The New
GROVE®
Dictionary of
OPERA

Volume Three

Lon-Rod

The New
GROVE®
Dictionary of
OPERA

Edited by

STANLEY SADIE

Managing Editor

CHRISTINA BASHFORD

Volume Three

Lon-Rod

MACMILLAN REFERENCE LIMITED, LONDON
GROVE'S DICTIONARIES OF MUSIC INC., NEW YORK, NY

© Macmillan Reference Limited, 1997

The New Grove and The New Grove Dictionary of Music and Musicians are registered trademarks in the United States of Macmillan Publishers Limited, London.

Macmillan Publishers Limited, London and its associated companies are the proprietors of the trademarks Grove's, The New Grove, and The New Grove Dictionary of Music and Musicians throughout the world.

The New Grove ® Dictionary of Opera

edited by STANLEY SADIE, in four volumes, 1992

First published in hardback 1992 by Macmillan Reference Limited, London.
In the United States of America and Canada, Macmillan Reference
has appointed Grove's Dictionaries of Music Inc.,
New York, NY, as sole distributor.

First published in paperback, 1998

Database creation and typesetting by Morton Word Processing Limited,
Scarborough, Great Britain

Printed and bound in Hong Kong by China Translation and Printing Services
Limited.

**British Library Cataloguing
in Publication Data**

New Grove Dictionary of Opera
  I.Sadie, Stanley
  782.103

Library of Congress Cataloguing in Publication Data

The New Grove dictionary of opera/edited by Stanley Sadie
  p. cm.
  "First published in hardback 1992 by Macmillan Reference
Limited, London" -
  - T.p. verso
    Includes bibliographical references.
    ISBN 1-56159-228-5 Paperback
    1. Opera - Dictionaries. I Sadie, Stanley
  ML102.O6N5 1992   92-36276
  782.1'03-dc20   CIP
                             MN

ISBN 0-333-73432-7   ISBN 1-56159-228-5

Contents

General Abbreviations

A	alto, contralto [voice]		bur.	buried
AB	Bachelor of Arts			
ABC	American Broadcasting Company; Australian Broadcasting Commission			
Abt.	Abteilung [section]		*c*	circa [about]
acc(s).	accompaniment(s); accompanied by		CA	California (USA)
AD	anno Domini		Cambs.	Cambridgeshire (GB)
add, addl	additional		cap.	capacity
add(s), addn(s)	addition(s)		carn.	Carnival
ad lib	ad libitum		cb	contrabass [instrument]
AK	Alaska (USA)		CBC	Canadian Broadcasting Corporation
AL	Alabama (USA)		CBE	Commander of the Order of the British Empire
Alta.	Alberta (Canada)			
AM	Master of Arts		CBS	Columbia Broadcasting System (USA)
a.m.	ante meridiem [before noon]		CBSO	City of Birmingham Symphony Orchestra
Amer.	American		CD	compact disc
AMS	American Musicological Society		cel	celesta
Anh.	Anhang [appendix]		cf	confer [compare]
anon.	anonymous(ly)		CG	Covent Garden, London
appx	appendix		CH	Companion of Honour
AR	Arkansas (USA)		chap.	chapter
arr(s).	arrangement(s); arranged (by/for)		Chin.	Chinese
ASCAP	American Society of Composers, Authors and Publishers		Cie	Compagnie
			cl	clarinet
attrib.	attribution, attributed to		cm	centimetre(s)
Aug	August		cmda	comédie mêlée d'ariettes
aut.	autumn		CNRS	Centre National de la Recherche Scientifique (F)
AZ	Arizona (USA)			
			CO	Colorado (USA)
			Co.	Company; County
			col(s).	column(s)
B	bass [voice]		coll.	collection, collected by
b	bass [instrument]		collab.	collaborator, in collaboration with
b	born		comp.	composer, composed
BA	Bachelor of Arts		conc.	concerto
bap.	baptized		cond.	conductor, conducted by
Bar	baritone [voice]		cont	continuo
bar	baritone [instrument]		contrib(s).	contribution(s)
BBC	British Broadcasting Corporation		Corp.	Corporation
BC	British Columbia (Canada)		CRI	Composers Recordings, Inc. (USA)
BC	before Christ		CSc	Candidate of Historical Sciences
bc	basso continuo		CT	Connecticut (USA)
Bd.	Band [volume]		Ct	countertenor
Berks.	Berkshire (GB)		CUNY	City University of New York
Berwicks.	Berwickshire (GB)		CVO	Commander of the Royal Victorian Order
BFA	Bachelor of Fine Arts		Cz.	Czech
bk	book			
BL	British Library			
BLitt	Bachelor of Letters; Bachelor of Literature			
BM	Bachelor of Music; British Museum		D	Deutsch catalogue [Schubert]
BME, BMEd	Bachelor of Music Education		*d*	died
BMI	Broadcast Music, Inc. (USA)		d.	denarius, denarii [penny, pence]
BMus	Bachelor of Music		Dan.	Danish
bn	bassoon		db	double bass
Bros.	Brothers		DBE	Dame Commander of the Order of the British Empire
BS, BSc	Bachelor of Science			
Bucks.	Buckinghamshire (GB)		dbn	double bassoon
Bulg.	Bulgarian		DC	District of Columbia (USA)

DE	Delaware (USA)		HMV	His Master's Voice
Dec	December		hn	horn
ded.	dedication, dedicated (to)		Hon.	Honorary; Honourable
Dept	Department		hpd	harpsichord
Derbys.	Derbyshire (GB)		HRH	His/Her Royal Highness
DFA	Doctor of Fine Arts		Hung.	Hungarian
dg	dramma giocoso		Hunts.	Huntingdonshire (GB)
dir.	director, directed by		Hz	Hertz [cycle(s) per second]
diss.	dissertation		IA	Iowa (USA)
DLitt	Doctor of Letters; Doctor of Literature		IAML	International Association of Music Libraries
DMA	Doctor of Musical Arts		ibid	ibidem [in the same place]
DMus	Doctor of Music		ID	Idaho (USA)
DPhil	Doctor of Philosophy		i.e.	id est [that is]
Dr	Doctor		IL	Illinois (USA)
DSc	Doctor of Science; Doctor of Historical Sciences		IMS	International Musicological Society
			IN	Indiana (USA)
			Inc.	Incorporated
			inc.	incomplete
			incl.	includes, including
E.	east, eastern		inst(s)	instrument(s); instrumental
EBU	European Broadcasting Union		int	intermezzo
ed(s).	editor(s); edited (by)		IRCAM	Institut de Recherche et de Coordination Acoustique/Musique (F)
edn(s)	edition(s)			
e.g.	exempli gratia [for example]		ISAM	Institute for Studies in American Music
elec	electric, electronic		ISCM	International Society for Contemporary Music
EMI	Electrical and Musical Industries		ISM	Incorporated Society of Musicians (GB)
Eng.	English		It.	Italian
eng hn	english horn			
ENO	English National Opera			
ens	ensemble			
esp.	especially		Jan	January
etc.	et cetera [and so on]		Jap.	Japanese
ex., exx.	example, examples		*Jb*	Jahrbuch [yearbook]
			Jg.	Jahrgang [year of publication/volume]
			jr	junior
f	forte			
f., ff.	folio, folios			
facs.	facsimile		K	Köchel catalogue [Mozart; no. after / is from 6th edn]
fasc.	fascicle			
Feb	February		kbd	keyboard
ff	following pages		KBE	Knight Commander of the Order of the British Empire
ff	fortissimo			
fff	fortississimo		KCVO	Knight Commander of the Royal Victorian Order
fig.	figure [illustration]			
FL	Florida (USA)		Kgl	Königlich [royal]
fl	flute		kHz	kilohertz [1000 cycles per second]
fl	floruit [he/she flourished]		km	kilometre(s)
fp	fortepiano		KS	Kansas (USA)
Fr.	French		KY	Kentucky (USA)
frag(s).	fragment(s)			
			£	libra, librae [pounds, pounds sterling]
GA	Georgia (USA)		LA	Louisiana (USA)
Ger.	German		Lancs.	Lancashire (GB)
Gk.	Greek		Lat.	Latin
Glam.	Glamorgan (GB)		Leics.	Leicestershire (GB)
glock	glockenspiel		lib(s).	libretto(s)
Gloucs.	Gloucestershire (GB)		Lincs.	Lincolnshire (GB)
GmbH	Gesellschaft mit beschränkter Haftung [limited-liability company]		LittD	Doctor of Letters; Doctor of Literature
			LlB	Bachelor of Laws
govt.	government		LlD	Doctor of Laws
GSM	Guildhall School of Music and Drama, London		LP	long-playing record
			LPO	London Philharmonic Orchestra
gui	guitar		LSO	London Symphony Orchestra
			Ltd	Limited
H	Hoboken catalogue [Haydn]			
Hants.	Hampshire (GB)		m	metre(s)
Heb.	Hebrew		M.	Monsieur
Herts.	Hertfordshire (GB)		MA	Master of Arts
HI	Hawaii (USA)		MA	Massachusetts (USA)
HMS	His/Her Majesty's Ship		mand	mandolin

mar	marimba	OM	Order of Merit
MBE	Member of the Order of the British Empire	Ont.	Ontario (Canada)
MD	Maryland (USA)	op	opera [genre]
ME	Maine (USA)	op., opp.	opus, opera
Met	Metropolitan Opera, New York	opt.	optional
Mez	mezzo-soprano	OR	Oregon (USA)
mf	mezzo-forte	orch	orchestra, orchestral, orchestration
MFA	Master of Fine Arts	orchd	orchestrated (by)
MI	Michigan (USA)	org	organ
MLitt	Master of Letters; Master of Literature	orig.	original(ly)
Mlle(s)	Mademoiselle(s)	ORTF	Office de Radiodiffusion-Télévision Française
MM	Master of Music	os	opera seria
M.M.	Metronome Maelzel	OUP	Oxford University Press
mm	millimetre(s)	ov(s).	overture(s)
Mme	Madame	Oxon.	Oxfordshire (GB)
MMus	Master of Music		
MN	Minnesota (USA)		
MO	Missouri (USA)		
mod	modulator	P	Pincherle catalogue [Vivaldi]
Mon.	Monmouthshire (GB)	*p*	piano
movt	movement	p., pp.	page, pages
MP	Member of Parliament (GB)	PA	Pennsylvania (USA)
mp	mezzo-piano	p.a.	per annum
MPhil	Master of Philosophy	PBS	Public Broadcasting Service (USA)
Mr	Mister	perc	percussion
Mrs	Mistress	perf(s).	performance(s); performed (by)
MS(S)	manuscript(s); Master of Science	pf	piano(forte)
MS	Mississippi (USA)	PhD	Doctor of Philosophy
MSc	Master of Science	pic	piccolo
MT	Montana (USA)	pl(s).	plate(s); plural
Mt	Mount	p.m.	post meridiem [after noon]
MusB, MusBac	Bachelor of Music	PO	Philharmonic Orchestra
MusD, MusDoc	Doctor of Music	Pol.	Polish
MusM	Master of Music	pop.	population
		Port.	Portuguese
		posth.	posthumous(ly)
		POW	prisoner of war
N.	north, northern	*pp*	pianissimo
nar	narrator	*ppp*	pianississimo
NBC	National Broadcasting Company (USA)	pr.	printed
NC	North Carolina (USA)	PRO	Public Record Office, London
ND	North Dakota (USA)	prol.	prologue
n.d.	no date (of publication)	PRS	Performing Right Society
NE	Nebraska (USA)	Ps, ps	psalm
NEA	National Endowment for the Arts (USA)	pseud.	pseudonym
NEH	National Endowment for the Humanities (USA)	pt(s)	part(s)
		pubd	published
NET	National Educational Television (USA)	pubn	publication
NH	New Hampshire (USA)		
NHK	Nippon Hōsō Kyōkai [Japanese national broadcasting system]		
NJ	New Jersey (USA)	qnt	quintet
NM	New Mexico (USA)	qt	quartet
no(s).	number(s)		
Nor.	Norwegian		
Northants.	Northamptonshire (GB)		
Notts.	Nottinghamshire (GB)	/R	(editorial) revision [in signature]
Nov	November	*R*	photographic reprint
n.p.	no place (of publication)	*r*	recto
nr	near	RAF	Royal Air Force
NSW	New South Wales (Australia)	RAI	Radio Audizioni Italiane
NV	Nevada (USA)	RAM	Royal Academy of Music, London
NY	New York State (USA)	RCA	Radio Corporation of America
NZ	New Zealand	RCM	Royal College of Music, London
		rec	recorder
		recit(s).	recitative(s)
		red.	reduction, reduced for
ob	opera buffa; oboe	repr.	reprinted
obbl	obbligato	Rev.	Reverend
OBE	Officer of the Order of the British Empire	rev(s).	revision(s); revised (by/for)
OC	Opéra-Comique [company]	RI	Rhode Island (USA)
oc	opéra comique [genre]	RIdIM	Répertoire International d'Iconographie Musicale
Oct	October		
OH	Ohio (USA)	RILM	Répertoire International de Littérature Musicale
OK	Oklahoma (USA)		

RISM	Répertoire International des Sources Musicales		U.	University
RMCM	Royal Manchester College of Music		UCLA	University of California at Los Angeles (USA)
RNCM	Royal Northern College of Music, Manchester		UHF	ultra-high frequency
RO	Radio Orchestra		UK	United Kingdom of Great Britain and Northern Ireland
Rom.	Romanian			
r.p.m.	revolution(s) per minute		Ukr.	Ukrainian
RPO	Royal Philharmonic Orchestra (GB)		unacc.	unaccompanied
RSFSR	Russian Soviet Federated Socialist Republic		unattrib.	unattributed
RSO	Radio Symphony Orchestra		UNESCO	United Nations Educational, Scientific and Cultural Organization
RTE	Radio Telefís Éireann (Ireland)			
RTF	Radiodiffusion-Télévision Française		UNICEF	United Nations International Children's Emergency Fund
Rt Hon.	Right Honourable			
Russ.	Russian		unperf.	unperformed
RV	Ryom catalogue [Vivaldi]		unpubd	unpublished
			US	United States [adjective]
			USA	United States of America
			USSR	Union of Soviet Socialist Republics
S	San, Santa, Santo, São [Saint]; soprano [voice]		UT	Utah (USA)
$	dollar(s)			
S.	south, southern			
s	soprano [instrument]			
s.	solidus, solidi [shilling, shillings]		v, vv	voice, voices
SACEM	Société d'Auteurs, Compositeurs et Editeurs de Musique (F)		*v*	verso
			v., vv.	verse, verses
Sask.	Saskatchewan (Canada)		VA	Virginia (USA)
sax	saxophone		va	viola
SC	South Carolina (USA)		vc	cello
SD	South Dakota (USA)		VHF	very high frequency
Sept	September		vib	vibraphone
ser.	series		viz	videlicet [namely]
Serb.	Serbian		vle	violone
sf, *sfz*	sforzando, sforzato		vn	violin
sing.	singular		vol(s).	volume(s)
SO	Symphony Orchestra		vs	vocal score, piano-vocal score
Sp.	Spanish		VT	Vermont (USA)
Spl	Singspiel			
SPNM	Society for the Promotion of New Music (GB)			
spr.	spring			
sq	square		W.	west, western
sr	senior		WA	Washington (USA)
SS	Saints		Warwicks.	Warwickshire (GB)
Ss	Santissima, Santissimo		WI	Wisconsin (USA)
SSR	Soviet Socialist Republic		Wilts.	Wiltshire (GB)
St	Saint, Sankt, Sint, Szent		wint.	winter
Staffs.	Staffordshire (GB)		WNO	Welsh National Opera
Ste	Sainte		WoO, woo	Werk(e) ohne Opuszahl [work(s) without opus number]
str	string(s)			
sum.	summer		Worcs.	Worcestershire (GB)
SUNY	State University of New York (USA)		WV	West Virginia (USA)
suppl(s).	supplement(s); supplementary		WW	woodwind
Swed.	Swedish		WY	Wyoming (USA)
sym(s).	symphony (symphonies); symphonic			
synth	synthesizer			
			xyl	xylophone
T	tenor [voice]			
t	tenor [instrument]			
timp	timpani		Yorks.	Yorkshire (GB)
TN	Tennessee (USA)			
tpt	trumpet			
Tr	treble [voice]			
tr	treble [instrument]		z	Zimmerman catalogue [Purcell]
trans.	translation, translated by		zar	zarzuela
transcr.	transcription, transcribed by			
trbn	trombone			
TV	television			
TX	Texas (USA)		*	autograph manuscript

Bibliographical Abbreviations

The bibliographical abbreviations used in this dictionary are listed below. Full bibliographical information is not normally supplied for national biographical dictionaries and general music reference works, or if details may be found elsewhere in this dictionary under the heading 'Dictionaries and guides' or 'Editions' (relevant items are indicated with D or E, respectively). General music periodicals are shown with dates only; for those in existence before 1980 full information may be found in the list forming part of the article 'Periodicals' in *The New Grove Dictionary of Music and Musicians*. Opera periodicals, listed in the present dictionary under the heading 'Periodicals', are shown here with an asterisk and serial number in brackets.

In this list, and throughout the dictionary, italic type is used for periodicals and reference works, and roman type for anthologies of music, series etc.

AcM	*Acta musicologica* (1928/9–)	BUCEM	*British Union-Catalogue of Early Music*, ed. E. Schnapper (London, 1957)
ADB	*Allgemeine deutsche Biographie* (Leipzig, 1875–1912)	BurneyFI	C. Burney: *The Present State of Music in France and Italy* (London, 1771, 2/1773); ed. P. A. Scholes, *Dr. Burney's Musical Tours in Europe* (London, 1959)
AllacciD	L. Allacci: *Drammaturgia* D		
AMe (AMeS)	*Algemene muziekencyclopedie* (and suppl.) (Antwerp and Amsterdam, 1957–63; suppl., 1972)		
AMf	*Archiv für Musikforschung* (1936–43)	BurneyGN	C. Burney: *The Present State of Music in Germany, the Netherlands, and United Provinces* (London, 1773, 2/1775); ed. P. A. Scholes, *Dr. Burney's Musical Tours in Europe* (London, 1959)
AMI	L'arte musicale in Italia E		
AMw	*Archiv für Musikwissenschaft* (1918/19–)		
AMZ	*Allgemeine musikalische Zeitung* (1798/9–1882)		
AMz	*Allgemeine Musik-Zeitung* (1874–1943)	BurneyH	C. Burney: *A General History of Music from the Earliest Ages to the Present* (London, 1776–89) [p. nos. refer to edn of 1935]
AnM	*Anuario musical* (1946–)		
AnMc	*Analecta musicologica* (some vols. in series Studien zur italienisch-deutschen Musikgeschichte), Veröffentlichungen der Musikabteilung des Deutschen historischen Instituts in Rom (Cologne, 1963–)		
		CBY	*Current Biography Yearbook* (New York, 1940–)
		CHM	*Collectanea historiae musicae* (in series Biblioteca historiae musicae cultores) (Florence, 1953–)
Baker6(–8)	*Baker's Biographical Dictionary of Musicians* (New York, 6/1978, 7/1984, 8/1992)	CMc	*Current Musicology* (1965–)
		CMI	I classici musicali italiani E
BAMS	*Bulletin of the American Musicological Society* (1936–48)	ČMm	*Časopis Moravského musea* [Journal of the Moravian Museum] (c1915–)
BDA	*A Biographical Dictionary of Actors, Actresses, Musicians, Dancers, Managers & Other Stage Personnel in London, 1660–1800* D	CMz	*Cercetări de muzicologie* (1969–)
		COJ	*Cambridge Opera Journal* [*Great Britain 27]
		CroceN	B. Croce: *I teatri di Napoli* D
BeJb	*Beethoven-Jahrbuch* (1953/4–)	ČSHS	*Československý hudební slovník* (Prague, 1963–5)
BMB	Bibliotheca musica bononiensis E		
BMw	*Beiträge zur Musikwissenschaft* (1959–)	CSPD	*Calendar of State Papers (Domestic)* (London, 1856–1972)
BNB	*Biographie nationale [belge]* (Brussels, 1866–86)		
BordasD	*Dictionnaire de la musique* (Paris: Bordas, 1970–76)		
Bouwsteenen: JVNM	*Bouwsteenen: jaarboek der Vereeniging voor Nederlandsche muziekgeschiedenis* (1869/72–1874/81)	DAB	*Dictionary of American Biography* (New York, 1928–36; 8 suppls., 1944–88)
		DAM	*Dansk aarbog for musikforskning* (1961–)
BSIM	*Bulletin français de la S[ociété] I[nternationale de] M[usique] [previously Le Mercure musical; also other titles]* (1905–14)	DBF	*Dictionnaire de biographie française* (Paris, 1933–)
		DBI	*Dizionario biografico degli italiani* (Rome, 1960–)

DBL	Dansk biografisk leksikon (Copenhagen, 1887–1905, 2/1933–)
DBP	Dicionário biográfico de músicos portuguezes (Lisbon, 1900–04)
DDT	Denkmäler deutscher Tonkunst E
DEUMM	Dizionario enciclopedico universale della musica e dei musicisti (Turin, 1985–8)
DJbM	Deutsches Jahrbuch der Musikwissenschaft (1957–)
DMV	Drammaturgia musicale veneta E
DNB	Dictionary of National Biography (London, 1885–1901, suppls.)
DTB	Denkmäler der Tonkunst in Bayern E
DTÖ	Denkmäler der Tonkunst in Österreich E
EDM	Das Erbe deutscher Musik E
EIT	Ezhegodnik imperatorskikh teatrov (1892–1915)
EitnerQ	R. Eitner: Biographisch-bibliographisches Quellen-Lexikon (Leipzig, 1900–04, 2/1959–60)
EitnerS	R. Eitner: Bibliographie der Musik-Sammelwerke des XVI. und XVII. Jahrhunderts (Berlin, 1877)
EMC	Encyclopedia of Music in Canada (Toronto, 1981)
EMc	Early Music (1973–)
EMDC	Encyclopédie de la musique et dictionnaire du Conservatoire (Paris, 1920–31)
ERO	Early Romantic Opera E
ES	Enciclopedia dello spettacolo D
EwenD	D. Ewen: American Composers: a Biographical Dictionary (New York, 1982)
FAM	Fontes artis musicae (1954–)
FasquelleE	Encyclopédie de la musique (Paris: Fasquelle, 1958–61)
FétisB (FétisBS)	F.-J. Fétis: Biographie universelle des musiciens (and suppl.) (Brussels, 2/1860–65; suppl., 1878–80)
FlorimoN	F. Florimo: La scuola musicale di Napoli e i suoi conservatorii (Naples, 1880–83)
FO	French Opera in the 17th and 18th Centuries E
GänzlBMT	K. Gänzl: The British Musical Theatre D
GerberL	E. L. Gerber: Historisch-biographisches Lexikon der Tonkünstler (Leipzig, 1790–92)
GerberNL	E. L. Gerber: Neues historisch-biographisches Lexikon der Tonkünstler (Leipzig, 1812–14)
GfMKB	Gesellschaft für Musikforschung Kongressbericht (1950–)
GiacomoC	S. Di Giacomo: I quattro antichi conservatorii musicali di Napoli (Milan and Naples, 1924–8)
GMB	Geschichte der Musik in Beispielen, ed. A. Schering (Leipzig, 1931)
GOB	German Opera 1770–1800, ed. T. Bauman E
Grove1(–5)	G. Grove, ed.: A Dictionary of Music and Musicians (London, 1878–90; 2/1904–10 ed. J. A. Fuller Maitland, 3/1927–8 and 4/1940 ed. H. C. Colles, 5/1954 ed. E. Blom with suppl. 1961, all as Grove's Dictionary of Music and Musicians)
Grove6	S. Sadie, ed.: The New Grove Dictionary of Music and Musicians (London, 1980)
GroveAM	H. W. Hitchcock and S. Sadie, eds.: The New Grove Dictionary of American Music (New York, 1986)
GroveI	S. Sadie, ed.: The New Grove Dictionary of Musical Instruments (London, 1984)
GSL	Grosses Sängerlexikon D
GV	Le grandi voci: Dizionario critico-biografico dei cantanti con discografia operistica D [where two authors are separated by a semi-colon, the second one compiled the discography]
HawkinsH	J. Hawkins: A General History of the Science and Practice of Music (London, 1776) [p. nos. refer to edn of 1853]
HayJb	Haydn-Jahrbuch/Yearbook (1962–71, 1975–8, 1980–)
HiFi	High Fidelity (1951/2–1965)
HiFi/MusAm	High Fidelity/Musical America (1965–87)
HJb	Händel-Jahrbuch (1928–33, 1955–)
HJbMw	Hamburger Jahrbuch für Musikwissenschaft (1975–)
HMT	Handwörterbuch der musikalischen Terminologie (Wiesbaden, 1972–)
HMw	Handbuch der Musikwissenschaft, ed. E. Bücken (Potsdam, 1927–) [monograph series]
HMYB	Hinrichsen's Musical Year Book (1944–61)
HPM	Harvard Publications in Music E
HR	Hudební revue (1908–20)
HRo	Hudební rozhledy (1948/9–)
HS	Handel Sources E
HV	Hudební věda (1961–)
IIM	Izvestiya na Instituta za muzika (1952–)
IMa	Instituta et monumenta E
IMSCR	International Musicological Society Congress Report (1930–)
IMusSCR	International Musical Society Congress Report (1906–11)
IOB	Italian Opera 1640–1770, ed. H. M. Brown E
IOG	Italian Opera 1810–1840, ed. P. Gossett E
IRASM	International Review of the Aesthetics and Sociology of Music (1971–)
IRMAS	The International Review of Music Aesthetics and Sociology (1970–71)
IRMO	S. L. Ginzburg: Istoriya russkoy muzïki v notnïkh obraztsakh (Moscow, 2/1968–70)
ISAMm	Institute for Studies in American Music, monograph series
JAMS	Journal of the American Musicological Society (1949–)
JbMP	Jahrbuch der Musikbibliothek Peters (1895–1941)
JbO	Jahrbuch für Opernforschung [*Germany 60]
JM	Journal of Musicology (1983–)
JMT	Journal of Music Theory (1957–)
JRBM	Journal of Renaissance and Baroque Music (1946–7)
JRMA	Journal of the Royal Musical Association (1987–)
JVNM	see Bouwsteenen: JVNM
KJb	Kirchenmusikalisches Jahrbuch (1886–1911, 1930–35, 1936/8, 1950–)
KM	Kwartalnik muzyczny (1911/13–1913/14, 1928/9–1933, 1948–50)
Kobbé10	G. Kobbé: Complete Opera Book (New York and London, 10/1987) D

LaborD	*Diccionario de la música Labor* (Barcelona, 1954)	*OM*	*Opus musicum* (1969–)
LaMusicaD	*La musica: dizionario* (Turin, 1968–71)	*ÖMz*	*Österreichische Musikzeitschrift* (1946–)
LaMusicaE	*La musica: enciclopedia storica* (Turin, 1966)	*ON*	*Opera News* [*USA 13]
LM	*Lucrări di muzicologie* (1965–)	*OQ*	*The Opera Quarterly* [*USA 28]
LoewenbergA	A. Loewenberg: *Annals of Opera 1597–1940* D	*OW*	*Opernwelt* [*Germany 42]
LS	*The London Stage, 1660–1800* D		
		PAMS	*Papers of the American Musicological Society* (1936–8, 1940–41)
		PÄMw	Publikationen älterer praktischer und theoretischer Musikwerke E
MA	*The Musical Antiquary* (1909/10–1912/13)		
MAS	Musical Antiquarian Society [Publications] E	*PBC*	Publicaciones del departamento de música de la Biblioteca de Catalunya E
MB	*Musica britannica* E		
MD	*Musica disciplina* (1948–)	*PEM*	*Pipers Enzyklopädie des Musiktheaters* D
ME	*Muzikal'naya entsiklopediya* (Moscow, 1973–82)	*PMA*	*Proceedings of the Musical Association* (1874/5–1943/4)
Mf	*Die Musikforschung* (1948–)	*PNM*	*Perspectives of New Music* (1962/3–)
MGG	*Die Musik in Geschichte und Gegenwart* (Kassel and Basle, 1949–68; suppl., 1973–9, index 1986)	*PRM*	*Polski rocznik muzykologiczny* (1935–6)
		PRMA	*Proceedings of the Royal Musical Association* (1944/5–1984/5)
MJb	*Mozart-Jahrbuch des Zentralinstituts für Mozartforschung* (1950–)	*PSB*	*Polskich słownik biograficzny* (Kraków, 1935)
ML	*Music and Letters* (1920–)		
MLE	Music for London Entertainment, 1660–1800 E	*QRaM*	*Quaderni della Rassegna musicale* (1964–72)
MM	*Modern Music* (1925–46)		
MMA	*Miscellanea musicologica* [Australia] (1966–70, 1972, 1975, 1977–)		
MMC	*Miscellanea musicologica* [Czechoslovakia] (1956–62, 1965–1971/3, 1975–)	*Rad JAZU*	*Rad Jugoslavenske akademije znanosti i umjetnosti* (Zagreb, 1867–)
MMg	*Monatshefte für Musikgeschichte* (1869–1905)	*RaM*	*La rassegna musicale* (1928–43, 1947–62)
MMR	*The Monthly Musical Record* (1871–1960)	*RBM*	*Revue belge de musicologie* (1946–)
MMS	Monumenta musicae svecicae E	*RdM*	*Revue de musicologie* (1917/19–1943, 1945–)
MO	*Musical Opinion* (1877/8–)	*RdMc*	*Revista de musicología* (1978–)
MQ	*The Musical Quarterly* (1915–)	*ReM*	*La revue musicale* (1920–40, 1946–)
MR	*The Music Review* (1940–)	*RHCM*	*Revue d'histoire et de critique musicales* (1901); *La revue musicale* (1902–11)
MS	*Muzikal'niy sovremennik* (1915/16–1916/17)		
MSD	Musicological Studies and Documents, ed. A. Carapetyan (Rome, 1951–)	*RicordiE*	*Enciclopedia della musica* (Milan: Ricordi, 1963–4)
MT	*The Musical Times* (1844/5–)	*RiemannL 11,12*	H. Riemann: *Musik-Lexikon* (Leipzig, 1882, 11/1929 rev. A. Einstein, 12/1959–75 rev. W. Gurlitt, H. H. Eggebrecht and C. Dahlhaus)
MusAm	*Musical America* (1898–1964, 1987–92)		
MZ	*Muzikološki zbornik* (1965–)		
		RIM	*Rivista italiana di musicologia* (1966–)
		RISM	*Répertoire international des sources musicales* (Munich and Duisburg, 1960–; Kassel, 1971–)
NA	*Note d'archivio per la storia musicale* (1924–7, 1930–43, 1983–)		
NAW	*Notable American Women* (Cambridge, MA, 1971; suppl., 1980)	*RMARC*	R[oyal] M[usical] A[ssociation] *Research Chronicle* (1961–)
NBJb	*Neues Beethoven-Jahrbuch* (1924–5, 1927, 1930, 1933, 1935, 1937–9, 1942)	*RMFC*	*Recherches sur la musique française classique* (1960–)
NBL	*Norsk biografisk leksikon* (Oslo, 1921–)	*RMG*	*Russkaya muzikal'naya gazeta* (1894–1917)
NDB	*Neue deutsche Biographie* (Berlin, 1953–)	*RMI*	*Rivista musicale italiana* (1894–1932, 1936–43, 1946–55)
NicollH	A. Nicoll: *A History of English Drama, 1660–1900* (Cambridge, 1952–9)		
NMA	W. A. Mozart: Neue Ausgabe sämtlicher Werke, ed. E. F. Schmid, W. Plath and W. Rehm (Kassel, 1955–91)	*RosaM*	C. de Rosa, Marchese di Villarosa: *Memorie dei compositori di musica del Regno di Napoli* (Naples, 1840)
NNBW	*Nieuw Nederlandsch biografisch woordenboek* (Leiden, 1911–37)	*RRAM*	Recent Researches in American Music E
		RRMBE	Recent Researches in the Music of the Baroque Era E
NÖB	*Neue österreichische Biographie* (Vienna, 1923)	*RRMCE*	Recent Researches in the Music of the Classical Era E
NOHM	*The New Oxford History of Music*, ed. E. Wellesz, J. A. Westrup and G. Abraham (London, 1954–)		
NRMI	*Nuova rivista musicale italiana* (1967–)	*SBL*	*Svenska biografiskt leksikon* (Stockholm, 1918–)
NZM	*Neue Zeitschrift für Musik* (1834–1943, 1950–74, 1979–)	*SchmidlD (SchmidlDS)*	C. Schmidl: *Dizionario universale dei musicisti* (and suppl.) (Milan, 1887–90, 2/1928–9; suppl., 1938)
		SCMA	Smith College Music Archives E
OC	*Opera in Canada* [*Canada 1]	*SeegerL*	H. Seeger: *Musiklexikon* (Leipzig, 1966)
OHM	*The Oxford History of Music*, ed. W. H. Hadow (Oxford, 1901–5, enlarged 2/1929–38)	*SH*	*Slovenská hudba* (1957–71)
		SIMG	*Sammelbände der Internationalen Musik-Gesellschaft* (1899/1900–1913/14)

SM	Studia musicologica Academiae scientiarum hungaricae (1961–)	VMw	Vierteljahrsschrift für Musikwissenschaft (1885–94)
SMA	Studies in Music (1967–) [Australia]	VogelB	E. Vogel: Bibliothek der gedruckten weltlichen Vocalmusik Italiens, aus den Jahren 1500 bis 1700 (Berlin, 1892); rev., enlarged, by A. Einstein (Hildesheim, 1962); further addns in AnMc, nos.4, 5, 9 and 12; further rev. by F. Lesure and C. Sartori as Bibliografia della musica italiana vocale profana pubblicata dal 1500 al 1700 (Geneva, 1978)
SML	Schweizer Musiker Lexikon (Zürich, 1964)		
SMN	Studia musicologica norvegica (1968, 1976–)		
SMP	Słownik muzyków polskich (Kraków, 1964–7)		
SMw	Studien zur Musikwissenschaft (1913–16, 1918–34, 1955–6, 1960–66, 1977–)		
SMz	Schweizerische Musikzeitung/Revue musicale suisse (1861–)		
SOI	Storia dell'opera italiana, ed. L. Bianconi and G. Pestelli (Turin, 1987–)		
SouthernB	E. Southern: Biographical Dictionary of Afro-American and African Musicians (Westport, CT, 1982)	WaltherML	J. G. Walther: Musicalisches Lexicon oder Musicalische Bibliothek (Leipzig, 1732)
SovM	Sovetskaya muzika (1933–41, 1946–)	WE	The Wellesley Edition E
StiegerO	F. Stieger: Opernlexikon D	WurzbachL	C. von Wurzbach: Biographisches Lexikon des Kaiserthums Oesterreich (Vienna, 1856–91)
STMf	Svensk tidskrift för musikforskning (1919–)		
TVNM	Tijdschrift van de Vereniging voor Nederlandse muziekgeschiedenis (1885–)	ZfM	Zeitschrift für Musik (1920–55)
		ZIMG	Zeitschrift der Internationalen Musik-Gesellschaft (1899/1900–1913/14)
		ZL	Zenei lexikon (Budapest, 1930–31, 2/1965)
VintonD	J. Vinton, ed.: Dictionary of Contemporary Music (New York, 1974)	ZMw	Zeitschrift für Musikwissenschaft (1918/19–1935)

Library Sigla

The system of library sigla in this dictionary follows that used in its publications (Series A) by Répertoire International des Sources Musicales, Kassel, by permission. Below are listed the sigla to be found; a few of them are additional to those in the published RISM lists, but have been established in consultation with the RISM organization. Some original RISM sigla that have now been changed are retained here.

In the dictionary, sigla are always printed in *italic*. In any listing of sources a national sigillum applies without repetition until it is contradicted.

Within each national list below, entries are alphabetized by sigillum, first by capital letters (showing the city or town) and then by lower-case ones (showing the institution or collection).

A: AUSTRIA

Gk(h)	Graz, Hochschule für Musik und Darstellende Kunst und Landesmusikschule
Gmi	——, Musikwissenschaftliches Institut der Universität
HE	Heiligenkreuz, Zisterzienserstift
KR	Kremsmünster, Benediktinerstift
LA	Lambach, Benediktinerstift
LIm	Linz, Oberösterreichisches Landesmuseum
M	Melk an der Donau, Benediktinerstift
Sca	Salzburg, Museum Carolino Augusteum
Sm	——, Mozarteum (Internationale Stiftung Mozarteum)
Ssp	——, St Peter (Erzstift oder Benediktiner-Erzabtei)
Su	——, Universitätsbibliothek
SPL	St Paul, Stift
ST	Stams, Zisterzienserstift
Wdtö	Vienna, Gesellschaft zur Herausgabe von Denkmälern der Tonkunst in Österreich
Wgm	——, Gesellschaft der Musikfreunde
Wm	——, Minoritenkonvent
Wn	——, Österreichische Nationalbibliothek, Musiksammlung
Wst	——, Stadtbibliothek, Musiksammlung

ARG: ARGENTINA

BAc	Buenos Aires, Teatro Colón

AUS: AUSTRALIA

CAnl	Canberra, National Library of Australia
Msl	Melbourne, State Library of Victoria
NLwm	Nedlands, Wigmore Music Library, University of Western Australia
Scm	Sydney, New South Wales State Conservatorium of Music
Sfl	——, Fisher Library, University of Sydney

B: BELGIUM

Aa	Antwerp, Stadsarchief
Aac	——, Archief en Museum voor het Vlaamse Culturleven
Ac	——, Koninklijk Vlaams Muziekconservatorium
Ba	Brussels, Archives de la Ville
Bc	——, Conservatoire Royal de Musique
Bcdm	——, Centre Belge de Documentation Musicale [CeBeDeM]
Bmichotte	——, Michotte private collection
Br	——, Bibliothèque Royale Albert 1er/ Koninklijke Bibliotheek Albert I
Gc	Ghent, Koninklijk Muziekconservatorium
Gu	——, Rijksuniversiteit, Centrale Bibliotheek
Lc	Liège, Conservatoire Royal de Musique
Lg	——, Musée Grétry

BR: BRAZIL

Rem	Rio de Janeiro, Escola Nacional de Música, Universidade do Brasil
Rn	——, Biblioteca Nacional

C: CANADA

HNu	Hamilton, McMaster University, Mills Memorial Library
Lu	London, University of Western Ontario, Lawson Memorial Library
On	Ottawa, National Library of Canada
Qsl	Quebec, Séminaire de Québec
Tp	Toronto, Metropolitan Toronto Library, Music Department
Tu	——, University of Toronto, Edward Johnson Music Library

CH: SWITZERLAND

Bu	Basle, Öffentliche Bibliothek der Universität, Musiksammlung
BEl	Berne, Schweizerische Landesbibliothek
E	Einsiedeln, Kloster
EN	Engelberg, Stift
Gc	Geneva, Conservatoire de Musique
Lmg	Lucerne, Allgemeine Musikalische Gesellschaft

Lz	——, Zentralbibliothek
LAcu	Lausanne, Bibliothèque Cantonale et Universitaire
MONbonynge	Montreux, Richard Bonynge, private collection
N	Neuchâtel, Bibliothèque Publique et Universitaire
Zschmitt	Zürich, Schmitt private collection
Zz	——, Zentralbibliothek

CS: CZECHOSLOVAKIA

Bm	Brno, Ústav Dějin Hudby Moravského Musea, Hudebněhistorické Oddělení
Bu	——, Universitní Knihovna
K	Český Krumlov, Pracoviště Státního Archívu Třeboň, Hudební Sbírka
KRa	Kroměříž, Státní Zámek a Zahrady, Historicko-Umělecké Fondy, Hudební Archív
KU	Kutná Hora, Oblastní Muzeum
Pk	Prague, Archív Státní Konservatoře v Praze
Pnd	——, Archív Národního Divadla
Pnm	——, Národní Muzeum, Hudební Oddělení
Pr	——, Československý Rozhlas, Hudební Archív Různá Provenience
Pu	——, Národní Knihovna v Praze, Universitní Knihovna

CU: CUBA

Hin	Havana, Instituto Nacional de la Música
Hn	——, Biblioteca Nacional

D: GERMANY

As	Augsburg, Staats- und Stadtbibliothek
Au	——, Universitätsbibliothek
ALa	Altenburg, Historisches Staatsarchiv
AN	Ansbach, Regierungsbibliothek
B	Berlin, Staatsbibliothek Preussischer Kulturbesitz, Musikabteilung
Ba	——, Amerika-Gedenkbibliothek (Berliner Zentralbibliothek); Deutsche Akademie der Künste
Bbb	——, Bote & Bock Archiv
Bdhm	——, Deutsche Hochschule für Musik Hanns Eisler
Bds	——, Deutsche Staatsbibliothek (formerly Königliche Bibliothek; Preussische Staatsbibliothek; Öffentliche Wissenschaftliche Bibliothek), Musikabteilung
Bdso	——, Deutsche Staatsoper
Bhbk	——, Staatliche Hochschule für Bildende Kunst
Bhm	——, Staatliche Hochschule für Musik und Darstellende Kunst
Bko	——, Komische Oper
Bmm	——, Märkisches Museum
Bp	——, Pädagogisches Zentrum
Bsommer	——, Sommer private collection
Bsp	——, Sprachkonvikt
BAs	Bamberg, Staatsbibliothek
BAL	Ballenstedt, Stadtbibliothek
BAR	Bartenstein, Fürstzu Hohenlohe-Bartensteinsches Archiv [in *NEhz*]
BB	Benediktbeuern, Pfarrkirche
BMs	Bremen, Staats- und Universitätsbibliothek
BNu	Bonn, Universitätsbibliothek
BS	Brunswick, Öffentliche Bücherei (Stadtarchiv und Stadtbibliothek)
Cl	Coburg, Landesbibliothek
Dl	Dresden, Bibliothek und Museum Löbau [in *Dlb*]
Dla	——, Staatsarchiv
Dlb	——, Sächsische Landesbibliothek
Ds	——, Staatstheater
DEl	Dessau, Stadtbibliothek (formerly Universitäts- und Landesbibliothek)
DI	Dillingen an der Donau, Kreis- und Studienbibliothek
DL	Delitzsch, Museum und Bibliothek
DO	Donaueschingen, Fürstlich Fürstenbergische Hofbibliothek
DS	Darmstadt, Hessische Landes- und Hochschulbibliothek
DT	Detmold, Lippische Landesbibliothek
DÜl	Düsseldorf, Landes- und Stadtbibliothek
Es	Eichstätt, Staats- und Seminarbibliothek [in *Eu*]
Eu	——, Universitätsbibliothek
Ew	——, Benediktinerinnen-Abtei St Walburg
EB	Ebrach, Katholisches Pfarramt
F	Frankfurt am Main, Stadt- und Universitätsbibliothek
FS	Freising, Dombibliothek
Ga	Göttingen, Staatliches Archivlager
Gs	——, Niedersächsische Staats- und Universitätsbibliothek
Hmb	Hamburg, Hamburger Öffentliche Bücherhallen, Musikbibliothek
Hs	——, Staats- und Universitätsbibliothek Carl von Ossietzky
HAmi	Halle an der Saale, Martin-Luther-Universität, Sektion Germanistik und Kulturwissenschaften, Fachbereich Musikwissenschaft (formerly Institut für Musikwissenschaft)
HAu	——, Universitäts- und Landesbibliothek
HG	Havelberg, Prignitz-Museum
HR	Harburg über Donauwörth, Fürstlich Oettingen-Wallerstein'sche Bibliothek [in *Au*]
HVl	Hanover, Niedersächsische Landesbibliothek
HVs	——, Stadtbibliothek
Ju	Jena, Universitätsbibliothek der Friedrich-Schiller-Universität
Kl	Kassel, Landesbibliothek und Murhardsche Bibliothek der Stadt
KA	Karlsruhe, Badische Landesbibliothek
KIl	Kiel, Schleswig-Holsteinische Landesbibliothek
KNha	Cologne, Historisches Archiv der Stadt Köln
KNu	——, Universitäts- und Stadtbibliothek
Lr	Lüneburg, Ratsbücherei und Stadtarchiv
LEm	Leipzig, Musikbibliothek der Stadt Leipzig
LEmi	——, Sektion Kulturwissenschaften und Germanistik der Karl-Marx-Universität, Wissenschaftsgebiet Musikwissenschaft (formerly Institut für Musikwissenschaft) [in *LEu*]
LEu	——, Universitätsbibliothek der Karl-Marx-Universität
LÜh	Lübeck, Bibliothek der Hansestadt
Mbm	Munich, Metropolitankapitel [in *FS*]
Mbn	——, Bayerisches Nationalmuseum
Mbs	——, Bayerische Staatsbibliothek
Mh	——, Staatliche Hochschule für Musik
Mo	——, Opernarchiv
Mth	——, Theatermuseum (Clara-Ziegler-Stiftung)
MEIr	Meiningen, Staatliche Museen mit Reger-Archiv
MGmi	Marburg an der Lahn, Musikwissenschaftliches Institut der Philipps-Universität
MGs	——, Staatsarchiv und Archivschule
MH	Mannheim, Wissenschaftliche Stadtbibliothek und Universitätsbibliothek
MHrm	——, Städtisches Reiss-Museum
MÜp	Münster, Diözesanbibliothek, Bischöfliches Priesterseminar und Santini-Sammlung
MÜs	——, Santini-Bibliothek [in *MÜp*]
MÜu	——, Universitätsbibliothek
Ngm	Nuremberg, Germanisches National-Museum
Nst	——, Stadtbibliothek
NEhz	Neuenstein, Hohenlohe-Zentralarchiv

OB	Ottobeuren, Benediktiner-Abtei
Rp	Regensburg, Bischöfliche Zentralbibliothek
Rtt	——, Fürst Thurn und Taxis Hofbibliothek
RH	Rheda, Fürst zu Bentheim-Tecklenburgische Bibliothek [in *MÜu*]
ROmi	Rostock, Institut für Musikwissenschaft der Universität
ROu	——, Wilhelm-Pieck-Universität, Universitätsbibliothek
RUl	Rudolstadt, Staatsarchiv
Sl	Stuttgart, Württembergische Landesbibliothek
SHs	Sondershausen, Stadt- und Kreisbibliothek
SHsk	——, Schlosskirche [in *SHs*]
SWl	Schwerin, Wissenschaftliche Allgemeinbibliothek (formerly Mecklenburgische Landesbibliothek)
SWth	——, Mecklenburgisches Staatstheater
Tu	Tübingen, Eberhard-Karls-Universität, Universitätsbibliothek
W	Wolfenbüttel, Herzog-August-Bibliothek
Wa	——, Niedersächsisches Staatsarchiv
WD	Wiesentheid, Musiksammlung des Grafen von Schönborn-Wiesentheid
WEY	Weyarn, Pfarrkirche [in *FS*]
WIbh	Wiesbaden, Breitkopf & Härtel, Verlagsarchiv
WRdn	Weimar, Deutsches Nationaltheater
WRl	——, Staatsarchiv (formerly Landeshauptarchiv)
WRtl	——, Thüringische Landesbibliothek, Musiksammlung [in *WRz*]
WRz	——, Zentralbibliothek der deutschen Klassik
WS	Wasserburg am Inn, Chorarchiv St Jakob, Pfarramt [in *FS*]
WÜsa	Würzburg, Stadtarchiv
ZI	Zittau, Stadt- und Kreisbibliothek

DK: DENMARK

Kk	Copenhagen, Det Kongelige Bibliotek
Kmk	——, Det Kongelige Danske Musikkonservatorium
Km(m)	——, Musikhistorisk Museum
Sa	Sorø, Sorø Akademis Bibliotek

E: SPAIN

Bc	Barcelona, Biblioteca de Cataluña
Bcd	——, Centro de Documentación Musical
Bim	——, Instituto Español de Musicología
Bit	——, Instituto del Teatro (formerly Museo del Arte Escénico)
Boc	——, Biblioteca Orfeó Catalá
Fbaudot	El Ferrol, G. Baudot-Puentes, private collection
La	León, Catedral
Mc	Madrid, Conservatorio Superior de Música
Mcns	——, Congregación de Neustra Señora
Mm	——, Biblioteca Municipal
Mn	——, Biblioteca Nacional
Mp	——, Palacio Real
Msa	——, Sociedad General de Autores de España
SC	Santiago de Compostela, Catedral
Zac	Saragossa, Archivo de Música del Cabildo

EIRE: IRELAND

Dam	Dublin, Royal Irish Academy of Music
Dtc	——, Trinity College

F: FRANCE

A	Avignon, Bibliothèque Municipale Livrée Ceccano (formerly Musée Calvet)

AG	Agen, Archives Départementales
AIXc	Aix-en-Provence, Conservatoire
AIXm	——, Bibliothèque Municipale, Bibliothèque Méjanes
AM	Amiens, Bibliothèque Municipale
BER	Bernay, Bibliothèque Municipale
BO	Bordeaux, Bibliothèque Municipale
BOLbrindejoint	Boulogne, Y. Brindejoint, private collection
CLO	Clermont-de-l'Oise, Bibliothèque
COGbuckley	Cognac, W. Buckley, private collection
COM	Compiègne, Bibliothèque Municipale
Dc	Dijon, Bibliothèque du Conservatoire
Dm	——, Bibliothèque Municipale
Lm	Lille, Bibliothèque Municipale
LYm	Lyons, Bibliothèque Municipale
Mc	Marseilles, Conservatoire de Musique et de Déclamation
MAC	Mâcon, Bibliothèque Municipale
ML	Moulins, Bibliothèque Municipale
MON	Montauban, Bibliothèque Municipale
NAc	Nancy, Conservatoire
NS	Nîmes, Bibliothèque Municipale
Pa	Paris, Bibliothèque de l'Arsenal
Pbourdon	——, M.-M. Bourdon, private collection
Pc	——, Fonds du Conservatoire National de Musique [in *Pn*]
Pcf	——, Comédie-Française, Bibliothèque
Pi	——, Bibliothèque de l'Institut de France
Pim	——, Institut de Musicologie de l'Université
Plambert	——, Lambert private collection
Pm	——, Bibliothèque Mazarine
Pmeyer	——, André Meyer, private collection
Pn	——, Bibliothèque Nationale
Po	——, Bibliothèque-Musée de l'Opéra
Poffenbach	——, P. Comte-Offenbach, private collection
Prt	——, Office de Radiodiffusion-Télévision Française
Psal	——, Editions Salabert
R(m)	Rouen, Bibliothèque Municipale
Sim	Strasbourg, Institut de Musicologie de l'Université
SA	Salins, Bibliothèque Municipale
SMcusset	St-Maud, F. Cusset, private collection
SRPalmeida	St-Rémy-de-Provence, A. de Almeida, private collection
TLm	Toulouse, Bibliothèque Municipale
V	Versailles, Bibliothèque Municipale

GB: GREAT BRITAIN

ABu	Aberystwyth, University College of Wales
ALb	Aldeburgh, Britten-Pears Library
Bu	Birmingham, University of Birmingham, Barber Institute of Fine Arts
BEL	Belton (Lincs.), Belton House
BRu	Bristol, University of Bristol Library
Ccl	Cambridge, Central Library
Cfm	——, Fitzwilliam Museum
Ckc	——, King's College, Rowe Music Library
Cmc	——, Magdalene College
Cpl	——, Pendlebury Library of Music
Cu	——, University Library
CDp	Cardiff, Public Libraries, Central Library [in *CDu*]
CDu	——, University of Wales College of Cardiff (formerly University College of South Wales and Monmouthshire)
DRc	Durham, Cathedral
En	Edinburgh, National Library of Scotland
Er	——, Reid Music Library, University of Edinburgh
Ge	Glasgow, Euing Music Library
Gm	——, Mitchell Library
Gu	——, University Library
Lam	London, Royal Academy of Music

Lbl	——, British Library (formerly *Lbm*, British Museum)
Lcm	——, Royal College of Music
Lfm	——, Faber Music
Lgc	——, Gresham College (Guildhall Library)
Lkc	——, University of London, King's College
Lmic	——, British Music Information Centre
Lpro	——, Public Record Office
Lu	——, University of London, Music Library
Lue	——, Universal Edition
Lva	——, Victoria and Albert Museum
Lwa	——, Westminster Abbey
LEbc	Leeds, University of Leeds, Brotherton Collection
LVp	Liverpool, Public Libraries, Central Library
Mp	Manchester, Central Public Library, Henry Watson Music Library
NWr	Norwich, Norfolk and Norwich Record Office
Ob	Oxford, Bodleian Library
Och	——, Christ Church
Ouf	——, University, Faculty of Music
SOp	Southampton, Public Library
T	Tenbury, St Michael's College [dispersed: now principally in *F-Pn*, *V*, *GB-Ob*]
TWmacnutt	Tunbridge Wells, Richard Macnutt, private collection
WC	Winchester, Chapter Library

GR: GREECE

Aels	Athens, Ethniki Lyriki Skini
Akounadis	——, Panayis Kounadis, private collection
Aleotsakos	——, George Leotsakos, private collection
Am	——, Mousseio ke Kendro Meletis Ellinikou Theatrou
An	——, Ethniki Vivliothiki tis Ellados [National Library of Greece]

H: HUNGARY

Bn	Budapest, Országos Széchényi Könyvtára
Bo	——, Állami Operaház

HV: CROATIA

Zu	Zagreb, Nacionalna i Sveučilišna Biblioteka

I: ITALY

Ac	Assisi, Biblioteca Comunale
Af	——, S Francesco [in *Ac*]
AC	Acicatena, Biblioteca Comunale
Baf	Bologna, Accademia Filarmonica
Bas	——, Archivio di Stato
Bc	——, Civico Museo Bibliografico Musicale
Bea	——, Biblioteca Comunale dell' Arciginnasio
Bsf	——, Convento di S Francesco
Bsp	——, Basilica di S Petronio
Bu	——, Biblioteca Universitaria
BAc(n)	Bari, Biblioteca Nazionale (Consorziale)
BAn	——, Biblioteca Nazionale Sagarriga Visconti-Volpi
BGc	Bergamo, Biblioteca Civica Angelo Mai
BGi	——, Civico Istituto Musicale Gaetano Donizetti
BRc	Brescia, Conservatorio di Musica
BRq	——, Biblioteca Queriniana
BZtoggenburg	Bolzano, Count Toggenburg, private collection
CAS	Cascia, Archivio di S Rita
CATc	Catania, Biblioteche Riunite Civica e Antonio Ursino Recupero
CATm	——, Museo Belliniano
CCc	Città di Castello, Biblioteca Comunale
CF	Cividale del Friuli, Archivio Capitolare
CHf	Chioggia, Archivio dei Padri Filippini
CMbc	Casale Monferrato, Biblioteca Civica

CNM	Civitanova-Marche, Biblioteca Comunale
CORc	Correggio, Biblioteca Comunale
CR	Cremona, Biblioteca Statale
Fa	Florence, Ss Annunziata
Fas	——, Archivio di Stato
Fbecherini	——, Becherini private collection
Fc	——, Conservatorio di Musica Luigi Cherubini
Fm	——, Biblioteca Marucelliana
Fn	——, Biblioteca Nazionale Centrale
Folschki	——, Olschki private collection
FAN	Fano, Biblioteca Comunale Federiciana
FEc	Ferrara, Biblioteca Comunale Ariostea
FEd	——, Duomo
FERc	Fermo, Biblioteca Comunale
FERd	——, Duomo
FOc	Forlì, Biblioteca Civica Aurelio Saffi
FZc	Faenza, Biblioteca Comunale
Gi(l)	Genoa, Istituto (Liceo) Musicale Paganini; see *Gl*
Gl	——, Conservatorio di Musica Nicolò Paganini
Gim	——, Istituto Mazziniano
Gu	——, Biblioteca Universitaria
IBborromeo	Isola Bella, Borromeo private archive
IE	Iesi, Biblioteca Comunale
La	Lucca, Archivio di Stato
Li	——, Istituto Musicale Luigi Boccherini (incl. Bottini Collection)
Ls	——, Seminario Arcivescovile
LI	Livorno, Biblioteca Comunale Labronica Francesco Domenico Guerrazzi
Mb	Milan, Biblioteca Nazionale Braidense
Mc	——, Conservatorio di Musica Giuseppe Verdi
Mcom	——, Biblioteca Comunale
Mr	——, Archivio Storico Ricordi
Ms	——, Biblioteca Teatrale Livia Simoni
Msartori	——, Claudio Sartori, private collection
Mt	——, Biblioteca Trivulziana e Archivio Storico Civico
MAav	Mantua, Accademia Virgiliana di Scienze, Lettere ed Arti
MAC	Macerata, Biblioteca Comunale Mozzi-Borgetti
MC	Monte Cassino, Biblioteca dell'Abbazia
MOa	Modena, Accademia Nazionale di Scienze, Lettere ed Arti
MOe	——, Biblioteca Estense
MOs	——, Archivio di Stato
Na	Naples, Archivio di Stato
Nc	——, Conservatorio di Musica S Pietro a Majella
Nf	——, Biblioteca Oratoriana dei Padri Filippini
Nlp	——, Biblioteca Lucchesi-Palli [in *Nn*]
Nn	——, Biblioteca Nazionale
OS	Ostiglia, Fondazione Greggiati
Pc	Padua, Biblioteca Capitolare
Pca	——, Biblioteca Antoniana, Basilica del Santo
Pci	——, Museo Civico, Biblioteca Civica e Archivio Comunale
Pi(l)	——, Istituto Musicale (Biblioteca del Liceo Musicale); see *Pl*
Pl	——, Istituto Musicale Cesare Pollini
PAc	Parma, Conservatorio di Musica Arrigo Boito
PAi	——, Istituto di Studi Verdiani
PAt	——, Teatro Regio
PAVu	Pavia, Biblioteca Universitaria
PCcon	Piacenza, Conservatorio di Musica Giuseppe Nicolini
PEc	Perugia, Biblioteca Comunale Augusta
PEl	——, Conservatorio di Musica Francesco Morlacchi
PEsp	——, S Pietro
PEA	Pescia, Biblioteca Comunale Carlo Magnani
PESc	Pesaro, Conservatorio di Musica Gioacchino Rossini
PESr	——, Fondazione Rossini
PIv	Pisa, Teatro Verdi

PLa	Palermo, Archivio di Stato
PLcom	——, Biblioteca Comunale
PLcon	——, Conservatorio Vincenzo Bellini
PS	Pistoia, Cattedrale
PSrospigliosi	——, Rospigliosi private collection
Rasc	Rome, Archivio Storico Capitolino
Rc	——, Biblioteca Casanatense
Rdp	——, Archivio Doria-Pamphili
Ria	——, Istituto di Archeologia e Storia dell'Arte
Rli	——, Accademia Nazionale dei Lincei e Corsiniana
Rmalvezzi	——, Malvezzi private collection
Rmassimo	——, Massimo princes, private collection
Rn	——, Biblioteca Nazionale Centrale Vittorio Emanuele III
Rp	——, Biblioteca Pasqualini [in *Rsc*]
Rps	——, Archivio dei Padri Scolopi (Chiesa di S Pantaleo)
Rrai	——, Radiotelevisione Italiana
Rrostirolla	——, Giancarlo Rostirolla, private collection
Rsc	——, Conservatorio di Musica S Cecilia
Rsp	——, Santo Spirito in Sassia
Rvat	——, Biblioteca Apostolica Vaticana
REm	Reggio Emilia, Biblioteca Municipale
RIM	Rimini, Biblioteca Civica Gambalunga
RVI	Rovigo, Accademia e Biblioteca dei Concordi
Sac	Siena, Accademia Musicale Chigiana
Sc	——, Biblioteca Comunale degli Intronati
SA	Savona, Biblioteca Civica Anton Giulio Barrili
SML	Santa Margherita Ligure, Biblioteca Comunale Francesco Domenico Costa
Tci	Turin, Biblioteca Civica Musicale Andrea della Corte
Tco	——, Conservatorio Statale di Musica Giuseppe Verdi
Tf	——, Accademia Filarmonica
Tmc	——, Museo Civico
Tn	——, Biblioteca Nazionale Universitaria
Tr	——, Biblioteca Reale
TAc	Taranto, Biblioteca Civica Pietro Acclavio
TLp	Torre del Lago, Museo Puccini
TOL	Tolentino, Biblioteca Comunale Filelfica
TRc	Trent, Biblioteca Comunale
TSmt	Trieste, Civico Museo Teatrale di Fondazione Carlo Schmidl
TVco	Treviso, Biblioteca Comunale
UDc	Udine, Biblioteca Comunale Vincenzo Soppi
Vas	Venice, Archivio di Stato
Vc	——, Conservatorio di Musica Benedetto Marcello
Vcg	——, Biblioteca Casa di Goldoni
Vgc	——, Biblioteca e Istituto della Fondazione Giorgio Cini
Vlevi	——, Fondazione Ugo Levi
Vmc	——, Museo Civico Correr
Vnm	——, Biblioteca Nazionale Marciana
Vqs	——, Fondazione Querini-Stampalia
Vs	——, Seminario Patriarcale
Vsm	——, Procuratoria di S Marco
Vt	——, Teatro La Fenice
VEc	Verona, Biblioteca Civica
VEs	——, Seminario Vescovile

J: JAPAN

Tn	Tokyo, Nanki Music Library, Ohki Collection [in Tokyo College of Music Library]

N: NORWAY

Ou	Oslo, Universitetsbiblioteket

NL: THE NETHERLANDS

At	Amsterdam, Toonkunst-Bibliotheek
DHgm	The Hague, Gemeentemuseum
DHk	——, Koninklijke Bibliotheek

NZ: NEW ZEALAND

Wt	Wellington, Alexander Turnbull Library

P: PORTUGAL

Em	Elvas, Biblioteca Municipal
EVc	Évora, Arquivo da Catedral
EVp	——, Biblioteca Pública
La	Lisbon, Palácio Nacional da Ajuda
Lan	——, Arquivo Nacional de Torre do Tombo
Lc	——, Conservatorio Nacional
Ln	——, Biblioteca Nacional
Lt	——, Teatro Nacional de S Carlos
VV	Vila Viçosa, Casa da Bragança, Museu-Biblioteca

PL: POLAND

CZp	Częstochowa, Klasztor OO. Paulinów na Jasnej Górze
Kc	Kraków, Muzeum Narodowe, Biblioteka Czartoryskich
Kj	——, Biblioteka Jagiellońska
Kp	——, Biblioteka Polskiej Akademii Nauk
KA	Katowice, Biblioteka Śląska
LA	Łańcut, Muzeum
Wn	Warsaw, Biblioteka Narodowa
Wtm	——, Biblioteka Warszawskiego Towarzystwa Muzycznego
Wu	——, Biblioteka Uniwersytecka
WRol	Wrocław, Biblioteka Ossolineum Leopoldiensis; see *WRzno*
WRzno	——, Polska Akademia Nauk Zakład Narodowy imienia Ossolińskich

R: ROMANIA

Bc	Bucharest, Biblioteca Centrală de Stat

RU: RUSSIA

KAu	Kaliningrad, Universitetskaya Biblioteka
Mcl	Moscow, Gosudarstvennïy Tsentral'nïy Literaturnïy Arkhiv
Mcm	——, Gosudarstvennïy Tsentral'nïy Muzey Muzïkal'noy Kul'turï imeni M. I. Glinki
Mk	——, Gosudarstvennaya Konservatoriya imeni P. I. Chaykovskogo, Nauchnaya Muzïkal'naya Biblioteka imeni S. I. Taneyeva
Mrg	——, Rossiyskaya Gosudarstvennaya Biblioteka (formerly *Ml*, Lenin Library)
SPan	St Petersburg, Biblioteka Rossiyskoy Akademii Nauk
SPia	——, Gosudarstvennïy Tsentral'nïy Istoricheskiy Arkhiv
SPil	——, Institut Russkoy Literaturï
SPit	——, Gosudarstvennïy Institut Teatra, Muzïki i Kinematografii
SPk	——, Biblioteka Gosudarstvennoy Konservatorii imeni N. A. Rimskogo-Korsakova
SPsc	——, Gosudarstvennaya Ordena Trudovogo Krasnogo Znameni Publichnaya Biblioteka imeni M. E. Saltïkova-Shchedrina
SPtob	——, Tsentral'naya Muzïkal'naya Biblioteka Gosudarstvennogo Akademicheskogo Mariinskogo Teatra Operï i Baleta

S: SWEDEN

L	Lund, Universitetsbiblioteket
Sdt	Stockholm, Drottningholms Teatermuseum
Sic	——, Informationscentral för Svensk Musik
Sk	——, Kungliga Biblioteket
Skma	——, Statens Musiksamlingar (formerly Kungliga Musikaliska Akademiens Bibliotek)
Sm	——, Musikhistoriska Museet [in Skma]
Smf	——, Stiftelsen Musikkulturens Främjande
Ssr	——, Sveriges Radio
St	——, Kungliga Teaterns Bibliotek [in Skma]
Uu	Uppsala, Universitetsbiblioteket

SF: FINLAND

A	Turku [Åbo], Sibelius Museum Musik-vetenskapliga Institutionen vid Åbo Akademi, Bibliotek & Arkiv
Hy	Helsinki, Helsingin Yliopiston Kirjasto

[SLN]: SLOVENIA

Lf	Ljubljana, Knjižnica Frančiskanškega Samostana
Lu	——, Narodna in Univerzitetna Knjižnica

UA: UKRAINE

Kan	Kiev, Tsentral'na Naukova Biblioteka, Akademii Nauk
LV	L'viv, Biblioteka Derzhavnoï Konservatorii imeni N. V. Lysenka

US: UNITED STATES OF AMERICA

AA	Ann Arbor, University of Michigan, Music Library
AUS	Austin, University of Texas
Bm	Boston, University, Mugar Memorial Library
Bp	——, Public Library, Music Department
BApi	Baltimore, Peabody Conservatory of Music; Peabody Institute
BAT	Baton Rouge, Louisiana State University Library
BE	Berkeley, University of California, Music Library
BLl	Bloomington, Indiana University, Lilly Library
BLu	——, Indiana University, School of Music Library
BUu	Buffalo, State University of New York at Buffalo
Chs	Chicago, Chicago Historical Society
Cn	——, Newberry Library
CA	Cambridge, Harvard University Music Libraries
CDs	Concord, New Hampshire State Library
CHH	Chapel Hill, University of North Carolina, Music Library
DN	Denton, North Texas State University, Music Library
Eu	Evanston, Northwestern University Libraries
FAlewis	Farmington (CT), Wilmarth S. Lewis, private collection
G	Gainesville, University of Florida Library, Rare Book Collection
I	Ithaca, Cornell University, Music Library

KBrobbin	Key Biscayne (FL), Leon Robbin, private collection
KC	Kansas City, University of Missouri, Kansas City Conservatory of Music
LAu	Los Angeles, University of California, Walter H. Rubsamen Music Library
LAuc	——, University of California, William Andrews Clark Memorial Library
LOu	Louisville, University, School of Music Library
MAhs	Madison, Wisconsin Historical Society
MED	Medford (MA), Tufts University Library
MSu	Minneapolis, University of Minnesota, Music Library
NH	New Haven (CT), Yale University, School of Music Library
NYbroude	New York, Broude private collection
NYcu	——, Columbia University, Music Library
NYgs	——, G. Schirmer, Inc.
NYj	——, Juilliard School of Music
NYlibin	——, Laurence Libin, private collection
NYp	——, Public Library at Lincoln Center, Library and Museum of the Performing Arts
NYpm	——, Pierpont Morgan Library
NYyellin	——, Victor Yellin, private collection
PHci	Philadelphia, Curtis Institute of Music
PHf	——, Free Library of Philadelphia
PHhs	——, Historical Society of Pennsylvania
PHlc	——, Library Company of Philadelphia
PHu	——, University of Pennsylvania Libraries (Otto E. Albrecht Music Library; Van Pelt Library; Rare Book Collection)
PRu	Princeton, University, Harvey S. Firestone Memorial Library
R	Rochester (NY), University, Eastman School of Music, Sibley Music Library
Su	Seattle, University of Washington, Music Library
SB	Santa Barbara, University of California at Santa Barbara Library
SFp	San Francisco, Public Library, Fine Arts Department, Music Division
SFsc	——, San Francisco State University (formerly State College) Library, Frank V. de Bellis Collection
SLug	St Louis, Washington University, Gaylord Music Library
SM	San Marino (CA), Henry E. Huntington Library and Art Gallery
SPmoldenhauer	Spokane (WA), Hans Moldenhauer, private collection
STu	Stanford, University, Division of Humanities and Social Sciences, Music Library
U	Urbana, University of Illinois, Music Library
Wc	Washington, DC, Library of Congress, Music Division
Ws	——, Folger Shakespeare Library
Wsi	——, Smithsonian Institution, Music Library
WM	Waltham (MA), Brandeis University Library, Music Library, Goldfarb Library
WS	Winston-Salem (NC), Moravian Music Foundation

YU: YUGOSLAVIA

(for libraries in the former republic of Yugoslavia, see also under HV, Croatia; and [SLN], Slovenia)

Bn	Belgrade, Narodna Biblioteka N. R. Srbije

L

CONTINUED

Lonati [Lunati, Leinati, Lainati, Leonati], **Carlo Ambrogio** [Ambrosio] (*b* Milan, *c*1645; *d* ?Milan, *c*1710–15). Italian composer, impresario and singer. He is first heard of in 1665–7 as a violinist of the royal chapel in Naples, where in 1667 he also sang the comic role of Lesbo in a production of Cavalli's *Scipione africano*, whose libretto refers to him as 'milanese'. The records of the Congregazione di S Cecilia show that by 1668 he was in Rome, where he participated in several Roman oratorio productions and (at least from 1673) also served the expatriate Queen Christina of Sweden as leader of her string orchestra. At this time he acquired the sobriquet 'Il gobbo della regina' ('the queen's hunchback'), by which he became widely known. In 1673 he sang the comic role of Vafrindo in Pasquini's *Amor per vendetta* at the Teatro Tordinona. Similar roles that call for a 'gobbo' or 'nano' in operas for the Tordinona (*Il novello Giasone*, 1671; *Eliogabalo*, 1673; *Massenzio*, 1673–4) may also point to his participation. Much speculation about his friendship with Stradella and the scandalous involvement which might have precipitated their departure from Rome in 1677 is based on Giazotto's romantic biography of Stradella (1962), which must be read with caution. In the 1677–8 season he acted as impresario and composer at the Teatro del Falcone in Genoa, where Stradella joined him. There he produced Pasquini's *dramma per musica L'Amor per vendetta* under the title *Amor stravagante* (1677), perhaps with additional music of his own, and his *Amor per destino* to a libretto by Minato. In 1682, after the murder of Stradella and the ensuing investigations, he was deported from Genoa; he applied unsuccessfully to return in 1683. A violinist named 'Gobbo' or 'Gobbetto' figures on the expenses list of S Luigi dei Francesi in Rome in 1682–3. He was definitely in the service of the dukes of Mantua as a 'virtuoso' in 1684–6, when he wrote his *Ariberto e Flavio regi de' Longobardi* for the Venetian Teatro S Salvatore and two works for the Modenese court, the opera *I due germani rivali* and the oratorio *L'innocenza di Davide*; he may also have been responsible for the revival there of Stradella's *Il trespolo tutore* in 1686. He collaborated in several Milanese productions in the 1680s and 90s. The additional arias in the Veronese score of Marc'Antonio Ziani's *Tullo Ostilio* may hint at an activity as reviser of others' operas in that period and region. In a letter from Milan (dated 2 January 1701, in *I-Bc*), the famous castrato Pistocchi mentions a 'scolara del Gobbo del Violino', so

Lonati may also have been a singing teacher. He apparently spent his late years in Milan. He should not be confused with Antonio, Angelo or Ascanio Lonati, who signed several Milanese librettos in the 1670s.

Although Lonati was noted for his violin playing and his instrumental composition, and was said to have been the teacher of Francesco Geminiani, he also made a significant contribution to opera, as both a performer and a composer. Whereas his activity as a singer was primarily in comic roles, his dramatic output belongs to the more serious branch of *dramma per musica*. His Genoese operas seem not to have been very successful despite fine musical writing, especially in those arias accompanied by string orchestra. Notwithstanding their lengthy da capo arias and a penchant for *stile concitato*, his later operas display skilful writing for such obbligato instruments as trumpet, violin and cello, thus revealing the adoption of some stylistic peculiarities developed in northern Italy.

dm – *dramma per musica*

Amor per destino (dm, prol., 3, after N. Minato: *Antioco*), Genoa, Falcone, 1678, *I-Rvat*; rev. as Antioco principe della Siria, Genoa, Falcone, 1690
Ariberto e Flavio regi de' Longobardi (dm, 3, R. Cialli), Venice, S Salvatore, aut. 1684, arias *MOe*
Enea in Italia (dm, 3, G. F. Bussani), Milan, Regio Nuovo, 1686, 2 arias *MOe*; collab. Magni and Ballarotti
I due germani rivali (dm, 3), Modena, Fontanelli, Oct 1686, *MOe*
Scipione africano (dm, 3, Minato), Milan, Regio, 1 Feb 1692, collab. Magni
L'Aiace (dm, 3, P. d'Averara), Milan, Regio, 1694, *US-Cn*; collab. Magni and Ballarotti

Music in: Tullo Ostilio, 1689; Arione, 1694; L'Etna festivo, 1696

*

HawkinsH
F. Raguenet: *Paralèle des italiens et des françois* (Paris, 1702; Eng. trans., annotated, as *A Comparison Between the French and Italian Musick and Operas*, 1709)
A. Bertolotti: *Musici alla corte dei Gonzaga in Mantova* (Milan, 1890)
R. Giazotto: *La musica a Genova* (Genoa, 1951)
A. F. Ivaldi: 'Teatro e società genovese al tempo di Stradella', *Chigiana*, xxxix (1982), 447–574
L. Bianconi and T. Walker: 'Production, Consumption and Political Function of Seventeenth-Century Italian Opera', *Early Music History*, iv, ed. I. Fenlon (Cambridge, 1984), 209–96
J. Lionnet: *La musique à Saint-Louis des Français de Rome au XVIIe siècle*, NA, new ser., iii–iv (1985–6), suppl.
N. Dubowy: 'Pollarolo e Ziani a Verona. Annotazioni in margine a tre partiture ritrovate', *Atti del terzo convegno internazionale sulla musica in area lombardo padana: Lenno-Como 1989* [forthcoming]
NORBERT DUBOWY

London. Capital of Great Britain, and by far the largest city in Europe. It has ancient musical traditions, deriving from its many ecclesiastical institutions, its importance as a court and centre of government and its commercial prosperity, and has been a magnet for musicians from Europe since the 17th century (and more recently the rest of the world, especially the British Commonwealth and the USA). From the 18th century onwards leading opera composers, among them Handel, Bononcini, Gluck, J. C. Bach, Sacchini, Weber, Verdi and Henze, have settled in or visited London to compose for the rich and appreciative audiences. Alongside this cosmopolitan tradition, a vernacular one has maintained an existence at varying levels of success and at a slightly different level of sophistication. The city has always attracted singers and also, since the later years of the 19th century, conductors and directors.

I. History. II. Institutions.

I. History

1. Introduction. 2. The masque tradition and Davenant. 3. 1671–1704: semi-operas and masques. 4. 1705–19: Vanbrugh's theatre and Italian opera. 5. 1719–38: the Royal Academies and their competitors. 6. 1739–78: Italian versus English. 7. 1778–92: the end of the first King's Theatre and the Pantheon. 8. 1792–1829: the second King's and its competitors. 9. 1830–90. 10. 1890–1940. 11. Since 1940.

1. INTRODUCTION. The early history of opera in London encompasses a double tradition. In 'English' form, opera finds its origins in the Stuart court masque and its first flowering in the half-sung, half-spoken 'semi-opera' that reached its zenith in the work of Henry Purcell in the early 1690s. By 1708 the transition to all-sung opera in English was well under way, but a government order temporarily separating operas from plays, along with the importation of high-priced Italian castratos, led rapidly to a tradition of performance in Italian. Unlike inhabitants of most other major opera centres in Europe, Londoners after 1710 saw their main form of opera in a language they could not understand.

A second major peculiarity of opera in London is its commercial basis. The Civil War and the execution of Charles I in 1649 terminated large-scale royal patronage. George I countenanced the establishment of the Royal Academy of Music in 1719 and provided a small subsidy, but his £1000 a year never supplied even as much as 10% of the company's costs. With the exception of a brief and ill-starred attempt to make the Pantheon a kind of court opera (1790–92), opera remained the province of commercial theatres and individual impresarios – aided by shaky season subscriptions and occasionally by individual patrons (notably Lord Middlesex in the early 1740s).

For more than a century the regular season consisted of twice-weekly performances, starting in December or January and totalling about 50 in all. The venue was almost always the King's (or Queen's) Theatre in the Haymarket. Against the grand and very expensive Italian opera, the straight theatres – Lincoln's Inn Fields (then, after 1732, Covent Garden) and Drury Lane – offered more popular fare in English. The ballad-opera boom inaugurated by Gay's *The Beggar's Opera* (1728) was followed by a craze for burletta afterpieces, and eventually by a tradition of native light opera that virtually dominated the English theatre in the late 18th century and early 19th.

From 1830 onwards, London's wealth, population and theatrical and musical resources continued to attract the most eminent performers even when British composers' contribution to the international repertory was small. As compared with orchestral and choral premières, actual first performances of non-British works were few and rarely important, but taste was lively enough to bring the new European repertory quickly across the Channel, at least up to the era of Puccini and Richard Strauss. Two parallel incentives can be seen – to present operas and performers of greatest international fame, and to encourage native talent and a vernacular repertory.

A peculiar (though hardly severe) British limitation on operatic performance was exerted by the compulsory submission of all stage work to the censorship of the Lord Chamberlain's office. Objection was not taken on political grounds, in the way that local Italian censorship had obstructed Verdi, but on the grounds of licentiousness and profanity. *La traviata* escaped a ban (though its source, Dumas' *La dame aux camélias*, did not). Prohibition of biblical events on stage compelled the masking of Verdi's *Nabucco* as *Nino* (the Assyrian king Ninus) in 1846 and would keep Saint-Saëns's *Samson et Dalila* off the British stage until 1900, 23 years after its Weimar première. In 1910 Beecham was unable to show John the Baptist's head in *Salome* and had to change the Baptist's name into one 'Mattaniah the Prophet'. Later Beecham was given the option, in Act 3 of *Der Rosenkavalier*, of either cutting the sung references to the bed or cutting out the bed (he chose the latter). The censor's office was not formally abolished until 1968.

2. THE MASQUE TRADITION AND DAVENANT. Most authorities treat William Davenant's *The Siege of Rhodes* (1656) as the first real opera in London, but it clearly derives both from continental influences and native English developments, particularly the court masque in which Davenant was heavily involved before the Civil War. The court masque itself apparently grew out of an ancient mumming tradition that merged with elaborate continental entertainments, presenting dance, spectacle and allegorical-poetical compliments to a king or noble patron. The masque rose to dizzying heights of spectacle and expense under James I and Charles I (1603–42). The most famous examples are those devised by Ben Jonson and Inigo Jones, notably *The Masque of Queens* (1609), in which the antimasque was first introduced, and *The Gypsies Metamorphosed* (1621). When Jones broke with Jonson in 1631, others filled the place of poet, including Davenant.

Masques are mixed entertainments stressing highly elaborate scenery and costumes and generally lacking much in the way of plot coherence and characterization. Their integral connection with what was to become opera, however, is evident by the time of *Lovers Made Men* (1617), for which the 1640 printing of Jonson's libretto states that 'the whole Masque was sung after the Italian manner, *Stylo recitativo*, by Master Nicholas Lanier' (none of Lanier's music survives). Davenant advanced the masque towards mid-century opera in his *Triumphs of the Prince d'Amour* (1636), with music by the Lawes brothers. All but a prologue is set to music, the work consisting of songs and dumb-show dances in the style of a French *ballet de cour*. Davenant's last masque, *Salmacida spolia* (1640), is similar in conception. Both seem to show the dramatist working towards a sophisticated multi-media form.

Masques were basically single-performance court entertainments employing scenery and machines of a sort virtually unknown in the public theatres. A few, such as the Inns of Court production of James Shirley's *Triumph of Peace* (1634), given at a cost reportedly approaching £10 000, were mounted by wealthy nobles or groups. Had the Civil War not intervened, such entertainments would probably have been transplanted into the public theatre. In 1639 Davenant received a royal patent permitting him to build a playhouse 'behind the Three Kings Ordinary in Fleet-street' and to perform not only plays but 'musical Presentments, Scenes, Dancing or other the like'. Obviously he hoped to present music and spectacle in a fully equipped public theatre, but the Civil War delayed his experiment.

During his Civil War exile, Davenant evidently saw some Italian court operas and *tragédies à machines* at the Théâtre du Marais in Paris. In May 1656, evading the Puritan ban on plays, he offered 'The First Dayes Entertainment at Rutland-House, by Declamations and Musick; after the manner of the Ancients'. At Rutland House, his home in Charterhouse Yard, Aldersgate Street, Davenant fitted up a stage with a curtain at one end of a long room. The prologue asked the audience to 'Think this your passage ... To our Elisian field, the *Opera*'. The following September he mounted *The Siege of Rhodes* in the same venue, with music by Charles Coleman, Henry Cook, Henry Lawes and George Hudson. John Webb provided designs for three 'shutter' scenes and two 'relieves' (the designs are now at Chatsworth House, in Derbyshire). Davenant mounted another such show, *Sir Francis Drake*, in 1659. Following the Restoration he obtained authority from Charles II and converted Lisle's tennis court in Portugal Street into a public theatre capable of scene changes, the first Lincoln's Inn Fields theatre, called the Duke's Theatre. Its exterior dimensions were approximately 23 metres by 9 (recent estimates of capacity vary from 350 to 500), and admission ranged from 1s. (gallery) to 4s. (boxes). The building opened in June 1661 with an expanded version (possibly without music) of *The Siege of Rhodes*, a triumph that forced the rival King's Company to abandon their non-scenic Vere Street theatre and build a theatre in Bridges Street (May 1663), on whose site Drury Lane was constructed in 1674 after a fire. Despite Davenant's fascination with opera, however, he did not mount more operas or semi-operas at Lincoln's Inn Fields before his death in 1668, probably because of its small size and minimal machinery.

3. 1671–1704: SEMI-OPERAS AND MASQUES. In November 1671 the Duke's Company opened their lavish new Dorset Garden Theatre (fig.1), a multi-purpose building designed to accommodate scenic spectacle and operatic extravaganzas. The theatre was on the river's edge, bordering Salisbury Court off Fleet Street; its exterior dimensions were about 17 metres by 45 (recent estimates of capacity hover around 820), and the construction cost amounted to £9000. Interior details have been hotly disputed from minimal evidence, but patterns of use by the United Duke's and King's companies in the 1680s and 90s show that Dorset Garden was a machine house very different from the £4000 Drury Lane of 1674 (about whose interior virtually nothing is known with any certainty).

At least 90% of the repertory at Dorset Garden consisted of ordinary plays (performance records are radically incomplete); semi-operas were a special effort and an occasional treat. The fancy ones required many

1. Engravings from Elkanah Settle, 'The Empress of Morocco' (London, 1673): (above) front elevation of the Dorset Garden Theatre (opened in 1671) where all Purcell's major semi-operas were first performed; (below) stage of the same theatre, with a scene representing a Hell; the setting gives some idea of the elaborate stagings for which this theatre was known (note the room for musicians above the proscenium arch)

2. Stage and proscenium of a theatre, possibly the Queen's/King's Theatre, Haymarket: wash drawing by an unknown artist, first half of the 18th century

months to prepare and investment totally beyond ordinary budgets (up to £3000–4000 against a total annual income of some £8000–10 000). The famous 1670s productions are *The Tempest* (1674), the Shadwell-Locke *Psyche* (1675) and *Circe* (1677). The specialness of these works is demonstrated by their long-standing use as showpieces for foreign dignitaries.

Theatrical hard times during the Exclusion Crisis, a period in the early 1680s when the succession from Charles II to James II was in doubt, delayed further extravaganzas until the Dryden-Grabu *Albion and Albanius* (1685), which was interrupted by Monmouth's invasion and lost at least £2000. Though it failed, *Albion and Albanius* is in fact the first full-length opera in English that survives. In 1690 the United Company mounted the triumphant Betterton-Purcell *Prophetess*, in 1691 the Dryden-Purcell *King Arthur* and in 1692 Purcell's *Fairy-Queen*. The last two were successful but not sufficiently so to justify their enormous costs.

The semi-opera tradition received a dire setback with the early death of Henry Purcell in 1695. In the same year, the actors' rebellion removed Thomas Betterton (the great champion of operatic spectacle) to the cramped old Lincoln's Inn Fields Theatre, reconverted from a tennis court. These two events contributed sub-stantially to the decline of semi-opera. The idea that new operas disappeared from the London stage until the advent of Italian opera and Handel is, however, entirely false. More than 20 new 'operatic' works were staged in this decade.

Between 1695 and 1701 the Patent Company under Christopher Rich mounted a series of semi-operas at Dorset Garden and Drury Lane – *The Indian Queen* (1695; Purcell's last opera), *Brutus of Alba* (1696), the long-popular *Island Princess* (1699), and a pair of original extravaganzas concocted by Elkanah Settle, *The World in the Moon* (1697) and *The Virgin Prophetess* (1701). Betterton fought back as best he could at Lincoln's Inn Fields with a series of musical masques by Peter Motteux and John Eccles, notably *The Loves of Mars and Venus* (1696), on which he collaborated with Godfrey Finger, and *Europe's Revels for the Peace* (1697). More theatrical hard times precluded new opera offerings between 1701 and 1704, but a rising tide of entr'acte songs and instrumental entertainments, and the growing popularity of concerts of all sorts in London, gave promise of renewed interest in opera as soon as an innovatory entrepreneur seized the opportunity. All-sung opera had flourished on the Continent; its importation into London could only be a matter of time.

4. 1705–19: VANBRUGH'S THEATRE AND ITALIAN OPERA.
In spring 1703 John Vanbrugh started plans for a new theatre of his own design (fig.2 and fig.16 below; for further illustration *see* THORNHILL, JAMES), the Queen's (from 1714 the King's) Theatre in the Haymarket. He obtained £100 from each of 30 subscribers (who were to have a lifetime right of free admission) and supplied an unknown amount of capital himself. His plan was to reunite the two theatre companies at his own theatre. As previously in London, opera would be mounted as an occasional treat by a company devoted primarily to plays.

The theatre had outside dimensions of about 18 metres by 40, with a normal capacity of about 760; packed full, it may have held as many as 940 (attendance estimates of up to 2000 in the 1730s were for oratorios, with stage and backstage space used for seating). Vanbrugh's architectural grandiosity and eccentricity were severely modified by alterations made in 1709 for acoustical reasons. With relatively minor changes, the 1709 building was to be London's principal opera house until it burnt down in June 1789.

Vanbrugh intended to open in early 1705 with Clayton's all-sung opera *Arsinoe* (in English), but Rich stole this novelty and mounted it successfully at Drury Lane. Vanbrugh countered with Jakob Greber's *Gli amori d'Ergasto* (in Italian), which struggled through five performances in April 1705. During 1705–6 Rich enjoyed a major triumph with Giovanni Bononcini's *Camilla* (in English); Vanbrugh riposted with two semi-operas (George Granville's *British Enchanters* was a moderate success) and one all-sung pastoral. Convinced that all-sung opera would prove a goldmine, and unable to arrange the 'union' he desired, Vanbrugh wangled an order from the Lord Chamberlain, restricting plays to Drury Lane under Rich and opera to the Haymarket (31 December 1707). Thus in spring 1708 a company tried for the first time in London to offer nothing but opera. The results were a fiasco: Vanbrugh was bankrupt within four months. He was offering translated pasticcios of no distinction, had a wholly inadequate repertory and owed large salaries to imported castratos who could not perform in English.

The operatic history of the next decade was stormy and complex, as managements transmogrified themselves in bewildering ways. Owen Swiney took over for 1708–9, gambling on a star system by bringing in expensive Italian singers. This led, inevitably, to performances given entirely in Italian, starting with *Almahide* (1710) – a practice attacked by Addison in the *Spectator* but impossible to discard if star singers were a *sine qua non*. That Swiney could have run the company profitably seems improbable, but he never really got a chance to try.

The Lord Chamberlain silenced Drury Lane in June 1709, thereby creating a dual company at the Haymarket for 1709–10. Four nights a week were devoted to English plays, two to Italian operas. In 1710–11 plays returned to Drury Lane, and opera held sway at the Haymarket under the dilettante management of William Collier and Aaron Hill. The major event of the season was the arrival of Handel in London and the première of his *Rinaldo* (24 February 1711). Handel's first London opera was a considerable success, but management was acutely unstable. Hill was summarily dismissed as manager after the third night of *Rinaldo*, and arguments over responsibility for debts to tradesmen for fabric and timber wound up in Chancery.

The company was so short of cash that Linike, the copyist, was allowed by the Lord Chamberlain to collect the parts and take them home after performances until he was paid the £26 he was owed. A major reorganization occurred in spring 1712 but proved short-lived. Owen Swiney resumed control at the Haymarket, then fled to the Continent the following January, bankrupt. The performers carried on as a cooperative, evidently with J. J. Heidegger as manager, but extant records show woefully short-paid salaries.

During the next four seasons (1713–17) the opera barely survived. Handel was available and Heidegger was a competent manager, but opera simply could not attract enough attendance to pay its costs. Ticket prices generally ran about double those for plays (8s. versus 4s. at the top mark). The first few performances of a new production were usually offered as a 'subscription', but even if fully taken up such subscriptions could not pay for an elaborate new production. Managers were caught in a double-bind: to attract a fashionable audience, fabulous salaries had to be paid to foreign stars (Nicolini got 800 guineas a season, plus a benefit), yet the prices necessary to support such salaries proved prohibitive. Meanwhile, the opera suffered from musical competition at the playhouses. The Lord Chamberlain never formally rescinded his prohibition on musical entertainments at Drury Lane, but it soon fell into disregard. Especially after 1714, when Lincoln's

3. Caricature of Francesca Cuzzoni (left) and Farinelli, with J. J. Heidegger the impresario (seated): etching (c1735) by Joseph Goupy after Marco Ricci

Inn Fields reopened, the straight theatres competed aggressively with each other and with the Haymarket opera, using musical works to do so.

During the last season of Italian opera in this initial period, 1716–17, Heidegger managed only 31 performances (including six by subscription and eight benefits), and his cashbook (now in the Essex Record Office) makes clear why he abandoned the cause as hopeless. Meanwhile, at Lincoln's Inn Fields, John Rich presented, besides plays, 36 performances of full-length operas (in English). The works included *The Island Princess*, *The Prophetess* and *Camilla* – that is, both semi-opera and all-sung opera in the new 'Italian' manner. Lincoln's Inn Fields' singers were not the biggest stars (though Margherita de L'Epine, Jane Barbier and Richard Leveridge were far from negligible), but at bargain rates they attracted audiences. Drury Lane, meanwhile, countered with musical masques as afterpieces, notably Pepusch's *Venus and Adonis* and *Apollo and Daphne*.

As of spring 1717 when Heidegger's company closed, the taste for Italian opera appeared to be a fad that had run its course. The logic of the situation suggested that 'serious' opera should migrate back to the regular theatres, which could use it as an occasional treat in English. The actual course of events was to be entirely different.

5. 1719–38: THE ROYAL ACADEMIES AND THEIR COMPETITORS. By January 1719 plans were afoot to re-establish Italian opera by obtaining letters patent for incorporating a joint-stock company under royal charter devoted to that purpose. A prospectus was circulated in about April, and in May George I granted a subsidy of £1000 a year. The royal charter was issued in July, by which time some 60 persons had taken at least one share of £200. Handel was dispatched to the Continent to hire singers. The patent (now in the Public Record Office) spells out the unique governance of this company, which was an odd amalgam of royal household entertainment and publicly held joint-stock company. The 'Governor' was to be the Lord Chamberlain, who held veto power in all matters, but each November stockholders were to elect 15–20 directors, on whom operational responsibility devolved. The company would have £10 000 in pledged capital (it actually obtained about £15 000 in pledges), but hoped to call no more than 20% of it. (The prospectus suggests that a subscriber might have to put up £40 and could expect a 25% annual return – a calculation reflecting prevalent South Sea speculative fever more than reality.) 'General Courts' of stockholders would be held at least every three months. The company rented Vanbrugh's Haymarket theatre. Its normal ticket price settled at a startling 10s. 6d. (5s. for the gallery); subscribers for season tickets paid £15

4. *'Masquerades and Operas'* (or *'The Bad Taste of the Town'*): engraving (1724) by Hogarth satirizing the prevailing taste for Italian music and architecture. On the left a fool leads an audience into the King's Theatre where Italian operas and masquerades were performed (the impresario J. J. Heidegger leans out of the window); in the foreground traditional works of English drama are wheeled away in a barrow. On the right crowds throng to a pantomime (the allusion is probably to 'Harlequin Dr Faustus', first performed at Rich's Lincoln's Inn Fields Theatre in 1715). The three figures in front of Burlington Gate link these examples of debased taste with the fashionable world of aristocratic patronage; one of them, Lord Burlington, patron of the new Palladian architecture, was also a patron of Handel and much involved in Italian opera.

(later £20) for 50–60 nights, while boxes, generally rented for the season, were extra. Performances were given twice a week from roughly December to June, on Tuesday or Wednesday and Saturday. Members of the royal family attended regularly.

The era of the 'First Academy' (1720–28) was artistically probably the pinnacle of opera in London. From 1720–21 to the collapse of the bankrupt company in 1728 Senesino was its principal performer. Francesca Cuzzoni joined in 1722–3 and Faustina Bordoni in 1725–6, giving the company three reigning international stars in addition to Handel. Unfortunately, rivalry between the two women and their supporters created severe tensions and even public disruption during a performance. Letters of the librettist Paolo Rolli and those of Owen Swiney (serving as continental agent and talent hunter) give a vivid idea of just how wracked by infighting the company was. Government by dilettante committee proved inefficient. The company quickly ran through all the pledged capital it could collect (and threatened defaulters with public exposure); in fact records contained in the Portland Papers (University of Nottingham) suggest that the venture was financially doomed from the start. But all such matters of infighting and insolvency pale into insignificance when considered against the artistic achievement of the company, however short-lived. The dozen operas Handel wrote for its eight and a half seasons represent one of the great achievements in the history of opera. Some of the highlights were *Radamisto* (1720), *Floridante* (1721), *Giulio Cesare in Egitto* and *Tamerlano* (1724), and *Tolomeo* (1728). By no means was the company devoted entirely to Handel's work: it opened in April 1720 with Rolli and Porta's *Numitore*, and in its early years both Handel and Bononcini had partisans among the directors.

No Italian opera was performed in London in 1728–9. A session of the remaining Royal Academy shareholders voted in January 1729 to let Handel and Heidegger have the use of their scenery and costumes for five years, and the so-called Second Academy opened in December 1729 – initially without Senesino, an effort at cost-cutting. The nature of its financial backing is unknown. The king continued his £1000 subsidy, and private patrons probably helped as well. The reconstituted company operated less lavishly, but artistically much as before. Handel's *Poro* (1731) and *Orlando* (1733) were among its offerings. What little is known of the number of performances and of box-office receipts is unimpressive. The venture had 170 subscribers in 1731–2, and only 140 in 1732–3 (of whom 122 seem to have paid in full). None the less, losses incurred by the Second Academy were probably not more than patrons could bear; its demise came about for other reasons.

Handel and Senesino came to an unfriendly parting of ways in June 1733, and mounting personal hostility to Handel in society circles produced one of the oddest developments in the chequered history of opera in London – the establishment of the Opera of the Nobility, a rival Italian opera company. If one company could not make ends meet, a second was definitely a bad idea, and both companies were to go dismally broke in the course of the next three seasons.

The Opera of the Nobility opened at the third Lincoln's Inn Fields Theatre (vacant since 1732) in December 1733 with Porpora's *Arianna in Nasso*; Handel riposted at the King's Theatre, Haymarket, with *Arianna in Creta* in January 1734. During this season Handel mounted 60 performances (including oratorios),

5. *Ticket for a performance of 'The Beggar's Opera' at Covent Garden (possibly on 15 March 1737) for the benefit of Thomas Walker who had created the role of Macheath at Lincoln's Inn Fields in 1728: engraving by J. Sympson (the younger) after Hogarth*

his rivals 52, with both companies insisting on performing on Tuesday and Saturday nights in direct and destructive opposition to each other. At the end of the year, in circumstances that remain mysterious, the Opera of the Nobility took over the King's Theatre, Haymarket, and Handel became a part-time tenant of John Rich's at Covent Garden. In 1734–5 the Opera of the Nobility hired the glamorous Farinelli and Handel was virtually beaten from the field – though he probably lost a lot less money. By the spring of 1737 Rich claimed to be unable to pay his ground rent on account of opera losses; Handel had a stroke in May; and the great opera war was over. Handel joined Heidegger and the remnants of the Opera of the Nobility at the King's Theatre, Haymarket, during 1737–8, but attempts to raise a subscription for 1738–9 failed, and the Italian opera collapsed for the third time in just over 20 years.

While Italian opera was experiencing artistic triumph but financial ruin, musical entertainment in English was for the most part flourishing. The popular English musical forms of the 1710s continued to thrive in the 20s, and *The Beggar's Opera* had a totally unprecedented success at Lincoln's Inn Fields in 1728, changing the whole face of London entertainment. Gay's oddity enjoyed a staggering 62 performances in its first half-season and spawned a tremendous boom in ballad opera in both mainpieces and afterpieces. Music virtually flooded the legitimate stage, mostly in decidedly popular forms. The suggestion that serious opera might improve its position by returning to English was put forward more than once. Aaron Hill urged Handel to 'deliver us from our *Italian bondage*' in a famous letter of 1732. Others had similar ideas, and the prospective availability of Lincoln's Inn Fields in 1732 helped generate some attempts at the establishment of an English opera company. Thomas Arne senior, styling himself 'Proprietor of the English Operas', staged several works including Lampe's *Amelia* (March 1732 at the Little Theatre in the Haymarket), J. C. Smith's *Teraminta* (November 1732) and his own son's *Rosamond* (March 1733). These experiments attracted little support: plenty of music was available at Drury Lane and Covent Garden, and English opera could not compete with the Italian in social glamour.

6. *Title-page of the first edition of Stephen Storace's 'The Siege of Belgrade' (London: Joseph Dale, 1791), showing Thomas Greenwood's design for Act 1 scene i in the original production at Drury Lane, 1 January 1791*

6. 1739–78: ITALIAN VERSUS ENGLISH. Handel abandoned Italian opera in 1741, and for the next 40 years the history of the form in London is a dizzying sequence of changing managements and a tale of artistic mediocrity. Throughout this period the King's Theatre in the Haymarket continued to serve as venue and the basic season remained as before – performances on Tuesday and Saturday from December to June, with a total of roughly 50–60 nights. Ticket prices remained at half a guinea, but managers could not afford the fabulous fees that had brought the likes of Senesino, Cuzzoni and Farinelli to London. Artistically the pasticcio reigned supreme. Music was provided by or filched from Galuppi, Pergolesi, Guglielmi, Hasse, J. C. Bach, Porpora, Veracini, Gluck, Sacchini, Paisiello and a host of others. The King's Theatre company rarely mounted more than ten operas a season, and a large majority were never revived. No more than 15% were newly composed for London, and as time went on, comic opera and ballet loomed increasingly large in the company's operations.

In this period, management was acutely unstable. In 1741 30 gentlemen pledged £6000 as a subsidy for four years, but the company lost about £3800 each season and survived only two. This venture was headed by Lord Middlesex, who tried to carry on by himself and did manage to bring Gluck to London for 1745–6. Middlesex's venture had collapsed by the end of 1749 and there was a hiatus until 1753, when Domenico Paradies and Francesco Vanneschi organized a company, surviving two years. 12 separate opera managements can be identified between 1741 and 1778, when the opera house, bought by Richard Brinsley Sheridan and Thomas Harris, entered, incredibly, on an even more unstable phase of its stormy history. Despite occasional rumours of substantial profits, there is no evidence that any of the impresarios made their expenses for long, let alone a surplus.

Meanwhile at Covent Garden and Drury Lane, musical entertainments in English were proving very profitable indeed. Although the Licensing Act of 1737 produced a lengthy drought in new works of all kinds, the enormous popularity of the Carey-Lampe afterpiece *The Dragon of Wantley* (1737) foreshadowed the English opera boom of the 1760s. This was inaugurated, ironically, by T. A. Arne's *Artaxerxes* (Covent Garden, February 1762), an all-sung English version of Metastasio's *Artaserse* that was regularly revived well into the 19th century. It was followed by lighter fare, with many of the librettos provided by Isaac Bickerstaff. *Love in a Village* (December 1762) was a pasticcio arranged by Arne from more than 15 sources, with some original music of his own. Other great successes at Covent Garden were the Bickerstaff-Arnold *Maid of the Mill* (1765; a charming musical treatment of Richardson's *Pamela* of 1740) and the Bickerstaff-Dibdin *Lionel and Clarissa* (1768). Sheridan's *The Duenna*, with music by the Linleys, ran a startling 75 times in 1775–6, and in the next two decades Storace concoctions such as *The Haunted Tower* (1789) and *The Siege of Belgrade* (1791) made enormous profits for Drury Lane. Such works had plenty of 'serious' Italian music in them, but were offered as part of the regular six-days-a-week theatrical repertory at the patent theatres, always in English and at less than half the price of Italian opera. In the third quarter of the 18th century opera was flourishing in London – but at the King's Theatre, Haymarket, it had become a decidedly sickly and uninspiring venture.

7. 1778–92: THE END OF THE FIRST KING'S THEATRE AND THE PANTHEON. In 1778 Thomas Harris and R. B. Sheridan, the principal owner-managers of Covent Garden and Drury Lane respectively, bought the King's Theatre for £22 000 (of which £12 000 was mortgaged). Their plans were not clear: reportedly they intended to use the dormant Killigrew patent of 1662 to authorize a third playhouse. As events fell out, their purchase was the first step into legal snarls from which neither the first King's Theatre nor its successor was to recover for more than half a century. G. A. Gallini bought the mortgage and tried to take over the theatre in 1780; Sheridan

bought out Harris and then sold his interest to William Taylor, who was to remain the evil genius of Italian opera in London until 1815. Gallini and Taylor spent the 1780s fighting for control of the theatre.

In 1782 Taylor had the interior of the building virtually gutted and rebuilt by Michael Novosielski. The result was a shallower working stage, a large pit and an auditorium with five shallow tiers in horseshoe form; the capacity was just over 1800. Taylor's artistic policy was not markedly different from that of his predecessors, but he was the first manager in many years to spend freely and promote aggressively. The immediate outcome was bankruptcy: he was arrested for debt in May 1783 and Gallini regained control at a sheriff's auction. Taylor then challenged the sale in court, and the theatre fell into the hands of trustees, including the profligate Novosielski. The affairs of the King's Theatre in the mid-1780s are a tangle of recriminatory pamphlets and Chancery actions no one has ever yet quite sorted out. Gallini managed the theatre from 1785 to 1789, despite Taylor's determined efforts to evict him.

When the King's Theatre burnt down on 17 June 1789 the situation became even more chaotic. Taylor and Gallini both wanted to rebuild but could not agree to cooperate. During summer and autumn 1789 at least four more schemes were proposed for the future of Italian opera in London. Unlike the other theatres, the King's had operated since 1740 entirely under short-term licences granted by the Lord Chamberlain: anyone who could cajole a licence (or better, a patent) out of the government could run an opera company. The scheme that found royal favour was officially put forward (most improbably) by an impecunious law clerk and amateur architect named Robert Bray O'Reilly; in fact he was simply front man for a cabal of nobles headed by the Duke of Bedford and the Earl of Salisbury (who happened to be Lord Chamberlain). They enjoyed the political, if not financial, support of the Prince of Wales. Salisbury arranged for a 31-year patent grant to O'Reilly, the plan being that the noble backers would erect a glamorous new theatre along French architectural lines on the north side of Leicester Square. (An architectural plan, of disputed authorship, is now in Sir John Soane's Museum, London.) The theatre was designed to hold only about 2300 people and had a staggering projected cost of £150 000. The scheme fell through because Taylor and shareholders in the King's Theatre violently protested at being deprived of the opera licence, and the Lord Chancellor refused to let the patent grant pass the Great Seal.

In summer 1790 affairs took a bizarre turn. Taylor scrounged up backers and commissioned Novosielski to rebuild the King's Theatre (fig.17 below), taking care to make the building extend substantially beyond the original site so he could not readily be dispossessed by the ground lessee when his sublease expired in 1803. Taylor proceeded with the new building – it opened in February 1791, measured about 28 metres by 52 and had a capacity of over 3000 – even though Salisbury awarded a four-year opera licence to O'Reilly for performance at another venue. This was the Pantheon in Oxford Street, erected by James Wyatt in 1772 as an elegant exhibition space and now hastily altered for use as an opera house at a cost of some £22 000. London had not managed to keep its one opera house out of bankruptcy and now it was going to have two expensive modern theatres built for the purpose, only one of which would have a licence. For the new King's Theatre Taylor

hired dancers and Joseph Haydn, used his new building as a concert hall, and bided his time. Haydn even composed an *opera seria* for London, *L'anima del filosofo* (though in the event it was never performed).

Until the recent discovery of the company's papers in the Bedford Estates Office, London, little was known about the rival Pantheon operation beyond the works it performed and the names of its principal performers – a strong company including Mara, Pacchiarotti and Didelot. In fact the enterprise was a deliberate attempt to change the nature of the opera establishment in England. The Pantheon was conceived as a kind of 'court opera', in which more of the financial burden was to be borne directly by noble patrons, thus freeing the company to pursue innovations in opera and ballet and to hire the best performers in Europe. To compete against Haydn at the King's, the Pantheon tried (unsuccessfully) to hire Mozart. Artistically its backers were committed to the old-fashioned *opera seria*, costly and tending to appeal to only a small, élite audience. But as the hastily mounted season of 1790–91 demonstrates, they were willing to support this preference with a second company devoted to *opera buffa*. Unfortunately very little went right. The company gave 55 performances during 1790–91 and lost a startling amount of money. The luckless O'Reilly was forced to flee to France, though some of his creditors successfully sued the lawyer who represented the invisible noble backers.

Four performances into the season of 1791–2, the Pantheon burnt to the ground under highly suspicious circumstances (the insurance company refused to pay), and the venture finished the spring in makeshift conditions at the Little Theatre in the Haymarket, a road house used primarily for variety entertainments and as a summer theatre. The highlight of the season was Paisiello's *La locanda*, specially composed for London. Evidence in the Bedford papers suggests that the Pantheon's backers killed it off when they realized that not even a princely subvention would be adequate to support *opera seria* in the fiercely competitive and highly pluralistic London theatre world. The Pantheon was an adventurous but doomed experiment, and it seems to have lost more than £40 000 in its two seasons.

8. 1792–1829: THE SECOND KING'S AND ITS COMPETITORS. The burning of the Pantheon solved the city's two-opera-house problem, and on 24 August 1792 a General Opera Trust Deed was signed, a kind of peace treaty intended to restore amity and fiscal responsibility. It did not work on either count. Trustees were to be appointed and any profits of the new King's Theatre in the Haymarket used to pay off the Pantheon's debts. The wily William Taylor somehow succeeded in evading the trustee provision. Taylor was anxious to build a large adjoining concert room and did so at a cost of some £35 000, obtaining the money by selling rights in 41 (later 68) boxes until 1825. The significant loss of income this entailed was partly offset by raising the annual subscription to 25 guineas for the usual total of 50 performances.

Management never stabilized. Taylor managed the theatre while technically in a debtors' prison (except between 1797 and 1802, when he was MP for Leominster). He was forced to sell part of his interest to Francis Gould in 1803 and 1804, but after Gould died in 1807 Taylor and Edmund Waters, Gould's executor, fought so viciously for control that they virtually paralysed the theatre. The King's was dark in 1813 while the rebuilt Pantheon tried to regain the Italian opera. Waters eventually bought and sued his way into control of the King's but went irretrievably bankrupt in 1820. Management was then assumed by John Ebers, whose artistically creditable but financially disastrous reign is chronicled in detail in his *Seven Years of the King's Theatre* (1828). The theatre lost £44 000 during Ebers's management, despite his steadfast refusal to pay the outrageous salaries demanded by top stars.

The artistic quality of King's Theatre productions varied widely in the early 19th century. The presence of Lorenzo da Ponte, house poet at the theatre, 1794–1804, promised much; but while he wrote a few original librettos for Martín y Soler, Bianchi and Winter, his gifts were squandered on producing substitute arias and pasticcios. Gradually pasticcios gave way to productions of successful foreign operas. Many works by Paisiello, Cimarosa, Sarti, Gazzaniga, Salieri and Portogallo were given for the first time in London, as well as the English premières of *Alceste, Iphigénie en Tauride, La clemenza di Tito, Così fan tutte, Die Zauberflöte, Le nozze di Figaro, Don Giovanni* (highly successful in 1817), Rossini's *Il barbiere di Siviglia, Elisabetta, regina d'Inghilterra, L'italiana in Algeri, La Cenerentola* and *Tancredi*. Leading singers continued to appear, including Banti, Kelly, Grassini, Naldi, Catalani (hired in 1807 by Gould, who had to pay her the unprecedented salary of £5250 for the season), Nicolas Levasseur, Pasta (making her London début in 1817), Ambrogietti, Angrisani, Camporese and Crivelli. Even under Ebers's solid management, however, no important new operas were commissioned. The emphasis was on Rossini – *La gazza ladra* was a success-

ful novelty in 1821 – though in 1825 Ebers's director, William Ayrton, mounted the first Meyerbeer opera to be heard in London, *Il crociato in Egitto*. Among the singers in this period were Brambilla, De Begnis, Pasta (making a second London début), Malibran and the castrato Velluti.

Throughout these three and a half decades the Italian opera was hamstrung by its own endless internecine disputes and its crippling mortgages: the wonder is that it kept going at all. Its competitors had their own troubles, but in general the economic status of English-language opera fared better. In 1792 Covent Garden had been expanded to seat some 3000 spectators, and Drury Lane was completely rebuilt by Henry Holland, expanding to a capacity of 3611 in 1794. These theatres burnt down in 1808 and 1809 respectively, and had to be replaced at mind-boggling cost. Robert Smirke's vast 1809 Covent Garden cost £188 000 and turned out to be a white elephant.

Both the patent theatres continued to feature music in their offerings. Their approach is typified in the work of Henry Bishop, who was musical director of Covent Garden between 1810 and 1824 and later worked at Drury Lane. His wholesale rewritings of Mozart and Rossini have made him the target of much derision in later histories of music, but they were successful at the time. Bishop popularized good music, and for his achievement he was knighted by Queen Victoria in 1842 – the first English musician to be so honoured. A description by a German visitor gives some idea of his *Marriage of Figaro* at Drury Lane in November 1826: 'Neither the Count, the Countess, nor Figaro sang; these parts were given to mere actors, and their principal songs, with some little alteration in the words, were

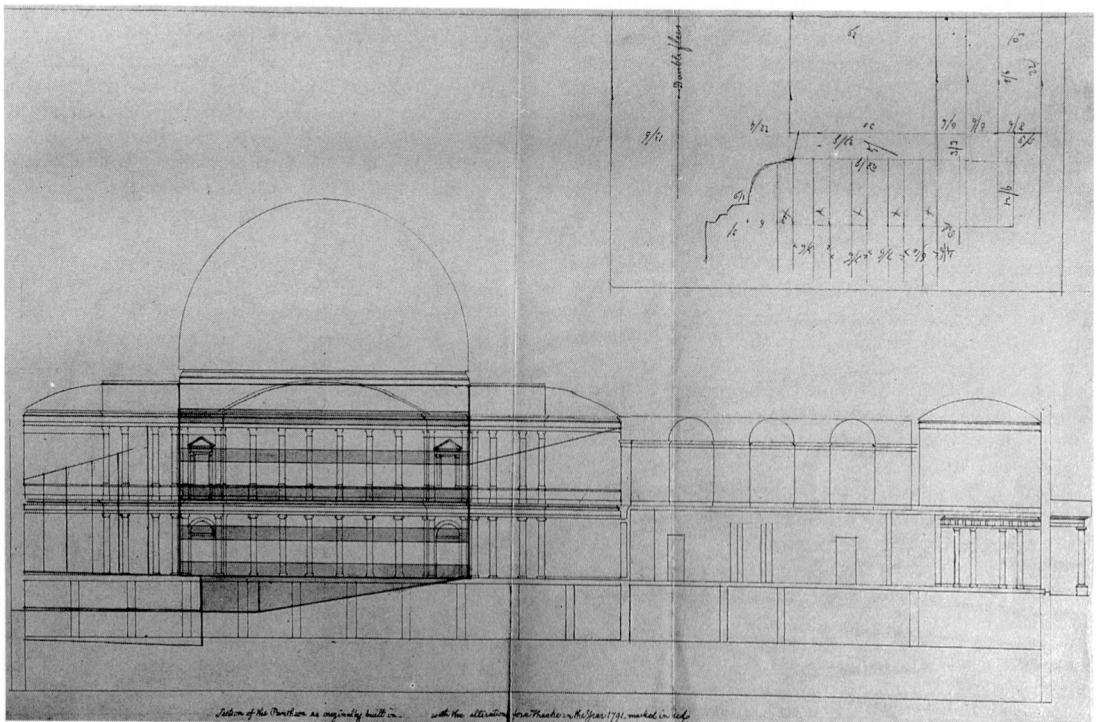

7. *Section of the Pantheon, London, showing proposed alterations for conversion to an opera house in 1791. The shaded areas indicate five tiers of boxes and (at basement level) the orchestra and a raked pit (stalls); the four vertical lines running up to a slanted line left of the dome suggest wing positions, and the slanted line right of the dome, a gallery. The single line above the fifth tier of boxes probably represents a ceiling added later to eliminate echo from the dome.*

8. Playbill for a production of Mozart's 'Così fan tutte', as 'Tit for Tat', at the Lyceum Theatre, 29 July 1828 (the second half of the evening consisted of a performance of George Rodwell's 'The Bottle Imp')

First Night of the New Grand Comick Opera.

Theatre Royal, English Opera House, Strand.

This Evening, TUESDAY, JULY 29th, 1828,

Will be performed (FIRST TIME) A NEW GRAND COMICK OPERA, The MUSICK from the masterly Compositions of MOZART,
to be called

TIT FOR TAT;
OR
THE TABLES TURNED!
ALTERED AND ADAPTED FROM THE
"COSÌ FAN TUTTE."

The whole of the MUSICK under the superintendance of Mr. HAWES, who will preside at the Piano-Forte.
The CHORUSSES conducted by Mr. J. T. HARRIS.—The new and Splendid SCENERY executed by Mr. TOMKINS and Mr. PITT.
The DRESSES by Mr. HEAD and Mrs. STILLMAN.

Ferrando, Guglielmo, } *Two Young Italian Officers,* { Mr. WOOD, Mr. THORNE,

Alfonso, Mr. H. PHILLIPS,

Masqueraders, Soldiers, Domestics, &c

Messrs. Birt, Bowman, Brady, East, Fuller, Green, Henshaw, Irwin, Jones, Lodge, Miller, G. Miller, Sherreff, Walsh, Willing, Wills.
Mesdames and Misses Barnett, Clarke, Ibbs, Jerrold, Lodge, Perry, Phillips, Rumens, Tennant, Walsh, Wills, Willmott.

Fiordiligi, Dorabella, } *Two Sisters,* { Miss BETTS, Miss CAWSE,

Despina, *(their Servant)* Madame FERON.

The following NEW SCENERY incidental to this Opera:

INTERIOR OF AN HOTEL, IN NAPLES.—Pitt.
VESTIBULE OF A VILLA, WITH A DISTANT VIEW OF THE BAY.—Tomkins. AN APARTMENT IN THE VILLA.—Pitt.
A GARDEN.—Tomkins. TERRACE OVERLOOKING THE BAY.—Tomkins. A PARK.—Tomkins. GRAND SALOON.—Tomkins and Pitt.
After which, (Twentieth Time) an entirely new OPERATIC ROMANCE, in Two Acts, called THE

sung by the other singers; to add to this, the gardener roared out some interpolated popular English songs'. Another famous 'Mozartian perversion' was the production of *Così* at the Lyceum in 1828 as *Tit for Tat*, translated by S. J. Arnold and with the music arranged by William Hawes (see fig.8). What could be heard quasi-authentic at the King's could be heard in cheaper and perhaps more accessible form at Covent Garden and Drury Lane, and increasingly elsewhere as well.

Technically the Licensing Act remained in force, but after 1800 the authorities became more lenient about tolerating various fringe and musical enterprises. Two theatres are particularly important. The Lyceum (on Wellington Street, off the Strand), built in the 1770s as an exhibition and concert hall, was licensed for musical works in 1809 and rebuilt in 1816 as the English Opera House, a function it served until it burnt in 1830 (to be rebuilt again, in 1834). The Royal Coburg on Waterloo Road (which was to become the Old Vic) opened in 1818. It served primarily as a venue for melodrama.

The early history of *Der Freischütz* in London shows how the theatres competed. Weber's opera had enjoyed a great triumph in Berlin in 1821. In February 1824 a version of it was given at the Royal Coburg as a 'legendary melodrama' under the title *The Fatal Marksman* – without mention of Weber in the playbill. The Lyceum mounted it in July as an opera, translated as *Der Freischütz, or The Seventh Bullet*, the music adapted by Hawes. In August and September it was given in different forms at the Royal Amphitheatre and the Surrey Theatre. Covent Garden mounted it in October in an adaptation by J. R. Planché with the music arranged by Barham Livius; Drury Lane's version (with additional music by Bishop) was presented in November. The popularity of all the adaptations led to Charles Kemble's invitation to Weber to compose an English opera for Covent Garden. Weber was too ill to accept Kemble's additional offer to become music director, though he wrote *Oberon* and conducted the première; he was frustrated by the demands of 'English' form, but still gave London its first important opera première in a very long time.

There is no precise dividing line between 18th- and 19th-century opera production in London, but by the end of the Ebers administration at the King's Theatre, quite different circumstances obtained from those at the turn of the century. Despite the importation of Mozart and Rossini by the Italian opera company, activity at the King's remained in many respects extremely old-fashioned and indeed increasingly derivative. The competition from English comic opera at the patent theatres increased sharply and threateningly after 1810. New venues sprang up, and the English theatres were aggressive in mounting current continental works as well as offering their own home-grown brand of opera. The ineffective competition put up by the King's Theatre is only partly attributable to the innate unprofitability of full-fledged opera: there were plenty of potential patrons who were never attracted. Much of the problem must be imputed to the impresario system and the horrible financial snarls from which the King's Theatre was never able to extricate itself.

9. 1830–90. The greatest prestige lay with 'the Royal Italian Opera' – a title properly belonging to an annual subscription season (by social custom confined to the summer months) and not to the theatre in which it was located. It was run, like all other British operatic enterprises, as a private speculation. Benjamin Lumley, manager of the Royal Italian Opera at Her Majesty's Theatre from 1842 to 1858, remarked in his *Reminiscences* on the difference from 'similar enterprises on the Continent, [where] the enormous expenses of operatic undertakings are often lightened to managers by Government subventions'.

Both at Her Majesty's (known as the King's Theatre until Victoria's accession in 1837) and at Covent Garden after the establishment of a rival Royal Italian Opera there in 1847, the staple diet was of Italian opera by living or recent composers – principally Rossini, Bellini, Donizetti and Verdi. Ballet was also included in the season. The Italian operas (which included the sole opera written by Verdi especially for London, the unsuccessful *I masnadieri*) were supplemented by other recent works in Italian translation, all sung by a company specially contracted for the season.

Thus it was in Italian that Berlioz's French opera *Benvenuto Cellini* had a single and disastrous performance at Covent Garden in 1853 under the composer's baton; in 1858 Balfe's popular English opera *The Bohemian Girl* had to become *La zingara* before it could enter the repertory of Her Majesty's. (Balfe had actually composed his *Falstaff* in Italian for Her Majesty's Theatre 20 years before.) Meyerbeer's *Les Huguenots* achieved its huge popularity at Covent Garden as *Gli Ugonotti*, both in a celebrated production of 1848 and later. Similarly, *Faust* was first heard in London (1863) in Italian; so was *Carmen* (1878). Wagner arrived in London in the shape of *L'olandese dannato* (as *Der fliegende Holländer* was billed in the Drury Lane production of 1870). There was also a demand for Mozart (Lumley noted this as evidence of English operatic sophistication), particularly *Le nozze di Figaro* and *Don Giovanni*. The occasional appearance of *Die Zauberflöte*, given as *Il flauto magico*, entailed the provision of Italian recitatives to replace the spoken dialogue; a similar surgery was performed for *Fidelio* and *Der Freischütz*.

9. *Giulia Grisi in the title role of Bellini's 'Norma' (Act 2 scene i), which she sang almost every season from 1837 until 1861 at both Her Majesty's Theatre and Covent Garden: lithograph from a contemporary sheet music cover*

The performers on what Lumley called 'the Anglo-Italian boards' were by no means all of Italian origin. The vocal distinction of Italians such as Grisi, Tacchinardi-Persiani, Rubini, Mario, Tamburini and Lablache (all of whom made London débuts in the 1830s) was equalled by that of Viardot, Lind and Tietjens (French, Swedish and German respectively, with débuts in 1839, 1847 and 1858). The leading British tenor and baritone, Reeves and Santley, likewise participated in Italian-language seasons. The 'queen' of opera in the second half of the century was Patti, who was only 18 when she made her London début in 1861 as Amina in *La sonnambula* and who became London's first Aida in 1876 (both at Covent Garden). The

conducting rested principally in Italian hands – notably those of Costa and Arditi, both of whom made England their home. Costa is credited with the firm establishment of the baton-conductor's command in London opera (replacing the old division of authority between key-boardist and first violin), and his decision to quit the Lumley administration at Her Majesty's was a major factor in the setting up of the new Covent Garden regime under his conductorship. The British composers Balfe and Benedict were also intermittently engaged as conductors.

The performance of French and German opera in their native tongues rested almost entirely on occasional visits by foreign companies. At the King's Theatre (still under that name), London's first season of German opera took place in 1832: performances were given of *Fidelio*, with Schröder-Devrient playing Leonore, and *Der Freischütz*. The impact of an intelligent, active chorus, instead of the usual 'scarecrows', was remarked on by the most celebrated critic of the time, Chorley (quoted by White 1983, p.258). The visit of a Brussels company to Covent Garden in 1845 is notable for showing the popularity of Auber's music up to this time: *La muette de Portici* and two other works by him were among the 11 operas staged. Short seasons of French opera were independently promoted at the St James's Theatre in 1854, at the Gaiety Theatre in 1885 (with the first London performance of Delibes' *Lakmé*), and at Her Majesty's in 1886.

Wagner in German arrived with performances of the *Ring* given at Her Majesty's in May 1882 by a German company under Seidl, followed in the same month by another German company with performances of *Lohengrin*, *Der fliegende Holländer* and *Tannhäuser* at Drury Lane, Richter conducting. The idea of an italianized repertory as enshrining the most precious traditions of opera was dead; the regime at Covent Garden, soon to change its title to Royal Opera (and from 1889 admitting languages other than Italian in performance) did no more than recognize the fact.

Various managements, without the prestige of the Royal (Italian) Opera but nevertheless with considerable support, pursued the promotion of opera in English. The history of these schemes has been set out in some detail by White (1951, 1983): the more important may be mentioned here, with further discussion under the respective companies and theatres. The rebuilt Lyceum Theatre was opened in 1834 as the English Opera House (a name it first acquired in 1816): works by Loder, Balfe and others were given up to 1840. At Drury Lane, Bunn as manager presented no less a star than Malibran in English versions of *Fidelio* and *La sonnambula* and then in Balfe's *The Maid of Artois* (1836); under Bunn's management more than 20 new British works were given at Drury Lane between 1835 and 1849, of which Balfe's *The Bohemian Girl* (1843) and Wallace's *Maritana* (1845) were long to remain popular.

The title of Royal English Opera (Queen Victoria's name appeared among the subscribers) was used by the Pyne-Harrison management for its winter seasons of opera in English at Covent Garden from 1858–9 until 1863–4. The company had played in the two previous seasons at the Lyceum and at Drury Lane. The greater part of its repertory was of new or recent operas by British composers, including the first production of Benedict's *The Lily of Killarney* (1862), supplemented by such works as Flotow's *Martha* and Verdi's *Il trovatore*. There was talk of a state subsidy for this company on the German example, supposedly with the encouragement of the Prince Consort; his death in 1861 removed the possibility and deprived English opera of an active patron. The Queen, whose first state visit to the opera had been to Balfe's *The Siege of Rochelle* at Drury Lane in 1837 shortly after her accession, ceased to attend theatres after the Prince Consort's death.

In 1873 the Carl Rosa Opera Company, after having taken opera in English on tour in the USA, began its British operation with performances in Manchester and gave its first London season (at the Princess's Theatre) in 1875. Its general repertory ran from Mozart to brand-new Massenet, the first British performance of *Manon* being included in its Drury Lane season of 1885. Up to Rosa's death in 1889 a substantial number of new works were commissioned from composers such as Cowen, Goring Thomas, Mackenzie and Stanford: none has remained in the repertory. But the company itself was to remain a chief national purveyor of opera in English until after World War II, its significance being that (unlike all the previous enterprises referred to) its basis was national touring with regular London visits.

In 1875, on the initiative of the impresario J. H. Mapleson, the foundation stone was ceremonially laid of a new 'Grand National Opera House', the programme of which was specifically to include 'the works of English composers, represented by English performers'. It was never built, the site eventually becoming that of New Scotland Yard. In the same year, a modest beginning was made to an enterprise that developed major proportions: at the Royalty Theatre, where Richard D'Oyly Carte was business manager, the one-act *Trial by Jury*, with words by W. S. Gilbert and music by Sullivan, was produced in support of the main-piece, Offenbach's operetta *La Périchole* (in English).

A succession of further pieces made Sullivan the best-known British theatrical composer, established the fortunes of the D'Oyly Carte Opera Company, and added to the capital's landscape the Savoy Theatre (fig.10) and the Savoy Hotel. Of these pieces *The Mikado* (1885) became the most-travelled English opera (or operetta) between *The Bohemian Girl* and *Peter Grimes*. Meanwhile Offenbach's own operettas, which had been presented in London in both French and English since 1857 (under theatrical rather than operatic management), remained popular. His *Whittington* was specifically written for the Alhambra Theatre as a Christmastide entertainment in 1874. The so-called comedy opera *Dorothy*, by Sullivan's associate Alfred Cellier, outstripped with 931 performances even the run of *The Mikado* and, as the inaugural production of George Edwardes's management of the Gaiety Theatre in 1886, heralded the theatrical genre now known as musical comedy.

10. 1890–1940. Whereas Mapleson had got no further than laying a foundation stone, Carte actually constructed a new theatre, named the Royal English Opera House, for the launching of Sullivan's one 'serious' opera, *Ivanhoe* (1891). He applied to that genre the principle hitherto attaching only to plays and operettas – that of uninterrupted nightly performances (with changing casts). Even a run of 160 performances did not sufficiently repay Carte's investment, nor did a subsequent English-language version of Messager's *La basoche* (a Parisian success from the Opéra-Comique), and in 1892 Carte sold the theatre, now the Palace

Theatre. (The buyer was Sir Augustus Harris, already the lessee of Covent Garden and Drury Lane.) Messager was to retain strong connections with London, not only as composer and conductor but as manager at Covent Garden (1901–7) on behalf of the Grand Opera Syndicate, which took control in 1896 after Harris's death.

In international seasons with (mainly) continental soloists, performances in the original language now gradually displaced the previous Italian, or italianized, performances. In 1892, when Covent Garden marked that displacement by a change in nomenclature from Royal Italian Opera to Royal Opera, Mahler appeared there at the head of a contingent from the Hamburg Opera and conducted the *Ring*. Throughout these decades Covent Garden remained, under successive changes of management, London's pre-eminent international house. Intermittent challenges came, however, from other theatres. At Covent Garden itself, moreover, the Royal Opera's own 'grand seasons' in summer were often equalled in importance by the presentations of other managements renting the theatre at other times of the year.

Singers heard during the grand seasons up to 1914 included such stars as Lilli Lehmann, Melba and (from 1901) Caruso, the last two a famous leading pair in *La bohème* (which had actually been introduced to Covent Garden by the Carl Rosa company, in English, at one of its 'subsidiary seasons' in 1897). Successive works by Puccini gained the public excitement which those of Verdi had formerly done, but this was also a period when the prestige of French opera was sustained in repeated performances of works by Bizet, Gounod (*Roméo et Juliette* as well as *Faust*), Massenet and Saint-Saëns. Both Debussy's *Pelléas et Mélisande* and Charpentier's *Louise* received their first London performances (at Covent Garden) in 1909. Exceptional in the grand seasons was the first production in English of the *Ring* in 1908 – at the direct instigation of the conductor, Hans Richter, who spoke proudly of '*our* English opera' and bitterly of the Covent Garden management's subsequent abandonment of it.

In 1910 Beecham arrived at Covent Garden – not in the grand season, but using his family wealth to present his own seasons on either side of it, some 17 weeks in all. His productions included the first performances in Britain of Strauss's *Salome* and *Elektra* and of Delius's *A Village Romeo and Juliet*. Already, in summer 1909, he had given the first British performance of Smyth's opera *The Wreckers* at His Majesty's (as that theatre had been renamed). In 1910, between his own two Covent Garden seasons, he went back to His Majesty's for a prodigious three-month summer season that embraced the first British performance of Strauss's *Feuersnot*, a revival of Stanford's *Shamus O'Brien* (1896) and three Mozart operas including *Così fan tutte*, then a considerable rarity.

A public plea by Stanford, in a paper of 1908, for the foundation of a new national opera house supported by public subsidy gained no official backing. But in 1911 London unexpectedly acquired a new opera theatre when the German-born American impresario Oscar Hammerstein (senior) built the London Opera House, which later became the Stoll Theatre. Two short seasons in 1911–12, with a roster of artists less lustrous than Covent Garden's, were financially disastrous and ended Hammerstein's venture. Beecham's challenge, however, continued in 1913 with a six-week season at Covent

10. Interior of the Savoy Theatre during the opening run of Sullivan's 'Patience' in 1881, showing the newly installed electric lighting

Garden, which brought the first British performances of *Der Rosenkavalier*, and a later season at His Majesty's with the first British performance of *Ariadne auf Naxos* (in its original version, Sir Herbert Beerbohm Tree's company giving the preceding performance of Molière's *Le bourgeois gentilhomme*).

Another important step was also taken on Beecham's initiative in 1913, though not involving him as conductor. Dyagilev, who had already created a sensation in London with his ballet performances (1911), brought a Russian opera company to Drury Lane, Shalyapin opening the season in the title role of *Boris Godunov* (in the Rimsky-Korsakov edition then in use), followed by *Khovanshchina* and *The Maid of Pskov* (under the name of *Ivan the Terrible*). Though Russian opera was not absolutely new to London (*A Life for the Tsar* had been given in Italian at Covent Garden in 1887, and *Yevgeny Onegin* in English at the Olympic Theatre in 1892), there had been nothing like this. Not only Shalyapin, 'but the whole company with its wonderful chorus and completely revolutionary style of operatic acting … made an impact on London such as had not been experienced since the first performances in England of the *Ring* and *Tristan* in the 1880s' (Rosenthal 1958, p.378).

While the Carl Rosa company continued its activity, giving the first performances in Britain of Humperdinck's *Hänsel und Gretel* at Daly's Theatre (no longer existent) in 1894, another touring enterprise, the Moody-Manners Company, led a shorter but vigorous existence from 1898 to 1916; it occasionally occupied Covent Garden for its London seasons. The most enduring of all ventures into giving opera in English had meanwhile begun in the 1880s at what was familiarly known as the Old Vic, where operatic performance was

at first confined (because of the limitations of a music-hall licence) to extracts and tableaux. With the succession of Lilian Baylis as acting manager from 1898 (and sole manager from 1912) came full operatic presentations, albeit with reduced orchestra. Edward J. Dent exercised beneficent influence both as one of its governing body and as a provider of outstandingly successful translations – an influence that continued when an expansion of the enterprise in 1931 took in the newly rebuilt Sadler's Wells Theatre.

At first opera and spoken drama were given at both theatres, but opera became concentrated at Sadler's Wells (where what became the Vic-Wells Ballet was also located). The repertory of Sadler's Wells Opera, as it was now called, embraced several Russian works, the original version of *Boris Godunov* receiving there its first performance in Britain (1935). Here too Holst's *Sāvitri* and Vaughan Williams's *Hugh the Drover*, though not new, encountered their first regular audiences, in a repertory which in the first six years extended to more than 50 operas.

Independently, two remarkable ventures ran successfully on the principle of nightly, uninterrupted performances. Rutland Boughton's opera *The Immortal Hour* (originally staged at the composer's own Glastonbury Festival in 1914) achieved 216 performances at the Regent Theatre, King's Cross, in 1922–3; *The Beggar's Opera* in a new musical edition by Frederic Austin opened at the Lyric Theatre, Hammersmith, in 1922 and broke records with its 1463 performances.

At Covent Garden the vicissitudes of operatic management between the wars were interlocked with the various enterprises of Beecham, including the British National Opera Company (BNOC) and the Imperial League of Opera. Under the latter's auspices at Covent

Garden (and not in the grand season), Beecham gave the first British performance of Delius's *Koanga* in 1935. Among international artists Bruno Walter became a well-loved figure (but Toscanini never conducted opera in London); Melba, Gigli and Pinza were adored stars in the Italian repertory and Lotte Lehmann, Elisabeth Schumann and Lauritz Melchior in the German. After Puccini's death (1924), Strauss became the only living composer whose place in this context was secure. (In 1936 Strauss himself conducted the visiting Dresden company in performances of *Ariadne auf Naxos* in its second version.) To the British composer-conductor Eugene Goossens was given the honour of writing a new work in George VI's coronation year, 1937 – but neither this *Don Juan de Mañara* nor Goossens's earlier *Judith* (1929) won success.

11. SINCE 1940. World War II silenced opera at Covent Garden from 1940 until 1945. Sadler's Wells Opera maintained rather more than a vestigial existence, with the New Theatre as a temporary home, and returned to its own theatre in 1945 with the historic first performance of *Peter Grimes* (Goodall conducting, Pears in the title role; fig.11). Covent Garden had a visit from the S Carlo Opera of Naples before its own combined opera and ballet companies presented Purcell's *The Fairy-Queen*. Ballet and opera henceforth shared the theatre equally. The new financial factor in British operatic promotion was the steady provision of state subsidy to opera through the Arts Council. Both the Covent Garden Opera Company (as the postwar company was called until its change in 1968 to Royal Opera) and Sadler's Wells Opera (in 1974 renamed English National Opera) remained dependent on it. A

11. Scene from the original production of Britten's 'Peter Grimes' (Act 1 scene ii) at Sadler's Wells in 1945, with Peter Pears in the title role

continuity of management was established for both companies, which henceforth dominated the London opera scene (their histories are given more fully below: see §II, 2, Covent Garden, and §II, 1, English National Opera).

There was hardly any challenge from speculative impresarios between the Stoll Theatre seasons of Italian opera of 1946–8 and the arena-style performances at Earls Court of *Aida* (1988) and *Carmen* (1989), to audiences exceeding 14 000. There were, however, a few short-term productions of a more specialized nature, including three importations of New York casts: a double bill of Menotti's *The Medium* and *The Telephone* at the Aldwych Theatre in 1948, Menotti's *The Consul* at the Cambridge Theatre in 1951, and Gershwin's *Porgy and Bess* at the Stoll in 1952. The work of other London-based operatic enterprises, smaller in scale and not competing with the two permanent companies, is described below in §II, 1 and 3.

The Sadler's Wells repertory established for opera in English a firmer foothold than ever before; at Covent Garden a brief indulgence in opera in English gave way to the pre-war ideal of international opera in (mainly) the original languages. The immediate postwar era brought stars such as Hotter (making his London début in 1947), Gobbi (1950), Callas (1952), Christoff (1949), Sutherland (1952) and Geraint Evans (1948); some notable black American artists emerged, including Dobbs (1954) and Bumbry (1963). Among conductors Kleiber, Solti, Kubelik and Kempe exercised decisive authority, as did the British conductors Colin Davis and Charles Mackerras, whose careers embraced both London opera houses. To Kubelik and Mackerras is particularly due the important British cultivation of Janáček, and Mackerras's conducting of *Le nozze di Figaro* at Sadler's Wells in 1965 was an early instance of what would later be called an 'early music' or 'authentic' approach to Mozart.

Above all, however, this was the era when the 'producer' (British opera companies generally retained this rather outdated term for stage director) took on an increasingly conspicuous role. At Covent Garden the arrival of the Italians Visconti (1958) and Zeffirelli (1962) had a notable impact, as did the work of Peter Hall from 1965. The greater freedom claimed by the producer (including the choice of stage designer) brought a widespread departure from the more or less literal staging that had previously been the norm. Successive stagings of the *Ring* at Covent Garden furnished remarkable examples of this, as also of the rapid obsolescence of productions. On the other hand, economy was served in having more and more productions there borrowed from, or shared with, other companies both British and foreign.

New operas by Britten, apart from those given under his own auspices by the English Opera Group, appeared at Covent Garden, which also took responsibility for *Peter Grimes* in two productions (1947, 1971) – Peter Pears and Jon Vickers singing the title role in the respective first-night casts. Among other composers whose new works were given, from Vaughan Williams to Peter Maxwell Davies, Tippett with four operas established the most conspicuous presence. Sadler's Wells (later ENO) gave new British works by Blake, Birtwistle and others. Of non-British composers after Stravinsky, Henze was the best represented in London, from *Boulevard Solitude* (New Opera Company, 1962) to *We Come to the River*, a Covent Garden commission produced in 1976. Homage to the Second Viennese School was paid with a belated first British staging of *Wozzeck* (1952, under Kleiber), and later of *Moses und Aron* (1965, under Solti) and of the complete *Lulu* (1981, under Colin Davis), all at Covent Garden.

Handel's operas, confined to rare and specialized revival in previous decades, now earned a more general exposure, from Covent Garden's *Alcina* with Sutherland (1962) to the ENO's *Giulio Cesare* with Janet Baker and Valerie Masterson (1979). At first, the heroic castrato parts were reallotted to tenors, Richard Lewis singing the title role in the Handel Opera Society's production of *Riccardo primo* in 1964. But by the mid-1970s such roles, along with the castrato roles in Mozart's *Idomeneo* and *La clemenza di Tito*, were usually restored to original pitch, either by female impersonation of the male characters or by the employment of countertenors, among whom James Bowman won prominence. In the operatic use of period instruments, however, London was slow to follow where Kent Opera had led, and Covent Garden's first hearing of such instruments was a Sunday performance of Rameau's *La princesse de Navarre* in 1977, one of the adventurous promotions of the English Bach Festival, which also used the historic Banqueting House in Whitehall for Handel's *Acis and Galatea* and other works.

An increased interest in Baroque opera by no means decreased the taste for Wagner. London was the only city in the world where two companies more or less simultaneously staged the *Ring*. The Sadler's Wells Opera production in Andrew Porter's English version brought particular acclaim for the conducting of Reginald Goodall and had been made possible by the company's move in 1968 to a much larger (and more central) location, the Coliseum. Another production that filled the large stage to no less splendid a musical effect was Prokofiev's *War and Peace* in 1972, translated and conducted by David Lloyd-Jones – the opera's first performance in Britain. Earlier acquaintance with important Soviet operas had come with Shostakovich's *Katerina Izmaylova* (at Covent Garden under Edward Downes, 1963) and Prokofiev's *The Fiery Angel* (New Opera Company under Leon Lovett, 1965).

The 1980s saw no new singers rivalling the international stars who had consolidated their reputations in earlier decades, among them Pavarotti, Domingo and the London-trained, part-Maori soprano, Kiri te Kanawa. To a greater degree than ever, the staging and design of opera was subjected to the imposition of directors' 'concepts', overlaying the original libretto: in 1989, a Napoleonic setting for Cherubini's *Médée* at Covent Garden (London's first staging with authentic French spoken dialogue) was an egregious and derided example. On the other hand, some equally drastic transformations at the ENO had artistic cogency and considerable success, including an updated *Hänsel und Gretel* (fig.12, page 20) and a 'de-Japanned' *Mikado*, the respective directors being David Pountney and Jonathan Miller.

The tightening of the national economy in the 1980s caused financial worries and an increased drive to find in private sponsorship what the state would not provide. Several new productions were postponed or abandoned, some smaller enterprises ceased and a promisingly launched New Sadler's Wells Opera (based on operetta) came to grief after a few seasons. The D'Oyly Carte Opera Company ceased operations in 1982 but was revived in 1988. As a whole, London opera remained richly varied. Covent Garden presented Stockhausen's *Donnerstag aus Licht* and Berio's *Un re in ascolto* and received important visits by the Kirov Opera from Leningrad and the Komische Oper from East Berlin. The ENO staged Ligeti's *Le Grand Macabre* and found one of its greatest box-office successes in Glass's *Akhnaten* (the only American opera to make an impact on London since Menotti's *The Consul*). A new stage capability at the Queen Elizabeth Hall accommodated productions by David Freeman's Opera Factory and a few other groups. The solidity at London's operatic centre was indeed happily supported by an irrepressible effervescence at its fringe. Unfamiliar Rossini sung in a suburban back garden to the accompaniment of period instruments – the achievement of Midsummer Opera – aptly exemplified this in 1989.

II. Institutions

1. Companies. 2. Theatres. 3. Miscellaneous institutions.

1. COMPANIES. Below are listed, in alphabetical order, opera companies active exclusively or principally in London. British companies active only occasionally in London, and possibly with an administrative base there, are listed in the dictionary under their own names: *see* BRITISH NATIONAL OPERA COMPANY; CARL ROSA OPERA COMPANY; CHELSEA OPERA GROUP; DENHOF OPERA COMPANY; ENGLISH OPERA GROUP; INTIMATE OPERA COMPANY; KENT OPERA; MOODY-MANNERS COMPANY; OPERA FOR ALL; OPERA RESTOR'D; and PHOENIX OPERA.

Beecham Opera Company. A company organized and largely financed by Sir THOMAS BEECHAM during World War I. Its nucleus was formed by British artists who had appeared in earlier Beecham seasons at His Majesty's Theatre and Covent Garden, including Perceval Allen, Agnes Nicholls, Frederic Austin, John Coates, Walter D'Oisly, Frederick Ranalow and Robert Radford, reinforced by members of the Denhof company, which Beecham took over in 1913 after its collapse. The company opened in October 1915 at the Shaftesbury Theatre: the première of Stanford's *The Critic* was conducted by Eugene Goossens and that of Smyth's *The Boatswain's Mate* by the composer. After a further London season at the Aldwych Theatre came one at the Queen's Theatre, Manchester, which, to quote Beecham, 'was the turning-point in the career of the company. Overnight it evolved from the chrysalis state of a smallish troupe of Opéra Comique dimensions into the full growth of a Grand Opera organization'. Seasons alternated between Manchester and London, with a move to the Theatre Royal, Drury Lane, in summer 1917. Having acquired scenery from the Dyagilev company in 1914, Beecham was able to give the first performances in English of such works as *Prince Igor*, *Boris Godunov* and *The Maid of Pskov* (as *Ivan the Terrible*). Other productions, variously in the original languages and in translation, embraced Mozart, Verdi (including *Otello* and *Falstaff*) and Wagner. In the casts were the singers Miriam Licette, Mignon Nevada, Frank Mullings and Norman Allin, the conductors (besides Beecham himself) being Aylmer Buesst, Albert Coates, Julius Harrison, Percy Pitt and both Eugène Goossens and his son Eugene Goossens.

Beecham as lessee of Covent Garden in 1920 brought his company to play there (with the first performance in English of *Parsifal*, 1919), but his unsuccessful 'grand season' with international singers compelled him to put the British company into voluntary liquidation. The BRITISH NATIONAL OPERA COMPANY succeeded it in 1922.

Betterton's Company. A theatre company based at the second Lincoln's Inn Fields Theatre, 1695–1705; led by Thomas Betterton and including Elizabeth Barry and Anne Bracegirdle, it was made up of actors rebelling against the tyranny of Christopher Rich at Drury Lane. Because Lincoln's Inn Fields was small and scenically inadequate, Betterton was unable to mount the fancy semi-operas for which he was famous. He did, however, produce a large number of small-scale masques and similar musical entertainments, most of them composed by John Eccles. One of the most successful was *The Loves of Mars and Venus* (1696), set by Eccles and Godfrey Finger. The company gave the public première of Purcell's *Dido and Aeneas*, interpolated into an adaptation of *Measure for Measure* in 1700. The actors transferred to Vanbrugh's elegant new Queen's Theatre in the Haymarket in April 1705, at which time Vanbrugh became the manager.

Covent Garden Opera Company. See §2, Covent Garden.

D'Oyly Carte Opera Company. The management under which the Gilbert and Sullivan operettas, and a few other works, were presented by RICHARD D'OYLY CARTE and his successors. Carte's association with W. S. Gilbert and Arthur Sullivan actually began (with *Trial by Jury*, 1875) when he was working under Selina Dolaro's management at the Royalty Theatre; he then, with others, formed the Comedy Opera Company, which presented *The Sorcerer* (1877) and *HMS Pinafore* (1878) at the Opera Comique Theatre. Thereafter Carte on his sole account contracted the librettist and composer. His new productions began with *The Pirates of Penzance* on the last day of 1879 in New York, Sullivan conducting a British cast that Carte had brought on a major tour of the USA and Canada. (His usual managerial form at that time was 'Mr R. D'Oyly Carte's Opera Company'.) Continuing success led to Carte's building of the Savoy Theatre, where he presented the later works of the pair (and a few by other librettists and composers). Extensive provincial touring meant that Carte had commonly several companies in being. Without interrupting the London run of *The Mikado* (1885, with a record 672 performances), he took a whole cast of soloists and chorus to give *The Mikado* in New York a few months after its London opening. In 1886 a continental tour embraced Vienna, where *The Mikado* drew Hanslick's enthusiasm.

On Carte's death the business was administered by his widow Helen and then by a son of a previous marriage, Rupert D'Oyly Carte. Under the latter, what had been a company for new productions (and a few revivals) was successfully turned into a repertory company, playing extensively on tour and in London seasons principally at the Prince's Theatre, 1919–26, and at a rebuilt Savoy Theatre. *Cox and Box* (words by F. C. Burnand) was admitted to the canon along with the Gilbert works. Successive recordings were made of the well-known pieces, many under Isidore Godfrey, musical director from 1929 to 1968. Leading artists remained with the company for many years, notably the comedian Henry Lytton from 1884 to 1934.

Directed after 1948 by Bridget D'Oyly Carte, Rupert's daughter, the company profited by a monopoly on British stage performances, which expired on the last day of 1961 (the year-end following the 50th anniversary of Gilbert's death). Thereafter challenges came in performances of the operettas by Sadler's Wells Opera and other companies. Though it was not true that the D'Oyly Carte company followed literally every element of staging in Gilbert's prompt-books, a stress on 'the tradition' remained. Anthony Besch's new production of *The Gondoliers* in 1968 (Saville Theatre, Shaftesbury Avenue) marked the company's first departure from certain older stage traditions. At a time when other opera companies received Arts Council support (the D'Oyly Carte never did), its commitment to year-round touring was no longer financially sustainable. The performing company disbanded in 1982, its final London season having taken place at the Adelphi Theatre. The management remained in being (servicing, as it always had, amateur societies) and was thus able to launch a new company in 1988, with Bramwell Tovey as musical director. After a tour, the first London season was at the Cambridge Theatre, the second (1989) at the Savoy. John Pryce-Jones became musical director in 1990, but was replaced by John Owen Edwards on the eve of the 1992 tour. The company moved its headquarters to Birmingham in 1991.

Duke's Company. A company founded in 1660 by Sir William Davenant with the patronage of the Duke of York under a royal patent granted by Charles II. It occupied the first Lincoln's Inn Fields Theatre from 1661 to 1671, when it moved into the new Dorset Garden Theatre. Davenant opened in 1661 with a revamped version of his own 'opera' *The Siege of Rhodes* (1656) and he employed large quantities of music, song and dance in his play productions, but not until after his death in 1668 did the company occupy a theatre in which its founder's lifelong penchant for spectacle and opera could be fully developed. Under the artistic management of Thomas Betterton in the 1670s the Duke's Company became famous for its 'multimedia spectaculars', notably *The Tempest* (1674), the Shadwell-Locke *Psyche* (1675) and *Circe* (1677). In 1682 the Duke's Company absorbed the rival King's Company, creating what is now generally called the United Company. Through Christopher Rich, who later became principal owner of the United Company, and his son John Rich, who built Covent Garden, the Covent Garden Theatre Royal of the 18th and 19th centuries can be traced as the direct lineal descendant of the Duke's Company.

English National Opera (ENO). A permanent company devoted to performance in English. Now a year-round operation drawing a state subsidy second only to that of Covent Garden, it traces its origins directly to the performances of operatic excerpts and tableaux at the Old Vic before 1900. The enterprise became firmly established as Sadler's Wells Opera in 1935, retaining that name until 1974 though it moved from Sadler's Wells Theatre to the Coliseum six years earlier.

Opera at the Old Vic was due to the management of Lilian Baylis, first assisting her aunt, Emma Cons, from 1898, and then on her own from 1912. The first complete opera given was *The Bohemian Girl* in 1900, and the Baylis regime was grounded on a sharing of the theatre by what became 'the opera company' (always performing in English) and 'the Shakespeare company'. Self-contained ballet was added only in 1928 (becoming the Vic-Wells Ballet, later the Sadler's Wells Ballet). In order to establish a north London counterpart to the

Old Vic (itself lying just south of Waterloo Bridge), a charitable enterprise was founded to buy the old Sadler's Wells Theatre and rebuild it. The new theatre opened in 1931, giving a mixed fare of opera, Shakespeare and ballet, just as happened at the Old Vic; but from the 1935–6 season, spoken drama was concentrated at the Old Vic while Sadler's Wells became the home of opera and ballet.

By 1931 the opera company had already built a repertory of nearly 30 operas. *The Bohemian Girl*, *Maritana* and *The Lily of Killarney* still kept their place alongside works such as *Il trovatore*, *Lohengrin* and *Tosca*; less familiar additions included *Dido and Aeneas*, *La fille du régiment*, *Les contes d'Hoffmann*, *Un ballo in maschera* and *Yevgeny Onegin*. The singers included Joan Cross, Edith Coates, Rose Morris, Constance Willis, Sumner Austin, Arthur Carron, Tudor Davies, Powell Lloyd and Henry Wendon. Charles Corri (1861–1941), who had worked at the Old Vic from 1895, continued as the company's musical director until 1935. He then retired in favour of Lawrance Collingwood, who had been associated with the Old Vic since 1920. Collingwood's long connection with opera in Russia (he had been Albert Coates's assistant in pre-war St Petersburg) led to the British premières of *The Snow Maiden*, *The Tale of Tsar Saltan* and (in 1935) the original version of *Boris Godunov*; his own opera *Macbeth* was produced in 1934.

Both the repertory and company grew apace until World War II, with excellent productions of *Fidelio*, *Die Meistersinger*, *Die Walküre*, *Der Rosenkavalier*, *Don Carlos* and *Falstaff*, this last much praised by Toscanini. British works produced up to the end of the 1938–9 season included Benjamin's *The Devil Take Her* and Smyth's *The Boatswain's Mate* (both, on occasion, conducted by Beecham), as well as *Hugh the Drover*, *The Wreckers* and *The Travelling Companion*. In 1933 when the orchestra was increased to 45 players, Warwick Braithwaite joined the conducting staff. Singers, recruited by the season but with strong continuity, included Janet Hamilton-Smith, Jeanne Dusseau, Audrey Mildmay, Ruth Naylor, Gladys Parr, Owen Brannigan, Redvers Llewellyn, Arnold Matters, Ronald Stear and John Wright. Occasional guest appearances were made by such outstanding British singers as Florence Austral, Florence Easton, Mary Jarred, Miriam Licette and Heddle Nash. Barbirolli and Albert Coates, as well as Beecham, were guest conductors.

From 1932 to 1934 Geoffrey Toye was co-director of opera with Lilian Baylis, and after Baylis's death in 1937 the operatic management devolved on a committee of conductors and directors. Amid the exigencies of war Tyrone Guthrie administered both Sadler's Wells and the Old Vic in 1939–45. Reduced to a small touring group, the opera company found a temporary base at Burnley and visited many towns; its repertory was drawn from *The Beggar's Opera* (with Joan Cross as Mrs Peachum and Edith Coates as Lucy), *Dido and Aeneas*, *Thomas and Sally*, *Le nozze di Figaro*, *Die Zauberflöte*, *La traviata* and *Madama Butterfly*. The company reappeared in London for two weeks in 1941 at the New Theatre (now the Albery, in St Martin's Lane), which became its London base until 1944, when it transferred to the Prince's Theatre. The tours and London seasons were helped financially by the Carnegie UK Trust and the recently formed Council for the Encouragement of Music and the Arts; and thus, imperceptibly, the idea of permanent state patronage for

opera in England took hold. By the time the company moved to the Prince's Theatre for its last wartime season, Joan Cross had become director of opera. During the war new productions had included *The Bartered Bride*, *Così fan tutte*, *Il tabarro* and *Gianni Schicchi*; among the new singers were Victoria Sladen, Anna Pollak, Owen Brannigan and Peter Pears, and the conductors included Peter Gellhorn and Reginald Goodall.

With victory in Europe (but not yet in the Far East), the opera company returned to Sadler's Wells Theatre in June 1945 with the first performance of *Peter Grimes*. Internal dissension led to the departure of Cross, Pears and some others, and to the eventual creation of the ENGLISH OPERA GROUP. Clive Carey took temporary charge of the company for the 1946–7 season, with James Robertson as musical director. Richard Lewis and Anna Pollak were among the new singers of the period. In 1948 Norman Tucker began his managerial association with the theatre; until 1953 he shared the direction with the conductors Robertson and Michael Mudie, then served with Robertson alone, and then (1954–66) was sole director. Robertson resigned as musical director in 1954 and was succeeded by Alexander Gibson (1957–9) and Colin Davis (1961–5).

Tucker decisively expanded the repertory and nourished its strengths in staging and ensemble, himself translating *Simon Boccanegra* for its first performance in Britain (1948) with James Johnston, Arnold Matters and Howell Glynne in the leading male roles; Mudie conducted, and John Moody (the company's principal director) staged the opera to the designs of John Piper. Also new to Britain (1947) was Wolf-Ferrari's *I quattro rusteghi*, translated by Dent as *The School for Fathers*: it was the first Sadler's Wells production by Dennis Arundell, later responsible for an outstanding *Fliegende Holländer* as well as for *Kát'a Kabanová* in its first British stage production (1951). Tucker's enthusiasm for Janáček led likewise to the first productions in Britain of *The Cunning Little Vixen* (1961) and *The Makropulos Affair* (with Marie Collier, 1964); *From the House of the Dead*, previously given by the Prague Opera at the Edinburgh Festival, followed in 1965. Amy Shuard, who sang the title role in *Kát'a*, was one of the company's singers who achieved an international career; others such as Derek Hammond-Stroud (joining in 1962, an outstanding Beckmesser in 1968), showed distinction mainly in long, varied service to the company itself.

New British works given in the 21 years after *Peter Grimes* were Antony Hopkins's *Lady Rohesia* (1947), Lennox Berkeley's *Nelson* (1954), John Gardner's *The Moon and Sixpence* (1957, the first opera produced by Peter Hall), Richard Rodney Bennett's *The Mines of Sulphur* (1965) and Malcolm Williamson's *The Violins of St Jacques* (1966). (Williamson's *Our Man in Havana* had been given at Sadler's Wells Theatre, but by a separate organization called Rostrum, in 1963.) Dvořák's *Rusalka* had its first professional British staging in 1959, with Joan Hammond as guest artist and with Vilem Tausky conducting; Colin Davis, soon after his appointment as musical director, displayed an even-handed brilliance in the 1962–3 season with the company's first-ever *Idomeneo* and the first British staging of Weill's *Aufstieg und Fall der Stadt Mahagonny*. A curiosity of 1965 was Monteverdi's *Orfeo* in Italian (conducted by Raymond Leppard): this departure from the opera-in-English principle was only rarely to be repeated. Among the most distinctive singers during these years were Elizabeth Fretwell, Pauline Tinsley, Patricia Kern (the first of a line of British coloratura mezzo-sopranos in the company's *La Cenerentola*), Ronald Dowd, William McAlpine, Peter Glossop, Thomas Hemsley, Alberto Remedios, David Ward and Alexander Young, with June Bronhill and Eric Shilling particularly successful in the brilliant operetta translations by Geoffrey Dunn and Christopher Hassall.

A financial crisis in 1958, involving the Carl Rosa company also, was surmounted and Sadler's Wells undertook the older company's touring function for a short time. A plan to create a new home for the company on the South Bank proved abortive, to Tucker's disappointment. In 1966, amid a strained relationship with the governing trust, he resigned. Stephen Arlen, who succeeded him, promoted the move to the Coliseum in 1968 and – in place of an unsatisfactory sharing of musical responsibilities by Bryan Balkwill and Mario Bernardi – engaged Mackerras as musical director, 1970–77. Mackerras had already established himself with the company, particularly in Janáček and in a pioneering restoration of 18th-century (and early 19th-century) musical practice to *Le nozze di Figaro* in 1965.

At the Coliseum, a production of the *Ring* in a new and admired translation by Andrew Porter was completed by 1973: it was acclaimed for the conducting of Reginald Goodall and for the vocal ensemble in which Rita Hunter sang Brünnhilde and Norman Bailey Wotan. In the previous year the company's quality was no less well displayed in the mustering of the enormous cast necessary for *War and Peace*, of which the first British production was staged by Colin Graham and conducted by Lloyd-Jones (who was also the translator): Bailey (as Kutuzov) and the chorus were triumphant. Josephine Barstow, John Brecknock and Valerie Masterson were among other admired singers of the 1970s, and Janet Baker sang memorably as Donizetti's Mary Stuart, as Charlotte in *Werther*, and as Handel's Julius Caesar. The company gave the first British performances of Penderecki's *The Devils of Loudun* (1973) and Henze's *The Bassarids* (1974), as well as the premières of Bennett's *A Penny for a Song* (1967), Williamson's *Lucky-Peter's Journey* (1969), Gordon Crosse's *The Story of Vasco* (1974) and David Blake's *Toussaint* (1977). The Earl of Harewood became managing director, succeeding Arlen, in 1972, two years before the company assumed the name of English National Opera. The affiliate it set up in Leeds, in 1978, was at first styled English National Opera North, but it soon became independent, as Opera North.

In the ENO's own history Sir Charles Groves's short and suddenly terminated musical directorship (1977–9) left small impression. But Mark Elder, succeeding to the position at the age of 32, brought flair and vigour to the regime in combination with David Pountney as director of productions (from 1982), with effective administrative backing from Harewood and his successor from 1985, Peter Jonas (whose title was changed in 1989 to general director). In Elder's first ten years no fewer than 68 new productions were added to the repertory, Elder himself conducting a wide range of works from Verdi's *Otello* and *Les vêpres siciliennes*, both with Plowright, to Tchaikovsky's *Mazepa* (first British performance, 1984) and Busoni's *Doktor Faust* (first British stage performance, 1986). In 1984 he added *Fate* (*Osud*) to the British tally of Janáček; it later made a double bill

with a staging of *The Diary of One who Disappeared*. Other conductors including Mackerras, Elgar Howarth, Simon Rattle and Paul Daniel have maintained a repertory stretching from Monteverdi and Handel to the first British performances of Ligeti's *Le Grand Macabre* (1982), Glass's *Akhnaten* (1985) and *The Making of the Representative for Planet 8* (1988) and Reimann's *Lear* (1989). Premières were given of Iain Hamilton's *Anna Karenina* (1981), Birtwistle's *The Mask of Orpheus* (1986) and Blake's *The Plumber's Gift* (1989). Prominent singers not already mentioned included Sally Burgess, Anne Evans, Helen Field, Lesley Garrett, Della Jones, Felicity Lott, Ann Murray, Jean Rigby, Sarah Walker, Kenneth Collins, Neil Howlett, Anthony Rolfe Johnson, Philip Langridge, Benjamin Luxon, Alan Opie, John Tomlinson, Richard Van Allan and, specially notable, the countertenors James Bowman and Christopher Robson.

The sold-out houses for both *Akhnaten* and *The Mikado* (in an adventurous 'de-Japanned' production by Jonathan Miller, 1986) testified to the company's success with its public. A like success was registered by Jonathan Miller's 'New York mafia' staging of *Rigoletto* (Elder conducting, with John Rawnsley in the title role), which the company ventured to take to New York and other American cities in 1984. Pountney was audaciously successful in imposing a new scenario on Dvořák's *Rusalka* and on *Hänsel und Gretel* (fig.12). Nicholas Hytner was another director who contributed much, notably a witty *Serse* that was taken on the company's visit to the USSR in 1990. Productions by David Alden, including the *Mazepa* already mentioned, had a deliberately savage or taunting approach, which stirred or infuriated the public. Vulgarized Offenbach and misfiring American works (Sondheim's *Pacific Overtures* in its first British staging, 1987, and Weill's *Street Scene* in 1989) were among the stumbles.

Though the company's singers have been nearly all native English-speakers, with a large and constantly changing Australian contingent, there have been exceptions. Sergey Leiferkus (having been conspicuously successful in the Kirov Opera's visit to Covent Garden) sang Escamillo in 1988. Foreign conductors have been regular guests, including the veteran Erede (in *Mosè in Egitto*, 1986), Serge Baudo, Albert Rosen and John Mauceri. Despite the convention that only original-language performances are acceptable on recordings, a number of ENO productions (including the *Ring*) were commercially recorded, thanks to benevolent sponsorship from the Peter Moores Foundation; videos appeared from the mid-1980s. In 1992 Dennis Marks was appointed general director and Sian Edwards music director, with effect from 1993.

Handel Opera. An organization founded in 1955 (as the Handel Opera Society), with the encouragement of Edward J. Dent, for 'reviving public interest in professional stage performances of Handel's dramatic works' – the latter term allowing it to embrace the staging not only of the Italian operas but of Handel's oratorios and other English-texted works of similar genre such as *Hercules*. (It gave a few non-Handel works as well, such as the first modern revival of J. C. Smith's *Ulysses* in 1963.) Charles Farncombe became its musical director in 1955 and remained so, enlisting a small professional orchestra (of modern instruments, with harpsichord) and an amateur chorus. Different stage directors were used for the annual productions, which moved to

Sadler's Wells Theatre in 1959. The Italian operas were usually, but not always, given in English, with translations by Farncombe himself, Dent, Arthur Jacobs and others. Notable appearances were made by artists on the brink of wider fame, Joan Sutherland singing the title role of *Alcina* in 1957 and Janet Baker the role of Eduige in *Rodelinda* in 1959. In all, 28 works were staged, and some productions were taken to Halle, Drottningholm and other continental centres. Dropping the word 'Society' in 1980, Handel Opera continued its valuable service until its position was weakened by the increasing diffusion of Handel operas elsewhere, as well as by a restrictive financial climate. Its last production was of *Rodrigo* (with newly recovered material) in 1985.

King's Company. A company founded by Thomas Killigrew in 1660 under a royal patent granted by Charles II. It initially occupied a small, non-scenic theatre in Vere Street, then in May 1663 opened a new theatre, capable of scene changes, in Bridges Street. When that building burnt down in 1672, the company erected Drury Lane (1674) on the same site. The group went broke and was absorbed by the Duke's Company in 1682, creating the United Company. Not an innovatory manager, Killigrew had relatively little to do with opera. He did produce Cambert and Perrin's *Ariane* at Drury Lane in March 1674, and the company mounted a series of hostile burlesques by Thomas Duffett, notably *The Mock-Tempest* (1674) and *Psyche Debauch'd* (1675), on the spectacular semi-operas of the rival Duke's Company.

Midsummer Opera. An occasional company organized by the husband-and-wife team of David and Lorelle Skewes (tenor and soprano, both Australian), which since 1987 has performed at St John's, Smith Square, as well as in the founders' back garden in the London suburb of Ealing. It has given Handel's *Rinaldo*, *Atalanta* and *Acis and Galatea* and (at the Donmar Warehouse, Covent Garden, as part of the London International Opera Festival, 1988) the première of Alison Bauld's *Nell*. Under its regular conductor, David Roblou, it produced Rossini's burletta *L'occasione fa il ladro* (in English, as *The Opportunist*) in 1989 – believed to be

the first British staging of a Rossini opera with an ensemble of period instruments.

Morley Opera. A student company (formerly called Morley College Opera Group) emanating from Morley College in Lambeth. The college, an adult education institute, was originally the Samuel Morley Memorial College for Working Men and Women, housed within the premises of the Old Vic, but moved to Westminster Bridge Road in December 1924. It has been distinguished for music since the days when Holst was music director (1907–28). In 1911 Holst conducted his Morley students in the first (concert) performance of Purcell's *The Fairy-Queen* since 1697, but public theatrical performances deriving from a specialized opera course did not reach importance until the 1950s. From then on, many young singers found the courses at Morley College an important stepping-stone, Janet Baker singing Gluck's *Orfeo* in 1958. Under Andrew Downie (director of opera, 1968–86), productions included the first British stage production of Tchaikovsky's *The Slippers* (1984). A cultivation of unusual works continued under Tom Hawkes's directorship, Cherubini's *Les deux journées* receiving a rare staging in 1987. Also in that year Morley Opera left its base to give London's first staged performance of Cavalieri's *Rappresentatione di Anima, et di Corpo* (at St Martin-in-the-Fields, in an English version by Arthur Jacobs) as part of the London International Opera Festival. At the 1988 festival, Morley Opera revived two Victorian operettas, Clay's *Ages Ago* and Macfarren's *Jessy Lea*.

New London Opera Company. The name given by the impresario Jay Pomeroy to his operatic enterprise at the Cambridge Theatre in 1946–8, transferring to the Stoll Theatre in 1949. See §2, Cambridge Theatre and Stoll Theatre.

New Opera Company. An organization which, stemming from the Cambridge University Opera Club's production of *The Rake's Progress* in 1956, mounted short London seasons from the following year, comprising unfamiliar 20th-century works. Its principal initiators were Leon Lovett (who remained musical

12. The dream pantomime from David Pountney's production of Humperdinck's 'Hänsel und Gretel' for the ENO, 1987 (designed by Stefanos Lazaridis); the characters, all dressed in white, are fantasy figures from the children's imagination

director), Peter Hemmings and Brian Trowell. Anthony Besch became director of productions in 1972. Productions were chiefly at Sadler's Wells Theatre, coordinated with the schedule of Sadler's Wells Opera up to the time of its quitting that theatre (1968). Later, within the schedule of the (renamed) English National Opera at the Coliseum, the New Opera Company was responsible for mounting important Ginastera and Martinů works, while continuing to give occasional independent productions elsewhere until its activities were frozen by the financial climate of the later 1980s. Its service to London opera in introducing new works, mostly in highly effective performances, was unparalleled.

The first London performance of *The Rake's Progress* shared the opening 1957 season with the stage première of Arthur Benjamin's *A Tale of Two Cities* (previously broadcast), and in 1964 Benjamin's (posthumous) *Tartuffe* had its première. There were premières also of Arnold Foster's *Lord Bateman* (1958); Maconchy's *The Departure* and Buxton Orr's *The Wager* (double bill, 1962); Daniel Jones's *The Knife* (1963); Phyllis Tate's *The What-d'ye-call-it* (in a double bill with Crosse's *Purgatory*, having its London première, 1966); Musgrave's *The Decision* (1967); John Joubert's *Under Western Eyes* (Camden Festival, 1969); Lutyens's *Time Off? – Not a Ghost of a Chance!* (in a double bill with Anthony Gilbert's *The Scene-machine*, in its first London performance, 1972); Lutyens's *Infidelio* (1973); and Nicola LeFanu's *Dawnpath* (1977).

Equally notable were the first British stage performances of Menotti's *The Unicorn, the Gorgon and the Manticore* and Egk's *Der Revisor* (1958), Dallapiccola's *Il prigioniero*, Orff's *Die Kluge* and Joubert's *In the Drought* (all 1959), Schoenberg's *Erwartung* (with Heather Harper) and Searle's *The Diary of a Madman* (1960), Francis Burt's *Volpone* and Joubert's *Silas Marner* (1961), Henze's *Boulevard Solitude* (1962), Prokofiev's *The Fiery Angel* with Marie Collier (1965), Hindemith's *Cardillac* (1970), Shostakovich's *The Nose* (1973), Goehr's *Arden Must Die* (1974), Szymanowski's *King Roger* (1975), Ginastera's *Bomarzo* (1976), Martinů's *Julietta* (1978), Nino Rota's *Il cappello di paglia di Firenze* (Camden Festival, 1980), and John Harbison's *A Full Moon in March* and Brian Howard's *Inner Voices* (1983).

A withdrawal of the Arts Council grant halted its work after a co-production with Opera North of Krenek's *Jonny spielt auf*, given at Sadler's Wells in 1984.

New Sadler's Wells Opera. A company founded in 1982, which from the following year presented seasons at Sadler's Wells Theatre and on tour. It specialized in operetta, giving Lehár's *Der Graf von Luxemburg* (its first professional London performances since the original run of 1911) as well as *Die lustige Witwe*, and also Imre Kálmán's *Die Csárdásfürstin* and *Gräfin Mariza*. Marilyn Hill Smith was the company's outstanding soloist, Nigel Douglas occasionally the director and the provider of stylish new English texts. The company took Gilbert and Sullivan's *Ruddigore* and (in 1988) Noël Coward's *Bitter Sweet* on tour and several of its productions were recorded. It failed financially, however, and closed in 1989 after playing *HMS Pinafore* in New York.

Opera Factory. A company founded in Sydney in 1973 by the director David Freeman; in 1976 it moved to Zürich, and in 1981 to London, where it became a successful vehicle for Freeman's intensely physical style of staging. Its most notable performers have included Omar Ebrahim and Freeman's wife Marie Angel. Paul Daniel was its usual conductor until 1990. In 1984 it joined forces with one of the most forward-looking of London concert organizations, the London Sinfonietta, and was renamed Opera Factory London Sinfonietta. The company's sexually audacious treatment of Cavalli's *Calisto* (1985) and its hilariously updated opera-on-a-beach version of *Così fan tutte* (1988) exemplify its style. These were among several productions given at the Queen Elizabeth Hall, where the company also gave the first British performance of Reimann's *Gespenstersonate* in 1989, in English. Nigel Osborne's *Hell's Angels* was given its first performance by the company at the Royal Court Theatre in 1986.

Opera of the Nobility. The name sometimes given to the company founded in 1733 as a rival to Handel and Heidegger's 'Second Royal Academy'. Burney states that it was headed by William, the second Earl Cowper. Artistic and financial decisions were made by a group of directors evidently including the Duke of Richmond, while a group of wealthy backers (among them the Duke of Bedford) paid 'calls' to meet deficits. The company spent its first season in the third Lincoln's Inn Fields Theatre (vacated in 1732 when John Rich moved his acting troupe to Covent Garden). Nicola Porpora was the principal composer and Paolo Rolli principal librettist. The directors hired Senesino and other singers away from Handel's company and for 1734–5 moved into the King's Theatre, Haymarket, while Handel had to become a part-time tenant at Covent Garden. Although the company hired Farinelli for this season, by 1735–6 audiences had fallen off and the venture was in dire trouble. Handel rejoined Heidegger at the King's Theatre for 1737–8, after which the company collapsed. The name 'Opera of the Nobility' (sometimes 'Nobility Opera') was not used at the time.

Opera Viva. A company based at an adult education institute in south-west London, and performing chiefly at Fulham Town Hall. On a mainly amateur basis but under the professional musical direction of Leslie Head, it has included a number of rarities among its stage productions since 1963 (other such works were given in concert performance, using the name Pro Opera). They include Puccini's *La rondine* (first British performance, 1965) and Havergal Brian's *Agamemnon* (with excerpts from *The Tigers*) in 1971. A recording on two LPs (taken from a concert of 1983) offers, uniquely in the record catalogue, excerpts from English operas by MacCunn, Naylor, Smyth, d'Erlanger, Corder, Stanford, Goring Thomas and Cowen, as well as Boughton and Delius.

Patent Company. A name commonly applied to the acting company that occupied Drury Lane (and occasionally performed at Dorset Garden) between 1695 and 1709. It succeeded the United Company, and was silenced by the Lord Chamberlain on 6 June 1709 for defiance of his orders. The company mounted some late semi-operas, notably Purcell's *Indian Queen* (1695), the Motteux-Daniel Purcell *Island Princess* (1699) and Elkanah Settle's *Virgin Prophetess* (1701). With Clayton's *Arsinoe* (1705) and Bononcini's highly successful *Camilla* (1706), it was the first company to present all-sung italianate opera in London (in translation).

Pyne-Harrison Opera Company. A company devoted to opera in English under the direction of the soprano Louisa Pyne and the tenor William Harrison. It was originally assembled in the USA about 1854, when Pyne and Harrison went to New York, and made tours along the eastern seaboard. On returning to England in 1857, the singers re-formed the company. It appeared at the Lyceum and Drury Lane theatres before embarking on regular seasons in the autumn and winter at Covent Garden from 1858, using the title Royal English Opera. Balfe's *Satanella* (1858), Wallace's *Lurline* (1860) and most notably Benedict's *The Lily of Killarney* (1862) were among the new works produced; *Martha, Il trovatore* and Meyerbeer's *Dinorah* (all by living composers) were among the works performed in translation. Despite early prosperity, the enterprise failed financially in 1864, and so in 1866 did another one formed to succeed it.

Royal Academy of Music. An opera company founded in 1719 under a 21-year patent granted by George I. The King provided a subsidy of £1000 a year. Managed by elected 'directors', the company was organized as a joint-stock venture in which more than 60 individuals pledged £200 each in capital. Handel was the foremost among several composers employed; the venue was the King's Theatre, Haymarket. The company opened in April 1720 and worked to the highest artistic standards. But despite massive subsidy, it collapsed in bankruptcy and acrimony in 1728. It employed some of the great singers of the day, including Senesino, Cuzzoni and Faustina Bordoni. Several of Handel's greatest operas were first presented by the Royal Academy, notably *Radamisto* (1720), *Tamerlano* (1724) and *Tolomeo* (1728). It was succeeded by the Second Royal Academy.

Royal English Opera. See Pyne-Harrison Opera Company.

Royal Italian Opera. The name given to an annual subscription season (normally in spring and summer) during the 19th century, consisting of Italian opera by living or recent composers, sung by a specially contracted company. By extension, the term has been applied to the companies so contracted and to the theatres in which they sang, including, at various times, Her Majesty's Theatre, Covent Garden, the Lyceum and Drury Lane.

Royal Opera. See §2, Covent Garden.

Sadler's Wells Opera. See English National Opera.

Second Royal Academy. An opera company founded in 1729 to revive the Royal Academy of Music. Often known simply as the 'Second Academy', it served principally as a showcase for Handel. Its ownership and finances remain unclear, but Handel and J. J. Heidegger had operational charge. Performances were given at the King's Theatre, Haymarket, and the company continued to receive the £1000 annual subsidy enjoyed by its predecessor. After four seasons the Second Academy was severely undercut by the foundation of the Opera of the Nobility at Lincoln's Inn Fields; in 1734 Handel moved to Covent Garden while his rivals occupied the King's Theatre and took over the royal subsidy. Despite the end of competition and Handel's return to the King's Theatre for 1737–8, the Second Academy could not make its expenses and it ceased operations in summer 1738.

Théâtre de Complicité. A theatre group founded in Paris in 1983. Shortly thereafter it moved its base to London and in 1988 extended its work to music theatre with the first stage performance of Gerard McBurney's *The Phantom Violin*, at the Almeida Festival. At the 1989 festival it presented Dmitry Smirnov's *The Lamentations of Thel* (after William Blake), the first London production of any opera by the younger generation of Russian composers.

Travelling Opera. A company founded in 1986 by the baritone Peter Knapp, who serves as translator, director and sometimes singer. Performing standard repertory in English, without chorus and with a reduced orchestra, it has become (with 136 performances in the 1990–91 season) probably the most active of small-scale British touring groups.

United Company. A company created in 1682 by the collapse of the King's Company and its absorption into the Duke's Company. It used both the Drury Lane and Dorset Garden theatres, preferring the latter when giving such scenically spectacular semi-operas as Dryden and Grabu's *Albion and Albanius* (1685) and Purcell's major semi-operas at the beginning of the 1690s, *Dioclesian, King Arthur* and *The Fairy-Queen.* Christopher Rich became principal owner of the company in 1693, but two years later the actors' rebellion of 1695 fragmented its membership. Thereafter it is usually known as the Patent Company.

2. THEATRES.

Adelphi Theatre. A theatre in the Strand originally called the Sans Pareil, opened in November 1806; it was renamed the Adelphi in October 1819, rebuilt in 1858, reconstructed in 1910 and again in 1930. In 1831 it housed the Lyceum's opera company after that theatre burnt down. Sullivan's *Cox and Box* was first publicly performed at the Adelphi in 1867, and the Carl Rosa company later gave occasional seasons there. Since 1908 it has been devoted mainly to musical comedy and the successors of that genre: productions by C. B. Cochran included the first London performance of Cole Porter's *Nymph Errant* in October 1933 (soon after its Manchester première) and the first performance of *Bless the Bride*, 1947 (music by Vivian Ellis). Jay Pomeroy's production of Musorgsky's *The Fair at Sorochintsï* was given there in 1942 after a provincial tour.

Alhambra Theatre. A theatre in Leicester Square that opened in 1854 as the Panopticon. It became London's main theatre for operetta of the more spectacular kind (always in English). Offenbach's *Le roi Carotte* (an *opéra bouffe-féerie*) was produced in 1872, only a few months after its Paris première, and an original score was commissioned from Offenbach for the Christmas holiday entertainment of 1874, *Whittington. Die Fledermaus* had its first British production there (similarly under conditions of nightly run, not in an operatic season) in 1876. From 1890 to 1914 the theatre was famous as a music hall presenting spectacular ballets, among them (1897) Sullivan's *Victoria and Merrie England.* It was demolished in 1936, the Odeon cinema then being erected on the site.

Cambridge Theatre. A theatre in Seven Dials, near Cambridge Circus, opened in 1930. In 1934 a season of *Hänsel und Gretel* was given. From June 1946 to May 1948, under Jay Pomeroy's management, it was the home of the New London Opera Company, under the musical and artistic direction of Alberto Erede and Dino Borgioli (which transferred in 1949 to the Stoll Theatre). Highly successful performances of *Don Pasquale*, *Don Giovanni*, *Rigoletto*, *Falstaff*, *Il barbiere di Siviglia*, *Bohème* and *Tosca* were given, the singers including Margherita Grandi, Ljuba Welitsch, Marko Rothmüller and Mariano Stabile. A number of young British singers began their operatic careers there, including Murray Dickie, Martin Lawrence and Ian Wallace. In 1951 the British première of Menotti's *The Consul*, with its original New York cast, was given. *The Black Mikado* (a version of *The Mikado*) was heard in 1975, *The Mikado* itself in a Plymouth Theatre Royal production in 1982 and in a new production by the revived D'Oyly Carte company in 1989 (its second London season, in tandem with *The Pirates of Penzance*).

Coliseum. A theatre in St Martin's Lane. Built by Sir Oswald Stoll as a music hall in 1904, it has the largest seating capacity of any London theatre (2354). It possesses the largest stage in London (17 metres wide and 28 deep) and was the first anywhere to be equipped with a revolving stage. In its days as a music hall it often included items by opera singers and ballet dancers; in June 1913 a series of living tableaux of *Parsifal*, designed by Glen Byam Shaw, were presented with Wagner's music arranged and conducted by Sir Henry Wood. In 1931 the music hall became a theatre for musical comedy, beginning with the long-running first British productions of *White Horse Inn* (Benatzky and Stolz) and of *Casanova* (Johann Strauss, arr. Benatzky) in 1932. After World War II came a parallel success with long-running American musicals including *Annie Get Your Gun* (1947), *Kiss Me Kate* (1949), *Guys and Dolls* (1953) and *The Most Happy Fella* (1960). The theatre then became a cinema, but was taken by Sadler's Wells Opera in April 1959 for productions of *Die Fledermaus* and *Das Land des Lächelns*, becoming the permanent home of that company (later the ENO) in

1968. In 1992 the ENO acquired the freehold.

Covent Garden. A theatre with a frontage on Bow Street, now known as the Royal Opera House; it has a seating capacity of 2186. The present theatre is the third on the site. The original Covent Garden was built by John Rich as a home for his acting company (which moved there from Lincoln's Inn Fields). He chose a site in the Covent Garden area which he leased from the Duke of Bedford; it had once been a 'convent garden' belonging to a Catholic church in Westminster. The theatre opened on 7 December 1732 with Congreve's *The Way of the World* and soon revived *The Beggar's Opera*. Rich raised the money for construction by selling £15 000 worth of 'renters' shares', making a large profit since the building only cost about £6000. It was designed by Edward Shepherd and, with exterior dimensions of some 19 by 36 metres, had a capacity of about 1400; as Rich specialized in pantomime with elaborate scenic effects, the theatre was adapted to accommodate such displays. In 1734–5 Handel joined Rich at Covent Garden, giving performances of Italian operas up to twice a week and a season of oratorios during Lent. His performers included Carestini, Anna Strada and John Beard, as well as the dancer Marie Sallé. This arrangement lasted three seasons, during which Handel wrote *Ariodante*, *Alcina*, *Atalanta*, *Arminio*, *Giustino* and *Berenice*. He continued on friendly terms with Rich after their partnership ended in 1737, and many of his oratorios were produced there over the next 20 years.

During the second half of the 18th century Covent Garden remained one of the two patent theatres in London, mounting productions of old and new plays roughly 200 nights a season. A growing proportion were designated 'opera', meaning works mixing speech and song in English, though most of these we would now dub 'comic operetta'. An exception was Arne's *Artaxerxes*, all-sung after the Italian manner and a tremendous success in 1762. Dozens of operas with spoken dialogue, by composers such as William Shield,

13. Interior of the Theatre Royal, Covent Garden, shown after the alterations carried out by Henry Holland in 1792: engraving by Springsguth

J. A. Fisher, Charles Dibdin and Thomas Linley (i), were put on at Covent Garden in this period. The theatre was substantially rebuilt (and lengthened by approximately 19 metres) in 1782, the alterations carried out by John Inigo Richards. At this time the capacity went up to about 2200. The building was used briefly for Italian opera in summer 1789 after the King's Theatre burnt down – notably for a production of Paisiello's *Barbiere di Siviglia* involving Nancy Storace, Francesco Benucci and Michael Kelly (Mozart's first Susanna, Figaro and Don Basilio). It was again used for Italian opera for a month in summer 1790, but the theatre remained primarily devoted to stage plays and English light opera.

A major alteration was carried out by Henry Holland in 1792 at the cost of some £25 000. Overall dimensions remained unchanged, but capacity was increased to about 3000. The 'first' Covent Garden burnt down on the night of 19 September 1808. The 'second' Covent Garden, designed by Robert Smirke, opened on 18 September 1809 with *Macbeth* and a musical afterpiece, *The Quaker*. The capacity was about 2800, and the building cost nearly £150 000. At this time management attempted to raise admission prices to a top of 7s., a move that provoked the 'Old Price' riots. Catalani had been hired for a series of concerts, and despite her popularity among operagoers the theatre audience objected violently to subsidizing her fabulous salary. After two months the managers were forced to revert to the usual charges.

Between 1810 and 1824 Henry Bishop was musical director for the theatre, and a significant part of its repertory consisted of his free adaptations (in English) of operas by Mozart, Rossini and other continental favourites. In 1819, for example, *The Marriage of Figaro* was advertised as having 'The Overture and Musick selected chiefly from Mozart's Operas' but with 'new Musick' composed by Bishop. These and similar arrangements by other composers (notably Rophino Lacy) remained in the theatre's repertory into the 1830s. *La Cenerentola* (in English in 1830 as *Cinderella, or The Fairy and the Little Glass Slipper*) had interpolations from three other Rossini operas. A change might have occurred when, in 1825, the manager Kemble invited Carl Maria von Weber to London and offered him the musical directorship; but Weber died shortly after the première of his *Oberon* at Covent Garden on 12 April 1826. Not until the next decade was any real attempt made to alter the nature of Covent Garden's operatic productions.

The management of Alfred Bunn brought integral and important opera productions from 1833. In that year Schröder-Devrient and Malibran were the stars of a company that gave *Die Zauberflöte*, *Fidelio*, *Der Freischütz* and the first performance in Britain of *Euryanthe*, all in German, plus *La sonnambula* in English. Charles Macready became manager in 1837, followed by Vestris and her husband from 1839 to 1842. Despite brilliant appearances by Adelaide Kemble in *Norma* and other works, these years were financially a failure. Bunn resumed management – and met failure also. Visits were paid by a German company in 1842 and by the Brussels Théâtre de la Monnaie company in 1845, whose performances included *Guillaume Tell*, *Les Huguenots* and *La muette de Portici*. Then, under the new management of Giuseppe Persiani (husband of the prima donna Fanny Tacchinardi-Persiani), the interior of the theatre was radically remodelled as an opera house – specifically to launch a Royal Italian Opera in rivalry to that at Her Majesty's Theatre. It duly opened in April 1847 with *Semiramide*, Giulia Grisi singing the title

14. *Caricature concerning the 'Old Price' riots that followed the opening of the new Covent Garden theatre, designed by Robert Smirke, in 1809: etching by George Cruikshank*

15. Interior of the third (present) Covent Garden theatre, designed by E. M. Barry and opened on 15 May 1858: engraving from 'The Illustrated London News' (10 July 1858)

role and Alboni making her London début as Arsace.

In 1851 Frederick Gye took over the management. A fire destroyed the theatre in 1856, but a third theatre (fig.15; *see also* SEATING) was opened on 15 May 1858 with *Les Huguenots* – the last act being unperformed in deference to Victorian Sabbatarianism (the opera's Saturday performance had overrun midnight). Gye remained manager until 1877, and his son Ernest succeeded him to 1884. After an interim when separate seasons of Italian opera were presented by the impresarios J. H. Mapleson and Lago, Augustus Harris (already managing Drury Lane) took over the lease of Covent Garden for 1887, determined 'to give grand opera a decent burial or resuscitate it'. The latter aim succeeded and Harris maintained his highly successful regime until his death in 1896. In 1892 he had discreetly changed the theatre's billing from Royal Italian Opera to Royal Opera, in recognition of some performances in French and of London's first performances of the *Ring*, given in that year by a Hamburg company, Mahler conducting.

During the second half of the century Covent Garden gave many Verdi operas their first British performances, from *Rigoletto* in 1853 to *Falstaff* in 1892. Patti was London's first Aida there (1876), and had been the first Juliet in Gounod's *Roméo et Juliette* (in Italian, 1867). Barely second to her in repute was the Canadian soprano Emma Albani (married to Ernest Gye), who sang Elsa when Covent Garden gave London its first *Lohengrin* (in Italian) in 1875. From the late 1880s the singers most admired included the De Reszke brothers and an Australian newcomer, Melba: she was Juliet, Jean de Reszke was Romeo and Edouard de Reszke was Friar Laurence in Gounod's revised version of his *Roméo et Juliette* in 1889 – in French, an early token of Harris's abandonment of the all-Italian basis. These performances all took place within the annual 'grand season' held each summer, usually for 11 weeks – but for 16 weeks in 1891, with 94 performances of 20 operas.

Occasional autumn seasons presented opera at cheaper prices, *Cavalleria rusticana* proving a hugely popular new work (21 performances) in 1892. In that year, similarly at reduced prices, Harris gave Christmas-tide 'concert recitals of opera in costume'. In 1893 *Pagliacci* with Melba (first London performance) was greatly successful; *Manon Lescaut*, the first Puccini opera to be heard in London (1894), was not. In that year, at one of the autumn promenade concerts which were held annually at Covent Garden under an independent management, *Samson et Dalila* had its first London hearing.

Harris was one of the commanding London managers of the old style, that is, in running a great business on his own account. From his death in 1896 until 1924, the running of the theatre, and with it the promotion of the grand season, was in the hands of a Grand Opera Syndicate that engaged salaried managers. Maurice Grau combined management of Covent Garden and the Metropolitan, New York, in 1897–1900; André Messager in 1901–4 similarly combined his posts at Covent Garden and at the Paris Opéra-Comique. Soon after 1900 Puccini's fame was confirmed, and Covent Garden gave the first British performances of *Tosca* (1900) and *Madama Butterfly* (1905), with singers such as Destinn, Caruso and Scotti. The ever-popular *La traviata*, however, was chosen for Tetrazzini's London début in 1907.

The theatre was also leased for short seasons of opera in English by the Moody-Manners Company in 1902 and 1903. But a much more powerful blow in that cause was struck in the determination of Hans Richter to perform the *Ring* in English. Richter had become the leading Wagner conductor at Covent Garden, with three cycles of the *Ring* (in German) in 1903, in a season in which Wagner took 29 out of 73 performances. Backed by Percy Pitt, who was musical adviser to the governing syndicate, Richter accomplished his aim – in the short term. The *Ring* was given in English in 1908 and repeated in 1909, and in 1909 *Die Meistersinger* was given in English as well. Audiences were crowded, but Richter's further aim to build a whole repertory in English was opposed by the syndicate, and opera-in-the-original remained the rule for grand seasons.

The year 1909 saw the first London performances of *Pelléas et Mélisande* and of *Louise*, and the first London staging of *Samson et Dalila*, all at Covent Garden. But from then until the outbreak of war in 1914, the theatre's most significant productions were those promoted outside the grand season by Beecham (see above, §I, 10). During the first Beecham season, 1910, Bruno Walter made his London début conducting *Tristan und Isolde*. The grand season of 1911, prolonged to 15 weeks with a certain magnificence to celebrate the coronation of George V, included the first London performance, in the presence of the composer, of Puccini's *La fanciulla del West*. An additional winter season early in 1914 served to give London its first staged *Parsifal*.

Closed during World War I, Covent Garden reopened in 1919. The ensuing 30 years were marked by the invigorating but sometimes hazardous activities of Beecham. The Beecham Opera Company held the lease of the theatre from November 1919 to July 1920, during which a winter and a spring season with British artists (and with the first performance in English of *Parsifal*) were successful but an international grand season in summer was not – despite the first London production of Puccini's *Trittico*. With Beecham consequently in financial difficulty, opera at Covent Garden from July 1920 to May 1922 was confined to two short seasons by the Carl Rosa company; the British National Opera Company then undertook both summer and supplementary seasons in 1922–4, mostly in English, including the *Ring*, and gave the first performance of Holst's *The Perfect Fool* and the first London performance of Smyth's *Fête galante*, both specially commissioned. The controlling syndicate of Covent Garden decided, however, to resume its own international grand seasons from 1924.

The country's financial depression reduced the 1932 grand season to four weeks of Wagner, with Beecham, at the syndicate's invitation, as principal conductor. The formation of a new syndicate with Beecham as artistic director placed him effectively in charge from then until 1939. But despite his personal eclecticism, a retrospective view of the Covent Garden schedules of the inter-war years shows a heavy dependence on a pre-existent and safe repertory, without the constant flow of new works that had animated the previous century. *Turandot* (first British performance, 1927) concluded the Puccini canon; *Ariadne auf Naxos* (second version) and *Arabella* had none of the impact of Strauss's earlier works. Concert audiences might sample the works of Berg, Hindemith, Prokofiev or Shostakovich, but not operagoers. The more progressive of British composers tended to favour ballet rather than opera. Eugene Goossens's one-act *Judith* and his full-length *Don Juan de Mañara* left no mark, nor did Albert Coates's *Pickwick* (this last in a separate season by a newly arisen and quickly dying British Music Drama Opera Company in 1936).

It was, nevertheless, a period of some distinguished performances. German opera prospered, interpreted by singers of the calibre of Leider, Lotte Lehmann, Lemnitz, Elisabeth Schumann, Olczewska, Flagstad, Melchior, Janssen, Schorr, Kipnis, Mayr and (in 1938) Tauber. Strauss conducted his own *Ariadne auf Naxos*

during a visit in 1936 by the Dresden Staatsoper, the first foreign company to visit for 30 years. The artistic cohesiveness of the ensemble made much impression but the visit was recognized as a political bid for friendship by the Nazi government; during the ensuing years, especially after the Anschluss in 1938, there were some uneasy confrontations when artists supportive of the Nazis confronted others who had been victimized by the Nazis or (like Kleiber, who had conducted in 1938) had voluntarily turned their back on them. The use of German for *The Bartered Bride* in 1939 could hardly fail to seem politically, as well as artistically, inept.

In the standard Italian repertory, with Barbirolli among the conductors, the performances by Turner (from 1928), Ponselle (from 1929) Gigli and Pinza (both from 1930) were among those particularly admired. During the 1934 and 1935 seasons Rossini's coloratura mezzo-soprano heroines in *La Cenerentola* and *L'italiana in Algeri* received new animation from Conchita Supervia. Russian opera was haphazardly given, *Prince Igor* being sung in German (1935) and in French (1937), with the participation of De Basil's Russian Ballet in the Polovtsian Dances. When not used for opera seasons (normally only for a few weeks each summer) Covent Garden functioned as a dance hall. That became its year-round function during World War II, when opera fell mute.

In 1944, however, to prevent a renewal of the dance-hall lease, the music publishers Boosey & Hawkes took over, and preparations for what became the Covent Garden Opera Trust were set in train. A 'permanent' opera company (as distinct from one based on short-term seasonal engagement) would be set up, sharing a year-round season with the already renowned Sadler's Wells Ballet. That company was renamed the Royal Ballet in 1957; the Covent Garden Opera Company did not become the Royal Opera until 1969. Members of the opera and the ballet company combined to open the new regime with Purcell's *The Fairy-Queen*, conducted by Constant Lambert, in November 1946, following an eight-week season given by the company of the Teatro S Carlo, Naples.

An annual Arts Council grant of £50 000 was made to the combined opera and ballet companies; by 1989 it had risen to nearly £13.5 million (for the Royal Opera, the Royal Ballet and its junior company, the Sadler's Wells Royal Ballet), a 40-fold increase in real terms. David Webster (knighted in 1960) as general administrator of the house had authority over the ballet wing as well, but the fact that the ballet company already had fame and momentum and the opera company had to develop its own meant that his decision-making was more strongly felt on the operatic side. He remained until 1970, and was succeeded by John Tooley. The title was later changed to general director, Jeremy Isaacs succeeding to the post in 1988.

The first appointment as musical director of the new opera company went not to the obvious choice, Beecham, nor to either of two other operatically seasoned British conductors, Goossens and Barbirolli, but to an Austrian refugee musician, Karl Rankl. Remaining until 1951, he at least laid the foundations of a company with a reasonably broad repertory, in which British singers were perceived not as a special breed for special seasons but as members of an international team. Whereas few British singers of previous generations enjoyed international operatic careers (Eva Turner was exceptional), the postwar Covent Garden seasons nurtured many who became well known in other major houses and, the newest measure of success, in internationally cast recordings. Geraint Evans was the first, appearing at Covent Garden as early as 1948. Among others (listed alphabetically) were Ryland Davies, Murray Dickie, Peter Glossop, Adele Leigh, Donald McIntyre, Amy Shuard, Josephine Veasey and David Ward, to whom may be added the British-trained Joan Sutherland and Kiri te Kanawa.

After the opening season of the new company (1946–7), an important visit by the Vienna Staatsoper (September 1947) introduced Elisabeth Schwarzkopf, Ljuba Welitsch, Irmgard Seefried, Hilde Gueden, Sena Jurinac, Erich Kunz and Hans Hotter to London opera audiences in performances of *Don Giovanni*, *Le nozze di Figaro*, *Così fan tutte* (two of them in German) and *Fidelio*. At one performance Tauber, who had made London his home after his Jewishness had cut him off from the Vienna Staatsoper, rejoined the company as Don Ottavio to give his last performance on any stage. The visit was immediately followed by that of the English Opera Group in *Albert Herring* and *The Rape of Lucretia*.

The function of stage director was highlighted by the appointment of the 25-year-old Peter Brook in 1948 as director of productions; he resigned in the following year after some outraged reaction to his *Salome* with designs by Salvador Dali. Continuity in supervision of staging was thereafter sporadic. Among Brook's other stagings was Bliss's *The Olympians*, the first new opera presented by the company; neither this in the 1949–50 season nor Vaughan Williams's *The Pilgrim's Progress* in the next had the potential for revival inherent in Britten's *Billy Budd*, first seen in the 1951–2 season.

Whether and in what circumstances to perform in translation remained a lively issue. English was at first preferred, and in that language Hans Hotter sang with some unease in *Die Meistersinger* in early 1948. But *Tristan*, with Flagstad, followed immediately in German. Where all principals were foreign (as in a 1948 *Bohème* with Schwarzkopf, Welitsch, Schock and Silveri) the awkwardness with English became apparent; some performances in mixed languages were artistically still less defensible. By the mid-1950s a shift in language policy was perceptible, French, German and Italian operas now being normally given in the original. *Die Zauberflöte* was for a time an exception, and it was in English that *Die schweigsame Frau* had its first British performance in 1961. English remained longer in favour for Russian and Czech works, though Boris Christoff had exceptionally sung the title role of *Boris Godunov* in Russian in 1949 amid an otherwise English-singing cast. Cotrubas made her Covent Garden début as an enchanting English-singing Tatyana in *Yevgeny Onegin* in 1971, under Solti. Later, Russian and Czech works were given in the original, sometimes with hardly a native speaker of those languages in the cast.

In 1953 Britten's *Gloriana* antagonized those who had expected a celebratory opera for the coronation. Other new British works by prominent composers were Walton's *Troilus and Cressida* (1954) and Tippett's *Midsummer Marriage* (1955), *King Priam* (1962, with a preliminary showing in Coventry), *The Knot Garden* (1970) and *The Ice Break* (1977). Searle's *Hamlet* (originally given in German at Hamburg) arrived in 1969, with younger composers represented by Richard Rodney Bennett (*Victory*, 1970) and Peter Maxwell Davies (*Taverner*, 1972). New operas from abroad were

few: Poulenc's *Dialogues des Carmélites* in 1958, Henze's *We Come to the River* (a Covent Garden commission, with English text by Edward Bond) in 1976, Stockhausen's *Donnerstag aus Licht* in 1985 and Berio's *Un re in ascolto* in 1989.

Musical directors after Rankl, with some gaps, were Kubelik (1955–8), Solti (1961–71), Colin Davis (1971–86) and Haitink (from 1988). A zealous proponent of opera in the vernacular, Kubelik gave London's first performance of *Jenůfa* (1956) and of *Les Troyens* (1957) in English. Solti's high energy was admired in the *Ring*, in Verdi and Strauss, and in London's first staging (in English) of *Moses und Aron*. Davis's sympathies for Mozart, Berlioz and Tippett were evident. Other conductors who contributed notably to the postwar decades included Kleiber, especially for the belated first British production of *Wozzeck*, in 1952; Kempe, with a famous *Ring* in 1956; and Klemperer, especially for a *Fidelio* in 1961 in which he was his own stage director. Barbirolli was the conductor in 1953 for the *Orfeo* (Gluck) in which Ferrier made her last appearances. No less significant were the services of Edward Downes, as a member of Covent Garden's staff until 1969 and a frequent conductor thereafter; in 1991 he was appointed music director and principal conductor. He was the translator as well as conductor of *Katerina Izmaylova* (its first British production) in 1963. Pritchard was also a frequent and successful conductor.

Giulini, a rare visitor, conducted a memorable *Don Carlos* (in Italian) in 1958, with Christoff (King Philip), Gobbi (Posa), Vickers (Don Carlos) and Brouwenstijn (Elisabeth de Valois). Gobbi had made his first appearance with the Covent Garden company in 1953, the combination of his Scarpia with Callas's Tosca in 1964 making a special impact. Callas herself first sang at Covent Garden in *Norma* (1952), with outstanding success. She came in her fullest maturity: Joan Sutherland progressed through small and larger roles before arriving in 1959 at the *Lucia di Lammermoor* that established her major celebrity.

Visconti's staging of *Don Carlos* and Zeffirelli's of *Lucia*, much praised, both maintained a traditional adherence to historical eras and locations as perceived by librettist and composer. A similar approach underlay Peter Hall's productions of the *Moses und Aron* and *Yevgeny Onegin* already mentioned. Wagner was the ground on which a newer freedom in stage direction was asserted, as in Covent Garden's 1974–6 production of the *Ring* by Götz Friedrich, whose authority was such that he held the post of principal director from 1976 to 1981. The superimposition of a director's 'concept' thereafter became common, as in Nuria Espert's redating of *Madama Butterfly* (1988) to a shabby 20th-century tenement, and Mike Ashman's Napoleonic setting for Cherubini's *Médée* (1989, a production almost universally derided).

A number of important visits to Covent Garden have been made by foreign companies. That of La Scala in 1950, with De Sabata as principal conductor, introduced Tagliavini and Gobbi to London; in 1976 the Covent Garden and Scala companies carried out an exchange of visits. The Stockholm Royal Opera made a sensational impact in 1960 with a *Ballo in maschera* restored to its intended Swedish setting and with Blomdahl's 'space opera' *Aniara*. Later visitors have included the Kirov Opera of Leningrad in 1987, and both the Hungarian State Opera and the Komische Oper

(East Berlin) in 1989. The WNO presented a *Ring* cycle in 1986.

In 1988–9 the Royal Opera itself promoted a series of productions of new works, competitively selected, at the Donmar Warehouse Theatre in Earlham Street, near Covent Garden. Known as the 'Garden Venture', the series was generally regarded as disappointing in the composers' achievement.

The adoption of surtitles, at first for selected performances and then from 1988 for all non-English-language performances, provoked cries of outrage from some leading critics, who were nonetheless unable to deny the management's assertion that most patrons welcomed them.

It was announced in 1989 that, subject to civic planning approval, the theatre would undergo a partial rebuilding during 1993–6 to improve facilities for both performers and audiences.

Daly's Theatre. A theatre in Cranbourn Street, Leicester Square, built for the American manager Augustin Daly (1839–99) and opened in 1893. During a season given there by the Carl Rosa company in 1894, *Hänsel und Gretel* received its first performance in Britain. But it was under the theatre's own management that the première was given of Sidney Jones's *The Geisha* (1896), an operetta that was to achieve international celebrity. Other operettas followed, including *Die lustige Witwe* (1907) and *The Maid of the Mountains* (1916), with book by Frederick Lonsdale and music by H. Fraser-Simson. The theatre was pulled down in 1937.

Dorset Garden Theatre. A theatre built on land owned by the Earl of Dorset on the bank of the Thames at the bottom of Salisbury Court, Fleet Street (see fig.1 above); it was opened by the Duke's Company on 9 November 1671 with Dryden's *Sir Martin Mar-all.* The theatre cost the then enormous sum of £9000 and is believed to have accommodated some 800 spectators. Sir Christopher Wren is often said to have been the architect, but there is no good evidence for this ascription, and Robert Hooke has been suggested as a more plausible candidate. The theatre was designed for elaborate machine display, suiting the spectacular semi-operas and tragedies in which the company's co-manager, Thomas Betterton, specialized. Some notable productions were an operatic *Macbeth* with music by Locke (1673), the operatic Dryden-Davenant-Shadwell *Tempest* with music by several composers (1674), Shadwell's *Psyche* with music by Locke and Baptiste Draghi (1675), Charles Davenant's *Circe* with music by Banister (1677), and Nathaniel Lee's *Theodosius* with music by Henry Purcell (1680). Purcell's major semi-operas all received their premières at Dorset Garden: *Dioclesian* in 1690, *King Arthur* in 1691 and *The Fairy-Queen* in 1692. After the theatrical union of 1682 Dorset Garden was used principally for operas and machine-plays. Between the accession of James II (1685) and the death of Queen Mary (1694) it was occasionally called the Queen's Theatre, but it fell increasingly into disuse and disrepair by the end of the century. The Eccles-Finger-Daniel Purcell-Weldon competition of settings for the masque *The Judgment of Paris* was held there in spring 1701. No performances are known after 1706, and the theatre was demolished in 1709.

Drury Lane. Properly called the Theatre Royal, Drury Lane, it is historically one of London's two patent theatres, Covent Garden being the other. The first

theatre on the site was known as the Bridges Street Theatre. Opened by the King's Company on 7 May 1663, it burnt down on 25 January 1672. The 'second' Drury Lane opened on 26 March 1674 and presented Cambert and Perrin's *Ariane* four days later. Described by Dryden as 'a plain-built house', this theatre lasted until 1791, when it was demolished. Little is known of its interior arrangements or capacity, except that alterations, carried out in 1696 and later, gradually expanded capacity from perhaps 700 to perhaps 2300. In the late 17th century the theatre was used almost entirely for straight plays: productions with music were mounted at Dorset Garden, which permitted more elaborate staging. The second Drury Lane was, however, where much of Purcell's incidental music was first performed, and in 1705 it was the venue for *Arsinoe*, the first all-sung opera staged in London (in translation). Bononcini's *Camilla*, also in English, was put on in the next year with enormous success.

The 'third' Drury Lane, Henry Holland's enormous new theatre of 1794, cost £151 000 and seated 3611. It burnt down on 24 February 1809 and was replaced by the fourth theatre on the site, designed by Benjamin Dean Wyatt and opened on 10 October 1812. By this time the exterior dimensions had expanded considerably, to some 39 by 71 metres. The contract cost was stipulated at £150 000, and the capacity was 3106 (plus private boxes), with 1286 of the seats in public boxes and 920 in the pit. Gas lighting was installed in 1817.

During the second half of the 18th century and the early decades of the 19th Drury Lane's repertory was similar to that of Covent Garden – a mixture of English plays and dialogue opera. Arne, Dibdin, Linley and Storace all wrote extensively for the theatre in the 18th century. Until it was taken over in 1879 by the impresario Augustus Harris (who became known as 'Druriolanus'), its record in the 19th century was one of unsuccessful management, bankruptcy and at least one suicide. Henry Bishop was musical director from 1806 to 1809 before decamping to Covent Garden. Tom Cooke (principal tenor, 1813–35) served as music director in the 1820s, adapting foreign operas in the style of Bishop. Alfred Bunn became manager in 1831; under his regime Malibran sang Leonore in *Fidelio* and Amina in *La sonnambula* (in English). Between 1835 and 1847 Bunn attempted to make Drury Lane a permanent home for English opera, staging the premières of works such as Balfe's *Bohemian Girl*, Benedict's *Gypsy's Warning* and *The Brides of Venice* and Wallace's *Maritana*. A number of these works (including *The Bohemian Girl*) had librettos by 'the poet Bunn', as he was derisively known. But the English opera venture failed to pay and it had to be abandoned.

Both plays and operas were thereafter given; among the latter was the first British performance of Verdi's *Les vêpres siciliennes* (in Italian) in 1854. The burning down of Her Majesty's Theatre in 1867 led to the transfer of its Royal Italian Opera seasons to Drury Lane from 1868 to 1877, in the course of which *Der fliegende Holländer* became the first Wagner opera to be heard in Britain (1870), 27 years after its Dresden première. Augustus Harris's regime (1879–96) was famous chiefly for spectacular plays (explosions, earthquakes, shipwrecks and chariot races included) and pantomimes, but in 1882 a German company under the guidance of the Hamburg Opera director, Bernhard Pollini, with Hans Richter as musical director, presented London with its first performances of *Tristan und Isolde* and *Die Meistersinger* (as well as *Lohengrin*, *Der fliegende Holländer*, *Fidelio* and *Euryanthe*).

Drury Lane also accommodated annual seasons by the Carl Rosa company (Augustus Harris for a time being a business partner of Rosa), which enjoyed considerable success. First performances were given of Goring Thomas's *Esmeralda* (1883) and *Nadeshda* (1885), Mackenzie's *Colomba* (1883) and *The Troubadour* (1886), Stanford's *The Canterbury Pilgrims* (1884) and Cowen's *Thorgrim* (1890). Harris himself engaged leading stars such as the De Reszke brothers for a season of Italian opera (including Italian-language performances of *Lohengrin*) in 1887. From the following year he transferred his main operatic base to Covent Garden. But, continuing to run Drury Lane, he used it when the demand for particular operas exceeded his seasonal capacity at Covent Garden, as with the Wagner operas given under Mahler's conductorship in 1892.

With Harris's death at the age of 45 in 1896, opera disappeared from Drury Lane until the Dyagilev seasons of ballet and opera in 1913 and 1914 (see above, §I, 10). Beecham furnished the orchestra for both seasons, the second of which went beyond the Russian repertory to include *Die Zauberflöte*, *Der Rosenkavalier* and Joseph Holbrooke's *Dylan* (first performance), all conducted by Beecham himself. The Beecham Opera Company took Drury Lane for its London seasons from 1917 to 1919. Musical comedy and operetta prospered with shows such as Friml's *Rose Marie* (1925) and Kern's *Show Boat* (1928); in 1931 Lehár's *Das Land des Lächelns* counted as a failure (71 performances) despite the participation of Tauber, making his first London appearance.

After World War II a succession of spectacular American musicals began with Rodgers and Hammerstein's *Oklahoma!* in 1947. Opera returned briefly in 1958 when the impresario S. A. Gorlinsky presented an Italian company for a two-month season, which gave the first London performance since 1830 of *Guillaume Tell* (in Italian). In 1982 Joseph Papp's Broadway production of *The Pirates of Penzance* (maintaining Sullivan's harmonies, but subjecting the music to reorchestration and microphoned sound) captured London's theatrical public as it had that of New York.

Duke's Theatre. The home of the Duke's Company; from 1661 to 1671 the term refers to the first Lincoln's Inn Fields, and from 1671 to 1682 it denotes Dorset Garden.

English Opera House. See Lyceum.

Gaiety Theatre. A theatre that stood in the Strand (in an area now part of the Aldwych): it opened in 1864 and closed in 1903 when that area of London underwent reconstruction. From 1868 it achieved celebrity as a theatre of light entertainment under the management of John Hollingshead (1827–1904), whose boast was to keep alive 'the sacred lamp of burlesque'. In that category fell *Thespis* (1871), the first stage collaboration of W. S. Gilbert and Arthur Sullivan, of which the music is now lost. George Edwardes (1852–1918), a name as famous as Hollingshead's in London theatrical management, took over in 1886, opening with Alfred Cellier's *Dorothy*, which achieved a longer run (931 performances) than any of Gilbert and Sullivan's pieces and is sometimes said to have inaugurated the genre of musical comedy.

Gallery of Illustration. Situated in Regent Street, this was never referred to as a theatre, and indeed, for respectability's sake, avoided all theatrical connotations. Opened in 1856 by Thomas German Reed (1817–88) and his wife Priscilla (1818–95), it presented small-scale dramatic representations with music, of which W. S. Gilbert's *Ages Ago* (1869; music by Frederic Clay) anticipates Gilbert's work with Sullivan.

Goodman's Fields Theatre. A theatre built by Thomas Odell in 1729 on Ayliffe Street in Goodman's Fields, just east of the City near what is now Aldgate. Nothing is known of the building's dimensions, capacity or cost. It housed a resident repertory company that came to specialize in 'modern classic' plays (Vanbrugh, Farquhar, Steele and other turn-of-the-century writers). Built in the theatrical boom that followed the triumph of *The Beggar's Opera* in 1728, Goodman's Fields naturally included ballad operas among its mainpieces and afterpieces. The company flourished, and in 1731 Odell sold out to Henry Giffard, a highly competent manager. Giffard persuaded investors to fund a better theatre, designed by Edward Shepherd (architect of Covent Garden). The second Goodman's Fields opened on 2 October 1732. It cost at least £2300 and had a capacity estimated at about 700. Giffard mounted relatively little ballad opera in the 1730s, but in 1735 he revived the Dryden-Purcell *King Arthur* for a spectacular run of 35 nights. After the Licensing Act of 1737 Goodman's Fields was used only briefly in 1740–42 before the authorities closed it permanently and it became a chapel, then a warehouse. It is now remembered largely as the theatre in which David Garrick made his London début in 1741. The second Goodman's Fields must be distinguished from the New Wells Theatre in Leman Street, Hooper's Square, Goodman's Fields, which had a pump room and taphouse and was home to various fringe theatre entertainments from 1739 to 1752.

Haymarket Theatre. See King's Theatre and Little Theatre in the Haymarket.

Her/His Majesty's Theatre. A theatre in the Haymarket (there have been four successive buildings on approximately the same site). It was originally the Queen's Theatre, having opened in 1705 in the reign of Queen Anne. Later called the King's Theatre, it became Her Majesty's on Victoria's accession in 1837. (For the theatre's early history see below, King's Theatre.) The second building, which opened in 1791, was briefly the largest theatre in Britain (cap. 3300): it burnt down in 1867, and a new theatre, built in 1869, came into use in 1874. It was demolished in 1890 (though the neighbouring Royal Opera Arcade survives). The present building (cap. 1260) was opened in 1897. It has been His or Her Majesty's, according to the royal succession, ever since. Particularly when under the management of John Ebers between 1820 and 1827, of Pierre Laporte in 1828–31 and 1833–41, of Benjamin Lumley between 1842 and 1858, and J. H. Mapleson in 1862–7, 1877–81, 1887 and 1889, the theatre had major operatic importance. The Carl Rosa Company gave seasons there from 1879 to 1882, and in 1882 Angelo Neumann's Wagner company, under the musical direction of Anton Seidl, gave the first performances in England of the *Ring*. A French opera season in 1886 included notable performances by Galli-Marié as Carmen, a role she had created in Paris 11 years earlier. In 1887 Patti made her only appearance there. Important British premières under Mapleson's management included *Faust*, *Die lustigen Weibe von Windsor* (in Italian as *Falstaff*), *Médée*, *La forza del destino*, *Carmen*, *Mefistofele* and *Les pêcheurs de perles*.

The fourth (and present) theatre was built by the actor-manager Herbert Beerbohm Tree, whose reign lent it distinction from 1897 to 1915. Among later presentations were the long-running musical comedy (1916–21) *Chu Chin Chow* (words by Oscar Asche, music by Frederick Norton), J. E. Flecker's play *Hassan* with music by Delius (1923), and the first British production of Theo Mackeben's *Die Dubarry* (1932, after Millöcker). Bernstein's *West Side Story* ran from 1958 to 1961. The much-praised productions of *HMS Pinafore* and *The Pirates of Penzance* by Tyrone Guthrie's company from Stratford, Ontario, in 1962 marked the earliest London performances of those works outside the repertory of the D'Oyly Carte company, whose monopoly of the British performing right had expired in 1961. Lloyd Webber's *Phantom of the Opera* opened in 1987.

King's Theatre. A theatre which, under various names in four different buildings on approximately the same site (in the Haymarket), played a leading part in London's operatic life from 1705 to 1910. The original theatre was built by John Vanbrugh on the west side of the Haymarket and opened in April 1705 (fig.16, and fig.2 above). Until the death of Queen Anne in 1714 it was known as the Queen's Theatre; later in the century it was generally called the King's Theatre, Haymarket (and must be distinguished from the Little Theatre in the Haymarket, on the east side of the street). From 1708 to the 1840s it was London's principal Italian opera house. Vanbrugh built the theatre as an elegant home for what he hoped would be a single company with a monopoly on both plays and operas in London. But despite early alterations, the building proved acoustically more suitable for opera, and after 1710 it was devoted almost entirely to that purpose. Vanbrugh raised £3000 from among the nobility and gentry (30 persons contributing £100 each); the total cost of the first theatre is unknown. The exterior dimensions were approximately 18 by 40 metres, and normal capacity was about 850. (Reports of 1500 and 2000 in the 1730s are for concert performances in which large numbers of people sat on the stage and in backstage space.) Throughout the 18th century the theatre normally offered two opera performances a week (on Tuesday and Saturday) during a season extending from November or December to June.

The great castrato Nicolini was engaged at the astonishing salary of 800 guineas in 1708, and Handel's *Rinaldo* had its première at the theatre in 1711. But artistically glorious and socially glamorous though the theatre was, even the foundation of the Royal Academy of Music (1719) did not long establish the opera company on a secure financial basis. Among the works first performed in the 1720s and early 30s were Handel's *Amadigi*, *Radamisto*, *Ottone*, *Giulio Cesare*, *Tamerlano*, *Rodelinda*, *Scipione*, *Admeto*, *Partenope*, *Poro*, *Sosarme* and *Orlando*. In 1734 the theatre was taken over by the rival Opera of the Nobility, importing Farinelli and featuring the music of Porpora. Handel rejoined the King's Theatre for 1737–8, but the company collapsed at the end of the season. In the 1740s Lord Middlesex ran a financially ill-fated company, employing Galuppi (1741–3) and Gluck

(1745–6). Gluck's *Orfeo* was first given in 1770, with additional music by J. C. Bach and Guglielmi. The opera company was in rocky shape in the 1750s and early 60s but stabilized between about 1765 and 1778. Composers included Cocchi (from 1758), Giardini (head of the band and briefly theatre manager), J. C. Bach (from 1763), Guglielmi (from 1768) and Sacchini (from 1773). After R. B. Sheridan and Thomas Harris bought the company in an ill-advised leveraged takeover in 1778, it descended rapidly into a permanent condition of insolvency. Nevertheless the 1780s were artistically splendid: the castratos Pacchierotti, Rubinelli and Marchesi were imported, and Noverre became ballet-master for 1781–2.

Major alterations in 1782 increased the theatre's capacity to about 1800 (at a cost of some £10 000), but despite larger box-office receipts the manager William Taylor went bankrupt in spring 1783. He went to prison and turned the theatre over to six trustees, headed by the architect and machinist Michael Novosielski. After two more disastrous seasons G. A. Gallini, formerly a dancer and ballet-master, took over as manager and kept the venture afloat until the theatre burnt down on 17 June 1789. At that time there was a major battle over the future of Italian opera in London: the accumulated debts of the King's Theatre approached £100 000, and the Lord Chamberlain announced that in future, opera would be given at the Pantheon by a company of which he was secretly a principal backer. William Taylor nonetheless succeeded in rebuilding the King's Theatre and opened it in February 1791 as a concert and dance venue, in defiance of the authorities. When the Pantheon burnt down in January 1792 the King's Theatre was the logical place for opera to find a home, and the following year it returned there. (The King's was used by Drury Lane performers between September 1791 and June 1793 while that theatre was being rebuilt.)

The second King's Theatre (fig.17), Haymarket, was designed by Novosielski and cost at least £73 000. It was built on a larger site (about 28 by 51 metres) and held some 3300 people, making it the largest theatre in London until Holland's new Drury Lane was completed in 1794. After the 'General Opera Trust Deed' of August 1792 the theatre regained both its licence and its Italian opera monopoly, but management continued stormy and finances precarious. Taylor fought with a succession of partners (Francis Gould, Edmund Waters) until forced out of the business by the Lord Chamberlain in 1814. Early in the century the theatre engaged Catalani at the staggering salary of £5250, with her benefits guaranteed at £1000 more. Escalating salaries for other singers as well drove up seat prices and led to public protest. During these years work by Paisiello, Cimarosa, Sarti, Gazzaniga, Martín y Soler, Salieri and Portogallo were performed, as were, in their English premières, *Alceste*, *Iphigénie en Tauride*, *La clemenza di Tito*, *Così fan tutte*, *Die Zauberflöte*, *Le nozze di Figaro*, *Don Giovanni*, and Rossini's *Barbiere di Siviglia*, *Elisabetta, regina d'Inghilterra*, *L'italiana in Algeri*, *La Cenerentola* and *Tancredi*. Principal singers included Teresa Belocchi, Giorgi-Banti, Mrs Billington, Catalani, Fodor-Mainville, Grassini, Mara, Ambrogietti, García, Kelly, Levasseur and Naldi.

Between 1821 and 1827 the company was managed by John Ebers, whose *Seven Years of the King's Theatre* (1828) gives a vivid picture of the artistic aspirations and financial difficulties that led to the loss of £44 000. Ebers mounted more Rossini, in addition to Spontini

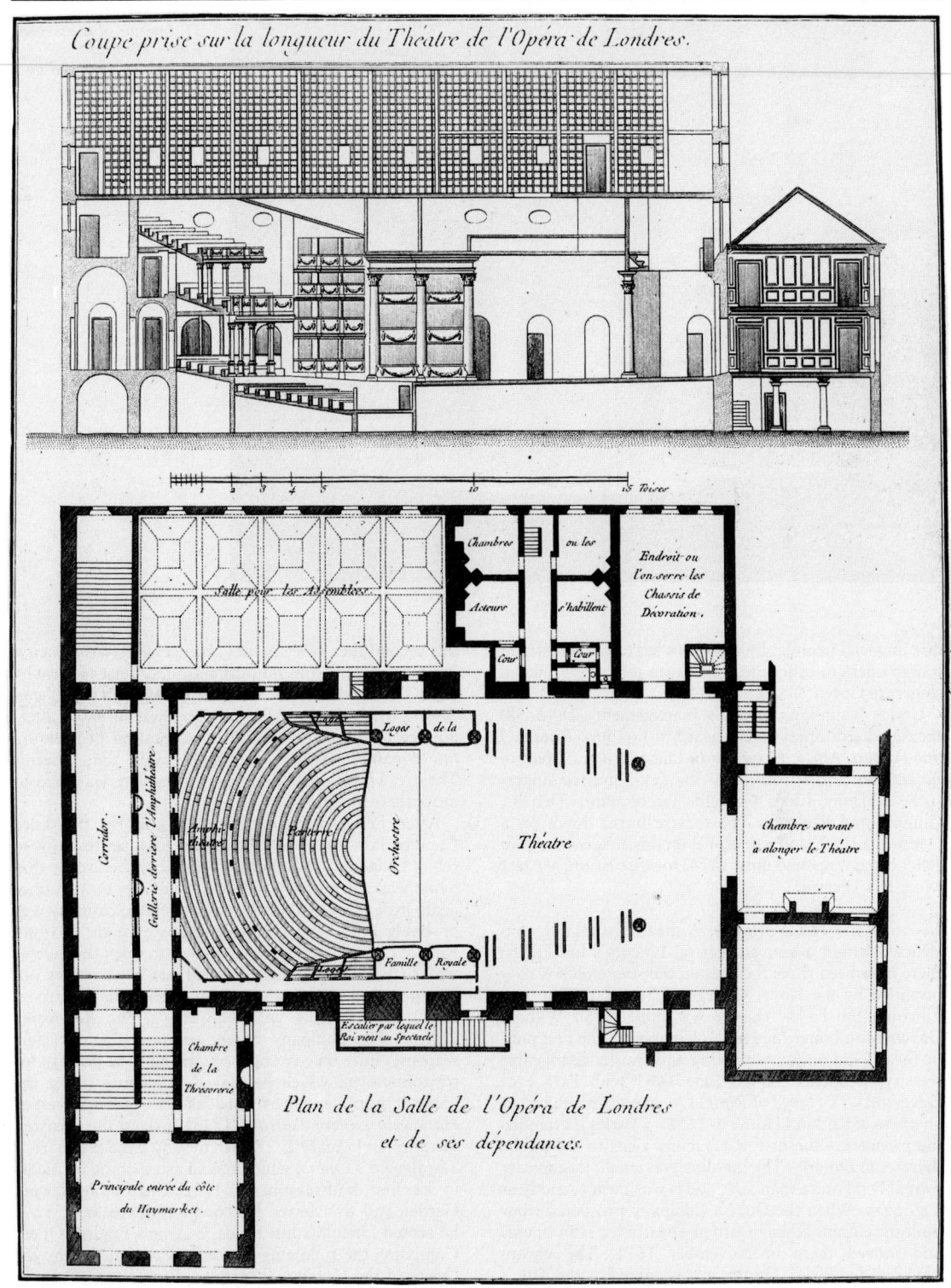

Coupe prise sur la longueur du Théatre de l'Opéra de Londres.

Plan de la Salle de l'Opéra de Londres et de ses dépendances.

16. *Plan and section of the first King's Theatre, designed by John Vanbrugh in 1703 (altered 1709): engraving from 'Parallèle de plans des plus belles salles de spectacles d'Italie et de France' (c1764) by G. Dumont*

and *Il crociato in Egitto*, the first Meyerbeer opera given in England. His singers included Brambilla, Camporese, Caradori, De Begnis, Pasta and Velluti. Ebers was succeeded by Pierre Laporte (1828–31, 1833–41) who brought the works of Bellini and Donizetti to London. His company included Grisi, Tacchinardi-Persiani, Viardot, Rubini, Mario and Lablache, and the noted conductor Michael Costa. When Victoria became queen in 1837 the theatre was renamed Her Majesty's and the company called the Royal Italian Opera. Increasingly

31

17. *Interior of the second King's Theatre, Haymarket, designed by Michael Novosielski and opened in 1791: engraving (1709) by Pugin after Rowlandson, aquatinted by Black*

dire financial troubles by the 1840s led to the transfer of Italian opera to other theatres. Costa took the principal singers to Covent Garden in 1847.

Under Benjamin Lumley's management (1842–58) the first Verdi operas were heard in London: *Ernani, I due Foscari, Attila, I Lombardi, Luisa Miller, Nabucco, La traviata* and *Il trovatore*. Lumley imported singers such as Jenny Lind, Cruvelli, Piccolomini, Tietjens, Giuglini and Ronconi. The theatre burnt down on 6 December 1867, and a new one, on this site, was built in 1869 but not opened until 1874; for discussion, see Her Majesty's Theatre.

Lincoln's Inn Fields Theatre. A theatre originally constructed within a tennis court on Lincoln's Inn Fields; there have been three theatres on the site, which is now occupied by the Royal College of Surgeons. The first Lincoln's Inn Fields Theatre was built by Sir William Davenant to house the Duke's Company. The first public theatre in London with wing-and-shutter changeable scenery, it opened on 28 June 1661 with Part 1 of Davenant's *The Siege of Rhodes* (originally produced as an opera at Rutland House in 1656). Charles II attended the première – the first of his many visits to the public theatres in London. The building was small, its capacity probably no more than 500, and it was meant strictly as a stopgap. When the Duke's Company prospered, they built the elegant Dorset Garden Theatre for semi-operas and moved there in November 1671. The vacant Lincoln's Inn Fields Theatre was occupied by the King's Company between January 1672 and March 1674 and then reverted to a tennis court.

In 1695 the rebel actors who left the United Company needed a theatre. Led by Thomas Betterton, they obtained contributions from the gentry and reconverted the Lincoln's Inn Fields tennis court. By the standards of Drury Lane and Dorset Garden it was very small and woefully inadequate for the elaborate plays and operas Betterton loved to stage. Virtually nothing is known of this second theatre's internal arrangements or capacity. It mounted numerous musical masques, most of them by John Eccles, the house composer. Purcell's *Dido and Aeneas* received its public première there in 1700, interpolated between the acts of an adaptation of *Measure for Measure*. When Vanbrugh built the Queen's Theatre, Haymarket, Betterton's company was glad to move there in 1705.

After his silencing at Drury Lane by the Lord Chamberlain in 1709, Christopher Rich set to work to rebuild Lincoln's Inn Fields. The third theatre of that name was a drastically different structure, though once again little is known of its internal details; capacity was probably at least 1000 and perhaps as high as 1400. Rich obtained George I's permission to open the theatre under Charles II's patent, but did not live to carry out his intentions. His son John Rich opened the theatre on 18 December 1714 with Farquhar's *The Recruiting Officer.* The company barely survived the next few seasons, but the younger Rich had a genius for pantomime (in which he played Harlequin under the name of 'Lun'), and shows such as *The Necromancer, or Harlequin Doctor Faustus* (1723) revived the theatre's fortunes. In January 1728 Rich mounted the première of *The Beggar's Opera*, which ran an astonishing 62 nights in its first half-season. In 1732 Rich built Covent Garden and transferred his company there. In 1732–3 he rented Lincoln's Inn Fields to Arne's English Opera Company; the following season it was occupied by the Opera of the Nobility. Thereafter Rich was left to rent out the old theatre night by night when he could. Handel used it occasionally from November 1739, when he gave a series of concerts as well as *Alexander's Feast* and *Acis and Galatea*; his last two operas, *Imeneo* and *Deidamia*, were first performed there in 1740 and 1741. The theatre was used occasionally for balls and concerts until 1756, when it became a barracks and subsequently an auction room and a china warehouse. It was demolished in 1848.

Little Theatre in the Haymarket. A small theatre built by John Potter in 1720 on the east side of the Haymarket, opposite the King's Theatre. Its interior arrangements are unknown but capacity was probably about 550. For its first eight seasons it was basically a road house for visiting French troupes and amateurs. After the theatre boom started by *The Beggar's Opera* in 1728 it housed a variety of pickup companies, one of which promptly mounted a pirate production of Gay's ballad opera. Henry Fielding used the theatre in 1730–31 and 1736–7, staging his wildly popular *Author's Farce*, *Pasquin* and *Historical Register* there, as well as some ballad operas. The Little Theatre in the Haymarket (sometimes known as the New Theatre in the Haymarket, or simply as the Little Haymarket) was used by J. F. Lampe in 1732 for several 'English Operas after the Italian manner', notably Lampe's own *Amelia* and *Britannia* and a private production of Handel's *Acis and Galatea* in which Thomas Mountier, Susanna Arne (later Mrs Cibber) and Gustavus Waltz took the principal parts. An opera season was given in winter and spring 1740 but Burney states that the singers were on half pay and the performances poor. In 1747 the actor Samuel Foote took over the theatre as a summer venue, receiving a royal patent in 1766 after a practical joke in the presence of the Duke of York cost him a leg. The theatre was thereafter called the Theatre Royal, Haymarket (often shortened simply to 'Haymarket Theatre'). Foote (and later others) expanded the theatre; by the 1790s it held about 1500. Foote's repertory included plays and burlettas. George Colman (i) took over management in 1777 and produced several of Samuel Arnold's operas, notably *The Spanish Barber* (1777).

Following the destruction of the King's Theatre by fire in 1789, the Italian opera company moved into the Little Haymarket for the period 7 January to 12 June 1790. Works by Cimarosa, Nasolini, Paisiello and others were given by singers as eminent as Mara, Storace and Kelly. Italian opera was staged at the Pantheon in 1790–91, but when it burnt down on 14 January 1792 the company took refuge in the Little Haymarket for the rest of the spring, performing *opera buffa* alone. The theatre was too small to support a full-scale Italian opera company, and in 1792–3 the opera returned to the rebuilt King's Theatre.

The Little Theatre in the Haymarket is often confused with the King's (sometimes Queen's) Theatre in the Haymarket (later His or Her Majesty's). They were near neighbours on opposite sides of the street, but there is no other connection. The original Little Theatre was demolished in 1820; the present Haymarket Theatre was built on approximately the same site and opened in 1821.

London Hippodrome. It opened in 1900 as a circus; later it became a restaurant-cabaret. In 1911 and 1912 Leoncavallo conducted performances of his *Pagliacci* and the première of his *Zingari* there; and in 1912 Mascagni conducted his *Cavalleria rusticana*.

London Opera House. See Stoll Theatre.

Lyceum. A theatre in Wellington Street, off the Strand. It opened in 1772 and served as a venue for exhibitions and occasional concerts. In 1792 Samuel Arnold attempted to obtain a licence for opera and other musical entertainments there but was unsuccessful, and the theatre was used for circuses, panoramas and (in 1802) Mme Tussaud's first waxworks show. In 1809 Drury Lane burnt down and the acting company, with its licence for musical works, took temporary refuge in the Lyceum. When they returned to the rebuilt Drury Lane in 1812 Dr Arnold's son, Samuel James Arnold, managed to retain the licence and give English opera performances during the summer (3 June to 3 October). In 1815 he obtained a 99-year lease on the premises and engaged Samuel Beazley to rebuild and improve the theatre. In 1817 it was one of the first two London theatres to install gas lighting (the other being Drury Lane). As the English Opera House between 1816 and 1830 it staged works by Bishop, Braham, Reeve and Loder, among others. In July 1824 *Der Freischütz* received its first performance in England, in English and with the music arranged by William Hawes. In 1828 the house mounted the first English version of *Così fan tutte* (as *Tit for Tat, or The Tables Turned*). The theatre burnt down in 1830. The company performed at the Adelphi and Olympic theatres while Beazley designed and built a replacement, also known as the English Opera House, on the same site; it opened in July 1834 with Loder's *Nourjahad*, followed by Barnett's *The Mountain Sylph*. Between 1835 and 1838 came new works by Balfe, Loder, Macfarren and others. Balfe himself took over the management in 1840 but his hopes of a regular English opera repertory got no further than an inaugural run of his own *Keolanthe* in 1841. The Licensing Act of 1843 enabled the Lyceum to mount spoken drama as well, and in that direction its future mainly lay. Nevertheless a brief occupation of the theatre by the Pyne-Harrison company in 1857 included a success for Balfe's *The Rose of Castille*, which achieved its 100th performance in less than a year. The Royal Italian Opera from Covent Garden also gave seasons in 1856–8 during the rebuilding of its own theatre.

In rivalry with Covent Garden, the impresario J. H. Mapleson took the theatre for an operatic summer season in 1861, his sopranos including Tietjens but not Patti, as he had hoped. In that season he presented the first performance in Britain of *Un ballo in maschera*. During the theatre's management by the American H. L. Bateman, seasons by the Carl Rosa company took place in 1876 and 1877. Bateman gave a leading place in his company to the young Henry Irving, under whose own management from 1878 to 1901 the theatre enjoyed its most famous (non-operatic) period. In 1889 the company of La Scala, Milan, visited the Lyceum to give the first performances in Britain of Verdi's *Otello*, with Tamagno and Maurel in their original roles.

In 1931 Beecham gave the last of his seasons of Russian opera there, with the Zereteli-Basil company. Once again, as formerly at Drury Lane, the star was Shalyapin; the repertory provided the first performances in Britain of *Sadko*, *Rusalka* (Dargomïzhsky), *Ruslan and Lyudmila* and *The Tsar's Bride*. George Lloyd's *Iernin*, first given in Penzance in 1934, was brought to the Lyceum in 1935. In 1945 the theatre, closed during World War II, became a dance hall, and has rarely been reclaimed for theatrical use.

Lyric Theatre (Hammersmith). A theatre in Hammersmith, west London (not to be confused with the Lyric Theatre, Shaftesbury Avenue, in central London). Opened as the Lyric Hall in 1888 and reconstructed in 1895, it had a poor reputation until Nigel Playfair (actor, producer, manager) took it over in 1914, remaining until 1932. His production of *The Beggar's Opera*, musically edited by Frederic Austin, opened in 1920 and ran nightly for 1463 performances, often claimed as the longest-ever operatic run. (But the work is really of the operetta class and should be compared with modern, even longer-running musicals.) In an attempt (such as has scarcely been made since) to build a British light-opera repertory outside the Gilbert and Sullivan canon, Playfair proceeded in 1924 to revive Sheridan's play *The Duenna* with its original music by the 18th-century Linleys arranged by Alfred Reynolds. In the following year came Dibdin's opera *Lionel and Clarissa*. In 1926 Arne's *Thomas and Sally* was combined with Reynolds's new one-act comic opera *The Policeman's Serenade* to form the show *Riverside Nights*; in 1928 the 18th-century pasticcio *Love in a Village* ran for 124 performances. A. P. Herbert, having been the librettist for *The Policeman's Serenade*, functioned likewise for Thomas Dunhill's *Tantivy Towers* and Reynolds's *Derby Day*, respectively given their first performances at the Lyric in 1931 and 1932. The theatre's subsequent fare has been mixed, but not operatic.

Mermaid Theatre. A conversion of a former school hall in St John's Wood into a small Elizabethan-style theatre (borrowing the name of a famous Elizabethan playhouse) at the instigation of the actor-manager Bernard Miles and his wife Josephine Wilson. Seating 200, it opened in September 1951 with *Dido and Aeneas*, conducted by Geraint Jones, in which Kirsten Flagstad and Maggie Teyte sang as Dido and Belinda. A permanent Mermaid Theatre was established in 1958 by the Thames, under Miles's continuing management, mainly for straight theatre.

New Middlesex Theatre of Varieties. See Winter Garden Theatre.

Old Vic. A theatre in the Waterloo Road. It was built in 1817–18 by the impresario Joseph Glossop as the Royal Coburg Theatre, and led a successful existence as a home of drama and melodrama. In 1833 it was redecorated and renamed the Royal Victoria Theatre (from which its familiar nickname arose). It closed in spring 1880, but later that year the social reformer Emma Cons reopened it as a temperance amusement hall under the name of Royal Victoria Hall and Coffee Tavern. The beginning of opera performances there, from 1900, and the development into Britain's oldest continuous opera-in-English company are described above in §1, English National Opera. After opera left its repertory in 1935, the Old Vic Theatre continued to be an important repertory centre for spoken drama until 1963, then became the temporary home of the new National Theatre company until 1976. Bought by the Canadian impresario Ed Mirvish in 1982, it was completely refurbished and reopened in 1983. Presentations have included the Stratford, Ontario, production of *The Mikado* in 1984 and Bernstein's *Candide* in a joint production with Scottish Opera in 1988.

Olympic Theatre. A theatre that opened in 1805 in what is now the Aldwych area. It was rebuilt in 1818 and again in 1850 but closed in 1899. The extraordinary singer-actress Lucia Vestris was its lessee in 1831–8, presenting spoken drama, farces and burlesques by Planché and others. The impresario Lago used it for a season in 1892 during which he produced the first performance in Britain of *Yevgeny Onegin* (conducted by Henry Wood).

Opera Comique. A theatre in the Strand, opened in 1870 and closed in 1899. (Its name was not generally spelt in proper French fashion as 'Opéra'.) It was first occupied by French drama companies, at a time when the turmoil following the Franco-Prussian War drove many French as refugees to London, including Gounod. The theatre had little success before Richard D'Oyly Carte announced its 'reopening' in November 1877 with the presentation by his own Comedy Opera Company of Gilbert and Sullivan's *The Sorcerer*. Its success led to the première of *HMS Pinafore* there in 1879, followed by *The Pirates of Penzance* (1880, after the New York première) and the first performance of *Patience* in 1881. The unattractiveness of the Opera Comique was often remarked on, and Carte's subsequent transfer of operations to his own newly built Savoy Theatre signified the prosperity of his enterprise. Subsequent presentations at the theatre (under other managements) have been historically dwarfed by Gilbert and Sullivan's fame, but a run of 116 performances for *Carina*, a comic opera by Julia Woolf (1888), should not be ignored. The last opera produced there was Stanford's *Shamus O'Brien* (1896), conducted by Henry Wood.

Palace Theatre. A theatre in Cambridge Circus built by Richard D'Oyly Carte as the Royal English Opera House, specifically for the first production of Sullivan's sole serious opera, *Ivanhoe*, in January 1891. Mounted in successive performances with changing casts, it achieved 160 performances, but neither this nor Messager's *La basoche* later in the year (with which *Ivanhoe* was revived in alternating performances) was sufficient to recoup Carte's investment; his losses were reported at £36 000. He sold the theatre to Augustus Harris, who at the time controlled Covent Garden, Drury Lane, Her Majesty's and the Olympic. Harris reopened it as the Palace Theatre of Varieties in 1892. Its later function (as the Palace from 1911) has been chiefly in musical comedy and its successors, though there was a brief opera season by an Italian company in 1955. Rodgers and Hammerstein's *The Sound of Music* (1961) achieved 2386 performances, the longest-running American musical in British stage history. The eight-year run of Andrew Lloyd Webber's *Jesus Christ Superstar* from 1972 (3358 performances) was even more remarkable. Lloyd Webber himself has been the owner of the theatre since 1983.

Pantheon. A theatre converted from an elegant exhibition hall built by James Wyatt and opened in 1772; it was located on the south side of Oxford Street just west of Poland Street, on a site now occupied by the Marks and Spencer department store and still labelled 'The Pantheon'. Used for masquerades and concerts in the 1770s and 80s, it was one of the venues for the Handel festival in 1784; it became an opera house in 1790. After the destruction of the King's Theatre, Haymarket, by fire in June 1789 a battle developed over where Italian opera should be staged. The Duke of Bedford and the Earl of Salisbury decided to create a kind of English court opera with themselves as secret backers and Robert Bray O'Reilly as front man; they acquired the lease of the Pantheon and had Wyatt convert it into a small but glamorous opera house (fig.7, page 10). The exterior dimensions of the stage and auditorium area were approximately 29 by 37 metres; the capacity was 1500 or slightly higher, including some 850 box seats. Mount Edgcumbe called the Pantheon 'one of the prettiest, and by far the most genteel and comfortable theatre I ever saw, of a moderate size and excellent shape, and admirably adapted both for seeing and hearing'. A starry company headed by Pacchierotti and Mara was assembled to perform both *opera seria* and *opera buffa* for the 1790–91 season. It opened on 17 February 1791 with a pasticcio based on Sacchini's *Armida*, and on 16 June gave the première of Paisiello's *La locanda*, specially composed for London. Unfortunately the company lost far more money than its backers expected, and O'Reilly (the scapegoat) was forced to flee to Paris. Four nights into the second season the theatre burnt down in suspicious circumstances (arson was suspected) and the performers finished the season at the Little Theatre in the Haymarket. The Pantheon was rebuilt by April 1795, after which it was again used for concerts and masquerades. In 1812 it was elaborately refitted for theatrical purposes and an attempt was made by discontented singers at the King's Theatre to occupy it, but a licence was refused. A move to turn it into an English opera house in 1813 was likewise quashed, and the building was not thereafter used as a theatre. It was demolished in 1937.

Prince's Theatre. A theatre in Shaftesbury Avenue, built in 1911. Though primarily used for spoken drama, it successfully mounted Messager's operetta *Monsieur Beaucaire* in 1919. In the same year, it was chosen by the D'Oyly Carte Opera Company for the resumption of its London seasons and was often used by that company thereafter. During World War II it was three times damaged by enemy action but managed to stay open, and in 1944–5 accommodated the Sadler's Wells opera and ballet companies. It was the location of the Carl Rosa company's last London season (1960), followed by an ad hoc Italian company in *Rigoletto* and *Tosca*.

The name Prince's Theatre was also occasionally used for the St James's Theatre, King Street, in its early years.

Princess's Theatre. A theatre near Oxford Circus, opened in 1840. After some unsuccessful promenade concerts it underwent alterations and was reopened in 1842 with *La sonnambula* in English. The performances of Rossini's *Tancredi* in 1843 and *L'italiana in Algeri* in 1844 were the first ever to be given in English. Works by Balfe were also given, and likewise the premières of Loder's *The Night Dancers* (1846) and Macfarren's *King Charles II* (1849). Thereafter the theatre mainly housed spoken drama, though in 1870 Offenbach's *La Périchole* was staged there by a French company with Hortense Schneider in the title role, and in 1875 the Carl Rosa company chose it for its first London season. In 1900 the theatre became a warehouse, demolished in 1931.

Queen's Theatre. See Dorset Garden Theatre, King's Theatre and Scala Theatre.

Regent Theatre. A theatre on Euston Road, opened in 1900 as the Euston Palace of Varieties, becoming the Regent in 1922. It was then run by the celebrated impresario Barry Jackson, who brought to it his Birmingham Repertory Company production of Rutland Boughton's opera *The Immortal Hour* in 1922. Here it achieved a total of 216 consecutive performances – the longest such run for any 'serious' opera in London. The theatre later became a cinema and was demolished in 1971.

Royal Coburg Theatre. See Old Vic.

Royal English Opera House. See Palace Theatre.

Royal Opera House, Covent Garden. See Covent Garden.

Royalty Theatre. A theatre in Dean Street, Soho (not related to an earlier and a later theatre of that name elsewhere in London); it opened in 1840 and closed in 1939. Offenbach's *La Périchole*, having been already staged in French at the Princess's Theatre, was given its first performance in English in January 1875 with the actress-singer-manager Selina Dolaro in the title role; in March, on the suggestion of Dolaro's assistant Richard D'Oyly Carte, the newly written *Trial by Jury* by W. S. Gilbert and Arthur Sullivan was added to the bill (opening, in effect, the Gilbert-Sullivan-Carte partnership).

Royal Victoria Theatre. See Old Vic.

Sadler's Wells Theatre. A theatre in Rosebery Avenue, Islington, on the site of a 17th-century Music House built to entertain patrons of Mr Sadler's well-spring. It was converted into a theatre in 1746, and later became famous for various spectacles from aquatic drama to Shakespeare; it was then a music hall and a cinema, before closing in 1906. Rebuilt with a capacity of 1548, it was reopened in 1931 on the initiative of Lilian Baylis, the manager of the Old Vic Theatre, who wished to establish a north London counterpart to the Old Vic. Initially, as at her first theatre, the Baylis presentations at Sadler's Wells embraced classic drama as well as opera and ballet, but soon concentrated on the last two. (For details of the company and the repertory, see §1 above, English National Opera.) Sadler's Wells Opera became firmly established in 1935–6 and retained that title through its wartime exile to other venues, through the theatre's reopening almost at the war's end (1945) with *Peter Grimes*, and even for the first few years after the company quit the theatre for good in 1968, moving to the much larger, more centrally located Coliseum.

On a similar point of nomenclature, from 1945 the Sadler's Wells Ballet moved its main establishment to Covent Garden and in 1956 was renamed the Royal Ballet. A junior troupe continued, when not touring, to have Sadler's Wells as its London base: for a period it was detached from the theatre, but in 1976 it was relocated there as the Sadler's Wells Royal Ballet. In 1990 it moved to Birmingham as the Birmingham Royal Ballet.

Even before Sadler's Wells Opera left the theatre for good in 1968, its schedule allowed occasional guest seasons to be given at the theatre by other companies. Among these visitors were London-based groups such as the Handel Opera Society and the New Opera Company, but also others such as the WNO (five visits, 1955–62) and the Frankfurt Opera, whose visit in 1963 included a rare London performance of Lortzing's *Zar und Zimmermann*. After 1968, other visiting companies included the Cologne Opera (first British performance of Henze's *Der junge Lord*, 1969), the D'Oyly Carte Opera Company, the English Opera Group and (1973) the Royal Northern College of Music. The prestige of the theatre's name was lent to an operetta-based enterprise, the New Sadler's Wells Opera (see §1 above), from 1982 to 1989. In 1988 a small subsidiary auditorium was opened under the name of the Lilian Baylis Theatre.

St James's Theatre. A theatre in King Street, Covent Garden, which opened in 1835. It was built for the singer John Braham, who began with an 'operatic burlesque', *Agnes Sorel*, followed by two short farces. Losing money, he sublet the theatre to a French company early in 1836 but returned in the autumn. Among his productions that year were two with texts by Dickens – the two-act farce *The Strange Gentleman*, and the ballad opera *The Village Coquettes* with music by John Hullah. In 1875, in a triple bill with two plays, Sullivan's operetta *The Zoo* received its first performance. The theatre closed in 1957 and was then demolished.

Savoy Theatre. A theatre in Savoy Hill, between the Strand and the Embankment, built by Richard D'Oyly Carte for Gilbert and Sullivan operettas. It opened in October 1881 with a transfer of *Patience* from the Opera Comique, and was the first theatre in London to be entirely lit by electric light (fig.10, page 14). All the later Gilbert and Sullivan operettas were first produced there, beginning with *Iolanthe* in 1882, as also were Sullivan's later operettas with other librettists. Under the same management (Helen Carte being active during her husband's last years and taking over after his death in 1901), other operettas including Edward German's *Merrie England* (1902) and *A Princess of Kensington* (1903) were given. The name 'Savoy Operas' was originally applied by Carte to them all. In the 20th century the theatre's fare has been diversified. From 1909 to 1929 no Gilbert and Sullivan was given. Spoken drama predominated, though in 1910 and 1911 the mezzo-soprano Marie Brema organized three seasons of opera distinguished by her portrayal of the title role in Gluck's *Orfeo* in her own production. The old Savoy was closed in December 1928 and the present theatre (cap. 1122) opened ten months later with *The Gondoliers*. A rare operatic enterprise in wartime was Jay Pomeroy's presentation of Musorgsky's *The Fair at Sorochintsï* in October 1941 (later given at the Adelphi Theatre). Among the D'Oyly Carte company's later seasons at the Savoy was a celebration (1975) of the centenary of the first Gilbert and Sullivan work under Carte's management, *Trial by Jury*. On this anniversary a complete cycle of the operettas was given, including, for the occasion only, *Utopia Limited*, and, in concert performance, *The Grand Duke*. After the company had dissolved in 1982 and was later reconstituted, the Savoy housed its second London season (1989). The theatre was gutted by a fire in 1990.

Scala Theatre. A theatre in Charlotte Street, Soho, opened in 1905 on the site of a previous theatre known at different times as the Queen's, the Fitzroy and, from 1865, the Prince of Wales's. In 1832 it housed the first performance of the 18-year-old G. A. Macfarren's operetta *The Maid of Switzerland* (the theatre, at that time the Queen's, was under the management of the composer's father). It did not regularly accommodate opera but was the site of the remarkable London Opera Festival, which ran from 30 December 1929 into the following month. The programme included Monteverdi's *Orfeo* (in its first London staging, being the Oxford 1925 production), conducted by J. A. Westrup, and Handel's *Giulio Cesare*, conducted by Gervase Hughes, both in English translations by R. L. Stuart, as well as *Der Freischütz* conducted by Beecham. In the Handel opera, Nirenus was played by a male alto, described by Richard Capell in the *Monthly Musical Record* (1930) as 'a voice that should never in any circumstance be heard as a solo'. The Scala was used by

the D'Oyly Carte Opera Company in 1938 and by amateur companies after World War II, and also by the English Opera Group for its tenth anniversary season in 1956, during which the première of Lennox Berkeley's *Ruth* was given. The theatre closed in 1969 and was demolished in the following year.

Shaftesbury Theatre. The first theatre to be built in Shaftesbury Avenue (it opened in 1888). It was taken by the impresario Lago for a season of Italian opera in October–November 1891, during which the first production in Britain of *Cavalleria rusticana* was so successful that it was given nightly (with extracts from other Italian operas) for a further fortnight. The theatre also housed the Beecham Opera Company's seasons in 1915–16, including premières of Stanford's *The Critic* and Ethel Smyth's *The Boatswain's Mate*. It was destroyed by bombing in April 1941.

Stoll Theatre. A theatre built by the elder Oscar Hammerstein at the southern end of Kingsway, originally called the London Opera House. It opened in 1911 with the first performance in Britain of Jean Nouguès's *Quo vadis?*. The season continued until 2 March 1912 with an emphasis on the French repertory, including *Les contes d'Hoffmann*, *Faust*, *Louise*, *Hérodiade* and *Le jongleur de Notre-Dame*. Artists included Lina Cavalieri, Marguerite d'Alvarez and Maurice Renaud. A second season, from 22 April to 13 July 1912, coincided with the regular grand opera season at Covent Garden and was financially disastrous; it included the première of Holbrooke's *Children of Don*, conducted by Arthur Nikisch, and the British première of Massenet's *Don Quichotte*. The theatre was then used for films, revues and pantomime, though from May to July 1915 a season of Russian, French and Italian opera was given under the direction of Vladimir Rosing; it included the first productions in England of *The Queen of Spades*, in which Rosing himself sang Hermann, and Rakhmaninov's *Aleko*, as well as *Yevgeny Onegin*, *Lakmé* and *Madama Butterfly*. In 1916 the theatre was bought by Oswald Stoll and renamed the Stoll Theatre, offering variety entertainment and films.

Jay Pomeroy presented his New London Opera Company (from the Cambridge Theatre) in a two-month season in summer 1949, for which Clemens Krauss returned to London as an operatic conductor. Between 1952 and 1955, under the joint management of Eugene Iskoldoff and Peter Daubeny, three seasons of Italian opera were given with artists including Margherita Carosio, Magda Olivero, Virginia Zeani, Carlo Bergonzi, Tito Gobbi, Gianni Raimondi and Ferruccio Tagliavini; orchestral and production standards were poor.

In 1952 a New York company brought the first performances in England of *Porgy and Bess*, with Leontyne Price and William Warfield. A short season by the Zagreb Opera and Ballet included Jakov Gotovac's *Ero the Joker* (1955). In 1957 Sandor Gorlinsky mounted a successful season of Italian opera that brought *Lucia di Lammermoor* back to the London stage for the first time since 1925 and introduced Renata Scotto and Alfredo Kraus to London audiences. The theatre closed in 1957 and was demolished.

Strand Theatre. A theatre originally named Rayner's New Subscription Theatre in the Strand, functioning between 1832 and 1905, on a site now covered by the Aldwych Underground station. On a different site, the present theatre was built by the Shubert Brothers of New York and opened in 1905 as the Waldorf; it was renamed the Strand Theatre in 1909. It opened with a season of Italian opera organized by Henry Russell, brother of Sir Landon Ronald. The repertory included *La sonnambula*, *L'elisir d'amore* and *L'amico Fritz*, and Bonci, De Lucia, Ancona and Pini-Corsi were among the singers. The performances alternated with appearances by an Italian drama company. In March 1942 a company made up of British and refugee musicians put on a season of *Les contes d'Hoffmann* conducted by Walter Susskind.

Theatre Royal, Covent Garden. See Covent Garden.

Theatre Royal, Drury Lane. See Drury Lane.

Theatre Royal, Haymarket. See Little Theatre in the Haymarket.

Waldorf Theatre. See Strand Theatre.

Winter Garden Theatre. Opened in 1911 as the New Middlesex Theatre of Varieties, this theatre in Drury Lane was renamed the Winter Garden in 1919. It housed many musical comedies, among them the first British performances of *Sally* (1921; music by Jerome Kern) and *The Vagabond King* (1927; music by Rudolf Friml). The theatre closed in 1959.

3. MISCELLANEOUS INSTITUTIONS.

Almeida Festival. An annual festival, in June, concentrating on contemporary music and music theatre, begun in 1981. Most of its events are held at the Almeida Theatre, Islington, or the nearby Union Chapel, but during the 1988 festival the Queen Elizabeth Hall was used for the first British performance of Kagel's 'music-epic' *Oral Treason* (three actors and instrumental ensemble), given to an English text by Christopher Logue. Other first British performances have included Claude Vivier's *Kopernikus* (1985), Rihm's *Jakob Lenz* (1986) and Michael Finnissy's *The Undivine Comedy* (1988); the première of John Casken's *Golem* was given in 1989. The group Théâtre de Complicité has presented music-theatre works at the festival.

Camden Festival. A municipally financed festival held each spring, inaugurated as the St Pancras Festival in 1954 by the then existing Borough of St Pancras. Renamed on that borough's amalgamation (1965) into the Borough of Camden, it continued until 1987 to play an important role in widening London's available repertory. Mostly using the St Pancras Town Hall, the Jeannetta Cochrane Theatre, Holborn, and the Collegiate (later named the Bloomsbury) Theatre, Gordon Street, the Camden Festival promoted small companies in presentations of unfamiliar works, chosen with regard to the moderate orchestral and scenic facilities available and often using amateur chorus. Exceptional was the festival's use of Sadler's Wells Theatre for a staging of Delius's *Koanga* (in collaboration with the Delius Trust) in 1972. Among British stage premières given at the festival were those of Haydn's *L'infedeltà delusa* (Handel Opera Society, 1964), Storace's *Gli equivoci* (Opera Rara, 1974) and Weill's *Der Silbersee* (Abbey Opera, 1987). No less significant in operatic exploration were early London revivals of works such as Rossini's *Il turco in Italia* (Handel Opera Society, 1965) and Donizetti's *Maria Stuarda* (staged by Opera Concerts Ltd, 1966).

City of London Festival. A festival founded in 1962, now occurring in July, and funded by the City of London (i.e. the local government body covering the City, the capital's financial area). The festival's operatic activities included a staging of Gilbert and Sullivan's *The Yeomen of the Guard* at the Tower of London in 1962 and some later years and an imaginative use of the quasi-baroque features of Christ Church, Spitalfields, for productions of Handel's *Alcina* (1985) and Monteverdi's *L'incoronazione di Poppea* (1989).

Earl's Court Stadium. A steel and concrete building in south-west London, opened in 1937. Though capable of seating 20 000, it has been used mainly as an exhibition hall. In 1988 special seating was used when the promoter Harvey Goldsmith brought Vittorio Rossi's production of *Aida* (originally designed for the Verona Arena in 1976). It was given with multiple casts on successive nights including a Sunday; Martina Arroyo and Carlo Cossutta were among the singers and microphoned amplification was employed. Nightly audiences, including many who were new to opera, exceeded 14 000, bringing a commercial success that led to a similar production (not an import, but a new staging by Steven Pimlott) of *Carmen* in 1989, with Maria Ewing.

English Bach Festival. A festival founded and directed by Lina Lalandi, which originally (1963) functioned in Oxford, but was extended to London and since the 1970s has been rooted there. (The works of Bach have become increasingly peripheral to its importance.) Its opera performances not only brought Baroque and other rarities to London, but emphasized the observance of historically correct style and the employment of period instruments. In particular it beneficially tilted the balance, in public perception, of 18th-century period stage performance away from an Anglo-Italian towards a French repertory. More than any other British institution it was responsible for the revival, on a suitably large scale, of Baroque dance, both in independent ballets and as part of opera. Festival productions have been taken to Athens, Versailles, Madrid and elsewhere. Some works were given in concert performance (chiefly at the Banqueting House, Whitehall, or the Queen Elizabeth Hall), including Rameau's *Les Indes galantes* (1974), Handel's *Rinaldo* and Vivaldi's *Griselda* (both 1978) and a double bill of Cavalli's *Ercole amante* and its counterpart, Lully's *Hercule amoureux* (1980). But starting with Rameau's *La princesse de Navarre* in 1977, the festival's most remarkable accomplishment has been its single-night staged performances at Covent Garden, with specially engaged casts and an orchestra of period instruments (usually Jean-Claude Malgoire's La Grande Ecurie et la Chambre du Roy). Further such presentations have included Rameau's *Hippolyte et Aricie* (1978, 1979) and *Castor et Pollux* (1981), for the first time in London, and a rare hearing (1988) of Gluck's *Orfeo ed Euridice* in its Paris version, followed in 1989 by Gluck's *Alceste*. Critical opinion recognized musical and scenic imperfections in these performances but saluted the enlightened impetus behind them. The festival was also responsible for the first British (concert) performance of Roussel's *Padmâvatî*, given at the Coliseum in 1969.

Guildhall School of Music and Drama (GSM). An institute of higher musical and dramatic education, founded in 1880 by the Corporation of the City of London (i.e. the local government body for the capital's financial centre) and until 1935 called simply the Guildhall School of Music. Originally sited in the Blackfriars area, it moved in 1977 to premises adjoining the new Barbican Arts Centre, which included a purpose-built (but ill-designed) theatre. Its courses catered chiefly for amateurs until Landon Ronald became principal in 1911, but it had already staged operas by Gounod and others, including (in 1909) an important revival of Gluck's *Iphigénie en Tauride*. Edric Cundell, principal in 1938–59, heightened the school's operatic activity and conducted many of its productions – an impetus sustained by later appointments as director of opera, including those of Brian Trowell (1963–7), Vilem Tausky (1967–86) and Anthony Besch (1986–9). A wide range of works included the first British performance of Rossini's *Il viaggio a Reims* (1987). In 1989 both music and drama students from the school performed in a production of Purcell's *The Fairy-Queen* at the Middle Temple Hall in the City, one of the Inns of Court used for masques in the 17th century; it was conducted by William Christie, with Baroque instrumentalists from the Royal Conservatory of Music at The Hague.

Henry Wood Promenade Concerts. An annual series of summer concerts, begun by the impresario Robert Newman and the conductor Henry Wood in 1895 as the Queen's Hall Promenade Concerts; the BBC became proprietor in 1926, and since 1944, the year of Wood's death, the series has borne his name. In 1941 the destruction of Queen's Hall by wartime bombing forced the transfer of the concerts to the Royal Albert Hall. The practice began 20 years later of including one or more performances of opera each season – not a mere concert performance with soloists enlisted ad hoc, but an opera company's own performance under its own conductor. Glyndebourne, able to offer performances fresh from its summer festival, gave the first such presentation (*Don Giovanni*) in 1961; with *L'incoronazione di Poppea* in 1963 and Cavalli's *Ormindo* in 1968 Glyndebourne spread the range wider, as with Haydn's *La fedeltà premiata* in 1979. The Royal Opera House, the ENO, the WNO, Scottish Opera and Kent Opera were later called on. From the start, gestures and positioning imitative of the original stage performances served to enhance the enjoyment of listeners present (if not of the primary radio audience), and later an increased dramatic element justified the description of performances as 'semi-staged' – or even 'staged', as with Britten's *Curlew River* in 1987. A semi-staged *Pelléas et Mélisande* exhibited the Opéra de Lyon under John Eliot Gardiner in 1988. Likewise semi-staged, though crudely, was the historic revival organized in the following year by the Consort of Musicke under Anthony Rooley's direction. A single evening comprised performances of Congreve's text *The Judgment of Paris* in settings by Daniel Purcell, Weldon and Eccles – settings that had originally competed for a contemporary audience's favour (along with another setting by Godfrey Finger) in 1701. Weldon's setting was then preferred, but that of Eccles in the 'judgment by clapometer' (measuring volume and warmth of applause) in 1989.

John Lewis Partnership Music Society. An amateur society whose opera productions, under professional guidance and with some professional soloists, have cultivated a unique repertory. It is based on, and subsidized by, the chain of stores whose name it bears. An unbroken run of annual performances (in English) began in 1947 at an auditorium within the Oxford Street store, remaining there until a move to the Britten Opera House within the Royal College of Music in 1989. Hugo Cole's *The Tunnel*, specially commissioned, was given its first performance in 1960. The group's standards were safeguarded for a long period (1960–81, 1984–6) by James Robertson as principal conductor. In a wide range of works, the society gave the first British stage performances of Dvořák's *Rusalka* (1950) and *Šelma sedlák* (as *The Peasant a Rogue*, 1963). Cherishing operetta and *opéra comique* at a time of their general neglect, the society performed not only Offenbach but also Adam, Bizet, Chabrier, Planquette, Lecocq (*La fille de Madame Angot* in 1972 and *Giroflé-Girofla* in 1988), Messager and Suppé. Tom Hawkes and Sally Gilpin were particularly successful as director and choreographer, extending their work to Millöcker's *Der Bettelstudent* at the new location in 1989.

London International Opera Festival. An annual event of about five weeks (from 1986), in May–June, aimed at capturing a new audience with a programme partly of unusual works and of standard works offered at discounted prices for young people at the main opera houses. In 1989 the ENO production of Blake's *The Plumber's Gift* was included alongside such small-scale enterprises as that of Midsummer Opera and student productions. A wide range of locations is used. A change of name to London Opera Festival was announced in 1992. See also §1, Morley Opera.

London Opera Centre. An institute for operatic training, set up in 1963 with an Arts Council grant. Musical and dramatic training was given, but not individual singing lessons. It was housed in the former Roxy Cinema in the Commercial Road, East London, premises that also served as a rehearsal stage for the Covent Garden Opera Company. It was meant to succeed, and improve on, the National School of Opera, but the directorate with Sir David Webster in charge declined to appoint either Joan Cross or Anne Wood (who had run that school) to direct it. Humphrey Procter-Gregg was given the position, with Cross and Wood assisting. Both of them resigned in 1964 over policy, in a public argument extending to Parliamentary questions. Procter-Gregg also resigned after that year and was succeeded by James Robertson, who directed the centre until it closed in 1978. Under Robertson's direction the students (who included Kiri te Kanawa and Ann Murray) participated in public opera productions, some at the Collegiate Theatre, Bloomsbury, and Sadler's Wells, which were generally well received. These included the first British performance of Lortzing's *Die Opernprobe* (1969). Finally in 1978 at the Collegiate a triple bill was given of Haydn's *La canterina*, Vaughan Williams's *Riders to the Sea* and Puccini's *Gianni Schicchi*, with Robertson and Peter Gellhorn sharing the conducting. The winding-up of the centre was accompanied by a recognition that its activities had been over-ambitiously planned in an inconvenient location. Its function, considerably reduced, was then allotted to the much smaller National Opera Studio under the direction of Michael Langdon and later, from 1986, of Richard Van Allan.

National Opera Studio. See London Opera Centre.

National School of Opera. An institution for operatic training, originally named the Opera Studio, founded in 1948 by the singers Joan Cross and Anne Wood. It changed its name (and moved to new premises at

Morley College) in 1959. Its end was signalled in 1963 by the foundation of the new, larger London Opera Centre.

Royal Academy of Music (RAM). An institute for specialized musical education, founded in 1822 (when students, mostly boarders, were aged between 10 and 15). It moved to its present site in Marylebone Road in 1912. With the raising of the student age, full-fledged opera performance became possible. Sir George Macfarren as principal (1875–87) took students to perform his *Jessy Lea* at the Haymarket Theatre in January 1886. The academy gave the first performances of *The Cricket on the Hearth* by another principal, Mackenzie, in 1914, and of Dunhill's *The Enchanted Garden* in 1928; it gave the first British performance of Wolf's *Der Corregidor* in 1934. After World War II, even before the opening of the new Sir Jack Lyons Theatre in 1977, the academy's opera performances attained a high level (especially under John Streets, director of opera 1965–84). Notable were a performance in 1965 of *The Cappemakers* by John Tavener when he was still a student, an early British performance of Verdi's *Giovanna d'Arco* in 1966 and the first London stage performance of Monteverdi's *L'incoronazione di Poppea* in 1969, the first performance in Britain of Henze's *Moralities* in 1970 and, in 1971, a remarkable arena-style production of *Die Zauberflöte* in the Auden-Kallman translation. John Gardner's *Tobermory* had its première in 1977 and Weill's *Street Scene* its first British production in 1984.

For the Handelian Royal Academy and its successor the 'Second Academy', see §1, above.

Royal Albert Hall. A large circular hall sited in Kensington. Named after the late Prince Consort, it was opened in 1871 with seating for up to 8000 people and has always been used for both musical and non-musical events. *Parsifal* was first heard in Britain in a concert performance conducted by Joseph Barnby in 1884, nearly 30 years before the expiry of Bayreuth's self-proclaimed monopoly of stage performances (1913). In 1922 Thomas Fairbairn produced *Cavalleria rusticana* and scenes from *Faust* in the central arena, winning a success that led to his celebrated pageant productions of Coleridge-Taylor's *Hiawatha* (with the Royal Choral Society), beginning in 1924 and repeated in later years up to World War II. The destruction of Queen's Hall by wartime bombing in 1941 led to the transfer to the Royal Albert Hall of the Henry Wood Promenade Concerts, the programmes of which were later to embrace semi-staged opera productions.

Royal College of Music (RCM). An institute of higher musical education founded in 1883 and located in Kensington. A distinguished record of opera performances owed its initial impetus to the encouragement of Stanford, who was a professor from the college's beginning until his death in 1924. Stanford himself directed the historic revival of *Dido and Aeneas* given by students at the Lyceum Theatre in 1895. The college was responsible for the first performances in English of Schumann's *Genoveva* (1893), Delibes' *Le roi l'a dit* (1894), Weber's *Euryanthe* (1900) and Goetz's *Francesca von Rimini* (1908); and the British operas it has produced include Smyth's *Entente cordiale* (1925), Vaughan Williams's *The Shepherds of the Delectable Mountains* (1922), *Hugh the Drover* (1924), *Sir John in Love* (1929) and *Riders to the Sea* (1937),

and Arthur Benjamin's *The Devil Take Her* (1931) – all first performances. After World War II the college joined in the new enthusiasm for opera training, with Clive Carey as director of opera, 1948–53, and Richard Austin, 1955–76. Productions have ranged from Handel to Offenbach and 20th-century works such as Granados's *Goyescas* (1951, the first British production) and Roussel's *Le testament de la tante Caroline* (1963). The Britten Opera Theatre (named after a composer who had found little encouragement as a student there) was opened in 1986 with mixed 'gala' performances, followed the next year by *Albert Herring*. James Lockhart became head of the Opera School in 1986. In 1989 the first performance of *The Fisherman* by Paul Max Edlin, a recent student, was given on the eve of the composer's 26th birthday.

South Bank Halls. The name given to the three concert halls forming part of the arts complex on either side of Waterloo Bridge on the south side of the Thames. The Royal Festival Hall (cap. 2895) was opened in 1951 as part of the Festival of Britain celebrations; the Queen Elizabeth Hall (cap. 1094) and, in the same building, the Purcell Room (cap. 368) were opened in 1967. The Royal Festival Hall has been occasionally used for staged operatic productions, the Stuttgart Opera's visit in 1955 being notable for Wieland Wagner's staging of *Fidelio* – the first time London had seen the 'new Bayreuth' approach to such a work, dispensing with traditional action. Many concert performances of opera have been given, among them Busoni's *Doktor Faust* conducted by Boult in 1959, with Fischer-Dieskau and Richard Lewis. Such concert performances, described in *Opera* (xix, 1968, p.1015) as 'all the rage just at present', included several conducted by Klemperer. Montserrat Caballé made her London début in a 1968 concert performance of *Lucrezia Borgia* under the management of Denny Dayviss, whose other promotions included the first British (concert) performances of Donizetti's *Caterina Cornaro* (1973) and of Bloch's *Macbeth* (1975). In 1988 Messiaen's *Saint François d'Assise* received its first London hearing in a staged performance under the auspices of the LPO.

The Queen Elizabeth Hall has likewise accommodated both staged opera and concert performances, the English Bach Festival using it in both categories from 1977. The Handel Opera Society gave many concert performances there between 1967 and 1974. In 1986 the hall underwent special modification of its platform and technical facilities to permit a theatre-like staging, an early beneficiary being Birtwistle's *Yan Tan Tethera*, given its first performance by Opera Factory London Sinfonietta in 1986. The same organization gave Reimann's *Die Gespensterstonate* (in tandem with Strindberg's play from which it is derived) in 1989. Other companies presenting staged performances have included Kent Opera (Judith Weir's *A Night at the Chinese Opera*, 1987), Glyndebourne Touring Opera (Nigel Osborne's *The Electrification of the Soviet Union*, 1987), Wexford Festival Opera (Mercadante's *Elisa e Claudio*, 1988; Mozart's *Mitridate, re di Ponto*, 1989), Opera Restor'd and Travelling Opera.

University College Opera Group. A college society which, under professional musical direction and using some professional soloists, became known from the mid-1950s for presenting a number of rarities, including Moniuszko's *Halka* (1961, the first British performance). Between 1962 and 1976, performances under George Badacsonyi included the première of Peter Wishart's *Clytemnestra* (1974) as well as the first British performances of Wagner's *Das Liebesverbot* (1965), Erkel's *Bánk bán* (1968) and Verdi's *Stiffelio* (1973). Later musical directors have been Guy Woolfenden and Christopher Fifield. Performances began within the college, part of the University of London, and moved in 1968 to the Collegiate (now the Bloomsbury) Theatre in Gordon Street.

*

Burney H; LS; NicollH

The Case of the Opera-House Disputes, Fairly Stated (London, 1784)
   A. Le Texier: *Ideas on the Opera, offered to the Subscribers, Creditors, and Amateurs of that Theatre* (London, 1790)

R. B. O'Reilly: *An Authentic Narrative of the Principal Circumstances relating to the Opera-House in the Haymarket* (London, 1791)

W. Taylor: *A Concise Statement of Transactions and Circumstances respecting the King's Theatre, in the Haymarket* (London, 1791)

Opera House: a Review of this Theatre (London, c1815)

R. Mount Edgcumbe: *Musical Reminiscences of an Old Amateur, containing an Account of the Italian Opera in England from 1773* (London, 1824)

E. W. Brayley: *Historical and Descriptive Account of the London Theatres* (London, 1826)

M. Kelly: *Reminiscences of Michael Kelly, of the King's Theatre, and Theatre Royal, Drury Lane* (London, 1826, 2/1826); ed. R. Fiske (London, 1975)

J. Ebers: *Seven Years of the King's Theatre* (London, 1828)

W. T. Parke: *Musical Memoirs* (London, 1830)

G. Hogarth: *Memoirs of the Musical Drama* (London, 1838, 2/1851 as *Memoirs of the Opera*)

H. F. Chorley: *Thirty Years' Musical Recollections* (London, 1862, rev. 2/1926 by E. Newman)

B. Lumley: *Reminiscences of the Opera* (London, 1864)

J. H. Mapleson: *Memoirs* (London, 1888); ed. H. Rosenthal as *The Mapleson Memoirs: the Career of an Operatic Impresario* (London, 1966)

H. Klein: *Thirty Years of Musical Life in London, 1870–1900* (London, 1903)

H. Saxe Wyndham: *The Annals of Covent Garden Theatre from 1732 to 1897* (London, 1906)

C. Forsyth: *Music and Nationalism: a Study of English Opera* (London, 1911)

W. H. Cummings: 'The Lord Chamberlain and Opera in London, 1700–1740', *PMA*, xl (1913–14), 37–72

H. Klein: *The Reign of Patti* (London, 1920)

S. J. Adair-Fitzgerald: *The Story of the Savoy Opera: a Record of Events and Productions* (London, 1924)

E. J. Dent: *Foundations of English Opera* (Cambridge, 1928)

G. Cecil: *The History of Opera in England* (Taunton, 1930)

T. Beecham: *A Mingled Chime: Leaves from an Autobiography* (London, 1944)

D. Shawe-Taylor: *Covent Garden* (London, 1948)

Opera (1950–)

E. W. White: *The Rise of English Opera* (London, 1951)

M. Stapleton: *The Sadler's Wells Opera* (London, 1954)

W. C. Smith: *The Italian Opera and Contemporary Ballet in London, 1789–1820* (London, 1955)

D. Arundell: *The Critic at the Opera* (London, 1957)

H. Rosenthal: *Two Centuries of Opera at Covent Garden* (London, 1958)

J. M. Knapp: 'Handel, the Royal Academy of Music, and its First Opera Season in London (1720)', *MQ*, xlv (1959), 145–67

P. Lord: 'The English-Italian Opera Companies, 1732–3', *ML*, xlv (1964), 239–51

D. Arundell: *The Story of Sadler's Wells* (London, 1965)

S. Hughes: *Glyndebourne: a History of the Festival Opera* (London, 1965, 2/1981)

E. A. Langhans: 'The Dorset Garden Theatre in Pictures', *Theatre Survey*, vi (1965), 134–46

——: 'Pictorial Material on the Bridges Street and Drury Lane Theatres', *Theatre Survey*, vii (1966), 80–100

P. Hartnoll, ed.: *The Oxford Companion to the Theatre* (London, 1967, 4/1983)

H. Rosenthal: *Opera at Covent Garden: a Short History* (London, 1967)

E. A. Langhans: 'The Vere Street and Lincoln's Inn Fields Theatres in Pictures', *Educational Theatre Journal*, xx (1968), 171–85

R. Mander and J. Mitchenson: *The Lost Theatres of London* (London, 1968)

E. Haun: *But Hark! More Harmony: the Libretti of Restoration Opera in English* (Ypsilanti, MI, 1971)

E. A. Langhans: 'A Conjectural Reconstruction of the Dorset Garden Theatre', *Theatre Survey*, xiii (1972), 74–93

D. Nalbach: *The King's Theatre, 1704–1867* (London, 1972)

R. Fiske: *English Theatre Music in the Eighteenth Century* (London, 1973, 2/1986)

R. Leacroft: *The Development of the English Playhouse* (London, 1973)

R. Jarman: *A History of Sadler's Wells Opera* (London, 1974)

M. Haltrecht: *The Quiet Showman: Sir David Webster and the Royal Opera House* (London, 1975)

J. Milhous: 'New Light on Vanbrugh's Haymarket Theatre Project', *Theatre Survey*, xvii (1976), 143–61

Earl of Drogheda: *Double Harness* (London, 1978)

J. Milhous and R. D. Hume: 'Box Office Reports for Five Operas Mounted by Handel in London, 1732–1734', *Harvard Library Bulletin*, xxvi (1978), 245–66

C. A. Price: 'The Critical Decade for English Music Drama, 1700–1710', *Harvard Library Bulletin*, xxvi (1978), 38–76

N. Tucker: *Norman Tucker, Musician: an Autobiography* (London, 1978)

E. A. Langhans: 'The Theatres', *The London Theatre World, 1660–1800*, ed. R. D. Hume (Carbondale, IL, 1980), 35–65

F. C. Petty: *Italian Opera in London, 1760–1800* (Ann Arbor, 1980)

Earl of Harewood: *The Tongs and the Bones* (London, 1981)

D. H. Laurence, ed.: *Shaw's Music: the Complete Musical Criticism* (London, 1981)

N. Temperley, ed.: *Music in Britain: the Romantic Age, 1800–1914* (London, 1981)

R. D. Hume: 'The Nature of the Dorset Garden Theatre', *Theatre Notebook*, xxxvi (1982), 99–109

E. A. Langhans: 'Conjectural Reconstructions of the Vere Street and Lincoln's Inn Fields Theatres', *Essays in Theatre*, i (1982), 14–28

J. Milhous and R. D. Hume: 'Handel's Opera Finances in 1732–3', *MT*, cxxv (1982), 86–9

——, eds.: *Vice Chamberlain Coke's Theatrical Papers, 1706–1715* (Carbondale, IL, 1982)

Royal Opera House Retrospective, 1732–1982 (London, 1982)

A. Saint and others: *A History of the Royal Opera House, Covent Garden, 1732–1982* (London, 1982)

G. F. Barlow: *From Tennis Court to Opera House* (diss., U. of Glasgow, 1983)

J. Milhous and R. D. Hume: 'New Light on Handel and the Royal Academy of Music in 1720', *Theatre Journal*, xxxv (1983), 149–67

E. W. White: *A History of English Opera* (London, 1983)

——: *A Register of First Performances of English Operas and Semi-Operas from the 16th Century to 1980* (London, 1983)

R. D. Hume: 'Opera in London, 1695–1706', *British Theatre and the Other Arts, 1660–1800*, ed. S. S. Kenny (Washington DC, 1984), 67–91

J. M. Knapp: 'Eighteenth-Century Opera in London before Handel, 1705–1710', ibid, 92–104

J. Milhous: 'The Multimedia Spectacular on the Restoration Stage', ibid, 41–66

——: 'The Capacity of Vanbrugh's Theatre in the Haymarket', *Theatre History Studies*, iv (1984), 38–46

——: 'Opera Finances in London, 1674–1738', *JAMS*, xxxvii (1984), 567–92

C. A. Price: *Henry Purcell and the London Stage* (Cambridge, 1984)

R. D. Hume: 'Handel and Opera Management in London in the 1730s', *ML*, lxvii (1986), 347–62

J. Milhous and R. D. Hume: 'The Charter for the Royal Academy of Music', *ML*, lxvii (1986), 50–58

L. Foreman: *From Parry to Britten: British Music in Letters, 1900–1945* (London, 1987)

F. Donaldson: *The Royal Opera House in the Twentieth Century* (London, 1988)

R. D. Hume: 'The Sponsorship of Opera in London, 1704–1720', *Modern Philology*, lxxxv (1988), 420–32

L. Langley: 'Italian Opera and the English Press, 1836–1856', *Periodica musica*, vi (1988), 3–10

G. F. Barlow: 'Vanbrugh's Queen's Theatre in the Haymarket, 1703–9', *EMc*, xvii (1989), 515–21

J. Milhous and R. D. Hume: 'The Haymarket Opera in 1711', *EMc*, xvii (1989), 523–37

C. Price: 'Italian Opera and Arson in Late Eighteenth-Century London', *JAMS*, xlii (1989), 55–107

C. Price, J. Milhous and R. D. Hume: 'A Royal Opera House in Leicester Square (1790)', *COJ*, ii (1990), 1–28

R. Fiske and H. D. Johnstone, eds.: *Music in Britain: the Eighteenth Century* (Oxford, 1990)

C. Price, J. Milhous and R. D. Hume: 'The Rebuilding of the King's Theatre, Haymarket, 1789–1791', *Theatre Journal*, xliii (1991), 423–44

——: 'A Plan of the Pantheon Opera House', *COJ*, iii (1991), 213–46

——: *The Impresario's Ten Commandments: Continental Recruitment for Italian Opera in London 1763–64* (London, 1992)

ROBERT D. HUME, ARTHUR JACOBS

London [Burnstein, Burnson], **George** (*b* Montreal, 30 May 1920; *d* Armonk, NY, 24 March 1985). American bass-baritone. In 1941 he made his opera début, as George Burnson, singing Dr Grenvil (*La traviata*) at the Hollywood Bowl. His international career began in 1949 when he sang Amonasro in Vienna. Engagements followed at Glyndebourne, La Scala, the Metropolitan Opera, Bayreuth and the Bol'shoy, where he was the first non-Russian to sing Boris (1960). A long collaboration with Wieland Wagner culminated in London's singing Wotan in the complete *Ring* in Cologne (1962–4). His repertory also included Don Giovanni and Count Almaviva, Gounod's Méphistophélès, Escamillo, the multiple villains in *Les contes d'Hoffmann*, the Dutchman, Scarpia, Mandryka and the title role in Menotti's *Le dernier sauvage*. At the height of his career London's performances were distinguished by a rare dramatic individuality and vocal power. From 1968 he concentrated on arts administration, serving successively at the Kennedy Center, Washington, DC, the National Opera Institute and the Opera Society of Washington. He was also active as a producer: he staged the first complete English-language *Ring* in the USA (1975, Seattle), a production that forswore Wieland Wagner's modernism in favour of storybook realism.

*

GV [with discography by R. Vegeto and C. Williams]

J. Wechsberg: 'The Vocal Mission', *New Yorker* (26 Oct, 2 Nov 1957)

T. Page: Obituary, *New York Times* (26 March 1985)

T. Stewart: 'George London', *ON*, l/1 (1985–6), 32–3

MARTIN BERNHEIMER

London Opera House. Theatre built in 1911 and renamed the Stoll Theatre in 1916; see LONDON, §II, 2.

Long, John Luther (*b* Hanover, PA, 1 Jan 1861; *d* Clifton Springs, NY, 31 Oct 1927). American writer. In 1897 his story *Madame Butterfly* appeared in the *Century Magazine*. Based partly on a true incident told him by his sister, Mrs Irwin Corell, wife of a missionary at Nagasaki, and partly on Pierre Loti's popular 'conte' *Madame Chrysanthème*, it created such a sensation that two famous American actresses, Maude Adams and Julia Marlowe, at once sought his permission to turn it into a play. This, however, was eventually granted to the playwright David Belasco, whose one-act *Madame Butterfly*, written with Long's assistance, so impressed Puccini when he saw it in London in 1900 that he determined to make a full-length operatic version. Giuseppe Giacosa even published an Italian translation of the original story in *La lettura* to coincide with the première of *Madama Butterfly* in February 1904. Long collaborated with Belasco in five further plays, the most successful of which, *The Darling of the Gods*, also has a Japanese setting. During a visit to Philadelphia in 1907 Puccini for the first time met Long himself, who suggested to him another operatic subject; but what it was remains unknown, and in any case Puccini failed to take it up.

*

D. Belasco: *The Theatre through the Stage Door* (New York, 1918)

JULIAN BUDDEN

Long Beach. American city in southern California, 28 miles south of Los Angeles. The first operatic ensemble to blossom was the Singers' Workshop, founded in 1950 and renamed the Long Beach Civic Light Opera in 1959. It has specialized in American musicals and some European operetta, with Hollywood stars in the leading roles. It functions throughout the year in the Terrace Theater (3054 seats) at the Long Beach Convention and Entertainment Center, where it staged the Los Angeles première of Sondheim's *Sunday in the Park with George* in 1986. The first traditional opera in Long Beach was performed by Pacific Opera Theater, a workshop founded in 1967 by the singing teacher Josephine Lott. The company presented two or three operas a year with two-piano accompaniment in the Community Playhouse (99 seats). In 1972 the company closed because of lack of funds. In 1978 Michael Milenski formed the Long Beach Grand Opera, the oldest existing opera company in the metropolitan Los Angeles region; the enterprise was backed by civic leaders who wanted an opera company for the new Convention and Entertainment Center. The first production, Verdi's *La traviata*, was performed at the Terrace Theater. In 1981 the company turned away from strictly conventional productions to more avant-garde conceptions with such directors as Christopher and David Alden and Peter Mark Schifter. Renaming itself the Long Beach Opera, it began using the smaller Center Theater (800 seats) for most performances. Notable productions have included Britten's *Death in Venice* in 1983, followed the next year by the first American performance of Monteverdi's *L'incoronazione di Poppea* using historically informed performance practices. In 1985 Christopher Alden's staging of Mozart's *Die Entführung* altered the ending to include a palace coup and the assassination of Selim, led by the servant Osmin. In 1986 Krenek's *Jonny spielt auf* was billed as the first American performance since the Metropolitan Opera production (1929). In the same year the company reunited Cesare Siepi and Jerome Hines in Verdi's *Don Carlos*, which they had sung together at the Metropolitan in 1950. In 1988 the company gave the West Coast première of Udo Zimmermann's *Die weisse Rose* and the American company première of Szymanowski's *King Roger*.

NANCY MALITZ

Long Christmas Dinner, The [*Das lange Weihnachtsmahl*]. Opera in one act by PAUL HINDEMITH to a libretto by Thornton Wilder after his play; Mannheim, Nationaltheater, 17 December 1961.

The action, in one continuous scene, covers 90 years in the life of the Bayard family, somewhere in the American West. The stage is dominated by a dining-table set for Christmas dinner, and succeeding generations of Bayards assemble around it throughout the years. Doors to the left and right denote birth and death, and the various characters pass through them as their time comes. A door at the back is used for actual entrances and exits. A stage direction reads: 'Throughout the play the characters continue eating imaginary food with imaginary knives and forks'. Apart from one rebellious son, appearing towards the end, there is no dramatic conflict: the conversation is of everyday occurrences, but we gather from it that over the years the Bayard family and firm, already quite solid at the start, have prospered, and the town they helped to build has grown.

Wilder worked closely with Hindemith to adapt his conversational and deliberately repetitive play to the composer's need for musical forms. Each of the 11 characters (five male, six female) is treated at some point as a soloist, and overlong stretches of recitative are largely avoided. The restrained musical setting with its mild asperities counteracts to some extent the rather cloying complacency of the family members.

Scored for a chamber orchestra, including harpsichord, the opera opens with a working of the Christmas carol, 'God rest ye merry, gentlemen', which returns briefly at the end. The rest of the music is divided into eight sections, each cast in a single (though not too rigidly applied) musical form (e.g. jig, minuet, passacaglia, fugue). Of the set pieces the most extended are an attractive love duet, 'Light is her step on the stair and floor', between a young Bayard and his bride, and a powerful sextet, 'We talk of the weather', the climactic point of the work before another young Bayard, off to fight in the war, passes through the door denoting death.

Hindemith set Wilder's English words to music and translated them himself simultaneously into German. The first performance in English was on 13 March 1963 at the Juilliard School of Music in New York, with Hindemith conducting.   GEOFFREY SKELTON

Loomis, Clarence (*b* Sioux City, SD, 13 Dec 1889; *d* Aptos, CA, 3 July 1965). American composer. As a child he studied the piano and music theory with T. C. Tjaden. At the American Conservatory in Chicago he studied the piano with Heniot Levy and composition with Adolph Weidig. In 1914 he joined the theory and composition faculty of the conservatory, remaining there until 1929. While on leave in Vienna in 1918–19 he studied the piano with Leopold Godowsky and composition with Franz Schreker. Loomis subsequently taught in the USA from 1929 to 1956. A prolific composer, he wrote exclusively in a tonal, chromatic idiom. Chiefly interested in opera, he sought consciously to subordinate the music to the text, which led him to eschew virtuosity in both vocal and instrumental writing. His operas make use of American material, notably poems of Edgar Allan Poe and melodies by Stephen Foster. *Yolanda of Cyprus*, the best-known of his operas, was performed 22 times in four cities and in 1926 was awarded the David Bispham Medal.

Dun an Oir, 1923 (H. M. Barnes)
Yolanda of Cyprus, 1919–26 (3, C. Y. Rice), Hamilton, Ont., 6 April 1929
Susanna Don't You Cry (theatre piece, E. Ferguson, after S. Foster), 1931
A Night in Avignon (1, Rice), concert perf., Indianapolis, IN, Claypole Hotel, 7 July 1932
The White Cloud (1), 1935
The Fall of the House of Usher (1, E. Ferguson, after E. A. Poe), concert perf., Indianapolis, IN, Block's Auditorium, 11 Jan 1941
Revival (1), Los Angeles, KWFB Radio, 3 April 1942
The Captive Woman (1), 1953

'Notes of Chicago Musicians', *Musical Leader*, li/14, (1926), 10
E. E. Hipsher: *American Opera and its Composers* (Philadelphia, 1927), 298–301   SEVERINE NEFF

Loos, Karel (*b* c1723–4; *d* Tuchoměřice, nr Prague, 2 March 1772). Czech composer. He was the choirmaster, school rector and organist at the Jesuit house in Tuchoměřice (1747–72), and most of his works are for the church, although it is possible that his string trio *Lamentazione del doctore Fausto* was written as an overture to a play on the Faust subject. Several dramatic works were attributed to him, but the only one known today is *Opera bohemica de camino a caementariis luride aedificato, seu Pugna inter patrem familias et murarios* (date of composition unknown). It was the first Czech opera to take as its subject the lives of artisans and is a Baroque allegory on the transient nature of worldly things. In its style of composition the opera derives from the Jesuit school plays. The music is late Baroque in character, uncomplicated yet refined, with occasional references to Italian *opera buffa* and to folk music. It is possible, on the other hand, that some of the numbers were so popular that they became in effect folksongs: it is known that 19th-century collectors found them being sung in Bohemia.

J. Němeček: *Lidové zpěvohry a písně z doby roboty* [Folk Operas and Songs from the Time of Serfdom] (Prague, 1954)
J. Trojan: *České zpěvohry 18. století* [Czech Operas of the 18th Century] (Brno, 1981)   MICHAELA FREEMANOVÁ

Loose, Emmy (*b* Ústí nad Labem, 22 Jan 1914; *d* Vienna, 14 Oct 1987). Czech soprano. She studied in Prague, making her début in 1939 at Hanover as Blonde. In 1941 she sang Aennchen at the Vienna Staatsoper, where she was engaged for 25 years. She made her Covent Garden début in 1947 with the Staatsoper as Despina and Zerlina, returning to sing Susanna and Sophie with the Royal Opera (1949–50). At Salzburg she sang Aennchen (1948) and at Glyndebourne Blonde (1953). She also appeared in Italy, France and Germany. Although her repertory included Elisetta (*Il matrimonio segreto*), Clorinda (*La Cenerentola*), Pamina and Micaëla, her delightful voice and charming personality were best displayed in soubrette roles.   ELIZABETH FORBES

Lope de Vega (Carpio), Félix (*b* Madrid, 25 Nov 1562; *d* Madrid, 27 Aug 1635). Spanish dramatist, virtual founder of the Spanish theatre and the first Spanish opera librettist. His LA SELVA SIN AMOR, performed at court before Philip IV on 18 December 1627, was a one-act 'pastoral eclogue', wholly sung to music (now lost) by Filippo Piccinini (a Bolognese musician in the employ of the Spanish royal chapel) and Bernardo Monanni (secretary of the Tuscan embassy in Madrid), staged in spectacular style by Cosimo Lotti. This is the earliest record of a wholly-sung drama in Spain, but Lope seems not to have written other such librettos, nor is there any record of any further such operas before the performance of LA PÚRPURA DE LA ROSA by Hidalgo and Calderón de la Barca in Madrid in 1660. Since the composers and the stage designer of *La selva* were all Italian, Calderón's claim that *La púrpura* was the first wholly-sung drama in Spain was not without some justification. Lope de Vega also wrote a study of dramaturgical theory (1609).

S. B. Whitaker: 'Florentine Opera Comes to Spain: Lope de Vega's *La selva sin amor*', *Journal of Hispanic Philology*, ix (1984), 43–66

A. Cardona, D. Cruickshank and M. Cunningham: *Pedro Calderón de la Barca, Tomás de Torrejón y Velasco, 'La púrpura de la rosa'* (Kassel, 1990), 128–44   JACK SAGE

López Buchardo, Carlos (*b* Buenos Aires, 12 Oct 1881; *d* Buenos Aires, 21 April 1948). Argentine composer. He first studied the piano and composition in Buenos Aires, then lived in Paris (1909–13), where he studied composition with Roussel at the Schola Cantorum. After his return to Buenos Aires, he served as president of the Wagnerian Association and directed the music school at the Teatro Colón. From 1924 until his death he directed the National Conservatory of Music, which today is named in his honour. For several years he served on the board of directors of the Teatro Colón.

López Buchardo is recognized as one of the leading nationalist composers of Argentina. His works reveal a deep affinity for *criollo* music (newly created Argentine music derived from Hispanic traditions). His lyrical, melodic style finds its perfect expression in his songs, many of which were written for his wife, Brígida Frías de López Buchardo. His early fairy-tale opera, *Il sogno di Alma* (1914), signalled the arrival of a talented young composer; later, the delightful musical comedies *Madama Lynch* (1932), *La Perichona* (1933) and *Amalia* (1935) earned enthusiastic praise for their spontaneous sense of humour and agreeable *criollo* flavour. López Buchardo also composed incidental music for the theatre; his *Comentarios musicales para Romeo y Julieta* (1934) is a work of uncommon timbral delicacy.

Il sogno di Alma (fantasía lírica, 3, S. Benelli, after E. Prins: *En la país violenta*), Buenos Aires, Colón, 4 Aug 1914, *US-Wc* (microfilm of MS)
Madama Lynch (comedia lírica, 3, E. García Velloso and A. Remón), Buenos Aires, Odeón, 25 June 1932
La Perichona (comedia musical, 3, García Velloso and Remón), Buenos Aires, Ateneo, 31 May 1933
Amalia (comedia musical, García Velloso and P. M. Obligado, after J. Marmol), Buenos Aires, Odeón, 1935
Santos Vega, begun ?1935 (leyenda lírica, 1, G. Caraballo, after R. Obligado), inc.
La bella Otero, begun ?1940 (comedia musical, A. Berruti and Remón), inc., collab. M. Torroba

*

A. Jurafsky: *Carlos López Buchardo* (Buenos Aires, 1966)
M. Kuss: *Nativistic Strains in Argentine Operas Premiered at the Teatro Colón (1908–1972)* (diss., UCLA, 1976)
DEBORAH SCHWARTZ

López-Cobos, Jesús (*b* Toro, 25 Feb 1940). Spanish conductor. He graduated in philosophy from Madrid University, then studied in Italy with Franco Ferrara and in Vienna with Hans Swarowsky. His operatic début was at La Fenice, Venice, with *Die Zauberflöte* in 1969, followed in 1970 by *La bohème* at the Deutsche Oper, Berlin, where he was engaged on a five-year contract before being appointed music director, 1981–90. His American début was at San Francisco (*Lucia di Lammermoor*, 1972), and was followed by débuts at the Opéra (*Il trovatore*, 1975) and Covent Garden (*Carmen*, 1975), and at the Metropolitan (*Adriana Lecouvreur*, 1978). In 1987 he conducted the first *Ring* cycle staged in Japan (with the Deutsche Oper). His recordings include Rossini's *Otello* from the autograph score and the original version of *Lucia di Lammermoor*. In opera his conducting favours a Latin liveliness of spirit (in the German repertory as well) with clarity of texture achieved through care for instrumental detail.

NOËL GOODWIN

Lorand [née Grauaug], **Colette** (*b* Zürich, 7 Jan 1923). Swiss soprano. She studied in Hanover, making her début in 1946 at Basle as Marguerite (*Faust*). Engaged at Frankfurt in 1951, she also sang at Zürich and made her Covent Garden début in 1954 as Violetta. In 1960 she moved to the Hamburg Staatsoper. Her repertory ranged from the Queen of Night, Konstanze and Donna Anna to Olympia, Salome and Emilia Marty, which she sang in Basle in 1982. In 1969 she made her American début at New York in Orff's *Prometheus* and sang Lavinia in the European première of Levy's *Mourning Becomes Electra* at Dortmund. She created Mary Stuart in Fortner's *Elisabeth Tudor* (1972, Berlin), took part in the first performance of Orff's *De temporum fine comoedia* (1973, Salzburg) and created Regan in Reimann's *Lear* (1978, Munich), a part she sang for the last time in 1982 at the Paris Opéra. The extreme agility of her voice, with its impeccable sense of pitch, and her extraordinary dramatic gifts were demonstrated by such roles as Jeanne (*The Devils of Loudun*) and Orff's Antigone.

ELIZABETH FORBES

Lorca, Federico García. *See* GARCÍA LORCA, FEDERICO.

Lord Byron. Opera in three acts by VIRGIL THOMSON to a libretto by Jack Larson; Juilliard Theater, New York, 20 April 1972.

Set in Westminster Abbey in 1824, Act 1 opens with mourning for the poet and freedom-fighter, whose body has just been returned from Greece. Dead poets including Shelley (baritone) lament their colleague. A committee led by John Hobhouse (bass-baritone) and including Thomas Moore (baritone), Byron's sister Mrs Leigh (soprano) and his estranged wife (mezzo-soprano) petition for Byron's burial in the Abbey. The ship bringing the corpse also contains a statue as well as Byron's memoirs, both accompanied by Byron's last love, the Contessa Guiccioli (soprano) and her brother (baritone). The statue arrives and as the stage freezes in admiration, Byron (tenor) enters as a shade and sings a 'satirical apostrophe' to the city of London.

Act 2 begins with the friends still admiring the statue. Some argue for the destruction of the potentially damaging memoirs, but Moore insists that they be read. Four memory scenes follow. At a garden party at Lady Melbourne's (soprano) in 1812, Byron meets Annabella Millbank, his future wife. During a victory ball in 1814, Byron proposes to Miss Millbank to quieten the scandal regarding the pregnancy of his sister. At Lady Melbourne's house, the women apprehensively hope for the best while Byron and his male friends play out a mock marriage at his club. Byron denounces women in a drunken frenzy, and both groups come 'close to hysteria'.

Act 3 opens in Byron's sister's country house in 1815. Now Lady Byron is pregnant, and discovers brother and sister in amorous embrace. Byron urges his sister to elope with him to Europe, but she lacks courage and 'accepts Annabella as her moral counsellor'. In despair, Byron flees family and country. Back in the Abbey, Hobhouse burns Byron's memoirs. The Dean of the Abbey (bass), seeing this suppression of the facts, denounces Byron's impiety and refuses him burial. The Contessa and her brother scorn British hypocrisy. The statue is put back in its crate. All lament until Shelley brings in Byron, whom the poets welcome in a 'joyous madrigal finale'.

Thomson's third and last opera was the only one not to a libretto by Gertrude Stein. Larson's libretto is more conventional and straightforward than those of Stein, and Thomson matched it with music of greater romantic effusiveness (which also suits the title character and period). *Lord Byron* has suffered from relative neglect despite the composer's affection for it. In an effort to encourage performances, Thomson made misguided cuts in the early 1980s. A recording from a concert performance in New Hampshire was made in 1991.

JOHN ROCKWELL

Lord Inferno. Radio opera in one act by GIORGIO FEDERICO GHEDINI to a libretto by Franco Antonicelli after Max Beerbohm's novella *The Happy Hypocrite* (1896); broadcast, RAI, 22 October 1952 (staged as *L'ipocrita felice*, Milan, Piccola Scala, 10 March 1956).

Though slighter and more subdued in tone than his operatic masterpiece *Le baccanti*, Ghedini's last opera is an evocative and highly characteristic work. It is heard to best advantage in its original version for radio (joint winner of the Italia Prize), which contains an important part for a speaking narrator – replaced, in the stage version, by an obviously less essential tenor.

The plot closely follows Beerbohm's lighthearted 'fairy tale for tired men' about the redeeming power of love. Lord Inferno (baritone) – Lord George Hell in the original – is an early 19th-century playboy who unexpectedly, and quite literally, falls victim to the dart of Cupid (soprano) while watching a stage performance by the young actress Jenny Mere (soprano). He at once falls for her; but she refuses him, saying that she can love only a man with 'the face of a saint'. After pensively wandering the streets all night, Inferno finds a makeshift solution in the form of a saintly mask, bought from the shop of the ingenious Mr Aeneas (bass). Thus transformed into 'Lord Paradiso', he easily wins the heart of Jenny, who has herself been struck by one of Cupid's arrows. A blissfully happy marriage follows, which is only momentarily disturbed when Inferno's embittered former mistress La Gambogi (mezzo-soprano) intervenes and tears off his mask. Such, however, is love's transforming power that his real face is now as saintly as his disguise.

The incidents and characters in this quaint tale are portrayed with the help of terse, incisive musical imagery, vivid enough to make stage presentation seem superfluous. These overtly pictorial elements are presented against an intermittent but pervasively atmospheric backcloth of more sustained, usually rather solemn linear textures, whose cumulative effect (notably in the nocturnal street scene) is to transform what might otherwise have seemed a mere *jeu d'esprit* into a fundamentally serious meditation on the vagaries of human nature and destiny.   JOHN C. G. WATERHOUSE

Loreley. *Azione romantica* in three acts by ALFREDO CATALANI to a libretto by Angelo Zanardini and others after CARLO D'ORMEVILLE's libretto for Catalani's *Elda* (1880, Turin); Turin, Teatro Regio, 16 February 1890.

The action takes place on the shores of the Rhine in 1300. Although he is in love with the young Loreley (soprano), Walter von Oberwesel (tenor), encouraged by his friend Baron Hermann (baritone), intends to keep his promise to marry Anna von Rehberg (soprano),

niece of the Margrave of Biberich (bass). Instead of seeking revenge, Loreley offers her life to Albrich, god of the Rhine, who allows her to plunge into the river and emerge more beautiful. She appears as a mirage to Walter as the wedding is about to be celebrated, and he is overwhelmed with love for her. He leaves his bride to follow Loreley and feels remorse only when he sees the funeral procession of Anna, who has died of a broken heart. For a short time Loreley abandons herself to Walter's embrace, but the spirits remind her of her pact with the god and she bids her love farewell for ever. In despair Walter throws himself into the river to follow her.

A reworking of the four-act *dramma fantastico Elda*, Catalani's second opera, *Loreley*, reaches greater artistic heights because of improvements in the libretto (Zanardini, Giuseppe Depanis and d'Ormeville all contributed, along with Giuseppe Giacosa and Luigi Illica) as well as in the composer's capabilities. The third act is particularly interesting, containing some of the most important descriptive writing in the stage music of the period, such as the dance of the water-spirits and the funeral march for the dead Anna.   MICHELE GIRARDI

Loreley, Die. *Grosse romantische Oper* in four acts, op.16, by MAX BRUCH to a libretto by Emanuel Geibel; Mannheim, 14 June 1863.

The opera is set in the wine-producing heart of the Rhineland. Ever since a chance meeting, Count Otto (tenor) has been obsessed with the peasant girl Lenore (soprano). She returns his love, unaware of his identity and of his forthcoming marriage to Countess Bertha (soprano). Lenore's father Hubert (bass) is supervising a shipment of wine for the wedding feast when Lenore arrives and is chosen by the villagers to present a symbolic goblet to Otto and his bride. As the wedding procession passes, Lenore recognizes her lover, but he promptly denies her. She summons Evil from the depths of the Rhine: to gain revenge she sells her soul to the river spirits in exchange for an irresistible sensual beauty. During the wedding feast Otto is angry with the ballad singer Reinald (baritone) and calls for the wedding cup. He is confronted once again by Lenore, is immediately enchanted by her and, having renounced his bride, claims her hand. The Archbishop of Mainz (bass) condemns Lenore as a witch, but in court her charms prevail and she is acquitted. Bertha vainly attempts to win back Otto, but he curses her, whereupon he is banished from the court. The tragedy reaches its climax as the broken-hearted Bertha dies. Her funeral is seen by the penitent Otto, still ensnared by the bewitching Lenore. She awaits him on a rock above the Rhine and almost forgives him, but cannot escape the fate she has chosen for him and herself. Otto flings himself into the river, and the Rhine spirits claim Lenore for themselves.

Bruch's music derives from Beethoven, Mozart, Weber and Spohr, the last two having a discernible influence in the most effective and dramatic scene, during which Lenore's pact with the river spirits is made. Though Bruch's harmonic language, rooted in the Classical tradition, is conservative, his opera is deftly orchestrated and full of beautiful melodies.

CHRISTOPHER FIFIELD

Lorengar, Pilar [García, Pilar Lorenza] (*b* Saragossa, 16 Jan 1928). Spanish soprano. She studied in Madrid, making her début in zarzuelas in 1949. In 1955 she sang

Cherubino at Aix-en-Provence, Rosario in a New York concert performance of *Goyescas* (her American début) and Violetta at Covent Garden, where she returned as Donna Anna, Countess Almaviva, Fiordiligi and Alice. She sang Pamina at Glyndebourne (1956) and Buenos Aires (1958), and Ilia (*Idomeneo*) at Salzburg (1961). She sang at San Francisco (1964–5) as Desdemona, Liù, Mélisande and Eva. In 1966 she made her Metropolitan début as Donna Elvira, later singing Elsa, Eva, Agathe and Butterfly. She appeared in most major European opera houses, but it was at the Deutsche Oper, Berlin, where she was engaged from 1958 for over 30 years, that she chiefly made her career, broadening her repertory to include Regina (*Mathis der Maler*), Elisabeth de Valois, Mařenka, Tatyana, Jenůfa, Mimì, Tosca, Manon Lescaut, Valentine (*Les Huguenots*) and Queen Isabella in the German première of Falla's *Atlántida* in 1961. Her last new role was Maddalena (*Andrea Chénier*), which she sang at Lyons (1989). She retired from the Deutsche Oper in 1991. With a beautiful pearly-toned voice and exquisite phrasing, she could encompass, despite her placid temperament, strong dramatic as well as lyrical music.

W. Elsner and M. W. Busch: *Pilar Lorengar – ein Portrait* (Berlin, 1985)
HAROLD ROSENTHAL/R

Lorentzen, Bent (*b* Stenvad, 11 Feb 1935). Danish composer. He studied at Århus University and then at the Royal Danish Conservatory, from which he graduated as a music teacher in 1962. From that year he taught theory at the Jutland Conservatory at Århus and in 1967–8 held a scholarship to study at the electronic studio in Stockholm. He settled in Copenhagen in 1971, and has since won various composition prizes.

In his creative work Lorentzen quickly turned away from convention and, stimulated by what he had learnt at the Darmstadt summer courses of 1965, devoted much of his attention to electronic music. In addition to purely musical works, he has interested himself in a theatrical form that seeks to voice a protest against capitalist society and its sophisticated musical life. In his opera *Euridice*, which won the 1970 Italia Prize, the underworld is viewed through the eyes of the title character.

Stalten Mette [Haughty Mette] (Lorentzen), Århus, 17 Nov 1963; rev. 1972; rev. (television op), televised, Copenhagen, Danish Radio, 1982
Dissonances (1), 1964, Brunswick, 28 Jan 1975
Die Schlange, 1964 (Lorentzen); rev. version, Brunswick, Staats, Jan 1975
Euridice, 1965 (radio op, Lorentzen), Danish Radio, 16 Dec 1969; stage, Hamburg, 6 Aug 1977
Die Musik kommt mir äusserst bekannt vor!, Kiel, 3 May 1974
Eine wundersame Liebesgeschichte (5), Munich, Bayerische Staats, 2 Dec 1979
Klovnen Toto [Toto the Clown], 1982, Copenhagen, Kongelige, aut. 1985
Fackeltanz, 1986

*

B. Lorentzen: 'Die Musik kommt mir äusserst bekannt vor!', *Dansk Musiktidsskrift*, xlix (1974–5), 4–8
M. Bonnesen: 'Stalten Mette – noter til en fjernsynsopera', *Dansk Musiktidsskrift*, lvi (1981–2), 248–53
JENS BRINCKER

Lorenz, Alfred (Ottokar) (*b* Vienna, 11 July 1868; *d* Munich, 20 Nov 1939). German musicologist and conductor. A pupil of Spitta in Berlin, he worked as a conductor from 1893, notably at Coburg and Gotha, before studying musicology under Bauer at Frankfurt and then

taking a teaching post at Munich University. His four-volume *Das Geheimnis der Form bei Richard Wagner* (1924–33) laid the foundation for all subsequent Wagnerian analysis and is still unsurpassed in scope. Cognizant of Wagner's mention in *Oper und Drama* (1851) of the tonally unified 'dichterisch-musikalische Periode', Lorenz divided his post-*Lohengrin* works into such periods, each internally articulated by recurring forms such as *Bar* and *Bogen*. He was the first Wagner analyst to systematize musical procedures beyond the purely referential web of leitmotif, endeavouring to defend the works from accusations of 'formlessness' and to prove their worth as absolute music. This musical focus to the exclusion of dramatic study presupposes acceptance of his idea that 'musical form is the sculptress of the dramatic structure'. Lorenz subsequently elevated his formal analysis into a universal principle: the 'eternal rules of form'. Their applicability to other composers was demonstrated by studies of the early operas of Alessandro Scarlatti and Mozart's operatic finales as well as of instrumental pieces by Bach, Beethoven, Bruckner and Strauss.

Lorenz's analytical method is firmly rooted in his time. Criticism has only recently recognized the influence of contemporary German intellectual trends, ranging from organicism to incipient Nazism; its historical context provides a fuller understanding of its significance. Lorenz edited Weber's early operas (1926) and published a collection of Wagner's letters and other writings (1938); he also composed an opera, *Helges Erwachen* (1896).

'Parsifal als Übermensch', *Die Musik*, i (1902), 1876–82
Gedanken und Studien zur musikalischen Formgebung in Richard Wagners Ring des Nibelungen (diss., U. of Frankfurt, 1922)
Das Geheimnis der Form bei Richard Wagner (Berlin, 1924–33) Eng. trans. in R. Wagner: *Prelude and Transfiguration from 'Tristan und Isolde'*, ed. R. Bailey (New York, 1985), 204–23 [incl. analysis of *Tristan* prelude]
Alessandro Scarlattis Jugendoper: ein Beitrag zur Geschichte der italienischen Oper (Augsburg, 1927)
'Das Finale in Mozarts Meisteropern', *Die Musik*, xix (1927), 621–32
'Die Religion des Parsifal', *Die Musik*, xxv (1933), 342–7

Articles in *Bayreuther Festspielführer*: on musical form in Wagner (1924, pp.138–50†), *Meistersinger* (1925, pp.131–5*†), *Tristan und Isolde* (1927, pp.177–86; 1938, pp.139–45*†), dramatists and composers (1928, pp.117–22), *Tannhäuser* (1930, pp.58–62), *Parsifal* (1933, pp.161–8*†), *Lohengrin* (1936, pp.189–98*), the *Ring* (1937, pp.112–16), *Der fliegende Holländer* (1939, pp.102–8)

* – Eng. trans. in *Wagner*, ii (1981), 21–5, 40–44, 74–7; iv (1983), 9–13
† – orig. in *Das Geheimnis* (1924–33)

*

H. A. Grunsky: 'Neues zur Formenlehre', *ZMw*, xvi (1933–4), 84–91
——: 'Einer der uns fehlt: dem Gedanken von Alfred Lorenz', *Neue Wagner-Forschungen* (Karlsruhe, 1943), 35–42
C. Dahlhaus: 'Formprinzipien in Wagner's "Ring des Nibelungen"', *Beiträge zur Geschichte der Oper*, ed. H. Becker (Regensburg, 1969), 95–129
W. J. Darcy: *Formal and Rhythmic Problems in Wagner's 'Ring' Cycle* (diss., U. of Illinois, Urbana-Champaign, 1973)
E. Voss: 'Noch einmal: des Geheimnis der Form bei Richard Wagner', *Theaterarbeit an Wagners 'Ring'* (Munich, 1978), 251–67; Eng. trans. in *Wagner*, iv (1983), 66–79
R. van der Lek: 'Zum Begriff Übergang und zu seiner Anwendung durch Alfred Lorenz auf die Musik von Wagners *Ring*', *Mf*, xxxv (1982), 129–47
J. Deathridge: 'Grundzüge der Wagner-Forschung', *Richard Wagner Handbuch* (Stuttgart, 1986), 803–30; Eng. trans. in *Wagner*, viii (1987), 92–114

S. McClatchie: 'The Warrior Foil'd: Alfred Lorenz's Wagner Analyses', *Wagner*, xi (1990), 3–12

——: *Alfred Lorenz as Theorist and Analyst* (diss., U. of Western Ontario, in preparation) [with comprehensive list of writings and bibliography]   STEPHEN McCLATCHIE

Lorenz, Max (*b* Düsseldorf, 10 May 1901; *d* Vienna, 12 Jan 1975). German tenor. After studying in Berlin he made his début at the Dresden Staatsoper as Walther (*Tannhäuser*), becoming a principal tenor in 1928. From 1933 he was at the Berlin Staatsoper, and he also appeared at the Metropolitan, making his début as Walther (*Die Meistersinger*) in 1931 and singing there until 1934 and again in 1947–50; he also sang at Bayreuth (from 1933 and in 1952) and Covent Garden (1934, 1937). He joined the Vienna Staatsoper in 1937 and appeared at many Salzburg festivals, creating roles in such new works as von Einem's *Der Prozess* (Josef K., 1953), Liebermann's *Penelope* (1954) and Wagner-Régeny's *Das Bergwerk zu Falun* (1961). Lorenz was a prominent Wagnerian tenor, celebrated as Tristan, Siegfried and Walther in particular; he was also a notable Florestan, Otello, Bacchus (Strauss's *Ariadne*) and Herod.

GV (L. Riemens; R. Vegeto)   PETER BRANSCOMBE

Lorenzaccio. *Melodramma romantico danzato* in five acts by SYLVANO BUSSOTTI to a libretto by the composer and Fred Philippe, based on Alfred de Musset's drama *Lorenzaccio* (1834) and on a collage of European literature; Venice, La Fenice, 7 September 1972.

The opera is set in a multiple time frame, with the action taking place in Medici Florence (1537), in Venice at the time of the visit of George Sand (mezzo-soprano) and Alfred de Musset (spoken) in 1834, and in the composer's Rome of 1968. The action of the first three acts follows the outlines of Musset's drama, but changes the order of events. Act 1 depicts the corruption at the Medici court under Duke Alessandro (spoken), who tries to abduct Uliva (dancer), the daughter of Maffio Salviati (baritone). The second act concentrates on the relationship between Lorenzino de' Medici, called Lorenzaccio (spoken), the future murderer of Duke Alessandro, and his mother Maria Soderini (soprano). Lorenzaccio dreams that he will be killed by followers of the duke in Venice. He then murders the duke, who is succeeded by the new duke, Cosimo I. The last two acts consist of Bussotti's *Rara Requiem* (1970), which accompanies Musset's farewell to the characters of his imagination.

The presence of Alfred de Musset on stage within his own drama reflects Bussotti's desire to show any action on stage as his personal dream of self-identification with creative artists of the past. (Bussotti himself played the author's role at the première.) The music contains quotations from other composers as well as from Bussotti's own earlier works. By giving instructions in the score for adding or subtracting parts of a given musical texture, Bussotti developed a system of composition and de-composition which allowed the notation of large musical units on one page of full score. Apart from this, which recalls the techniques of musical graphics, the score of *Lorenzaccio* marks Bussotti's return to a more traditional approach to musical notation. His visual creativity was confined to the numerous sketches for stage designs and costumes that are interwoven with the music throughout the score (see illus-tration opposite). The use of these visual elements is mandatory for any performance.   JÜRGEN MAEHDER

Lorenzi, Giambattista [Giovanni Battista] (*b* Naples, 1719; *d* ?Naples, Dec 1805). Italian librettist. He was one of the outstanding librettists of Neapolitan comic opera in the second half of the 18th century. He began his career as a dilettante actor reciting comedies in private homes, playing the role of the lover in Neapolitan dialect. His talent for improvisation led to his appointment in 1768 as director of improvised comedies for the king of Naples. A year later, he was appointed director for the Teatrino di Corte, for which he provided improvised and written comedies. He also began his long association with the Teatro S Carlo.

Lorenzi was initially reluctant to write librettos for musical comedies because of the rigidity of the contemporary Neapolitan *opera buffa* conventions, which left the librettist little room for imaginative invention (see the preface to Lorenzi's collected works, *Opere teatrali*, Naples, 1806–20). However, he eventually wrote more than 30 librettos, mainly set by Paisiello, Cimarosa and Piccinni. His characters represent middle-class citizens, often including low-ranking nobility from the countryside. Marital disagreements and contemporary moral values are frequent objects of humour. Buffoonery, slapstick, disguise, mistaken identities, broken French phrases and Turkisms are Lorenzi's humorous devices. The most successful and colourful personalities are characters using Neapolitan dialect, with whom local audiences could easily empathize. Neapolitan characters from the *commedia dell'arte* such as Pulcinella, Pantaleone and Coviello appear in a number of librettos. There is a strongly delineated improvisatory element in Lorenzi's work, resulting from his experience as an actor.

The late 18th-century Neapolitan comic libretto was to a great extent derived from the comedies of Goldoni, Gozzi's fables and the sentimental romances of English and French playwrights. Lorenzi's output was no exception: a number of his works derive from Molière, Shakespeare, Addison, Marmontel, Lamotte and Nivelle de la Chaussée.

commedie per musica unless otherwise stated
Le gelosie, N. Piccinni, 1755; *Il trionfo di Camilla* (dramma per musica, after S. Stampiglia), N. Porpora, 1760; *Tra i due litiganti il terzo gode*, G. Astarita, 1766 (G. Paisiello, 1772, as Gli amanti comici); *L'idolo cinese*, Paisiello, 1767; *Il furbo malaccorto*, Paisiello, 1767; *La luna abitata*, Paisiello, 1768; *La finta maga per vendetta*, Paisiello, 1768; *Don Chisciotte della Mancia*, Paisiello, 1769; *Gelosia per gelosia*, Piccinni, 1770; *La Corsara*, Piccinni, 1771; *Le trame zingaresche*, Piccinni, 1772; *Il tamburro*, Paisiello, 1773; *Don Taddeo in Barcellona* (commedia), A. Pio, 1774; *Il divertimento dei numi* (farsa), Paisiello, 1774
Il duello, Paisiello, 1774; *La pazzia giudiziosa* [*Il dottorato di Pulcinella*], Pio, 1774 (G. Farinelli, 1792, as Il dottorato di Pulcinella); *Socrate immaginario* (? with F. Galiani), Paisiello, 1775; *La fuga*, G. Monti, 1777; *Li tre Eugenie*, F. Lenzi, 1778 (P. Casella, 1804, as L'equivoco); *Il geloso sincerato* (farsa), Monti, 1779; *L'infedeltà fedele*, D. Cimarosa, 1779 (Haydn, 1781, as La fedeltà premiata); *Il convitato di pietra* [*Don Giovanni Tenorio*] (farsa), G. Tritto, 1783 (V. Fabrizi, 1787); *Li due gemelli* (dramma giocoso per musica), Tritto, 1783
L'apparenza inganna, o sia La villeggiatura, Cimarosa, 1784; *La scuffiara* (farsa), Tritto, 1784 (Paisiello, 1787, as La modista raggiratrice); *La finta zingara* (farsa), P. A. Guglielmi, 1785; *Il marito disperato* (dramma giocoso per musica), Cimarosa, 1785; *Nina, o sia La pazza per amore* (commedia in prosa e verso, after B.-J. Marsollier des Vivetières), Paisiello, 1789; *Le vane gelosie*, Paisiello and S. Palma, 1790; *La serva onorata* (dramma giocoso per musica, after L. da Ponte: *Le nozze di Figaro*), Piccinni, 1792;

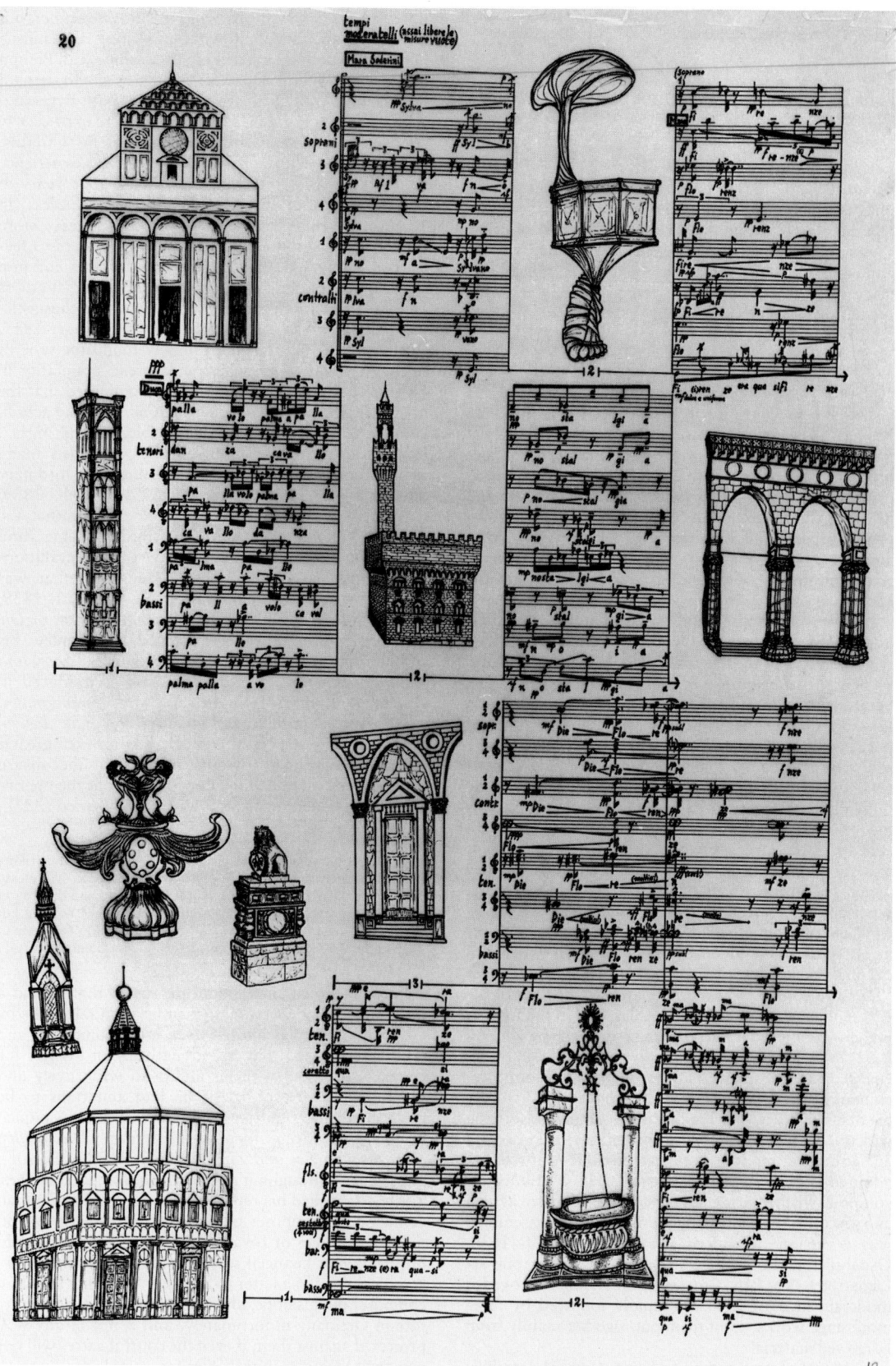

'Lorenzaccio' (Bussotti): page 20 from the full score of Act 1, with sketches for stage designs by the composer

La pietra simpatica, Palma, 1795; *Gli amanti ridicoli*, Palma, 1797; *Le ninfe di Diana*, Palma, 1805, as Le seguaci di Diana
GORDANA LAZAREVICH

Lorenzo Fernândez, Oscar. *See* FERNÂNDEZ, OSCAR LORENZO.

Lortzing, (Gustav) Albert (*b* Berlin, 23 Oct 1801; *d* Berlin, 21 Jan 1851). German composer. His comic operas, from *Die beiden Schützen* (1837) to *Die Opernprobe* (1851), are his most characteristic, showing a vivid personal vein of sentimental humour which, although limited in range, was popular in appeal and made him the most inventive composer of opera with spoken dialogue in Germany in the middle of the 19th century.

1. Early years. 2. Later career.

1. EARLY YEARS. Shortly before Lortzing's birth, his father Johann Gottlob had taken over the family hide business. There were, however, pronounced theatrical tendencies in the family; Johann Gottlob's younger brother, Friedrich Maler Lortzing, was an admired professional actor, while Johann Gottlob himself and his wife Charlotte Sophie were keen amateurs. As a child Lortzing had his first stage roles in the Berlin amateur theatre company, Urania, of which his parents were members. During the economic upheavals accompanying the Napoleonic campaigns, the family hide business collapsed and the Lortzings turned their hobby into a profession. Over the next few years they were members of theatre companies in Breslau, Coburg, Bamberg, Strasbourg, Freiburg and Baden-Baden, before joining Josef Derossi's ABC Theatre Company. Lortzing's father played mainly comic and sentimental parts, while his mother had a good enough voice to take soubrette and comic roles in operas. Lortzing himself was sometimes given children's roles. Despite the difficulties of their unsettled life, Lortzing's parents made considerable efforts to further their son's musical education; he learnt the violin, cello, guitar and piano, and received some desultory tuition in music theory which he supplemented by his own assiduous study, especially of Albrechtsberger's *Gründliche Anweisung zur Composition*. He made a number of early attempts at composition, and during his late teens wrote incidental music (lost) for August von Kotzebue's *Der Schutzgeist*. In 1823 he married a fellow member of the ABC company, Rosina Regina Ahles, and in the following year composed his first opera, a one-act Singspiel *Ali Pascha von Janina*. Two years later he and Rosina were engaged as members of the Detmold Hoftheater company, which performed *Ali Pascha* in 1828. During his first five years with the Detmold company, Lortzing widened his stage experience considerably; he possessed an attractive tenor voice and became particularly admired for his comic portrayals. He continued to compose, writing incidental music for the theatre as well as a few other pieces; among the Singspiels he assembled was a version of Hiller's *Die Jagd* of 1770 (1830, Osnabrück). In 1832 he compiled the one-act Liederspiel *Der Pole und sein Kind*, which enjoyed a moderate success. This was rapidly followed by three more stage works, all of them put together mainly from borrowed material.

In 1833 Lortzing moved to Leipzig, where *Der Pole und sein Kind* was again staged. Ambitious to produce something more substantial, he began to sketch a libretto based on Wilhelm Vogel's *Der Amerikaner*, but ultimately abandoned it without writing any music. During this period he struck up friendships with Philipp Reger and Philipp Düringer which were to remain important to him for the rest of his life. Both Reger and Düringer (later Lortzing's biographer) were to be closely connected with the writing of many of his librettos. Lortzing gained further valuable theatrical experience by working as a director for his first four years in Leipzig, but after his first great operatic success, in 1837, he gave up this side of his activities to leave more time for composition. He had begun work on his three-act comic opera *Die beiden Schützen* in 1835 and in a short time finished both libretto and music. Various factors delayed its production, but it was enthusiastically received when eventually staged in February 1837. With this work Lortzing had finally found the style of opera that was to gain him widespread popularity in Germany. A contemporary reviewer remarked that the opera pleased the audience through its 'amusing action, comic characters and easily graspable, natural music', even though the music undeniably contained many reminiscences of other composers and was 'ordinary almost to the point of triviality' (*AMZ*, xli, 1839, cols.723–4); this writer went on to observe that the comic ensembles, particularly the third-act Septet, and the folklike lieder were more effective than the traditionally handled arias and duets, a judgment that was echoed by other contemporaries (see *NZM*, x, 1839, p.151). Spurred on by the favourable reception of *Die beiden Schützen*, Lortzing hastened to complete his second three-act comic opera *Zar* (originally *Czaar*) *und Zimmermann*, and was able to have it produced in December of the same year. *Zar und Zimmermann*, which shows significant advances on *Die beiden Schützen* in its structural control, was an even greater triumph. Lortzing's brilliant portrayal of the absurd burgomaster van Bett contributed greatly to the opera's success. After its première, a writer commented (*AMZ*, xl, 1838, col.30):

> With such a burgomaster the piece, which with its many striking effects is entirely tailored to the tastes of the moment, will please everywhere. Herr Lortzing understands the theatre and the way of the world, and with clever diligence gives the public nothing but what is to its taste ... He knows only too well that on the German stage nothing a German does can succeed unless it unites pleasure with amusing taste.

Lortzing's own correspondence shows that he had a refreshingly modest estimation of his own talent; he by no means regarded himself as a great composer, and clearly recognized that his strength lay in his gift for comedy combined with his ability to write lively and tuneful music. Nevertheless, he had ambitions to be more than a mere tunesmith and was sometimes piqued by the patronizing tone of his critics. *Die beiden Schützen* and *Zar und Zimmermann*, which were soon performed throughout German-speaking countries, firmly established his reputation as the leading German comic-opera composer of the day. Since there was no regulated system of royalties, however, his success did not bring him financial security. On 19 February 1840 he complained in a letter to a friend: 'On what should a composer pin his hope when he is so poorly paid, at any rate in Germany unfortunately, and is not in any way protected against theft, if even the court theatres will not pay their debts to him?'. Similar complaints were to resurface regularly in his correspondence for the rest of his life.

The next few years saw a steady stream of stage works. In 1839 he arranged E.-P. Prévost's *opéra bouffon Cosimo* as *Caramo*, a *grosse komische Oper*; this was followed in 1840 by *Hans Sachs* (for which Philipp Reger was principal librettist), in 1841 by *Casanova* and in 1842 by *Der Wildschütz*. With the last he repeated the triumph of *Die beiden Schützen* and *Zar und Zimmermann*. The comments *Der Wildschütz* elicited from the *Allgemeine musikalische Zeitung* reviewer (*AMZ*, xlv, 1843, col.527) indicate a growing appreciation of Lortzing's talent; the somewhat patronizing tone of earlier reviews is replaced here by genuine, unstinted admiration. The writer began by reconsidering *Die beiden Schützen* and *Zar und Zimmermann*, saying:

These two works, which have been received with enthusiastic acclamation, are characterized above all by good nature and natural cheerfulness, and since [Lortzing] has employed these universally welcome but yet so rare gifts with such ease, with such simple means, so unpretentiously and spontaneously, this has led to his successful vocation for the almost abandoned German comic opera. It is not the unprecedented or the astonishing that has made his works prosper, rather something much friendlier, more enduring; it is that good, healthy humour, that playful unaffectedness – ennobled in the appropriate places by simple, truthful feeling – that has opened stages, ears and hearts to him and his cheerful creations.

In many respects *Der Wildschütz* is Lortzing's comic masterpiece. The characters, particularly the hilarious figure of Baculus, the schoolmaster-cum-poacher, are delineated with an acute eye for the absurd, and Lortzing's ability to enhance the comic potential of solos and ensembles through musical means seems, if anything, heightened: the billiard table quintet 'Ich habe Num'ro eins' and Baculus's solo 'Fünftausend Thaler' are among the finest examples of their kind in Lortzing's output.

2. LATER CAREER. Following the enthusiastic reception of *Der Wildschütz*, Lortzing's fortunes seemed in the ascendant; he had played a leading role in the Leipzig company for some time, and on the retirement of the Kapellmeister, Ringelhardt, at Easter 1844, Lortzing was appointed in his stead. At about the same time, he began to plan his next opera, *Undine*, freely adapted from the tale by Friedrich de la Motte Fouqué which had provided the basis for Hoffmann's *Undine* of 1816 as well as for long-forgotten operas by Seyfried (1817) and C. F. J. Girschner (1830). Lortzing's *Undine* differs significantly from his earlier operas. The comic element is not absent (indeed Lortzing introduced two comic characters who do not appear in Fouqué's original), but does not play a pervasive part. The principal characters in the opera are wholly serious and, though Lortzing modified the tragic ending, the style of the opera as a whole is much closer to the German Romantic tradition. He himself described it in a letter of 16 May 1844 as 'a grand lyric, romantic opera with all kinds of nastinesses'. The writing of an essentially serious libretto posed problems for Lortzing, and he approached Düringer for assistance with some of the versification. Despite the fact that Lortzing was in poor health at this time, he completed the opera in early 1845 and conducted it in Hamburg on 25 April. (Because of delays in mounting the Hamburg production, the première had actually taken place four days earlier in Magdeburg.) Despite deficiencies in the Hamburg production the opera had a warm reception, but as before, critics regarded the opera's serious portions as less successful than the comic ones. Lortzing himself seems not to have been entirely satisfied with some parts

of the work and he made substantial changes for a Vienna production shortly afterwards.

At the beginning of May 1845, just after his return from Hamburg, Lortzing received notice of dismissal from his post at the Leipzig theatre (along with many of the other personnel). But the blow was somewhat softened later in the month by an approach from Pokorny, lessee of the Theater an der Wien in Vienna, with a proposal that he become Kapellmeister of a reconstituted opera company there. By February 1846 negotiations with Pokorny were completed and he signed a three-year contract. He took his newly completed comic opera, *Der Waffenschmied*, with him to Vienna and directed its première there on 30 May 1846. Benefiting perhaps from *Undine*, *Der Waffenschmied* is more richly orchestrated than the earlier comic operas and contains some attractive serious music; the comedy is effective, but not so disarmingly genial as in *Der Wildschütz*.

Though the Vienna post gave Lortzing a degree of material security, he was not happy there. The finances of the theatre soon became precarious and he could not be sure how long his position would be tenable; in addition, the lack of suitable singers made it virtually impossible for him to mount any of his own operas. The taste of the Viennese public, too, made his operas far less popular than they were in northern Germany. He wrote to his friend Philipp Reger on 29 May 1847:

I have had the sad experience of discovering that Vienna is no place for me (as an opera composer). The people cannot talk or play. It is a real misery. In general there is the most depraved musical taste here. Italian music holds sway. German operas, such as those of Spohr and Marschner, are certainly put on occasionally for appearance's sake, but immediately disappear again because they find no appreciation. There is only doodling, always doodling and trilling! And that in a city where Mozart, Beethoven, Gluck and other such men lived and worked.

At the time he wrote this, Lortzing was working on another comic opera, *Zum Grossadmiral*, which, since it was impossible to stage it in Vienna, had its first performance in Leipzig in December 1847. It enjoyed a moderate success, but despite many attractive qualities did not arouse the same admiration as the best of his earlier comic operas. Reviewing the vocal score in 1848, the *Allgemeine musikalische Zeitung* observed that the work was not so convincingly structured as the earlier operas; and, while admiring the attractiveness and skill of the comic numbers, the journal echoed criticism of earlier works by noting that though the more serious sections were pleasant enough, they did not achieve genuine power of expression. The writer remarked on Lortzing's musical style in general (*AMZ*, l, 1848, col.389):

As a composer, Lortzing is not driven by the power of genius and deep musical erudition to aspire for higher ideals. He is led by a more cheerful view of art; being merely gifted with a lucky talent he aims for the easily graspable and does not call for a deep understanding of art in the listener, and he usually achieves his aim.

Lortzing's next operatic venture, *Regina*, is a curiosity in his output. Its libretto is based on real events associated with the revolutionary unrest in Vienna in March 1848. It incorporates choruses and libertarian songs Lortzing had recently composed, and the libretto shows clearly that he shared many of the liberal sentiments of the time. Unlike all his other extant operas it is entirely serious; this obviously resulted from the nature of the subject, but it may also have owed something to his desire to show people such as the reviewer of *Zum*

Grossadmiral that he was capable of tackling a serious subject successfully. As he wrote to Philipp Reger on 18 September: 'I am already looking forward to hearing how the musicians who wish to appear learned will exclaim: "if only the man would stick to his comic music", but I cannot help them, these poor-spirited creatures, who are unable to do anything themselves but criticize everything else – they will have to swallow my latest work.' But his choice of subject matter proved fatal to the opera's prospects, and by December he was beginning to receive rejections from theatres to which he offered it. His publishers, too, refused it, and Lortzing had finally to concede that it would be neither performed nor published. Whether, had it been staged, it would have convinced his critics is highly doubtful.

The expiry of his contract at the Theater an der Wien again left Lortzing without a post. Before leaving Vienna, however, he hastened to complete another opera, *Rolands Knappen*, of which he had already composed the first act when he wrote to Reger about *Regina* in September 1848. He finished *Rolands Knappen*, a 'romantic magic opera' in which the comic element was again prominent, during the next few months and the première took place on 25 May 1849 in Leipzig. This opera gives evidence of Lortzing's growing maturity and assurance as a musician and of his continued striving to show that he could write music of substance in the German Romantic tradition; its handling of chromaticism, especially, shows a thorough and flexible command of the musical idiom that had been established by Spohr and Weber. *Rolands Knappen* was cordially received (though it was not to achieve long-term popularity), but Lortzing was again in financial difficulties which not even successful productions could alleviate. In search of another post he unsuccessfully approached various opera houses. He wrote the libretto of another three-act comic opera, *Cagliostro*, but did not compose music for it. For a while it seemed that he might remain in Leipzig as Kapellmeister, but that too came to nothing. Eventually, in April 1850, he accepted a rather poorly paid appointment as Kapellmeister at the Friedrich-Wilhelmstadt Theater in Berlin, a second-rate theatre where little substantial opera was performed. Berlin proved hardly better than Vienna for Lortzing, and he was constantly short of money. He managed to compose one more opera during this period, the one-act *Die Opernprobe*, but he never saw it performed. Its première took place in Frankfurt on 20 January 1851 while the composer lay ill. On the following morning he died.

Lortzing occupies a curious position in the history of German Romantic opera. He admired Mozart above all, but was also deeply appreciative of the operas of Spohr, Weber and Marschner, and did not hesitate to use elements of their styles in his own music. His own musical style is undeniably derivative, but because his works enjoyed such extensive popularity he played a major role in familiarizing a wider theatre-going public with the early German Romantic operatic idiom, if only in a somewhat diluted version. His position today is equivocal. On the one hand (according to Subotnik 1976) his operas have been more frequently performed in Germany in the third quarter of the 20th century than those of any other German-speaking composer except Mozart; on the other, perhaps because their humour does not travel well, Lortzing's operas are seldom performed outside the German-speaking countries.

See also BEIDEN SCHÜTZEN, DIE; HANS SACHS; UNDINE (ii); WAFFENSCHMIED, DER; WILDSCHÜTZ, DER; and ZAR UND ZIMMERMANN.

librettos by the composer unless otherwise stated

Ali Pascha von Janina, oder Die Franzosen in Albanien, 1824 (Spl, 1), Münster, Stadt, 1 Feb 1828, vs (Leipzig, 1904)

Der Pole und sein Kind, oder Der Feldwebel vom IV. Regiment (Liederspiel, 1), Osnabrück, 11 Oct 1832, vs (Regensburg, ?1832)

Der Weihnachtsabend 'Launige Scene aus dem Familienleben und Vaudeville' (Spl, 1), Münster, 21 Dec 1832

Andreas Hofer, 1832 (Spl, 1, after K. Immermann: *Trauerspiel in Tyrol*); arr. E. N. von Reznicek, Mainz, 14 April 1887

Szenen aus Mozarts Leben, 1832 (Spl, 1), unperf.

Der Amerikaner, ?1833–4 (after W. Vogel), only lib. sketched

Die beiden Schützen, 1835 (komische Oper, 3, after G. Cords: *Die beiden Grenadiere*), Leipzig, Stadt, 20 Feb 1837, vs (Leipzig, 1837)

Die Schatzkammer des Ynkas, 1836 (tragische Oper, R. Blum), unperf., only a Festmarsch survives

Czaar [Zar] und Zimmermann, oder Die zwei [beiden] Peter (komische Oper, 3, after G. C. Römer: *Der Bürgermeister von Saardamm, oder Die zwei Peter*), Leipzig, 22 Dec 1837, D-Bds; vs (Leipzig, 1838), full score (Leipzig, 1900)

Caramo, oder Das Fischerstechen (grosse komische Oper, 3, after A. Vilain de St Hilaire and P. Duport: *Cosimo*), Leipzig, 20 Sept 1839 [arr. of E.-P. Prévost: Cosimo]

Hans Sachs (komische Oper, 3, P. Reger, Lortzing and P. J. Düringer, after J. L. F. Deinhardstein), Leipzig, Stadt, 23 June 1840, vs (Leipzig, 1840); rev. version, Mannheim, National, 25 May 1845

Casanova (komische Oper, 3, after A. Lebrun), Leipzig, 31 Dec 1841, vs (Leipzig, 1842)

Der Wildschütz, oder Die Stimme der Natur (komische Oper, 3, after A. von Kotzebue: *Der Rehbock, oder Die schuldlosen Schuldbewussten*), Leipzig, 31 Dec 1842, vs (Leipzig, 1843), full score (Leipzig, 1928)

Undine (romantische Zauberoper, 4, after F. de la Motte Fouqué), Magdeburg, 21 April 1845, vs (Leipzig, 1845), full score (Leipzig, 1925)

Der Waffenschmied [Der Waffenschmied von [zu] Worms] (komische Oper, 3, after F. W. von Ziegler: *Liebhaber und Nebenbuhler in einer Person*), Vienna, An der Wien, 30 May 1846, vs (Leipzig, 1846), full score (Leipzig, 1922)

Zum Grossadmiral (komische Oper, 3, after A. W. Iffland: *Heinrich des Fünften Jugendjahre*), Leipzig, 13 Dec 1847, vs (Leipzig, 1848)

Regina, 1848 (3), Bds, vs (Leipzig, 1954); arr. A. L'Arronge as Regina, oder Die Marodeure, Berlin, 21 March 1899, vs (Berlin, 1899)

Rolands Knappen, oder Das ersehnte Glück (komische romantische Zauberoper, 3, Lortzing, G. Meisinger and K. Haffner, after G. A. Musäus: *Rolands Knappen*), Leipzig, 25 May 1849, vs (Lund, Berlin and Leipzig, 1920)

Cagliostro, 1849–50 (komische Oper, 3, after E. Scribe and J.-H. Vernoy de Saint-Georges), only lib. written

Die Opernprobe, oder Die vornehmen Dilettanten (komische Oper, 1, after J. F. Jünger: *Die Komödie aus dem Stegreif*), Frankfurt, 20 Jan 1851 (Leipzig, 1899)

*

ADB (M. Schletterer)

A. Lortzing: *Albert Lortzings komische Opern* (Leipzig, 1847)

P. J. Düringer: *Albert Lortzing: sein Leben und Wirken* (Leipzig, 1851)

H. Welti: 'Lortzing und Wagner', *Richard Wagner-Jb* 1886, 229–38

H. Wittmann: *Lortzing* (Leipzig, 1890, 2/1902)

R. Bürner: *Lortzing in Detmold, Pyrmont, Münster und Osnabrück* (Detmold, 2/1900)

E. von Komorzynski: 'Lortzings "Waffenschmied" und seine Tradition', *Euphorion*, viii (1901), 340–50

G. R. Kruse: 'Ein Mozart-Singspiel von Lortzing', *Mitteilungen für die Mozartgemeinde in Berlin*, xii (1901), 71–5

——, ed.: *A. Lortzing: gesammelte Briefe* (Leipzig, 1902, enlarged 2/1913, 3/1947)

L. Eisenberg: *Grosses biographisches Lexicon der deutschen Bühne im XIX. Jahrhundert* (Leipzig, 1903)

A. Fritz: 'Die Künstlerfamilie Lortzing an rheinischen Bühnen', *Archiv für Theatergeschichte*, i (1904), 160

K. M. Klob: *Beiträge zur Geschichte der deutschen komischen Oper* (Berlin, 1904)

G. R. Kruse: 'Albert Lortzing und seine "Regina"', *NZM*, Jg.79 (1912), 677–9

——: *Albert Lortzing: Leben und Werk* (Leipzig, 1914, 2/1947)

J. Schwermann: *Albert Lortzings Bühnentexte* (Wattenscheid, 1914)

H. Laue: *Die Operndichtung Lortzings* (Würzburg, 1932)

S. Goslich: *Beiträge zur Geschichte der deutschen romantischen Oper* (Leipzig, 1937; rev. 1975 as *Die deutsche romantische Oper*)

R. Butschek: *Die musikalischen Ausdrucksmittel in den Opern Lortzings* (diss., U. of Vienna, 1938)

M. Loy: *Lortzings 'Hans Sachs': ein Beitrag zur Geschichte und zum Stil der komischen Oper im 19. Jahrhundert* (diss., U. of Erlangen, 1940)

G. Dippel: *Albert Lortzing: ein Leben für das deutsche Musiktheater* (Berlin, 1951)

W. Schramm: *Albert Lortzing während seiner Zugehörigkeit zur Detmolder Hoftheatergesellschaft 1826–1833* (Detmold, 1951)

——: 'Lortzing in Detmold: bisher Unveröffentlichtes aus dem Schaffen Lortzings', *NZM*, Jg.112 (1951), 11–15

E. Sanders: 'Oberon and Zar und Zimmermann', *MQ*, xl (1954), 521–32

M. Hoffmann: *Gustav Albert Lortzing, der Meister der deutschen Volksoper* (Leipzig, 1956)

J. Lodemann: *Lortzing und seine Spielopern: deutsche Bürgerlichkeit* (diss., U. of Freiburg, 1962)

E. Wulf: '"Die Opernprobe" von G. A. Lortzing', *Untersuchungen zum Operneinakter in der Mitte des 19. Jahrhunderts* (diss., U. of Cologne, 1963)

H. Schirmag: *Das erste Auftreten des Proletariats als Klasse in der deutschen Opernliteratur des 19. Jahrhunderts: neue Aspekte für die Gewinnung eines realistischen Lortzingsbildes aus der Sicht der Lortzing-Oper 'Regina'* (diss., Pädagogische Hochschule, Potsdam, 1967)

A. Goebel: *Die deutsche Spieloper bei Lortzing, Nicolai und Flotow* (diss., U. of Cologne, 1975)

R. R. Subotnik: 'Lortzing and the German Romantics: a Dialectical Assessment', *MQ*, lxii (1976), 241–64

J. Schläder: 'Die Dramaturgie in Lortzings komischen Opern', *Oper als Text: romanistische Beiträge zur Libretto-Forschung*, ed. A. Gier (Heidelberg, 1986), 249–75

S. Johns: *Das szenische Liederspiel zwischen 1800 und 1830* (Frankfurt, 1988)
CLIVE BROWN

Los Angeles. City in California, ranked second largest in the USA. Its first taste of opera came from troupes travelling between Mexico City and San Francisco. On 21 and 23 November 1865 the Gerardo López del Castillo company performed at the Temple Theater one act of Verdi's *Attila* in Spanish between the acts of a Tomás Rodríguez Rubí play. Completed in 1860, the theatre had a stage measuring 15 by 12 metres, a two-tiered gallery, two private boxes and a parquette. At Childs' Grand Opera House, opened in 1884 and accommodating 1500 in a horseshoe-shaped auditorium, Emma Abbott's English Opera Company performed works from the standard repertory in February 1885 and again in January 1887. Later in 1887, the National Opera Company presented seven operas, including Anton Rubinstein's *Nero*, at the newly opened Hazard's Pavilion, a wooden building seating 4000 with upper and lower balconies on three sides. The following year, a Hispano-Mexican opera company brought zarzuelas by F. A. Barbieri and Joaquín Gaztambide to the Armory Hall.

Emma Nevada and Adelina Patti visited Los Angeles in 1885 and 1887, singing single scenes from operas, and in the late 1880s various troupes (Bijou, Carleton, Hazard's American and Pike) satiated the city with Gilbert and Sullivan and Viennese operettas. Touring opera increased still further in the next decade. Emma Juch's company staged *Guillaume Tell* at Childs' in January 1890, and the Los Angeles Theater (opened 14 December 1888) saw appearances by Abbott's group in December. The Columbia Opera Company gave the Los Angeles première of *Cavalleria rusticana* on 19 November 1891 and, the next year, the Arcaraz Spanish Grand Opera Company at Childs' performed works ranging from *Carmen* to *La tempestad* (Chapí) and *La gran vía* (Chueca). The Alesandro Salvini and Del Conte companies gave the American premières of *L'amico Fritz* in 1892 and *La bohème* in 1897. It was, however, in Milan that the first local resident to become an operatic soloist, Mamie Perry, made her début, in Petrella's *La contessa d'Amalfi*, under the name of 'La Perrini'; she had first appeared in her home town at Turnverein Hall in 1882 in a programme of arias.

Hazard's Pavilion was razed in 1905 and replaced a year later by a venue known variously as The Auditorium (1906–15), Clune's (1915–19) and the Philharmonic Auditorium (1919–64); the building was demolished in 1985. Seating 2600, in what was then the largest reinforced concrete building in California, it opened on 7 November 1906 with a Lambardi production of *Aida*. Horatio Parker's prize-winning *Fairyland* received its première there on 1 July 1915. Other operas to have had world premières in Los Angeles include Joseph Carl Breil's *Der Asra* (1925), Mary Carr Moore's *Los rubios* (1931), *David Rizzio* (1932) and *Flutes of Jade Happiness* (1934), Villa-Lobos's *Magdalena* (1948), Antheil's *Volpone* (1953), Roy Travis's *The Passion of Oedipus* (1968) and Eugene Zador's *The Inspector General* (1971).

The city's opera history in the 20th century has, however, revolved mostly around traditional repertory mounted by visiting companies. On its first visit to the West Coast (9–10 November 1901), the Metropolitan Opera Company gave *La bohème* and the mad scene from *Lucia* (with Melba), *Roméo et Juliette* and *Lohengrin* at Hazard's Pavilion; the company returned in 1902, but losses during the San Francisco earthquake forced the cancellation of their 1906 visit and they did not revisit Los Angeles until 1948. There were visits from the San Carlo Opera Company in 1907 (with Lillian Nordica singing *La Gioconda* at a matinée and *La traviata* the same evening), and the Henry Savage company (at the Mason Opera House) in 1908. In April 1908 the Edgar Temple company began a three-week engagement, advertising itself as the first professional organization to use local singers in leading roles. Bringing 27 different stage settings from France, the Paris Grand Opera played from 9 January to 3 February 1912.

The Los Angeles Grand Opera Association was formed in 1924, after the model of the San Francisco Opera founded a year earlier by Gaetano Merola. At first Merola tried staging the same repertory in both cities, a month apart. But he was replaced in Los Angeles by Richard Hageman, who in 1925 presented *Aida* a week before Merola's company did. Such competition proved harmful and the Los Angeles Association was returned to Merola's direction from 1926 to its dissolution in 1932.

From 1939 to 1962, 13 short-lived organizations attempted to form resident grand opera companies; meanwhile, the Los Angeles Civic Light Opera flourished at the Philharmonic Auditorium, 1938–65, usually presenting Broadway musicals such as *Blossom Time*, *New Moon* and *Roberta* (with Bob Hope and Carol Landis) as well as *Porgy and Bess* (1943). Under Hugo Strelitzer in the 1940s and 50s, Los Angeles City Opera Workshop gave works ranging from Hindemith's *Hin und zurück*, Douglas Moore's *The Devil and Daniel Webster* and Ibert's *Angélique* to *Boris Godunov*. Walter Ducloux conducted the University of Southern

California student opera, 1953–68, and was followed in 1974 by Natalie Limonick, who had conducted Rameau's *Les Indes galantes* at UCLA in 1969. In 1932, 1934 and every autumn from 1937 to 1965, the San Francisco Opera gave a season of several weeks at the massive Shrine Auditorium, holding 6000. Subsequently the New York City Opera appeared, beginning its three-week season in 1967 with Ginastera's *Don Rodrigo*. By 1974 the annual season had extended to 24 performances in four weeks, including a production of *I puritani* staged at the Dorothy Chandler Pavilion, Music Center (cap. 3200), before its New York run. The company's repertory attempted to accommodate all tastes, embracing Mozart, Rossini, Menotti, Weill (*Street Scene*) and Romberg (*The Student Prince*).

In 1984, apart from the visiting Royal Opera, which gave 11 performances in the Chandler Pavilion, the short-lived Los Angeles Opera Theater staged *Der Rosenkavalier* in English at the Wilshire Ebell Theater and, after a 12-year hiatus, the Hollywood Bowl (holding 17 619) was the site of a production of *La bohème*. With Peter Hemmings as Executive Director, Music Center Opera ('Los Angeles's first truly professional opera company') launched its long-awaited inaugural season in 1986 with Domingo in *Otello* at the Chandler Pavilion. In January 1989 the company announced a deficit of $3 million; their February staging of *Tancredi*, with Marilyn Horne, was a co-production with Chicago Lyric Opera. Among further productions, several of which have included Domingo as either singer or conductor, may be mentioned *Salome* and *Tosca* (both with Maria Ewing) in 1989; *Don Carlos*, *Idomeneo* (with Siegfried Jerusalem), *Fidelio* and Gluck's *Orfeo* (with Marilyn Horne) in 1990; *Elektra*, *The Turn of the Screw*, *Madama Butterfly* (with Ewing) and *Les Troyens* (conducted by Charles Dutoit) in 1991; and the première of Sallinen's *Kullervo*, a joint venture with Finnish National Opera, in February 1992.

*

S. W. Earnest: *An Historical Study of the Growth of Theatre in Southern California* (diss., U. of Southern California, 1947)

R. L. Karson: *Music Criticism in Los Angeles 1895–1919* (diss., U. of Southern California, 1964)

N. E. Wilson: *A History of Opera and Associated Educational Activities in Los Angeles* (diss., Indiana U., 1967)

A. Jacobs: 'The California Experience', *Opera*, xx (1969), 587–92

J. Sanders: 'Los Angeles Grand Opera Association: the Formative Years, 1924–1926', *Southern California Quarterly*, lv (1973), 261–302

M. Bernheimer: 'The Royal Opera at the Olympics', *Opera*, xxxv (1984), 1101–4

H. Rosenthal: ' "Salome" Triumphs in L.A.', *Opera*, xxxvii (1986), 1350–51
ROBERT STEVENSON

Los Angeles, Victoria de (*b* Barcelona, 1 Nov 1923). Spanish soprano. She comes of a musical family and studied piano, guitar and singing at home as well as at the Barcelona Conservatory. After her operatic début at Barcelona (1941, Mimì), she soon became a leading opera and concert singer, internationally as well as in Spain. Having been invited by the BBC to sing Salud in a 1948 studio broadcast of Falla's *La vida breve*, she made her début at Covent Garden in 1950, and at the Metropolitan in the following year, and sang regularly in both houses until 1961. Although she successfully tackled the lighter Wagnerian roles, such as Eva and Elsa, she excelled as the more lyrical heroines of *La bohème*, *Madama Butterfly* and *Manon*. At the Metropolitan she was especially admired in her début

Victoria de los Angeles in the title role of Massenet's 'Manon'

role of Marguerite, and as Mélisande and Desdemona; and in two successive years (1961 and 1962) she appeared at Bayreuth as Elisabeth. During the later 1960s she took part in several productions at the Teatro Colón, Buenos Aires, and she sang in *Otello* at Dallas in 1969. By that time, however, she had already confined her appearances mainly to the concert platform, where her personal and vocal charms have made her a great and continuing favourite. In her best years the timbre of her voice was exceptionally sweet, and she was a most communicative artist in both song and opera. Among the best of her many recordings is that of *La bohème*, conducted by Beecham.

*

GV (R. Celletti; S. Smolian)

C. Hardy: 'Victoria de los Angeles', *Opera*, viii (1957), 210–16

G. Moore: *Am I too Loud?* (London, 1962), 168ff

A. Natan: *Prima Donna: Lob der Stimmen* (Basle, 1962), 86ff [with discography, 117ff]

B. James: 'Victoria de los Angeles', *Audio & Record Review*, ii/6 (1963), 12–15 [with discography by F. F. Clough and G. J. Cuming]

J. B. Steane: *The Grand Tradition* (London, 1974), 367ff

L'avant-scène opéra, no.78 (1985) [whole issue]
DESMOND SHAWE-TAYLOR

Lost in the Stars. Musical tragedy by KURT WEILL to a libretto by Maxwell Anderson after Alan Paton's novel *Cry, the Beloved Country*; New York, Music Box Theatre, 30 October 1949.

In South Africa in 1949, a black preacher, Stephen Kumalo (bass-baritone), is anxious about his son Absalom (spoken), who is working in the mines to pay for his education; Stephen has not heard from him for nearly a year. Stephen's wife, Grace (spoken), senses trouble, but Stephen has faith, expressed in the song 'Thousands of Miles'.

Stephen agrees to take their meagre savings and look for their son in the city ('Train to Johannesburg'). At the station he sees Arthur Jarvis (spoken), son of a British planter, who is bemused by his own son's sympathy for black people. Unsuccessful in his search for Absalom, Stephen agrees to look after his sister's son Alex (treble) back in his 'Little Gray House' in Ndotsheni. Absalom is living in a shanty-town with his friend Irina (mezzo-soprano), who is pregnant; he listens to 'Who'll Buy', the brazen song of the entertainer Linda (mezzo-soprano). Desperate for a better life, he plans to take part in a gang robbery. Irina loves him, but is anxious about her 'Trouble Man'. During the robbery Absalom shoots a white man in panic. It is James (spoken), Arthur Jarvis's son. The double chorus, split into black and white halves, comments with 'Fear'. When Absalom is arrested, Stephen's faith is shaken: 'Sometimes it seems God's gone away ... And we're lost ... in the stars'.

Stephen prays to God ('O Tixo, Tixo, Help Me!') and persuades his son to confess to the crime. Irina reaffirms her commitment ('Stay Well'), while the chorus casts doubt on the judicial system ('The Wild Justice'). Absalom's accomplices are acquitted on lack of evidence; Absalom tells the truth and receives the death penalty. The chorus laments: 'Cry the beloved country! The wasted childhood, the wasted youth, the wasted man!'.

Back in his church, Stephen announces his intention to resign. Man is like a 'Bird of Passage'. Alex, meanwhile, has befriended Jarvis's grandson Edward (spoken). Jarvis censures their friendship. As Absalom is about to be executed, Jarvis overcomes his hatred. He and Stephen seal their friendship.

Although Paton's novel was first published in 1948, Weill drew some of the material for his last completed work from an earlier collaboration with Maxwell Anderson: the unfinished musical *Ulysses Africanus*, which was begun in 1939 and fleetingly resuscitated in 1945. The resulting 'musical tragedy', composed between February and September 1949, is a hybrid of a type Weill was keen to cultivate, mixing straight play and sung musical, with stretches of dialogue accompanied by the orchestra in the manner of Hollywood melodrama à la Douglas Sirk. It is much more, however, than an agglomeration of separate numbers. Weill creates a whole network of thematic associations, based on melodic and harmonic motifs. Three elements are particularly pervasive: a descending chromatic bass figure, which provides a kind of fate motif; the melody that expresses Stephen's faith; and the Wagnerian tetrachordal harmonies of 'Trouble Man'. At the beginning of the double chorus 'Fear', for example, all three elements help create the uneasy atmosphere of the entire piece.

Weill's orchestration, involving just 12 players, is unusual for a Broadway musical and required special dispensation from the Musicians' Union. At the première, whose cast took part in a gramophone recording, the role of Stephen was taken by Todd Duncan, the star of the original *Porgy and Bess*. A 'Concert Sequence' by David Drew, entitled *Cry, the Beloved Country* and with connecting texts taken from the novel, received its première in New York in 1988. It comprises 11 numbers, among them the unpublished 'Gold' and the original setting of 'Bird of Passage'.   STEPHEN HINTON

Lotario ('Lothair', 'Lotharius'). Opera in three acts by GEORGE FRIDERIC HANDEL to a libretto anonymously adapted from ANTONIO SALVI's *Adelaide* as revised for Venice (1729); London, King's Theatre, 2 December 1729.

Lotario opened the first season of the so-called 'Second Academy' period of opera in London, when the Royal Academy of Music ceded to Handel and his manager Heidegger the right to promote operas in London. The cast, newly gathered by Handel on a European trip, consisted of the castrato Antonio Bernacchi (Lotario), Anna Strada del Pò (Adelaida), Annibale Pio Fabri (Berengario), Francesca Bertolli (Idelberto), Antonia Merighi (Matilda) and Johann Gottfried Riemschneider (Clodomiro). It had only moderate success (ten performances) and was never revived by Handel, though he re-used several numbers of the score in the pasticcio *Oreste* and revivals of other operas (*Scipione, Rinaldo, Rodelinda, Poro, Il pastor fido*); two numbers also reappear without musical change in the oratorio *The Triumph of Time and Truth* (1757). The only revival before 1992 was given by Unicorn Opera at the Kenton Theatre, Henley-on-Thames, on 3 September 1975 (repeated at Goldsmiths' Hall, London, on 12 July 1976); it was the last in the series of Handel revivals by this pioneering group.

The historical background (which overlaps that of Handel's *Ottone*) is the events following the death of Lothair II of Italy in 950. The usurper Berengar captured Lothair's widow Adelaide, intending to force her to marry his son Adalbert and thus secure the Italian crown for his descendants. On an appeal from Adelaide, King Otho I of Germany advanced into Italy, rescued Adelaide and married her. In Salvi's libretto these characters appear as Berengario, Idelberto, Adelaide and Ottone, but Handel renamed the last character Lotario during the course of composition, avoiding confusion with his earlier opera but muddling the historical connections.

The action is set in and around Pavia, where Adelaida (soprano) has taken refuge; it is under siege by Berengario, Duke of Spoleto (tenor), who has murdered Adelaida's former husband. Idelberto (contralto), Berengario's son, reports Adelaida's rejection of his proposal of marriage; Berengario orders him to storm the city. Berengario's general Clodomiro (bass) brings news of the advance of the German king Lotario (alto castrato). Berengario's wife Matilda (contralto) explains a plan to take Pavia by night. Idelberto begs Berengario to spare Adelaida (whom he loves); Berengario agrees, if she will marry Idelberto, who resolves to protect her. Adelaida is visited by Lotario, who declares his love; she promises to marry him if he restores peace. Clodomiro offers her marriage to Idelberto or war with Berengario; she refuses any connection with his family. Berengario takes Pavia and Matilda takes charge of Adelaida.

Act 2 opens by a bridge over the river Ticino. Berengario has been defeated by Lotario and taken prisoner. Adelaida is presented by Clodomiro with a choice of two bowls, one containing a dagger and poison, the other a sceptre and crown: she must choose death or marriage to Idelberto. She seizes the dagger and poison but Idelberto intervenes: he presents the dagger to Matilda and demands death at her hand; then, as Adelaida attempts to drink the poison, he threatens to stab himself and die with her. Matilda snatches the poison and the dagger; her fury is further incensed by Clodomiro's announcement of Berengario's capture.

She appears on the walls by Lotario's camp and threatens to kill Adelaida: in answer Lotario says he will kill Berengario. Idelberto offers himself as a hostage and Lotario sends Berengario under guard to get Matilda to yield the city and release Adelaida, or Idelberto will die.

In Act 3 Berengario and Matilda offer freedom to Adelaida if she will ask Lotario to allow them to keep their kingdom; she refuses. Lotario attacks Pavia and breaches the walls, but his advance is halted by Clodomiro's exposure of Adelaida to the battle. Lotario puts Berengario, unarmed, at the front of his troops. When Idelberto offers to take his father's place, Lotario tells him to secure Adelaida's safety. Lotario is welcomed by the people of Pavia. Matilda rejects Idelberto's pleas for Adelaida, but on hearing that she has been freed and that Pavia has been taken, she attempts to turn her sword on herself. Adelaida, united with Lotario, accepts Idelberto's plea for mercy for his parents and gives him his father's throne.

*　*　*

Handel's friend and admirer Mrs Delaney reported that the opera was disliked because it was 'too much studied' – which may be taken as a reference to a paucity of instantly memorable melody. The arias incline to tenderness or vocal virtuosity, sometimes dissipating rather than reinforcing the dramatic tensions. In particular the potentially dominating character of Matilda emerges more in recitative than in her arias, and it is Berengario, with several expansive and expressive songs, who comes through more strongly in the music. Adelaida's final aria in Act 1 ('Scherza in mar la navicella') is a brilliant piece though dramatically inapt; her aria of defiance in Act 3 ('Non sempre invendicata') gets the balance right. Idelberto's arias, notably 'Per salvarti, idolo mio', have considerable charm.

ANTHONY HICKS

Lothar, Mark [Hundertmark, Lothar] (*b* Berlin, 23 May 1902; *d* Munich, 6 April 1985). German composer. He was a pupil of Schreker and Juon at the Berlin Hochschule für Musik and studied composition privately with Wolf-Ferrari, who exercised a considerable influence on his musical development. After the success of his operas *Tyll* (1928) and *Lord Spleen* (1930), he was engaged by Max Reinhardt to become music director at the Deutsche Theater, Berlin, in 1933 and from 1934 to 1944 worked under Gustaf Gründgens at the Preussische Staatstheater. After the war, he moved to Munich where he held a similar position at the Bayerische Staatstheater. In 1956 he retired from public life to devote himself exclusively to composition.

Although Lothar wrote music in a variety of different genres, his long association with the theatre as well as his penchant for composing lieder gave him the necessary experience to write technically fluent and dramatically convincing operas. He judiciously avoided tackling psychologically complex subjects, preferring to offer the public vivid portrayals of lovable if eccentric outsiders such as Tyll Eulenspiegel (*Tyll*), Anton Wibbel (*Schneider Wibbel*) or the Irish priest of *Der widerspenstige Heilige*. In this respect, he attempted a renewal of the traditions of German Singspiel much in the manner of Lortzing, whose *Casanova* he arranged for performance at the Berlin Staatsoper in 1944. Of his 11 operas, the most successful were *Schneider Wibbel* (1938), which enjoyed over 200 performances in German opera houses up to 1944, and *Rappelkopf* (1958). Both are notable for their swiftly moving action, skilful characterization and sense of atmosphere.

In *Rappelkopf*, Lothar sought to bring Raimund's musical play up to date and free it from the conventions of Viennese popular theatre. Yet despite the music's evident charm, the score seems to lack the melodic memorability needed to ensure it a permanent place in the repertory.

Tyll op.12 (3, H. F. Königsgarten), Weimar, 14 Oct 1928, vs (Berlin, 1928)
Lord Spleen op.17 (2, Königsgarten, after B. Jonson), Dresden, 11 Nov 1930 (Berlin, 1931)
Münchhausen op.20 (3, W. M. Treichlinger), Dresden, 6 June 1933, vs (Berlin, 1933)
Das kalte Herz (Funkoper, 1, G. Eich), Berlin Radio, 24 March 1935
Schneider Wibbel op.34 (4, H. Müller-Schlosser), Berlin, Staatsoper, 12 May 1938, vs (Berlin, 1938)
Rappelkopf op.56 (2, Treichlinger, after F. Raimund), Munich, 20 Aug 1958, vs (Berlin, 1958)
Der Glücksfischer op.62 (2, W. Brandin), Nuremberg, 16 March 1962, vs (Hamburg, 1962)
Liebe im Eckhaus op.70 (Spl, 2, A. Cosmar)
Der widerspenstige Heilige op.73 (3, Lothar, after P. V. Carrol), Munich, Gärtnerplatz, 8 Feb 1968, vs (Berlin, 1968)
Momo und die Zeitdiebe op.84 (M. Ende), Coburg, Landes, 19 Nov 1978
La bocca della verità: Hommage à Baldassare Galuppi op.93, Munich, 1982

*

H. Tessmer: 'Hat die deutsche Oper eine Zukunft?', *ZfM*, c (1933), 1000–03
J. Kapp: 'Über Mark Lothars Opernschaffen', *Blätter der Staatsoper Berlin* (1938)
W. Zentner: 'Mark Lothar', *ZfM*, cxiii (1952), 282–4
A. Ott, ed.: *Mark Lothar: ein Musikerporträt* (Munich, 1968)
Mark Lothar, Ausstellung zum 75. Geburtstag: Bayerische Staatsbibliothek Musiksammlung, 12. Mai–15. Juli 1977 (Munich, 1977) [exhibition catalogue]
A. L. Suder, ed.: *Mark Lothar* (Tutzing, 1986)　　ERIK LEVI

Loti, Pierre [Louis-Marie-Julien Viaud] (*b* Rochefort, 14 Jan 1850; *d* Hendaye, 10 June 1923). French novelist and travel writer. Born into a Protestant family, he joined the French navy, was posted to a variety of stations around the world and retired as 'capitaine de vaisseau' in 1906, returning later for war service. He was elected to the Académie Française in 1891. Although *Mon frère Yves* (1883) is set in Brittany, *Pêcheur d'islande* (1886) in northern waters and *Ramuntcho* (1897) in the Basque region, most of his stories reflect experiences, or perhaps dreams of experiences, in the Levant and the Far East. Exoticism and eroticism mingle in picturesque settings until the call of duty brings things to a gently melancholic end; Delibes' *Lakmé* (1883), with a libretto based on Loti's novel *Rarahu*, is typical. Messager's *Madame Chrysanthème* (1893), with a libretto by Georges Hartmann and André Alexandre after Loti's tale of the same name, has situations that were to be developed more powerfully in a similar setting by Puccini in *Madama Butterfly*, and in 1897 Lucien Lambert set Loti's *Le Spahi* to music (libretto by Louis Gallet and Alexandre). Loti collaborated with Hartmann and Alexandre on the libretto of *L'île du rêve*, a three-act 'Polynesian idyll' set by Reynaldo Hahn. Stefano Donaudy's setting of *Ramuntcho* (libretto by Stefano and Alberto Donaudy) was first performed in 1921.

*

M. G. Lerner: *Pierre Loti* (New York, 1974)

CHRISTOPHER SMITH

Lott, Felicity (*b* Cheltenham, 8 May 1947). English soprano. She studied at the RAM and made her début in 1973 with Unicorn Opera, Abingdon, as Seleuce (*Tolomeo*). In 1975 she sang Pamina with the ENO, for whom her subsequent roles have included Natasha (*War and Peace*), Roxana (Szymanowski's *King Roger*) and Fiordiligi. In 1976 she made her Covent Garden début in Henze's *We Come to the River* and sang the Countess (*Capriccio*) for Glyndebourne Touring Opera. She has also sung Jenifer (*The Midsummer Marriage*) and the Governess (*The Turn of the Screw*) for the WNO, Anne Trulove, Octavian and Helena (*A Midsummer Night's Dream*) at Glyndebourne, and has appeared in Hamburg, Munich, Florence, Paris, Brussels and Chicago. Her roles include Handel's Cleopatra, Donna Elvira, Countess Almaviva, Louise, Blanche (*Dialogues des Carmélites*), Ellen Orford and Eva, her first Wagnerian role, which she sang at Covent Garden in 1990, the year of her Metropolitan début as the Marschallin. With a beautiful voice and superb diction, she excels in Strauss, most notably as the Marschallin, Countess Madeleine, Christine Storch and Arabella, which she sang at La Scala in 1992. She was made a CBE in 1990.

*

E. Forbes: 'Felicity Lott', *Opera*, xl (1989), 1174–80

ELIZABETH FORBES

Lottchen am Hofe ('Lottchen at Court'). *Comische Oper* in three acts by JOHANN ADAM HILLER to a libretto by CHRISTIAN FELIX WEISSE, after CHARLES-SIMON FAVART's *opéra comique La caprice amoureux, ou Ninette à la cour*; Leipzig, Theater am Rannstädter Thore, 24 April 1767.

To punish her fiancé Gürge (bass), the country girl Lottchen (soprano) agrees to go off to court with Astolph, Duke of Lombardy (bass), who has designs on her although betrothed to Emilie (soprano). After complications and jealousies at court, the women join forces (as in Da Ponte's *Figaro*). In a darkened room Lottchen, pursued by Astolph, substitutes Emilie for herself; exposure brings him to his senses. Musical emphasis rests on the many short songs of the rustic pair, but all the characters are drawn with fairly modest musical means. Weisse did not transfer the action to Germany, which may account for the text's strong ridicule of courtly artificiality as well as the concluding *divertissement* of several danced entrées.

THOMAS BAUMAN

Lotti, Antonio (*b* Venice or Hanover, *c*1667; *d* Venice, 5 Jan 1740). Italian composer. By 1683 at the latest he had settled in Venice and was studying with Legrenzi, and soon was deeply involved in the musical life of the city. He was among the first to join the musical fraternity of S Cecilia when it was established on 25 November 1687 at St Mark's, where he served as an extra singer. From 30 May 1689 he was employed as a regular alto. He followed C. F. Pollarolo in his rise through the hierarchy of St Mark's: when Pollarolo was appointed second organist (13 August 1690) Lotti was his assistant, and two years later, when Pollarolo was appointed vice-*maestro di cappella*, Lotti replaced him as second organist (23 May 1692). On 17 August 1704 Lotti became first organist. Except for two works of the 1690s, his operas for Venice were written between 1706 and 1717. During this decade of continuous activity he wrote first for the Teatro S Cassiano for two seasons (1706–8) before beginning in 1709 a long association with the Teatro S Giovanni Grisostomo, the most important Venetian theatre of the day. During Carnival 1715, when the S Giovanni Grisostomo was closed, he

wrote for the Teatro SS Giovanni e Paolo. During the 1709–10 season his *Ama più chi men si crede* and *Il comando non inteso et ubbidito* at the S Giovanni Grisostomo framed the production of Handel's *Agrippina*; according to contemporary reports, Lotti's two operas were at least as successful as Handel's.

During a visit of the Crown Prince of Saxony to Venice that extended from spring 1716 to autumn 1717, Lotti was invited to assemble an opera company for the elector at Dresden. Shortly before he received permission to leave Venice on 22 July 1717, he married the soprano Santa Stella, who accompanied him to Dresden along with several musicians from St Mark's, the librettist A. M. Lucchini, the violinist Veracini and the alto castrato Senesino. The theatre architect and set designer Alessandro Mauro, who had acted as impresario at the S Giovanni Grisostomo since 1715, also joined the new operatic enterprise in Dresden. From 1717 to 1719 the Dresden opera under Lotti constituted one of the finest opera establishments in Europe.

Lotti and his wife found their stay in Dresden financially rewarding. After returning to Venice in autumn 1719 Lotti chose to devote himself to sacred music: the increasing prominence of young composers cultivating a new style may have influenced his decision to withdraw from opera. He resumed his position as first organist at St Mark's, and on 2 April 1736 was appointed *maestro di cappella*. He was highly esteemed as an opera composer in Venice, but his works never enjoyed the wide diffusion of those of his chief rival, Gasparini.

Lotti worked with the leading librettists of his day – Silvani, Piovene, S. B. Pallavicino, Zeno and Pariati – whose librettos are distinguished from *seicento* librettos in their clearly motivated plots, extensive recitatives and consistently high moral tone. Lotti composed comic intermezzos (one a collaboration with Gasparini) for at least two of the four serious operas he wrote for the S Cassiano. The aria was his central focus, and his surviving scores do not have the finely crafted shaping of recitative (both simple and accompanied) for which Gasparini was famous. Each serious opera has 30 or more arias; most are in da capo form and are accompanied by upper melodic instruments with continuo. Like his Venetian colleagues, Lotti retained the focus on the voice in spite of the increased use of instruments. He usually lightened the texture during vocal statements, and cultivated a smooth vocal line, eschewing the extremes of his younger contemporary Handel. The stylistic distance between the two is clearly evident in Lotti's writing for the bass Giuseppe Boschi, which avoids the wide leaps and extended vocal range that Handel required of him.

The instrumental forces for Lotti's Venetian operas vary. *Alessandro Severo* has minimal requirements: two oboes, strings and basso continuo. *Foca superbo* also requires two trumpets, and *Polidoro* two recorders, two trumpets and two horns. (Bassoons, though not indicated in the surviving Venetian scores, may have doubled the continuo.) His operas for Vienna and Dresden employ flutes, recorders and oboes as solo instruments, as well as two bassoons. He also used horns in his Dresden operas. An aria in *Costantino* calls for a chalumeau, and one in *Teofane* requires a mandolin or archlute.

See also ALESSANDRO SEVERO (i) and TEOFANE.

drammi per musica in three acts, first performed in Venice, unless otherwise stated

VC – *Venice, Teatro S Cassiano*
VGG – *Venice, Teatro S Giovanni Grisostomo*

Il trionfo dell'innocenza (R. Cialli), S Angelo, carn. 1693, arias *I-CCc* and *Rvat*

Tirsi [Act 1] (dramma pastorale, 5, A. Zeno), S Salvatore, 3 Nov 1696 arias *B-Bc*; collab. A. Caldara and A. O. Ariosti

Sidonio (5, P. Pariati), VC, aut. 1706

Achille placato (tragedia per musica, 5, U. Rizzi), VC, 12 Feb 1707, perf. with Le rovine di Troja [Dragontata e Policrone] (int), *Br*(*R: DMV*, x, forthcoming)

Teuzzone (Zeno), VC, 27 Dec 1707, perf. with Catulla e Lardone (int); rev. G. Vignola, as L'inganno vinto dalla ragione, Naples, Fiorentini, 19 Nov 1708

Il vincitor generoso (F. Briani), VGG, 10 or 11 Jan 1709

Ama più chi men si crede (melodramma pastorale, 3, F. Silvani), VGG, 23 Nov 1709

Il comando non inteso et ubbidito (Silvani), VGG, 8 Feb 1710, arias *D-WD*

La ninfa Apollo (scherzo comico pastorale, 3, F. de Lemene), VC, 4 March 1710, collab. F. Gasparini

Isacio tiranno (Briani), VGG, 24 Nov 1710, arias *WD*

Il tradimento traditor di se stesso (Silvani), VGG, 17 Jan 1711; rev. F. Mancini, as Artaserse, re di Persia (with prol.), Naples, Palazzo, 1 Oct 1713, arias *B* and *WD*

La forza del sangue (Silvani), VGG, 14 or 15 Nov 1711; rev. Vignola, Naples, S Bartolomeo, 26 Oct 1712

L'infedeltà punita (Silvani), VGG, 15 Nov 1712, arias *Dlb*; collab. C. F. Pollarolo

Porsenna (A. Piovene), VGG, 4 Feb 1713; rev. A. Scarlatti, Naples, S Bartolomeo, 19 Nov 1713

Irene augusta (Silvani), VGG, 22 Nov 1713, arias *Dlb*

Polidoro (tragedia per musica, 5, Piovene), SS Giovanni e Paolo, carn. 1715, *I-Nc*

Foca superbo (A. M. Lucchini), VGG, carn. 1716, *D-Dlb*

Ciro in Babilonia (Pariati), Reggio Emilia, Pubblico, May 1716

Costantino (Pariati ?and Zeno), Vienna, Hof, 19 Nov 1716, *A-Wgm*, *Wn*; ov. by Fux, intermezzos and licenza by Caldara, arias and dances by N. Matteis

Alessandro Severo (Zeno), VGG, carn. 1717, *D-Dlb* (*R1977: IOB*, xx)

Giove in Argo (melodramma pastorale, Lucchini), Dresden, Redoutensaal, 25 Oct 1717; rev., Dresden, Neues Opernhaus, 3 Sept 1719; *B*, *Dlb*, *Mbs*

Ascanio, ovvero Gli odi delusi dal sangue (Lucchini), Dresden, Redoutensaal, Feb 1718, *B*, *Dlb*

Teofane (S. B. Pallavicino), Dresden, Neues Opernhaus, 13 Sept 1719, *B*, *Dlb*

Li quattro elementi (carosello teatrale), Dresden, palace garden, 15 Sept 1719

*

M. Fürstenau: *Zur Geschichte der Musik und des Theaters am Hofe zu Dresden* (Dresden, 1861–2)

C. Spitz: *Antonio Lotti in seiner Bedeutung als Opernkomponist* (diss., U. of Munich, 1918)

——: 'Die Opern *Ottone* von G. F. Händel (London, 1722) und *Teofane* von A. Lotti (Dresden, 1719): ein Stilvergleich', *Festschrift zum 50. Geburtstag Adolf Sandberger* (Munich, 1918), 265–71

——: 'Eine anonyme italienische Oper um die Wende des 17. zum 18. Jahrhunderts', *ZMw*, ii (1919–20), 232–5

——: 'Die Entwicklung des "Stile recitativo"', *AMw*, iii (1921), 237–44

R. L. Holden: *The Six Extant Operas of Antonio Lotti (1667–1740)* (diss., U. of Washington, 1970)

R. Strohm: 'Italienische Opernarien des frühen Settecento: 1720–1730', *AnMc*, no.16 (1976) [whole vol.]

C. E. Troy: *The Comic Intermezzo: a Study in the History of the Eighteenth-Century Italian Opera* (Ann Arbor, 1979)

R. Strohm: 'Manoscritti di opere rappresentate a Venezia, 1701–1740', *Informazioni e studi vivaldiani*, iii (1982), 45–51

HARRIS S. SAUNDERS

Lotti, Santa. *See* STELLA, SANTA.

Lottini, Antonio (*b* Pistoia; *fl* 1717–65). Italian bass. He was a pupil of A. F. Carli and later of the composer Francesco Gasparini, in whose *Intermezzi in derisione della setta maomettana* he made his first appearance (1717, Rome). Until Carnival 1729 he performed serious as well as comic roles in both southern and northern Italy. After 1729 he sang almost exclusively in Tuscany (perhaps because he had entered the service of the Grand Duchess of Tuscany), confining himself to the comic repertory. His permanent partner in intermezzos was A. Faini, with whom he visited London (perhaps summoned by Handel) and introduced a number of comic intermezzos, which were not well received. While in London he also sang minor roles in works by Handel (Teobaldo in *Faramondo*, Elviro in *Xerxes*) and others before returning to Tuscany and resuming his career there. He was a singer of solid technique with perhaps greater agility than power.

*

S. Fassini: 'Il melodramma italiano a Londra ai tempi del Rolli', *RMI*, xix (1912), 35–74, 575–636

F. Piperno: 'Appunti sulla configurazione sociale e professionale delle "parti buffe"', *Antonio Vivaldi: teatro musicale, cultura e società: Venice 1981*, 483–97

——: 'F. Gasparini, le sue abitazioni romane, i suoi allievi coabitanti', *Esercizi: arte, musica, spettacolo*, iv (1981), 104–15

——: 'Buffe e buffi', *RIM*, xviii (1982), 240–84

FRANCO PIPERNO

Loughran, James (*b* Glasgow, 30 June 1931). Scottish conductor. He organized and conducted music while at school and, on the advice of Karl Rankl, went to Germany in 1958 to gain experience as a répétiteur at the Bonn Opera, then with the Netherlands Opera and in various Italian centres. After winning a Philharmonia Orchestra competition for conductors in 1961 he made his operatic début conducting the première of Malcolm Williamson's *Our Man in Havana* at the Sadler's Wells Theatre (1963), and in 1964 made his débuts with Sadler's Wells Opera (*La traviata*) and at Covent Garden (*Aida*). He also worked with the English Opera Group (1966) and with Scottish Opera (first in *The Gondoliers*, 1968). Since then his work has been almost entirely in concerts, including an influential period with the Hallé Orchestra, from 1971 to 1983, when he was named conductor laureate.

NOËL GOODWIN

Louise. *Roman musical* in four acts by GUSTAVE CHARPENTIER to a libretto by the composer or by Saint-Pol-Roux; Paris, Opéra-Comique (Salle Favart), 2 February 1900.

Charpentier began *Louise* in Rome while, as winner of the Prix de Rome, he was at the Villa Medici, having reluctantly departed from Paris in 1887. Originally, it was planned that Hartmann, the music publishers, would obtain a libretto on which he could write an opera, but, tired of waiting, Charpentier began writing a text himself. Although he vehemently denied suggestions that others had collaborated, there is now strong evidence to suggest that the poet Saint-Pol-Roux, godfather to his eldest son, was paid outright by the composer to supply the complete text. Whatever the case, Charpentier was advised to incorporate more lyrical elements beside the extended realistic scenes. It is this Zolaesque naturalism, transferred into operatic terms, that most strongly characterizes the work: Charpentier himself explained that he wished to capture the thought of his generation. He finally completed the work in 1896, and though timid in promoting it, he made several attempts to interest opera houses in it.

Léon Carvalho, director of the Opéra-Comique, disliked the sordid realism of the Montmartre setting, suggesting a substitution of the epoch of Louis XV and the incorporation of a happy ending, where Julien

Julien *a young artist*	tenor
Louise	soprano
Her Mother	contralto
Her Father	bass
A Young Rag Picker	mezzo-soprano
A Coal Gatherer	mezzo-soprano
A Noctambulist *later dressed as the King of the Fools*	tenor
A Newspaper Girl	soprano
A Rag Picker	bass
A Milkwoman	soprano
Two Policemen	baritones
An Arab Street Vendor	soprano
A Street Sweeper	mezzo-soprano
A Painter	bass
A Songwriter	baritone
A Student	tenor
A Young Poet	baritone
Two Philosophers	tenor and bass
A Sculptor	baritone
An Apprentice	baritone
Blanche	soprano
Marguérite	soprano
Suzanne	contralto
Gertrude	contralto
Irma	soprano
Camille	soprano
An Errand Girl	soprano
Madeleine	contralto
An Old-clothes-man	tenor
A Dancer	silent
An Old Bohemian	baritone
A Forewoman	mezzo-soprano
Elise	soprano

Street vendors, vegetable sellers, beggars, Bohemians, working girls, women etc.

Setting The Montmartre district of Paris

would suddenly appear through a window to embrace Louise, to the accompaniment of a benediction by her father. Charpentier, however, would accept no such compromises. In 1898 Albert Carré accepted the work unaltered, scheduling it as the first production of the new century. He directed the production himself, André Messager conducted, and the sets were by Lucien Jusseaume: the team who two years later were to inaugurate Debussy's *Pelléas*. Marthe Rioton was the first Louise and was succeeded by Mary Garden, who made the role one of her greatest successes. The work itself was a success, performed a hundred times during the first season and a thousand times by 1935.

ACT 1 *A room in the mansard of a working man's tenement* Through the window is the balcony of a neighbouring house where a young poet, Julien, sings lyrically of spring in Paris and of his love for Louise. Louise soon joins him, and he explains that he has written to her parents asking for her hand. If they refuse again, he says, she must elope with him. But Louise is torn: 'I love you so much', she tells Julien, 'but I love them too'. Julien accuses her of timidity, and encourages her to be brave and free. As each tells how they fell in love with the other, the music becomes more lyrical. 'There's no madonna of Vinci who has a smile like you', says Julien. As they sing together in octaves, her mother

enters, shuts Louise in the kitchen, and goes to the window to scold Julien.

In scene iii Louise's mother mocks the loving words of Julien and scolds Louise, calling Julien a good-for-nothing, a drunkard and a debaucher. Louise's remark that he might go to the bar less often if he had a woman provokes bitter laughter from her mother. Taunting her mother, Louise prides herself on having won Julien's heart and inflames her still further in an exchange highlighted by Charpentier with unconventional chromatic harmony (ex.1).

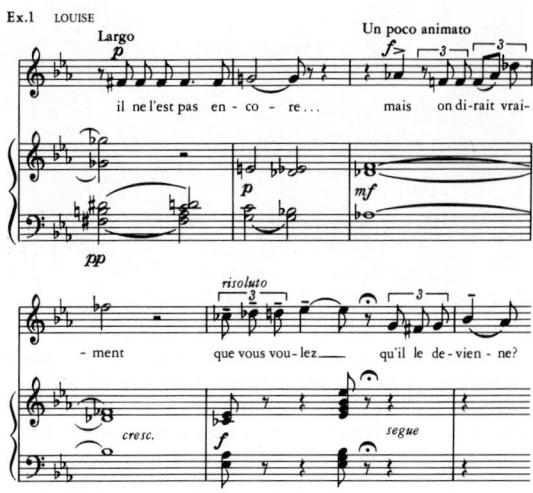

Ex.1 LOUISE

['It is not done as yet, but one might well suppose that you would like to have me do it.']

In scene iv Louise's father returns from work with words which characterize him as the archetype of the French working-class husband: 'La soupe est prête?' ('Is the soup ready?'). He has a letter which he lays on the table. Louise's mother brings up the subject of idlers, rich enough to fall in love and spend all their lives on holiday. 'L'égalité, les grands mots' ('Equality? Just big words'), says her father, in the first of many such statements with political overtones: 'when you don't have an income, you have to be content to earn one for someone else'. But underneath he seems happy, affectionately calling his wife an old goose, dancing with her and kissing Louise. Louise finds the letter which she knows to be from Julien and confronts her father with it. A row ensues, in which Charpentier gradually increases the musical tension, as the father admires the eloquence of the letter while Louise's mother pours scorn on Julien. Louise collapses in tears: the pretext for a tender scene between father and daughter. 'How does one choose a good husband?', asks Louise. 'Experience', replies her father, adding the remark, shocking for its time, that 'second marriages are generally happier'.

ACT 2 *An open thoroughfare at the foot of Montmartre* The prelude to the act is entitled 'Paris awakes' and is bound together by a simple motif heard at the outset. The various street vendors and waste gatherers form the basis of the scene. The noctambulist dwells on the readiness of the poor working girls for better things, love included. More political questions are put into the mouths of the various vendors: 'Shouldn't soft beds and fine clothes, like the sun, belong to everyone?' The milkwoman has never had time for love. Others talk of paradise. 'Give me the address', asks the Arab. 'Why', replies the vendor, 'it's Paris'.

*'Louise' (Gustave
Charpentier), Act 2 scene
i of the original
production at the Opéra-
Comique (Salle Favart), 2
February 1900, with sets
designed by Lucien
Jusseaume: from 'Le
théâtre' (April 1900)*

In the next two scenes Julien and his Bohemian friends look for the place where Louise works. Julien plans to catch her when her mother isn't looking, while the others have the idea of making her their muse. A discussion on class ensues. 'The one hope in life', explains a philosopher, 'is to become middle-class'. The street vendors reappear, and Julien is once again drunk with the beauty of Paris. Coming out of work, the girls chatter about their fancies and conquests. Eventually Louise arrives with her mother, who is suspicious, but Julien manages to pull Louise aside. With the street vendors' cries as a background they once again argue, Louise still attached to her parents, Julien encouraging her to break free.

After an interlude, the scene changes to a seamstress's workroom, where the girls are busy at work, singing to the sound of the sewing-machine. Louise looks sick with love. The girls provocatively remark that she is too much under her mother's spell and that when she is slapped she should slap her in return. One of the errand girls, in Paris argot, explains how, when her father spanks her, she tells him to try her mother, who has a larger behind. They extol the virtues of love and the delirium of kissing. Julien appears in the courtyard and sings a serenade, accompanied on a guitar. The girls and Louise are delighted, but after a little flirting they all get bored with the ardour of his song. Louise, overcome, decides to leave work. The act ends with the stupefaction of the girls and forewoman at this gesture of defiance.

ACT 3 *A little garden on the side of Montmartre* The act begins with a prelude, 'Towards the distant city', followed by 'Depuis le jour'. Louise sings to Julien of her love for him: she seems to have broken free and she recalls the constraints of her home. 'Each soul has a right to be free', says Julien, with conviction and dignity, again extolling the wonders of the city of Paris as they contemplate its lights from the hill: 'city of joy, city of Love'. An extended love scene ensues, followed by the entry of children, Bohemians and the people of the *quartier* following a carnival procession. The noctambulist is dressed as the King of the Fools.

In scene iii Louise is crowned muse of Montmartre. After a while, her mother appears, looking unhappy and falling into Julien's arms. She explains that she has not come to quarrel but to announce that Louise's father is ill and needs his daughter to cure him. Louise explains to Julien that when she returns she will have her freedom. Reluctantly she leaves, handing back the shawl with which she has been crowned.

ACT 4 *As Act 1* Louise's father, who has been idle for 20 days, has become bitter, 'crushed beneath a yoke imposed by fate'. Louise looks out of the window to a tenderly orchestrated reminiscence of 'Depuis le jour'. Her father continues by recounting the pain a family feel when their daughter, whom they have cared for, runs off with a stranger, taking away their one joy in life and changing her too into a stranger. Her mother, calling her into the kitchen, tells her that, despite her promise, she cannot go back to Julien. 'Free love', mocks her mother, 'just an excuse to get out of marriage'. Her father pretends she is a little girl again. 'Baby would be quiet', sings Louise, 'if her father had not caused so much sorrow'. She talks of his 'misguided affection'. Voices are heard; 'Paris is calling', says Louise, preparing to leave. Her father, angry, tries to bar the way, but eventually she breaks out, and her father, now distraught, curses Paris, shaking his fist.

*   *   *

Even before the première, the work had become something of a *cause célèbre*: rumours circulated about the immorality of the subject matter as well as about the revolutionary nature of the score. In fact it is far from unconventional, owing much to Gounod and Massenet; and Massenet admired it. There are, however, moments of originality, such as the highly effective end to the first tableau of Act 2, where the voice of the street vendor, plying his fresh green artichokes, forms an unresolved added ninth chord, perfectly capturing the continuity of Montmartre street life (ex.2). The work's allegiance to the realist cause, its rich orchestral palette – which includes instruments as different as the viola d'amore (perhaps used by a sentimental Montmartre busker) and the sewing-machine (foreshadowing the use of everyday

Ex.2

STREET VENDOR

A la___ ten - dress'!___ la ver - du -

dim. poco a poco

- ress'! . . .

['So sweet and green!']

'instruments' such as the typewriter in Satie's *Parade*) – and the memorability of the set-piece 'Depuis le jour' have assured it a unique place in the repertory.

For further illustration *see* PARIS, fig.23.

RICHARD LANGHAM SMITH

Louis Riel. Opera in three acts by HARRY SOMERS to a libretto by Mavor Moore and Jacques Languirand; Toronto, O'Keefe Centre, 23 September 1967.

The opera is set in the time of the Indian and Métis uprisings of 1869–70 and 1884–5 and deals with the death of Louis Riel (baritone), who became the natural leader of the French-speaking half-breeds of the West. Riel had killed the Orangeman Thomas Scott, saying that he could not allow one man to stand in the way of a whole nation. 15 years later the Prime Minister Sir John A. Macdonald (baritone) had Riel executed on the same grounds. The opera covers the circumstances which link these two events and includes other characters such as Riel's mother and sister (sopranos), his wife Marguerite (soprano), Bishop Tache (bass), Baptiste Lépine (tenor) and William McDougall (bass). Although artistic licence leads to some changes and omissions, the larger issues still resonate, causing a reviewer to comment that 'as long as the French and English in Canada keep plaguing each other, the story of Louis Riel will have topical appeal' (*The Telegram*, 25 September 1967).

Riel is portrayed as a mixture of rebel and visionary, lunatic and leader. His music is distinguished by long, lyrical, melismatic melodies in the arias and flexible parlando recitative. The text is a mixture of English, French, Cree and Latin. Somers distinguishes among the personages by the type of singing style. He himself describes *Louis Riel* as a multi-level work, which incorporates several distinct styles, namely folk music, as in Marguerite's aria in Act 3 scene i, 'Kuyas' (Cree for 'Long ago'), which is an actual song of a Wolfhead chief of a Nass River tribe; contemporary Western popular song (as in 'Orangemen unite', Act 2.iv); abstract atonal orchestral writing, 'for dramatic intensity and to create a platform of orchestral sound on top of which the singing is entirely apart' (Somers); familiar diatonic writing; and electronically produced sounds (created in

collaboration with Lowell Cross in the Electronic Music Studio at the University of Toronto), in which Somers says he has aimed for 'a sound totally unfamiliar to the audience in order to gain a certain kind of impact' (as in the battle scene, Act 1.i). These styles are juxtaposed or superimposed in subtle ways so as to reaffirm the message of Somers's own voice in the abstract atonal writing.

GAYNOR G. JONES

Louisville. American city in Kentucky. Some of the earliest operatic performances in Louisville were given at Mozart Hall by such travelling troupes as Kunkel's Nightingale (1853) and Cooper's Celebrated (1859). The Louisville Theatre (built 1846) also presented short seasons of opera, by the Strakosch and Arditi companies among others. After a fire in 1866, the theatre was rebuilt and by 1869 was renamed the Louisville Opera House. Within a few years it was eclipsed by Macauley's Theatre (1873–1925), which received week-long visits from the Emma Abbott Grand English Opera Company and the Scotti Grand Opera Company. After several successful visits of Lotti's and Grau's German opera troupes, the Liederkranz, a German singing society (1848–77), ventured two seasons of opera in German at their hall, transforming it into the Liederkranz Opera House in 1873–4, first with the Franosch 30-member troupe in residence, and then with the Garay-Lichtmay company, who performed the first Wagner opera in Louisville.

By 1891 the impresario Daniel Quilp was presenting the Abbey and Grau Grand Italian Opera Company, with stars such as the de Reszkes, in the Louisville Auditorium. The first opera to be performed in Louisville's new Memorial Auditorium was Clarence Loomis's *Yolanda of Cyprus*, given by the American Opera Company in 1929. Enthusiastic amateur groups, such as the Louisville Opera Club, presented Gilbert and Sullivan from 1892.

The Kentucky Opera Association can trace its beginnings to the 1948 amateur production of *Le nozze di Figaro*, mounted by the University of Louisville School of Music, which had sponsored local productions since 1933. Dwight Anderson, Dean of the School, invited Moritz von Bomhard to produce several operas; in 1952, after several successful productions, it became a professional company with Bomhard as artistic director. He joined the Louisville Philharmonic Society in commissioning, producing and recording operas such as Peggy Glanville-Hicks's *The Transposed Heads* (1954), Richard Mohaupt's *Double Trouble* (1954), Rolf Liebermann's *The School for Wives* (1955) and others by George Antheil and Lee Hoiby. Throughout this period a strong Kentucky Opera Chorus was developed and formal ties established with the Louisville Orchestra. After 30 successful seasons, Bomhard was succeeded in June 1981 by Thomson Smillie, who has continued to build on the support given by the Friends of the Opera, the Louisville Fund for the Arts and other major local and national grants. The Association is continuing its emphasis on new work, having jointly commissioned Philip Glass's *The Fall of the House of Usher*, which received its première at the Kentucky Opera in 1988. Partly in recognition of its statewide touring programme, it was named the State Opera of Kentucky in 1986.

*

J. J. Weisert: *Mozart Hall 1851–1866* (Louisville, 1962)

MARION KORDA

Louis XIV (*b* Saint-Germain, 5 Sept 1638; *d* Versailles, 1 Sept 1715). King of France and patron of opera. He was a minor when his father, Louis XIII, died in 1643, and did not accede to the throne until 1661. At his court J.-B. Lully, with his librettist Philippe Quinault, created a lavish, panegyric form of *tragédies en musique* (or *tragédies lyriques*), in which Louis XIV was implicitly identified with the hero and the achievements of his reign allegorized in the prologues.

Louis XIV's interest in opera was fostered by Cardinal Mazarin, the Italian first minister during his minority, when the finest Italian composers and singers were imported to entertain the court. Lully came to his attention as early as 1652, but it was to the writer Pierre Perrin that, on 28 June 1669, Louis XIV granted *lettres patentes* to establish 'Académies d'opéra ou représentations en musique en langue française sur le pied de celles d'Italie'. Despite the success of Perrin's first production, *Pomone* (1671), with music by Robert Cambert, the Académie foundered financially; Lully acquired the rights and new *lettres patentes* (13 March 1672), and a year later obtained use of the Palais Royal theatre with rights to all the profits. He consulted the king on the subjects of his operas and was careful that he was first to see each completed score. As premières were usually attended by the king they were often given at Saint-Germain or Versailles before the opera opened in Paris. Subsequent performances before Louis XIV were often held in special outdoor theatres within larger *spectacles* mounted to mark a royal birth or military victory. Only *Isis* (1677) proved problematic, though it was Quinault who bore the brunt of royal displeasure when his unflattering portrayal of Juno too closely resembled Mme de Montespan, the royal mistress. In the year after the queen's death in 1683 Louis eschewed opera, but allowed public performances of *Amadis* during Carnival (January 1684). His favourite Lully opera was said to be *Atys* (1676).

After Lully's death (1687), the Académie continued in the hands of his heirs. Operas for the court were given at Marly and Fontainebleau as well as Saint-Germain and Versailles; after the turn of the century they were increasingly open only by invitation. Meanwhile, members of Louis XIV's family (the Grand Dauphin and the Duke and Duchess of Burgundy) regularly attended the Opéra in Paris. The king was often heard singing excerpts from Lully's operas and within hours of the death of his brother in 1701 was listening from an anteroom to opera prologues. In his last years, because of his health, he contented himself with private performances of scenes.

*

J.-L. Le Cerf de la Viéville: *Comparaison de la musique italienne et de la musique françoise* (Brussels, 1704–6)

M. de Sévigné: *Lettres de sa famille et de ses amis* (Paris, 1820)

C. Masson: 'Journal du Marquis de Dangeau', *RMFC*, ii (1961), 193–223

F. Robert: 'La musique à travers le "Mercure galant"', ibid, 173–90

L. Norton, ed. and trans.: *Historical Memoirs of the Duc de Saint Simon* (London, 1968)

A. Ducrot: 'Les représentations de l'Académie Royale de Musique à Paris au temps de Louis XIV, 1671–1715', *RMFC*, x (1970), 19–55

N. Dufourcq: *La musique à la cour de Louis XIV et de Louis XV d'après les mémoires de Sourches et Luynes, 1681–1758* (Paris, 1970)

J. R. Anthony: *French Baroque Music from Beaujoyeulx to Rameau* (London, 1973, 2/1978)

R. M. Isherwood: *Music in the Service of the King: France in the Seventeenth Century* (Ithaca, 1973)

J. de La Gorce: *L'opéra sous le règne de Louis XIV: le merveilleux ou les puissances surnaturelles, 1671–1715* (diss., U. of Paris-Sorbonne, 1978)

——: 'L'opéra et son public au temps de Louis XIV', *Bulletin de la Société de l'histoire de Paris et de l'Ile-de-France*, cviii (1981), 27–46

F. Bluche: *Louis XIV* (Paris, 1984; Eng. trans., 1990)

R. Fajon: *L'opéra à Paris du Roi-Soleil à Louis le Bien-aimé* (Geneva, 1984)

B. Coeyman: 'Theatres for Opera and Ballet during the Reigns of Louis XIV and Louis XV', *EMc*, xviii (1990), 22–37

JULIE ANNE SADIE

Lourié, Arthur (**Vincent**) (*b* St Petersburg, 2/14 May 1892; *d* Princeton, 12 Oct 1966). Russian composer. He studied at the St Petersburg Conservatory, but soon abandoned formal studies to experiment with dodecaphonic and serial techniques. From 1918 he was music commissar for three years before leaving for Berlin, where he met Busoni, with whose broad cultural interests and philosophical ideas he found himself in sympathy. He moved to Paris in 1924 and there met Stravinsky, an acquaintance that later developed into a strong friendship. Lourié left for the USA in 1941 and became an American citizen six years later.

Although Lourié wrote much orchestral and chamber music, he considered his two stage pieces, *The Feast during the Plague* (composed 1935) and *The Blackamoor of Peter the Great* (composed 1949–61), his most important works. The action of *The Feast*, a two-act opera-ballet based on Pushkin's 'little tragedy' after John Wilson's dramatic poem *The City of the Plague* (1816), takes place in England. The musical idiom is pandiatonic. The later opera, in three acts, concerns an episode in the life of Ibrahim Hannibal, an African who was a great-grandfather of Pushkin, and is based on the poet's unfinished novel. Irina Graham was the librettist. Lourié described the opera's style as 'Russian Baroque'. The music has some Byzantine overtones; the story, while it depicts scandal and romantic intrigue with echoes of the *commedia dell'arte*, also contains what Lourié characterized as 'epic and historic elements relating to the creation of St Petersburg, the new capital of Russia, often described as half European, half barbaric, waking up from her Asiatic slumber and immobility'. Lourié compiled two suites from the operas; the suite from *The Feast* was first performed in Boston on 5 January 1945, but neither opera has been staged. The libretto of *The Blackamoor* has been published in its English version by Irina Graham (in D. Gojowy, ed.: *Studien zur Musik des XX. Jahrhunderts in Ost- und Ostmitteleuropa*, Berlin, 1990, pp.129–82). Lourié contributed essays to music journals and published the book *Sergei Koussevitzky and his Epoch* (New York, 1931).

GIOVANNI CAMAJANI/DETLEF GOJOWY

Loutherbourg, Philip James de (*b* Strasbourg or Fulda, 31 Oct or 1 Nov 1740; *d* London, 11 March 1812). German designer active in London. He studied in Paris, and obtained an introduction to Garrick at Drury Lane in 1771. The most influential and innovative scene designer of 18th-century England, he was mainly responsible for the replacement of architectural and formal scenery by romantic and picturesque landscapes. His chief reform was the breaking up of the rigid back-flat and wing system by the introduction of separate raking pieces which could be set at angles affording several perspectives, and the use of ground rows to fill the central spaces between the wings, thus increasing flexibility (*see* STAGE DESIGN, fig.10). He also used coloured silks on the side scenes which, when pivoted, threw colour on the wing behind, thus adding to the range of lighting effects; in his first pantomime, *A Christmas Tale*, he astonished the audience by a sudden transition of forest foliage from green to red. He also made use of gauze for effects of mist. Of 380 pieces listed in the sale catalogue of his work in 1812, all that remains are a few incomplete maquettes, and sketches for *Richard III* in the Theatre Museum, London.

Loutherbourg designed the scenery for five comic operas: *The Maid of the Oaks* (music by Barthelemon, 1774), *The Camp* (by the elder Thomas Linley, 1778), *The Artifice* (M. Arne, 1780), *The Lord of the Manor* (Jackson, 1780) and Linley's *The Carnival of Venice* (1781). He left Drury Lane in 1781 owing to disputes about his salary.

W. H. Pyne: *Wine and Walnuts* (1824), i, 281–304

W. J. Lawrence: 'The Pioneers of Modern English Stage-Mounting: Phillipe Jacques de Loutherbourg, R. A.', *Magazine of Art* [London] (1895), 172–7

H. A. Dobson: 'Loutherbourg, R. A.', *At Prior Park, and Other Papers* (London, 1912), 94–117

S. Rosenfeld: 'The Eidophusikon Illustrated', *Theatre Notebook*, xviii (1963–4), 52–4   SYBIL ROSENFELD

Love, Shirley (*b* Detroit, 6 Jan 1940). American mezzo-soprano. She studied in Detroit and with Margaret Harshaw in New York. After her début at the Metropolitan in 1963, she appeared in New York for 20 seasons, notably as Dorabella, Rosina, Angelina, Carmen, Delilah, Fricka and Amneris. Guest appearances took her to Europe (Germany and Italy) and to Baltimore, Chicago and Philadelphia. Among her modern repertory were roles in Kagen's *Hamlet* and Bernstein's *Trouble in Tahiti*.   DAVID CUMMINGS

Love for Three Oranges, The [*Lyubov' k tryom apel'sinam*; *L'amour des trois oranges*]. Opera in a prologue and four acts, op.33, by SERGEY PROKOFIEV to his own libretto after CARLO GOZZI's *fiaba L'amore delle tre melarance* (1761), adapted (1913) by Vsevolod Meyerhold, Vladimir Solov'yov and Konstantin Vogak; Chicago, Auditorium, 30 December 1921 (as *L'amour des trois oranges*, French translation by the composer and Vera Janacopoulos).

Prokofiev's second completed opera (juvenilia apart) and the first to achieve performance, *The Love for Three Oranges*, was written in New York, where the composer had settled after emigrating from Russia in the wake of the revolution. Immediately before his departure, in spring 1918, Vsevolod Meyerhold, the great director, made Prokofiev a gift of the first issue of his journal *The Love for Three Oranges*, containing a Russian adaptation (by Meyerhold with two collaborators) of the eponymous theatrical tale by the Venetian nobleman and satirist Carlo Gozzi (1720–1806). Gozzi had cast the work in the form of a *commedia dell'arte* scenario, seeing in the slapstick comedy of masks an antidote to the heavy melodrama and the petty naturalism that were (he thought) degrading the contemporary theatre. A century and a half later Meyerhold felt the same way. He expressed the hope that Prokofiev would derive a prose libretto from the scenario and set it in the fleet, flexible and resolutely 'anti-operatic' manner of his earlier opera, *The Gambler*, which Meyerhold had hoped to produce in the last pre-revolutionary Petrograd season. By the time Prokofiev docked in San Francisco he had a draft libretto in hand.

The King of Clubs *king of an imaginary kingdom where everyone dresses as a playing-card*	bass
The Prince *his son*	tenor
Princess Clarice *the king's niece*	contralto
Leander *prime minister, costumed as the King of Spades*	baritone
Truffaldino *jester*	tenor
Pantalone *courtier, the king's confidant*	baritone
Celio *sorcerer, the king's protector*	bass
Fata Morgana *witch, Leander's protector*	soprano
Linetta ⎫	contralto
Nicoletta ⎬ *princesses in the oranges*	mezzo-soprano
Ninetta ⎭	soprano
Cook	hoarse bass
Farfarello *a devil*	bass
Smeraldina *a black slave girl*	mezzo-soprano
Master of Ceremonies	tenor
Herald	bass
Trumpeteer	bass trombone

Ten Cranks (five tenors, five basses), Tragedians (basses), Comedians (tenors), Lyricists (sopranos, tenors), Empty Heads (altos, basses), imps (basses), doctors (tenors, baritones), courtiers (full chorus)

Silent roles: monsters, drunks, gluttons, watchmen, servants, four soldiers

Setting The world of make-believe, once upon a time

Gozzi had derived his *fiaba*, a ludicrous parody of the standard quest motif, by conflating two stories in Giambattista Basile's *Pentamerone*, subtitled *Lo cunto de li cunti* ('The Tale of Tales'), the earliest (1634) printed collection of European folk and fairy-tales. Hav-

Title-page from the first issue of Vsevolod Meyerhold's journal, 'The Love for Three Oranges' (the theatrical tale which gave the journal its name inspired Prokofiev's opera)

ing launched a pamphlet war on both the reigning dramatists of the mid-18th-century Venetian stage – Carlo Goldoni, the paragon of bourgeois realism, and Pietro Chiari, a specialist in highflown melodrama – Gozzi was challenged by Goldoni to do better. He boasted that he could ruin his antagonists by dramatizing the most ridiculous story in the world in the very manner Goldoni and Chiari most despised. As enacted by the celebrated troupe of Antonio Sacchi during the Venetian carnival of 1761, *L'amore delle tre melarance* redeemed its author's boast: Goldoni beat a retreat the next year to Paris.

Owing to the conventions of the *commedia dell'arte*, Gozzi made room in his adaptation for a large number of traditional masks: Tartaglia (the Prince), Pantalone, Smeraldina, Brighella (a character dropped by Prokofiev) and above all Truffaldino, a species of Arlecchino, the mask worn by Sacchi himself. The folksy Celio and the bombastic Fata Morgana were stand-ins for Goldoni and Chiari respectively. Their parts, written out in full, consisted of parodies of their literary prototypes. Erudite burlesque reached its height in a little set piece in Act 2, entitled the 'quarrel trio' (*contrasto in terzo*), in which three characters fall into a dispute about dramatic values. Clarice declares her preference for 'tragic performances, in which you find characters hurling themselves from windows or turrets'; Leandro plumps for comedies of manners; Brighella pleads for 'the improvised comedy of masks, an innocent popular diversion'.

This little quarrel trio grew in Meyerhold's adaptation to become, both temporally and spatially, the frame of the entire play. The spatial frame was to consist of twin turrets on opposite sides of the stage, housing a collection of clowns representing aesthetes of various antagonistic persuasions. The action was to begin with a parade, in which the actors portraying the aesthetes, divided into 'Realistic Comedians' and 'High Tragedians', would enter duelling with quills; the fight was to be broken up by a trio of Cranks. Thus joined, the battle would continue in an undertone, with frequent eruptions, throughout the play; the aesthetes' constant comment on the action, and their strenuous exhortations to the actors, would furnish the temporal frame. This was one of the very earliest applications of illusion-destroying 'art as art' gimmickry, soon to become such a modernist cliché. What makes it historically significant is the clarity of its descent from an 18th-century aristocratic model. Even if Prokofiev had never set it, Meyerhold's *Love for Three Oranges* would have been a prime document of the emergent modernist sensibility and of its sources.

Thanks to Prokofiev, it is more than a document. Having secured a commission from Cleofonte Campanini, the director of the Chicago Grand Opera, who had wanted to produce *The Gambler* but was unable to obtain the materials from revolutionary Petrograd, the composer went to work on the music early in 1919 and delivered the completed score on 1 October. But it took more than two years before the opera achieved production, first because of Campanini's sudden death but second because of Prokofiev's impossible demands (he insisted on compensation for the delay in implementing the contract). Mary Garden, who took over the directorship of the Chicago company, finally agreed to his terms, and the opera was given under his baton, with Nina Koshetz as Fata Morgana. Its enormously successful Soviet premières took place in 1926

(Leningrad, Academic Theatre, formerly and now the Mariinsky, with Ivan Yershov as Truffaldino) and 1927 (Moscow, Bol'shoy Theatre under Golovanov, with Nadezhda Obukhova as Clarice and Antonina Nezhdanova as Ninetta). These triumphs played a significant role in persuading Prokofiev to return to his homeland in the 1930s.

Compared with Meyerhold's scenario, Prokofiev's opera shows the usual streamlining and minor alterations. The most noteworthy difference is the hugely expanded role Prokofiev accorded the 'Greek chorus' of onstage spectators – the very thing Meyerhold and his colleagues had already so significantly expanded from Gozzi's little 'quarrel trio'. To Meyerhold's Comedians, Tragedians and Cranks (the latter numbering three in the scenario, ten in the opera), Prokofiev added groups of 'Lyricists', forever demanding 'romantic love, moons, tender kisses', and 'Empty Heads', bent on 'entertaining nonsense, witty double-entendres, fine costumes'. In this way he thought to cover every sort of standard operatic situation and cliché (what in Russian is still called *vampuka* after a famous grand-opera lampoon first produced at a St Petersburg cabaret in 1909). The Comedians, Tragedians, Lyricists and Empty Heads are continually breaking in on the action of Prokofiev's opera as it approaches one or another of their pet stereotypes to egg it on. His Cranks, eager to foil all factions (but particularly the Tragedians), do more than that: they actually intervene in the plot, Pirandello-fashion (but before Pirandello!), change its course and utterly destroy all stage illusion. The play, literally, is their plaything. (And art, the composer implies, is ours.) When Prokofiev's forgotten opera was given its earliest postwar revivals (especially the Ljubljana revival of 1956 that travelled to the Holland Festival and was recorded there), critics were struck by the mutually validating affinity between the ironically detached, constantly interrupted antics on stage and the characteristically discontinuous structure of the music. That remains the most authentic of the opera's virtues.

PROLOGUE *A grand proscenium with towers on either side, each with little balconies and balustrades* The opening skirmish between the Cranks on the one hand and the Tragedians, the Comedians, the Lyricists and the Empty Heads on the other. As the Cranks announce the beginning of the play, the Trumpeteer gives the signal (bass trombone in the orchestra) for the curtain to go up. (This scene provides the material for the first movement, 'Cranks', in the concert suite from *The Love for Three Oranges*, op.33/*bis*.)

ACT 1.i *The royal palace* The King consults with his physicians over the Prince's hypochondria. Only laughter, he is advised, will cure his son. He decides, with Pantalone and Leander (the latter secretly plotting with Clarice against the Prince), to arrange entertainments and charges Truffaldino to oversee them.

1.ii *Before a cabbalistic drop curtain* Celio and Fata Morgana, protectors respectively of the King of Clubs and his arch-enemy the King of Spades (Leander), play three rounds of cards while their attendant imps frolic about. Celio loses all three hands, to the Cranks' dismay. (This scene provides the material for the second movement, 'Infernal Scene', of the suite.)

1.iii *The royal palace* Leander and Clarice plot to worsen the Prince's hypochondria, thus paving Clarice's way to the throne. She advises 'opium or a bullet'; Leander retorts that booming 'Martellian verses' (the one surviving – and possibly unwitting – reference in Prokofiev's libretto to the old Venetian disputes) will do.

ACT 2.i *The bedroom of the hypochondriac Prince* Truffaldino tries in vain to get the Prince to laugh by dancing, then forcibly rouses him for the entertainments (heralded offstage by the first of several versions of the March; the fully elaborated March that forms the third movement in the suite is a conflation of all the versions heard in the opera, but is based chiefly on the reprise that forms the entr'acte between this scene and the next).

   2.ii *The great courtyard of the royal palace* The Prince is singularly unamused by Truffaldino's entertainments (a mock battle of monsters with enormous heads, and a pair of fountains pouring forth oil and wine – the latter a survival from Gozzi's scenario, where the oil and wine, both rancid, had stood for Goldoni and Chiari). Fata Morgana enters to make sure the Prince does not laugh. Truffaldino collides with her, causing her to fall back and expose her knobbly knees and withered behind. At this the Prince goes into gales of laughter, represented in the music by a little set piece over an ostinato (and with the Prince's 'Ha-ha-ha-ha' inevitably parodying the opening unison in Beethoven's Fifth). Enraged, Fata Morgana curses the Prince with a fatal passion for three oranges, which he must seek to the ends of the earth. He rushes off with Truffaldino to find them, the devil Farfarello propelling them with his magic bellows.

ACT 3.i *A desert* Celio intervenes on the Prince's behalf. He conjures up Farfarello, who blows the Prince and Truffaldino on stage. Celio informs them that the oranges they seek are in the kitchen of the palace of the witch Creonta, guarded by a cook with a lethal ladle. He gives Truffaldino a ribbon to distract the cook, and warns that when the oranges have been secured they must be opened only in the presence of water. Farfarello blows up a storm, which carries the pair off towards Creonta's palace. (The orchestral scherzo symbolizing their flight serves as an entr'acte in the opera and as the fourth movement of the suite.)

   3.ii *The courtyard of Creonta's palace* Having distracted the cook with Celio's ribbon, the Prince and Truffaldino sneak into the kitchen (offstage) and make off with the oranges. They are transported back to the desert (so the next entr'acte tells us) by a reprise of the scherzo.

   3.iii *The desert* The oranges have grown to enormous size. Weary of lugging them, the Prince and Truffaldino lie down to sleep. Truffaldino is too thirsty to sleep. He cuts one of the oranges to get some juice. Instead a fairy princess emerges, calling for water. Truffaldino opens a second orange to get juice for the two of them. A second princess emerges, also calling for water. The two princesses die of thirst; the horrified Truffaldino rushes offstage in a panic. The Prince awakens and finds the bodies. He nonchalantly orders four passing soldiers to bury them. Then he cuts into the third orange. Princess Ninetta emerges and is about to share the fate of her predecessors, but the Cranks lower a pail of water from their turret and save her life. A great love duet seems imminent, only to be spoilt by the Lyricists, who break into a paean in praise of love duets. (The thirst music, the recognition music and the aborted love music furnish the materials for the fifth movement, 'The Prince and the Princess', of the suite.) Ninetta

refuses to go with the Prince without suitable clothes. He goes off to fetch them for her. Fata Morgana now enters with Smeraldina in tow. By means of a magic pin they turn Ninetta into a rat and Smeraldina takes her place. The King and his retinue accompany the Prince back to the desert to the strains of the familiar March. They are dismayed to discover Smeraldina, but the King commands his son to proceed with the wedding.

ACT 4.i *The drop curtain (as 1.ii)* Celio and Fata Morgana have it out: the latter gets the upper hand, but the Cranks come once again to the rescue, abduct her to their tower and bid Celio turn the rat back into Ninetta.

   4.ii *The throne room of the royal palace* The King and his retinue enter to one last reprise of the March. When the curtains around the Princess's throne are drawn back the rat is discovered. Pandemonium ensues, during which Celio manages to turn the rat back into Ninetta. Truffaldino arrives out of nowhere to expose Smeraldina; she is sentenced to hang, along with Clarice and Leander. As the rope is prepared, they all make a run for it. (The music accompanying their breakout forms the basis of the final suite movement, entitled 'Flight'.) Fata Morgana appears and opens a trap door for them into which they (and she) disappear. The remaining *dramatis personae* hail the Prince and the Princess.

*   *   *

Like *The Gambler*, *The Love for Three Oranges* is basically in what Prokofiev called a 'declamatory' style; but ('taking American tastes into account', as he put it in his autobiography) the composer provided a few more obviously lyrical moments cast in fugitive rounded forms, and there are a couple of diverting instrumental showpieces (the March in Act 2, the Scherzo in Act 3). The musical style as such derives from Rimsky-Korsakov's *Golden Cockerel* by way of Stravinsky's *Petrushka*. Its nub and essence is the exploitation of the harmonic possibilities of paired triads with roots a tritone apart. These harmonies function variously as a cadential succession (as in the opening announcement, in the prologue, of the start of the show), as a vertical 'polychord' (at moments of horror; e.g. the curse music in Act 2 scene ii) or as the governors of a bipolar tonal plan (as in the Act 3 Scherzo).

For a set design for the original production *see* ANISFELD, BORIS IZRAYELEVICH.   RICHARD TARUSKIN

Love in a Village. Comic opera in three acts, composed or arranged by THOMAS AUGUSTINE ARNE to a libretto by ISAAC BICKERSTAFF after Charles Johnson's *The Village Opera* (1729); London, Covent Garden, 8 December 1762.

The work is a pasticcio of 42 items, of which five were newly composed by Arne and 13 borrowed from his earlier works. The new overture was by C. F. Abel and the remainder adapted from other composers, including Geminiani and Galuppi. In his *English Theatre Music* (2/1986) Fiske gives a list of attributions (Appendix E).

Rosetta (soprano), the heroine, has run away from home to avoid an unhappy marriage and taken a position as chambermaid in the house of Justice Woodcock (bass). Thomas (tenor), the son of Sir William Meadows, in a similar predicament, takes the post of gardener to the household. The two young people fall in love. Their position appears hopeless until Sir William's arrival reveals that Rosetta was Thomas's intended bride all the time. Other characters are Lucinda

A scene from Arne's 'Love in a Village' with Edward Shuter as Justice Woodcock (left), John Beard as Hawthorne (centre) and John Dunstall as Hodge: painting by Johann Zoffany (1734/5–1810)

(soprano), Woodcock's daughter, and Farmer Hawthorne (tenor), originally played by John Beard.

The opera was immediately successful, with 40 performances in its first season, and had many revivals, including a version by Alfred Reynolds at the Lyric Theatre, Hammersmith, on 19 April 1928. The published vocal score (1763) contains 18 songs by Arne, and a MS full score, partly in the composer's hand, also survives (in *GB-Lcm*). Arne's song 'The traveller benighted', written for Miss Brent as Rosetta, has some coloratura passages, but most of the music avoids vocal display.

For the playbill for the original production *see* PASTICCIO.

JOHN A. PARKINSON

Loving [*Toi*; *Loving/Toi*]. Opera (or 'audio-visual poem') in one act by R. MURRAY SCHAFER to a text by the composer; Montreal, CBC TV French Network, 3 February 1966.

Commissioned by CBC Television, *Loving* is an allegorical music drama, in an unspecified setting, which focusses on relations between a woman, who speaks English, and a man, who speaks French (both speaking roles). Thus contrasting the two sexes and the two official languages of Canada, it analyses various aspects of the female personality, represented by four singers, three who sing principally in English – Modesty (soprano), Vanity (mezzo-soprano) and Eros (mezzo-soprano) – and one who sings principally in French – Ishtar (mezzo-soprano). Each is given an extended aria. The score features percussion and electronic sounds prominently, while the vocal writing demands a variety of articulations, extended range, improvisation and elements of jazz. The television première consisted of a truncated version of the score; the complete work received a semi-staged performance in Toronto on 11 March 1978.   STEPHEN J. ADAMS (with KIRK MACKENZIE)

Lovini, Domenico. *See* LUINI, DOMENICO.

Lowe, Thomas (*d* London, 1 March 1783). English tenor. He joined the Drury Lane company in 1740, as a singing actor, and for many years appeared with success in ballad operas and other light theatre pieces. He also sang in Arne's more serious stage works, including *Comus, Rosamond, The Judgment of Paris* and *Alfred*, both in London and Dublin, where he spent the 1743–4 season. He moved to Covent Garden in 1748 and back to Drury Lane in 1760, on each occasion succeeding Beard, with whom he alternated as Macheath in *The Beggar's Opera* and in the tenor parts of Handel's later oratorios, several of which were written for him. In his last years he sang mostly in pleasure gardens, and declined in voice, fortune and character. More naturally gifted than Beard, he fell far below him in intelligence and application. According to Burney, 'with the finest tenor voice I ever heard in my life, for want of diligence and cultivation, he could never be safely trusted with any thing better than a ballad, which he constantly learned by his ear'. To judge from the parts Handel composed for Lowe, he must have commanded at least an adequate florid technique.   WINTON DEAN

Lualdi, Adriano (*b* Larino, Campobasso, 22 March 1885; *d* Milan, 8 Jan 1971). Italian composer. He studied music in Rome and then in Venice under Wolf-Ferrari. After gaining his diploma in 1907, he began a career as a conductor. In the 1920s he also became active as a music critic: among his numerous writings *Viaggio musicale in Italia* (Milan, 1927) is particularly valuable for the light it throws on the Italian musical world of the time, while *Serate musicali* (Milan, 1928) includes many thought-provoking opera reviews. An ardent fascist, Lualdi was 'elected' to parliament in 1929 as representative of the Sindacato Nazionale dei Musicisti. He was an organizer of the first few Venice Festivals (1930–34) and director of the conservatories of Naples (1936–44) and Florence (1947–56).

Lualdi's association with fascism, which conditioned his teaching and organizing activities as well as his polemics, led to his being overrated in the 1930s, but in due course aroused such antagonism that his reputation may have suffered unfairly. Undoubtedly he was an imperfect composer, who rarely achieved stylistic unity and could sink to the abysmal level of the ballet *Lumawig e la saetta* (1936). Yet the best pages of *Le nozze di Haura* and *La figlia del re* (e.g. Damara's invocation to the night and the whole of Act 3 scene i in the latter work) show that his evocative powers and sense of colour were considerable. Comparable qualities still appear in some later operas, such as *La luna dei Caraibi*, with its recurrent use of an offstage negro spiritual, or the very eclectic *Il testamento di Euridice*, where the search for appropriate picturesque detail led him to use the ancient Greek *Epitaph of Seikilos* as a leitmotif. In comic and satirical works, too, Lualdi was resourceful: the small-scale and unpretentious *Le furie di Arlecchino* remained close enough to Wolf-Ferrari to win easy and widespread success; but the freakish libretto of *Il diavolo nel campanile* (freely based on Poe) is matched by a wilfully heterogeneous score that aroused much controversy.

See also DIAVOLO NEL CAMPANILE, IL and FIGLIA DEL RE, LA.

2 early operas, 1902–3, unperf.
Le nozze di Haura, 1908, rev. 1913 (1, L. Orsini), Italian Radio, 19 Oct 1939; stage, Rome, Opera, 18 April 1943
La figlia del re, 1914–17 (3, Lualdi), Turin, Regio, 18 March 1922
Le furie di Arlecchino (1, Orsini), Milan, Carcano, 7 May 1915; rev. Buenos Aires, Colón, 19 June 1925 (or ?1924)
Il diavolo nel campanile, 1919–23 (grottesco, 1, Lualdi, after E. A. Poe: *The Devil in the Belfry*), Milan, Scala, 21 April 1925; rev. 1952, Florence, Comunale, 21 May 1954
La grançeola (1, Lualdi, after A. Bacchelli), Venice, Goldoni, 10 Sept 1932
Eurydikes diatheke [Il testamento di Euridice], ? *c*1940–62 (4, Lualdi, after Gk. and Lat. poems), RAI, 22 Nov 1962
La luna dei Caraibi, 1944 (1, Lualdi, after E. O'Neill: *The Moon of the Caribbees*), Rome, Opera, 29 Jan 1953
Tre alla radarstratotropojonosferaphonotheca del Luna Park, ? *c*1962 (commedia da concerto, 1, Lualdi), unperf.
Il cabaret della maga senza pena, ? early 1960s (3, Lualdi), ?inc., unperf.

A. Della Corte: 'La figlia del re (tragedia musicale di A. Lualdi)', *Arte e vita* [Turin], iii (1922), 210–17
F. B. Pratella: 'La figlia del re di Adriano Lualdi', *Pensiero musicale*, ii (1922), 108–9, 220–27
C. de Mohr: 'Il diavolo nel campanile di Adriano Lualdi alla Scala', *Musica e scena*, ii/5 (1925), 3–7
A. Veretti: 'Adriano Lualdi', *RMI*, xxxv (1928), 105–23
F. Abbiati: 'Musicisti contemporanei: Adriano Lualdi', *Emporium* [Bergamo], lxx (1929), 231–8
G. Confalonieri: *L'opera di Adriano Lualdi* (Milan, 1932)
G. Cogni: 'Le opere teatrali di Adriano Lualdi', *Retroscena* [Palermo], xx/2–3 (1953), 22–3, 30–32
G. Confalonieri: 'Il diavolo nel campanile', *XVII maggio musicale fiorentino* (Florence, 1954), 7–9
R. Smith Brindle: 'Current Chronicle: Italy', *MQ*, xl (1954), 585–7 [on *Il diavolo nel campanile*]
J. C. G. Waterhouse: *The Emergence of Modern Italian Music (up to 1940)* (diss., U. of Oxford, 1968), 530–33
A. Lualdi, M. Morini and others: *La bilancia di Euripide* (Milan, 1969) [incl. libs. and press criticisms]

JOHN C. G. WATERHOUSE

Luart [Lawaert], Emma (*b* Brussels, 14 Aug 1892; *d* Brussels, 26 Aug 1968). Belgian soprano. She trained at the Brussels Conservatoire and after singing in the summer season at Ostend made her official début at The Hague the following year. From 1918 to 1922 she sang at the Monnaie in Brussels, appearing mostly in lyric roles such as Louise, Mélisande and Manon which became her most famous part. She then transferred to the Opéra-Comique in Paris where she remained till World War II. Her début role there was Lakmé, and premières in which she took a leading part included Samuel-Rousseau's *Le bon roi Dagobert* and Gabriel Pierné's one-act *Sophie Arnould*. At Monte Carlo in 1923 she sang in the first performances outside Russia of Musorgsky's *The Fair at Sorochintsï* with John McCormack. On her retirement she taught singing in Brussels. A characteristically bright 'French' voice is heard in her recordings along with a touching expressiveness, especially in the excerpts from *Manon*.

J. B. STEANE

Lübeck. City and port in northern Germany. The first opera was given in 1701. In 1752–3 the city had its first permanent theatre built, the Ebbesche Theater in der Beckergrube; drama is still performed on the same site. Designed with opera in mind, the theatre was opened on 19 February 1753, and over the next few years many famous troupes appeared there, including F. L. Schröder's Hamburg company and that of the actor and dramatist Iffland. Eventually the house built up a permanent company with its own repertory. The theatre's shortcomings however led to the erection of a new building on the same site in 1858, known as the Theater der Casino-Gesellschaft; it opened on 3 March with a performance of *Der Freischütz*. In 1907 it was demolished because of fire hazards and replaced by a new theatre in the *art nouveau* style, which survived World War II and is still in use. This building opened on 1 October 1908, and the first operatic performance, Wagner's *Lohengrin* with Karl Erb in the title role, took place on 5 October. Between 1911 and 1915 the conductors Wilhelm Furtwängler and Hermann Abendroth worked in Lübeck. In the 1920s Walter Felsenstein acted here. Directly after the war the Intendant Otto Karsten organized a society for opera enthusiasts called the 'Lübecker Besucher-Ring'. It was a great success and was imitated in many other big cities. There are three stages in the complex: the Grosses Haus (913 seats), the Kammerspiele (325 seats) and the Studio (*c*90 seats), all run by the civic authorities. Music directors at Lübeck have included Gerd Albrecht (1963–6) and Bernhard Klee (1966–73). In the Grosses Haus both music theatre and large-scale plays are performed. The season generally lasts from September to the end of June. High points in the activity of the theatre include the staging of the *Ring* cycle at the beginning of the 1980s. Premières since then have included *Die Piratinnen* by Niels Frédéric Hoffmann in 1984 and a revival of *Dafne* by Bontempi and Peranda in 1988.

C. Stiehl: *Geschichte des Theaters in Lübeck* (Lübeck, 1902)

SABINE SONNTAG

Lubin, Germaine (Léontine Angélique) (*b* Paris, 1 Feb 1890; *d* Paris, 20–27 Oct 1979). French soprano. She studied at the Paris Conservatoire (1909–12) and with Litvinne and Lilli Lehmann. She made her début as Antonia in *Les contes d'Hoffmann* at the Opéra-Comique, where she also sang Strauss's Ariadne, Fauré's Penelope, Charlotte, Louise and Camille (*Zampa*). At the Opéra (1916–44) she sang a very varied repertory, at first lyric roles such as Marguerite (Gounod and Boito), Juliet, Thaïs, Aida and Reyer's Salammbô; later, heavier roles including Agathe, Fidelio, Cassandra, Elsa, Eva, Elisabeth, Sieglinde, Electra, Octavian and the Marschallin. She created Nicéa in d'Indy's *La légende de Saint Christophe* (1920), Empress Charlotte in

Germaine Lubin as Ariane in Dukas' 'Ariane et Barbe-bleue'

Milhaud's *Maximilien* (1932) and Gina, Duchess Sanseverina in Sauguet's *La chartreuse de Parme* (1939). She was admired for her classical dignity and repose in Gluck's *Alceste* and *Iphigénie en Aulide*, as Telaira in Rameau's *Castor et Pollux* (Maggio Musicale, 1935) and for her singing of Dukas' Ariane in the local première at Covent Garden in 1937.

Lubin's friendship with the Wagners and her sympathy with Germany (though she described herself as 'a quarter Polish, a quarter Arab and half Alsatian') brought her career to an abrupt close in 1944 during the German occupation of Paris. She was imprisoned for three years and thereafter sang only in recitals (1952 and 1954).

H. Barnes: 'Germaine Lubin Discography', *Recorded Sound*, no.19 (1965), 367
M. de Schauensee: 'Lubin Revisited', *ON*, xxx/12 (1965–6), 27–8
N. Casanova: *Isolde 39 – Germaine Lubin* (Paris, 1974) [with discography by G. Mannoni]

MARTIN COOPER/ELIZABETH FORBES

Luca, Giuseppe de. *See* DE LUCA, GIUSEPPE.

Luca, Severo de. *See* DE LUCA, SEVERO.

Lucas, Clarence (*b* Smithville, Ont., 19 Oct 1866; *d* Paris, 1 July 1947). Canadian composer and conductor. After studying in Montreal and Paris, he taught in Toronto and at the Utica Conservatory; in 1892 he went back to Europe. From 1893 he worked in London as a freelance journalist and editor and conducted the first performance of his own comic opera *The Money Spider* in London in 1897. In 1904 he composed and conducted the Irish musical play *Peggy Machree* and was also at this time a conductor for George Edwardes's touring musical comedies. A period in the USA

followed, in which Lucas conducted Grieg's *Peer Gynt* music for Richard Mansfield's production. He moved once more to Europe in 1923 and worked at a variety of musical jobs in Paris and London until his death. A prolific and sometimes imaginative exponent of an uncomplicated, conservative style, Lucas worked best in small formal units. His music was highly successful in its day, and was performed by Sir Henry Wood, Theodore Thomas and other leading conductors. He seems to have written at least three other stage works, including *Anne Hathaway* (before 1898), *Arabia* and *Semiramis*, none of them performed.

EMC (S. L. Hall)   CARL MOREY

Lucca. City in Tuscany, Italy; it is the provincial capital of Lucca. There is evidence that *intermedi* were performed there from the last decades of the 16th century under the auspices of the Accademia degli Oscuri. In 1628 *Esione*, a 'favola per musica per intermedii', ushered in a period of intensive production of *favole* and *drammi per musica*, most of them by the librettist Francesco Sbarra in collaboration with the composer Marco Bigongiari and promoted by the academies of the Oscuri and the Accesi. Sbarra also directed Breni's *Psiche* (1645). Companies such as the Febiarmonici (1645 and 1650) also performed in Lucca. The main buildings used for performances were the hall of the Palazzo dei Borghi, where a wooden theatre with boxes was erected at public expense (from at least as early as 1653 entrance was by the purchase of 'bullettini'), halls in the Palazzo Pubblico, the Seminary, and private palazzos and villas.

In 1672 the Republic of Lucca constructed a purpose-built theatre near the church of S Girolamo. The Teatro Pubblico, designed by Francesco Buonamici and built by Giovanni Maria Padredio, with three tiers of boxes supported by stone columns, opened on 14 January 1675 with Antonio Sartorio's *La prosperità di Elio Seiano*. The 48 boxes, assigned by drawing lots, were supplemented by seats in the stalls, which were sold for an evening or for a series of performances. The theatre was destroyed by fire in 1688 and rebuilt with four tiers of boxes (67 in all), reopening in 1693 (see illustration). The principal season was in autumn (approximately 15 August to 31 October), when two operas, usually *opere serie*, were given some 40 performances, four evenings a week. There were less intensive seasons in Carnival, spring and summer. The Teatro Pubblico was managed by the magistracy of the Republic (after 1754 by a specific Cura sopra il Teatro); the impresarios were mainly noblemen. The productions, which were fairly lavish and involved some of the most celebrated singers and dancers of the day, were mostly brought from elsewhere, but there were also first performances such as Giuseppe Scarlatti's *Ezio* (1744), *Olimpiade* (1745) and *Artaserse* (1747). Pasticcios by local composers were often performed.

The Teatro Pubblico was renamed the Teatro Nazionale during the years of the Democratic Republics installed by the French (1799–1805). After a closure of ten years and restoration to plans by Giovanni Lazzarini, consisting of a new façade and 83 boxes in four tiers, as well as a gallery, it reopened as the Teatro del Giglio in August 1819 with Simon Mayr's *La rosa bianca e la rosa rossa*. For 30 years from 1819 the impresario Alessandro Lanari staged productions of high quality, including the Italian première of Rossini's

Guillaume Tell (1831). The theatre continues to function in substantially the same building. In 1985 it was officially recognized as a 'teatro di tradizione'.

The most important among the other theatres were the Castiglioncelli and the Pantera. Both were privately managed (with occasional contributions from public funds) and staged mostly comic opera, alternating with drama and other kinds of entertainment and using promotional events such as tombola to encourage attendance. The Castiglioncelli, built in 1752 by the Accademia 'Magis Vigent' in via del Moro and radically altered in 1772 to plans by Ottaviano Diodati, was smaller than the Teatro Pubblico but very elegant. It was restored and reopened in 1808, and for a decade functioned as the only theatre in the city. First performances there included that of Domenico Puccini's *Il ciarlatano* (1815). From 1829 to 1840 it was called Teatro Nota, and from 1872 to the end of the 19th century Teatro Goldoni.

The Teatro Pantera, designed by Michele Lippi with four tiers of boxes and a gallery, was built on the initiative of the Accademia dei Collegati in 1770 and financed by contributions from box-holders. It had fallen into disrepair by the beginning of the 19th century but was reopened in 1817 and throughout the century functioned as the city's second theatre. After considerable reconstruction it is now a cinema.

From the second half of the 19th century, after Lucca ceased to be an independent state, the quality and frequency of productions declined. Nevertheless, the fine musical tradition of the city may have influenced two of its natives, Alfredo Catalani and Giacomo

Puccini. Since 1978 the Festival Internazionale di Marlia, held during July and August, has included opera performances.

*
L. Nerici: *Storia della musica in Lucca* (Lucca, 1879)
C. Sardi: *Lucca e il suo ducato* (Florence, 1912)
A. Pellegrini: *Spettacoli lucchesi nei secoli XVII–XIX* (Lucca, 1914) [index and bibliography ed. E. Amico Moneti (Lucca, 1959)]
F. Ciancaglini: *Il Teatro del Giglio nella sua vita tre volte secolare* (Pescia, 1941)
B. Paoli Catelani: *Il Teatro comunale del Giglio di Lucca* (Pescia, 1941)
E. Moneti: 'Gli spettacoli teatrali in Lucca nei secoli XVII–XIX e la Cronistoria di Almachilde Pellegrini', *Bollettino storico lucchese*, xiv (1942), 61–79
L. Bianconi and T. Walker: 'Dalla "Finta pazza" alla "Veremonda": storie di Febiarmonici', *RIM*, x (1975), 379–454
P. Cristofani: *Francesco Sbarra, librettista lucchese del '600* (diss., U. of Pisa, 1976)
J. Rosselli: *The Opera Industry in Italy from Cimarosa to Verdi: the Role of the Impresario* (Cambridge, 1984)
M. T. Quilici: *Spettacoli lucchesi nella seconda metà del '700* (diss., U. of Pisa, 1986)   GABRIELLA BIAGI RAVENNI

Lucca, Francesco (*b* Cremona, 1802; *d* Milan, 20 Nov 1872). Italian music publisher. He began as an apprentice music engraver to Ricordi but left in 1825 to start his own shop and establish himself as a publisher. Though he commissioned two early Verdi operas and acquired the rights to a third, his tactlessness alienated the composer, who thereafter preferred Ricordi. With the help of his wife Giovannina, née Strazza (*b* Cernobbio, 1814; *d* Cernobbio, 19 Aug 1894), the stronger personality, Lucca countered by publishing works by Marchetti, Gomes and Catalani and, in particular, by securing the Italian rights to important operas by foreign composers (Halévy, Meyerbeer, Gounod), culminating in the complete works of Wagner, who said of Signora Lucca: 'Nature originally intended to make a man, until it realized that in Italy the men were not much use, and quickly corrected itself'. War between Lucca and Ricordi, ostensibly over 'Wagnerism', went on with much mutual vilification until, in 1888, the aging widow sold out to her rival.

*
ES (M. Morini)
F. Schlitzer: *Mondo teatrale dell'ottocento* (Naples, 1954)
C. Gatti: *Il Teatro alla Scala nella storia e nell'arte (1778–1963)*, i (Milan, 1964), 141–4
M. Gregor-Dellin and D. Mack, eds.: *C. Wagner: Diaries* (London, 1978–80)
L. Jensen: *Giuseppe Verdi and Giovanni Ricordi: with Notes on Francesco Lucca* (New York, 1989)   JOHN ROSSELLI

Lucca, Pauline (*b* Vienna, 25 April 1841; *d* Vienna, 28 Feb 1908). Austrian soprano. She studied in Vienna, joining the chorus at the Hofoper, where she sang the Second Boy (*Die Zauberflöte*) in 1859. Engaged at Olomouc, she made her début there as Elvira (*Ernani*), and in 1860 she sang in Prague as Valentine (*Les Huguenots*) and Norma. She sang at the Berlin Hofoper from 1861, and made her Covent Garden début as Valentine in 1863, returning in 1864 as Marguerite (*Faust*). She sang Sélika at the first London and Berlin performances of *L'Africaine* (1865), and during the 1866 Covent Garden season she sang Léonore (*La favorite*), Zerlina (*Fra Diavolo*) and Cherubino. She was Elisabeth de Valois in the first London performance of *Don Carlos* (1867). After two seasons in Russia, she returned to London to sing Angèle (Auber's *Le domino noir*), Zerlina, Pamina and Agathe. In 1872

Teatro Pubblico, Lucca: design (1724) by Filippo Juvarra showing the theatre adapted for a festival of dance

Pauline Lucca as Marguerite in Gounod's 'Faust'

she broke her contract in Berlin and went to New York, where she sang at the Academy of Music. Returning to Europe in 1874, she was engaged at the Vienna Hofoper, where she remained until her retirement in 1889, appearing in Boito's *Mefistofele* (1882) and Ponchielli's *La Gioconda* (1885). In 1882, after a ten-year absence, she returned to Covent Garden, where she sang Carmen and Leonora (*Il trovatore*). Her voice ranged two and a half octaves, and she was especially admired in dramatic roles.

*

A. Ehrlich: *Berühmte Sängerinnen der Vergangenheit und Gegenwart* (Leipzig, 1895)

A. Jansen-Mara and D. Weisse-Zahrer: *Die Wiener Nachtigall* (Berlin, 1935)

J. Kapp: *Geschichte der Staatsoper Berlin* (Berlin, 1937)

H. Rosenthal: *Two Centuries of Opera at Covent Garden* (London, 1958)

H. Kralik: *The Vienna Opera* (Vienna, 1963)

ELIZABETH FORBES

Lucchesi [Luchesi], Andrea (*b* Motta di Livenza, nr Treviso, 23 May 1741; *d* Bonn, 21 March 1801). Italian composer. While still in his early teens, he studied in Venice (perhaps with Cocchi and others). He composed his first operas there in 1765–7. Early in 1771 the Mozarts met him in Venice; later that year he probably supervised the production of his last comic opera for Venice, before leaving for Bonn as director of a travelling opera company. Here he enjoyed considerable success for a time, and by late 1773 he had directed revivals of two of his Venetian operas, as well as three new theatrical works, of particular interest because Beethoven's father and grandfather sang in them.

After Beethoven's grandfather died, Lucchesi was awarded his position as court Kapellmeister in 1774, and the Italian opera troupe returned to Italy. But in 1779, when the Nationaltheater in Bonn was established, C. G. Neefe became its musical director. Except for ballet music in 1774, Lucchesi's theatrical works

ceased to be performed in the city. In 1783 he was granted leave to visit Italy, and the following year he directed his first *opera seria*, *Ademira*, in Venice. He returned to Bonn probably in late 1784, though his prestige gradually declined; with the departure of the court and the occupation of Bonn by the French in 1794, his income nearly disappeared. The libretto of his last opera, *L'amore e la miseria* (1794), names him as *maestro di cappella* and director of the Accademia Musicale de' Tedeschi in Venice.

As well as stage works, Lucchesi composed a large amount of sacred and instrumental music. Burney described him as 'a very pleasing composer'.

L'isola della fortuna (dg, G. Bertati), Venice, S Samuele, aut. 1765, *P-La*

Le donne sempre donne (dg, P. Chiari), Venice, S Moisè, 27 Feb 1767, *I-MOe, P-La*

Il giocatore amoroso (int, A. Salvi), Venice, private perf., 13 Feb 1769; Bonn, Hof, 1772

Il matrimonio per astuzia (dg), Venice, S Benedetto, Oct 1771, *I-MOe* (orch pts), *P-La*

L'inganno scoperto, overo Il conte Caramella (dg, 3, C. Goldoni), Bonn, Hof, 13 May 1773, *I-MOe* (ov.)

L'improvisata, ossia La galanteria disturbata (azione comica teatrale, G. Dolfin and Lucchesi), Bonn, Hof, wint. 1773–4

Die Liebe für das Vaterland (prol.), Frankfurt am Main, 22 April 1783

Ademira (os, 3, ? F. Moretti), Venice, S Benedetto, 2 May 1784, *P-La, I-Mc* (ov. and aria)

L'amore e la miseria guadagnano il giuoco (operetta giocosa, D. Friggieri), Passau, spr. 1794

*

BurneyGN; EitnerQ

J. B. de La Borde: *Essai sur la musique ancienne et moderne*, iii (Paris, 1780), 199

C. G. Neefe: 'Nachricht von der churfürstlich-cöllnischen Hofcapelle zu Bonn', *Magazin der Musik*, i (1783), 377–96

A. Henseler: 'Andrea Luchesi, der letzte Bonner Hofkapellmeister zur Zeit des jungen Beethoven: ein Beitrag zur Musik- und Theatergeschichte des 18. Jahrhunderts', *Bonner Geschichtsblätter*, i (1937), 225–364

E. Forbes, ed.: *Thayer's Life of Beethoven*, i (Princeton, 1964, 2/1967), 34, 68

M. Braubach: 'Die Mitglieder der Hofmusik unter den vier letzten Kurfürsten von Köln', *Colloquium amicorum: Joseph Schmidt-Görg zum 70. Geburtstag* (Bonn, 1967), 26–63

N. Jers: 'Luchesi, Andrea', *Beiträge zur rheinischen Musikgeschichte*, xcvii: *Rheinische Musiker*, vii (1972), 77–81

SVEN HANSELL

Lucchesina, La. *See* MARCHESINI, MARIA ANTONIA.

Lucchesino, Il. *See* PACINI, ANDREA.

Lucchini [Luchini], Antonio Maria (*fl* 1716–30). Italian librettist. He was a member of the Venetian middle class (*cittadinanza*); his first known libretto was *Foca superbo* (1716), for which Lotti composed the music. After providing the text for Vivaldi's *Tieteberga* (1717), he went with Lotti to Dresden, where he was engaged as court librettist at a salary of 1000 thalers. The future Elector of Saxony (Friedrich August II) commented in a letter that Lucchini was not in the top flight of poets but would serve well enough to write texts for oratorios, serenatas and cantatas or to make 'adjustments' to existing opera librettos. Nevertheless, Lucchini provided two original opera librettos for Dresden, both set by Lotti: *Giove in Argo* (1717) and *Ascanio, overo Gli odi delusi dal sangue* (1718). His activity in Dresden was abruptly curtailed when a scandal involving a local woman forced him to flee. He wrote four more librettos for the Venetian stage: *Ermengarda, Gli sforzi d'ambizione e d'amore, Dorilla in Tempe* and *Selim, gran Signor de'*

Turchi. His most successful libretto, however, was *Farnace* (1724), written for the Teatro Alibert, Rome; first set by Vinci, it also achieved wide circulation through Vivaldi's much-revived setting (1727). Lucchini's gifts as a librettist are perhaps greater than the prince allowed, though his approach is entirely conventional.

Foca superbo, Lotti, 1716; *Tieteberga*, Vivaldi, 1717; *Giove in Argo*, Lotti, 1717 (Handel, 1739); *Ascanio, overo Gli odi delusi dal sangue*, Lotti, 1718; *L'inganno tradito dall'amore*, Caldara, 1720; *Ermengarda*, Albinoni, 1723; *Gli sforzi d'ambizione e d'amore*, Porta, 1724; *Farnace*, Vinci, 1724 (Vivaldi, 1727); *Dorilla in Tempe*, Vivaldi, 1726; *L'Adaloaldo furioso*, Maccari, 1727; *Selim, gran Signor de' Turchi*, pasticcio, 1730

*

M. Fürstenau: *Zur Geschichte der Musik und des Theaters am Hofe zu Dresden* (Dresden, 1861–2)
F. Tàmmaro: 'Il "Farnace" di Vivaldi: problemi di ricostruzione', *Studi musicali*, xv (1986), 213–56   MICHAEL TALBOT

Luccio, Francesco. *See* LUCIO, FRANCESCO.

Lucerna ('The Lantern'). Musical fairy-tale in four acts, op.56, by VÍTĚZSLAV NOVÁK to a libretto by Hanuš Jelínek after the play by Alois Jirásek; Prague, National Theatre, 13 May 1923.

A young Miller (baritone) is in love with his foster-daughter Hanička (soprano), but the water-sprite Michal (tenor) also eyes her lovingly. Although long ago released from serfdom, the millers still have a duty to accompany the lords to the forest hunting-lodge with a lantern. The Steward (bass), who wants Hanička to serve at the mansion, plans to curb the Miller's freedom by cutting down his ancient linden tree. In Act 2 the Miller is undaunted by the passionate Countess (soprano), but he cannot refuse to accompany her to the hunting-lodge. In Act 3 she flirts with the headstrong Miller; they are disturbed by a comic band of musicians led by Zajíček (tenor). Michal appears, but is caught by Klásková (contralto), the wife of one of the musicians, who makes him carry her own lantern to the lodge. An interlude follows in which another water-sprite, Ivan (bass), is met by the Countess and the Miller, whom the Countess has almost won for herself, followed by Klásková, who warns him of the Steward's intentions. The Miller hastens to defend his rights. Act 4 shows Hanička hiding from the bailiffs in the tree. The Miller rushes to protect it, but a magic glow appears in it and Hanička walks out of its trunk. The Countess grasps the tree's significance as the guardian and witness of the struggle for freedom, and she breaks the lantern, thus releasing the Miller from his bond.

Novák presented *The Lantern* as an idyllic fairy-tale, radiating a sense of well-being, lyricism and gentle humour. The central theme of the Miller's defiance of authority is stressed, but not dramatically underlined, and the almost kaleidoscopic variety of characters and moods is reflected by a wide expressive palette, from simple folklike arioso to ecstatic declamation, from clearcut arias to melodrama, from simple harmony to polyphony. A number of motifs are used to characterize personalities and events. Novák used sounds colouristically, adding illustrative elements and playful quotations (e.g. from Mendelssohn's Wedding March). In its detail and character, *The Lantern* looks back to his subjective Romantic works. There are more reminiscences of Smetana and Dvořák than in Novák's earlier operas: evidently he wanted to emphasize the national tradition in the postwar years. This provoked criticism from

young musicians, though the opera was well received by audiences and has had some 20 productions in Czech theatres.   EVA HERRMANNOVÁ

Lucerne (Ger. Luzern). City in central Switzerland. Musical theatre was first given in the Obrigkeitliche Comödienhaus, built in 1741 for the Jesuit order in Lucerne and handed over to the city authorities in 1773. *Wilhelm Tell*, an opera-pantomime by Ignaz Gspan, received its première there in 1779. The present Stadttheater (cap. 564) was built in 1839, renovated in 1867 and closed from 1924 to 1926 because of fire damage; it was modernized in 1970 and 1984. In 1974 the theatre staged the first of several joint productions with the Lucerne International Music Festival which have included Heinrich Sutermeister's *Die schwarze Spinne* (1985). In 1982 Schoeck's comic opera *Don Ranudo de Colibrados* was revived, using a score reconstructed from war-damaged fragments. Performances are given on most nights from September to June, with up to six new opera productions each season. The theatre has its own ensemble for opera, ballet and drama, and draws on the services of the orchestra of the Allgemeine Musikgesellschaft Luzern. Singers who began their careers in the theatre include Inge Borkh, Edith Mathis and Fritz Uhl.

ANDREW CLARK

Luchetti, Veriano (*b* Viterbo, 12 March 1939). Italian tenor. Early operatic assignments of significance were at Wexford as Alfredo (1965) and at Spoleto in Donizetti's *Il furioso all'isola di San Domingo* (1967). He has performed throughout the world, making notable appearances at the Maggio Musicale, Florence, in *L'Africaine* (1971) and Spontini's *Agnes von Hohenstaufen* (1974). He made his La Scala début in May 1975, in *Attila*; for the company's 1976 London season he sang Gabriele Adorno (*Simon Boccanegra*), having earlier appeared at Covent Garden as Pinkerton (1973) and Rodolfo (1974–5). A singer of robust build and strong, firmly knit voice, encompassing roles such as Rodolfo, Don Carlos and Don José with equal authority, his performances are marked by a manly style in which intelligence and sensitivity play a notable part.

MAX LOPPERT

Lucia, Fernando de. *See* DE LUCIA, FERNANDO.

Lucia di Lammermoor ('Lucy of Lammermoor'). *Dramma tragico* in three acts by GAETANO DONIZETTI to a libretto by SALVADORE CAMMARANO after WALTER SCOTT's novel *The Bride of Lammermoor*; Naples, Teatro S Carlo, 26 September 1835.

Before Cammarano adapted Scott's novel, it had been the basis of three earlier Italian librettos – by Giuseppe Balocchi for Michele Carafa's *Le nozze di Lammermoor* (1829, Paris), Calisto Bassi for Luigi Rieschi's *La fidanzata di Lammermoor* (1831, Trieste) and Pietro Beltrame for Alberto Mazzucato's *La fidanzata di Lammermoor* (1834, Padua). Like nearly all the Scott operas, Donizetti's *Lucia* departs from its model in several ways. Cammarano made the original characters Frank Hayston, Laird of Bucklaw, Ailsie Gourlay and the Reverend Peter Bide-the-Bent into, respectively, Lord Arturo Bucklaw, Alisa and Raimondo Bidebent, conflating Lucy's father Sir William Ashton and her elder brother Colonel Sholto Ashton into Enrico Ashton. (Some English adaptations use the names Sir

Lucia   soprano
Enrico Ashton *Laird of Lammermoor,*
    Lucia's brother   baritone
Edgardo *Laird of Ravenswood*   tenor
Lord Arturo Bucklaw *Lucia's bridegroom*   tenor
Raimondo Bidebent *a Calvinist chaplain*   bass
Alisa *Lucia's companion*   mezzo-soprano
Normanno *huntsman, a retainer of Enrico*   tenor
    Retainers and servants, wedding guests

Setting The grounds and hall of Lammermoor and of
Ravenswood, and the graveyard of the Ravenswoods;
Scotland, during the reign of William and Mary (late
17th century)

*Fanny Tacchinardi-Persiani as Lucia in the first London
production of Donizetti's 'Lucia di Lammermoor' (Her
Majesty's Theatre, 5 April 1838): lithograph (1839) by
Edward Morton*

Arthur Bucklaw, Alice, Raymond Bide-the-Bent and Sir
Henry Ashton.) Although Scott's most memorable
villainess, Lucy's mother, is left out altogether, much of
the powerful plot survives.

The opera was first performed with a remarkable cast,
Fanny Tacchinardi-Persiani (Lucia), Gilbert Duprez
(Edgardo), Domenico Cosselli (Enrico) and Carlo Porto
(Raimondo). Adelaide Kemble and Napoleone Moriani
sang in the La Scala première, on 1 April 1839; at the
French première (Paris, Théâtre Italien, 12 December
1837) Tacchinardi-Persiani and Rubini sang, as they did
at the English première (London, Her Majesty's, 5 April
1838). The French version by Donizetti himself (to a
translation by Alphonse Royer and Gustave Vaëz, with
the music adjusted and altered at many points) was first
given at the Théâtre de la Renaissance, Paris, on 6
August 1839, with Sophie Anne Thillon and Achille
Ricciardi. This version entered the Opéra repertory in
1846, with Maria Nau and Duprez, and became a staple
of the repertory of French provincial theatres; and it was
in this version that the opera was introduced to the USA,
at New Orleans, with Julia Calvé and Auguste Nourrit,
on 28 December 1841. The Italian original's first hearing in the USA was also at New Orleans, given by a
touring company from Havana, on 1 March 1842. Since
these beginnings the role of Lucia has been central in the
repertory of every soprano with a gift for *fioritura*;
among the most famous are Patti, Gerster, Di Murska,
Albani, Sembrich, Melba, Tetrazzini, Galli-Curci, Dal
Monte, Pons, Callas, Sutherland, Sills and Gruberová.

Act 1.i *The grounds of Ravenswood Castle* After a
short B♭ minor prelude, punctuated by ominous
drumrolls, mournful horn phrases and a dirge-like
march, the curtain rises on Normanno and the other
huntsmen, who are about to explore the nearby ruins of
the castle belonging to Enrico's hated enemy (chorus,
'Per correte le spiagge vicine'). The huntsmen leave, and
Normanno, seeing that Enrico is troubled, learns from
him that the Lammermoor fortunes are in jeopardy;
only Lucia can save them, by means of an expedient
marriage. The chaplain reminds Enrico that she is still
grieving for her mother, who has recently died, and that
the girl is not ready to love. At that, Normanno declares
that she has been on fire with love for Edgardo, meeting
him every morning ever since he rescued her from a
rampaging bull. Enrico is enraged (Larghetto, 'Cruda,
funesta smania'). The huntsmen return to report that
Edgardo is nearby; Enrico swears to destroy his enemy
(cabaletta, 'La pietade in suo favore'). The chorus and
the double aria for the baritone form the impetuous

climax to the extended *introduzione*, the transitional
material held together by frequent arioso passages built
on motivic ideas.

1.ii *The park at Lammermoor Castle, with a
fountain* The scene begins with an elaborate harp solo
(which at least one Lucia, Ernesta Grisi, was enterprising enough to perform herself). Impatiently, Lucia
awaits a tryst with Edgardo. She looks at the fountain,
where an ancestor of the Ravenswoods jettisoned the
corpse of a Lammermoor lass he had slain in a jealous
rage; she is frightened because she has recently seen the
girl's ghost. She describes the episode vividly to Alisa
(Larghetto, 'Regnava nel silenzio'), mentioning that the
water had turned blood-red. This aria is a fine example
of Donizetti's gift of using vocal ornament to dramatic
ends: the embellishments he wrote out vividly convey
the heroine's unstable state. Alisa declares that Lucia's
love for Edgardo is beset with difficulties and urges her
to renounce him. Lucia, however, believes in his constancy (cabaletta, 'Quando rapito in estasi';
Tacchinardi-Persiani was not fond of Lucia's entrance
arias and substituted ones from the role of Rosmonda,
from Donizetti's *Rosmonda d'Inghilterra*, 1834, which
had been written for her – that Donizetti approved of
the substitution is evident from his incorporation of the
Rosmonda scena into the French *Lucie de
Lammermoor*).

Edgardo arrives and Alisa goes to watch for intruders.
He tells Lucia that he has been called to the Stuart cause
in France and must leave next morning. Before he goes
he wants to extend the hand of friendship to Enrico,
despite the longstanding feud between their families.
Lucia, frightened of her brother's furious temper, begs
Edgardo to keep their love secret. He reminds her that
he swore, by his father's grave, that he would be

avenged, and although their love has quenched his anger his oath remains unfulfilled. Lucia calms him, and he places a ring on her finger, claiming that henceforth they are as married; Lucia accepts this, giving him a ring in return. She begs him to write to her, telling him that he will hear the echo of her sighs, even in France, and he reassures her before he departs (duet, 'Verranno a te sull'aure', a melody that will be of strategic importance in her later mad scene as she imagines her formal marriage).

ACT 2.i *Enrico's apartments in Lammermoor Castle* Enrico discusses with Normanno the marriage he has hastily arranged between Lucia and Arturo, and is worried that she may oppose it. Normanno has been intercepting Edgardo's letters and has forged one to say that Edgardo loves another woman – leaving her no reason to hold back from the proposed marriage. Taking the forged letter, Enrico sends Normanno to welcome Arturo. Lucia enters, listless; Enrico comments on her pallor, to which she responds that he knows why she grieves (duet, 'Il pallor funesto'). She protests at his inhuman severity, but he claims that his strong fraternal feelings prompt his wish to see her appropriately married. When she says that she already considers herself Edgardo's wife, Enrico hands her the forged letter; the shock of reading it causes her to stagger as though she had received a blow. Enrico reproaches her with folly, but Lucia is numbed at the thought of Edgardo's infidelity. Sounds are heard of the welcome for Arturo. Lucia wants only to die, not to marry; but Enrico stresses the perils of his political situation, from which only an alliance with the Bucklaws can save him. He ruthlessly tells her that without her cooperation he will surely be executed, and she will be responsible. This powerful duet scene with its three contrasting sections represents a touchstone of Donizetti's skill as a musical dramatist, in his characterization of the successive stages of the estrangement between brother and sister.

Enrico hurries out to greet Arturo. Lucia turns to Raimondo, who tells her that, although he knows her letters to Edgardo were intercepted, he managed to have one of them securely delivered. Believing Edgardo has never replied, the chaplain is convinced of his infidelity and tells Lucia that the exchange of rings has no validity in God's eyes. Despite his persuasiveness, Lucia confesses she loves Edgardo still. He urges the impressionable girl to remember a sister's duty and her obligation to her dead mother (aria, 'Ah! cedi, cedi'), and goes on to assure her that her reward will be in heaven. (This episode was traditionally omitted, but its importance in charting Lucia's crumbling resistance is now generally recognized.)

2.ii *The Great Hall of Lammermoor Castle* Wedding guests are assembled to greet Arturo ('Per te d'immenso giubilo': a rousing unison chorus with a solo interlude); Arturo smugly claims that the fortunes of the house will now undoubtedly improve. Enrico tells him not to be surprised at Lucia's sad demeanour as she is still grieving for her mother. Arturo questions Enrico about the rumours of Edgardo, but Lucia's entrance saves him from answering. The marriage contract awaits the requisite signatures: half-fainting, Lucia signs her name, but to her the document is like her own death warrant. Suddenly there is uproar as Edgardo unexpectedly appears: he wonders what power restrains him as he confronts his enemy, and Enrico fears that he has betrayed his sister. The famous sextet in Db, 'Chi mi frena in tal momento', expands the shock of Edgardo's arrival, developing a groundswell of conflicting emotions, twice rising to climaxes. Its structure is simple (A–A'–B–B'), but no small measure of its effectiveness comes from the skilful *crescendo* of forces: first tenor-baritone, then soprano-bass with tenor and baritone in the background, and only in the B sections engaging all six soloists and chorus. Lucia is bereft; Raimondo is touched by her pitiable state. Their swords drawn, Arturo and Enrico order Edgardo away, but he defies them, insisting on his right to be present: Lucia, he claims, is his bride. Raimondo now shows him the contract; Edgardo asks if Lucia herself has signed it and when she confesses he tears off her ring and tramples on it, cursing the moment he fell in love with her and vowing eternal hatred. Enrico, Arturo and the guests demand his instant departure. Lucia sinks to her knees, praying for deliverance; but Edgardo throws down his sword, bares his breast and declares he has no more desire to live. The *tempo di mezzo* of this concerted finale brings back, in Rossinian fashion, the accompanying tune that had underlain the earlier conversation between Arturo and Enrico in the *tempo d'attacco*. This uneasy attempt at civilized discourse breaks down when Raimondo produces the marriage contract, an episode accompanied by misremembered echoes of Lucia's entrance music earlier in this scene, providing thereby a clue to her mental agitation. Edgardo's curse (a moment made famous by Duprez) precipitates the D major *stretta*, which develops in the usual fashion: a thrusting unison for the furious Enrico and his followers, succeeded by a shift in texture dominated by phrases for the soprano and tenor in octaves, leading through an interlude of harmonic restlessness to a reinforced statement of the earlier material, capped by an emphatic coda.

ACT 3.i *The dilapidated hall of the Ravenswoods* A fierce storm rages; Edgardo, alone, expresses the wish that the storm foretell the end of the world. Unexpectedly, Enrico enters; he gloats that, even as he speaks, Lucia is entering her bridal chamber with Arturo (duet, 'Qui del padre ancor respira') and declares that he has come to challenge Edgardo to a duel the following dawn in the Ravenswoods' graveyard. (In the mid-19th century this Tower Scene was regarded as one of the great dramatic moments of the opera; and there was once a near-riot at the Théâtre Italien when it was omitted because of a singer's indisposition. The scene was later often omitted as the opera came to be regarded primarily as a prima donna's vehicle and the rest of the cast was second string; but with singers who understand the art of dramatic declamation in bel canto opera, the Tower Scene can still produce a strong impression.)

3.ii *The Great Hall at Lammermoor* The wedding guests dance to celebrate Lucia's wedding (chorus, 'D'immenso giubilo'). Suddenly Raimondo, badly shaken, appears, ordering them to stop their merriment. In a grisly narrative (Larghetto, 'Dalle stanze ove Lucia', over a restlessly modulating accompaniment), he tells that he heard a cry from the bridal chamber; hastening there, he was aghast to see Arturo dead on the floor, with Lucia, holding a bloodstained dagger, smiling at him, enquiring where her bridegroom was. The guests are stunned (chorus, 'Oh! qual funesto avvenimento!').

At Lucia's entrance her mental disorder is suggested by the flute (Donizetti had originally planned to use a glass harmonica here; for a page of the autograph score, *see* DONIZETTI, GAETANO) playing a distorted variant of 'Regnava nel silenzio'. She is wearing a white gown, now spattered with blood, and believes she is ready for her wedding to Edgardo. Trembling, she urges him to let her rest by the fountain in the park (the melody of 'Verranno a te' makes it clear that in her confusion she thinks their exchange of rings was a true plighting); then she remembers the ghost that arose from the fountain. Next, imagining they are before an altar, she believes she hears their wedding hymn, and sees the ceremony taking place ('Ardon gl'incensi'). This is the Larghetto of the Mad Scene; her hallucination is appropriately cast as a theme and variations, and it is capped today by an extensive cadenza with flute obbligato. That this now traditional effect does not appear in the score indicates that Donizetti evidently trusted Tacchinardi-Persiani, whose powers of improvisation were legendary, to insert her own cadenza at this point.

Enrico, returning from his encounter with Edgardo, is at first furious at her apparent vindictiveness; but Raimondo points out that her mind has failed. Her declaration that she is the victim of her brother's cruelty fills Enrico with contrition; foreseeing her death, Lucia assures the imagined Edgardo that heaven will be beautiful for her only when he joins her there (cabaletta, 'Spargi d'amaro pianto'). Enrico bids Alisa lead his stricken sister away and urges Raimondo to attend her. Raimondo sternly rebukes Normanno for the bloodshed he has caused.

3.iii *The graveyard of the Ravenswoods* Edgardo appears, early for his appointment to duel with Enrico. The thought of dying on Enrico's sword is not unwelcome to him as the whole universe seems a desert. He thinks of Lucia as a joyous bride as he confronts the prospect of his death. He bids farewell to the earth, thinking of his own neglected, unwept grave (Larghetto, 'Fra poco a me ricovero') and wishing Lucia would at least pay heed to the tomb of one who died for love of her.

The Lammermoor retainers approach, remarking how a day that dawned in gladness has ended in grief. Edgardo demands their meaning: they tell him that Lucia lies near death and is calling for him. A funeral knell tolls. Edgardo is determined to try to see her once more but Raimondo restrains him, assuring him that Lucia is indeed already dead. Edgardo thinks of her in heaven; although they were separated on earth, they shall be united before God (cabaletta, 'Tu che a Dio spiegasti l'ali'). He is determined to die. Raimondo and the others try to restrain him, but he draws his dagger and stabs himself. His dying thoughts are of Lucia.

* * *

In the days of exigent prima donnas, the famous Mad Scene was regarded as the sole raison d'être for *Lucia's* survival, but today, thanks to the example of Callas as much as anyone, its eerie persuasiveness, heightened by melodic and harmonic allusions to earlier parts of the score, as well as its musico-dramatic distinction, has obtained it recognition as a good deal more than a soprano's warhorse. Besides allowing a soprano to demonstrate her technical prowess, the Mad Scene is extraordinarily forward-looking and filled with adroit psychological touches. It gives the effect of being through-composed although in fact it consists of two major episodes: the choruses before and after Raimondo's narrative, and the extended recitative and double aria for the soprano. But so cannily are the sec-

tions joined and overlapped (for instance, Lucia continues the recitative while the orchestra introduces the melody of her Larghetto) that the traditional sequence of segments succeed each other without any sense of disruption. Most surprising of all, perhaps, is the mirroring of Lucia's disorientation in the distorted versions of melodies heard earlier in the opera. Significantly, the one melody she manages to keep straight in her muddled head is 'Verranno a te'.

The Tomb Scene is in effect a second aria-finale, but it conveys a true Romantic frisson with its setting, its atmosphere of foreboding succinctly created in a brief prelude with prominent horn parts. Both of Edgardo's solos, in D major, and the B major chorus that separates them evoke a sense of tragic loss that seems inconsistent with the major mode. One fine touch (which Duprez claimed he suggested to Donizetti) was to have the initial phrases of the repetition of the *moderato* cabaletta, following Edgardo's stabbing himself, divided between the cello and the voice. For many the Tomb Scene is the high point of the whole score.

Both historically and artistically, *Lucia* deserves its reputation. When it was new it was regarded as the apogee of high Romantic sensibility. The clear plot, which trims away much of Scott's accessory detail, possesses the stark tautness of a tale by Poe. It is no coincidence that Flaubert employed it as an important point of reference in the downward course of Emma Bovary, that quintessential victim of Romantic illusions.

Although all the principal roles are vocally challenging, their music is uniformly grateful. The score contains scant sign of the unevenness that afflicts a number of Donizetti's works. Cammarano's libretto moved him deeply and, inspired by his recent first exposure to Paris, Donizetti produced what is certainly his masterpiece. That *Lucia* used to be regarded as an unlikely survivor of an outmoded style derives from the fact that it was usually performed with many damaging cuts (sometimes even the Tomb Scene would be omitted). Today the value of the work is more easily grasped as it has fortunately become customary to perform it complete, and the many revivals of other bel canto operas in recent years have helped in the appreciation of its true stature.

WILLIAM ASHBROOK

Lucile. *Comédie mêlée d'ariettes* in one act by ANDRÉ-ERNEST-MODESTE GRÉTRY to a libretto by JEAN FRANÇOIS MARMONTEL; Paris, Comédie-Italienne (Hôtel de Bourgogne), 5 January 1769.

The character names were carried over by Marmontel from his moral tale *L'école des pères*, but the story is different. It is Lucile's wedding morning, in the house of her supposed father, the rich Timante (tenor). Lucile (soprano) sings of future happiness. Her fiancé, Dorval *fils* (tenor), does likewise, and Timante and Dorval *père* (bass) join them. In the celebrated quartet 'Où peut-on être mieux' they hymn the virtues of hearth and home. Then they welcome Blaise (baritone), a working man, widower of Lucile's wet-nurse. He is left alone, and sings of a misdeed committed by his wife that is on his conscience ('Ah! ma femme!'). It transpires that Timante's true daughter died as a baby, and that Lucile – Blaise's daughter – was exchanged for her. Blaise confesses this to Lucile, who sees that she is of no class to marry Dorval. In a dramatic ensemble, Lucile's unhappiness is made apparent to her maid Julie (soprano) and Dorval *fils*; he challenges Blaise, but Lucile herself reveals the situation to Timante and to her fiancé.

Timante, elderly and generous, would keep Lucile. He undertakes to persuade his friend, Dorval *père*, to accept matters. Cleverly, he makes it morally difficult for Dorval *père* to refuse Lucile as a daughter. Blaise is accepted into the house, and the lovers are united. The piece concludes with villagers dancing and singing.

Lucile was Grétry's most popular *opéra comique* for more than ten years. Its sentimental solutions to problems of social inequity tapped enormous resources of public sympathy; audiences could identify with either party, still be satisfied, and emerge both 'weeping and enchanted' (as described by Louis Petit de Bachaumont in his *Mémoirs secrets*, iv, 1787, pp.208–9). The music spans a considerable range of feeling and drama, with Blaise's F minor character portrait 'Ah! ma femme!' as the linchpin of the whole.   DAVID CHARLTON

Lucio [Luccio, Luzzo], **Francesco** (*b* Venice, *c*1628; *d* Venice, 1 Sept 1658). Italian composer. He spent his life in Venice. In his second book of motets (1650) he is described as a pupil of G. A. Rigatti and singing master at the Ospedale degli Incurabili; he was probably appointed to replace his teacher, who died on 25 October 1649. At the time of his death (from a sword wound) he was attached to the church of S Martino, where he was buried. Apparently he was also employed at the Ospedale della Pietà, to which he left all his music. He was notable primarily as a composer of opera. The attribution to Lucio of *L'Orontea* (traditionally acknowledged as the work of Cesti, whose later version survives) is found in a letter by P. A. Ziani dated 30 January 1666. The widest survey of Lucio's operatic work is contained in the *Arie* of 1655; the arias are close to Cavalli in form and in style of vocal writing, but they are perhaps more striking in their sometimes angular melodic style and more inclined to chromatic harmony. Some of the arias of *Il Medoro* are notable for their unusual formal design.

See also MEDORO.

all performed in Venice; exact dates are of dedication

L'Orontea (drama musicale, prol., 3, G. A. Cicognini), SS Apostoli, 20 Jan 1649 [music traditionally attrib. Cesti, but see Bianconi and Walker; music lost, unless the score of the 1654 Naples performance (*I-Nc*, at least partly by Cirillo) contains some of the orig. music]
Gl'amori di Alessandro Magno e di Rossane (dramma musicale, prol., 3, Cicognini, completed by an unknown librettist), SS Apostoli, 24 Jan 1651, arias in Arie (1655/*R*1984: DMV, iv)
Pericle effeminato (drama per musica, 3, G. Castoreo), S Apollinare, 7 Jan 1653, arias in Arie (1655/*R*1984: DMV, iv), 1 in *GB-Lbl*
L'Euridamante (drama regio, prol., 3, G. dall'Angelo), S Moisè, 20 Jan 1654, arias in Arie (1655/*R*1984: DMV, iv)
Il Medoro (drama per musica, prol., 3, A. Aureli, after L. Ariosto), SS Giovanni e Paolo, 11 Jan 1658, *I-Vnm*/*R*1984: DMV, iv; 1 aria ed. in Worsthorne, 3 ed. in Rosand

*

S. T. Worsthorne: *Venetian Opera in the Seventeenth Century* (Oxford, 1954)
T. Walker: 'Gli errori di "Minerva al tavolino": osservazioni sulla cronologia delle prime opere veneziane', *Venezia e il melodramma nel seicento: Venice 1972*, 7–20
L. Bianconi and T. Walker: 'Dalla *Finta pazza* alla *Veremonda*: storie di Febiarmonici', *RIM*, x (1975), 379–454
G. Morelli: 'Fare un libretto: la conquista della poetica paraletteraria', DMV, iv (1984), pp.ix–lvii
T. Walker: ' "Ubi Lucius": Thoughts on Reading *Medoro*', DMV, iv (1984), pp.cxxxi–clxiv
E. Rosand: *Opera in Seventeenth-Century Venice: the Creation of a Genre* (Berkeley, 1991)   THOMAS WALKER, BETH L. GLIXON

Lucio Silla (i) ('Lucius Sulla'). *Dramma per musica* in three acts, K135, by WOLFGANG AMADEUS MOZART to a libretto by GIOVANNI DE GAMERRA; Milan, Regio Ducal Teatro, 26 December 1772.

Lucius Sulla *dictator of Rome*	tenor
Giunia [Junia] *daughter of Caius Marius, betrothed to Cecilius*	soprano
Cecilio [Cecilius] *exiled Roman senator*	soprano castrato
Lucio [Lucius] Cinna *his friend, a conspirator*	soprano
Celia *sister of Sulla*	soprano
Aufidio [Aufidius] *tribune, friend of Sulla*	tenor

Guards, nobles, senators, people of Rome

Setting Rome, 79 BC

The contract for *Lucio Silla*, dated 4 March 1771, required Mozart to deliver the recitatives in October 1772 and to be in Milan by November to compose the arias and rehearse 'with the usual reservations in case of theatrical misfortunes and Princely interventions (which God forbid)'.

The primo uomo Venanzio Rauzzini (Cecilius) arrived only on 21 November, the prima donna Anna de Amicis-Buonsolazzi (Junia) still later. Bassano Morgnoni (Sulla) was a last-minute replacement (so his role is relatively simple). The other singers were Felicità Suardi (Cinna), Daniella Mienci (Celia) and Giuseppe Onofrio (Aufidius). Mozart had to make alterations in the light of Metastasio's comments on the libretto. Archduke Ferdinand's letter-writing delayed the première two hours; it was immensely long (there were three ballets), but nevertheless was followed by 25 more performances, a major triumph. The libretto was set by other composers including J. C. Bach (1775, Mannheim), but Mozart's opera was not revived until 1929 (Prague, in German).

The successful general Lucius Sulla seized total power in Rome but unexpectedly laid it down the year before his death. Some of the characters are historical, but the plot is fiction.

ACT 1 *A neglected grove* The banished Cecilius reappears secretly in Rome and learns from Cinna that Sulla, declaring him dead, proposes to marry Junia. Cecilius may see her when she goes to mourn her father; love promises a better future ('Vieni ov'amor t'invita'). Cecilius is prey to fear and joyful anticipation (the first of many fine obbligato recitatives) as well as feelings of tenderness ('Il tenero momento').

In Sulla's palace Celia agrees to persuade Junia to accept Sulla (in minuet style, 'Se lusinghiera speme'); no girl will resist for the sake of the dead. Junia rejects the tyrant who has deposed her father and banished her lover. Sulla, at first not unkind, says the price of obstinacy may be death. Junia responds ('Dalla sponda tenebrosa'): in an *adagio* section she invokes her father and lover, then (*allegro*) pours scorn on his love. Sulla decides he must overcome the weakness of affection and, like a true tyrant, condemn her (obbligato recitative and aria, 'Il desio di vendetta').

The mausoleum The rest of Act 1 uses no simple recitative. After the fiery D major of Sulla's aria, Mozart sets the new scene by sombre music which modulates obliquely to C minor. Cecilius's mixed feel-

73

ings bring varied figurations and rapid tempo changes. Junia enters with mourners; within their funeral chorus she sings a G minor lament ('O del padre ombra diletta'). Cecilius is taken for a ghost. Their duet ('D'Eliso in sen m'attendi'), a moving Andante and brilliant Allegro, ends the act on a note of hope.

ACT 2 *A military arch* Aufidius tells Sulla that as Junia has many supporters in Rome he should publicly declare her his wife ('Guerrier, che d'un acciaro'). Sulla permits Celia's betrothal to Cinna. Cecilius pursues Sulla with a sword but Cinna restrains him; rashness will gain nothing. Cecilius mingles hope and despair in snatches of obbligato recitative, but his aria ('Quest'improviso tremito'), a concise Allegro in D, shows his fierce desire for revenge. Celia tries to declare her love for Cinna but is tongue-tied (an appealing Grazioso, 'Se il labbro timido'). Cinna is more concerned with plotting; but Junia refuses to marry Sulla and murder him in bed. He must care for Cecilius (obbligato recitative), whose danger freezes her heart. Her aria ('Ah se il crudel periglio') is a grandiose Allegro of stunning virtuosity. Cinna decides that he must take communal vengeance upon himself (obbligato recitative and a vigorous aria, 'Nel fortunato istante').

Hanging gardens Struggling with contradictory feelings, Sulla again assures Junia that refusal means death. His aria ('D'ogni pietà mi spoglio') explodes without ritornello. Drained of pity, he will assuage his hurt by killing. In a short middle section he is overcome by tenderness towards her, quickly suppressed. Cecilius tells Junia that he must kill the tyrant; if he dies his shade will watch over her ('Ah, se a morir mi chiama'). Exceptionally, the main section is Adagio, nobly arching in wide leaps (up to a 15th), and the middle section a tender Andante. Celia urges Junia to marry Sulla ('Quando sugl'arsi campi'). Her cheerful A major is followed by the tragic D minor of Junia's soliloquy on the conflict of duty and love. She will kill herself rather than submit, and gasps out her despair in an agitated aria ('Parto, m'affretto') with a daring harmonic shift (Eb from G, the tonic being C) at the reprise.

The Capitol The chorus hopes that Sulla's glory will be crowned by love ('Se gloria il crin ti cinse'). Sulla publicly claims Junia as the token of civil peace; she is prevented from killing herself when Cecilius vainly attacks Sulla. In a trio ('Quell'orgoglioso sdegno') Sulla declares that he will humble his enemies, Cecilius is defiant, and Junia, joined by Cecilius, anticipates the consolation of death.

ACT 3 *Before the prison* Cinna excuses his failure to support a futile assassination attempt. He agrees to marry Celia if she can persuade her brother to have mercy; she promises to achieve this whatever storms arise ('Strider sento la procella'). Cinna expresses optimism (Cecilius has supporters) in a heroic aria in D ('De' più superbi il core'). Junia appears for a last farewell; she will not save Cecilius by yielding to Sulla. Aufidius comes to take Cecilius to public judgment; in a melting, rondo-like aria ('Pupille amate') in minuet tempo he says her tears will make him die too soon; his soul will return, dissolved in a sigh. Junia is left to her premonitions, her obbligato recitative richly scored and anticipating the motif of the aria ('Frà i pensier più funesti'), in which she imagines Cecilius dead, lamenting over a throbbing muted accompaniment; then with a determined Allegro she runs after her lover.

A hall in the palace The denouement takes place in simple recitative. Even as Sulla condemns Cecilius, Junia publicly proclaims her betrothal. Baffled, even moved, the tyrant decides to forgive her and permit the two couples to marry. He retires from public life (finale); the chorus praises his devotion to Rome, and the soloists sing of love and freedom.

* * *

Mozart constructed the first two acts cleverly, gradually abandoning the conventionally formed and very long arias liked in Milan for more flexible designs perhaps suggested by Gluck's *Alceste*. Despite the magnificent mausoleum scene, *Lucio Silla* remains an unreformed type of *opera seria*. Several D major arias with trumpets and drums are contrasted with remarkable richness of expression in the splendid roles of Cecilius and Junia, while Celia's lightly scored music provides relief.

'Lucio Silla' (Mozart), first scene of Act 1 (a neglected grove): design by Fabrizio Galliari for the original production at the Regio Ducal Teatro, Milan, 26 December 1772

Although its plot is turgid and its denouement unconvincing, *Lucio Silla* is musically the finest work Mozart wrote in Italy, and ranks with *opera seria* by the greatest masters of the time. JULIAN RUSHTON

Lucio Silla (ii) ('Lucius Sulla'). *Dramma per musica* in three acts by JOHANN CHRISTIAN BACH to a libretto by GIOVANNI DE GAMERRA adapted by MATTIA VERAZI; Mannheim, Hoftheater, 5 November 1775.

Two years after Mozart wrote his setting of *Lucio Silla* for Milan, Bach was commissioned to write an opera on the same libretto for Carl Theodor's court. But before the opera could be sent from London, part of the score was apparently lost by the palatine ambassador to England. The première was cancelled and the elector went to Rome in November 1774. A year later the opera was performed for the name-day of Carl Theodor, and although *Lucio Silla* was not as successful as Bach's earlier work for Mannheim, *Temistocle*, it was revived in November 1776 and was the last Italian *opera seria* given there before the court moved to Munich in 1778.

The libretto was adapted to the composer's needs, and the court poet, Verazi, made a number of improvements to the plot. The first and third acts were largely the same as in the original version, but the second was substantially revised to achieve a more logical sequence of events. The role of Sulla was expanded from two arias to four, because at Mannheim Bach had at his disposal the experienced tenor Anton Raaff. Bach's setting includes a new penultimate aria for Sulla, 'Se al generoso ardire', which is similar in position and scope to 'Torna la pace al core', Mozart's last aria for Raaff in *Idomeneo* (cut before the première). The opera featured all but one of the same singers as *Temistocle*: Raaff (Sulla), the sopranos Dorothea (Junia) and Elisabeth Wendling (Celia), Roncaglia (Cecilius) and G. B. Zonca (Cinna). In many details, *Lucio Silla* is similar in design to *Temistocle*. There are several concertante arias, and in general the writing for wind instruments is especially rich and varied. Although the work was not performed during his visit to Mannheim, Mozart was able to borrow a copy of the opera from G. J. Vogler.

The differences between the two settings of Cecilius's Act 3 aria 'Pupille amate', his supposed farewell to his beloved, are revealing: both, originally sung by soprano castratos, are in A major and 3/8 metre, but whereas Mozart's (ex.1*a*) is in a tender and pathetic style, Bach's

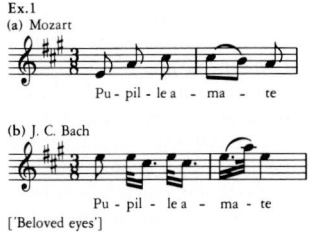

Ex.1
(a) Mozart

Pu - pil - le a - ma - te

(b) J. C. Bach

Pu - pil - le a - ma - te
['Beloved eyes']

is decorative and rather artificial (ex.1*b*). This may have been in Vogler's mind when he called it 'ridiculous' (see Mozart's letter of 13 November 1777).

PAUL CORNEILSON

Lucio Vero ('Lucius Verus'). Libretto by APOSTOLO ZENO, first set by C. F. Pollarolo (1700, Venice) and much re-used under a variety of titles.

The plot, taken from Roman history, deals with the Emperor Lucius Verus in Ephesus. He is promised to Lucilla, daughter of his co-emperor Marcus Aurelius, but is in love with his captive, Berenice, Queen of Armenia. Berenice is faithful to her betrothed, Vologeso [Vologeses], King of the Parthians, who was taken in battle. When Vologeses appears in the gladiatorial arena, she joins him. A lion threatens her, and Verus throws a sword to Vologeses, who kills it; Lucilla realizes that Verus loves Berenice. In Act 2, urged on by his friend Aniceto [Anicetus], Verus tries to separate the pair; Berenice would rather have Vologeses dead than become Verus's wife. Verus orders Vologeses' death, and Berenice resolves to die with him. Infuriated, Lucilla returns to Rome with her counsellor Claudio [Claudius] and enlists the Roman army against Verus. Act 3 begins in the Roman camp with military games in the form of a ballet. Meanwhile, Verus's servant Niso [Nisus] brings Berenice a basin covered with a black cloth. She believes it contains Vologeses' head, but as she lifts the cover the gloomy scene changes to a brilliant throne room: the basin contains a crown and sceptre. When Berenice still refuses Verus's advances, Verus orders Vologeses' death. Nisus reports that the people have turned against Verus, and that Lucilla is leading the Roman army in an attack; Verus stops the execution and is reconciled with Lucilla. Meanwhile Berenice, believing Vologeses dead, goes mad and is about to kill herself when Vologeses enters. He has uncovered a plot devised by Anicetus to gain Lucilla for himself. Verus apologizes and wishes the faithful couple well. The characters depart in separate ships during an antiphonal *coro* with sections for each pair.

Zeno's *Lucio Vero* was set at least 15 times under its original title (e.g. C. F. Pollarolo, 1700; Albinoni, 1713; Francesco Gasparini, 1719; Araia, 1735; Jommelli, 1754). G. E. Luccarelli's reworking for Rinaldo di Capua (1739, Rome) generated a series of librettos entitled *Vologeso* or *Vologeso re de' Parti* (Galuppi, 1748; Sarti, 1754; P. A. Guglielmi, 1775; Martín y Soler, 1783). As with others of Zeno's enduring librettos, the text was modified to conform with mid-century theatrical conventions. His aria texts of irregular lengths and the many short duets were replaced with conventional arias of two quatrains. Recitatives were shortened, the plot simplified and the number of arias reduced. Luccarelli shortened Act 3, though expanding Berenice's mad scene with the basin, and the sudden scene change becomes the climactic point, after which the plot quickly resolves to a concluding quintet. The scenes and arias following the amphitheatre scene in Act 1 are telescoped into a quartet for Verus, Berenice, Vologeses and Anicetus, and Act 2 ends with a duet for Vologeses and Berenice. Verazi's reworking for Jommelli (1766, Ludwigsburg), also called *Vologeso*, was based on the Luccarelli version; he heightened the mounting horror of Act 3 with two mad scenes for Berenice, the first when Verus sends Anicetus for Vologeses' head, the second with the basin. Vologeses appears with the Roman consul and army just as Berenice is refusing the crown and sceptre. Other settings of the libretto (or of reworkings of it) have been entitled *Lucio Vero, imperator di Roma* (Ariosti, 1727), *Lucius Verus* (Keiser, 1728) and *Berenice* (Perez, 1762).

For a list of settings *see* ZENO, APOSTOLO; *see also* VOLOGESO [Jommelli].

MARITA P. McCLYMONDS

Łuciuk, Juliusz (*b* Brzeźnica, nr Radomsko, 1 Jan 1927). Polish composer. He studied composition with Stanisław Wiechowicz in Kraków (1947–56) and with Max Deutsch and Nadia Boulanger in Paris. To some extent he has been left on the sidelines by more single-minded compatriots, even though his music has displayed many of the features of postwar avant-garde techniques, as well as anticipating the more recent return to diatonic elements. His predominantly lyrical talent has led to several works for vocal forces, such as the oratorio *St Francis of Assisi* (1976). His opera-ballet *Miłość Orfeusza* ('The Love of Orpheus', 1973) and the opera *Demiurgos* (1976) show his variegated musical personality. In *The Love of Orpheus* (in two parts, libretto by A. Świrszczyńska; Wrocław, State Opera, 23 February 1980), Łuciuk's lyric impulse is traditionally harnessed, although the four characters (Persephone, Eurydice, Orpheus and Hermes) are deliberately distinguished by carefully differentiated melodic lines. On the other hand, *Demiurgos* (one act, libretto by the composer) moves less conventionally in and out of the fantastic world of stories by Bruno Schulz (like Zbigniew Rudziński's *Manekiny*), absorbed in the power of creation and the dangerous consequences of heresy.   ADRIAN THOMAS

Lucius Papirius. Libretto subject popular in the 18th century.

Operas on the subject have been entitled *Lucio Papirio* and also *Quinto Fabio*. Livy, not the most reliable of the Roman historians, gives a unique account (vi.29–35) of a conflict between Lucius Papirius Cursor, military dictator during the second Samnite war, and Quintus Fabius Maximus Rullianus, his Master of Horse (*c*325 BC). Papirius left the field of battle briefly to retake the auguries in Rome, and though he left clear orders with Quintus Fabius neither to leave his post nor to engage the enemy, the youthful leader took advantage of the enemy's laxity and attacked, winning a great victory. Papirius, learning of those events, declared his will breached and military discipline at danger; he condemned Fabius to death. Fleeing first to the Roman Senate with his father (and former Roman dictator) Marcus Fabius, then pleading his case to the Roman people, Quintus Fabius sought to escape the dictator's wrath. In this he was supported by the army (the soldiers unsympathetic towards the merciless dictator) and the voice of the populace, but only when both father and son showed humility and pleaded for mercy did Papirius at last relent.

Two distinct versions of this account gained particular popularity as opera librettos during the 18th century: Antonio Salvi's *Lucio Papirio* (first set in 1714 by Francesco Gasparini for Rome) and Apostolo Zeno's *Lucio Papirio dittatore* (Caldara, 1719, Vienna). Besides the three principal characters, each supplied a dictator's daughter (Emilia in Salvi's libretto, Papiria in Zeno's), betrothed to Quintus Fabius, and other ancillary roles. In Salvi's drama each character is propelled by an uncompromising and sometimes tragic duty; Lucius Papirius himself mourns his chastisement of Quintus Fabius, and even minor characters (such as Appius, a tribune in love with Emilia) consistently temper their passions with virtue. At least 14 productions portrayed Salvi's poetry (including Leo's 1735 Naples setting, ascribed to Zeno). In Zeno's drama (whose outline generally follows Salvi's), Quintus Fabius is clearly constrained more by circumstance than

propelled by ambition; the enemy attacks and only on the advice of close counsellors does he finally repel and conquer the opposing army. The Zeno drama was the more popular, with over 20 productions (for illustration see BELLAVITE, INNOCENTE). In the 1770s another libretto, apparently adapted from both earlier versions, became particularly popular under the title *Quinto Fabio*, and was set by Anfossi, Bertoni and others.

See also QUINTO FABIO [Bertoni].   DALE E. MONSON

Lucrezia Borgia. *Melodramma* in a prologue and two acts by GAETANO DONIZETTI to a libretto by FELICE ROMANI after VICTOR HUGO's play *Lucrèce Borgia*; Milan, Teatro alla Scala, 26 December 1833.

One of the major successes of Donizetti's career, *Lucrezia Borgia* reflects Donizetti's interest in powerful melodramatic tragedy. He was attracted to the subject by the scene in Hugo's play in which the six coffins of Lucrezia's victims were suddenly revealed. The Milanese censors refused to allow the inclusion of this episode in the opera; indeed, the subject was at first regarded as so suspect that three years elapsed between the successful opening run at La Scala (with Henriette Méric-Lalande as Lucrezia, Marietta Brambilla as Orsini, Francesco Pedrazzi as Gennaro and Luciano Mariani as Alfonso) and its second production. For a time the work was given under a number of aliases; in one version the action was transferred to a non-Christian country.

For its second production at La Scala, in January 1840, Donizetti revised the final scene, adding an arioso for the dying Gennaro and eliminating Lucrezia's final cabaletta, as he thought it dramatically incongruous for a mother to sing a brilliant aria over a son whose death she has, albeit unwittingly, caused. From 1840 on, *Lucrezia Borgia* became one of the central works of the repertory, its vogue lasting until the end of the century. Famous Lucrezias have included Karoline Unger, Giulia Grisi, Therese Tietjens and, more recently, Montserrat Caballé. A number of complete recordings have reawakened interest in this powerful, if dated, work.

Gennaro (tenor) has come to Venice with his friends, among them Maffio Orsini (mezzo-soprano), Liverotto (tenor) and Vitellozzo (bass), to celebrate Carnival. His companions leave Gennaro behind; he lies down on a bench to rest. A masked woman enters and admires the sleeper affectionately (aria, 'Com'è bello!'), revealing that he is her son, although he is unaware of their relationship. When he awakens she questions him about his past; but when Gennaro's friends return he is horrified to learn from them that this beautiful creature is the infamous Lucrezia Borgia (soprano).

In Ferrara, Duke Alfonso (bass-baritone), Lucrezia's fourth husband, hopes to avenge his honour, having learnt from a spy that Gennaro is suspected of being Lucrezia's lover. Gennaro and his friends have come to Ferrara for adventure, but when he sees Lucrezia's crest on the façade of her palace he lops off the 'B', causing the emblem to read ORGIA. Indoors Lucrezia, furious at this insult, bids Alfonso avenge her. When Gennaro is brought in, Lucrezia fears for his safety, but she pretends to go along with her husband's plan of poisoning Gennaro, knowing that she has an antidote. When Alfonso leaves, Lucrezia gives her son the antidote and orders him to leave Ferrara at once. But before he can go, Maffio Orsini insists that he attend a ball at the

Princess Negroni's. There Orsini's carefree drinking song (brindisi, 'Il segreto per esser felici') is interrupted by sinister voices singing of death. Gennaro and his companions rush to the doors to escape but discover they are locked in. Clad in black, Lucrezia suddenly appears, declaring she has poisoned their wine to avenge the insult to her family crest. Believing that he had left Ferrara, she is horrified to see Gennaro among her victims. The others are led off, leaving Lucrezia with her son. She swears she never meant to harm him and pleads with him to drink an antidote (aria, 'M'odi, ah, m'odi'); Gennaro refuses, even when she reveals their relationship to him. He dies, and she swoons by his corpse.

In a number of significant ways *Lucrezia Borgia* anticipates Verdian *melos*. A dialogue duet over a sombre melody anticipates the scene between Rigoletto and Sparafucile. The interplay of the voices in the trio for Lucrezia, Gennaro and Alfonso looks forward to a number of Verdian terzettos, and the arioso for the dying Gennaro, 'Madre, se ognor lontano', prefigures the phrases of the dying Ernani.　　WILLIAM ASHBROOK

Ludi caesarei (Lat.: 'imperial games'). Type of Baroque theatre performed for the Habsburg court by the Viennese College of Jesuits; it was imitated by ecclesiastical establishments that supported schools throughout the Holy Roman Empire from the 17th century to the middle of the 18th. Its Latin dramas were in four or five acts, each consisting of two to seven scenes, the whole of which was enclosed by a prologue and epilogue. The plots of the principal plays, which were mostly spoken, dealt allegorically with world affairs or with ancient or modern history, and often contained patriotic elements. The prologue–epilogue would be sung and had its own separate cast of singers, as well as its own exegetic or 'parallel' plot. The additional insertion of *intermedia* between the acts of the main play resulted in three independent but synchronized plots slotted into one another. Music was confined to songs, choruses and ballets that were interspersed within, but mostly between, the acts; Mozart's *Apollo et Hyacinthus* K38, composed in 1767 for the Benedictine University theatre in Salzburg, is a late example.

O. Teuber and A. von Weilen: *Die Theater Wiens* (Vienna, 1896–1909)
W. Flemming: *Geschichte des Jesuitentheaters in den Landen deutscher Zunge* (Berlin, 1923)
G. Schünemann: *Geschichte der deutschen Schulmusik* (Leipzig, 1928)
F. Hadamowsky: 'Barocktheater am Wiener Kaiserhof, mit einem Spielplan (1625–1740)', *Jb der Gesellschaft für Wiener Theaterforschung, 1951–2*, 7–117
W. Flemming: *Das Ordensdrama* (Hildesheim, 2/1965)
H. Kindermann: *Das Theater der Barockzeit* (Salzburg, 2/1967)
V. Keil-Bodischowsky: *Die Theater Wiens* (Vienna, 1983)
　　　　　　　　　　　　　　ROBERT N. FREEMAN

Ludikar [Vyskočil], **Pavel** (*b* Prague, 3 March 1882; *d* Vienna, 19 Feb 1970). Czech bass. He trained first as a pianist, then studied singing with Jean Lassalle in Paris. From Prague, where he made his début in 1904 as Sarastro, he went to Vienna and then Dresden. At La Scala in 1911 he sang Ochs in the Italian première of *Rosenkavalier*; other roles there included Bluebeard in *Ariane et Barbe-bleue*, Falstaff in *Die lustigen Weiber von Windsor* and Pogner in *Meistersinger*. From 1913 until his return to Prague as director of the opera in 1935, his career was based in the Americas: he sang Hans Sachs in Boston, enjoyed considerable success at

the Colón, Buenos Aires, and was at the Metropolitan from 1926 to 1932. The great achievement of his later years in Prague was in Krenek's *Karl V* at its première in 1938. The few recordings of his voice have come to light have character but no great beauty of sound.

　　　　　　　　　　　　　　　　J. B. STEANE

Ludwig, Christa (*b* Berlin, 16 March 1928). German mezzo-soprano. The daughter of the singers Anton Ludwig and Eugenia Besalle, she studied with her mother and Felice Hüni-Mihaczek, making her début in 1946 as Orlovsky at Frankfurt, where she sang until 1952. After engagements at Darmstadt and Hanover, she joined the Vienna Staatsoper in 1955 and remained there for more than 30 years, creating Miranda in Martin's *Sturm* (1956) and Claire Zachanassian in Einem's *Besuch der alten Dame* (1971). Having first sung at Salzburg in 1954 as Cherubino, she took part in Liebermann's *Die Schule der Frauen* (1957) and returned there until 1981, when she sang Mistress Quickly. She made her American début in Chicago in 1959 as Dorabella. At the Metropolitan (1959–90) her roles included Cherubino, the Dyer's Wife, Dido in the first New York production of *Les Troyens* (1973), Fricka, Waltraute, Ortrud, Kundry, the Marschallin, Charlotte and Clytemnestra. At Bayreuth she sang Brangäne (1966) and Kundry (1967). She made her Covent Garden début in 1968 as Amneris, returning as Carmen (1976). She also appeared at Hamburg, Munich, Rome, San Francisco, La Scala and the Paris Opéra. Her repertory has included Leonore (*Fidelio*) and Lady Macbeth, as well as Monteverdi's Octavia, Eboli and Marie (*Wozzeck*). Her voice is rich, eventoned and expressive, and she is a compelling actress. Her many recordings include Dorabella under Böhm, Venus and Kundry for Solti and Ortrud for Kempe. From 1957 to 1971 she was married to the bassbaritone Walter Berry.

P. Lorenz: *Christa Ludwig, Walter Berry* (Vienna, 1968)
　　　　　　　　　　　　　　　　ALAN BLYTH

Ludwig, Leopold (*b* Witkowitz, Moravia, 12 Jan 1908; *d* Lüneburg, 24 April 1979). Austrian conductor. After studies at the Vienna Conservatory, his first engagements were in south Germany and at Brno. In 1936 he became music director of the Oldenburg Staatsoper and began to be a frequent guest in Berlin. He was appointed principal conductor of the Vienna Staatsoper in 1939 and principal conductor of the Berlin Städtische Oper in 1943. The appointment that brought him the widest international repute came in 1950, when he was appointed Generalmusikdirektor of the Hamburg Staatsoper, where he remained until 1971. He helped to broaden the company's repertory and also took it to the Edinburgh Festival in 1952 and to the Lincoln Center Festival, New York, in 1967; he made his American début with the San Francisco Opera in 1958 and conducted *Parsifal* at the Metropolitan in 1970. Ludwig conducted the first Glyndebourne production of *Der Rosenkavalier* in 1959. His performances of *Mathis der Maler* in 1967 reflected many of his virtues and failings: they evoked gratitude for the championship of a neglected and attractive work, admiration for the ability to build impressive orchestral effects and balance them skilfully with the stage action, but also astonishment at cuts so drastic that they changed the entire meaning of at least one crucial scene.　　BERNARD JACOBSON

Ludwig, Walter (*b* Bad Oeynhausen, 17 March 1902; *d* Lahr, 15 May 1981). German tenor. He studied singing while at Königsberg University and made his operatic début in 1928. At Schwerin he created the title role in *Friedemann Bach* by Graener (1931). He was the leading lyric tenor at the Berlin Städtische Oper, being particularly admired as Belmonte and Tamino, roles he sang at Glyndebourne (1935) and Salzburg (1948–50). Guest appearances took him to Paris, London, Barcelona and Vienna; other roles were Don Ottavio, Idomeneus, Loge and Wilhelm Meister. He taught singing in Berlin from 1952 to 1969.   DAVID CUMMINGS

Ludwig II (*b* Nymphenburg, nr Munich, 25 Aug 1845; *d* Lake Starnberg, nr Munich, 13 June 1886). King of Bavaria and patron of Richard Wagner (*see* WAGNER family, (1)). On ascending the Bavarian throne in 1864, at the age of 18, he befriended Wagner – whose works he admired with a passion bordering on neurosis – and initiated the generous financial support that allowed the composer not only to devote his energies to his ambitious projects (and to execute them without need for artistic compromise) but also to live in a state of luxury to which he had not previously been accustomed. There was indisputably an element of opportunism in Wagner's relationship with the king, and Ludwig's obsession with Wagner and his music was one reason for his neglect of affairs of state and resulting unpopularity. His patronage should, however, be put in perspective: the total amount received by Wagner over the 19 years of their acquaintance – including stipend, rent and the cash value of presents – was 562 914 marks, or less than one seventh of the annual Civil List.

G. von Böhm: *Ludwig II. König von Bayern* (Berlin, 1922)
O. Strobel, ed.: *König Ludwig II. und Richard Wagner: Briefwechsel*, v: *Neue Urkunden zur Lebensgeschichte Richard Wagners, 1864–1882* (Karlsruhe, 1939)
W. Blunt: *The Dream King: Ludwig II of Bavaria* (London, 1970)
M. and D. Petzet: *Die Richard Wagner-Bühne König Ludwigs II.* (Munich, 1970) [incl. correspondence with Ludwig's court secretary, Düfflipp]
C. McIntosh: *The Swan King: Ludwig II of Bavaria* (London, 1982)
S. Spencer and B. Millington, eds.: *Selected Letters of Richard Wagner* (London, 1987) [incl. 58 letters from Wagner to Ludwig in Eng. trans.]
            BARRY MILLINGTON

Ludwigsburg. Town in south-west Germany, 10 km north of Stuttgart, formerly the residence of the dukes of Württemberg (*see also* STUTTGART). The first court theatre opened in 1728, and under the Oberkapellmeister Giuseppe Antonio Brescianello occasional performances of Italian operas took place there. The period of greatest brilliance was during the reign of Duke Carl Eugen (from 1744), who maintained the highest artistic standards. The Schlosstheater was extended and renovated in 1752. With Jommelli as head of the opera company (1753–69) and Jean-Georges Noverre in charge of the ballet (1760–66), Ludwigsburg's fame quickly spread, the more so after a new opera house, one of the largest in Europe, was inaugurated in 1765. Here Jommelli's *Vologeso* (1766) and *Fetonte* (1768) were first performed. The court transferred back to Stuttgart in 1775, and the opera house was closed and later demolished, but during the summer occasional opera performances were given at the court theatre by members of the Stuttgart court opera. In 1810 the court theatre was completely rebuilt by the well-known architect Nikolaus Thoret. Opera performances were rare and petered out in the 1850s. Only in 1954, after a complete renovation of the court theatre (cap. 500), did opera become the backbone of the Ludwigsburger Schlossfestspiele. Special emphasis is laid on the operas of Mozart, given in German-language productions with young casts and conducted by the festival's artistic director Wolfgang Gönnenwein. A bigger theatre and concert building was felt necessary when the festival, which now lasts from May to early October, extended its scope. Hence the Forum am Schlosspark was built with two halls, of which the larger has 1248 seats and a stage with the same dimensions as that of the Stuttgart Staatsoper. Opened in 1988, it has presented productions of *Der Freischütz* and Philip Glass's *Einstein on the Beach*. During the winter it houses touring opera and ballet companies.

N. Stein: 'Ludwigsburg als Festspielstadt: ein Rückblick auf vergangene Höhepunkte ihres Musik- und Theaterlebens', *Almanach Ludwigsburger Schlossfestspiele: Internationale Festspiele Baden-Württemberg 1985*, 14–33
M. Strässner: *Die Ludwigsburger Schlossfestspiele* (Stuttgart, 1987)
            HORST KOEGLER

Ludwigshafen. City in south-west Germany, on the Rhine. It was founded in 1859. Its operatic history began in 1928 with the building of the Pfalzbau, which soon became a cultural centre, though dramatic performances were few at first. The Pfalzbau was destroyed in 1944, and for over 20 years theatrical performances took place in a former concert hall, until the new Pfalzbau was opened in 1968. The auditorium, with stalls and two circles, has 1171 seats, and the season runs from mid-September to early June. Until recently the Pfalzbau theatre had no company of its own, but staged guest performances. Since 1988 it has also presented its own productions, with a team specially engaged for opera. Opera performances occupy some 25 evenings a season; as a rule the repertory includes one modern and one or two Baroque or early Classical works. The city finances the theatre, with additional regional funding from the Rhineland-Palatinate for the Pfalzbau's own productions.   GÁBOR HALÁSZ

Luening, Otto (Clarence) (*b* Milwaukee, 15 June 1900). American composer and conductor. He began composing as a child under his father's tutelage, and then studied in Munich and Zürich before returning to the USA in 1920. In Chicago he conducted the American Grand Opera Company in Charles Wakefield Cadman's *Shanewis* and other works, which led to his appointment as executive director of the opera department at the Eastman School (1925–8). In Rochester he was also conductor of the American Opera Company, which commissioned his three-act opera *Evangeline* for the 1931 season. The company's disbandment prevented a production, but excerpts were given at the Arts Club of Chicago on 29 December 1932, when the opera was awarded the Bispham Medal. Luening later taught at the University of Arizona, Bennington College in Vermont, Barnard College, Columbia University, and the Juilliard School in New York. As director of opera production at Columbia, he conducted the premières of Menotti's *The Medium* and Thomson's *The Mother of Us All*, and the first complete performance of *Evangeline*, a revised version in a reduced orchestration, on 5 May 1948 at Brander Matthews Theater. Luening's large oeuvre includes orchestral, chamber, vocal and electronic music.

The long narrative poem by Longfellow on which Luening based his libretto for *Evangeline* follows the fortunes of two lovers separated when the British evicted the Acadians from Nova Scotia in the mid-1700s. *Evangeline* has much in common with other Americanist scores of the 1920s and 30s, though its roots lie in 19th-century grand opera rather than folk opera. Luening described it as 'a kind of documentary opera'. Two Guggenheim fellowships (1930–32) enabled him to retrace the wanderings of the exiled Acadians and study their music, snatches and echoes of which permeate his effusively lyrical score. One of the most vivid scenes, in which the priest urges the Acadians not to resist their deportation, skilfully incorporates the plainsong melody 'Ave maris stella'. Modal harmonies, mild dissonances and metrical instability help create what Henry Cowell, in a full and sympathetic analysis of the opera, called 'a tissue of small surprises'. In 1974 Luening added a narration and further revised the score for publication. The After Dinner Opera Company performed this version in New York on 8 February 1985.

H. Cowell: 'Current Chronicle', *MQ*, xxxiv (1948), 599–603

V. Thomson: 'Luening's "Evangeline" ', *New York Herald Tribune* (16 May 1948)

O. Luening: *The Odyssey of an American Composer* (New York, 1980), 307–19, 465–8
HARRY HASKELL

Lugo. Town in the Romagna region of northern Italy. Its first documented opera performances were in the period 1711–20, during the important annual commercial fair in August–September, possibly in a temporary theatre. Benedetto Marcello mentioned the town in his satirical pamphlet *Il teatro alla moda* (1720), and other seasons are documented for the period 1752–5. It was perhaps this intensification of activity that persuaded the municipality to construct a permanent theatre; the shell was built in 1758–9 by Francesco Petrocchi and it was equipped with 38 temporary boxes in two tiers. Pasquale Bondini's company performed *Il mercato di Malmantile* there during the 1759 fair season. The definitive furnishing of the auditorium on a bell-shaped plan (stage and scenographic equipment, 59 boxes in four rows and a gallery) was completed in 1761 by Antonio Galli-Bibiena. It opened during the fair that year with Florian Gassmann's *Catone in Utica*, and thereafter the opera season coincided with the fair. In 1819 Leandro Marconi dismantled the auditorium and built four rows of boxes (67 in all) and a stonework gallery on a truncated oval plan. Originally called the Teatro dell'Unione, or Pubblico (since it was communal property), in February 1859 it took the name of Rossini. It was restored and reopened in the late 1980s.

M. Rossi: *Cento anni di storia del teatro di Lugo, la patria di Rossini* (Lugo, 1916)

M. Rossi Ferrucci: *Cronistoria del teatro di Lugo, la patria di Rossini* (Imola, 1970)

C. Verlicchi: *Il 'Teatro Rossini' di Lugo* (diss., U. of Bologna, 1970–71)

D. Lenzi: 'Alcune note sull'attività di Antonio Galli Bibiena in Romagna', *Studi romagnoli*, xxiii (1972), 359–73

F. Farneti and S. Van Riel: *L'architettura teatrale in Romagna, 1757–1857* (Florence, 1975)

P. Fabbri: 'Teatri settecenteschi della Romagna estense: Lugo', *Romagna arte e storia*, iii (1983), 55–76

O. Savioli: *Cento anni di vita del Teatro Rossini di Lugo (1761–1861)* (diss., U. of Bologna, 1983–4)

G. Manzoni: *Spettacoli teatrali e altre manifestazioni culturali e folkloristiche in Lugo di Romagna dal 1711 al 1920* (Lugo, 1984)

P. L. Cervellati: *Il Rossini di Lugo: sul restauro di un celebre teatro* (Bologna, 1986)
PAOLO FABBRI

Lugo, Giuseppe (*b* Isola della Scala, nr Verona, 2 Nov 1898; *d* Milan, 18 Sept 1980). Italian tenor. After military service he emigrated to Belgium, where he was heard singing in a café and subsequently encouraged to study in Italy. Through his Belgian connections he made his début at the Opéra-Comique in Paris (1930) and remained a prime favourite there throughout the decade. Appearances at Bologna in 1936 led to an engagement at La Scala, where he sang till 1940. During the war he had considerable success throughout Italy and in films. His premature decline has been attributed to a disharmony between Italian and French methods, but personal difficulties and disappointments appear to have contributed. Recordings show a voice of fascinating quality; they and his short-lived triumph in *Tosca* at Covent Garden in 1936 suggest that promise exceeded achievement.
J. B. STEANE

Luigini, Alexandre (Clément Léon Joseph) (*b* Lyons, 9 March 1850; *d* Paris, 29 July 1906). French conductor and composer of Italian descent. He won the *second prix* for violin at the Paris Conservatoire in 1869 and from that year led the orchestra of the Grand-Théâtre at Lyons; he was appointed its chief conductor in 1877. In 1897 he became a conductor of the Opéra-Comique in Paris. His one-act *opéra-comique Les caprices de Margot* (to a libretto by Coste) was given at the Grand-Théâtre, Lyons, on 13 April 1877, and the operetta *Faublas* (in three acts, libretto by E. Cadol and G. Duval) at the Théâtre Cluny, Paris, on 25 October 1881. He also composed many ballets, orchestral music and chamber works.

G.-M.-J. Vuillermoz: *Cent ans d'opéra à Lyon* (Lyons, 1932)
DAVID CHARLTON

Luigino, Il. *See* ALBARELLI, LUIGI.

Luik (Flem.). LIÈGE.

Luini [Luino, Loini, Luvini, Lovini], **Domenico** (*b* ?Brescia, *fl* 1748–73). Italian soprano castrato. He made his début in secondary roles in *opera seria* at Rome in Carnival 1748, then sang in Italy up to Carnival 1755, sometimes as primo uomo, sometimes as secondo. He may then have been at Bayreuth and in Berlin, returning for Italian engagements early in 1759, before going to Russia as primo uomo of the court opera, where Casanova found him 'handsome and extremely agreeable', though quarrelling incessantly with his mistress, the prima donna Colonna. Luini was in Russia until at least 1769, but by July 1770 he was back in Brescia, where Burney met him, rich but gambling heavily. He returned to the Italian stage in autumn 1772 (Florence) and for Carnival 1773 (Turin).
DENNIS LIBBY

Luisa Fernanda. Lyric comedy in three acts by FEDERICO MORENO TORROBA to a libretto by FEDERICO ROMERO and GUILLERMO FERNÁNDEZ SHAW; Madrid, Teatro Calderón, 26 March 1932.

The action is set in the mid-19th century, in the troubled time of Isabella II, during the strife between royalists and republicans. Luisa Fernanda (mezzo-soprano) is being courted by Vidal (baritone), a rich landowner, but is in love with Javier (tenor), a young philanderer from the locality who has risen to the rank of colonel in the royal hussars. Vidal joins the republican cause so as to oppose his rival. When Javier's wayward fancy is taken by the queen's lady-in-waiting, the duchess Carolina (soprano), Luisa decides to accept Vidal, who genuinely loves her. In a brief revolt the republicans and Vidal capture Javier and call for his death, but Luisa pleads for him, and shortly afterwards the arrival of his hussars saves him. In Act 3 Luisa is at Vidal's estate in Extremadura preparing for her marriage when news arrives that the queen has been dethroned and has fled, with the duchess Carolina, to Portugal. Javier, now humbled, appears and pleads his love anew; Luisa cannot stifle her feelings, and Vidal, saddened, relinquishes her to exile with Javier.

Considered one of the finest of 20th-century zarzuelas, *Luisa Fernanda* has also been one of that repertory's greatest successes, receiving over a thousand performances before the outbreak of the Spanish civil war. Apart from the many attractions of the score, including the Act 1 duet for Javier and Carolina, the Act 2 mazurka, a romance for Vidal and the final duet 'Subir, subir', the work owed its initial popularity to its topical parallel, appearing as it did only a year after the declaration of the 1931 Republic.　　　　LIONEL SALTER

Luisa Miller. *Melodramma tragico* in three acts by GIUSEPPE VERDI to a libretto by SALVADORE CAMMARANO after FRIEDRICH VON SCHILLER's play *Kabale und Liebe*; Naples, Teatro S Carlo, 8 December 1849.

Count Walter	bass
Rodolfo *his son*	tenor
Federica *Duchess of Ostheim, Walter's niece*	contralto
Wurm *Walter's steward*	bass
Miller *a retired old soldier*	baritone
Luisa *his daughter*	soprano
Laura *a peasant girl*	mezzo-soprano
A Peasant	tenor

Federica's ladies-in-waiting, pages, retainers, archers, villagers

Setting The Tyrol, in the first half of the 17th century

Verdi's relationship with Naples, never entirely happy, continued inauspiciously during the late 1840s: in 1848, despite his efforts to withdraw, the Neapolitan authorities held him to a longstanding contract for a new opera at the S Carlo. The librettist was to be Salvadore Cammarano, resident poet at the theatre and a man of vast experience in both the practical and the artistic side of operatic production. Verdi's first idea was for a setting of Francesco Guerrazzi's recent historical novel, *L'assedio di Firenze*, a large-scale subject designed to suit the dimensions of the S Carlo and, one imagines, intended to follow the line of Verdi's current preoccupation, *La battaglia di Legnano*. However, by April 1849 this idea – hardly surprisingly given the counter-revolutionary political climate – had been rejected by the Neapolitan censors. Cammarano then suggested using Schiller's *Kabale und Liebe*, a play Verdi himself had earlier considered. The composer accepted, although not without asking for a considerable number of structural alterations to the synopsis Cammarano sent him (not all of which the poet, who was no Piave in matters of acquiescence, agreed to).

Negotiations had thus far been undertaken with Verdi in Paris. In the late summer of 1849 he returned to Italy to work on *Luisa Miller* (as Schiller's play had been retitled); he arrived in Naples in late October to supervise the staging of the opera, first performed some five weeks later. The première, whose cast included Marietta Gazzaniga (Luisa), Achille De Bassini (Miller), Antonio Selva (Walter) and Settimio Malvezzi (Rodolfo), was probably a success (press reports are lacking), but even though the opera received a respectable number of revivals it never attained the popularity of *Nabucco* or *Ernani* and faded from the repertory later in the century. *Luisa* was 'rediscovered' in the 1920s as part of the German Verdi 'renaissance' and has subsequently become – with *Nabucco*, *Ernani* and *Macbeth* – one of the few Verdi scores written before 1850 to enjoy a firm place in the international repertory.

The overture, in C minor, is unlike any other Verdi wrote in that it is monothematic and built primarily around a process of modulation rather than on a succession of contrasting melodies; the composer's clear intention was to emulate a Germanic, 'symphonic' movement rather than the usual, Italian potpourri type. Moments such as the feint towards G minor in the exposition, or the unusual modulations of the retransition, show that Verdi was perfectly able to understand and reproduce such symphonic devices when the mood took him.

ACT 1: 'Love'

1.i *A pleasant village* A pastoral atmosphere is immediately created by the orchestra's 6/8 movement and prominent wind writing, and is confirmed by the chorus's simple, rocking melody 'Ti desta, Luisa', which bids Luisa awake on a beautiful April dawn. Miller and Luisa enter, Miller casting doubts on his daughter's relationship with 'Carlo', an unknown young man who has arrived with the new Count. Luisa expresses her naive love in the cavatina 'Lo vidi, e 'l primo palpito', which is simple and cabaletta-like, continuing elaborate woodwind effects in the accompaniment. Villagers present Luisa with flowers and 'Carlo' (Rodolfo in disguise) emerges from the crowd. The lovers join Miller in a closing terzetto, 'T'amo d'amor ch'esprimere', Miller avoiding the main melody to mutter his suspicions and discontent in a staccato counter-theme.

As the stage clears, Miller is detained by Wurm, who angrily demands Luisa's hand in marriage. In the spacious, conventionally organized Andante, 'Sacra la scelta è d'un consorte', Miller insists that his daughter will make her own choice of husband. But Wurm reveals the true identity of 'Carlo' and Miller bursts into a cabaletta of rage and grief, 'Ah! fu giusto il mio sospetto!'.

1.ii *A room in Walter's castle* Walter and Wurm are in mid-conversation, Wurm having told the Count of Rodolfo's involvement with Luisa. When Wurm leaves, Walter releases his confused paternal feelings in the minor–major *romanza* 'Il mio sangue, la vita darei', another expanded form in which the major section takes an unexpected plunge back into minor reflections. Rodolfo appears and his father orders him to marry the recently widowed Duchess Federica. Before Rodolfo can explain his predicament Federica appears, heralded by a delicate chorus, 'Quale un sorriso d'amica sorte'. Federica and Rodolfo are left alone, and the Duchess admits her love in the first movement of a two-movement duet (the Andante 'Dall'aule raggianti'),

which begins lyrically but diverts into fragmentary dialogue as Rodolfo admits he loves another. The ensuing cabaletta, 'Deh! la parola amara', confirms their divided position.

1.iii *A room in Miller's house* An offstage chorus tells of a hunt in progress. Luisa is anxiously awaiting 'Carlo' but is instead confronted by her father, who reveals her lover's true identity and his forthcoming marriage. Rodolfo intervenes to swear his continuing love, telling Miller he knows a terrible secret that will protect them from the Count's wrath. Walter himself arrives to precipitate the first movement of the concertato finale, an Allegro dominated by a driving violin melody reminiscent of the overture theme. Walter summons soldiers and orders the arrest of Miller and his daughter, ignoring both the protests of Miller and Rodolfo and the entreaties of Luisa. The ensuing Andantino, the central lyrical movement 'Fra' mortali ancora oppressa', allows the principals to present their differing reactions with unusual definition. The act then quickly comes to a close: in an arioso of gathering intensity Rodolfo pleads with his father and, at the climax, threatens to reveal the dreadful secret. Walter immediately frees Luisa, the chorus thanks heaven, and the curtain falls with no concluding stretta.

ACT 2: 'The Intrigue'

2.i *A room in Miller's house* (as 1.iii) Villagers rush on and in a formal narrative tell Luisa that her father has been taken to prison. As they disperse Wurm enters and tells Luisa that, to save her father, she must write a letter to Wurm's dictation, saying that she never loved Rodolfo and now wishes to elope with Wurm. Before signing the letter, Luisa offers a prayer, the famous 'Tu puniscimi, o Signore', an Andante agitato remarkable for its lack of formal repetition. Wurm continues his demands: that she will swear the letter is her own and that she loves Wurm. She closes the scene with

a cabaletta, 'A brani, a brani, o perfido', that swings from minor to major as she moves from anticipation of death to the thought that her father will be at hand to minister to her final moments.

2.ii *Walter's room in the castle* Walter, brooding, is joined by Wurm, who tells him of the progress of their plot against Luisa. They join in a narrative duet, 'L'alto retaggio non ho bramato', recalling their murder of the old Count and Rodolfo's discovery of the secret. The duet begins with an objectivity typical of operatic narrative, but becomes increasingly fragmented as the description of events unfolds, culminating in the cabaletta-like 'O meco incolume' in which Walter vows to protect Wurm or accompany him to the gallows.

Federica appears and Wurm is dismissed. Walter tells her that Rodolfo is now ready to marry, and produces Luisa who in a dialogue movement controlled by orchestral melody denies Rodolfo and declares her love for Wurm. This last statement precipitates the lyrical Andante 'Come celar le smanie', unusual in its complete lack of orchestral accompaniment.

2.iii *The castle gardens* Rodolfo now has Luisa's infamous letter, and sorrowfully reminisces in the famous Andante 'Quando le sere al placido', an early example of Verdi's use of the French *couplet* form. Wurm appears and Rodolfo challenges him to an immediate duel, which Wurm evades by firing his pistol into the air and rushing off. Walter appears with some followers and, after Rodolfo has told him of Luisa's 'betrayal', Walter persuades his son to marry Federica as revenge. Rodolfo, in a confusion of distress, closes the act with the cabaletta 'L'ara, o l'avello apprestami'.

ACT 3: 'The Poison'

A room in Miller's house (as 1.iii) An orchestral reminiscence of past themes introduces 'Come in un giorno solo', in which the villagers lament Luisa's sorrowful countenance. Luisa, who exchanges words with the chorus while writing a letter, is joined by Miller, who has learnt from Wurm the true nature of her sacrifice. Their ensuing duet is in the usual four movements, during the first of which Miller discovers that Luisa's letter proposes a suicide pact with Rodolfo. In the second movement, the Andantino 'La tomba è un letto', Luisa returns to her naive, first-act musical style as she looks forward to an innocent grave while Miller counters with an impassioned plea in the parallel minor. The movement ends with Luisa tearing up the letter; there is a heartfelt reconciliation, and father and daughter join in a cabaletta, 'Andrem, raminghi e poveri', in which they look forward to leaving the village to live a simple, wandering existence.

As Miller departs, Luisa hears an organ from a nearby church; she kneels in prayer. Rodolfo enters and in a long, passionate recitative full of violent orchestral interjections forces her to admit to writing the letter; then he shares with her a drink which he has surreptitiously poisoned. The duet moves into regular musical periods at the Andante, 'Piangi, piangi, il tuo dolore', whose lyricism seems all the more intense for having so long been denied in the duet. Rodolfo admits that he has poisoned them both; Luisa at last feels free to confess her deception, and they join in the stretta, 'Maledetto il dì ch'io nacqui', Rodolfo cursing the day he was born, Luisa trying to comfort him. The arrival of Miller, who quickly discovers all, leads to a terzetto finale, 'Padre, ricevi l'estremo addio', at the close of which Rodolfo, seeing Luisa fall dead, kills Wurm before himself collapsing by the side of his beloved.

*   *   *

For that perceptive early critic of Verdi, Abramo Basevi, *Luisa Miller* marks the beginning of Verdi's 'second manner', one in which he drew more on Donizetti's example and less on Rossini's, and in which his musical dramaturgy took on a more subtle and varied form. Modern commentators have sometimes endorsed this judgment, signalling the opera as an important step towards *Rigoletto*. However, while the rustic ambience of the opera undoubtedly called forth from Verdi a new and compelling attention to local colour, it is difficult to see in the formal aspect of *Luisa* an essential stylistic turning-point, particularly when compared with *Macbeth*, which had appeared two years earlier. Nevertheless, few would argue about the opera's important position among pre-*Rigoletto* operas: not so much for its formal experiments as for its control of conventional musical forms, especially the grand duet. And in this respect, the middle-period work *Luisa* most resembles is not *Rigoletto* but *Il trovatore*, whose driving energy within conventional contexts is apparent through much of the earlier opera, in particular in its final act.

ROGER PARKER

Lulier, Giovanni Lorenzo [Giovanni del Violone, Giovanni del Violoncello] (*b* Rome, *c*1665; *d* Rome, *c*1704). Italian composer. His dramatic compositions include at least six operas (four of which were collaborations). The first, *L'Agrippina*, was planned for performance at the Tordinona theatre in Rome during the 1691 carnival, but the production was cancelled because of the death of Pope Alexander VIII. According to Pitoni (*c*1725; see Ruini), Lulier was 'a Roman who studied counterpoint [before 1680] with Pier Simone Agostini, played the cello superbly, served Ottoboni as a chamber composer and died soon after 1700 at an early

age [*in età fresca*]'. He was admitted to the Accademia di S Cecilia in 1679 and from March 1681 to March 1690 was the manager (*aiutante di camera*) of Cardinal Pamphili's musical establishment. He entered the service of Cardinal Ottoboni in 1690 and was still there in 1700, according to the title-page of the *componimento drammatico La Gloria, Roma e Valore* (1700, Rome; *D-Hs*; written in collaboration with G. M. Pertica). While in the service of these cardinals he played the continuo or concertino cello part in works by Corelli and his other colleagues. His own compositional style is similar to Corelli's, in that his relatively brief arias are tuneful with contrapuntal accompaniments.

[L'Agrippina], 1691 (?3, dramma per musica, G. De Totis), ?unperf., arias *D-MÜs*, *I-Fc*, *Rli*, *Rvat*
La Santa Genuinda overo L'innocenza difesa dall'inganno [Act 1] (dramma sacro per musica, 3, ? P. Ottoboni), Rome, Palazzo della Cancelleria, ?carn. 1694, *D-Mbs*, *F-Pc*, *GB-Lbl* [Act 2 by A. Scarlatti, Act 3 by C. F. Pollarolo]
Il Clearco in Negroponte [Act 2] (dramma, 3, after A. Arcoleo), Rome, Capranica, 18 Jan 1695, arias *D-MÜs*, *I-Bmalvezzi*, *Rc*, *US-NYlibin* [Act 1 by B. Gaffi, Act 3 by C. F. Cesarini]
L'amore eroico fra pastori [Act 2] (favola pastorale for puppets, 3, Ottoboni), Rome, Palazzo della Cancelleria, Feb 1696 [Act 1 by Cesarini, Act 3 by G. Bononcini]; rev. A. Scarlatti as La pastorella, also for puppets, Rome, Palazzo del Ambasciator di Venezia, 5 Feb 1705, arias *GB-Lbl*; rev. P. A. Motteux and V. Urbani as Love's Triumph, London, Queen's, 26 Feb 1708, 70 arias (London, 1708)
Fausta restituita al impero (dramma per musica, 3, after N. Bonis: Odoacre), Rome, Tordinona, 19 Jan 1697, arias *D-MÜs*, *GB-Lbl*, *Ob*, *I-Rc*
Temistocle in bando [Act 1] (dramma per musica, 3, after A. Morselli), Rome, Capranica, 2 Feb 1698, arias attrib. Lulier *Bc*, anon. arias *B-Br*, *F-Pc*, *Pn*, *GB-Lbl*, *Lcm*, *Ob* [Act 2 by ? M. A. Ziani, Act 3 by Bononcini]

*

Grove6 (O. Jander); *MGG* (H. J. Marx)

L. Montalto: *Un mecenate in Roma barocca: il Cardinale Benedetto Pamphili (1653–1730)* (Florence, 1955)
H. J. Marx: 'Die Musik am Hofe Pietro Kardinal Ottobonis unter Arcangelo Corelli', *AnMc*, no.5 (1968), 104–77
—— : 'Die "Giustificazioni della Casa Pamphili" als musikgeschichtliche Quelle', *Studi musicali*, xii (1983), 145–61
S. Franchi: *Drammaturgia romana: repertorio bibliografico cronologico dei testi drammatici pubblicati a Roma e nel Lazio, secolo xvii* (Rome, 1988)
C. Ruini, ed.: *G. O. Pitoni: Notitia de' contrapuntisti e compositori di musica* [MS, *c*1725] (Florence, 1988), 339
F. Carboni, T. M. Gialdroni and A. Ziino: 'Cantate ed arie romane del tardo seicento nel Fondo Caetani della Biblioteca Corsiniana: repertorio, forme e strutture', *Studi musicali*, xviii (1989), 58–9, 115–17
H. J. Marx: '"… da cantarsi nel Palazzo Apostolico": Römische Weihnachtsoratorien des 17. Jahrhunderts', *Musikkulturgeschichte: Festschrift für Constantin Floros* (Wiesbaden, 1990), 415–24

LOWELL LINDGREN

Lully. French family of composers.

(1) Jean-Baptiste Lully [Lulli, Giovanni Battista] (*b* Florence, 29 Nov 1632; *d* Paris, 22 March 1687). French composer of Italian birth. He was the first important composer of French opera, the omnipotent director of the Paris Opéra, and the creator of the *tragédie en musique*.

1. Life and achievements. 2. *Tragédies en musique*: (i) Components of dramatic scenes (ii) Larger-scale organization (iii) *Divertissements* and prologues.

1. LIFE AND ACHIEVEMENTS. Lully was a miller's son, who perhaps studied the guitar as a child in Florence. He was taken to Paris in 1646 to serve as a *garçon de chambre* for the king's young cousin Mlle de Montpensier, who wished to practise speaking Italian.

While employed at her court, located at the Tuileries, he was exposed to a full range of cultural activities and had the opportunity to meet and study with important musicians, both French and Italian. He may have attended the production of Luigi Rossi's *Orfeo* at the royal court in 1647. By the time he left Mlle de Montpensier's employ in 1652 to take a position at the court of King Louis XIV, he had certainly become a virtuoso violinist and accomplished dancer and had perhaps studied composition and keyboard instruments.

In March 1653 Louis appointed Lully *compositeur de la musique instrumentale*; Lully thus began a fruitful career as composer of court ballets, in which he also danced alongside the king and courtiers. At first he composed only the instrumental portions, but that arrangement quickly changed. His numerous ballets, most of which were written in collaboration with the poet Isaac de Benserade, date mainly from between 1657 and 1671. (The two ballets from the 1680s – *Le triomphe de l'Amour* and *Le temple de la Paix* – are more operatic in structure than the early ones and were performed at the Paris Opéra as well as at court.) On three occasions Lully and Benserade composed ballet entrées to occur between the scenes of Italian operas produced at court: in 1654 (in collaboration with other composers) for Caproli's *Le nozze di Peleo e di Theti*; in 1660 for Cavalli's *Xerse*; and in 1662 for Cavalli's *Ercole amante*. Very early in his court career, before 1656, Lully took control of the string ensemble called the 'petits violons' or 'petite bande', an offshoot of the '24 violons du Roi', and taught the players a type of group discipline virtually unknown previously; he thus took an important step towards the invention of the modern orchestra.

On the strength of these various successful activities Lully was able to consolidate his power at court: in 1661 (the year he became a naturalized French citizen) he was appointed both *surintendant* and *compositeur de la musique de la chambre du roi*; and in 1662 he acquired the succession to the post of *maître de la musique de la chambre*. At the time of this last appointment he married Madeleine Lambert, daughter of his long-time mentor, the composer Michel Lambert. He now turned his attention to a new genre: from 1664 to 1670, while continuing to write ballets with Benserade, he collaborated with Molière on a series of *comédies-ballets*, which combined spoken comedy with singing and dancing. Virtually all the musical elements that would later make up his operas may be found in the ballets and *comédies-ballets* of the 1660s. Lully's first motet also dates from 1664, though he apparently composed most of his religious music during the 1680s.

Lully was thus a senior member of the court's artistic establishment when, in 1669, the poet Pierre Perrin obtained a royal monopoly to form an Académie d'Opéra (later known as the Académie Royale de Musique) for the purpose of producing operas in Paris. At first Lully was unconcerned. According to the unsuccessful legal suit that Perrin's associates would later bring against him, Lully had 'always claimed that opera was something particular to Italy and impossible to execute in our language'. The 'claim' was perhaps disingenuous. It is more likely that Lully's reluctance to compose operas had stemmed from the French courtiers' lack of interest in the Italian operas that Cardinal Mazarin had brought to France; only the machines, scenery and added French ballet entrées had held their attention. At all events, when Lully saw that

the initial production by the new Académie was an enormous success he changed his mind.

Lully had little difficulty convincing the king to withdraw the monopoly from Perrin and give it to him, and Perrin offered no resistance: thanks to the unscrupulous dealings of his business partners, he was in a debtors' prison, and the possibility of selling his right to run the Académie offered a way to regain his freedom. The transfer occurred in March 1672 and was followed by four months of unsuccessful legal challenges by Perrin's associates.

According to the terms of Lully's *lettres patentes* from the king, the primary purpose of the Académie was the king's personal entertainment; in theory, all the operas were to be staged first at court, then before the public in Paris. In practice, for a variety of reasons, about half of Lully's operas received their premières in Paris and were heard only later at court. The court productions, which involved a combination of the king's musicians and performers from Lully's Paris troupe, were in well-equipped theatres at St Germain-en-Laye and Fontainebleau and in temporary theatres at Versailles. In Paris, Lully started out in a temporary location, but in 1673 he received permission to move into the theatre in the Palais Royal that had previously been occupied by Molière's troupe (Molière himself had just died). Despite the Académie's nominal financial independence, Lully paid the court no rent for use of the theatre in the Palais Royal; and the scenery and machines prepared for court productions, at royal expense, were re-used in Paris.

From the time he received the monopoly until his death 15 years later, the main thrust of Lully's professional activity was the composition and production of operas, approximately one per year. Although he largely left the costumes, scenery and machinery to specialists (Carlo Vigarani and Jean Bérain), he insisted on controlling every activity at the Académie, including even the romantic liaisons of his singers. Le Cerf de la Viéville claimed that Lully taught the singer Beaupui to act one of his roles 'gesture by gesture', that he showed his dancers what he wanted by demonstrating the dances himself, and that he had the final word on the content of the librettos. According to Dubos, he composed his own steps and figures for the chaconne in *Cadmus et Hermione*, having rejected the choreography supplied by his ballet-master, Pierre Beauchamps. Ironically, one activity Lully was willing to entrust to his secretaries (again according to Le Cerf) was the composition of the inner parts in homophonic textures, except in particularly 'important' pieces.

Lully's insistence on military precision in the orchestra, including the famous 'premier coup d'archet' (the first bowstroke at the beginning of the overture), was reported by Georg Muffat and others. Le Cerf cited the rhythmically difficult 'Entrée des songes funestes' from *Atys* as Lully's standard audition piece for violinists. Le Cerf and others also reported Lully's violent intolerance of added ornamentation by either instrumentalists or singers, a situation exacerbated by his willingness to allow his father-in-law Michel Lambert, who was famous for writing *airs* with ornamental *doubles*, to coach the singers.

The Paris Opéra (the familiar name for the Académie Royale de Musique) became a fashionable gathering place, where opera enthusiasts returned to see their favourite works over and over again. According to Titon du Tillet, Lully's tunes were whistled on the Pont

Neuf, and Le Cerf claimed that 'every cook in France' could sing 'Amour, que veux-tu de moi' from *Amadis*. Starting in 1677, each new opera (except *Psyché*) was published under the composer's direction, *Isis* in part-books and the others in full score. It was during this period of enormous public success that Lully was allowed to purchase the office of *secrétaire du roi*, thereby acquiring noble rank; from 1681 he gave his surname as 'de Lully'.

From immediately after his death and continuing well into the 18th century, Lully's operas were produced in numerous cities all over Europe. At the Paris Opéra they remained in the repertory until the 1770s.

2. TRAGÉDIES EN MUSIQUE. Lully and his librettist, PHILIPPE QUINAULT, invented a new genre, the *tragédie en musique* (which came to be called *tragédie lyrique* around the mid-18th century). It shares certain superficial characteristics with French spoken tragedy of the time, notably its five-act structure and heroic (i.e. noble) characters, usually from ancient mythology, who work out their problems in conversations with their confidants. However, it is far closer in spirit to the 17th-century French *pastorale*. Some of the librettos have sad endings, but few even pretend to focus on such tragic themes as the conflict between love and duty (*Roland* and *Armide* are two such). In fact all the plots revolve around the vicissitudes of love, and their love intrigues are worked out in an atmosphere laden with magic, divine intervention and scenic transformation. Yet these operas were judged by the standards of tragedy. Comic scenes, like those of Italian opera, were deemed so unseemly that they disappeared after 1675. The routine violation of unity of place was tolerated, but only because the *merveilleux* (the supernatural element) made normal questions of verisimilitude irrelevant: gods on stage machinery could go anywhere during the entr'actes.

The *tragédie en musique* was a veiled allegory of life at court. Louis XIV is overtly praised only in the prologues (where, however, he is never explicitly named), yet nearly every hero can be understood as a symbol for the king. In dedicating *Persée* to Louis XIV, Lully referred to the hero as 'the image of Your Majesty'. (The king had chosen the subject of *Persée*; he also chose those for the three librettos, *Amadis*, *Roland* and *Armide*, based on tales of medieval chivalry.) The costumes worn by the female protagonists were little more than court dress with exotic decoration. The oblique reference to the court led to Quinault's disgrace in 1677, when two ladies (the king's mistress in particular) saw themselves portrayed unflatteringly in *Isis*; Lully was obliged to collaborate temporarily with Thomas Corneille until Quinault returned to favour.

(i) Components of dramatic scenes. At the heart of Lully's operatic style is a supple, expressive type of recitative, which combines characteristics of Italian recitative, French *airs de cour* and French theatrical declamation. The melodic contour is a gentle singsong that superficially resembles that of mid-17th-century Italian recitative. The harmonic support, however, is different: Lully's bass line makes genuine counterpoint with the voice, usually in a fast harmonic rhythm. Even a slow-moving bass supporting an extended arpeggio in the voice is likely to move through several harmonies in a tonally directed fashion (compare exx.1 and 2).

Although French spoken tragedies were written en-

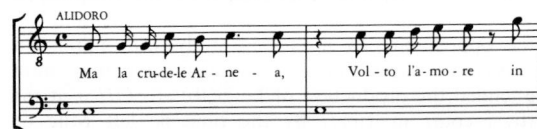

Ex.1 Antonio Cesti: *Orontea*, Act 1 scene ix

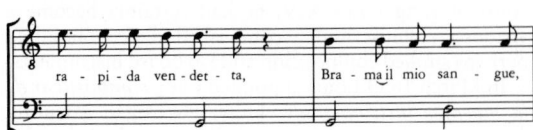

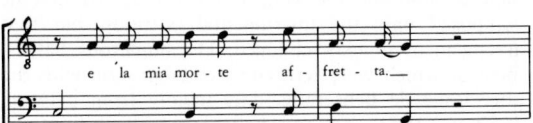

['But the cruel Arnea, changing from love to raging vengefulness, longed for my blood and hastened my death.']

Ex.2 Lully: *Cadmus et Hermione*, Act 1 scene iii

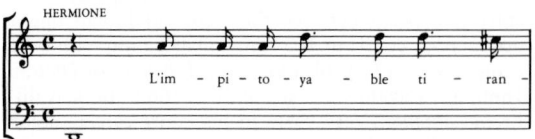

['The relentless tyranny whose barbarous laws I flee, does not forbid fondness for song and harmony.']

tirely in 12-syllable alexandrines, opera librettos used *vers libres*, a free mixture of lines of different lengths. Lully placed the fixed poetic accents – that is, the final rhyming syllables in all lines and the internal caesuras in long lines (see the asterisks in the examples) – on notated strong beats, usually downbeats. Only feminine rhyme coinciding with a strong cadence routinely violates this rule (see, in ex.2, 'harmo*nie*', rhyming with 'tiran*nie*'). While the fixed accents in the poetry nearly always coincide with points of metrical stress in the music, the mobile secondary accents might be brought out in the recitative by pitch or by agogic, harmonic or metric accents of varying strength (in ex.3 compare 'Ah', 'bien', 'moy' in bar 4, and '(char)mans'). The expressive nature of this recitative lies in its subtle variety. In ex.4, for instance, the cowardly First Prince

Ex.3 *Roland*, Act 3 scene ii

['Ah! At least allow me the one good thing left to me; allow me the fatal sweetness of seeing such delightful charms.']

Ex.4 *Cadmus et Hermione*, Act 3 scene i

['It serves you right to be prudent.']

Ex.5 *Roland*, Act 4 scene iv

['To the place where Médor was dying alone, Angélique directed her steps. She knew how to use a skill whose power protected Médor from death.']

responds to a longwinded warning of danger with two clipped cadential motifs; in context their dismissive effect is humorous.

In setting *vers libres* to music Lully followed the tradition of the 17th-century *air de cour*, in which frequent alternation between bars of duple and triple metre, even in the middle of phrases, reflects a virtual absence of metrical regularity in the poetry. Since the bar-lines are determined by the irregular accentuation of the verse, it is not surprising that passages of recitative designed to approximate to speech rhythms are notated with frequent changes of metre. The metrical fluctuations are not, as is sometimes said, purely notational – the bars notated in triple metre contain music in triple metre – but the subtle interplay of fixed and secondary accents in the poetry means that the listener usually cannot tell where the bar-lines come.

On the other hand, the changing line-lengths of the poetry in no way necessitate changing musical metre: in many passages Lully chose to adjust the surface rhythms in order to impose metrical regularity on the music despite its absence from the poetry, and he did so without violating his rules of bar-line placement (see ex.5, in which alexandrines and octosyllables alternate). The recitative is normally categorized according to metrical regularity, using terminology proposed by Pierre Estève in 1753: *récitatif simple* (more declamatory, with fluctuating metre) and *récitatif mesuré* (more lyrical, with regular metre). Frequent hemiola, a general trait of Lully's music, often has implications for text expression (e.g. ex.5, bars 10–12).

In general, the interpretation of the fluctuating metres is based on the principle of the equivalence of beats (stated by Etienne Loulié, *c*1696), which applies to vocal music only. This is illustrated by ex.3, where the crotchets in 3 and C and the minims in 2 are all equal in length. There are, however, numerous passages in Lully's recitatives and *airs* in which the juxtaposition of

the signatures 2 and ₵ or 3 and 3/2 apparently indicates some sort of tempo change, or in which an apparently unnecessary metrical change appears at a moment of surprise or other dramatic disjunction, perhaps simply to encourage a change of character in the interpretation (see Rosow, 'The Metrical Notation of Lully's Recitative', 1987).

Le Cerf de la Viéville's claim that Lully compared his recitative to the declamation of the actress La Champmeslé must be understood in the light of the known chronology of his works: Lully had developed his operatic recitative in the ballet *récits* and *comédies-ballets* of the 1660s, well before La Champmeslé came to prominence in 1670; the essential traits of the style existed by 1668. Whatever he learnt from her must represent a late refinement. Anecdotal evidence suggests that the dramatist Racine, who occasionally emphasized the mobile secondary accents in an alexandrine more strongly than the fixed caesura, taught La Champmeslé to exploit the anomalous accentuation of such verses when declaiming them. Lully and his librettists occasionally did the same. In ex.6, where the structural

Ex.6 *Acis et Galatée*, Act 2 scene i

['He is leaving me! Stop, Acis, I command you.']

caesura occurs at 'arrestez' and the mobile accents at 'quitte' and 'Acis', the poet left the phrasing ambiguous (is it 'arrestez, Acis' or 'Acis, je vous ordonne'?); Lully used metre and other forms of accentuation, including the introduction of a rest that prevents the normal elision of 'quitte' to 'arrestez', to resolve the ambiguity. Whatever the significance of Le Cerf's remark, it is only one of several 18th-century anecdotes comparing Lully's recitative to good tragic declamation.

Lully's attitude towards syllable 'quantity' needs further investigation. 'Long' and 'short' syllables (see Tunley 1984) usually receive appropriate relative weight in both *airs* and recitatives, but there are occasional exceptions, and they involve such pronounced accentuation of 'short' syllables and occur in such prominent positions – a recurring refrain, for instance – that the attempt by Grimarest (*Traité de récitatif*, 1707) to explain them away as unintentional faulty text-setting is unconvincing (e.g. *'Et vous me laisserez mourir'*, *Atys*, 1.vi; or *'De la felicité parfaite'*, *Armide*, 4.ii).

The term 'air', not adequately defined in early writings about Lully's operas, is generally understood to refer to brief passages that are tonally unified and involve text repetition, usually in a binary, ternary or rondeau pattern. The tables of *airs à chanter* preceding Henri de Baussen's editions of Lully's operas (1708–11) support this definition but also include a few important passages of solo recitative, whether monologues or extended speech within dialogues (e.g. *Armide*, 'Un songe affreux', 1.i; 'Enfin il est en ma puissance', 2.v; 'Il m'aime', 3.ii; Baussen, of course, meant to serve the practical needs of amateur singers). The difficulty in defining 'air' is exacerbated by the stylistic similarity of *airs* and recitatives: just as the recitatives tend to be lyrical, the *airs* tend to be declamatory. The first few tragedies include some *airs* with delicately ornamental melodies (ex.7) – and occasionally even recitatives are

Ex.7 *Alceste*, Act 1 scene iv

['To see a girl who changes her mind']

ornamented this way for word-painting purposes (end of ex.2) – but from the late 1670s onwards nearly all *airs* were entirely syllabic, apart from melismas for word-painting (e.g. 'chaîne') and melismas on the so-called 'privileged' words 'triomphe' and 'gloire'. Early commentators often avoided the question of categorizing a particular passage as 'recitative' or 'air' by using the general term *récit*, meaning any passage for solo voice or voices.

Lully borrowed the form of the so-called extended binary *air* from Italian composers such as Luigi Rossi: a quatrain of poetry is extended by the repetition, with different music, of the last two lines. The resulting three-phrase form, which sometimes covers more than four lines of poetry (see ex.8), may be represented by *ABb*, where *B* and *b* have the same words but *B* ends in a secondary key and *b* returns to the tonic. (The form is usually shown as *ABB'*. The use of the lower-case *b* to indicate poetic but not musical identity with *B*, adopted by Renée Girardon in her writings on Destouches' operas, is more accurate: since they contain the same words, *B* and *b* are virtually identical in rhythm, but the melody is not always similar.) Brief extended binary *airs*

Ex.8 *Amadis*, Act 5 scene i

['It is carrying perseverance too far to obey such severe laws without resisting; sometimes Cupid takes offence at too much obedience.']

are ubiquitous in Lully's dramatic dialogue. Equally common is a variant in which the initial phrase is repeated literally: *AABb*. Other binary formulae appear as well. Though binary *airs* are usually metrically regular and often evoke dance rhythms, they occasionally contain shifts in metre to accommodate poetic accentuation.

Brief conversational *airs* in ternary and rondeau forms appear occasionally during dialogues, but the most important *airs* in these forms occur in monologues, where they are usually weightier than Lully's other *airs*. Lully often used ternary and rondeau forms for emotional outpourings and invocations by distressed protagonists (e.g. ternary form in *Armide*, 3.i; rondeau in *Isis*, 5.i). The refrains are metrically regular and very short (usually one or two phrases), while the episodes are longer and declamatory – indeed, no different rhythmically from *récitatif simple*. Internal instrumental ritornellos, as in some of Cavalli's ternary-form arias, occur only rarely.

Ensembles are generally through-composed and just a few phrases in length. The great majority are duets, using various combinations of voice-types. Of these the most expressive are the love duets, usually between soprano and *haute-contre*. (Ex.9 shows an ironic use of

Ex.9 *Amadis*, Act 2 scene v

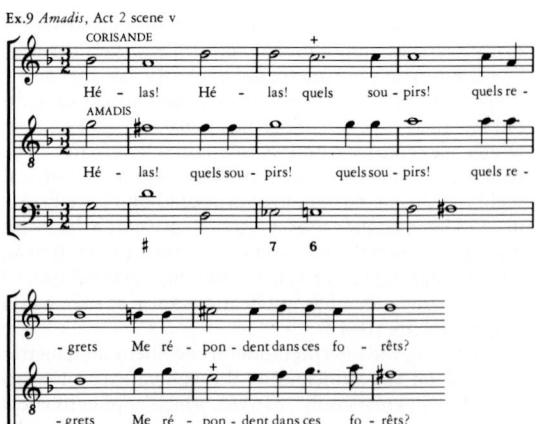

['Alas! Alas! What sighs, what sorrows echo mine in this forest?']

the genre: the lovesick participants' sighs are not about each other, and the two characters identify each other only after the duet has ended.) Some scenes made up of solo and duet fragments (e.g. *Cadmus et Hermione*, 4.vi; *Alceste*, 2.viii; *Armide*, Prologue) show the influence of the *airs de cour* in dialogue form by Lambert and others. Elsewhere, like-minded pairs of characters, such as Doris and Idas in *Atys*, 3.ii, might speak together in homorhythmic duet fragments throughout a recitative scene.

Instrumental passages occur mainly in two textures: a trio for two treble parts (woodwind or violins) and continuo, emphasizing parallel 3rds or 6ths between the upper parts; and five-part homophony. The five-part orchestra, based on the '24 violons du Roi', used violins and *basses de violon* (an 8' instrument) as the outer voices, with violas in three sizes for the harmonic filling; double reeds usually doubled the outer voices, though recorders occasionally substituted for the oboes (or shawms) in the treble part. Lully's continuo group included harpsichord, theorbos, *basses de violon* and bass viols.

Introductory three-part instrumental pieces are usually called *ritournelles*; those in five parts are usually called *préludes*. These introductions, despite their brevity, are often highly expressive and introduce the emotional content of the ensuing vocal passages, for instance by using jagged rhythms and wide intervals in a moment of high drama, as in *Armide*, 2.v. Concerning the noble gestures and facial expressions of Lully's greatest soprano, Marthe Le Rochois, Titon du Tillet wrote that 'she understood marvellously well what is called the *ritournelle*, which is played during the time that the actress enters and presents herself to the theatre'. If the character who enters is a deity, the *ritournelle* or *prélude* might accompany a descent by a machine (e.g. Mercury's entrance, *Proserpine*, 1.ii). Sometimes a *prélude* prefigures the music of the *air* that follows.

The orchestral imagery associated mainly with *divertissements* often spills over into dramatic scenes. In *Persée*, 4.ii, for instance, the dialogue is interrupted by a tempest, and the rising waves are painted in a *symphonie*, the undulating bass line of which continues during the ensuing duet (where it becomes a rising melisma on 'soulève').

In the early operas solo voices are virtually always accompanied by continuo alone. The only exception is the 'doubled continuo *air*' (after M. F. Bukofzer, *Music in the Baroque Era*, 1947), in which two treble instruments and continuo accompany a sung bass line. The resulting trio texture admits a wide range of expressive possibilities; in *Alceste*, for instance, Charon's humorous circle-of-5ths shopkeeper's chant 'Donne, passe' (4.i) and Aeolus's soothing undulation in the highest part of the *basse-taille* range (1.ix) both belong to this genre. Later, starting tentatively with brief passages in *Bellérophon* and *Proserpine* (1679–80), Lully often accompanied important *airs* and passages of recitative with the string orchestra (without woodwind doubling). The last few operas contain occasional lengthy scenes that rest on a seamless orchestral underpinning, with accompanied recitative or *air* flowing directly into *symphonie*. In one case the use of continuous accompaniment led Lully to experiment with form: Renaud's monologue *air de sommeil* in *Armide*, 2.iii, is in a miniature ritornello form with modulating vocal episodes. (He had tried something similar, using only an instrumental trio, in Mercury's *air de sommeil* in *Persée*, 3.ii.)

It has been incorrectly implied that *récitatif mesuré* is routinely accompanied by the orchestra. The confusion probably results from Estève's definition of 1753, which claimed that this more lyrical sort of recitative was used to give vent to strong emotion. The statement is inapplicable to Lully's operas, where there is no consistent relationship between metrical regularity and emotional content in the recitative. In 18th-century scores and parts, 'mesuré' (not 'récitatif mesuré') was used simply to indicate a metrically regular passage where the singer was expected to maintain a steady beat. In Lully's works these passages might or might not involve heightened emotion, and might or might not have orchestral accompaniment.

After Lully's death there developed the unfortunate practice of publishing and copying his operas in *partition réduite*, with inner parts omitted except at imitative entries (trio passages were given in full). Whether composed by Lully or, as Le Cerf de la Viéville claimed, by his secretaries, the inner parts are often expressive in their textural flexibility (ex.10) and are certainly not dispensable.

Ex.10 *Thésée*, Act 2 scene vi

(ii) Larger-scale organization. Lully's dramatic dialogue is typically set as a fluid mixture of brief *airs* and passages of recitative, along with occasional short duets or other ensembles. Monologues, though more likely to consist of single *airs* or single extended passages of recitative, might also mix the two settings. Brief instrumental passages introduce and occasionally punctuate the scenes, and there might be choral interjections as well. Not only the brevity of *airs* and *symphonies* but also the frequency of cadences makes this a shortbreathed style.

Lully's music is in a virtually constant state of gentle modulation (see exx.2, 3 and 5). However, because of the brevity of musical units – *airs*, passages of recitative marked by important points of articulation, instrumental passages – the music always returns to the home key after very few phrases. The affective nature of some of Lully's modulatory progressions, when coupled with his tendency to place the third of the triad in the top voice at certain moments of harmonic resolution, results in a characteristic sweetness (see ex.10, bars 3–4).

Despite some use of contrasting closely related keys, a single key generally dominates a scene. A dramatic turning-point, which might occur within an individual scene but which usually occurs at the entrance or exit of characters to mark the beginning of the next scene, will be accompanied by definitive modulation to a new home key, often announced by a brief descent in the bass line (ex.11) or perhaps by a slightly longer 'prélude' for con-

Ex.11 *Armide*, Act 4 scenes i to ii

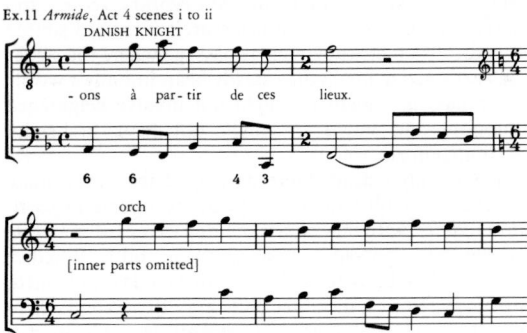

['(He will urge us) to leave this place.']

tinuo alone. These connecting links in the bass are an evocative musical realization of the requirement of scene 'liaison' in French classical drama, usually met by keeping at least one character on stage as others enter and exit.

Because of the stylistic similarity between *airs* and recitatives (and the frequency of cadences in both), it is often hard to distinguish the beginning of an *air* from the preceding recitative. In some cases the start of the *air* is clearly marked by metre; texture marks the beginning of a doubled continuo *air*. Often, however, one perceives the closed formal unit only in retrospect. The ambiguity is enhanced by Lully's frequent use of the *Bb* closing formula of the extended binary *air* simply to close off several phrases of recitative, bringing the passage back to its opening key (e.g. *Amadis*, 1.ii, Florestan's lines 'Fils d'un Roy ... pas tant aimé'); and by his frequent use of widely spaced recurring cadential phrases, evocative of rondeau refrains, to give a coherent structure to long passages of recitative (e.g. *Alceste*, 1.i, Alcides' hemistich 'Je partiray trop tard'; *Atys*, 1.vi, Attis's lines 'Vous me condamnerez vous même/Et vous me laisserez mourir').

Equally ambiguous is the division of labour between recitatives and *airs* within dialogues. There is no italianate suspension of time during the *airs*; a conversation consisting of a series of clearcut ideas might well be made up of several adjacent *airs*. Paul-Marie Masson (*L'opéra de Rameau*, 1930) gave the name 'maxim *airs*' to the many little statements of principle, usually facile, that are normally sung by secondary characters (ex.8); these *airs* routinely occur as part of conversations. The observation that jilted lovers represented by basses sing doubled continuo *airs* when they are most deceived (Howard 1989) might be mentioned in this context: when they are most deceived, they sing one-dimensional, over-simplistic ideas, just the sort usually represented in brief *airs*. Elsewhere, however, Lully used the contrast between *air* and recitative within dialogue to highlight central themes of the drama: in *Armide*, 5.i, the lovers' differing opinions of Glory as Armide's rival are stated as a pair of adjacent *airs* in C major, preceded and followed by recitative in C minor.

Lully used his short-breathed units to build large-scale scenes with coherent shape and clearly highlighted dramatic moments. He did so by clever placing of strong cadential phrases, whether isolated or recurring; closing formulae involving text repetition; beginnings both vague and clearly marked (the latter perhaps by the repeated phrase at the start of an *AABb air* or perhaps by a metrical or textural change); brief *symphonies* (which occasionally recur); and recurring choral or solo fragments within the dialogue.

(iii) Divertissements and prologues. Each act of a *tragédie en musique* contains an event that serves as an excuse for pure spectacle, a 'diversion' from the dramatic dialogue. The *divertissements* are miniature ballet scenes: their musical, dramatic and spectacular components were borrowed from the court ballet tradition, which, in turn, borrowed from both French pastoral drama and Italian opera. Among the topics are mythological events (such as Pan's pursuit of Syrinx, *Isis*, Act 3) and other purely pastoral scenes, civic and heroic ceremonies, battle scenes, weddings and other festive celebrations, invocations leading to magical ceremonies, funerals and underworld scenes. The stock participants include not only shepherds, citizenry, major and minor deities, magicians, priests and ghosts but allegorical figures such as Sleep, Hatred, the Hours of the Day, Baleful Dreams and personifications of winds and rivers. Certain musical images occur repeatedly: the *sommeil* (sleep piece) with murmuring recorders and strings; the invocation sung in wide, jagged intervals; monsters and Furies, presented in fast runs and dotted rhythms; the image of water, painted by undulating strings; that of wind, painted by imitative strings in running semiquavers; martial imagery using trumpets and timpani; and rustic imagery using oboes and bassoons. Sometimes a small number of costumed instrumentalists joined the singers and dancers on stage. Grotesque female figures were represented by male performers; thus, Hatred in *Armide* is a tenor role. Before 1681, the year professional female dancers first appeared on the stage of the Paris Opéra, all the dancers were men, including those representing attractive females.

The lengthy prologues to Lully's tragedies, which praise Louis XIV (referring to him only as an unnamed 'Hero') and refer to topical political events, are essentially extended *divertissements* in content and structure. Their characters (e.g. Victory, Peace, Felicity, Abundance) often explore the king's virtues in dialogues consisting of solo and duet fragments. The prologues of *Atys*, *Psyché*, *Persée*, *Amadis*, *Roland* and *Armide* include poetic references to the tragedies themselves. Other prologues include indirect references; for instance, the Sun (understood to represent Louis XIV) in the Prologue to *Cadmus et Hermione* expresses impatience with grand sacrifices, as does Mars in the tragedy (3.vii).

Most dance pieces in Lully's tragedies are in binary form; many are rondeaux. Contrary to common misperception, phrases of irregular length are common. The dances are written in the same two orchestral textures as the *ritournelles* and *préludes*, and alternation between the five-part orchestra and a three-part woodwind ensemble often occurs during individual dance pieces. The titled dances include bourrées, canaries, chaconnes, gavottes, gigues, loures, marches, minuets, passacailles, passepieds, rigaudons and sarabandes; by far the most frequent are minuets and gavottes. Another common genre, though usually untitled, is the *entrée grave*, danced to music resembling the opening section of a French overture. Untitled dances, labelled simply 'air' or 'entrée', are very common. These were often the basis for pantomime, described in the librettos (e.g. 'The followers of Hatred zealously break and burn Cupid's weapons', *Armide*, 3.iv). Dubos commented on this 'jeux muet' in Lully's *divertissements*, saying that gesture and demonstration replaced ordinary dance steps. Since masks were a normal part of the dancers' costumes, the gestures were never facial.

Dancing also occurred during the choruses. The members of the chorus, who neither gestured nor occupied centre stage, provided the voices of collective characters whose actions were represented by the dancers. The large soprano section, composed of women, falsettists and boys, dominated the four-part chorus. The three lower sections were composed entirely of men: *hautes-contre* (very high tenors), low tenors and basses. The typical large-scale choral piece involves a free alternation between two essentially homophonic choral textures – four-part with orchestral doubling and three-part with continuo, the latter made up of first sopranos, second sopranos and *hautes-contre* – along with occasional interludes for instrumental trio. Brief pieces labelled 'petit choeur' use the high-pitched trio texture alone. Choreography might reflect these textural changes, as in the first chorus in the Prologue to *Armide*, where the trio phrases were danced by females representing 'followers of Wisdom' and the four-part phrases by males representing 'followers of Glory'. There are occasional double choruses (e.g. *Isis*, 3.vi), in which not merely two textures but two separate groups of singers alternate, perhaps overlapping at phrase endings. Finally, there are some four-part all-male choruses, the highest part being for *hautes-contre* (e.g. the choir of 'divinitez infernales' in *Proserpine*, 2.ix).

Airs and duets in *divertissements* are often in fully symmetrical closed forms, such as binary with both sections repeated literally, and many are strophic. Just as *airs de scène* (dramatic *airs*) tend to share characteristics with recitative, *airs* in *divertissements* usually have the rhythmic traits of dance pieces. According to Le Cerf de la Viéville, the music for many of these dance-songs preceded their texts. Lully wrote 'canevas' for them – verses outlining the rhythm to guide the poet. In some cases, both sung and purely instrumental versions exist side by side (e.g. *Persée*, Prologue, passepied 'La grandeur brillante').

The action of the *divertissements* is always fully integrated into the drama itself, but the necessity for that action varies: in *Armide* the civic festival celebrating Armide's beauty and power (Act 1) could easily be omitted, whereas Hatred's preparations to 'remove the Love from Armide's breast' (Act 3) are essential to the plot. Some *divertissements* are entirely self-contained, while others seem to spill over into the dramatic action; the entire fourth act of *Isis* is structured as a series of small *divertissements* alternating with small dramatic passages.

Lully's manner of building long scenes out of a mosaic of tiny units, some of which recur, takes on a particularly high degree of symmetry and unity in many of the *divertissements* and prologues. Recurring passages and patterns of scoring (such as *récit* followed by chorus followed by dance) combine to make large-scale complex designs, for example the *sommeil* scene of *Atys* (3.iv) and the Prologue to *Isis*. The entire pattern of small units is sometimes superimposed on variations in paired phrases over a ground bass, as in the *passacaille* of *Armide* (5.ii). The normal reprise of the overture at the end of the Prologue further demonstrates Lully's concern for large-scale symmetry.

See also Acis et galatée; Alceste (i); Amadis; Armide (i); Atys (i); Cadmus et hermione; Fêtes de l'amour et de bacchus, les; Isis; Persée; Phaëton; Proserpine; Psyché; Roland (i); and Thésée; *see further* Bellerophon.

Editions: *Les chefs-d'oeuvres classiques de l'opéra français*, ed. T. de Lajarte (Paris, 1878–83) [L]
         J.-B. Lully: Les oeuvres complètes, ed. H. Prunières (Paris, 1930–39) [P]
         French Opera in the 17th and 18th Centuries, ed. B. Brook (New York, 1984–) [FO]
         J.-B. Lully: Collected Works, ser. 3: *Major Dramatic Works*, ed. C. B. Schmidt (in preparation)
Catalogues: *Chronologisch-thematisches Verzeichnis sämtlicher Werke von Jean-Baptiste Lully*, ed. H. Schneider (Tutzing, 1981) [LWV]
         A Catalogue Raisonné of the Literary Sources for the Tragédies Lyriques of Jean-Baptiste Lully: Lully Livret Catalogue, ed. C. B. Schmidt (New York, in preparation) [LLC]

Principal MS sources are in *F-Pc*, *Pn*, *Po* and *V*; those formerly in *GB-T* are now in *F-Pn*, *V*, *US-STu* and elsewhere. For specific source information see LWV, LLC and Schmidt (1987–8). For arrangements of instrumental and vocal airs see LWV.

tragédies en musique, in a prologue and five acts, unless otherwise stated; printed works published by Ballard in Paris, unless otherwise stated

LWV	title (genre, acts)	libretto	performances	publication; edition; remarks
47	Les fêtes de l'Amour et de Bacchus (pastorale, prol., 3)	P. Quinault, I. de Benserade and President de Périgny, after Molière and Lully (LWV 33, 38, 42, 43)	Paris, Jeu de Paume de Béquet, ?10 Nov 1672	full score (1717); FO ii
49	Cadmus et Hermione	Quinault, after Ovid: *Metamorphoses*	Paris, Jeu de Paume de Béquet, 27 April 1673	full score (1719); L xx, P i
50	Alceste, ou Le triomphe d'Alcide	Quinault, after Euripides: *Alcestis*	Paris, Opéra, 19 Jan 1674	reduced score (Baussen, 1708; 1727); L xvi, P ii
51	Thésée	Quinault, after Ovid: *Metamorphoses*	St Germain-en-Laye, 11 Jan 1675; Paris, Opéra, April 1675	full score (1688), reduced score (Baussen, 1711); L xxvi
53	Atys	Quinault, after Ovid: *Fasti*	St Germain-en-Laye, 10 Jan 1676; Paris, Opéra, April 1676	full score (1689), reduced score (Baussen, 1708); FO iii, L xviii
54	Isis	Quinault, after Ovid: *Metamorphoses*	St Germain-en-Laye, 5 Jan 1677; Paris, Opéra, Aug 1677	part books (1677), full score (1719); L xxi

LWV	title (genre, acts)	libretto	performances	publication; edition; remarks
56	Psyché	T. Corneille, after Apuleius: The Golden Ass	Paris, Opéra, 19 April 1678	full score (1720); L xxv, ed. in Turnbull (1981)
57	Bellérophon	Corneille and B. le Bovier de Fontenelle, after Hesiod: Theogeny	Paris, Opéra, 31 Jan 1679	full score (1679), reduced score (1714); L xix
58	Proserpine	Quinault, after Ovid: Metamorphoses	St Germain-en-Laye, 3 Feb 1680; Paris, Opéra, 15 Nov 1680	full score (1680), reduced score (1715); L xxiv
60	Persée	Quinault, after Ovid: Metamorphoses	Paris, Opéra, 17 or 18 April 1682	full score (1682), reduced score (Baussen, 1710); FO v, L xxii
61	Phaëton	Quinault, after Ovid: Metamorphoses	Versailles, 6 Jan 1683; Paris, Opéra, 27 April 1683	full score (1683), reduced score (Baussen, 1709); L xxiii
63	Amadis	Quinault, after Montalvo, adapted by N. Herberay des Essarts, Amadis de Gaule	Paris, Opéra, 18 Jan 1684	full score (1684), reduced score (Baussen, 1711); P iii
65	Roland	Quinault, after L. Ariosto: Orlando furioso	Versailles, 8 Jan 1685; Paris, Opéra, 8 or 9 March 1685	full score (1685), reduced score (Baussen, 1709)
71	Armide	Quinault, after T. Tasso: Gerusalemme liberata	Paris, Opéra, 15 Feb 1686	full score (1686), reduced score (Baussen, 1710); FO vi, L xvii, ed. F. Martin (Geneva, 1924)
73	Acis et Galatée (pastorale-héroïque, prol., 3)	J. G. de Campistron, after Ovid: Metamorphoses	Anet, 6 Sept 1686; Paris, Opéra, 17 Sept 1686	full score (1686)
74	Achille et Polyxène [ov. and Act 1]	Campistron, after Homer: Iliad	Paris, Opéra, 7 Nov 1687	full score (1687); collab. P. Collasse [prol., Acts 2–5]

Comédies-ballets etc. (collab. Molière unless otherwise stated; principal sources in *D-B, Sl, F-B, Pa, Pc, Pn, Po, V, GB-Cfm, Lbl, US-BE*, see also LWV): Le mariage forcé (comédie-ballet, 1), Paris, Louvre, 29 Jan 1664; La princesse d'Elide (comédie-ballet, 5), Versailles, 8 May 1664; L'Amour médecin (comédie-ballet, prol., 3), Versailles, 14 Sept 1665; La pastorale comique (comédie-ballet, 1), St Germain-en-Laye, 5 Jan 1667; Le sicilien, ou L'Amour peintre (comédie-ballet, 1), St Germain-en-Laye, 14 Feb 1667; George Dandin (comedy with ballet intermèdes, 3), Versailles, 18 July 1668; La grotte de Versailles (eclogue, 1, Quinault), Versailles, Aug 1668 (Paris, Opéra, Nov 1685, as Eglogue de Versailles); Monsieur de Pourceaugnac (comédie-ballet, 3), Chambord, 6 Oct 1669; Les amants magnifiques (comédie-ballet, 5), St Germain-en-Laye, 7 Feb 1670; Le bourgeois gentilhomme (comédie-ballet, 5), Chambord, 14 Oct 1670; Psyché (tragédie-ballet, 5, Molière, Quinault and P. Corneille), Paris, Tuileries, 17 Jan 1671; Le triomphe de l'Amour (ballet, 20 entrées, Quinault and Benserade), St Germain-en-Laye, 21 Jan 1681 (Paris, Opéra, 10 May 1681); Idylle sur la paix (divertissement, 1, J. Racine), Sceaux, 16 July 1685 (Paris, Opéra, Nov 1685); Le temple de la paix (ballet, 6 entrées, Quinault), Fontainebleau, 20 Oct 1685 (Paris, Opéra, Nov 1685)

GENERAL

Grove6 (J. R. Anthony); *PEM* (H. Schneider)

Recueil général des opéra, i–iii (Paris, 1703)

J. L. Le Cerf de la Viéville: *Comparaison de la musique italienne et de la musique françoise* (Brussels, 1704–6)

C. Parfaict and F. Parfaict: *Histoire de l'Académie royale de musique* (MS, 1741, *F-Pn* nouv. acq. fr.6532) [1835 copy with annotations by L.-F. Beffara, *Pn* fr.12.355]

——: *Dictionnaire des théâtres de Paris* (Paris, 1756, 2/1767 with G. d'Auguerbe)

L.-F. Beffara: *Dictionnaire de l'Académie royale de musique* (MS, 1783–4, *Po* Rés.602)

T. de Lajarte: *Bibliothèque musicale du théâtre de l'Opéra*, i (Paris, 1878)

H. Prunières: *Lully* (Paris, 1909, 2/1927)

L. de La Laurencie: *Lully* (Paris, 1911, 2/1919)

R. Rolland: *Musiciens d'autrefois* (Paris, 3/1912, Eng. trans., 1915, as *Some Musicians of Former Days*)

L. de La Laurencie: *Les créateurs de l'opéra français* (Paris, 1921, 2/1930)

E. Gros: *Philippe Quinault* (Paris, 1926)

E. Borrel: 'Jean-Baptiste Lully', *Euterpe: cahier bimestriel*, no.7 (1949), 1–109

A. M. Nagler: 'Lully's Opernbühne', *Kleine Schriften der Gesellschaft für Theatergeschichte*, xvii (1960), 9–26

A. Ducrot: *Recherches sur Jean-Baptiste Lully (1632–1687) et sur les débuts de l'Académie royale de musique* (diss., Ecole de Chartes, 1961)

J. R. Anthony: *French Baroque Music from Beaujoyeulx to Rameau* (London, 1973, 2/1978)

N. Dufourcq: 'Lully: l'oeuvre, à la diffusion, l'héritage', *XVIIe siècle*, nos. 98–9 (1973), 109–21

R. Scott: *J.-B. Lully: the Founder of French Opera* (London, 1973)

P. Howard: *The Operas of Lully* (diss., U. of Surrey, 1974)

——: 'The Académie Royale and the Performances of Lully's Operas', *The Consort*, xxxi (1975), 109–15

P.-M. Masson: 'French Opera from Lully to Rameau', *NOHM*, v (London, 1975), esp. 206–26

J. E. W. Newman: *Jean-Baptiste de Lully and his Tragédies Lyriques* (Ann Arbor, 1979)

L. Rosow: *Lully's Armide at the Paris Opéra: a Performance History, 1686–1766* (diss., Brandeis U., 1981)

T. M. Turnbull: *A Critical Edition of Psyché: an Opera with Words by Thomas Corneille and Philippe Quinault, and Music by Jean-Baptiste Lully* (diss., U. of Oxford, 1981)

L. Bianconi: *Il seicento* (Turin, 1982; Eng. trans., 1987, as *Music in the Seventeenth Century*)

S. Pitou: *The Paris Opéra: an Encyclopedia of Operas, Ballets, Composers, and Performers*, i (Westport, CT, 1983)

R. Fajon: *L'Opéra à Paris du Roi Soleil à Louis le Bien-Aimé* (Geneva, 1984)

L'avant-scène opéra, no.94 (1987) [*Atys* issue]

W. Brooks: 'Lully and Quinault at Court and on the Public Stage, 1673–86', *Seventeenth-Century French Studies*, no.10 (1988), 101–21; suppl. note, no.11 (1989), 147–50

SOURCES

L. de La Laurencie: 'Une convention commerciale entre Lully, Quinault et Ballard en 1680', *RdM*, ii (1920–21), 176–82

P. Mélèse: *Répertoire analytique des documents contemporains ... concernant les théâtres à Paris sous Louis XIV* (Paris, 1934)

H. M. Ellis: 'The Sources of Jean-Baptiste Lully's Secular Music', *RMFC*, viii (1968), 89–130

M. Benoit: *Musiques de cour: chapelle, chambre, écurie, recueil de documents, 1661–1733* (Paris, 1971)

L. Rosow: 'Lallemand and Durand: Two Eighteenth-Century Music Copyists at the Paris Opéra', *JAMS*, xxxiii (1980), 142–63

H. Schneider: 'Dokumente zur französischen Oper von 1659 bis 1699', *Quellentexte zur Konzeption der europäischen Oper im 17. Jahrhundert*, ed. H. Becker (Kassel, 1981)

P. Cadell: 'La musique française classique dans la collection des comtes de Panmure', *RMFC*, xxii (1984), 50–58

R. Harris-Warrick: 'Contexts for Choreographies: Notated Dances Set to the Music of Jean-Baptiste Lully', *Lully: Heidelberg and St Germain-en-Laye 1987*, 433–55

J. de La Gorce and others: *Lully, musicien soleil* (Versailles, 1987) [exhibition catalogue]

M. Turnbull: 'The Sources for the Two Versions of Psyché (1671 and 1678)', *Lully: Heidelberg and St Germain-en-Laye 1987*, 349–56

C. Schmidt: 'Newly Identified Manuscript Sources for the Music of Jean-Baptiste Lully', *Notes*, xliv (1987–8), 7–32

J. de La Gorce: *De la naissance à la gloire: Louis XIV à Saint-Germain, 1632–1682* (St Germain-en-Laye, 1988) [exhibition catalogue]

——: *Lully, un âge d'or d'opéra français: catalogue Drouot-Montaigne 1991–1992* (Paris, 1991) [exhibition catalogue]

SOCIAL CONTEXTS, RECEPTION

J. de La Fontaine: 'Epitre xii: Sur l'Opéra' (1677), *Oeuvres complètes*, new edn, vii (Paris, n.d.), 121–31

J. N. du Tralage: *Notes* (MS, c1687–96); ed. Jacob as *Notes et documents sur l'histoire des théâtres de Paris au XVIIe siècle* (Paris, 1880)

E. Titon du Tillet: *Le Parnasse françois* (Paris, 1732–43)

J.-B. Durey de Noinville: *Histoire du théâtre de l'Académie royale de musique en France* (Paris, 1753, 2/1757)

C. Nuitter and E. Thoinan: *Les origines de l'opéra français* (Paris, 1886)

H. Prunières: 'La Fontaine et Lully', *ReM*, ii/10 (1921), 98–112

——: 'L'Académie royale de musique et de danse', *ReM*, vi (1925), 3–25; Eng. trans. as 'Lully and the Académie de Musique et de Danse', *MQ*, xi (1925), 528–46

F. Torrefranca: 'La prima opera francese in Italia?: l'*Armida* di Lulli, Roma 1690', *Musikwissenschaftliche Beiträge: Festschrift für Johannes Wolf* (Berlin, 1929), 191–7

P. Mélèse: *Le théâtre et le public à Paris sous Louis XIV, 1659–1715* (Paris, 1934)

D. J. Grout: 'Seventeenth Century Parodies of French Opera', *MQ*, xxvii (1941), 211–19, 514–26

B. Champigneulle: 'L'influence de Lully hors de France', *ReM*, xxii (1946), 26–35

T. Dart: 'The Cibell', *RBM*, vi (1952), 24–30

C. L. Cudworth: '"Baptist's Vein" – French Orchestral Music and its Influence from 1650 to 1750', *PRMA*, lxxxiii (1956–7), 29–47

C. Masson: 'Journal du Marquis de Dangeau 1684–1720', *RMFC*, ii (1961–2), 193–223

L. Hibberd: 'Mme de Sévigné and the Operas of Lully', *Essays in Musicology: a Birthday Offering for Willi Apel* (Bloomington, 1968), 153–63

A. Ducrot: 'Les représentations de l'Académie royale de musique à Paris au temps de Louis XIV, 1617–1715', *RMFC*, x (1970), 19–55

M. Benoit: *Versailles et les musiciens du Roi: étude institutionnelle et sociale, 1661–1733* (Paris, 1971)

R. M. Isherwood: *Music in the Service of the King: France in the Seventeenth Century* (Ithaca, NY, and London, 1973)

A. I. Borowitz: 'Lully and the Death of Cambert', *MR*, xxxv (1974), 231–9

J. de La Gorce: 'L'Opéra et son public au temps de Louis XIV', *Bulletin de la Société de l'histoire de Paris et de l'Ile-de-France*, cviii (1981), 27–46; repr. in *The Garland Library of the History of Western Music*, xi (New York, 1986)

C. Visser: 'French Opera and the Making of the Dorset Garden Theatre', *Theatre Research International*, vi (1981), 163–71

H. Schneider: *Die Rezeption der Opern Lullys im Frankreich des Ancien Regime* (Tutzing, 1982) [based on diss., U. of Mainz, 1976]

——: 'Die französische Kammersuite zwischen 1670 und 1720', *Jacob Stainer und seine Zeit: Innsbruck 1983*, 163–73

N. Zaslaw: 'At the Paris Opéra in 1747', *EMc*, xi (1983), 515–16

J. de La Gorce: 'L'opéra français à la cour de Louis XIV', *Revue de la Société d'histoire du théâtre*, xxxv (1983–4), 387–401

H. Schneider: 'La parodie spirituelle de chansons et d'airs profanes chez Lully et chez ses contemporains', *La pensée religieuse dans la littérature et la civilisation du XVIIe siècle en France: Bamberg 1984*, 69–91

W. Weber: '*La musique ancienne* in the Waning of the Ancien Regime', *Journal of Modern History*, lvi (1984), 58–88

W. Braun: 'Lully und die französische Musik im Spiegel der Reisebeschreibungen', *Lully: Heidelberg and St Germain-en-Laye 1987*, 271–85

J. Cheilan-Cambolin: 'La première décentralisation des opéras de Lully en province: la création de l'Opéra de Marseille au XVIIe siècle', ibid, 529–38

D. Fuller: 'Les arrangements pour clavier des oeuvres de Lully', ibid, 471–82

B. Gustafson: 'The Legacy in Instrumental Music of Charles Babel, Prolific Transcriber of Lully's Music', ibid, 495–516

F. Karro: 'L'Empire ottoman et l'Europe dans l'opéra français et viennois en temps de Lully', ibid, 251–69

J. de La Gorce: 'Lully's First Opera: a Rediscovered Poster for *Les fêtes de l'Amour et de Bacchus*', *EMc*, xv (1987), 308–14

F. Moreau: 'Lully en visite chez Arlequin: parodies italiennes avant 1697', *Lully: Heidelberg and St Germain-en-Laye 1987*, 235–50

F. Noske: 'L'influence de Lully en Hollande (1670–1700)', ibid, 591–8

M. Rollin: 'Les oeuvres de Lully transcrites pour le luth', ibid, 483–94

L. Rosow: 'From Destouches to Berton: Editorial Responsibility at the Paris Opéra', *JAMS*, xl (1987), 285–309

W. Weber: 'Lully and the Rise of Musical Classics in the Eighteenth Century', *Lully: Heidelberg and St Germain-en-Laye 1987*, 581–90

R. Harris-Warrick: '*La Mariée*: the History of a French Court Dance', *Jean-Baptiste Lully and the Music of the French Baroque: Essays in Honor of James R. Anthony* (Cambridge, 1989), 239–58

P. Rice: *The Performing Arts at Fontainebleau from Louis XIV to Louis XVI* (Ann Arbor, 1989)

L. Rosow: 'How Eighteenth-Century Parisians Heard Lully's Operas: the Case of *Armide*'s Fourth Act', *Jean-Baptiste Lully and the Music of the French Baroque: Essays in Honor of James R. Anthony* (Cambridge, 1989), 213–38

C. Schmidt: 'The Geographical Spread of Lully's Operas during the Late Seventeenth and Early Eighteenth Centuries: New Evidence from the Livrets', *Jean-Baptiste Lully and the Music of the French Baroque: Essays in Honor of James R. Anthony* (Cambridge, 1989), 183–212

H. Schneider: 'The Amsterdam Editions of Lully's Orchestral Suites', *Jean-Baptiste Lully and the Music of the French Baroque: Essays in Honor of James R. Anthony* (Cambridge, 1989), 113–30

STYLE, AESTHETICS

C. [or P.] Perrault: *Critique de l'opéra, ou Examen de la tragédie intitulée 'Alceste ou Le triomphe d'Alcide'* (Paris, 1674)

F. Raguenet: *Parallèle des italiens et des françois, en ce qui regarde la musique et les opéra* (Paris, 1702; Eng. trans., 1709, repr. in *MQ*, xxxii, 1946, pp.411–36)

J.-B. Dubos: *Réflexions critiques sur la poësie et sur la peinture* (Paris, 1719, 7/1770; Eng. trans. of 5/1746 as *Critical Reflexions on Poetry, Painting and Music*, 1748)

G. B. Mably: *Lettres à madame la Marquise de P ... sur l'opéra* (Paris, 1741)

R. de Saint-Mard: *Réflexions sur l'opéra* (The Hague, 1741)

J.-J. Rousseau: *Lettre sur la musique françoise* (n.p., 1753)

J.-P. Rameau: *Observations sur notre instinct pour la musique* (Paris, 1754)

G. Lote: 'La déclamation du vers français à la fin du XVIIe siècle', *Revue de phonétique*, ii (1912), 313–63

E. Borrel: 'L'interprétation de Lully d'après Rameau', *RdM*, x (1929), 17–25

L. Maurice-Amour: 'Comment Lully et ses poètes humanisent dieux et héros', *Cahiers de l'Association internationale des études françaises*, xvii (1965), 59–95

H. M. Ellis: *The Dances of J. B. Lully (1632–1687)* (diss., Stanford U., 1967)

——: 'Inventory of the Dances of Jean-Baptiste Lully', *RMFC*, ix (1969), 21–55

Y. Giraud: 'Quinault et Lully ou l'accord de deux styles', *Marseille*, no.95 (1973), 195–212

P. Howard: 'Lully's *Alceste*', *MT*, cxiv (1973), 21–3

E. C. Verba: 'The Development of Rameau's Thoughts on Modulation and Chromatics', *JAMS*, xxvi (1973), 69–91

R. Fajon: 'Proposition pour une analyse rationalisée du récitatif de l'opéra lullyste', *RdM*, lxiv (1978), 55–75

L. E. Brown: 'Oratorical Thought and the *Tragédie-lyrique*: a Consideration of Musical-Rhetorical Figures', *Symposium*, xx (1980), 99–116

W. Hilton: *Dance and Music of Court and Theatre: the French Noble Style, 1690–1725* (Princeton, NJ, 1980)

J.-C. Malgoire: 'L'analyse ramiste du monologue d'*Armide*', *Jean-Philippe Rameau: Musique raisonnée*, ed. C. Kintzler and J.-C. Malgoire (Paris, 1980), 201–15

D. Muller: 'Aspects de la déclamation dans le récitatif de Jean-Baptiste Lully', *Basler Studien zur Interpretation der alten Musik*, ed. H. Oesch, ii (Winterthur, 1980), 234–51

C. Wood: *Jean-Baptiste Lully and his Successors: Music and Drama in the 'tragédie en musique', 1673–1715* (diss., U. of Hull, 1981)

——: 'Orchestra and Spectacle in the *tragédie en musique, 1673–1715*: Oracle, *sommeil* and *tempête*', *PRMA*, cviii (1981–2), 25–46

H. Schneider: 'Tragédie et tragédie en musique: querelles autour de l'autonomie d'un nouveau genre', *Komparatistische Hefte*, v-vi (1982), 43–58

L. Rosow: 'French Baroque Recitative as an Expression of Tragic Declamation', *EMc*, xi (1983), 468–79

M. Turnbull: 'The Metamorphosis of "Psyché"', *ML*, lxiv (1983), 12–24

F. Reckow: '"Cacher l'Art par l'Art même": Jean-Baptiste Lullys "Armide"-Monolog und die "Kunst des Verbergens"', *Analysen: Beiträge zu einer Problemgeschichte des komponierens: Festschrift für Hans Heinrich Eggebrecht zum 65. Geburtstag* (Stuttgart, 1984), 128–57 [suppls. to *AMw*, xxiii]

D. Tunley: 'The Union of Words and Music in Seventeenth-Century French Song: the Long and the Short of It', *Australian Journal of French Studies*, xxi (1984), 281–307

H. Schneider: '"Canevas" als Terminus der lyrischen Dichtung', *AMw*, xlii (1985), 87–101

W. Hilton: 'Dances to Music by Jean-Baptiste Lully', *EMc*, xiv (1986), 51–63

C. Kintzler: 'De la pastorale à la tragédie lyrique: quelques éléments d'un système poétique', *RdM*, lxxii (1986), 67–96

C. V. Palisca: 'The Recitative of Lully's *Alceste*: French Declamation or Italian Melody?', *Actes de Baton Rouge: Biblio 17: Papers on 17th-Century French Literature*, xxv (1986), 19–34

H. Schneider: 'Chaconne und Passacaille bei Lully', *Studi Corelliani IV: Fusignano 1986*, 319–34

J. R. Anthony: 'The Musical Structure of Lully's Operatic Airs', *Lully: Heidelberg and St Germain-en-Laye 1987*, 65–76

——: 'Lully's Airs – French or Italian?', *MT*, cxxviii (1987), 126–9

H. Schneider: 'Strukturen der Szenen und Akte in Lullys Opern', *Lully: Heidelberg and St Germain-en-Laye 1987*, 77–98

——: 'Les monologues dans l'opéra de Lully', *XVIIe siècle*, xl (1988), 353–64

P. Howard: 'Lully and the Ironic Convention', *COJ*, i (1989), 45–59

C. Massip: 'Michel Lambert and Jean-Baptiste Lully: the Stakes of a Collaboration', *Jean-Baptiste Lully and the Music of the French Baroque: Essays in Honor of James R. Anthony* (Cambridge, 1989), 25–40

M.-F. Christout: 'Ballets de cour et comédies-ballets: sources d'inspiration pour les tragédies lyriques de Lully', *La tragédie lyrique*, ed. P. Van Dieren (Paris, 1991), 123–7

J. Duron: 'L'instinct de M. de Lully', *La tragédie lyrique*, ed. P. Van Dieren (Paris, 1991), 65–119

P. Howard: 'The Influence of the Précieuses on Content and Structure in Quinault's and Lully's Tragédies Lyriques', *AcM*, lxiii (1991), 57–72

C. Massip: 'L'air dans la tragédie lyrique', *La tragédie lyrique*, ed. P. Van Dieren (Paris, 1991), 119–31

L. Rosow: 'Making Connections: Thoughts on Lully's Entr'actes', *EMc*, (forthcoming)

PERFORMING PRACTICE, PERSONNEL, THEATRES, MISE-EN-SCÈNE

A. Levinson: 'Notes sur le ballet au XVIIe siècle: les danseurs de Lully', *ReM*, vi/5 (1925), 44–55

E. Borrel: *L'interprétation de la musique française (de Lully à la Révolution)* (Paris, 1934)

M. Pincherle: 'L'interpretazione orchestrale di Lulli', *L'orchestra* (1954), 139–52

J. Eppelsheim: *Das Orchester in den Werken Jean-Baptiste Lullys* (Tutzing, 1961)

K. Cooper and J. Zsako: 'Georg Muffat's Observations on the Lully Style of Performance', *MQ*, liii (1967), 220–45

F. Lesure: *L'opéra classique français: XVIIe et XVIIIe siècles* (Geneva, 1972)

A. Ducrot: 'Lully créateur de troupe', *XVIIe siècle*, nos.98–9 (1973), 91–107

M. Seares: 'Aspects of Performance Practice in the Recitatives of Jean-Baptiste Lully', *SMA*, viii (1974), 8–16

N. Zaslaw: 'The Enigma of the Haute-Contre', *MT*, cxv (1974), 939–41

J. de La Gorce: *L'Opéra sous le règne de Louis XIV: le merveilleux ou les puissances surnaturelles, 1671–1715* (diss., U. of Paris-Sorbonne, 1978)

R. P. Wolf: 'Metrical Relationships in French Recitative of the Seventeenth and Eighteenth Centuries', *RMFC*, xviii (1978), 29–49

G. Sadler: 'The Role of the Keyboard Continuo in French Opera, 1673–1776', *EMc*, viii (1980), 148–57

D. Barnett: 'La rhétorique de l'opéra', *XVIIe siècle*, xxxiii (1981), 336–55

J. de La Gorce: 'L'Opéra sous le règne de Louis XIV: recherches et méthodes pour une étude comparative entre les arts du décor et la musique', *Aspects de la recherche musicologique*, ed. CNRS (Paris, 1984), 131–9, pls.i–vi

J.-P. Pinson: 'L'action dans le récitatif pathétique de Lully: la déclamation', *Canadian University Music Review*, v (1984), 152–78

J. de La Gorce: 'Three Designs for Lully's *Armide*', *Torquato Tasso* (Bologna, 1985), 335–8 [exhibition catalogue]

——: *Bérain: dessinateur du Roi Soleil* (Paris, 1986)

T. Boucher: 'Un haut lieu de l'opéra de Lully: la salle de spectacles du château de Saint-Germain-en-Laye', *Lully: Heidelberg and St Germain-en-Laye 1987*, 457–67

L. Rosow: 'The Metrical Notation of Lully's Recitative', *Lully: Heidelberg and St Germain-en-Laye 1987*, 405–22

——: 'Performing a Choral Dialogue by Lully', *EMc*, xv (1987), 325–35

L. Sawkins: 'For and Against the Order of Nature: Who Sang the Soprano?', *EMc*, xv (1987), 315–24

D. Tunley: 'Grimarest's *Traité du récitatif*: Glimpses of Performance Practice in Lully's Operas', *EMc*, xv (1987), 361–4

N. Zaslaw: 'Lully's Orchestra', *Lully: Heidelberg and St Germain-en-Laye 1987*, 539–79

J. de La Gorce: 'Some Notes on Lully's Orchestra', *Jean-Baptiste Lully and the Music of the French Baroque: Essays in Honor of James R. Anthony* (Cambridge, 1989), 99–112

B. Coeyman: 'Theatres for Opera and Ballet during the Reigns of Louis XIV and Louis XV', *EMc*, xviii (1990), 22–37

R. Harris-Warrick: 'A Few Thoughts on Lully's *hautbois*', *EMc*, xviii (1990), 97–106

(2) Louis Lully (*b* Paris, 4 Aug 1664; *d* Paris, 1 April 1734). Composer, eldest of three sons of (1) Jean-Baptiste Lully. He was frequently in debt and not very talented. After the death of his brother (3) Jean-Louis, the post of *surintendant de la musique de la chambre du roi* (and later that of *compositeur*) went not to Louis but to Lalande. Louis composed operas, occasional pieces and *airs*; some of his works were written in collaboration with his brothers and Marin Marais.

Zéphire et Flore (opéra, prol., 3, M. Du Boullay), Paris, Opéra, 22 March 1688 (Paris, 1688), collab. J.-L. Lully; rev. Destouches, 1715, F-Po

Orphée (tragédie en musique, prol., 3, Du Boullay), Paris, Opéra, 8 April 1690 (Paris, 1690)

Alcide [La mort d'Hercule, La mort d'Alcide] (tragédie en musique, prol., 5, J. G. de Campistron), Paris, Opéra, 3 Feb 1693, Pn, collab. M. Marais

(3) Jean-Louis Lully (*b* Paris, 23 Sept 1667; *d* Paris, 23 Dec 1688). Composer, youngest son of (1) Jean-Baptiste Lully. In June 1687 he acquired the posts of *surintendant* and *compositeur de la musique de la chambre du roi*, both vacated on his father's death. (JEAN-NICOLAS DE FRANCINE, Jean-Louis' brother-in-law, took over the directorship of the Paris Opéra.) Between his father's death in 1687 and his own premature death in 1688 he composed one opera and three occasional pieces, all in collaboration with his brother (2) Louis. A few *airs* are attributed to him as well.

T. de Lajarte: *Bibliothèque musicale du théâtre de l'Opéra*, i (Paris, 1878)

J. Ecorcheville: 'Lully gentilhomme et sa descendance: les fils de Lully', *BSIM*, vii/6 (1911), 1–27

J. Chailley: 'Notes sur la famille de Lully', *RdM*, xxxiv (1952), 101–8

L. Rosow: 'From Destouches to Berton: Editorial Responsibility at the Paris Opéra', *JAMS*, xl (1987), 285–309
LOIS ROSOW

Lulu (i). Romantische Oper in three acts by FRIEDRICH KUHLAU to a libretto by Carl Christian Frederik Güntelberg after A. J. Liebeskind's fairy-tale '*Lulu, oder Die Zauberflöte*' in CHRISTOPH MARTIN WIELAND's collection *Dschinnistan*; Copenhagen, Det Kongelige Teater, 29 October 1824.

This 'magic' opera (in Danish 'Trylleopera'), which is strictly a Singspiel with spoken dialogue, is based on the same source as Mozart's and Schikaneder's *Die Zauberflöte*, but the transposition of the evil and good characters (Sarastro and the Queen of Night) made in that opera is not followed. The plot deals with the oriental prince Lulu (tenor), who decides to set free Sidi (soprano), a princess captured by the evil wizard Dilfeng (bass); to this end he is given a magic flute by Sidi's mother, the fairy Periferihme (spoken part). In Dilfeng's subterranean cave Lulu, disguised as an old man, enchants the wizard and his son, the malicious dwarf Barca (tenor), and his witches and spirits by his flute-playing. He manages to free Sidi and her friend Vela (soprano) and to cause the ruin of Dilfeng and his magic powers.

Kuhlau's setting, though strongly influenced by Mozart, Rossini and Weber, shows much originality in its catchy tunes. The richly coloured harmony, impressive ensembles and choruses, and many dramatic situations, make it not only his major opera, but also one of the most important in Danish musical history.

GORM BUSK

Lulu (ii). Opera in a prologue and three acts by ALBAN BERG to his own libretto after FRANK WEDEKIND's plays *Erdgeist* and *Die Büchse der Pandora*; Zürich, Stadttheater, 2 June 1937 (Acts 1 and 2); Paris, Opéra, 24 February 1979 (three-act version, completed by FRIEDRICH CERHA).

Lulu	high soprano
Countess Geschwitz	dramatic mezzo-soprano
A Theatrical Dresser/A High-School Boy/A Groom	contralto
The Professor of Medicine (spoken)/The Banker/The Professor (silent)	high bass
The Painter/A Negro	lyric tenor
Dr Schön *editor-in-chief*/Jack the Ripper	heroic baritone
Alwa *Dr Schön's son, a composer*	young heroic tenor
Schigolch *an old man*	high character bass
An Animal Tamer/An Athlete	heroic buffo bass
The Prince/The Manservant/The Marquis	buffo tenor
The Theatre Manager	low buffo bass
A Clown	silent
A Stagehand	silent
The Police Commissioner	spoken
A Fifteen-year-old Girl	opera soubrette
Her Mother	contralto
A Woman Artist	mezzo-soprano
A Journalist	high baritone
A Manservant	lower baritone

Setting A German city, Paris and London, in the late 19th century

Berg began to prepare an operatic treatment of Wedekind's two Lulu plays in 1928, when his negotiations to secure the rights to Hauptmann's *Und Pippa tanzt* came to nothing. He had known the text of *Erdgeist* at least since the early 1900s, and in 1905 had attended a private production by Karl Kraus in Vienna of *Die Büchse der Pandora*. Although Berg did not finalize his agreement with Wedekind's widow until the following year, the libretto of *Lulu* was completed by the end of 1928 together with musical drafts of early scenes, which carried over some of his sketches for *Und Pippa tanzt*. Work on the opera occupied him until his death in 1935; he interrupted it twice to fulfil commissions, in 1929 for the concert aria *Der Wein* (which served as a study for some aspects of the sound-world of *Lulu*) and in the first half of 1935 for the Violin Concerto.

By 1934 the short score of *Lulu* was virtually complete, but under the Nazi regime the possibility of a German or Austrian opera house's daring to mount the première became increasingly remote. To encourage a production further afield Berg prepared a five-movement concert suite from the opera, the *Symphonische Stücke aus der Oper 'Lulu'*, consisting of the rondo, Film Music and Lied der Lulu from Act 2, together with the interlude between Act 3 scenes i and ii, and the final Adagio; these became the first portions of the score to be orchestrated, and the suite received its first performance, conducted by Erich Kleiber, in Berlin on 30 November 1934. Berg then began to orchestrate *Lulu* from the beginning, incorporating those sections already scored for the suite. By the time of his death Acts 1 and 2 were complete, as well as the first 360 bars of Act 3, together with its interlude and the final Grave taken over from the Adagio of the suite. Of the remaining short score four brief passages (87 bars out of a total of 1326 in Act 3) remained to be fully notated, with accompanimental or subsidiary vocal lines still to be added.

After Berg's death his widow, Helene, was at first keen to see the opera completed; it was generally agreed that such a completion would be possible without the need for any new music to be composed. Schoenberg and Webern were asked to carry out the task but both declined, and after the première of the first two acts in Zürich (conducted by Robert Denzler, with Nuri Hadzic in the title role, Maria Bernhard as Geschwitz, Asger Stig as Dr Schön and Peter Baxevanos as Alwa) Helene Berg became increasingly unwilling to allow the score to be finished by another hand; in 1937 political pressure halted the engraving of the vocal score of Act 3.

After World War II concert performances in Vienna in February and April 1949, conducted by Herbert Hafner with Ilona Steingruber as Lulu, were followed in September by a staging at La Fenice, Venice, conducted by Nino Sanzogno and directed by Giorgio Strehler. Productions at Essen in 1953 conducted by Gustav König, and at Hamburg in 1957 conducted by Leopold Ludwig with Helga Pilarczyk in the title role and Toni Blankenheim as Schön, renewed the debate over the completion of the score, and during the next decade Berg scholars including Hans Redlich and George Perle argued strongly in favour of such a treatment. But by 1960 Helene Berg's prohibition had become complete: no-one was to be allowed access to the Act 3 material, a decision repeated in her will made in 1969 and published after her death in 1976. In 1962, however, shortly after the Viennese stage première on 9 June (conducted by Karl Böhm with Evelyn Lear as Lulu, Gisela Litz as Geschwitz, Rudolf Schock as Alwa and Paul Schöffler as Schön), Universal Edition had allowed Friedrich Cerha to begin a study of the sketches and short score with a view to completing the work. After Helene Berg's death the Alban Berg Foundation took legal action to prevent the performance of Cerha's version, but the première of the three-act *Lulu* eventually took place in Paris in February 1979, conducted by Pierre Boulez and staged by Patrice Chéreau. Teresa Stratas sang Lulu, Yvonne Minton Geschwitz; Kenneth Riegel was Alwa and Franz Mazura Schön. The same forces subsequently made a commercial recording. There followed a rapid sequence of new productions of the three-act version. The American première took place at Santa Fe in July 1979 in English translation (by Arthur Jacobs) and conducted by Michael Tilson Thomas, with Nancy Shade in the title role. Covent Garden staged the British première on 16 February 1981, conducted by Colin Davis and directed by Götz Friedrich; Karan Armstrong was Lulu.

'Lulu' (Berg): scene from the original production at the Stadttheater, Zürich, 2 June 1937, with Emmerich as the Animal Tamer and Nuri Hadzic as Lulu

PROLOGUE To a flourish in the orchestra the Animal Tamer welcomes the audience and invites them to inspect his menagerie. As each animal is introduced the orchestra identifies it thematically with a character in the opera. The snake appears last; assistants carry Lulu on, and the orchestra introduces the music that will accompany each of her entrances in the opera.

ACT 1.i *A spacious but shabby painter's studio* Dressed as a pierrot and watched by Dr Schön, Lulu is having her portrait painted. Alwa arrives to take his father to the dress rehearsal of his new ballet, asking after Lulu's husband, the Professor of Medicine (Recitative). The Painter seduces Lulu; he calls her 'Nelly' and later 'Eva' (Introduction–Canon–Coda). The Professor is heard knocking at the door; he enters and collapses with a heart attack (Melodrama). While the Painter goes

to fetch help, Lulu tries unsuccessfully to urge her husband back to life, accompanied by a saxophone (Canzonetta). On his return, the Painter questions Lulu's motives (Recitative–Duet): does she love anything or anyone? Lulu's response is always the same: she does not know. She goes off to change her clothes, and the Painter worries about what a future with her might hold (Arioso). An orchestral interlude then develops the music first heard in the Canzonetta and Canon.

1.ii *An elegant salon in the Painter's house* Lulu and the Painter have married. They discuss the morning's mail; Lulu is astonished by the announcement of Dr Schön's engagement. The Painter celebrates Lulu's beauty and his good fortune in marrying her (Duettino); the sound of the doorbell (a vibraphone tremolando) interrupts them. The visitor is a beggar, and the Painter leaves Lulu to deal with him. It is Schigolch, an old friend of Lulu's – perhaps her father, perhaps a former lover (Chamber Music I, for wind nonet). He calls her Lulu; she says, 'I have not been called Lulu in the memory of man'. The doorbell sounds again, and Schigolch leaves as Dr Schön enters.

The remainder of the act is dominated by a large-scale sonata form, the elements of which symbolize Lulu's relationship with Schön. Its first theme is introduced with Schön's opening words as he shows his distaste for Schigolch. He is surprised by the Painter's blindness to Lulu's behaviour (exposition transition), but the purpose of his visit is to insist that Lulu stop seeing him (second subject: gavotte and musette). Lulu's love for Schön is crystallized in a Mahlerian *lento* theme that forms the coda of the exposition, all the elements of which are repeated as their argument goes back over the same ground. The Painter returns and Lulu leaves. The reprise of the exposition coda is interrupted by a passage dominated by an obsessive, steadily accelerating rhythmic figure, the opera's *Hauptrhythmus*, which signifies death and destruction and which had previously appeared at the death of the Professor of Medicine (Monoritmica). Schön tells the Painter of Lulu's past; appalled, the latter rushes off and cuts his throat. Lulu reappears and Schön realizes what has happened; Alwa arrives and together they discover the body. The music now begins to decelerate as Schön telephones the police to report the suicide. The doorbell announces their arrival, and Lulu tells Schön that she will still marry him. The orchestral interlude picks up the sonata coda at the point at which it was broken off; it gives way to the sound of a jazz band to introduce the following scene.

1.iii *A theatre dressing room* Lulu is changing for her performance as a cabaret dancer. She asks Alwa whether Dr Schön will be in the audience and tells him of her latest admirer, a prince, who wants to take her to Africa as his wife. When she goes on stage Alwa wonders whether he could write an opera about her, but decides it would be too incredible. The Prince's conversation with Alwa (Chorale Variations) is interrupted by an alarm, and Lulu storms in (Ragtime): she has seen Schön in the audience with his fiancée. Schön soon follows and tries to make her return to the stage (Sextet); the Theatre Manager gives Lulu five minutes to compose herself, and everyone leaves except Schön.

The sonata movement resumes with a development section as Schön pleads with Lulu not to stop his forthcoming marriage. But when she tells him of her plan to marry the Prince, he realizes that he is incapable of severing his links with her. As the sonata finally reaches its recapitulation Schön breaks down, and Lulu, triumphant, dictates a letter for him to send, breaking off his engagement.

ACT 2.i *A large living-room in Schön's house* Lulu has married Schön but continues to attract admirers. She welcomes one of them, the lesbian Countess Geschwitz, who invites her to a ball for women artists (Recitative). Geschwitz's music has strong pentatonic associations, harmonized in bare 5ths. As she leaves, Schön regrets that such people are now part of his 'family circle' (Ballade). Against Lulu's wishes he goes off to the Stock Exchange (Cavatina); Geschwitz returns, followed by the Athlete, Schoolboy and Schigolch (Ensemble). As they settle down for the day, Lulu greets them. All three declare their love for Lulu and their wish to marry her (Canon); they panic when 'Herr Doktor Schön' is announced (Recitative) and rush to hide, but it is Alwa who enters, not his father.

Alwa's declaration of love for Lulu begins the rondo that will dominate this act (just as the sonata form dominates the first one), representing his own obsessive dependence on her. The main theme, highly lyrical, is heard first as Alwa enters. Its course is constantly interrupted, first by two Chorales as the Manservant brings hors d'oeuvre and returns to clear the plates. Schön's return goes unnoticed, until the Athlete sees him brandishing a gun (Tumultuoso); Alwa is taken off by his father, and the Athlete takes the opportunity to hide again. In a five-strophe aria Schön then rounds on Lulu, accusing her of disgracing him and offering her the revolver to kill herself and save his face. He searches the room, discovering Geschwitz's hiding-place. Before his final strophe Lulu offers her first apologia: in her Lied, whose high tessitura and elaborate figuration crystallize her vocal character in the opera, she disclaims responsibility for the men who have died for love of her. Schön knew her character when he married her, and she has never pretended to be other than she is; he may have sacrificed his position for her, but she has offered her youth to him. Resuming his aria, Schön threatens Lulu with the gun, but a noise from the Schoolboy distracts him, and Lulu fires five shots into her husband. As he dies he catches sight of Geschwitz – 'the devil!'. Lulu begs Alwa to save her from arrest (Arietta); the scene ends as the police knock on the door.

The palindromic orchestral interlude is the turning-point in the opera, the division in Wedekind's drama between *Erdgeist* and *Die Büchse der Pandora*; Lulu's remorseless climb to success and social status in the first half will be mirrored by her fall in the second. The music accompanies a silent film that portrays her arrest, trial for Schön's murder and imprisonment, and then, during the retrograde, the plans for her escape (to be effected by catching cholera from Geschwitz and changing places with her in an isolation hospital).

2.ii *The same living-room, a year later* Alwa, Geschwitz and the Athlete await Schigolch (Recitative). He brings plans for Lulu's rescue and leaves with the Countess, who is to take Lulu's place in the hospital (Largo). The Schoolboy arrives, having escaped from a correction centre. He has his own plan to rescue Lulu, but the Athlete convinces him that she has died in prison and throws him out. Lulu appears with Schigolch and slowly descends the stairs; the Athlete is appalled by her wasted appearance and leaves, threatening to betray her to the police. When Lulu is finally left alone with Alwa, she regains her former vitality and celebrates her freedom (Melodrama). The music of the rondo surfaces again as Alwa declares his love, praising her beauty in minute detail and musical metaphors (Hymn). As the couple fall on to the sofa, Lulu observes that it might be the very spot where his father bled to death.

ACT 3.i *Paris, a spacious salon* The Athlete proposes a toast to the assembled company in honour of Lulu's birthday in the first of three large-scale ensembles that dominate the scene (each is cast in ternary form with material based on the circus music of the Prologue, which returns on each occasion with increasing frenzy). The Banker is questioned about the prospects for the Jungfrau Railway shares that everyone has bought, and the crowd drifts off to the gambling tables. Lulu is threatened by the Marquis: he is blackmailing her, but instead of demanding money intends to instal her in a Cairo brothel (Concertante Chorale Variations I and II). In his Procurer's Song (Intermezzo I) a solo violin quotes for the first time a Wedekind cabaret song (the *Lautenlied*), which will form the basis of the subsequent orchestral variations and articulate the final scene. Lulu refuses (Intermezzo II) in an aria that recapitulates her Lied from Act 2 scene i, and the Marquis threatens to reveal her to the police as the murderer of Doctor Schön (Variations III–XII).

The crowd returns, on its way to supper; the Jungfrau shares are booming (Ensemble II). The Athlete again tries to blackmail Lulu, and as the Banker is told of the collapse of the Jungfrau shares, Schigolch too asks Lulu for money; together they make plans to dispose of the Athlete (Pantomime). In a spoken dialogue over a cadenza for solo violin and piano the Marquis warns off the Athlete, and in a dialogue that mixes speech, Sprechgesang and lyrical arioso Lulu first convinces the Athlete that Geschwitz is in love with him, then persuades Geschwitz (who is horrified by the prospect) to spend a night with the Athlete. The Athlete and Geschwitz leave for Schigolch's lodgings, while Lulu arranges to exchange clothes with the Groom. There is uproar as the news spreads of the Jungfrau collapse: everyone is ruined (Ensemble III). In the chaos Lulu manages to escape just before the Marquis brings the police to arrest her.

The orchestral interlude is a set of four variations on Wedekind's *Lautenlied*, first heard during the Marquis's Procurer's Song in the preceding scene. At the end of the interlude the tune is crudely harmonized and played on seven woodwind to simulate the sound of a barrel organ. The tune will reappear three times in the course of the next scene.

3.ii *London, a windowless garret in the East End* Alwa and Schigolch await Lulu's return on her first night as a prostitute. They hide as she enters with her first client, the Professor; the music associated with her first husband, the Professor of Medicine – the Melodrama and Canzonetta of Act 1 scene i – returns. As Lulu and her silent client go into an adjoining room Alwa and Schigolch rifle his pockets, finding nothing but a devotional book. They hide again as he leaves, but the next visitor proves to be Geschwitz, carrying Lulu's pierrot portrait which has dogged her throughout the opera. When it is nailed to the wall, Lulu and her three admirers contemplate its beauty and how their fate has been bound up with it (Quartet). Lulu is unable to bear the memory of her past and leaves again for the street, followed by Geschwitz, as the fourth variation from the interlude is recalled in the orchestra.

A reprise of the second variation accompanies the conversation of Schigolch and Alwa, who hide again as Lulu returns with her second client, a Negro. As they argue about money, the music associated with the Painter in Act 1 (the Monoritmica and Duettino) is evoked; Alwa intervenes and the Negro clubs him to death. Lulu leaves again; Schigolch drags off Alwa's body as the third variation is heard. Geschwitz considers suicide, but Lulu appears with another client: Jack the Ripper. Music associated with Dr Schön from the Act 1 sonata and Act 2 Cavatina is recalled as Lulu begs Jack to stay the night and then argues about money. As the couple go off into the next room there is a final quotation of the music that has accompanied Lulu's entrances throughout the opera. Geschwitz contemplates Lulu's portrait and a return to Germany (Nocturno). There is a scream off stage, and a death cry (to a 12-note chord) as Jack kills Lulu. He then stabs the Countess as she goes to help her. Jack washes his hands and leaves the dying Countess to her *Liebestod*, and to a final cadence based upon chords associated with Alwa, Schön and herself.

*   *   *

Although *Lulu* lacks the easily comprehended musical symmetry of *Wozzeck*, its large-scale structure is completely reliant on closed forms in a way that invokes the 'number opera', even though those formal divisions do not always coincide with the dramatic divisions into acts and scenes. Each scene is built up from more or less self-contained units, carefully defined in the score; Berg's terminology is not wholly consistent, and the unfinished Act 3 left some of the forms untitled. The first two acts are dominated by the sonata and rondo structures respectively, the third by the theme and variations that first appear in its orchestral interlude; the entire structure is unified further by the increasing tendency of the music to recapitulate earlier material, until the final scene contains little that has not been heard earlier in widely differing dramatic contexts.

Berg's use of 12-note technique in *Lulu* is very much tailored to his own dramatic ends, and differs from classical Schoenbergian method in several respects. Although all its note rows are ultimately derived by permutation from the single basic set that represents Lulu's innate sexuality, in practice the score is based on a collection of interrelated rows used both as ordered pitch sets and as tropes, and whose distinct melodic shapes function as character motifs throughout the opera: they portray Lulu's protean nature (indicating how each of her admirers has a different concept of her), Schön's conformist inflexibility, Alwa's lyrical idealism, Geschwitz's selfless love and so on. Material derived from several rows may be combined in harmonic complexes with strong tonal tendencies. Perle (1985) offers a masterly dissection of the structural intricacies of Berg's musical language.   ANDREW CLEMENTS

Lumley [Levy, Levi], Benjamin (*b* ?Birmingham, 1810; *d* London, 17 March 1875). English impresario. His father was Lion or Sion Levi (later Louis Levy), a Canadian merchant resident in Birmingham. The boy attended King Edward's School, Birmingham, 1823–6, and left to work as clerk to an attorney in London, adopting the name Lumley about the same time. In 1832 he became a solicitor and three years later was hired to resolve the bankruptcy of P. F. Laporte, manager of the Italian opera at the King's Theatre (renamed Her Majesty's in 1837). From 1836 Lumley oversaw all the opera's finances and in 1842, after Laporte's death,

reluctantly succeeded him. The new manager dealt coolly with the *vieille garde* of Grisi, Persiani, Rubini, Tamburini and Lablache, and with Michael Costa the conductor. In 1846–7 all but Lablache left him to set up their own (successful) company at Covent Garden, the 'Royal Italian Opera'. Jenny Lind's appearances at Her Majesty's, 1847–9, together with aristocratic support (Lumley gave annual fêtes for them at his villa on the Thames), briefly strengthened the manager's position, but for the seasons 1853–5 he had to close. Reopening in 1856 – Covent Garden had burnt down on 4/5 March – he struck a notable success with Piccolomini in the first London performances of *La traviata*. Thereafter receipts went down. In August 1858 the Earl of Dudley, by then Lumley's creditor and the theatre's lessee, took possession (unfairly according to Lumley), and the manager retired. He resumed his law practice and later wrote two books of fiction and two on his operatic experiences; the last are particularly valuable for their discussion of the opera house as legal property in England and of the weaknesses of the commercial finance system.

Although Lumley may be credited with introducing Lind, Johanna Wagner, Tietjens and other singers to London, as well as with the London premières of *Linda di Chamounix* and *Don Pasquale* (1843), *Ernani* (1845), *Nabucco* and *I Lombardi* (1846), and *Traviata*, he is also associated with some outstanding failures, including Costa's *Don Carlos* (1844), Verdi's *I masnadieri* (1847; commissioned by Lumley and conducted by the composer) and Thalberg's *Florinda* (1851). He seems to have suffered from a combination of bad luck (Verdi's withdrawal from a proposed *King Lear* in 1846), bad judgment (too much emphasis on the ballet; the choice of Balfe as a replacement for Costa) and hostility from certain sections of the press (notably Chorley in the *Athenaeum*).

*

DNB (L. M. Middleton); *Grove4* (W. H. Husk)

B. Lumley: *The Earl of Dudley, Mr. Lumley, and Her Majesty's Theatre: a Narrative of Facts* (London, 2/1863)

——: *Reminiscences of the Opera* (London, 1864)

Obituary, *The Times* (19 March 1875)

R. Bledsoe: 'Henry Fothergill Chorley and the Reception of Verdi's Early Operas in England', *Victorian Studies*, xxviii (1984–5), 631–55   LEANNE LANGLEY

Luna (y Carné), Pablo (*b* Alhama de Aragón, Saragossa, 21 May 1879; *d* Madrid, 28 Jan 1942). Spanish composer. He studied harmony and composition at the music school in Saragossa, then worked as a conductor of various zarzuela companies before becoming conductor at the Teatro de la Zarzuela in Madrid in 1908. There he did much to further the music of Spanish composers such as Falla, Turina, Guridi and Millán. At the same time he was making a name with his own stage works, not least those that moved the zarzuela away from traditional settings, such as *Molinos de viento* (1910), set in the Netherlands. There followed *Los cadetes de la reina* (1913), *El niño judío* (1918) and *La pícara molinera* (1928), all of which displayed Luna's fluent and insinuating melodic invention and command of atmosphere to good effect. He composed more than 170 stage works, including operettas and revues.

selective list; first performed in Madrid unless otherwise stated; most published in vocal score in Madrid shortly after production

La escalera de los duendes (zar, M. Navarro), Bilbao, Campos Elíseos, 12 Feb 1904; La rabalera (zar, M. Urbano), Saragossa, Pignatelli, 29 Sept 1904; El oso blanco (zar, Urbano), Saragossa, *c*1904; Musetta (opereta, 1, L. P. Frutos), Ideal Polistilo, 13 July 1908; Fuente escondida (1, E. de la Vega), Apolo, 1908; ¡A.C.T! ... ¡Qué se va al tío! (epitafio cómico lírico, 1, M. Fernández Palomero and E. Córdoba), Zarzuela, 27 Feb 1909, collab. T. Barrera

Pura, la cantaora (zar, 1, E. Montesinos and F. Porset), La Latina, 25 June 1909; Las once mil virgénes, Tívoli, 28 June 1909; Vida de príncipe (revista, A. López Monís and R. Asensio Más), Príncipe Alfonso, 6 Oct 1909, collab. L. Foglietti; El club de las solteras (M. Fernández de la Puente and Frutos), Zarzuela, 14 Oct 1909, collab. Foglietti; La reina de los mercados (opereta, G. Perrín and M. de Palacios), Gran, 3 Dec 1909; Molinos de viento (opereta, 1, Frutos), Seville, Cervantes, 2 Dec 1910

Huelga de criadas (apropósito, A. Martínez Viergol), Novedades, 20 Dec 1910; El dirigible (2, F. Noriega and J. Tellaeche), Martín, 13 Feb 1911; Sangre y arena (arreglo lírico-dramático, J. Jover, after V. Blasco Ibáñez), Apolo, 26 April 1911, collab. P. Marquina; Las hijas de Lemnos (fantasía cómico lírica, 1, Frutos and Fernández de la Puente), Apolo, 2 Sept 1911; La canción húngara (opereta, 1, P. Muñoz Seca and P. Pérez Fernández), Seville, Cervantes, 23 Sept 1911

El paraguas del abuelo (cuento fantástico, 1, Perrín and Palacios), Gran, 22 Nov 1911, collab. Barrera; Canto de primavera (opereta, 2, Frutos), Saragossa, Circo, 26 March 1912; Los cuatro gatos (viaje fantástico de espectáculo, Candela and Nieto), Cómico, 11 Jan 1913; Los cadetes de la reina (opereta, 1, J. Moyrón), Price, 18 Jan 1913; La cucaña del Sotanillo (1, Muñoz Seca and S. Alonso Gómez), Apolo, 21 Jan 1913

La alegría del amor (opereta romántica, 1, J. J. Cadenas and R. Asensio Más), Apolo, 24 May 1913; La gloria del vencido (opereta, 1, E. González del Castillo), Bilbao, Arriaga, Dec 1913, collab. M. Amenázabal; La corte de Risalia (obra bufa, 2, C. Arniches, E. García Alvarez, A. Paso and J. Abati), Apolo, 11 April 1914; El rey del mundo (zar, 2, J. M. Martín), Zarzuela, 11 April 1914; El potro salvaje, Cómico, June 1914, collab. Valverde *hijo*; Salambó, o Los ojos de mi morena (zarzuela cómico, 2, Paso and Abati), Zarzuela, 24 Dec 1914

La boda de Cayetana, o Una tarde en Amaniel (1, A. Torres dell Alamo and A. Asenjo), Apolo, 28 April 1915; El patio de los naranjos (zar andaluza, 2, J. Fernández del Villar and J. Pellicer), Apolo, 11 Feb 1916; El asombro de Damasco (zar, 2, Paso and Abati, after *The Thousand and One Nights*), Apolo, 20 Sept 1916; El sapo enamorado (pantomima, T. Borrás), Eslava, 2 Dec 1916; La casa de enfrente (sainete, 1, S. Alvarez Quintero and J. Alvarez Quintero), Apolo, 20 March 1917

Los postineros (sainete, 1, Asenjo and Torres del Álamo), Apolo, 2 Nov 1917, collab. Foglietti; El niño judío (zar, 2, Paso and García Alvarez), Apolo, 5 Feb 1918; El aduar (zar, 2, Pellicer), Apolo, 11 May 1918; Trini, la Clavellina (zar, 1, Fernández del Villar), Apolo, 29 June 1918; Los calabreses (zar, 2, J. Jackson Veyan and G. del Castillo), Apolo, 19 Oct 1918; Muñecos de trapo (farsa cómico-lírica, Paso and A. Fanosa), Cómico, 22 Feb 1919

La menanógrafa (opereta, 2, Fernández de la Puente), Centro, 7 May 1919; Pancho Virondo (zar, 2, García Alvarez and Paso), Apolo, 31 Oct 1919; ¡Llévame al Metro, mamá! (Asenjo and Torres del Alamo), Cómico, 29 Nov 1919; El suspiro del moro (López Monís and López Núñez), Martín, 19 Dec 1919; Una aventura en París (opereta, 3, R. López Montenegro and R. Peña), Centro, 21 Feb 1920; Las Venus de las pieles (sainete, 1, Torres del Alamo and Asenjo), Eslava, 9 April 1920

Su alteza se casa (opereta, S. Delgado), Infanta Isabel, 19 Jan 1921; Los papiros (zar, 3, S. Alvarez Quintero and J. Alvarez Quintero), Reina Victoria, 25 Feb 1921; Ojo por ojo (húmorada lírica, 1, Paso and J. Rosales), Martín, 15 Oct 1921; El sinvergüenza en palacio (zar bufa, 3, Muñoz Seca and Pérez Fernández), Apolo, 28 Oct 1921, collab. A. Vives; Los dragones de París (zar, 1, A. Olivares and J. M. Castelví), Zarzuela, 15 April 1922

Los apuros de Pura (farsa matrimonial, 1, Paso), Martín, 5 Oct 1922; La tierra de Carmen (revista, 3, Paso, Borrás and C. Primelles), Apolo, 10 Feb 1923, collab. Valverde *hijo*; Benamor (opereta, 3, Paso and R. González del Toro), Apolo, 12 May 1923; La moza de campanillas (drama lírico, Paso and González del Toro), Zarzuela, 10 Oct 1923; Su Majestad (historieta cómico lírica, 2, Rodríguez Avecilla and M. Merino), Price, 12 Oct 1923

Rosa de fuego (revista, 3, Paso and Borrás), Apolo, 22 March 1924; La joven Turquía (zar, 2, C. Palencia *hijo* and González del Castillo), Barcelona, Sept 1924; Calixta la prestamista, o El niño de Buenavista (sainete, 1, García Alvarez and F. Luque), Apolo, 15 Oct 1924; El anillo del sultán (zar, bufa, L. Blanco and J.

Lloret), Apolo, 6 Feb 1925; La paz del molino (zar, 2, L. Manzano and M. de Góngora), Pavón, 9 May 1925; Sangre de reyes (zar, 2, Torres del Alamo and Asenjo), Pavón, 3 June 1926, collab. F. Balaguer

Los ojos con que me miras (humorada lírica, Paso and González del Toro), Martín, 10 Sept 1925; El torpiezo de la Nati, o Bajo una mala capa (sainete, 2, Arniches and A. Estremera), Pavón, 29 Oct 1925; Las espigas (zar, 2, E. Parados and E. Jiménez), Pavón, 18 Dec 1925, collab. E. Brú; Las musas del Trianón (zar, 3, F. García Pacheco and J. Ramos Martín), Zarzuela, 20 Oct 1926; La pastorela (zar, 3, Luque and Calonge), Novedades, 10 Nov 1926, collab. F. Moreno Torroba

Las mujeres son así, o Amor con amor se gana (sainete, 2, Paso and González del Toro), Apolo, 12 Nov 1926; El fumadero (Luque and F. de Torres), Martín, 1 Dec 1927, collab. Moreno Torroba; La manola del portillo (zar, 3, E. Carrère and García Pacheco), Pavón, 21 Jan or Feb 1928; La chula de Pontevedra (sainete, 2, J. Jiménez and Paradas), Apolo, 27 Jan or Feb 1928, collab. E. Brú; La pícara molinera (zar, 3, Torres del Alamo and Asenjo, after A. Camín: *La Carmona*), Saragossa, Circo, 28 Oct 1928

¡Ris Ras! (húmorada, 1, Torres del Alamo and A. Paso *hijo*), Martín, 4 Dec 1928, collab. M. Penella; La ventera de Alcalá (zar, 1, J. M. Granada and D. San José), Zarzuela, 1928/9, collab. R. Calleja; El antojo (revista, Paso and Borrás), Romea, 13 March 1929; El caballero del guante rojo (zar, 2, González del Castillo and J. Pérez López), Centro, 4 May 1929; La mujer de su marido (sainete, 1, Fernández del Villar), Chueca, 6 Sept 1929

La ventera de Alcalá (zar, D. San José and J. M. Granada), Zarzuela, 7 Nov 1929; Flor de Zelanda (zar cómica, 2, Carreño and Fernández de Sevilla), Alcázar, 9 Jan 1930; La moza vieja (zar, 3, F. Romero and G. Fernández Shaw), Calderón, 8 April 1931, rev. as El pregón del riojana (1); ¡Como están las mujeres! (húmorada lírico-bailable, 2, F. Loygorri), Maravillas, 26 March 1932; Los moscones (sainete, Carreño and P. Llabrés), Ideal, 25 Nov 1932

Las peponas (revista, E. Povedano and M. Ligero), Maravillas, 22 Feb 1934; Al cantar el gallo (opereta bufa, F. R. de Castro and J. L. Mayral), Romea, 28 Feb 1935; Quién te quiso petenera, o Una copla hecha mujer (opereta, 3, J. Silva Aramburu), Calderón, 30 Jun 1939; Currito de la Cruz, o El chavalillo (zar, Silva Aramburu, after A. Pérez Lugín), Calderón, 15 July 1939; La gata encantada, o Flor del cerezo (opereta, 2, Tellaeche and Silva Aramburu), Calderón, 21 Oct 1939

Los calatravas (comedia romántica, 3, Romero and Tellaeche), Alcázar, 17 Sept 1941; El Pilar de la victoria (zar, 2, M. Machado), Saragossa, Principal, 12 Oct 1944, completed J. Gómez

*

'Luna y Carné (Pablo)', *Enciclopedia universal ilustrada europeo-americana* (Barcelona, 1907–30), xxxi, 803; appx vi (1932), 1327–8; suppl. 1942–4 (1950), 279

A. Fernández-Cid: *Cien años de teatro musical en España (1875–1975)* (Madrid, 1975)

A. Sagardía: *Pablo Luna* (Madrid, 1978)

J. Arnau and C. M. Gomez: *Historia de la zarzuela* (Madrid, 1979)

R. Alier and others: *El libro de la zarzuela* (Barcelona, 1982, 2/1986 as *Diccionario de la zarzuela*)   ANDREW LAMB

Lunati, Carlo Ambrogio. *See* LONATI, CARLO AMBROGIO.

Lüneburg. City in north Germany. Theatre companies first visited Lüneburg in 1739; the Seyler company appeared in 1769, and the Stöffler troupe often performed Singspiels and operettas. In 1822 Lüneburg acquired a permanent company. Lortzing visited the city for performances of his *Zar und Zimmermann* and *Die beiden Schützen* in 1850. The Stadttheater (626 seats), built in 1945 and initially used as a cinema, was planned as a theatre and was eventually taken over for that purpose in 1961. Only small- and medium-scale operatic performances can be given, as the stage is among the smallest music-theatre stages in Germany; large-scale productions of works by Wagner, Verdi or Strauss are not feasible. The season begins in September and ends in June.

*

P. A. von Magnus: *Die Geschichte des Theaters in Lüneburg bis zum Ende des 18. Jahrhunderts* (Lüneburg, 1961)

SABINE SONNTAG

Lunn, (Louise) Kirkby (*b* Manchester, 8 Nov 1873; *d* London, 17 Feb 1930). English mezzo-soprano. She studied in Manchester and then at the RCM with Visetti. While still a student she sang Margaretha in the English première of *Genoveva* (1893) and the Marquise de Montcontour in *Le roi l'a dit*. She sang Nora in *Shamus O'Brien* at the Opéra-Comique in 1896, then joined the Carl Rosa company, where her roles included Julia in Sullivan's *Martyr of Antioch* and Ella in the première of MacCunn's *Diarmid*, both at Covent Garden (1897). In 1901 she reappeared there as the Sandman in *Hänsel und Gretel* and Siébel in *Faust*; she continued to sing at Covent Garden until 1914, appearing in several London first performances, notably as Pallas in *La belle Hélène* and in the title role in *Hérodiade* (both 1904), Hate in Gluck's *Armide* (1906) and Delilah (1909), as well as Orpheus, Ortrud, Brangäne, Fricka, Carmen, Olga (*Yevgeny Onegin*) and Amneris. She appeared at the Metropolitan (1902–3 and 1906–8). She sang Kundry in English in Boston (1904), and later with the British National Opera Company at Covent Garden (1922). She possessed a large, rich voice, which was under complete control, and ranged from g to bb″; her stage performances were considered rather cool.

J. B. Richards: 'Louise Kirkby Lunn', *Record Collector*, xix (1970–71), 101–43
——: 'The Kirkby Lunn Recordings', *Record Collector*, xix (1970–71), 172–88 [discography]   HAROLD ROSENTHAL/R

Lupi, Roberto (*b* Milan, 28 Nov 1908; *d* Dornach, Solothurn, 17 April 1971). Italian composer. He was a pupil of Arrigo Pedrollo at the Milan Conservatory, where he studied composition, piano and cello. He taught at the Florence Conservatory from 1941. In 1950 he won the Premio Roma with his cantata *Orpheus*.

A strongly individual musician, he developed and used from 1936 a theory of harmony which he called 'gravitational' because it was based on an analogy with Newtonian principles. This system has something in common with Hindemith's *Unterweisung im Tonsatz*, but at the same time the structural principles are associated with theosophical ideas and symbolism influenced by Rudolf Steiner's eurhythmics, as Lupi explained in his books *Armonia di gravitazione* (Rome, 1946) and *Il mistero del suono* (Rome, 1955). He applied it in his theatre music from the time of his *sacra rappresentazione La danza di Salomè* (1952), but even more markedly in the *mistero melodrammatico La nuova Euridice* (1957), in which he borrowed from Steiner's theories.

La danza di Salomè (sacra rappresentazione, 1, after a 14th-century Umbrian text), Perugia, S Domenico, Sept 1952 (Rome, 1952)
La nuova Euridice (mistero melodrammatico, 3, M. Della Quercia), Bergamo, Donizetti, 3 Oct 1957 (Rome, 1957)
Persefone (12 immagini sceniche), Florence, 1970 (Florence, 1970)

F. D'Amico: 'Lupi, Chailly, Bucchi', *I casi della musica* (Milan, 1962), 362, 363
C. Dall'Argine: 'Armonia di gravitazione', *Rassegna di studi musicali* (1975)   RAFFAELE POZZI

Luria, Juan [Lorié, Johannes] (*b* Warsaw, 20 Dec 1862; *d* Auschwitz, 1943). Polish baritone. He studied with Josef Gänsbacher in Vienna. He then sang in Stuttgart from 1885 and appeared at the Metropolitan Opera in the 1890–91 season as Nevers, Pizarro, Gunther and Alberich. In 1893 he sang Wotan in the Italian première

of *Die Walküre*, at La Scala. At Elberfeld in 1901 he sang in the première of Pfitzner's *Die Rose vom Liebesgarten*. At the Theater des Westens, Berlin, and in Paris, Brussels, Genoa and Turin he appeared in operas by Wagner, Verdi and Strauss. He fled to the Netherlands during the rise of the Nazis but was arrested and transported to Auschwitz.   DAVID CUMMINGS

Lurline. Grand romantic opera in three acts by VINCENT WALLACE to a libretto by EDWARD FITZBALL after the Lorelei legend; London, Covent Garden, 23 February 1860.

Lurline, the Nymph of the Rhine (soprano), has fallen passionately in love with Count Rudolph (tenor). She interrupts a banquet at his castle and places a ring on his finger. Under its spell, he returns her love and joins her in her coral caves beneath the Rhine. He is granted permission to return to his companions for a short time, and is given a treasure chest to take with him by Rhineberg, the River King (baritone). Rudolph's former lover, Ghiva (mezzo-soprano), steals his ring, and throws it into the Rhine, where it is discovered by Zeelick, the gnome (bass), who presents it to Lurline. She determines to revenge herself on Rudolph and denounces him for his supposed treachery. Rudolph's companions, meanwhile, have decided to murder him for his treasure. On discovering this, Lurline's affection returns; she destroys the assassins by the fatal power of her magic harp, and she and Rudolph are reunited.

Lurline was initially comissioned for performance at the Paris Opéra in August 1848. Wallace began it in 1847, but was delayed by illness. The opera is said to have been staged as *Loreley* in Germany in 1854, and Wallace is thought to have subsequently revised the score. On 18 March 1859 he assigned all rights in the work to the Pyne-Harrison company for ten shillings, which he gallantly presented to a stage-carpenter, and had the chagrin of seeing the management net over £50 000. *Lurline* marks a considerable advance on the musical style of *Maritana*, being more ambitious in its conception and more refined in its execution. It was last revived, at Drury Lane, on 12 April 1890.

NIGEL BURTON

Lussan, Zélie de. *See* DE LUSSAN, ZÉLIE.

Lustige Beylager, Das ('The Merry Wedding'). Singspiel in two acts by WENZEL MÜLLER to a text by JOACHIM PERINET adapted from Philipp Hafner's play *Der beschäftigte Hausregent*; Vienna, Theater in der Leopoldstadt, 14 February 1797.

The wedding day of Graf Höllerblüh and Fräule Fanille turns out disastrously: the death of the bride is reported, the groom goes mad and dies; as do several members of the household; the horrified major-domo and a servant find it fitting that they too should die, or at least faint. As one of the characters in Hafner's prologue disingenuously remarks: 'We must choose something comic, something mixed with arias, for that makes the play still more lively.' – 'Yes, especially when they are arias that people can sing at home afterwards.' This exchange was certainly justified by Müller's setting of Perinet's words in *Das lustige Beylager*: with the emphasis more firmly placed on farce than on tragic-comedy, and with Müller's songs and ensembles adding tuneful charm and wit, the Singspiel was performed nearly one hundred times at the Theater in der Leopoldstadt in 28 years, and was successfully mounted in many other towns. PETER BRANSCOMBE

Lustigen Weiber von Windsor, Die ('The Merry Wives of Windsor'). *Komische-fantastische Oper* in three acts by OTTO NICOLAI to a libretto by SALOMON HERMANN MOSENTHAL after WILLIAM SHAKESPEARE; Berlin, Königliches Opernhaus, 9 March 1849.

Frau Fluth [Mrs Ford]	soprano
Frau Reich [Mrs Page]	mezzo-soprano
Herr Fluth [Ford]	baritone
Herr Reich [Page]	bass
Jungfer Anna Reich [Anne Page]	soprano
Junker Spärlich [Slender]	tenor
Dr Caius	bass
Fenton	tenor
Sir John Falstaff	bass
First Citizen	tenor
Innkeeper, Waiter, Second, Third and Fourth Citizens	spoken

Citizens, women and children

Setting Windsor in the early 17th century

In 1841, having written four Italian operas with mixed success, Nicolai took up the post of Kapellmeister at the Vienna Hofoper, where he was expected to compose German opera. He seems to have searched continuously for a suitable libretto for a German opera, but was unable to find a subject that satisfied him. In the meantime he revised two of his Italian operas, *Il proscritto* (as *Die Heimkehr des Verbannten*, 1844) and *Il templario* (as *Der Tempelritter*, 1845). In about 1845 he finally decided on *The Merry Wives of Windsor*, though not without misgivings about his ability to do justice to it. When he offered *Die lustigen Weiber von Windsor* for production at the Hofoper it was turned down and he resigned his post. In 1847 he went to Berlin as Kapellmeister at the cathedral and at the Hofoper; there he conducted the highly successful première of *Die lustigen Weiber von Windsor* two years later. Nicolai did not live long to enjoy his triumph, dying of a stroke just two months after the première; however, the opera has never lost its place on the German stage, and the charming overture is still popular in the concert hall.

ACT 1.i *Between the houses of Ford and Page* Mrs Ford is reading a love letter from Falstaff; Mrs Page joins her and they realize that he has sent them identical letters. The repeated quaver patterns in their duet 'Nein das ist wirklich doch zu keck!' neatly characterize their reaction to the effrontery of the fat old knight, and they plan to take revenge on him. In the following dialogue Page tells Ford, Slender and Dr Caius that he hopes to wed his daughter, Anne, to Slender, though Dr Caius and Fenton both want to marry her. In the recitative and duet 'So geht indes hinein', Fenton urges his suit in vain; his ardent melodic line is effectively contrasted with Page's busy semiquaver patterns as he gloats over Slender's wealth.

1.ii *Inside Ford's house* Mrs Ford considers what she will say to Falstaff when he visits her; the fine recitative and aria 'Nichts sei zu arg' skilfully develops her character as a quick-witted, resourceful and charming woman. Mrs Page enters and in dialogue they dis-

cuss their plan to make Falstaff hide in a washing basket and then have him thrown in the river. Mrs Page conceals herself and as the finale begins Falstaff arrives. His portliness contrasts amusingly with the tripping figures that Nicolai gives him to sing as he begins his courting of Mrs Ford. Mrs Page bursts in as planned with the news that Ford is coming, and the two women get Falstaff into the basket. Ford, accompanied by his neighbours, enters in a fury and searches the house (he has been informed, anonymously, by his own wife of Falstaff's assignation with her). Meanwhile, the washing basket is removed by two servants, and Mrs Ford and Mrs Page laugh together, in a delightful duet, at the lessons they are teaching the men. When Ford returns from the search, his wife roundly scolds him for his unworthy suspicions; as the curtain falls, she simulates a fainting spell.

ACT 2.i *The Garter Inn* In a dialogue scene Falstaff is gossiping with his cronies; he has been invited to a further meeting with Mrs Ford. He and his friends sing a tuneful drinking song, 'Als Büblein klein'. In another short section of dialogue the waiter tells Falstaff that a certain Sir Brook (or 'Bach' in the German), actually Ford in disguise, is waiting to speak to him. The following recitative and comic duet 'O! Ihr beschämt mich', in which Ford tries to discover the truth about Falstaff's relationship with Mrs Ford, amusingly depicts the increasingly furious Ford's struggles to maintain the character of Sir Brook while Falstaff boasts of his success with Mrs Ford.

2.ii *Page's garden* It is evening and Anne's three suitors have the idea of serenading her. Nicolai blends this succession of scenes into a musically continuous number. Slender enters with comic fearfulness ('Dies ist die Stunde') but hides on the arrival of Dr Caius, whose comical mixture of French and mispronounced German increases the humour of the situation. Hearing Fenton approaching, he too hides. Fenton, thinking he has the garden to himself, sings the Romanze 'Horch, die Lerche singt im Hain!', which is full of charming melodic invention with a smooth, expressive string accompaniment and bird-like trills on piccolo and flute. When Anne appears, they sing the duettino 'Kannst du zweifeln'; an elaborate violin solo enriches the orchestral colour and the section closes with an ingenious cadenza for the two voices and solo violin. In the concluding quartettino, the lovers pledge themselves to each other while Slender and Dr Caius comment in suppressed fury from their hiding places.

2.iii *Inside Ford's house* In a dialogue scene Falstaff is again courting Mrs Ford. As before, Mrs Page interrupts them with the news that Ford is coming. This time they disguise Falstaff as an old woman. Ford and his wife confront each other in the duet 'So jetzt hätt' ich ihn gefangen' and she mocks his jealous fury. The finale follows without a break as Slender, Dr Caius and Page arrive; Falstaff is smuggled out under their very noses and they again search the house fruitlessly.

ACT 3.i *Page's house* The scene begins in dialogue. Mrs Ford and Mrs Page have explained the situation to their husbands; Ford is penitent. They plan to teach Falstaff a lesson he will not forget, and Mrs Page sings the ballad of Herne the Hunter, 'Vom Jäger Herne'. Mrs Page privately tells Anne (in dialogue) that she has arranged for her to marry Dr Caius that night: then Page tells Anne that he has arranged for her to marry Slender. Anne, alone, vows to confound both of them and marry

Fenton, affirming her determination to outwit them in the aria 'Wohl denn! Gefasst ist der Entschluss'.

3.ii *Windsor Park* The moon rises during the orchestral introduction and Ford, Page and their neighbours sing the chorus 'O süsser Mond' as they prepare for Falstaff's arrival. Falstaff enters dressed as Herne the Hunter and in the terzettino 'Die Glocke schlug schon Mitternacht' Mrs Ford and Mrs Page flirt teasingly with him. Then follows a ballet and chorus of the neighbours dressed as elves ('Ihr Elfen weiss und rot und grau'), and a harp solo announces the arrival of Anne dressed as Titania and Fenton as Oberon. Page appears dressed as Herne, and in the *Mückentanz* (Midges' Dance) 'Mücken, Wespen, Fliegenchor' the terrified Falstaff is further tormented. In the meantime, Slender and Dr Caius go off with each other, disguised as elves, both thinking that they are with Anne, and Anne and Fenton hurry away to get married; there is then a general dance and chorus, 'Er gesteht noch immer nicht'. In a final dialogue, Anne reconciles her parents to her marriage with Fenton, and the opera concludes with a charming terzettino for the 'merry wives', Mrs Ford and Mrs Page, with Anne.

* * *

The criticisms of Italian influence in Nicolai's work, which had been levelled at his earlier operas by German writers, continued to be directed against *Die lustigen Weiber von Windsor*, though less aggressively. A reviewer of the overture, writing in the *Neue Zeitschrift für Musik* in 1850, appreciated its 'obvious avoidance of trivialities', but also noted that 'Italian reminiscences, even if only distant and somewhat ennobled, are clearly recognizable'. However, it is arguable that such criticism was motivated by narrow nationalistic feeling, and that in this opera Nicolai had found a highly effective balance between the German and Italian elements in his musical makeup; it was a balance which the young Wagner, almost 20 years earlier, seems to have envisaged in his first published article, 'Die deutsche Oper' (1834), and which he tried unsuccessfully to achieve in *Das Liebesverbot* (1836). In *Die lustigen Weiber von Windsor*, Nicolai's German background is apparent in the importance given to the orchestra, in his concern to match form and structure to the dramatic situation, and in the range of the harmonic language. The Italian element shows in his liking for vocal decoration and in the nature of much of the melodic material; his Italian experience enabled him to treat the comic elements in the opera with a lightness and charm which few German composers of his generation were able to rival.

CLIVE BROWN

Lustige Witwe, Die ('The Merry Widow'). *Operette* in three acts by FRANZ LEHÁR to a libretto by VICTOR LÉON and LEO STEIN after HENRI MEILHAC's *L'attaché d'ambassade*; Vienna, Theater an der Wien, 30 December 1905.

Offered first to Heuberger, the libretto of *Die lustige Witwe* inspired Lehár's first international success and the most commercially successful operetta of its day. It has held the stage ever since and is now firmly recognized as a part of the operatic repertory. It was first performed with Mizzi Günther (Hanna), Louis Treumann (Danilo), Siegmund Natzler (Baron Zeta), Annie Wünsch (Valencienne) and Karl Meister (Camille). Lehár composed two additional numbers for London in 1907, and various numbers were interpolated for Berlin revue productions of the 1920s, but

Baron Mirko Zeta *Pontevedrin envoy in Paris*		baritone
Valencienne *his wife*		soprano
Count Danilo Danilowitsch *cavalry lieutenant, secretary to the legation*		*buffo* tenor
Hanna Glawari		soprano
Camille de Rosillon		tenor
Vicomte Cascada		baritone
Raoul de St Brioche		baritone
Bogdanowitsch *Pontevedrin consul*		baritone
Sylviane *his wife*		soprano
Kromow *counsellor to the Pontevedrin legation*		baritone
Olga *his wife*		mezzo-soprano
Pritschitsch *retired Pontevedrin colonel*		baritone
Praskowia *his wife*		mezzo-soprano
Njegus *clerk at the Pontevedrin legation*		spoken
Lolo, Dodo, Jou-Jou, Frou-Frou, Clo-Clo, Margot *grisettes*		sopranos

Parisian and Pontevedrin society, musicians, servants

Setting Contemporary Paris

the definitive score is essentially unchanged from 1905. In effect the first two acts of Meilhac's play were compressed into the first act of the operetta and Meilhac's third act developed into Acts 2 and 3. Pontevedro is a thinly disguised representation of Montenegro.

Franz Lehár (right) with Mizzi Günther and Louis Treumann, who created the roles of Hanna and Count Danilo in the original production of 'Die lustige Witwe' at the Theater an der Wien, Vienna, 30 December 1905

ACT 1 *The Pontevedrin legation in Paris* A party is in progress to mark the birthday of the ruling prince of the Balkan state. Vicomte Cascada, an aristocratic French guest, proposes a vote of thanks and a toast ('Verehrteste Damen und Herren') to which the envoy, Baron Mirko Zeta, replies. The Baron is delighted to see his young wife, Valencienne, acting the perfect hostess to another French aristocrat, Camille de Rosillon, never suspecting that Camille is expressing his love for her. Valencienne seeks to rebuff Camille with the assurance that she is a respectable wife ('Ich bin eine anständ'ge Frau').

Njegus, the clerk of the legation, announces the arrival of the young Pontevedrin widow, Hanna Glawari, whose ex-banker husband has just left her a considerable fortune. The Baron is determined that her millions shall not be lost to the impoverished Pontevedrin nation by her remarrying, but all the French noblemen swoon over her as she sweeps glamorously in ('Bitte meine Herr'n!'). Hanna responds to the Baron's welcome by inviting everyone to a Pontevedrin party at her home the following day. Meanwhile Zeta sees the saviour of the Glawari millions in the secretary to the legation, an eligible bachelor named Danilo, whom Njegus has tracked down at his favourite night-spot, Maxim's. Danilo arrives protesting that he does enough for the fatherland by day without having to give up his nocturnal pleasures with the girls ('Da geh' ich zu Maxim').

Short of sleep and full of champagne, Danilo seeks to grab forty winks, but his snores are overheard by Hanna. It transpires that the two are former lovers, but he swears that he will never now utter the words 'I love you' since it will class him with all the other men after her money. When Baron Zeta catches up with Danilo and explains his plan for Danilo to marry Hanna and save her millions for the state, Danilo recoils. 'Never!' he exclaims.

In the ballroom a ladies' choice is announced, and the men clamour to be Hanna's chosen partner ('Damenwahl!'). Danilo seeks to get them away by arriving with a bevy of girls ('O kommet doch, o kommt, Ihr Ballsirenen'). However, the pressure on Hanna is complicated further when Valencienne promotes the claims of Camille. Hanna seeks to resolve her problem by choosing the one man who ignores her, namely Danilo. Perversely he declines, adding that, if the dance belongs to him, he will offer it for ten thousand francs for charity. The other men immediately lose interest, leaving Hanna and Danilo to sweep into the dance together.

ACT 2 *In the garden of Frau Glawari's palace* At her party the following day Hanna is an attentive hostess. To entertain her guests, a company of singers and dancers in Pontevedrin costume perform a national dance, a *kolo*. Then Hanna tells a traditional national folk tale of a maid of the woods and a huntsman's unrequited love ('Es lebt' eine Vilja, ein Waldmägdelein'). To the Baron's concern, Hanna is rumoured to be intending to marry Camille. Njegus reports that Camille is known to be in love with a married woman, and the Baron suggests that the lady's ass of a husband should give her up for the sake of the fatherland. Hanna meanwhile accuses Danilo of avoiding her, but he explains that he is merely reconnoitring like the true former cavalry officer he is ('Dummer, dummer Reitersmann'). Cascada and St Brioche continue to clamour after

Hanna, and Danilo mischievously stirs things up. With Zeta, they join in an animated discussion on how to handle women ('Ja, das Studium der Weiber ist schwer!').

Camille is still reluctant to take 'no' for an answer from Valencienne, and she consents to give him her fan as a souvenir, on which she writes the words 'I am a respectable wife'. She tells him to be sensible and urges him to turn his attention to Hanna. He merely reiterates the passion that blossoms in his heart like a rosebud in May ('Wie eine Rosenknospe') and persuades Valencienne to join him in the summerhouse ('Sieh' dort den kleinen Pavillon'). The two are spotted by Njegus and, when Baron Zeta approaches the summerhouse, he hurriedly reports that it is already occupied by Camille and a lady. Anxious to discover the lady's identity, the Baron resorts to looking through the keyhole. To his horror he spies his wife, but in the ensuing confusion Njegus manages to enter the summerhouse by a back door and substitute Hanna for Valencienne. Camille and Hanna step out, asking what the fuss is all about. Zeta is persuaded that he was mistaken over the identity of the lady, and Camille repeats his passionate declaration of love – this time to Hanna ('Wie eine Rosenknospe').

Hanna seeks to explain events by announcing her engagement to Camille, and Danilo cannot disguise his disgust. Hanna provokes him by vowing to live in the liveliest Parisian style ('Ein flotter Ehestand soll's sein'). Furious, Danilo tells a parable about a prince who kept silent about his love for a princess, only for her to repay him by giving her hand to another ('Es waren zwei Königskinder'). Then he turns on his heel and storms off to the place where he really feels at home – Maxim's. Hanna is now sure that he loves her.

ACT 3 *Inside Frau Glawari's palace* For Danilo's benefit the inside of Hanna's residence has been decked out as a cabaret spot. Valencienne appears and performs a cancan with Lolo, Dodo, Jou-Jou, Frou-Frou, Clo-Clo and Margot, the girls from Maxim's ('Ja, wir sind es, die Grisetten'). Danilo seeks to forbid Hanna to marry Camille and is relieved when she tells him that she never did have a rendezvous with Camille in the summerhouse. Now they can no longer disguise their love for each other ('Bei jedem Walzerschritt'). To the Baron's consternation, Valencienne's fan is found in the summerhouse, but she pacifies her husband by pointing to the words 'I am a respectable wife' written on it. Everyone reflects afresh on the difficulty of understanding women ('Ja, das Studium der Weiber ist schwer!').

* * *

In the field of operetta, *Die lustige Witwe* remains a masterpiece. It has a fund of marvellous melodies that remain astonishingly fresh – ever inventive, ever graceful. Comparing *Die lustige Witwe* with any previous Viennese operetta – by Suppé, Johann Strauss, Millöcker, Zeller or Heuberger – one cannot help but be struck by the novel turns the score takes at almost every point. It is evident at once in the exhilarating opening passage that sets the scene of glamour and bustle of a Parisian embassy with orchestral colouring that shows Lehár's awareness of the innovations of Puccini, Debussy and Richard Strauss. In Hanna's entrance song the tremors of male expectation and the glamour of her personality are all there in the music, while in Danilo's entrance song the shifting keys of the single verse instantly depict his unreliability, with the glowing orchestration of the refrain portraying the joy he finds at Maxim's. Surely no operetta before or since has had such original entrance numbers for its leading characters! Elsewhere, in the scene in Act 2 where the relationship between Camille and Valencienne reaches a tempestuous height, the writing has an almost Wagnerian grandeur. In countless places there are delicious orchestral touches, as for instance in the Balkan *kolo* at Hanna's party and in the refrain of the 'Vilja Song' where Lehár avoids banality by accompanying the vocal line with solo violin supported by rocking pizzicato strings supplemented by tamburizzas. Not least, Lehár's writing contains an eroticism unprecedented in operetta, as in the celebrated waltz duet of Act 3 where solo violin and cello symbolically intertwine.   ANDREW LAMB

Lutyens, (Agnes) Elisabeth (*b* London, 9 July 1906; *d* London, 14 April 1983). English composer. A daughter of the architect Sir Edwin Lutyens, she first studied the violin before beginning serious music studies in 1922 at the Ecole Normale, Paris. At the RCM (1926–30) she studied composition with Harold Darke and the viola with Ernest Tomlinson. By 1939 Lutyens found her way independently to serial technique in the manner of Webern, though his music was little known in Britain then. Her Chamber Concerto no.1 (1939), with other chamber works, heralded her mature style and led her to discard some 50 earlier compositions as unworthy. She pursued an uncompromising and often lonely creative development before obtaining wider recognition in the 1950s. Her belief that composing was a craft, and her ability to work to order, resulted in music for over 200 radio plays and a number of film scores, but her operatic works achieved only limited performances, some none at all. She was twice married: to Ian Glennie, the singer, and to Edward Clark, conductor and BBC music organizer, who died in 1962. She was appointed CBE in 1969.

Lutyens's first opera was *The Pit* (1947), which was commissioned by William Walton and staged for the ISCM at Palermo (1949), having received an earlier concert performance in London (1947); a drama about trapped miners, it uses a note-series also found in the Chamber Concerto no.1. Her next dramatic work, *Penelope* (1950), a radio opera, was left unorchestrated and *The Numbered* (1965–7), on Elias Canetti's parable of potential longevity and written for large vocal and orchestral forces, remained unperformed.

Infidelio (1954), commissioned by the Institute of Contemporary Arts, traces a love affair back from the girl's suicide to the first meeting; in some ways it anticipated the vogue for music theatre that had developed by the time it was staged by the New Opera Company in 1973, in a double-bill with her *Time Off? Not a Ghost of a Chance!*, first given by the same company the previous year. *Time Off?* obtained a measure of success by its topical references and verbal virtuosity; it explores the nature of time using an assemblage of puns, riddles and quotations set as a musical collage that employs parody, quotation and chance elements within a serial idiom. *Isis and Osiris* (1969–70), a mythic ritual, like a tomb-painting brought to life, is notable for expressive choral dances; the work was given its première at Morley College in 1976. *The Linnet from the Leaf* (1972), a short music-theatre work expressing passionate feelings against racism, was broadcast in 1979. *The Waiting Game* (1973), a chamber opera about women always waiting for husbands, lovers or

babies, sought unsuccessfully to provide a setting for colloquial speech. *The Goldfish Bowl* (1975), alluding to the title of Lutyens's autobiography (London, 1972), was a ballad opera exploring the conflict between conventional values and student protest; Lutyens finished it, called it 'awful' and destroyed it.

In none of these works did Lutyens's vocal music approach the best of her concert works, but on the basis of poetic assurance and instrumental (as well as intellectual) brilliance *Time Off?* merits further attention.

completed works published in facsimile in London

The Pit op.14 (dramatic scene, W. R. Rodgers), concert perf., London, Wigmore Hall, 18 May 1947; stage, Palermo, Massimo, 24 April 1949

Penelope, 1950 (music drama for radio, Lutyens), unorchd

Infidelio op.29, 1954 (7 scenes, T. E. Ranselm [Lutyens]), London, Sadler's Wells, 17 April 1973

The Numbered op.63, 1965–7 (prol., 2, M. Volonakis, after E. Canetti: *Die Befristeten*), unperf.

Time Off? Not a Ghost of a Chance! op.68, 1967–8 (charade, 4 scenes and 3 interruptions, Lutyens), London, Sadler's Wells, 1 March 1972

Isis and Osiris op.74, 1969–70 (lyric drama, Lutyens, after Plutarch), London, Morley College, 26 Nov 1976

The Linnet from the Leaf op.89, 1972 (music-theatre work, Lutyens), BBC, 11 Nov 1979

The Waiting Game op.91, 1973 (3 scenes, Lutyens), unperf.

One and the Same op.97, 1973–4 (scena, Lutyens), York, 21 June 1976

The Goldfish Bowl op.102, 1975 (ballad op, Lutyens), unperf., destroyed

Like a Window op.109 (after letters of V. Van Gogh), BBC, 24 Nov 1977

R. M. Schafer: 'Elisabeth Lutyens', *British Composers in Interview* (London, 1963), 103–11

S. Bradshaw: 'The Music of Elisabeth Lutyens', *MT*, cxii (1971), 653–6

R. R. Bennett: 'Time off? Not a Ghost of a Chance!', *Opera*, xxiii (1972), 102–5

L. East: 'Time Off? … With Lis Lutyens', *Music and Musicians*, xx/6 (1971–2), 18, 20

S. Walsh: ' "Time Off" and "The Scene Machine" ', *MT*, cxiii (1972), 137–9 [interview]

M. Harries and S. Harries: *A Pilgrim Soul: the Life and Work of Elisabeth Lutyens* (London, 1989)   NOËL GOODWIN

Luxon, Benjamin (*b* Redruth, Cornwall, 24 March 1937). English baritone. He studied at the GSM and in 1963 joined the English Opera Group, for which his roles included Britten's Sid, Tarquinius and Demetrius, and Purcell's King Arthur (1970). He created the title role in Britten's television opera *Owen Wingrave* (1971), as well as the Jester, Death and Joking Jesus in Maxwell Davies's *Taverner* at Covent Garden (1972). Other roles he sang there included Owen Wingrave, Yevgeny Onegin, Wolfram, Marcello, Falke (*Fledermaus*) and Diomede (*Troilus and Cressida*). At Glyndebourne (1972–80) he sang Monteverdi's Ulysses, Count Almaviva, Don Giovanni, Papageno, the Forester (*The Cunning Little Vixen*) and Ford. With the ENO (1974–90) he sang Posa, Papageno, Falstaff and Gianni Schicchi. He sang Wozzeck in Glasgow (1983), Sherasmin (*Oberon*) in Edinburgh (1986), Captain Balstrode in Philadelphia (1987) and Wozzeck again in Los Angeles (1988), where he returned as Falstaff (1990). His strong personality and warm, expressive voice were as effective in contemporary works as in his most famous role, Yevgeny Onegin, which he sang at the Metropolitan (1980), Frankfurt (1984), La Scala, Geneva (1986), Amsterdam, Paris and Prague. He was made a CBE in 1986.   ALAN BLYTH

Luzern (Ger.). LUCERNE.

Luzzo, Francesco. *See* LUCIO, FRANCESCO.

L'viv (Russ. L'vov; Pol. Lwów; Ger. Lemberg). City in Ukraine. From 1340 until 1772 it belonged to Poland; from 1773 to 1918 it was the capital of the Austrian province of Galicia. After World War I the city was returned to Poland, but in 1939 it became part of the Ukrainian SSR (under German occupation, 1941–4). From 1776 various Austrian theatre companies performed works there by Gluck, Piccinni, Salieri, Dittersdorf, Haydn (*Armida* and *Orlando paladino*, 1794) and Mozart (*Figaro* and *Die Zauberflöte*, 1792; *Don Giovanni*, 1794); from 1801 performances took place in the Municipal Theatre. Polish theatre companies played there from 1780, giving operas, Singspiels and vaudevilles under the direction of Tomasz Truskolaski (1780–83), Wojciech Bogusławski (1789, 1794–9), Józef Elsner (1792–9), Karol Lipiński (1810–14) and Jan Nepomucen Kamiński (1809–30). In both the Polish and Austrian theatres after 1795 operas in the current international repertory were given, including works by Cimarosa, Paisiello, Salieri, Sarti, Dittersdorf, Grétry, Elsner, Gaetano, Holland, Kurpiński, Stefani, Weber (*Der Freischütz*, 1827), Hérold, Rossini (*La donna del lago*, 1819; *Zelmira*, 1823), Bellini, Donizetti (*L'elisir d'amore*, *Belisario*, *Lucia di Lammermoor*, all 1838) and Auber (*Le maçon*, 1828). In the second half of the century, the repertory was enlarged with works by Meyerbeer (*L'Africaine*, Polish première in 1874), Verdi (*Nabucco*, 1850; *Rigoletto*, 1854), Wagner (Polish premières of *Tannhäuser*, 1867, and *Lohengrin*, 1877), Offenbach (from 1859), Moniuszko (*Halka*, 1867), Stanisław Duniecki, Henryk Jarecki, Mieczysław Sołtys and Władysław Żeleński.

Under the successive direction of Jarecki (1874–1900), Tadeusz Pawlikowski (1900–06) and Ludwik Heller (1906–18) the Polish theatre in L'viv became, after Warsaw, the most important Polish opera house. Internationally famous singers such as Marcella Sembrich, Salomea Krusceniski, Aleksander Myszuga, Aleksander Bandrowski-Sas, Modest Mentsyns'ky and Adam Didur were educated in the city and started their careers there. There were frequent guest appearances by outstanding singers from abroad – Battistini, Bellincioni, Caruso, Dal Monte, Patti, Slezak – and by many eminent Polish soloists. The ambitious repertory continued to include Polish premières, among them *Parsifal* (1904) and the *Ring* (1911), as well as works by Musorgsky (*Boris Godunov*, 1912), Rubinstein (*The Demon*, 1907), Mascagni (*Cavalleria rusticana*, 1892), Giordano (*Andrea Chénier*, 1907), Paderewski (*Manru*, 1901) and Różycki (*Bolesław Śmiały*, 1909). From 1875 almost every year until 1913 the opera company gave a summer season in Kraków. In 1900 a new building was opened, the Velykyy Teatr Opery ta Baletu (Grand Theatre of Opera and Ballet; 'Teatr Wielki' in Polish, 'Bol'shoy Teatr' in Ukrainian; cap. 1060), designed by Z. Gorgolewski. During the interwar period the Grand Theatre was one of three opera houses in Poland that remained permanently open (along with Warsaw and Poznań).

In October 1939 L'viv was incorporated into the Ukrainian SSR following the Hitler–Stalin pact, under which western Ukraine was absorbed into Soviet territory. The Grand Theatre was renamed the L'vivs'kyy Derzhavnyy Teatr Opery ta Baletu (L'viv State Theatre of Opera and Ballet) and reopened on 21 September 1940, staging 11 works (among them *Yevgeny Onegin*, *Carmen*, *Aida* and Lysenko's *Natalka Poltavka*) in the ensuing years. Productions continued during the German occupation, when the theatre was known as the L'vivs'kyy Opernyy Teatr. Ironically, it was during this period that Ukrainian opera was free from external artistic interference. Under the direction of Andry Petrenko, with principal stage director Volodymyr Blavats'ky and conductor Lev Turkevych, the theatre endeavoured to present mainstream operatic repertory on a level comparable to that of European theatres with works such as *La traviata*, *Tosca*, *Carmen*, d'Albert's *Tiefland* and Lysenko's *Noktyurn* ('Nocturne'). The theatre also produced operettas under the musical direction of composer-conductor Yaroslav Barnych. With the return of Soviet rule, it again became the L'viv State Theatre of Opera and Ballet and in 1956 was renamed the L'vivs'kyy Akademichnyy Teatr Opery ta Baletu imeni I. Franka (Franko Academic Theatre of Opera and Ballet) and, together with similar theatres in Kiev, Kharkiv and Odessa, became one of the most important in Ukraine. During its rather turbulent years since the resumption of productions in 1945 with Gulak-Artemovsky's *Zaporozhets za Dunayem* ('A Cossack beyond the Danube'), it took the lead with a number of important Soviet premières, including Smetana's *Dalibor* (1950) and Verdi's *Ernani* (1970). Premières of Ukrainian operas there have included Oskar Sandler's *V stepakh Ukraïny* ('In the Steppes of Ukraine', 1954), Vitaly Kyreyko's *Lisova pisnya* ('Forest Song', 1958), Yuly Meytus's *Ukradene shchastya* ('Stolen Happiness', 1960) and *Rikhard Zorge* (1976), the revised version of Borys Lyatoshyns'ky's *Zolotyy obruch* ('The Golden Ring', 1970), the world première of Volodymyr Zahortsev's *Maty* ('Mother', 1985) and Mark Karmins'ky's *Vsego odin den'* ('One Day Left', 1987).

ME ('L'vov', L. Z. Mazepa; also 'L'vovskiy teatr operï i baleta')
S. Pepłowski: *Teatr polski we Lwowie, 1780–1881* [The Polish Theatre in Lwów] (Lwów, 1889–91) [with suppl. covering 1881–90]
H. Cepnik and W. Kozicki: *Scena lwowska 1780–1929* [The Lwów Stage, 1780–1929] (Lwów, 1929)
F. Pajączkowski: *Teatr lwowski pod dyrekcją Tadeusza Pawlikowskiego 1900–1906* [The Lwów Theatre under the Direction of Tadeusz Pawlikowski, 1900–06] (Kraków, 1961)
B. Lasocka: *Teatr lwowski w latach 1800–1842* [The Lwów Theatre in 1800–42] (Warsaw, 1967)
J. Got: *Na wyspie Guaxary: Wojciech Bogusławski i teatr lwowski 1789–1799* [On the Island of Guaxara: Bogusławski and the Theatre in Lwów, 1789–99] (Kraków, 1971)
O. Palamarchuk and V. Pylypiuk: *L'vovskiy gosudarstvenniy akademicheskiy teatr operï i baleta im. Ivana Franko* (Kiev, 1988)
Yu. Stanyshevs'ky: *Opernyy teatr Radyans'koï Ukraïny* [The Opera Theatre of Soviet Ukraine] (Kiev, 1988)
O. Palamarchuk and T. Eder: *L'vivs'kyy teatr opery ta baletu imeni Ivana Franka* (L'viv, 1989)
A. Tereshchenko: *L'vivs'kyy derzhavnyy akademichnyy teatr opery ta baletu imeni Ivana Franka* (Kiev, 1989)
VIRKO BALEY, KORNEL MICHAŁOWSKI

L'vov, Alexey Fyodorovich (*b* Reval [now Tallinn, Estonia], 25 May/5 June 1798; *d* Roman', nr Kovno [now Kaunas, Lithuania], 16/28 Dec 1870). Russian composer, great-nephew of N. A. L'vov. He was the outstanding Russian violin virtuoso of his time, though his high social and military rank prevented a public career except abroad, where he was admired by

Mendelssohn, Meyerbeer, Spontini and Schumann. His appointment as director of the court chapel choir, a post he inherited from his father Fyodor Petrovich L'vov (1766–1836) and held from 1837 to 1861, stimulated his creative ambitions. He arranged the music of the liturgy (but delegated the actual conducting to assistants, Glinka among them), and eventually turned his attention to the stage.

L'vov's first opera, *Bianca und Gualtiero*, a lyric drama set in 15th-century Italy and peopled by Sforzas and Malatestas, was originally written to a French libretto by Joseph Guillou but performed only in translation – first in German, and then, for St Petersburg, in Italian. Rubini, Tamburini and Viardot took the leading roles, but the work nevertheless lasted for only two performances in the Russian capital, amid complaints that the repertory of the Imperial Italian Opera was being diluted with cheap domestic products. L'vov's second effort, *Undina*, a romantic opera in Russian, had better luck. First performed in St Petersburg in 1848, it lasted in repertory into the 1860s; as *Die Tochter der Wellen* it was performed in Vienna in 1852. (Tchaikovsky re-used the libretto in 1869 for his ill-fated second opera.) Also in 1848 L'vov's one-act operetta *Varvara, yaroslavskaya kruzhevnitsa* ('Barbara, the Lace-Maker from Yaroslavl') was performed at the Russian dramatic theatre (the Alexandrinsky) as a vehicle for the company's leading lady, N. V. Samoylova. His last work for the musical stage was a comic opera on a subject drawn from the Patriotic War of 1812: *Starosta Boris, ili Russkiy muzhichok i frantsuzskiye marodyori* ('Old Man Boris, or The Russian Peasant and the French Marauders'), with the great bass Osip Petrov in the title role.

L'vov was a legend in his own day for his old-fashioned eclecticism, his operatic style being wholly derived from Mozart and the older Italians (Rossini, Bellini, Donizetti). He is best remembered for his operas but for his new melody to the Tsarist hymn *Bozhe, tsarya khrani* ('God Save the Tsar', 1833, previously sung to the tune of the British national anthem), which has become familiar to concert audiences through symbolic quotations by Tchaikovsky in the *1812* Overture and the Slavonic March.

Bianca und Gualtiero (2, J. Guillou), Dresden, Oper, 13 Oct 1844; as Bianca e Gualtiero, St Petersburg, Bol'shoy, 28 Jan/9 Feb 1845
Undina (3, V. Sollogub, after La Motte Fouqué), St Petersburg, Bol'shoy, 8/20 Sept 1848; as Die Tochter der Wellen, Vienna, 1852
Starosta Boris, ili Russkiy muzhichok i frantsuzskiye marodyori [Old Man Boris, or The Russian Peasant and the French Marauders] (comic op, 3, N. Kulikov), St Petersburg, Alexandrinsky, 19 April/1 May 1854

*

A. Vol'f: *Khronika peterburgskikh teatrov*, i (St Petersburg, 1877)
'N. F.' [N. Findeyzen]: 'Avtor gimna "Bozhe, tsarya khrani" A. F. L'vov: biograficheskiy ocherk' [A. F. L'vov, Author of the Hymn 'God Save the Tsar': a Biographical Essay], *Russkaya muzikal'naya gazeta* (1895), no.7, p.397; no.8, p.452
V. Cheshikhin: *Istoriya russkoy operï (s 1674 po 1903 g.)* (Moscow, 1905)
M. Montagu-Nathan: 'The Composer of the Russian National Anthem', *MT*, lvi (1915), 82–4
A. Gozenpud: *Russkiy operniy teatr XIX veka (1836–1856)* (Leningrad, 1969)
RICHARD TARUSKIN

L'vov, Nikolay Alexandrovich (*b* Nikol'skoye Cherenchitsï, nr Tver', 4/15 March 1751; *d* Moscow, 21 or 22 Dec 1803/2 or 3 Jan 1804). Russian poet and folksong collector. He came of a noble family distinguished in arts and letters. In addition to his literary and musical activities, he was a draughtsman, architect, geologist and engraver. One of the earliest Russian connoisseurs of peasant culture, he compiled one of the first collections of folksongs to contain the tunes (notated and arranged by the Bohemian pianist and composer J. G. Pratsch) as well as the texts. Its first edition, with 100 songs, appeared in 1790. In its second, expanded edition (St Petersburg, 1806, repr. 1987), the L'vov-Pratsch anthology, entitled *Sobraniye narodnïkh russkikh pesen* ('Collection of Russian Folksongs'), with over 150 items, has remained a perennial source for composers of art music. Songs from it have found their way into operas by Arensky (*Son na Volge*), Cavos (*Ivan Susanin*), Dargomïzhsky (*Rusalka*), Davïdov (*Rusalka*), Musorgsky (*Boris Godunov*), Nápravník (*Dubrovsky*), Rimsky-Korsakov (*The Snow Maiden*, *The Tsar's Bride*, *The Tale of Tsar Saltan*), Rubinstein (*Kupets Kalashnikov*), Serov (*Rogneda*, *Vrazh'ya sila*), Tchaikovsky (*Mazepa*) and Verstovsky (*Gromoboy*). Many songs that later went into the collection can be found in Fomin's comic opera *Yamshchiki na podstave* ('The Postal Coachmen at the Relay Station', 1787), for which L'vov wrote the libretto.

*

F. L'vov: *O penii v Rossii* [On Singing in Russia] (St Petersburg, 1834)
A. Veys: 'Novïye materialï dlya biografii i tvorchestva N. A. L'vova' [New Data on the Biography and Works of N. A. L'vov], *XVIII vek*, iii (Moscow and Leningrad, 1958)
N. Bachinskaya: *Narodnïye pesni v tvorchestve russkikh kompozitorov* [Folksongs in the Works of Russian Composers] (Moscow, 1962)
Yu. Keldïsh: 'K istorii operï "Yamshchiki na podstave"', *Ocherki i issledovaniya po istorii russkoy muziki* (Moscow, 1978), 130–40
M. Mazo: Introduction and appendices to N. Lvov and I. Prach: *A Collection of Russian Folk Songs* (Ann Arbor, 1987)
RICHARD TARUSKIN

Lwów (Pol.). L'VIV.

Lyatoshyns'ky, Borys Mykolayovych [Lyatoshinsky, Boris Nikolayevich] (*b* Zhitomir, 22 Dec 1894/3 Jan 1895; *d* Kiev, 15 April 1968). Ukrainian composer. He studied composition with Glier, first privately, then at the newly opened Kiev Conservatory, where he later taught (1919–68, as professor from 1935). He was head of the State Association of Contemporary Music (1922–5) and of the Ukrainian Composers Union (1939–41) and also held the chair of orchestration at the Moscow Conservatory (1935–7). During World War II he taught at the Saratov Conservatory (1941–3) and again in Moscow (1943–4). After the war he travelled extensively throughout Europe.

Following the social and cultural changes in European music after World War I Lyatoshyns'ky wrote his first opera, *Zolotyy obruch* ('The Golden Ring'), also known as *Berkuty*, to a libretto by Yakiv Mamontov, after a novel by Ivan Franko. One of the most significant works to come out of the Soviet Union in the early 1930s, this four-act opera, first performed in Odessa on 28 March 1930, is considered the first Ukrainian music drama and owes much to Berg's *Wozzeck*. The composer revised the work between 1965 and 1968, and this three-act version was staged at the Franko State Academic Theatre of Opera and Ballet, L'viv, on 29 April 1970. In the late 1930s Lyatoshyns'ky wrote *Shchors*, which concerns the exploits of the Soviet partisan leader Mykola Shchors during the Ukrainian Revolution of 1917–20. Written in five acts with an epilogue to a libretto by Ivan

Kocherha and Maxym Rïls'ky, the opera had its première in Kiev on 1 September 1938; a revised version entitled *Polkovodets* ('The Commander') was first performed in Kiev on 18 February 1970. In this opera, as in most of his works written between 1936 and the early 1960s, Lyatoshyns'ky simplified his language to conform to the style of socialist realism. There is genuine beauty in the music, but his natural bent towards continual variation and his expressionist laconicism do not wear well in a work that essentially aspires to fulfil political requirements.

See also ZOLOTYY OBRUCH.

*

I. Belza: *B. M. Lyatoshyns'ky* (Kiev, 1947; Russ. trans., 1947)

A. Malozyomova: 'Stanovleniye geroicheskikh chert v ukrainskoy sovetskoy opere 20–30 godov' [The Appearance of Heroic Features in Ukrainian Soviet Opera in the 1920s and 30s], *Ukrainskoye muzïkovedeniye* (Kiev, 1966), 86–116 [incl. analysis of *Shchors*]

L. Arkhimovych: *Shlyakhy rozvytku ukraïns'koï radyans'koï opery* [On the Development of Ukrainian Soviet Opera] (Kiev, 1970), 61ff, 145ff

S. Pavlishin: 'Geroicheskaya natsional'naya drama' [Heroic National Drama], *SovM* (1970), no.8, pp.36–8

V. Samokhvalov: *B. Lyatoshyns'ky* (Kiev, 1970, 2/1974)

——: *Cherti muzikal'novo mishleniya B. Lyatoshinskoho* [Features of Lyatoshyns'ky's Musical Thought] (Kiev, 1970)

M. D. Kopytsa, ed.: *Boris Nikolayevich Lyatoshinskiy: sbornik statey* [Collected Articles] (Kiev, 1987)   VIRKO BALEY

Lyceum. London theatre built in the late 18th century, rebuilt in 1816 and 1834; see LONDON, §II, 2.

Lyod i stal' ('Ice and Steel'). Opera in four acts by VLADIMIR MIKHAYLOVICH DESHEVOV to a libretto by B. A. Lavrenyov; Leningrad, Academic Theatre of Opera and Ballet, 17 May 1930.

The action takes place at the time of the Kronstadt rebellion in 1921. Counter-revolutionary agents spread anti-Soviet propaganda and succeed in tempting some workers; news of the Kronstadt rebellion, however, banishes any doubts and unites the proletariat. Brigades of workers are created which go to the defence of Soviet power. The opera ends with the assault on the fortress at Kronstadt and its capture by Red Guards.

Ice and Steel achieved notoriety chiefly as one of the first attempts to treat the revolutionary theme in Soviet opera in a serious, yet modern manner. Peopled with a large and colourful cast of loyal tsarists, peasants, workers, soldiers and sailors, it is the opera's mass scenes which were intended to dominate, and no individual hero stands out. The music, which made much of the sound potential of the contemporary environment – the bustling market (Act 1), the metal factory (Act 2) and the assault on the fortress (Act 4) – was compared with the 'realism' of Musorgsky and the 'naturalism' of Berg. Despite several early productions in Moscow as well as Odessa, critics even potentially sympathetic to the modern musical approach found Deshevov's treatment of the heroic subject to be emotionally and dramatically shallow, emphasizing grotesque caricature and melodrama. With the advent of Socialist Realism and the more conservative aesthetic atmosphere of the 1930s, *Ice and Steel* was branded as an inevitable failure of formalism.   LAUREL E. FAY

Lyons (Fr. Lyon). City in France, situated at the confluence of the Rhône and Saône rivers. Opera there dates from the foundation, after Lully's death in 1687, of an Académie royale de musique, which had a three-year privilege granting performing rights (on payment to Lully's heirs) of *tragédies lyriques* already performed in Paris. The first director was Jean-Pierre Leguay (*c*1655–1731). His principal singers included the Lyonese Jean Journet and his daughters, Andrée ('Drion') and Françoise; the chorus numbered about 25, mostly male (only the top part was sung by women), and there were eight full-time dancers. In addition to 20 strings, the orchestra had five wind players plus continuo instruments – two bass viols (Pierre Bellon and Jean Rebel, the latter doubling on theorbo) and harpsichord (J. B. Duplessis, who was répétiteur). The first musical director was Philippe Delacroix, replaced in September 1688 by Pierre Gautier; Leguay continued to organize the choreography and administration. Performances of Lully's operas (*Phaëton*, *Bellérophon*, *Armide* and *Atys*) were given four times a week before the first opera house, a former tennis court in the rue Pizay, was destroyed by fire on 29 November 1688. Performances continued at the home of the governor, the Duke of Villeroy, and a nine-year privilege was granted in December 1690 to Nicolas le Vasseur, who built a theatre in stables in the Place Bellecour. Meanwhile the company mounted productions at Aix-en-Provence, Avignon, Châlon, Dijon, Grenoble and Marseilles. Leguay resumed direction in 1694 with works by Lully and Desmarets. When in 1699 the theatre walls collapsed, the troupe toured Provence, introducing works by Campra (*L'Europe galante*, 1701; *Les fêtes vénitiennes*, 1710) and Destouches (*Issé*, 1709). After the Treaty of Utrecht (1713) the Lyons town council accepted responsibility for a permanent opera.

Under the direction of Antoine-Michel Desbargues (1714–22), Campra's *Iphigénie* and Destouches' *Callirhoé* were mounted at the Hôtel du Gouvernement. After another financial failure Leguay was recalled between 1716 and 1722, but he mounted only comedies and ballets. From 1722 to 1739 the opera was dominated by the Desmarais (Eucher) family. With the chorus cut from 25 to 17 and the dancers from 17 to 13, *comédie-ballets* and *opéra-ballets* by Lully, Bourgeois, Campra, Destouches, Francoeur and Rebel were performed alongside potpourris by local musicians such as François Henri Desmarais. Numerous changes in management reflect the opera's constant financial difficulties, though by 1750 the company had increased to 32 singers and 16 dancers. A high point was reached with the presence of the dancer and choreographer J. G. Noverre during the 1750s. In 1756 a new theatre was constructed behind the Hôtel de Ville by J.-G. Soufflot; under the direction of the actress Michelle Poncet-Destouches (1752–60, 1764–79), the company presented *opere buffe* in translation, as well as *opéras comiques* by Philidor, Monsigny and Duni. Michelle's half-sister Marie Dunant-Destouches was director between 1782 and 1785, when new works by Gluck, Piccinni and Grétry appeared. Probably the first work to be given its first performance in the city was *Pygmalion* by Coignet and Rousseau, performed privately in 1770 at the Hôtel de Ville. N. C. Bochsa's festive opera *Trajan* was composed for Napoleon's visit in 1805.

A new and larger house, the Grand Théâtre, now known as the Lyons Opéra (1800 seats), was built by Chenavard and Pollet opposite the Hôtel de Ville and inaugurated on 1 July 1831 with *La dame blanche*. In order to improve the dull acoustics a fourth balcony was added in 1837 (this gives the present Opéra one of the best acoustics in France). The restored theatre was opened with *Les Huguenots*. Although in the second half of the 19th century and in the early 20th, French opera was the backbone of the repertory, with premières of Saint-Saëns' *Etienne Marcel* in 1879 and Antoine Mariotte's *Salomé* in 1908, the company's Wagner productions became famous after the local premières of *Lohengrin* (1891), *Tannhäuser* (1892), *Die Walküre* (1894) and *Die Meistersinger* (1896; also the national première), all sung in French. In 1912 *Boris Godunov* was given its first performance in the city.

In 1989 the Opéra was closed for renovation and enlargement (to be reopened in 1993 with Debussy's *Rodrigue et Chimène*), while the company continued to perform in other locations. The Opéra Studio, directed by Louis Erlo and Eric Tappy, is attached to the Opéra as a training school for young singers, making Lyons one of the few French houses with the basis of a permanent company. The Opéra has been lucky in its choice of music directors in recent years: Theodor Guschlbauer, Serge Baudo, John Eliot Gardiner – who formed the present opera orchestra after the Orchestre National de Lyon, formerly attached to the Opéra, became a permanent symphony orchestra – and, from 1988, Kent Nagano. Several of the most successful productions of the Gardiner era have been recorded. Since 1975 the company has also performed in the Auditorium Maurice Ravel, a large (2055 seats) modern concert hall and opera house situated in the modern district, La Part Dieu. From 1955 to 1970 the Lyons Opéra was administered by Paul Camerlo; he was followed in 1970 by his nephew, the director Louis Erlo, who has made it one of the best-run and most adventurous opera companies in France. Since 1981 Erlo has also directed the Aix-en-Provence Festival and arranged a system of successful co-productions between Aix and Lyons. In summer, performances are sometimes given at the Roman theatre of Fouvières. The Lyons Berlioz Festival (biennially in October), which presented Berlioz's operas in the Ravel Auditorium, was transformed into the Biennale de la Musique Française in 1991.

*

A. Sallès: *L'opéra italien et allemand à Lyon au XIXe siècle (1805–1882)* (Paris, 1906) [collection of articles from *Revue musicale de Lyon* (1–16 Dec 1906)]

L. Vallas: *Un siècle de musique et de théâtre à Lyon, 1688–1789* (Lyons, 1932)

G.-M.-J. Vuillermoz: *Cent ans d'opéra à Lyon: le centenaire du Grand-Théâtre de Lyon, 1831–1931* (Lyons, 1932)

Trois siècles d'opéra à Lyon (Lyons, 1982)

F. Poudru: 'L'opéra à Lyon de 1945 à 1969', *Le théâtre lyrique français 1945–1985*, ed. D. Pistone (Paris, 1987), 311–18

N. Moulinier: 'La création contemporaine à l'Opéra de Lyon 1969–1986', ibid, 319–27   FRANK DOBBINS, CHARLES PITT

Lyric Opera. American company in CHICAGO; founded as the Lyric Theatre in 1954, it was renamed Lyric Opera of Chicago in 1956.

Lyric Opera of Queensland. Australian company founded in 1982 and based in BRISBANE.

Lyric soprano (Fr. *soprano lyrique*; Ger. *lyrische Sopran*; It. *soprano lirico*). This is the central, 'standard' type of soprano voice, one whose range covers the two octaves from c' to c''' with something over at either end, whose power and fullness are sufficient to take her out of the class of LIGHT SOPRANO while not extending to the demands of heavy roles open to the DRAMATIC SOPRANO, and whose appeal lies not so much in the agility of her

florid singing as in the beauty of tone she is able to bring to her singing of the melodic line. Typical roles for the lyric soprano are Countess Almaviva (*Le nozze di Figaro*), Agathe (*Der Freischütz*), Marguerite (*Faust*), Tatyana (*Yevgeny Onegin*) and Mimì (*La bohème*). Examples of the lyric soprano in the 20th century are Geraldine Farrar, Ninon Vallin and Kiri Te Kanawa. Many have extended their repertory so as to include roles which are better defined as lyric-dramatic, such as Amelia (*Un ballo in maschera*), Elsa (*Lohengrin*) and the title roles of *Tosca* and *Madama Butterfly*. Into this somewhat heavier category come singers such as Elisabeth Rethberg, Renata Tebaldi and Cheryl Studer.

See also SOPRANO.   J. B. STEANE

Lyric tenor (Fr. *ténor lyrique*; Ger. *lirischer Tenor*; It. *tenore lirico*). Tenors of the lighter sort will not be required to contend with heavy orchestration or to raise their voices in strenuous declamation, and therefore (the theory goes) can concentrate on the production of beautiful tone and evenness of line. In this way they will bring grace to the composer's melodies: hence 'lyric'. (The lighter kind of lyric tenor is also known as TENORE DI GRAZIA.) As the tenor became increasingly important in opera during the latter half of the 18th century, he found himself having two main dramatic functions to fulfil, those of hero and lover. Where the role was largely confined to the part of lover it fell essentially to the lyric tenor; so Ferrando and Don Ottavio (but not Idomeneus) in Mozart are taken by the lyric tenor, as also Almaviva, Lindoro and Don Ramiro (but not Arnold or Otello) in Rossini. Tenors who specialize in operas of this period and who include in their repertory parts such as Arturo in *I puritani* need both technical skill in florid work and an extensive upper range. A notable exponent in recent times has been Alfredo Kraus, who also sings lyric roles in later operas such as *Faust*, *Werther* and *La bohème*. Two earlier tenors, Fernando De Lucia and Tito Schipa, were more limited in vocal range, though the first had a voice of considerable dramatic power and the second brought a special grace and personal charm to the best of his singing. Many, such as Caruso and Pavarotti, have begun as lyric tenors and then developed towards the lyric-dramatic repertory. Some have crossed repertories in surprising ways: at Monte Carlo in 1900 Francesco Tamagno could be found singing the lyric role of Alfredo in *La traviata* within two days of his famous part as Verdi's Otello, the most dramatic of all.

See also TENOR.   J. B. STEANE

Lyrique. (1) Company based in Paris from 1851 to 1872 which, between 1862 and 1871, also lent its name to the theatre it occupied; *see* PARIS, §4(vi).

(2) The name under which several late 19th-century theatrical enterprises operated; *see* PARIS, §5(iv).

Lysenko, Mykola Vitaliyovych [Lïsenko, Nikolay Vital'yevich] (*b* Hrynky, nr Kremenchug, Poltava district, 10/22 March 1842; *d* Kiev, 24 Oct/6 Nov 1912). Ukrainian composer. He is regarded as the founder of his native region's national school. After music study at home, in Kharkiv and in Kiev (and after two years in the civil service), Lysenko spent two years (1867–9) at the Leipzig Conservatory with E. F. Richter (theory and composition) and Carl Reinecke (piano). While at Leipzig he began setting the work of the Ukrainian national poet Taras Shevchenko and publishing folk-song arrangements, of which he was to issue seven volumes between 1868 and 1911. He returned home a committed musical nationalist.

From 1869 to 1874 Lysenko lived in Kiev, teaching the piano, working for the local branch of the Imperial Russian Musical Society (with which he later broke over the national question) and composing. His first opera (*Chernomortsy*, 'Black Sea Sailors') was completed in 1873. From 1874 to 1876 he was in St Petersburg, receiving instruction in orchestration from Rimsky-Korsakov and hobnobbing with other members of The Five or the 'mighty Kuchka' (especially Musorgsky, who was then working on *The Fair at Sorochintsï*, his Ukrainian opera). While in the capital Lysenko directed choral performances and organized appearances for the minstrel Ostap Veresay, from whom he had collected many songs.

Lysenko reached the summit of his creative career around 1890 with his two most important stage works: the popular peasant comedy *Natalka Poltavka* (origin-ally conceived as incidental music to Kotlyarevsky's play) and the grandly epic *Taras Bulba* (after Gogol's story), on which he laboured ten years and which Tchaikovsky greatly admired. No Ukrainian house being capable of handling *Taras Bulba* in the 19th century, it was not published until after the composer's death (in Russian translation), and had to wait until Soviet times for its première (orchestrated anew, as most recent productions of Lysenko's operas have been). In addition to Gogol's Ukrainian tales, Lysenko was attracted to fables as subjects and composed a number of children's operas. In 1904 he helped found a school of music and drama in Kiev (named after him in 1918) at which many Ukrainian-Soviet composers were trained.

Harkushka, 1864 (after Storozhenko), frag.
Andrashiada, 1866 (op-satire, M. Starytsky and Drohomanov), frag.
Utoplena, abo Mays'ka nich [The Drowned Maiden, or May Night], 1871–83 (lyric-fantastic op, 3, Starytsky, after Gogol: *May Night*), Odessa, Russian, 2/14 Jan 1885, vs (Leipzig, 1900)
Chernomortsy [Black Sea Sailors], 1872–3 (operetta, 3, Starytsky, after Kukharenko: *Chernomorskiy bit na Kubani* [Life on the Black Sea in the Kuban]), orch. I. David, Kharkiv, Opera House, 1/13 June 1883, vs (Leipzig, 1886)
Rizdv'yana nich [Christmas Eve], 1877–82 (comic-lyric op, 4, Starytsky, after N. Gogol), Kharkiv, Opera House, 27 Jan/8 Feb 1883, vs (Leipzig, 1883)
Taras Bulba, 1880–91 (historical op, 5, Starytsky, after Gogol), orch. L. Shteynberg, Kharkiv, Opera House, 4 Oct 1924, vs (Kiev, 1913)
Koza-Dereza [The Nanny-Goat], 1888 (comic op for children, 1, Dneprovaya Chayka [L. A. Vasil'yevskaya]), Kiev, Hall of Commerce, 8/21 April 1901, vs (Kiev, 1891)
Natalka Poltavka (3, Starytsky, after I. Kotlyarevs'ky), Odessa, Russian, 12/24 Nov 1889, vs (Kiev, 1953)
Pan Kots'kiy [Sir Cat], 1891 (comic op for children, 4, Dneprovaya Chayka), orch. V. Nakhabin, Kharkiv, Opera House, 8 May 1955, vs (Kiev, 1945)
Zima i vesna, abo Snigova kralya [Winter and Spring, or The Snow Maiden], 1892 (fantastic op for children, 2, Dneprovaya Chayka), Kiev, 29 June 1956, vs (Kiev, 1913)
Volshebnïy son [The Magic Dream], 1894 (musical fairy-tale, Starytsky)
Sappho, 1896–1900 (Starytsky)
Eneída [Aeneid] (musical comedy, 3, M. Sadovsky, after Kotlyarevs'ky), Kiev, Literacy League, 23 Nov/6 Dec 1910, vs (Kiev, 1911)
Letney nochyu, 1912, inc.
Noktyurn [Nocturne], 1912 (op-miniature, 1, L. M. Starytskaya-Chernyakhovskaya), Kiev, Municipal, 3/16 Feb 1914, vs (Kiev, 1912)

M. Starytsky: *K biografii N. V. Lïsenko: vospominaniya* [Toward a Biography of Lïsenko: Reminiscences] (Kiev, 1904)
A. Gozenpud: *N. V. Lïsenko i russkaya muzikal'naya kul'tura* (Moscow, 1954)
A. Gudzenko: *Narodno-pesennïye osnovï opernogo tvorchestva N. V. Lïsenko* [The Folksong Foundations of Lysenko's Operas] (Kiev, 1955)
O. Lysenko: *Mikola Lïsenko: vospominaniya sïna* [Memoirs of his Son] (Moscow, 1960)
L. Arkhimovich, A. Shreyer-Tkachenko, T. Sheffer and T. Karïsheva: *Muzikal'naya kul'tura Ukraïni* (Moscow, 1961)
N. Andrievska: *Dityacha opera M. V. Lysenka* [Lysenko's Child-ren's Operas] (Kiev, 1962)
I. Durnev: 'Narodnaya osnova Tarasa Bul'bï' [The Folk Source of *Taras Bulba*], *SovM* (1962), no.10, pp.58–66
L. Arkhimovych and M. Hordiychuk: *M. V. Lysenko* (Kiev, 1963)
RICHARD TARUSKIN

Lyster, W(illiam) S(aurin) (*b* Dublin, 21 March 1827; *d* Melbourne, 27 Nov 1880). Australian impresario. Born into an impoverished Irish gentry family, he was a soldier of fortune before turning to the stage in Boston, Massachusetts. In 1858 he became manager of a New Orleans-based touring opera company assembled by his brother Frederick. After recruiting the Americans Lucy Escott and Henry Squires, former stars of J. H. Tully's National English Opera, the company had successful seasons in California before leaving for Melbourne, which they reached on 1 March 1861. Intending only a short tour, instead they remained in Australia until August 1868, the continent's first permanent opera organization. During that period they gave 1459 performances of a repertory containing 42 operas. Among their landmarks were 26 performances of *Les Huguenots* during the 1862–3 Melbourne season, and an 11-night run of *Guillaume Tell* given in the same city in honour of the 1867 royal visit. From August 1864 to February 1865 the company toured New Zealand. Lyster's brother was a *buffo* baritone in the company and acted as singing coach and conductor; Frederick also composed works for the stage, including *Alfred the Great* (1878) in collaboration with Alfred Plumpton.

Between 1870 and his death in 1880, Lyster created an intercolonial touring chain, the forerunner of the J. C. Williamson organization. He oversaw the tours of several visiting Italian companies while paying his way with seasons by a permanent *opéra bouffe* troupe. A star of many performances was the locally trained tenor, Armes Beaumont, who was denied an international career as a result of being blinded in a shooting accident. In 1877 at the Prince of Wales Opera House, Melbourne, Lyster gave the Australian premières of *Lohengrin* (19 performances) and *Aida* (nine performances) with Pietro Paladini and Antonietta Link. Lyster's success arose from resilience, opportunism and a cheerful scorn for difficulties (of which he faced many), but also reflects the rich musical and theatrical culture of colonial Australia.

*

H. Love: *The Golden Age of Australian Opera* (Sydney, 1981)
——: 'W. S. Lyster's 1861–8 Opera Company: Seasons and Repertoire', *Australasian Drama Studies*, ii (1983–4), 112–24
HAROLD LOVE

Lytton [Jones], Sir H(enry) A(lbert) [Henri] (*b* London, 3 Jan 1865; *d* London, 15 Aug 1936). English baritone. In 1884, with his wife 'Louie Henri', he joined the chorus of the D'Oyly Carte company touring Sullivan's *Princess Ida*. In 1887 he deputized at the Savoy Theatre as Robin Oakapple in *Ruddigore*, and during the 1890s appeared at the Savoy in Gilbert and Sullivan revivals, playing mostly heavier baritone roles. He created roles for Sullivan and German in *The Rose of Persia* (1899), *The Emerald Isle* (1901), *Merrie England* (1902) and *A Princess of Kensington* (1903) before appearing in musical comedy. In 1906–7 and 1908–9 he again appeared at the Savoy under Gilbert, and then from 1909 until 1934 toured with the D'Oyly Carte company in the principal comedy roles. He was a versatile performer, with a sound baritone and winning stage presence. He was knighted in 1930.

H. A. Lytton: *The Secrets of a Savoyard* (London, 1922)
——: *A Wandering Minstrel* (London, 1933)   ANDREW LAMB

Lytvynenko-Vol'hemut, Mariya (Ivanovna) (*b* Kiev, 1/13 Feb 1892; *d* Kiev, 3 April 1966). Ukrainian soprano. She studied with M. Alexeyeva-Yunevich and M. Ivanitsky, graduating from the Kiev Conservatory in 1912. She joined M. Sadovs'ky's theatre company, making a successful début as Oxana in Gulak-Artemovsky's *Zaporozhets za Dunayem* ('A Cossack beyond the Danube'). She sang at the Music Drama Theatre in Petrograd (1914–16), and at the Kharkiv Opera (1923–5) and the Kiev Opera (1935–51). Her voice was expressive and rich and her excellent technique was complemented by a talent for character portrayal in a wide repertory, notably as Natasha in Dargomïzhsky's *Rusalka*, Lisa in Tchaikovsky's *The Queen of Spades*, Tosca and Aida. Among her roles in Ukrainian operas were Varvara (Dan'kevych's *Bohdan Khmel'nyts'ky*), Nastya (Lysenko's *Taras Bulba*) and Hanna (Verykivs'ky's *Naymichka*).

A. Polyakov: *M. I. Lytvynenko-Vol'hemut* (Kiev, 1956)
T. Shvachko: *Mariya Lytvynenko-Vol'hemut* (Kiev, 1972)
                    I. M. YAMPOL'SKY

Lyubimov, Yury (Petrovich) (*b* Yaroslavl', 17/30 Sept 1917). Israeli director of Russian origin. He began his career as an actor in Moscow, first with the Second Studio of the Moscow Arts Theatre, and then at the Vakhtangov Theatre, with which he toured Europe in 1957. From 1964 to 1984 he was artistic director of the Taganka Theatre, Moscow. His opera productions include *The Queen of Spades* at the Paris Opéra, *Boris* and *Khovanshchina* at La Scala, *Don Giovanni* at Budapest, *Tristan* at Bologna and *Rigoletto* in Florence. His British operatic début was with *Jenůfa* (Covent Garden, 1986), a simple but stunningly theatrical staging in which large black and white side panels reflected the conflicting emotions and oppressive social conventions of Czech folk life. His *Rheingold* (Covent Garden, 1988) offered some similarly striking images, but the lack of a clearly unified conception precluded the continuation of the cycle.   BARRY MILLINGTON

Lyubov' k tryom apel'sinam. Opera by Sergey Prokofiev; *see* LOVE FOR THREE ORANGES, THE.

M

Maag, (Ernst) Peter (Johannes) (*b* St Gall, 10 May 1919). Swiss conductor. He attended the universities of Zürich, Basle and Geneva and from 1943 to 1946 was engaged at the Biel-Solothurn civic theatre, moving from répétiteur to principal conductor. After assisting Furtwängler and Ansermet, Maag became principal conductor at Düsseldorf (1952–5), then general director at Bonn (1955–9), where he encouraged the performance of unfamiliar works such as *Genoveva* and *Rappresentatione di Anima, et di Corpo* as well as 20th-century operas. His British opera débuts were at Covent Garden in *Die Zauberflöte* and at Glyndebourne in *Le nozze di Figaro*, both in 1959. He conducted *Così fan tutte* at the Chicago Lyric Opera in 1961 and was principal conductor at the Vienna Volksoper from 1964 to 1968. His Metropolitan début was with *Don Giovanni* in 1972, and in Italy he held short-term appointments as artistic director at the Teatro Regio, Parma (1972), and the Teatro Regio, Turin (1974), as well as becoming a regular guest at La Scala, Milan. He has appeared at the Teatro Colón, Buenos Aires, and at major European festivals. He received the Toscanini Medal at Parma (1969), the Verdi Medal (1973) and the Toscanini 'Presentation Baton' (1975). He is renowned chiefly as a Mozart conductor, usually accompanying the recitatives himself, and giving performances that combine natural grace with Classical brio. He is also accomplished in the mainstream Italian repertory, his recordings of which include Verdi's *Luisa Miller* (1975) and Paer's *Leonora* (1976 and 1979).

JÜRG STENZL, NOËL GOODWIN

Maas, Joseph (*b* Dartford, Kent, 30 Jan 1847; *d* London, 16 Jan 1886). English tenor. He studied with Bodda-Pyne in London and San Giovanni in Milan. He made his début as Babil in Boucicault's spectacle *Babil and Bijou* at Covent Garden in 1872, after which he toured the USA with Clara Louise Kellogg's English Opera Company. In 1878 he sang Gontran in the first performance in England of *Das goldene Kreuz* (Adelphi Theatre) and was engaged by the Carl Rosa company. He sang the title role in the English première of *Rienzi* (1879), Wilhelm Meister and Radames in the first English-language performances of *Mignon* and *Aida* (1880), and Des Grieux in the first London performance of *Manon* (1885). In 1883 he sang Lohengrin at Covent Garden, and his repertory included Faust and Donizetti's Edgar. He was an indifferent actor, but his voice was said to be of a pure and beautiful quality.

Obituary, *The Athenaeum* (23 Jan 1886)
Obituary, *MT*, xxvii (1886), 93
G. Hauger: 'Joseph Maas: a Centenary Memoir', *Opera*, xxxvii (1986), 136–41
HAROLD ROSENTHAL/R

Maazel, Lorin (Varencove) (*b* Neuilly-sur-Seine, 6 March 1930). American conductor. He studied privately in Los Angeles and Pittsburgh and began conducting as a child, at Los Angeles in 1938 and at the New York World's Fair in 1939, later earning Toscanini's commendation. After further study at Pittsburgh University and a spell as a violinist, he made his adult conducting début in Catania (1953) while in Italy on a Fulbright scholarship to research Baroque music, and this was followed by performances elsewhere in Europe. In 1960 he was the first American conductor at Bayreuth (in *Lohengrin*) and he returned for the *Ring* in 1968 and 1969. His début at the Metropolitan Opera was with *Don Giovanni* in 1962. He both produced and conducted *Yevgeny Onegin* at Rome in 1965, and that year became artistic director at the Deutsche Oper, Berlin; he remained there until 1971, conducting some 20 operas, including the première of Dallapiccola's *Ulisse* (1968), and was admired for his forceful, secure musical direction.

While music director of the Cleveland Orchestra (1972–82), he brought staged opera into the seasonal repertory there, and described his approach to the organization and performance of opera in *Opera News* ('A Brave New World for Opera', xl/5, 1975–6, pp.18–21). His Covent Garden début was not until 1978 with Verdi's *Luisa Miller*, which he recorded the next year with Katia Ricciarelli, Domingo and the Royal Opera House forces. In 1982 he became the first American to take the dual post of artistic and general director at the Vienna Staatsoper on a four-year contract, but political and other problems led to this being curtailed in 1984. Since 1988 he has been music director of the Pittsburgh Symphony Orchestra.

At La Scala he opened the season in 1983 and since then his operatic activity has mainly been based there, including a Puccini series with the 1985 production of *Madama Butterfly* available in video recordings. He has been increasingly involved in filmed opera, conducting for Joseph Losey's production of *Don Giovanni*,

Francesco Rosi's *Carmen* and Zeffirelli's *Otello*, among others. His other opera recordings total more than a dozen, and include a much-admired performance of Ravel's *L'enfant et les sortilèges* (1961); *Fidelio* (1964) and *Tosca* (1966) both with Birgit Nilsson; the first fully operatic version of *Porgy and Bess* with Houston Grand Opera (1976); Massenet's *Thaïs* with Beverly Sills (1976); *Aida* (1985) with Pavarotti; and *Otello* (1986) with Domingo.

In opera Maazel has shown himself to be a bold, vigorous but variable conductor, unafraid of indulging expressive sentiment and sometimes crude orchestral colour. His numerous honours include the Légion d'honneur and the German Federal Cross of Merit.

ARTHUR JACOBS, NOËL GOODWIN

Mabellini, Teodulo (*b* Pistoia, 2 April 1817; *d* Florence, 10 March 1897). Italian composer and conductor. His father was a wind instrument maker. His first teachers (in Pistoia) included Giuseppe Pilotti, who had studied under Stanislao Mattei. In 1833 he moved to Florence, where he completed his studies at the Istituto Musicale in 1836. The same year he made his début as a composer with the opera *Matilde e Toledo*, the success of which earned him a scholarship from the Grand Duke Leopold II. He then studied under Mercadante in Novara, and in 1840 produced *Rolla*, his most successful opera, in Turin. He returned to Pistoia, but in 1843 settled in Florence, where he became director of the orchestra of the Società Filarmonica; this involved him in directing (1863–80) the Concerti Popolari promoted by Abramo Basevi. In 1847 Mabellini was appointed *maestro di cappella* to the grand ducal court and in 1848 became conductor at the Teatro della Pergola. He held the chair of composition at the Istituto Reale Musicale 'L. Cherubini' from 1859 and taught until 1887. The city of Pistoia built a theatre in his honour and gave it his name.

As a composer Mabellini had many strong qualities, notably an ability to work successfully in different genres, a mastery of counterpoint and orchestration, a solid musical grounding, a sure technique and a conscious adherence to the great Classical tradition. But none of these could redeem his numerous works from the fundamental lack of an individual, original and genuinely creative musical personality, and they are now forgotten. His output included eight masses and other sacred and secular vocal works, and orchestral and other instrumental pieces.

Matilde e Toledo (os, 2), Florence, Alfieri, 27 Aug 1836
Rolla (os, 2, G. Giacchetti), Turin, Carignano, 12 Nov 1840, *I-Mr**, vs (Milan, 1841)
Ginevra degli Almieri [Ginevra di Firenze] (os, 3, L. Guidi-Rontani), Turin, Carignano, 13 Nov 1841
Il conte di Lavagna (tragedia lirica, 4, F. Guidi), Florence, Pergola, 4 June 1843, vs (Milan, ?1844)
I veneziani a Costantinopoli (os, 2), Rome, Apollo, spr. 1844
Maria di Francia (dramma tragico, 3, Guidi), Florence, Pergola, 14 March 1846
Il venturiero (ob, 2, A. de Lauzières), Livorno, Rossini, carn. 1851, collab. L. Gordigiani
Il convito di Baldassarre (os, 3, G. de Toscani), Florence, Pergola, Nov 1852
Fiammetta (ob, 3, G. B. Canovai), Florence, Pergola, 12 Feb 1857, excerpts, pf acc. (Milan, n.d.)

*

DEUMM (F. Bussi)   FRANCESCO BUSSI

McAlpine, William (*b* Stenhousemuir, 3 Dec 1922). Scottish tenor. He made his début in 1951 as First Jew (*Salome*) at Covent Garden, then sang Jaquino, Don Basilio, Andres (*Wozzeck*), the Holy Fool (*Boris Godunov*), Gastone (*La traviata*) and many other minor roles. He created the Novice in *Billy Budd* (1951) and the Spirit of the Masque in *Gloriana* (1953). Moving in 1956 to Sadler's Wells, he sang lyric roles, including Don Ottavio, Rinuccio, Tamino, Alfredo, Fenton, Belmonte, Lensky and Boris (*Kát'a Kabanová*). At Glyndebourne (1956–9) he sang Idamantes, the Italian Singer (*Der Rosenkavalier*) and Bacchus. For Sadler's Wells (1961–74) he took on heavier roles such as Cavaradossi, Rodolfo, Pinkerton, Hermann (*The Queen of Spades*), Hoffmann and Erik. Meanwhile he sang at Berlin, Hamburg, Paris, Florence, Aix-en-Provence and Vancouver. For Scottish Opera (1965–74) he sang Faust, Cassio, Grigory and Robert Boles (*Peter Grimes*). Later roles at Covent Garden (1960–75) included Alfredo, Hoffmann, Grigory and Walther von der Vogelweide. A lyric tenor with an attractive, ringing timbre, he found the heavier roles in his repertory a strain in larger theatres.   ELIZABETH FORBES

Macbeth (i). Musical scenes by RICHARD LEVERIDGE for WILLIAM SHAKESPEARE's play with words by Thomas Middleton and WILLIAM DAVENANT; London, Drury Lane, 21 November 1702.

Songs from Middleton's *The Witch*, with music by Robert Johnson, were added to the witches' scenes in Acts 3 and 4 of *Macbeth* very early in the play's history. In his adaptation of the play in the 1660s Davenant doubled the amount of music by adding a scene for the witches to the end of Act 2; his composer was Matthew Locke. Pepys (19 April 1667) liked the 'variety of dancing and music', and John Downes in *Roscius anglicanus* (London, 1708) remembered a spectacular production for the new Dorset Garden Theatre: 'it being all Excellently perform'd, being in the nature of an Opera, it Recompenc'd double the Expence; it proves still a lasting Play'.

On 21 November 1702, Drury Lane staged *Macbeth* with 'Vocal and Instrumental Musick, all new Compos'd by Mr. *Leveridge*, and perform'd by him and others'. Leveridge's score, no doubt influenced by Locke's version, became the standard *Macbeth* music and continued in use even when Davenant's other additions were discarded. It held the stage until 1875 and was much admired. In her edition of *Macbeth* (*c*1800) Mrs Inchbald wrote of 'this grand tragic opera' with its 'awful, yet inspiring music', and George Hogarth (1851) praised the music at length, calling it 'one of the noblest and most beautiful works that has ever been produced by an English musician'. The music was not published until 1770, when William Boyce edited *The Original Songs Airs & Choruses which were introduced in the Tragedy of Macbeth*. By this time the name of the composer of the frequently used score was forgotten and Boyce ascribed the music to Matthew Locke. Later, attempts were made to prove Henry Purcell's authorship. However, an early 18th-century manuscript (*GB-Cfm*) clearly ascribes the music to Leveridge and contains the names of singers who were in the Drury Lane company in 1702.

Leveridge was the theatre's leading bass and a successful composer of songs, so it is not surprising that the music in *Macbeth* is dramatically effective and contains important bass solos. Leveridge sang the First Witch in Act 2 and Hecate in Acts 3 and 4 for over 40 years. In Act 2 the witches celebrate the murder of

Duncan ('We should rejoice when good kings bleed'), gloat over crimes to come and dance on the heath. The soprano solo 'Let's have a dance' was the only part of the music published before 1770, in a songsheet naming Kitty Clive as the singer (*c*1750). At the climax of the scene in Act 3 Hecate flies off on a machine singing 'Now I go, and now I fly', and the chorus concludes with 'We fly by night 'mongst troops of spirits'. In Act 4 singing witches add extra ingredients to the cauldron. The distribution of the solos and size of the chorus varied according to the singers employed by the theatre company, but numbers tended to increase. At Drury Lane in April 1794 Michael Kelly was one of 23 advertised singers, and 20 years later he supervised even larger forces: 'It was a rare and novel sight, to see so great a body of English chorus singers on the stage, full of appropriate and animated action.'

OLIVE BALDWIN, THELMA WILSON

Macbeth (ii). Opera in four acts by GIUSEPPE VERDI to a libretto by FRANCESCO MARIA PIAVE (with additional material by Andrea Maffei) after WILLIAM SHAKESPEARE's play; Florence, Teatro della Pergola, 14 March 1847 (revised version, with libretto translated by CHARLES-LOUIS-ETIENNE NUITTER and Alexandre Beaumont, Paris, Théâtre Lyrique, 21 April 1865).

Duncano [Duncan] *King of Scotland*		silent
Macbeth	} *Generals in Duncan's army*	baritone
Banco [Banquo]		bass
Lady Macbeth *Macbeth's wife*		soprano
Lady-in-waiting to Lady Macbeth		mezzo-soprano
Macduff *a Scottish nobleman, Lord of Fife*		tenor
Malcolm *Duncan's son*		tenor
Fleanzio [Fleance] *Banquo's son*		silent
A Servant of Macbeth		bass
A Doctor		bass
A Murderer		bass
The Ghost of Banco [Banquo]		silent
A Herald		bass

Witches, messengers of the King, Scottish nobles and exiles, murderers, English soldiers, bards, aerial spirits, apparitions

Setting Scotland and the Anglo-Scottish border

Verdi's contract of 1846 with the impresario Alessandro Lanari and the Teatro della Pergola of Florence stipulated no particular opera, and in the summer various possibilities, including *I masnadieri* and *Macbeth*, were under consideration. The final decision, Verdi made clear, would depend on the singers available. *Macbeth* would have no tenor lead but needed a first-class baritone and soprano; *I masnadieri*, on the other hand, was dependent on a fine tenor. By late September the cast had been secured, notably with the engagement of Felice Varesi, one of the finest actor-singer baritones of the day; accordingly, the choice fell on *Macbeth*. By this time, Verdi had already drafted the broad dramatic lines of the opera and had written encouraging letters to his librettist, Piave, emphasizing that this, his first Shakespearean subject, was to be a special case: 'This tragedy is one of the greatest creations of man! If we can't do something great with it, let us at least try to do something out of the ordinary ... I know the general character and the *tinte* as if the libretto were already finished'.

As the première drew near, Verdi again and again demonstrated his particular interest in the opera: by bullying Piave into producing exactly the text he required; by engaging his friend Andrea Maffei to retouch certain passages; by taking unusual time and care in making sure the production was well rehearsed and true to his intentions; and by endlessly coaching the leading singers – in particular Varesi and the Lady Macbeth, Marianna Barbieri-Nini – to ensure that their every nuance was as he wished. The première was a great success and the opera soon began to be performed around Italy; Verdi often advised those responsible for revivals of the special attention that the opera needed.

In 1864 the French publisher and impresario Léon Escudier asked Verdi to add ballet music for a revival of the opera at the Théâtre Lyrique, Paris. The composer agreed but also stated that he wanted to make substantial changes to some numbers that were 'either weak or lacking in character'. As well as the additional ballet and major or minor retouchings to various numbers, this revision eventually included: a new aria for Lady Macbeth in Act 2 ('La luce langue'); substantial alterations to Act 3, including a new duet for Macbeth and Lady Macbeth ('Ora di morte'); a new chorus at the beginning of Act 4 ('Patria oppressa'); and the replacement of Macbeth's death scene with a final 'Inno di vittoria'. The Paris première, which included Jean-Vital Ismael Jammes (Macbeth) and Amélie Rey-Balla (Lady Macbeth), was largely unsuccessful. The reception puzzled Verdi and, although the original version of the opera continued to be performed for some time in Italy, it is clear that he wished the 'Paris' version to supersede it. In spite of a recent revival of interest in the 1847 version, and in spite of the fact that it is clearly more unified stylistically, the later version is the one generally heard today. In the discussion below, the most substantial revisions will be considered as they appear.

The prelude is made up of themes from the opera. First comes a unison woodwind theme from the witches' scene at the start of Act 3, then a passage from the apparition music in the same act. The second half is taken almost entirely from Lady Macbeth's Act 4 'sleepwalking' scene.

ACT 1.i *A wood* The witches' chorus that opens the act divides into two parts, the first ('Che faceste?') in the minor, the second ('Le sorelle vagabonde') in the parallel major. Both partake of the musical 'colour' associated throughout with the witches, among which are prominent woodwind sonorities (both dark and shrill), mercurial string figures and a tendency for rhythmic displacement. Macbeth and Banquo enter and are hailed by the witches with their threefold prophecies, darkly scored and with prominent tritones in the harmonic progression. A brisk military march then introduces messengers, who inform Macbeth of Cawdor's death and hence the fulfilment of part of the prophecy. As Verdi admitted to his principal baritone, Varesi, this sequence would traditionally have called for a double aria for Macbeth, but instead the composer supplied a one-movement duettino for Macbeth and Banquo, 'Due vaticini', full of broken lines and suppressed exclamations as the two men examine their consciences. The witches' closing stretta, 'S'allontanarono', is far more conventional, though it does find room for yet more 'characteristic' colour.

1.ii *A room in Macbeth's castle* Lady Macbeth's cavatina generates great dramatic power from a conventional outward form. After a stormy orchestral introduction, she enters to read a letter from her husband describing the events we have just witnessed. The first part of her double aria, 'Vieni! t'affretta!', bids Macbeth hurry home so that she can instil in him her bloody thoughts; it is remarkable for its avoidance of formal repetition and for its tightly controlled but distant harmonic excursions. A messenger announces that Macbeth and Duncan are expected that night, and Lady Macbeth exults in the cabaletta 'Or tutti sorgete', whose moments of agility are tightly woven into the restricted formal structure. The cabaletta over, Macbeth appears and in a brief recitative Lady Macbeth unfolds her plans for Duncan. The couple are interrupted by the arrival of the king himself, whose parade around the stage is accompanied by a 'rustic' march from the *banda*.

The 'Gran Scena e Duetto' that follows begins with Macbeth's extended arioso 'Mi si affaccia un pugnal?!', during which he sees a vision of a dagger and steels himself to murder Duncan. The passage is extremely rich in musical invention, as sliding chromatic figures jostle with distorted 'religious' harmonies and fugitive reminiscences of the witches' music; it will set the tone for the great free recitatives of Verdi's later career. Macbeth enters the king's room, and Lady Macbeth appears, soon to be rejoined by her husband. Macbeth's neighbour-note motif at 'Tutto è finito!' ('All is finished!') furnishes the accompaniment material for the first movement of the four-movement duet, the Allegro 'Fatal mia donna! un murmure'. This first movement involves a rapid exchange between the characters, with musical continuity mostly supplied by the orchestra. As Macbeth describes the inner voice that has forever denied him sleep, the second, more lyrical movement, 'Allor questa voce', begins: the singers again have dissimilar musical material, although they eventually come together for an extended passage in 3rds and 6ths. A short transitional movement, 'Il pugnal là riportate', sees Lady Macbeth return the dagger to the king's room and emerge with blood on her hands. The duet closes with a much-curtailed cabaletta, 'Vieni altrove! ogni sospetto', which in the 1847 version quickly turns to the major mode but which in 1865 Verdi revised to keep subdued and in the minor throughout.

The first-act finale begins with the arrival of Macduff and Banquo, the latter singing a solemn apostrophe to the night. Macduff calls everyone on stage and announces the murder of Duncan. The news launches the Adagio concertato, 'Schiudi, inferno': a tutti outburst of group anguish, a quiet unaccompanied passage in which all pray for God's guidance, and a final soaring melody in which divine vengeance is called down upon the guilty one. Following the pattern of the preceding duet, the final stretta is extremely short, functioning more as a coda than as a movement in its own right.

ACT 2.i *A room in the castle* An orchestral reprise of part of the Act 1 grand duet leads to a recitative between Macbeth and his wife. Malcolm has fled and is suspected of Duncan's murder, but Macbeth, obsessed by the witches' prophecy that Banquo's sons will be kings, decides that more blood must flow. In the 1847 version, Lady Macbeth closes the scene with the cabaletta 'Trionfai! securi alfine', a conventional two-verse aria in the manner of Elvira's music in *Ernani*. In

1865 Verdi replaced this with 'La luce langue', a multi-sectional aria whose advanced chromaticism is consistently that of his later style.

2.ii *A park* The quiet, staccato chorus of murderers, 'Sparve il sol', in Verdi's traditional manner of depicting sinister groups, leads to a *romanza* for Banquo, in the coda of which the assassins strike him down but cannot prevent Fleance from escaping.

2.iii *A magnificent hall* Lively festive music underpins the assembling of noble guests, after which Macbeth summons his wife to sing a brindisi (drinking song). She obliges with 'Si colmi il calice', and (as will happen in Act 1 of *La traviata*) is answered by the unison chorus. The closing strains of the song still echo in the orchestra as Macbeth learns from an assassin of Banquo's death and Fleance's escape. The festive music resumes, but Macbeth has a horrible vision of Banquo at the banquet table (this and the second hallucination were revised and chromatically intensified in the 1865 version). Lady Macbeth calms him and repeats her brindisi, but the vision returns. The king's terror precipitates the concertato finale, 'Sangue a me', which is led off and dominated by Macbeth, though with frequent interjections from his wife, who tries to calm him. There is no formal stretta, the act ending with the general sense of stunned surprise still intact.

ACT 3 *A dark cavern* After a stormy orchestral introduction, the witches' chorus, 'Tre volte miagola', brings back the opening idea of the prelude as the first of a series of increasingly lively, rhythmically bumpy 6/8 melodies, ones clearly intended to depict the 'bizarre' element of the supernatural. The ballet that follows, written for the 1865 Paris version, is broadly in three movements. In the first, various supernatural beings dance around the cauldron to an Allegro vivacissimo. Hecate is called forth and, in an Andante second movement full of the rich chromaticism of Verdi's later style, mimes that Macbeth will come to ask of his destiny and should be answered (Verdi insisted that this section be mimed rather than danced). The final movement is a sinister waltz, the spirits dancing even more wildly around the cauldron.

The Apparition Scene, substantially revised in the 1865 version to intensify its harmonic and orchestral effect, has little sustained melodic writing and consists of brief but telling musical episodes. The first introduces the three apparitions (who make their predictions of Macbeth's fate); then, to Macbeth's arioso 'Fuggi, regal fantasima', come the eight kings, the last of whom is in the form of Banquo and precipitates Macbeth's 'Oh! mio terror! dell'ultimo', at the end of which he faints. A gentle chorus and dance of the aerial spirits, 'Ondine e silfidi', precedes the finale, which was completely rewritten for 1865. In the 1847 version the act finished with an Allegro risoluto cabaletta for Macbeth, 'Vada in fiamme', very much in the early Verdi mould though with an unusual minor–major key scheme. In 1865 the composer replaced this with a duettino for Macbeth and Lady Macbeth, 'Ora di morte e di vendetta', in which, however, the added subtlety of articulation results in a loss in sheer rhythmic power.

ACT 4.i *A deserted place on the borders of England and Scotland* The original 1847 version of the opening chorus, 'Patria oppressa', not least in its lamenting of the 'lost' homeland, is somewhat reminiscent of the 'patriotic' choruses that became so famous in Verdi's early operas, although the minor mode gives it a

'Macbeth' (Verdi), the witches' cavern in Act 3: sepia drawing presented to Verdi by Countess Clara Maffei after the first production at the Teatro della Pergola, Florence, 14 March 1847

different colour. The 1865 replacement is one of the composer's greatest choral movements, with subtle details of harmony and rhythm in almost every bar. Macduff's 'Ah, la paterna mano', which follows, is a conventional minor–major *romanza*, and the scene is rounded off by a cabaletta-like chorus, 'La patria tradita', as Malcolm's troops prepare to descend on Macbeth.

4.ii *A room in Macbeth's castle* (as 1.ii) Lady Macbeth's famous 'sleepwalking' aria, 'Una macchia', is justly regarded as one of the young Verdi's greatest solo creations. Preceded by an atmospheric instrumental depiction of Lady Macbeth's guilty wandering, the aria itself is distinguished by its expanded formal and harmonic structure and – most important – by a marvellously inventive orchestral contribution.

4.iii *Another room in the castle* A noisy orchestral introduction leads to Macbeth's confessional Andante sostenuto 'Pietà, rispetto, amore', an effective slow aria with some surprising internal modulations. The aria concluded, soldiers rush on to announce the seeming approach of Birnam Wood; a pseudo-fugal orchestral battle ensues during which Malcolm overcomes Macbeth in single combat. In 1847 the opera ended with a short, melodramatic scene for Macbeth, 'Mal per me', full of declamatory gestures that recall motivic threads from earlier in the drama. For 1865 Verdi replaced this with a Victory Hymn, 'Macbeth, Macbeth ov'è?', a number in his most modern style, with more than a hint of Offenbach in its dotted rhythms, and perhaps even a hint of the *Marseillaise* in its final bars.

*   *   *

There is no doubt that Verdi's frequently voiced perception of the 1847 *Macbeth* as an especially important work, ennobled by its Shakespearean theme, was one that he successfully converted into dramatic substance. Much of the opera shows an attention to detail and sureness of effect unprecedented in earlier works. This holds true as much for the 'conventional' numbers, such as Lady Macbeth's opening aria or the subsequent duet with Macbeth, as for formal experiments like the Macbeth-Banquo duettino in Act 1. What is more, the

new standard set by *Macbeth* was one that Verdi rarely retreated from in subsequent works.

The 1865 revisions undoubtedly enrich the score, supplying several of its most effective pieces, notably 'La luce langue' and the opening chorus of Act 4. Clearly the sense of stylistic disparity the revisions create did not concern Verdi; indeed, for the most part he made little attempt to match the replacement numbers with the main body of the score, instead producing pieces that are among the most harmonically advanced of his later career. Nor should such disparity unduly concern us: we may well overestimate the importance of stylistic consistency in opera, and the 1865 revision will surely continue to be the most commonly performed version of this magnificent work. ROGER PARKER

Macbeth (iii). Lyric drama in a prologue and three acts by ERNEST BLOCH to a libretto by Edmond Fleg after WILLIAM SHAKESPEARE's play; Paris, Opéra-Comique (Salle Favart), 2 November 1910.

The libretto, in French, follows the play quite closely. Lucienne Bréval, to whom the opera was dedicated, sang Lady Macbeth in the première. For a later version in English, by Bloch and Alex Cohen, the composer altered certain rhythms in an effort to make the English text conform as closely as possible to Shakespeare's. For the first Italian performance, at S Carlo, Naples, 5 March 1938, an Italian libretto was prepared by Maria Tibaldi-Chiesa. In an effort to make the action more concise, the murder of Lady Macduff and her son was deleted from this production. Important revivals of the opera took place in Rome and Trieste (1953), Brussels (1957, La Monnaie) and Milan (1960, La Scala). The first major American performance was at the University of California at Berkeley (1960); a student production in English had been presented at Karamu House in Cleveland in 1957.

Macbeth shows evidence of Bloch's emerging originality: frequent changes of metre, tempo and tonality, melodic use of the augmented and perfect 4th at crucial moments, modal flavour, dark instrumentation, many ostinatos and pedal points and ever-present cyclic formal procedures. As in *Pelléas*, the vocal lines are essentially declamatory. There are dialogues among the principals rather than traditional duets, words are not repeated, and ensembles are limited to the witches and the crowds (at moments of climax). The understatement that permeates the opera, notable in the subtle metamorphoses of the several leitmotifs, is no better illustrated than in Lady Macbeth's 'sleepwalking' scene. Instead of a full-blown aria, Bloch provides the dishevelled Queen with pitches more closely associated with the speaking voice, allowing Shakespeare's words to be the focus of attention. This approach, far removed from the high drama accorded this scene in Verdi's version, makes all the more powerful the tremendous climax that follows.   DAVID Z. KUSHNER

McBurney, Mona (*b* Douglas, Isle of Man, 29 July 1862; *d* Melbourne, 4 Dec 1932). Australian composer. She studied privately with Alexander Mackenzie in Edinburgh before settling in Australia. Having matriculated at the University of Melbourne in 1881, she became the first female graduate of the University Conservatorium and the fourth BMus in Australia. Though she wrote orchestral works, chamber music and songs, she was most famous in her lifetime for her three-act opera *The Dalmatian* (subtitled *An Idyl of Murano*; composed 1905), which received its première in a concert performance on 10 December 1910 and was first staged in 1926 (Melbourne, Playhouse, 25 June). The libretto is an adaptation by McBurney of Francis Marion Crawford's novel *Marietta: a Maid of Venice* (1901). Set in Venice in 1470, it has as its major themes family rivalry, romance and conflict between the state and a Venetian secret brotherhood. A late-Romantic influence is reflected in the opera's set pieces (which include choruses and liturgical chants), its lyric style and the picturesque Venetian settings which exploit the romance, mystery and intrigue of the plot. There is some Wagnerian quotation, and the principal musical ideas are structured thematically on the conflict between good and evil. A striking feature of the work is the choral writing.

F. Patton: 'McBurney, Mona', *Australian Dictionary of Biography*, ed. B. Nairn and G. Serle (Melbourne, 1983)
——: 'Rediscovering our Musical Past: the Works of Mona McBurney and Florence Ewart', *Sounds Australian*, no.21 (1989), 10–12   FAYE E. PATTON

Maccabäer, Die ('The Maccabees'). Opera in three acts by ANTON GRIGOR'YEVICH RUBINSTEIN to a German libretto by SALOMON HERMANN MOSENTHAL after the tragedy by Otto Ludwig (1854); Berlin, Königliches Theater, 17 April 1875 (Russian première, as *Makkavei*, St Petersburg, Mariinsky Theatre, 10/22 January 1877).

Written in Vienna in 1872–4 (with many interruptions because of the composer's concert tours in Europe and America), this monumentally conceived if somewhat coarsely executed work was Rubinstein's most successful opera during his lifetime, achieving repertory status on both the German and the Russian stages. The widely praised libretto focussed on the family drama of the Maccabees – Judas (baritone), leader of the revolt against the Syrians, his brother Eleazar (tenor), who betrays his people for love of the Syrian princess Cleopatra (soprano), and their mother Leah (contralto) – against a background of political and religious struggle in which the chorus (divided into groups of Israelites, Syrian warriors and priests, and Greek slaves)

assumed the leading role. Each act culminates in a huge ensemble with chorus; that in the second act (a victory hymn during which Eleazar's treason is gradually revealed to fine ironic effect) is based on the melody of a Jewish song the composer learnt as a child from his mother. According to Berlin reviewers, the opera's opening night was the greatest triumph the city had witnessed since that of *L'Africaine* ten years before. After the Vienna première (1878), Hanslick attempted to set *Die Maccabäer* up as the antidote to the Wagnerian method. The Berlin cast included Marianne Brandt (Leah) and Franz Betz (Judas), the St Petersburg cast Alexandera Men'shikova (Cleopatra), Wilhelmina Raab (Naomi), Josef Paleček (Antiochus), Bogomir Korsov (Judas) and Osip Petrov (Simeon). The most recent production was in 1925, in Jerusalem, in Hebrew.   RICHARD TARUSKIN

McCabe, John (*b* Huyton, 21 April 1939). English composer. During his early years when ill-health kept him from school, he came to know music through records and the piano and had written 13 symphonies by the time he went to the Liverpool Institute at the age of 11. He studied composition with Proctor Gregg at Manchester University, with Thomas Pitfield at the RMCM and with Harald Genzmer at the Munich Hochschule. On his return to Britain he was resident pianist at Cardiff University (1965–8) and then moved to London, remaining active as a pianist. From 1983 to 1990 he was principal of the London College of Music.

McCabe's first opera, *The Lion, the Witch and the Wardrobe* (4, G. Larner, after C. S. Lewis), was commissioned for the 1969 Manchester Cathedral Festival and first performed by Chetham's Hospital School in the cathedral on 29 April 1969. The cast consists of two adult singers with a minimum of nine children. Much of the dialogue is set in arioso recitative, though some use is made of *Sprechgesang*. As in Humperdinck's *Hänsel und Gretel*, sophisticated music and fairy-story here find a common level, exceptional compositional skill being used so self-effacingly that we are rarely aware of the art that lies behind the charming surface of the music. The chamber opera *The Play of Mother Courage* (5 scenes, M. Smith, after H. J. C. von Grimmelhausen) was commissioned by Opera Nova and first performed in Middlesbrough on 3 October 1974.

G. Larner: 'The Lion, the Witch and the Wardrobe', *MT*, cx (1969), 372
M. Kennedy: Review of 'The Lion, the Witch and the Wardrobe', *MT*, cx (1969), 656   HUGO COLE

Maccari [Macari], Giacomo (*b* Rome, *c*1700; *d* ?Venice, after 1744). Italian composer. His Roman origin is asserted by Goldoni, who knew him, but Maccari was in Venice at least by 15 December 1720, when he became a *musico tenore* for the ducal chapel at St Mark's. He may have been related to the sisters Antonia and Costanza Maccari, both opera singers from Rome; Costanza was popular in Venice (where she led a scandalous private life) between 1715 and 1718.

Maccari wrote an early serious opera, *Adaloaldo furioso* (1727), but most of his theatrical work, like that of Salvatore Apolloni, his colleague at St Mark's, was connected with Giuseppe Imer's company at the Teatro di S Samuele from 1734 to 1743. During these years he is known to have composed two intermezzos, *La pupilla* (C. Goldoni) and *Il conte Copano* (A. Gorì and G.

Imer), both performed at S Samuele in 1734, and he is also thought to have written other comic works for Imer and his amateur singers (one of whom was Zanetta Casanova, mother of the writer and amorist). However, it is unlikely that the settings of Goldoni intermezzos considered by Ortolani to be possibly by Maccari are the composer's work (or the work of Apolloni); the authorship of these intermezzos is not known, although the opera *Aristide* has been attributed to Lotavio Vandini (an anagram of the name Antonio Vivaldi; Weiss considered it highly improbable that Vivaldi could be the composer). None of this music survives, but Goldoni said that its 'easy, clear style was well adapted to the needs of those performing it'. He also had some repute as a contrapuntalist, but a solo cantata indicates only a middling talent. In 1744 he contributed some arias to the pasticcio *La finta schiava*.

first performed at S Samuele, Venice, unless otherwise stated

Adaoaldo furioso (melodramma, A. Lucchini), S Moisè, carn. 1727
Ottaviano trionfante di Marc'Antonio (dramma comico, P. Miti), S Salvador, carn. 1735
La fondazione di Venezia (divertimento per musica, prol. and 11 scenes, C. Goldoni), aut. 1736
Lucrezia Romana in Constantinopoli (dramma comico, 3, Goldoni), carn. 1737
La contessina (commedia per musica, 3, Goldoni), carn. 1743

Doubtful: La birba (os, Goldoni), carn. 1735; L'ippocondriaco (int, Goldoni), Oct 1735; Aristide (Goldoni), aut. 1735 [also attrib. Lotavio Vandini]; Monsieur Petiton (int, Goldoni), carn. 1736; La bottega da caffè (int, Goldoni), Oct 1736; L'amante cabala (int, Goldoni), aut. 1736

ES ('Macari, Giacomo'; P. Petrobelli)
T. Wiel: *I teatri musicali veneziani del settecento* (Venice, 1897)
G. Ortolani, ed.: *Tutte le opere di Carlo Goldoni* (Milan 1935–56), i, 717, 727 and passim on Imer's troupe; notes here and in vol. x passim
P. Weiss: 'Venetian Commedia dell'Arte "Operas" in the Age of Vivaldi', *MQ*, lxx (1984), 195–217

Macchi, Egisto (*b* Grosseto, 4 Aug 1928). Italian composer. He studied in Rome, where his composition teachers were Roman Vlad and Heinrich Scherchen. He also studied literature and medicine at Rome University. In 1959 he collaborated with Domenico Guaccero in founding *Ordini: studi sulla nuova musica*, a periodical devoted to contemporary music, and in 1965 joined the Compagnia del Teatro Musicale di Roma. He was a founder member of the Roman musical society 'Nuova Consonanza' (1960).

Macchi flirted briefly with serialism in the orchestral *Composizione 2* of 1959, but in *Composizione 3* (1960) he started on a technique of his own, in direct opposition to post-Webern pointillism. His first theatre composition, *Anno Domini* (1962), for large orchestra, four *recitanti* voices, three sopranos and four choirs to texts inspired by the Auschwitz holocaust, is indicative of the search for a sound continuum which he began in *Composizione 3* and marked the first clear change of interest towards vocal music, which was henceforth to be the centre of his creative activity.

After *Parabola* (1963, incomplete) for voices, instruments and a tape of 'concrete music', to texts inspired by Joan of Arc as a symbol of the heroine needed in our time, Macchi wrote *A(lter) A(ction)* (1966), a chamber opera centred on the personality of Antonin Artaud, divided among four characters. The title derives from the initials of the actor-dramatist, and the texts are taken from his *Lettres de Rodez*.

Macchi returned to composition for the theatre in the 1980s with two chamber works, *Venere e il leone* (1985) for voice and piano (first version) to texts by Petrarch, inspired by the sacrifice of Mussolini's mistress Claretta Petacci, and *'A Matra* (1987), based on the trial in 1946 of the murderess Leonarda Cianciulli, the libretto in each case being provided by Nicola Badalucco. Both confirm the central role played by the voice in Macchi's works for the theatre.

Anno Domini, 1962 (composizione per teatro, 1, A. Titone), Palermo, Biondo, 1965, (Florence, 1965)
Parabola, 1963 (composizione per teatro, 1, Titone), inc.
A(lter) A(ction) (composizione per teatro, 1, A. Artaud and M. Diacono), Rome, Olimpico, 15 June 1966, vs (Florence, 1966)
Venere e il leone, 1985 (melodramma da camera, 1, N. Badalucco), unperf., unpubd
'A Matra, 1987 (melodramma da camera, 1, Badalucco), unperf., unpubd

D. Guaccero: 'Studio per *A(lter) A(ction)*', *Marcatre*, nos. 26–9 (1966), 16
R. Vlad and D. Guaccero: '*A(lter) A(ction)* di Egisto Macchi', *Collage*, vii (1967), 92   RAFFAELE POZZI

Macchi, Maria de (*b* Peruzzaro, Italy, Jan 1870; *d* Milan, 16 Jan 1909). Italian soprano. She trained in Milan as a mezzo-soprano, making her début as Laura in *La Gioconda* at Brescia in 1889. Turning then to the dramatic soprano repertory she appeared in Italy, Russia, Spain and Portugal, and in 1901 sang the title role in Karl Goldmark's *Die Königin von Saba* under Toscanini at La Scala. Caruso recommended her to the Metropolitan, where she sang with him in *Lucrezia Borgia* (1904); her other operas there were *Aida*, *Cavalleria rusticana*, *La Gioconda* and *Les Huguenots*, in which she sang Valentine. Her final appearance was at Rome in 1908 as Lucrezia Borgia. Her recordings, few and rare, show her as an accomplished artist with a voice of remarkable beauty in the middle register.

J. B. STEANE

Maccioni, Giovanni Battista [Giambattista] (*b* ?Orvieto; *d* ?Rome, *c*1678). Italian composer and librettist. Quadrio and Allacci stated that the libretto of a *commedia* of 1615 entitled *I pazzi prudenti* was 'by Giambattista Maccioni of Orvieto'. Rudhart and others assumed that this Maccioni was the same person who arrived in Munich on 12 May 1651 and received an appointment as court chaplain and harpist. In the following year the Elector Ferdinand Maria married Princess Adelaide of Savoy, who enthusiastically supported Italian artistic endeavours in Bavaria. Maccioni soon won Adelaide's favour and became an important cultural adviser. He not only collaborated with her in the preparation of several librettos but also taught her the harp. In August 1653 the Emperor Ferdinand III was honoured during a visit to Munich by the performance of a brief allegorical composition, *L'arpa festante*, for which Maccioni wrote both text and music (in *A-Wn*; three extracts ed. in Schiedermair 1903–4, pp.461ff). Librettos by him for at least four other works performed in Munich survive (in *D-Mbs*): introductions for three occasional pieces and a *dramma musicale Ardelia* (1660), all inspired by Adelaide. J. K. Kerll appears to have composed the music for *Ardelia*, whose libretto shows Venetian influence, but it has not survived. Lipowsky (who has been followed by others) indicated that Maccioni also wrote the libretto for an *opera pastorale* entitled *Celaroso*, allegedly performed at Munich in 1657, but no evidence has been found that an opera with this title was actually staged. Maccioni seems to have left Munich about 1661. By 1662 he was in Rome, where he served as an envoy for Munich and became a resident at the papal court. Correspondence between him and Ferdinand Maria, dating from 1662 to 1674, reveals his influence in securing musicians for the Munich court; they included the castratos Ferrucci and Boni and the composer Ercole Bernabei.

Maccioni's *L'arpa festante* marks the beginning of opera at the Munich court, where Italian dramatic music flourished for the rest of the Baroque era. It consists of a single extended scene. The music calls for five soloists and includes brief recitatives, arias and duets and a final chorus. The florid arioso patterns and snatches of melodic chromaticism indicate that Maccioni was familiar with contemporary techniques.

*

AllacciD

F. Quadrio: *Della storia, e della ragione d'ogni poesia*, iii (Bologna, 1744)

F. Lipowsky: *Baierisches Musik-Lexikon* (Munich, 1811)

F. Rudhart: *Geschichte der Oper am Hofe zu München* (Freising, 1865)

K. von Reinhardstöttner: 'Über die Beziehungen der italienischen Literatur zum bayrischen Hofe und ihre Pflege an demselben', *Jb für Münchener Geschichte*, i (1887), 93–172

H. Riemann: *Opern-Handbuch: Repertorium der dramatisch-musikalischen Litteratur* (Leipzig, 1887)

J. Mantuani: *Tabulae codicum manu scriptorum praeter Graecos et Orientales in Bibliotheca Palatina Vindobonensi Asservatorum*, ix (Vienna, 1897)

L. Schiedermair: 'Künstlerische Bestrebungen am Hofe des Kurfürsten Ferdinand Maria von Bayern', *Forschungen zur Geschichte Bayerns*, x (1902), 82–148

——: 'Die Anfänge der Münchener Oper', *SIMG*, v (1903–4), 442–68

R. Brockpähler: *Handbuch zur Geschichte der Barockoper in Deutschland* (Emsdetten, 1964)   LAWRENCE E. BENNETT

McClymonds, Marita (Martha) P(etzoldt) (*b* St Louis, MO, 4 Dec 1935). American musicologist. She studied at Culver-Stockton College and became a schoolteacher; then she opened a music studio and became a bassoonist, singer and pianist. She returned to academic studies, under Heartz, Curtis and others at Berkeley, California, in 1969 (MA 1971, PhD 1978); there she founded Commedia dell'Opera. She became a professor at the University of Virginia in 1981.

Her PhD dissertation, published as *Niccolò Jommelli: the Last Years, 1769–1774* (Ann Arbor, 1980), proved to be the starting-point for extensive, wide-ranging studies on 18th-century Italian opera, in particular treating the innovations and modifications in *opera seria* during the second half of the century (the subject of many of her writings and congress papers); these studies have thrown new light on the background to the operas of Mozart, Haydn and Gluck, and have focussed scholarly attention on the librettist Mattia Verazi. McClymonds has prepared a performing edition of Jommelli's *La schiava liberata* which has been given at European and American centres and promoted interest in Jommelli generally. She was founder of the RISM libretto project in the USA.

McCormack, John (*b* Athlone, 14 June 1884; *d* Dublin, 16 Sept 1945). Irish tenor, later naturalized American. He began his studies in Dublin, and in 1905 went to Milan to take further lessons with Vincenzo Sabatini.

He made his stage début under the assumed name of Giovanni Foli in 1906 in Mascagni's *L'amico Fritz* at the Teatro Chiabrera in Savona, near Genoa, after which he returned to England and appeared at Covent Garden, at first as Turiddu in the autumn season of 1907, also in *Rigoletto* and as Don Ottavio. In the following year he appeared in the international summer season, returning every year until World War I. He made both his New York début (with Oscar Hammerstein's Manhattan Opera Company in 1909) and his Metropolitan Opera début (1910) as Alfredo in *La traviata*; between 1910 and 1918 he appeared six times with the Metropolitan during five seasons, and more often with the Boston and Chicago companies. By his own admission a poor actor, he soon abandoned the stage and devoted himself to hugely successful recitals. He made numerous recordings; most of the operatic items were recorded during his short operatic period, and show the sweetness of his tone and the perfection of his style and technique in his prime.

*

L. A. G. Strong: *John McCormack* (London, 1941)

L. F. X. MacDermott Roe: *John McCormack: the Complete Discography* (London, 1956, 2/1972)

P. W. Worth and J. Cartwright: *John McCormack: a Comprehensive Discography* (New York and London, 1986)   DESMOND SHAWE-TAYLOR

McCoy, Seth (*b* Sanford, NC, 17 Dec 1928). American tenor. He studied singing with Pauline Thesmacher in Cleveland and Antonia Lavanne in New York and opera with Goldovsky. He sang in concert performances, as Belmonte, Florestan and Don Ottavio, and in the American premières of *Kát'a Kabanová*, Steffani's *Il Tassilone* and Joplin's *Treemonisha*; his stage début was in 1979 as Tamino at the Metropolitan Opera, where in the same season he appeared as the Italian Singer (*Der Rosenkavalier*). A singer of expressive warmth and scrupulous musicianship and diction, he pursues his career chiefly in the concert hall.   CORI ELLISON

McCracken, James (Eugene) (*b* Gary, IN, 16 Dec 1926; *d* New York, 29 April 1988). American tenor. His début was as Rodolfo in *La bohème* at Central City, Colorado, in 1952. He made his Metropolitan Opera début on 21 November 1953 as Parpignol in the same opera and took many other comprimario roles before leaving for Europe in 1957. He was engaged at Bonn as Max, Radames and Canio.

The turning-point in his career was an engagement as Otello with the Washington (DC) Opera in 1960; it became, and remained, his most celebrated role. He sang in most of the world's leading houses, and his repertory included Florestan, Don José, Calaf, Manrico and Don Alvaro, Bacchus (*Ariadne auf Naxos*), Hermann, Samson and John of Leyden. A powerful and convincing actor, McCracken had an emotional intensity and a dark-timbred tenor of exceptional fervour. He married the mezzo-soprano Sandra Warfield, with whom he collaborated on an autobiography, *A Star in the Family* (New York, 1971).

*

A. Williamson: 'James McCracken', *Opera*, xviii (1967), 7–14

S. Wadsworth: 'Finding Tannhäuser', *ON*, xlii/11 (1977–8), 14–15, 32

J. Hines: 'James McCracken', *Great Singers on Great Singing* (Garden City, NY, 1982), 156

B. Paolucci: 'America's Heroic Tenor: James McCracken', *Ovation*, vi/8 (1985), 15–17, 30
MARTIN BERNHEIMER

McCredie, Andrew D(algarno) (*b* Sydney, 3 Sept 1930). Australian scholar and teacher. A graduate of the University of Sydney, he also studied at the New South Wales State Conservatorium of Music before leaving for Europe. He studied musicology in Copenhagen (1955–6), Stockholm (1956–7) and Hamburg (1960–63), where he took the doctorate in 1963 with a dissertation on German Baroque opera. Returning to Australia in 1965, he became a senior research fellow in musicology at the University of Adelaide, where he was later appointed to a chair in musicology. His writings include studies of Graupner and Keiser and also Australian composers.
DAVID TUNLEY

MacCunn, Hamish (James) (*b* Greenock, 22 March 1868; *d* London, 2 Aug 1916). Scottish composer, conductor and teacher. The son of a wealthy ship-owner, he inherited his precocious musical gifts from his mother, who was a talented amateur musician. At 15 he won a composition scholarship to the RCM, and he remained in London for the rest of his life. In 1887 he produced the work by which he is now best known, the concert overture *The Land of the Mountain and the Flood*, following it with a series of secular cantatas on Scottish subjects. These successes led in 1889 to his being commissioned to compose an opera for the Carl Rosa Opera Company: *Jeanie Deans*, based on Scott's *The Heart of Midlothian*, was completed less than two months before its première in 1894. It was successful, and led to the commission of a second opera for the Carl Rosa company, *Diarmid* (1897). Both works remained in the repertory until World War I.

The production of his operas also established MacCunn's reputation as an able conductor, and for financial reasons he turned increasingly to operatic conducting from 1898 onwards. He directed *Siegfried* and the English première of *Tristan* for the Carl Rosa company, and worked with the Moody-Manners Company before conducting operetta at the Savoy Theatre until 1905. Possibly as a result of this experience he wrote a light opera, *The Golden Girl* (1905). Thereafter he conducted for various touring companies, and for the Beecham Opera Company in 1910 and 1915. He taught composition privately and at the GSM (from 1912), where he also directed the opera class; he had previously been professor of harmony at the RAM (1888–94). In 1914 he was nominated principal of the proposed musical academy in Edinburgh, but the war put an end to the project.

Jeanie Deans is MacCunn's masterpiece and the finest serious opera of the late Victorian period. The narrative force of Scott's novel was strong enough to sweep away much of the dust from Joseph Bennett's usual poetic style, though the libretto retains much native dialect. There is a gaunt wildness and an inner strength about the music which marks it as uniquely MacCunn's. There can be no doubt that these qualities are derived from the landscape and the people of Scotland, for *Jeanie Deans* is as deeply yet unobtrusively imbued with the spirit of its native country as are the operas of Tchaikovsky. Such external influences as can be detected are usually Teutonic: traces of Weber and Mendelssohn are evident, though each is transfigured. MacCunn's orchestration mirrors every nuance of his characters' feelings by means of a kaleidoscopic multiplicity of colours which

reveals his emotional debt to Wagner. His use of folksong (both authentic and composed) now sounds surprisingly modern, and his ability to conceive whole scenes at a time is prophetic of the musico-dramatic methods of 20th-century British opera.

Diarmid, a vast but undramatic Celtic music-poem, advances MacCunn's harmonic language to a point where it anticipates the operatic style of Delius. Thereafter he adopted a more cosmopolitan outlook; his obituary in *The Musical Times* noted: 'it seemed evident that his desire to compose serious artistic music became chilled by his realisation of things as they are in this country'. The conventional wisdom that MacCunn's songs and light music did not fulfil the promise of his youth is in one sense true, but it is now apparent that the extent of his achievement in *Jeanie Deans* has for too long been underestimated.

See also JEANIE DEANS.

Jeanie Deans (grand op, 4, J. Bennett, after W. Scott: *The Heart of Midlothian*), Edinburgh, Lyceum, 15 Nov 1894, *GB-Lcm**, vs (London, 1894)
Diarmid op.34 (grand op, 4, Duke of Argyle, after Celtic legends), London, CG, 23 Oct 1897, *Gu**, vs (London and New York, 1897)
Breast of Light (Duke of Argyle), *Gu**, inc.
The Masque of War and Peace (masque, L. Parker), London, Her Majesty's, 13 Feb 1900, *Gu**, vs (London, 1900)
The Golden Girl (light op, B. Hood), Birmingham, Prince of Wales, 5 Aug 1905, lost
Prue (light op, 3, C. H. Taylor), inc., lost
The Pageant of Darkness and Light (stage pageant in 6 episodes, J. Oxenham), 1908, *Gu**, vs (London, 1908)

Music in: H. E. Haines: The Talk of the Town, 1905; A Waltz Dream, 1908–9

*
DNB (C. Aveling); *LoewenbergA*; *StiegerO*
'Hamish MacCunn's "Jeanie Deans"', *MT*, xxxv (1894), 816–17
J. D. Brown and S. S. Stratton: *British Musical Biography* (London and Birmingham, 1897)
J. Bennett: *Forty Years of Music 1865–1905* (London, 1908), 377–9
The Dunedin Magazine, ii/2 (1914), 65–78
Obituary, *MT*, lvii (1916), 410
G. B. Shaw: *London Music in 1888–89* (London, 1937), 110–13
A. M. Henderson: *Musical Memories* (Glasgow, 1938), 65–72
H. G. Farmer: *History of Music in Scotland* (London, 1947), 519–21
E. W. White: *The Rise of English Opera* (London, 1951), 118–19, 126
N. Burton: 'Opera: 1865–1914', *Music in Britain: the Romantic Age, 1800–1914*, ed. N. Temperley (London, 1981), 330–57, esp. 351–2
E. W. White: *A Register of First Performances of English Operas and Semi-Operas* (London, 1983)
D. Johnson: Review of 'Jeanie Deans', *MT*, cxxvii (1986), 401
NIGEL BURTON

McDaniel, Barry (*b* Lyndon, KS, 18 Oct 1930). American baritone. He studied at the Juilliard School and in Stuttgart. After engagements at Mainz (1954), Stuttgart (1957) and Karlsruhe (1960), he joined the Deutsche Oper, Berlin, in 1962. He created the Secretary in Henze's *Der junge Lord* (1965) and Lusignan in Reimann's *Melusine* at Schwetzingen (1971), repeating the part in Edinburgh. He sang at Vienna, Munich and the Metropolitan, where his only role was Pelléas (1972). His repertory included many Mozart roles, Weber's Sherasmin (*Oberon*), and the 20th-century parts in which he specialized: the Barber (*Die schweigsame Frau*), Olivier (*Capriccio*), Harlequin (*Ariadne*) and the Husband (*Les mamelles de Tirésias*). He took part in Blacher's *Abstrakte Oper no. 1* at the Academy of Arts, Berlin (1987). He had a warm, mellifluous voice and was an excellent actor.
ALAN BLYTH

Macdonald, Hugh (John) (*b* Newbury, Berks., 31 Jan 1940). English musicologist. He studied at Pembroke College, Cambridge, from 1958 to 1966 and was awarded the PhD in 1969. He has held university appointments at Cambridge, Oxford and Glasgow and at Washington University, St Louis, from 1987. His chief area of work has been the music of the 19th century, especially in France. In addition to his editions of *Les Troyens* (1969–71) and *Béatrice et Bénédict* (1980), he has published singing translations of *Pelléas et Mélisande* (1981), *Mireille* (1983) and *Les Troyens* (1986), as well as a number of articles on 19th-century French opera.   DAVID SCOTT

McDonall, Lois (*b* Larkspur, Alta., 7 Feb 1939). Canadian soprano. She made her début in 1969 with the Canadian Opera Company in Wolf-Ferrari's *Il segreto di Susanna*. After a year at Flensburg, where she sang Tosca, Elsa and Konstanze, she was engaged by Sadler's Wells Opera, later the ENO, making her first appearance in 1970 as Handel's Semele. She also sang Konstanze, Countess Almaviva, Fiordiligi, Freia, Massenet's Manon, Rosalinde, Jenny (Bennett's *The Mines of Sulphur*) and the Marschallin. She made her Covent Garden début in 1975 as a solo voice in *Die Frau ohne Schatten*. In 1981 she created the title role in Hamilton's *Anna Karenina* at the ENO. Endowed with a handsome stage presence and a naturally beautiful voice, she had great facility in florid music as well as fine breadth of phrasing.   ELIZABETH FORBES

McDonnell, Tom [Thomas] (**Anthony**) (*b* Melbourne, 27 April 1940). Australian baritone. After studying in Melbourne, he sang Belcore (*L'elisir d'amore*) in Brisbane. He joined Sadler's Wells Opera (later the ENO) in 1967. His first major role was Mozart's Figaro and in 1968 he sang Marcel Sciocca in Williamson's *The Violins of St Jacques*. In 1969 he sang Yevgeny Onegin with Glyndebourne Touring Opera. His roles with the ENO include Germont, Schaunard, Escamillo, Papageno and Andrey, which he sang at the first London performance of Prokofiev's *War and Peace* (1972) and at the opening of the Sydney Opera House (1973). He also sang Wolfram (*Tannhäuser*) with Australian Opera. In 1974 he created Lieutenant September in Crosse's *The Story of Vasco* and sang the Captain (Adonis) in the first London stage performance of Henze's *The Bassarids*. He made his Covent Garden début in the première of Henze's *We Come to the River* (1976) and created Yuri in Tippett's *The Ice Break* (1977); for the ENO he created Atahuallpa in Hamilton's *The Royal Hunt of the Sun* and at the Collegiate Theatre he sang in the première of LeFanu's *Dawnpath* (1977). For Opera Factory he sang Faber (*The Knot Garden*), Don Alfonso and Seneca and took part in the first performance of Osborne's *Hell's Angels* (1986). A powerful actor, he excels in dramatic roles.
                            ELIZABETH FORBES

Macedonia. Region in northern Greece, the southeastern part of the former Yugoslavia and of western Bulgaria. For discussion of operatic activity in the area *see* SALONICA and SKOPJE.

Macerata. City in the Marches region of central Italy. In July and August an open-air opera season is held in the Arena Sferisterio, built in 1829 for the game of pallone and restored in 1966. Its stage is 90 metres long, and the semicircular auditorium can hold 6000. Count Pier Alberto Conti organized the first seasons of opera in 1921 and 1922 which included *Aida* and *La Gioconda*. Since 1967 there has been a regular summer season centred on the main operas of the standard repertory (*Aida*, *Tosca*, *Carmen*, *Rigoletto*, *La bohème*) that has attracted famous singers such as Pavarotti, Sherrill Milnes and Montserrat Caballé.   ARRIGO QUATTROCCHI

Macfarren, Sir **George Alexander** (*b* London, 2 March 1813; *d* London, 31 Oct 1887). English composer and teacher. In 1829 he entered the RAM, where he studied composition with Cipriani Potter. On completing his studies there in 1836 he taught at a school in the Isle of Man, but he returned to the RAM as professor of harmony and composition in 1837. He resigned this position in 1847 when his adherence to Alfred Day's theory of harmony was condemned by the other professors but was reinstated in 1851. He founded the Society of British Musicians in 1834 and the Handel Society in 1844, and in 1845 he became conductor at Covent Garden. In his later years many honours and appointments were bestowed on him: in 1875 he became principal of the RAM and professor of music at Cambridge; he received the honorary MusD from Cambridge in 1875, from Oxford in 1876 and from Dublin in 1887; and he was knighted with Sullivan and Grove in 1883.

Although he wrote prolifically in all the major musical genres it was Macfarren's lifelong ambition to be recognized as a successful operatic composer. He seemed to thrive on difficulties: his eyesight troubled him from 1823 onwards, and when it finally failed in 1860 he was compelled to dictate his compositions to amanuenses. Several of his operas were never performed: *Caractacus* (*c*1834) was rejected by the censor on grounds of historical inaccuracy; *El Malhechor* (1837–8) and *Allan of Aberfeldy* (*c*1850) were accepted by several managements which later went bankrupt; and *Kenilworth* (1880) was cancelled by the management that had commissioned it. Macfarren's graphic account of the problems he overcame in seeing *The Devil's Opera* (1838) through to its production makes it seem remarkable that some early Victorian operas ever reached the stage at all.

Macfarren had a predilection for English dramatic subjects, and many of his operas are invested with genuine English nationalism. *King Charles II* (1849), one of his most successful works, shows him to be in a direct line of descent from the 18th-century ballad opera. Despite his worship of Mozart, his musical personality possessed a strength and determination that frequently recall Beethoven. He was a true intellectual: his operatic overtures are formally ingenious (the 'Illustrated Overture' to *Helvellyn*, 1864, especially so), his musical characterizations are always sharply drawn (*An Adventure of Don Quixote* of 1846 is masterly in this respect), and his intricacies of word-setting often anticipate Sullivan (see, for instance, the ballad 'She shines before me like a star' from *King Charles II*).

Robin Hood (1860) is probably Macfarren's best opera and merits revival, even though Oxenford's libretto detrimentally alters the traditional story and has a weak final denouement. The work is indebted to Weber's *Oberon* in the variety of its individual numbers, in the fully operatic writing for the principal soprano, tenor and baritone, and in its musical distinction between their social position and that of the secondary characters. The inclusion of male-voice partsongs, a feature common to many 19th-century British operas, derives from the glee tradition. Macfarren's handling of the orchestra is bright, uncluttered and masculine; his brass writing is notably good, being less garish than Wallace's and more confident than Sullivan's.

Jessy Lea (1863) and *The Soldier's Legacy* (1864), both designated 'opera di camera' and requiring only piano and harmonium accompaniment, demonstrate Macfarren's operatic style at the peak of its maturity. Both are innovatory in their economy of means, *The Soldier's Legacy* also in its use of folk material. The vital ingredient lacking in Macfarren's operas is melodic inspiration; this is why the works of Balfe and Wallace, though less endowed with intellect and polished musical technique, have been deservedly more successful.

unless otherwise stated, first performed in London, printed works published in vocal score in London , and MSS in GB-Cfm

LCG – *Covent Garden*   LDL – *Drury Lane*
LHM – *Her Majesty's*
LLY – *Lyceum Theatre (English Opera House)*

Genevieve, or The Maid of Switzerland (operetta, 1, Mrs C. Baron-Wilson), Queen's, Charlotte St, 1832, *Gb-Lbl**
The Prince of Modena, 1833
Caractacus, *c*1834 (G. Macfarren sr), inc., unperf.
I and my Double (farce, 2, J. Oxenford), LLY, 16 June 1835
Innocent Sins, or Peccadilloes (operetta, Macfarren sr), Coburg Theatre, Aug 1836
El Malhechor, 1837–8 (2, Macfarren sr), unperf.
The Devil's Opera (2, Macfarren sr), LLY, 13 Aug 1838 (1838)
Agnes Bernauer, the Maid of Augsburg (romance, 2, T. J. Serle), LCG, 20 April 1839
Emblematical Tribute on the Queen's Marriage (masque, Macfarren sr), LDL, 10 Feb 1840, no MS
An Adventure of Don Quixote, 1841 (ob, 2, Macfarren sr, after M. de Cervantes), LDL, 3 Feb 1846 (1846)
King Charles II (2, M. D. Ryan, after J. H. Payne: *Charles II*), Princess's, 27 Oct 1849, selections (1849)
The Sleeper Awakened (serenata, 1, Oxenford, after *The Thousand and One Nights*), LHM, 15 Nov 1850 (1850)
Allan of Aberfeldy, *c*1850 (Oxenford), unperf.
Robin Hood (3, Oxenford), LHM, 11 Oct 1860 (1860)
Freya's Gift (allegorical masque, 1, Oxenford), LCG, 10 March 1863 (1863)
Jessy Lea (op di camera, 2, Oxenford, after E. Scribe: *Le philtre*), Gallery of Illustration, 2 Nov 1863 (1863)
She Stoops to Conquer (3, E. Fitzball, after O. Goldsmith), LCG, 11 Feb 1864 (1864)
The Soldier's Legacy (op di camera, 2, Oxenford), Gallery of Illustration, 10 July 1864 (1873)
Helvellyn (4, Oxenford, after S. H. Mosenthal: *Der Sonnenwendhof*), LCG, 3 Nov 1864 (1870)
Kenilworth, 1880 (It. op), unperf.

*
DNB (R. H. Legge); *Grove6* (N. Temperley); *LoewenbergA*
Obituary, *MT*, xxviii (1887), 713
W. Spark: *Musical Memories* (London, 1888), 269–79
J. Sims Reeves: *My Jubilee* (London, 1889), 189–93
H. C. Banister: *George Alexander Macfarren* (London, 1891)
W. Macfarren: 'George Alexander Macfarren', *RAM Magazine*, no. 1 (1900), 14–18
J. A. Fuller Maitland: *English Music in the XIXth Century* (London, 1902), 107–10
G. B. Shaw: *London Music in 1888–89* (London, 1937), 106–9
N. Temperley: 'The English Romantic Opera', *Victorian Studies*, ix (1966), 300–01
[C. L. Cudworth]: MS list of Macfarren MSS in *GB-Cfm, Cpl*
M. Hurd: 'Opera: 1834–1865', *Music in Britain: the Romantic Age, 1800–1914*, ed. N. Temperley (London, 1981), 307–29, esp. 312–13, 318
E. W. White: *A History of English Opera* (London, 1983)
——: *A Register of First Performances of English Operas and Semi-Operas* (London, 1983)   NIGEL BURTON

Macfarren [née Andrae], **Natalia** [Clarina Thalia] (*b* Lübeck, 1827; *d* Bakewell, 9 April 1916). British

translator and editor. She became a pupil of G. A. Macfarren in London at the RAM; they were married in 1844. From the 1870s she translated choral texts, solo songs and operas (chiefly from German and Italian) into English with considerable flair. She was among the first translators of *Lohengrin* (1872), *Tannhäuser* (1873) and *Rigoletto* (1872). Her other translations include *Fidelio*, *Martha*, *The Bartered Bride* and *Der Freischütz*. The Novello vocal score of *Le nozze di Figaro* (1872) is among those she not only translated but also edited, with a useful indication of orchestration given in the piano part. She had a concert career as a contralto and appeared in the première of her husband's opera *King Charles II* (1849).   ARTHUR JACOBS

McFerrin, Robert (*b* Marianna, AR, 19 March 1921). American baritone. After appearing in 1949 in Weill's *Lost in the Stars*, in William Grant Still's *Troubled Island* at the New York City Opera and as Amonasro in *Aida* with the National Negro Opera Company, he joined the New England Opera Company in 1950. He was the first black male to join the Metropolitan company, making his début on 27 January 1955 as Amonasro; his other roles were Valentin and Rigoletto. After a period in Naples at the Teatro S Carlo, he was chosen to sing the role of Porgy (played by Sidney Poitier) in the soundtrack of the film of Gershwin's *Porgy and Bess* (1959). He toured internationally as a recitalist, and was also active as a teacher.

*
SouthernB
P. Turner: *Afro-American Singers* (Minneapolis, 1977)
                    DOMINIQUE-RENÉ DE LERMA

Mácha, Otmar (*b* Mariánské Hory, nr Ostrava, 2 Oct 1922). Czech composer. He studied composition at the Prague Conservatory (1945–8) while working as a director and adviser to Czechoslovak radio (1942–62). He is a prolific composer whose style springs from Moravian folk melody and from the legacy of Janáček, which he gradually enriched with late 20th-century elements. He has presented important issues in his operas. *Jezero Ukereve* ('Lake Ukereve'), set in an area of equatorial Africa troubled by sleeping sickness and colonial oppression, expresses the humanitarian responsibility of European civilization for all people. Mácha employs elements of traditional European music, avoiding African folk styles; the melodies derive from the intonation of colloquial speech, and the rhythms are intensified by the use of tapes within the orchestral texture. *Růže pro Johanku* ('A Rose for Johanka') is an artistic reportage of the assassination of the Nazi Reinhard Heydrich and reflects the mental state of people fighting for freedom. Reality is interwoven with past events in a dynamic succession of contrasting verbal and dramatic scenes, often with characteristics of other musical genres. The vocal writing ranges from speech to expressive cantabile lines.

Using procedures specific to television, Mácha worked in close cooperation with a television crew in the production of *Proměny Prométheovy* ('Prometheus's Metamorphoses'), in which man's never-ending fight against evil is expressed in three historical parallels with Prometheus, Giordano Bruno and Albert Einstein, using rich, expressive music full of dramatic tension; this won first prize in the 1983 Golden Prague television festival. In a different mould is *Polapená nevěra* ('Infidelity Unmasked'), a pithy neo-classical farce on the eternal-triangle theme, here concerning an old merchant, his young wife and her lover. Composed in neo-Renaissance style, it treats operatic clichés with irony and takes the form of a *commedia dell'arte* using anti-illusionary theatrical principles. The modern comic folk opera *Svatba naoko* ('The Mock Wedding') gave Mácha the opportunity to use folksongs and a duel between a bagpipe band and a rock band, which represent the two greedy families of the engaged couple. He has also composed a comic fairy-tale opera for children, *Zvířátka a loupežníci* ('The Little Animals and the Robbers').

Polapená nevěra [Infidelity Unmasked] (operatic farce, prol., 5 scenes, epilogue, Mácha, after Old Cz. anon. text, 1608), Prague, D 34, 21 Nov 1958
Jezero Ukereve [Lake Ukereve], 1960–63 (5, Mácha, after V. Vančura), Prague, National, 27 May 1966
Růže pro Johanku [A Rose for Johanka], 1971–4 (ballad and musico-dramatic fantasy, 2, J. Pávek), Brno, Janáček, 8 Jan 1982
Svatba naoko [The Mock Wedding], 1974–7 (comic op, 4, V. Trapl and S. Kinzl), unperf.
Proměny Prométheovy [Prometheus's Metamorphoses] (television music drama, J. Kolařík), Czechoslovak TV, 1982
Zvířátka a loupežníci [The Little Animals and the Robbers] (sung fairy-tale, V. Šefl), Prague, spr. 1986

*

ČSHS
V. Pospíšil: 'Jezero Ukereve', *HRo*, xix (1966), 402–3
J. Volek: 'Jezero Ukereve', *Kulturní tvorba*, iv/22 (1966), 12
J. Brožovská: 'O věrnosti a zradě' [On Fidelity and Betrayal], *Scéna*, vii/4 (1982), 4
J. Majer: 'Brněnská premiéra nové opery' [Première of a New Opera in Brno], *HRo*, xxxv (1982), 313–14
V. Pospíšil: 'Mácha a Pauer v Ústí' [Mácha and Pauer at Ústí], *HRo*, xxxvi (1983), 251–2
L. Šíp: *Česká opera a její tvůrci* [Czech Opera and its Composers] (Prague, 1983), 324–8
H. Havlíková: 'Humor v ústecké opeře' [Humour at the Ústí Opera House], *Tvorba* (1987), no.49, p.7   HELENA HAVLÍKOVÁ

Machado, Augusto (de Oliveira) (*b* Lisbon, 27 Dec 1845; *d* Lisbon, 26 March 1924). Portuguese composer. He studied in Lisbon, and in 1867 went to Paris, intending to become a pianist, and studied with Lavignac. On his return to Lisbon he was unhappy with the predominance of the Italian style in Portuguese music, and went back to Paris (1873), where he studied with Danhauser and was in contact with Saint-Saëns and Massenet. From 1893 he taught singing at the Lisbon Conservatory and between 1901 and 1910 he was also director there.

Machado composed many operettas in Portuguese, such as *O espadachim do outeiro* and *A triste viuvinha*, and tried to create a national operetta based on historical themes, as in *Maria da Fonte*. In his most important opera, *Lauriane*, to a French libretto, Machado wrote in the French style; it was successfully produced in Marseilles (1883), Lisbon (in Italian, 1884) and Rio de Janeiro (1886). A few years later, however, he returned to the earlier Italian tradition, using librettos by Ghislanzoni, Leoncavallo and Golisciani in his operas *I Doria* (1887), *Mario Wetter* (1898) and *La borghesina* (1909).

first performed in Lisbon unless otherwise stated

O sol de Navarra (operetta, 3, A. Athayde), Trindade, 25 Dec 1870
A cruz de Ouro (operetta, 2, Athayde and R. de Lima), Trindade, 22 Oct 1873
O desgelo (operetta, 3, A. de Quental and J. B. Reis), Trindade, 9 Oct 1875
Os frutos de Ouro (mágica, 3, F. Palha and C. Leoni), Trindade, 6 Oct 1876
A guitarra (comic op, 1, E. Leal), Trindade, 28 March 1878

Maria da Fonte (operetta, 3, G. Lobato, Reis and Leal), Trindade, 5 May 1879
Lauriane (4, A. Guiot and J.-J. Magne, after P. Meurice and G. Sand: *Les beaux messieurs de bois doré*), Marseilles, Grand, 9 Jan 1883
I Doria (drama lírico, 4, A. Ghislanzoni, after F. von Schiller: *Fiesco*), S Carlos, 15 Jan 1887
Piccolino (comic op, 3, E. Garido), Trindade, 27 March 1889
A leitora da infanta (comic op, 3, Leal), Trindade, 18 Feb 1893
Os filhos do Capitão mor (3, E. Schwalbach), Trindade, 8 July 1896
Mario Wetter (3, R. Leoncavallo), S Carlos, 7 Feb 1898
O tição negro (farsa lírica, 3, H. Lopes de Mendonça), Avenida, 18 Jan 1902
O rapto de Helena (operetta, 3, A. Antunes), Avenida, 12 Nov 1902
Venus (pièce fantastique, Antunes), Dona Amélia, 29 Dec 1905
La borghesina (3, E. Golisciani), S Carlos, 12 March 1909
O espadachim do outeiro (comic op, 3, Lopes de Mendonça), Trindade, 18 Jan 1910
Vida mundana (revista), ? Casa Abecassis, Jan 1914
Rosas de todo o ano (comédia, 1, J. Dantas), S Luiz, July 1920
Paula Vicente (4, Ghislanzoni), ?unperf.
A triste viuvinha (operetta, 3, after D. João da Câmara), inc., unperf.

*

F. F. Benevides: *O Real Theatro de S. Carlos de Lisboa: memórias 1883–1902* (Lisbon, 1902)
J. Freitas Branco: *História da música portuguesa* (Lisbon, 1959)
          LUISA CYMBRON

Machavariani, Alexey Davidovich (*b* Gori, 10/23 Sept 1913). Georgian composer. He graduated in 1936 from the Tbilisi Conservatory, where he pursued postgraduate studies and taught from 1940. Other posts he has held include those of artistic director of the Georgian State SO (1956–8) and deputy to the Supreme Soviet of the USSR (1962–70); he has received many honours. He has conducted his own works and contributed many articles on contemporary music to the Georgian and all-Union press.

The characteristics of Machavariani's style are those of a composer formed under the combined influences of Georgian national art and contemporary musical trends. Among the features that appeared in his works of the 1930s are a distinctive interpretation of Georgian folk intonation, a development of rhythmic and other elements of Georgian folk music and an endeavour to embody lofty, ethical themes.

During the 1940s he composed refined, lyrical chamber pieces as well as large-scale works, such as the patriotic opera *Deda da shvili* ('Mother and Son', 1944; Machavariani, after I. Chavchavadze), based on the struggle for independence in the Caucasus; the work received its première in Tbilisi on 1 May 1945. His ballet *Otello* (1957) brought him his greatest success. His second opera, *Gamlet*, to his own libretto, after I. Machabeli's translation of Shakespeare's *Hamlet*, was first performed in Tbilisi in 1965.

          YEVGENY MACHAVARIANI

Machinery. The various mechanical devices used on, below or above a stage to move scenery or people or to create special effects.

1. Introduction. 2. Rolling or sliding devices. 3. Flying devices. 4. Elevating devices. 5. Revolving devices. 6. Special effects.

1. INTRODUCTION. The ancient Greeks seem to have invented most of the machines we find in theatres today: a device that rolls or slides (*ekkeklema*), one that flies things through the air like a boom crane (*mekane*), one that raises and lowers like an elevator (*anapeismata*) and one that revolves (*periaktos*). The basic scene-shifting machinery at the Metropolitan Opera House and most other opera houses in the world consists of

1. Two sets of painted scenery flats (a park setting on stage, an interior off stage), designed by Jan Wetschel and Leo Märkl, standing in grooves on the stage of the theatre (1767) at Český Krumlov, southern Bohemia

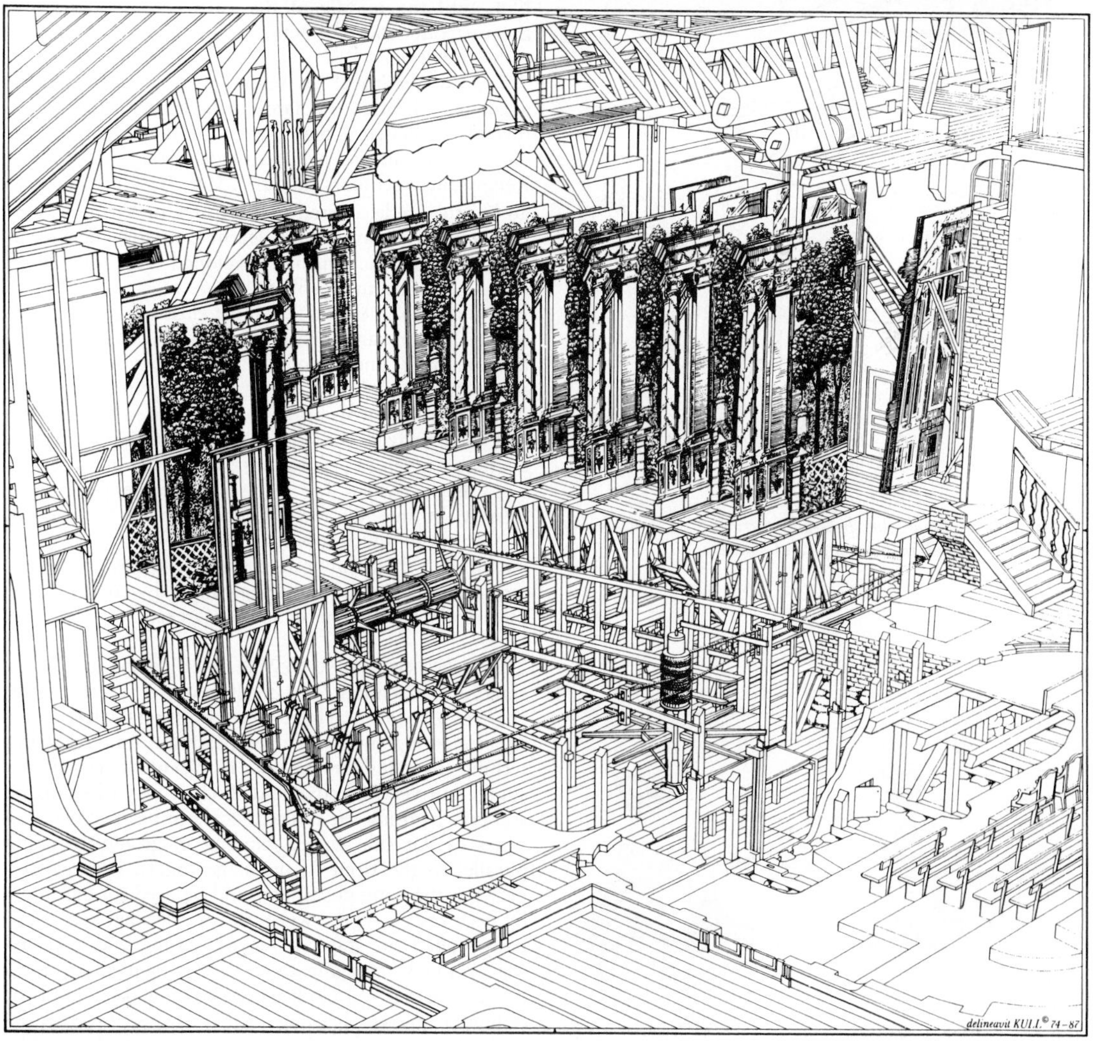

2. Cutaway diagram through the stage of the Drottningholm court theatre (1766) showing the machinery below stage for changing the wing flats: drawing by Gustaf Kull

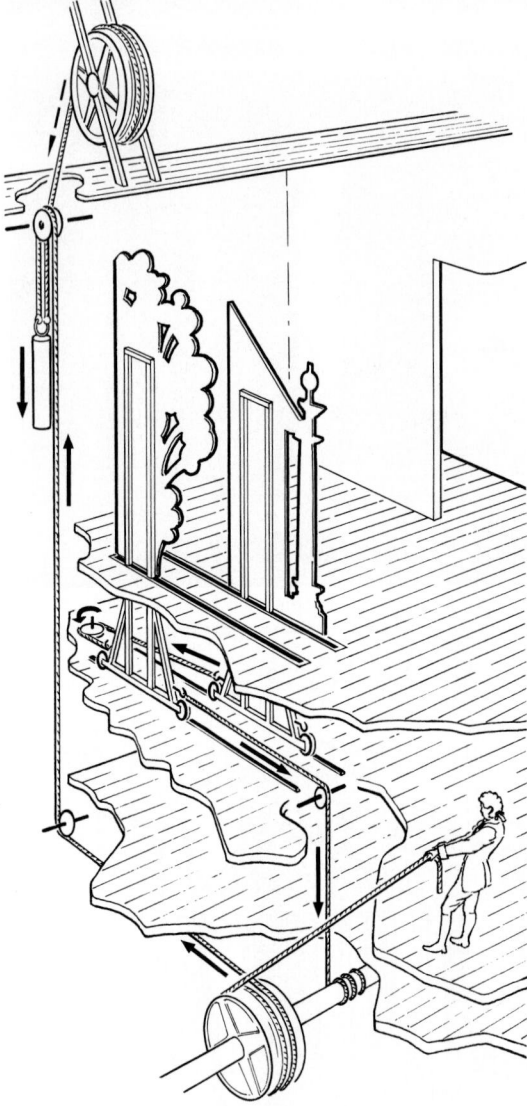

3. *Diagram showing the pole-and-carriage, or pole-and-chariot system for changing wings and shutters*

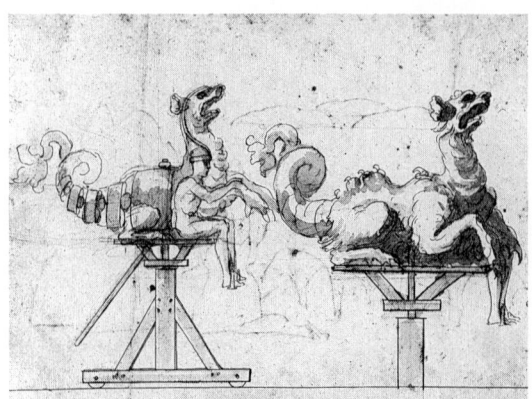

4. *French dragon machine on wheels: drawing, 17th century*

wagon stages, one of which contains a revolve, segments of the stage floor on elevators, and a rigging system (*see* THEATRE ARCHITECTURE, fig.12). Present-day machines are elaborate, sophisticated and electronically controlled, but it was the ancients who developed the basic ideas. We do not know if the Egyptians in 3000 BC, the date of the first recorded play production, had already invented the same devices, but they certainly had the necessary technical knowledge. The Romans borrowed Greek stage machinery almost wholesale; indeed, our sources of information on Greek scenes and machines are from the Roman period: Vitruvius's *De architectura* dating from between 16 and 13 BC, and Pollux's *Onomastikon* from the 2nd century AD.

When theatrical activity resumed after the so-called dark ages it was the unsophisticated amateurs putting on religious plays, not the professional players, who made use of elaborate stage machinery. They probably did so without knowing anything about the theatrical work of the ancient Greeks and Romans. If a biblical story called for a miracle, the amateurs worked out how to stage one; if Christ was to fly down from heaven, they devised machinery to allow him to do so (to the ancients this was a *deus ex machina*, 'god out of the machine'). Not until the middle of the 16th century did court theatres, out of which opera developed, begin using such elaborate devices.

Typical theatrical presentations at court and in academic theatres in late 15th-century Italy were revivals of classical plays; most of them required no change of locale and hence a single setting sufficed. But Renaissance scholars about 1500, seeking classical authorities, rediscovered the writings of Vitruvius and Pollux (and Aristotle) and learnt that the ancients in their stage productions had developed ways for rolling, flying, elevating and revolving.

About the same time that these classical writers were studied, Renaissance artists mastered the art of perspective painting and recognized the possibility of its application in theatrical presentations. When song-and-dance entertainments began to be presented between the acts of a revived classical play not only were courtly audiences given two shows instead of one, but a reason was also provided for using changeable perspective scenery. In time, the revived classical plays became less interesting to spectators than the *intermezzi* (or *intermedii*) with their elaborate costumes, scenes, machines, music and dance, the same elements that were present in theatrical presentations in ancient Greece.

2. ROLLING OR SLIDING DEVICES. Not all operas call for elaborate machines, but most require, at the least, changes of locale and hence scene-shifting devices. After experimenting with revolving scenic units, theatre technicians in Italy in the early 17th century settled on a simple but very effective and efficient way of changing scenery: painting the desired locale in perspective on a series of flat side wings standing in grooves running parallel to the front of the stage (fig.1). Passageways between the wing positions could be used for entrances by performers. As the wings for one setting were manually pulled off stage, a second setting was revealed (figs. 2 and 3). Hanging above each wing position was a painted border – a cloth piece showing sky, clouds or ceiling beams, etc. Closing off the prospect towards the back of the stage were painted shutters, which could be slid on from each side to meet at the centre line of the stage (fig.13 below). In England in the early 17th

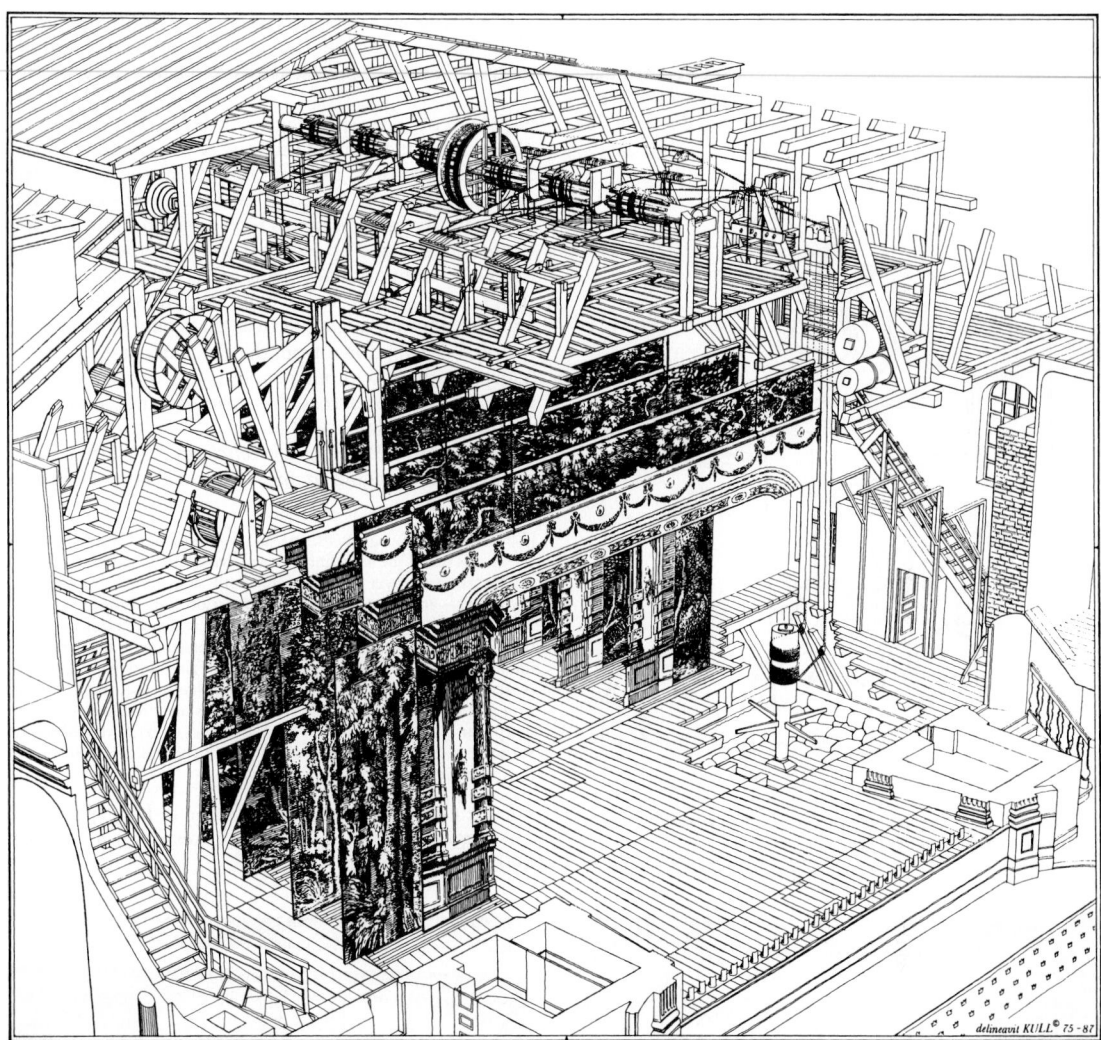

5. Diagram of the Drottningholm court theatre (1766) showing the machinery in the roof space for raising and lowering the hanging borders: drawing by Gustaf Kull

century the designer-architect Inigo Jones (1573–1652) devised a two-level upstage scenic area covered by shutters which could open to reveal upper and/or lower performing spaces. To mask the backstage area from the view of the audience, a frontispiece or picture frame (called a 'proscenium', since it was in front of the scenery) was set up (see THEATRE ARCHITECTURE, fig.2).

By the middle of the 17th century the designer-machinist-architect Giacomo Torelli (1608–78) had invented a mechanical method (the wheeled pole-and-carriage or pole-and-chariot system) for changing the wings and shutters (fig.3). Though not much used in England, the system was standard in continental theatres up to the end of the 19th century. Whether the manual or the mechanical system was used for changing scenery, shifts normally took place in full view of the spectators (a vista) and were part of their visual pleasure. The system made possible an infinite number of changes of locale, since settings in their offstage positions could be removed from their grooves or poles and replaced by new ones. The changes took only a matter of seconds and had the visual effect of a dissolve in modern films.

Until the early 18th century the side wings were lined up along each side of the stage, but when designers began to use multiple vanishing points running off at angles (scena per angolo) the slots or grooves in stage floors were extended across the width of the stage, allowing wings to be placed not just along the side but at virtually any point on the floor (see GALLI-BIBIENA, fig.1). Ground rows (profiled pieces of scenery representing such things as hills, embankments, rocks etc.) could also be slid onstage, as could rolling cross-stage platforms or steps between wing positions, so that performers could appear to walk on higher ground. The rolling or sliding side wings were standard features of theatres until near the end of the 19th century, when three-dimensional (and difficult-to-shift) scenery began replacing flat surfaces painted in perspective and new methods of scene shifting were needed. Putting wheels on scenic units (or putting the units on wagons – boat trucks) was one solution. This was not new, for a drawing exists that shows a 17th-century French dragon machine attached to a wheeled platform (fig.4; for further illustration see RHEINGOLD, DAS). Today many opera houses have full-stage rolling wagons (the new Bastille opera house in

Paris has eight, working in a circulatory system) upon which can be erected complete stage settings. Huge backstage spaces – sizable wings and/or a large upstage space – are required when wagons are part of a theatre's design; the Bastille stage can be opened to a depth of 75 metres. Wagons can be moved on stage or off mechanically, making possible fast changes of heavy settings within an opera or between operas in a repertory.

3. FLYING DEVICES. Drawing scenic borders up and down above the wings and shutters was the simplest of the flying mechanisms used in the Renaissance. Painted drops could also be raised or lowered; by the end of the 17th century these began to replace sliding shutters, for drops did not take up valuable space on the stage floor and could be hung at any plane of the stage. Borders and drops were simple flown units (fig.5). Machinists invented elaborate rigging devices that could bring people (painted or live) down from the sky, show a 'heaven' or 'glory' (with or without people in it), or fly a winged beast and chariot across the stage, up and down, and round and round (figs.6–8).

The London *Morning Chronicle* of 20 March 1851 described the rigging at the King's Theatre (Nalbach, p.150):

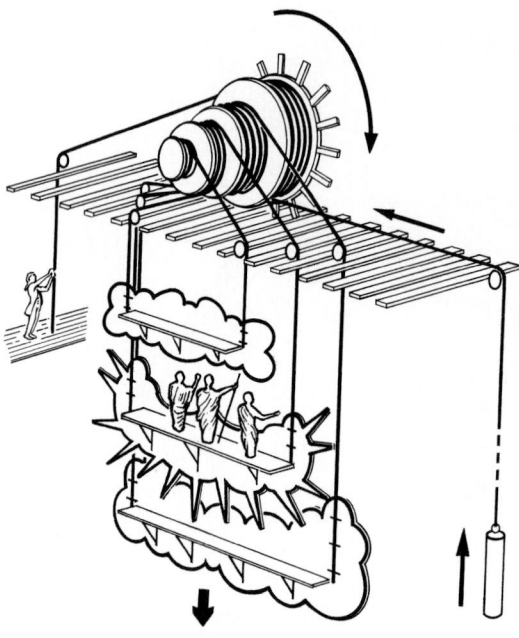

6. *Diagram of a rigging device for raising and lowering a cluster of clouds forming a 'glory'*

[T]he scenes of this great theatre are worked from below the stage on what is called the Mezzanine floor – from three ranges of 'flies' or platforms rising over the stage, on both sides of the theatre, tier above tier – and from a still higher elevation, called the barrel loft, which is in the roof. In all these stations, which amount to eight, there is communication with the scenic machinery by means of immense numbers of ropes and cords of all sizes and lengths, which work upon 'barrels' … Of course every line has its use, and the precision and rapidity with which scenic effects are produced – castles disappear, and palaces open, and clouds descend, or retire to make way for some glorious vision – speak of the power and completeness of the machinery.

For the elaborate enchantment scene in Halévy's opera *La tempestà* (1850, based on Shakespeare) a crew of 100 men was needed.

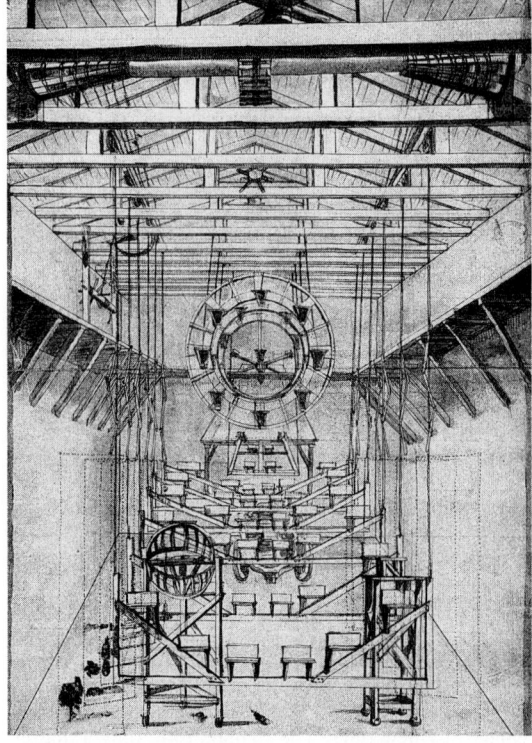

7. *Decorated (left) and undecorated (right) 'glory' machinery (possibly designed by Francesco Santurini) for Legrenzi's 'Germanico sul Reno' in the original production at the Teatro S Salvatore, Venice, 1676: drawing*

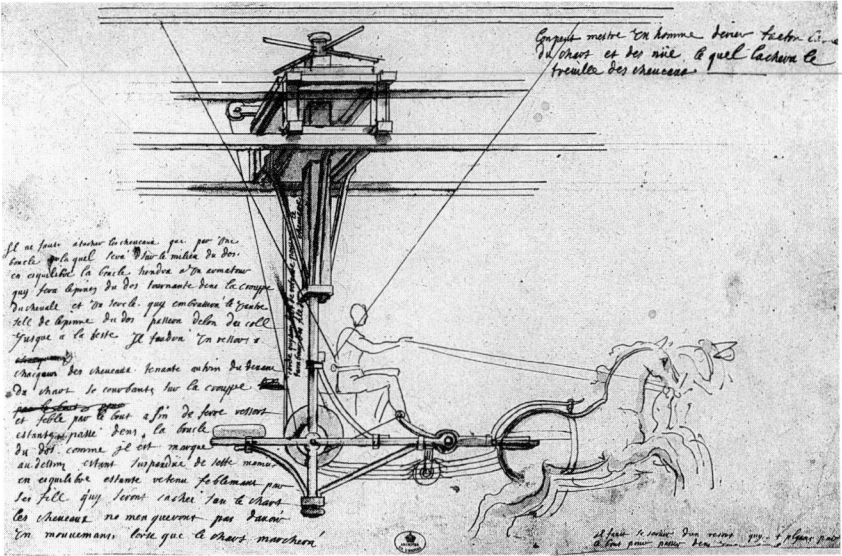

8. Design by Jean Berain for Phaëthon's chariot in Lully's 'Phaëton', Paris, 1683: the annotations describe how, by means of a system of wheels of different diameter, the chariot is made to fall from the sky in the final scene of the opera (see TRAGÉDIE EN MUSIQUE, *fig.2)*

Hanging in the flies above a present-day opera stage can be seen built scenic units (even complete 'box' sets), curtains and draperies of many sizes and shapes, battens (pipes, barrels) with lighting instruments and their electrical cables, catwalks, a curved sky cyclorama, painted drops, flat or three-dimensional chandeliers, projection machines and screens – indeed, virtually anything capable of being hauled up and down manually or mechanically. In some theatres the rigging system may consist of electronically controlled individual lines, mechanically operated sets of lines or traditional hand lines, or a combination of all three (fig.9). Not often today does one find a theatre without a fly tower – that towering structure rising above the main stage space that contains the theatre's rigging system (fig.10; *see also* THEATRE ARCHITECTURE, figs.7, 9 and 11). The fly tower is an identifying architectural feature of most proscenium theatres, and virtually all opera houses fall into this category.

4. ELEVATING DEVICES. Descended from the ancient practice of raising things into the audience's view are the variety of traps and elevator mechanisms that were developed during the Renaissance. Entertainments at court theatres in the 16th century were often given in banquet halls specially fitted up for theatrical shows (and often for a single performance). That meant that a stage was designed or redesigned for a particular production and had whatever technical features the show demanded. For an entertainment calling for three ghosts to appear from below the stage, machinists would provide a trap and an elevator large enough to work the effect.

When permanent Renaissance theatres were built (perhaps as early as 1532 in Ferrara) architects tried to anticipate the variety of demands that might be placed on the stage and provide accordingly. Many stage plans show three traps, two small ones (for single-person appearances) downstage left and right and a larger 'grave' trap at centre stage. Some plans show a second set of three traps upstage of those. A few 19th-century stages had six different types of aperture in the stage floor, including stage-wide slots for raising flat pieces of scenery (Southern, p.284); lockable hinged flaps or

plugs could close such openings. Theatres today are designed to cover every possible contingency, and in some the entire stage floor is trapped and a hole of any size can be opened up. Below such a stage must be steps or ladders for performers to climb or portable elevators to raise people or things through an opened trap.

Elevators were operated by stage hands below the stage, usually with some mechanical advantage – winches and counterweights (fig.11). The most effective appearance from below was through a 'star' trap, devised with triangular hinged flaps that allowed such a character as Erda in Wagner's *Ring* to appear as though through solid ground.

By the late 19th century, opera houses were being built with sizable segments of the stage floor on hydraulic lifts (Aspheleia stages) that were designed not so much for effecting sudden appearances as for creating different levels and ramps on stage (fig.12). Huge elevators and wagons become necessary when scenery is heavy and three-dimensional, and when multiple settings are required in order to operate in repertory – as

9. Grid and rigging at the Paris Opéra (Salle Garnier)

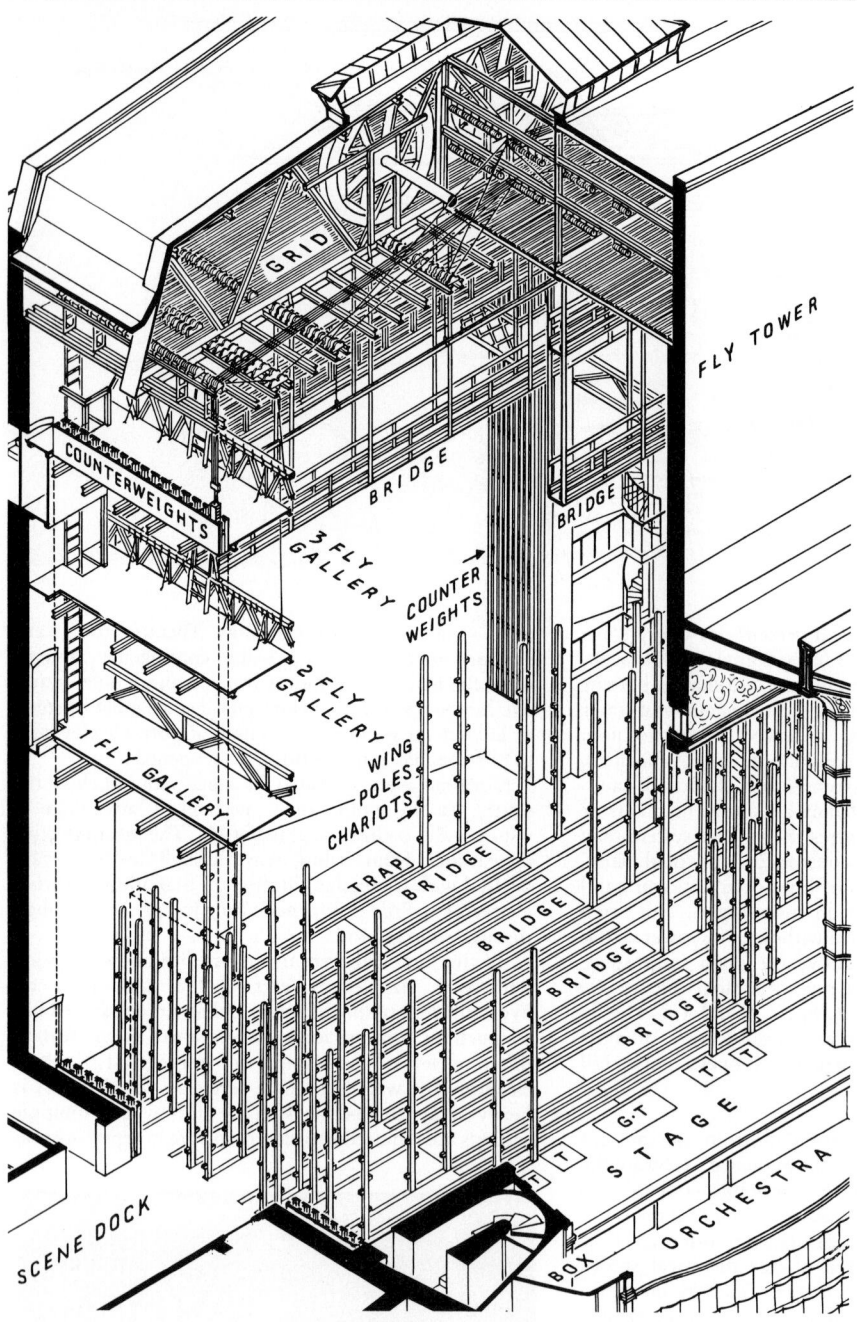

10. Cutaway diagram of the fly tower at the New English Opera House, London, 1891: drawing by Richard Leacroft

most opera companies do. When the new Metropolitan Opera House opened in 1966 *Architectural Record* described 'The Met's Amazing Stage' (*see* THEATRE ARCHITECTURE, fig. 12). The elevator machinery is typical of that found in late 20th-century opera theatres:

Each of the seven main hydraulically operated stage lifts is 60 feet across and eight feet deep, with the long dimension parallel to the audience. They move individually or can be locked together in any combination. For part of their rise they can be elevated in increments of 6 inches and for the remaining part, 12 inches. The lifts can move at speeds of 13, 27 or 40 feet per minute. Six of the lifts are double-decked. With three of these the decks are 28 feet apart and the rise is 29 feet, permitting one set of scenery to be used while a second is in readiness on the top deck. The single deck lift travels 20 feet and the remaining three lifts have ten feet between decks and travel 24 feet

… The first three lifts are equipped with two fly pipes for hanging drops and one border light pipe, all manually operated. All lift decks have floor pockets for portable electric equipment.

Sophisticated as that may sound, even by today's standards, nevertheless the Madison Square Theatre, designed in 1879 by Steel MacKaye (1842–94), had a similar double stage: two full stages, each complete in itself, stacked one on top of the other.

5. REVOLVING DEVICES. The revolve used by the Greeks was a simple three-sided scenic unit which (presumably along with others) could be turned one third to show a new painted surface to the audience and thus indicate a change of locale (fig. 13). It is thought that such a *peri-*

aktos painted with a jagged design could be spun to show a lightning effect. The Romans borrowed the idea, and in the 16th and 17th centuries designers experimented with but finally gave up *periaktoi* in favour of sliding wings. They did not, however, abandon the principle of rotating scenic units. Inigo Jones, for the English court masque *Hymenaei* (1606), had a turning globe out of which performers stepped, and a plan for the masque *Candy Restored* (1641) shows revolving flat wings (Nicoll, 63, 151).

In 1896 Carl Lautenschläger (1843–1906), over a century after the Japanese had invented the revolving stage (in 1758), developed a circular, wheeled stage floor upon which (usually) three three-dimensional

settings could be built (fig.14). Spectators saw the scenery through the traditional proscenium arch. The rotating floor could be turned one third to bring a new setting into view. The chief problem with such a stage is that, if more than three settings are needed, a set facing backstage must be dismantled and another erected. Since a revolve will not go away (like a wagon), modern practice has been to construct a revolving stage (or two smaller revolves, or a combination of revolves and wagons) specially for a particular production. A repertory company, if it has a revolving stage, will want it as part of a wagon stage that can be moved off when not needed; the Metropolitan revolve is built into the upstage-downstage wagon.

11

12

11. *Star trap, or 'trappe anglaise': from G. Moynet, 'La machinerie théâtrale: trucs et décors' (Paris, 1893)*

12. *Hydraulic lifts (Aspheleia stages) and sky cyclorama at the Budapest Opera House in 1884: from G. Moynet, 'La machinerie théâtrale: trucs et décors' (Paris, 1893)*

13. *Diagram showing the use of three-sided units (periaktoi) as side wings, and sliding shutters as backdrop*

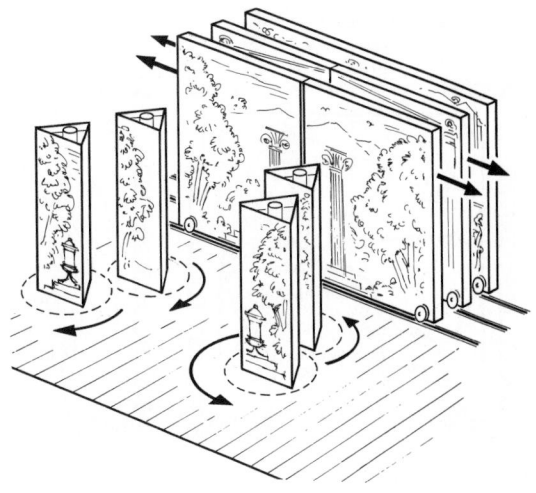

13

The principle of a rotating device has been used in other ways. The original *periaktos* idea of revolving three-sided scenic units lends itself to some stage designs. The New York production of the musical theatre piece *Chess* involved 12 *periaktoi* moving through 47 complicated major scene shifts with the assistance of a computer program. Double-sided scenic flats can be put on a vertical or horizontal pivot and flipped to show the back face; this in the 19th century was called a pivot trap, used for sudden appearances through a wall. The vertical pivot arrangement is not unlike the 1641 device used in *Candy Restored*.

A different kind of rotating device has been used to simulate the ocean. As early as the 17th century machinists used a series of rotating horizontal pillars, sculpted and painted to look like water and foam, set near the stage floor behind a low masking piece (*see* DROTTNINGHOLM, figs.2 and 3). There exists a colour film of the Drottningholm court theatre that shows their sea machine in action, and the effect is remarkably believable. Another variant on the rotating device is the panorama or diorama – a painted backcloth that unrolls from a vertical cylinder at one side of the stage and rolls on to another on the opposite side. Wagner called for such a machine for the two transformation scenes in *Parsifal* (for illustration *see* PARSIFAL).

A very complicated elevator-revolve was designed by Josef Svoboda for the 1974–6 *Ring* at Covent Garden: a platform measuring 11.3 × 9.75 × 0.6 metres that could rise, sink, tilt and rotate (*see* PRODUCTION, fig.23 and STAGE DESIGN, fig.26). 'It can be a static area virtually indistinguishable from the regular stage level at Covent Garden; it can interact kinetically with the performers and the music; it can become one or several staircases; it can function as a giant mirror reflecting action beneath the level of the stage; it can become a surface for projections' (Burian, 57). The platform was supplemented with other scenographic elements, especially intense laser projections. A detailed analysis of the Svoboda *Ring*, with many photographs and diagrams of the remarkably versatile machine, is provided by Burian.

Not to be outdone, in 1983 at Bayreuth William Dudley (*b* 1947), working with the director Peter Hall, concocted a similar and very expensive rotating concave-convex platform (fig.15) that moved hydraulically forwards, back, up and down, so that when raised it could suggest a cave and when lowered it could serve as a mountain top. The horror stories concerning its development are chronicled by Fay and Wood, a useful reminder that elaborate theatre machinery can sometimes create as many problems as it solves.

6. SPECIAL EFFECTS. Sometimes called machines are devices for creating such special effects as explosions, fire, smoke, thunder, lightning, rain, snow, crashes, sun or moon effects, magical appearances and disappearances, ghosts, rocking boats, monsters, guided missiles (like Klingsor's spear or the dying swan in *Parsifal*), trick properties (Siegfried's anvil) etc. (figs.16–19). Sebastiano Serlio (*Architettura*, 1545; quoted in Nagler 1952, pp.79–80) was one of the earliest to describe such stage tricks: 'Sometime it may chance that you must make some thing or other [such as a building] which should seem to burne, which you must wet throughly with excellent good Aquavite [like modern lighter fluid]; and setting it on fire with a candle it will burne all over' – presumably without actually consuming the scenery.

Serlio also described lightning bolt effects using skyrockets guided on wires stretched across the stage. Lightning flashes were accomplished by risking the safety of a stagehand:

there must be a man placed behind the Scene ... in a high place with a boxe in his hand, the cover whereof must be full with holes, and in the middle of that place there shall be a burning candle placed, the boxe must be filled with powder of vernis or sulphire, and casting his hand with the boxe upwards the powder flying in the candle, will shew as if it were lightning.

The creation of fire effects in the 20th century (for the finale of *Die Walküre*, for example) has ranged from fan-blown strips of coloured cloth or paper to tinted steam to film projections. One of the most effective was in a Covent Garden production in 1954–5 that used a film projection of flames that began on the sky cyclorama and moved to the downstage end of it and on to a scrim stretched across the proscenium opening, then across the front of the stage and again on to the cyclorama to create what appeared to be flames fully encircling the performers.

Most of the operas calling for special effects belong to the 19th century, when stage technology made so many

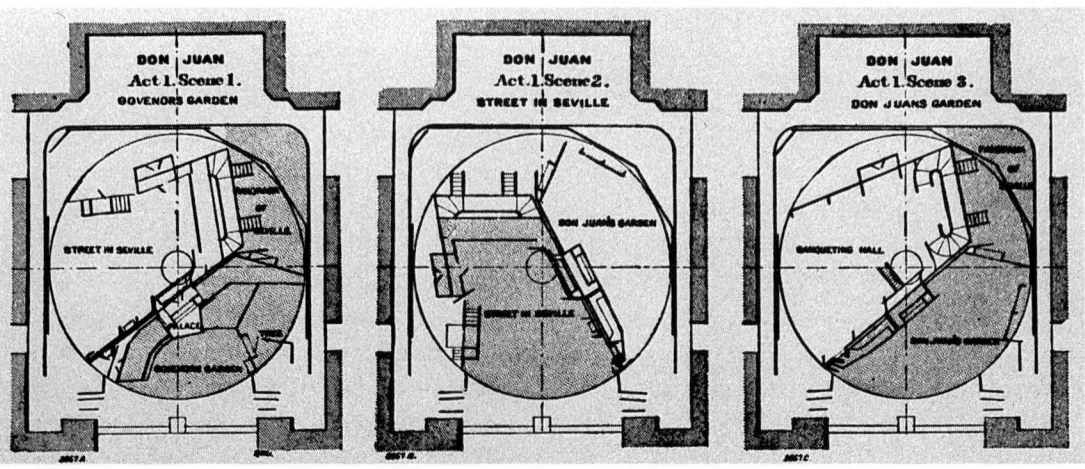

14. Karl Lautenschläger's revolving stage, with settings for Act 1 scenes i–iii of Mozart's 'Don Giovanni' for a production at the Residenztheater, Munich, 1896: from E. O. Sachs and E. A. E. Woodrow, 'Modern Opera Houses and Theatres', iii (London, 1898)

15. William Dudley's hydraulically operated concave-convex platform designed for the 1983 'Ring' production at Bayreuth: (a) convex form

15. (b) Cross section of the stage at Bayreuth showing various positions of the platform in Wagner's 'Die Walküre'

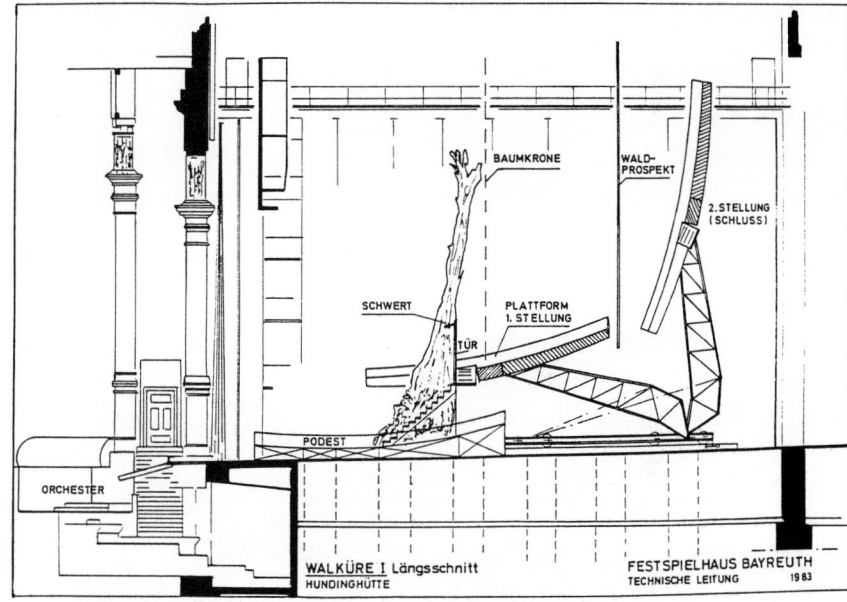

advances. But an examination of operas from Monteverdi's *Orfeo* to Stockhausen's *Donnerstag aus Licht* shows that few call for much beyond standard stage settings that any theatre would have on hand or for machinery beyond that needed to shift the settings. Wagner asked for so many interesting effects that his requirements have frequently been used here as examples (fig.17).

Operas and melodramas from the 19th century used a variety of special effects, many of which were pictured and explained in M. J. Moynet's *L'envers du théâtre* and G. Moynet's *Trucs et décors*. In 1865 Meyerbeer, in Act 3 of *L'Africaine*, asked for the setting to show Don Pedro's ship. This could have been done with a standard ship setting, and the ship rocking in the storm could have been suggested by the performers swaying (as in Orson Welles's 1955 production of *Moby Dick*). But at the Paris Opéra they created a cross-section of a huge three-dimensional ship and a machine to make the whole thing rock (fig.19). Designers and stage technicians sometimes enjoy doing things the hard way. Audiences were thrilled with the effect, and that kind of literalism made them thirst for more and more complicated staging.

The effects Wagner asked for in *Der fliegende Holländer* and the *Ring* present interesting challenges to designers and machinists. The composer-librettist did not request anything that in 1876 could not be staged. He even questioned technical experts to make sure he was not asking for the impossible. In his kind of wing-and-drop theatre the transformation of Alberich into a *Wurm* could have been accomplished quite easily: a painted cut-out monster could be thrust upward through a stage floor slot or onstage in a groove from the side, directly in front of Alberich, concealing him. Seldom today do designers and directors try to do things so simply.

Audiences love special effects and stage spectacle, but they are also quite capable of using their imaginations, if asked. One of the most frightening dragons in any production of *Siegfried* was simply inky blackness at the back of the stage, with the hero, his back to the audience, battling against an unseen menace. Less sometimes does mean more.

(a)

(b)

16. (a) Steam machine used to simulate smoke for a fire effect in the original production of Massenet's 'Le mage' (Paris Opéra, 1891); (b) hinged flaps to simulate the collapse of a building: both from A. Hopkins, 'Magic, Stage Illusions and Scientific Diversions' (London, 1897)

17. Backstage view of the dragon in Wagner's 'Siegfried' in the first Paris production (Opéra, 1902): from the 'Scientific American' (29 March 1902), supplement 1369

19. (a) Storm scene in Act 3 scene vi of the original production of Meyerbeer's 'L'Africaine' (Paris Opéra, 1865): from 'L'illustration' (6 May 1865)

(a)

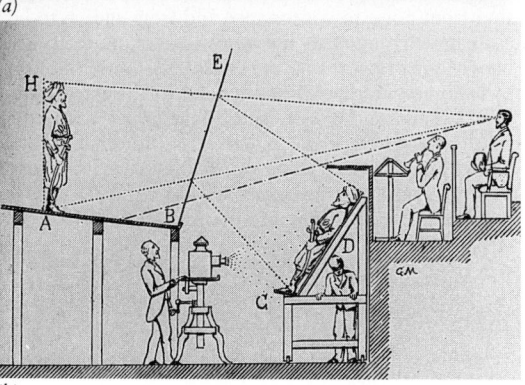

(b)

19. (b) Machinery used to simulate the storm scene in Act 3 of Meyerbeer's 'L'Africaine': from M. J. Moynet, 'L'envers du théâtre' (Paris, 1873)

18. Ghost effect: (a) as seen from the audience; (b) how the effect is achieved using an unsilvered sheet of glass (BE) with an intense light source: from G. Moynet, 'La machinerie théâtrale: trucs et décors' (Paris, 1893). A similar principle was used at Bayreuth in 1983 to give the impression that the Rhinemaidens were swimming in real water.

C. Contant and J. de Filippi: *Parallèle des principaux théâtres modernes de l'Europe et des machines théâtrales françaises, allemandes et anglaises* (Paris, 1860)

M. J. Moynet: *L'envers du théâtre* (Paris, 1873; Eng. trans., enlarged, as *French Theatrical Production in the Nineteenth Century*, ed. M. A. Carlson, 1976)

A. Pougin: *Dictionnaire historique et pittoresque du théâtre et des arts qui s'y rattachent* (Paris, 1885)

G. Moynet: *La machinerie théâtrale: trucs et décors* (Paris, 1893)

E. O. Sachs and E. A. E. Woodrow: *Modern Opera Houses and Theatres* (London, 1896–8)

F. Kranich: *Bühnentechnik der Gegenwart* (Munich, 1929)

E. Carrick: 'Theatre Machines in Italy, 1400–1800', *Architectural Review*, lxx/416 (1931), 9–14, 34–6

A. Beijer: *Court Theatres of Drottningholm and Gripsholm* (Malmö, 1933)

A. Nicoll: *Stuart Masques and the Renaissance Stage* (London, 1937)

A. M. Nagler, ed.: *Sources of Theatrical History* (New York, 1952)

R. Southern: *Changeable Scenery* (London, 1952)

S. T. Worsthorne: *Venetian Opera in the Seventeenth Century* (Oxford, 1954, enlarged 2/1968)

O. K. Larson: *Italian Stage Machinery* (diss., U. of Illinois, Urbana-Champaign, 1956)

B. Hewitt, ed.: *The Renaissance Stage: Documents of Serlio [1545], Sabbattini [1638] and Furttenbach [1628, 1640, 1663]* (Coral Gables, FL, 1958)

P. Bjurström: *Giacomo Torelli and Baroque Stage Design* (Stockholm, 1961, 2/1962)

M. Hampe: *Die Entwicklung der Bühnendekoration von der Kulissenbühne zum Rundhorizont-System* (diss., U. of Vienna, 1961)

J. Hawley and A. Jackson: 'Scene Changing at the Palais Royal (1770–1781)', *The Ohio State University Theatre Collection Bulletin*, viii (1961), 9–23

A. M. Nagler: *Theatre Festivals of the Medici 1539–1637* (New Haven, CT, 1964)

R. M. Wren: 'Groves and Doors on the Seventeenth and Eighteenth Century Dutch Stage', *Theatre Research*, vii (1965), 56–7

M. Baur-Heinold: *Theater des Barock: Festliches Bühnenspiel im 17. und 18. Jahrhundert* (Munich, 1966; Eng. trans., 1967)

G. Isgrò: *Fortuny e il teatro* (Palermo, 1966)

'The Met's Amazing Stage', *Architectural Record*, cxl/3 (1966), 156–60

B. Gascoigne: 'Shuffling the Schouwburg Scenes', *Theatre Research*, ix (1968), 88–104

R. W. Gutman: *Richard Wagner: the Man, his Mind, and his Music* (New York, 1968, 2/1972), 382

Theatre Architecture and Stage Machines (New York, 1969) [engravings from the *Encyclopédie*, 1762–72]

D. Nalbach: *The King's Theatre 1704–1867* (London, 1972)

S. Orgel and R. Strong: *Inigo Jones: the Theatre of the Stuart Court* (Berkeley, CA, 1973)

F. C. Mohler: *Spectacular Effects on the Seventeenth-Century Continental Stage* (diss., Ohio State U., 1976)

C. F. Baumann: *Bühnentechnik im Festspielhaus Bayreuth* (Munich, 1980)

C. T. Ault: *Design, Operation and Organization of Stage Machinery at the Paris Opéra: 1770–1873* (diss., U. of Michigan, 1983)

J. Burian: *Svoboda: Wagner* (Middletown, CT, 1983)

S. Fay and R. Wood: *The Ring* (London, 1984)

B. Cohen-Stratyner, ed.: *Scenes and Machines from the 18th Century: the Stagecraft of Jacopo Fabris [1760] and Citoyen Boullet [1809]* (New York, 1986)

C. T. Ault: 'Baroque Stage Machines for Venus and Mars from the Archivo di Stato, Parma', *Theatre Survey*, xxviii/2 (1987), 27–39

G. Kull: *Drottningholms Slottsteater: Scenmaskineriet* [Drottningholm Court Theatre: the Stage Machinery] (Härnösand, 1987)

O. K. Larson: *The Theatrical Writings of Fabrizio Carini Motta* (Carbondale, IL, 1987)

G. C. Izenour: *Theater Technology* (New York, 1988)

M. Loeffler and M. Sommers: 'Sets of Chess: Breaking the CAD [Computer Assisted Design] Barrier', *Theatre Crafts*, xxii/8 (1988), 70–78

'The Stage and its Machinery [at Covent Garden]', *About the House*, viii/1 (1988), 40–47

R. Hughes: 'Paris à la Mitterand', *Time* (18 Sept 1989)

A. Clark: 'The Bastille – "Vision fugitive"?', *Opera*, xl (1989), 406–12

EDWARD A. LANGHANS

Machlis, Joseph [Selcamm, George] (*b* Riga, 11 Aug 1906). American translator, of Latvian birth. He has written novels under the name of George Selcamm. Machlis has translated more than 15 operas, many for NBC, including *Rigoletto*, *Fidelio*, *Cavalleria rusticana* and, for the first American performance (on television), Prokofiev's *War and Peace* (1957). His published English version of Poulenc's *Dialogues des Carmélites* was used to good effect in the first American and first British performances of the opera (1957, San Francisco; 1958, Covent Garden); he also translated Poulenc's *La voix humaine*. His translation of Puccini's *Il tabarro* was printed in Mario Parenti's revised musical edition (1960). ARTHUR JACOBS

Machover, Tod (*b* New York, 24 Nov 1953). American composer. He studied the cello as a child and at an early age encountered the most advanced music of the 1960s, including that of Berio and Stockhausen; he was also drawn to rock music and briefly led his own band. After two years at the University of California, Santa Cruz, in 1973 he went to Florence to study with Dallapiccola; while there he met Boulez. Later at the Juilliard School (BM 1975, MM 1977), Machover studied with Roger Sessions and Elliott Carter. In 1975–6 he was principal cellist of the National Opera of Canada, Toronto, and in 1978 he was invited to IRCAM in Paris as a guest composer; two years later the position of Director of Musical Research was created for him there. He left in 1985 to join the faculty of the Massachusetts Institute of Technology, where, as director of the Experimental Media Facility (from 1986), he has been on the cutting edge of research into computer-instrumental interactions ('hyperinstruments').

Machover's training provided him with an unusually rigorous technical background, subsumed however within a Europeanized compositional outlook that he did not fully succeed in overcoming until 1987. His works of the 1980s display an extraordinarily rapid and sustained stylistic growth, culminating in the opera *Valis* (Paris, 1 December 1987). This work, commissioned by the Centre Georges Pompidou in celebration of its tenth anniversary, caused a considerable stir both at its première and when issued as a recording the following year. The opera employs computer technology with unprecedented sophistication to multiply, shadow and alter instrumental and vocal sounds in real time with genuine ensemble responsiveness. Each of the 22 continuous numbers is in a different style, ranging from rock and new-age music to serialism and pure noise, unified by motivic links and an overall progression from noise to consonance and from speech to lyricism. In keeping with the work's dramatic theme, the lines of theatrical reality are constantly blurred not only by computer manipulations but also by the extensive use of video and audio tape, and by the appearance of the conductor in a crucial, if wordless, dramatic role. In 1988 Machover revised the opera and issued a recording of the revised version on the Bridge label; this too polarized critical opinion, though laudatory notices strongly outnumbered negative ones. The new version was given a concert performance in Boston in 1989.

See also VALIS.

T. Machover: 'Etre compositeur aujourd'hui', *InHarmoniques*, no. 1 (1987), 211–36

——: record notes, *Valis* (Bridge BCD 9007, 1988)

R. Dyer: 'At MIT, Tod Machover finds music's deepest connections', *Boston Globe* (11 June 1989)
A. Stiller: '"Valis" Unveiled', *MusAm/Opus*, cix/2 (1989), 75–6
J. Wierzbicki: 'Machover: Valis', *HiFi*, xxxix/2 (1989), 62–3
R. H. Kornick: *Recent American Opera: a Production Guide* (New York, 1991), 180–83   ANDREW STILLER

Macías. Opera in three acts by FELIPE GUTIÉRREZ ESPINOSA after Mariano José de Larra's historical drama; San Juan, Puerto Rico, Teatro Tapia, 19 August 1977.

The authorship of the libretto remains a matter of conjecture despite attributions to Alejandro Tapia y Rivera and Martín J. Travieso. A strong possibility, based by Batista on evidence found in the autograph score, is that the libretto was made by the composer himself.

The courtly legend of *Macías* had received several dramatic treatments before Larra's romantic play (1834), going back as far as the 16th century. The Gutiérrez version reduces Larra's four acts to three but retains all of his numerous roles and adds a large chorus. The opera is set in the palace of Don Enrique de Villena in Andújar, Spain, in 1406; the entire action occurs in one day. The troubadour Macías (tenor) having been sent deliberately on a mission, his beloved Elvira (soprano) is forced to marry Fernán Pérez (baritone). Macías returns, finds Elvira married, challenges Fernán to a duel and is imprisoned. Elvira's companion Beatriz (mezzo-soprano) bribes the guard; Elvira enters Macías's cell and urges him to flee. Macías refuses, insisting on going ahead with the duel, but is mortally wounded by assassins sent by Fernán. Fernán arrives in time to witness Elvira's suicide. Elvira and Macías thus fulfil their vow to die together, as Fernán proclaims that his marital honour has been avenged.

Macías earned its composer a gold medal at the Puerto Rico Exposition in 1871; the autograph score then disappeared until 1970, when it came to light at the library of the Royal Palace, Madrid, bearing a dedication in the composer's hand to King Alfonso XII, dated 1877. It was given its first known performance in 1977, and is the only extant opera written in Puerto Rico in the 19th century. In it, Gutiérrez's style and technique compare favourably with those of works composed in Europe during the third quarter of the century, reflecting the composer's immersion in contemporaneous European, and especially Italian, music as conductor at the San Juan Teatro Municipal (now the Tapia) during that period.   DONALD THOMPSON

McIntyre, Donald (Conroy) (*b* Auckland, 22 Oct 1934). British bass-baritone of New Zealand birth. He studied in London and made his début in 1959 with the WNO as Zaccaria (*Nabucco*). At Sadler's Wells (1960–67) he sang over 30 roles, including Mozart's Figaro, Attila, the Dutchman, Caspar and Pennybank Bill in the first British staging of *Mahagonny* (1963). He made his Covent Garden début in 1967 as Pizarro, later singing Barak, Golaud, Shaklovity (*Khovanshchina*), Balstrode, Escamillo, Nick Shadow, Scarpia, John the Baptist, Orestes, Axel Heyst in the première of Bennett's *Victory* (1970), Sarastro, Count des Grieux, Kurwenal and Wotan, the role of his Metropolitan début in 1975. At Bayreuth (1967–80) he sang Telramund, Amfortas, the Dutchman and Wotan in the 1976 centenary *Ring* cycle. He has appeared at Vienna, Munich, Berlin, Chicago, La Scala and Paris. He first sang Gurnemanz with the WNO (1981) and Hans Sachs at Zürich (1984), and

sang Prospero in the British première of Berio's *Un re in ascolto* (1989, Covent Garden). With his strongly projected, full-toned voice and fine stage presence, he is a compelling singing actor. He was appointed OBE in 1977.

A. Blyth: 'Donald McIntyre', *Opera*, xxvi (1975), 529–36
A. Simpson and P. Downes: *Southern Voices: International Opera Singers of New Zealand* (Auckland, 1992), 132–47
ALAN BLYTH

Macintyre, Margaret (*b* India, 1865; *d* London, April 1943). British soprano. She studied in London with the younger Manuel Garcia and made her début in 1888 as Micaëla at Covent Garden, where she sang regularly until 1897. Her roles included Donna Elvira, Inès (*L'Africaine*), Mathilde (*Guillaume Tell*), Aida, Marguerite (*Faust*), Marguerite de Valois (*Les Huguenots*), Elsa, Senta, Elisabeth (*Tannhäuser*), Desdemona, Leonora (*Il trovatore*) and Santuzza. She created Rebecca in Sullivan's *Ivanhoe* at the Royal English Opera House (1891); she sang Sieglinde at La Scala in the first Milan performance of *Die Walküre* (1892), and made her only Metropolitan appearance as Margherita (*Mefistofele*) in 1901.   ELIZABETH FORBES

Mackenzie, Sir **Alexander** (Campbell) (*b* Edinburgh, 22 Aug 1847; *d* London, 28 April 1935). Scottish composer and conductor. By the age of 18 he had undergone musical training in Germany, at Sondershausen, and in London at the RAM, and returned to Edinburgh as a professional violinist and conductor. In 1879 he moved to Florence, where he was able to concentrate on composition, producing choral works and his first opera, *Colomba* (1883). He returned to Britain in 1885 and from 1888 to 1924 was principal of the RAM, where administration, teaching and conducting constituted the core of his life's work. He continued to compose and have his works performed, but they failed to make a distinctive enough contribution to the British musical renaissance for them to survive in the repertory.

His early operas suffer from old-fashioned librettos and cosmopolitan sympathies, ranging from Gounod to Liszt, which override rather than stimulate a personal voice. *Colomba* reached Hamburg and Darmstadt as well as London, but its dramaturgical similarity to *Carmen* – it is based on a story by Mérimée about a vendetta between two Corsican families – sets an impossible comparison; like *Guillem the Troubadour* (1886), a story of tragic love between Guillem de Cabestanh and the wife of a Provençal noble (which was damned by Hanslick though taken up for a piano fantasia by Liszt just before his death), it is grand in conception but predominantly effete in execution. His commercial operettas must be measured by different yardsticks. *His Majesty* (1897) ran in London for only 61 performances; its music, though surprisingly well judged for the lightness of the genre, was insufficiently memorable to overcome a confused Gilbertian book and the disastrous comeback of George Grossmith in the title role. *The Knights of the Road* (1905) is short, containing only six numbers, and trivial; Mackenzie saw it as 'an attempt … to stimulate an interest in operetta on the music-hall stage'.

Like Stanford, in two of his last works for the stage Mackenzie turned from grand opera and operetta to something closer to fairy-tale and pastoral (though *The Cricket on the Hearth*, composed 1900, was revised as a light opera). *The Eve of St John*, written during World War I as a 'recreation and distraction', begins to explore a world of midsummer night's madness, with its testing of the values of love and fidelity, themes developed later in the work of Bliss and Tippett. Childhood innocence in *The Cricket on the Hearth*, with its burgeoning solos and ensembles, might earn it a niche as a Christmas piece. In both these works there is a musical freshness which almost turns the tables from conservatism to neo-classicism.

Colomba op.28 (lyrical drama, 4, F. Hueffer, after P. Mérimée), London, Drury Lane, 9 April 1883, vs (London, 1883); rev. version (3, C. Aveling), London, Her Majesty's, 3 Dec 1912; *GB-Lam*

Guillem the Troubadour op.33 (4, Hueffer), London, Drury Lane, 8 June 1886, *Lam*, vs (London, 1886)

Phoebe op.51 (comic op, B. C. Stephenson), unperf., unpubd

His Majesty, or The Court of Vingolia op.56 (comic op, 2, F. C. Burnand and R. C. Lehmann, addl lyrics A. Ross), London, Savoy, 20 Feb 1897, vs (London, 1898)

The Cricket on the Hearth [Das Heimchen am Herde] op.62, 1900 (3, J. Sturgis, after C. Dickens), London, RAM, 6 June 1914; rev. version (light op), Glasgow, Royal, 13 Aug 1923; *Lam*, vs (Leipzig, 1901)

The Knights of the Road op.65 (operetta, H. A. Lytton), London, Palace, 27 Feb 1905, vs (London, 1905)

The Eve of St John [St John's Eve] op.87, 1919 (1, E. Farjeon), Liverpool, 16 April 1924, *Lam*, vs (London, 1923)

*

GänzlBMT

C. Willeby: *Masters of English Music* (London, 1893), 103–72

H. Klein: *Thirty Years of Musical Life in London 1870–1900* (London, 1907), 141–6, 148

A. C. Mackenzie: *A Musician's Narrative* (London, 1927)

F. Howes: *The English Musical Renaissance* (London, 1966), 63

N. Burton: 'Opera: 1865–1914', *Music in Britain: the Romantic Age, 1800–1914*, ed. N. Temperley (London, 1981), 330–57, esp. 346–7

E. W. White: *A History of English Opera* (London, 1983)

S. Banfield: 'British Opera in Retrospect', *MT*, cxxvii (1986), 205–7

——: 'The Early Renaissance: Mackenzie, Stanford and Smyth', *British Opera in Retrospect* (n.p., 1986) [pubn of the British Music Society], 63–8
STEPHEN BANFIELD

Mackerras, Sir (Alan) Charles (MacLaurin) (*b* Schnectady, NY, 17 Nov 1925). Australian conductor. He studied in Sydney and began conducting while principal oboist with the Sydney SO. After coming to Britain in 1947, he received a British Council scholarship to study with Václav Talich in Prague, where he formed an enthusiasm for Janáček. He made his début at Sadler's Wells in 1948 (*Die Fledermaus*) and remained a staff conductor until 1954, giving the first stage production of Janáček in Britain with *Kát'a Kabanová* in 1951. From 1956 he was the main conductor for several seasons with the English Opera Group. His Covent Garden début was in 1963 with *Katerina Izmaylova*, and he returned frequently to conduct Mozart, Puccini and Verdi. His interest in period-style interpretation brought a production of *Le nozze di Figaro* at Sadler's Wells (1965) where his appoggiaturas and added ornamentation had a lasting influence; his intentions are explained in 'What Mozart Really Meant' (*Opera*, xvi, 1965, pp.240–46).

Mackerras was chief conductor at the Hamburg Staatsoper, 1966–9. His wide repertory there included *Rappresentatione di Anima, et di Corpo*, recorded in 1970. He returned to London as music director for Sadler's Wells Opera (which became the English National Opera during his tenure, 1970–77), exercising a strong influence on both style and standards of ensemble performance and broadening the repertory to in-clude works from Handel to Janáček. In 1972 he made his début at the Metropolitan in Gluck's *Orfeo ed Euridice* (of which he had made and recorded his own edition in 1966) and in 1973 conducted the inaugural concert and *Die Zauberflöte* at the Sydney Opera House. He moved to the Welsh National Opera as music director from 1987 to 1992, when he was appointed Conductor Emeritus; his version of *Lucia di Lammermoor* (1989) was based on a facsimile of the autograph and with the orchestral players arranged in early 19th-century manner behind as well as in front of him.

In 1990, Mackerras was named principal guest conductor at San Francisco Opera, conducted *Serse* with the ENO in the USSR, made his Glyndebourne début in *Falstaff* and gave his reflections on over 40 years in opera in an interview (*Opera*, xli, 1990, pp.169–74). He conducted *Don Giovanni* at the reopening in November 1991 of the renovated Estates (Tyl) Theatre in Prague, where the opera was first performed in 1787. His recordings include a major Janáček series from *Kát'a Kabanová* (1976) to *Jenůfa* (1982) in Czech; English-sung performances by the ENO of *Maria Stuarda* (1983) and Handel's *Giulio Cesare in Egitto* (1985), both with Janet Baker; and Martinů's *The Greek Passion* (1981). His influence on the British opera scene, as a conductor both scholarly and mettlesome, has been significant. He was made CBE in 1974 and knighted in 1979.

*

N. Phelan: *Charles Mackerras: a Musician's Musician* (London, 1987)
STANLEY SADIE, NOËL GOODWIN

McLaughlin, Marie (*b* Hamilton, Lanarks., 2 Nov 1954). Scottish soprano. She studied in Glasgow and London, making her début in 1978 as Anna Gomez (*The Consul*) with the ENO. She made her Covent Garden début in 1981 as Barbarina and has subsequently sung Zerlina, Iris (*Semele*), Susanna, Marzelline, Adina, Norina, Titania, Zdenka and Nannetta there. At Glyndebourne she has sung Micaëla (1985) and Violetta (1987), and she made her Metropolitan début (1986) as Marzelline which she also sang at Salzburg (1990). She has also sung in Paris, Vienna, Berlin, Munich, Aix-en-Provence, Rome, Hamburg, Salzburg, Chicago and at La Scala; among her roles are Despina, Ilia, Gilda and Stéphano (*Roméo et Juliette*). In 1989 she sang Tatyana for the ENO, and in 1992 Jenny (*Mahagonny*) at Geneva. She has a beautiful, flexible voice and a charming stage presence.

ELIZABETH FORBES

Maclean, Alick [Alexander Morvaren] (*b* Eton, 20 July 1872; *d* London, 18 May 1936). English composer and conductor. He was born and later educated at Eton, where his father, Charles Maclean, was director of music. He began operatic composition early. Recognition came in 1895 with the Covent Garden production of *Petruccio*; an early example in England of *verismo* (it was paired with *Cavalleria rusticana* at its first performance), it won the Moody-Manners prize for a one-act British opera. Maclean pursued a successful career in the theatre, as musical director to Charles Wyndham (1899–1912), for whose production of *Cyrano de Bergerac* he wrote the music, and to the Spa Company at Scarborough (1912–35); he also conducted at Chappell's Ballad Concerts (1915–23). But operatic exposure was sporadic, and like Stanford he found more support in Germany before World War I than in England. The belated production in 1920 of the revised

Quentin Durward was the first by the Carl Rosa company of a 'new' British opera since the 1890s.

See also PETRUCCIO.

all to librettos by Sheridan Ross

Crichton, *c*1892 (comic op, 3), ?unperf.
Quentin Durward, 1892–3 (3, after W. Scott), vs (London, 1894); Newcastle upon Tyne, Theatre Royal, 13 Jan 1920
Petruccio (1), London, CG, 29 June 1895, vs
The King's Price, London, Royalty, 29 April 1904
Die Liebesgeige [The Hunchback of Cremona] (2, after F.-J.-E. Coppée: *Le luthier de Crémone*), Mainz, Stadt, 15 April 1906
Maître Seiler, London, Lyric, 20 Aug 1909
Die Waldidylle (after Erckmann-Chatrian), Mainz, Stadt, April 1913

A. Eaglefield-Hull: 'Maclean, Alick', *A Dictionary of Modern Music and Musicians* (London, 1924)
K. Young: 'Alick Maclean: the "God of Scarborough"', *Music's Great Days in the Spas and Watering Places* (London, 1968), 78–107
J. Mitchell: 'Maclean's *Quentin Durward*', *The Walter Scott Operas* (Birmingham, AL, 1977), 289–300
N. Burton: 'Opera: 1865–1914', *Music in Britain: The Romantic Age, 1800–1914*, ed. N. Temperley (London, 1981), 330–57, esp. 347
STEPHEN BANFIELD

McLeod, Jenny [Jennifer] (**Helen**) (*b* Wellington, 12 Nov 1941). New Zealand composer. She studied at Victoria University and was later professor there (1971–6); she also studied with Messiaen and Stockhausen. An interest in ancient Maori creation poetry led to the work which established her reputation, *Earth and Sky* (1968), based on the Maori legend of Rangi and Papa. A music-theatre experiment for children and amateurs, it involved almost the entire community of the small city of Masterton at its first performance. *Under the Sun* (1971), for similar forces, commissioned by the city of Palmerston North, was partly in a rock idiom and depicted the eventual extinction of life on earth by the sun. McLeod returned to New Zealand in 1980 after some time in the USA, and more recently has worked on the development of a new harmonic theory originally formulated by the Dutch composer Peter Schat.

M. Cull: 'Earth and Sky', *Ascent*, i/3 (1969), 30–34
H. McNaughton: 'Earth and Sky', *Landfall*, no.25 (1971), 176–81
F. Page: 'Ambitious Work for Children', *Opera*, xxii (1971), 911–12 [on *Under the Sun*]
M. Lodge: *New Zealand Music Theatre, especially 1920–1970* (research essay, Victoria U. of Wellington, 1981)
E. Kerr: 'Jenny McLeod', *Music in New Zealand* (spr. 1988), 7–13 [interview]
J. M. Thomson: *Biographical Dictionary of New Zealand Composers* (Wellington, 1990)   J. M. THOMSON

McMaster, Brian (**John**) (*b* Hitchin, Herts., 9 May 1943). English administrator. He studied law at Bristol University and qualified as a solicitor before taking employment with EMI in 1968. After five years there he was made controller of opera planning at the ENO and then, in 1976, general administrator (later managing director) of the WNO.

McMaster did much to establish the WNO as one of Britain's finest opera companies, first by reorganizing its management structure and reducing its touring commitments, and then by engaging foreign directors, many of them from eastern Europe, to put on adventurous, if sometimes controversial, productions of both standard repertory and unusual operas. He was also successful in securing sponsorship to allow the company to show its productions in London and abroad.

Between 1984 and 1989 McMaster combined his work in Cardiff with an appointment as artistic director of the Vancouver Opera. He resigned from the WNO in 1991 to become artistic director of the Edinburgh Festival.

See also CARDIFF.

R. Fawkes: *Welsh National Opera* (London, 1986)
MALCOLM BOYD

MacNeil, Cornell (*b* Minneapolis, 24 Sept 1922). American baritone. He studied with Friedrich Schorr and made his début in 1950 at Philadelphia as John Sorel in the première of *The Consul*. Engaged by New York City Opera (1953–5) he made his début as Germont. He first appeared at San Francisco in 1955 as Escamillo and at Chicago in 1957 as Puccini's Lescaut. In 1959 he sang Don Carlo (*Ernani*) at La Scala, and made his Metropolitan début as Rigoletto, continuing to sing with the company until 1987; his roles included Nabucco, Amonasro, Luna, Gérard, Barnaba (*La Gioconda*), the Dutchman, Boccanegra, Guy de Montfort (*Les vêpres siciliennes*), Carlo (*La forza del destino*), Iago and Trinity Moses (*Mahagonny*). He appeared at the Paris Opéra, the Vienna Staatsoper, Covent Garden (1964) as Macbeth, and Florence (1966) as Miller (*Luisa Miller*). For much of his career a magnificent Verdi singer with fine legato and a secure top register, but little dramatic involvement, he later developed into a powerful interpreter of *verismo* roles such as Gianciotto (*Francesca da Rimini*), Tonio, Michele (*Il tabarro*) and, above all, Scarpia.

H. E. Phillips: 'Backstage with Boccanegra', *ON*, xxxiii/7 (1968–9), 26–7
E. C. Mordden: 'Big Mac', *ON*, xxxix/19 (1974–5), 16–17
J. Hines: 'Cornell MacNeil', *Great Singers on Great Singing* (Garden City, NY, 1982), 144–55
RICHARD BERNAS/ELIZABETH FORBES

Maconchy, Dame **Elizabeth** (*b* Broxbourne, Herts., 19 March 1907). English composer of Irish descent. She studied at the RCM (1923–9) with Charles Wood and Vaughan Williams, and later in Prague with Karel Jirák; there her first major work, the Piano Concertino, was performed in 1930. During the 1930s Maconchy became known mainly as a chamber music composer in England and abroad. She was made a CBE in 1977 and a DBE in 1987.

Maconchy's later output includes operas designed for professionals, for amateur groups and for children, as well as the dramatic cantata *Heloise and Abelard* which could well be staged. The three one-act operas *The Three Strangers*, *The Departure* and *The Sofa*, which have been performed as a triple bill, illustrate the breadth of her dramatic interests, the first being a ghost story based on Hardy, the second a domestic tragedy, the third a lighthearted and fantastic comedy. Most of the operas were written for special occasions, often for particular performers. *The Jesse Tree*, a 'church opera', was first performed at the Dorchester Festival with a professional cast led by Philip Langridge. *The Birds*, commissioned by Bishop's Stortford College, was performed by the students of the college; *Johnny and the Mohawks* was written for junior classes at the school where her daughter Nicola LeFanu was teaching music; *The King of the Golden River* includes both adults and children in the cast. While the string quartets are perhaps the most personal and concentrated of

135

Maconchy's works, she exhibits in the later operas, and in *Heloise and Abelard*, a sure instinct for dramatic effect, and a hitherto latent gift for the direct and often passionate expression of extreme emotions.

The Sofa, 1956–7 (1, U. Vaughan Williams), London, Sadler's Wells, 13 Dec 1959
The Three Strangers, 1958–67 (1, Maconchy, after T. Hardy), Bishop's Stortford College, 5 June 1968
The Departure, 1960–61 (1, A. Ridler), London, Sadler's Wells, 16 Dec 1962
The Birds, 1967–8 (1, Maconchy, after Aristophanes), Bishop's Stortford College, 5 June 1968 (London, 1974)
Johnny and the Mohawks (children's op, 1, Maconchy), London, Francis Holland School, March 1970 (London, 1970)
The Jesse Tree (church op, 1, Ridler), Dorchester Abbey, 7 Oct 1970
The King of the Golden River (1, Maconchy, after J. Ruskin), Oxford, University Church of St Mary, 29 Oct 1975

*

E. Maconchy: 'The Birds', *Music in Education*, xxxiii (1969), 24–5
E. Maconchy and A. Ridler: 'The Jesse Tree', *MT*, cxi (1970), 995–7
HUGO COLE

McSwiney, Owen. *See* SWINEY, OWEN.

Macurdy, John (*b* Detroit, 18 March 1929). American bass. He served in the US Air Force before studying with Avery Crew and Boris Goldovsky. After appearances in New Orleans and Santa Fe, he joined the New York City Opera in 1959 and moved to the Metropolitan Opera in 1962 (début as Samuel in *Un ballo in maschera*); his roles there included King Mark, Hagen, Sarastro, Gounod's Méphistophélès and Ezra Mannon in the première of Levy's *Mourning Becomes Electra* in 1967. In addition to engagements with leading orchestras and opera companies in the USA, he sang widely in Europe, appearing at Aix-en-Provence (Arkel, 1972), in Paris (Arkel, 1973) and at La Scala (Pizarro, 1974). Although Macurdy sometimes seemed temperamentally bland, his singing was notable for its breadth of range and dynamics as well as evenness and warmth.
MARTIN BERNHEIMER

Madagascar. Island in the Indian Ocean. In 1883 the French occupied the port of Tamatave (now Toamasina), and although the UK formally recognized the French protectorate of the island in 1890, the country was not completely conquered until 1897. By 1898 there was a Théâtre Municipal in Tamatave (seating 360) and one in the inland capital Tananarive (now Antananarivo; capacity 542). They were run by French impresarios, with companies from France resident for three months of the year in Tananarive and two in Tamatave. At first they played both spoken theatre and opera (including *opéra comique*), but after 1902 they became mainly operatic. The stage sets and musicians commuted between the two towns by stage coach until the railway was built in 1913. In the 1930s the Théâtre de Tananarive was destroyed by fire, and performances were transferred to the Maison de la Culture; after that decade there was no longer a resident troupe, although French lyric companies continued to perform in both towns until Madagascar became an independent state in 1960.
CHARLES PITT

Madama Butterfly ('Madam Butterfly'). *Tragedia giapponese* in two acts by GIACOMO PUCCINI to a libretto by GIUSEPPE GIACOSA and LUIGI ILLICA after DAVID BELASCO's play *Madame Butterfly*, itself based on JOHN LUTHER LONG's short story, which in turn was based partly on PIERRE LOTI's tale *Madame Chrysanthème*;

Milan, Teatro alla Scala, 17 February 1904 (revised version, Brescia, Teatro Grande, 28 May 1904).

Cio-Cio-San [Madam Butterfly]	soprano
Suzuki *her maid*	mezzo-soprano
F. B. Pinkerton *Lieutenant in the United States Navy*	tenor
Sharpless *United States consul at Nagasaki*	baritone
Goro *a marriage broker*	tenor
Prince Yamadori	tenor
The Bonze ⎱ *Cio-Cio-San's uncles*	bass
Yakuside ⎰	bass
The Imperial Commissioner	bass
The Official Registrar	bass
Cio-Cio-San's mother	mezzo-soprano
The Aunt	soprano
The Cousin	soprano
Kate Pinkerton	mezzo-soprano
Dolore ('Trouble') *Cio-Cio-San's child*	silent

Cio-Cio-San's relations and friends and servants

Setting Nagasaki, the beginning of the 20th century

Puccini was seized with the subject after seeing Belasco's play performed in London in June 1900, and he immediately applied to Belasco for the rights. These, however, were not officially granted until September of the following year. In the meantime Puccini had sent a copy of Long's story to Illica, who drew up a scheme in two parts. The first, originally intended as a prologue, derived exclusively from Long and showed the wedding of Pinkerton and Cio-Cio-San (called Butterfly by her friends); the second covered the action of Belasco's play and was divided into three scenes, the first and last being set in Butterfly's house and the second in the American consulate. As Giacosa proceeded with the versification the prologue expanded into Act 1 and the first scene of the second part into Act 2, while Illica's intention of retaining Long's ending (with Butterfly's suicide interrupted by the arrival of her child and the maid Suzuki who bandaged her wounds) was overruled in favour of Belasco's final catastrophe. Not until November 1902 was the libretto complete, whereupon Puccini decided in spite of strenuous opposition from Giacosa to abolish the scene in the American consulate, and with it the contrast between a Japanese and a Western ambience desired by Illica. Instead the two remaining scenes of the second part were to be fused into a single act lasting an hour and a half. So convinced was Giacosa of the folly of this arrangement that he wanted the text of the missing scene to be printed in the libretto; but Ricordi refused. The composition was interrupted in February 1903 by a motor accident from which Puccini made a long and painful convalescence. The score was completed by December and the première fixed for February the following year with an outstanding cast: Rosina Storchio (Butterfly), Giovanni Zenatello (Pinkerton) and Giuseppe de Luca (Sharpless). The conductor was Cleofonte Campanini. Although the singers and orchestra showed much enthusiasm, the first night was a disaster. Puccini was accused of plagiarism of himself and other composers. He at once withdrew the opera, and although convinced of its merits he made alterations to the score before allowing it to be performed elsewhere. He discarded several details involving Butterfly's relations in Act 1, divided the long second act into two

1. *'Madama Butterfly' (Puccini), Act 1 (a hill near Nagasaki; in the foreground a Japanese house with terrace and garden): design by Vittorio Rota for the original production at La Scala, Milan, 17 February 1904*

parts separated by an interval and added the arietta 'Addio, fiorito asil' for Pinkerton. The second performance took place on 28 May that same year at the Teatro Grande, Brescia, Salomea Krusceniski replacing Rosina Storchio among the original cast. This time the opera enjoyed a triumph. Nonetheless further modifications were to follow, mainly affecting Act 1. These ended with the Paris première, which was given by the Opéra-Comique on 28 December 1906, and formed the basis of the definitive printed edition. At the suggestion of Albert Carré, the theatre director and husband of the prima donna, Puccini further softened Pinkerton's character, eliminating his more xenophobic utterances, and avoided the confrontation between Butterfly and Kate, who thus emerges as a more sympathetic character. Earlier that year, however, Ricordi had already brought out a vocal score in which many of the original passages can be found. Three of them, all from Act 1, were reinstated with Puccini's sanction for a revival at the Teatro Carcano, Milan, shortly after World War I (they were not, however, reprinted). Joachim Herz's production of *Madama Butterfly* in 1978 restored some of the original music from the autograph, and the earliest version was given complete at La Fenice in 1982 and at Leeds in 1991. Outstanding exponents of the title role have included Geraldine Farrar, Toti dal Monte (Toscanini's favourite interpreter), Victoria de los Angeles, Elizabeth Vaughan (in English), and later Renata Scotto and Mirella Freni, as well as several Japanese singers.

ACT 1 *A hill near Nagasaki; in the foreground a Japanese house with terrace and garden* An orchestral fugato sets a scene of bustling activity as Goro leads Lieutenant Pinkerton out of the house, demonstrating its various appurtenances, in particular the sliding panels – so ridiculously fragile, the lieutenant thinks.

The domestic staff are presented to him: a cook, and his future wife's maid, Suzuki, who at once begins to bore Pinkerton with her chatter. While Goro is reeling off the list of wedding guests, Sharpless enters out of breath, having climbed the hill from Nagasaki. A characteristic motif establishes his benign, good-humoured presence. At Goro's bidding servants bring drinks and wicker chairs for Sharpless and his host. Pinkerton explains that he has bought the house on a 99-year lease which may be terminated at a month's notice. In his solo 'Dovunque al mondo', framed by the opening strain of *The Star-Spangled Banner* (later used as a recurrent motif), Pinkerton outlines his philosophy – that of the roving 'Yankee' who takes his pleasure where he finds it ('an easy-going gospel', observes Sharpless). After sending Goro to fetch the bride, Pinkerton dilates on her charms and his own infatuation. Sharpless recollects having heard her voice when she paid a visit to the consulate. Its ring of simple sincerity touched him deeply and he hopes that Pinkerton will never hurt her. Pinkerton scoffs at his scruples, so typical of unadventurous middle age. Both drink a toast to America (*The Star-Spangled Banner* again) and, in Pinkerton's case, to the day when he will take home an American wife. Goro announces the arrival of Butterfly and her friends, heralded by the distant sound of humming female voices. As the procession draws nearer the orchestra unfolds a radiant theme that begins with a series of rising sequences, each phrase ending on a whole-tone chord, then evolves into an extended periodic melody to which an essentially pentatonic motif of Japanese origin (ex.1) forms a hushed coda. Butterfly, whose voice has been heard soaring above those of the female throng, has by now appeared. She bows to the two men. Sharpless questions her about her family and background. He learns that her people were once wealthy but have since fallen on hard times, so that she has been forced to earn

Ex.1

her living as a geisha. She is 15 years old. Sharpless repeats his warning to Pinkerton. More guests arrive, including Butterfly's mother, a Cousin, an Aunt and Uncle Yakuside, who immediately asks for wine. Meanwhile the women exchange impressions of the bridegroom (not all of them favourable) until at a sign from Butterfly they all kowtow to Pinkerton and disperse. Butterfly shows Pinkerton her treasures and mementos, which she keeps concealed in her voluminous sleeves – a clasp, a clay pipe, a girdle, a pot of rouge (which she throws away in response to Pinkerton's mocking glance) and a narrow sheath which she hurriedly carries into the house. Goro explains that it holds the dagger with which Butterfly's father killed himself by the emperor's command. Re-emerging, she produces puppets that represent the spirits of her forebears. But she adds that she has recently visited the American mission to renounce her ancestral religion and embrace that of her husband. Goro calls for silence; the Imperial Commissioner proclaims the wedding and all join in a toast to the couple's happiness, 'O Kami! O Kami!'. (At this point in the original version there was a drunken arietta for Yakuside, who broke off to chastise a badly behaved child.) The festivities are interrupted by the Bonze, who bursts in denouncing Butterfly for having forsworn her faith. As her relations scatter in horror the orchestra embodies their curse in a whole-tone motif (ex.2). Alone with his bride Pinkerton comforts her,

Ex.2

while Suzuki can be heard muttering her evening prayers to the gods of Japan. There follows an extended duet for the lovers ('Viene la sera') woven from several melodic threads, now rapturous, now tender and delicate. Twice the 'curse' motif intrudes, first as Butterfly recalls how her family has cast her off, then when she remembers how the most beautiful butterflies are often impaled with a pin. The duet concludes with a grandiose reprise of the theme which accompanied her first appearance.

ACT 2 Part i *Inside Butterfly's house* Three years have gone by. Butterfly is alone with Suzuki, who is praying to the Japanese gods that her mistress's sufferings may soon end. Butterfly retorts that such gods are lazy; Pinkerton's God would soon come to her aid if

2. Rosina Storchio as Cio-Cio-San and Giovanni Zenatello as Pinkerton in the original production of Puccini's 'Madama Butterfly' at La Scala, Milan, 17 February 1904

only He knew where to find her. Their funds are nearly exhausted and Suzuki doubts whether Pinkerton will ever return. Furious, Butterfly reminds her how he had arranged for the consul to pay the rent, how he had put locks on the doors, and how he had promised to return 'when the robins build their nests'. In a celebrated aria ('Un bel dì vedremo') she pictures the scene of Pinkerton's return and her own joy. Goro arrives with Sharpless, who brings a letter from the lieutenant. Butterfly gives him a cordial welcome, and asks him how often the robins build their nests in America. Sharpless is evasive. Prince Yamadori enters and makes Butterfly an offer of marriage, which she mockingly rejects: she is a married woman according to the laws of America, where divorce, she says, is a punishable offence. Yamadori leaves and Sharpless begins to read the letter, breaking the news that Pinkerton intends to go out of Butterfly's life for ever, but she misunderstands the letter's drift and he abandons the task. He asks what she would do if Pinkerton were never to return, and she replies that she could resume her profession as a geisha, but that she would rather die by her own hand. Sharpless angers her by advising her to accept Yamadori's offer, but then she hurries to fetch her son by Pinkerton; astonished and moved, Sharpless promises to inform the father and leaves. Suzuki drags in Goro, whom she has caught spreading slanderous rumours about the child's parentage. Butterfly threatens to kill him, then dismisses him with contempt. The harbour cannon signals the arrival of a ship. To an orchestral reprise of 'Un bel dì' Butterfly seizes a telescope and makes out the name *Abraham Lincoln* – Pinkerton's man-of-war. She and Suzuki proceed to deck the house with blossom in a duet

('Scuoti quella fronda di ciliegio'). After adorning herself 'as on our wedding day' she, Suzuki and the child settle to a night of waiting, while an unseen chorus of wordless voices, recalling the theme to which Sharpless attempted to read Pinkerton's letter, evokes the slowly fading light.

ACT 2 Part ii An interlude, originally joined to the previous humming chorus, depicts Butterfly's restless thoughts; then, to the distant cries of the sailors the sun rises to disclose Butterfly, Suzuki and the child seated as before. Butterfly sings a lullaby and takes the boy to another room, where she quickly falls asleep. Pinkerton appears with Sharpless. Suzuki catches sight of a woman in the garden and Sharpless tells her that it is Pinkerton's wife, Kate. Their concern, he tells her, is to ensure the child a good American upbringing. He reproaches the lieutenant for his heartlessness. Pinkerton pours out his grief and remorse in the *romanza* that Puccini added for Brescia ('Addio, fiorito asil') and leaves, unable to face the bride he has betrayed. Butterfly enters, to confront Sharpless, Suzuki and Kate. When the situation is explained to her she bids them retire and return in half an hour. She takes a last farewell of her child and stabs herself behind a screen with her father's dagger. Pinkerton is heard desperately calling her name.

* * *

No other Puccini opera testifies more strongly to his ability to discern the possibilities for music drama in a trivial play performed in a language of which he hardly understood a word. In *Madama Butterfly* he and his librettists (working as always under his own direction) fleshed out Belasco's pathetic but ridiculous puppet into a genuine figure of tragedy who proceeds during the action from child-like innocence to an adult understanding and a calm acceptance of the destiny which her code of honour enjoins upon her. Butterfly is the apotheosis of the frail suffering heroine so often encountered in Puccini's gallery; and he would return to her only once more in the slave-girl Liù in *Turandot*.

By making use of at least seven Japanese folk melodies the composer both evoked the Far Eastern ambience and enlarged his musical vocabulary, since every one of them is assimilated into his own personal and by now highly sophisticated style. The scale of musical thought is likewise grander than ever before, the love duet in Act 1 being the longest and most elaborate that Puccini ever wrote. Though the organization remains for the most part motivic the motifs are no longer always referential in the Wagnerian manner. Ex.2, as already mentioned, is not always associated with the Bonze, while ex.1 receives its fullest treatment where Butterfly tells Pinkerton about her visit to the American mission in order to embrace her husband's religion ('Io seguo il mio destino') – an event that has no bearing on the theme's first appearance. In his later operas Puccini tended more and more to use motifs without hard and fast associations.
JULIAN BUDDEN

Madame Favart. *Opéra comique* in three acts by JACQUES OFFENBACH to a libretto by Alfred Duru and HENRI CHARLES CHIVOT; Paris, Folies-Dramatiques, 28 December 1878.

The 18th-century actress Madame Favart (soprano) is forced to adopt various disguises in support of her husband Charles-Simon Favart (baritone). He is in hiding from the military leader, Marshal de Saxe, who has been pressing his attentions on Madame Favart. She finally appears triumphantly in her husband's play *La chercheuse d'esprit*, staged to celebrate victory at Fontenay, and regains favour for herself and her husband. A satire on 18th-century manners and morals, with a lively and varied score, the work featured Juliette Simon-Girard as Madame Favart and her husband, Simon-Max, as the police official Hector de Boispréau (tenor).
ANDREW LAMB

Madame Sans-Gêne ('Madame Carefree'). Opera in three acts by UMBERTO GIORDANO to a libretto by RENATO SIMONI based on the comedy of the same title by VICTORIEN SARDOU and Emile Moreau; New York, Metropolitan Opera, 25 January 1915.

Set in Paris in August 1792, Act 1 opens outside the laundry of Caterina Hubscher (soprano), known as Madame Sans-Gêne, where all is confusion. Soldiers of the Revolution are attacking the Tuileries. Caterina arrives, having run the gauntlet of an amorous patrol, all of whom exacted a kiss ('Mentre andavo via leggera'). Fouché (baritone), a supporter of the insurgents, takes shelter at the laundry while the fighting lasts. Caterina dispatches one of her girls with a bundle of clothes to an impoverished officer, telling her not to demand payment. His name is Napoleon Bonaparte. She then sends for Sergeant Lefèbvre (tenor) – her lover, she tells Fouché, ever since he rescued her from the attentions of a would-be seducer at Vauxhall ('Lo conobbi son due mesi'). News comes that the Tuileries has fallen and Fouché leaves to join the victorious troops. An enemy soldier knocks at the door begging for shelter; he is the Austrian Count of Neipperg (tenor), gravely wounded in the fight. Caterina conceals him in an adjoining room. Lefèbvre arrives and joyfully recounts his exploits ('Alle giubbe scarlatte diam la caccia'). Caterina is unable to prevent him from entering the room where Neipperg is hidden. He reappears to announce that the fugitive is dead. But this is merely a ruse to discover whether the man is Caterina's lover. Satisfied with her reaction, he commends the wounded man to her care.

Act 2 takes place at the Château de Campiègne in September 1811. Napoleon is now emperor and Lefèbvre, married to Caterina, has been created Duke of Danzig. A tailor, a valet and a ballet-master are lamenting the bygone days of aristocratic elegance. When Caterina enters they try without success to instruct her in manners and deportment befitting her newly acquired status. Lefèbvre arrives much preoccupied; the Emperor has suggested that he should divorce Caterina and marry a lady of high society, but he declares that Caterina is the only wife for him ('Questa tua bocca profumata e pura'). They are joined by a distressed Neipperg, banished from the Emperor's court under suspicion of a scandalous intrigue. After he has left, supposedly to return to Vienna, guests arrive, among them Napoleon's sisters, Elisa Bacocchi, Grand Duchess of Lucca (soprano), and Carolina, Queen of Naples (soprano). Caterina's language and behaviour cause them disdainful amusement, whereupon she proclaims herself a true daughter of the Revolution and refers pointedly to their own humble origins. Furious, they vow revenge. Caterina receives a summons to the Emperor's presence.

The imperial cabinet is the setting for Act 3. Napoleon (baritone) reproaches Caterina for having compromised the dignity of his court; she answers by producing his laundry bill, outstanding for 19 years.

Napoleon is delighted to recognize his creditor and offers to repay her in more than currency; but this she virtuously refuses. As he is about to have her escorted home, he learns that the secret door to the empress's apartment is open. He summons his guards, who arrive in time to arrest the Count of Neipperg. The prisoner insists that he was exercising his right to salute the daughter of his sovereign before returning to Austria; but Napoleon suspects otherwise. He sends for Lefèbvre and Fouché, now Minister of Police, to sign Neipperg's death warrant. Lefèbvre is heartbroken at the prospect ('Ah non guardarmi e taci'). Neipperg is saved by a subtle stratagem of Napoleon's devising, which involves the interception of a letter proving the Count's innocence. Amid general rejoicing the Emperor and his entourage depart on a hunting expedition.

The première featured Geraldine Farrar (Caterina), Giovanni Martinelli (Lefèbvre) and Pasquale Amato (Napoleon); the conductor was Toscanini, who directed the first Italian performance at La Scala in 1922. The opera's most recent revival took place again at La Scala in 1967 on the centenary of the composer's birth. *Madame Sans-Gêne* is Giordano's only full-length comedy. His idiom is therefore more vigorous and robust here than in his other works, with fewer excursions into passionate lyricism. The first act makes abundant use of the traditional French Revolutionary songs to be found in *Andrea Chénier*, beginning with *La Carmagnole* (later interwoven with 'Ah, ça ira') and ending with a full-blooded choral statement of the *Marseillaise*. Especially attractive is Caterina's account of her first meeting with Lefèbvre at Vauxhall, set to a fife-and-drum-style melody *à l'anglaise*. The highlight of Act 2 is Lefèbvre's solo protesting his love for Caterina. Towards the end of Act 3 the complexities of the plot result in a dilution of the musical interest.

JULIAN BUDDEN

Mädchen aus der Feenwelt, Das [*Das Mädchen aus der Feenwelt, oder Der Bauer als Millionär* ('The Girl from the Fairy World, or The Peasant as Millionaire')]. 'Romantisches Original-Zaubermärchen mit Gesang' in three acts by JOSEPH DRECHSLER to a text by FERDINAND RAIMUND; Vienna, Theater in der Leopoldstadt, 10 November 1826.

The most successful of Raimund's plays in his lifetime and thereafter (207 performances in the Leopoldstadt alone up to 1859, and performed widely in Germany and Austria, where it continues to be given regularly), *Der Bauer als Millionär*, as it is usually called, perfectly met the expectations of its audiences. The story, a deft blend of magic and realism, depicts the peasant Fortunatus Wurzel (tenor) learning the lesson that riches do not bring happiness: his arrogant refusal to let his stepdaughter marry her fisherman boyfriend leads to his being turned prematurely old and impoverished. When he repents his folly, he regains his former state. Joseph Drechsler's score of 14 numbers, the musical ideas for some of which were Raimund's, contains one piece that has become one of the best-loved 'folksongs', the soprano and tenor duet 'Brüderlein fein', in which the allegorical figure of Youth (soprano; first sung by Therese Krones) bids farewell to the newly rich Wurzel (Raimund's own role). Wurzel's other solos include the 'Aschenlied' ('Dustman's Song') 'So mancher steigt herum', with its haunting refrain 'Ein Aschen', and the finale, 'Vergessen ist schön'. The overture and six of the

most popular numbers were published by Diabelli in vocal score.

PETER BRANSCOMBE

Maddalena. Opera in one act, op.13, by SERGEY PROKOFIEV to his own libretto; concert performance, Manchester, 22 December 1978; staged Graz, Opernhaus, 28 November 1981.

Maddalena was composed in 1911, partly orchestrated in 1912 and revised in 1913; the libretto is after a privately published (1905) play in blank verse by 'Baron Liven' (Magda Gustavovna Liven-Orlova), which is evidently modelled on Oscar Wilde's *A Florentine Tragedy*. (Prokofiev's music, *mutatis mutandis*, followed suit: in the opinion of Nikolay Myaskovsky, its dedicatee, it 'calls to mind the operas of Richard Strauss, but it lacks Strauss's banalities'.) The plot, set in 15th-century Venice, concerns a love triangle involving a painter (Genaro, tenor), his wife (Maddalena, soprano) and an alchemist (Stenio, baritone); the two men kill each other in a duel over the indifferent woman. Prokofiev at first hoped to have the opera performed by the St Petersburg Conservatory's opera workshop, but it proved too difficult. Later it was accepted for production by the Moscow Free Theatre. When that short-lived institution closed down, the composer abandoned work on the piece, which he had been revising, leaving only the first scene orchestrated. He brought the score out of Russia in 1927, but left it with his publisher in Paris when he returned permanently to the USSR. It was rediscovered in 1953 by Hans Swarsenski, but owing to unresolved legal questions involving ownership and performance rights no move was then made towards completing the orchestration. When Prokofiev's widow Lina emigrated from the USSR, in 1976, she claimed the manuscript and gave it to Edward Downes for completion. The opera's first performance took place under Downes's baton in Manchester, in a concert reading (22 December 1978) for a BBC broadcast (25 March 1979) with Jill Gomez, Arthur Davies and Terence Sharpe in the main roles. The stage première, also conducted by Downes, took place three years later. The vocal score was published in 1990.

RICHARD TARUSKIN

Madeira [née Browning], **Jean** (*b* Centralia, IL, 14 Nov 1918; *d* Providence, RI, 10 July 1972). American contralto. She studied at the Juilliard School and under the name Jean Browning made her début in 1943 at the Chautauqua Summer Opera as Nancy (*Martha*). In 1947 she was chosen by Menotti to alternate with Marie Powers in the European tour of *The Medium*. She joined the Metropolitan in 1948, making her début as the First Norn. From 1955 she sang mostly in Europe: she appeared as Clytemnestra, one of her greatest roles, at Salzburg (1956), as Carmen at Vienna and Aix-en-Provence and as Erda at Covent Garden, Bayreuth and Munich. She created Circe in *Ulisse* (1968, Berlin) and continued to sing until 1971. She had a rich, dark voice and was a compelling figure on the stage.

HAROLD ROSENTHAL/R

Maderna, Bruno (*b* Venice, 21 April 1920; *d* Darmstadt, 13 Nov 1973). Italian composer. After an early life of great turmoil, and adolescent years when, as 'Brunetto', he appeared as conductor with major Italian orchestras, Maderna's formal musical education was with Alessandro Bustini and later G. F. Malipiero. It was from Malipiero that Maderna gained an intense and lasting passion for Renaissance and Baroque music, while through the guidance of Hermann Scherchen after the war he began to move towards serial composition. Maderna first visited the Darmstadt summer courses in 1950, and he later settled there, but also travelled widely as a conductor in Europe and America, as well as founding with Berio the Studio di Fonologia Musicale in Milan.

Alongside his electronic pieces, Maderna explored composition through more traditional means, and as early as 1950 planned a stage work to be based on Kafka's novel *Der Prozess*: this was quickly modified to the *Studi per 'Il processo' di Kafka* for soprano, speaker and orchestra. His first completed dramatic work was *Don Perlimplin*, a radiophonic opera based on Lorca's play and written for Italian radio in 1962, which won the Italia Prize. The nature of radio presentation determined the work's character, with a protagonist whose 'voice' is heard only through a solo flute, and with imaginative use of radiophonic effects.

Hyperion, given first in Venice in 1964 and in new versions in Brussels and Bologna in 1968, was described as a 'poem in staged form'; this brought together elements from several existing works, and centred on the attempts of a flautist to perform an expressive solo. The later versions introduced new elements: in Brussels the work was given a Vietnamesque war-setting, and in Bologna a version of Domenico Belli's *Orfeo dolente* was placed among the 'scenes' of the original *Hyperion*, but all three versions culminated in the expressive *Aria* for soprano and orchestra.

Satyricon is a partly improvisational work hovering between music theatre and number opera: its 16 sections may be performed in varying order, and taped sections may if wished be placed between them, the dramatic 'action' consisting of bawdy and knockabout in the *commedia dell'arte* tradition. Large sections of the score are formed from pastiche and quotation, and Maderna created here a model of music theatre which has influenced many composers.

See also DON PERLIMPLIN; HYPERION; and SATYRICON.

Don Perlimplin (radiophonic op, 1, Maderna, after F. García Lorca), RAI, 12 Aug 1962
Hyperion (poem in staged form, 1, Maderna and V. Puecher, after F. Hölderlin, phonemes by H. G. Helms), Venice, Fenice, 6 Oct 1964; rev. as Hyperion en het geweld [Hyperion and Violence], Brussels, Monnaie, 17 May 1968; rev. as Hyperion–Orfeo dolente, Bologna, Palazzo Bentivoglio, 18 July 1968
Satyricon (1, Maderna and I. Strasfogel, after Petronius), Scheveningen, 16 March 1973

L. Pestalozza: 'Orfeo e Hyperion', *Rinascita*, xxv/31 (Rome, 1968), 23
L. Pinzauti: 'A colloquio con Bruno Maderna', *NRMI*, vi (1972), 545–52
I. Strasfogel: 'Nieuwe impulsen voor het muziektheater', *Opera journaal* (1973)
M. Mila: *Maderna musicista europeo* (Turin, 1976)
A. Gentilucci: 'Gestualità drammatica nel teatro musicale italiano nel dopoguerra', *Musica/realtà*, no.3 (1980), 81–93
A. Giubertoni: 'Le fonti poetiche dell'Hyperion di Bruno Maderna', *NRMI*, xv (1981), 197–205
F. Magnani: 'Considerazioni sul rapporto tra musica e testo nell'opera di Bruno Maderna', *Ricerche musicali*, no.5 (1981), 6–25
M. Baroni and R. Dalmonte, eds.: *Bruno Maderna: documenti* (Milan, 1985)
R. Fearn: *Bruno Maderna* (London, 1990)   RAYMOND FEARN

Madetoja, Leevi (Antti) (*b* Oulu, 17 Feb 1887; *d* Helsinki, 6 Oct 1947). Finnish composer. Following studies with Sibelius (1906–10), d'Indy and Fuchs, and at Helsinki University and in Berlin, he worked mainly as an orchestral conductor until 1916. In Helsinki he taught at the music institute (later academy) from 1916 to 1939 and was music critic of the *Helsingin Sanomat* (1916–32); he also spent some time in France. Madetoja was a leading member of the Finnish national romantic school which followed Sibelius. He made use of the folktunes of Ostrobothnia, dark and heavy melodies tinged by church modes; at the same time he was influenced by contemporary French music. His orchestration was particularly skilful, approaching the clarity and balance of chamber music, but in harmony and rhythm his means were more limited. His two operas were both performed at the Finnish Opera in Helsinki: *Pohjalaisia* ('The Ostrobothnians' op.45; 3, Madetoja, after A. Järviluoma) on 25 October 1924, and *Juha* (op.74; 2, A. Akté and Madetoja, after J. Aho) on 17 February 1935. Madetoja's output also includes three symphonies and much vocal music.

See also JUHA *and* POHJALAISIA.   HANNU ILARI LAMPILA

Madrid. Capital city of Spain. It became the capital in 1561, in the reign of Philip II. Its early role as the focus of Spanish court life greatly assisted its development as a centre of operatic activity, and for more than a century nearly all opera in the country was performed in Madrid theatres.

1. To 1700. 2. The 18th century. 3. After 1800.

1. TO 1700. The Spanish tradition of musical drama is well known, in both its religious and its secular aspects (*églogas*, *entremeses*, *autos sacramentales*, mystery plays etc.), and during the 16th century performances combining music and poetry on the stage were frequent. The process of establishing melodrama in Madrid began in the first decades of the 17th century, helped by the presence of visiting Florentine companies. Linked to the Renaissance court *fiesta*, with its *bailes*, *máscaras* and *saraos*, another type of entertainment developed, based on the dramatic madrigal, with individualized characters, recitative, choruses, dances and instrumental interludes. An example of this new form was the 'invención' of the Count of Villamediana, *La gloria de Niquea*, first performed in 1622 in the Real Sitio de Aranjuez (a royal palace near Madrid), with scenery by Giulio Cesare Fontana. This was not quite an opera as the word was by then understood in Italy, but Lope de Vega's *La selva sin amor* certainly was: it was staged on 18 December 1627 at the Coliseo del Buen Retiro, the royal palace theatre, by Cosimo Lotti, a Florentine designer imported by Philip IV. The composer of this first Spanish opera is unknown, and the music is lost.

Until the middle of the 17th century a succession of entertainments treating mythological and legendary themes appeared in a variety of genres: spoken verse with musical interventions, *ballet de cour*, allegorical sea battles, and all kinds of variations on the new form of opera with choral, solo, instrumental or dance elements. One such was *El mayor encanto, Amor*, first performed in summer 1635 on the lake of the Buen Retiro palace, with machinery by Lotti and text by Pedro Calderón de la Barca; this was followed by Bocángel's *El nuevo Olimpo* and Calderón de la Barca's *Los tres mayores prodigios* and *El jardín di Falerina*. Through such works as these – often with music by Juan Hidalgo, José Marín, Carlos Patiño, Juan del Vado, Cristóbal Galán or José Peiró – the transition was made from the recited to the acted style, a particular vocal style was defined and, above all, a sumptuous conception of staging evolved. Specifically Spanish preferences, the result of musical and theatrical tradition, aesthetic feeling and idiosyncratic taste, meanwhile led to the development of the zarzuela, so called after the royal palace on the outskirts of Madrid where they were originally performed. The first 'fiestas de zarzuela', *El laurel de Apolo* and *El golfo de las sirenas*, both with texts by Calderón de la Barca, were performed in Madrid in 1657 and are characterized by the alternation of sung and spoken parts, a feature of all zarzuelas.

The operatic tradition begun by Lope de Vega was continued by Calderón de la Barca as librettist of two new operas by Hidalgo performed in 1660: *La púrpura de la rosa* (Teatro del Buen Retiro, probably 17 January) and *Celos aun del aire matan* (Salón of the Palacio Real, probably 5 December); the music of the latter has survived. Hidalgo is also the composer of the earliest surviving zarzuela, *Los celos hacen estrellas*, to a libretto by Juan Vélez de Guevara, first performed in 1672 for the birthday of the queen mother (fig.1). The arrival in 1691 of Sebastián Durón provided a fresh stimulus for the creation of operas and zarzuelas with a more fluid musical line and abundant repetition, making for greater vocal brilliance. A clear change of taste became evident in the work produced by Durón and his successor Antonio Literes under Italian influence about 1700, when the Habsburg dynasty was replaced by the Bourbons.

2. THE 18TH CENTURY. Relations between Spain and Italy had been particularly close during the 16th and 17th centuries, and the presence in Madrid of actors, technicians and theorists such as Vincenzo Giustiniani, Giulio Rospiglioso, G. B. Doni and Vaggio del Bianco, in addition to Lotti and Fontana, helped keep the Spanish capital well informed of the newest developments in Italy. But though accepted, Italian opera had failed to impose itself definitively in the 17th century, unlike the zarzuela, which was more varied and gained wider popular acceptance. Certainly it was due to the successive kings (and their Italian wives) in the first half of the 18th century that the Italian style gained ground in Madrid, to the detriment of the native genre, naturally less appealing to a court of foreign origin. An Italian comic troupe, the Trufaldines, brought to Madrid in January 1703 by Philip V (who could not even speak Spanish) soon won the monopoly for performances in the Coliseo del Buen Retiro, which drew protests from the other Madrid theatres, the Príncipe and the Cruz. But the Italians, under the protection of Cardinal Alberoni, acquired further favours and exemptions, culminating in 1716 with a licence to perform in the Caños del Peral theatre. The arrival of Annibale Scotti three years later marked an even greater predominance of the Italian repertory and more privileges for the Trufaldines in their rivalry with Spanish companies, including that of receiving their salaries from the royal household.

The year 1737 was particularly significant for the decision to reform the Caños del Peral 'in the Italian style'. Although not an especially active theatre, it became one of the most distinguished in Europe, as did the Coliseo del Buen Retiro, 'reformed' the following year to enable it to present new operas from Italy. 1737 also saw the arrival in Madrid of the celebrated castrato Farinelli, who dominated Spanish music for more than two decades until his departure in 1759. A personal friend of Metastasio's, Farinelli persuaded the librettist to write works appropriate for the Madrid court even though they could not be attributed to him because of his exclusive contract with the Viennese court. At this period, Italian opera with its spectacles of dazzling

1. Scene from 'Los celos hacen estrellas' by Juan Hidalgo, the earliest surviving zarzuela, performed at the Alcázar Palace, Madrid, for the birthday of the queen mother in 1672: frontispiece from a manuscript copy of the work

2. *Masked ball in the Teatro del Príncipe, Madrid: painting (c1770) by Luís Paret y Alcázar*

sumptuousness definitively took root in Madrid and began to spread to other Spanish cities.

In the capital some Spanish composers such as Literes, José de Nebra and José Lidón attempted to compete in a field in which Italian composers were dominant. Not surprisingly, a revival of the zarzuela began in the last third of the century, during the reign of the enlightened Charles III, partly as a logical reaction and partly because of the new monarch's lack of enthusiasm for operatic spectacle. The librettist Ramón de la Cruz and composers such as Antonio Rodríguez de Hita, Pablo Esteve and Antonio Palomino succeeded in re-establishing the original Spanish tradition of musical drama. The new zarzuela was unmistakably directed towards a wider audience than the court entertainments, and although showing signs of French and Italian influence it was suited to the new age: it was more realistic, abandoning themes from myth and legend, and maintained a balance between alternating spoken and musical numbers and cohesion of music with drama, besides containing a variety of choruses, arias, duets, ensembles and orchestral interludes as well as frequent references to popular music. Where Italian opera had attracted Spanish composers, the resurrected zarzuela now interested composers such as Luigi Boccherini, who lived in Madrid from 1769 to 1805 and set Cruz's libretto *La Clementina* in 1786.

While the zarzuela was developing from a line running back to Florentine melodrama, in the last decades of the 18th century a purist reaction produced a strange minor genre, the *tonadilla escénica*, originating in the *sainetes*, *entremeses* and dances that had enlivened old play performances and which bore a certain kinship to *opera buffa*. It was made up of short comic sketches for an unsophisticated audience, with few characters and simple music, no chorus and uncomplicated structure. Once again Madrid provided the stage on which this genre was established, presented by companies such as that of Manuel Martínez. The Biblioteca Municipal holds more than 2000 *tonadilla* titles, giving an idea of the genre's extraordinary popularity.

3. AFTER 1800. The royal decree which from January 1800 forbade performance in Spain by non-Spanish artists and of works in foreign languages did not make a great difference to operatic activity in Madrid: barely eight years later Italian was sung again in the Caños del Peral. This theatre closed in 1810 because of its dilapidated condition, and was finally demolished in 1817. The first third of the century was marked by the Peninsular War and subsequent political instability, but after the return of Ferdinand VII Madrid was filled with enthusiasm for the Rossinian style and once more dominated by Italian singers, conductors, composers and impresarios. In 1837 work began on a royal theatre on the site of the Caños del Peral. Modelled on La Scala, the Teatro Real was finally inaugurated in 1850 with Donizetti's *La favorite*, followed in the first season by *I puritani*, *La sonnambula*, *Beatrice di Tenda*, *Il barbiere di Siviglia*, *L'elisir d'amore*, *La Cenerentola*, *Otello*, *La fille du régiment*, *Ernani*, *Linda di Chamounix*, *Maria di Rohan*, *Don Pasquale* and *Lucia di Lammermoor*. Only in 1854 were there two performances – the last of the season – of a Spanish work, *Ildegonda*, with music by Emilio Arrieta and libretto by Temistocle Solera, sung in Italian. Of the 126 operas performed up to 1900 in the Teatro Real only 17 were by Spanish composers, several of them with Italian texts.

As well as the Teatro Real (which held 2404 spectators) other theatres devoted to musical drama, either opera or, more usually, zarzuela, flourished during the 19th century. Chief among them were the Rossini (cap. 2750), the Príncipe Alfonso (2500), the Apolo (2200), the Bufos (2147), the Novedades (1778), the Zarzuela (1766), and smaller ones such as the Variedades, Capellanes, Recreo and Marsella (each with some 700 seats). Other halls, such as the Teatro del Circo, the Liceo Artístico y Literario, the Museo and the Comedia, occasionally staged opera and zarzuela.

Throughout the century there was much impassioned discussion of the need for a national opera, and both the conservatory and the Real Academia de Bellas Artes proposed measures to achieve it. In Madrid over a dozen music periodicals were dedicated to the praise and defence of Spanish opera. But in reality the moneyed classes of Madrid society clearly favoured Italian opera, while the populace preferred the zarzuela of the old tradition, revived once again in the middle of the century by Barbieri, Oudrid, Gaztambide and others. The strong nationalist attitude alive in other European countries was manifest in Spain as mere traditionalism, perfectly reflected in the zarzuelas that were produced in their thousands to supply the theatres and fill the needy pockets of Spanish composers. Once again the zarzuela found in Madrid fertile ground for new development, which was to reach the furthest corners of the Spanish-speaking world; it is in zarzuela rather than opera that the best composers of the time are to be found. In the last decades of the 19th century the so-called *género chico* appeared, a short zarzuela generally in a single act, portraying picturesque figures and scenes of everyday Madrid life. The librettos have an undoubted sociological value, while some of the scores are of considerable musical worth, such as Tomás Bretón's *La verbena de La Paloma* (1894), Ruperto Chapí's *La revoltosa* (1897) and Federico Chueca's *Agua, azucarillos y aguardiente* (1897), all still performed.

The presence in Madrid of Rossini (1831), Verdi (1863) and Puccini (1892) accentuated the preference for Italian opera rather than French or German (the last rarely seen), although taste was becoming increasingly conservative. The final years of the 19th century and the first third of the 20th were characterized by a falling off of musical activity in general and opera in particular, with the possible exception of the opening of the Teatro Lírico in 1902; it was dedicated to promoting Spanish opera but went bankrupt after only three productions. Conrado del Campo was fortunate enough to see some of his operas staged in the Teatro Real, but composers such as Albéniz and Granados had to find other cities (and even other countries) to have their operas performed. The closure of the Real in 1925 because of structural decay marked the beginning of a dark age of almost 70 years during which Madrid had no opera house.

During the Republic (1931–9) new developments were planned and begun, and even during the Civil War (1936–9), in a Madrid under bombardment by the rebel forces, there were performances in the Teatro Pardiñas in 1938 of *Rigoletto*, *Butterfly* and four Spanish operas: Chapí's *Margarita la Tornera*, Barbieri's *El diablo en el poder*, Usandizaga's *Las golondrinas* and Bretón's *La Dolores*. For many years after the war Madrid had no regular opera season, only a few very occasional and unpredictable performances at the Teatro Calderón and, after 1955, the Zarzuela. In 1964 the so-called Madrid Opera Festival was begun, consisting of a few performances in the spring. The Teatro Real reopened in 1966, but only for concerts, and closed again in 1988 for restoration to its original status as an opera house. Meanwhile the only operatic activity has been that promoted by the management of the Teatro de la Zarzuela: it has undertaken the laudable step of commissioning operas by contemporary Spanish composers, among which *Kiú* by Luis de Pablo (1983) made a particular mark. These works have a vitality which augurs well for the future.

F. A. Barbieri: *Il Teatro real y el Teatro de la Zarzuela* (Madrid, 1877)

L. Carmena y Millán: *Crónica de la ópera italiana en Madrid desde el año 1738 hasta nuestros días* (Madrid, 1878; suppls. 1879, 1880)

A. Peña y Goñi: *La ópera española y la música dramática en España en el siglo XIX* (Madrid, 1881)

R. Mitjana: 'Historia del teatro musical español', *Revista musical catalana*, iii (1906)

F. Borrell: *El wagnerismo en Madrid* (Madrid, 1912)

E. Cotarelo y Mori: *Origen y establecimiento de la ópera en España hasta 1800* (Madrid, 1917)

M. Zurita: *Historia del género chico* (Madrid, 1920)

M. Muñoz: *Historia del Teatro real* (Madrid, 1946)

A. Martínez Olmedilla: *Los teatros de Madrid* (Madrid, 1947)

J. Deleito y Piñuela: *Origen y apogeo del género chico* (Madrid, 1949)

J. Subirá: *Historia y anecdotario del Teatro real* (Madrid, 1949)

——: *El teatro del Real palacio (1849–1951), con un bosquejo preliminar sobre la música palatina desde Felipe V hasta Isabel II* (Madrid, 1950)

A. M. Coe: *Carteleras madrileñas 1677–1792, 1819* (Mexico City, 1952)

J. Subirá: 'Evocaciones en torno a las óperas madrileñas', *Revista de la biblioteca, archivo y museo* (1954)

——: 'Repertorio teatral madrileño y resplandor transitorio de la zarzuela (años 1763 a 1771)', *Boletín de la Real academia española*, xxxix (1959), 429–62

——: *Temas musicales madrileños* (Madrid, 1971)

R. Andioc: *Teatro y sociedad en el Madrid del siglo XVIII* (Madrid, 1976, 2/1988)

A. Gallego: 'Introducción al estudio de la ópera española en el siglo XIX', *Cuadernos de música*, ii (1982), 93–103

N. D. Shergold and J. E. Varey: *Fuentes para la historia del teatro en España*, i: *Representaciones palaciegas: 1603–1699* (London, 1982)

El teatro de Madrid (1583–1925): del Corral del Príncipe al Teatro de Arte (Madrid, 1983)

M. Agulló y Cobo, ed.: *El teatro en Madrid (1583–1925)* (Madrid, 1983)

J. Torres: *La prensa musical española* (Madrid, 1990)

JACINTO TORRES

Madrigal comedy. A loosely defined genre developed in late Renaissance Italy. It drew both on contemporary forms of entertainment (the *mascherata*, the *commedia dell'arte*) and on recent trends in secular music, both serious (madrigal cycles, the 'dialogue'-madrigal) and 'popular' (the *canzone villanesca alla napolitana* and its derivatives).

Alessandro Striggio (*c*1540–1592) depicted chattering washerwomen in *Il cicalamento delle donne al bucato* (1567): the programmatic tendencies perhaps derive from Janequin. Other musical miscellanies – such as the *Selva di varia ricreatione* (1590) and *Il convito musicale* (1597) by Orazio Vecchi (1550–1605), and Giovanni Croce's *Triaca musicale* (1595) – exhibit similar traits, evoking the high spirits of the *commedia dell'arte* with dialect texts, nonsense rhymes and humorous musical effects. But the term 'madrigal comedy' is best reserved for more unified collections such as Vecchi's *L'Amfiparnaso* (perhaps written in collaboration with the Bolognese poet Giulio Cesare Croce), first performed in Modena in 1594 (published 1597; ed. C. Adkins, Chapel Hill, NC, 1977). This three-act 'comedia harmonica' (or 'comedia musicale') deals with the lives and loves of stock *commedia dell'arte* figures through a sequence of polyphonic madrigals. *L'Amfiparnaso* could be (and has been) acted and/or mimed, but Vecchi's prologue says that the comedy is for the ear rather than the eye.

The technique was followed in three madrigal comedies by Adriano Banchieri (1568–1634) – *La pazzia senile* (1598), *Il metamorfosi musicale* (1601) and *Prudenza giovenile* (1607) – as well as in Vecchi's *Le veglie di Siena* (1604): Banchieri recommends that a narrator should help keep track of the 'plot', but again staging is neither implied nor intended.

The genre was short-lived, declining in tandem with the madrigal. It might be associated with the new impulses to match music with drama in late 16th-century Italy, and Vecchi's approval of early Florentine opera is noted in the preface to Jacopo Peri's *Euridice* (1601). But the view of the madrigal comedy as a significant precursor of opera is both old-fashioned and untenable.

*
A. Einstein: *The Italian Madrigal* (Princeton, 1949)
N. Pirrotta: 'Commedia dell'Arte and Opera', *MQ*, xli (1955), 305–24; repr. in N. Pirrotta: *Music and Culture in Italy from the Middle Ages to the Baroque* (Cambridge, MA, 1984), 343–60
J. Haar: 'On Musical Games in the 16th Century', *JAMS*, xv (1962), 22–34
W. Kirkendale: 'Franceschina, Girometta and their Companions in a Madrigal "a diversi linguaggi" by Luca Marenzio and Orazio Vecchi', *AcM*, xliv (1972), 181–213
M. Farahat: 'On the Staging of Madrigal Comedies', *Early Music History*, x (1991), 123–43
TIM CARTER

Mad scene (Fr. *scène de folie*; Ger. *Wahnsinnszene*; It. *scena di pazzia*). An operatic scene in which a character, usually the soprano heroine, displays traits of mental collapse, for example through amnesia, hallucination, irrational behaviour or sleepwalking. The mad scene, which became particularly popular during the early 19th century – a symptom of the post-Revolutionary treatment of hitherto taboo topics – supplies a brilliant vehicle for the display of a singer's histrionic and vocal talents. It traditionally involved elaborate coloratura writing and commonly the participation of a wind instrument, often the flute or, in particular, the english horn. The mad scene of Donizetti's *Lucia di Lammermoor* (1835) is generally regarded as the *locus classicus*.

The treatment of heightened states of emotion has always been central to opera. In 17th-century opera the lament was a favourite device for a heroine *in extremis*, from Monteverdi's Ariadne to Purcell's Dido. In some works of this period fully-fledged loss of reason is displayed, for example in Cavalli's *Egisto* (1643), *Giasone* (1649; a treatment of the Medea legend) and *Pompeo magno* (1666), where there is a 'Balletto dei pazzi'. Feigned madness was also depicted on the stage, as in Sacrati's *La finta pazza* (1641). In the early 18th century, there are a number of mad scenes in Handel's dramatic works, notably for Ariodante (1735) and Orlando (after Ariosto, 1733), whose mental disintegration is portrayed in a long scene with broken, disjunct phrases, irregular formal organization and brief passages in quintuple metre. In this period, however, madness was widely regarded as comic rather than tragic and it often featured in comic operas, sometimes feigned but often real. Two characters briefly appear mad in Mozart's *La finta giardiniera* (1775), a device to extricate them from an unmanageable dramatic situation. The contemporary trend of depicting sensibility, in literature and reality, is reflected in settings of the Nina story, in which a young woman is prevented by her father from selecting her own spouse; this, combined with the belief that her beloved is dead, causes her to become unhinged. Settings include one by Dalayrac (1786) and a highly popular one by Paisiello (1789).

This story influenced later works such as Paer's *Agnese* (1809) and Adam's ballet *Giselle* (1841, in which ballet acrobatics serve the same function as operatic fioritura). In Berton's *Le délire* (1799), the recurrent insanity of a young man is depicted by recurring musical motifs.

The great age of the mad scene began in the 1820s. Sleepwalking is explored in Carafa's *Il sonnambulo* (1824), and Hérold wrote a ballet on the subject to a scenario by Scribe (1827). The two best-known sleepwalking heroines are Bellini's Amina (*La sonnambula*, 1831) and Verdi's Lady Macbeth (1847); wandering in mind and body is symbolized through the abandonment of melodic periodicity in the former (in 'Ah, non credea mirarti') and in the latter through unfocussed tonalities, while coloratura writing takes on a dramatic-psychological quality, its range and speed suggesting vulnerability and instability. Bellini had earlier depicted madness in *Il pirata* (1827), writing a very spare line for the victim, Imogene, and reserving coloratura outbursts for her most severe attacks; an english horn portrays her tortured thoughts. He also wrote a mad scene for Elvira (*I puritani*, 1835), in which much is made of ghostly offstage voices, imagined nuptials, storm scenes to indicate mental turmoil and vocal virtuosity.

Walter Scott's novel *The Bride of Lammermoor* provided the basis for many mad-scene operas, beginning with Carafa's *Le nozze di Lammermoor* (1829), of which the most famous is Donizetti's (1835). He used vocal acrobatics and high tessitura, with an obbligato flute (he had originally intended to use a glass harmonica, whose eerie sound and vibrations had the reputation of causing madness in those who played it; for illustration *see* DONIZETTI, GAETANO). This was not his first mad scene: there is a mock mad scene in his *I pazzi per progetto* (1830), one for Anne Boleyn in *Anna Bolena* (1830), where to external military sounds and enacting imagined nuptials she slips in and out of reality in the last moments before her execution, and another in *Torquato Tasso* (1833), which falls to the baritone name-part. A tenor is the victim of madness in his *Maria Padilla* (1841), singing a *romanza* introduced by english horn over harp arpeggios. *Linda di Chamounix* (1842) also includes a mad scene, in which the heroine's recurring song eventually effects her cure.

Verdi wrote no mad scene as such, the sleepwalking scene in *Macbeth* apart, but in several of his operas characters experience disturbance through dreams, visions or hallucinations. Macbeth, for example, sees Banquo's ghost; Joan of Arc (1845) and Jacopo Foscari, the hero of *I due Foscari* (1844), have visions; Francesco has a dream in *I masnadieri* (1847); while Giselda in *I Lombardi* (1843) sings a cabaletta marked 'quasi colpita di demenza'. Verdi did not ultimately set *King Lear*, but Cagnoni's opera (1893) has a mad scene in which Regan sees spectres. Boito's *Mefistofele* (1868) includes a mad scene for Margherita. There are no mad scenes in Wagner; the nearest approach comes in Sieglinde's tormented visions in *Die Walküre* at the sound of Hunding's dogs. Among French operas, Halévy's *Charles VI* (1843) has an extended mad role as the king's personal traumas are played out against events of state. Meyerbeer's *Dinorah* (1859) addresses ghostly visions in coloratura outbursts. The mental collapse of Musorgsky's Boris (1874) is captured by an ostinato figure; this opera also features the traditional Russian figure of the idiot in the crowd.

If the mad scene was largely obsolete by 1875, madness as an operatic preoccupation only became more pronounced after that date, with obsession, *Angst* and paranoia playing a central part in many operas, such as *Salome*, *Elektra*, *Erwartung* and *Wozzeck*. The moon, a symbol of lunacy, is a significant presence in the first and last of these. There is a parody mad scene in Britten's *A Midsummer Night's Dream* (1960), for Thisbe, in a *Lucia*-like idiom; coloratura pyrotechnics abound in Menotti's *La loca* (1979) and Argento's *Miss Havisham's Fire* (1979).

*

A. Garlington: *The Concept of the Marvelous in French and German Opera, 1770–1840: a Chapter in the History of Opera Esthetics* (diss., U. of Illinois, Urbana-Champaign, 1965)

L. Florua: 'Der Wahn und seine Darstellung in Verlauf der Musikgeschichte', *Confinia psychiatrica*, xvii (1974), 69–93

S. Döhring: 'Die Wahnsinnszene', *Die 'couleur locale' in der Oper des 19. Jahrhunderts*, ed. H. Becker (Regensburg, 1976), 279–314

J. Mitchell: *The Walter Scott Operas: an Analysis of Operas Based on the Works of Sir Walter Scott* (Birmingham, AL, 1977)

G. Schmidgall: *Literature as Opera* (New York, 1977)

P. Fabbri: 'Alle origini di un "topos" operistico: la scena di follia', *L'opera tra Venezia e Parigi: Venice 1986*, ii

G. Morelli: 'La scena di follia nella *Lucia di Lammermoor*: sintomi, fra mitologia della paura e mitologia della libertà', *La drammaturgia musicale*, ed. L. Bianconi (Bologna, 1986), 411–34

S. Willier: *Early Nineteenth-Century Opera and the Impact of the Gothic* (diss., U. of Illinois, Urbana-Champaign, 1987)

——: 'Madness, the Gothic, and Bellini's *Il pirata*', *OQ*, vi/4 (1988–9), 7–23

——: 'Through Dooms of Love', *ON*, liii/11 (1988–9), 12–14, 46

E. Rosand: 'Operatic Madness: a Challenge to Convention', *Music and Text: Critical Inquiries*, ed. S. P. Scher (Cambridge, 1992), 241–87

STEPHEN A. WILLIER

Maestra, La ('The Schoolmistress'). *Opera buffa* in three acts by GIOACCHINO COCCHI to a libretto by ANTONIO PALOMBA; Naples, Teatro Nuovo, spring 1747 (revised versions, *La scuola moderna, o sia La maestra di buon gusto*, Venice, autumn 1748; *La scaltra governatrice*, Paris, 1753; Venice, 1754).

Fazio (tenor), a rich bourgeois, is in love with Drusilla (soprano), the wily governess of his daughter Leonora (soprano). Drusilla loves, and is loved by, Fazio's servant Pistone (tenor, in the original production a Neapolitan-dialect role). Leonora is loved by Ottavio and Flaminio (sopranos), but loves only Ottavio. Through Drusilla's wiles, the two unmatched couples are brought together, Flaminio marries elsewhere and Fazio renounces love. Among the comic highlights are various lesson scenes (an alphabet aria, a French-lesson aria) and a sneezing scene. As *La scuola moderna*, with additional music by Vincenzo Ciampi and others and new lines by Goldoni, the work reappeared at Venice the following year. Cocchi himself reintroduced it there in 1754, in a version closer to the original. Meanwhile, as *La scaltra governatrice*, it had become a part of the repertory of Bambini's Bouffons in Paris and from 1752 to 1754 was the only full-length comic opera given by them. The opera, Cocchi's most successful, maintained itself into the 1760s, albeit much altered and mutilated.

PIERO WEISS

Maestro concertatore (It.). A person who played keyboard continuo in performances and was in charge of individual preparation of singers and of orchestral rehearsals. *See also* RÉPÉTITEUR.

Maestro di cappella, Il ('The Music Director'). Comic monologue by DOMENICO CIMAROSA, composed *c*1786–92.

The Music Director (bass) is conducting a rehearsal of a large orchestra of flutes, oboes, horns and strings. The musicians are undisciplined: they do not pay attention to the Music Director, entering on the wrong beat and playing incorrect notes. The violins are at odds with the violas and oboes, the flutes with the basses, causing the Music Director to lose his patience. Finally, by imitating the melodic passage of each instrument, he manages to get them to play correctly, melodiously and, eventually, in harmony.

It is not clear whether the piece was intended as a humorous cantata, an intermezzo for solo voice (an uncharacteristic genre for the period) or an arrangement of an aria. Parodies of music teachers, music directors, impresarios and prima donnas abound in 18th-century comic works: Sarro's intermezzo *L'impresario delle Canarie* (1724), Haydn's *La canterina* (1766) and Mozart's *Der Schauspieldirektor* (1786) are notable examples. Cimarosa's monologue can be viewed within this context, with its caricaturing of the music master and the musicians, and may indeed be related to his popular *L'impresario in angustie* (1786).

Il maestro di cappella is a continuous, through-composed unit in which accompanied recitative alternates with aria-like material. The music is extremely witty, featuring passages for solo instruments; the third-related harmonic movement reflects Cimarosa's mature style of composition.

GORDANA LAZAREVICH

Maestro direttore (It.). The leader of the first violins in an opera orchestra, who might also be in charge of the orchestra's administrative arrangements and of hiring and paying the players.

Maeterlinck, Maurice (*b* Ghent, 29 Aug 1862; *d* Nice, 6 May 1949). Belgian playwright. He is best known by musicians for his play *Pelléas et Mélisande* (1892), set as an opera by Debussy. Maeterlinck's reputation was established around 1890 when he was hailed in Paris as the 'Belgian Shakespeare'. He became the leading playwright of the Symbolist movement with a series of plays with medieval settings, culminating in *Ariane et Barbe-bleue* (1907), written to be set as an opera which, after several composers including Grieg had been approached, was eventually composed by Paul Dukas.

Maeterlinck's work has inspired many musicians to write incidental music, symphonic poems, songs and operas. Debussy was the first composer to approach Maeterlinck directly. He had considered setting *La princesse Maleine* (1889) but obtained Maeterlinck's permission to set *Pelléas* after he had seen the single Paris performance of the play in 1893, and having heard that Satie was considering a setting of the earlier play. Debussy and Maeterlinck later quarrelled, when Debussy would not allow Maeterlinck's mistress Georgette Leblanc to take the role of Mélisande. However, much later in his life, long after his liaison with Leblanc had ended, Maeterlinck confessed that Debussy had been 'entirely right'.

plays unless otherwise stated

La princesse Maleine (1889), L. Boulanger, 1918, inc.; *L'intruse* (1890), Pannain, 1940; *Pelléas et Mélisande* (1892), Debussy, 1902; *Alladine et Palomides* (1894), sketched by Webern, 1908 (Burian, 1923; Chlubna, 1925; Burghauser, 1944); *La mort de Tintagiles* (1894), Nouguès, 1905 (Collingwood, 1950); *Monna Vanna* (1902), Ábrányi, 1907 (Rakhmaninov, 1907, inc.; Février, 1909; *Soeur Béatrice* (1902), Grechaninov, 1912 (A. A. Davidov, 1912; A. Wolff, 1914; Mitropoulos, 1920; Rasse, 1944; A. Marquès Puig; Hoiby, 1959); *Joyzelle* (1903), A. Tcherepnin,

1926; *Ariane et Barbe-bleue* (opera, 1907), Dukas, 1907; *L'oiseau bleu* (1908), A. Wolff, 1919

*

R. Orledge: *Debussy and the Theatre* (Cambridge, 1982)
D. Grayson: *The Genesis of Debussy's 'Pelléas et Mélisande'* (Ann Arbor, 1986)
R. Nichols and R. Langham Smith: *Pelléas et Mélisande* (Cambridge, 1989)   RICHARD LANGHAM SMITH

Maffoli, Vincenzo (*b* Iesi or Pesaro, *c*1760; *d* ?Vienna, 1794/5). Italian tenor. After beginning his career with a few comic roles in the early 1780s, he quickly rose to fame as a serious tenor in the mid-1780s with roles in operas by Bertoni, Francesco Bianchi and Tarchi. His triumph in Rome in 1788 was complete, according to Gerber; audiences were 'full of wonder and enthusiasm' at his singing. In 1791 he was engaged by Emperor Leopold II as part of a plan to reintroduce *opera seria* to the Burgtheater in Vienna, and his Viennese début was a great success. Benedetto Frizzi lamented Maffoli's early death:

Maffoli, who was taken from us in the flower of his youth, deserved the sincerest esteem both for his profound knowledge of harmony and for the grace of his cantabile, and even his nasal voice; even this imperfection, in some *adagio* passages, gave his voice a pleasing quality. He won the special admiration of the Viennese for several years.

*

B. Frizzi: *Dissertazione di biografia musicale* (Trieste, 1805)
J. A. Rice: *Emperor and Impresario: Leopold II and the Transformation of Viennese Musical Theater, 1790–1792* (diss., U. of California, Berkeley, 1987)   JOHN A. RICE

Magagnoli, Maria Ginevra (*b* Bologna, *fl* 1740–52). Italian soprano. She first appeared at Alessandria in 1740 (in Buini's *Il savio delirante*) with established *buffo* singers including Anna Maria Querzoli and in the same year began to collaborate with Domenico Cricchi in performing comic intermezzos (e.g. Pergolesi's *La serva padrona* and *Amor fa l'uomo cieco*). After singing in Latilla's *La finta cameriera* in Venice and Livorno in Francesco Baglioni's company, she joined that of Pietro Mingotti (1743–5) and sang in Hamburg, Leipzig and Prague. In autumn 1745 she was again in Italy performing intermezzos with Cricchi and also comic operas, including Giuseppe Scarlatti's *Il giocatore*. Müller's reference to her presence in Copenhagen in 1748 is due to a misinterpretation of programmes printed in Copenhagen in that year.

*

E. H. Müller: *Angelo und Pietro Mingotti* (Dresden, 1917)
F. Piperno: 'Gli interpreti buffi di Pergolesi', *Studi pergolesiani*, i (1986), 166–78   FRANCO PIPERNO

Magdeburg. City in Germany, capital of Saxon-Anhalt. Musical and theatrical events began in 1755, when Otto Ackermann's touring company staged the ballet *Die Eifersucht des Bauern*; in 1771 that of K. G. Döbbelin performed Singspiels by J. A. Hiller. Italian operas were given in 1769 and 1772, including works by Galuppi, Ciampi and Pergolesi. With Döbbelin as its first director, the Magdeburg Nationaltheater opened on 27 March 1795 in the building designed by Erdmannsdorf and known as 'Zu den drei Engeln'. The French occupation brought the public into contact with contemporary French works. Weber's *Der Freischütz* was given in 1821, the year of its first production, but the company began to flourish again only after 1825, when it performed works by Mozart, Rossini, Paer, Paisiello, Cimarosa and Beethoven. Richard Wagner was Kapellmeister in 1834–6 under H. E. Bethmann's direction, and the first performance of *Das Liebesverbot* was given in 1836. In 1845 Lortzing's *Undine* had its première there.

The new Stadttheater, with 1200 seats, opened on 6 May 1876; Herman Zumpe, its first influential musical director (1878–9), was a Wagnerian, as were his successors, who directed the *Ring* and *Tristan*. A Mozart cycle was given in 1895. In 1932 Mark Lothar's revision of Haydn's *Il mondo della luna* had its first performance at Magdeburg in collaboration with the Schwerin opera company. In 1944 the Stadttheater was destroyed; it was replaced by the Maxim-Gorki-Theater, which opened in 1950 and is now the city's chief venue for operatic performances. The main auditorium, the Grosses Haus, has 904 seats. Operas are also given in the studio theatre, or Kleines Haus, with 314 seats. The Magdeburg Telemann Festival has, since its inception in 1962, contributed to the revival of Telemann's operas, which, with those of Mozart and Wagner, form the mainstay of the present-day repertory.

*

M. Hasse: *Festschrift des Richard-Wagner-Verbandes* (1913)
M. Widmann: 'Geschichte des Magdeburger Theaterwesens', *Montagsblatt der Magdeburger Zeitung* (1925)
M. Hasse: '50 Jahre Stadttheater', *Montagsblatt der Magdeburger Zeitung* (1926)
B. Sommerlad: *Nachrichten über das Geschlecht Pitterlin* (Leipzig, 1929)
O. Riemer: *Musik und Musiker in Magdeburg* (Magdeburg, 1937)
W. Hobohm: 'Magdeburg', *Bedeutende Musiktraditionen der Bezirke Halle und Magdeburg*, ii (Halle and Magdeburg, n.d.)   DIETER HÄRTWIG

Maggi, Carlo Maria (*b* Milan, 3 May 1630; *d* Milan, 22 April 1699). Italian poet and playwright. He was the son of a merchant of luxury goods, studied law at Bologna and travelled throughout Italy before becoming in 1661 secretary to the senate of Milan, a post he held for the rest of his life. From 1664 he was lecturer in Latin and Greek at the Scuole Palatine and from 1691 a member of the Accademia d'Arcadia. He is known primarily for his comedies in Milanese dialect (e.g. *I consigli di Meneghino*), performed with great success at the Collegio dei Nobili beginning in 1695: the servant characters (who speak in dialect) have a monopoly of sententious and proverb-laden wisdom, which, consistent with the author's declared pessimistic moralism, compensates for and neutralizes the caricatured social, economic and cultural corruption of the ruling-class characters. The calculation for a Milanese audience and the 'maravigliosa imitazione di costumi' (in the sense, for example, of Molière's comedy of manners) of this comic theatre, which verges on the 'popular', are already apparent in Maggi's opera librettos, which he repudiated after his turn to moral and elevated subjects for poetry, to which the *Rime varie* of 1688, rich in cantatas 'per musica', bear witness. L. A. Muratori nonetheless published three librettos in his edition of Maggi's works; they were friends and both criticized the shortcomings of musical theatre, sharing a concept of theatre committed to urban society. Maggi may have been the unnamed author of the parts in Milanese dialect in Carlo Righenzi's comic opera *La farsa musicale* (1664, Milan). The 'favola pastorale' *Lucrina* was written in 1666 for the visit of the future Empress Margareta Theresa of Austria to Milan on her way to Vienna; the music is attributed to G. A. Celidone (in *I-*

Rvat Ottob. lat.2480, ff.24–8). For the theatre of Count Vitaliano Borromeo on Isola Bella, Lake Maggiore (opened *c*1667–8), he wrote *Bianca di Castiglia*, first performed in October 1669, and at the Regio Ducal Teatro, Milan, in 1674 and 1676. Also for Count Borromeo's theatre he wrote *Gratitudine umana*, *Irene di Salerno* and *Ben venga maggio*, *Irene di Salerno* and *Ben venga maggio*, *o sia La ninfa guerriera*. In the winter of 1672–3 his *Il trionfo d'Augusto in Egitto* and *Amor tra l'armi, overo Corbulone in Armenia* were performed at the Regio Ducal Teatro, Milan. *Ippolita reina delle amazzoni* has also been attributed to him. Scores of *Ben venga maggio* and *Il trionfo d'Augusto in Egitto* and music fragments of *Bianca di Castiglia*, *Gratitudine umana* and *Irene di Salerno* are held at the Borromeo family archive in Stresa, Italy (*I-IBborromeo*).

In all these 'opere in musica' (the nomenclature is intentionally closer to the tradition of the *commedia dell'arte* than the normal 'dramma per musica' would be) the author of the text, though never mentioned by name on the title-page, is often present for the purpose of satire or criticism in the characters of servants or ministers or through transparent allusions to Milanese state and cultural events or to his own biography (e.g. the secretary Alfonso, the principal male character in *Bianca di Castiglia*). The romance-like intrigue, often of Spanish inspiration, is rigorously realistic (with abundant use of such mundane props as clocks, handkerchiefs and rings). The style is plain and clear, with a good deal of banter against metaphorical, high-flown language. The moralism is conveyed by the great number of terse 'mezz'arie', particularly for the secondary characters. Precisely because their comedy and morality were rooted in a specifically Milanese social reality, Maggi's works were never performed outside Milan, although they must be reckoned among the finest Italian librettos of the 17th century: the very structure of the mainstream of Italian opera ruled out any attempt at moral and stylistic regeneration such as that undertaken by Maggi, who after 1673 was reduced to supplying 'arie aggiunte' for imported dramas (e.g. *Girello*, 1674, and *Attila*, 1677; scores at *IBborromeo*).

Lucrina (favola pastorale), G. A. Celidone, 27 Sept 1666; *Bianca di Castiglia*, F. Rossi, 1669; *Gratitudine umana*, Borzio and Magni, 1670 [also as *Affari ed amori*, 1675]; *Amor tra l'armi, overo Corbulone in Armenia*, Busca, 1672–3; *Il trionfo d'Augusto in Egitto*, 1672–3; *Ben venga maggio, o sia La ninfa guerriera*, B. Castelli and G. Rivolta, before 1673; *Irene di Salerno*, ?Gerolamo or ?Angelo Zanetti, before 1673

Doubtful: *Ippolita reina delle amazzoni*, Busca, P. S. Agostini and P. A. Ziani, 1670

*

ES (R. Rebora)

L. A. Muratori, ed.: *Rime varie* (Milan, 1700)

L. A. Muratori: *Vita di Carlo Maria Maggi* (Milan, 1700)

——: 'Vita di Carlo Maria Maggi milanese, detto Nicio Meneladio', *Le vite degli Arcadi illustri*, ed. G. M. Crescimbeni (Rome, 1708), i, 79–88

G. Machio, ed.: *Poesie miscellanee* (Milan, 1729)

A. Cipollini: *Per Carlo Maria Maggi* (Milan, 1900), 75ff

D. Isella, ed.: *Il teatro milanese* (Turin, 1964)

D. Isella: 'Le rime milanesi di Carlo Maria Maggi', *Studi secenteschi*, vi (1966), 67–264; pubd separately, enlarged (Pistoia, 1985)

A. Petrella: 'Carlo Maria Maggi's Theory of Comedy', *Italian Quarterly*, xii (1968), 223–37

G. Mazzocchi: 'El teatro español en Lombardía a fines del siglo XVII', *El teatro español a fines del siglo XVII*, iii (Amsterdam, 1989), 691–714

P. Fabbri: *Il secolo cantante: per una storia del libretto d'opera nel seicento* (Bologna, 1990)   LORENZO BIANCONI

Maggio Musicale. Summer festival, in May and June, inaugurated in Florence in 1933; several opera premières have been given under its auspices. *See* FLORENCE, §8.

Maggiore, Francesco (*b* ?Naples, *c*1715; *d* ?Netherlands, ?1782). Italian composer. He was said by contemporaries to be talented but, as far as is known, he never achieved regular employment, and his life was unusually peripatetic. He studied in Naples, and after the production of a comic opera there in 1737 he spent a number of years in the Veneto and elsewhere in northern Italy, obtaining occasional musical and composing jobs; librettos of the time call him a *maestro di cappella*. For Carnival 1742 he contributed arias to a pasticcio, *Nerone* (A. Piovene), in Gorizia; in the same year he directed the music at the newly rebuilt theatre in Verona. The next year he was director of the opera in Reggio Emilia, adding at least seven arias to a production of Gluck's *Demofoonte*, and seems also to have been in Ferrara. Similarly, in Venice in 1751 he helped put together a revival of *Statira* (C. Goldoni), providing the recitatives and several arias; other arias (according to Piovano) were chosen by the singers. He is of historical interest as having been among the first Naples-trained composers to write an *opera buffa* for Venice (*I rigiri delle cantarine*, 1745), contributing to the new popularity of the form there. He travelled extensively throughout Europe giving concerts and directing operas. He had a singular gift for mimicking in his music the natural sounds of animals and birds. Although La Borde considered this a 'low and undesirable' species of entertainment, chroniclers agree that he amused his audiences well. He is said to have settled in the Netherlands by 1764 and to have died there in poverty.

Maggiore's surviving arias show compositional ability. Melodic lines, frequently setting conventional texts, are fresh, take unexpected turns and exhibit an unusual degree of expressive chromatic detail which however does not obscure the solid harmonic structure.

Lo Titta (ob), Naples, Pace, 1737

Il Demetrio (os, P. Metastasio), Verona, Accademia Filarmonica, or Graz, 1742, possibly collab. others

Il Temistocle (os, Metastasio), Ferrara, 1743

Siface (os, Metastasio), Rovigo, Manfredini, 10 Oct 1744

Caio Marzio Coriolano (os, P. Pariati), Livorno, aut. 1744

I rigiri delle cantarine (dg, B. Vitturi), Venice, S Cassiano, aut. 1745

Artaserse (os, Metastasio), Trent, 1747

Il non so che (ob), Bergamo, 1757, *D-Bds*

Gli scherzi d'amore (int, 3), Venice, S Angelo, 2 Feb 1762, perf. between acts of a spoken comedy

Arias in *A-Wn*, *D-Dlb*, *F-Pn*, *I-Nc*, *Pca*, *Vmc*

Doubtful: Il quartiere fortunato (int, C. Goldoni), ? Rimini, Jan 1744

*

J.-B. de La Borde: *Essai sur la musique ancienne et moderne* (Paris, 1780), iii, 200

F. Piovano: 'Un opéra inconnu de Gluck', *SIMG*, ix (1907–8), 231–81   JAMES L. JACKMAN

Magic Flute, The. Opera by W. A. Mozart; *see* ZAUBERFLÖTE, DIE.

Magic Fountain, The. Lyric drama in three acts by FREDERICK DELIUS to his own libretto; London, BBC Radio, 20 November 1977.

In addition to the legend of a magic fountain, Delius's second opera (1893–5) treats of Spanish wrongs to the American Indians of Florida. About this time he considered a trilogy of operas: the first to treat of Indians, the second of black slaves (the eventual *Koanga*) and the third of gypsies (an important element in *A Village Romeo and Juliet*).

The work opens on shipboard, with the Spanish nobleman Solano (tenor) poring over his books and charts, obsessed with finding gold and the Magic Fountain which can confer eternal youth. Sailors bewail the lack of wind and their slender chance of seeing home again. A breeze fills the sails and gradually develops into a full-scale storm during which the ship founders. The scene changes to the shore of Florida, where Solano lies insensible. The Indian girl Watawa (soprano), a Seminole princess, discovers him, and the chieftain Wapanacki (bass) has him carried to his camp.

In Act 2 Solano and the Indians are smoking round a fire. Wapanacki asks Solano why he has come; Solano replies it was to find the Magic Fountain. Only the sage Talum Hadjo knows its secrets, he is told. Solano, anxious to be on his way, offers gold for safe guidance. Wapanacki is about to leave on the war-path but hands Solano over to Watawa who, nursing revenge for the death of her father and the rest of her people at the Spaniards' hands, determines to lead Solano to his doom. The Indians begin a war dance, and Solano is astonished he is to have so fair a guide. The scene is now the Everglades, where Solano and Watawa make their way through the undergrowth towards the hut of Talum Hadjo (bass), who hails Watawa as last of her kin. Watawa asks whether she should slay Solano with her poisoned knife. The seer questions her about Solano's mission and expounds the folly of his trying to acquire instantly at the Magic Fountain the wisdom it had taken him 50 years to gain; if she wishes Solano's death, she need only let him drink at the Magic Fountain, since it will poison any who come unprepared. Watawa returns to Solano, who is more than ever struck by her beauty, and they continue to the inner depths of the Everglades.

At the start of Act 3 Watawa communes with herself, torn between revenge against the white man and her growing love for Solano. When he appears and declares his passion, she tells him of her dilemma but yields to him. Spirits of the Magic Fountain praise the god of wisdom, and Solano wakes to find his goal before him. As the fountain turns a lurid red, Watawa warns him of danger. He refuses to listen. Watawa hastens so that she drinks first of the waters and instantly faints into Solano's arms, dying. In his agony he drinks too and falls dead upon Watawa's breast.

Delius's verse in the libretto, though often clumsy, has more freedom and variety than in the previous *Irmelin*. The dramatic stakes are much higher, the action swifter, and the music responds appropriately, from the fierce impact of the storm in Act 1 to the Act 3 love duet, the more passionate for the sullen racial tension that has preceded it. Delius made some use in the opera of his 1888 *Florida* suite, inspired by personal experience of the area. The voice parts are more eloquent than in *Irmelin*, more directly following the inflexions of the libretto. If the love duet has too many octaves, the virtuosity of the orchestral writing almost demands them. A recording was issued of the 1977 BBC broadcast performance. ROBERT ANDERSON

Magic Opal, The. Comic opera in two acts by ISAAC ALBÉNIZ to a libretto by Arthur Law; London, Lyric Theatre, 19 January 1893.

The story opens in the marketplace of the Greek town of Karakatol, in the late 19th century. Lolika (soprano),

adopted daughter of the wealthy banker Arristippus (bass), is to wed Alzaga (tenor), son of the mayor of Karakatol, Carambollas (bass). Trabucos (baritone), chief of a gang of bandits, serenades Lolika beneath her window but she turns him away. Informed by his lieutenant Curro (baritone) that if he does not win Lolika he will lose face with his men, Trabucos remembers the magic opal, a ring with the power to make any member of the opposite sex who touches its wearer immediately fall in love with that person. But first he must steal it from the mayor, who has taken it from the museum to give as a wedding present to Lolika. In the meantime, Alzaga arrives to serenade his bride and is kidnapped by the bandits. Day breaks and the villagers arrive to celebrate the wedding. Lolika appears, looking for Alzaga. Trabucos and his sister Martina (contralto) enter disguised as pedlars, Martina with a replica of the magic opal which she plans to substitute for the real one. Trabucos tries to charm Lolika, who once again rebuffs him and leaves. Carambollas arrives and Martina manages to switch her false ring for Carambollas's real one. In trying to evict the pedlars, the mayor pushes Martina and falls in love with her. Just then, news arrives that Alzaga has been captured by the bandits.

The second act is set in an abandoned monastery where the bandits are holding Alzaga for ransom. They are celebrating the recovery of the magic ring, which originally belonged to their former chief. Olympia (mezzo-soprano), an elderly spinster in love with Trabucos, manages to secure the opal. Carambollas appears, looking for Martina, but on touching Olympia directs his affection towards the spinster. Lolika arrives with her father and the villagers in search of Alzaga and Carambollas. Olympia then touches Trabucos who, falling in love with her, renounces Lolika, free at last to marry her Alzaga.

The opera continued to play at the Lyric for more than a month, and after some revisions (notably the conflation of Martina and Olympia into one role, that of Martina, a female bandit enamoured of Trabucos) it reopened at the Prince of Wales Theatre on 11 April 1893 under the title of *The Magic Ring*, Albéniz conducting. Originally the composition of *The Magic Opal* was to be a joint effort by Albéniz and his friend the violinist Enrique Fernández Arbós, but Arbós withdrew, finding his knowledge of English inadequate. Albéniz's score was quickly composed, but despite its pastiche quality, contemporary critics compared it favourably with works by Gilbert and Sullivan, particularly praising its lyricism and refined orchestration. Translated into Spanish by Eusebio Sierra as *La sortija*, it was performed in Madrid at the Teatro de la Zarzuela on 23 November 1894. FRANCES BARULICH

Magic opera. ZAUBEROPER.

Magic Ring, The. Opera by Isaac Albéniz; *see* MAGIC OPAL, THE.

Magini-Coletti, Antonio (*b* Iesi, 17 Feb 1855; *d* Rome, 7 July 1912). Italian baritone. He studied in Rome at the Accademia di S Cecilia, and, having made his baritone début at the Teatro Costanzi in 1880, was retrained as a tenor. This proved unsuccessful and he quickly returned to the baritone repertory, becoming associated throughout Italy with the role of Escamillo. In 1885 he had a considerable success in Lisbon, appearing in rarities such as Rossini's *Matilde di Shabran* and Donizetti's *Poliuto*. Two years later he established himself as a favourite at La Scala, where in 1889 he created the role of Frank in Puccini's *Edgar*, and in 1901 appeared in the première there of Mascagni's *Le maschere*. He also sang Méphistophélès in the first Italian performances of *La damnation de Faust*. His wide-ranging repertory included Wagnerian roles such as Kurwenal, Telramund and Wotan (*Die Walküre*). Though his career centred on Italy, where he was engaged by most of the major houses, he sang regularly in South America, travelling also to Russia and Poland. He made his Metropolitan début in 1901 as Nevers (*Les Huguenots*) with Albani and the De Reszke brothers. His last stage appearance was as Iago at Reggio Emilia in 1910. From 1902 to 1908 he made many recordings, showing to advantage his resonant, evenly produced voice, wide in its range and authoritative and dramatic in use.   J. B. STEANE

Magli, Giovanni Gualberto (*fl* 1604–25). Italian castrato. A Florentine, he was a pupil of Giulio Caccini and entered Medici service on 23 August 1604. In 1607 he was lent to Prince Francesco Gonzaga of Mantua for the first performances of Monteverdi's *Orfeo*: he played Music, Proserpine and perhaps Hope, acquitting himself well despite the difficulty of learning the music. Magli then performed in the wedding festivities for Prince Cosimo de' Medici and Maria Magdalena of Austria in 1608. He came under the protection of Don Antonio de' Medici, who arranged two years' paid leave (from 18 October 1611) to study vocal and instrumental technique in Naples. Magli again left Florence in October 1615, perhaps to serve the Margrave of Brandenburg, but his salary payments had resumed by September 1622. He disappears from Florentine court records in early January 1625.

*

T. Carter: 'A Florentine Wedding of 1608', *AcM*, lv (1983), 89–107
——: Communication, *EMc*, xi (1983), 577
J. Whenham, ed.: *Claudio Monteverdi: 'Orfeo'* (Cambridge, 1986)
                                                TIM CARTER

Magnard, (Lucien Denis Gabriel) Albéric (*b* Paris, 9 June 1865; *d* Baron, Oise, 3 Sept 1914). French composer. His father was Francis Magnard, the wealthy editor of *Le Figaro*. Despising the life of ease that was his for the taking, and after hearing *Tristan und Isolde* at Bayreuth, he devoted himself to music with a zealous idealism, studying at the Conservatoire and then privately with d'Indy. As well as symphonic and chamber works, he wrote three operas to his own librettos, the most original being *Guercoeur*. In his lifetime Magnard's works had few performances and little success. Apart from publishing them at his own expense he hesitated to promote them, preferring to compose at his house near Baron. There, early in World War I, he died fighting German soldiers, who burnt the house and with it his early opera *Yolande* and parts of *Guercoeur*.

The music long had a reputation for excessive austerity, but modern performances have revealed the hand of a passionate polyphonist and luminous orchestrator, together with the burning sincerity and spirituality of a French Bruckner. Magnard's conception of opera was shaped by Wagner – 'the style', as he wrote in the preface to *Bérénice*, 'best adapted to my classical tastes and wholly traditional culture'. Yet his thought is more formally symphonic, his harmony less chromatic, and his leitmotifs delineate emotional and spiritual states, never objects. Moreover, his cultivation of an aristocratic style of tragic simplicity reveals a kinship with both Gluck and Berlioz, manifest especially in the statuesque interior drama of his masterpiece *Bérénice*.

See also BÉRÉNICE and GUERCOEUR.

Yolande op.5 (drame en musique, 1, Magnard), Brussels, Monnaie, 27 Dec 1892, vs (Paris, 1892)
Guercoeur op.12, 1897–1901 (tragédie en musique, 3, Magnard), Act 3 perf. in concert, Nancy, Conservatoire, 23 Feb 1908, Act 1, Paris, Concerts Colonne, 18 Dec 1910; complete perf. Paris, Opéra, 24 April 1931, with parts reconstructed by J. G. Ropartz; vs (Paris, 1904)
Bérénice op.19 (tragédie en musique, 3, Magnard, after J. Racine), Paris, OC (Favart), 15 Dec 1911, vs (Paris, 1909)

*

M. Boucher: *Albéric Magnard* (Lyons, 1919)
G. Carraud: *La vie, l'oeuvre et la mort d'Albéric Magnard* (Paris, 1921)
M. Cooper: *French Music from the Death of Berlioz to the Death of Fauré* (London, 1951)
B. Bardet: *Albéric Magnard, 1865–1914* (Paris, 1966)
F. Ducros: *L'oeuvre vocal d'Albéric Magnard* (Paris, 1984)
                                        MALCOLM MacDONALD

Magni, Paolo (*b* ?Milan, *c*1650; *d* Milan, 21 Feb 1737). Italian composer. He was active throughout his career at Milan, where he was an organist of the cathedral from 1686 to 1716. For most of that period he was also *maestro di cappella* of the Milanese court, with the composition of operas, often in collaboration with others, as one of his chief functions. The preface to *Il Radamisto* (1695) first names him as occupying this post; from 1718, because of his age, his duties were carried out by Giuseppe Vignati, though he retained his title.

music lost unless source given; first performed at Milan, Ducal, unless otherwise stated
Gratitudine umana (C. M. Maggi), Isola Bella, Lake Maggiore, Dec 1670; as Affari ed amori, sum. 1675, frags. *I-IBborromeo*, lib. *Mc*; collab. Borzio
Enea in Italia (G. F. Bussani), Milan, Regio Nuovo, 1686, 2 arias *MOe*, pubd lib. *Bc*; collab. Lonati and Ballarotti (? C. Pallavicino)
Scipione africano (N. Minato, rev.), 1 Feb 1692, collab. Lonati
Endimione [Act 1] (F. de Lemene), Lodi, 24 Nov 1692, pubd lib. *Bc* [last 2 acts by Griffini]
L'Aiace (P. d'Averara), 1694, collab. Lonati and Ballarotti, *US-Cn*
Il Radamisto, overo La Fede nelle sventure (P. F. Manfredo Trecchi), 1695
L'Etna festivo (introduzione al ballo), Milan, 1696, collab. 19 other composers
L'Amfione, 26 Dec 1697
Ariovisto (d'Averara), 1699, collab. Perti and Ballarotti
Cleopatra regnante, Novi Ligure, S Giacomo, 1700 (cited in Schmidl)
Admeto re di Tessaglia (d'Averara), 1702
L'Agrippina, 1703, rev. of Perti: Nerone fatto Cesare
Il Meleagro, Pavia, 1705, collab. Martinenghi and Sabadini
Il Teuzzone (A. Zeno), 1706, ? arias *E-Mn*; collab. Monari
Tito Manlio (M. Noris, rev.), 8 Feb 1710, *A-Wn*, ? collab. Fiorè

*

AllacciD; *EitnerQ*; *RicordiE*; *SchmidlDS*   THOMAS WALKER

Maguenat, Alfred (*b* *c*1880; *d* 1928 or later). French baritone. He joined the Opéra-Comique in 1908, making his début as Baron Douphol in *La traviata*. His regular roles there and elsewhere included Rossini's Figaro and Pelléas, but he soon acquired a large and varied repertory. At Nice in 1911 he sang Sebastiano in the French première of d'Albert's *Tiefland*, and in 1914 was in the première of Massenet's *Cléopâtre* at Monte Carlo. He first sang at Covent Garden in 1913 as Pelléas and repeated the part in 1914 and 1920. In the British première of *L'heure espagnole* (1919) he sang Ramiro; he returned in that role for his last season there in 1926, when some deterioration was noted. From 1915 to 1919 he was with Mary Garden in Chicago, but thereafter sang mostly at the Opéra in Paris. Some excerpts from *Pelléas et Mélisande* recorded in 1928 show his clear diction but, by then, somewhat dry, unromantic tone; earlier recordings suggest a firm-voiced, serviceable artist, but not a singer of notable charm or individuality.

J. B. STEANE

Mahagonny (i). 'Songspiel' in three parts by KURT WEILL after poems from BERTOLT BRECHT's *Hauspostille*; Baden-Baden, Kurhaus, Grosser Bühnensaal, 17 July 1927.

On receiving a commission in March 1927 for an experimental 'short opera' (*Kurzoper*) to be performed at the festival Deutsche Kammermusik Baden-Baden in July of the same year, Weill at first demurred. Only after the publication of the 'Mahagonny-Gesänge' from Brecht's *Hauspostille* in April did he have the idea of composing a 'Songspiel': a pun, of course, on 'Singspiel', the central ingredient being the American-influenced 'song' rather than operatic arias. (The other new *Kurzopern* on the programme were Toch's 'musical fairy-tale' *Die Prinzessin auf der Erbse*, Milhaud's 'minute opera' *L'enlèvement d'Europe* and Hindemith's 'sketch' *Hin und zurück*.) Brecht gave his consent and added the finale ('Dieses ganze Mahagonny'); and the pidgin-English 'Alabama-Song' and 'Benares-Song' were moved from the end of the cycle to the first part (Prologue) and the second part (Life in Mahagonny) respectively. The melody of the 'Alabama-Song' may have originated in the setting that Brecht and the composer Franz S. Bruinier had included in the *Hauspostille*; but since the similarities are largely rhythmic, any creative influence is negligible. As well as composing the 'Mahagonny-Gesänge', Weill provided four instrumental interludes for the ten-piece orchestra. There is no dialogue, either spoken or sung. Nor are the members of the cast given any individual identity, except for the names used to distinguish the six vocal parts (sopranos, Jessie and Bessie; tenors, Charlie and Billie; basses, Bobby and Jimmy). The autograph score was finished less than two months before the première.

The pleasure city Mahagonny has four main attractions – whisky, women, horses and poker (first 'Mahagonny-Song'). But nothing goes without 'the next little dollar' ('Alabama-Song'). The attractions cost at least five dollars a day (second 'Mahagonny-Song'). When the whisky, money and girls run out, the inhabitants are at a loss ('Benares-Song'). God comes to Mahagonny and orders them to hell. But they revolt: 'because we have been in hell all along' (third 'Mahagonny-Song'). The 'paradise' city only exists because everything is so bad: 'there is nothing to hold on to'. In fact, 'Mahagonny is just a made-up word'.

The programme contained the following note:

In his more recent works Weill is moving in the direction of those artists of all art forms who predict the liquidation of arts engendered by established society. The small epic piece *Mahagonny* merely takes the logical step from the inexorable decline of existing social structures. It already addresses an audience that naively demands its fun in the theatre.

Generically, the Songspiel can best be described as an 'anti-opera'. It was set in a boxing ring, and incorporated 'lowbrow' jazz music and intentional vulgarity. Many of the musical gestures are taken from familiar tonal contexts (foxtrots, waltzes and marches) but are spiced with surrealistic dissonance. If it was intended to shock, then *Mahagonny* certainly achieved

that aim. The première was a *succès de scandale*. Since Weill and Brecht soon resolved to expand the 25-minute work into the full-length opera AUFSTIEG UND FALL DER STADT MAHAGONNY, the Songspiel was effectively suppressed, with just one more staged production (in Hamburg) and a few concert performances before the composer emigrated to the USA. The 'Paris version' of 1932, repeated in London and Rome the following year, included four numbers from the full-length work. A show entitled 'Das kleine Mahagonny', arranged by members of the Berliner Ensemble, was first performed at their theatre in 1963. Discredited by Weill's heirs, this 'theatre version' bears little relation to the Songspiel; it has also led to confusion because the Songspiel, too, is sometimes referred to as 'Das kleine Mahagonny' to distinguish it from the full-length opera. Apart from the 'Alabama-Song', which appeared separately in a harmonically simplified version in 1927, the Songspiel itself was not published until 1963.

STEPHEN HINTON

Mahagonny (ii). Name used to refer to the opera *AUFSTIEG UND FALL DER STADT MAHAGONNY*. It should be confused with the Songspiel *MAHAGONNY* (i).

Mahler, Gustav (*b* Kalischt [now Kalište], Bohemia, 7 July 1860; *d* Vienna, 18 May 1911). Austrian composer and conductor. Celebrated as a composer of symphonies and orchestral songs, he derived his primary income, throughout his life, from operatic conducting. In his youth he also embarked on a number of stage works, although his completion of Weber's *Die drei Pintos* (1888) is the only surviving example of an opera in any way attributable to him. Carl von Weber, the composer's grandson, invited Mahler to produce a performable score. This he did by orchestrating the sketches, composing linking material and adapting existing works by Weber, who had abandoned the opera in 1821 after drafting seven out of 17 numbers. His theatrical conducting career represented an odyssey through the world of late 19th-century European opera in search of a position in which he might assert his Wagnerian idealism over the pressures of a constantly changing weekly repertory. After early experience in small provincial theatres, Mahler was second conductor at Kassel (Hofoper, 1883–5), Prague (Deutsches Landestheater, 1885–6) and Leipzig (Neues Stadttheater, 1886–8) before becoming director of the Royal Hungarian Opera in Budapest (1888–91). He was then first conductor at the Stadttheater in Hamburg (1891–7) until he attained his goal in the position of director of the Hofoper in Vienna (1897–1907). His only subsequent operatic work was as a guest conductor at the Metropolitan Opera House in New York (1908–10).

Legendary stories of Mahler's idealism are associated with his stormy reign in Vienna, valuably documented by Specht. Many relate to his hostility to audience noise and latecomers, his insistence on lowering the house lights during performances and his opposition to the 'claque'. In effect, his aim was to transform the opera house from a place of singer-orientated social entertainment into a serious showplace of musical drama. He rejected the cuts in Wagner's works and took as leading a role as the antiquated imperial-opera administration permitted in all aspects, scenic as well as musical, of the works he directed. Particularly alive to the relationship between music and drama (he would occasionally engage in judiciously limited re-composition of works he wished to champion), Mahler presented not only

Wagnerian and new post-Wagnerian works (by Zemlinsky and Pfitzner, for example) but also staged Smetana, Tchaikovsky and Puccini in Vienna, while reviving Mozart and Gluck in model productions with his chosen stage designer Alfred Roller (1864–1935). Their *Tristan und Isolde* (1903), *Don Giovanni* (1905) and *Iphigénie en Aulide* (1907) were celebrated long after anti-Semitism and the intrigues of disgruntled singers had led to Mahler's resignation in 1907 and the dismantling of the integrated company of singers he had trained (including Anna Bahr-Mildenburg and Marie Gutheil-Schoder).

See also DREI PINTOS, DIE.

Herzog Ernst von Schwaben (? J. Steiner, after Uhland), *c*1875–9, unfinished, lost

Rübezahl, *c*1879–83 (Mahler, after German legend), Act 1 partly completed, lost, lib. private collection, USA

Die Argonauten, *c*1880 (Mahler, ? after Grillparzer), ? only a prelude composed, lost

Die drei Pintos (comic op, 3, T. Hell, after C. L. Seidel), Leipzig, 20 Jan 1888 [rev. of C. M. von Weber]

*

G. Adler: '"Euryanthe" in neuer Einrichtung', *ZIMG*, v (1903–4), 267–75

R. Specht: *Gustav Mahler* (Berlin, 1913, 18/1925)

G. Brecher: *Oberon, König der Elfen: neue Bühneneinrichtung von Gustav Mahler* (Vienna, 1914)

L. Hartmann: *Opernführer: Die drei Pintos* (Leipzig, n.d.)

A. Jemnitz: 'Gustav Mahler als kgl. ung. Hofoperndirektor', *Der Auftakt*, xvi (1936), 7–11, 63–7, 183–8

E. Stein: 'Mahler and the Vienna Opera', *Opera*, iv (1953), 4–13, 145–52, 200–07, 281–5

H. Holländer: 'Gustav Mahler vollendet eine Oper von Carl Maria von Weber: vier unbekannte Briefe Mahlers', *NZM*, Jg.116 (1955), 130–32

H. J. Schaefer: 'Gustav Mahlers Wirken in Kassel', *Musica*, xiv (1960), 350–57

D. Kučerová: 'Gustav Mahler ǎ Olomouc', *HV*, v (1968), 627–40

J. Warrack: *Carl Maria von Weber* (London, 1968, 2/1976) [incl. chap. on reconstruction of *Die drei Pintos*]

D. Cvetko: 'Gustav Mahlers Saison 1881/1882 in Laibach (Slovenien)', *Musik des Ostens*, v (1969), 74–83

M. L. von Deck: *Gustav Mahler in New York: his Conducting Activities in New York City, 1908–11* (diss., New York U., 1973)

H. L. de la Grange: *Mahler* (London, 1974)

V. Lébl: 'Gustav Mahler als Kapellmeister des Deutschen Landestheaters in Prag', *HV*, xii (1975), 351–71

R. Werba: 'Il "Don Giovanni" nella interpretazione di Gustav Mahler', *NRMI*, ix (1975), 515–40

S. Wiesmann, ed.: *Gustav Mahler und Wien* (Stuttgart and Zürich, 1976; Eng. trans., 1976)

H. L. de la Grange: *Gustav Mahler: chronique d'une vie* (Paris, 1983–4)

Z. Roman: *Gustav Mahler's American Years 1907–11: a Documentary History* (New York, 1989)   PETER FRANKLIN

Mahler-Kalkstein, Menahem. *See* AVIDOM, MENAHEM.

Mahomayev, (Abdul) Muslim (*b* Groznïy, 6/18 Sept 1885; *d* Nal'chik, 28 July 1937). Azerbaijani composer. He studied at the teachers' seminary in Gori (1899–1904) together with his friend Hajibeyov, playing the violin and the clarinet in orchestras and studying Azerbaijani folklore. From 1905 to 1911 he taught; on moving to Baku he began an unbroken involvement with the musical stage. At the opera theatre, later the Azerbaijan State Theatre, he was successively an orchestral player, conductor and director. In 1916 he composed his first large work, the opera *Shakh Ismail* (M. Ismail-zade and Mahomayev), which was first performed in Baku in 1919; it remains among his best achievements. In the first version, *mugam* improvisation predominated, musical numbers alternating with spoken dialogue, but in the second (1920–23) and third (1930–32) versions Mahomayev notated many of the improvisatory passages and introduced recitatives.

Mahomayev was artistic director and conductor of the musical theatre (from 1924) and in 1929 was appointed musical director of the Azerbaijani Radio Centre. In the same year he began to compose the musical comedy *Khoruz-bey*, but it was left unfinished. His last major composition was the opera *Nergiz* (M. Ordubadï), which concerns the struggle of the peasants against their oppressors; it was first performed in Baku on 24 December 1935. All the music is notated, yet the result is a truly national work, demonstrating Mahomayev's development of the genre from *mugam* opera to works freely using European forms.

S. Mamedova: *Puti razvitiya azerbaydzhanskogo muzikal'nogo teatra* [The Paths of Development of the Azerbaijani Musical Theatre] (Moscow, 1931)

Nergiz (Baku, 1935–8) [collections of articles]

K. Kasimov: *Kak sozdavalsya Shakh Ismail* [How *Shakh Ismail* was Created] (Baku, 1965)

S. Kasimova: *Opera 'Nergiz' M. Mahomayeva* (Baku, 1967)

G. Ismailova: *Muslim Magomayev* (Baku, 1975)   YURY GABAY

Mahón (Sp. Máo). Principal city of Minorca, an island off the south-east coast of Spain. For most of the 18th century (1708–56, 1763–81 and 1798–1802) the island was under British rule, and there is consequently little record of theatrical activity in Mahón except for the successful and repeated performances of *The Beggar's Opera*. The Teatro Principal, built in 1829 and seating 1500, seems to have functioned during the 19th century in conjunction with that of Palma, on the neighbouring island of Mallorca, coinciding with the replacement of opera in public favour by the zarzuela. In 1854 the baritone Lorenzo Pagàns made his début there, and in February 1873 *Romeo y Julieta*, by the local composer Antonio Mercadal y Pons (1850–73), had its première. The theatre is the oldest surviving opera house in Spain; a short season of two or three operas is given each spring.   XOÁN M. CARREIRA, CHARLES PITT

Maid of Orléans, The [*Orleanskaya deva*]. Opera in four acts by PYOTR IL'YICH TCHAIKOVSKY to his own libretto after FRIEDRICH VON SCHILLER's tragedy translated by VASILY ANDREYEVICH ZHUKOVSKY, JULES BARBIER's *Jeanne d'Arc* and AUGUSTE MERMET's libretto for his own opera, after Barbier (1876), with various details adapted from Henri Wallon's biography of Joan of Arc; St Petersburg, Mariinsky Theatre, 13/25 February 1881.

Tchaikovsky's most ambitious opera, in which he vied belatedly for Scribian laurels with Verdi, Meyerbeer and Rubinstein, was written in just nine months beginning in late November 1878. Actual composition took place entirely in western Europe (Florence, Paris, Vaudois Switzerland) and was finished 'down to the smallest detail' by the end of February 1879. Orchestration, which took longer, was carried out during the spring and summer months on various southern Russian and Ukrainian country estates belonging to the composer's friends and relations, and finished in late August. From the beginning Tchaikovsky envisaged the work as 'the one that will make my name popular', and that it did. For the first time he experienced an unqualified success with a first-night audience; not only that, *The Maid of Orléans* was the first Tchaikovsky opera to be performed abroad (1882,

Joan of Arc	soprano/mezzo-soprano
King Charles VII	tenor
Agnès Sorel	soprano
Dunois *French knight*	baritone
Lionel *Burgundian knight*	baritone
Archbishop (Cardinal in first production)	bass
Raymond *Joan's betrothed*	tenor
Thibaut d'Arc *Joan's father*	bass
Bertrand *a peasant*	bass
Lauret	bass
A Soldier	bass
Voice from the Angelic Choir	soprano

Courtiers and ladies, French and English soldiers, knights, monks, gypsies, pages, buffoons, dwarfs, minstrels, jesters, clowns, crowd

Setting France, 1431

Prague). Thereafter the opera's fate was not happy. It fell victim to the curtailment of the theatrical season following the assassination of Tsar Alexander II, only two weeks after the première, and in the ensuing austerity it was not revived. It did not see the stage again until the 20th century, by which time it was something of a historical curio.

Compared to its chief literary source, *The Maid of Orléans* shows an enormous effort to popularize and simplify. Schiller's scenes of dissension and intrigue – and valour – among the English are eliminated; indeed, the English do not exist in the opera except as an on-rushing crowd in Act 4. On the other hand, the fleeting episode with Lionel is grossly magnified to provide the pretext for a love duet (and perhaps for deeper reasons; *see* TCHAIKOVSKY, PYOTR IL'YICH, §3). The beginning of the opera, a decorative genre scene, is borrowed from Mermet; the conclusion (Joan's martyrdom at the stake rather than on the battlefield as per Schiller) comes from Barbier. Along the way the composer made various alterations and interpolations on his own initiative: Lauret in Act 2, the final encounter with Lionel in Act 4 and virtually all the choral repliques.

The overture, a portrait of Joan as pure virginal being epitomized by a flute cadenza, culminates in a preview of the angelic music from the Act 1 finale.

ACT 1 *A forest near Domrémy* Maidens are celebrating a village festival. Thibaut enters with Raymond and upbraids them for making merry at a time of war; he urges Joan to marry Raymond for protection (scena and trio). Joan refuses, claiming to be following heaven's wish; Thibaut accuses her of alliance with the devil. Fire is seen; the tocsin rings; Bertrand enters with fleeing peasants and warns the villagers that an English attack is imminent. Joan reassures the crowd with a prophecy, asserting that the English commander, Salisbury ('Sa-lis-byú-ri'), has been slain. A French soldier rushes in and confirms this news and Joan is acclaimed a seer. All join her in a hymn of thanksgiving. Obedient to her calling, the Maid of Orléans sings farewell to her native region (aria, 'Prostite vï, kholmï, polya rodnïye': 'Farewell, O native hills and fields' – best known in French translation, 'Adieu, forêts'). Attended by a heavenly choir, she sets out to save France.

ACT 2 *The Castle of Chinon* After an entr'acte, based chiefly on the main theme of the hymn, minstrels entertain the anxious Charles VII (the chorus is Tchaikovsky's interpolation, based on the melody of *Mes belles amourettes*, included as 'Mélodie antique française' in his *Children's Album* for piano, op.39). Unconsoled, the king calls for his gypsies, dwarfs and clowns; each group does a dance. When Charles orders the entertainers be given rich rewards, his vassal Dunois reminds him that the treasury is empty; his mistress Agnès promises assistance and goes off to collect her jewels. Dunois exhorts the voluptuary monarch to renounce Agnès and lead an attack and briefly succeeds in rousing him. The dying Lauret rushes in with news of another French defeat, then expires; Charles, terrified, decides to retreat beyond the Loire, and Dunois, disgusted, forswears his allegiance and departs (compare their duet with that in Act 2 scene i of *Don Carlos*). Agnès returns and consoles the king (arioso and duettino; compare the latter with 'Tu m'aimes' in Act 4 of *Les Huguenots*). A chorus is heard off stage in praise

'The Maid of Orléans' (Tchaikovsky), Act 3 scene ii (cathedral square at Reims; Thibaut accuses Joan of sorcery) in the original production at the Mariinsky Theatre, St Petersburg, 13/25 February 1881: drawing by K. Brozh

153

of 'the maiden saviour' and Dunois comes rushing back with the news that the English have been miraculously defeated. The Archbishop enters and tells how a young girl took command of the battle and routed the enemy; the king changes places with Dunois to test her. Joan enters at the head of a throng; she picks out the king and to prove her vatic powers repeats to him his secret prayers; at the Archbishop's request she tells her story (Joan's narrative, 'Svyatoy otets, menya zovut Ioanna': 'Holy Father, they call me Joan' – compare Pimen's narrative in *Boris Godunov*, Act 4). Charles, believing in her, puts her at the head of the army amid general thanksgiving.

ACT 3.i *A battlefield near Reims* After a short introduction representing a battle with the English, Lionel rushes on stage pursued by Joan; they fight, and he yields, but just before slaying him she sees his face and is overcome with love. After at first taunting her weakness Lionel also falls in love. Dunois enters; Lionel surrenders to him and changes his allegiance to the French while Joan sinks back as if wounded.

3.ii *The cathedral square at Reims* Charles and his retinue enter the cathedral for his coronation. He reappears crowned, with Joan at his side. Thibaut, still persuaded that his daughter is in league with the devil, announces to Raymond his determination to expose her. King and crowd hail Joan as saviour; Thibaut accuses her of sorcery. She is silent; thunder is heard; the Archbishop demands that she affirm her holy mission and her purity. She remains silent, there is a louder thunderclap, and all express horror. During the ensuing ensemble with chorus Joan's voice is heard – to the audience alone – admitting guilt and requesting punishment. Lionel urges Joan to flee; she does so, but not before turning on him and calling him her enemy and destroyer.

ACT 4.i *A thick forest* Joan, distraught, admits her love for Lionel ('Kak! Mne lyuboviyu pïlat'?': 'What! me, inflamed with love?'). Lionel enters and after a short resistance she yields to his embrace; heavenly voices, heard by her alone, reproach Joan for failing and foretell pain and martyrdom, but eventual redemption. English troops enter, slay Lionel and take Joan prisoner.

4.ii *A square in Rouen* Joan is led to the stake to the strains of a lugubrious march. Onlookers at first mock the witch, but are then overcome with pity at her pale, luminous expression; English soldiers ward them off. Joan asks for a cross and a soldier breaks a stick in two, binds the pieces, and gives them to a priest for her (this episode was prohibited by the censor at the first production). The fire is lit and grows; the angels invite the transfigured Joan to her heavenly abode.

* * *

The first performance was conducted by Eduard Nápravník, to whom the opera was dedicated; Mariya Kamenskaya sang Joan, Fyodor Stravinsky Dunois, Ippolit Pryanishnikov Lionel and Wilhelmina Raab Agnès. The role of Joan exists in two versions (both included in the composer's complete works, vol.v): as originally written, for dramatic soprano, and as revised for Kamenskaya, a mezzo. Ever since the first production the role has been regarded primarily as a vehicle for star mezzos, notably Irina Arkhipova, for whose sake the opera was given a revival at the Bol'shoy in the 1970s, and recorded.   RICHARD TARUSKIN

Maid of Pskov, The [*Pskovityanka*]. Opera in three acts, op.4, by NIKOLAY ANDREYEVICH RIMSKY-KORSAKOV

to his own libretto after the drama by Lev Alexandrovich Mey (with additional text by Vsevolod Krestovsky and MODEST PETROVICH MUSORGSKY); St Petersburg, Mariinsky Theatre, 1/13 January 1873 (revised version, St Petersburg, Panayev Theatre, 6/18 April 1895; standard version, with prologue, Moscow, Bol'shoy Theatre, 10/23 October 1901).

Tsar Ivan Vasil'yevich ('The Terrible')	bass
Prince Yury Ivanovich Tokmakov *the tsar's viceroy and bailiff in Pskov*	bass
Boyar Nikita Matuta	tenor
Prince Afanasy Vyazemsky	bass
Bomelius *the tsar's physician*	bass
Mikhail Andreyevich Tucha *a bailiff's son*	tenor
Yushko Velebin *courier*	bass
Princess Ol'ga [Olga] Yur'yevna Tokmakova *the viceroy's daughter*	soprano
Boyarïnya Stepanida Matuta (Styosha) *Olga's bosom friend*	contralto
Vlas'yevna ⎱ *wet-nurses*	contralto
Perfil'yevna ⎰	mezzo-soprano
A Watchman's Voice	tenor

Commanders, judges, Pskovian boyars, bailiff's sons, royal forces and bodyguards, Moscow musketeers, immured maidens, urchins, populace, royal huntsmen

Setting Pskov, 1570

Rimsky-Korsakov began work on this, his first opera, in 1868; it was completed in 1872, dedicated 'To my dear Musical Circle' (i.e. the Balakirev circle or 'Mighty Kuchka') and given in St Petersburg at the beginning of 1873 under Eduard Nápravník, with Osip Petrov as Ivan, Yuliya Platonova as Olga, Ivan Mel'nikov as Tokmakov and Dar'ya Leonova as Vlas'yevna. He revised it in 1876–7, but this version was never published or performed (some of the music was salvaged as incidental music to the original play and given in 1882). The second revised version, of 1891–2, was first heard in an amateur performance under Ivan Davïdov in St Petersburg and later, on 12/24 December 1896, in Moscow, given by Savva Mamontov's Private Russian Opera Company at the Solodovnikov Theatre under Giuseppe Truffi, with Fyodor Shalyapin as Ivan. While working on the first revision, in 1877, Rimsky had composed a narrative scena based on the first act of Mey's drama. This eventually formed the basis of a one-act opera, *Boyarïnya Vera Sheloga* ('The Noblewoman Vera Sheloga'); its première was given by the Mamontov company at the Solodovnikov Theatre, Moscow, on 15/27 December 1898. The 'standard version' of *The Maid of Pskov*, with *Boyarïnya Vera Sheloga* as prologue, was given at the Bol'shoy Theatre, Moscow, in 1901, under Ippolit Al'tani, with Shalyapin (for whom Rimsky had composed an extra aria, to begin Act 3, in 1898). The opera was given as *Ivan le Terrible* at the Théâtre du Châtelet, Paris, during the first Dyagilev season, on 20 May 1909, conducted by Nikolay Tcherepnin, with Shalyapin and Yelizaveta Petrenko.

Written during the heyday of historical drama in Russia, *The Maid of Pskov* is based on a play that attempted not only to portray historical events but to explain them according to enlightened historiographical notions. Mey's *Pskovityanka* posed the question: why did Ivan the Terrible, at the height of a bloody campaign to consolidate his autocracy, lay waste to the old republican city of Novgorod but spare Pskov, Novgorod's sister city to the west? The play imagines that the tsar had fathered a love-child in Pskov on a visit 17 years earlier, and that confronting her softened his heart. The question may be arbitrary, the answer sentimental, and the action full of anachronisms (like the turbulent meeting of the Pskovian republican council, which by 1570 had been defunct for a century), but the play was taken seriously. It contained a great deal of didactic rumination of a kind then popular – much of it through the mouth of Ivan himself, who fairly paraphrases the writings of the liberal historian Sergey Solov'yov on the beneficial long-term effects of his Draconian policies. And in the figure of Olga, the love-child, torn fatally between inexplicable attraction for her secret father and love for the leader of a rebellion against the tsar, Mey invented an effective metaphor for Pskov itself, torn between its republican traditions and the historical imperatives that demanded submission to the unified autocratic state Ivan was in the process of forming.

PROLOGUE   As originally planned, *The Maid of Pskov* the opera dispensed with the playwright's first act, in which the circumstances of Olga's conception and birth were fully revealed. This is the basis of the 1877 scena, for Vera Sheloga, the noblewoman who bore Olga illicitly to Tsar Ivan the Terrible (she never identifies him, but the music does). The 1877 redaction of the opera having been scrapped as unworkable (and the opera given its definitive form in 1892), Rimsky went back after two decades to Vera's monologue, connected it with his even earlier setting (newly orchestrated) of her lullaby to the infant Olga, and filled in the gaps, relying heavily on existing leitmotifs. *Boyarïnya Vera Sheloga*, which could be called Rimsky-Korsakov's single essay in the *verismo* style, was meant to stand either alone or as prologue to the definitive ('third') version of *The Maid of Pskov*. In practice it has been employed almost exclusively in the latter capacity, though both the lullaby 'Bayu, Olen'ku moyu' ('Rock-abye, my little Olga') and the steamy monologue 'Shla zamuzh ya nevoley' ('I was married against my will') have been effectively detached for recital use.

ACT 1.i   *The garden of Prince Yury Tokmakov*   Olga and her friends are playing tag under the supervision of Vlas'yevna and Perfil'yevna. The nurses exchange news of Ivan's campaign of terror while the girls go berry-picking. When the girls return Vlas'yevna relates the 'Tale of Tsarevna Lada' (the first number composed in the summer of 1868). All exit. Tucha climbs over the garden wall. Olga rushes out to meet him and tells him that her father has promised her in marriage to old Matuta, her best friend's father; they sing a love duet (on the folksong 'Uzh tï, pole moyo': 'My fair field', from Balakirev's collection). Tucha flees and Olga hides as Tokmakov and Matuta enter. She overhears Tokmakov telling Matuta that she is not really his daughter but the child of his wife's sister by an unknown father. She exclaims in horror, but before the two men can find her the bell rings summoning a citizens' assembly (*veche*). (A powerful tam-tam concerto of an entr'acte follows here.)

1.ii   *Pskov, Kremlin square*   A messenger from the wiped-out city of Novgorod warns the assembled citizens of Pskov of the tsar's murderous approach.

Tokmakov exhorts them to submit and expect mercy. Tucha organizes defiance; he collects a rebel band and marches off singing (to the tune of 'Kak pod lesom, pod lesochkom': 'Beneath a wood, a little wood', from the Balakirev collection).

ACT 2.i   *The great square in Pskov*   The populace prepares to welcome the tsar. Olga appears with Vlas'yevna and bewails her orphan state. The crowd acclaims Ivan's entrance.

2.ii   *Tokmakov's house*   Ivan mocks Pskov's pretensions to independence and demands to be served by the lady of the house. When he sees Olga Yur'yevna he is shaken. There is a chorus of immured maidens (to an imitation folk text by Musorgsky, 'Iz-pod kholmika': 'From beneath a hill'). Alone with Tokmakov, Ivan learns that Olga is the daughter of Vera Sheloga; he stuns the reassembled company with a declaration that hostilities shall cease.

ACT 3.i   *A forest road*   After an orchestral hunt and storm, a chorus of maidens is heard (to another folklike text by Musorgsky, 'Akh tï, dubrava-dubravushka': 'O forest, leafy forest'). A rendezvous for Olga and Tucha is interrupted by Matuta; Tucha is beaten and Olga carried off.

3.ii   *The tsar's encampment*   Ivan, alone, muses on kingship. He learns of Olga's abduction; furious, he sends for her (when she arrives he addresses her inadvertently as Olga Ivanovna, forming the patronymic from his own name). She begs for protection from Matuta; Ivan promises to take her to Moscow. Just then Tucha's band, uninformed of the tsar's mercy, attacks; Olga, caught in the crossfire, is killed, and the tsar mourns. In a concluding chorus the fall of Pskov is proclaimed ('Sovershilosya! Voley Bozhiyey pal velikiy Pskov': 'It is fulfilled! Great Pskov has fallen by God's will').

*   *   *

An earnestness of purpose comparable to Mey's marked Rimsky-Korsakov's musical treatment, which strove for 'formlessness' in the name of truth. Actually the opera contains a fair number of set pieces, but their cadences are interrupted to maintain the scenic flow; and several whole scenes (including the council scene and those in which Ivan appears) are carried mainly by naturalistic recitative, including choral recitative. It is a formula obviously reminiscent of Musorgsky's exactly contemporaneous *Boris Godunov*: a serious historical theme; a complex, tortured royal personage who sings impassioned soliloquies (for which special dispensation had to be sought from the censor); declamatory writing over a texture of leitmotifs (including a dominant one that serves as an *idée fixe* – in *The Maid of Pskov* it is an ersatz ecclesiastical chant representing Ivan); unruly crowd scenes. The parallels extend further: orchestral tintinnabulations (the Coronation in *Boris*, the Council summons in *The Maid of Pskov*); folksongs *in situ* (and here out of context as well, as in the Act 1 love duet); old wet-nurses who tell stories and give comfort; in fact, Rimsky-Korsakov and Musorgsky were sharing a bachelor apartment at the time of writing, and the two operas definitely imitated one another.

What they also had in common was the unschooled technique of the early 'kuchkist' period. After Rimsky-Korsakov's heroic self-education he revised the opera twice (as he would later twice revise *Boris Godunov* – another parallel!). The first revision overloaded the opera with new scenes (including a prologue incorporating the action of Mey's Act 1 and a confrontation between tsar and holy fool that to no good dramatic purpose aped a favourite scene from *Boris*) and it was suppressed by the composer. The revision of 1891–2 reverted to the original action, and amounts to a thorough technical and stylistic overhaul of the earlier score. Both first and final versions have been published in Rimsky-Korsakov's collected works (though through an oversight only the superseded first was included in the Belwin-Mills reprint); comparison is an education.

RICHARD TARUSKIN

Maid of the Mill, The. Comic opera in three acts by TOMMASO GIORDANI to a libretto by ISAAC BICKERSTAFF after Samuel Richardson's novel *Pamela* and John Fletcher's and William Rowley's comedy *The Maid in the Mill*; Dublin, Smock Alley, 26 March 1765.

On 31 January 1765 the Theatre Royal, Covent Garden, began its run of the latest of Isaac Bickerstaff's highly successful comic operas, *The Maid of the Mill*, with music arranged and composed by Samuel Arnold, and with an overture by the Earl of Kelly. The plot is a common one concerning the gradual disentanglement of various people betrothed to partners with whom they are not in love. Eventually true love triumphs and, here, Lord Aimsworth marries Patty, the Miller's daughter, despite their difference in social standing. The success of the opera was such that by late March the two rival theatres in Dublin were both staging the work. Word-books of the opera were freely available, and the manager of the Crow Street theatre had procured a manuscript copy of Arnold's arrangements. Smock Alley, however, turned to Giordani, who, according to Hitchcock (1788; ii, 137), composed music to the entire opera 'in less than a fortnight'. Hitchcock reported that 'The opera pleased much. The music did infinite credit to the genius of Signior Giordani'. But the Irish success was a short-lived one: the opera ran at Smock Alley for nine nights (and just five at Crow Street). None of Giordani's music for this production survives.

IRENA CHOLIJ

Maikl, Georg (*b* Zell an der Ziller, 4 April 1872; *d* Vienna, 22 Aug 1951). Austrian tenor. He studied in Stuttgart and made his début in 1899 at Mannheim as Tamino. In 1904 he joined the Hofoper (later Staatsoper) in Vienna, remaining there for 40 years and giving over two thousand performances in about a hundred roles. He sang Don Ottavio at Salzburg (1906) and took part in the première of the second version of *Ariadne auf Naxos* (1916, Vienna). Other roles included Pinkerton in *Madama Butterfly* (1907), the Italian Singer in *Der Rosenkavalier* (1911), Narraboth in *Salome* (1918), Victorin in *Die tote Stadt* (1921) and the Captain in *Wozzeck* (1930), all first performances in Vienna. At first a lyrical singer specializing in Mozart, he developed into a very fine character tenor.

ELIZABETH FORBES

Maillart, Aimé [Louis] (*b* Montpellier, 24 March 1817; *d* Moulins-sur-Allier, 26 May 1871). French composer. From 1833 he was a pupil at the Paris Conservatoire, where he studied with Halévy, Leborne, Elwart and Guérin. In 1841 he won the Prix de Rome. On his return to Paris he began writing operas, the first of which, *Gastibelza, ou Le fou de Tolède*, was the opening work at the Opéra National (later the Théâtre Lyrique) in 1847; it later appeared in New Orleans and Buenos

Aires. His most successful opera was *Les dragons de Villars* (1856) which became popular throughout Europe, reaching New Orleans in 1859 and New York in 1868; it is still occasionally performed in France and Germany. His last two operas, *Les pêcheurs de Catane* and *Lara*, proved less enduring, though the latter was performed in Belgium, Spain, Germany, England and Poland. Maillart's music is characterized by graceful melodies, a colourful, theatrical style and skilful instrumentation.

all works published in Paris in year of first performance

Gastibelza, ou Le fou de Tolède (opéra dramatique, 3, A. P. d'Ennery and E. Cormon, after ballade *Le fou de Tolède*), Paris, Opéra National, 15 Nov 1847
Le moulin des tilleuls (oc, 1, J. de Maillan and Cormon), Paris, OC (Favart), 9 Nov 1849
La croix de Marie (oc, 3, Lockroy [J. P. Simon] and d'Ennery), Paris, OC (Favart) 19 July 1852, vs
Les dragons de Villars (oc, 3, Cormon and Lockroy), Paris, Lyrique, 19 Sept 1856; Ger. trans. as Das Glöckchen des Eremiten, Berlin, Friedrich-Wilhelmstädtisches, 29 Nov 1860
Les pêcheurs de Catane (drame lyrique, 3, Cormon and M. Carré), Paris, Lyrique, 19 Dec 1860
Lara (oc, 3, Cormon and Carré, after Byron), Paris, OC (Favart), 21 March 1864

ES (B. Horowicz); *LoewenbergA*
F. Clément and P. Larousse: *Dictionnaire lyrique, ou Histoire des opéras* (Paris, 1867–81, 3/1905)

Mainpiece. Term formerly used to refer to the principal work in a London theatrical programme when more than one item was presented. Like the term 'afterpiece', its application was contextual; if there was only one work in the programme, the term was redundant. The development of the multiple-bill programme, erratic during the early years of the 18th century, accelerated in the 1714–15 season, when the competition between theatres led to a sharp increase in the number of double bills presented; the number next increased significantly with the introduction of pantomime in the 1723–4 season. The bulk of the repertory used as mainpieces was serious drama such as Shakespeare's plays, Cibber's tragedies or Sheridan's comedies; full-length operas were rarely given with afterpieces. Masques such as James Dalton's version of Milton's *Comus* (1738) and Richard Cumberland's *Calypso* (1779) and burlettas such as Kane O'Hara's *Midas* (1760) and George Colman's *The Portrait* (1770), were also performed as mainpieces. However, the comparatively few performances recorded of these works suggests that their style and subjects were unsuitable in an extended form, and it is significant that *Comus* and *Midas* also had their greatest success when cut to two-act afterpieces.

MICHAEL BURDEN

Mainvielle-Fodor, Joséphine. See FODOR-MAINVIELLE, JOSÉPHINE.

Mainz. German city on the confluence of the Rhine and the Main, capital of the Rhineland-Palatinate. A court theatre, the Mainzer Adelstheater, was established in 1711, introducing French musical taste; the first Italian opera was given in 1758 in the Redoutensaal. Italian opera was subsequently given in the Komödienhaus (built in 1767 on the Grosse Bleiche) by the Kurfürstliche Bühne, including Gluck's *Alceste* and *Orfeo ed Euridice*, and between 1783 and 1786 Mozart operas were presented by G. F. W. Grossmann. The Mainz-Frankfurt Nationaltheater opened in Frankfurt on 17 April 1788, but the collaboration between the two cities seems to have been unsatisfactory, for Elector Karl Joseph of Erthal, with Vincenzo Righini as his Kapellmeister, founded the separate Mainz Nationaltheater the same year. It opened on 5 November in the Komödienhaus, and only a few months later the first performance in German of *Don Giovanni* was given there. The Komödienhaus was destroyed in 1793 when the Prussians bombarded Mainz, and performances moved to the electoral Reithalle (the riding school). The city was under French rule from 1797 to 1814, following the Peace of Rastatt; German and French companies used the Reithalle in turn, and the repertory was predominantly French. From 1817, after the end of French occupation, it was run as a municipal theatre, the Grossherzogliches Hessisches Nationaltheater, managed jointly by Mainz and Wiesbaden and receiving a grant from Grand Duke Ludwig I of Hess. In 1833 the Theater der Landeshauptstadt Mainz (the Stadttheater), designed by Georg Moller and built in the Gutenbergplatz, opened on 21 September with *La clemenza di Tito*; it continued in use until World War II.

The theatre was damaged and closed in 1944, reopening in 1951 after renovation. The auditorium comprises stalls and two circles with about 900 seats. The season, usually beginning in early September, provides 66 evening performances spread over ten months; each year the repertory contains five operas, including a modern opera and a *Spieloper*. Since 1990 the theatre has been under state control: it is now called the Staatstheater Mainz, and the *Land* of Rhineland-Palatinate and the city share its funding.

Notable artists who have worked at the Mainz theatre include the composers Conradin Kreutzer (1844–5), Emil Nikolaus von Reznicek (1887–8) and Hans Pfitzner (Kapellmeister, 1893–5) and the conductors Emil Steinbach (1877–1909), Karl Elmendorff (1920–23) and Gerd Albrecht (1961–3). Pfitzner conducted the first performance of his opera *Der arme Heinrich* in Mainz in 1895.   GÁBOR HALÁSZ

Maison, René (*b* Frameries, 24 Nov 1895; *d* Mont d'Or, France, 11 July 1962). Belgian tenor. He studied in Brussels and Paris, and made his début in 1920 at Geneva, as Rodolfo. His reputation grew with three successive seasons, beginning in 1925, at Monte Carlo, where his roles included Faust, Hoffmann and Huon in *Oberon*. From 1928 to 1931 he was a member of the company at Chicago, undertaking heavier roles such as Lohengrin, Florestan and Parsifal. In Paris he sang at the Opéra-Comique and at the Opéra, where in 1934 he created the role of Eumolpus in Stravinsky's *Perséphone*. From 1934 to 1937 he was principal dramatic tenor at the Colón; he also had a career at the Metropolitan from 1935 to 1943. One of his greatest successes there was as Julien in *Louise*, which he also sang at Covent Garden in 1935. His only other London role was Lohengrin in 1931, when his acting and physical presence (he was 6 feet 4 inches in height) impressed, though his singing was criticized for roughness in the loud passages and 'a rather falsetto character of voice' in the soft (Ernest Newman in the *Sunday Times*). On retirement he taught in New York and Boston, his pupils including Ramón Vinay. Recordings show an expressive style and a strong voice which remains attractive despite the somewhat pinched quality of his high notes.   J. B. STEANE

Maître de chapelle, Le [*Le maître de chapelle, ou Le souper imprévu* ('The Chapelmaster, or The Unexpected Supper')]. *Opéra comique* in two acts by FERDINANDO PAER to a libretto by Sophie Gay after Alexandre Duval's *Le souper imprévu, ou Le chanoine de Milan*; Paris, Théâtre Feydeau, 29 March 1821.

Paer's only opera to enjoy any longevity, *Le maître de chapelle* was performed occasionally throughout the 19th century (usually in a truncated, one-act version as part of a double bill), not only in France but also in Italy, Germany, England and the USA, often in Italian translation with the spoken dialogues of the original set as recitatives. Paer's elegant, charming music has contributed considerably to its continued appeal.

The action takes place in 1797, in and around the house of Barnabé (bass), the *maestro di cappella* of a small town near Milan. The best-known, short version of the opera is all taken from the first act and includes only three numbers and three characters: Barnabé, his French cook Gertrude (soprano) and his cowardly nephew Benetto (tenor). The first scene is a trio, 'Paix! Chut! entendez-vous ce bruit?', in the form of a Rossinian comic ensemble. After Barnabé worries that the French will steal the score of his new opera *Cleopatra* and Benetto boasts of his courage, the annoyed Gertrude frightens them by pretending to hear (and imitating) the sounds of cannon and trumpets and suggesting that the French army is attacking their village. After she sets them straight, Barnabé sends Benetto out for wine and takes the opportunity to sing a freely constructed, episodic *air* ('Ah! quel bonheur de pressentir sa gloire') in which he envisages his opera being staged in Milan, imitates various instruments, performs one of the dances from the opera, enacts the death of Cleopatra and revels in his anticipated fame. In the longer version, he then decides to call on his pupil Coelénie (soprano) while his supper cooks, but before leaving he has Gertrude join him in reading through a duet from his opera. Barnabé begins this duet with a duet ('Comment voulez-vous que je chante?') by humming its ritornello while Gertrude ponders the motivations of her character. Eventually – and with considerable effort – he teaches her how to pronounce the Italian text correctly.

The full score published in Paris by Petit (?1821) and the vocal score published there by Columbier (?1854) preserve the musical numbers (without the intervening dialogues) of the second act. This includes six additional scenes: a trio 'Oh ciel! quel temps affreux', a quartet 'Des brigands, que dis-tu', an *air* for Coelénie ('Non, je n'en fais pas mystère'), a quintet 'Oh ciel, puis-je vous croire?', *couplets* for Benetto ('La jeune Ermance, dans Férare') and a finale. It introduces Firmin (tenor), captain of a brigade of hussars, and Sans Quartier (bass), one of his men, and unites them with their lovers Coelénie and Gertrude respectively, despite the objections of Barnabé, who wants them arrested.

SCOTT L. BALTHAZAR

Maître Pathelin [*Maître Pathelin, oder Die Hammelkomödie* ('Master Pathelin, or The Comedy of the Sheep')]. Opera in eight scenes by RAINER KUNAD, to his own libretto after Horst Ulrich Wendler's comic play *Wer zuletzt lacht*, based on a French farce of 1465; Dresden, Staatsoper, 30 April 1969.

The plot centres on a piece of 'fine blue cloth' which the lawyer Pathelin (tenor) tricks out of an avaricious cloth merchant (tenor) for his wife (contralto). Two riotous comic plot lines develop: one concerns the cloth and one a shepherd (bass) who is to be hanged on suspicion of sheep stealing. In the conventionally constructed trial scene Pathelin saves his client by a simple trick: the accused man answers all questions with 'Baa!', causing hopeless confusion. But when the clever lawyer demands an extortionate fee he gets the same answer, much to the amusement of the people. The moral is: 'He who laughs last laughs longest.' Apart from the rather over-intense love story between the shepherd and the woman cloth seller (soprano), with its contrived naivety, *Maître Pathelin* is an accomplished comic work of music drama, combining production, text and music in an indissoluble whole in accordance with Kunad's conception of 'functionality'. The range of the dodecaphonically constructed score extends from recitative in free rhythm through cluster to chanson, from murmuring and yawning to hissing, and the work has proved remarkably effective on stage in over 20 productions.

JOCHEN SCHÖNLEBER

Majewski, Andrej (*b* Warsaw, 15 June 1936). Polish stage designer and painter. He is one of several leading designers who have kept Poland in the forefront of contemporary stage design. He studied at the Kraków Academy of Fine Art under Karol Frycz and made his operatic and theatrical début in Kraków in 1959. Two years later his *Hamlet* won international attention and a prize at the Festival des Nations in Paris. He was awarded a gold medal for costume design at the 1967 Prague Quadriennale. In 1962 he designed Honegger's *Judith* for the Wielki Theatre, Warsaw, where he eventually became resident designer. Significant productions there have included *Elektra* (1971), the sets for the theatre's first Italian-language *Lucia* in the 20th century (1972), the first Polish production of *The Devils of Loudon* and a monumental staging of *Halka* (both 1975), *King Roger* (1983), Kunad's *Der Meister und Margarita* (1988) and, with the director August Everding, costumes to Günther Schneider-Siemssen's sets for the first *Ring* in Poland (1988–9). Majewski had earlier worked with Everding at Covent Garden with a decadent and much revived *Salome* (1970). They went on to complete an innovatory *Elektra* (1973, Hamburg; 1974, Paris), the première of Orff's *De temporum fine comoedia* at Salzburg (1973), *Khovanshchina* (1974, Hamburg) and a staged performance of the oratorio *Die Schuldigkeit des ersten Gebots*, by Mozart and others (1980, Berlin).

In Munich he designed a magnificent *Andrea Chénier* (1975) for Kurt Pscherer and a staid *Rigoletto* (1980) for Jean-Claude Riber. For Bonn Opera he also designed *Wozzeck* (1982) and *Tannhäuser* (1989) for Riber and *Les vêpres siciliennes* for Giancarlo Del Monaco. Majewski has worked at major opera houses in Buenos Aires (*King Roger*, 1981), Cologne (*Samson et Dalila*, 1968, and sets for *Yevgeny Onegin*, 1974), Geneva (Cherubini's *Médée*, 1978), Lisbon (*Ariadne auf Naxos*, 1981), Łódź (the Kurpiński pasticcio *Henryk VI na łowach* ['Henry VI Goes Hunting'], 1972), Trieste (*Jenůfa*, 1965), Turin (*Les contes d'Hoffmann*, 1973) and Zürich (Giordano's *Fedora*, 1982).

Majewski is not identified with any particular school of design. His work is suggestive, often surrealistic and highly textured, and he makes symbolic use of realistic detail. At the same time he can, when required, produce highly individual Baroque settings and costumes of visual splendour.

DAVID J. HOUGH

Majo [Maio], **Gian Francesco de** [di] ['Ciccio'] (*b* Naples, 24 March 1732; *d* Naples, 17 Nov 1770). Italian composer, son of Giuseppe de Majo. He studied with his father, his uncle Gennaro Manno and his great-uncle Francesco Feo. As a boy he assisted his father in the royal chapel in Naples as *organista soprannumerario* without salary. In 1750, on the death of Pietro Scarlatti, he was appointed to a salaried position, though still on the same supernumerary basis, at one ducat per month, and by 1758 he was second organist, with a salary of eight ducats. His first opera, *Ricimero, re dei goti*, was given in Parma and Rome (1759). Goldoni, in his memoirs, recorded Majo's overwhelming reception in Rome: 'A part of the pit went out at the close of the entertainment to conduct the musician home in triumph, and the remainder of the audience staid in the theatre, calling out without intermission, Viva Majo! till every candle was burnt to the socket'. Early in 1760 an attack of tuberculosis forced him to renounce the commission to set Stampiglia's libretto *Il trionfo di Camilla* for the Teatro S Carlo, Naples. Seemingly restored to health after several months' cure at Torre del Greco, he returned to the court at Naples, where he resumed his duties in the royal chapel. Shortly thereafter he set *Astrea placata*, a *componimento drammatico* performed at the S Carlo in June 1760 with Raaff, Manzuoli and Spagnuoli. With the enthusiastic reception of *Cajo Fabrizio* at the S Carlo in November his fame was firmly established, and he was called on to compose operas for Livorno, Venice and Turin.

During his stay in northern Italy (April 1761 to February 1763) Majo studied with Padre Martini, although an apologetic letter (in *I-Bc*) to Martini implies that his studies were erratic because of amorous distractions. After another brief stay in Naples he left in 1764 for Vienna, where he was invited to compose an opera to celebrate the coronation of Joseph II as Holy Roman Emperor. From Vienna he proceeded to Mannheim, where his *Ifigenia in Tauride* was presented, and further invitations from Turin, Mannheim and Madrid prolonged his journey until 1767. Beset by his old illness he returned to Naples, where he sought to strengthen his position at court so as to succeed his father as *primo maestro*; Piccinni had also returned to Naples and was competing for the post. Discouraged by the king's procrastination and constrained by financial need, Majo was forced to undertake further trips to northern Italy to fulfil commissions for new operas. Again in Naples in January 1770 he resumed his activities as second organist and composer of church music. In that year the Teatro S Carlo's new impresario Tedeschi commissioned him to set *Eumene* to celebrate the queen's birthday on 4 November, but by September he was so weak that the opera had to be postponed until the following January. He rallied long enough only to complete the first act, and the opera was finished by Insanguine (Act 2) and Errichelli (Act 3). He died a year and a day before his father, leaving a large family destitute.

Mozart, on hearing Majo's music in a church in Naples, described it, in a letter to his sister, as 'bellissima'. The poet Heinse chose Majo as his favourite composer, preferring his melodies to those of Gluck and Pergolesi. In studies of 18th-century opera Majo is often mentioned together with Jommelli and Traetta as one of the three Italian composers who attempted to infuse into *opera seria* those elements of reform now associated with Gluck. Although he accepted the traditional structure of *opera seria*, he was successful in augmenting its dramatic value through an expressive intensification of the music, and through modifications of the aria form. He frequently shortened the da capo aria by omitting a portion of the *A* section on its return, or by completely writing out an abbreviated *ABA* form. The *B* section thus gains a more important position both in proportion and in dramatic interest, while ritornellos are greatly varied and at times omitted. The arias become more realistic through the use of recitative-type declamation and scrupulous word-setting. Melodies are predominantly lyrical, with long lines made sensuous by a pervading chromaticism – a characteristic that may have influenced Mozart. The second themes in the arias are often instrumentally conceived. Although the orchestral accompaniment never assumes a Jommellian complexity, Majo went a long way towards making it independent of the voice, at times elaborating a motif throughout the aria. Viola and woodwind acquire greater prominence, and there is an increased attention to orchestration that is not evident in the works of most of his contemporaries.

In Vienna and Mannheim Majo had the opportunity to work with librettists whose texts approach the reform ideal of Gluck. In *Alcide negli orti esperidi* by Coltellini (1764, Vienna) and *Ifigenia in Tauride* by Verazi (1764, Mannheim) Majo made liberal use of orchestrally accompanied recitative to heighten dramatic intensity and to make fluid connections between numbers. In contrast with traditional *opera seria*, these operas contain lavish spectacle and many choruses and ensembles, often welded into large composite scenes. In *Ifigenia in Tauride* the movements of the sinfonia are used as introductory scenes, a device later employed in Gluck's *Iphigénie en Tauride* (1779, Paris). Majo's *Motezuma*, to a libretto by Cigna-Santi, is one of the few 18th-century operas with a tragic ending. When Majo returned to Italy his operas again became primarily 'singers' operas', cast in the traditional structure of alternating recitative and aria. This same flexibility of purpose is evident in the operas of Jommelli, Traetta, J. C. Bach and even Gluck, and suggests that the opera reform commonly attributed to Gluck was as much the result of national taste as of the composer's vision.

See also ALCIDE NEGLI ORTI ESPERIDI; IFIGENIA IN TAURIDE (ii); and MOTEZUMA.

opere serie in three acts unless otherwise stated

Ricimero, re dei goti (P. Pariati and A. Zeno: *Flavio Anicio Olibrio*), Parma, Ducale, 7 Feb 1759, *D-Dlb, Hs, GB-Lbl, I-Rc, US-Wc*; Rome, 1759, *D-MÜs, P-La*
Cajo Fabrizio (Zeno), Naples, S Carlo, 29 Nov 1760, *La*
Almeria (M. Coltellini), Livorno, S Sebastiano, spr. 1761, *B-Br*
Artaserse (P. Metastasio), Venice, S Benedetto, 30 Jan 1762, *D-B, P-La, US-Wc*
Catone in Utica (Metastasio), Turin, Regio, carn. 1763, *P-La* (2 copies)
Demofoonte (Metastasio), Rome, Argentina, Feb 1763, *B-Bc, D-B, F-Pn, P-La*
Alcide negli orti esperidi (2, Coltellini), Vienna, Privilegiato, 9 June 1764, *A-Wn, US-Wc*
Ifigenia in Tauride (M. Verazi), Mannheim, Hof, 5 Nov 1764, *D-B, US-Wc*
Motezuma (V. A. Cigna-Santi, after A. de Solis: *La conquista del Messico*), Turin, Regio, carn. 1765, *P-La, US-Wc*
La constancia dichosa (L. Fontana), Madrid, Duke of Medinaceli's residence, 1765
Alessandro [nell'Indie] (Verazi, after Metastasio), Mannheim, Hof, 5 Nov 1766, *D-B* (arias only)
Antigono (Metastasio), Venice, S Benedetto, 26 Dec 1767, *P-La*
Antigona (G. Roccaforte), Rome, Dame, carn. 1768, arias in *B-Lc, I-Mc, PAc, Rc*
Ipermestra (Metastasio), Naples, S Carlo, 13 Aug 1768, *Nc, P-La*

Adriano in Siria (Metastasio), Rome, Dame, carn. 1769, *B-Bc, P-La, US-Wc*
Didone abbandonata (Metastasio), Venice, S Benedetto, carn. 1770, *D-Mh, P-La*
Eumene (Zeno), Naples, S Carlo, 21 Jan 1771, completed by G. Insanguine and P. Errichelli, *I-Nc, P-La*

Doubtful: Ifigenia in Aulide (Zeno), Naples, S Carlo, aut. 1762; Ezio (Metastasio), Venice, S Benedetto, carn. 1769; Ulisse, Rome, 1769; L'eroe cinese (Metastasio), Naples, S Carlo, aut. 1770

Arias in pasticcios, all perf. London: Ezio, King's, 1764 (London, 1765); Solimano, King's, 1765 (London, 1765); Eumene, King's, 1766; The Golden Pippin, Covent Garden, 6 Feb 1773

FlorimoN
S. Arteaga: *Le rivoluzioni del teatro musicale italiano* (Venice, 1783–8, 2/1785)
A. Marx: *Gluck und die Oper* (Berlin, 1863)
H. Müller: 'Wilhelm Heinse als Musikschriftsteller', *VMw*, iii (1887), 561–605
H. Abert: *W. A. Mozart* (Leipzig, 1919–21, 3/1955–66)
W. Vetter: 'Gluck und seine italienischen Zeitgenossen', *ZMw*, vii (1924–5), 609–46
G. Barblan: *Mozart in Italia* (Milan, 1956)
D. DiChiera: *The Life and Operas of Gian Francesco de Majo* (diss., UCLA, 1962)
H.-B. Dietz: 'A Chronology of Maestri and Organisti at the Cappella Reale in Naples, 1745–1800', *JAMS*, xxv (1972), 379–406
M. McClymonds: 'Mattia Verazi and the Opera at Mannheim, Stuttgart, and Ludwigsburg', *Studies in Music from the University of Western Ontario*, vii (1982), 99–136
S. Henze: 'Opera seria am kurpfälzischen Hofe', *Mannheim und Italien: zur Vorgeschichte der Mannheimer: Mannheim 1983*, 78–96

DAVID DiCHIERA, MARITA P. McCLYMONDS (with NICOLE BAKER)

Majo, Giuseppe de [Maio, Giuseppe di] (*b* Naples, 5 Dec 1697; *d* Naples, 18 Nov 1771). Italian composer. From 1706 to 1718 he studied at the Turchini conservatory in Naples, where his teachers included Nicola Fago and Andrea Basso. His first stage work, the *opera buffa Lo finto laccheo*, was performed at the Teatro Fiorentini in 1725. He was *organista soprannumerario* in the royal chapel in Naples from 9 May 1736, promoted to pro-vice-*maestro* in August 1737 and to vice-*maestro* in 1744. After the death of the *primo maestro* Leo in 1744, Majo competed for the post the following year against Porpora, Fago and Durante. Of the four judges (Hasse, Jommelli, Perti and Constanzi), only Hasse supported Majo, but the influence of Queen Maria Amalia prevailed, and on 9 September 1745 he became *primo maestro*. In this post, which he held until his death, his activities as a composer were devoted primarily to sacred music, while his operatic output was sporadic and not marked by any important successes. Only *Il sogno d'Olimpia*, a serenata celebrating the birth of the heir to the throne, was highly acclaimed, perhaps partly because the cast included the renowned singers Tesi, Caffarelli, Conti ('Gizziello') and Babbi. It was on this gala occasion that Majo's son Gian Francesco made his first public appearance, at the second harpsichord.

For illustration *see* SEATING, fig.1.

all first performed in Naples

Lo finto laccheo (commedia, 3), Fiorentini, 1725
Lo vecchio avaro (commedia, 3, F. A. Tullio), Fiorentini, carn. 1727
La milorda (commedia, 3), Nuovo, wint. 1728
Erminia (commedia, B. Saddumene, after T. Tasso: *Gerusalemme liberata*), Nuovo, wint. 1729
La baronessa, ovvero Gli equivoci (commedia, Saddumene), Fiorentini, 10 Dec 1729
Arianna e Teseo (os, 3, P. Pariati), S Carlo, 20 Jan 1747, *I-Nc*

Il sogno d'Olimpia (serenata, R. de' Calzabigi, after L. Ariosto: *Orlando furioso*), Palazzo Reale and Teatro S Carlo, 6 Nov 1747, *F-Pn*

Semiramide riconosciuta (os, 3, P. Metastasio), S Carlo, 20 Jan 1751

Il napolitano nelli fiorentini (farsa), *I-Nc*

H.-B. Dietz: 'A Chronology of Maestri and Organisti at the Cappella Reale in Naples, 1745–1800', *JAMS*, xxv (1972), 379–406, esp. 379, 385

DAVID DiCHIERA (text), MARITA P. McCLYMONDS (work-list)

Major, Malvina (*b* Hamilton, New Zealand, 28 Jan 1943). New Zealand soprano. She studied in Auckland, then at the London Opera Centre and with Ruth Packer at the RCM. She had an early success at the Camden Festival, London, in 1968 as Matilda in Rossini's *Elisabetta, regina d'Inghilterra*, and went on to sing Rosina at the Salzburg Festival in 1968 and 1969. She returned to New Zealand in 1969 to sing Mozart's Konstanze. Her rare appearances since her marriage have been received with enthusiasm. She sang Butterfly with the New Zealand National Opera in Auckland (1984), Donna Elvira at the Brighton Festival (1987), and Konstanze with the Wellington City Opera (1988) and Australian Opera (1989).

A. Simpson and P. Downes: *Southern Voices: International Opera Singers of New Zealand* (Auckland, 1992), 214–17

FREDERICK PAGE

Majorano, Gaetano. *See* CAFFARELLI.

Majorca [Mallorca]. For discussion of opera in Mallorca, *see* PALMA DE MALLORCA.

Making of the Representative for Planet 8, The. Opera in three acts by PHILIP GLASS to a libretto by Doris Lessing; Houston, Grand Opera, 8 July 1988.

By the time *Akhnaten* was first presented, Glass was much in demand. He had recently collaborated with Robert Wilson on *Civil Wars* (1983) and with Robert Moran on *The Juniper Tree* (1985) and had undertaken a host of other projects before setting to work with the novelist Doris Lessing in 1985 on his fourth large opera. It was co-commissioned by Houston Grand Opera (which had presented the American première of *Akhnaten*), the ENO, the Muziektheater Foundation, Amsterdam, and Kiel Opera. Lessing adapted the text from her 1982 novel of the same name (book 3 of the 'Canopus in Argos: Archives' series).

Marking a change from his three previous large-scale operas, Glass's main concern in *Representative* was to set the text so that the words could be understood as fully as possible. The plot tells of a planet entering an ice-age through what Lessing calls a 'cosmological disaster', gradually losing the heat of the sun. Threatened with extinction, the people are guided by extra-terrestrial overlords to overcome their fate by evolving into a 'representative' of the planet – a collective soul that transcends the deaths of individuals. Many have treated the story as plain science fiction but Glass sees it as an allegory, acknowledging the power of allegory in allowing people to discuss objectively things that are difficult to talk about or are close to the heart. Thus the opera suggests different ways of dying.

Despite the apocalyptic qualities of the story, the opera can seem curiously undramatic. Indeed, it has many of the qualities of an oratorio; it might also, with some justification, be compared to a secular passion play. Certainly, heart-in-mouth entertainment it is not,

nor was it meant to be. Having met with adverse criticism at its première, it has not been revived or recorded; it is currently the least well known of the major Glass operas.

Yet it contains much that is meritorious: a recurring SATB chorus (used like the chorus of a Greek play) conveys a visceral sense of tragedy. Glass's harmonic language is more dense than in any of the earlier operas and he often substitutes rapid-fire chord progressions for his trademark arpeggios. The motivic construction is tight, the orchestration sure (if idiosyncratic), and Glass displays a much more acute understanding of the English language than in *The Juniper Tree* or the cycle *Songs from Liquid Days*. There is a continuing exploration of the mating of music with spoken word – not only in the narration that begins and ends the opera but in much of the drama as well, including choral passages that are spoken collectively rather than sung. It is possible that *Representative* will ultimately be taken to heart for the very quality that was lamented in it at its first production – its grave, sustained, peculiarly elevated expression of a mood beyond despair.

TIM PAGE

Makino, Yutaka (*b* Tokyo, 5 July 1930). Japanese composer. He inherited a style based on German Romanticism from his teacher, Kósçak Yamada, which he modified with characteristic Japanese idioms. A prolific composer, he has won the government-sponsored Art Festival prizes several times and the Argentine Music Festival Prize (1955). His first opera, *Ayame* ('Iris'), written for radio and later revised for the stage, won a *grand prix* at the 1960 national Art Festival and a Spanish Radio Prize in 1962. Many of his operas are based on subjects taken from Japanese folktales, noh drama or the *kyōgen* (comic theatre). *Shishi-odori no Hajimari* ('The Origin of the Deer Dance', 1967) was the first opera scored entirely for Japanese instruments. *Ugetsu monogatari* ('The Tale of Ugetsu', 1990) was commissioned by the National Cultural Bureau.

Ayame [Iris] (radio op, 1, H. Mizuo, after Y. Mishima), CBS, Oct 1960; rev. version for stage, Tokyo, Toshi Centre Hall, Dec 1967

Kusabira [Mushrooms] (comic op, 1, K. Ikeda, after a *kyōgen* play), Tokyo, Suidobashi Noh, 30 Nov 1961

Funa Benkei [Benkei in the Boat] (1, M. Chiya, after a noh play), Tokyo, Sankei Kokusai Kaigijō, 14 Nov 1962

Hanjo (1, Mizuo, after Mishima and a noh play), Tokyo, Sabō Hall, 31 Oct 1963

Yuki-onna [Snow-Woman] (Mizuo, after L. Hearn), Yokohama, Shimin Hall, Feb 1964

Shishi-odori no Hajimari [The Origin of the Deer Dance] (1, Mizuo, after K. Miyazawa), Tokyo, National Small, 16 Nov 1967

Ayaginu-chōja [The Millionaire Ayaginu] (comic op, 1, A. Sugano), Tokyo, Hatsumei Hall, 30 Nov 1968

Kurozuka (1, T. Takechi, after a noh play by Zeami), Tokyo, Bunkyō Kōkaidō, 27 Feb 1974

Anju to Zushi-ou [Anju and Zushi-ou] (1, J. Maeda, after O. Mori), Tokyo, Toshi Centre Hall, 14 Sept 1979; rev. version for radio, NHK, 1984

Ugetsu monogatari [The Tale of Ugetsu] (3, Maeda, after S. Ueda), Oct 1990

MASAKATA KANAZAWA

Makropulos Affair, The [*The Makropulos Case*; *Věc Makropulos*]. Opera in three acts by LEOŠ JANÁČEK to his own libretto after KAREL ČAPEK's comedy *Věc Makropulos*; Brno, National Theatre, 18 December 1926.

Janáček saw Karel Čapek's play on 10 December 1922 in Prague a few weeks after its première and was immediately struck by it. His approaches to Čapek in

Emilia Marty *a famous opera singer*	soprano
Dr Kolenatý *a lawyer*	bass-baritone
Albert Gregor *Dr Kolenatý's client*	tenor
Vítek *Dr Kolenatý's clerk*	tenor
Kristina *Vítek's daughter, a young opera singer*	soprano
Baron Jaroslav Prus *a lawyer and Gregor's legal adversary*	baritone
Janek *Prus's son*	tenor
Cleaning Woman	contralto
Stage Technician	bass
Hauk-Šendorf *an old, half-witted ex-diplomat*	tenor
Chambermaid	contralto
Doctor	silent role

Offstage male chorus

Setting Prague in 1922: Kolenatý's chambers, the empty stage in a theatre, a hotel room

February 1923 were discouraged because of possible copyright problems, but nevertheless Janáček took a copy of the play with him on his holiday in Slovakia in July that year together with another play, Šalda's *Dítě* ('The Child'), as possible texts for his next opera (he was in the final stages of revising *The Cunning Little Vixen*). By the time he returned to Brno he had decided firmly in favour of *Makropulos*. Further negotiations with Čapek in August and September found a way round the problems and on 11 November 1923 Janáček began work on his eighth opera.

Janáček adapted the text himself, adhering to Čapek's three-act plan, but avoiding the scene change in Act 3. He completed the opera on 12 November 1925. His pupil Ludvík Kundera made the vocal score, which was sent to Universal Edition on 19 June 1926 and published a few days before the Brno première (under František Neumann) on 18 December; the Prague première under Ostrčil took place on 1 March 1928. Despite the great demands of the piece, both productions were successful and Janáček was delighted with the warm reception of what was to be his last new opera given during his lifetime. However, he took exception to the freedom with which Max Brod translated the text into German and insisted on many changes before the final text was approved. The German première took place at Frankfurt under Joseph Krips on 14 February 1929, six months after Janáček's death.

Čapek's play is essentially a thriller: the gradual uncovering of the mystery surrounding the opera singer Emilia Marty, who is in possession of detailed information about events long past, and who exerts a strange fascination on all who meet her. Her arrival in Prague coincides with the final stages of the protracted lawsuit between Albert Gregor and Jaroslav Prus.

The overture is one of Janáček's most formal and depends in essence on the conflict between a lyrical theme introduced in the ninth bar and a disruptive ostinato background, which occasionally overwhelms it. A further element is an offstage trumpet fanfare against a dotted motif on the timpani.

ACT 1 *A room in Dr Kolenatý's chambers* Vítek's ruminations on the Gregor–Prus case are interrupted by the plaintiff, Albert Gregor, asking for news of it. Gregor is optimistic about the outcome; Vítek, who has seen Gregor's father shoot himself, less so. The arrival of Vítek's daughter Kristina breaks into their arguments. A quiet, richly harmonized chordal motif evokes her bemused state: she is infatuated with the beauty and the artistry of the singer Emilia Marty, whom she has just heard rehearsing at the theatre. Suddenly (and simultaneously with Dr Kolenatý) Emilia Marty appears in the chambers (a stage direction specifies a 'strange light'). Kristina and her father withdraw. Emilia Marty wishes to hear details of the case and at a rattling speed (sometimes no more than a single-note parlando), Kolenatý proceeds to expound it. The case concerns the attempt of the Gregor family to prove their claims to the profitable Loukov estate, which they believe Ferdinand Karel Gregor should have inherited from Baron Josef Ferdinand Prus, who died intestate and without issue in 1827. Prus had informed the head of the academy where Ferdinand Gregor was a pupil of his intention to leave his estate to Gregor; Prus's relatives contested this on the grounds that no written will was found and that on his deathbed Baron Prus had proclaimed he was leaving his estate to a certain 'Mach Gregor'. Emilia Marty startles Kolenatý by asserting that 'Mach Gregor' was in fact Ferdinand Gregor, the son of the Scottish singer Elian MacGregor, and that a will does exist – she describes its whereabouts in the present Baron Prus's house. The reluctant and disbelieving Kolenatý is sent off there.

Emilia Marty and Albert Gregor are left alone together. The substantial scene between them, one of the many virtuoso dialogues of the opera, shows Gregor bewitched by Emilia Marty and tantalized by her revelations. His passion is depicted in a new surging motif in the orchestra and by his high-lying tenor part. Emilia Marty is immune to his ardour, treating him like a child though she softens a little when asked about Elian MacGregor. She becomes strangely perturbed, however, when he knows nothing about a 'Greek document' that she believes he has inherited.

Kolenatý returns with Prus. They have found the will, though Prus dampens excitement by insisting that more evidence is needed to prove that Josef's 'son Ferdinand' is in fact Ferdinand Gregor. Emilia Marty offers to provide it, to the further bemusement of Kolenatý. An orchestral postlude – one of Janáček's longest – concludes the act.

ACT 2 *The empty stage of a theatre after a performance* A Stage Technician and a Cleaning Woman discuss Emilia Marty's triumph and the effect the singer has had on them. Prus comes on, looking for Emilia Marty. Hearing that she will soon return, he stands on one side. The Technician and the Cleaning Woman leave, and Kristina and Prus's son Janek steal on to the stage, Kristina alternately teasing and encouraging her tongue-tied admirer. When he attempts to kiss her, his father comes forward. Emilia Marty enters; her questions to Janek make him even more silent and embarrassed. Gregor appears, followed by Vítek, and gives Emilia Marty a bouquet containing a present. She discards both and insults him further by giving him money. When Vítek offers his congratulations by comparing her to 'Strada', Emilia Marty delivers her contemptuous opinion of Strada and other long-dead singers. She then turns her attention to Janek and Kristina, cuddling in the corner, and asks if they have been 'in paradise' yet. Emilia Marty declares that it is not really worth it, to a striking passage

'The Makropulos Affair' (Janáček): set design by Josef Čapek for the first Prague performance, 1 March 1928

(ex.1) based on a four-note motif (taken from the postlude to Act 1) against a side-drum roll. When asked what is worth it, she replies, chillingly: 'Nic! zhola nic!' ('Nothing, absolutely nothing!').

The group is joined by Hauk-Šendorf, to a fidgety little flourish in the orchestra. He has come to see the woman who has reminded him of his lover of 50 years earlier. Against a dance motif with castanet rhythms, he describes the Spanish gypsy Eugenia Montez: since losing her he has also lost his reason. Emilia Marty, who has comprehensively insulted everyone else, is strangely kind-hearted towards the madman, kisses him and addresses him in Spanish to a fast, grotesquely scored version of the dance tune. Suddenly the flourish returns and Hauk withdraws. Emilia Marty asks all to leave her except Prus, suggesting to the eager Gregor that he return later.

In her crucial encounter with Prus, Emilia Marty learns two things: that in addition to the will he has found a sealed envelope; and that in the parish register 'Ferdinand' is referred to not as 'Ferdinand Gregor', but as 'Ferdinand Makropulos', his mother given as 'Elina Makropulos'. The mention of this name sets off a version of ex.1 in the orchestra, and Emilia Marty's angry surprise cuts into the courteous pace of the interview. Unless a 'Mr Makropulos' comes forward, the sealed document will remain with Prus. When she suggests he might sell it to her, he turns away.

Prus is followed by Gregor. He must go, she says, to Kolenatý to get back the document she gave him, to be replaced with another in the name of Makropulos. She is totally indifferent to his passionate declarations; in fact she falls asleep. Gregor's frustration is only averted by the entrance of the Cleaning Woman. When Emilia Marty wakes up it is Janek who stands before her. Like the others, he is bewitched by her. She persuades him to do a 'heroic deed': to steal the envelope for her. But the scene has again been witnessed by his father, who imperiously dismisses him. Janek retires, crestfallen. Emilia Marty steps up close to Prus and again asks for the envelope. To a brief but powerful climax – a dotted rhythm ending in a cymbal roll – Prus agrees to hand it over that evening.

Act 3 *A hotel room* A lively prelude accompanies 'motions of dressing', shadows thrown on the transparent curtain of the bedroom. Emilia Marty emerges in a peignoir, Prus in evening dress, but without a collar. He silently hands over an envelope, which Emilia Marty reads and declares genuine. But Prus feels he has been defrauded: she was like a corpse. They are interrupted by a Chambermaid with the message that Prus's servant urgently needs to speak to him. When Prus returns, he makes Emilia Marty send the girl away: his son has killed himself. Emilia Marty is unmoved. As Prus goes off, Hauk comes in. He has stolen his wife's jewels and proposes fleeing to Spain with Emilia Marty. Surprisingly, she consents, but the Chambermaid returns to announce company: Gregor, Kolenatý, Vítek, Kristina, Prus and a doctor, who removes Hauk. The document dated 1836 which Emilia Marty sent Kolenatý turned out to be written with modern ink and is thus a forgery. They have come to interrogate her.

She goes to change, while in a short interlude the others go through her trunk in which they find a variety of documents and names, but all with the same initials 'E.M.'. When Emilia Marty returns, elaborately dressed and slightly drunk, she answers their questions by insisting that her name is Elina Makropulos, born in Crete in 1585, and that her father was Hieronymus Makropulos, physician to the Holy Roman Emperor Rudolf II. She also admits to the alias of Elian MacGregor, the mistress of Josef Prus and the mother of Ferdinand Gregor. She had lent Josef Prus the Makropulos document (now in the sealed envelope) – a formula devised by her father for Rudolf to give him 300 years' life. Rudolf had insisted that Makropulos first try it out on his daughter. Elina fell sick; her father was imprisoned as a charlatan, but Elina recovered and escaped with the formula. Kolenatý continues to insist that she is lying, but Emilia Marty is fast becoming beyond the reach of words and begins to recite the opening of the Lord's Prayer in Greek, her mother tongue. When Kolenatý again demands to know her real name she collapses with the words 'Elina Makropulos' as ex.1 returns. At last Kolenatý believes she is telling the truth. Emilia Marty is carried to the bedroom, and a doctor summoned.

An interlude follows, at first fast and shrill with piccolos and percussion, then slow with high violins as a new lyrical tune emerges. When Emilia Marty appears again, it is 'as a shadow' supported by a doctor. She has felt the hand of death upon her, and 'a green light fills the stage and the theatre'. In chorus the men ask her forgiveness. By now, however, for her they are only 'things and shadows'; living and dying are all the same to her. The other-worldly atmosphere is heightened by an off-stage male chorus which repeats Emilia Marty's words. One mustn't live so long, she declares; only for those with normal short lives can life have meaning. Then to a final version of ex.1 (now in harmonics) Emilia Marty reaches the climax of her *scena*, sung against a gentle rocking motif in the orchestra, a slow waltz theme which modulates through several keys against high sustained chords. Asked why she came, she replies that it was for the document, and the pace increases as she reads its opening words. She no longer wants it, and gives it to Kristina – she can live 300 years, she can be famous, she can sing like Emilia Marty. Kristina, however, takes the document and holds it above a flame until it burns. A red light fills the stage. With the words 'Pater hemon' Emilia Marty collapses. The orchestra concludes with a grandiose version of the rocking theme.

* * *

The Makropulos Affair was his last operatic première that Janáček lived to see; despite the complexities of the score (which caused considerable worries during rehearsals) both the Brno and Prague productions were triumphs. It has never enjoyed the same affection as his other late operas, although among them it is his most perfectly constructed; no one doubts the power of the wonderful finale with some of Janáček's grandest music or the virtuosity of the characterization, from its stunning central portrait down to the smallest subsidiary characters, all memorably alive. But the elaborate lawsuit, explained in the first act at some length, the great demands of the orchestral parts and the need for outstanding singing actors have all inhibited performances. When given with total conviction by an outstanding cast, such as the durable Sadler's Wells production with which Charles Mackerras introduced the piece to British audiences (1965), the work with its strange amalgam of passion, mystery and eccentricity comes across as one of the most powerful operas of the 20th century.

JOHN TYRRELL

Makropulos Case, The. Opera by Leoš Janáček; *see* MAKROPULOS AFFAIR, THE.

Maksakova [Maxakova], **Mariya Petrovna** (*b* Astrakhan, 26 March/8 April 1902; *d* Moscow, 11 Aug 1974). Russian mezzo-soprano. The pupil and wife of the opera singer, producer and teacher Maximilian Maksakov, she joined an Astrakhan opera company in 1919, made her début as Amneris at the Bol'shoy in 1923, sang with the Leningrad Academy Opera (formerly the Mariinsky), 1925–7, and then again at the Bol'shoy, 1927–53. Her noble voice, exceptional technique and vivid enunciation were most dramatically displayed as Carmen, Marina (*Boris Godunov*), and Marfa (*Khovanshchina*) and Lyubasha (*The Tsar's Bride*). Her other roles included Princess Clarice (*The Love for Three Oranges*), Stesha (Shaporin's *The Decembrists*), Ortrud, Delilah and Urbain (*Les Huguenots*).

M. L'vov: *M. P. Maksakova* (Moscow and Leningrad, 1947)

I. M. YAMPOL'SKY

Malagigi. See PASQUALINI, MARC'ANTONIO.

Malaniuk, Ira (*b* Stanislav, 29 Jan 1923). Austrian mezzo-soprano of Ukrainian birth. She studied with Adam Didur in L'viv and with Anna Bahr-Mildenburg in Vienna. After making her début in Graz in 1945 she sang at the Zürich Opera from 1947, appearing in the local première of *The Rake's Progress*. She was a member of the Munich Opera from 1952, singing Adelaide (*Arabella*) when the company visited Covent Garden in 1953. She sang at Salzburg and elsewhere as Mozart's Marcellina, Dorabella and Vitellia. Her recordings include Waltraute in *Götterdämmerung* (1953, Bayreuth).

DAVID CUMMINGS

Malanotte, Adelaide (*b* Verona, 1785; *d* Salò, 31 Dec 1832). Italian contralto. She made her début in 1806 at Verona, then sang in Turin and at the Teatro Valle, Rome, in the first performance of Manfroce's *Alzira* (1810). She repeated *Alzira* in Monza (1811), sang in Florence (1812), then created the title role of Rossini's *Tancredi* (1813) at La Fenice, scoring a great success. She later sang Tancredi in Ferrara and Bologna and, in 1818, at the S Carlo, where she was heard by Ferdinand Hérold. He did not like the timbre of her voice but thought her style, taste and intonation perfect.

ELIZABETH FORBES

Malas, Spiro (*b* Baltimore, 28 Jan 1933). American bass. He made both his stage début (at the Baltimore Civic Opera in 1959) and his first appearance with the New York City Opera (5 October 1961) in comprimario roles in *Gianni Schicchi*. In 1965 he toured Australia with the Sutherland-Williamson International Grand Opera Company. For his Covent Garden début in 1966 he played Sulpice, the role in which he made his début at the Metropolitan (1983); with this company he subsequently appeared in *Manon Lescaut* and *Tosca*. A leading singer with the City Opera, he has appeared as General Boum (*La Grande-Duchesse de Gérolstein*), Falstaff (both Verdi's and Nicolai's), Mozart's Figaro and Leporello, and Frank (*Die Fledermaus*). With Scottish Opera he sang Frank

Maurrant in the UK première of *Street Scene* in 1989, and in the same year Isaac Mendoza in *Betrothal in a Monastery* at Wexford. Malas's voice is not large, but it has a natural beauty that overcomes the lack of impact. The lowest notes tend to be lost in large houses, but his well-thought-out characterizations compensate for this.

Q. Earon: 'Spiro Malas', *ON*, xxxiv/26 (1969–70), 12
RICHARD LeSUEUR

Malát, Jan (*b* Starý Bydžov, Bohemia, 16 June 1843; *d* Prague, 2 Dec 1915). Czech composer. He studied at the organ school in Prague and from 1876 onwards taught singing at schools in Prague. He made his name as an adaptor and harmonizer of folksongs and did much to popularize the works of Czech composers, particularly the operas of Smetana, in the form of piano miscellanies. His own compositions are marked by eclecticism and superficiality, but he achieved some success as a composer of operas with two comic works. The one-act *Slavnost sv. Floriána* ('The Feast of St Florian', later performed as *Stáňa*, the name of the main character) has a libretto by Karel Kádner based on a play by Josef Štolba. It is a folk opera following the models of Smetana and Blodek and was first performed in the National Theatre, Prague, on 29 June 1899. His second opera, *Staří blázni* ('Old Fools'; also known as *Veselé námluvy*, 'Merry Wooing'), pleased audiences with its fresh, lively music. It was first performed at the Vinohrady Theatre, Prague, on 12 January 1908.

V. Vycpálek: *Jan Malát* (Prague, 1946)
JAN TROJAN

Mala vita ('Underworld'). Opera in three acts by UMBERTO GIORDANO to a libretto by Nicola Daspuro based on a story by SALVATORE DI GIACOMO; Rome, Teatro Argentina, 21 February 1892 (revised version, as *Il voto*, Milan, Teatro Lirico, 10 November 1897).

Act 1 is set in a square in the Basso Porto district of Naples. Vito Amante (tenor), a dyer, suffers from tuberculosis. Encouraged by his neighbours Marco (bass) and Nunzia (mezzo-soprano) he vows to the Saviour to rescue a woman from a life of sin in return for a cure ('O Gesù mio d'amore'), much to the distress of his mistress Amalia (mezzo-soprano), wife of the loose-living Annetiello (baritone). His choice falls on a local prostitute, Cristina (soprano), whom he promises to marry. When Act 2 opens, Amalia, alone in her house, determines to win her lover back. She sends for Cristina and attempts to bribe her into giving up the marriage and even threatens her with a knife, but to no avail. With Vito himself she is more successful; and once more he declares his love for her. In Act 3, in the square, Vito prepares to join his companions, including Annetiello, on a visit to the song festival at Piedigrotta. Sorrowfully Cristina returns to her old life.

Giordano's first full-length opera, *Mala vita* is closely modelled on Mascagni's *Cavalleria rusticana*, both in its heavy rhetorical style and crude scoring and in the design of its numbers. The local ambience is evoked by a tarantella and several canzone in popular vein, including a song in Neapolitan dialect ('Ce sta, ce sta nu mutto ca dice') sung by Annetiello in Act 3. Though the opera enjoyed a temporary vogue in Germany and Austria, its subject proved too shocking for Italian audiences. Nor were its fortunes improved by the revision of 1897, in which Annetiello is removed and the heroine commits suicide. At the first performance, the roles of Cristina and Vito were taken by Gemma Bellincioni and Roberto Stagno.

For illustration *see* VERISMO.
JULIAN BUDDEN

Malcher, José Cândido da Gama (*b* Belém, 2 Nov 1853; *d* Belém, 17 Jan 1921). Brazilian composer. After studying the piano with Henrique Eulálio Gurjão (1834–85), the founder of the Pará group of opera composers, he enrolled as an engineering student at Lehigh University, Pennsylvania, in 1877, but left the USA that year to study harmony, counterpoint and composition at the Milan Conservatory with Michele Saladino (1835–1912). Returning home in 1881 he invited Carlos Gomes to direct *Il Guarany* and *Salvator Rosa* at Belém the following year and, as artistic director of the newly formed Gomes Leal opera company, saw his own *Bug-Jargal* (4, V. Valle, after V. Hugo) produced at the Teatro da Paz, Belém, on 17 December 1890. It was repeated with the same singers at the Teatro São José, São Paulo, on 30 December 1890, and because of its appropriate subject – the plot deals with the 1791 slave uprising in Santo Domingo – it was staged at the Teatro Fênix in Rio de Janeiro on 25 February 1891 at a gala honouring the founder of the Brazilian republic, Deodoro da Fonseca. In 1892 Malcher became professor of choral singing at the Liceu Paraense and in 1895 organized a symphony orchestra that accompanied the première of his second opera, *Iara*, on 20 March 1895 at the Teatro da Paz, Belém. In three acts and to Malcher's own libretto, based on a poem by Count Stradelli, this concerns an implacable Amazon river god who seduces the young Begiuquira; she follows him into the river depths and the nuptials take place in a resplendent lighted blue chamber. Malcher deposited his manuscript score (there is also a printed vocal score; Milan, 1894) at the Instituto Carlos Gomes at Belém; that of *Bug-Jargal* is housed at the University of Rio de Janeiro (*BR-Rem*).

L. H. Corrêa de Azevedo: *Relação das óperas de autores brasileiros* (Rio de Janeiro, 1938), 53–4
Enciclopédia da música brasileira (São Paulo, 1977), i, 442
ROBERT STEVENSON

Maldere, Pierre van (*b* Brussels, 16 Oct 1729; *d* Brussels, 1 Nov 1768). South Netherlands composer. He may have received his earliest teaching at the royal chapel in Brussels where, from 1746, he is listed as a violinist. In that period the chapel musicians were required to perform whenever Prince Charles of Lorraine, governor-general of the Netherlands, had music at dinner or held a concert. The prince, impressed by van Maldere's talent and charm, furthered his career. On his authority van Maldere spent two seasons in Dublin (1751–3) conducting the 'Philarmonick Concerts'. On 15 August 1754 he played in the Paris Concert Spirituel and around that time was appointed director of the prince's concerts.

In July 1756 van Maldere's first *opéra comique*, *Le déguisement pastoral*, was also performed in Vienna, at Schönbrunn, and on 5 November 1758 *Les amours champêtres*, another *opéra comique*, was also performed there. The next day the prince returned to the Netherlands, and he demonstrated his personal attachment by appointing van Maldere 'valet de chambre'. He continued his career in the prince's entourage, accompanying him on his travels. In 1762 he obtained a seven-year contract as director of the Brussels Grand Théâtre; there he conducted, and was in charge of choosing the repertory: tragedies and comedies of the French theatre, as well as *opéras comiques* which he had composed (*La bagarre*), arranged (Desbrosses' *Les soeurs rivales*) or written in collaboration (*Le soldat par amour*). Overwhelmed by work and by financial worries, he eventually resigned in 1767.

Though a significant composer, he is known mainly as a pioneer of the classical symphony and for his sonatas and trio sonatas.

Le déguisement pastoral (oc), Vienna, Schönbrunn, 12 July 1756, A-Wn
Les amours champêtres (oc), Vienna, Schönbrunn, 5 Nov 1758, lost
La bagarre (opéra bouffon, 1, J. F. Guichard and A. A. H. Poinsinet), Paris, Italien, 10 Feb 1763 (Paris, 1763), lost
Le soldat par amour (opéra bouffon, 2, J.-F. Bastide), Brussels, Grand, 4 Nov 1766, lost; collab. I. Vitzthumb
Le médecin de l'amour (oc, 1, L. Anseaume), 1766 (Brussels, 1766), lost

*

BurneyGN
Mercure de France (1754), Sept; (1764), May, July; (1769), May
J. Isnardon: *Le Théâtre de la Monnaie* (Brussels and Paris, 1890)
H. Liebrecht: *Histoire du théâtre français à Bruxelles au XVIIe et au XVIIIe siècle* (Paris, 1923)
S. Clercx: *Pierre van Maldere: virtuose et maître des concerts de Charles de Lorraine (1729–1768)* (Brussels, 1948)

SUZANNE CLERCX-LEJEUNE

Malec, Ivo (*b* Zagreb, 30 March 1925). Croatian composer and conductor. He studied with Zaun and Cipra at the Zagreb Academy of Music. After a brief period as director of the Rijeka Opera (1952–3) he lived in Paris from 1955 and studied composition with Messiaen. He met Pierre Schaeffer, with whom he collaborated in the Groupe de Recherches de la Musique Concrète (1956–60), and in 1960 he began working with the Groupe des Recherches Musicales. He became professor of composition at the Conservatoire in 1972.

Malec revealed anti-Romantic tendencies even in his earliest works, and has been open in his adherence to the avant garde since 1959. His one stage work, the 'scenic poster collage' *Victor Hugo – un contre tous*, for two reciters, chorus, orchestra and tape, was first performed at Avignon on 1 August 1971; it shows his interest in electrically modifying the sound of the human voice and in divided ensembles. Various autonomous groups at contrasting levels of volume and intensity illustrate the 'collage' aspect, with superimposed blocks of sound on the tape. The libretto, taken from Hugo's political speeches, was prepared by Roger Pillaudin. Malec has also written ballet scores, incidental music, and music for radio plays and musical fairy-tales.

*

U. Stürzbecher: *Werkstattgespräche mit Komponisten* (Cologne, 1971)
I. Malec: 'Sam protiv svih ili glazbeni plakat' [One Against All, or A Musical Poster], *Novi zvuk, izbor tekstova o suvremenoj glazbi* [New Sounds, Textual Options in Contemporary Music], ed. P. Selem (Zagreb, 1972), 295–7
P. Selem: 'Ivo Malec ili zrenja vremena' [Ivo Malec, or the Maturing of Time], ibid, 249–53
J. Andreis: *Music in Croatia* (Zagreb, 1974)

KORALJKA KOS

Malfitano, Catherine (*b* New York, 18 April 1948). American soprano. After making her début at the Central City Opera in 1972 as Nannetta, she sang Rosina with the Minnesota Opera Company (1972–3). From 1973 to 1979 she sang regularly with the New York City Opera. She made her European début as Susanna at the 1974 Holland Festival, her Metropolitan Opera début as Gretel (1979) and her Vienna Staatsoper début as Violetta (1982). She has performed with most of the principal American companies, and sang the leading roles in the premières of Conrad Susa's *Transformations* (1973), Floyd's *Bilby's Doll* (1976) and Pasatieri's *Washington Square* (1976). In 1980 she appeared as Servilia in Ponnelle's film of *La clemenza di Tito*. She sang Konstanze at the Paris Opéra (1984), the title roles in *Lulu* (1985) and *Daphne* (1988) at the Munich Festival and Butterfly at Covent Garden (1988). In May 1989 she sang Poppaea at La Monnaie, repeating it in Geneva in the autumn, together with Manon. Her first Salome was with the Deutsche Oper, Berlin, under Sinopoli in 1990; she sang it again with the WNO in Tokyo at the end of the year. In 1991 she appeared in *Der ferne Klang* in Vienna, followed by an arresting portrayal of Cleopatra in the Chicago Lyric Opera's production of Barber's revised *Antony and Cleopatra*. She took the title role in the *Tosca* filmed with Domingo in Rome in 1992 and is scheduled to appear in the world première of William Bolcom's *McTeague* in Chicago. Malfitano has a pure, rich voice remarkable for its ease of phrasing, which makes her especially suited to such roles as Violetta, Liù and Mimì, as well as to the dramatic parts of recent seasons.

MICHAEL WALSH

Malgoire, Jean-Claude (*b* Avignon, 25 Nov 1940). French conductor. He studied in Avignon and at the Paris Conservatoire, where he won a *premier prix* for oboe playing and another for chamber music. Besides founding La Grande Ecurie et la Chambre du Roy (1966) for the performance of Baroque music, he formed L'Atelier du Tourcoing (in north-east France) as a base for staging and touring Baroque opera by Campra, Lully, Rameau and others. He made several visits to London to direct performances for the English Bach Festival, including Rameau's *Les Indes galantes* at the Whitehall Banqueting House (1974), *Hippolyte et Aricie* at Covent Garden (1978) and *Platée* at Sadler's Wells (1983). He conducted Campra's *Tancrède* at the Aix-en-Provence festival in 1986 and elsewhere, and recorded it, and in 1988 gave performances of Salieri's five-act *Tarare* at Schwetzingen and Kreutzer's *Paul et Virginie* at Tourcoing. At St Etienne in 1989 he revived Elisabeth-Claude Jacquet de la Guerre's *Céphale et Procris*, the first French opera composed by a woman. His recordings also include Rameau's *Platée* from Tourcoing and Handel's *Rinaldo* (1977) and *Serse* (1979). Malgoire has played a significant role in the early music and period instrument movement in France, and although his performances have been criticized for instrumental inconsistency and his sometimes erratic delineation and control of rhythm, they have won wide acceptance for their vigour, colour and committed enthusiasm.

NOËL GOODWIN

Malherbe, Charles (Théodore) (*b* Paris, 21 April 1853; *d* Cormeilles, Eure, 5 Oct 1911). French musicologist and composer. He first studied law and was later a pupil of A. L. Danhauser and Massenet. From 1885 to 1893 he contributed to various journals and collaborated with Albert Soubies in several books, two on Wagner (1886, 1892) and two on the history of the Opéra-Comique (1887, 1892–3); he also later wrote a book on Auber (1911). From 1896 he assisted Charles Nuitter, archivist-librarian of the Opéra; succeeding him in 1899, he improved the organization of the library and bequeathed to the Conservatoire collection (now part of the Bibliothèque Nationale) a magnificent collection of autographs. He wrote the historical notes for 16 volumes of Rameau's collected works, beginning in 1895, and with Felix Weingartner began an edition of the works of Berlioz. Malherbe's own compositions, which are of little importance, include four *opéras comiques*: *L'amour au camp* (1905, Le Mans), and *L'ordonnance*, *Les trois commères* and *La barbière de Cetteville* (all unperformed). He supplied recitatives and an entr'acte for Bizet's *Don Procopio*, and made several piano transcriptions.

J. Ecorcheville: 'Charles Malherbe: 1853–1911', *BSIM*, vii/11 (1911), 1–4
E. Lebeau: 'Un Mécène de la musique, Charles Malherbe', *Humanisme actif: mélanges ... offerts à Julien Cain*, ii (Paris, 1968), 91–9   ELISABETH LEBEAU

Malheurs d'Orphée, Les ('The Misfortunes of Orpheus'). Chamber opera in three acts, op.85, by DARIUS MILHAUD to a libretto by Armand Lunel; Brussels, Théâtre de la Monnaie, 7 May 1926.

Orpheus (baritone), a simple peasant, lives in a village in the Camargue, absenting himself from time to time to tend sick animals. He tells his village friends that he plans to marry Eurydice (soprano), one of four gypsies recently arrived in the village. Suddenly Eurydice enters, pursued by her nomadic relatives; they are appalled at the prospect of her marriage and determine to reclaim her. The lovers seek refuge in the mountains, but Eurydice is smitten by a mysterious disease that even Orpheus cannot cure. She dies after commending her husband to the animals who, singing a funeral chorus, carry her away. Orpheus returns home and confides that his heart still bleeds. The Bohémiennes, Eurydice's three sisters (mezzo-soprano and two sopranos), accuse him of causing their sister's death and stab him. As he expires, yearning towards his beloved, they realize their mistake.

Composed in 1924, *Les malheurs d'Orphée* was the first of Milhaud's chamber operas and lasts about 35 minutes. The libretto is in the form of short scenes with separate arias, duets and choruses, and the orchestra requires 13 players. The most inspirational moments include the 'Dernières recommendations d'Eurydice aux animaux' and Eurydice's funeral cortège (both in Act 2).

CHRISTOPHER PALMER

Malibran [née García], **Maria**(-Felicia) (*b* Paris, 24 March 1808; *d* Manchester, 23 Sept 1836). Spanish mezzo-soprano. She was the daughter of the elder Manuel García and sister of the mezzo-soprano Pauline Viardot. She studied with her father, a rigorous teacher whose harshness towards her was notorious, and made her London début at the King's Theatre in June 1825 as Rosina (*Il barbiere*); subsequently she sang Felicia in the first British performance of Meyerbeer's *Il crociato in Egitto*. *Il barbiere* opened the García family's season at the Park Theatre, New York, in 1825. (*Tancredi*, *Otello*, *Il turco in Italia* and *La Cenerentola*, *Don Giovanni* and two pieces by García were also in the repertory.) After the failure of her marriage to Eugène Malibran she returned to Europe in 1827. She made her Paris début at the Théâtre Italien in *Semiramide* in 1828, reappeared at the King's Theatre in 1829 in *Otello*, and then sang alternately in Paris and London until 1832, when she went to Italy. At Bologna she sang in Bellini's *I*

Maria Malibran with symbols of her two most famous roles: the helmet (title role of Rossini's 'Tancredi') and the harp (Desdemona in his 'Otello'); lithograph by Focosi

Capuleti e i Montecchi and at Naples in 1833 appeared in *La sonnambula*, which she then sang in English at Drury Lane. In 1834 she sang Norma in Naples and for her début at La Scala. In 1835 she sang in *Fidelio* in English at Covent Garden and returned to La Scala to sing the title role in Donizetti's *Maria Stuarda*, causing a famous scandal by ignoring some changes that the Milanese censors had insisted upon. Bellini adapted the role of Elvira in *I puritani* (1835, Paris) for her to sing in Naples, but the opera was turned down by the management and she never sang it.

Her first marriage having eventually been annulled, she married the violinist Charles de Bériot in March 1836, and at Drury Lane in May of that year created the title role in Balfe's *The Maid of Artois*, which he had written for her. A riding accident when she was pregnant resulted in her death during the Manchester Festival. To judge from the parts adapted for her by both Donizetti and Bellini, the compass (g to *e'''*), power and flexibility of Malibran's voice was extraordinary. Her early death turned her into something of a legendary figure with writers and poets during the later 19th century.

An Amateur: *Memoirs, Critical and Historical, of Madame Malibran de Bériot* (London, ?1836)
G. Barbieri: *Notizie biografiche di M. F. Malibran* (Milan, 1836)
I. Nathan: *Memoirs of Madame Malibran de Bériot* (London, 1836)
Memoirs of the Public and Private Life of the Celebrated Madame Malibran (London, 1836)
Countess M. Merlin: *Madame Malibran* (Brussels, 1838)
——: *Memoirs of Madame Malibran* (London, 1840)
W. H. H.: *Templeton and Malibran: Reminiscences of these Renowned Singers, with Original Letters and Anecdotes* (London and Brighton, 1880)
E. Legouvé: *Maria Malibran* (Paris, 1880)
E. Heron-Allen: *Contributions towards an Accurate Biography of de Bériot and Malibran* (London, 1894)
A. Pougin: *Marie Malibran: histoire d'une cantatrice* (Paris, 1911; Eng. trans., 1911)
P. Larionoff and F. Pestellini: *Maria Malibran e i suoi tempi* (Florence, 1935)
D. Bielli: *Maria Malibran* (Castelbordino, 1936)

M. Lorenzi de Bradi: *La brève et merveilleuse vie de la Malibran* (Paris, 1936)

H. Malherbe [pseud. of H. Croisilles]: *La passion de la Malibran* (Paris, 1937)

D. Milačić: *Marija Malibran* (Belgrade, 1954)

S. Desternes and H. Chandet: *La Malibran et Pauline Viardot* (Paris, 1969)

A. Fitzlyon: *Maria Malibran* (London, 1987)

ELIZABETH FORBES

Malipiero, Gian Francesco (*b* Venice, 18 March 1882; *d* Treviso, 1 Aug 1973). Italian composer and musicologist. Although very uneven, and less influential than Casella and Pizzetti, he was the most original and inventive Italian composer of his generation – not least in his often wildly unconventional theatre works.

1. Life. 2. Stage works up to 1929. 3. Later stage works.

1. LIFE. Born into a family of musicians of aristocratic origin, he was the grandson of the opera composer Francesco Malipiero (1824–87) and the uncle of Riccardo Malipiero. His childhood was restless and troubled: after the break-up in 1893 of his parents' marriage, his father Luigi, a pianist and conductor, took him to Trieste, Berlin and eventually Vienna, where the boy studied briefly at the conservatory (1898–9). But in 1899 he returned to his mother's house in Venice, where he entered the Liceo Musicale, learning counterpoint from Marco Enrico Bossi, who at first had a low opinion of him. After Bossi's move to Bologna (1902), Malipiero continued his composition studies on his own. It was then that an important new experience transformed his musical outlook: in 1902, without any external encouragement, he discovered and began to transcribe the long-forgotten early Italian music (Monteverdi, Merulo, Frescobaldi etc.) in the Biblioteca Marciana. By 1904, when he too moved to Bologna, his composition technique had matured sufficiently to win Bossi's approval and a diploma at that city's Liceo Musicale.

Soon afterwards Malipiero became amanuensis for a while to the blind opera composer Smareglia, a disciple of Wagner. Later he claimed that he learnt more, especially about orchestration, from that experience than from all his formal studies. He gained nothing significant from the few of Bruch's classes that he attended in Berlin in 1908: more important were his discovery, around that time, of the music of Debussy (including *Pelléas et Mélisande*) and his enthusiastic response to the first performance of Strauss's *Elektra* – an enthusiasm which did not, however, last very long. A visit to Paris in 1913 came as another landmark in his development: it was there that he formed a lasting friendship with Casella, at whose suggestion he attended the première of *The Rite of Spring*; the experience woke him, as he later put it, 'from a long and dangerous lethargy'. As a result he soon decided to suppress nearly all his compositions written up to that time, although, contrary to what he consistently gave the world to understand, he did not destroy most of the manuscripts.

Though again based in Venice after his return from Bologna in 1905, Malipiero spent more and more time from 1910 onwards in the little Veneto hill town of Asolo. But before he could settle there permanently the Retreat of Caporetto forced him and his family to flee, in November 1917, to Rome, arriving there with shattered nerves. He later wrote of this tormented time: 'In 1914 the war disrupted my whole life, which remained, until 1920, a perennial tragedy. The works of

these years perhaps reflect my agitation; however, I consider that if I have created something new in my art (formally and stylistically) it happened precisely in this period' (see Scarpa 1952, p.224). Rome remained his base until 1921 and he was associated, while there, with Casella's Società Italiana di Musica Moderna. The two again collaborated, in 1923, in founding the Corporazione delle Nuove Musiche; but Malipiero was less practical and extroverted than Casella, and played a less central part in the campaign to modernize Italian music. Nevertheless it is surely no coincidence that the first few of his idiosyncratically experimental stage works, which have aroused so much controversy, date from these years.

In 1921 Malipiero was appointed professor of composition at the Parma Conservatory, but he resigned three years later, by which time he had bought (late in 1922) the house in Asolo that remained his home until his death. Having thus stabilized his life as never before, he embarked, in 1926, on his edition of all Monteverdi's works. The fruits of these labours, completed in 1942, have been justly criticized, but their importance as a major step forward in Monteverdi studies is unquestionable. Moreover, frankly neo-Monteverdian elements can be discerned in several of his own theatre works, especially in the 1920s, 30s and 40s. In 1932 Malipiero again became a professor of composition, this time at the Venice Liceo Musicale (Conservatory from 1940), which he directed from 1939 to 1952. After his retirement from the conservatory, he continued to teach privately and to preside over the Istituto Italiano Antonio Vivaldi, editing many volumes in the series of Vivaldi's complete instrumental works. But these activities, like their equivalents in earlier periods, always remained secondary to his irrepressible urge to compose, which continued unabated right up to 1971.

2. STAGE WORKS UP TO 1929. Malipiero was slower in finding a personal voice in his stage works than in his best instrumental pieces. Whereas the *Poemetti lunari* for piano (1909–10) and the first set of orchestral *Impressioni dal vero* (1910–11) show that even before his visit to Paris he was capable of a refined, luminous expressiveness of striking individuality, his pre-1917 operas are less sure-footed, and he subsequently repudiated most of them (although only *Schiavona* seems actually to have been destroyed). The most interesting of these early operatic ventures – and the only one that has been performed since World War I – is *Sogno d'un tramonto d'autunno*, in which a cut version of one of D'Annunzio's more controversial plays is set to an appropriately restless score, evidently reflecting Malipiero's current enthusiasms for French music (notably Dukas) and for certain more turbulent aspects of Strauss. Moreover the dissonant outbursts that erupt as the drama approaches its lurid (albeit offstage) climax are probably an immediate, as yet rather naive response to his recent experience of *The Rite of Spring*.

Malipiero's breakthrough into a more radically innovatory type of music theatre did not come, however, until the formidable crisis (personal and creative) through which he passed in the later war years. The most hectically intense expression of this crisis was *Pantea* – the first and still perhaps the clearest of his frankly symbolic stage works, in which he made as decisive a break with traditional operatic methods as he did with orthodox thematic processes in his instrumental music. The only figures on the stage are the

167

protagonist, represented by a mute dancer, and, briefly near the end, an apparition of Death; the only voices are those of a hidden, largely wordless chorus with baritone soloist, symbolizing the unattainable freedom and beauty for which Pantea yearns. The work's conception as a monodrama, in which a woman is haunted by hallucinations and false hopes before being confronted with the brutal finality of death, led Piero Santi (*L'approdo musicale*, 1960) to make interesting comparisons with *Erwartung*. But there is nothing Schoenbergian about the music, for all its quasi-expressionist turbulence. Indeed, the anticipations, in more abstract terms, of the basic idea of *Il prigioniero* are just as noteworthy, especially as Dallapiccola revered Malipiero greatly.

Sette canzoni, too, rebels against established operatic traditions, but in a totally different manner, recalling the 'panel' construction of Malipiero's orchestral piece *Pause del silenzio I* (1917). Seven miniature operas, without any unifying plot and lasting about 45 minutes in all, are threaded together like beads on a string. Each presents (like *Pantea*, but in ostensibly more realistic terms) a head-on collision between incompatible forces, uncomplicated by dramatic elaboration. Each has a song as its musical nucleus but is otherwise largely mimed. The total result, for all its eccentricity, is still regarded in Italy as a supreme example of 20th-century experimental music theatre.

In the early 1920s the restless, tormented vision of the works of 1917–19 tended to give place to more serene, even exuberantly humorous expressions, though without reverting towards more conventional methods. On the contrary, the two extraordinary little operas that Malipiero composed during 1919–22 as companion pieces to *Sette canzoni*, in the oddly heterogeneous triptych *L'Orfeide*, show his iconoclastic approach to music theatre in a particularly extreme form. Perhaps the richest expression of the comic-grotesque side of his genius is to be found, however, in the *Tre commedie goldoniane*, in which the composer's idiosyncratic, extremely compressed treatment of events and characters taken from well-known Goldoni plays is only marginally more 'traditional' in effect than *L'Orfeide*. An apparently more drastic departure from his own preceding methods can be seen in *San Francesco d'Assisi*, in which his longstanding interest in early music, from plainsong to Monteverdi, is reflected in a much more thoroughgoing manner than it had been in parts of *Sette canzoni*. Yet the resultant antique, Giottoesque calm does not preclude violent episodes: there are echoes of *Pantea* in the 'fire' scene. Moreover, the colourful post-Debussian qualities of Malipiero's orchestration are not noticeably inhibited, however much they may be redirected, by the new austerity in his basic approach. Though originally conceived for stage presentation, *San Francesco* has nearly always been performed in the concert hall, becoming, in effect, a cantata.

Malipiero's music of the later 1920s could be said to follow on from *San Francesco* in that, while not rejecting his pre-1920 style outright, it is marked by an ever closer interaction between archaic and early 20th-century idioms. Ostinato devices are now less frequent; contrapuntal textures become more expansive and elaborate, though almost never strictly organized for more than a few seconds at a time; but modal archaisms still rub shoulders with acrid false relations, sudden outcrops of convulsive dissonance and the like. The process is clearly seen in a further series of highly unconven-

tional operas, whose symbolism as such, however, lacks the lucidity of that of *Pantea*, having instead the perplexing irrationality of dreams. It is perhaps understandable, though unjust, that *Filomela e l'Infatuato* and *Merlino mastro d'organi* had to wait until 1972 before being staged in Italy. *Merlino*, for instance, features a huge magic organ which kills all men who hear it, until a deaf mute kills the organist and then becomes articulate in the 'purifying fire' of the stake, revealing himself as his victim's reincarnation. To add to the confusion, the librettos of both operas (like those of *Sette canzoni* and several other works) include many quotations, with or without modification, from old Italian texts, sometimes introduced in situations which would have startled the original authors. *Filomela* and *Merlino*, for all their musical qualities, are best regarded as transitional – preparing the way for the hauntingly enigmatic *Torneo notturno*, another of Malipiero's supreme achievements, in which the obsessively recurring 'canzone del tempo' evokes the inexorable destructiveness of time.

The triptych *Il mistero di Venezia* stands a little apart from the frankly 'symbolic' operas of the 1920s: even more overtly than the *Tre commedie goldoniane*, the work is a celebration of Malipiero's native city – ending with a ferocious (though musically disappointing) diatribe against the Serenissima's tourist-infested degeneracy in modern times. The most impressive 'panel' in this triptych is undoubtedly *Le aquile di Aquileia* – resplendent in its pageant-like celebration of the founding of Venice, with quasi-oriental phrases mingling with the archaisms in a way that recalls the architecture of St Mark's.

3. LATER STAGE WORKS. It was hardly to be expected that Malipiero's recklessly unconventional theatre works of 1917–29 would find easy acceptance in conservative, provincial Italy: most of them had their premières abroad, especially in pre-Nazi Germany. Nor is it surprising that during the 1930s, when his musical style on the whole became more euphonious and stable in effect, his theatrical methods, too, became less aggressively nonconformist. In *La favola del figlio cambiato* he even collaborated, for the first time for nearly two decades, with a librettist, rather than devising and assembling the text himself. However, his collaborator on this occasion was the far from conventional Luigi Pirandello, in whom Malipiero evidently recognized a kindred spirit. *La favola*, whose best parts again show Malipiero at the height of his powers, won considerable success at its German première but was suppressed by the Nazis a few months later; moreover in Italy Mussolini banned it after a single performance. After that experience, Malipiero naturally preferred to turn, in his next few operas, to much more safely traditional methods and subjects: in *Giulio Cesare* – a rather oddly proportioned and undercharacterized (though musically inventive) adaptation of Shakespeare's play – there is even an unmistakable obeisance to the Duce at the end. During 1936–41 Malipiero based three further operas on existing dramas, by Euripides and Calderón de la Barca as well as Shakespeare: the results, though far from valueless, are undeniably disappointing after the boldness of his previous stage works.

Malipiero's urge to experiment could not, however, be suppressed for long. In 1942 he returned to the kind of quirkily anarchic subject matter that naturally suited him, in *I capricci di Callot*, which is derived (with typically Malipierian freedom) from parts of E. T. A. Hoffmann's *Prinzessin Brambilla* and, beyond it, from the bizarre world of Callot's engravings. The purely orchestral preludes and ballet scenes in particular have a colourful verve which makes this musically his finest opera of 1935–50, although *Vergilii Aeneis*, a work primarily intended for the concert hall that may also be staged, reaches perhaps still greater heights in its superb first part, 'La morte di Didone'. Also worthy of mention in this period is *L'allegra brigata*, which consists of a series of operatic vignettes analogous to those in *Sette canzoni* – this time held together by a *Decameron*-like frame.

Despite such partial reversions to the theatrical methods of some of his earlier works, Malipiero remained true, throughout most of the 1940s, to the expansively lyrical, basically diatonic musical idiom which he had adopted at the beginning of the 1930s (and which also flowered in his numerous instrumental pieces of the time). After this long, relatively stable middle period of his career, *Mondi celesti e infernali* marks the moment of transition to his final phase. Here he took a major step into a more complex, pervasively chromatic idiom, culminating, as early as the end of Act 1, in a complete 12-note chord. The opera's transitional nature is revealed in its inconsistent approach, both musically and dramatically, and it is decidedly uneven in quality. But it remains an important link in the chain leading towards the intense world of the best parts of *Venere prigioniera*: here Malipiero's new chromatic language, in which modal and whole-tone outlines often interact so closely that they are barely identifiable as such, reached full maturity.

The quality of Malipiero's last-period operas is extremely variable: too often their vocal writing seems contrived and unmemorable compared with that of his best earlier works from *Sette canzoni* to *La favola del figlio cambiato*. However, *Il capitan Spavento* and especially *Il marescalco* use his new chromatic style with abundant comic energy, reviving something of the sparkle of the *Tre commedie goldoniane* in new, more angular terms; while *Le metamorfosi di Bonaventura* recaptures some of the enigmatic, dreamlike quality previously encountered in *Torneo notturno*, helped now by the composer's discovery of another kindred spirit in the mysterious anonymous author of *Die Nachtwachen des Bonaventura* (1804/1805). Moreover, the covertly autobiographical *Uno dei Dieci* shows that even at the age of 88 Malipiero could still create a strangely moving operatic miniature, pervaded by a characteristic mixture of self-deprecating satire and nostalgia for the Venetian past.

A place apart is occupied by the surprisingly successful compilation *Gli eroi di Bonaventura*, which consists largely of individual scenes salvaged (with only minor modifications) from various earlier Malipiero operas, from *Giulio Cesare* to *Le metamorfosi di Bonaventura*. The work is held together by an ingenious theatrical and musical frame, again involving the figure of Bonaventura, whom the composer had evidently come to see as an 'alter ego'. Structurally *Gli eroi* (like *L'allegra brigata* and *Mondi celesti e infernali*) is a recognizable descendant of *Sette canzoni*, even if the operas from which it directly draws material are of more recent vintage. After the première Fedele D'Amico unequivocally declared that this strange composite opera was superior to any of its sources. Certainly it pulls together many different threads from Malipiero's previous operatic experience, in a way that adds up to more than the sum of its parts.

See also CAPRICCI DI CALLOT, I; FAVOLA DEL FIGLIO CAMBIATO, LA; MARESCALCO, IL; ORFEIDE, L'; TORNEO NOTTURNO; TRE COMMEDIE GOLDONIANE; UNO DEI DIECI; and VENERE PRIGIONIERA.

all stage works involving voices, whether classifiable as operas in the traditional sense or not, are listed

Elen e Fuldano, 1907–9 (3, S. Benco), unperf., unpubd

Canossa [La notte dei penitenti], 1911–12 (1, Benco), Rome, Costanzi, 24 Jan 1914, unpubd

Schiavona, ? c1912, unperf., unpubd, probably destroyed

Sogno d'un tramonto d'autunno, 1913[?–14] (1, after G. d'Annunzio), RAI, 4 Oct 1963; staged Mantua, Sociale, 4 Oct 1988, unpubd

Lancelotto del lago, 1914–15 (prol., 3, A. de Stefani), unperf., orch frags., Per una favola cavalleresca (Milan, 1921)

Pantea, 1917–19 (dramma sinfonico, 1, Malipiero), Venice, Goldoni, 6 Sept 1932, vs (London, 1920)

Sette canzoni, 1918–19 (7 espressioni drammatiche, 1, Malipiero, using poems by A. Poliziano, Jacopone da Todi and others), Paris, Opéra, 10 July 1920, vs (London, 1919) [pt 2 of L'Orfeide; triptych perf. complete, Düsseldorf, Stadt, 5 Nov 1925]

Orfeo, ovvero L'ottava canzone, 1919–20 (rappresentazione musicale, 1, Malipiero, using old It. poems), Düsseldorf, Stadt, 5 Nov 1925, vs (London, 1922) [pt 3 of L'Orfeide]

San Francesco d'Assisi, 1920–21 (mistero, 1, Malipiero, after *Fioretti di San Francesco* and Jacopone da Todi), New York, Carnegie Hall, 29 March 1922 (concert perf.); staged Perugia, 22 Sept 1949, vs (London, 1921)

La morte delle maschere, 1922 (1, Malipiero, using old It. poems), Düsseldorf, Stadt, 5 Nov 1925, vs (London, 1922) [pt 1 of L'Orfeide]

Tre commedie goldoniane (triptych, Malipiero, after C. Goldoni), Darmstadt, Hessisches Landes, 24 March 1926, vs (Milan, 1924), orch frags. (Milan, 1925)
  La bottega da caffè 1922, (1)
  Sior Todero brontolon, 1922 (1)
  Le baruffe chiozzotte, 1920 (1)

Filomela e l'Infatuato, 1925 (dramma musicale, 3 scenes, Malipiero, using old It. poems), Prague, Neues Deutsches, 31 March 1928, vs (Vienna, 1926)

Il finto Arlecchino, 1925 (commedia musicale, 1, Malipiero), Mainz, Stadt, 8 March 1928, vs (Boston and New York, 1927) [pt 2 of Il mistero di Venezia; triptych perf. complete, Coburg, Landes, 15 Dec 1932]; orch frags., unpubd

Merlino mastro d'organi, 1926–7 (dramma musicale, 2 scenes, Malipiero, after old It. poems), Rome Radio, 1 Aug 1934; staged Palermo, Massimo, 28 March 1972, vs (Vienna, 1928)

Le aquile di Aquileia, 1928 (dramma musicale, 3 scenes, Malipiero, using old It. poems), Coburg, Landes, 15 Dec 1932, vs (Vienna, 1929) [pt 1 of Il mistero di Venezia]

I corvi di San Marco, 1928 (dramma musicale senza parole, 1, Malipiero, after old It. poems), Coburg, Landes, 15 Dec 1932, vs (Vienna, 1929) [pt 3 of Il mistero di Venezia]

Torneo notturno, 1929 (7 notturni, 1, Malipiero, using old It. poetry), Munich, National, 15 May 1931, orch frags. and vs (Berlin, 1930)

I trionfi d'Amore, 1930–31 (triptych, Malipiero)
  Castel smeraldo (1), unperf., unpubd
  Mascherate (commedia, 1, after G. G. de' Rossi), as Il festino, Turin Radio, 6 Nov 1937; staged Bergamo, Donizetti, 2 Oct 1954, vs (Milan, 1936)
  Giochi olimpici (1), unperf., unpubd

La favola del figlio cambiato, 1932–3 (3, L. Pirandello), Brunswick, Landes, 13 Jan 1934 (Milan, 1933), orch frags. (Milan, 1935)

Giulio Cesare, 1934–5 (dramma musicale, 3, Malipiero, after W. Shakespeare), Genoa, Carlo Felice, 8 Feb 1936 (Milan, 1935)

Antonio e Cleopatra, 1936–7 (dramma musicale, 3, Malipiero, after Shakespeare), Florence, Comunale, 4 June 1938 (Milan, 1938), orch frags. (Milan, 1939)

Ecuba, 1938–40 (tragedia, 3, Malipiero, after Euripides: *Hecuba*), Rome, Opera, 11 Jan 1941 (Milan, 1940)

La vita è sogno, 1940–41 (3, Malipiero, after P. Calderón de la Barca), Breslau, Opernhaus, 30 June 1943, vs (Milan, 1942)

I capricci di Callot, 1941–2 (commedia, prol., 3, Malipiero, after E. T. A. Hoffmann: *Prinzessin Brambilla*), Rome, Opera, 24 Oct 1942 (Milan, 1942)

L'allegra brigata, 1943 (6 novelle in 1 dramma, 3, Malipiero, after

F. Sacchetti, M. Salernitano, S. degli Arienti and M. Bandello), Milan, Scala, 4 May 1950, vs (Milan, 1950)

Vergilii Aeneis, 1943–4 (sinfonia eroica, 2 pts, Malipiero, after Virgil, trans. A. Caro), RAI, 21 June 1946; staged Venice, Fenice, 6 Jan 1958 (Milan, 1946)

Mondi celesti e infernali, 1948–9 (3, Malipiero, after Shakespeare: *Romeo and Juliet*, Euripides: *Medea*, D. Cavalca and others), RAI, 12 Jan 1950; staged Venice, Fenice, 2 Feb 1961, vs (Milan, 1950)

El mondo novo [La lanterna magica], 1950–51 (ballet incl. one operatic scene, 1, Malipiero, after G. D. Tiepolo and N. de Fatouville), Rome, Argentina, 16 Dec 1951 (concert perf.), unpubd

Il figliuol prodigo, 1952 (1, P. Castellano Castellani), RAI, 25 Jan 1953; staged Florence, Pergola, 14 May 1957, vs (Milan, 1954)

Donna Urraca, 1953–4 (commedia musicale, 1, Malipiero, after P. Mérimée: *Le ciel et l'enfer*), Bergamo, Donizetti, 2 Oct 1954, vs (Milan, 1955)

Il capitan Spavento, 1954–5 (mascherata eroica, 1, Malipiero, partly after Ruzante [A. Beolco] and Fatouville), Naples, S Carlo, 16 March 1963, vs (Milan, 1958)

Venere prigioniéra, 1955 (commedia musicale, 2, int, Malipiero, after E. Gonzales: *Giangurgolo*), Florence, Pergola, 14 May 1957, vs (Milan, 1958)

Rappresentazione e festa di Carnasciale e della Quaresima, 1961 (op with dances, 1, Malipiero, after Florentine text of 1558), Venice, Fenice, 20 April 1962 (concert perf.); staged Venice, Fenice, 20 Jan 1970 (Milan, 1962)

Don Giovanni, 1962 (2, Malipiero, after A. S. Pushkin: *The Stone Guest*), Naples, Auditorium della RAI, 21 Sept 1963 (staged), vs (Milan, 1964)

Le metamorfosi di Bonaventura, 1963–5 (3, Malipiero, after anon. *Nachtwachen des Bonaventura*), Venice, Fenice, 4 Sept 1966, vs (Milan, 1970)

Don Tartufo bacchettone, 1966 (2, Malipiero, after Molière: *Le Tartuffe* and G. Gigli: *Don Pilone*), Venice, Fenice, 20 Jan 1970, vs (Milan, 1971)

Il marescalco, 1960–68 (commedia, 2, Malipiero, after P. Aretino), Treviso, Comunale, 22 Oct 1969, vs (Milan, 1970)

Gli eroi di Bonaventura, 1968 (2, Malipiero), Milan, Piccola Scala, 7 Feb 1969, unpubd [mostly anthology of excerpts from earlier Malipiero ops]

Uno dei Dieci, 1970 (1, Malipiero), Siena, Rinnuovati, 28 Aug 1971, vs (Milan, 1972)

L'Iscariota, 1970 (1, Malipiero, after anon. *Iscariot's Bitter Love*), Siena, Rinnuovati, 28 Aug 1971, vs (Milan, 1972)

EDITIONS

C. Monteverdi: *L'Orfeo* (London, 1923)

Tutte le opere di Claudio Monteverdi (Asolo, Gardone Riviera and Vienna, 1926–42, 2/1954)

C. Monteverdi: *Combattimento di Tancredi e Clorinda* (London, 1931)

C. Monteverdi: *L'Orfeo*, 1943 (Milan, 1950) [adapted to orig. 1607 Mantuan lib.]

WRITINGS

Teatro (Bologna, 1920, 2/1927) [libs. of his own stage works]

I profeti di Babilonia (Milan, 1924) [selection of 18th-century writings and satires criticizing opera]

Il filo d'Arianna: saggi e fantasie (Turin, 1966)

L'armonioso labirinto: teatro da musica 1913–1970, ed. M. Pieri (Venice, 1992) [collected libs. of stage works]

Articles in periodicals, newspapers etc., some repr. in *Il filo* or in books mentioned below

*

MONOGRAPHS AND COLLECTIONS OF ESSAYS

F. Alfano, A. Casella, M. Castelnuovo-Tedesco and others: *Malipiero e le sue 'Sette canzoni'* (Rome, 1929)

RaM, xv (1942), 37–112 [Malipiero issue; most important contributions repr. (some rev.) in Scarpa (1952), 81–146]

F. Ballo: *'I "capricci" di Callot' di G. F. Malipiero* (Milan, 1942)

M. Bontempelli and R. Cumar: *G. Francesco Malipiero* (Milan, 1942) [incl. some writings by Malipiero]

G. Scarpa, ed.: *L'opera di Gian Francesco Malipiero* (Treviso, 1952) [incl. many writings by Malipiero]

Approdo musicale, no.9 (1960) [Malipiero issue, incl. P. Santi: 'Il teatro di Gian Francesco Malipiero', 19–112; chronology of life and works, ed. A. Mantelli, 163–204]

Omaggio a Malipiero: Venice 1972 [Studi di musica veneta, iv, ed. M. Messinis (Florence, 1977); incl. L. Alberti: 'L'interpretazione registica e scenografica', 55–77]

G. F. Malipiero e le nuove forme della musica europea: Reggio Emilia 1982 [*Quaderni di Musicalrealtà*, iii, ed. L. Pestalozza (1984); incl. F. Degrada: 'Strutture musicali del "Torneo notturno"', 66–82; R. Dalmone: 'Le fonti letterarie del teatro malipieriano (L'Orfeide)', 95–111; G. Livio: 'I testi e le forme del teatro malipieriano: La favola del figlio cambiato', 112–36; C. Orselli: 'Fantasmi goldoniani nel teatro di Malipiero', 175–87]

M. T. Muraro and J. C. G. Waterhouse, eds.: *Malipiero, scrittura e critica*, Studi di musica veneta, viii (Florence, 1984) [incl. proceedings of conference held at Venice and Asolo, 1982, and some of Malipiero's previously uncollected articles]

J. C. G. Waterhouse: *La musica di Gian Francesco Malipiero* (Turin and Rome, 1990)

ARTICLES ON SPECIFIC WORKS

G. Barini: '"Canossa" di Silvio Benco e G. Francesco Malipiero', *Nuova antologia*, no.253 (1914), 538–41

S. A. Luciani: 'Una nuova forma di dramma musicale (le espressioni drammatiche di G. F. Malipiero)', *Ars nova* [Rome], iii/1 (1918), 4–6 [on *Sette canzoni*]

G. M. Gatti: 'Le "espressioni drammatiche" di G. F. Malipiero (Sette canzoni)', *RMI*, xxvi (1919), 690–712

L. Laloy: 'Les Sept chansons de Malipiero', *Comoedia* [Paris] (12 July 1920); repr. in Scarpa (1952), 3–6

F. B. Pratella: '"L'Orfeide" di G. Francesco Malipiero', *Pensiero musicale*, iii (1923), 7–10, 28–32

H. F. Redlich: 'G. F. Malipiero und die neue Oper', *Musikblätter des Anbruch*, xi (1929), 325–30

G. Rossi-Doria: 'Il teatro musicale di G. F. Malipiero', *RaM*, ii (1929), 354–64; Fr. trans. in *Musique* [Paris], iii (1929–30), 100–04, 168–71

S. Goddard: 'Malipiero's "L'Orfeo"', *The Chesterian*, xii (1930–31), 33–8

M. Bruschettini: 'Il "Torneo notturno" di G. F. Malipiero', *Italia musicale* [Genoa], iv/8 (1931), 1–3

H. F. Redlich: 'Francesco Malipiero: dramaturge lyrique', *ReM*, no.120 (1931), 300–04

L. [F.] D'Amico: 'Il "Torneo" di Malipiero a Roma', *Italia letteraria* [Rome], iv/50 (1932), 5

D. de' Paoli: 'Lettera da Coburgo', *RaM*, vi (1933), 59–62 [on *Il mistero di Venezia*]

G. Rossi-Doria: 'Musica', *Nuova antologia*, no.366 (1933), 312–14 [on *Il finto Arlecchino*]

G. M. Gatti: 'Malipiero and Pirandello at the Opera', *MM*, xi (1934), 213–16 [on *La favola del figlio cambiato*; serious errors in Eng. trans.]

H. Prunières: 'Un opéra de Pirandello et Malipiero', *ReM*, no.144 (1934), 207–11 [on *La favola*]

G. Rossi-Doria: 'Lettera da Roma', *RaM*, vii (1934), 228–31 [on *La favola*]

H. H. Stuckenschmidt: 'Zu Malipieros Bühnenwerken', *Melos*, xiii (1934), 47–51; It. trans. in Scarpa (1952), 71–5

H. Malherbe [pseud. of H. Croisilles]: 'Malipiero's *Pantéa*', *The Chesterian*, xvii (1935–6), 26–8

A. Mantelli: 'Lettera da Firenze: "Antonio e Cleopatra" di Malipiero', *RaM*, xi (1938), 239–41

A. Gasco: 'Canzoni e burrasche al Teatro Reale (1929)' [on *Sette canzoni*] and '"La favola del figlio cambiato" al Teatro Reale (1934)', *Da Cimarosa a Strawinsky* (Rome, 1939), 422–6, 427–34

H. Fleischer: 'Pour l'étranger: "L'allegra brigata" de G. F. Malipiero', *Il diapason* [Rome], i/6–7 (1950), 26–8

F. D'Amico: 'La farsa degli equivoci nella "Favola del figlio cambiato"', *Vie Nuove* [Rome], viii/33 (1952), 19; enlarged in *Cinquant'anni del Teatro dell'Opera 1928 Roma 1978*, ed. J. Tognelli (Rome, 1979), 207–9

M. Mila: 'L'*Eneide* in bassorilievo', *Cronache musicali 1955–1959* (Turin, 1959), 173–5

F. D'Amico: '"Mondi celesti e infernali" di G. F. Malipiero', *Musica d'oggi*, new ser., iv/1 (1961), 34–5

G. Gavazzeni: 'Le "Sette canzoni" di G. Francesco Malipiero', *RaM*, xxxii (1962), 143–50

F. D'Amico: 'I vestiti che cantano', *L'espresso* [Rome], xiv/4 (1968), 22 [on *I capricci di Callot*]

——: 'Bonaventura vestito da Arlecchino', *L'espresso*, xv/7 (1969), 22 [on *Gli eroi di Bonaventura*]

——: 'Malipiero al Comunale di Treviso: un angelo nell'alcova', *L'espresso*, xv/44 (1969), 30 [on *Il capitan Spavento* and *Il marescalco*]

L. Pinzauti: 'Malipiero and his "Sette canzoni"', *Opera*, xx (1969), 670–73

J. C. G. Waterhouse: 'Malipiero's "Sette canzoni"', *MT*, cx (1969), 826–8

L. Alberti: 'Annotazioni drammaturgiche sul più recente Malipiero', *Chigiana*, xxviii (1971), 263–70 [principally on *Il figliuol prodigo*, *Uno dei Dieci* and *L'Iscariota*]

F. D'Amico: 'La settimana senese: Giuda e i suoi ciceroni', *L'espresso*, xvii/37 (1971), 23 [on *Il figliuol prodigo*, *Uno dei Dieci* and *L'Iscariota*]

——: 'Malipiero a Palermo: melodie prima del diluvio', *L'espresso*, xviii/15 (1972), 22 [on *Filomela*, *Merlino* and *Uno dei Dieci*]

C. Orselli: 'La favola del figlio cambiato' and G. Gualerzi: 'Cenni sul teatro di Malipiero in Italia', *La favola del figlio cambiato* (Palermo, Teatro Massimo, 1979–80) [programme notes]

F. D'Amico: 'Idiota sì, ma con lo scettro', *L'espresso*, xxvi/17 (1980), 188–94 [on *La favola*]

L. Pestalozza: 'Gian Francesco Malipiero: le canzoni del silenzio', *Musica italiana del primo novecento: la generazione dell'80: Florence 1980*, 311–22 [on *Sette canzoni*]

G. Petrocchi: 'Il carteggio Pirandello-Malipiero', *Ariel* [Rome], i/3 (1986), 126–38 [on *La favola*]

R. Tedeschi: 'D'Annunzio-Malipiero: un "sogno" durato tre quarti di secolo', *Rivista del Museo teatrale alla Scala*, i/1 (1988–9), 58–9 [on *Sogno d'un tramonto d'autunno*]

J. C. G. Waterhouse: 'Between Opera and Music Theatre: Gian Francesco Malipiero's Rebellion against the Italian Operatic Establishment, 1917–29', *ATI Journal*, no.56 (1989), 27–38 [Association of Teachers of Italian pubn]

OTHER LITERATURE

G. M. Gatti: 'Musicisti italiani: G. Francesco Malipiero', *Critica musicale*, i (1918), 40–47; repr. in G. M. Gatti: *Musicisti moderni d'Italia e di fuori* (Bologna, 1920, 2/1925), 75–86

H. Prunières: 'Le renouveau musical en Italie: G. Francesco Malipiero', *Mercure de France*, cxxxiii (1919), 212–30; Eng. trans. as 'G. Francesco Malipiero', *MQ*, vi (1920), 326–41

L. Henry: 'Contemporaries: G. Francesco Malipiero', *MO*, xliii (1919–20), 954–5; repr. in Scarpa (1952), 7–15

G. M. Gatti: 'Musica: Italia: aspetti dell'arte di Malipiero', *L'esame* [Milan], ii (1923), 823–31; rev. as 'Musicisti contemporanei: G. Francesco Malipiero', *Il pianoforte*, vi (1925), 147–57; repr. in Scarpa (1952), 25–39; Eng. trans., further rev., as 'Malipiero: Romantic and Classic', *MMR*, lxv (1935), 54–6

H. Prunières: 'G. Francesco Malipiero', *ReM*, viii/3 (1927), 5–25; repr. in Scarpa (1952), 40–60

G. Bastianelli: 'Gian Francesco Malipiero', *Solaria* [Florence], ii/2 (1927), 50–57; repr. in Scarpa (1952), 61–5; variant version in G. Bastianelli: *Il nuovo dio della musica*, ed. M. de Angelis (Turin, 1978), 143–7

D. de' Paoli: *La crisi musicale italiana* (Milan, 1939), esp. 215–51

——: 'Gabriele d'Annunzio, la musica e i musicisti', *Nel centenario di Gabriele d'Annunzio* (Turin, 1963), 41–125, esp. 114–18 [RAI pubn]

J. C. G. Waterhouse: *The Emergence of Modern Italian Music (up to 1940)* (diss., U. of Oxford, 1968), esp. 388–504

A. Gentilucci: *Guida all'ascolto della musica contemporanea* (Milan, 1969), esp. 250–55

F. Nicolodi: 'L'opera lirica del '900 in Italia: considerazioni e aspetti inediti', *Quarant'anni di spettacolo in Italia attraverso l'opera di Maria de' Matteis* (Florence, 1979), 19–37, esp. 20–22, 34

J. C. G. Waterhouse: 'I lavori "distrutti" di Gian Francesco Malipiero: brani da un "Work in Progress"', *NRMI*, xiii (1979), 564–602

——: 'G. F. Malipiero's Crisis Years (1913–19)', *PRMA*, cviii (1981–2), 126–40

F. Nicolodi: *Musica e musicisti nel ventennio fascista* (Fiesole, nr Florence, 1984), esp. 200–35, 348–70

J. C. G. Waterhouse: *G. F. Malipiero's 'Chester Period'* (London, 1985) [leaflet on works pubd by Chester and Wilhelm Hansen]

N. Fortune: 'The Rediscovery of "Orfeo"' and appxes 1 and 2, *Claudio Monteverdi: Orfeo*, ed. J. Whenham (Cambridge, 1986), 78–118, 173–81

R. Tedeschi: 'Gian Francesco Malipiero: il sogno', *D'Annunzio e la musica* (Scandicci, nr Florence, 1988), 108–15

JOHN C. G. WATERHOUSE

Malipiero, Giovanni (*b* Padua, 20 April 1906; *d* Padua, 10 April 1970). Italian tenor. He studied at Padua and made his début at Cremona in 1931 as the Duke in *Rigoletto*. He first appeared at La Scala in 1937 and was among the artists who sang under Toscanini at the reopening of the theatre after the war. Here he repeated the success he had had on records, partnering Lina Pagliughi in *Lucia di Lammermoor*. He also won critical esteem with his characterizations as Jean in Massenet's *Le jongleur de Notre Dame* and as Sancho Panza in Frazzi's *Don Chisciotte* in 1952. Heard and admired in lyric and later comprimario roles throughout Italy, he also sang in South America and in most European countries, though never in England. Records show a clear, well-trained voice and a technique which Italians recognized as being of the old school.

J. B. STEANE

Malipiero, Riccardo (*b* Milan, 24 July 1914). Italian composer. Besides studying with his uncle, Gian Francesco Malipiero, he took a diploma in piano at the Milan Conservatory in 1932 and in composition at the Turin Conservatory in 1937. He then devoted his attention to composing and, from 1945 to 1966, to music criticism; he gave lessons, lectures and courses in Latin America and the USA, and from 1969 to 1984 he was director of the Liceo Musicale in Varese.

Malipiero's first opera, *Minnie la candida* (1942), was also his first important work. His use in it of atonality shows cultural affinities with Dallapiccola's *Volo di notte*, which he then knew only from broadcasts. Malipiero's taste for experiment, lucid intellectual control and expressive reticence, combined with a free lyrical impulse, are already evident in *Minnie*. His choice of Massimo Bontempelli as the source for a libretto is significant: in Bontempelli's 'magic realism' the play of intelligence and irony can produce fantasy and unreality from everyday events. Minnie (soprano) takes seriously a friend's joking remark that some people are made artificially to the point that she comes to believe that she is artificial and commits suicide. Malipiero's vocalization favours a flexible declamatory line (in which the influence of his uncle is evident) over limpid and elegant orchestral writing. Some parts of *Minnie la candida* reveal an unconscious adoption of the 12-note scale, which Malipiero was one of the first Italian composers to use.

He returned to the theatre with the comic opera *La donna è mobile* (1954) to a libretto by Guglielmo Zucconi, freely based on Bontempelli's comedy *Nostra Dea*. The adventures of the protagonist, Dea (soprano), who changes her mood as she changes her clothes, is the pretext for simple, humorous entertainment. The elaborate score features varied, changing 'iridescences' through a flexible use of the 12-note scale and, when justified by the action, parodic treatment of Puccini and 19th-century melodrama. A mixture of the dramatic and the grotesque, of irony and obsession characterizes Malipiero's third opera, *Battono alla porta* (1962), in which the châtelaine of an aristocratic villa, Countess Matilde (mezzo-soprano), refuses to take action against the hurricane that eventually destroys her home.

Minnie la candida (3, Malipiero, after M. Bontempelli), Parma, 19 Nov 1942

La donna è mobile, 1954 (comic op, 1, G. Zucconi, after Bontempelli: *Nostra Dea*), Milan, Piccola Scala, 22 Feb 1957

Battono alla porta (television op, 1, D. Buzzati), RAI, 12 Feb 1962; stage, Genova, 24 May 1963

*

C. Sartori and P. Santi: *Due tempi di Riccardo Malipiero* (Milan, 1964)

PAOLO PETAZZI

Maliponte, Adriana (*b* Brescia, 26 Dec 1938). Italian soprano. Her teachers included Suzanne Steppen in

Mulhouse and Carmen Melis in Como. In 1958 she made her stage début at the Teatro Nuovo, Milan, in *La bohème*, and in 1960 won the Geneva International Competition. She made her Paris Opéra début as Micaëla in March 1962 and attracted international attention when she created Sardula in Menotti's *Le dernier sauvage* at the Opéra-Comique (1963). She first appeared at La Scala in 1970 as Massenet's Manon and made her Metropolitan Opera début in 1971 as Mimì. Subsequent New York roles have included Gluck's Eurydice, Pamina, Gounod's Juliet, Luisa Miller, and Micaëla in the posthumously re-created production of *Carmen* (1972) conceived by Göran Gentele. Maliponte first appeared at Covent Garden in February 1976, as Nedda. She sang Gemma di Vergy at Bergamo (1987) and Luisa Miller at Turin (1990). A remarkably versatile singing actress, she balances lyrical finesse with dramatic intensity in a manner that lends individuality to her roles.
MARTIN BERNHEIMER

Maliszewski, Witold (*b* Mogilev Podol'skiy, 8/20 July 1873; *d* Zalesie, nr Warsaw, 18 July 1939). Polish composer. He graduated in medicine at St Petersburg (1897), then studied at the conservatory with Rimsky-Korsakov (1898–1902). In Odessa he taught at the conservatory (1908–21) and conducted the symphony orchestra, then moved to Warsaw as professor of its conservatory and director of the Chopin School. He won several composition prizes, including the Paris (1923) and the Geneva (1928). Maliszewski was a Romantic, whose music shows the influence of Rimsky-Korsakov and Glazunov in orchestration and melody, and, after his return to Poland, of Polish folktunes and rhythms. He wrote two four-act opera-ballets during the period when his talent had fully matured, both first performed at the Wielki Theatre, Warsaw. *Syrena* ('The Mermaid') op.24, to a libretto by L. M. Rogowski, based on the fairy-tale by Hans Andersen, was first performed on 21 April 1928; *Boruta* op.26, to a libretto by A. Oppman, on 15 March 1930. In both, ballet scenes predominate and perform a descriptive function, sometimes hardly connected with the plot: the vocal scenes provide the dramatic intensity. *The Mermaid* is distinguished by a keen theatrical sense and colourful orchestration.
ZOFIA CHECHLIŃSKA

Maliy Opera Theatre. Theatre in ST PETERSBURG, used for opera from 1918.

Mallinger [née Lichtenegger], **Mathilde** (*b* Zagreb, 17 Feb 1847; *d* Berlin, 19 April 1920). Croatian soprano. After studying at the Prague Conservatory with Gordigiani and in Vienna with Loewy, she was engaged at the Hofoper, Munich, where she made her début in 1866 as Norma. While at Munich she sang Elsa, Elisabeth (*Tannhäuser*) and Eva at the first performance of *Die Meistersinger* (1868). She was then engaged at the Hofoper, Berlin, making her début as Elsa (1869) and remaining there until her retirement in 1882. She took part in the first Berlin performances of *Die Meistersinger* (1870) and *Aida* (1874), and her repertory also included Leonore, Agathe, Sieglinde, Valentine (*Les Huguenots*) and Mozart's Pamina, Donna Anna and Countess Almaviva. Her voice, essentially a lyric soprano, was not large but so well schooled that she could sing heavier, dramatic roles without strain.

A. Ehrlich: *Berühmte Sängerinnen der Vergangenheit und Gegenwart* (Leipzig, 1895)
J. Kapp: *Geschichte der Staatsoper Berlin* (Berlin, 1937)
H. Fetting: *Die Geschichte der Deutschen Staatsoper* (Berlin, 1955)
H. Wagner: *200 Jahre Münchner Theaterchronik 1750–1950* (Munich, 1958)
ELIZABETH FORBES

Mallorca. For discussion of opera in Mallorca *see* PALMA DE MALLORCA.

Malta. Island in the Mediterranean. It was ceded in 1530 by the Emperor Charles V to the Knights of Rhodes, later the Knights of St John of Jerusalem. In the 17th century, masques, pageants and operas were performed by the knights and their employees. The Grand Master, Antonio Manuel de Vilhema, built the Teatro Pubblico, inaugurated on 9 January 1732 with the tragedy *Merope* by Scipione Maffei. The theatre later became the Teatro Real, then, in 1866, the Manoel Theatre (in honour of its founder); it was run by a senior knight (the 'Protettore'). Italian operas by Jommelli, Piccinni, Galuppi, Paisiello and others were produced during the next 60 years. During the period of Napoleon's holding the island, 1798–1800, the Maltese composer Nicolas Isouard became director. The island was ceded to the British in 1814. In 1811 and 1834 the theatre was enlarged, to about 480 seats; the season lasted from September to May and the impresario was obliged to present at least 12 operas each season, five of them new to Malta. By the 1860s, 32 of Donizetti's works had been staged and almost all Verdi's to date.

Because of the success of opera with the garrison, the fleet, the islanders and the increasing number of tourists, the Real became inadequate and in 1860 a new theatre was planned: it was built by Edward M. Barry, the architect of Covent Garden (1858), and inaugurated as the Royal Opera House on 9 October 1866 with *I puritani*. In 1873, during a rehearsal of Privitera's *La vergine del castello*, it burnt down. The Manoel was put back to service during the rebuilding; the new theatre, seating 1095 with 200 standing places, was inaugurated on 11 October 1877 with *Aida* (in the presence of the Duke of Edinburgh). Until World War II it was run as one of the principal Italian opera houses, with all works, including Wagner and the French and Russian repertories, being sung in Italian by leading singers, among them Albani, Scotti and Stabile. New Italian works were often given within months of their premières.

On 7 April 1943, in an air raid, the Royal Opera House was reduced to rubble, and the Manoel was again pressed back into service. Plans to rebuild the Royal Opera came to nothing, and in 1961 the Manoel was acquired by the government and restored as the Maltese National Theatre. Italian opera returned, subsidized by the Italian government during the period 1966–8 and in 1972. The seasons, often given by smaller Italian and Bulgarian as well as local companies, are more modest than in the past. In the summer, open-air performances are given in the theatre on Manoel Island.

The Manoel Theatre (Valletta, n.d.)
J. Bonnici and M. Cassar: *The Royal Opera House* (Valletta, 1990)
C. Pitt: 'L'opéra à Malte', *Opéra international* (forthcoming)
CHARLES PITT

Malta, Alexander (*b* Visp, 28 Feb 1942). Swiss bass. He studied in Zürich and in Italy, making his début in 1966

at Stuttgart as the Monk in *Don Carlos*. Engaged at Munich, he appeared at Cologne, Berlin, Vienna, Zürich, Geneva, Milan and Florence, where in 1983 he sang the Landgrave (*Tannhäuser*). He made his American début in 1976 at San Francisco, later appearing at Chicago and Philadelphia; in 1985 he sang Zuniga at Salzburg and made his Covent Garden début as Tippett's King Priam. His wide repertory includes Osmin, Masetto, Don Pasquale, Fasolt, Colline, Golaud, Orestes, Count Waldner, Isaac (*Betrothal in a Monastery*) and Animal-Tamer/Athlete (*Lulu*), which he sang at Brussels in 1988. A fine character actor with a strong voice, he excels in roles such as the Doctor (*Wozzeck*).
ELIZABETH FORBES

Malten [Müller], Therese (*b* Insterburg, Prussia, 21 June 1855; *d* Neuzschieren, nr Dresden, 2 Jan 1930). German soprano. After studying with Gustav Engel in Berlin, she made her début in 1873 as Pamina at the Dresden Hofoper, where she was engaged for the next 30 years. Wagner heard her as Senta there in 1881 and invited her to Bayreuth the following summer to share the role of Kundry with Materna and Brandt in the first performance of *Parsifal*. She also sang Kundry at Munich in the private performances given for King Ludwig and at the Albert Hall, in the first concert performance in London (1884). She had previously made her London début at Drury Lane in 1882 as Leonore (*Fidelio*), a role she repeated in Munich. At Dresden she sang Isolde, Brünnhilde and many other roles in French, Italian and German operas, ranging from Gluck's *Armide* to *Cavalleria rusticana*. Returning to Bayreuth she sang Isolde (1886), Eva (1888) and Kundry for the last time in 1894. She also took part in the *Ring* cycles presented by Angelo Neumann in St Petersburg and Moscow (1889). Her voice was notable for its extensive compass; its middle register was rich and powerful with the higher and lower notes equally strong and pleasing.

A. Ehrlich: *Berühmte Sängerinnen der Vergangenheit und Gegenwart* (Leipzig, 1895)
E. Newman: *The Life of Richard Wagner* (London, 1933–47)
G. Skelton: *Wagner at Bayreuth* (London, 1965)
ELIZABETH FORBES

Malvezzi. Theatre in BOLOGNA, built by Marquess Francesco Pirro Malvezzi in 1653 and burnt down in 1745.

Mamedova, Shevket (Hassan-kïzi) (*b* Tbilisi, 6/18 April 1897). Azerbaijani soprano. She studied first at the Kiev Conservatory (1917–21) with Shperling, then in Milan and Paris (1927–9). She made her début in 1921 as Violetta at the Azerbaijan State Theatre, Baku, where she sang until 1948. Mamedova was one of the founders of opera in Azerbaijan, combining European culture and technique with her characteristic national style, and her performances were noted for integrity and taste. She sang Guchokhra in Hajibeyov's *The Travelling Salesman* in 1922, and created Glier's Shakh-Senem (1934) and Mahomayev's Nergiz (1936); she also sang Gyul'sara in Mahomayev's *Shakh Ismail* in 1940. Her career took her to Moscow, Leningrad and Kiev, to France and to Iran. She organized the first drama school in Azerbaijan (1923), and published *Puti razvitiya azerbaydzhanskogo muzïkal'nogo teatra* ('Paths of Development of Azerbaijani Music Theatre', Moscow, 1931).

E. Abasova: 'Shevket-Khanum Mamedova', *SovM* (1959), no.11, pp.121–4
L. Karagicheva: 'Shevket-Khanum Mamedova', *Azerbaydzhanskaya muzïka*, ed. J. Hajiyev and others (Moscow, 1961), 337–43
L. Bretanitskaya: 'Shevket Mamedova', *Muzïkal'naya zhizn'* (1967), no.11, pp.18–19
I. M. YAMPOL'SKY

Mamelles de Tirésias, Les ('The Breasts of Tiresias'). *Opéra bouffe* in a prologue and two acts by FRANCIS POULENC to his own libretto after Guillaume Apollinaire's play; Paris, Opéra-Comique (Salle Favart), 3 June 1947.

Apollinaire's text was written in 1903 but revised and first performed in 1917. In his introduction to the play he coined the word 'surrealist' and its plot encapsulates everything that has come to be understood by that term. Familiar settings and realistic behaviour are turned on their heads, reshuffled and juxtaposed, producing effects and events which, though recognizable, become variously hilarious, impossible and disturbing. Nonetheless the published version has serious reverberations. It was revised in time of war and its message, the need to repopulate and re-establish France, was equally real for Poulenc in the years 1940–44 when he was planning and shaping his opera.

The work seems to open seriously with the Theatre Director (baritone) addressing the audience in front of the curtain, exhorting them to 'make children – like you never have before'. The curtain rises on 'Zanzibar', a location which Poulenc, in his own mind at least, changed to Monte Carlo (he frequently needed to 'locate' a work precisely, even down to a particular Parisian street, before he could write a note of music). A vertiginous presto introduces Thérèse (soprano), who declares that she is bored with being a woman, and would rather be a soldier, waiter, president of the republic. We hear her husband (baritone; sometimes sung by a tenor) off stage demanding his bacon ('donnez-moi du lard!') while Thérèse, a self-styled feminist, comments that 'he only thinks of love'. She grows a beard, opens her gown to release her breasts (two coloured balloons) and sings a ravishing *café-concert* waltz as they fly away. A new moustache completes her metamorphosis, which is so convincing that when her husband enters he assumes that an assassin has killed her and put on her clothes. She tries to explain: she is Thérèse yet no longer a woman, thus no longer his wife and henceforward to be called Tirésias. She prepares to move out, as the husband comments 'La situation devient grave', but is interrupted: a comic polka à la Prokofiev announces Presto (baritone) and Lacouf ('Trial' tenor), two old friends who are having an argument over whether they are in Paris or Zanzibar. They draw guns and kill each other (but reappear, on roller-skates, for the Act 1 finale). The mood shifts again as the chorus sing epitaphs for the two men. The setting of the magic words 'Seine' and 'Paris', even in this absurd context, suffuses the music with a Ravelian lyricism. (Poulenc was, in 1944, in self-imposed exile from his beloved city, then under Nazi occupation.) A policeman (baritone) arrives, scenting a crime. He pays extravagant court to the husband, by now dressed in his wife's discarded clothes. In a solemn aria the husband declares that since the women of Zanzibar wish to have political rights, the men must

'Les mamelles de Tirésias' (Poulenc): Act 1 finale, from the original production at the Opéra-Comique (Salle Favart) in Paris, 3 June 1947, designed by Erté

make babies themselves. He promises to show the policeman how.

Act 2 opens with an entr'acte of Stravinskian severity leading to a mysterious dance in which couples glide around to a strange syncopated sarabande: Ravelian harmonies rendered by a music-hall band in the pit replete with overblown piano part. The band is asked to sing a yowling chorus portraying the 40 049 children that the husband has produced in one day. This bizarre effect is only one of many tricks – falsetto notes, sneezes, laughs and quirky accents – with which Poulenc peppers the piece in an attempt to reproduce Apollinaire's 'sound score' of odd noises off.

A journalist arrives from Paris (another sad swoon from the orchestra) to ask the secret of the husband's success. Surely he must be rich? The husband admits that the children support him, rather than the other way round. Joseph, for example, has already written a best-selling novel. The journalist, impressed, asks for a loan and is thrown out. Deciding to make a journalist of his own, the husband pours ink and glue into one of the cradles that are filling the stage, and adds a pair of scissors. A son is born, a fully-fledged journalist. Unfortunately he is from the gutter press and in a rapid patter tries to blackmail his father. He exits in order to make up tomorrow's news. To feed his flock the husband requires ration cards, available (where else?) from the Cartomancer. She is none other than Thérèse/Tirésias in a further disguise, iterating the husband's doctrine of fecundity. She is arrested by the policeman, whom she strangles; she then reveals herself to her husband. The policeman revives. To restore her full femininity the husband fetches balloons which Thérèse looses, amid lyrical music, into the night sky. A nonsense finale ('sing night and day – scratch yourself if you itch') wraps up the proceedings suitably rumbustiously.

Poulenc's music reflects the delight and love he found in Apollinaire's play; it is bursting with melodic invention and unfeigned charm. Having chosen his medium, the *opéra bouffe*, he then ransacked French musical history from 1870 to 1920. There are numerous echoes of Offenbach, Messager, Chabrier's *L'étoile* and Ravel's *L'heure espagnole*, not to mention numerous comic operas by lesser-known composers such as Maurice Yvain and Henri Christiné which were all the rage in 1916 and whose 'tinkly' pianos and seductive trumpets haunt Poulenc's score. Despite this abundance of comic music, the composer's restraint and taste win the day. There are obvious influences, but it could only have been written by Poulenc: in the exalted company of his great secular cantata *Figure humaine* and his *Stabat mater* he considered it one of his most 'authentic' works.

Poulenc prepared a transcription of the score for two pianos which was used for a performance at Aldeburgh on 13 June 1958, conducted by Charles Mackerras with Benjamin Britten and Viola Tunnard playing the pianos.

JEREMY SAMS

Mamiya, Michio (*b* Asahikawa, 29 June 1929). Japanese composer. He studied composition privately with Ikenouchi, and later at the Tokyo Geijutsu Daigaku (National University of Fine Arts and Music), 1948–52. About 1952 he began to show a particular interest in Japanese folk music, notating tunes and using some of them in instrumental compositions. He continued field studies in collaboration with the singer Ruriko Uchida, subsequently writing songs and choral works in which he makes effective use of folk music. His first opera, *Mukashibanashi Hitokai Tarobei* ('The Old Tale: Tarobei, the Slave Dealer', 1959), also uses folk materials successfully, as well as the vocal style of traditional Japanese music. In his next opera, *Nihonzaru Sukitoorime* ('Clairvoyant Monkey Painter', 1965), a satirical drama about a monkey world, Mamiya employs a full orchestra, with Renaissance ensemble, a bagpipe and organ. His third opera, *Narukami* (1974), a television opera for four singers, male chorus and chamber orchestra, based on a kabuki play (a theatrical form popular since the 17th century) of the same title, won a *grand prix* at the Salzburg Opera Festival.

Mukashibanashi Hitokai Tarobei [The Old Tale: Tarobei, the Slave Dealer] (radio op, 1, I. Wakabayashi, after folktale), NHK, June 1959; stage, Tokyo, Sōgetsu Kaikan, 19 June 1961
Nihonzaru sukitoorime [Clairvoyant Monkey Painter] (radio op, 1, H. Kijima), NHK, 21 March 1965; stage, Tokyo, Metropolitan Festival Hall, 14 March 1966
Narukami (television op, 1, Mamiya, after kabuki play *Narukami* and noh play *Ikkakusennin*), NHK, June 1974

MASAKATA KANAZAWA

Mamontov, Savva Ivanovich (*b* Yalutorovsk, 3/15 Oct 1841; *d* Moscow, 6 April 1918). Russian impresario, director of the MOSCOW Private Russian Opera Company from 1885.

Manaus. City in north-western Brazil, on the Amazon River 1450 km upstream from the Atlantic Ocean. It was founded in 1660 and became the state capital of Amazonas in 1850. After 1890 the wealth brought by the rubber boom resulted in the erection of the ornate 1000-seat Teatro Amazonas, inaugurated on 31 December 1896 with a programme of miscellaneous Italian opera excerpts. During the apogee of its imported seasons, the Companhia Lírica Italiana, contracted by José Fernandes de Carvalho, opened its 1901 season on 29 June with *La Gioconda*, followed by *La bohème*, *Rigoletto*, *Il trovatore*, *Un ballo in maschera*, *Aida*, *Il barbiere di Siviglia* and *Cavalleria rusticana* with *Pagliacci*. On 23 July the same company gave Carlos Gomes's *Il Guarany*. Other standard operas continued until 15 August. In September a zarzuela company arrived; directed by the Mexican impresario Gustavo de María Campos, it brought 28 zarzuelas, four operettas and four operas (including as a novelty Arrieta's *Marina*). The following year Carvalho brought 19 soloists, a chorus of 32 and an orchestra of 16; to the six operas given in 1901, his company added *Ernani*, *Faust*, Gomes's *Fosca* and ten operettas.

Opera seasons, interspersed with concerts by travelling virtuosos, continued until 1907; in that year local premières were given of *La favorite*, *Les Huguenots*, *L'Africaine*, and *La Juive*. Between 1909 and 1937 the Teatro Amazonas was no longer host to touring opera companies. Rebuilt in 1929 and restored in 1974 and again during 1987–9, the theatre (now with 685 seats) was used about once a month for plays. On 17 March 1990, opera returned with an all-Brazilian programme, which included selections from Gomes's *Lo schiavo* and *Il Guarany*. An international season followed, beginning with *Carmen* on 29 March.

*

M. Ypiranga Monteiro: *Teatro Amazonas* (Manaus, 1965)
'Chronicle', *New York Times* (12 March 1990)
'Arias grace the Amazon once again', *New York Times* (19 March 1990)

ROBERT STEVENSON

Manchester. City in north-west England. A centre of commerce and industry, it has had a thriving musical life since the 18th century and is the home of the Hallé Orchestra, although it has never succeeded in establishing its own opera company. Various attempts have proved abortive or short-lived, one of the first involving Charles Hallé in 1854–5, before he founded his orchestra. In 1916 and 1917 Sir Thomas Beecham financed two memorable seasons, with the Hallé Orchestra in the pit. Their success impelled him to offer to build an opera house in the city on condition that he be allowed to direct it, but the matter was not pursued

and Beecham shortly afterwards retired temporarily from the musical scene because of personal financial problems. In 1978 the Palace Theatre was bought by a Manchester businessman and extensively refurbished in the expectation that the Royal Opera would make it a second home. Two visits were made, in 1981 and 1983, but the Arts Council turned its back on touring by the major London companies. Since then Manchester's professional opera has consisted of regular visits by Opera North, Glyndebourne Touring Opera and, occasionally, other regional companies.

For many years Manchester was a regular venue for touring opera companies such as the Carl Rosa, who gave the British première of *La bohème* in 1897, at the Comedy Theatre, and that of *Andrea Chénier* in 1903. Between the two world wars the British National Opera Company and its successor, the Covent Garden English Opera Company, visited Manchester frequently. In 1925, at the theatre called the Opera House, the British National gave the first performance of Holst's *At the Boar's Head*. In the 20 years following World War II, the Covent Garden and Sadler's Wells companies performed in Manchester almost every year.

Manchester's reputation as an opera centre lies principally, therefore, in its educational establishments. Performance of opera was a feature of the Royal Manchester College of Music almost from its foundation, by Hallé, in 1893. At first, concert performances were given: in *Don Giovanni* in 1902 the roles of Masetto and the Commendatore were doubled by a former student, Charles Walton, father of the composer. In 1907 Hallé's successor as principal, Adolph Brodsky, conducted Verdi's *Un ballo in maschera*. But the college's operatic fame dates from Frederic Cox's appointment as principal in 1953. He was a noted singing teacher and under his tutelage ambitious productions were mounted, including *Parsifal*, *Guillaume Tell*, *Pelléas et Mélisande* and *Der Corregidor*, and notable singers emerged from among the students. When the Royal Manchester College amalgamated with the Northern School of Music in 1972 to become the Royal Northern College of Music, the new college had a splendidly equipped opera theatre; the performances staged there have become famous internationally for their high standards.

MICHAEL KENNEDY

Mancia [Manza], Luigi (*b* ?Brescia, ?c1665; *d* after 1708). Italian composer. Quadrio (1744) termed him Brescian, and the last libretto that names him is that for the performance of his opera *Partenope* at Brescia in 1710. His first known dramatic composition, *Paride in Ida*, was for the electoral court in Hanover in 1687. He had gone there in that year with the singer Ferdinando Chiaravalle and presumably remained to perform in productions at the Elector Ernst August's new opera house, which opened in 1689. Mancia contributed one aria to *Arione* (1694, Milan), a pasticcio which celebrated the emperor's birthday, but had probably returned to Italy by 1695, when his opera *Giustino* was performed in Rome on 8 January; he composed two further operas for Rome, which were both performed early in 1696. He was in Hanover for a summer production in 1697, and in Berlin by October, where he sang at a concert for the Electress (later Queen) Sophie Charlotte.

He returned to Italy to compose operas for the Spanish viceregal theatre at Naples in 1698–9. Consequently he has been identified with the 'Signor

Mancini, formerly Servant to the late King of Spain' (*BDA*), who sang at the Theatre Royal in London on 31 January 1701. He cannot, however, have been that Mancini, as on 15 January 1702 he wrote to the violinist Nicola Cosimi, who was then in London, asking him for news of the reception given to Italian music in England, for 'I have not yet seen that fine land, but I hope to greet you there shortly'. In fact, from 1701, Mancia was in Düsseldorf where he was *consigliere della camera* to the Elector Palatine Johann Wilhelm, according to the inscription on the score (in *A-Wn*) of the serenata he wrote for Karl III, the Austrian claimant to the Spanish throne, who travelled through Düsseldorf in mid-October 1703. He wrote the text as well as the music for this work and for several of his cantatas.

In 1707 he accompanied the Venetian ambassador to London, but stayed only briefly and in 1708 was back in the Veneto. He composed a serenata in honour of Karl III's wife who passed through Brescia in May of that year, and wrote his last known works. He sought also to become one of Queen Anne's musicians in London, according to a letter of 13 March 1708 to the Duchess of Marlborough written by Charles Montagu, Duke of Manchester and ambassador extraordinary in Venice (London, 1864).

Mancia's opera of 1687 has very brief arias that are not in da capo form. While later works contain da capo arias, even in these arias the *A* sections are unusually brief, because syllabic text setting with little word repetition predominates. Their texture can be rich, in five or six parts, with two viola parts, as in *Partenope* (1699). Such traits ally his style to that of his elders (Legrenzi and Stradella) rather than to that of his contemporaries (Ariosti, Gasparini and Alessandro Scarlatti).

three-act operas unless otherwise stated

Paride in Ida (N. Nicolini), Hanover, Hof, 1687; ? as Gl'amori di Paride ed Ennone in Ida, Salzthal, c1697; ? with text rev. F. Mazzari and addnl music by A. B. Colletti, Venice, S Angelo, aut. 1706 [see G. C. Bonlini, *Le glorie della poesia e della musica* (Venice, 1731), 149]; *GB-Lbl*

Giustino (after N. Beregan), Rome, Tordinona, 8 Jan 1695, arias in *D-MÜs*, *I-Bc*, *Bmalvezzi*, *Msartori*, *Rc*, *Rli* and *US-NYlibin*

Flavio Cuniberto (after M. Noris), Rome, Capranica, c25 Jan 1696, arias in *F-Pn*, *GB-Ob*, *I-Rc* and *Rvat*

Il re infante (after Noris), Rome, Capranica, Feb 1696, *Fc*, arias in *F-Pn*, *GB-Ob* and *I-Rvat*

La costanza nelle selve (O. Mauro), Hanover, Hof, sum. 1697; as La costanza trionfante, Salzthal, 12 Sept 1715; *GB-Lbl*

Tito Manlio (after Noris), Naples, S Bartolomeo, carn. 1698, *D-Dlb* (comic scenes only), arias in *I-Nc*

Partenope (S. Stampiglia), Naples, S Bartolomeo, carn. 1699, *D-Dlb* (comic scenes only), *I-Nc*

Alessandro in Susa (5, G. Frigimelica Roberti), Venice, S Giovanni Grisostomo, 28 Jan 1708, *D-W*

Doubtful: L'innocenza difesa (G. Gigli), Milan, 1700

*

BDA; *MGG* (C. Sartori)

F. S. Quadrio: *Della storia e della ragione d'ogni poesia*, iii/2 (Milan, 1744), 517, 519

C. Sartori: 'Il dilettante Luigi Mancia, dignitario dell'imperatore', *RMI*, lv (1953), 404–25

R. Freeman: 'The Travels of *Partenope*', *Studies in Music History: Essays for Oliver Strunk* (Princeton, 1968), 356–85

C. E. Troy: *The Comic Intermezzo: a Study in the History of Eighteenth-Century Italian Opera* (Ann Arbor, 1979)

L. Lindgren: 'Nicola Cosimi in London, 1701–1705', *Studi musicali*, xi (1982), 237

H. S. Saunders jr: *The Repertoire of a Venetian Opera House (1678–1714): the Teatro Grimani di San Giovanni Grisostomo* (diss., Harvard U., 1985)

A. Chiarelli: *I codici di musica della Raccolta Estense: ricostruzione dall'inventario settecentesco*, Quaderni della *RIM*, xvi (Florence, 1987)

LOWELL LINDGREN

Mancinelli, Luigi (*b* Orvieto, 6 Feb 1848; *d* Rome, 2 Feb 1921). Italian conductor and composer. He had music lessons from his brother, and later studied in Florence with Mabellini. He was a cellist in the Orvieto *cappella* (1862) and later in the Pergola theatre orchestra, Florence, then (1874) at the Teatro Morlacchi in Perugia, where he was also assistant *maestro concertatore*; he made his conducting début in *Aida*, taking over at short notice from Usiglio. The impresario Jacovacci was present and engaged him for the Teatro Apollo, Rome, where he appeared until 1881.

A success from the beginning, Mancinelli soon attained great authority as a conductor; in 1877 Boito called him the ideal interpreter of *Mefistofele*, and the publisher Giovannina Lucca, holder of the Wagner copyrights in Italian, saw him as Mariani's successor as a Wagner conductor. He also began to be known as a composer through his incidental music for Cossa's tragedies *Messalina* (1876) and *Cleopatra* (1877). In 1878 he conducted concerts in Paris, Milan, and in Bologna, where he was a founder and director of the Società del Quartetto and initiated the popular concerts at the Teatro Brunetti; he also conducted the opera season at the Comunale. From 1881 he taught at Bologna Conservatory and was *maestro di cappella* at S Petronio. In January 1883 he conducted at a concert in honour of Liszt and Wagner in Venice.

His first opera, *Isora di Provenza*, was successful in Bologna in 1884, but failed in Naples in 1886. On returning from that production, Mancinelli resigned his posts in Bologna and left the city. Gui stated that 'under the threat of a disgraceful lawsuit ... he had to leave Italy and live an exile for many years'. However, Mancinelli conducted in Bologna in 1887 and elsewhere in Italy in 1892. Augustus Harris engaged him as sole conductor of a season of Italian opera at Drury Lane in spring 1887 and as chief conductor at Covent Garden in 1888, a post he held until 1905. In 1888 he went with Harris to Bayreuth in preparation for *Die Meistersinger* with Jean de Reszke. He was chief conductor at the Madrid opera, 1887–93, and at the new Metropolitan, New York, 1893–1903, taking leave when he was composing his operas *Ero e Leandro* (1895–6) and *Paolo e Francesca* (1901–2). He conducted opera in Italy until 1911 and seasons at the S Carlos, Lisbon, from 1901 to 1919–20. In 1905 he was at the Rio de Janeiro opera and in 1908 inaugurated the Teatro Colón, Buenos Aires, returning there in 1909, 1910 and 1913. He often conducted in Spain.

Mancinelli was probably the most important Italian conductor of the generation between Faccio and Toscanini, of whom in many ways he was a forerunner: both were authoritarian, charismatic figures, put great emphasis on fidelity to the score, which they often conducted from memory, and had little patience with singers' whims and conceits. In London and New York Mancinelli conducted a wide range of operas, seldom with adequate rehearsal. In Italy and Spain he was celebrated as a champion of Wagner and Beethoven, but in London and New York his authority in this area was not undisputed. Shaw wrote of his *Lohengrin* (1889) that his

Italian temperament came repeatedly into conflict with the German temperament of the composer. Where the music should have risen to its noblest and broadest sweep he hurried on in the impetuous self-assertive Southern way that is less compatible than any other manner on earth with the grand calm of the ideal Germany.

Weingartner, on the other hand, found Mancinelli's *Meistersinger*

astonishingly good … I could never have thought that an Italian could so thoroughly master so German a score. He conducted with so much temperament and energy … and such subtle understanding of where the orchestra should dominate and where it should be subordinate, and yet without neurotics or the petty tricks of the fatal *tempo rubato*, that I could wish many a German conductor could take a lesson from him.

In his early years in London and New York Mancinelli conducted much Wagner, tailored to an Italian pattern (parts of the Trial and Prize Songs and the first part of 'Wahn, wahn', were cut for the 1889 *Meistersinger*). During his time, however, Wagner began to be sung in the original language, with Germans engaged to conduct it, and by 1900 Mancinelli was shut out of the German repertory.

Mancinelli had been judged a composer of great promise on the basis of his early incidental music and his first opera. He was placed among the progressives of the young Italian school and suffered the usual critical assessment of Wagnerism, without justification in spite of occasional superficial reminiscences. He saw Wagner as an isolated genius and himself as following the true path for Italian opera marked out by *Otello* and *Falstaff*. After becoming a busy international conductor in the late 1880s he composed little and sporadically. His promise was never realized, nor did his style develop significantly. The enthusiasm for his most important opera, *Ero e Leandro*, at its first performance in Madrid (1897) did not survive the work's transference to Italian theatres (Turin, Venice, Rome, 1898), and it had a lukewarm reception in London and New York in spite of star casts. *Paolo e Francesca* had even less success in 1907. Mancinelli was embittered by this failure, which was probably caused partly by a dramatic temperament strongly at variance with the dominating currents in Italian opera at the time, as manifested in the *verismo* school and Puccini. Mancinelli tended in his choice of librettos towards the idealism and classicism of Boito, author of *Ero e Leandro*. This is evident also in his rather abstract treatment of his characters, a tendency emphasized by his lack of facility in creating memorable melodies. This failing was often pointed out by critics, who from the 1890s usually passed him off as a conductor who dabbled in composition and who, while admirable for his fastidious and elegant craftsmanship, especially his orchestration, lacked the essential gift of individuality. He was at his best in the creation of atmosphere and background. From this derived his success in incidental and descriptive music and the appropriateness of his late ventures into film music (*Frate Sole*, 1918, and *Giuliano l'apostata*, 1920). His operas are full of excellent passages of this sort, but they tend to overwhelm the dramatic core. His greatest success was the orchestral suite *Scene veneziane* (1888); Shaw called it 'a very pretty piece of promenade music', indicating how far Mancinelli's achievements fell below his aspirations. His output also included sacred music and songs.

Isora di Provenza (dramma romantico, 3, A. Zanardini, after V. Hugo: *La légende des siècles*), Bologna, Comunale, 2 Oct 1884, vs (Milan, 1885)

Ero e Leandro (tragedia lirica, 3, A. Boito), Norwich Festival, 8 Oct 1896, vs (London and New York, 1896)

Paolo e Francesca (dramma lirico, 1, A. Colautti, after Dante: *Commedia*), Bologna, Comunale, 11 Nov 1907, vs (Milan, 1907)

Sogno di una notte d'estate, 1915–17 (fantasia lirica, 3, F. Salvatori, after W. Shakespeare), excerpts, Rome, 1922, vs (Bologna, 1922)

*

DBP ('Mancinelli, Marino')

A. K. 'Weingartner on Covent Garden and Bel Canto', *Musical Standard*, lv (1898), 20

L. Mancinelli: *Ero e Leandro: Analysis by the Composer* (New York, n.d.)

G. Orefice: *Luigi Mancinelli* (Rome, 1921)

G. B. Shaw: *Music in London 1890–94* (London, 1932)

L. Silvestri: *Luigi Mancinelli: direttore e compositore* (Milan, 1966)

V. Gui: 'Ricordo di Luigi Mancinelli', *NRMI*, v (1971), 242–8

DENNIS LIBBY

Mancini, Francesco (*b* Naples, 16 Jan 1672; *d* Naples, 22 Sept 1737). Italian composer. His work has its roots in the theatrical world of the late 17th century and reflects the salient features of late Baroque *melodramma* in its evolution towards the Classical style. Educated at the Conservatorio di S Maria della Pietà dei Turchini in Naples from 1688, he was taught by Francesco Provenzale and Gennaro Ursino. He held the post of first organist of the royal chapel from 1704 to 1706 and was briefly its director in 1708. With the arrival of Alessandro Scarlatti, Mancini became vice-*maestro* and remained in that post until Scarlatti's death in 1725, when he again took up the post of director. At the Conservatorio di S Maria di Loreto (of which he was director from 1720 to 1735), Mancini was responsible for training a new generation of composers, among them David Perez.

The gaps in the scores of Mancini's operas make it impossible to trace clearly the evolution of his compositional style, but a few distinguishing characteristics of his technique may be singled out. Prominent in his treatment of *secco* recitative (to judge by sources from 1705 to 1713; the recitatives for the 1735 production of Metastasio's *Demofoonte* are in fact by Giuseppe Sellitto, not Mancini) is his constant close attention to the relationship between music and text, with textual parentheses or punctuation often clearly reflected in *soste* (pauses) in the music; and the melodic line is used to great effect for descriptive purposes. A notable instance of recitative literally inserted between the A and B sections of an aria is that of Livia's aria 'Oh Dio che pena è questa' (*Turno Aricino*, Act 2 scene iii).

An interesting feature of the arias is that they are predominantly monothematic in the early operas, bithematic after the 1710s and polythematic from 1705 (sometimes taking the form of a lament, accompanied by an ostinato bass formed from a descending tetrachord). The duets and ensemble pieces fully reflect the characteristic tripartite structure of the arias; the choruses are used mostly for scenes of jubilation among the people, groups of soldiers, etc. and appear in the finales (in binary or da capo form, with prevalently homorhythmic writing in which the instruments double the voices) or in tripartite form in prayer scenes involving people or priests.

Particularly significant was the 1710 staging at the Queen's Theatre in the Haymarket, London, of Mancini's opera *Hydaspes* (reworked from *Gl' amanti generosi*, produced five years earlier at the Teatro S Bartolomeo); the performance, with its mock fight with a lion in the third act, was harshly attacked by the satirical journalist Joseph Addison.

A sign of Mancini's central position in Neapolitan opera after the early years of the 18th century is the presence of arias and intermezzos by him in operas by composers of such fame as G. M. Orlandini (*Artaserse*,

1708), Giovanni Bononcini (*Abdolomino*, 1711) and particularly Handel (*Agrippina*, 1713). Equally significant is the fact that his last opera, *Demofoonte* (1735), was written in collaboration with Domenico Sarro and Leonardo Leo, both rising composers on the Neapolitan operatic scene, the first destined to succeed Mancini as director of the royal chapel, the second to become, on his death, its vice-*maestro*.

See also AMANTI GENEROSI, GL'.

performed in Naples unless otherwise stated

NB – *Teatro S Bartolomeo*
dm – *dramma per musica*

Il nodo sciolto e ligato dall'affetto, o vero L'obbligo e 'l disobbligo vinti d'amore (dm boscareccio, 3), Rome, 1696

Alfonso [prol. and ints] (G. D. Pallavicini), Collegio dei Nobili, 20 Oct 1697

Ariovisto (dm, 3), NB, 15 Nov 1702

[Lucio] Silla (melodramma, 3, A. Rossini), NB, ?27 Jan 1703; for musical source of Act 2 scene xxiv see Romagnoli (1987), i, 33–5

La costanza nell'onore (commedia, 3, F. Passarini), NB, 1st week of June 1704

Gl'amanti generosi (dm, 3, G. Candi, rev. G. Convò and S. Stampiglia), NB, ?carn. 1705, *I-Mc* (R1978: IOB, li) [see also Hydaspes, 1710]

La serva favorita (melodramma, 3, G. C. Villifranchi and Convò), NB, 1705, *Mc*

Alessandro il Grande in Sidone (dm, 3, A. Aureli and Convò), NB, 1706, Act 1 *Nc*, arias in *Nc* and *D-MÜs*

Turno Aricino (dm, 3, Stampiglia and F. Falconi), Fiorentini, 4 Feb 1708, *MÜs*

Melissa Schernita (int), Palazzo Reale, 1708

Engelberta, ossia La forza dell'innocenza [Act 3 and part of Act 2] (dm, 3, A. Zeno and P. Pariati), Palazzo Reale, 4 Nov 1709, *A-Wn* (listed as Pimpinone), perf. with int Pimpinone by T. Albinoni [Act 1 and part of Act 2 by A. Orefice]

Hydaspes [L'Idaspe fedele] (3, ? rev. Nicolini), London, Queen's, 23 March 1710, *GB-Lbl*, *I-Rsc*, arias (London, 1710) [rev. of Gl'amanti generosi, 1705]

Mario fuggitivo (dm, 3, Stampiglia), NB, 27 Dec 1710

La Semele (favola per musica, N. Giuvo), Piedimonte, Palazzo Ducale, Nov 1711

Selim re d'Ormuz (dm, 3, G. D. Pioli), NB, 23 Jan 1712

Artaserse re di Persia (dm, 3, F. Silvani and others), Palazzo Reale, 8 Oct 1713

Il gran Mogol (dm, 3, D. Lalli and A. Birini), NB, 26 Dec 1713, *MC*

Il Vincislao (dm, 3, Zeno), NB, 26 Dec 1714, aria *Nc*

Alessandro Severo (dm, 3, Zeno), Rome, Alibert, carn. 1718, arias in *D-MÜs*

La fortezza [forza] al cimento (melodramma, 3, Silvani), NB, 16 Feb 1721

Trajano (dm, 3, ?Biavi), NB, 17 Jan 1723; with int Colombina e Pernicone, *I-Nc* (R ed. E. Gallico, Milan, 1989)

L'Oront[e]a (dm, 3, N. Stampa or G. A. Cicognini), NB, carn. 1729; with int Perichitta e Bertone

Il cavalier Bardone [Bertone] e Mergellina (int, ? A. Belmuro), Turin, Carignano, 1730

Alessandro nell'Indie (dm, 3, P. Metastasio), NB, carn. 1732, aria *D-B*

Don Aspremo [14 arias] (commedia, 3, D. Caracajus), Nuovo, wint. 1733, lib. *I-Rn*

Demofoonte [6 arias] (dm, 3, Metastasio), NB, 20 Jan 1735, Act 1 *MC*, Act 2 *Nc*, collab. Sarro, Leo and Sellitto

Addl music for: G. M. Orlandini: Artaserse, 1708; G. Bononcini: Abdolomino, 1711; Handel: Agrippina, 1713

Music in: F. Gasparini: Ernelinda, 1713 [rev. of La fede tradita e vendicata, 1704]; Il ritorno del figlio con l'abito più approvato, 1730

Doubtful: Il cavalier Brettone (int) Conservatorio di S Maria di Loreto, 1720 [see Florimo]

*

*Croce*N; *ES* (H. Hucke); *Florimo*N; *Giacomo*C; *MGG* (H. Hucke); *Rosa*M

U. Prota-Giurleo: 'Breve storia del teatro di corte e della musica a Napoli nei secoli XVII e XVIII', *Il teatro di corte del Palazzo reale di Napoli* (Naples, 1952), 19–146

G. Lazarevich: *The Role of the Neapolitan Intermezzo in the Evolution of Eighteenth-Century Musical Style: Literary, Symphonic and Dramatic Aspects, 1685–1735* (Ann Arbor, 1973)

G. Hardie: 'Comic Operas Performed in Naples, 1707–1750', *MMA*, viii (1975), 56–81, esp. 65

R. Strohm: 'Italienische Opernarien des frühen settecento', *AnMc*, no.16 (1976) [whole issue]

R. Pecman: 'Ein italienisches Opernlibretto über König Vaclav', *Mf*, xxxiii (1980), 319–22

R. Strohm: 'Metastasios "Alessandro nelle Indie" und seine frühesten Vertonungen', *Probleme der Händelschen Oper (insbesondere am Beispiel 'Poro')* (Halle, 1982), 40–61

G. Hardie: 'Neapolitan Comic Opera, 1707–1750: some Addenda and Corrigenda for *The New Grove*', *JAMS*, xxxvi (1983), 124–7

G. J. Buelow: 'Handel's Borrowing Techniques: some Fundamental Questions derived from a Study of *Agrippina*', *Göttinger Händel-Beiträge*, ii (1986), 105–28

A. Romagnoli: *Francesco Mancini: i melodrammi* (diss., U. of Pavia, 1987)

C. Sartori: *I libretti italiani a stampa dalle origini al 1800* (Cuneo, 1990–)

T. Griffin: *Musical References in the 'Gazetta di Napoli', 1681–1725* (Berkeley, forthcoming)

A. Romagnoli: 'Il Turno Aricino di Silvio Stampiglia nelle versioni musicali di Giovanni Bononcini e Francesco Mancini', *Gli affetti convenienti all' idee*, ed. R. Cafiero, M. Caraci Vela and A. Romagnoli (Naples, forthcoming)

ROSA CAFIERO (work-list with ELEANOR SELFRIDGE-FIELD)

Mancini, Giovanni Battista [Giambattista] (*b* Ascoli Piceno, 1 Jan 1714; *d* Vienna, 4 Jan 1800). Italian castrato, author of an influential treatise on singing. He studied at Naples with Leonardo Leo, then at Bologna with Antonio Bernacchi and (for counterpoint and composition) G. B. Martini (with whom he remained in touch, helping him in 1778 to arrange a Bologna performance of Gluck's *Alceste*). Mancini sang in Italy and Germany from about 1730, never, it seems, as more than a second-rank singer, though no doubt a musicianly one (he became a member of the Accademia Filarmonica in Bologna). He also made a name as a singing teacher, and in 1757 was called to Vienna to teach the Empress Maria Theresa's daughters; there he remained for the rest of his life.

Mancini's treatise, *Pensieri, e riflessioni pratiche sopra il canto figurato* (Vienna, 1774), was largely a more systematic version of Pier Francesco Tosi's *Opinioni de' cantori antichi e moderni* (1723); both writers shared a belief in the need for singers to undergo prolonged training and to work out their own ornamentation, since this could not be definitively written down. But Mancini went beyond Tosi in assuming no practical difference between operatic and other singing, and in endorsing without qualms the cult of agility; he was himself soon embroiled in controversy with Vincenzo Manfredini, who preferred the value of utterance 'from the heart' to the artificiality of trills. Mancini's account of Italian schools of singing and their decadence, which he blamed on the modern rush to get pupils on to the stage, was a partial one; lamenting the lost golden age was commonplace among authors of treatises on singing. The *Pensieri* was published in English translation, as *Practical Reflections*, in 1967.

*

Burney GN; *ES* (R. Celletti)

C. Ricci: *I teatri di Bologna* (Bologna, 1888)

A. Della Corte: *Canto e bel canto* (Turin, 1933) [reprints most of Mancini's book]

B. Ulrich: *Die altitalienische Gesangsmethode* (Leipzig, 1933)

R. Celletti: *Storia del belcanto* (Fiesole, 1983, 2/1986; Eng. trans., 1991)

S. Durante: 'Il cantante', *SOI*, iv (1987), 378–9, 390–91

JOHN ROSSELLI

Mandac, Evelyn (*b* Malaybalay, Mindanao, 16 Aug 1945). Filipina soprano. She studied in Manila, and at the Juilliard School with Jennie Tourel. She has specialized in lyric roles in Washington, DC (where she made her opera début as Mimì in 1969), San Francisco (where she was Inès in the 1972 revival of *L'Africaine*), Geneva, Rome, Amsterdam, Glyndebourne (début 1974) and Salzburg (début 1975). Her Metropolitan Opera début was on 19 December 1975 as Lauretta in *Gianni Schicchi*, and she returned as Gretel. She sang Mélisande at Santa Fe in 1977, and Lisa in a televised production of *The Queen of Spades*; she also appeared in the American premières of Berio's *Passaggio* and Bennett's *The Mines of Sulphur* (Jenny) and the world premières of Pasatieri's *Black Widow* (Berta) and *Ines de Castro* (Ines). A singer of considerable refinement and charm, she is especially well cast in Mozart's soubrette roles.   MARTIN BERNHEIMER

Mandanici, Placido (*b* Barcellona, Sicily, 1798; *d* Genoa, 6 June 1852). Italian composer. He studied at the Palermo Conservatory and, from 1824, with Pietro Raimondi in Naples. *L'isola disabitata* (1829), based on a libretto by Metastasio, was the first of his four operas for Naples; Mandanici also composed several ballets for that city's royal theatres. Further operas, mainly *melodrammi*, were given in Turin and Milan (where he had moved to teach singing and composition). He visited Palermo in 1843 for performances of his last known opera, *Maria degli albizzi*. Throughout his life he was active as a teacher, and wrote instrumental and religious music in addition to his stage works.

L'isola disabitata (2, P. Metastasio), Naples, Fondo, 1829, excerpts (Milan, n.d.)
Argene (R. Barresi), Naples, S Carlo, Feb 1832
La moglie di mio marito e il marito di mia moglie (G. Ceccherini), Naples, Nuovo, 23 Nov 1833
La fedeltà alla prova (G. Schmidt), Naples, Fondo, 1835
Il segreto (2, F. Romani), Turin, Carignano, 12 Nov 1836
Il rapimento (melodramma buffa, G. Rossi), Milan, Scala, 26 Sept 1837
Il buontempone di Porta Ticinese, ovvero Sabato, Domenica e Lunedì (melodramma buffa, 3, C. Bassi), Milan, Scala, 16 June 1841, vs (Milan, 1841)
Maria degli albizzi (melodramma, 3), Palermo, Carolino, 21 Jan 1843, vs (Milan, 1843)

Mandeville, Félicité. Stage name of Marie-Jeanne Trial, wife of Antoine Trial; *see* TRIAL (i) family, (2).

Mandini. Family of singers.

(1) **Stefano Mandini** (*b* 1750; *d* ?*c*1810). Italian baritone. He appeared at Venice in 1775–6 and at Parma in 1776, described as 'primo buffo mezzo carattere'. In 1783 he and his wife were engaged by Joseph II for his new Italian opera company in Vienna; Stefano was a leading member during its finest period. There is some confusion between Stefano and his younger brother (3) Paolo. Stefano made his Vienna début on 5 May 1783 as Milord Arespingh in Cimarosa's *L'italiana in Londra*; that season he appeared as Mingone in Sarti's *Fra i due litiganti*, Don Fabio in Cimarosa's *Il falegname* and Count Almaviva in Paisiello's *Il barbiere di Siviglia*; in the last, Zinzendorf noted, he excelled in all four disguises in Almaviva's role. The following season he sang in *Le vicende d'amore* (P. A. Guglielmi), *La finta amante* and *Il re Teodoro in Venezia* (Paisiello) in which he created the title role, and *La vendemmia* (Gazzaniga). In

1785 he created Artidoro in Storace's *Gli sposi malcontenti* and Plistene in Salieri's *La grotta di Trofonio*.

Mandini created three roles in 1786: the Poet in Salieri's *Prima la musica e poi le parole*, Count Almaviva in Mozart's *Le nozze di Figaro* (on 1 May) and Lubino in Martín y Soler's *Una cosa rara*. He also sang in Sarti's *I finti eredi* and Paisiello's *Le gare generose*. In 1787–8 he appeared as Leandro in Paisiello's *Le due contesse* and created Doristo in Martín y Soler's *L'arbore di Diana* and Biscroma in Salieri's *Axur, re d'Ormus*. He was then released to go to Naples. Later he sang at the Théâtre de Monsieur in Paris, having considerable success in *Il barbiere di Siviglia*, *Una cosa rara* and *La villanella rapita*, and in Venice (1794–5), then returned to Vienna for Piccinni's *La Griselda* and Paisiello's *La molinara*; he then went to St Petersburg, where the painter Elisabeth Vigée Le Brun remarked that he was an excellent performer and sang wonderfully. Nothing is known for certain of his later career, though it was probably he rather than Paolo who appeared in Berlin in 1804. An extremely versatile singer, he acquitted himself well both as the comic servant (e.g. Doristo) and as the serious lover (e.g. Lubino). His wide range permitted him to create Count Almaviva as a tenor for Paisiello and as a baritone for Mozart.

(2) **Maria Mandini** (*fl* 1783–7). French soprano, wife of (1) Stefano Mandini. The daughter of a Versailles court official, she was engaged with her husband in the Italian opera company in Vienna; she made her début there in 1783 as Madama Brillante in Cimarosa's *L'italiana in Londra* and then sang Countess Belfiore in Sarti's *Fra i due litiganti*. She is known to have created three roles, all small parts: Marina in Martín y Soler's *Il burbero di buon cuore* (1786), Marcellina in *Le nozze di Figaro* (1786) and Britomarte in Martín y Soler's *L'arbore di Diana*. In 1787 she appeared in Cimarosa's *Le trame deluse* and sang Livietta in Paisiello's *Le due contesse*. Nothing is known of her later career. She was apparently an attractive but poor singer. Zinzendorf wrote of her performance as Marina: 'La Mandini let us see her beautiful hair'. As Britomarte she was said to sound 'like an enraged cat' and the performing score contains a pencilled comment at the head of her only aria: 'canta male'.

(3) **Paolo Mandini** (*b* Arezzo, 1757; *d* Bologna, 25 Jan 1842). Italian tenor and baritone, brother of (1) Stefano Mandini. He is sometimes confused with Stefano because, like him, Paolo had a wide range and sang both tenor and baritone roles. A pupil of Saverio Valente, he made a successful début at Brescia in 1777 and sang at La Scala in 1781 and subsequently in Turin, Parma, Bologna and Rome. He was active in Haydn's company at Eszterháza, 1783–4, appearing as Don Fabio in Cimarosa's *Il falegname*, Gianetto in Anfossi's *I viaggiatori felici*, Armidoro in Cimarosa's *L'amor costante*, the Marquis in Sarti's *Le gelosie villane* and the Count in Bianchi's *La villanella rapita*. Haydn wrote Idreno for him in *Armida*. For the 1785–6 season he was engaged in Vienna, making his début in Anfossi's *I viaggiatori felici* as Gianetto and singing Paulino in Bianchi's *La villanella rapita*. He achieved greater success in Venice in 1787, in Cimarosa's *L'amor costante* among other operas. In 1788–9 he sang the title role of Paisiello's *Il rè Teodoro in Venezia* in Parma, Milan and Bologna, and appeared in Martín y Soler's *L'arbore di Diana* as Silvio (Milan) and *Una cosa rara*

(Parma). He then returned to Vienna, where he created Sandrino in Salieri's *La cifra*. His subsequent career is uncertain; he and his brother were in St Petersburg in 1796.

O. E. Deutsch: 'Mozart in Zinzendorfs Tagebüchern', *SMz*, cii (1962), 211–18

P. Branscombe: Review of L. Finscher, ed.: *W. A. Mozart: Le nozze di Figaro* (NMA II:5/xvi), *ML*, lvi (1975), 426–8

R. Paissa: '"Questi è il conte, alla voce il conosco": Stefano Mandini prima di Mozart (1774–1783)', *RIM*, xxii (1987), 145–82   CHRISTOPHER RAEBURN

Mandragola, La ('The Mandrake Root'). *Commedia musicale fiorentino* in a prologue and two acts, op.20, by MARIO CASTELNUOVO-TEDESCO to his own libretto after Niccolò di Bernardo dei Machiavelli's play; Venice, Teatro La Fenice, May 1926; revised two-act version in German, Wiesbaden, Staatsoper, 1928.

Callimaco (tenor) tells his servant Siro (tenor) of his fascination with the beautiful Lucrezia (soprano), who is married but childless. The parasite Ligurio (baritone) offers to bring the two together, for a price, using a potion concocted from a mandrake root: he informs Lucrezia and her husband Nicia (bass) that the potion cures infertility, but that the first person to sleep with one who has taken it will die within 12 hours. The couple therefore agree to substitute Callimaco as Lucrezia's partner for one evening. The thought of a grandchild pleases Lucrezia's mother, Sostrata (mezzo-soprano), though Fra' Timoteo (baritone), Lucrezia's confessor, has to be bribed into agreeing to the action. Lucrezia and Callimaco sing a rapturous duet ('Ecco gia vien la fredda notte') and when dawn breaks, everyone contented, the opera concludes with an ebullient grand finale. *La mandragola* is one of Castelnuovo-Tedesco's most inventive and original operas, a satirical comedy full of youthfulness, freshness and sparkling lyricism.

NICK ROSSI

Manelli [Mannelli], **Francesco** [? 'Il Fasolo'] (*b* Tivoli, 1595–7; *d* Parma, before 27 Sept 1667). Italian composer, singer and impresario. Together with Benedetto Ferrari he was instrumental in establishing the tradition of public opera at Venice.

Manelli began his musical career about 1605 as a chorister at Tivoli Cathedral, where he was later employed as a *cantore ordinario*, from 1609 until February 1624. His father then sent him to Rome to pursue an ecclesiastical career. Instead he married a Roman singer, Maddalena, and returned to Tivoli, where he worked as choirmaster of the cathedral from 1627 until the end of January 1629. In 1629–30 the Manellis were again living in Rome, where they lodged at Stefano Landi's house. From 18 May 1630 to before September 1631 Manelli was choirmaster of the Arciconfraternita di S Maria della Consolazione, Rome. It is not known how long the Manellis stayed in Rome after 1631, though Maddalena's presence there was noted in a letter, dated 3 December 1633, from Fulvio Testi to Francesco I of Modena. By 1636 she had moved to northern Italy. On 11 April 1636 she sang the roles of Minerva and Cibele in the performance at Padua of *Ermiona*, an 'introduction to a torneo' with libretto by Pio Enea degli Obizzi and music by G. F. Sances, and later the same year she published at Venice a collection of her husband's music, *Musiche varie, libro quarto* (1636), which she dedicated to the English ambassador, Viscount Basil Feilding.

By 1637 at the latest Manelli had joined his wife at Venice, where he became associated with the composer and librettist Benedetto Ferrari. His setting of Ferrari's *Andromeda* was performed in 1637 for the inauguration of the Teatro S Cassiano, the first of the Venetian public opera houses. In this production Manelli himself took the roles of Neptune and Astarco, while his wife sang the prologue and the title role. (The opera was revived at Modena in 1656, presumably at Ferrari's instigation, for the opening of another public theatre, the Teatro della Speltà.) Following the success of *Andromeda* Manelli and Ferrari collaborated again in 1638 to produce the opera *La maga fulminata*, and Manelli and his wife again sang in it. On 3 October 1638 he was admitted to the choir of St Mark's, Venice, as a bass singer. His employment there did not curtail his operatic activity. In 1639 he collaborated with Giulio Strozzi to produce *Delia* for the opening of the Teatro SS Giovanni e Paolo, and later in the same year he wrote the music for *Adone*, an opera once attributed to Monteverdi. He subsequently wrote only one more opera for Venice, *Alcate* (1642). In the intervening years, however, he may have been active in a touring company which performed Venetian operas at Bologna; in 1640, according to Osthoff (1958) and Petrobelli (1967), he acted as impresario for performances there of *Delia* and Monteverdi's *Il ritorno d'Ulisse in patria*. These performances were celebrated in a published collection of sonnets which reveals that his wife sang the roles of Venus in *Delia* and Minerva in *Il ritorno d'Ulisse* and that their young son Costantino also appeared in *Delia* in the role of Cupid.

In 1645 the Manelli family moved to Parma; Francesco and Costantino were admitted on 23 March to the choir of S Maria della Steccata, and Maddalena became a singer at the ducal court on 1 April. Francesco continued to work at the Steccata, certainly until 1665 and probably until his death. During his years at Parma he wrote a number of dramatic works for performance at the Farnese court theatre, including three for official court celebrations (see Mamczarz 1988). Of these, *Le vicende del tempo*, with its lavish spectacle and episodic structure, owes much to the tradition of the *intermedio*; and each of its three sections ends with a ballet. *La Filo*, written for the marriage of Ranuccio II Farnese to Margherita Violante of Savoy, has a more coherent plot, with well-developed characters, some of whom introduce an element of comedy; its three acts, based on events in the career of Hercules, are framed by four celestial *intermedi* which parallel and explicate the earthly events of the main drama.

In a preface to the libretto for *Le vicende del tempo* (1652) and again on the title-page of the libretto for *La Licasta* (1664) Manelli is described as *maestro di cappella* to the Duke of Parma. Pelicelli stated that he succeeded to this post on 1 March 1653, but, according to Petrobelli (1967), in the sole surviving official document for this date both he and his wife were described simply as 'musicians' in the service of the duke.

Manelli was a key figure in the early development of Venetian public opera. Since, however, his operatic scores are lost, his achievement in this respect cannot properly be assessed. His surviving vocal music, mainly strophic arias and dance-songs, is written in a fresh, lively style and shows a penchant for ostinato basses. One such setting, 'O sfortunata, chi mi consola?' (*La Luciata*), a lament which uses the descending tetrachord ostinato, was published in his *Musiche varie, libro quarto* (Venice, 1636) but now survives only in manuscript (in *D-Bds*). This features a dialogue between two *commedia dell'arte* characters, Cola (Coviello) and Lucia, who are joined by a third voice for the imitative refrain and final ensemble. An earlier setting of the same text was published at Rome in 1628 in *Il carro di Madama Lucia … rappresentato* by 'Il Fasolo' (Il Retirato in the Accademia de' Capricciosi). It is possible that 'Il Fasolo' was Manelli's pseudonym.

See also ANDROMEDA.

L'Andromeda (B. Ferrari), Venice, S Cassiano, 1637, before 25 Feb, lib. ded. 6 May 1637 (Venice, 1637)
La maga fulminata (favola, Ferrari, after L. Ariosto), Venice, S Cassiano, lib. ded. 6 Feb 1638 (Venice, 1638)
La Delia, o sia La sera sposa del sole (poema drammatico, G. Strozzi), Venice, SS Giovanni e Paolo, lib. ded. 20 Jan 1639 (Venice, 1639)
L'Adone (tragedia, P. Vendramino), Venice, SS Giovanni e Paolo, lib. ded. 21 Dec 1639 (Venice, 1640)
L'Alcate (drama, M. A. Tirabosco), Venice, Novissimo, lib. ded. 13 Feb 1642 (Venice, 1642)
Le vicende del tempo (dramma fantastico musicale, 3, with 3 ballets, B. Morando), Parma, Farnese, 1652; lib. (Parma, 1652)
Il ratto d'Europa (dramma, E. Sandri [P. E. Fantuzzi]), Piacenza, Ducale, 1653; lib. (Parma, 1653)
La Filo, overo Giunone repacificata con Ercole (F. Berni), da cantarsi … col motivo ad un torneo [I sei gigli], che dovrà seguire un'altra sera, Parma, Farnese, *c*17 May 1660
La Licasta (dramma, Ferrari, after L'inganno d'Amore), Parma, Collegio dei Nobili, 1664; lib. (Parma, n.d.)

Other dramatic: L'Ercole nell'Erimanto (ballet, Morando), Piacenza, Ducale, carn. 1651, lib. (Piacenza, 1651); I sei Gigli (torneo, Berni), Parma, Farnese, 1660, lib. (Parma, 1660)

*

ES (W. Osthoff)
F. Caffi: *Storia della musica sacra nella già cappella ducale di S. Marco in Venezia (dal 1318 al 1797)* (Venice, 1854–5); ed. E. Surian (Florence, 1987)
P.-E. Ferrari: *Spettacoli drammatico-musicali e coreografici in Parma dall'anno 1628 all'anno 1883* (Parma, 1884)
G. Radiciotti: *L'arte musicale in Tivoli nei secoli XVI, XVII e XVIII* (Tivoli, 1907, enlarged 2/1921), 41ff
N. Pelicelli: 'Musicisti in Parma nel secolo XVII', *NA*, ix (1932), 239; x (1933), 122, 124, 234
A. A. Abert: *Claudio Monteverdi und das musikalische Drama* (Lippstadt, 1954)
W. Osthoff: 'Zur Bologneser Aufführung von Monteverdis "Ritorno d'Ulisse" im Jahre 1640', *Anzeiger der phil.-hist. Klasse der Österreichischen Akademie der Wissenschaften*, xcv (1958), 155–60
P. Kast: 'Biographische Notizen zu römischen Musikern des 17. Jahrhunderts', *AnMc*, no.1 (1963), 48
P. Petrobelli: 'L'"Ermiona" di Pio Enea degli Obizzi ed i primi spettacoli d'opera veneziani', *QRaM*, iii (1965), 125–41
——: 'Francesco Manelli: documenti e osservazioni', *Chigiana*, xxiv (1967), 43–66
M. L. Doglio, ed.: *F. Testi: Lettere* (Bari, 1967), i, 495–6
T. Antonicek: 'Zum 300. Todestag von Francesco Manelli', *ÖMz*, xxiii (1968), 617
E. Ferrari Barassi: '"La Luciata" di Francesco Manelli: considerazioni su una perduta stampa della Biblioteca municipale di Breslavia, l'esemplare di un manoscritto berlinese, e un componimeno del "Fasolo"', *2° incontro con la musica italiana e polacco: Bologna 1970*, 211–42
L. Bianconi and T. Walker: 'Dalla *Finta pazza* alla *Veremonda*: storie di Febiarmonici', *RIM*, x (1975), 379–454
J. Whenham: *Duet and Dialogue in the Age of Monteverdi* (Ann Arbor, 1982)
L. Stefani: *Francesco Mannelli (1595–1677)* (Tivoli, 1985)
J. Lionnet: 'La musique à "Santa Maria della Consolazione" au 17ème siècle', *NA*, new ser., iv (1986), 153–202
I. Mamczarz: *Le Théâtre farnese de Parme et le drame musical italien (1618–1732)* (Florence, 1988)
J. Southorn: *Power and Display in the Seventeenth Century: the Arts and their Patrons in Modena and Ferrara* (Cambridge, 1988)
P. Fabbri: *Il secolo cantante: per una storia del libretto d'opera nel seicento* (Bologna, 1990)
E. Rosand: *Opera in Seventeenth-Century Venice: the Creation of a Genre* (Berkeley, 1991)
JOHN WHENHAM

Manelli, Maddalena. Italian singer, wife of FRANCESCO MANELLI.

Manén, Juan (*b* Barcelona, 14 March 1883; *d* Barcelona, 26 June 1971). Spanish (Catalan) violinist and composer. Precociously gifted, he learnt solfège and piano with his father from the age of three, and at five began to study the violin, on which he rapidly attained astonishing technical mastery, touring as a virtuoso from the age of nine. Almost entirely self-taught as a composer, in 1900 he conducted a concert of his own works in Barcelona, where two years later the Liceu presented his first opera, *Juana de Nápoles*; it was well received, and in 1903 he followed it up with *Acté*, for which (as for all his later operas) he wrote his own libretto. He then spent some time in Germany, where he acquired an admiration for Wagner and Richard Strauss which can be observed in his orchestral writing.

Manén was a prolific composer, writing symphonic and concertante as well as some chamber works, but he later destroyed or disowned everything he had composed before 1907. This led him to revise *Acté* – or rather almost completely to rewrite it, increasing the complexity of the texture – as *Neró i Acté*; in 1928 it was produced in German (as had been his three-act 'theatre symphony' *Cami del sol* in Leipzig 15 years earlier) and enjoyed performances in several German cities before it was given in Catalan (in 1933) in Barcelona. The 'opera romanesca' *Soledad* is set in Seville in 1765, the diptych *Don Juan* in Spain at the turn of the 16th century. In this ambitious work (never performed and calling for a cast of 15, as against the four plus a mute character of *Soledad*), the Comendador's daughter is a not unwilling victim to Don Juan; her fiancé and her father pursue him to Seville and attack him at a masked ball (in which a gypsy dance is featured), only for him to kill them both.

librettos by Manén unless otherwise stated

Juana de Nápoles (1, M. Chassang), Barcelona, Liceu, Jan 1903
Acté (4), Barcelona, Liceu, 3 Dec 1903, vs (Leipzig, 1908)
Der Fackeltanz (2), Frankfurt, Stadt, spr. 1909
Heros (3), unperf.
Neró i Acté (4), Karlsruhe, 28 Jan 1928, vs (Leipzig, 1928)
Don Juan (comedia trágica, 7, epilogue), unperf., vs (Acts 1–3) (Madrid, 1944)
Soledad (op romanesca, 3), Barcelona, Liceu, 1952, vs (Barcelona, 1951)

*

J. Manén: *Variaciones sin tema* (Barcelona, 1955)
F. Sopeña: *Historia de la música española contemporánea* (Madrid, 1958)
J. Subirá: *La ópera en los teatros de Barcelona* (Madrid, 1960)
J. Manén: *El jóven artista* (Barcelona, 1964)
A. Fernández-Cid: *Cien años de teatro musical en España 1875–1975* (Madrid, 1975)
LIONEL SALTER

Manent, Nicolau (*b* Mahón, Baleares, 22 June 1827; *d* Barcelona, 1887). Spanish composer. He was educated by Benito Andreu, choirmaster in Mahón, and at 19 was in the orchestra of the theatre in Mahón as a flautist and later as a double-bass player. In 1842 he became organist of the church of S Francisco and, after moving to Barcelona in 1845, he was professor of flute and organ, as well as playing the double bass in the orchestra of the Teatro Liceu and acting as choirmaster at the parish church of S Jaime Apostel. With his stage works he became one of the most prolific and popular Catalan composers of his day.

Gualterio di Monsenis (It. op, 3, Cortada), Barcelona, Liceu, 23 May 1857

Zarzuelas (all first performed Barcelona): Buen viaje, señor don Simón, Liceu, 1853, collab. various composers; La tapada del Retiro (3, V. Balaguer and Lerossa), Liceu, March 1853; Tres para una (3, F. Camprodón), Principal, Nov 1853; María (1), Liceu, Aug 1866; El convidado da piedra (3, after J. Zorrilla: Don Juan Tenorio), Circo, 1875; La pou de la veritat (Colomé), Circo, March 1875; Lo cant de la Marsellesa (3, N. Campmany and J. Molas), Circo, 1877; Lo rellotge de Montseny, Tívoli, 24 July 1878; De la tierra al sol (3, Campmany and Molas), Circo, Sept 1879; El gran conquistador, 1881; Cargar con el muerto, 1883; Laura (3, Campmany), 1885

*

StiegerO
Enciclopedia universal ilustrada europeo-americana (Barcelona, 1907–30), xxii, 788–9
A. Fernández-Cid: Cien años de teatro musical en España (1875–1975) (Madrid, 1975)   ANDREW LAMB

Manfredini, Vincenzo (b Pistoia, 22 Oct 1737; d St Petersburg, 5/16 Aug 1799). Italian composer and writer on music. His teachers included Perti in Bologna and Fioroni in Milan. In 1758 his elder brother Giuseppe, a castrato, went to Moscow in Locatelli's opera troupe, and Vincenzo went with him, possibly as one of the troupe. Moving to St Petersburg, he became maestro di cappella to Peter Fedorovich, who on becoming emperor in 1762 made him maestro of the court's Italian opera company. Confirmed in this post by Catherine II, he composed operas and occasional works, but on Galuppi's arrival in 1765 he was relegated to composing the ballets performed with Galuppi's operas; in 1769 he returned with a pension to Bologna. After two further attempts at opera, Manfredini devoted himself mainly to writing, notably on the proper method of teaching singing; he also published some instrumental music. Although he answered the new emperor's summons to St Petersburg in 1798, he took up no post and died the next year.

In April 1785 Manfredini reviewed the first volume of Arteaga's Le rivoluzioni del teatro musicale (Bologna, 1783) in the Giornale enciclopedico di Bologna. In his third volume Arteaga reprinted extracts from this critique with acerbic commentary, leading Manfredini to publish his Difesa della musica moderna (Bologna, 1788), a commentary on Arteaga's commentary. This work is one of the period's most direct (though rather superficially argued) attacks on the widespread line of reformist thinking that saw the weakness of contemporary opera in the decadent over-elaborateness of its music (always contrasted with the simplicity, expressiveness and moral effect assumed to have been present in that of ancient Greece).

Manfredini's daughter Antonia Elisabetta (b ?1786) had a highly successful career as a prima donna during the Rossinian period. Autobiographical material by Manfredini is held at the Accademia Filarmonica, Bologna.

Semiramide riconosciuta (dramma per musica, 3, P. Metastasio), Oranienbaum, sum. 1760
Olimpiade (Metastasio), Moscow, 13/24 Nov 1762, 6 arias, 1 duet (Nuremberg, n.d.), 2 arias in Recueil lyrique d'airs choisis (Paris, 1772)
Carlo Magno (L. Lazzaroni), St Petersburg, 1763; rev. 1764
La finta ammalata, St Petersburg, 1763
La pupilla (int, C. Goldoni), St Petersburg, 1763
Armida (J. Durandi, after T. Tasso: Gerusalemme liberata), Bologna, Comunale, May 1770

Artaserse (Metastasio), Venice, S Benedetto, Jan 1772, F-Pn, P-La

*

R.-A. Mooser: Annales de la musique et des musiciens en Russie au XVIIIme siècle (Geneva, 1948–51)   DENNIS LIBBY

Manfredini-Guarmani, Elisabetta (b Bologna, 1790; d after 1817). Italian soprano. After making her début in 1809 at Bologna, she created roles in four operas by Rossini: Amira in Ciro in Babilonia (1812) at Ferrara; Amenaide in Tancredi (1813) at La Fenice; Aldimira in Sigismondo (1814) at La Scala; and the title role of Adelaide di Borgogna (1817) at the Teatro Argentina, Rome. She also sang in Turin. To judge from the music composed for her by Rossini, she had a voice of exceptional flexibility.   ELIZABETH FORBES

Manfroce, Nicola Antonio (b Palmi Calabro, 20 Feb 1791; d Naples, 9 July 1813). Italian composer. He was a pupil of Giovanni Furno and Tritto at the Conservatorio dei Turchini, Naples, from 1804 and then of Zingarelli in Rome. He was active in Naples (then under French rule), and his first work was a cantata for Napoleon's birthday, La nascita di Alcide, performed at the Neapolitan court on 15 August 1809. His first opera, Alzira (1810, Rome), was followed by his masterpiece, Ecuba (1812, Naples), commissioned by the impresario Barbaia. His librettist was Giovanni Schmidt, whose translation from Sophocles had been used by Sacchini for Oedipe à Colone, performed in Naples at the S Carlo in 1808 and one of the most spectacular examples of the new style favoured in Murat's Naples. Manfroce's subject was taken from a tragedy by Milcent, a version of the Achilles and Polyxena episode in the Trojan war, and is explicitly a derivation from the French operatic tradition. It was a courageous choice for the young composer to make, in preference to the Neapolitan tradition represented by his master Zingarelli. According to Florimo, he was perhaps influenced by hearing the Naples performance of Spontini's La vestale in 1811. Ecuba, in spite of the characteristic unevenness of the first work of a young composer, shows that he would have been capable of great achievement, had he not died so young. Progressive features of his style include the use of recitatives, always with accompaniments including wind instruments, and the bipartite aria, often producing great dramatic concision (in spite of the inferior quality of the libretto). Arias and duets come within the acts, not at the end of them; and choruses are used in such a way as to heighten the tragedy of the individual characters by giving it wider resonance.

Alzira (dramma per musica, 2, G. Rossi), Rome, Valle, 10 Sept 1810, I-Nc, Rsc
Ecuba (tragedia per musica, 3, G. Schmidt), Naples, S Carlo, 13 Dec 1812, Nc, Rsc

*

FlorimoN
D. Ferraro: N. A. Manfroce (Naples, 1978)
G. Carli-Ballola: 'Presenza e influssi dell'opera francese nella civiltà melodrammatica della Napoli murattiana: il "caso" Manfroce', Musica e cultura a Napoli dal XV al XIX secolo: Naples 1982, 307–15 [Quaderni della RIM, ix (1983)]   RENATO BOSSA

Mango, Hieronymus [Gerolamo] (b ?Italy, c1740; d Rome, 1790). Italian composer. After the première of his first opera in Rome (1760), he moved to Eichstätt as Kapellmeister for Prince Bishop Raimondo Anton von Strassoldo on 29 March of that year. There he composed, on Metastasian texts, at least one serenata or *opera seria* a year between 1764 and 1768; he also exerted considerable influence throughout Bavaria. He was associated with the renowned singers and instrumentalists of the St Walburg monastery, who performed cantatas and small Italian operas for neighbouring courts. After his dismissal from Eichstätt in 1773, Mango returned to Rome, where he concentrated his efforts on *opera buffa*. His music is representative of the type favoured in Bavarian courts during the years 1750–1800.

Il paese della cuccagna (ob, C. Goldoni), Rome, Capranica, Jan 1760
Ciro riconosciuto (os, 3, P. Metastasio), Eichstätt, 1767
Adriano in Siria (os, 3, Metastasio), Eichstätt, 1768
L'eroe cinese (os, 3, Metastasio), ?Eichstätt, 1771
L'imbroglio fortunato (ob, G. Mancinelli), Rome, Tordinona, 9 Jan 1773
La maga per amore (ob, G. Donadini), Rome, Tordinona, 3 Jan 1776
La disfatta di Turmo (ob, F. Ballani), Florence, Pallacorda, spr. 1794

Doubtful: La serva spiritosa (ob, Mancinelli), Rome, Tordinona, Feb 1770

EitnerQ; MGG ('Eichstätt'; O. Kaul)
M. Schuler: 'Das Noteninventar der Kollegiat- und Pfarrkirche St. Stephan in Konstanze', *KJb*, lviii–lvix (1974–5), 85–103
R. Münster: *Die ehemaligen Musikhandschriftensammlungen der königlichen Hofkapelle und der Kurfürstin Maria Anna in München* (Munich, 1982)   LISA SZEKER-MADDEN

Mangold, Carl (Ludwig) Amand (*b* Darmstadt, 8 Oct 1813; *d* Oberstdorf im Allgäu, 4 Aug 1889). German conductor and composer, the most important member of a family of musicians active in Hesse from the 17th century. He studied in Paris (1836–9), directed several Darmstadt choirs and was court music director from 1848 to 1869. He wrote five operas including *Tanhauser*, composed independently of Wagner's *Tannhäuser* and initially more favourably received. Mangold's *Tanhauser* omits the song contest, incorporates elements from the Pied Piper legend and ends happily with the collapse of the Venusberg and the hero's marriage. It was revived in 1892 as *Der getreue Eckart*, with a new libretto by Ernst Pasqué. Mangold also composed choral music, songs, and orchestral and chamber music.

all MSS in D-DS; all completed works first performed in Darmstadt
Das Köhlermädchen, oder Das Tournier zu Linz (Wilke), 1843
Die Fischerin (Spl, J. W. von Goethe), 1845
Tanhauser (4, E. Duller), 17 May 1846
Dornröschen (fairy-tale with ballet, Duller), 1848
Gudrun (4, after Old Ger. heroic saga), 1851, vs (Darmstadt, 1851)

Inc.: Fiesko; Rübezahl, begun 1848

T. Rode: 'Mangold, Karl Amand', *Musikalisches Conversations-Lexikon*, ed. A. Reissmann, vii (Berlin, 1877)
W. Mangold: 'Mangold, Carl Amand: Komponist und Dirigent, 1813–1889', *Hessische Biographien*, ed. H. Haupt, ii (Darmstadt, 1927), 10
H. Mendl-Schrama: 'The Other *Tanhäuser*', *Wagner*, vii (1986), 83   PHILIP ROBINSON

Mangold, (Johann) Wilhelm (*b* Darmstadt, 19 Nov 1796; *d* Darmstadt, 23 May 1875). German violinist and composer. He studied with Vogler, and in Paris with Kreutzer and at the Conservatoire (1815–18). In 1819 he was appointed leading violinist at the court in Darmstadt, where he was Kapellmeister from 1825 to 1857. He did much to improve orchestral standards and conditions and also widened the operatic repertory there, being an early sponsor of the works of Spontini

and Gluck, the classical subject matter of which was reflected in his own opera *Merope*. His other dramatic works include two comic operas, incidental music and overtures.

Merope (grosse Oper, 3), Darmstadt, Grossherzogliche Hof, 15 June 1823
Vergebliche Vorsicht (komische Oper, 1), Darmstadt, Hof, 2 March 1834
Graf Ory (komische Oper, 1), unperf.

StiegerO
T. Rode: 'Mangold, Wilhelm', *Musikalisches Conversations-Lexikon*, ed. A. Reissmann, vii (Berlin, 1877)
W. Mangold: 'Mangold, Johann Wilhelm: Hofkapellmeister und Komponist, 1796–1875', *Hessische Biographien*, ed. H. Haupt, i (Darmstadt, 1918), 414–16   PHILIP ROBINSON

Manhattan Opera Company. A company founded by OSCAR HAMMERSTEIN I; it rivalled the Metropolitan Opera, 1906–10. *See also* NEW YORK, §3.

Manila. Capital of the Philippine Islands. The first opera known to have been given there was *La favorite*, produced in summer 1865 by a French company from Indo-China en route to Batavia. They performed at the Teatro Quiapo and the Teatro Principe Alfonso (built 1862; destroyed 1878), which was to be the primary opera house in Manila for some years. Other theatres used for opera in the 19th century were the Teatro Variedades, the Teatro del Tondo and the Teatro Zorilla. The first Italian company arrived in August 1867 and gave ten works, and another performed in spring and summer 1868; both had visited the city in the course of much larger tours, but their success was such that by 1871 it was financially feasible to engage artists just for Manila: they would stay for a full season and then return to Italy. This became the standard practice, although in the last two decades of the century some companies split the season with Batavia while others visited Mindanao and possibly other islands. Some 20 to 25 works were normally given during a season, with new operas within 10 to 20 years of their premières. The repertory was wide, even including *Don Carlos* (1887); *Aida* was given in April 1888, before Glasgow or Manchester, and the Manilese heard *La Gioconda* many years before the Parisians. The first Tagálog opera was *Sandugong Panaginip*, composed by Ladislaw Bonus and given at the Teatro Zorilla on 2 August 1902.

Operatic activity continued well into the 20th century and was not halted by World War I, although it slowed down after the Japanese occupation and independence. The first locally produced opera was *Aida*, given at the Grand Opera (built 1907; burnt down 1943) in 1933; more works followed later that year.

The Cultural Center of the Philippines was built in 1969 with a specially commissioned zarzuela among the inaugural works. In 1979 *Tosca* was given by the Opera Guild of the Philippines, with Eva Marton. Further performances have been given by the Los Angeles Opera and the Ambassadors of Opera.

R. C. Banas: *Pilipino Music and Theater* (Quezon City, 1975)   TOM KAUFMAN

Manina [Fletcher, Seedo], Maria (*fl* 1712–36). Italian soprano. She played Eucharis in Galliard's *Calypso and Telemachus* at the Queen's Theatre, London, in 1712 and Almirena in Handel's *Rinaldo* in 1713, a part she may have taken the previous year. She probably sang

Celia in Handel's *Silla* (1713). In 1714 she sang in the pasticcios *Ernelinda* and *Arminio* at the Queen's, and in 1717 (and later) G. Bononcini's *Camilla* and the pasticcio *Thomyris*. She was at the Lincoln's Inn Fields theatre in 1726 in *Camilla* and was employed there until 1732, singing in pantomime afterpieces and Purcell's *Dioclesian* (1731) and taking the male lead in revivals of Pepusch's *Venus and Adonis* and *Myrtillo* (1730). Manina sang in the first performances of Lampe's *Britannia* (New Haymarket, 1732) and Seedo's masque *Venus, Cupid and Hymen* (Drury Lane, 1733). She married twice, using her husbands' names, Fletcher (from *c*1715) and Seedo (from 1727), and left for Potsdam in 1736. WINTON DEAN

Manitoba Opera Association. Opera company formed in 1969 and based in WINNIPEG.

Mann, Thomas (*b* Lübeck, 6 June 1875; *d* Kilchberg, 12 Aug 1955). German writer. His father was a merchant; his mother, who was musically gifted, was of South American descent. Mann's most characteristic literary subject matter questioned bourgeois values while holding music, especially Wagner's, in high esteem. His novels and stories, from *Buddenbrooks* (1901) to *Doktor Faustus* (1947), make much of music's blend of the mathematical and the magical – he once defined it as 'both calculated order and chaos-breeding irrationality' – and while his essays often celebrate Wagner's genius, he also perceived the relationship between that genius and social and political developments in Germany during the 1930s. His lecture 'Leiden und Grösse Richard Wagners', first delivered in Munich in February 1933, provoked such hostility that he was forced into exile, first to Switzerland and then to the USA.

Mann felt that 'there is, in Wagner's bragging, his endless holding-forth … an unspeakable arrogance that prefigures Hitler', and he summed up his own attitude to Wagner as 'enthusiastic ambivalence'. Wagner was for him primarily 'a great narrative artist', whose techniques as well as spirit were relevant to the writing of fiction. Hence his confession in 1927 that 'the traces of my early and continuing experience of Wagner's work are manifest in everything I have written'. (A collection of Mann's essays, translated by A. Blunden, was published as *Pro and Contra Wagner*, London, 1985.) Mann initially held the music of Pfitzner in high regard: with others he founded a Pfitzner society and in 1918 included a detailed discussion of *Palestrina* in his *Betrachtungen eines Unpolitischen*.

Mann's post-Nietzschean consciousness of a culture in decline is expressed with particular power in *Der Tod in Venedig* (1911), the story of a writer destroyed by a forbidden, inexpressible love. *Doktor Faustus* is the study of a composer, Adrian Leverkühn, whose pact with the Devil is the ultimate, self-destructive embrace of decadence. Mann's account of Leverkühn's music owes much to the philosopher (and Berg pupil) T. W. Adorno's understanding of Schoenberg's 12-note method, and Schoenberg was furious at the way in which Mann, whom he regarded as a friend, refused to exclude something very like the 12-note technique from his vision of cultural crisis.

Despite this concern with music, Mann's intricate literary style and the complex plotting and psychology of his fiction have not encouraged musical treatment. By far the best-known composition based on his work is Britten's last opera, *Death in Venice* (1973). There is also an opera-oratorio by Hilding Rosenberg, *Josef och hans bröder* (1946–8), an opera-ballet, *The Transposed Heads* (1949), by Peggy Glanville-Hicks, three works by Franco Manino, *Mario e il mago* (1956), *Luisella* (1969) and *Le teste scambiate* (composed 1988), Stephen Oliver's one-act opera, *Mario ed il mago* (1988) and Henry Somers's opera *Mario and the Magician* (1992).

*

P. Carnegy: *Faust as Musician: a Study of Thomas Mann's Novel Doctor Faustus* (London, 1973)
——: 'The Novella Transformed: Thomas Mann as Opera', *Benjamin Britten: Death in Venice*, ed. D. Mitchell (Cambridge, 1987), 168–77 ARNOLD WHITTALL

Mann, William S(omervell) (*b* Madras, 14 Feb 1924; *d* Bath, 5 Sept 1989). English music critic. He was educated at Winchester, and studied in London with Ilona Kabos (piano) and Seiber (composition) and at Cambridge, 1946–8. He then joined the music staff of *The Times*, succeeding Frank Howes as chief critic in 1960; he retired in 1982. He was a vigorous and prolific writer, with a deep knowledge of the human voice and wide sympathies in opera production; besides criticism he wrote many programme and sleeve notes and record and book reviews, and he was also a regular broadcaster. His strongest operatic sympathies lay in 19th-century Germany and the 20th century. He wrote two substantial books on opera, *Richard Strauss: a Critical Study of the Operas* (London, 1964) and *The Operas of Mozart* (London, 1977), of which the former was especially well received; both are critical studies of the works in the context of their composers' development and incorporate detailed discussion of the music in relation to character and drama. STANLEY SADIE

Manna, Gennaro (*b* Naples, 12 Dec 1715; *d* Naples, 28 Dec 1779). Italian composer. He studied at the Conservatorio di S Onofrio in Naples where his uncle Francesco Feo was *primo maestro* and Ignazio Prota *secondo maestro*. His first *opera seria*, *Tito Manlio*, was performed on 21 January 1742 in Rome. Its immediate success led to a commission from the Teatro S Giovanni Grisostomo, Venice, for which he wrote *Siroe, re di Persia* for Carnival 1743. After returning to Naples, he collaborated with N. B. Logroscino in composing a *festa teatrale* to celebrate the birth of Princess Maria Elisabetta Borbone (autograph in *I-Nf*); the work was never performed, since an outbreak of the plague caused the festivities planned for July 1743 to be cancelled. Manna then revised Leonardo Vinci's *Artaserse* for a production at the Teatro S Carlo in November 1743, and in January 1745 presented a new work of his own there, the *opera seria* *Achille in Sciro*. Its enthusiastic public reception instantly made him the most sought-after composer in Naples. The French ambassador ordered a serenata for his soirée on 3 August 1745 honouring the marriage of Louis, dauphin of France and Maria Teresa of Spain (autograph in *I-Nf*), and the S Carlo theatre quickly commissioned two additional operas from Manna, *Lucio Vero* for December 1745 and *Arsace* for Carnival 1746. Invitations from theatres in other Italian cities followed. Between 1747 and 1754, Manna composed six new *opere serie*, one each for Ferrara, Messina, Rome and Venice, and two for Turin. In 1755, he joined Pietro Antonio Gallo as co-*maestro* of the Neapolitan conservatory S Maria di Loreto, and also become music director for various local churches. His last theatrical works were *Enea in Cuma*, a serenata written for a fête given by the ambassador of the Maltese Knights on 4 September 1760 (*I-Nf*), and (according to some sources) the *opera seria Temistocle*, performed in Piacenza during Carnival 1761. He then retired from the operatic scene. After the death of Francesco Feo in January 1761, Manna succeeded him as *maestro* of the Ss Annunziata church, and on 9 May of the same year resigned from the Loreto conservatory, citing his many duties which included that of *maestro* of the metropolitan cathedral. On his name-day, 19 September 1762, he was celebrated with the performance of a cantata written in his honour by Vincenzo Bidognietti (*GB-Lbl*). He remained active and revered as a composer of sacred music and oratorios until his death.

Unlike Jommelli, Latilla, Abos and other Neapolitan composers of his generation, Manna apparently never ventured into the field of *commedia per musica*, but dedicated himself exclusively to *opera seria*. He expanded the *galant* tendencies of Francesco Feo and consolidated pre-classical characteristics. Many of his arias are guided by the sonata principle and exhibit varying textures, crescendo, judicious scoring for wind, and strong forward movement to cadences. Arias in major keys often mark the introduction of the secondary tonal area with contrasting phrases in minor keys. The success of Manna's operas rested on his arias, which his contemporaries praised for their spirit, vivacity and delicacy. Although his contributions to opera belong primarily to the first 12 years of his career, they established his fame as one of the most important composers of his time. It is interesting to note that Manna gave up writing for the stage when his nephew Gian Francesco Majo came on the scene, just as his uncle Francesco Feo had done when Manna embarked on his career some 20 years earlier. His cousin, Cristoforo Manna (*b* 1704), was the author of a lost comic opera, *Lo trionfo d'ammore o pure chi dura vence* (to a text by C. Di Palma), performed at the Teatro dei Fiorentini in Naples in spring 1729.

opere serie unless otherwise indicated

Tito Manlio (3, G. Roccaforte), Rome, Argentina, 21 Jan 1742, arias in *A-KR* and *D-SWl*, Acts 2 and 3 *I-Nf**
Siroe re di Persia (3, P. Metastasio), Venice, S Giovanni Grisostomo, carn. 1743, Act 3 *Nf**
Artaserse (3, Metastasio), Naples, S Carlo, 4 Nov 1743, aria *GB-Lbl* [rev. of L. Vinci]
Achille in Sciro (3, Metastasio), Naples, S Carlo, 20 Jan 1745, *D-Hs*, *MÜs*
Lucio Vero, ossia Il Vologeso (3, A. Zeno), Naples, S Carlo, 19 Dec 1745, ?*I-Nf**, *Rsc*
Arsace (3), Naples, S Carlo, carn. 1746, aria *A-Wn*
La clemenza di Tito, Messina, carn. 1747 [according to *StiegerO*]
Adriano placato, Ferrara, Bonacossi, carn. 1748, aria *I-Nc*
Lucio Papirio dittatore (3, Zeno), Rome, Dame, carn. 1748, *D-B*, Acts 1 and 2 *I-Nf**
Eumene (3, Zeno), Turin, Reggio, carn. 1750
Didone abbandonata (3, Metastasio), Venice, S Giovanni Grisostomo, carn. 1751, *D-Hs*, *MÜs*
Demofoonte (3, Metastasio), Turin, Reggio, carn. 1754, Acts 2 and 3 *I-Nf**
Temistocle (3, Metastasio), Piacenza, Ducale, carn. 1761

Arias in *I-MAav*, *Mc* and *Nc*

BurneyH; *ES*; *FlorimoN*; *StiegerO*
M. F. Robinson: *Naples and Neapolitan Opera* (Oxford, 1972), 115–21   HANNS-BERTOLD DIETZ

Mannelli, Francesco. *See* MANELLI, FRANCESCO.

Manners, Charles [Mansergh, Southcote] (*b* London, 27 Dec 1857; *d* Dundrum, Co. Dublin, 3 May 1935). Irish bass and impresario. He studied in Dublin, at the RAM and in Italy. He joined the chorus of the D'Oyly Carte company in 1881 and made his solo début in 1882 at the Savoy Theatre, London, creating the role of Private Willis in *Iolanthe*. He then joined the Carl Rosa company and in 1890 was engaged at Covent Garden, where he sang Bertram in *Robert le diable*. Two years later he sang Prince Gremin in the first performance in England of *Yevgeny Onegin* at the Olympic Theatre, London. In 1896–7 he toured South Africa with his wife, the soprano FANNY MOODY; in 1898 they formed the Moody-Manners Company, which lasted until 1916.

P. Graves: 'The Moody-Manners Partnership', *Opera*, ix (1958), 558–64   HAROLD ROSENTHAL/R

Mannheim. City in Baden-Württemberg, Germany. It was founded by the Elector Palatine Friedrich IV in 1606 as a fortress at the confluence of the Rhine and Neckar rivers.

1. 1720–78. 2. After 1778.

1. 1720–78. Soon after the Elector Palatine Carl Philipp moved his court from Heidelberg to Mannheim in November 1720, the town was transformed by an extensive building programme that included a palace, the largest Baroque complex in Germany. No operas, however, were performed before 1742; in that year the Hoftheater, designed by Alessandro Galli-Bibiena, was completed (see illustration overleaf). Located in the west wing of the palace, it was destroyed in the siege of 1795. The auditorium had a conventional U-shape with six tiers of boxes; the stage was approximately 10 metres wide (at the proscenium) and 30 deep. Contemporary accounts praised it as one of the most beautiful theatres of Europe. Burney, and others, claimed that it was capable of holding 5000 people. Townspeople as well as foreigners were admitted free of charge, but boxes were reserved for visiting dignitaries and court officials. The first opera, C. P. Grua's *Meride* (to a libretto by G. C. Pasquini), was performed on 18 January 1742 as part of the festivities for the marriage of Elisabeth Augusta, the granddaughter of Carl Philipp, to his heir, Carl Theodor.

Within a year the 18-year-old Carl Theodor succeeded Carl Philipp, who died on 31 December 1742 at the age of 81. A celebrated patron of the arts and sciences, Carl Theodor vigorously cultivated music at Mannheim. The famous orchestra, led by Stamitz and Cannabich, established a reputation for virtuoso and disciplined playing. Singers, both German and Italian, rivalled the excellence of the orchestra; notable among the company were the castratos Mariano Lena, Tonarelli, Silvio Giorgetti and Roncaglia, the tenor Raaff, his pupils Ludwig Fischer and Hartig, and the bass G. B. Zonca. The prima donnas included Rosa Gabrielli-Bleckmann, Dorothea Wendling and Franziska Danzi.

Opera assumed an important role in court festivals, and from 1748 until 1778 new works were given almost every year. The season began on 4 November, the elector's name-day, and continued until Shrove Tuesday. Performances resumed after Easter when the court retired to SCHWETZINGEN for the summer. Operas were normally given twice a week, alternating with spoken drama, ballets and concerts, and masked balls during Carnival. Burney reported that each new production cost £4000, but there were rarely more than one or two

Cross-section of the Hoftheater in the west wing of the electoral palace, Mannheim, designed by Alessandro Galli-Bibiena and dedicated in 1742: drawing destroyed in World War II

new operas in a single year. The repertory included as many as seven or eight operas in a season. The productions contained plenty of visual spectacle, provided by the theatrical designers Stefan Schenck and Lorenzo Quaglio. In addition, ballets or ballet pantomimes were given between acts of operas.

During Holzbauer's tenure as Kapellmeister (1753–78), some of the best composers of the day were commissioned to write operas for Mannheim. Located between Paris and Vienna, Mannheim absorbed the latest cross-currents in operatic reform. The electoral court poet Mattia Verazi blended French and Italian elements in his librettos. The most important premières of the period were Jommelli's *Cajo Fabrizio* (1760), Traetta's *Sofonisba* (1762), Majo's *Ifigenia in Tauride* (1764), Piccinni's *Catone in Utica* (1770) and J. C. Bach's *Temistocle* (1772). Italian comic operas were presented at Mannheim and Schwetzingen, including Galuppi's *Il filosofo di campagna* (1756, 1771), Piccinni's *La buona figliuola zittella* (1769), Sacchini's *La contadina in corte* (1772), and Salieri's *La fiera di Venezia* (1772) and *La secchia rapita* (1774). In an attempt to promote serious German opera, the Marchand company performed Wieland and Schweitzer's *Alceste* in 1775. Its success prompted the commission of Holzbauer's *Günther von Schwarzburg* (1777) and Schweitzer's *Rosamunde* (1778), although the latter was postponed when the elector of Bavaria died on 30 December 1777 and was not performed until 1780 at the Nationaltheater. In autumn 1778, Carl Theodor transferred his court to Munich, and opera performances at the Hoftheater in Mannheim virtually ceased. Mozart, who had hoped to receive an appointment at the palatine court during his visit in 1777–8, wrote *Idomeneo* (1781, Munich) for many of the musicians he had met during his visit to Mannheim.

2. AFTER 1778. The Nationaltheater in Mannheim, built by Quaglio, was founded in 1779 by Carl Theodor as a German-language theatre, on the model of those in Vienna and Hamburg, to act as a counterweight to the court theatres dominated by the French and Italian languages. The building was destroyed in an air raid during World War II. From 1945 the Universum and later the Schauburg, a former cinema, served as

temporary theatres until the present Nationaltheater in the Goetheplatz, built to plans by Gerhard Weber, opened on 13 January 1957 with *Der Freischütz*. The opera house, which is now (like the theatre) in urgent need of renovation, has 1154 seats; its auditorium contains stalls, a balcony at the back and seven boxes on each of the two sides.

The Nationaltheater has an honourable tradition behind it. The first Intendant, Heribert von Dalberg, established a fine reputation, performing Schiller's and translations of Shakespeare's early plays in addition to German Singspiel. Barely a decade after it was opened, Mozart conducted the first performance in Mannheim of *Le nozze di Figaro*. The first great surge in the fortunes of the Mannheim Opera came towards the middle of the 19th century with the brothers Franz and Vinzenz Lachner, its first truly professional conductors. Vinzenz, the younger brother, built up a repertory of some 65 operas between 1836 and 1873, and began the tradition of the great conductors of the Nationaltheater; later conductors included Felix Weingartner (1889–91), Emil Nikolaus von Reznicek in the 1890s (appointed in preference to Richard Strauss) and Wilhelm Furtwängler (1915–20). Furtwängler worked in collaboration with the administrator Carl Hagemann, an operatic director of the first rank. His two periods of administration, 1906–10 and 1915–20, when the theatre had excellent companies, are among the peaks of theatrical history in Mannheim. Other conductors were Erich Kleiber in the 1920s, Karl Elmendorff (1936–42), Eugen Szenkar in the 1950s, Horst Stein (1963–70) and Peter Schneider (1985–7).

As guests, Albert Lortzing conducted his *Undine* and Hans Pfitzner his *Palestrina* in Mannheim. A concert conducted by Richard Wagner in 1871 instituted a contact with Bayreuth which exists to this day. Emphasis has always been placed on the works of Wagner in the repertory, and singers and musicians from Mannheim are well represented at the Bayreuth Festival. In the 1970s and 80s they included Hannelore Bode, Astrid Schirmer, Gabriele Schnaut, Jean Cox, Franz Mazura and Philip Kang in leading roles, and Horst Stein, Hans Wallat and Peter Schneider as conductors.

An important occasion in the history of the Nationaltheater was the first performance of Wolf's *Der*

Corregidor (7 June 1896). A significant period of development began after World War II, when Hans Schüler was administrator (1951–63); there were notable premières of works by Hindemith, Blacher and Egk, including Hindemith's opera *The Long Christmas Dinner* in 1961 with the composer conducting. Two first performances of a later date should also be mentioned: Giselher Klebe's *Der jüngste Tag* in 1980, and Wolfgang Rihm's *Hamletmaschine* in 1987.

With more than 40 operas, the repertory of the Nationaltheater is still one of the most extensive in the German-speaking countries, or indeed anywhere. It includes two or three modern works and around 12 to 15 *Spielopern*; the theatre is also committed to children's opera. Mannheim offers between 170 and 180 operatic performances during the season, which lasts for at least ten months. The city and the *Land* of Baden-Württemberg provide the finance.

*

BurneyGN

A. Pichler: *Chronik des Grossherzoglichen Hof- und Nationaltheaters in Mannheim* (Mannheim, 1879)

F. Walter: *Geschichte des Theaters und der Musik am kurpfälzischen Hofe* (Leipzig, 1898)

——: *Das Archiv und Bibliothek des Grossh. Hof- und Nationaltheaters in Mannheim, 1779–1839* (Leipzig, 1899)

——: *Das Mannheimer Schloss* (Karlsruhe, 1922, 2/1927)

K. Sommerfeld: *Die Bühneneinrichtungen des Mannheimer Nationaltheaters unter Dalbergs Leitung, 1778–1803* (Berlin, 1927)

E. L. Stahl: *Das europäische Mannheim: die Wege zum deutschen Nationaltheater, die klassische Zeit des Mannheimer Theaters* (Mannheim, 1940)

F. Walter: *Aufgabe und Vermächtnis einer deutschen Stadt* (Frankfurt, 1952)

D. Heartz: 'The Genesis of *Idomeneo*', *MQ*, lv (1969), 1–19; repr. in *Mozart's Operas*, ed. T. Bauman (Berkeley, 1990), 15–35

P. Mertz and W. Magin: *Das Nationaltheater Mannheim 1779–1970* (Mannheim, 1970)

E. K. Wolf and J. K. Wolf: 'A Newly Identified Complex of Manuscripts from Mannheim', *JAMS*, xxvii (1974), 379–437

R. Würtz: *Verzeichnis und Ikonographie der kurpfälzischen Hofmusiker zu Mannheim nebst darstellenden Theaterpersonal, 1723–1803* (Wilhelmshaven, 1975)

S. Pflicht: *Kurfürst Carl Theodor von der Pfalz und seine Bedeutung für die Entwicklung des deutschen Theaters* (Reichling, 1976)

T. A. Bauman: *Music and Drama in Germany: a Traveling Company and its Repertory, 1767–1781* (diss., U. of California, Berkeley, 1977)

R. Würtz, ed.: *Das Mannheimer Mozart-Buch* (Wilhelmshaven, 1977)

H. Meyer: *Das Nationaltheater Mannheim 1929–79* (Mannheim, Vienna and Zürich, 1979)

O. Fambach: *Das Repertorium des Hof- und Nationaltheaters in Mannheim 1804–32* (Bonn, 1980)

K. Heinz and H. Schönfeldt: *200 Jahre Nationaltheater Mannheim: Geschichte und Jubiläum* (Mannheim, 1980)

H. E. Valentin and others: *Die Wittelsbacher und ihre Künstler in acht Jahrhunderten* (Munich, 1980)

H. Huth, ed.: *Die Kunstdenkmäler des Stadtkreises Mannheim* (Munich, 1982)

M. McClymonds: 'Mattia Verazi and the Opera at Mannheim, Stuttgart, and Ludwigsburg', *Studies in Music from the University of Western Ontario*, vii/2 (1982), 99–136

S. Henze: 'Opera seria am kurpfälzischen Hofe', *Mannheim und Italien: zur Vorgeschichte der Mannheimer: Mannheim 1983*, 78–96

G. Ebersold: *Rokoko, Reform und Revolution: ein politisches Lebensbild des Kurfürsten Karl Theodor* (Frankfurt, 1985)

L. Finscher, ed.: *Die Mannheimer Hofkapelle im Zeitalter Carl Theodors* (Mannheim, 1991)

P. Corneilson: *Opera at Mannheim, 1770–1778* (diss., U. of North Carolina, 1992)   PAUL CORNEILSON (1), GÁBOR HALÁSZ (2)

Mannino, Franco (*b* Palermo, 25 April 1924). Italian composer. He studied at the Rome Conservatory.

Composition prizes he has won include the Dyagilev award in France in 1956 for the best new work of the year, his *azione coreografica Mario e il mago* (his first work for the theatre). In 1969–70 he was artistic director at the S Carlo in Naples; in 1990 he was appointed head of the Accademia Filarmonica in Bologna.

In *Mario e il mago* the singing roles are doubled by dancers. The story is based on Thomas Mann and centres on Mario, a shy young waiter in love with Silvestra, who in turn loves Renato. A magician arrives in the town and involves Mario in one of his tricks. Unaware that it is an illusion, Mario experiences the realization of his dreams; but when in his dream he approaches Silvestra to kiss her the spell is broken and the crowd laughs. Mario kills the magician and is taken to prison. The libretto was by Luchino Visconti, for whom Mannino also wrote film music.

Mannino wrote two other works based on Mann: *Luisella* (1963) and *Le teste scambiate* (1988, as yet unperformed). In *Luisella* the beautiful Amra Jacoby plots with her lover, the musician Alfredo Läutner, against her husband Cristiano, who is physically repulsive and completely ruled by his wife. She compels him to sing at the end of a party the song 'Luisella', composed by Alfredo. Cristiano accepts this humiliation, but during the performance dies of a heart attack. The composer's liking for melodramatic subjects of a *verismo* type is confirmed in *Vivì* (1955). Vivì, a celebrated soubrette, falls in love with an English airman, but he betrays her and marries someone else. Realizing she cannot win him back, she kills him.

Mannino has been attracted to a wide variety of dramatic subjects, from the strong melodramatic *La speranza* (in which, against the background of the declaration of World War II, two stepbrothers discover that one of them is the son of a Jewess) to the irony of the intermezzo *Il quadro delle meraviglie*, a fable after Cervantes. There is a similar disparity between two Wilde operas: the decadent *Il ritratto di Dorian Gray* (1973) and the fantastic and magical *Il principe felice* (1981). *La stirpe di Davide* (1958) has a biblical subject, while *Il diavolo in giardino* (1962), set in the court of Louis XVI, concerns the intrigues surrounding the sale of a precious jewel to Marie Antoinette. A smaller scale (involving an effective doubling of the characters) is common to *Le notti della paura* (1960), a monologue in which the narrative is given to a *recitante* voice and reminiscences to three sopranos, and to the 'liederopera' *Le notti bianche* (1987), based on Dostoyevsky.

Mannino's wide range of subjects and dramatic situations is accompanied by facility of invention and an eclectic style, partly the result of his study of works of the past and his conservative concern not to alienate the public. Stylistic innovations are used within a conception of opera that affirms Italian post-*verismo* and, in a wider context, late Romantic musical tradition.

Mario e il mago, 1952 (azione coreografica, 2, L. Visconti, after T. Mann), Milan, Scala, 25 Feb 1956 (Milan, 1956)

Vivì, 1955 (dramma lirico, 4, P. Masino and B. Missiroli), Naples, S Carlo, 28 March 1957 (Milan, 1957)

La speranza, 1956 (melodramma, 3, L. Malerba and E. Visconti), Trieste, Verdi, 14 Feb 1970 (Milan, 1969)

La stirpe di Davide, 1958 (tragedia, 2, V. Viviani), Rome, Opera, 19 April 1962 (Milan, 1962)

Le notti della paura, 1960 (melodramma, 1, M. Binazzi), Lecco, Sociale, 26 June 1969 (Milan, 1969)

Il diavolo in giardino (commedia, 3, L. Visconti, F. Sanjust and E. Medioli), Palermo, Massimo, 28 Feb 1963 (Milan, 1962)

Il quadro delle meraviglie (int, 1, A. Camilleri, after M. de Cervantes), Rome, Opera, 24 April 1963 (Milan, 1963)

Luisella, 1963 (dramma, 4, Masino, after Mann), Palermo, Massimo, 28 Feb 1969 (Milan, 1968)

Il ritratto di Dorian Gray, 1973 (dramma, 2, Masino and B. de Tomasi, after O. Wilde), Catania, Bellini, 12 Jan 1982 (Milan, 1981)

Il principe felice, 1981 (fiaba, 3, M. S. Sernas, after Wilde), Milan, Scala, 7 July 1987 (Milan, 1987)

Soltanto il rogo (dramma, 3, E. Mann Borgese), Agrigento, Pirandello, 21 Oct 1987 (Rome, 1987)

Le notti bianche, 1987 (liederopera, 2, B. Cagli, after F. M. Dostoyevsky), Rome, Accademia Nazionale di S Cecilia, 14 April 1989 (Milan, 1989)

Le teste scambiate, 1988 (leggenda indiana, 3, A. Giubertoni Mila, after Mann), unperf. (Milan, 1988)

De Colombo a Broadway, 1991 (musical, 2, Mannino, after F. Kafka: Amerika), unperf.

*

A. della Corte: 'Mario e il mago, balletto di Luchino Visconti e Franco Mannini', Nuova stampa (26 Feb 1956)

F. Abbiati: 'Vivì di Franco Mannino', Corriere della sera (29 March 1957)

F. D'Amico: 'Vivì e i fumetti', Il contemporaneo (6 April 1957)

E. Valente: 'Tre prime all'Opera', L'unità (20 April 1962)

M. Mila: 'La signora è da bruciare', La stampa (22 Oct 1987)

RAFFAELE POZZI

Manolov, Emanuil (*b* Gabrovo, 7 Jan 1860; *d* Kazanlak, 2 Feb 1902). Bulgarian composer. After the liberation of Bulgaria from Turkish domination in 1878 he studied for about two years at the Moscow Conservatory, returning to Bulgaria in 1885. He composed the first Bulgarian opera, *Siromachkinya* ('The Poor Woman'), to his own libretto after a poem by Ivan Vazov. Although unfinished, the opera was performed by an amateur company in Kazanlak in December 1900; the score was later completed by others and staged by the Bulgarian Opera Society in Sofia on 25 November 1910. *The Poor Woman* is in a conventional Italian style and its melodies show the influence of urban folk romances.

*

I. Kamburov: *Emanuil Manolov* (Sofia, 1933)
A. Balareva: *Emanuil Manolov* (Sofia, 1961)

LADA BRASHOVANOVA, MAGDALENA MANOLOVA

Manon. *Opéra comique* in five acts by JULES MASSENET to a libretto by HENRI MEILHAC and PHILIPPE GILLE after ANTOINE-FRANÇOIS PRÉVOST's novel *L'histoire du chevalier des Grieux et de Manon Lescaut* (1731); Paris, Opéra-Comique (Salle Favart), 19 January 1884.

Manon Lescaut	soprano
Poussette ⎱	mezzo-soprano
Javotte ⎰ *actresses*	mezzo-soprano
Rosette ⎰	mezzo-soprano
Chevalier des Grieux [Des Grieux]	tenor
Count des Grieux *his father*	bass
Lescaut *Manon's cousin*	baritone
Guillot de Morfontaine *a nobleman*	tenor
Brétigny *a tax farmer*	baritone
Innkeeper	baritone
Two Guardsmen	tenor, baritone
A Maid	mezzo-soprano

Citizens of Amiens, travellers, gamblers, the Parisian beau monde, worshippers, soldiers

Setting Amiens, Paris and the road to Le Havre, early 18th century

Massenet suggested setting Abbé Prévost's novel to Meilhac, with whom he had collaborated on the one-act trifle *Bérangère et Anatole* in 1876 (destroyed by the composer); Meilhac was separated from his usual partner Halévy, and working at this time with Philippe Gille.

Prévost (1697–1763) was briefly a member of a strict Benedictine order, and having left it spent the rest of his life in exile. The novel known nowadays simply as *Manon Lescaut* is the seventh and last part of a sequence entitled *Mémoires et aventures d'un homme de qualité*; it was written in London and published in Amsterdam. A narration within a narration – the storyteller meets Des Grieux, who recounts the story of Manon – it is similar in structure to Mérimée's *Carmen*. The action is set during the regency of Philippe d'Orléans, which followed the death of Louis XIV in 1715, a period of notorious corruption in public life; a possible parallel with the Second Empire may have appealed to Massenet and his librettists, whose adaptation is altogether more faithful to the original than that of Auber and Scribe (1856). Inevitably the plot is simplified (Manon leaves Des Grieux three times in the novel, but only once in the opera) and any element of social criticism is avoided in the interests of providing a conventional, highly competent and lightly licentious libretto acceptable to Opéra-Comique audiences. The main changes are turning Lescaut into Manon's cousin rather than her brother, and transferring the scene of her death from the swamps of Louisiana to the road to Le Havre.

Massenet worked closely with his librettists in spring 1882, completed the piano score later that year, and

Marie Heilbronn as Manon and Jean-Alexandre Talazac as Des Grieux, in the original production of Massenet's 'Manon' at the Opéra-Comique, Paris, 19 January 1884

finished the orchestration in summer 1883. He had the score printed before rehearsals started at the Opéra-Comique, as was his practice to minimize opportunities for interference from Léon Carvalho. The première was a success with the public and most of the press, and *Manon* remained in the Opéra-Comique repertory until 1959, reaching over 2000 performances.

The leading roles were sung by the Flemish soprano Marie Heilbronn (1851–86) and Jean-Alexandre Talazac (1851–96), who also created Hoffmann and Gérald (*Lakmé*). Heilbronn was not the first choice: Massenet wanted (and rehearsed with) a soprano under contract to another theatre whose manager would not release her, while Talazac pressed the claims of one of his protégées. Heilbronn had sung in Massenet's first piece for the Opéra-Comique, *La grand'tante* (1867), and temporarily retired from the stage following her marriage into the aristocracy. She died young, only two years after the première. Almost exactly a year later (17 January 1885) the Carl Rosa Opera Company gave the British première, in Liverpool, and the work was soon being played throughout Europe and the Americas (December 1885, New York, with Minnie Hauk). In 1887 Massenet met the Californian soprano Sibyl Sanderson, whom he coached for her début in the title role (2 February 1888, The Hague, under the pseudonym of 'Ada Palmer' as a publicity gimmick) and for whom he made alterations subsequently incorporated in the 'definitive' score published in 1895. Further post-première additions include the third-act entr'acte, Manon's Gavotte (added in 1884 for Marie Roze, who created the title role in London, and adapted from the song 'Sérénade de Molière' dating from 1880), the reprise of 'N'est-ce plus ma main' in the finale, and in 1894 an alternative to the Gavotte, the 'Fabliau', in all probability composed for Georgette Bréjean-Silver, who sang the role in a major revival at the Opéra-Comique (Carvalho had temporarily dropped *Manon* from the repertory following Sanderson's defection to the Opéra). Since then the leading roles have been sung by all leading singers: Melba, Garden, Edvina, Teyte, Heldy, Vallin, Los Angeles, Jurinac, Ansseau, Caruso, De Lucia, Schipa, McCormack, Gigli, Piccaver, Gedda, Kraus and Vanzo are represented in an exhaustive discography.

ACT 1 *The courtyard of an inn in Amiens* Guillot, Brétigny and the three 'actresses' impatiently await their dinner. The coach from Arras arrives, and curious townspeople are joined by Lescaut, who is meeting his 15-year-old cousin Manon on her way to a convent on the orders of her parents. She arrives, breathless with wonder at her first journey away from home ('Je suis encore tout étourdie'). While Lescaut leaves to search for her luggage, Guillot sees her and offers her money 'for a word of love', is rebuffed, and mocked by his companions. He nevertheless tells Manon that his coach is at her disposal. Lescaut witnesses the end of the conversation and reproaches Manon for her lack of discretion, which threatens the family honour ('Ne bronchez pas'), before retiring to gamble with his cronies. Left alone once more, Manon casts envious glances at the actresses and their fine clothes, but realizes sadly that prospects of a life of luxury will be shut off by the convent door ('Voyons, Manon, plus de chimères'). Des Grieux enters to await the coach that will take him to his father ('J'ai marqué l'heure du départ'). He sees Manon and falls in love with her at first sight. She

receives his compliments gracefully, and admits that it is her taste for pleasure that has led to her family sending her to the convent. Des Grieux will have none of this, and Manon sees her chance of escape: Guillot's postilion is standing by his coach. The lovers flee joyfully ('Nous vivrons à Paris'). Lescaut and Guillot return to find the bird has flown. Guillot, publicly humiliated, swears revenge.

ACT 2 *The apartment of Manon and Des Grieux in the rue Vivienne, Paris* Des Grieux writes a letter to his father asking permission to marry Manon, who reads it back to him ('On l'appelle Manon'). She inquires thoughtfully whether it is not enough for them just to be lovers. Des Grieux asks about a bunch of flowers; Manon answers that it was thrown anonymously through the window from down in the street. The maid announces two soldiers: one is Lescaut and the other, she whispers to Manon, is Brétigny in disguise. Brétigny pretends to restrain Lescaut from avenging insults to the family honour – the latter is deflated when Des Grieux shows him the letter – and tells Manon aside that Des Grieux's father is having him abducted that same evening. This is her chance of escape to a better life. The intruders leave, and Des Grieux goes to post the letter. Manon tells herself that though she loves Des Grieux, she is not worthy of him, and she knows she is unable to resist Brétigny's offer. She bids sentimental farewell to the domestic scene ('Adieu, notre petite table'). Des Grieux returns and tells her of his dream of the rustic retreat they will share in wedded bliss ('En fermant les yeux'). Noise is heard at the door. Manon begs her lover not to go to it, in vain. He is abducted.

ACT 3.i *The Cours-la-Reine* Lescaut and the three actresses are among the tradesmen and pleasure-seekers (Lescaut: 'A quoi bon l'économie … O Rosalinde'). The actresses pointedly snub Guillot, who in turn provokes the possessive and jealous Brétigny; he has heard that Manon asked her protector to invite the company from the Opéra to perform at her home, and he refused. Guillot makes plans. Manon enters on Brétigny's arm, at the summit of her fame ('Je marche sur tous les chemins'; Gavotte: 'Obéissons quand leur voix appelle'). Manon then overhears a conversation between Brétigny and the Count des Grieux, the Chevalier's father, who reveals that his son is taking holy orders and is to preach his first sermon at St Sulpice later in the day. Manon asks the Count if his son has forgotten the cause of his misery, and he answers in the affirmative. Guillot returns in triumph with the ballet troupe from the Opéra. After the fourth entrée, Manon abruptly orders her coach to take her to St Sulpice. Guillot is publicly humiliated once more.

3.ii *The parlour of the seminary at St Sulpice* Pious female worshippers comment admiringly on the qualities of the new abbé. The Count des Grieux tries to dissuade his son from taking the final step ('Epouse quelque brave fille') and, seeing that he is adamant, promises to make over part of his inheritance. Alone, Des Grieux prays for peace of mind ('Ah! fuyez, douce image'). He leaves for the holy Office. Manon enters and asks the porter if she may see Des Grieux, and while waiting prudently prays God for forgiveness in advance. Des Grieux angrily dismisses her. She admits her guilt, begs for forgiveness, and asks him only to remember their past love ('N'est-ce plus ma main'). Her physical touch overcomes Des Grieux's scruples: the lovers are reunited.

ACT 4 *The Hôtel de Transylvanie* Lescaut and the actresses join gamblers and professional card-sharpers. Guillot entertains them with a suggestive ditty about the regent. Manon enters with Des Grieux, a fish out of water yet still under her spell ('Manon, sphinx étonnant'). She reminds him that his inheritance has nearly run out: he must gamble for more money. Unwillingly he accepts a challenge from Guillot, while Manon and the actresses sing rapturously of what money will bring them ('Ce bruit de l'or'). Guillot loses repeatedly and suddenly breaks off the game, hinting that Des Grieux has cheated – a charge hotly denied. As Guillot leaves, Manon urges Des Grieux to follow suit, but he feels that if he does, then the charge will be believed. Guillot returns with the police and orders the arrest of Des Grieux and his accomplice. The Count des Grieux also enters to lead the final ensemble and support the order for his son's arrest. Manon collapses as she is led away.

ACT 5 *On the road to Le Havre* Manon has been sentenced to deportation to the colonies, and Lescaut's and Des Grieux's plot to rescue her has foundered on the desertion of their accomplices. But Lescaut bribes the sergeant of the escort to let him speak to his cousin. He leaves the lovers alone. Manon, broken in body and spirit, begs Des Grieux's forgiveness for the shame she has brought him (duet: 'Tu pleures?' 'Oui, de honte sur moi') before expiring amid a flurry of reminiscences from the earlier acts.

*　　*　　*

Manon may be Massenet's best-known and most popular opera but, an early work, it is by no means unflawed. The Meilhac-Gille libretto is prolix and over-reliant on narrative values; the result is nearly three hours of music – longer than *Carmen* – and the score is seldom performed uncut in the theatre. The first act, especially, takes a long time to get going, a crucial fault. In the interests of producing a conventional libretto tailor-made for Opéra-Comique audiences – opportunities for a church scene, two street scenes and a gambling scene, all stock material at the Favart, must have attracted Massenet to the novel – the authors softened the material significantly. Lescaut, in the novel Manon's brother and pimp, becomes her cousin and is turned into a standard *opéra comique* swashbuckler, blandly characterized by the music. There is some confusion about why he talks so proudly of the Lescaut family honour in the first two acts; in the original version of the novel the Lescauts were of some substance, but in Prévost's revision of 1753 they were taken down a social peg. Massenet and his librettists presumably preferred the original, but the degree of irony intended is not made clear. Des Grieux is similarly watered down. In the novel he does indeed cheat at cards, and is taught how to by Lescaut, who with some awkwardness in the opera has to combine military bluffness with some of the functions of Des Grieux's faithful friend in the novel, Tiberge. In both instances the aura of moral corruption in Prévost's story is compromised, just as no one would know from the opera alone that Brétigny is a tax farmer. In post-1871 Paris even Offenbach's satire was blunted, and any hint of social criticism was unwelcome.

The designation 'opéra comique' is misleading: there are only a few lines of spoken dialogue. But in their place there is much *mélodrame*, faultlessly handled at a technical level. The first meeting of Manon and Des Grieux is presented this way under a 9/8 phrase on solo violin later to become the lovers' main motif, and the scene for the Count and his son at St Sulpice, which moves from dialogue to *mélodrame* to arioso and back again, is another perfectly crafted passage. (Massenet left among his papers a score in which both dialogue and *mélodrame* were set vocally without any changes to the accompaniment; this revision was first given at the Metropolitan Opera in New York in 1988.)

Less satisfying are the moments when convention takes over. The sinister atmosphere of the gambling den, laced with the hysterical hedonism of 'Ce bruit de l'or', gives way to the stock concerted finale, complete with the Count des Grieux, who has no business to be there save to underline a calculated echo of *La traviata*; similarly, the desolation of the last act with its perky song for the military escort and swooning 9/8 Andante espressivo for the lovers dissolves into a cynically laid-out series of reprises. Massenet's post-première insertion of the reminiscence of 'N'est-ce plus ma main' effectively sinks the ship, and is one of the rare examples of his second thoughts definitely not being for the better.

Yet in general it is hard not to admire the charm of the 18th-century pastiche, the suavely composed bustle of the crowd scenes, the genuine dramatic power of the St Sulpice confrontation with its heady charge of sex-and-religion, or the deft delineation of the principal characters. Des Grieux may remain the undeveloping mooncalf lover – a fault of the adaptation – yet three solos of the varied quality of the second-act Dream, 'Ah! fuyez' and 'Manon, sphinx étonnant' are reward enough for both singer and audience.

But in Manon herself Massenet created a portrait of the eternal feminine to rank with Mélisande and Lulu, and it is on this that the opera's appeal rests. Maupassant wrote of Prévost's heroine's 'instinctive perfidy', describing her as 'sincere in her deception and frank in her infamy', and Massenet caught the contradictions perfectly. This is, to be sure, a male view of seductive womankind: the generous, ambitious, pleasure-loving good-time girl who delivers the goods and expires of nothing so much as sheer exhaustion, but not before having repented of the sins required of her and sworn eternal constancy to her faithful (male) lover. Yet this somewhat one-sided view has not prevented all lyric sopranos of note queuing up to sing the role, encompassing as it does a string of well-contrasted showpieces, from the shy, hesitant 'Je suis encore tout étourdie' (an example of supremely perceptive musical characterization), through the regretful 'Voyons, Manon', the skittish charm of the Letter Scene, the pure sentiment of the farewell to the *petite table*, the glittering confidence of the Gavotte, the irresistible 'N'est-ce plus ma main' (the shimmering violins at the moment of physical contact is one of operatic literature's great X-rated effects) to the mournful repentance of the finale. They add up to a formidable and teasingly enigmatic whole, and a rewarding challenge to singing-actresses. In the final analysis *Manon* is by way of being a 'highlights' opera, lacking the cohesion and economy of more mature Massenet works, but those highlights were seldom surpassed in the composer's oeuvre.

RODNEY MILNES

Manon Lescaut (i). *Opéra comique* in three acts by DANIEL-FRANÇOIS-ESPRIT AUBER to a libretto by EUGÈNE SCRIBE after ANTOINE-FRANÇOIS PRÉVOST's novel *L'histoire du chevalier des Grieux et de Manon Lescaut*

(1731); Paris, Opéra-Comique (Salle Favart), 23 February 1856.

The Marquis d'Hérigny (baritone) is seeking access to Manon (soprano) with the help of her cousin, Lescaut (bass). Manon wants to lead a life of luxury. Her lover, the Chevalier des Grieux (tenor), has acquired money to dine with her at the café of Madame Bacelin (soprano). Lescaut joins them and gambles away the money Des Grieux has entrusted to him. Threatened, because he cannot pay the bill, Des Grieux signs a contract to serve in Hérigny's regiment. Manon performs as a café singer and earns a large sum of money, but she is too late to free Des Grieux from his pledge. In Act 2 Manon, now living in Hérigny's villa, asks his permission to see Des Grieux, but he has already deserted. He enters and tries to flee with Manon, but Hérigny confronts him. In the ensuing duel, Hérigny is severely wounded, and Des Grieux is recaptured and sentenced to death. In Act 3 Manon is deported to America with a group of women convicts. Des Grieux, who has secretly followed her on the ship, bribes Renaud (bass), the overseer, to let him embrace Manon. The couple escape with the help of Manon's friend Marguerite (soprano) and Marguerite's fiancé Gervais (tenor). In the desert of Louisiana the exhausted Manon dies in the arms of Des Grieux.

Scribe was 65 and Auber 74 when *Manon* had its première. The collaborators, so successful in the past, now had to prove themselves in a new type of music drama, already represented by Verdi's *Les vêpres siciliennes* (1855; Bizet's *Le Docteur Miracle* followed in 1857). These circumstances account, at least in part, for the special position *Manon* holds in the history of *opéra comique*; and the tragic death of the heroine – the first in the genre – foreshadows *Carmen*. Scribe freely adapted Prévost's novel, but retained two of Manon's characteristics: her fidelity to Des Grieux and her desire to live in luxury. He avoided 18th-century allusions, depicting the society of his own time in the first two acts and the colonial ambitions of the Second Empire (with occasional echoes of Offenbach) in the third. The classification of the work as 'a descendant of the vaudeville' (Kämper and Knabe) is untenable; the demanding role of Manon (written for Marie Cabel) would be unthinkable in a vaudeville.

Several themes heard in the overture play an important part in the opera: the horn theme at the beginning (a reference to Manon's origins), two motifs from the café scene, including the chorus 'C'est la guinguette', and a subject taken from the third-act quartet that recurs in the finale. Auber thus draws attention to the two climactic points in the opera: the café scene and the death of Manon.

The complex duet in Act 1 between Manon and Marguerite is divided into a letter scene followed by Marguerite's *couplets*, a short dialogue, a melody for Marguerite and two virtuoso arias in the shape of a cavatina and a cabaletta. The café scene, with its galop-like chorus and Manon's appearance as a singer, evokes the society of the Second Empire. The climax of the finale is the 'Bourbonnaise' 'C'est l'histoire amoureuse', which became popular throughout Europe. The original *couplets* for Hérigny at the beginning of Act 2, in two contrasting sections, are followed by his duet with Manon, ending with a virtuoso cabaletta.

In Act 3, Auber injects exotic local colour in the introduction and later in a Creole song. An original feature is the trio for Manon, Marguerite and Des Grieux, in which Renaud counts the minutes he has granted the lovers for their conversation, while the orchestra moves the action forward. The final tableau (which is entirely sung) opens with a short melodrama, a complete contrast of musical language. The accompaniment to Manon's *romanza* 'Je crois encore de ce tigre sauvage' is more like a recitative than an aria; its distinctive chromatic 'death' motif (in C minor) has already been heard in the introduction. The key changes to E major for Manon's duet with Des Grieux, 'Je ne souffre plus', with its moving prayer, 'Mon dieu, jette sur nous un regard favorable', accompanied by a romantically harmonized chorale. The shift of the melody to the orchestra and the reduction of the voice to declamation on a single note point to late Verdi. The recurrence of the music of the quartet after Manon's death brings the work full circle with the theme first heard in the overture.   HERBERT SCHNEIDER

Manon Lescaut (ii). *Dramma lirico* in four acts by GIACOMO PUCCINI to a libretto by Domenico Oliva and LUIGI ILLICA after ANTOINE-FRANÇOIS PRÉVOST's novel *L'histoire du chevalier des Grieux et de Manon Lescaut*; Turin, Teatro Regio, 1 February 1893 (revised version, Milan, Teatro alla Scala, 7 February 1894).

Manon Lescaut	soprano
Lescaut *her brother, Sergeant of the Royal Guards*	baritone
The Chevalier des Grieux	tenor
Geronte de Revoir *Treasurer General*	bass
Edmondo *a student*	tenor
The Innkeeper	bass
A Singer	mezzo-soprano
The Dancing Master	tenor
A Lamplighter	tenor
Sergeant of the Royal Archers	bass
A Naval Captain	bass

Singers, old beaux and abbés, girls, townsfolk, students, courtesans, archers and sailors

Setting France and America during the second half of the 18th century

Of all Puccini's operas *Manon Lescaut* had the most tormented genesis. His publisher Ricordi tried to dissuade him from a subject which had already achieved great popularity in Massenet's setting of 1884, as yet unperformed in Italy. Puccini remained firm in his decision to undertake it, declaring that 'Manon is a heroine I believe in and therefore she cannot fail to win the hearts of the public. Why shouldn't there be two operas about her? A woman like Manon can have more than one lover.' Dissatisfied with the bizarre pseudo-philosophical pretensions of the 'scapigliato' Ferdinando Fontana, who had written the librettos for *Le villi* and *Edgar*, Puccini first turned to the playwright Marco Praga as a possible librettist. But Praga had never attempted an opera libretto before and insisted on bringing in the young poet Domenico Oliva, with whom he had already collaborated on a literary and artistic journal, to do the versification. Both authors were contracted by Ricordi during the summer of 1889. By the beginning of the next year they had produced a libretto in four acts set respectively in Amiens, in the lovers' humble apartment in Paris, in Geronte's town house and in the Louisiana desert where Manon dies. Puccini professed himself satisfied and managed to complete the first act by March 1890. But by June he was complaining that the libretto was driving him to despair and that it would have to be re-done. He particularly wanted an entire scene at the end of Act 3 showing the embarkation at Le Havre. Rather than alter his original scheme Praga preferred to bow out. Ricordi then turned to Ruggero Leoncavallo, who drafted out a new scheme for Act 2, leaving Oliva to fill out the lines; then he too retired from the project, owing to pressure of other work. Finally, in autumn 1891 Luigi Illica was called in to overhaul the entire text in accordance with Puccini's requirements. He re-worked the scene at Le Havre into its present form, adding the song of the Lamplighter, while Giulio Ricordi contributed the quatrain in which the ship's captain agrees to take Des Grieux aboard. Puccini himself supplied 11 unmetrical lines for the duet between Lescaut and Manon in Geronte's town house; a further two were provided by Leoncavallo for the conclusion of Des Grieux' solo in the same scene. Some time during the summer of 1892 the original Act 2 was dropped altogether and replaced by what had until then been Act 3 part 1, now suitably expanded. Thus the embarkation scene became a separate act, prefaced by an intermezzo. By this time Oliva no longer wanted to be associated with the opera; but as much of his work exists in the finished product, Illica tactfully withheld his own name from the title-page, so that the published libretto remains to this day without an attribution. Later Oliva maintained that the fourth act was exactly as he had originally written it. The score was finished in October 1892, Act 3 being completed last. Puccini, as he often did, drew on previous material: the Agnus Dei from the *Messa di gloria* (1880) for the 'madrigal' of Act 2; the student exercise *Mentìa l'avviso* (1883) for the melody of Des Grieux' aria 'Donna non vidi mai'; a minuet for string quartet (1884) speeded up for the opera's opening; and the elegy *Crisantemi* (1890), also for quartet, for certain moments in Act 3 and Act 4.

As La Scala was occupied at the time with rehearsals for Verdi's *Falstaff*, Ricordi chose the Teatro Regio, Turin, for the première. The performance was conducted by Alessandro Pomè with Cesira Ferrani (Manon), Achille Moro (Lescaut), Giuseppe Cremonini (Des Grieux), Alessandro Polonini (Geronte), Elvira Ceresoli (the Singer) and Roberto Ramini (Edmondo, the Dancing Master and the Lamplighter). *Manon Lescaut* was Puccini's first and only uncontested triumph, acclaimed by critics and public alike. Ricordi took advantage of the favourable reception to link its hire with that of *Falstaff*, so that neither opera could be given without the other. Before the published vocal score appeared Puccini made, at Illica's suggestion, a radical change to the finale of Act 1, replacing a conventional *pezzo concertato*, based on the melody of 'Donna non vidi mai', by an exchange between Lescaut and Geronte and a reprise of the melody of Des Grieux' 'Tra voi belle' entrusted to Edmondo and the students. The new finale was first performed on 7 February 1894 at La Scala, where the cast included Olga Olghini (Manon), Tieste Wilmant (Lescaut), Vittorio Arimondi (Geronte) and the original Des Grieux, Cremonini. The London première (Covent Garden, 14 May 1894), with Olghini (Manon), Antonio Pini-Corsi (Lescaut) and Umberto Beduschi (Des Grieux), prompted Bernard Shaw to hail Puccini as Verdi's most probable heir among Italian composers. The opera established itself at the Metropolitan, New York (18 January 1907), with Lina

Cavalieri (Manon), Antonio Scotti (Lescaut) and Enrico Caruso (Des Grieux). Outstanding exponents of the title role have included Lucrezia Bori, who introduced the opera to Paris in 1910, and Lotte Lehmann, who sang it in Vienna in 1923 with Alfred Piccaver as Des Grieux. In the score, the role of Geronte de Revoir is described as for 'basso brilliante'.

Puccini continued to modify *Manon Lescaut*, in particular omitting for many years the heroine's aria in Act 4, 'Sola, perduta, abbandonata'. He finally reinstated it with a slightly altered ending for the 30th-anniversary performance, given at La Scala (1 February 1923) under Toscanini with Juanita Caracciolo in the title role. Toscanini himself suggested certain alterations to the scoring, all of which have since been incorporated in the current version of the opera.

ACT 1 *A public square in Amiens* Outside an inn soldiers, students and townsfolk are enjoying the fine summer evening. Edmondo leads the company in a 'madrigal' ('Ave sera gentil'). The students welcome Des Grieux, who addresses a group of girls with ironical gallantry ('Tra voi belle, brune o bionde'). Manon arrives on the stage coach from Arras accompanied by Lescaut and Geronte, who orders lodgings for the night; the two men go into the inn. The crowd disperse leaving Manon alone with Des Grieux. She tells him that she is bound for a convent, but agrees to meet him later. When she has left, Des Grieux pours out his feelings in the soliloquy 'Donna non vidi mai'. Edmondo overhears Geronte summoning a carriage to leave for Paris within the hour and warns Des Grieux. He and Manon sing a love-duet ('Vedete? io son fedele') before making their escape. Lescaut assures the mortified Geronte that his sister will soon need a rich protector.

ACT 2 *An elegant salon in Geronte's house* Manon, installed as Geronte's mistress, is in the hands of her hairdresser when Lescaut enters. She asks for news of Des Grieux, recalling nostalgically the humble apartment in which they were happy together and contrasting it with her present luxurious surroundings ('In quelle trine morbide'). Lescaut tells her that he has turned the young man into a gambler, so that he may win enough money to provide her with the luxury she cannot do without. A group of singers perform a madrigal in her honour ('Sulla vetta tu del monte'), after which Lescaut goes to fetch Des Grieux. Geronte arrives with friends who offer bouquets and trinkets. A dancing master teaches her the minuet. Manon takes leave of the company with a brief 'pastoral' ('L'ora, o Tirsi, è vaga e bella'), promising to join them later on the boulevards. Des Grieux appears at the door. In their duet ('Tu, tu, amore') he begins by reproaching her, but she soon overcomes his resistance and Geronte returns to find them in each other's arms. Manon parries his ironic thrusts by holding a mirror to his face. He retires, threatening that they will meet again. The lovers prepare to flee; but Manon is sad at having to relinquish so much wealth, as Des Grieux observes with dismay ('Ah, Manon, mi tradisce il tuo folle pensier'). To a brisk orchestral fugato Lescaut bursts in to tell them that Geronte is on his way back with the city guards. Manon's insistence on gathering up the jewels causes a fatal delay. As Geronte and the guards enter the jewels spill out of her cloak, and she is arrested for theft.

ACT 3 *Le Havre, a square near the harbour* An intermezzo based on previously heard themes covers the

time of Manon's imprisonment and the journey to the French port. She is housed in a barracks with prostitutes awaiting deportation to America. Lescaut plans to procure her escape by bribing a guard. As Manon appears at a grille, she and Des Grieux exchange words of love and hope while a lamplighter passes by on his rounds. A shot is heard, indicating that Lescaut's plan has miscarried. One by one the prostitutes and Manon are taken to the ship, while a sergeant-at-arms calls their names and the crowd comment on the appearance of each. Des Grieux prevails upon the ship's captain to take him aboard in a solo, 'Guardate, pazzo son, guardate', and with a reminiscence of the Act 2 duet, he falls into Manon's arms.

ACT 4 *A vast desert near the outskirts of New Orleans* Manon, in flight with Des Grieux from the son of the French governor, is at the end of her strength. She sends Des Grieux to look for shelter for the night, then breaks out in an agonized lament, 'Sola, perduta, abbandonata'. Des Grieux returns to find her dying.

* * *

Manon Lescaut placed Puccini firmly in the front rank of contemporary composers. Bernard Shaw correctly drew attention to the symphonic element in Act 1, while the *grand tableau* in the third act represents something new in Italian musical dramaturgy – a *pezzo concertato* in which time is never frozen. No less remarkable is Puccini's skill in depicting the dawning of young love, first with an orchestral anticipation of Des Grieux' aria 'Donna non vidi mai', then in the course of the duet 'Vedete? io son fedele', in which shy conversational exchanges gradually flower into an ecstatic lyricism. Thematic recurrence is used with a new flexibility, exemplified by the various transformations undergone by the motif associated with the heroine (ex.1).

On the debit side, the elimination of the lovers' Parisian idyll not only leaves an awkward gap in the action but also precludes a full portrayal of Manon's character. Indeed, as late as 1903 a letter to Illica shows Puccini toying with the notion of an additional act showing the lovers living happily together in Paris. The chief difficulty lay in finding a sufficiently original end-

Two pages from the disposizione scenica (production book) for the original production of Puccini's 'Manon Lescaut' at the Teatro Regio, Turin, 1 February 1893: (above) the setting for Act 3 (Le Havre, a square near the harbour), with (below) some of the accompanying stage directions (the prostitutes are ordered on board ship; the serried ranks of chorus serve as a reminder of this act's function as a grand concertato finale, with the private passions of Manon and Des Grieux played out in a public place)

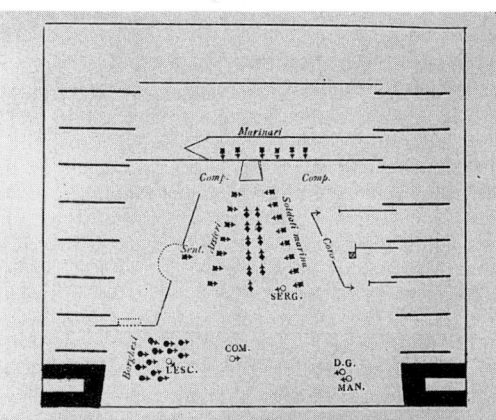

Quando **Des Grieux** vede il **Comandante**, prorompe in uno straziante singhiozzo: l'emozione lo vince, e le braccia che stringevano **Manon** si sciolgono: **Des Grieux** fa due passi verso il **Comandante**, il quale gli volge allora le spalle.

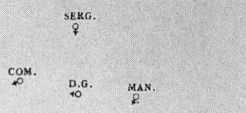

Il **Sergente** ordina alle Cortigiane di avviarsi verso la nave: esse si incamminano lentamente a capo basso, passando fra le due file dei Soldati: di mano in mano che salgono sulla nave, volgono a destra verso prora e spariscono, sotto la guida dei Marinai. Intanto il **Sergente** si è avvicinato a **Manon** e la spinge verso le altre: **Manon** s'incammina piangendo disperatamente, quasi cadendo ad ogni passo: poi ad un tratto si svincola e tenta correre presso **Des Grieux**: ma il **Sergente** di nuovo la trascina verso la nave, assieme alle altre condannate. Si raccomanda molto all'attrice questa controscena. La folla guarda silenziosa, con un senso di profonda pietà.

Ex.1
(a) Act 1

ing. Also unsatisfactory is the concentration of all the gaiety into Acts 1 and 2 and all the gloom into Acts 3 and 4. But any such weaknesses are amply made good by the abundance of youthful vitality, which has enabled Puccini's opera to hold its own against Massenet's technically more adroit setting of the same subject.

JULIAN BUDDEN

Manowarda, Josef von (*b* Kraków, 3 July 1890; *d* Berlin, 24 Dec 1942). Austrian bass of Polish birth. He studied in Graz, where he sang from 1911 to 1915. Then, after three years at the Vienna Volksoper and a further period of study, he made his début at the Staatsoper as the Spirit Messenger in the première of *Die Frau ohne Schatten* (1919). He continued to sing regularly in Vienna even after 1934, when he moved to Berlin. At Salzburg he was heard first in 1922 and at Bayreuth in 1931; he became closely associated with both festivals, his Mozart roles including Osmin in *Die Entführung*, while at Bayreuth he sang most of the Wagnerian bass parts. Elsewhere he also took the bass-baritone roles of Wotan and Hans Sachs. Recordings, some from actual performances, capture something of the authority and power of his stage performances but also expose unevenness in his voice production.

J. B. STEANE

Mansouri, Lotfi [Lotfollah] (*b* Teheran, 15 June 1929). American director and administrator of Iranian birth. After graduating from UCLA in 1953 with a degree in psychology, he turned to opera direction, serving as resident stage director for the Zürich Opera (1960–65) and the Geneva Opera (1965–75). In 1976 he was named general director of the Canadian Opera Company in Toronto, leaving that post in 1988 to become general director of the San Francisco Opera. As a freelance director, Mansouri has staged a wide range of works for companies throughout North America. Although seldom startlingly novel or theatrically experi-

mental, his smartly professional productions can be relied on to represent the work at hand in a tasteful and traditional manner.

PETER G. DAVIS

Mantelli, Eugenia (*b* Italy, 1860; *d* Lisbon, 3 March 1926). Italian mezzo-soprano. She studied at the Milan Conservatory and made her début at Lisbon as Urbain in *Les Huguenots* in 1883. Touring widely throughout Europe and South America, she developed a repertory that included soprano parts, even Brünnhilde in *Die Walküre*, as well as the normal mezzo roles. At Covent Garden she appeared first in 1896 as Léonor in *La favorite*, and this was also her most successful part at the Metropolitan, where she sang from 1894 to 1899, returning briefly in 1903. In both countries she met with a mixed reception, some critics finding her style forced and her production uneven. For a time she sang in vaudeville, but returned to the S Carlo in Lisbon where she later taught. Her recordings, made around 1905, show a warm, flexible voice without notable powers of characterization.

A. Wolf: 'Eugenia Mantelli', *Record Collector*, iv (1949), 66–71

J. B. STEANE

Mantius, Eduard (*b* Schwerin, 18 Jan 1806; *d* Ilmenau, Thuringia, 4 July 1874). German tenor. He studied in Leipzig and made his début in 1830 as Tamino at the Berlin Hofoper, where he was engaged until 1857. In 1849 he created Slender in Nicolai's *Die lustigen Weiber von Windsor*. His repertory of over 150 roles included Adolar (*Euryanthe*), Raoul (*Les Huguenots*), Arnold (*Guillaume Tell*), Pylades (*Iphigénie en Tauride*) and Florestan, which he sang at his farewell performance in Berlin. He had a powerful, brilliant voice as effective in Mozart as in heavier German or French roles.

ELIZABETH FORBES

Mantovanina, La. *See* ORLANDI, CHIARA.

Mantua (It. Mantova). Northern Italian city. It was a principal centre of dramatic performance in the Renaissance and early Baroque. By the early 16th century, plays with incidental music and *intermedi* were being given at the court of the ruling Gonzaga family. Under Dukes Vincenzo (1587–1612), Francesco (1612), Ferdinando (1613–26) and Vincenzo II (1627) a lively interest in theatre and the monodic style gave impetus to splendid spectacles, among them Guarini's *L'idropica* (1608), with *intermedi* by Chiabrera, choreography and eight scene changes, and Hercole Marliani's *Le tre costante* (1622), in which more than 50 stage machines were used. Casts often exceeded 60, and included the celebrated singers Francesco Rasi, Adriana and Margherita Basile, Settimia Caccini and Francesco Campagnolo. Giaches de Wert, G. G. Gastoldi, Salomone Rossi, Monteverdi, Santi Orlandi and Alessandro Ghivizzani contributed songs and concerted dances, and Antonio Maria Viani and Gabriele Bertazzolo designed sets, staging and machines.

Despite the city's musical rivalry with the Medici and the papacy, opera had not been imported until a decade after its appearance in Florence. Monteverdi's *Orfeo* (1607), staged in a palace room before the Invaghiti academy and then again for 'the principal ladies of the city', was the first Mantuan opera. Of its novelty the court official Carlo Magni reported, 'all the personages will speak musically', while the brother of the librettist

Alessandro Striggio called it 'something new ... not before ... heard in a similar form of singing'. Marco da Gagliano's *Dafne* (1608), composed for Ferdinando's elevation to a cardinalate, and Monteverdi's *Arianna* (1608), for the nuptials of Francesco and Margherita of Savoy, followed. For the latter, a temporary structure seating 6000 spectators was erected in the palace grounds. Operatic production declined sharply thereafter. Some works were commissioned, but documents point to only three that reached performance up to 1630: one in 1614, Orlandi's *Gli amori di Aci e Galatea* in 1615 (mounted again in 1617 on the occasion of Ferdinando's marriage to Caterina de' Medici) and Monteverdi's *Andromeda* in 1620.

Most productions were staged in the ducal theatre situated in the Corte Nuova, adjacent to S Giorgio castle. Constructed in the mid-16th century by G. B. Bertani, it had semicircular tiers ascending almost to the ceiling at the back and sides, and a decorated backdrop showing a city perspective with palazzos, towers, temples and human figures. This building was destroyed by fire in 1588 and 1591. A new theatre was built on the same site by Viani in 1596 and stood until early in the 18th century. Tiers provided seating for the women, benches were at floor level for the men, and a platform, raised about 45 cm above the ground, accommodated the royal family. The central floor space was also used for dances or for instrumentalists, sometimes seated on a platform or in a box. The stage was elevated, with a room underneath accessible by a trap-door. Besides the modest Teatro dei Comici, theatrical spaces in Mantua included the loggia of the synagogue, for productions by the Jewish community, palace rooms and private residences, and outdoor locations: the Piazza S Pietro (now Piazza Sordello) in front of the palace, and the courtyard of the Palazzo del Te, where tournaments and jousts incorporating scenery and sometimes musical interludes were held.

A city plan of 1628 shows the public theatre, the Teatro dei Comici (or 'Piccolo di Corte'), adjoining the ducal palace, close to what is now Piazza Arche. It accommodated travelling troupes and appears to have had boxes even before the restructuring of 1688–9 (designed by Fabrizio Carini Motta, with 104 boxes in six tiers, one of which was at ground level). In the second half of the 17th century operatic entertainments were staged there, as well as at the old Teatro Grande di Corte and the Teatro Fedeli (built by Carini Motta in the present vicolo Canove, with 54 boxes in three tiers and a gallery, inaugurated in 1669 with Antonio del Gaudio's *L'Eudosia*). Patronized by Ferdinando Carlo, the last Gonzaga duke (1665–1707), the operas were mainly revivals of Venetian productions given by a mixed management of impresarios and the court. They were perhaps encouraged by the policy of 'licences', a form of patronage conferred by the duke (probably for purposes of diplomacy and prestige) on many singers working in the Po region, centred in Venice. Antonio Caldara was Ferdinando Carlo's *maestro di cappella* from 1699 to 1707 and was involved in the vicissitudes of the ducal court and its operatic activity during the war of succession.

In 1706, two years before he was deposed, Ferdinando Carlo commissioned from Ferdinando Galli-Bibiena the reconstruction of the ducal theatre. Although the arrival of an Austrian governor in 1708 and the siege of the city by Philip of Hessen-Darmstadt in 1714 held up this project, opera production continued as before at the Teatro dei Comici (one or two a year). Vivaldi worked there when he was in the city as *maestro di cappella da camera* to the Landgrave (1718–20), which involved the supervision of all secular music and activity as impresario (1732). During those seasons his *Teuzzone* (1718), *La Candace, o siano Li veri amici* (1720) and *Semiramide* (1732) received their first performances. The Regio Ducal Teatro Nuovo (64 boxes in four tiers, subscribed by the local aristocracy) was finally built in 1732 by Andrea Galluzzi and opened with a *Cajo Fabrizio*. It was accorded the monopoly of operatic productions in the city – a somewhat fictitious monopoly, however, as in practice both *opera seria* and comic opera, as well as drama, continued to be presented at the Teatro dei Comici (now known as the Teatro Vecchio) until it was dismantled in 1797, at the time of the Napoleonic siege. The Teatro Nuovo was destroyed by fire in 1781 and almost at once rebuilt by Giuseppe Piermarini, opening in 1783 with Sarti's *Il trionfo della pace*. It housed first performances of Cherubini's *Alessandro nell'Indie* (1784) and Angelo Tarchi's *Arminio* (1785) and *Artaserse* (1788). Under the Republic (from 1797) it was named the Nazionale and then became the Regio about 1805.

After the Restoration some city notables formed a syndicate (1817) to build a new theatre, not without opposition from the proprietors of the Teatro Regio (where Donizetti's *Le nozze in villa* was first performed in 1820). The present Teatro Sociale was designed by Luigi Canonica (78 boxes in four tiers) and opened on 26 December 1822 with Mercadante's 'new opera' *Alfonso ed Elisa*. Rivalry between the theatres meant that the Sociale was prohibited from mounting opera seasons at the same time as the Regio's traditional ones (carnival and spring–summer). But the newer theatre soon predominated – as early as 1826–7 – and continued to operate almost unchanged until the final years of Austrian rule (1859–66); there were fixed carnival and spring seasons (with a ratio of 7:1 in the value of the respective endowments, being guaranteed half by the owning syndicate and half by the municipality), and sporadic summer seasons (without subsidy). With the exceptions of Alessandro Lanari, 1846–7, and Luciano Marzi, 1852–3, managerial contracts were awarded to minor or local impresarios. When the Sociale could no longer function, the Teatro Andreani came into existence (1862); it was a small house in which carnival seasons were organized, supplementing the city's limited operatic activities, a role it played whenever the Sociale encountered difficulties.

At the beginning of the 20th century both theatres were opened to other forms of entertainment, including film (from 1912 at the Sociale). Operas were produced almost solely for the carnival season, with no continuity of programming and, in the 1930s, with a decline in public interest. The ownership and managerial arrangements of the Teatro Sociale remained unchanged even after the war. A 'teatro di tradizione' (one that is only partly funded by the state) from 1967, with seasons usually beginning in February, the Sociale continues to suffer the financial and artistic uncertainties of an 'impresarial' management.

*

A. Bertolotti: *Musici alla corte dei Gonzaga in Mantova dal secolo XV al XVIII* (Milan, 1890)

E. Lui and A. Ottolenghi: *I cento anni del Teatro sociale di Mantova* (Mantua, 1923)

C. Romani: *Cronistoria dei teatri mantovani del settecento* (diss., Catholic U. of Milan, 1959)

——: 'I teatri di Mantova nel secolo XVIII', *Città di Mantova*, viii (1964), 23–34

G. Amadei: *I 150 anni del Sociale nella storia dei teatri di Mantova* (Mantua, 1973)

P. Carpeggiani: 'Teatri e apparati scenici alla corte dei Gonzaga tra cinque e seicento', *Bollettino del Centro internazionale di studi di architetture Andrea Palladio*, xvii (1975), 101–8

C. Gallico: 'Vivaldi dagli archivi di Mantova', *Vivaldi veneziano europeo: Venice 1978*, 77–88

I. Fenlon: *Music and Patronage in Sixteenth-Century Mantua* (Cambridge, 1980)

——: 'The Mantuan *Orfeo*', *EMc*, xii (1984), 163–72

N. Pirrotta: *Music and Culture in Italy from the Middle Ages to the Baroque* (Cambridge, MA, 1984), 254–7

G. Ricci: 'Note sull'attività di Fabrizio Carini, architetto teatrale e scenotecnico', *Il seicento nell'arte e nella cultura con riferimenti a Mantova* (Milan, 1985), 148–63

L. Cataldi: 'I rapporti di Vivaldi con il "Teatro detto il Comico" di Mantova', *Informazioni e studi vivaldiani*, vi (1985), 88–110

——: 'Alcuni documenti relativi alla permanenza di Vivaldi a Mantova', 'La rappresentazione mantovana del "Tito Manlio" di Antonio Vivaldi', *Informazioni e studi vivaldiani*, viii (1987), 13–22, 52–88

——: 'L'attività operistica di Vivaldi a Mantova', *Nuovi studi vivaldiani* (Florence, 1988), 131–45

P. Besutti: *La corte musicale di Ferdinando Carlo Gonzaga ultimo duca di Mantova: musica, cantanti e teatro d'opera tra il 1665 e il 1707* (Mantua, 1989)

S. Parisi: *Ducal Patronage of Music in Mantua, 1587–1627: an Archival Study* (diss., U. of Illinois, 1989)

SUSAN PARISI, ALESSANDRO ROCCATAGLIATI

Mantzaros [Halikiopoulos], Nikolaos (*b* Corfu, 26 Oct 1795; *d* Corfu, 12 April 1872). Greek composer and teacher. Of noble descent, he studied with Cavalier Barbatti in Corfu; from 1821 he was strongly influenced by what was to be a lifelong friendship with Zingarelli in Naples. Mantzaros declined the directorships of both the Naples and the Milan conservatories, preferring instead to settle in Corfu as a teacher. In 1840 he helped to found the first Greek conservatory, the Società Filarmonica di Corfù, where most of the Ionian opera composers (including Xyndas, Padovanis and Edouardos Lambelet) were his pupils. His one-act *azione comica Don Crepuscolo* is the earliest extant Greek opera. A youthful work, it is an interesting example of *buffo* style on the threshold of Rossini's *Il barbiere di Siviglia*. The première took place at the S Giacomo theatre, Corfu, in 1815. Mantzaros also left some arias and duets. Beneath their flowing melodic lines these pieces reveal an accomplished technique.

*

S. G. Motsenigos: *Neoelliniki moussiki* [Modern Greek Music] (Athens, 1958)

G. Leotsakos: 'Nikolaos Halikiopoulos-Mantzaros (1795–1872): ya ena mikro tou engolpio' [Halikiopoulos-Mantzaros: a Short Guidebook on the Composer], *Moussikologhia*, v–vi (Salonica, 1987), 228–71   GEORGE LEOTSAKOS

Manuguerra, Matteo (*b* Tunis, 5 Oct 1924). French baritone of Tunisian birth. He settled in Argentina after World War II and at 35 entered the Buenos Aires Conservatory. In 1963 he returned to France to accept a three-year contract as first baritone in Lyons. He moved to the Paris Opéra in 1966, singing in *Faust*, *Rigoletto*, *La traviata*, *Carmen* and *Lucia di Lammermoor*. Engagements throughout Europe followed. His American début was in Seattle in 1968 (*Andrea Chénier*), and he joined the Metropolitan Opera as Enrico Ashton in *Lucia* in 1971. He attracted special attention the next year in a concert performance of *L'Africaine* in New York, and became known for Verdi roles such as Renato, Don Carlo (*La forza del destino*) and Macbeth. He sang Rigoletto at Chicago (1977), Houston (1983)

and Buenos Aires (1986), and Renato (*Un ballo in maschera*) at Naples in 1989. A baritone of uncommon fervour, taste and versatility, Manuguerra has brought equal authority to the French and Italian repertories.

MARTIN BERNHEIMER

Manza, Luigi. *See* MANCIA, LUIGI.

Manzoni, Alessandro (*b* Milan, 7 March 1785; *d* Milan, 22 May 1873). Italian novelist, poet and dramatist. An admirer of Walter Scott, he was one of the founders of Italian Romanticism; a prevalent theme of his works is victimization, accepted with resignation and surmounted by faith. His poetic drama *Adelchi*, set by Apolloni in 1852, deals with the tragic figure of Adelchi at the time of the defeat of the Longobards by Charlemagne's Frankish forces. Manzoni is best known, however, for his historical drama *I promessi sposi* (1828), set in 17th-century Lombardy, which was the subject of at least six operas; its plot, when simplified, was particularly apt for melodramatic treatment. The best-known setting is Ponchielli's (1856); the first performance of Petrella's opera, at Lecco (the original setting for the novel), was attended by Manzoni. Verdi wrote his Requiem Mass in memory of Manzoni.

Adelchi (poetic drama, 1822): Apolloni, 1852

I promessi sposi (novel, 1828): P. Bresciani, 1833; L. Gervasi, 1834; Gläser, 1849, as *Brylluppet ved Como-Søen* ('The Wedding by Lake Como'); Ponchielli, 1856; A. Traventi, 1858; E. Petrella, 1869

*

A. Colquhoun: *Manzoni and his Times* (London, 1954)

BARBARA REYNOLDS

Manzoni, Giacomo (*b* Milan, 26 Sept 1932). Italian composer. After several years of self-tuition he began formal musical study at the age of 16, when his family moved to Messina. His own sense of musical identity was crucially shaped by his encounter with Schoenberg's *Pierrot lunaire* at the Palermo ISCM Festival in the following year. In 1950 he returned to Milan to study at the university and conservatory. His first theatre piece, *La legge*, was submitted for his composition diploma at the conservatory in 1955, but it was rejected, and remained unperformed. A story of Sicilian peasants vainly struggling to gain land, it anticipated future work both in its subject matter and in its expressionist musical idiom.

Having taken his degree in languages in 1955, and obtained his composition diploma a year later, Manzoni embarked on a career that combined journalism, translation and composition. In 1962 he began to teach at the Milan Conservatory, transferring to Bologna in 1964. When, from 1969, he became professor of composition at Bologna, he quickly created a considerable reputation: both at Bologna and at Milan, where he returned in 1974, he has taught many of the most gifted young Italian composers.

Manzoni himself has defined theatre as the central point into which all his other work flows. With Luigi Nono he has proved the most forceful exponent of a theatre of political debate in postwar Italian music. Given his first opportunity by a commission from the Teatro delle Novità festival, Bergamo, in 1959, he collaborated with Emilio Jona on a parable of Brechtian cut, *La sentenza*, produced for the festival in the following year by Virginio Puecher. Less Brechtian was Manzoni's resolutely dodecaphonic idiom: a marriage

Giovanni Manzuoli as Theseus, fighting the Minotaur in Ponzo's 'Arianna e Teseo', performed at the Regio Ducal Teatro, Milan, January 1762: engraving by Marc'Antonio dal Re after Fabrizio Galliari

of musical and political radicalism that he, like Nono, was to maintain throughout his theatre work.

The collaboration with Jona and Puecher was reactivated for *Atomtod* (1963–5), and with Puecher for *Per Massimiliano Robespierre* (1974–5). *Atomtod*, in particular, raised a considerable furore. Written at a time when nuclear war seemed a distinct possibility, and the right of the rich and powerful to build their own private bunkers was hotly debated, it provoked interventions from political and ecclesiastical authorities determined to prevent its performance.

If *Atomtod* stood at the boundaries of operatic narrative, *Per Massimiliano Robespierre* moved beyond them. Puecher had originally proposed a scenography rich in incident and imagery, with many historical characters represented. Manzoni instead chose to scrutinize our own ambivalences in the face of Robespierre's thought and achievement. The work's use of blocks of complex vocal and instrumental sound owed a good deal to Manzoni's major works for chorus and orchestra of the late 1960s and early 70s, especially *Parole da Beckett* (1971), which won the UNESCO prize. This fascination with sound materials (in part influenced by Varèse) gave way in *Doktor Faustus* (1984–8) to a strikingly rich melodic vein, contrasting sharply with Manzoni's still rather undifferentiated harmonic palette. This, coupled with the work's renewed attention to concise, graphic narrative gestures – at times recalling the Verdian tradition of the *parola scenica* – has made *Doktor Faustus* the most accessible of Manzoni's theatre works.

See also ATOMTOD; DOKTOR FAUSTUS; PER MASSIMILIANO ROBESPIERRE; and SENTENZA, LA.

La sentenza (1, E. Jona), Bergamo, Donizetti, 13 Oct 1960
Atomtod (2, Jona), Milan, Piccola Scala, 27 March 1965
Per Massimiliano Robespierre (prol., 2, int, Manzoni and V. Puecher, after M. Robespierre and others), Bologna, Comunale, 12 April 1975
Doktor Faustus (2, G. Manzoni, after T. Mann), Milan, Scala, 16 May 1989

G. Manzoni, L. Pestalozza and V. Puecher: *Per Massimiliano Robespierre: testo e materiali per le scene musicali* (Bari, 1975)
G. Morelli: 'Per Massimiliano Robespierre', *RIM*, xi (1976), 126–37
J. Noller: *Engagement und Form: Giacomo Manzonis Werk in kulturtheoretischen und musikhistorischen Zusammenhängen* (Frankfurt, 1987)
——: 'Sprachkomposition und neuer Vokalstil des Komponisten Giacomo Manzoni', *NZM*, Jg.148, no.3 (1987), 19–22
H. W. Heister: 'Experiment v. Engagement: zu einigen Werken von Giacomo Manzoni', *Musiktexte*, xxiii/Feb (1988), 6–9
F. Dorsi: *Giacomo Manzoni* (Milan, 1989)
J. Noller: 'Musica e drammaturgia del "Doktor Faustus"', *Sonus*, i/1 (1989)
G. C. Taccani: 'Scena, musica, società', *Sonus*, ii/1 (1990), 69
E. Girardi: 'Doktor Faustus: un nuovo rigore di ordine drammaturgico nella continuità della scrittura musicale di Giacomo Manzoni', *Quaderni della Civica scuola di musica di Milano* (Dec 1991)
G. Manzoni: *Scritti* (Florence, 1991)
L. Pestalozza: *L'opposizione musicale* (Milan, 1991), 185–92
P. Santi: 'Musica del diavolo per Dottor Faust dei nostri tempi', *Civiltà musicale* (Feb 1991), 23–46   DAVID OSMOND-SMITH

Manzuoli, Giovanni (*b* Florence, *c*1720; *d* Florence, 1782). Italian soprano castrato, later contralto. After appearances in operas in Florence (1731) and Verona (1735) he settled in Naples until late 1748, occasionally performing in Rome and Venice. By the mid-1740s he was singing leading parts at S Carlo. After Carnival 1749 at Milan he performed in ten productions in Madrid (1749–52). He left after an incident occasioned by his arrogant temperament, and sang in Parma in Carnival 1754, but was in Lisbon for the opening of the Teatro de los Paços Ribeira in 1755 and briefly back in Madrid. He returned to Italy and remained there until 1764 except for a trip to Vienna, where his performance in Hasse's *Alcide al bivio* (1760) made him the idol of the city, according to Metastasio. In the 1764–5 season Manzuoli, a fine actor whose voice was 'the most powerful and voluminous soprano that had been heard … since the time of Farinelli' (Burney), drew 'a universal thunder' of applause at the King's Theatre, London; there he became acquainted with the Mozart family and sang in the première of J. C. Bach's *Adriano in Siria*. He retired to Florence in 1768 after three successful seasons in Italy (Verona, Turin, Venice and Milan), but sang again in Rome in 1770 and in Milan the next year in Hasse's *Ruggiero* and Mozart's *Ascanio in Alba*.

KATHLEEN KUZMICK HANSELL

Manzuolino, Il. *See* NERI, MICHELE ANGIOLO.

Maometto II ('Mahomet II'). *Dramma* in two acts by GIOACHINO ROSSINI to a libretto by Cesare della Valle after his *Anna Erizo*; Naples, Teatro S Carlo, 3 December 1820.

Maometto II, later revised by Rossini as LE SIÈGE DE CORINTHE (1826, Paris), is his penultimate Neapolitan opera and one of his grandest pieces of musical architecture, the two 90-minute acts built from a handful of huge interlocking musical units. It is one of Rossini's most powerfully scored works, with a large brass contingent used to darken textures and add a declamatory element to much of the writing; equally, Rossini appears to have lavished particular care on the accompanied recitatives, particularly in Act 2 where one of the most striking moments – Anna's consecration of her soul to her mother's spirit before Mahomet's fateful entry – is expressed in recitative.

The setting is the mid-15th-century Venetian colony of Negroponte in Greece which is being besieged by the Turkish army. General Condulmiero (tenor) advises the governor, Paolo Erisso (tenor), to meet the demands of Mahomet (bass) and open the gates; but the younger General Calbo (contralto) persuades the military council to fight to the end. Meanwhile Erisso, concerned for the safety of his daughter Anna (soprano), wishes to speed her marriage to Calbo despite the fact that she has been smitten with a man she met in Corinth (in reality, Mahomet on a spying mission for his father). When it becomes clear that the man was an impostor, the huge 867-bar *terzettone* is launched, a movement that embraces moral outrage, a military engagement as the Turks attack, a prayer and a leave-taking as Erisso ushers Anna and the women of the citadel to safety. The remaining two movements of Act 1 bring Mahomet and his followers to the fore; they rout the outer citadel and take Erisso and Calbo captive. They refuse to sanction the opening of the gates and are led away to be tortured. Rushing to intervene, Anna is recognized by Mahomet. She is promised a life of luxury if she is still faithful to him. Act 2 is dominated by Anna – Isabella Colbran in the original production – as she is courted by Mahomet before escaping to the citadel's burial vaults where her father and Calbo have taken refuge. In the trio 'In questi estremi' she asks her father to marry her to Calbo at the family tomb. She gives the two men a seal Mahomet has entrusted to her. Inspired by the reappearance of their two leaders, the Venetians put the Turks to flight but Anna has remained in the funeral vault. There she is hunted down by Mahomet and his broken band of followers, but before they can wreak their revenge she stabs herself to death in front of her mother's tomb.

RICHARD OSBORNE

Mapleson, James Henry (*b* London, 4 May 1830; *d* London, 14 Nov 1901). English impresario. He studied in London at the RAM and joined the orchestra of the Royal Italian Opera at Her Majesty's Theatre as a violinist (1848–9). After three years of vocal study under Mazzucato in Milan he sang briefly at Lodi and Verona under the name of Enrico Mariani. In 1856 he opened a musical agency, and in 1858 managed E. T. Smith's season at Drury Lane. In 1861 he began his own career as impresario at the Lyceum, and in his opening season produced *Un ballo in maschera* for the first time in England. He managed Her Majesty's, 1862–7, and in 1868 was at Drury Lane. He joined Gye at Covent Garden for the famous 'coalition seasons' of 1869 and 1870, and was again at Drury Lane, 1871–6. He reopened Her Majesty's in 1877 and continued to give seasons there until 1881. His last London seasons were in 1887 and 1889.

In 1878 Mapleson's company offered simultaneous seasons in London and New York, and the American group went on tour in the East and Mid-west. Its success brought Mapleson a three-year contract with the Academy of Music in New York, where from 1879 to 1883 he presented opera in an unprecedentedly glamorous style. The company also went on tour to Detroit, Cleveland, Buffalo, Pittsburgh, Indianapolis, Chicago and St Louis, and gave an annual opera festival in Cincinnati. When Henry Abbey opened the Metropolitan Opera in New York in 1883, he and Mapleson battled for singers and patrons. Mapleson abandoned his New York season early, barely managing to survive an ambitious tour that ranged as far west as San Francisco. In 1884–5 the 'opera war' drained Mapleson's resources further; the 1885–6 season and tour were a fiasco, with Mapleson being hounded by sheriffs and lawyers from San Francisco to London. His American career was effectively ended, although he returned briefly to the Academy of Music in 1896.

Besides being a flamboyant and resourceful promoter in the USA, Mapleson produced many operas for the first time in England, including *Faust*, *Carmen*, *La forza del destino*, *Les vêpres siciliennes*, *Mefistofele* and *Médée*, and brought to London many famous artists, including Christine Nilsson, Lillian Nordica and Jean de Reszke. He was popularly known as 'the Colonel'; his memoirs give an entertaining, if not altogether accurate, account of his activities.

See also TRAVELLING TROUPES, §5(v).

*
J. H. Mapleson: *The Mapleson Memoirs* (London, 1888); ed. H. Rosenthal (London, 1966)
J. F. Cone: *First Rival of the Metropolitan Opera* (New York, 1983)

WILLIAM BROOKS, HAROLD ROSENTHAL

Mara [née Schmeling], **Gertrud Elisabeth** (*b* Kassel, 23 Feb 1749; *d* Reval [now Tallinn], 20 Jan 1833). German soprano. Her father, a wandering violinist, trained her to play; to this she attributed her pure intonation, accurate timekeeping and coloratura made expressive through accentuation. After studying singing and theory as she moved about London, the Netherlands and Germany, she made her operatic début at Dresden (1767) in *Talestri*, by the Electress Maria Antonia. From 1771 prima donna at Frederick the Great's court opera in Berlin, she chafed at his bullying (he let her marry the disreputable cellist Johann Baptist Mara only if she agreed to stay on permanently) and left in 1779. At her peak she sang in Paris (1782–4) and, with forays to Turin and Venice, London (1784–1802): she triumphed particularly in Handel roles, such as Cleopatra (*Giulio Cesare*, 1787). In her decline, besides much concert work, she took to ballad opera (e.g. Polly in *The Beggar's Opera*, Covent Garden, 1797). Her later, impoverished years were spent in Estonia. Mara was the type of florid singer who could command vocal pathos as well as extraordinary speed and brilliance, but she was regarded as a poor actress.

*

BDA; *BurneyH*; *ES* (F. Serpa)

G. C. Grossheim: *Das Leben der Künstlerin Mara* (Kassel, 1823)

Lord Mount-Edgcumbe: *Musical Reminiscences* (London, 1824, 4/1834)

F. Rochlitz: *Für Freunde der Tonkunst*, i (Leipzig, 1824, 3/1868)

L. Schneider: *Geschichte der Oper und des königlichen Opernhauses in Berlin* (Berlin, 1852)

C. F. Pohl: *Mozart und Haydn in London* (Vienna, 1867), 339–47

O. von Riesemann, ed.: 'Eine Selbstbiographie der Sängerin Gertrud Elisabeth Mara', *AMZ*, new ser., x (1875), 497–609 *passim*

R. Kaulitz-Niedeck: *Die Mara* (Heilbronn, 1929)

O. Anward: *Die Prima Donna Friedrichs des Grossen* (Berlin, 1931)

A. Yorke-Long: *Music at Court* (London, 1954), 138–42

F. C. Petty: *Italian Opera in London 1760–1800* (Ann Arbor, 1980)

JOHN ROSSELLI

Marais, Marin (*b* Paris, 31 May 1656; *d* Paris, 15 Aug 1728). French composer and viol player. Son of a Parisian master cobbler, Vincent Marais, he showed at an early age an exceptional talent for music. After singing as a choirboy at St Germain-l'Auxerrois, he soon became one of the best viol players of his time, and is said to have surpassed his master, the celebrated Sainte-Colombe, after only six months of study. His outstanding gifts as an instrumentalist ensured him a brilliant future at court, where he was appointed in 1679 to the post of *ordinaire* of the Musique de la Chambre du Roi.

In 1676 Marais had become a member of the orchestra that performed Lully's operas at the royal court in St-Germain-en-Laye. For performances of *Atys* in 1676 and 1682, he played the viol on stage dressed as one of the 'Songes' (Dreams). It was probably from Lully, then *surintendant* of the Musique du Roi, that he learnt composition; he certainly absorbed the fine dramatic style displayed in the older composer's *tragédies en musique*. Marais's first dramatic work, *Idylle dramatique*, was a small-scale *divertissement* in three scenes with no plot, given a concert performance at Versailles in 1686 (libretto published in *Mercure galant*, April 1686). This was followed by four *tragédies en musique*, including *Alcide* (1693), written in collaboration with Louis Lully, and *Alcyone* (1706), his own masterpiece. Meanwhile, in 1705, Marais had succeeded Campra as *batteur de mesure* (orchestral conductor) at the Opéra.

His operas are in the Lullian tradition, as can be seen from the five-act structure of the *tragédie en musique* as well as from the dance forms chosen for the *divertissements*. But he was also aware of innovations introduced into the orchestra around 1690 by Collasse, such as writing independent parts for solo instruments: the oboe is used in *Alcyone*, the trumpet and the German (transverse) flute in *Sémélé*. He further excelled in *symphonies* describing such phenomena as storms and earthquakes, and, as in *Ariane et Bacchus*, in passages imitating birdsong or evoking the ethereal character of Love. In *Sémélé* he introduced *musettes*, adapting himself, like Campra, to the pastoral fashion later adopted by Rameau, a composer he also anticipated through his subtle harmonic writing, through the use of suspensions creating interesting dissonances, and by his use of 7ths.

See also ALCYONE.

all tragédies en musique, first performed at the Paris Opéra

Alcide [La mort d'Hercule, La mort d'Alcide] (prol., 5, J. G. de Campistron), 3 Feb 1693, collab. L. Lully, *F-Pn*

Ariane et Bacchus (prol., 5, Saint-Jean), 8 March 1696, *Pn*; (Paris, 1696)

Alcyone (prol., 5, A. H. de Lamotte), 18 Feb 1706, *Pn*; (Paris, 1706)

Sémélé (prol., 5, Lamotte), 9 April 1709, *Pn*; (Paris, 1709)

*

E. Titon du Tillet: *Le Parnasse françois* (Paris, 1732)

M. Barthélemy: 'Les opéras de Marin Marais', *RBM*, vii (1953), 136–46

F. Lesure: 'Marin Marais: sa carrière, sa famille', *RBM*, vii (1953), 129–36

J. de La Gorce: 'Some Notes on Lully's Orchestra', *Jean-Baptiste Lully and the Music of the French Baroque: Essays in Honor of James R. Anthony* (Cambridge, 1989), 99–112

S. Milliot and J. de La Gorce: *Marin Marais* (Paris, 1991)

JÉRÔME DE LA GORCE

Mařák, Otakar (*b* Esztergom, Hungary, 5 Jan 1872; *d* Prague, 2 July 1939). Czech tenor. He studied at the Prague Conservatory with Paršova-Zikešová. In 1899 he made his début at Brno as Faust and from 1900 he appeared at the New German Theatre, Prague. He sang under Mahler at the Vienna Hofoper and created Gennaro in Wolf-Ferrari's *I gioielli della Madonna* (1911, Berlin). In 1913 he was the first London Bacchus (*Ariadne auf Naxos*), and the following year he sang in Chicago as Parsifal in the local première of Wagner's opera. He was principal tenor at the Prague National Theatre from 1914 and retired from the stage in 1934.

DAVID CUMMINGS

Marazzoli, Marco [Marco dell'Arpa] (*b* Parma, *c*1602–8; *d* Rome, 25 Jan 1662). Italian composer. Although little is known of his life before his association with the Barberini family, Wolfgang Witzenmann (1986) has noted his arrival in Rome in 1626. Marazzoli's earliest known association with Cardinal Antonio Barberini dates from 1631 in conjunction with an entourage taken to Urbino. In 1634 the benefice he received in the Roman basilica of S Maria Maggiore was probably a result of Barberini favour, and an inventory of 1636–40 lists Cardinal Antonio's 'arpa grande' as being in Marazzoli's possession. By 1637 the musician-priest was serving as the cardinal's 'aiutante di camera'; in the same year, he resigned a benefice at the cathedral in Parma and the Barberini placed him in the Sistine Chapel choir. There he retained a permanent post as tenor from March 1640 until his death. Over a 25-year period Marazzoli composed some 400 cantatas, besides sacred dialogues, motets, 11 oratorios and eight, perhaps ten, operas. Between 1637 and 1656 he set five dramas for the Barberini, collaborating in 1637 with Virgilio Mazzocchi and in 1654 with Antonio Maria Abbatini. A sixth opera was first presented in 1641 in Ferrara. He spent one operatic season in Venice (1642) and, at Cardinal Mazarin's invitation, was in residence at the court of France from 1644 to the spring of 1645. This service earned him an annual pension from the crown. He died a *bussolante* to Pope Alexander VII and a rich man.

Chi soffre speri is one of the earliest known operas with comic characters, though its *commedia* scenes are balanced by a complex of romantic pastoral plots. Exactly which portions of its three acts Marazzoli composed in 1637 is not known. The payment record assigns him 34% of the copying expenses. Later collaborations in Rome distribute blocks of continuous scenes to each composer, usually whole but sometimes half acts. On this model, Marazzoli might have been assigned the whole of the original second act and its subsequent *intermedio*, since two arias early in Act 3 can be

'La Vita humana' (Marco Marazzoli): design by Giovanni Francesco Grimaldi for the Prologue and Act 1 in the original production at the Teatro Barberini, Rome, 31 January 1656; engraving by G. B. Galestruzzi

attributed to Mazzocchi. Scenes were shifted, added and replaced for lavish restaging in 1639, in which all three original *intermedi* were supplanted. Only the rearranged musical version of 1639 has survived. Marazzoli's estate included a separate copy of *La fiera di Farfa*, the 1639 *intermedio* to Act 2, which has therefore been attributed to him. He may also have been responsible for the new first *intermedio*, because its opening dances bear titles that match the main dances in the Barberini's 1638 ballet *L'acquisto di Durindana*, a production in which Marazzoli was involved.

A more secure assessment of his style may be made from his next three undertakings. An eight-month sojourn in Ferrara culminated in the performance of *L'Amore trionfante dello Sdegno* (also known as *Armida*) to celebrate a wedding in February 1641. To the episode between the sorceress Armida and the crusader Rinaldo d'Este from Tasso's epic *Gerusalemme liberata*, the librettist added a host of personifications (the sopranos La Curiosità [Curiosity], La Prudenza [Prudence], L'Amore [Love], Lo Sdegno [Disdain], La Fortuna [Fortune], Il Genio [Genius], La Lascivia [Lasciviousness] and the contralto Il Valore [Valour]), thereby transforming the story into an allegory of love. Like Homeric gods, Love and Disdain compete to control Armida's feelings towards the crusader, and Love wins. The score reveals traits that mark Marazzoli's style in this period: male characters sung by tenors and basses rather than castratos; functional rather than lyric recitative; arias in increasingly elaborate strophic variations, fluid madrigalian duets (seven in *Armida*) and an unobtrusive building of musical tension where required.

After nine months in Rome, Marazzoli returned to Ferrara in November 1641. Despite being sick with fever, or because of it, he presented *Armida* again in January 1642. In the following months two collaborations with Oratio Persiani were given at the Teatro SS Giovanni e Paolo in Venice: his revision or rewriting of Filippo Vitali's *Narciso et Ecco immortalati* and his

festa teatrale with 16 characters, a 'prodigious crow' and various choruses, *Gli amori di Giasone e d'Isifile*. By March he had composed *Le pretensioni del Tebro, e del Po*, again for Ferrara. More spectacle than drama, and filled with vocal ensembles, this work presents Pluto (bass) presiding over dancing demons, and a *combattimento*, or mimed battle, between the forces of the rivers of Rome (bass) and Ferrara (bass), an implicit reference to the War of Castro between the papacy and Parma. Taddeo Barberini as *generalissimo* of the Church is extolled, and Giove (Jupiter, bass, standing for Urban VIII) has the battle halted in favour of peace.

In contrast, *Il giuditio della Ragione tra la Beltà e l'Affetto* of 1643 is animated more by the ridiculous humour and quips of Francesco Buti's allegorical light comedy than by musical invention. Bellezza [Beauty] has fallen in love with Capriccio [Caprice]. To conquer his capriciousness, she tries to win him through Gelosia [Jealousy] by appearing to return to Vero Amore [True Love]. In the end, Tempo [Time] and Ragione [Reason] reconcile Beauty and True Love. The opera calls for eight sopranos and two mute characters. The successful carnival performances at the house of the Count of Marciano no doubt relied on the neat rhymes of the insouciant dialogue and on the humorous situations, with enchanted fleas, an 'instrumental' serenade given by Martello (one of the mute characters), and Time as a vendor of spectacles that help people see differently. The unobtrusive recitative is responsive to the rhythms of comic speech. Unlike *Chi soffre speri*, *Il giuditio* is pure comedy, without pathos or personalized emotion. The work is attributed to Marazzoli because most of Act 1 of the sole surviving score, which was in his possession at his death, is in his hand. Pier Maria Capponi hypothesized a 1643 performance at the French Embassy in Rome, followed by a revival in Paris in 1645, when Marazzoli was certainly there. But as late as 14 February 1643 the French ambassador had not yet settled into permanent quarters in Rome; moreover, contemporary Roman reports do not mention the French in connection with the work, and *Il giuditio* would have been most uncharacteristic as a vehicle to test French reaction to Italian opera.

The changing operatic trends of the 1650s had little effect on Marazzoli's last three musical dramas, undertaken for the Barberini. As in most of his earlier scores, male characters are sung by lower voices, and all but two of the personifications in *La Vita humana* (1656) are sopranos. He mostly retained the rhythms and melodic contours of his earlier recitative, though with an increased boldness in the use of leaping intervals, and never moved towards the quicker, *secco* style. Rather, a broadened harmonic rhythm allowed a faster tempo. His harmonies became more chromatic and darker, relying increasingly on series of cadential progressions and loose sequential gestures. He discarded some old aria forms and replaced them with newer refrain forms, such as the *estriviglio*, which he called *intercalare* (refrain, strophe 1, refrain, strophe 2, refrain etc.). His fondness for ostinato patterns continues to underlie these newer arias, as in those he wrote for *Dal male il bene*, of which he set the whole of Act 2, and Act 3 scenes i–ix. The three new librettos themselves did less to inspire these developments than did Marazzoli's experience in writing chamber cantatas.

Although Giulio Rospigliosi modelled both *Dal male il bene* (1654) and *Le armi e gli amori* (1656) on existing Spanish plays, the scores do not have any obvious Spanish-style music, though there was dancing in Spanish style. Both 'Spanish' works have few arias and ensembles compared with the amount of recitative dialogue, a result of the intricate romantic plots based on undeclared love, mistaken infidelities and hot-headed defences of honour. *Le armi e gli amori* tangles three romantic heroes (two tenors and a high tenor in alto clef) with two resourceful heroines (two sopranos, sung by castratos), an interfering father (bass) and four comic servants (soprano, mezzo-soprano, tenor and baritone).

The morality play *La Vita humana* was judged thin on plot in favour of 'a collection of arias held together by a few recitatives' by one contemporary observer. L'Innocenza [Innocence] (soprano) and La Colpa [Guilt] (soprano) aided by Il Piacere [Pleasure] (tenor) battle for control over La Vita Humana [Life] (soprano), a rather spoilt young Everyman. Though warned by Innocence, Life chooses Pleasure, while his companion L'Intendimento [Understanding] (contralto) falls victim to pain, confusion and a sleeping potion. Believing that Understanding is dead, Life is shocked into penitence. After the deceptions are unmasked, Life resolves to follow the path of virtue. This simple parable received some of Marazzoli's most ambitious music. Extended arias and duets are supported by expansive phrasing, virtuoso melodic ornamentation bordering on the motivic, and the darkened colour of his later harmonic style. Polychoral music, long unused in Roman opera, appears in the static festive scenes, reminiscent of oratorio. Some listeners thought the work tedious, a 'sermon in music', 'more suited for church than theatre', according to a contemporary newssheet. (The first modern performance, given in Glasgow in 1990, proved its musical viability.) The work was written to celebrate the Lutheran Queen of Sweden's conversion to Roman Catholicism. The pope himself had given Marazzoli charge of the music for the celebrations as early as two months before the queen's arrival in Rome at the end of 1655. Indeed Marazzoli appears to have become

Alexander VII's unofficial palace composer in 1656, when he is first listed in the pope's household among the *camerieri extra*. Although Queen Christina also named him one of her *virtuosi da camera*, the composer retained his ties to the Barberini, who subsidized the publication of *La Vita humana* in 1658, with its splendid plates (see illustration).

Marazzoli set more operas than Stefano Landi or Luigi Rossi. Yet despite the quantity of his surviving works, a comprehensive assessment of his musical personality is still lacking. Not an outstanding melodist, contrapuntist or harmonist, Marazzoli can be credited with mere facility, perhaps on the basis of his presumed skills in instrumental improvisation. But this judgment underrates the vivacity and validity of his most satisfactory work, especially his duets or what may be termed vocal trio sonatas. Imitative upper textures counterbalance the harmonic patterning – ostinatos and shadows of ostinato procedure – in the basso continuo. His style was perhaps reassuringly conventional and stable, without literary heavy-handedness, calling up the necessary amount of musical virtuosity and fantasy, or 'bizzaria', that his courtly audiences required.

See also CHI SOFFRE SPERI and DAL MALE IL BENE.

Chi soffre speri [L'Egisto; L'Alvida] (commedia musicale, 3, Giulio Rospigliosi, after G. Boccaccio: *Il decamerone*), Rome, Palazzo Barberini, 12 Feb 1637, lost, argomento (Rome, 1637); rev., Rome, Teatro Barberini, 27 Feb 1639, *I-Rvat* (*R1982*: IOB, lxi); collab. V. Mazzocchi [referred to as *Il falcone* in Ademollo 1888, p.25]

La fiera di Farfa (intermedio to Act 2 of Chi soffre speri), Rome, Teatro Barberini, 27 Feb 1639, *Rvat* (*R1982*: IOB, lxi)

L'Amore trionfante dello Sdegno [L'Armida] (operetta drammatica, 5, A. Pio di Savoia, after T. Tasso: *Gerusalemme liberata*), Ferrara, Sala Grande, Feb 1641, *Rvat* (mostly autograph)

Gli amori di Giasone e d'Isifile (festa teatrale, 3, O. Persiani), Venice, SS Giovanni e Paolo, 22 Feb 1642, lost, lib. (Venice, 1642)

Le pretensioni del Tebro, e del Po (Pio di Savoia), Ferrara, 4 March 1642, *Rvat**

Il giuditio della Ragione tra la Beltà e l'Affetto [La Bellezza amata; Il Capriccio] (dramma in musica, 3, F. Buti), Rome, Palazzo Roberti, before 7 Feb 1643, MS lib. *Rvat*

Dal male il bene (dramma musicale, 3, Giulio and Giacomo Rospigliosi, after A. Sigler de Huerta: *No ay bien sin ageno daño*), Rome, Palazzo Barberini, 12 Feb 1654, *D-MÜs* (Act 1), *I-Bc*, *IBborromeo*, *Rsc* (Acts 2–3), *Rvat*; collab. A. M. Abbatini

La Vita humana, ovvero Il trionfo della pietà (dramma musicale, 3, Giulio Rospigliosi), Rome, Teatro Barberini, 31 Jan 1656, *IBborromeo*, *Rvat* (Rome, 1658)

Le armi e gli amori (dramma per musica, 3, Giulio Rospigliosi, after J. Pérez de Montalbán), Rome, Palazzo Barberini, 20 Feb 1656, *Rvat*

Doubtful: L'Arianna (commedia in musica), lost; Narciso et Ecco immortalati (op drammatica, 3, Persiani), Venice, SS Giovanni e Paolo, 30 Jan 1642, lost [rev. of F. Vitali: Narciso et Ecco immortalati, also lost]

*

G. Tetio: *Aedes barberinae ad Quirinalem* (Rome, 1642), 18, 35, 150

G. Gualdo Priorato: *Historia della sacra real maestà di Cristina Alessandra, regina di Svezia* (Modena, 1656)

A. Ademollo: 'Una rappresentazione celebre nel Teatro Barberini (1639)', *Rassegna settimanale*, no.177 (1881), 333–5

——: *I teatri di Roma nel secolo decimosettimo* (Rome, 1888)

H. Goldschmidt: *Studien zur Geschichte der italienischen Oper im 17. Jahrhundert*, i (Leipzig, 1901)

H. Prunières: *L'opéra italien en France avant Lulli* (Paris, 1913)

U. Rolandi: 'La prima commedia musicale rappresentata a Roma nel 1639', *Nuova antologia*, no.62 (1927), 523–8

R. Rolland: *Les origines du théâtre lyrique moderne: histoire de l'opéra en Europe avant Lully et Scarlatti* (Paris, 1931), 160–62

H. Prunières: 'Les musiciens du Cardinal Antonio Barberini', *Mélanges de musicologie offerts à M. Lionel de la Laurencie* (Paris, 1933), 117–22

U. Rolandi: *Il libretto per musica attraverso i tempi* (Rome, 1951), 57–9, pls. 30–31, 44

P. M. Capponi: 'Marco Marazzoli e l'oratorio *Christo e i Farisei*', *Chigiana*, x (1953), 101–6

S. Reiner: 'Collaboration in *Chi soffre speri*', *MR*, xxii (1961), 265–82

A. Beijer: 'Une maquette de décor récemment retrouvée pour le "Ballet de la prospérité des armes de France" dansé à Paris, le 7 fevrier 1641', *Le lieu théâtral à la Renaissance: CNRS Royaumont 1963*, 377–403

P. Bjurström: *Feast and Theatre in Queen Christina's Rome* (Stockholm, 1966)

G. Masson: 'Papal Gifts and Entertainments in Honour of Queen Christina's Arrival', *Analecta reginensia*, i (1966), 244–61

W. Holmes: 'Comedy – Opera – Comic Opera', *AnMc*, no.5 (1968), 92–103

I. Küffel: *Die Libretti Giulio Rospigliosis: ein Kapitel frühbarocker Operngeschichte in Rom* (diss., U. of Vienna, 1968)

P. Kast: 'Unbekannte Dokumente zur Oper *Chi soffre speri* von 1637', *Helmuth Osthoff zu seinem 70. Geburtstag* (Tutzing, 1969), 129–34

W. Witzenmann: 'Autographe Marco Marazzolis in der Biblioteca Vaticana', *AnMc*, no.7 (1969), 36–86; no.9 (1970), 203–94

T. Walker: 'Gli errori di "Minerva al tavolino"', *Venezia e il melodramma nel seicento: Venice 1972*, 7–20

W. Witzenmann: 'Die römische Barockoper *La Vita humana, ovvero Il trionfo della pietà*', *AnMc*, no.15 (1975), 158–201

F. Hammond: 'Girolamo Frescobaldi and a Decade of Music in Casa Barberini: 1634–1643', *AnMc*, no.19 (1979), 94–124

M. Murata: 'The Recitative Soliloquy', *JAMS*, xxxii (1979), 45–73

——: *Operas for the Papal Court* (Ann Arbor, 1981)

L. Bianconi and T. Walker: 'Production, Consumption and Political Function of Seventeenth-Century Opera', *Early Music History*, iv (1984), 209–96

K. Andrae: *Ein römischer Kapellmeister im 17. Jahrhundert: A. M. Abbatini* (Herzberg, 1986)

G. Ciliberti: *A. M. Abbatini e la musica del suo tempo (1595–1679): documenti per una ricostruzione bio-bibliografica* (Selci-Umbro, 1986)

W. Witzenmann, ed.: *Cantatas by Marco Marazzoli, c.1605–1662* (New York, 1986), pp.v–x

S. Franchi: *Drammaturgia romana: repertorio cronologico dei testi drammatici pubblicati a Roma e nel Lazio, secolo XVII* (Rome, 1988)

N. Zaslaw: 'The First Opera in Paris: a Study in the Politics of Art', *Jean-Baptiste Lully and the Music of the French Baroque: Essays in Honor of James R. Anthony* (Cambridge, 1989), 7–23

P. Fabbri: *Il secolo cantante: per una storia del libretto d'opera nel seicento* (Bologna, 1990)   MARGARET MURATA

Marcel [Wasself], Lucille (*b* New York, 1877; *d* Vienna, 22 June 1921). American soprano. She studied in New York and later in Vienna and with Jean de Reszke in Paris. Her début was as a last-minute replacement for Anna Bahr-Mildenburg in the Vienna première of *Elektra* at the Staatsoper in 1908; she remained there until 1910, when she resigned in order to marry the company's director, Felix Weingartner, and later sang in Darmstadt, Hamburg and Paris. She was a member of the Boston Opera Company, 1911–14, where she performed Tosca and the title role in the American première of Bizet's *Djamileh* in 1912. A voice combining power and beauty enabled her to sing such roles as Marguerite, Eva and Aida.   CORI ELLISON

Marcello, Benedetto (*b* Venice, 24 June or 24 July 1686; *d* Brescia, 24 July 1739). Italian composer and satirist. He was the youngest child of the Venetian nobleman Agostino Marcello and the poet Paolina Capello, and the brother of Alessandro Marcello (1668–1747), a composer of chamber music. Although he is widely said to have died on his 53rd birthday, parish records give 24

June as his date of birth. His father taught him to play the violin, but later discouraged his developing interest in singing and counterpoint, wanting him to pursue a legal career. He was elected in 1706 to serve on the Grand Council of the Republic, which led to a succession of important posts in the civil service; he also practised as an advocate and magistrate. He joined the Arcadian Academy of Rome in October 1711 and was admitted to the Accademia Filarmonica of Bologna in December 1711. In 1728 he was secretly married within the church to Rosanna Scalfi, one of his pupils; after his death she appeared in one opera, Paganelli's *Artaserse*, in a performance at S Salvatore in spring 1742.

Marcello composed approximately 700 works, of which roughly 500 are secular works for one or two voices and continuo, 100 are instrumental, and 50 are the celebrated Psalms of David published in eight elegant instalments by Domenico Lovisa (*Estro poetico-armonico*, Venice, 1724–6); he also wrote four oratorios. No operas can now be attributed to him, although he composed several serenatas. Among operas previously attributed to Marcello, an *Engelberta* in Turin (1704) is now credited to Fiorè, and *La fede riconosciuta* (1707) to C. F. Pollarolo. *La Dorinda* (1729) is considered a revision of *La fede riconosciuta* by Baldassare Galuppi and Pescetti. Marcello was the composer of two *intrecci scenichi*: *Psiché* (*c*1711) and *Arianna* (*c*1727), on librettos by Vincenzo Cassani. The libretto of the *pastorale ad uso di scena*, *Calisto in orsa* (*c*1725) is anonymous. All three works were for private performance. The libretto of *Arato in Sparta* (1709, music by Ruggieri) was by Minato.

Marcello's literary interests, inherited from his mother, developed into a penchant for merciless criticism and satire. His noble background and his conscientious study of antiquity, which is documented in the prefaces to the Psalms, predisposed him to revere tradition and academic rigour and to deride virtuosity and self-indulgence. In *Il teatro alla moda* (Venice, October 1720), a satire on opera that was published anonymously but can be securely attributed to him on the basis of censors' records, the composer railed against both musical customs and social foibles particular to his time. Among the things he attacked were excessive ornamentation, unprepared dissonances, haughty prima donnas and chattering stage mothers. As a composer Marcello was occasionally guilty of some of the sins he enumerated. He might have been surprised to find the work taken as seriously as it has been; later editions of it include 13 in Italian, four in French, one in German (Alfred Einstein, *c*1917) and one in English (Reinhard Pauly in the *Musical Quarterly*, xxxiv, 1948).

Marcello was also a successful teacher and was preoccupied with the cultivation of good taste in singing. He seems to have been an early teacher of Faustina Bordoni, who was born in his parish and brought up under the protection of him and his brother Alessandro. In response to the widespread casting of castratos in Venetian opera, Marcello weighed the moral vice of castration against its artistic benefits in the comic madrigals 'No' che lassù' and 'Si che laggiù', published by Bortoli in 1715. In the satirical letter cantata, 'Carissima figlia', which was addressed to Vittoria Tesi in about 1719, he mimicked the singing styles of a host of opera stars, including Tesi, Bordoni, Francesca Cuzzoni and Gaetano Berenstadt. The two madrigals and the cantata are apparently set to Marcello's own texts. With *Il teatro alla moda*, these works provide valuable insight into operatic practices of the time.

*

R. Giazotto: 'La guerra dei palchi', *NRMI*, v (1971), 1034–52

F. Della Seta: 'I Borghese (1691–1731): la musica di una generazione', *NA*, new ser., i (1983), 139–208

N. J. Clapton: 'RISM Notes', *EMc*, xi (1983), 295

C. Vitali: '*Il teatro alla moda* ha finalmente un editore', *NA*, new ser., i (1983), 245–50

G. Vio: 'Una satira sul teatro veneziano di Sant'Angelo datata "febbraio 1717"', *Informazioni e studi vivaldiani* (1989), 103–30

E. Selfridge-Field: *The Music of Benedetto and Alessandro Marcello: a Thematic Catalogue with Commentary on the Composers, Repertory, and Sources* (Oxford, 1990)

ELEANOR SELFRIDGE-FIELD

Marcello da Capua. *See* BERNARDINI, MARCELLO.

Marchand, Theobald Hilarius (*b* Strasbourg, 1741; *d* Munich, 22 Nov 1800). German singer and theatre manager. He went to Paris as a 17-year-old to study medicine, but the *opéras comiques* he heard excited him and he became a singer and actor. He was a member of Sebastiani's troupe in the Rhineland in 1764; the repertory included many Italian and French operas. By 1771 Marchand was manager of the company, which performed mainly in Mainz, but also in Strasbourg, Mannheim and Frankfurt. In 1772 Gotter translated Poinsinet's *Tom Jones* for him, and André and Faber also provided him with versions of mainly French works. In 1774 he staged the Wieland-Schweitzer *Alceste*. In 1775 he went to Mannheim, with such success that the Elector Carl Theodor decided to open a German National Theatre, with Marchand as its first director. When the elector moved to Munich in 1778 he took Marchand's company with him. Marchand retired in 1793 but continued to take the roles of comic fathers until shortly before his death.

Marchand was a pioneer in the performance of French light operas in German translation; three volumes of librettos were published: *Sammlung der komischen Operetten … unter der Direktion des Herrn Marchand aufgeführt* (Frankfurt, 1772). His company had fine actor-singers, including Magdalena Brochard (later Marchand's wife), Huck and Brandl; Maria Henriette Wilhelmine Stierle (née Mierk) and Johann Nouseul, later to create Monostatos in *Die Zauberflöte*, were also members for a time. Not the least of Marchand's claims to attention is the fact that Goethe owed his introduction to and love of French opera to the performances he heard that company give, at Frankfurt and probably Strasbourg, during his most impressionable years; he wrote warmly of Marchand in his autobiography *Dichtung und Wahrheit* (pt iv, bk 17).

Marchand's daughter Margarethe was a singer and composer; *see* DANZI family, (3).

*

ADB (J. Kürschner)

C. H. Schmid: *Chronologie des deutschen Theaters* (Leipzig, 1775); ed. P. Legband in *Schriften der Gesellschaft für Theatergeschichte*, i (Berlin, 1902)

E. Devrient: *Geschichte der deutschen Schauspielkunst* (Leipzig, 1848–61, 2/1967 rev. R. Kabel and C. Trilse)

F. Walter: *Geschichte des Theaters und der Musik am kurpfälzischen Hofe* (Leipzig, 1898)

E. Pies: *Prinzipale: zur Genealogie des deutschsprachigen Berufstheaters vom 17. bis 19. Jahrhundert* (Ratingen, 1973), 235–8

PETER BRANSCOMBE

Marchand de Venise, Le ('The Merchant of Venice'). *Opéra* in three acts by REYNALDO HAHN to a libretto by Miguel Zamacoïs after WILLIAM SHAKESPEARE's play; Paris, Opéra, 25 March 1935.

The libretto follows the outline of the play but omits all the comic scenes with the character of Lancelot Gobbo; it transposes lines and speeches freely, as well as adding a certain amount of new material, for instance Shylock's recitative at the finale of Act 1, 'La vengeance est un plat de roi,/Qui peut très bien se manger froid'.

The opera is set in five tableaux. Act 1 is in Venice, before Shylock's house, and introduces the characters of Graziano and Lorenzo (tenors), Jessica (soprano), Shylock (bass), Bassanio (baritone) and Antonio (bass); it includes the sealing of the bond and the abduction of Jessica and has three notable arias, 'Portia … lorsque l'on prononce ces accents', sung by Bassanio, Shylock's tirade against the Christians, 'Que je le hais', and the serenade in front of Shylock's house, sung by a masker, 'Bel oiseau, quittez votre cage'. Act 2 concerns itself entirely with the courtship of Portia (soprano) and Bassanio; it has a long scene with the entrance music in comic style for the Princes of Morocco (bass) and Aragon (tenor) and the most celebrated passage in the opera, the quartet 'L'amour qui pourtant n'est pas bête'. The third act is divided into two tableaux, the first in the Court of Justice in Venice, with Portia's monologue, 'La sentence, nous y venons', and Shylock's aria, 'Frustré! Dépouillé!'. The final scene reunites the three pairs of lovers in Portia's palace in Belmont.

An attempt by Hahn to create what he described as a Mozartian entertainment (he began to compose it while at the front during World War I), it was originally envisaged as a vehicle for Mary Garden. The romantic music and the music for the entrance of the princes are in the familiar style of Hahn's best *mélodies* or ballets, but Shylock's dramatic outbursts fit uneasily beside the rest, and the timing of the first performance, when the rise of National Socialism in Germany had triggered off a wave of anti-Semitism in France, can only have added to Hahn's difficulties.

At the first performance the roles of Portia, Nérissa [Nerissa] (mezzo-soprano) and Jessica were sung by Fanny Heldy, Renée Mahé and Odette Renaudin; Bassanio, Antonio and Graziano by Martial Singher, Paul Cabanel and Le Clezio, and Shylock by André Pernet, in a production designed by Yves Alix and conducted by Philippe Gaubert. The opera has been revived occasionally, notably at the Opéra-Comique in 1979, conducted by Manuel Rosenthal.

PATRICK O'CONNOR

Märchenoper (Ger.: 'fairy-tale opera'). The origins of *Märchenoper* were traced by Schmidt back to such works as Baldassare Galuppi's *Il paese della Cuccagna* (1750), Laruette's *Cendrillon* (1759) and F.-A. D. Philidor's *Le soldat magicien* (1760). But the term, and variants such as 'Feenmärchen', 'Märchenspiel', 'Volksmärchen' and 'Feerie', more strictly refer to a genre which acquired considerable popularity among German composers of the 19th and early 20th centuries, typical examples being written by Drechsler, Schnyder von Wartensee, Riotte, August Conradi, Sommer, Humperdinck and Siegfried Wagner. Fairy-tale operas were written in other languages too (*see* OPÉRA FÉERIE), though the appeal to the German Romantic imagination was uniquely powerful.

Fairies as such are not an obligatory feature of the *Märchenoper*: an element of the supernatural, the oriental or the irrational may suffice. Simplicity and naivety of treatment, in the manner of a children's story, are characteristic, though the works are not necessarily intended for a young audience; indeed, the content of the tales is often symbolic and bears a moral message. Occasionally the borderline between fairy-tale and myth or legend is blurred: a work such as *Siegfried*, which contains fairy-tale elements, is clearly close to *Märchenoper*, as are *Oberon* and *Hans Heiling*, though they are not so designated by their composers. There is also an affinity with such genres as *Zauberspiel* and *Zauberoper*.

L. Schmidt: *Zur Geschichte der Märchen-Oper* (Halle, 2/1896)

J. C. Daninger: *Sage und Märchen im Musikdrama: eine ästhetische Untersuchung an der Sagen- und Märchenoper des 19. Jahrhunderts* (Prague, 1916)

O. Daube: *Siegfried Wagner und die Märchenoper* (Leipzig, 1936)

H. Stier-Somlo: *Das Grimmsche Märchen als Text für Opern und Spiele* (Berlin and Leipzig, 1936)

P. Gossett: 'Fairy-Tale and *Opera Buffa*: the Genre of Rossini's *La Cenerentola*', *La Cenerentola*, ed. N. John (London, 1980) [ENO Opera Guide]   BARRY MILLINGTON

Marchesi. Family of singers.

(1) **Salvatore Marchesi** Cavaliere de Castrone, Marchese della Rajata (*b* Palermo, 15 Jan 1822; *d* Paris, 20 Feb 1908). Italian baritone and singing teacher. He studied in Palermo, and in Milan with Lamperti. In 1848 he made his début in New York as Don Carlo (*Ernani*). On returning to Europe he studied further with Garcia in London, where in 1850 he met the German mezzo-soprano Mathilde Graumann. After their marriage in 1852 he appeared at the Berlin Opera in *Ernani*, *Il barbiere di Siviglia* and *Lucrezia Borgia*. Further engagements in Germany followed, and in 1853 he sang at Ferrara, again in *Ernani*. After a period spent teaching at the Vienna Academy, in 1863 he returned briefly to the stage. He sang Leporello and Méphistophélès (*Faust*) both in Italian and in English at Her Majesty's Theatre. He translated several French and German opera librettos into Italian, including three by Wagner, and wrote *A Vademecum for Singing-Teachers and Pupils* (New York, 1902).

(2) **Mathilde (de Castrone) Marchesi** [née Graumann] (*b* Frankfurt, 24 May 1821; *d* London, 17 Nov 1913). German mezzo-soprano and teacher, wife of (1) Salvatore Marchesi. She studied in Frankfurt, Vienna and in Paris with Garcia. A concert singer, she made a single stage appearance, as Rosina (*Il barbiere*), at Bremen in 1852, the year of her marriage. In 1854 she began to teach, in Vienna, Paris, Cologne and again Vienna. In 1881 she founded her own school of singing in Paris, where her pupils included Emma Calvé, Gabrielle Krauss, Nellie Melba, Sibyl Sanderson, Emma Eames, Katharina Klafsky, Selma Kurz, and her daughter (3) Blanche Marchesi. She retired in 1908. She published numerous sets of vocal exercises, mostly under the title *L'art du chant*, with various opus numbers, from the 1850s onwards, and an *Ecole Marchesi: méthode de chant théorique et pratique* (Paris, 1886; Eng. trans., 1896, 1903) as well as a book of memoirs.

(3) **Blanche Marchesi** (*b* Paris, 4 April 1863; *d* London, 15 Dec 1940). French soprano, daughter of (1) Salvatore and (2) Mathilde Marchesi. She studied with her mother in Paris and made her operatic début in 1900 at Prague, as Brünnhilde (*Die Walküre*). For several seasons she sang with the Moody-Manners Opera Company, appearing at Covent Garden in 1902 as Elisabeth (*Tannhäuser*), Elsa, Isolde, Leonora (*Il trovatore*) and Santuzza. She taught singing for many years in London and wrote her memoirs and a *The Singer's Catechism and Creed* (London, 1932).

M. de Castrone Marchesi: *Erinnerungen aus meinem Leben* (Vienna, 1877, enlarged 4/1889 as *Aus meinem Leben*; Eng. trans, enlarged, 1897 as *Marchesi and Music*)

B. Marchesi: *A Singer's Pilgrimage* (London, 1923)
                                    ELIZABETH FORBES

Marchesi [Marchesini], **Luigi** (*b* Milan, 8 Aug 1755; *d* Milan, 14, 15 or 18 Dec 1829). Italian castrato and composer. He studied with the tenor Albuzzi and the castrato Caironi, entering the Milan cathedral choir in 1765. He made his theatrical début in Rome's Teatro delle Dame, singing female roles in three comic operas (1773–4); he never again appeared in either female or comic roles. During Carnival 1775 he took minor roles at the Regio Ducal Teatro, Milan, and later sang in Venice and Treviso; in Carnival 1776 he began a six-year contract with the Munich court, but sang there for two seasons only. His emergence as one of the foremost singers in Italy dates from his engagement at S Carlo, Naples (1778–9) where he appeared in five operas by Mysliveček, Platania and Martín y Soler. He sang other works by Mysliveček (1779, Venice; 1780, Milan) and in 1779 at Florence began an important association with the composers Bianchi and Sarti. He appeared in works by Martín y Soler, Jommelli, Schuster and Bianchi at S Carlo, then, after appearances in Genoa and Florence (1781), made a triumphant return to Milan at Carnival 1782.

Following a sensational performance of Bianchi's *Il trionfo della pace* in Turin, he was appointed singer to the court, remaining there until 1798. With leave to travel nine months of the year, he sang in premières in Turin, Rome, Lucca, Padua, Sinigaglia, Florence and Mantua between 1782–4. In 1785 he appeared in Sarti's *Giulio Sabino* in Vienna (for illustration *see* GIULIO SABINO) and Warsaw, then went to St Petersburg, where he sang Sarti's *Armida e Rinaldo* to inaugurate the Hermitage Theatre (1786). From 1788–90 he divided his time between Italy and London, where his greatest success was his début in Sarti's *Giulio Sabino* (1788; see Mount Edgcumbe). He remained in Italy for the rest of his career apart from short trips to Vienna in 1798 and 1801 (for Mayr's *Ginevra di Scozia*). He spent four Carnival seasons in Venice between 1791 and 1798 and appeared at Carnivals in Turin and Milan, where he last sang publicly in Mayr's *Lodoiska* (1805).

Marchesi was indisputably one of the greatest castratos of his age. Burney found him 'not only elegant and refined to an uncommon degree, but often grand and full of dignity' though he later criticized his excessive embellishment of recitative. With his range of *g* to *d'''*, Marchesi was known as the most celebrated castrato of *opera seria*. He also composed several vocal works.

BurneyH; *EitnerQ*; *ES* (R. Celletti)

C. F. Cramer, ed.: *Magazin der Musik*, ii (Hamburg, 1784), 559–68, 572–8

Lodi caratteristiche del celebre cantore Luigi Marchesi (Siena, 1791)

C. Burney: *Memoirs of the Abbate Metastasio*, iii (London, 1796), 387

Lord Mount Edgcumbe: *Musical Reminiscences* (London, 1824, 4/1834), 60ff, 64ff, 72

M. Kelly: *Reminiscences*, i (London, 1826, 2/1826), 44f, 229

E. Greppi and A. Giulini, eds.: *Carteggio di Pietro e di Alessandro Verri*, xi (Milan, 1923), 21, 27

E. Haböck: *Die Kastraten und ihre Gesangskunst* (Stuttgart, 1927), 101, 225, 297, 419ff

A. Heriot: *The Castrati in Opera* (London, 1956), 156ff, 170

SVEN HANSELL

Marchesini, Maria Antonia ['La Lucchesina'] (*fl* 1736–9). Italian mezzo-soprano. She sang in three operas at the Teatro Nuovo, Naples, in 1736 and was engaged for London by the Opera of the Nobility, making her début at the King's Theatre in the pasticcio *Sabrina* in 1737. She next appeared in Duni's *Demofoonte*, and Heidegger re-engaged her for the autumn season when she sang in the pasticcios *Arsace* and *Alessandro Severo*, Handel's *Faramondo* and *Serse*, Pescetti's *La conquista del vello d'oro* and Veracini's *Partenio*. Still in London in 1739, she sang in Pescetti's *Angelica e Medoro* at Covent Garden and may have appeared in Handel's *Giove in Argo*. She probably created the Witch of Endor in Handel's oratorio *Saul*. Her parts in *Faramondo* (Rosimonda) and *Serse* (Arsamenes) suggest a singer of limited accomplishments; the compass is *a* to *g″*, with a low tessitura. She took male roles in *Demofoonte*, *Serse* and several other operas.

WINTON DEAN

Marchesini, Santa (*b* Bologna, *fl* 1706–39). Italian contralto. She was probably trained in Bologna, but nothing is known of her career before 1706, when she sang as an intermezzo performer – a genre in which she specialized – for the first time at the Teatro S Cassiano, Venice, in Lotti's *Grimora e Erbosco*, with the famous *buffo* Giovanni Battista Cavana. In 1709 she moved with Cavana to Naples, where she also worked with Gioacchino Corrado; between 1711 and 1716 she sang alternately with both of them, acting as an important intermediary between the expertise and repertories of the two principal *bassi buffi* in successive generations. In 1725 she and Corrado took to Venice Sarro's *L'impresario delle Canarie* which they had created in Naples in 1724. After Venice Marchesini began a new career as an itinerant performer with other basses including Antonio Lottini and Pietro Gaggiotti; she ended her career at the Spanish court.

E. Cotarelo y Mori: *Origines y establecimiento de la opera en España hasta 1800* (Madrid, 1917)

C. E. Troy: *The Comic Intermezzo* (Ann Arbor, 1979)

F. Piperno: 'Appunti sulla configurazione sociale e professionale delle "parti buffe"', *Antonio Vivaldi: teatro musicale, cultura e società: Venice 1981*, 483–97

——: 'Buffe e buffi', *RIM*, xviii (1982), 240–84

R. Strohm: 'P. Pariati librettista comico', in G. Gronda: *La carriera di un librettista* (Bologna, 1990)

FRANCO PIPERNO

Marchetti, Filippo (*b* Bolognola, Macerata, 26 Feb 1831; *d* Rome, 18 Jan 1902). Italian composer. At the age of 12 he began to study music privately with Bindi and in 1850 he entered the Naples Conservatory, then directed by Mercadante: his teachers there included Lillo and Carlo Conti. His first attempt at an opera was *Gentile da Varano*, to a libretto by his brother Raffaele, performed in 1856 at the Teatro Nazionale, Turin. Its success led the impresario to secure the rights of his next opera, *La demente*, which, staged at the Carignano in Turin the same year and repeated in Rome in 1857, was a failure. Marchetti was consequently unsuccessful in finding an impresario willing to accept his third work, *Il paria*, which remained unperformed and unpublished.

For some years he lived in Rome, where he taught singing and composed *romanze*. In 1862, encouraged by his brother, he moved to Milan. There the young poet Marcelliano Marcello persuaded him to compose *Romeo e Giulietta*, which he had adapted from Shakespeare. Produced at the Teatro Grande, Trieste (1865), it had a lukewarm reception, but two years later achieved a resounding success at the Teatro Carcano, Milan, in spite of competing with Gounod's *Roméo et Juliette*, given at La Scala the same season.

With *Ruy Blas* Marchetti reached the apogee of his career. Despite the modest interest its first performance aroused at La Scala in April 1869, the opera was acquired by the publisher Lucca (then searching for a counterpart to the success of Verdi at Casa Ricordi) and was repeated at the Teatro Pagliano, Florence, with a sensational result. Within a few years it had been staged in over 50 Italian theatres and many foreign ones, including a revival at La Scala in 1873 where it reached 21 performances (a number at the time surpassed only by *Aida*). One of the few Italian operas to win real fame during the period of Verdi's domination, the work has a few points of merit; but it reveals rather more shortcomings in its lack of variety and its weakness of invention and dramatic tension.

Those limitations became more evident in Marchetti's next two operas, *Gustavo Wasa* (1875) and *Don Giovanni d'Austria* (1880), which met with a cold reception and ended his short operatic career. When the last was repeated in Rome, Verdi pointed out the 'lungaggini' ('tedious writing') in a letter to Giorgio Arrivabene (11 December 1885). After leaving the stage Marchetti was elected president of the Accademia di S Cecilia, Rome, in 1881 and in 1886 became director of the affiliated Liceo Musicale, a position he held until 1901. In 1889 he was a member of the selection committee of the competition promoted by the publisher Sonzogno for a one-act opera; he insisted on awarding the first prize to Mascagni's *Cavalleria rusticana*.

Marchetti is now virtually forgotten. His operas reflect a generalization of the Verdian model, which he assimilated in a formal way, reducing it to standard procedures. Like Verdi, he chose subjects based on strong psychological and ethical oppositions and adopted a complex articulation of scenes and arias, but without Verdi's energetic sense of theatre and variety of characterization. Marchetti's dramatic model contrasts with his main distinctive musical features: an inclination to the elegiac and a certain melodic over-sweetness. These tendencies, as well as his skill in creating atmosphere and local colour, mark a point of transition on the line that was to lead to Catalani and the *verismo* of Puccini, though in fact he was for the most part always a little conservative in style.

See also RUY BLAS.

published in Milan unless otherwise stated

Gentile da Varano (opera semiseria, 3, R. Marchetti), Turin, Nazionale, Feb 1856, unpubd

La demente (os, 2. G. Checchetelli), Turin, Carignano, 27 Nov 1856, *I-Mr**, unpubd

Il paria (Checchetelli), 1859, unperf., unpubd

Romeo e Giulietta (dramma lirico, 4, M. Marcello, after W. Shakespeare), Trieste, Grande, 25 Oct 1865, *Mr**, vs (1865)

Ruy Blas (dramma lirico, 4, C. D'Ormeville, after V. Hugo), Milan, Scala, 3 April 1869, *Mr**, vs (1869)

Gustavo Wasa (dramma lirico, 4, D'Ormeville), Milan, Scala, 7 Feb 1875, *Mr**, vs (1875)

205

Don Giovanni d'Austria (dramma lirico, 4, D'Ormeville), Turin, Regio, 11 March 1880, Mr*, vs (1880)

*

Gazzetta musicale di Milano, xxxv (1880), 110–11; lvii (1902), 43, 82

C. D'Ormeville: 'Filippo Marchetti', Il teatro illustrato e La musica popolare, i/11 (1881), 2–3

P. Mascagni: 'Filippo Marchetti', Cronache musicali e drammatiche, iii (1902), 28–9

S. Procida: 'Filippo Marchetti', Rivista teatrale italiana, iii/Feb (1902), 102–6

J. Nicolaisen: Italian Opera in Transition, 1871–1893 (Ann Arbor, 1980)

T. G. Kaufman: 'Filippo Marchetti', Verdi and his Major Contemporaries: a Selected Chronology of Performances with Casts (New York and London, 1990), 61–76   ANDREA LANZA

Marchetti Fantozzi [née Marchetti], **Maria** (?**Vincenza**) (b ?1760; d ? after 1800). Italian soprano. She was one of the leading singers of opera seria during the 1780s and 90s. Around 1783 (earlier than 1788, the date given by Abert) she married the tenor Angelo Fantozzi and thereafter usually identified herself as Maria Marchetti Fantozzi. She was praised throughout Italy for her acting as well as her singing, particularly in Naples, where she performed in at least seven different operas in 1785–6. Marchetti was a specialist in the portrayal of passionate, tragic heroines like Semiramide and Cleopatra; she was thus ideally suited to create the role of Vitellia in Mozart's La clemenza di Tito. The music that she sang in that opera shows her to have been an extraordinary virtuoso, with a large range and a capacity for difficult coloratura.

*

H. Abert: W. A. Mozart (Leipzig, 1919–21, 3/1955–6)

J. A. Rice: W. A. Mozart: La clemenza di Tito (Cambridge, 1991)   JOHN A. RICE

Marchi, Antonio (fl 1692–1725). Italian librettist. Described in librettos as a Venetian, he was the author of eight drammi per musica performed on the Venetian stage between 1692 and 1725 (discounting revivals). His La costanza trionfante degli amori e degli odi, set by Vivaldi for the Venetian theatre of S Moisè in 1716, was revived at least three times: in Venice as Artabano, re de' parti (1718) and L'odio vinto dalla costanza (1731) and in Prague as Doriclea (1732). To judge from his Zenobia, regina de' palmireni (1694), whose music was composed by Albinoni, Marchi had scant pretensions as a poet and did not scruple to depart from the historical record in the construction of his plots; but he at least showed a lively theatrical sense and a welcome resistance to the neat symmetries favoured by the 'reform' current in the opera of his day.

Rosalinda, M. A. Ziani, 1692 (pasticcio, 1710, as L'Erginia immascherata); Zenobia, regina de' palmireni, Albinoni, 1694 (pasticcio, ? with some music by Vivaldi, as Il vinto trionfante del vincitore, 1717); Zenone, imperatore d'Oriente, Albinoni, 1696; Radamisto, Albinoni, 1698; Demetrio e Tolomeo, A. Pollarolo, 1702; L'ingannatore ingannato, Ruggieri, 1710; La costanza trionfante degli amori e degli odi, Vivaldi, 1716; Alcina delusa da Ruggero, Albinoni, 1725 (as Gli evenimenti di Ruggero, 1732)

*

M. Talbot: Tomaso Albinoni: the Venetian Composer and his World (Oxford, 1990)   MICHAEL TALBOT

Marchi, Emilio de. See DE MARCHI, EMILIO.

Marchisio. Family name of two Italian singers. Barbara Marchisio (b Turin, 6 Dec 1833; d Mira, 19 April 1919), contralto, studied with her brother Antonino and with Fabbrica in Turin, making her début in 1856 at

Carlotta (left) and Barbara Marchisio as Semiramide and Arsace in Rossini's 'Semiramide' (Her Majesty's Theatre, London, 1862): lithograph from a contemporary sheet music cover, which also names all the Rossini and Verdi operas they sang together

Vicenza as Adalgisa and then appearing in Madrid as Rosina. Her sister Carlotta Marchisio (b Turin, 8 Dec 1835; d Turin, 28 June 1872), soprano, also studied with their brother and Fabbrica, and made her début in 1856 at Madrid as Norma. The sisters first sang together at Turin in 1858 in Rossini's Matilde di Shabran (Carlotta as Matilde, Barbara as Edoardo), Guillaume Tell (as Mathilde and Jemmy) and Semiramide (as Semiramide and Arsace); the same year they appeared at Trieste in Rossini's Otello (as Emilia and Desdemona) and in Norma, then made their début at La Scala, Milan, in Semiramide. They both took part in the première of Petrella's Il duca di Scilla (1859). The following season they sang in Il trovatore (as Leonora and Azucena), La Cenerentola (as Clorinda and Cenerentola) and La sonnambula (as Amina and Teresa).

In 1860 they sang in the first performance of their brother Antonino Marchisio's Piccarda Donati at Parma, then made their début at the Paris Opéra in Semiramide (in French) and also appeared in Guillaume Tell. Their London début was at Her Majesty's Theatre in 1862 in Semiramide (see illustration), and Carlotta also sang Isabelle (Robert le diable). They appeared in La forza del destino (given as Don Alvaro) at Rome in 1863 as Leonora and Preziosilla. The sisters appeared together for the last time in 1871 at Rome in Otello and Il trovatore. The following year Carlotta died at the age of 36. Barbara sang in Mercadante's Il giuramento at La Scala in 1872 and in Il barbiere di Siviglia at Venice in 1876, then retired to teach. Both sisters, with voices that were even throughout the scale and unusually flexible, excelled in the florid music of Rossini.

*

P. Cambiasi: La Scala 1778–1906 (Milan, 1906)

E. Gorin-Marchisio: Le sorelle Marchisio (Milan, 1930)

U. Tegani: *Cantanti di una volta: le brute e belle sorelle Marchisio* (Milan, 1945)
C. Gatti: *Il Teatro alla Scala nella storia e nell'arte (1778–1963)* (Milan, 1964)
H. Weinstock: *Rossini: a Biography* (New York and London, 1968)
ELIZABETH FORBES

Marco Attilio Regolo ('Marcus Atilius Regulus'). *Dramma per musica* by Alessandro Scarlatti (*see* SCARLATTI family, (1)); Rome, Teatro Capranica, Carnival 1719.

The opera is set in Carthage in 250 BC, the point of departure for the plot being the historical account of how the consul Marcus Atilius Regulus, held captive at Carthage, was sent on parole to Rome to negotiate a peace or to exchange himself for the Carthaginian prisoners, but urged the very opposite before returning to Carthage, as he had promised, to face death. The departure from historical truth is, however, as radical as in other heroic operas of the period, the libretto being filled out with love intrigues involving Marcus's wife Fausta and daughter Emilia (soprano castratos), his Spartan conqueror Santippo [Xanthippus] (tenor), the Carthaginian dictator Amilcare [Hamilcar] (alto castrato), and Hamilcar's lover Eraclea [Heraclia] (soprano castrato). The comic scenes, more prominent in this opera than usual, are played out by Emilia's maid, Eurilla (alto castrato), and Heraclia's servant, Leonzio (bass), and a happy ending is contrived in which Marcus (soprano castrato) regains both his freedom and his wife, while the four other principal characters are suitably paired off.

The main source for *Marco Attilio Regolo*, a manuscript score in the British Library, London, states that it is Scarlatti's 112th opera – a total which presumably includes at least some of the *rifacimenti* of other composers' operas that Scarlatti prepared for the Neapolitan stage. As in his other mature operas, the basic musical constituent after the 'Italian' overture is the recitative-aria unit. Except for Marcus's 'Nella procella che agita l'alma' in Act 3 scene i, all the complete arias sung by the six serious characters are in the customary ternary (da capo or dal segno) form. A particular feature of the opera is that no fewer than six arias are left incomplete, in one case because the character falls asleep, in the others because he or she is interrupted by the entrance of another. This enhances the musical and dramatic continuity of the work, as also do some particularly effective passages of accompanied recitative.

MALCOLM BOYD

Marcolini, Marietta (*b* Florence, *c*1780; *d* 1814 or later). Italian contralto. In 1800 she was singing at the Teatro S Benedetto, Venice; in 1803 she took part in the first performance of P. C. Guglielmi's *La serva bizzarra* at the Teatro Nuovo, Naples. In 1806 she sang at Livorno and Pisa, then at the Teatro Argentina, Rome, in the premières of Tritto's *Andromaca e Pirro* and Nicolini's *Traiano in Cacia* (1807). She made her début at La Scala in the first performances of Bigatti's *L'amante prigioniero* and of Ercole Paganini's *Le rivali generose* (1809). She created roles in five operas by Rossini: Ernestina in *L'equivoco stravagante* (1811) at Bologna; the title role of *Ciro in Babilonia* (1812) at Ferrara; Clarice in *La pietra del paragone* (1812) at La Scala; Isabella in *L'italiana in Algeri* (1813) at the Teatro S Benedetto; and the title role of *Sigismondo*

(1814) at La Fenice. She was also a renowned exponent of Rossini's *Tancredi*.

ELIZABETH FORBES

Marcoux, Vanni [Jean Emile Diogène]. *See* VANNI-MARCOUX.

Mardones, José (*b* Fontecha, Spain, 1869; *d* Madrid, 4 May 1932). Spanish bass. He studied in Madrid, where he made his début. His first notable success came in 1891 in South America. In 1908 he joined the Lisbon S Carlos Opera and in 1909 made his North American début in *Aida* with the new Boston Opera. His best role in the most flourishing years of his career was Boito's Mefistofele, which he repeated at the Metropolitan in 1920. He had become leading bass there in 1917, remaining until 1926 and singing in the first performances there of *Luisa Miller*, *Le roi de Lahore* and Spontini's *La vestale*. Returning to Spain, he continued singing and made some fine recordings when nearly 60. His reputation was that of an indifferent actor with one of the most magnificent voices of the age. The voice is mightily impressive on recordings, which are also by no means wooden or characterless as interpretations.

J. B. STEANE

Maréchal, Adolphe (Alphonse) (*b* Liège, 26 Sept 1867; *d* Brussels, 1 Feb 1935). Belgian tenor. He studied at the Liège Conservatory and made his début at Dijon in 1891. After singing for some years in provincial French houses he was engaged by the Opéra-Comique in 1895, where he sang in several premières, most notably those of *Louise* in 1900 and *Grisélidis* in 1901. This led to another important Massenet première, at Monte Carlo, where in 1902 he created the title role in *Le jongleur de Notre Dame*, playing 'his difficult role with infinite address and virtuosity', according to the *Journal de Monaco*. He made his Covent Garden début in 1902 as Don José, acting with 'marked and picturesque power' (*Musical Times*). He also appeared in *Faust*, *Manon* and the première, under Messager, of Herbert Bunning's *The Princess Osra*, with Mary Garden in the title role and the English libretto translated into French. He retired after a crisis of voice and health in 1907. Among his few and rare recordings is a solo from *Le jongleur* which shows a finely tutored voice and an eloquent style.

J. B. STEANE

Maréchal, (Charles) Henri (*b* Paris, 22 Jan 1842; *d* Paris, 12 May 1924). French composer. After studying literature, he began his musical training in 1859; later he studied with Massé and Chauvet at the Conservatoire. In 1867 he became chorus master of the Théâtre Lyrique and in 1870 won the Prix de Rome. He gained recognition with his 'sacred poem' *La nativité* in 1875, and the next year established himself in the theatre, where his real ambitions lay, with *Les amoureux de Catherine*, which reached its 100th performance in 1889 and was still being performed in the 1920s. In 1876 he wrote *La taverne des Trabans*, which was awarded the Mombinne prize but was not produced until 1881. He wrote six further operas, a ballet and incidental music and works in many other genres.

all printed works published in Paris

Les amoureux de Catherine (oc, 1, J. Barbier, after Erckmann-Chatrian), Paris, OC (Favart), 8 May 1876 (1876)
La taverne des Trabans, 1876 (oc, 3, Erckmann-Chatrian and Barbier), Paris, OC (Favart), 31 Dec 1881 (1882)

L'étoile (idylle-opéra, 1, P. Collin), Paris, Société Chorale d'Amateurs, 12 March 1881 (1881)

Déidamie (2, E. Noël), Paris, Opéra, 15 Sept 1893 (1893)

Calendel (4, P. Ferrier, after Mistral), Rouen, Arts, 21 Dec 1894 (1885)

Ping-Sin, 1895 (drame lyrique, 2, L. Gallet), Paris, OC (Favart), 23 Jan 1918 (1917)

Daphnis et Chloé (3, J. and P. Barbier), Paris, Lyrique, 8 Nov 1899 (1895)

Autour d'un tiare (drame lyrique, Melliet) (n.d.)   JOHN TREVITT

Maréchal ferrant, Le ('The Blacksmith'). *Opéra comique* in two acts by FRANÇOIS-ANDRÉ DANICAN PHILIDOR to a libretto by Antoine François Quétant after Giovanni Boccaccio's *Decameron*; Paris, Opéra-Comique (Théâtre de la Foire St Laurent), 22 August 1761.

Marcel (baritone), village blacksmith and surgeon, sings of his trade. La Bride (tenor), coachman at the nearby castle, is indifferent about whom he loves. Claudine (soprano) loves Colin (tenor), who is secretly betrothed to Marcel's daughter Jeannette (soprano). Marcel warns La Bride against the anaesthetic potion prepared for amputating a man's leg. He boasts of his medical skill and dictates an outrageous invoice for the castle. Colin drinks the potion and after a chromatic *air* falls into a deathlike sleep. Jeannette makes the peasants Bastien (tenor) and Eustache (bass) hide the 'body' in the cellar.

In Act 2 Jeannette laments her loss. Marcel and La Bride are the worse for drink; La Bride sings of his *métier*, illustrating his actions with tongue-clicking, rolling r's and whooping glissandos. In his excitement he embraces Claudine, who decides she prefers him after all. Colin wakes up and sings a recitative and aria which parody serious opera; Eustache takes him for a ghost; Marcel takes Eustache for a burglar. The resulting confusion is resolved and the two couples are united.

Quétant preceded the libretto with an essay claiming that *opéra comique* requires as much skill as tragedy. His blend of sentiment and farce is robustly supported by the composer in his most colourful *opéra comique*, enlivened by mixed metres, parody, onomatopoeia and inventive ensemble writing. An astounding success, *Le maréchal ferrant* was played before 1800 all over Europe and in the New World.   JULIAN RUSHTON

Marescalchi, Luigi (*b* Bologna, 1 Feb 1745; *d* after 1805). Italian composer and music publisher. He studied composition with Padre Martini; his first opera was written in 1765 for Madrid. About 1770 he began publishing in Venice, where he issued some 60 engraved publications, evenly distributed between vocal pieces (mainly scores and parts of single numbers from operas performed in Venice) and instrumental works (including opera overtures). In 1775 he probably visited Lisbon for a revival of his *Il tutore ingannato*; during the next ten years he was active primarily as a composer, writing three further operas for Venice, Piacenza and Rome.

On 15 November 1785 Marescalchi obtained an exclusive royal licence for printing music in Naples and in 1786, with his brother Francesco, began to publish many operatic excerpts, notably by Bianchi, Cimarosa, P. A. Guglielmi and Paisiello. He also reprinted (as separate numbers) most of Sarti's *Giulio Sabino* from the plates of the Vienna first edition of about 1782 and issued a second edition of Millico's *La pietà d'amore*, his largest publication. From about 1793 his output diminished, but up to January 1799 the librettos of operas given at the S Carlo and Fondo theatres still announced that the music could be obtained from him. His business was destroyed in June 1799; possibly this was the doing of Neapolitan music copyists, whose livelihood had been affected by the licence given him.

Marescalchi's *opera seria Alessandro nell'Indie* (1778, Venice) contains an early example of an extensive final sextet, incorporating the action in the libretto at the close of Act 3; it begins in the last scene, just as Cleofide is about to stab herself. Although the conflict is resolved during the sextet, the text suggests a formal ensemble rather than an action finale (the music is lost). *Andromeda e Perseo* (1784, Rome) involves some machinery when Perseus rescues Andromeda from a sea monster; this scene closes with a trio that becomes a quartet. The opera begins with a chorus and concludes with a chorus with ensembles of soloists. In Marescalchi's comic operas the musical interest centres on the arias and on ensemble finales with increasing numbers of personnel; each opera has one or two additional duets or trios.

Marescalchi was far more prolific as a composer of ballets; he wrote at least 30, mainly for Venice and Rome (mostly choreographed by Onorato Viganò). During this period, when opera librettos normally do not mention composers of ballet music, Marescalchi's name appears even when the composer of the opera goes unmentioned. Many of these pieces are extensive, multi-partite pantomime ballets.

Il proseguimento del chiarlone (dg, 3, G. Fiorini), Madrid, wint. 1765, arias (Venice, n.d.)

Il tutore ingannato (dg, 3, ? C. Mazzolà), Venice, S Samuele, carn. 1774, ov. (Venice, 1774)

Alessandro nell'Indie (os, 3, P. Metastasio), Venice, S Benedetto, 27 May 1778

I disertori felici (dg), Piacenza, Ducale, carn. 1784, duet (Venice, n.d.)

Andromeda e Perseo (os, 3), Rome, Argentina, carn. 1784

*

Grove6 (R. Macnutt)

A. Mazarella, ed.: *Biografia degli uomini illustri del Regno di Napoli … compilato da diversi letterati nazionali* (Naples, 1819), 47

U. Prota-Giurleo: *La prima calcografia musicale a Napoli* (Naples, 1923)

C. Sartori: *Dizionario degli editori musicali italiani* (Florence, 1958), 6, 96–7   MARITA P. McCLYMONDS

Marescalco, Il ('The Marshal'). *Commedia* in two acts by GIAN FRANCESCO MALIPIERO to his own libretto after Pietro Aretino's comedy; Treviso, Teatro Comunale, 22 October 1969.

L'Aretino's famous 16th-century comedy, from which Malipiero took nearly all the words of his libretto (albeit with huge cuts and much transference of material from one scene to another), is a sparklingly satirical conversation piece rather than a substantial drama. The misogynistic Marshal of the title (baritone) is made to believe he is being forced to marry; only when the 'wedding' has taken place is the whole affair revealed as a practical joke. This slender plot provides a pretext for a delightful gallery of grotesque character sketches – the most memorable, perhaps, being that of the Pedant (tenor), who talks in a macaronic mixture of Latin and pompous Italian, and whose Gregorian-inflected theme stands out with wilful incongruity amid the spiky angularities of Malipiero's later style. Though slight compared with the composer's best earlier theatre works, and more distinguished orchestrally than vocally, *Il marescalco* is arguably the most satisfying of his postwar operas. A first version of the score was completed in 1960, but Malipiero rewrote the ending in 1968.   JOHN C. G. WATERHOUSE

Maretzek, Max (*b* Brno, 28 June 1821; *d* New York, 14 May 1897). American conductor, impresario and composer of Czech birth. After working as a conductor and composer in central Europe and Paris he became chorus master at Covent Garden in 1844. In 1848 Edward Fry invited him to conduct Italian opera at the Astor Place Opera House in New York. In 1849 Maretzek began a career as impresario, initially with the Astor Place company, conducting and managing companies in New York (principally at the Academy of Music), and touring the USA, Cuba and Mexico. He managed to engage excellent singers and conducted the American premières of *La traviata* (1856) and *Don Carlos* (1877). His managerial policies helped to establish continuing popular support for opera in New York. In 1878 Maretzek retired from management, though he continued to conduct and teach. He composed an opera, *Sleepy Hollow, or The Headless Horseman* (1879), and wrote two volumes of reminiscences: *Crotchets and Quavers* (New York, 1855) and *Sharps and Flats* (New York, 1890), both reprinted in 1968 as *Revelations of an Opera Manager in 19th Century America*.

WILLIAM BROOKS

Margaritov, Athanas (*b* Kharmanli, 25 Jan 1912). Bulgarian conductor and violinist. He studied at the Sofia State Academy of Music, and was principal violinist at the Sofia National Opera, 1933–6. After studying with Felix Weingartner at the Vienna Conservatory, he made his conducting début in 1938 in *Carmen* with the Sofia Opera, where he was a resident conductor from 1940 (principal conductor, 1964–6). He has toured in other European countries and the USSR. The hallmark of Margaritov's conducting is an innate musicality and sense of style based on careful preparation. His many records include Musorgsky's *Khovanshchina* with the Sofia National Opera (issued in Britain in 1975).

LADA BRASHOVANOVA

Margot la rouge. Lyric drama in one act by FREDERICK DELIUS to a libretto in French by Berthe Gaston-Danville ('Mme Rosenval'); St Louis, Missouri, Opera Theatre, 8 June 1983.

The scene is a Paris café, where the latest affair of Margot la rouge (soprano) is under discussion. Soldiers enter and have animated exchanges with the girls. Thibault, their sergeant (tenor), holds back, realizing that Margot was previously his own lover. At Margot's entry they sing a passionate duet. When her present lover (baritone) enters, a quarrel ensues. Margot sticks by Thibault, and the lover attempts to stab her, but Thibault receives the wound and is killed. Margot seizes Thibault's bayonet and runs her lover through. A police officer (bass) arrests her as the curtain falls.

Delius's fifth opera was composed in 1902 and entered for the Concorso Melodrammatico Internazionale of 1904, sponsored by the Milan publisher Sanzogno. The competition was an attempt to rival Ricordi's successful venture of 12 years previously, when Mascagni's *Cavalleria rusticana* had taken the prize. Though Delius lost to Lorenzo Filiasi, whose *Manuel Menendez* was eventually performed in Milan, he clearly had the Italian *verismo* market in mind, with much onstage violence and parlando recitative against a light orchestral background in the manner of Puccini. A vocal score was prepared by Ravel (1905) but it did not lead to a performance. The reason is not far to seek. Delius was out of his element in the more sensational parts of the action; it is the lyrical music that has his characteristic stamp. This he later reworked for the *Idyll* (1932), to words adapted from Walt Whitman by Robert Nichols, thus salvaging more than a third of the opera. The manuscript full score of *Margot la rouge* passed into the Beecham collection and came to the Delius Trust only in 1982. The Trust had earlier commissioned from Eric Fenby a reconstruction based on the vocal score and hints from the *Idyll*; this version was broadcast by the BBC, 21 February 1982, and issued on LP.   ROBERT ANDERSON

Maria Antonia Walpurgis, Electress of Saxony (*b* Munich, 18 July 1724; *d* Dresden, 23 April 1780). German princess, composer, singer and patron. The eldest daughter of the Elector Karl Albert of Bavaria (later Emperor Karl VII) and of Archduchess Maria Amalia of Austria, she received her first musical training in Munich from Giovanni Ferrandini and Giovanni Porta. After her marriage in 1747 to Friedrich Christian, later Elector of Saxony, she continued her studies in Dresden with Porpora and Hasse. With the Seven Years War and the death of the elector in 1763 the cultural life at the Dresden court declined. Her lively exchange of letters with Frederick the Great of Prussia from 1763 to 1779 bears witness to her increasing sense of personal and artistic isolation; the musical ideals she had grown up with as a pupil and devotee of Hasse and a correspondent of Metastasio lost their validity, and new music, in particular the new Neapolitan operatic style, found no favour with her.

Maria Antonia Walpurgis was also a patron of Hasse, Porpora and J. G. Naumann, and the singers Mingotti and Mara (who made her début in *Talestri* in 1767), and was herself an active participant in the arts. She frequently performed at court as a singer or keyboard player; Burney warmly praised her singing. She took leading roles in court performances of her own operas – *Il trionfo della fedeltà* (Dresden, summer 1754) and *Talestri, regina delle amazoni* (Nymphenburg, 6 February 1760) – both to her own texts. They were published by Breitkopf, performed in other European capitals and translated into several languages. Their texts are clearly modelled on Metastasio (who made alterations to *Trionfo*), and their music on Hasse, who may have had a hand in the composition of *Trionfo*. The published score of *Trionfo* included her self-portrait, engraved by Giuseppe Canale, on the title-page. Many other compositions in manuscript in Dresden bear her name, but cannot be authenticated; in many cases her name merely indicates ownership. Among the compositions attributed to her are arias, a pastorale, intermezzos, meditations and motets.

BurneyGN; *EitnerQ*; *GerberL*

J.-D.-E. Preuss, ed.: *Correspondence de Frédéric avec l'Electrice Marie-Antonie de Saxe*, Oeuvres de Frédéric le Grand, xxiv (Berlin, 1854)

J. Petzholdt: 'Biographisch-litterarische Mittheilungen über Maria Antonia Walpurgis von Sachsen', *Neuer Anzeiger für Bibliographie und Bibliothekwissenschaft* (1856), 336, 367 [incl. list of her works and those dedicated to her]

C. von Weber: *Maria Antonia Walpurgis, Churfürstin zu Sachsen* (Dresden, 1857) [incl. list of works, writings and paintings]

F. M. Rudhart: *Geschichte der Oper am Hofe zu München* (Freising, 1865)

M. Fürstenau: 'Maria Antonia Walpurgis, Kurfürstin von Sachsen: eine biographische Skizze', *MMg*, xi (1879), 167–81

W. Lippert, ed.: *Kaiserin Maria Theresia und Kurfürstin Maria Antonia von Sachsen: Briefwechsel 1747–1772* (Leipzig, 1908)

H. Drewes: *Maria Antonia Walpurgis als Komponistin* (Leipzig, 1934)

A. Yorke-Long: *Music at Court: Four Eighteenth Century Studies* (London, 1954), 73–93

For illustration *see* DRESDEN, fig.3 and PUBLISHING, fig.3.

GERHARD ALLROGGEN

Maria d'Alessandria ('Mary of Alexandria'). Opera in three acts by GIORGIO FEDERICO GHEDINI to a libretto by Cesare Meano; Bergamo, Teatro delle Novità, 9 September 1937.

Although written in 1936, when he was over 40, this first of Ghedini's operas to reach the stage is still in some respects immature; yet it contains many premonitions of the strong individuality that was to emerge in his best works of the 1940s. The libretto, like that of Respighi's *Maria egiziaca* (1932), is based on the story of St Mary of Egypt – the Alexandrian prostitute whose life was transformed after she boarded a ship taking pilgrims to the Holy Land, and who ended up as a hermit in the desert. In Ghedini's opera, however, the treatment is far more melodramatic than in Respighi's, with many details invented by the librettist. Act 2 in particular, which is set on board the ship, shows Maria (soprano) giving free rein to her formidable feminine charms, thus creating havoc among the crew and even among the pilgrims. At the end of the act's second scene, a pilgrim who is identified simply as 'the father' (baritone) tries to kill Maria with an arrow; but instead he kills his own son (tenor) who, out of obsessive love for her, has shielded her with his body. Profoundly moved by this self-sacrifice, Maria prays to Christ to make her 'capable of love, of purity'. Her prayer is answered, and she alone survives when the ship is wrecked in a storm.

The music of *Maria d'Alessandria* is relatively mild in its dissonances by the composer's later standards, and a debt to Pizzetti is at times conspicuous. Yet Ghedini's more personal qualities come through strongly in (above all) the music associated with the sea, which was also to be the main inspiration behind what is commonly regarded as his masterpiece, the *Concerto dell'albatro* (1945). Despite its mixed style and lurid plot, *Maria d'Alessandria* was deemed worthy of revival in Turin as recently as 1984–5.

JOHN C. G. WATERHOUSE

María del Carmen. Opera in three acts by ENRIQUE GRANADOS to a libretto by José Feliu Codina after his play of the same title; Madrid, Teatro Parish, 12 November 1898.

The setting is the countryside of Murcia. Javier (tenor) is wounded in a fight by Pencho (baritone), the fiancé of María del Carmen (soprano), and Pencho flees to avoid arrest. Attempting to obtain a pardon for Pencho, María del Carmen nurses Javier, who falls in love with her. When news of this reaches Pencho he returns to claim María del Carmen, who renounces her love for him in the hope of influencing Javier to pardon him. Pencho challenges Javier to a duel and mortally wounds him. When Javier realizes the depth of Pencho's love for María del Carmen, he pardons Pencho as the authorities come to arrest him, protecting the couple and giving them his blessing.

María del Carmen was Granados's first great success. After the première there were other well-received productions in Barcelona (1899) and later in Valencia. Although the opera, which has been compared to *Lakmé*, might seem from its subject and year of composition to belong to the *verismo* style, it is clearly in the spirit of Spanish Romanticism. It is rich in orchestral colour and, like many of Granados's works, filled with profound lyricism. The melodies are in folk style and may have been collected by Granados during travels in Murcia. Outstanding are the tense monologue of María del Carmen (Act 1), Pencho's dramatic entrance (Act 2), and the aria of the peasant girl Fuensanta (mezzo-soprano) in Act 2.

DOUGLAS RIVA

Maria de Rudenz ('Maria of Rudenz'). *Dramma tragico* in three acts by GAETANO DONIZETTI to a libretto by SALVADORE CAMMARANO after A. Bourgeois, J.-G.-A. Cuvelier and J. de Mallian's play *La nonne sanglante*, derived from an episode in Matthew Lewis's novel *The Monk*; Venice, Teatro La Fenice, 30 January 1838.

The opening run at the Fenice, with Karoline Unger in the title role, consisted of just two performances, but later in the 1840s it was put on in a number of Italian cities. It then fell into total oblivion until it was revived at the Fenice in 1981 and proved modestly successful. That revival, starring Katia Ricciarelli, is preserved on a commercial recording.

The overdrawn plot deals with the misdeeds of Corrado (baritone) who has eloped with Maria (soprano) and abandoned her. Now he schemes to marry her sister Matilde (soprano), an heiress; his brother Enrico (tenor) also loves Matilde. Maria has secretly returned to Rudenz, still loving Corrado in spite of his ill-treatment, but when she discovers that Corrado is to marry Matilde she determines to be avenged. She orders him away as a usurper and plans to banish Matilde to a convent. Enrico pleads for Matilde, but Maria suggests that Corrado is not in fact his brother. She confronts Corrado, saying that it does not matter to her that he is an assassin's son since she loves him passionately; but he must renounce Matilde. When he refuses, she opens a trapdoor, pointing to Matilde's tomb; the enraged Corrado stabs her. Apparently with her last breath, she says she is dying; Enrico challenges Corrado to a duel but is killed by him. But Maria has only feigned death, and now steals into Matilde's room and stabs her. She confesses to Corrado and, saying that she has reopened her wounds, dies, proclaiming her love for him; he is left to live with his conscience.

With its highly romantic plot, unusual in involving a heroine who apparently dies twice, *Maria de Rudenz* marks the extreme of Donizetti's interest in 'strong' subjects. It has often been remarked that the libretto's violent plot, and its reliance on past events to move the action on, is more than a little reminiscent of Cammarano's later *Il trovatore*. The score contains much fine music, including a mellifluous *sortita* for the baritone, a notable Larghetto to the Act 1 finale (later incorporated into *Poliuto* and *Les martyrs*), several powerful duets with contrasting melodies for the participants (particularly effective is the one for Maria and Corrado in Act 2), a moving aria-finale for the heroine and, extraordinarily, in the prelude to Act 2, an extended solo for bass clarinet.

WILLIAM ASHBROOK

Maria di Rohan ('Maria of Rohan'). *Melodramma tragico* in three acts by GAETANO DONIZETTI to a libretto by SALVADORE CAMMARANO after Lockroy and Badon's play *Un duel sous le Cardinal de Richelieu*; Vienna, Kärntnertortheater, 5 June 1843.

The original cast included Eugenia Tadolini (Maria) and Giorgio Ronconi (Chevreuse). For the Paris première of the work, at the Théâtre Italien in November 1843, Donizetti made a number of revisions in the score, adding a cabaletta for Grisi in Act 3 ('Benigno il cielo arridere') and altering the role of Gondì from a tenor to a mezzo-soprano *en travesti*.

When Act 1 opens, set in the reign of Louis XIII, Maria (soprano) has secretly married the Duke de Chevreuse (baritone), who has killed Cardinal Richelieu's nephew in a duel. She begs Riccardo, Count de Chalais (tenor), her former lover, to intercede on Chevreuse's behalf; his willingness to do so reawakens her former love. One of the courtiers, Armando di Gondì (mezzo-soprano), makes a slighting reference to Maria, whereupon Riccardo challenges him to a duel. Chevreuse, released from prison, arrives to thank his friend and intercessor, and when he hears of the impending duel with Gondì offers to be Riccardo's second.

'Maria di Rohan' (Donizetti), Act 3: scene from the original production at the Kärntnertortheater, Vienna, 5 June 1843, with Eugenia Tadolini (Maria), Giorgio Ronconi (Chevreuse) and Carlo Guasco (Count de Chalais); engraving after Cajetan

In Act 2 Riccardo is in his room, writing Maria a farewell note, to be delivered only if he dies in the duel. She comes secretly to warn him that Richelieu is angry at his intercession, but she is forced to hide when Chevreuse arrives to accompany Riccardo to the duelling ground. When he leaves, Maria emerges from her hiding-place and, now having heard of the impending duel, begs Riccardo not to run such danger, confessing her love for him. When word is brought that, because of Riccardo's delay, Chevreuse is about to take his place in the duel, he tears himself away from Maria and departs.

At the opening of Act 3, Chevreuse has fought the duel and sustained a wound in his arm. Riccardo comes to Maria at Chevreuse's hôtel; while there he learns

from Aubry (tenor) that Richelieu's men have pillaged his room and carried off documents, his farewell letter to Maria among them. Knowing that discovery is at hand, he begs Maria to run off with him. Chevreuse, unaware of these developments, returns and shows Riccardo a secret passageway that will help him elude his enemies. Before he goes into it, Riccardo whispers that if Maria does not join him before the clock next strikes, he will return for her. The letter is delivered to Chevreuse who, overcome with jealousy, accuses Maria, who does not deny her guilt. The clock strikes; Riccardo returns; Chevreuse challenges him and they rush off through the secret door. Soon Chevreuse returns to announce that Riccardo has turned his pistol on himself. When Maria begs her husband to kill her, he condemns her to a life of disgrace.

The most tautly constructed of Donizetti's romantic *melodrammi*, *Maria di Rohan* shows clear signs, particularly in Act 3, that Donizetti was moving towards the effect of unbroken musical continuity, abandoning the closed patterns of conventional 'number' opera. Even in Act 1, the usual succession of 'entrance' arias is given new force and dynamism by Donizetti's tendency to reduce the fixed forms to their minimum, and to inject vivid musical characterization. It is a work that calls for accomplished singers who are also powerful actors, particularly for the baritone role of Chevreuse. Chorley described the powerful effect produced by Giorgio Ronconi in this part.

Maria di Rohan contains some of Donizetti's most expressive music. The soprano's first-act aria, 'Cupa, fatal mestizia', suggests *Un ballo in maschera*. The tenor's aria at the beginning of Act 2, 'Alma soave e cara', is one of a number of fine single-movement tenor arias from the final years of Donizetti's output that reveal how effectively he wrote for this range of voice. The baritone's scene in Act 3, 'Bella e di sol vestita', has been eloquently recorded by Mattia Battistini.

WILLIAM ASHBROOK

Maria egiziaca ('The Egyptian Mary'). *Trittico per concerto/Mistero* in three episodes by OTTORINO RESPIGHI to a libretto by CLAUDIO GUASTALLA after Domenico Cavalca's *Le vite dei santi padri* (14th century); New York, Carnegie Hall, 16 March 1932 (concert première, semi-staged), Venice, Teatro Goldoni, 10 August 1932 (stage première).

Although it was soon transferred to the operatic stage, where it naturally belongs, *Maria egiziaca* was conceived in response to an unusual commission for a so-called 'concert opera'. The première, though on a concert platform, was in costume, with simple scenery consisting of a painted screen in the form of a triptych depicting the three episodes. In devising his libretto, Guastalla wished to create a modern equivalent of a medieval mystery play, and to model his affectedly archaic language on that of Fra' Domenico Cavalca, whose life of St Mary of Egypt was his main source.

St Mary (soprano) is first seen as a young Alexandrian prostitute who suddenly feels an urge to sail to the Holy Land, paying for her passage with her body. In the second episode she finds herself unable to enter the temple until she has repented, and an angel tells her to retire into the desert and become a hermit. Finally we see her still in the desert in old age: when the time is ripe for her to die, a lion digs a grave for her.

Respighi matched Guastalla's consciously archaic libretto with an austerely evocative score in which

211

Gregorian, Renaissance and Monteverdian influences are evident. The small orchestra even includes a harpsichord, which occasionally accompanies recitatives on its own. These 'archaizing' tendencies are not as thoroughgoing as in, say, the *Lauda per la Natività del Signore* (among the composer's non-operatic works): the opera's first orchestral interlude even begins with an incongruous, albeit fleeting, echo of Richard Strauss. Yet at its best – for example, in Mary's magnificent aria 'O bianco astore', addressed to the angel in the central episode – the music rises to heights of calm, dignified spirituality that are rare in Respighi. Highlights of this calibre help to explain why *Maria egiziaca*, uneven though it is, has become his most frequently performed opera in Italy.　　　　　　　　　　JOHN C. G. WATERHOUSE

Mariage aux lanternes, Le ('The Wedding by Lantern-Light'). Operetta in one act by JACQUES OFFENBACH to a libretto by MICHEL CARRÉ and Léon Battu; Paris, Théâtre des Bouffes-Parisiens (Salle Choiseul), 10 October 1857.

The piece is a revised version, with identical plot and some different musical numbers, of Offenbach's *Le trésor à Mathurin*, produced in concert at the Salle Herz in May 1853. Guillot, a young farmer (tenor), is desired by two young widows, the more so when he receives a letter from his Uncle Mathurin, announcing that Guillot will find a treasure beneath a large tree on his farm as the angelus sounds that evening. To the widows' dismay, as the angelus sounds and the villagers gather by lantern-light, the 'treasure' arranged by Mathurin turns out to be Guillot's orphaned cousin Denise (soprano).
　　　　　　　　　　　　　　　　ANDREW LAMB

Mariages samnites, Les ('The Samnite Marriages'). *Drame lyrique* in three acts by ANDRÉ-ERNEST-MODESTE GRÉTRY to a libretto by Barnabé Farmain de Rosoi after JEAN FRANÇOIS MARMONTEL's moral tale; Paris, Comédie-Italienne (Hôtel de Bourgogne), 12 June 1776.

Agathis (tenor) and Parmenon (tenor) are friends and comrades in arms. Both are in love, but a Samnitic law forbids disclosing the identity of the beloved before the annual marriage ceremony, except to a parent. They are preparing for a battle against the Romans in which Eumene (bass), Agathis's father, wishes to fight. Agathis tells him that he is in love with Céphalide (soprano), who separately reveals her love for Agathis to her mother Euphémie (soprano). A march summons the soldiers to battle. In Act 2 Céphalide's friend Eliane (soprano) is distressed by the thought that the man she loves may die in battle. When she demands the right to participate in the fighting, she is reproached by Céphalide and Euphémie. Agathis brings his wounded father back from the battlefield, where the Samnites are on the brink of defeat. As Eliane has disappeared, Céphalide is lonely and in Act 3 appeals to the goddess of love. The victorious Samnitic soldiers return and Agathis, Parmenon and Eliane, who fought in the battle and saved a general's life, are decorated by the Samnite chief for their bravery. To the delight of the two male heroes, they have chosen different women so that Agathis can marry Céphalide and Parmenon Eliane.

Les mariages samnites is an expanded and revised version of a one-act opera which Grétry had written to a libretto by Pierre Légier in 1767, but which had remained unperformed. Despite further revisions after the première in 1776 it never became a great success, and Grétry blamed this failure on the public's inability

to enjoy serious plots played by actors known for their comic roles. The plot's ancient setting was chosen to promote friendship, family loyalties, equality of women and the crucial role of law in society, yet these ideas are not successfully adapted in this opera as the women have no right to choose a husband and the lovers cannot address each other. The focus on different characters in each act (Agathis and Parmenon, Eliane, and the Samnite chief) weakens the dramatic continuity, and the often *larmoyant* and metaphorical language has a detrimental effect on the musical expression. The substantial score (24 arias, ensembles, choruses and closing vaudeville) demonstrates for the first time Grétry's ambition to emulate the style of Gluck's *tragédies* in the *opéra comique* genre. The scoring of some pieces is exceptionally rich (requiring the services of military musicians) and their structural design varied. The repeated use of a motif links different parts of the opera, and the chorus march 'Dieu d'amour' formed the theme for Mozart's piano variations in F K352.　　　　MICHAEL FEND

Mariani, Angelo (Maurizio Gaspare) (*b* Ravenna, 11 Oct 1821; *d* Genoa, 13 June 1873). Italian conductor and composer. During the winter of 1844–5, he became first violinist and *maestro concertatore* in Messina, returning as conductor after visiting Mercadante in Naples. He made his Milan début in Verdi's *I due Foscari* (Teatro Re, 1846) and was so successful that Verdi wanted him to conduct the première of *Macbeth*, but negotiations came to nothing because his fees were too high. Moving to the Teatro Carcano in Milan he conducted *I Lombardi alla prima crociata*, and in 1847 his *Nabucco* almost set off a political riot. He directed the winter season at the court theatre in Copenhagen, 1847–8, and then made his début as conductor and director at the Teatro Carlo Felice in Genoa with *Robert le diable* in 1852. He held this post until his death and enlarged and improved the Genoa orchestra, making it the best in Italy. He conducted many notable performances of Meyerbeer operas but was equally competent in Rossini, Spontini, Cimarosa, Bellini, Donizetti and Verdi. After working with Verdi on *Aroldo* in Rimini in 1857 the two became intimate friends; Mariani made his début as conductor at the Teatro Comunale in Bologna with *Un ballo in maschera* (1860) and followed it with other Verdi operas, notably *Don Carlos* (1867). He subsequently conducted the Italian premières there of *Lohengrin* (1871) and *Tannhäuser* (1872).

Mariani made each opera a unified, integrated work involving orchestra, singers and stage personnel in a concentrated effort. He was dedicated to the theatre, and letters to him from Meyerbeer, Rossini, Mercadante, Verdi and Wagner show the gratitude and esteem that composers felt for him. Verdi urged many impresarios in Italy and abroad to engage him, and he wanted him to conduct the world première of *Aida* in Cairo. Mariani, however, was unable to accept the invitation on account of illness, and this led to a falling out with Verdi which caused Mariani great suffering. During his last season in Genoa Mariani conducted Petrella's *Manfredo*, *La favorita* and Marchetti's *Ruy Blas*.

A. Ghislanzoni: 'Angelo Mariani', *Gazzetta musicale di Milano*, xxiii (1868)

S. Busmanti: *Cenni su Angelo Mariani* (Ravenna, 1887)

T. Mantovani: *Angelo Mariani* (Rome, 1921)

U. Zoppi: *Angelo Mariani, Giuseppe Verdi e Teresa Stolz in un carteggio inedito* (Milan, 1947)

F. Walker: *The Man Verdi* (New York, 1962)

S. Martinotti: 'Angelo Mariani, direttore e musicista, nel suo tempo', *Studi musicali*, ii (1973), 315–39

G. Vecchi: 'Note sul Angelo Mariani: II: Angelo Mariani, l'arte e gli artisti e gli amici accademici bolognesi', *Quadrivium*, xiv (1973), 321–51   MARY JANE PHILLIPS MATZ

Mariani, Luciano (*b* Cremona, 1801; *d* Castell'Arquato, Piacenza, 10 June 1859). Italian bass. In 1823 he was singing at La Fenice, where he created Oroe in *Semiramide*. He sang Olivo (Donizetti's *Olivo e Pasquale*) at the Teatro della Cannobiana, Milan (1830). He created Rodolfo in *La sonnambula* at the Teatro Carcano, Milan (1831), and Alfonso in *Lucrezia Borgia* at La Scala (1833). At the Teatro Comunale, Bologna, he sang Oroveso (*Norma*) and Rodolfo (1834). His sister Rosa Mariani (*b* Cremona, 1799; *d* after 1832) was a coloratura contralto who created Arsace in *Semiramide* (1823, Venice) and later made a speciality of the role. She appeared at the King's Theatre, London, in 1832.   ELIZABETH FORBES

Mariani, Tommaso (*fl* Naples, 1728–39). Italian librettist. He lived in Naples, where he wrote intermezzos and comic operas in Neapolitan dialect, as well as one *opera seria* (*Il castello d'Atlante*, 1734). Biographical details are lacking, although his nickname 'romano' suggests a Roman origin; Napoli Signorelli claimed he was educated in Naples. One libretto (appropriately, *L'impresario di teatro*, 1730) shows that Mariani was impresario of the Teatro Nuovo in that year. Scherillo maintained that Mariani's comedies lacked the essential spirit of Neapolitan dialect comedy and that they failed to provoke laughter; nevertheless, his intermezzo *La contadina astuta* (1734), under various titles, was performed frequently throughout Europe until 1757. Mele and Scherillo regarded *Il baron della Trocciola* (1736), based on Molière's *Georges Dandin*, as Mariani's best comedy. His librettos display a gradual movement of locale and character away from the prevailing focus on Naples and Neapolitans: over half the comedies are set in Rome, Pistoia, Pisa, Antignano and 'addo le pejace'. Also, as Simonelli pointed out, in *Il finto pazzo* (1735) the alternation between language and dialect begins to be resolved in favour of language, with the dialect confined, in this case, to only two characters.

Lo cecisbeo coffeato (commeddeia redicola pe museca), Roberto, 1728; *La pastorella commattuta* (chelleta redicola pe museca), Leo, 1728; *Lo matremmoneio pe' mennetta* (commeddeia redicola pe museca), Araia, 1729; *La schiava per amore* (comedia per musica), Leo, 1729; *L'impresario di teatro* (comedia per musica), dell'Anno and unknown composer, 1730; *Lo ggeluso chiaruto* (chelleta redicola, pe mmuseca), Speltra, 1731; *Il castello d'Atlante* (os), 1734; untitled, with characters Nerina and D. Chisciotto (int), 1734 (perf. with Il castello d'Atlante); *La contadina astuta* (int), Pergolesi, 1734 (perf. with Pergolesi: Adriano in Siria)

La franchezza delle donne (int), Sellitto (perf. with Sellitto: Siface re di Numidia), 1734; *Chi dell'altrui si veste presto si spoglia* (comedia per musica), Aurisicchio, 1734; *Gl'amanti generosi* (comedia per musica), Sarro, 1735; *Il finto pazzo per amore* (comedia per musica), Sellitto, 1735; *La vedova ingegnosa* (int), Prota (perf. with Leo: Emira), 1735; *La maga per vendetta, e per amore* (int) (perf. with La nemica amante), 1735; *Il baron della Trocciola* (comedia per musica), Fischietti, 1736; *Fingere per godere* (comedia per musica), Sarro, 1736; *L'inganno felice* (comedia per musica), Logroscino, 1739

*

P. Napoli Signorelli: *Vicende della coltura nelle Due Sicilie*, vi (Naples, 1786), 110

M. Scherillo: *L'opera buffa napoletana durante il settecento: storia letteraria* (Naples, 1883, 2/1917), 194ff

E. Mele: 'Monzù Moliero', *Flegrea*, iv (1900), 145–6

C. Troy: *The Comic Intermezzo* (Ann Arbor, 1979)

P. Simonelli: 'Lingua e dialetto nel teatro musicale napoletano del '700', *Musica e cultura a Napoli dal XV al XIX secolo*, ed. L. Bianconi and R. Bossa (Florence, 1983), 217–37, esp. 235   GRAHAM HARDIE

Maria Padilla. *Melodramma* in three acts by GAETANO DONIZETTI to a libretto by GAETANO ROSSI and Donizetti after François Ancelot's play; Milan, Teatro alla Scala, 26 December 1841.

The plot deals with the wooing of Maria Padilla (soprano, originally sung by Sophie Loewe) by the disguised King Pedro the Cruel of Spain (baritone; originally Giorgio Ronconi). He comes to abduct her, and she, knowing his true identity, is willing to go with him if he promises to make her his queen; he glibly swears he will. Maria tries to persuade her sister Ines (mezzo-soprano) to reconcile their aged father Don Ruiz (tenor) to her temporarily compromised position. But Ruiz, his honour stung, storms to court to demand satisfaction, and for his pains receives a bastinado, an ordeal which causes the old man to lose his mind. The distressed Maria shows him a letter from Pedro in which he states his intention to legitimize his relationship with her; when Ruiz finally understands the import of the document, he tears it up. But courtiers, opposed to the pretensions of the Padilla family, force Pedro into a marriage with a French princess; and when the bride arrives Maria, finding herself rejected, snatches the crown from her rival's head and kills herself.

One of the most unfairly neglected of Donizetti's mature operas, *Maria Padilla* contains a wealth of brilliant and dramatically powerful music. Especially noteworthy is the duet between Maria and her father in Act 3 scene i, which goes through a wide emotional gamut and possesses searing intensity, while the Act 2 duet for Maria and her sister Ines consists of a touching slow movement followed by a very brilliant cabaletta.

WILLIAM ASHBROOK

Maria Stuarda ('Mary Stuart'). *Tragedia lirica* in two or three acts by GAETANO DONIZETTI to a libretto by GIUSEPPE BARDARI after Andrea Maffei's translation (1830) of FRIEDRICH VON SCHILLER's *Maria Stuart*; Milan, Teatro alla Scala, 30 December 1835.

This work was originally intended by Donizetti as a vehicle for his favourite prima donna, Giuseppina Ronzi De Begnis, but when it was in rehearsal at the S Carlo, Naples, the king personally forbade its performance. Donizetti cobbled much of the score into a work with a different plot, *Buondelmonte*, with new recitatives and other changes, given at Naples on 18 October 1834. But Malibran became enthused with the subject of Mary Stuart and insisted on appearing in the opera at La Scala, where she ignored the censor's changes and caused the opera to be banned by the local authorities. In sanitized form, the work was given occasionally in Italy in the ensuing years. Its first 20th-century revival was at Bergamo in 1958 and it speedily re-entered the repertory. The discovery of the missing autograph in Sweden (now in *S-Smf*) made possible the preparation of a more authentic edition, in two acts, which was revived at Bergamo in 1989.

The critical edition based on the recovered autograph reveals an interesting example of Donizetti's practice of self-borrowing. Two numbers from *Maria Stuarda*, which Donizetti seems to have given up as a lost cause some time after its suppression in Milan, were later re-used in *La favorite*: the opening chorus at Westminster and the stretta to the first finale. After *Stuarda*, this ensemble at one time formed part of an apparently never-completed project, *Adelaide*, and from there it went into *L'ange de Nisida* before coming to rest at the end of Act 3 of *La favorite*. For the *rifacimento* of *Maria Stuarda* at S Carlo in 1865 these numbers were replaced, as they were now familiar from their context in *La favorite*. It is in this inaccurate version that the opera has become widely known in the 20th century.

Act 1 opens with Elisabetta [Queen Elizabeth] (soprano) mulling over the possibility of marriage to the Dauphin of France, but she cannot forget her love for Leicester (tenor). When he arrives at court, Leicester is taken aside by Talbot (bass), who gives him a portrait and a letter from Mary Stuart (soprano) in which she requests an interview with the English queen. Leicester's love and sympathy for the imprisoned Mary are rekindled. Later, Elizabeth confronts Leicester, who hands her the letter, thereby arousing her jealousy; but he persuades her to agree to meet Mary.

Act 1 scene ii (in most 20th-century performances entitled Act 2) is set at Fotheringay, where Mary thinks nostalgically of freedom, envying the clouds that can skim towards France (cavatina, 'O nube che lieve'). Leicester arrives to prepare her for Elizabeth's coming, but Mary is both resentful and afraid. (Their love duet was added – via *Buondelmonte* – for the 1835 Milan performance, and was later judged 'intrusive' by Donizetti.) Elizabeth, infuriated at the sight of the proud, beautiful Mary, treats her with contempt and disdain; stung, Mary calls Elizabeth a 'vil bastarda' and a stain on the honour of England. Elizabeth summons the guards and swears to be avenged.

In Act 2, back at Westminster, Cecil (bass) tries to persuade Elizabeth to sign Mary's death warrant while Leicester pleads that she be spared. Offended by Leicester's obvious preference for the Scottish queen, Elizabeth tells him that she has already signed the document and orders him to witness the execution. At Fotheringay, Mary receives her sentence from Cecil without flinching. Revealing a cassock beneath his cloak, Talbot hears her confession and absolves her. Mary asks her faithful friends to join her in praying for forgiveness for all who have wronged her; and Leicester can only stand helplessly by as Mary is led towards the executioner.

* * *

There are a number of interesting features in this score. The extended Act 1 finale (the scene of the confrontation – historically untrue, of course – between the two queens) is unusual in that the middle section, the *materia di mezzo*, is longer than the Larghetto and the stretta combined; it shows more clearly perhaps than anywhere else in Donizetti's output his intense interest in dramatic immediacy and potency. The Larghetto of this finale, a canonic sextet, is the source of a remarkably similar passage in Verdi's *Nabucco*. One of the most impressive numbers in *Maria Stuarda* is the eloquent prayer in the final scene; extensively revised, this melody was to form the basis for the ensemble at the end of Act 1 of *Linda di Chamounix*. Mary's confession duet with Talbot and her aria-finale are among the most affecting moments in the opera – indeed, in Donizetti's entire output.   WILLIAM ASHBROOK

Maria Tudor ('Mary Tudor'). *Opera seria* in four acts by CARLOS GOMES to a libretto by Emilio Praga after VICTOR HUGO's play; Milan, Teatro alla Scala, 27 March 1879.

The action takes place in London in the 1550s. Giovanna (mezzo-soprano), a young orphan, is the fiancée of Gilberto (bass) but has been seduced by a young man whom she knows as Lionel. Lionel is in fact Count Fabiano Fabiani (tenor), whose scandalous relationship with Queen Mary is the subject of gossip. Don Gil (baritone) warns Gilberto that he has a rival but Gilberto disbelieves him. Fabiano arrives and Giovanna runs to him, thinking it is Lionel. Seeing them, Gilberto becomes furious and tries to seize Fabiano, who flees. In despair, Gilberto tells Giovanna that her lover is the favourite of Queen Mary. Giovanna faints and Don Gil intimates that he can help Gilberto to avenge his honour and his love.

In the royal palace, Mary Tudor (soprano) appears for a reception. Once alone with her, Fabiano expresses his resentment against Don Gil, the ambassador of Philip II, King of Spain, who intends to marry the Queen, but Mary affirms her love for Fabiano. Don Gil requests an audience with the Queen and Fabiano leaves. Don Gil reveals Fabiano's treason and his infidelity. Giovanna enters; Mary, forcing her to confess that her lover Lionel is actually Fabiano, swears revenge. During a reception at the court, Fabiano becomes worried at the Queen's cold attitude. After she has accepted an engagement ring sent by the King of Spain, Mary asks Don Gil to bring Gilberto to her. She has Fabiano and Gilberto arrested and sent to the Tower of London on the pretext that Fabiano ordered Gilberto to kill her. Giovanna begs for clemency.

In the tower, Don Gil reads the royal decree that orders the execution of Fabiano but spares Gilberto. Mary, however, still intends to save Fabiano and makes a pact with Don Gil: that the latter place the convict's hood on Gilberto's head so that Fabiano can be saved, in return for which Don Gil will be made a duke. Giovanna enters to thank the Queen for sparing Gilberto, but, in a fit of jealousy and anger, Mary tells her that the convict with the black hood who is passing is really Gilberto. The cannon shot announcing the execution is heard. Mary asks that the remaining prisoner be brought to her. The guards bring Gilberto. Mary Tudor realizes then her disgrace and Don Gil's treason, and faints in tears.

The work was not well received in 1879 by the Milan audience despite a cast that included the great voices of Francesco Tamagno, Anna d'Angeri, Giuseppe Kaschmann and Edouard de Reszke. Several divergent explanations have been offered for that failure, among them the work's lack of originality, or the anti-French feeling prevalent in Italy at the time (exacerbated in Hugo's play by the negative attributes of the Italian Fabiano). The work adheres closely to the obsolescent and predictable formulae of the grand opera of the period and, despite some very effective musical passages (including the prelude and various arias), lacks dramatic impact and balance.   GERARD BÉHAGUE

Maribor. Town in northern Slovenia, formerly Marburg, Austria. There was no opera before the founding of the Stadttheater in 1785; and from then until 1919, opera was provided only by visiting companies who were all German troupes that leased the theatre for a few seasons. The theatre had to fight for its existence, so the repertory understandably included works of wide appeal like farces and musical comedies. However, in the second half of the 18th century and the first half of the 19th the town's amateur dramatic society also played an important role, presenting the first opera produced in Maribor, Bellini's *Norma*, in 1843 and urging the construction of a new theatre. Still in use today, it opened in 1852 with Flotow's *Martha*, performed by a troupe from Graz. The lack of a permanent musical ensemble in the town prevented the establishment of a serious repertory; in the later 19th century most musical works staged there were operettas. Conductors included Robert Stolz (1898–9), who composed his first works for theatre, including one operetta, in Maribor and Max Schönherr (1917–18). The theatre remained in German hands until 1919 and was thus inaccessible to the Slovene-speaking part of the population. Regular opera performances by the Slovene National Theatre began after World War I.

With the engagement of the conductor Andro Mitrović (1922–5 and 1926–8), Slovene works were added to the standard repertory, especially those of Viktor Parma, honorary Kapellmeister of the theatre for four years. After 1955 the opera director Jakov Cipci began to produce modern operas and to focus on Slovene works. His successors worked on similar principles, endeavouring to achieve a balance between old and new works in the repertory. The Maribor opera house staged the first Yugoslav performances of Weill's *Down in the Valley* (as *Im Tal*) and Wolf's *Der Corregidor*, and gave the premières of eight operas or similar projects by Danilo Švara, Darijan Božič, Pavle Merkù and other composers. The opera and ballet company performs regularly at other Yugoslav opera houses and festivals, and abroad.

Yugoslav and foreign singers who have appeared at Maribor include Peter Dvorsky, Ruža Baldani and Tomislav Neralić. In the mid-1980s operetta was re-introduced (*Die Fledermaus*, *Die lustige Witwe*) and some musicals were also produced.   MANICA ŠPENDAL

Marie Antoinette [Maria Antonia Josefa Johanna] (*b* Vienna, 2 Nov 1755; *d* Paris, 16 Oct 1793). Queen of France and patron of opera. The daughter of Emperor Franz I of Austria, she received her early tuition from Gluck (clavecin and singing) and Noverre (dance and deportment). As dauphine (1770) and later queen of France (1774), she supported a great many artists working within the field of opera. The success of Gluck's *Iphigénie en Aulide* at the Opéra in 1774 was due largely to the presence of the entire court at the première and to the dauphine's enthusiastic applause for individual numbers. Accused of favouring Austrian interests too overtly, she was obliged to welcome Piccinni to Paris, and later favoured Sacchini until further criticism forced her to support native composers: for celebrations at Fontainebleau in 1786 Lemoyne's *Phèdre* was staged in preference to Sacchini's *Oedipe à Colone*. Works by Grétry (*Les deux avares* and *L'amitié à l'épreuve*) received their premières as part of her wedding celebrations; Grétry was given a royal pension as a result of *Zémire et Azor* (1771) and eventually became the queen's director of music. Dalayrac also enjoyed her support, particularly during the early years of his operatic career. Voltaire, Marmontel and Sedaine were among librettists who benefited from her patronage in the form of official positions at court, and generous pensions were granted to numerous singers, including Arnould, Saint-Huberty and Caillot. At her private theatre in the Trianon, Marie Antoinette staged *opéras comiques* by leading composers of the day, and performed title roles such as Jenny (in Monsigny's *Le roi et le fermier*) and Colette (in Rousseau's *Le devin du village*). Her attractive and graceful stage presence apparently compensated for certain vocal shortcomings.

A. Jullien: *La cour et l'opéra sous Louis XVI: Marie-Antoinette et Sacchini, Salieri, Favart et Gluck* (Paris, 1878)

E. Goncourt and J. Goncourt: *Histoire de Marie-Antoinette* (Paris, 1879), 176–81

A. Jullien: *La cour et la ville au XVIIIe siècle* (Paris, 1881)

F. Boysse, ed.: *L'administration des Menus: journal de Papillon de la Ferté … (1756–1780)* (Paris, 1887)   ELISABETH COOK

Marié de l'Isle, (Claude Marie) Mécène (*b* Château-Chinon, 1811; *d* Paris, 1882). French tenor, later baritone. He sang in the chorus of the Opéra-Comique, Paris, then in 1838 made his début as a soloist at Metz. Returning to the Opéra-Comique, he sang Albert in the first performance of Clapisson's *La symphonie* (1839) and created Tonio in Donizetti's *La fille du régiment* (1840). Engaged at the Opéra in 1841, he sang Eléazar (*La Juive*), Max (*Der Freischütz*), Arnold (*Guillaume Tell*), Raoul (*Les Huguenots*), Fernand (*La favorite*) and Robert le diable. He then became a baritone and, after singing in Italy, in 1848 he returned to the Opéra, where he sang the title role of *Guillaume Tell*, Nevers (*Les Huguenots*), Alphonse (*La favorite*) and Raimbaud (*Le comte Ory*). After retiring from the stage he taught in Paris, his best-known pupil being his daughter, Célestine Galli-Marié, who created Carmen.   ELIZABETH FORBES

Mariinsky. Theatre in ST PETERSBURG, built in 1860; it was known as the State Academic Theatre of Opera and Ballet from 1917 and as the Kirov Theatre from 1935. In 1991 it reverted to the name Mariinsky.

Marilyn. 'Scenes from the fifties' in two acts by LORENZO FERRERO to texts by the composer and Floriana Bossi; Rome, Teatro dell'Opera, 23 February 1980.

These 'scenes from the fifties, after documents from American life' brought Ferrero wide public attention in Italy. Interleaved with episodes from the life of Marilyn Monroe (coloratura soprano), unstable and unhappy even at her most successful, are summary portraits of the society that surrounded her. In Act 1 these emphasize the violence of official culture: the Korean War, the McCarthy investigations and the prosecution of the psychoanalyst Wilhelm Reich (tenor), with whom Marilyn closes the act in a sort of long-distance duet. The second act focusses on sub-cultures: Ginsburg and the beat poets, peace marches, and Timothy Leary discussing LSD with students. By contrast with these relatively peaceable images, Monroe's own life disintegrates. At last we see her corpse on stage: the tableau of 'American life' with which the work began resumes its momentum around her. In *Marilyn* the eclectic stylistic mixture that has become Ferrero's trademark is already apparent. Neo-tonal materials, already adumbrating the synthesis of 19th-century opera and postwar popular music typical of his later works, are mixed with modernist orchestral textures. In retrospect, therefore, it has been seen as heralding the wave of post-modern and eventually populist and neo-tonal operas that followed from Ferrero and others in the 1980s.

DAVID OSMOND-SMITH

Marina. Zarzuela in two acts by PASCUAL EMILIO ARRIETA to a libretto by Francisco Camprodón; Madrid, Teatro del Circo, 21 September 1855.

The plot is a simple story set in a Catalan fishing village. Marina (soprano), an orphan, has been brought up by the family of Jorge (tenor), now a ship's captain, and is secretly in love with him. He has never declared his love for his childhood companion, and when she is misled into believing that his affections lie elsewhere she is heartbroken and agrees to marry, instead, the shipwright Pascual (bass). He, however, becomes insanely jealous when Alberto, an old sea-captain (baritone), sends her a letter which had been written by her dead father. A quarrel ensues, misunderstandings are finally sorted out, and the true lovers are united.

Though coolly received initially, *Marina* quickly won wide popularity, and Arrieta was persuaded to supply recitatives, add extra numbers, and turn it into a three-act opera (the text being revised by Miguel Ramos Carrión), in which form it was produced at the Teatro Real in Madrid on 16 March 1871. The opening fishermen's chorus was taken from Arrieta's early unfinished opera *Pergolesi*. Despite the inclusion of a seguidilla and a tango, the predominant flavour of *Marina* is Italian, from the coloratura of Marina's romance 'Pensar en él' to the flagrant imitation of Donizetti's *Lucia di Lammermoor* at the end.

LIONEL SALTER

Marinari, Gaetano (*b* Italy; *fl* 1764–*c*1844). Italian scene painter active in London. He succeeded Michael Novosielski at the King's Theatre in 1785–6 and remained with the company as painter and machinist until 1794–5, when he was replaced by Novosielski. He worked on six operas by Cimarosa, including *Il matrimonio segreto*, for which he supplied new scenes and dresses as well as the theatre decorations, and on several by Paisiello, notably *La locanda* (1791) at the Pantheon, with scenery by Simon Frédéric Moench, and at the Little Theatre in the Haymarket in 1792 (after the Pantheon burnt down), with scenery by Marinari. He was also the scenographer for Cherubini's *Ifigenia in Aulide* (1789). After the reconstruction of the King's Theatre (1789–91), Marinari designed and executed the new scenery, machinery and decorations for the pasticcio *Le nozze di Dorina* (1793). His fire effects in Gazzaniga's *Don Giovanni* (1794) were greatly admired. After Novosielski's death in 1795, he returned to the King's but as theatre decorator, his designs being taken from Italy. From October 1794 to May 1799 he also worked at Drury Lane as house painter. He was engaged on such comic operas as Hook's *Jack of Newbury* (1795), Storace's *Mahmoud* (1796) and Arnold's *Zorinski* (1795, Haymarket, with Rooker). Later he returned to the King's (1802–3), went to Dublin (1809) and worked sporadically at Drury Lane (1812–13). He was accounted one of the leading scene painters in Europe and, with his classical approach, produced some of the first specimens of architectural scenery.

S. Rosenfeld and E. Croft-Murray: 'A Checklist of Scene Painters Working in Great Britain and Ireland in the 18th Century (4)', *Theatre Notebook*, xix (1964–5), 133–45, esp. 134–6

SYBIL ROSENFELD

Marinelli, Gaetano (*b* Naples, 3 June 1754; *d* after 1820). Italian composer. He was a pupil of Manna and P. A. Gallo at the Loreto conservatory, Naples, and then from 1772 at the Pietà dei Turchini conservatory, where he studied under Cafaro and Lorenzo Fago and became a *maestrino*. In 1776 his intermezzo *Il barone di Sardafritta*, perhaps a student work, was performed at a Naples convent. His first known comic opera was *I tre rivali*, for the Teatro della Pace, Rome, in Carnival 1784 (an earlier work for that theatre is considered doubtful). The next year he wrote *Gli uccellatori* for the Teatro della Pergola, Florence.

In 1786 he married in Naples and went to Madrid, where he lived until 1789, working as a singing teacher. In Carnival 1790 two comic operas were performed in Naples, *La contadina semplice* and *La bizzarra contadina*, in December another, *Gli accidenti inaspettati*, and on 30 May 1791 he achieved the S Carlo with his first *opera seria*, *Lucio Papirio*. This led to a contract for the spectacle opera *La vendetta di Medea*, given in Venice in 1792, a year in which he wrote a total of four operas. Thereafter he wrote two or three a year, mainly for Naples and Venice, but after 1796, when Napoleon invaded Italy, his output dropped, with some apparently barren years. Marinelli is said to have been in the service of the Duke of Bavaria, so one or more visits to Munich may account for the apparent gaps in his output. However, there is no evidence that he was still working in Munich in 1811, as is sometimes stated. Marinelli had moved to Portugal by 1817, when he composed a wedding cantata for the crown prince, Dom Pedro. He was said to have been teaching singing at Oporto about 1820. According to Gerber, several numbers from Marinelli's operas were popular with amateurs, and Gervasoni called him an 'excellent composer' who 'has a style that is very expressive and of a particular newness'.

While Marinelli's serious operas for Naples consist primarily of recitatives and arias with one or two duets, *La vendetta di Medea* exhibits the radical departures from traditional Italian practice then taking place in Venice. Elements formerly found only in French-inspired operas, such as scene complexes and choruses, here co-exist with multi-sectional ensemble finales hitherto the province of comic opera. Many scenes are realized entirely in obbligato recitative. The Act 1 solo scena for Medea (soprano) involves a chorus of Furies that acts as a second character. Marinelli explores the textural options of obbligato recitative, solo with chorus, a cavatina with interruptions by the Furies, and finally an aria with a tutti closing. Staged death, new to Italian opera, takes repugnant form at the end of the opera, when Medea, enraged at the treachery of Giasone [Jason] (soprano castrato), murders their children on stage and exits in a flying carriage, leaving the palace in ruins and calling down a rain of fire. *Issipile* and *Germanico* are equally notable for their use of the chorus, ensembles and unusual constructions. Some of Marinelli's sinfonias (in one movement) have slow introductions. Wind instruments, including english horn, are used in recitatives as well as in arias and ensembles, and Marinelli exploits contrasts of key (as in the finale of *Medea*) and tempo as well as timbre for expressive purposes. Arias in either rounded ternary or rondò forms often have two tempos and even two metres. In the comic operas of the 1790s some of the larger ensembles incorporate extensive action in constructions similar to the finale.

Il barone di Sardafritta (int), Naples, Convento della Maddalena, 1776, *I-Nc**

I tre rivali, ossia Il matrimonio impensato (int, 2, C. A. Casini), Rome, Pace, carn. 1784

Gli uccellatori (dg, C. Goldoni), Florence, Pergola, 28 March 1785, *F-Pn* (Act 1)

Il trionfo d'Arianna (azione teatrale, P. Tagliazucchi), Florence, Pergola, ?1785–6

La bizzarra contadina in amore [La villanella semplice] (ob, 2, G. Palomba), Naples, Nuovo, carn. 1790, *I-Nc**

La contadina semplice (ob, 2), Naples, Fondo, carn. 1790, *Nc**

Gli accidenti inaspettati (dg, 2, Palomba), Naples, Fiorentini, 4 Dec 1790, *Nc**

Lucio Papirio [Quinto Fabio] (os, 3, after A. Zeno), Naples, S Carlo, 30 May 1791, *Nc*

La vendetta di Medea (os, 2), Venice, S Samuele, carn. 1792, *B-Bc*

Amore aguzza l'ingegno (ob, 2), Naples, Fondo, carn. 1792

Arminio (os, 3, F. Moretti), Naples, S Carlo, 13 Aug 1792; as Germanico (2), Venice, S Benedetto, 4 Feb 1797

Lo sposo a forza (ob, 2, Palomba), Naples, Fiorentini, 1792, *I-Nc**

I vecchi delusi (ob, 2, Palomba), Naples, Fiorentini, July 1793

Attalo, re di Bitinia (os, 3, F. Casorri), Naples, S Carlo, 13 Aug 1793

L'interesse gabba tutti (dg, 2, C. Mazzini), Florence, Pergola, June 1795, *Fc*

I vecchi burlati (dg, 2, after Palomba), Venice, S Samuele, 12 Oct 1795

La finta principessa (dg, 2, F. Livigni), Venice, S Samuele, carn. 1796

Issipile (os, 3, P. Metastasio), Venice, Fenice, 12 Nov 1796

Li due vecchi amanti delusi (dg, Palomba), Corfu, S Giacomo, 1796

Le due fratelli Castracani (dg), Padua, Obizzi, 1798

Le quattro mogli (dg, 2, G. Rossi), Venice, S Benedetto, carn. 1799; as Il concorso delle spose, Milan, Carcano, spr. 1806

Bajazette (os, 2, A. Piovene), Venice, S Benedetto, May 1799

La morte di Cleopatra (os, S. A. Sografi), Venice, Fenice, May 1800

Rocchetta in equivoco (farsa giocosa, G. Foppa), Venice, S Moisè, carn. 1802

La sposo contrastato (melodrama giocoso), Milan, Novara, carn. 1808

Il trionfo d'amore, Cremona, Sociale, 1808, *Mr**

Alessandro in Efeso (os, F. Marconi), Milan, Carcano, 25 Oct 1810

I quattro rivali in amore (commedia), Milan, Carcano, Nov 1810

L'equivoco fortunato (azione comica, 2, L. Prividali), Milan, Scala, 21 June 1811, *Mc**

Music in: La disfatta di Dario, Naples, 1790

Doubtful: La semplice ad arte (ob, Casini), Rome, Pace, carn. 1783; Lo sposo contrastato, ossia Il letterato alla moda (ob, Mocenigo), Florence, Pergola, 1786; I quattro rivali in amore, Naples, 1795; I diversi accidenti (G. Artusi), Venice, 1804

ES (U. Prota-Giurleo); *FlorimoN*; *GerberNL*
C. Gervasoni: *Nuova teoria di musica* (Parma, 1812)
B. Gutierrez: *Il teatro carcano* (Milan, 1916)
U. Prota-Giurleo: *Nicolo Logroscino* (Naples, 1927), 34–5
DENNIS LIBBY, MARITA P. McCLYMONDS

Marini, Ignazio (*b* Tagliuno, Bergamo, 28 Nov 1811; *d* Milan, 29 April 1873). Italian bass. He made his début in 1832 at Brescia and was then engaged at La Scala, where he created Guido in Donizetti's *Gemma di Vergy* (1834), sang Talbot in *Maria Stuarda* (1835), created the title role of Verdi's *Oberto* and sang in the first performance of Donizetti's *Gianni di Parigi* (1839). At the Teatro Apollo, Rome, he sang the title role of *Marino Faliero* (1840) and created Arnoldo in Donizetti's *Adelia* (1841). In 1846 he created the title role of *Attila* at La Fenice. Engaged at Covent Garden, 1847–9, he sang Silva (*Ernani*), Marcel (*Les Huguenots*), Bertram (*Robert le diable*), Mozart's Figaro and Leporello. His vast repertory included Rossini's Moses, Elmiro (*Otello*) and Mustafà; Bellini's Oroveso, Rodolfo (*La sonnambula*), Filippo (*Beatrice di Tenda*) and Giorgio (*I puritani*); and Donizetti's Belisarius, Nottingham (*Roberto Devereux*) and Félix (*Poliuto*). He sang in New York, Havana and St Petersburg, where in 1862 he appeared as the Alcalde in the

Marini's designs for demons and furies for Pasquale Anfossi's 'Armida' performed at the Teatro Regio, Turin, 1770: title page from 'Abiti dell'Armida' (Turin, 1770), engraving by Gizzardi

first performance of *La forza del destino*. His wife, the soprano Antonietta Marini-Rainieri, created Leonora in *Oberto* (1839) and the Marchesa del Poggio in *Un giorno di regno* (1840) at La Scala.   ELIZABETH FORBES

Marini, Leonardo (*b* Turin, *c*1735; *d* Turin, after 1806). Italian costume designer. He succeeded his father, Giuseppe Stefano Marini, as costume designer of the Regio and Carignano theatres in Turin, where he worked until 1798–9 with stage designers such as the Galliari brothers and, in 1770, Innocente Colomba. At the same time he had a successful career as designer of furniture and furnishings for the royal family and for rich and aristocratic clients in Turin. In 1775 he was appointed 'royal designer' of uniforms for the Savoy army. He also contributed a treatise, *Ragionamento intorno alla foggia degli abiti teatrali*, to the collection of engravings entitled *Abiti antichi di diverse nazioni d'Europa e d'Asia* (Turin, 1771), which shows the influence of the ideas of Francesco Algarotti and Diderot's *Encyclopédie* (Paris, 1745–72). Since plentiful evidence of his work as theatre costumier survives both in volumes (Turin, Biblioteca Reale, and private collections) and as single sheets (Canberra, Australian National Gallery and Christie's sale, 1989), it is possible to follow the development of his style, in which the pursuit of verisimilitude (which he declared in the *Ragionamento* to be his aim) was no impediment to a brilliant display of inventiveness and fantasy.

M. Viale Ferrero: 'Scene e costumi dei Galliari e del Marini', *Antichità viva*, i/9–10 (1963), 31–44
——: *La scenografia del '700 e i fratelli Galliari* (Turin, 1963)

——: *Storia del Teatro Regio di Torino*, iii: *La scenografia dalle origini al 1936* (Turin, 1980)
Old Master Drawings: Christie's, 11 January 1989 (New York, 1989), pls.77–91 [sale catalogue]   MERCEDES VIALE FERRERO

Marino Faliero. *Tragedia lirica* in three acts by GAETANO DONIZETTI to a text by GIOVANNI EMANUELE BIDERA with revisions by Agostino Ruffini, after Casimir Delavigne's tragedy; Paris, Théâtre Italien, 12 March 1835.

The Doge, Marino Faliero (bass), is furious when Steno (bass) accuses the Dogaressa Elena (soprano) of adultery. Captain Ismaele (baritone) joins Faliero in a conspiracy against the Council. Elena breaks off with the Doge's nephew Fernando (tenor), giving him her scarf as a memento. She accuses Steno of hounding her, and Fernando challenges him; but Fernando is borne in, dying, and his last request is to be buried with Elena's scarf. Faliero comes to tell Elena of Fernando's death, but the conspiracy has been betrayed and he is arrested; before the Council, Faliero tears off his Doge's cap and tramples on it. At a final interview with Elena, he shows her the scarf and requests that it be used to shroud both his and Fernando's faces. Shaken, Elena confesses her infidelity; but as death is near, the Doge, though enraged, forgives her. He is led away; Elena watches the execution from the window and at the sound of the executioner's blow she screams and collapses.

Donizetti's first opera for Paris, performed late in the season that introduced Bellini's *I puritani*, *Marino Faliero* contains a beautiful barcarolle and a powerful musical portrait of the aged Doge. (There are obvious resemblances to two Verdi operas, *I due Foscari* and *Simon Boccanegra*.) The original cast included Grisi (Elena), Lablache (Faliero), Rubini (Fernando) and Tamburini (Ismaele).   WILLIAM ASHBROOK

Marinuzzi, Gino (i) (*b* Palermo, 24 March 1882; *d* Milan, 17 Aug 1945). Italian conductor and composer. He showed an early aptitude for music and at the age of 12 won first prize in a competition with a cantata which he himself conducted. At 18 he completed his studies at the Palermo Conservatory, where he was taught composition by G. Zuelli and composed a requiem mass on the death of Umberto I that was performed in 1900 at the Pantheon in Palermo. In 1901 he made his first appearance as conductor at the Teatro Massimo, Palermo, in Verdi's *Rigoletto*, the beginning of a career that brought him international renown, and critical acclaim for his excellent technique. He built up a wide repertory including contemporary music, especially that of Richard Strauss, whose music he was one of the first to make known in Italy, and of Puccini, conducting the première of *La rondine* at Monte Carlo in 1917. He succeeded Busoni as director of the Bologna Conservatory in 1916, but resigned in 1918. In 1920–21 he was artistic director of the Chicago Opera Association. From 1928 to 1934 he was permanent conductor and artistic director of the Rome Opera, from where he went to La Scala, Milan; he remained there until 1945, acting also as sovrintendente during his last years.

Considered one of the foremost Italian interpreters of Wagner and an excellent exponent of the lesser-known operas of Donizetti and Bellini, he often appeared at the Maggio Musicale in Florence. His compositions include three operas: *Barberina* (1903, Palermo), *Jacquerie* (1918, Buenos Aires) and *Palla de' Mozzi* (1932, La

Scala). In 1982 a study conference was organized at La Scala to mark the centenary of his birth.

*

F. Balilla Pratella: 'Jacquerie di Gino Marinuzzi', *Pensiero musicale*, ii (Bologna, 1922)
L. P. Cei: *Il Signore del Golfo Mistico* (Florence, 1982)
LEONARDO PINZAUTI

Marinuzzi, Gino (ii) (*b* New York, 7 April 1920). Italian composer, son of Gino Marinuzzi (i). He studied at the Milan Conservatory. From 1946 to 1951 he was deputy conductor at the Rome Opera. In 1956 he was a founder member of the studio di fonologia at the Accademia Filarmonica Romana, and he continued to be involved in electronic music throughout the 1960s. From 1964 Marinuzzi was concerned mainly with composing music for the theatre, films and television.

Initially influenced by Hindemith, in *Due improvvisi* for orchestra (1959) he began to explore other directions that led him towards electronic music: it is to this phase that his radio opera *La signora Paulatim* belongs. To a libretto by Italo Chiusano, influenced by Hindemith's *Hin und zurück* and based on a story by Italo Calvino, it tells of the mutual infidelity (but with a happy outcome) of Signor and Signora Paulatim. Without any predetermined stylistic system the music faithfully follows the twists of the narrative. Parodic elements, hints of musical commonplaces from the operatic tradition, and the resources of electronic music when factory, city and bird sounds are required, are juxtaposed, in line with the pragmatic and anti-intellectual aesthetic characteristic of the composer. The opera was first broadcast from Turin in spring 1964 by RAI (who also printed a vocal score that year); it was staged in Naples in the RAI auditorium in October 1966 as part of the Autunno Musicale Napoletano.

*

F. L. Lunghi: '*La signora Paulatim* di Gino Marinuzzi jr', *Giornale d'Italia* (17–18 Oct 1966)
A. Quattrocchi: *Storia dell'Accademia filarmonica romana* (Rome, 1991)
RAFFAELE POZZI

Mario, Giovanni Matteo, Cavaliere de Candia (*b* Cagliari, 17 Oct 1810; *d* Rome, 11 Dec 1883). Italian tenor. He was an army officer but was forced to desert and go into exile because of his association with Mazzini's 'Young Italy' party. He studied in Paris with Ponchard and Bordogni and was coached by Meyerbeer himself for his Opéra début as Robert le diable (1838); he also sang the title role of *Le comte Ory*. His London début, as Gennaro (*Lucrezia Borgia*), was at Her Majesty's (1839); Lucrezia was sung by Giulia Grisi, his stage partner for the next 22 years and his lifelong companion. He also appeared as Nemorino and Pollione. He returned to Paris to make his début at the Théâtre Italien as Nemorino and sang in the first performance of Halévy's *Le drapier* at the Opéra.

Thereafter, Mario and Grisi divided their time between Paris and London. In winter 1840–41 Mario transferred to the Théâtre Italien. He sang Orombello in *Beatrice di Tenda*, the first of ten new roles, including Almaviva, that year. He began to take over parts written for Rubini or habitually sung by him, among them Arturo (*I puritani*) and Elvino. He took on four Donizetti roles during the next two years, Edgardo, Percy (*Anna Bolena*), Carlo (*Linda di Chamounix*) and Ernesto in the première of *Don Pasquale*. In 1843 he sang four Rossini roles, Otello, Gianetto (*La gazza ladra*), Lindoro (*L'italiana in Algeri*) and Don Ramiro

(*La Cenerentola*). During the next three seasons in London he created the title role of Costa's *Don Carlos* (1844) and sang Paolino in *Il matrimonio segreto*, Ferrando, and Oronte in *I Lombardi*. In Paris he took over Gualtiero, a favourite Rubini role, in *Il pirata* (1844) and appeared in *I due Foscari* (Verdi wrote a cabaletta especially for him).

In 1847 Mario and Grisi transferred from Her Majesty's Theatre to Covent Garden, where he sang with the Royal Italian Opera every season (except 1869) until his retirement in 1871. During the winters he appeared at St Petersburg (1849–53, 1868–70), Paris (1853–64), New York (1854) and Madrid (1859, 1864). He was able to return to Italy but never sang there professionally. At Covent Garden his roles included James (*La donna del lago*), Fernand (*La favorite*), Raoul (*Les Huguenots*), Masaniello (*La muette de Portici*), John of Leyden (*Le prophète*), Raimbaut (*Robert le diable*), Eléazar (*La Juive*) and Tamino; he also sang the Duke in the London première of *Rigoletto* (1853).

In St Petersburg he sang in Alary's *Sardanapale* (1852) and in New York Idreno (*Semiramide*). At the Théâtre Italien he appeared as Manrico, Alfredo and Lyonel (*Martha*). On 15 May 1858 he sang in *Les Huguenots* at the reopening of Covent Garden after the 1856 fire. He attempted the title role of *Don Giovanni* but soon reverted to the part of Ottavio. He appeared in the Paris première of *Un ballo in maschera* (1861); his last new roles at Covent Garden were in Gounod's *Faust* (1864) and *Roméo et Juliette* (1867).

Mario's voice was a lyric tenor of great sweetness and beauty, with a range from *c* to *c″*; for the roles he inherited from Rubini he added a falsetto extension up to *f″*. Nemorino, Ernesto and Gennaro were the successes of his earlier years, while the Duke of Mantua, Raoul and Faust were the most admired roles of his maturity. Almaviva, which he sang more than a hundred times in London alone, personified for 30 years his vocal charm and dramatic grace.

For illustration *see* DON PASQUALE; FAUST (ii), fig.1; and ROMÉO ET JULIETTE (ii).

*

Castil-Blaze: *L'opéra italien de 1548 à 1856* (Paris, 1856)
T. Gautier: *L'histoire de l'art dramatique en France depuis vingt-cinq ans* (Paris, 1858–9)
H. F. Chorley: *Thirty Years' Musical Recollections* (London, 1862)
B. Lumley: *Reminiscences of the Opera* (London, 1864)
[J. E. Cox]: *Musical Recollections of the Last Half-Century* (London, 1872)
L. Engel: *From Mozart to Mario* (London, 1886)
W. Beale: *The Light of Other Days* (London, 1890)
W. Kuhe: *My Musical Recollections* (London, 1896)
Mrs G. Pearse and F. Hird: *The Romance of a Great Singer: a Memoir of Mario* (London, 1910)
H. Rosenthal: *Two Centuries of Opera at Covent Garden* (London, 1958)
E. Forbes: 'The Purloined Cabaletta', *About the House*, iv/3 (1973), 51
——: *Mario and Grisi* (London, 1985)   ELIZABETH FORBES

Mario [Tillotson], **Queena** (*b* Akron, OH, 21 Aug 1896; *d* New York, 28 May 1951). American soprano. To earn money for singing lessons, she wrote women's columns for newspapers in New York. She studied with Oscar Saenger and later with Marcella Sembrich; she was twice turned down by the Metropolitan, but with the help of Caruso was engaged by the San Carlo Opera Company, making her début in *Les contes d'Hoffmann* in 1918. After two seasons with that company and another two with the Scotti Grand Opera Company, Mario made her Metropolitan début as Micaëla in 1922. For the next 17 seasons she sang lyric and coloratura parts there, enjoying her greatest success as Humperdinck's Gretel, a role she also performed in the first complete opera broadcast live from the Metropolitan stage (Christmas Day, 1931) and at her farewell performance with the company (1938). She also sang with the San Francisco Opera (1923–4, 1929–30, 1932), notably as the Child in the American première of Ravel's *L'enfant et les sortilèges* (1930). She was especially admired for her sensitivity to word inflections and for silvery tone. In her later years she devoted herself to teaching; her pupils included Rose Bampton and Helen Jepson.   PHILIP LIESON MILLER

Marion Delorme. *Melodramma* in four acts by AMILCARE PONCHIELLI to a libretto by ENRICO GOLISCIANI after VICTOR HUGO's play; Milan, Teatro alla Scala, 17 March 1885.

The action takes place in France in 1638. Marion Delorme (soprano), former actress and demi-mondaine, lives with Didier (tenor), who knows nothing of her past. He rescues the Marquis de Severny (baritone) from a band of cut-throats, but suspects him of designs on Marion and challenges him publicly to a duel, for which Cardinal Richelieu has ordained the death penalty. Severny escapes arrest by feigning death, while Didier is imprisoned as his murderer. Marion procures Didier's escape, and they join a company of strolling players headed by Lelio (mezzo-soprano). Laffemas (bass), spy of Richelieu, decides to entrap the lovers by ordering a performance at the cardinal's palace. Severny, present in disguise, reveals Marion's true identity and his own previous involvement with her. In disgust Didier gives himself up. His example is gallantly followed by Severny. Laffemas offers to save Didier's life in return for Marion's favours. Reluctantly she yields. For this she is savagely denounced by Didier; but they are finally reconciled before he and Severny are taken away to be executed.

In his last opera Ponchielli moved away from grandeur to a lighter style that owes much to French *opéra comique*. The textures are more airy, especially in the ensembles, where the voices often chatter and there is a good deal of high woodwind figuration. Not until the finale to Act 3 where first Didier and then Severny surrender to Richelieu's 'arcieri' is there a reversion to the old-style massive concertato, launched by a savagely declaimed melody from Didier. Lelio, a brilliant travesty role, is entirely *à la française*, his music suggesting a sophisticated Auber. Severny, one of those likable danger-loving rogues common in Hugo (compare Rochester in *Cromwell*, Don César in *Ruy Blas*), is limned in suitably swaggering rhythms. The villainy of Laffemas is conveyed less by harmonic means than by depth of vocal register. The love music, two of whose themes are quoted in the prelude, abounds in italianate lyrical flourishes; but it is Gounod who stalks the lovers' final encounter, with its many sequences and melting harmonies. There is even a hint of Bizet in the march-like motif that dominates the Act 4 intermezzo, recurring twice in the course of the action. Some solos (e.g. Didier's *romanza* in the same act) reach out tentatively to a new freedom of design; but the sureness of touch that marks *La Gioconda* is lacking.   JULIAN BUDDEN

Marionette opera. *See* PUPPET OPERA.

Mariotte, Antoine (*b* Avignon, 22 Dec 1875; *d* Paris, 22 Dec 1944). French conductor, composer and administrator. He abandoned a naval career to study composition under d'Indy at the Schola Cantorum and held conducting posts as well as teaching the piano in the conservatories at Lyons and Orléans. From 1936 to 1939 he was director of the Opéra-Comique. His first opera, *Salomé*, was composed before that of Richard Strauss but was not performed until after the première of Strauss's opera. Disputes over the rights to Wilde's play, which Mariotte's opera sets in the original French, hindered productions of the opera, though it was well received. His works use the full range of operatic effects including imaginative choral writing, especially in *Esther*, which has oriental set pieces punctuating the unfolding of the drama, treated with striking rhythmic power. His work as a whole shows him to have been familiar with various contemporary styles. *Le vieux roi* tells a tale of Celtic honour and adultery, while the lighter *Gargantua* is set in four self-contained tableaux.

Salomé (tragédie lyrique, 1, O. Wilde), Lyons, Grand, 30 Oct 1908, vs (Paris, 1910)
Le vieux roi (tragédie lyrique, 1, R. de Gourmont), Lyons, Grand, 28 Feb 1913, vs (Paris, 1913)
Léontine soeurs (comédie musicale, 3, A. Acremant), Paris, Trianon Lyrique, May 1924
Esther, princesse d'Israël (tragédie lyrique, 3, André Dumas and S.-C. Leconte), Paris, Opéra, 1 May 1925, vs (Paris, 1925)
Gargantua (scènes rabelaisiennes, 4, d'Armory and Mariotte), Paris, OC (Favart), 17 Feb 1935, vs (Paris, 1935)
Nele Dooryn (3, C. Mauclair), Paris, OC (Favart), 17 Oct 1940

*

M. Emmanuel: 'Albert Roussel, Jean Cras, Antoine Mariotte', *Le théâtre lyrique en France*, iii (Paris, 1937–9), 234–41 [pubn of Poste National/Radio-Paris]
P. Landormy: *La musique française après Debussy* (Paris, 1943)
G. Samazeuilh: *Musiciens de mon temps* (Paris, 1947)
A. Thomazi: *Trois marins compositeurs* (Paris, 1948)
RICHARD LANGHAM SMITH

Marischka, Hubert (*b* Vienna, 27 Aug 1882; *d* Vienna, 4 Dec 1959). Austrian tenor and director. He made his début in St Pölten in 1904, was discovered in Brno by the librettist Victor Léon, and made his début at the Theater an der Wien in 1908 in Strauss's *Wiener Blut*. After moving to the Carltheater, he returned to the Theater an der Wien in 1912 as principal tenor. He married Léon's daughter in 1908; after her death in childbirth, he married the daughter of Wilhelm Karczag, from whom he inherited the directorship of the Theater an der Wien (1923–35) as well as that of the Wiener Stadttheater and the Raimundtheater. Operettas in which he created principal tenor roles included Fall's *Die geschiedene Frau* (1908) and *Die Rose von Stambul* (1916), Lehár's *Zigeunerliebe* (1910), *Die ideale Gattin* (1913), *Endlich allein* (1914), *Die blaue Mazur* (1920), *Frasquita* (1922) and *Die gelbe Jacke* (1923), Kálmán's *Gräfin Mariza* (1924) and *Die Zirkusprinzessin* (1926), and Eysler's *Die gold'ne Meisterin* (1927). His appeal lay as much in his stage presence as in his somewhat constricted voice. He later became a film director. His brother Ernst Marischka (*b* 1893) was an operetta librettist and film director; the two collaborated on the libretto of Kreisler's operetta *Sissy* (1932).

*

GSL; StiegerO   ANDREW LAMB

Maritana. Grand opera in three acts by VINCENT WALLACE to a libretto by EDWARD FITZBALL after Adolphe Philippe d'Ennery and Philippe François Pinel Dumanoir's drama *Don César de Bazan*; London, Drury Lane, 15 November 1845.

Act 1 is set in a square in Madrid, where the handsome gypsy, Maritana (soprano) attracts the attention of the disguised King of Spain, Charles II (bass). Don José de Santarem (baritone), an unscrupulous courtier who is enamoured of the queen, observes this and hopes thereby to further his own designs. He is accosted by Don Caesar de Bazan (tenor), a penniless, devil-may-care nobleman famed for his duelling victories. It is Holy Week, and the king has decreed that anyone who fights with the sword will be hanged as a felon instead of being shot as a gentleman. At that moment, Lazarillo (mezzo-soprano), a young apprentice who is fleeing from his master, rushes into the square pursued by the guards. In order to give the youth a chance to escape Don Caesar challenges the Captain (baritone) to a duel; he wounds him, but is himself arrested.

In Act 2 scene i Don José decides to advance his plans by marrying Maritana to a nobleman. He undertakes to ensure that Don Caesar shall be shot, not hanged, if he will first agree to wed a veiled lady. Eager to escape the rope, Don Caesar consents, and his marriage to Maritana duly takes place. So, apparently, does his execution; but the faithful Lazarillo has secretly removed the bullets from the firing squad's rifles. Finding himself still alive, Don Caesar resolves to discover his wife's identity. In scene ii Maritana has been taken to the palace of the Marquis de Montefiori (bass), where the king pretends to be her husband. She rejects his advances, telling him that she loves Don Caesar. Meanwhile, Don Caesar arrives at the palace, but the quick-thinking Don José presents the aged Marchioness (mezzo-soprano) to him as his wife. Don Caesar is about to sign away his claim to his wife when he hears Maritana's voice and realizes that he is being tricked. Don José has him rearrested.

As Act 3 opens Don Caesar, who has escaped from prison again, forces an entry into his own villa, knowing that Maritana has been taken there. He is met by the king, who claims to be Don Caesar de Bazan. In response, Don Caesar pretends to be the king; in the wrangle that ensues, he learns that he has already been pardoned. Left alone with Maritana, he convinces her that he is her husband. Don José is about to reveal the king's intended infidelity to the queen, but Don Caesar runs him through. Moved by this devotion, the king appoints Don Caesar governor of Valencia and all ends happily.

Wallace had not long returned from his extensive travels abroad when, in 1845, he was introduced to the dramatist Edward Fitzball. Fitzball was impressed by Wallace's compositions, and gave him the libretto of *Maritana* which he had just completed. In setting it, Wallace made use of music he had composed in Australia (1835–8), though Maritana's song 'The harp in the air' is said to have been inspired by his future first wife's playing during a harp lesson at the convent of Thurles in 1830. The opera was produced under Bunn's management at Drury Lane with Emma Romer as Maritana and William Harrison as Don Caesar, and it was Wallace's greatest triumph (running for more than 50 consecutive nights). The words of two of its most popular numbers, Don José's 'In happy moments' and Maritana's 'Scenes that are brightest', were written by Bunn 'at the request of the author and composer'. The opera was an international success and was performed in Dublin and Philadelphia (1846), New York and

Vienna (1848) and, in Italian with recitatives by Mattei, in Dublin (1877) and at Her Majesty's, London (1880). It was revived at the Lyceum, London (1925), and at Sadler's Wells (1931) and remained in the repertory of British touring companies until World War II. Stylistically it is characterized by youthful spontaneity, uninhibited tunefulness and brash, but effective, orchestration. NIGEL BURTON

Marito disperato, Il ('The Desperate Husband'). *Melodramma giocoso* in two acts by DOMENICO CIMAROSA to a libretto by GIAMBATTISTA LORENZI; Naples, Teatro dei Fiorentini, 1785.

Gismonda (soprano) is married to the insanely jealous Don Corbolone (baritone), who believes that his wife should be kept locked in the house. Her maid Dorina (soprano), who cannot tolerate his jealousy, attempts to avenge her mistress by falsely accusing Corbolone of mistreating her in front of Gismonda's father, the Marchese Castagnacci (bass). Dorina encourages Gismonda to play a ruse on Corbolone by pretending to be in love with the foolish and affected Count Fanfalucci (baritone), who yearns to be Gismonda's companion.

Gismonda is visited by her widowed friend Eugenia (soprano), who loves Valerio (tenor). She believes that he is unfaithful to her, but he is innocent of any wrongdoing. Misunderstandings are compounded when Corbolone, about to ask his wife's forgiveness, encounters Valerio leaving his house. Shortly thereafter Fanfalucci, not recognizing Corbolone, praises Gismonda's beauty and maligns him. The plot also involves a mock duel between Fanfalucci and Valerio, antagonism between Corbolone and Castagnacci and a scene of mistaken intentions in a garden labyrinth. In the final nocturnal scene, in which Fanfalucci is enticed into Gismonda's house during a storm, Corbolone realizes his foolishness and his wife's innocence, and is cured of his jealousy.

Although this is not one of Lorenzi's best librettos, Cimarosa successfully characterized the shrewd Dorina, the jealous Corbolone and the infatuated Count in the music. The ensembles, especially the quartet 'Ah queste stoccate' (Act 2) and the nocturnal septet 'Ohime, son morta', are masterly depictions of contrasting situation and mood. Cimarosa's predilection for Neapolitan folk elements is seen in Corbolone's siciliano-like cavatina 'Moglierema nostra' (Act 2). The opera was performed in a number of Italian cities, as well as at Eszterháza (1788), where Haydn made some minor adjustments to it. In the original version the role of Corbolone was entirely in Neapolitan dialect, but for performances outside Naples the dialect part was rewritten in high Italian. A number of different titles (e.g. *Die bestrafte Eifersucht*, *Il marito geloso*, *L'amante disperato*) were appended to it over the years. GORDANA LAZAREVICH

Marito giocatore e la moglie bacchettona, Il ('The Gambler Husband and the Bigoted Wife'). Intermezzo in three parts by GIUSEPPE MARIA ORLANDINI to a libretto by ANTONIO SALVI; Verona, May 1715, as *Bacocco e Serpilla*.

The work tells the story of Bacocco (tenor), an inveterate gambler, and his wife Serpilla (soprano), who after a quarrel is determined to divorce him (Part 1). In court Bacocco, disguised as a judge, promises Serpilla to favour her cause if she will become his mistress. Serpilla accepts and Bacocco, having revealed his identity, shames her and drives her from his house (Part 2).

Serpilla, dressed as a pilgrim, is reduced to begging and Bacocco threatens to kill her, but finally the two are reconciled (Part 3). In later editions Serpilla softens his heart by reminding him of their past love. The work has also been known as *Bajocco e Serpilla* (1729, Paris), *Il giocatore* and *Serpilla e Bacocco*.

In the version given in Venice in Carnival 1719 (with the third part considerably modified), initially performed by Rosa Ungarelli and Antonio Ristorini, the intermezzo was successful throughout Europe. Revived in Paris in August 1752 as a pasticcio, it contributed to the famous Querelle des Bouffons: the supporters of Italian music praised its naturalness and vivacity, manifested in simple arias in syllabic style with frequent repeated notes and wide vocal leaps, and in the orchestral accompaniment, which followed the singing and gestures of the actors. FRANCESCO GIUNTINI

Mariya Styuart ('Mary Stuart'). Opera-ballade in three acts by SERGEY MIKHAYLOVICH SLONIMSKY to a libretto by Ya. A. Gordin after the novel by STEFAN ZWEIG; Kuybïshev (now Samara), Opera and Ballet Theatre, 31 January 1981.

Zweig's documentary novel on Mary Stuart gave Slonimsky the impetus for his third opera, a number opera on the conflict between love and power. Although he made a careful study of music in period manuscripts, Slonimsky did not quote from original sources. Instead, he imbued the modern idiom with period details as well as dance and song forms, all of which contribute to a highly stylized evocation of Elizabethan atmosphere.

The opera is set in Scotland and England in the 16th century. Two bards, one sad (baritone), the other merry (tenor), comment on the action in the manner of a Greek chorus. A song of the sad bard opens the opera: 'Tot, kto ot smertnogo rozhdyon' ('He who is born of mortal'). The residents of Edinburgh welcome their new queen, Mary Stuart (soprano), who reveals her apprehension in an arietta, 'Otchego tak stranno' ('Why is it so strange'). While the Protestant lord Bosuel [Bothwell] (bass) vows to defend the Catholic queen, Dzhon Noks [John Knox] (bass), head of the Scottish Reformed Church, warns of the encroaching threat. Mary discloses her true purpose, to claim her rightful place and unite the Scottish and English crowns, in her arioso, 'Shotlandiya ubogaya i zlaya' ('Scotland is wretched and evil'). Elizaveta [Elizabeth], Queen of England (mezzo-soprano/contralto), comments on the proceedings and reflects on the duties and tribulations of power, to stylized harpsichord accompaniment.

During a ball at Mary's castle, the French court poet Shatelyar [Châtelard] (tenor) sings a sonnet to the queen and, while dancing with her, rashly declares his undying passion. He is arrested. Knox preaches woe to the impious, and the crowds demand the execution of Châtelard. He is led away by Rutven [Ruthven] (bass), a Scottish baron, to echoes of his lyrical farewell aria, 'Kogda tot, kto tebe poklonyalsya vsyu zhizn'' ('When the one who worshipped you throughout his life'). In a sharp change of mood, Meri Seton [Mary Seton] (mezzo-soprano), Mary's attendant, and her friends sing a folklike song, at first unaccompanied and later with trumpet fanfares to herald the wedding of Mary and Darnley (baritone), an English lord. Richcho [Riccio] (tenor), an Italian musician and Mary's secretary, makes an eternal enemy of Darnley when he reminds him that the marriage does not make him king.

221

Riccio entertains Mary with a lilting canzona to imitated lute accompaniment, 'Volnï lazurnïe b'yutsya o skalï' ('Azure waves beat against the crags'), and reminds her of her duty to return Scotland to the Catholic faith. Bothwell swears to uphold all that brings glory to Scotland. Left alone, Mary sings a folklike evening song, 'O posmotri, dusha moya' ('Look, O my soul'), to strummed accompaniment.

Knox summons the Protestant faithful to fight the Catholic enemy. Ruthven and the first and second barons (baritone and tenor) resolve to strike against Riccio and easily subvert Darnley to their purpose. Against a reprise of Riccio's canzona, the barons burst into Mary's chamber with drawn swords and murder Riccio. Only Bothwell stands with Mary, who vows revenge for two deaths.

Mary Seton's pastoral duet with the sad bard, 'Song of Scotland', which opens Act 2, bears a striking resemblance to an American revival hymn. Disaffected barons conspire to install Bothwell on the throne in place of the despised Darnley. Bothwell reflects in a ballade on his decision to seize power. He confronts Mary with a proposal of love; in a sonnet, she puts herself and Scotland in his hands. Mary, while voicing doubts in a monologue accompanied by solo flute, prepares to summon Darnley to Edinburgh to ask for a divorce. Darnley is afraid to return, but Mary beguiles him into doing so. A festive choral reprise of the 'Song of Scotland' accompanies the procession. Suddenly flames are seen and Bothwell announces that Darnley has been killed in the fire. Elizabeth writes to Mary advising her to bring the murderer to justice, which Mary rejects defiantly.

In the prelude to Act 3, the sad bard foresees Mary's inevitable death. As the fanfares for her wedding to Bothwell ring out, Knox predicts that the Day of Judgment is at hand, and Elizabeth expresses horror at Mary's rashness. Ruthven, sent by the barons, demands that Mary banish Bothwell. She refuses, and Bothwell suggests that the conflict should be settled in battle. Against Mary's protests, he takes up his sword, 'Ya volk!' ('I am a wolf!'), but his followers flee. Mary pleads in vain with her subjects; eventually she surrenders to save Bothwell and is led away as the crowd clamours for her execution. In her English prison, Mary upholds her claims and waits for Bothwell to save her. Imprisoned in Denmark, Bothwell loses his sanity. Elizabeth, supported by Knox, remains firm in her decision to execute Mary. In a lullaby, 'Spi, usni, dalyokiy drug' ('Sleep, … distant friend'), Mary bids farewell to Bothwell and life before being led to the scaffold. The sad bard and chorus repeat the opera's opening 'He who is born of mortal'.   LAUREL E. FAY

Marliani, Count **Marco Aurelio** (*b* Milan, Aug 1805; *d* Bologna, 8 May 1849). Italian composer. Born into a wealthy family, he studied philosophy at Siena, and at the same time studied music privately. He graduated in 1830 and moved to Paris the same year, partly for political reasons. He was a singing teacher in Paris, where Giulia Grisi was among his pupils; he was also appointed consul-general of Spain. Meanwhile he made progress in composition, benefiting from Rossini's teaching, and made his début as an opera composer with *Il bravo* in 1834. He returned to Italy in 1847, and the following year joined the army as captain; for his acts of courage he was promoted to the rank of major. He died during a battle against the Austrians. Marliani's best

known and most successful opera, *La xacarilla*, is musically clear, fluent and elegant, though it owes its success partly to Scribe's skilful libretto.

See also Xacarilla, la.

Il bravo (dramma tragico, 3, A. Berrettoni), Paris, Italien, 1 Feb 1834
Le marchand forain (commedia, 3, E. Planard and P. Duport), Paris, OC (Bourse), 1 Oct 1834
Ildegonda (os, 3, P. Giannone), Paris, Italien, 7 March 1837
La xacarilla (3, E. Scribe), Paris, Opéra, 28 Oct 1839; as Lazzarillo, o I contrabbandieri (ob, 2, Berrettoni), Venice, S Benedetto, 23 Feb 1842
Gusmano il buono, o L'assedio di Tarifa (tragedia lirica, 3, G. C. Mattioli), Bologna, Comunale, 7 Nov 1847   FRANCESCO BUSSI

Marmontel, Jean François (*b* Bort, Corrèze, 11 July 1723; *d* Abloville, Eure, 31 Dec 1799). French librettist and writer. Educated by Jesuits at Mauriac and Clermont-Ferrand, he was at first destined for the church. His success as *lauréat des jeux floraux* at Toulouse (1746, 1747) and the encouragement of Voltaire led him to Paris. His first tragedy, *Denys le tyran* (1748), was exceptionally well received, but its successors failed and he abandoned the genre.

Marmontel was befriended by La Pouplinière and through him met Rameau, for whom he wrote four librettos. He was, however, already in sympathy with Encyclopedist musical preferences, which were then turning towards Italy. As a friend of Diderot and D'Alembert he contributed literary and musical articles to the *Encyclopédie*, including one on declamation and another on criticism. He also contributed to the *Mercure de France*, of which he was editor from 1758 to 1760. He could usually count, in later years, on a friendly reception from the *Mercure* towards his collaborations with musicians. He was elected to the Académie Française in 1763 and became its permanent secretary in 1783. His literary works include the *Contes moraux*, some of which (*La bergère des alpes, Annette et Lubin, Les mariages samnites, L'amitié à l'épreuve*, for example) were made into operas by Marmontel and others, and novels, of which *Les Incas* provided the subject of Méhul's *Cora*.

Marmontel's librettos for Rameau include the charming *La guirlande* and other pastoral pieces, or single acts for *opéras-ballets*. He wrote his first *tragédie lyrique* for Dauvergne as part of an attempt to regenerate French opera by a modest admixture of Italian music. His principal librettos, however, were for Grétry and Niccolò Piccinni. *Le Huron*, in 1768, established Grétry's reputation, and was followed by successful comedies and the ambitious magic opera *Zémire et Azor*. The basis in fairy-tale is characteristic of the author of the *Contes*, and the varied emotions of the Beauty and the Beast story stimulated Grétry to his most ambitious score to date. Even without the later setting by Spohr, this became Marmontel's most widely performed work. The poem of *Céphale et Procris* was blamed for the opera's comparative failure, which led to a falling-out with the composer.

Piccinni became Marmontel's pupil in French language and accentuation. Marmontel wrote the most abrasive of Piccinnist pamphlets, *Essai sur les révolutions de la musique en France*, in which he compared the melodic truth of the periodic style established by Vinci with the alleged barbarity of Gluck. The *Essai* was printed twice in 1777 and reprinted, with profuse criticisms, in Leblond's 1781 collection, *Mémoires pour*

Marriage

servir à l'histoire de la révolution dans la musique (it is also reprinted in Lesure). Marmontel responded to the sallies of Arnaud with a satirical poem, *Polymnie*, which was widely circulated but not printed until 1820.

Marmontel wanted to reform French opera along Encyclopedist lines, keeping its design while using Italian music. The music he encouraged was 'reformed', paradoxically, on lines suggested by Gluck, being free of lengthy ritornellos and showy roulades. Following work on *Bellérophon* in 1773, he turned to the father of the *tragédie lyrique*, becoming known as 'le savetier de Quinault'. According to Ginguené he adapted *Thésée*, *Isis*, *Roland*, *Atys*, *Amadis* and *Persée*. He retained the choruses and *divertissements* and most of the recitative, but made space for arias and ensembles; he also condensed the action into three acts, with drastic results in *Persée*. Only three adaptations were used; Gossec's *Thésée* and J. C. Bach's *Amadis* were 'marmontelisés', as Grimm put it, by others. *Atys* is the most satisfactory adaptation, with nearly all the action retained, but it was spoilt on its revival by a contrived happy ending. Marmontel also adapted Metastasio's *Demofoonte* for Cherubini, again dangerously simplifying the plot.

Of Marmontel's original librettos, the comedies and pastorals are attractively written, while *Didon* and *Pénélope* are distinguished tragedies; the former, coming at the height of Piccinni's popularity, was Marmontel's second most enduring theatrical work. Out of sympathy with the Revolution, Marmontel retired to the country, where he enjoyed enough peace to write his memoirs (published in *Oeuvres posthumes*, i–iv, 1804). In these he gave a full, if naturally biased, account of his theatrical career and his collaborations with composers. The accounts of his own youth and of French society make this book perhaps his most enduring achievement.

oc – *opéra comique* tl – *tragédie lyrique*

La guirlande, ou Les fleurs enchantées (acte de ballet), Rameau, 1751; *Acante et Céphise, ou La sympathie* (pastorale-héroïque), Rameau, 1751; *Les sybarites* (entrée de ballet), Rameau, 1753 (also in revival of Rameau, Les surprises de l'Amour, 1757); *Lysis et Délie* (pastorale), Rameau, comp. 1753; *Hercule mourant* (tl), Dauvergne, 1761; *Annette et Lubin* (comédie, with C.-S. Favart), La Borde, 1762 (1768, as La nouvelle Annette); *La bergère des alpes* (pastorale), Kohaut, 1766

Le Huron (oc, after Voltaire: L'ingénu), Grétry, 1768; *Lucile* (comédie), Grétry, 1769; *Silvain* (comédie, after S. Gessner: Erast), Grétry, 1770 (Ger., Benda, 1776); *L'ami de la maison* (comédie), Grétry, 1771; *Zémire et Azor* (comédie-ballet, after J. M. Le Prince de Beaumont: La belle et la bête), Grétry, 1771 (Spohr, 1819); *Bellérophon* (after T. Corneille and B. le Bovier de Fontenelle), Lully, arr. P.-M. Berton and L. Granier, 1773; *Céphale et Procris, ou L'amour conjugal* (tl, after Ovid), Grétry, 1773

La fausse magie (oc), Grétry, 1775; *Roland* (tl, after P. Quinault), N. Piccinni, 1778; *Atys* (tl, after Quinault), N. Piccinni, 1780, rev. 1783; *Persée* (tl, after Quinault), Philidor, 1780; *Le Sigisbée, ou Le fat corrigé*, 1782 (comédie), L. Piccinni, 1804; *Didon* (tl), N. Piccinni, 1783; *Le dormeur éveillé* (oc), N. Piccinni, 1783; *Pénélope* (tl), N. Piccinni, 1785; *Démophoön* (tl, after P. Metastasio), Cherubini, 1788; *Antigone* (opéra lyrique), Zingarelli, 1790

*

J. F. Marmontel: *Oeuvres complètes … revues et corrigées par l'auteur*, i–xvii (Paris, 1787); *Oeuvres posthumes*, i–xi (Paris, 1804–6)
A. E. M. Grétry: *Mémoires, ou Essais sur la musique*, i (Paris, 1789)
P. L. Ginguené: *Notice sur la vie et les ouvrages de Nicolas Piccinni* (Paris, 1800–01)
F. M. Grimm: *Correspondance littéraire, philosophique et critique* (Paris, 1812–14); ed. M. Tourneux (Paris, 1877–82)
J. Ehrard, ed.: *De l'Encyclopédie à la contre-révolution: Jean-François Marmontel (1723–1799): études réunies* (Clermont-Ferrand, 1970)
K. Pendle: 'The Opéras Comiques of Grétry and Marmontel', *MQ*, lxii (1976), 409–34
F. Lesure: *Querelle des Gluckistes et des Piccinnistes*, i (Geneva, 1984)
JULIAN RUSHTON

Marriage [*Zhenit'ba*]. A projected 'experiment in dramatic music in prose' by MODEST PETROVICH MUSORGSKY, consisting of a verbatim setting in continuous recitative of a two-act comedy by NIKOLAY VASIL'YEVICH GOGOL; St Petersburg, Suvorin Theatre School, 19 March/1 April 1908.

Marriage concerns (to quote Vladimir Nabokov) 'the hesitations of a man who has made up his mind to marry, has a swallowtail suit made, is provided with a fiancée – but at the last moment makes a fenestral exit'. During summer 1868 Musorgsky managed to compose and revise one act in piano-vocal score – it corresponds to the first 11 scenes of Gogol's Act 1 – before casting the project aside in favour of *Boris Godunov*.

Undertaken at the suggestion of Alexander Dargomïzhsky and César Cui, Musorgsky's 'opéra dialogué' (as he informally christened it) was an attempt to pursue to its limits a radical realist aesthetic he had derived in part from the example of Dargomïzhsky's opera *The Stone Guest* (then in progress) and in part from *Händel und Shakespeare* (Leipzig, 1868), a treatise by the German literary historian Georg Gottfried Gervinus. Gervinus's theory was an application of the Aristotelian concept of imitation to music, according to which the highest natural object of musical imitation is emotion, and the method of imitating emotion is to mimic speech (emotion's outward manifestation), especially in its paralexical aspects – contour, pitch-level, volume, tempo.

This much was nothing new for operatic theory; it went all the way back to Galilei, if not further. What was new was the dogged literalism with which Musorgsky was prepared to carry out the theory's naturalistic implications in practice. Acting more as a sort of exalted régisseur than as a composer in the usual sense, Musorgsky clothed Gogol's laconic prose in music so completely formed in tempo, in rhythm, and in melodic contour on the patterns of conversational speech that it loses all import and coherence when divorced from the words. His anti-lyricism extended even to the point of eschewing normal melodic intervals. The vocal line, and the attendant harmonies as well, are saturated with tritones and diminished 4ths; the music is notated without key signatures and remains tonally suspensive, with functional cadences reserved (as in some Wagner) to underscore moments of declarative emphasis in the text. Most un-Wagnerian, however, is the accompaniment, which (despite a few skimpy leitmotifs and one long speech set to a moto perpetuo) is basically punctuation, as if to *recitativo secco*.

It is doubtful whether Musorgsky seriously intended *Marriage* for performance. In any case, it was not performed (except at 'kuchkist' gatherings) until 1908. (Published the same year in a typically toned-down version by Rimsky-Korsakov, it immediately prompted Ravel to emulate its manner, in *L'heure espagnole*.) Musorgsky's single completed act has been orchestrated by Alexander Gauk (1917), Marguerite Béclard d'Harcourt (Monte Carlo, 1930), Antoine Duhamel (for a 1954 recording under René Leibowitz) and Gennady Rozhdestvensky (for his own recording, 1982). In 1931, an anniversary year for Musorgsky, Soviet Radio commissioned Ippolitov-Ivanov not only to orchestrate the existing act but to finish the setting of Gogol's play (in four acts, as it turned out). An independent setting was made by Alexander Grechaninov (1946).

RICHARD TARUSKIN

Marriage of Figaro, The. Opera by W. A. Mozart; *see* *NOZZE DI FIGARO, LE* .

Marschner, Heinrich August (*b* Zittau, 16 Aug 1795; *d* Hanover, 14 Dec 1861). German composer. He was the most important exponent of German Romantic opera in the generation between Weber and Wagner.

1. Life and works. 2. Style.

1. LIFE AND WORKS. Marschner's father was a master craftsman, working with horn and ivory. Although both parents possessed musical talent, Marschner's father encouraged him to pursue music only as an amateur and to choose a more stable career. From 1804 to 1813, therefore, the boy undertook courses in liberal studies at the gymnasium in Zittau and in nearby Bautzen. Some musical instruction was permitted, however, and his teachers included Karl Gottlieb Hering, August Bergt and Friedrich Schneider. His first stage work, *Die stolze Bäuerin*, was a ballet performed successfully in Zittau in 1810.

In spring 1813, Marschner left Zittau for Prague, where he met Tomášek. From there he went on to Leipzig to study law, but his interests seemed to centre less on legal studies than on his evening association with such men as the publisher Friedrich Hofmeister, the music critic J. A. Wendt and Friedrich Rochlitz, founder of the *Allgemeine musikalische Zeitung*. It was at this time that he began to develop an interest in opera and tried his hand at setting Caterino Mazzolà's adaptation of Metastasio's *La clemenza di Tito*, which he obtained from a copy of Mozart's version. Although he completed the work, it was never staged and apart from a few bars of one aria it is lost. In 1815 Marschner visited Karlsbad (now Karlovy Vary), where he spent much time in the company of the pianist Count Thaddeus Amadé de Varkony of Vienna (later a patron of Liszt). Varkony took him to Vienna, where he secured him an audience with Beethoven, and then to Hungary; there he met Count Johann Nepomuk Zichy, who employed him as domestic music teacher.

Soon after settling at Zichy's estate in Pressburg (now Bratislava), Marschner composed *Der Kiffhaeuser Berg* (1816). Based on Thuringian legends set in the Harz Mountains, near Goslar, this work, really a typical Viennese Singspiel, is a bourgeois comedy that centres on the efforts of two young peasants to obtain permission to marry, the girl's father having disappeared 20 years before as the victim of a dwarf's potion. Although the work is engaging and contains a clever sextet for pipe smokers ('Krik! krik! krik!'), it suffers from many supernatural digressions that contribute nothing to the plot. For this reason, it never caught on. The same can be said of Marschner's next Singspiel, *Saidar und Zulima* (1818), now lost. In his autobiography of 1818, Marschner mentions beginning work on *Das stille Volk*, a Zauberspiel by August Gottlieb Hornbostel, a physician and not insignificant amateur playwright, but no sketches have survived. After these disappointments, Marschner abandoned the Singspiel in favour of the historically based 'rescue opera', then popular in

Vienna. *Heinrich IV und D'Aubigné*, whose libretto Hornbostel based rather loosely on the exploits of Henry IV of France (a Catholic) and his Huguenot equerry, Théodore-Agrippa d'Aubigné, at least gave Marschner some exposure in the musical mainstream, for Weber had the work performed in Dresden in 1820. Yet it lacked significant dramatic events and bored its audiences. Marschner was married twice during this period, first to Emilie von Cerva (1817), who died only six months later, then to Eugenie Franziska Jaeggi (1820). This marriage produced one son, Alfred, who emigrated to America in 1848.

Dissatisfied with the anonymity that cultural life in Pressburg appeared to promise him, Marschner moved in 1821 to Dresden, where Heinrich von Könneritz, director of the Saxon Hoftheater, introduced him to court circles and secured him a commission to compose incidental music to Heinrich von Kleist's *Prinz Friedrich von Homburg*, a historical drama surrounding the Battle of Fehrbellin (1675) with characters motivated by emotion rather than the rationalism popularized by the German dramatist Gotthold Lessing. The première with Marschner's music (1821, Dresden) was reviewed favourably by Ludwig Tieck and the play was given with limited success in other cities. Late in 1822 Marschner began a collaboration with Friedrich Kind, a leading literary figure in Dresden after the Berlin success of Weber's *Der Freischütz*, for which Kind had provided the libretto. First Marschner wrote incidental music for Kind's *Schön Ella* (1823, Dresden), a romantic tragedy based on G. A. Bürger's ballad *Lenore*, which, like *Der Freischütz*, makes use of supernatural intervention to drive home a moral. Unlike *Der Freischütz*, however, *Schön Ella* is severely flawed in its drama. An even greater fiasco was Carl Gottfried Theodor Winkler's play *Ali Baba, oder die 40 Räuber*, for which Marschner also provided incidental music (1823, Dresden).

Towards the end of 1823 Weber began to suffer from tuberculosis, and both of his assistants had been ill as well, so he petitioned the court for additional help. Through the machinations of Könneritz, Marschner was appointed over Weber's objections, and he ended up directing both the Italian and the German companies. During the next two years he was so busy that he had time to compose only one opera and incidental music for two plays. To a libretto by Kind, he wrote *Der Holzdieb* (1823), a rustic, countrified Singspiel in one act, devoid of supernatural elements and conceived in a style reminiscent of Schenk's *Der Dorfbarbier* and Weigl's *Die Schweizerfamilie*. Its well-integrated action demands that most of the six characters be on stage throughout the work, providing Marschner with an opportunity to develop the techniques of ensemble writing that were to characterize his mature works. Considerable mystery, however, surrounds the incidental music that Marschner wrote at this time. Fresh from successes in Berlin, Carl Eduard von Holtei, a distinguished journalist and actor, brought to the Dresden stage in 1825 his Liederspiel *Die Wiener in Berlin*, a dialogue farce (*Mundartsoper*) in the Viennese style of Adolf Bäuerle and Meyer von Schauensee. Much of the music derives from pre-existing sources, but additional songs were provided by Marschner and others. In 1826 Dresden audiences also saw *Alexander und Darius* by Friedrich von Uechtritz, a five-act historical drama in the style of Schiller. *Alexander's Feast*, which Handel wrote for Dryden's *Ode for St Cecilia's Day*, accompanied the first three acts, and since the narrative of Dryden's poem overlapped approximately the same portion of Uechtritz's drama, it was necessary for Marschner to write additional music only for the remaining two acts. Notable is the melodrama in which Alexander and the slave girl Thaïs use firebrands to burn the palace of Darius at Persepolis (Act 5 scene viii).

The year 1826 saw the death of Weber, and since Könneritz's successor, Wolf von Lüttichau, had no interest in hiring Marschner to replace him, Marschner was forced to travel, hoping to make a living by free-lance appearances with his third wife, the singer Marianne Wohlbrück, whom he had married (1826) shortly after the death of Eugenie in 1825. After stops in Berlin and Breslau (now Wrocław) the couple arrived in Danzig (now Gdańsk), where they obtained a six-month contract with Marschner as music director and Marianne as leading soprano. Here Marschner completed and produced his first through-composed opera, *Lucretia* (1820–26), based on Sextus Tarquinius's supposed rape in 509 BC of Lucretia Collatinus and her subsequent suicide. A weak attempt to emulate Spontini, *Lucretia* slipped into oblivion after only three performances.

When their contract expired in Danzig, the couple travelled to Magdeburg, where Marschner became acquainted with his brother-in-law Wilhelm August Wohlbrück, a popular actor. The two seized upon the idea of collaborating on an opera involving vampires. Such a topic fitted into the short-lived literary movement in Germany called the 'Schauerromantik', then at its peak of popularity. The first of Marschner's three famous operas, *Der Vampyr* (composed in 1827) focusses on the efforts of the vampire to secure another year of life on earth in exchange for the murder of three virgins. Wohlbrück constructed an effective libretto from multiple literary sources and the work has held the interest of the opera-going public ever since the resounding success of its Leipzig première in 1828. Called a romantic opera, it is in many respects similar in musical construction to Weber's *Der Freischütz*.

Wohlbrück and Marschner decided next to write an opera based on a novel by Sir Walter Scott after Marschner attended a performance in Leipzig of Joseph von Auffenberg's *Löwe von Kurdistan*, based on Scott's *The Talisman*. The result was a setting of the Ivanhoe story, *Der Templer und die Jüdin* (1829). Wohlbrück adapted his libretto from Johann Reinhold Lenz's *Das Gericht der Templer*, which in turn was based on one or more of the many plays that appeared in England after the publication of Scott's novel. The original story seemed to be eminently stageworthy, and Wohlbrück's libretto follows it rather closely. This time Marschner's model was Weber's *Euryanthe*, and many numbers from *Der Templer*, notably 'Wer ist der Ritter hochgeehrt', were later sung as concert pieces. Following phenomenal success in Leipzig, the opera was performed throughout Europe but is rarely revived owing to the cost of the sets and properties.

By 1830 Marschner was in demand throughout Europe, but his interests centred on the Königstädtisches Theater in Berlin, whose director, Karl Friedrich Cerf, had invited him to write a comic opera. The result, *Des Falkners Braut* (1832), an italianate piece in the style of Rossini, failed, mainly because Wohlbrück had tried to create a comic libretto from a tragic model (A. J. K. Spindler's short story of the same name). Worse, there is clearly not enough material for three acts and the plot, lacking any compelling humour, is sterile; when the

work was revived in England in 1838, the libretto was replaced by one about Robin Hood.

Despite international recognition, the Marschners were forced to support themselves in Leipzig through Marianne's singing engagements and his occasional conducting contracts and royalties. At the end of 1830, however, Marschner obtained the permanent position of Hofkapellmeister in Hanover and moved his family there the following year. Shortly thereafter, he received a libretto entitled *Hans Heiling* from the famous actor, playwright and theatre historian Eduard Devrient, who had developed it from several legends surrounding the Hans Heiling Cliffs. Hewn from the mountains by the River Eger (now Ohře) in Bohemia, these formations were popularly thought to have been created when Hans Heiling, king of the earth spirits, turned an entire wedding procession to stone. For the first time, Marschner was dealing with a librettist who really understood the exigencies of drama. Though they were separated geographically, an exchange of letters between the two indicates a constant flow of adjustments between music and text until both were satisfied that a theatrically functional work had been constructed. The resulting romantic opera was an overwhelming success.

Although Marschner lived for nearly 30 years after the première of *Hans Heiling* (1833), it represented the zenith of his creative powers, and not one stage work that he produced after it enjoyed any popularity. The first of these, a romantic opera entitled *Das Schloss am Aetna* (1836) and set to a libretto by August von Klingemann, Generaldirektor of the Brunswick Hoftheater, was a confused rehash of the dramatic themes present in *Der Freischütz*. It was followed by the comic opera *Der Bäbu* (1838; *bäbu* means 'nobleman' in parts of India). An oriental spoof reminiscent of Mozart's *Die Entführung aus dem Serail*, Wohlbrück's rambling libretto is cluttered with disparate elements that simply fail to hang together. Nonetheless, the opera contains some beautiful melodies, and parts of it have been broadcast by German radio. In *Kaiser Adolph von Nassau* (1845) and *Austin* (1852), Marschner returned to the realm of the historical narrative in an apparent attempt to emulate French grand opera. Heribert Rau based his libretto for *Kaiser Adolph* on the life of Adolph of Nassau (?1250–1298), King of Frankfurt, who amassed so many territories through conquest, purchase and political intrigue that the Electors deposed him in favour of Albert I, who killed him in battle and defeated his armies. With the exception of some memorable choruses, the music is banal, and Wagner, who conducted the première in Dresden, claimed to have brought a stillborn child into the world. Marianne Wohlbrück-Marschner's libretto to *Austin* concerns the events surrounding Ferdinand the Catholic's annexation in 1512 of Navarre, a strategically important buffer state between France and Spain. To acquire the territory, Ferdinand poisoned the young Navarrese king, Francisco I (nicknamed 'Austin'), bringing to the throne Francisco's sister and, through marriage to her, his own son.

In 1854 Marianne died, but Marschner soon fell in love with a singer 31 years his junior, Theresa Janda. After their marriage (1855), he turned again to dramatic composition. Considerably more successful than his previous few operas was his incidental music for Julius Rodenberg's rustic comedy *Waldmüllers Margret* (1855, Hanover) and for Salomon Hermann von

Mosenthal's *Der Goldschmied von Ulm* (1856, Dresden), a folk legend with supernatural overtones similar to those he had treated so successfully in *Hans Heiling*. His last opera, *Sangeskönig Hiarne, oder Das Tyrsingschwert* (composed in 1857–8), was not a success. It is based on a libretto which Wilhelm Grothe adapted from Esaias Tegnér's poetical version of the medieval saga of Fridthjof, a Viking who longs to marry Ingeborg but fails to do so because he is a mere vassal to her father, Bele, while Bele's ancestry derives from the god Odin. In this final effort, Marschner attempted to emulate Wagner, but the libretto suffers for want of a well-defined hero. Attempts to have the work performed in Germany during Marschner's lifetime were unsuccessful, and although he interpolated ballets to 'qualify' it for production at the Paris Opéra during the time *Tannhäuser* was being performed there, nothing came of this either. Thanks, however, to the invention of an electrical sword for special effects, several performances took place towards the end of the century. In 1859 the Hanoverian court chose to retire Marschner, rather against his wishes, and he died two years later.

In addition to operas and incidental music, Marschner wrote three operatic *Gelegenheitgedichte* (pageants) entitled *Festspiel zur Feier der Vermählung des Kronprinzen von Hannover und der Prinzessin Marie von Altenburg* (1843), *Der Zauberspiegel* (1850) and *Natur und Kunst* (1852). All were intended for private performance at the Hanoverian court. Outside opera, he is best known for his choral music, particularly the *Männergesänge* he wrote in the 1820s.

2. STYLE. Marschner was a great eclectic, for he systematically worked through all major genres of opera from Mozart onwards. Much of the time the result was an unequivocal failure, but this was not the case with his German Romantic operas. With the Singspiel and Weber as points of departure, he broke new ground that was eventually exploited by Wagner, first evident in *Der fliegende Holländer*. His most important contribution was formal expansion. In the 18th century the typical Singspiel had been a series of fairly short, numbered songs in predictable forms connected by spoken dialogue. This changed little in the early 19th century, even when the Singspiel developed into Romantic opera on the one hand and the post-Mozartian comic opera of the Biedermeier group on the other, despite some through-composed exceptions. Marschner enlarged the individual forms of Singspiel and combined them into what may be termed 'ensemble complexes', containing multiple numbered subsections and nearly always one or more ensembles. Weber had done this in a few places (such as the Wolf's Glen Scene in *Der Freischütz*), but with Marschner it became the rule. The ensemble complex helped to organize the action through musical and formal means into dramatically complete and self-contained subsections – which could be described as through-composed 'sub-operas'. Some became so large that one might reasonably ask why Marschner did not simply write out his operas entirely in through-composed form. Certainly there were precedents for this, not only in Spohr's *Faust* and Hoffmann's *Undine* (both landmarks of 1816) but also in his own *Lucretia*. The reason is that structurally these works were based on Italian and French models, and Marschner, having inveighed vehemently and frequently against the encroachment of foreign styles upon German opera, was attempting to retain the essentially German formal character of serious Romantic opera, which required spoken dialogue to connect musical sections. Consequently, when in *Der fliegende Holländer* Wagner eliminated the last vestiges of speech, he created a work that was transitional between Romantic opera and his later music dramas, rather than a pure example of the former. Of course, Wagner's efforts to impose a second level of organization on *Der fliegende Holländer* by creating a symmetrical formal scheme around Senta's ballad, in order to frame it as the psychological apex of the drama, exceeded any of Marschner's attempts at formal innovation, but Marschner's ensemble complexes had provided Wagner with the building blocks.

Marschner developed the psychological aspects of Romantic opera and thus added a new dimension to its dramatic organization. Whenever the supernatural was present in Singspiel, its function was typically to facilitate plot development: divine intervention could be invoked to make almost anything happen without need of explanation. Supernatural characters in Zauberspiel might even approach mortal characters in number and possess similar foibles and weaknesses. In *Der Freischütz*, this changed. Here both good and bad supernatural characters had power transcending that of mortals, and they used it to try to swing the tide of the drama towards their own objectives. Except for Max, whose moral weakness made him vulnerable to manipulation, each main character, mortal or supernatural, statically represented either good or evil. But Marschner placed the attributes of Weber's separate good and evil personages inside a single, centrally significant character. This device allowed Marschner's dramas to become all the more complex, since the psychological conflict within one character could be worked out in the larger dimensions and external action of the drama as a whole. Because this kind of character is closely related to the title role in Mozart's *Don Giovanni*, it is not surprising that Marschner made him invariably a dramatic baritone, but it is notable that he can be either supernatural or mortal. Cast as the vampire Ruthven in *Der Vampyr*, the Templar Bois-Guilbert in *Der Templer und die Jüdin* and Heiling himself in *Hans Heiling*, this complex figure with built-in foil migrated through Marschner's operas directly into the title role in Wagner's *Der fliegende Holländer*.

Marschner employed additional dramatic techniques to support the generally sombre ambience of his romantic operas. One was melodrama. Ever since the experimental days of Rousseau and Benda, speaking or acting against orchestral accompaniment had proved an effective means of heightening dramatic tension. Mozart, Beethoven and Weber had all used it, and in Marschner it became particularly important. Instances include the passage in which the light of the moon revives the murdered vampire in *Der Vampyr* and the scene in *Hans Heiling* where Gertrude must weather a summer storm in her hut. On the other hand, comic relief is necessary to keep operas of this sort from becoming overwhelming. Particularly successful examples of this in *Der Vampyr* are the drinking-song and the antics of Suse Blunt, who jumps on to a table to castigate her husband and his cronies for drunkenness.

In general, Marschner worked within the common-practice musical style of his contemporaries, but he excelled in some techniques that were advanced for his day. First, he increased the scope of the opera orchestra, adding particularly to the low brass. Where Weber would have favoured horns, Marschner liked the texture of three trombones, whose effect, perhaps indebted to the temple scene in *Die Zauberflöte*, can be considerably more sombre than that which horns would have provided. Second, while Weber stuck primarily to the conventional harmonies of German folksong, Marschner extended the bounds of tonality with chromatic lines in both melody and bass – sometimes to accomplish a rapid modulation to a remote key, sometimes (like Wagner) to avoid a cadence altogether, and occasionally just to convey a mood of foreboding. In general, his music is considerably more difficult to divorce from the drama than Weber's, since he intended to write music that would bind intimately with the drama. As a result, he is accused of being a poor melodist, and the closed forms in his operas do not possess the accessible, folklike charm of Weber's. In consequence, there will probably never be a thoroughgoing resurgence of interest in Marschner's operas, although several revivals of *Hans Heiling* and *Der Vampyr* have taken place from the 1970s onwards in Germany, Great Britain and America.

See also HANS HEILING; HOLZDIEB, DER; TEMPLER UND DIE JÜDIN, DER; and VAMPYR, DER (i).

grosse romantische Opern unless otherwise stated
La clemenza di Tito, 1816 (os, 3, C. Mazzolà, after P. Metastasio), unperf., lost
Der Kiffhaeuser Berg, 1816 (romantische Oper, 1, A. von Kotzebue), Zittau, 2 Jan 1822, *D-Bds**, vs as op.89 (Hamburg, ?1834)
Heinrich IV und D'Aubigné, 1817–18 (grosse Oper, 3, Alberti [A. G. Hornbostel]), Dresden, Hof, 19 July 1820, *Dlb**
Saidar und Zulima, oder Liebe und Grossmut (3, Hornbostel), Pressburg, Schauspielhaus, 26 Nov 1818, lost
Das stille Volk (Zauberspiel, Hornbostel), planned 1818 but abandoned
Lucretia, 1820–26 (Oper, 2, J. A. Eckschlager), Danzig, Danziger, 17 Jan 1827, *Bds** (Act 1 only), ov. as op.67 (Leipzig, ?1834), excerpts (Hanover, n.d.), ballet as op.51[a] (Halberstadt, n.d.) and in Mühling's *Museum*, iii/9, no.36
Der Holzdieb, 1823 (Spl, 1, J. F. Kind), Dresden, Hof, 22 Feb 1825, *US-Wc*, vs in *Polyhymia, ein Taschenbuch* (Dresden, 1825); rev. as Geborgt, Berlin, 21 April 1853, vs (Berlin, 1853)
Die Wiener in Berlin (Liederspiel, 1, C. E. von Holtei), Dresden, am Linckeschen Bade, 24 Aug 1825, pasticcio, items by Marschner in *D-ZI**
Der Vampyr (2, W. A. Wohlbrück, after C. Nodier, P. F. A. Carmouche and A. de Jouffroy; J. R. Planché; and H. L. Ritter), Leipzig, Stadt, 29 March 1828, *B-Bc, D-Dlb, LEm, DK-Kk, US-Wc*, vs as op.42 (Leipzig, 1828); rev. H. Pfitzner, Stuttgart, 24 May 1924, vs (Berlin, 1925)
Der Templer und die Jüdin (Wohlbrück, after W. Scott: *Ivanhoe*, via J. R. Lenz and others), Leipzig, Stadt, 22 Dec 1829, *B-Bc, D-Dlb, HVs** (Act 2 only), *DK-Kk, F-Pc, S-St, US-Wc*, vs as op.60 (Leipzig, ?1830); rev. R. Kleinmichel, vs (Leipzig, 1896); rev. H. Pfitzner, vs (Leipzig, 1912)
Das Schloss am Aetna, 1830–35 (3, E. A. F. Klingemann), Leipzig, Stadt, 29 Jan 1836, *DK-Kk, US-Bp*, vs as op.95 (Leipzig, 1836)
Des Falkners Braut (komische Oper, 3, Wohlbrück, after A. J. K. Spindler), Leipzig, Stadt, 10 March 1832, *D-Ds, Mbs*, vs as op.65 (Leipzig, ?1832); also pubd as La sposa promessa del falconiere
Hans Heiling (prol., 3, E. Devrient), Berlin, Hofoper, 24 May 1833, *HVs, DK-Kk, S-St*, vs as op.80 (Leipzig, ?1833); rev. G. Kogel, *D-HVs*, full score (Leipzig, 1892)
Der Bäbu (komische Oper, 3, Wohlbrück), Hanover, Hof, 19 Feb 1838, *Bds**, vs as op.98 (Leipzig, 1837)
Kaiser Adolph von Nassau (grosse Oper, 4, K. Golmick [H. Rau]), Dresden, Kgl Sächsisches Hof, 5 Jan 1845, *Dlb**, vs as op.130 (Hanover, 1845)
Austin (4, M. Wohlbrück-Marschner), Hanover, Hof, 25 Jan 1852, *Dlb**, *F-Pc*, Krönungsmarsch (Hanover, 1891)
[Der] Sangeskönig [Sängerkönig] Hiarne, oder Das Tyrsingschwert, 1857–8 (4, W. Grothe, after E. Tegnér), Frankfurt, National, 13 Sept 1863, *D-Mbs**, *LEm, US-Wc*

'Marschners neue Oper *Austin*', *Signale für die musikalische Welt*, x (1852), 65–7
E. Genast: *Aus dem Tagebuche eines alten Schauspielers* (Leipzig, 2/1862)
H. Borges: 'Heinrich Marschner's Oper *Hiarne*', *NZM*, lxxix (1883), 165–7, 173–4, 197–9
E. Danzig: 'Heinrich Marschner in seinen minder bekannten Opern und Liedern', *NZM*, lxxxvi (1890), 369–71
J. Rodenberg: 'Erinnerungen aus der Jugendzeit: Heinrich Marschner', *Deutsche Rundschau*, xxii (1895), 257–72, 418–33
M. E. Wittmann: *Marschner* (Leipzig, 1897)
G. Münzer: *Heinrich Marschner* (Berlin, 1901)
E. Istel: 'Aus Heinrich Marschners produktivster Zeit: Briefe des Komponisten und seines Dichters Eduard Devrient', *Süddeutsche Monatshefte*, vii (1910), 774–820
C. Preiss: *Templar und Jüdin* (Graz, 1911)
H. Gaartz: *Die Opern Heinrich Marschners* (Leipzig, 1912)
G. Fischer: *Marschner-Erinnerungen* (Hanover, 1918)
G. Becker: 'Eine Erzgebirgssage als romantische Oper, Marschners *Hans Heiling*', *Sächsische Heimat*, v (1922–3), 289–91
H. Pfitzner: 'Zu meiner *Heiling*-Inszenierung am Dresdner Staatstheater im März 1923', *Die Scene*, xiii (1923), 65–71
——: 'Marschners *Vampyr*', *Neue Musik-Zeitung*, xlv (1924), 133–9
J. F. A. Bickel: *Heinrich Marschner in seinen Opern* (diss., U. of Erlangen, 1929)
A. Gnirs: *Alte Sagen aus dem Elbogener Ländchen* (Karlsbad, 1930)
——: *Hans Heiling: die Sagen und die Geschichte der Felsen im Elbogener Egertale bei Karlsbad* (Karlsbad, 1930)
A. Saft: 'Das Zauberbuch in *Hans Heiling*', *Bühnentechnische Rundschau* (1930), no.3, pp.15–16
G. Abraham: 'Marschner and Wagner', *MMR*, lxx (1940), 99–104
V. Köhler: *Heinrich Marschners Bühnenwerke* (diss., U. of Göttingen, 1956)
Z. H[rabussay]: 'Heinrich Marschner (1795–1861) a Bratislava', *SH*, v (1961), 551
K. Günzel: 'Heinrich Marschner – ein Zittauer Musiker', *Sächsische Heimatblätter*, viii (1962), 65–70
V. Köhler: 'Heinrich Marschner [gestorben] 14.12.1861: Festrede zur Marschner-Ehrung 1961', *Hannoversche Geschichtsblätter*, new ser., xvi (1962), 229–42
I. Killmann: *Heinrich Marschner: eine Personalbibliographie mit besonderer Berücksichtigung der Bühnenwerke und seiner Instrumentalmusik* (thesis, Bibliothekarschule der Freien und Hansestadt Hamburg, 1963)
A. S. Garlington, jr: *The Concept of the Marvelous in French and German Opera, 1770–1840: a Chapter in the History of Opera Esthetics* (diss., U. of Illinois, 1965)
I. E. Reid: *Some Epic and Demonic Baritone Rôles in the Operas of Weber and Marschner* (diss., U. of Boston, 1968)
V. Köhler: 'Rezitativ, Szene und Melodram in Heinrich Marschners Opern', *GfMKB: Bonn 1970*, 461–4
R. Kloiber: *Handbuch der Oper* (Kassel, 1973), esp. i, 281–5 [on *Hans Heiling*]
J. Mitchell: *The Walter Scott Operas* (Birmingham, AL, 1977), esp. 156–66 [on *Der Templer*]
A. D. Palmer: *Heinrich August Marschner, 1795–1861: his Life and Stage Works* (Ann Arbor, 1980)
J. Moriarty: 'Exhuming a Vampire', *Opera Journal*, xiv/4 (1981), 4–12
H. A. Neunzig: *Lebensläufe der deutschen Romantik: Komponisten* (Munich, 1984), esp. 48–73
P. C. White: 'Two Vampires of 1828', *OQ*, v/1 (1987), 22–57
A. DEAN PALMER

Marseilles (Fr. Marseille). French city on the Mediterranean coast. It was founded in the 6th century BC by a Phoenician colony. In 1685 Pierre Gautier, a pupil of Lully, obtained the right by royal charter to open an Académie de Musique, making Marseilles one of the first provincial centres to have an opera house. On 28 January he presented his *Le triomphe de la paix*. A second theatre, in the rue Vacon, existed between 1733 and 1787; operas by Rameau, Gluck, Grétry and Boieldieu were presented there, with first performances in Marseilles often following Paris premières within a year. According to contemporary accounts the company was excellent; the public was demanding and often noisy.

The present opera house, built on the site of the old galley slaves' barracks at the behest of the Prince of Beauvau, was inaugurated on 31 October 1787 with Champein's *La mélomanie*. In the early 19th century, as the Grand Théâtre, it gave many performances of ballets and operas, featuring in particular the works of Meyerbeer and Halévy. Opera was given there until 1919 when it was destroyed by fire, only the original colonnade façade surviving. Behind this façade the architects Castel, Ebrard and Raymond built a new theatre (1786 seats) in the *art déco* style, assisted with the decoration by Carrera, Bourdelle and other leading artists of the time. This building, now called the Opéra Municipal, in the rue Molière, was inaugurated in 1924 with *Sigurd* by the Marseilles composer Ernest Reyer. Although the city council has owned the theatre since 1882, it is only since 1945 that it has been run as a municipal service. The company has given the premières of Kenton Coe's *Sud* (1965), Daniel-Lesur's *Andrea del Sarto* (1969), Louis Saguer's *Miriana Pineda* (1970) and Milhaud's *Christophe Colomb* (1984; French stage première), and the first French performances of *Lulu* (1963), *The Turn of the Screw* (1965), *The Devils of Loudon* (1972) and Dvořák's *Rusalka* (1982). Artistic directors have included Michel Leduc, Bernard Lefort and Reynaud Giovaninetti; from 1989 productions have been directed by Jacques Karpo. The season runs from October to June, when some 12 productions are each given four to six performances. During the summer, popular operas are performed in the courtyard of La Charité (before 1990 they were given in the courtyard of the 18th-century Château de Borély). The public favours Italian opera sung by international stars.

V. Combarnous: *L'histoire du Grand Théâtre de Marseille 1787–1919* (Marseilles, 1922)
J. Cheilan-Cambolin: *Un aspect de la vie musicale à Marseille au XVIIIe siècle: cinquante ans d'opéra* (diss., U. of Aix-en-Provence, 1972)
F. Ducros: '1945–1985: quarante années de théâtre lyrique à Marseille', *Le théâtre lyrique français 1945–1985*, ed. D. Pistone (Paris, 1987), 329–38
A. Ségond: *L'Opéra de Marseille 1787–1987* (Marseilles, 1987)
MARCEL FRÉMIOT, CHARLES PITT

Marsh, Stephen Hale (*b* London, *c*1805; *d* San Francisco, *c*1888). Australian composer. He studied the harp with Bochsa in London and emigrated to Australia (with his brother Henry, a music seller and composer) in 1842. He became established in Sydney as a harp teacher, recitalist and concert organizer. In 1852 he moved to Melbourne, possibly to escape the influence of his rival, the composer Isaac Nathan. Marsh left Australia in 1872 and after two years in Japan settled in San Francisco.

His three-act opera *The Gentleman in Black*, to a libretto by Edward Searle after James Dalton's novel, was composed about 1847 (perhaps in emulation of Nathan's *Don John of Austria*) and first staged by the Lyster Opera Company at the Theatre Royal, Melbourne, on 24 July 1861. Set during the French Revolution it shows how the 'Gentleman in Black' of the title (bass) lures a young merchant, Maxwell (tenor), into a Faustian pact and then attempts to ensnare Adele (mezzo-soprano), Maxwell's beloved. The story ends happily, however: Adele burns the document of the pact and is liberated from prison by Max and the local *sans-culottes*. The work combines many conventions of opera (a masked fête, spectacular machinery) with those of melodrama (spoken dialogue interspersed between set musical numbers) and incorporates comedy, satire and the supernatural into a traditional 'rescue' plot. The score is believed to have been destroyed in the San Francisco earthquake of 1906.

E. Wood: *Australian Opera 1842–1970* (diss., U. of Adelaide, 1979)
H. Love: *The Golden Age of Australian Opera: W. S. Lyster and his Companies, 1861–1880* (Sydney, 1981)
THÉRÈSE RADIC

Marshall, Lois (Catherine) (*b* Toronto, 29 Jan 1924). Canadian soprano. She sang in Beecham's recording of *Die Entführung aus dem Serail* and made her London concert début under his direction in 1956, later touring widely. Though partly paralysed by polio, she appeared as the Queen of Night in Toronto, in *La bohème* and *Tosca* in Boston, and as Ellen Orford in a television production of *Peter Grimes*. In its prime her voice was a lyric soprano of power, warmth and unusual flexibility, and she was a singer of strong emotional commitment. In the mid-1970s she began performing works from the alto and mezzo-soprano repertories. She sang the title role in Massenet's *Thérèse* in Toronto in the late 1970s, and has taught in the Faculty of Music, University of Toronto, since 1976.
JOHN BECKWITH

Marshall, Margaret (*b* Stirling, 4 Jan 1949). Scottish soprano. She studied in Glasgow, and later with Hans Hotter. In 1978 she sang Gluck's Eurydice with Muti in Florence and Gardiner in London. Since 1982 she has appeared regularly with Muti at Salzburg, singing Countess Almaviva, Fiordiligi and Ilia. In 1979 she made her début at La Scala in Vivaldi's *Tito Manlio*, and in 1980 at Covent Garden as Countess Almaviva. With Scottish Opera she has sung Pamina, Ilia and in 1985 the Countess in *Capriccio*. Her first performance as the Marschallin, at Cologne in 1986, was followed by others at Zürich. She has also sung at the Staatsoper in Vienna, the Deutsche Oper, Berlin, the New York State Theatre and Glyndebourne, and as Fiordiligi at Covent Garden in 1989 and at Salzburg in 1990. Recordings include *Orfeo ed Euridice* and *Così fan tutte*; as with her stage appearances, there is a limited range of dramatic expression, but her musicianship and warm, evenly produced voice give much pleasure.
J. B. STEANE

Marshall-Hall, George W(illiam) L(ouis) (*b* London, 28 March 1862; *d* Melbourne, 18 July 1915). Australian composer of English birth. In 1883, after study in Berlin and a short time as a teacher, he gained admission to the RCM, where he was taught composition by Hubert Parry and counterpoint by Frederick Bridge. Subsequently he held a post as an organist, and in 1888, after an unsuccessful attempt to establish himself as a composer in London, he became director of the orchestra and choral society at the London Organ School and College of Music. In 1890 Marshall-Hall left England for Melbourne as the first Ormond Professor of Music at the university.

He was to become a controversial figure of lasting importance in the development of music in Australia, teaching composition, founding two conservatories, becoming the centre of a public debate over freedom of speech (which led to his dismissal from the university in

1900 and the establishment of his own conservatory), founding an orchestra which bore his name and composing, among other works, seven operas. Three of these pre-date the Australian years. *Harold*, an opera on the subject of the last Saxon king, was probably written before February 1888, for though the scores are undated, the scene from it known as *The Defence of Earl Godwin before the Witan* was introduced by Charles Santley at the 11th concert of the LSO under George Henschel. Both *Dido and Aeneas* and *Leonard*, his next two operas, appear in John Tower's *Dictionary-Catalogue of Operas and Operettas* (New York, 1910) as having 'been performed upon the public stage', but no details of any such performances survive.

Alcestis, his first opera to be composed in Australia, was originally intended as incidental music for a university performance of the Euripides play, but it evolved into an operatic work, much to the chagrin of the director, Alexander Leeper, whose enmity became a major factor in Marshall-Hall's confrontation with the university. It had its European première at the Stadttheater of Meissen in 1913. *Aristodemus* (completed 11 August 1902) has never been performed, although the libretto was published in 1900. *Stella*, a one-act opera with an Australian setting, is signed on the final page of the score: 'finished in the tail of Halley's comet 12 May 1910'. After its first performance in Melbourne, it was given in London in 1914 at the Palladium in a heavily reduced version. *Romeo and Juliet* uses an arrangement of Shakespeare's play as its libretto. One scene was performed in Melbourne in 1912, but the projected full-scale London production did not eventuate.

In 1915 Marshall-Hall was reinstated as Ormond Professor and returned to Australia, having spent the previous two years in England. Six months later he died. None of his operas achieved a full production, and after his death his entire output fell into neglect. In the 1930s Percy Grainger bought the manuscripts from Marshall-Hall's widow, the first he acquired in setting up the Australian collection of the Grainger Museum in the grounds of the University of Melbourne.

A Marshall-Hall Trust, endowed by the composer's grandson, aims to foster interest in the analysis, performance and recording of Marshall-Hall's music, his operas in particular.

Harold, ?before 1888 (4, Marshall-Hall), 1 scene, London, 2 Feb 1888

Dido and Aeneas, ?before 1890 (5), ?perf.

Leonard, ?perf., lost

Alcestis (3, Marshall-Hall, after Euripides), Melbourne, Town Hall, 22 June 1898

Aristodemus, 1902 (25 sections, Marshall-Hall), unperf., lib. (Melbourne, 1900)

Stella, 1910 (1, Marshall-Hall), Melbourne, Her Majesty's, 4 May 1912

Romeo and Juliet (4, Marshall-Hall, after W. Shakespeare), 1 scene, Melbourne, Her Majesty's, 14 Dec 1912

*

W. Bebbington: *The Operas of G. W. L. Marshall-Hall* (diss., U. of Melbourne, 1977)

T. Radic: *Some Historical Aspects of Musical Associations in Melbourne 1888–1915* (diss., U. of Melbourne, 1978)

——: 'A Man Out of Season: G. W. L. Marshall-Hall', *Meanjin*, ii (1980), 195–211

E. Wood: *Australian Opera, 1842–1970* (diss., U. of Adelaide, 1980)

T. Radic: *G. W. L. Marshall-Hall: Portrait of a Lost Crusader* (Nedlands, 1982)

J. W. Rich: *His Thumb unto his Nose* (diss., U. of Melbourne, 1986)

THÉRÈSE RADIC

Marsick, Armand (Louis Joseph) (*b* Liège, 20 Sept 1877; *d* Haine-St Paul, Hainaut, 30 April 1959). Belgian composer. He studied composition with Ropartz at the conservatory in Nancy and completed his studies with d'Indy in Paris. In 1908 he was appointed conductor and professor of composition at the Athens conservatory; he was later director of the Bilbao conservatory (1922–7), then professor of harmony at the Liège conservatory (1927–42). His operas, notably *Lara*, are in the *verismo* tradition, and his orchestration is powerfully suggestive. Among his other works are a radio score, incidental music and orchestral and instrumental pieces.

Cybélia (songe antique, P. Gusman and P. Géraldy), Paris, private perf., 1908
La Jane (vendetta corsa, 1, F. Beissier), Rome, Adriano, 1912
Lara, 1913 (3, Kloster, after Byron), Antwerp, Koninklijke Vlaamse Opera, 3 Dec 1929
L'anneau nuptial, 1920 (3, U. Fleres), Brussels, Monnaie, 3 March 1928
HENRI VANHULST

Marsigli [Marsiglio, Marsili], **Giuseppe** (*b* Bologna; *fl* 1677–1727). Italian tenor. He studied in Bologna. In 1677 he sang Floro in Legrenzi's *Germanico sul Reno* in Modena. Between 1677 and 1727, although not continuously, he was in the choir of S Petronio, Bologna, but he also took other appointments; from 6 September 1686 until at least 1700 he was a virtuoso of Duke Ferdinando Carlo Gonzaga of Mantua, and when he performed in Bologna in L. A. Predieri's *Partenope* (1710) and A. Giannettini's *Artaserse* (1711) he designated himself 'virtuoso of Prince Cesare Ignazio d'Este'. He also sang in Milan, Reggio Emilia, Turin and Genoa.

*

S. Durante: 'Alcune considerazioni sui cantanti di teatro del primo settecento e la loro formazione', *Antonio Vivaldi: teatro musicale cultura e società: Venice 1981*, ii, 427–81

P. Besutti: *La corte musicale di Ferdinando Carlo Gonzaga ultimo duca di Mantova: musici, cantanti e teatro d'opera tra il 1665 e il 1707* (Mantua, 1989)
PAOLA BESUTTI

Marsollier des Vivetières, Benoît-Joseph (*b* Paris, 1750; *d* Versailles, 21 or 22 April 1817). French librettist. The son of a wealthy merchant, he was destined for a career as a magistrate but early turned his attention to writing for the stage. During the 1770s he produced a number of comedies and *opéras comiques* under the pseudonym D[u] G[rand] N[ez]. The stunning success of *Nina* (1786) caused him to abandon the spoken theatre in favour of *opéra comique*, and he wrote librettos for leading composers such as Méhul, Gaveaux, Berton and Isouard. His greatest and most enduring successes were the 20 pieces he wrote with Dalayrac, a collaboration that spanned nearly 25 years. Although Marsollier held a civil-service position before the Revolution, he lost it and most of his fortune during the conflict, and he was imprisoned for a time following the discovery that he had corresponded with some émigrés who had fled to England. Yet he soon returned to public favour, and in 1814 was made a Chevalier of the Légion d'honneur.

Marsollier's librettos are marked less by refined writing than by a sure theatrical sense and a gift of portraying realistic characters in lifelike situations. He was particularly noted for his ability to juxtapose tearful, sentimental scenes and genuinely comic ones and to create tastefully sensitive situations. Like *Nina*, most of his librettos are in one act and reflect the popular trends of the time: sentimental comedy (*Nina*); comedy of manners (*Adolphe et Clara*, 1799); 'rescue opera' (*Camille*, 1791); political commentary (*La pauvre femme*, 1795); exoticism (*Gulnare*, 1798); and combinations of rescue themes with features of sentimental comedy or adventure (*La maison isolée*, 1797, and *Deux mots*, 1806). Thus in many ways Marsollier continued the lines of development begun around 1770 by Grétry and his librettists Sedaine and Marmontel. Marsollier's characters are always contemporary, and in his politically orientated works (e.g. *La pauvre femme*) they speak out against the Terror in no uncertain terms. The psychology of Nina, his finest heroine, seems modern even today. A generous, modest man, Marsollier was always ready to assist younger authors and to give credit to those who had helped or influenced him, particularly Dalayrac.

opéras comiques unless otherwise stated

Le bal masqué, Darcis, 1772; La fausse peur, Darcis, 1774 (Dalayrac, 1797, as La leçon, ou La tasse de glaces); La fausse délicatesse, P. J. Hinner, 1776; Les deux aveugles de Bagdad, Fournier, 1782; Théodore, Davaux, 1785; Nina, ou La folle par amour, Dalayrac, 1786; Les deux petits Savoyards, Dalayrac, 1789; Camille, ou Le souterrain, Dalayrac, 1791; Asgill, ou Le prisonnier de guerre, Dalayrac, 1793 (rev. 1795, as Arnill, ou Le prisonnier américain)

Les détenus, ou Cange, commissionaire de Lazare, Dalayrac, 1794; La pauvre femme, Dalayrac, 1795; Adèle et Dorsan, Dalayrac, 1795; Marianne, ou L'amour maternel [La tendresse maternelle], Dalayrac, 1796; La maison isolée, ou Le vieillard des Vosges, Dalayrac, 1797; Le traité nul, Gaveaux, 1797; Gulnare, ou L'esclave persanne, Dalayrac, 1797; Alexis, ou L'erreur d'un bon père, Dalayrac, 1798; Primerose [Roger, ou Le sage] (with E.-G.-F. Favières), Dalayrac, 1798

Adolphe et Clara, ou Les deux prisonniers, Dalayrac, 1799; Emma, ou Le soupçon, E. Fay, 1799; Laure, ou L'actrice chez elle, Dalayrac, 1799; Le rocher de Leucade, Dalayrac, 1800; Une matinée de Catinat, ou Le tableau, Dalayrac, 1800; Léhémann, ou La tour de Neustadt, Dalayrac, 1801; L'irato, ou L'emporté, Méhul, 1801; Joanna, Méhul, 1802; Le concert interrompu (with Favières), H.-M. Berton, 1802; Léonce, ou Le fils adoptif, Isouard, 1805

Deux mots, ou Une nuit dans la forêt, Dalayrac, 1806 (Ger., C. Kreutzer, 1808; L. Gordigiani, 1854); Les deux aveugles de Tolède, Méhul, 1806; Elise-Hortense, ou Les souvenirs de l'enfance, Dalayrac, 1809; Le testament, Daussoigne-Méhul, 1818; Edmond et Caroline, ou La lettre et la réponse, Kreubé, 1819

*

Comtesse d'Hautpoul, ed.: *Oeuvres choisies de Marsollier* (Paris, 1825)

K. Pendle: 'Marsollier and Dalayrac: a Working Friendship', *ML*, lxiv (1983), 44–57   KARIN PENDLE

Martello [Martelli], **Pier Jacopo** (*b* Bologna, 28 April 1665; *d* Bologna, 10 May 1727). Italian poet and writer on opera. He wrote a number of librettos for operas performed at Bologna in the 1690s, among them *Perseo* and *Tisbe* (both Malvezzi, 1697), set by various composers, *L'Apollo geloso* (Perti, Formagliari, 1698) and a pastorale *Gli amici* (Albergati, Malvezzi, 1699). He then turned to spoken tragedy, using 14-syllable rhyming lines imitative of alexandrines and later known as *versi martelliani*, which were little admired though occasionally used by Goldoni and others. He went to Rome in 1708 as secretary of the Bolognese embassy, and was in Paris, 1713–14. There he wrote *L'impostore: dialogo sopra la tragedia antica e moderna* (Paris, 1714), revised as *Della tragedia antica e moderna* (Rome, 1715, 2/1735) with a dialogue on opera. This has been described as 'the opening salvo in that long, often highly amusing series of satirical writings produced in Italy during the ... eighteenth century', with its 'humorous, sometimes savage, tirades against many

of the excesses of opera and its practitioners' (Weiss 1980). The dialogue, with 'Aristotle' as the mentor, shows Martello on the side of reform (he had connections with the Arcadian Academy), pressing the claims of the mythological plot above the historical and satirizing opera-house abuses.

*

P. J. Martello: *Scritti critici e satirici*, ed. H. S. Noce (Bari, 1963), 270–96

C. Gallico: 'P. I. Martello e "la poetica di Aristotile sul melodramma"', *Scritti in onore di Luigi Ronga* (Milan, 1973), 225–32

P. Weiss: 'Pier Jacopo Martello on Opera (1715): an Annotated Translation', *MQ*, lxvi (1980), 378–403

R. Freeman: *Opera Without Drama: Currents of Change in Italian Opera, 1675 to 1725* (Ann Arbor, 1981), 35–51

Martens, Frederick Herman (*b* New York, 6 July 1874; *d* Mountain Lakes, NJ, 18 Dec 1932). American writer on music and librettist. He was educated by tutors and studied music privately in New York. He wrote texts for operettas, cantatas and songs, and his many translations include Rimsky-Korsakov's *The Snow Maiden* (1921), Massenet's *Le roi de Lahore* (1923), Falla's *La vida breve* (1925), Spontini's *La vestale* (1925), Stravinsky's *The Nightingale* (1925), Thomas' *Mignon* (1927) and Krenek's *Jonny spielt auf* (1928). From 1907, however, his main occupation was the writing of books and essays, including *The Art of the Prima Donna and Concert Singer* (New York, 1923), *The Book of the Opera and the Ballet and History of the Opera* (New York, 1925) and *A Thousand and One Nights of Opera* (New York, 1926).   PAULA MORGAN

Martha [*Martha, oder Der Markt zu Richmond* ('Martha, or The Market at Richmond')]. Romantic comic opera in four acts by FRIEDRICH FLOTOW to a libretto by W. FRIEDRICH after an idea by JULES-HENRI VERNOY DE SAINT-GEORGES; Vienna, Kärntnertortheater, 25 November 1847.

Lady Harriet Durham *maid of honour to Queen Anne*	soprano
Sir Tristan Mickleford *her cousin*	bass
Plumkett *a young farmer*	bass
Lyonel *his foster brother*	tenor
Nancy *waiting-maid to Lady Harriet*	mezzo-soprano
Sheriff	bass
Three Manservants	tenor, basses
Three Maidservants	soprano, mezzo-sorpanos

Courtiers, pages, ladies, hunters and huntresses, farmers

Setting In and near Richmond, *c*1710

It was after the success of *Alessandro Stradella* in Vienna in 1845 that Flotow received a commission from the Vienna Hofoper to write a new opera. He decided to extend his music from the ballet *Lady Harriette, ou La servante de Greenwich* of 1844 into a full-length opera. For the libretto he again approached Friedrich, who had written the text of *Alessandro Stradella*. Friedrich was well versed in the new plot, having already written a libretto on the subject for Eduard Stiegmann's opera *Lady Harriet*, performed in Hamburg in 1846. Working in close collaboration, Flotow and Friedrich created their most successful opera, *Martha*, which has held its place in the repertory until the present day. (The same plot was also set to music that year by the Irish

'Martha' (Flotow), Act 2 (the spinning scene) with the principals of the original production at the Kärntnertortheater, Vienna, 25 November 1847: engraving by A. Geiger after Cajetan

composer Michael Balfe as *The Maid of Honour*, performed in London a month later than *Martha* with no success.) The celebrated aria 'Letzte Rose' is the Irish folksong, 'The last rose of summer', as it appeared in Thomas Moore's *Irish Melodies* in 1813, although the tune was adapted by Moore from earlier sources.

Act 1.i *Lady Harriet Durham's boudoir* Lady Harriet is tired of life at court and longs for true love. Her maid, Nancy, tries in vain to raise her spirits; to make things worse Lady Harriet has to ward off the amorous approaches of her foppish cousin, Lord Tristan. On hearing the local peasant girls singing on their way to the annual Richmond Fair, she decides all three should dress up as peasants and mingle with the common folk to watch the merriment, for it is at this fair that the maids commit themselves for one year to the service of the bidding farmers. To ensure anonymity, Lady Harriet will call herself 'Martha', Nancy will be known as 'Julia' and Lord Tristan must answer to the name of 'Bob'.

1.ii *The market square of Richmond* Plumkett and Lyonel arrive in the hope of finding two servant-girls. They reminisce on how Lyonel's fugitive father had brought him as a child to Plumkett's parents, where they found refuge, until the father died, without ever revealing his name or standing. He did, however, leave Lyonel his ring, saying that if he were ever in danger he should show it to the queen. The Sheriff formally opens the fair and proclaims the royal decree that any maid who takes on service has to remain with her new master for one year. The farmers have no difficulty in finding willing maids, while Plumkett and Lyonel remain undecided. Lady Harriet and Nancy arrive, dragging 'Bob' behind them. He insists they go home immediately, and as their discord starts to attract attention, Lady Harriet pretends that 'Bob' is trying to force her into service on his farm. The indignant commoners point out that there are enough willing maids to serve him, and a group of girls who have not yet found employment descend on

him. Left alone with Plumkett and Lyonel the ladies, highly diverted, hire themselves off as servants for the pittance now paid in advance. The joke over, they try to get Lord Tristan to take them home, but the Sheriff confirms that they have entered into a one-year agreement of service, and their new masters drag them off to their cart while Tristan is held back by the angry farmers.

Act 2 *Plumkett's farmhouse* The farmers try putting the girls to work, but they protest that they are unversed in household chores. While the two exasperated men show them how to spin flax, Nancy flees the room and Plumkett runs after her, leaving Lyonel and 'Martha' alone. Lyonel confesses his tender feelings, offering to overlook her assumed low standing and to marry her. Amused, Lady Harriet declines, but accedes to his request to sing a simple folksong ('Letzte Rose'), in which she hints at her loneliness. It is now midnight. The girls are locked into their room, and the men retire. When all are sleeping a knock is heard on the girls' window. It is Lord Tristan. Overjoyed, Harriet and Nancy escape through the window before their new masters, woken by the noise, can stop them.

Act 3 *A forest near Richmond* Queen Anne is hunting, watched by Plumkett and a group of peasants. Nancy arrives fully accoutred for the royal hunt and accompanied by her huntresses. She and Plumkett recognize each other, and he attempts to take her back to the farm by force. Nancy denies ever having known him and has him chased away by her formidable companions. Lyonel appears, lamenting the loss of Lady Harriet, whom he loves in the guise of his absconded maid Martha, and sings the aria 'Ach, so fromm'. Deep in thought, he fails to notice Lady Harriet enter with Lord Tristan. The latter is still trying to win her heart, but she sends him away, admitting to herself that she is actually pining for Lyonel. On hearing her voice, Lyonel falls to her feet, professing his love, but she disavows him, for fear of the scandal any knowledge of her adventure would cause at court. Lyonel becomes angry and Lady Harriet, alarmed, calls Lord Tristan and the hunting party. Lyonel is not believed when he relates how Lady Harriet had tricked her way into his house by posing as a servant. She declares that he has lost his mind, and he is arrested. The act ends with the quintet with chorus 'Mag der Himmel euch vergeben'. As Lyonel is led away, he gives Plumkett the ring he had received from his father with the request that it reach the queen.

ACT 4.i *Plumkett's farmhouse* The ring has now been identified by the queen as that of the unjustly banished Earl of Derby. Lady Harriet comes to reveal to Lyonel who he really is, but also to ask his forgiveness and to offer him her hand in marriage. Lyonel angrily rejects her. Plumkett has already forgiven Nancy, and Harriet now enlists the loving couple's assistance in her plan to win Lyonel back.

4.ii *In front of Plumkett's farmhouse* Peasants and servants set up a replica of the Richmond Fair, with one of the farmers dressed as the Sheriff. Lady Harriet and Nancy appear as 'Martha' and 'Julia' in peasant costume to meet Plumkett as he leads the heartbroken Lyonel to the mock fair. The two girls, re-enacting the events of the real fair in Act 1, offer themselves once again to Plumkett and Lyonel, who can no longer resist their offer of love and dedication. The two couples embrace to the jubilation of the crowd.

* * *

From the point of view of the intrinsic merit of the work, the success of *Martha* was surely inevitable. The libretto, couched in succinct and witty couplets, tells a tale that is well constructed, exciting, amusing and sentimental. The bustling folk scenes, the rough-and-ready situation at the farm, the magnificence of the royal hunt and the sophistication of court life and, in particular, the depth of the emotions of the principal characters, find fitting expression in Flotow's music. Although this implies a certain degree of eclecticism (which was indeed common in France at the time), the stylistic unity of the work is manifest. For example, the motifs of the theme of the highly operatic and heroic 'Mag der Himmel euch vergeben' are derived from those in the simple folksong 'Letzte Rose'. Flotow also included numerous well-placed repetitions of the reminiscence themes ('Letzte Rose' is repeated five times).

PETER COHEN

Martin, Frank (*b* Geneva, 15 Sept 1890; *d* Naarden, 21 Nov 1974). Swiss composer. The tenth and youngest child of a Calvinist minister, he went to the normal schools of Geneva, but had private lessons in composition from Joseph Lauber. After World War I he lived in Zürich, Rome and Paris but returned in 1926 to Geneva, where he taught rhythmic theory and improvisation at the Jaques-Dalcroze Institute. Martin was active as a pianist and harpsichordist, lectured on chamber music at the conservatory and was director of the private music school Technicum Moderne de Musique. From 1942 to 1946 he was president of the Swiss Musicians' Union. In 1946 he moved to the Netherlands, from where he held a composition class at the Cologne Hochschule für Musik (1950–57). After 1957 he devoted himself to composing and to the performance of his works.

Martin was familiar with theatre from early childhood (his parents were amateur musicians who encouraged entertainments for family festivities) and he was increasingly drawn to the stage. Besides the well-known operas he wrote a dozen works connected with the theatre, including *La nique à Satan* (1931), a *spectacle populaire* on folk themes for baritone, choruses (male, female and children's), wind instruments, two pianos, percussion and double bass, from which 18 songs were extracted for independent performance and publication. The secular oratorio *Le vin herbé* (1938–41), based on part of Joseph Bédier's *Roman de Tristan et Iseut*, was first staged at Salzburg in 1948 and has been produced many times since, though it does not need dramatic performance to make its effect.

Despite Martin's considerable output of vocal and choral works he set to work on his first opera only at the age of 60. *Der Sturm* (1952–4), a three-act adaptation of Shakespeare's *The Tempest* in Schlegel's German translation, is more of a musical setting of the play, whose fairy-tale atmosphere seems to call for music. Martin abridged the text very little. His music does not divide into recitatives and arias but flows without a break. The harmonic structure is appropriately fluid: the key-scheme moves through a cycle of 5ths, with scenes beginning and ending in different keys. Ernest Ansermet conducted the work's première at the Vienna Staatsoper on 17 June 1956. *Le mystère de la Nativité* (1957–9), from a part of the late medieval mystery play by Arnoul Greban, is not an opera in the general sense of the word; the three levels of the stage – heaven, the human world in the middle and hell, populated by humorously rowdy devils – correspond with three kinds of music. The music for heaven is of particular simplicity, and the scenes in hell are written in free 12-note style with rich instrumental colouring. *Le mystère* was first staged at Salzburg on 15 August 1960 with Heinz Wallberg as conductor. *Monsieur de Pourceaugnac* (1963), Martin's last opera, follows the entire text of Molière's play; although its music is less independent it enabled the composer to display his sense of humour. In three acts, this *comédie mise en musique* received its first performance at the Grand Théâtre, Geneva, on 23 April 1963 with Ansermet conducting.

*

R. Klein: *Frank Martin: sein Leben und Werk* (Vienna, 1960)

A. Koelliker: *Frank Martin: biographie, les oeuvres* (Lausanne, 1963)

J. A. Tupper: *Stylistic Analysis of Selected Works by Frank Martin* (diss., Indiana U., 1964)

J.-C. Piguet and F. Martin: *Entretiens sur la musique* (Neuchâtel, 1967)

E. Ansermet: 'Frank Martins historische Stellung', *ÖMz*, xxiv (1969), 137–41

B. Billeter: *Frank Martin: ein Aussenseiter der neuen Musik* (Frauenfeld, 1970)

——: *Die Harmonik bei Frank Martin: Untersuchungen zur Analyse neuerer Musik* (Berne, 1971)

B. Martin: *Frank Martin ou la réalité du rêve* (Neuchâtel, 1973)

A. Surchamp: *Entretiens avec Frank Martin* (St Léger-Vauban, 1975)

B. Billeter: 'Die letzten Vokalwerke von Frank Martin', *SMz*, cxvi (1976), 344–51

——: 'Werkverzeichnis Frank Martin', *SMz*, cxvi (1976), 378–81

J.-C. Piguet: *Ernest Ansermet–Frank Martin: correspondance* (Neuchâtel, 1976)

C. Regamey: 'Les éléments flamenco dans les dernières oeuvres de Frank Martin', *SMz*, cxvi (1976), 351–9

M. Martin, ed.: *Un compositeur médite sur son art* (Neuchâtel, 1977)

B. Billeter: 'Frank Martins Bühnenwerke', *Schweizer Theaterjahrbuch*, xlv (1983), 92–108

M. Martin, ed.: *A propos de …: commentaires de Frank Martin sur ses oeuvres* (Neuchâtel, 1984)

P. Sulzer: *Frank Martin: lettres à Victor Desarzens* (Lausanne, 1988)

BERNHARD BILLETER

Martin, Janis (*b* Sacramento, CA, 16 Aug 1939). American mezzo-soprano, later soprano. She made her début in 1960 singing minor roles at the San Francisco Opera. By 1966 she had graduated to Marina (*Boris Godunov*), Venus and Meg Page. In 1968 she sang the Composer (*Ariadne auf Naxos*) in Munich, and Magdalene and Fricka at Bayreuth. Engaged for a year at Nuremberg, she added Hänsel and Octavian to her repertory. In the early 1970s she began to sing soprano roles, appearing as Tosca, Eva, Sieglinde and Kundry in leading European houses, and at San Diego and Chicago. She made her London début at Covent Garden in 1973 as Marie (*Wozzeck*), a role she repeated a year later at the Metropolitan. Her repertory also includes Brangäne, Senta, Ortrud, Adriano (*Rienzi*), Isolde, Yaroslavna (*Prince Igor*), Ariadne, Judith (*Bluebeard's Castle*), the Woman in Schoenberg's *Erwartung*, which she sang at La Scala (1980), Electra, Leonore and Brünnhilde (*Die Walküre*), which she sang at Bayreuth (1989) and San Francisco (1990). The rich middle register characteristic of the mezzo-soprano voice was not lost when she became a dramatic soprano.

ELIZABETH FORBES

Martin, Jean Baptiste (*fl* 1748–57). French costume designer. Few facts are known about him: he was the immediate successor of François Boucher at the Paris Opéra from July 1748 until 1757 or 1758, and his initial wage of 1200 livres was doubled in 1750. He designed costumes for *opéras-ballets* by Rameau and revivals of Lully and Charpentier. The *Mercure* reported, in July 1763, the appearance of Martin's *Collection de figures theatrales* (20 coloured engravings), 'six years after he retired'. They portray Driade, Indienne, Incas, Hercule, Flore, Paysan, Paysanne, Suivante de Flore, Suivante de Zéphire, Zéphire, Africain, Apollon, Démon, Faune, Furie, Médée, Neptune, Paysan galant, Paysanne galante and Thétis. The last ten were reworked to conform to the fashion 16 years later and, with six new designs (Chinois, Chinoise, Silphide, Silphe, Reine des sylphes, Vénus), were printed in *Gallerie des modes et costumes français, dessinés d'après nature* (1779). Martin's work inspired many later designers; C. W. Beaumont considered him 'Berain's only peer'.

For illustration *see* COSTUME, fig.7.

*

M. von Boehm: *Das Bühnenkostüm in Altertum, Mittelalter und Neuzeit* (Berlin, 1921), 351–62
C. Fischer: *Les costumes de l'opéra* (Paris, 1931), 69–80
F. Rapp: 'Zu J. B. Martin', *Essays presented to Fritz Saxl* (London, 1937), 295–311, pls.78–81
C. W. Beaumont: *Ballet Design Past & Present* (London, 1946), pp.xx, 19–21
L. Kirstein: *Movement & Metaphor: Four centuries of Ballet* (New York, 1970) [incl. illustrations]   SIDNEY JACKSON JOWERS

Martin, (Nicolas-)Jean-Blaise [Blès] (*b* Paris, 24 Feb 1768; *d* Ronzières, nr Lyons, 28 Oct 1837). French baritone. He made his début at the Théâtre de Monsieur in 1789 in *Le marquis de Tulipano*, a French version of a Paisiello opera. In 1794 he moved to the Théâtre Favart, remaining until it merged with the Feydeau to form the Opéra-Comique in 1801. He specialized in comic servant roles in new operas by Dalayrac, Boieldieu, Méhul, Isouard and others. He retired from the Opéra-Comique in 1823 but returned briefly in 1826 and 1833, when he appeared in Halévy's *Les souvenirs de Lafleur*, a pasticcio incorporating songs from his most successful roles. Martin's voice combined the range and quality of a tenor and a baritone, spanning two and a half octaves ($E\flat-a'$) with an additional octave in falsetto. His exceptional range influenced vocal characterization in *opéras comiques* for over a century, and high-lying 'baryton-Martin' roles are found in operas by Hérold (*Zampa*), Gounod (Valentin in *Faust*), Bizet (Escamillo, Ernesto in *Don Procopio*, the Duke of Rothsay in *La jolie fille de Perth*, Splendiano in *Djamileh*), Debussy (Pelléas) and Ravel (Ramiro in *L'heure espagnole*). Martin was also noted for his facility in rapid vocalization. He composed a one-act *opéra comique*, *Les oiseaux de mer* (1796, Théâtre Feydeau).

*

ES (B. Horowicz)
J. A. de la Fage: 'Blaise Martin', *Revue et gazette musicale de Paris* (19 Nov 1837)
A. Barraud, ed.: *Galerie théâtrale* (Paris, 1873)

PHILIP ROBINSON

Martin, Riccardo [Whitefield, Hugh] (*b* Hopkinsville, KY, 18 Nov 1874; *d* New York, 11 Aug 1952). American tenor. He studied in Paris, making his début in 1904 at Nantes as Faust; after further study in Italy, he sang Andrea Chénier at Verona, then made his American début in 1906 at New Orleans as Canio. He toured with the San Carlo Opera Company and in 1907 made his Metropolitan début as Boito's Faust; he remained with the company until 1915, creating Quintus in Horatio Parker's *Mona* (1912) and Christian in Walter Damrosch's *Cyrano* (1913), and singing Pinkerton, Cavaradossi and Rodolfo. He made his Covent Garden début in 1910 as Pinkerton, also singing Puccini's Des Grieux, Radames, Faust, Cavaradossi, Angel Clare (*Tess*) and, in 1911, Canio and Dick Johnson. He appeared at Boston and in Chicago (1920–23) as Radames, Nicias (*Thaïs*) and Don José. He had a voice of great beauty, though lacking in individuality, and a fine presence, but he suffered comparison with Caruso throughout his career.

*

O. Thompson: *The American Singer* (New York, 1937), 278–80
M. de Schauensee: 'A Tribute to Riccardo Martin', *ON*, xvii/6 (1952–3), 12–13   RICHARD LeSUEUR/ELIZABETH FORBES

Martin, Thomas (Philipp) (*b* Vienna, 28 May 1909; *d* New York, 14 May 1984). American translator and conductor. From 1944 to 1956 he conducted at the New York City Opera, and from 1958 to 1965 was assistant chorus master at the Metropolitan Opera. He is chiefly known for the many opera translations he made in collaboration with his wife Ruth (née Ruth Berenice Kelley; *b* 1914). Both were awarded a medal of honour, first class, by the Austrian government in 1981, principally in recognition of their versions of Mozart's five most popular operas. Of these, *Die Zauberflöte* was given at the Metropolitan under Bruno Walter in 1941. Apart from works of the standard repertory, their translations included Dvořák's *Rusalka*, Lortzing's *Der Wildschütz* and *Der Waffenschmied*, and Korngold's *Der Ring des Polykrates*. Many of their translations were published in vocal score.   ARTHUR JACOBS

Martina Franca. Town in Apulia, south-east Italy. Its cultural and musical history is closely connected with its geographical position – it was formerly part of the kingdom of Naples – and with its architectural status as one of the finest southern Baroque towns. The Palazzo Ducale, designed by G. A. Carducci, was begun by Duke Petraccone V Caracciolo in 1668. Musical activity in the town benefited from the patronage of the Caracciolo dukes and the proximity of the Naples conservatories. In the 18th century one of its most famous native musicians was the castrato Giuseppe Aprile. But even in the heyday of its Baroque architectural development, the town had no opera house. Its importance for opera lies rather in a modern festival. In 1975 a group of interested local individuals and musicians (including Paolo Grassi, director of La Scala, Milan, 1970–75) instituted the Festival della Valle d'Itria, which takes place over a fortnight in July and August, in the splendid setting of the great courtyard of the Palazzo Ducale. Its aim is the rediscovery and historical performance of operatic and sacred works of the 18th and early 19th centuries. As well as works by composers born in southern Italy, those who spent a long time in Naples, such as Rossini, Bellini and Donizetti, are also represented. Other Italian and European institutions have used productions first staged at Martina Franca as models, notably *Tancredi* (1976); *Norma* (1977), the first performance of the original version with Adalgisa as a soprano role; *I Capuleti e i Montecchi* (1980) and Mercadante's *Il giuramento* (1984), the first complete modern performances; *I puritani* (1985), the first complete Italian performance; and Rossini's *Adelaide di Borgogna* (1984), the first complete performance anywhere. The festival has been used as a laboratory for musicological research, and there have been live broadcasts by the RAI and recordings of festival performances. Internationally celebrated singers (Bruscantini, Cortez, Olivero, Bumbry, Ricciarelli, Pavarotti, Raimondi, Kabaivanska and Valentini-Terrani) have often appeared, but at the same time much new talent, both Italian and foreign, has been discovered. The stage of the Palazzo Ducale has seen the débuts of Lella Cuberli, Martine Dupuy, Luciana Serra, Dano Raffanti and Daniela Dessì. In 1985 the festival was awarded the coveted Premio Abbiati by Italian music critics in recognition of its achievements in the re-evaluation of 18th- and 19th-century traditions of opera and bel canto. Between 1975 and 1989 the festival staged 30 operas and presented 16 sacred compositions. In 1986 it gave the first modern performance of Traetta's *Ifigenia in Tauride*. More recently the scope has been extended to Baroque opera, with productions of Monteverdi's *L'incoronazione di Poppea* (1988) and Handel's *Giulio Cesare in Egitto* (1989).

PIERFRANCO MOLITERNI

Martinelli, Caterina (*b* Rome, 1589 or 1590; *d* Mantua, bur. 7 March 1608). Italian singer. She was brought into the service of the Gonzagas at Mantua in August 1603; she lodged with Monteverdi, whose wife may have been her teacher, until September 1606. She sang Venus (and possibly also the title role, though scholarly opinion is divided), in Marco da Gagliano's *Dafne*, given at Mantua in February 1608. A few weeks later, when about to create the title role in Monteverdi's *Arianna*, she died of smallpox. Monteverdi wrote the part with her in mind, and in her memory he wrote his fine madrigal cycle *Lagrime d'amante al sepolcro dell'amata* (1614). She was buried with some pomp in the Carmelite church and had ferial Requiem Masses endowed by the Duke of Mantua as well as the Office of the Dead said for her every month.

*

A. Bertolotti: *Musici alla corte dei Gonzaga in Mantova dal secolo XV al XVIII* (Milan, 1890)

S. Reiner: 'La vag'Angioletta (and Others)', *AnMc*, no.14 (1974), 44, 47ff
E. Strainchamps: 'The Life and Death of Caterina Martinelli: New Light on Monteverdi's "Arianna"', *Early Music History*, v (1985), 155–86
DENIS ARNOLD

Martinelli, Gaetano (*fl* 1764–95). Italian librettist. He first appears as the author of the successful *dramma giocoso Li rivali placati*, set by P. A. Guglielmi for Venice in 1764. Three similar works followed in quick succession, drawing him to the attention of Duke Carl Eugen, who engaged him in 1766 to produce comic opera for his new theatre at Ludwigsburg (near Stuttgart). There Martinelli wrote five works for Jommelli, who had not composed comic opera for over ten years. In 1768 Jommelli arranged to work for the Portuguese court theatre *in absentia*, sending Martinelli as his representative. During his early years in Lisbon, Martinelli directed Jommelli revivals, including the French-inspired *Fetonte*. He also provided Jommelli with a reworked version of Metastasio's *Ezio* and a new semi-serious magic opera, *Le avventure di Cleomede*, both produced in Lisbon in 1772. For Perez, the Portuguese *mestre da capela real*, he wrote the French-inspired *Creusa in Delfo* (1774, Lisbon). After the death of King José I in 1777, he began writing short operas and serenatas for six Portuguese composers of italianate music, some of whom were trained in Naples.

The elegant buffoonery, aristocratic ambience and amorous intrigues of his plots identify Martinelli as a disciple of Goldoni, although he began writing libretto for Venice after Goldoni had left. The *introduzioni*, the minimal number of ensembles, the bipartite arias and action-filled finales are all characteristic of Goldoni's structural designs. At Ludwigsburg, the singers of *opera seria* also performed in the comic operas, allowing Martinelli unusual latitude in blending these normally quite separate genres to produce librettos like the semi-serious *La schiava liberata* (a direct precursor of Mozart's *Die Entführung aus dem Serail*), which has enjoyed a successful 20th-century revival. The Portuguese librettos were short, staged pieces of one or two acts on serious subjects with one or more ensembles and choruses.

Li rivali placati (dg), P. A. Guglielmi, 1764; *Il ratto della sposa* (dg), Guglielmi, 1765; *Le nozze disturbate* (dg), Paisiello, 1766; *Lo spirito di contradizione* (dg), Guglielmi, 1766 (Lima, 1772); *La critica* (commedia) Jommelli, 1766; *Il matrimonio per concorso* (dg), Jommelli, 1766 (Alessandri, 1767); *Il cacciatore deluso, ovvero La Semiramide in bernesco* (op seria-comica), Jommelli, 1767; *La schiava liberata* (op seria-comica), Jommelli, 1768 (Schuster, 1777); *Le avventure di Cleomede* (op seria-comica), Jommelli, 1772; *Creusa in Delfo* (os), Perez, 1774
Ati e Sangaride (serenata), Santos, 1779; *Perseo* (serenata), Carvalho, 1779; *Testoride Argonauta* (os), Carvalho, 1780; *Edalide e Cambise* (serenata), Silva, 1780; *Seleuco, re di Siria* (os), Carvalho, 1781; *Enea in Tracia* (os), Lima, 1781; *Palmira di Tebe* (serenata), Santos, 1781; *Everardo II, re di Lituania* (os), Carvalho, 1782; *Calliroe in Siria* (serenata), Oliveira, 1782; *Bireno ed Olimpia* (serenata), Moreira, 1782; *Penelope nella partenza da Sparta* (os), Carvalho, 1782; *Siface e Sofonisba* (os), Moreira, 1783
Teséo (os), Lima, 1783; *Tomiri, amazzone guerriera* (os), Carvalho, 1783; *Adrasto rè degli Argivi* (os), Carvalho, 1784; *Cadmo* (os), Oliveira, 1784; *Esione* (serenata), Santos, 1784; *Il ratto di Proserpina* (os), Silva, 1784 (Asioli, 1785); *Archelao* (os), Silva, 1785; *Alcione* (os), Carvalho, 1787; *Artemisia, regina di Caria* (os), Moreira, 1787; *Megara tebana* (os), Silva, 1788; *Gli eroi spartani* (os), Moreira, 1788; *Bauce e Palemone* (os), Silva, 1789; *Numa Pompilio II, re de' Romani* (serenata), Carvalho, 1789; *Lindane e Dalmiro* (op seria-comica), Silva, 1789

M. McClymonds: *Niccolò Jommelli: the Last Years, 1769–1774* (Ann Arbor, 1980)

——: 'Jommelli's Last Opera for Germany: the Opera Seria-Comica *La schiava liberata* (Ludwigsburg, 1768)', *CMc*, no.39 (1985), 7–20

M. C. de Brito: *Opera in Portugal in the Eighteenth Century* (Cambridge, 1989)   MARITA P. McCLYMONDS

Martinelli, Giovanni (*b* Montagnana, 22 Oct 1885; *d* New York, 2 Feb 1969). Italian tenor. After study in Milan, he made his stage début there at the Teatro Dal Verme in Verdi's *Ernani* in 1910. In the following year he sang Dick Johnson in *La fanciulla del West* at Rome under Toscanini, later his 'passport role' to many theatres. He appeared at Covent Garden during five seasons between 1912 and 1937, singing over 90 performances in 15 operas, among which the *Otello* and *Turandot* of his last season were particularly memorable. The Metropolitan Opera, however, became the centre of his career for 31 consecutive seasons from 1913, with a few still later appearances in 1945. He sang with the company in 926 performances in a total of 38 operas.

Over the years he developed an unimpeachable technique and scrupulous style, and after the death of Caruso became the leading exponent of such dramatic and heroic roles as Verdi's Manrico, Radames, Don Alvaro, and eventually Otello. The clarion ring of his upper register, the distinctness and purity of his declamation and the sustained legato phrasing made possible by remarkable breath control were the outstanding features of his mature style; he retained his vocal powers to an advanced age. His many records well display his splendid tone and style.

Giovanni Martinelli in the title role of Verdi's 'Otello'

J. B. Richards and J. A. Gibson: 'Giovanni Martinelli', *Record Collector*, v (1950), 173–93 [with discography]

W. J. Collins: 'Giovanni Martinelli', *Record Collector*, xxv (1979–80), 149–215, 221–55 [with discography]

DESMOND SHAWE-TAYLOR

Martinenghi, Antonio Francesco (*fl* 1677–1705). Italian composer. He held the rank of Cavaliere and worked in Milan and Pavia. Of three operas he is known to have written, the librettos alone survive: *La fedeltà mascherata* (Pavia, 1677, by G. B. Novarese), *L'Arsiade* (Milan, 1700, P. d'Averara) and *Il Meleagro* (Pavia, 1705); the last was a collaboration with Paolo Magni and Bernardo Sabadino. A Francesco Martinenghi of Pavia, who together with Perti and Vanelli reset Minato's *La prosperità di Elio Sejano* (1699, Milan), is probably identical with this composer.   SERGIO LATTES

Martínez Valls, Rafael (*b* Onteniente, Valencia, 13 Oct 1887 or 1897; *d* Barcelona, 27 Dec 1946). Spanish composer. He studied first with his father and brother and, after studying medicine at Valencia University for two years, pursued his musical studies with Juan Pastor (composition) and José María Úbeda (organ). He obtained his first professional position as director of the Valencia provincial band and later became chorus master and organist at the Teatro Real, Madrid. He then moved to Barcelona, where he was for seven years choirmaster and organist of the church of S José Oriol. During this time he composed a considerable amount of religious and chamber music, but found lasting acclaim with zarzuelas composed to Catalan librettos, most notably his *Cançó d'amor i de guerra* (1926).

Zarzuelas: La mosquetera (3), Barcelona, Tívoli, 1925; Así canta mi amor (1, G. A. Mantua), *c*1925; Cançó d'amor i de guerra (2, L. Capdevila and V. Mora), Barcelona, Victoria, 26 April 1926; Charivari (revue, J. M. de Sagarra), Barcelona, 1927; El perdón del rey (Asenjo, Torres del Álamo), *c*1927; La ventera de Ansó (Vidal, Planas and Ballesteros de Martos), *c*1928–9, collab. Godes; La legió d'honor (2, Mora), Barcelona, Nueva, 26 Feb 1930; La duquesita (Prada and Calva), *c*1931; L'aliga roja (Mora), Paril, 1932; La aldeanita; Boris d'Eukalia; La cigarrona; Fray Jerónimo; Paz en la guerra; Princesita; Rosaleda; Soy una mujer fatal

*

Enciclopedia universal ilustrada europeo-americana (Barcelona, 1907–30), appx vii (1932), 82   ANDREW LAMB

Martini, Giovanni Battista [Padre Martini] (*b* Bologna, 24 April 1706; *d* Bologna, 3 Aug 1784). Italian composer, teacher and writer on music. One of the outstanding figures in 18th-century music, he was revered in his day as a teacher, his pupils including J. C. Bach, Bertoni, Grétry, Jommelli, Mozart and Neumann. Also a prolific historian and theorist, he corresponded with eminent musicians throughout Europe, building up a library that became the basis of the Civico Museo Bibliografico Musicale in Bologna. His own music consists of a quantity of sacred music and many chamber works, mostly in the homophonic style, and five operatic works. The first, an untitled *azione teatrale*, reveals the influence of contemporary Venetian opera. The rest are all intermezzos in the Neapolitan tradition. *Il maestro di musica* contrasts the two modes of singing, the old (expressive) and the new (virtuoso); *La Dirindina* and *L'impresario delle Canarie* satirize contemporary musical and theatrical practices. *Don Chisciotte* is a curious conflation of Cervantes and the Alcina story, with an incantation scene notable for its mercurial music. Martini also left some 22 arias, some evidently intended to be staged. One of these, 'Freme il mar', was written for the castrato Tedeschi for interpolation in a performance of Caldara's *Temistocle* at the Pergola in Florence in spring 1739.

all in I-Bc
Untitled azione teatrale (3 pts), Feb 1726
La Dirindina (int, G. Gigli), 1731
L'impresario delle Canarie (int, P. Metastasio), 1744, lib. (Bologna, 1744)
Don Chisciotte (int), 1746
Il maestro di musica (int), 1746

*

ES (L. F. Tagliavini)
F. Vatielli: 'Le opere comiche di G. B. Martini', *RMI*, xl (1936), 450–76

Martini, Jean-Paul-Egide [Martin, Johann Paul Aegidius; Schwarzendorf; Martini il Tedesco] (*b* Freystadt, Bavaria, 31 Aug 1741; *d* Paris, 10 Feb 1816). French composer of German birth. Son of the organist Andreas Martin, he was trained first by his father and later at the Jesuit seminary in Neuburg. In 1758 he began studies in philosophy at the University of Fribourg, supporting himself by playing the organ at the local Franciscan convent. During this period he was known as Schwarzendorf. In 1760 he arrived destitute in Nancy, where his musical gifts soon brought him to the attention of two influential patrons: in Fléville the Marchioness of Desarmoises, who held what was reputed to be the most aristocratic and witty salon in the provinces, and in Lunéville Stanislas I, the exiled King of Poland, Duke of Lorraine and father-in-law of Louis XV. After Stanislas's death in 1766 Martini went to Paris, where his instrumental works including much military music began to appear under the name 'Martini il Tedesco' to distinguish him from G. B. Martini.

Thanks probably to his Lorraine patrons, Martini had introductions to important courtiers; he began to collaborate with the court-connected librettists Pierre Laujon and Barnabé Farmian de Rosoi. He acted as secretary to the Marquis of Chamborant and as first equerry to the Prince of Condé, and later became the prince's music director; his first two operas were written to commemorate special occasions for this house. The Duchess of Bourbon lent her support to *Le fermier cru sourd* – to no avail. At Louis XVI's court his *L'amant sylphe* was performed despite the strong objections of the *sociétaires* of the Comédie-Italienne; they resisted later pressure to stage it in Paris. His printed score of *Annette et Lubin* is dedicated to the Count of Artois (later Charles X), whose music director he had become. In 1789 he became general director of the Théâtre de Monsieur (later the Théâtre Feydeau).

The fall of the monarchy (1792) brought financial disaster, and Martini risked arrest as a supporter of the *ancien régime*; he left the capital for Lyons and returned only with the end of the Terror (late 1794). With the Thermidorian Reaction he again benefited from official support, through a special government grant in 1795 and an appointment as *inspecteur* to the new Conservatoire (he assumed duties in 1798 and retired in 1802). Martini adapted skilfully to the changing regimes. His cantata in honour of Napoleon's marriage in 1810 to Marie-Louise of Austria (text by the Princess von Salm) includes representations of classical Greece (Sapho), the French heritage (Corneille) and the emperor's favourite bard ('Ossian'). Yet with the Restoration of the Bourbons he insisted on – and received – his appointment as *surintendant de la musique du Roi*

(to which in 1788 he had been named *en survivance*, next in line after the death of the current holder). His last compositions were written for the royal chapel.

L'amoureux de quinze ans, Martini's best opera, achieved a long-lived popularity unusual for a work that began as a *pièce de circonstance*. The sentimental libretto lent itself well to brief *airs*, duets, marches and dances, allowing his gift for melodies in a gracious and simple style to come to the fore. *Le droit du seigneur* was also successful; *Annette et Lubin*, on the other hand, could not compete with the popularity of the original vaudeville work (1762). When Martini turned to the farcical, as in *Le rendez-vous bien employé*, he failed miserably because his music was too 'noble', not matching the broadly humorous requirements of the *parade* (according to contemporary reviews of unusual severity).

The première of *Henri IV* marked an important innovation in the repertory of the Comédie-Italienne in that the plot centres on historical events and has a king as a central figure; although the libretto was justly condemned, the opera was a precedent for later works on historical subjects. Rosoi sought to use the genre for didactic purposes, in this case to teach the lesson of good monarchical government. The composer responded with a score in which fanfares, marches and heroic vocal pieces dominate; in addition, he made effective use of traditional *airs* ('Charmante Gabrielle' and 'Vive Henri IV'). The emphasis on spectacle and the hiring of wind players as extras for the military music, unusual at the Comédie-Italienne, added to the work's impact. In *Sapho* Martini maintained a generally Classical *tragédie lyrique* style (the choruses, for example, follow Gluck's precedents), but, learning from more recent developments, he also paid close attention to details in orchestration, such as establishing the night atmosphere at the beginning of Act 3 with solo viola and cello accompanied by lower strings. To illustrate dramatic moments, particularly the heroine's suicide, Martini introduced extensive modulations and striking dissonances (see Charlton 1985 and *Pÿpers Enzyklopädie des Musiktheaters*).

Martini's friend and collaborator, the Princess von Salm, ranked him among the innovators of French opera. This is perhaps an exaggeration; nonetheless, in *Henri IV* and *Sapho* he contributed to the broadening of subjects and styles thought suitable for secondary theatres, and in his two most successful *opéras comiques* (*L'amoureux de quinze ans* and *Le droit du seigneur*) he proved himself a worthy contemporary of Grétry and Dalayrac. He also wrote symphonies and chamber works; his church music and theoretical writings (both original and translations and adaptations of German ones) were well regarded in his time, but he is best remembered now for his song 'Plaisir d'amour'.

La convalescence de Thémire (divertissement, 1, Gaultier), Fléville, private perf., 20 Feb 1765, *F-Pn* [for the Marchioness of Desarmoises; probably not fully staged]
L'amoureux de quinze ans, ou La double fête (cmda, 3, P. Laujon), Paris, Comédie-Italienne (Bourgogne), 18 April 1771 (Paris, 1771) [for the marriage of the Duke of Bourbon]
Le nouveau-né (cmda, 3, Laujon), Chantilly, private perf., Nov 1772 [for the birth of the Duke of Enghien]
Le fermier cru sourd, ou Les méfiances (cmda, 3, Laujon), Paris, Comédie-Italienne (Bourgogne), 7 Dec 1772
Le rendez-vous bien employé (comédie-parade, 1, L. Anseaume), Paris, Comédie-Italienne (Bourgogne), 10 Feb 1774
Henri IV [Henri IV, ou La bataille d'Ivry] (drame lyrique, 3, B. F. de Rosoi), Paris, Comédie-Italienne (Bourgogne), 14 Nov 1774

(Paris, 1775/R: FO, lxiv [forthcoming]) [for the accession of Louis XVI]

Le droit du seigneur (cmda, 3, F. G. Desfontaines and Laval), Fontainebleau, 17 Oct 1783 (Paris, 1784)

L'amant sylphe, ou La féerie de l'amour (cmda, 3, A.-F. Quétant), Fontainebleau, 24 Oct 1783, lib. Pn; (Paris, 1783)

Annette et Lubin (oc, 1, M.-J.-B. Favart, J. F. Marmontel, J. B. Lourdet de Santerre and C.-S. Favart), Fontainebleau, 6 Feb 1789, Pn; (Paris, 1789)

Sapho (tragédie lyrique, 3, C. M. Pipelet de Leury [later the Princess von Salm-Reifferscheid-Dyck], Paris, Amis de la Patrie [Louvois], 12 Dec 1794 (Paris, 1795); rev. c1805 (?1805), unperf.

Ziméo (opéra, 3, Lourdet de Santerre), Paris, Feydeau, 16 Oct 1800, lib. in Paris, Archives Nationales; (Paris, 1800)

Sophie, ou Le tremblement de terre de Messine, c1800 (opéra, 3), unperf. [cited in Salm-Reifferscheid-Dyck 1841–2]

La maison louée, ou La maison à deux maîtres (cmda, 3, Desfontaines), OC (Feydeau), 30 Aug 1806, lib. in Paris, Archives Nationales

Chanson in Beffroy de Reigny and Chardiny: L'histoire universelle, 1790

Choruses in: Le couvent, ou Le bienfait de la loi [Amélie, ou Le couvent] (drame, 2, J. B. Pujoulx), Feydeau, 3 March 1791

Spurious: Camille, ou Le souterrain, 1796, Pn [attrib. 'Martini', probably by Martín y Soler]; Le poëte supposé, ou Les préparatifs de la fête [lib. of Le nouveau né, rev. Laujon, set by S. Champein, 1782]; La partie de campagne [by L.-E. Jadin, 1810]; Les rendez-vous nocturnes [Fr. trans. of title of play, in It., in repertory of Comédie-Italienne 1740–79, sometimes wrongly confused with Le rendez-vous bien employé]

FétisB; PEM (E. C. Bartlet)

B. Farmian de Rosoi: Dissertation sur le drame lyrique (Paris and The Hague, 1775 [1776])

C. M. von Salm-Reifferscheid-Dyck: Mes soixante ans, ou mes souvenirs politiques et littéraires (Paris, 1833)

——: 'Eloge de Martini', Oeuvres complètes (Paris, 1841–2), iv, 113–28

A. Pougin: 'Martini', Revue et gazette musicale de Paris, xxx (1863), 387–8, 394–5, 401–03; xxxi (1864), 12–13, 19–20, 27–8, 35–6, 67–8; pubd separately (Paris, 1864)

G. Widenbauer: 'J. P. Ägid Martini ein vergessener Oberpfälzer Tondichter', Unser Bayern, iii/10 (1954), 76

D. Charlton: 'The Tragic Seascape: Sapho and its 12-Note Chord', JbO, i (1985), 46–72

M. ELIZABETH C. BARTLET

Martinoty, Jean-Louis (b Etampes, 20 Jan 1946). French producer and administrator. He worked as a radio producer for ORTF, and as a music and dance critic for the newspaper L'humanité, before taking up stage direction as an assistant to Jean-Pierre Ponnelle. Since 1975 he has staged many productions for French and German opera companies, obtaining early critical recognition for his stagings of Baroque operas. His production of Strauss's Ariadne auf Naxos for the Paris Opéra (1983) was also staged at Covent Garden. He was the last administrateur-général of the Paris Opéra at the Palais Garnier (1986–9) before the opening of the Opéra Bastille.

ANDREW CLARK

Martinů, Bohuslav (Jan) (b Polička, east Bohemia, 8 Dec 1890; d Liestal, Switzerland, 28 Aug 1959). Czech composer. He eschewed the ethos of both Czech national opera and Wagnerian music drama in favour of more traditional forms of music theatre such as the commedia dell'arte and medieval mystery plays; in his best-known full-length operas, Julietta and The Greek Passion, he nevertheless produced memorable dramas which sit comfortably in the eclectic operatic tradition of the 20th century. His fascination with experiment led him at an early stage to address film, radio and television as suitable media for opera. Although his operas have not acquired the popularity of those of his older contemporary Janáček, Martinů remains one of the chief representatives, and one of the most prolific composers, of Czech 20th-century opera.

1. Early years and first operas. 2. The experiments of the 1930s. 3. The USA and Europe, 1940–59.

1. EARLY YEARS AND FIRST OPERAS. Martinů's enduring interest in the theatre dated from his earliest years in Polička, the small town on the border of Bohemia and Moravia where he was born. His father, Ferdinand Martinů, drew the young Bohuslav into his enthusiasm for amateur dramatics at the town theatre, whose performance traditions stretched back to the early 19th century and whose repertory, by 1900, included plays in Czech and opera and operetta performed by travelling companies. Folk music, songs and carols also formed a vital part of Martinů's childhood. The composer himself attested to the importance of the view of life gained from the top of the church tower of Polička, where he lived for his first 11 years. The sound of the organ from the church below and the 'church processions and festivals, the fair and the Sundays when people from all around flocked to church' had an effect on such works as Hry o Marii ('The Plays of Mary') and the ballet Špalíček ('The Little Chapbook').

In 1907 Martinů went to Prague, where he studied for two years at the conservatory and one at the Organ School, from which he was expelled in 1910. Far more stimulating for the young composer was the musical and cultural life of the Czech capital. Carmen proved an early love and Martinů developed a liking for Tannhäuser and Der fliegende Holländer, though not for the Ring. He also became familiar with the classics of the Czech repertory and took an interest in Strauss; but one of the most important influences in these early years was his encounter, in 1908, with Debussy's Pelléas et Mélisande performed at the German Theatre.

After gaining a teaching diploma on the violin in 1912, Martinů spent the next few years teaching and playing. To a growing pile of compositions he added a number of melodramas and ballets, including Noc ('Night', 1913–14), a meloplastic scena influenced by the performances of Olga Gzowska at the Prague National Theatre in 1912 and 1914. In 1912 Martinů made sketches for an opera based on Stanisław Przybyszewsky's De profundis which, however, along with later interests in stories by Julius Zeyer and Alois Jirásek, came to nothing. 1917 saw the production of a substantial four-act ballet entitled Koleda ('Christmas Carols'), which anticipated Špalíček in subject matter and the use of voices. Martinů continued to produce a steady stream of ballets including Istar (1924), Kdo je na světě nejmocnější? ('Who is the most powerful in the world?', 1925) and Vzpoura ('The Revolt', 1928), all of which were staged in Prague or Brno.

Martinů's first opera dates from his early years in Paris, where he settled in 1923 and, with the exception of long holidays in Czechoslovakia, remained until June 1940. By the early 1920s his musical style was heavily influenced by that of Debussy, to which was added in 1922 a profound respect for the polyphony of the Elizabethan and Jacobean madrigal. Martinů's move to Paris was not made simply to pursue musical interests but, in the composer's own words, 'to find the real foundations on which Western culture rests'. From November 1923 he studied with Roussel; although his compositional style developed considerably under the French composer's tutelage, there is little sign of direct influence. Stravinsky's music, in particular *The Wedding*, had a more palpable effect on Martinů's musical style, which continued to reflect his influence as late as the last act of *The Greek Passion*.

From August 1926 to 19 June 1927, Martinů worked on his first opera, *Voják a tanečnice* ('The Soldier and the Dancer'), to a libretto based on Plautus's *Pseudolus* by J. L. Budín (pseudonym of Jan Löwenbach). *The Soldier and the Dancer* already epitomized the eclectic kind of theatre Martinů was to favour in a number of later operas, incorporating elements of operetta, dance-band music and jazz alongside appearances from the authors Plautus and Molière, *buffo* intermezzos and the interference of a critic at the end of the first act. Martinů's developing friendship with the French poet Georges Ribemont-Dessaignes led to the surreal one-act opera *Les larmes du couteau* (composed in 1928). Both the orchestration of the work, including saxophone and banjo, and the musical language reflect a continuing pre-occupation with jazz. The grotesque aspects of the scenario, dominated by Satan in a number of guises including those of a racing cyclist and a hanged man, reveal the composer's interest in parody and film techniques.

In 1928 Martinů and Ribemont-Dessaignes began work on a far more practical collaborative operatic project, *Les trois souhaits, ou Les vicissitudes de la vie*, known in Czech as *Trojí* (or *Tři*) *přání*. Film provides a large part of the action and motivation for this full-length opera in which surreal elements blend with tableaux depicting scenes from everyday life. The score still shows strong jazz influences and a flexible technique that blends a wide range of elements including neo-classical pastiche, dance-band music and barbershop singing. A further project with Ribemont-Dessaignes, *La semaine de bonté*, on which Martinů and the poet worked in 1930, was never completed.

2. THE EXPERIMENTS OF THE 1930s. The chief theatre project of the early 1930s, a time when Martinů was turning to chamber music, was the folk ballet *Špalíček*, composed in 1931–2 and revised in 1940, an extended and brilliant evocation of folk customs that includes episodes amounting to miniature operas. *The Plays of Mary*, a sequence of medieval miracle plays, led directly on from *Špalíček* in its use of a nationally inflected musical style. Composed in 1933–4, *The Plays of Mary* was a deliberate attempt to extend the range of Czech opera by reference to medieval drama. Martinů's successful blend of national elements and a tight musical-dramatic structure was recognized by the award of a Czechoslovak state prize in October 1935.

Martinů continued to explore the possibilities of new media for opera in two works composed in 1935 to commissions from Czechoslovak Radio, *Hlas lesa* ('The Voice of the Forest') and the work that was to become one of his most popular operas, *Veselohra na mostě* ('The Comedy on the Bridge'). These vivid scores provide a brilliant evocation of the subject matter of the two operas. The simplicity of means and effective characterization, in particular in Klicpera's farce *Veselohra na mostě*, fulfil perfectly the requirements for radio opera.

In between composing the two radio operas, Martinů began work in June 1935 on *Divadlo za branou* ('The Suburban Theatre') to his own libretto. Completed the following year, the work was based on ideas from Molière and Jean Gaspard Debureau and on Czech folk-song texts. The work is a further extension of operatic technique by reference to earlier theatrical traditions, this time *commedia dell'arte*. *The Suburban Theatre* was also Martinů's last opera to make use, by direct quotation, of Czech folk elements. His next opera, *Julietta*, was a significant departure from the directness and simplicity of the other theatre works written in the 1930s. Martinů worked on *Julietta* throughout the second half of 1936, completing the opera in January 1937. Neveux was deeply impressed by the theatrical instinct Martinů displayed in reducing his original play, a reaction echoed by others of the composer's collaborators, including Nikos Kazantzakis in the 1950s. Martinů returned to the *opera buffa* elements of *The Suburban Theatre* in a short one-act opera, *Alexandre bis*, composed in 1937 to a libretto by André Wurmser.

The successful première of *Julietta* at the National Theatre in Prague in 1938 marked the end of an intensive decade of operatic endeavour. During the same period Martinů's style had acquired a national dimension, a greater urgency of utterance and a convincing energy under the influence of the Baroque concerto grosso, displayed at its finest in the Double Concerto for two string orchestras, piano and timpani of 1938. Throughout these years of considerable compositional activity, Martinů had resisted offers of a teaching post in Brno. Extended visits to Czechoslovakia and strong links with influential musical figures such as Václav Talich ensured an effective relationship with the musical institutions of his native land. The outbreak of World War II not only cut Martinů off from family and friends, it denied him ready access to theatrical production. In July 1940 he fled with his wife, Charlotte, to Provence and finally, in March 1941, via Marseilles and Lisbon, arrived in New York.

3. THE USA AND EUROPE, 1940–59. The war years in the USA were at first marked by considerable financial difficulty for the Martinůs until their circumstances were improved by commissions, notably from Koussevitzky. Partly because of these orchestral commissions, Martinů devoted most of his energies in the USA to the composition of his first five symphonies, written between 1942 and 1946. He had certainly intended to return to Czechoslovakia after the war, but the Communist takeover in his native land in 1948 and the machinations of unfriendly parties in Prague set him against such a move. Although opportunities arose and Martinů expressed a desire on more than one occasion to return to Czechoslovakia, he remained an exile for the rest of his life. On 25 July 1946 his personal circumstances took a further downturn when he suffered a serious head injury as the result of a fall. His slow and expensive recuperation led to further economic hardship and delays to plans for a return to Europe.

Martinů gradually recovered his earlier productivity and, supported by composition and teaching, continued to live in the USA until 1952. He did not return to opera until 1951, the year in which, beginning on 28 May, *The Comedy on the Bridge* had a highly successful run of performances in New York. A setting of Tolstoy's story *What Men Live By*, composed in 1951–2 to an English libretto by the composer, was presented on television in New York in May 1953. This was followed by a setting of Gogol's *The Marriage*, once again to an English libretto by the composer, for television performance in New York.

A seven-month stay in Europe in 1952, including visits to France, Italy and Austria, prefaced a permanent return in 1953. A further visit to Italy in 1954 led to the composition of the orchestral *Fresky Piera della Francesca* of 1955 and the three-act opera *Mirandolina*, based on Goldoni's *La locandiera*, composed between December 1953 and July 1954. Before beginning work on *Mirandolina* Martinů had made a substantial start on an opera based on Neveux' *Plainte contre inconnu*, in Nice during October 1953, but the work was never completed.

In September 1954 Martinů expressed a strong desire to write an opera based on Czech subject matter, but he was diverted by his enthusiasm for the work of Nikos Kazantzakis. He first considered *Alexis Zorba* as a possible libretto but settled on *Christ Recrucified*, which became *The Greek Passion* (*Řecke pašije*). The composition of the opera occupied Martinů from February 1956 until January 1959, the year of his death. While at work on it he also composed, in May–June 1958, the one-act opera *Ariane* based on Neveux' play *Le voyage de Thésée*. Although Martinů followed news of the first production of *Mirandolina* in Prague, on 17 May 1959, he did not attend the première. In his last year he showed a renewed interest in Jirásek's play *Lucerna* as a possible operatic subject, but after the completion of the final revision of *The Greek Passion* his operatic activities were confined to a French translation of *Julietta*. He died on 28 August 1959 in a sanatorium in Liestal, near Pratteln, Switzerland.

Martinů's operatic creativity attests to the breadth and variety of his literary interests as well as to his own abilities as a librettist. The style of his operas developed in tandem with his interests outside music and reflects a preoccupation with folk idioms in the mid-1930s to which he returned in *What Men Live By* and *The Greek Passion*. Whereas the early works show a lively interest in the music of the world around him, including jazz and dance-band music, those of the late 1930s, in particular *Julietta*, benefit from Martinů's attraction to the motoric power of the Baroque concerto grosso. Skilled in pastiche and the evocation of older operatic forms, as for example in *The Suburban Theatre*, *Alexandre bis* and the coloratura aria in *Ariane*, Martinů was also capable of producing natural declamation, in particular when setting Czech, but frequently also in his librettos in French, Italian and English. While there are passages in his operas that share a tendency with some of the instrumental works to craftsmanship which can at times seem routine, Martinů always shows a keen theatrical instinct and an understanding of drama which place his finest operas among the most effective of the century.

See also ARIANE (ii); GREEK PASSION, THE; HRY O MARII; JULIETTA; MIRANDOLINA; TROIS SOUHAITS, LES; and VESELOHRA NA MOSTĚ.

H – no. in Halbreich

Voják a tanečnice [Soldier and Dancer] H162 (3, J. L. Budín [J. Löwenbach], after Plautus: *Pseudolus*), Brno, National, 5 May 1928

Les larmes du couteau [Slzy nože] H169, 1928 (1, G. Ribemont-Dessaignes), Brno, State, 22 Oct 1969

Les trois souhaits, ou Les vicissitudes de la vie [Trojí (Tří) přání] H175, 1928–9 (film op, prelude, 3, postlude, Ribemont-Dessaignes), Brno, State, 16 June 1971

Hry o Marii [The Plays of Mary] H236 (4-pt operatic cycle), Brno, Provincial, 23 Feb 1935
  Prolog: Panny moudré a panny pošetilé [The Wise and Foolish Virgins] (V. Nezval, after 12th-century Fr.)
  Mariken z Nimègue [Mary of Nijmegen] (V. Závada, after 15th-century Flemish, trans. H. Ghéon)
  Narození Páně [The Nativity of Our Lord] (Moravian folk poetry)

Sestra Paskalina [Sister Pasqualina] (Martinů, after J. Zeyer and folk poetry)

Hlas lesa [The Voice of the Forest] H243 (radio op, 1, Nezval), Czech Radio, Prague, 6 Oct 1935

Divadlo za branou [The Suburban Theatre] H252 (ballet pantomime [Act 1], ob [Acts 2–3], 3, Martinů, after folk poetry, Molière and J. G. Debureau), Brno, Zemské, 20 Sept 1936

Veselohra na mostě [The Comedy on the Bridge] H251 (radio op, 1, Martinů, after V. K. Klicpera), Czech Radio, Prague, 18 March 1937

Alexandre bis H255, 1937 (1, A. Wurmser), Mannheim, National, 10 Feb 1964

Julietta [Snář (The Book of Dreams)] H253 (3, Martinů, after G. Neveux: *Juliette, ou La clé des songes*), Prague, National, 16 March 1938

What Men Live By [Čím lide žijí] H336, 1951–2 (1, Martinů, after L. Tolstoy), televised, New York, May 1953

The Marriage [Ženitba] H341, 1952 (Martinů, after N. Gogol), NBC TV, New York, 7 Feb 1953

Mirandolina H346, 1953–4 (3, Martinů, after C. Goldoni: *La locandiera*), Prague, National, 17 May 1959

Ariane [Ariadna] H370, 1958 (1, Martinů, after Neveux: *Le voyage de Thésée*), Gelsenkirchen, 2 March 1961

The Greek Passion [Řecké pašije] H372, 1956–9 (4, Martinů, after N. Kazantzakis: *Christ Recrucified*), Zürich, Stadt, 9 June 1961

Unfinished: La semaine de bonté [Týden dobročinnosti] H194 (3, Ribemont-Dessaignes, after I. Erenburg); Plainte contre inconnu [Žaloba proti neznámému] H344, 1953 (Martinů, after Neveux) [1 act sketched]

M. Šafránek: *Bohuslav Martinů: the Man and his Music* (London, 1946)

——: 'Martinů und das musikalische Theater', *Musica* (1959), no.12

——: *Bohuslav Martinů: his Life and Works* (London, 1962)

J. Mihule: *Bohuslav Martinů v obrazech* [Martinů in Pictures] (Prague, 1964)

R. Pečman: *Stage Works of Martinů* (Prague, 1967)

H. Halbreich: *Martinů: Werkverzeichnis, Dokumentation und Biographie* (Zürich, 1968)

J. Bajer: 'Martinů a evropska divadelní avantgarda', *HRo*, xxiv (1971), 365

C. Martinů: *Ma vie avec Bohuslav Martinů* (Prague, 1971; Eng. trans., 1978)

J. Mihule: *Martinů* (Prague, 1972)

B. Large: *Martinů* (London, 1975)

——: 'Martinů's Julietta', *Opera*, xxix (1978), 352–6

M. Šafránek: *Divadlo Bohuslava Martinů* (Prague, 1979)

Bohuslav Martinů: Prague 1981 [incl. R. Pečman: 'Bohuslav Martinůs Musiktheater und seine Beziehung zur Welt der Antike', 78–85; R. Vonásek: 'Gesang und Schauspielkunst in den Opern von Bohuslav Martinů', 95–9; J. Bajer: 'Zur Frage der Beziehungen von Bohuslav Martinů zur europäischen Theateravantgarde', 152–6; E. Vítová: 'Zur Tradition der Inszenierung von Bohuslav Martinůs Opern auf der Bühne des Staatstheaters in Brno', 283–9]

JAN SMACZNY

Martinucci, Nicola (*b* Taranto, 28 March 1941). Italian tenor. He studied in Milan and made his début at the Teatro Nuovo there in 1966 as Manrico, which he repeated at La Scala. Engagements followed at principal Italian centres, including the Florence Maggio Musicale, where he sang King Philip in a revival of Spontini's *Agnese von Hohenstaufen*. A *spinto* tenor of much elegance, firmness and body, with clear diction and secure if sometimes inflexible delivery, he has appeared elsewhere in Europe, in New York and Buenos Aires, and made his Covent Garden début in 1985 as Dick Johnson in *La fanciulla del West*, returning in 1990 as Calaf (*Turandot*). Puccini, Verdi, Mascagni and Bizet have been central to his developing repertory, which also includes Pollione and Turiddu; among his recordings are the title role in *Poliuto* and Calaf (both 1989).

NOËL GOODWIN

Martín y Soler, (Atanasio Martín Ignacio) Vicente (Tadeo Francesco Pellegrin) [Martini, Vincenzo, lo Spagnuolo (il Valenziano); Martini, Ignaz] (*b* Valencia, 2 May 1754; *d* St Petersburg, 30 Jan/10 Feb 1806). Italian composer.

1. LIFE. Born and raised in Valencia, he entered the service of the Prince of Asturias, the future Charles IV of Spain, in about 1776, the year in which his first opera was probably given in Madrid. By November 1777 he was working in Naples, where he wrote ballets and then serious operas for Ferdinand I of the Two Sicilies, brother of the Prince of Asturias, and Maria Carolina, sister of Emperor Joseph II; among them was the festive opera on the state visit in 1782 of Paul Petrovich, the future Paul I of Russia.

Martín moved to Venice in 1782 and henceforth, with a single exception, he wrote only comic operas. He may have become acquainted with Nancy Storace in Venice, but she did not sing in either of his Venetian operas (as Kelly reports). In 1783 the court theatre in Turin chose Martín's *In amor ci vuol destrezza* (retitled *L'accorta cameriera*) for the state visit of Archduke Ferdinand, Joseph II's brother. Another court commission came from the Duke of Parma, cousin of the Prince of Asturias, and his consort Maria Amalia, sister of Emperor Joseph II. In 1785 Martín moved to Vienna, where he received three commissions for comic operas from the court theatre. This period represents the peak of his career, as well as the high point in the Italian opera established by Joseph; *Il burbero di buon cuore* (1786), *Una cosa rara* (1786) and *L'arbore di Diana* (1787) are artistic triumphs associated with Joseph's regime. The second and third were immensely popular, and *L'arbore di Diana* was the most performed Italian opera of the 70 given at the Burgtheater between 1783 and 1792. Da Ponte credited the launching of his career as a librettist to his first collaboration with Martín.

Before the première of *L'arbore di Diana*, Martín had been appointed Kapellmeister to the Russian court, a position apparently created for him by Catherine the Great. Felicitious though the appointment was in terms of prestige and financial security, it spelt the end of his artistic growth; except for his brief excursion to London, he composed nothing further of any consequence. Cimarosa was the court opera composer, so when Martín took up his position in 1788 he had no association with the Italian opera company but provided music for the royal residence. This included productions of *Una cosa rara* and *L'arbore di Diana* in Russian, and also commissions for comic operas in Russian. In 1789 Martín wrote a comic opera in Russian to a libretto by Catherine herself (a satire on her enemy, the Swedish King Gustavus III), and another the following year. His apparent success in setting the Russian language led to a four-year contract in October 1790 as director and composer of the Russian opera, but in the event he wrote only ballets. In 1793 Sarti replaced Cimarosa as the principal Italian opera composer, and Martín left St Petersburg in August 1794.

His destination was London, where he resumed collaboration with Da Ponte, now librettist at the King's Theatre. Martín composed two operas for the 1794–5 season. The first, *La scuola dei maritati*, was one of the most frequently performed operas that season. The second, *L'isola del piacere*, fared less well; Da Ponte recounted that during composition their collaboration

broke down, and it received only four performances. For its second performance, a benefit concert for himself, Martín assembled an intermezzo *Le nozze de' contadini spagnuoli*, performed only once and consisting of nine numbers including the overture of *L'arbore di Diana* and five pieces from *Una cosa rara*. By early 1796 Martín was back in St Petersburg. He wrote his last opera for Paul I, who had succeeded Catherine, and thereafter supported himself with teaching and administrative work until his death.

2. OPERAS. Martín's contemporaries perceived a distinctive quality in his music. The term 'song style' perhaps captures the essence of his personal manner: its main features are melody-dominated, three-voice texture, periodicity in rhythm, phrasing and form, and above all a non-dramatic or lyrical nature. Within the limitations of this style, he shows a much-admired skill for variety and unexpected charm, devising endless patterns of textual and musical repetition, particularly in combination with underlying dance rhythms. Here his music departs from what Dent describes as the 'pretty 6/8 tunes of the "Here we go round the mulberry bush" type'. Perhaps most striking is his blending of styles, his ability to impart varying degrees of lyricism to the *buffo* and *seria* numbers while staying within their conventions. His contemporaries consistently used the words 'sweet' and 'graceful' to describe his music. The melodies take the shape of an arch or a turn, remain solidly diatonic and often rely on the structural interval of a 3rd (ex.1) or a recurring pitch that functions as a

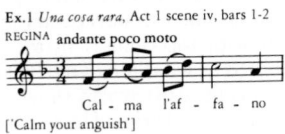

Ex.1 *Una cosa rara*, Act 1 scene iv, bars 1–2
REGINA andante poco moto

Cal - ma l'af - fa - no
['Calm your anguish']

Ex.2 *Una cosa rara*, Act 1 scene v, bars 11–15
PRINCIPE
andantino amoroso

Più bian - ca di gi - glio più fres - ca di ro - sa
['Whiter than a lily, fresher than a rose']

brief internal pedal point (ex.2). This, and elsewhere drones, suggest a pastoral quality in the music. Many of his melodies are in the 'rustic' metres of the contredanse or in 6/8 time, as in Mozart's allusion to Martín's style in the dinner music of *Don Giovanni*. The composer's fondness for delicate orchestral colouring finds gratification in the characteristic *amoroso* winds of the pastoral.

Martín's operatic style developed in collaboration with Da Ponte, who provided him with librettos suitable to his lyrical genius. But this was not as yet the case in their first joint effort, *Il burbero di buon cuore*. For this libretto, after a Goldoni comedy of character (revolving around Ferramondo, an impatient bachelor with a bankrupt nephew and a marriageable niece, whose poor communication skills give rise to humorous complications of plot), Martín provided a conventional musical setting with a mixture of *buffo* and *seria* numbers and two arias in song style. But with their second opera, *Una cosa rara*, they found their formula for success. Da Ponte promoted the use of song style by expanding on the pastoral tendencies of his literary model, and Martín experimented with the blending of styles in addition to traditional *buffo* and *seria* numbers. Encouraged by the opera's overwhelming success, Da Ponte constructed *L'arbore di Diana* as a typical pastoral, and Martín composed almost all the numbers in song style and blended style. Along with the increasing use of song style, the proportion of ensembles to solo numbers increased over the course of the three operas. As the number of ensembles increases, so does the number of single-tempo ensembles. Many of them are in song style, in the manner of an aria *a 3* for example, or a chorus of voices in the same range. In *L'arbore di Diana* like-voice grouping is built into the libretto; the characters are presented in sets of three nymphs and three youths, which recombine to form other sets. Such groupings form the basis of the ensemble writing in the opera, either as trios or as the nucleus of larger ensembles. A quartet, for example, is conceived as a three-voice chorus to which an independent fourth voice is added.

For their London opera *La scuola dei maritati*, Da Ponte wrote a Goldoniesque comedy of character about the marriage of an older man to a young, second wife whose capriciousness and vanity make him and his household miserable. Martín composed half the numbers in a lyrically modified *buffo* style and half in song style. For *L'isola del piacere*, Martín and Da Ponte produced a pastoral opera modelled on *L'arbore di Diana*. This time Arcadia is located on a Turkish island, giving rise to some 'Turkish' music. As in *L'arbore*, the like-voice groupings again account for the nature of the ensemble writing as well as the large number of ensembles.

Martín's contemporaries uniformly identified him as a composer for the amateur, usually approvingly. That he catered to the taste of the public, whose approbation in turn encouraged him to develop his lyrical style, is borne out by the publication of favourite numbers which were uniformly in song style. These included the vocal canons, the presence of which in *Una cosa rara*, *L'arbore di Diana* and *La scuola dei maritati* can be understood in this context.

See also ARBORE DI DIANA, L', and COSA RARA, UNA.

La Madrileña, o Tutor burlado (zar), ?Madrid, 1776

Ifigenia in Aulide (dramma per musica, 3, L. Serio), Caserta, 12 Jan 1779, *I-Nc, P-La*

Ipermestra (os, 3, P. Metastasio), Naples, S Carlo, 30 May 1780, *I-Nc, P-La*

Andromaca (dramma per musica, 3, A. Zeno), Turin, Regio, 26 Dec 1780

Astartea (os, 3), Lucca, Pubblico, carn. 1782

Partenope (componimento drammatico, 2, Metastasio), Naples, Accademia, Feb 1782

L'amor geloso (azione teatrale comica, 2), Naples, Fondo, sum. 1782

In amor ci vuol destrezza (ob, 2, C. Lanfranchi-Rossi), Venice, S Samuele, aut. 1782; as L'accorta cameriera (dg), with prol. La dora festeggiata (C. Oliveri), Turin, Regio, Sept 1783; *La, US-Wc*

Vologeso (dramma per musica, 3, Zeno, rev. A. Cigna), Turin, Regio, carn. 1783, *P-La*

Le burle per amore (dg, 2, M. Bernardini), Venice, S Samuele, carn. 1784, *B-Bc*

La vedova spiritosa (dg, 2), Parma, Ducale, carn. 1785, *A-Wgm, US-Wc*

Il burbero di buon cuore (dg, 2, L. da Ponte, after C. Goldoni: *Le bourru bienfaisant*), Vienna, Burg, 4 Jan 1786, *A-Wn, B-Bc, D-Dlb, Rtt, F-Pc, RU-SPtob, US-Bp, Wc* (2 copies)

Una cosa rara, o sia Bellezza ed onestà [Lilla, oder Schönheit und Tugend] (dg, 2, Da Ponte, after Vélez de Guevara: *La luna della Sierra*), Vienna, Burg, 17 Nov 1786, *A-KR, Wgm, Wn* (2 copies), *B-Bc, Br, C-Lu, D-Bds, Dlb* (3 copies), *SWl, SWth, WRdn, DK-Kk, F-Pc, Pn, R(m), GB-Lbl, Lcm, I-Fc* (2 copies), *Mc, MOe, Nc, PAas, PAc, NL-At* (2 copies), *P-La, RU-SPtob, S-Sk, US-Wc* (2 copies), vs (Vienna, 1786; Munich, *c*1790; Bonn, n.d.), ed. G. Allroggen (Munich, 1990)

L'arbore di Diana [Der Baum der Diana] (dg, 2, Da Ponte), Vienna, Burg, 1 Oct 1787, *A-Ee, Wgm, Wn* (3 copies), *B-Bc, Br, D-Bds, Dlb, Ds, SWth, EIRE-Dtc, F-Pc, GB-Lbl, Lcm, I-Fc* (2 copies), *Gl, P-La, RU-SPtob, US-NYp, R, Wc*, vs (Vienna, 1787; Bonn, 1796)

Gorebogatïr Kosometovich [The Sorrowful Hero Kosometovich] (play with music, 5, Catherine II and A. V. Khrapovitsky), St Petersburg, Hermitage, 29 Jan/9 Feb 1789, *RU-SPtob*, vs (St Petersburg, 1789)

Pesnolyubie [Melomania] (play with music, 3, Khrapovitsky), St Petersburg, Hermitage, 7/18 Jan 1790, *SPtob* (orch pts)

Fedul s det'mi [Fedul and his Children] (play with music, 1, Catherine II and Khrapovitsky), St Petersburg, Hermitage, 16/27 Jan 1791, *SPtob*, vs (Moscow, 1895), collab. Pashkevich

La scuola dei maritati [La capricciosa corretta; Gli sposi in contrasto; La moglie corretta] (comic op, 2, Da Ponte), London, King's, 27 Jan 1795, *A-Wn, D-Ds, I-Fc* (2 copies), *Gl, Nc, US-Wc*, vs (Vienna, 1796; Bonn, 1797)

L'isola del piacere [L'isola piacevole] (comic op, 2, Da Ponte), London, King's, 26 May 1795, *B-Bc, I-Fc* (2 copies)

Camille, ou Le souterrain (comédie mêlée de musique, 3, B.-J. Marsollier des Vivetières), St Petersburg, private perf., 19Feb/1 March 1796, *F-Pn* [attrib. 'Martini', probably Martín y Soler]

La festa del villaggio (op comica, 2, ? F. Moretti), St Petersburg, Hermitage, 15/26 Jan 1798, *A-Wn, I-Fc, RU-SPtob*

*

L. da Ponte: *Memorie* (New York, 1823–7, enlarged 2/1829–30); Eng. trans., ed. L. A. Sheppard (London, 1929)

M. Kelly: *Reminiscences of the King's Theatre* (London, 1826, 2/ 1826); ed. R. Fiske (London, 1975)

F.-J. Fétis: 'Noticias biográficas de D. Vicente Martín', *Gaceta musical de Madrid*, i (1855), 45

B. Saldoni: 'Apuntes biográficos del célebre maestro español Don Vicente Martín conocido … por Martini lo Spagnuolo', *Heraldo de las artes, de las letras y de los espectáculos* [Madrid] (14 Dec 1871)

R. G[enée]: ' "Una cosa rara" in Mozarts "Don Juan" ', *Mitteilungen für die Mozart-Gemeinde Berlin*, i (1900), 63–5

'Vinzenz Martín, der Komponist von "Una cosa rara" ', *Mitteilungen für die Mozart-Gemeinde Berlin*, ii (1906), 23–5

E. Walter: 'Mozarts Nebensonnen', *Mitteilungen der Salzburger Festspielhausgemeinde*, iv/5–6 (1921), 5–8; repr. in *Der Auftakt*, v (1925), 102–4

R. A. Mooser: 'Un musicien espagnol en Russie', *RMI*, xl (1936), 432–49

I. Salvat: 'Vicenç Martín i Soler i la seva òpera "Una cosa rara o sia bellezza ed onestà" ', *Revista musical catalana*, xxxiii (1936), 144–9

A. Loewenberg: 'Lorenzo da Ponte in London', *MR*, iv (1943), 171–89

R.-A. Mooser: *Annales de la musique et des musiciens en Russie au XVIIIme siècle* (Geneva, 1948–51)

U. Prota-Giurleo: 'Del compositore spagnuolo Vincente Martín y Soler', *Archivi*, xxvii (1960), 145–56

R. Jesson: 'Una cosa rara', *MT*, cix (1968), 619–21

O. Michtner: *Das alte Burgtheater als Opernbühne: von der Einführung des deutschen Singspiels (1778) bis zum Tod Kaiser Leopolds II (1792)* (Vienna, 1970)

R. Jesson: 'Martín y Soler's "L'arbore di Diana" ', *MT*, cxiii (1972), 551–3

D. Link: 'The Viennese Operatic Canon and Mozart's "Così fan tutte" ', *Mitteilungen der Internationalen Stiftung Mozarteum*, xxxviii (1990), 111–21

——: *The Da Ponte Operas of Vicente Martín y Soler* (diss., U. of Toronto, 1991)   DOROTHEA LINK

Marton [née Heinrich], **Eva** (*b* Budapest, 18 June 1943). Hungarian soprano. She studied in Budapest, making her début there in 1968 as the Queen of Shemakha. From 1972 to 1977 she was engaged at Frankfurt; she made her Metropolitan début in 1976 as Eva, and at Bayreuth sang Elisabeth and Venus (1977–8). She has appeared in Vienna, Florence, Berlin, Paris, Brussels, Zürich, Hamburg, Chicago and Verona, and at La Scala and Covent Garden, where she made her début as Turandot (1987). In 1982 she sang Leonore at Salzburg and in 1985 Brünnhilde at San Francisco; among her other roles are Donna Anna, Elsa, Ortrud, Aida,

Elisabeth de Valois (*Don Carlos*), Leonora (*Il trovatore* and *Forza del destino*), La Gioconda, Maddalena (*Andrea Chénier*), Fedora, Tosca, Chrysothemis, Strauss's Electra, the Empress (*Die Frau ohne Schatten*) and Dyer's Wife, which she sang at Salzburg in 1992. She has a powerful voice with a gleaming top register and can sing Italian and German music with equal facility.

A. Blyth: 'Eva Marton', *Opera*, xli (1990), 276–82

ELIZABETH FORBES

Marttinen, Tauno (*b* Helsinki, 27 Sept 1912). Finnish composer. He studied with Selim Palmgren and Wladimir Vogel, and thereafter worked in Hämeenlinna as conductor of the city orchestra (1949–59) and director of the music school (1950–75). An energetic composer, he writes fluently; although some of his work is lightweight, at its best it has an individual imaginativeness, and in the operas the flowing quality is balanced by a feeling for the dramatic. The operas reach from a humorous Finnish national romantic style (*Kihlaus, Tulitikkuja lainaamassa*) to a Bergian psychological expressionism (*Poltettu oranssi*).

selective list

Päällysviitta [The Cloak] (television op, 1, after N. V. Gogol), 1964, Finnish TV
Kihlaus [The Engagement] (oc, 1, A. Kivi), Helsinki, 12 June 1966
Tulitikkuja lainaamassa [Borrowing Matches] (oc, 3, M. Lassila), Helsinki, 20 Aug 1966
Lea (2, Kivi), Turku, 19 Sept 1968
Poltettu oranssi [Burnt Orange] (television op, 3, E.-L. Manner), Finnish TV, 6 Oct 1971; stage, Helsinki, Finnish National Opera, 3 Nov 1975
Mestari Patelin [Master Patelin], 1974 (2, after an old Fr. tale) Hämeenlinna, 31 July 1983
Psykiatri [The Psychiatrist] (1, Marttinen), Bayreuth [opera course], 1975
Laestadiuksen saarna [The Sermon of Laestadius] (3, N. Out-akoski), Oulu, 29 April 1976
Meedio [The Medium] (chamber op, 1, Marttinen), Hämeenlinna, 1978
Jaarlin sisar [The Sister of a Jarl] (ballad op, 2, V. Isomäki), Hämeenlinna, 3 April 1979
Suuren joen laulu [The Song of a Big River] (2, T. Yrjänä), Kemi, 2 May 1982
Faaraon kirje [The Letter of the Pharaoh] (3, E. Mutru), Tampere, 18 Oct 1982
Häät [The Wedding] (chamber op, 1, A. Tšehov), Helsinki, 31 Jan 1986

T.-M. Lehtonen and P. Hako, eds.: *Kuninkaasta kuninkaaseen* [From King to King] (Juva, 1987), 199–217

ERKKI SALMENHAARA

Martyr [née Thornton], **Margaret** (*d* London, 7 June 1807). English soprano and actress. Margaret Thornton sang at Vauxhall Gardens before making her stage début as Rosetta in *Love in a Village* (1779). She married in 1780 and appeared regularly at Covent Garden until 1804. Hailed by Bellamy as 'Catley's pupil – Catley's boast', she imitated that singer's arch manner and staccato style of singing. Her trim figure and 'black rolling eye' fitted her for breeches roles and she acted (with a song by Shield) the Cherubino part in *The Follies of a Day: or, The Marriage of Figaro* (1784). She was Phoebe in the première of Shield's *Rosina* and Dolly in his *The Woodman*. Her husband died in a debtors' prison in 1783 and she lived with the oboist W. T. Parke from 1784.

BDA; LS
A. Pasquin [pseud. of J. Williams]: *The Children of Thespis*, iii (London, 1788, 13/1792)
T. Bellamy: *The London Theatres* (London, 1795)
J. Roach: *Authentic Memoirs of the Green Room* (London, 1796)
C. H. Wilson: *The Myrtle and Vine* (London, 1802)

OLIVE BALDWIN, THELMA WILSON

Martyrdom of St Magnus, The. Chamber opera in nine scenes by PETER MAXWELL DAVIES to his own libretto after George Mackay Brown's novel *Magnus*; Kirkwall, St Magnus Cathedral, 17 June 1977.

Davies's treatment of the historical events that led to the death of Orkney's patron saint was composed for the first St Magnus Festival, Orkney, of which Davies was artistic director. It follows Mackay Brown's novel in making Magnus (baritone) a universalized victim, an idealist sacrificed to satisfy the demands of collective brutality and political expediency. His death at the hands of his rival, Hakon, Earl of Orkney (baritone), is charted from the schematic Battle of Menai Strait (where Magnus's pacifist instincts are first revealed) to the peace conference on the island of Egilsay and Hakon's planning of the murder. The action then moves forward to the present day so that the execution can become that of a political prisoner prepared to die for his beliefs. The opera returns to the 12th century for the final scene, which records the first miracle at Magnus's tomb, when Blind Mary (soprano), the seer-prophetess who throughout the opera has represented the conscience and spirit of the people of Orkney, has her sight restored, and Magnus is accorded his place among the northern saints.

Davies requires five singers to take 26 roles: the accompanying ensemble consists of 11 instrumentalists. After the expressionist extremes of his music-theatre works of the later 1960s, the cool, restrained vocal writing, continually coloured by plainchant, and the lucid, precise scoring of this chamber opera reflect the influence of Orkney on his style in the 1970s. Britten's church parables are one distant stylistic mode, while Eliot's verse dramas suggest a theatrical precedent, though echoes of earlier phases in Davies's development (the persistent use of plainchant transformations and the musical parodies that signal the progress from the 12th century to the present) emerge in the course of the work.

ANDREW CLEMENTS

Martyrs, Les. Opera by Gaetano Donizetti; *see* POLIUTO.

Marusin, Yury (*b* Perm', 8 Dec 1947). Russian tenor. He studied in St Petersburg, where he made his début at the Maliy Theatre in 1972. After further study in Milan (1977–8) he joined the Kirov Opera, making his British début in 1987 with that company at Covent Garden as Lensky, also singing Hermann and Grigory. He has sung the Tsarevich (*The Tale of Tsar Saltan*) at La Scala and Reggio Emilia (1988), Golitsïn (*Khovanshchina*) at the Vienna Staatsoper (1989), Anatol Kuragin (*War and Peace*) at the Kirov and in San Francisco, and Prince Andrey Khovansky at Edinburgh (1991). His roles also include Faust, Rodolfo, Pinkerton, the Duke, Alfredo, Don Carlos, Don Alvaro and Vaudémont (*Iolanta*). Although the strong beat in his voice is not to all tastes he is a powerful singing actor, specially effective as Hermann, which he has sung in Toronto, Nice, Turin, Madrid and at Glyndebourne (1992).

ELIZABETH FORBES

Maruxa. *Egloga lírica* in two acts by AMADEO VIVES to a libretto by Luis Pascal Frutos; Madrid, Teatro de la Zarzuela, 28 May 1914.

One of Vives's greatest successes, this pastoral is set in Galicia; it uses Galician elements such as the *gaita*, the local form of bagpipe, and some characters sing not in Spanish but in the Galician dialect, but apart from a *muñeira* danced by country folk in Act 2 there is no quotation of folk music. The story is an intrigue in which the shepherdess Maruxa (soprano) and the shepherd Pablo (baritone) are in love, but Rosa (soprano), the young owner of an estate, though engaged to her cousin Antonio (tenor), wants Pablo for herself. Antonio hopes to arouse her jealousy by pursuing Maruxa, whom Rosa takes into her service. Ostensibly on Maruxa's behalf, Rosa writes a note to the now separated Pablo, asking for a meeting; but the factor Rufo (bass), determined to prevent a scandal, so arranges matters that Rosa and Antonio (who have both disguised themselves) embrace each other by mistake in the dark, while Maruxa and Pablo go off happily together. Most of the opera's highlights are in Act 2: the orchestral prelude, the folk-dancing and storm, and Pablo's romance 'Aquí, n'este sitio'.   LIONEL SALTER

Mary, Queen of Scots. Opera in three acts by THEA MUSGRAVE to her own libretto after Amalia Elguera's play *Moray*; Edinburgh, King's Theatre, 6 September 1977.

The opera is set in Scotland at the time of Mary's reign (1561–8). In Act 1, Mary (soprano) arrives from France to be met by her half-brother, the Earl of Moray (baritone), and by the Scottish baron Bothwell (tenor). They contend for influence at court, but Mary favours the Englishman Darnley (tenor), heir to both English and Scottish thrones. At Holyrood, Bothwell and his men disrupt courtly dances with a lusty Scottish reel. Bothwell quarrels with the queen's minstrel, Riccio (tenor), and is banished from court, while Moray retires in anger at the queen's decision to marry Darnley. In Act 2, Darnley's familiars, Morton (baritone) and Ruthven (tenor), incite him to demand the crown. Darnley, led to believe that Riccio is the father of Mary's child, murders Riccio. Moray attempts to seize power, but Mary wins the people's support and banishes Moray. In the final act, Mary sends for Bothwell to put down a revolt led by Moray. She lets him ravish her as the price for his help. Darnley is murdered; the people turn against Mary and she is forced to escape to England leaving her child behind to be proclaimed king.

Following Elguera, Musgrave allowed herself a good deal of freedom in extracting a workable libretto from the confused events of Mary's reign. Moray is portrayed as an Iago-like figure whose ruthless ambition is contrasted with Mary's fatal indecisiveness. As in Verdi's great historical operas, tragic destinies are worked out against a background of pageantry and intrigue, the plot allowing for much tender and intimate music as well as a fine sequence of courtly dances (in Act 1), fully integrated into the score.   HUGO COLE

Masagniello [*Masagniello (Masaniello) furioso [oder] Die neapolitanische Fischer-Empörung* ('Masaniello the Mad, or The Neapolitan Fisherman's Rebellion')]. *Drama musicale* in three acts by REINHARD KEISER to a libretto by BARTHOLD FEIND; Hamburg, Theater am Gänsemarkt, June 1706; revised by GEORG PHILIPP TELEMANN, Hamburg, 1727.

The libretto deals with an insurrection that took place in Naples in 1647. Masagniello (bass), a fisherman, incites the people to rebel against their Spanish rulers because of an oppressive tax. He intimidates the viceroy, the Duke of Arcos (contralto), into agreeing to his demands but finally goes mad and is shot by his own supporters. Around this essentially historical core Feind constructed a pair of amorous plots involving noble characters. Don Pedro (tenor) secretly loves Aloysia (soprano), the wife of his cousin Don Velasco (tenor), while she is torn between love for Pedro and loyalty to her husband. Arcos loves Marianne (soprano), but her heart belongs to Antonio (bass). When Antonio is arrested by the rebels she persuades his guard to let her take his place, but, once free, Antonio does nothing to obtain her release. Ransomed by Arcos, Marianne returns to discover Antonio making advances to Aloysia, leading him to attempt suicide, and Don Velasco catches Aloysia and Don Pedro in an apparently compromising situation. In the end the viceroy succeeds in reconciling Marianne with Antonio and Velasco with Aloysia, while Pedro decides to withdraw from the world. Some comic relief in this prevailingly severe drama is provided by Bassian (tenor), a fruit-seller.

Feind, who himself played a revolutionary role in the turbulent Hamburg politics of the period, produced a libretto of remarkable originality and dramatic power, which drew a strong response from Keiser. The brutal Masagniello is one of the most extraordinary character studies in Baroque opera, and Marianne is perhaps the most affecting of the composer's suffering heroines.

JOHN H. ROBERTS

Mascagni, Pietro (*b* Livorno, 7 Dec 1863; *d* Rome, 2 Aug 1945). Italian composer and conductor. His precocious musical talent was identified by Alfredo Soffredini, his first teacher, who encouraged him in a musical career against the wishes of Mascagni's father, a baker. His first compositions, a four-part mass and the cantata *In filanda* (1881), from which he extracted the dramatic idyll *Pinotta* in 1883, won him financial support from Count Florestano de Larderel and enabled him to go to the Milan Conservatory, where he studied with Ponchielli and Saladino and lived a bohemian student life, sharing a room with Puccini. He was incapable of following a regular course of study for long, and he left in April 1885, finding work at once with the company of Dario Acconci, who had already staged his operetta *Il re a Napoli* that year. He toured Italy as a conductor with various companies until he arrived at Cerignola, in Apulia, for Carnival 1886, where he settled as teacher to the local philharmonic society, partly because his wife, Lina, was expecting their first child. In 1888 he abandoned the first version of *Guglielmo Ratcliff*, on which he had been working since 1882, in order to enter the Sonzogno competition. His *Cavalleria rusticana* greatly impressed the jury, which included Giovanni Sgambati and Amintore Galli, and he was awarded the prize over 72 rivals, among them Bossi and Giordano. The opera was enormously successful from its first performance at the Costanzi in Rome in 1890. From then on Mascagni spent the rest of his long career treating a wide variety of subjects, almost as a demonstration of his many-sided talents. His next opera, *L'amico Fritz* (1891), consolidated his success with the Roman audiences, revealing a lyrical vein particularly in the numbers that have become famous, such as the Cherry Duet. This fluent rustic comedy was successful particularly because the melodic vitality – the outstanding merit of *Cavalleria* – was combined with a more elegant harmonic idiom.

Concerned to make his music widely known, Mascagni soon acquired a high reputation as a conductor outside Italy. In 1892 he had a great personal success in Vienna and Paris and in the following year in London, where he conducted his operas in Covent Garden's Italian season. These included *I Rantzau*, a bitter story of love between cousins but with a happy ending, which had been well received in Florence in 1892 with fine performances by singers including Battistini, Darclée and De Lucia. The critics were also favourable, the opera being hailed as 'a real music drama', and the Germans particularly praised its orchestration. Meanwhile Mascagni had succeeded in finishing *Ratcliff*, and it was performed at La Scala in 1895 with moderate success. The opera was rather dated, using old-fashioned mannerisms from Verdi and melodies reminiscent of Ponchielli which jarred after the novelties of *Manon Lescaut* and *Falstaff*. To satisfy Sonzogno Mascagni also had to write *Silvano* in a great hurry for the same season, and this was savaged by audience and critics alike.

In 1895 Mascagni was also appointed director of the Liceo Musicale of Pesaro, where his one-act opera *Zanetto* (1896) was performed, but his commitments to the operatic seasons prevented him from fulfilling his academic duties adequately, and he had to resign after he went on a long tour of the USA and Canada in 1902–3. *Iris*, with its Japanese setting, which had its première in Rome (1898) and was then performed, with minor revisions, at La Scala with considerable success, inaugurated the vogue for *fin-de-siècle* exotic opera. At the height of his popularity, Mascagni produced a resounding failure in *Le maschere* (1901), which opened simultaneously at seven Italian theatres and was a fiasco at all of them except in Rome, where it was saved by the composer's presence as conductor. The fault was laid on his falling into mannerism, but it was due rather to the impossibility of a reconciliation of Illica's wish to revive the *commedia dell'arte* with the natural vitality of the composer which was unsuited to sophisticated intellectual attempts at reviving it.

He was more successful at Monte Carlo in 1905 with *Amica*, to a French libretto by the publisher Paul de Choudens, which signalled a return to *verismo* and a renewed attention to orchestral models. At the many Italian performances of it that he conducted Mascagni included Tchaikovsky's Sixth Symphony in the programme. True success, however, returned with *Isabeau* (1911), written as a South American answer to Puccini's recent début at the New York Metropolitan with *La fanciulla del West*. Enthusiastically welcomed by the Italian community in Buenos Aires, its triumph was repeated in Milan and Venice, where it received its European première. But this voluntary return to a romantic atmosphere made it evident that Mascagni's inventiveness was exhausted and that he was acquiring a mannered style which could be reinvigorated only by his constantly seeking new subjects for treatment. His momentous collaboration with D'Annunzio, a risky partner whom Puccini had carefully avoided, resulted in *Parisina*, a 'cultured' opera which the critics unhesitatingly condemned. The following year Mascagni continued to experiment by writing for the cinema – a *Rapsodia satanica* for the film of the same name by Nino Oxilia (1915).

With *Lodoletta*, by Ouida (1917), he returned to the sentimental lyrical genre in close rivalry with Puccini's *La rondine*, and with *Sì* he made another foray into the world of operetta. Their more successful workmanship confirms Mascagni's propensity towards a balance of lyricism and drama, but feeling he had won his way back into public favour he returned to *verismo* with *Il piccolo Marat* (1921). Probably realizing at this juncture that his career was leading him inexorably to regress, he shut himself up, in spite of the work's success, in almost total seclusion, interrupted only by a revival of his youthful *Pinotta* in 1932, the 'symphonic vision' *Guardando la Santa Teresa del Bernini* and finally *Nerone* (1935). Mascagni hoped that this last work, written for himself and refused by every publisher, represented a new direction dictated by genuine inspiration, believing that he had created through the metaphor of history a new relationship with reality. His fame was briefly revived, largely through the Fascist regime which was responsible for its elaborate première at La Scala in which Aureliano Pertile shone in the leading role. It was Mascagni's last battle against the modernism of his times, and the regime was probably grateful to him for it. Celebrating the 50th anniversary of *Cavalleria*, the priest and musician Licinio Refice defined him as 'the musical lymph of pure Italianity; flame of the intact Italian tradition of melodrama; a vigilant sword to protect the artistic strength of the Italian race'. He died in 1945, in a Rome now free from totalitarianism and full of the ghosts of his triumphs.

See also AMICO FRITZ, L'; CAVALLERIA RUSTICANA (i); GUGLIELMO RATCLIFF; IRIS; ISABEAU; PARISINA (ii); and PICCOLO MARAT, IL.

printed works published in Milan unless otherwise stated

title	genre, acts	librettist	first performance	publication; remarks
Il re a Napoli	operetta, 3		Cremona, Municipale, 18 March 1885	
Cavalleria rusticana	melodramma, 1	G. Targioni-Tozzetti and G. Menasci, after G. Verga	Rome, Costanzi, 17 May 1890	1890
L'amico Fritz	commedia lirica, 3	P. Suardon [N. Daspuro], after Erckmann-Chatrian	Rome, Costanzi, 31 Oct 1891	vs, 1891
I Rantzau	4	Targioni-Tozzetti and Menasci	Florence, Pergola, 10 Nov 1892	vs, 1893
Guglielmo Ratcliff	tragedia, 4	after H. Heine: *William Ratcliff*, trans. A. Maffei	Milan, Scala, 16 Feb 1895	vs, 1895; comp. 1882–8, rev. and orchd 1894
Silvano	dramma marinaresco, 2	Targioni-Tozzetti, after A. Karr: *Romano*	Milan, Scala, 25 March 1895	vs, 1895

title	genre, acts	librettist	first performance	publication; remarks
Zanetto	1	Targioni-Tozzetti and Menasci, after F. Coppée: Le passant	Pesaro, Liceo Rossini, 2 March 1896	vs, 1896
Iris	melodramma, 3	L. Illica	Rome, Costanzi, 22 Nov 1898	vs, 1898; score, 1911
Le maschere	commedia lirica e giocosa, parabasi, 3	Illica	Rome, Costanzi; Milan, Scala; Venice, Fenice; Turin, Regio; Genoa, Carlo Felice; Verona, Filarmonico: 17 Jan 1901; Naples, S Carlo, 19 Jan 1901	vs, 1901
Amica	dramma, 2	P. Bérel [de Choudens], trans. Targioni-Tozzetti	Monte Carlo, Casino, 16 March 1905	vs, Paris, 1905
Isabeau	leggenda drammatica, 3	Illica, after Lady Godiva legend	Buenos Aires, Coliseo, 2 June 1911	vs, 1910
Parisina	tragedia lirica, 4	G. D'Annunzio	Milan, Scala, 15 Dec 1913	vs, 1914; reduced to 3 acts after 1st perf.
Lodoletta	3	G. Forzano, after Ouida: Two Little Wooden Shoes	Rome, Costanzi, 30 April 1917	vs, 1917
Sí	operetta, 3	C. Lombardo and A. Franci	Rome, Quirino, 13 Dec 1919	vs, 1919
Il piccolo Marat	dramma lirico, 3	Forzano	Rome, Costanzi, 2 May 1921	1921
Pinotta	idillio, 3	Targioni-Tozzetti	Sanremo, Casinò, 23 March 1932	?1975; comp. 1882–3; based on cantata In filanda, 1881
Nerone	3	Targioni-Tozzetti, after P. Cossa	Milan, Scala, 16 Jan 1935	vs, Rome, 1934

E. Hanslick: Die moderne Oper (Berlin, 1891–3) [incl. Cavalleria rusticana, vi, 171–80; Freund Fritz, vii, 37–46; I Rantzau, vii, 70–79]

V. F. Dwelshauvers-Dry: Die 'Cavalleria rusticana' und ihre Bedeutung für Deutschland (Leipzig, 1892)

P. Mascagni: Aus dunklen Tagen: Lebensabriss (Vienna, 1893)

R. Streatfeild: Masters of Italian Music (London, 1895)

L. Torchi: 'Guglielmo Ratcliff', RMI, ii (1895), 287–311

G. Monaldi: Pietro Mascagni: l'uomo e l'artista (Rome, 1898)

L. Torchi: 'Iris', RMI, vi (1899), 71–118

——: 'Le maschere', RMI, viii (1901), 178–80

G. Bastianelli: Pietro Mascagni (Naples, 1910)

R. De Rensis: 'Il connubio Mascagni-D'Annunzio per una trilogia italiana', Musica [Rome], in (1910)

G. Barini: 'Isabeau di Pietro Mascagni', Nuova antologia, no.161 (1912), 550–7

E. Pompei: Pietro Mascagni nella vita e nell'arte (Rome, 1912)

G. Cogo: Il nostro Mascagni: da Cavalleria a Parisina (Milan, 1914)

M. A. Barrenechea: 'Pietro Mascagni y sus dos últimas obras', Musica y literatura (Valencia, 1916)

G. Scuderi: Pietro Mascagni, 'Iris': guida attraverso il dramma e la musica (Milan, 1923)

G. M. Gatti: 'Gabriele D'Annunzio and Italian Opera-Composers', MQ, x (1924), 263–88

G. Orsini: Vangelo d'un Mascagnano (Milan, 1926)

G. Pannain: 'L'opera italiana', Il pianoforte, viii (1927)

A. De Donno: Modernità di Mascagni (Rome, 1932)

M. Rinaldi: Musica e verismo (Rome, 1932)

T. W. Adorno: 'Mascagnis Landschaft: zum 70. Geburtstag', Vossische Zeitung, vii (1933), 7

'Bibliografia delle opere di Pietro Mascagni', Bollettino bibliografico musicale, viii (1933)

W. Altmann: 'Pietro Mascagni', Die Musik, xxvi (1933–4), 185–8

L. Kárpáth: 'Das Dioskurenpaar Mascagni-Leoncavallo', Begegnung mit dem Genius (Vienna, 1934), 365–74

G. Orsini: Pietro Mascagni e il suo 'Nerone' (Milan, 1935)

L. Tomelleri: 'Gabriele D'Annunzio: ispiratore di musicisti', RMI, xliii (1939), 161–233, esp. 213–19 [on Parisina]

G. Cenzato, ed.: Nascita e gloria di un capolavoro italiano: cinquantenario della 'Cavalleria rusticana': le lettere ai librettisti durante la creazione del capolavoro (inedite) (Milan, 1940)

R. De Rensis: 'I cinquant'anni di Cavalleria rusticana', Musica d'oggi, xxii (1940), 123–5

A. Jeri: Mascagni (Milan, 1940)

C. Fratta Cavalcabò: Mascagni e Puccini (Parma, 1942)

F. Bonavia: Pietro Mascagni (London, 1952)

G. Pannain: 'Il cinquantenario di un successo', Ottocento musicale italiano (Milan, 1952)

G. Gavazzeni: Non eseguire Beethoven e altri saggi (Milan, 1954) [incl. 'Proposito di rilettura del Nerone, 113–16; 'Indicazioni per ascoltare l'Iris', 134–9]

——: 'Il teatro di Mascagni nel suo tempo e nel nostro', La musica e il teatro (Pisa, 1954)

W. Klein: 'Mascagni and his Operas', Opera, vi (1955), 623–31

A. Anselmi: Pietro Mascagni (Milan, 1959)

J. W. Klein: 'Pietro Mascagni and Giovanni Verga', ML, xliv (1963), 350–57

M. Morini: 'Illica e Mascagni nell'esperienza dell'Iris', Musica d'oggi, new ser., vi (1963), 58–66

Pietro Mascagni: contributi alla conoscenza della sua opera nel 1° centenario della nascita (Livorno, 1963)

K. Geitel: 'Der unbekannte Mascagni', Theater und Zeit, xi (1963–4), 106–10

M. Morini, ed.: Pietro Mascagni (Milan, 1964)

D. Cellamare: Pietro Mascagni (Rome, 1965)

M. Morini: 'Mascagni e Rossini', L'opera, iv/12–13 (1968), 45–54

R. Giazotto: 'Quattordici lettere inedite di Pietro Mascagni', NRMI, iv (1970), 493–513

A. Alexander: G. Verga: a Great Writer and his World (London, 1972)

R. Stivender, ed. and trans.: The Autobiography of Pietro Mascagni (New York, 1975)

H. Goetz: 'Die Beziehungen zwischen Pietro Mascagni und Benito Mussolini', AnMc, no.17 (1976), 212–53

R. Mariani: Verismo in musica (Florence, 1976)

J. R. Nicolaisen: Italian Opera in Transition, 1871–1893 (diss., U. of California, Berkeley, 1977)

N. Benvenuti: Pietro Mascagni nella vita e nell'arte (Livorno, 1981)

L'avant-scène opéra, no.50 (1983) [Cavalleria rusticana and Pagliacci issue]

F. Nicolodi: Musica e musicisti nel ventennio fascista (Fiesole, 1984)

Mascagni (Milan, 1984)

C. Orselli: 'Panneggi medievali per la donna decadente: Parisina e Francesca', Chigiana, xxxvii (1985), 135–50

A. Csampai and D. Holland, eds.: Pietro Mascagni, Cavalleria rusticana/R. Leoncavallo, Der Bajazzo: Texte, Materialen, Kommentare (Reinbek, 1987)

R. Jovino: Mascagni, l'avventuroso dell'opera (Milan, 1987)

H. Sachs: Music in Fascist Italy (London, 1987)

J. Maehder: 'The Origins of Italian Literaturoper: Guglielmo Ratcliff, La figlia di Iorio, Parisina, and Francesca da Rimini', Reading Opera, ed. A. Groos and R. Parker (Princeton, 1988), 92–128

M. Morini and P. Ostali, eds.: Mascagni e l'Iris fra simbolismo e floreale (Milan, 1989)

Cavalleria rusticana 1890–1990: cento anni di un capolavoro (Milan, 1990)

Il piccolo Marat: storia e rivoluzione nel melodramma verista (Milan, 1990)

MICHELE GIRARDI

245

Mascheroni, Edoardo (*b* Milan, 4 Sept 1852; *d* Ghirla, 4 March 1941). Italian conductor and composer. He made his début in 1880 at Brescia with *Macbeth* and *Un ballo in maschera*, and after further conducting in the Italian provinces he worked in Rome from 1884, mainly at the Teatro Apollo. He gave the Italian première of *Fidelio* at the Apollo in 1886, and the first performances in Rome of *Tannhäuser* and *Der fliegende Holländer* in successive seasons (1886–7) and of *Manon Lescaut* (1893) and *La bohème* (1896). In 1891 and 1893 he also introduced the two Wagner operas at La Scala, where, with the support of Verdi and Boito, he was engaged as chief conductor (1891–4). There he conducted the premières of Catalani's *La Wally* (1892) and, at Verdi's request, *Falstaff* (1893). Verdi called him the 'third author' of *Falstaff* and entrusted him with productions elsewhere in Italy and in Austria and Germany. In 1898 Mascheroni inaugurated the Teatro Adriano, Rome. Between 1887 and 1922 he conducted several other premières of operas by Catalani (the revised *Loreley*, 1890), Bustini, Donaudy, Falchi, Alberto Franchetti and Vallini. Although he was generally held in high esteem, he did not receive the support of younger composers such as Puccini and Mascagni. Mascheroni retired about 1925, having composed two requiems, chamber music and two operas, both to librettos by Luigi Illica: *Lorenza* (3), staged at the Teatro Costanzi, Rome, on 13 April 1901, and revised for a performance in Brescia on 3 September 1901, and *La Perugina* (4), favourably received at the S Carlo, Naples, on 24 April 1909.

*

'Edoardo Mascheroni ed il "Falstaff"', *Musica d'oggi*, xxiii (1941), 175
CLAUDIO CASINI

Maschinist Hopkins ('Hopkins the Engineer'). Opera in a prologue and three acts, op.11, by MAX BRAND to his own libretto; Duisburg, Stadttheater, 13 April 1929.

Bill *an engineer*	tenor
Hopkins *chief engineer*	baritone
Jim *foreman at the Lixton works*	bass
Nell *Jim's wife and the boss's secretary*	soprano
Bertier *theatre director*	bass
Stage Manager	bass
Cloakroom Attendant	contralto
Band-Leader	baritone
Secretary	baritone
Chief of Personnel	bass
Three Factory Workers	contralto, tenor and bass
Young Girl	soprano
Two Men	tenor and bass-baritone
Fireman	bass
Clerk	spoken
Official	silent
Six Negroes	two tenors and four basses
Main-Switch	contralto
Two Voices	soprano and baritone

Sprechstimmen spoke, two wheels, belt-drive, axle, cog-wheels, piston

Sprechchor ladies and gentlemen, workers, actors, dancers, whores and pimps

Setting An industrial city in America, in the mid-1920s

With *Maschinist Hopkins*, his first opera, Brand aimed for a substantial success, writing it to finance medical treatment for his wife. The work was selected for the Allgemeiner Deutscher Musikverein festival by a jury which included Berg, who was extremely impressed (similarities between the opera and his *Lulu* may be more than coincidental). Composed in a period which saw an unprecedented number of new operas staged in Germany, the work's contemporary metropolitan setting and 'American' characters were much in vogue. Brand's theme – the relationship between humanity and technology – was familiar through such works as Fritz Lang's film *Metropolis* (1926) and was the focus of experiments at the Bauhaus. Brand, like Krenek, Weill and Hindemith, advocated a regeneration of opera by means of a 'vertical résumé of the most characteristic features of the epoch'. Posing social and humanitarian questions in a mélange of thriller and romance, Brand presents events cinematically, using colourful orchestration to enhance the emotional impact of the drama, fully exploiting the stylistic palette of his day. The original cast included Robert von der Linde (Jim), Hildegard Bieber-Baumann (Nell), Hanns Bohnhoff (Bill) and Wilhelm Trieloff (Hopkins). Its tremendous success (25 different productions in 41 opera houses between 1929 and 1932) was short-lived for political reasons. Unperformed thereafter for more than 40 years, it was given in a shortened concert version in Graz in 1973. It was not revived on the stage until 1984 at Bielefeld, in a production which, with some cuts and reordering, interpreted Hopkins's regime as prophetic of the evolving fascist state. In 1986, BBC Radio 3 produced a complete English version; a full German concert version was given in Vienna in 1988.

PROLOGUE i *An alley in a poor working-class district of a large industrial city* Bill hastens out of Bondy's Bar, irritated by Jim who is inciting the Lixton workers to industrial action. Bill has his own plans for taking over the means of production and with the help of his mistress, Jim's wife, Nell, steals the master key to the factory from Jim's home.

ii *The machine hall the same night* The brooding machines tell in *Sprechstimme* of their neglected state, using four different methods of declamation, which Brand based on the technique developed by Schoenberg in *Die glückliche Hand*. Jim disturbs Bill and Nell who are on the point of securing the secret production formula. In the ensuing fight over Nell, Jim is caught up in the machinery and is crushed to death as Nell accidentally operates the Main-Switch. The futuristic music vividly evokes the industrial scene, and its force underlines the message that machines control the human dilemma.

ACT 1.iii *Bill's luxurious modern office* Five years later Bill has set up as a successful rival to Lixtons. Haunted by Jim's murder, he wishes to buy the firm out, close it down and bury the evidence. Hopkins, on whom Bill has relied as an informer, sympathizes with the workers' dissatisfaction and Bill sacks him. Nell, now married to Bill, persuades him to let her pursue a singing career.

1.iv *An exclusive business restaurant with a garden terrace* The Brand New Band strikes up with an authentic Black Bottom routine to a nonsense text in English by George Antheil. Nell signs her contract to the background of a tango and during the celebrations Bill learns from his Clerk, declaiming over the mayhem, that Lixton shares have plummeted.

'Maschinist Hopkins' (Brand), scene ii (the machine hall): set design by Johannes Schröder for the original production at the Stadttheater, Duisburg, 13 April 1929

1.v   *On the terrace steps*   Following a dodecaphonic introduction, Bill and Nell indulge in a love duet charged with late Romantic erotic lyricism (and notable for its use of the celeste). This is the most human part of the opera, with Bill and Nell near to a state of perfect oblivion.

ACT 2.vi   *The machine room at Lixtons*   As a siren sounds the news of closure, the desperate workers spread the rumour that their new boss murdered his wife's first husband there. Hopkins, now in charge on the shop-floor, recognizes a chance to get his revenge on Bill and to secure the workers' future.

2.vii   *Nell's dressing room*   Hopkins, now an electrician at the theatre, forces Nell to confess.

2.viii   *In the wings*   Following a brief comic interlude, when the theatre personnel vie for Nell's attention (although she has agreed to follow Hopkins), Bill's world falls apart. Hopkins blackmails him with Nell's confession and he learns of her numerous infidelities from the back-stage Fireman.

ACT 3.ix   *A deserted street, one year later*   The music returns to the opening, mirroring the events of the Prologue, but the original motivations and emotions of the characters have changed. Hopkins, cold and hard as iron, has no further use for Nell now that he has avenged himself.

3.x   *Bondy's Bar*   Hopkins proclaims to the unemployed that Lixtons will reopen. The bawdy singing (which Bill overhears) about Nell, now a prostitute, is replaced by a jubilant hymn to work, food and warmth. Enraged, Bill storms out.

3.xi   *An alley as in Prologue i*   Bill reflects on how events have turned full circle. Through Nell's window he sees her, naked and with a client, and in a fit of madness goes in and murders her.

3.xii   *The machine room at night*   Bill, in a deranged state, tries to regain control. The machines refuse to submit and he sets out to destroy them. Just as he is about to grasp the Main-Switch (which sings out in Nell's ghostly voice) to short-circuit the entire plant, he falls into the machinery and is mangled to death to a parodistic imitation of the Magic Fire music from Wagner's *Die Walküre*. This leaves Hopkins, master of machines and workers' leader, at the control panel of his industrial temple – himself now an automaton. Against a relentlessly thunderous background the workers, crying 'Arbeit!', take up their places on the production line and a new working day dawns.

*   *   *

Contemporary critical opinon enthused about the effective injection of everyday reality into the rarefied world of opera and praised the consequent broadening of the musical and theatrical accessibility of the *Zeitoper*. Debate centred on the expressionist spirit of the work and on the symbolism inherent in the violent victimization of humanity by technology, represented both by the finely tuned robotic ensemble of machines that seem to throb with the rhythm of a life of their own and by the protagonist Hopkins with his virtually inhuman make-up. The driving force behind *Hopkins*, making for uncompromisingly exhilarating theatre, is that promiscuous modernism, also characteristic of Krenek's *Jonny spielt auf* and rooted in *fin-de-siècle* Viennese culture, which had blossomed in Weimar Berlin through the work of Franz Schreker and other cultural émigrés. The music resounds with original combinations of textures and skilful thematic cross-referencing, and its mechanistic sonorities seem to contain the seeds of subsequent electronic composition. The questions it raises about the relationship between technology and progress remain relevant today.   CHARLOTTE PURKIS

Masi [Massi], **Giovanni** (*b* Florence, *c*1730; *d* after 1776). Italian composer. His first known opera, *Il gran conte di Cordanova*, was performed in Rome in Carnival 1754. Six years later he was invited to compose an *opera seria*, *Muzio Scevola*, for Florence. The libretto for his *La scuffiara* (1765) identifies him as *maestro di cappella napolitano*, though he is *maestro di cappella fiorentino* in that for *I tre amanti burlati* (1766). By 1774, according to the librettos of his last two operas, he had become *maestro di cappella romano*. He was probably related to, or even possibly the same person as,

Girolamo Masi, a *maestro di cappella romano* at S Giacomo de' Spagnoli, who set the *farsa Lo sposalizio per puntiglio* (1768, Rome, Valle). Manuscript copies of this, as well as of the intermezzo *Il governo dell'isola passa* (1765, Rome), survive (*I-Baf*); though attributed to 'Pater Felice Masi' they are apparently works of Girolamo (or Giovanni) Masi.

Il gran conte di Cordanova (commedia, 2, G. Aureli), Rome, Saponari, carn. 1754
Muzio Scevola (os, 3, C. Lanfranchi-Rossi), Florence, Cocomero, spr. 1760, aria *I-Fc*
La scuffiara, o La caccia della bufala (int, 2, A. Pioli), Rome, Tordinona, carn. 1765
I tre amanti burlati (commedia, P. Mililotti), Naples, Fiorentini, spr. 1766
La disfatta di Dario (os, 3, Morbilli), Turin, Regio, carn. 1774, *P-La*
Vologeso re dei Parti (os, 3, A. Zeno), Rome, Argentina, carn. 1776, *I-Rsc*
La montecarina (int, 2), *Fc*   MARITA P. McCLYMONDS

Masini, Angelo (*b* Terra del Sole, Forlì, 28 Nov 1844; *d* Forlì, 26 Sept 1926). Italian tenor. He studied with Gilda Minguzzi and made his début in 1867 at Finale Emilia as Pollione, a role he repeated at Mantua in 1869. The following year he appeared at La Fenice, Venice, in Donizetti's *Lucrezia Borgia* and Pacini's *Saffo*. In 1871 he sang in *Faust* in Rome and Donizetti's *Dom Sébastien* at Bologna. He was heard as Radames at Florence (1874) and Don Alvaro (*La forza del destino*) at the Teatro Apollo, Rome (1875). He spent the winter of 1875–6 in Cairo, singing in Donizetti's *Maria di Rohan* and *La favorite*, *I puritani* and *Aida*. In 1876 he sang in the first Paris performance of *Aida* at the Théâtre Italien. He also appeared in Moscow, St Petersburg, Madrid, Lisbon and Buenos Aires. His repertory ranged from Mozart (Don Ottavio) to Wagner (Lohengrin), from Rossini (Almaviva) to Meyerbeer (Raoul and Vasco da Gama), and his vocal technique was considered outstanding. He made his last appearance in 1905 in *Il barbiere di Siviglia* at the Théâtre Sarah Bernhardt, Paris.

C. Rivalta: *Il tenore Angelo Masini e Faenza* (Faenza, 1927)
                                        ELIZABETH FORBES

Masini, Galliano (*b* Livorno, 7 Feb 1896; *d* Livorno, 15 Feb 1986). Italian tenor. He studied in Milan, making his début in 1924 at Livorno as Cavaradossi (*Tosca*). From 1930 to 1950 he was engaged at the Rome Opera. He also appeared regularly at La Scala, where he sang Paco in the first Milan performance of Falla's *La vida breve* (1934) and Turiddu in the 50th-anniversary performance of *Cavalleria rusticana* (1940). He was engaged at Chicago (1937–8) and at the Metropolitan (1938–9), where his roles included Edgardo, Turiddu and Radames. Another favourite part was Loris (*Fedora*). He retired in 1957.   ELIZABETH FORBES

Maskarade ('Masquerade'). Comic opera in three acts by CARL NIELSEN to a libretto by Vilhelm Andersen after Ludvig Holberg's play *Mascarade* (1724); Copenhagen, Royal Theatre, 11 November 1906.

Attracted by the element of masque comedy in Holberg's play and by the character of Henrik – a forerunner of Beaumarchais' Figaro – Nielsen worked out the plot for *Maskarade* on his own and then turned to Vilhelm Andersen, a literary historian and acknowledged expert on Holberg; the two worked on the libretto in April and May 1904. After his resignation

from the Royal Theatre orchestra early in 1905, Nielsen's work on *Maskarade* progressed rapidly, and the composition was largely complete by October 1905, although production was postponed until 1906.

After a lighthearted overture the curtain goes up on a room in the house of Jeronimus, a citizen of Copenhagen. The year is 1723. It is 5 p.m., and Leander (tenor), Jeronimus's son, and his servant Henrik (bass-baritone) are feeling the after-effects of the previous night's revelry. Leander has fallen in love and exchanged rings with an unknown girl he met at the dance; Henrik points out that this may conflict with Jeronimus's plans for Leander to marry the daughter of fellow-citizen Leonard. Henrik's amusing charade depicting the likely legal consequences is interrupted by the arrival of Leander's mother Magdelone (mezzo-soprano). In a delightful dance scene she inquires whether 'old women' can also go to the masquerade, and she entrances the two men with a *folie d'Espagne*. Jeronimus (bass) bursts in, upbraids his wife, forbids all present to leave the house that evening, dismisses Leander and Henrik, and delivers a denunciatory monologue on the evils of masquerading. Leonard (tenor/baritone) enters. His daughter has also fallen in love, and the two citizens compare notes on miscreant offspring.

A tenderly beautiful prelude introduces the second act. The Nightwatchman (bass) passes. Alone outside the house, the superstitious Arv (tenor) is confronted by a 'ghost' and confesses to various petty thefts including, finally, 'the kitchen-maid's virginity'. The 'ghost' reveals himself as Henrik, who can now blackmail Arv into letting him and Leander pass. Groups of students, officers and girls start to assemble for the masquerade. Leander sees his beloved Leonora (soprano) and an ecstatic love duet ensues, mildly inconvenienced by the gentle mocking of Henrik and Pernille (soprano), Leonora's maid. Jeronimus has discovered Leander and Henrik's absence and he goes with Arv to the masquerade. The Nightwatchman returns as the distant sounds of the masquerade are heard.

Interspersed with set-piece dances (the best-known being 'Hanedansen': 'Dance of the Cockerels') the comedy unfolds in the third act. Leander and Leonora reveal their names and pledge faithfulness; Henrik and Pernille also confess their mutual attraction; Leonard and Magdelone indulge in a mild flirtation, interrupted by Jeronimus. Henrik tells his master of Jeronimus's presence and connives with the students' leader (baritone), an elderly don, in getting the old man drunk. The tipsy Jeronimus makes a fool of himself dallying with a ballerina. The time for unmasking arrives (a sublime bittersweet moment in Nielsen's setting). With various degrees of delight and amazement the main characters recognize their partners, and Jeronimus is the last to realize that all is well, since Leonora is after all Leonard's daughter. After an exit-dance Henrik addresses the audience and solicits applause.

Maskarade quickly established itself as the most successful Danish opera and is coming to be recognized as one of the most engaging of all 20th-century comic operas. Andersen's adaptation was initially criticized for its extensive rhyming and for coarsening some of Holberg's characters (notably the killjoy Jeronimus). The rhyme-schemes admittedly present something of an obstacle to successful translation, but the characterization, even in the most burlesque scenes, stops well short of malice; and the humanity of Nielsen's setting enables *Maskarade* to touch lightly on such fundamental issues as liberty, equality and mortality.

Nielsen's earliest musical experiences were his mother's simple songs and his father's amateur fiddling and cornet-playing, and the music of *Maskarade* is rarely far from these in spirit. The many memorable tunes inaugurate a phase in Nielsen's career which was to make him the most popular and influential figure in the history of Danish song, while the *joie de vivre* of the dances and the affectionate good humour of the duets brings to mind Johann Strauss's *Die Fledermaus*. Nielsen was uncertain about the disposition of his second and third acts. He allowed a number of cuts and made some last-minute changes before the first performance. Nonetheless, his technique is remarkably assured and almost certainly owes something to his acquaintance with *Die Meistersinger* (his favourite Wagner opera) and Verdi's *Falstaff*, as well as to his determination to outdo the many vaudeville comedies and ballets which he found so tedious as a violinist in the Royal Theatre.   DAVID FANNING

Mask of Orpheus, The. Lyric tragedy in three acts by HARRISON BIRTWISTLE to a libretto by Peter Zinovieff; London, Coliseum, 21 May 1986.

Orpheus:	
The Man	high baritone
The Hero	mime
The Myth/Hades	high baritone
Eurydice:	
The Woman	lyric mezzo-soprano
The Heroine	mime
The Myth	lyric mezzo-soprano
Aristaeus:	
The Man	tenor
The Hero	mime
The Myth	tenor
The Oracle of the Dead/Hecate	high soprano
The Troupe of Ceremony/Judges of the Dead:	
The Caller	bass-baritone
First Priest	bright tenor
Second Priest	baritone
Third Priest	basso profondo
The Three Women/	soprano,
Furies	mezzo-soprano, contralto
The Troupe of Passing Clouds	mimes
The Voice of Apollo	pre-recorded tape

Setting Mythic Greece

Birtwistle was first commissioned by the Royal Opera House, Covent Garden, to write an opera on the Orpheus myth after the success of the première of *Punch and Judy* in 1968. He began work on the score in 1973 but the initial project foundered, and the commission passed first to London Weekend Television and then to Glyndebourne before lapsing altogether in 1976, at which point Act 1 and much of Act 2 had been completed. In 1981 the ENO revived the commission, and between 1982 and 1984 Birtwistle completed the second act and the whole of the third, as well as compiling the electronic tapes at IRCAM in Paris with the help of Barry Anderson. The staging at the ENO was conducted by Elgar Howarth and directed by David Freeman with designs by Jocelyn Herbert; Philip Langridge sang the role of Orpheus Man, Jean Rigby Eurydice Woman, Tom McDonnell Aristaeus Man; Marie Angel

was the Oracle of the Dead. Despite its critical success the work has not been revived since 1986 because of the formidable production costs; a concert performance of Act 2 was given by the BBC SO at the Barbican, London, in January 1988.

The essence of the dramatic organization of *The Mask of Orpheus* is its rejection of linear narrative and of a goal-directed treatment of dramatic time. Birtwistle's presentation of the bundle of myths surrounding the central story of Orpheus and Eurydice involves the parallel presentation of different, often contradictory, versions of the events; episodes are overlaid and repeated from different perspectives, and the threefold representation of each of the main characters by singer, mime and puppet (whose words are delivered by an off-stage singer), allows simultaneous presentation of such perspectives. What is already a highly complex formal structure is interrupted on six occasions by electronic interludes in which a mime troupe enacts myths associated with (but not related directly to) the Orpheus story; these violent 'Passing Clouds of Abandon' and lyrical 'Allegorical Flowers of Reason' are inserted at points of maximum calm or crisis in the main action, and while they are being portrayed all other action is frozen.

PARODOS Speaking in his own invented language, Apollo oversees the birth of Orpheus, giving him the gifts of speech, poetry and music. Orpheus's first memory is of voyaging with Jason and the Argonauts.

ACT 1.i Orpheus falls in love with Eurydice; she agrees to their marriage.
(Passing Cloud: Dionysus)
In the wedding ceremony, Hymen is invoked and the Troupe of Ceremony ritually questions the lovers; the omens are bad as Eurydice stumbles over her answers. Orpheus's love song fails to lift the gloom.

1.ii Two versions of Eurydice's death are presented simultaneously.
(Passing Cloud: Lycurgus)
Aristaeus as Man and Hero makes love to Eurydice Woman and Heroine as she walks by the river; in one version she resists, in the other she does not; in both she dies from the bite of a water snake.
(Allegorical Flower: Anemone)
Aristaeus tells Orpheus of his wife's death.

1.iii First time-distortion: Orpheus imagines he, and not Aristaeus, watched Eurydice's death. During the funeral ceremony the Troupe of Ceremony asks Hermes to guide Eurydice to the Underworld, while elements of the earlier love duet are recalled. Orpheus cannot accept that he was powerless to save his wife and consults the Oracle of the Dead. The Oracle offers him three clues to the Underworld in exchange for his gift of music, but when she attempts to imitate his song produces only screams and shrieks. Orpheus imagines he can find his way to the Underworld. He describes the 17 arches of the aqueduct that connects the mountain of the living to that of the dead; Eurydice is transformed into myth.

ACT 2 The structure of Act 2 follows the progress of Orpheus Myth across the 17 arches of the aqueduct, while Orpheus Man watches as in a dream and sings, offstage, a 17-verse Song of Magic. Each arch represents a different attribute of the world of the living which Orpheus is leaving behind, and all the characters he encounters are distorted versions of those he met in Act 1.

*'The Mask of Orpheus'
(Birtwistle): scene from
the original production at
the Coliseum, London, 21
May 1986, with Nigel
Robson as Orpheus Myth
(centre)*

This act begins, though, with the second time-distortion: Eurydice's death is presented again; she is killed by two giant snakes.

Arch 1 *Countryside* Orpheus sings to Charon as he crosses the River Styx.

Arch 2 *Crowds* Orpheus's music moves the Furies.

Arch 3 *Evening* Orpheus's death is foretold; he sees a vision of Eurydice.

Arch 4 *Contrasts* He drinks from the pool of memory but refuses the pool of forgetfulness; he has a second vision.

Arch 5 *Dying* He sees those tormented in the Underworld.

Arch 6 *Wings* His magic overcomes all dangers.

Arch 7 *Colour* Orpheus reaches the centre of the Underworld and confronts its rulers, Hades, Persephone and Hecate. He does not notice that they mirror himself, Eurydice and the Oracle.

Arch 8 *Secrecy* Orpheus continues his singing.

Arch 9 *Glass* He makes his escape.

Arch 10 *Buildings* He is surrounded by shadows of Eurydice.

Arch 11 *Weather* The shadows dance before him but he does not select one.

Arch 12 *Eyes* Orpheus begins his return, thinking Eurydice is following him, but it is Persephone.

Arch 13 *Knives* Persephone stumbles and another Eurydice replaces her. As Orpheus overcomes all the dangers she tries to leave the Underworld, but cannot; Apollo urges Orpheus to sing.

Arch 14 *Animals* Orpheus crosses the Styx. Charon refuses to carry Eurydice and she falls away. As Orpheus meets the sunlight the memory of Eurydice fades.

Arch 15 *Ropes* Orpheus has lost Eurydice for ever.

Arch 16 *Order* Orpheus realizes his journey was a dream, and re-enacts it as Orpheus Hero.

Arch 17 *Fear* Orpheus mourns Eurydice, rejecting three offers of marriage.

(Allegorical Flower: Hyacinth)

Orpheus hangs himself.

ACT 3 The dramatic structure of the act is based upon the movements of the tides, as it explores Orpheus's reputation, the beginnings of Orphism and his destruction by Apollo. Nine episodes of the myth are presented in a time-sequence that begins by moving backwards, then moves into the future and finally returns to the past. Between the episodes, Orpheus sings the verses of his Song of Magic, eventually challenging Apollo. The act begins with the third time-distortion: Orpheus Hero is rejected by the Underworld and re-created as a myth.

Episode 1 Orpheus Hero re-enacts his return from the Underworld and his suicide.

Episode 2 Orpheus Man sings of his descent to the Underworld.

Episode 3 Eurydice's death is viewed by Orpheus Man and Hero.

(Allegorical Flower: Lotus)

Episode 4 Orpheus Hero re-enacts his journey from the Underworld, with the same result.

Episode 5 Aristaeus is punished by his bees and is consoled by Orpheus; Zeus kills Orpheus with a thunderbolt for daring to reveal divine mysteries through his art.

Episode 6 Orpheus Myth is dismembered by the Dionysiac women.

Episode 7 His head floats down the river Hebrus.

Episode 8 Orpheus Myth has become an oracle, consulted by Aristaeus. Apollo eventually silences him for challenging his own Delphic oracle.

(Passing Cloud: Pentheus)

Episode 9 The sacrifice of Orpheus Myth is resumed from Episode 6, as the women eat his flesh.

EXODOS The myth of Orpheus decays.

*   *   *

Complicated as the dramatic structure of *The Mask of Orpheus* is, its musical structure is substantially more intricate. Like Birtwistle's *Punch and Judy* it is designed as a 'number opera' but one in which the closed forms are interlocked and superimposed, and the components of which owe very little to traditional notions of operatic structure. In the second act, for example, each verse of Orpheus's Song of Magic is itself broken down into four sections: a dream (aria), fantasy (recitative), nightmare (speech) and finally silence. As the journey progresses, however, the verses contract and their proportions alter, until at the 15th Arch the nightmare element takes over completely. Such careful plotting is built into each section of the opera, and it is underpinned by an independent orchestral structure that is, as Birtwistle describes it, 'through-composed'; 'the orchestra, even though it responds to the events on stage, has a life of its own'. The structures of the stage music and the orchestral music coincide only once, at the climax of the work in the third act, when the principal characters are represented only by puppets. The electronic elements, for the voice of Apollo and the interludes of the mime troupe, add yet another independent layer.

ANDREW CLEMENTS

Masnadieri, I ('The Bandits'). *Melodramma* in four parts by GIUSEPPE VERDI to a libretto by Andrea Maffei after FRIEDRICH VON SCHILLER's play *Die Räuber*; London, Her Majesty's Theatre, 22 July 1847.

Massimiliano, Count Moor	bass
Carlo *his son*	tenor
Francesco *brother to Carlo*	baritone
Amalia *orphan, the Count's niece*	soprano
Arminio *the Count's treasurer*	tenor
Moser *a pastor*	bass
Rolla *a companion of Carlo Moor*	tenor

Wayward youths (later bandits), women, children, servants

Setting Germany, at the beginning of the 18th century

The lucrative contract to compose an opera for Her Majesty's Theatre in London was an important sign of Verdi's burgeoning international reputation, and the occasion allowed him to write for some of the most famous singers of the age. More than that, the librettist was his friend Andrea Maffei, a distinguished man of letters with a reputation far above that of Piave or Solera, who had supplied most of Verdi's earlier librettos. However, all this notwithstanding, *I masnadieri* had a troublesome birth: Maffei's lack of experience in theatrical matters was a considerable trial; Verdi quarrelled with the publisher of the opera, Francesco Lucca (with whom he never had the generally cordial relations he enjoyed with the rival firm, Ricordi); and when he arrived in London to supervise the production, he seems to have been oppressed beyond all reason by the detested English weather. The première was a magnificent gala occasion – Queen Victoria headed the guests of honour – and a triumphant success. The famous soprano Jenny Lind played Amalia, Italo Gardoni was Carlo, Filippo Coletti was Francesco, and Luigi Lablache, one of the great names of the previous generation of Italian singers, played Massimiliano. But the enthusiastic reception was short-lived, and the opera fared rather badly in Italy. Modern revivals are not uncommon, but they remain special occasions: it seems unlikely that the work will find a permanent place in the international repertory.

A lachrymose cello solo, written expressly for Piatti, principal cellist at Her Majesty's Theatre, forms a brief but effective prelude.

ACT 1.i *A tavern on the frontier of Saxony* In a formally conventional, carefully crafted double aria with chorus, Carlo muses on his distant homeland and his beloved Amalia (the Andante 'O mio castel paterno') before learning, through a letter from his brother, that he is forbidden to return home. He and his friends decide to become bandits and swear an oath of blood brotherhood (the cabaletta 'Nell'argilla maledetta').

1.ii *Franconia: a room in Massimiliano's castle* A rapid change of locale is effected for a second double aria, this time for Carlo's wicked brother, Francesco. In the angular Andante sostenuto, 'La sua lampada vitale', Francesco threatens to hasten the end of his father's life. He then orders that Massimiliano be told of Carlo's death in battle, hoping that shock and grief will finish the old man off. In a forceful cabaletta, 'Tremate, o miseri!', he eagerly looks forward to assuming power.

1.iii *A bedroom in the castle* After a prelude in which solo woodwind are prominent, Amalia looks at the sleeping Massimiliano and thinks back over past joys in 'Lo sguardo avea degli angeli'. The aria was clearly written with Jenny Lind in mind: it is far more highly ornamented than the usual Verdian model and, to accommodate the free flow of decoration, formally far more discursive. Massimiliano awakes and, in a short duet movement with Amalia, 'Carlo! io muoio', laments that he will die without seeing his favourite son. Arminio and Francesco enter to deliver the false news of Carlo's death, saying that Carlo's dying words accused his father and instructed Amalia to marry Francesco. This revelation precipitates the quartet 'Sul capo mio colpevole': Massimiliano is both repentant and furious with Francesco; Amalia (joined by a reformed Arminio) offers religious consolation; Francesco eagerly looks forward to his triumph. It is a powerfully effective clash of emotions, and ends as Massimiliano, seemingly lifeless, falls to the ground.

ACT 2.i *An enclosure adjoining the castle chapel* Time has passed, and Francesco is lord of the castle. Amalia visits Massimiliano's grave and in a simple Adagio, 'Tu del mio Carlo al seno', imagines him and Carlo together in heaven. Arminio rushes in to reveal that Carlo and Massimiliano are both alive. Amalia rejoices in a jubilant and distinctly old-fashioned cabaletta, 'Carlo vive?', which again gave ample opportunity for Jenny Lind to demonstrate her famed agility. Francesco enters to declare his love for Amalia and they launch into a four-movement soprano-baritone confrontation duet, a type of dramatic situation at which Verdi almost always succeeded magnificently. But for once the format proves disappointing: the Andantino 'Io t'amo, Amalia' dissolves too quickly into routine rhythmic unison at the 3rd or 6th, and the cabaletta 'Ti scosta, o malnato', in which Amalia defies Francesco's attempts to take her by force, deals unimaginatively with the clash of tessituras that many of Verdi's best examples exploit so powerfully.

*'I masnadieri' (Verdi):
final scene in Act 4 in the
original production at
Her Majesty's Theatre,
London, 22 July 1847,
with Jenny Lind as
Amalia (centre) and Luigi
Lablache as Massimiliano
(right): engraving from
'The Illustrated London
News' (31 July 1847)*

2.ii *The Bohemian forest near Prague* The 'Scena e Coro' offers a typical slice of bandit life, though the choral writing is more complex than Verdi usually ventured. Rolla, condemned to be hanged, is rescued by Carlo and his followers, who rejoice in their carefree life. They leave Carlo alone to lament his outcast state in a fine minor–major *romanza*, 'Di ladroni attorniato'. His companions return to report that they are under attack and all join in a warlike chorus.

ACT 3.i *A deserted place adjacent to the forest near Massimiliano's castle* Amalia has escaped from Francesco but is now alone and terrified to hear the sound of bandits nearby. She begs for mercy from the first man she sees: miraculously, he turns out to be Carlo, and the lovers are blissfully united in a duet. The first lyrical movement, 'Qual mare, qual terra', is perhaps a trifle dull, although colouristic vocal effects in part make up for a lack of the usual confrontational tension. Amalia tells Carlo of his father's death, and of Francesco's attempts on her virtue. They join in a closing cabaletta, 'Lassù risplendere', in which Amalia has yet more opportunity to display her trills and agility.

3.ii *Inside the forest* A further, rather jaunty bandits' chorus introduces the 'Finale Terzo'. Carlo wrestles with his Byronic soul and even contemplates suicide, but is interrupted by Arminio, whom he sees delivering food to someone imprisoned in a deserted tower. Carlo intervenes, bringing forth from the tower an emaciated old man who reveals himself as Massimiliano. In an impressive minor–major narrative, 'Un ignoto, tre lune or saranno', Massimiliano (who has not recognized his son) tells how Francesco had him confined there after he recovered from his collapse. Carlo is outraged, and calls on his fellow bandits to join him in swearing a solemn oath of vengeance against Francesco.

ACT 4.i *A suite of rooms in Massimiliano's castle* Francesco's 'Pareami che sorto da lauto convito' describes a frightening vision of divine retribution in a movement that prefigures the great soliloquies of Verdi's middle-period operas. He summons Moser and asks forgiveness for his sins: only God can grant forgiveness, the pastor answers. Prompted by signs that the castle is under attack, Francesco rushes off to meet his fate.

4.ii *The forest (as 3.ii)* Carlo will not reveal his identity to Massimiliano but nevertheless asks for 'a father's blessing'. In a gentle duet, 'Come il bacio d'un padre amoroso', father and son are vocally united. The robbers appear, having captured Amalia, and very soon Carlo's identity is revealed. In a final trio 'Caduto è il reprobo!', reminiscent of the parallel number in Act 4 of *Ernani*, Carlo rails against his commitment to the life of crime while Amalia offers to stay with him no matter what may befall. But Carlo's robber companions are near at hand, impossible to ignore: in a final declamatory passage, he stabs Amalia and rushes off to the gallows that await him.

* * *

I masnadieri is one of the most intriguing of Verdi's early works. It should have been a great success: a foreign commission of great prestige, a high Romantic basis in Schiller (one of the composer's favourite sources), a distinguished man of letters as the librettist, a cast of international standing. What is more, Verdi and his librettist consciously tried to break with certain longstanding traditions in order to make their creation more romantically intense: no other early opera dispenses with an opening chorus, for example, or with a concertato finale. But all these ingredients proved problematic. Verdi felt out of touch and out of sympathy with the English environment and may have been unsure of the audience's taste and requirements; the drama proved somewhat unwieldy, particularly in its lack of opportunities for character confrontation; Maffei, in spite of his poetic skills and willingness to experiment, was unsure of himself in dramatic pacing; and the cast, Jenny Lind in particular, inspired music which, though distinguished enough on its own, proved difficult to subsume under an overall dramatic colour, the achievement of which was so crucial to Verdian success.

For further illustration *see* LIBRETTO (i), fig.5.

ROGER PARKER

Mason, Edith (**Barnes**) (*b* St Louis, 22 March 1893; *d* San Diego, 26 Nov 1973). American soprano. She studied in Cincinnati and made her début in 1912 at Boston as Nedda. After further study in Paris she made her European début in 1914 at Nice. She made her Metropolitan début in 1915 as Sophie, then sang Micaëla, Gretel and Musetta and took part in the première of De Koven's *The Canterbury Pilgrims* (1917). In Paris (1920) she sang Juliet, Marguerite and Gilda at the Opéra, and Massenet's Manon at the Opéra-Comique. At Monte Carlo (1920–21) she sang Thaïs, Salome (*Hérodiade*), Antonia, Marguerite de Valois and Butterfly. She appeared at La Scala (1923) as Mimì; at Covent Garden (1930) as Martha, Juliet and Gilda; and at Florence (1933) and Salzburg (1935) as Nannetta. At Chicago (1921–39) her roles included Snow Maiden, Sophie, Boito's Margherita, Thaïs, Elsa, Fiora, Butterfly and Desdemona, which she sang at her farewell; she returned for one performance of Mimì in 1941. Her beautiful voice, even in tone and easily produced, was used with taste, and she was a fine, if restrained, actress.

O. Thompson: *The American Singer* (New York, 1937), 351

A. E. Knight: 'Edith Mason', *Record Collector*, x (1955–6), 75–87 [with discography]

RICHARD D. FLETCHER/ELIZABETH FORBES

Masque. A kind of English court entertainment which flourished from the last quarter of the 16th century until 1640; also a self-contained, opera-like entertainment found in late 17th- and early 18th-century English plays, either included within the acts themselves or performed as a separate afterpiece to the play.

The early masque, which is said to have reached England from Italy in 1512, seems to have added a novel feature to the existing types of seasonal mummery: the masked and costumed aristocratic participants danced with members of the audience as well as performing their own numbers. The masque came of age in the reign of James I. By then the masks had been largely discarded, spectacular scenic effects were in vogue, and speaking characters, taken by professional actors, were used to outline a simple allegorical or mythological plot in praise of the royal or aristocratic sponsor. A typical Jacobean court masque had five dance episodes or 'entries'. The aristocratic 'masquers' danced three of these, and took partners from the audience for a fourth, the 'revels', a variable and often indeterminate number of social dances (branles, corantos, pavins, galliards etc.). The fifth, the comic 'antimasque', first introduced in Jonson's *The Masque of Queens* (1609), was a separate, self-contained entertainment executed entirely by professionals, which preceded the main masque as 'a foil or false masque'. The performers were often grotesquely (or 'antiquely') dressed, and the themes were low life, comic or simply bizarre.

The early masques had a general theme (ranging from Purity to the Virtues of Tobacco) to which all the entries were related; the later Jacobean masques, especially those with scenarios written by Ben Jonson (Master of the Revels and the first poet laureate), have complex, allegorical plots designed to flatter the king and glorify the court and state. Each masque was designed for a particular occasion and was normally presented only once, almost always in honour of the king or another member of the royal family. The usual venue was the Banqueting House of Whitehall Palace or one of the Inns of Court; stage and scenery were specially constructed for each show. In spite of the participation of leading court composers, such as Robert Johnson, Thomas Campion, Alfonso Ferrabosco II and John Coprario, and the introduction of monody (or 'recitative musick', as it was called) by Nicholas Lanier perhaps as early as 1617, the masque was never really set to become opera, because at the heart of every masque were the revels. The intermingling of fantasy and reality during the revels (and after which the formal entries could continue) distinguishes the masque from other kinds of early Baroque music drama.

The early masques were, apart from the instrumental music, performed mostly by the courtiers themselves, who rehearsed for weeks, even months before the single performance. As masques became longer and dramatically more complex, professional singers and dancers played larger roles. The antimasques in particular became musically and choreographically more adventurous, and specially invented dances called 'the measures', rather than familiar ballroom types, predominated. The masque was brought to a pinnacle of sophistication by Jonson and Inigo Jones during the period 1605–15. But Jonson's desire for literary coherence and poetic beauty was incompatible with Jones's concern for visual spectacle. Productions became increasingly lavish, and the architect and designer brilliantly adopted and improved upon the new single-point perspective scenery first developed in Italy; transformations were effected instantaneously by use of complicated and expensive machinery. The two men finally fell out and Jonson withdrew, being replaced after 1631 by Aurelian Townshend, Thomas Carew and William Davenant.

The Jacobean masque possessed nearly all the essential ingredients of true opera except a consistent, coherent plot and continuous music. Jonson's *Lovers made Men* (1617) seems to have satisfied even these criteria: the title-page of the 1640 edition of the libretto states that it was *'sung after the Italian manner, stilo recitativo'* by Lanier who also composed the music. Unfortunately, none of the music of what may have been the first English opera survives. The musical remains of the Stuart masque in general are meagre, consisting mostly of the treble parts of dances which are difficult to ascribe to specific works. The multi-media splendours of these works would thus seem irrecoverable.

The masques of the reign of Charles I, with texts by Shirley and Davenant, grew decadent in content and ever more expensive; their extravagance was severely criticized in the massive tract *Histrio-Mastix* (1633) whose author William Prynne, a barrister, was punished by the removal of his ears. The last Stuart masque was *Salmacida Spolia* (1640). Any further court entertainment of this scale was rendered impossible by the Civil Wars and the execution of Charles I. But the masque tradition survived into the Commonwealth and after the Restoration with *Cupid and Death* (1653), a moral fable in five entries, and John Crowne's *Calisto* (1675), which, including the Princesses Mary and Anne (future queens of England) in the speaking *dramatis personae*, was essentially a pastoral-ballet with masque-like entr'actes. Many Restoration plays included entertainments of music and dance which are called 'masques', but they are merely theatrical representations of the court masque, rarely comprise more than one entry and lack the revels. John Blow's *Venus and Adonis*, which was composed for the private entertainment of Charles II (*c*1683), was also called a masque, though it is a true opera; and Purcell's *Dido and Aeneas*, which is also an

opera, includes many masque-like elements, particularly the witches' scenes which are much indebted to the anti-masque. All-sung works, such as those entered for the 1701 competition to set Congreve's *The Judgment of Paris* or Handel's *Acis and Galatea* (1718), were sometimes called masques even though they did not feature dancing – perhaps because they were in English and had mythological subjects; true masques, with speech, music and dance, continued to be written from time to time for special occasions well into the 19th century.

For further illustration *see* JONES, INIGO and THEATRE ARCHITECTURE, fig.2.

*

E. Welsford: *The Court Masque* (Cambridge, MA, 1927)

E. J. Dent: *Foundations of English Opera: a Study of Musical Drama in England during the Seventeenth Century* (Cambridge, 1928)

A. Nicoll: *Stuart Masques and the Renaissance Stage* (London, 1938)

J. P. Cutts: *La musique de scène de la troupe de Shakespeare* (Paris, 1959, 2/1971)

A. J. Sabol: *Songs and Dances for the Stuart Masque* (Providence, RI, 1959, enlarged 2/1978)

R. Fiske: *English Theatre Music in the Eighteenth Century* (London, 1973, 2/1986)

S. Orgel and R. Strong: *Inigo Jones: the Theatre of the Stuart Court* (London, 1973)

A. J. Sabol, ed.: *Four Hundred Songs and Dances from the Stuart Masque* (Hanover, NH, 1978, 2/1982)

M. Chan: *Music in the Theatre of Ben Jonson* (London, 1980)

D. Lindley, ed.: *The Court Masque* (Manchester, 1984)

PETER HOLMAN, CURTIS PRICE

Designs by Inigo Jones for characters from masques by Ben Jonson, performed at the Banqueting House of Whitehall Palace, London: (above) the masquer Lady Anne Winter as Candace in 'The Masque of Queens', 1609, and (below) the dwarf postilion's lackeys from the first antimasque in 'Chloridia', 1631

Massarani, Renzo (*b* Mantua, 26 March 1898; *d* Rio de Janeiro, 28 March 1975). Italian composer and critic. He studied in Rome under Respighi, and in the early 1920s was associated with Labroca and Rieti in the group I Tre (named in imitation of Les Six). For a time he was music director of Vittorio Podrecca's famous puppet theatre Il Teatro dei Piccoli, with which he travelled widely during the mid-1920s. Between the wars he also sometimes wrote for the newspaper *L'impero*. When Mussolini adopted Hitler's race policies, however, his works were banned and much material was destroyed during World War II. He emigrated to Brazil, where he wrote music criticism; but after his traumatic experiences he preferred to forget about his own music, forbade its republication and performance, and refused access to the manuscripts. Only since his death have his many unpublished pieces (which include the successful puppet ballet *Guerin detto il meschino* as well as several operas) again become available, at least for inspection; and some of them were not brought back to Italy until 1991.

In the 1920s and 30s Massarani was highly regarded by some of the most intelligent Italian critics. For instance, Rossi-Doria (1924) wrote of 'compositions saturated with life and with warm, red, very Italian blood like that of our rough Lombard craftsmen'. Among the long-concealed operas, *Il pozzo* and *La donna nel pozzo* are indeed full of explicitly Lombard local colour; but probably the most interesting (and certainly the most widely performed) part of Massarani's output consists of the works that he wrote specifically for Podrecca's puppets. The brief 'intermezzo grottesco' *Bianco e nero* (also described as an 'operina') is an amusing early example; but it was with *Guerin detto il meschino* that he came to international notice. Though not strictly speaking an opera, the work contains extensive vocal narrations (alternately lyrical and rapidly declamatory) which introduce the danced action and owe something to Falla's *El retablo de maese Pedro*. The freshness of the melodic invention, and the well-judged excursions into irregular barring and polytonality as foils to the simple ostinatos of other passages, suggest a composer of real if unassuming individuality, already clearly foreshadowed in *Bianco e nero*. The other available theatre works, though variable in quality, confirm the impression that Massarani was potentially the most original of I Tre though not always the best at giving his ideas coherent shape. His ballet *Boè* (1937, Bergamo), whose success was tragically cut short by anti-Semitic persecution, shares many of the best qualities of *Guerin* while being much more complex and sophisticated. The manuscript of the unfinished last opera *Eliduc* reveals how abruptly Massarani's urge to compose was stifled by his personal tragedy: Act 1 seems to be complete apart from the orchestration; Act 2 consists only of fragmentary sketches in pencil. Massarani's critical writings include booklets on Verdi, *Lohengrin*, *Tristan*, *Don Pasquale* and *L'elisir d'amore*.

La vittoria, perf. 1921, ?lost
Noi due, 1922 (3, Massarani), ?unperf.
Bianco e nero (int grottesco, 1, A. Pagan), Rome, Palazzo Odescalchi, 1923
Le nozze di Takiù (operina), Rome, 1927
Il pozzo, 1928 (op contadina, 1), ?unperf.
Guerin detto il meschino (puppet ballet with sung narrative), Paris and Darmstadt, 1928
Gibetto e Gherminella, 1928–9 (operina, 3, R. Bartolozzi), Rome, 1929
I dolori della principessa Susina (operina, C. Pavolini), Rome, Circolo delle Arti, via Margutta, 1929
La donna nel pozzo (notturno paesano, 1, A. Rossato), 19 Dec 1930
Eliduc, 1938 (C. Meano), inc.

*

G. Rossi-Doria: 'Labroca-Massarani-Rieti', *Il pianoforte*, v (1924), 303–9
——: 'Lettera da Roma', *RaM*, ii (1929), 332 [on *Guerin detto il meschino*]
J. C. G. Waterhouse: *The Emergence of Modern Italian Music (up to 1940)* (diss., U. of Oxford, 1968), 670, 674–9

JOHN C. G. WATERHOUSE

Massard, Robert (*b* Pau, 15 Aug 1925). French baritone. After studying in Pau and Bayonne, he made his début on 8 June 1952 as the High Priest in *Samson et Dalila* at the Paris Opéra, remaining with the company until 1976. His big, easy baritone established him from the outset as a favourite for repertory parts throughout France. He has sung in many leading houses, his roles including Thoas, Enrico Ashton, Ramiro (*L'heure espagnole*), Valentin and Escamillo. But it is in the important revivals of Gluck and Berlioz that he has proved indispensable: his Orestes with the Covent Garden Opera at the 1961 Edinburgh Festival was praised as stylish, vigorous and impassioned; by contrast, his slow-witted Fieramosca (*Benvenuto Cellini*) was a clever character study. Massard created the Harpist in Barraud's *Numance* in 1955 and sang the Count in the first Opéra-Comique production of *Capriccio* (1957), as well as Orpheus in Milhaud's *Les malheurs d'Orphée* and Nero in *L'incoronazione di Poppea* at Aix. In the 1970s he added Massenet roles to his repertory at the Opéra. ANDRÉ TUBEUF

Massary, Fritzi [Massarik, Friederike] (*b* Vienna, 21 March 1882; *d* Beverly Hills, CA, 30 Jan 1969). Austrian soprano. She made her name in variety in Vienna before achieving success in revues at the Metropoltheater, Berlin. She starred in many Berlin productions of operettas by Lehár, Fall, Kálmán and Offenbach, including a revue version of *Die lustige Witwe* (1928, Metropol). In 1918 she married the *buffo* bass Max Pallenberg (1877–1934), with whom she occasionally appeared. Works in which she created leading roles included Fall's *Der liebe Augustin* (1912), *Die Kaiserin* (1915), *Die spanische Nachtigall* (1921) and *Madame Pompadour* (1922), Straus's *Der letzte Walzer* (1920), *Die Perlen der Kleopatra* (1923), *Der Tanz um die Liebe* (1924), *Die Teresina* (1925), *Die Königen* (1926) and *Eine Frau, die weiss was sie will* (1932), and Coward's *Operette* (1938, London). Although considered less a pure soprano than a *diseuse*, with a captivating stage presence and ability to put a song over, Massary sang Adele in *Die Fledermaus* in performances conducted by Richard Strauss and, at Salzburg in 1926, Bruno Walter.

*

ES (O. Schneidereit)
O. Bie: *Fritzi Massary* (Berlin, 1920)
'Pem': *Und der Himmel hängt voller Geigen: Glanz und Zauber der Operette* (Berlin, 1955)
O. Schneidereit: *Berlin wie es weint und lacht* (Berlin, 1968)
P. Rose: *Berlins grosse Theaterzeit* (Berlin, 1969)
O. Schneidereit: *Fritzi Massary* (Berlin, 1970)
P. O'Connor: 'Fritzi Massary', *Opera*, xxxiii (1982), 467–74

ANDREW LAMB

Massé, Victor [Félix Marie] (*b* Lorient, 7 March 1822; *d* Paris, 5 July 1884). French composer. He moved to Paris as a child, and entered the Conservatoire in October 1834. After some years of study with Halévy, he won the Prix de Rome in 1844 for his cantata *Le rénégat de Tanger*. In Rome he composed a mass and an opera, *La favorita e la schiava* (*c*1845). After returning to Paris, having travelled through Italy and Germany, he composed many songs and romances, but found little success in opera until *La chanteuse voilée* (1850), followed by the more ambitious *Galathée* (1852). The following year he obtained a major success with *Les noces de Jeannette*, in which his recent bride Marie Miolan appeared in the title role, as also in *La reine Topaze* (1856), in which Massé incorporated (in Act 2) variations on Petrella's *Il carnevale di Venezia* for flute.

In 1860 Massé became chorus master at the Opéra, earning Wagner's approval for his work on *Tannhäuser*. The idea in 1864 of an operatic setting of Mérimée's *Carmen* came to nothing. In 1866 he was appointed professor of advanced composition at the Conservatoire, his duties leaving him little time to write himself. However, an opera, *Paul et Virginie*, was produced in 1876, in which year a nervous disease forced him to give up his position at the Conservatoire; it eventually confined him to his home. He was made a Chevalier of the Légion d'honneur in 1856 and Officier in 1877, and was elected to the Institut in 1872. The opera *Une nuit de Cléopâtre* was in the preliminary stages of preparation when he died. As with *Paul et Virginie*, however, *Cléopâtre* suggests that Massé was inclined to aim above his talents, which are perhaps best represented by the unassuming *Les noces de Jeannette*, among the most delightful of one-act *opéras comiques*.

See also NOCES DE JEANNETTE, LES.

unless otherwise stated, opéras comiques, first performed and published (vocal score) in Paris
La favorita e la schiava, *c*1845 (op), Venice, 1855, ?unpubd
La chambre gothique (1, P. F. A. Carmouche), Folies-Dramatiques, 1849, ?unpubd

La chanteuse voilée (1, E. Scribe and A. de Leuven), OC (Favart), 26 Nov 1850 (1852)

Galathée (2, J. Barbier and M. Carré), OC (Favart), 14 April 1852 (1854)

Les noces de Jeannette (1, Barbier and Carré), OC (Favart), 4 Feb 1853 (1853)

La fiancée du diable (3, Scribe and H. Romand), OC (Favart), 5 June 1854 (1854)

Miss Fauvette (1, Barbier and Carré), OC (Favart), 13 Feb 1855 (1854)

Le prix de famille (opérette, 1, J. Méry), unperf. (1855)

Les saisons (3, Barbier and Carré), OC (Favart), 22 Dec 1855 (1856)

La reine Topaze (3, Lockroy [J. P. Simon] and L. Battu), Lyrique, 27 Dec 1856 (1857)

Le cousin de Marivaux (saynète, 1, Battu), Baden-Baden, 15 Aug 1857, ?unpubd

Les chaises à porteurs (1, P. F. Dumanoir and Clairville), OC (Favart), 28 April 1858 (1858)

La fée Carabosse (prol., 3, Lockroy and Cogniard), Lyrique, 28 Feb 1859 (1859)

Mariette la promise (? oc, 1), St Petersburg, Imperial, Aug 1862, ?unpubd

La mule de Pedro (opéra, 2, Dumanoir), Opéra, 6 March 1863 (1863)

Fior d'Aliza (4, Carré and H. Lucas, after A. de Lamartine), OC (Favart), 5 Feb 1866 (1866)

Le fils du brigadier (3, E. M. Labiche and A. Delacour), OC (Favart), 25 Feb 1867 (1868)

Les enfants de Perrette (opérette, 1), unperf. (1872)

La petite soeur d'Achille (1), unperf. (1873)

La trouvaille (1, Mme Rocheblanc), unperf. (?1873)

Paul et Virginie (opéra, 3, Barbier and Carré, after B. de Saint-Pierre), Opéra National Lyrique, 15 Nov 1876 (1877)

Une loi somptuaire (opérette, 2, P. Dubourg), unperf. (1879)

Une nuit de Cléopâtre (3, Barbier, after T. Gautier), OC (Favart), 25 April 1885 (1885)

*

G. Ropartz: *Victor Massé* (Paris, 1887)

H. Delaborde: *Notice sur la vie et les ouvrages de M. Victor Massé* (Paris, 1888)

L. Gallet: *Notes d'un librettiste* (Paris, 1891)   ANDREW LAMB

Massenet, Jules (Emile Frédéric) (*b* Montaud, St Etienne, 12 May 1842; *d* Paris, 13 Aug 1912). French composer, the leading figure in French opera of the late 19th century and composer of two works that remain central to the repertory.

1. Life: to 1880. 2. Life: after 1880. 3. Personality, reputation. 4. Style. 5. Achievement.

1. LIFE: TO 1880. Massenet was born of solid bourgeois stock, the 12th and last child of a master-founder by his second marriage. His mother was musical; after her husband's business failed and the family moved to Paris when the composer was six, she provided valuable financial support by giving piano lessons. Her son was one of her pupils, and gained admission to the piano class at the Paris Conservatoire on his second attempt in 1853. The following year the family moved once more, to Chambéry, and the 12-year-old boy demonstrated his determination to pursue a musical career by running away from home, being recaptured by chance by a family friend on Lyons railway station. He was thereupon allowed to return to Paris in the care of an elder sister. He won a *premier prix* for piano at the Conservatoire in 1859, having given his first public recital the previous year. He supported himself by giving lessons, and by playing the piano in cafés and in the percussion section in theatre orchestras; he almost certainly played in the première of *Faust* at the Théâtre Lyrique in 1859, but it is more doubtful if, as legend has it, he was in the orchestra at the *Tannhäuser* fiasco at the Opéra two years later.

Massenet started harmony and composition classes at the Conservatoire in 1860, receiving particular en-couragement from the director, Ambroise Thomas. He won the Prix de Rome, again at his second attempt, in 1863 with the active support of Berlioz. He composed prolifically but unoperatically during his two years at the Villa Medici and met Liszt, who recommended Louise-Constance de Gressy ('Ninon') to him as a piano pupil; they married in 1866 and Juliette, their only child, was born two years later.

The late 1860s were a time of great, if not profitable, activity, although his association with the publisher Georges Hartmann provided a certain stability. *La grand'tante*, his first work for the stage to be performed, had a respectable success at the Opéra-Comique in 1867 (the cast included Marie Heilbronn, later to create Manon). More ambitious projects included *La coupe du roi de Thulé*, *Esmeralda* (after Hugo), the *opéra comique Florentin*, *Manfred* (after Byron), *Les templiers* and *Méduse*, few of them completed and none performed. In the Franco-Prussian War he served in the national guard with his friend Bizet.

After the Commune, *Don César de Bazan* (based on the same Hugo play as Wallace's *Maritana*) enjoyed a fair success at the Opéra-Comique (1872). But fame came decisively in 1873 with his incidental music to Leconte de Lisle's *Les érinnyes* (one section of which, the Elégie for cello, has proved durable) and with the oratorio *Marie-Magdeleine*, which Pauline Viardot promoted and in which she sang the leading role. Another oratorio, *Eve*, followed in 1875 with scarcely less success, and these, together with various orchestral pieces, earned him the Légion d'honneur in 1876. The early death of Bizet the previous year left him without rival in his generation of composers for the stage, a position confirmed by the triumphant reception of his Meyerbeerian opera *Le roi de Lahore* at the Palais Garnier in 1877. The success was repeated in Turin the following year and led to the joint commissioning of *Hérodiade* by Hartmann and Tito Ricordi. Also in 1878 Thomas appointed him professor of composition at the Conservatoire – a post he filled with scrupulous integrity for 18 years – and he was elected to the Académie Française in preference to Saint-Saëns, which the senior composer found it hard to forgive. Massenet had been an active member of Saint-Saëns' Société Nationale de Musique since 1871, but their relationship was never easy.

2. LIFE: AFTER 1880. A change of management at the Opéra led to the withdrawal of *Le roi de Lahore* from the repertory and the rejection of *Hérodiade*, which was first heard in Brussels in 1881 and always more popular in the French provinces than in the capital. The *opéra comique Manon* restored the balance in 1884, and the revival of *Hérodiade* at the Théâtre Italien the same year together with the première of *Le Cid* (a *grand opéra* in all but name) in 1885 marked Massenet's first period of success in Paris. But *Werther*, which was conceived as early as 1882, was turned down by the Opéra-Comique and *Manon* temporarily withdrawn from the repertory in 1886. *Werther* received its belated première, in Vienna, only in 1892, following the success of *Manon* at the Hofoper there.

Meanwhile, in 1887 Massenet met the Californian soprano Sibyl Sanderson, for whom he revised *Manon* and wrote *Esclarmonde* (1889). There followed a period of discernible crisis: the five-act *Le mage* was a failure at the Opéra in 1891; the same year *Amadis* was sketched but abandoned for 20 years (Massenet took it up again for the object of his second *amitié amoureuse*, Lucy Arbell); Hartmann went bankrupt, and his business was taken over by Heugel. Massenet wrote little of substance for nearly four years, and not until after the success of *Werther* in Vienna (and indeed in France outside Paris, where it was withdrawn from the repertory of the Opéra-Comique after only a year) did he regain his full creative powers, first with *Thaïs* (1894), which marked the end of his association with Sanderson, then with the *verismo* two-acter *La Navarraise*, an appreciable success in London the same year.

When Ambroise Thomas died in 1896, Massenet declined the directorship of the Conservatoire (and did so again in 1905) and resigned from the chair of composition to devote himself full-time to the theatre. *Sapho* (1897) and *Cendrillon* (1899) were modestly successful with the public at the Opéra-Comique, where Albert Carré's new regime was in place, and Massenet substantially revised *Thaïs*, which was nevertheless no more warmly received at the Opéra in 1898 than it had been four years earlier. In 1901 *Grisélidis*, which had been on the stocks for seven years, was coolly treated at the Opéra-Comique, where the musical director Messager had *Pelléas* in his sights (it followed five months later). The approach from Raoul Gunsbourg of the Monte Carlo Opéra, then, was timely for the 59-year-old composer: not only did *Le jongleur de Notre-Dame* have its première there in 1902, but *Chérubin* (1905), *Thérèse* (1907), *Don Quichotte* (1910) and *Roma* (1912) were commissioned, revivals of many other works were mounted, lavishly cast, and all – thanks to one of the great entrepreneurs of operatic history – equally lavishly publicized. The triumph of Lina Cavalieri in *Thaïs* both at La Scala (1905) and at the Opéra (1907), in addition to revivals of *Werther* and *Sapho* at the Opéra-Comique that ensured their place in the repertory, made up for disappointments elsewhere – the failures of *Ariane* (1906) and *Bacchus* (1909) at the Opéra. The Rabelais-based *Panurge* had its première posthumously (Théâtre de la Gaité, 1913), as did *Cléopâtre* (1914) and *Amadis* (1922), both at Monte Carlo.

The last years of Massenet's life were dominated by his relationship with the mezzo-soprano Lucy Arbell, for whom he wrote *Thérèse* as well as roles in *Ariane*, *Bacchus*, *Don Quichotte*, *Roma* and – according to her – the title roles of *Cléopâtre* and *Amadis*. The composer was 62 when they met in 1904 (she was 40 years younger) and their association caused Mme Massenet more upset than had that with Sanderson. According to eye-witnesses, Arbell's demands on the composer tested even his infatuation, and after his death she pursued his widow and his publishers with lawsuits over exclusive rights to his posthumous oeuvre – hence the long-delayed premières of *Cléopâtre* and *Amadis*. Massenet himself started to suffer from chronic uraemia in 1900, and died of cancer in August 1912, having barely had the strength to attend the Monte Carlo première of *Roma* six months earlier.

3. PERSONALITY, REPUTATION. Massenet's extravagantly misleading 'autobiography' (*Mes souvenirs*, 1912; in fact dictated to a journalist) has unfortunately been followed by most writers on the composer in English. Through it he sought to establish the legend of a composer who wrote with supreme ease and enjoyed an unbroken string of successes with the public – 'the dear public, which is rarely deceived' – if not with jealous colleagues and critics. As the above summary would suggest, this is far from the truth. His successes at the Opéra were few and far between, and he had several set-backs at the Opéra-Comique. Without Gunsbourg, his career could well have come to a premature end, though it is true that he followed the pattern of so many French composers in seeing his works appreciated more abroad than at home. The most misleading section of the book concerns the gestation of *Werther*, leading all commentators until recently to suppose that he wrote the piece after rather than before *Esclarmonde*, and this may have been a deliberate attempt to cover up the un-productive crisis years of 1889–93.

The legend he successfully created has ultimately proved extremely counterproductive in the matter of his posthumous reputation. It has been all too easy for commentators to follow the summings-up of writers like Debussy, whose obituary in the *Revue blanche* included the eminently quotable lines about his colleagues finding it hard to forgive Massenet's 'ability to please', and the somewhat snobbish observation that females among the working classes of Paris hummed tunes from *Manon* and *Werther* when they got up in the morning rather than those from the *St Matthew Passion*. Massenet's systematic destruction of sketches and revisions, part of his aim to establish 'definitive' scores to be published before first productions in order to minimize opportunities for interference from managements – he was well aware of the havoc wrought by Carvalho on Gounod's operas – has led to accusations of facileness in addition to cynical opportunism: it was felt that there was something altogether too 'easy', too superficial, about the way he worked. But what little can be established about his methods, particularly in the case of post-production revisions (which were substantial), indicates both shrewdness and a near-faultless sense of theatrical shape and effect – something that not even his detractors can deny. But in general he covered his tracks too efficiently for the good of his reputation.

His essential shyness led, as is so often the case, to an overwhelming desire to be liked, adding to the picture of a composer seeking above all to please rather than provoke. Yet the *Souvenirs* cannot help revealing a decidedly feline personality, one adept at settling old scores under a cloak of sugary bonhomie and copious flattery (there can be no doubt, for instance, of his opinion of Shalyapin's Don Quichotte, as if the Russian bass's records are not enough to demonstrate why). He did nothing to counter his reputation as a successful womanizer, although external evidence would suggest sex in the head rather than in the bed; Sibyl Sanderson had a domineering mother and her interests probably lay in other directions, and there is something rather sad about the aging Massenet's relationship with the gold-digging Lucy Arbell, a relationship surely reflected in *Don Quichotte*. Indeed, it is hard to accept without question that a composer whose greatest strength lay in writing about unfulfilled erotic obsession – Charlotte and Werther, Herod and Salome, Thaïs and Athanaël – matched the legendary facility of his compositions in other departments. But Massenet scholarship is still in its infancy: a chronology of his life has only recently been established (see Gillis 1990) and the first serious biography of the composer is awaited with some impatience.

4. STYLE. 'La fille de Gounod', one of the unflattering phrases coined by his contemporaries, is a convenient

starting-point for a discussion of his style. Gounod was important if only in that he liberated French opera from the domination of foreigners – from Cherubini, Spontini and Rossini to Meyerbeer, Donizetti and Verdi – and Massenet continued the process, as well as being a successful exporter of the product. Like Gounod, he was not shy of melody, and like Gounod he developed a gift for long-breathed tunes in 9/8 and 12/8, the so-called 'phrase Massenétique', which in his hands never limped or faltered. Unlike Gounod's, perhaps, his tunes were seldom there for their own sake, save of course in the dance interludes; they were part of his stock-in-trade of characterization through music, whether of the long, rhapsodic, potentially unending variety of the Méditation from *Thaïs*, or of the sort built out of the repetition and development of a single phrase, like Don Quichotte's Serenade or the little fragments that make up Herod's outpourings in *Hérodiade*. Both kinds have an obsessive, introverted quality well suited to dramatic needs. His use of pastiche, whether of the Spanish forms so beloved of French composers, of 18th-century dances or medieval patterns, has charm as well as ingenuity.

There is no reason to disbelieve Massenet's own account of his habitually memorizing his librettos over a period of weeks before starting to set them, given the way words and notes in his melodic phrases are so much part of each other that one cannot imagine the lines being set in any other way; Cendrillon's much-repeated 'Vous êtes mon Prince Charmant' is one, and the whole opening scene of *Grisélidis* (the shepherd Alain's hymn of love) is another. It is surely in word-setting that Massenet's greatest achievement lies. Whereas Gounod and to some extent Bizet used the natural stress-flexibility of the French language to constrain it within regular musical phrases, Massenet reversed the process and used that flexibility to achieve maximum musical freedom. Add his meticulously detailed stress marks – no previous composer had annotated his scores so liberally or so purposefully – and instructions for rubato, and the result is richly expressive, full of verbal cross-rhythms to complement natural or expected musical ones. *Thaïs* is especially rich in this respect (see ex.1). The use Massenet makes of musico-verbal detail for the purpose of characterization through music might have earned him a further nickname, 'La belle-soeur de Bizet', since he shares that composer's infallible knack of placing his characters precisely the moment they appear: Manon's hesitant 'Je suis encore tout étourdie', for example, Cendrillon's wistful 'Reste au foyer', or Werther's just sufficiently selfconsciously rapturous 'Je ne sais si je rêve'.

If Massenet was less innovatory in his use of harmony, he still knew his Wagner, like all French composers of his generation, and profited. His taste, developed early, for enharmonic modulation and comparatively chaste chromatic progression earned d'Indy's remark about his 'discreet eroticism', though in operas in his middle period the adjective becomes redundant: the eroticism of some of the love music in *Esclarmonde* or the masterly mystical marriage in *Cendrillon* is agreeably indiscreet. In the later works his harmony grows more simple yet no less expressive, as does his instrumentation. From earliest days there was a diaphanous quality, a fastidious economy to Massenet's orchestra even amid the bombast of the traditional *grands opéras*, which developed in the middle period into something more characteristic, in particular a shimmering, sparkling effect notable in the

Ex.1 *Thaïs*, Act 1 scene ii

['Tell me that I am beautiful, and that I will be beautiful, for evermore. That nothing will blight the roses of my lips']

Mendelssohnian fairy music in *Cendrillon*, or – his first truly memorable (and erotic) orchestral effect – the accompaniment to the 'N'est-ce plus ma main' duet in *Manon*. The delicacy is tempered by a sometimes daring use of instrumental colour: he wrote frequently and effectively for the saxophone (*Le roi de Lahore*, *Hérodiade*, *Werther*). His taste for voices in unison with strings in early works, an idea seized upon eagerly by the Italian *veristi*, gave way later to, as it were, opposing unisons, in which voices are heard in counterpoint with often single instrumental lines, harking back to opera in its purest form and forward, curiously, to moments in Britten.

This was part of the general refinement of his compositional technique developed through a wide variety of works: traditional *grands opéras*, which he virtually abandoned after *Le Cid* in 1885 (significantly *Le mage*, *Ariane* and *Bacchus*, later works written for the Opéra, were all failures); *opéras comiques*, in which he skilfully used *mélodrame* to stand in for spoken dialogue; attempts at *verismo*, of which *Sapho* is by far the most interesting; and – a genre to which *Sapho* also belongs – sung plays (*Chérubin*, *Don Quichotte*). There is a sub-genre of medieval romances that are among Massenet's most appealing and delicate works for the stage, launched by the deceptively neo-grand *Esclarmonde*, and continued with *Grisélidis*, *Le jongleur de Notre-Dame* and *Amadis*. These are part of the general *fin-de-siècle* medieval revival: Burne-Jones is specifically cited for a sylvan visual effect in *Amadis*, the first act of which is composed entirely as *mélodrame*, a daring experiment, and a successful one.

From *Esclarmonde* onwards, the process of refinement, of increasing economy of means, grows ever more marked. In that work, the way the complicated plot is dispatched in order to leave room for lyrical expansion is extremely impressive from a purely technical point of view (this fine work has been sadly misrepresented in its few revivals). In *Thaïs*, Massenet finally mastered motivic reminiscence, hitherto rather blatantly deployed (his use of it in the last act of *Manon*, including the misguided post-première addition of 'N'est-ce plus ma main', is what leads one ultimately to withhold the term 'masterpiece' from the work); indeed, the manipulation of musical motifs in *Thaïs*, the sly development of Athanaël's erotic-fantasy music from his original *Hymns-Ancient-and-Modern* diatonicism and their subsequent interplay, is managed with a subtlety unsurpassed by any composer working within Wagnerian parameters.

This does not preclude humour, an aspect of Massenet's output all too easily overlooked. In *Thaïs*, the quartet in which the slave girls attempt (unsuccessfully) to undress Athanaël and generally tidy him up before his first meeting with the heroine, is Gallic humour at its sauciest, and the suave tune is yet another – and extremely witty – transformation of the monk's basic erotic-fantasy theme. Humour of an altogether gentler kind centred upon Brother Boniface defuses the potentially over-gluey religious sentiment of *Le jongleur*, and the tender-hearted, downtrodden Pandolfe in *Cendrillon* is drawn with a ruefulness in perfect contrast to the broader strokes with which his termagant wife is painted. The Devil in *Grisélidis* and Sancho Panza are both richly rounded comic portraits, and it is no coincidence that all these roles, along with that of Le Philosophe in *Chérubin*, were written with the great bass-baritone Lucien Fugère in mind, as much a muse to Massenet as Sanderson or Arbell (neither of whom was a great singer). If sentiment is Massenet's Achilles' heel, then humour is his saving grace.

5. ACHIEVEMENT. It is difficult to assess Massenet's achievements and importance in the history of opera. The critical approach to his work so far – or rather, the lack of it – means that not necessarily the best of it has survived in the game of chance that still largely determines the operatic repertory. Yet whatever the stature of his works, he was the most successful composer of opera in France, if not in Europe, in the quarter-century between the death of Bizet and the première of *Pelléas*. His technical mastery and his craftsmanship are undeniable. He was also a complete man of the theatre, assiduously attending to every detail in the staging of his works – scenery, costumes and lighting, as well as orchestral – and their revivals throughout Europe. In this respect he was as much a 'producer' as Wagner.

His influence as exemplar and teacher was far-reaching. It was his early works, unfortunately, that were aped by the *veristi* as a necessary alternative inspiration to the brooding example of Verdi: would that they had waited to listen more carefully to his later ones. His pupils at the Conservatoire included Bruneau, Pierné, Charpentier, Rabaud, Hahn and Chausson, and more than one of them recalled the trouble he took drawing out their own ideas, never seeking to impose his own. Romain Rolland's image of 'a slumbering Massenet' in the heart of every subsequent French composer has more than a ring of truth to it: it is palpably true. In word-setting alone, all French musicians profited from the freedom he won from earlier restrictions. Rolland himself, echoed later by Poulenc, wrote of Massenet's influence on *Pelléas* (one reason, perhaps, for Debussy's decidedly equivocal attitude to his predecessor) and it is not necessary to delve far to discover the slumbering Massenet in, say, *La cathédrale engloutie* (the second-act entr'acte in *Le jongleur*) or the chorus of shepherds in *L'enfant et les sortilèges* (the minuet in *Thérèse*).

Massenet's reputation sank to its lowest ebb in the period after World War II. His major works lapsed from the repertory in France, not so much because of any lack of merit, more because the French operatic world itself collapsed, and Anglo-Saxon critics fell upon its remains with glee. The fifth edition of *Grove's Dictionary* (1954) said that his operas were fit only for a public 'which regards music as an agreeable after-dinner entertainment'. Martin Cooper in *The New Grove* was scarcely less dismissive, writing of a 'popularity and corresponding financial success that reveal how faithfully his music reflected the ideas, prejudices, anxieties and preoccupations of his contemporaries'. The key word is 'reflected'.

In terms of a post-Wagnerian, German-dominated critical aesthetic, one that ideally would sanction performances of operas by only about half a dozen composers, one in which all art has to be 'great' art, those views have a certain validity. But as we start to struggle out from underneath that uncompromising edifice, its natural lifespan artificially prolonged by political events that delayed reasoned reaction to it, they have less validity. 'Small' art, too, has its place in any civilized society, and a lively interreaction between stage and audience is perhaps more interesting than passively worshipping at the altar of great art.

Now that even serious musicians recognize that some quite important things have been said in the Broadway commercial theatre, they might be prodded into recognizing the same about the similarly commercial French operatic institutions of the 19th century. Gershwin, Weill and Rodgers at their best do more than just 'reflect' the anxieties and preoccupations of their audiences: they tease and provoke them from a consciously humanist and moralistic standpoint. So did Massenet. The agonies of Werther and Charlotte as they decline to challenge bourgeois taboos, the trials and tribulations of the medieval heroes and heroines striving to live within a strictly circumscribed set of values (and failing, but usually being forgiven), the dignity of Don Quichotte upholding traditional ways in a changing world – these do more than reflect the prejudices of their audience: they challenge them, and the compassion that Massenet shows for all his victims, whether willing or unwilling, is a tacit instruction to audiences to go and do likewise.

Massenet had the added advantage of working in that most fascinating of operatic periods, the decades preceding the publication of Freud's *The Interpretation of*

Dreams – a time in which his language of music, like that of Tchaikovsky and even the unworldly Dvořák, paved the way, in keeping with the *Zeitgeist*, for Freud's theories. Athanaël is an astoundingly sophisticated (and compassionate) psychological portrait, even today, and the sophistication is entirely expressed in the music.

Following the near-obligatory 50 years of flux after any composer's death, Massenet has been left with two operas secure in the international repertory (*Manon* and *Werther*); three re-establishing a toehold (*Cendrillon*, *Thaïs* and *Don Quichotte*); many more awaiting serious re-evaluation through repeated performance (*Esclarmonde*, *Grisélidis*, *Amadis* and *Sapho*); and a handful simply awaiting rediscovery (*Panurge* and *Ariane*). It would be absurd to claim that he was anything more than a second-rate composer; he nevertheless deserves to be seen, like Richard Strauss, at least as a first-class second-rate one.

See also CENDRILLON (ii); CHÉRUBIN; CID, LE; DON QUICHOTTE; ESCLARMONDE; GRISÉLIDIS; HÉRODIADE; JONGLEUR DE NOTRE-DAME, LE; MANON; NAVARRAISE, LA; ROI DE LAHORE, LE; SAPHO (ii); THAÏS; THÉRÈSE (i); and WERTHER.

printed works are full scores published in Paris, unless otherwise stated; principal MSS in F-Pc, Po

MCO – *Monte Carlo, Opéra* PO – *Paris, Opéra* POC – *Paris, Opéra-Comique*
POD – *Paris, Théâtre de l'Odéon* PPM – *Paris, Théâtre de la Porte St Martin*

title	genre, acts	libretto	première	publication	remarks
Esmeralda	opéra	after V. Hugo: *Notre-Dame de Paris*			comp. *c*1865, unperf., lost
La coupe du roi de Thulé	opéra, 3	E. Blau and L. Gallet			comp. *c*1866, unperf.
La grand'tante	opéra comique, 1	J. Adenis and C. Granvallet,	POC (Favart), 3 April 1867	vs, 1867	
Manfred	opéra	after Byron			comp. *c*1869, inc.
Méduse	3	M. Carré			comp. 1870, inc.
Don César de Bazan	opéra comique, 4	A. d'Ennery, P. P. Dumanoir and J. Chantepie, after Hugo: *Ruy Blas*	POC (Favart), 30 Nov 1872	vs, 1872 [2nd version, 1888]	2 versions: 1st destroyed by fire, rev. and reorchd 1888
L'adorable Bel'-Boul	opérette, 1	Gallet	Paris, Cercle des Mirlitons, 17 April 1874		destroyed
Les templiers					comp. *c*1875, inc., lost
Bérangère et Anatole	sainete, 1	H. Meilhac and P. Poirson	Paris, Cercle de l'Union Artistique, Feb 1876		
Le roi de Lahore	opéra, 5	Gallet	PO, 27 April 1877	n.d., inc.; vs, 1877	Act 3 based on Act 2 of La coupe du roi de Thulé; 3 versions
Robert de France	drame lyrique				comp. *c*1880, unperf., lost
Les Girondins	opéra				comp. 1881, lost
Hérodiade	opéra, 4	P. Milliet and H. Grémont [G. Hartmann], after G. Flaubert: *Hérodias*	Brussels, Monnaie, 19 Dec 1881 [in 3 acts]; rev. in 4 acts, Paris, Italien, 1 Feb 1884 [in It.]	1900 [4-act version]; vs 1882 [3-act], 1884 [4-act]	It. trans. by A. Zanardini
Manon	opéra comique, 5	Meilhac and P. Gille, after A.-F. Prévost: *L'histoire du chevalier des Grieux et de Manon Lescaut*	POC (Favart), 19 Jan 1884	Leipzig, 1930; vs, 1884	
Le Cid	opéra, 4	D'Ennery, E. Blau and Gallet, after P. Corneille	PO, 30 Nov 1885	*c*1895; vs, 1885	
Esclarmonde	opéra romanesque, 4	A. Blau and L. de Gramont	POC (Lyrique), 14 May 1889	?1889	
Le mage	opéra, 5	J. Richepin	PO, 16 March 1891	?1891	2 versions
Werther	drame lyrique, 4	E. Blau, Milliet and Hartmann, after J. W. von Goethe: *Die Leiden des jungen Werthers*	Vienna, Hofoper, 16 Feb 1892, in Ger.; Fr., POC (Lyrique), 16 Jan 1893	1892	comp. 1887
Thaïs	comédie lyrique, 3	Gallet, after A. France	PO, 16 March 1894; rev., PO, 13 April 1898	1894 [2nd version, 1898]	
Le portrait de Manon	opéra comique, 1	G. Boyer	POC (Lyrique), 8 May 1894	?1894	
La Navarraise	épisode lyrique, 2	J. Claretie and H. Cain, after Claretie: *La cigarette*	London, Covent Garden, 20 June 1894	1894	
Amadis	opéra légendaire, 4	Claretie	MCO, 1 April 1922	1921	comp. *c*1895

title	genre, acts	libretto	première	publication	remarks
Sapho	pièce lyrique, 5	Cain and A. Bernède, after A. Daudet	POC (Lyrique), 27 Nov 1897; rev., POC, Jan 1909	?1909; vs, 1898 [2nd version, 1909]	2 versions
Cendrillon	conte de fées, 4	Cain, after C. Perrault	POC (Favart), 24 May 1899	1898	
Grisélidis	conte lyrique, prol., 3	A. Silvestre and E. Morand	POC (Favart), 20 Nov 1901	1901	
Le jongleur de Notre-Dame	miracle, 3	M. Léna, after France: L'étui de nacre	MCO, 18 Feb 1902	1901	
Chérubin	comédie chantée, 3	F. de Croisset and Cain	MCO, 14 Feb 1905	1904	
Ariane	opéra, 5	C. Mendès	PO, 31 Oct 1906	1906	
Thérèse	drame musical, 2	Claretie	MCO, 7 Feb 1907	1906/7	
Bacchus	opéra, 4	Mendès	PO, 5 May 1909	vs, 1909	
Don Quichotte	comédie-héroïque, 5	Cain, after J. Le Lorrain: Le chevalier de la longue figure	MCO, 19 Feb 1910	1909/10	
Roma	opéra tragique, 5	Cain, after A. Parodi: Rome vaincue	MCO, 17 Feb 1912	1912	
Panurge	haulte farce musical, 3	M. Boukay and G. Spitzmüller, after Rabelais: La vie inestimable de Gargantua and Faits et dits héroïques du grand Pantagruel	Paris, Gaîté, 25 April 1913	vs, 1912	
Cléopâtre	opéra, 4	L. Payen [A. Liénard]	MCO, 23 Feb 1914	1915	
L'écureuil du déshonneur	opérette burlesque				n.d. [early], unperf., lost
Montalte	?opéra				n.d., unperf., lost

WRITINGS AND LETTERS

Discours prononcé à l'inauguration de la statue de Méhul à Givet, le 2 octobre, 1892 (Paris, 1892)

'Autobiographical Notes by the Composer Massenet', *Century Magazine*, xlv/Nov (1892), 122–6

Discours prononcé aux funérailles d'Ernest Guiraud (Paris, 1892)

'Souvenirs d'une première', *Le Figaro* (29 Aug 1893)

Preface to G. Bonnal: *Dictionnaire des connaissances musicales* (Paris, 1898)

Reply to 'Confidences d'hommes arrivés', *La revue* (15 March 1904)

'La musique d'aujourd'hui et de demain', *Comoedia* (4 Nov 1909

Mes souvenirs (1848–1912) (Paris, 1912; Eng. trans., 1919; Ger. trans., 1982)

'19 lettres inédites de Massenet à Ernest Van Dyck', *Le ménestrel*, xciv (1927), 45, 57, 69

E. de Bertier de Sauvigny, ed: *Quelques photographies et lettres inédites de Gounod, Massenet et Saint-Saëns* (La Jourdane, 1980)

*

OBITUARIES, COMMEMORATIVES AND RECOLLECTIONS

R. Batka: 'Jules Massenet', *Der Kunstwart*, xxvi (1912), 393

C. Debussy: 'Massenet n'est plus', *Le matin* (14 Aug 1912); repr. in *Monsieur Croche et autres écrits*, ed. F. Lesure (Paris, 1971), 203–4

H. Güttler: 'Jules Massenet', *NZM*, lxxix (1912), 477–8

H. Heugel: 'Les dernières heures', *Le ménestrel*, lxxviii (1912), 260

Musica [Paris] (Sept 1912) [Massenet issue]

A. Pougin: 'Jules Massenet', *Le ménestrel*, lxxviii (1912), 257–9

R. Specht: 'Jules Massenet', *Der Merker*, iv (1912), 627–8

J. Tiersot: 'Souvenirs', *Le ménestrel*, lxxviii (1912), 267–8

R. Bouyer: 'A la mémoire de Massenet', *Le ménestrel*, lxxix (1913), 259–60

A. de Guichard: 'Appreciation of Massenet', *Musician*, xviii (1913), 207

C. Saint-Saëns: *Ecole Buissonnière* (Paris, 1913; Eng. trans., 1921, as *Musical Memories*), chap.19

R. de Rigné: 'Souvenirs de Massenet', *Mercure de France*, cxlvi (1921), 325–6

J. Bruyr: 'En parlant de Massenet avec son petit-fils', *Guide du concert* (26 Feb 1937)

L. Laloy: 'Jules Massenet', *Revue des deux mondes* (1 May 1942)

J. W. Klein: 'A Centennial Appreciation', *MO*, lxv (1941–2), 337–8

R. Berthelot: 'Il y a cinquante ans, mourait "Monsieur" Massenet', *Musica* [Paris], no.103 (1962), 42

A. N. Verveen: 'Jules Massenet op bedevaart in Den Haag', *Mens en melodie*, xxii (1967), 177

LIFE AND WORKS

E. de Solenière: *Massenet: étude critique et documentaire* (Paris, 1897)

L. Schneider: *Massenet: l'homme, le musicien* (Paris, 1908, 2/1926)

H. T. Finck: *Massenet and his Operas* (London and New York, 1910)

O. Séré: *Massenet* (Paris, 1911)

A. Soubies: *Massenet* (Paris, 1912)

A. Pougin: *Massenet* (Paris, 1914)

C. M. Widor: *Notice sur la vie et les travaux de Massenet* (Paris, 1915)

C. Bouvet: *Massenet* (Paris, 1929)

M. Delmas: *Massenet: sa vie, ses oeuvres* (Paris, 1932)

A. Bruneau: *Massenet* (Paris, 1935)

A. Morin: *Jules Massenet et ses opéras* (Montreal, 1944)

J. Bruyr: *Massenet* (Geneva, 1948)

——: *Massenet, musicien de la belle époque* (Lyons, 1964)

A. Coquis: *Jules Massenet: l'homme et son oeuvre* (Paris, 1965)

E. Bouilhol: *Massenet: son rôle dans l'évolution du théâtre musical* (St Etienne, 1969)

Yu. A. Kremlyov: *Zhyl' Massne* (Moscow, 1969)

J. Harding: *Massenet* (London, 1970)

O. Salzer, ed.: *The Massenet Compendium* (Fort Lee, NJ, 1984)

P. Gillis: 'Biographie de Massenet' [chronology], *St Etienne Massenet Festival 1990* [programme book]

CRITICISM OF WORKS
General

C. Debussy: 'D'*Eve* à *Grisélidis*', *Revue blanche* (1 Dec 1901); repr. in *Monsieur Croche et autres écrits*, 58–60

——: Interview in *Revue bleue* (2 April 1904); repr. as 'L'état actuel de la musique française' in *Monsieur Croche et autres écrits*, 272–3

A. Pougin: 'Le répertoire dramatique de Massenet', *Le ménestrel*, lxxviii (1912), 283–4

C. Bouvet: 'L'idée de la mort chez Massenet', *Le ménestrel*, xcii (1930), 361–2

G. Fauré: 'Massenet', *Opinions musicales* (Paris, 1930)

P. Godfrey: 'Massenet and French Opera', *MO*, lvi (1932–33), 770

R. Hahn: 'Autour de Massenet et d'Alphonse Daudet', 'Autour de Massenet et de Marcel Proust', 'Mort de Massenet', *Candide* (Sept 1935)

A. Boschot: 'Bruneau et Massenet', *Le ménestrel*, xcix (1937), 53–4

P. Landormy: *La musique française de Franck à Debussy* (Paris, 1943)

N. Boyer: *Trois musiciens français: Gounod, Massenet, Debussy* (Paris, 1946)

M. Cooper: *French Music from the Death of Berlioz to the Death of Fauré* (London, 1951)

J. W. Klein: 'A Plea for Massenet', *MO*, lxxv (1951–2), 277–9

R. Berthelot: 'Massenet, musicien de la belle époque', *Vie musicale*, ii (1952), 13

C. Smith: 'The Operas of Massenet', *Opera*, vi (1955), 226–33

J. Budden: 'Massenet and the French Tradition', *The Listener* (18 Dec 1969), 865

——: 'Puccini, Massenet and Verismo', *Opera*, xxxiv (1983), 477–81

D. A. De Sanctis: *Literary Realism and Verismo Opera* (diss., City U., New York, 1983)

D. E. Baxter: *Women's Voice Classifications in Selected Operas of Jules Massenet: Computer Analyzation and Anecdotal Study* (diss., U. of Missouri, 1989)

Manon

E. Hanslick: *Aus dem Tagebuche eines Musikers* (Berlin, 1892), 137ff

R. Batka: 'Jules Massenet: "Manon"', *Aus der Opernwelt* (Munich, 1907)

J. F. Cooke: 'Massenet's Manon', *Etude*, xl (1922), 127

J. Loisel: *Manon de Massenet: étude historique et critique* (Paris, 1922)

C. Bellaigue: 'A travers le répertoire lyrique (IX): "Manon"', *Revue universelle* (1 Oct 1922), 59

L. Schneider: 'Le centenaire de Manon', *Le ménestrel*, xcvi (1934), 25–7

M. Carner: 'The Two Manons', *MMR*, lxvii (1937), 176–8

P. Colson: *Massenet: Manon* (London, 1947)

C. S. Hiss: *Abbé Prévost's 'Manon Lescaut' as Novel, Libretto and Opera* (diss., U. of Illinois, 1967)

A. Jefferson: 'Impressions of Manon', *Music and Musicians*, xvii/4 (1968–9), 28–9

C. Barda: '"Manon"', *About the House*, vii/9 (1984–8), 32–5

J. Kestner: 'Reign of Pleasure', *ON*, li/12 (1986–7), 16–19, 39

L'avant-scène opéra, no. 123 (1989) [*Manon* issue]

Werther

E. Hanslick: *Fünf Jahre Musik* (Berlin, 1896), 23ff

C. Debussy: 'Une renaissance de l'opéra bouffe: reprise de *Werther* à l'Opéra-Comique', *Gil Blas* (27 April 1903); repr. in *Monsieur Croche et autres écrits*, 154–8

H. Béraud: '*Werther* au phonographe', *Le ménestrel*, xciv (1932), 9–10

Earl of Harewood: 'Massenet's *Werther*', *Opera*, iii (1952), 69–74

J. Commons: 'Genesis of *Werther*', *Music and Musicians*, xiv/10 (1965–6), 18–19

J. Harding: 'Massenet's *Werther*', *The Listener* (30 June 1966), 958

L. L. Stocker: *The Treatment of the Romantic Literary Hero in Verdi's 'Ernani' and in Massenet's 'Werther'* (diss., Florida State U., 1969)

L'avant-scène opéra, no. 61 (1984) [*Werther* issue]

U. Wand: 'Werther as a Tenor', *Theater der Zeit*, xxxix (1984), 14–15

'Massenet's "Werther"', *ON*, lii/15 (1987–8), 25–6

J. W. Hansen: '*Werther*'s Way', *ON*, liii/13 (1988–9), 18–21, 40

Other operas

E. Hanslick: *Musikalische Stationen* (Berlin, 1885), 86ff [on *Le roi de Lahore*]

——: *Musikalisches und Litterarisches* (Berlin, 1889), 79ff [on *Le Cid*]

C. Malherbe: *Notice sur 'Esclarmonde'* (Paris, 1890)

E. Hanslick: *Fünf Jahre Musik* (Berlin, 1896), 140ff [on *La Navarraise*]

Willy-Bréville: 'A propos de Sapho', *Revue blanche*, xiv (1897), 457–61

S. Stojowski: 'Grisélidis von Massenet', *Die Musik*, i (1901–2), 513–14

H. T. Finck: 'Massenet, Thaïs and Farrar', *The Nation*, civ (1917), 223

D. C. Parker: 'Thérèse', *Musical Standard*, xcvi (1919), 223

R. Augenot: *Esclarmonde ou Une forme divine de l'expression musicale au théâtre* (Brussels, 1939)

R. Wilson: '"Esclarmonde"', *About the House*, vi/11 (1980–84), 44–7

A. Gier: '"Thaïs": a Novel by Anatole France and an Opera by Jules Massenet', *Romanistische Zeitschrift für Literaturgeschichte*, v (1981), 232–56

R. Crichton: '"Mireille" and "Esclarmonde"', *Opera*, xxxiv (1983), 1293–9

L'avant-scène opéra, no.63 (1986) [*Don Quichotte* issue]

G. A. Capik: *La vie de Thais: Prolegomena* (diss., U. of Chicago, 1986)

L'avant-scène opéra, no. 109 (1988) [*Thaïs* issue]

RODNEY MILNES (text)
KENNETH THOMPSON, STELLA J. WRIGHT (work-list)

Massimilla Doni. Opera in four acts, op.50, by OTHMAR SCHOECK to a libretto by Armin Rüeger after Honoré de Balzac's novel; Dresden, Staatsoper, 2 March 1937.

Set in the artistic world of Venice in the 1830s, the opera contrasts spirited aesthetic debate with amorous intrigue, candid soprano monologues with conversational lyricism. Massimilla Doni (soprano), a young noblewoman, is engaged to the aging and impotent Duke Cattaneo (tenor) but loves Emilio Memmi (tenor), a poor young man suddenly enriched by inheritance. Cattaneo and his friend Capraja (bass) argue and pontificate about art, and each champions a young hopeful. Cattaneo's protégé, the coloratura soprano Tinti, is beautiful, calculating and technically brilliant. Capraja's is the lyric tenor Genovese, all feeling and passion. Tinti lures Emilio away from Massimilla; and during a rehearsal at the Fenice theatre of an opera about Europa and the Bull, she distracts Genovese so that he begins to bellow like an animal. Thanks to her own cunning and the help of Emilio's older friend Vendramin (baritone), Massimilla eventually sorts everything out to her own advantage.

Karl Böhm conducted the première in Dresden (where the first performances of three other operas by Schoeck, *Don Ranudo*, *Penthesilea* and *Vom Fischer un syner Fru* had also been given). The Swiss première was given the same month in Zürich. The work was revived in Berne and Zürich in 1956 as part of Schoeck's 70th birthday celebrations. A recording conducted by Gerd Albrecht, with Edith Mathis in the title role, was issued to coincide with a concert performance at the Lucerne Festival in 1986, and Ferdinand Leitner conducted a staging in Zürich the following year. The music is distinguished by its grateful vocal writing and broad canvas of instrumental detail. ANDREW CLARK

Massimo. Theatre in PALERMO, opened in 1897; it is the third largest opera house in Europe, after those in Vienna and Paris.

Massimo Bellini. Theatre in CATANIA, Bellini's birthplace; it opened in 1866 as the Arena Nuovoluce, was renamed Arena Pacini in 1869 and enlarged as the Teatro Massimo Bellini in 1890.

Massol, Jean-Etienne August [Eugène Etienne Auguste] (*b* Lodève, 23 Aug 1802; *d* Paris, 30 Oct 1887). French baritone. He made his Opéra début as a tenor, singing Licinius in *La vestale* (17 November 1825), but Nourrit's pre-eminence restricted him to secondary roles until the mid-1830s, when he began to appear, with increasing success, in baritone roles such as William Tell. In 1840 he created Sévère in Donizetti's *Les martyrs*. In 1845 he left the Opéra for Brussels, where he returned in 1848–9 as director of La Monnaie. He made his London début in 1846 as Nevers (*Les Huguenots*) at Drury

Lane, and appeared with the Royal Italian Opera at Covent Garden, 1848–50, most impressively as Alphonse (*La favorite*), Pietro (*La muette de Portici*) and Nevers. In 1850 he returned to the Opéra as principal baritone and created Reuben in Auber's *L'enfant prodigue*, repeating the role at Her Majesty's Theatre in the following season. Massol's imposing physique and voice made him a most effective 'heavy' baritone. His last notable creation at the Opéra was Ahasuerus in Halévy's *Le Juif errant* (1852).

B. Lumley: *Reminiscences of the Opera* (London, 1864), 303

PHILIP ROBINSON

Masson, Diego (*b* Tossa, Spain, 21 June 1935). French conductor. He studied at the Paris Conservatoire and conducting with Pierre Boulez. Active in contemporary music circles, he formed his own ensemble, Musique Vivante, in 1966. For some years he was music director at the Marseilles Opera (where his repertory included a *Ring* cycle), and of Ballet-Théâtre Contemporain, formed at Amiens in 1968 and from 1972 based at Angers, where it was combined with the opera company under his direction as the Théâtre-Musical d'Angers. They staged a spectacular opera-ballet production of *The Nightingale* at Angers in 1973 and took it to Sadler's Wells Theatre that year. Masson later conducted the ENO productions of *La damnation de Faust* (1980–81), *Die Zauberflöte* (1982) and *Carmen* (1983), the première of Edward Harper's *Hedda Gabler* for Scottish Opera in 1985, Puccini's *La bohème* for Opera North in 1988 and the première of Saxton's *Caritas* for the same company in 1991. He has also conducted opera at the Paris Châtelet, Netherlands Opera and elsewhere, but his work is mainly in the concert repertory.

PAUL GRIFFITHS, NOËL GOODWIN

Masson, Paul-Marie (*b* Sète, Hérault, 19 Sept 1882; *d* Paris, 27 Jan 1954). French musicologist. He was educated at Sète, Montpellier and Paris, where he attended Rolland's courses at the Sorbonne. He then taught for the Institut Français, from 1910 at Florence and after World War I at Naples. In 1931 he joined the staff of the Sorbonne, where he succeeded Pirro in 1943; in 1951 he established the Institut de Musicologie at the University of Paris. Although his early research was in 16th- and 17th-century music, his preferred sphere was the 18th, in particular opera and its related forms. His dissertation *L'opéra de Rameau*, published in 1930, was the first serious assessment of Rameau's operas and remains the fundamental study. Masson's other writings on opera treat works by Campra and Méhul.

Master i Margarita ('The Master and Margarita'). Chamber opera in three acts by SERGEY MIKHAYLOVICH SLONIMSKY to a libretto by Yury Dimitrin and V. Fialkovsky after the novel by MIKHAIL AFANAS'YEVICH BULGAKOV; Moscow, Mossovet Theatre, 11 February 1991 (completed in 1972, first performed in concert, Moscow, Bol'shoy Hall of the Conservatory, 20 May 1989).

Slonimsky's chamber opera was one of the most notorious musical victims of repressive cultural policy under Brezhnev. Composed after the Soviet publication, in 1966, of Bulgakov's controversial masterpiece of 1938, it was not intended as a challenge to prevailing aesthetic strictures. Act 1 was performed by members of the Kirov Theatre at a closed hearing in 1972. After virulent attacks by the cultural bureaucracy in Leningrad, who found in it ideological shortcomings, among other flaws, the opera was suppressed and the composer hid the manuscript. When the work was unveiled publicly 17 years later, the event was hailed as a milestone in the cultural rehabilitation spurred by Gorbachov's policy of *glasnost'*.

Slonimsky's opera retains the dual narrative strands of the literary original: on the one hand, it retells the biblical story of the confrontation between Ponty Pilat [Pontius Pilate] (bass) and Iyeshua [Jesus] (baritone), leading to the Crucifixion; on the other, the escapades of the satanic Voland [Woland] (baritone) and his comic entourage on a visit to Moscow serve to illuminate a scathing satire of Russian society, especially its cultural politics, a satire which had lost none of its pungency by the 1970s. Providing a lyrical focus for the drama are the figures of the Master (baritone), the tragically fated author, and his faithful and loving Margarita (soprano).

The musical texture of Slonimsky's opera is fine-spun and intimate, emphasizing the philosophical reflectiveness of the novel over its more obvious potential for spectacle. The two planes of the drama proceed simultaneously, bringing the similarities between the issues of moral conflict into sharp relief. The vocal writing – using a wide range of techniques but frequently consisting of melodic recitative with free or relative rhythmic values – is set off by the colours of solo instruments, which serve to refine the characterizations: Margarita's tenderness towards the Master, for instance, is underscored by violin, and Iudas [Judas] (tenor) is identified with the tuba. Woland's two mischievous sidekicks, Korov'yev and the cat Begemot [Behemoth], are silent roles associated respectively with the bassoon and the piccolo.

LAUREL E. FAY

Master iz Klamsi ('The Master of Clamecy'). Opera by Dmitry Kabalevsky; *see* COLAS BREUGNON.

Mastersingers of Nuremberg, The. Opera by Richard Wagner; *see* MEISTERSINGER VON NÜRNBERG, DIE.

Masterson, (Margaret) Valerie (*b* Birkenhead, 3 June 1937). English soprano. She studied in Liverpool, at the RCM and with Adelaide Saraceni in Milan. In 1963–4 she made her début at the Landestheater, Salzburg, singing Frasquita, Nannetta, Fiorilla (*Il turco in Italia*) and in *Der Schauspieldirektor*. She then joined the D'Oyly Carte company, taking most principal Gilbert and Sullivan soprano roles (1966–70). After singing Konstanze at the Coliseum in 1971, she joined the Sadler's Wells Opera, later ENO; her roles have included Adèle (*Le comte Ory*), the Countess, Cleopatra (*Giulio Cesare*), Romilda (*Xerxes*), Violetta, Oscar, Manon, Sophie, the Marschallin, Louise, Mireille, Juliet, Pamina and Adele (*Die Fledermaus*). At Aix-en-Provence (1975–9) she has sung Matilde (*Elisabetta, regina d'Inghilterra*), Fiordiligi, Morgana (*Alcina*) and Countess Almaviva. At Covent Garden she has sung Marguerite, Semele, Micaëla and The Anne who Steals in the British première of *The King Goes Forth to France* (1987), and she created the Wife of the Second Soldier in *We Come to the River* (1976). She made her début at the Opéra in 1978 as Marguerite, followed by Drusilla (*L'incoronazione di Poppea*) and Cleopatra (1987). In 1980 she made her American début, in San Francisco, as Violetta and first appeared at Glyndebourne, as Konstanze. In 1991 she returned to Aix as Mercy in

Mozart's *Die Schuldigkeit des ersten Gebots*. To her clean, forward, smooth vocal production with its ease and lustre in high phrases are added excellent diction and an attractive stage presence.

H. Rosenthal: 'Valerie Masterson', *Opera*, xxx (1979), 1128–34
HAROLD ROSENTHAL/R

Mastilović, Danica (*b* Negotin, 7 Nov 1933). Serbian soprano. She studied with Nikola Cvejić in Belgrade, where as a student she sang in the operetta theatre (1955–9). Engaged at Frankfurt, she made her début there as Tosca in 1959 and remained for 25 years. She sang Gerhilde at Bayreuth (1966) and then began to sing the heavier Wagner and Strauss roles, establishing a reputation throughout Europe as Senta, Ortrud, Kundry, Brünnhilde, Strauss's Electra, the Dyer's Wife and Turandot, which she sang at Torre del Lago in 1974 to commemorate the 50th anniversary of Puccini's death. She made her American début as Abigaille (*Nabucco*) at Chicago in 1963 and her Covent Garden (1973) and Metropolitan (1975) débuts as Electra. In 1987 she sang Clytemnestra at the Landestheater, Salzburg. Her voice was large, at times unwieldy, and always exciting.   HAROLD ROSENTHAL/R

Mastini, Giovanni Battista (*b* Panne, San Giovanni di Macerata, *c*1700; *d* Fermo, 20 Feb 1771). Italian composer. In spring 1726 (according to a libretto) he was musical director of the Teatro de Nobili in Perugia; at about the same time he was *maestro di cappella* of Fermo Cathedral. In these years he wrote the following operas: *Li tre fanciulli resuscitati* (1723, Fermo); *Cartoccio speziale* (carn. 1725, Perugia); *L'amor fra gl'impossibili* (G. Gigli; 1727, Ancona); and *Massimo Puppieno* (A. Aureli; 1729, Macerata). The music is lost, though some of Mastini's sacred works survive. From 1733 until his death he abandoned theatrical composition, having taken the position of organist at the S Casa, Loreto.   JAMES L. JACKMAN

Mastromei, Giampietro [Gian-Piero] (*b* Camaiore, 1 Nov 1932). Italian baritone. After his family settled in Buenos Aires he made his début at the Teatro Colón in 1952 and sang principal roles for 13 seasons. His European début, at Marseilles in 1966, was followed by engagements elsewhere in France and in Italy and frequent appearances at the Vienna Staatsoper (from 1969). He sang Amonasro in the centenary *Aida* at Verona and for his Covent Garden début in 1973. After appearing as Renato at La Scala that year, he toured with the company to Moscow in 1974. He has sung in major American centres from Philadelphia to San Francisco and has returned often to South America. Possessing a ringing baritone of virile character, he has a repertory encompassing more than a hundred operas from Scarlatti and Pergolesi to Dallapiccola and Menotti, most of them Italian.   NOËL GOODWIN

Masur, Kurt (*b* Brieg, Silesia [now Brzeg, Poland], 18 July 1927). German conductor. He studied at Breslau and the Leipzig Conservatory, and in 1948 joined the Landestheater, Halle, as répétiteur and conductor. He was appointed chief conductor at the city theatres of Erfurt (1951–3) and Leipzig (1953–5), then music director at the Mecklenburg Staatstheater, Schwerin (1958–60). In 1960 he was engaged by Walter Felsen-stein as music director at the Komische Oper, Berlin, where he remained until 1964; his varied repertory included Felsenstein's epochal production of Britten's *A Midsummer Night's Dream* in 1961.

From 1970 Masur was a renowned conductor of the Leipzig Gewandhaus Orchestra, where his work also embraced opera performances in the theatre, and he succeeded Zubin Mehta as music director of the New York PO in 1991. His recordings (mainly symphonic) include Schumann's *Genovera*, and *Ariadne auf Naxos* with Leipzig forces and guest principals in 1988. The same year he conducted a notable concert performance in London of *Fidelio* with the LPO. A member of the Academy of Arts in the former German Democratic Republic and recipient of several national arts prizes and honorary doctorates, Masur has undertaken world-wide conducting tours. He is deeply admired for his musical insight, dynamic spirit and emotional expression, especially in the German Romantic repertory.

DIETER HÄRTWIG, NOËL GOODWIN

Matačić, Lovro von (*b* Sušak, 14 Feb 1899; *d* Zagreb, 4 Jan 1985). Slovene conductor. He studied at the Vienna Hochschule für Musik and after a period as chorus master of the Cologne Opera, where he made his conducting début in 1919, he joined the music staff of the Salzburg Festival. On returning to Yugoslavia he appeared at Ljubljana and Zagreb, and then in 1938 became music director of the Belgrade Opera. After World War II he helped to establish the festivals of Dubrovnik and Split, as well as working to build up the new opera company in Skopje between 1948 and 1952. From 1956 to 1958 he was Generalmusikdirektor at Dresden and, jointly with Konwitschny, at Berlin, then in 1961 he succeeded Solti at Frankfurt, where he remained until 1966. He made guest appearances with the Chicago Opera (1959), at La Scala and the Vienna Staatsoper and conducted the Frankfurt company at Sadler's Wells (1963) in *Salome* and *Die Entführung aus dem Serail*. His programmes suggested a preference for large-scale Romantic scores but his sparkling recording of Lehár's *Die lustige Witwe* with Schwarzkopf demonstrated an ability to set off sumptuousness with lighter qualities.   BERNARD JACOBSON

Materna(-Friedrich), Amalie (*b* St Georgen, 10 July 1844; *d* Vienna, 18 Jan 1918). Austrian soprano. She made her début in 1865 at Graz and then appeared in operetta at the Carltheater, Vienna. In 1869 she first sang at the Vienna Hofoper, as Sélika (*L'Africaine*), and was engaged there for 25 years. She sang Amneris in the first Vienna performance of *Aida* (1874) and created the title role of Goldmark's *Die Königin von Saba* (1875). Her voice grew to be immensely powerful, but never lost its youthful bright timbre and was ideal for Brünnhilde, which she sang in the first complete *Ring* cycle at Bayreuth (1876; for illustration *see* COSTUME, fig.23*a*), in the first Vienna performances of *Die Walküre* (1877) and *Siegfried* (1878), and in the first Berlin *Ring* at the Victoria Theatre (1881). In 1882 she sang Kundry at Bayreuth in the first performance of *Parsifal*, repeating the role there at every festival until 1891. She made her début at the Metropolitan in 1885 as Elisabeth (*Tannhäuser*), and also sang Valentine (*Les Huguenots*), Rachel (*La Juive*) and Brünnhilde (*Die Walküre*). She gave her final performance in Vienna as Elisabeth in 1894.

A. Ehrlich: *Berühmte Sängerinnen der Vergangenheit und Gegenwart* (Leipzig, 1895)

G. Skelton: *Wagner at Bayreuth* (London, 1965)

ELIZABETH FORBES

Mathes, Rachel (*b* Atlanta, GA, 14 March 1941). American soprano. She studied in Birmingham, Alabama, then in Vienna, Düsseldorf and New York. After winning competitions in Washington and Baltimore she made her début at Basle in 1965, as Aida. She was a member of the Deutsche Oper am Rhein, Düsseldorf, from 1966 and made guest appearances in Cologne, Stuttgart, Munich, Geneva, Zürich and Glasgow (with Scottish Opera). She has been most admired in such spinto roles as Leonora (*Il trovatore*), Donna Anna, Amelia (*Un ballo in maschera*) and Ariadne. More dramatic repertory includes Senta, Electra (*Idomeneo*), Venus and Elisabeth. Her Metropolitan Opera début was in 1973, as Donna Anna. In 1986 she appeared as Leonore in *Fidelio* (Greenville, SC).

DAVID CUMMINGS

Matheson, (Henry) John (Parke) (*b* Seacliff, Otago, 14 May 1928). New Zealand conductor. He studied at Otago University and, after moving to London in 1950, at the RCM. He joined the Carl Rosa Opera in 1952 as chorus master, then the Sadler's Wells Opera as a répétiteur, making his conducting début in 1953 with *Le nozze di Figaro*. That year he joined the staff at Covent Garden, first conducting *The Bartered Bride* in 1955; he remained there until 1960. He was a staff conductor with the Sadler's Wells Opera (1961–71), and after that was a regular conductor with the company and at Covent Garden. He also appeared in 1967 at the Stratford (Ontario) Festival, where he conducted *Così fan tutte* and Britten's *Albert Herring*.

Matheson's conducting of a wide repertory in London showed consistent reliability and expressive character, and during the 1970s he was admired for well-paced and dramatically cogent performances of Verdi (notably *Falstaff* and *Simon Boccanegra*) and Berg's *Wozzeck*. At Sadler's Wells he added Verdi's *Attila* and Ravel's *L'enfant et les sortilèges* to the English repertory. A special interest in French 19th-century opera was reflected in first British (concert) performances with the Chelsea Opera Group of the French originals of Rossini's *Guillaume Tell* and *Moïse*, and Verdi's *Don Carlos*, during 1970–72, and in 1981 the original version of *La forza del destino* at a Promenade concert.

By this time Matheson was increasingly active abroad; he conducted both Berg operas at Lisbon, and introduced Walton's *The Bear* to Oslo. In 1983 he conducted Gluck's *La rencontre imprévue* at the Piccola Scala, Milan, and worked with Ken Russell on controversial productions of Puccini operas at the Spoleto festivals in Italy and at Charleston, South Carolina. Later he returned to New Zealand and Australia, where he was music director for the Lyric Opera of Queensland (Brisbane) in 1989 and the following year was named principal guest conductor and music adviser with that company.

NOËL GOODWIN

Mathias, William (James) (*b* Whitland, Carmarthenshire, 1 Nov 1934; *d* Menai Bridge, Gwynedd, 29 July 1992). Welsh composer. Educated at the University College of Wales, Aberystwyth, and in London at the RAM, where he studied with Lennox Berkeley, he was professor of music at the University College of North Wales, Bangor, 1970–88, and artistic director of the North Wales Festival from 1972.

Mathias's early reputation was established with instrumental works. The hallmarks of his style are rhythmic propulsion and lyrical warmth, expressed in a tonally rooted but chromatically flexible language. The earliest works to incorporate an element of drama were the masque-like cantata *St Teilo* (1962) and the children's entertainment *Culhwch ac Olwen* (1966). His first opera was written for the WNO, to a libretto by Iris Murdoch based on her play *The Servants and the Snow* (1970). Work on *The Servants* began in 1977 and it was first performed at the New Theatre, Cardiff, on 15 September 1980. The opera is set in the 1900s, in a large central-European country house. The old despotic landlord has died and his idealistic son attempts to inaugurate a democratically enlightened order. His dream fades as the hideous crimes of the past emerge to suffocate his liberalism and the servants welcome the return of a tyranny they understand and need. Alongside this quasi-political and philosophical backdrop a characteristically intense series of emotional and sexual entanglements is acted out. Mathias creates a vivid cast of characters with strongly individual musical personalities, whose interaction on stage is convincingly caught. Encompassing scenes of intimacy and confrontation among vast tableau-like choruses, the opera impresses through its unity of tone and purpose and the identifiable world it inhabits. Critical response was mixed but audience reaction was uniformly enthusiastic.

Mathias's 'musical morality' *Jonah*, to a text by Charles Causley, was first performed at Guildford Cathedral (6 July 1988). Three fully operatic roles, Jonah, a Storyteller and a Shipmaster, interact with school forces in a fresh telling of the Bible story, with considerable dramatic scope for movement and dance. *Jonah* has all the immediacy of Mathias's large-scale choral works, such as *This Worldes Joie*, and culminates in a moving setting of the Welsh hymn *St Denio* for the whole company which draws the audience into the drama as a congregation.

GERAINT LEWIS

Mathieu, Emile (Louis Victor) (*b* Lille, 18 Oct 1844; *d* Ghent, 20 Aug 1932). Belgian composer. His father was a singer and a director of the theatre at Antwerp; his mother was a singing teacher at the Académie des Beaux-Arts in Louvain. Mathieu was to have studied medicine, but after the death of his parents devoted himself to music, studying with Dupont, Bosselet and Fétis at the Brussels Conservatory. In 1867 he became a teacher at the music school in Louvain. He won the Belgian Prix de Rome in 1869, 1871 and 1873. He conducted the orchestra of the Théâtre du Châtelet in Paris, 1873–5; returning to Brussels, he became an accompanist at the Théâtre Royal de la Monnaie. In 1881 he became director of the music school in Louvain and was director of the Ghent Conservatory 1898–1924. Most of Mathieu's operas were composed to his own librettos; though possessing a certain elegance and charm, they are also somewhat academic in nature and have seldom been revived.

L'échange (oc, 1, Mathieu), Liège, Royal, 25 April 1863

Georges Dandin (oc, 2, Coveliers, after Molière), Brussels, Monnaie, Dec 1877

La bernoise (oc, 1, L. Solvay), Brussels, Monnaie, 1 April 1880

Richilde (tragédie lyrique, 4, Mathieu), Brussels, Monnaie, 12 Dec 1888

L'enfance de Roland (légende lyrique, 3, Mathieu, after Uhland), Brussels, Monnaie, 16 Jan 1895, vs (Leipzig, 1895)

La reine Vashti (biblical op), Brussels, 1905, vs (Mainz, 1905)

ANNE-MARIE RIESSAUW

Mathis, Edith (*b* Lucerne, 11 Feb 1938). Swiss soprano. After studying at Lucerne she made her début there in 1956 as the Second Boy (*Die Zauberflöte*). She appeared in 1959 at the Cologne opera, then, in 1963, at the Deutsche Oper, Berlin. She first sang at Salzburg in 1960 as Ninetta (*La finta semplice*), returning regularly. She took part in the première of Einem's *Der Zerrissene* (1964, Hamburg) and created Luise in Henze's *Der junge Lord* (1965, Berlin). At Glyndebourne she sang Cherubino (1962–3) and Sophie (1965). She made her Covent Garden début in 1970 as Susanna, a role she recorded for Böhm, later singing Sophie and Despina. At the Metropolitan (1970–76) her roles included Pamina, Marzelline, Aennchen and Zerlina. She sang in Vienna and Munich, where she created Queen Mary in Sutermeister's *Le roi Bérenger* (1985). Her repertory has also included Nannetta, Zdenka, Mélisande, Agathe, which she sang at Barcelona (1986), and the Marschallin, which she sang for the first time in 1990 at Berne. She has a fresh, pure-toned voice and an attractive simplicity of manner on stage.   ALAN BLYTH

Mathis der Maler ('Mathis the Painter'). Opera in seven scenes by PAUL HINDEMITH to his own libretto; Zürich, Stadttheater, 28 May 1938.

The action takes place at the time of the Peasants' War in 16th-century Germany. In Scene 1, Mathis (baritone) is working on a fresco in a monastery when the peasants' leader, Schwalb (tenor), who is wounded, bursts in with his young daughter Regina (soprano). Schwalb reproaches Mathis for spending his time painting while his fellow beings are fighting for their lives. A cavalry group led by Sylvester (tenor) comes in search of Schwalb, and Mathis helps him and Regina escape. In Scene 2, the citizens of Mainz, Catholics and Protestants, are quarrelling as they wait in the Martinsburg for the cardinal archbishop's return. Cardinal Albrecht (tenor), after acknowledging their greetings, dismisses them, retaining only Riedinger, a rich Protestant citizen (bass), and Ursula, Riedinger's daughter (soprano). Mathis joins them and, while the cardinal is engaged with Riedinger, he and Ursula reveal their love. Riedinger complains to the cardinal of a Catholic order to burn Lutheran books, and Albrecht, who is dependent on Riedinger for money, countermands the order. After Riedinger's departure, however, he is persuaded by the dean of Mainz cathedral, Pommersfelden (bass), to allow the burning. Sylvester enters and, recognizing Mathis, denounces him for letting the peasant leader escape. When Mathis pleads for the peasants, Albrecht tells him not to meddle in political matters. Mathis, asserting that he cannot paint while his fellow men go in fear, demands his release from Albrecht's service. Pommersfelden orders Mathis's arrest, but Albrecht decides he should be allowed to go in peace.

Scene 3 opens in Riedinger's house where Lutherans are hiding books; a fire can be seen burning outside in the market-place. Their attempts are foiled by Albrecht's counsellor Capito (tenor), and soldiers carry off the books. Capito overcomes the Lutherans' anger by producing a letter from Luther to the cardinal, urging him to marry a Protestant, thus bringing reconciliation to his people. Ursula, entering, is asked whether she would be prepared to serve the cause by marrying a man chosen for her. Left alone, Ursula is full of foreboding and, when Mathis enters, she begs him to take her away with him. Despite his love, Mathis declines, since he is going to join the rebel peasants. As they sing their farewells, Lutherans and Catholics in the market-place exchange insults; the books burn.

In Scene 4, set in a ruined village, peasants have captured Count and Countess Helfenstein. As the Count (silent) is led off to execution, they threaten the Countess (contralto) with rape. They scorn Mathis's efforts to restrain them and finally strike him down. Schwalb, entering with Regina, puts an end to the quarrel by warning them of approaching troops. In the ensuing battle Schwalb is killed. The army leader, Truchsess von Waldburg (bass), wants to arrest Mathis, but the Countess pleads for him. Mathis is left alone with Regina, weeping over her father's body. In Scene 5, in the cardinal's office, Capito attempts to persuade Albrecht to marry a rich heiress: the alternative is bankruptcy. Albrecht, discovering that his intended bride is Ursula, reproaches her for taking part in an 'ignoble bargain'. She replies that she consented to the marriage because she saw in him an enlightened prince who alone had the power to reconcile the warring people, and she begs him to devote himself to this cause. Albrecht, his conscience roused, vows to do so, but within his church, eschewing both riches and marriage. Ursula makes a similar renunciation.

In Scene 6 Mathis and Regina, fleeing from the fighting, have taken refuge in a forest. After singing the child to sleep, Mathis muses bitterly on his abject state. He experiences a series of visions, in which he, as St Anthony, is confronted with figures from his past: the Countess (representing luxury); Ursula (successively as beggar, prostitute and martyr); Schwalb (warlord); Capito (man of learning); and Pommersfelden (merchant). A chorus of demons, as depicted in Grünewald's Isenheim altarpiece, torments him, to be succeeded by another scene from the Isenheim altar: the meeting of St Paul and St Anthony. St Paul (Albrecht) encourages Mathis to return to his painting and use the gift God gave him for the betterment of mankind.

In Scene 7 Mathis sits in his studio in Mainz surrounded by his pictures and drawings, while Ursula watches over Regina, who is dying. Her death is followed by an orchestral interlude. When the lights come up, Mathis is alone in his studio, now bare except for a table containing his last few possessions and an empty chest. Albrecht comes to visit him. Mathis tells him that his work is done, and all that now remains for him is 'like a beast in the forest to seek a place to die'. After Albrecht has gone, Mathis begins quietly to pack the chest.

Hindemith spent two years (July 1933 to July 1935) composing the words and music of the opera, and its related symphony. It was the result of his desire, already heralded by his *Gebrauchsmusik* period, to write in a more popular way. Consequently *Mathis*, though composed in numbers, is contrapuntally less rigid than *Cardillac*, and the music is based to a large extent on folksong and church choral music, though only occasionally are these quoted directly. Another unifying factor lies in the tonal relationships, based on ideas which Hindemith developed while teaching in Berlin and subsequently expounded in his book *Unterweisung im Tonsatz* (Mainz, 1937–70; Eng. trans. of vols.i and ii, 1941–2). However, there is nothing academic about the opera, which is a powerful expression, clearly autobiographical, of the dilemma of an artist in times of political strife. Both words and music are skilfully used to present the main characters (Mathis, Albrecht, Ursula, Regina) as living human beings, and the lyrical scenes are as touching as the more spectacular ones (the book burning, the temptation of St Anthony) are dramatically exciting. *Mathis der Maler* is without doubt Hindemith's operatic masterpiece. Difficulties with the Nazis prevented its production in Germany until 1946, since when it has become well established in the operatic repertory.   GEOFFREY SKELTON

Matho, Jean-Baptiste (*b* Brittany, *c*1660; *d* Versailles, 16 March 1746). French composer. The only important Breton musician of the 17th and 18th centuries, he held various appointments at the French court from 1684. He provided several ballets and *divertissements* for court entertainments; others were presented for the Duchess of Maine at Châtenay, near Sceaux. His opera *Arion* (1714) was a failure, and was withdrawn from the repertory after five performances. Matho's music, in the Lullian tradition, has been praised for its skilful orchestration.

Tircis et Célimène (pastorale, A. Morel), 1687, *F-Pc*
Le palais de Flore (ballet, Lalande), Versailles, 1689
Coronis (tragédie, Morel), Fontainebleau, 18 Sept 1699, *Pa*
Philémon et Baucis (divertissement, N. de Malézieu), Château de Châtenay, 5 Aug 1703
Le prince de Cathay (divertissement, Malézieu), Château de Châtenay, 17 Aug 1704
La Tarentole (comédie-ballet, 3, Malézieu), Château de Châtenay, 10 Aug 1705
La fine mouche (comédie, Malézieu), Clagny, 8 March 1706
L'hôte de Lemnos (comédie, 5, Malézieu), Château de Châtenay, 8 Aug 1707
Arion (tragédie lyrique, prol., 5, L. Fuzelier), Paris, Opéra, 10 April 1714 (Paris, 1714)

*

C. Masson: 'Journal du marquis de Dangeau, 1684–1720: extrait concernant la vie musicale à la cour', *RMFC*, ii (1961–2), 193–228
H. Corbes: 'Le doyen des compositeurs bretons: Jean-Baptiste Matho (1660–1746)', *Bulletin de la Société archéologique du Finistère*, xcii (1968), 62
M. Benoit: *Versailles et les musiciens du roi 1661–1733* (Paris, 1971)
R. Machard: 'Les musiciens en France au temps de Jean-Philippe Rameau d'après les actes du Secrétariat de la Maison du Roi', *RMFC*, xi (1971), 6–117   VIVIEN LO

Matilde di Shabran [*Matilde di Shabran, ossia Bellezza, e cuor di ferro* ('Matilde of Shabran, or Beauty with a Heart of Iron')]. *Melodramma giocoso* in two acts by GIOACHINO ROSSINI to a libretto by JACOPO FERRETTI after F.-B. Hoffman's libretto for Méhul's *Euphrosine* (1790, Paris) and J. M. Boutet de Monvel's play *Mathilde*; Rome, Teatro Apollo, 24 February 1821.

Paganini conducted the first performance of this opera which, even by the usual standards of the mixed comic-melodramatic genre, is one of Rossini's most unpredictable, if at times undeniably brilliant, scores. The story centres on the exploits of the choleric misogynist Corradino (tenor) and Matilde (soprano), the shrewish daughter of a deceased friend whom Corradino has promised to look after. Corradino's temper can be gauged in the opening scene when an innocent itinerant poet, Isidoro (*buffo* bass), is thrown into the castle prison along with Edoardo (contralto), the son of Corradino's arch-enemy. When Matilde arrives at the castle she is admitted but studiously ignored by Corradino. Provoked by this intended slight, she determines to seduce him, though her plan brings her into conflict with the Contessa d'Arco (mezzo-soprano), who also has designs on Corradino. Mayhem ensues at the end of the first act when the castle is surprised by Edoardo's father, Raimondo (bass). At the start of Act 2 Isidoro, now Corradino's official war poet, is chronicling the defeat of Raimondo and Edoardo. In the confusion, however, Edoardo has escaped and he believes he owes his freedom to Matilde. The idea that Matilde is Edoardo's ally is further exploited by the jealous Contessa. Convinced by this farrago of calumny and coincidence, Corradino orders Isidoro to murder Matilde by throwing her from a nearby height into the torrent below; but Isidoro cannot bring himself to do so. Meanwhile, when Matilde's innocence and the Contessa's wiles are revealed to Corradino he is filled with remorse and determines to jump to his death from the same treacherous height. Before he takes the fatal step, Matilde, Edoardo and Raimondo arrive to save him. Amid general rejoicing, a triumphant Matilde points the moral – that women are born to rule.

RICHARD OSBORNE

Matinée. In opera as in the straight theatre, matinées (extra afternoon performances) became possible when the main performance time shifted from early afternoon to about 7 p.m. or later, in the second half of the 18th century. Opera matinées were, however, long seen as fit only for plebeian audiences. In Naples, the Bourbon government forbade them at the leading theatre, the S Carlo; but from 1817 at least they were common at small opera houses with lower-class audiences, not only on Sundays (when the working population was most likely to be free) but as part of a twice-daily schedule on other days. In Paris, the Sunday matinée became established from 1868 as the occasion for family visits to the national theatres, opera houses included; it has generally been favoured in continental and Latin American countries. In the English-speaking countries, where Sunday performances have at most times been ruled out by custom or by law, American opera companies have been readier than British to put on Saturday and sometimes other matinée performances of heavyweight works; the New York Metropolitan gave in 1933 an uncut *Götterdämmerung* followed in the evening by *L'amore dei tre re*.

*

ES ('Orario')
I-Na, Teatri, f.146
A. Piaget: 'Matinée', *Grande encyclopédie* (Paris, 1887–98)
I. Kolodin: *The Metropolitan Opera* (New York, 1936), 207, 217, 332, 372, 435
J. Rosselli: *The Opera Industry in Italy from Cimarosa to Verdi* (Cambridge, 1984), 171   JOHN ROSSELLI

Matka ('The Mother'). Quarter-tone opera in ten scenes, op.35, by ALOIS HÁBA to his own libretto; Munich, Staatstheater am Gärtnerplatz, 17 May 1931 (in German).

The roots of the action and of the music lie in rural Moravian society. After the death of his first wife, the cottager Křen (heroic tenor) marries the noble-minded, loving and wise Maruša (soprano). She considers her vocation to be to bring up her children and stepchildren, while trying to moderate her husband's coarse, domineering and passionate sexual nature. As the

Mother of the title, she is the physical and moral heroine of the opera; the other soloists and the chorus serve to characterize episodes.

Like Janáček, Hába considered the dominant component of opera to be singing, accompanied by the orchestra, which also serves to support the intonation of difficult quarter-tone parts. *Matka* is neither a music drama in the Wagnerian sense nor a 'song-opera' like Slavic folk operas; its musical flow is smooth and its form athematic, with no recurrence of motifs. Any independent numbers are prompted by the demands of the action. The funeral of Křen's first wife, for example, which uses traditional prayers and folk dirges, forms an authentic folk scene. In addition to the instruments conventionally used for quarter-tone music (strings, trombones), quarter-tone instruments of Hába's own invention appear (clarinets, trumpets, harmonium). The orchestration has a chamber music feel to it, which corresponds to the work's broadly lyrical atmosphere.

Hába composed *Matka* between March 1927 and October 1929; it was not given in Czech until after the war, when it was conducted by Karel Ančerl in Prague (23 May 1947). It was given a second performance in Czech in Prague and Florence (1964), conducted by Jiří Jirouš.

JIŘÍ VYSLOUŽIL

Mátray, Gábor (*b* Nagykáta, 23 Nov 1797; *d* Budapest, 17 July 1875). Hungarian administrator and writer on music. He studied music and law in Pest. From 1817 until 1830 he was a tutor in the service of Count Lajos Széchényi in Vienna. He returned to Pest in 1830 and in 1833 was made a corresponding member of the Hungarian Academy of Science. As musical director (appointed 1837) of the Hungarian National Theatre in Pest he made an important contribution to the operatic life of the country. In 1840 he was elected director of the music school of the Pestbuda music society (from 1867 the National Conservatory).

Mátray wrote the first account of the music history of his country, and his informed music criticism was profoundly influential. He was also a composer: his incidental music for István Balog's historical play *Csernyi György* (1812), characterized by elements of *verbunkos* and of Hungarian, Serbian and Turkish folk and popular music, is the earliest surviving Hungarian work connected with the stage.

*

P. Várnai: 'Egy magyar muzsikus a reformkorban: Mátray Gábor élete és munkássága a szabadságharcig' [A Hungarian Musician in the Reform Era: the Life and Work of Mátray until the War of Independence], *Zenetudományi tanulmányok*, ii (1954), 231

——: 'Mátray Gábor élete és munkássága a szabadságharctól haláláig' [Life and Work of Mátray from the War of Independence to his Death], *Zenetudományi tanulmányok*, iv (1955), 163

FERENC BÓNIS

Matrero, El ('The Artful Knave'). Opera in three acts by FELIPE BOERO to a libretto by Yamandú Rodriguez; Buenos Aires, Teatro Colón, 12 July 1929.

The opera begins during a party at the farm of Don Liborio (baritone). The guests discuss a *matrero* who is terrorizing the district. Pontezuela (mezzo-soprano), Liborio's daughter, has heard a noise on the outskirts of the estate. She says that her horse stumbled over the fallen nest of an *hornero* (ovenbird), and Liborio explains that the *hornero* is the symbol of the hard-working farmer, the opposite of the vagrant *matrero*. A serenade is addressed to Pontezuela by a wandering singer, Pedro Cruz (tenor). Pontezuela does not want to let him in, but

Liborio welcomes him in accordance with the time-honoured tradition of hospitality.

In the second act Pedro woos Pontezuela. Liborio doubts that a homeless strolling singer will find favour with his daughter, but Pedro promises to prove his worth. Farm workers from the surrounding area gather to hunt down the *matrero*. All the men leave except Pedro, who stays behind with Liborio. At the beginning of Act 3 Pontezuela rejects her father's suggestion that she marry the vagabond; she confesses to Pedro that her masculine ideal is the *matrero*, a man of unconstrained freedom. Pedro promises to bring her bridegroom to her, but he is injured in a burning stubble field. Returning, he declares that he is the *matrero* and dies in Pontezuela's arms.

Rooted in local tradition, *El matrero* is undoubtedly the most typically indigenous Argentinian opera. Its seamless blending of native elements into the texture is somewhat unusual in Spanish American music. Boero's music is based on clearly defined leitmotifs, and rhythms and melodies from folk music can be discerned. He uses some well-known dances (*La media caña*) and songs (in particular, the *Guaraní* song in the prelude to Act 3), and makes use of the *gaucho* dialect in the text. Several numbers became very popular after the première.

JUAN PEDRO FRANZE

Matrimonio segreto, Il ('The Secret Marriage'). *Melodramma giocoso* in two acts by DOMENICO CIMAROSA to a libretto by GIOVANNI BERTATI, after George Colman the elder (*see* COLMAN family, (2)) and DAVID GARRICK's play *The Clandestine Marriage*; Vienna, Burgtheater, 7 February 1792.

Carolina		soprano
Elisetta	*Geronimo's daughters*	mezzo-soprano
Paolino *young clerk to Geronimo*		tenor
Geronimo *a rich merchant*		bass
Fidalma *his sister*		contralto
Count Robinson		bass

Setting Geronimo's house in 18th-century Bologna

Leopold II, who attended the première, was so impressed that, after offering dinner to all the performers, he had them repeat the opera in a private performance on the same day. This was a considerable feat considering that, according to contemporary reports, the première lasted close to three hours because of public acclamation and the repetition of arias and ensembles.

The opera's initial success was partly due to the cast, which included Dorothea Bussani (Fidalma), Irene Tomeoni (Carolina), and the particularly happy combination of Giambattista Serafino Blasi (as Geronimo) and Francesco Benucci (Count Robinson), whose Act 2 duet 'Se fiato in corpo avete' brought the house down at the première. Giuseppina Nettelet (Elisetta) and Santi Nencini (Paolino), who went to Vienna in 1790 from Eszterháza, where he had performed in several of Cimarosa's operas, completed the cast.

Bertati's text found a perfect match in Cimarosa's music. The unfavourable comments of Bertati's fellow poets are clearly biased. A letter from Giambattista Casti to Da Ponte exemplifies the intrigues and backstabbings prevalent in operatic circles at the Viennese court: 'Last evening came the première of *Il matrimonio segreto*. The music is marvellously beautiful, but the words fell very far below expectations, and everyone is dissatisfied, particularly the singers' (L. da Ponte, *Memorie*, Eng. trans., 1954, p.225). Da Ponte, to whom Casti had also sent a copy of the libretto, replied: 'Bertati's verses are what they might have been expected to be. Let Vienna swallow them' (this from a man who fashioned his own *Don Giovanni* after Bertati's text set to music by Gazzaniga).

The plot of *Il matrimonio segreto* derives in part from the elder Colman and Garrick's *The Clandestine Marriage* (1766, London), which in turn was inspired by William Hogarth's series of etchings *Marriage à la mode*. Two earlier operas on the same topic might have influenced Bertati: the French comedy with music *Sophie, ou Le mariage caché* (1768, Paris), with text by Mme Riccoboni and music by Josef Kohaut; and the one-act comic opera *Le mariage clandestin* (1790, Paris), with text by Joseph Alexandre Pierre de Ségur and music by François Devienne.

Cimarosa's opera, given in Vienna exactly two months after Mozart's death, enjoyed a greater success than any of Mozart's operas, with the possible exception of *Così fan tutte*. Up to the end of the century it had over 70 performances in Vienna alone and was still being given there in 1884, with revisions by J. N. Fuchs. Hanslick wrote that the opera was 'full of sunshine … it had that genuine light golden colour, which is the only fitting one for a musical comedy'.

The opera attained instant international fame, and in the first two years after its première was presented in Leipzig, Dresden, Berlin, Paris, Milan, Florence, Naples, Turin, Madrid and Lisbon, among other cities. In the first half of the 19th century it was performed in German, French, Spanish, Danish, Swedish, Polish, Dutch, Russian, English and Czech, often reworked with titles such as *Die heimliche Ehe*, *Le mariage secret*, *Der adelsüchtige Bürger*, *Il segreto e l'intrigo della lettera*, *Lo sposalizio segreto* and *Il matrimonio notturno*. It was even performed in Calcutta (1870). It was given on 23 April 1933 at the Library of Congress, Washington, DC, and is one of the few late 18th-century *opere buffe* to receive occasional revivals.

Some celebrated singers also furthered its fame throughout the 19th century. The bass Luigi Lablache sang the role of Geronimo at the King's Theatre, London, and the Théâtre Italien, Paris, in 1830. Maria Malibran's Carolina, Tamburini's Count and Rubini's Paolino were also noteworthy. While the opera conquered Paris audiences throughout the 1830s and 40s, Berlioz found it tiring. Schumann considered it masterly in its writing and instrumentation but musically uninspiring.

ACT 1 The musical world of Mozart has already been re-created in the Largo of the overture with three initial D major chords. The brilliant orchestration of flutes, oboes, clarinets, horns, trumpets, timpani and strings not only provides a festive atmosphere but shows a melodic effusiveness and inventiveness full of verve, vitality and exuberance. The light, whirling string figures that open the Allegro moderato sections recall the beginning of the overture to *Le nozze di Figaro*.

As the curtain rises Paolino and Carolina, who have been secretly married for several months, are discussing how they will break their news to her father without antagonizing him too much. They hope that Geronimo, who aspires to join the ranks of the nobility, will be appeased through the wedding of his elder daughter, Elisetta, to Count Robinson. Paolino has arranged this match in the hope that, when Geronimo learns of the secret wedding of Paolino and Carolina, he will forgive them. The duet 'Cara non dubitar', followed by a recitative and the duet 'Io ti lascio', present a continuous opening scene, unified by the recurrence of the initial string figures of the overture which are combined with witty interjections for solo oboe. It is a remarkably tender and touching love duet.

Paolino delivers the Count's letter to Geronimo, whose deafness is a source of humour. Once he realizes that the Count is asking for Elisetta's hand, Geronimo rejoices at the prospect of his daughter becoming a countess in the aria 'Udite tutti, udite'; it begins Andante maestoso, but changes to an Allegro of unbridled enthusiasm, with dotted rhythms and leaps in the orchestral parts depicting Geronimo's joy at the words 'Che saltino i dinari'. The aria is a wonderful portrayal of the varying moods of the dramatic situation, ranging from sections in rapid parlando to a slower pacing at Geronimo's realization that Elisetta does not share his joy, and a sudden recovery of the original joyful mood (with a shift in tonality from A major to B♭ major), with a *più mosso* ending at 'La festa si prepara'. This was one of the most popular numbers at the opera's première.

Elisetta, quickly assuming the airs of a countess, accuses her younger sister of treating her with disrespect. The ensuing agitated trio for Carolina, Elisetta and Fidalma, 'Le faccio un inchino', another highlight of the opera, is an excellent characterization of the verbal aggression between the sisters: Carolina ridicules Elisetta in a parlando line, and Fidalma attempts to act as peacemaker. Despite Fidalma's good life with her brother, her state of widowhood does not please her; she too has nuptial intentions, and the object of her affections is Paolino.

The plot is complicated by the Count's pompous entrance and his attempt to identify his bride. He approaches Carolina, then Fidalma and, when he finds out that the least attractive, Elisetta, is to be his spouse, he is shocked and disappointed. The ensuing quartet, 'Sento in petto un freddo gelo', for Carolina, Fidalma, Elisetta and the Count, is an excellent depiction of four disparate sets of thoughts and sentiments. The situation is now quite out of hand for Carolina and Paolino; not only will the Count have nothing to do with Elisetta but he wants to marry Carolina instead. Pandemonium breaks out in the Act 1 finale as Elisetta accuses her younger sister of seducing the Count, while Geronimo's deafness prevents him from hearing or understanding the commotion.

ACT 2 A duet for Geronimo and the Count, 'Se fiato in corpo avete', cleverly depicts their differences, as the Count tells Geronimo that he will not marry Elisetta, while Geronimo insists that he will. There is a complete change in the character of the music when the Count's proposal to marry Carolina for only half the original dowry is met with enthusiasm. The young lovers' misfortune worsens with Fidalma's declaration of love for Paolino. In a beautiful bel canto aria with clarinet solo ('Pria che spunti in ciel aurora') Paolino decides that he and Carolina must run away. The finale is a nocturnal scene, in which each character emerges from his or her bedroom and catches the lovers in the act of escaping. Paolino and Carolina admit that they are married; the

Count, in a quick about-face, decides to marry Elisetta; and Geronimo accepts and forgives.

* * *

The directness, exuberance, spontaneity, gracefulness and musical sincerity of this opera gave it an international appeal. With a libretto that presents the action in clear strokes, uncomplicated by disguises and mistaken identities, it successfully depicts the misfortunes of a young couple who dare to contradict the established social codes. A sentimental comedy along the lines of Samuel Richardson's *Pamela* (1740), it celebrates the naturalness popularized by Rousseau. Though not a satire, it is an expression of contemporary values and social mores. The aristocrat, Count Robinson, is a laughable, comic figure, as is Geronimo, whose aristocratic aspirations override paternal concern for his daughter's feelings. The music is at times almost Romantic in expression, especially in Paolino's 'Pria che spunti in ciel aurora'. In its clever use of parlando as a comic device it bridges the gap between the 18th-century *intermezzo comico per musica* and the operas of Rossini and Donizetti.   GORDANA LAZAREVICH

Mattei, Colomba (*b* ?Rome; *fl* 1743–78). Italian soprano. She began in comic opera at Naples in 1743–4 and Palermo in 1745–6, becoming a pupil of the composer Perez. In 1748 she was in service at Bayreuth and in 1749–50 she was seconda donna in *opera seria* at Vienna, where she made an impression on Metastasio, who praised her eyes, figure and voice (range approximately *b*♭ to *b*♭''), although he considered both her voice and stature too small for a prima donna. However, she sang as prima donna in Italy from 1751 and during the period 1757–62 in London, at the King's Theatre, where, with her husband Trombetta, she was also manager, 1757–63; it was she who engaged J. C. Bach in 1762 to write for the theatre. She was not seconda donna there in 1754–6, as Burney averred; this was probably Camilla Mattei, possibly a relative. She then retired and in 1778 was living in Milan with children and a husband named Diletti. Burney praised her acting and judged her singing 'amiable and pleasing' but 'not quite in the *grand gusto*'. This is reflected in her music by a lack of emphasis on the extremes, either of bravura or of cantabile.   DENNIS LIBBY

Mattei, Saverio (*b* Calabria, 1742; *d* Naples, 1795). Italian librettist and writer on music. A Neapolitan lawyer, he published works of poetry, biography, jurisprudence and religion; his biography of Jommelli is one of the most important contemporary descriptions of the composer, who, during his last years, was an intimate friend of Mattei's. Mattei also greatly enlarged the library of the Naples conservatory. His writings on dramatic poetry and opera continue the calls for reform voiced throughout the 18th century by such literati as Muratori (1706), Algarotti (1755) and Arteaga (1783), although Mattei was an ardent admirer of Metastasio's *drammi*. He wrote a single serenata libretto, *Il natal d'Apollo*, set to music by Pasquale Cafaro for Naples in 1775.

WRITINGS

Saggio di poesie latine, ed italiane (Naples, 1774); repr. as 'Elogio del Jommelli o sia il progresso della poesia, e musica teatrale', *Memorie per servire alla vita di Metastasio* (Colle, 1785), 59–135

'La filosofia della musica o sia la riforma del teatro per musica', *Opere del Signor Abate Pietro Metastasio*, iii (Naples, 1781); repr. as *Filosofia della musica ossia riforma del teatro* (Nice, 1785)

Vita di Benedetto Marcello, patrizio veneto, con l'aggiunta delle risposte alle censure (Venice, 1788)   DALE E. MONSON

Matters, Arnold (*b* Adelaide, 11 April 1904; *d* Adelaide, 21 Sept 1990). Australian baritone. He studied in Adelaide with Frederick Bevan and Clive Carey and in London with W. Johnstone Douglas. From 1932 to 1939 he sang with Sadler's Wells Opera, making his début as Valentin in Gounod's *Faust*. He combined a fine voice with admirable histrionic art: his Falstaff, in particular, was a ripe and humorous study, and his repertory included Don Giovanni, Sarastro, Hans Sachs and Wotan. He also sang small roles during the international seasons at Covent Garden. During the war he returned to Australia. He rejoined Sadler's Wells in 1944 and sang the title role in the English première of *Simon Boccanegra* in 1948, as well as Don Alfonso, Germont and Sharpless. He created Pilgrim in *The Pilgrim's Progress* (1951) and Cecil in *Gloriana* (1953) at Covent Garden, and Sir William Hamilton in the première of Berkeley's *Nelson* (1954, Sadler's Wells). He sang Procida (*Les vêpres siciliennes*) for the WNO in 1955, then returned to Adelaide to teach.

For illustration *see* PILGRIM'S PROGRESS, THE.

*

A. Blyth: 'Arnold Matters (1903–90)', *Opera*, xli (1990), 1311–12   HAROLD ROSENTHAL/R

Matteuccio. *See* SASSANO, MATTEO.

Mattheson, Johann (*b* Hamburg, 28 Sept 1681; *d* Hamburg, 17 April 1764). German composer, singer, critic and theorist. He was the third and only surviving son of Johann Mattheson, a Hamburg tax collector, and Margaretha Höling of Rendsburg (Holstein). Details of his life come largely from his autobiography found in his *Grundlage einer Ehren-Pforte* (Hamburg, 1740). He was educated at the Johanneum, where he received a substantial grounding in the liberal arts, including musical instruction from the Kantor, Joachim Gerstenbüttel. At six he began private music lessons, studying the keyboard and composition as well as taking singing lessons and instruction on the gamba, violin, flute, oboe and lute. At nine he was a child prodigy, performing on the organ and singing in churches. Gerhard Schott, manager of the Hamburg opera, asked him to join the company, and he sang in J. W. Franck's opera *Aeneas*. Realizing that the opera was a 'musical university' he decided not to pursue formal education after completing the Johanneum curriculum in 1693. Three years later he made his solo début in female roles when the opera company visited Kiel in 1696. By the following year his voice had changed, and he began to take tenor roles, in which he had considerable success up to 1705. He enjoyed a rich musical life during his 15 years with the Hamburg opera; he sang and conducted rehearsals under such composers as J. G. Conradi, J. S. Kusser and Reinhard Keiser. He said he learnt the new, Italian manner of singing from Kusser. In 1699 he wrote and had performed his first opera, *Die Plejades*.

During his career Mattheson not only performed in some 65 new operas but wrote several of his own. One of them, *Cleopatra*, involved the well-known altercation between him and his friend Handel, who had come to Hamburg in 1703. In 1704 Mattheson's opera was performed with the composer singing the role of Antonius [Antony]. Handel conducted from the harpsichord while Mattheson was on the stage. However, after Antony's suicide in the middle of Act 3, Mattheson returned to the orchestra, intending to take his place at the keyboard, but Handel refused to yield. An argument between the two young musicians led to the duel described by Mattheson in his *Ehren-Pforte*; according to him, Handel's life was spared by a large button on his coat that Mattheson struck with his sword. Apparently, however, the two were soon reconciled, and Mattheson claimed he sang leading roles in Handel's *Almira* and *Nero* at Hamburg in 1705. He also later reported that he had influenced Handel's musical development, particularly by teaching him how to compose in the operatic style.

In 1704 Mattheson became a tutor to Cyrill Wich, son of the English ambassador to Hamburg, Sir John Wich. This position was the turning-point in his career, offering him employment with social status and a considerable salary. In 1706 he was made secretary to the ambassador, a position he retained for most of his life, continuing with the same responsibilities when Wich's son was appointed his father's successor in 1715. In 1709 Mattheson married Catharina Jennings (*d* 8 Feb 1753), daughter of an English minister. In 1715 he became music director of Hamburg Cathedral, a post of particular importance for which he composed many sacred works, including more than two dozen oratorios. During the extraordinarily productive years between 1715 and 1740 he produced not only numerous important scores and treatises but also many translations from English of books, pamphlets and articles primarily connected with his secretarial duties to the English ambassador. On 25 April 1764 he was buried in the crypt of the Michaeliskirche, to which he had donated the bulk of his considerable fortune. *Das fröhliche Sterbelied*, which Mattheson had composed for his funeral, was conducted by Telemann.

Mattheson documented in unparalleled detail the musical world of those critical years in the 18th century when musical styles and values changed radically in the transition from the Baroque period to the Classical. His reputation as a composer is impossible to assess fully because most of his music, including six complete operas, was apparently lost in the destruction of the Hamburg Stadtbibliothek in World War II. Only one opera survives, *Cleopatra*, which, though an early work, is evidence of his talent. While the opera is famous particularly for its connection with the Mattheson–Handel duel, its real significance lies in the supporting musical evidence it contributes to Mattheson's theoretical doctrines, codified several years later. Former opinions that Mattheson as a composer was insignificant and merely imitated the style of Keiser can be disproved by this opera. He is clearly distinguishable from Keiser, particularly in his melodic writing: his melodies are usually more conjunct in motion and therefore less angular than Keiser's; he generally achieved simpler melodic expressivity, taking more care than Keiser over maintaining poetic metres, and usually avoiding the long, more italianate melismatic passages characteristic of Keiser's arias. There is a striking emphasis on folklike songs, often strophic in form, at times in Hamburg dialect. The folk element was a tradition of earlier Hamburg operas, and Mattheson employed it to special advantage in comic scenes. He was the first musical genius that Hamburg had produced, and this is of the utmost importance when considering the substance and validity of his aesthetic and musical theories and critical judgments. He wrote

about music from the vantage point of enormous practical experience not only as an observer but also as a trained professional.

In Mattheson's numerous writings about music, opera is often discussed as both an art form and a cultural necessity for the educated citizen (in his words the *galant homme*). Vocal music remained for him as for most Baroque composers the foundation of all important aspects of composing, and he devoted major theoretical discussions to it in various works. He even considered opera essential to civic pride and a metropolitan necessity, as the following passage from *Der musicalische Patriot* (p.176) suggests:

Through celebrated performances [of an opera theatre] great princes and lords are often persuaded to stay and to bring their households to stay in a city, procuring for them frequent foodstuffs. Scholars, artists, artisans come along too, and the city takes on the kind of eminence with a good opera that it has with good banks. For the latter are for service, the former give pleasure; the latter serve to give security, the former [serve] to instruct. It is almost always true that where the best banks are found, so too are found the best opera houses.

Mattheson expressed his belief in the intrinsic worth of opera even more eloquently in *Die neueste Untersuchung der Singspiele* (pp.86–7):

A good opera theatre is nothing less than an academy of many of the fine arts – architecture, perspective, painting, mechanics, dancing, acting, ethics, history, poetry, and especially music – where all together and at once they are most agreeably conjoined and continuously experimented with anew for the pleasure and edification of distinguished and intelligent audiences. … However, without such a well-planned nursery like opera as described here, the best as well as the worst music must finally be spoilt and become extinct. Indeed, even in the church it will no longer have an enduring place. The downfall of opera causes the downfall of the very essence of music.

See also CLEOPATRA (i).

Die Plejades, oder Das Sieben-Gestirne (Spl, F. C. Bressand), Hamburg, 1699
Der edelmüthige Porsenna (Spl, 4, Bressand), Hamburg, 1702
Victor, Hertzog der Normannen [Act 2] (3, H. Hinsch), Hamburg, 1702 [Act 1 by J. C. Schieferdecker, Act 3 by G. Bronner]
Cleopatra [Die unglückselige Cleopatra, Königin von Egypten, oder Die betrogene Staats-Liebe] (drama per musica, 3, F. C. Feustking), Hamburg, 20 Oct 1704, *US-Wc*; ed. in EDM, lxix (1975)
Le retour du siècle d'or, das ist Die Wiederkehr der güldnen Zeit ('Operetgen', Countess Löwenhaupt), Nehmten and Perdoel, Holstein, 1705
Boris Goudenow, oder Der durch Verschlagenheit erlangte Trohn, (drama per musica, 3, Mattheson), Hamburg, 1710
Die geheimen Begebenheiten Henrico IV, Königs von Castilien und Leon, oder Die getheilte Liebe (5, J. J. Hoë), Hamburg, 9 Feb 1711

WRITINGS

Das neu-eröffnete Orchestre (Hamburg, 1713)
Das beschützte Orchestre (Hamburg, 1717)
Critica musica (Hamburg, 1722–5)
Der musicalische Patriot (Hamburg, 1728)
Der vollkommene Capellmeister (Hamburg, 1739; Eng. trans., Ann Arbor, 1981)
Die neueste Untersuchung der Singspiele, nebst beygefügter musicalischen Geschmacksprobe (Hamburg, 1744)

*

H. Schmidt: *Johann Mattheson, ein Förderer der deutschen Tonkunst* (Leipzig, 1897)
B. C. Cannon: *Johann Mattheson, Spectator in Music* (New Haven, CT, 1947)
H. C. Wolff: *Die Barockoper in Hamburg* (Wolfenbüttel, 1957)
G. J. Buelow: 'Johann Mattheson, the Composer, an Evaluation of his Opera Cleopatra (Hamburg, 1704)', *Studies in Eighteenth Century Music: a Tribute to Karl Geiringer* (London and New York, 1970)
H. J. Marx, ed.: *Johann Mattheson: Lebensbeschreibung des Hamburger Musikers, Schriftstellers und Diplomaten* (Hamburg, 1982)

G. J. Buelow: 'Johann Mattheson and the Invention of the *Affektenlehre*', *New Mattheson Studies*, ed. G. J. Buelow and H. J. Marx (Cambridge, 1983), 393–407

J. M. Knapp: 'Mattheson and Handel: their Musical Relations in Hamburg', ibid, 307–326

G. Flaherty: 'Mattheson and the Aesthetics of Theater', ibid, 75–99

W. Dean: 'Mattheson's Arrangement of Handel's *Radamisto* for the Hamburg Opera', ibid, 169–78   GEORGE J. BUELOW

Matthus, Siegfried (*b* Mallenuppen, East Prussia, 13 April 1934). German composer. He studied conducting (1952–8) at the Städtisches Konservatorium in Berlin, where from 1956 he also studied composition with Wagner-Régeny. He was in Eisler's masterclass at the Akademie der Künste until 1960 and from then until 1964 he worked in Berlin as a freelance composer. Apart from extensive and diverse compositional activity, he was resident Dramaturg at the Komische Oper in Berlin, a post that served to sharpen his sense of music drama.

In the early 1960s Matthus experimented with various means of organizing form and pitch in the search for a new style. The works of Schoenberg, Webern and Eisler influenced the maturing of his tonal language, which is characterized by the incorporation of new techniques and methods of composition, though he remains concerned that his music be accessible to his audience:

In my music I want to show what I am thinking, what I am feeling, what changes I would like to see … my greatest wish is to use the technical achievements of contemporary musical language to make statements that will be understood without the hearer's needing to grasp the craftsmanship and technique behind them, as if learning grammar or a foreign language. I want to speak to my audience in a language it can easily understand.

Those aims are supported by Matthus's increasing involvement as a conductor in performances of his works.

The 1970s saw a phase in which Matthus turned to traditional models, culminating in the concerto for orchestra, *Responso* (1977), after which he adopted a combination of pre- and post-serial forms, turning increasingly to contemporary human problems for subject matter. His use of motifs, themes and tonal colour serves emotional purposes, and is characteristic of his musical language. *Die Weise von Liebe und Tod des Cornets Christoph Rilke* has a psychologically complex plot and was one of the works given its première at the opening of the rebuilt Semper Oper in Dresden in 1985. This was followed by the expressive dramatic work *Judith*, the revolutionary opera *Graf Mirabeau*, dedicated to the 200th anniversary of the French Revolution and, in 1992, *Desdemona und ihre Schwestern*.

Matthus's work is at its most impressive in his contributions to music drama but is also of considerable significance in other genres. His international success confirms him as the most important composer of his time to come from East Germany.

Der Professor kommt um sechs (musical for children, after J. Hall and M. Lwowski), Rostock, 4 April 1963

Lazarillo vom Tormes, oder Spanische Tugenden (7 scenes, H. Seeger), Karl-Marx-Stadt, Städtisches, 23 May 1964

Die Heimkehr des Odysseus (adapted from C. Monteverdi: Il ritorno d'Ulisse in patria), Berlin, Komische Oper, 19 April 1966, collab. G. Bahner and V. Rohde

Der letzte Schuss (2, Matthus and G. Friedrich, after B. Lawrenjow: *Der Einundvierzigste*), Berlin, Komische Oper, 5 Nov 1967

Der Barbier von Berlin (Altberliner Posse, 1, adapted M. Vogler), Berlin, Komische Oper, 7 June 1970

Herr Ohnezeit (operatic scene, G. Branstner), Berlin, Komische Oper, 15 Dec 1970

Noch einen Löffel Gift, Liebling? (komische Kriminaloper, prol., 3, P. Hacks, after S. O'Hara: *Heiraten ist immer ein Risiko*), Berlin, Komische Oper, 16 April 1972

Omphale (3, Hacks), Weimar, National, 7 Sept 1976; rev. Cologne, 1979

Die Weise von Liebe und Tod des Cornets Christoph Rilke (Opernvision, Matthus, after R. M. Rilke), Dresden, Staatsoper, 16 Feb 1985

Judith (2, Matthus, after F. Hebbel and the Old Testament), Berlin, Komische Oper, 28 Sept 1985; in Eng., Santa Fe, 28 July 1990

Graf Mirabeau (2, Matthus, from historical documents), Berlin, Staatsoper, and Karlsruhe, Badisches Staatstheater, 14 July 1989

Desdemona und ihre Schwestern (Opernmonologe, Matthus, after C. Brückner and the Old Testament), Schwetzingen, 12 May 1992

*

MGG (D. Härtwig)

F. Hennenberg: 'Dialektische musikdramaturgische Verfahren in der Oper "Der letzte Schuss" ', *Jb der Komischen Oper Berlin*, viii (1967–8)

Musik in der DDR [pubn of the Akademie der Künste], Arbeitsheft 13 (Berlin, 1973), 41–8, 147

H. Döhnert: *Siegfried Matthus: für Sie porträtiert* (Leipzig, 1979)

U. Liedtke: *Siegfried Matthus: Tendenzen im Schaffen eines Komponisten der DDR* (diss., U. of Leipzig, 1985)

G. Belkius and U. Liedtke, eds.: *Musik für die Oper? Gespräche mit Komponisten* (Berlin, 1990)

U. Liedtke: 'Oper als Welttheater: zum Opernschaffen von S. Matthus', *Oper heute*, xiii, ed. H. Seeger and W. Lange (Berlin, 1990)   DIETER HÄRTWIG

Mattila, Karita (Marjatta) (*b* Somero, 5 Sept 1960). Finnish soprano. She studied in Helsinki, appearing while still a student at Savonlinna as Donna Anna (1981) and Lady Billows (1982), then made her début with the Finnish National Opera as Countess Almaviva in 1983. In 1985 she sang Donna Elvira with Scottish Opera, and in 1986 she made her Covent Garden début as Fiordiligi, returning to sing Pamina, Countess Almaviva and Agathe. She sang Emma in Schubert's *Fierrabras* in Vienna in 1988, and has also appeared in Brussels, Washington, DC, Houston and the Metropolitan, where she sang Donna Elvira (1990). Her other roles include Eva and Rosalinde (*Fledermaus*), but her bright-toned, well-focussed voice is heard to best advantage in Mozart.   ELIZABETH FORBES

Mattioli, Andrea (*b* Faenza, *c*1620; *d* Mantua, 2 Oct 1679). Italian composer. He was a beneficed priest and *maestro di cappella* of Imola Cathedral in 1646. Later he was described as a vicar of S Romano, Ferrara. By early 1650 he was *maestro di cappella* of the Accademia dello Spirito Santo at Ferrara, the city for which he composed most of his operas, nearly all performed with machinery by Carlo Pasetti; he was succeeded late in 1654 by Giuseppe Tricarico. From at least 1656 until his death he was court *maestro di cappella* to the Duke of Mantua; in 1658 he was listed among the foreigners living in the parish of St Peter, Rome. Little survives of his operas and other secular music.

La palma d'amore (Berni), Ferrara, S Lorenzo, carn. 1650

Il ratto di Cefalo (F. Berni), Ferrara, Sala, 1650

L'esiglio d'amore (Berni), Ferrara, Cortile, 20 Feb 1651, collab. Filiberto Laurenzi

Gli sforzi del desiderio (ricreazione dramatica musicale, Berni), Ferrara, Palazzo Miroglio, 1652

L'Antiopa (Berni), Ferrara, Sala, 1653

Oritia (A. Passarelli), Ferrara, 1655

La Didone (P. Moscardini), Bologna, 25 April 1656

L'Artabano (A. Lanzoni), Mantua, Castello, 1662

La Filli di Tracia (? E. Pinamonte Bonacossi), Ferrara, S Stefano, 17 Feb 1664

Perseo (A. Aureli), Venice, SS Giovanni e Paolo, 1665

New arias in F. Provenzale and F. Cavalli: *Ciro* (G. C. Sorrentino), Venice, SS Giovanni e Paolo, 4 Feb 1665, *I-Vnm*

EitnerQ; *FétisB*; *GerberNL*; *MGG* (O. Mischiati); *SchmidlD*; *WaltherML*

A. Bertolotti: *Musici alla corte dei Gonzaga in Mantova dal secolo XV al XVIII* (Milan, 1890)

G. Gaspari: *Catalogo della Biblioteca del Liceo musicale di Bologna*, i–iv (Bologna, 1890–1905); v, ed. U. Sesini (Bologna, 1943)

T. Walker: 'Gli sforzi del desiderio: cronaca ferrarese, 1652', *Studi in onore di Lanfranco Caretti* (Modena, 1987), 45–75

THOMAS WALKER

Matti per amore, Li ('The Fools for Love'). *Opera buffa* in three acts by GIOACCHINO COCCHI to a libretto by CARLO GOLDONI after GENNARO ANTONIO FEDERICO's libretto *Amor vuol sofferenza*; Venice, Teatro S Samuele, autumn 1754 (revised version, *Il signor Cioè*, Modena, 1755).

Goldoni, writing as 'Polisseno Fegejo', is identified as the author on the title-page of some (not all) prints of the original libretto. The plot involves two *parti serie*, Eugenia (soprano) and Lelio, and five *parti buffe*, Fazio Tondi (tenor), Lisetta (soprano), Mosca (bass), Camilla and Ridolfo. In its inaugural run, the opera benefited from a brilliant cast: Francesco Baglioni played Fazio, a fool whose every other sentence is punctuated with 'cioè' ('that is'); his daughters Giovanna and Clementina played Eugenia and Lisetta, and Francesco Carattoli was Mosca. Cocchi's music, to an undistinguished libretto featuring three sets of lovers at cross-purposes, is competent without being innovatory. The work enjoyed a few revivals elsewhere.
PIERO WEISS

Mattocks, George (*b* 1734/5; *d* Edinburgh, 14 Aug 1804). English tenor, actor and theatre manager. As a boy he sang at the London fairs and then had three seasons at Drury Lane (1749–52), creating the role of Palaemon in Boyce's *The Chaplet*. His adult singing career was principally at Covent Garden, where he appeared every year from 1757 to 1784. O'Keeffe remembered him as 'tall and well made' and Hugh Kelly admired his 'tender strain, so delicately clear'. He sang many romantic leading roles in English operas, retaining most of them until the early 1780s. He was the first Thomas in *Love in a Village*, Lord Aimsworth in *The Maid of the Mill*, Tom in *Tom Jones* and Ferdinand in *The Duenna*. Mattocks often sang with his wife, formerly Isabella Hallam, with whom he had eloped in 1765. He managed summer seasons in the provinces for many years and in 1784 turned completely to provincial management.

BDA; *LS*

H. Kelly: *Thespis*, ii (London, 1767)

Theatrical Biography, ii (London, 1772)

J. O'Keeffe: *Recollections*, ii (London, 1826)

OLIVE BALDWIN, THELMA WILSON

Mattocks [née Hallam], Isabella (*b* London, bap. 25 May 1746; *d* Kensington, 25 June 1826). English actress and soprano. In 1752 her father fled from his debts to become a theatre manager in America and she was brought up by her aunt, the actress Mrs Barrington. She was on stage from a very early age and made her 'adult' début as an actress as Juliet at Covent Garden in 1761. She remained there until her retirement in 1808, apart from two years in Liverpool with her husband George Mattocks, with whom she also appeared in provincial summer seasons. Initially performing in a wide variety of plays and English operas, she became a much admired comic actress, specializing in sprightly ladies and pert chambermaids. As a young woman she had an 'exceeding good natural voice, improved by a knowledge of music' (*Theatrical Biography*) and created Lucinda in *Love in a Village*, Theodosia in *The Maid of the Mill* and Louisa in *The Duenna*.

BDA; *DNB* (J. Kennedy); *LS*

H. Kelly: *Thespis*, ii (London, 1767)

Theatrical Biography, ii (London, 1772)

T. Bellamy: *The London Theatres* (London, 1795)

'Biographical Sketch of Mrs Mattocks', *Monthly Mirror*, ix (1800), 323–4

R. Fiske: *English Theatre Music in the Eighteenth Century* (London, 1973, 2/1986)

OLIVE BALDWIN, THELMA WILSON

Matuszczak, Bernadetta (*b* Toruń, 10 March 1933 or 1937). Polish composer. She studied at the conservatories of Poznań and Warsaw with Tadeusz Szeligowski and Kazimierz Sikorski, then with Nadia Boulanger in Paris. Her music, which reflects the general trends of Polish music since the early 1960s, is dominated by vocal genres and by her six operatic works, although only one (*Mysterium Heloizy*, 1973–4) is full-length. Matuszczak displays concern for integrated theatre, as in *Julia i Romeo*, composed in 1967, where the instrumental parts play a supporting role and detailed instructions are included in the score for lighting and other effects. She also uses tape and film projection in her stage pieces. In these two works, and also in *Pamiętnik wariata* ('The Diary of a Madman', composed 1975–6), Matuszczak explores the theatrical device of triple characterization of the principal roles (i.e. as actor, dancer and singer). The issues of war and peace, seen in the works of other Polish composers of her generation, surface in her two radio operas, in which multilingual narration plays an important part. *Humanae voces* (1970–71) is presented in the hybrid form of a documentary drama and is characterized by austere recitative and choral chant.

unpublished unless otherwise stated

Julia i Romeo, 1967 (chamber op, 5 scenes, Matuszczak and J. Iwaszkiewicz, after W. Shakespeare), Warsaw, Wielki, 19 Nov 1970 (Kraków, 1979)

Humanae voces, 1970–71 (radio op-oratorio, texts from *Genesis*, *St John*, Mahatma Gandhi, A. Frank, letters from Majdanek and Hiroshima etc.), Polish Radio, 1972

Mysterium Heloizy, 1973–4 (Matuszczak, after P. Abelard), unperf.

Pamiętnik wariata [The Diary of a Madman], 1975–6 (operatic monodrama, Matuszczak, after N. Gogol), Warsaw Chamber Op, 5 Sept 1978

Apocalypsis, 1976–7 (radio op-oratorio, Matuszczak, after *Revelation*), Polish Radio, 3 July 1979 (Kraków, 1982)

Prometheus, 1981–2 (chamber op, after Aeschylus), unperf.

H. Schiller: 'Romeo and Juliet by Bernadetta Matuszczak' *Polish Music* (1969), no.4, pp.18–20 [also in Ger.]

T. Marek: 'Composer's Workshop: Bernadetta Matuszczak', *Polish Music* (1974), no.4, pp.24–7 [on *Mysterium Heloizy*; also in Ger.]

ADRIAN THOMAS

Matzenauer, Margaret(e) (*b* Temesvár [now Timişoara, Romania], 1 June 1881; *d* Van Nuys, CA, 19 May 1963). American contralto of German parentage. She had already appeared in opera before studying in Graz with Georgine von Januschowsky-Neuendorff and in Berlin with Antonia Mielke and Franz Emerich. She made her début in Strasbourg as Puck in *Oberon* in 1901 and made guest appearances with many companies, including that of Bayreuth in 1911 (Waltraute, Flosshilde and the First Norn). Later that year she sang for the first time at the Metropolitan, as Amneris under Toscanini. During her 19 seasons there, she took part in many new productions and revivals, notably *Fidelio*, *Samson et Dalila* and *Le prophète* (both with Caruso), and *Jenůfa*. She appeared at Covent Garden in 1914, as both Kundry and Ortrud. Enthusiastically praised for her acting, Matzenauer had a photographic memory (she undertook Kundry at 24 hours' notice having never sung the part before), and her musicianship was exceptional. Although her voice was a sumptuous contralto, she often sang soprano roles and her repertory was vast. In a single season in the 1920s, she sang Isolde, Brünnhilde, Delilah, Azucena and Amneris, and although her ventures into the soprano repertory took their toll on her voice, it retained its contralto richness. She is known to have made 85 recordings. Her second husband was the tenor Edoardo Ferrari-Fontana.

GV (R. Celletti; L. Riemens)
P. L. Miller: 'Margaret Matzenauer', *Record Collector*, xxiii (1976–7), 5–47 [with discography]   PHILIP LIESON MILLER

Mauceri, John (*b* New York, 12 Sept 1945). American conductor. He graduated from Yale University, studied at Tanglewood and made his operatic début with Menotti's *The Saint of Bleecker Street* at Wolf Trap in 1973. His European début followed the same year with Bernstein's *Mass* at Vienna (first European performance). He introduced Britten's *Death in Venice* to San Francisco (1975), where the next year he conducted the première of Andrew Imbrie's *Angle of Repose*. His Metropolitan début was *Fidelio* in 1976, and performances at New York City Opera, 1977–82, ranged from Monteverdi to a new version of Bernstein's *Candide*. He was music director of Washington Opera, 1980–82, and co-produced *On your Toes* (Rodgers and Hart) in New York and London. His British début was with the WNO (*Don Carlos*, 1974), and was followed by débuts at Scottish Opera (*Otello*, 1976), the ENO (*La forza del destino*, 1983) and with the Covent Garden company (*Madama Butterfly*, 1983, in Manchester). He succeeded Sir Alexander Gibson as music director of Scottish Opera in 1987, where his work included the first professional staging in Britain of Weill's *Street Scene* (1989), and the first performance in Europe of Marc Blitzstein's *Regina*, in its revised form (1991). A volatile, dynamic conductor, he brings an almost missionary fervour to his performances.

NOËL GOODWIN

Maupin [first name unknown] (*b* 1670; *d* Provence, 1707). French soprano. She was the daughter of a Sieur d'Aubigny, secretary to the Count of Armagnac. Her physical beauty and natural talent were said to have compensated for a lack of musical training. She made her début at the Opéra in 1690 as Pallas in a revival of Lully's *Cadmus et Hermione* (1673), but her career flourished only from 1698 (when Marthe le Rochois retired) until 1705. During that time she sang in new productions by Collasse, Destouches, Campra and their contemporaries as well as in revivals of Lully *tragédies lyriques*. She made her last appearance in Michel de La Barre's *La vénitienne* (1705). The Marquis of Dangeau wrote in his journal of a performance at Trianon of Destouches' *Omphale* (1701), describing Maupin's as 'the most beautiful voice in the world'. Campra is supposed to have written the first *bas-dessus* (contralto)

role for her, that of Clorinde, in *Tancrède* (1702); in fact the part never descends below *d'* (at one time however she wanted to sing Lully's Armida a tone below its original pitch). In that same year she performed chamber music accompanied by Couperin (*Mercure galant*, 7 July 1702), and she replaced Mlle Desmatins in the title role of Bouvard's *Médus, roi de Mèdes*, receiving considerable acclaim. She was especially popular in comic roles.

Maupin was a colourful, tempestuous figure, fond of masquerading as a man and capable of duelling to the death with as many as three men at a time. Le Cerf (*Comparaison*, ii (1705), 123) remarked on her success in roles in which she abandoned her hairdo and fan for a helmet and lance, noting however that her lively and cavalier manner and her unusually strong voice offended neither decency nor verisimilitude. After marrying young, she left her husband and became the mistress of the Elector of Bavaria and others; she returned to him in her last years. Attracted to women as well as to men, she attempted suicide when her love for the soprano Fanchon Moreau was spurned. These and Maupin's other adventures are chronicled by La Borde and Campardon.

J.-B. de La Borde: *Essai sur la musique* (Paris, 1780), iii, 519ff
T. de Lajarte: *Bibliothèque musicale du Théâtre de l'Opéra* (Paris, 1876)
E. Campardon: *L'Académie royale de musique au XVIIIe siècle* (Paris, 1884), ii, 177ff
G.-J.-A.-P. Letainturier-Fradin: *La Maupin (1670–1707): sa vie, ses duels, ses aventures* (Paris, 1904)
M. Barthélemy: *André Campra: sa vie et son oeuvre* (Paris, 1957), esp. 76, 102   JULIE ANNE SADIE

Maurel, Victor (*b* Marseilles, 17 June 1848; *d* New York, 22 Oct 1923). French baritone. He studied at

Victor Maurel in the title role of Verdi's 'Falstaff', which he created at La Scala, Milan, 9 February 1893

Marseilles, then at the Paris Conservatoire with Vauthrot and Duvernoy. He made his début in 1867 at Marseilles in *Guillaume Tell* and appeared at the Paris Opéra in the following season as Nevers and Count di Luna. After appearances in St Petersburg, Cairo and Venice, he made his début at La Scala as Cacico in the première of Gomes's *Il Guarany* (1870). He returned to the Opéra in 1879 in the title role of Thomas' *Hamlet* and sang there regularly until 1894 as Don Giovanni, Méphistophélès and Alphonse (*La favorite*). At La Scala he sang the title role in the revised version of *Simon Boccanegra* (1881); his performance led Verdi to choose him to create Iago (1887) and Falstaff (1893; see illustration). He sang at Covent Garden (1873–9, 1891–5 and 1904), where he was the first London Telramund and Wolfram and the first Covent Garden Dutchman. He sang Amonasro in the American première of *Aida* (Academy of Music, New York, 1873) and later appeared at the Metropolitan Opera (1894–6, 1898–9). He created the role of Tonio in *Pagliacci* (1892, Milan). Maurel was outstanding less for the timbre or resonance of his voice than for his perfect breath control and skill as an actor. He wrote books on the staging of *Otello* (Rome, 1888) and *Don Juan* (Paris, 1896) as well as treatises on singing.

*

GV (R. Celletti; R. Vegeto)

V. Maurel: *Dix ans de carrière* (Paris, 1897) [memoirs]

M. Strakosch: *Souvenirs d'un imprésario* (Paris, 1887)

H. de Curzon: *Croquis d'artistes* (Paris, 1898)

F. Rogers: 'Victor Maurel: his Career and his Art', *MQ*, xii (1926), 580–601

D. Shawe-Taylor: 'Victor Maurel', *Opera*, vi (1955), 293–7

HAROLD ROSENTHAL/R

Maurer, Ludwig (Wilhelm) (*b* Potsdam, 8 Feb 1789; *d* St Petersburg, 13/25 Oct 1878). German violinist and composer. He was a pupil of Carl Haack, Frederick the Great's Konzertmeister. He played in the royal chapel in Berlin from 1803, and on its dissolution in 1806 travelled eastwards. In Riga he met P. Baillot and P. Rode, with whom he studied the French violin style. After playing in St Petersburg (where A. N. Verstovsky was one of his pupils) he went to Moscow, where Baillot recommended him as director of Count Vsevolozhsky's orchestra. In 1817 he left and toured through Germany to Paris (1820). From 1824 to 1833 he directed concerts and opera in Hanover, but toured annually, at the same time collaborating on the writing of *opéras-vaudevilles*, particularly with Verstovsky and A. A. Alyab'yev. In 1833 he returned to Vsevolozhsky (now in St Petersburg), where he became director of the French opera in 1835. Various other appointments continued his musical activities into old age.

Maurer's violin style, on the evidence of his compositions, was at times highly virtuoso, and he wrote much music for the instrument. Of his operatic works, *Aloise* (1828) was the most successful, but *Der neue Paris* (1826) was taken up in Riga, London (1828) and Moscow (1829).

Maurer's son Vsevolod (1819–92) was a violinist, later director of the Italian opera in St Petersburg.

L'amant jaloux, St Petersburg, *c*1815

Alonzo, *c*1819

Heinrich und Angoline, Hanover, ?1819

La fourberie découverte [Die entdeckte Betrügerei] (opérette), St Petersburg, *c*1820

Novaya shalost', ili Teatral'noye srazheniye [A Novel Prank, or A Theatrical Battle] (opéra-vaudeville, 1, N. I. Khmelnitsky), St

Petersburg, Bol'shoy, 12/24 Feb 1822, collab. A. N. Verstovsky, A. A. Alyab'yev

Der neue Paris (1, opérette), Hanover, 27 Jan 1826

Aloise (2, historische-romantische Oper, F. I. von Holbein, after F. Wodomerius), Hanover, 16 Jan 1828, vs *GB-Lbl*

Die Runenschrift (2, Holbein), Hanover, Feb 1830

Muzh i zhena [Man and Wife] (opéra-vaudeville, 1, D. T. Lensky, from Fr.), Moscow, Bol'shoy, 23 May/4 June 1830, collab. Verstovsky, F. Shol'ts

Stariy gusar, ili Pazhi Fridrikha II [The Old Hussar, or The Pages of Frederick II] (opéra-vaudeville, 3, Lensky, from Fr.), Moscow, Bol'shoy, 5/17 June 1831, collab. I. I. Genisha, Alyab'yev, Shol'ts, addns from N. Isouard

Die Müllerin von Marly (1, komische Oper), Hamburg, 11 Sept 1843

Die beiden Diebe [Der entdeckte Diebestahl], St Petersburg, Deutsches Opernhaus, 1846

*

FétisB; *StiegerO*

Obituary, *Signale für die musikalische Welt*, lviii (1878)

G. Fischer: *Musik in Hannover* (Hanover, 1903)

S. Goslich: *Die deutsche romantische Oper* (Tutzing, 1975)

Mauri (Esteve), José (*b* Valencia, 12 Feb 1855; *d* Havana, 11 July 1937). Cuban composer of Spanish birth. His parents emigrated to Cuba when he was three months old. He began his career as a violinist at the age of ten. His first composition for the theatre was the zarzuela *El sombrero de Felipe II* (1874). Mauri visited France, Belgium, Spain (where he worked as a violinist in the orchestra of the Royal Opera), and various Latin American countries, returning to Cuba in 1901. In 1914 he founded a conservatory, the Instituto Musical de la Habana, and thereafter devoted himself to teaching. His most important work is the three-act opera *La esclava* (libretto by Tomás Juliá). This was first performed in the National Theatre in Havana on 6 June 1921, and with its Cuban dances (habanera, *criolla*, *danzón* and rumba) is considered by some critics to be the best Cuban opera. Mauri also composed orchestral music and sacred choral pieces.

See also ESCLAVA, LA.

*

J. Ardevol: *Introducción a Cuba: la música* (Havana, 1969)

A. Carpentier: *La música en Cuba* (Havana, 1979)

J. A. González: *La composición operística en Cuba* (Havana, 1987)

JORGE ANTONIO GONZÁLEZ

Maurice, Pierre (*b* Allaman, 13 Nov 1868; *d* Geneva, 25 Dec 1936). Swiss composer. He studied composition with Massenet at the Paris Conservatoire (1891–9); he was influenced by his teacher and by Fauré, but above all by Wagner, particularly in his operas. His attraction to German music led him to settle in Munich, and his operas had considerable success in Germany: *Misé Brun* was given in Stuttgart, Aachen and Graz. In 1917 he returned to Geneva, becoming known in his native land largely through his numerous songs, though he also composed in other genres, vocal and instrumental. His work is characterized by formal perfection and a sensitive handling of instruments in music that is essentially contemplative. Although he was a disciple of Wagner, he turned his back on Romantic indulgence in his later works, but his synthesis of German and French traditions remains a valuable achievement.

Misé Brun, 1902–4 (drame lyrique, 4, Maurice), Stuttgart, 15 Nov 1908

Le drapeau blanc [Die weisse Flagge] (oc, P. Maurice); Kassel, 1903

Lanval, 1907 (opéra, 2, Maurice), Weimar, 9 Nov 1913

Andromède, 1912 (opéra, 3, M. Maurice, after Seneca), Basle, 23 April 1924

Arambel, 1912 (mimodrama, I. Ravina), 1923

La nuit tous les chats sont gris [Bei Nacht sind alle Katzen grau] (oc,
after M. Bandello), Munich, 1924
Le mystère de la Nativité, Yverdon, 1933
La vengeance du pharaon, 1934–5 (oc), unperf.

Undated: Kalif Storch; Spes   PIERRE MEYLAN

Mauritius. Island in the Indian Ocean. A prosperous
sugar-producing colony under French rule since 1715, it
became a British colony in 1814 and achieved independence in 1968. In 1790 Joseph Laglaine brought
his lyric troupe – 45 orchestral players and singers –
from France to Port Louis, the capital. Early
performances were in makeshift premises but in 1797
the first permanent theatre was built in the Jardin de la
Compagnie (des Indes) where the Laglaine company
performed operas, operettas, vaudevilles and plays, until
the theatre was destroyed in the cyclone of 1818. It was
replaced by the present Théâtre Municipal, which
opened on 11 June 1822 with an amateur creole group
who performed a play and Dalayrac's opéra comique
Maison à vendre, Laglaine's promised French troupe not
having arrived in time. With its 900 seats (today reduced
to 600), it showed the important place that theatre held
in Port Louis, then a town of 25 000 people, and is the
oldest surviving lyric theatre in the southern hemi-
sphere. The names of 14 composers from Mozart to
Weber, Boieldieu and Auber to Bizet, Gounod and
Meyerbeer, Rossini and Donizetti to Verdi, are inscribed
around the wooden dome. It was let out to impresarios
who ran it as a typical French provincial theatre with
French and local artists – the latter including the tenor
Max Moutia, who after a successful career with the
Paris Opéra-Comique ran the Mauritian company in
1938–9 and 1945–50. In 1933 the Théâtre du Plaza
(1300 seats) was built in the town of Rosehill as part of
the town hall complex by the architect Pierre de
Coulhac Mazerieux, with technical help from Louis
Tharaud, a French singer established in Mauritius. From
1986 the Théâtre Municipal was closed because of
flooding during cyclones, but operas, one or two each
year, are still given at the Théâtre du Plaza by Mauritian
singers with young European and American artists.

*

P. Renaud and G. Raynal: Histoire et légendes d'un théâtre (Port
Louis, 1972)
C. Pitt: 'L'opéra de Port Louis', Opéra international (Feb 1991),
11–13   CHARLES PITT

Mauro. Italian family of stage designers. They had a
crucial influence on the stage production of Italian opera
in the 17th and 18th centuries. The first members to
achieve significance as stage designers and designers of
peòte (ceremonial barges for Venetian theatrical
regattas) were the engineers and architects Gaspare (fl
1657–c1719) and Pietro (fl 1669–c1697) and the painter Domenico (i) (fl 1669–1707), all supposed to have
been sons of Francesco Mauro, a carpenter active in
Munich in 1662. They are known to have worked at the
Venice opera houses of S Apollinare (Gaspare, 1657),
S Cassiano (Gaspare, 1658; Domenico, 1707),
SS Giovanni e Paolo (Gaspare, 1659–c1674; Pietro,
1669; Domenico, 1694–6), S Moisè (Domenico, 1673),
S Salvatore (Gaspare and Domenico, 1675) and S
Giovanni Grisostomo (Gaspare, 1679–c1719;
Domenico, 1697), and at theatres throughout Italy and
in Munich. Developing the ideas of Torelli and
Giovanni Burnacini, the Mauros, often working in part-
nership, became leading exponents with Francesco
Santurini (i) and Mazzarini of a style of stage design that

attempted to realize visually the middle-class aspects of
Venetian opera in the later 17th century: the powerful
'affects' of the emotions, the renunciation of mythology
and allegory in favour of history and everyday life, and
such elements of parody, comedy and realism as are
found in the works of Cavalli, Cesti, Antonio Sartorio,
Legrenzi, P. A. Ziani and others. Gaspare and Pietro did
much to adapt traditional apparatus to the new requirements. They were involved in new Venetian techniques
of illusion including split backcloths, quasi-enclosed
rooms, naturalistically outlined properties and other
devices aiming at a naturally structured stage layout.
Their work was enhanced by Domenico's theatre painting. In the sketches ascribed to him for Legrenzi's La
divisione del mondo (1675, Venice; I-PAc) and the engravings of his stage designs for Steffani's Servio Tullio
(1686, Munich), Sabadini's Il favore degli dei (1690,
Parma; see illustration) and Pignatti's Sigismondo primo
al diadema (1696, Venice), there are indications of a
new approach, notably the emphasis on verticals in the
often multi-storey stage buildings and the inclusion of
the higher parts of the stage in the setting. Two
vanishing-points, one above the other, and experiments
with angled perspective show alternatives to the traditional central perspective all'infinito. They achieved a
realistic, pictorially conceived stage design only in landscapes, in which contemporary painting and scenes from
everyday life served as models.

Domenico's sons Antonio (i) (fl 1692–c1733),
Gerolamo (i) (fl 1692–1719), Romualdo (fl 1699–1756)
and Alessandro (i) (fl c1709–48), and Gaspare's sons
Giuseppe (fl 1699–1722) and Antonio (ii) (fl
c1709–1738), continued their fathers' work for the
Venetian opera houses. Their work was inspired by the
themes and structure of opera seria: spectacular mechanical devices were abandoned in favour of illusion
techniques derived from painting, sometimes preserving
the central perspective and sometimes adapting new
techniques of illusionist wall-painting (angular perspective, diagonal view, worm's-eye view etc.). The most
important member of this generation was Alessandro
(i), who worked as a stage designer and architect in
Venice, Dresden, Rome, Turin and probably Paris with
such composers as Lotti, Leo, Porpora and above all
Hasse. By integrating the techniques of perspective
wall-painting into picturesque designs intended to
suggest mood and setting, he introduced formal elements of bourgeois realism into opera seria.

In the later 18th century the family tradition passed to
Alessandro's sons Domenico (ii) (fl 1733–80) and
Gerolamo (ii) (b ?Venice, 1725; d Venice, 4 March
1766) and Romualdo's son Gerolamo (iii) (fl 1750–88).
Although they carried out a prodigious amount of work
at all the Venetian opera houses, its quality was no longer uncontested (see Croce 1891). It seems to have been
beyond them to keep up with the multiplicity of requirements for the later forms of opera seria, as well as for
opera buffa and related forms by composers like
Galuppi, Gassmann, Bertoni, Piccinni, Anfossi etc.
Antonio (ii) (fl 1774–1807), son of Domenico (ii), was
the last member of the family to become a stage designer
of any importance. He was responsible for more than a
hundred productions for the opera houses of Venice and
other north Italian theatres.

Two other Venetian artists of unknown origin bore the
name of Mauro: Alessandro (ii) (fl 1782) was a painter of
decorations at official banquets, and Gaetano (fl
1806–20) a stage designer in Venice, Padua and Milan.

Stage design by Domenico Mauro for Sabadini's 'Il favore degli dei' performed at the Gran Teatro dei Farnese in Parma, 1690: engraving

For further illustration *see* DRESDEN, fig.2; MUNICH, figs.1 and 2; and TURIN, fig.1.

CroceN; ES (E. Povoledo)

A. Neisser: *Servio Tullio: eine Oper aus dem Jahre 1685 von Agostino Steffani* (diss., U. of Munich, 1900), 140ff

L. Livan: *Notizie d'arte tratte dai notatori o dagli annali del N. H. Pietro Gradenigo* (Venice, 1942)

E. Povoledo: 'La scenografia architettonica del settecento a Venezia', *Arte veneta*, v (1951), 126–30

G. Löwenfelder: *Die Bühnendekoration am Münchner Hoftheater von den Anfängen der Oper bis zur Gründung des National-theaters 1651–1778* (diss., U. of Munich, 1955), 54ff, 136

C. Molinari: 'Disegni a Parma per un spettacolo veneziano', *Critica d'arte*, new ser., xii/70 (1965), 47–64

A. Baudi di Vesme: 'Mauri', *Schede Vesme: l'arte in Piemonte dal XVI al XVIII secolo*, ii (Turin, 1966), 664

P. Bjurström, ed.: 'Unveröffentlichtes von Nicodemus Tessin d.J: Reisenotizen über Barocktheater in Venedig und Piazzola', *Kleine Schriften der Gesellschaft für Theatergeschichte*, xxi (1966), 14–41

C. Molinari: *Le nozze degli dei: un saggio sul grande spettacolo italiano nel seicento* (Rome, 1968), 145ff, 204ff

L. Zorzi, M. T. Muraro, G. Prato and E. Zorzi: *I teatri pubblici di Venezia (secoli XVII–XVIII)* (Venice, 1971)

F. Mancini, M. T. Muraro, E. Povoledo: *Illusione e pratica teatrale: proposte per una lettura dello spazio scenico dagli intermedi fiorentini all'opera comica veneziana* (Vicenza, 1975)

C. B. Schmidt: 'An Episode in the History of Venetian Opera: the Tito Commission (1665–1666)', *JAMS*, xxxi (1978), 442–66

H. Leclerc: *Venise et l'avénement de l'opéra public à l'âge baroque* (Paris, 1987)
MANFRED BOETZKES

Mauro, Ermanno (*b* nr Trieste, 29 Jan 1939). Canadian tenor of Italian birth. He emigrated to Canada at the age of 19 and made his operatic début at Edmonton in 1962 as Tamino and Manrico, then won a scholarship to the Toronto Royal Conservatory, singing with the Canadian Opera Company and regional companies from 1965. He joined the Covent Garden Opera in 1967, making his début in a small role in *Manon Lescaut* the next year and later graduating to such major roles as Gabriele Adorno, Alfredo, Cavaradossi, Edgardo (*Lucia*) and Rodolfo. He returned often to Canada, and made his American début in 1974 as Cavaradossi at San Diego and his New York début with the City Opera in 1975 as Calaf. He sang his first Otello at Dallas (1985), repeating the role in San Francisco and Toronto. At the Metropolitan he has sung Maurizio (*Adriana Lecouvreur*, 1987), Calaf, Turiddu, Canio, Manrico and Gounod's Faust (1990). Other roles have included Radames, Chénier, Luigi (*Il tabarro*), and Des Grieux (*Manon Lescaut*) which he sang in Buenos Aires in 1991. He is a forceful singer, stronger in vocal resource than in variety of colour.
NOËL GOODWIN

Mauro, (Bartolomeo) Ortensio (*b* Verona, 1632–3; *d* Hanover, 14 Sept 1725). Italian librettist. He was secretary and councillor to the dukes of Hanover from at least 1663, a priest and *abbate* from 1675 and a central figure in the Catholic community at Hanover. He was particularly highly regarded by Duke Ernst August (1679–98) and Duchess Sophie and their circle (including Leibniz), and given diplomatic responsibility. He wrote the librettos of probably all but one of the operas performed at Hanover from 1689 to 1697, the heyday of the form at the court. Six three-act operas, with music by Steffani, were translated into German by Gottlieb Fiedler and given at Hamburg from 1695 to 1699, at Wolfenbüttel, Stuttgart and elsewhere, and thus became widely known. Mauro also furnished two librettos for performance in Berlin under the Electress Sophie Charlotte, a former Hanoverian princess, and probably wrote that of Steffani's *Enea o Amor vien dal destino* (1709, Düsseldorf) for a performance at Hanover in the 1690s that never took place. Mauro wrote poetry in Latin, Italian and French and provided texts for other musical entertainments at court. Some of his Latin verse was published posthumously in editions by J. T. Roenick (1749 and 1751) and J. A. Weissenbach (1782).

Alceste (drama per musica), M. Trento, 1679; *Henrico Leone* (dramma), A. Steffani, 1689; *La lotta d'Hercole con Acheloo* (divertimento drammatico), Steffani, 1689; *La superbia d'Alessandro* (drama), Steffani, 1690; *Orlando generoso* (drama), Steffani, 1691; *Le rivali concordi* (drama), Steffani, 1692; *La libertà contenta* (drama), Steffani, 1693; *Il Turno* (drama), Steffani, 1709, as Enea o Amor vien dal destino; *I trionfi del fato* (drama), Steffani, 1695; *Baccanali* (?divertimento), Steffani, 1695; *La costanza nelle selve* (favola pastorale), Mancia, 1697; *Atys, o L'inganno vinto dalla costanza* (pastorale), Ariosti, 1700; *Le fantôme amoureux* (with Count F. Palmieri), Ariosti, 1702

Doubtful: *Anfione*, 1698

J. Hawkins: *Memoirs of the Life of Agostino Steffani* (London, c1750); repr. in *Gentleman's Magazine*, xxxi (1761), 489–92

J. C. F. Hoefer, ed.: *Nouvelle biographie générale*, xxxiv (Paris, 1852–66), 427

F. W. Woker: 'Der Tondichter Agostino Steffani', *Der Katholik*, lxvii (1887), 312–29

G. Fischer: *Musik in Hannover* (Hanover, 1903)

G. Croll: 'Zur Chronologie der "Düsseldorfer" Opern Agostino Steffanis', *Festschrift Karl Gustav Fellerer zum sechzigsten Geburtstag* (Regensburg, 1962), 82–7

P. Keppler: 'Agostino Steffani's Hannover Operas and a Rediscovered Catalogue', *Studies in Music History: Essays for Oliver Strunk* (Princeton, 1968), 341–54

R. E. Wallbrecht: *Das Theater des Barockzeitalters an den welfischen Höfen Hannover und Celle* (Hildesheim, 1974)

C. Sartori: *I libretti italiani a stampa dalle origini al 1800*, i (Cuneo, 1990)

COLIN TIMMS

Mauro, Tommaso de (*fl* Naples, 1701–9). Italian composer. He is historically important in early *opera buffa*. Prota-Giurleo called him a dilettante rather than a professional musician. When Carlo II died in Naples in December 1700 and the usual carnival festivities were cancelled and the theatres closed, a hastily prepared comic opera, *La donna sempre s'appiglia al peggio* (text by C. de Petris), was produced with puppets in the Largo del Castello – the first such work in Naples in the 18th century. Mauro wrote the music; the libretto says that he was already known to the audience, and was 'a young man, and the elder practitioners of his profession vie with each other to imitate, if not to equal him'.

This pioneer work was not in fact imitated, although Mauro's own pioneering continued; when the Teatro dei Fiorentini converted from spoken to musical theatre in October 1706 he was chosen to set the first opera: another comedy, *Ergasto*, again with text by Petris, and probably performed in part by comedians. In autumn 1709 at the Fiorentini the first publicly performed Neapolitan dialect comic opera – *Patrò Calienno della costa*, text by 'Agasippo Mercotellis' (possibly Nicolò Corvo), music by Antonio Orefice – was followed by a similar work, *Lo spellecchia*, with Mauro and Petris again collaborating. Dramatically this opera is superior to *Patrò Calienno*, showing a firmer grasp of the possibilities inherent in the *commedeja pe' mmuseca* form, with a better balance and a better rhythm established between recitatives and musical numbers. Although no scores survive, it can be inferred that the numbers were short (the opera contained at least 62); arias were often strophic and, as far as the libretto indicates, never da capo; ensemble numbers were frequent and concluded each act. Six of Mauro's pieces are in manuscript cantata-aria miscellanies in the British Library, London.

CroceN

M. Scherillo: *L'opera buffa napoletana durante il settecento: storia letteraria* (Naples, 1883, 2/1916), 93–5

U. Prota-Giurleo: *Nicola Logroscino: 'il dio dell'opera buffa'* (Naples, 1927), 16

V. Viviani: *Storia del teatro napoletano* (Naples, 1969), 264–6

JAMES L. JACKMAN

Mavra. *Opéra bouffe* in one act by IGOR STRAVINSKY to a libretto by BORIS YEVGEN'YEVICH KOCHNO after ALEXANDER SERGEYEVICH PUSHKIN's narrative poem *Domik v Kolomne* ('The Little House at Kolomna', 1830); Paris, Opéra, 3 June 1922 (previously given in a concert version, Paris, Hôtel Continental, 27 May 1922).

Parasha	soprano
Her Mother	contralto
A Neighbour	mezzo-soprano
Vasily *a hussar*	tenor

Setting Parasha's house in Kolomna, a town near Moscow

Although first performed by Dyagilev, Stravinsky's little musical skit seems to have been originally intended for Le Théâtre de la Chauve-Souris à Moscou (known in English as 'The Bat Theatre of Moscow'), Nikita Baliyev's international cabaret, with one of whose dancers (Zhenya Nikitina) the composer was having a brief affair. He actually modelled his work on a number of existing Chauve-Souris routines, particularly *Graf Nulin* ('Count Nulin', 1915), a one-act comic sketch after another humorous verse narrative by Pushkin, with music by Alexander Arkhangel'sky, Baliyev's staff composer. The text, by Dyagilev's teenage secretary Boris Kochno (who also had Chauve-Souris connections through the painter Sergey Sudeykin and his wife Vera, who later married Stravinsky), was an elegant adaptation of Pushkin's text to the requirements of a cabaret medley: seven numbers, running a gamut of stereotyped genres ('chanson populaire russe', 'duetto sentimentale', 'mélopée tzigane' etc.), with the action taking place in between as a series of 'set-ups'.

The plot as such can be summarized in a sentence: Parasha smuggles her lover, the hussar Vasily, into her house in the guise of a new cook named Mavra; her mother discovers the ruse when she returns home unexpectedly and finds the 'girl' shaving. In the synopsis below, the musical numbers are designated by numerals, the set-ups indented.

1. 'Chanson russe' (Parasha). The text, 'Drug moy miliy' ('Sweetheart mine'), is that of an imitation folksong that had been transcribed by Pushkin and first published in 1910. Unquestionably the hit tune from *Mavra*, this number was arranged by Stravinsky for voice and orchestra (1923), and also (in collaboration with Samuel Dushkin and Dmitry Markevich respectively) as instrumental solos for violin and cello.

2. Hussar's gypsy song, 'Kolokol'chiki zvenyat' ('Bells are jangling'), adapted from an untitled Pushkin lyric of 1833, composed in polonaise style. The sequence of these two numbers – melancholy (slow) giving way to exuberance (fast) – follows the stereotyped performance practice of professionalized folk singing.

Dialogue: Parasha and the Hussar arrange a tryst.

Dialogue: her mother sends Parasha out to find a new cook to replace the deceased Fyokla (text partly Pushkin's).

3. Mother's aria, 'Net, ne zabït' vo veki mne pokoynitsu' ('No, I'll never forget the departed'). An italianate stylization of the Russian 'drawn-out song'

'Mavra' (Stravinsky): set design by Léopold Survage for the original production by the Ballets Russes at the Opéra in Paris, 3 June 1922

genre, composed in imitation of Antonida's cavatina in Glinka's *A Life for the Tsar*.

Dialogue: a neighbour drops in.

4. Gossip-duet, 'Takaya, v koi veki raz, pogoda nam dayotsya' ('We've never had such perfect weather'). A polka composed in imitation of Dargomïzhsky's *Rusalka*.

Dialogue: Parasha returns with 'Mavra' (text partly Pushkin's).

5. Quartet (all *dramatis personae*, text partly Pushkin's). Parody of Tchaikovsky à la ragtime (this number was later arranged by Jack Hylton, with Stravinsky's help, and recorded with the former's jazz band in 1931).

Dialogue: Neighbour takes her leave, Mother exits after her.

6. Love duet, culminating in a slow salon waltz of a type that was *de rigueur* in early 19th-century opera, 'Pokhodit vsyo na novïy son' ('All becomes a blissful dream').

Dialogue: Mother and daughter go out.

7. Aria for 'Mavra', with trumpet obbligato, 'Ya zhdu pokorno' ('I wait obediently'). Parody of a 'cruel' cabaret romance.

Dialogue: shaving scene and denouement (a famously calculated anticlimax).

*   *   *

Despite its trivial subject matter and its featherweight music, *Mavra* was a milestone in Stravinsky's creative development. Through it he europeanized his 'Russian' style and prepared the way for his long neo-classical period. As the critic Boris de Schloezer noted shrewdly in 1929, it was the first of Stravinsky's notorious 'type-works' of the 1920s, to be followed immediately by the Octet for wind instruments (with which, minus the voices, its music betrays an enormous affinity) and later by the Concerto for piano and wind instruments, the Sonata for piano and so on. With its intriguingly off-centred tonal cadences, achieved by the use of dual ostinatos that go in and out of phase, the opening 'chanson russe' is particularly a neo-classical paradigm, as many young composers (including Poulenc, who wrote a very perceptive review) recognized at the time of the stage première, which was conducted by Grzegorz Fitelberg with Oda Slobodskaya playing Parasha.

With the larger public *Mavra* was a colossal flop, Stravinsky's first. In part this was due to the incongruity between its cabaret scale and the vast spaces of its original setting, the Palais Garnier. But underlying that was a fundamental discrepancy between the expectations of the Ballets Russes audience, for whom Stravinsky was the pre-eminent purveyor of modernistic Slav exotica in the tradition of The Five, and a musical evocation of a European Russia in which the French high-art public had no interest. The Dyagilev-sponsored concert in which the work was previewed, with piano accompaniment played by the composer, was pointedly entitled 'La musique russe en dehors des "Cinq"'.

Mavra has remained something of a Stravinskian stepchild. The full score was not published until 1969, and then only after the octogenarian composer had begged his publisher:

Of course the music is not and will never be a success and there may be no demand or justification for printing it; and if I say that worse music than *Mavra* is performed you may say that better music is also not performed. Still, I would like to see the work in print.

RICHARD TARUSKIN

Maw, (John) Nicholas (*b* Grantham, 5 Nov 1935). English composer. He studied composition with Lennox Berkeley and harmony and counterpoint with Paul Steinitz at the RAM (1955–8), during which time his first acknowledged work, *Eight Chinese Lyrics*, was performed at an SPNM concert. A French Government scholarship took him to Paris in 1958 where he studied with Nadia Boulanger and Max Deutsch. His *Scenes and Arias* (1962) for three women's voices and large orchestra established Maw as a gifted craftsman in an idiom of multiple tonality and rich harmonic resonance, with an instinct for word-setting and melodic writing in the tradition of Britten and Tippett. Two operas followed during this increasingly productive decade, for part of which he had a fellowship at Trinity College, Cambridge (1966–70). The comic opera *One Man Show* (2, A. Jacobs), based on Saki's story 'The Background', was commissioned by the London County Council for the opening of the Jeannetta Cochrane Theatre on 12 November 1964. *The Rising of the Moon* (3, B. Cross) was commissioned for the Glyndebourne Festival, opened there on 19 July 1970 and was repeated in 1971. Both operas were published (London, 1970), *One Man Show* in a revised version. Although the first opera was staged at Pittsburgh (1975) and the second at Graz and Bremen (both in 1978), Maw has since preferred to write for concert performance. His later works

Set design by Ita Maximowna for a production of Donizetti's 'Viva la mamma', at La Fenice, Venice, 1970

include much rewarding vocal music and *The World in the Evening* (1988), commissioned for the Royal Opera House Orchestra.

See also ONE MAN SHOW and RISING OF THE MOON, THE.

A. Jacobs: 'Notes Before an Opera', *MT*, cv (1964), 818–19

A. Payne: 'Nicholas Maw's "One Man Show"', *Tempo*, new ser., no.71 (1964–5), 2–14

B. Northcott: 'Nicholas Maw', *Music and Musicians*, xviii/9 (1970), 34–8

S. Walsh: 'Nicholas Maw's New Opera', *Tempo*, new ser., no.92 (1970), 2–15

B. Cross: 'The Rising of the Moon: Game-Pie and Panache', *Glyndebourne Festival 1970*, 62–3 [programme book]

N. Maw: 'The Rising of the Moon: Designed for Pleasure', ibid, 64–5

A. Whittall: 'Nicholas Maw', *British Music Now*, ed. L. Foreman (London, 1975), 97–107   NOËL GOODWIN

Maxakova, Mariya Petrovna. *See* MAKSAKOVA, MARIYA PETROVNA.

Maximilian III Joseph, Elector of Bavaria (*b* Munich, 28 March 1727; *d* Munich, 30 Dec 1777). German patron of music. He played the violin, the cello and the gamba, and studied composition with Andrea Bernasconi. He was a patron of chamber music and opera at the Munich court, and it was during his reign (begun in 1745) that a new opera house, the Residenztheater, was built by François Cuvilliés (1751–3). Gluck and Hasse wrote works celebrating his marriage by proxy at Dresden in 1747. In addition to the works by his court Kapellmeisters Porta, Ferrandini and Bernasconi, he commissioned operas by Sales, Traetta, Sacchini and Mysliveček; Mozart's *La finta giardiniera* received its première at the Salvatortheater on 13 January 1775.

BurneyGN

R. Münster, H. Schmid and F. Göthel, eds.: *Musik in Bayern*, i–ii (Tutzing, 1972), 196, 351–2   HANS SCHMID

Maximowna, Ita [Schnakenburg, Ita Maximovna] (*b* St Petersburg, 18/31 Oct 1914; *d* Berlin, 8 April 1988). Russian painter and stage designer. She studied in Paris and Berlin and spent most of her life in Germany. Her first designs for opera, Blacher's *Preussisches Märchen* (1952, Berlin), were praised for their atmospheric authenticity and elegance and attracted the attention of Günther Rennert, with whom she subsequently collaborated in more than 50 productions. In these she demonstrated her intelligent eclecticism, designing, with equal skill, in the Romantic tradition, as in *Un ballo in maschera* (1962–3, New York, Metropolitan), or the expressionist idiom, in Dallapiccola's *Il prigionero* (1974, La Scala). Her virtuoso handling of colour and particular sympathy with the 18th century were features of Rennert's Mozart productions at Salzburg – outstanding was *Così fan tutte* (1972), with costumes in bleached Neapolitan ice-cream colours against dominant black – and her vein of playful fantasy was delightfully displayed in Donizetti's *Viva la mamma* (*Le convenienze teatrali*; 1970, La Fenice), with its skewed, picture-book perspective (see illustration). Maximowna was responsible for over two hundred productions, which included many plays and other works for the musical theatre. In 1987 she retired, to concentrate on painting.

ES (I. A. Chiusano)

Ita Maximowna: Bühnenbilderbuch (Tübingen, 1982)

MARINA HENDERSON

Maxwell, Donald (*b* Perth, 12 Dec 1948). Scottish baritone. He studied in Edinburgh, making his début in 1977 as Morton in Musgrave's *Mary, Queen of Scots* with Scottish Opera, with which he also sang Rossini's Figaro, Zurga, Enrico Ashton, Ipparco (*Egisto*), the Poacher (*The Cunning Little Vixen*) and Šiškov (*From the House of the Dead*). With the WNO he has sung Ned Keene, Marcello, Renato, Rigoletto, Iago, Don Carlo (*Ernani*) and Falstaff (which he also sang at La Scala); with the ENO, Yeletsky, Leander (*The Love for Three Oranges*), Baron Prus (*The Makropulos Affair*) and Wozzeck (1990); and with Opera North, Riccardo (*I puritani*), Germont, Scarpia, Escamillo and the Dutchman. He appeared as Belfiore in *Un giorno di* *regno* at Wexford (1981) and as Maître Jean in Gounod's *La colombe* at Buxton (1983). He made his Covent Garden début as the English Archer in *The King Goes Forth to France* in 1987, returning as Kothner, Alidoro and Gunther (1991). A role such as Baron Prus perfectly suits his strong voice and powerful personality.

ELIZABETH FORBES

Mayboroda, Heorhy Ilarionovych (*b* Pelekhovshchyna, Poltava province, 18 Nov/1 Dec 1913). Ukrainian composer. He studied at the Kiev Conservatory with Levko Revuts'ky, graduating in 1941, and was its head from 1950 to 1958. He was also head of the Composers' Union of Ukraine in 1967–8. He became an Outstanding Artist of the Ukrainian SSR in 1957, People's Artist of the USSR in 1960 and in 1963 he received the coveted Shevchenko Prize. A profoundly conservative composer, his harmonic and melodic language is deeply rooted in the 19th century with just a hint of harmonic expansiveness that suggests certain aspects of Delius. Influenced by Ukrainian folklore and the Russian romantic style, he has written pieces that have immediate appeal. His most important compositions have been his operas, each one a carefully written work that projects an individual, if narrow, personality. Though *Yaroslav mudryy* ('Yaroslav the Wise', 1975) is considered Mayboroda's most ambitious opera, *Taras Shevchenko* (1964) is his most successful and exhibits his strengths: a wonderful melodic gift, succinct and clear musical structures, a good, if conventional, understanding of the orchestra and a firm knowledge of stage dramaturgy.

Milana, 1955 (A. F. Turchynska), Kiev, 1957, vs (Moscow, 1960)
Arsenal (A. Levada and A. Malyschko), Kiev, 1960, vs (Kiev, 1960)
Taras Shevchenko (Mayboroda), Kiev, 1964, vs (Kiev, 1968)
Yaroslav mudryy [Yaroslav the Wise], 1973 (Mayboroda), Kiev, 1975

*

M. Hordiychuk: *Heorhy Ilarionovych Mayboroda: narodnyy artyst URSR* (Kiev, 1963)
O. Zin'kevych: *Heorhy Mayboroda* (Kiev, 1973)   VIRKO BALEY

Mayer, Josepha. *See* HOFER, JOSEPHA.

Mayer, William (Robert) (*b* New York, 18 Nov 1925). American composer. He studied at Yale, principally with Richard Donovan and Herbert Baumgartner. In 1949 he spent the summer studying composition with Sessions and from 1949 to 1952 worked with Felix Salzer at Mannes College. He has won various awards, including a Guggenheim Fellowship (1966), a Ford Foundation recording grant (1969) and an NEA composition fellowship (1977); he has also received commissions, including one from the Minnesota Opera Company for *A Death in the Family* (1982). Based on James Agee's novel, and Tad Mosel's dramatization of it as *All the Way Home*, this was cited as the outstanding new American opera or musical theatre work of 1983 by the National Institute for Musical Theater. Musically, its style is conservative but effective and dramatically apt, with some weaving in of American folk idioms. Mayer has also composed three other operas, a ballet, orchestral pieces, chamber music and vocal works.

Hello, World! (children's op, 1, S. Otto), New York, Little Orchestra Society, 10 Nov 1956
One Christmas Long Ago (1, Mayer), New York, Little Orchestra Society, 9 Nov 1962

Brief Candle (micro-opera, 3, M. Feist), New York, New School for Social Research, 22 May 1967
A Death in the Family (Mayer, after J. Agee and T. Mosel), Minneapolis, 11 March 1983; rev. version, St Louis, 6 April 1986

*

R. H. Kornick: *Recent American Opera: a Production Guide* (New York, 1991), 183–5   DAVID COPE

May Night [*Mayskaya noch'*]. Opera in three acts by NIKOLAY ANDREYEVICH RIMSKY-KORSAKOV to his own libretto after NIKOLAY VASIL'YEVICH GOGOL's story 'Mayskaya noch', ili Utoplennitsa' ('May Night, or The Drowned Maiden') from his collection *Evenings on a Farm near Dikanka* (i, 1831); St Petersburg, Mariinsky Theatre, 9/21 January 1880.

Village Head	bass
Levko *his son*	tenor
Hanna	mezzo-soprano
Charcoal Burner	baritone or high bass
Village Clerk	bass
Distiller	tenor
Sister-in-law *of the Village Head*	contralto
Pannochka-Rusalka ('Little Lady Water Nymph')	soprano
Brood-hen } *water nymphs*	
Raven } *(coryphées)*	mezzo-sopranos
Stepmother }	

Lads, girls, bailiff's men, water nymphs (spirits of drowned maidens)

Setting A Ukrainian village; the time is unspecified

Gogol's early Ukrainian tales, full of evocative song and dance, and peopled with characters borrowed from the folk puppet theatre and the vaudeville stage, are little operas in search of a composer. *May Night*, in particular, the subject of planned or finished operas by Serov and Lysenko in addition to Rimsky-Korsakov, embodies a theme originating in German folklore but well known to urban Russians in the early 19th century in the form of a celebrated Singspiel, Kauer's *Das Donauweibchen*. As Russified – or rather, 'Little-Russianized' – by Stepan Davïdov under the title *Lesta, ili Dnevprovskaya rusalka* ('Lesta, or The Dnepr Water Nymph'), it played the Russian stage in various versions between 1803 and 1854 and was at its height of popularity in the early 1830s when Gogol wrote his tale. The way *May Night* begins already shows how reminiscences of operas and Singspiels were guiding the author's pen:

A ringing song flowed like a river down the streets of the village. It was the hour when, weary from the cares and labours of the day, the lads and girls gather together in the glow of the clear evening to pour out their gaiety in strains never far removed from melancholy. The brooding evening dreamily embraced the dark blue sky, transforming everything into vagueness and distance. It was already dusk, but the singing did not cease. Levko, a young Cossack, son of the Village Head, slipped away from the singers with a bandura in his hands. He was wearing an astrakhan cap. He walked down the street thrumming on the strings and dancing to it. At last he stopped quietly before the door of a cottage surrounded with low-growing cherry trees. Whose cottage was it? Whose door was it? After a few moments of silence, he began playing and singing:

Solntse nizen'ko,	The sun is low,
vechir blizen'ko,	the evening's nigh,
Viidi do mene,	Come out to me,
moyo serden'ko!	my little heart!

In the space of a paragraph we have a chorus, a dance to the bandura and a solo song. No wonder, as Rimsky-Korsakov tells us in his memoirs, his wife kept insisting that he compose an opera on this subject, until in 1877 he gave in. Rimsky allowed Gogol for the most part to dictate the succession of musical numbers, and wherever possible he drew on authentic folk materials, particularly the collection of Ukrainian folksongs published in 1872 by his St Petersburg Conservatory colleague Alexander Rubets, from which he chose eight songs. With its feast of folksong, *May Night* was not only a faithful counterpart to its literary prototype. It was also a fulfilment of Gogol's own prophecy – made in 1836, the year of *A Life for the Tsar* – that Glinka's example would lead to opera made out of 'our national life'.

The first performance was conducted by Eduard Nápravník, with Fyodor Stravinsky as the Village Head and Ivan Mel'nikov as the Charcoal Burner.

ACT 1 *A village street* The curtain rises on a group of lads and lasses enacting a ritual game song about planting ('A mï proso seyali': 'Ah, the millet did we sow', incorporating tunes from three collections, those of Rubets, Balakirev and Rimsky himself). Levko enters, singing to his bandura the song quoted above (set to a Rubets tune). Hanna comes to the door; they banter, Levko announcing his determination to marry her over his father's objections; they confess their love. At Hanna's request, Levko tells the tale of the old Squire's House (narrative, 'Davno eto bïlo': 'It happened long ago'): a widowed lieutenant had lived there with a beautiful daughter; he took a wife who was a witch; turned out by her stepmother, the little lady had hurled herself into the lake and become a water nymph; with her companions, she dragged the evil stepmother into the lake and drowned her, but the stepmother also became a water nymph, and no one knows which. Levko and Hanna part as the girls' voices are heard off stage singing a Whitsun song (recitative and Trinity

song, based on a Rubets tune). The Charcoal Burner staggers out, dead drunk, trying to dance the hopak and find his house; the girls send him to the Village Head's house instead (hopak, 'Hop! Hop! Hop! Tra-la!'). The Village Head approaches Hanna's house and tries to woo her; he is rebuffed, but his son Levko is infuriated and resolves to make a fool of his old dad (trio and chorus). He gathers some lads together and teaches them a scurrilous song about the Head.

ACT 2.i *The interior of the Village Head's cottage* The Head, his Sister-in-law and a Distiller, who is to set up shop in the old Squire's House, discuss their affairs (in a trio, based on two Rubets tunes). The Charcoal Burner enters, thinking he is home; he curses the Village Head to himself; the Head is about to throw him out when a stone comes through the window; the Head curses the thrower, but is stopped by the Distiller, who tells a story of a curse that backfired on his mother-in-law. Levko and his friends strike up their 'Song about the Head' from the street. The Head rushes out and comes back with Levko, disguised as a devil, with sooted face and sheepskin coat turned inside out, showing the black hide. The light suddenly goes out. Levko's friends rescue him and substitute the Sister-in-law, whom the Head locks up in a store-room. When the Clerk enters (to the strains of a Rubets tune) and informs him that they have captured the black-faced devil, the Head looks inside the store-room and discovers his indignant Sister-in-law, who departs muttering a stream of imprecations. The Head, the Clerk and the Distiller rush out, vowing to settle with the boys.

2.ii *The street, before the village lock-up* After deliberating, the Head, the Clerk and the Distiller decide to burn the lock-up and the devil within. The Clerk decides that if whatever is within agrees to make the sign of the cross then it is not the devil. They open the door and out comes the Sister-in-law again, more furious than ever: she had been seized by the boys and again substituted for Levko. The village bailiffs rush in with the culprit – only it turns out to be the tipsy Charcoal Burner. Beside himself, the Head sends everyone out again in pursuit (finale).

ACT 3 *The banks of the lake, before the old Squire's house* After an orchestral prelude evoking night in the Ukraine, Levko enters, pensive, and sings of Hanna ('Spi, moya krasavitsa, sladko spi': 'Sleep, my beauty, sleep sweetly'). To keep awake he strikes up another song, but is interrupted by Pannochka-Rusalka, soon joined by her water-nymph companions, who sing and dance a *khorovod*. She asks Levko's help in discovering her stepmother, which he succeeds in doing by watching them play the game 'Who shall be Raven?'. The nymphs turn on the culprit and drag her down. In gratitude, Pannochka-Rusalka hands Levko a letter to the Head. Levko, who cannot read it, wonders what it contains. At sunrise the Head, Clerk, Distiller and bailiffs enter in pursuit and are about to lock Levko up when the Clerk reads the letter, which is in the handwriting of the local commissar and which orders the Head to marry his son to Hanna at once (choral Whitsun songs, *Rusal'niye*, based on Rubets tunes). Hanna enters in rapture, and the lads and lasses sing the praises of the bridal pair.

RICHARD TARUSKIN

Mayr, Richard (*b* Salzburg, 18 Nov 1877; *d* Vienna, 1 Dec 1935). Austrian bass. Having first studied medicine in Vienna, he was persuaded by Mahler to adopt the career of a singer. After several years' work at the Vienna Academy, he made his début in 1902 at Bayreuth, as Hagen, and was at once engaged by Mahler for the Vienna Opera. Making his début there as Silva (*Ernani*), he sang at Vienna for more than 30 successive

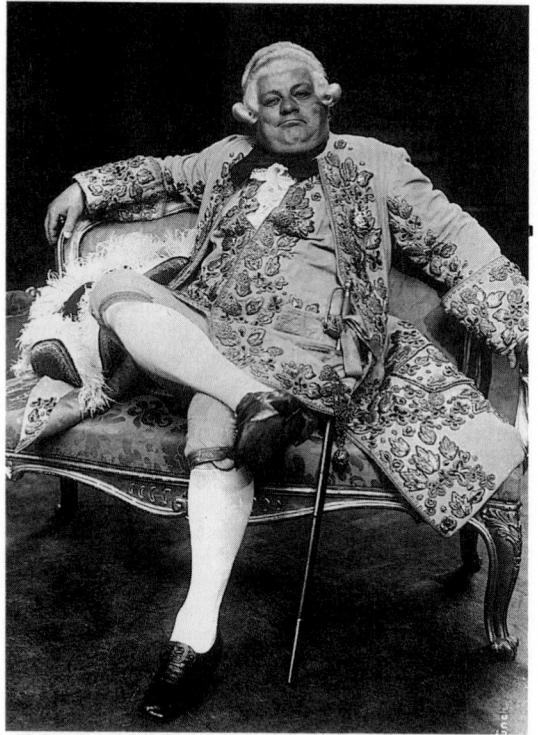

Richard Mayr as Ochs in 'Der Rosenkavalier' by Richard Strauss

years; he displayed amazing versatility in a round of leading parts of various schools, serious and comic, extending from Wotan, Gurnemanz and Sarastro to Figaro, Leporello and Ochs. The Strauss-Hofmannsthal correspondence shows that both men would have preferred Mayr for the original Dresden production of *Der Rosenkavalier*; he played the role a few months later in the Vienna première, and was soon recognized everywhere as the ideal exponent of a part which he sang to perfection and played with inimitable gusto and virtuosity (see illustration). It was as Ochs that he made his first Covent Garden appearance, in 1924, in the famous cast that included Lehmann, Delia Reinhardt and Schumann with Bruno Walter as conductor; he often returned to London in this and other roles. He made his Metropolitan début as Pogner in 1927, soon adding *Der Rosenkavalier* to his New York repertory, and remaining for three seasons with the company. In Vienna he sang Barak in the première of *Die Frau ohne Schatten* in 1919. He was naturally a mainstay of the Salzburg festivals, taking part in every one between 1921 and 1934. The most important of his records is the abridged *Rosenkavalier* of 1933, which gives a capital impression of the ripeness and spontaneity of his style and the richness of his voice.

GV (L. Riemens; S. Smolian)   DESMOND SHAWE-TAYLOR

*

Mayr [Mayer], **(Johann) Simon** [Giovanni Simone] (*b* Mendorf, nr Ingolstadt, Bavaria, 14 June 1763; *d* Bergamo, 2 Dec 1845). German composer, teacher and writer on music. He was a leading figure in the development of *opera seria* in the last decade of the 18th century and the first two decades of the 19th.

1. LIFE. Johann Simon, the second child of Josef Mayr, a schoolteacher and organist, and Maria Anna Prantmayer, a brewer's daughter from Augsburg, received his early musical education from his father. By the age of seven and a half he was an able sight-singer and by nine an accomplished pianist and budding composer of songs. Around this time his father refused the offer of a now unknown patron to provide him with further training in Vienna and instead sent him to the Jesuit seminary at nearby Ingolstadt, where he received a traditional education funded by a scholarship for his singing. In 1781 he began to study law and theology at the University of Ingolstadt, where he taught himself various orchestral instruments and supported himself by playing the organ. His first published work, *Lieder bei dem Clavier zu singen*, appeared in Regensburg in 1786.

In 1787, through a connection at the university, Mayr's talent was recognized by the lawyer Thomas von Bassus, who took him first to Poschiavo, a Swiss town close to the Italian border where he owned a printing business, and to nearby Tirano, then to Bergamo in 1789 to study with Carlo Lenzi, *maestro di cappella* of the basilica of S Maria Maggiore. This arrangement proved unsatisfactory for Mayr, and he would have returned to Bavaria except that the canon of the basilica, Count Pesenti, arranged for him to continue his studies in Venice with Ferdinando Bertoni, *maestro di cappella* of St Mark's, a composer of opera and sacred music. Mayr's stay in Venice provided an ideal opportunity to hear a broad range of Italian sacred, theatrical and instrumental music and enabled him to have his first oratorio and several cantatas performed between 1791 and 1794.

During this period Mayr was encouraged by Niccolò Piccinni and Peter Winter to begin composing theatrical works. His first opera, *Saffo* (1794), was written for La Fenice, where he had probably been a viola player for several years. His next opera, *La Lodoiska*, also performed at La Fenice (1796), was sufficiently successful to earn him a reputation immediately as one of the best Italian composers, a position reinforced by the subsequent popularity of his first *opera buffa*, *Un pazzo ne fa cento* (1796, Venice, S Samuele), performed 17 times in Vienna during the next year. Mayr's fame enabled him to marry one of his pupils, Angiola Venturali, daughter of a wealthy Venetian merchant, whose death in childbirth in 1797 was followed a month later by the death of their baby. In 1804 Mayr married Angiola's sister Lucrezia, who bore him one child, Nina, in 1805.

Mayr's early successes in Venice established a fruitful relationship with that city which was to last throughout his career. In fact, his first 17 operas were originally written for theatres in Venice, as were 14 others in later years. Throughout his career Mayr's activities continued to centre on north Italian theatres. The first of his operas to be given at La Scala was a revised version of *La Lodoiska*, in 1799, and he composed his first new opera for that city, *L'equivoco*, in 1800. In all he wrote 13 operas for Milanese theatres, as well as single operas for Trieste, Piacenza, Bologna, Brescia and Turin. His influence spread more slowly and less decisively to southern Italy. His first opera for Florence, *I due viaggiatori*, was produced at the Teatro Risoluti in 1804, and led to only one later commission; for Rome he wrote *I cherusci* (1808) and four later works, and for Naples *Medea in Corinto* (1813), also followed by four later operas.

Mayr was an active force in the community of Bergamo, helping to found several important civic and cultural institutions. In 1805 he spearheaded the establishment of a free school of music (the Lezioni Caritatevoli di Musica, which replaced the long-standing Collegio Mariano, dissolved in 1802 by Napoleonic law), primarily to provide choirboys and string players for the basilica. Mayr became the director and professor of music theory and composition and wrote and translated numerous exercises and treatises for the school. Donizetti enrolled in the first class of students in 1806 and remained for eight years, returning from his studies with Padre Mattei in Bologna to study with Mayr again from 1819 to 1821. Other successful pupils of the school included Marco Bonesi, Antonio Dolci, and Giovanni Battista Rubini. In 1809 Mayr founded the Pio Istituto Musicale, a charitable organization for the relief of impoverished music teachers and their widows and orphans. In 1822 he helped to organize the Unione Filarmonica – an association of professors of music, distinguished amateurs, and advanced students, which sponsored several 'academies' each year at which music of the Viennese masters was often performed. In 1823 he was elected president of the Ateneo di Scienze, Lettere, ed Arti, a position he was to hold for ten years.

Mayr's loyalty to his community and his apparent affection for its tranquil way of life led him to refuse numerous prestigious appointments in larger cities, among them directorships of the imperial theatres and concerts in Paris (1805, a position later accepted by Paer) and of the Italian theatres in St Petersburg, Lisbon and London (all in 1807), the post of Kapellmeister in Dresden (to replace Paer in 1808), that of *maestro di cappella* in Novara (1823) and the directorship of the Liceo Musicale in Bologna (1825). His distaste for the operatic life of the major Italian centres is also evident from his contemplation of retirement twice during his career, first in 1805 when he was victimized by a slanderous intrigue against him at La Scala during the production of *Eraldo ed Emma* (1805), and again after the failure of *I cherusci* at the Teatro Argentina in 1808. Mayr withdrew from the theatre after the production of his last opera, *Demetrio*, in 1824, devoting his time to composing religious music for the basilica, arranging performances of works by the Viennese masters, writing historical essays, contributing to the *Gazzetta musicale di Milano* and serving as a consultant for the Casa Ricordi. The end of his operatic career may have been hastened in part by the onset of cataracts in at least his left eye, beginning in the 1820s, although the resulting partial loss of sight did not entirely prevent him from composing. His operas continued to receive a modest number of performances in Europe and the USA after his retirement, and on a trip to Bavaria in 1838 to visit his sister he was welcomed enthusiastically by the press and the musical community. The year after the death of his second wife in 1844, Mayr died at his home in Bergamo at the age of 82.

2. WORKS. Mayr's operas have long been regarded as one of the most important links between 18th-century *opera seria* and 19th-century *melodramma*, and between the styles of German and French composers and those of such later figures as Donizetti and Verdi. Mayr's colourful instrumentation and rich harmonies are particulary indebted to Mozart, Haydn, Gluck and the French operas of composers such as Spontini. His skilful contrapuntal writing for concertato woodwind and horn and the expressive clarinet and oboe cantilenas in the instrumental introductions of his lyric numbers, as well as the evocative, non-traditional combinations of instruments heard in some of his accompaniments (his use of obbligato harp with solo cello but without second violins, violas, flutes or oboes in the 'Aria con arpa di Elfrido' in Act 2 of *Alfredo il grande* is one example), are extraordinary for turn-of-the-century Italian opera, and they had a clear influence on Rossini and other later composers. Orchestrally dominated action passages, in which a motif or short phrase is repeated over shifting harmonies as a background for vocal declamation, allowing the characters to interact flexibly and putting the dramatic and musical emphasis squarely on the action, are frequent in Mayr's ensembles. His rich, Germanic harmonic vocabulary allowed him to make abrupt shifts of tonal focus in both accompanied recitatives and lyric numbers – sudden modulations to the Neapolitan and flat submediant are particularly common – to emphasize new lines of thought, to underscore turning-points in the action or simply to maintain musical intensity in the codas of his arias. His exacting declamation of the text in dialogues (particularly in recitatives) and manipulation of orchestral and vocal texture to produce sharp dynamic changes often combine to create musico-dramatic effects of remarkable intensity for their time. Mayr avoided exaggeration, however. In fact, in his *Zibaldone* (1837; see Gazzaniga 1977) he disparaged much of the opera written in the 1820s and 30s as degenerate for relying on excessive dramatic effects and lamented the expan-

sion of the orchestra to include such trivial instruments as the triangle.

Mayr also bridged the 18th and 19th centuries through his treatment of form in his serious operas. Although they still consist of discrete numbers, they break with tradition in abandoning the exit convention in many scenes as early as *La Lodoiska* (1796); in including a high proportion of active, multipartite duets and ensembles; and in incorporating many expansive choral numbers, a reflection of Gluck's influence. Mayr's arias display a broad range of forms and may include as many as four movements (see the aria for Elfrido/Alfredo cited above), although one- or two-movement designs are the norm. His single-movement arias are the most traditional, generally adhering to the types of shortened da capo structures that were common at the end of the 18th century. His multi-movement arias, on the other hand, move towards Rossinian designs. In many cases their texts are longer than the conventional Metastasian pairing of quatrains and they often include sections in which the principal soloist interacts with other soloists or a chorus. Moreover, they minimize recapitulations and instead allow the music to unfold in conjunction with the emotional progress of the character's thoughts as an asymmetrical series of new ideas. Some, though by no means all, of Mayr's closing fast movements even include repetitions of their principal themes, like those found in Rossini's cabalettas.

Mayr's duets also provide models for the later Rossinian form in four sections (for example, Telemachus and the Mentor's duet in Act 3 of *Telemaco*, 1797), although many contain fewer independent movements and resemble instead earlier duets by Mozart or Cimarosa. Mayr has been credited with adapting the comic central finale to serious opera, and, while his role in this development has yet to be established definitively, the complex designs of his finales do in many cases show their comic origins by beginning with an extended series of active and reflective sections or even independent movements. Yet these finales also anticipate Rossinian conventions by normally including a slow concertato movement (though it rarely attains the length of Rossini's), an active transition and a stretta-like final tutti.

Mayr's sinfonias, like those of his predecessors and Rossini, have no specific thematic relationship to the body of the opera which they precede, but several (e.g. the Venetian *Lodoiska*, *Ginevra di Scozia*, 1801, and *Tamerlano*, 1813) include melodies which evoke their locales. In most cases they consist of a slow introduction followed by a fast movement in some version of sonata form, normally with the development section or the reprise of the first theme group truncated or eliminated. However, Mayr also experimented with non-traditional designs, for example the theme and variations movement of the sinfonia for *Zamori* (1804), the two dance movements of the sinfonia for the Venetian *Lodoiska* and the rondo-like allegro of the sinfonia for *I misteri eleusini* (1802).

Although Mayr's contribution as a melodist was less distinguished, at their best his melting cantilenas can be moving and his cabalettas exciting. He anticipated an important aspect of Rossini's melodic style by moving towards the later composer's broad spectrum of lyric types, which ranges from his 'open' melodies – freely constructed, additive series of short phrases having an almost improvisatory character – to 'closed' tuneful

themes, although in Mayr's style these extremes are somewhat less pronounced than in Rossini's operas. However, in their less vigorous profiles his melodies still adhere closely to the more refined language of such late 18th-century composers as Piccinni, Cimarosa and (to a lesser extent) Mozart.

Mayr was well regarded by such later Italian composers as Bellini and Giovanni Pacini. Rossini credited him with being 'among the first to cause the *dramma musicale* to progress with dignity' and praised him for 'using the instruments with abandon rather than with diffidence dictated by the rules'. Donizetti, whose high regard for his teacher is evident in many of his letters, composed a cantata for the public celebration of Mayr's 78th birthday. Verdi attended his funeral. Although Mayr has not shared in the continued fame of his best-known successors, his musico-dramatic creativity and his importance for the development of Italian opera at the turn of the century are evident throughout his works. Far beyond his role in the musical education of Donizetti, Mayr played a crucial part in the transition from 18th-century to 19th-century opera. Moreover, his interest in and cultivation of the music of northern composers paralleled the aim of progressive aestheticians to invigorate Italian theatre through the study and assimilation of foreign culture. Thus he was one of the first musicians to adapt the ideals of nascent Italian Romanticism to operatic practice.

See also AMOR CONIUGALE, L'; GINEVRA DI SCOZIA; LODOISKA (ii); MEDEA IN CORINTO; and ROSA BIANCA E LA ROSA ROSSA, LA.

NC – *Naples, Teatro di S Carlo*   VB – *Venice, Teatro S Benedetto*
VF – *Venice, Teatro La Fenice*   VM – *Venice, Teatro S Moisè*

dm – *dramma per musica*   f – *farsa*
mels – *melodramma serio*

Saffo, o sia I riti d'Apollo Leucadio (dm, 2, A. Sografi), VF, 17 Feb 1794, *I-BGc* *, *US-Bp*, *Wc*
La Lodoiska (dm, 3, F. Gonella), VF, 26 Jan 1796; rev. version (2), Milan, Scala, 26 Dec 1799; *I-Bc*, *BGc** (1796 perf.), *Fc*, *Gl*, *Mc* (1799 version), *Nc*, *Pi*, *PAc* (1799 version), *US-Bp*
Un pazzo ne fa cento [I rivali delusi; La contessa immaginaria] (dg, 2, G. Foppa, after D. Somigli: *Il conte villano*), Venice, S Samuele, 8 Oct 1796, *I-BGc**, *Fc*, *OS*
Telemaco nell'isola di Calipso (dm, 3, Sografi), VF, 16 Jan 1797, *BGc**, *US-Bp*
Il segreto (farsa giocosa, 1, Foppa), VM, 24 Sept 1797, *GB-Lbl*, *I-BGc**, *Fc*, *Nc*, *PAc*, *US-Bp*
L'intrigo della lettera [il pittore astratto] (farsa giocosa, 1, Foppa), VM, 22 Oct 1797, *I-BGc**, *Fc*, *Nc*
Avviso ai maritati (dg, 2, Gonella), Venice, S Samuele, 15 Jan 1798, *BGc**
Lauso e Lidia (dm, 2, Foppa), VF, 14 Feb 1798, *BGc*
Adriano in Siria (dm, 3, P. Metastasio), VB, 23 April 1798
Che originali [Il trionfo della musica; Il fanatico per la musica; La musicomania] (f, 1, G. Rossi), VB, 18 Oct 1798, *Fc*, *Gl*, *Mc*, *Nc*, *Pi*, *US-Bp*
Amor ingegnoso (f, 1, C. Mazzolà), VB, 27 Dec 1798, *I-BGc**
L'ubbidienza per astuzia (f, 1, Mazzolà), VB, 27 Dec 1798, *BGc**
Adelaide di Guesclino (dm, 2, Rossi, after Voltaire), VF, 1 May 1799, *BGc**, *Fc*, *PAc*, *US-Bp*, *Wc*
Labino e Carlotta (f, 1, Rossi), VB, 9 Oct 1799, *I-BGc*
L'accademia di musica (f, 1, Rossi), Venice, S Samuele, aut. 1799
L'avaro (f, 1, Foppa), VB, Nov 1799, *GB-Lbl*, *I-BGc**, *Fc*
Gli sciti (dm, 2, Rossi, after Voltaire: *Les scythes*), VF, Feb 1800, *BGc**, *Fc*, *Mc*, *Nc*, *US-Bp*
La locandiera (f, 1, Rossi, after C. Goldoni), Vicenza, Berico, spr. 1800, *I-BGc**, *Gl*, *Nc*
Il carretto del venditore d'aceto (f, 1, Foppa), Venice, S Angelo, 28 June 1800, *Bc*, *BGc*, *Fc*, *Gl*, *Nc*, *Pi*, *PAc*, *Rsc*, *Tn*, *Vnm*, *US-Wc*
L'equivoco, ovvero Le bizzarrie dell'amore (dg, 2, Foppa), Milan, Scala, 5 Nov 1800, *I-BGc*, *Fc*, *Mc*, *US-Bp*
L'imbroglione e il castiga-matti (farsa giocosa, 1, Foppa), VM, 9 Dec 1800

Ginevra di Scozia (dramma serio eroico per musica, 2, Rossi, after L. Ariosto: *Orlando furioso*), Trieste, Nuovo, 21 April 1801 [for the inauguration of the theatre]; as Ariodante, Frankfurt, 26 Dec 1802; *I-Bc*, *BGc*, *Fc*, *Gl*, *Mc*, *Mr**, *Nc*, *OS*, *Pi*, *PAc*, *PLcon*, *Rmassimo*, *Rsc*, *Us-Bp*, *LOu*; vs (Vienna, ?1801)

Le due giornate [Il portatore d'acqua] (dramma eroicomico per musica, 3, Foppa, after J. N. Bouilly: *Les deux journées*), Milan, Scala, 18 Aug 1801, *I-BGc*, *Fc*, *Mr**, *Nc*, *Pi*

I virtuosi [I virtuosi a teatro] (f, 1, Rossi), Venice, S Lucca, 26 Dec 1801, *BGc**

Argene (dramma eroico per musica, 2, Rossi), VF, 28 Dec 1801, *BGc*

Elisa, ossia Il monte S Bernardo (dramma sentimentale per musica, 1, Rossi), ? Malta, Manoeel, 1801, Venice, S Benedetto, 5 July 1804, *Bsf*, *Fc*, *Gl*, *Li*, *Mc*, *Nc*, *OS*, *Pi*, *PAc*, *PIv*, *Rc*, *Rsc*, *Vnm*, *US-Bp*, *LOu*

I misteri eleusini [Polibete] (dm, 2, G. Bernardoni), Milan, Scala, 6 Jan 1802, *I-BGc*, *Fc*, *Mc*, *Mr*, *Nc*, *PAc*, *US-Bp*, *LOu*

I castelli in aria, ossia Gli amanti per accidente (f, 1, Foppa), VB, May 1802

Ercole in Lidia (dm, 2, G. De Gamerra), Vienna, Burg, 29 Jan 1803, *I-Fc*

Gl'intrighi amorosi (dg, 2, G. Bertati), Parma, Ducale, carn. 1803

Le finte rivale (melodramma giocoso, 2, L. Romanelli), Milan, 20 Aug 1803, *Bc*, *BGc*, *Fc*, *Nc*, *US-Bp*

Alonso e Cora (dm, 2, Bernardoni, after J. F. Marmontel: *Les Incas*), Milan, Scala, 26 Dec 1803; rev. as Cora (2, M. Salfa-Berico), NC, 1815; *I-BGc*, *Fc*, *Mr**

Amor non ha ritegno [La fedeltà delle vedove] (melodramma eroicomico, 2, F. Marconi), Milan, Scala, 18 May 1804, *BGc*, *Fc*

I due viaggiatori (dg, 2, Foppa), Florence, Risoluti, sum. 1804

Zamori, ossia L'eroe dell'Indie (dm, 2, L. Prividali), Piacenza, Municipale, 10 Aug 1804 [for the inauguration of the theatre], *BGc*

Eraldo ed Emma (dramma eroico per musica, 2, Rossi), Milan, Scala, 8 Jan 1805, *Fc*, *PAc*, *US-Bp*

Di locanda in locanda e sempre in sala (f, 3, L. G. Buonavoglia), Venice, 5 June 1805, *I-BGc*

L'amor coniugale [Il custode di buon cuore] (farsa sentimentale, 1, Rossi, after Bouilly: *Léonore, ou L'amour conjugal*), Padua, Nuovo, 26 July 1805, *Bc*, *BGc**, *Gl*, *Mc*, *Mr*, *Nc*, *PAc*, *Rsc*, *Vnm*, *US-Bp*, *LOu*; ed. A. Gazzaniga (Bergamo, 1967)

La roccia di Frauenstein (melodramma eroicomico, 2, Rossi, after A. Anelli: *I fuorusciti*), VF, 26 Oct 1805, *GB-Lbl*, *I-Mc*, *Nc*

Gli americani [Idalide] (melodramma eroico, 2, Rossi), VF, carn. 1806, *BGc*

Adelasia e Aleramo (mels, 2, L. Romanelli), Milan, Scala, 26/28 Dec 1806, *GB-Lbl*, *I-BGc*, *CMbc*, *Fc*, *Mc*, *Nc*, *OS*, *PAc*, *US-Bp*, *Cn*, vs (Milan, 1807/R1990: IOG, xi)

Palmira, o sia Il trionfo della virtù e dell'amore (dm, 1), Florence, Pergola, 1806, *PAc*

Il piccolo compositore di musica (f, 2), VM, 1806, *BGc*

Nè l'un, nè l'altro (dg, Anelli), Milan, Scala, 17 Aug 1807, *BGc**

Belle ciarle e tristi fatti [L'imbroglio contro l'imbroglio] (dg, 2, Anelli), VF, Nov 1807, *Mr**

I cherusci (dm, 2, Rossi), Rome, Argentina, carn. 1808

Il vero originale (burletta per musica, 2, M. A. Brunetti), Rome, Valle, carn. 1808, *I-BGc*, *Rsc*

La finta sposa, ossia Il barone burlato (dg, 2, Brunetti), Rome, Valle, spr. 1808

Il matrimonio per concorso (dg, 2), Bologna, Comunale, carn. 1809

Il ritorno di Ulisse (azione eroica per musica, 2, Prividali), VF, carn. 1809, *BGc**

Alcide al Bivio (festa teatrale, Metastasio), Bergamo, Istituto Filarmonico, 1809

Amor non soffre opposizione (dg, 2, Foppa), VM, carn. 1810, *BGc**

Raùl di Créqui (mels, 2, Romanelli), Milan, Scala, 26 Dec 1810, *BGc*, *Mr**

L'amor figliale [Il disertore] (farsa sentimentale, 1, Rossi), VM, carn. 1811, *BGc**

Il sacrifizio d'Ifigenia [Ifigenia in Aulide] (azione seria drammatica per musica, 2, G. Arici, after M. F. L. G. L. Roullet), Brescia, Grande, carn. 1811, *Mc*, *PAc*, *PS*, *Tf*, frags. *BGc**; as Il ritorno di Jefte (o sia Il voto incauto (J. Ferretti), concert perf., Rome, 1814

Tamerlano (mels, 2, Romanelli, after Voltaire: *L'orphelin de la Chine*), Milan, Scala, 26 Dec 1812, *I-BGc*, *Mr**

La rosa bianca e la rosa rossa (melodramma eroico, 2, F. Romani, after R. C. G. de Pixérécourt: *La rose blanche e la rose rouge*), Genoa, S Agostino, 21 Feb 1813; as Il trionfo dell'amicizia, NC,

spr. 1819; *BGc*, *Fc*, *Nc*, *Rsc*, *US-Bp*; vs (Florence, n.d.); (Bergamo, 1963)

Medea in Corinto (melodramma tragico, 2, Romani after Euripides), NC, 28 Nov 1813, *I-Bc**, *BGc*, *Fc*, *Nc*, *Rmassimo*, *US-Bp*, *NYp*, vs (Paris, 1823/R1986: IOG, xii)

Elena [Elena e Costantino] (dramma eroicomico per musica, 2, A. Tottola), Naples, Fiorentini, carn. 1814, *Bc*, *BGc**, *Fc*, *Mc*, *Nc*, *OS*, *US-Bp*

Atar, o sia Il serraglio d'Ormus (mels, 2, Romani), Genoa, S Agostino, June 1814, *I-Mr**

Le due duchesse, ossia La caccia dei lupi [Le due amiche] (dramma semiserio per musica, 2, Romani), Milan, Scala, 7 Nov 1814, *BGc*, *Mr**

La figlia dell'aria, ossia La vendetta di Giunone (dm, 3, Rossi), NC, Lent 1817, *Nc**

Mennone e Zemira (dm, 3, Rossi), NC, 22 March 1817

Amor avvocato (commedia per musica, 1), Naples, Fiorentini, spr. 1817, *Nc*

Ifigenia in Tauride (azione sacra drammatica per musica, 3, after A. Zeno), Florence, Pergola, spr. 1817

Lanassa (melodramma eroico, 2, Rossi and B. Merelli, after A. M. Lemierre: *La veuve du Malabar*), VF, 26 Dec 1817

Alfredo il grande (mels, 2, Merelli), Rome, Argentina, Feb 1818, *BGc**, *Fc*, *Mc*

Le danaide [Danao] (mels, 2, Romani), Rome, Argentina, carn. 1819, *Fc*, *Mr**

Fedra (mels, 2, Romanelli), Milan, Scala, 26 Dec 1820, *Mc*, vs (Milan, 1821)

Atalia (dramma sacro per musica, 2, Romani), NC, Lent 1822, *NC**

Demetrio (dm, 2, after Metastasio), Turin, Regio, carn. 1824, *Tf*, frags. *BGc**

*

DEUMM (A. Gazzaniga)

L. Schiedermair: *Beiträge zur Geschichte der Oper um die Wende des 18. und 19. Jahrhunderts: Simon Mayr* (Leipzig, 1907–10)

A. Meli: *Giovanni Simone Mayr sulla linea musicale Baviera-Bergamo* (Bergamo, 1963)

M. Carner: 'Simone Mayr and his 'L'amor coniugale', *ML*, lii (1971), 239–58; repr. in *Major and Minor* (New York, 1980), 148–71

J. Freeman: 'Johann Simon Mayr and his *Ifigenia in Aulide*', *MQ*, lvii (1971), 187–210

A. Gazzaniga: 'Su "L'amor coniugale" di Simone Mayr', *NRMI*, v (1971), 799–826

J. S. Allitt: 'Mayr's *L'amor coniugale*', *Donizetti Society Journal*, i (1974), 58–79

——: 'The Notebooks of Giovanni Simone Mayr', ibid, 141–8

N. Jenkins: 'Giovanni Simone Mayr's *Medea in Corinto*', ibid, 80–90

J. S. Allitt: 'Mayr's *La passione*', *Donizetti Society Journal*, ii (1975), 294–313

——: 'Mayr's *Samuele*', ibid, 314–15

'Le lezione caritatevoli', ibid, 275–93 [Eng. trans. of speech given by Mayr, 1805]

'Mayr expresses some Thoughts on Italian Opera and in particular on Rossini's Comic Operas', ibid, 316–17

A. Gazzaniga: *Giovanni Simone Mayr: Zibaldone, preceduto dalle pagine autobiografiche*, i (Bergamo, 1977) [reviewed by F. Lippmann, *NRMI*, xiii (1979), 900–02]

C. Sartori: 'Antonio Bazzini e i suoi maestri', *NRMI*, xi (1977), 606–21

V. Gibelli: 'Twórczość operowa Simone Mayra i jego poglądy na dramat muzyczny' [Concerning the Operas of Simon Mayr and his Conception of the Musical Drama], *Pagine*, iv (1980), 93–101 [incl. summary in It.]

W. Witzenmann: 'Grundzüge der Instrumentation in italienischen Opern von 1770 bis 1830', *AnMc*, no.21 (1982), 276–332

F. Lippmann: 'Mozart und die italienischen Komponisten des 19. Jahrhunderts', *MJb 1980–83*, 104–13

P. Gossett: Introduction to S. Mayr: *Medea in Corinto*, IOG, xii (1986)

L. T. Sisk: *Giovanni Simone Mayr (1763–1845): his Writings on Music* (diss., Northwestern U., 1986)

S. Balthazar: 'Mozart, Mayr, Rossini and the Development of the opera seria Duet', *I vicini di Mozart: Venice 1987*, 377–98

J. S. Allitt: *J. S. Mayr: Father of 19th Century Italian Music* (Shaftesbury, 1989)

S. Balthazar: 'Mayr, Rossini, and the Development of the Early Concertato Finale', *JRMA*, cxvi (1991), 236–66

SCOTT L. BALTHAZAR

Mayskaya noch'. Opera by N. A. Rimsky-Korsakov; see MAY NIGHT.

Mayuzumi, Toshirō (*b* Yokohama, 20 Feb 1929). Japanese composer. He studied with Tomojirō Ikenouchi and Akira Ifukube at the Tokyo National University of Fine Arts and Music, from which he graduated in 1951. He went to Paris (1951–2) to study at the Conservatoire with Aubin and familiarized himself with the activities of Messiaen and Boulez and with *musique concrète*. Returning to Tokyo he founded (with Akutagawa and Dan) the Sannin no Kai (Group of Three) and began composing in earnest. He consistently experimented with new ideas and techniques, introducing many of the new trends in postwar European music into Japan. The more important of his works in those years include the orchestral *Bacchanale* (1953) and *X, Y, Z* (1955), the first Japanese example of *musique concrète*.

With his *Nehan Kōkyōkyoku* ('Nirvana Symphony') in 1958 Mayuzumi began to show particular interest in traditional Japanese music, in this case Buddhist music. The Buddhist influence is notable in subsequent works, including his only opera *Kinkakuji* ('The Golden Pavilion' or 'Der Tempelbrand'), in three acts, which was first performed at the Deutsche Oper, Berlin, on 23 June 1976. Mayuzumi often composed for such theatrical groups as the Bungaku-za or the Haiyū-za, and also collaborated with the novelist Mishima. Their joint projects included a drama, *Bara to kaizoku* ('Roses and Pirates', 1958), and a version of Wilde's *Salome* (1960), as well as *Kinkakuji*, which Mayuzumi set to a libretto in German by Claus Henneberg based on Mishima's novel. He has also composed much music for films, including *Akasen-chitai* ('Red District', the first Japanese film with electronic music), *Tokyo Olympic* and *The Bible* (1965).

See also KINKAKUJI.   MASAKATA KANAZAWA

Mazarin, Cardinal Jules [Mazzarini, Giulio Raimondo] (*b* Pescina, Aquila, 14 July 1602; *d* Vincennes, nr Paris, 9 March 1661). French politician of Italian birth. He is important in the history of music for his advocacy of Italian opera in France. In his youth he was exposed to Roman opera while serving Cardinal Antonio Barberini: he attended, and perhaps participated in, Landi's *Sant'Alessio* in 1632. From 1634 to 1636 he was in Paris as papal nuncio. He became a naturalized Frenchman in 1639, cardinal in 1641 (though he held only minor orders) and first minister in 1643 during Anne of Austria's regency. He saw Italian opera in France as a potential source of secret agents and as a smokescreen for political manoeuvres. He therefore brought Italians to Paris: in 1643 the composer Marco Marazzoli, in 1644 the singers Leonora Baroni and Atto Melani, in 1645 the designer Giacomo Torelli and in 1646 the composer Luigi Rossi. Moreover, by the end of 1646 Cardinal Barberini and his secretary, the poet Francesco Buti, had found refuge at the French court from papal vicissitudes.

Through the efforts of Mazarin, seven Italian operas were introduced to Paris audiences between 1645 and 1662. The first of these appears to have been Marazzoli's *Il giuditio della Ragione tra la Beltà e l'Affetto*, performed on 28 February 1645 (see Zaslaw). This was followed on 14 December 1645 by Sacrati's *La finta pazza*; Cavalli's *Egisto* was given on 13 February

1646. Except for their complicated machinery ('up to now unknown in France', *Gazette de France*), these first three productions excited little interest; but Rossi's *Orfeo*, opening on 2 March 1647 (eight performances), at last provided the image of Italian opera that Mazarin so badly needed. *Orfeo* also gave anti-Mazarin forces a *cause célèbre* which the French parliament used to minimize its fiscal problems by exploiting the admittedly exorbitant costs of the production. Public opinion, as reflected in satirical 'mazarinades', blamed the economic miseries of the state on the cost of an Italian opera staged by an Italian designer and sponsored by an Italian-born cardinal. The Fronde (1648–53) forced Mazarin into exile and threatened with imprisonment those Italians who remained in France. However, with the defeat of the Fronde, and Mazarin's return in February 1653, plans were immediately undertaken for the next opera, Caproli's *Le nozze di Peleo e di Theti*, which opened in Paris on 14 April 1654 (nine performances). By 1659, when he was at the peak of his power, Mazarin was still unable to establish a permanent Italian opera company in France: after each opera the Italian troupe disbanded and left. His letters to Buti show a stubborn commitment to his ideal in which money was no object: 'I would rather have such [outstanding] performers and spend more money than have those of ordinary talent at a cheaper price' (letter of 8 August 1659). To celebrate the marriage of Louis XIV he commissioned Cavalli to compose *Ercole amante*, to a text by Buti. It was to be performed in a *théâtre à machines* that Gaspare Vigarini and his two sons were to build. Neither opera nor theatre was ready by the time the king and his bride returned to Paris in August 1660, and Cavalli hastily substituted his *Xerse*, which was performed many times beginning on 22 November 1660. Mazarin was dead before *Ercole amante* was eventually performed on 7 February 1662 (at least five performances).

Mazarin had been forced to compromise with French taste. He saw the operas he had championed interlarded with ballets and prefaced by panegyric prologues. Because of the failure of these works over a period of nearly 20 years, Lully was discouraged from trying to establish French opera at the time of Mazarin's death, but when he eventually did so after the Académie d'Opéra was established in 1669 Italian opera left its mark on it (*see* TRAGÉDIE EN MUSIQUE).

H. Prunières: *L'opéra italien en France avant Lulli* (Paris, 1913)
J. Cain, ed.: *Mazarin* (Paris, 1961) [catalogue of exhibition at *F-Pn*]
N. Demuth: *French Opera* (Horsham, Sussex, 1963)
J. R. Anthony: *French Baroque Music from Beaujoyeulx to Rameau* (London, 1973, 2/1978)
R. M. Isherwood: *Music in the Service of the King* (Ithaca, NY, and London, 1973)
C. Massip: *La vie des musiciens de Paris au temps de Mazarin (1643–1661)* (Paris, 1976)
M. Laurain-Portemer: *Etudes Mazarines* (Paris, 1981)
N. Zaslaw: 'The First Opera in Paris: a Study in the Politics of Art', *Jean-Baptiste Lully and the Music of the French Baroque: Essays in Honor of James R. Anthony* (Cambridge, 1989), 7–23
                                        JAMES R. ANTHONY

Mazepa ('Mazeppa'). Opera in three acts by PYOTR IL'YICH TCHAIKOVSKY to a libretto by Victor Burenin, revised by the composer and with an Act 2 insert aria for the title character to words by Vasily Kandaurov, after ALEXANDER SERGEYEVICH PUSHKIN's poem *Poltava*; Moscow, Bol'shoy Theatre, 3/15 February 1884.

A simultaneous production by the Mariinsky Theatre had its first performance three days after the première. The Bol'shoy performance was conducted by Ippolit Al'tani, with Bogomir Korsov in the title role and Emiliya Pavlovskaya as Mariya; Eduard Nápravník conducted at St Petersburg, with Ippolit Pryanishnikov in the title role, Ivan Mel'nikov as Kochubey, Fyodor Stravinsky as Orlik and Mariya Kamenskaya as Lyubov'.

Tchaikovsky's was the second opera to be based on Pushkin's poem about the notorious 17th-century Ukrainian separatist. (The first, by a noble dilettante named Boris Viettinghoff-Schell, had been composed in 1858 and was performed the next year at the St Petersburg Bol'shoy Theatre.) The libretto, meant originally for the cellist-composer Karl Davïdov, largely ignores the historical and military circumstances. The operatic Mazeppa (baritone) does his dirt on a personal rather than political plane. He surprises his friend Vasily Kochubey (baritone), a cossack judge, by demanding the hand of the latter's daughter Mariya (soprano) with whom he has reached an understanding despite the vast difference in their ages (Act 1 scene i). To avenge what he sees as a dishonouring theft, Kochubey denounces Mazeppa's separatist scheme to the tsar (1.ii). Disbelieved, he is remanded by Peter to Mazeppa, who has him tortured and condemned. Act 2 scene i consists of an extended prison monologue followed by an interrogation by Mazeppa's henchman Orlik (bass), all based in large part on Pushkin's original verses. Act 2 scene ii, also based closely on the poem, consists of a scene in which Mazeppa hints to Mariya of his ambition and exacts from her a pledge of devotion, followed by one in which Kochubey's wife Lyubov' (mezzo-soprano) warns her daughter of the impending execution. In Act 2 scene iii, Kochubey and his friend Iskra (tenor) are beheaded before a crowd, Mariya and Lyubov' arriving a heartbreaking instant too late to prevent the act. In Act 3 the routed Mazeppa finds Mariya deranged and abandons her.

While this plot has all the makings of a pompous historical spectacle along the lines of *The Maid of Orléans*, the Joan of Arc opera that preceded it in Tchaikovsky's output, the composer chose to make *Mazepa* a more inward lyric drama. Only the execution scene is handled in the grand manner, replete with *banda*. Elsewhere, heavy emphasis is placed on an unhappy romantic intrigue that was in part fabricated ad hoc. One of the central characters – the tenor Andrey, a young cossack lad in love with Mariya – has no counterpart in Pushkin. He sings two duets with his beloved, both of them at strange cross-purposes. In the first scene he confesses his love to her, while she responds by confessing love for Mazeppa. In the last scene he makes an attempt on Mazeppa and is mortally wounded, dying in the arms of the crazed Mariya, who mistakes him for an infant and sings him a lullaby that brings the opera to a striking *pianissimo* conclusion. This was in fact a brilliant second thought, replacing a more conventional finale published in the original vocal score (Moscow, 1883) in which Mariya met an Ophelia-like end accompanied by a chorus of horrified onlookers. Another such second thought was Mazeppa's Act 2 aria, in which he leaves no doubt that for all his amorality his love for Mariya is sincere.   RICHARD TARUSKIN

Mazura, Franz (*b* Salzburg, 12 April 1924). Austrian bass-baritone. He studied in Detmold, making his début in 1949 at Kassel and then singing in Mainz, Brunswick and Mannheim. In 1961 he was engaged with the Deutsche Oper, Berlin; later he appeared in Hamburg and Vienna. At Bayreuth (1971–86) he sang Gunther, Alberich, Klingsor and Biterolf. He sang Moses in *Moses und Aron* at the Israel Festival in Caesarea (1974) and Dr Schön in the first three-act performance of *Lulu*, at the Opéra (1979); he made his Metropolitan début, also as Dr Schön, in 1980, then sang the Doctor (*Wozzeck*), Rangoni, Creon (*Oedipus rex*), Gurnemanz and the Messenger (*Die Frau ohne Schatten*) there. His wide range has allowed him to sing both bass and baritone roles, including Scarpia, John the Baptist and Orestes as well as Pizarro, Wotan and King Mark. A powerful actor, he has been particularly effective in 20th-century works.   ELIZABETH FORBES

Mazurok, Yury (Antonovich) (*b* Krasnik, 18 July 1931). Polish baritone. He studied in Moscow, and in 1963 he joined the Bol'shoy Theatre, where he later became a soloist. He won prizes in competitions at Prague (1960), Bucharest (1961) and Montreal (1967). His performances are noted for his firm, beautiful tone, vivid temperament and imposing stage presence, although he has been criticized for a lack of wholehearted commitment in his acting and for his limited range of gesture and expression. His roles include Yevgeny Onegin and Yeletsky, Andrey and Tsaryov (*War and Peace* and *Semyon Kotko*), and Rossini's Figaro. In 1975 he made his Covent Garden début as Renato, and in 1978 his Metropolitan début as Germont. He has frequently sung at the Vienna Staatsoper, including Escamillo in Zeffirelli's 1979 production of *Carmen*. In 1987 he sang Scarpia at Wiesbaden. He is also a noted interpreter of Russian songs.   I. M. YAMPOL'SKY

Mazza, Giuseppe (*b* Lucca, 3 March 1806; *d* Trieste, 20 June 1885). Italian composer. His first music lessons were in Lucca with Domenico Quilici; later he studied harmony and counterpoint at Bologna with Stanislao Mattei, the teacher of Rossini and Donizetti. He returned to Lucca, where his first opera was produced; the warm reception accorded *La vigilanza delusa* won him commissions to compose for Florence and Naples. His subsequent works were less successful and he turned to conducting operas. He finally found a secure niche when he was appointed *maestro di cappella* and organist at S Antonio Taumaturgo in Trieste, where he won a reputation as an excellent teacher of singing; he held this post until his death. His operas are now forgotten, with the curious exception of *La prova di un'opera seria* (1845; not to be confused with F. Gnecco's 1805 opera of the same title). A work in the tradition of Cimarosa's *Il maestro di cappella*, it was revived in Spanish in 1903 as *El maestro campanone*, revised by Vicente Lleó, in which form it was later recorded on LP under the Spanish conductor Ataúlfo Argenta, featuring Pilar Lorengar. Besides his operas, Mazza composed much sacred music.

La vigilanza delusa, ossia Amor le vince (dg, 3), Lucca, Pantera, carn. 1826

L'albergo incantato (dg, 2, F. Marconi), Florence, Immobili, 26 Dec 1827; rev. as Monsieur de Montenail, Naples, Nuovo, 1835

Monsieur de Chalumeaux (ob, 2, J. Ferretti), Naples, Nuovo, 1828

Elena de Malvina (melodramma, 3, F. Romani), Rome, Valle, Sept 1834; as La dama irlandese, Naples, Fondo, 1835

Caterina di Guisa (melodramma, 3, Romani), Treviso, Dolfin, 26 May 1837

L'orfanella di Lanissa (melodramma, 2, L. A. Paladini), Milan, Re, 17 Aug 1838

Leocadia (melodramma, 2, Romani, after E. Scribe and Mélesville), Venice, Apollo, 30 Aug 1843

La prova di un'opera seria (dg, 2, G. Rossi), Fiume, Comunale, spr. 1845; rev. V. Lleó as El maestro campanone (zar, 1), 1903

Jefte (dramma biblico, 2, Boccabadati-Francaluca), Venice, S Benedetto, 26 Feb 1851

La sacerdotessa d'Iside (os, 3, S. Torelli), Milan, Carcano, 30 March 1852

La sciocca per astuzia (dg, 2, L. Romanelli), Trieste, Mauroner, 7 July 1855

La Sorrentina, Bologna, 1857

Unperf.: Chiara di Salency; Il primo amore; Il divorzio persiano (Romani); Arsinoe

WILLIAM ASHBROOK (with ANDREW LAMB)

Mazzanti, Ferdinando (*b* ?Pescia, *c*1725; *d* London, ?1805). Italian soprano castrato. A pupil of Bartolomeo Nucci of Pescia, he is first found in *opera seria* at Berlin, 1741–2, after which he returned to Italy. He had no operatic engagements in 1745–8 but re-emerged in 1751 as a primo uomo notable for high-register singing (rising to *d′′′*) and bravura of a highly instrumental figuration. He sang in leading Italian houses up to 1769, also at Munich in 1755, in Vienna (in Gluck's *Il rè pastore*) in 1756 and in Jommelli's company at Stuttgart in 1759–60. With his voice in decline (Burney in 1770 described it as only a 'thread' but 'extremely flexible'), he sang as secondo uomo at Rome in 1772 and in a comic company there in 1774. He held court appointments at Stuttgart, *c*1772–82, and was then a music teacher in London, sinking into extreme poverty.

DENNIS LIBBY

Mazzanti, Rosaura (*b* Florence or Bologna; *fl* 1710–34). Italian contralto, half-sister of Antonio Ristorini. Her first known appearance was in the minor role of Zaida in Francesco Gasparini's *Tamerlano* in Venice in 1710. She sang in three operas in Florence in 1712–14, playing a trouser role in one of them. She was the prima donna in every other opera in which she is known to have appeared – nine in Venice in 1720–25, four in Florence in 1725–7, one in Naples in 1730 and three more in Florence in 1733–4. Among these she sang the title roles of Orlandini's *Griselda* (1720) and Vivaldi's *Ipermestra* (1727).

A. L. Bellina, B. Brizi and M. G. Pensa: *I libretti vivaldiani: recensione e collazione dei testimoni a stampa* (Florence, 1982)

COLIN TIMMS

Mazzi, Prospero (*fl* 1674–89). Italian composer. He was a Benedictine prior and the composer of two operas: *Il prencipe corsaro* (G. B. Giardini), given in Modena on 11 November 1674, and *Laerte Porsenna* (Mantua, 25 April 1689). The scores of these and other vocal works are in the Biblioteca Estense at Modena.

A. Gandini: *Cronistoria dei teatri di Modena dal 1539 al 1871* (Modena, 1873)

Mazzinghi, Joseph (*b* London, 25 Dec 1765; *d* Downside, nr Bath, 15 Jan 1844). English composer of Corsican origin. A pupil of J. C. Bach and Sacchini, he was appointed harpsichordist at the King's Theatre in the Haymarket for the 1784–5 season in succession to Clementi, and worked under the house composer Anfossi and the violinist Wilhelm Cramer, who led the orchestra. The first opera Mazzinghi directed was an adaptation of Cimarosa's *Il pittore parigino* (25 January 1785). During the next season he composed and arranged music for a ballet and provided substitute arias for Salieri's *La scuola de' gelosi*, which he also directed.

For the 1786–7 and 1787–8 seasons Mazzinghi was engaged formally as house composer at the King's. In addition to providing ballet music and directing operas (including works by Cimarosa, Paisiello, Sarti and Martín y Soler), he was primarily responsible for arranging pasticcios. Perhaps his most ambitious undertaking during these years was *Gli schiavi per amore* (24 April 1787), based on Paisiello's *Le gare generose*. Although this was not attributed to Mazzinghi and included arias by Mengozzi and Bianchi, as well as Paisiello, one must assume that Mazzinghi provided most of the new numbers, including some ensembles. He continued to work for the King's until its destruction in June 1789, but he was overshadowed by the other house composers Storace and Tarchi.

In the autumn of 1790 Mazzinghi was engaged by the Pantheon Opera House, where he directed and arranged works mostly by Paisiello, the house composer *in absentia*, who was appointed after Mozart declined the post. Mazzinghi received £250 for conducting every opera and ballet performance of the season, arranging pasticcios and composing a comic opera, *Zaffira*, which he never finished. He and Cramer are said to have reconstructed the score of Paisiello's *La locanda* from memory after the original was destroyed in the Pantheon fire in 1792. Thereafter, Mazzinghi worked only sporadically for the Italian theatre in London. He arranged and contributed arias to an adaptation by Da Ponte of Monsigny's *La belle Arsène* (as *La bella Arsena*, 12 December 1795) and also set Da Ponte's libretto *Il tesoro* (14 June 1796). From as early as 1791 Mazzinghi had contributed to English operas at Covent Garden, and in 1798 he collaborated with William Reeve on the music for Cobb's very successful *Ramah Droog*. Mazzinghi's own operatic music is slight, fashionably tuneful but harmonically bland. He was, however, a skilful arranger and could produce faithful imitations of Anfossi, Sarti, Martín y Soler and Paisiello; he also published a quantity of ballet music and several collections of piano and chamber music.

*

BDA

F. C. Petty: *Italian Opera in London 1760–1800* (Ann Arbor, 1980)

R. Fiske: *English Theatre Music in the Eighteenth Century* (London, 2/1986)

C. Price: 'Italian Opera and Arson in Late Eighteenth-Century London', *JAMS*, xlii (1989), 55–107

——: 'Unity, Originality and the London Pasticcio', *Harvard Library Bulletin*, ii/4 (1991), 17–30   CURTIS PRICE

Mazzocchi, Domenico (*b* Civita Castellana, bap. 8 Nov 1592; *d* Rome, 21 Jan 1665). Italian composer. He became a Roman citizen in 1614 and by 1619 was both priest and Doctor of Laws; he entered the household of Cardinal Ippolito Aldobrandini in 1621, though not specifically as a musician. The cardinal's brother Giovanni Giorgio, prince of Rossano, commissioned Mazzocchi's only surviving opera, *La catena d'Adone* (*favola boscareccia*, prol., 5, O. Tronsarelli), performed in Rome at the Palazzo Conti on 12 February 1626. After the cardinal's death in 1638, Mazzocchi stayed in the service of his niece and sole heir, Olimpia Aldobrandini Borghese (later Pamfili).

Nothing is known of Mazzocchi's musical training, nor is he ever mentioned as *musico* or *maestro*. His only known compositions before his opera are two canzonettas and a motet. If the composer Sigismondo d'India is to be believed, Mazzocchi was given the opera commission only after he himself fell ill and could not fulfil it (see Reiner). In fact d'India derided Mazzocchi's inexperience and suggested that *La catena d'Adone* was defective because it was 'completely stuffed with canzonettas'. However, Mazzocchi noted that his many *mezz'arie* – brief passages in aria style – 'break the tedium of the recitative'. Simple, fluid recitative dialogue, monologues with judicious harmonies, tuneful arias and 'half-arias' are further contrasted by large choral ensembles with dancing at the ends of each of the five brief acts. The scenic effects, executed by Francesco de Cuppis, were the most elaborate yet staged for musical drama in Rome. The opera (or a portion of it) was performed again later in the same year during Cardinal Aldobrandini's sojourn in Parma. Mazzocchi dedicated the published score (Venice, 1626) to Aldobrandini's nephew, the 14-year-old Duke of Parma.

In his later works, including dramatic sacred dialogues and vocal chamber music, Mazzocchi often shifts into the pathos of the full-blown middle Baroque style. His forays into chromatic harmony and microtonal inflections (all notated) and his careful marking of dynamics and expression make regrettable the loss of his last dramatic work, a sacred opera based on the deaths of four Christian martyrs, *Il martirio de' Santi Abundio prete, Abundantio diacono, Marciano, e Giovanni suo figliuolo cavalieri romani*. It was first performed in the cathedral of Civita Castellana on 16 September 1641; its libretto, also by Tronsarelli, was later published in Rome.

See also CATENA D'ADONE, LA.

*

M. Pagani: *La selva incantata* (Rome, 1626)

H. Goldschmidt: *Studien zur Geschichte der italienischen Oper im 17. Jahrhundert*, i (Leipzig, 1901), 8–29 [incl. musical exx.]

A. Cardinali: *Cenni biografici di Domenico e Virgilio Mazzocchi* (Subiaco, 1926)

N. Pirrotta: 'Falsirena e la più antica delle cavatine', *CHM*, ii (1956–7), 355–66; Eng. trans. in idem: *Music and Culture in Italy from the Middle Ages to the Baroque* (Cambridge, MA, 1984)

J. Bossert: *A Modern Edition of D. Mazzocchi's 'La catena d'Adone'* (thesis, Cornell U., 1965)

S. Reiner: ' "Vi sono molt'altre mezz'Arie ..." ', *Studies in Music History: Essays for Oliver Strunk* (Princeton, 1968), 241–58

W. Witzenmann: *Domenico Mazzocchi, 1592–1665: Dokumente und Interpretationen*, AnMc, no.8 (1970)

C. Gianturco: 'Nuove considerazioni su *Il tedio del recitativo* delle prime opere romane', *RIM*, xviii (1982), 212–39

MARGARET MURATA

Mazzocchi, Virgilio [Virginio] (*b* Civita Castellana, bap. 22 July 1597; *d* Civita Castellana, 3 Oct 1646). Italian composer, brother of Domenico Mazzocchi. He went to Rome some time before 1627 and in 1629 settled into a lifelong appointment as *maestro* of the Cappella Giulia at St Peter's. Cardinal Francesco Barberini became arch-priest of the basilica in 1633 and began to rely on Mazzocchi to provide musical performances at the various Roman establishments of which he was protector or patron. It was Barberini who paid the expenses for several boys who boarded and studied music with Mazzocchi and who performed in the musical dramas he wrote for the cardinal. In 1640 he composed comic *intermedi* for the Barberini, three to texts by Giulio Rospigliosi, and set the choruses to

Seneca's *Troades* for a performance *all'antico* sponsored by Cardinal Francesco. Rospigliosi was also the librettist for Mazzocchi's four operatic works. The composer collaborated with Marco Marazzoli on *Chi soffre speri* (1637; rev. 1639), probably setting originally the first and third acts (the extant score is of the 1639 version). His *San Bonifatio*, staged four times in 1638 and 1639, and *L'innocenza difesa* (better known as *La Genoinda*), mounted twice in 1641, were written for boys; *Sant'Eustachio*, performed in 1643, probably was also. (Of six 'cantatas' credited to Mazzocchi, five are excerpts from the operas.)

The three later operas are full-scale serious dramas with 13–16 solo roles; they present lofty moral dilemmas and tests of Christian virtue, few or no special stage effects, and contain a minimum of choral writing. *Bonifatio* was to be learnt by boys who were not yet in their teens; appropriately, the roles are less lyric or pathetic than those in *Chi soffre speri* and are all scaled for young, high soprano voices. Mazzocchi avoided exaggerated melodic expression and set the large amount of recitative over slow harmonic rhythm, relying mostly on differences in character to provide variety. Apart from the prologue, there are only seven closed pieces, the last an elaborate final duet akin to an early trio sonata *da chiesa*. Two internal comic *intermedi* offer a distinct contrast, being patently more juvenile in characters and tone. The changes of style in *Genoinda* and *Eustachio* suggest that the youthful troupe matured musically, even as it included new singers. *Genoinda* has 11 solo arias, five duets or trios and some intensely emotional characters. In *Eustachio* there are two roles in tenor clef and one each in alto and mezzo-soprano range, next to ten solo soprano roles. Both the madrigalian choral writing and the solo music express the pain of a family of four facing martyrdom by pagan Romans. Mazzocchi's three surviving scores all show straightforward declamation, the effective use of arioso and a strong, intelligent handling of harmonic progressions, giving the music a transparency that perhaps meets a playwright's ideal for a *dramma in musica*.

See also CHI SOFFRE SPERI.

Chi soffre speri [L'Egisto; L'Alvida] (commedia musicale, 3, G. Rospigliosi, after G. Boccaccio: *Il decamerone*), Rome, Palazzo Barberini, 12 Feb 1637, lost, argomento (Rome, 1637); rev., Rome, Teatro Barberini, 27 Feb 1639, *I-Rvat* (*R*1982: IOB, lxi); collab. M. Marazzoli

San Bonifatio (rappresentazione spirituale, 3, Rospigliosi), Rome, Palazzo della Cancelleria, 7 Feb 1638, *Rvat*, 1 duet in RISM 1640², 1st intermedio ed. in AMI, v (1897/*R*1968)

L'innocenza difesa [La Genoinda] (op musicale, 5, Rospigliosi), Rome, Cancelleria, 29 Jan 1641, music lost except for 3 arias, in *F-Pn*, *I-Bc*, *MOe*, *Rc* and *US-CA*

Il Sant'Eustachio (attione in musica, 3, Rospigliosi), Rome, Palazzo Campeggi in Borgo Nuovo, 10 Feb 1643, *I-Tn*

*

A. Ademollo: *I teatri di Roma nel secolo decimosettimo* (Rome, 1888), 25ff

H. Goldschmidt: *Studien zur Geschichte der italienischen Oper im 17. Jahrhundert* (Leipzig, 1901), 89–96, 312–24

A. Cardinali: *Cenni biografici di Domenico e Virgilio Mazzocchi* (Subiaco, 1926)

U. Rolandi: 'La prima commedia musicale rappresentata a Roma nel 1639', *Nuova antologia*, no.62 (1927)

S. Reiner: 'Collaboration in *Chi soffre speri*', *MR*, xxii (1961), 265–82

I. Küffel: *Die Libretti Giulio Rospigliosis: ein Kapitel frühbarocker Operngeschichte in Rom* (diss., U. of Vienna, 1968)

P. Kast: 'Unbekannte Dokumente zur Oper *Chi soffre speri* von 1637', *Helmuth Osthoff zu seinem 70. Geburtstag* (Tutzing, 1969), 129–34

W. Witzenmann: *Domenico Mazzocchi, 1592–1665: Dokumente und Interpretationen*, AnMc, no.8 (1970), 30–32

M. Murata: 'Rospigliosiana ovvero, gli Equivoci innocenti', *Studi musicali*, iv (1975), 131–6

——: *Operas for the Papal Court, 1631–1668* (Ann Arbor, 1981)

F. Hammond: 'Girolamo Frescobaldi and a Decade of Music in Casa Barberini: 1634–1643', *AnMc*, no.19 (1979), 94–124

MARGARET MURATA

Mazzolà, Caterino (*b* Longarone, 18 Jan 1745; *d* Venice, 16 July 1806). Italian poet and librettist. About 1767–8 his family moved to Venice, where Caterino's firm grounding in Latin and the classics began at a Jesuit school before he moved on to a Somaschi institution in Treviso. By the time he married, in 1780, his career as a librettist had already begun. He had also become a known figure in the houses of men of letters in Venice, where he met Casanova in 1774 and Lorenzo da Ponte in 1777. The following year the composer Joseph Schuster helped to secure his appointment as court poet at Dresden, a position Mazzolà held from 1780 to 1796. For six months in 1780 Mazzolà was joined in Dresden by Da Ponte who, in addition to gaining insight into the work of a librettist, received from his host a letter of introduction to Salieri which led to his first appointment in Vienna as librettist to the newly revived Italian opera. That the inaugural performance (1783) was a production of the Salieri-Mazzolà opera *La scuola de' gelosi* was probably no mere coincidence. From 1790 Da Ponte began to fall from favour in Vienna, and it is likely that both he and Salieri were instrumental in gaining the position of court poet for Mazzolà for a brief period early in 1791 through their influence with Count Rosenberg, the court theatre director. Rosenberg was replaced, however, and Giovanni Bertati was subsequently named to the position. Mazzolà is described as a generous and gracious man who seems to have been much appreciated by his employer in Saxony. When he left Dresden in 1796, Friedrich August III obtained diplomatic work in Venice for him and also requested that some of his writings be sent back to the Saxon court each year.

Most of Mazzolà's librettos are of the *opera buffa* type, set mainly by the Dresden composers Naumann, Schuster and Seydelmann. Salieri's interest in his friend's texts was to be expected, but Mazzolà librettos were also set by other important composers of the time. Da Ponte described him as 'possibly the first to know how to write a comic libretto', and *La scuola de' gelosi* bears a striking resemblance to *Le nozze di Figaro*, not only in its similarities of plot and characters but also because of its rapid pace, clear delineation of characters and sectional Act 1 finale. Mazzolà's masonic opera *Osiride* was known to Mozart, with whom Mazzolà may have discussed *Die Zauberflöte* while in Vienna from May to July 1791. His collaboration with Mozart in adapting Metastasio's *La clemenza di Tito* for Prague in 1791 produced a libretto that vividly reflects contemporary trends in the content and structure of Italian serious opera. These trends, often originating in *opera buffa*, include the two-act structure, opening duet, medial ensembles, rapid pace and directness of emotional expression, characteristics to be found in Mazzolà's earlier librettos. *Il mostro*, a text that antedates *Tito* by six years, provides a particularly clear example.

opere buffe unless otherwise stated

Ruggiero (os), P. A. Guglielmi, 1769; *Il tutore ingannato*, Marescalchi, 1774; *Il marito indolente*, Santi, 1778 (Astarita, 1778; J. Schuster, 1782; Rust, 1784); *La scuola de' gelosi*, Salieri, 1778; *Bradamante* (os), Schuster, 1779; *L'isola capricciosa*, Rust, 1780; *Elisa* (os), Naumann, 1781; *Osiride* (os), Naumann, 1781; *Il capriccio corretto*, F. Seydelmann, 1783; *Il pazzo per forza*, Schuster, 1784 (Weigl, 1788); *La villanella di Misnia*, Seydelmann, 1784; *Il governatore dell'isole Canarie* (int), S. Ghinassi, 1785 (Accorimboni, 1785)

Tutto per amore, Naumann, 1785 (N. N. Mussini, 1797); *Lo spirito di contraddizione*, Schuster, 1785; *Il mostro, ossia Da gratitudine amore*, Seydelmann, 1785; *Gli avari in troppola*, Schuster, 1787; *Il turco in Italia*, Seydelmann, 1788 (Süssmayr, 1794, as *Il musulmano in Napoli*); *Rübezahl ossia Il vero amore*, Schuster, 1789; *La dama [donna] soldato*, Naumann, 1791 (Gazzaniga, 1792; Valentino Fioravanti, 1806; F. Orlandini, 1808; F. Rutini, 1817, as *Il campo militare*)

Il trionfo d'amore, P. Dutillieu, 1791; *Amore giustificato* (festa teatrale), Naumann, 1792; *Il servo padrone, ossia L'amor perfetto*, Schuster, 1793 (Piccinni, 1794; Pavesi, 1808; Generali, 1814); *La capricciosa ravveduta* [later version of *Il turco in Italia*], Bianchi, 1794; *Gli avventurieri* (after G. B. Casti: *Il rè Teodoro in Venezia*), Portugal, 1795; *Il mondo alla rovescia* [later version of *L'isola capricciosa*], Salieri, 1795; *Amor ingegnoso*, S. Mayr, 1798; *L'ubbedienza per astuzia*, Mayr, 1798; *La prova indiscreta*, C. Mellara, 1804; *Il bizzarro capriccio*, Mellara, 1806

G. Moschini: *Della letteratura veneziana del secolo XVIII fino à nostri giorni*, ii (Venice, 1806–8), esp. 103ff

P. Molmenti: *Carteggi Casanoviani: lettere di Giacomo Casanova e di altri a lui* (Naples, 1918)

A. Livingston, ed.: *Memoires of Lorenzo Da Ponte*, trans. E. Abbott (Philadelphia, 1929)

M. Calzavara: *Caterino Mazzolà: poeta teatrale alla corte di Dresda dal 1780 al 1796* (Farri, 1964)

P. Chiara: 'Deux notules Casanoviennes, 2: Un ami de Casanova: Caterino Mazzolà', *Casanova Gleanings*, viii (1965), 29–31, esp. 30–31

W. Pross: 'Neulateinische Tradition und Aufklärung in Mazzolà/ Mozarts *La clemenza di Tito*', *Die österreichische Literatur: ihr Profil an der Wende vom 18. zum 19. Jahrhundert (1750–1830)*, ed. H. Zeman, i (Graz, 1979), 379–401   DON NEVILLE

Mazzoleni, Ester (*b* Sebenico, Dalmatia, 12 March 1883; *d* Palermo, 17 May 1982). Italian soprano. She studied with the soprano Amelia Pinto and made her début in 1906 in *Il trovatore* at the Costanzi, Rome. She became well known throughout Italy, appearing at La Scala first in 1908. Her roles there included Medea in the first Italian performances of Cherubini's opera (1909) and the heroines of Spontini's *La vestale* and *Fernando Cortez*. She also sang Isolde, Norma and a wide range of dramatic roles, travelling occasionally to Spain, France and Hungary. In 1913 she sang Aida at the opening of the Verona Arena, to which she returned for the commemorative ceremonies 50 years later. She retired in 1926 and then taught in Palermo. She sang and acted in a highly charged, emotional style, her voice vibrant and her treatment of the vocal line emphatic, so that her many recordings offer some excitement as well as instructive demonstration of the methods of another age.

*

GV (R. Celletti)

M. Scott: *The Record of Singing*, ii (London, 1979)

L. Rasponi: *The Last Prima Donnas* (London, 1984)

J. B. STEANE

Mazzoleni, Ettore (*b* Brusio, Switzerland, 18 June 1905; *d* Toronto, 1 June 1968). Canadian conductor and teacher of Swiss-Italian parentage. Educated in England (Oxford and the RCM), he moved to Toronto in 1929 where he became principal of the conservatory (now the Royal Conservatory of Music of Toronto) in 1945, holding the post until his death in a traffic accident. A reorganization of the conservatory put the opera school under his vigorous direction, and out of this came the

Opera Festival of Toronto, the forerunner of the Canadian Opera Company. Their productions ranged from *Les contes d'Hoffmann* (1958) and *The Bartered Bride* (1961) to contemporary works, Mazzoleni conducting the North American premières of Arthur Benjamin's *A Tale of Two Cities* (in 1954) and Willan's *Transit through Fire* and *Deirdre*. Mazzoleni's second wife was the mezzo-soprano Joanne Ivey.

GODFREY RIDOUT

Mazzoni, Antonio (Maria) (*b* Bologna, 4 Jan 1717; *d* Bologna, 8 Dec 1785). Italian composer. A pupil of L. A. Predieri, he presented his first composition, a sacred work, in 1735. In 1736 he was admitted to the Accademia Filarmonica as a singer (tenor) and was later promoted to composer. His first opera, *Siroe, re di Persia*, was performed in Fano in 1746; two years later he was there as *maestro di cappella*. In 1751 he held the same position at S Giovanni in Monte, Bologna. He was coadjutor to Angelo Caroli at the cathedral of S Pietro in 1757, and became *maestro* in 1759. He served as *principe* of the Accademia Filarmonica in 1757, 1761, 1771, 1773 and 1784, and was one of the examiners of the young Mozart when he was admitted to that institution. A letter to Padre Martini places him in Lisbon in 1753, where he was called to assist David Perez in composing two operas for the opening of the magnificent new Teatro dos Paços da Ribeira in 1755; some of the greatest singers and theatrical personnel in Europe were present. Since Mazzoni provided the opera for the autumn, he was undoubtedly still in Lisbon on 1 November, when a great earthquake destroyed most of city, reducing the new theatre to a pile of rubble. He was back in Italy by 1756 to prepare an opera for Treviso. There is no evidence to substantiate reports that he travelled to Russia. In 1763 he was *primo maestro al cembalo* at the inauguration of the Teatro Comunale in Bologna for the production of Gluck's *Il trionfo di Clelia*. At this time Dittersdorf heard his sacred music and pronounced it not equal to Mazzoni's reputation as an opera composer. Burney, on hearing one of Mazzoni's *Magnificat* settings during his visit to Bologna in 1770, said 'He is said to have great fire and fancy, but in this performance, which was all chorus, they were not discoverable'.

Mazzoni enjoyed fame and reputation however, notably as an opera composer. His works show originality and a graceful, elegant style. Both the comic and the serious operas consist mainly of recitatives and arias, and are representative of mid-century classical style. The serious works follow Metastasian texts closely, with some arias cut or replaced, and may include choruses, depending on the theatre; the comic works incorporate modest introductions and finales. The late works in both genres generally include a few ensembles. *Arianna e Teseo* (1758, Naples) reveals a willingness to move beyond the ordinary: wind instruments have solos within arias and appear in obbligato recitatives, sometimes occupying entire scenes; and the march provides genuine programmatic 'battle' music.

Siroe, re di Persia (os, 3, P. Metastasio), Fano, Fortuna, July 1746
Issipile (os, 3, Metastasio), Macerata, Comunale, carn. 1748
Didone abbandonata (os, 3, Metastasio), Bologna, Formagliari, 26 Dec 1752
Demofoonte (os, 3, Metastasio), Parma, Ducale, carn. 1754
Achille in Sciro (os, 3, Metastasio), Piacenza, Ducale, 1754
L'astuzie amorose (ob), Piacenza, Ducale, 1754

La clemenza di Tito (os, 3, Metastasio), Lisbon, Paços da Ribeira, 6 June 1755, *P-La*
Antigono (os, 3 Metastasio), Lisbon, Paços da Ribeira, aut. 1755, *La*
Ifigenia in Tauride (os, 3, M. Coltellini), Treviso, Dolfin, Oct 1756
Il viaggiatore ridicolo (ob, 3, C. Goldoni), Parma, Ducale, carn. 1757
Il re pastore (os, 3, Metastasio), Bologna, Marsigli-Rossi, 11 July 1757, *I-Bc, P-La*
Arianna e Teseo (os, 3, P. Pariati), Naples, S Carlo, 20 Jan 1758, *La*
Eumene (os, 3, A. Zeno), Turin, Regio, carn. 1759, *I-Tf*
L'astuto ciarlatano (int, 2), Bologna, Sala, carn. 1760
Le stravaganze del caso (int, 2), Bologna, Sala, carn. 1760, *P-La*
Adriano in Siria (os, 3, Metastasio), Venice, S Samuele, 14 May 1760
Il mercanto fallito (farsetta, A. Boschi), Rome, Pace, carn. 1762
Nitteti (os, 3, Metastasio), Naples, S Carlo, 30 May 1764, *La*
L'inglese in Italia (dg), Bologna, Formagliari, 7 Jan 1769

*

BurneyFI
C. D. von Dittersdorf: *Lebensbeschreibung* (Leipzig, 1801; Eng. trans., 1896)
N. Morini: *La R. Accademia filarmonica di Bologna: monografia storica* (Bologna, 1930)
L. F. Tagliavini: 'Accademico filarmonico', *Mozart in Italia*, ed. G. Barblan and A. Della Corte (Milan, 1956), 108–22
A. Schnoebelen: *Padre Martini's Collection of Letters in the Civico Museo Bibliografico Musicale in Bologna: an Annotated Index* (New York, 1979)
M. McClymonds: *Niccolò Jommelli: the Last Years* (Ann Arbor, 1980)   MARITA P. McCLYMONDS, ANNE SCHNOEBELEN

Mazzucato, Alberto (*b* Udine, 28 July 1813; *d* Milan, 31 Dec 1877). Italian composer, conductor and singing teacher. He studied mathematics, intending to become an astronomer, but gave it up to study music at the Padua Conservatory. In 1834 while he was still a student his first opera, *La fidanzata di Lammermoor*, was performed in Padua with some success; it was followed in 1836 by *Don Chisciotte* in Milan. According to Fétis, he then visited Paris, where performances of Beethoven, the French operas of Meyerbeer and Halévy's *La Juive* made a deep impression on him; this is reflected in his next operas, *Esmeralda* (1838) and *I corsari* (1840). Some critics had considered his earlier works too modern, and the more conservative ones now accused him of writing noisy, difficult music lacking in melody. Public reaction was mixed: *Esmeralda* was widely performed but not always well received, while *I corsari* was a fiasco at La Scala. Fétis attributed his abandonment of operatic composition in the 1840s to the advent of Verdi. His other works include sacred music and songs.

From 1839 Mazzucato taught singing at the Milan Conservatory, and later composition, music history, aesthetics and instrumentation; he was director from 1872 until his death. Among his pupils were Boito, Amintore Galli and Gomes. He translated treatises by Garcia, Berlioz and Fétis and was on the editorial staff of the *Gazzetta musicale di Milano*, as editor from 1856 to 1858. From 1859 to 1868 he covered the positions of both *maestro concertatore* and *direttore* at La Scala, preparing the way for the introduction of the modern figure of a conductor. In 1871 he was a member of the commission headed by Verdi for the reform of musical institutions.

La fidanzata di Lammermoor (dramma per musica, 2, P. Beltrami, after W. Scott), Padua, Nuovissimo, 24 Feb 1834, *I-Mr*, excerpts, pf acc. (Milan, 1836)
Don Chisciotte (melodramma giocoso, 2, G. Crescini, after M. de Cervantes), Milan, Cannobiana, 26 April 1836, *Mr*, excerpts, pf acc. (Milan, 1836)

Esmeralda (dramma serio, 2, F. De Boni, after V. Hugo: *Notre-Dame de Paris*), Mantua, Sociale, 10 Feb 1838, *Mr**, vs (Milan, 1838)

Coro dei penitenti (incidental music, A. Somma: *Parisina*), Trieste, Filodrammatico, 6 July 1838

I corsari (melodramma semiserio, 2, F. Romani), Milan, Scala, 15 Feb 1840, *Mr**, excerpts, pf acc. (Milan, 1840)

I due sergenti (melodramma, 2, Romani: *Chiara e Serafina*), Milan, Re, 27 Feb 1841, *Mr**, vs (Milan, 1841)

Luigi V, re di Francia (os, 3, Romani), Milan, Re, 25 Feb 1843, excerpts, pf acc. (Milan, n.d.); rev. in 4 pts, Scala 26 Dec 1852

Hernani (dramma serio, 2, D. Bancalari, after Hugo), Genoa, Carlo Felice, 26 Dec 1843

Alberico da Romano (dramma serio, 2, C. Berti), Padua, Nuovo, aut. 1847

Fede, unperf.

Music in: *La vergine di Kermo* (1870)   ANDREA LANZA

Meader, George (*b* Minneapolis, 6 July 1888; *d* Hollywood, CA, 19 Dec 1963). American tenor. While studying law at Minnesota, he studied singing with Anna Schoen-René, whom he accompanied to Germany after graduating. He later studied with Pauline Viardot in Paris and made his début in Leipzig in 1911 as the Steersman in *Der fliegende Holländer*. A year later he joined the Stuttgart Opera, where he created Scaramuccio in *Ariadne auf Naxos* (1912). In 1919 he returned to the USA, making his début at the Metropolitan as Victorin in Korngold's *Die tote Stadt* in 1921, later singing David (*Meistersinger*), Mime, Vašek and Ferrando in the company's first *Così fan tutte*. In 1931 he left to sing in Kern's *The Cat and the Fiddle* and other light operas and musicals on Broadway, then went to Hollywood, where he taught singing and took character parts in several films. Meader's voice was limited in power but of an ingratiating quality, and he used it with consummate art. Because of his slight build, he was best suited to character roles; many of his portrayals were considered among the greatest of his time.   PHILIP LIESON MILLER

Meale, Richard (Graham) (*b* Sydney, 23 Aug 1932). Australian composer. He is considered a dominant figure in Australian music, with a reputation both local and international. Although he attended the NSW State Conservatorium of Music for nearly nine years until 1955 and became a virtuoso pianist, he neither studied composition nor graduated. However, he studied ethnomusicology at the University of California, Los Angeles, and was later an observer at the Juilliard School, at the San Francisco Conservatory and at the University of California, Berkeley. For two years he was a record buyer for a Sydney department store. After working for the ABC (1962–9) he was appointed a lecturer at the Elder Conservatorium of Music, University of Adelaide, in 1969 (senior lecturer, 1972; reader, 1978).

For long the acknowledged pace-setter in Australian music, Meale made a public declaration of independence from the modern music establishment in 1980 at the time of the première of his Second String Quartet at the Adelaide Festival and the commissioning of *Voss* by the Australian Opera. Once before, in 1960, he had retreated into silence and reappraisal, withdrawing all former compositions and disowning the influence of Bax, Bartók and Stravinsky in favour of Boulez and Stockhausen. During the next 20 years he built a formidable reputation with music based on the structural premises of the very modernists he declared outmoded in 1980. With *Voss*, an opera in two acts and an epilogue to a libretto by David Malouf after Patrick White's novel (Adelaide, Festival Centre, 1 March 1986), he did a complete about-face, espousing melodic shapes, rhythmic structures and forms reminiscent of the romantics. A highly accessible opera on a complex theme, which speaks deeply to the Australian experience – man against the elements which prove to be as much internal as external – *Voss* has entered the repertory of the Australian Opera, a rare distinction.

See also VOSS.

E. Wood: 'Richard Meale', *Australian Composition in the 20th Century*, ed. F. Callaway and D. Tunley (Melbourne, 1978), 159–72

R. Covell: 'Richard Meale: Intuitions of a Solitary Modernist', *Sounds Australian* (1988), no.20, pp.5–9   THÉRÈSE RADIC

Mechem, Kirke (*b* Wichita, KS, 16 Aug 1925). American composer. After receiving degrees from Stanford and Harvard universities, where he studied with Walter Piston and Randall Thompson, Mechem spent three years in Vienna refining his compositional skills. A composer of more than 150 works in nearly all genres, Mechem is particularly renowned for his choral works. His musical style, characterized by melodiousness, lyricism, tonal clarity, wit and humour, is free of any specific compositional school.

Mechem's first opera, *Tartuffe*, is a three-act comic opera set to a libretto by the composer after the Molière play. Cast in traditional operatic forms and exuding a lighthearted, Falstaffian spirit, *Tartuffe* shows strong melodic and orchestral invention, skilled ensemble writing and text setting, and clearly drawn characterizations; it abounds in musical jokes, parody, caricature, satire and puns. First performed on 27 May 1980 by the San Francisco Opera's American Opera Project, conducted by David Agler and directed by Nancy Rhodes, *Tartuffe* became, in its first decade, one of the most frequently performed full-length American operas.

Mechem's second opera, *John Brown*, a highly dramatic, three-act historical epic, also to a libretto by the composer, was completed in 1989. It traces the career of the 19th-century white abolitionist John Brown, whose execution helped bring about the American Civil War and, ultimately, the end of slavery. To help re-create the era musically, spirituals and other American folk elements are employed.

Occasionally staged as a one-act opera is Mechem's dramatic cantata *The King's Contest* (1962; rev. 1974), for mixed chorus and four soloists, based on a text from the Old Testament Apocrypha.

K. Mechem: 'An American Opera Network', *Perspectives: Creating and Producing Contemporary Opera and Music Theater* (New York, 1983)

R. H. Kornick: *Recent American Opera: a Production Guide* (New York, 1991), 186–7   MARY LOU HUMPHREY

Měchura [Miechura], Leopold Eugen (*b* Prague, 2 Feb 1804; *d* Votín, nr Klatovy, 11 Feb 1870). Bohemian composer. He was a lawyer by profession, and studied music with Tomášek and B. D. Weber. Almost the whole of his life was spent in the countryside of southern Bohemia. His orientation was towards German culture, and until he was 60 he composed music only to German texts, but he was on good terms with the Czechs (in 1827 he became the brother-in-law of the renowned historian František Palacký) and during the last years of his life also set Czech texts. He was interested in Wagner, but his music is more obviously influenced by Weber, Mendelssohn and Bellini. His operas bear traces of insufficient experience of an orchestra and the theatre. His first stage work, the romantic fairy opera *Hiorba*, remained unfinished; its one completed act contains noteworthy passages of melodrama for the witch Hiorba. In 1845 Měchura's three-act knightly opera *Der Schild* modelled on Weber's *Euryanthe*, was performed privately at Klatovy. Ebert tried to get it performed at the Munich conservatory, but Měchura rejected the idea. In 1869 he wrote a three-act opera in Czech, *Marie Potocká*, to a libretto based on a poem by Pushkin; it was the first Czech opera on a Russian subject and was given an unsuccessful première in Prague, conducted by Smetana.

Hiorba op.21, 1837 (J. Ritter von Rittersberg, after F. C. van der Veld), inc., unperf., *CS-Pnm**
Der Schild (3, K. E. Ebert), Klatovy, 1845 (private perf.), vs *Pnm**; rev. 1850
Marie Potocká, 1869 (3, J. Kolář, after A. S. Pushkin: *The Fountain of Bakchisarai*), Prague, Provisional, 13 Jan 1871, *Pnm*

M. Očadlík: 'Opery L. E. Měchury', *Sborník prací k padesátým narozeninám Profesora Dra Zdeňka Nejedlého* (Prague, 1928), 129–60
A. Smolák: *Leopold Evžen Měchura* (Klatovy, 1939), 26–7, 34, 36–41, 52–75
JITKA LUDVOVÁ

***Medea* (i).** Melodrama in one act by Georg Benda (*see* BENDA family, (1)) to a text by FRIEDRICH WILHELM GOTTER; Leipzig, Theater am Rannstädter Tor, 1 May 1775.

Medea owes its existence to Sophie Seyler's jealousy over the triumph of her rival Charlotte Brandes in Benda's first melodrama, *Ariadne auf Naxos*. Wieland's *Teutscher Merkur* praised *Medea* as Gotter's 'dramatic masterpiece' in its structure and 'sublime simplicity' of language. Medea reflects on her lost happiness and prays to Juno for revenge. The sight of Jason with his new bride Kreusa [Creusa] inflames her jealousy and she determines to murder the children she bore him. Her resolve melts in a first attempt, but after invoking a storm from Hecate she succeeds. From her cloud-chariot she taunts an anguished Jason, who falls on his own sword.

With *Medea* Benda brought the nascent German melodrama to perfection. Less dependent on obbligato recitative, it explores a broader emotional palette than *Ariadne* and uses recurring motifs more pervasively and to greater effect; the shape is stronger owing to march episodes and aria-like sections (including dal segno indications), all without sacrifice of dramatic momentum. Passages of simultaneous declamation and music are more abundant, a technique that for Mozart, who saw Sophie Seyler perform *Medea* in Mannheim in 1778, made 'the most splendid effect' (letter of 12 November).
THOMAS BAUMAN

***Medea* (ii).** *Melodramma tragico* in three acts by GIOVANNI PACINI to a libretto by Benedetto Castiglia; Palermo, Real Teatro Carolino, 28 November 1843; revised, Vicenza, Teatro Eretenio, 1845.

In Castiglia's version of the myth, Medea (soprano), exiled for betraying her father and killing her brother, has disguised herself as Creusa to everyone but her husband Giasone [Jason] (tenor). When she discovers that Jason will soon marry Glauce (soprano), daughter of King Creon (bass), she demands without success that Creon prevent Jason's remarriage for the sake of his

children, whom she is now raising under her new identity. Calcante [Calchas] (bass) and the other priests plan to annul Jason's marriage to Medea, but she interrupts their ceremony, forcing Jason to reveal her true identity and causing her children to be taken from her. Later, by agreeing to immediate exile, she tricks Creon and Jason into returning them. Amid preparations for Jason's wedding to Glauce, she avenges herself by killing the children, his bride-to-be and herself.

In his memoirs Pacini recalled that he had been tremendously moved by the story, which excited both 'loathing and compassion' for the title character. Initially he had hesitated to set again a subject which had already been successfully treated by Cherubini, Mayr and 'other great geniuses', but was inspired by their example to complete the project. Although his audience was apparently bewildered by the opera at the première, after its second performance it was acclaimed as Pacini's best work to date. Thus it capped a triumphant year-long visit to Palermo during which a statue of the composer was erected alongside one of Bellini. In its music *Medea* represents a partial retreat from the innovations of *Saffo* (1840). Nonetheless, it contains many moments of great intensity, notably in Medea's duet with Jason, the concertato finale of Act 2 and the slow movement of the heroine's aria finale in Act 3.
SCOTT L. BALTHAZAR

Medea in Corinto ('Medea in Corinth'). *Melodramma tragico* in two acts by SIMON MAYR to a libretto by FELICE ROMANI after EURIPIDES; Naples, Teatro S Carlo, 28 November 1813.

Medea was the first opera that Mayr composed for Naples following a long string of successes in such north Italian centres as Venice and Milan. During the previous year he had paved the way with productions at the Teatro del Fondo of four of his earlier operas – *Che originali*, *Elisa*, *La roccia di Frauenstein* and *Amor non ha ritengo*. He was to follow *Medea* with three other Neapolitan operas – *Elena* (1814), *La figlia dell'aria* and *Amor avvocato* (both 1817) – none of which would equal the success of *Medea*, which marked the high point of Mayr's efforts at conquering this southern operatic stronghold.

Mayr apparently began composing *Medea* while still at his home in Bergamo. Upon arriving in Naples in September he was surprised to find that the director of the theatre insisted on an opera in the French style, with orchestrally accompanied recitatives. Consequently the text had to be shortened hurriedly by a local poet, and the recitatives which Mayr had already scored for continuo needed to be rewritten. According to evidence cited by Ludwig Schiedermair, Mayr may also have had to adjust the part of Jason from a mezzo-soprano to a tenor role.

Mayr's librettist, Felice Romani, had made his début earlier in the same year with another opera for Mayr, *La rosa bianca e la rosa rossa*. In the new opera he treated Euripides' version of the myth with a freedom characteristic of the period. In the first act Medea (soprano), a sorceress who has killed her brother and betrayed her father to obtain the Golden Fleece for her husband Giasone [Jason] (tenor), is to be exiled as the price of peace between her king, Creonte [Creon] (bass), and his enemy Acasto, although her two children are to be left with Jason. Her troubles multiply when she learns that Jason loves Creon's daughter, Creusa (soprano), and intends to dissolve their marriage so that

'Medea in Corinto' (Simon Mayr): Giuditta Pasta as Medea and Alberico Curioni as Jason in Act 1 of the first London production at the King's Theatre, 1 June 1826; lithograph by John Hayter

1826) and Milan (1829), probably in one of the early Neapolitan versions.

Mayr's score contains many noteworthy numbers. Among them Medea's and Jason's first confrontation in their Act 1 duet, 'Cedi al destin Medea', reveals Mayr's talent, seldom acknowledged by his critics, for writing beautiful and impassioned melodies at appropriate moments. Medea's *gran scena e scongiura* in Act 2, 'Antica notte, Tartaro profondo', makes the most of Mayr's emotionally vivid musical language by carrying the free arioso style of the initial recitative into the lyric text of the sorceress's incantation. Jason's aria in the same act, 'Amor per te penai', like many of Mayr's arias, anticipates the infusion of action into the later *tempo di mezzo* by having the chorus announce Creusa's death in an extended middle movement set in *parlante* and *declamato* textures. And Medea's final scena and aria, 'Ah! che tento! ... Oh figli miei!', is but one example of the range of moods that Mayr was capable of evoking through his rich harmonic vocabulary, his responsive orchestration and his flexible melodic style. According to Gossett, manuscript sources for *Medea* (though not the Parisian vocal score) show consistently that Mayr connected most of the opera's lyric numbers to the following recitatives with very short modulatory passages, making the music largely continuous within acts. Thus *Medea* foreshadows later efforts by such composers as Mercadante, Donizetti and Verdi at better integrating large-scale operatic structure.

SCOTT L. BALTHAZAR

Médecin malgré lui, Le ('The Doctor Despite Himself'). *Opéra comique* in three acts by CHARLES-FRANÇOIS GOUNOD to a libretto by JULES BARBIER and MICHEL CARRÉ after MOLIÈRE's play; Paris, Théâtre Lyrique, 15 January 1858.

The woodcutter Sganarelle (baritone), mistaken for a doctor, is recruited to cure Lucinde (soprano), daughter of the wealthy Géronte (bass), of her inability to speak. Lucinde's lover, the impoverished Léandre (tenor), soon explains to Sganarelle that Lucinde has feigned dumbness merely in order to avoid an undesirable marriage to another. Sganarelle makes Léandre his apothecary so that Léandre may gain entry into Géronte's house and arrange an elopement with his beloved. The two are successful. Géronte's anger is subdued at the conclusion when Léandre explains that he is the beneficiary of a large inheritance from an uncle.

Gounod received the commission for *Le médecin* at the beginning of 1857 from Léon Carvalho, director of the Théâtre Lyrique, to make up for a postponement of the *Faust* première. Because Molière's prose is used for all of the spoken dialogue and the verse set to music is also based closely on the play, the Comédie-Française tried unsuccessfully to block performance of the work. Vocal highlights include Sganarelle's Act 1 *couplets*, 'Qu'ils sont doux', and Léandre's serenade, 'Est-on sage dans le bel âge?'. Gounod shows a real talent for comedy in *Le médecin*; although it has been sporadically revived in France as well as England and Germany, alone among his lesser-known operas it deserves more performances than it has received. STEVEN HUEBNER

he can marry the princess. Creusa herself has broken her betrothal to Egeo [Aegeus] (tenor), King of Athens, who arrives in Corinth unexpectedly, prior to her wedding to Jason. In the finale of Act 1 the wedding ceremony is disrupted when Medea bursts in and, invoking the Furies, overturns the altar, while Aegeus has his men abduct Creusa.

Subsequently Jason's and Creon's men defeat Aegeus and rescue Creusa. At the beginning of Act 2 Aegeus has been imprisoned, awaiting punishment by Creon, while Jason has been left to decide Medea's fate. Before he can act she sets about her revenge, enlisting the Furies to poison a jewelled robe to be given to Creusa. Feigning repentance, she persuades Creusa to accept the gift and enlists her help in recovering her children. She also uses her magic to free Aegeus, so that he can return to Athens and eventually provide asylum for her. Having killed Creusa, Medea turns the Corinthians against Jason by blaming him for the princess's death. When she reveals that she has murdered her children, the crowd must restrain Jason from committing suicide, while she escapes by flying off in a chariot drawn by dragons.

Medea was a huge success at its première. The leading roles were performed by important singers whose status in Naples continued throughout the next decade: Isabella Colbran (later Rossini's first wife) created the role of Medea, Andrea Nozzari played Jason and Manuel García played Aegeus. A revival, for which Mayr made minor changes, apparently tailoring parts to new singers, was mounted in summer 1814. The composer revised the score more thoroughly for a later revival at La Scala in 1823, at which Teresa Belloc-Giorgi sang the role of Medea, 'modernizing' it by providing true cabalettas for the arias and replacing the short detached phrases of his earlier melodies with more expansive lyrical periods. *Medea* enjoyed continued attention in the 1820s as a vehicle for Giuditta Pasta, who performed the opera in Paris (1823), London (from

Médée (i) ('Medea'). *Tragédie mise en musique* in a prologue and five acts by MARC-ANTOINE CHARPENTIER to a libretto by THOMAS CORNEILLE; Paris, Opéra, 4 December 1693.

Medea *princess of Colchis*	soprano
Nérine *her confidante*	soprano
Jason *prince of Thessaly*	haute-contre
Arcas *confidant to Jason*	tenor
Créon [Creon] *King of Corinth*	bass
Oronte *prince of Argos*	baritone
Créuse [Creusa] *daughter of Creon*	soprano
Cléone *confidante to Creusa*	soprano

Corinthians, Argians, Love's captives, demons, phantoms

Setting Corinth in antiquity

Médée, Charpentier's only work for the Académie Royale de Musique, was perhaps the most important opera produced there in the decade after the death of Lully. Sébastien de Brossard considered it 'the one opera without exception in which one can learn the things most essential to good composition'. Campra later included portions of the music in his pastiche opera *Télémaque*. Louis XIV personally complimented Charpentier on the work, and the king's brother and his eldest son attended several performances. The *Mercure galant* favourably mentioned the Italian songs (2.vii) and praised in particular the performance of Marthe Le Rochois in the title role:

The passions are so vivid, particularly in Medea, that when this role was but declaimed it did not fail to make a great impression on the listeners. Judge for yourself if, having given rise to beautiful music, Mlle Rochois, one of the best singers in the world and who performs with warmth, finesse and intelligence, shone in this role and made the most of its beauties. All of Paris is enchanted with the way that this excellent singer performs Medea, and one cannot fail to admire her.

Creusa was sung by Mlle Moreau, Creon by Dun and Jason by Du Mesny, and Jean Bérain designed the scenery and costumes. While Titon du Tillet and others proclaimed *Médée* a critical success, Brossard pointed out that it was not successful with the public. The *Journal de l'Opéra* lists no performances after 15 March 1694, but it was revived at Lille on 17 November 1700.

In the prologue rustics and shepherds praise Louis XIV. They summon to earth La Victoire [Victory], Bellone, goddess of war, and La Gloire [Glory] (all sopranos). Victory, who has long lived in France, will not favour those who envy Louis' fame: they seek to prolong war, while Louis wishes to bring peace to his kingdom.

ACT 1 *A public place* The sorceress Medea has gained Jason's love in return for help in obtaining the golden fleece; they scheme to have King Pelias of Thessaly murdered, and when they are discovered they flee to Corinth. When the act begins Medea complains that Jason now loves the princess Creusa who is betrothed to Oronte, prince of Argos. She needs the protection of Oronte and King Creon of Corinth to fend off the impending attack by Thessaly. She reveals her dreadful revenge should Creusa steal Jason's heart. Jason tells Medea that their children are safe in the care of Creusa. In return, Medea agrees to give her superb robe to the princess. Jason, alone with Arcas, weighs his debt to Medea against his love for Creusa. A fanfare heralds Oronte's arrival. The Corinthian and Argian soldiers enact in song and dance their battle with the Thessalians.

ACT 2 *A vestibule* Creon tells Medea he will fight her enemies, but she must be banished. Medea sadly relinquishes her children into Creusa's care. Once she is gone, Creon plans to keep both Jason and Oronte near to defend his kingdom by means of their love for Creusa. Jason and Creusa sing a love duet; they are joined by Oronte, and a chorus of Love's captives sings of the pains and pleasures of love.

'Médée' (M.-A. Charpentier), Act 3 scene v: design by Jean Berain for the original production at the Paris Opéra (Académie Royale de Musique), 4 December 1693

ACT 3 *A place set aside for Medea's evocations* Oronte offers asylum in Argos to Medea and Jason, but Medea tells him of Jason's love for Creusa. Medea and Oronte together vow revenge and Jason reassures Medea that he will join her after the battle. In a grand monologue Medea laments her unjust fate. When Creon decrees the marriage of Creusa and Jason, Medea prepares a poison with which to saturate Creusa's robe.

ACT 4 *A palace with a magnificent garden* Medea and Oronte plot their revenge. Creon arrives to confront Medea, who uses her sorcery to summon madness. Left alone, Creon is overwhelmed by delusions.

ACT 5 *Medea's palace* Creusa begs Medea to return Creon's reason, but a chorus of Corinthians announces that Creon has murdered Oronte and then turned his sword upon himself. Creusa vows revenge on Medea, but Medea activates the poison contained within her robe and she dies in Jason's arms. Medea then reveals the full extent of her vengeance: she has murdered their children.

* * *

Corneille's libretto presents a complicated love quadrangle between Medea, Jason, Glauce and Oronte which, together with a struggle between Corinth and Thessaly, slows the opera's pace for the first three acts. But when Medea begins her holocaust of revenge the dramatic tension intensifies. Especially striking is Charpentier's depth of musical characterization in the monologues of Medea, which run the gamut of passions from seething rage (1.i) to motherly love (2.ii), lamentation (3.iii), vengeance (3.iv and 4.v) and horror at her own actions (5.i). Corneille's libretto includes stock situations common to both French and Italian opera of the time, such as Creon's mad scene (4.ix) and Medea's incantation scene (3.v), alongside elements of the *ballet de cour*: the *divertissement* of Love's captives (2.vii) and the choruses and dances of the demons and furies (3.v–vii). Charpentier's music is a virtual compendium of instrumental and vocal forms (overture, *passacaille*, chaconne, recitative, arioso, *air*, lament, ensemble and chorus), and the attention he devotes to details of instrumentation, tempo and dynamics could serve as a guide to 17th-century orchestration.   JOHN S. POWELL

Médée (ii) ('Medea'). *Opéra comique* in three acts by LUIGI CHERUBINI to a libretto by FRANÇOIS-BENOÎT HOFFMAN; Paris, Théâtre Feydeau, 13 March 1797.

Jason *leader of the Argonauts*	tenor
Médée [Medea] *his wife*	soprano
Néris [Neris] *her confidante*	mezzo-soprano
Créon [Creon] *King of Corinth*	bass
Dircé [Dirce] *his daughter*	soprano
First attendant	soprano
Second attendant	mezzo-soprano

Dirce's attendants, Argonauts, Corinthian citizens

Setting Creon's palace and its surroundings in Corinth, in mythological ancient Greece

---

At the première the title role was sung by Julie-Angélique Scio, who was acclaimed for her interpretations of difficult declamatory parts and whose early death from tuberculosis was attributed to excessive vocal gymnastics in roles such as Medea. The first Jason

was Pierre Gaveaux, also a renowned composer of *opéras comiques*. Although it received critical approval, *Médée* enjoyed only a *succès d'estime*, disappearing after 20 performances. Paris did not see another production until the mid-20th century. However, the Germans were taken with the work, performing it on numerous occasions throughout the 19th century. Margarete Schick was Medea in the first Berlin production (17 April 1800), for which the *Allgemeine musikalische Zeitung* published an extensive analysis; it was still being performed there in 1880. Franz Paul Lachner set the spoken dialogue to Wagnerian-style recitative in 1854 for a production in Frankfurt in 1855. This became the opera's standard form until the 1980s. *Médée* was introduced to Vienna in 1803, and it would appear that performances there in 1809 were the occasion for Cherubini to make extensive cuts of about 500 bars which were incorporated into a published edition of the period. It was revived again in 1812 for Anna Milder-Hauptmann and was still in repertory in 1871.

The opera's destiny in England and Italy was less fortunate. It was presented in London at Her Majesty's Theatre, Haymarket, on 6 June 1865 with Thérèse Tietjens in the title role and recitatives by Luigi Arditi. It was repeated on 30 December 1870 at Covent Garden. In Italy, it was not staged until 30 December 1909 at La Scala, in a translation by Carlo Zangarini; the edited score remained the standard Italian version until the 1980s. The reception was lukewarm, and there were no further performances until the 16th Maggio Musicale Fiorentino in 1952, when Maria Callas sang the title role and ensured the opera's renewed success in the 20th century. The original French version, with reduced spoken dialogue, was given at the Buxton Festival on 28 July 1984 and at Covent Garden on 6 November 1989.

ACT 1 *A gallery in Creon's palace* Dirce's attendants are trying to assure her that she is right to marry Jason. Finally convinced, Dirce calls on Hymen to bless the forthcoming union ('Hymen, viens dissiper une vaine frayeur'). Creon promises Jason protection for his sons and Jason begs Dirce to accept the Argonauts' gifts. The March of the Argonauts follows, but the sight of the Golden Fleece brings back Dirce's earlier forebodings. Rather than stop the music at the end of the march, Cherubini maintains the scene's momentum by having Dirce and Jason sing their first words concerning the fleece to musical accompaniment. Jason tries to calm Dirce by stating that Medea is probably dead. Creon incites her to have faith in the gods' generosity, and everyone invokes Hymen to bless the marriage in a hymnlike chorus. A stranger is announced and, entering, reveals herself to be Medea. She claims Jason but incurs the wrath of Creon, who orders her to depart. The act ends with a prolonged duet between Jason and Medea in which Medea alternately cajoles and threatens in an effort to persuade Jason to return to her ('Vous voyez de vos fils la mère infortunée'). Jason refuses, and both deplore the influence of the Golden Fleece on their lives ('O fatale Toison'). This scene is set almost entirely to music which closely follows the emotions of the participants, contributing to a profound understanding of their characters and motivation.

ACT 2 *A wing of Creon's palace* After a short orchestral introduction the enraged Medea enters cursing Jason for preventing her from seeing her children. She summons the deities of Hades to help her wreak

Title-page of the full score of Cherubini's 'Médée' (Paris: Imbault, 1797), showing a scene from Act 3

vengeance as Neris runs in, imploring her to hide from Creon's wrath. Medea, however, confronts him, pleading with him, in the first vocal music of the act, to allow her one day's respite to take leave of her children ('Ah! du moins à Médée accordez un azile'). In an extended ensemble in which the music faithfully mirrors everyone's passions, Creon, after much hesitation, grants Medea's wish. Medea lost in contemplation, Neris laments the fate of her mistress ('Ah! nos peines seront communes'). Medea revives to plot her revenge. Jason reveals his affection for their sons. She begs to see them one last time ('Chers enfants'), to which Jason agrees as he leaves for pre-marriage ceremonies in the temple. Medea instructs Neris to have her children give a poisoned robe, crown and jewels as presents to Dirce. The curtain descends as the prayerful strains of the off-stage ceremony to Hymen ('Fils de Bacchus descend des cieux') are punctuated by the onstage mutterings of Medea's vengeance.

ACT 3 *A meadow in front of the temple* The final act is preceded by an orchestral interlude depicting the storm raging both in nature and in Medea's heart. She invokes the help of the gods as Neris enters with the children. Except for the dialogue concerning Dirce's acceptance of the gifts, the rest of the action is set to music of a forcefulness unheard of at this period. After Neris leaves, Medea curses her maternal weakness ('Eh quoi, je suis Médée') and, under cover of cries from the palace, where Dirce is consumed by the flames of the presents, drags the children into the temple to murder them. Jason rushes in with the people of Corinth but too late. Medea, wielding her knife and surrounded by the three Eumenides, appears in the temple doorway. She prophesies that Jason will wander homeless for the rest of his life and will meet her in Hades. As she rises into

the air, the temple bursts into flames and the people, terror-stricken, flee as the curtain falls.

* * *

In its unmitigated horror, this opera has few equals. Its savage fury ties it closely to its Greek ancestry. Hoffman took one sentiment, revenge, and one action, murder, and expanded them into three hours of unrestrained emotion such as the French lyric stage had never seen. He provided excellent characterizations with which Cherubini could work, portraying the two principal characters in depth. Because of the spoken dialogue, *Médée* is classed as an *opéra comique*, although the first edition labels it simply *opéra*. There are no comic interludes, and most of the musical numbers are ensembles (nine, to three arias). In fact, the music of *Médée* gave way to mid-19th-century French and German grand opera, and not until Bizet's *Carmen* did it find a successor in style and form. As Brahms said: 'This *Médée* is the work we musicians recognize among ourselves as the highest peak of dramatic music.'

STEPHEN C. WILLIS

Médée et Jason ('Medea and Jason'). *Tragédie en musique* in a prologue and five acts by JOSEPH-FRANÇOIS SALOMON to a libretto by SIMON-JOSEPH PELLEGRIN after OVID's *Metamorphoses*, book 7; Paris, Opéra, 24 April 1713.

Médée et Jason, although a conventional *tragédie en musique* in most respects, offers an unusual conclusion in which good does not triumph over evil; rather the opera ends with the deaths of two innocents. Salomon's score, too, reflects the changing character of the *tragédie en musique* during the early decades of the 18th century. Although there are no fully fledged *ariettes*, the vocal writing is italianate in style, particularly in the *airs* of the *divertissement* scenes. Further, a number of orchestral *symphonies*, designed to link successive scenes, are vividly descriptive and dramatically effective.

Médée et Jason merited four revivals in all: in 1713 (with significant alteration to the original), 1727, 1736 and 1749. On the occasions of the 1727 and 1736 revivals, parodies of the opera were created by the Comédie-Italienne.

LESLIE ELLEN BROWN

Medek, Tilo (*b* Jena, 22 Jan 1940). German composer. The son of the composer and chamber musician Willy Müller-Medek (1897–1965), he studied musicology with Walther Vetter, E. H. Meyer and Georg Knepler at the University of Berlin (1959–64). He also studied composition with Rudolf Wagner-Régeny (1963–9) at the Hochschule für Musik in Berlin, and was Wagner-Régeny's leading pupil at the Akademie der Künste (1964–7). In 1977 he lost his East German citizenship and subsequently moved to the Federal Republic of Germany, where he received many international distinctions.

Medek's work embraces many musical genres, from chamber music to choral works for large vocal ensembles. Apart from an early phase (1962–6) during which he was influenced by dodecaphonic styles, his music has been determined by tonal elements. Medek has frequently distanced himself from the avant garde, associating himself with the school of the 'new tonality'. His music is distinguished by an individual style that aims at intelligibility and sets out to create a close relationship with the audience. Medek has called himself a 'narrative composer'; he has devoted himself to opera since 1969, specializing in chamber opera: *Icke und die Hexe Yu* has a cast of three, and *Appetit auf Frühkirschen* only two. He has also written an operatic scene for children, *Gritzko und der Pan* (1987), a ballet (*David und Goliath*, 1972) and many scores for the theatre, cinema and television.

His most important dramatic work, composed between 1984 and 1986, is the full-length *Katharina Blum*, for large cast and orchestra. Dorothea Medek, the composer's wife, wrote the libretto, adapting Heinrich Böll's novella *Die verlorene Ehre der Katharina Blum*, published in 1974. The librettist concentrates the action into five acts or 'days'; Böll's primarily political and moral intentions move on a more personal plane in the opera. *Katharina Blum* is a 'crime opera' telling of a woman who remains faithful to the terrorist Ludwig Götten (baritone) after a single meeting with him, although a popular newspaper mounts a smear campaign against her. The simple domestic servant Katharina (mezzo-soprano) can defend herself only by shooting the journalist Tötges (baritone) who has slandered her. Through her personal tragedy, the heroine rises above the heated political climate, and the various reactions of those around her are a major component of the action.

Medek sets the material with intentional reference to German opera of the 1920s, writing in a stylized, indeed a 'gestural', manner. An important feature is a hurried ostinato, impelling the action onward with insistent staccatos, its repeated appearances varied by the instrumentation. The music of *Katharina Blum* is reminiscent of 1920s cinema, and the separate scenes are linked by preludes or postludes suggesting 'fade-ins' and 'fade-outs'. The choruses of newspaper readers might be seen as part of this fade-out technique; they represent the power of manipulated public opinion, a variant of the chorus in Greek tragedy. Several 'arias' stand out from the breakneck haste of the action, although they are still integral components of the drama, which is conceived as an opera of separate numbers. As outbursts of human feeling or memories (for example, Katharina's 'rain aria'), they counterbalance the chorus of newspaper readers and the social consensus it propagates.

Einzug (Kurzoper, Medek, after I. Babel), Potsdam, Hans-Otto-Theater, 11 Oct 1969

Icke und die Hexe Yu (Spl, M. Streubel), broadcast, Berliner Welle, 30 March 1971; stage, Dresden, Staatsoperette, 1 Dec 1971

Appetit auf Frühkirschen (Spl, A. Osiecka, after S. Kirsch), Potsdam, Hans-Otto-Theater, 27 Jan 1972

Katharina Blum, 1984–6 (5, epilogue, D. Medek, after H. Böll: *Die verlorene Ehre der Katharina Blum*) Bielefeld, Bühnen der Stadt, 20 April 1991 [in Eng. version by R. Maxym]

Gritzko und der Pan (operatic scene for children, D. Medek, after a Ukrainian folktale), Berlin, Musikschule Neukölln, 1987

*

F. K. Prieberg: *Musik im anderen Deutschland* (Cologne, 1968)

U. Stürzbecher: *Komponisten in der DDR: 17 Gespräche* (Hildesheim, 1979)

Tilo Medek: eine Dokumentation, ed. Musikbücherei der Stadt Düsseldorf (Düsseldorf, 1980)

F. Reinighaus: 'Tilo Medek ("Man muss wissen, was man schreibt, wofür und wann")' *NZM*, Jg.145, no.3, (1984), 20–24

C. F. Schröer: 'Der Komponist und seine Böll-Oper "Katharina Blum"', *Rheinischer Merkur* (18 Sept 1987)

REINHARD ERMEN

Meder, Johann Valentin (*b* Wasungen, nr Meiningen, bap. 3 May 1649; *d* Riga, end of July 1719). German composer. Born into a musical family, he studied theology but soon became a professional singer, holding court posts at Gotha (1671), Bremen (1672–3), Hamburg (1673), Copenhagen and Lübeck (1674). From 1674 to 1680 he was Kantor at the gymnasium at Reval (now Tallinn). After a sojourn in Riga in 1685–6 he became Kapellmeister at Marienkirche, Danzig, in 1687. In 1698 Danzig city council refused to allow a performance of his opera *Die wiederverehligte Coelia*. He had it performed instead in the neighbouring town of Schottland, which led to his being dismissed from his post. After briefly being employed as Kantor at the cathedral at Königsberg, he went in 1700 to Riga, where he held a similar position until his death.

According to Mattheson, Meder was a singer of repute, an excellent organist and a notable composer. He knew Italian in his youth and was familiar with the music of Italian composers such as Carissimi and Cesti. As a composer of sacred music Meder shows to some extent the influence of Buxtehude. Of four stage works he is known to have written (including an *opéra-ballet*, *Die befreyete Andromeda*, 1688), only the opera *Die beständige Argenia* survives (*S-Sk*; ed. in EDM, 1st ser., lxviii (1973)), performed in Reval in 1680 by the students of the gymnasium. Dedicated to the newly married Swedish king, Carl XI, and his queen, it reveals his skilful handling of recitative and arioso and of strophic songs, which predominate over larger forms such as the through-composed aria. His *Nero* was the first German opera to be performed in Danzig, in November 1695; it was indebted to N. A. Strungk's opera of the same name (1693), for he used not only the same text (by G. C. Corradi, after C. Pallavicino) but also a few of Strungk's arias.

*

J. Mattheson: *Grundlage einer Ehren-Pforte* (Hamburg, 1740); ed. M. Schneider (Berlin, 1910)

J. Bolte: 'Johann Valentin Meder', *VMw*, vii (1891), 43–52

Å. Vretblad: 'Johann Valentin Meder och hans opera "Die beständige Argenia"', *STMf*, xix (1937), 65–79

C.-A. Moberg: 'Drag i Östersjöområdets musikliv på Buxtehudes tid' [Sketch of Musical Life in the Östersjö area in Buxtehude's Day], *STMf*, xxxix (1957), 15–88   ERIK KJELLBERG

Mederitsch(-Gallus), Johann (Georg Anton) (*b* Vienna, bap. 27 Dec 1752; *d* Lemberg [now L'viv], 18 Dec 1835). Austrian composer. After study with Wagenseil he became Kapellmeister of the Olmütz (Olomouc) theatre (1781–2), then returned to Vienna, where he was a double bass player in the orchestra of the German theatre as late as 1792. His years in Vienna saw the successful production of a number of Singspiels, and in about 1800 he was piano teacher to the poet Grillparzer, then nine years old. He was Kapellmeister at Ofen (Buda), 1793–4, possibly until 1796, and in 1798, and from 1817 he lived at Lemberg. The poverty and sadness of Mederitsch's old age were touchingly described in a letter to Moscheles from Mozart's son, written on 25 October 1827; his summary of Mederitsch ('perhaps the greatest contrapuntist of our age') may be set against his father's frivolous comments (letter of 5 February 1783). Mederitsch's gratitude to the younger Mozart is attested by his bequeathing to him the autograph scores of his works, some 80 in all, which after Mozart's death passed to the Mozarteum, Salzburg. Mederitsch was well known and respected in his day: his incidental music to *Macbeth* (1793–4, Pest; Vienna, Kärntnertor, 13 February 1808) was known even in London. However, he is now remembered mainly as the composer of Act 1 of *Babylons Pyramiden* (Act 2 was by Winter), one of the works in which

Schikaneder tried in vain to repeat the success of *Die Zauberflöte*.

first performed in Vienna unless otherwise stated

Der redliche Verwalter (J. F. Schmidt), Bauernfeindscher Saal, 26 Aug 1779

Arkatastor und Illiane (melodrama, F. Zawitzer), Bauernfeindscher Saal, 14 Oct 1779, lib. *A-Sm*

Der Schlosser, Olomouc, 1781

Rose, oder Pflicht und Liebe im Streit (Spl, 3, G. Stephanie the younger), Burg, 9 Feb 1783, *Sm**

Der letzte Rausch, ?1788 (2), 1795 [place of perf. unknown], *Sm*

Babylons Pyramiden [Act 1] (grosse heroisch-komische Oper, 2, E. Schikaneder), Weiden, 25 Oct 1797, *Sm**, vs (Vienna, 1797) [Act 2 by Winter]

Krakus, Fürst von Krakau, oder Frauengrosse und Vaterliebe (romantische Sage mit Chören, 5, J. Hirschfeld), Leopoldstadt, 30 March 1811

Die Heirat durch die Wiener Zeitung (Posse)

Doubtful: Der Seefahrer [Der grossmüthige Seefahrer] (after Ilein), Leopoldstadt, 14 Oct 1782; Die Rekruten, wobei Kasperl einen lustigen Bauernjungen und Rekruten spielt, Leopoldstadt, 6 Dec 1782

*

E. K. Blümml and G. Gugitz: *Alt-Wiener Thespiskarren: die Frühzeit der Wiener Vorstadtbühnen* (Vienna, 1925)

G. Gugitz: 'Der seltsame Herr Gallus-Mederitsch', *ÖMz*, vii/1 (1952), 15–22

W. Hummel: *W. A. Mozarts Söhne* (Kassel, 1956), 151ff, 332

F. Grillparzer: *Selbstbiographie*, Sämtliche Werke, iv (Munich, 1965), 15, 25, 30, 52–3

W. Binal: *Deutschsprachiges Theater in Budapest* (Vienna, 1972)

T. Aigner: *Johann Gallus Mederitsch (1752–1835): Leben und thematisches Verzeichnis der Werke* (diss., U. of Salzburg, 1973; thematic index, Wilhelming, 1974)   PETER BRANSCOMBE

Medici. Italian family of opera patrons, the ruling family of Florence. Their wealth and influence in the 15th-century Republic culminated in their being elevated to the status of dukes (after 1570, Grand Dukes) of Tuscany from 1532 until the extinction of the line in 1737. Cosimo I (ruled 1537–74), Francesco I (1574–87) and Ferdinando I (1587–1609) were adept rulers, ensuring the security of their state in difficult political and economic times. They used court entertainments adroitly, developing the *intermedi* as a potent symbol of Medici supremacy: those for the wedding of Ferdinando I and Christine of Lorraine in 1589 marked the pinnacle of the genre. Opera, however, was less suited to their tastes – although Peri's *Euridice* was performed for a Medici wedding in 1600, it was provided by a private individual, Jacopo Corsi – and in the 17th century the court generally preferred more spectacular forms of indoor and outdoor entertainment. The early death of Cosimo II (1609–21) and the regency before the reign of Ferdinando II (1621–70) marked a notable decline in the Medici's artistic interests save for political expediency. However, Medici princes, including Mattias (1613–67) and Giovanni Carlo (1611–63), remained patrons of Florentine academies. The latter, Cosimo II's second son, who became a cardinal in 1645, was protector of the Sorgenti academy, in the new Cocomero Theatre by 1654, and of the Immobili, whose theatre, the Pergola, was built at the cardinal's expense. As official guardian of Queen Christina of Sweden he attended performances of *Dal mal il bene* in 1656 and this may have led him to induce the Immobili to stage five comic operas in the period 1657–63 (music by Jacopo Melani and in one case Anglesi); the first, *Il potestà di Colognole*, inaugurated the Pergola. These works played a role in the establishment of the genre. In the reign of Cosimo III (1670–1723), Prince Ferdinando (1663–1713) re-established opera at the Cocomero,

promoted opera in other Tuscan cities (notably Livorno) and prepared the way for the reopening in 1717 of the Pergola. He also mounted operas almost yearly at his Pratolino villa, supervising productions, engaging his singers personally and corresponding with composers, librettists and others (the correspondence, in *I-Fas*, represents an important source for the study of Baroque opera practices). He at first favoured pastorals (the composers include Buonaventura Cerri and Alessandro Melani) and comic operas (Melani, Pagliardi, G. B. Benini, possibly A. Scarlatti) but turned in 1685 to serious operas (De Castris, Martino Bitti, Pagliardi, C. F. Pollarolo and especially Perti and Scarlatti).

*

A. Ademollo: *I primi fasti del teatro di via della Pergola (1657–1661)* (Milan, 1885)

R. Lustig: 'Per la cronistoria dell'antico teatro musicale: il teatro della Villa Medicea di Pratolino', *RMI*, xxxvi (1929), 259–66

H. Acton: *The Last Medici* (New York, 1958)

R. L. Weaver: *Florentine Comic Operas of the Seventeenth Century* (diss., U. of North Carolina, 1958)

M. Fabbri: *Alessandro Scarlatti e il Principe Ferdinando de' Medici* (Florence, 1961)

——: 'Nuova luce sull'attività fiorentina di Giacomo Antonio Perti, Bartolomeo Cristofori e Giorgio F. Haendel', *Chigiana*, xxi (1964), 143–90

R. Weaver: 'Opera in Florence: 1646–1731', *Studies in Musicology in Memory of Glen Haydon* (Chapel Hill, 1969), 60–71

E. Cochrane: *Florence in the Forgotten Centuries 1527–1800* (Chicago and London, 1973)

J. R. Hale: *Florence and the Medici: the Pattern of Control* (London, 1977)

R. L. Weaver and N. W. Weaver: *A Chronology of Music in the Florentine Theater 1590–1750* (Detroit, 1978)

TIM CARTER, ROBERT LAMAR WEAVER

Medici, I ('The Medici'). *Azione storica* in four acts by RUGGERO LEONCAVALLO to his own libretto; Milan, Teatro Dal Verme, 9 November 1893.

The opera covers the events between 1471, the year in which Sixtus V was elected pope, and 1478, when Lorenzo de' Medici (baritone) became Signore of Florence, having escaped assassination in the Pazzi conspiracy. Giuliano de' Medici (tenor) falls in love with Simonetta Cattanei (lyric soprano), who learns about the conspiracy and tries to warn Giuliano but is fatally wounded by Montesecco (bass), a murderer hired by the pope. The next day Giuliano is killed in S Reparata, but Lorenzo, with the help of the poet Poliziano (baritone), manages to escape and wins the support of the crowd, who lynch the conspirators.

In his plan to compose a trilogy of operas to be called *Crepusculum*, Leoncavallo sought to use the Italian Renaissance as a metaphor to illustrate the values of the Italian past. The other two parts of the trilogy, however, were never begun. Leoncavallo is free with the sequence of historical events, and borrows well-known operatic devices and settings, such as the septet in the third act, reminiscent of the inn scene in *Rigoletto*, and the flower given as a pledge of love (as in *La traviata*). In spite of the technical proficiency of the orchestration and the choral writing, the opera had little success, and never became part of the repertory.   MICHELE GIRARDI

Mediņš, Jānis (*b* Riga, 9 Oct 1890; *d* Stockholm, 4 March 1966). Latvian composer, brother of Jāzeps Mediņš. He graduated from the First Riga Musical Institute (piano, violin and cello) in 1909. From 1913 to 1915 he was a viola player and conductor at the Latvian Opera in Riga, later becoming opera conductor of the Latvian National Opera (1920–28) and chief conductor of the Latvian Radio SO and artistic director of Latvian Radio (1928–44). He also taught at the Latvian State Conservatory. From 1944 to 1948 he lived in Germany, then in Stockholm.

A composer of characteristically national neo-Romantic tendency, Mediņš achieved particular success in opera and ballet, symphonic music and solo song. Alongside Alfrēds Kalniņš, he was one of the first composers of opera in Latvia. His symbolic music drama *Uguns un nakts* ('Fire and Night') concerns the people's struggle for freedom; its powerfully drawn heroes are characterized both vocally and orchestrally. Struggle against the idea of despotism is expressed in his music drama *Dievi un cilvēki* ('Gods and Men'), which includes some original experiments in Egyptian colouring. *Sprīdītis* ('Tom Thumb'), a lively opera for children, is based on characters from folktales, and his last opera, *Luteklīte* ('The Little Darling'), is also for children. His *Mīlas uzvara* ('Love's Victory', 1935) was the first Latvian ballet. After Mediņš's death his manuscripts were donated to 14 libraries in Europe and North America (see Dunkele).

Uguns un nakts [Fire and Night], 1913–19 (2 operas, after J. Rainis), Riga, 26 May 1921; rev. (4), Riga, 2 Feb 1924
Dievi un cilvēki [Gods and Men] (4, after L. Paegle), Riga, 23 May 1922
Sprīdītis [Tom Thumb] (1, A. Brigadere), Riga, 22 Jan 1927
Luteklīte [The Little Darling] (children's op, A. Ozola, 1), Riga, 21 Dec 1939

*

I. Dunkele: *Latvju mūzika*, ii (Kalamazoo, MI, 1969), 170, 172
V. Briede-Bulavinova: *Latviešu opera* (Riga, 1975)
——: *Opernoye tvorchestvo latyshskih kompozitorov* [Operas of Latvian Composers] (Leningrad, 1979)

JĒKABS VĪTOLIŅŠ, ARNOLDS KLOTIŅŠ

Mediņš, Jāzeps (*b* Kaunas, 13 Feb 1877; *d* Riga, 12 June 1947). Latvian composer, brother of Jānis Mediņš. He graduated from the First Riga Musical Institute in 1896 (violin, cello and piano) and then became a teacher and director of that institute. Subsequently he worked as a conductor at the Riga Latvian Theatre (1906–11) and the Baku town opera theatre (1916–22), and as répétiteur and conductor at the Latvian National Opera in Riga (1922–5). Ill-health compelled him to give up his work, but he taught the piano at the Latvian State Conservatory from 1945 to 1947, as professor from 1946. As a composer he showed a gift for lyrical drama and colourful orchestration. His greatest work was the five-act opera *Vaidelote* ('The Priestess', 1922–4; after Aspāzija [E. Plickšāne]), a lyrical, psychological music drama in late Romantic style; it was first performed at the Latvian National Opera in Riga in 1927. His opera *Zemdegi* ('The Zemdegs Family', 1947; 3, P. Vīlips) was completed by Marǧeris Zariņš. Its theme is the resistance against the occupation army during World War II; it has recitative-like solo lines supplemented by large choral scenes. The opera was first performed on Latvian Television in 1960. Mediņš was also one of the first notable Latvian symphonists.

*

L. Viduleja: *Latviešu padomju opera* [Latvian Soviet Opera] (Riga, 1973)
L. Mūrniece: *Jāzeps Mediņš* (Riga, 1977)

JĒKABS VĪTOLIŅŠ, ARNOLDS KLOTIŅŠ

Medium, The. Tragic opera in two acts by GIAN CARLO MENOTTI to his own libretto; New York, Brander Matthews Theater, Columbia University, 8 May 1946

(revised version, New York, Heckscher Theatre, 18 February 1947).

Both acts take place in Madame Flora's parlour, where she holds séances. On the left is a stairway coming up from street level; on the right are a small puppet theatre with a white curtain and a small trunk. After a short instrumental introduction the curtain rises on Toby (dancer), a mute teenager, making up costumes from items in the trunk, and Madame Flora's daughter, Monica (soprano), combing her hair and singing a song ('Where, oh, where is my new golden spindle and thread?'). They are interrupted by Madame Flora, called Baba (contralto), who comes in and scolds Toby for playing with her possessions. They prepare for a séance and the participants arrive: Mr and Mrs Gobineau (baritone and soprano) and Mrs Nolan (mezzo-soprano). They sit round a table with only the light of a candle near a small statue of the Virgin Mary. Monica, in a white dress, is the voice and apparition of Mrs Nolan's dead child. Suddenly Baba turns on the light and screams that a hand touched her. In hysterics, she sends the people away and pours herself a drink. She blames Toby, who was behind the puppet theatre, and attacks him, but Monica intervenes and tries to comfort her with a song whose refrain is 'O black swan, where, oh, where is my lover gone?'. A ghostly offstage voice sings what Monica, as the apparition, had sung earlier. Baba sends Toby to see if someone is outside, but there is no one. Monica recapitulates her song, now to the words 'O black wave' and Baba recites the 'Ave Maria' as the curtain falls.

Act 2 opens with the same dramatic and arresting music that opened Act 1. Toby is finishing a puppet show with Monica as the audience. She sings to him and soon comes to realize that he loves her. She changes the words of her song to what he probably wants to say, but cannot ('Monica, Monica, can't you see, that my heart is

'The Medium' (Menotti): still from the film (1951) directed by the composer, with Leo Coleman as Toby and Maria Alberghetti as Monica

bleeding, bleeding for you?'). Baba enters, bottle in hand, and accuses Toby of touching her in the dark; she becomes enraged when he will not confess and whips him. He is saved by the arrival of Mr and Mrs Gobineau and Mrs Nolan expecting a séance. They are incredulous when Baba tells them that she is a fraud. Angrily she sends them and Toby away. Alone, in a drunken stupor, she sings a final aria ('Afraid, am I afraid?') and falls asleep. Toby returns and accidentally makes a loud noise which wakes Baba. He hides behind the puppet theatre, but Baba shouts 'Who's there?' and, taking a revolver from a drawer, shoots several times at the curtain. Toby's hands are seen grabbing the curtain from behind and blood appears on it. The curtain rod breaks and he falls forward into the room. 'I've killed the ghost!' Baba screams as Monica rushes in and cries for help.

In the notes to a recording of the opera Menotti wrote: 'Despite its eerie setting and gruesome conclusions, The Medium is actually a play of ideas. It describes the tragedy of a woman caught between two worlds, a world of reality which she cannot wholly comprehend, and a supernatural world in which she cannot believe'. After the initial performances Menotti revised the work and composed a comic curtain-raiser, The Telephone, to be paired with it. The two were performed together by Lincoln Kirstein's Ballet Society from 18 to 20 February 1947. The Broadway directors Chandler Cowles and Efrem Zimbalist, jr were so impressed that they moved the production to the Ethel Barrymore Theatre, where from 1 May 1947 it ran for 211 performances. The Medium received hundreds of performances in Europe and in 1951 was made into a film, directed by Menotti and starring Marie Powers as Baba, who had played the role on Broadway. The same year, The Telephone and The Medium toured Europe, under the auspices of the State Department. Many consider The Medium, with its gripping music and memorable tonal-modal, folklike melodies, to be Menotti's finest work.   BRUCE ARCHIBALD

Medley overture [potpourri overture]. An OVERTURE consisting of a series of passages excerpted from numbers in the work it introduces. The medley overture should be distinguished from the fully worked-out overture on themes from the opera as found in Beethoven and Weber, but a medley overture may show some concern for formal construction without resorting to sonata procedures.

An English collection of Six Medley or Comic Overtures, by Charke, Arne and Lampe, appeared in 1763, but these are not medley overtures in the later sense since they quote from a variety of sources and are not confined to music used in the rest of the works they originally introduced. The overture to Monsigny's Le déserteur (1769) is on the way to becoming a true medley overture, though most of its seven little sections evidently do not derive from the opera. Dibdin was using medley overtures by the late 1770s (Poor Vulcan, 1778; The Touchstone, 1779). What may be a criticism of the medley overture already appears in Iriarte's La música (Madrid, 1779, p.84). The overture to Reichardt's Die Geisterinsel (1798) is one of the first to show the substantial closing section in quick tempo that is a common feature of many later works. Medley overtures became extremely common in the 19th century, particularly in comic opera and operetta (notably

Offenbach and Sullivan); they continue to be standard in the musical.

R. Fiske: *English Theatre Music in the Eighteenth Century* (London, 1973, 2/1986)   STEPHEN C. FISHER

Medonte, re di Epiro ('Medonte, King of Epirus'). *Opera seria* in three acts by GIUSEPPE SARTI to a libretto by GIOVANNI DE GAMERRA; Florence, Teatro della Pergola, 8 September 1777.

Medonte (tenor), King of Epirus, is engaged to Selene (soprano), Princess of Argos, although she and Arbace (soprano castrato), Prince of Dodone and Medonte's general, are secretly in love. Medonte learns of this and pretends to relinquish Selene to Arbace. He then takes Arbace prisoner and tries to force Selene to marry him, but she chooses death instead. Medonte challenges Arbace on the field of battle, but Arbace returns triumphant with his opponent in chains. The lovers plan to depart for Argos, leaving Epirus in the hands of its chastened tyrant.

Based on one of De Gamerra's most conservative librettos, Sarti's setting enjoyed a popularity to rival the most successful of comic operas. A traditional *opera seria*, it includes a duet for the lovers at the end of Act 1 and a confrontational trio between the lovers and Medonte at the end of Act 2 — conventional features of operas of the late 1770s. A simple *coro* concludes Act 3. The only unusual feature is Arbace's cavatina at the beginning of the opera, precursor of the introduction (borrowed from comic opera) that was to become a component of operas in the 1790s. The reason for the success of *Medonte*, then, can only be the enormous appeal of Sarti's music, which nevertheless seems conservative when compared with some of his other works.

MARITA P. McCLYMONDS

Medoro. *Drama per musica* in a prologue and three acts by FRANCESCO LUCIO to a libretto by AURELIO AURELI after LUDOVICO ARIOSTO's *Orlando furioso*; Venice, Teatro SS Giovanni e Paolo, 1658 (libretto dedicated 11 January 1658).

Medoro centres on two couples, Angelica (soprano) and Medoro (alto), and Auristella (soprano) and Brimarte (alto), along with their unsatisfied admirers Sacripante (tenor) Leomede (tenor), and Miralba (soprano). Angelica, Queen of Cataio, has returned home with her beloved Medoro. The city is surrounded by the forces of Sacripante, King of Circassia, who hopes to prevent Angelica's impending marriage and win her himself. Leomede, the leader of Angelica's army, had also hoped to woo her; stung by her betrothal, he resolves to aid Sacripante, who also enjoys the protection of the sorcerer Atlante (bass). Medoro unwittingly saves the life of Sacripante. Atlante's attempts to harm Medoro and Brimarte, Prince of Assyria and an ally of Angelica, are thwarted by the power of Angelica's magic ring; Leomede's actions are more damaging: he leads Angelica to believe that Medoro loves Auristella, Angelica's sister, causing much confusion among the two couples. Just as their differences are resolved they learn that Sacripante's forces have entered the city. Miralba, Brimarte's sister, disguised in Medoro's armour, is wounded by Leomede, who is then killed by Brimarte. Sacripante finds the disguised Miralba; he immediately falls in love with her, believing it is she who had earlier saved his life. Captured by Brimarte and brought before Medoro and

Angelica, he is once again spared by Medoro. Miralba agrees to marry him, and the opera ends happily for the three couples.

Aureli's libretto completes the tale of Medoro and Angelica left open-ended by Ariosto in *Orlando furioso*; most of the characters are newly invented by him. *Medoro*, Lucio's last opera and only extant score, is notable for its chromaticism and its large number of martial ariosos, arias and instrumental pieces. It is enhanced by Lucio's use of arioso at important dramatic moments.

See also ANGELICA E MEDORO.   BETH L. GLIXON

Meester, Louis de (*b* Roeselare, West Flanders, 28 Oct 1904; *d* Ghent, 12 Dec 1987). Belgian composer. He began his career playing in bars and nightclubs and working with touring operetta companies; as a composer he was self-taught. From 1933 to 1937 he was director of the Meknes Conservatory, Morocco. He later became a radio sound engineer and in 1962 artistic director of the Institute for Electronic Music and Psychoacoustics attached to Ghent University. He used his knowledge of electronics in a major work for the first time in his radio opera *De grote verzoeking van St Antonius* ('The Great Temptation of St Anthony', 1957), which won the 1957 Italia Prize; his other dramatic works include the television opera *Twee is te weinig, drie is te veel* ('Two is not Enough, Three is too Many', 1966), the opera *Paradijsgeuzen* ('Birds of Paradise', 1967), and much incidental music for radio, television, theatre and cinema. De Meester was an outgoing composer, using novel techniques to express his feelings.

De grote verzoeking van St Antonius [The Great Temptation of St Anthony], 1957 (M. de Ghelderode, Dutch trans. J. Boon), Antwerp, Koninklijke Vlaamse Opera, 11 Nov 1961
Twee is te weinig, drie is te veel [Two is not Enough, Three is too Many] (ob, T. Brulin), Brussels Television, Sept 1966
Paradijsgeuzen [Birds of Paradise] (K. Locufier), Ghent, Koninklijke Vlaamse Opera, 2 April 1967   CORNEEL MERTENS

Mefistofele ('Mephistopheles'). Opera in a prologue, five acts and an epilogue by ARRIGO BOITO to his own libretto after JOHANN WOLFGANG VON GOETHE's play *Faust*; Milan, Teatro alla Scala, 5 March 1868 (revised version in four acts, Bologna, Teatro Comunale, 4 October 1875; second revised version, Venice, Teatro Rossini, 13 May 1876).

Mephistopheles	bass
Faust *a scholar*	tenor
Wagner *Faust's pupil*	tenor
Margherita *a simple girl*	soprano
Marta *Margherita's neighbour*	mezzo-soprano
Elena [Helen of Troy]	soprano
Pantalis *Helen's companion*	mezzo-soprano
Nereo *a Greek elder*	tenor

Heavenly host, cherubim, penitents, hunters, villagers, students, witches, warlocks, coryphaei and warriors

Setting The empyrean, Frankfurt in the 16th century, and the banks of the Peneois

The first performance of *Mefistofele* was a fiasco for several reasons, among them Boito's inexperience, the unworkable length of his 'reform' libretto and a largely inadequate cast. In addition, the advance promotion of the work by Boito's partisans and a few influential cri-

tics hoping for changes in conventional Italian opera antagonized a large sector of the conservative Milanese public and musical press. Only the Prologue in heaven was well received, but that came early in a stormy evening that lasted until well after midnight. Boito thoroughly revised and shortened the work. He eliminated two episodes that aroused particular opposition at the première: the scene at the emperor's court and an orchestral Battle Symphony. He recast the women's chorus, 'La luna immobile', as a duet for soprano and contralto, and shortened the dialogue between Faust and Wagner in Act 1; he inserted the duet 'Lontano, lontano' in the Prison Scene, taking it from his discarded score of *Ero e Leandro*; he revised the arias for Faust and Margherita; and with the assistance of Dominiceti he modified the orchestration. Later he expanded the choral fugue at the end of the Brocken Scene. Indeed, there are few pages of the autograph, a veritable palimpsest, that do not show modifications introduced over the space of a decade or more.

The revised version of 1875, performed at Bologna and sung by a notable cast including Erminia Borghi-Mamo, Italo Campanini and Romano Nannetti, aroused enthusiasm. For the next production of the work, at the Teatro Rossini, Venice, in 1876, Boito added, for Borghi-Mamo, Margherita's 'Spunta l'aurora pallida'. It is this definitive version that is described below. The opera was first given in London at Her Majesty's Theatre on 6 July 1880, with Christine Nilsson, Campanini and Nannetti. Its first performance (in English) in the USA was at Boston on 16 November 1880, with Marie Roze, Perugini and Conley. Eight days later it was given in New York in Italian with Alwina Valleria, Campanini and Franco Novara. The work returned to La Scala on 25 May 1881, this time to great approval, sung by Mariana-Masi, Marconi and Nannetti and conducted by Faccio. In all these productions the roles of Margherita and Helen of Troy were performed by the same singer, as Boito sought thereby to stress the concept of 'die ewige Weibliche'.

Revivals of *Mefistofele* in the 20th century have usually been associated with famous bass singers. The first was at La Scala on 16 March 1901, with Fyodor Shalyapin making his first appearance outside Russia, and with Caruso as Faust. The same role served for Shalyapin's North American début at the Metropolitan on 20 November 1907, with Farrar as Margherita. In the 1920s Nazzareno De Angelis was an impressive Mephistopheles, and he recorded the role. Pinza sang the part rarely, but it was often performed by his contemporary, Tancredi Pasero. Since 1969 the work has been staged with some regularity at the New York City Opera, where the title role has been associated principally with Norman Treigle and Samuel Ramey.

PROLOGUE *The empyrean* After echoing trumpet-calls the phalanxes of heaven praise the Lord. Mephistopheles offers to wager that he can gain the soul of Faust (aria, 'Ave Signor'). A Chorus Mysticus gives the Lord's assent. Mephistopheles vanishes, whereupon cherubim, penitents and finally the whole heavenly host resume their canticle of praise.

ACT 1.i *The square at Frankfurt* As merry-makers celebrate Easter Sunday, the elector and his retinue pass. Contemplating the arrival of spring, Faust is joined by his stuffy student, Wagner, who finds the crowds boring. They watch the dancing of a vigorous Obertas. As

'Mefistofele' (Boito): design by Carlo Ferrario for the Prologue (the empyrean) in the original production at La Scala, Milan, 5 March 1868

evening descends, Wagner superstitiously thinks of evil spirits, but Faust's attention is soon caught by a grey friar (rather than Goethe's poodle), who moves in mysterious circles. Wagner claims it to be a figment of Faust's imagination, but Faust observes the friar closely, apparently murmuring prayers, telling his rosary.

1.ii *Faust's study, later that evening* Faust enters, followed by the friar, who hides. The peaceful evening turns Faust's thoughts to God (aria, 'Dai campi, dai prati'). When he opens the Gospels a cry reveals the presence of Mephistopheles. Faust demands to know who his visitor is, and is informed that this is the Spirit of Denial (aria, 'Son lo spirito che nega sempre'). Mephistopheles offers to serve Faust in exchange for his soul. Faust agrees because if he can once think 'Stop, fleeting moment, you are beautiful' he will die without thought of the hereafter. The pact is quickly signed, the Devil spreads his cloak and off they fly.

ACT 2.i *Marta's garden* Faust courts the shy Margherita while Mephistopheles teases her neighbour, Marta. Margherita asks Faust if he believes in God; he replies that he seeks a deeper truth, an ecstasy that he defines as 'Nature, Love, Mystery'. When he declares his love she replies that she sleeps with her mother, who slumbers lightly, whereupon Faust provides her with a narcotic, assuring her that no harm will ensue. In a breathless, syncopated quartet the two couples proclaim their contrasting approaches to love.

2.ii *A rugged mountain-top in the Harz* A blood-red moon illuminates the scene as Faust and Mephistopheles climb up, accompanied by will-o'-the-wisps. Witches and warlocks arrive to celebrate the Witches' Sabbath. Mephistopheles seats himself on a rocky throne, seizes a globe of glass and tells Faust of the Earth's vileness (aria, 'Ecco il mondo'). Laughing, he shatters the globe. The witches begin a wild dance. Faust sees a vision of Margherita, a blood-red necklace about her throat. The dance in celebration of the Witches' Sabbath grows more frenzied.

ACT 3 *A prison cell* Margherita, her mind wandering, lies in chains. She thinks of the baby she is accused of drowning and of her mother, with whose death by poisoning she is charged. Mephistopheles has led Faust to her cell and withdraws as Faust pleads with her to flee. Upset by Faust's impatience, she wonders why he does not kiss her. She confesses her crimes, telling him how she wants the graves of her victims arranged. Again he urges her to escape, and they imagine fleeing to an enchanted isle in the duet 'Lontano, lontano'. When Mephistopheles announces the dawn, Margherita confuses him with the headsman come to lead her to her death; then she recognizes him as the Devil himself. Praying for forgiveness, she rejects Faust as she dies. Heavenly voices proclaim her salvation as Mephistopheles drags Faust away.

ACT 4 *A flowery mead by the banks of the Peneios* Helen of Troy and Pantalis greet the full moon, summoning sylphs and nereids. They withdraw as Faust and Mephistopheles appear, the former enchanted with his surroundings, the latter uneasy and unmoved by the dancing. Helen returns, obsessed by the burning of Troy. Faust addresses her in idealized terms, neatly rhymed, beguiling her with the way he fits sound to sound. They sing of their rapture in the duet 'Amore, misterio celeste' and retire to the grotto.

EPILOGUE *Faust's study* The aged Faust thinks of the emptiness of his experience. Now death is nigh he has a final dream: to rule over a prosperous populace in peace (aria, 'Giunto sul passo estremo'). Mephistopheles fears that Faust may yet elude him. While Faust clasps the Gospels, praying for salvation, Mephistopheles spreads his cloak, urging Faust to seek new adventures. As Faust dies, celestial voices welcome his soul to Heaven.

*　　*　　*

Boito's music is curiously uneven, often revealing his difficulty in developing ideas. It attains its greatest momentum in the Prison Scene (Act 3), in its revised form. The chorus of the heavenly phalanxes, 'Ave, Sign-or', from the Prologue returns at the end of the Prison

Scene and again at the conclusion of the opera, thereby endowing the work with an underlying coherence that it would not otherwise possess. Shaw (*London Music in 1888–89*, p.133) summed up his reaction to *Mefistofele* in these terms: 'The whole work is a curious example of what can be done in opera by an accomplished literary man without original musical gifts, but with ten times the taste and culture of a musician of only ordinary extraordinariness'. WILLIAM ASHBROOK

Megaro Moussikis Athinon (Athens Concert Hall). Multi-purpose performance complex opened in 1991 and including two auditoriums suited to opera; *see* ATHENS.

Mehta, Zubin (*b* Bombay, 29 April 1936). Indian conductor. The son of Mehli Mehta, founder-conductor of the Bombay SO, with whom he studied as a child, he later abandoned medical studies to work with Hans Swarowsky at the Vienna Academy. In 1958 he won the major prize for British and Commonwealth entrants in an international conductors' competition in Liverpool, giving him a year as musical assistant with the Liverpool PO. He quickly won success elsewhere which led to his joint appointment with the Montreal SO and Los Angeles PO in the 1970s, during which time he made his opera début at Montreal in *Tosca* (1964) and the same year in Europe with *La traviata* in Florence. He first appeared at the Metropolitan in *Aida* (1965), and returned regularly until 1971, mainly to conduct Italian repertory but also including the première of M. D. Levy's *Mourning Becomes Electra* (1967).

Mehta has formed a close association with the Israel PO (becoming musical adviser to the orchestra in 1970 and music director for life in 1981), and from 1976 to 1991 he was music director of the New York PO. His Covent Garden début was not until 1977 (*Otello*), but he appeared in opera more frequently in Vienna and Florence, where he was artistic director of the Maggio Musicale in 1986. In July 1990 at the Baths of Caracalla in Rome he conducted the 'three tenors' concert (with Carreras, Domingo and Pavarotti) which was televised worldwide. His performances generally favour bold attack, rhythmic vigour, voluptuous sonority and romantic expression, reinforced by boundless self-confidence. His recordings include *Aida* (1966) with Birgit Nilsson and Franco Corelli; *Tosca* (1968) with Régine Crespin, and again in 1973 with Leontyne Price; *Il trovatore* (1969), also with Price; *Turandot* (1973) with Sutherland and Pavarotti; and *La fanciulla del West* (1977). He has received Padma Bhushan (Order of the Lotus, 1967), the Indian government's highest cultural award, was appointed Commendatore by the Italian government and awarded the gold medal of the City of Paris.

R. Yockey and M. Bookspan: *Zubin: the Zubin Mehta Story* (New York, 1978) NOËL GOODWIN

Méhul, Etienne-Nicolas (*b* Givet, Ardennes, 22 June 1763; *d* Paris, 18 Oct 1817). French composer. He was one of the leading composers in Paris during the Revolution, Consulate and Empire. His works for the Opéra-Comique increased the range in subject and tone of the theatre's repertory; the serious lyric *drames*, in particular, were influential models for his contemporaries and praised by later composers such as Weber, Berlioz and Wagner.

1. LIFE. Méhul was the son of the Count of Montmorency's *maître d'hôtel*, Jean-François Méhul. After studying the organ locally at the Franciscan convent, he took the opportunity to continue lessons with Wilhelm Hanser (who also taught him counterpoint) at the nearby abbey of Laval-Dieu. Soon he became Hanser's assistant. For an ambitious provincial musician the lure of Paris was strong: Méhul arrived there in 1778 or 1779. He was fortunate to have an introduction to the harpsichordist and opera composer Jean-Frédéric Edelmann, with whom he studied while supporting himself by teaching keyboard instruments and probably playing the organ. Under his teacher's aegis, Méhul arranged popular opera *airs*, set one of Jean-Baptiste Rousseau's *odes sacrées*, which was performed at the Concert Spirituel in 1782, and wrote a set of keyboard sonatas (1783). By the mid-1780s he had made influential friends. He became a member of the distinguished society of professional musicians and amateurs, the Société des Enfans d'Apollon, which performed several of his dramatic *scènes*. Another two works for the Concert Spirituel (1789) and a second set of sonatas (1788) brought him some public attention. His first major opportunity to follow a career in opera came in 1785 when Valadier offered him his prize-winning libretto *Cora*. By the end of the following year Méhul had finished the score, and the opera composer Jean-Baptiste Lemoyne and the royal censor Jean-Baptiste Suard, one of Gluck's staunchest defenders, agreed to recommend it to the Opéra administration in January 1787. Adjudications, revisions (involving a change of title from *Alonzo e Cora* to *Cora* during the work's preparation for the stage; this often happened with Méhul's titles) and other circumstances (including competition with another work on the same subject, *La fête du soleil*, by Henri-Montan Berton, son of a former Opéra director) delayed its première until 1791.

By then Méhul had met FRANÇOIS-BENOÎT HOFFMAN, already a well-established librettist, who became his favourite partner for more than a decade. Their initial collaboration, *Euphrosine, ou Le tyran corrigé* (1790), was the composer's operatic début; its success was such that Méhul was quickly recognized as a leading figure in the Parisian musical scene. Although *Cora* was a failure and *Adrien* (planned for 1792) was banned for political reasons (as metaphorically favouring France's enemy, the Austrian Emperor), other substantial works performed during the 1790s at the Comédie-Italienne (from 1793 the Opéra-Comique), among them *Stratonice* (1792), *Mélidore et Phrosine* (1794) and *Ariodant* (1799), confirmed and increased the public's high opinion of him. To triumph on the stage of 'le premier théâtre lyrique' (the Opéra) remained Méhul's goal. The critical and popular acclaim for the second setting of *Adrien* (1799) must have pleased him, but the success proved short-lived: it was suspended after the fourth performance, again for political reasons (this time for promoting the monarchy, in spite of revisions making the title hero a mere general).

During the Revolution Méhul became widely known as a composer of patriotic songs and choruses, many of them government commissions. *Le chant du départ* (words by Marie-Joseph Chénier, a member of the National Convention) was the rallying cry for the new Republic and for a while rivalled the *Marseillaise* in popularity. Méhul also wrote the overture and choruses for Chénier's *Timoléon*, the frequently performed ballet *Le jugement de Pâris*, a symphony, an overture for wind band, and several romances and other songs.

Official recognition soon came for Méhul. In 1795 he became a founder-member of the Institut de France, the first composer and the second youngest person to be named to that body, membership of which represented the highest government honour for scholarship at that time. The Ministre de l'Intérieur in a public proclamation (1796) praised him for his contribution to Revolutionary *fêtes*. Méhul's friend in the Directoire, Louis Marie de Larevellière-Lépeaux, cited him as a model for composers (*Essai sur ... les fêtes nationales*, Paris, 1797, pp.15–16). In 1795 the government appointed him one of the five inspectors of the newly reorganized Conservatoire, the most senior members of the staff responsible for overseeing the institution. The Opéra-Comique expressed esteem for Méhul in a tangible way. To ensure his fidelity to their theatre, the *sociétaires* (the leading singers who owned the enterprise) paid him a special pension, over and above the performance honoraria legally due, beginning in April 1794. This was a most unusual step for them since, unlike the other prolific composer-pensioners Grétry and Dalayrac, Méhul had only three works in repertory by then.

By the time of Consulate (1799–1804), Méhul was the undisputed master of serious opera with spoken dialogue, and he continued to prefer dramatic librettos for major works. But Parisian tastes had shifted in favour of lighter, truly comic operas. Significantly, the *drame*-influenced *Héléna*, for example, was more popular elsewhere in Europe than in the French capital, while his shorter *opéras comiques* written to current fashions, *L'irato* and *Une folie* for instance, were well received everywhere. Méhul also wrote two more ballets for the Opéra (*La dansomanie*, given in 1800, was the theatre's most successful one of the period), incidental music for Alexandre Duval's play *Les Hussites* (1804), songs and other minor works, although the operatic genre remained the composer's principal concern.

Méhul benefited from the friendship and support of the First Consul, Napoleon Bonaparte, to whom he dedicated the printed score of *L'irato*. Bonaparte commissioned from him several large-scale works for public festivals, among them the impressive *Chant national* for soloists, three choirs and three orchestras, to celebrate the victory of Marengo and Bastille Day in 1800, and *Domine salvum fac rempublicam* for two choruses and two orchestras for the Mass following the signing of the Concordat (re-establishing Catholicism as the state religion) in 1802. His brother Lucien Bonaparte, as Ministre de l'Intérieur, personally intervened in 1800 to lift the interdiction of *Adrien*. In 1804 Méhul was named a member of the newly created Légion d'Honneur. His marriage in 1800 to Marie-Thérèse-Joséphine Gastaldy proved unhappy; by 1808 at the latest they had separated. Afterwards Méhul formed a common-law relationship with Marie-Françoise Tourette, sister of Cherubini's wife.

During the Empire (1804–1814/15) he continued to write mainly for the Opéra-Comique, although he seldom achieved the artistic or popular successes of his best works of the 1790s. Two experimental and atypical scores given premières in 1806 and 1807 (and not often performed in Paris during his lifetime) are his best-known works to modern scholars: *Uthal* (written during the Consulate), in which he tried to capture the Ossianic mood by an unusual orchestration emphasizing the sombre timbres of the violas and cellos and omitting violins altogether, and *Joseph*, whose pious subject and intentionally austere and pseudo-religious atmosphere made it a respected work throughout the 19th century, particularly in Germany.

As well as writing songs and several occasional cantatas in Napoleon's honour, Méhul composed four symphonies, 1808–10. He broke off composition of the fifth symphony in this set on receiving commissions for two cantatas, a *chant triomphal*, the ballet *Persée et Andromède* and the opera *Les troubadours, ou La fête au château* as part of the festivities to celebrate the Emperor's marriage to Marie-Louise of Austria (1810). Napoleon rewarded the composer handsomely for his efforts with gifts and a pension from the imperial household accounts (the only one for a musician not directly involved in private music for the court). Furthermore, in 1810, on the recommendation of an Institut committee, Napoleon gave the prize for the best work at the Opéra-Comique during the past ten years to *Joseph*. The following year, Méhul wrote three more cantatas (one jointly with his Conservatoire colleagues Cherubini and Catel) for the birth of the Emperor's son.

In spite of imperial patronage, 1810–11 was a period of crisis for Méhul. The lukewarm reception of his symphonies, some public criticism of the choice of *Joseph* for the prize, his disappointment at not seeing *Les troubadours* and *Valentine de Milan* performed, owing to factors beyond his control, and the poor state of his health after contracting tuberculosis all led to a severe depression. Problems in revising extensively his serious opera *Les amazones*, which he hoped would be the pinnacle of his career, and in rehearsing it aggravated the situation. Its failure in 1811 was the worst blow that the composer experienced. For a while he renounced writing for the theatre. Encouragement from friends later persuaded him to compose two more *opéras comiques*, but he left incomplete the *tragédie lyrique Sésostris*. His contribution to *L'oriflamme*, a *pièce de circonstance* commissioned by the government during the final days of the Empire when France was under attack, was limited.

Even though Méhul had close ties to Napoleon and his government, on the Restoration his pre-eminence ensured him a place in the new regime. He was named *surintendant honoraire de la musique du Roi*, and among his last works was a cantata celebrating the Bourbons' return (spring 1816). Terminally ill by this time, he fought hard for the preservation of the Conservatoire ('tainted' as an institution of the Revolution and Empire); its reduction to Ecole de Musique, rather than its outright abolition as advocated by influential members of the government, was due in part to his efforts. His death was mourned by friends, colleagues, students (including his nephew Louis Joseph Daussoigne-Méhul and Ferdinand Hérold) and the opera-going public of Paris. Cherubini, his close friend and sometime collaborator, paid a warm tribute to his generosity, fine character and great talent, summing up his style as 'sweeping and clear tending towards strong gestures rather than those requiring merely grace and sweetness; he was rather the Michelangelo than the Raphael of music' (Pougin 1909).

2. WORKS. For Berlioz (*Les soirées d'orchestre*, ed. Guichard, 1968) Méhul's operas were his greatest contribution to music. Dramatic truth was the paramount goal:

He believed that theatrical music ... must be directly correlated to the sentiments expressed by the words, that it must sometimes even

... seek to reproduce the intonation of speech, the declamatory accent ... He believed that for certain human emotions there are special melodic accents which can alone express them in all their essence, and that it is necessary at all cost to find them; otherwise the results would be false, inexpressive, cold, and fail to achieve the supreme end of art. Furthermore, he never doubted that for truly dramatic music, when the interest of a situation merits such sacrifices, between a pretty musical effect foreign to the emphasis of the scene or to the nature of the characters, and a series of [dramatic] strokes, true but not conducive to a frivolous pleasure, there was no reason at all to hesitate. He was convinced that musical expression ... did not reside only in the melody, but that everything combined to give it life or to destroy it: melody, harmony, modulations, rhythm, orchestration, choice of high or low registers of voices and instruments, degree of speed or slowness in the performance and various nuances in sound production. He knew ... that the true masters of dramatic art have always been endowed to a greater or lesser extent with very musical talents united with sentiment of expression.

Berlioz was right. The tremendous variety among Méhul's operas and his frequently daring and innovative approaches result in part from consistently putting the requirements of the drama first.

Méhul's works of the 1790s for the Opéra-Comique were the mainstay of the Paris repertory and were often performed elsewhere. As a group they show better than the output of any other French composer the stylistic break with the works of the previous generation (best represented by Grétry), the developments contributing to their far greater dramatic impact and the musical innovations that proved to be influential precedents for Romantic music.

Cora and the *scènes lyriques* demonstrate not only his indebtedness to the 'reform' operas of Gluck and Salieri, but also his awareness of symphonic style (particularly Haydn's) and his interest in dynamic, large-scale ensembles – both of which are unusual for the period. In these early works Méhul experimented with new techniques that he was to use later with greater expertise.

Literary trends are also significant. The lighthearted *comédie mêlée d'ariettes* type of libretto in vogue during the *ancien régime* gradually gave way to the serious *drame lyrique*. In the 1780s developments in operas on 'chevaleresque' subjects anticipated directions that Revolutionary opera was to take. Nevertheless, Hoffman's librettos for *Euphrosine* (1790), set at the time of the Crusades, and *Stratonice* (1792), on a classical legend, mark a turning-point. Drawing on techniques in dramatic construction, characterization and versification from the spoken *comédie* and *drame*, he produced a richer, more varied and flexible form.

The change in the style and content of the libretto presented a musical challenge. The texts of individual numbers were no longer merely incidental to the plot (as was often the case in the *comédie mêlée d'ariettes*); rather, they were an integral part and frequently had a crucial dramatic function. As a result, the music became more important. Drawing in part on earlier traditions of both the Comédie-Italienne and the Opéra, Méhul provided a highly original solution to the problems that the libretto set. Though uneven, the score of *Euphrosine* is in strong contrast to those of his most gifted predecessors Grétry and Dalayrac: the melodically orientated *ariette* style, which dominates in even the exceptional works of the previous decade (such as Grétry's *Richard Coeur-de-lion* and Dalayrac's *Raoul, sire de Créqui*), is passé. For the best pieces in *Euphrosine* – significantly those with the strongest dramatic impact – Méhul developed new and more extended forms (especially in the finales of Acts 1 and 2 and the confrontation duet), a greater role for the orchestra (which at times becomes the voice's equal and even superior), an expressive recurring motif symbolizing jealousy, and a broader range of effects (achieved, for example, through a larger harmonic vocabulary, remote modulations and deliberately unmelodic writing for the voice when justified by the exigencies of the text).

Cherubini's favourite Méhul opera, *Stratonice*, shows the consolidation and polishing of techniques and approaches evident in *Euphrosine*. The result is a consistent, mature work in which attention to balance and nuance within a modern style belies common assumptions about Revolutionary music. Méhul matched the classical subject with music in a noble style inspired by Opéra models. The *air* 'Versez tous vos chagrins dans le sein paternel' with its long, lyric phrases remained a favourite with tenors throughout the 19th century. The quartet containing, as a contemporary critic noted, almost half the music of the opera is an impressive dramatic rendering of the most important scene in the work where symphonic techniques, motivic symbolism, contrasting characterizations of the individuals through their melodies, effective orchestration and an extended form akin to the sonata-rondo all serve to heighten the theatrical impact.

Méhul's experiments of the mid-1790s demonstrate how daring he was, particularly in a sometimes shocking use of dissonance, the deliberate incompletion of formal expectations for dramatic effect and the orchestral expression of extreme psychological states to a degree surpassing previous works. In *Mélidore et Phrosine* the composer achieved a musical unification through themes and motifs, tonal structures and modulation schemes not hitherto attempted in the genre. *Ariodant* is Méhul's best work of the decade and a high point of Revolutionary opera. Another 'chevaleresque' work, it is in a serious and sentimental style throughout. The music is in turn nostalgic (the bard's *romance* 'Femme sensible', for example), intensely dramatic (the villain's outburst 'O démon de la jalousie' and the Act 2 finale) and mixed (the heroine's air, 'O des amans le plus fidèle', expressing her hopes and fears as her lover faces the villain's challenge). In spite of its fate *Adrien* contains much fine music, and its extensive use of chorus and ensemble as well as solos in long scene complexes set significant precedents for Spontini and for Empire opera.

Méhul's serious works for the Opéra-Comique during the Consulate and Empire (for instance *Joanna* and *Héléna*) are less experimental in terms of form, melodic style, harmony, modulation and motivic treatment than those of the 1790s, although he often refined and consolidated his earlier procedures. For the frankly comic works (*Une folie* and *L'irato*, for example), Méhul studied the then popular Italian-influenced *opéras comiques* of Isouard and others, as well as Paisiello's *opere buffe*, and distilled from them a lighter, more tuneful melodic approach. This he integrated so thoroughly into his more complex, symphonic style that to speak of imitation would be misleading. Sometimes, however, as Cherubini noted, the humour was more calculated than natural, and in places too heavy-handed.

The composer's quest for an appropriate translation of the dramatic situation and his growing interest in French music history led him occasionally to adapt traditional melodies for symbolic reasons, for example the *airs* 'Charmante Gabrielle' and 'Vive Henri IV' in

Gabrielle d'Estrées and the *forlane* from Campra's *L'Europe galante* in *Les troubadours*. Contemporary references could serve his purpose, too. Critics remarked how well the audience appreciated the bolero theme in the overture to *Les deux aveugles de Tolède* as an introduction to the work's Spanish setting.

More often, Méhul created his own unique musical atmosphere in a work through distinctive orchestrations. Sometimes he used instruments not commonly found in the opera orchestra, such as the harp, the serpent and the tuba curva, for their extra-musical associations as well as their sonorous qualities (as in *Joseph*). But more importantly, as he had begun to do in his earlier works, he emancipated whole sections of the orchestra. No longer was the violin always dominant, with treble winds occasionally providing contrast. Instruments of the tenor range, the horn, the viola and the cello in particular, were imaginatively handled and assigned prominent roles. To describe *Uthal* as 'the opera without violins', though accurate, is misleading; rather, the sombre qualities of an expanded viola section, as well as an emphasis on male voices, reeds, horns and cellos, give the score a suitably misty and dark cast for the Ossianic subject. His achievements in this domain had a marked influence on others. Beethoven's trumpet call in *Fidelio* was inspired by Méhul's *Héléna*;

Berlioz cited examples by Méhul as models several times in his treatise on orchestration, and echoes of the older composer's procedures can be heard in the *Symphonie fantastique*, the *Grande Messe des morts* and *L'enfance du Christ*, among other works.

Méhul was an innovator. He was far bolder than his compatriots at the time. Le Sueur, in his works for the Théâtre Feydeau, lacked the skill to develop occasionally interesting passages; without extension they sound odd rather than convincing. Furthermore, many of Le Sueur's pieces belong to the Grétry-Dalayrac aesthetic approach. Cherubini, a superior composer technically to his contemporaries, remained more traditional: he synthesized elements from Italian *opera buffa* and *opera seria* with French aspects. When the plot required an intense dramatic treatment, he learnt from Méhul (to whom he dedicated the score of *Médée*), but he tempered the latter's more extreme ideas. In places, Méhul's scores are flawed; sometimes he tried for effects beyond his reach, and although he invented striking figures, by repetition they quickly became clichés. But the successes are more numerous and above all more significant. In them he left a remarkably rich creative legacy to the 19th century.

See also ARIODANT; *JEUNE HENRI, LE*; *JOSEPH*; *MÉLIDORE ET PHROSINE*; and *UTHAL*.

For detailed information on sources, revisions and arrangements, see Bartlet (*Etienne Nicolas Méhul and Opera*, 1982 and 1992).

first performed and published in Paris unless otherwise stated

title	genre, acts	libretto	first performance	remarks and sources
Cora [orig. Alonzo et Cora]	opéra, 4	Valadier, after J. F. Marmontel: *Les Incas*	Opéra, 15 Feb 1791	comp. 1785–6, later rev.; *F-Pn** (inc.), Acts 1 and 3 with autograph adds *Pn*, inc. pts *Po*
Euphrosine, ou Le tyran corrigé [from 1795 Euphrosine et Coradin]	comédie mise en musique, 5	F.-B. Hoffman, after *Conradin*	Comédie-Italienne (Favart), 4 Sept 1790	in 4 acts, 11 Sept 1790; in 3 acts, 31 Oct 1790 (1791/ R1980: ERO, xxxviii); with new Act 3, 13 Aug 1791, *Pn*, *Po*, new Act 3 *Pn* (R1980: ERO, xxxviii); 4 nos. deleted from 5-act version *Pn**
Adrien, empereur de Rome	opéra, 3	Hoffman, after P. Metastasio: *Adriano in Siria*	unperf.	comp. 1790–91; première planned for March 1792 but forbidden by the Commune of Paris; Acts 1 and 3 *Pn** (inc.), Acts 2 and 3 *Pn*; some material reused in Adrien, 1799
Le jeune Henri [orig. La jeunesse de Henri IV]	drame lyrique, 2	J.-N. Bouilly	OC (Favart), 1 May 1797	comp. 1791, rev. 1797; *Pn** (lacks ov., 1 no.), ov. (1797)
Stratonice	comédie-héroïque, 1	Hoffman, after *De Dea Syria* [attrib. Lucian] and T. Corneille: *Antiochus*	Comédie-Italienne (Favart), 3 May 1792	rev. of 1 air *Pn**; (1792/R1992: FO, lxxii)
Le jeune sage et le vieux fou	comédie mêlée de musique, 1	Hoffman	OC (Favart), 28 March 1793	4 nos. *Pn**; (1793); rev. version, OC (Feydeau), 18 Dec 1801, 1 no. *Pn**
Horatius Coclès	opéra, 1	A.-V. Arnault	Opéra, 18 Feb 1794	*Po*; (1794)
Le congrès des rois	cmda, 3	Desmaillot [A. F. Eve]	OC (Favart), 26 Feb 1794	collab. H.-M. Berton, Blasius, Cherubini, Dalayrac, Deshayes, Devienne, Grétry, Jadin, Kreutzer, Solié and Trial; Berton's duo *Pn**; suspended after second perf., later banned

title	genre, acts	libretto	first performance	remarks and sources
Mélidore et Phrosine	drame lyrique, 3	Arnault, after P.-J. Bernard: *Phrosine et Mélidore*	OC (Favart), 6 May 1794	minor revs. to lib. by G. M. J. B. Legouvé; sketches *Pn**, 1 no. *S-Smf*; (?1794/*R*1990: FO, lxxiii)
Doria, ou La tyrannie détruite	opéra héroïque, 3	Legouvé and C. J. L. Davrigny	OC (Favart), 12 March 1795	ov., 6 nos., frags. *F-Pn**, excerpts from 1 no. *Po**
La caverne	comédie mise en musique, 3	N. J. Forgeot	OC (Favart), 5 Dec 1795	*Mc*, 6 nos. (1 in 2 versions) *Pn**
Le pont de Lody [orig. La prise du pont de Lody]	fait historique, 1	E. J. B. Delrieu	Feydeau, 15 Dec 1797	written to celebrate the French victory at Lodi (10 May 1796) and the Italian campaign (1796–7); not commissioned by Bonaparte as sometimes assumed; *Pn* (with autograph revs.; lacks 1 no.)
La taupe et les papillons	comédie lyrique, 1	A. E. X. Poisson de La Chabeaussière	unperf.	comp. 1797–8; perf. planned for April 1799 at the Montansier did not take place; 6 nos. (3 of which in 2 versions), sketches, *Pn**
Adrien	opéra, 3	Hoffman, after Metastasio: *Adriano in Siria*	Opéra, 4 June 1799	reuses some material from the 1790–91 setting with revs.; banned after the second perf.; revived 4 Feb 1800 and (with further revs.) 26 Dec 1801; *B-Bc*, *F-Pn** (nearly complete), *Pn*, *Po*, *US-COu*
Ariodant [orig. Ina]	drame mêlé de musique, 3	Hoffman, after L. Ariosto: *Orlando furioso*	OC (Favart), 11 Oct 1799	3 nos., sketches, frags. *F-Pn**; (1800/*R*1978: ERO, xxxix); rev. with new Act 2 finale, 30 Oct 1800, *Pn**
Epicure	opéra, 3	C. A. Demoustier	OC (Favart), 14 March 1800	collab. Cherubini; rev. version (2), 20 March 1800; 1 no., sketches *Pn**, Cherubini's autograph of ov., 6 nos. *D-Bds*
Bion	comédie mêlée de musique, 1	Hoffman, after E. F. de Lantier: *Voyages d'Anténor*	OC (Favart), 27 Dec 1800	1 no. *F-Pn**; (1801); rev. version, 21 Dec 1802, printed score with MS adds *Pn*
L'irato, ou L'emporté	comédie-parade, 1	B.-J. Marsollier des Vivetières	OC (Favart), 17 Feb 1801	1 unperf. no. *Pn**; (1801); an orig. work although claimed to be trans. from an opera buffa by 'Fiorelli'
Une folie	comédie mêlée de chants, 2	Bouilly	OC (Feydeau), 5 April 1802	3 nos., sketches *Pn**; (1802)
Le trésor supposé, ou Le danger d'écouter aux portes	comédie mêlée de musique, 1	Hoffman	OC (Feydeau), 29 July 1802	ov., 8 nos., sketches, arrs. *Pn**; (1802); rev. version, ? 7 July 1807, 2 nos. *Pn**
Joanna	opéra, 2	Marsollier, after his lib. *Emma, ou Le soupçon* [orig. set by E. Fay]	OC (Feydeau), 23 Nov 1802	complete score, sketches *Pn**, ov. pts (?1803)
Héléna	opéra, 3	Bouilly	OC (Feydeau), 1 March 1803	(1803)
Le baiser et la quittance, ou Une aventure de garnison	opéra-bouffon, 3	L. B. Picard, C. de Longchamps and J.-M.-A.-M. Dieulafoy, after Polier de Bottens: *L'heureuse gageure*	OC (Feydeau), 18 June 1803	collab. Boieldieu, Kreutzer and Isouard; *B-Ba*, *Bc*, *F-Pn* (3 MSS), *R(m)*
L'heureux malgré lui	opéra-bouffon, 1	C. G. d'A. de Saint-Just	OC (Feydeau), 29 Dec 1803	complete score, frags. *Pn**
Les deux aveugles de Tolède	oc, 1	Marsollier, after *The Thousand and One Nights* and his lib. *Les deux aveugles de Bagdad* [orig. set by A. J. Fournier]	OC (Feydeau), 28 Jan 1806	ov., 1 unused no., sketches, frags. *Pn**, frags. *S-Smf**; (1806)
Uthal [orig. Malvina]	opéra, 1	J. M. B. Bins de Saint-Victor, after J. Macpherson: *Berrathon* from the Ossian collection	OC (Feydeau), 17 May 1806	comp. 1803; 1 inc. no. *F-Pn**, 2 rev. nos., inc. *US-NYpm**; (1806)

title	genre, acts	libretto	first performance	remarks and sources
Gabrielle d'Estrées, ou Les amours d'Henri IV	opéra, 3	Saint-Just	OC (Feydeau), 25 June 1806	F-Pn* (lacks ov., no. 3), sketches, frags. Pn*); (1806); probably banned after the 6th perf.
Joseph	drame mêlé de chants, 3	A. Duval, after Genesis xxxvii–xlvi	OC (Feydeau), 17 Feb 1807	comp. 1805; 8 nos., sketches Pn*, ov. Po*
Valentine de Milan	drame lyrique, 3	Bouilly	OC (Feydeau), 28 Nov 1822	begun 1807, finished by ?1808, rev. 1815, posth. rev. by Méhul's nephew L. J. Daussoigne-Méhul, who added 4 nos.; frag. D-Bds*, complete score, sketches, unused nos. F-Pn*, frag. GB-Lbl*, 1 unused no. US-NYpm*; (1823)
Les troubadours, ou La fête au château [orig. Laurette; also as Les deux troubadours]	oc, 1	Duval	unperf.	comp. 1810, written for Napoleon's marriage to Marie-Louise of Austria, 2 April 1810; in rehearsal at the OC June 1810 but not perf.; see Bartlet (1984); ov., all but 2 nos. F-Pn*
Les amazones, ou La fondation de Thèbes [orig. Amphion]	opéra, 3	V.-J. Etienne de Jouy	Opéra, 17 Dec 1811	Pn* (nearly complete), sketches, frags., Po (Pn* lacks some of the material deleted after the première)
Sésostris	tragédie lyrique, 3	Arnault and Jouy		comp. 1812; intended for the Opéra, inc. on composer's death; Act 3 lacking final scene Po*, Act 2 sketched
Le prince troubadour, ou Le grand trompeur de dames	oc, 1	Duval	OC (Feydeau), 24 May 1813	Pn* (lacks 2 nos.), sketches, frags. Pn*; (1813); not to be confused with Les troubadours, 1810
L'oriflamme [orig. L'oriflamme de Charles Martel]	opéra, 1	C.-G. Etienne and L. P.-M.-F. Baour-Lormian	Opéra, 1 Feb 1814	written as a 'pièce de circonstance'; collab. H.-M. Berton, Kreutzer and Paer; Méhul wrote music for scene i and reused ov. from Horatius Coclès, 1794 (see Bartlet 1986); Po; (1814)
La journée aux aventures	oc, 3	P. D. A. Chapelle and L. Mézières-Miot	OC (Feydeau), 16 Nov 1816	F-Pn* (lacks ov.), sketches, unused nos. Pn*; (1817)

Wrongly attributed: Agar au désert [lib. submitted to Opéra in 1806 but rejected]; L'Amour et Psyché [Psyché; set by Mondonville in 1758, Saint-Amans in 1778, Candeille in 1781 and Lenoble in 1784]; Anacréon [set by Rameau in 1757, rev. by Legros in 1781]; Arminius [lib. submitted to Opéra in 1794, intended for Méhul but not set by him]; Hypsipile [lib. submitted to Opéra in 1787, intended for Méhul but not set by him]; Mézence, ou Lausus et Lydie [lib. submitted to Opéra in 1788, intended for Méhul but not set by him]; Scipion à Carthage [lib. submitted to Opéra in 1794, set by J. N. Le Froid de Méreaux in 1795–6 (unperf.)]; Tancrède et Mélizinde [Tancrède, Tancrède et Clorinde; lib. submitted to Opéra in 1795, set by G. Bergancini in 1806–7 (unperf.)]

FétisB

A. C. Quatremère de Quincy: Funérailles de M. Méhul, Institut royal de France (Paris, 1817)

——: 'Notice historique sur la vie et les oeuvres de M. Méhul', Institut royal de France: séance publique de l'Académie royale des beaux-arts du 2 octobre 1819 (Paris, 1819); also pubd in Quatremère de Quincy: Recueil de notices historiques (Paris, 1834)

Castil-Blaze: De l'opéra en France (Paris, 1820, 2/1826)

A. V. Arnault: Souvenirs d'un sexagénaire (Paris, 1833)

Castil-Blaze: Théâtres lyriques de Paris, [iii]: Histoire de l'Opéra-Comique (MS, 1857, F-Po Rés.660)

P. A. Vieillard: Méhul, sa vie et ses oeuvres (Paris, 1859)

J.-B. Weckerlin: 'Les quatre versions de la romance de Joseph, opéra de Méhul', Revue et gazette musicale de Paris, xlii (1875), 252–3 [suppl. incl. music examples]

P. Jacquinet: François Benoît Hoffman: sa vie, ses oeuvres (Nancy, 1878)

M. Dietz: Geschichte des musikalischen Dramas in Frankreich während der Revolution bis zum Directorium, 1787 bis 1795, in künstlerischer, sittlicher und politischer Beziehung (Vienna, 1885, 2/1893)

R. Wagner: Gesammelte Schriften und Dichtungen, iii: Oper und Drama (Leipzig, 1887; Eng. trans., London, 1893)

E. Hanslick: Die moderne Oper, v: Musikalisches und Literarisches (Berlin, 1889), 241–65

A. Pougin: Méhul: sa vie, son génie, son caractère (Paris, 1889, 2/1893)

——: L'Opéra-Comique pendant la Révolution de 1788 à 1801 (Paris, 1891)

H. Parent de Curzon: 'Méhul, sa vie et son oeuvre', Musiciens du temps passé (Paris, 1893), 117–72

A. Pougin: 'Méhul et Pleyel', Le ménestrel, lx (1894), 266–8

H. Quittard: 'L'Uthal de Méhul', La revue musicale ... de J. Combarieu, viii (1908), 295–300

A. Pougin: 'Notice sur Méhul par Cherubini', RMI, xvi (1909), 750–71

R. Brancour: Méhul (Paris, 1912)

H. Strobel: 'Die Opern von E. N. Méhul', ZMw, vi (1923–4), 362–402

E. Bücken: Der heroische Stil in der Oper (Leipzig, 1924)

J. Tiersot, ed.: Lettres de musiciens écrites en français du XVe au XXe siècle, i (Turin, 1924)

C. Barzel: 'Notes et documents de musique: la jeunesse et le roman de Méhul', *Mercure de France* (15 Sept 1932), 730–40

P.-M. Masson: 'L'oeuvre dramatique de Méhul', *Annales de l'Université de Paris*, xii (1937), 523–48

M. Pincherle, ed.: *Musiciens peints par eux-mêmes* (Paris, 1939)

G. Knepler: 'Die Technik der sinfonischen Durchführung in der französischen Revolutionsoper', *BMw*, i (1959), 4–22

——: *Musikgeschichte des 19. Jahrhunderts* (Berlin, 1961)

F. Schnapp, ed.: *E. T. A. Hoffman: Schriften zur Musik: Nachlese* (Munich, 1963, 2/1978)

W. Dean: 'Opera under the French Revolution', *PRMA*, xciv (1967–8), 77–96

L. Guichard, ed.: *Hector Berlioz: Les soirées d'orchestre* (Paris, 1968)

P. Citron, ed.: *Hector Berlioz: Correspondance générale*, i (Paris, 1972)

B. Deane: 'The French Operatic Overture from Grétry to Berlioz', *PRMA*, xcix (1972–3), 67–80

D. Charlton: *Orchestration and Orchestral Practice in Paris, 1789–1810* (diss., U. of Cambridge, 1973)

——: 'Motive and Motif: Méhul before 1791', *ML*, lvii (1976), 362–9

E. J. Dent: *The Rise of Romantic Opera*, ed. W. Dean (Cambridge, 1976)

R. C. C. de Cordes: *Etienne-Nicolas Méhul's 'Euphrosine' and 'Stratonice': a Transition from 'Comédie mêlée d'ariettes' to 'Opéra-comique'* (diss., U. of Southern California, 1979)

R. T. Laudon: *Sources of the Wagnerian Synthesis: a Study of the Franco-German Tradition in Nineteenth-Century Opera* (Munich and Salzburg, 1979)

G. Strobel and W. Wolf, eds.: *Richard Wagner: Sämtliche Briefe*, iv: *Briefe der Jahre 1851–52* (Leipzig, 1979)

J. Warrack, ed.: *Carl Maria von Weber: Writings on Music* (Cambridge, 1981)

M. E. C. Bartlet: *Etienne Nicolas Méhul and Opera during the French Revolution, Consulate, and Empire: a Source, Archival and Stylistic Study* (diss., U. of Chicago, 1982)

——: 'Opera as Patriotic Ceremony: the Case of L'Oriflamme', *IMSCR, xiii Strasbourg 1982*, i, 327–38

W. Dean: 'French Opera', *The Age of Beethoven (1790–1830)*, NOHM, viii (Oxford, 1982), 26–119

M. D. Grace: 'Méhul's *Ariodant* and the Early Leitmotif', *A Festschrift for Albert Seay: Essays by his Friends and Colleagues* (Colorado Springs, 1982), 173–93

M. E. C. Bartlet: 'A Newly Discovered Opera for Napoleon', *AcM*, lvi (1984), 266–96

J. Mongrédien: *La musique en France des lumières au romantisme (1789–1830)* (Paris, 1986)

M. E. C. Bartlet: 'Revolutionschanson und Hymne im Repertoire der Pariser Oper, 1793–1794', *Die französische Revolution als Bruch des gesellschaftlichen Bewusstseins*, ed. R. Reichardt and R. Koselleck (Munich, 1988), 479–507

——: 'Bonaparte et Méhul', *Ardenne wallonne* [Cercle d'histoire régionale de la pointe de Givet et terres limitrophes], no. 37 (1989), 57–77; no. 38 (1989), 43–58

——: 'On the Freedom of the Theatre and Censorship: the *Adrien* Debate (1792)', *Musique, histoire, démocratie: Paris 1989*

G. Buschmeier: *Die Entwicklung von Arie und Szene in der französischen Oper von Gluck bis Spontini* (Tutzing, 1991)

M. E. C. Bartlet: *Etienne Nicolas Méhul and Opera: Source and Archival Studies of Lyric Theatre during the French Revolution, Consulate, and Empire*, Studien zur französischen Oper des 19. Jahrhunderts/Etudes sur l'Opéra français du XIXe Siècle, iii (Saarbrücken, 1992)

——: 'The New Repertory of the Opéra during the Reign of Terror: Revolutionary Rhetoric and Operatic Consequences', *Music and the French Revolution*, ed. M. Boyd (Cambridge, 1992), 107–56

M. ELIZABETH C. BARTLET

Meier, Johanna (*b* Chicago, 13 Feb 1938). American soprano. She studied in New York and made her début in 1969 as the Countess (*Capriccio*) with the New York City Opera, with which her later roles included Louise, Donna Anna, Senta and Tosca. After her Metropolitan début in 1976 as Gounod's Marguerite she appeared as Ariadne, the Marschallin, Leonore, Ellen Orford, Chrysothemis and Elisabeth (*Tannhäuser*). In 1981 she sang Isolde at Bayreuth. She has sung widely in the USA, her repertory including Countess Almaviva, Agathe, Elsa, Sieglinde, Brünnhilde, the Dyer's Wife and Turandot; her powerful, full-toned voice is heard to best advantage in Wagner and Strauss. ELIZABETH FORBES

Meier, Jost (*b* Solothurn, 15 March 1939). Swiss conductor and composer. He studied the cello, conducting and composition at the Berne Conservatory and later became a private pupil of Frank Martin in the Netherlands. He was chief conductor at Biel (1969–79) and Kapellmeister in Basle (1980–83). His first opera, *Sennentuntschi* (1983), is a dramatic legend in five scenes based on a play by the contemporary Swiss author Hansjörg Schneider and has a cast of four. Meier's next opera, *Der Drache* (1985), is his longest, with more than three hours of heavily scored music. It is based on a play by the Russian writer Yevgeny Schwarz caricaturing political dictatorship and society's acceptance of it. *Augustin* (1988) is more concise and altogether more successful. With a libretto adapted from another play by Schneider, it is a parable about the plague, drawing parallels between society's reactions to epidemics in medieval and modern times. The opera is set in the present and the music is notable for its sparing use of a large 'dreamy' post-*Wozzeck* orchestra to considerable effect. The four main scenes, linked by interludes for a chorus singing Latin chant, are dominated by the bass-baritone part of Augustin, a lazy down-and-out busker who throws into relief society's hypocrisy and empty moralizing. Meier has also written a short opera, *Der Zoobär* (1987), as well as numerous symphonic works. He writes sympathetically for the voice, and uses a variety of means, including spoken dialogue, Sprechgesang and long, lyrical monologues, for expressive effect. His instrumentation and use of the orchestra bear a large debt to the second Viennese school, particularly Berg. An opera, *Dreyfus*, to a libretto by George Whyte, is commissioned for performance in Berlin in 1994, directed by Götz Friedrich.

Sennentuntschi (dramatic legend, 5 scenes, M. Markun, after H. Schneider), Freiburg, Stadt, 23 April 1983

Der Drache (2, Markun, after Ye. Schwarz), Basle, Stadt, 24 May 1985

Der Zoobär (4 scenes, Markun, after K. Schwitters), Zürich, Konservatorium, 11 June 1987

Augustin (introduction, 4 scenes, Markun, after Schneider: *Der liebe Augustin*), Basle, Stadt, 21 April 1988

*

H. Steinbeck and W. Labhart, eds.: *Schweizer Komponisten unserer Zeit* (Zürich, 1975, enlarged 2/1983) ANDREW CLARK

Meier, Waltraud (*b* Würzburg, 9 Jan 1956). German mezzo-soprano. She studied in Cologne, then joined the chorus at Würzburg, where she made her solo début in 1976; her roles included Cherubino, Nicklausse and Concepcion. Engaged next at Mannheim and Dortmund, she sang Fricka, Carmen, Octavian and Santuzza. In 1983 she appeared as Kundry at Bayreuth, where she later returned to sing Brangäne and Waltraute. She made her Covent Garden début as Eboli in 1984, and has also sung in Cologne, Hamburg, Stuttgart, Munich, Vienna, Paris and Dallas. Her repertory includes Azucena, Venus, Ortrud, Tchaikovsky's Joan and the Composer. She has a warm, vibrant voice and a powerfully dramatic presence.

*

A. Clark: 'Waltraud Meier', *Opera*, xlii (1991), 886–91

ELIZABETH FORBES

Mei-Figner [née Mei], **Medea** (*b* Florence, 4 April 1859; *d* Paris, 8 July 1952). Russian soprano of Italian birth. She married the tenor Nikolay Figner in 1889. She studied (as a mezzo) in Florence and made her début (?1875, Sinalunga) as Azucena, later singing in Turin (the Queen in *Hamlet* with Maurel), Florence, Odessa, Barcelona and Madrid. She sang in South America with Tamagno and Figner, and by 1886 was singing soprano roles. In April 1887 she sang Valentine (*Les Huguenots*) with Figner at the Imperial Theatre, St Petersburg. After opening the summer season at Covent Garden with Gayarre and D'Andrade in *La favorite*, she and Figner returned to the St Petersburg Opera where they reigned until their divorce (1904) and where she remained until 1912. She was the first Lisa in *The Queen of Spades* (1890) and the first Iolanta (1892). She appeared in the premières of Nápravník's *Dubrovsky* (1895) and *Francesca da Rimini* (1902). Her repertory included Tatyana, Natal'ya (*Oprichnik*), Marguerite, Carmen, Violetta, Desdemona, La Gioconda, Mimì, Tosca, Elsa, Elisabeth and the three Brünnhildes. Admired for her handsome presence, she combined a high degree of musicianship with a rich flexible voice. Between 1901 and the late 1920s she made at least 23 recordings.

For illustration *see* QUEEN OF SPADES, THE.

*

GV (R. Celletti; R. Vegeto)

M. Figner: *Moy vospominaniya* [My Recollections] (St Petersburg, 1912)

E. Stark: *Peterburgskaya opera i eyo mastera, 1890–1910* [The St Petersburg Opera and its Stars] (Leningrad, 1940)

J. Dennis: 'Medea Mei-Figner', *Record Collector*, iv (1949), 51–3 [with discography]   HAROLD BARNES

Meilhac, Henri (*b* Paris, 21 Feb 1831; *d* Paris, 6 July 1897). French playwright and librettist. He was educated at the Lycée Louis-le-Grand in Paris and then worked as a bookseller, but this did not hold his interest for long and he found more congenial employment writing and drawing for *Le journal du rire* (1852–5). He turned next to the theatre. Of his numerous plays and librettos, which were nearly all collaborative works, by far the most important are the *opéra comique* librettos which he and Ludovic Halévy provided for Offenbach during some 20 years. Another significant but somewhat less typical product of their association was the libretto after Mérimée for Bizet's *Carmen*. Both writers recorded that their cooperation was easy and friendly; Meilhac displayed the freer imagination and the more unbridled comic verve in the creation of shameless parody and uproarious satire, while Halévy developed ideas within a craftsmanlike dramatic framework. Meilhac was elected to the Académie Française in 1888.

Les bourguignonnes, L. P. Deffès, 1861; *Le café du roi*, Deffès, 1861; *José Maria* (with E. Cormon), J. Cohen, 1866; *L'élixir du docteur Cornélius* (with A. Delavigne), E. Durand, 1868; *La pénitente* (with W. Busnach), Mme de Grandval, 1868; *Vert-vert* (oc, with C.-L.-E. Nuitter), Offenbach, 1869; *Bérengère et Anatole* (opérette, with P. Poirson), Massenet, 1876; *Madame le diable* (with A. Mortier and A. Millaud), G. Serpette, 1882; *Manon* (with P. Gille), Massenet, 1884; *Le cosaque* (with Millaud and Blum), F. Herré, 1884; *Rip!* [Fr. version of Rip van Winkle] (with Gille), Planquette, 1884; *Kassya* (with Gille), Delibes, 1893; *Panurge* (oc, with A. de Saint-Albin), Planquette, 1895

See also HALÉVY, LUDOVIC for librettos written in collaboration.
                                                    CHRISTOPHER SMITH

Meissner, August Gottlieb (*b* Bautzen, 3 Nov 1753; *d* Fulda, 18 Feb 1807). German librettist. He studied law during the early 1770s but showed a strong penchant for the theatre and poetry. In response to his widowed mother's pleas he gave up the theatre, although he did supply several adaptations of French and Italian librettos to local composers while Privy Chancellor in Dresden; and the impresario Abel Seyler prevailed on him to write the melodrama *Sophonisbe* (1776) for his wife, the great tragic actress Sophie Seyler. In 1785 Meissner went to Prague as professor of aesthetics and classical literature.

Das Grab des Mufti (komische Oper), Baumgarten, 1776 (Hiller, 1779); *Sophonisbe* (musikalisch Drama), Neefe, 1776; *Der Alchymist* (Operette), Schuster, 1778 (André, 1778); *Arsene* (Spl), Seydelmann, 1779; *Die wüste Insel* (Spl), Schuster, 1779
                                                    THOMAS BAUMAN

Meistersinger von Nürnberg, Die ('The Mastersingers of Nuremberg'). Music drama in three acts by Richard Wagner (*see* WAGNER family, (1)) to his own libretto; Munich, Königliches Hof- und Nationaltheater, 21 June 1868.

Hans Sachs *cobbler*		bass-baritone
Veit Pogner *goldsmith*		bass
Kunz Vogelgesang *furrier*		tenor
Konrad Nachtigal *tinsmith*		bass
Sixtus Beckmesser *town clerk*		bass
Fritz Kothner *baker*		bass
Balthasar Zorn *pewterer*	Mastersingers	tenor
Ulrich Eisslinger *grocer*		tenor
Augustin Moser *tailor*		tenor
Hermann Ortel *soapmaker*		bass
Hans Schwarz *stocking weaver*		bass
Hans Foltz *coppersmith*		bass
Walther von Stolzing *a young knight from Franconia*		tenor
David *Sachs's apprentice*		tenor
Eva *Pogner's daughter*		soprano
Magdalene *Eva's nurse*		soprano
A Nightwatchman		bass

Citizens of all guilds and their wives, journeymen, apprentices, young women, people

Setting Nuremberg; about the middle of the 16th century

Wagner conceived *Die Meistersinger* in 1845 as a comic appendage to *Tannhäuser*, in the same way that a satyr play followed a Greek tragedy. His first prose draft for the work was written in Marienbad (Mariánské Lázně) in July that year, using Georg Gottfried Gervinus's *Geschichte der poetischen National-Literatur der Deutschen* of 1835–42 for historical background. Other relevant volumes in Wagner's Dresden library include Jacob Grimm's *Über den altdeutschen Meistergesang* (1811), J. G. Büsching's edition of Hans Sachs's plays (1816–19) and Friedrich Furchau's life of Sachs (1820). The second and third prose drafts date from November 1861 (the former probably 14–16 November, the latter, containing minor revisions, prepared on 18 November for Schott). At this point, Wagner found J. C. Wagenseil's Nuremberg Chronicle of 1697 a particularly rich source of information on the ancient crafts and guilds and on other aspects of Nuremberg. Also evident are motifs from such contemporary stories as E. T. A. Hoffmann's *Meister Martin der Küfner und seine Gesellen*, which is set in 16th-century Nuremberg.

Wagner completed the poem of *Die Meistersinger* on 25 January 1862 and began the composition in March or April. The full score was not completed until October 1867.

On one level, *Die Meistersinger* is a glorious affirmation of humanity and the value of art, as well as a parable about the necessity of tempering the inspiration of genius with the rules of form. The work may also be regarded, however, as the artistic component in Wagner's ideological crusade of the 1860s: a crusade to revive the 'German spirit' and purge it of alien elements, chief among which were the Jews. It can further be argued that anti-Semitism is woven into the ideological fabric of the work and that the representation of Beckmesser carries, at the very least, overtones of anti-Semitic sentiment (see Millington 1991).

Even after the immensely successful première under Bülow in Munich, *Die Meistersinger* was taken up first by theatres of medium size, such as Dessau, Karlsruhe, Dresden, Mannheim and Weimar (all in 1869). The court operas of Vienna and Berlin followed in 1870. The work was first given at Bayreuth in 1888 under Richter. The first performance in England was also under Richter, at the Theatre Royal, Drury Lane, in 1882, and in the USA under Seidl, at the Metropolitan in 1886. Notable exponents of the role of Hans Sachs have included Edouard de Reszke, Van Rooy, Schorr, Janssen, Hotter, Theo Adam, Stewart, Fischer-Dieskau, Bailey, Ridderbusch, Sotin and Weikl. Walther has been sung by Jean de Reszke, Lorenz, Svanholm, Jess Thomas, James King, Remedios, René Kollo, Cox, Domingo, Peter Hofmann, Jerusalem and Heppner. Eva has been sung by Eames, Destinn, Gadski, Rethberg, Lotte Lehmann, Schumann, Donath, Bode, Häggander and Marton. Notable conductors, besides Richter and Seidl, have included Muck, Mottl, Bodanzky, Leinsdorf, Bruno Walter, Barbirolli, Goodall, Beecham, Kempe, Solti, Karajan, Jochum and Varviso.

The prelude opens the work in an emphatic, magisterial C major, with a theme that celebrates the dignity of the Masters, at the same time possibly hinting at their air of self-importance (ex.1). A more pensive idea (ex.2) gives

Ex.1

Ex.2

Ex.3

Ex.4

way to a pair of themes (exx.3 and 4), the first, of a fanfare-like nature, standing for the Masters and their guild. An elaborate modulation to E major introduces

Ex.5

Walther and the theme of his passion (ex.5), later to form a part of his Prize Song. After an episode in E♭ (based on ex.1) depicting the chattering, bustling apprentices, three of these themes (exx.1, 3 and 5) are expansively combined before a grandiloquent coda.

ACT 1 *Inside St Katharine's Church* The act opens with the congregation singing a sturdy C major chorale (of Wagner's invention), the phrases of which are interrupted by ex.2: Walther is urgently trying to communicate with Eva. At the end of the service, the church empties and Walther addresses Eva. He wishes to know whether she is betrothed, and though Eva sends away Magdalene to find first her handkerchief, then the clasp, and then her prayer-book, she never quite manages to stem Walther's impassioned flow with an answer. Magdalene finally tells him that Eva will marry the mastersinger who wins the song contest to be held the next day. Walther is left to be instructed in the rules of the mastersingers by David, Sachs's apprentice, with whom Magdalene is in love.

In scene ii David, after some ribbing from his fellow apprentices, proceeds to initiate Walther into the secrets of his own master's art: a properly fashioned song is, after all, he says, like a well-made pair of shoes. His catalogue of the tones that have to be learnt ('Mein Herr!'), along with the appropriate rules (mostly taken by Wagner from Wagenseil) overwhelms Walther, but he sees that his only hope of winning Eva is by composing a mastersong in the approved manner. The apprentices, who have erected the wrong stage, put up the right one under David's supervision, to the accompaniment of their bustling semiquavers.

Eva's father, Pogner, now enters with the town clerk, Beckmesser (scene iii). Two tiny motifs are heard here, later much repeated both together and individually (ex.6). Pogner assures Beckmesser of his good will and

Ex.6

welcomes Walther to the guild, surprised as he is that Walther wishes to seek entry. Kothner calls the roll, to a contrapuntal working-out of ex.6. Pogner then announces the prize he intends to award to the winner of the song contest the next day ('Nun hört, und versteht mich recht!'). The first part of his address is based entirely on a new motif, ex.7. Then he changes to the style

Ex.7

of an old-fashioned recitative, accompanied by sustained chords, to tell how burghers such as they are regarded in other German lands as miserly. Returning to ex.7 and to an important idea derived from fig.*x* of ex.1, he proposes to counter this slander by offering all his goods, as well as his only daughter, Eva, to the winner of the song contest. His proviso that she must approve the man is not welcomed by all the Masters. Sachs's proposal, however, that the winner be chosen by the populace, as a means of renewing the traditional rules with the good sense and natural instincts of the common people, is laughed out of court.

Walther is introduced by Pogner and asked about his teacher. His reply ('Am stillen Herd') is that he learnt his art from the poetry of Walther von der Vogelweide and from nature itself. In formal terms, the song is a piece of gentle mockery, on the composer's part, of the *Bar*-form so prized by the Masters. Of the three stanzas, A-A-B, the last (*Abgesang*) is intended to be a variation of the others (*Stollen*), but in 'Am stillen Herd' the variation is so florid that no one is able to contradict Beckmesser's opinion that it is but a 'deluge of words'.

Beckmesser withdraws into his Marker's box, ready to pass judgment on the young knight's formal attempt to enter the guild. The syncopated motif accompanying him both here and elsewhere is a churlish version of the dotted motif that first introduced Walther, as befits Beckmesser's cantankerous character. The rules of the *Tabulatur* are read out by Kothner in a style that (as Robert Bailey has pointed out) parodies that of Handelian opera, complete with coloratura (given, unusually, to a bass, for comic effect).

For his Trial Song, Walther takes up the command of the Marker: 'Fanget an! So rief der Lenz in den Wald'. A passionate celebration of the joys of spring and youthful love, it again fails to find favour with the Masters. It is, in fact, a complex *Bar*-form in which each *Stollen* is in two parts – A-B-A'-B'-C – though Beckmesser interrupts after A', assuming that the form is ternary (A-B-A). Beckmesser's critical scratching of chalk on slate provokes Walther's angry outburst about envious Winter lying in wait in the thorn-bush. (That this is intended as a reference to the Grimm brothers' anti-Semitic folktale *Der Jude im Dorn* is clear from the parallel situation: in the Grimm tale a bird flies into the thorn-bush, in Walther's song it flies out again in an image of liberation. The matter is put beyond doubt by Wagner's pun 'Grimm-bewährt', which suggests both 'guarded with anger' and 'authenticated by Grimm'. The identification here of Beckmesser with the stereotypical Jew of folklore has profound implications for the interpretation of the character and of the work as a whole; see Millington 1991.)

Beckmesser leads the chorus of opposition to Walther; only Sachs admires his originality. Walther mounts the singer's chair (a gross breach of etiquette) to complete his song. The hubbub increases as he does so: the Masters, by an overwhelming majority, reject his application to the guild, while the apprentices revel in the commotion. With a gesture of pride and contempt, Walther strides from the stage, leaving Sachs to gaze thoughtfully at the empty singer's chair.

ACT 2 *In the street in front of the homes of Pogner and Sachs* The orchestral prelude takes up the main theme of Pogner's Address (ex.7) in a joyous celebration of midsummer's eve: trills and glissandos abound. The curtain rises to reveal a street and a narrower adjoining alley in Nuremberg. Of the two corner houses presented, Pogner's grand one on the right is overhung by a lime tree and Sachs's simpler one on the left by an elder. The apprentices are tormenting David once again.

Magdalene asks him how Eva's paramour fared at the Song School and is vicariously disconsolate at the bad news. Sachs arrives and instructs David to set out his work for him by the window. Pogner and Eva return from an evening stroll and sit on a bench under the lime tree. The new motif (ex.8) to which he expresses his

Ex.8

satisfaction with Nuremberg and its customs is reminiscent rhythmically of ex.7. Pogner belatedly realizes that Eva's questions about the knight are no idle curiosity.

As Eva follows her father inside, Sachs has his work bench set up outside his workshop. The tender reminiscences of a phrase from Walther's Trial Song (ex.9) suggest that the knight's celebration of spring and

Ex.9

his embodiment of vital youthful passion have made a great impression on him. Sachs's relishing of the scent of the elder in this solo, 'Was duftet doch der Flieder', has given it the name of the 'Flieder Monologue': it develops into an exquisite evocation of the joys of spring.

Eva approaches Sachs's workshop (scene iv) and, in a long, delicately woven exchange, tries to elicit from him the likely winner of the next day's contest. Sachs playfully parries her questions until Magdalene enters to tell her that her father is calling, and that Beckmesser intends to serenade her.

Walther now turns the corner (scene v) and an impassioned duet ensues, based largely on a demonstrative variant of one of the themes from the previous scene. They are at a loss as to how to obviate her father's conditions for obtaining her hand. Walther suggests eloping, but he gets carried away by his loathing of the Masters' pedantry until he is interrupted by the sound of the Nightwatchman's horn: a single blast on an F♯ that launches an exquisite transition to the B major of the Midsummer Magic music. Although an F♯ is sustained over many bars as a dominant pedal, the Nightwatchman's warning to the citizenry, when it starts, is in a conflicting F major. A second blast of F♯ on his horn then re-establishes B major. Eva has meanwhile followed Magdalene into the house and now re-emerges, having changed clothes with her.

Eva and Walther are about to make their escape when Sachs, who has realized what is afoot, allows his lamp to illuminate the alley they are in. They hesitate and are then pulled up short by the sound of Beckmesser tuning his lute. Walther is for settling his score with the Marker and has to be restrained by Eva: 'What trouble I have with men!', she sighs. She persuades him to sit quietly under the lime tree until Beckmesser has finished his song. But Sachs has other ideas, launching into a noisy, vigorous song of his own ('Jerum! Jerum!'). A simple, ballad-like structure with augmented harmonies spicing the basic B♭ major, Sachs's song is permeated with references to the biblical Eve and to shoemaking that are not entirely lost on the listeners. Beckmesser has less time for the poetic subtleties; seeing what he believes to be the object of his wooing come to the window (in fact Magdalene in Eva's clothes), he begs Sachs to stop his clattering. Reminding him that he had been critical of his workmanship earlier in the day, Sachs suggests that both would make progress if Beckmesser were to serenade while he, Sachs, marked any faults with his cobbler's hammer. (The coloratura of Beckmesser's Serenade 'Den Tag seh' ich erscheinen' is a parody of an old-fashioned bel canto aria (see Voss 1981). It is also notable for its obvious and stilted rhymes and its grotesque violations of metre and misplaced accents. Clearly Beckmesser provided a target for Wagner's ill-will towards what he perceived as hostile, insensitive critics – not least Eduard Hanslick, whose name was commandeered for the Marker in the 1861 prose drafts – and other reactionary practitioners. But Beckmesser's artistic failings are also precisely those ascribed to the Jews in *Das Judenthum in der Musik*, and it may be argued that the serenade is also a parody of the Jewish cantorial style.)

The commotion caused by Sachs's hammering and Beckmesser's attempts to make himself heard above it brings the populace out on to the streets. A riot ensues (scene vii), during which David, under the impression that he is courting Magdalene, cudgels Beckmesser. The music of the Riot Scene, which takes up the theme of Beckmesser's Serenade, and which contains more than a dozen polyphonic lines, is notoriously difficult to perform; a simplified version, initiated by Toscanini, is used in many houses. At the height of the pandemonium, the Nightwatchman's horn is heard again. Everybody disperses, and by the time he arrives on the scene the streets are empty; he rubs his eyes in disbelief.

ACT 3.i–iv *Sachs's workshop* The prelude to the third act, familiar as a concert item, opens with a broadly phrased theme on the cellos, taken up contrapuntally by the violas and, in turn, second and first violins; the theme (ex.10) has earlier been heard as a counter-

Ex.10

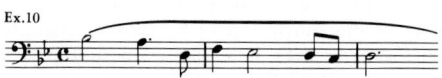

melody to Sachs's 'Jerum! Jerum!' in Act 2. The horns and bassoons then intone the solemn chorale that is to become the ode of homage to Sachs sung by the assembled townsfolk at the end of the opera. Announced by the characteristic semiquavers of the apprentices, David enters the workshop. Sachs, deep in thought, at first ignores him but then asks him to sing the verses he has learnt for the festival of St John, celebrated on midsummer's day. His mind still on the events of the previous evening, David begins his ditty to the tune of Beckmesser's Serenade and has to start again: 'Am Jordan Sankt Johannes stand'. David belatedly realizes that it is also his master's name-day (Hans = Johannes). When the apprentice has left, Sachs resumes his philosophical meditation on the follies of humanity: 'Wahn! Wahn! Überall Wahn!' (The concept of *Wahn*, which includes the notions of illusion, folly and madness, lies at the heart of *Die Meistersinger*: by the 1860s, Wagner had come to believe that all human endeavour was underpinned by illusion and futility, though art, he considered, was a 'noble illusion'.) The 'Wahn Monologue', as it is often known, begins with

ex.10; ex.8 is heard as Sachs's thoughts turn to Nuremberg and its normally peaceful customs. The memory of the riot returns, but the agitated quavers are banished by the serene music of the Midsummer Magic. The last part of the Monologue, the dawning of midsummer's day, brings back ex.7.

The end of Sachs's reverie, and the beginning of scene ii, is signified by a modulation with harp arpeggios, rather in the manner of a cinematic 'dissolve'; similar gestures occur later too in connection with dreams and reveries. Walther appears and tells Sachs of a wonderful dream. Sachs urges him to recount it as it may enable him to win the Master's prize. (Wagner had readily become a convert to the Schopenhauerian view that creativity originates in the dream-world.) Walther's resistance to the demands of the Masters is overcome in the name of love, and he embarks on his Morning Dream Song – what is to become the Prize Song: 'Morgenlich leuchtend in rosigem Schein'. He produces one *Stollen* and then, at Sachs's bidding, another similar, followed by an *Abgesang* (ex.5). Under Sachs's instruction, Walther goes on to produce another three stanzas. The last part of the overall structure (A-A-A), each section of which is in *Bar*-form (A-A-B), is not supplied until scene iv.

In the third scene, Beckmesser appears alone in the workshop. After his beating the night before, he is limping and stumbling, and prey to nightmarish memories and imaginings. All this is depicted in a 'pantomime' notable for its anarchically progressive musical style. Picking up Walther's freshly penned song, he pockets it on Sachs's re-entry. He adduces it as proof that Sachs means to enter the song contest, but Sachs denies such a plan and offers him the song. Beckmesser's suspicions are eventually allayed, and he delightedly retires in order to memorize the song.

Eva enters (scene iv) and under the cover of a complaint about the shoes Sachs has made for her, she expresses her anxieties about Walther and the coming contest. Sachs affects not to understand, and pretends not to notice Walther's arrival, in spite of Eva's passionate cry and the orchestra's thrilling tonal shift on to a dominant 9th chord in B major. Walther delivers the final section of his song and Eva, moved to tears, sobs on the shoulder of Sachs, until the latter drags himself away, complaining about the lot of the cobbler. Eva, emotionally torn between the avuncular shoemaker and her younger lover, draws Sachs to her again. Sachs reminds her of the story of Tristan and Isolde and says he has no wish to play the role of King Mark; the themes of the opening of Wagner's *Tristan* and of King Mark are recalled here.

Magdalene and David arrive, and Sachs, with a cuff on his ear, announces David's promotion to journeyman, in time to witness the baptism of 'a child' (the themes of the Masters and of the opening chorale are heard at this point). The progeny turns out to be Walther's new song. The music moves to a plateau of Gb major, a tritone from the C major of the surrounding scenes, for Eva's introduction to the celebrated quintet, 'Selig, wie die Sonne'.

3.v *An open meadow on the Pegnitz* The themes associated with Nuremberg (ex.8) and midsummer's day (ex.7), along with fig.*x* of ex.1, effect a transition to the fifth scene. The townsfolk are all gathered and, to the accompaniment of fanfares on stage, greet the processions of the guilds: first the shoemakers, then the tailors and bakers. A boat brings 'maidens from Fürth'

*'Die Meistersinger von
Nürnberg' (Wagner):
model of Heinrich Döll's
set for Act 3 scene v (an
open meadow on the
Pegnitz) for the original
production at the
Königliches Hof- und
Nationaltheater, Munich,
21 June 1868*

and the apprentices begin dancing with them; David, at
first reluctant, is drawn in.

At last the Masters arrive, to the music of the first-act
prelude. Sachs is hailed by the populace with the chorale
from the third-act prelude to the words with which the
historical Sachs greeted Luther and the Reformation:
'Wach auf, es nahet gen den Tag'. Sachs modestly
acknowledges the homage and exhorts people and
Masters to accord the coming contest and prize their
due worth. Beckmesser, who has frantically been trying
to memorize Walther's song, is led first to the platform.
His rendering of the song, to the tune of his own
Serenade, is marked by grotesque misaccentuations and
violations of metre, but it is his garbling of the words,
producing an absurd, tasteless parody of the original,
that provoke a crescendo of hilarity in the audience. He
presses on in confusion, but only makes a greater fool of
himself. Finally he rushes from the platform, denouncing Sachs as the author.

Sachs refutes that honour and introduces the man
who will make sense of it for them. Walther's Prize
Song, 'Morgenlich leuchtend in rosigem Schein',
compresses his earlier dry run into a single *Bar*-form of
three stanzas (*A-A-B*) but with each stanza expanded. In
several details, including the heartwarming plunge into
B major (from a tonic of C) in the second stanza,
Walther's prize-winning entry is a greater infraction of
the rules than ever. But the Masters are evidently swept
away by Walther's artistic integrity and impassioned
delivery, for he is awarded the prize by general consent.

When Pogner proffers the Master's chain to Walther,
he impetuously refuses, and Sachs delivers a homily (to
exx.1 and 3, together with the Prize Song) about the art
that the Masters have cultivated and preserved throughout Germany's troubled history: 'Verachtet mir die
Meister nicht'. Sachs's address concludes with a celebration of the sovereignty of the German spirit – a theme
dear to Wagner's heart in the 1860s; that spirit, it is
proposed, can never be exterminated so long as the great
German art that sustains it is respected. The salient
themes of the opera's prelude, notably ex.4, are recalled
for the final choral apostrophe to Sachs and 'holy German art'.

* * *

The only comedy among Wagner's mature works, *Die
Meistersinger* is a rich, perceptive music drama widely
admired for its warm humanity but regarded with suspicion by some for its dark underside. Its genial aspect is
immensely enhanced by the technical mastery displayed
by Wagner at the height of his powers.

BARRY MILLINGTON

Meister und Margarita, Der (i) ('The Master and
Margarita'). *Romantische Oper* in 10 scenes by RAINER
KUNAD to a libretto by Heinz Czechowski after MIKHAIL
AFANAS'YEVICH BULGAKOV's novel; Karlsruhe, Staats-
theater, 9 March 1986.

The opera is set in Moscow around 1930. The Master
(tenor), author of a novel about Jesus and Pilate,
despairs of the conclusion of his work. Persecuted by
Stalinist *apparatchiks*, he collapses, despite psychiatric
treatment; the Devil (bass) and his assistants (soprano,
tenor, baritone), however, ensure that the novel
becomes known in Moscow, while the Master and his
lover Margarita (mezzo-soprano) eventually find the
solution of all problems in their 'eternal house'. This
second of Kunad's operas on a Faustian theme, which
requires vast musical forces, deals with subjects ranging
from the most banal of bureaucrats through human love
and the doings of the Devil to Christ himself. In moving
from avant-garde music towards a 'new' tonality,
Kunad employs typically 'romantic' methods such as
dominant 7ths, the aria, a quartet of soloists and *secco*
recitative. But in the same way as the Devil cuts a
sympathetic figure in this work, helping good to prevail,
the traditional associations of musical methods are
switched in line with Kunad's paradoxical formula of
'aggressive harmoniousness and conciliatory dissonance'. Commissioned for Weimar, the opera was unable to have its première there because of Kunad's emigration to West Germany. The Karlsruhe première, with
its explosive subject matter, was staged by the exiled
Soviet director Yuri Lyubimov. This production, and a
televised performance at the Warsaw Autumn festival in
the presence of prominent political figures, created a

considerable sensation in what was then the Eastern bloc.

JOCHEN SCHÖNLEBER

Meister und Margarita, Der (ii) ('The Master and Margarita'). Opera in two acts by YORK HÖLLER to a libretto by the composer after MIKHAIL AFANAS'YEVICH BULGAKOV's novel; Paris, Opéra, 20 May 1989.

Commissioned by the Paris Opéra and the Hamburg Staatsoper, Höller's operatic version of Bulgakov's surreal allegory of Stalinism, in which the Devil and his retinue wreak havoc in 1930s Moscow, filters out the main narrative strands of the teeming novel while preserving its most spectacularly 'operatic' episodes. Woland (baritone), accompanied by the giant cat Behemoth (mezzo-soprano), bring disaster to everyone who crosses their path, and only the Master (baritone), a writer, and his lover Margarita (soprano) can survive the exploitation of their basest instincts. The Master has been incarcerated in a psychiatric hospital for writing a novel about Pontius Pilate in which he has explored the relationship between power and responsibility, and scenes from this retelling of the Crucifixion story are interspersed with the main narrative.

In the opera's most spectacular set pieces – Woland's appearance at the music hall, Margarita's night flight over the rooftops of Moscow, the Satanic Ball in which she is crowned queen of the underworld and the lovers' final journey to peaceful eternity – Höller uses a wide range of musical resources, including extensive use of pre-recorded tapes (realized at IRCAM in Paris and in Cologne) married to live orchestral textures, and musical collage, 'time-travelling' from the Renaissance to present-day rock (for the Satanic Ball). If such techniques of synthesis reveal a debt to his teacher B. A. Zimmermann, the vocal writing, often highly wrought and expressive, more clearly suggests Berg's *Lulu* as its model.

ANDREW CLEMENTS

Mekler, Mani (*b* Haifa, 2 July 1949). Israeli soprano. She studied in Italy and in 1976 sang Leonora (*Il trovatore*) in Stockholm. She also sang Leonora with the WNO (1977) and the First Lady at Glyndebourne (1978); at Wexford (1978–9) she sang Marta (*Tiefland*) and Julia (*La vestale*). In 1979 she was engaged at the Deutsche Oper am Rhein, Düsseldorf, where she sang Jenůfa, Chrysothemis, Míla (*Osud*) and Katerina Izmaylova. She has also appeared at Drottningholm, Zürich, Louisville and Long Beach and at La Scala, where she created Elizabeth in Testi's *Riccardo III* (1987). Her repertoire includes Gluck's Alcestis, Fiordiligi, Senta, Ariadne, Salome, Mimì, Tosca, Manon Lescaut, Butterfly and Goneril in Reimann's *Lear*, the last an example of the kind of powerfully dramatic part in which she excels.

ELIZABETH FORBES

Melani. Italian family of musicians. In addition to their individual contributions, the seven sons and two daughters of Domenico Melani, bellringer of Pistoia, were remarkable for their success in the church, opera and politics of the 17th century. (1) Jacopo, (2) Atto and (3) Alessandro, all important to opera, are discussed separately below. The others (who were born and died in Pistoia, except where otherwise stated) included Francesco Maria (Padre Filippo) (*b* 1628; *d* ? Florence, *c*1703), a soprano who sang a leading role in Cavalli's *Xerse* (1660, Paris) and, while serving the Medici (1672–1700), in Cerri's *Con la forza d'amor si vince*

amore (1679, Pratolino); Bartolomeo (*b* 1634; *d* 1703), organist, *maestro di cappella* of Pistoia Cathedral and singer in Jacopo's *Ercole in Tebe* (1661, Florence), and in other operas at the Pergola and Cocomero theatres; and Vincentio Paolo (*b* 1637; *d* before 1667), soprano in *Ercole in Tebe*.

(1) **Jacopo Melani** (*b* Pistoia, 6 July 1623; *d* Pistoia, 18 Aug 1676). Composer. He worked as organist of Pistoia Cathedral, and from 1657 to 1667 as *maestro di cappella* there, also composing music for Prince Mattias de' Medici. He wrote his first known dramatic works between 1655 and 1657 as a member of the Sorgenti, an academy of common citizens who occupied the newly constructed theatre in via del Cocomero in Florence. His fame and historical importance, however, rest primarily on his comic operas produced during the carnivals between 1657 and 1662 by the Accademia degli Immobili, a dramaturgical society of the nobility, in their new theatre in via della Pergola. Only the first and most famous of the four has survived, *Il potestà di Colognole*, written for the inauguration of the Pergola. The Immobili also mounted his *festa teatrale Ercole in Tebe*, for the wedding of Cosimo III de' Medici and Marguerite Louise of Orléans, in the Pergola in July 1661. This opera set the style for the coronation operas for Louis XIV (Cavalli's *Ercole amante*, 1662) and Leopold I of Austria (Cesti's *Il pomo d'oro*, 1668).

After resigning his positions in Pistoia and moving to Rome, Melani composed *Girello*, which was performed in 1668 at the Palazzo Colonna with a prologue by Alessandro Stradella. This *dramma musicale burlesco*, a rare example of operatic political satire, inaugurated a second period of Roman comic opera and was followed by works by Alessandro Melani, Bernardo Pasquini, Stradella and others. One of the most frequently performed operas of the century, it was staged throughout Italy between 1669 and 1676 by a touring troupe of *comici*, of which Melani may well have been a member (see below). For Carnival 1663 Melani prepared a *dramma civile*, *Amor vuol inganno*, but because of Cardinal Giovanni de' Medici's death (22 January) it was not staged until 1680 as *La vedova*. His next two operas, *Il ritorno d'Ulisse* (1669) and *Enea in Italia* (1670), were performed in Pisa during the annual February sojourn of the Medici court. Both were intended to entertain Marguerite Louise of Orléans and consequently featured ballets in which the princess (and Prince Cosimo in *Enea*) danced with her court. They thus anticipate aspects of Lully's French operas. Melani's final work was another *dramma civile*, *Tacere et amare*, performed in 1674 at the Cocomero by the Infuocati, whose members danced in the ballets and the *abbattimento*.

Melani's music is tuneful, graceful and, especially in the lovers' parts, tinged with sweet melancholy. Within the basic contrast between the elegant, irregular style of the serious roles and the folklike, more regular comic style, he maintained subtle distinctions between individual characters. A model for Tuscan composers of the next century, his music established melodic prototypes which, through the revival of his comic operas early in the 18th century, informed the styles of Ferdinando Rutini, Giuseppe Moneta and Michele Neri Bondi. By the third quarter of the century that style had merged harmoniously with the Florentine taste for farces 'in the French manner'.

See also GIRELLO *and* POTESTÀ DI COLOGNOLE, IL.

Intermedi with La donna più costante, Florence, Cocomero, wint. 1655–6

Il potestà di Colognole [La Tancia] (dramma civile rusticale, 3, G. A. Moniglia), Florence, Pergola, 5 Feb 1657, *D-Bds, I- Fc, Rvat,* excerpts in Goldschmidt

Scipione in Cartagine (dramma musicale, 3, Moniglia), Florence, Cocomero, 25 Nov 1657, lib. *Bc*

Il pazzo per forza (dramma civile rusticale, 3, Moniglia), Florence, Pergola, 20 Feb 1658, lib. *Fn*

Il vecchio balordo [burlato] (dramma civile, 3), Florence, Pergola, carn. 1659, lib. *Fn*

Ercole in Tebe (festa teatrale, 3, Moniglia), Florence, Pergola, 8 July 1661, *B-Bc, F-Pn, I-PSrospigliosi, Rvat, US-Wc*

Amor vuol inganno (dramma civile, 3, Moniglia), for carn. 1663 but unperf.; as La vedova, ovvero Amor vuol inganno, Florence, garden of Marchese Bartolomeo Corsini, 1680, lib. in Moniglia: Poesie dramatiche, iii (Florence, 1689)

Il Girello (dramma musicale burlesco, prol., 3, F. Acciaiuoli), Rome, Palazzo Colonna, 4 Feb 1668, *GB-Lbl, I-MOe, Nc, Rvat, STborromeo* [prol. by A. Stradella]

Il ritorno d'Ulisse (dramma musicale, 3, Moniglia), Pisa, Palazzo dei Medici, Feb 1669, lib. in Moniglia: Poesie dramatiche, i (Florence, 1689)

Enea in Italia (dramma musicale, 3, Moniglia), Pisa, Palazzo dei Medici, Feb 1670, *Fn* (lacking ballet music)

Tacere et amare (dramma civile musicale, 3, Moniglia), Florence, Cocomero, 7 Jan 1674, lib. *Bc* and *Mb*

(2) Atto Melani (*b* Pistoia, 31 March 1626; *d* Paris, 1714). Alto castrato. He was the first of the brothers to attain an international status. At about 15 years of age he entered the service of Prince Mattias de' Medici, who sent him to Rome in March 1644 to study with Luigi Rossi and Marc'Antonio Pasqualini. In the autumn he and Jacopo performed in an unknown Italian opera in Paris, and his singing attracted the attention of Queen Anne and her minister Mazarin. He returned to the French court in 1647 to sing in Rossi's *Orfeo* and again in Cavalli's *Xerse* in 1660, meanwhile serving Mazarin as a courier and spy and travelling extensively in Europe. Implicated in the embezzlement perpetrated by the minister of finance, Fouquet, he was banished from France in 1661 and spent his exile mostly in Rome. After receiving a pardon in 1679 he returned to France, where he remained for the rest of his life. His extant compositions include 15 solo cantatas and one duet.

(3) Alessandro Melani (*b* Pistoia, 4 Feb 1639; *d* Rome, 3 Oct 1703). Composer. Known primarily for his oratorios and liturgical music, he held a series of posts as *maestro di cappella*, notably at S Luigi dei Francesi, Rome (from 1672); he also wrote a number of operas. He moved with his brother Jacopo from Pistoia to Rome in 1667 to enjoy the favourable conditions of the Rospigliosi papacy, and on 2 February 1668 was paid by the Rospigliosi for an opera 'performed in the past Carnival'. The brothers were engaged to write two operas for Maria Mancini Colonna (Mazarin's niece, mistress of the young Louis XIV and later the unwilling wife of Lorenzo Colonna), who had also been such a close friend of Atto in Paris that their relationship caused gossip. The two operas were *Girello* (1668) by Jacopo (see above) and *L'empio punito* (1669) by Alessandro, on a subject taken by Filippo Acciaiuoli from Tirso de Molina's *El burlador de Sevilla* and converted into verse by G. F. Apolloni. The latter, chiefly known as the first opera on the subject of Don Juan, openly represented Maria Mancini's anger at being married to a notorious womanizer and is a satire on philanderers. But when Maria deserted her husband in 1672, after a performance at the Tordinona of Cesti's *La Dori* (which concerns the escape of a Christian princess from a harem), Alessandro was apparently barred from writing operas for production in Rome, a sign probably of the displeasure of Roman secular society, if not of Lorenzo Colonna himself; afterwards, the only dramatic work to which he contributed there was a sacred opera, *Santa Dimna* (1687), for which he composed Act 1.

Outside Rome, however, Alessandro Melani's operas continued to be in demand. His most successful *dramma per musica* was *Il carceriere di se medesimo*, with a libretto by Lodovico Adimari, first performed by the Infuocati at the Cocomero theatre in Florence in 1681. It is distinguished by having two distinct plots presented in alternating groups of scenes, a form anticipating the parallel plots of serious dramas with intervening comic scenes around 1700. It was subsequently performed in Reggio Emilia in 1684 and in Bologna in 1697. At a time when the vogue for the genre was waning, Melani composed three pastoral operas notable for elaboration and length. One, *Ama chi t'ama* (best known as *Gli amori di Lidia e Clori*), is classified in the published libretto (Siena, 1682) as a *dramma per musica* apparently only because of its full three-act format, since the plot and characters are typical of the pastorale. It may have been composed for Pope Clement X, whose death in 1676 prevented its performance in Rome; it was eventually staged in Siena in 1682 and revived in Bologna in 1688 and 1691.

In addition to the patronage of several noble Roman families and of three successive popes, Melani cultivated an impressive list of secular patrons elsewhere, of whom the most continuous were Cardinal Francesco and especially Prince Ferdinando de' Medici. Melani served the prince as an agent for recruiting Roman opera singers and composed at least one comic opera (*Il finto chimico*, 1686) for his theatre in Pratolino; the Florence performance in 1691 of his *Sospetto senza fondamento* was offered as a birthday celebration to Ferdinando by the Accademici Oscuri. For the cardinal he may have written *Il conte d'Altamura* in July 1695. Later in the same year, in recognition of services rendered, Ferdinando bestowed his protection on Melani.

Ergenia [?Eugenia], ? Rome, carn. 1668

L'empio punito (dramma musicale, 3, F. Acciaiuoli and G. F. Apolloni, after Tirso de Molina: El burlador de Sevilla y confidado de piedra), Rome, Palazzo Colonna, 17 Feb 1669, *I-Rvat*

Le reciproche gelosie (operetta in musica, 3, F. B. Nencini), Siena, 27 Feb 1677, *Rvat* (entitled Scherzo pastorale a 5); as Il sospetto senza fondamento (dramma pastorale), Florence, 9 Aug 1691; as Il sospetto non ha fondamento, o vero La costanza negli amori, Florence, sum. 1699

Il trionfo della continenza considerato in Scipione Affricano (dramma per musica, 3), Fano, Fortuna, 26 May 1677, arias *D-MÜp*

Il Corindo (favola boschereccia, 2, Giacomini), Villa di Pratolino, nr Florence, aut. 1680, lib. *I-Fc* and *US-Wc* [reworking with addns by L. Cattani]

Il carceriere di se medesimo (dramma per musica, 3, L. Adimari, after T. Corneille: Geôlier de soi-mesme), Florence, Cocomero, 24 Jan 1681, *I-Bc*; as La calma fra le tempeste, ovvero Il prencipe Roberto fra le sciagure felice, Reggio Emilia, Comunità, 28 April 1684; as Roberto, overo Il carceriere di sé medesimo, Bologna, Malvezzi, 28 Jan 1697

Ama chi t'ama (dramma per musica, 3, Nencini), Siena, carn. 1682; as Gli amori di Lidia e Clori, Bologna, 1688 and 1691, *Bc* (entitled Chi geloso non è amar non sa), *STborromeo*

L'innocenza vendicata, overo La Santa Eugenia (dramma per musica, 3, G. Bussi), Viterbo, ? Nobili, 6 March 1686, *F-LYm* (classified as oratorio)

Il finto chimico (dramma per musica, 3, G. C. Villifranchi), Villa di Pratolino, nr Florence, 10 Sept 1686, lib. *Fc* and *US-Wc*

Santa Dimna [Dinna], figlia del re [Principessa] d'Irlanda [Act 1] (commedia per musica or tragedia per musica, 3, B. Pamphili),

Rome, Palazzo Pamphili, carn. 1687 [Act 2 by B. Pasquini, Act 3 by A. Scarlatti]
Arsinda (dramma), Act 1 only, lost, formerly *MOe*
L'Idaspe (pastoral, 3), *Rvat*

Other works: L'Europa (introduttione), Vienna, Cortina, *c*1667, *A-Wn*; Troiani herois Aeneae iter ad elysium (cantata, Pamphili), Rome, 26 Nov 1676, music lost, lib. *I-Rvat*; Armida (cantata), *GB-Lbl* (as intermedio), *F-Pc*

Doubtful: Il conte d'Altamura, ovvero Il vecchio geloso (dramma musicale, 3), Florence, Casino di S Marco, lib. *I-Bc*

*

AllacciD; *ES* (P. M. Caponi)
A. Ademollo: 'Un campanajo e la sua famiglia', *Fanfulla della domenica* (1883), no.52
——: *I primi fasti della musica italiana a Parigi* (Milan, 1884)
——: *La storia del 'Girello'* (Milan, 1890)
H. Goldschmidt: *Studien zur Geschichte der italienischen Oper im 17. Jahrhundert* (Leipzig, 1901–4)
H. Prunières: *L'opéra italien en France avant Lulli* (Paris, 1913)
A. Damerini: 'La partitura dell'*Ercole in Tebe* di Jacopo Melani con appendice sui musicisti fratelli di Jacopo', *Bollettino storico pistoiese*, xix (1917), 45
L. Montalto: *Un mecenate in Roma barocca* (Florence, 1955)
R. L. Weaver: *Florentine Comic Operas of the Seventeenth Century* (diss., U. of North Carolina, 1958)
——: '*Il Girello*, a 17th-Century Burlesque Opera', *Quadrivium*, xii/2 (1971), 141–63
L. Bianconi and T. Walker: 'Dalla *Finta pazza* alla *Veremonda*: storie di Febiarmonici', *RIM*, x (1975), 379–454
C. Gianturco: 'Evidence for a Late Roman School of Opera', *ML*, lvi (1975), 4–17
J. W. Hill: 'Le relazioni di Antonio Cesti con la corte e i teatri di Firenze', *RIM*, xi (1976), 27–47
R. L. Weaver: 'Materiali per le biografie dei fratelli Melani', *RIM*, xii (1977), 252–95
R. L. Weaver and N. W. Weaver: *A Chronology of Florentine Theater 1590–1750* (Detroit, 1978)
R. Zanetti: *La musica italiana nel settecento* (n. p., 1978)
ROBERT LAMAR WEAVER

Melartin, Erkki [Erik] **(Gustav)** (*b* Käkisalmi, 7 Feb 1875; *d* Pukinmäki, 14 Feb 1937). Finnish composer. He studied music in Helsinki and Vienna and art history at Basle. A man of wide cultural interests, he regarded himself principally as a symphonist, but he was also a musical educator of great distinction. Musically, he veered from one style to another, but traditional late Romanticism predominates in his large and varied output. His only opera, Aino (2, J. Finne; Helsinki, National, 5 December 1907), is loosely based on the *Kalevala* and is permeated by a kind of Wagnerian mysticism. Wagnerian influences can also be found in the extensive use of leitmotifs. *Aino* is regarded as charmingly lyrical, though lacking in dramatic impact, and it was one of the works that laid the foundations for the subsequent development of opera in Finland.
ERKKI ARNI

Melba, Dame Nellie [Mitchell, Helen Porter] (*b* Richmond, Melbourne, 19 May 1861; *d* Sydney, 23 Feb 1931). Australian soprano of Scottish descent. She had already had some training and concert experience before 1886, the year she left Australia for further study in Europe. She studied in Paris with Mathilde Marchesi, and made her operatic début on 13 October 1887 at the Théâtre de la Monnaie, Brussels, as Gilda; in the following year she appeared at Covent Garden as Lucia and at the Paris Opéra as Ophelia. Her rare beauty of tone and finish of technique created an instant stir, and these virtues soon began to be matched by equivalent qualities of taste and musicianship, notably as the Gounod heroines, Juliet and Marguerite. Her Lucia in 1893 began an association with the Metropolitan Opera that lasted irregularly until 1910; she also sang for Hammerstein's Manhattan Opera, and in Chicago, and organized occasional operatic seasons in Australia. But Covent Garden always remained, as she said, her 'artistic home'; she sang there almost every year until World War I, and occasionally thereafter, making her farewell appearance in a mixed programme on 8 June 1926 – when direct recordings were made of the emotional occasion. After the brilliant French and Italian roles of her early career, she had come to concentrate increasingly on the role of Puccini's Mimì. Although her timbre was often called silvery, it also possessed in her prime what the American critic W. J. Henderson described as 'a clarion quality', adding that 'from B flat below the clef to the high F ... the scale was beautifully equalized throughout and there was not the smallest change in the quality from bottom to top'. These virtues are well exemplified in the best of her numerous recordings.

For illustration *see* COSTUME, fig.12.

*

N. Melba: *Melodies and Memories* (London, 1925)
W. Hogarth: Discography, *Record Collector*, xxvii (1981–3), 72–87
W. R. Moran, ed.: *Nellie Melba: a Contemporary Review* (Westport, CT, 1984) [with bibliography and discography]
T. Radic: *Melba: the Voice of Australia* (Melbourne, 1986)
DESMOND SHAWE-TAYLOR

Melbourne. Australian city, capital of the south-eastern state of Victoria. Founded in 1835, it was a provincial trading city and port until the gold rushes of the 1850s created sudden increases in wealth and population. From being a staging-post on the Empire opera troupe circuit, the town rapidly became the cultural centre of the country. Beginning in 1856 the entrepreneur George Coppin controlled most of the theatres and the ebb and flow of the many visiting opera troupes, enlisting touring singers and eventually recruiting his own soloists in Europe. In March 1861 the impresario William Saurin Lyster arrived, bringing a rival company from the USA, and opened his first season at the Royal Theatre with *Lucia di Lammermoor*. For the next seven years his company was to function in all but name as Australia's first national opera company. On Lyster's death in 1880 his mantle passed to J. C. Williamson; this organization continued to dominate theatre and opera performance for the next 80 years. When Nellie Melba toured Australia in 1911, 1924 and 1928, she relied on Williamson for organizational support. The Melba-Williamson seasons became legendary, but after Melba's death in 1931 the standard of Williamson's productions began to decline; the Benjamin Fuller companies, often performing with Florence Austral, gained prominence in the 1930s.

In 1935 Gertrude Johnson founded the Australian National Theatre Movement in Melbourne. Her intention, inspired by Lilian Baylis in London, was to keep Australian artists from being lost to the larger European and American markets. The ANTM acted as a training ground for young artists, though Australian opera composers received little recognition until the 1990s. In 1954 the Australian Elizabethan Theatre Trust was formed with strong government support; the Elizabethan Trust Opera Company began performing in 1956, drawing attention away from the ANTM, though an increase in living standards at this time boosted interest in the arts generally. The 1956 Mozart opera season, which coincided with the Melbourne Olympic Games, exposed the need for concert, theatre and opera venues capable of accommodating full-scale productions of works from the European repertory. As a result, the Elizabethan Trust Opera Company, which had at last achieved acceptable standards and a touring network after an erratic start, was re-named Australian Opera in 1970 and moved to the newly built Sydney Opera House in 1973. During the 1970s and 80s commercial dominance also shifted to Sydney, and with cuts in government funding curtailing the national company's touring operations, the small Victorian Opera Company, founded in Melbourne in 1962 by Leonard Spirs and developed from 1972 by its music director Richard Divall, began to blossom. In 1974 it became the Victoria State Opera, and in 1984 it moved to the newly opened State Theatre of the Victorian Arts Centre (cap. 2000), an acoustically superb underground complex.

*

A. Orchard: *Music in Australia* (Melbourne, 1952)
A. Bagot: *Coppin the Great* (Melbourne, 1965)
R. Covell: *Australia's Music: Themes of a New Society* (Melbourne, 1967)
I. G. Dicker: *J. C. W.: a Short Biography of James Cassius Williamson* (Sydney, 1974)
H. Love: *The Golden Age of Australian Opera* (Sydney, 1981)
H. H. Guldberg: *The Australian Music Industry* (Sydney, 1987)
A. Gyger: *Opera for the Antipodes* (Sydney, 1990)

THÉRÈSE RADIC

Melbye, Mikael (*b* Frederiksberg, nr Copenhagen, 15 March 1955). Danish baritone. He studied at the Royal Conservatory in Copenhagen and made his début with the Royal Opera there in 1978 as Guglielmo while still a student, joining the company the next year. He quickly acquired a repertory of some 30 lyric baritone roles, becoming specially associated with those of Mozart, Rossini and Donizetti. He was a member of the Hamburg Staatsoper from 1982, making his British début with the company as Papageno at the 1983 Edinburgh Festival. His Covent Garden début was as Figaro (*Barbiere*) in 1986; he sang the title role in Sallinen's *The King Goes Forth to France* at Santa Fe the same year and at Covent Garden in 1987. That year he rejoined the Danish Royal Opera as principal baritone, and in 1988 made his Vienna Staatsoper début, as Papageno. His fluent vocal technique is matched to a versatile, witty sense of character.　　NOËL GOODWIN

Melcer-Szczawiński, Henryk (*b* Kalisz, 21 Sept 1869; *d* Warsaw, 18 April 1928). Polish composer. He studied mathematics at the university in Warsaw and music at the institute there, with Rudolf Strobl (piano) and Zygmunt Noskowski (composition). After gaining his diploma (1890) he toured Russia as an accompanist. After further study, with Leschetizky in Vienna, he gave concerts in many European cities. In 1895 he won prizes at the Anton Rubinstein competition for performances of his own works and subsequently taught piano at the conservatories of Helsinki (1895), Lwów (*c*1896–1899), Vienna (from 1903) and Warsaw (1919–28, director 1922–7). From 1910 to 1912 he conducted the Warsaw PO and in 1915–16 the Warsaw Opera. His prize-winning opera *Maria* (3, S. Szczawiński, after a poem by A. Malczewski) was first performed in Warsaw on 16 February 1904.

Melcer-Szczawiński's compositions are in a late Romantic style, in the tradition of Chopin and Schumann. His instrumentation, harmony and forms draw on some of the advances made by Liszt and Tchaikovsky (in their transcriptions and piano concertos), by Wolf and Reger (in their songs), and by Wagner, the latter most notably in his unfinished opera *Protesilas i Laodamia* (composed 1902; S. Wyspiański). Melcer-Szczawinski wrote only three fragments of this work; they were performed in Poland several times (the first in 1902 in a concert performance), and then on 11 June 1925 at the Polish music festival in Paris.

BARBARA CHMARA-ŻACZKIEWICZ

Melchert, Helmut (*b* Kiel, 24 Sept 1910). German tenor. He studied in Hamburg, making his début in 1939 at Wuppertal. In 1943 he was engaged at the Hamburg Staatsoper, remaining there for over 30 years. In 1957 he sang Aaron in the first stage performance of Schoenberg's *Moses und Aron* at Zürich. He repeated the role many times, in Berlin, Paris, Milan, Rome and Buenos Aires. Though a fine Florestan, Loge and Shuysky, he specialized in 20th-century works. In 1966 he created Tiresias in Henze's *The Bassarids* at Salzburg and sang in the premières of Blacher's *Zwischenfälle bei einer Notlandung* and Schuller's *The Visitation* at Hamburg. In 1969 he created roles in Werle's *Resan* and Penderecki's *The Devils of Loudun* at Hamburg. His vast repertory included Aegisthus (*Elektra*), Herod (*Salome*), the Captain and the Drum Major (*Wozzeck*), Novagerio (*Palestrina*), Robespierre (Einem's *Dantons Tod*) and Stravinsky's Oedipus.　　ELIZABETH FORBES

Melchior, Lauritz [Hommel, Lebrecht] (*b* Copenhagen, 20 March 1890; *d* Santa Monica, CA, 18 March 1973). Danish tenor, later naturalized American. He studied at the Royal Opera School, Copenhagen, and made his début at the Royal Opera on 2 April 1913 as Silvio in *Pagliacci*, going on to sing various other baritone roles. The advice of Mme Charles Cahier and subsequent

Lauritz Melchior in the title role of Wagner's 'Lohengrin'

studies with Vilhelm Herold revealed the true nature of Melchior's voice, and he made a second début at the same theatre on 8 October 1918 in the title role of *Tannhäuser*. With the help of Hugh Walpole, who heard him sing in London in 1919, Melchior was enabled to study the Wagner repertory intensively with Anna Bahr-Mildenburg and others and made a third, or 'international', début at Covent Garden on 14 May 1924 as Siegmund. Later that year he sang Siegmund and Parsifal at Bayreuth, where he returned regularly until 1931. From 1926 to 1939 he appeared every year at Covent Garden, where he quickly became a mainstay of the Wagner repertory; Otello was his only non-Wagnerian London role. He was a regular singer in Berlin, 1925–39, and in Hamburg, 1927–30.

Melchior's Metropolitan début on 17 February 1926, as Tannhäuser, and subsequent appearances in 1926–7, were not outstandingly successful; his great New York period began only with his return, after a year's absence and further study (mainly with Egon Pollak in Hamburg), to sing Siegfried and Tristan in 1929. Thenceforward his activities centred on this house, until disagreements with the Bing regime caused him to take his leave, as Lohengrin, on 2 February 1950. During those years he made frequent guest appearances in Europe and in Buenos Aires. Latterly he scored some success in Broadway shows and films, but made occasional concert and radio appearances in his old repertory, even singing Siegmund with the Danish Radio Orchestra to celebrate his 70th birthday.

In his later years Melchior sang little but Wagner, and concentrated on the heaviest roles, in each of which he appeared over 100 times (as Tristan, over 200). These figures suggest something of the stamina and endurance that made him the only Wagner tenor of recent times who could still sound fresh in the last acts of *Tristan* and *Götterdämmerung*. A certain baritonal warmth remained a welcome characteristic, but there was no corresponding constriction in his top notes; Siegfried's lusty high C always rang thrillingly. These virtues, coupled with vivid and expressive enunciation, induced his admirers to overlook his dramatic limitations and even some musical defects – vagueness in rhythm and note values – which caused him to avoid the more lyrical and musically complex role of Walther. The heroic scale of his singing, even as experienced through recordings, marks him as the outstanding Heldentenor of the century.

From 1913 Melchior recorded extensively. His best pre-war years are documented by his Siegmund (with Lotte Lehmann and Bruno Walter) and by a composite but almost complete account of the young Siegfried's music, supplemented by extracts from *Götterdämmerung*, *Tristan*, *Lohengrin* and *Parsifal*, with Frida Leider or Kirsten Flagstad (1939–40). There are also many privately issued Wagner recordings, mainly from Metropolitan broadcasts.

*

H. Hansen: *Lauritz Melchior: a Discography* (Copenhagen, 1965, 2/1972)

S. Emmons: *Tristanissimo* (New York, 1990) [with discography by H. Hansen]   DESMOND SHAWE-TAYLOR

Melchissédec, Léon (*b* Clermont-Ferrand, 7 May 1843; *d* Paris, 23 March 1925). French baritone. He studied in Paris, where he made his début in 1866 at the Opéra-Comique in Auber's *Le châlet*. He took part in the first performances of Massé's *Paul et Virginie* (1876) and

Saint-Saëns' *Le timbre d'argent* (1877) at the Théâtre Lyrique, then in 1879 transferred to the Opéra, making his début as Nevers (*Les Huguenots*). His repertory included Alphonse (*La favorite*), William Tell, Amonasro, Valentin, Mercutio, Nélusko (*L'Africaine*), Rigoletto and Gunther (*Sigurd*). He sang the King at the première of Massenet's *Le Cid* (1885) and Méphistophélès in the first staged performance of *La damnation de Faust* at Monte Carlo (1893). He had a fine voice and a magnificent technique.   ELIZABETH FORBES

Mele, Giovanni Battista [Melle; Juan Bautista] (*b* Naples, ?1701; *d* ?Naples, after 1752). Italian composer. Modern sources state that he was born in 1701, since he entered the Neapolitan conservatory Poveri di Gesù Cristo on 25 November 1710 and is said to have remained there for 10 to 12 years, his fellow student for a time being Leonardo Leo. However, a signed affidavit of 1750 gives his date of birth as 1694. By 1735 he was in Madrid. The following year his opera *Por amor y por lealtad*, a Spanish translation and adaptation of Metastasio's *Demetrio*, was given, and he soon joined Francesco Corradini and Francesco Corselli as a successful composer of new operas in Italian style for the theatres in Madrid. He also became associated with the court of Philip V and in 1744 composed two Italian serenatas for court events. After the ascent of Ferdinand VI to the Spanish throne in 1746, Mele was engaged by Farinelli to serve with Corselli and Corradini as a composer of Italian operas and conductor of the orchestra at the Nuovo Real Teatro in the palace of Buen Retiro. For Carnival 1747 the composers collaborated on a setting of Metastasio's *La clemenza di Tito*, to a Spanish adaptation by Luzán y Suelves.

Mele's first independent work for Buen Retiro was *Angélica y Medoro*, written for the birthday celebrations of the music-loving Queen Maria Barbara on 4 December 1747. His last known opera, *Armida placata*, was performed at Buen Retiro in 1750 and revived there the next year. Performed during the festivities surrounding the wedding of the Infanta Maria Antonia, it was one of the most elaborate, spectacular and successful productions ever to be staged by Farinelli at Buen Retiro. In an unusually detailed description of the performance, the *Gazeta de Madrid* on 21 April even honoured the composer by mentioning his name. In 1752 Mele asked the king for permission to return to Naples, possibly because despite the success of his *Armida* he had not been charged with writing operas for the 1751 and 1752 seasons (the commissions went instead to the younger Conforto and Jommelli). The petition was granted together with a gratuity of 400 doblones. His fate thereafter is unknown.

Mele's *opere serie* have an affinity to the styles of Feo, Pergolesi and Terradellas. His surviving music is characterized by brilliant vocal writing, rhythmic vitality, sensitive harmonic colouring and a strong overall direction, and displays notable pre-Classical tendencies: the instrumental *introduzione* of his 1744 serenata (in *F-Pn*), written to celebrate the wedding of the Infanta Maria Theresa to the Dauphin of France, features a viola part in Alberti-bass style.

performed at the Coliseo del Buen Retiro, Madrid, unless otherwise stated

Por amor y por lealtad recobrar la majestad (os, 2, D. V. de Camacho, after P. Metastasio: *Demetrio*), Madrid, Cruz, 31 Jan 1736

Amor constancia y mujer (os, 2), Madrid, Caños del Peral, carn. 1737

La clemencia de Tito [Act 3] (os, I. de Luzán y Suelves, after Metastasio), carn. 1747 [Act 1 by F. Corselli, Act 2 by F. Corradini]

Angélica y Medoro (festa teatrale, Metastasio, after L. Ariosto), 1747, *I-Nc*

El Polifemo [Act 3] (os, P. Rolli), carn. 1748 [Act 1 by Corselli, Act 2 by Corradini]

El vellón de oro conquistado (os, Pico della Mirandola), 23 Sept 1748

Armida placata (os, G. A. Migliavacca), 12 April 1750

Music in: El Artajerjes [recits. and arias] (os, after Metastasio), carn. 1749

L. Carmen y Milan: *Cronica de la ópera italiana en Madrid desde el año 1748 hasta nuestros dias* (Madrid, 1878)

E. Cotarelo y Mori: *Orígenes y establecimiento de la ópera en España hasta 1800* (Madrid, 1917)

J. Subirá: *Historia de la música teatra en España* (Barcelona, 1945), 103, 105–6

R. Kirkpatrick: *Domenico Scarlatti* (New York, 1953), 110–12

A. Mondolfi: 'Giovanni Battista Mele, musicista felice', *Gazzetta musicale di Napoli*, ii (1956), 94–7

C. Morales Borrero, ed.: *Fiestas reales en el reinado de Fernando VI: manuscrito de Carlos Broschi Farinelli* (Madrid, 1972), 23–4

W. M. Bussey: *French and Italian Influences on the Zarzuela 1700–1770* (Ann Arbor, 1982), 11, 62–3, 113, 171–2

HANNS-BERTOLD DIETZ

Mélesville [Duveyrier, Anne-Honoré-Joseph] (*b* Paris, 13 Dec 1787; *d* Marly, 7 Nov 1865). French dramatist and librettist. He initially embarked on a career in law, entering the magistrature after only two years' practice as an advocate. He resigned his position in 1815 to devote himself to writing for the Paris stage, having already enjoyed some success at the Théâtre de l'Impératrice with his one-act comedy *L'oncle rival* in 1811. Like many of the French dramatists of the day he adopted a pseudonym, although it is doubtful whether many would have been unaware of the true identity of 'Mélesville'. Over a period of no less than half a century he wrote some three hundred plays of every description: comedies, *comédies-vaudevilles*, *mélodrames* (generally described as being *à grand spectacle*), *mélodrames comiques*, historical romances and others. They were all forms of popular dramatic entertainment with music that gave Parisian audiences an evening's undemanding, ephemeral entertainment. He was always willing to work with various collaborators, among whom by far the most prominent was Eugène Scribe. Scribe was also the most distinguished of the librettists with whom Mélesville was associated when he turned to devising opera and *opéra comique* librettos for composers such as Auber, Adam and Offenbach.

opéras comiques unless otherwise stated

La jeune tante, F. Kreubé, 1820; *La meunière* (with E. Scribe), M. García, 1821 (Monpou, 1838, as Perugina, la meunière); *Les projects de la sagesse*, L. Maresse, 1821; *La bonne mère* (after Florian), E. Douay, 1822; *Le paradis de Mahomet, ou La pluralité des femmes* (with Scribe), Kreubé and R. Kreutzer, 1822; *La petite lampe merveilleuse* (opéra-féerique, with Scribe), L. A. Piccinni, 1822; *Leicester, ou Le château de Kenilworth* (with Scribe), Auber, 1823; *Le valet de chambre* (with Scribe), M. Carafa, 1823

Le concert à la cour, ou La débutante (with Scribe), Auber, 1824; *Léocadie* (op, with Scribe), Auber, 1824; *Le lapin blanc* (with P. Carmouche), Hérold, 1825; *La lettre posthume* (with Scribe), Kreubé, 1827; *Le mal du pays, ou La batelière de Brientz* (with Scribe), A. Adam, 1827; *Le prisonnier d'état*, D. A. Batton, 1828;

Les rencontres (with Vial), G. Catrufo and J. F. A. Lemière de Corvey, 1828; *L'Amazone* (with Scribe, Delastre and Poirson), L. J. A. de Beauplan, 1830; *Zampa, ou La fiancée de marbre*, Hérold, 1831

Ali-Baba, ou Les quarante voleurs (op, with Scribe), Cherubini, 1833; *La maison du rampart, ou Une journée de la Fronde*, Carafa, 1833; *Le châlet* (with Scribe), Adam, 1834 (Donizetti, 1836, as Betley; S. Moniuszko, 1852, as Bettly); *Le mariage impossible* (with P. F. A. Carmouche), A. Grisar, 1834; *La grande duchesse* (op, with Merville and P. F. Camus), Carafa, 1835; *Sarah, ou L'orpheline de Glencoe*, A. Grisar, 1836; *L'an mil* (with P. Foucher), Grisar, 1837; *Le lac des fées* (op, with Scribe), Auber, 1839

La jeunesse de Charles Quint (with C. Duveyrier), A. Montfort, 1841; *Lambert Simnel* (with Scribe), Monpou and Adam, 1843; *La charbonnière* (op, with Scribe), Montfort, 1845; *Le trompette de Monsieur le Prince*, F. Bazin, 1846; *La nuit de la Saint-Sylvestre* (op, with M. Masson), Bazin, 1849; *Les dames capitaines* (op), Riber, 1857; *Le chatte métamorphosée en femme* (oc, with Scribe), Offenbach, 1858; *La voix humaine* (op), G. Alary, 1861; *La permission de dix heures* (with Carmouche), Offenbach, 1867; *Les soufflets* (op), H. M. J. Duveyrier de Mélesville jr, 1867

CHRISTOPHER SMITH

Mélidore et Phrosine ('Mélidore and Phrosine'). *Drame lyrique* in three acts by ETIENNE-NICOLAS MÉHUL to a libretto by Antoine-Vincent Arnault after Pierre-Joseph Bernard's poem *Phrosine et Mélidore*; Paris, Opéra-Comique (Salle Favart), 6 May 1794.

Phrosine (soprano) loves Mélidore (*haute-contre*), but her brother Aimar (baritone) presses her to marry a wealthier and more suitable husband of their rank. She hopes that her other brother Jules (tenor) will support her, but is shocked by his reaction on hearing her wishes. In fact, he loves her incestuously. Mélidore begs her to leave. Surprised by Aimar, he is forced to fight and then to flee, when his opponent is seriously wounded. Mélidore reaches a nearby island and assumes the identity of the resident hermit who has recently died. Jules, accompanied by Phrosine, asks the 'hermit's' advice on how to cure his sister of her affection. Mélidore profits from the opportunity to plan with his beloved her escape that night. Jules and Phrosine leave. Later, guided by Mélidore's light, the heroine swims towards the island in spite of a storm. In a jealous rage, Jules follows in a boat and tries to drown her. When he confesses his actions to the 'hermit', Mélidore, horrified, goes to her rescue and brings her ashore. Jules then realizes the enormity of his crime, begs his sister's forgiveness and forswears his incestuous love. All rejoice at the happy outcome.

The theme of incest cut short the opera's Parisian run (the Opéra-Comique turned to lighter fare during the Thermidorian Reaction and the Directoire) and prevented its performance elsewhere. However, the opera merits attention as Méhul's most experimental score of the mid-1790s. The composer sought to unify the work in spite of the divisions inherent in a genre using spoken dialogue. Act 3, for example, is virtually continuous, and includes an extended complex made up of the *air* 'Astre d'amour, heureux flambeau', a *mélodrame*, a storm in *récitatif obligé*, brief spoken dialogue and the *air* and ensemble 'D'un objet de honte et d'effroi'. Also important are Méhul's symbolic use of keys (particularly D minor and D major to represent extreme jealousy and its consequences, as in the duet 'Livrez ce Mélidore à mon juste courroux') and his tonal architecture for the opera as a whole, sometimes reinforced by unusual, formally incomplete endings for numbers, which are then resolved in some fashion by the next. In *Mélidore* recurring themes and motifs are employed much more extensively than in earlier operas. Those associated with the brothers' anger and its potential for violence (introduced in the overture and defined dramatically in the opening duet, 'Non, non, cessez de l'espérer') are prominent at later moments of crisis. The vehemence of the action on stage is often paralleled by shocking dissonances and abrupt modulations or shifts to remote tonal areas. Although not always successful, these experiments, developed further by the composer in works such as *Ariodant*, set significant precedents for later Romantic operas.

M. ELIZABETH C. BARTLET

Melik-Pashayev, Alexander Shamil'yevich (*b* Tbilisi, 10/23 Oct 1905; *d* Moscow, 18 June 1964). Georgian conductor and composer. He studied with Nikolay Tcherepnin at the Tbilisi Conservatory before becoming conductor at the Tbilisi Opera in 1924. After further studies at the Leningrad Conservatory he returned to Tbilisi in 1930 as chief conductor. From 1931 he was conductor, and from 1953 chief conductor, at the Bol'shoy Theatre in Moscow, where he remained until 1962. An outstanding conductor of opera, he was much admired for his control and shaping of large-scale Romantic works with careful attention to detail and to the balance of musical and dramatic character. As well as conducting memorable productions of operas by Verdi, Meyerbeer, Tchaikovsky and Rimsky-Korsakov, he introduced new operas by Chishko, Dzerzhinsky, Kabalevsky, Shaporin and others to the Bol'shoy Theatre repertory. He made his British début in a revival of Tchaikovsky's *The Queen of Spades* at Covent Garden in 1961.

WRITINGS

'Mïsli opernogo dirizhyora' [Thoughts of an Operatic Conductor], *SovM* (1951), no.12, pp.17–23

'Pikovaya dama v Kovent-Gardene' [*The Queen of Spades* at Covent Garden], *SovM* (1962), no.4, pp.85–9

*

'Pamyati Aleksandra Shamil'yevicha Melik-Pashayeva' [In Memory of Melik-Pashayev], *SovM* (1964), no.9, pp.73–6

I. M. YAMPOL'SKY

Melis, Carmen (*b* Cagliari, 16 Aug 1885; *d* Longone al Segino, nr Como, 19 Dec 1967). Italian soprano. Her teachers included Antonio Cotogni and Jean de Reszke. She made her début as Thaïs at Novara in 1905 and had a great success at Naples the following year in Mascagni's *Iris*; she also sang in Rome and toured Russia and Poland in 1907. From 1909 to 1913 she was with Hammerstein's company at the Manhattan, New York, where she was admired for her Latin temperament as well as for her voice. In Boston her roles included Desdemona and Helen of Troy, with the Puccini heroines at the centre of her repertory. She sang at Covent Garden in 1913, appearing in *Pagliacci* and *La bohème* with Caruso, and giving her part in *I gioielli della Madonna* 'all its romance and savagery' (*The Times*). On her return in 1929 the voice had faded, and she contributed an overplayed Musetta and an undersung Tosca. She remained a favourite for many years at La Scala, where in 1924 she sang in the première of Giordano's *La cena delle beffe*, and in Buenos Aires where she undertook more unexpected roles such as the Marschallin and Sieglinde. She later taught, numbering Renata Tebaldi among her pupils. Her recordings, which include a complete *Tosca* (1929), show a voice of beautiful quality in the middle register, with warmth and imagination in its usage.

J. B. STEANE

Melis, György (*b* Szarvas, 2 July 1923). Hungarian baritone. He studied at the Budapest Academy of Music, making his début at the Budapest Opera House in 1959 as Moralès (*Carmen*). He has taken both lyric- and heroic-baritone roles, notably in Mozart and Verdi operas, to which he brings subtle technique, colourful acting ability and a confident sense of style. As Don Giovanni he has appeared internationally – at Glyndebourne and in Brussels, Vienna, Berlin, Moscow and South America. In 1989 he sang Bartók's Bluebeard with the Hungarian State Opera at Covent Garden. His recordings include Bluebeard (conducted by Ferencsik), Rigoletto and Gianni Schicchi.

A. Rajk: *Melis György* (Budapest, 1983)

PÉTER P. VÁRNAI

Melk. Lower Austrian town with a Benedictine abbey (founded in 1089). Evidence of musical theatre at the abbey is documented from 1686, but only about 50 productions can be traced before 1785, a small number that must be attributed partly to the intense construction activity there after 1700. A theatre was built early in the rule of Abbot Berthold Dietmayr (1700–39), although it was not used until 1736. The productions were occasional, associated with events at the cloister school, celebrations surrounding the prelate and entertainment for visiting nobility. The repertory in the first half of the 18th century consisted of *ludi caesarei* (Latin dramas with incidental music), German *intermedi* (including Viennese popular comedy) and Singspiels, usually created by poets and composers resident at the abbey; a few were commissioned from Viennese court composers such as Fux (1701, *Neo-exoriens phosphorus*). The productions were subject to rigorous censorship of content, style of text, and staging.

In the second half of the century the Enlightenment made itself felt in the gradually changing repertory, subject matter, manner of censorship, shorter duration of performances, limited number of performers and smaller costs of production. By mid-century the Baroque *ludi caesarei* had disappeared and new categories such as *applausi musici* (secular choral cantatas) and Viennese-type Singspiels took their place. The century-old theatrical tradition was discontinued when the abbey's cloister school was transferred to St Pölten in 1789, following the reforms of Emperor Joseph II.

A second period of intense theatrical activity occurred in the years corresponding roughly to the rule of Abbot Alexander Karl (1875–1909). The principal outlets were the carnival performances, established in the 1870s. The productions took place annually in the Konvikts-Theater (boarding-school theatre) and consisted of full-length plays with incidental music. Later there was a tendency to present three one-act comedies, scenes or farces by composers such as J. N. Nestroy. The actors and musicians were students from the abbey's Gymnasium, and the musical direction was by members of the music faculty. This period continued until 1914.

Since 1960 musical theatre at the abbey has again flourished, in the form of annual summer festivals supported by local, state and federal cultural organizations. Unlike the practice of earlier times, however, the productions have employed entirely professional personnel. The mainstay of the repertory of these open-air performances has been Viennese popular theatre (Nestroy and Raimund), given with the original music by Adolf Müller, Drechsler and others.

E. Schuster and others: *25 Jahre Melker Sommerspiele 1961–1985* (Melk, 1985)

R. N. Freeman: 'Musik und Theater im Stift Melk: 1587–1989', *900 Jahre Benediktiner in Melk* (Zell am See, 1989), 415

——: *The Practice of Music at Melk Abbey, Based upon the Documents, 1681–1826*, Österreichische Akademie der Wissenschaften, Sitzungsberichte der philosophisch-historischen Klasse, dxlviii (Vienna, 1989)　　　ROBERT N. FREEMAN

Mellari [Mellara], **Girolamo** (*b* ?Reggio Emilia; *fl* 1677–1708). Italian soprano castrato. He sang Caligula in Legrenzi's *Germanico sul Reno* in Modena in 1677. He was later active in Reggio Emilia, where he took part in Freschi's *L'onor vindicato* (1681) and P. A. Ziani's *Il talamo preservato* (1683), and in Bologna, appearing in *Alba soggiogata dai Romani* (composer unknown; 1694) and Carlo Pallavicino's *Vespasiano* (1695). From 5 May 1691 until 1708 he is listed among the paid singers in the choir of St Mark's, Venice, as a soprano.

PAOLA BESUTTI

Mellini [Melini], **Vienna** ['La Vienna'] (*fl* 1706–28). Italian singer. She was probably Bolognese and perhaps a relation of Salvatore Mellini, a virtuoso at the court of Mantua and active in Vienna (1698–1711). During the same period other singers with the same surname included Barbara, Grazia and Eligenia (the last also known as Mellini-Fanti). She appears in librettos from at least 1703 as a *virtuosa* of the Duke of Modena. A singer who often performed with the best companies but rarely took principal roles, she made her career mainly in northern Italy until 1728, reaching what was probably the height of her popularity around the 1712 Venice season, when she sang as prima donna with the celebrated Nicolini at the S Cassiano theatre in Albinoni's *Le gare generose*.　　　SERGIO DURANTE

Mellini Scalabrini [née Mellini], **Grazia** (*b* Bologna, 1720; *d* 1781). Italian soprano. Her first appearance was in Faenza in 1741 in Latilla's *La finta cameriera*, with a company directed by the famous Roman *buffo* Francesco Baglioni. In 1742 she sang *opera seria* roles in Bologna (Cleartes in Caroli's *Andromaca*) but from 1743 she returned to *opera buffa* in Baglioni's company and shared in the success of Neapolitan, Roman and Florentine *commedie per musica* in Venice and other northern Italian cities. In Latilla's *La finta cameriera*, for example, she sang the roles of Betta and Gioconda in Vicenza, Venice, Bologna, Alessandria, Turin and Mantua between 1741 and 1747. In 1748 she married the composer Scalabrini, with whom she joined Pietro Gaggiotti's company and toured in northern Europe. She performed comic intermezzos in Hamburg and Copenhagen until 1758, and from 1749 was a *virtuosa* to the King of Denmark.

E. H. Müller: *Angelo und Pietro Mingotti* (Dresden, 1917)

C. E. Troy: *The Comic Intermezzo* (Ann Arbor, 1979)

FRANCO PIPERNO

Mellon, Agnès (*b* Epinay-sur-Seine, 17 Jan 1958). French soprano. She studied with Nicole Fallien and Jacqueline Bonnardot in Paris, and with Lilian Loran in San Francisco. Later she became a member of the Paris Opéra; she has also appeared at the Opéra-Comique. She has established an international reputation in Renaissance and Baroque music, her roles including Tibrino and Love in Cesti's *Orontea* (1986, Innsbruck), Eryxene in Hasse's *Cleofide* (1987) and Telaira in

Rameau's *Castor et Pollux* (1991, Aix-en-Provence). Her natural-sounding declamation, carefully controlled vibrato and purity of tone make for a rewarding partnership with period instruments. She has participated in recordings of Cavalli's *Serse*, Lully's *Atys*, Charpentier's *Actéon*, *Les arts florissants*, *Medée* and *David et Jonathas*, Rameau's *Anacréon* and *Zoroastre*, Hasse's *Cleofide* and Rossi's *Orfeo*.　　　NICHOLAS ANDERSON

Mellon, Alfred (*b* London, 7 April 1820; *d* London, 27 March 1867). English conductor. He was a violinist in Birmingham before moving to London, where he became leader of the Covent Garden orchestra. He wrote songs for plays and farces, and directed orchestras at the Haymarket and Adelphi theatres. In 1857 he became music director for the newly-formed Pyne-Harrison Company; during the next decade he conducted premières of more than a dozen operas by Balfe, Benedict, Macfarren, Wallace and others, and his own three-act *Victorine* (1859). The Pyne-Harrison Company, registered in 1864 as the Royal English Opera Company Ltd, was closed in 1866 through lack of funds. Mellon was subsequently conductor for the Liverpool Philharmonic Society.　　　NOËL GOODWIN

Mel'nik – koldun, obmanshchik i svat. Opera by M. M. Sokolovsky; *see* MILLER, THE.

Mel'nikov, Ivan Alexandrovich (*b* St Petersburg, 21 Feb/4 March 1832; *d* St Petersburg, 25 June/8 July 1906). Russian baritone. He studied in St Petersburg and Italy, singing at Kiev in the period 1865–7 (in such roles as Valentin and Luna), and made his début in 1867 at St Petersburg as Riccardo (*I puritani*); he was immediately acclaimed as an artist of the highest order. He appeared regularly at the Mariinsky Theatre, with particular success in Russian opera. His best-known roles included the Miller in Dargomïzhsky's *Rusalka*, Prince Igor, Méphistophélès, Ruslan (in 1871 Stasov described him as its greatest interpreter) and Boris, which he created in 1869 (for illustration *see* BORIS GODUNOV, fig.1). He sang in every opera, except *Iolanta*, by Tchaikovsky, who greatly admired his gifts. He was, however, unsuccessful as Yevgeny Onegin, which he sang when his voice was past its best, but remained a favourite with St Petersburg audiences until he retired after a farewell performance in *Prince Igor* in 1890. Mel'nikov went to the Russian stage at a time when standards were generally low; Modest Tchaikovsky remarked that he excelled in declamatory passages and cantilena, and his artistry revived the interest of composers and audiences in opera. After his retirement he was a director at the Mariinsky Theatre (1890–92).

A. E. Molchanov: 'Perechen' roley I. A. Mel'nikova, ispolnennïkh im v techeniye 25 let evo stsenicheskoy deyatel'nosti' [A List of the Roles Performed by Mel'nikov during his 25 Years on Stage], *EIT 1892–3*, 363–4

N. Findeyzen: 'Vmetso nekrologa pevtsa' [Instead of an obituary of a singer], *RMG* (1906)

I. A. Mel'nikov: 'Avtobiografiya', *RMG* (1906)

M. Montagu-Nathan: 'Shaliapin's Precursors', *ML*, xxxiii (1952), 232–8

Melodrama (from Gk. *melos*, *drama*; Fr. *mélodrame*; It. *melologo*; Ger. *Melodram*; Sp. *melólogo*). The technique of using short passages of music in alternation with or accompanying the spoken word to heighten its dramatic effect, often found within opera, or as an independent genre, or as a sporadic effect in spoken drama. The term is also used to designate a dramatic genre, popular in the 19th century, which used the technique of musical melodrama. In common usage the term has lost its musical meaning through its association with the popular Victorian dramatic entertainment, with its sentimental and sensational plots and life-and-death rescues characteristic of that genre (deriving from the French 'mélodrame à grand spectacle' associated with such writers as René-Charles Guilbert de Pixérécourt and the Théâtre de la Porte St Martin, Paris, c1800–30), whether accompanied by music or not. This article concerns primarily the origins of the musical technique in independent works of the 1770s and 80s, and the use of melodrama in opera from the 1770s onwards.

It is commonly agreed that Jean-Jacques Rousseau's *scène lyrique*, *Pygmalion*, probably written in 1762, and first performed in Lyons in 1770, with musical interludes by Horace Coignet and an overture and Andante possibly by Rousseau himself, was the first explicit melodrama in which the spoken phrase (in Rousseau's words) 'was announced and prepared by the musical phrase', although other uses of speech and music had undoubtedly been heard; one such from the 1750s is J. E. Eberlin's *Sigismundus*. After numerous performances in France, Rousseau's text for *Pygmalion* reached Vienna, where it was set by Franz Asplmayr (1772), and Germany, where it was set by Anton Schweitzer (1772) and Georg Benda (1779), as well as Spain and Italy. Benda had already used the technique in his two most famous melodramas, *Ariadne auf Naxos* and *Medea*, both written in 1775 (*Medea* was extensively revised in 1784). Benda usually employed the Rousseau model of speech alternating with passages of music reflecting the rapidly changing moods of the prose text, the text unnotated as to pitch and rhythm, although its

Charlotte Brandes as Ariadne in Georg Benda's 'Ariadne auf Naxos': engraving from the Gotha 'Theater-Kalender' (1776)

placement within the confines of a rest or a bar indicated the duration of each passage. However, in both *Ariadne* and *Medea* an occasional especially dramatic passage is read during the music; in *Ariadne* he directed that this music conform to the text underlay ('die Musik richtet sich nach den untergelegten Worten'). These techniques were taken up in the 1770s and 80s, largely by composers active in Austria and Germany, such as Neefe, Reichardt, Zimmerman, Vogler, Winter, Rust, B. A. Weber, Danzi, Cannabich and Zumsteeg, as well as the Spanish composer Iriarte; it was also much used by French composers of *opéra comique* in the 1790s, for example Méhul (*Mélidore et Phrosine*, 1794). Most of their works, like the original *Pygmalion*, were short, independent pieces, often with only one or, as in Benda's *Ariadne auf Naxos*, two characters (*see* MONODRAMA and DUODRAMA).

As a technique within opera, the first good examples are by Mozart, who, from enthusiastic accounts in letters to his father, seems to have been inspired by his attendance at Benda's duodramas *Ariadne* and *Medea* in Mannheim in 1778. For the 1779–80 season in Gotha he was commissioned to write a full-length melodrama, *Semiramis*, with text by Gemmingen, but no score survives and, although he claimed to have composed at least some of it, it is not clear whether it was ever begun. However, in the same years, melodrama scenes in his incomplete Singspiel, *Zaide*, and for the play by T. P. Gebler, *Thamos, König in Ägypten*, were written.

Zaide (K334/336b, 1779–80), to a libretto by J. A. Schachtner, includes melodrama in Act 1 scene ii and Act 2 scene i. At times the orchestra plays recitative-style chords between the speeches, but often there is melodic content, albeit discontinuous (ex. 1). In the melodrama provided for the opening monologue of the heroine, Sais, at the beginning of the fourth act of *Thamos, König in Ägypten* (K345/336a, ?1776–9) Mozart uses the technique of speech over accompanying music, again with abundant mood and tempo changes. In neither work is there rhythmic or pitch notation of the speech.

These two forms of melodrama – spoken word between and over music – continue in incidental music and in operas of the 19th century, with additional refinements. In Weber's incidental music to P. A. Wolff's *Preciosa* (1820), the Act 1 scene ii monologue for Preciosa uses notated rhythms in combination with unnotated forms, both between and over the rapidly changing orchestral passages, while in scene iv the words are unnotated and occur mostly during rests. Preciosa's last monologue in Act 4 is entirely unnotated. In *Der Freischütz* (1821), the famous Wolf's Glen Scene, Act 2 scene ii, combines singing by Caspar and unnotated melodramatic speech by Samiel, the two forms showing differentiation between human and supernatural. Later in the scene, in a section subtitled 'Melodram', Caspar symbolically joins the supernatural in his long unnotated speeches over held notes and slow trills, with spoken echoes following each count as he numbers the bullets.

Besides the uses of melodrama in incidental music to plays or as independent forms – among them, Busby's music for Holcroft's *A Tale of Mystery* (1802), Beethoven's music for *Egmont* (1809–10), Meyerbeer's *Gli amori di Teolinda* (1816), Schubert's *Die Zauberharfe* (1820), Mendelssohn's music for *Antigone* (1841) and *Oedipus at Colonos* (1845), Wagner's song *Melodram Gretchens*, Berlioz's *Lélio* (1855), Fibich's trilogy *Hippodamie* (1892), R. Strauss's *Enoch Arden*

Ex.1 W. A. Mozart, *Zaide*, Act 1 scene ii Melologo

GOMATZ O wehe! wie entkräftet fühle ich mich am ganzen Körper – wie entkräftet am ganzen Gemüte!

[Gomatz: 'O woe! How weak I feel in my whole body – how weak in my entire soul! . . . Oh, if only I could succeed in getting a short nap! . . . Only a short, mild reprieve! . . . The reward for all my sufferings. . . . I will try.' (he lies down)]

(1897) and *Das Schloss am Meere* (1899) and Humperdinck's *Königskinder* (1897, revised as an opera in 1910) – many operas of the 19th century and the early 20th include at least one passage using melodrama, even when not so designated: Cherubini's *Les deux journées* (1800), Beethoven's *Fidelio* (1805), J. Bray's *The Indian Princess* (1808), Schubert's *Des Teufels Lustschloss* (comp. 1814) and *Fierabras* (comp. 1823), Rossini's *La gazza ladra* (1815), Auber's *La muette de Portici* (1828); Marschner's *Hans Heiling* (1833), Verdi's *Macbeth* (1847, rev. 1865) and *La traviata* (1853), Smetana's *The Two Widows* (1874), Massenet's *Manon* (1884) and *Werther* (1892), Mascagni's *Cavalleria rusticana* (1890), Leoncavallo's *Pagliacci* (1892), Puccini's *La bohème* (1896), Strauss's *Salome* (1905) and the revised version of *Ariadne auf Naxos* (1916) and Britten's *Peter Grimes* (1945). Wagner's name is absent from the operatic list, though his so-called Sprechgesang may be seen as an extension of melodramatic techniques. His opinion of the use of actual spoken word with music, found in *Oper und Drama*, Part II, is that the wish of actors to declaim with music as backdrop shows the same egotistical spirit that solo piano virtuosity does; he describes melodrama as 'Genre von unerquicklichster Gemischtheit' ('a genre of the most disagreeable mixture').

While independent forms of melodrama enjoyed popularity in concert form in the early years of the 20th century, especially as performed by E. von Possart and L. Wüllner in Germany and D. Bipsham in England and America, it was in the expressionist dramas of Schoenberg and Berg that the use of varieties of spoken sound, usually given the title of Sprechstimme or Sprechgesang, was brought to a high point. While not operas, the following dramatic works show important stages in the development of melodramatic techniques: Schoenberg's early choral work *Gurrelieder* (1900–11) uses notated pitch and rhythm for spoken parts, much as in the original melodramatic form of Humperdinck's *Königskinder*; in the melodrama cycle *Pierrot lunaire* (1912) the notation is further refined to indicate whispered versus spoken words, and in the unfinished oratorio *Die Jakobsleiter* (1917–22) the entire chorus recites in Sprechgesang. The late works, *Kol Nidre* (1938), *Ode to Napoleon* (1942) and *A Survivor from Warsaw* (1947), employ simpler notation systems; the latter differentiates only between low, medium and high pitches. Schoenberg's incomplete opera *Moses and Aron* (1930–32) uses Sprechgesang tellingly to differentiate between the communicative powers of the two title characters, Moses as tongue-tied speaker and Aaron as the eloquent lyric tenor. Alban Berg's *Wozzeck* is full of both unnotated and rhythmically notated speech, as well as his version of Schoenberg's most developed style of Sprechgesang, where rhythm, approximate pitch and timbre are notated. In his directions to performers for *Lulu* (1929–35) Berg outlines the full spectrum of vocal styles from unaccompanied dialogue through Sprechstimme to fully sung (ex. 2).

Melodrama has continued as an independent form in 20th-century Europe and America; examples include Milhaud's *Les choéphores* (1916), Walton's *Façade* (1923), Weill's *Happy End* (1929), Honegger's *Amphion* (1931), *Sémiramis* (1933) and *Mille et une nuits* (1937), Stravinsky's *Perséphone* (1934), Copland's *Lincoln Portrait* (1942), Blitzstein's *The Airborne Symphony* (1944–6), Henze's *Das Wundertheater* (1948), Boulez's *Le visage nuptial* (1948), Floyd's *Flower and Hawk* (1972), Rochberg's *Phaedra* (1974) and (with taped speech) Reich's *Different Trains* (1988).

Ex.2 Alban Berg: directions to the performer from the score of *Lulu* (in English translation).

The text should be interpreted in six ways:
1. as unaccompanied dialogue
2. as free prose (accompanied)
3. rhythmically fixed by stems and beams without noteheads
4. as *Sprechstimme* in high, middle and low range*; notes indicated with ♪
5. half sung: notes indicated with ♪
6. complete sung; with normal stems

*Here see Arnold Schoenberg's foreword to his Pierrot-melodrama and the directions referring to this in the score of *Die glückliche Hand*

From the works of Schoenberg and Berg onwards, the emphasis has shifted away from the exaggerated sentiment of the 19th-century form back to the narrower interpretation of the term articulated by Rousseau – that of music that announces and prepares for the spoken phrase. In recognition of this change, composers of the later 20th century have for the most part shed the title 'melodrama' and have called their works 'recitations' or 'narrations'.

*

J. Marsan: 'Le mélodrame et Guilbert de Pixérécourt', *Revue d'histoire littéraire de la France*, vii (1900), 196–202

E. O. Nodnagel: 'Das naturalistische Melodram', *Jenseits von Wagner und Liszt* (Königsberg, 1902), 155

F. Brückner: 'Zum Thema "Georg Benda und das Monodram"', *SIMG*, vi (1904–5), 496–500

E. Istel: *Die Entstehung des deutschen Melodrams* (Berlin, 1906)

F. Helfert: 'K dejinam melodramatu' ('On the History of Melodrama'), *Dalibor*, xxx (1908), 296–302

A. Pitou: 'Les origines du mélodrame français à la fin du XVIIIe siècle', *Revue d'histoire littéraire en France*, xviii (1911), 256–96

J. F. Mason: *The Melodrama in France from the Revolution to the Beginning of Romantic Drama, 1791–1830* (Baltimore, 1912)

M. Steinitzer: *Zur Entwicklungsgeschichte des Melodrams und Mimodrams* (Leipzig, c1919)

E. C. van Bellen: *Les origines du mélodrame* (Utrecht, 1927)

H. Martens: *Das Melodram* (Berlin, 1933)

L. Granisch: *Die Erscheinungsformen des melodramatischen Stils im 19. Jahrhundert* (Vienna, 1936)

J. Subirá: *El compositor Iriarte (1750–1791) y el cultivo español del melólogo (melodrama)* (Barcelona, 1949–50)

J. van der Veen: *Le mélodrame musical de Rousseau au romantisme: ses aspects historiques et stylistiques* (The Hague, 1955)

R. Stephan: 'Zur jüngsten Geschichte des Melodrams', *AMw*, xvii (1960), 183–92

A. Winsor: *The Melodramas and Singspiels of Georg Benda* (diss., U. of Michigan, 1967)

E. V. Garrett: 'Georg Benda, the Pioneer of the Melodrama', *Studies in Eighteenth-Century Music: a Tribute to Karl Geiringer on his Seventieth Birthday* (New York, 1970), 236–42

J. L. Smith: *Melodrama* (London, 1973)

E. F. Kravitt: 'The Joining of Words and Music in Late Romantic Melodrama', *MQ*, lxii (1976), 571–90

A. D. Shapiro: 'Action Music in American Pantomime and Melodrama, 1730–1913', *American Music*, ii (1984), 49–72

ANNE DHU SHAPIRO

Melodramma (It.). A standard 19th-century term for opera with reference to text rather than music. It has no connection with the popular Victorian dramatic entertainment called 'melodrama', nor with MELODRAMA in the sense of words spoken over music, for which the Italian term is *melologo*.　　　　JULIAN BUDDEN

Melólogo (Sp.). MELODRAMA.

Melosio, Francesco (*b* Città della Pieve, 1609/10; *d* Città della Pieve, 2 March 1670). Italian poet and librettist. His works are distinguished by extravagant puns and metaphors in the style of Giambattista Màrino. Though more active in and around Rome as an author of cantata texts, Melosio supplied librettos for Cavalli and Nicolò Fontei in Venice. The first, *Orione*, was written in 1641 but was not set by Cavalli until 1653, when it was staged in Milan. In the preface to his other libretto, *Sidonio e Dorisbe*, set by Fontei (1642, Venice), Melosio explained that *Orione* had not been set for lack of time; Pirrotta, however, suggested that the real reason lay in its excessive similarity to contemporary librettos. Both librettos were printed at the time of first production. *Orione* also appears in Melosio's posthumously published *Poesie e prose* (Rome, 1672); *Sidonio e Dorisbe* was added in an enlarged edition (Bologna, 1674). Two other poems refer to Melosio's difficulties in receiving payment for his work and also contain the information that Càvalli, the object of the poet's complaint, was active as impresario at the Teatro S Moisè in Venice.

*

D. Gnoli: 'Un freddurista nel seicento', *Nuova antologia*, no. 26 (1881), 575–95

N. Pirrotta: 'The Lame Horse and the Coachman: News of the Operatic Parnassus in 1642', *Music and Culture in Italy from the Middle Ages to the Baroque* (Cambridge, MA, 1984), 324–34

R. Holzer: *Music and Poetry in Seventeenth-Century Rome* (diss., U. of Pennsylvania, 1990), 340–413

E. Rosand: *Opera in Seventeenth-Century Venice: the Creation of a Genre* (Berkeley, 1991)　　　　ROBERT R. HOLZER

Melton, James (*b* Moultrie, GA, 2 Jan 1904; *d* New York, 21 April 1961). American tenor. He studied in New York with Enrico Rosati, making his début in 1938 as Pinkerton with the Cincinnati Opera. In 1942 he sang at the Metropolitan as Tamino, conducted by Bruno Walter, and remained there until 1950, appearing as Don Ottavio, Alfredo, Wilhelm Meister (*Mignon*) and Pinkerton. He also sang with the San Carlo Opera Company (1938–9) and the Chicago Opera (1938–42). A handsome man with a confident stage presence, Melton had a voice of great beauty but limited power. His recording of excerpts from *Madama Butterfly* with Albanese is justly admired.　　　　RICHARD LeSUEUR

Meltzer, Charles Henry (*b* London, 7 June 1852; *d* New York, 14 Jan 1936). American critic and translator. He studied informally at the Sorbonne in 1875 and was music critic in Paris for the *Musical Standard and Bohemia* (1870–75) and the *Chicago Tribune* (c1875–8); drama and music critic and general reporter for the *New York Herald* (1878–93), transferring to New York in 1890; drama critic for the *New York World* (1893–6); 'official librettist, secretary and publicity director' (his own words) to two successive directors of the Metropolitan Opera, Maurice Grau and Heinrich Conried (1902–7); and critic, first in music (1907–14), then in drama (1914–16), for the *New York American*. Meltzer also wrote on music (particularly opera), drama, art and politics for numerous journals. Many of these articles reveal him to be a passionate, eloquent and convincing advocate of opera in English translation, the establishment of a national American conservatory and opera house, and the production of more operas by American composers. He had a substantial correspondence with several composers (now in *US-Wsi* and at the College of Charleston, Charleston, SC).

A gifted and experienced translator of plays and librettos, he was commissioned in the 1920s by Edith Rockefeller McCormick to translate 22 standard operas (none was published; 13 of the typescripts are now in

US-Wc). Meltzer also approached as librettist such noted composers of his day as Elgar and Gershwin, and worked on operatic projects with Debussy (*Un rêve d'Isis*), Henry Kimball Hadley (*The Garden of Allah*) and, in a lengthy and sometimes turbulent collaboration, CARL RUGGLES (*The Sunken Bell*), none of which came to fruition.   ROBERT YOUNG McMAHAN

Melville, Herman (*b* New York, 1 Aug 1819; *d* New York, 28 Sept 1891). American novelist, short-story writer and poet. He went to sea in 1839 and spent one year in the US Navy (1843), then returned to New York to begin his writing career. As a sailor he was steeped in sea ballads, songs and shanties, and his novels include many songs that he either wrote himself, borrowed directly, or adapted. Almost all settings of his works were composed after 1940, following a revival of interest in his writings.

Melville's often highly cadenced prose is well suited to musical treatment. The few operatic adaptations are derived chiefly from the short story *Bartleby the Scrivener*, and from the novella *Billy Budd* (begun in 1888, but still in manuscript at Melville's death), notably that by Benjamin Britten. Others have been made from the novel *Moby Dick*, the short story *The Bell Tower* and the novel *The Confidence Man*; the last was set by George Rochberg and given at Santa Fe in 1982.

Moby Dick, or The Whale (novel, 1851): J. Low, 1955
Bartleby the Scrivener (short story, 1853): W. Flanagan, 1961; W. Aschaffenburg, 1964; M. Niehaus, 1967
The Bell Tower (short story, 1856): Krenek, 1957
The Confidence Man: his Masquerade (novel, 1857): Rochberg, 1982
Billy Budd, Foretopman (novella, 1924): Ghedini, 1949; Britten, 1951

*

W. Aschaffenburg: 'Random Notes on "Bartleby" ', *Opera Journal*, ii/3 (1969), 4–10
J. Fougerousse: *Billy Budd from Novel to Opera: a Comparative Study of Herman Melville's 'Billy Budd, Sailor' and Benjamin Britten's Opera, 'Billy Budd'* (diss., U. of Innsbruck, 1975)
L. M. Freibert: 'A Checklist of Musical Compositions Inspired by Herman Melville's Works', *Extracts*, xxiii (1975), 3
                MICHAEL HOVLAND

Memphis. American city in Tennessee. From 1857 travelling opera companies performed at the New Memphis Theatre (cap. 1000); the Greenlaw Opera House (cap. 1600), built in 1866, was destroyed by fire in 1884. The Metropolitan Opera visited Memphis on its annual tours from the 1950s, and in 1956 Opera Memphis, the only professional opera company in the American mid-South, was founded. Its annual season consists of eight performances of four productions at the Orpheum Theatre (2300 seats) in downtown Memphis. The company was supplemented by an amateur chorus and the Memphis SO. In 1984 Opera Memphis began sharing productions with the Indianapolis Opera to save costs. Four years later the National Center for the Development of American Opera was formed as a subsidiary of Opera Memphis and Memphis State University to receive and catalogue new operas by American composers. The centre has hosted readings of staged excerpts of new operas or operas in progress, providing an annual audition forum for composers and directors. Among its first projects was Christopher Drobney's *Kissing and Horrid Strife*, based on the poetry of D. H. Lawrence.   NANCY MALITZ

Ménageot, François-Guillaume (*b* London, 9 July 1744; *d* Paris, 4 Oct 1816). French painter and costume designer. He went to Paris in about 1759 and entered the Académie des Beaux-Arts, where his teacher was François Boucher. He was awarded the Prix de Rome for painting in 1766. After five years in Rome, where he was a fellow student of Jean-Simon Berthélémy at the Académie de France, he returned to Paris in 1774. He subsequently had a brilliant career as a painter. On 4 April 1785 he joined the administrative committee of the Opéra, and became assistant to the architect Pierre-Adrien Pâris, chief stage designer at the theatre, and to Louis-René Boquet, the costume designer. When Ménageot was appointed professor at the Académie de France in Rome, and then its director, he resigned his post at the Opéra, vacating it in September 1787 in favour of his friend Berthélémy. He left Rome in 1793, stayed in Italy for some time, and resumed his post of professor at the Ecole Nationale de Peinture in Paris in about 1801. In 1808 Berthélémy, whose health was very precarious, reinstated him as costume designer at the Opéra. Ménageot worked there from 1808 until November 1815, when the post was abolished for economic reasons. During his second period at the Opéra he designed costumes for Rodolphe Kreutzer's *Aristippe* (1808); Le Sueur's *La mort d'Adam* and Spontini's *Fernand Cortez* (1809); Luigi Piccini's *Hippomène et Atalante* (1810); Vincenzo Fiocchi's *Sophocle* and Méhul's *Les amazones* (1811); H.-M. Berton's ballet *L'enfant prodigue* and Persuis' *Jerusalem délivrée* (1812); the pasticcio *Le laboureur chinois* and Cherubini's *Les abencérages* (1813). His sketches are preserved in the Opéra library.

*

N. Willk-Brocard: *François-Guillaume Ménageot* (Paris, 1976)
                NICOLE WILD

Mendelsohn, Alfred (*b* Bucharest, 17 Feb 1910; *d* Bucharest, 9 May 1966). Romanian composer. He studied in Vienna (1927–31) with Franz Schmidt, Joseph Marx, Egon Wellesz and Robert Zach, completing his composition studies with Mihail Jora in Bucharest (1931–2), where he later taught at the Egizzio Massini and Ciprian Porumbescu conservatories and became conductor at the Romanian Opera. He was one of the most prolific Romanian composers and worked in all genres. As well as incidental music for plays by Molière, among others, and the operetta *Anton Pann*, he wrote three operas, in which his dramatic temperament is evident. Post-Romantic in idiom, eclectic and intensely chromatic, with references to Jewish and Romanian folk material, the operas are distinguished by the melodic invention of the arias, the polyphony of the choruses and by excellent orchestration.

Meşterul Manole [Master Manole], 1949 (lyrical drama, 3, A. Jar, after folktale)
Anton Pann (operetta, 3, I. Roman and R. Albala), Bucharest, 10 Dec 1963
Michelangelo, 1964 (3, Mendelsohn, after A. Kiriţescu), Timişoara, 29 Sept 1968
Spinoza, 1966 (6 scenes, P. Sterian)

*

R. Negreanu: *Alfred Mendelsohn* (Bucharest, 1978)
                VIOREL COSMA

Mendelson (Prokof'yeva), Mira Alexandrovna (*b* Kiev, 26 Dec 1914/8 Jan 1915; *d* Moscow, 8 June 1968). Soviet poet and librettist. The second wife of Prokofiev, she was co-author with him of the librettos of *War and*

Peace and *The Story of a Real Man*; she also wrote the verses for the arias and ensembles in *Betrothal in a Monastery* (*The Duenna*), of which the text was otherwise the composer's. Both Prokofiev and Myaskovsky wrote songs (including propagandistic 'mass songs') on her poems.

Mendelson's relationship to Prokofiev was disputed by the composer's first wife, the singer Carolina Codina (1897–1989, stage name Lina Llubera), whom he left for Mendelson in 1941. According to his official biographer, Prokofiev divorced Codina and married Mendelson in that year. According to a document shown to and described by an American biographer, the wedding took place on 13 January 1948. According to Codina, she and Prokofiev were never divorced.

*

I. V. Nest'yev: *Prokof'yev* (Moscow, 1957; Eng. trans., 1960)

M. Mendelson (Prokof'yeva): 'O Sergeye Sergeyeviche Prokof'yeve', *S. S. Prokof'yev: materialï, dokumentï, vospominaniya*, ed. S. I. Shlifshteyn (Moscow, 2/1961), 370–97

——: 'Posledniye dni' [Last Days], *Sergey Prokof'yev: stat'i i materialï*, ed. I. V. Nest'yev and G. Y. Edelman (Moscow, 2/1965), 281–92

G. Bernandt and I. Yampol'sky: *Kto pisal o muzike* [Writers on Music], ii (Moscow, 1974), 307–8

D. Henahan: 'Is she the only wife of Serge Prokofiev?', *New York Times* (20 Dec 1976)

H. Robinson: *Sergei Prokofiev: a Biography* (New York, 1987)

RICHARD TARUSKIN

Mendelssohn, Arnold (Ludwig) (*b* Ratibor [now Racibórz], Silesia, 26 Dec 1855; *d* Darmstadt, 19 Feb 1933). German composer, son of a second cousin of Felix Mendelssohn. After studying law (1877), he was a composition pupil of Taubert and others at the Institut für Kirchenmusik in Berlin (1877–80). He then occupied a series of increasingly important posts as a teacher, organist and music director; from 1891 to 1912 he was professor at the conservatory in Darmstadt and from 1912 taught at Frankfurt Conservatory, where one of his pupils was Hindemith. Although most important for his church music, he composed two operas: *Elsi, die seltsame Magd* op.8 (H. Wette, after J. Gotthelf), performed in Cologne in 1896 and published in Berlin the same year; and *Der Bärenhäuter* op.11 (Wette), given in Berlin in 1900 (Berlin, 1897). He tried, with only partial success, to avoid Wagnerian influence by writing the first as a number opera with closed units and the second as a comic opera (based on a fairy-tale by the Grimm brothers). A man of impressive cultural breadth, Mendelssohn wrote essays, edited music and was well-versed in literature, theology and philosophy.

*

E. O. Nodnagel: 'Arnold Mendelssohn', *Jenseits von Wagner und Liszt* (Königsberg, 1902), 37–64   EDWARD F. KRAVITT

Mendelssohn(-Bartholdy), (Jakob Ludwig) Felix (*b* Hamburg, 3 Feb 1809; *d* Leipzig, 4 Nov 1847). German composer. He showed an early enthusiasm for opera and composed six substantial dramatic works before he reached the age of 21. The brilliant successes of his maturity, however, were achieved in other fields and he never realized his frequently expressed ambition to complete an operatic masterpiece.

Mendelssohn's rich and cultured family background was of the greatest importance to his development as a musician. His remarkably precocious talent was fostered by the best available teaching, and at the same time his general artistic and intellectual education was carefully nurtured. In his earliest years he showed marked abilities not only in music but in drawing and poetry, and it is perhaps hardly surprising that at an early stage he should have been drawn towards drama, in which musical, poetic and scenic elements were combined.

Mendelssohn's earliest surviving compositions, preserved in manuscripts in the Deutsche Staatsbibliothek, Berlin, date from 1820. They include a number of pieces which reveal the 11-year-old boy's interest in dramatic music; there are several passages of instrumental recitative, an incomplete vocal scene for two characters and a 'Singspiel in 3 Szenen' of which only the first scene and part of a second (deleted by Mendelssohn) seem to have been composed. This little domestic piece, generally known by its opening words, *Ich, J. Mendelssohn*, was written to celebrate his father's 44th birthday; the main characters are Mendelssohn's father Abraham (bass) and uncle Joseph (tenor), joint proprietors of the family banking and import business.

Later in the same year Mendelssohn embarked on a more ambitious operatic project, composing a one-act Singspiel, *Die Soldatenliebschaft*, to a text by a family friend, Dr Johann Ludwig Casper, who was also to provide Mendelssohn's next three librettos; all four seem to have been based on French originals. The score, which consists of an overture and 11 numbers (including an extended finale), indicates that Mendelssohn was familiar with the conventional treatment of stock operatic characters, that he already had more than a passing acquaintance with Mozart's operas and that his training in counterpoint with C. F. Zelter, which had begun a year earlier, was beginning to bear fruit.

1821 saw a considerable increase and diversification in Mendelssohn's compositional activity. Apart from setting a second Casper libretto, *Die beiden Pädagogen*, he composed among other things the first six of his symphonies for strings and a piano sonata in G minor. The opera shows some remarkable advances on its predecessor, particularly in characterization and in the musical enhancement of situations. Mendelssohn's rapidly advancing maturity at this stage of his development is illustrated by the continually growing scope of his output in 1822 and 1823; more string symphonies, several concertos, chamber works (including the piano quartet published in 1823 as his op.1), sacred music for large forces and two further operas were added to his list of compositions. Casper's libretto for the one-act Singspiel *Die wandernden Komödianten* of 1822 is somewhat unbalanced, and the finished opera reflects this deficiency, but Mendelssohn's score is more ambitious and in many respects more polished than that of *Die beiden Pädagogen*; the overture and the ingeniously constructed finale, in particular, are striking. The dialogue is not, as was previously believed, lost, but is in the Bodleian Library (Deneke Collection), Oxford.

The last Mendelssohn-Casper collaboration, *Der Onkel aus Boston, oder Die beiden Neffen*, of 1823, is in three acts and thus on an altogether larger scale. Although the music continues to give evidence of real advances in Mendelssohn's musical and dramatic technique, the deficiencies of the libretto, with its lengthy dialogue in Act 1 and rather static action later, make it an even less satisfactory opera than its immediate predecessor. A full appraisal, however, is hindered by the loss of the dialogue to the third act (the dialogue to Acts 1 and 2 is also in the Bodleian Library). *Der Onkel aus Boston* was rehearsed for the first time with orchestra at the Mendelssohns' house in Berlin on

3 February 1824, Mendelssohn's 15th birthday, and was given two performances before invited guests.

At about the time of these performances Mendelssohn seems to have begun to consider the composition of his next opera, *Die Hochzeit des Camacho*. The librettist, about whose identity various suggestions have been made over the years, was probably an obscure Hanover author, Friedrich Voigt (see Elvers). A letter written by Mendelssohn to Voigt early in 1824, which discusses structure and characterization in *Camacho* with maturity and perspicacity, appears to be a response to the receipt of the libretto. Mendelssohn, whose self-critical faculties were by now developing rapidly, proceeded unusually slowly with the composition of the music, and the opera was not finished until 10 August 1825, just a few weeks before he completed the magnificent String Octet op.20, his first undoubted masterpiece.

Camacho was the first and only Mendelssohn opera to receive a fully public performance in his lifetime. Despite the Berlin Generalmusikdirektor Spontini's disapproval, it was produced at the Berlin Schauspielhaus on 29 April 1827 and greeted with enthusiastic applause, at least from the portion of the audience sympathetic to the young composer. Mendelssohn himself was far from satisfied with the mediocre performance and with the work itself, which he felt he had outgrown; he made little effort to secure further performances.

By this time Mendelssohn had already made several journeys that broadened his experience and brought him into contact with many leading figures in music and the other arts. He had met Goethe in Weimar in 1821 and in 1825 had been encouraged by Cherubini in Paris. After a period attending the University of Berlin in 1827–8 he was sent by his father on a series of European travels that were to occupy much of the next few years and were to take him as far north as Scotland and as far south as Naples. During a trip to England in 1829 he composed his last completed operatic work, the Liederspiel *Die Heimkehr aus der Fremde*, to a text by his friend Karl Klingemann. A gift to his parents on their silver wedding anniversary, it was performed in the family home in Berlin on 26 December 1829.

Despite his failure to complete another opera, Mendelssohn never entirely lost interest in dramatic composition. In the aftermath of *Camacho* he wrote to his father:

I shall not stop looking everywhere for a librettist, and sooner or later I am bound to find one. ... I have blazed a path for myself in instrumental music ... but in other areas I have yet to do so. I know that I shall be able to do so in the genre of opera, but I am also convinced that I have only just begun to in the area of instrumental music; therefore I shall continue working until I find the opportunity to bring my ideas about opera into the open.

Four years later, in 1831, he remarked to the singer Eduard Devrient:

Put a real opera [libretto] into my hands and in a few moments it will be composed, for every day I long anew to write an opera. ... I will not set a text that does not suit me. If you know a man who is able to write a libretto, for Heaven's sake tell me about him: I look for nothing else.

But though he was to live for another 16 years and to consider many operatic projects, he never finished another; he began work on several, but seldom proceeded far. Among the subjects he considered were Shakespeare's *Tempest* in 1831, Wieland's *Pervonte* in 1834 and an English opera on the siege of Calais (with

Planché, librettist of Weber's *Oberon*). Towards the end of his life he composed a first-act finale and 'Vintners' Chorus' for Emanuel Geibel's libretto *Die Loreley*, a text that Max Bruch was later to set with limited success.

Mendelssohn's completed operas belong to the German tradition of opera with spoken dialogue. The works from *Ich, J. Mendelssohn* to *Der Onkel aus Boston* are firmly in the lightweight Singspiel tradition, though the latter shows a growing awareness of the possibilities of musical continuity, especially in the finales. *Die Heimkehr aus der Fremde* has much greater musical substance and contains many delicate Romantic touches, but is also within the same tradition. Only in *Die Hochzeit des Camacho* did Mendelssohn show any marked inclination to emulate the more substantial and serious type of German opera that was currently being developed in the works of Spohr and Weber. *Camacho* is in fact a remarkable testimony to the 15-year-old Mendelssohn's awareness of and response to contemporary trends; in the mid-1820s, just as he enthusiastically devoured the new musical language of Beethoven's late quartets (even if he did not fully understand them), so he was powerfully moved by Weber's *Der Freischütz* and Spohr's *Jessonda*. Unmistakable echoes of these works can be heard in *Camacho*. The use of musical motif, a symbolic key structure, the creation of sophisticated scene complexes and a greatly enhanced awareness of the possibilities of chromatic harmony and orchestral sonority for creating atmosphere and drama, all reveal a particular debt to these two operas. It is hardly surprising that the employment of such resources did not of itself enable the young Mendelssohn to create a great opera, but his skilful use of them shows that even at the age of 15 he fully appreciated what the two older composers were attempting to achieve. *Die Heimkehr aus der Fremde* represents a retreat from this position, and its modest aims may have been one reason why Mendelssohn was unwilling to allow it to be publicly produced. By the time he came seriously to consider a more substantial operatic venture, the wave of enthusiasm that had swept Spohr's and Weber's operas to popularity had almost spent its force; German opera was already sinking into the doldrums that it was to occupy until Wagner raised a storm of controversy in the 1840s. Marschner's success with *Hans Heiling* in 1833 marked the end of an era, and the only really successful German operas during the next 15 years were the deftly composed but modest Singspiels of Lortzing. The morbidly self-critical Mendelssohn, however much he may have wished to write a German opera, was well aware of the daunting obstacles that he would have had to overcome.

In fact, Mendelssohn's dramatic interests found a more fruitful outlet in other types of music, both instrumental and choral, in such works as the 'Reformation' (1832), the 'Italian' (1833) and 'Scottish' (1843) symphonies, the concert overtures *A Midsummer Night's Dream* (1826), *Meeresstille und glückliche Fahrt* (1828), *Die Hebriden* (1830–32), and *Die schöne Melusine*, the cantata *Die erste Walpurgisnacht* (1832) and the incidental music to Calderón's *Der standhafte Prinz* (1833), Hugo's *Ruy Blas* (1839), Sophocles' *Antigone* and *Oedipus at Colonos* (1841 and 1845), Shakespeare's *A Midsummer Night's Dream* (1842) and Racine's *Athalie* (1845). But above all he seems to have found his true dramatic métier in the oratorios *St Paul* (1836) and *Elijah* (1846).

See also BEIDEN PÄDAGOGEN, DIE; HEIMKEHR AUS DER FREMDE, DIE; HOCHZEIT DES CAMACHO, DIE; and SOLDATENLIEBSCHAFT, DIE.

Ich, J. Mendelssohn (Spl, 3 scenes [only 1 complete], ?Mendelssohn), private perf., Berlin, 1820, D-Bds*
Die Soldatenliebschaft (Spl, 1, J. L. Casper, ? after a French source), private perf., Berlin, ?1820; stage, Wittenberg, 28 April 1962; Bds*, dialogue GB-Ob
Die beiden Pädagogen (Spl, 1, Casper, after E. Scribe: Les deux précepteurs, ou Asinus asinum fricat), private perf., Berlin, ?1821; stage, Berlin, 27 May 1962; D-Bds*, lib. GB-Ob
Die wandernden Komödianten (Spl, 1, Casper, ? after a French source), private perf., Berlin, 1822, D-Bds*, lib. GB-Ob
Der Onkel aus Boston, oder Die beiden Neffen (Spl, 3, Casper), private perf., Berlin, 1824, D-Bds*, lib. GB-Ob
Die Hochzeit des Camacho op.10 (2, ? F. Voigt, after M. de Cervantes: Don Quixote), Berlin, Schauspielhaus, 29 April 1827; rev. version, Oxford, Playhouse, 24 Feb 1987; D-Bds*, draft lib. GB-Ob, vs (Berlin, 1829), full score (Leipzig, 1876)
Die Heimkehr aus der Fremde op.89 (Liederspiel, 1, K. Klingemann), private perf., Berlin, 26 Dec 1829; stage, Leipzig, 10 April 1851
Die Loreley [frag., incl. finale of Act 1 and Vintners' Chorus] op.98, 1847 (3, E. Geibel), Birmingham, 8 Sept 1852

*

Thematisches Verzeichnis im Druck erschienener Compositionen von Felix Mendelssohn Bartholdy (Leipzig, 1846; new edn, 1853, 3/1882)
E. Devrient: Meine Erinnerungen an Felix Mendelssohn Bartholdy und dessen Briefe an mich (Leipzig, 1869, 3/1891; Eng. trans., 1869)
S. Hensel: Die Familie Mendelssohn 1729–1847, nach Briefen und Tagebüchern (Berlin, 1879, 18/1924; Eng. trans., 1882)
G. Schünemann: 'Mendelssohns Jugendopern', ZMw, v (1922–3), 506–45
B. L. Richmond: Felix Mendelssohn (Molenbeek and Brussels, 1946)
B. Bartels: Mendelssohn Bartholdy: Mensch und Werk (Bremen, 1947)
K. H. Wörner: Felix Mendelssohn Bartholdy: Leben und Werk (Leipzig, 1947)
A. Koole: Felix Mendelssohn Bartholdy (Haarlem, 1953)
P. Radcliffe: Mendelssohn (London, 1954, 3/1990)
H. C. Worbs: Felix Mendelssohn Bartholdy (Leipzig, 1956, 2/1957)
S. Jemnitz: Felix Mendelssohn Bartholdy (Budapest, 1958)
H. C. Worbs: Felix Mendelssohn Bartholdy: Wesen und Wirken im Spiegel von Selbstzeugnissen und Berichten der Zeitgenossen (Leipzig, 1958)
H. E. Jacob: Felix Mendelssohn und seine Zeit: Bildnis und Schicksal eines Meisters (Frankfurt, 1959–60; Eng. trans., 1963)
K.-H. Köhler: 'Zwei rekonstruierte Singspiele von Felix Mendelssohn Bartholdy', BMw, ii/3–4 (1960), 86–93
——: 'Das Jugendwerk Felix Mendelssohns: die vergessene Kindheitsentwicklung eines Genies', DJbM, vii (1962), 18–35
M. F. Schneider: 'Felix Mendelssohn Bartholdy: Herkommen und Jugendzeit in Berlin', Jb der Stiftung Preussischer Kulturbesitz 1963, 157–63
E. Werner: Mendelssohn: a New Image of the Composer and his Age (New York, 1963)
E. Rudolph: Der junge Felix Mendelssohn: ein Beitrag zur Musikgeschichte der Stadt Berlin (diss., Humboldt U., Berlin, 1964)
K.-H. Köhler: Felix Mendelssohn Bartholdy (Leipzig, 1966, 2/1972)
A. S. Kurtzman: Mendel'son (Moscow, 1967)
M. Hurd: Mendelssohn (London, 1970)
W. Reich: Felix Mendelssohn im Spiegel eigener Aussagen und zeitgenössischer Dokumente (Zürich, 1970)
G. R. Marek: Gentle Genius: the Story of Felix Mendelssohn (New York, 1972)
P. Ranft: Felix Mendelssohn Bartholdy: eine Lebenschronik (Leipzig, 1972)
Y. Tiénot: Mendelssohn: musicien complet (Paris, 1972)
R. Elvers: 'Nichts ist so schwer gut zu componieren als Strophen': zur Entstehungsgeschichte des Librettos von Felix Mendelssohn-Bartholdys Oper 'Die Hochzeit des Camacho', Veröffentlichung der Mendelssohn-Gesellschaft, iv (Berlin and Basle, 1976)
W. Kunold: Felix Mendelssohn-Bartholdy und seine Zeit (Regensburg, 1984)
J. Warrack: 'Mendelssohn's Operas', Essays in Honour of Winton Dean, ed. N. Fortune (Cambridge, 1987), 263–97

S. Johns: Das szenische Liederspiel zwischen 1800 und 1830 (Frankfurt, 1988)
CLIVE BROWN

Mengal, Martin-Joseph [l'aîné] (b Ghent, 27 Jan 1784; d Ghent, 4 July 1851). Belgian composer. He entered the Paris Conservatoire in 1804 and after playing the horn in the orchestra at the Odéon he became principal horn at the Opéra-Comique and remained there for 13 years. He studied composition with Reicha and wrote a number of operas and instrumental works as well as sacred music. Most of his stage works, which are light and attractive, enjoyed a modest success. In 1825 he became director of the theatre in Ghent but soon resigned and after the 1830 Revolution became a conductor in Antwerp and The Hague. Finally, in 1835, he obtained the directorship of the new conservatory in Ghent, where his pupils included Gevaert and Van Duyse.

all MSS in B-Gc

Une nuit au château (oc, 1, P. de Kock), Paris, OC (Feydeau), 5 Aug 1818 (Paris, 1818)
L'île de Babilary (oc, 3, de Kock), Paris, OC (Feydeau), 27 March 1819
Les infidèles (oc, 1, de Kock), Paris, OC (Feydeau), 2 Jan 1823; ?rev. (3), Ghent, 1825
Apothéose de Talma (scène dramatique), Ghent, 1826
Le vampire (oc, 1), Ghent, 1826
Un jour à Vaucluse (oc, 1, C. Durant), Ghent, 1 May 1830

*

BNB (P. Bergmans)
E. Fétis: 'Notice sur Martin-Joseph Mengal', Annuaire de l'Académie royale des sciences, des lettres et des beaux-arts de Belgique, xxv (1859), 167–76
E. Grégoir: Les artistes-musiciens belges au XVIIIme et au XIXme siècle (Brussels, 1885)
P. Bergmans: Variétés musicologues (Ghent, 1891), 45–50

Mengozzi [Mengocci, Mingozzi], **Bernardo** (b Florence, 1758; d Paris, Feb or March 1800). Italian composer and singer. He studied singing in Florence with Guarducci and at St Mark's in Venice with Potenza. His name appears in two librettos for Sarti's Le gelosie villane, performed in 1777 in Florence and in 1784 in Naples. His London début was in February 1787 as a tenor in the Haymarket company, to which his wife, the soprano Anna Benini, also belonged. The Mengozzis went to Versailles during the summer of 1787 with other singers from the Haymarket for performances of Italian opera buffa; they then settled in Paris, and in 1789 joined the company of the Théâtre de Monsieur, where Mengozzi became famous both as a singer and as the composer of many substitute arias. His Isola disabitata is a landmark in the history of opera in France, being the first serious opera performed in Italian in Paris since Cavalli's Ercole amante. The most successful of his French operas seem to have been Isabelle de Salisburi and Selico, principally because of their spectacular element. Under the Directory Mengozzi spent some time in Bordeaux, and then returned to Paris to teach singing at the Conservatoire; he took an active part in the writing of the Méthode de chant du Conservatoire de Musique (1804) in collaboration with Garat, Cherubini and Langlé.

performed in Paris unless otherwise stated

L'isola disabitata (azione teatrale, 1, P. Metastasio), Florence, 1783; in 2 acts, Paris, Monsieur, 22 Aug 1789; 1 air (Paris, 1783)
Aujourd'hui, ou Les fous supposés (3, Bouyon), Montansier, 3 Feb 1791
Isabelle de Salisburi (comédie-héroïque et lyrique, 3, P. F. N. Fabre d'Eglantine, after F.-T. Arnaud: Salisbury), Montansier, 20 Aug 1791, collab. G. G. Ferrari

Les deux vizirs (prol., 3, P. Desforges), Montansier, 10 March 1792
Pourceaugnac (after Molière), Montansier, 25 Jan 1793
L'amant jaloux (3, T. d'Hèle), Montansier, 2 Feb 1793
Selico, ou Les nègres (cmda, 3, Saint-Just), National, 5 Oct 1793
Une faute par amour (cmda, 1, Vial), Feydeau, 16 May 1795
Les habitans de Vaucluse (1, Montanclos), Montansier, 1 June 1799
Brunet et Caroline, ou Le chansonnier impromptu (1, Ségur jeune), Jardin-Egalité [Montansier], 5 July 1799
La dame voilée, ou L'adresse de l'amour (oc, 1, Ségur jeune), OC (Favart), 28 Nov 1799

*

ES; StiegerO
Calendrier musical universel, i (1788), 112, 119
Almanach des spectacles de Paris (1800–01), 43–5

MICHEL NOIRAY

Menicuccio. *See* RICCI, DOMENICO.

Mennini, Louis (Alfred) (*b* Erie, PA, 18 Nov 1920). American composer. He studied composition at the Eastman School with Bernard Rogers and Howard Hanson. Between 1949 and 1983 he taught at various institutions, including Eastman (1949–65), and Mercyhurst College, Erie (1973–83). His many awards and commissions include a grant from the National Institute of Arts and Letters (1949), two commissions from the Koussevitzky Foundation (one for *The Rope*) and an NEA grant (1979). Mennini's *The Well*, to his own libretto, was first performed at Rochester, New York, on 8 May 1951. His chamber opera *The Rope* (1, Mennini, after E. O'Neill) had its première at the Berkshire Music Festival in Lenox, Massachusetts, on 8 August 1955. Though somewhat conservative in harmony, his music shows an expert command of contrapuntal texture, strong rhythmic drive and a lyrical, flowing melodic line.

*

EwenD
J. S. Harrison: 'What it Takes to Write Opera', *New York Herald-Tribune* (7 Aug 1955)
H. Taubman: 'Premiere of "Rope" at Lenox', *New York Times* (9 Aug 1955)

PAUL C. ECHOLS

Menorca [Minorca]. For a discussion of opera in Minorca *see* MAHÓN.

Menotti, Gian Carlo (*b* Cadegliano, 7 July 1911). American composer and librettist of Italian birth.

1. Up to 1950. 2. 1951–72. 3. From 1973. 4. Style.

1. UP TO 1950. The sixth of ten children, he was born in a country town on Lake Lugano. His father was a prosperous businessman and his mother a talented amateur musician. He had already written two operas when he entered the Milan Conservatory at the age of 13. In 1928 he began studies with Rosario Scalero at the Curtis Institute, where a close friendship with his fellow student Samuel Barber began. The two spent several summers in Europe attending opera performances in Vienna and in Italy. It was in Vienna, having received his diploma with honours from the Curtis Institute in 1933, that Menotti began the libretto for a one-act *opera buffa*, *Amelia al ballo*. He completed the orchestration on his return to the USA in 1935; the opera received its première in an English translation by George Mead as *Amelia Goes to the Ball*. A few days later it was performed in New York with such success that the Metropolitan Opera accepted it for the following season.

The success of *Amelia* brought Menotti a commission from the NBC for a radio opera. Using the *opera buffa* tradition of set numbers, Menotti wrote his first libretto in English, *The Old Maid and the Thief* (1939). His next opera, *The Island God* (1942), was poorly received. Menotti remained in the USA during World War II but retained his Italian citizenship.

A commission by the Alice M. Ditson Fund led to the very successful opera *The Medium* (1946), a tragedy in two acts for five singers, a dance-mime role, and a chamber orchestra of 14 players. The melodramatic story is the 'tragedy of a woman caught between two worlds, a world of reality which she cannot wholly comprehend, and a supernatural world in which she cannot believe'. The work is theatrically effective and the music, often quite dissonant, conveys an eerie, morbid atmosphere. Typical of the Italian operatic tradition, *The Medium* has memorable melodies such as the folklike 'O, black swan'. The opera had a run of 211 performances during 1947–8 at the Ethel Barrymore Theatre on Broadway. As a curtain-raiser for these performances (and a striking contrast), Menotti wrote a light one-act comedy, *The Telephone*, subtitled *L'amour à trois*. The State Department organized a European tour of these works in 1955. In 1951 Menotti directed a successful film version of *The Medium*.

Menotti's versatile dramatic skills, as director, librettist and composer, brought him a contract from Metro-Goldwyn-Mayer to write film scripts. Although his scripts were never filmed, one contained the seeds of his first full-length opera, *The Consul* (1950), considered by many to be his greatest work. It uses the *verismo* of Puccini's day to treat a contemporary situation: the impossibility of obtaining a visa to leave a police state. Music and stage techniques combine to communicate strongly and directly. The New York première at the Ethel Barrymore Theatre on 15 March 1950 (after try-outs in Philadelphia from 1 March 1950) was a great success and performances continued there for about eight months. The work received the Pulitzer Prize and the Drama Critics' Circle Award. It has been translated into 12 languages and has been performed in over 20 countries. With *The Consul* and his next two operas, Menotti seemed at the height of his powers and of public acclaim.

2. 1951–72. *Amahl and the Night Visitors* (1951), commissioned by NBC, was the first opera written expressly for American television. In writing it, Menotti was influenced by *The Adoration of the Magi* of Hieronymus Bosch. The work was first televised on Christmas eve 1951 and has been broadcast annually. The roles, particularly the main part for boy soprano, are skilfully conceived so that they can be performed by amateurs. The charm and clear diatonicism of the work have helped to make it one of the most frequently performed operas of the 20th century. Menotti's next opera, *The Saint of Bleecker Street* (1954), is a full-length piece in the broad and serious style of *The Consul*. It is an effective drama set in contemporary New York and concerned with the conflict of the physical and spiritual worlds. Again a contemporary plot is set in a Puccinian manner. The opera received the Drama Critics' Circle Award for the best play, the New York Music Critics' Circle Award for the best opera and the Pulitzer Prize in music for 1955.

Choral music was an important element in *Amahl* and *The Saint of Bleecker Street*; it is basic to the 'madrigal fable' *The Unicorn, the Gorgon and the Manticore*. Commissioned by the Elizabeth Sprague Coolidge Foundation, it is one of Menotti's most charming works. The model was the late Renaissance madrigal comedy (such as Vecchi's *L'amfiparnaso*), and the work consists of an introduction, 12 madrigals (some *a cappella*), and six instrumental interludes. At about the same time Menotti wrote the text for Barber's opera *Vanessa*.

Menotti's next opera, *Maria Golovin*, was commissioned by NBC. It was performed in New York in November 1958, but with little success, and later broadcast by NBC. From 1958 much of Menotti's time was taken up by the Spoleto Festival of Two Worlds, which he founded and directed. Thomas Schippers became music director in 1967, but Menotti continued as president. However, new works began to appear again in 1963: *Labyrinth*, written for NBC television, exploits the possibilities of special camera techniques; *Le dernier sauvage* was written for the Paris Opéra. The première of the latter work in fact was given by the Opéra-Comique, and it was later given a lavish production at the Metropolitan Opera in New York.

A CBS commission for the 1964 Bath Festival was fulfilled by a church opera in one act, *Martin's Lie*. Other works of this period include a song cycle on Menotti's own texts for Elisabeth Schwarzkopf; *Help, Help, the Globolinks!*, a 70-minute 'opera in one act for children and those who like children' commissioned by the Hamburg Staatsoper; and a New York City Opera commission, *The Most Important Man*. A drama without music, *The Leper*, was first performed in Tallahassee, Florida, on 22 April 1970.

3. FROM 1973. In 1973 Menotti and Barber sold their house in Mount Kisco, New York, where they had lived since 1943. Menotti, with his adopted son, moved to Scotland. In 1977 he expanded the Spoleto Festival to Charleston, South Carolina (the other of its Two Worlds). In spite of the festival's claims on his time, which included directing plays as well as operas, he maintained an active creative career. As an elaborate farewell vehicle for Beverly Sills he wrote the opera *La loca* (1979), which tells the story of the daughter of Isabella and Ferdinand of Spain. His non-operatic works include a symphony, 'The Halcyon' (1976), which he said represents 'the most sincere and optimistic days of my youth, when the horizon [was] unclouded', and the *Missa O pulchritudo*. His later operas are directed towards children, both as subjects and as performers: *The Egg* (a companion piece to *Martin's Lie* for a Washington Cathedral performance, 1976), *The Trial of the Gypsy*, *Chip and his Dog*, *A Bride from Pluto* and *The Boy who Grew too Fast*. In 1984 Menotti was awarded a Kennedy Center Honor for lifetime achievement in the arts.

4. STYLE. Menotti cares about his audience and about the human voice. He wrote: 'There is a certain indolence towards the use of the voice today, a tendency to treat the voice instrumentally, as if composers feared that its texture is too expressive, too *human*' (1963–4). Like Puccini he is sensitive to new musical techniques that will serve his dramatic purpose: a high, sustained dissonant chord in *The Consul* as Magda turns on the gas stove to commit suicide; the 12-note music used to parody contemporary civilization (and indirectly the avant-garde composer) in Act 2 of *Le dernier sauvage*; or electronic tape music to represent the invaders from outer space in *Help, Help, the Globolinks!*. Also like Puccini he gives first place to the human voice and the effective theatrical moment. Menotti's melodies are

tonal, sometimes with a modal flavour, and often easily remembered. Sequence and repetition are common, but aria-like passages tend to be brief so as not to interrupt the dramatic flow. The continuous, recitative-like passages set the text with naturalness and clarity. His harmony is tonal, sometimes using parallel chords over a clear and simple tonal basis. Many of his more commanding musical gestures, such as the opening of *The Medium*, reflect his avowed fondness for Musorgsky. His orchestration tends to be light and open and he writes particularly well for small instrumental ensembles. His rhythms, even when metrical irregularities are used, are natural and easily grasped by performer and listener.

Critical appraisal of Menotti's works has ranged from sincere appreciation (Sargeant) to bitter denunciation (Kerman). His techniques are traditional and conservative, and while some have faulted his style as sentimental or even dull, his best works can be powerful (*The Consul*) or charming (the Scarlattian Piano Concerto, *Amahl and the Night Visitors*). The best summary of his achievement is by Hitchcock: 'Menotti combined the theatrical sense of a popular playwright and a Pucciniesque musical vocabulary with an italianate love of liquid language and a humane interest in characters as real human beings; the result was opera more accessible than anyone else's at the time.'

See also AMAHL AND THE NIGHT VISITORS; AMELIA AL BALLO; CONSUL, THE; HELP, HELP, THE GLOBOLINKS!; MEDIUM, THE; OLD MAID AND THE THIEF, THE; SAINT OF BLEECKER STREET, THE; and TELEPHONE, THE.

all librettos by Menotti

Amelia al ballo (ob, 1), Philadelphia, Academy of Music, 1 April 1937 as Amelia Goes to the Ball; San Remo, 1938 [in It.]; vs (Milan, 1952)

The Old Maid and the Thief (radio op, 1), NBC, 22 April 1939; stage, Philadelphia, 11 Feb 1941, vs (New York, 1943)

The Island God (1), New York, Met, 20 Feb 1942

The Medium (tragic op, 2), New York, Columbia U., Brander Matthews, 8 May 1946; rev., New York, Heckscher, 18 Feb 1947; vs (New York, 1947)

The Telephone, or L'amour à trois (ob, 1), New York, Heckscher, 18 Feb 1947, vs (New York, 1947)

The Consul (musical drama, 3), Philadelphia, Shubert, 1 March 1950; official première, New York, Ethel Barrymore, 15 March 1950, vs (New York, 1950)

Amahl and the Night Visitors (television op, 1), NBC, 24 Dec 1951; stage, Bloomington, IN, Indiana U., 21 Feb 1952, vs (New York, 1952)

The Saint of Bleecker Street (musical drama, 3), New York, Broadway Theatre, 27 Dec 1954, vs (New York, 1955)

The Unicorn, the Gorgon and the Manticore, or The Three Sundays of a Poet (madrigal ballet or madrigal fable), Washington DC, Library of Congress, Coolidge Auditorium, 21 Oct 1956, vs (New York, 1957)

Maria Golovin (musical drama, 3), Brussels, International Exposition, American Pavilion, 20 Aug 1958

Labyrinth (television op, 1), NBC, 3 March 1963

L'ultimo selvaggio (opéra-bouffe, 3), Paris, OC (Favart), 21 Oct 1963 as Le dernier sauvage; as The Last Savage, New York, Met, 23 Jan 1964; vs (New York, 1973)

Martin's Lie (children's church op, 1), Bristol, Cathedral, 3 June 1964

Help, Help, the Globolinks! (children's op, 1), Hamburg, Staatsoper, 21 Dec 1968 as Hilfe, Hilfe, die Globolinks!; Santa Fe, Opera, 1 Aug 1969 [in Eng.]; vs (New York, 1969)

The Most Important Man, New York, 12 March 1971

Tamu-Tamu (chamber op, 2), Chicago, 5 Sept 1973

The Egg (children's church op), Washington DC, Cathedral, 17 June 1976

The Hero (comic op), Philadelphia, Academy of Music, 1 June 1976

The Trial of the Gypsy (children's op), New York, Alice Tully Hall, 24 May 1978

Chip and his Dog (children's op), Guelph, U. of Guelph, War Memorial Hall, 6 May 1979, vs (New York and London, 1979)

La loca (3), San Diego, Civic, 3 June 1979

A Bride from Pluto (children's op), Washington DC, Kennedy Center, Terrace, 12 April 1982

The Boy who Grew too Fast (children's op), Wilmington, DE, Grand, 24 Sept 1982

Goya (3), Washington DC, Kennedy Center, 11 Nov 1986

The Wedding (comic op, 2), Seoul, 16 Sept 1988

Librettos: *A Hand of Bridge*, Barber, 1960; *Introductions and Goodbyes*, Foss, 1961; *Vanessa*, Barber, 1964

*

CBY 1979; EwenD

J. Kerman: *Opera as Drama* (New York, 1956)

W. Sargeant: 'Orlando in Mount Kisco', *New Yorker*, xxxix (4 May 1963), 49–89

C. Menotti: 'I am the Savage', *ON*, xxviii/13 (1963–4), 8–12

R. Tricoire: *Gian Carlo Menotti: l'homme et son oeuvre* (Paris, 1966)

D. Ewen: 'Gian Carlo Menotti', *The World of Twentieth-Century Music* (Englewood Cliffs, NJ, 1968), 481ff

H. W. Hitchcock: *Music in the United States: a Historical Introduction* (Englewood Cliffs, NJ, 1969, 2/1974), 211f

L. Grieb: *The Operas of Gian Carlo Menotti, 1937–1972: a Selective Bibliography* (Metuchen, NJ, 1974)

J. Gruen: *Menotti: a Biography* (New York, 1978)

J. Ardoin: 'A Welcome Gift', *ON*, xlv/20 (1981), 9–11, 16

——: *The Stages of Menotti* (Garden City, NY, 1985)

J. Honig: 'The Menotti Theorem', *ON*, lv/17 (1991), 13–15, 51

R. H. Kornick: *Recent American Opera: a Production Guide* (Columbia, NY, 1991)   BRUCE ARCHIBALD

Menucci, Tomasso. *See* ANELLI, ANGELO.

Menzinsky, [Mentsyns'ky], **Modeste** (*b* Novosiolki, Galicia, 29 April 1875; *d* Stockholm, 11 Dec 1935). Polish tenor of Russian parentage. He studied with Julius Stockhausen at Frankfurt, making his début in 1902 at Elberfeld. Engaged at the Royal Opera, Stockholm (1904–10), he sang Siegfried in the Swedish premières of *Siegfried* (1905) and *Götterdämmerung* (1907). At Covent Garden (1905) he sang Walther, Lohengrin and Tannhäuser. Having moved to Cologne (1910), he created Nan in Schreker's *Irrelohe* (1924), conducted by Klemperer. His repertory also included Florestan, Manrico, Otello and other dramatic roles. After his retirement in 1926, he taught in Stockholm.

ELIZABETH FORBES

Mérante, Louis (François) (*b* Paris, 25 July 1828; *d* Courbevoie, 16 July 1887). French choreographer. Engaged as a dancer at the Paris Opéra in 1848, he eventually succeeded Lucien Petipa as principal male dancer, retaining that position until his death. From 1869 he was also *premier maître de ballet*. A highly competent rather than an inspired choreographer, he worked in the style of Joseph Mazilier and Arthur Saint-Léon, whom he had observed at work in his earlier days. Besides independent ballets, he produced a number of *divertissements* for operas including Gounod's *Polyeucte* (1878) and *Le tribut de Zamora* (1881), Massenet's *Le roi de Lahore* (1877) and *Le Cid* (1885), Thomas' *Françoise de Rimini* (1882), Saint-Saëns' *Henry VIII* (1883) and the revival at the Opéra of *Aida* (1880).

*

I. Guest: *The Ballet of the Second Empire* (London, 1974)

——: *Le ballet de l'Opéra de Paris* (Paris, 1976)   IVOR GUEST

Mercadante, (Giuseppe) Saverio (Raffaele) (*b* Altamura, nr Bari, bap. 17 Sept 1795; *d* Naples, 17 Dec 1870). Italian composer. After Rossini, Bellini and Donizetti he was the most important composer of Italian opera in the period immediately preceding Verdi, on whom his influence was considerable.

1. LIFE. Mercadante was an illegitimate child. In later life, when he had become the Grand Old Man of Neapolitan music, he insisted that he had been born in Naples, but in fact he first went there at the age of 11. In 1808, in order to secure a free place at the Naples Conservatory, his first Christian name and the place and date of his birth were falsified, and as a result some early works of reference date his birth at Naples in 1797 or even 1798.

At the Conservatory he studied with Giovanni Furno and Giacomo Tritto (both of whom taught Bellini a few years later) and from 1816 to 1820 composition with the director, Niccolò Zingarelli, whose favourite pupil he became. Entrusted with the direction of the students' orchestra, he wrote for it a considerable number of compositions including several concertos and sinfonias. It was two of these that Rossini heard on a visit to the conservatory at about this time; embracing Mercadante warmly, he turned to Zingarelli and said, 'Maestro, my compliments; I see that your students are beginning where we leave off'. Unusually for an Italian composer at this period, but also perhaps significantly in view of his own later development, Mercadante's predominant interest until the age of 23 was instrumental music. In 1818, however, when he produced the music for three ballets at the Teatro S Carlo, at least one critic urged the young composer to 'abandon his sterile symphonies' and give 'more splendid proof of his talents in vocal music'; as it happened, he had in the same year scored a notable success with a cantata in honour of the ex-king Charles IV of Spain, and in 1819 (no doubt with the encouragement of Rossini, then music director of the S Carlo) he was invited to compose his first opera for that theatre. *L'apoteosi d'Ercole* was enthusiastically received and in 1820, the year he completed his studies with Zingarelli, he produced four more, two in Naples and two in Rome. From then on he concentrated exclusively on operatic composition. His fame spread rapidly and during the next seven years he turned out an average of three operas a year, at one point actually producing five within 11 months.

Mercadante's first big success came in 1821 with his seventh opera, *Elisa e Claudio*, given at La Scala, Milan, on 30 successive nights and repeated six months later for a further 28. With this work he established a European reputation: it was performed in London, Barcelona and Paris in 1823, and Vienna in 1824. Mercadante himself directed the Viennese performances and stayed on to write three further operas for the Kärntnertortheater, but these were poorly received and the composer returned at the end of the year to Italy, where a new triumph followed in Venice with *Caritea, regina di Spagna* (more often known as *Donna Caritea*), a work which marks an important new step in Mercadante's style. At about this time he was offered a contract to write a series of operas for the Italian theatre in Madrid, but the arrangement fell through and he was back in Turin for a new opera in February 1827. A few months later he was in Spain again: the details of Mercadante's life at this period are not clear, but it seems likely that one opera, *I due Figaro*, was written for performance in Madrid but banned on political grounds (it was eventually given there in 1835). In any case, by August the composer had moved on to Lisbon, where he produced three or possibly four operas during the next 12 months. Of these, *Gabriella di Vergy* later had considerable success in Italy. By autumn 1829 he was in Cádiz, where he interested himself in the Italian opera and produced two comic operas of his own, and in 1830 he returned to Madrid, where his *Francesca da Rimini* was given during Carnival 1830–31.

In spite of various negotiations, no solid contract materialized in Spain, and at the beginning of 1831 Mercadante finally returned to Italy. This was the period of Bellini's greatest Italian successes and of Donizetti's first fame: after so long an absence from the Italian scene Mercadante seems to have felt the need to reconsider his style, and though *Zaira*, his first work at Naples for over six years, had only a moderate reception, he scored a triumph at Turin in 1832 with *I normanni a Parigi*. At the beginning of 1833 he succeeded Pietro Generali as *maestro di cappella* at the cathedral of Novara, an appointment which lasted for seven years and occasioned the composition of a good deal of church music, without unduly interrupting his operatic career.

In 1835 Rossini, from Paris, invited Mercadante (as he already had Bellini and Donizetti) to write an opera for the Théâtre Italien. Mercadante arrived in Paris in September but the libretto, which Romani was to provide, never turned up, and at the end of November he was obliged to accept another, of inferior quality, and set it to music in a hurry. In spite of the singing of Grisi, Rubini, Tamburini and Lablache, *I briganti* was a failure. Nevertheless, Mercadante's Paris visit was of decisive importance for the contact it gave him with a new and more sophisticated musical world, and for the music he heard there – particularly that of Meyerbeer, whose *Les Huguenots* had its first performance at the Opéra in February 1836.

The example of Meyerbeer is evident in Mercadante's next opera, *Il giuramento*, which was produced at La Scala 11 months after his return from Paris. It was received with enthusiasm, and has remained his best-known work ever since. With it Mercadante finally broke away from his earlier manner and began the programme of operatic reform with which his name has been chiefly associated in the history of Italian opera. The four operas that followed, *Le due illustri rivali*, *Elena da Feltre*, *Il bravo* and *La vestale*, maintained and developed the ideals of this reform and are among his best works. By this time conditions in Italy were more favourable to Mercadante: Rossini's operatic career was over, Bellini was dead, and Donizetti, though still active, was increasingly drawn to Paris and Vienna; at home, among a mass of minor figures, only Giovanni Pacini (an altogether less substantial composer) was a serious rival, and by 1840 Mercadante was certainly the most respected figure on the purely Italian operatic scene. In this year he was invited to succeed his old master, Zingarelli, as head of the conservatory in Naples; he took up the appointment in October and retained it until his death 30 years later. His theatrical career continued, however: another important opera, *Il reggente*, followed at Turin in 1843; in August 1844 he made a ceremonial visit to his birthplace at Altamura, returning to Naples for another success with *Leonora* at the end of the year; and in 1846 he scored a spectacular triumph at the S Carlo with *Orazi e Curiazi*.

But with the passing of the years Mercadante's operatic output began to slow down. One reason was certainly his position at the conservatory and his growing preoccupation, in that capacity, with instrumental works, sacred music and teaching. But another may well have been jealousy of the young Verdi. At an early stage in their relations Verdi seems to have respected

Mercadante, asking him to supervise the choice of artists for the first Neapolitan *Macbeth* in 1848. But later Mercadante fought bitterly to block Verdi's success in Naples. At the time of the first performance of *Il trovatore* at the S Carlo in 1853 he is said to have used all his influence with the Neapolitan authorities to get only the first two acts of the opera allowed – though in the end without success. Relations between the two men were eventually patched up, and in 1868, when Mercadante was old and blind, Verdi put him 'even for a few bars' at the head of his list of contributors to the projected Requiem in memory of Rossini.

The last complete opera composed by Mercadante was *Pelagio* in 1857. *Virginia*, which followed in 1866, was an earlier work that had fallen foul of the censor; it gave him his last great public success. By this time he had become a venerable figurehead in Italian musical life. While he was at Novara he had lost the sight of one eye, and about the middle of 1862 he became completely blind; yet he still managed to compose, by dictation to pupils, a number of orchestral works, as well as an immense hymn for the inauguration of Rossini's statue at Pesaro, and at his death he left the manuscript of yet another opera dictated as far as the middle of the finale of the first act.

2. WORKS. Mercadante's 60 operas span an active half century of Italian operatic history: the first was performed only three years after *Il barbiere di Siviglia* and the last a year before *Don Carlos*. In the early part of his career, like virtually all his contemporaries, Mercadante was a follower of Rossini, and of this period *Elisa e Claudio* is the outstanding example, a neat and brilliantly written work in a style that was sure of success and had not yet become weighed down by the conscious elaboration of the later operas. But Mercadante's temperament, like Verdi's, was more naturally drawn to serious subjects. Many of his earlier librettos draw on classical themes redolent of 18th-century *opera seria* (four are actually by, or after, Metastasio), giving way, as his dramatic instinct developed in the direction of the later 19th century, to the Romantic melodramas of Romani and Cammarano. Here, too, Rossini was the point of departure, but *Donna Caritea* in 1826 added a distinctive new element: the florid manner of Rossinian lyric drama is deployed with greater regard for the dramatic action, and there is more of the lyrical pathos that is associated with Bellini or Donizetti rather than Rossini (though *Caritea* antedates all the characteristic works of both these composers). But by 1832, after Mercadante's absence in Spain, the boot was on the other foot and it was certainly the examples of Donizetti's *Anna Bolena* and Bellini's *Norma* that prompted the new seriousness of purpose, the original touches of harmony and inventive instrumentation, which help out the otherwise rather creaking structure of *I normanni a Parigi*.

It was *Il giuramento* which marked the crucial turning-point of Mercadante's career, and which has been generally regarded as his masterpiece. Its libretto, after Hugo's *Angelo* (the same subject as Ponchielli's *Gioconda*), is a tolerably good one, and the composer made a genuine attempt to set it as a drama rather than a theatrical entertainment, discarding conventions when he felt it necessary to do so and creating a real interplay of characters in a seriously considered, if not always consistent, musical framework. That much of the improvement is due to the example of Meyerbeer can hardly be doubted – but it remains an example and not an influence, and there is little or no direct trace of the Meyerbeerian idiom to dilute the essentially Italian quality of Mercadante's melodic style.

Il giuramento and the best of the operas that follow it are of the greatest interest and importance in the history of 19th-century Italian music; more than any others of the period, they provide the link between Rossini, Bellini and Donizetti on the one hand, and Verdi and the later 19th-century melodrama on the other. Mercadante himself was quite aware of what he was doing. In a much quoted letter to Florimo, written during the composition of *Elena da Feltre*, he put it clearly:

I have continued the revolution I began with *Il giuramento*; forms varied, trivial cabalettas banished, crescendos out, vocal lines simplified, fewer repeats, more originality in the cadences, proper regard paid to the drama, orchestration rich but not so as to swamp the voices, no long solos in the ensembles – they only force the other parts to stand idle to the detriment of the action –, not much bass drum and a lot less brass band.

Besides eliminating in this way the external weaknesses of the older lyric drama, he deliberately attempted to loosen its basic schematic patterns in a new approach, combining musical intelligence and greater dramatic fluency with the strong melodic impulse that is the motive power behind all 19th-century Italian opera. With varying success he tried to balance the claims of music and drama in a way that not even Donizetti had done before him, using calculated repetition to weld whole scenes into dramatic unity (the opening scenes of *Il giuramento* and *Il bravo* are examples) and linking the closed numbers with scenas that blend declamation, arioso and orchestral melody – very much in the manner that Verdi was later to develop. It must be said that he nowhere achieves the dramatic momentum of Donizetti, still less of Verdi. Yet the harmonic interest and range of modulation in these works are well ahead of anything else in the period: the treatment of the orchestra is imaginative, sometimes almost over-elaborate; accompaniments are varied and the ensemble writing is masterly, whether at the solo level (*Le due illustri rivali* offers some fine examples) or in the massive and imposing finales. He could not always keep it up. In every opera there are lapses into rhetoric and convention, particularly in the arias (where he still had to content his singers); the melodic ideas are not always characteristic or memorable in themselves; and the ensembles are so carefully worked out that spontaneity is lost and the result can be laboured and heavy-handed. Nevertheless, the general level is still far above that of the minor figures who proliferated around him, as Liszt noted in an otherwise critical account of the current Italian scene:

Exception must always be made for Mercadante. He has the wisdom to write slowly, and revises his compositions with care … Several of the ensemble pieces are really remarkable. The latest works of Mercadante are without question the most seriously thought out of the contemporary repertory.

Mercadante had written 45 operas and was at the height of his fame when Verdi opened his career: at the very time when the younger composer was struggling to get *Oberto* put on at La Scala, *Il bravo* was receiving its brilliantly successful first performance at the same theatre. Verdi had many opportunities to see Mercadante's works on the stage, and the operas of this central period, often fresh from the maestro's pen, could not fail to make a profound impression on his developing ideas about music and drama. In the long run it was the overall influence of Mercadante's style and approach that was of importance in the development of Verdian melodrama, though musicologists have not failed to point out, at a more specific level, the similarities between the title role of *Il bravo* and the roles of both Rigoletto and Sparafucile in Verdi's opera, or the curious parallels (amounting even to a literal quotation) that undoubtedly exist between *La vestale* and *Aida*.

La vestale was another of Mercadante's more successful dramatic achievements, and has been regarded by some as his best work. The only subsequent opera that can still be regarded as falling into the 'reform' group is *Il reggente*, a finely written piece on the same subject as Verdi's *Un ballo in maschera*. But in the later operas the ideals of reform tend to get forgotten. The forms are more conventional, with much repetition; vocalization reappears as an end in itself, the scoring is heavy and there is a tendency to deploy great energy for little result. Even so, a work like *Orazi e Curiazi*, where the power of the orchestra and the heroic scale of the vocal writing are to some extent justified by the subject, must certainly be counted among his best: the exhilarating finale of Act 1 is a worthy summing up of all that is good in the ensemble writing of the period. Mercadante's last two operas, *Virginia* and *Pelagio*, both contain fine music, and the latter at least one aria (for Bianca in Act 4) of an almost Verdian intensity and pathos.

After his death, Mercadante's reputation suffered a rapid decline. By the standards of his time his best work had been serious and thoughtful: its weaknesses, at least from *Il giuramento* onwards, are not the negative ones of so many of his contemporaries, but rather a tendency to over-elaboration and too much care. As a result his operas can be impressive, noble, passionate and physically exciting, with passages of beauty, but seldom spontaneous or directly personal – and beside the powerful, comprehensive genius of Verdi they inevitably appeared old-fashioned and lacking in human appeal. Nevertheless it has for too long been an easy commonplace of Italian musical history that Mercadante's sole importance was having, in Amintore Galli's phrase, 'served as a footstool [sgabello] for Verdi'. The fact that he contributed to the development of a much greater composer does not invalidate his own achievement. Revivals of his operas in connection with the centenary of his death in 1970 showed that, with all his faults, Mercadante clearly demands consideration as a composer in his own right.

See also BRAVO, IL; BRIGANTI, I; ELISA E CLAUDIO; GIURAMENTO, IL; REGGENTE, IL; and VESTALE, LA (ii).

references to I-Nc are from Florimo (1869–71): exact nature of the material not always certain, some autograph

NC – *Naples, Teatro di S Carlo*   TR – *Turin, Teatro Regio*   VF – *Venice, Teatro La Fenice*

dm – *dramma per musica*   mel – *melodramma*   mels – *melodramma serio*
melss – *melodramma semiserio*   tl – *tragedia lirica*

title	genre, acts	libretto	first performance	sources and remarks
L'apoteosi d'Ercole	dm, 2	G. Schmidt	NC, 19 Aug 1819	*F-Pn, I-Fc, Mr, Nc, US-Bp, Wc*, vs excerpts (Milan, *c*1821; Naples, n.d; R1989: IOG, xiv)
Violenza e costanza, ossia I falsi monetari	dramma giocoso, 2	A. L. Tottola	Naples, Nuovo, 19 Jan 1820	*I-Bc, Fc, Mr, Nc*, vs excerpts (Naples, 1822); as Il castello dei spiriti, Lisbon, 1825
Anacreonte in Samo	dm, 2	Schmidt, after J.-H. Guy: *Anacréon chez Polycrate*	NC, 1 Aug 1820	*F-Pn, I-Fc, Mr, Nc*
Il geloso ravveduto	mel buffo, 2	B. Signorini	Rome, Valle, Oct 1820	*Fc*
Scipione in Cartagine	mels, 2	J. Ferretti	Rome, Argentina, 26 Dec 1820	*Fc, Mr, US-Wc*, vs excerpts (Milan, 1821)
Maria Stuarda regina di Scozia	dramma serio, 2	G. Rossi, after F. von Schiller: *Maria Stuart*	Bologna, Comunale, 29 May 1821	*I-Mr*; also as Maria Stuart
Elisa e Claudio, ossia L'amore protetto dall'amicizia	melss, 2	L. Romanelli, after F. Casari: *Rosella*	Milan, Scala, 30 Oct 1821	*B-Bc, GB-Lbl, I-Bc, Fc, Mr*, Nc, US-Bp, Wc*, vs (Milan, 1821–2/R1989: IOG, xiv; Paris, 1823)
Andronico	mel tragico, 2	G. Kreglianovich ('Dalmiro Tindario')	VF, 26 Dec 1821	*I-Mr*, vs excerpts (Milan, 1821–4)
Il posto abbandonato, ossia Adele ed Emerico	melss, 2	F. Romani	Milan, Scala, 21 Sept 1822	*Mr**, vs excerpts (Milan, 1823); rev. 1828/9, ? for perf. in Spain
Alfonso ed Elisa	mels, 3	after V. Alfieri: *Filippo*	Mantua, Nuovo, 26 Dec 1822	as Aminta ed Argira, Reggio Emilia, 1823
Amleto	mel tragico, 3	Romani, after W. Shakespeare	Milan, Scala, 26 Dec 1822	*Mr*, Nc*
Didone abbandonata	dm, 2	P. Metastasio	TR, 18 Jan 1823	*F-Pn, I-Fc, Mr, Nc, US-Wc*, vs excerpts (Milan, 1823)
Gli sciti	dm, 2	Tottola, after Voltaire: *Les scythes*	NC, 18 March 1823	vs excerpts (Milan, 1823/4)
Costanzo ed Almeriska	dm, 2	Tottola	NC, 22 Nov 1823	*I-Nc*, vs excerpts (Naples, ?1824)
Gli amici di Siracusa	mel eroico, 3	Ferretti	Rome, Argentina, 7 Feb 1824	
Doralice	dramma ?semiserio, 2		Vienna, Kärntnertor, 18 Sept 1824	
Le nozze di Telemaco ed Antiope	azione lirica, 3	C. Bassi	Vienna, Kärntnertor, 5 Nov 1824	? incl. music by others
Il podestà di Burgos, ossia Il signore del villaggio	melss, 2	Bassi	Vienna, Kärntnertor, 20 Nov 1824	as Il signore del villaggio, Naples, Fondo, 28 May 1825 (in Neapolitan dialect); *Nc*
Nitocri	mels, 2	A. Zeno, rev. Conte Piosasco	TR, 26 Dec 1824	*Mr*, vs excerpts (Milan, 1826)
Ipermestra	dramma tragico, 2	L. Ricciuti, after Metastasio	NC, ?carn. 1824–5	*Mr*, Nc*; probably rev., ?Spain, *c*1828–30; perf. ?Genoa, Carlo Felice, 26 Dec 1832; vs excerpts (Milan, ?1833)
Erode, ossia Marianna	dramma tragico, 2	Ricciuti	VF, 27 Dec 1825	*Mr*, Vt*
Caritea, regina di Spagna, ossia La morte di Don Alfonso re di Portogallo	mels, 2	P. Pola	VF, 21 Feb 1826	usually as Donna Caritea; *GB-T, I-Bc, Fc, Mr*, Nc, Vt, US-Wc*, vs (Milan, 1827; Paris, n.d.)
Ezio	dm, 3	Metastasio	TR, 2 Feb 1827	vs excerpts (Milan, 1827)
Il montanaro	mel comico, 2	Romani	Milan, Scala, 16 April 1827	*I-Mr*
La testa di bronzo, ossia La capanna solitaria	mel eroico comico, 2	Romani	Lisbon, private theatre of Barone di Quintella at Laranjeiras, 3 Dec 1827	*GB-Lbl, I-Mr*, vs (Paris, ?1828)
Adriano in Siria	dramma serio, 3	A. Profumo, after Metastasio	Lisbon, S Carlos, 24 Feb 1828	

title	genre, acts	libretto	first performance	sources and remarks
Gabriella di Vergy	mels, 2	Profumo, partly after Tottola	Lisbon, S Carlos, 8 Aug 1828	rev. (E. Bidera), Genoa, spr. 1832; *Mr**, *Nc*, vs (Milan, n.d.; Naples, n.d.)
La rappresaglia	opera buffa, 2	Romani	Cádiz, Principal, ? 20 Nov 1829	*US-Wc*
I due Figaro	mel buffo, 2	Romani, after H.-A. R. Martelly	Madrid, Principe, 26 Jan 1835 [1st known perf.]	probably comp. *c*1827–9
Don Chisciotte alle nozze di Gamaccio	opera buffa, 2	after M. de Cervantes	Cádiz, Principal, ? carn. 1829–30	*I-Nc*
Francesca da Rimini	mel, 3	Romani, after Dante: *Commedia*	?unperf.	comp. *c*1830
Zaira	mel tragico, 2	Romani, after Voltaire	NC, 31 Aug 1831	*F-Pn, I-Nc**, vs excerpts (Milan, *c*1831)
I normanni a Parigi	tl, 4	Romani	TR, 7 Feb 1832	*Bc, Fc, Mr, Nc, US-Bp*, vs (Milan, 1832)
Ismalia, ossia Amore e morte	mels fantastico, 3	Romani	Milan, Scala, 27 Oct 1832	*I-Mr**, vs (Milan, *c*1832)
Il conte di Essex	mel, 3	Romani	Milan, Scala, 10 March 1833	*Mc, Mr**, vs excerpts (Milan, ?1833)
Emma d'Antiochia	tl, 3	Romani	VF, 8 March 1834	*Mr**, *Nc, Vt*, vs excerpts (Milan, 1835)
Uggero il danese	mel, 2	Romani	Bergamo, Riccardi, 11 Aug 1834	*Mr*, vs (Milan, 1839)
La gioventù di Enrico V	mel, 4	Romani, partly after Shakespeare	Milan, Scala, 25 Nov 1834	*Mr**, vs excerpts (Milan, ?1835)
Francesca Donato, ossia Corinto distrutta	melss, 3	Romani, after Byron	TR, 14 Feb 1835	rev. (S. Cammarano), NC, ? Jan 1845; *Mr, Nc**, vs excerpts (Milan, ?1845)
I briganti	mel, 3	J. Crescini, after Schiller: *Die Räuber*	Paris, Italien, 22 March 1836	*Fc, Mr*, vs (Milan, 1836); rev. with adds, probably NC, 1853, *Mr**, *Nc*
Il giuramento	mel, 3	G. Rossi, after V. Hugo: *Angelo*	Milan, Scala, 11 March 1837	*Fc, Mr**, *Nc, US-Wc*, vs (Milan, 1837/*R*1986: IOG, xviii; 2/1860; Paris, 1859); as Amore e dovere, Rome, 1839
Le due illustri rivali	mel, 3	Rossi	VF, 10 March 1838	*I-Nc, Vt*, vs (Milan, ?1838; Leipzig, *c*1840); rev. Scala, 26 Dec 1839, vs (Milan, 1839)
Elena da Feltre	dramma tragico, 3	S. Cammarano	NC, 1 Jan 1839 [not 26 Dec 1838]	*Fc, Mr, Nc*, vs (Milan, 1839/*R*1985: IOG, xx; Naples, n.d.)
Il bravo, ossia La veneziana	mel, 3	Rossi and M. M. Marcello, after J. F. Cooper and A. A. Bourgeois	Milan, Scala, 9 March 1839	*F-Pn, GB-Lbl, I-Mr**, *Nc*, vs (Milan, 1839/*R*1989: IOG, xxi; 2/?1888; Naples, n.d.; Paris, n.d.)
La vestale	tl, 3	Cammarano	NC, 10 March 1840	*Fc, Mr, Nc*, vs (Milan, 1840/*R*1986: IOG, xxii; Paris, n.d.); as Emilia, Rome, aut. 1842; as San Camillo (azione sacra), Rome, 1851
La solitaria delle Asturie, ossia La Spagna ricuperata	mel, 5	Romani	VF, 12 March 1840	*Mr**, *Vt*
Il proscritto	mel, 3	Cammarano, after F. Soulié	NC, 4 Jan 1842	*Nc*, vs excerpts (Milan, 1842)
Il reggente	dramma lirico, 3	Cammarano, after E. Scribe: *Gustave III*	TR, 2 Feb 1843	*Mr**; rev. with adds, Trieste, 11 Nov 1843, vs (Milan, 1843; Paris, n.d.)
Leonora	melss, 4	M. d'Arienzo	Naples, Nuovo, 5 Dec 1844	*Mr**, *Nc*, vs (Milan, n.d.; Paris, n.d.) [see also I cacciatori delle Alpi, doubtful, 1859]
Il Vascello de Gama	mel romantico, prol., 3	Cammarano	NC, 6 March 1845	*Mr**, *Nc*, vs excerpts (Milan, 1845)
Orazi e Curiazi	tl, 3	Cammarano	NC, 10 Nov 1846	*Bc, Mr**, *Nc*, vs (Milan, 1846; Naples, n.d.)
La schiava saracena, ovvero Il campo di Gerosolima	mel tragico, 4	F. M. Piave	Milan, Scala, 26 Dec 1848	orig. Il campo de' crociati; rev. NC, ?1850; *Mr**, *Nc*, early autograph draft *US-NYpm*, vs (Milan, *c*1849–51)

title	genre, acts	libretto	first performance	sources and remarks
Medea	tl, 3	Cammarano, after Romani	NC, 1 March 1851	*I-Mr**, *Nc*, vs (Milan, ?1864; Rome, n.d.)
Virginia	tl, 3	Cammarano, after Alfieri	NC, 7 April 1866	comp. 1845/?1851, perf. not allowed; *Mr*, *Nc**, vs (Milan, ?1845; Naples, n.d.)
Statira	tragedia, 3	D. Bolognese, after Voltaire: *Olympie*	NC, 8 Jan 1853	*Nc*, vs (Paris, 1853; Naples, n.d.)
Violetta	mel, 4	Arienzo	Naples, Nuovo, 10 Jan 1853	*Mr*, *Nc**, vs (Milan, n.d.)
Pelagio	tl, 4	Arienzo	NC, 12 Feb 1857	*Mr*, *Nc**, vs (Milan, n.d.)
L'orfano di Brono, ossia Caterina dei Medici		Cammarano	unperf.	inc., *Nc* (dictated to middle of Finale, Act I)
Giovanna I				scene i only, *Nc**

Doubtful: Les noces de Gamache (opéra bouffon, 3, J. H. Dupin and T. Sauvage, after Cervantes: *Don Quixote*), Paris, Odéon, 9 May 1825, music arr. Guénée, full score (Paris, ?1825) [presumably pasticcio or other adaptation]; Pietro il grande, Lisbon, 1827 [mistaken reference to Vaccai's opera]; Eduardo ed Angelica [De Napoli cites announcement of benefit perf. of Act 1, Naples, Nuovo, 9 Aug 1828]; Parisina [presumably a confusion with Donizetti's opera]; I cacciatori delle Alpi (?1), Mantua, 1859 [De Napoli gives Ferrara, Buonacossi, 12 Oct 1859 and states that lib. is extract, with changed names etc., of Leonora (see above, 1844)]

ES (M. Rinaldi)

I. Tranchini and L. Tarantini: *Omaggio a Mercadante* (Naples, 1844)

A. Pomè: *Saggio critico sull'opera musicale di S. Mercadante* (Turin, 1925)

G. de Napoli: *La triade melodrammatica altamurana: Giacomo Tritto, Vincenzo Lavigna, Saverio Mercadante* (Milan, 1931), 67–256

F. Schlitzer: *Mercadante e Cammarano* (Bari, 1945)

F. Walker: 'Mercadante and Verdi', *ML*, xxxiii (1952), 311–21; xxxiv (1953), 33–8

G. Roncaglia: 'Il giuramento', *La Scala*, lxi (1954), 81–4

B. Notarnicola: *Verdi non ha vinto Mercadante* (Rome, 1955)

F. d'Amico: 'Il ballo in maschera prima di Verdi', *Verdi: bollettino dell'Istituto di studi verdiani*, i/3 (1960), 1251–328

F. Lippmann: *Vincenzo Bellini, und die italienische Oper seria seiner Zeit*, AnMc, no.6 (1969), esp. 328–40

G. Carli Ballola: 'Incontro con Mercadante', *Chigiana*, xxvi-xxvii (Florence, 1969–70), 465–500

——: 'Mercadante e *Il bravo*', *Il melodramma italiano dell'ottocento: studi e ricerche per Massimo Mila* (Turin, 1977)

S. Palermo: *Saverio Mercadante: biografia, epistolario* (Fasano, 1985)

P. Gosset: Introductions to: *Elena da Feltre*, IOG, xx (1985); *Il giuramento*, IOG, xviii (1986); *La vestale*, IOG, xxii (1986); *L'apoteosi d'Ercole*, IOG, xiv (1989); *Il bravo*, IOG, xxi (1989); *Elisa e Claudio*, IOG, xiv (1989)

K. M. Bryan: 'Mercadante's experiment in form: the cabalettas of *Elena da Feltre*', *Donizetti Society Journal*, vi (1988), 37–56

T. G. Kaufman: 'Saverio Mercadante', *Verdi and his Major Contemporaries* (New York, 1990), 61–76

S. Perna: '*La vestale*' di Saverio Mercadante: approdo romantico di un mito neoclassico (Brindisi, 1990)   MICHAEL ROSE

Mercato di Malmantile, Il ('The Market of Malmantile'). *Dramma giocoso per musica* in three acts by DOMENICO FISCHIETTI to a libretto by CARLO GOLDONI; Venice, Teatro Grimani di S Samuele, 26 December 1757.

At a colourful marketplace not far from the castle of Malmantile the peasants Berto (tenor), Lena (contralto) and Cecca (soprano) are selling poultry and eggs. Rubiccone (tenor) is a quack, who in a 'catalogue' aria describes all the ailments he has cured. Lampridio (bass), governor of the Malmantile district, is in love with Lena. Lena, whom Berto wishes to marry, is not averse to marrying someone of Lampridio's higher social standing. The Conte della Rocca (alto castrato), betrothed to the widowed Marchesa Giacinta (soprano), is inspecting the market, and is attracted by Lampridio's daughter Brigida (soprano). When Giacinta discovers

this, she swears revenge. She forces the count to renounce Brigida, who promptly develops an interest in Rubiccone, who has made her believe that he is rich and has numerous titles. Lampridio is deposed from the governor's post, and Rubiccone is exposed as a charlatan. Resigned to their fates, Brigida decides to marry Rubiccone, Lena accepts Berto and the count pledges his vows to Giacinta.

Goldoni's popular libretto is notable for the colourful personalities of Lampridio and Rubiccone. Two librettos for Carnival 1758 performances at the S Samuele list the same cast, but attribute the music to different composers, one to Fischietti and the other to Giuseppe Scarlatti. Most contemporary sources list Scarlatti as the first composer to set the text to music, for a performance in Vienna in 1757 or 1758, but no libretto or score of this exists. According to Lowenberg's *Annals of Opera 1597–1940* (London, 1943, 3/1978), the music was originally to be composed by Scarlatti, as his name occurs in the original libretto, but this is overpasted with a slip bearing Fischietti's name. In 1766, a year after Fischietti replaced Hasse as Kapellmeister in Dresden, he presented *Il mercato di Malmantile* in a considerably revised version. At its 1761 London performance the opera included some substitute arias by Galuppi. Fischietti, who shows a stylistic affinity with Galuppi, incorporated into his operas Neapolitan and Venetian elements. The second finale in *Il mercato* serves as an example of rondo-finale technique.   GORDANA LAZAREVICH

Merchant Kalashnikov, The. Opera by Anton Rubinstein; see KUPETS KALASHNIKOV.

Merchant of Venice, The [*Il mercante di Venezia*]. Opera in three acts op.181 by MARIO CASTELNUOVO-TEDESCO to his own libretto after WILLIAM SHAKESPEARE's play; Florence, Teatro Comunale, 25 May 1961; in original English version, Los Angeles, Shrine Auditorium, 13 April 1966.

Bassanio (baritone) persuades his friend Antonio (baritone), a merchant of Venice, to finance his trip to Belmont where he plans to win the hand of Portia (mezzo-soprano). Since Antonio's assets are tied up in sea-vessels, he borrows from Shylock (bass), a rich Jewish money-lender, pledging as a bond a pound of his flesh. Meanwhile Lorenzo (tenor) elopes with Shylock's daughter Jessica (lyric soprano). In Act 2, at Belmont, Portia's suitors attempt to win her hand by guessing in which of three caskets her picture may be found. The princes of Morocco and Aragon (both mimes) fail, but Bassanio guesses correctly. News arrives that Antonio's fortunes have been lost at sea. Act 3 takes place in the Court of Justice in Venice where Shylock demands his pound of flesh. Portia, disguised as a lawyer, eloquently invokes some legal technicalities, making Shylock's demands impossible. He departs, outdone and dejected.

Lush and late romantic in style, *The Merchant* is essentially through-composed. The scoring for large orchestra places heavy demands on the soloists, especially Shylock. Much of the opera's melodic interest derives from motifs found in the overture (composed 30 years earlier).   NICK ROSSI

Méreaux, Nicolas-Jean Le Froid de (*b* Paris, 1745; *d* Paris, 1797). French composer. He was educated in Paris by various French and Italian musicians. By 1767 he was organist at St Sauveur, Paris, and later organist of the Petits Augustins and of the royal chapel. He was unusual in his social context for working so consistently both in sacred and secular *milieux*. Besides oratorios and motets given at the Concert Spirituel, for example, he had two *scènes lyriques* given at the Société Académique des Enfants d'Apollon.

Méreaux's publicly performed *opéras comiques* were not very successful. D'Origny detected dramatic shortcomings in the music for *Le retour de tendresse*, but *Laurette* had an early flurry of enthusiasm. The libretto of *Alexandre aux Indes* was criticized for overzealous limitation of love interest, and the music was deemed derivative. It certainly echoes the gestures of Gluck, but remains lyrical; there is extensive use of the clarinet, and brief use of an Indian cymbal ('Ind. cimbale') and a 'Gros tambour' in Act 1. *Oedipe et Jocaste* (known under various titles) was well received and contains music of great vigour, especially the D minor trio for Jocaste, Oedipe and Phorbas in Act 2. Méreaux wrote parts for the new ceremonial Revolution instruments (tuba curva and buccin), but they were not copied for use by the Opéra staff.

first performed in Paris unless otherwise stated

PCI – *Comédie-Italienne*

La meunière enrichie, ou Le gascon puni (oc, 2, P. L. Moline), private perf., ?Paris, 1767

La ressource comique, ou La pièce à deux acteurs (cmda, 1, L. Anseaume, after C. F. Panard: *L'armoire*), PCI (Bourgogne), 22 Aug 1772 (Paris, 1773)

La rencontre imprévue (compliment de rentrée, Anseaume), PCI (Bourgogne), 11 April 1774

Le retour de tendresse (cmda, 1, Anseaume, after La Ribadière: *La réconciliation villageoise*), PCI (Bourgogne), 1 Oct 1774 (Paris, 1774)

Le duel comique (opéra bouffon, 2, Moline [parody of Paisiello: Il duello]), PCI (Bourgogne), 16 Sept 1776

Laurette (oc, 1, Danzel de Malzéville, after J. F. Marmontel), PCI (Bourgogne), 23 July 1777 (Paris, 1777)

La réduction de Paris par Henri IV (opéra, C. L. Ducrest), private theatre of Mme de Montesson, 1781

Alexandre aux Indes (opéra, 3, E. Morel de Chédeville), Opéra, 26 Aug 1783 (Paris, c1784)

Dormenon et Beauval, ou Le fils corrigé (cmda, 2), PCI (Favart), 15 Sept 1787

Grisélide, ou La vertu à l'épreuve (comédie-héroïque, 3, P. J. B. C. Desforges), PCI (Favart), 8 Jan 1791, *F-Pc*

Oedipe et Jocaste [Oedipe à Thèbes] (tragédie lyrique, 3, P. A. Duprat de la Touloubre), Opéra, 30 Dec 1791, *Pn*, *Po*

Fabius (tragédie lyrique, 3, M. J. D. M. Barouillet), Opéra, 9 Aug 1793, *Pc*, *Po*

Unperf.: Les Thermopyles, *Pc*; Scipion à Carthage, 1795–6 (3, J. Lacombe) [listed in *FétisB*]

FétisB

A. D'Origny: *Annales du Théâtre Italien depuis son origine jusqu'à ce jour* (Paris, 1788)

A. Choron and F. Fayolle: *Dictionnaire historique des musiciens* (Paris, 1810–11)

C. D. Brenner: *A Bibliographical List of Plays in the French Language* (Berkeley, 1947, 2/1979)

——: *The Théâtre Italien: its Repertory, 1716–1793* (Berkeley and Los Angeles, 1961)

C. Pierre: *Histoire du Concert Spirituel 1725–1790* (Paris, 1975)

M. E. C. Bartlet: 'Revolutionschanson und Hymne im Repertoire der Pariser Oper 1793–1794', *Die Französische Revolution als Bruch des gesellschaftlichen Bewusstseins*, ed. R. Koselleck and R. Reichardt (Munich, 1988), 479–508

M. Noiray: 'Les créations d'opéra à Paris de 1790 à 1794: chronologie et sources parisiennes', *Orphée phrygien: les musiques de la Révolution*, ed. J.-R. Julien and J.-C. Klein (Paris, 1989), 193–203   DAVID CHARLTON

Mère coupable, La ('The Guilty Mother'). Opera in three acts, op.412, by DARIUS MILHAUD to a libretto by Madeleine Milhaud after PIERRE-AUGUSTIN BEAUMARCHAIS' play; Geneva, Grand Théâtre, 13 June 1966.

The play is the last in the cycle that includes *Le barbier de Séville* and *Le mariage de Figaro*. The characters are older, wiser and, according to the composer, 'perhaps more human'. Beaumarchais introduced a villain, Begaers (baritone), who tries to make his fortune by ruining Count Almaviva (baritone) and is finally worsted by Figaro (baritone). The libretto contrasts drama between Rosine (soprano) and Begaers with wit in the characters of Suzanne (mezzo-soprano) and Figaro and features a love affair between Léon (tenor), son of Rosine and Chérubin (who does not appear in the opera), and Florestine (coloratura soprano), Almaviva's illegitimate daughter.

Milhaud was convinced that the play would adapt well to operatic treatment, but his touch was a little on the heavy side. His strengths were acerbic and violent rhetorical grandeur on the one hand and sustained lyrical sweetness on the other: *La mère coupable* offers little scope for either. Much of the musical interest is in the orchestra, which inevitably obscures the words; but the plot is so complicated that to lose the words is disastrous. Added to this, the predominance of dialogue over action means that *La mère coupable* probably fares better on record or radio than on the stage.

CHRISTOPHER PALMER

Merelli, Bartolomeo (*b* Bergamo, 1794; *d* Milan, 10 April 1879). Italian librettist and impresario. The son of the steward to a noble Bergamo family, he was intended for a career in law but attended Simon Mayr's composition class together with Donizetti, for whose earliest operas he was to write librettos. In 1812 he was arrested and charged with attempted theft, but, after a few months in gaol, was released for lack of evidence. He found work with a theatrical agent in Milan. Between then and the late 1820s his own opera agency became one of the busiest. Like Alessandro Lanari, he engaged singers and dancers on long-term contracts at fixed salaries and sought to profit by selling their services to managements, or by managing seasons himself throughout a large network of theatres, mainly in north Italian towns.

From 1829 to 1850 Merelli managed La Scala, originally in partnership with others; when Giuseppe Crivelli died during rehearsals, Merelli was responsible for the staging of *Norma* (1831). From 1836 he also assisted with the Kärntnertortheater, Vienna, where his partner, Carlo Balochino, was in charge. At La Scala he staged Verdi's first opera, *Oberto*, and its three successors. Verdi's story of how Merelli helped him overcome depression after the deaths of his wife and children by giving him the libretto of *Nabucco* is inaccurate in some ways but may be substantially true. Verdi, however, turned against Merelli after *Giovanna d'Arco* (1845), as did Donizetti after Viennese performances of his operas. Both complained bitterly of careless, shabby productions and cavalier treatment of their scores, and Verdi refused to let Merelli give the first performance of any more of his works. During the 1848 revolution Merelli, openly pro-Austrian, was suspected of spying; he spent part of the 1850s in Vienna but was able to run La Scala again in 1861–3. He kept up a gentlemanly manner, spent much time and money trying to prove his own noble origins, and lived on a grand scale; but he was often regarded as shifty or dishonest. After losing much of his money he retired to the hills above Bergamo. His son Eugenio was an impresario in Venice, Vienna and Paris.

L'idolo Birmanno, P. Brambilla, 1816; *Lanassa* (melodramma eroico, with G. Rossi), S. Mayr, 1818; *Alfredo il grande* (melodramma serio), Mayr, 1818; *Enrico conte di Borgogna* (op semiseria), Donizetti, 1818; *Una follia* (farsa), Donizetti, 1818; *Il lupo d'Ostenda* (op semiseria), Vaccai, 1818; *Le nozze in villa* (ob), Donizetti, 1820–21; *Zoraide di Grenata* (os), Donizetti, 1822; *Pietro il grande, ossia Un geloso alla tortura* (ob), Vaccai, 1824; *La pastorella feudataria* (op semiseria), Vaccai, 1824; *Il precipizio, ossia Le fucine di Norvegia* (melodramma semiserio), Vaccai, 1826; *Don Desiderio ovvero Il disperato per ecceso di buon cuore* (ob), Morlacchi, 1829; *Emma, ossia Il protettore invisibile*, J. Benoni, 1851

*

Correspondence: I-Fn Carteggi Vari 395–6, Ms
F. Regli: *Dizionario biografico dei più illustri poeti e artisti melodrammatici* (Turin, 1860)
[B. Merelli]: *Cenni biografici di Donizetti e Mayr raccolti dalle memorie di un ottuagenario dilettante di musica* (Bergamo, 1875)
G. Monaldi: *Impresari celebri del secolo XIX* (Rocca S Casciano, 1918)
G. Zavadini: *Donizetti* (Bergamo, 1948), 696, 815
F. Schlitzer: *Mondo teatrale dell'ottocento* (Naples, 1954), 186–7
F. Abbiati: *Giuseppe Verdi* (Milan, 1959), i, 539–46, 604–5; ii, 654–5
F. Walker: *The Man Verdi* (London, 1962)
J. Rosselli: *The Opera Industry in Italy from Cimarosa to Verdi* (Cambridge, 1984)
L. Jensen: *Giuseppe Verdi and Giovanni Ricordi* (New York, 1989)

JOHN ROSSELLI

Méric, Joséphine de. See DE MÉRIC, JOSÉPHINE.

Méric-Lalande [née Lamiraux-Lalande], **Henriette (Clémentine)** (*b* Dunkirk, 4 April 1799; *d* Chantilly, 7 Sept 1867). French soprano. She sang in French provincial towns from 1814 to 1822, when she joined the Théâtre du Gymnase-Dramatique in Paris, taking lessons with the younger García before making her appearance on 3 April 1823 in a pasticcio by Castil-Blaze. She then went to Italy, studying further in Milan and singing in the première of Meyerbeer's *Il crociato in Egitto* (1824, Venice); she also created four Bellini roles: Bianca (*Bianca e Gernando*; 1826, Naples), Imogene (*Il pirata*; 1827, Milan), Alaide (*La straniera*; 1829, Milan) and the title role in *Zaira* (1829, Parma). Her London début was at the King's Theatre on 17 April 1830 in *Il pirata* but, according to Chorley, her voice was past its best. Later that year she appeared at the Théâtre Italien, and in 1831 she again sang in London and Paris, where she was admired as Semiramide. She continued to sing in Italy and Spain, but retired shortly after creating the title role in *Lucrezia Borgia* (1833, Milan). In her prime she was a brilliant dramatic singer, with a fine technique and a powerful stage presence.

Merighi, Antonia Margherita (*b* Bologna; *fl* 1714–40; *d* before 1764). Italian contralto. She sang in five operas at Florence (1714–16) and regularly in Venetian theatres (1717–21, 1724–6, 1732–3), appearing in 19 operas, the first of them Vivaldi's *Tieteberga*. In 1718 she was in Vivaldi's *Armida al campo d'Egitto* at Mantua. She had a great success in Bologna in Gasparini's *Sesostri* (1719), and sang in at least 18 operas in Naples (1721–4, 1728–9), often in male roles, in Parma and Florence in 1725, Turin in 1726 and Bologna again in 1727. In 1729 Handel engaged her for London where she was advertised as 'a Woman of a very fine Presence, an excellent Actress, and a very good Singer – A Counter Tenor', and remained for two seasons. She created Matilda in *Lotario* (her début in December 1729), Rosmira in *Partenope* and Eryxene in *Poro*, and was also heard in *Giulio Cesare*, *Tolomeo*, *Scipione*, *Rinaldo* and probably *Rodelinda*, often in soprano parts adapted for her. That she stood high in Handel's favour is clear from the size and quality of all his parts for her. Rolli paid tribute to her intelligence in *Lotario*; Mrs Pendarves wrote that 'her voice is not extraordinarily good or bad … she sings easily and agreeably'. Burney dismissed her, quite wrongly, as 'a singer of the second or third class'.

Merighi was singing in Florence in 1731–2 and Modena in 1735; she returned to London in 1736 for the unsuccessful final season of the Opera of the Nobility and sang at the King's Theatre in operas by Hasse, Riccardo Broschi, Pescetti, Veracini and Duni. The following season she appeared in pasticcios, further operas by Pescetti and Veracini, and in Handel's *Faramondo* and *Serse* as the original Gernando and Amastris. By then she had declined and her compass had narrowed: from ab to f'' in her earlier Handel parts to no more than c' to d'' in *Serse*. She is last heard of in two operas during Carnival 1740 at Munich. She married the tenor Carlo Carlani (1716–76) but was dead by 1764 when he remarried.

WINTON DEAN

Merighi, Giorgio (*b* Ferrara, 20 Feb 1939). Italian tenor. He studied at Pesaro and made his début at Spoleto in 1962 as Riccardo (*Un ballo in maschera*). He sang throughout Italy and in 1968 took the title role in *Robert le diable* at Florence. He made his American début in 1970 at Dallas as Luigi (*Il tabarro*) and his Covent Garden début in 1971 as Riccardo, returning in 1974 as Cavaradossi. He sang Alfredo and Rodolfo at Chicago (1972) and Puccini's Des Grieux at San Francisco (1974); in 1978 he made his Metropolitan début as Manrico. His roles included Tebaldo (*I Capuleti e i Montecchi*), Pollione, Fernand (*La favorite*), Boito's Faust, Chénier, Enzo Grimaldi (*La Gioconda*), Loris (*Fedora*), Maurizio (*Adriana Lecouvreur*), Pinkerton and Luigi. A good actor, he has a powerful voice best suited to the *verismo* style.

ELIZABETH FORBES

Merikanto, Aarre (*b* Helsinki, 29 July 1893; *d* Helsinki, 29 Sept 1958). Finnish composer, son of Oskar

Merikanto. He studied in Leipzig with Reger and in Moscow with Vasilenko. He worked at the Sibelius Academy, Helsinki, from 1936 to 1958, as professor of composition from 1951. Using unorthodox methods he was responsible for the training of many Finns who became well-known composers.

Merikanto began to improvise and to compose as a young child. When he was 18 his one-act opera *Helena*, for voices and piano, to a libretto by J. Finne, was given a student gala performance in Helsinki on 16 March 1912, his father playing the piano. Critics dubbed the work 'atonal' and the composer subsequently destroyed the score. After his death, music for the two leading roles was discovered; a substantial part of the score was reconstructed and the music was then considered to be Puccinian. The most decisive musical influence on Merikanto, however, was the harmonic and orchestral effects of Skryabin. His mature style may be seen as a fusion of chromatic polyphony, Russian 'mystical' colour and Finnish folkdance rhythms; he was one of the pioneers of highly chromatic and highly coloured writing in Finland, and for many years his endeavours were not understood. Many works remained unperformed at his death, including the three-act opera *Juha* (1920–22; A. Ackté, after J. Aho); rejected as too modern, it was neglected – partly as a result of personal conflicts within the Finnish Opera, partly because of its novel style – until Finnish radio gave a concert performance on 3 December 1958, and it received its stage première at Lahti on 28 October 1963. This was the period when Merikanto's music was rediscovered, and *Juha* was soon regarded as the best Finnish, and probably the best Nordic, opera. Stylistically comparable with Janáček, the opera describes with dramatic power and strong colour the conflict between the inflexibility of the Finnish character and the liveliness of the east Karelian milieu. Merikanto's other compositions include nine concertos, orchestral and chamber works.

See also JUHA.

K. Maasalo: *Suomalaisia sävellyksiä*, ii (Porvoo and Helsinki, 1969), 209–49

T. Teerisuo: *Aarre Merikannon ooppera Juha* (diss., U. of Helsinki, 1970)

H. Suilamo: 'A. M. – a Battered Genius', *Finnish Music Quarterly*, no.1 (1986), 46–59

T.-M. Lehtinen and P. Hako, eds.: *Kuninkaasta kuninkaaseen* [From King to King] (Helsinki, 1987), 113–20

ERKKI SALMENHAARA

Merikanto, (Frans) Oskar (*b* Helsinki, 5 Aug 1868; *d* Oitti, 17 Feb 1924). Finnish composer. He studied briefly at the Leipzig Conservatory and in Berlin. His activities in church music education and in initiating professional opera performances were of great importance in the development of Finnish musical life in the early 20th century; he also appeared as an opera conductor and was an excellent accompanist. His *Pohjan neiti* (1899) was the first opera in Finnish. It is Singspiel-like in character but not very convincing as drama; the two later operas are dramatically more ambitious. Merikanto owed his wide popularity to his numerous folksong-influenced salon romances.

See also POHJAN NEITI.

Pohjan neiti [The Maid of the North], 1899 (3, A. Rytkönen, after the Kalevala), Viipuri, Song Festival, 19 June 1908

Elinan surma [Elina's Death] (5, J. Finne), Helsinki, National, 17 Nov 1910

Regina von Emmeritz (5, Z. Topelius), Helsinki, Finnish Opera, 30 Jan 1920

ERKKI SALMENHAARA

Mérimée, Prosper (*b* Paris, 28 Sept 1803; *d* Cannes, 23 Sept 1870). French novelist and short-story writer. Inheriting a taste for the picturesque and the grotesque from his father, Léonor Mérimée, a drawing master at the Ecole Polytechnique, he began his literary career with *Le théâtre de Clara Gazul*, a collection of plays never intended for stage performance. He discovered the literary form best suited to his temperament in a series of short stories that first appeared in the *Revue de Paris*. *Tamango*, for instance, presents a mutiny by slaves on board a ship, while the subject of *Mateo Falcone* is a Corsican father's bitter punishment of his son's lapse from honour; there are several operatic versions of the latter. Mérimée was fond of strong, strange situations, exotic settings and blazing emotions, but an ironic tendency predisposed him to distance himself from this violence even as he presented it. There is a reflection of his attitude in his language, precise in description and laconic to the point of indifference in narrative. Paradoxically, the style enhances the impact of the narrative because the reader feels impelled to respond. *Colomba*, a short novel set in Corsica, attracted a number of composers including Sir Alexander Mackenzie (1883), but none had the success that Bizet enjoyed with *Carmen*. This story of unbridled passion in Spain was first published in the *Revue des deux mondes* in 1845, and the opera, to a libretto by Meilhac and Halévy, had its première in 1875. Its success silences criticism, but the difference in style between the opera and its literary source is striking. Mérimée's work in his later years reflects his many travels. He also translated works by Pushkin, Gogol and Turgenev; Scribe's libretto for Halévy's *La dame de pique* is partly based on Mérimée's translation.

Inès Mendo, ou Le préjugé vaincu (play, 1825): Erlanger, 1897

Le carrosse du Saint-Sacrement (saynète, 1829): Offenbach, 1868, as La Périchole; Berners, 1923; Büsser, 1948

Mateo Falcone (novella, 1829): Zöllner, 1893; T. Gerlach, 1898; Cui, 1907; Ewart, 1932; P. Fejko, 1987

La Vénus d'Ille (story, 1837): Schoeck, 1922, as Venus; H. H. Wetzler, 1928, as Die baskische Venus; Büsser, 1964

Colomba (story, 1840): G. Pacini, 1842, as La fidanzata corsa; A. K. W. Grandjean, 1882; Mackenzie, 1883; V. Radeglia, 1887; Büsser, 1921

Carmen (novel, 1845): Bizet, 1875

Le ciel et l'enfer (play, written 1825): G. F. Malipiero, 1954, as Donna Urraca

L'occasion (play, written 1829); Durey, comp. 1923–5

A. W. Rait: *Prosper Mérimée* (London, 1970)

M. A. Smith: *Prosper Mérimée* (New York, 1972)

CHRISTOPHER SMITH

Merkù, Pavle (*b* Trieste, 12 July 1927). Slovene composer. He studied philology at the University of Ljubljana and literature at Rome University, and took private composition lessons in Trieste. After a period as a schoolteacher he worked for the Slovene section of RAI, Trieste, becoming deputy director of Slovene programmes. He has also been active as a music critic and ethnomusicologist. He has written only one opera, in two languages, Italian and Slovene: *La libellula* (*Kačji pastir*, 'The Dragonfly'; 1976, Trieste, Comunale, in Italian; 1985, Maribor, in Slovenian). This work, in two acts, is basically expressionist, and the music is well suited to the theme of the libretto (by S. Makarovič), which depicts from various viewpoints the human endeavour to survive. Merkù has also composed incidental music for a number of plays.   MANICA ŠPENDAL

Merli, Francesco (*b* Milan, 27 Jan 1887; *d* Milan, 12 Dec 1976). Italian tenor. He studied in Milan with Negrini and Borghi, and began his career in 1916 as a second tenor in Buenos Aires, then sang Alvaro in *Fernand Cortez* at La Scala. He was soon singing larger roles, and in 1918 he sang Elisero (*Mosè in Egitto*) and created Fausto in Favara's *Urania* at La Scala, where he continued to appear until 1942, sharing the dramatic tenor roles in the repertory with Pertile. He sang at Covent Garden between 1926 and 1930 and was the first London Calaf in *Turandot*. His appearances at the Metropolitan, where he made his début as Radames in 1932, were dogged by ill-health and he was never re-engaged. He participated in numerous revivals of works by Franchetti, Gomes, Catalani and Zandonai and continued to sing until 1948. Merli had a powerful and resonant voice and his feeling for words was notable. His acting was never less than adequate and often, in roles congenial to him such as Don José, Dick Johnson and Samson, rather more than that.

*

GV (R. Celletti; R. Vegeto)
R. Celletti: 'Francesco Merli', *Discoteca* (1967), no.71, p.35 [with discography by R. Vegeto]   HAROLD ROSENTHAL/R

Mermet, Auguste (*b* Brussels, 5 Jan 1810; *d* Paris, 4 July 1889). French composer. He was destined for a military career but abandoned that for music, having studied the flute and later composition privately with Le Sueur and Halévy. Most of his small output was for the stage. His first opera, *La bannière du roi*, was performed in 1835 and his *Le roi David* was staged at the Opéra in 1846 with Rosine Stoltz singing David's part. A long gap intervened before *Roland à Roncevaux* in 1864 and yet another between that and *Jeanne d'Arc* in 1876. *Roland à Roncevaux* enjoyed considerable if short-lived success (65 performances by 1867) owing to its patriotic tone and its appeal to the spectacular; Mermet's Napoleonic connections (his father was a colonel in Napoleon's army) served him well under the Second Empire and he exploited the same patriotic vein, with less success, in *Jeanne d'Arc*, the first new work presented at Garnier's Opéra (opened in 1875). Both of these works told of stirring episodes in French history; the music was modelled closely on Meyerbeer and Halévy, and his own librettos were modelled on those of Scribe, but Mermet lacked their imaginative sweep. His music is direct, attractive, unadventurous and noisy. He filled canvases too large for his slender musical skills but knew how to make a direct appeal to certain sectors of Parisian taste, with a special fondness for martial and rousingly rhythmic music. The failure of *Jeanne d'Arc* has been seen as the close of Meyerbeer's domination of French opera. The libretto was one of Tchaikovsky's sources for *The Maid of Orléans*.

La bannière du roi (oc, 2, P. F. A. Carmouche), Versailles, April 1835
Le roi David (opéra, 3, A. Soumet and F. Mallefille), Opéra, 3 June 1846
Roland à Roncevaux (4, Mermet), Paris, Opéra, 3 Oct 1864 (Paris, ?1865)
Jeanne d'Arc (opéra, 4, Mermet, after J. Barbier), Paris, Opéra, 5 April 1876, vs (Paris, 1876)
Pierrot pendu (opéra bouffe, 1), unperf.
Bacchus dans l'Inde, unperf.

*

FétisBS

H. Blanchard: 'David de M. Mermet', *Revue et gazette musicale*, xiii (1846), 177–8
P. Smith: 'Théâtre Impérial de l'Opéra: Roland à Roncevaux', *Revue et gazette musicale*, xxxi (1864), 321–3
A. Dupeuty: 'A. Mermet (notes intimes)', *Chronique musicale*, xi (1876), 57–63
A. Jullien: 'Théâtre National de l'Opéra: Jeanne d'Arc', *Revue et gazette musicale*, xliii (1876), 113–15   HUGH MACDONALD

Merola, Gaetano (*b* Naples, 4 Jan 1881; *d* San Francisco, 30 Aug 1953). American conductor and impresario of Italian birth. After studying at the Naples Conservatory he became assistant conductor at the Metropolitan Opera in 1899. He toured with Henry Savage's opera company, became associated with Oscar Hammerstein's two companies (the Manhattan Opera and the London Opera) and then conducted the San Carlo Opera in San Francisco between 1918 and 1922. A year later he founded the San Francisco Opera, and as its first general director conducted the inaugural performance, *La bohème*, at the Civic Auditorium. In the 30 years he held the position, the San Francisco Opera became one of America's leading companies. Merola used singers primarily from the Metropolitan, and staged operas from the standard European repertory almost exclusively. Nevertheless, he introduced the *Ring* to San Francisco (1935), gave the American première of *L'enfant et les sortilèges* (1931) and presented contemporary rarities such as Franco Vittadini's *Anima allegra* (1925), Giordano's *La cena delle beffe* (1927) and Henri Rabaud's *Mârouf* (1931). From 1924 to 1931 he was also the general director of the Los Angeles Grand Opera Association. He died while conducting at the Stern Grove Festival.

*

W. Zakariasen: 'Fior d'Italia', *ON*, xxxvii/4 (1972–3), 16–18
C. Bishop: *The San Carlo Opera Company, 1913–1955* (Santa Monica, CA, 1978)
A. Bloomfield: *The San Francisco Opera: 1922–1978* (Sausalito, CA, 1978)   ALLAN ULRICH

Merope. Libretto subject used chiefly in the 18th and 19th centuries. Its source is Greek history, in particular EURIPIDES' lost tragedy *Cresphontes*.

The story is set in the kingdom of Messenia in the Greek Peloponnese, ruled by Cresphontes, a descendant of Hercules, and his queen, Merope, princess of neighbouring Arcadia. In an insurrection of the Messenian nobles Cresphontes is deposed by Polyphontes and executed along with two of his three sons. Merope sends the youngest son, Aepytus, into hiding in Arcadia. When he reaches manhood he returns to avenge his father's murder; arriving in disguise, he announces that he has killed the long-missing third son of Cresphontes. Merope, whom Polyphontes has forced to become his wife, learns that Aepytus is no longer in Arcadia and orders the stranger put to death. Aepytus's true identity is revealed before the execution; mother and son are reunited. Aepytus kills Polyphontes and assumes his rightful place on the throne.

There are two major variants of the story. In its earliest version, by Zeno (1712), Merope has not yet been forced to marry Polifonte [Polyphontes]. Zeno also adds a love interest for Epitide [Aepytus] in the Arcadian princess Argia, taken hostage by Polyphontes. Polyphontes forces Anassandro [Anasander], the executioner of Cresofonte [Cresphontes] and his sons, to accuse Merope in public of having commissioned the act. Merope learns Aepytus's true identity only near the end of the opera, having believed him executed at her request. Later *Merope* librettos tell a somewhat different version, based primarily on Scipione Maffei's drama (1713). Aepytus (renamed Egisto) is at first unaware of his true identity. He is brought to Messenia accused of murder and is believed by Merope (who recognizes items found at the scene as her son's) to be her son's murderer. The truth is revealed at the last moment and mother and son are reunited. Polyphontes arrests Egisto and forces Merope to choose between marriage and her son's death; but Egisto is rescued and kills the tyrant.

The most successful *Merope* libretto, Zeno's, was first set by Francesco Gasparini (1712) and had at least 28 new settings over the next 75 years, notably by Giacomelli (1734), Jommelli (1741), Terradellas (1743), Perez (1750), Gassmann (1757) and Traetta (1776). Zeno considered the libretto one of his 'least poor' dramas. *Merope* is also noteworthy among Zeno's texts because large portions of the original recitative text survived the revision process late into the century. None of the later *Merope* librettos – by Giampietro Tagliazucchi for C. H. Graun (1756), Mattia Botturini for Sebastiano Nasolini (1796), or Salvadore Cammarano for Giovanni Pacini (1847) – achieved Zeno's success.

See also MEROPE below.   PAUL CAUTHEN

Merope. *Dramma per musica* in three acts by DOMÈNECH MIGUEL BERNABÉ TERRADELLAS to a libretto by APOSTOLO ZENO; Rome, Teatro delle Dame, 3 January 1743.

Terradellas's opera dramatizes a case of intrigue at the court of the Queen of Messenia, Merope (soprano), who has been wrongfully accused of killing her husband and two elder children. Polifonte [Polyphontes] (tenor), the mastermind behind the murders, has seized power and is sheltering Anassandro [Anasander] (contralto), who committed them. The unsuspecting prime minister, Trasimede [Thrasymedes] (contralto), is giving Polyphontes halfhearted support. To consolidate his power Polyphontes plans to marry Merope and kill her third son, Epitide [Aepytus] (soprano), who has taken shelter in the neighbouring kingdom of Etolia. By kidnapping Argia (contralto), the king's daughter and Aepytus's fiancée, Polyphontes induces the king to send his ambassador, Licisco [Lyciscus] (contralto), to Messenia to save her. Aepytus comes too, disguised as 'Cleon', resolved to uncover the truth about the murders. In recompense for killing a wild boar threatening Messenia he is promised the hand of Argia by Polyphontes, who manipulates a public trial of Merope to get her condemned to death. Having discovered Cleon's identity, Polyphontes persuades Merope that Cleon has killed Aepytus in exile, so she commands Thrasymedes to assassinate the young man. Anasander now reveals Polyphontes' treachery. Thrasymedes spares Aepytus's life and supports him as he successfully claims the throne. Merope is absolved from blame, and Polyphontes is sent away to be executed.

Because of the law preventing women acting on the public stage in Rome, the original cast of *Merope* consisted of six castratos and one tenor. The difference in their capabilities is revealed in the treatment Terradellas gave each part. Merope and Polyphontes are the only two characters with accompanied recitatives. Merope and Aepytus have the most technically difficult arias with the most turbulent music. Many of the arias in lighter styles, usually for the other characters, have lilting melodies of the kind found in much Neapolitan opera of the period. The aria accompaniments tend to have busy top and bottom string parts. The wind are sparingly though effectively used in a few arias and in the accompanied recitatives.

See also MEROPE above.   MICHAEL F. ROBINSON

Merrem-Nikisch, Grete (*b* Duren, 7 July 1887; *d* Kiel, 12 March 1970). German soprano. She studied in Cologne and at Leipzig, where she made her début in 1910. At the Berlin Hofoper (1911) she sang the Goose girl (Humperdinck's *Königskinder*). In 1913 she joined the Dresden Hofoper (later Staatsoper), remaining there until 1930 and creating Arsinoe in Eugen d'Albert's *Die toten Augen* (1916) and the Lady in *Cardillac* (1926). Her roles included Sophie (*Der Rosenkavalier*), Eva (which she sang in 1914 at Covent Garden, conducted by her father-in-law, Arthur Nikisch); and Christine, which she took over from Lotte Lehmann at the second performance of *Intermezzo*. She had a bright-toned, flexible voice and sang Adele on a recording of the Act 2 finale of *Die Fledermaus* with Lehmann and Richard Tauber.   ELIZABETH FORBES

Merrie England. Operetta in two acts by EDWARD GERMAN to a libretto by BASIL HOOD; London, Savoy Theatre, 2 April 1902.

Essentially a pseudo-historical pageant, the operetta portrays a fictitious episode in which Queen Elizabeth I (contralto) becomes jealous of the love Sir Walter Raleigh (tenor) displays for Bessie Throckmorton (soprano), revealed through the machinations of Raleigh's rival, the Earl of Essex (baritone). Designed to exploit German's 'olde English' style, popularized through his incidental music, the work also exhibits his gift for the ballad, both lyrical ('The English Rose', 'O Peaceful England') and patriotically robust ('The Yeomen of England'). Bessie's sparkling waltz-song, 'O who shall say that love is cruel!', contrasts with the poignancy of her own 'She had a letter from her love' and the solos for Jill-All-Alone (mezzo-soprano).

Professional revivals have been few: for one, by Sadler's Wells (1960), the libretto was revised; for another, under the title of *Elizabeth of England* (1945), the original story was jettisoned altogether. Nonetheless, the work can probably claim more performances than any other 20th-century British opera or operetta, its enormous popularity with amateurs – there were hundreds of productions in the year of Queen Elizabeth II's coronation – having declined only with the fading myth of England's merriness in days of yore, a once potent element in English self-perception which German's operetta itself helped to sustain.

DAVID RUSSELL HULME

Merrill, Nathaniel (*b* Newton, MA, 8 Feb 1927). American director. He was a pupil of Boris Goldovsky at the New England Conservatory of Music, and also gained experience in Europe with Carl Ebert, Herbert Graf, Günther Rennert and Friedrich Schramm. He made his début in Boston in 1952, when he directed the American première of Lully's *Amadis*. In 1955 he joined the Metropolitan, and remained as resident stage director for two decades; he took charge of more than a dozen new productions, many of them in collaboration with the designer Robert O'Hearn. He also worked for the Opéra du Rhin, Strasbourg, in the same capacity, and has directed operas in Vancouver and for the open-air Arena in Verona. He excels in the deployment of large forces on stage, as in *Aida*, *Die Meistersinger* and *Les Troyens*, all of which he staged at the Metropolitan.

N. Merrill: 'The Making of a Director', *ON*, xxxii/16 (1967–8), 8–12
FRANK MERKLING

Merrill, Robert (*b* Brooklyn, New York, 4 June 1917). American baritone. He studied with Samuel Margolis in New York. He based his career at the Metropolitan Opera, where he sang all the major baritone roles of the Italian and principal French repertories. In vocal endowment, technical security and longevity he was unequalled among baritones of his generation at the Metropolitan, where he made his début as Germont on 15 December 1945 and remained until 1974–5. He first appeared in Europe, also as Germont, at La Fenice in 1961 and at Covent Garden (in the same role) in 1967. His numerous complete opera recordings include *La traviata* and *Un ballo in maschera* under Toscanini. In 1975 he made his London concert début, winning praise for the generosity, if not the subtlety, of his singing. For all the natural beauty and healthy resonance of his voice, he was never highly regarded as an imaginative interpreter or a compelling actor.

GV (L. Riemens; S. Smolian)
R. Merrill and S. Dody: *Once More from the Beginning* (New York, 1965)
H. Rosenthal: 'Robert Merrill', *Great Singers of Today* (London, 1966)
H. E. Phillips: 'Merrill's Milestone', *ON*, xxxv/11 (1970–71), 14–16
R. Merrill and R. Saffron: *Between Acts* (New York, 1977)
PETER G. DAVIS

Merriman, Nan [Katherine-Ann] (*b* Pittsburgh, 28 April 1920). American mezzo-soprano. She studied in Los Angeles with Alexia Bassian, and in 1942 made her début at Cincinnati as La Cieca (*La Gioconda*). Toscanini engaged her for his broadcasts and recordings of Gluck's *Orfeo* (as Orpheus), *Falstaff* (as Meg Page), *Rigoletto* (as Maddalena) and *Otello* (as Emilia). She sang Dorabella at Aix-en-Provence (1953, 1955, 1959), the Piccola Scala (1955–6) and Glyndebourne (1956). She played Baba the Turk in the British première of *The Rake's Progress* at Edinburgh (1953), and Laura in Dargomïzhsky's *The Stone Guest* at the Piccola Scala (1958). Merriman retired in 1965 while her appealingly vibrant mezzo-soprano was still at the height of its powers.
HAROLD ROSENTHAL/R

Merritt, Chris (Allan) (*b* Oklahoma City, OK, 27 Sept 1952). American tenor. After studying in Oklahoma, he became an apprentice at the Santa Fe Opera. He made his début in 1978 as Lindoro at the Landestheater, Salzburg. At Augsburg (1981–4) he sang Tamino, Idomeneus, Julien (*Louise*) and Rodolfo. A Rossini specialist, he has sung Erisso (*Maometto II*), Capellio (*Bianca e Falliero*), Pyrrhus (*Ermione*) and Otello at Pesaro; James (*La donna del lago*) for his début (1985) and Idreno (*Semiramide*) at Covent Garden; Count Libenskof (*Il viaggio a Reims*) in Vienna; Aménophis (*Moïse et Pharaon*) at the Paris Opéra; Antenore (*Zelmira*) in Venice and Rome; Argirio (*Tancredi*) in Los Angeles and Chicago; and Arnold (*Guillaume Tell*) at La Scala, Paris, Covent Garden (1990) and other theatres. He has also appeared in Madrid, San Francisco, Florence, Naples and Parma. His roles in-clude Gluck's Pylades, Arturo (*I puritani*), Percy (*Anna Bolena*), Nemorino, Léopold (*La Juive*), Cellini, Aeneas (*Les Troyens*), Arrigo (*Les vêpres siciliennes*), Admetus (*Alceste*) and Leukippos (*Daphne*). His voice, resonant and expressive in its lower ranges, has a powerful upper extension to *d''*, allowing him to sing high-lying roles without strain.
ELIZABETH FORBES

Merry Widow, The. Operetta by Franz Lehár; *see* *LUSTIGE WITWE, DIE.*

Merry Wives of Windsor, The. Opera by Otto Nicolai; *see* *LUSTIGEN WEIBER VON WINDSOR, DIE.*

Merveilleux (Fr.: 'marvellous'). A term used extensively in the discussion of French opera of the 17th and 18th centuries to describe spectacular and decorative effects of staging involving elaborate machinery, derived from earlier *ballets de cour* and *tragédies aux machines*. A typical embodiment of *le merveilleux* is the arrival of gods among mortals in the *tragédie en musique*, a feature present in Lully's first opera, *Cadmus et Hermione*, and sustained in Rameau's work (the first and last acts of *Hippolyte et Aricie*, for example) and beyond. *Le merveilleux* was also a vital element of supernatural and magical scenes and for those depicting transformations, battles and other spectacular events; audiences were challenged to suspend their disbelief, enter an enchanted world inhabited by an assortment of divinities, allegorical figures and humans, and accept that this constituted *vraisemblance* in the *tragédie en musique*.

See also TRAGÉDIE EN MUSIQUE, §3.

V. Delaporte: *Du merveilleux dans la littérature française sous le règne de Louis XIV* (Paris, 1891)
E. Friedrich: *Die Magie im französischen Theater des XVII. und XVIII. Jahrhunderts* (Leipzig, 1908)
A. S. Garlington: 'Le merveilleux and Operatic Reform in 18th Century French Opera', *MQ*, xlix (1963), 484–97
M. F. Christout: *Le merveilleux et le 'théâtre du silence' en France à partir du XVIIe siècle* (The Hague and Paris, 1965)
J. de La Gorce: *L'opéra sous le règne de Louis XIV: le merveilleux ou les puissances surnaturelles, 1671–1715* (diss., U. of Paris-Sorbonne, 1978)
M. Hobson: *The Object of Art* (Cambridge, 1982)
M. Pineda: *Magie et phénomènes surnaturels dans l'opéra lullyste* (diss., U. of Paris-Sorbonne, 1986)

Méry, (François-)**Joseph**(-Pierre-André) (*b* Aygalades, nr Marseilles, 21 Jan 1797; *d* Paris, 17 June 1865). French playwright and librettist. He studied law at the University of Aix-en-Provence before turning to political journalism, expressing his hatred of the Restoration regime with a violence that led to a brief period of imprisonment. After a visit to Turkey he moved to Paris where he wrote for *Le nain jaune* and attacked the July Monarchy. A prolific author of fiction, verse, drama and essays, he also wrote a number of librettos, generally in collaboration with others. His most significant association with opera came when he started work with Camille Du Locle on the adaptation of Schiller's *Don Carlos* for Verdi, but he died before he had finished his task. It was completed by Du Locle, who also devised the libretto for *Aida*, as well as revising that of *Don Carlos* in the 1880s.

Maître Wolfram (oc, with T. Gautier), Reyer, 1854; *Entrez, messieurs, mesdames* (prol., with L. Halévy), Offenbach, 1855; *Le prix de famille* (opérette), Massé, comp. 1855; *Herculanum* (opéra, with T. Hadot), F. David, 1859; *Erostate* (opéra, with E.

Pacini), Reyer, 1862; *Jeanne d'Arc* (opéra, with E. Duprez), G. Duprez, 1865; *Valse et menuet* (oc, with J. Adenis), P.-L. Deffès, 1865; *Le fantôme du Rhin* (oc, with Adenis), Deffès, 1866; *La comédie en voyage* (oc), Deffès, 1867; *Don Carlos* (opéra, with C. Du Locle), Verdi, 1867   CHRISTOPHER SMITH

Mesplé, Mady (*b* Toulouse, 7 March 1931). French soprano. She studied at the Toulouse Conservatory and in 1953 joined the Liège Opera, making her début as Lakmé. After three seasons she was engaged at La Monnaie, singing Lucia and the Queen of Night. In 1956 she joined the Opéra-Comique, where she created the title role in Henri Tomasi's *Princesse Pauline* (1962) and Kitty in Menotti's *Le dernier sauvage* (1963). At Aix-en-Provence she sang Zémire (*Zémire et Azor*; 1956) and Zerbinetta (1966). She made her début at the Opéra as Sister Constance of St Denis in the French première of *Dialogues des Carmélites* (1958). Her repertory included Mireille, Philine (*Mignon*), Ophelia, Norina, Oscar, Gounod's Juliet, Sophie (*Werther*), and The Fire, The Princess and The Shepherdess (*L'enfant et les sortilèges*). She sang throughout Europe and the USA, making her Metropolitan début as Gilda (1973). A high soprano of rare distinction, she had an individuality of timbre and a refinement of phrase beyond the usual coloratura singer. She has recorded Mme Herz (Mozart's *Der Schauspieldirektor*), in addition to several French operatic roles.

MAX LOPPERT, ELIZABETH FORBES

Mesquita, Henrique Alves de (*b* Rio de Janeiro, 15 March 1830; *d* Rio de Janeiro, 12 July 1906). Brazilian composer. He received his training at the Imperial Conservatory of Music and, on a government scholarship, studied with Bazin at the Paris Conservatoire. His symphonic overture *L'étoile du Brésil* was performed in Paris in 1861, while he was there, as was his comic opera *Une nuit au château*. Mesquita's most important work was the opera *O vagabundo* or *A infidelidade, sedução e vaidade punidas*, in three acts with a prologue, to a libretto by Luiz Vicente de Simoni, first performed at the Teatro Lírico Fluminense, Rio, on 24 October 1863. Called a 'semi-serious melodrama' in the 1863 publication of the libretto, the work was received at the time as a 'monstrous drama'. The action takes place in France at the beginning of the 17th century. The Count of Savigny, nicknamed 'the Vagabond', seduces a young woman, Adèle, who commits suicide shortly after her forced wedding to the Baron of Marcey. 18 years later, Savigny encounters Marcey in the company of Isaura, who he thinks is Marcey's lover. In his wish to avenge himself, Savigny plans to kidnap and seduce Isaura, but shortly before the execution of his plan the Baron reveals that Isaura is really Savigny's daughter. This was the last opera by a Brazilian composer to be produced by the Imperial Academia de Música e Opera Nacional, founded in 1857. In 1869 Alves de Mesquita became the regular conductor of the Teatro Fénix Dramática, which specialized in operettas, and for which he wrote some successful pieces including *Ali Babá* and *Coroa de Carlos Magno*.

*

L. H. Corrêa de Azevedo: *Relação das óperas de autores brasileiros* (Rio de Janeiro, 1938)

——: *150 anos de música no Brasil (1800–1950)* (Rio de Janeiro, 1956)

A. de Andrade: *Francisco Manuel da Silva e seu tempo, 1808–1865*, ii (Rio de Janeiro, 1967)

B. Kiefer: *História da música brasileira* (Porto Alegre, 2/1977), 103–4   GERARD BÉHAGUE

Messa di voce (It.: 'placing of the voice'). The singing or playing of a long note so that it begins quietly, swells to full volume, and then diminishes to the original quiet tone. The *messa di voce* was at first looked upon as an ornament and was described by Giulio Caccini in *Le nuove musiche* (1601/2) as 'il crescere e scemare della voce'. P. F. Tosi (*Opinioni de' cantori antichi e moderni*, 1723) defined it briefly and advised that it should be used sparingly. G. B. Mancini (*Pensieri, e riflessioni pratiche sopra il canto figurato*, 1774), on the other hand, devoted a short chapter to the subject, specifying that the *messa di voce* should be used 'at the beginning of an aria and on any note with a fermata. Similarly it is necessary at the beginning of a cadenza. A truly accomplished singer, however, will use it on every long note that occurs in a cantilena'. During the 18th century the *messa di voce* acquired such importance in Italian singing that it was turned into a vocal exercise. Domenico Corri, the principal transmitter of the pedagogical method of his teacher, Nicola Porpora, set forth as the first lesson in his *The Singer's Preceptor* (1810) the singing of the *messa di voce* on different notes of the scale with piano accompaniment. The term is also found in 19th-century scores, for example in Act 1 scene vi of Bellini's *Norma* (1831), where the first note of Adalgisa's phrase, 'Lo, l'obbliai', is to be sung 'con messa di voce assai lunga'. The first note of Leonora's aria 'Pace, pace, mio Dio' from *La forza del destino* is often used for practice in exercising the skill.

OWEN JANDER, J. B. STEANE

Messager, André (**Charles Prosper**) (*b* Montluçon, 30 Dec 1853; *d* Paris, 24 Feb 1929). French composer. Following his formal musical education at the Ecole Niedermeyer, and lessons with Saint-Saëns, he succeeded Fauré as *organiste de choeur* at S Sulpice before beginning a career as a stage composer at the Folies Bergère in the late 1870s. He had by this time already composed a symphony, awarded a prize by the Société des Auteurs et Compositeurs de Musique in 1875, and two cantatas, one of which (*Don Juan et Haydée*) brought him to the attention of Auguste Vaucorbeil, the director of the Paris Opéra, who subsequently commissioned (May 1884) Messager's ballet *Les deux pigeons*. Messager's interest in Wagner also seems to date from the 1870s, probably under the influence of Saint-Saëns and Fauré, with whom he improvised the skittish *Souvenirs de Bayreuth*, regularly performed as a party piece by the two composers, but probably first conceived around 1880. Messager left the Folies Bergère at the end of the 1870s, and was engaged for a season as conductor at the Eden Théâtre in Brussels. An important opportunity to have his work performed in Paris presented itself in 1883, when William Enoch (who had already published a number of Messager's songs) asked him to complete Firmin Bernicat's *opéra comique François les bas-bleus*, left unfinished at Bernicat's death. Messager completely orchestrated the work, and composed about 12 numbers for it.

After further praise for his ballet *Les deux pigeons* in October 1886, Messager wrote a number of stage works until the end of the 1880s as well as vocal and piano compositions. His first attempt to write in a more serious vein was the unsuccessful nationalist work, *Le bourgeois de Calais* (1887). Three subsequent projects also ended in failure: *Isoline* (Christmas 1888); incidental music for *Colibri*, a one-act comedy (June

1889); and *Le mari de la reine* (December 1889), which Gauthier-Villars ('Willy') noted had fallen completely flat (*La paix*, 20 December 1889), and which Messager at the time called 'the best of my failures'. Part of this failure was probably due to an influenza epidemic at the end of 1889, and the departure of visitors to the Exposition Universelle by the time of the work's première.

The 1890s began to bring success both in France and England, beginning with *La Basoche* (produced in England as *The King of the Students*). *Mirette* (1894) was written for London, and Messager later resisted attempts to have it performed in France. *Madame Chrysanthème* (1893, the earliest musical setting of the story by Pierre Loti later set by Puccini as *Madama Butterfly*) was another attempt to write a less lightweight work, but it met with little success, as did *Le chevalier d'Harmental* (1896), another serious piece, whose failure led Messager to consider retirement from the stage. He moved to Maidenhead, Berkshire, and lived there with his second wife, Alice Maude Davis (known professionally as the composer Hope Temple). This self-imposed exile was brought to an end by the brilliant success of *Les p'tites Michu* in 1897, and by his being appointed (by Albert Carré) musical director of the Opéra-Comique, a position Messager held until 1904. This meant that he composed fewer works during the period 1898–1904, concentrating instead on bringing the works of others (including Debussy's *Pelléas et Mélisande*, of which he was joint dedicatee) to the stage. From 1901 to 1907 he was also employed at Covent Garden, where much of his time seems to have been spent on administration. He consequently conducted few works – Saint-Saëns' *Hélène* with Melba and *Don Giovanni* with Caruso were rare examples.

None of Messager's own works was performed either by the Opéra-Comique or at Covent Garden during his time with those institutions; but his next dramatic work, *Fortunio* (1907), was performed by the Opéra-Comique with great success. The title role was played by Jean Périer, who had already appeared in Messager's *La fiancée en loterie* and *Véronique*, and in *Pelléas*. Messager was then named director, with Frederick Broussan, of the Opéra. The partnership lasted until 1914 but was only moderately successful, owing to shortage of funds for new productions and constant disputes with staff. Highlights of the period included Fauré's *Pénélope*, Rameau's *Hippolyte et Aricie* (1908), Ravel's *L'heure espagnole* and Musorgsky's *Boris Godunov*. Wagner was also popular, and on the strength of his experience in this area Messager was appointed conductor of the Société des Concerts du Conservatoire in 1908, a position he had failed to obtain seven years earlier. During World War I he took the orchestra on a number of foreign propaganda tours, including an expedition to Argentina (1916), where his performances of Wagner made him some enemies at home. Further trips followed, to Switzerland (1917) and the USA (1918–19), at the end of which Messager resigned his post because of disputes with members of the orchestra, especially with his deputy conductor Philippe Gaubert.

Messager's most significant stage work from the war years was *Béatrice* (1914), a quasi-Wagnerian piece, whose première was moved from Paris to Monte Carlo at the outbreak of war; it received no French performances until 1917 and was not successful, much to Messager's disappointment. He conducted a performance in Bordeaux in 1926, and a few months before his death was still hopeful of a performance in Darmstadt that was being negotiated with Robert Brussel. April 1919 saw the première of *Monsieur Beaucaire*, although Messager was suffering from sciatica and was unable to attend the first nights in either Birmingham or London. He took on the musical directorship of the Opéra-Comique for the 1919–20 season, conducting among other items the first complete French performance of *Così fan tutte*.

Six stage works followed, two of them for Sacha Guitry and his wife, Yvonne Printemps; the second of these, *Deburau*, is dedicated to Fauré's memory. Although asked to record extracts from *L'amour masqué* (his other collaboration with Guitry) he did not do so, and few recordings survive of him as performer or conductor.

He was elected President of the Société des Auteurs et Compositeurs Dramatiques in 1926, the first composer to hold this office, and in 1927 was made a Commandeur of the Légion d'honneur. His health began to decline steadily (a serious illness in 1921 had led to his being reported dead at that time) and he died in February 1929.

In spite of the fact that his greatest successes were stage works of a lightweight character, Messager claimed in his memoirs that his intention had always been to write *opéra comique* in the tradition of composers such as Boieldieu. Albert Carré also considered Messager to have had higher aspirations; he suggested that the composer should have been producing works of the stature of *Pénélope* and *Pelléas*, and gave as a reason for his failure to do so Messager's early first marriage (1883) and the consequent need for a guaranteed living from the stage, which was more easily gained from the operettas, ballets and incidental music he composed in the 1880s and early 1890s than from more serious work. Carré also thought that by the time Messager had made enough money to fulfil his ambitions, the public expected nothing but operetta from him. There may be substance in this latter argument, since Messager's four operas – *Le bourgeois de Calais*, *Madame Chrysanthème*, *Le chevalier d'Harmental* and, above all, *Béatrice* – did follow periods of artistic and financial success. Whether conducting the great works of the operatic repertory composed by others compensated Messager for his own disappointments cannot be known; but there is no evidence to show that he found operetta composition irksome, even if he may privately have felt it to be demeaning.

Messager's style is characterized by fine orchestration (evident also in the ballet music), a gift for easy-flowing melody, often in a waltz rhythm, and a skill in writing music of a dance-like character. His own experience of operetta came through the works of Offenbach, Hervé and Lecocq, and he was regarded by some as the last of this line. His biographer and pupil Henry Février claimed that *La Basoche* was the last great French *opéra comique* of the 19th century, and Messager's next *opérettes*, especially *Les p'tites Michu* and *Véronique*, certainly show a difference in style from the earlier works, bringing an altogether fresher approach to the genre. Nevertheless, none of the stage works has been able to hold its popularity, with the possible exception of *Fortunio*, occasionally revived in France. Although the best music is still interesting, the 'precious' nature of many of the plots, and especially the attitudes shown towards women, may make some of the pieces at best unbelievable, at worst unacceptable, condemning them to obscurity along with much other light music of the period. Only *Véronique*, *Fortunio* and *Coups de roulis* have been recorded complete. Nonetheless, Messager's contribution to French music, both through his own works and as conductor and promoter of opera, is undeniable, and was recognized as such by his musical contemporaries in many countries.

See also MONSIEUR BEAUCAIRE; P'TITES MICHU, LES; and VÉRONIQUE.

first performed, and published in vocal score, in Paris unless otherwise stated

Les païens (opérette, H. Meilhac), *c*1876, collab. G. Serpette, Widor, Massenet and Delibes, lost

François les bas-bleus (oc, 3, E. Dubreuil, E. Humbert and P. Burani), Folies-Dramatiques, 8 Nov 1883 (1883); completion of work begun by F. Bernicat

Gisèle, *c*1884–5 (opérette, 3, F. Oswald and M. Boucheron), lost

La fauvette du temple (oc, 3, Humbert and Burani), Folies-Dramatiques, 17 Nov 1885 (1885)

La Béarnaise (oc, 3, E. Leterrier and A. Vanloo), Bouffes-Parisiens, 12 Dec 1885 (1886)

Le bourgeois de Calais (oc, 3, Dubreuil and Burani), Folies-Dramatiques, 6 April 1887 (1887)

Les premières armes de Louis XV (oc, 3, A. Carré), Menus-Plaisirs, 16 Feb 1888, unpubd; enlarged version of F. Bernicat: Les beignets du roi, 1882, addl music by Messager

Isoline (conte des fées, 3, C. Mendès), Renaissance, 26 Dec 1888 (1888)

Le mari de la reine (opérette, 3, E. Grenet-Dancourt and O. Pradels), Bouffes-Parisiens, 18 Dec 1889 (1890)

La Basoche (oc, 3, A. Carré), OC (Lyrique), 30 May 1890 (1890)

Hélène (drame lyrique, 4 [5 tableaux], P. Delair), Vaudeville, 15 Sept 1891 (1891)

Madame Chrysanthème (comédie-lyrique, prol., 4, epilogue, G. Hartmann and A. Alexandre, after P. Loti), Renaissance, 30 Jan 1893 (1893)

Miss Dollar (opérette, 3, Clairville (L. Lhérie) and A. Vallin), Nouveau, 22 Dec 1893 (1894)

Mirette (3, M. Carré, Eng. lyrics by F. E. Weatherley, H. Greenbank and A. Ross), London, Savoy, 3 July 1894 (London, 1894); ? collab. H. Temple

La fiancée en loterie (opérette, 3, C. de Roddaz and A. Douane), Folies-Dramatiques, 13 Feb 1896 (1896), collab. P. Lacome

Le chevalier d'Harmental (oc, 5, P. Ferrier, after A. Dumas *père* and A. Maquet), OC (Sarah Bernhardt), 5 May 1896 (1896)

La montagne enchantée (pièce fantastique, 5 [12 tableaux], A. Carré and E. Moreau), Porte-St-Martin, 12 April 1897 (1897); ? collab. X. Leroux

Les p'tites Michu (opérette, 3, G. Duval and Vanloo), Bouffes-Parisiens, 16 Nov 1897 (1897); as The Little Michus, rev. H. Hamilton and P. Greenbank, London, Daly's, 29 April 1905

Véronique (oc, 3, Duval and Vanloo), Bouffes-Parisiens, 10 Dec 1898 (1898)

Les dragons de l'impératrice (oc, 3, Duval and Vanloo), Variétés, 13 Feb 1905 (1905)

Fortunio (comédie lyrique, 4 [5 tableaux], G.-A. de Caillavet and R. de Flers, after A. de Musset: Le chandelier), OC (Favart), 5 June 1907 (1907)

Béatrice (légende lyrique, 4, Caillavet and Flers, after C. Nodier), Monte Carlo, 21 March 1914 (1914)

Monsieur Beaucaire (romantic op, 3, A. Rivoire and P. Veber, after B. Tarkington), Eng. version by F. Lonsdale and A. Ross, Birmingham, Prince of Wales, 7 April 1919 (London, 1918); in Fr., Paris, Marigny, 21 Nov 1925

Cyprien, ôte ta main de là! (fantaisie, 1, M. Hennequin), Concerts Mayol, 1920 (1920)

La petite fonctionnaire (comédie musicale, 3, A. Capus and X. Roux), Mogador, 14 May 1921 (1921)

L'amour masqué (comédie musicale, 3, S. Guitry), Edouard VII, 15 Feb 1923 (1923); completion of work begun by I. Caryll

Passionnément (comédie musicale, 3, Hennequin and A. Willemetz), Michodière, 16 Jan 1926, full score (1926)

Deburau (comédie, prol., 4, Guitry), Sarah Bernhardt, 9 Oct 1926 (1926)

Coups de roulis (opérette, 3, Willemetz, after M. Larrouy), Marigny, 29 Sept 1928 (1928)

Music in: Miousic, 1914, ?lost

Musica, lxxii (1908) [Messager issue]

O. Séré: *Musiciens français d'aujourd'hui* (Paris, 1911, 2/1921)

P. B. Gheusi: *Guerre et théâtre 1914–1918* (Paris, 1919)

——: *L'Opéra-Comique pendant la guerre* (Paris, [1919])

L. Schneider: *Les maîtres de l'opérette française* (Paris, 1924)

L. de Rohozinski, ed.: *Cinquante ans de musique française* (Paris, 1925) [incl. Messager's memoirs in vol.ii]

C. Bellaigue: 'André Messager', *Revue des deux mondes* (15 March 1929), 459–62

H. de Curzon: *L'opérette: Figaro artistique illustré* (Paris, 1931)

R. Dumesnil: *Les maîtres d'histoire: portraits de musiciens français* (Paris, 1938)

J. André-Messager, ed.: *L'enfance de Pelléas: lettres de Claude Debussy à André Messager* (Paris, 1938)

L. Beydts: *Le théâtre lyrique en France depuis les origines jusqu'à nos jours* (Paris, 1938–9)

E. Berteaux: *En ce temps-là* (Paris, 1946)

P. Lalo: *De Rameau à Ravel: portraits et souvenirs* (Paris, 1947)

G. Samazeuilh: *Musiciens de mon temps* (Paris, 1947)

H. Février: *André Messager: mon maître, mon ami* (Paris, 1948)

A. Carré: *Souvenirs de théâtre* (Paris, 1950)

M. Augé-Laribé: *André Messager: musicien de théâtre* (Paris, 1951)

H. Büsser: *De Pelléas aux Indes galantes* (Paris, 1955)

G. Hughes: *Composers of Operetta* (London, 1962)

F. Bruyas: *Histoire de l'opérette en France, 1855–1965* (Lyons, 1974)

J. Harding: *Folies de Paris: the Rise and Fall of French Operetta* (London, 1979)

J. Wagstaff: *André Messager: a Bio-Bibliography* (Westport, CT, 1991)

JOHN WAGSTAFF

Messaline ('Messalina'). *Tragédie lyrique* in four acts (five tableaux) by ISIDORE DE LARA to a libretto by Paul Armand Silvestre and Eugène Morand; Monte Carlo, Casino Municipal, 21 March 1899.

The setting is Rome, AD 45. The Empress Messalina (mezzo-soprano) ensnares the poet Harès (baritone), but soon tires of his devotion. His brother, the handsome gladiator Hélion (tenor), arranges to meet Harès in a city brothel; he is observed there by Messalina, and they fall violently in love. Harès determines to kidnap Messalina for her infidelity, but she forestalls this by having him thrown into the Tiber. He is rescued by the river boatmen and vows revenge. The final scene takes place in the Imperial box at the Circus. Confronted by Hélion, Messalina confesses that she is the cause of his brother's estrangement from him. Harès has meanwhile entered stealthily; he attempts to kill Messalina, but is struck down by Hélion. Realizing that he has murdered his brother, Hélion rushes to his death in the arena. Messalina, for the first time in her life, is overcome by grief and remorse.

Messaline was de Lara's most successful opera, and exhibits all the characteristics of *fin-de-siècle* decadence. It was given in London, 1899; New York, 1902; Paris, 1903; Warsaw, 1904; and Cairo, 1907. In 1901 it became the first opera by an Englishman to be performed at La Scala, Milan; it survived on the French stage until 1943.

NIGEL BURTON

Messel, Oliver (*b* London, 13 Jan 1904; *d* Bridgetown, Barbados, 13 July 1978). English stage designer. He attended the Slade School of Art (1922–4), and became apprenticed to the portrait artist and landscapist John Wells in 1925. After a Dyagilev commission in the same year, in 1926 he began a long and successful association with C. B. Cochran and the London Pavilion Revues. His many masks were noted for their 'suggestive physiognomy', his costumes and sets for their 'lavish picturesqueness'. His white-on-white designs for the Cochran-Max Reinhardt *Helen!* in 1932 became the fashion in interior design. Five years later he designed the ballet *Francesca da Rimini* for the de Basil company. His most famous and important ballet design was *The Sleeping Beauty* (1946) for Sadler's Wells Ballet, revived many times in some 1200 performances.

Die Zauberflöte (1947, Covent Garden) was Messel's first opera commission. He began an influential partnership with Glyndebourne in 1950 with a lavish *Ariadne auf Naxos*; this was followed by a much revived *Idomeneo* (1951), *La Cenerentola* (1952), a Goyainspired *Il barbiere* and *Le comte Ory* (both in 1954), *Figaro* (1955), *Die Entführung* (1956) and *Der Rosenkavalier* (1959). He also designed a number of memorable stage productions and films, working with Tyrone Guthrie, Alexander Korda, Gabriel Pascal and Peter Brook. He was made a CBE in 1958. Not since Inigo Jones has there been an English designer to match Messel's baroque combination of splendour, fantasy, spaciousness and extravagance. His sense of colour was unmatched. And no designer ever commanded such high fees or such contractual control over productions.

For illustration *see* COSTUME, fig.17 and STAGE DESIGN, fig.23.

*

O. Messel: *Stage Designs and Costumes* (London, 1933)
S. Hughes: *Glyndebourne: a History of the Festival Opera* (London, 1965, 2/1981)
R. Pinkham: *Oliver Messel* (London, 1983) [exhibition catalogue]
C. Castle: *Oliver Messel* (London, 1986)   DAVID J. HOUGH

Messiaen, Olivier (Eugène Prosper Charles) (*b* Avignon, 10 Dec 1908; *d* Paris, 28 April 1992). French composer. He studied at the Paris Conservatoire with Dukas and others (1920–30) and later taught there (1941–78), his pupils including Boulez and Stockhausen. Though the theatre played a large part in his creative formation (as a boy he amassed a library of operatic vocal scores by Mozart, Gluck, Berlioz, Wagner and Debussy which he played through at the piano), he was attracted to a greater theatre, that of the church. From 1931 he played the organ regularly at La Trinité in Paris and his roots lay in Debussy and in the French organ tradition. During the 1930s, 40s and 50s he consistently added new things to his non-developing musical style: Indian modes and rhythms, 12-note speculations, vivid orchestral colours suggested by stained glass or electronic music (the simultaneity of medieval and modern is characteristic), and birdsong. Most of his works are religious, often taking the form of cycles of meditations on moments of divine intervention. *Saint François d'Assise* (Paris, Opéra, 28 November 1983) is his largest and longest work and his only opera, commissioned by Rolf Liebermann in 1975. Messiaen's interpretation of theatre as ceremonial and liturgy, his openness to Asian forms of music, dance and drama, and his insistence on a correspondence between sound and colour (having, of course, important implications for stage design and lighting) may thus be felt as much in Stockhausen's *Licht*, for example, as in the work he chose to crown his own oeuvre.

See also SAINT FRANÇOIS D'ASSISE.

*

O. Messiaen: 'Ariane et Barbe-Bleue de Paul Dukas', *ReM*, musicale, no.166 (1936), 79–86
C. Samuel: *Entretiens avec Olivier Messiaen* (Paris, 1967; Eng. trans., London, 1976)
C. Pitt: 'Messiaen's "St Francis"', *Opera*, xxxv (1984), 145–8
P. Griffiths: *Olivier Messiaen and the Music of Time* (London, 1985)   PAUL GRIFFITHS

Messidor. *Drame lyrique* in four acts by ALFRED BRUNEAU to a libretto by EMILE ZOLA; Paris, Opéra, 19 February 1897.

The opera takes its name from that of the harvest month in the French revolutionary calendar. On the surface it is a story of simple mountain folk, but on a symbolic level it examines political and moral questions raised by capitalist industrialism. Gaspard (bass) has diverted a stream for his gold-refining factory, depriving the villagers of their share of gold dust and water. As a despairing family fruitlessly tries to work the land,

'Messidor' (Alfred Bruneau): design by Amable for Act 3 scene ii of the original production at the Paris Opéra (Salle Garnier), 19 February 1897

Guillaume (tenor) has to share his meagre meal with his cousin Mathias (baritone). Véronique (soprano), Guillaume's widowed mother, thinks it was Gaspard who killed her husband, and when he approaches with his daughter, Hélène (soprano), she refuses to give them water. But Guillaume, in love with Hélène, gives her some. Véronique recalls an old legend telling of a cathedral filled with gold: when someone finds it, all the gold in the world will vanish.

The centrepiece of the opera, 'La légende de l'or', is a ballet. Two groups of dancers try in vain to take a golden image and having failed, they fight. Suddenly Véronique enters and in a clap of thunder the vision disappears.

The opera returns to the factory where a new machine has been installed, but a shepherd warns Gaspard that armed villagers are coming to close it. An avalanche is heard and the machine grinds to a halt. In Act 4 Gaspard is ruined while the villagers' land shows renewed fertility. Véronique announces that her magic necklace has been stolen but the villagers have caught the thief, Mathias, who, after confessing to the theft and to being the murderer of Véronique's husband, throws himself off a rock. The opera ends with a religious procession, forming the background to a reconciliation, and with a celebration of the disappearance of all gold from the land.

The dialogue, like that of Charpentier's *Louise*, is frequently the vehicle for the discussion of moral and political questions. Mathias curses the laziness of the rich but Gaspard too is allowed to put his case: why should he not be rewarded for working harder than anyone else and using his initiative?

Zola and Bruneau leave little doubt that the quest for gold – symbolizing an excess of wealth rather than wealth itself – is ultimately destructive. The work suggests a return to religion and to the power of folk legend as possible solutions to the problems of industrialization, urbanization and the enterprise culture.

RICHARD LANGHAM SMITH

Messina. Italian city in north-east Sicily. From 1552 the Jesuits produced tragedies, comedies and sacred plays in the theatre of their Collegio Mamertino, in which singing and musical intermezzos had an increasingly important part. In 1579, by order of the Senate, a theatre was built in a former arsenal, and hence was known as the Teatro del Senato or della Munizione. Opera properly so called reached Messina and Palermo from Venice through Naples; the first opera known to have been performed in Messina was Olivo's *Il ratto di Elena*, which reached the city in 1657 after having been produced in Piacenza in 1646 and in Naples in 1655. The Messina printer noted that the opera had been adapted for performance there, the text by Vincenzo Montana and the music by Vincenzo Tozzi.

In 1664, a year earlier than Naples, Messina staged Cesti's *Dori*, as well as an *Adone* probably by Manelli. In 1681 there was a performance of Domenico Scorpione's *Giulio Cesare in Egitto*, followed by works of Giacomo Facco and C. I. Monza (who were working in Messina), David Perez, Girolamo Abos and Baldassare Galuppi. Between 1750 and 1815 the principal composers represented were Guglielmi, Cimarosa, Paisiello and Fioravanti; they were then eclipsed by Rossini, Donizetti, Bellini and Verdi. The Teatro della Munizione was restored and enlarged many times (1724, 1747–54, 1831, 1867, 1895, 1905). By the mid-19th century it had five tiers of boxes and 216 seats as well as some standing room, and could hold up to a thousand. During the second half of the century it was used by secondary companies and for other types of entertainment.

A second theatre, the Santa Elisabetta (after 1860 the Vittorio Emanuele II), was designed by Pietro Valente with a horseshoe-shaped interior, four tiers and a gallery, holding about 950. It was inaugurated on 21 January 1852 with Donizetti's *Marino Faliero*, performed under the title of *Pascià di Scutari* for reasons of censorship and conducted by Angelo Mariani. 48 more seasons followed, comprising mainly Italian operas (predominantly Verdi) and a few foreign ones (including *Lohengrin* in 1870). Opera and ballet seasons lasted from autumn to spring, interspersed with drama. The open-air theatre of Arena Peloro was inaugurated in 1878 and was active in the summer months.

The 1908 earthquake, which almost completely destroyed the city, spared the Teatro Vittorio Emanuele, although it was seriously damaged, but totally destroyed the Teatro della Munizione. On 8 July 1910, only 18 months after the disaster, the new Teatro Mastroieni opened with *Il trovatore* and at once became the centre of the musical life of the city. Designed by Vincenzo Vinci, it had two tiers of boxes and a capacity of about 1200. The chronology of its presentations bears witness to the Messina audiences' increasing interest in operetta.

In addition to the damage caused by the earthquake, the Vittorio Emanuele also suffered from bombing in World War II; it did not reopen until 1984. It now seats 1024 and has a stage of 600 square metres. The theatre ceiling has large panels of oil paintings by the scene painter Renato Guttuso, depicting the myth of Colapesce. In September 1989, having previously been under the direct control of the municipality of Messina, the theatre became an independent public company. With no chorus or orchestra of its own, it organizes short opera seasons with productions brought in from other Italian or foreign theatres. The first opera presented after its reopening, on 7 January 1986, was *Aida* – which was the last to be performed before the 1908 earthquake – in a production from Poland with soloists, chorus and orchestra of the Grand Theatre of Łódź.

*

N. Scaglione: *La vita artistica del Teatro Vittorio Emanuele dal 12 gennaio al 28 dicembre 1908* (Messina, 1921)

——: *I teatri minori* (Messina, 1932)

——: *La vita del Teatro Vittorio Emanuele* (Messina, 1933)

Accademia filodrammatica e filoarmonica di Messina: calendario musicale messinese e le prime del Teatro Vittorio Em. II dalle sue origini al suo silenzio (Messina, 1956)

S. Papalia Jerace: *Storia del Teatro Mastroieni e dello spettacolo a Messina* (Messina, 1957)

R. Pagano: 'La vita musicale a Palermo e nella Sicilia del seicento', *NRMI*, iii (1969), 439–66

G. Donato: *Il Teatro Vittorio Emanuele di Messina* (Messina, 1979)

G. La Corte Cailler: *Musica e musicisti in Messina*, ed. A. Crea and G. Molonia (Messina, 1982)

G. Donato: 'Su alcuni aspetti della vita musicale in Sicilia nel seicento: i rapporti con Napoli: influenze, autonomie, analogie', *La musica a Napoli durante il seicento: Naples 1985*, 567–623

G. Uccello: *Lo spettacolo nei secoli a Messina* (Palermo, 1986)

G. Corsi: *Il Teatro Mastroieni nella Messina delle baracche* (Messina, 1989)

G. Molonia: *L'archivio storico del Teatro Vittorio Emanuele* Messina, 1990)

GIUSEPPE FERRARO

Metaphor aria. *See* SIMILE ARIA.

Metastasio [Trapassi], **Pietro** (**Antonio Domenico Bonaventura**) (*b* Rome, 3 Jan 1698; *d* Vienna, 12 April 1782). Italian poet and librettist. His fame rests chiefly with his 27 *opera seria* librettos written between 1723 and 1771. In settings by over 300 composers, adapted versions of these texts span a period of over a hundred years that stretches well into the 19th century.

1. Life: to 1730. 2. Life: from 1730. 3. Librettos. 4. Purpose, philosophy. 5. Editions.

1. LIFE: TO 1730. Metastasio's father, Felice Trapassi, came to Rome from Assisi; his mother, Francesca Galastri, from Bologna. Trapassi first joined the papal regiment but later set up a small grocery business with his wife. The family was poor, and the early education of both Pietro and his brother, Leopoldo, was arranged by Pietro's godfather, Cardinal Pietro Ottoboni. In 1708, Pietro's education was taken over by Gian Vincenzo Gravina, a jurist and a man of letters who, impressed by the boy's intelligence and ability at verse improvisation, adopted him and directed his studies in the classics, projecting for him a career in law. He also introduced his new ward to influential members of society and, until such time as the boy's delicate health seemed in jeopardy, encouraged him to recite at social gatherings and to participate in improvisation contests. Under Gravina's supervision, Pietro Trapassi wrote, in 1712, his only tragedy, *Giustino*, a work conceived in strict imitation of ancient models and published five years later with a collection of poems under the title *Poesie di Pietro Metastasio*. (The name change from 'Trapassi' to 'Metastasio', the hellenized equivalent, was engineered by Gravina in 1715.) It was also in 1712 that the 14-year-old boy was taken, via Naples, to Scalea in Calabria where, for several months, he studied with Gravina's cousin, Gregorio Caloprese, a noted scholar of Cartesian philosophy. Upon his return to Rome, Metastasio studied jurisprudence while maintaining his interest in poetry, an interest that now extended, un-beknown to Gravina, to the lyrical works of Guarini, Tasso and Marini. He took minor orders at the Lateran Basilica in 1714.

When Gravina died in January 1718, Metastasio was left well educated, well connected and well provided for. The young man honoured the memory of his guardian with the 'reverie' *La strada della Gloria*, recited one month later when, as Artino Corasio, he was admitted to the Arcadian Accademia Aletina in Naples. Free from tutelage and unprepared for the responsibility of financial independence, Metastasio soon squandered most of the 15 000 scudi left him by Gravina and had to find employment. In this respect he was disappointed at the papal court and at the University of Turin, in addition to which he was also disappointed in love when Rosalia Gasparini, daughter of Francesco, a musician at the Lateran Basilica, passed him over for another early in 1719. Metastasio moved to Naples where he found work in a law office. He also found recognition in aristocratic circles as a poet. For the wedding, in 1721, of Antonio Pignatelli, Prince of Belmonte, and Anna Pinelli di Sangro, Metastasio wrote a lengthy nuptial ode and offered the *azione teatrale Endimione*. This *azione* had been written during the previous year and was now dedicated to the groom's sister, Marianna Pignatelli, Countess of Althann, a lady-in-waiting to the Empress Elizabeth, consort of the Austrian emperor, Charles VI. The countess was to remain a close and valuable friend. Over the next two years, Metastasio

fulfilled further aristocratic commissions with two more odes and another three *azioni*, two of which were performed in Naples as birthday celebrations to honour the Empress Elizabeth, *Gli orti esperidi* (1721) and *Angelica* (1722).

In 1723 Metastasio's first opera libretto, *Siface re di Numidia*, was brought to the stage in a setting by Feo. The text, a reworking of Domenico David's *La forza del virtù*, was subsequently viewed by Metastasio as a mere adjunct to his oeuvre. His first original libretto, *Didone abbandonata*, launched his career in Naples the following year in a setting by Sarro. While writing this work Metastasio lived in the home of Giuseppe Bulgarelli and his wife, the singer-actress Maria Anna Benti ('La Romanina'), who probably influenced the shape of the work, fully aware that she was to create the title role. She had sung the part of Venus in *Gli orti esperidi*, and the fascination that she and Metastasio shared for each other led to his regular presence in her salon, where he met the composers who first set his early works and where he began his lifelong friendship with the castrato Farinelli (Carlo Broschi). The Romanina and the first Aeneas, the castrato Nicolini (Nicolo Grimaldi), sub-sequently appeared in settings of *Didone abbandonata* in both Reggio and Venice in 1725. They were thus in Venice to take the leading roles in Metastasio's second original drama, *Siroe re di Persia* (1726), with music by Vinci. When *Catone in Utica* opened in Rome two years later, again in a setting by Vinci, Metastasio had the satisfaction of seeing his first three original texts given successively in the three major opera centres in Italy. Following the première of *Ezio* (1728, Venice), three more dramas opened in Rome during the period 1729–30, all in settings by Vinci: *Semiramide riconosciuta* in February and, for the following carnival season, the two librettos that were to gain the greatest popularity of all Metastasio's works, *Alessandro nell'Indie* and *Artaserse*.

2. LIFE: FROM 1730. When, in 1729, Metastasio received an invitation to take up the position of Caesarian court poet in Vienna, he was already known to the imperial household, and his reputation as a poet and dramatist was fully established. Recommendations for this appointment were volunteered by Marianna Pignatelli and by Apostolo Zeno, the reigning court poet at the time. Metastasio moved in April 1730 to Vienna, where over the next ten years he wrote, in addition to other smaller works, another 11 dramas, including *L'olimpiade*, *Demofoonte* and *La clemenza di Tito*, seven oratorios and 11 texts for occasional pieces. In general, the oratorios were performed at Easter and the operas and occasional pieces were given to cele-brate either the birthday of the Empress Elizabeth (28 August) or the name-day of the emperor (4 November). The Archduchess Maria Theresa and her sister, Maria Anna, performed in three of Metastasio's occa-sional pieces in 1735 and another in 1740, *Il natal di Giove*. This presentation was given on 1 October, the birthday of Charles VI. For the emperor's name-day Metastasio had written *Attilio Regolo*; Charles, however, died on 19 October, and the work was not seen on the opera stage until Hasse set it for Dresden in 1750.

As the new empress, Maria Theresa exercised her authority from 1740 until her death in 1780. Her con-sort, Francis of Lorraine, became Holy Roman Emperor in 1745, and their eldest son, Joseph, was elected to that office on the death of Francis in 1765, at which time he was also made co-regent with his mother. In 1764 Joseph was crowned as successor to the empire. Changes in Austrian affairs of state and theatre policy worked against Metastasio, as did the personal preferences of the monarchs. Maria Theresa's reign was beset by wars with Prussia, the first of which broke out two months after she ascended the throne at the age of 23. This crisis, together with concerns over internal politics and the debt inherited from her predecessors, relegated new opera commissions to a low priority. From 1740 to 1746 Metastasian operas in Vienna were mainly first stagings of works already written, followed by a preponderance of new settings of existing texts over the next four years. From the early 1750s to the mid-1760s, Metastasian opera representations at the court theatres dwindled almost to nothing. These dates coincide with the support given to French theatre in Vienna by the imperial rulers and, as from 1752–3, by the new chancellor, Wenzel Kaunitz. During the next two decades, the French theatre and its offshoots drew upon the talents of Giacomo Durazzo and Giuseppe d'Afflisio, theatre directors under Kaunitz, Gluck and Calzabigi, and the ballet-masters Gasparo Angiolini and Jean-Georges Noverre, the latter's ballet company remaining in Vienna until 1776. Theatre repertory lists from 1764 also reflect the preference of Joseph II for *opera buffa* over *opera seria* until, in 1776, he established first the German Nationaltheater and then the National Singspiel.

Between 1740 and 1782 several of Metastasio's best works had premières outside Vienna, while at home the imperial court's demands of him were for in-house entertainments and works to honour only the most special royal events. In addition to smaller works, he produced, during this 42-year period, texts for 16 occasional pieces and only eight designated dramas for the *opera seria*. *Antigono* (1743) and *Nitteti* (1756), his most successful opera librettos from this time, had their premières at the courts of Dresden and Madrid respectively. The Spanish court was also the recipient of four occasional pieces, including the *azione teatrale L'isola disabitata*, a text that subsequently caught the attention of such composers as Jommelli, Paisiello, Perez, Traetta and Joseph Haydn. Two operas, *Romolo ed Ersilia* (1765) and *Ruggiero* (1771), were performed for Habsburg weddings in Innsbruck and Milan, and five works, including the opera *Ipermestra* (1744) and the elaborately staged *feste teatrali*, *Alcide al bivio* (1760) and *Partenope* (1767), honoured royal weddings in Vienna. Another, *Egiria* (1764), was written for Joseph II's coronation. On a more lowly level, the two operas *Il re pastore* (1751) and *L'eroe cinese* (1752) were performed by court personnel, and seven occasional pieces were prepared for performances by the archduchesses. Metastasio's renown, after 1750, was chiefly proclaimed by the number of editions of his works produced, the continued settings and imitations of his texts, and the literary commentaries with Metastasio as subject that proliferated outside the imperial capital.

In comparison with the period 1723–40, the second half of Metastasio's career in Vienna was anti-climactic, overshadowed by the death of the Countess d'Althann in 1755 but brightened by the close relationship that developed with Marianna Martinez. She was the daughter of Metastasio's landlord, Niccolò Martinez, master of ceremonies to the papal nuncio. The Martinez house was Metastasio's only place of residence in Vienna. It stands at the corner of Kohlmarkt and the Michaelerplatz, where it once overlooked the 'altes Hofballhaus' which, in 1742, was inaugurated as the Burgtheater. Metastasio died in 1782, at the age of 84, from a cold that turned to a fever. His revealing essay on Aristotle's *Poetics* was in the press at the time and appeared posthumously.

3. LIBRETTOS. As with all stage texts designated for musical settings at the time, each of Metastasio's librettos for the *opera seria* is labelled 'dramma' or 'dramma musicale', and together they exhibit certain fundamental characteristics. Generally, the plots concern six or seven characters of royal or noble birth, their interrelationships and their complex dilemmas, which are intensified as the action proceeds and finally resolved in a *lieto fine*. The dramas divide into three acts, and each act into an average of 12 scenes, defined according to the entry or exit of a character. A series of scenes will often be linked by a character common to all of them (the *liaison de scène* technique), and a change of location will often follow at the end of such a series. Apart from the occasional duet, almost always for the principal couple, the usual set musical piece is the aria which, if included in a scene, has its expected place at the end. Opening scenes usually begin with a situation already in progress; each of the first two acts will generally conclude with a climactic scena for a principal character or a duet; and the third will normally end with a united 'coro' for all the *dramatis personae*. Although these generalities occur with some consistency, they are quite rudimentary and often underlie considerable variation. *Didone abbandonata*, *Catone in Utica* and *Attilio Regolo*, for example, lack happy endings; duets are not always confined to the act conclusions; and three of the later operas, *Antigono*, *Il re pastore* and *Nitteti*, contain an ensemble, as does *Catone in Utica*, an unexpected early example. Several works include one or more short arias that do not conclude the scenes in which they occur, and more than a third of the librettos call for a chorus in addition to the final 'coro' for the principal singers.

Half of Metastasio's dramas received over 30 different musical settings during the 18th and early 19th centuries: *Artaserse*, his most popular, close to 90, *Romolo ed Ersilia* and *Ruggiero*, his least, only two each. Whatever the number, only the first composer to set any given text actually did so as Metastasio wrote it, and a setting by any one composer given in a different location could also be subject to further changes. Although such alterations may suggest a mere response to the whims of singers, individual theatre librettists or composers, they also reflect local conditions and changes in what an audience expected of an *opera seria*. At the peak of its popularity from the 1730s to the 1760s, Metastasian opera stretched across Europe from Lisbon to St Petersburg, London and Copenhagen to Naples, thus encountering theatres, stages and theatre companies of considerably varied sizes and capabilities, and addressing local tastes, from those of a ruler and his select audiences to those of an entrepreneur and his paying public. Further, Metastasio's first drama appeared in 1723 and his works did not completely fade from the stage in Italy until the 1830s, during which time the aria forms of the 'aria' opera changed and later became more varied within any one work, and the *opera seria* itself became a genre that contained duets, ensembles and act-ending finales along with the arias. Rewriting of the original dramas was thus made essential by operatic evolution, which also incorporated a move from the emotional decorum of Metastasio's original characters to the less controlled emotional displays of their later counterparts.

Curtailments, particularly to the recitatives, became an almost automatic type of alteration in response to Metastasio's librettos being literary dramas, complete in text alone. As such, they could be read at a salon or performed on stage as spoken dramas, a practice that Metastasio preferred to poor musical settings. As a ward of Gravina, Metastasio encountered the literary side of the Arcadian movement at an early age. Gravina was a founding member of the first Arcadian Academy, the Accademia degli Arcadi, established in Rome in 1690 by members of the intellectual circle that had gathered around Queen Christina of Sweden, resident in Rome after her abdication in 1654. The Arcadian 'reform' gave impetus to an existing literary trend that had made itself felt in Italy around 1675 and stressed a return to the simplicity of antiquity.

This return to antiquity manifested itself in several different ways. The ancients, for example, acknowledged only three forms of drama: tragedy, comedy and satyr plays. Many of Metastasio's contemporary commentators therefore lauded his works as profound tragedies, proclaiming Metastasio at least the equal of Sophocles and Euripides and a rival to the French supremacy in spoken tragedy established by Pierre Corneille and Jean Racine. Such encomia, however, placed greater expectations upon the dramas than their form or content could support and paved the way for subsequent detractors to criticize the texts for not being what they were never intended to be. In uninformed hands, the return to antiquity led to rule-making and mimicry. Ideas derived particularly from the Aristotle *Poetics* and the Horace *Ars poetica* had, by the second half of the 17th century, already been codified into a rigid set of mandates. Literary commentators, therefore, could substitute for any real knowledge of ancient sources the 'rules' gleaned from the writings of others and pass superficial judgments. For Gravina, and subsequently for Metastasio, return to antiquity presupposed a first-hand knowledge of the ancient philosophers and historians and the Greek dramas as well as the literary-dramatic commentaries that included Aristotle and Horace. It was upon such knowledge that Metastasio drew for his general classical imagery, the plots for his dramas and occasional pieces, and for his prose works: the annotated translation of the *Ars poetica* (1749), the *Osservazioni sul teatro greco* (1768) and the lengthy *Estratto dell'arte poetica d'Aristotile* (1772, published 1782). Far from being a lexical or syntactical study of the *Poetics*, the *Estratto* simply provides a justification of the *opera seria* in Aristotelian terms, freely interpreted by the author with insights brightly coloured by his experience with imperial court drama. For Metastasio, for his two Arcadian predecessors in Vienna, Zeno and Antonio Moniglia, and for other Arcadian-approved librettists, Aristotle could lend substance and direction to their work. Blind obedience to the rules of modern Aristotelianism, however, was folly. Thus, hindered by those who saw his dramas as inimitable classical tragedies, angered by the artificial rule makers and equipped with a thorough grounding in classical studies, Metastasio steered a course between operatic practic-

ability and Aristotelianism towards the establishment of the opera libretto as a viable literary genre in its own right.

4. PURPOSE, PHILOSOPHY. Metastasio once stated that he had 'wasted his entire life in order to instruct mankind in a pleasing way'. He held that 'pleasures that do not succeed in making impressions on the mind and on the heart are of short duration'. Thus emerges his aim, which was to instruct under the guise of giving pleasure, and to reinforce the moral issue by arousing the emotions for the sake of the moral purpose. This principle of 'pleasurable instruction' stretches back to Horace and Plato, less directly to Aristotle, and leads to a clear division between poetry as pleasurable in itself and poetry as a means of instruction.

The creation of pleasure in poetry for its own sake meant exercising care over the basic construction of a dramatic work as well as its poetic style. Aristotle and Horace had advice to offer on the first of these considerations, which included the choice of events and the interest created in them, the conduct of the characters and the probability of their actions, and the exploitation of the dramatic elements of conflict, contrast and accumulated intensity. Arcadia had much to say about the manipulation of poetic elements. For example, such matters as choice of words, versification, figures of speech and eloquence of style that are topics of discussion in several of Metastasio's letters are discussed as items of 'external' beauty by Giovanni Crescimbeni, the first president of the Accademia degli Arcadi, and as elements of 'corporeal' beauty by Lodovico Muratori, a friend of Zeno and an associate of the Accademia degli Accesi in Bologna.

Metastasio's verses are concise, economical and mellifluous, and, for all his claims towards literary drama, his musical education allowed him to hear his verses mentally as operatic vocal lines as he wrote them. He possessed an unmatched facility to express the subtle nuances of a vast range of human emotions while conveying the meaning vividly and in a few words which, in combination, could exploit the consonance, assonance and rhythm appropriate to the emotion of the moment. In addition, in writing arias for da capo settings, he generally supplied two stanzas (mostly quatrains), mindful of the appropriate vowel placement for coloratura extensions.

Poetry as a means of instruction meant, to Metastasio, the process of 'inducing, by way of pleasure, the love of virtue so necessary for general happiness'. For Crescimbeni this was the area of 'internal' beauty, for Muratori that of 'incorporeal' beauty, and it included matters of profundity, hidden mysteries, philosophy and theology. Metastasio's poetry, however, was to prove the example *par excellence* of what Crescimbeni called 'mixed' beauty, the highest achievement of all, with its emphasis on internal matters without losing sight of 'external' considerations. His leanings towards 'internal' beauty established his texts as moral dramas that realized on stage the principles set out in René Descartes' treatise on moral philosophy, *Les passions de l'âme*.

In 1649, the year in which *Les passions de l'âme* was published, Descartes went to Stockholm as tutor to Christina of Sweden. Her abdication and removal to Rome thus provided a direct link from Descartes to the Arcadian movement and hence to Metastasio. Further contacts with Cartesian philosophy came from his studies with Caloprese in Scalea in 1712 and from his knowledge of French 17th-century drama, particularly that of Corneille, which also carried the Cartesian stamp. Burney acknowledged Metastasio a master at unfolding and displaying 'all the passions of the human heart', and it is upon this subject that Descartes' philosophy focusses. Metastasio saw passions as 'the necessary winds by which one navigates through the sea of life', and was at one with Descartes in the belief that all the passions are 'good in themselves' and that 'we have nothing to avoid but their evil uses or excesses'. Indeed, morality was seen to exist, above all, in the power of the individual to gain control over the desires that arise from human passions and so prevent the actions to which these passion-incited desires may lead. In demonstrating such a process, Metastasio drama became a drama of moral forces personified by specified characters who are differentiated by emotionally charged actions and reactions that drive them towards either personal moral victory or moral self-defeat. At the centre is a moral hero or heroine, like Titus or Semiramide, who must not only triumph over his or her own spontaneous desires but also uphold a moral vision against the onslaughts of the morally weak who fall victim to their personal desires. For the sake of the veiled exhortation to moral endurance, the moral crusader must succeed in the *lieto fine*, and the power of the achievement will be marred if the antagonists are not brought to moral truth (along with the audience) by the example.

At court performances, the moral hero served to set before the monarch the ideal of the morally inspired ruler. It was also intended that the audience would equate the monarch with the moral hero, and a final *licenza* usually ensured that the association was not missed. And last, the state of well-being brought about by the triumph of virtue encouraged general support for the political status quo. Here, also, were ideals to set before the young, a practice in educational establishments that explains, for example, Beltrami's Metastasio settings for the Vescovile seminary in Verona, and the existence of both Latin and Polish translations of Metastasian texts printed in Warsaw during the mid-18th century. Although Metastasio was aware of his court responsibilities, it is difficult to ascertain the extent to which calculated propaganda ruled his thinking. The dramas advocate universal moral conditions rather than the principles of a specific regime, yet political conduct had much to gain by association with the moral principles extolled. For Metastasio, however, the demands of a personal moral commitment appear to have had the upper hand upon his powers as both a dramatic and a lyric poet.

The distinction between his dramas, his occasional pieces and his oratorios is largely one of degree with regard to the emotional energy expended over the central moral conflicts. The oratorios, at times, may plumb the emotional depths of the dramas, but the dilemmas will progress from ethical to spiritual considerations. With the occasional pieces, increased lyricism will often compensate for the lack of dramatic intensity, and with the *festa* works, spectacle will also lend a hand. In all cases, Metastasio's literary precision and clarity constantly enabled his works to satisfy Muratori's definition of the beautiful object as 'that which, when seen, heard or understood, pleases us and excites within us sweet sensations and love [for the cause]'.

5. EDITIONS. Metastasio's oeuvre, in addition to the librettos, the oratorio texts and other poetic works, also includes prose items and the collection of over 2600 letters that make up the 'epistolario'. Further, two 'authentic' versions exist for five of the dramas (*Adriano in Siria, Alessandro nell'Indie, Catone in Utica, Didone abbandonata* and *Semiramide riconosciuta*), and *L'asilo d'Amore* was subsequently revised as *Il trionfo d'Amore*. *Tutte le opere di Pietro Metastasio*, edited by Bruno Brunelli (Milan and Verona, 1943–54), remains the only edition to embrace this entire output and to attempt the type of extensive commentary that it generates. The publication of the Mario Fubini edition, *Teatro di Pietro Metastasio* (Turin, 1977), has also made readily accessible the selection of works with textual commentary that was first published as *Pietro Metastasio: opere* (Milan and Naples, 1968). Other recent editions of selected works include those of Riccardo Bacchelli (Turin, 1962), Elena Sala Di Felice (Milan, 1965), Franco Gavazzeni (Turin, 1968) and Franco Mollia (Milan, 1979).

With the notable exception of Sebastiano d'Ayala's edition of *Opere postume* (Vienna, 1795), the *Lettere* were generally published, in part, in separate editions from the other writings that appeared under the titles *Opere, Opere dramatiche* or *Poesie del … Pietro Metastasio*. Altogether, over 40 Metastasio editions were published during the poet's lifetime. Many of these he condemned: several complaints are expressed in the correspondence generated by the editions of Giuseppe Bettinelli, which began their complex history in Venice in 1733. The editions themselves assume particular historical significance as reflections of Bettinelli's responses both to Metastasio's directions and to his censure. Also important, particularly to the history of Metastasio criticism and reception, are the commentaries on the poet's life and works that accompany many of the editions. The *Opere* published in Nice (1783–5) contain a wealth of such writings, and several important essays are to be found in Camillo Antona-Traversi's edition of *Lettere disperse e inedite* (Rome, 1886) in addition to the editor's customary preface. Calzabigi's well-known 'Dissertazione' in the first volume of the *Poesie del … Pietro Metastasio* (Paris, 1755) and Giuseppe Baretti's 'Prefazione' in the last (1769) also form a part of this tradition, which has continued through such offerings as Francesco Reina's *Opere scelte* (Milan, 1820) and Giosuè Carducci's *Lettere disperse e inedite* (Bologna, 1883) to the editions of the present time.

Visiting Milan in 1770, Leopold Mozart and his son were presented with what had been published of yet another important edition of the *Poesie*, that of Turin (1757–88). A reliable and handsomely illustrated *Opere* was published by the firm of Antonio Zatta (Venice, 1782–4) and dedicated to Catherine II of Russia. This publication was preceded by the equally handsome Hérissant edition edited by Giuseppe Pezzana (Paris, 1780–82) and dedicated to Marie Antoinette. Prepared, save for the last volume, in direct consultation with Metastasio, and the first to contain the commentary on the Aristotle *Poetics*, the Hérissant edition has remained the definitive early source.

See also ACHILLE IN SCIRO; ADRIANO IN SIRIA; ALESSANDRO NELL'INDIE; ANTIGONO; ARTASERSE; ATTILIO REGOLO; CATONE IN UTICA; CIRO RICONOSCIUTO; CLEMENZA DI TITO, LA; DEMETRIO; DEMOFOONTE; DIDONE ABBANDONATA; EROE CINESE, L'; EZIO; IMPRESARIO DELLE CANARIE, L'; IPERMESTRA; ISSIPILE; NITTETI; OLIMPIADE, L'; RE PASTORE, IL;

Romolo ed ersilia; Ruggiero; Semiramide riconosciuta; Siface re di numidia; Siroe re di persia; Temistocle; Trionfo di clelia, il; and Zenobia.

OPERAS

Achille in Sciro

Caldara, 1736; Sarro, 1737; G. Arena, 1738; Chiarini, 1739; Leo, 1740; Corselli, 1744; Manna, 1745; G. Verocai, 1746; Meyer, ?1747 (as Il trionfo della gloria); G. B. Runcher, 1747; Jommelli, 1749; ?Sciroli, 1751; Mazzoni, 1754; Hasse, 1759; Sarti, 1759; Bertoni, 1764; Monza, 1764; Agricola, 1765; Gassmann, 1766; Naumann, 1767; Jommelli, 1771; A. Amicone, 1772; Anfossi, 1774; Sales, 1774; Paisiello, 1778; Sarti, 1779; Gazzaniga, 1780; Pugnani, 1785; Bernardini, 1794; Coppola, ?1825

Adriano in Siria

Caldara, 1732; Giacomelli, 1733; Pergolesi, 1734; Sandoni, 1734; Broschi, 1735; Duni, 1735; Veracini (rev. Corri), 1735; Ferrandini, 1737; Hasse, ?1737; Nebra, 1737; Porta, 1737; Ristori, 1739; Galuppi, 1740; Giai, 1740; Lampugnani, 1740; Giaino, 1741; ?Logroscino, 1742; Verocai, 1745 (as Die getreue Emirena); Abos, 1746; Graun, 1746; Latilla, 1747; V. Ciampi, 1748 (rev. 1750); Scalabrini, 1749; Pampani, 1750; Pescetti, 1750 (as Farnaspe); Adolfati, 1751; Hasse, 1752; Perez, 1752; G. Scarlatti, 1752; Valentini, 1753; Conforto, 1754 (rev. 1757); Scolari, 1754; Bernasconi, 1755; Brusa, 1757; Uttini, 1757; Galuppi, 1758; Rinaldo di Capua, 1758; Borghi, 1759; Mazzoni, 1760; Colla, 1762; Schwanenberger, 1762; M. Wimmer, 1764; J. C. Bach, 1765; Guglielmi, 1765; Mango, 1768; Holzbauer, 1768 or 1769; Majo, 1769; Monza, 1769; Tozzi, 1770; Sacchini, 1771; Insanguine, 1773; Monti, 1775; Mysliveček, 1776; Anfossi, 1777; Sarti, 1778; Alessandri, 1779; Rust, 1781; Cherubini, 1782; Nasolini, 1789; Méhul, comp. 1790–91 (rev. F.-B. Hoffman as Adrien, empéreur de Rome; rev. and perf. 1799); Mayr, 1798; ? V. Migliorucci, 1811; P. Airoldi, 1821; Mirecki, ?1826 (inc.); Mercadante (rev. A. Profumo), 1828

Alessandro nell'Indie

Vinci, 1729; Handel, 1731 (as Poro re dell'Indie); Hasse, 1731 (as Cleofide; rev. 1736, 1738, 1743); Porpora, 1731 (as Poro); Predieri, 1731; Mancini, 1732; Pescetti, 1732; Bioni, 1733; Lucchini, 1734; Schiassi, 1734; Corselli, 1738; Galuppi, 1738; Brivio, 1742; Sarro, 1743; Uttini, 1743; Gluck, 1744; Graun, 1744 (as Alessandro e Poro); Jommelli, 1744; Perez, 1744; Chiarini, 1745; Pelegrini, 1746; Abos, 1747; Wagenseil, 1748; Scalabrini, 1749; Scolari, 1749 (rev. 1759); Rutini, 1750; Fiorillo, 1752; Latilla, 1753; G. Scarlatti, 1753; Agricola, 1754 (as Cleofide); Galuppi, 1754; Araia, 1755; Galuppi, 1755; Perez, 1755; Piccinni, 1758; Holzbauer, 1759; Jommelli, 1760 (rev. Silva, 1776); Cocchi, 1761; Dal Barba, 1761; Sarti, 1761 (rev. 1766); J. C. Bach, 1762; Traetta, 1762; G. Brunetti, 1763; Sacchini, 1763 (rev. 1768); Fischietti, 1764; Sciroli, 1764; Majo, 1766; Gatti, 1768; Naumann, 1768; Bertoni, 1769; J. Kozeluch, 1769; ?Felici, 1771; Anfossi, 1772; Paisiello, 1773; Corri, 1774; Piccinni, 1774; Monza, 1775; Rust, 1775; Marescalchi, 1778; Mortellari, 1778; Vincenti, 1778; A. Calegari, 1779; Cimarosa, 1781; Cherubini, 1784; Bianchi, 1785; V. Chiavacci, 1785; Caruso, 1787; Sarti, 1787; Tarchi, 1788 (rev. C. F. Badini, 1789, as Le generosità di Alessandro, rev. 1798); Guglielmi, 1789; Gnecco, 1800; Ritter, 1811 (as Alexander in Indien); Pacini (rev. A. L. Tottola), 1824

Antigono

Hasse, 1743 or 1744 (rev. 1744, 1753, as Alessandro, re d'Epiro); Scalabrini, 1744; Bernasconi, 1745; Galuppi, 1746; Jommelli, 1746; Conforto, 1750; Wagenseil, 1750; Bertoni, 1752; ?Cocchi, 1754; Sarti, 1754 (rev. 1765); Mazzoni, 1755; Gluck, 1756; Pampani, 1756; Re, 1757; Ferradini, 1758; Durán, 1760; Galuppi, 1762; Piccinni, 1762 (rev. 1771); Traetta, 1764; Zannetti, 1765; Scolari, 1766; Guglielmi, 1767; Majo, 1767; Schwanenberger, 1768; Felici, 1769; Sales, 1769; Cafaro, 1770 (rev. 1774); Monza, 1772; Anfossi, 1773; Latilla, 1775; Mortellari, 1777; Bachschmidt, 1778; Gazzaniga, 1779; Mysliveček, 1780; Gatti, 1781; Paisiello, 1785; Zingarelli, 1786; Caruso, 1788 (rev. 1794); ?Rossi, 1788; ?Parenti, comp. 1780s; F. Ceracchini, 1794; Santis, 1798; Poissl, 1808; A. Gandini, 1824

Artaserse

Vinci, 1730 (rev. Manna, 1743); ?Chiocchetti, 1730; Hasse, 1730 (rev. 1740, 1760); D. Zamparelli, 1731; Bambini, 1733; Bioni, 1733; R. Broschi and Hasse, 1734; Corradini, 1736 (as Dal er ser el hijo al padre); Paganelli, 1737; F. Poncini Zilioli, 1737; Schiassi, 1737; Araia, 1738; Brivio, 1738; Ferrandini, 1739; Adolfati, 1741; Arena, 1741; Chiarini, 1741; Gluck, 1741;

Graun, 1743; Scalabrini, 1743; Duni, 1744; Terradellas, 1744; Abos, 1746; Bernasconi, 1746 (rev. 1763); V. Ciampi, 1747; Maggiore, 1747; G. Scarlatti, 1747 (rev. 1763); Carcani, 1748; Perez, 1748; Smith, 1748 (inc.); Galuppi, 1749; Jommelli, 1749; Lampugnani, 1749; Mele, 1749; G. Bollano, 1750; Pampani, 1750; Dal Barba, 1751; Galuppi, 1751; Pescetti, 1751; Fischietti, 1754; Cocchi, 1755; O. Mei, 1755; Peretti, 1755; Gasparini, 1756; Jommelli, 1756; Pampani, 1756; ? G. Quagliattini, 1757; Scolari, 1757; J. C. Bach, 1760; Sarti, 1760; Arne, 1762; Majo, 1762; Piccinni, 1762 (rev. 1772); Fiorillo, 1765; Sertori, 1765; Ponzo, 1766; Boroni, 1767; Sacchini, 1768; Paisiello, 1771; Vento, 1771; Manfredini, 1772; Mysliveček, 1774; Borghi, 1775; Bertoni, 1776; Guglielmi, 1777; Re, 1777; Ullinger, 1777–81; Bertoni, 1779; Caruso, 1780; Rust, 1781; Zannetti, 1782; Alessandri, 1783; Cimarosa, 1784; Schacht, 1785; Bianchi, 1787; Anfossi, 1788; Bertoni, 1788 (? rev. of 1776); Tarchi, 1788; Andreozzi, 1789; Zingarelli, 1789; ?Parenti, comp. 1780s; Isouard, 1794; Ceracchini, 1795; Nicolini, 1795; Portugal, 1806; Lucas, 1840 (as The Regicide)

Attilio Regolo

Hasse, 1750; Jommelli, 1753 (rev. 1761); Monza, comp. 1777; Beltrami, 1780

Catone in Utica

Vinci, 1728; Leo, 1729; Hasse, 1731; Marchi, 1733; Torri, 1736; Vivaldi, 1737; Duni, 1740; Rinaldo di Capua, 1740 (rev. 1748); Verocai, 1743 (as Cato); Graun, 1744; Scalabrini, 1744; Latilla, 1747; Ferrandini, 1747; Höpken, 1753; Jommelli, 1754; G. Ballabene, 1755; V. Ciampi, 1756; Poncini Zilioli, 1756; J. C. Bach, 1761; Gassmann, 1761; Majo, 1762; Piccinni, 1770; Ottani, 1777; F. Antonelli Torres, 1784; Andreozzi, 1786 (rev. 1789); Nasolini, 1789; Paisiello, 1789; Winter, 1791

Ciro riconosciuto

Caldara, 1736; Rinaldo di Capua, 1737; Leo, 1739; Chiarini, 1743; Jommelli, 1744; Galuppi, 1745; Smith, comp. 1745; Verocai, 1746; Jommelli, 1747; Duni, 1748; Jommelli, 1749 (rev. 1751, 1758); Hasse, 1751; Fiorillo, 1753; Sarti, 1754; G. Meneghetti, 1758; Cocchi, 1759; Galuppi, 1759; Piccinni, 1759; Petrucci, 1765; Puppi, 1765; Mango, 1767; P. Persicchini, 1779; Tarchi, 1796; Capotorti, 1805; Mosel, 1818 (rev. M. von Collin as Cyrus und Astyages)

La clemenza di Tito

Caldara, 1734; ?Chiocchetti, 1735; Hasse, 1735 (as Tito Vespasiano, rev. 1738, 1759); Leo, 1735; F. Peli, 1736; Marchi, 1737; Veracini (rev. Corri), 1737; Arena, 1738; Wagenseil, 1746; Camerloher, 1747; Corradini, Corselli and Mele, 1747 (rev. I. de Luzán y Suelves); Grua, 1748; Pampani, 1748; Perez, 1749; Correia, c1750; Gluck, 1752; Adolfati, 1753; Jommelli, 1753; Valentini, 1753; Mazzoni, 1755; V. Ciampi, 1757; C. Cristiani, 1757; Holzbauer, 1757; G. Scarlatti, 1757; A. Caputi, ?1750s; Cocchi, 1760; Galuppi, 1760; Jommelli, 1765 (rev. Silva, 1771); Franchi, 1766; Plantania, 1766; Bernasconi, 1768; Anfossi, 1769; Naumann, 1769; Sarti, 1771; Mysliveček, 1773; Bachschmidt, 1776; Beltrami, 1779; Apell, ?1787; Santos, ?1780s; Mozart, 1791; Nicolini, 1797; Ottani, 1798; Del Fante, 1803

Demetrio

Caldara, 1731; Bioni, 1732; Giai, 1732; Hasse, 1732 (rev. 1734 [as Cleonice], 1737, 1740 [as Demitrio (Dresden), Cleonice (Venice)], 1747); Leo, 1732 (rev. 1735, 1741); Pescetti, 1732; Schiassi, 1732; Mele, 1736 (rev. D. V. de Camacho as Por amor y por lealtad recobrar la majestad); Giacomelli, 1737; Perez, 1741; Carcani, 1742; Caroli, 1742; Gluck, 1742 (as Cleonice); Lampugnani, 1744 (rev. P. A. Rolli as Alceste); A. Duni, ?1746; Wagenseil, 1746; Galuppi, 1748; D. Naselli (Lasnel), 1748; Jommelli, 1749 (rev. 1751); Pulli, 1749; Piazza, 1750; Gibelli, 1751; Pallavicini, 1751; G. Scarlatti, 1752; Fiorillo, 1753; Ferrandini, 1756 or 1758; S. Perillo, 1758; Insanguine, 1759; Ponzo, 1759; Eberlin, 1760; Galuppi, 1761; Sala, 1762; Perez, 1766; Pampani, 1768; Monza, 1769; Piccinni, 1769; Paisiello, 1771; Bernasconi, 1772; Guglielmi, 1772; Mysliveček, 1773; Bianchi, 1774 (rev. 1780); Bachschmidt, 1777; G. Giordani, 1779; Mysliveček, 1779; Paisiello, 1779; Gresnick, 1786 (rev. Badini as Alceste); Tarchi, 1787; Mayr, 1824; A. Gandini, 1828; Saldoni, 1840 (as Cleonice, regina di Siria)

Demofoonte

Caldara, 1733; Chiochetti, 1735; F. Ciampi, 1735; Sarro, Mancini, Sellitto and Leo, 1735; Schiassi, 1735; Duni, 1737; Ferrandini, 1737; Brivio, 1738; Lampugnani, 1738; Latilla, 1738;

Bernasconi, 1741 (rev. 1766); Verocai, 1741; L. Vinci, 1741; Gluck, 1743; Jommelli, 1743; Graun, 1746; Hasse, 1748 (rev. 1749, 1758); Galuppi, 1749; Fiorillo, 1750; Uttini, 1750; Perez, 1752; Jommelli, 1753; Cocchi, 1754; Manna, 1754; Mazzoni, 1754; Sarti, 1755 (rev. 1771, 1782); Pampani, 1757; Ferradini, 1758; Galuppi, 1758; Traetta, 1758; P. Vinci, 1758; Eberlin, 1759; A. Brunetti, 1760; Piccinni, 1761; Majo, 1763; Jommelli, 1765; Petrucci, 1765; Vento, 1765; Guglielmi, 1766; Mysliveček, 1769; Jommelli, 1770 (rev. Silva, 1775); Vanhal, 1770; J. Kozeluch, 1772; Anfossi, 1773; Berezovsky, 1773; Mysliveček, 1775; Paisiello, 1775; Monza, 1776; Schuster, 1776; Rust, 1780; Anfossi and Bianchi, 1781; Gazzaniga, 1782; A. Pio, 1782; Alessandri, 1783; Prati, 1786; Tarchi, 1786; Gatti, 1787; Pugnani, 1787; Vogel, 1789 (rev. Desriaux as Démophon); Federici, 1790 (as L'usurpatore innocente); Trento, 1791; Portugal, 1794 (rev. 1808); Horn, 1821 (as Dirce, or The Fatal Urn); G. M. Sborgi, 1836

Didone abbandonata

Sarro, 1724; Albinoni, 1725; Porpora, 1725; Vinci, 1726; Schiassi, 1735; Brivio, 1739; Duni, 1739; Lampugnani, 1739 (rev. 1753); Galuppi, 1740; Bernasconi, 1741 (rev. 1756); Rinaldo di Capua, 1741; Hasse, 1742 (rev. Logroscino, 1744, rev. 1752, 1753); Scalabrini, 1744; Adolfati, 1747; Jommelli, 1747; Bertoni, 1748; Chiarini, 1748; Jommelli, 1749; Terradellas, 1750; Fiorillo, 1751; Manna, 1751; Perez, 1751; Bonno, comp. 1752 (?unperf.); Mazzoni, 1752; Poncini Zilioli, 1752; Scolari, 1752 (rev. 1763); V. Ciampi, 1754; G. Fioroni, 1755; Traetta, 1757; F. Zoppis, 1758; Auletta, 1759; A. Brunetti, 1759; Ferradini, 1760; Sarti, 1762; Jommelli, 1763 (rev. 1777–83); Galuppi, 1764; Schwanenberger, 1765; Zannetti, 1766 (rev. 1781); Boroni, 1768; Celoniati, 1769; Majo, 1769; Insanguine, 1770; Piccinni, 1770; Mortellari, 1772; Colla, 1773; Anfossi, 1775; Mombelli, 1776; Schuster, 1776; Holzbauer, 1779 (as La morte di Didone, rev. 1780 as Der Tod der Dido); Ottani, 1779; Astarita, 1780; Piticchio, 1780 (rev. 1784); Sarti, 1782; Andreozzi, 1784; Gazzaniga, 1787; Paisiello, 1794; L. Kozeluch, 1795; Marino, 1799; Fioravanti, 1810; Paer, 1810; Klein, 1823 (rev. L. Rellstab as Dido); Mercadante, 1823; Reissiger, 1824

L'eroe cinese

Bonno, 1752; Galuppi, 1753; Hasse, 1753 (rev. 1773 as Der chinesische Held); Perez, 1753; Conforto, 1754; Ballabene, 1757; Piazza, 1757; Uttini, 1757; T. Giordani, 1766; ?Majo, 1770; Sacchini, 1770; Colla, 1771; Mango, 1771; Bertoni, 1774 (as Narbale); Bachschmidt, 1775; Checchi, 1775; Cimarosa, 1782; V. Rauzzini, 1782

Ezio

Porpora, 1728; Auletta, 1728; Hasse, 1730 (rev. 1755); ?Predieri, 1730; Broschi, 1731; Handel, 1732; Lampugnani, 1737 (rev. 1743); Jommelli, 1741; Sarro, 1741; ?Contini, 1742; G. Scarlatti, 1744 (rev. 1754); Pescetti, 1747; Jommelli, 1748; Bernasconi, 1749; Bonno, comp. 1749; Gluck, 1750; Perez, 1751; Ferradini, 1752; Conforto, 1754; Traetta, ?1754; Graun, 1755; Galuppi, 1756; Jommelli, 1758; Latilla, 1758; Gassmann, 1761 (rev. 1770); Gluck, 1763; Schwanenberger, 1763; Rutini, 1763; Alessandri, 1767; Bertoni, 1767; ?Majo, 1769; Guglielmi, 1770; Jommelli, 1771 (rev. Silva, 1772); Sacchini, 1771; Gazzaniga, 1772; Mysliveček, 1775; Mortellari, 1777; Anfossi, 1778; Bachschmidt, 1780; Levis, 1782; Calvi, 1784; Gabriele Prota, 1784; Pio, 1785; Tarchi, 1789 (rev. 1792); Mercadante, 1827

L'impresario delle Canarie

Sarro, 1724 (as Dorina e Nibbio, rev. 1730); Albinoni, 1725; Chiocchetti, 1726; Orlandini, ?1729; Leo, 1741; Martini, 1744

Ipermestra

Hasse, 1744 (rev. Palella, 1746, rev. 1751); Gluck, 1744; Bertoni, 1748; Duni, 1748; Jommelli, 1751; Adolfati, 1752; Perez, 1754; Re, 1755; Galuppi, 1758; Fiorillo, 1759; Cafaro, 1761 (rev. 1763); Sarti, 1766; Majo, 1768; Mysliveček, 1769; Piccinni, 1772; Fortunati, 1773; Naumann, 1774; ?R. Mei, 1778; Martín y Soler, 1780; Rispoli, 1785; Astarita, 1789; Paisiello, 1791; Mercadante (rev. L. Ricciuti), 1825 (rev. 1828–30, perf. 1832); Saldoni, 1838; Carnicer, 1843

Issipile

F. Conti, 1732 (rev. 1737); Bioni, 1732; Hasse, 1732 (rev. Leo, 1742, rev. Cafaro 1763); Porta, 1732; Feo, 1733; Porpora, 1733; Sandoni, 1735; Galuppi, 1737; Chiarini, 1740; K. Bellermann, ?1741; Smith, comp. 1743; Verocai, 1743 (as Hissifile); Mazzoni, 1748; Galuppi, 1750; Gluck, 1752; Errichelli, 1754; Holzbauer,

1754; Cocchi, 1758; Gassmann, 1758; G. Scarlatti, 1760; Sarti, 1761; Schwanenberger, 1766 (rev. 1767); Anfossi, 1784; Marinelli, 1796; Poissl, comp. 1818; ?Ellerton, ?1825

Nitteti

Conforto, 1756; Cocchi and Piccinni, 1757; Traetta, 1757; Fiorillo, ?1758 (rev. 1771); Hasse, 1758 (rev. 1762); Holzbauer, 1758; Jommelli, 1759 (rev. Silva, 1770); Sarti, 1760 (rev. 1765); Mazzoni, 1764; Fischietti, 1765 (rev. 1775); Adlgasser, 1766; Carvalho, 1766; Petrucci, 1766; Czeyka, 1768; Mysliveček, 1770; Rutini, 1770; Anfossi, 1771; Monza, 1771; Gatti, 1773; Sacchini, 1774; Accorimboni, 1777; Paisiello, 1777; Rispoli, 1782; Curcio, 1783; Parenti, 1783; G. Giordani, 1784; Nasolini, 1788; Bertoni, 1789; Bianchi, 1789; Benincori, ?1797; Pavesi, 1811; Poissl, 1817

L'olimpiade

Caldara, 1733; Vivaldi, 1734; Pergolesi, 1735; Brivio, 1737; Leo, 1737; ?Orlandini, 1737; Corradini, 1745 (as La más heroica amistad y el amor más verdadero); Fiorillo, 1745 (rev. 1749 as Die olympischen Spiele); G. Scarlatti, 1745; Galuppi, 1747; Scolari, 1747; Lampugnani, 1748; Wagenseil, 1749; Pulli, 1751; Latilla, 1752; Logroscino, 1753; Perez, 1753; Uttini, 1753; Duni, 1755; Hasse, 1756 (rev. 1761, 1764); Carcani, 1757; Monza, 1758; Traetta, 1758; Sciroli, 1760; Jommelli, 1761 (rev. Silva, 1774); Piccinni, 1761; Manfredini, 1762; Fischietti, 1763; Guglielmi, 1763; Sacchini, 1763 (rev. 1777 as L'olympiade, ou Le triomphe de l'amitié); Bernasconi, 1764; Gassmann, 1764; Arne, 1765; Bertoni, 1765; Brusa, Guglielmi and Pampani, 1766; Zanotti-Cavazzoni, 1767; Piccinni, 1768; Cafaro, 1769; Anfossi, 1774; Gatti, 1775; Rosetti, 1777; Mysliveček, 1778; Sarti, 1778; Bianchi, 1781; Andreozzi, 1782; Schwanenberger, 1782; Cherubini, 1783; Sarti, 1783; Borghi, 1784; Cimarosa, 1784; Paisiello, 1786; Minoja, 1787; Federici, 1789; Reichardt, 1791; Tarchi, 1792; Poissl, 1815 (as Der Wettkampf zu Olympia, oder Die Freunde)

Il re pastore

Bonno, 1751; Höpken, 1752; Sarti, 1752; Hasse, 1755 (rev. 1760 or 1762); Uttini, 1755; Gluck, 1756; Agnesi, ?1756; Mazzoni, 1757; Lampugnani, 1758; Piccinni, 1760; Zonca, 1760; Galuppi, 1762 (rev. 1766); Richter, 1762; Jommelli, 1764 (rev. Silva, 1770); Rush, 1764 (rev. R. Rolt as The Royal Shepherd); Giardini, 1765; ?Tozzi, 1766–7; Guglielmi, 1767; Sarti, 1771; Bachschmidt, 1774; Mozart, 1775; T. Giordani, 1778; Platania, 1778; M. Rauzzini, 1784; ?Parenti, comp. 1780s; Sales, 1780s; Santos, 1797

Romolo ed Ersilia

Hasse, 1765; Mysliveček, 1773

Ruggiero

Hasse, 1771; A. Gandini, ?1820

Semiramide riconosciuta

Vinci, 1729; Porpora, 1729; Giacomelli, 1730; Leo, 1730; Porta, 1733; Araia, 1738; Porpora, 1739; Aliprandi, 1740; Jommelli, 1741; Lampugnani, 1741; Hasse, 1744 (rev. 1747, 1760); Terradellas, 1746; Gluck, 1748; Galuppi, 1749; Perez, 1750; Giuseppe de Majo, 1751; G. Scarlatti, 1751; Rutini, 1752 (rev. 1780); Cocchi, 1753 (rev. 1771); Jommelli, 1753; Brusa, 1756; Fischietti, 1759; Manfredini, 1760; Jommelli, 1762; Sarti, 1762 (rev. 1768); Sacchini, 1764; Bernasconi, 1765; Mysliveček, 1765; Traetta, 1765; Bertoni, 1767; Guglielmi, 1776; Salieri, 1782; Meyerbeer (rev. G. Rossi), 1819

Siface re di Numidia

Feo, 1723; Porpora, 1725, 1726; G. N. R. Redi, 1729 (as Viriate); Porpora, 1730; G. M. Nelvi, 1732; Leo, 1737; Hasse, 1739 (as Viriate); Maggiore, 1744; Cocchi, 1749; Fiorillo, 1752; Fischietti, 1761; Valentini, 1761 (as Viriate); Galuppi, 1762 (as Viriate)

Siroe re di Persia

Vinci, 1726; Porta, 1726; Porpora, 1727; Sarro, 1727; Vivaldi, 1727; Handel, 1728; Fiorè, 1729; Bioni, 1732; Hasse, 1733 (rev. 1747, 1763); Latilla, 1740; Perez, 1740; G. Scarlatti, 1742 (rev. 1747); Manna, 1743; Scalabrini, 1744; Mazzoni, 1746; Wagenseil, 1748; Cocchi, 1750; Conforto, 1752; Uttini, 1753; Galuppi, 1754; Lampugnani, 1755; Errichelli, 1758; Piccinni, 1759; Raupach, 1760; G. B. Cedronio, ?1760; Boroni, 1764; Guglielmi, 1764; Tozzi, 1766–7; Traetta, 1767; Franchi, 1770; Borghi, 1771; Sarti, 1779; Beltrami, 1783; Ubaldi, 1810

Temistocle

Caldara, 1736; Chinzer, 1737; Latilla, 1737; Orlandini, 1737; Pampani, 1737 (as Artaserse Longimano); Ristori, 1738; Poncini Zilioli, 1739; Bernasconi, 1740 (rev. 1744, 1754, 1762); Maggiori, 1743; Porpora, 1743; Costantini, 1744; Finazzi, 1746; Jommelli, 1757 (rev. 1765); Manna, 1761; Durán, 1762; Schwanenberger, 1762; Uhde, 1762; Monza, 1766; J. C. Bach, 1772; G. Brunetti, 1776; Ullinger, 1777; Beltrami, 1780; Pacini (rev. P. Anguillesi), 1823

Il trionfo di Clelia

Hasse, 1762 (rev. 1763); Gluck, 1763; Mysliveček, 1767; Bertoni, 1769; Vanhal, 1770; Borghi, 1773; Jommelli, 1774 (rev. Silva, 1774); Michl, 1776; Urbani, 1784–5; Tarchi, 1786

Zenobia

Predieri, 1740; Porpora, 1740 (as Tiridate); G. Sbacchi, 1740; Pellegrini, 1741; Poncini Zilioli, 1741; Latilla, 1742 (as Zenobia und Radamistus); Verocai, 1742; Michieli, 1746; Pulli, 1748; Perez, 1751; Uttini, 1754; Piccinni, 1756; Cocchi, 1758; G. B. Zingoni, 1760; Hasse, 1761; Pescetti, 1761; Sala, 1761; Traetta, 1761; Schwanenberger, 1765; Tozzi, 1773; G. Calegari, 1779; F. Sirotti, 1783; Mount Edgcumbe, 1800

FESTE, AZIONI, COMPONIMENTI

Alcide al bivio

Hasse, 1760; Conforto, 1765; Bortnyansky, 1778; Santos, 1778; L. Xavier, 1778; Paisiello, 1780; Righini, 1790 (rev. 1804); Mayr, 1809

Amor prigioniero

Predieri, 1732; Reutter, 1741; Beringer, ?1740s; Perez, 1751; Araia, 1755; Colla, 1762; Bonno, date unknown (?unperf.); Ferrandini, 1781; Bevilacqua, 1784; Musenga, 1789; Ottani, 1789; Schuster, 1801; S. Cristiani, 1803; Vogler, comp. 1804; Apell, 1815

Angelica

Porpora, 1720; G. F. Milano, 1740; Fiorillo, 1744; Scalabrini, 1746; Mele, 1747; Brusa, 1756; Zonca, 1758; Carvalho, 1778; Moneta, 1780; ?Cimarosa and Millico, ?1783; Andreozzi, 1792 [? or 1783]; Mortellari, 1796; Cinque, c1800; ?Valero, 1843

L'ape

No settings known

L'asilo d'Amore

Caldara, 1732; Paganelli, 1732; Pescetti, 1738; Hasse, 1742; comp. unknown, Vienna, 1743; Corselli, 1750; Jommelli, 1758; Gassmann, 1765 (also as Il trionfo dell'onore); Sarti, 1769 (rev. Deschamps as L'asile de l'amour); P. A. Skokov, 1787; Schicht, 1789; Bierey, 1797

Astrea placata

Predieri, 1739 (also as La felicità della terra); Schürer (rev. B. Campagnari), 1746; J. M. Breunich, ?1749; Majo, 1760; Sarti, 1760; Mango, 1765; Traetta, 1770; Anton of Saxony, 1785

L'Atenaide [Gli affetti generosi]

Bonno, comp. 1762

Le cinesi

Caldara, 1735; Conforto, 1751 (as La festa cinese); Gluck, 1754; Holzbauer, 1756; Misón, 1757 (as La festa chinese); Sales, 1757; Jommelli, 1765; Perez, 1769; Astarita, 1773; Colla, 1781; Anton of Saxony, 1784; ?Cedronio, 1789; Millico, ?1780s; García, ?1825

La contesa de' numi

Vinci, 1729; Gluck, 1749

La corona

Gluck, comp. 1765; De Mora, 1815

Egeria

Hasse, 1764; ?Ottani, 1789; Tantari, 1800

Endimione

Sarro, 1721; Bioni, 1727; Buini, 1729; Alberti, 1737; Pescetti, 1739 (as Diana e Endimione); ?Treu, 1741; Bernasconi, 1742 (rev. 1766); Hasse, 1743; Mele, 1749; N. Conti, 1752; Fiorillo, 1754 (rev. 1763 as Diana ed Endimione); Sabatini, 1758; Jommelli, 1759; Conforto, 1763; A. Rugarli, 1769; Sigismondo, comp. 1760s; J. C. Bach, 1770 (rev. Jommelli, 1774); Schmittbaur, 1772; M. Haydn, ?1778; Jommelli, 1780; Guglielmi, 1781 (rev. Serio as Diana amante); Carvalho, 1783; G. Rugarli, 1795

La Galatea

Comito, 1722; Alberti, 1738; C. Nichelmann, 1740; Schürer, 1746; Uttini, 1755; Zoppis, 1760; Brunetti, 1762; Schwanenberger, 1763; J. C. Bach, 1764; Mango, 1767; A. da Silva, 1779; Bertoni, ?1781; Sclart, 1789; B. Furlanetto, 1780s; Santos, comp. 1780s; Benincori, comp. 1804; L. Kozeluch, ?1806

La gara

Reutter, 1755

Le grazie vendicate

Caldara, 1735; ?Ferrandini, 1753; Reutter, 1758; Santos, 1762; Anton of Saxony, 1784

L'isola disabitata

Bonno, 1754; Holzbauer, 1754; Uttini, 1755; Sales, 1758 (as Die unbewohnte Insel); Sarti, 1760; Fischietti; Jommelli, 1761; Schmittbaur, 1762 (as Die wüste Insel); Sigismondo, 1766; Perez, 1767; Traetta, 1768; Calegari, 1770; Astarita, 1773; Coccia, ?1773; Naumann, 1773; Anton of Saxony, 1775; Boroni, 1775; Bologna, 1777; ?Garbi, 1779; Haydn, 1779; Schuster, 1779 (as Die wüste Insel); Jommelli, 1780; Michl, 1780; Millico, ?1780s (unperf.); Gatti, 1783; Mengozzi, 1783 (rev. 1789); ?F. Benda, ?1789; ?Musenga, 1789; Lanza, 1792; G. Rugarli, 1794; García, ?1824

Il natal di Giove

Bonno, 1740; Hasse, 1749; Plá, 1752; Latilla, 1757; Santos, 1766; Lucchesi, ?1744; J. da Silva, 1778; A. L. Fracassini, date unknown

Gli orti esperidi

Porpora, 1721; Conforto, 1751; Santos, 1764; Lima, 1779; Vannacci, 1802

La pace fra la virtù e la bellezza

Predieri, 1738; Bioni, ?1739; Adolfati, 1746; Galuppi, 1766; Perez, 1777

La pace fra le tre dee

Conforto, 1765

Il palladio conservato

Reutter, 1735; Meyer von Schauensee, 1743; Santos, 1771; ? F. Robuschi, c1805

Il Parnaso accusato e difeso

Reutter, 1738; Mango, 1766; Schwanenberger, 1768; Colla, 1786; Ottani, 1790

Il Parnaso confuso

Gluck, 1765; Sarti and ?Bertoni, 1766; Rust, 1778

Partenope

Hasse, 1767 (rev. 1775); Martín y Soler, 1782; Benelli, 1798; ?G. Farinelli, 1814; ?Pacini, 1826; ?Cordella, 1840

La rispettosa tenerezza

Reutter, 1750

La ritrosia disarmata

comp. unknown, 1759; ?Elsner, ?1825

Il sogno

Reutter, 1756

Il sogno di Scipione

Predieri, 1735; Porta, 1744 (as Der Traum des Scipio); Nichelmann, 1746; ?Sciroli, 1752; Llussa, 1753; Sarti, 1755; Bernasconi, 1765 (as Il trionfo della costanza); ?Hasse, 1758; Cinque, 1750s; Bonno, comp. 1763; Mango, 1764; Uttini, 1764; Santos, 1768; Mozart, 1772

Il tempio dell'Eternità

Fux, 1731 (also as Enea negli Elisi); comp. unknown, 1772; ?Tritto, 1793; Liverati, 1810

Tributo di rispetto e d'amore

Reutter, 1754

Il trionfo d'Amore

Gassmann, 1765; Portugal, 1817

Il vero omaggio

Bonno, 1743; J.W. Hertel, ?1761; Anton of Saxony, 1783

*

F. Rosellini [E. Edisimo]: *Considerazioni sopra il 'Demofoonte' dell'abate Metastasio, scritte in una lettera* (Palvino, 1735); repr. in P. A. Paravia: *Vita di Alfonso Varano* (1820)

F. Algarotti: *Saggio sopra l'opera in musica* (privately printed, 1754; Livorno, 1755); repr. in *Opere varie del conte Francesco Algarotti*, ii (Venice, 1757), 277–364, and in *Illuministi italiani*, ii, ed. E. Bonora (Milan, 1969), 433–509

R. de' Calzabigi: 'Dissertazione su le poesie drammatiche del signor abate Pietro Metastasio', *Poesie del signor abate Pietro Metastasio*, i (Paris, 1755), pp.xvii–cciv; repr. in *Poesie*, i (Turin, 1757), pp.iii–ccxiv, and in *Poesie*, ii (Livorno, 1774)

D.-J. de Villeneuve: *Lettre sur le méchanisme de l'opéra italien* (Naples, 1756)

G. Baretti: 'Opere drammatiche dell'abate Pietro Metastasio poeta cesareo', *La frusta letteraria di Aristarco Scannabue*, i/3 (Roveredo, 1763), 30–35; repr. in *Poesie del signor abate Pietro Metastasio*, ed. R. de' Calzabigi, x (Paris, 1769), pp.vi–xxvii, and in *Poesie del signor abbate Pietro Metastasio, poeta e bibliotecario cesareo*, i (Paris, 1773), pp.iii–xviii; also in repr. of *La frusta letteraria, Opere scelte di Giuseppe Baretti*, ed. B. Maier (Turin, 1972), 124–32

F.-J. de Chastellux: *Essai sur l'union de la poésie et de la musique* (Paris, 1765)

A. Planelli: *Dell'opera in musica* (Naples, 1772)

G. Baretti: 'Prefazione', *Poesie del signor abbate Pietro Metastasio, poeta e bibliotecario*, i (Paris, 1773)

P. Giovannini: *Alcune critiche dissertazioni sui drammi del Metastasio* (Forlì, *c*1775)

P. Napoli-Signorelli: *Storia critica de' teatri antichi e moderni*, iii (Naples, 1777)

F. Franceschi: *Apologia delle opere drammatiche di Pietro Metastasio* (Lucca, 1778)

S. Bettinelli: 'Discorso sopra la poesia italiana', 'Discorso sopra il teatro italiano', *Opere dell'abate Saverio Bettinelli* (Venice, 1780–82), v, 1–64, vi, 1–36; repr. in *Illuministi italiani*, ii, ed. E. Bonora (Milan, 1969), 1057–1111, 1113–45

J. von Retzer: *Metastasio: eine Skizze für seinen künftigen Biographen* (Vienna, 1782)

G. Taruffi: *Elogio accademico del Metastasio* (Rome, 1782)

J. Andrés: 'Delle belle lettere', 'Della poesia', *Dell'origine, progressi e stato attuale d'ogni letteratura*, ii–iii (Parma, 1782–99)

M. Aluigi: *Storia dell'abate Pietro Trappasi Metastasio poeta drammatico* (Assisi, 1783)

S. Arteaga: *Le rivoluzioni del teatro musicale italiano dalla sua origine fino al presente*, i (Bologna, 1783)

G. Moreschi: 'Riflessioni di Giambatista Alessandro Moreschi intorno le feste ed azioni teatrali di Pietro Metastasio', *Opere del signor abate Pietro Metastasio*, xii (Nice, 1783), pp.iii–xxxiv

A. de' Giorgi Bertolà: 'Osservazioni sopra Metastasio con alcuni versi', *Operette in verso e in prosa*, ii (Bassano, 1784), 177–229

S. Mattei: 'Memorie per servire alla vita del Metastasio in una lettera dell'abate Giuseppe Orlandini', *Opere drammatiche del signor abate Pietro Metastasio*, xiii (Naples, 1784); repr. as 'Memorie per servire alla vita del Metastasio raccolte da Saverio Mattei', *Metastasio e Jommelli* (Colle, 1785), 1–57

S. Arteaga: 'Difetti del signor Abate Metastasio', *Opere del signor abate Pietro Metastasio*, xlv (Nice, 1785), pp.iii–xlv

C. Cristini: 'Vita dell'abate Pietro Metastasio', *Opere del signor abate Pietro Metastasio*, i (Nice, 1785), pp.ix–ccxiv; repr. in *Opere dell'abate Pietro Metastasio*, i (London, 1813), pp.i–lxxii

S. Mattei: 'La filosofia della musica o sia la riforma del teatro', *Opere del signor abate Pietro Metastasio*, iii (Nice, 1785), pp.iii–xlviii

'Osservazioni' di vari letterati sopra i drammi dell'abate Pietro Metastasio', *Opere del signor abate Pietro Metastasio* (Nice, 1785)

J. A. Hiller: *Über Pietro Metastasio und seine Werke* (Leipzig, 1786)

F. Altanesi: *Vita di Pietro Metastasio* (Naples, 1787, 2/1807)

S. D'Ayala: 'Ristretto della vita del Metastasio', *Opere postume dell'abate Pietro Metastasio*, iii (Vienna, 1795), 311–48

J. Andrés: 'Le belle lettere', *Dell'origine, progressi e stato attuale d'ogni letteratura*, ii–iii (Parma, 1795–7); corrections in viii (Parma, 1822), 47–151

C. Burney: *Memoirs of the Life and Writings of the Abate Metastasio* (London, 1796)

J. C. Walker: *Historical Memoir on the Italian Tragedy* (London, 1799)

A. W. Schlegel: *Über dramatische Kunst und Literatur*, ii/1 (Heidelberg, 1809), 1–300; (Eng. trans., 1815, 2/1840), 277–324

G. Corniani: 'Pietro Metastasio', *I secoli della letteratura italiana dopo il suo risorgimento*, ix (Brescia, 1813), 340–68; (2/1833, rev. S. Ticozzi), ii/1, 272–9

J.-C. Simonde de Sismondi: 'Dix-huitième siècle: Métastase', *De la littérature du midi de l'Europe*, ii (Paris, 1813), 298–345; (3/1829)

Stendhal [H. Beyle]: *Vies de Haydn, de Mozart et de Métastase* (Paris, 1817; Eng. trans., 1818 and 1972)

F. Reina: 'Vita di Pietro Metastasio', *Opere scelte di Pietro Metastasio* (Milan, 1820), pp.ix–lv

G. Maffei: *Storia della letteratura italiana dall'origine della lingua fino al secolo XIX* (Milan, 1824, 2/1834)

P. Emiliani Giudici: 'Poesia drammatica: Pietro Metastasio–Carlo Goldoni', *Storia delle belle lettere in Italia* (Florence, 1844), 993–1036; (2/1855), ii, 287–321; repr. in *Opere di Paolo Emiliani-Giudici* (Florence, 1863), ii, 287–321

C. Cantù: 'Letteratura italiana', *Storia universale*, xvii (Turin, 1845), esp. 740–41; (10/1883–91), xvii

——: 'Letteratura', 'Belle arti', *Storia universale*, xviii (Turin, 1846), esp. 832, 915; (10/1883–93), xvii

F. Cicconetti: 'Di Cesare Cantù giudice di Pietro Metastasio', *Giornale arcadico*, cviii (1846), 346–51

P. Gennarelli: 'Pietro Metastasio giudicato da C. Cantù', *Saggiatore*, iii (1846), 243–56

G. Torelli: 'Tradizioni del pensiero italiano: Metastasio', *Rivista europea* (Oct–Nov 1846), 457–96

V. Faguet: *Metastasio considéré comme critique* (Poitiers, 1856)

T. von Karajan: *Aus Metastasios Hofleben* (Vienna, 1861)

C. Cantù: 'Il teatro', *Storia della letteratura italiana* (Florence, 1865), 484–7; (2/1887)

L. Settembrini: 'Del melodramma: il Metastasio, il Lorenzi', *Lezioni di letteratura italiana dettate nell'Università di Napoli* (Naples, 1866–72), iii, 129–41; repr. (Turin, 1927), iii, 123–34

F. de Sanctis: 'La nuova letteratura', *Storia della letteratura italiana*, ii (Naples, 1870), 381–402; repr. in *Opere di Francesco de Sanctis*, ix, ed. N. Gallo (Turin, 1966), 853–79; material on Metastasio enlarged as 'Pietro Metastasio', *Nuova antologia*, no.16 (1871), 807–25

M. Landau: *Der italienische Literatur am österreichischen Hofe* (Vienna, 1879)

V. Paget [V. Lee]: *Studies on the Eighteenth Century in Italy* (London, 1880)

G. Carducci: 'Pietro Metastasio', *Domenica letteraria* (16 April 1882); repr. in *Opere*, xix (Bologna, 1909), 63–93, and *Edizione nazionale delle opere di Giosuè Carducci*, xv (Bologna, 1955), 237–67

A. Mussafia: *Pietro Metastasio* (Vienna, 1882)

O. Tommaseo: 'Pietro Metastasio e lo svolgimento del melodramma italiana', *Nuova antologia*, no.33 (1882), 17–60; repr. in *Scritti di storia e critica* (Rome, 1891), 153–222

G. Carducci: 'Metastasiana', *Cronaca bizantina* (16 June 1883); repr. in *Opere*, xi (Bologna, 1902), 254–68, and *Edizione nazionale delle opere di Giosuè Carducci*, xv (Bologna, 1955), 269–85

——: Preface to *Lettere disperse e inedite di Pietro Metastasio*, ed. G. Carducci (Bologna, 1883), pp.i–xxiv; repr. in *Opere*, xi (Bologna, 1902), 269–80, and *Edizione nazionale delle opere di Giosuè Carducci*, xv (Bologna, 1955), 287–301

L. Falconi: *Pietro Metastasio alla corte di Carlo VI e di Maria Teresa e sua rinomanza ne' secoli XVIII e XIX* (Vienna, 1883)

C. Antona-Traversi: Preface to *Lettere disperse e inedite di Pietro Metastasio*, ed. C. Antona-Traversi (Rome, 1886), pp.xv–cviii [incl. repr. articles first pubd 1882–3: G. Cugnoni: 'Metastasio e l'Arcadia', 477–501; R. Fornaciari: 'Pietro Metastasio', 457–76; M. Landau: 'Pietro Metastasio', 503–19; L. Morandi: 'Il Metastasio critico e prosatore', 521–44; A. Moroni: 'Osservazioni intorno a una edizione sconosciuta della vita e delle opere del Metastasio', 435–55; A. Moroni: 'Un mistero nella vita del Metastasio a Roma', 405–24]

E. Masi: 'Pietro Metastasio', *Parrucche e sanculotti nel secolo XVIII* (Milan, 1886), 1–31

C. Dejob: 'Les amoureux éconduits ou transis dans Corneille et dans Racine, dans Apostolo Zeno et dans Metastasio', *Revue d'histoire littéraire de la France*, iv (1897), 393–406

——: *Etudes sur la tragédie* (Paris, 1897)

A. Donadoni: *Dalla 'Didone' all''Attilio Regolo': osservazioni sulla struttura del melodramma metastasiano* (Rome, 1897)

M. Landau: 'Das Musikdrama', *Geschichte der italienischen Litteratur im achtzehnten Jahrhundert* (Berlin, 1899), 518–58

P. Arcari: *L'arte poetica di Pietro Metastasio* (Milan, 1902)

B. Peroni: 'I melodrammi e le teorie drammatiche di Pietro Metastasio', *Rivista teatrale italiana*, ii (1902), 305–19

C. Levi: 'Il Metastasio sulle scene', *Rivista teatrale italiana*, ix (1904–5), 113–21

J. M. Baroni: 'La lirica musicale di Pietro Metastasio', *RMI*, xii (1905), 383–406

A. Wotquenne: *Alphabetisches Verzeichnis der Stücke in Versen aus den dramatischen Werken von Zeno, Metastasio, und Goldoni* (Leipzig, 1905)

I. Vecchia: *La varia fortuna di Pietro Metastasio* (Turin, 1907)

C. Levi: 'La critica metastasiana in Italia', *Rivista teatrale italiana*, xii (1907–8), 147–51, 187–8, 209–11, 250–51, 310–11, 369–70; xiii (1909), 40–43, 218–20; repr. as *La critica metastasiana in Italia* (Florence, 1911)

E. M. Leonardi: *Il melodramma del Metastasio e la sua fortuna nel secolo XVIII* (Naples, 1909)

A. de Gubernatis: *Pietro Metastasio: corso di lezioni fatte nell'Università di Roma nell'anno scolastico 1909–1910* (Florence, 1910)

R. Rolland: 'Métastase, précurseur de Gluck', *Mercure musical*, viii (1912), 1–10; repr. in *Voyage musical au pays du passé* (Paris, 1919), 155–77; trans. B. Miall as 'Metastasio: the Forerunner of Gluck', *A Musical Tour through the Land of the Past* (New York, 1922), 145–62

A. D'Angeli: 'Niccolò Jommelli e Gluck nel giudizio di Metastasio', *Cronaca musicale* (1914)

A. De Sanctis: *Le imitazioni del Metastasio dal teatro di Pierre Corneille* (Gaeta, 1914)

G. A. Borgese: 'La comicità del Metastasio', *Studi di letteratura moderna* (Milan, 1915), 29–37

L. Russo: *Pietro Metastasio* (Pisa, 1915, 3/1945)

G. Natali: 'Pietro Metastasio', *Giornale storico della letteratura italiana*, lxviii (1916), 434–40; repr. in *Idee, costumi, uomini del settecento* (Turin, 1926), 213–21

M. Callegari: 'Il melodramma e Pietro Metastasio', *RMI*, xxvi (1919), 518–44; xxvii (1920), 31–59, 458–76

A. Della Corte: 'Appunti sull'estetica musicale di Pietro Metastasio', *RMI*, xxviii (1921), 94–119

——: *Settecento italiana: Paisiello*, ii: *L'estetica musicale di Pietro Metastasio* (Turin, 1922)

A. Costa: *Pagine metastasiane* (Palermo, 1923)

G. Natali: *La vita e le opere di Pietro Metastasio* (Livorno, 1923); enlarged in 'Il melodramma', *Il settecento*, ed. G. Natali (Milan, 1929, 3/1950), 773–851

L. Tonelli: *Il teatro italiano dalle origini ai giorni nostri* (Milan, 1924), 280–94

R. Gerber: 'Die Dramen Pietro Metastasios nach Form und Inhalt', *Der Operntypus Johann Adolf Hasses und seine textlichen Grundlagen* (Leipzig, 1925), 1–26

F. de Sanctis: *Teoria e storia della letteratura*, ed. B. Croce (Bari, 1926), i, 141–2; ii, esp. 34–8, 167–70; see also *Opere di Francesco de Sanctis*, iii: *Lezione: Purismo illuminismo storicismo*, ed. A. Marinari (Turin, 1975), i, 601–2, 734–40; ii, esp. 1516–21 [lectures given in Naples, 1839–48; reconstructed by B. Croce and orig. pubd in instalments in *La critica* (1915–19)]

M. Apollonio: *Metastasio* (Milan, 1930)

A. Bonaventura: 'Pietro Metastasio musicista', *Musica d'oggi*, xiv (1932), 8–12

C. Culcasi: *Pietro Metastasio* (Turin, 1935)

M. Fubini: Review of E. Sponagno: *Ugo Foscolo: l'homme et le poète* (Paris, 1934), *Annali della Scuola normale superiore di Pisa*, iv (1935), 191–6; repr. with corrections as 'Dall'Arcadia all'Illuminismo', *Dal Muratori al Baretti: studi sulla critica dal settecento* (Bari, 1946), 125–32

G. Gervasoni: *Metastasio, Goldoni, Alfieri* (Turin, 1935, 3/1950 as *Il teatro italiano nel settecento: Metastasio*)

A. Momigliano: 'L'arcadia e il Metastasio', *Storia letteraria d'Italia*, ii (Milan, 1935, 8/1954), 314–27

G. Roncaglia: *Il melodioso settecento* (Milan, 1935), esp. 35–50

A. Vullo: *Confronto fra i melodrammi di Zeno e di Metastasio* (Agrigento, 1935)

A. Capri: 'Melodramma e opera comica', *Il settecento musicale in Europa* (Milan, 1936), 19–33, 42–92

F. Torrefranca: 'Il melodramma', *Storia del teatro italiano*, ed. S. d'Amico (Milan, 1936), 135–63

M. Fubini: 'Pietro Metastasio', *I classici italiani*, ed. L. Russo, ii: *Dal cinquecento al settecento* (Florence, 1939), 459–94

B. Brunelli: 'Grandezza e decadenza della riforma metastasiana', *Rivista italiana del dramma*, iv (1940), 30–54

F. Flora: 'Pietro Metastasio', *Storia della letteratura italiana*, ii/2: *Il seicento, il settecento* (Milan and Verona, 1942, 13/1962), 15–49

B. Brunelli: 'Pietro Metastasio', 'Bibliografia', *Tutte le opere di Pietro Metastasio*, ed. B. Brunelli (Milan, 1943–54), i, pp.xi–xli; v, 827–37

M. Apollonio: 'Metastasio', *Storia del teatro italiano*, i/3: *Il teatro dell'età barocca* (Florence, 1946), 179–223

M. Fubini: 'Arcadia e illuminismo', *Problemi ed orientamenti critici di lingua e di letteratura italiana*, ed. A. Momigliano, iii: *Questioni e correnti di storia letteraria* (Milan, 1948), 503–95; repr. in *Dal Muratori al Baretti* (Bari, 2/1954), 292–395; (4/1975), 335–425; summarized as 'Dall'Arcadia all'Illuminismo', *Critica sociale*, xliv (1952), 488–92, 509–11

B. Croce: 'Il giudizio del De Sanctis sul Metastasio', *La letteratura italiana del settecento* (Bari, 1949), 15–23

R. Giazotto: 'Zeno, Metastasio e la critica del 700', *RMI*, li (1949), 43–66

C. Calcaterra: *Il barocco in Arcadia e altri scritti sul settecento* (Bologna, 1950)

C. Varese: *Saggio sul Metastasio* (Florence, 1950)

A. Trigiani: *Il teatro raciniano e i melodrammi di Pietro Metastasio* (Turin, 1951)

F. Hadamowsky: 'Barocktheater am Wiener Kaiserhof, mit einem Spielplan (1625–1740)', *Jb der Gesellschaft für Wiener Theaterforschung 1951–2*, 7–117

R. Giazotto: *Poesia melodrammatica e pensiero critico nel settecento* (Milan, 1952)

R. Bacchelli: 'Vocazione teatrale del settecento italiano', *Teatro e immagini del settecento italiano*, ed. R. Bacchelli and R. Longhi (Turin, 1953), 9–59, esp. 48–52

M. Fubini: 'Il giudizio di De Sanctis sul Metastasio e una questione di storia letteraria', *Romanticismo italiano* (Bari, 1953), 181–94; (new edn, 1965), 235–48

H. Kunz: 'Höfisches Theater in Wien zur Zeit der Maria Theresia', *Jb der Gesellschaft für Wiener Theaterforschung 1953–4*, 3–113

A. M. Nagler: 'Metastasio poeta di corte e regista', *Arena* [Rome] (1954), 175–87

N. Burt: 'Opera in Arcadia', *MQ*, xli (1955), 145–70

S. Romagnoli: 'Pietro Metastasio', *I classici italiana nella storia della critica*, ed. W. Binni, ii (Florence, 1955, 2/1961), 43–88

A. Yorke-Long: 'A Defence of Metastasio', *Opera*, vi (1955), 154–62

W. Weichlein: *A Comparative Study of Five Musical Settings of 'La clemenza di Tito'* (diss., U. of Michigan, 1956)

E. Scuderi: 'Metastasio teorico di poesia', *Ausonia* [Siena], xii (1957), 45–8

J. Fucilla: 'Nuove lettere inedite del Metastasio', *Convivium*, xxvi/5 (1958), 586–93

M. Fubini: Introduction to *Lirici del settecento*, ed. B. Maier (Milan, 1959), pp.xxviii–xxx

R. Giazotto: 'Canto semplice e canto composto nell'aria di Metastasio', *Musurgia nova* (Milan, 1959), 169–205

W. Vetter: 'Deutschland und das Formgefühl Italiens: Betrachtungen über die metastasianische Oper', *Deutsches Jb der Musikwissenschaft 1959*, 7–37

S. Towneley: 'Metastasio as a Librettist', *Art and Ideas in Eighteenth-Century Italy* (Rome, 1960), 133–45

M. Vani: *Metastasio: poeta cesareo e cittadino di Roma* (Turin, 1960)

B. Brunelli: 'Pietro Metastasio', *Letteratura italiana*, iii: *I minori*, iii (Milan, 1961), 1941–58

R. Bacchelli: Preface to *Teatro di Pietro Metastasio*, ed. R. Bacchelli (Turin, 1962), pp.vii–xxxvii

A. Buck: 'Eroi e pastori nella poesia italiana del settecento', *Lettere italiane*, xiv/3 (1962), 249–64

Problemi di lingua e letteratura italiana del settecento: Mainz 1962 [incl. W. Binni: 'Poetica e poesia nel settecento italiano', 3–25; A. Buck: 'Eroi e pastori nella poesia italiana del settecento', 25–38; M. Fubini: 'La poesia settecentesca nella storia delle forme metriche italiane', 38–56; P. Renucci: 'Irradiazione eroica e impostazione psicologica nei drammi del Metastasio', 56–70]

W. Binni: *L'Arcadia e il Metastasio* (Florence, 1963)

U. Casari: *Una lettera inedita di Pietro Metastasio* (Mirandola, 1964)

F. Gavazzeni: *Studi metastasiani* (Padua, 1964)

E. Sala Di Felice: Preface to *Pietro Metastasio: opere* (Milan, 1965)

M. Zorić: 'Dieci lettere inedite di Pietro Metastasio', *Studia romanica et anglica*, xxi–xxii (1966), 321–36

R. Freeman: *Opera without Drama: Currents of Change in Italian Opera, 1675 to 1725, and the Roles Played therein by Zeno, Caldara, and Others* (diss., Princeton U., 1967)

W. Binni: 'Il melodramma', 'Pietro Metastasio', *Storia della letteratura italiana*, vi: *Il settecento* (Milan, 1968), 455–60, 461–508

H. Bösch: *Die Opernaufführungen des Abate Pietro Metastasio am*

Wiener Kaiserhof nach Zeugnissen aus seinen Briefen (diss., U. of Vienna, 1968)

M. Fubini: 'Introduzione a Metastasio', *Pietro Metastasio: opere*, ed. M. Fubini (Milan, 1968), 3–27; repr. in *Pietro Metastasio: teatro*, ed. M. Fubini, i (Turin, 1977), pp.xxxv–lix

F. Gavazzeni: 'Introduzione', *Opere scelte di Pietro Metastasio* (Turin, 1968)

G. Luzzatto: 'Metastasio e la musica', *Rivista trimestrale di cultura*, xvii (1968), 102–8

E. Raimondi: ' "Ragione" e "sensibilità" nel teatro di Metastasio', *Sensibilità e razionalità nel settecento*, ed. V. Branca, i (Florence, 1968), 249–68; repr. as 'Il teatro allo specchio', *Il concerto interrotto* (Pisa, 1979), 23–44

L. Ronga: 'L'opera metastasiana', *Pietro Metastasio: opere*, ed. M. Fubini (Milan, 1968), pp.vii–xxxiii; repr. in *Pietro Metastasio: teatro*, ed. M. Fubini, i (Turin, 1977), pp.vii–xxxiii

C. Galimberti: 'La finzione del Metastasio', *Lettere italiane*, xxi (1969), 155–70

H. Kramer: 'Pietro Metastasio in Wien', *Archiv für Kulturgeschichte*, lii (1970), 49–64

H. C. Wolff: 'Das Märchen von der neapolitanischen Oper und Metastasio', *AnMc*, no.9 (1970), 94–111; trans. as 'The Fairy-Tale of the Neapolitan Opera', *Studies in Eighteenth-Century Music: a Tribute to Karl Geiringer* (London, 1970), 401–6

A. Ragni: *Incontri e scontri con Metastasio* (Campobasso, 1971)

B. Brizi: 'Metrica e musica verbale nella poesia teatrale di Pietro Metastasio', *Atti dell'Istituzione veneziana di scienze, lettere ed arti*, cxxxi (1972–3), 679–740

C. Halusa: *Metastasio und sein Freundeskreis in Wien* (diss., U. of Vienna, 1972)

M. Robinson: *Naples and Neapolitan Opera* (Oxford, 1972)

K. Hortschansky: Preface to J. A. Hasse: *Ruggiero, ovvero L'eroica gratitudine* (Cologne, 1973), pp.ix–xxiv

G. Nicastro: *Metastasio e il teatro del primo settecento* (Rome and Bari, 1973)

E. Paratore: 'L' "Andromaque" del Racine e la "Didone abbandonata" del Metastasio', *Scritti in onore di Luigi Ronga* (Milan, 1973), 515–47

Venezia e il melodramma nel settecento: Venice 1973–5, i [incl. D. Heartz: 'Hasse, Galuppi and Metastasio', 309–39; E. Surian: 'Metastasio, i nuovi cantanti, il nuovo stile: verso il classicismo', 341–62; B. Brizi: 'La "Didone" e il "Siroe", primi melodrammi di Pietro Metastasio a Venezia', 363–88, and 'Le componimenti del linguaggio melodrammatico nelle "Cinese" di Pietro Metastasio', 389–406; K. Hortschansky: 'Die Rezeption der Wiener Dramen Metastasios in Italien', 407–20]

C. Galimberti: 'Pietro Metastasio', *Dizionario critico della letteratura italiana*, ii (Turin, 1974), 601–9

R. Moberly: 'The Influence of French Classical Drama on Mozart's *La clemenza di Tito*', *ML*, lv (1974), 286–98

C. Varese: 'Parola, ideologia, spettacolo nel teatro illuministico del settecento', *Bollettino del Centro internazionale di studi di architettura Andrea Palladio*, xvii (1975), 175–86

R. Monelle: 'The Rehabilitation of Metastasio', *ML*, lvii (1976), 268–91

D. Heartz: 'Les lumières: Voltaire and Metastasio; Goldoni, Favart and Diderot', *IMSCR*, xii: *Berkeley 1977*, 233–8

A. Lanfranchi: 'La librettistica italiana del settecento, 3: Il Metastasio e i suoi imitatori', *Storia dell'opera*, ed. G. Barblan and A. Basso (Turin, 1977), iii, esp. 64–75

G. Santangelo: 'Modernità del Metastasio', *Arcadia: atti e memorie*, vii/4 (1977), 97–117

J. Schütze: ' "Prima la musica?", Betrachtungen zu Fragen des Opernlibrettos', *Jb zu Wittheit zu Bremen*, xxi (1977), 149–78

R. Angermüller: 'Mozart und Metastasio', *Mitteilungen der Internationalen Stiftung Mozarteum*, xxvi (1978), 12–36

J. Joly: *Les fêtes théâtrales de Métastase à la cour de Vienne (1731–1767)* (Clermont-Ferrand, 1978)

P. Renucci: 'Irradiazione eroica e impostazione psicologica nei drammi del Metastasio', *Revue des études italiennes*, i–iii (1978), 228–49

W. Dürr: 'Zur Dramaturgie des *Titus*: Mozarts Libretto und Metastasio', *MJb 1978–9*, 55–60

M. L. Astaldi: *Metastasio* (Milan, 1979)

C. S. Demmel: *A Comparison of Five Musical Settings of Metastasio's Artaserse* (diss., UCLA, 1979)

N. Merola: 'Un'ipotesi sul classicismo settecentesco: l'Arcadia e Metastasio', *Il Veltro*, xxiii (1979), 644–8; xxiv (1980), 105–9

F. Mollia: 'Pietro Metastasio', *Pietro Metastasio: opere*, ed. F. Mollia (Milan, 1979), pp.v–xxvii

E. Sala Di Felice: 'Storicità del Metastasio', *Problemi*, lvi (1979), 288–303

R. Strohm: *Die italienische Oper im 18. Jahrhundert* (Wilhelmshaven, 1979)

P. Gallarati: 'L'estetica musicale di Ranieri de' Calzabigi: il caso Metastasio', *NRMI*, xiv (1980), 497–538

J. L. Jorgensen: *Metastasio: Revaluation and Reformulation* (diss., U. of Minnesota, 1980)

F. Portinari: 'Per un Eden burocratico', *Paragone*, xxxi, nos.360–62 (1980), 30–58

J. Fucilla: *Three Melodramas by Pietro Metastasio* (Lexington, KY, 1981) [trans.]

Crosscurrents and the Mainstream of Italian Serious Opera, 1730–1790: London (Ontario) 1982 [*Studies in Music from the University of Western Ontario*, vii (1982)] [incl. N. Pirrotta: 'Metastasio and the Demands of his Literary Environment', 10–21; D. Neville: 'Moral Philosophy in the Metastasian Dramas', 28–46; M. Robinson: 'The Ancient and the Modern: a Comparison of Metastasio and Calzabigi', 137–47]

E. Fubini: 'Razionalità e irrazionalità nel melodramma metastasiano', *Musica/Realtà* (1982), no.9, pp.73–85

Metastasio e il melodramma: Cagliari 1982 [incl. C. Varese: 'Metastasio scrittore in prosa', 11–38; E. Fubini: 'Razionalità e irrazionalità nel melodramma metastasiano', 39–53; E. Sala Di Felice: 'Virtù e felicità alla corte di Vienna', 55–87; P. Gallarati: 'Zeno e Metastasio tra melodramma e tragedia', 89–104; R. Chiesa: 'Metastasio e Mozart', 105–30; M. Delogu: '*La clemenza di Tito* tra Metastasio e Mozart', 131–60; I. Ciani: 'La *Didone* rivisitata', 209–23; M. Teresa Marcialis: 'Il melodramma o le trasgressioni della tragedia', 225–46; L. Sannia Nowé: 'Una voce sul melodramma nelle discussioni del primo settecento (S. Maffei)', 247–70]

E. Sala Di Felice: 'Metastasio: la parola e la scena', *Problemi*, lxv (1982), 264–87

P. Weiss: 'Metastasio, Aristotle, and the Opera Seria', *JM*, i (1982), 385–94

J. K. Wilson: *L'Olimpiade: Selected Eighteenth-Century Settings of Metastasio's Libretto* (diss., Harvard U., 1982)

Il centenario della morte di Metastasio: convegno linceo, lxv: *Rome 1983* [incl. G. Giarrizzo: 'L'ideologia di Metastasio tra cartesianesimo e illuminismo', 43–77; G. Muresu: 'Metastasio e la tradizione poetica italiana', 111–46; C. Varese: 'Tempo e struttura nel dramma metastasiano', 147–66; F. della Corte: 'Metastasio e l' "Arte poetica" d'Orazio', 167–86; G. Santangelo: 'Vita e letteratura nell' "Epistolario" del Metastasio', 187–97; R. Macchioni Jodi: 'Metastasio, Assisi e l'Arcadia umbra', 223–4; N. Pirrotta: 'I musicisti nell'Epistolario di Metastasio', 245–55; J. Joly: 'Le didascalie per la recitazione nei drammi del Metastasio', 227–91; A. Wandruska: 'Pietro Metastasio e la corte di Vienna', 293–300]

G. Folena: 'Una lingua per la musica', *L'italiano in Europa: esperienze linguistiche del settecento* (Turin, 1983), esp. 272–81, 307–9

J. Joly: 'Metastasio e le sintesi della contraddizione', P. Anfossi: *Adriano in Siria*, DMV, xxiv (1983), pp.lviii–lxiv

H. Lühning: '*Titus*'-Vertonungen im 18. Jahrhundert: Untersuchungen zur Tradition der opera seria von Hasse bis Mozart* (Volkach, 1983)

N. Merola: 'La tragedia congetturale: nota su Metastasio', *Studi romani*, xxxi (1983), 161–72

E. Sala Di Felice: *Metastasio: ideologia, drammaturgia, spettacolo* (Milan, 1983)

R. Wiesend: 'Metastasios Revisionen eigener Dramen und die Situation der Opernmusik in den 1750er Jahren', *AMw*, xl (1983), 255–75

P. Gallarati: *Musica e maschera: il libretto italiano del settecento* (Turin, 1984)

G. Gronda: 'Metastasiana', *RIM*, xix (1984), 314–32

——: 'Le passione della ragione', *Studi sul settecento* (Pisa, 1984)

G. P. Maragoni: *Metastasio e la tragedia* (Rome, 1984)

G. Muresu: 'Metastasio e la tradizione poetica italiana', *Rassegna della letteratura italiana*, lxxxviii (1984), 24–51

M. Saccenti, ed.: 'Metastasio e altro settecento', *Italianistica*, xiii/1–2 (1984) [incl. N. Mangini: 'Il teatro italiano tra seicento e settecento: primi tentativi di riforma', 11–20; C. Carese: 'Metastasio scrittore in prosa', 21–39; E. Sala Di Felice: 'Metastasio sulla scena del mondo', 41–70; M. Accorsi: 'Metastasio e l'idea dell'amore', 71–123; A. Bellina: 'Metastasio in Venezia: appunti per una "recensio" ', 145–73; J. Joly: 'Dall' "Adriano in Siria" metastasiano all' "Adrien" di Méhul',

211–22; J. Da Costa Miranda: 'Sul teatro di Metastasio nel settecento portoghese', 223–7]
Metastasio e il mondo musicale: Venice 1985 [incl. P. Weiss: 'Metastasio e Aristotile', 1–12; D. Goldin: 'Per una morfologia dell'aria metastasiana', 13–37; E. Sala Di Felice: 'Il desiderio della parola e il piacere delle lacrime nel melodramma metastasiano', 39–97; M. Viale Ferrero: 'Le didascalie sceniche del Metastasio', 133–49; R. Wiesend: 'Le revisioni di Metastasio di alcuni suoi drammi e la situazione della musica per melodramma negli anni '50 del settecento', 171–97; R. Weaver: 'Metastasio a Firenze', 199–206; D. Heartz: 'Metastasio, "maestro dei maestri di cappella drammatici"', 315–38
N. Pirrotta: 'Metastasio e i teatri romani', *Le muse galanti: la musica a Roma nel settecento*, ed. B. Cagli (Rome, 1985), 23–34
R. Strohm: *Essays on Handel and Italian Opera* (Cambridge, 1985)
R. di Benedetto: 'Parole e musica: il settecento e l'ottocento', *Teatro, musica, tradizione dei classici* (Turin, 1986), 365–410
P. Galimberti: 'Pietro Metastasio', *Dizionario critico della letteratura italiana*, iii (Turin, 1986), 162–9
R. Herklotz: *Die opera seria und die Ideen der Aufklärung: eine Untersuchung zum Menschenbild Pietro Metastasios* (diss., Leipzig U., 1986)
E. Kanduth: 'Das Libretto im Zeichen der Arcadia, paradigmatisches in den Musikdramen Zenos, Pariatis und Metastasios', *Oper als Text: romanistische Beiträge zur Libretto-Forschung*, ed. A. Gier (Heidelberg, 1986), 33–53
D. Neville: *Mozart's La clemenza di Tito and the Metastasian Opera Seria* (diss., U. of Cambridge, 1986)
I vicini di Mozart: Venice 1987, i: *Il teatro musicale tra sette e ottocento*
G. Mangini: 'Le passioni, la virtù e la morale nelle concezioni tardo-settecentesca dell'opera metastasiana', *RIM*, xxii (1987), 114–44
E. Taddeo: 'Metastasio da Marino a Seneca, I & II', *Giornale storico della letteratura italiana*, clxiv (1987), 321–64, 481–508
D. Neville: 'Aesthetic Considerations in Metastasio's Dramatic Theories', *Musica antiqua*, viii Bydgoszcz 1988, 723–45
——: 'Cartesian Principles in Mozart's "La clemenza di Tito"', *Studies in the History of Music*, ii: *Music and Drama* (New York, 1988), 97–123
M. Accorsi: 'Vent'anni di studi metastasiani (1968–88)', *Lettere italiane*, xli/4 (1989) 604–27
D. Heartz: 'The Poet as Stage Designer: Metastasio, Goldoni, and Da Ponte', *Mozart's Operas* (Berkeley, 1990), 89–105
P. Alatri: 'Metastasio nel quadro politico e culturale dell'Europa', *Musica senza aggettivi: studi per Fedele d'Amico* (Florence, 1991), i, 145–64
D. Neville: 'Metastasio's Reinterpretation of Aristotle', *Musica antiqua*, ix Bydgoszcz 1991
M. McClymonds: 'The Myth of Metastasian Dramaturgy', *Patrons, Politics, Music, and Art in Italy 1738–1859* (forthcoming)

DON NEVILLE

Metcalf, John (*b* Swansea, 13 Aug 1946). Welsh composer. He was educated at University College, Cardiff, and Goldsmiths' College, and also studied privately with Don Banks. After founding the Vale of Glamorgan Festival in 1969, he taught at Atlantic College (1971–81), where he was also artistic director of the Arts Centre (1975–86). In 1986 he went to Banff, Alberta, as composer-in-residence and associate artistic director at the School of Fine Arts. He returned to Wales in 1991 and has since worked as a freelance composer. His first opera, *The Journey*, was commissioned by the WNO and first performed at the Sherman Theatre, Cardiff (12 June 1981). John Hope Mason's enigmatic libretto is shaped to some extent by the Chinese *I Ching*, Metcalf's music (again to some extent) by middle-period Tippett. Metcalf's next stage work, *The Crossing* (Cardiff, Chapter Arts Centre, 20 September 1984), is a more economical and dramatically much stronger piece, incorporating dance and mime as well as singing. The libretto, by the composer, after the play by Geoff Gilham, is based on an incident in the life of the painter George Grosz, during an Atlantic crossing in 1932. In *Tornrak*, a two-act opera to a libretto by Michael

Wilcox (Cardiff, New Theatre, 19 May 1990, after previews in Banff), Metcalf drew on the technique of Inuit throat singing to heighten the dramatic clash between Eskimo culture and that of industrial Britain during the mid-19th century.

*

M. Boyd: 'Metcalf and *The Journey*', MT, cxxii (1981), 369–71
R. Fawkes: *Welsh National Opera* (London, 1986), 236–8

MALCOLM BOYD

Metropolitan Opera Company. Although based in New York, at the Metropolitan Opera House (*see* NEW YORK, §2), it also toured regularly from its inception in 1883 until 1986.

At its height, the company used the railways to take productions to a dozen cities during the spring, these accounting for a fifth of its annual performances, a quarter of its audience, and sporadic profit. In December 1883, two months into the Metropolitan's inaugural season under Henry Abbey, the company headed for Boston by rail to recoup some of its mounting debt with productions that included *Faust*, in Italian, with Christine Nilsson and Italo Campanini, and *Lucia di Lammermoor*, starring Marcella Sembrich, two works that had opened the season in New York the previous October. The company also toured to Brooklyn, Philadelphia, Chicago, St Louis, Washington, Baltimore and Cincinnati, where a flood of the Ohio River prompted a benefit concert on 17 February to aid victims; this concluded with the Act 1 finale of *Lohengrin*, staged as a pageant, with the roles of Elsa, Ortrud, Lohengrin, Friedrich and Heinrich sung at quadruple strength by leading artists, backed by a chorus of 100, military band and full orchestra.

Tour losses contributed to the company's $250 000 debt from the first season, but it continued to travel and missed only four seasons in its first hundred years. Operas were given in German on tours from 1884–5 to 1888–9, first under Walter Damrosch, followed by tours in 1885–6 and 1888–9 under the musical direction of Anton Seidl; Italian opera was reinstated during the 1889–90 season, however, the company travelling as far as San Francisco and Mexico on this tour. During the 1888–9 season *Ring* cycles were presented for the first time in Philadelphia, Boston, Milwaukee, Chicago and St Louis, under the direction of Anton Seidl, with Lilli Lehmann as Sieglinde and Brünnhilde. Tours were often used to try out works that would later appear in the New York season: the US première of *Werther*, for example, starring Jean de Reszke, took place in Boston on 29 March 1894. Except for the 1890–91, 1892–3 and 1897–8 seasons, the Metropolitan company made extensive tours each year; by the end of the century the touring loop included eight cities with special prominence given to Chicago, where the company's 1898–9 season began with Ernestine Schumann-Heink making her company début as Ortrud in *Lohengrin*. Many other artists made their Metropolitan débuts out of town. During the 1899–1900 season the company, under the management of Maurice Grau, undertook a five-month tour during which it gave performances in 23 cities (some visited twice), including such small towns as New Haven, Utica, Syracuse and Portland (Maine); the company's 1901–2 season was launched with a tour that encompassed 21 cities and delayed the New York opening until 23 December. In 1906 the company was caught in the San Francisco earthquake, abruptly ending its April tour when all the sets and costumes and most of the orchestral instruments were lost, although there were no casualties among the artists, who included Caruso, Eames and Sembrich. In 1910, the second year of Giulio Gatti-Casazza's reign as general manager, the company travelled without its orchestra to Paris, opening on 21 May with Destinn and Caruso in *Aida*. Lucrezia Bori made her company début there as Manon Lescaut on 9 June, with Toscanini conducting musicians from the Colonne and Lamoureux orchestras. In 1913, while on tour in Philadelphia, Caruso sang a bass role for the only time in his career (the aria 'Vecchia zimarra') when the Colline, Andrés de Segurola, became hoarse.

With the arrival of the Great Depression the company's tours were drastically shortened and a system of local guarantees developed to make up any deficit; these measures led to a period of financially viable tours that lasted several decades. On 26 May 1952 the company made its début in a new Toronto hockey arena, the Maple Leaf Gardens (cap. 12 000), reaching 43 344 people in four performances. By 1955 it travelled to 16 cities using a special 18-carriage train that carried 320 people and stage equipment, covering 113 600 km in seven weeks. Four years later requirements had increased to two Pullman passenger trains and 20 baggage cars filled with costumes and props.

During the 1960s the world's leading singers were still accompanying the Metropolitan Opera on its tours; throughout the 1960s and early 1970s tours continued to make money for local sponsors and the company was able to cast stars such as Joan Sutherland and Marilyn Horne as the rival Druid priestesses in *Norma*. By the late 1970s, however, major singers began to prefer European engagements and lucrative recording contracts in the spring. Most sponsors were forced to raise substantial sums to supplement waning box-office receipts. In Detroit in 1961 ticket sales had exceeded the Metropolitan's guarantee by $47 000; by 1981 the shortfall had reached $115 000. Meanwhile, union costs, inflation and jet travel increased touring costs drastically. At the same time, elaborately constructed sets replaced painted drops, further straining the company's resources. In 1984, the touring repertory included *Francesca da Rimini*, *Ernani*, *Rinaldo* and *Peter Grimes*, which was tentatively received in the cities visited. In 1985 the company's guarantee, which had been $608 000 in 1981, rose to $856 000, for a season that offered only one star, the baritone Sherrill Milnes as Simon Boccanegra. By then, regional opera companies routinely offered the better casts: in 1985 the Washington Opera gave 72 performances of 16 operas including a new Jean-Pierre Ponnelle production of *Così fan tutte* shared with the Paris Opéra; likewise the Dallas Opera was offering Alfredo Kraus in *Traviata* and finishing the construction of its own *Ring* cycle. In 1986 only four sponsoring agencies in Atlanta, Minneapolis, Cleveland and Boston had not baulked at a guarantee that had increased to $915 000. The Metropolitan Opera's president, Bruce Crawford, announced the cessation of touring as an annual ritual after 1986, citing television productions as a more efficient method of reaching the national public and regional opera as an alternative for local audiences. The final tour performance on 31 May 1986, in Minneapolis, was *La traviata* with Barbara Daniels and Dennis O'Neill.

NANCY MALITZ

Metropolitan Opera Guild. Organization founded in 1935 to support the Metropolitan Opera through educational and publishing programmes; *see* NEW YORK, §2.

Metropolitan Opera House. The most important New York opera house, built in 1883; a new house opened at Lincoln Center for the Performing Arts in 1966. *See* NEW YORK, §2.

Metternich, Josef (*b* Hermühlheim, nr Cologne, 2 June 1915). German baritone. He studied in Cologne and Berlin, and sang with the Cologne and Bonn choruses. His solo début was in 1941 in *Lohengrin* with the Berlin Städtische Oper, to which he returned in 1945 as Tonio (*Pagliacci*), winning esteem in the Italian as well as the German repertory. He made his Covent Garden début in 1951 as the Dutchman and also sang at La Scala and the Vienna Staatsoper; his first appearance at the Metropolitan Opera was in 1953 as Don Carlo (*La forza del destino*), and he returned in both Italian and German roles. In 1954 he became a member of the Staatsoper in Munich, where he created Johannes Kepler in Hindemith's *Die Harmonie der Welt* (1957) and later sang Kothner (*Die Meistersinger*) under Keilberth at the reopening of the rebuilt Nationaltheater (1963). He was a powerful and reliable if not always very imaginative singer. His recordings include John the Baptist under Moralt (1952) and Mandryka under Matačić with Schwarzkopf (1955). NOËL GOODWIN

Metz. Town in Lorraine, eastern France, on the Moselle river. The present Théâtre de Metz, adjoining the governor's palace (today the Préfecture) on the Ile de Saulcy, was built between 1738 and 1751 by Jacques Oger to replace the Jeu de Paume theatre which had fallen into disrepair. It was inaugurated in February 1752 with a public ball before the interior decoration had been completed and, six days later, with a performance of Rousseau's *Le devin du village*. Run by impresarios in the 18th and 19th centuries, it is the oldest opera house still active in France. The seating capacity was once as high as 1380; now it is 750, in stalls and three galleries. A company was formed during the German occupation of Alsace-Lorraine from 1870 to 1918, but since 1950 the house has been a municipal theatre. The season runs from October to June, with productions of five operas and five operettas each given three or four performances (Friday evenings for opera, Saturday evenings for operetta, and Sunday matinées, besides midweek performances).

L. J. Brote: 'A propos du répertoire lyrique des théâtres français', *Le théâtre lyrique français 1945–1985*, ed. D. Pistone (Paris, 1987), 51–73 CHARLES PITT

Metzger(-Lattermann), Ottilie (*b* Frankfurt, 15 July 1878; *d* Auschwitz, ?Feb 1943). German contralto. She was a pupil of Selma Nicklass-Kempner in Berlin, and made her début at Halle in 1898. After three years at Cologne she became the leading contralto at the Hamburg Opera, and when Caruso appeared as guest artist she sang with him in *Carmen* and *Aida*. In 1901 she appeared for the first time at Bayreuth, where she was heard last in 1912, her great roles being Erda and Waltraute in *Götterdämmerung*. She also sang at Hamburg in the premières of S. Wagner's *Bruder Lustig* (1905), Blech's *Versiegelt* (1908) and d'Albert's *Izegl*

(1909). From 1916 to 1921 she sang with the Dresden Staatsoper. Though her career centred on Germany, she was also heard in Vienna, St Petersburg and New York, where she sang under Blech with the German Opera Company which toured the USA in 1922 and 1923. At Covent Garden she made her début in 1902, singing in *Die Meistersinger*, *Siegfried* and *Tristan*. In 1910 she appeared as Clytemnestra in *Elektra* and later that year as the first London Herodias in *Salome*; she also made a strong impression as Carmen. Following her second marriage, to the bass-baritone Theodor Lattermann, she used the composite name of Metzger-Lattermann and developed a distinguished career as a concert singer, her accompanists including Richard Strauss and Pfitzner. She later taught in Berlin until the Nazis came to power when, as she was Jewish, she took refuge in Brussels, only to be deported to Auschwitz in 1942. Her recordings, made between 1904 and 1910, show a strong, deep tone, ideally suited to Erda's scene in *Siegfried*.

J. B. STEANE

Meulemans, Arthur (*b* Aarschot, 19 May 1884; *d* Etterbeek, Brussels, 29 June 1966). Belgian composer. He studied at the Lemmens Institute, Mechelen (1900–06), and was a professor there until 1914. From 1916 to 1930 he was director of the organ and song school at Hasselt; he was then made conductor, and later director, of Belgian radio. He left this position in 1942 to devote his time to composition; he received numerous awards for his works. Although his most important compositions are for orchestra, his output included the operas *Vikings* (composed 1919), *Adriaen Brouwer* (1926) and *Egmont* (1944), and smaller instrumental and vocal works.

all first performed in Antwerp, Koninklijke Vlaamse Opera
Vikings, 1919 (tragédie lyrique, 3 tableaux, E. Buskens), 27 Nov 1937
Adriaen Brouwer, 1926 (3, F. de Witt-Huberts), 26 Nov 1947
Egmont, 1944 (drame lyrique, 3, J. van Rooy), 24 May 1960

CORNEEL MERTENS

Mexico. Mexico's first opera, *La Partenope*, was sung at the viceregal palace in Mexico City on 1 May (the name-day of Philip V) 1711. The music was by a native of Mexico City, Manuel de Zumaya, but the libretto (which was printed in bilingual form and testifies to the patronage of Fernando de Alencastre Noroña y Silva, the Mexican viceroy) was by the Neapolitan Silvio Stampiglia and the opera was sung in Italian. However, as soon as operas and other sung stage pieces began to be given for a paying public at the Coliseo Nuevo (inaugurated on 23 December 1753), Spanish was their language.

During the 19th century Italian opera dominated the Mexican musical scene. At first the genres cultivated were of Spanish origin – zarzuela, *tonadilla escénica*, *sainete* – and they were sung in Spanish. Cimarosa's *Il fanatico burlato* was given as a 'zarzuela bufa' under the title *El filósofo burlado* on 25 October 1805 (*Diario de México*, i, 100) and Paisiello's *Il barbiere di Siviglia* as *El barbero de Sevilla* on 4 and 9 November 1806. Unaware of local bias, Manuel García began his first Mexico City season on 29 June 1827 with Rossini's *Il barbiere* sung in Italian. To teach him a lesson a large part of the audience, who had already heard it done in Spanish by Andrés Castillo's company in 1823, walked out. (Rossini's *Tancredi*, *La gazza ladra* and *Otello* had also won over the Mexican public sung in Spanish.) As a result García had to capitulate with numerous translations, to the disgust of the Italians accompanying him from New York City.

Later companies singing in Italian fared better. Nonetheless, to coax local sympathies the touring Italian company headed by Eufrasia Borghese found it expedient to give a native of Mexico City, María de Jesús Zepeda y Cossío, leading roles in *Lucrezia Borgia*, *Beatrice di Tenda* and *La sonnambula* in 1844. In 1852 the Stefanone-Maretzek company presented the Mexican contralto Eufrasia Amat as Arsace in *Semiramide*. Eclipsing the success of all previous Mexican divas, Angela Peralta returned home after European triumphs to star in three operas composed by Mexicans – Melesio Morales's *Ildegonda* (1865) and Gino Corsini (1877) and Aniceto Ortega's *Guatimotzín* (1871) – and to barnstorm the entire republic with her own company of about 80 (most of them Italian). At Guadalajara on 13 September 1866 she inaugurated the Teatro Alarcón (later renamed the Degollado) with *Lucia*. San Miguel Allende named a newly built theatre after her which she inaugurated on 11 May 1873 by appearing in *Rigoletto*. At Veracruz she sang opera excerpts when scenery was lacking and at La Paz, Baja California, she sang in an enclosed sand-pit. She appeared in her last *Trovatore* at Mazatlán on 23 August 1883 and died (as did nearly all the members of her company) of yellow fever a week later.

Among the better-known Mexican opera composers of the 19th century, in addition to Morales and Ortega, were Luis Baca (1826–55) and Cenobio Paniagua y Vasques. Ortega's *Guatimotzín* is considered the first serious attempt to incorporate some elements of indigenous music within the framework of prevailing Italian models, but it did not give rise to any strong native tradition in opera. 20th-century Mexican composers have concentrated their efforts much more on concert music, and the most influential of them, Carlos Chávez, composed only one opera, *Panfilo and Lauretta* (1957, New York). The fervour for Italian opera, too, could not outlast the Porfirian epoch, and after 1911 no Italian companies visited Mexico for a decade. Instead, a local composer, Arnulfo Miramontes, saw his *Anahuac* given its première on 15 June 1918 at Guadalajara's Teatro Degollado with Mexican singers in the leading roles. Italians returned to Guadalajara with repertory works in short seasons in 1920–21, and in subsequent years Monterrey, Puebla and Veracruz were visited by second-rate troupes until cinema drove out all touring companies.

While Mexican composers since then have shown little interest in opera, a number of Mexican singers have established international reputations. Placido Domingo, who moved to Mexico from Madrid at the age of nine, sang in *Madama Butterfly* with Montserrat Caballé at Puebla in 1965 and appeared the following year in *Lucia* and *Il barbiere di Siviglia* at Guadalajara. Most of Mexico's leading native opera singers have been women: Fanny Anitua, María Romero, Irma González and Oralia Dominguez. Like Peralta, they consolidated their operatic reputations outside Mexico.

For further information on operatic life in the country's principal centre see MEXICO CITY.

*

E. Olavarría y Ferrari: *Reseña histórica del teatro en México, 1538–1911* (Mexico City, 1895, 3/1961)
A. de María y Campos: *Angela Peralta, el ruiseñor mexicano* (Mexico City, 1944)

R. Stevenson: *Music in Mexico: a Historical Survey* (New York, 1952)

C. Díaz Du-Pond: *Cincuenta años de ópera en México: testimonio operístico* (Mexico City, 1978)

B. Mora: *Notas para la historia del teatro en Jalisco* (Guadalajara, 1985)
ROBERT STEVENSON

Mexico City. Capital of Mexico. Founded in 1325 as Tenochtitlán, capital of the Aztecs, it became known as Ciudad de México following its conquest by the Spanish in the 16th century. The first full opera to be performed there, on Philip V's name-day, 1 May 1711, was also the first to be composed in North America, *La Partenope*. Based on a libretto by Silvio Stampiglia (later used in modified form by Handel), it was set by Manuel de Zumaya (*c*1678–1755), a native of Mexico City, and given in the viceregal palace at the expense of Fernando de Alencastre Noroña y Silva, Duke of Linares. The bilingual libretto was published in 1711, but the music, which may be presumed to have been of the same italianate cast as that of Zumaya's extant solo cantatas of 1715, does not survive.

Public opera performance, at the Coliseo Nuevo (opened 1753; rebuilt in 1806), dates from the first decade of the 19th century. Italian works, such as Cimarosa's *Il fanatico burlato* (called a 'zarzuela bufa' in the *Diario de México* of 25 October 1805) and Paisiello's *Il barbiere di Siviglia* (4 December 1806), were translated into Spanish. There were native works as well: 1805 saw the premières of two stage pieces by the director of music at Puebla Cathedral, Manuel Arenzana (*fl* 1791–1821), the two-act comedy *El extrangero* (25 November), and a week later, *Los dos ribales en amor*. After independence was won, the first opera composed in Mexico and given at the Coliseo (renamed the Teatro Principal in 1826) was Stefano Cristiani's three-act *El solitario*. It was repeated several times following its première on 2 December 1824. In 1826 a company headed by Rita González de Santa Marta performed four Rossini operas in Spanish. Andrés del Castillo of the same company sang the first Mexican *Otello* in 1827 at the remodelled Teatro de los Gallos (opened 21 August 1825 and known alternatively as the Teatro Provisional).

Italian opera sung in the original language had to await the arrival from New York of Manuel García, who on 29 June 1827 sang Almaviva, the part he had created in 1816 in Rossini's *Il barbiere di Siviglia*. But so intense was the resentment of the Mexican public crowded into the Teatro de los Gallos on the Calle de las Moras because the opera was not sung in Spanish, that a large number left in the middle of the first act. García was meanwhile forced by order of the town council to halve ticket prices for the best seats. After the première of his own *Abufar, ossia la famiglia araba* in Italian (13 July 1827), he supervised the translation of the recitatives of several operas including *Don Giovanni* and Rossini's *Semiramide*; he also translated into Spanish the libretto of at least one of his own operas, *L'amante astuto* (15 May 1828). Nevertheless, his troubles in getting the soprano Carolina Pellegrini and others in his company to sing in Spanish (he defended his conviction that operas should be sung in the language in which they are set in a long article published in *El Sol*), together with mounting resentment against *gachupines* (Spanish nationals) following the recent achievement of independence from Spain, caused his departure in November or December 1828.

Later touring companies met less resistance. The troupes of Filippo Galli (1831–7), Anaida Castellan di Giampietro (1841–4), Barilli-Valtellina (1850) and Max Maretzek (1852) were able to perform in Mexico City in Italian. In 1854 two companies competed with each other, those of Pedro Carvajal and of the French immigrant René Masson; the latter brought Henriette Sontag (who died there on 17 June), and Giovanni Bottesini as orchestra director. Throughout the century members of the opera orchestras were mostly Mexico City residents.

As a rule the native Mexicans who succeeded in having their operas mounted at Mexico City before 1900 were forced to set Italian librettos and to have them sung by touring companies. Cenobio Paniagua's *Catalina di Guisa*, the première of which was given on 29 September 1859 by members of the Amilcare Roncari Company, was both the first and the most successful of its type (its libretto was by Felice Romani). Dedicated to the Mexican president Miguel Miramón (shot in 1867 beside the Emperor Maximilian), it concerned a 16th-century rivalry that to the audience mirrored the contemporary struggle between Juárez and Miramón's partisans. It had a further four performances in the Teatro Nacional and was revived two years later during another visit to the capital by Maretzek's troupe.

As a result of the triumph of his first opera, Paniagua succeeded in organizing the first Mexican opera company. Active in 1862, 1863 and the first part of 1864, the Compañía Mexicana presented the première of his own second opera *Pietro d'Abano* on 3 May 1863 and also gave the premières of works by two other Mexican composers: *Clotilde di Coscenza* by Octaviano Valle (19 July 1863) and *Agorante rè della Nubia* by Miguel Meneses (12 July 1864).

Four operas by Melesio Morales reached the [Gran] Teatro Nacional (known as the [Gran] Teatro Imperial from 1865 to 1867) before 1900: *Giulietta e Romeo* (1863), *Ildegonda* (1865; the first Mexican opera to be performed abroad), *Gino Corsini* (1877) and *Cleopatra* (1891). In contrast to these works, written in Italian, Aniceto Ortega's *Guatimotzín*, first performed at the Nacional on 13 September 1871 with Enrico Tamberlik in the role of Cuauhtémoc, was the sole Mexican opera of its century dealing with a native subject. Even so, Ortega – a devotee of Beethoven – gave the Tarascans in his one-act opera a dance echoing the third movement of Beethoven's Seventh Symphony.

The leading female roles in *Ildegonda*, *Gino Corsini* and *Guatimotzín* were sung by Angela Peralta, the foremost Mexican soprano of the century. After spectacular success in her European débuts, she returned to organize her own company, and with it toured the nation, singing in *Lucia* 166 times and *Sonnambula* 122 times.

Between 1885 and 1910 the Mexican opera-going public heard all the Italian novelties of the epoch: *La Gioconda* (14 October 1885) at the Teatro Principal, *Mefistofele* (14 November 1888), *Falstaff* (7 October 1893), *Manon Lescaut* (11 October 1894) and *La bohème* (21 August 1897) at the Teatro Nacional, *Tosca* (27 July 1901) at the Teatro Arbeu and *Adriana Lecouvreur* (5 May 1903) at the Teatro del Renacimiento. The first taste of Wagner was given there, as almost everywhere else in Latin America, with *Lohengrin*, sung in Italian by the Napoleon Sieni Company on 8 November 1890. *Tannhäuser* came next (20 March 1891), then *Der fliegende Holländer* (3 April) and *Die Walküre* (11 April). *Der Freischütz* was performed on 1 April and *Fidelio* on 22 April. But all these offerings, sung in German by the Emma Juch Company, were tolerated rather than hailed.

Massenet, the most frequently presented French opera composer, influenced Gustavo E. Campa's *Le roi poète* (given at the Teatro Principal by the López-Pizzoni Company on 9 November 1901), despite the fact that its protagonist was a 15th-century Texcoco ruler. Better success had attended the première on 20 January 1900 in the Teatro del Renacimiento of a similar attempt at evoking Mexico's indigenous past in Ricardo Castro's *Atzimba*, on a Tarascan subject (it was revived in August 1935 in the newly opened Palacio de Bellas Artes). The aura of his European triumphs assured Castro's second opera, *La légende de Rudel* (21 June 1906), even heartier applause.

After the downfall in 1911 of Porfirio Díaz, the next decade was one of instability, and saw a marked decline in visits by foreign companies. These were replaced in 1915 by the local Compañía Impulsora de Opera, organized by the singing teacher José Pierson. Although various Mexicans continued writing operas, 20th-century Mexican opera composers failed to achieve the recognition that contemporary Argentinians were receiving at the Teatro Colón.

Maria Callas made her début at Mexico City on 23 May 1950 in *Norma*, singing with the Opera Nacional (founded by Fanny Anitúa in 1943; dissolved in 1953, and restarted in 1955). After two more triumphant seasons she sang her farewell on 1 July 1952 in *Tosca*. During her third season, when she sang in five operas (*I puritani, Traviata, Lucia, Rigoletto, Tosca*), she received the highest amount ever paid to a singer in Mexico. Placido Domingo, who began his career in Mexico, was the piano accompanist for the 1959 Metropolitan Opera Auditions at Mexico City; in 1961 he sang the lover in Menotti's *Amelia al ballo*, Prince Shuysky and the Holy Fool in *Boris Godunov*, Goro in *Butterfly*, and finally Arturo in *Lucia*. That same season he and his future wife, Marta Ornelas, also took the leads in José F. Vásquez's *El último sueño*. In 1971 he and Irma González sang *Andrea Chénier* at Mexico City, and *Carmen* on 29 July 1972. The concert hall of the Palacio de Bellas Artes (cap. 3500, opened 29 September 1934), the city's leading opera venue, has not up to the present housed a stable Mexican opera company.

*

E. de Olavarría y Ferrari: *Reseña histórica del teatro en México 1538–1911* (Mexico City, 1895, 3/1961)

L. Castillo Ledon: 'Los mexicanos autores de óperas', *Anales del Museo nacional de arqueología, historia y etnología*, ii (1910), 313–54

M. Mañón: *Historia del Teatro principal de México 1753–1931* (Mexico City, 1932)

F. Monterde: *Bibliografía del teatro en México* (Mexico City, 1934), 603–13

R. Stevenson: *Music in Mexico: a Historical Survey* (New York, 1952)

C. Díaz Du-Pond: *Cincuenta años de ópera en México, testimonio operístico* (Mexico City, 1978)

C. Díaz Du-Pond, A. López Mancera and others: *Cincuenta años de ópera en el Palacio de bellas artes* (Mexico City, 1986).
ROBERT STEVENSON

Mey, Guy de. *See* DE MEY, GUY.

Meyer, Ernst Hermann (*b* Berlin, 8 Dec 1905; *d* Berlin, 22 Oct 1988). German composer and musicologist. After leaving school he worked in an office for three years, then supported himself with part-time jobs while studying music in Berlin and Heidelberg; his teachers included Eisler and Hindemith. Under the Nazi regime he was obliged to emigrate to England (1933), where he was active as a conductor, a lecturer and a composer, especially of music for documentary films. In 1948 he was invited back to Berlin as professor and director of the institute for musicology at the Humboldt University (he retired in 1970); he was also president of the East German Association of Composers and Musicologists. The leading musician of the German Democratic Republic, he composed prolifically, and was awarded national prizes in 1950, 1952 and 1963.

In 1966, encouraged by a commission from the state opera of East Berlin, Meyer began to consider the subject of what was to be his only opera, *Reiter der Nacht*. Günther Deiche prepared a libretto based on *The Path of Thunder* (1946), a novel by the South African author Peter Abrahams. This powerful, emotional indictment of the South African political system appealed to Meyer, whose interest in liberationist music was furthered by immigrant black South Africans in Berlin, from whom he learned contemporary folksongs of protest. These left their mark on the score, composed between 1970 and 1972 and first performed at the Staatsoper, Berlin, on 17 November 1973. In this work, Meyer created a significant role for the orchestra and strengthened the musical structure with familiar instrumental forms, in the manner of Berg. The final chorus recalls the ending of Meyer's dramatic *Mansfelder Oratorium* of 1950.

*

E. H. Meyer: *Kontraste, Konflikte: Erinnerungen, Gespräche, Kommentare*, ed. D. Brennecke and M. Hansen (Berlin, 1979)
PERCY M. YOUNG

Meyer, Kerstin (Margareta) (*b* Stockholm, 3 April 1928). Swedish mezzo-soprano. She studied in Stockholm, at the Salzburg Mozarteum, and in Siena, Rome and Vienna. She made her début in 1952 as Azucena with the Swedish Royal Opera and became permanently associated with that company. She sang Carmen (1959) at Hamburg, where she also created Mrs Claiborne in Schuller's *The Visitation* (1966), Alice Arden in *Arden Must Die* (1967) and Gertrude in Searle's *Hamlet* (1968). In 1960 she sang Dido (*Les Troyens*) at Covent Garden, later appearing as Octavian and Clytemnestra. After her début as Carolina in the first English-language performances of *Elegy for Young Lovers* (1961), she became a favourite at Glyndebourne; her roles there included Debussy's Geneviève, Monteverdi's Octavia, Clairon (*Capriccio*), Elisabeth in the première of Maw's *The Rising of the Moon* (1970) and Claire in the first British performance of *Der Besuch der alten Dame* (1973), a role she also sang in Stockholm (1976). At Salzburg she created Agave in *The Bassarids* (1966); she also appeared at the Metropolitan (1960–63) and Bayreuth (1962–5). She created Spermando (Amando) in Ligeti's *Le Grand Macabre* (1978, Stockholm). Her voice, though not large, was used with skill; of strikingly handsome presence, she exhibited a remarkable dramatic flair.

HAROLD ROSENTHAL/R

Meyer, Krzysztof (*b* Kraków, 11 Aug 1943). Polish composer. His prolific and eclectic output reflects the influences of his teacher, Penderecki, and particularly of Lutosławski. Shostakovich, the other major influence, is the subject of an authoritative study by Meyer (Kraków, 1973). His book anticipated his completion of

Shostakovich's *Igroki* ('The Gamblers', 1980–81), an outstanding achievement of patchworking (including elements from Shostakovich's Third and Fourth Symphonies) and strict pastiche. Meyer's own opera, *Cyberiade* ('Cyberiada', 1967–70) is a comic science fiction story in three acts after Stanisław Lem. It won the Grand Prix at the Prince Rainier III Competition in 1970 and has since been successful both at home and abroad (the first, partial, performance was on Polish TV in 1970; the full stage première took place in Wuppertal on 11 May 1986). *Cyberiade* is a good example of Meyer's ability to weld together disparate materials into a convincing whole: the plot's thread is provided by Trull, an inventor of three tale-telling machines, and the humorous and grotesque nature of the story is vividly brought to life with Meyer's references to a range of idioms from 12-note textures to jazz. Meyer's next opera *Klonowi bracia* ('The Klonowi Brothers'), in two acts to his own libretto, after the story by Yevgeny Schwartz, received its première on 3 March 1990 at the Grand Theatre, Poznań.

*

M. Jabłoński: 'Opera ludens: Poznańska prapremiera *Klonowych braci* Krzysztofa Meyera', *Ruch muzyczny*, xxxvi/7 (1990), 1, 5

ADRIAN THOMAS

Meyerbeer [Beer], **Giacomo** [Jakob Liebmann Meyer] (*b* Vogelsdorf, nr Berlin, 5 Sept 1791; *d* Paris, 2 May 1864). German composer. He was among the most important writers of French grand opera in the 19th century.

1. Life to 1831. 2. Life, 1831–64. 3. Operatic style and influence.

1. LIFE TO 1831. The Beer family was among the wealthiest in Berlin at the end of the 18th century. Meyer was the eldest son of Juda Herz and Amalia Beer and brother to the playwright Michael Beer; in 1810 the composer conflated his given and family names into Meyerbeer. He received a complete humanistic education from family tutors; music instruction came from the court pianist Franz Lauska, the theorist Abbé Vogler (who also taught Weber) and Carl Zelter (Mendelssohn's teacher). Meyerbeer soon distinguished himself as a pianist, winning public acclaim for a performance of Mozart's Piano Concerto in D minor at the age of 11, a notoriety gained (in an age replete with child prodigies) partly from a certain 'exotic' appeal of his Jewish background. His religion drew considerable (and sometimes adverse) attention throughout his career but, in accordance with a formal commitment to his family, he never contemplated conversion.

After completing numerous piano pieces and a short ballet score, Meyerbeer composed his first large-scale work in 1811, the oratorio *Gott und die Natur* to a libretto by Alois Schroeber. In May of that year it was successfully performed and favourably reviewed in Berlin papers, though Meyerbeer wryly noted to his friend Gottfried Weber that the critics 'do not even know how to praise someone effectively'; he already showed keen awareness of the power of the press and sought to ensure that carefully tapered stories were planted in some newspapers. The positive reception accorded the oratorio encouraged Meyerbeer to turn to the stage. Collaborating with Schroeber again, he composed the biblical opera *Jephtas Gelübde* in 1812. Through connections that Vogler enjoyed with the royal family in Munich, Meyerbeer was able to obtain a production at the court opera later that year. It was evidently well received and the queen presented the composer with a diamond ring after the second performance, but the work did not enter the repertory of the house and was never revived. During the rehearsal period Meyerbeer completed *Wirth und Gast*, a Singspiel to a libretto by the Munich actor Johann Gottfried Wohlbrück. Meyerbeer travelled to Stuttgart for the première (which was unsuccessful) only two weeks after that of *Jephtas Gelübde*. With a plot from *The Thousand and One Nights*, *Wirth und Gast* follows in a long line of Singspiels on a Turkish theme to which Meyerbeer's friend, Carl Maria von Weber, made a contribution two years later with *Abu Hassan*. During an 18-month stay in Vienna in 1813–14 Meyerbeer arranged to have the work mounted at the Kärntnertortheater, but it was again unsuccessful, as it was when Weber took it up in Prague in 1815 and (as *Alimelek*) in Dresden five years later.

Meyerbeer considered first-hand experience with French and Italian operatic culture to be indispensable in the training of a complete dramatic musician. To gain this he spent most of 1815 in Paris, and in the next year moved to Italy. He travelled from centre to centre, paying great attention to the works he saw (particularly those of Rossini, whose popularity was rapidly spreading over the entire peninsula) but even greater attention to the singers. He did not set a libretto until 1817; this was *Romilda e Costanza* by the prolific Gaetano Rossi. Typically for the Italian operatic milieu of this period, and in contradistinction to his later French operas, he composed the work in little over a month, signing a contract with the Teatro Nuovo in Padua on 1 June and overseeing the première on 19 July. *Romilda e Costanza* was moderately successful, receiving subsequent performances in Venice and Munich. Other Italian operatic commissions with Rossi followed: *Semiramide riconosciuta* in 1819 and *Emma di Resburgo*, his first major success, later the same year at the Teatro S Benedetto, Venice. Receiving 74 performances during its first run, *Emma* far eclipsed a new pasticcio by Rossini, *Eduardo e Cristina*, that received its première in Venice around the same time and left little doubt that Meyerbeer was the Italian composer's chief rival. But when the work made its way north of the Alps, German critics, including Weber, remarked grimly that a composer who had promised such originality in his early works now seemed to have been transformed into a slavish imitator of Rossini.

Meyerbeer's next opera, *Margherita d'Anjou*, was even more successful, achieving many performances throughout Europe over the next two decades. *L'esule di Granata* was less well received, but a subsequent commission from La Fenice for Carnival 1824 brought Meyerbeer's greatest Italian triumph, *Il crociato in Egitto*, a work which also bears the distinction of being the last major opera with a castrato role. In most critical quarters Meyerbeer's compositional style was now seen to have, in some respects, transcended that of Rossini. With reference to *Il crociato* an English observer noted in the preface to the first English edition of the libretto:

Meyerbeer is the one who most happily combines the easy flowing and expressive melodies of Italy with the severer beauties, the grander accompaniments of the German school; to which I would add that he unites the still greater merit of painting the passions with perfect truth, and of producing a pure instrumentation entirely in unison with the character of the melody which it is made to invigorate and enforce. It is in this department of the art that the modern Italian composers, are so defective.

Meyerbeer's much coveted entrée into the Parisian operatic world occurred when he was invited in 1825 to supervise a production of *Il crociato* at the Théâtre Italien; the work was greeted with critical acclaim in what the composer, despite a few misgivings, held to be an improved version overall. The following year he married his cousin Minna Mosson, a happy union that produced three children who lived beyond infancy, Blanka, Caecilie and Cornelie. The stability of his family at least spared him later attacks on the moral front by a frequently hostile press and perhaps assisted his rise to favour in the eyes of French officialdom, inasmuch as the order of his own life harmonized with works that were taken as models of operatic order.

Meyerbeer befriended the director of the Opéra-Comique, Guilbert de Pixérécourt, and turned to that house early in 1827 with his first French opera project, *Robert le diable* to a libretto by Scribe and Delavigne. The diabolical subject matter and medieval setting were timely: Goethe's *Faust* had been translated for the first time into French in the 1820s and popularized adaptations of it, as well as other *diableries*, multiplied on French boulevard stages later in the decade; the gothic novel imported from England was finding much favour with French readers; and the scene entitled 'Holyrood Chapel by Moonlight' at Jacques Daguerre's newly opened diorama had great appeal and may have influenced the cloister set in the opera. Pixérécourt relinquished the directorship of the Opéra-Comique and Meyerbeer looked elsewhere for a production. The success of Auber's *La muette de Portici*, with a lavish *mise-en-scène* featuring a volcanic eruption, may have been instrumental in steering Meyerbeer towards the Opéra and its impressive resources. At the end of 1829 he signed a contract with Emile Lubbert, the director of the house. The July Revolution of 1830 brought a change in the directorship and Lubbert's successor, Louis Véron, took up the work. *Robert le diable* proved to be the repertorial mainstay of his administration and a reason why he was one of the few Opéra directors in this period to turn a profit. The voice of the critic F.-J. Fétis was prominent in the dithyrambic reception accorded the work: 'The score of *Robert le diable* is not only the masterpiece of M. Meyerbeer but it is also a remarkable document in the history of art'. Fétis and others were particularly impressed by the great musical and scenic variety in the production. A host of arrangements based on the opera, including a duo for piano and cello by Chopin, soon flowed from the pens of composers eager to capitalize on Meyerbeer's success.

2. LIFE, 1831–64. Much of Meyerbeer's time in the following months was spent supervising productions of *Robert* at various centres, but within a year of the première he embarked upon a new operatic project, *La Saint Barthélemy*, which became *Les Huguenots*. An agreement with Véron was signed in October 1832 stipulating delivery of the entire score by December of the following year, with a penalty of 30 000F to be levied for any violation of the contract. The death of Meyerbeer's brother Michael in March 1833, a subsequent illness of his wife and numerous other family matters prevented completion of the score by the required date. Véron proceeded to seek payment of the penalty, as well as to ensure that Meyerbeer would deliver the work to the Opéra. Offended by Véron's rapacity, the composer angrily delivered the sum while telling the director at the same time that the score would

never be performed at his house; Meyerbeer even considered adapting the work for the Opéra-Comique, which he regarded as inferior to the Opéra. It soon became clear that the dispute was advantageous to neither party and, following a trip to Italy in summer 1834 during which he made substantial changes to *Les Huguenots*, Meyerbeer agreed to complete the score for the Opéra by April 1835 in return for repayment of the 30 000F penalty. The rehearsal period brought the usual upheavals; objections from the censor about the political reverberations of some scenes and from the singers about the moral implications of others caused some revision. Nonetheless, the première on 29 February 1836 was an even greater triumph than that of *Robert*. The bass Nicolas Levasseur, in particular, drew attention for his portrayal of the Protestant die-hard Marcel; Meyerbeer had befriended Levasseur many years before and shortly before the first performance of *Les Huguenots* dedicated two of his most famous *mélodies*, *Le moine* and *Rachel à Nephtali*, to him.

New operatic projects followed closely on the heels of the *Les Huguenots* première: *Cinq-Mars* with the librettist Saint-Georges, and *Le prophète* and *L'Africaine* with Scribe. The first opera was soon abandoned and *L'Africaine* was temporarily set aside in 1838 after Meyerbeer had written one act. He went on to compose most of *Le prophète* during the next three years, but his dissatisfaction with the cast at the Opéra and mistrust of the new director, Léon Pillet, fuelled by his generally suspicious nature, prevented the opera from moving quickly to rehearsal. In the meantime *Les Huguenots* traversed the length and breadth of Europe, though it was given with an altered setting and plot where local censors felt that the libretto might exacerbate religious tensions or offend church authorities. In Meyerbeer's native Berlin, where his music had not received the enthusiastic response it had elsewhere, censors delayed a production of the opera until 1842. He had enough supporters, however, to be named Prussian Generalmusikdirektor when Gasparo Spontini was dismissed from the post that year. Meyerbeer, previously in the habit of regularly displacing himself either for professional commitments or for reasons of his own or his wife's health, settled in Berlin and mixed freely with the local aristocracy. As part of his responsibilities he directed the court orchestra, organized concerts and wrote occasional pieces. These included a masque, *Das Hoffest von Ferrara*, to words by Ernst Raupach (after Tasso), produced at a masked ball on 28 February 1843, and the Singspiel *Ein Feldlager in Schlesien*, a patriotic work written for the reopening of the court opera in 1844 following a fire. At the request of King Friedrich Wilhelm, Meyerbeer also composed incidental music to *Struensee*, a play by his brother Michael Beer which was revived posthumously in 1846.

Casting problems surrounding a production of *Le prophète* were not resolved until the directorship of the Opéra passed from Pillet to Roqueplan and Duponchel in 1847. Meyerbeer could afford to be excessively cautious, but he was also anxious to score a new triumph in the light of Verdi's recent rise to prominence. The desired success was achieved during the first run of *Le prophète* in 1849, with Pauline Viardot and Gustave Roger in the principal roles. A particular sensation was the ballet in which the effect of ice skating was simulated by equipping the dancers with roller-skates. The political turbulence in the previous year gave the libretto a relevance not imagined when it was written more than a decade before: some critics read analogies to recent events into the work, arguing that Anabaptist revolt in the opera (like 'communist' insurgency during the June days) demonstrated that insurrection around demagogues could result only in the complete destruction of social and moral order.

With *Le prophète* launched on its lucrative career, Meyerbeer turned his attention to *L'Africaine*, entirely recasting that work from a draft he had completed several years before. Reacting to what he perceived to be hostility towards him in circles connected to the Opéra, he abandoned *L'Africaine* again in 1853 and took up with the Opéra-Comique. That house had clamoured for a French adaptation of *Ein Feldlager* since 1846 but, given the nationalistic tone of the libretto, something more than a mere adaptation was required: Scribe rewrote the book entirely into *L'étoile du Nord* and Meyerbeer composed a good deal of new music. In a production of unusual lavishness for that house, the work was given its première on 16 February 1854, the composer having characteristically brought success 'to the boil six months before the event in the cauldrons of the press' (in the words of Alexandre Dumas). Meyerbeer then briefly considered returning to the Opéra with a setting of a Scribe libretto entitled *Judith* but, much to the annoyance of his customary librettist, he ultimately chose to make another appearance at the Opéra-Comique in 1859 with *Le pardon de Ploërmel* (later more commonly known as *Dinorah*), a libretto by Jules Barbier and Michel Carré. That *L'Africaine* continued to lie somnolent drew perennial barbs from the press. Meyerbeer finally took the work up in 1860 with a view to an imminent production. The essentials of the score were completed by November 1863, but as rehearsals began the composer was struck with a sudden illness and died. With great publicity his body was transported to Berlin and interred in the Jewish cemetery there. Fétis was placed in charge of the remaining rehearsals of *L'Africaine* and a brilliant première, attended by many Second Empire notables, took place on 28 April 1865. Though the reception in the press was more divided than it had been for any of Meyerbeer's earlier grand operas, many concurred with the critic G. Spada that the work 'bears the stamp of that proud genius who has left such a bright mark on contemporary musical art'.

3. OPERATIC STYLE AND INFLUENCE. The partnership of Meyerbeer and Scribe contributed substantially to the definition of French grand opera as a genre. One of the principal characteristics of grand opera is that, in the words of Véron, 'it brings into play great passions of the human heart and powerful historical forces'. The composer's task involved not only the creation of numbers with pomp, ritual, *couleur locale* and large chorus to project the historical dimension, and intimate arias and duets for the more personal aspects, but also the inclusion of *divertissements* in the form of incidental vocal pieces, ballet and scenic coups. The tone of the discourse, both musical and verbal, extends from high seriousness to comedy. In short, Meyerbeerian grand opera is extraordinarily variegated; the genre has not lost its appeal on that level even today, but it is no longer possible to subscribe to the critical position of the 19th century that saw such variety as the essence of works embracing a wide spectrum of human existence.

Part of the problem for today's listener is that the grand operas have a distinctly mannered quality, whereby particular melodic, harmonic and instrumental effects often draw attention to themselves for their own sake rather than serving a higher dramatic end called for by the historical or personal premise of the libretto. For example, Meyerbeer's contrapuntal combination of music first exposed separately in the third act of *Les Huguenots* seems little more than an exhibition of compositional virtuosity at the service of scenic spectacle; there can be little complaint about this on the level of *divertissement* but, given that the two opposing factions in the opera are involved, the result is a certain trivialization of the historical framework. Moreover, character development is not well integrated into the whole in Meyerbeer's works; it competes with too many other parameters to yield an operatic experience that touches upon universality. Meyerbeer rarely brings his characters to truly intense lyricism, and at crucial dramatic points the expression is wont to fall flat. To cite one instance: after Berthe learns of the death of John of Leyden in her duet with Fidès in Act 4 of *Le prophète*, the section 'Dernier espoir, lueur dernière' leaves more the impression of an exercise in varied vocal articulations and coloratura than an outpouring of pathos. Meyerbeer's melodies are often shortwinded because he failed to connect two-bar building blocks into phrases that have direction on a higher level.

On the other side of the critical ledger, however, Meyerbeer sometimes does use coloratura to potent dramatic effect, for example in Fidès's heroic invocation for divine intervention, 'Comme un éclair'. The combination of the martial and the heroic is usually presented with great verve and supplies some truly memorable moments, as in Robert le diable's 'Des chevaliers de ma patrie' or Vasco da Gama's 'Je viens à vous' in Act 3 of *L'Africaine*. Meyerbeer was also especially successful in bringing the chorus to life through extensive use of chorus singers in small solo parts, making it into an active participant in, instead of a backdrop to, the action. The strongest scenes in Meyerbeerian grand opera occur when personal drama unfolds against a canvas of mass ritual, as in the encounter between Robert and Bertram in Act 5 of *Robert*, between Fidès and John in Act 4 of *Le prophète* or between Sélika and Vasco da Gama in Act 4 of *L'Africaine*.

Meyerbeer's notes and correspondence bear ample witness to a concern for characterization. Like German Romantic opera composers, he associated specific instrumental colours with certain figures – Bertram in *Robert le diable* and Marcel in *Les Huguenots* for example – and he was also particularly successful at translating *buffo* character traits as well as the grotesque and macabre. Meyerbeer's skill as an orchestrator has been widely acknowledged and he was responsible for many ingenious and innovative effects, among them the creation of dark timbres through the subdivision of low strings, the presentation of a complete melody by four timpani, the use of the organ and scoring for evocative instrumental combinations such as piccolo, bassoons, double basses, bass drum and cymbal in Marcel's 'Chanson huguenote' or english horn and tenor voice in Raoul's *cavatine*, 'Tu l'as dit', in *Les Huguenots*.

It has frequently been noted that Meyerbeer effected a conflation of Italian and French operatic practices in his grand operas. Cross-fertilization between these two national traditions was nothing new, and Meyerbeer's immediate predecessors in this were Auber and Rossini.

The nature of the conflation was not always the same. Unlike Rossini in *Guillaume Tell*, for example, Meyerbeer did not duplicate Cherubini's monumental choral style achieved through slow harmonic rhythm and carefully planned crescendos. Yet in another respect he adhered more closely to indigenous French practice than did Rossini in his French operas, by supplying a large amount of measured music between set pieces instead of long stretches of unmeasured declamation. Meyerbeer also used thematic reminiscence to a modest degree in his grand operas, a practice ultimately derived from the *opéra comique* repertory. Thematic recall sometimes enhances continuity across a single act: in Act 3 of *Robert*, for example, material from the demons' chorus is brought back between the strophes of Alice's *couplets* and in the subsequent scene, where the *couplets* are also recalled. Continuity is, on occasion, further enhanced by the avoidance of closure at the end of set pieces, although this is never carried on across an entire act. For many arias, duets and finales Meyerbeer appropriated from Italy multipartite forms containing a slow section and a *cabalette* or *strette* separated by a more open-ended transition (the original shapes are sometimes obscured by cuts). He achieved structural enlargement of the prototype by expanding individual sections into ternary form and generally avoided commonplaces of the Italian repertory, such as extended passages of parallel singing or the long crescendo over a dominant preparation for the *cabalette* or *strette*. Strophic pieces appear more often than in the Italian repertory, particularly in his *opéras comiques* and *Robert* (initially conceived as an *opéra comique*), and Meyerbeer was often structurally inventive within the rigid constraints of the form, changing the position of the refrain from the end to the beginning or supplying new music for a portion of the second strophe. Meyerbeer remained conservative in his set pieces inasmuch as those that are brought to a complete textural close are also tonally closed. The apogee of his musical influence was the 1830s and 40s, subsequent composers such as Verdi and Wagner adapting some of the premises of grand opera to a much richer musico-dramatic conception.

See also AFRICAINE, L'; CROCIATO IN EGITTO, IL; DINORAH; ETOILE DU NORD, L'; FELDLAGER IN SCHLESIEN, EIN; HUGUENOTS, LES; PROPHÈTE, LE; and ROBERT LE DIABLE.

title	genre, acts	libretto	first performance	sources and remarks
Jephtas Gelübde	3	A. Schraeber	Munich, Hof, 23 Dec 1812	*GB-Lbl*, duet (Munich, ?1812)
Wirth und Gast, oder Aus Scherz Ernst	Lustspiel, 2	J. G. Wohlbrück	Stuttgart, 6 Jan 1813	as Die beyden Kalifen, 1814; as Alimelek, 1820, arr. pf 4 hands (Milan, n.d.)
Das Brandenburger Tor	Spl	E. Veith	unperf.	comp. for Berlin, 1814
Romilda e Costanza	melodramma semiserio, 2	G. Rossi	Padua, Nuovo, 19 July 1817	*I-Bc, Fc, Mr*, excerpts (Milan, n.d.)
Semiramide riconosciuta	dramma per musica, 2	Rossi, after P. Metastasio	Turin, Regio, March 1819	excerpts pubd
Emma di Resburgo	melodramma eroico, 2	Rossi	Venice, S Benedetto, 26 June 1819	as Emma di Leicester, 1820; *Fc, Mr*, vs (Berlin, ?1820)
Margherita d'Anjou	melodramma semiserio, 2	F. Romani, after R. C. G. de Pixérécourt	Milan, Scala, 14 Nov 1820	rev. Paris, 1826; *Mr*, vs (Paris, 1826)
L'Almanzore		Rossi	unperf.	intended for Rome, Argentina, carn. 1821, probably unfinished
L'esule di Granata	melodramma serio, 2	Romani	Milan, Scala, 12 March 1821	*Mr*, excerpts (Milan, n.d.)
Il crociato in Egitto	melodramma eroico, 2	Rossi	Venice, Fenice, 7 March 1824	rev. Paris, 1825; *GB-Lbl, I-Bc, Mr*, (VtlR1979: ERO, xviii); *US-Bp, Cu, Wc*, vs (Milan, 1824; Bonn and Cologne; Paris, 1826)
Robert le diable	grand opéra, 5	E. Scribe and G. Delavigne	Paris, Opéra, 21 Nov 1831	*PL-Kj**; (Paris, 1831/R1980: ERO, xix); scene and prayer added for Mario's début, 1839; rondo for Mme Alboni added to It. version
Les Huguenots	grand opéra, 5	Scribe and E. Deschamps	Paris, Opéra, 29 Feb 1836	*Kj**; (Paris, 1836/R1980: ERO, xx)
Ein Feldlager in Schlesien	Spl, 3	Scribe, trans. L. Rellstab and C. Birch-Pfeiffer	Berlin, Hof, 7 Dec 1844	as Vielka, 1847
Le prophète	grand opéra, 5	Scribe	Paris, Opéra, 16 April 1849	begun 1836; *Kj**; (Paris, 1849/R1978: ERO, xxi); ov., Berthe's cavatina and barcarolle added c1850
L'étoile du nord	oc, 3	Scribe, partly after his ballet La cantinière	Paris, OC (Favart), 16 Feb 1854	based on the music of Ein Feldlager in Schlesien (Paris, ?1854/R1980: ERO, xxii)
Dinorah, oder die Wallfahrt nach Ploërmel	oc, 3	J. Barbier and M. Carré, after Carré: Les chercheurs de trésor	Paris, OC (Favart), 4 April 1859	first per. as Le pardon de Ploërmel; also known as Le chercheur du trésor (Paris, ?1859/R1981: ERO, xxiii)
L'Africaine	grand opéra, 5	Scribe, F. J. Fétis and others	Paris, Opéra, 28 April 1865	also known as Vasco da Gama; begun 1837, final revisions by Fétis; *Kj**; (Paris, 1865/R1980: ERO, xxiv); 22 pieces and frags. not used in final version, ed. Fétis in vs (Paris, 1865)

Opera frags.: Abu Hassan, comp. 1810, Darmstadt, unperf.; Der Admiral, oder Der verlorene Prozess, comp. 1811, Darmstadt, unperf.; Le bachelier de Salamanque, ?1815, inc.; Ines de Castro 1824 (Rossi), inc.; Malek Adel 1824 (Rossi), inc.; La nymphe de Danube, 1826 (T. Sauvage), inc.; Le portefaix, 1831 (Scribe), inc.; Les brigands (A. Dumas *père*), planned 1832, not begun; Cinq mars, Dec 1837 (J.-H. Vernoy de Saint-Georges and E. de Planard, after A. de Vigny), inc.; Noëma, ou Le repentir [L'ange au exil] (Scribe and Saint-Georges), contract signed 15 Jan 1846, inc.; Judith, 1854 (Scribe), inc.

Other dramatic works: Der Fischer und das Milchmädchen, oder Viel Lärm um einen Kuss [Le passage de la rivière, ou La femme jalouse; Le pêcheur et la laitière] (divertissement, 1, E. Lauchery), Berlin, Königliches Opernhaus, 26 March 1810; Gli amori di Teolinda [Thecelindens Liebschaften] (monodrama, Rossi), Verona, 1816, *A-Wgm*

GENERAL

E. de Mirecourt: *Meyerbeer* (Paris, 1854)

A. Pougin: *Meyerbeer: notes biographiques* (Paris, 1864)

H. Blaze de Bury: *Meyerbeer et son temps* (Paris, 1865)

H. Mendel: *Giacomo Meyerbeer* (Berlin, 1868)

J. Schucht: *Meyerbeers Leben und Bildungsgang* (Leipzig, 1869)

A. Kohut: *Meyerbeer* (Leipzig, 1890)

E. Destranges: *L'oeuvre théâtral de Meyerbeer* (Paris, 1893)

J. Weber: *Meyerbeer* (Paris, 1898)

J. Combarieu: 'Meyerbeer', *RHCM*, iv (1904), 434

H. de Curzon: *Meyerbeer* (Paris, 1910)

H. Eymieu: *L'oeuvre de Meyerbeer* (Paris, 1910)

L. Dauriac: *Meyerbeer* (Paris, 1913, 2/1930)

G. R. Kruse: 'Meyerbeers Jugendopern', *ZMw*, i (1918–19), 399–413

H. Strelitzer: *Meyerbeers deutsche Jugendopern* (diss., U. of Münster, 1920)

R. Haudek: *Scribes Operntexte für Meyerbeer: eine Quellenmuntersuchung* (diss., U. of Vienna, 1928)

H. Abert: 'Giacomo Meyerbeer', *Gesammelte Schriften und Vorträge*, ed. F. Blume (Halle, 1929), 397–420

J. Kapp: *Giacomo Meyerbeer* (Berlin, 8/1932)

H. Becker, ed.: *Giacomo Meyerbeer: Briefwechsel und Tagebücher* (Berlin, 1960–) [with additional bibliography in each vol.]

J. W. Klein: 'Giacomo Meyerbeer (1791–1864)', *MR*, xxv (1964), 142–8

S. Döhring: *Formgeschichte der Opernarie* (diss., U. of Marburg, 1969)

H. Becker: 'Giacomo Meyerbeers Mitarbeit an den Libretti seiner Opern', *GfMKB, Bonn 1970*, 155–62

C. Frese: *Dramaturgie der grossen Opern Giacomo Meyerbeers* (Berlin, 1970)

J. L. Thomson: *Meyerbeer and his Contemporaries* (diss., Columbia U., 1972)

——: 'Giacomo Meyerbeer: the Jew and his Relationship with Richard Wagner', *Musica judaica*, i (1975–6), 55–87

H. Becker: 'Die Couleur locale als Stilkategorie der Oper', *Die Couleur locale in der Oper des 19. Jahrhunderts*, ed. H. Becker (Regensburg, 1976), 23–45

C. Dahlhaus: 'Motive der Meyerbeerkritik', *Jb des Staatlichen Instituts für Musikforschung* (1978), 35–42

P. A. Bloom: 'Friends and Admirers: Meyerbeer and Fétis', *RBM*, xxxii–xxxiii (1978–9), 174–87

K. Pendle: *Eugène Scribe and French Opera of the 19th Century* (Ann Arbor, 1979)

H. Becker: *Giacomo Meyerbeer in Selbstzeugnissen und Bilddokumenten* (Reinbek, 1980)

C. Chabot: 'Ballet in the Operas of Eugène Scribe: an Apology for the Presence of Dance in Opera', *SMA*, v (1980), 7–14

J. Fulcher: 'Meyerbeer and the Music of Society', *MQ*, lxvii (1981), 213–29

J. Budden: 'Verdi and Meyerbeer in Relation to "Les vêpres siciliennes"', *Studi verdiani*, i (1982), 11–20

S. Döhring: 'Die Autographen der vier Hauptopern Meyerbeers: ein erster Quellenbericht', *AMf*, xxxix (1982), 32–63

H. Becker: 'Zwischen Oper und Drama: zu Meyerbeers Konzeption der dramatischen Szene', *Wagnerliteratur und Wagnerforschung: Bericht über das Wagner-Symposium: Munich 1983*, 86–94

S. Döhring: 'Giacomo Meyerbeer: Grand Opera als Ideendrama', *Lendemains*, viii/31–2 (1983), 11–22

——: 'Meyerbeers Konzeption der historischen Oper und Wagner Musikdrama', *Wagnerliteratur und Wagnerforschung: Bericht über das Wagner-Symposium: Munich 1983*, 95–100

H. Becker: 'Setkani v Boulogne-sur-mer: Wagner a Meyerbeer' [Encounter in Boulogne-sur-Mer: Wagner and Meyerbeer], *HV*, xxi (1984), 293–302

J. Ludvova: 'Meyerbeer na prazsken nemeckem jevisti 1815–1935'

[Meyerbeer on the German Stage in Prague, 1815–1935], ibid, 365–74

M. Ottlova and M. Posbisil: 'Smetanüv Meyerbeer' [Smetana's Meyerbeer], ibid, 355–64

B. Srba: 'Scenicke vypravy Meyerbeerovych oper da ceskem jevisti' [The Sets for Meyerbeer Operas at the Czech Theatre], ibid, 376–85

B. Wessling: *Meyerbeer: Wagners Beute – Heines Geisel* (Düsseldorf, 1984)

H. Becker: 'Meyerbeers Wiener Reisetagebuch 1813', *Festschrift für Rudolf Elvers zum 60. Geburtstag* (Tutzing, 1985), 29–47

C. Dahlhaus: 'Wagner, Meyerbeer und des Fortschritt: zur Opernästhetik des Vormärz', ibid, 103–16

N. Miller: 'Grosse Oper als Historiengemälde: Uberlegungen zur Zusammenarbeit von Eugène Scribe und Giacomo Meyerbeer', *Oper und Opertexte* (Heidelberg, 1985), 45–79

H. Becker: 'Eine "Undine" Oper Meyerbeers für Paris', *Festschrift Martin Ruhnke* (Neuhausen-Stuttgart, 1986), 31–44

M. Brzoska: 'Historisches Bewusstsein und musikalische Zeitgestaltung', *AMw*, xlv (1988), 50–66

A. Everett: '"Bewitched in a Magic Garden": Meyerbeer in Italy', *Donizetti Society Journal*, vi (1988), 163–92

H. Weinland: 'Wagner und Meyerbeer', *Musik-Konzepte*, lix (1988), 31–72

S. Huebner: 'Italianate Duets in Meyerbeer's Grand Operas', *Journal for Musicological Research*, viii (1989), 203–58

A. Gerhard: 'Meyerbeer und das "juste milieu"', *Die Verstädterung der Oper* (Stuttgart, 1992)

INDIVIDUAL OPERAS

Robert le diable

H. Tardel: *Die Sage von Robert dem Teufel in neueren deutschen Dichtungen und in Meyerbeers Oper*, Forschungen zur neueren Literaturgeschichte, xiv (Berlin, 1900)

C. Rosen: Introduction to: *Robert le diable*, ERO, xix (1980)

L'avant-scène opéra, no.76 (1985) [*Robert le diable* issue]

H. R. Cohen, ed.: *The Original Staging Manuals for Twelve Parisian Operas/Douze livrets de mise en scène lyrique datant des créations parisiennes* (Stuyvesant, NY, 1991) [incl. production book for *Robert le diable*]

Les Huguenots

J. G. Prod'homme: 'Die Hugenotten-Première', *Die Musik*, iii/1 (1903–04), 187–200

E. Istel: 'Act IV of Les Huguenots', *MQ*, xxii (1936), 87–97

H. Frederichs: 'Das Rezitativ in den Hugenotten G. Meyerbeers', *Beiträge zur Geschichte der Oper*, ed. H. Becker (Regensburg, 1969), 55–76

H. Becker: '… der Marcel von Meyerbeer', *Jb des Staatlichen Instituts für Musikforschung* (1979), 79–100

C. Rosen: Introduction to: *Les Huguenots*, ERO, xx (1980)

M. Walter: 'Zwei Hugenotten-Bearbeitungen des 19. Jahrhunderts', *JbO*, i (1985), 122–43

Le prophète

A. Morel: *Le prophète: analyse critique de la nouvelle partition de Giacomo Meyerbeer* (Paris, 1849)

E. O. Lindner: *Meyerbeers 'Prophet' als Kunstwerk beurtheilt* (Berlin, 1850)

J. Schladebach: *Meyerbeers Prophet (unter besonderer Berücksichtigung der Dresdner Aufführung)* (Dresden, 1850)

C. Rosen: Introduction to: *Le prophète*, ERO, xxi (1978)

A. Armstrong: *Meyerbeer's Le prophète: a History of its Composition and Early Performances* (diss., Ohio State U., 1990)

H. R. Cohen, ed.: *The Original Staging Manuals for Twelve Parisian Operas/Douze livrets de mise en scène lyrique datant des créations parisiennes* (Stuyvesant, NY, 1991) [incl. production book for *Le prophète*]

L'Africaine

G. Servières: 'Les transformations et tribulations de *L'Africaine*', *RMI*, xxxiv (1927), 80–99

J. H. Roberts: *The Genesis of Meyerbeer's 'L'Africaine'* (diss., U. of California, Berkeley, 1977)

C. Rosen: Introduction to: *L'Africaine*, ERO, xxiv (1980)

Others

M. Loppert: 'An Introduction to "L'étoile du nord"', *MT*, cxvi (1975), 130–33

H. Schneider: 'Die Bearbeitung des "Pardon de Ploërmel" von G. Meyerbeer im Jahre der Uraufführung', *Festschrift Heinz Becker* (Laaber, 1982), 152–61

P. Gossett: Introduction to: *Il crociato in Egitto*, ERO, xviii (1979)

C. Rosen: Introduction to: *L'étoile du nord*, ERO, xxii (1980)

——: Introduction to: *Le Pardon de Ploermel*, ERO, xxiii (1981)

STEVEN HUEBNER

Meyerowitz, Jan [Hans-Hermann] (*b* Breslau [now Wrocław, Poland], 23 April 1913). American composer of German birth. He studied at the Hochschule für Musik, Berlin, with Walther Gmeindl and Alexander Zemlinsky; in 1933 he went to Rome and became a composition pupil of Respighi and Casella. He emigrated in 1946 and became an American citizen in 1951. A strong believer in the role of music in education, he held teaching positions at the opera department of the Berkshire Music Center (1948–51) and at Brooklyn and City colleges, CUNY (1954–80). His awards include two Guggenheim fellowships (1956, 1958) and an NEA grant (1977).

As a composer, Meyerowitz has adhered to tonality and attempted to build his own style on Classic-Romantic traditions. Although occasionally his music betrays the influences of Schoenberg and Berg, the lyric expressionism of his operas testifies to 19th-century ideals (Meyerbeer, Verdi, Ponchielli). Without abandoning the European substance of his style, he has utilized typically American idioms in his operas on American topics. *The Barrier*, to a libretto by Langston Hughes dealing with the racial problems in the South, was performed on Broadway (1950) and revived by the Teatro S Carlo, Naples (1971). As well as operas Meyerowitz has composed choral pieces, works for orchestra and chamber music.

The Barrier (2, L. Hughes), New York, 10 Jan 1950

Simoon (P. Stephens, after A. Strindberg), Tanglewood, 2 Aug 1950

Eastward in Eden (5 scenes, D. Gardner), Detroit, 16 Nov 1951, renamed Emily Dickinson

Bad Boys in School (Meyerowitz, after J. N. Nestroy), Tanglewood, 17 Aug 1953

Esther (3, Hughes), U. of Illinois, 17 May 1957

Port Town (1, Hughes), Tanglewood, 4 Aug 1960

Godfather Death (3, Stephens), New York, 2 June 1961

Winterballade (3, after G. Hauptmann), Hanover, 29 Jan 1967

SIEGMUND LEVARIE

Meyer von Schauensee, Franz Joseph Leonti (*b* Lucerne, 10 Aug 1720; *d* Lucerne, 2 Jan 1789). Swiss composer. A member of an aristocratic family, he was taught the organ, cello and violin (the last in Milan). From 1742 to 1744 he served in a mercenary regiment in Sardinia and on his return worked in public life in Lucerne until 1752. He then became organist at the seminary of St Leodegar in Lucerne and in 1768 founded the Helvetische Konkordiagesellschaft. He was one of the first Swiss musicians to become known beyond the boundaries of his own country.

Meyer von Schauensee wrote chiefly stage works and church music. According to Koller his works show him to be a representative of the late Neapolitan style, revealing many points of similarity with Hasse, Sammartini and Pergolesi, as well as Handel's influence.

Die Parnassische Gesandschaft (ob), 1746

Hans Hüttenstock (ob), 1769, *CH-EN*

Angenehmer und wohllautender Streit dreyer Polizeiständen (Spl), 1773

Die Engelbergische Talhochzeit (ob), 1781, *EN*

Heli (Spl), 1785

Iphigenie (Spl), 1785, *Lmg*

E. Koller: *Franz Joseph Leonti von Schauensee* (Frauenfeld and Leipzig, 1922) [with complete list of works and thematic index]

J. E. Saladin: *Die Musikpflege am Stift St. Leodegar in Luzern* (Stans, 1948)

W. Jerger: 'Zur Musikgeschichte der deutschsprachigen Schweiz im 18. Jahrhundert', *Mf*, xiv (1961), 303–12   WILHELM JERGER

Meytus, Yuly Sergeyevich (*b* Yelizavetgrad [now Kirovograd], 15/28 Jan 1903). Ukrainian composer of Turkmenian descent. In 1931 he graduated from the Kharkiv Music and Drama Institute where he had studied composition with Bogatïryov. In 1923–4 he was rehearsal pianist with the Kharkiv Opera Theatre and from 1926 he worked as a professional composer. He became a member of the executive committee of the Composers' Union of the Ukraine in 1939 and of the USSR in 1957. He has received most of the honours available to a successful Soviet artist. Meytus is noted for having composed, with Alexander Mosolov, one of the first constructivist pieces, *Na Dniprobudi* ('The Building of the Dnieper Dam'), in 1929. Although he wrote works in other genres, he is best known for his operas. As part of the new dogma of socialist realism and aesthetic collectivization imposed by Stalin, Meytus and the Ukrainian composers M. D. Ribal'chenko and M. D. Tits collaborated on two operas: *Perekop* (1939) and *Gaydamaky* (1943). His first big success, *Moloda hvardiya* ('The Young Guard'), concerns the struggle for existence of the early Soviet regime; it retains a folk-like quality even while outlining the official Soviet aesthetic. Meytus is an interesting composer in that he is very much a synthesis of Turkmenian, Ukrainian and Russian influences; indeed his output includes two Turkmenian operas: *Leyli i Medzhun* ('Leyli and Medzhun') and *Makhtumkuli*. He began as a fairly experimental composer with eclectic interests and a diversity of styles. In *Ukradene shchastya* ('Stolen Happiness'), which is still in the repertory of the L'viv Opera, he was able to conform to the requirements of socialist realism without becoming 'faceless'. This drama of Galician village life is enhanced by 'national' colouring and an excellent libretto by the poet Maksym Ryl'skyy, after a strong drama by Ivan Franko. Stylistically, Meytus is a conservative composer whose works integrated easily into the mainstream of the Soviet musical establishment.

Perekop, 1918–20, Kiev, 20 Jan 1939, collab. V. P. Ribal'chenko and M. D. Tits

Gaydamaky, 1941, Ashkhabad, 15 Oct 1943, collab. Ribal'chenko and Tits

Abadan, Ashkhabad, Turkmenia Theatre of Opera and Ballet, 1943, collab. A. Kuliyev; rev. 1946–7

Leyli i Medzhun [Leyli and Medzhun] (4, K. Burunov), Ashkhabad, Turkmenia Theatre of Opera and Ballet, 2 Nov 1946, collab. D. Ovezov

Moloda hvardiya [The Young Guard] (4, A. Malyshko, after A. Fadayev), Kiev, Shevchenko Academic Theatre of Opera and Ballet, 7 Nov 1947; rev., Leningrad, 1950; ov and excerpts (Moscow, 1951–2)

Zarya nad Dvinoy [Dawn Over the River Dvina] (4, V. Rozhdestvensky), Kiev, 5 July 1955; rev. as Severnïye zori [Northern Dawns], 1957 (trans. M. Ryl'skyy)

Ukradene shchastya [Stolen Happiness], 1958–9 (Ryl'skyy, after I.

Franko), L'viv, Ivan Franko State Academic Theatre of Opera and Ballet, 10 Sept 1960

Makhtumkuli (3, A. Karliyev and B. Kerbabayev), Ashkhabad, Turkmenia Theatre of Opera and Ballet, 29 Dec 1962

Vitrova don'ka [The Daughter of the Wind] (prol., 3, A. Vasyl'yeva and V. Zubar, after Zubar), Odessa, 1965, vs (Kiev, 1972)

Braty Ul'yanovy [The Brothers Ul'yanov] (3, Vasyl'yeva and D. Pavlychko), Ufa, 25 Nov 1967; rev., Alma Ata, 1970

Anna Karenina, 1969–70 (3, Vasyl'yeva and L. Smirnov, after L. N. Tolstoy)

Yaroslav mudryy [Yaroslav the Wise] (3, Vasyl'yeva, after M. Kocherha), Donets'k, 3 March 1973

Rikhard Zorge (prol., 3, Vasyl'yeva and Smirnov), L'viv, 1976

Mar'yana Pineda [Mariana Piena], 1977 (3, Vasyl'yeva, after F. García Lorca)

Ivan Groznyy [Ivan the Terrible], 1980 (3, Vasyl'yeva, after Tolstoy)

Mariya Volkonskaya, 1988 (historical op, 3, Vasyl'yeva)

Yu. Malyshev: *Yu. S. Meytus. Ocherk tvorchestva* [Survey of Works] (Moscow, 1962)

L. Bas: *Yuly Meytus* (Kiev, 1973)

B. Yarustovsky: 'Entuziast sovremennoy temï' [Enthusiast of Contemporary Themes], *SovM* (1974), no.11, pp.7–10

I. Nemtsov: 'Dramaturhiya opery Yu. Meytus a "Braty Ul'yanovy"', *Ukraïns'ke muzykoznavstvo*, x (1974), 258–73

VIRKO BALEY

Mezzo-contralto. Term used in the 19th century for a particular style of voice with affinities with both the mezzo-soprano and the contralto. Singers to whom it has been applied include Maria Malibran, Rosine Stoltz, Marie Delna and Lucy Arbell, noted for their wide range and weight of tone.

Mezzo-soprano [mezzo] (It.: 'medium soprano'; Fr. *mezzo-soprano*, *bas-dessus*, *second dessus*; Ger. *Mezzosopran*, *tiefer Sopran*). A female voice, intermediate in pitch between the contralto and the soprano, usually written for in the range *a* to *g″*, which may be extended at either end.

1. Terminology, early usage, voice types. 2. The 19th century: singers and roles: (i) Italian, French and Russian opera (ii) German opera. 3. The 20th century: singers and roles.

1. TERMINOLOGY, EARLY USAGE, VOICE TYPES. The distinction between soprano and mezzo-soprano (or simply mezzo, as in common usage) came to be made only towards the middle of the 18th century. In the 17th, most music for the soprano voice lay within the range *c′* to *g″* (at current pitch levels, generally a whole tone or a semitone lower than today), which by later criteria would be deemed appropriate for a mezzo-soprano. During the first half of the 18th century, however, composers began to write parts that not only slightly extended the upper range (often to *a″*) but lay in a somewhat higher tessitura and were characterized by florid writing in the upper octave. Alongside this trend came an awareness of the somewhat weightier mezzo-soprano voice, which was unsuited to roles of this kind. The term itself was used by J. J. Quantz, writing of Faustina Bordoni; he is quoted by Burney (*History*, iv, 1789, pp.318ff) as saying that she had 'a less clear than penetrating mezzosoprano voice', with the range *b* to *g″*; he also used the term of the castrato Senesino: 'a penetrating, clear, even and pleasant deep soprano voice (mezzoSoprano)' (see his autobiography in F. W. Marpurg, *Historisch-kritische Beyträge zur Aufnahme der Musik*, i, 1754–5, pp.213, 240f).

The term was little used in the later 18th century, though the voice itself was common. It is clear from the range of many roles nominally for soprano that in modern terminology they would be described as for mezzo; examples are Mozart's Cherubino (written for Dorothea Bussani, 1786), Dorabella (for Louise Villeneuve, 1790) and in *La clemenza di Tito* (1791) Annius (Carolina Perini) and arguably Vitellia (Maria Marchetti Fantozzi). In French music, where the terms *bas-dessus* or *second dessus* were used for the female voice lower than the soprano, there were few solo roles (*see* BAS-DESSUS).

It was the extension of demands upon the upper voice, used increasingly for strenuous dramatic purposes in the early years of the 19th century, that left many singers who in previous decades would have been simply 'soprano' to take the classification of mezzo-soprano; at the other end of the range, the contralto came to denote a more specialized (and in some degree less popular) type. The disappearance of the castrato, who generally occupied a very similar pitch range, gave further impetus to the development of the place of the mezzo-soprano in opera, and indeed many of the important mezzo roles in the first decades of the 19th century are heroic, travesty ones. In this period, and later, the mezzo-soprano's range may often be no less extensive than the soprano's, but, with a voice generally deeper in timbre, a slightly lower tessitura is found more comfortable (and composers realized that the dramatic mezzo, as used by Verdi and Wagner, could more comfortably surmount the heavier orchestration of the period than many soprano voices). Thus in Verdi's *Don Carlos* (1867) the topmost note for both the soprano (Elisabeth de Valois) and the mezzo (Princess Eboli) is *b″*, the distinction between the voices being observed by the composer's calling more upon the upper half of the voice with the one and the lower with the other. Earlier the difference may be less clearcut. In Bellini's *Norma* (1831) the role of Adalgisa presupposes a voice that will still match the soprano's; though the lower line is assigned to Adalgisa when they sing together, there are imitative passages in which equal demands are made upon the voices, suggesting that the conception of the mezzo-soprano here (if indeed anything other than soprano was in Bellini's mind at all) is at any rate further removed than Verdi's from association with the contralto. It is in any case impossible to be specific in establishing the distinctions between voice-types; there are singers who are sometimes described as soprano and at others as mezzo, or as contralto and as mezzo. Equally, there are roles that are susceptible to performance by one voice or another, for example Kundry (a mezzo or a dramatic soprano), Saint-Saëns' Delilah (mezzo or contralto) and Santuzza (open to a dramatic soprano). Perhaps the greatest of all mezzo roles, though often described as soprano, is Carmen (1875), which has also been sung by true sopranos and true contraltos. The central mezzo repertory includes, in Italian opera, Amneris, Eboli and Azucena; in German, Ortrud, Fricka (particularly in *Die Walküre*), Brangäne, Octavian and Hänsel; in French, Carmen, as well as Charlotte in *Werther* and the title role in *Mignon* (both lyric mezzo roles); and in Russian, the shepherd Lel' (*The Snow Maiden*), Marina (*Boris Godunov*) and Olga (*Yevgeny Onegin*), though the latter is also considered a contralto role. The term MEZZO-CONTRALTO has also been used, seemingly for voices of unusual richness.

In recent times the Rossini revival has encouraged the mezzo-soprano to acquire a technique that can cope with rapid passage-work over a secure two-octave range. Rossini himself wrote for his wife Isabella Colbran, and the coloratura mezzo or contralto never became completely extinct as a species in Italy; even so, the appropriation by coloratura sopranos of the leading female role in the most popular of Rossini's operas was an indication of the general movement away from the lower to the higher voices. This has also added to the temptations for a mezzo to attempt full soprano roles. A foretaste of the possibilities, both in the voice-types and in the Rossini operas themselves, was provided for a few years before her early death in 1936 by Conchita Supervia; but it was not until the 1960s with singers such as Marilyn Horne and Teresa Berganza that the revival prospered, and in the following decades it became far more mandatory that the mezzo-soprano should make herself available for work in this type of repertory, including many operas such as Rossini's *Tancredi* and *Semiramide* and Bellini's *I Capuleti e i Montecchi* that had hitherto been rarities.

2. THE 19TH CENTURY: SINGERS AND ROLES.

(i) Italian, French and Russian opera. An important early interpreter of Rossini's mezzo roles was Teresa Belloc-Giorgi, who created Isabella in *L'inganno felice* (1812), the third opera of Rossini to be produced, and Ninetta in *La gazza ladra* (1817). She was engaged in 1819 in London, under the name Teresa Bellochi; after her début as Isabella in the British première of *L'italiana in Algeri*, the *Times* critic wrote that she had 'an agreeable and flexible voice … it is of the class called mezzo-soprano, but combines in a remarkable degree many of the peculiar qualities and facilities of the soprano'. Bellochi also sang Rosina (*Il barbiere*) and Mozart's Zerlina, Susanna and Pamina; the following year she scored a particular success in the London premières of *Cenerentola* and *Tancredi*. Another gifted coloratura mezzo, Marietta Marcolini, was the first Isabella in *L'italiana* (1813) and created four other Rossini roles in the years 1811–14, including Clarice in *La pietra del paragone*.

The only major mezzo-soprano role in Bellini's operas is Romeo in *I Capuleti e i Montecchi*, which was first sung by Giuditta Grisi, elder sister of Giulia Grisi; Giuditta also sang Alaida, the protagonist, in the London première of *La straniera*. Bellini adapted Elvira in *I puritani* for Maria Malibran (sometimes described as a mezzo-contralto), but she never sang the role and that version was not heard till the 1980s. Malibran was greatly admired in an adaptation of *La sonnambula*, which she sang in English in London. She also sang the title role of *Maria Stuarda* at La Scala.

In his early Italian operas Donizetti provided few leading mezzo roles (Jane Seymour in *Anna Bolena*, now usually sung by a mezzo, was intended for a light soprano), but later, when he was working for the Paris Opéra, he wrote two rewarding parts for the French mezzo Rosine Stoltz, Léonor in *La favorite* (1840) and Zayda in *Dom Sébastien* (1843). Stoltz, sometimes called a mezzo-contralto and possessor of a particularly rich as well as flexible voice, also created Ascanio in *Benvenuto Cellini* (1838), and Halévy wrote Catarina Cornaro in *La reine de Chypre* (1841) and Odette in *Charles VI* (1843) for her. There are leading mezzo roles in Verdi's first two operas, *Oberto* (1839) and *Un giorno di regno* (1840), both written for Antonietta Ranieri-Marini. The dramatic nature of Lady Macbeth's role has often led to its being sung by a mezzo-soprano. Beginning with Azucena in *Il trovatore* (1853), Verdi composed a long series of magnificent mezzo parts. Both Maddalena (*Rigoletto*) and Ulrica (*Un ballo in maschera*) were originally intended for contralto' but have usually been sung by a mezzo-soprano.

Preziosilla (*La forza del destino*, 1862) was created by Constance Nantier-Didiée who, generally considered a first-class seconda donna rather than a principal, became the first Maddalena in London, where she also sang Azucena, Ulrica, Nancy (*Martha*) and the travesty roles Maffio Orsini (*Lucrezia Borgia*), Urbain (*Les Huguenots*), Ascanio (*Benvenuto Cellini*), Isolier (*Le comte Ory*) and Siébel (*Faust*). Princess Eboli in *Don Carlos*, Verdi's finest role for mezzo, was first sung (in Paris) by Pauline Guéymard-Lauters (1867), whose very wide compass and powerful upper register also enabled her to sing many soprano roles; at the Italian première of *Don Carlos* Eboli was sung by Giuseppina Pasqua, whose strength lay more in her middle register; later she created Mistress Quickly in *Falstaff* (1893). Maria Waldmann, the Austrian mezzo who became the first Italian Amneris, made her début as Pierotto in *Linda di Chamounix*; at La Scala she sang Maffio Orsini and Preziosilla with particular success.

At the Opéra, Guéymard-Lauters also created Balkis in Gounod's *La reine de Saba* (1862) and Queen Gertrude in Thomas' *Hamlet* (1868), in which she was especially effective in the fine Closet scene. At the Opéra-Comique, Célestine Galli-Marié had created the title role of Thomas' best-known opera, *Mignon* (1866). Subsequently Galli-Marié, who had a vibrant but not over-large voice, sang Lazarillo at the première of *Don César de Bazan* (1872), Massenet's second opera, and in 1875 achieved immortality by creating Carmen, returning in 1883 to sing in the 100th performance of Bizet's opera. According to Modest Tchaikovsky she 'managed to combine with the display of unbridled passion an element of mystical fatalism'.

Marietta Biancolini-Rodriguez, who sang Laura in the première of *La Gioconda* (1876), did not have the huge, heavy voice usually heard in the part, but was famous for her performances of Rossini's mezzo and contralto coloratura roles, being specially admired as Arsace (*Semiramide*). Sofia Scalchi, whose large, imposing voice had a range of *f* to *b″*, sang Azucena, Amneris and other Verdi mezzo roles with great success and was Siébel at the performance of *Faust* with which the Metropolitan opened. Zélia Trebelli, a vibrant, flexible French mezzo, was the first London Preziosilla and sang Frédéric (a role created by a tenor) in the first London performance of *Mignon* (given in Italian); Thomas composed the rondo-gavotte 'In veder l'amata stanza' for her.

(ii) German opera. In Germany during the 19th century the lines dividing the three categories of female voice become ever more difficult to distinguish. Eglantine, the villainess of Weber's *Euryanthe*, though written for a mezzo was created by the soprano Therese Grünbaum (1823); Adriano (*Rienzi*, 1842) and Venus (*Tannhäuser*, 1845) were first sung by a soprano, Wilhelmine Schröder-Devrient; these three roles and also Ortrud (*Lohengrin*), Magdalene (*Die Meistersinger*) and Brangäne (*Tristan und Isolde*) were all introduced to the Metropolitan by Marianne Brandt, the contralto whose enormous range allowed her to sing any part from the coloratura role of Astaroth (Goldmark's *Die Königin von Saba*) to Kundry (*Parsifal*), which she shared with Materna and Malten (both sopranos) at Bayreuth in 1882. Fortunata Tedesco, an Italian contralto who was Venus at the disastrous Paris

première of *Tannhäuser*, sang the soprano roles of Elvira and Odabella in the American premières of *Ernani* and *Attila*; her wide range and excellent coloratura technique helped her in parts as different as Léonor (*La favorite*) and Fidès (*Le prophète*).

The mezzo role of Fricka (*Das Rheingold*) was created in Munich by a soprano (1869–70), Sophie Stehle, and it again fell to a soprano, Frederike Grun, at Bayreuth in the first complete *Ring* cycle. Later the Liverpool-born mezzo Marie Brema, who made her début as Lola in the London première of *Cavalleria rusticana*, was much praised as Fricka; she also sang Ortrud and Kundry at Bayreuth. In the first London *Ring* Fricka was sung by Hedwig Reicher-Kindermann, another mezzo with an extraordinary compass, who had sung Erda in the first cycle at Bayreuth; later she became a magnificent Brünnhilde before dying in her 30th year.

3. THE 20TH CENTURY: SINGERS AND ROLES. Lucy Arbell, the inspiration of Massenet's last years, first sang in one of his works at the Opéra in 1906, creating the secondary role of Persephone in *Ariane*. Massenet then wrote *Thérèse* (1907) for Arbell, the title role of which was perfectly suited to her strong, vibrant mezzo-contralto and vivacious personality. She created Queen Amahelli in *Bacchus* (1909; the sequel to *Ariane*); then, in his last unequivocal success, *Don Quichotte* (1910), Massenet provided her with another tailor-made role, Dulcinée. She sang in two more Massenet premières, as Postumia in *Roma* (1912) and, after the composer's death, as Colombe in *Panurge* (1913).

Arbell was renowned for her interpretation of Charlotte in *Werther*. Another fine Charlotte, who had sung the role in the first Paris performance of Massenet's opera, Marie Delna, was also a mezzo-contralto with a wide range and a generous-toned voice. Having sung Dido in *Les Troyens à Carthage* at the Opéra-Comique, she became the first Paris Cassandra in *La prise de Troie* at the Opéra; she also sang Léonor (*La favorite*), Fidès and Delilah. Delilah, a role seized upon by mezzos and contraltos alike, figured largely in the repertory of Louise Kirkby Lunn, the great English mezzo who was equally at home in French, Italian and German opera; a notable Ortrud, Fricka and Brangäne, she sang Kundry in the first production of *Parsifal* in English at Boston in 1904. She was also greatly admired as Gluck's Orpheus.

Puccini wrote only minor or character mezzo roles, with the possible exception of Suzuki in *Madama Butterfly*. Richard Strauss, on the other hand, introduced several superb mezzo characters, usually older women, into his operas. Herodias in *Salome* and Clytemnestra in *Elektra* are the obvious examples; though the latter role was created by a contralto, Ernestine Schumann-Heink, many mezzos have excelled in both parts. Maria Olczewska and Margarete Klose, also admired in Verdi, Wagner and as fiery interpreters of Carmen, used their generous voices to magnificent effect as Clytemnestra. Dramatic sopranos who can no longer manage the role of Electra have taken to singing Clytemnestra, not always with satisfactory results. Two sympathetic travesty roles in operas by Strauss, Octavian in *Der Rosenkavalier* and the Composer in *Ariadne auf Naxos*, both written for and created by a soprano, are now usually sung by mezzos, whose voices sound more like that of a boy. The finest Octavian and Composer in the post-World War II period was Sena Jurinac who, though she later became a soprano, retained the mezzo timbre to her voice.

In the mid-1930s, the Spanish mezzo Conchita Supervia initiated a renewal of interest in the comic operas of Rossini by singing the title roles of *La Cenerentola* and *L'italiana in Algeri* at Covent Garden (Rosina in *Il barbiere* remained the property of high sopranos, including Lily Pons). The Rossini revival later broadened to include his serious operas and new singers had to be found for the immensely florid music; the Spanish mezzo Teresa Berganza was greatly admired in the comic operas, particularly in *La Cenerentola*, while Marilyn Horne displayed amazing virtuosity and style as Arsace (*Semiramide*) and Malcolm (*La donna del lago*). Even Giulietta Simionato, a dramatic mezzo primarily renowned in heavy roles such as Amneris and Eboli, sang Bellini's Romeo and Adalgisa, Donizetti's Jane Seymour and several Rossini coloratura roles with equal facility.

Meanwhile composers continued to write new roles and to adapt old ones for specific singers; Britten composed Kate in *Owen Wingrave* for Janet Baker, for whose mezzo Walton altered the role of Cressida (originally for soprano). Baker enjoyed huge success in *Maria Stuarda*; another role in which she excelled was that of Dido in *Les Troyens*. The challenge offered to a dramatic mezzo in a complete performance of Berlioz's vast epic was taken up by Josephine Veasey and Sarah Walker in addition to Baker (among British singers); others to have sung the role include Régine Crespin, Shirley Verrett and Christa Ludwig. Technically a soprano, Crespin also sang Cassandra, as did Verrett, a mezzo who became a soprano; Ludwig, another mezzo who sang soprano roles, used her rich, even middle register to particularly good effect as Dido, which she sang at the Metropolitan.

The Russian repertory offers the mezzo many opportunities. The Australian mezzo Yvonne Minton found two rewarding roles in Marina (*Boris Godunov*) and Marfa (*Khovanshchina*); she also appeared in two of Tippett's operas, creating Thea in *The Knot Garden* and singing Helen in *King Priam*. Among Minton's finest roles was the castrato role of Sextus in *La clemenza di Tito*.

See also SOPRANO.

For bibliography *see* SINGING: A BIBLIOGRAPHY and SOPRANO.
                    OWEN JANDER, J. B. STEANE, ELIZABETH FORBES

Miami. American city, in Florida. The Greater Miami Opera (originally the Opera Guild of Miami) was launched with a production of *Pagliacci* on 14 February 1942 in the auditorium of Miami High School. Its founder was the Italian immigrant Arturo di Filippi, who sang Canio and who remained the guiding force behind the opera company until his death in 1972. From these humble beginnings the Greater Miami Opera has grown into a world-class company, attracting such singers as Birgit Nilsson, Beverly Sills, Jussi Björling and Placido Domingo, as well as featuring the American début, in, 1965, of Luciano Pavarotti in *Lucia di Lammermoor*, with Joan Sutherland. The conductor Emerson Buckley (1916–89) became music director in 1950, following a period as conductor of the New York City Opera; he succeeded Di Filippi as artistic director in 1973. Willie Anthony Waters succeeded him as conductor in 1984. Robert Herman, formerly Bing's assistant at the New York Metropolitan Opera, became manager in 1973 and guided the Greater Miami Opera to international prominence until his retirement in

1985, when he was succeeded by Robert Heuer (formerly of the Michigan Opera).

R. Herman: *The Greater Miami Opera: from Shoestring to Showpiece 1941–1985* (Miami, 1985)
RAYMOND A. BARR

Míča [Micza, Mischa, Mitscha], **František Adam** [Jan Adam František de Paula] (*b* Jaroměřice nad Rokytnou, Moravia, 11 Jan 1746; *d* Lwów, 19 March 1811). Czech composer, nephew of František Antonín Míča. After law studies at Vienna he became a government official there, and later in Styria (*c*1786–96) and in the Austrian provinces of Poland (from 1796). He devoted himself to music as an amateur, mostly while in Vienna (to 1785). He played several instruments, and his orchestral and chamber music enjoyed considerable esteem, notably with W. A. Mozart and Emperor Joseph II. The music of his two Singspiels, *Bernardon, die Gouvernante* (2, J. Kurz-Bernardon) and *Adrast und Isidore, oder Die Nachtmusik* (2, C. F. Bretzner, after Molière; Vienna, Burg, 26 April 1781), is all lost. A manuscript biography of Míča, including a detailed though incomplete list of his works, is in the library of the Gesellschaft der Musikfreunde in Vienna, and was partly published in Veselý.

ČSHS; WurzbachL
'Nachricht vom Leben des Franz Adam von Mitscha', *Monatbericht der Gesellschaft der Musikfreunde* (1829), no.8, pp.113–24
J. Racek: 'František Adam Jan Míča', *Zprávy Bertramky* (1961), no.25 [with bibliography]
O. Veselý: 'Rod Míčů' [Míča Family], *HV*, v (1968), 264–95
O. Michtner: *Das alte Burgtheater als Opernbühne* (Vienna, 1970), 97–8, 117, 373, 466
MILAN POŠTOLKA

Míča [Micza, Mitscha], **František Antonín (Václav)** (*b* Třebíč, 5 Sept 1694; *d* Jaroměřice nad Rokytnou, 15 Feb 1744). Czech composer and conductor. He was taken as a child to Jaroměřice. After studying music as Count Questenberg's page in Vienna (1711), he was Kapellmeister of the count's orchestra from about 1722. He conducted performances of operatic works by Caldara, F. B. and I. M. Conti, D. N. Sarro, Vinci, Leo, Hasse and others, occasionally with insertions and adaptations of his own, and frequently sang the tenor parts.

Míča's only extant opera, *L'origine di Jaromeriz in Moravia* (*A-Wn*; aria ed. in DČHP, 1958, no.122), was first performed with two intermezzos (text by Bonlini) in Jaroměřice in December 1730. It exists in both a two-act version, with Italian text by Nicodeno Blinoni and Czech text by A. F. Dubravius, and a three-act one with a German text by H. Bademin. The work's late Baroque idiom resembles that of Caldara; in the first allegro of the Italian fast-slow-fast type overture there are elements of the pre-Classical sonata. Other operas (some in Czech) and intermezzos, written between 1723 and 1738, are lost (see Helfert 1916).

ČSHS; MGG (J. Bužga)
V. Helfert: *Hudební barok na českých zámcích* [Musical Baroque in Bohemian Castles] (Prague, 1916), 154–67 [with list of works]
——: *Hudba na jaroměřickém zámku* [Music in Jaroměřice Castle] (Prague, 1924)
O. Veselý: 'Rod Míčů' [The Míča Family], *HV*, v (1968), 264–94
V. Telec: 'Stará libreta a míčovská otázka' [Old Librettos and the Míča Problem], *OM*, ii (1970), 239–47
T. Straková: 'Jaroměřice nad Rokytnou', *OM*, v (1973), 57–60
J. Trojan: 'Jak to dopadlo v Jaroměřicích: německý tisk libreta opery L'origine di Jaromeriz in Moravia' [A German Printing of the Libretto of the Opera L'origine di Jaromeriz in Moravia], *OM*, vi (1974), 82–5

——: 'Čeština na zámecké scéně v Jaroměřicích' [The Czech Language on the Stage of Jaroměřice Castle], *OM*, xvi (1984), 101–5
J. Tyrrell: *Czech Opera* (Cambridge, 1988), 14, 18, 206
MILAN POŠTOLKA

Michaelis, Johann Benjamin (*b* Zittau, 31 Dec 1746; *d* Halberstadt, 30 Sept 1772). German librettist. He was a student at Leipzig during the ascendancy of the comic operas of C. F. Weisse and J. A. Hiller. In 1770 he moved to Hamburg, where Lessing recommended him to the Seyler company as theatrical poet. He left the company in 1771 owing to its impending financial ruin and was taken in by the poet J. W. L. Gleim. Michaelis died, not yet 26, a year later. In contrast to Weisse's, his librettos make artful use of the low comic, and several favour mythological plots.

Walmir und Gertraud (Operette), Schweitzer, 1769; *Je unnatürlicher, je besser!* (komische Oper), 1769; *Herkules auf dem Oeta* (Operette), Schmittbaur, 1771; *Amors Guckkasten* (Operette), Neefe, 1772 (Reichardt, 1772); *Der Einspruch* (Operette), Neefe, 1772
THOMAS BAUMAN

Michailova, Maria. *See* MIKHAYLOVA, MARIYA.

Michalesi, Aloyse. German singer of Czech origin, wife of KARL AUGUST KREBS.

Micheau, Janine (*b* Toulouse, 17 April 1914; *d* Paris, 18 Oct 1976). French soprano. She studied in Toulouse and at the Paris Conservatoire, and made her début in 1933 at the Opéra-Comique as the Newspaper Girl in *Louise*. In 1935 in Amsterdam she sang Mélisande, which she later repeated elsewhere in Europe and in San Francisco. Her French roles at the Paris Opéra-Comique (1933–56) included Mireille, Olympia and Bizet's Leïla; she was the first French Zerbinetta in 1943 and Anne Trulove in 1953. At the Opéra (1940–56) she sang Juliet, Gilda, Violetta, Pamina, Sophie (*Der Rosenkavalier*), and Creusa in Milhaud's *Médée*, and created the role of Manuela in his *Bolivar* (1950). She made her Covent Garden début as Micaëla in 1937 and sang Violetta and Micaëla in Chicago in 1946. She retired in 1968. In all her roles Micheau was admired for the care, skill and taste with which she used a characteristically French voice, light and flexible with a wide range and conspicuously even production.
MARTIN COOPER

Micheletti, Gaston (*b* Tavaco, Corsica, 5 Jan 1892; *d* Ajaccio, 21 May 1959). Corsican tenor. He studied at the Paris Conservatoire, made his début at Rheims as Faust (1922), and three years later joined the Opéra-Comique where he remained until his retirement in 1946. During this period he sang a large repertory of lyric-dramatic roles, appearing on such occasions in the company's history as the 500th performance of *Les contes d'Hoffmann* (1927) and the 1000th of *Carmen* (1930). Among world premières in which he took a leading part were those of Raoul Laparra's *Le joueur de viole* (1925) and Camille Fournier's *Le chevalier de Mauleon* (1927). He also appeared in Brussels, Nice and Monte Carlo. On records he is most widely remembered in excerpts from *Carmen* with Conchita Supervia, whom he partnered on stage in 1930; but his worth as a fine singer on his own account is well attested by solo recordings, many of which are as pleasing for their stylistic qualities as for the resonance of his full-bodied, securely placed voice.
J. B. STEANE

Micheli, Benedetto (*b* Rome, ?*c*1700; *d* after 15 Sept 1784). Italian composer. He studied painting until he was 15; then his attention turned to music, where it remained until at least 1739. As a young man he appears to have enjoyed the patronage of Cardinal Alvaro Cienfuegos, who between 1722 and 1734 ordered five *componimenti*. During that period he also wrote for Rome an *opera seria*, *L'Oreste* (G. Barlocci; Sala Capranica, 1723) and the *dramma sacro S Contardo* (A. Ruspoli; 1725), and contributed Act 1 and intermezzos to the *opera seria La virtù trionfante dell'amore, e dell'odio, ovvero Il Tigrane* (Capranica, carn. 1724; Act 2 by Vivaldi, Act 3 by Romaldo). But these cannot have been greatly successful, for no further commissions ensued. His main interest to music history derives from his activities in about 1736–8. By his own recollection early in 1736 he was requested to compose a *farsetta* 'ad uso d'Intermezzi … in una Tragicomedia' for the Teatro di Valle, which met with such applause that two more were commissioned for the autumn season, and another pair, now to his own librettos, for Carnival 1737. Similar work followed for the Teatro di Torre Argentina; in *Don Frullone marchese di Lupino* (1737) he introduced characters speaking Roman dialect, a novelty that captured the local fancy. Thereafter he worked for some time in the Roman theatres, writing other such intermezzos and adapting *opere buffe* by such composers as Gaetano Latilla, Rinaldo da Capua, Pietro Auletta and Nicolò Conforti to meet the new taste (Narducci suggested that the Roman production of Latilla's popular *La finta cameriera*, Teatro di Valle, spring 1738, may have been one of these). This represents the northern adaptation of a comic device which, although it continued for many years to have a following in Naples, had already passed its peak of popularity there.

In 1740 Micheli became a member of the Accademia di S Cecilia as 'organista e maestro'; he apparently made part of his living by teaching. In later years he composed several occasional pieces, conducted others, and was also active as a flautist. Librettos attest to his having written some new arias for Auletta's *Il marchese di Spartivento*, performed at the Teatro di Valle in 1747, and the intermezzo *La gelosia non giova*, for the Teatro de Granari, Rome, in 1748. By 1749 misfortune had overtaken him; no further music is known from him though he continued to write poetry. Almost all his works, including the operas, are lost.

AllacciD

J.-B. de La Borde: *Essai sur la musique ancienne et moderne* (Paris, 1780), iii, 204

Abbate Cancellieri: *Le due nuove campane di Campidoglio* (Rome, 1806), 124–5

E. Narducci: 'Di Benedetto Micheli, poeta, musico e pittore romano del secolo XVIII e di un suo poema inedito in dialetto romanesco intitolato *La libbertà romana*', *Reale accademia dei lincei*, cclxxv, 3rd ser.: *Memorie della Classe di scienze morali, storiche e filologiche*, ii (Rome, 1878)   JAMES L. JACKMAN

Michigan Opera Theatre. Company based in DETROIT, founded in 1971.

Michl [Michel, Michelini], **Joseph** (**Christian**) **Willibald** (*b* Neumarkt, 9 July 1745; *d* Neumarkt, 1 Aug 1816). German composer. By the beginning of 1771 at the latest he was in the service of Elector Maximilian III Joseph. In 1774–5 he stayed in Italy at the elector's expense, and in 1776 he wrote the carnival opera *Il trionfo di Clelia* for the Munich court. With the succession of the new elector, Carl Theodor, in 1778 Michl was dismissed. From about 1784 to September 1803 he lived with his brother-in-law, Johann Baptist Moser, a judge at the Augustinian prebendary institute at Weyarn, and wrote sacred works as well as symphonies and school dramas for the monastery.

Michl was a talented composer, known particularly for his sacred works. Much of his music is lost, including numerous works for school theatres, written between 1767 and 1777.

Il barone di Torre Forte (ob, 2), Munich, Salvator, 23 March 1772, *D-Rtt*

L'amante deluso (ob), Munich, 27 Nov 1773

Milton und Elmire (Spl, 1, H. Spaur), Frankfurt, Schauspielhaus im Junghofe, 1773; Munich, 6 June 1785

Il trionfo di Clelia (os, 3, P. Metastasio), Munich, Hof, 8 Jan 1776, *Mbs*

Johann Faust (Spl, 5, P. Weidmann), Munich, Salvator, 16 May 1776

Der König und der Pächter, Munich, 1777

Fremore und Meline (Spl, 3, Spaur), Mainz, An der grossen Bleichen, Jan 1778

Die reisenden Komödianten (Spl, 3, G. W. Burmann), Munich, 1778

Der Jahrmarkt (Spl, 2, F. W. Gotter), Mannheim, National, 13 Feb 1780; with music by G. Benda

L'isola disabitata (azione teatrale, 1, Metastasio), Munich, 1780

Regulus, der Patriot (os), Weyarn, 3 Sept 1781, frag. *WEY*

Der König auf der Jagd (Spl), Munich, 8 Aug 1785

*

F. J. Lipowsky: *Baierisches Musik-Lexikon* (Munich, 1811)

P. Legband: *Münchner Bühne und Literatur im 18. Jahrhundert* (Munich, 1904)

A. Zehelein: *Joseph Michl* (Munich, 1928)

R. Münster: *Oberpfälzische Komponisten zur Zeit Mozarts* (Regensburg, 1963)   ROBERT MÜNSTER

Middlesex, Earl of [Sackville, Charles; later 2nd Duke of Dorset] (*b* London, 6 Feb 1711; *d* London, 6 Jan 1769). English impresario. He made his first European 'grand tour', 1731–3, and undertook a second continental visit, 1737–8. He is best known as the extravagant young aristocrat who took up the direction of Italian opera at the King's Theatre in 1739 just when Handel dropped the form altogether. Under his direction, Galuppi, Lampugnani and the soprano castrato Angelo Maria Monticelli were invited to appear in London from 1739 to 1745. Londoners also heard Pergolesi's music on the stage for the first time in 1741–2 (*L'Olimpiade*), and Lord Middlesex undoubtedly had a hand in bringing Gluck in 1745–6. Middlesex engaged a complete *buffo* company from Italy for the coming seasons, before withdrawing from direct involvement in the opera management in autumn 1748. Francesco Vanneschi, Middlesex's chief poet and assistant manager, ultimately took over as impresario in 1753.

Middlesex was more than usually susceptible to opera's attractions, but to his love of music and social distinction there was added an unfortunate mixture of recalcitrance, impetuosity and managerial ineptitude. He reinvigorated London with enthusiasm for Italian opera but failed to find a way to meet its costs. He tried the patience of his subscribers and his company, suing the former for subscription arrears in 1744 and being sued by one of the latter (Monticelli) for salary arrears in 1748. The Italian Opera, in decline in the 1730s, struggled through the 1740s largely as a result of his energies, and it may have owed its further decline to his incompetence; it could be argued that opera struggled on for so long in the face of changes in taste, because of the selfless commitment of Middlesex and his colleagues; but a sounder and more professional director might have accommodated the genre to public taste, and kept it in being until the 1760s when the London appetite for Italian opera revived.

BDA ('Sackville, Charles')
S. Klima, ed.: *Joseph Spence: Letters from the Grand Tour* (Montreal, 1975)
C. Taylor: 'From Losses to Lawsuit: Patronage of the Italian Opera in London by Lord Middlesex, 1739–45', *ML*, lxviii (1987), 1–20
——: 'Handel's Disengagement from the Italian Opera', *Handel: a Tercentenary Collection*, ed. S. Sadie and A. Hicks (London, 1987), 165–81   CAROLE TAYLOR

Midsummer Marriage, The. Opera in three acts by MICHAEL TIPPETT to his own libretto; London, Covent Garden, 27 January 1955.

Mark *a young man of unknown parentage*	tenor
Jenifer *his betrothed, a young girl*	soprano
King Fisher *Jenifer's father, a businessman*	baritone
Bella *King Fisher's secretary*	soprano
Jack *Bella's boy-friend, a mechanic*	tenor
Sosostris *a clairvoyant*	alto
He-Ancient *Priest of the Temple*	bass
She-Ancient *Priestess of the Temple*	mezzo-soprano

Chorus of Mark's and Jenifer's friends

Dancers attendant on the Ancients

Strephon *one of the dancers*

Setting A clearing in a wood with a ruined temple and steps leading away on either side; the present time

Tippett had written a folksong opera in 1934 and two children's operas in 1938–9; a first full-scale opera was to be the goal of his first decade of mature composition and the completion of a long-term strategy. He considered a range of ideas, and others developed during this period but were then discarded. A crucial stage in the journey towards his operatic vision was his war-time oratorio *A Child of our Time* (1939–41), for which, acting on the advice of T. S. Eliot, he wrote his own text. With this achievement as a foundation he embarked on the creation of an operatic scenario. This began as a vision in his mind's eye:

I *saw* a stage picture ... of a wooded hilltop with a temple, where a warm and soft young man was being rebuffed by a cold and hard young woman ... to such a degree that the collective, magical archetypes take charge – Jung's *anima* and *animus* – the girl, inflated by the latter, rises through the stage flies to heaven, and the man, overwhelmed by the former, descends through the stage floor to hell. But it was clear they would soon return.

In acknowledging the strong Jungian resonance of his starting-point, Tippett points to the crux of the opera – the search for wholeness. In *A Child of our Time* the scapegoat figure sings 'I would know my shadow and my light, so shall I at last be whole', and Tippett later described the sentence as 'the only truth I will ever utter'. *The Midsummer Marriage* (1946–52) is the dramatic realization of this dream achieved by means of a modern comedy with a mythic backdrop.

ACT 1: 'Morning'

The young man and woman of the initial stage-picture are Mark and Jenifer. He is an orphan, of mysterious birth, a child of nature in touch with the elements and of a warm generous nature. Jenifer is the cold, idealistic daughter of a modern tycoon, King Fisher. The strong Celtic, and specifically Cornish, connotations of these names already touch upon a deeper dimension which is immediately present in visual terms as the curtain opens on mist, which as it clears in the rising sun reveals a ruined temple. The trigger for the action is the runaway marriage eagerly anticipated by Mark in the opening scene and furiously opposed by King Fisher. This conflict in itself might have delivered only comedy. The key to the opera's sequence of events is Jenifer's arrival and surprising announcement that she wants to postpone the wedding – the rebuff of Tippett's first vision.

The music of these first scenes has a symphonic breadth, and even before Jenifer's dramatic entry the opera's supernatural substructure has emerged. It is immediately apparent that Tippett is in full command of the musico-dramatic stage. The buoyant exhilaration of the orchestral prelude gently recedes and in so doing creates a sense of space and distance to which the off-stage voices of the chorus calling to each other lend enchantment.

These are Mark's and Jenifer's friends, who are gathering to celebrate the marriage. When they emerge in full view they sing a radiant hymn to the sun, but as the music fades, mysterious sounds invade the air and the ruined temple becomes the focus of attention. From its portals, to the accompaniment of a charming little march, a procession of dancers emerges. As an audience we seem to be observing, through the eyes of the silent chorus, the actions of another world. This ritual is interrupted by Mark's unexpected arrival. He remonstrates with the guardians of the temple, the He- and She-Ancients, whom he clearly knows of old, and asks for a 'new dance'. They do not oblige him and quickly disappear to the same little march which heralded their mysterious arrival.

Mark now greets his friends and sings a passionate love-reverie ('And like the lark I sing for joy because I love'). At the height of his rapture he sees Jenifer arrive, but his joy fades when he observes that her dress is not that of a bride. Her rejection of Mark is couched in lofty, spiritual terms ('It isn't love I want, but truth ... For me the light! For you the shadow'). She climbs up some stone steps as if to heaven and disappears. The chorus cannot cheer up the crestfallen Mark, who responds to her challenge by descending through a set of gates, as if to Hell. By this climactic gesture the plighted pair begin their journey of spiritual discovery.

Coming in hot pursuit of his daughter the bluff, brazen King Fisher arrives on stage. Having seen Mark run away, he assumes that Jenifer has gone with him. After the accumulation of tension at the end of the previous scene, Tippett now introduces a welcome touch of comedy. King Fisher is accompanied by his charmingly dutiful secretary, Bella. Thwarted by the closure of the gates, King Fisher demands to have them opened, and so encounters the Ancients, who treat him with aloof contempt. Tippett's delineation of musical characterization is beautifully handled here. Bella eventually suggests that she should get her boy-friend, the mechanic Jack, to open the gates and King Fisher agrees. In the meantime he exhorts the male and female chorus in turn to help him search for Mark and Jenifer. He resorts to offering money, which the men cheerfully accept but the women angrily reject as a bribe. This encounter is cast as a sturdy strophic set piece which allows for the rejection to emerge very effectively as the upsetting of a musical scheme.

The atmosphere again lightens with the arrival of Jack. He and Bella emerge immediately as the down-to-earth counterbalance to Mark and Jenifer. In some of Tippett's most delightfully loose-limbed writing they sing easily of their comfortable love for each other. But when an attempt is made to break open the gates a powerful unseen voice warns King Fisher not to tamper. His arrogance forces another confrontation which is again thwarted by the voice. An urgent ensemble of confusion ensues in which King Fisher urges Jack to try again, while Bella, frightened by the voice, tries to draw him back. As this conflict grows to heights of musical passion, the issue at stake is swept aside by the sudden re-emergence of a transfigured Jenifer at the top of the steps. Time seems to stand still: having now mastered the ebb and flow of his dramatic presentation so far with such skill, it is as if Tippett can summon up from the depths of the psyche whatever music is required.

Jenifer's dazed utterance on 'returning to the world' provokes a confrontation with her father, and this acts as a cue for Mark's return. At length the two relate their separate experiences. Jenifer's aria is an exalted visionary expression of spiritual radiance. Mark sings of earthy passion – it is a conflict of spirit and senses. Ecstatic with spiritual purity, Jenifer asserts her superiority, only to be broken by Mark's revelation. This action provokes a reversal of their earlier journeys, and as they run off in opposite directions to continue their spiritual exploration the threads of the act are stirringly pulled together in a chorus recalling the symphonic opening in key (Bb) and gesture, and which comments on the ordeal of individuation to be endured by Mark and Jenifer.

Act 2: 'Afternoon'

Mark and Jenifer are absent throughout this act, yet its crux is an enactment of their trials. Tippett frames the act with a glowing evocation of a balmy summer's afternoon in which the glistening, shimmering heat is virtually palpable. The whole is constructed symmetrically but with an unerring dramatic curve. The chorus inhabit the landscape with madrigal-like bursts of song and wander off into the woods, leaving Jack and Bella to sing a love duet in which they map out the course of their married life with touching intimacy and predictability. They also disappear into the woods, and the stage is suddenly alive with unseen presences.

What follows, at the very heart of the opera, is the celebrated sequence of Ritual Dances. Three are enacted here: 'The Earth in Autumn' (in which the hound hunts the hare), 'The Waters in Winter' (where the otter chases the fish) and 'The Air in Spring' (the hawk shadows the bird). This ballet is a predatory struggle between the female and the male. The vulnerable male is represented throughout the animal transformations by Strephon, the leading dancer from the temple, who acts as Mark's 'shadow'. In the third dance the violence of the chase (every move in the music is graphically portrayed) threatens to overwhelm the stage, and the bird is nearly killed. Bella, who is watching, screams, and we are back in the everyday world of the opera. She is comforted by Jack, the chorus pass by merrily, and the act ends as it started, but scarred by the undercurrent of menace.

Act 3: 'Evening and Night'

The act opens at sunset with a choral tableau of rejoicing and festivity. King Fisher arrives to announce that he is bringing a private clairvoyant, Madame Sosostris, to unravel the mystery. Sending the chorus off to greet her, he tangles again with the Ancients, whom he challenges to a contest. He is warned by them again ('You meddle with powers you cannot gauge, courting a risk you do not understand. Should you persist, there's mortal danger to your person'). But King Fisher is now beyond such sober instruction. The entry of Madame Sosostris seems a bit of a romp, and she turns out at first to be Jack in disguise, a trick which only serves to deepen the apprehension of awe as the presence of Sosostris herself becomes apparent.

She emerges as a 'huge contraption of black veils of roughly human shape, though much more than life-size' – her face is never seen. A crystal bowl is placed before her and there follows a magnificent extended aria which forms the still centrepiece of the final act. Sosostris is not however a mere modern clairvoyant, for Tippett invests her with divine insight – oracular power achieved at the expense of her womanhood. Her aria is a profound exposition of the seer's self-sacrifice, which outlines the

'The Midsummer Marriage' (Tippett), Act 3: final scene from the original production at Covent Garden, London, 27 January 1955, with Joan Sutherland and Richard Lewis as Jenifer and Mark (centre) flanked by Edith Coates and Michael Langdon (standing, left and right) as the Ancients and with the dancer Pirmin Trecu as Strephon kneeling before them (set by Barbara Hepworth)

ordeal of the oracle in hearing divine inspiration. She is therefore a metaphor for the very source of creativity: 'I am what has been, is and shall be. No mortal ever lifted my garment'. This great apostrophe is the transcendent lodestar of the opera, quoting from an essay by Schiller which Beethoven kept framed over his desk. The aria draws from Tippett his most overwhelmingly moving and visionary music – a supreme moment in the whole literature of opera.

After the aria King Fisher rejects Sosostris's lyrical vision of Jenifer about to unite with Mark, and he is moved to tear the veils which surround her, only to reveal the lotus flower in which Mark and Jenifer are seen in 'radiant transfiguration, in reds and gold, posed in mutual contemplation. Sosostris has vanished'. Her vision vindicated, King Fisher is blinded by it, and when he tries to shoot Mark, he dies himself, as predicted, and we realize that the earlier warning voice had been Sosostris's. The requiem which follows releases the energy of rebirth for the fourth and final ritual dance, 'Fire in Summer' (the voluntary human sacrifice).

Strephon and a fellow dancer prepare for the rite of the summer solstice with ritual fire, and as he holds the 'freely burning stick above his head' we see Mark and Jenifer assume a pose of 'vigour and ecstasy' in symbolic union within the lotus petals. They sing an ecstatic duet as Strephon collapses at their feet in a final gesture of sacrifice, to be wholly consumed as the incandescent spiritual fire transfigures the stage. As the chorus join the celebration of divine and physical love the lotus leaves rise to cover the three figures and the bud finally bursts aflame. Although Strephon is dead, Mark and Jenifer are reborn to their life of fulfilment and psychic equilibrium, and as the fire dies away and the magical 'second dawn' breaks they return to the everyday world to marry at last.

* * *

The Midsummer Marriage represents the musical and philosophical culmination of Tippett's extended first period of composition. Its richly coloured harmonic language, often based on chords built from networks of 4ths and 5ths, is the foundation for a profusion of lyrical expression unparalleled in Tippett's output. The writing for chorus and orchestra is warmly homogeneous but accommodates an effortless range of Tippett's rhythmic and contrapuntal devices. The distinctive musical world of the opera was to linger briefly in three major works: the Corelli Fantasia (1953), the Piano Concerto (1953–5) and the Second Symphony (1956–7). For many it represents the quintessential Tippett. The magnificence of Tippett's conception in every respect has assured the work a unique position in 20th-century opera. Nevertheless its initial reception was very mixed, even hostile. The dramatic confusion of the production and the common perception of Tippett's libretto as a clumsy hotchpotch obscured the reaction to the music. Its self-sufficient strength was revealed in a crucial studio broadcast in 1963, which led to a superior production at Covent Garden in 1968; but even this did not entirely rehabilitate the work as a dramatic entity. The production by Welsh National Opera in 1976 finally revealed the score to be a universal masterpiece, and it has since been produced all over the world to general recognition as a source of musical and theatrical enrichment.   GERAINT LEWIS

Midsummer Night's Dream, A. Opera in three acts, op.64, by BENJAMIN BRITTEN to a libretto by him and

PETER PEARS, after WILLIAM SHAKESPEARE's play; Aldeburgh, Jubilee Hall, 11 June 1960.

Oberon *King of the Fairies*	countertenor (or contralto)
Tytania [Titania] *Queen of the Fairies*	coloratura soprano
Puck	acrobat, speaking role
Theseus *Duke of Athens*	bass
Hippolyta *betrothed to Theseus*	contralto
Lysander ⎱ *in love with Hermia*	tenor
Demetrius ⎰	baritone
Hermia *in love with Lysander*	mezzo-soprano
Helena *in love with Demetrius*	soprano
Bottom *a weaver*	bass-baritone
Quince *a carpenter*	bass
Flute *a bellows-mender*	tenor
Snug *a joiner*	bass
Snout *a tinker*	tenor
Starveling *a tailor*	baritone
Cobweb ⎱	treble
Peaseblossom ⎪ *fairies*	treble
Mustardseed ⎪	treble
Moth ⎰	treble

Chorus of fairies

Setting A wood near Athens, then Theseus's palace

Britten's *A Midsummer Night's Dream* was something of a rush job, conceived and created between August 1959 and April 1960 for performance at the 1960 Aldeburgh Festival, in celebration of rebuilding work at the Jubilee Hall, the festival's only theatre until the opening of the Maltings at Snape in 1967. The cast for the première included Alfred Deller as Oberon, Jennifer Vyvyan as Titania and Owen Brannigan as Bottom. In 1960 Britten's reputation stood high and the new opera was soon taken up elsewhere. In 1961 alone it was seen at Covent Garden (in the Aldeburgh production) and in Hamburg, Berlin, Milan, San Francisco, Zürich and Tokyo. It was the first Britten opera to be staged at Snape (1967) and among many successful subsequent productions the English Music Theatre Company's 1980 staging, also first seen at Snape, transferred to Covent Garden in 1986. A fine production at Glyndebourne by Peter Hall (1981) was televised and a recording conducted by Britten and with many of the original cast was released in 1967.

ACT 1 *The wood, deepening twilight* At the start the orchestra evokes the mystery and magic of the wood by moving through a succession of all 12 major triads, the string glissandos suggesting the breathing of a dreamer in a deep sleep. The fairies appear and their first song, 'Over hill, over dale', has the direct, fresh melodic use of scale patterns that is a familiar yet never hackneyed Britten fingerprint. Puck enters to what will prove his characteristic accompaniment of trumpet and drum, speaking rather than singing, and preparing for the entrance of Oberon and Titania. The King and Queen of the Fairies are angry with each other, their music ('Ill met by moonlight') almost extravagantly intense as they quarrel over possession of the 'lovely boy stol'n from an Indian king'. After Titania's departure, Oberon summons Puck and orders him to fetch a magic herb that will enable him to have his own way. Now the quartet of Athenian lovers approach: first Hermia and Lysander, who swear undying love; then Helena and

'A Midsummer Night's Dream' (Britten): scene from the original production at Jubilee Hall, Aldeburgh, 11 June 1960, with Alfred Deller as Oberon and Jennifer Vyvyan as Titania

Demetrius in a very different state, she making frank advances, he spurning them. As the lovers move away, Oberon returns. Puck brings him the flower and Oberon charges him to use it to 'cure' Demetrius of his dislike of Helena. Britten sets Oberon's lines 'I know a bank' to a sinuous melody in a suitably exotic orchestral garb, celesta prominent. Here the justification for what might have seemed a risk – the choice of the countertenor voice for Oberon – is clear and complete: there is an air of Baroque fantasy in the music, which nevertheless remains entirely Britten's.

Next the Rustics (as Britten designates the Athenian craftsmen) appear, to decide on the cast for the play they are offering for the Duke's wedding celebrations. For the broad comedy of this scene Britten adopts an appropriately jaunty style, with a gawky solo trombone, making sure that the words have every chance of being heard, and that Bottom achieves the necessary prominence, with his desire to 'play the lion'. As the Rustics depart, Lysander and Hermia return, still in love but weary. They fall asleep and Puck, in error, squeezes the herb's juice into Lysander's eyes. Then Helena and Demetrius arrive, still fighting. Left alone, Helena wakes Lysander, whose instant declaration of love she interprets as mockery. They run off, and Hermia awakes alone, bewildered and afraid. The act ends with the events which, in Shakespeare, happen earlier. To a repeat of the initial forest music, Titania asks her attendants to sing her to sleep. After the lullaby ('Ye spotted snakes') has done its work, Oberon enters and squeezes the juice into her eyes, with the final admonition 'Wake when some vile thing is near'.

ACT 2 *The wood, dark night* The act begins with four quiet orchestral chords (using all 12 notes) like a chromatic version of the harmonies that begin Mendelssohn's famous overture. Titania is asleep, and does not wake as the Rustics rehearse their play. Puck

observes them, resolving to make mischief – so, when Bottom returns after an exit, he wears an ass's head and his colleagues flee in terror. Bottom sings a loud, coarse song ('The woosel-cock, so black of hue'), waking Titania and inspiring her instant devotion. She summons her fairies with a gentle, florid waltz ('Be kind and courteous') and the fairies, complete with an on-stage band of sopranino recorders, small cymbals and woodblocks, entertain the couple until they both fall asleep. Oberon is at first well satisfied with Puck's doings, but when Demetrius and Hermia appear Puck's mistake is all too clear. After Demetrius has fallen asleep Oberon uses the magic herb on him, singing 'Flower of this purple dye' to a reminiscence of 'I know a bank'. But the lovers' main scene of conflict is yet to come. When Lysander and Helena enter, Demetrius awakes and immediately declares his passion for Helena. Hermia returns and there is an extended quartet of argument and recrimination, reaching a climax when Lysander and Demetrius leave to fight. Oberon is in a rage with Puck, but the trouble-maker makes amends, manoeuvring the lovers about the forest until they collapse exhausted. The fairies sing a touching lullaby to the four 'magic' chords ('On the ground sleep sound') and Puck squeezes an antidote into Lysander's eyes.

ACT 3 *The wood, early next morning* Oberon explains to Puck that he now has the Indian boy who was the cause of his dispute with Titania. He releases Titania from the spell, and causes Bottom's ass's head to disappear. To a solemn dance ('quasi Saraband') the King and Queen of the Fairies anticipate their midnight visit to Theseus's palace. As offstage horns take over from the 'morning lark', the lovers wake and are at last fully reconciled, Helena with Demetrius, Hermia with Lysander. Still in a daze they set off for Athens. Bottom only wakes when the other Rustics come in search of him with the exciting news that 'our play is preferred'.

After a lively ensemble they hurry away to make their own preparations. During an orchestral interlude based on increasingly urgent statements of the horn-call music, the scene changes to the ducal palace. Theseus sings the praises of his bride Hippolyta, and after hearing the two pairs of lovers tell of their reconciliation he announces that they shall be married alongside his own wedding. The play is called for, and 'The most Lamentable Comedy and most Cruel Death of Pyramus and Thisby' is presented. Britten's music adds splendid point to this notably unpatronizing farce of confusion and incompetence; even his parody of a Donizetti mad-scene with obbligato flute for Thisby makes its point without over-emphasis. The performance ends with a robust Bergomask dance. Then midnight strikes and a more solemn mood supervenes. At Theseus's bidding – 'Lovers to bed' – the stage empties. Then the fairies appear, with Puck, Titania and Oberon. 'Now, until the break of day' is a haunting song of blessing, as serenely poised as anything in Britten. But, as in Shakespeare, the last words go to Puck, the last sounds to the brisk divisions of his trumpet and drum.

*   *   *

The nocturnal theme of Shakespeare's play was an obvious attraction to Britten: only the year before he had concluded his *Nocturne* with a setting of a Shakespeare sonnet. Moreover, the play had been a favourite at least since he had played the viola in Mendelssohn's incidental music as a 15-year-old. It was a particular challenge to start with a text other than a custom-made libretto, and Shakespeare's play had to be cut by half. The shift of emphasis is clear in that, while the play begins at Theseus's court, Britten begins in the wood, with Act 2 scene i. Nevertheless, only one line is added to Shakespeare: in Act 1 of the opera Lysander explains Hermia's plight in the face of the ruling, 'compelling thee to marry with Demetrius'. In all three acts the music is continuous and there are no scene-divisions marked in the score, although Act 3 has an extended interlude to facilitate the change of scene. In style the music relates to Britten's other major works of the 1950s and early 60s: the language is essentially tonal, the vocabulary essentially triadic; although there is a high degree of chromaticism, consequent on the presence of 12-note features, these are by no means as extensive as in some of the later works.

ARNOLD WHITTALL

Mierzwiński, Władysław (*b* Warsaw, 21 Oct 1850; *d* Paris, ?14 July 1909). Polish tenor. He studied at Warsaw, Naples and Milan, and made his début at the Paris Opéra as Raoul in *Les Huguenots*. His appearance in London in 1880 marked the beginning of an immensely successful career. He appeared on all the principal European and American stages, singing the leading roles in *Guillaume Tell*, *Les Huguenots*, *Robert le diable* and *Il trovatore*. His voice was distinguished by its wide range, great strength and fine sound, and he was considered one of the most outstanding tenors of his time. A throat disease forced him to retire prematurely, and he died in poverty and obscurity.

*

'Władysław Mierzwiński i jego występy na scenie warszawskiej w Hugonotach, Robercie Diable i Wilhelmie Tellu' [Władysław Mierzwiński and his performances on the Warsaw stage in *Les Huguenots, Robert le diable* and *Guillaume Tell*], *Echo muzyczne* (1881), 130–32

Z. Noskowski: 'Władysław Mierzwiński', *Echo muzyczne, teatralne i artystyczne*, no.431 (1892), 1–3

A. Dobrowolski: 'Władysław Mierzwiński: wspomnienie pośmiertne' [Posthumous Recollections], *Tygodnik ilustrowany*, xxx (1909), 598

R. Koczalski: 'Wspomnienie o Władysławie Mierzwińskim', *Scena i sztuka* (1911), no.8, p.4; no.9, pp.3–4   ZOFIA CHECHLIŃSKA

Migenes [Migenes-Johnson], **Julia** (*b* New York, 13 March 1945). American soprano. As a child she appeared as Dolore in *Madama Butterfly*, at the Metropolitan. After graduating from the High School of Music and Art in New York she appeared on Broadway and made her New York City Opera début as Annina in *The Saint of Bleecker Street* (1965). In the early 1970s she went to Europe; she studied in Vienna and became a popular performer with the Vienna Volksoper (1973–8), where her roles included Despina, Susanna, Blonde, and Toinette, which she created in Wolpert's *Der eingebildete Kranke* (1975). She sang Musetta with the San Francisco Opera in 1978; her first appearance with the Metropolitan Opera was the following year as Jenny in *Aufstieg und Fall der Stadt Mahagonny*, followed by Nedda, Musetta and Lulu, a role she also sang at the Vienna Staatsoper (1983). She sang Salome in Geneva, and Offenbach's Eurydice at the Deutsche Oper, Berlin (1983). Her Covent Garden début, in 1987, was as Massenet's Manon, and she sang Olympia, Antonia and Giulietta (*Les contes d'Hoffmann*) at Los Angeles in the following year. In 1984 she performed the title role in Francesco Rosi's film *Carmen*. Her most successful stage role has been as Lulu in the Metropolitan Opera production (1980–81, then 1985), for which both her singing and acting were highly praised.

*

F. Gannon: 'Carmen Chameleon: a Profile of Julia Migenes-Johnson', *Saturday Review*, xi/2 (1985), 26–30, 59

KATHLEEN HAEFLIGER, ELIZABETH FORBES

Migliavacca, Giovanni Ambrogio (*b* Milan, *c*1718; *d* Dresden, Vienna or Milan, after 1787). Italian librettist. His academic name was 'Filodosso'. Nothing is known of his life before his appointment as imperial secretary to the vicariate in Vienna some time before the mid-1740s. Presumably, he became amanuensis to the court poet Pietro Metastasio at about the same time. The fullest sources of information on Migliavacca are a dozen letters written by Metastasio to him between 1750 and 1771, and as many more to Farinelli and others from the late 1740s to the 1760s. Metastasio recommended Migliavacca to the Dresden court, where the latter was court poet from 1752 until perhaps the mid-1780s, and wrote to Migliavacca generally with respect and kindness, although several of his letters to Farinelli and others are critical of Migliavacca's talent and person.

Metastasio seems to have had mixed feelings for his assistant, and many of his compliments hide veiled insults. He described Migliavacca as able to write 'an attractive *canzone, cantata, scenetto* and things that require no great skill in managing the passions or delineating characters' but also as 'questo gocciolone' ('this big drip'; 7 December 1748), and as inconsiderate and 'not more rich in abilities than deficient in judgment' (5 July 1749).

In evaluating Migliavacca for a position at the Lisbon court, Metastasio reported (in a letter to A. L. Laugier, 2 September 1752) that he liked some of the works he had read, and added that the poet should function well in a theatre where cutting and adding verses, serving composers and adjusting to the moment, place and pleasure of his patron were vital.

Metastasio also wrote to Migliavacca about *Solimano* (on 13 January 1753), alternately praising and criticizing aspects, but concluding that the spectacle of the production would distract the audience from its shortcomings. Nevertheless, it enjoyed relatively wide popularity, and was revived and reset by many composers. He was complimentary the following year (16 February 1754) about *Artemisia*: vicissitudes of fortune portrayed reflect Migliavacca's increased output and experience, but expressions of passion and characterization do not match Metastasio's own high level of invention.

In time, Migliavacca came to be hailed as the worthy successor to Metastasio, and was described in a letter of 18 May 1761 from Count Giacomo Durazzo to Favart as the Italian poet who best imitated the style of Metastasio.

Migliavacca may have settled in Vienna, but he received letters in Milan in 1771, and in 1768 was described as court poet and political functionary at Dresden. His last datable work, *La reggia d'Imeneo*, to mark the wedding of the Saxon prince Anton and the duchess Maria Theresa, was set by Johann Gottlieb Naumann and performed in Dresden in 1787. Since it appears not to be a revival, it seems likely that Migliavacca was then living in Dresden and still official poet to the Saxon court.

See also SOLIMANO.

Armida placata (os), Mele, 1750 (Mysliveček, 1778); *Solimano* (os), Hasse, 1753 (Fischietti, 1755; M. Valentini, 1756; Pescetti, 1756; D. Perez, 1757; Errichelli, 1757; A. Ferradini, 1757; Traetta, 1759; B. Galuppi, 1760; Schwanenberger, 1762; Sciroli, 1766; J. G. Naumann, 1773; Astarita, 1777; Curcio, 1782); *Artemisia* (os), Hasse, 1754 (G. Calegari, 1782); *Tetide* (serenata), Gluck, 1760; *Armida* (azione teatrale, with G. Durazzo), Traetta, 1761; *Prometeo assoluto* (serenata), Wagenseil, 1762; *Acide e Galatea* (festa teatrale), Haydn, 1763; *La reggia d'Imeneo* (festa teatrale), J. G. Naumann, 1787

*

P. Napoli-Signorelli: *Storia critica de' teatri antichi e moderni* (Naples, 1787–90), vi, 286
C. Burney: *Memoirs of the Life and Writings of the Abate Metastasio* (London, 1796) [incl. 6 letters about Migliavacca]
C.-S. Favart: *Mémoires*, i (Paris, 1808), 152
M. Fürstenau: *Zur Geschichte der Musik und des Theaters am Hofe zu Dresden* (Dresden, 1861–2), ii, 274–80, 294
C. Mennicke: *Hasse und die Brüder Graun als Symphoniker* (Leipzig, 1906), 417
B. Brunelli, ed.: *Tutte le opere di Pietro Metastasio*, iii–v (Milan, 1951–4)   SVEN HANSELL

Mignatti [Mignatta], **La**. *See* MUSI, MARIA MADDALENA.

Mignon. *Opéra comique* in three acts by AMBROISE THOMAS to a libretto by JULES BARBIER and MICHEL CARRÉ, after JOHANN WOLFGANG VON GOETHE's novel, *Wilhelm Meister Lehrjahre*; Paris, Opéra-Comique (Salle Favart), 17 November 1866.

Mignon was an immediate success, in large measure because of the performance of Célestine Galli-Marié (who later created Carmen) in the title role. Although she did not have an outstanding voice, Galli-Marié was a fine singing actress and possessed exactly the waifish charm that the part required. In Goethe's novel Mignon is not the main character, but Barbier and Carré, often blamed for their cavalier treatment of literary masterpieces (in Gounod's *Faust* and Thomas' *Hamlet*, for instance), here showed extremely sound theatrical judg-

Mignon	mezzo-soprano
Wilhelm Meister *a student*	tenor
Philine *an actress*	soprano
Lothario *a wandering minstrel*	bass
Laerte *an actor*	tenor
Jarno *a gypsy*	bass
Frédéric *Philine's admirer*	tenor or contralto
Antonio *castle retainer*	bass

Townspeople, gypsies, actors and servants

Setting Germany and Italy in the late 18th century

ment in their adaptation of a work not, on the surface, suitable as the basis of an opera libretto. Even the obligatory happy ending seems right in the context (in the novel Mignon dies; it was another nine years before *Carmen* overturned the convention of a happy ending at the Opéra-Comique).

The original cast of *Mignon* also included Marie Cabel as Philine, Léon Achard as Wilhelm Meister, Eugène Battaille as Lothario and Joseph-Antoine-Charles Couderc as Laerte. The opera reached its hundredth performance at the Comique in eight months, and its 1000th in 28 years. Its British première took place at Drury Lane on 5 July 1870 where it was sung in Italian and Thomas provided recitatives to replace the spoken dialogue. He also adapted the title role for the soprano Christine Nilsson; the part of Frédéric, hitherto sung by a buffo tenor, was taken by the contralto Zélia Trebelli, for whom Thomas wrote the rondo-gavotte, 'In veder l'amata stanza'. Nilsson also sang Mignon in the first New York performance at the Academy of Music on 22 November 1871 and at the Metropolitan in 1883.

It was in this version that *Mignon* became popular outside France, especially in Italy and the USA. Notable soprano interpreters of the title role have included Emma Albani (who was Covent Garden's first Mignon in 1874), Geraldine Farrar and Lucrezia Bori; among the mezzo-soprano Mignons, Risë Stevens, Ebe Stignani, Giulietta Simionato, Marilyn Horne and Frederica von Stade should be mentioned. Cynthia Clarey was a poignant Mignon at the Wexford Festival in 1986, when the original *opéra comique* version of the score was used. Lily Pons made a spectacular Philine, while Gigli and Schipa both found Meister a rewarding role. The first commercially sponsored broadcast of opera from the Metropolitan in 1933 was *Mignon*, with Bori, Pons, Schipa and, as Frédéric, Gladys Swarthout.

ACT 1 *The courtyard of an inn in a small German town* Townspeople and travellers drink and are entertained by the wandering minstrel Lothario, who sings 'Fugitif et tremblant' to his own harp accompaniment. Philine and Laerte, members of a troupe of actors, look on as the gypsies dance. Jarno, their chief, threatens to beat Mignon when she refuses to dance, but Lothario and Wilhelm Meister, a student, come to her help. In gratitude she divides her bunch of wild flowers between them. Wilhelm tells Laerte, in 'Oui, je veux, par le monde', that he is 20 years old, comes from Vienna and is wandering the world in search of adventure. Greatly impressed by Philine's beauty, he does not protest when Laerte takes the flowers that Mignon gave him and presents them to the actress. Philine and Laerte leave; Wilhelm questions Mignon about her childhood, but she has only a vague memory, before she was kidnapped

*Poster by Jules Chéret for Thomas'
'Mignon', printed at the time of the
original production at the Opéra-
Comique, Paris, in 1866*

by gypsies, of a foreign land, warmer than Germany
('Connais-tu le pays?'). Deciding to purchase Mignon's
freedom, Wilhelm negotiates the price with Jarno.
Lothario comes to say goodbye to Mignon; he is travelling southward, like the swallows, and together they
sing 'Légères hirondelles'. Lothario would like Mignon
to go with him, but she wants to stay with Wilhelm.
Philine enters, followed by her young admirer Frédéric,
but she is interested only in Wilhelm. The actors have
received an invitation from Baron de Rosenberg
(Frédéric's uncle) to perform at his castle and they are
about to set off there. Mignon, by now deeply in love
with Wilhelm, is upset to see the flowers that she gave
him in the hands of Philine.

ACT 2.i *Philine's boudoir in Rosenberg castle* After
an entr'acte, the tune of which is used for Frédéric's
rondo-gavotte, Philine expresses great pleasure in the
luxury of her present surroundings. The voice of Laerte
is heard outside in praise of Philine's charms. He ushers
in Wilhelm and Mignon, who pretends to be asleep as
Wilhelm and Philine sing a duet, 'Je crois entendre les
doux compliments'. When they have left, Mignon tries
on one of Philine's costumes and, sitting at the mirror,
makes up her face. She is consumed with jealousy. She
goes out, Frédéric enters and, in the version for contralto, sings the gavotte. When Wilhelm returns looking
for Mignon he is confronted by Frédéric; as they are
about to fight, Mignon rushes between them. Frédéric
laughs to see her in Philine's dress, but Wilhelm realizes
that she cannot stay with him and says goodbye to her.

He goes off arm-in-arm with Philine, who mocks
Mignon's appearance in her borrowed finery.

2.ii *The park of the castle* Mignon, eaten up by
jealous rage, sings 'Elle est là, près de lui?'. She is about
to throw herself in the lake when she hears the strains of
a harp. It is Lothario and he comforts the girl in a duet,
'As-tu souffert? As-tu pleuré?'. Applause for Philine is
heard from the conservatory where the actors are
performing *A Midsummer Night's Dream*. Crying out
that she wishes the building could be struck by lightning
and set on fire, Mignon rushes away. Lothario, muttering 'Fire, fire' to himself, wanders off towards the conservatory. Philine, elated by success, sings the brilliant
polonaise 'Je suis Titania' as the actors and the guests
come out into the park. When Mignon reappears, she is
greeted so warmly by Wilhelm that Philine sends her
into the conservatory to fetch the flowers given to
Wilhelm the previous day. Smoke and flames are seen
coming from the building that Lothario has obediently
set on fire. Wilhelm rushes inside and emerges with
Mignon unconscious in his arms, the scorched flowers
still in her hand.

ACT 3 *The gallery of a castle in Italy* Wilhelm has
brought Mignon and Lothario to Italy, where Mignon is
recuperating under the watchful care of the old man,
who prays for her complete recovery. Antonio, one of
the servants, tells the sad story of the castle's previous
owners: the young daughter believed drowned, the
mother dead from grief and the father, driven mad by
these events, in exile. The castle, he informs Wilhelm, is

now up for sale and could be bought quite cheaply. Wilhelm tells Lothario that, as the Cipriani palace has contributed so greatly to Mignon's recovery, he intends to buy it for her. At the name 'Cipriani' Lothario goes to one of the gallery doors and disappears. Wilhelm, though curious at this response, returns to the contemplation of Mignon, who is unable to believe that her love for him is returned. A letter from Laerte arrives, warning Wilhelm that Philine is nearby. Mignon awakens and in a duet with Wilhelm, 'Je suis heureuse! l'air m'enivre', she expresses her love for this strange yet oddly familiar place, while he assures her that he loves her. The sound of Philine's voice outside causes Mignon to faint; on regaining consciousness she sees Lothario, richly dressed, coming towards them. He formally welcomes the two young people to his palace and hands Mignon a small box. On opening it she finds a book belonging to Sperata, the daughter of the house. She starts to read the prayer inside, then continues to recite it by heart. Mignon is Sperata, and Lothario, his reason once more restored, is her father. With Wilhelm they sing of their happiness at being reunited in a trio whose melody recalls that of 'Connais-tu le pays?'.

* * *

The character of Mignon inspired Thomas to write his finest and most dramatic music. Every note that she sings comes from the heart, ensuring that her feelings of passionate love for Wilhelm and her murderous jealousy of Philine are made perfectly clear, while the less violent emotions raised by the clouded memories of her childhood and by the familiarity of the Italian landscape are equally well conveyed. The shallow, frivolous Philine, so beautifully caught in her polonaise, the youthful and genuinely sincere student Wilhelm and the noble, gentle and bewildered figure of Lothario are all firmly and individually drawn, but none of them has the depth of Mignon, in whom pathos and strength of will are balanced to a hair's breadth. Without in any way flouting the strict conventions of opéra comique at that time, Thomas achieved a freedom of emotional and dramatic expression in his score that Bizet, when he wrote Carmen, was able to achieve only by shattering those conventions.   ELIZABETH FORBES

Mignone, Francisco (Paulo) (b São Paulo, 3 Sept 1897; d Rio de Janeiro, 18 Feb 1986). Brazilian composer and conductor. The son of an Italian immigrant musician and music teacher, he began flute and piano studies with his father. He continued his studies, including composition, at the São Paulo Conservatory with Agostino Cantù, graduating in 1917. In 1920 he went to the Milan Conservatory and studied for two years under Vincenzo Ferroni, himself a composer of operas, and a former pupil of Massenet; the composition of Mignone's first opera O contratador de diamantes in 1921 was supervised by Ferroni. A ballet, Congada, taken from the second act, became quite famous. His second opera L'innocente received its première at Rio in 1928 with great success. These two works reveal a strong affinity with late 19th-century Italian and French opera.

Mignone's definitive return to São Paulo took place in 1929, when he became a harmony teacher at the Conservatory. He also worked as a répétiteur and played for Gigli and Schipa during their Brazilian tours. At the end of 1932 he moved to Rio de Janeiro, succeeding Walter Burle Marx as the official conductor and conducting teacher at the Instituto Nacional de Música. He

remained at that institution until his retirement in 1967. He also taught privately for many years. After a European conducting tour (1937–8) he visited the USA for the first time in 1942. In New York the League of Composers had some of his works performed, and he conducted the NBC and CBS orchestras in concerts of his music. During the next two decades he held many different appointments, among them the music directorships of the Teatro Municipal, Radio Ministério da Educação e Cultura and Radio Giobo, all in Rio.

Many of Mignone's earlier works are Romantic in structure and harmony, although he also composed several popular-music pieces under the pseudonym of Chico Bororó. From the 1930s to about 1960 his music was strongly nationalistic, influenced by the ideas propounded by Mário de Andrade who had been a severe critic of Mignone's early Italianate works. Only in the 1970s did Mignone return to opera. His lifelong adherence to musical nationalism (with the exception of the decade of the 1960s) made him select Brazilian historical and literary themes in his last two operas. O chalaça (1976) deals with a historical character at the court of the Emperor Pedro I, and is probably one of the best works of the contemporary operatic repertory in Brazil. O sargento de milícias (1978), to a libretto by Humberto Mello Nóbrega after the 1854 novel of Manuel Antonio de Almeida, was commissioned by the Rio Theatre Foundation for the re-opening of the Teatro Municipal after a substantial remodelling of the theatre's interior. In two acts with a prologue and three tableaux, the opera outlines characters typical of colonial Brazil, in an attractive social and human depiction of Rio de Janeiro around 1800. The libretto does not present a plot in the traditional operatic mould, so that the work appears more like a comedy of social customs and habits. In addition to exploring 20th-century compositional techniques, Mignone incorporates an old Portuguese song, a Bahian streetvendor's cry and Brazilian sentimental love songs (modhinas). The last tableau depicts a feast day, and the street dancing of a sarambeque (supposedly the forerunner of the samba) by black people, celebrating the wedding of three couples. Thus Mignone comments effectively on the social atmosphere of the period through generic musical means.

See also CHALAÇA, O; CONTRATADOR DE DIAMANTES, O; and INNOCENTE, L'.

O contratador de diamantes, 1921 (3, G. Bottoni, after A. Arinos), Rio, Municipal, 20 Sept 1924
L'innocente (3, A. Rossato, after C. Espina Tagle), Rio, Municipal, 5 Sept 1928
Mizú (operetta), 1937
O chalaça, 1973 (2, H. Mello Nóbrega), Rio, Cecília Meireles, 27 Nov 1976
O sargento de milícias (2, Mello Nóbrega, after M. A. de Almeida), Rio, Municipal, 15 Dec 1978

*

Francisco Mignone: catálogo de obras (Brasilia, 1978)
B. Kiefer: Mignone, vida e obra (Porto Alegre, 1983)
Z. Baptista Filho: A opera (Rio de Janeiro, 1987)
                                        GERARD BÉHAGUE

Migot, Georges (b Paris, 27 Feb 1891; d Levallois, nr Paris, 5 Jan 1976). French composer. He studied orchestration with d'Indy and music history with Emmanuel at the Paris Conservatoire, and won three successive composition prizes (1918–20). In 1921 he was awarded the Blumenthal Foundation Prize for French Thought and Art. The years 1920 to 1939 were ones of constant struggle against the neo-classical aesthetic which dominated music in Paris; always an independent spirit, Migot took nothing from this or any other fashionable movement. From 1949 to 1961 he was keeper of the Museum of Instruments at the Paris Conservatoire. He was an officer of the Légion d'honneur.

A prolific composer in many genres, Migot wrote several stage works, among them the chamber opera Le rossignol en amour (composed 1926–8), two ballets, and four pieces combining elements of opera and ballet: the Japanese Hagoromo (1920–21), La belle et la bête (1938), Mystère orphique (1948) and Le zodiaque (1958–60). He wrote his own librettos, insisting on a close spiritual link between text and music. What distinguishes him from his contemporaries – Hindemith or Les Six, for example – is the uncompromisingly polyphonic style that he progressively developed, and in his mature works he achieved a line completely free from rigid metrical restriction and from tonal function; while the melody is strictly diatonic, any suggestion of definite tonality is avoided – a technique he described as 'permodality'. Migot's melodic style is one of the most characteristic features of his music, but his use of timbre is also highly individual. The flowing quality of the music sets it in the tradition of Couperin, Rameau and Debussy. Migot was also a successful painter, poet and writer on music.

librettos by Migot unless otherwise stated

Hagoromo (symphonie lyrique et chorégraphique, with L. Laloy), Monte Carlo, 9 May 1922 (Paris, 1922)
Le rossignol en amour, 1926–8 (chamber op), Geneva, 2 March 1937
La belle et la bête, 1938 (opéra chorégraphique)
Mystère orphique, 1948 (polyphonie chorégraphique), Strasbourg, 18 March 1964
Le zodiaque, 1958–60 (chorégraphie lyrique, 4)

I. Schwerke: 'Georges Migot', *The Dominant*, ed. E. Evans (London, 1928)
P. Wolff: *La route d'un musicien: Georges Migot* (Paris, 1933)
M. Honegger: 'Georges Migot on "Le retour de la musique à ses origines vocales"', *SMz*, xciv (1954), 329–31
M. Pinchard: *Connaissance de Georges Migot* (Paris, 1959)
M. Honegger: 'Georges Migot', *Réforme* (25 Feb 1961)
J. Roy: *Présences contemporaines* (Paris, 1962)
M. Honegger: 'Introduction à Georges Migot, musicien', *Profils*, iii (1963), 42 [repr. in *SMz*, cv (1965), 348–56]
M. Honegger, ed.: *Catalogue des oeuvres musicales de Georges Migot* (Strasbourg, 1977)   MARC HONEGGER

Miguéz, Leopoldo (Américo) (*b* Niterói, 9 Sept 1850; *d* Rio de Janeiro, 6 Sept 1902). Brazilian composer. Born of a Spanish father and a Brazilian mother, he was educated in Portugal after spending some years in Spain. He studied the violin with Nicolau Medina Ribas and composition with the Italian Giovanni Franchini in Oporto. When 21 he returned to Brazil with his family and went into business with his father. He remained active in amateur music and was frequently asked to play or to conduct amateur ensembles. In 1881 he went with his wife to Europe; he spent two years living in Brussels, observing new developments in music and studying the techniques of the foremost composers of the time, particularly Wagner. On his return to Brazil in 1884, Miguéz became the leading personality in Brazilian musical life, as both a composer and a conductor. He was the first director of the young republic's Instituto Nacional de Música, established in 1889; in the same year he won a competition to select a new

Brazilian national anthem, but his entry was not adopted.

Miguéz's only opera, Os saldunes (3; Rio de Janeiro, Lírico, 20 Sept 1901; vs, Leipzig, 1901 or 1902), was composed in collaboration with Coelho Neto, one of the best Brazilian writers of the period; the première was of the Italian version, I salduni. The action takes place in the time of Julius Caesar's campaign in Gaul. The saldunes are two friends who go to war against Caesar, bound together by chains and by an oath that neither one will survive his friend's death. Both love the same woman and one lover decides to accept death in battle to oblige the other to follow him.

Miguéz also composed occasional music for Pelo amor!, a dramatic poem in two acts, also by Neto (1897).   LUIS HEITOR CORRÊA DE AZEVEDO

Mihalovich, Ödön [Edmund] **(Péter József de)** (*b* Feričance, Slovenia, 13 Sept 1842; *d* Budapest, 22 April 1929). Hungarian composer. From 1855 he lived in Pest, where he studied with Mosonyi. In 1865 he took composition lessons with Moritz Hauptmann in Leipzig and he completed his education with Peter Cornelius in Munich in 1868; thereafter he lived mainly in Pest. He was president of the Wagner Society in Pest from 1872 and in 1881 was appointed director of the Színitanoda (School of Dramatic Arts), which had an opera department. He succeeded Liszt as head of the music academy (1887–1918).

Both Wagner and Liszt strongly influenced his career. Wagner's influence began in 1863 when he gave concerts in Pest. In 1865 Mihalovich met Wagner in Munich when Tristan und Isolde was first performed and two months later he was in Pest for the première of an oratorio by Liszt, conducted by the composer; he became a close friend and admirer of Liszt. Despite his profound musical knowledge and his mastery of orchestral writing his operas are overwhelmed by Wagnerian traits, and for this reason had little success – with the exception of Toldi szerelme ('Toldi's Love', composed 1888–90). In spite of the impact of Wagner's own music, audiences were not interested in works by other composers in a similar style.

By 1868 Mihalovich already had the libretto for his first opera, Hagbarth und Signe; he began to compose it the following year, but did not complete it until 1874. It is based on a drama (1814) by the Danish writer Adam Oehlenschlaeger, derived from a romantic saga: Hagbarth, king of Trondheim, and Signe, princess of Seeland, fall in love at first sight; Signe saves Hagbarth from death by giving her own life, but he kills himself in despair. Mihalovich called this opera a 'Musikdrama', and composed it in a continuous declamatory style, with leitmotifs. It was not produced until 1882, in Dresden, in a revised version, and was further revised in 1886 for Budapest, where it received only five performances. Wieland der Schmied, based on an abandoned dramatic sketch by Wagner (1849), was never performed. Eliana (composed 1885–7), set to a free adaptation of Tennyson's account of the story of King Arthur, Lancelot and Guinevere, includes leitmotifs and employs melodic patterns close to those of Lohengrin. It was first produced in Budapest (in translation) in 1908 and in German in Vienna in 1909.

Mihalovich's last completed opera, Toldi szerelme, has a medieval Hungarian setting and it was the first opera in which he used Hungarian melodic and rhythmic patterns. Although it is dominated by its

Wagnerian orchestral background, it includes powerful music in the choruses and in a sextet and a duet. It was acclaimed at its première (1893) and remained in the repertory for eight years.

Hagbarth und Signe, 1869–74 (3, A. Stern, after A. Oehlenschlaeger), rev., Dresden, 17 Jan 1882; rev., Budapest, 17 Jan 1886; *H-Bn*
Wieland der Schmied, 1876–8 (3, Stern, after R. Wagner), unperf.
König Fjalar, 1880–84 (O. Schlemm), inc.
Eliana, 1885–7 (3, H. Herrig, after A. Tennyson: *The Idylls of the King*), in Hung., Budapest, 16 Feb 1908 (Budapest, 1908); in Ger., Vienna, 17 April 1909; *Bn*
Toldi szerelme [Toldi's Love], 1888–90 (3, G. Csiky and Ábrányi, after J. Arany), Budapest, 18 March 1893; rev., 1893–4, Budapest, 27 Nov 1911 (Budapest, 1895); rev. 1904; *Bn*
A tihanyi visszhang [The Echo of Tihany], 1903 (G. Moravcsik), inc.

*

E. Major: 'Mihalovich Ödön', *Muzsika* (June 1929), 7–25 [with work-list and bibliography]
K. Szerző: 'Eine Oper der ungarischen Wagner-Schule: Edmund von Mihalovich: Eliana', *SM*, xix (1977), 109–60   DEZSŐ LEGÁNY

Mihalovici, Marcel (*b* Bucharest, 22 Oct 1898; *d* Paris, 12 Aug 1985). French composer of Romanian origin. He studied harmony with Cuclin in Bucharest and composition with d'Indy at the Schola Cantorum, Paris; he also received advice from his compatriot Enescu. Mihalovici remained in the French capital, drawing in his music on a wide range of current trends. Harmonic fantasy and continuous rhythmic variations give his music freshness and dynamism, and his dramatic solutions are simple and austere (in *Krapp*, there is only one character and a magnetic tape). For the stage he composed operas, ballets and incidental music; his output also includes orchestral, chamber and vocal works.

L'intransigeant Pluton, 1928 (1, J.-F. Regnard), RTF, 3 April 1939 (Paris, 1937)
Phèdre (5 scenes, Y. Goll, after J. Racine), RTF, 18 April 1950; stage, Stuttgart, 9 June 1951 (Paris, 1949)
Die Heimkehr (1, K. H. Ruppel, after G. de Maupassant), Düsseldorf, 9 Nov 1954 (Berlin, 1954); rev., Hamburg, 23 Jan 1955 (Berlin, 1955)
Krapp ou La dernière bande (1, S. Beckett), Bielefeld, 25 Feb 1961 (Paris, 1960)
Les jumeaux (ob, 3, C. Rostand, after Plautus: *Menechemes*), Brunswick, 23 Jan 1963 (Paris, 1962)

*

G. Beck: *Marcel Mihalovici: esquisse biographique* (Paris, 1954)
'Marcel Mihalovici', *Le courrier musical de France*, lx/4 (1977) [biographical list of works]   VIOREL COSMA

Mikado, The [*The Mikado; or, The Town of Titipu*]. Operetta in two acts by ARTHUR SULLIVAN to a libretto by W. S. GILBERT; London, Savoy Theatre, 14 March 1885.

Nanki-Poo (tenor) has fled the court of his father, the Mikado of Japan (bass), to avoid marrying the unattractive Katisha (contralto). Disguised as a wandering minstrel he is reunited in Titipu with his new love, Yum-Yum (soprano). Their union is thwarted, however, by her betrothal to Ko-Ko (baritone) who, condemned to death under the Mikado's severe anti-flirting laws, has been appointed Lord High Executioner on the principle that he cannot execute anyone before decapitating himself. Compelled to stage an execution to satisfy the Mikado, Ko-Ko permits the marriage of Yum-Yum and Nanki-Poo when the latter consents to be beheaded in return. No blood is spilt, however, as Ko-Ko, aided by Pitti-Sing (mezzo-soprano) and the self-important Pooh-Bah (baritone), convinces the emperor that the deed has been done. On discovering that the victim was his son, the Mikado sentences those responsible but he relents when Nanki-Poo reappears.

The Mikado is widely regarded as the finest Gilbert and Sullivan operetta. Certainly it is the only one to have gained significant popularity outside the English-speaking world. Gilbert's play is brilliantly constructed, and the ingenuity and variety of his lyrics provided unfailing inspiration to the composer. There are specific musical jokes, such as the wind interpolations in 'The criminal cried' and the quotation from Bach's G minor organ fugue in 'A more humane Mikado', but more fundamental is the vein of pure good humour which infects the score. Nowhere did Sullivan write more wittily than in 'Three little maids from school', 'So please you, sir' and 'Here's a how-de-do!'; and where verbal humour is to the fore, as in 'As someday it may happen' and 'There is beauty in the bellow of the blast', the musical support is impeccable.

Gilbert and Sullivan excel in their portrayal of girlish innocence, and their inspiration is at its happiest in the choruses and sparkling ensembles for the schoolgirls. Yum-Yum's solo, 'The sun whose rays', is a tour de force of subtle rhythmic treatment and expressive vocal contour. 'A wand'ring minstrel I' – a miniature compendium of ballad styles – and 'On a tree by a river' are among the most celebrated Savoy numbers, but ultimately the achievement of composer and librettist in *The Mikado* goes beyond the creation of a succession of individually brilliant musical pieces and dialogue scenes. It is the work's complete artistic cohesion that places it among the greatest operettas ever written.

DAVID RUSSELL HULME

Mikhaylov, Maxim Dormidontovich (*b* Kol'tsovka, nr Kazan', 13/25 Aug 1893; *d* Moscow, 30 March 1971). Russian bass. He studied singing with F. Oshustovich in Kazan' and V. Osipov in Moscow. He was a soloist at the Bol'shoy from 1932, singing mainly in Russian operas, his great parts being Susanin, Konchak, Pimen (which he sang in the film of *Boris*, 1955) and the Viking Guest (*Sadko*). His rare power and tonal beauty were impressive in heroic-epic roles, while in a part such as Chub (Tchaikovsky's *Cherevichki*) he displayed a sharp sense of comedy.

*

V. Yendrzheyevsky and E. Osipov: *M. Mikhaylov* (Moscow, 1957)
I. M. YAMPOL'SKY

Mikhaylova [Michailova], **Mariya** [Maria] **(Alexandrovna)** (*b* Kharkiv, 22 May/3 June 1866; *d* Molotov [now Perm'], 18 Jan 1943). Russian soprano. She studied in St Petersburg, Paris and Milan, and made her début in 1892 as Marguerite de Valois (*Les Huguenots*) at the Imperial Opera, St Petersburg; she remained there until 1912, making frequent tours in Russia and one each to Prague (1903) and Tokyo (1907). She was the first Electra in Taneyev's *Oresteya* (1895); her repertory also included Mozart's and Auber's Zerlina, Aennchen (*Der Freischütz*), Carolina (*Il matrimonio segreto*), Berthe (*Le prophète*), Juliet, Nannetta (*Falstaff*), Gilda, Lakmé, Micaëla, Tamara (*The Demon*) and Glinka's Lyudmila and Antonida (*A Life for the Tsar*). With a pure, musical voice, she was the first singer to achieve world fame through the gramophone alone.

*

E. Stark: *Peterburgskaya opera i eyo mastera, 1890–1910* [St Petersburg Opera and its Stars] (Leningrad, 1940)
A. Favia-Artsay: 'Marie Michailowa', *Hobbies* (June 1954), 22–5

H. Barnes: 'Maria Michailova', *Recorded Sound*, no.33 (1969), 354–80 [including discography]   HAROLD BARNES

Mikhaylov-Stoyan [Mikhaylov], **Konstantin Ivanovich** (*b* Golyam Boyalak, Bessarabia, 25 March 1853; *d* Sofia, 13 June 1914). Bulgarian tenor. He toured Russia with various opera companies, and from 1888 sang as a soloist at the Bol'shoy Theatre, Moscow, until 1899, when he first visited Bulgaria. He returned to Russia as guest artist in different opera houses (in 1902 together with Shalyapin). The success of his concerts in Bulgaria in 1907 with two other Bulgarian singers from Bessarabia led to the foundation that year of the Operna Druzhba (Opera Association) which marked the beginning of opera in Sofia. Mikhaylov-Stoyan's repertory included roles in leading operas by Verdi, Wagner, Gounod, Mascagni and above all by Russian composers. He staged several operas in Sofia and wrote a book on the foundation of the Bulgarian National Opera, *Po vaprosa za osnovavaneto na Balgarskata narodna opera* (Sofia, 1907).   LADA BRASHOVANOVA

Miki, Minoru (*b* Tokushima, Shikoku, 16 March 1930). Japanese composer. He was born into a musical family, several members of which were skilled in performance on Japanese instruments. He had his first encounter with European music as a member of a choral group at high school and began to study the piano and harmony at the age of 20. He was taught composition by Akira Ifukube and Tomojirō Ikenouchi at the Tokyo National University of Fine Arts and Music from 1951 to 1955. In 1953 he won a prize in a Japanese radio competition for orchestral works. He founded the Nihon Ongaku Shūdan (Ensemble Nipponia, later Pro Musica Nipponia), an ensemble of Japanese traditional instruments, in 1964. In autumn 1972 he led the group on a European tour, the first of several foreign visits.

In 1963 Miki composed *Mendori teishu* ('The Henpecked Husband'), a satirical chamber opera, which was well received by the public, revived several times and also performed in Europe. Another minor theatrical success was *Kikimimi* (1967), a musical drama for children, which quickly became a regular repertory work for schoolchildren. His first serious opera, *Shunkin-shō* ('The Story of Shunkin'), based on a novel by Tanizaki, was written to a commission from the Japan Opera Society and was given a successful première in 1975. The opera tells of the mutual devotion of a beautiful blind girl, Shunkin, and a young clerk, Sasuke, who works at her father's drug store; their love is so strong that Sasuke finally blinds himself in order to be closer to his sweetheart. Although the opera is written in a European style and accompanied by a Western orchestra, Miki managed to recreate in it the atmosphere of traditional Japanese theatre. It forms the first part of a trilogy completed by *Ada* ('An Actor's Revenge', 1979), written for the English Music Theatre, and *Jōruri* (1985), commissioned by the Opera Theatre of St Louis; both use Japanese instruments together with a Western-style orchestra, and their international success is due primarily to the composer's skill in blending elements of European and Japanese music in a way both natural and subtle. Miki founded a music-theatre ensemble, Utayomi-za, in 1986 to develop his ideas on musical drama further.

See also ADA *and* JŌRURI.

Mendori teishu [The Henpecked Husband] (chamber op, 1, T. Kawano and H. Matsumoto, after G. de Maupassant), Tokyo, Bunkyo Public Hall, Oct 1963, vs (Munich, n.d.)
Kikimimi (children's musical play, 1, A. Fujita), NHK TV, 27 Feb 1968
Shunkin-shō [The Story of Shunkin] (3, J. Maeda, after J. Tanizaki), Tokyo, 24 Nov 1975, vs (Tokyo, 1985)
Ada [Revenge] (2, J. Kirkup, after O. Mikami); as An Actor's Revenge, London, Old Vic, 5 Oct 1979, vs (London, 1989)
Tōge no mukō ni naniga aruka (choral op, 2 parts), Nagoya, 1983
Utayomizaru [The Monkey Poet] (musical, 2, M. Kawamura), 1983, vs (Tokyo, n.d.)
Jōruri (3, C. Graham, after M. Chikamatsu), St Louis, Loretto Hilton, 30 May 1985, vs (Tokyo, 1989)
Hanazono nite [At the Flower Garden] (mini-op, 1, Fujita), Tokyo, Toshi Centre Hall, 1 Aug 1985
Yomigaeru, 1989 (musical, 2, H. Terazaki and Fujita, after S. Kusano)   MASAKATA KANAZAWA

Mikley-Kemp, Barbara. *See* KEMP, BARBARA.

Mila, Massimo (*b* Turin, 14 Aug 1910; *d* Turin, 26 Dec 1988). Italian music critic and writer. For his degree from Turin University (where he studied with Alberto Gentili) he wrote a thesis on Verdi (1931). In all his works he was much influenced by Benedetto Croce's aesthetics. He was imprisoned for anti-fascist activities before and during World War II; afterwards he helped in reorganizing the government. He taught music history at Turin Conservatory (1954–73) and University (1962–75) and was music critic of *L'unità* (1946–67), *L'espresso* (1955–67) and *La stampa* (1967–74). From 1967 he was co-director of *Nuova rivista musicale italiana*. He wrote extensively on Mozart and Verdi.

Il melodramma di Verdi (Bari, 1933, repr. 1980 as *L'arte di Verdi*)
Cent'anni di musica moderna (Milan, 1944, 2/1981)
Saggi mozartiani (Milan, 1945)
W. A. Mozart (Turin, 1945, 2/1985)
'*La carriera d'un libertino' di Strawinsky* (Milan, 1952)
Cronache musicali 1955–1959 (Turin, 1959) [essays]
'*I vespri siciliani' di Verdi* (Turin, 1973)
La giovinezza di Verdi (Turin, 1974)
Lettura delle 'Nozze di Figaro' (Turin, 1979)
I costumi della Traviata (Pordenone, 1984)

*

H. Sachs: 'Massimo Mila (1910–88)', *Opera*, xl (1989), 673–5   CAROLYN GIANTURCO

Milan (It. Milano; Ger. Mailand). Italian city, capital of Lombardy. It is not only the home of the most famous Italian opera house, the Teatro alla Scala, but has also been a principal centre of Italian opera since the late 18th century, when it was the main city from which northern Italy was governed.

1. Up to 1700. 2. The 18th century. 3. The 19th century. 4. The 20th century.

1. UP TO 1700. Religious processions with music and dialogue are known in Milan from the 14th century, and stage entertainments with music, song and dancing became popular at court during the 15th and 16th centuries. An important forerunner of opera was the eclogue *Arminia* by Giambattista Visconte, performed on 18 July 1599 in honour of the Infanta Isabella and her husband Archduke Albert of Austria; the *intermedi*, by Camillo Schiaffenati, were perhaps the first in Milan to include music in recitative style. This spectacle and others were performed in the Salone Margherita, the theatre in the ducal palace named after Archduchess Margherita of Austria, wife of Philip III of Spain, and inaugurated in her presence in 1598. The Teatro Ducale in the palace courtyard, first built as a rectangle and later

387

modified into horseshoe form, had three tiers of boxes and a gallery, with 12 boxes on each side. Light entered through large windows in the upper gallery. The palace also contained the little Teatrino della Commedia, or Teatro di Corte, near the via delle Ore, which was used by travelling companies. Boxes in the Salone Margherita were private so that nobles could sit separately from the lower classes (who were in the stalls), and they were also used as parlours to entertain friends during the theatre seasons. Profits from all entertainments in the city went to the Collegio delle Vergini Spagnole, an institution founded in 1578 to house the orphans of Spanish officials and soldiers stationed in occupied Milanese territory, a privilege that continued even after the end of Spanish rule.

At the beginning of the 17th century Milan could offer few original theatrical productions, but it was ready to welcome those from other cities. After the plague of 1630 the Teatro Ducale opened with works from Venice. The librettos of Francesco Manelli's *Andromeda* (1637, Venice) and *La maga fulminata* (1638, Venice) were reprinted in Milan in 1644 by Ramellati. It is not certain that they were therefore performed in Milan – the librettos mention only the Venetian performances – but it is certain that in the following years many other Venetian operas were staged at the Ducale: Benedetto Ferrari's *Il pastor regio* in 1646, Manelli's *Delia* (libretto by Giulio Strozzi) in 1647 and Cavalli's *Giasone* in 1650. The first and last of these were performed by the Febiarmonici, who also gave Strozzi and Francesco Sacrati's enormously successful *La finta pazza* in about 1650. The score of this opera, long thought to have been lost, is in the Borromeo archives on Isola Bella, Lake Maggiore, where that noble Milanese family had its own theatre; it was probably performed there. In 1652 G. B. Andreini presented his *Maddalena lasciva e penitente* and in 1653 *Orione*, an opera specially written for Milan by Cavalli. This was followed by *Bradamante* in 1658 (attributed to Cavalli), Cesti's *Alessandro vincitor di se stesso* in 1659 and Cavalli's *Xerse* in 1665; in 1661 two operas by Pietro Andrea Ziani, *Le fortune di Rodope e Damira* and *Antigona delusa da Alceste*, were performed, and in 1662 Cesti's *Orontea*.

Soon, however, the predominance of Venetian works in Milan gave way to operas by local composers. Francesco Rossi, organist at S Celso, composed several including in 1663 *Crispo* (libretto by Carlo Righenzi), in 1664 *La farsa musicale* (Righenzi) and in 1674 *Bianca di Castiglia* (Carlo Maria Maggi). Rossi, Lodovico Busca and P. S. Agostini wrote an act each of *La regina Floridea* (?1669); another collaborative work was *Ippolita, regina delle amazzoni* (1670), with music by Busca, Agostini and Ziani. This libretto too was by Maggi, secretary to the senate and professor of Latin and Greek at the Palatine Schools, who also wrote poetry in Milanese dialect and included in his librettos some comic and salacious scenes reminiscent of the *lazzi* of the *commedia dell'arte*. Other works for which he wrote the libretto were *Amor tra l'armi, overo Corbulone in Armenia* (1673, music by Busca) and *Affari ed amori* (1675, music by Paolo Magni and Carlo Borzio). The latter had been performed in Count Vitaliano Borromeo's little theatre on Isola Bella and includes scenes constituting one of the earliest satires against singers and the opera audience.

In the following years there was a return to the Venetian repertory, with operas by Ziani, Badia, Antonio Sartorio and Giovanni Legrenzi; works by Bolognese composers such as Domenico Gabrielli, G. A. Perti and Giovanni Bononcini were also performed, and in 1674 *Il Girello* by Jacopo Melani, who worked in Rome. In the last decade of the 17th century Paolo Magni returned to composing operas, including *Scipione l'africano* (1692) in collaboration with Lonati, a celebrated violinist, *Aiace* (1694) with Lonati and Francesco Ballarotti of Bergamo, *Amfione* (1698), and *Ariovisto* (1699) with Perti and Ballarotti.

Performances in the Salone Margherita were distinguished by the high quality of the singing and the magnificence of the scenery, supervised by the Galli-Bibiena and the Mauro brothers. For years the theatre was managed by Lonati, who was succeeded in 1676 by the Piantanida brothers. Damaged by fire in 1695, the theatre was restored and enlarged in 1699 by Federico Pietrasanta, and given the name of Regio Ducal Teatro Nuovo. Performances there included F. A. Vanelli's *La prosperità di Elio Seiano* (1699) and C. F. Pollarolo's *L'inganno di Chirone* (1700). In 1700 the Piantanida handed over management to Giacomo Cipriotti, who was also a librettist. Under Prince Vaudémont, governor from 1698, French taste began to infiltrate Milan, both in music, commissioned from A. S. Fiorè, *maestro di cappella* to the Duke of Savoy in Turin, for *La casta Penelope* and *La Svanvita* (1707), and in choreography and dances, entrusted to L'Evêque and to Michel Pignolet de Montéclair for Pollarolo's *Ascanio re del Lazio*. This opera, together with *Angelica nel Catai*, celebrated the visit of Philip V of Spain in 1702.

2. THE 18TH CENTURY. Spanish rule came to an end with the departure of the Spanish governor from Milan on 24 September 1706, and his place was taken by Eugène of Savoy, the first representative of the Austrian government. This was the beginning of a new age of prosperity and peace which lasted until 1796 and saw a flowering of culture and the arts and an increasing addiction to spectacles and entertainments. Relations between Milan and Vienna were close and continuous, with exchanges of operas, musicians and singers. The Regio Ducal Teatro Nuovo, however, was destroyed by fire on the night of 5 January 1708, and until a new theatre was built on the same site, as Vienna had decreed, opera was staged on a smaller scale in the Teatrino della Commedia near the via delle Ore. For the most part these were revivals of Venetian operas by Albinoni, Gasparini, Lotti, Caldara, Pollarolo and Giovanni Bononcini. In 1716 a group of Milanese noblemen proposed that the Regio Ducal Teatro should be rebuilt at their expense in exchange for ownership of the boxes. Permission was given by the governor, Löwenstein, in 1717 and in a few months a new theatre (sometimes called the Regio Ducal Teatro and sometimes the Teatro Regio Ducale) was built by the architect Giovan Domenico Barbieri (see fig.1; for further illustration *see* BARBIERI, GIOVAN DOMENICO). It had five tiers of boxes, each with an anteroom where servants could prepare refreshments. Gaming was permitted in a room set aside for the purpose, and profits still went to the Collegio delle Vergini Spagnole (this right continued until 1755, when it passed to the impresario). Although larger than its predecessor and one of the largest in Italy, the new theatre had the defect of being too long and narrow, providing a poor view of the stage. The last work staged at the Teatrino was Alessandro Scarlatti's *Mitridate Eupatore*, the only opera of his to be performed in Milan.

1. *Interior of the Regio Ducal Teatro, Milan, during the ball held in celebration of the birth of Peter Leopold, future Archduke of Austria, in 1747: engraving by Marc'Antonio dal Re*

The new theatre was inaugurated on 26 December 1717 with Gasparini's *Costantino* (libretto by Pariati and possibly Zeno). For 59 years, until 25 February 1776 when it in turn burnt down, this was the centre of musical and social life in Milan. The city was still not a creative or dynamic force in opera, but rather an eclectic and receptive centre open to widely varying tendencies. Its productions, whether important revivals or works written for it by composers from elsewhere, shone for the scenery of the Galliaris, who had succeeded the Bibienas, for the ballets in the intermezzos, arranged by fine choreographers such as Le Picq, Noverre and Angiolini, and for the singers, who were among the best in Italy: the castratos Carestini, Bernacchi, Tenducci and Farinelli and the prima donnas Tesi, Bordoni, Gabrielli and Aguiari. In about 1740 the orchestra numbered 45. From the beginning comic intermezzos had been inserted between the acts of operas, as in Naples and Venice. Some of these were in Milanese dialect, as is evident from the *Raccolta copiosa d'intermedi* (Amsterdam [*recte* Milan], 1723), the first printed collection of intermezzos, but after 1738 they were usually replaced by ballets. During carnival (26 December to February) two *opere serie* were performed; Löwenstein began a tradition, which proved to be lasting, of a third opera in August. The years following brought operas by local composers (in 1719 *Ambleto* by Giuseppe Vignati, Carlo Baliani and Giacomo Cozzi and *Porsena* by Vignati), alternating with revivals of operas by Gasparini, Fiorè and Orlandini, while public interest centred mainly on the singers.

The first opera by Porpora and Metastasio to be performed in Milan was *Siface* in 1725, composed for the Regio Ducal Teatro. In 1730 Hasse's *Arminio* was presented with his wife Faustina Bordoni and Carestini in the leading roles. In Carnival 1732 *Candace*, the first work by one of the foremost Milanese opera composers, G. B. Lampugnani, was performed at the Regio Ducal Teatro, and in 1734 *L'ambizione superata dalla virtù* by the Milanese symphonic composer G. B. Sammartini. In 1733 Milan had passed to Carlo Emmanuele of Savoy, King of Sardinia, but in 1737 the Austrians returned and the new governor, Count Abensperg, entrusted the management of the theatre to a council of 'Cavalieri Direttori'. For Carnival 1738 Lampugnani's *Angelica* was performed with intermezzos from Pergolesi's *La serva padrona* sung by Domenico Cricchi and Francesca Fabiani, who also performed Hasse's intermezzo *La contadina* in the summer of that year. G. F. Brivio's *La Germania trionfante in Arminio* celebrated a visit of the Archduchess Maria Theresa in 1739.

Gluck was in Milan from 1737 as a guest of Count Antonio Maria Melzi to study with Sammartini, whose influence is evident in his early work, in particular *Le nozze d'Ercole e d'Ebe* and *La contesa de' numi*. Four of his operas were first performed in Milan: *Artaserse* (1741), *Demofoonte* (1743), *Sofonisba* (1744) and *Ippolito* (1745). Sammartini's second opera, *Agrippina moglie di Tiberio*, was performed in 1743. Comic opera was popular in Milan and from 1745 had its own spring season. Later the *opera buffa* season was fixed in the autumn (from the beginning of August to October or November) and three different operas were produced, so that comic opera acquired the same importance as *opera seria*, two of which were performed between 26 December and the last day of the Ambrosian carnival,

the Saturday after Ash Wednesday. For several years from 1744 works by Galuppi were almost continually in performance at the Regio Ducal Teatro. His *opere serie* were usually to texts by Metastasio: *Ricimero* (1744, libretto by Silvani), *Ciro riconosciuto* (1745), *L'olimpiade* (1747), *Semiramide riconosciuta* (1749), *Ezio* (1757) and *Ipermestra* (1758). Galuppi's comic operas, mostly to librettos by Goldoni, were given in spring and autumn: *L'Arcadia in Brenta* (1750), *Il mondo della luna* (1751), *Arcifanfano re dei matti* (1753), *Il filosofo di campagna* (1755) and *Le nozze* (1756).

Maria Theresa, who acceded to the imperial throne in 1740, did not enjoy music or spectacular entertainment, but realized that the theatre was a social necessity in Italy and thought it wise to allow opera in Milan. The arrival of Francesco III d'Este, Duke of Modena, as governor of Milan in 1754, and even more the active presence of his minister plenipotentiary Count Firmian and the supreme chancellor Wenzel von Kaunitz, ensured a central role in city life for the Regio Ducal Teatro, which had been restored and improved at the expense of the Cavalieri Direttori in 1752. Operas included works by Andrea Bernasconi (*Antigono*), Jommelli (*Demofoonte* and *Lucio Vero*, 1754) and G. A. Fioroni, *maestro di cappella* at Milan Cathedral, as well as Lampugnani's *Il re pastore* (1758) and comic operas by him to Goldoni librettos (*Le cantatrici*, 1758; *La contessina* and *Il conte Chicchera*, both 1759). Caterina Gabrielli and Tenducci sang with distinction.

Lampugnani, who had spent some time in London, returned to Milan in 1758 as harpsichordist at the Regio Ducal Teatro, where Mozart was to meet him. J. C. Bach was in Italy from 1754 as a guest of Count Agostino Litta in Milan and a pupil of Padre Martini in Bologna. His style was influenced by Sammartini and other Milanese composers, and he in turn had some influence on Mozart. In 1760 he obtained one of the two organists' posts at Milan Cathedral, and in 1762 his opera *Catone in Utica*, written for Naples the year before, was repeated at the Regio Ducal Teatro.

In the second half of the 18th century Milan was one of the most enlightened of Italian cultural centres, with thinkers and men of letters such as the Verri, Cesare Beccaria and Giuseppe Parini; in instrumental music the innovations of Sammartini heralded Viennese Classicism. In opera, however, Milanese taste was still narrowly traditional, with little room for the innovatory ideas of Gluck and Calzabigi, whose *Orfeo* was received with admiration in Vienna in 1762. When the Cavalieri Direttori decided to produce *Alceste*, Gluck's music was rejected and a new score composed by P. A. Guglielmi. Parini had the task of revising Calzabigi's libretto, adding irrelevant arias to please the singers and trivializing the plot. Calzabigi was indignant, and Parini defended himself by saying that he had done the work 'to suit the unavoidable present circumstances of our theatre', which according to Calzabigi meant 'to draw out the performance to the ridiculous length of five hours and to be able to have supper during the performance' (see Donà).

The custom of inserting ballets between the acts of serious and even comic operas went back to about 1738. There were usually two or three of them, and the titles, choreographer, dancers and plot were written into the opera's libretto. The first was usually a pantomime ballet, a danced narrative representing a historical, mythological or fantastic event; the second was a *divertissement*, a succession of picturesque scenes such as working peasants or country festivals. The final ballet was a chaconne in the Italo-French 'ballo nobile' tradition. Choreographers included Gaetano Grossatesta, François Sauveterre, the Salamonis (father and son), Vincent Saumier, Pierre Allouard, Jean Favier, Vincenzo Galeotti, Charles Le Picq, Giuseppe Canziani, P. B. Michel, J. B. Martin and Francesco Clerico. But the most distinguished were Jean-Georges Noverre and Gasparo Angiolini, who were rivals not only on the stage but also in polemical writing on the aesthetics of dance: their lively arguments entranced the Milanese.

This was the atmosphere in Milan when the young Mozart visited the city for the first time early in 1770. At the palace of Count Firmian he met many musicians, including Sammartini, and was commissioned to write an opera for the Regio Ducal Teatro. He returned to Milan to conduct the opera, *Mitridate, re di Ponto*, on 26 December. There was an orchestra of 60, with Lampugnani at the harpsichord, and the singers included Antonia Bernasconi and Guglielmo Ettore. Mozart's next visit to Milan (21 August–5 December 1771) was in connection with the important commission he had received for a *festa teatrale, Ascanio in Alba*, to a text by Parini on the occasion of the marriage of Archduke Ferdinand of Austria and Maria Ricciarda Beatrice d'Este of Modena. The main work was *Il Ruggiero* by the 72-year-old Hasse to a libretto by the elderly Metastasio, performed in the Regio Ducal Teatro on 17 October 1771; *Ascanio in Alba* was given with greater success the following evening by Giovanni Manzuoli and Antonia Maria Girelli. Mozart was in Milan for the last time in 1772–3, when the third opera he wrote for the theatre, *Lucio Silla* to a libretto by De Gamerra (who had been appointed the theatre's poet in 1771), was performed on 26 December 1772, with Anna De Amicis and Venanzio Rauzzini.

In the last four years of the Regio Ducal Teatro operas by Paisiello, Anfossi, Guglielmi, Gazzaniga, Monza, Gassmann, Felice (or Luigi) Alessandri and Traetta were performed. It was Traetta's *Merope* that was staged on 24 February 1776, only a few hours before a fire broke out which completely destroyed the theatre. Arson was suspected; in any case the need had long been felt for a more elegant and modern theatre. Until it was built a temporary wooden theatre, the Teatro Interinale, was erected to a design by Giuseppe Piermarini in the garden of the palace that had belonged to Bernabò Visconti; it had 32 boxes in three tiers but no gallery. Between September 1776 and Carnival 1777–8 operas by Astarita, Anfossi, Bertoni, Mortellari and Paisiello were performed there. Meanwhile, on 15 July 1776, the box holders of the old Regio Ducal Teatro received permission from Maria Theresa to erect a new theatre, which was called the Regio Ducal Teatro alla Scala because it was built on the site of the suppressed church of S Maria della Scala (itself named after Beatrice della Scala, the wife of Bernabò Visconti). The architect was again Piermarini, the interior was painted by Giuseppe Levati and Giuseppe Reina and the curtain, depicting Parnassus (at Parini's suggestion), was the work of Domenico Riccardi. The theatre was inaugurated on 3 August 1778 with Salieri's *L'Europa riconosciuta*, written for the occasion to a libretto by Verazi. The singers included Marina Balducci and Gasparo Pacchiarotti, and scenery was by the Galliari brothers (see fig.3). The ballets were *Pafio e Mirra, o sia I prigionieri di Cipro*, with music by Salieri and choreography by Claudio Legrand, and *Apollo placato*, with music by Luigi de Baillou and choreography by Canziani. The horseshoe-shaped theatre, had five tiers of 194 boxes, a large royal box opposite the stage, gallery and stalls; each box had an anteroom as a cloakroom. Visibility and acoustics were excellent from every point. The foyer was a large saloon with side rooms which at first served for gaming. The exterior had a façade of three orders with a pediment, central project-

3. Design by the Galliari brothers for the inaugural performance of Salieri's 'L'Europa riconosciuta' (Act 1 scene i) at the Regio Ducal Teatro alla Scala, Milan, 3 August 1778

ion and three-arched portico with a terrace above. The theatre overlooked a narrow street; it was only in 1857 that the piazza was opened out to its present size.

The Teatro alla Scala (as it came to be known) soon became the most famous opera house in Italy and the principal centre for the development of Italian opera. It was also central in Italian social and political history: in 1793 it housed the festivities for the birth of an heir to the Emperor Franz II; at the end of Austrian rule and the foundation of the Cisalpine Republic in 1797 Napoleon's arrival was celebrated there. Ballets such as *Guglielmo Tell*, *Lucio Giunio Bruto*, *Il generale Colli in Roma* and *Silvio, o Il vero patriota* were inspired by patriotic subjects, while operas in 1797 included A. Tarchi's *La congiura pisoniana* (libretto by Francesco Salfi). On 1 June 1805 a *Cantata per l'incoronazione di Napoleone imperatore e re d'Italia*, with music by Vincenzo Federici to a text by Vincenzo Monti, was performed in the presence of the emperor. During the Napoleonic era older operas alternated with celebratory cantatas.

Almost contemporary with La Scala, the smaller Teatro della Cannobiana (sometimes 'Canobbiana') had been inaugurated on 21 August 1779 (see fig.4). Also designed by Piermarini, it was built on a site adjoining the schools founded in 1554 by Paolo da Cannobio; it held 2000 spectators, had four tiers of boxes and a gallery, and opened with Salieri's *La fiera di Venezia* and *Il talismano* by Salieri and Giacomo Rust. The Cannobiana also staged drama and ballet and, during the Republic, patriotic displays and festivities. It was used chiefly for comic and semiserious opera, especially when La Scala was closed.

In the first years of activity at La Scala the chief composers were Guglielmi, Zingarelli, Cimarosa, Paisiello, Paer and Nicolini. From 1798 the most important was Simon Mayr, 27 of whose operas were performed before 1813, of which 14 were new works, including *Le due giornate* (1801), *I misteri eleusini* (1802) and *Alonso e Cora* (1803).

3. THE 19TH CENTURY. At the turn of the century Milan began to develop into a modern city based on the activity of a prosperous middle class, which eventually turned it into the most important industrial centre of Italy. Lombardy was returned to Austrian control in 1815; renewed Viennese connections resulted in a large patrician and upper class supporting cultural life.

A new era began with the success of Rossini (*La pietra del paragone*, 1812), who quickly came to dominate Italian opera along with Donizetti and Bellini; from then on, Milan's musical history became virtually identified with that of Italian opera, of which La Scala was perhaps the most notable centre (it was also at that time that cycles of Mozart operas began to be mounted there). Important operas had their premières at La Scala and helped to establish the theatre's reputation: Rossini's works dominated the period 1812–20 (including *Aureliano in Palmira*, 1813; *Il turco in Italia*, 1814; *La gazza ladra*, 1817; and *Bianca e Falliero*, 1819); Meyerbeer had successes with *Margherita d'Anjou* (1820) and *L'esule di Granata* (1821); Mercadante with *Elisa e Claudio* (1821), *Il giuramento* (1837) and *Il bravo* (1839); Donizetti with *Lucrezia Borgia* (1833) and others; and Bellini had three successes particularly important for the theatre, *Il pirata* (1827, commissioned by Barbaia and initiating the composer's fruitful collaboration with the librettist Romani), *La straniera* (1829) and, after an initial failure, *Norma* (1831).

By the 1830s La Scala was one of the leading opera houses in Europe; 40 premières were given in that decade and in 1839 Verdi's first opera, *Oberto, conte di San Bonifacio*, was performed there. Ricordi bought the publishing rights, and the theatre's director, Bartolomeo Merelli, commissioned three more operas from the young composer. The first, *Un giorno di regno*, was a failure and was withdrawn after its first performance in 1840, but *Nabucco* (1842) and *I Lombardi alla prima crociata* (1843) were great successes; in fact, *I Lombardi* came to represent the drive towards unification, and the patriotic choruses often incited demonstrations in the theatre. Although Verdi is closely associated with La Scala, his career there was chequered, and his works un-

4. *Interior of the Teatro della Cannobiana (designed by Giuseppe Piermarini; inaugurated 21 August 1779) during a festival of dance: engraving (1825)*

5. Design by Alessandro Sanquirico for the final scene of Pacini's 'L'ultimo giorno di Pompei' in the 1827 production at La Scala, Milan

til *Otello* in 1887 had their premières elsewhere (with the exception of revisions); there was hissing and chatter during the Milan performances of *La forza del destino*, *Un ballo in maschera* and *Aida*, and Milanese critics accused Verdi of not knowing how to write for singers and of imitating Wagner. The Requiem, written for Manzoni, was given at La Scala in 1874 only a few days after its first performance at S Marco, and Verdi did return to La Scala with the premières of his last two operas, *Otello* (1887) and *Falstaff* (1893). Many other Italian composers were presented at La Scala during the second half of the 19th century, including Petrella, Faccio, Marchetti, Boito, Ponchielli and Catalani. The works of foreign composers were also brought to the theatre and, after initial failure, Wagner's operas were enthusiastically received under Franco Faccio's direction.

The best Italian singers performed at La Scala throughout the century, while the most notable conductors were Alberto Mazzucato (1859–68), Faccio (1871–89) and Toscanini (1898–1903). Alessandro Sanquirico was the theatre's leading stage designer and scene painter from 1817 to 1832; besides setting new standards of design in Rossini's *opere serie* and the operas of Mozart, Bellini, Donizetti and Meyerbeer, he influenced opera stage design throughout the 19th century and into the 20th. Carlo Ferrario, who was the leading Milanese scene painter of the second half of the 19th century, worked at other theatres as well as at La Scala, making a return to more realistic design. Ballets were produced there by such great choreographers as Salvatore Viganò and Gaetano Gioja.

Throughout the 19th century alterations and improvements were made to the theatre, the most important of which were the enlargement of the stage in 1807, the overall restoration in 1838, and the removal in 1857 of the tall houses that had made it impossible to

have a perspective view of the façade. Gas lighting was installed in 1860 and electric lighting in 1883. There have traditionally been four annual seasons: Carnival to Lent (initially reserved for *opere serie*), and autumn, spring and summer, when *opere buffe* were mounted. The administration of La Scala had at first been supported by the proceeds of the dramatic company which used the theatre until 1803, but from 1806 to 1918 the theatre was supported, with varying success, by its joint owners: the state, then the city, box holders, impresarios and patrons. During the Austrian Restoration, the administration was in the hands of the government, but afterwards the theatre attracted such adventurous impresarios as Domenico Barbaia (1826–32) and Bartolomeo Merelli (1835–50 and 1861–3). In 1897 the city withdrew its subsidy and Duke Guido Visconti di Modrone formed a syndicate to take over the theatre's management, appointing Toscanini artistic director in 1898, with Giulio Gatti-Casazza as manager.

There were several minor Milanese theatres that mounted opera during the 19th century. Despite several substantial interruptions the Teatro della Cannobiana continued its activities, particularly when La Scala was closed. Many works by second-rate composers had their premières there, as did Donizetti's *L'elisir d'amore* (1832). In 1894, under the ownership of the publisher Sonzogno, the theatre was renamed the Teatro Lirico Internazionale and opened with the Greek composer Spyridon Samaras's *La martyre*. It was later known simply as the Teatro Lirico and passed into other hands. In 1897 Caruso made his Milan début there in the première of Cilea's *L'arlesiana*. The Teatro Carcano, modelled on La Scala, was built by Giuseppe Carcano in 1803 and opened that year with *La Zaira*, sometimes attributed to Vincenzo Federici but more probably by Francesco Federici. Of the operas that had their premières there, few were memorable, though Donizetti's *Anna Bolena* (1830) and Bellini's *La sonnambula* (1831) were notable exceptions. In 1882 the first concert of Wagner's music in Milan was given there by Faccio. The Carcano had largely lost its importance by the mid-century and by 1900 it was no longer used for music. The Teatro di S Radegonda was opened in 1803 in a Benedictine convent, remodelled to accommodate drama and opera; it was demolished in 1882. The Teatro Lentasio opened in 1801 as a marionette theatre but also presented opera and drama from 1805 to 1853. The Teatro Re was built by Carlo Re, opening in 1813 with Rossini's *Tancredi*; after the 1848 revolution it was used primarily for drama, though operas were occasionally mounted until its demolition in 1872, the final performance being Rossini's *Il barbiere di Siviglia*. In 1815 the Teatro Fiando was opened, offering a variety of entertainments including marionette plays, drama, opera and ballet; the building was demolished in 1868, rebuilt and renamed the Teatro Gerolamo. The Teatro Manzoni (so called from 1873) was built in 1872 as the Teatro della Commedia to replace the Teatro Re. It initially concentrated on performances of drama and music, particularly *opere buffe* and operettas, and over the next 50 years gradually raised its standards to occupy an important place in the city's theatrical life; however, soon after 1900 its musical activity ceased. The Politeama Ciniselli, a private theatre, was acquired by Count Francesco Dal Verme, demolished and rebuilt, reopening in 1872 with Meyerbeer's *Les Huguenots* as the Teatro Dal Verme. The most modern theatre of its time, it primarily gave drama and grand opera; first performances there included Puccini's first opera *Le villi* (1884) and Leoncavallo's *Pagliacci* (1892).

4. THE 20TH CENTURY. Milan continued to grow as a thriving industrial city supporting a wide range of musical activity. La Scala further expanded its prestige and, in addition to presenting the standard repertory and works by Puccini, Franchetti, Leoncavallo and Giordano, mounted the first Italian productions of many foreign works, including Tchaikovsky's *Yevgeny Onegin* (1900), Strauss's *Salome* (1906), *Elektra* (1908) and *Rosenkavalier* (1911), Debussy's *Pelléas et Mélisande* (1908), Musorgsky's *Boris Godunov* (1909) and Falla's *La vida breve* (1934). After World War II several important works had their premières there, for instance J. J. Castro's *Proserpina e lo extranjero* (1952), Poulenc's *Dialogues des Carmélites* (1957), Pizzetti's *L'assassinio nella cattedrale* (1958) and *Il calzare d'argento* (1961), Stockhausen's *Donnerstag aus Licht* (1981), *Samstag aus Licht* (1984; see fig.7) and *Montag aus Licht* (1988), Berio's *La vera storia* (1982), Bernstein's *A Quiet Place* and *Trouble in Tahiti* (1984), Donatoni's *Atem* and Testi's *Riccardo III* (1987). Many other operas had their Italian premières in Milan, including Britten's *Peter Grimes* (1947), Prokofiev's *The Love for Three Oranges* (1947), Walton's *Troilus and Cressida* (1956) and Janáček's *The Cunning Little Vixen* (1958).

In 1920 the theatre had become a self-governing body, Ente Autonomo del Teatro alla Scala; Toscanini was reappointed artistic director and established a reputation for consistent excellence in performances during what was called 'the great Toscanini period'. He formed a new orchestra of 100 players and a chorus of 120; while the stage and auditorium were being reconstructed he took the company on a tour of Italy, the USA and Canada. His regime culminated in the

6. *Interior of the Teatro alla Scala, Milan, with (inset) a view of the façade: engraving from 'Il teatro illustrato' (25 August 1882)*

7. Interior of the Palazzo dello Sport, Milan, during rehearsals for the original La Scala production of Stockhausen's 'Samstag aus Licht', 25 May 1984

company's visit to Vienna and Berlin in 1929. His eventual resignation had many causes, including political ones. Artistic directors succeeding him have included Erardo Trentinaglia (appointed 1931), Jenner Mataloni (1935), Carlo Gatti (1941), Gino Marinuzzi (i) (1944), Antonio Ghiringhelli (1948), Victor De Sabata (1953), Francesco Siciliani (1957), Gianandrea Gavazzeni (1967), Massimo Bogianckino (1972), Claudio Abbado (1977), Siciliani again (1979), Cesare Mazzonis (1982) and Alberto Zedda (1992). Conductors have included De Sabata, Giulini, Abbado and Muti. The La Scala company has also visited Munich (1937), London, (Covent Garden, 1950 and 1976), Johannesburg (1957), Edinburgh (1957), Brussels (1958), Moscow (1964), Montreal (1967), Washington, DC (1976), Japan (1981), Berlin (1987), Paris (1988), Korea (1988) and the USSR (1989).

After being seriously damaged by bombing in 1943, La Scala was one of the first buildings in Milan to be rebuilt after the war. It was reconstructed to the original designs (capacity now 3000) and was reopened on 11 May 1948 with a concert conducted by Toscanini including works by Rossini, Verdi, Boito and Puccini. In 1955 the Piccola Scala (cap. 600) was built next to La Scala for performances of early opera and small-scale contemporary works, opening with Cimarosa's *Il matrimonio segreto*. It closed down in 1983.

The Museo Teatrale alla Scala (opened 1913) has a large collection of musical autographs and manuscripts, letters and portraits of composers, opera librettos and drawings and etchings by important stage and set designers. It often has exhibitions illustrating particular periods and aspects of the theatre's history, and from 1988 has published a quarterly *Rivista illustrata del Museo teatrale alla Scala*.

*

G. Chiappari: *Serie cronologica delle rappresentazioni ... dei principali teatri di Milano dall'autunno 1776 sino all'intero autunno 1818* (Milan, 1818–25)

L. Romani: *Teatro della Scala* (Milan, 1862)

P. Cambiasi: *Rappresentazioni date nei reali teatri di Milano 1778–1872* (Milan, 1872, 3/1882 as *Teatro alla Scala 1778–1881*, 5/1906 as *La Scala 1778–1906*)

A. Paglicci-Brozzi: *Contributo alla storia del teatro: il teatro a Milano nel secolo XVII* (Milan, 1892)

——: *Il R. Ducal Teatro di Milano nel secolo XVIII* (Milan, 1894)

G. de Saint-Foix: 'Les débuts milanais de Gluck (l'élève de Sammartini)', *Gluck-Jb*, i (1913), 28–46

B. Gutierrez: *Il Teatro Carcano (1803–1914)* (Milan, 1914)

G. Marangoni and E. Vanbianchi: *La Scala* (Bergamo, 1922)

G. Macchi: *La Scala, dalle origini all'ordinamento attuale* (Milan, 1927)

V. Ramperti: *Per la storia del teatro milanese* (Milan, 1929)

G. M. Ciampelli and B. Gutierrez: *La Scala nel 1830 e nel 1930* (Milan, 1930)

G. Morazzoni: *I palchi del Teatro alla Scala* (Milan, 1930)

C. A. Vianello: *Teatri, spettacoli, musiche a Milano nei secoli scorsi* (Milan, 1941)

F. Abbiati and others: *La Scala (3.8.1778–11.5.1946)* (Milan, 1950)

F. Armani and G. Bascapé: *La Scala: breve biografia 1778–1950* (Milan, 1951)

G. Barblan and A. Della Corte: *Mozart in Italia* (Milan, 1956)

G. Barblan: 'Le orchestre in Lombardia all'epoca di Mozart', *Kongressbericht: Wien Mozartjahr 1956*, 18–21

——: 'Il teatro musicale in Milano nei secoli XVII e XVIII', *Storia di Milano*, xii (Milan, 1958), 947–96

——: 'L'ottocento e gli inizi del secolo XX', *Storia di Milano*, xvi (Milan, 1962), 661–711

C. Gatti: *Il Teatro alla Scala nella storia e nell'arte (1778–1963)* (Milan, 1964)

Il Museo teatrale alla Scala 1913–1963 (Milan, 1964)

F. Armani, ed.: *La Scala 1946–1966* (Milan, 1966)

L. Rossi: *Il ballo alla Scala, 1778–1970* (Milan, 1972)

M. Donà: 'Dagli archivi milanesi: lettere di Ranieri de' Calzabigi e di Antonia Bernasconi', *AnMc*, no.14 (1974), 268–300

E. Ferrari-Barassi: 'Milano e la Lombardia', *Storia dell'opera*, ed. A. Basso and G. Barblan (Turin, 1977), i, 488–505

K. K. Hansell: *Opera and Ballet at the Regio Ducal Teatro of Milan, 1771–1776: a Musical and Social History* (diss., U. of California, Berkeley, 1980)

C. Sartori: *I libretti italiani a stampa dalle origini al 1800* (Cuneo, 1990–)

MARIANGELA DONÀ

Milanov [née Kunc; Ilić], **Zinka** (*b* Zagreb, 17 May 1906; *d* New York, 30 May 1989). Croatian soprano. She studied at the Zagreb Academy of Music, and with Milka Ternina, Maria Kostrenčić and Fernando Carpi, making her début as Leonora (*Il trovatore*) at Ljubljana in 1927; she was the leading soprano at the Zagreb Opera from 1928 to 1935, singing such roles as Sieglinde, the Marschallin, Rachel and Minnie. After appearances at the Deutsches Theater, Prague, in 1937 she began a long association with the Metropolitan Opera, making her début as Leonora (*Il trovatore*) and appearing every season (except for 1941–2 and 1947–50) until her farewell performance as Maddalena de Coigny (*Andrea Chénier*) in 1966; with the company she gave 424 performances in 14 works – notably as the principal Verdi and Puccini heroines, but also as Norma, Donna Anna and La Gioconda. She appeared at the Teatro Colón (1940–42), San Francisco and Chicago, but her European performances after 1939 were few: as Tosca at La Scala (1950), and as Tosca and Leonora at Covent Garden (1956–7).

Milanov's voice was one of translucent beauty as well as great power, and she was able to spin out the most exquisite *pianissimo* phrases. She was a handsome and stately figure on the stage, relying mostly on her voice to achieve dramatic effects.

GV (L. Riemens; S. Smolian)

E. K. Einstein, jr: 'Zinka Milanov: a Discography', *Grand Baton*, v/2 (1968), 7–16, 21

R. Jacobson: 'The Most Beautiful Voice in the World', *ON*, xli/22 (1976–7), 11–15

L. Rasponi: *The Last Prima Donnas* (New York, 1982), 216–22

A. Blyth: 'Zinka Milanov: an Appreciation', *Opera*, xl (1989), 929–32   HAROLD ROSENTHAL/R

Milashkina, Tamara (Andreyevna) (*b* Astrakhan', 13 Sept 1934). Russian soprano. She studied with Yelena Katul'skaya at the Moscow Conservatory; while still a student, she was engaged as a soloist at the Bol'shoy Opera (1958). She became the first Soviet singer to appear at La Scala, as Lida in Verdi's *La battaglia di Legnano* (1962). She has a voice of distinctive timbre and unusual warmth and beauty; reserve and emotional depth combine to lend her stage portrayals particular sensitivity. Notable among her many roles are the Tchaikovsky heroines Tatyana, Lisa and Mariya (*Mazepa*), Fevroniya (Rimsky-Korsakov's *Legend of the Invisible City of Kitezh*, filmed in 1966), Prokofiev's Natasha (*War and Peace*) and Lyubka (*Semyon Kotko*), Leonora (*Il trovatore*), Elisabeth de Valois, Aida and Tosca. She has sung throughout Europe, and appeared at the Metropolitan Opera during the Bol'shoy company's visit in 1975. In 1973 she was made a National Artist of the USSR.

B. Pokrovsky: 'Tamara Milashkina', *Teatr* (1961), no.1, p.70

I. Tumanov: 'Chetïre goda spustya' [Four Years Later], *Teatr* (1965), no.1, p.85

G. Baranova: 'Solistka Bol'shogo: Tamara Milashkina', *Molodïye golosa* [Young Voices] (Moscow, 1966), 26ff
                                        I. M. YAMPOL'SKY

Milcheva, Alexandrina (*b* Shumen, 27 Nov 1936). Bulgarian mezzo-soprano. She studied in Sofia, making her début in 1961 at Warna as Dorabella and then joining the Bulgarian National Opera in 1968. She has sung in Vienna, Munich, Hamburg, Berlin, Paris, Chicago, Geneva, Zürich and Moscow and at La Scala, where she created Ada in Berio's *La vera storia* (1982). Her repertory includes Carmen, Delilah, Azucena, Preziosilla, Eboli, Laura (*La Gioconda*), Princess of Bouillon and the Princess (*Suor Angelica*), which she sang in Florence (1983). She also sings such Russian roles as Marina, Marfa and Konchakovna (*Prince Igor*), while her smooth, flexible voice is particularly effective in the part of Adalgisa.   ELIZABETH FORBES

Milde, Hans (Feodor) von (*b* Petronell, nr Vienna, 13 April 1821; *d* Weimar, 10 Dec 1899). Austrian baritone. He studied in Vienna and with the younger Manuel García in Paris. From 1845 to 1884 he was engaged at the Hofoper, Weimar, where in 1850 he sang Telramund in the first performance of *Lohengrin*, con-

ducted by Liszt. He also sang the Dutchman and, later, Hans Sachs and Kurwenal. He took part in the revival of Berlioz's *Benvenuto Cellini* (1852), created the title role of Cornelius's *Der Barbier von Bagdad* (1858) and Ruy Diaz in the same composer's *Der Cid* (1865). He sang the High Priest in the first stage performance of *Samson et Dalila*, at Weimar (1877).   ELIZABETH FORBES

Milde-Agthe, Rosa von [née Agthe, Rosa] (*b* Weimar, 25 April 1825; *d* Weimar, 25 Jan 1906). German soprano. She studied in Weimar, where she was engaged at the Hofoper from 1845 to 1867. Under the name of Rosa Agthe, in 1850 she sang Elsa in the first performance of *Lohengrin*, conducted by Liszt. The following year she married the baritone Hans von Milde. She created Margiana in Cornelius's *Der Barbier von Bagdad* (1858) and Chimène in the same composer's *Der Cid* (1865). Her repertory also included Lucia, Pamina, both of Gluck's Iphigenias, Leonore (*Fidelio*) and Lady Harriet (*Martha*).   ELIZABETH FORBES

Mildenburg, Anna. *See* BAHR-MILDENBURG, ANNA.

Milder-Hauptmann, (Pauline) Anna (*b* Constantinople, 13 Dec 1785; *d* Vienna, 29 May 1838). Austrian soprano. She studied in Vienna with Salieri, making her début in 1803 at the Theater an der Wien as Juno in Süssmayr's *Der Spiegel von Arkadien*. She sang Leonore in all three versions of *Fidelio* (1805, 1806 and 1814). She created the title role of Cherubini's *Faniska* (1806) and sang in the first Vienna performance of his *Médée* (1814). Moving to Berlin, she made her début there in 1816 as Emmeline in Weigl's *Die Schweizerfamilie*. While Spontini was music director of the Hofoper she sang Statira in the first Berlin performance of *Olympie* (1821) and created Namouna in *Nurmahal* (1822) and Irmengard in *Agnes von Hohenstaufen* (1829). Then she quarrelled with Spontini and returned to Vienna, where she sang until her retirement in 1836. A strongly dramatic singer, she was a noble interpreter of Gluck's heroines. Her voice, at ease in florid music, was rich, powerful and penetrating.   ELIZABETH FORBES

Mildmay, (Grace) Audrey (Louise St John) (*b* Herstmonceux, Sussex, 19 Dec 1900; *d* London, 31 May 1953). English soprano. She studied in London and in Vienna with Jani Strasser, then toured Canada and the USA as Polly in 1927–8. On her return to England she joined the Carl Rosa company, singing such roles as Zerlina, Gretel, Micaëla, Olympia, Musetta and Nedda and remaining with the company until her marriage to John Christie in 1931. With her husband she helped found the Glyndebourne Festival where, between 1934 and 1939, her Susanna, Zerlina and Norina were much admired for their vivacity and charm. In 1940 she sang Polly on Glyndebourne's wartime tour. She retired from the stage in 1943 after singing Susanna in Montreal.

S. Hughes: *Glyndebourne* (London, 1965)
                                        HAROLD ROSENTHAL/R

Miles, Philip Napier (*b* Shirehampton, Glos., 21 Jan 1865; *d* King's Weston, 19 July 1935). English composer. He studied in Dresden, and in England with Hubert Parry and Edward Dannreuther, and later did much to foster music in the Bristol region. *Westward Ho!* (in three acts, to a libretto by E. F. Benson, after Charles Kingsley) was given at the Lyceum Theatre,

London, in 1913, and parts of another extended work, *Queen Rosamond*, were performed at Shirehampton. The one-act *Markheim* (after R. L. Stevenson) was performed in Bristol, then London (1923); it shows a surer technique than Miles's large-scale operas. He also composed *Good Friday*, a church opera after John Masefield (London, 1933), and *Demeter* (T. S. Moore). Miles lent support to the Glastonbury festivals scheme and organized a number of performances in Bristol including the first public stage performance of Falla's *El retablo de maese Pedro* at Clifton in 1924.

Milhaud, Darius (*b* Aix-en-Provence, 4 Sept 1892; *d* Geneva, 22 June 1974). French composer. Born into a well-to-do Jewish family, he studied composition with Gédalge in Paris but was also powerfully influenced by writers and painters, especially Francis Jammes and Paul Claudel. That he was drawn to practitioners of other arts was significant in the light of his lifelong commitment to dramatic music in general and to the theatre in particular.

Milhaud's first major works included the incidental music to Claudel's *Protée* (three versions, 1913–19) and the opera *La brebis égarée* (composed 1910–15). When war broke out he was rejected for military service on medical grounds. The following year he composed incidental music to Claudel's *Les choëphores*, establishing polytonality as the norm of his harmonic language. In 1913 he had begun his settings of Claudel's translation of the *Oresteia* with *Agamemnon*, in which he shunned traditional techniques of incidental music and effected a novel type of transition from speech to song. He employed the same basic procedures in *Les choëphores* and later in *Les euménides* (1917–22); the former also contains the fruits of his research into every aspect of polytonality. The polytonal elements in his harmony and the way he used them are responsible above all else for the distinctive profile of his music. They are present throughout his work, but later there was some abatement in the intellectual rigour and consistency with which he applied them.

Milhaud spent the years 1916–18 in Rio de Janeiro as Claudel's secretary. On his return to Paris he was drawn into Cocteau's circle and became one of Les Six. Jazz dominated his interests in the early 1920s, but in 1925 he turned to opera. *Les malheurs d'Orphée* (1926) was the first of his chamber operas, all of short duration and economically scored: others were *Le pauvre matelot* (1927) and the trilogy of one-act operas to Henri Hoppenot librettos, *L'enlèvement d'Europe*, *L'abandon d'Ariane* and *La délivrance de Thésée* (1927–8); the total duration of the three is 27 minutes. In contrast, the most imposing of the Claudel-Milhaud collaborations is *Christophe Colomb* (1930), a work of Berliozian proportions that would be inordinately expensive to produce today.

Throughout the 1920s and 30s Milhaud combined a high rate of composition with extensive travels. *Maximilien* (1932), based on the true story of the reluctant Habsburg and the Mexican War, was the first of his operas to be staged at the Paris Opéra; *Médée* (1939) was one of the last produced there before the fall of France (it was performed on 8 May 1940). In 1940 he fled from the Nazis and settled in America for the duration of the war. *Bolivar* was his only opera of the war years; the subject appealed on account of its vigour and action and its masculine hero, but most of all because its central theme, liberation and freedom, was uppermost in every exile's thoughts in the 1940s.

Milhaud returned to Europe in 1947 but continued to visit the USA every year (he had connections both with Mills College, Oakland, California, and with the music school at Aspen, Colorado) until late in life, and despite his severely disabling rheumatoid arthritis he maintained a full, active schedule of teaching, composing and travelling until shortly before his death. His biggest postwar opera was *David*, composed at Koussevitzky's instigation for the Festival of Israel in 1954 in honour of the 3000th anniversary of King David's founding of Jerusalem. In 1964–5 he composed *La mère coupable*, for which Madeleine Milhaud adapted Beaumarchais. Finally, in 1970, *Saint Louis* appeared, an opera-oratorio marking the 700th anniversary of the death of St Louis, King of France, and described by Milhaud as 'une oeuvre austère, sans pittoresque': the action is confined to four principals and a 'madrigal' of 16 who take all the subsidiary roles, accompanied by an instrumental group of 13 positioned in the corner of the stage; the main orchestra and chorus, in the pit, perform only between the scenes and at the end of each act.

Milhaud's commitment to dramatic music was extensive: as well as 15 operas he produced dozens of ballets, theatre, film and radio scores, as well as music for stage spectacles and *son et lumière* shows. He worked quickly and tirelessly, both advantageous in the theatre; but his protean musical personality was suited to the medium in less prosaic ways. Stylistic diversity and contradictions are of the essence in his operas: his music is by turns euphonious and cacophonous, tender and violent, spiritual and earthy, sensuous and austere, pastoral and urban, colourful and monochrome. Italian on his mother's side, he was a great entertainer, and the spirit of *commedia dell'arte* is perhaps never far away. He drew heavily on 'entertainment' music of all kinds, as well as on folksong and dance from different parts of the world. As his autobiography, *Notes sans musique* (1949), reveals, he had a powerful visual sense, a keen response to art and literature and a passionate interest in people, places and new experiences. All his operas have strong subjects, and the music shows that he identified with them all. Nor did he ever abandon direct communication with his audience: even his most *recherché* polyharmonic experiments are carried out within the framework of the tonal system. His musical personality is unmistakable and charismatic, a particular advantage for an opera composer.

See also CHRISTOPHE COLOMB; MALHEURS D'ORPHÉE, LES; MÈRE COUPABLE, LA; and PAUVRE MATELOT, LE.

Esther de Carpentras op.89, 1910–14 (comic op, 2, A. Lunel), Radio Rennes, May 1937; stage, Paris, OC (Favart), 1 Feb 1938

La brebis égarée op.4, 1910–15 (3, F. Jammes), Paris, OC (Favart), Dec 1923

Les malheurs d'Orphée op.85 (chamber op, 3, Lunel), Brussels, Monnaie, 7 May 1926

Le pauvre matelot op.92 (complainte, 3, J. Cocteau), Paris, OC (Favart), 16 Dec 1927

L'enlèvement d'Europe op.94 (1, H. Hoppenot), Baden-Baden, July 1927 [pt 1 of trilogy]

L'abandon d'Ariane op.98 (1, Hoppenot), Wiesbaden, April 1928 [pt 2 of trilogy]

La délivrance de Thésée op.99 (1, Hoppenot), Wiesbaden, April 1928 [pt 3 of trilogy]

Christophe Colomb op.102 (2 pts, P. Claudel), Berlin, Staatsoper, 5 May 1930; rev. Graz, Oper, 27 June 1968

Maximilien op.110 (3, R. S. Hoffman, after F. Werfel), Paris, Opéra, 5 Jan 1932

Médée op.191 (1, M. Milhaud), Antwerp, Opéra Flamand, 7 Oct 1939

Bolivar op.236, 1943 (3, M. Milhaud, after J. Superveille), Paris, Opéra, 12 May 1950

David op.320 (5, Lunel), concert perf., Jerusalem, 1 June 1954; stage, Milan, La Scala, 2 Feb 1955

Fiesta op.370 (1, B. Vian), Berlin, Städtische Oper, 3 Oct 1958

La mère coupable op.412 (3, M. Milhaud, after P.-A. Beaumarchais), Geneva, Grand, 13 June 1966

Saint Louis, roi de France op.434 (opera-oratorio, 2 pts, Claudel), RAI, 18 March 1972; stage, Rio de Janeiro, Municipal, 14 April 1972

*

D. Milhaud: *Etudes* (Paris, 1927)

P. Collaer: *Darius Milhaud* (Paris, 1947, 2/1982; Eng. trans., 1988)

G. Beck: *Darius Milhaud* (Paris, 1949)

D. Milhaud: *Notes sans musique* (Paris, 1949; Eng. trans., 1952; enlarged as *Ma vie heureuse*, 1974; Eng. trans., 1992)

Entretiens avec Claude Rostand (Paris, 1952)

Correspondance Paul Claudel–Darius Milhaud, Cahiers Paul Claudel, iii (Paris, 1961)

J. Roy: *Darius Milhaud* (Paris, 1968)

R. Crichton: Obituary, *MT*, cxv (1974), 684

E. Helm: 'Darius Milhaud und seine moderne Musik südlicher Impressionen', *Universitas*, xxix (1974), 1177

CHRISTOPHER PALMER

Mililotti, Pasquale (*fl* Naples, 1755–82). Italian librettist. He worked exclusively at the Teatro dei Fiorentini and the Teatro Nuovo in Naples.

commedie per musica unless otherwise stated

L'amore alla moda (with A. Palomba), Sellitto, 1755; *La francese brillante*, P. A. Guglielmi, 1763 (Paisiello, 1764); *La vedova di bel genio*, Paisiello, 1766; *Le 'mbroglie de la Bajasse* (commedia musicale), Paisiello, 1767 (Paisiello, 1769, as *La serva fatta padrona*); *La finta semplice, o sia Il tutore burlato*, Insanguine, 1769; *L'arabo cortese*, Paisiello, 1769; *I sposi perseguitati*, N. Piccinni, 1769; *La somiglianza de' nomi*, Paisiello, 1771

Le stravaganze del conte, Cimarosa, 1772; *Il vagabondo fortunato*, Piccinni, 1773; *I viaggiatori*, Piccinni, 1775 (Valentino Fioravanti, 1796, as *I viaggiatori amanti*); *I matrimoni in ballo* (farsetta per musica), Cimarosa, 1776; *La frascatana nobile*, Cimarosa, 1776; *I sposi incogniti*, Latilla, 1779; *I commedianti fortunati*, A. Amicone, 1779; *Il rè alla caccia*, Tarchi, 1780; *Il trionfo de' pupilli oppressi*, Rispoli, 1782

*

CroceN

P. Napoli-Signorelli: *Storia critica de' teatri antichi e moderni* (Naples, 1787–90)

C. Baseggio: 'Mililotti, Pasquale', *Biografia degli italiani illustri nelle scienze, lettere ed arti del sec. XVIII e de' contemporanei, compilata da letterati italiani di ogni provincia*, ed. E. de Tipaldo (Venice, 1845), x, 167

M. Scherillo: *L'opera buffa napoletana durante il settecento* (Palermo, 1916)

F. de Filippis and R. Arnese: *Cronache del Teatro di S Carlo (1737–1960)* (Naples, 1961)
PATRICIA LEWY GIDWITZ

Milinkovič, Georgine von (*b* Prague, 7 July 1913; *d* Munich, 26 Feb 1986). Czech mezzo-soprano of Croatian parentage. She studied in Zagreb and Vienna, making her début in 1937 at Zürich. In 1940 she was engaged in Munich, in 1945 at Prague, then from 1948 to 1968 she sang at the Vienna Staatsoper. In 1952 she created Alkmene in Strauss's *Die Liebe der Danae* at Salzburg. She sang at Bayreuth (1954–7) as Fricka, Grimgerde, Second Norn and Magdalene. During the 1957–8 season at Covent Garden she sang Fricka and Strauss's Clytemnestra, two of her finest roles, which splendidly displayed her rich voice as well as her fiery temperament.

ELIZABETH FORBES

Mill, Arnold van (*b* Schiedam, 26 March 1921). Dutch bass. He studied at the conservatories of Rotterdam and The Hague. After his début at the Théâtre de la Monnaie, Brussels, in 1946 he sang at the Royal Opera, Antwerp, until 1950. He was a member of the Hamburg Staatsoper from 1953, visiting Edinburgh with the company in 1956 and appearing in the 1969 première of Penderecki's *The Devils of Loudun*. At Bayreuth (1955–60) he was heard as Daland, Titurel, Fafner and Fasolt. His authoritative art is well preserved in his King Mark, in the Solti recording of *Tristan*.

DAVID CUMMINGS

Millán, Rafael (*b* Algeciras, 24 Sept 1893; *d* 8 March 1938). Spanish composer. His early studies were with his father, a military musician. After initial activities as a violinist and a conductor, and as composer of various forms of music, he gravitated towards composing for the theatre. He moved to Madrid and began a sequence of about 40 zarzuelas that demonstrated fluent melody and sound technique and placed him in the front rank of zarzuela composers of the time. Most successful was *La dogaresa* (1920), performed in Barcelona with Emilio Sagi-Barba and in Madrid with Marcos Redondo. A progressive ailment cut short his career.

selective list; zarzuelas unless otherwise stated

El príncipe bohemio (M. Merino and M. González de Larra), Madrid, Zarzuela, 1914

El chico de las pañuelas (C. Arniches), Madrid, Apolo, 1915

La famosa (L. Navarro), Madrid, Novedades, 1915

Las alegras chicas de Berlin (Merino and C. R. Avecilla), Madrid, Zarzuela, 1916

Los piratas (M. Garrido), Madrid, Novedades, 1916

El preceptor de su alteza (L. García Conde and A. Paso), Madrid, Apolo, 1916

La dogaresa (2, A. López Monís), Barcelona, Tívoli, 17 Sept 1920

El pájaro azul (2, López Monís), Barcelona, Tívoli, 5 March 1921

Glorias del pueblo (op), Barcelona, 1921

El dictator (F. Romero and G. Fernández Shaw), Barcelona, Apolo, 1923

La severa [La morería] (Romero and Fernández Shaw, after J. Dantas), Barcelona, 1925

Date unknown: La mujer indecisa; La mala tarde (Merino and Avecilla); Los burladores de oro (A. G. Rendón)

*

A. Fernández-Cid: *Cien años de teatro musical en España (1875–1975)* (Madrid, 1975)

J. Arnau and C. M. Gomez: *Historia de la zarzuela* (Madrid, 1979)

R. Alier and others: *El libro de la zarzuela* (Barcelona, 1982, 2/1986 as *Diccionario de la zarzuela*)
ANDREW LAMB

Miller, Arthur (*b* New York, 17 Oct 1915). American writer. A prolific writer in many genres, he is best known for four award-winning plays produced between 1947 and 1955, including *The Crucible* (1953). Many critics have seen parallels between this play, based on the late 17th-century Salem witch trials, and the McCarthy hearings of the 1950s (to which Miller was called to testify). The only operatic adaptations of Miller's work are Jef van Durme's *La mort d'un commis-voyageur* (after *Death of a Salesman*; composed 1954–5), Renzo Rossellini's *Uno sguardo dal ponte* (after *A View from the Bridge*; 1961) and Robert Ward's setting of *The Crucible* (1961), to a libretto by Bernard Stambler. Closely based on the original play, the latter won a Pulitzer Prize and the New York Music Critics' Circle Award in 1962.

MICHAEL HOVLAND

Miller, Jonathan (**Wolfe**) (*b* London, 21 July 1934). English director. A polymath whose achievements in both the sciences and the arts are prolific and extraordinarily varied, he studied medicine at Cambridge. As one of the four co-authors and performers of the Cambridge revue *Beyond the Fringe* (1961) he became widely known in London and later New York; regular television appearances added to his reputation, as subsequently did theatrical productions, of Shakespeare, Chekhov, Beaumarchais and other classic authors.

Miller's first venture in opera was with the British première (New Opera Company, 1974) of Alexander Goehr's *Arden must Die*; this led to Glyndebourne (*The Cunning Little Vixen*, 1975), and thence to particularly close associations with Kent Opera and the ENO. For Kent, Miller and the conductor Roger Norrington collaborated on performances of operas by, among others, Mozart (*Così fan tutte*), Verdi (*La traviata*, *Falstaff*), Monteverdi (*L'Orfeo*) and Tchaikovsky (*Yevgeny Onegin*), which had as their common factor an imaginative avoidance of all extraneous decorative effect and, often, a compelling economy of physical movement. For the ENO, Miller's stagings, which have included *Le nozze di Figaro*, *The Turn of the Screw*, *Arabella*, *Otello*, *Il barbiere di Siviglia* and *Tosca*, have been on the whole somewhat more uneven in quality – although his transplantations of *Rigoletto* in a 1950s New York setting (1982) and *The Mikado* in that of an English 1920s hotel (1986) proved among the most celebrated and popular productions in the company's history. A criticism of Miller's work which was heard more frequently in the 1980s was that the many fertile intellectual ideas and cultural associations on which he was able to draw (and which he expounded with peculiar vividness in articles or interviews) sometimes failed to enliven the actual stagings, which could seem stiff and insecure in command of a large stage or theatrical space. Miller has later undertaken regular work in Italy and the USA; his 1991 début at the Metropolitan was with *Kát'a Kabanová*.

*

M. Romain: *A Profile of Jonathan Miller* (Cambridge, 1992)

MAX LOPPERT

Miller, Lajos (*b* Szombathely, 23 Jan 1940). Hungarian baritone. He studied in Budapest, making his début there in 1968 with the Hungarian State Opera as Horatio (Szokolay's *Hamlet*). He has also sung in Munich, Cologne, Prague, Brussels, Geneva, Turin, Rome, Florence and at La Scala. His repertory includes Gluck's Orestes, Enrico Ashton, Wolfram, Valentin, Scarpia, Yeletsky, Yevgeny Onegin and Grigory (*The Tsar's Bride*), but his keenly focussed, warm-toned voice is best employed in Verdi, as Luna, Renato, Miller, which he sang at the Metropolitan (1989), Macbeth, Don Carlo (*Ernani*), Germont, Boccanegra, Nabucco, Iago and Rolando (*La battaglia di Legnano*). He sang Ivo in Berio's *La vera storia* at the Paris Opéra in 1985 and Basilio in Respighi's *La fiamma* at Buenos Aires in 1987.

ELIZABETH FORBES

Miller, The [*Mel'nik – koldun, obmanshchik i svat* ('The Miller who was a Wizard, a Cheat and a Matchmaker')]. Comic opera in three acts by MIKHAIL MATVEYEVICH SOKOLOVSKY to a libretto by Alexander Onisimovich Ablesimov; Moscow, Maddox's Theatre, 20/31 January 1779.

Ablesimov (1742–83), a minor journalist and satirical fabulist, cast his libretto in racy rustic dialect. It tells of a miller named Faddey (bass) who, posing as a fortune teller and conjuror of spirits, tricks Ankudin (baritone) and Fetin'ya (soprano), the parents of the clever Anyuta (soprano), into consenting to her choice of a suitor. Though obviously beholden to Rousseau's *Le devin du*

village, which had played in Moscow only the year before (in a Russian adaptation called *Derevenskog vorozheya*, 'The Village Soothsayer', with music by Ivan Kerzelli), Ablesimov muted the social message and stretched his play out to three modest acts by means of a large infusion of genre detail, including the first theatrical representation of a peasant bride's party (*devichnik*), which was so often emulated that a *devichnik* became practically *de rigueur* for Russian operas up to and including those of Glinka.

The music, consisting of 19 numbers separated by spoken dialogue, is the only known work by Sokolovsky, who is not named in the original published libretto (Moscow, 1782; early librettos rarely carried a composer's name). During the 19th century the score was misattributed to Yevstigney Fomin and first published in vocal score under the latter's name (Moscow, 1884), with a spurious overture later identified as the first movement of a symphony on Russian folk themes by Arnošt Vančura. That it was published so long after its première testifies to *The Miller*'s extraordinary popularity; it is the only Russian musical play of the 18th century to have held the stage throughout the 19th and beyond, albeit chiefly in provincial and amateur productions, and often heavily abridged or in updated instrumentation (a version by Alexander Tcherepnin was performed in Paris in 1929).

Although the original libretto and contemporary performance materials refer to *The Miller* as an opera, the genre to which it belongs is rather somewhere between the *comédie-vaudeville* and the *comédie mêlée d'ariettes* in the style of Favart. 13 numbers are sung to the tunes of folk music and popular songs (nine of them specified by Ablesimov), so that all Sokolovsky had to do was arrange them, which in addition to harmonizing and orchestrating them meant composing ritornellos. Even the numbers that do not actually quote folk material are demonstrably in a 'peasant dialect' as pronounced as that of the libretto: thus the Miller's song in Act 3 (no.18), through which the plot is resolved, is in the characteristic rhythm of the famous *Kamarinskaya* dance tune. The score, reconstructed by Irina Sosnovtseva from the earliest surviving source material (a set of parts dating from 1806), was published in 1984.

See also VANČURA, ARNOŠT.

RICHARD TARUSKIN

Millico, (Vito) Giuseppe (*b* Terlizzi, nr Bari, 19 Jan 1737; *d* Naples, 2 Oct 1802). Italian soprano castrato and composer. He worked at the Russian court, 1758–65, then returned to Italy; at Parma in 1769 he sang Orpheus in *Le feste d'Apollo* by Gluck, who took him to Vienna, where he created Paris in *Paride ed Elena* (1770). In 1772 he went to London and again appeared as Orpheus; he was with Gluck in Paris in 1774, and in Zweibrücken and Mannheim. He was in Berlin before his final return to Italy in 1780, when he was appointed 'virtuoso di camera e della Regia Cappella' in Naples. He composed several operas, including *Le cinesi* and *L'isola disabitata* for the Bourbon princesses Teresa and Luisa. The published score of his opera *La pietà d'amore* bears an acknowledgment to Gluck and his ideals in the foreword, addressed to the opera's librettist, Antonio Lucchesi.

Ipermestra (3, R. de' Calzabigi or P. Metastasio), Palermo, S Cecilia, spr. 1781

La pietà d'amore (2, A. Lucchesi), Naples, Fiorentini, 1782 (Naples, 1782)

Angelica e Medoro (dramatic cantata, Metastasio), ?1783, collab. Cimarosa
La Zelinda, Naples, Fondo, 17 April 1786
Le cinesi (1, Metastasio), ?Naples, Real Palazzo, ?1780s
L'isola disabitata (1, Metastasio), ?Naples, Real Palazzo, ?1780s
L'avventura benefica (G. S. Poli), Naples, Real Palazzo, 14 July 1797

Doubtful: Ecuba e Climene; Achille in Sciro (Metastasio)

*

BurneyH; FétisB; GerberL; GerberNL; RiemannL 12
M. Bellucci La Salandria: *Vito Giuseppe Millico* (Bari, 1951)
L. Finscher: 'Der Opernsänger als Komponist: Giuseppe Millico und seine Oper *La pietà d'amore*', *Opernstudien: Anna Amalie Abert zum 65. Geburtstag* (Tutzing, 1975), 57–90   GERHARD CROLL

Milligan, James (*b* Halifax, Nova Scotia, 5 April 1928; *d* Basle, 27 Nov 1961). Canadian bass. He studied at the Royal Conservatory of Music, Toronto, 1948–55. In 1955 he became the first Canadian to win the Geneva Competition, and the same year he made his operatic début, in Toronto. 1960 brought débuts at Glyndebourne as Arbaces in *Idomeneo* and at Covent Garden as Escamillo. He was much admired as the Wanderer in *Siegfried* at his Bayreuth début in 1961, and also enjoyed great success as a concert singer. At the time of his early death from a heart ailment he was a member of the Basle Opera.   CORI ELLISON

Millo, Aprile [April] (*b* New York, 14 April 1958). American soprano. Brought up in Los Angeles, she received her musical education primarily from her parents, who were both opera singers; she later studied with Rita Patanè in New York. While a student at the San Diego Opera Center (1977–80), she sang the High Priestess in *Aida*, but then resolved to accept only leading roles. She won prizes in Busseto (1978) and Barcelona (1979). Her first major role was Aida, in Salt Lake City in 1980, followed by Elvira (*Ernani*) at La Scala in 1982. She made her Metropolitan Opera début in 1984 as Amelia in *Simon Boccanegra*, replacing an ill colleague. She has since made the company her artistic home, singing the Verdi heroines in which she specializes: Aida, Desdemona, Elisabeth de Valois, Elvira and Leonora (*Il trovatore*), as well as Liù. She also worked with Eve Queler's Opera Orchestra of New York, and has sung in concert performances of *Andrea Chénier*, *La battaglia di Legnano*, *I Lombardi*, *Il pirata* and *La Wally* at Carnegie Hall. In Europe, she has sung in Bologna, Bonn, Rome, where she sang Luisa Miller, Verona and Vienna. She possesses a spinto voice of power, warmth and temperament which should prove to be one of the glories of her generation.   CORI ELLISON

Millöcker, Carl (*b* Vienna, 29 April 1842; *d* Baden, nr Vienna, 31 Dec 1899). Austrian composer. The son of a goldsmith, he studied the flute and theory at the Vienna Conservatory (1855–8). In 1858 he played at the Theater in der Josefstadt and in 1864, on the recommendation of Suppé (from whom he had received some practical tuition), he became conductor at the Thalia-Theater in Graz. There his first one-act pieces, somewhat in the style of Offenbach, were produced in 1865, and there he also married one of the theatre's singers, whose name was Kling. In 1866 he obtained a position as conductor at the Theater an der Wien, but because of the lack of opportunities he moved to the Harmonie-Theater, where another short operetta, *Diana*, was produced.

In 1868 Millöcker was appointed conductor at the Deutsches Theater in Budapest and in 1869 returned to the Theater an der Wien as second conductor. In the course of his duties there he composed songs and incidental music for many short theatrical pieces, gaining particular attention with his score for *Drei Paar Schuhe* (1871). From 1873 to 1876 he edited the *Musikalische Presse*, a monthly magazine of piano music and articles. He also began writing full-length operettas, his first real success being *Das verwunschene Schloss* (1878) which, like his later major works, starred the leading Viennese operetta singer of the time, Alexander Girardi. His greatest success came with *Der Bettelstudent* (1882), and in 1883 he was able to give up his conducting position to concentrate on composition. *Gasparone* and *Der Feldprediger* (both 1884) were almost as well received, while the most successful of his later operettas was *Der arme Jonathan* (1890). Set partly in the USA, it was produced in London with additional numbers by Isaac Albéniz and proved particularly popular in the USA itself. In 1894 Millöcker suffered the first of several strokes, which partly paralysed him and eventually led to his death. He was twice married.

Millöcker's successes in the late 1870s and the 1880s established him with Johann Strauss and Suppé as one of the three leading exponents of Viennese operetta. His music lacked the vigorous appeal of Suppé's and the melodic facility of Strauss's, as a result of which he has remained the least known abroad. Yet, at its best, his music combines much of the qualities of both, especially in *Der Bettelstudent*, which remains a repertory piece in Austria and Germany. Several numbers from other operettas are familiar, notably 'Dunkelrote Rosen' and 'Er soll dein Herr sein' from *Gasparone* (which also became popular in Germany in bastardized form as 'Mutter der Mann mit dem Koks ist da') and 'Ich bin der arme Jonathan' from *Der arme Jonathan* (both for Girardi). Unfortunately, other than in *Der Bettelstudent*, Millöcker's music is frequently represented in arrangements that grossly distorted his style to suit the tastes of the 1930s. *Die Dubarry* (1931), to a totally new libretto, had a score arranged by Theo Mackeben from *Gräfin Dubarry* and other pieces, with alien structures and orchestration, while a 1932 revision of *Gasparone* by Ernst Steffan also introduced other material and reduced the scale of Millöcker's comic-opera structures. Millöcker's theatrical expertise remains clearly evident, however, in *Der Bettelstudent*, a work that admirably displays his rich invention and accomplished theatrical workmanship.

See also BETTELSTUDENT, DER (ii).

operettas, first performed in Vienna, Theater an der Wien, unless otherwise stated; most published in vocal score in Vienna around time of first performance; many MSS in A-Wst

Der tote Gast (1, L. Harisch), Graz, Thalia, 11 Feb 1865
Die beiden Binder (1, G. Stoltze), Graz, Thalia, 21 Dec 1865
Diana (1, J. Braun), Vienna, Harmonie, 2 Jan 1867
Der Dieb (1, A. Berla), Budapest, 1868/9
Die Frau=insel [Die verkehrte Welt] (3, after Cogniard), Budapest, Deutsches, 1868/9
Der Regimentstambour (3), Vienna, Josefstadt, 23 Oct 1869
Abenteuer in Wien (3, Berla), 20 Jan 1873
Das verwunschene Schloss (5, Berla), 30 March 1878
Gräfin Dubarry (3, F. Zell and R. Genée), 31 Oct 1879
Apajune, der Wassermann (3, Zell and Genée), 18 Dec 1880
Die Jungfrau von Belleville (3, Zell and Genée), 29 Oct 1881
Der Bettelstudent (3, Zell and Genée, after E. Bulwer-Lytton: *The Lady of Lyons* and V. Sardou: *Les noces de Fernande*), 6 Dec 1882
Gasparone (3, Zell and Genée), 26 Jan 1884

Der Feldprediger (3, H. Wittmann and A. Wohlmuth), 31 Oct 1884
Der Vice-Admiral (3, Zell and Genée), 9 Oct 1886
Die sieben Schwaben (3, Wittmann and J. Bauer), 29 Oct 1887
Der arme Jonathan (3, Wittmann and Bauer), 4 Jan 1890
Das Sonntagskind (3, Wittmann and Bauer), 16 Jan 1892
Der Probekuss (3, Wittmann and Bauer), 22 Dec 1894
Nordlicht, oder Der rote Graf (3, Wittmann), 22 Dec 1896

Music for about 40 other theatrical pieces, mostly for Theater an der Wien, incl. Drei Paar Schuhe (1871), Die schlimmen Töchter (1876), Ein Blitzmädel (1878), Ihr Korporal (1878), Die Näherin (1880), Ihre Familie (1881) [list in StiegerO]

*

StiegerO
C. Preiss: 'Versuch einer Biographie Carl Millöckers', Wochenschrift für Kunst und Musik, iii (1905), 18
R. Holzer: Die Wiener Vorstadtbühnen: Alexander Girardi und das Theater an der Wien (Vienna, 1951)
E. Nick: Vom Wiener Walzer zur Wiener Operette (Hamburg, 1954)
G. Hughes: Composers of Operetta (London, 1962)
F. Racek: 'Das Tagebuch Carl Millöckers', Wiener Schriften, iii (1969), 137–230
R. Traubner: Operetta: a Theatrical History (New York, 1983)
ANDREW LAMB

Milnes, Rodney [Blumer, Rodney Milnes] (b Stafford, 26 July 1936). English critic. Educated at Rugby and Oxford, he worked initially in publishing, and in 1968 became music critic for Queen magazine (later Harpers and Queen) and two years later opera critic for the Spectator; he remained in both positions for more than 20 years. He became opera critic of the London Evening Standard in 1990 and of The Times in 1992. Milnes began to write for Opera in 1971, and became associate editor in 1976 and editor, in succession to Harold Rosenthal, in 1986. A trenchant and entertaining writer, with a strong background in literature and theatre, and wide musical sympathies, he has had a considerable influence on opera staging in Britain. He is an accomplished linguist and has prepared translations, under his original name, of a large number of operas, among them Dvořák's Rusalka and The Jacobin, Janáček's Osud, Giovanna d'Arco, the Riccis' Crispino e la comare, Almeida's Spinalba, Grétry's Zémire et Azor, Lortzing's Undine and Tannhäuser.

Milnes, Sherrill (Eustace) (b Hinsdale, IL, 10 Jan 1935). American baritone. After studies at Drake and Northwestern universities, and with Rosa Ponselle, he became an apprentice at Santa Fe, then made his début with the touring Boston Opera company as Masetto (1960). In 1961 he sang Gérard (Andrea Chénier) with the Baltimore Civic Opera, and in 1964 Rossini's Figaro at the Teatro Nuovo, Milan. With New York City Opera (1964–6) he sang Valentin, Ruprecht in the American première of The Fiery Angel, John Sorel (The Consul) and, in 1982, Thomas' Hamlet. He made his Metropolitan début in 1965 as Valentin, remaining with the company for more than 25 years; in 1967 he created Adam Brant in Levy's Mourning Becomes Electra. His repertoire includes Escamillo, Tonio, Don Giovanni, Barnaba, Jack Rance, Scarpia, Athanaël (Thaïs), Alphonse (La favorite), Sir Riccardo Forth (I puritani) and the leading Verdi baritone roles, in particular Amonasro, Carlo (Ernani and La forza del destino), Boccanegra, Rigoletto, Iago and Montfort. In 1971 he made his Chicago début as Posa and first sang at Covent Garden as Renato, returning in 1983 as Macbeth. He sang Falstaff for the first time in 1991. Milnes's brilliant top voice, general fervour and command of legato have led to comparisons with Lawrence Tibbett, Leonard Warren and Robert Merrill.

*

S. Milnes: 'A Role in Hand', ON, xxxvi/2 (1971–2), 12–14
W. Sargeant: 'Sherrill Milnes', New Yorker (29 March 1976), 36ff
J. Spong: The First Forty-Five (West Des Moines, LA, 1978)
T. Lanier: 'Sherrill Milnes', Opera, xxxi (1980), 538–44
J. Hines: 'Sherrill Milnes', Great Singers on Great Singing (Garden City, NY, 1982), 173–81
MARTIN BERNHEIMER, ELIZABETH FORBES

Milona [Mylonas], **Costa** [Costas] (b Keratea, Attica, 3 Feb 1889; d London, 27 March 1949). Greek tenor. The son of a poor farmer, he worked in the lead mines of Lavrion, Attica, until a patron heard him sing and financed his training at the Athens Conservatory, first in Byzantine chant (1908–13), then in Western singing. He graduated in 1920 with a scholarship to the Milan Conservatory and is reported to have lived in Milan and Rome. About 1925 he settled in Berlin; there he made hundreds of operatic recordings, including arias by Boito, Puccini, Verdi, Donizetti, Ponchielli, Mascagni, Massenet, Weber and Wagner, as a result of which he became known abroad as 'the pocket Caruso'. He was short in stature and appeared infrequently on the stage, but he is known to have sung at Monte Carlo in 1923 in minor roles in Tristan und Isolde, and at the Deutsche Oper, Berlin, as Rodolfo and Canio in 1938. (Reported appearances with the Vienna Staatsoper in 1932 and at Frankfurt an der Oder have not yet been documented.) In June 1946 he left Berlin for London, intending to emigrate to the USA, but his hopes were never realized and three years later he died in poverty. Milona's powerful and dark-timbred voice was used effectively in both lyrical and dramatic roles, and his performances were always informed by a keen sense of musical style.

*

G. Leotsakos: Elliniko Lyriko Theatro, 100 chronia, 1888–1988 (YP 4–6, A/A 14564–6, 1988), 128–33 [record notes]
GEORGE LEOTSAKOS (with STATHIS ARFANIS)

Milwaukee. American city, in Wisconsin. Visiting troupes had provided its first operatic productions, including La sonnambula, La fille du régiment and Le postillon de Lonjumeau, by 1850, often in a combination of English and Italian. The American première of Lortzing's Zar und Zimmermann (8 April 1853), presented by the newly established Milwaukee Musical Society under the direction of Hans Balatka, was the first complete opera given by local performers. Der Waffenschmied also received its American première, by the same organization, in 1853. During the next 20 years the society presented 24 operas, many barely performed before in America, including Der Freischütz, Die Zauberflöte, Norma, Alessandro Stradella, La traviata (in German), Il trovatore, Fra Diavolo and Méhul's Joseph. Its last opera performance was of Gluck's Orfeo ed Euridice (1890). Operatic activity subsequently declined, although the city had been included in the 1889 Metropolitan tour as one of only five to be treated to a complete Ring. Local composers included Eduard Sobolewksi, a pupil of Weber whose opera Mohega, die Blume des Waldes received its première on 11 October 1859. The only Polish opera company in the USA was based in Milwaukee; it staged the American première of Halka on 13 May 1923.

Concert halls and opera houses in the city included Hustis Hall, 1840 (cap. 650; burnt down 1853); Young's Hall, 1852 (burnt down shortly after comple-

Scene from the American première of Lortzing's 'Zar und Zimmermann', performed by the Milwaukee Musical Society, 8 April 1853

tion, was rebuilt in 1853, burnt down again 1859); Albany Hall, 1859 (also called 'Academy of Music'; burnt down 1862); and Music Hall, 1865 (cap. 1500, remodelled and renamed Academy of Music, 1872). The Nunemacher Grand Opera House, 1871 (cap. 855; burnt down 1893), and the Pabst Theater on the same site, 1895 (cap. 1820; still in regular use), were the other principal centres for opera. In 1933 John Anello sr founded the local Florentine Opera, which presents four productions a year of the standard repertory, using imported soloists and members of the Milwaukee SO, at Uihlein Hall of the Performing Arts Center (cap. 2331) and the Pabst Theater. A more experimental group is Skylight Opera, founded in 1960 by Claire Richards, and later co-directed by Steven Wadsworth and Francesca Zambello (1985–90), which presents both Baroque (Monteverdi, Cavalli, Purcell) and 20th-century works (Weill, Orff, Argento, Kurka, Johann Strauss, and Gilbert and Sullivan). The Opera Theater Department of the Music Department of the University of Wisconsin-Milwaukee (Corliss Phillabaum, director) mounts a full-scale production each year in the Fine Arts Theater of the university (cap. *c*500), as well as programmes of excerpts twice a year.

*

R. A. Koss: *Milwaukee* (Milwaukee, 1871) [in Ger.]

H. L. Conard, ed.: *History of Milwaukee from its First Settlement to the Year 1895* (Chicago, 1895)

O. Burkhardt: *Der Musikverein von Milwaukee, 1850–1900: eine Chronik* (Milwaukee, 1900)

J. G. Gregory: *History of Milwaukee, Wisconsin* (Chicago, 1931)

J. J. Schlicher: 'Hans Balatka and the Milwaukee Musical Society', *Wisconsin Magazine of History*, xxvii (1943–4), 40–55

——: 'The Milwaukee Musical Society in Time of Stress', *Wisconsin Magazine of History*, xxvii (1943–4), 178–93

T. Schleiss: *Opera in Milwaukee, 1850–1900* (thesis, U. of Wisconsin, Milwaukee, 1974)

A. B. Reagan: *Art Music in Milwaukee in the Late Nineteenth Century, 1850–1900* (diss., U. of Wisconsin, Milwaukee, 1980), 31   FRANKLIN S. MILLER

Milyutin, Yury Sergeyevich (*b* Moscow, 5/18 April 1903; *d* Moscow, 10 June 1968). Russian composer. He studied with Vasilenko and A. N. Alexandrov in the Moscow Regional College of Music. His first work for the stage was incidental music for Gogol's *Christmas Eve* at the Moscow Satirical Theatre (1927); he went on to become a leading exponent of operetta in the USSR.

His operettas were staged in many theatres in and outside the Soviet Union; most are concerned with the lives of ordinary Soviet people, and their musical language is direct and derived from folksong. *Trembita*, treating the Soviet liberation of Transcarpathia, uses Huzul folk themes (the trembita is a Huzul instrument); *Pervaya lyubov'* ('First Love') is about collective farm life.

first performed in Moscow, Operetta Theatre, unless otherwise stated

Zhizn' aktyora [An Actor's Life] (3, K. Finn and V. Gusev), 11 Jan 1941, lost

Devichiy perepolokh [Alarm among the Girls], 1944 (3, M. Gal'perin and V. Tipot, after V. Krïlov), Leningrad, Musical Comedy Theatre, 20 Sept 1950, vs (Moscow, 1961); rev. version, 1972

Bespokoynoye schast'e [Uneasy Happiness]/Tayozhnïy solovey [The Nightingale of the Taiga] (4, Tipot, E. Pomeshchikov and N. Rozhkov, after the film *Skazanie o zemle Sibirskoy* [A Tale of the Land of Siberia]), 24 March 1948

Trembita (3, V. Mass and M. Chervinsky), 12 Nov 1949, vs (Moscow, 1958)

Pervaya lyubov' [First Love]/Lynbushka (3, Pomeshchikov and Tipot), 20 Nov 1953

Grushen'ka, 1955 (I. Shtok, after N. Leskov: *Ocharovannïy Strannik*), lost

Potseluy Chanitï [Chanita's Kiss] (3, E. Shatunovsky), 25 Dec 1957, vs (Moscow, 1959)

Fonari-fonariki [Lanterns, Lamps] (3, Shatunovsky), 17 May 1958

Tsirk zazhigayet ogni [The Circus Lights the Lamps] (3, Ya. Ziskind), 7 June 1960, vs (Moscow, 1965)

Anyutinï glazki [Pansies] (3, Ziskind), Sverdlovsk, Musical Comedy Theatre, 20 Oct 1964

Tikhaya semeyka [A Quiet Little Family] (2, G. Fere and S. Obraztsov, after L. Velle: *Kafe 'Lunnik'* [The Moon Rocket Café]), 16 August 1968, vs (Moscow, 1981)

Obruchal'nïye kol'tsa [The Engagement Rings] (3, Shatunovsky), Volgograd, Musical Comedy Theatre, June 1970

*

K. Petrova: 'Operettï Yu. Milyutina', *SovM* (1951), no.8, pp.23–9

A. Medvedev: *Yury Milyutin* (Moscow, 1956)

O. Fel'tsman: 'Yu. S. Milyutin', *SovM* (1963), no.4, pp.142–3

Yu. S. Milyutin: notobibliograficheskiy sbornik [Milyutin: Musico-bibliographical Handbook] (Moscow, 1984)

GALINA GRIGOR'YEVA

Minato, Count **Nicolò** (*b* Bergamo, *c*1627; *d* Vienna, 28 Feb 1698). Italian librettist, impresario and poet, later resident in Austria. His prodigious career as a librettist, attested by an extant output of over 200 works, began in 1650 with *Orimonte* and continued until the year of his death. His activity fell into two distinct periods: the

Venetian years, from 1650 to 1669, and the longer Viennese period, from then until his death. In Venice he was a member of the Accademia degli Imperfetti, formed in 1649 and dedicated to the study of jurisprudence, history and the classics; Giacomo dall'Angelo, Aurelio Aureli and G. F. Busenello were other librettists who belonged to it. Minato was also a member of the older Accademia dei Discordanti; poems by him were printed in publications of these institutions (1651 and 1655). The prefaces to his earliest libretto indicate that he was a lawyer by profession and that he initially viewed his writing as an avocation. By the mid-1660s, however, he was fully committed to the theatre as both librettist and impresario, a combination characteristic of the careers of several other Venetian librettists, including Giovanni Faustini and Aureli. By 1665 he was involved in the management of the Teatro di S Salvatore, an involvement reaffirmed by a three-year contract in 1667. His departure for Vienna in 1669 to become court poet to the Emperor Leopold I thus provoked a lawsuit for breach of contract by the Vendramin family, owners of the theatre. In the dedication of Il ratto delle sabine (1674) Minato mentioned nine libretto that he had written for Venice, but he actually wrote at least 11. His chief musical collaborator there was Cavalli, though Antonio Sartorio provided the music for his last three Venetian libretto.

Minato's duties in Vienna included the provision of texts for a wide range of theatrical events, sacred as well as secular, on the occasion of weddings, royal visits, royal birthdays and name-days, carnival and the important Lenten celebrations. During his 29-year period at the Viennese court he wrote more than 170 secular libretto (variously labelled 'dramma per musica', 'festa teatrale', 'invenzione', 'introduzione ad un balletto' or 'serenata') and approximately 40 sacred texts (labelled 'rappresentazione sacra' or 'oratorio'). He averaged about five texts a year and occasionally – in 1678, for example – produced as many as ten. Most of his Viennese works were collaborations with the court composer Antonio Draghi and the court designer Ludovico Burnacini. His election to the exclusive Academy of the Emperor and the posthumous republication in 1700 of two volumes of his sacred texts indicate the high esteem in which he was held. Revived throughout Italy, as well as in France and Germany, his works were set by many composers, among them Leopold I himself, Pederzuoli, Sances, Pistocchi, Legrenzi, Giovanni Bononcini, M. A. Ziani, Albinoni, Hasse and Telemann.

Most of Minato's texts, like those of such contemporaries as Aureli and Matteo Noris – but unlike the pseudo-historical and mythological libretto of Giovanni Faustini, his chief predecessor in Venice – exploit and embroider events of ancient history, with particular emphasis on the military and moral stature of the hero. Although these subjects suggested parallels between the virtues of ancient Rome and those of the Venetian republic, political symbolism became more overt in the Viennese libretto, many of which contain detailed allegorical elucidations identifying the hero with the Emperor Leopold I. Unlike those of his contemporaries, Minato's multi-act libretto contain an equal number of scenes in each act, 20 in the Venetian texts, usually fewer in those written for Vienna. The growing public demand for arias in Venice after about 1650 is reflected in the increased formal and functional distinction he made between recitative and aria as well

as in his ingenious manipulation of situations and characters to create plausible opportunities for arias. Although they afforded a means of integrating both arias and scenic display within the drama, his elaborate secondary plots and mixture of comic and serious elements earned him the scorn of late 17th-century opera reformers.

first set by Draghi unless otherwise stated

dm – *dramma per musica* fm – *festa musicale*
idb – *introduzione d'un balletto* ttm – *trattenimento musicale*

Orimonte (dm), Cavalli, 1650; Xerse (dm), Cavalli, 1654/5 (Provenzale, 1657; Bologna, 1657; G. Bononcini, 1694; Handel, 1738); Artemisia (dm), Cavalli, 1656/7 (Provenzale, ?1658; Ger., J. F. Braun, 1716); Antioco (dm), Cavalli, 1658/9; Elena (dm, completion of G. Faustini's text), Cavalli, 1659/60; Scipione africano (dm), Cavalli, 1664 (addns by Stradella, 1671; rev. Viviani, 1678; Ger., J. P. Krieger, 1690, as Der grossmütige Scipio)

Mutio Scevola (dm), Cavalli, 1665 (Monari, 1692; G. Bononcini, 1695; comp. unknown, Florence, 1696); Pompeo Magno (dm), Cavalli, 1666 (A. Scarlatti, 1683; rev. Ravenna, 1685; Perti, 1691); Seleuco, Sartorio, 1666 (Draghi, 1675, as Zaleuco; comp. unknown, Naples, 1688, as Zaleuco; Ger., Löhner, 1687, as Der gerechte Zaleukus); La prosperità di Elio Sejano (dm), Sartorio, 1667 (Draghi, 1671; Pisa, 1672; Perti, A. Vanelli and Martinenghi, 1699; Albinoni, 1707; Lapis and Cordans, 1729, as La generosità di Tiberio); La caduta di Elio Sejano (dm), Sartorio, 1667

Tiridate (rev. of ?H. Bentivoglio: Zenobia e Radamisto), Legrenzi, 1668; Atalanta (dm), 1669; Aristomene Messenio (dm), Sances, 1670 (comp. unknown, Padua, 1699, ? as Elmira); Le risa di Democrito (ttm), 1670 (Pistocchi, 1700; Ger., Telemann, 1703); Leonida in Tegea (dm), 1670 (rev. M. A. Ziani, 1676); Iphide Greca (dm), 1670 (Partenio, Freschi and G. Sartorio, 1671; Partenio, Freschi, Sartorio and G. P. Fusetto, 1672; rev. Partenio, Freschi, Sartorio and Spinazzari, 1675; comp. unknown, Bologna, 1675); Penelope (dm), 1670

L'avidità di Mida (ttm), 1671; La gara dei genij (festa teatrale), 1671; Cidippe (dm), 1671; Gl'atomi d'Epicuro (dm), 1672; Gundeberga (dm), 1672; Sulpitia (dm), 1672; Il gioir della speranza (introduzione ad un balletto), 1673; Batto convertito in sasso (musica di camera), 1673; Provare per non recitare (composizione per musica), 1673; Gl'incantesimi disciolti (idb), 1673; La Tessalonica (dm), 1673 (Pasquini, 1683); La lanterna di Diogene (dm), 1674

Le staggioni ossequiose (idb), 1674; Il ratto delle sabine (dm), 1674 (P. S. Agostini, 1680; G. Bononcini and others, 1692, as Eraclea); Il trionfatore de' centauri (fm), 1674; Il fuoco eterno custodito dalle vestali (dm), 1674; La nascità di Minerva (fm), 1674; I pazzi Abderiti (dm), 1675; Pirro (dm), 1675; Turia Lucretia (dm), 1675; Sciegliere non potendo adoprare, 1676; Hercole acquistatore dell'immortalità (dm), 1677; Chilonida (dm), 1677 (M. A. Ziani, 1709), carn. 1677; Il silentio di Harpocrate (dm), 1677 (?Pasquini, 1686)

Adriano sul Monte Casio (dm), 1677; Le maghe di Tessaglia (fm), 1677; Rodogone (dm), 1677; Creso (dm), Leopold I, 1678; La conquista del vello d'oro (festa teatrale), 1678; Leucippe Phestia (dm), 1678; Il tempio di Diana in Taurica (fm), 1678; La monarchia latina trionfante (fm), 1678; Enea in Italia (dm), 1678; Li favoriti dalla fortuna (fm), 1678; Baldracca (dm), 1679; La svogliata (ttm), carn. 1679; L'osequio di Flora (introduzione a un balletto di giardinieri), carn. 1679

Curzio (dm), intended for 1679; I vaticinij di Tiresia Tebano (fm), 1680; La patienza di Socrate con due mogli (scherzo dramatico per musica), 1680 (G. Reutter and Caldara, 1731; F. A. de Almeida, 1733; Ger., Telemann, 1721, as Der geduldige Socrates); La forza dell'amicitia (dm), 1681; Temistocle in Persia (dm), 1681; La rivalità nell'ossequio (ttm), 1681; L'albero del ramo d'oro (introduzione d'un ballo), 1681; Gli stratagemi di Biante (dm), 1682; La chimera (drama fantastico musicale), 1682

Il tempio d'Apollo in Delfo (idb), 1682; Il monte Chimera (ttm), Pederzuoli, 1682; Il giardino della virtù, 1683; Lo smemorato (ttm), 1683; La lira d'Orfeo (ttm), 1683; Gl'elogii (idb), 1684; Tullio Hostilio, aprendo il tempio di Giano (fm), 1684; I varii effetti d'amore (introduzione ad un balletto), 1685; Didone costante (compositione per musica), Pederzuoli, carn. 1685; La più generosa Spartana (introduzione ad un balletto), 1685; Musica, Pittura, e Poesia (ttm), Pederzuoli, 1685

Il Palladio in Roma (dm), 1685; *Il rissarcimento della ruota della Fortuna* (introduzione ad un balletto), 1685; *Lo studio d'amore* (introduzione ad un balletto), 1686; *Le scoccagini degli Psilli* (ttm), 1686; *Il nodo gordiano* (festa teatrale), 1686; *Le ninfe ritrose* (idb), 1686; *Il ritorno di Teseo dal labirinto di Creta* (idb), 1686; *La grotta di Vulcano* (idb), 1686; *La vendetta dell'Honestà* (rappresentazione musicale), 1687; *La Gemma Ceraunia d'Ulissipone hora Lisbona* (dramma musicale), 1687

La vittoria della fortezza (idb), 1687; *La fama addormentata e risvegliata* (idb), 1687; *Il marito ama più* (fm), 1688; *Tanisia* (dm), 1688; *La moglie ama meglio* (fm), 1688; *Pigmaleone in Cipro* (fm), 1689; *La regina de' volsci* (dm), 1690; *Scipione preservatore di Roma* (ttm), 1690; *Li tre stati del tempo: passato, presente, e venturo* (idb), 1691; *Il Ringiovenito* (fm), 1691; *Il pellegrinaggio delle Gratie all'oracolo dodoneo* (invenzione per una serenata), 1691; *Le attioni fortunate di Perseo* (festa), 1691

Fedeltà e Generosità (festa teatrale), 1692; *Le varietà di fortuna in L. I. Bruto* (festa per musica), 1692; *Il vincitor magnanimo T. Quintio Flaminio* (dm), 1692; *L'amore in sogno, overo Le nozze d'Odati, e Zoriadre* (dm), 1693; *La madre degli dei* (fm), 1693; *Pelopida tebano in Tessaglia* (festa teatrale), 1694; *L'industrie amorose in Filli di Tracia* (dm), 1695; *La chioma di Berenice* (fm), 1695 (intended for 1690); *Le piramidi d'Egitto* (ttm), 1697; *La tirannide abbatuta dalla virtù* (fm), 1697

*c*50 one-part dramatic vocal chamber works set by Draghi, Pederzuoli, Badia and F. T. Richter

Doubtful: *Il merito uniforma i genii* (idb), 1692

Archivio Vendramin, 42 F 6/2 (*I-Vcg*) [papers concerning Minato's relationship to the Teatro di S Salvatore]

M. Maylender: *Storia delle accademie d'Italia*, ii (Bologna, 1927), 185–6; iii (1929), 175–6

S. T. Worsthorne: *Venetian Opera in the Seventeenth Century* (Oxford, 1954)

F. Hadamowsky: 'Barocktheater am Wiener Kaiserhof', *Jb der Geschichte für Wiener Theaterforschung 1951–2* (1955), 7–96

H. S. Powers: 'Il *Serse trasformato*', *MQ*, xlvii (1961), 481–92; xlviii (1962), 73–92

R. Brockpähler: *Handbuch zur Geschichte der Barockoper in Deutschland* (Emsdetten, 1964)

M. N. Clinkscale: *Pier Francesco Cavalli's 'Xerse'* (diss., U. of Minnesota, 1970)

H. S. Powers: 'Il "Mutio" tramutato, Part I: Sources and Libretto', *Venezia e il melodramma nel seicento: Venice 1972*, 227–58

N. Hiltl: *Die Oper am Hofe Kaiser Leopolds I. mit besonderer Berücksichtigung der Tätigkeit von Minato und Draghi* (diss., U. of Vienna, 1974)

L. Bianconi: 'Funktionen des Opernttheaters in Neapel bis 1700 und die Rolle Alessandro Scarlattis', *Colloquium Alessandro Scarlatti: Würzburg 1975*, 13–111

J. Glover: *Cavalli* (London, 1978)

H. Seifert: *Neues zu Antonio Draghis weltlichen Werken* (Vienna, 1978)

R. L. Weaver and N. W. Weaver: *A Chronology of Music in the Florentine Theater, 1590–1750* (Detroit, 1978)

E. Rutschman: *The Minato-Cavalli Operas: the search for Structure in Libretto and Solo Scene* (diss., U. of Washington, 1979)

——: 'Minato and the Venetian Opera Libretto', *CMc*, no.27 (1982), 84–91

L'opera italiana a Vienna prima di Metastasio: Venice 1984 [incl. M. Hager: 'La funzione del linguaggio poetico nelle opere comiche di Amalteo, Draghi e Minato', 17–30; E. Rutschman: '"Orimonte": Anatomy of a Failure', 31–41; N. Pirrotta: 'Note su Minato', 127–63]

H. Seifert: *Die Oper am Wiener Kaiserhof* (Tutzing, 1985)

C. Sartori: *I libretti italiani a stampa dalle origini al 1800* (Cuneo, 1990–)

E. Rosand: *Opera in Seventeenth-Century Venice: the Creation of a Genre* (Berkeley, 1991)   ELLEN ROSAND, HERBERT SEIFERT

Minchejmer [Münchheimer], **Adam** (*b* Warsaw, 23 Dec 1830; *d* Warsaw, 27 Jan 1904). Polish composer and conductor. He studied composition in Warsaw with Achim Freyer and, briefly, in Berlin with A. B. Marx. At the Wielki Theatre, Warsaw, he was first violin (1850–64), music director and manager of the ballet (1858–72), conductor (1872–82), director of the opera

(1882–90) and librarian (1890–1902). He also taught at various institutions in Warsaw. His large output includes four operas, which are eclectic in character and stylistically immature. The first three are in the manner of Meyerbeerian grand opera. In *Mazepa* national and folk dances are used; *Mściciel* was influenced by early Wagner.

Otton łucznik [Otto the Archer] (5, J. Chęciński, after A. Dumas *père*), Warsaw, 8 Dec 1864, *PL-Wtm*; vs (Warsaw, 1870)
Stradiota (5, J. S. Jasiński), Warsaw, 14 Dec 1876, *Wtm*
Mazepa (4, M. Radziszewski, after J. Słowacki), Warsaw, 1 May 1900, vs (Warsaw, 1899)
Mściciel [The Avenger] (W. Miller), Warsaw, 7 May 1910

Album Münchheimera (MS, *PL-WRol* 5836) [collection of press cuttings, photographs and other documents]

L. T. Błaszczyk: *Dyrygenci polscy i obcy w Polsce działający w XIX i XX wieku* [Polish and Foreign Conductors Working in Poland in the 19th and 20th Centuries] (Kraków, 1964)

KATARZYNA MORAWSKA

Minelli, Giovanni Battista (*b* Bologna, ?1687; *d* after 1735). Italian contralto castrato. He is first found in opera in 1705 but did not begin a sustained career in Italy until 1711. In 1722–4 he was in service at Munich; he then resumed Italian engagements until 1729, after which he was in the imperial service in Vienna, creating the title role in Metastasio's first Vienna opera, *Demetrio* (1731; music by Caldara). He retired from the stage after singing at Genoa and Bologna in 1735 and is said to have become a monk. His singing (range approximately *g* to *e″*) was praised for its finish and its mastery of all the vocal genres, and this is reflected in the arias written for him, which require a musician of subtlety and intelligence.   DENNIS LIBBY

Mines of Sulphur, The. Opera in three acts by RICHARD RODNEY BENNETT to a libretto by Beverley Cross; London, Sadler's Wells, 24 February 1965.

The action takes place in the mid-18th century in a decaying manor house in the west of England. Boconnion (tenor), a deserter, aided and abetted by Tovey (baritone), a tramp, and Rosalind (mezzo-soprano), a gypsy, murder the landowner Braxton (bass-baritone) in order to steal the wealth they feel he has done nothing to deserve. Their celebrations (during which they don grand clothing found in the house) are interrupted by the arrival of a troupe of actors seeking shelter for the night: Jenny (soprano), Leda (contralto), Fenney (tenor) and Tooley (baritone), together with the actor-manager Sherrin (bass-baritone, doubling the murdered Braxton) and Trim (mime-dancer), a mute. Boconnion agrees, in return for a performance of their latest play, *The Mines of Sulphur*. This tells of a wealthy count who is persuaded by his valet to seek the hand of a beautiful girl. Alas, the girl falls in love with the valet, and when the count fails to carry out his threat to kill them both she hands the knife to her lover, daring him to turn the tables on her husband. All this is too much for the audience of Braxton's killers. As they shout for the play to stop, it is seen that the actress Jenny has fainted; escorting her upstairs, Tooley finds Braxton's body together with Boconnion's discarded army uniform. Realizing that the game is up, Boconnion plans to confine the theatrical troupe to the cellar before setting fire to the house and making good his escape with Rosalind and Tovey. The ailing Jenny reappears and, just as the evil trio are about to leave, she reveals the dreadful truth that there can be no escape: she is infected with the plague.

The Mines of Sulphur, Bennett's first full-length opera, composed in 1963, is scored for large orchestra, including piano, harpsichord, celesta and harp; it shows the composer's mastery of a 'personalized' 12-note idiom that owes as much to Britten as to Schoenberg, as much to Bennett's essential Englishness as to European influences. His use of ostinato focusses on recurring thematic elements – including a quasi-folktune, memorably bleak and sorrowful, and the increasing menace of an action-stopping horn call – that evoke the changing circumstances of each of the three acts in a manner both atmospheric and intensely dramatic.   SUSAN BRADSHAW

Ming Cho Lee (*b* Shanghai, 3 Oct 1930). Chinese-American set designer. He studied traditional Chinese landscape painting before attending Occidental College and UCLA (1950–54). In 1955 he began a five-year apprenticeship in New York with Joe Mielziner, eventually becoming his assistant. In 1958 he designed *The Infernal Machine* and *The Crucible* for the Phoenix Theatre. Ming's ballet sets include work for the choreographers Martha Graham and Alvin Ailey. For the Peabody Arts Theatre in Baltimore (1959–63) he designed opera sets for *Il turco in Italia*, *Aufstieg und Fall der Stadt Mahagonny*, *La bohème*, *Les pêcheurs de perles*, *Werther* and *Hamlet*. Other opera designs include *Peter Ibbetson* and *Kát'a Kabanová* (1960) and *Les pêcheurs de perles* (1961) for the Empire State Music Festival in New York; *Tristan und Isolde* for the Baltimore Civic Opera and *Madama Butterfly* for the Opera Company of Boston (1962).

In 1961 Ming was appointed art director and resident designer at the San Francisco Opera. The next year he became Joseph Papp's principal designer for the New York Shakespeare Festival in Central Park. From 1964 to 1970 he was principal designer at the Juilliard School. For the Metropolitan Opera his set designs include *Madama Butterfly* (and costumes, 1965), *Figaro* (1966), *Boris Godunov* (1974), *Lohengrin* (1976) and *Khovanshchina* (1985), and for the Opera Society of Washington, DC, *Faust*, the première of *Bomarzo*, and *Roberto Devereux* (1970). He designed *Giulio Cesare* (1969) and *Lucia di Lammermoor* (1971) for the Hamburg Staatsoper, and has also worked for the Teatro Colón, Buenos Aires. He has taught set design at New York University (1967–9) and at the Yale Drama School (from 1968). Ming Cho Lee has described his sets (he rarely designs costumes) as 'the abstract essence of a dramatic statement'. They are noted for their skeletal but suggestive use of modern materials, especially metals, and their painterly use of lighting to achieve sculptural effects.

For illustration *see* BOMARZO.   DAVID J. HOUGH

Mingotti, Pietro (*b* Venice, *c*1702; *d* Copenhagen, 28 April 1759). Italian impresario active in Austria, Germany and Denmark. His brother Angelo Mingotti (*b c*1700; *d* after 1767) formed an Italian opera company in Prague around 1732, consisting of three male and five female singers, a typical configuration. The troupe performed frequently at Brno, inaugurating a new opera house, the Theater in der Tafern, in 1734, and joined Pietro's company at Graz from 1736 to 1740. During the following decade both troupes performed in various German and Austrian centres, occasionally together,

presenting some *opere buffe* along with the mainstay of *opere serie*. Pietro's company, the more distinguished of the two, performed for the coronation of Franz I, Maria Theresa's husband, at Frankfurt in 1745 and for a royal wedding at Dresden in 1747. On the latter occasion Gluck apparently conducted his own *festa teatrale Le nozze d'Ercole e d'Ebe*, replacing the company's music director, Paolo Scalabrini. Pietro's wife Regina was recruited by the Dresden court opera at this time at an annual salary of 2000 thalers.

In December 1747 the troupe performed by royal invitation in Copenhagen, their first of many seasons. Gluck was still with the company there and in Hamburg in 1748. Most of the serious operas that made up its repertory were by Scalabrini, who was appointed Kapellmeister by the Danish court in 1748. In December 1752 Giuseppe Sarti joined Pietro's troupe as music director, by which time its repertory consisted of both serious operas and ballets. Financial reverses led Pietro to seek dissolution of his contract with the Danish court in 1755. His property was seized and sold to cover his considerable debts, and he died penniless in Copenhagen. Little is known of Angelo's later career, although he performed at Bonn in 1764 and 1767.

*

E. H. Müller [von Asow]: *Die Mingottischen Opernunternehmungen: 1732 bis 1756* (Leipzig, 1915)
——: *Angelo und Pietro Mingotti* (Dresden, 1917)
——: 'Gluck und die Brüder Mingotti', *Gluck-Jb*, iii (1917), 1–14
THOMAS BAUMAN

Mingotti [née Valentin(i)], **Regina** [?Caterina] (*b* Naples, 16 Feb 1722; *d* Neuburg an der Donau, 1 Oct 1808). Italo-German singer. Her early life is known almost wholly from her account to Burney in 1772, which is inaccurate in at least one important respect. According to this, she was the daughter of a German officer in the Austrian service at Naples and was educated in a convent at Grätz in Silesia (not Graz, as sometimes stated). She attributed her firm intonation to the abbess, who made her practise scales without keyboard accompaniment. According to Prota-Giurleo she was the sister of the composer Michelangelo Valentini, hence presumably Italian, and may have had an early, undocumented Italian career. She was at all events trilingual in German, Italian and French. Her first recorded appearance was in the mixed entertainment *Il tempio di Melpomene* (Hamburg, 31 Jan 1747), as a leading member of a notable company run by the impresario Pietro Mingotti, whom she married but soon parted from. She scored an immediate success in Dresden (1747), where she was kept on by the Saxon court and studied with Porpora. She sang in Naples, Prague, Madrid (1751–3), Paris and London (1754–5); in the 1756–7 and 1763–4 London seasons she took over the management of the King's Theatre together with the leader of the orchestra, Felice Giardini, and incurred much obloquy. Her retirement was spent at Dresden, then Munich, and finally Neuburg, where her son Samuel von Buckingham was inspector of forests; he was apparently born (in London) of a liaison with a Piedmontese nobleman. Burney called her 'perfect mistress of her art', 'always grand' in her style though lacking in grace and softness; her practical musical intelligence, he wrote, was equal to that of any composer he had known. She was admired as an actress, particularly in the breeches roles she often sang (for illustration *see* ATTILIO REGOLO).

BDA; BurneyH; BurneyGN; MGG (U. Prota-Giurleo)
M. Fürstenau: *Zur Geschichte der Musik und des Theaters am Hofe zu Dresden* (Dresden, 1861–2), ii, 251–3
E. H. Müller [von Asow]: *Angelo und Pietro Mingotti* (Dresden, 1917)
——: 'Regina Mingotti: eine italienische Primadonna aus österreichischer Familie', *Musikblätter*, no.4 (1950), 79–82
                                                                JOHN ROSSELLI

Minneapolis and St Paul. Cities (known as the Twin Cities) in Minnesota, on the Upper Mississippi. They received frequent visits from the early travelling companies, but local opera production did not get under way until 1930 with a Minneapolis-based enterprise, the Twin Cities Opera. The company mounted an inaugural summer season of 'grand opera' (*Martha*, *Il trovatore*, *Carmen*, *Cavalleria rusticana*) and in April 1932 made its winter-season début with *Faust*; performances were sung in English. However, the Minneapolis enterprise quickly faded on the founding of the St Paul Civic Opera, which opened with *Samson et Dalila* on 8 December 1933. The new company normally presented three standard works each season; under the directorship of Leo B. Kopp (1938–68), these gave way to two operettas or musicals and one opera.

With the accession of George M. Schaefer as general manager in 1968, and with Igor Buketoff as conductor, the St Paul Opera (as it was now known) engaged distinguished American singers, commissioned Lee Hoiby's *Summer and Smoke* (1971) and undertook more ambitious programmes, usually given only a few weeks after the Metropolitan Opera's spring visit. The company failed to win sufficient public support and went out of business in 1975, its remnants officially merging with Minnesota Opera.

Minnesota Opera began as Center Opera in 1964 with the première of Dominick Argento's *The Masque of Angels* at the Tyrone Guthrie Theater, Minneapolis. This production launched a series of commissions including Argento's *Postcard from Morocco* (1971), *The Voyage of Edgar Allan Poe* (1976) and *Casanova's Homecoming* (1985), Conrad Susa's *Transformations* (1973), Libby Larsen's *Frankenstein* (1990) and Robert Moran's *From the Towers of the Moon* (1992). The company has presented on average one world première each season, and complemented the Metropolitan Opera Tours, which from 1945 had given a season at the 4800-seat Northrop Auditorium on the University of Minnesota campus (where the company was officially known as the Metropolitan Opera in the Upper Midwest). Minnesota Opera gradually moved away from 20th-century opera to focus increasingly on traditional repertory, particularly after the annual Metropolitan visits ended in 1986. Presenting such staples as *Carmen* and *La bohème*, while venturing into *Rusalka* and *A Midsummer Night's Dream*, the company at last won larger audiences and increased in financial strength. Operas began to be sung in their original languages with surtitles, and avant-garde music-theatre pieces were mostly relegated to a secondary stage.

In the late 1970s and early 80s, productions were given at the O'Shaughnessy Auditorium (on the campus of the College of St Catherine) in St Paul and at the Orpheum Theater in Minneapolis. On the opening of the 1800-seat Ordway Music Theatre in 1985, the company found a base in St Paul. However, in September 1990 it moved its operations to three renovated warehouses in Minneapolis and in autumn 1991 began to perform in the restored State Theatre, as well as at other venues. With Kevin H. Smith as general director and George Manahan as principal conductor, the standard repertory predominates, although the company continues to commission new operas, maintains an experimental New Music-Theater Ensemble and undertakes an annual national tour (formerly as the Midwest Opera Theater).   MARY ANN FELDMAN

Minnesota Opera. Company, formerly Center Opera, in MINNEAPOLIS AND ST PAUL.

Minoja, Ambrogio (*b* Ospitaletto Lodigiano, nr Piacenza, 22 Oct 1752; *d* Milan, 3 Aug 1825). Italian composer. He studied in Lodi and with Nicola Sala in Naples, and was *maestro al cembalo* at La Scala and the Teatro della Cannobiana in Milan from 1784 until 1802. While at La Scala, he represented his colleagues in negotiations with impresarios and was secretary-general of a musicians' union that sponsored Lenten concerts there; he also worked as *maestro di cappella*. Minoja composed two operas, *Tito nelle Gallie* (after P. Giovannini: *Giulio Sabino*; Milan, Scala, 26 Dec 1786, *F-Pn*, *P-La* [Act 1]) and *Olimpiade* (P. Metastasio; Rome, Argentina, 26 Dec 1787). Although these brought no commissions from other cities, he was called upon to compose cantatas and instrumental music for state occasions in Milan. When the city came under Austrian rule, Minoja replaced Bonifazio Asioli as censor of the Milan Conservatory, the highest teaching position there.

EitnerQ; FétisB; FlorimoN; GerberNL
P. Cambiasi: *Rappresentazioni date nei reali teatri di Milano, 1778–1872* (Milan, 1872), 115   SVEN HANSELL

Minorca. For discussion of opera in Minorca *see* MAHÓN.

Minsk. Capital of Belarus'. There are no indications of musical stage works in the city until the 1830s, when there are records of plays with incidental music. The most notable activity during the middle part of the century is associated with Stanisław Moniuszko, who was born near Minsk. His operetta *Loteria* ('The Lottery') was first produced in Minsk, in 1843; other stage works by him, such as *Pobór rekrutów* ('Conscription'), *Sielanka* ('Idyll') and the vaudeville *Nocleg w Apeninach* ('A Night's Lodging in the Apennines'), were also presented. In 1865 the Society of Nobles in Minsk opened a theatre which performed operas by Donizetti, Lysenko, Verstovsky and others. The theatre also presented touring Italian troupes performing Russian and west European opera and operetta. A ballet troupe was added in 1890.

The Belorusskaya Gosudarstvennaya Studiya Operï i Baleta (Belorussian State Opera and Ballet Studio), opened in 1930, was replaced by the Belorusskiy Teatr Operï i Baleta in 1933; the repertory of the first season included *Prince Igor*, *Rigoletto* and Dzerzhinsky's *Tikhiy Don* ('Quiet Flows the Don'). The first Belorussian national operas, Tikotsky's *Mikhas' Podgornïy*, Bogatïryov's *V pushchakh Poles'ya* ('In the Virgin Forests of Poles'ye') and Turenkov's *Tsvetok schast'ya* ('The Flower of Happiness'), were all first performed there in 1939–40. The opera house, designed by I. Langrad, was finished in 1938 but has been remodelled twice, in 1947 and 1967, when the stage was reconstructed. The Gosudarstvennïy Teatr

Muzïkal'noy Komedii (State Theatre of Musical Comedy), which also performs operettas, opened in 1971.

*

ME (I. Nisnevich)

I. G. Nisnevich: *Ocherki po istorii sovetskoy belorusskoy muzïkal'noy kul'turï* [Studies in the History of Soviet Belorussian Musical Culture] (Leningrad, 1969)

G. C. Glushchenko and others: *Gistoriya belaruskay sovetskay muzïki* (Minsk, 1971)

——: *Istoriya belorusskoi muzïki* (Moscow, 1976)

P. U. Brovka and others: *Minsk: entsiklopedicheskii spravochnik* [Minsk: an Encyclopedic Guide] (Minsk, 1980)

MITCHELL MORRIS

Minter, Drew (*b* Washington DC, 11 Jan 1955). American countertenor. He attended Indiana University and studied privately with Marcy Lindheimer, Myron McPherson, Rita Streich and Erik Werba. Early in his career he was a member of early music ensembles, including the Waverly Consort in New York. His stage début was in the title role of Handel's *Orlando* at the St Louis Baroque Festival in 1983. He has since appeared in Boston, Brussels, Los Angeles, Milwaukee and Omaha, where his clear, ringing voice has won praise, particularly in operas by Handel, Landi and Monteverdi. In 1989, he made his Santa Fe Opera début as the Military Governor in the American première of Weir's *A Night at the Chinese Opera* and also sang Endymion (*Calisto*).

CORI ELLISON

Minton, Yvonne (Fay) (*b* Sydney, 4 Dec 1938). Australian mezzo-soprano. She studied at the Conservatorium in Sydney and in 1960 moved to London, where she began a concert career before making her operatic début in 1964 as Britten's Lucretia in a City Literary Institute production; the same year she created Maggie Dempster in Maw's *One Man Show*. She then joined the Covent Garden company and over the next 12 years sang more than 30 major roles, creating Thea in *The Knot Garden* (1970) and having notable success as Octavian, the role of her débuts at Chicago (1970), the Metropolitan Opera (1973) and the Paris Opéra (1976); she also recorded it under Solti. Her appearance as Brangäne at Bayreuth in 1974 was followed by Fricka and Waltraute in the centenary *Ring*, and she sang Kundry at Covent Garden in 1979. Also in 1979 she sang Countess Geschwitz in the first three-act *Lulu* in Paris, which she also filmed and recorded. Other recordings include Dorabella under Klemperer (1971), Mozart's Sextus (1976) under Colin Davis and Geneviève (*Pelléas*) under Boulez (1970). Her warm fullness of tone and striking stage personality are combined with interpretative skill and imagination. She was made a CBE in 1980. After a short period of retirement she sang Leokadja Begbick (*Mahagonny*) at Florence in 1990 and Clytemnestra at Adelaide in 1991.

H. Rosenthal: 'Yvonne Minton', *Opera*, xxviii (1977), 834–41

J. Burnie: 'Singing a Different Song', *Sunday Times Magazine* (27 Oct 1985)

NOËL GOODWIN

Miolan-Carvalho, Marie Caroline. See CARVALHO, MARIE CAROLINE.

Mion, Charles-Louis (*b* 1698; *d* Versailles, 12 Sept 1775). French composer. He was a great-nephew of Michel-Richard de Lalande, and his professional life focussed on the court. He was named as a singer in the royal chapel in 1727, taught singing to Mme de Pompadour and composed at least five occasional stage works, including a *ballet héroïque, Julie et Ovide,* for the Prince of Condé. With his *opéra-ballet L'année galante* (1747), Mion received an annual royal pension of 2000 livres and by 1750 was named *compositeur du ballets du roi*. His only *tragédie lyrique, Nitétis,* was performed at the Paris Opéra in 1741. By 1765 he was suffering from paralysis and had ceased composing. He was buried in Notre Dame de Versailles.

Bouquets de Mlle de G*** à sa mère (idylle, 3, P. de Morand), Versailles, 12 Dec 1735

Nitétis (tragédie lyrique, prol., 5, J.-L.-I. de La Serre), Paris, Opéra, 11 April 1741 (Paris, 1741)

Les quatre parties du monde (opéra-ballet, P.-C. Roy), Versailles, 1745

L'année galante (opéra-ballet, prol., 4, Roy), Versailles, 13 Feb 1747 (Paris, 1747)

Julie et Ovide (ballet héroïque, after L. Fuzelier: *Les amours déguisés*), Paris, 11 June 1753

*

FétisB

Mercure de France (Feb 1728), 386; (June 1753), 164

Almanach parisien (Paris, 1767), ii, 131

M. Brenet: *Les musiciens de la Sainte-Chapelle du Palais* (Paris, 1910)

N. Dufourcq, ed.: *Notes et références pour servir à une histoire de Michel-Richard Delalande* (Paris, 1957)

BARBARA COEYMAN

Miramontes, Arnulfo (*b* Tala, 18 July 1882; *d* Aguascalientes, 1960). Mexican composer. He studied in Guadalajara, Mexico City and Berlin, and left an output that includes three symphonies, two string quartets, a piano concerto, a cantata, two oratorios and diverse solo and chamber music. His style is conservative and mostly features a complex linear counterpoint. He also wrote three operas, the first two referring to pre-Hispanic Mexico: *Anahuac* (libretto by Nicolas Bracho, first performed in Mexico City in 1918), from which he extracted the material for his symphonic poem *La leyenda de los volcanes,* and *Cihuatl* (composed in 1922; unperformed), which tells the story of the Aztec goddess of the same name. The third opera, *Juana de Asbaje,* with a libretto by Bracho, is based on the life of the 18th-century poet Sor Juana Inés de la Cruz (date of composition unknown; unperformed).

RICARDO MIRANDA-PÉREZ

Miranda, Lalla (*b* Melbourne, 1874; *d* Edinburgh, 25 Feb 1944). Australian soprano. She became principally active in France and Belgium in such parts as Ophelia, Lucia and Lakmé, and as an early interpreter of the Fairy Godmother in Massenet's *Cendrillon,* but also took leading roles at Covent Garden (Gilda, Marguerite de Valois, 1900; Gilda, Zerlina, 1907) and at the Manhattan Opera House, New York, opening the 1910 season there as Lucia and returning to London to partner McCormack in *Lakmé* and *La traviata*.

Noted for her vocal range, light-toned consistency and highly developed coloratura technique in Melbourne in the 1890s, she made her European début at The Hague in 1898 as Marguerite de Valois in *Les Huguenots,* later appearing as Gilda with Caruso in Belgium. Under contract to the Paris Opéra, she was given permission to return to Australia with the Quinlan touring company in 1912, relearning her parts in English for the occasion and opening the season as Olympia in *Les contes d'Hoffmann*. Thereafter she continued to base her career in Europe.

ROGER COVELL

Mirandolina. Comic opera in three acts by BOHUSLAV MARTINŮ to a libretto by the composer after CARLO GOLDONI's play *La locandiera*; Prague, National Theatre, 17 May 1959.

Martinů had wanted to set a Goldoni text since the mid-1930s. While working on the *commedia dell'arte*-influenced opera *Divadlo za branou* ('The Suburban Theatre') in 1935–6 he considered using texts by Goldoni in place of scenes from *Le médecin volant* (by Molière). The opportunity to compose *Mirandolina* arose from a Guggenheim Foundation award intended to support him while writing an opera after his return to Europe from the USA in 1953. He contemplated variously Neveux's *Plainte contre inconnu* and Dostoyevsky's *The Devils*. Shortly before returning to Europe he had thought of setting Goldoni's *La locandiera* as a television opera for New York in 1952, but had abandoned it in favour of Gogol's *The Marriage*.

Martinů understood enough Italian to fashion the libretto from Goldoni's original himself. Work on the opera, which he found far more congenial than his efforts with *The Devils*, began on 15 December 1953 in Nice; the first act was completed on 14 March 1954. A car journey through Italy briefly interrupted work but also fuelled Martinů's enthusiasm for things Italian; the second act was finished by 7 May and the entire opera by 1 July 1954.

The story follows Goldoni's tale of Mirandolina (soprano), the mistress of an inn, who beguiles three suitors, the Count of Albafiorita (tenor), the Marquess of Forlimpopoli (bass; originally Forlipopoli) and the misogynist Baron [Cavaliere] of Ripafrata (bass). While Mirandolina gently torments the main servant of the establishment, Fabrizio (tenor), having turned the heads of all three suitors, she eventually agrees to marry him and change her ways.

The music of *Mirandolina* is suffused with the warmly original tonal language cultivated by Martinů in the 1950s. The composer himself admitted that the work was 'in Czech style and not in Italian', but he suggested local colour quite effectively with orchestral interludes, most notably the saltarello which opens Act 3 (often performed as a separate piece) and Mirandolina's brilliant coloratura aria in Act 1 scene vi.

JAN SMACZNY

Mirate, Raffaele (*b* Naples, 3 Sept 1815; *d* Sorrento, Nov 1895). Italian tenor. He studied with Crescentini and made his début in 1837 at the Teatro Nuovo, Naples, in Donizetti's *Torquato Tasso*. After singing at the Théâtre Italien, Paris, in 1840 he sang Amenophis (*Mosè in Egitto*) at La Scala. In 1845 he sang Jacopo (*I due Foscari*) and Charles VII (*Giovanna d'Arco*) at the Teatro Argentina, Rome; in 1847 he sang Ruiz (*Maria Padilla*) in Vienna. He created the Duke in *Rigoletto* at La Fenice in 1851. He appeared in Boston and New York (1856), then sang Leicester in *Maria Stuarda* (1865) and took part in the first performance of Mercadante's *Virginia* (1866) at S Carlo.

ELIZABETH FORBES

Mirecki, Franciszek (*b* Kraków, bap. 31 March 1791; *d* Kraków, 29 May 1862). Polish composer. He came from a musical family and received his first lessons from his father, an organist. Between 1814 and 1816 he studied with Hummel in Vienna, and after 1817 with Cherubini in Paris. He spent a few months in Venice,

where he studied the principles of Italian singing. From 1822 to 1838 he was again in Italy, first in Milan, where he made friends with Ricordi (later publisher of several of his works, including some of the operas), then in Genoa, where he conducted opera and taught singing. In the 1825–6 season he performed with an Italian opera troupe in Lisbon, France and England. Returning to Kraków in 1838, he founded a school of singing where he trained singers for the Kraków opera, which he conducted from 1844 to 1850.

All his life Mirecki upheld the Classical style and took a stand against Romanticism. The ideas expressed in his treatise *Pogląd na muzykę* ('Opinion on Music', Prague, 1860) are borne out in his music, which includes a symphony, several chamber works, songs, ballets and, most importantly, Polish and Italian operas connected with his work as a conductor. Following Rossinian models, they were popular in their time and won him a considerable reputation. The charlatan Bombalo in *Nocleg w Apeninach* ('A Night in the Apennines') is similar to Dulcamara in Donizetti's *L'elisir d'amore*. One of the most eminent Polish opera composers before Moniuszko, Mirecki brought the Italian large-scale virtuoso aria into Polish opera, and was the first Polish composer whose operas were staged in Italy.

Puławski, before 1822, lost
Cyganie [The Gypsies] (Spl, 3, after F. D. Kniaźnin), Warsaw, National, 23 May 1822, ov. and vs (Warsaw, n.d.)
Piast (J. U. Niemcewicz), Warsaw, National, 22 Nov 1822, lost
Evandro in Pergamo (os, 2, A. Peracchi), Genoa, S Agostino, 26 Dec 1824, vs (Milan, n.d.)
Adriano in Siria, c1826, inc.
I due forzati (os), Lisbon, March 1826, ov. *PL-Kj*, excerpts vs (Milan, 1840)
Cornelio Bentivoglio (os), Milan, Scala, 18 March 1844 (Milan, n.d.)
Nocleg w Apeninach [A Night in the Appenines] (oc, 2, N. Ekielski, after A. Fredro), Kraków, Miejski, 11 April 1845, vs (Milan, 1850)
Rajmund mnich [Raymond the Friar] (after Fredro), inc., excerpts vs (Lwów, c1860)

*

W. Spodenkiewicz: 'Nocleg w Apeninach', opera Franciszka Mireckiego (diss., Jagiellonian U., 1947)
W. Sandelewski: 'Francesco Mirecki, campione polacco del melodramma italiano', *RMI*, lv (1953), 426–33
K. Herman: 'Franciszek Mirecki w setną vocznicę śmierci', *Ruch muzyczny*, xviii/11 (1962), 1
M. Bristiger: 'Włoskie i klasyczne momenty argumentacji muzycznej Franciszka Mireckiego / Riflessi italiani e classici nel pensiero musicale di Francesco Mirecki', *Pagine*, iii (1979), 199–218

ZOFIA CHECHLIŃSKA

Mireille. *Opéra* in five acts by CHARLES-FRANÇOIS GOUNOD to a libretto by MICHEL CARRÉ after FRÉDÉRIC MISTRAL's epic poem *Mirèio*; Paris, Théâtre Lyrique, 19 March 1864.

The appearance of the epic *Mirèio* in 1859 (in a bilingual edition, with the Provençal text matched by a French prose translation on facing pages) brought the Provençal poet Frédéric Mistral to the attention of the Parisian literary establishment for the first time. Gounod probably knew the epic by the end of 1861 and, after receiving permission from Mistral for an operatic adaptation, began to work seriously on the project at the beginning of 1863. Gounod gave the poet regular progress reports, admitting early on that the dramatic requirements of the stage had forced the elimination of much local detail. Shorn of its forays into such things as the intricacies of olive cultivation and silk weaving, the essentials of Mistral's plot are reproduced faithfully by

Mireille *daughter of Maître Ramon*	soprano
Vincent *son of Maître Ambroise*	tenor
Ourrias *a bull-tamer*	baritone
Maître Ramon *a wealthy farmer*	bass
Maître Ambroise *a peasant*	bass
Vincenette *Vincent's sister*	soprano
Taven *a sorceress*	contralto
Clémence *a friend of Mireille*	soprano
A Ferryman	bass
Andreloux *a shepherd*	contralto

Mulberry gatherers, townspeople, spirits of the Rhône, farmhands, pilgrims to the chapel of the Saintes-Maries

Setting Provence, 19th century

Carré, with some re-ordering of events: Mistral gives the great scene in which Mireille confronts her father with her love for Vincent after Vincent is wounded by Ourrias; in the opera that scene occurs before the duel, to create a situation where Vincent's wound provides dramatic justification for Mireille to undertake the dangerous journey to the Saintes-Maries.

Preparations for the first production by the Théâtre Lyrique began in October 1863; the work Gounod first brought to rehearsal was radically modified before the première. Changes included the elimination of a duet for Mireille and Ourrias in Act 2, an abbreviation of Mireille's Act 4 'Air de la Crau' and resultant composition of her Act 2 *air* (not, as is frequently said, the Act 4 *ariette* 'Heureux petit berger', which had been planned from the start), and the composition of Andreloux's *chanson* in Act 5. *Mireille* was poorly received at its première, with Caroline Carvalho unsuccessful in certain passages of the title role and François Morini ineffective as Vincent. In an attempt to improve its fortunes, major changes in the order of events in Acts 3 and 4 were hastily improvised after the second performance, but these do not seem to have prolonged the run appreciably. Neither was *Mireille* a success at Covent Garden in July 1864, for which Gounod supplied recitatives in place of the original spoken dialogue and created a happy ending. Further changes were made for a new production at the Théâtre Lyrique in December 1864: the work was regrouped into three acts (with elimination of much material in the original Acts 3, 4, and 5), a new duet for Mireille and Vincent was added to bring down the final curtain, and a *valse-ariette* was written for Carvalho. *Mireille* still did not take hold. An additional unsuccessful attempt to make the work profitable – with numerous new changes not sanctioned by the composer – was made in 1874 at the Opéra-Comique. Finally in 1889 the work was well received in a new production at the Opéra-Comique that used a version very similar to the three-act one of December 1864.

Mireille became a staple of the Opéra-Comique repertory for the next 75 years and the aim of new productions subsequent to that of 1889 became to restore the score as it was first performed in March 1864. This was only partly achieved in 1901 and 1939. The composer-conductor Henri Busser produced an edition of *Mireille* based upon the latter production that purported to be as close to the version of the première as documentation would allow; all complete recordings of the work have used this text. Unfortunately his score is founded on misreadings of the early editions and newly uncovered manuscript source material permits a more accurate reconstruction.

ACT 1 *A mulberry orchard* While a group of girls gathers mulberry leaves, the good sorceress Taven sadly notes that some of them will experience sorrow in love. Clémence (originally listed, like the role of Vincenette, as a 'dugazon' voice; *see* DUGAZON, LOUISE-ROSALIE) retorts that this will not happen to her because she will be taken from Provence by a handsome prince to live in a splendid castle. Mireille modestly confesses that she would be satisfied simply if a lad declared love to her in complete sincerity ('Et moi, si par hasard'); her melodic line, in contrast to Clémence's exuberant music, is dominated by conjunct motion and a naturalistic flow between durational and metrical accents. Mireille's friends playfully mock her, and after they leave she tells Taven that the rumour of her love for Vincent, a boy below her station, is true. Taven warns her that wealth and poverty are ill-matched. Vincent himself passes by and Mireille engages him in conversation. He tells her that she is even more attractive than his sister in a duet ('Vincenette a votre âge'), which starts casually in B♭ but later grows in lyrical intensity with a section in D♭; an instrumental refrain containing syncopated rhythms in 6/8 supplies Mediterranean *couleur locale*. Before parting they agree that if misfortune should befall either of them, the other will make a pilgrimage to the shrine of the Saintes-Maries to pray for assistance.

ACT 2 *At the entry to the arena at Arles* After a Provençal *farandole*, Mireille appears with her friends, followed shortly by Vincent. When bystanders suggest a love song, Mireille and Vincent oblige with the Chanson de Magali ('La brise est douce et parfumée'), featuring elegant alternation between 6/8 and 9/8 and many musical details that effectively evoke the nature-based metaphors for love in the poetry. The revellers take up the *farandole* again and enter the arena. Mireille stays behind and is gently warned by Taven that at this time of year she will be approached by suitors (*chanson*, 'Voici la saison mignonne'). In response, Mireille sings of her love for Vincent in a large *air* ('Trahir Vincent') with a heartfelt slow section followed by a mechanistic *cabalette*. As Taven predicted, the bull-tamer Ourrias declares his love for Mireille in *couplets* pervaded by dotted rhythms that communicate his resolve. Mireille leaves hastily. When her father, Maître Ramon, steps out of the arena Ourrias complains that Mireille has not been receptive to his suit. At that moment, Vincent and his father, Maître Ambroise, also appear. To a declaimed melodic line, Ramon asserts that fathers must wield an iron fist over their families and that no one in his household would dare defy him (finale, 'Un père parle en père').

Mireille reappears and reveals that she is in love with Vincent. Ramon orders her to forswear her attachment to him. He is about to strike Mireille when she falls on her knees to beg for understanding in the ternary slow section of the finale ('A vos pieds hélas me voilà'); she evokes the memory of her mother with a shift from minor to major coloured by an expressive clarinet counterpoint to the vocal line. But her plea falls on deaf ears: Ramon angrily curses Vincent and his father and in the *strette* ('Oui que l'enfer de vous s'empare') vows that he will not let Mireille see the lad again. Mireille and Vincent sing in unison that the attempt to separate them is vain; Ambroise replies to Ramon's verbal abuse in

'Mireille' (Gounod): final scene in Act 2 (at the entry to the arena at Arles) of the original production at the Théâtre Lyrique, Paris, 19 March 1864; lithograph by Caillot after Auguste Lamy

similar terms; the assembled crowd deplores Ramon's insensitivity.

ACT 3.i *The Val d'enfer, near Taven's cave* After an elfin orchestral entr'acte redolent of Mendelssohn, Ourrias tells his friends to return home without him; he is still distressed by Mireille's rejection and intends to take revenge upon Vincent (duet, 'Ils s'éloignent'). Vincent appears and is surprised by Ourrias, who accuses him of having used sorcery to obtain Mireille's affection. Ourrias ignominiously strikes the unarmed lad with his trident. Hearing the moans of the wounded Vincent, Taven rushes out from her cave and curses Ourrias.

3.ii *The banks of the Rhône* The waters are lit by a full moon. Ourrias, plagued by remorse and fear ('Ah! que j'ai fait!'), calls on the ferryman to transport him to the opposite bank. Suddenly, as the orchestra gives forth eerie chromatic progressions, white phantoms emerge from the depths of the river. A distant bell sounds midnight. String arpeggios translate the effect of ghosts floating on water. Terrified, Ourrias renews his call to the ferryman. He jumps on to the boat when it finally appears. As it sets off the waters become agitated. The ferryman reminds Ourrias of Vincent. The boat sinks; Ourrias drowns.

ACT 4.i *The interior courtyard of Ramon's farm on St John's Eve; bonfires light the scene* Ramon and his farm hands celebrate the harvest, but Mireille is despondent and leaves. Her father bemoans the fact that the laws of nature have made his daughter so unhappy. Mireille opens her window and dreamily remembers the Chanson de Magali. As day begins to break, the shepherd boy Andreloux appears playing his pipes (*chanson*, 'Le jour se lève'). Mireille envies him for his blissful existence (*ariette*, 'Heureux petit berger'). Vincenette rushes on to tell Mireille what has happened to Vincent (duet, 'Ah! parle encore'). To a grand chordal accompaniment in triplets, Mireille resolves to undertake the perilous pilgrimage across the Crau desert to the Saintes-Maries. The music assumes a much more intimate character as she gathers her jewels as a humble offering and the two girls pray for Vincent's recovery.

4.ii *The Crau desert – a vast rocky and arid plain; midday* Mireille is exhausted and disorientated (*air*, 'En marche'). She sees a mirage of a splendid city on the edge of a lake as the orchestra sounds an augmented version of the 'Sainte ivresse' music (to be heard at the end of the opera). Mireille collapses in despair when it disappears. The shepherd's pipes in the distance revive her and she pushes on to her destination.

ACT 5 *Outside the chapel of the Saintes-Maries* The faithful cross the stage and enter the chapel, calling for divine protection. Vincent appears and looks for Mireille; he prays for her safety (*cavatine*, 'Anges du paradis'). Mireille stumbles in, delirious and on the brink of death. She is ecstatic at being reunited with Vincent and has a vision of the sky opening to receive her ('Sainte ivresse! divine extase'). Ramon and others rush on. Mireille dies of sunstroke, but her soul is beckoned to eternal bliss in heaven by a celestial voice.

* * *

The role of Mireille stands far above the others in its musical characterization. This is partly because the other characters, with the exception of Vincent, are not developed through sustained presence: Vincenette, Taven, Ourrias, and even Ramon, serve almost as episodic figures in the unfolding story. Vincent sings fine music in the Act 1 duet and the Chanson de Magali (the best-known number from the opera) but a pale *cavatine* in the last act. *Mireille* was noteworthy in its day for presenting class differences entirely within the context of agrarian, rural society and some early reviewers had difficulty accepting that a 'mere' country girl could sing an aria with heroic cut such as 'En marche'.

STEVEN HUEBNER

Miricioiu, Nelly (*b* Adjud, 31 March 1952). Romanian soprano. She studied in Bucharest and Milan, making her début in Iaşi as the Queen of Night. After an engagement with Braşov Opera (1975–8), in 1981 she sang Violetta and Tosca for Scottish Opera and made her Covent Garden début in 1982 as Nedda, returning as Musetta, Marguerite (*Faust*) and Antonia. She has also sung in San Francisco, San Diego, Toronto, Berlin,

Paris, Hamburg, Frankfurt, Verona and Rome and at La Scala. Her repertory includes Manon Lescaut, Butterfly, Mimì, Magda, Lucia, Olympia and Juliet; she sang Valentine (*Les Huguenots*) at Montpellier in 1990 and Gilda at Philadelphia in 1991. Her warm voice and the intensity of her temperament are specially well suited to the operas of Puccini.   ELIZABETH FORBES

Miró, Henri [Enrique] (*b* Tarrega, 13 Nov 1879; *d* Montreal, 19 July 1950). Canadian composer and conductor of Spanish birth. He studied at the monastery of Monserrat in Catalonia and at the Barcelona conservatory. In 1898 he went to France as a conductor of opera, and in 1901 to Montreal, where he at first conducted the orchestra of the Eldorado café. He was soon conducting opera (including, in 1914, his operettas *Miss Meg* and *Le roman de Suzon*) and from 1916 to 1921 he also directed the Berliner Gramophone Co. and the Compo record company. In 1930 he conducted a series of operas and operettas for the Canadian national radio station. Miró was inspired by folk music, particularly from his native Spain. His compositions won him the first competition of the Société des Concerts Symphoniques de Montréal (1936) and the Prix Lallemand.

operettas, first performed in Montreal
Miss Meg (3, A. Robi), Nouveautés, 2 March 1914
Le roman de Suzon (3, L. Rad), Princess, 15 June 1914
La petite milliardaire (3, Robi), Canadien Français, 1 May 1916
Lolita (radio operetta, 3, Robi), CKAC Radio Station, 9 Oct 1928

*

EMC (G. Potvin)   MIREILLE BARRIÈRE

Miroglio, Francis (*b* Marseilles, 12 Dec 1924). French composer. He attended the conservatories of Marseilles and Paris, studying with Milhaud at the latter. From 1959 to 1961 he worked in the electronic music studios of the ORTF and in 1965 founded the annual summer arts festival Nuits de la Fondation Maeght at St Paul de Vence, which he also directed. Many of his compositions are mobile in form, variable in instrumentation and ornately fashioned. His opera *'Il faut rêver' dit Lénine* (1, R. Pillaudin) was first performed at the Cloître des Célestins, Avignon, on 15 July 1972. Based on a quotation from Lenin it tells of a choral society who, inspired by the song of a lark, transform a dark inhospitable place into one of light and joy. A second opera, *Inferno di gelo*, also in one act, is set to a passage from Dante adapted by the composer for singer and actor. It is accompanied by nine instruments whose players are required to take part in the action.

*

'Francis Miroglio', *Les cahiers du CREM* [Centre de Recherches en Esthétique Musicale], nos.6 and 7 (1987–8) [2 Miroglio issues]
PAUL GRIFFITHS, RICHARD LANGHAM SMITH

Miroshnichenko, Yevgeniya (Semyonovna) (*b* Kharkiv district, 12 June 1931). Ukrainian soprano. She studied at the Kiev Conservatory and in 1957 joined the Kiev Opera. She won second prize at the 1958 Toulouse Competition. Her voice is of light and beautiful timbre, particularly clear in the upper register, and aided by a sparkling coloratura technique. In a repertory including Violetta, Gilda, Rosina, Musetta, Venera (Lysenko's *Eneida*), Yolan (Mayboroda's *Milana*) and Stasya (Zhukovsky's *First Spring*), her performances are distinguished by their liveliness of musical colour and dramatic expression. She was made People's Artist of the USSR in 1965.   I. M. YAMPOL'SKY

Miry, Karel (*b* Ghent, 14 Aug 1823; *d* Ghent, 3 Oct 1889). Belgian composer. He studied with M. J. Mengal at the Ghent Conservatory and at the Brussels Conservatory where he was a fellow pupil of Gevaert. In 1845 he composed the song *De vlaamse leeuw* to words by his uncle, H. van Peene; it became popular and remains the national hymn of the Flemish people. In 1857 Miry become professor at the Ghent Conservatory and in 1871 assistant director; he was later an inspector of music at schools and conservatories.

Miry was one of the first Belgian composers to set Flemish texts. Of his 21 operas and operettas, which are written in a conventional Romantic style, several are to librettos by van Peene. *Bouchard-d'Avesnes* was a great success when first produced in Ghent in 1864. He also composed in most other genres, notably choral music and songs, especially children's songs.

Wit en zwart (oc, 1, H. van Peene), Ghent, 18 Jan 1846
Brigitta (oc, 3, van Peene), Ghent, Minard, 27 June 1847
Anne Mie (1), Antwerp, 9 Oct 1853
La lanterne magique (oc, 3, van Peene), Ghent, 10 March 1854
Karel V (opéra national, 5, van Peene), Ghent, Grand, 29 Jan 1857
Bouchard-d'Avesnes (opéra national, 5, van Peene), Ghent, Grand, 6 March 1864
Maria van Boergondië (oc, 4, N. Destanberg), Ghent, Grand, 28 Aug 1866
De Keizer bij de Boeren (oc, 1, Destanberg), Ghent, 29 Oct 1866
De occasie maakt den dief (1, Destanberg), Ghent, Minard, 24 Dec 1866
Frans Ackermann (oc, 4, Destanberg), Brussels, National, 13 Oct 1867
Brutus en Cesar (oc, 1, P. Geiregat), Ghent, Minard, 14 Oct 1867
Le mariage de Marguerite (oc, 1, M. de Wille), Ghent, Grand, 27 Nov 1867
Een engel op wacht (1, Geiregat), Brussels, National, 8 Dec 1869
La Saint-Lucas (oc, 1, J. Story), Ghent, 17 Feb 1870
Het Driekoningenfeest (oc, 1, Geiregat), Brussels, National, 1870
De dichter en zijn droombeeld (grand op, 4, Conscience), Brussels, Maragy, 2 Dec 1872
De twee zusters (operetta, 1, Geiregat), Brussels, 1872
Muziek in t'huisgezin (1, Destanberg), 1873
Het arme kind (1, Story), Ghent, 1874
De kleine patriot (oc, 4, J. Hoste), Brussels, Alhambra, 23 Dec 1883
La Napolitaine (operetta, 1, J. de Bruyne), Antwerp, 25 Feb 1888

*

C. Bergmans: *Le conservatoire royal de musique de Gand* (Ghent, 1901)   ANNE-MARIE RIESSAUW

Mise en scène (Fr.). The term generally applied in France to the staging; the *livret de mise en scène* often described in minute detail how the opera should be staged. *See* PRODUCTION and PRODUCTION BOOK.

Miser, The [*Skupoy*]. Comic opera in one act by VASILY ALEXEYEVICH PASHKEVICH to a libretto by YAKOV BORISOVICH KNYAZHNIN after MOLIÈRE's *L'avare* and Alexander Sumarkov's *Opekun* ('The Guardian'); St Petersburg, Karl Knipper's Theatre, summer 1781.

The libretto itself contains the information (in the form of a discharge dictated by the title character) that it was composed in 1780. After its first performance in St Petersburg the piece was performed regularly at the Petrovsky Theatre, Moscow, until the theatre burnt down in 1805. The plot concerns the machinations of a young girl, Lyubima (soprano), together with her beloved, Milovid (tenor), and two of the latter's servants – Marfa (soprano) and Prolas (tenor), themselves a couple – to wangle her inheritance from her miserly uncle and guardian Skryagin (bass-baritone). For the most part a typical *comédie mêlée d'ariettes*, the piece is distinguished by one remarkable number: a lengthy and varied accompanied recitative that shows Skryagin, in a parody of the rhetoric of *opera seria*, struggling with the conflict between his cupidity and his love for a beautiful countess (Marfa in disguise).

The Miser was revived (and recorded) in 1974 by the Moscow Chamber Musical Theatre (a subsidiary of the Bol'shoy opera company), in a staging by Boris Pokrovsky, the Bol'shoy Theatre's director of production.   RICHARD TARUSKIN

Miserly Knight, The [*Skupoy rïtsar'*]. Opera in one act, op.24, by SERGEY VASIL'YEVICH RAKHMANINOV to the slightly shortened text of the 'little tragedy' (1830) by ALEXANDER SERGEYEVICH PUSHKIN; Moscow, Bol'shoy Theatre, 11/24 January 1906.

With this opera, the entire series of Pushkinian 'little tragedies' had been put to music after the fashion of Dargomïzhsky's *The Stone Guest*, the first such setting, in which the unaltered original dramatic text was adopted in lieu of libretto (the others were *Mozart and Salieri*, set by Rimsky-Korsakov, and *A Feast in Time of Plague*, set by Cui). Rakhmaninov's opera differs from the rest by virtue of its symphonic approach, which makes it one of the very few Russian operas in the tradition of Wagner's *Ring*. Its high dramatic pressure, demanding a maximum of virtuosity from both singers and orchestra, achieves near-expressionistic intensity at climaxes, belying the composer's reputation as a melancholic lyricist of limited expressive range.

The action revolves around the conflict between a miserly baron (baritone) and his spendthrift son Albert (tenor). The latter, having rejected the advice of a Jewish usurer (tenor) that he poison his father to receive his inheritance, lodges a complaint with the local duke (baritone). The father, summoned by the duke to appear and answer the son's charges of non-support, dies suddenly of apoplexy. The heart of play and opera alike is the second scene, a soliloquy for the baron in his subterranean vault, gloating over his fortune. As set to music (with Shalyapin in mind, though he did not sing in the original production, which was conducted by the composer in a double bill with his *Francesca da Rimini*) this 25-minute study in abnormal psychology is a tour de force for poet, composer and performer alike, unquestionably Rakhmaninov's finest operatic achievement. It has been effectively performed alone, in concert (by Shalyapin and Siepi, among others). The opera as a whole is probably unrevivable, due to the screechy monotony of the outer scenes, the absence of female roles and the offensive musical caricature of the Jew.
                                                RICHARD TARUSKIN

Mislivéček, Josef. *See* MYSLIVEČEK, JOSEF.

Misón [Missón], **Luis** (bap. Mataró, Barcelona, 26 Aug 1727; *d* Madrid, 13 Feb 1766). Spanish composer. On 27 June 1748 he became a flautist and oboist in the royal chapel at Madrid. In 1757 he provided music for a Spanish translation of Metastasio's *Le cinesi*. The Christmas play of 1761, presented in the Coliseo de la Cruz, included two of his tonadillas, the first entitled *Juego de la malilla*; the music is lost, but the published libretto calls him the 'delicado Orpheo de este siglo'. Misón's reputation rests on his tonadillas, nearly all to his own texts. Subirá catalogued approximately a hundred in the Biblioteca Municipal at Madrid and transcribed two. In *Una mesonera y un arriero* (*c*1757) both roles are assigned to women, Casimira Blanco ('La Portuguesa') and Maria Lavdenant. A tag line at the end

of each *copla* serves as refrain, and, as often elsewhere in his tonadillas, plucked strings imitate a strummed guitar. In *Los ciegos* (1758) three newsvendors hawk their wares, Relación selling true confessions, Gaceta recipes for cooking and other 'how-to' advice, and Diario lost-and-found notices and advertisements. The three publicize themselves in spoken texts above held string chords; a *jota* and seguidillas conclude the skit. Apart from tonadillas, Misón composed about a dozen *entremeses* and a similar number of *sainetes*, also in the Madrid Biblioteca Municipal. His zarzuelas are known only by their titles – *Eco y Narciso*, *Piramo y Tisbe* and *El tutor enamorado*; the libretto of the last (by Ramón de la Cruz, 1764) survives.

dates are of composition or first performance

TONADILLAS

Los ciegos, 1758; El novato, 1758; El puento [Ya llegó la fortuna], 1759; Las cabezas de peluca [El chasco de plasencia y Juan Manuel], 1760; La concinera, 1760; El examen de Espejo [pts 1 and 2], 1760; El gigante, 1760; No me llama Entramoro, 1760; El vejete disfrazato, 1760; La chinesca, 1761; El compositor, 1761; Los jardineros, 1761 (pubd in Hamilton); El maestro de baile, 1761; Los negros, 1761 [for the play *La Sivilla del Oriente*]; Un palurdo, un ganzo y una limera, 1761; La amorosa, 1762; Un arriero manchego y un hipócrita, 1762; El arriero y el miguelete [pt 2], 1762; Las campanas, 1762

El chasco del arriero y la mesonera, 1762; El chasco del peluquero [Peluquero burlado], 1762; Los cortejos, 1762; La criate y el pobre del hospicio, 1762; El discurso fingido, 1762; Doña Urraca [El tiempo de Doña Urraca], 1762; Una graciosa de compañia y un compositor de viejo, 1762; Una maja, un alcade, dos abogados y su escribano, 1762; Los mayordomos de Griñón, 1762; Nisena y Silvia [Un pastor y una pastora], 1762; Un pastor y una pastora, 1762; El peluquero burlado, 1762; Un petimetre de oficina, una dama y un paje, 1762; Los pillos y una dama [Los pillos y trompeteros], 1762

El sacrificio de indios, 1762; El sacristán, el payo y su mujer, 1762; El sastre borracho, 1762; El abandono, 1763; Los abogados, 1763; Las ciegas y un petimetre, 1763; Una dama, un paje y un ciego de los enigmas, 1763; Los doctores fingidos [El abogado; Letrados fingidos], 1763; El equivoco, 1763; El gallego fingido y enamorado y una dama fingida, 1763; El gracejo en la demanda, todo es un mogiganga, 1763; Un maestro de música y un copiante [Un maestro de música y un señorita], 1763; La maestra de niñas, 1763; Una maja, un albañil y una bollera, 1763; El médico de Fama, 1763

Un memorialista, un sargento y una dama, 1763; Mercader y hortera [Un arriero, un hortera y un mercader], 1763; Un pastor y una pastora [El sueño], 1763; La pastorelita, 1763, Los puetas de viejo, 1763; La queja de los mosqueteros, 1763; El relujero, 1763; Un tambor francés, 1763; La visita de Bastos, 1763; El chasco de la carta de Juan Aprieta, 1764; El mozo de compra disfrazado, 1764; No hallo consuelo [Una viuda, un caballero y una vieja], 1764; Una viuda, un caballero y una vieja, 27 April 1764; El sueño de los pastores, 1765; Los maestros, 1768 [perf. in the auto sacramental]

Dates unknown: A cantar va gustosa; La almohadilla; Un arriero, un hortera y un mercader; Un barquero y una pastora; Un calesero y dos mozas; El calesero y la peregrina; La carcel; La carta para el parte; El cartero y la criada; Los cazadores; El chasco del cofre; El corazón; El doctor; La estera [Mosquetero de la silla]; Lo que pasa en la calle de la Comadre el día de la Minerva [melody of the fandango pubd in J. Subirá: *La participación musical en el antiguo teatro español*, Barcelona, 1930]; Mal haya la fortuna; Una mesonera y un arriero (transcr. for vv and pf in Subirá 1928–30); Montes, llanos y prados; El mosquetero de la silla y la espuerta; Una mujer y dos sacristanes; Oigan cómo llora; Los pastores [Lesvia y Anfriso]; Una peregrina y un majo; La queja; Remedar a Mariana; Silencio a todos pide; La viuda; Un vizcaíno, un indiano, un gallego, un mercader, una tapada y un negro; Yo me acuerdo al algún día

ENTREMESES

Los celibatos (baile), 1760; Seguidillas de pajes, 1761; Los mayordomos de Griñón, 1762; La muda en el teatro, 1762 [for the play *El origen carmelitano*]; El tribuna de la moda, 1762; El alcalde chinela, 1763; Cantillana, 1763; Lo que fae antaño es hugaño (entremés/sainete), Christmas 1763; Los locos caseros, 1763; La jocura de Ayala, 1763; La visita de Mariano (baile), 1764

Dates unknown: Ande la broma [perf. with Easter play *La pramatica*]; Las máscaras

SAINETES

El festero ridículo, 1760; Contra gustos no hay disputas, 1761/2; Los molineros, 1762 [for the play *Orlando furioso*]; La residencia de las tonadillas, 1762 [for the play *Cumplir lo que ofrece el hado*]; La ronda de la verdad, 1762 [for *La Sirena de Tinacria*]; La codicia rompe el saco, 1763; El cumpleaños de Mariana y robo de Ayala, 1763; La ensaladilla, 1763 [for the play *Las mujeres*]; La tienda de café, 1763 [for the play *El docto Euclides*]

Dates unknown: El codicioso burlado; El gusto de la moda; La junta de payos

*

DEUMM (G. Bourligueux)

E. Cotarelo y Mori: *Orígenes y establecimiento de la ópera en España hasta 1800* (Madrid, 1917), 178, 196, 311

J. Subirá: 'Vida y obras de Don Luis Misón', *La música en la casa de Alba* (Madrid, 1927), 191–204

——: *La tonadilla escénica* (Madrid, 1928–30) [vol.iii appx incl. transcr. of *Una mesonera y un arriero*]

——: *Tonadillas teatrales inéditas* (Madrid, 1932) [appx incl. edn of *Los ciegos*]

M. L. Hamilton: *Music in Eighteenth Century Spain* (Urbana, IL, 1937), 50ff, 75–98 [transcr. of *Los jardineros*]

J. Subirá: *Catálogo de la sección de música de la Biblioteca Municipal de Madrid* (Madrid, 1965), 202–16, 349–55 [incl. catalogue of Misón's works in E-Mm]   ROBERT STEVENSON

Mississippi Opera. American company based in JACKSON, founded in 1945 as the Jackson Opera Guild.

Mistral, (Jean-Etienne-)Frédéric (*b* Maillane, Bouches-du-Rhône, 8 Sept 1830; *d* Maillane, 25 March 1914). Provençal poet and philologist. The son of a prosperous landowner, he devoted his life to the promotion of the cultural values of Provençal. His most famous work is the rural epic *Mirèio* (1859) which Michel Carré used as the basis for the libretto of the five-act opera (sometimes described as an 'opéra-dialogué') *Mireille*, set by Gounod. This was first performed in 1864 and subsequently remodelled. *Calendau* (1867) formed the basis of Henri Maréchal's opera *Calendel* (libretto by Paul Ferrier), which had its première in Rouen in 1894. Maurice Léna's libretto for C. M. Widor's opera *Nerto* (1924, Paris) was derived from Mistral's verse-tale of the same name. In 1904, half a century after the foundation of the pro-Provençal 'félibrige', the Nobel Prize for literature was awarded jointly to Mistral and the Spanish poet José Echegaray.

*

R. Lyle: *Mistral* (Cambridge, 1953)

R. Aldington: *Introduction to Mistral* (London, 1956)

S.-A. Peyre: *Essai sur Mistral* (Paris, 1959)

CHRISTOPHER SMITH

Miszuga, Ołeksandr. *See* MYSZUGA, ALEKSANDER.

Mitchell, Leona (*b* Enid, OK, 13 Oct 1949). American soprano. In 1971 she won first place in a study programme sponsored by the San Francisco Opera and in 1972 made her professional début as Micaëla at the San Francisco Spring Opera Theater. Her Metropolitan Opera début, also as Micaëla, took place in December 1975; that year she also sang Bess in Maazel's recording of Gershwin's opera. At the Metropolitan she has sung Pamina, the Prioress (*Dialogues des Carmélites*), Butterfly, Musetta, Leonora (*La forza del destino*) and Elvira (*Ernani*). She made her European début at the Geneva Opera (1976) as Liù, a role she repeated in 1980

at Covent Garden and the Paris Opéra. Her voice has been described as a cross between Price's husky chest tones and Freni's radiant upper register. Although Mitchell's early career was as a lyric soprano, in the early 1980s she started to move into the *spinto* repertory.

*

S. Wadsworth: 'Here to Sing: Soprano on the Rise: Leona Mitchell', *ON*, xliii/14 (1979), 10–13

E. Southern: *Biographical Dictionary of Afro-American and African Musicians* (Westport, CT, 1982)

H. Waleson: 'A Lyric Soprano Ventures into Heavier Fare', *New York Times* (20 March 1983)   MICHAEL WALSH

Mitchinson, John (*b* Blackrod, Manchester, 31 March 1932). English tenor. He studied in Manchester and made his début in 1959 with the Handel Opera Society as Jupiter (*Semele*). With Sadler's Wells Opera, later the ENO, 1972–8, he sang Oedipus, Idomeneus, Dalibor and Svatopluk Čech (*The Excursions of Mr Brouček*); he also created the Poet in Tal's *Masada 967* (1973, Jerusalem). During the years 1978–82 he worked with the WNO, singing Florestan, Aegisthus, Peter Grimes, Tristan, Manolios (Martinů's *The Greek Passion*) and Filka Morozov (*From the House of the Dead*). In 1983 he sang Max with Opera North and Gualtiero in Vivaldi's *Griselda* at Buxton. A very powerful singing actor, he made a superb Grimes and a fine Tristan.

ELIZABETH FORBES

Mithridates. Libretto subject used in the 17th and 18th centuries. Its source is Roman history as related in Florus, Appian of Alexandria and others; many librettos relied on JEAN RACINE's *Mithridate* (1673), a work favoured by Louis XIV.

Mithridates VI, King of Pontus (called 'the Great', 120–63 BC), was a popular subject in 18th-century operas. His conquests of Asia and wars against Rome, and particularly his despotic cruelty and sensuality, were usually condensed into a single cataclysmic event. Two sons of Mithridates, Pharnaces and Xiphares, hearing a false report of Mithridates' death, seek the hand of Mithridates' proclaimed queen, Monima. Mithridates returns alive and learns of Pharnaces' intentions towards Monima, as well as his alliance with Rome, and imprisons him. Next he discovers the mutual love between Xiphares and Monima. Pharnaces escapes and attacks with an approaching Roman army, but Xiphares rallies the king's army, defeats his brother, and is rewarded with Monima and the kingdom. Librettos by Vanstryp (set by Porpora, 1730, Rome), Cigna-Santi (as *Mitridate re di Ponto*; set by Quirino Gasparini, 1767, Turin, and Mozart, 1770, Milan), Pasqualigo (as *Mitridate re di Ponto vincitor di se stesso*; set by Capelli, 1723, Venice) and Villati (set by Graun, 1750, Berlin) all imitated this model, although details vary, particularly in the role taken by a foreign princess betrothed to Pharnaces (a character used only as a ruse by Racine).

Frigimelica Roberti's libretto in five acts (as *Mitridate Eupatore*; set by Alessandro Scarlatti, 1707, Venice) imitated, in a scattered and eclectic fashion, characters and situations in Aeschylus's *Choephoroe* and the *Electra* plays of Sophocles and of Euripides (with Mithridates as the Orestes figure, Stratonica as Clytemnestra, etc.). Stratonica, with her accomplice Farnace [Pharnaces], has assassinated her former husband and Eupatore's father, Mitridate Evergetes [Mithridates], and now rules Pontus. Eupatore and his wife Issicratea [Hypsicrateia], who appear in disguise as

Egyptian ambassadors, promise Stratonica that they will deliver Eupatore, dead or alive. Laodice, Eupatore's sister, learns of the plot and endeavours to stop them, but when she learns their true identities she joins them. Eupatore kills Pharnaces and presents his head to Stratonica, who pleads for her own death and is slain by Hypsicrateia. Eupatore takes the throne, though regretting his mother's death, and swears lasting enmity towards Rome. A third popular view of Mithridates' court was supplied by Zeno, also in five acts and set by Caldara (1728, Vienna). It was revised by anonymous librettists for Sarti (1779, Florence, as *Mitridate a Sinope*) and Sacchini (1781, London). In this version, Pharnaces, Mithridates' son by a previous wife, is secretly married to Aristia, a woman in the service of Mithridates' present wife, Ladice. Mithridates and Ladice ordain that Pharnaces shall marry Apamea, daughter of Ladice and Tigrane. Pharnaces tries to flee with Aristia but they are caught and condemned. Apamea intercedes and pleads for mercy; Aristia is discovered to be a long-lost princess, and in the end the couple is blessed. Other versions included librettos by Corbellini (1603, Turin), Maggi (as *Mitridate in Sebastia*, with music by Aldrovandini, 1701, Genoa), Andrea del Po (an altered version of Maggi set by Aldrovandini and Vignola, 1706, Naples), Vanneschi (set by Terradellas, 1746, London) and Sografi (as *La morte di Mitridate*, set by Nasolini, 1796, Trieste).

See also MITRIDATE, RE DI PONTO [Mozart] and MITRIDATE EUPATORE [A. Scarlatti]. For a list of operas based on Racine's *Mithridate*, see RACINE, JEAN.   DALE E. MONSON

Mitridate, re di Ponto ('Mithridates, King of Pontus'). *Dramma per musica* in three acts, K87/74*a*, by WOLFGANG AMADEUS MOZART to a libretto by VITTORIO AMEDEO CIGNA-SANTI after Giuseppe Parini's translation of JEAN RACINE's *Mithridate* (see MITHRIDATES); Milan, Regio Ducal Teatro, 26 December 1770.

Mitridate was commissioned for Carnival 1771; Mozart wrote the recitatives and overture while touring Italy in 1770. Reaching Milan on 18 October, he was forced to write and rewrite the arias quickly; the castrato Pietro Benedetti caused anxiety by his late arrival (1 December) and someone tried to persuade the prima donna to introduce arias from Gasparini's *Mitridate* (1767, Turin: with the same libretto). As in Vienna in 1768 there were those who condemned the work in advance because of Mozart's extreme youth. They were silenced by the first performance. Despite its length – six hours, with the ballet – *Mitridate* was repeated 21 times. Some music not by Mozart may have been included in the performances, and some lines of recitative are missing in every source. No further performances are known until the present century.

The setting is at Nymphaeum, in 63 BC; the scenes, for which designs by the brothers Galliani were applauded, include the palace, a temple, the port, hanging gardens and a military encampment. Mithridates, who long defended his empire against the Romans, and his son Pharnaces (who in Racine's play remains treacherous to the end) are historical personages; but the plot is fiction.

ACT 1 Mithridates (tenor, originally Guglielmo d'Ettore), twice married and with two sons, is betrothed to Aspasia (Racine's Monime; soprano, Antonia Bernasconi). He is reported dead resisting the Romans. Both his sons, Sifare [Xiphares] (soprano castrato, Benedetti) and the elder Farnace [Pharnaces] (alto castrato,

Giuseppe Cicognani) are in love with Aspasia; she reciprocates only the love of Xiphares. Thwarted ambition leads Pharnaces to conspire against his father with the Roman Marzio [Marcius] (tenor, Gaspare Bassano). Defeated by Pompey, Mithridates unexpectedly returns, bringing Ismene, a Parthian Princess betrothed to Pharnaces (soprano, Anna Francesca Varese; she does not appear in Racine). Mithridates fears he has returned to two ungrateful sons, but is reassured by Arbate [Arbates] (Governor of Nymphaeum; soprano castrato, Pietro Muschietti) concerning Xiphares. Mithridates' second aria, in a regal D major, ends the first act.

ACT 2 Pharnaces spurns Ismene; she complains to the King who says Pharnaces is worthy to die. Mithridates doubts Aspasia's fidelity; he has to leave to do battle with Pompey, but proposes to marry her first. His aria alternately thanks loyal Xiphares (*andante*) and hurls accusations at Aspasia (*allegro*). Xiphares decides he must leave Pontus and bids Aspasia a moving farewell ('Lungi da te, mio bene': one of the three extant versions has an obbligato horn part). Aspasia laments her fate in a soliloquy (aria in two tempos, 'Nel grave tormento'). When Mithridates accuses Pharnaces of treachery he admits his guilt ('Son reo: l'error confesso'), but betrays Xiphares's love for Aspasia. Mithridates imprisons both his sons; the lovers bid a last farewell (the only duet).

ACT 3 Mithridates prepares for his final battle ('Vado incontro al fato'; Gasparini's setting is the one in the standard Mozart scores). Spurned by Aspasia, he sends her poison, which she accepts (monologue: recitative framing a cavatina); but Xiphares prevents her from drinking it. He prepares for worthy death in battle ('Se il rigor d'ingrata sorte', a noble *Sturm und Drang* aria in C minor). As the Romans attack, Marcius frees Pharnaces; in a magnificent *scena* (aria, 'Già dagli occhi') he resolves to support his father and goes to burn the Roman fleet. Mithridates is victorious but mortally wounds himself; he unites Xiphares with Aspasia, and forgives Pharnaces, who marries Ismene.

*   *   *

Fitting the arias for demanding singers did not prevent Mozart introducing ample variety of expression. Aspasia's second aria is a powerful lament in G minor; Xiphares' second combines short *andante* sections with vehement *allegro* passages. All his, Aspasia's and Ismene's music is characterized by extreme virtuosity. Mozart skilfully abbreviated the required ternary forms and used a large number of arias in which contrasting affections are expressed by alternating tempos. The overture is a three-movement sinfonia in D major and the finale a very short 'coro' of soloists. *Mitridate* is an astonishing achievement for a boy of 14; it makes the best use of conventional forms of expression and presents a drama which, if artificial, contains scenes of real intensity.

JULIAN RUSHTON

Mitridate Eupatore ('Mithridates Eupator'). *Tragedia in musica* in five acts by Alessandro Scarlatti (see SCARLATTI family, (1)) to a libretto by GIROLAMO FRIGIMELICA ROBERTI; Venice, Teatro S Giovanni Grisostomo, 5 January 1707.

Although the characters are drawn from ancient history, the plot is based on Aeschylus's *Choephoroe*, and in particular on the *Electra* dramas of Euripides and Sophocles (see MITHRIDATES). Mithridates (soprano) and his wife Issicratea [Hypsicrateia] (alto), disguised as

Egyptian envoys, resolve to overthrow Farnace [Pharnaces] (tenor), who has seized the throne of Pontus and married Mithridates' mother, Stratonica (soprano), widow and murderer of Mithridates' father. To this end they offer to seal a pact between Pontus and Egypt by delivering to the usurpers the head of Mithridates, insisting only that the people be present to show their assent. When Mithridates' sister Laodice (soprano) hears of this, she and her husband Nicomede [Nicomedes] (soprano) detain the two 'envoys' until Mithridates promises to bring her proof of his good faith. When he returns with a casket supposedly containing his own head Laodice is overcome, but her grief turns to rejoicing when Mithridates reveals his true identity to her. Pharnaces enters to see the head, but is killed by Mithridates, and when Stratonica also comes to gloat over her victim it is Pharnaces' head she finds on the platter; she dies at Hypsicrateia's hand. Nicomedes announces to the populace the end of the tyrants' reign and Mithridates is crowned king by Laodice.

Mitridate Eupatore stands apart from Scarlatti's other extant operas. It is the only one in five acts and includes neither comic characters nor amatory intrigue. Disguise plays its part, but both plot and characterization are unusually consistent and convincing. Despite this, and despite some exceptionally fine music, noteworthy for its instrumental colour (Act 4 opens with a sinfonia in which muted trumpets in the pit are answered by stage trumpets on board ship) and expressive depth (Dent, 1905, considered Laodice's lament for her supposed dead brother, 'Cara tomba del mio diletto', to be 'worthy of J. S. Bach at his best'), the serious tone of *Mitridate Eupatore* was apparently not to the Venetians' taste and the opera was a dismal failure. It was revived only once during Scarlatti's lifetime (1717, Milan).

MALCOLM BOYD

Mitropoulos, Dimitri (*b* Athens, 1 March 1896; *d* Milan, 2 Nov 1960). American conductor and composer of Greek birth. He studied at the Athens Odeion Conservatory where his opera based on Maeterlinck, *Soeur Béatrice*, was produced in 1920. Continuing his studies at the Berlin Hochschule für Musik, 1921–4, he worked as répétiteur at the Staatsoper under Erich Kleiber. In 1937 he was appointed conductor of the Minneapolis SO, with which he gave concert performances of such operas as *Elektra*, *Erwartung*, *Wozzeck* and *Arlecchino* when they were rarely seen on the stage. He took American nationality in 1946. He conducted opera in the 1950s at the Florence Maggio Musicale, and from 1956 at Chicago Lyric Opera; his début at the Metropolitan Opera was in 1954 with *Salome*. He returned there each season until his death, giving the première of Barber's *Vanessa* (1958), which he introduced to Europe at the Salzburg Festival the same year. An ascetic by temperament, Mitropoulos had complete command of the music, using neither baton nor score; in spite of imprecise gestures he obtained impassioned, if sometimes unorthodox, performances.

NOËL GOODWIN

Mitternachtstunde, Die ('The Midnight Hour'). Singspiel in three acts by Franz Danzi (*see* DANZI family, (2)) to a libretto by Matthias Georg Lambrecht, after Dumaniant's *La guerre ouverte, ou Ruse contre ruse*; Munich, Hoftheater, 16 February 1798.

Die Mitternachtstunde was the most successful of Danzi's operas; Friedrich Rochlitz praised it as 'one of the best original German comic operas'. A captain, Don Fernando (tenor), is in love with Julie (soprano), the niece of General Don Gusmann (bass). However, following an old family custom, Julie must marry a rich sea captain at midnight. Fernando makes a proposal to Gusmann: he will attempt to kidnap Julie before midnight and, if successful, to marry her. Gusmann agrees and wagers him 1000 ducats that he will not get her out of the house. Bastian (bass), Fernando's valet, and Laura (soprano), Julie's chambermaid, assist the young lovers, while Gusmann employs Ambros (bass), Matthias (bass), Niklas (tenor) and the duenna Cecilia (soprano) to thwart them. After two failed attempts to rescue her, Julie disguises herself and escapes from her uncle's house with minutes to spare. Danzi's music ranges from simple lieder to artfully embellished composite arias. Eight of the 19 numbers are ensembles, including two extended *buffo* finales to the second and third acts.

PAUL CORNEILSON

Mitterwurzer, Anton (*b* Sterzing, Tyrol, 12 April 1818; *d* Döbling, Vienna, 2 April 1876). Austrian baritone. He studied in Vienna, making his début in 1838 at Innsbruck. From 1839 until his retirement in 1870 he was a member of the Dresden Hofoper, where he made his début as the Hunter in Conradin Kreutzer's *Das Nachtlager in Granada*, took part in the première of Marschner's *Kaiser Adolf von Nassau* and created Wolfram in *Tannhäuser* (1845). He also sang Kurwenal in the first performance of *Tristan und Isolde* (1865, Munich). His repertory included Aubry in *Der Vampyr*, Bois-Guilbert in *Der Templer und die Jüdin* and the title role of *Hans Heiling*. An intelligent singer with a powerful voice, he was also an excellent actor.

ELIZABETH FORBES

Mitusov, Stepan (Stepanovich) (*b* St Petersburg, 11/23 Sept 1878; *d* Leningrad, 25 Jan 1942). Russian librettist, pianist and conductor. He was the son of the opera singer Yevdokiya Vasil'yevna Golenishcheva-Kutuzova, through whom he was collaterally related to Musorgsky and to the painter Nikolay Roerich. Through his friendship with his exact contemporary Andrey Rimsky-Korsakov, the composer's son, Mitusov became a habitué of the bi-weekly Wednesday musical gatherings at the Rimsky-Korsakovs', where he met and befriended Stravinsky. A skilful versifier, he wrote the libretto for Stravinsky's opera *The Nightingale* (1908–14), which is dedicated to him, and also made the singing translations from Verlaine which Stravinsky set to music in 1910. In the twenties he championed Stravinsky's music as a performer. He died of hunger during the Leningrad blockade.

V. Yastrebtsev: *Vospominaniya o N. A. Rimskom-Korsakove* [Reminiscences of Rimsky-Korsakov], ii (Leningrad, 1960)

I. Stravinsky: *Selected Correspondence*, ed. R. Craft, ii (New York, 1984)

L. Kazanskaya: 'Stepan Mitusov', *SovM* (1990), no.12, pp.82–8

RICHARD TARUSKIN

Miura, Tamaki (*b* Tokyo, 22 Feb 1884; *d* Tokyo, 26 May 1946). Japanese soprano. She made her début in 1914 singing Santuzza in *Cavalleria rusticana* at Tokyo, and in the same year went to Europe. She studied in Germany, sang in concerts in London and elsewhere, and in 1915 was engaged to sing Butterfly in Boston. 'Fresher, more graceful in its joy and pathos than any other' (Q. Eaton: *The Boston Opera Company*, 1965, p.275), this 'authentic' portrayal brought her immediate fame in the USA, with Mascagni's *Iris* as her best alternative role. She sang in New York, San Francisco and Chicago, returning to England for performances of *Madama Butterfly* under Beecham, and in 1920 appeared at Monte Carlo and in Barcelona. Other operas in her repertory were Messager's *Madame Chrysanthème* and Aldo Franchetti's *Namiko-San*, both of which she sang at their American premières in Chicago. She took part in various tours and also sang in Italy before returning finally to Japan in 1932. Her voice sounds somewhat thin and unsupported on recordings, though she earns her place in history as the first internationally famous singer from Japan.   J. B. STEANE

Mizuno, Shūkō [Nobutaka] (*b* Tokushima, 24 Feb 1934). Japanese composer. He studied with Minao Shibata and Yoshio Hasegawa at the Tokyo Geijutsu Daigaku (National University of Fine Arts and Music) from 1958 to 1963. Together with Takehisa Kosugi he organized in 1958 the Group Ongaku (a music improvisation group). During the 1960s he experimented with other contemporary techniques such as tape music and graphic notation. Some of his works between 1967 and 1975 show the influence of jazz, and since 1975 he has frequently composed for Japanese instruments and percussion. He is notable as a composer for orchestra or instrumental ensemble, but he has also written some successful choral works. He was appointed to teach at Chiba University in 1968, and became a professor there in 1979; since 1971 he has also taught at Tokyo Geijutsu Daigaku.

His only opera, *Tenshu Monogatari* ('Tale of a Donjon'), was originally written as a television drama in 1977, based on a drama (1917) by the popular novelist Kyōka Izumi (1873–1939), which deals with the romantic love of a monster princess and a young handsome warrior. The work was turned into an opera with a libretto by Saburō Kanazawa, Jun Maeda and Mizuno himself. Its première, at the Tokyo Yūbin-chokin Hall (8 March 1979), proved to be a success, primarily owing to the composer's delicate treatment of the text in an expressive declamatory style and a successful combination of European and Japanese elements. The opera was revised for a performance at the Shinjuku Bunka Centre, Tokyo, on 25 May 1983, and has been revived since then.   MASAKATA KANAZAWA

Mlada (i). Opera-ballet in four acts by CÉSAR ANTONOVICH CUI (Act 1), MODEST PETROVICH MUSORGSKY and NIKOLAY ANDREYEVICH RIMSKY-KORSAKOV (Acts 2 and 3) and ALEXANDER PORFIR'YEVICH BORODIN (Act 4) to a libretto by VIKTOR ALEXANDROVICH KRĪLOV.

The work was commissioned by Stepan Gedeonov for the Mariinsky Theatre, St Petersburg, in January 1872. The music, which included ballets by Ludwig Minkus, was composed between February and April 1872, but the work was never performed, and most of the music was recycled into other works. The plot is drawn from the mythology of the Baltic Slavs (*see* MLADA (ii)).

Cui published his music for Act 1 almost 40 years after the commission (vocal score, Leipzig, 1911), 'in memory of my dear comrades A. P. Borodin, M. P. Musorgsky, and N. A. Rimsky-Korsakov'. Except for some conjuration music that was transferred to *Andzhelo* (1876), the music was all previously unknown. It fluctuates between three styles: all-purpose

lyric, for the interaction of human characters (cast in what Cui liked to call 'melodic recitative' à la Dargomïzhsky); fantastic/chromatic, for the conjuration of mythical beings (common-note progressions over pedals, etc.); and – rarity of rarities for Cui – folkish diatonic, for choruses of 'immured maidens', hunters and so on. Even though Act 1 was nominally Cui's, the wedding-dream theme was composed by Rimsky-Korsakov in the original version of 1872 (he later recycled it for the slow movement of his String Quartet op.12 and finally reinserted it in his own opera *Mlada*). Evidently Cui recomposed the passage for the publication of 1911.

Musorgsky's contribution was first published by Andrey Rimsky-Korsakov as a supplement to his collected edition of Musorgsky's letters (1932) and later in Lamm's edition of the collected works (iv/3, vii/1). It begins with a market scene to open Act 2, of which the main section later became the model for the opening chorus in *The Fair at Sorochintsï*. (For an elaborate triple chorus representing a fist-fight only part of the accompaniment was written down; this fits one of Musorgsky's early choruses for Ozerov's play *Oedipus in Athens*, which was recycled in *Salammbô*.) The next number, the 'Procession of Princes and Priests' (published only by Lamm), was based on a hauler's song from Balakirev's collection of 1866. It is in a conventional march and trio form; the opening section later saw duty in the orchestral *March with Trio alla Turca*, subtitled *The Capture of Kars* (1880); the original trio of 1872 was by Rimsky-Korsakov. The demoniac revel in Act 3 was a choral arrangement of the already twice-recycled *Night on Bald Mountain*; it went into *The Fair at Sorochintsï* unchanged.

Except for the trio to Musorgsky's march, already mentioned, none of Rimsky-Korsakov's music for the *Mlada* of 1872 has been published as such. Most of it was of course absorbed into his later setting of the whole, much expanded libretto. Scattered obiter dicta – in the composer's autobiography, in notes to it by his son Andrey and in the memoirs of Yastrebtsev – indicate that some of the fantastic music in *May Night* (1879) and *The Snow Maiden* (1881) derived from the earlier score.

Borodin's act, the most elaborate and acknowledged by all the collaborators as the best, was divided into eight discrete numbers, of which five were recycled back into *Prince Igor* (from which they had to some extent derived, since as of 1872 Borodin considered his epic opera an abandoned project ripe for recycling). A summary of these derivations appears in Table 1.

Rimsky-Korsakov's concert piece based on Borodin's nos.5–7 is a luxuriant essay in fantastic chromaticism à la Glinka: circles of 3rds, whole-tone scales, French sixths, pedals galore. The apotheosis, following long-standing tradition, is diatonic: a folklike melody (Mlada's leitmotif, according to Dianin) reminiscent of the Igor-Yaroslavna love theme in Borodin's magnum opus. The other numbers from Act 4 remain unpublished (MSS in *RU-SPsc*).

*

N. A. Rimsky-Korsakov: *Letopis' moyey muzïkal'noy zhizni* [Chronicle of my Musical Life] (St Petersburg, 1909; Eng. trans., 1924, as *My Musical Life*)

G. Abraham: 'The Collective "Mlada"', *On Russian Music* (London, 1939), 90–112

V. Yastrebtsev: *Nikolay Andreyevich Rimsky-Korsakov: vospominaniya*, ed. A. Ossovsky (Leningrad, 1959–60; Eng. trans., abridged, 1985)

Table 1: Borodin's music for *Mlada* (Act 4)

No.	Action	Later publication or use
1	Sacrificial chorus (priests and people)	Prologue (*Igor*): chorus of praise (also Symphony no.2, 4th movt)
2	Duet for High Priest and Yaromir	Partly from Yaroslavna's 'dream' arioso (*Igor*, 1.ii), otherwise unknown
3	'Apparition of the Phantoms'	*Igor*: eclipse (Prologue), Igor's aria (Act 2)
4	Duet for Yaromir and Voyslava	*Igor*: Escape Trio (Act 3, adapted by Glazunov)
5–7	Voyslava's appeal to Morena; Morena's vengeance: flood, storm, destruction of the temple; Mlada's apotheosis	*Finale de l'Opéra-Ballet inachevé "Mlada"*, arr. and orch. N. A. Rimsky-Korsakov (Leipzig, 1892)
8	Final chorus	*Igor*: final chorus

S. Dianin: *Borodin* (Moscow, 1960; Eng. trans., 1963)

RICHARD TARUSKIN

Mlada (ii). 'Magical opera-ballet' in four acts by NIKOLAY ANDREYEVICH RIMSKY-KORSAKOV to his own libretto based on VIKTOR ALEXANDROVICH KRÏLOV's libretto for *Mlada* (i); St Petersburg, Mariinsky Theatre, 20 October/1 November 1892.

Mstivoy *Prince of Retra*	bass
Voyslava *his daughter*	soprano
Yaromir *Prince of Arkon*	tenor
Veglasnïy *High Priest of Radegast*	baritone
Lumir *Czech singer*	contralto
Morena *goddess of the underworld*/	
Svyatokhna *Voyslava's nurse*	mezzo-soprano
Chernobog 12 to 16 basses singing into megaphones	
Kashchey the Deathless 12 to 16 tenors	
Novgorodian	tenor
His Wife	mezzo-soprano
Viking	baritone
Tiun	bass
Moor from Khalifat	tenor
Two Tradesmen	tenor, bass
Three Tradeswomen	soprano, mezzo-soprano, contralto

SILENT ROLES

Shade of Princess Mlada	mime
Shade of Queen Cleopatra	prima ballerina

Immured maidens, weapon-bearers and Mstivoy's retinue; tradespeople, pilgrims, peoples of various Slavonic lands; priests and priestesses of Radegast, trumpeters, Cherv (god of famine), Chuma (Plague), Topelets (god of floods and inundations), wood sprites, werewolves, kikimoras, witches, ghosts; shades of dancers and black slaves of both sexes in Cleopatra's retinue; apparitions of ancient heroes; slavonic deities

Setting The city of Retra, near the Laba (Elbe) in the Slavonic territories on the Baltic shore, 9th or 10th century

It was Anatoly Lyadov who, on a memorial visit to the deceased Borodin's apartment, suggested to Rimsky-Korsakov, his former teacher, that he finally set the abandoned *Mlada* libretto himself (*see* MLADA (i)). Rimsky's sudden attraction to Gedeonov's old white elephant, which had repelled him 17 years before, was triggered by belated contact with Wagner's *Ring*, given its first complete performances in Russia (by Angelo Neumann's Prague company, Carl Muck conducting) during the season 1889–90. Although the basic situation in *Mlada* was really just a stock ballet plot deriving

from Filippo Taglioni's *La sylphide* (by way, perhaps, of *Giselle*), it was served up with a heavy dose of ersatz mythology that chimed not only with the Wagnerian variety but with those atavisms of ancient Slavonic religion in which Rimsky had a longstanding interest. There were obvious if superficial plot parallels with Wagner's tetralogy: a fateful ring and a concluding apotheosis involving the destruction of hallowed property followed by an inundation (and, as Gerald Abraham pointed out, a 'hero temporarily in love with the wrong woman'). The most specific musical echo is the drawn-out introduction to the third act ('Starry Night'), all too obviously modelled on the prelude to *Das Rheingold*.

The title role in *Mlada* is assigned not to a singer but to a ballerina (danced at the première by Mariya Petipa, daughter of the legendary Mariinsky Theatre ballet-master), whose dramatic répliques are cast in terms of the old formal mime conventions, already archaic by the 1890s, as was the whole concept of opera-ballet, essentially a court spectacle of a type that had died out everywhere else but the one remaining European autocracy. The ethereal Fantastic Kolo in Act 3 was designed for the celebrated Mariinsky female *corps de ballet* – 80 tutu'd maidens in a row – in emulation of Marius Petipa's fabled 'Kingdom of the Shades' sequence from *La bayadère* (music by Minkus, who was to have supplied the episode in question for the original *Mlada* group project).

The curious if opulent hybrid was not successful, leaving the Mariinsky repertory after the sixth performance, and has had few revivals. (One took place in 1923 in the same theatre as the original production – by then the State Academic Theatre of Opera and Ballet – with sets and costumes by Alexandre Benois; the Moscow Bol'shoy Theatre staged *Mlada* for the first time in 1988.) Between 1899 and 1901 Rimsky-Korsakov abridged the third act and arranged it as a 'symphonic picture' for a somewhat reduced and normalized orchestra, without voices; it was performed in 1903 under the title *Noch' na gore Triglave* ('A Night on Mount Triglav') and first published in the Soviet edition of the composer's complete works. A more conventional suite from the opera was extracted in 1903 (its culminating showpiece is the popular Procession of the Princes from Act 2) and published the next year.

The première in 1892 was conducted by Eduard Nápravník and choreographed by Lev Ivanov and Enrico Cecchetti; Fyodor Stravinsky sang Mstivoy.

ACT 1 *Mstivoy's lands* After a short orchestral introduction ('Princess Mlada'), the curtain goes up to reveal a chorus of maidens weaving garlands for the midsummer holiday. Mstivoy's daughter Voyslava is

417

'Mlada' (Rimsky-Korsakov): design (1889) by Mikhail Il'yich Bocharov

troubled; her passionate love for the young Arkonian prince Yaromir has led her into wrongdoing – she has killed Mlada, Yaromir's bride. Faithful to the memory of his beloved, Yaromir has spurned her. She calls to Lada, the goddess of love, for assistance, but her crime has turned the beneficent deities against her. Her old nurse Svyatokhna promises help if Voyslava will pledge herself to Morena, goddess of the underworld. Voyslava agrees; thunder is heard, the scene is plunged into darkness, and before her stands not Svyatokhna but Morena herself, who calls upon the dark forces on Voyslava's behalf.

Yaromir arrives with his retinue to celebrate midsummer. Morena's spell begins to work: struck by Voyslava's beauty, Yaromir pledges his troth to her. Mstivoy orders a dance of celebration (a *redowa*). Yaromir falls into a charmed sleep, and in a vision sees how Voyslava had murdered Mlada with a poisoned ring. He awakes in confusion. Servants of Mstivoy summon him to the festival.

ACT 2 *A lakeside valley outside the Temple of Radegast* Tradespeople from many countries have gathered for the festival. A fight nearly breaks out between the Polabians and the Novgorod merchants, but the bard Lumir calms them, reminding them of their common enemy, the Teutonic Christians. The princes of the land assemble in a procession. The High Priest leads a divination rite. Mstivoy orders entertainment (Lithuanian Dance; Hindu Dance). The ritual of wreaths and idols now begins with a *khorovod* (based in part on a folksong from Balakirev's collection), in which couples kiss periodically. At each such moment, however, Mlada's shade materializes between Voyslava and Yaromir, separating them; Yaromir rushes off after the shade. Voyslava curses Morena, whose spell has proved weaker than Yaromir's love for her rival. Mstivoy leads his daughter away, commanding that the *khorovod* continue. It reaches its climax with the ritual casting of wreaths on the waters of the lake.

ACT 3 *A gorge at the summit of Mount Triglav (Three Peaks); night, lit by shooting stars* The shades of departed souls weave their midsummer garlands (Fantastic Kolo, wordless chorus and *corps de ballet*).

The moon rises, revealing Mlada leading Yaromir up the mountainside. He pleads with her to forgive him and admit him to the silent world of shades, but she disappears, telling him (by gesture) that he must first endure a trial. The moon turns crimson; subterranean thunder announces the beginning of a Witches' Sabbath. The bright shades disperse, to be replaced by Chernobog's entourage of monsters and demons (Hellish Kolo). Morena beseeches the evil god to break Lada's spell and let Voyslava gain Yaromir. At Chernobog's command the sorcerer Kashchey conjures up a vision of Cleopatra to seduce Yaromir (to Persian and Caucasian melodies, imparted to Rimsky-Korsakov by Balakirev). The cock's crow brings the orgy to a halt. Morning finds Yaromir asleep beneath a tall tree. Awakening, he decides to return to the Temple of Radegast and ask the priests to explain the meaning of his visions.

ACT 4 *The Temple of Radegast* Yaromir makes his way to the temple and watches the priests perform their ceremonies. The High Priest bids him await dark, when the shades of ancient heroes will appear to reveal the truth. Night falls; the shades arrive and tell him 'Voyslava has indeed poisoned Mlada; avenge her!'. Voyslava enters in pursuit; she confesses her crime but tries to excuse it by her love for Yaromir. But he seizes her by the hair and runs her through with his sword. Dying, she calls on Morena to avenge her. The goddess commands the dark forces to send storms and earthquakes to destroy the temple; the lake overflows and the city of Retra is submerged. When the storm subsides a rainbow lights the air, and the shades of Yaromir and Mlada are seen embracing atop the Holy Rock, surrounded by all the beneficent deities.

RICHARD TARUSKIN

Młynarski, Emil (*b* Kibarty, 18 July 1870; *d* Warsaw, 5 April 1935). Polish conductor and composer. He studied at the St Petersburg Conservatory with Leopold Auer (violin) and Lyadov (composition). From 1894 to 1897 he taught at a music school attached to the Imperial Musical Society in Odessa. He returned to Poland in 1898 and inaugurated regular orchestral concerts in

Warsaw. He was director of the Warsaw Conservatory, 1904–7 and 1919–22. As a conductor, he held appointments with the Scottish SO (1910–16) and at the Curtis Institute, Philadelphia (1929–31), and worked in London, Moscow (at the Bol'shoy Theatre between 1914 and 1917) and Paris, where he organized festivals of Polish music (1903, 1925). In Warsaw he was also director of the opera (1919–29) and was responsible for the premières of several important Polish stage works, among them Szymanowski's *Hagith* and *King Roger*.

Although he promoted new Polish music, Młynarski's own work follows the traditions of Moniuszko, Wieniawski and Paderewski, combining Romantic traits with folksong elements. His comic opera *Noc letnia* ('Summer Night', comp. 1914; 3, H. Friedendorff) was first performed on 29 March 1924, in Warsaw. The opera is dominated by dance and elements of pantomime, with a simple, naive plot. The music is fluent and graceful, the orchestration rich and colourful – a good example of 'Kapellmeister-Musik'.

*

A. Wach: *Życie i twórczość Emila Młynarskiego* [The Life and Works of Emil Młynarski] (diss., U. of Kraków, 1953)

W. Poźniak: 'Opera po Moniuszce' [Opera after Moniuszko], *Z dziejów polskiej kultury muzycznej*, ii (Kraków, 1966), 306–28

TERESA CHYLIŃSKA

Modena. City in Emilia Romagna, northern Italy. Venetian opera reached the court of Francesco I d'Este, in what were almost certainly private festive performances, with two *drammi musicali*, *Ersilla* in 1653 (libretto by Giovanni Faustini) and *Gli amori di Alessandro Magno e di Rossane* in 1654 (libretto by G. A. Cicognini; the music for this was perhaps adapted by Benedetto Ferrari, the duke's *maestro di cappella* from 1653). More effective for state prestige were the imposing Teatro Ducale di Piazza (built by G. Vigarani within the Palazzo Comunale, with terraces, columns and galleries) and the first operas staged there: Rima's *Sancio* (1656) and Ferrari's *L'Erosilda* (1658; libretto by Carlo Vigarani). After a break during the regency of Laura Martinozzi, operatic activity resumed in 1674, but Francesco II and Rinaldo I virtually abandoned the Teatro Ducale di Piazza and supported the public theatre on the corner of the present via Emilia and via Farini, a definite policy change. Erected in 1643, it was used for operas only after it had been rebuilt in stone following a fire in 1681 (166 boxes in six tiers, one at ground level). The first opera there was Carlo Pallavicino's *Vespasiano* in November 1685.

In the two centuries of its existence the theatre had a variety of owners and names: Teatro Valentini, then Fontanelli (1683), Rangoni (1705), via Emilia (1807), Comunale (1816) and Vecchio (1841). The Teatro di Corte (near the east wing of the ducal palace) was inaugurated in 1686 with a performance of *L'Eritrea, overo Gl'inganni della maschera* (G. B. Rosselli Genesini and Antonio Ferrari) by amateurs from the court. Its use for opera was at first sporadic, since the dukes preferred more popular spectacular productions.

At the beginning of the 18th century – with breaks, especially during the periodic wars of succession – opera flourished at two theatres, the one in via Emilia (at that time called Teatro Rangoni) and the Teatro Molza, which was constructed in the northern part of the Palazzo Comunale (with three rows of boxes) and inaugurated in 1713 with Francesco Gasparini's *La fede tradita e vendicata*. The Molza was used between 1720

and 1735, when the Rangoni, which was at the disposal of the court between 1724 and 1730, was not staging opera. In the second half of the century – which saw the decline of the Molza (it was dismantled in 1769) and the opening of the Teatro di Corte to the public – carnival seasons continued regularly at the Rangoni, where Venetian *opera giocosa* made an early appearance. There was another lull in its activity (1770–80) when there were seasons, mostly of *opera seria*, at the Teatro di Corte, with several first performances of Metastasian operas, including G. M. Rutini's *La Nitteti* (Carnival 1770), Paisiello's *Artaserse* (Carnival 1772) and *Alessandro nell'Indie* (Carnival 1774), and G. Giordani's *Demetrio* (Carnival 1780). The Palazzo Ducale theatre presented no opera between 1783 and 1800 (when it was renamed Teatro Nazionale, then, from 1804, Teatro Regio), being superseded by the Rangoni.

After 1815 the same two theatres alternated with operatic seasons – carnival and summer at the Comunale in via Emilia, autumn at the Teatro di Corte – until the Teatro Comunale Nuovo (designed by Francesco Vandelli; 114 boxes in four rows and gallery) was built in the Corso Canalgrande. This was inaugurated in 1841 with Alessandro Gandini's *Adelaide di Borgogna al castello di Canossa*; as the Municipale, 1859 to 1956, it became the leading theatre. Seasons of minor importance were given at the Teatro Aliprandi (constructed from the Teatro di Corte in 1862, burnt down 1881; it normally presented comedies and musical comedies), the Arena Goldoni (1866–90, originally an open-air theatre), and the Storchi, which opened in 1889 with Usiglio's *Le donne curiose* and was the most important opera house in the period between 1916 and 1921.

After World War II the standard of performance rose considerably, owing to the presence of such singers as Freni and Pavarotti, natives of Modena. The Teatro Comunale (accorded the status of 'teatro di tradizione', one that is only partly funded by the state, in 1967) embarked on an innovatory management strategy in 1956 – formalized with the foundation of the Associazione Teatri Emilia Romagna (ATER) in the 1970s – importing foreign productions and exchanging productions with other theatres within the region.

Documents in the State Archive and the musical collections of the Biblioteca Estense are of great importance for the history of opera in Modena and beyond in the 17th and 18th centuries. The sporadic theatrical activity in the 18th century at the summer residence of the Estense court at Sassuolo is of interest. A note of 1750 is significant: between August and November there were no fewer than 42 performances of Baldassare Galuppi's *Artaserse* – the Italian première – and of Leonardo Vinci's *Alessandro nell'Indie*.

*

A. Gandini: *Cronistoria dei teatri di Modena dal 1539 al 1871* (Modena, 1873)

G. Ferrari Moreni and V. Tardini: *Cronistoria dei teatri di Modena dal 1873 a tutto il 1881* (Modena, 1883)

V. Tardini: *I teatri di Modena* (Modena, 1899–1902)

L. Bianconi and T. Walker: 'Dalla *Finta pazza* alla *Veremonda*: storie di Febiarmonici', *RIM*, x (1975), 379–454, esp. 424–34

D. Benassati: 'Dalla sala teatrale all'arena: i teatri a Modena nell'800', *Teatri storici dell'Emilia Romagna* (Bologna, 1982), 127–38

L. Bianconi and T. Walker: 'Production, Consumption and Political Function of Seventeenth-Century Opera', *Early Music History*, iv (1984), 209–96, esp. 286–7

G. Martinelli Braglia: 'Il Teatro Fontanelli: note su impresari e artisti nella Modena di Francesco II e Rinaldo I', *Alessandro Stradella e Modena* (Modena, 1985), 139–59

A. Chiarelli: *I codici di musica della raccolta estense: Ricostruzione dall'inventario settecentesco* (Florence, 1987)

G. Gherpelli: *L'opera nei teatri di Modena* (Modena, 1988)

ALESSANDRO ROCCATAGLIATI

Modista raggiratrice, La ('The Swindling Milliner'). *Commedia per musica* in three acts by GIOVANNI PAISIELLO to a libretto by GIAMBATTISTA LORENZI after GENNARO ANTONIO FEDERICO's comedy *Il Filippo*; Naples, Teatro dei Fiorentini, autumn 1787.

A milliner, Madama Perlina (soprano), is in love with the pedantic teacher Don Gavino (bass), who talks in mock Latin when not using his native Neapolitan dialect. A fencing-master, Gianferrante (tenor), and an apothecary, Mitridate (bass), are both in love with Madama Perlina, but she ignores their affections. They, in turn, neglect their prospective brides: Mitridate's daughter Ninetta (soprano), betrothed to Gianferrante, and Gianferrante's sister Chiarina (soprano), betrothed to Mitridate. The plot revolves around Madama Perlina's tireless attempts to make Gavino appreciate her amorous feelings. Gavino is depicted as an ignorant fool, unaware and incapable of understanding the hints that she gives him. Her servant Cicco (bass), also a Neapolitan dialect role, adds to the comic confusion. In the first-act finale Gavino, Mitridate and Gianferrante each ask Madama Perlina to hide him. One by one she makes the men occupy the place of a mannequin in her workroom, covering each head with a cap. Ninetta and Chiarina, who watch the entire escapade in hiding, play at pulling Mitridate and Gianferrante's heads. Madama Perlina finally ensnares Gavino, and the other two couples also pair off.

Lorenzi's text, based on G. A. Federico's comedy *Il Filippo* (1735), was first set to music by Giacomo Tritto in 1784 as a one-act opera, *La scuffiara*. Paisiello's opera, revived in Naples several times (1791, 1796 and 1801), was also given in other Italian cities, as well as in Vienna, Madrid and Lisbon. In Rome (1788) it was given as *La scuffiara amante, o sia Il maestro di scuola napolitano*. As is typical of late 18th-century Neapolitan opera, *La modista raggiratrice* opens with an ensemble – a trio of women – and includes several cavatinas. Acts 1 and 2 conclude with extended chain finales, and Act 3 ends with a duet for Madama Perlina and Gavino.

GORDANA LAZAREVICH

Mödl, Martha (*b* Nuremberg, 22 March 1912). German soprano and mezzo-soprano. She studied at the Nuremberg Conservatory, made her début as Hänsel at Remscheid in 1942 and was then engaged at Düsseldorf (1945–9), singing Dorabella, Octavian, the Composer (*Ariadne auf Naxos*), Clytemnestra, Eboli, Carmen and Berg's Marie. In 1949 she joined the Hamburg Staatsoper and became a dramatic soprano. In 1950–51 she appeared as Lady Macbeth in Berlin and then added Kundry, Venus, Isolde and Brünnhilde (*Die Walküre*) to her repertory. In 1951 she sang Kundry at the first post-war Bayreuth Festival; she returned there regularly until 1967.

Mödl first appeared in England in the 1949–50 Covent Garden season, as Carmen. She sang at Edinburgh in 1952 with the Hamburg company and in 1958 with the Stuttgart Opera, which she had joined in 1953. In 1955 she sang Leonore at the reopening of the Vienna Staatsoper. She appeared at the Metropolitan

Martha Mödl as Kundry in Wagner's 'Parsifal' at Bayreuth, 1956

(1956–60) and sang the Nurse (*Die Frau ohne Schatten*) at the reopening of the Munich Nationaltheater (1963). She sang in the premières of Reimann's *Melusine* (1971, Schwetzingen), Fortner's *Elisabeth Tudor* (1972, Berlin), Einem's *Kabale und Liebe* (1976, Vienna) and Reimann's *Die Gespenstersonate* (1984, Berlin). Returning to the mezzo repertory, she continued to sing into her mid-70s roles such as the Housekeeper (*Die schweigsame Frau*), the Countess (*The Queen of Spades*, a role she repeated in Vienna when she was 80) and the Mother (Fortner's *Die Bluthochzeit*). An intensely dramatic singer, Mödl made her audiences forget the hint of strain at the top of her voice and concentrate on its warm and beautiful lower register.

*

GV (G. Gualerzi; R. Vegeto)

H. Rosenthal: *Sopranos of Today* (London, 1956)

A. Natan: 'Mödl, Martha', *Prima donna* (Basle and Stuttgart, 1962) [with discography]

H. Rosenthal: *Great Singers of Today* (London, 1966)

W. E. Shäfer: *Martha Mödl* (Hanover, 1967)

HAROLD ROSENTHAL/R

Moffo, Anna (*b* Wayne, PA, 27 June 1932). American soprano. She studied at the Curtis Institute, and in Rome with Luigi Ricci and Mercedes Llopart, making her début in 1955 as Norina. In 1956 she sang Zerlina at Aix-en-Provence and appeared throughout Italy, making her American début the following year as Mimì in Chicago. She joined the Metropolitan Opera in 1959, making her début as Violetta; she appeared regularly in New York during the 1960s and early 1970s in such roles as Pamina, Norina, Gilda, Luisa Miller, the four heroines of *Les contes d'Hoffmann*, Juliet, Gounod's Marguerite, Manon, Mélisande and the title role in *La Périchole*. She sang Gilda at Covent Garden (1964), and appeared in Vienna, Salzburg,

Berlin and elsewhere. A lyric soprano of warm, full, radiant tone, she also undertook coloratura parts. As Violetta she was internationally acclaimed, notably as a guest artist in Felsenstein's production at the Komische Oper, Berlin, the range and versatility of her voice, and her charming stage presence, being put to particularly good use. After a vocal breakdown in 1974–5 she made a fresh start in 1976, singing the title roles in *Thaïs* (1976, Seattle) and *Adriana Lecouvreur* (1978, Parma), as well as Kate in Giannini's *The Taming of the Shrew* (1979, Vienna, Virginia). She also made a number of recordings including *L'amore dei tre re* (Montemezzi), *Carmen* and *Hänsel und Gretel*.

J. Hines: 'Anna Moffo', *Great Singers on Great Singing* (Garden City, NY, 1982), 182–8   HAROLD ROSENTHAL/R

Moggi, Pietro. *See* MOZZI, PIETRO.

Mohaupt, Richard (*b* Breslau, 14 Sept 1904; *d* Reichenau, Austria, 3 July 1957). German composer. He began his music studies at Breslau University and subsequently worked as a vocal coach and conductor in the opera houses of Weimar, Breslau and Aachen. In 1932 he settled in Berlin where he spent several years as a composer and pianist for various film and theatre companies. Disagreements with the Nazi regime caused him to be expelled from membership of both the *Reichstheaterkammer* and the *Reichsmusikkammer* and in 1939 he left for New York. While in the USA, he continued to compose prolifically, receiving several commissions and achieving some success with film scores and music for the radio. He returned to Europe in 1955.

Mohaupt's first opera, *Die Wirtin von Pinsk*, commissioned by Karl Böhm and the Dresden Staatsoper for its 1937–8 season, enjoyed a rather chequered career. Like Strauss's *Die schweigsame Frau*, it was banned by the Nazis after only a few performances, but here it was the composer's political views and his non-Aryan wife, rather than the racial identity of the librettist, that provoked such action. The opera was revived by several German opera houses after the war, but despite receiving favourable reviews it failed to maintain a place in the repertory. On the other hand, *Die Bremer Stadtmusikanten* (composed 1944) proved extremely popular in the 1950s. It is a charming comic opera in which the composer provides some entertaining parodies of 19th-century music, including a dog performing sections of Tchaikovsky's Piano Concerto no.1 and a cat playing the fiddle with the skill of a Paganini. Mohaupt's third opera, *Double Trouble*, is notable for its use of a chorus whose role, as in a classical drama, is to comment upon the actions of the main characters. Both this work and the composer's final opera, *Der grüne Kakadu*, based on a play by Schnitzler, demonstrate the influence of Stravinsky in their rhythmic vitality and instrumental colouring. Yet their effectiveness on the stage is somewhat diminished by the lack of real individuality in the musical idiom.

Die Wirtin von Pinsk (3, K. Naue, after Goldoni: *Mirandola*), Dresden, Staatsoper, 10 Feb 1938, vs (Vienna, 1938)
Die Bremer Stadtmusikanten, 1944 (2, Mohaupt), Bremen, 15 June 1949
Double Trouble (Zwillingskomödie, 1, Mohaupt, after Plautus), Louisville, KY, 4 Dec 1954
Der grüne Kakadu (1, Mohaupt, after A. Schnitzler), 1956, Hamburg, 16 Sept 1958, vs (Vienna, 1957)
Boleslaw der Schamhafte, unperf.

R. Bilke: 'Richard Mohaupt', *Musica*, iv (1950), 324–6
H. Lindlar: 'Richard Mohaupt (3.7. [1957])', *Musica*, xi (1957), 581–2   ERIK LEVI

Möhring [Möring], **Monsieur** (*b* c1700; *d* after 1733). German tenor. He sang at the Hamburg Opera between 1722 and 1733, making his début as Mitrane in *Arsace*, by Orlandini and Amadei. He also sang Helmiges (Telemann's *Sieg der Schönheit*), Lope (Conti's *Don Chisciotte in Sierra Morena*) and Piritous (Keiser's *Ariadne*). The following year he sang only in *Muzio Scevola*, by Amadei, Bononcini and Handel. In 1725 Möhring performed in nine operas and prologues, his roles including Theobald in Keiser's *Bretislaus* and Nirenus in Handel's *Giulio Cesare*. The following year his roles included Mezzatin in Telemann's *Il capitano* and Henriques and Miecislaus in Keiser's *Jodelet* and *Mistevojus*.

Between 1727 and 1730 he sang almost exclusively in operas by Telemann, including *Calypso* (1727), *Die verkehrte Welt* (1728), *Flavius Bertaridus* and *Margaretha* (1730). Möhring's final season in Hamburg saw him singing Hephestion in Telemann's *Der Weiseste in Sidon* (1733).

L. Krüger: *Die Hamburgische Musikorganisation im XVII. Jahrhundert* (Leipzig, 1933), 142f
K. Zelm: 'Die Sänger der Hamburger Gänsemarkt-Oper', *HJbMw*, iii (1978), 59–61   HANS JOACHIM MARX

Moïse et Pharaon [*Moïse et Pharaon, ou Le passage de la Mer Rouge* ('Moses and Pharaoh, or The Crossing of the Red Sea')]. *Opéra* in four acts by GIOACHINO ROSSINI, derived from his MOSÈ IN EGITTO (1818–19), to a new libretto by Luigi Balocchi and ETIENNE DE JOUY; Paris, Opéra, 26 March 1827.

For the Paris version of his Moses opera, Rossini elaborated and reordered the musical and dramatic structures of *Mosè in Egitto*. In conformity with French taste of the time and the added resources of the Paris Opéra, the work is both grander and more spectacular than the original, at some cost to its essential freshness and cogency. Only three numbers are entirely new: the *scène et quatuor* 'Dieu de la paix' in Act 1, Anaï's *scène et air* 'Quelle horrible destinée' in Act 4 and the concluding and rarely performed *cantique* 'Chantons, bénissons le Seigneur'. The overture, introduction and Act 3 ballet all draw on material from Rossini's *Armida* (1817), though the ballet is substantially new. Reorderings include the transference of the famous 'Scene of the Shadows' from the start of the work to the opening of Act 2 and the dismembering of the original's important Act 2 finale. The death of Pharaoh's son is postponed and Elcia's 'Porgi la destra amata' is turned into an appeal by Pharaoh's wife to their lovelorn son. The Paris libretto also renames several leading characters: Pharaoh's son, Osiride, becomes Aménophis (tenor), Pharaoh's wife, Amaltea, becomes Sinaïde (soprano) and the young Hebrew girl Elcia becomes Anaï (soprano), daughter of Marie (mezzo-soprano), Moses's sister. Osiride (bass) is the Egyptian High Priest, originally Mambre (not to be confused with Prince Osiride in *Mosè in Egitto*).

In the opening scene the Israelites lament their oppression by the Egyptians; Moses (bass) promises that he will lead them to freedom. Eliéser [Aaron] (tenor) describes how he has threatened Pharaon [Pharaoh] with God's wrath, but it is the Queen of Egypt, Sinaïde [Sinais], sympathetic to the Israelite cause, who has prevailed upon Pharaoh to release Anaï [Anaïs] and her mother as a token of good faith. The Israelites are told of Anaïs's love for Pharaoh's son, but it soon becomes apparent that she plans to leave Egypt with the Israelites; Aménophis [Amenophis] is equally determined that they will stay. But his intervention brings catastrophe as Moses, angered by the Egyptians' duplicity, decrees that the country shall be plunged into darkness.

At the start of Act 2 the Egyptians plead with Pharaoh to resolve the crisis; he promises Moses freedom if light is restored. Moses complies, but then it is revealed that Pharaoh has arranged a marriage between his son and the daughter of the Assyrian king. Amenophis's grief is partly assuaged in an extended scene with his mother, Sinais, but he swears revenge on Moses. In Act 3 the Egyptians give thanks for their deliverance but the High Priest Osiride [Osiris] demands that the Israelites pay homage to Isis before they depart; Moses refuses. When the flame on the altar of Isis is suddenly extinguished both parties claim credit for the miracle. Pharaoh, tired of the crises, expels the Israelites but decrees that they shall leave in chains.

In the first scene of the final act Amenophis and Anaïs meet in the desert. He hopes that by allowing her to return to her people their love will be sanctioned but Anaïs prays for the moral strength to resist this. Outraged, Amenophis warns that Pharaoh and his army are in pursuit of the Israelites. Moses leads the Israelites in prayer and the Red Sea parts for them but not for the Egyptians, who are engulfed. After a gloomy orchestral postlude, derived from the more buoyant end to *Mosè in Egitto*, the Israelites sing a hymn of praise to God for their deliverance.

Like *Le siège de Corinthe* (1826), *Moïse et Pharaon* can be seen as an experiment in handling the resources of grand opera and, as such, an important stepping-stone towards the creation of Rossini's one wholly original work for the French stage, *Guillaume Tell* (1829). Houses with large choral resources and a ballet will continue to prefer it but the Neapolitan original, *Mosè in Egitto*, has been too little noted by smaller houses and companies to which it is admirably suited.

RICHARD OSBORNE

Mojica, José (*b* Mexico City, 14 Sept 1896; *d* Lima, 21 Sept 1974). Mexican tenor. Born in poverty and out of wedlock, but gifted with a fine voice and good looks, he joined the Chicago Opera Company in 1919 and remained until 1930, when he went into films, returning once more to sing Fenton in *Falstaff* in 1940. His parts ranged from Pelléas, which he sang opposite Mary Garden, to Don Basilio in *Le nozze di Figaro*. In 1921 he sang the Prince in the première of *The Love for Three Oranges*, in which he scored a further success the following year in New York. On his mother's death in 1943 he gave up his career and became Father José Francisco de Guadaloupe, a Franciscan priest, working as a missionary in Peru. He undertook a concert tour of Central America to raise funds in 1954, and later wrote his autobiography, *Yo pecador* (Mexico City, 1956). His recordings show an attractive lyric voice often used with skill and imagination. J. B. STEANE

Mojsisovics(-Mojsvár), Roderich Edler von (*b* Graz, 10 May 1877; *d* Graz, 30 March 1953). Austrian composer. He studied music and law (doctorate 1900) in Graz, then continued music studies in Cologne and Munich with Wüllner, Thuille and others. He worked

mainly as a teacher. From 1912 to 1931 he was director of the Steiermärkischer Musikverein (which became the Conservatory in 1920) in Graz, and after periods in Munich and Mannheim he returned there to teach operatic dramaturgy (1945–8). Although his main interest was in opera, his style belongs to the tradition of Reger. His stage works are marked by a strong theatrical sense and contain moments of colourful orchestration and expressive declamation, but they did not achieve wide popularity.

Die roten Dominos op.20 (2, Mojsisovics, after H. Hopfen: *Zehn oder elf*), Graz, Franzens, 24 April 1907
Ninion op.19 (Melodram, 1, E. Mayer and A. Weissmann), Pressburg, Stadt, 13 May 1907
Messer Ricciardo Minutolo op.50 (Musikkomödie, 4, Mojsisovics), Zürich, Serano, ? 1907
Tantchen Rosmarin (komische Oper, 4, K. H. Strobl, after Zschokke), Brno, Städtisches, 31 Jan 1913
Merlin (Märchenspiel, 3, E. Hoffer), Graz, Schauspielhaus, 19 Feb 1921
Der Zauberer op.60 (1, Mojsisovics, after M. de Cervantes: *La cueva de Salamanca*), Gera, Preussisches, 1 April 1926
Die Locke op.72 (musikalisches Lustspiel, 1, Mojsisovics), Knittelfeld, Steiermark, 10 July 1927
Die Lerche, Krefeld, 1928
Madame Blaubart op.62 (burleske Oper, 3, K. Mayer and E. Meier-Hahn), inc. radio perf., Breslau, 20 Sept 1934
Norden im Not (nordische Volksoper, 3, F. Stege), Leipzig, 25 June 1936
Anno domini op.75 (altdeutsche Oper, 2 scenes, Mojsisovics)

Unperf. (according to Gruber): Aspasia; Claudine von Villabella (after J. W. von Goethe); Erwin und Elmire; Viel Lärm um nichts (4, after W. Shakespeare); Vivat Allotria. Oedipus auf Kolonos (after Sophocles) mentioned by Stichtenoth

*

M. Morold: 'Roderich von Mojsisovics', *ZfM*, xcix (1932), 661–4
R. von Mojsisovics: 'Die Veränderungen der Ausdrucksfähigkeit einer Melodie bei "wandernden" Themen: ein musikdramaturgischer Versuch', *ZfM*, xcix (1932), 664–72
F. Stichtenoth: 'Roderich von Mojsisovics', *ZfM*, cix (1942), 202–5
K. Haidmayer: *Roderich von Mojsisovics: Leben und Werk* (diss., U. of Graz, 1951)
C. M. Gruber, ed.: *Opern-Uraufführungen: ein internazionales Verzeichnis von der Renaissance bis zur Gegenwart* (Vienna, 1978–)

Molchanov, Kirill Vladimirovich (*b* Moscow, 7 Sept 1922; *d* Moscow, 14 March 1982). Russian composer. He studied with Alexandrov at the Moscow Conservatory, graduating in 1949. He was active in the Moscow section of the Composers' Union, and worked as director of the State Academic Bol'shoy Theatre of the USSR. Molchanov's reputation rests mainly on his operas, which have been praised for their feeling for drama and staging, and for their lyricism; heroic, patriotic themes predominate and links with Russian musical traditions are evident, with considerable reliance on song. His first opera, *Kamennïy tsvetok* ('The Stone Flower'), is based on a famous fairy-tale from the Urals, and its approach has been compared with that of Rimsky-Korsakov; its successors, *Zarya* ('Daybreak') and *Ulitsa del' korno* ('Del Corno Street'), tackle political themes: the October Revolution in the former and Fascism in the latter. *Zori zdes' tikhiye* ('The Dawns are Quiet Here'), on a World War II theme, was performed by the Moscow Bol'shoy company in New York in 1975.

first performed and published in vocal score in Moscow, unless otherwise stated
Kamennïy tsvetok [The Stone Flower] (4, S. Severtsev, after P. Bazhov), Stanislavsky–Nemirovich-Danchenko Music Theatre, 1951 (1952)

Zarya [Daybreak] (4, Severtsev, after B. Lavrenyov: *Razlom* [The Rout]), Stanislavsky–Nemirovich-Danchenko Music Theatre, 1956 (1959)

Ulitsa del' korno [Del Corno Street] (3, S. Tsenin, after V. Pratolini: *Povest' o bednïkh vlyublyonnïkh* [A Tale of Poor Lovers]), Stanislavsky–Nemirovich-Danchenko Music Theatre, 1961 (1964)

Romeo, Dzhul'yetta i t'ma [Romeo, Juliet and the Darkness] (2, Molchanov, after J. Otčenášek), Leningrad, Malïy, 1963 (1968)

Neizvestnïy soldat [The Unknown Soldier]/Brestskaya krepost' [The Brest Fortress] (2, Molchanov), Bol'shoy, 1967 (1972)

Russkaya zhenshchina [The Russian Woman] (9 scenes, Molchanov, after Yu. Nagibin: *Bab'ye tsarstvo* [The Kingdom of Women]), Voronezh, 1970, unpubd

Odissey, Penelopa i drugiye [Odysseus, Penelope and Others] (musical comedy, after Homer), 1970, unpubd

Zori zdes' tikhiye [The Dawns are Quiet Here] (2, Molchanov, after B. Vasil'yev), Bol'shoy, 1973 (1978)

Vernost' [Faithfulness] (opera-poem, Molchanov, after V. Astaf'yev: *Pastukh i pastushka* [Shepherd and Shepherdess]), Sverdlovsk, 1980, unpubd

*

Yu. Korev: *Kirill Molchanov* (Moscow, 1971)

'Pamyati K. V. Molchanova' [In Memory of Molchanov], *SovM* (1982), no.6, p.143

Obituary, *Sovetskaya kul'tura*, no.22 (1982)

GALINA GRIGOR'YEVA, SVETLANA SARKISYAN

Moldova. For an account of operatic activity in Moldova *see* KISHINEU.

Moldoveanu, Eugenia (*b* Busteni, nr Sinaia, 19 March 1944). Romanian soprano. She studied at the Bucharest conservatory and made her début with the Romanian National Opera in 1968 as Donna Anna, later singing leading roles with this and other Romanian companies. She was a prizewinner at international singing competitions in Bucharest and Sofia (both 1968), in Toulouse (1970) and in the 'Butterfly' Competition at Tokyo in 1973. Since then she has appeared in centres in France, Germany, Italy, the Netherlands and the USA in *lirico spinto* roles, chiefly of Mozart, Puccini and Verdi.

NOËL GOODWIN

Moldoveanu, Vasile (*b* Constanţa, 6 Oct 1935). Romanian tenor. After beginning medical studies he turned to singing, at the Bucharest Conservatory, and made his début with the Romanian National Opera in 1966 as Rinuccio (*Gianni Schicchi*); later he took leading roles by Donizetti, Mozart, Puccini and Verdi and appeared in Belgium, Finland, the Netherlands and Spain. In 1972 he joined the Stuttgart Opera as principal tenor for the Italian repertory; he made his débuts with the state opera companies of Vienna and of Munich in 1976 and the Deutsche Oper in Berlin the next year. Also in 1977 he made his American début with the Metropolitan Opera (on tour) as Alfredo; in 1979 he sang with the Metropolitan in New York as Pinkerton, and the same year he sang at Covent Garden as Don Carlos, a role he had first sung in the Ponnelle production in Hamburg (1978). He is a frequent concert soloist.

NOËL GOODWIN

Molière [Poquelin, Jean-Baptiste] (*b* Paris, bap. 15 Jan 1622; *d* Paris, 17 Feb 1673). French playwright. Musically he is important for his 'comédies mêlées de danse et de musique' or *comédies-ballets*, many of which were set by Lully, which date from the last 12 years of his life, during which time he also wrote most of his best-known plays. The COMÉDIE-BALLET, which incorporated elements of the *ballet de cour* into spoken comedy, came

into existence almost accidentally. For festivities at the court of Louis XIV in August 1661 both a play by Molière (*Les fâcheux*) and a ballet by Lully were planned. However, only a small number of dancers were available, and in order to give them time for costume changes it was decided to place the ballet entrées between the acts of the play; then, as Molière explained in his preface, 'in order to not break the thread of the play by these *intermèdes*, we decided to link them with its subject as best we could and to make a single thing of the ballet and the play'.

Following *Les fâcheux* (with some music by Lully), Molière and Lully collaborated on a number of other *comédies-ballets* until 1671. Lully also composed the *tragédie-ballet Psyché* (1671) to a text by Molière, Philippe Quinault and Pierre Corneille. After becoming estranged from Lully, Molière asked Marc-Antoine Charpentier to revise parts of Lully's scores for *La comtesse d'Escarbagnas*, *Le mariage forcé* and *Les fâcheux* (summer and autumn 1672) and to compose the music for the work that was to be his last *comédie-ballet*, *Le malade imaginaire* (1673).

Besides ballet entrées and entr'acte *intermèdes* set to music, many *comédies-ballets* include songs and other musical *divertissements* within the play proper. The dramatic and musical components are integrated to varying degrees. They are most closely intertwined in *La princesse d'Elide*, *Monsieur de Pourceaugnac*, *Les amants magnifiques*, *Le bourgeois gentilhomme* and *Le malade imaginaire* – indeed, the last two culminate in musico-dramatic finales essential to the comedy.

Molière had no immediate successors in the genre of *comédie-ballet*, mainly because the king came to prefer Lully's operas to spoken plays. But Lully had devised and perfected his recitative in his work with Molière; the nature of Quinault's verse in his *tragédies lyriques* for Lully owes something to Molière; and the first real opera of Lully and Quinault, *Cadmus et Hermione* (1673), bears in general plan a considerable resemblance to the *comédie-ballet*. In addition to forming the basis for scores of ballets and operas in all centuries, including his own, Molière's plays have inspired a large number of orchestral pieces including much incidental music.

Le médecin volant (improvised comedy, *c*1650): Veretti, comp. 1923

Les précieuses ridicules (comedy, 1659): B. Galuppi, 1752, as Le virtuose ridicole; A. Goetzl, 1905, as Zierpuppen; Zich, 1926, as Precieźky; Lattuada, 1929; Behrend, 1949; G. Bush, 1956, as If the Cap Fits

Sganarelle, ou Le cocu imaginaire (verse comedy, 1660): Grosz, 1925; Wagner-Régeny, 1929; Kalmanoff, 1974; Pasatieri, 1974, as Signor Deluso; T. Sullivan, 1990, as The Imaginary Couple

L'école des maris (verse comedy, after Terence: *Adelphi*, 1661): Alessandri, 1781, as Il vecchio geloso; Bondeville, 1935

Les fâcheux (comédie-ballet, 1661): C.-L. Beauchamps and Lully, 1661

L'école des femmes (verse comedy, 1663): Liebermann, 1955

L'impromptu de Versailles (comedy, 1663): Lully, 1663, as Mascarade du capitaine

Le mariage forcé (comédie-ballet, 1664): Lully, 1664; André, 1796, as Der Bräutigam in der Klemme; F. Wart, 1928, as The Forced Marriage

La princesse d'Elide (comédie-ballet, 1664): Lully, 1664 [part of Les plaisirs de l'île enchantée]; A.-B. Lavergne, comp. *c*1700; Galuppi, 1749, as Alcimena principessa dell'Isole Fortunate

Le Tartuffe [L'imposteur] (comedy, 1664): J. Eidens, 1929; Haug, 1937; Kósa, 1952; Benjamin, 1964; Malipiero, 1970

L'amour médecin (comédie-ballet, 1665): Lully, 1665; Poise, 1880; Wolf-Ferrari, 1913; R. Werbergis, 1920; Bell, comp. 1930, as Doctor Love; Bentoiu, 1966, as Amorul doctor

Le médecin malgré lui (prose comedy, after medieval fabliau *Le vilain mire*, 1666): Désaugiers, 1792; Haibel, 1841, as

Hanswurst, Doctor nolens volens; Gounod, 1858; Poise, comp. 1887

Le misanthrope (comedy, 1666): Caldara, 1729, as I disingannati

La pastorale comique (pastorale-héroïque, 1666): Lully, 1667

Le sicilien, ou L'amour peintre (comédie-ballet, 1667): Lully, 1667; Kospoth, 1779, as Adrast und Isidore; Dauvergne, 1780; Mǐča, 1781, as Adrast und Isidore, oder Die Nachtmusik; L. C. L. Mezeray, 1825; Joncières, 1859; K. H. David, 1924; O. Letorey, 1930

Amphitryon (irregular verse comedy, after Plautus: *Amphitruo*, 1668): Grétry, 1786; Papandopulo, 1940; R. Oboussier, 1949

L'avare (prose comedy, after Plautus: *Aulularia*, 1668): Burghauser, 1950, as Lakomec

George Dandin (prose comedy, 1668): Lully, 1668; Mathieu, 1877; Gounod, inc.; Ollone, 1930

Monsieur de Porceaugnac (comédie-ballet, 1669): Lully, 1669; Orlandini, 1727; Haibel and Seyfried, 1809, as Rochus Pumpernickel; Castil-Blaze, 1827; Alberto Franchetti, 1897; F. Martin, 1963

Les amants magnifiques (comédie-ballet, 1670): Lully, 1670

Le bourgeois gentilhomme (comédie-ballet, 1670): Lully, 1670; Orlandini, 1722; M. Esposito, 1905

La comtesse d'Escarbagnas (comedy, 1671): M.-A. Charpentier, 1672

Les fourberies de Scapin (comedy, 1671): Falik, 1984, as Plutni Skapena

Psyché (tragédie-ballet, with P. Quinault and P. Corneille, 1671): Lully, 1671; Locke, 1675; Uttini, 1766

Le malade imaginaire (comédie-ballet, 1673): Charpentier, 1673; Orlandini, 1725; Napoli, 1939; Haug, 1946; Szőnyi, 1961; Wolpert, 1975; Hadjiev, 1987, as Mnimiyat bolen

*

Castil-Blaze: *Molière musicien* (Paris, 1852)

V. Fournel: *Les contemporains de Molière* (Paris, 1862–75)

E. Despois and P. Mesnard, eds.: *Oeuvres de Molière* (Paris, 1873–1900)

A. Pougin: *Molière et l'opéra-comique* (Paris, 1882)

L. de La Laurencie: *Lully* (Paris, 1911)

M. Pellisson: *Les comédies-ballets de Molière* (Paris, 1914)

J. Tiersot: *La musique dans la comédie de Molière* (Paris, 1922)

H. C. Lancaster: *A History of French Dramatic Literature in the Seventeenth Century* (Baltimore, 1936)

R. Brancour: 'Molière et la musique', *RMI*, xli (1937), 446–59

B. E. Young and G. P. Young, eds.: *Le Registre de La Grange, 1659–1685, reproduit en fac-similé avec un index et une notice sur La Grange et sa part dans le théâtre de Molière* (Paris, 1947)

A. R. Oliver: 'Molière's Contribution to the Lyric Stage', *MQ*, xxxiii (1947), 350–64

P. A. Touchard, ed.: *Oeuvres complètes* (Paris, 1962)

G. Mongrédien: *Recueil des textes et de documents du XVIIIe siècle relatifs à Molière* (Paris, 1965)

M.-F. Christout: *Le ballet de cour de Louis XIV, 1643–1672* (Paris, 1967)

L. Auld: *The Unity of Molière's Comedy-Ballets: a Study of their Structure, Meanings, and Values* (diss., Bryn Mawr College, 1968)

M. Benoit: *Musiques de cour: chapelle, chambre, écurie, 1661–1733* (Paris, 1971), 37–8

H. W. Hitchcock: 'Marc-Antoine Charpentier and the Comédie-Française', *JAMS*, xxiv (1971), 255–81

——: 'Problèmes d'édition de la musique de Marc-Antoine Charpentier pour *Le malade imaginaire*', *RdM*, lviii (1972), 3–15

H. Purkis: 'Les intermèdes musicaux de George Dandin', *Baroque*, v (1972), 63–9

J. R. Anthony: *French Baroque Music from Beaujoyeulx to Rameau* (London, 1973, 2/1978; Fr. trans., 1981)

E. B. Lance: 'Molière the Musician: a Tercentenary View', *MR*, xxxv (1974), 120–30

J. S. Powell: *Music in the Theatre of Molière* (diss., U. of Washington, 1982)

M. Turnbull: 'The Metamorphosis of *Psyché*', *ML*, lxiv (1983), 12–24

A. Parmley: *The Secular Stage Works of Marc-Antoine Charpentier* (diss., U. of London, 1985)

J. S. Powell: 'Charpentier's Music for Molière's *Le malade imaginaire* and its Revisions', *JAMS*, xxxix (1986), 87–141

——: 'Music, Fantasy and Illusion in Molière's "Le malade imaginaire"', *ML*, lxxiii (1992), 222–43

H. WILEY HITCHCOCK

Molinara, La [*L'amor contrastato, ossia La molinara* ('Doubtful Love, or The Maid of the Mill')]. *Commedia per musica* in three acts by GIOVANNI PAISIELLO to a libretto by GIUSEPPE PALOMBA; Naples, Teatro dei Fiorentini, autumn 1788.

In a villa on the outskirts of Naples a baroness, Eugenia (soprano), is supervising the progress of her marriage contract with Don Calloandro (tenor) which is being written by the notary Pistofolo (bass). Calloandro, Eugenia's vain and affected cousin, is more enthusiastic about the young and pretty owner of the adjacent mill, Rachelina (soprano), than about his cousin's marital intentions. Pretending to be modest, Rachelina manages to attract two other suitors: the elderly governor Don Rospolone (bass) and Pistofolo, who continually uses Latin words in normal conversation. In a scene full of slapstick action, Calloandro and Rospolone confess their love for Rachelina to the notary, who tries to hide the fact that all three are rivals; his life is eventually threatened by the other two when they discover the truth.

Determined to regain her bridegroom from her rival's clutches, Eugenia, along with a few of her friends, pursues Calloandro to Rachelina's mill, where he has been seen approaching with a notary. Rachelina quickly gets Calloandro to hide and to disguise himself as a gardener; she has the notary hide in another room and disguise himself as a miller. For a while she manages to fool Eugenia with this ruse, but Eugenia's two companions – Don Luigino (bass), who adores her, and Amaranta (soprano), her elderly maid – soon recognize the bluff and reveal it to her. Calloandro resorts to feigning madness, so successfully that Eugenia asks Rospolone to fetch three doctors to administer medication; Rospolone and two of his friends appear disguised as doctors, which results in a humorous slapstick scene. General chaos ensues as the notary and Rachelina also pretend to hallucinate. Miraculously cured, Calloandro promises to marry Eugenia, while the rejected Luigino contents himself with continuing as her admiring companion. In the short third act Rachelina decides to marry Pistofolo.

The libretto, not to be confused with Filippo Livigni's *La molinara* (music by Fischietti, 1778) or with *La molinarella* (music by Piccinni, 1766), was originally called *L'amor contrastato* but became more commonly known as *La molinara* (and was sometimes known as *La molinarella*). Paisiello's opera attained great popularity throughout Europe over a period of four decades, rivalling the fame of his *Il barbiere di Siviglia* (1782). It received over 160 performances between 1790 and 1809 in Vienna, where its initial success was due in part to the cast of singers, which included the soprano Adriana Ferrarese, the bass Francesco Benucci and Gasparo Bellentani (one of the best *buffo* tenors at the Burgtheater). Paisiello's *La molinara* was also the last opera performed by Haydn's troupe at Eszterháza before the dissolution of the opera company in 1790 and Haydn's trip to London.

The popularity of the work is also evident in the number of arrangements made of its music: these include one printed by Simrock for two clarinets, two horns and two bassoons and one printed by Schott for a flute, violin, viola and cello quartet. A number of composers wrote variations on popular arias. The Act 2 duet 'Nel cor più non mi sento' was used as a basis for variations by a number of composers, including J. N. Hummel and Beethoven (WoO70). Beethoven also composed a set of nine variations for piano (WoO69)

'La molinara' (Paisiello):
design by Antonio de
Pian for a production at
the Burgtheater, Vienna,
in 1790

'Quant'è più bello', an aria (not, however, by Paisiello) that was added for the revival of the opera in Vienna in 1795, which Beethoven probably heard. *La molinara* was also performed in German as *Die schöne Müllerin* and *Die streitig gemachte Liebschaft*, and in 1789 it was performed in Paris as *La molinarella*, with nine arias by Cherubini.

In this opera Paisiello proved himself a master of musical characterization. Rachelina's feigned modesty is depicted in her Act 1 cavatina 'La Rachelina, molinara', set as an *andante* in 2/4, with folk-like simplicity. The Act 3 duet for Rachelina and Pistofolo, 'Il mio garzone il piffaro sonava', is a siciliana in a lilting 12/8. Paisiello frequently introduced popular folk instruments into his operas, and in the quintet 'Il villan, che coltiva il giardino' (2.v) Calloandro and Pistofolo play a chitarrino (small guitar) and a colascione (small folk lute), while Rachelina accompanies with a tamburro (drum). The opera bristles with melodic invention, and Acts 1 and 2 are ensembles organized as skilfully constructed chain finales.   GORDANA LAZAREVICH

Molinari-Pradelli, Francesco (*b* Bologna, 4 July 1911). Italian conductor. He studied the piano at Bologna, then conducting with Bernardino Molinari at the Accademia di S Cecilia in Rome, graduating in 1938. He made his début the same year as a concert conductor but concentrated almost exclusively on opera from 1939, when he conducted *L'elisir d'amore* at Bologna, Bergamo and Brescia. After his first appearance at La Scala in 1946, he conducted regularly at leading Italian opera houses as well as making frequent tours in other countries. He first appeared at Covent Garden in 1955, conducting *Tosca* (with Renata Tebaldi), and returned to conduct the new production of Verdi's *Macbeth* in 1960. From 1957 he was a regular conductor at San Francisco, and from 1959 at the Vienna Staatsoper; he made his début at the Metropolitan Opera in 1966 with *Un ballo in maschera*, and conducted 16 other operas there in following seasons until 1973, mostly Verdi and Puccini but including Gounod's *Roméo et Juliette*. He recorded more than a dozen operas, of which the most notable are *La*

traviata and *Manon Lescaut* (both 1954) and *La forza del destino* (1955), all with Tebaldi; *Turandot* (1965) with Birgit Nilsson; *La rondine* (1967); and live performances from Naples of *Samson et Dalila* (1959) with Jean Madeira and Mario Del Monaco, and from Florence of *Maria Stuarda* (1967) with Leyla Gencer, Shirley Verrett and Ferruccio Tagliavini.

BERNARD JACOBSON, NOËL GOODWIN

Moline, Pierre Louis (*b* Montpellier, *c*1740; *d* Paris, 19 Feb 1821). French writer. He studied arts at Avignon and law in Paris, but adopted literature as a profession. With deplorable fecundity, he contributed to every fashionable stage genre, including tragedy, comedy of manners, bourgeois drama and Revolutionary *sansculottide*. He was advocate to the *parlement*, then secretary to the Convention (1792–4). Among his few, generally poor, librettos, two were outstandingly successful at the Opéra: the adaptation of Calzabigi for Gluck's *Orphée* (1774), and the most important stage work of J.-F. Edelmann, *Ariane dans l'isle de Naxos* (1782). He also wrote the texts for Edelmann's *L'Amour enchaîné par Diane* (1783) and Candeille's pastoral *Laure et Pétrarque* (1778); he adapted Vadé's text for a revision of Gluck's *L'arbre enchanté* (Versailles, 1775), and translated Paisiello's *Il re Teodoro in Venezia* for Fontainebleau (1786, as *Le roi Théodore à Venise*). He contributed to the Gluckist controversy in *Dialogue entre Lully, Rameau, et Orphée dans les Champs Elysées* (Amsterdam, 1774).

*

[?F.] Fayolle: 'Moline, (Pierre-Louis)', *Biographie universelle*, ed. L. G. Michaud (Paris, 1843–65)

J. C. F. Hoefer, ed.: *Nouvelle biographie générale* (Paris, 1852–66)
                                                                JULIAN RUSHTON

Moll, Kurt (*b* Buir, 11 April 1938). German bass. He studied at the Hochschule für Musik, Cologne, then privately with Emmy Mueller. He made his début as Lodovico (*Otello*) at Aachen, where he was engaged from 1961 to 1963, and then sang at Mainz and Wuppertal before joining the Hamburg Staatsoper in

1970. From 1972 he has been a regular guest at Munich, Vienna and Paris, and has also appeared at Salzburg and Bayreuth. His roles include most of the leading bass parts in Wagner's operas, his King Mark and Pogner being particularly vivid portrayals, and he uses his true, strong and flexible bass equally well in less serious roles such as Osmin, which he recorded with considerable success under Böhm. He is a noble Sarastro, with the low notes resonant and firm. He is also an appreciable interpreter of such Verdian roles as Fiesco and Padre Guardiano. He first appeared in the USA as Gurnemanz (1974, San Francisco). In 1975 he created the King in Bialas's *Der gestiefelte Kater* at the Schwetzingen Festival in the Hamburg Staatsoper production and added the title role in Massenet's *Don Quichotte* (given with the same company) to his repertory. He made his Covent Garden début as Caspar in Götz Friedrich's production of *Der Freischütz* in 1977, returning as Osmin in 1987, and his Metropolitan début as the Landgrave in 1978.   ALAN BLYTH

Mollet, Pierre (*b* Neuchâtel, 23 March 1920). Swiss baritone. He studied at Lausanne and Basle. At first a concert singer, he made his début at the Opéra-Comique in 1952 as Pelléas, his best-known role, which he also sang in Lisbon, Rome, Buenos Aires, Geneva and other cities. He sang Orestes (*Iphigénie en Tauride*) at Aix-en-Provence (1952) and created Eraste in Frank Martin's *Monsieur de Pourceaugnac* at Geneva in 1963, repeating the role at the Holland Festival. His repertory included Albert (*Werther*) and Mercutio (*Roméo et Juliette*). A stylish artist, he did not have a large voice, but sang with excellent diction and well-focussed tone.
                                        ELIZABETH FORBES

Molotov. See PERM'.

Molteni, Benedetta Emilia. *See* AGRICOLA, BENEDETTA EMILIA.

Mombelli, Domenico (*b* Villanova Monferrato, nr Alessandria, 17 Feb 1751; *d* Bologna, 15 March 1835). Italian tenor and composer. He began his career as organist at Crescentino, where in 1776 he staged his own three-act opera *Didone*, to a libretto by Metastasio. He came to prominence as a singer in 1780, when he first appeared in Venice in Anfossi's *Nitteti*; he returned there frequently until 1800. Although he sang in Rome, Turin, Reggio Emilia, Padua and Bologna during this period, his main centre of activity other than Venice was Naples, especially the S Carlo, where he first appeared in 1783 in Sarti's *Medonte* and Cimarosa's *Oreste*, and returned periodically until 1803.

Mombelli's first wife was Luisa Laschi, Mozart's first Countess Almaviva, with whom he sang in Vienna in 1786; she died in 1789. In 1791 he married the dancer Vincenza Viganò, a niece of Boccherini and sister of the choreographer Salvatore Viganò. They had 12 children of whom two, Ester (*b* Bologna, 1794) and Anna (*b* Milan, 1795), became singers (mezzo-soprano and contralto respectively); with them and a bass Mombelli formed a travelling company which appeared in Lisbon, Padua and Milan (1806–11).

In 1805 Mombelli became friendly with the 13-year-old Rossini, who composed for him the principal role in *Demetrio e Polibio* to a text by Vincenza Mombelli. The work was performed in 1812 at the Teatro Valle, Rome, with Domenico as Demetrius, Ester as Lisinga and Anna

as Siveno. For some years Mombelli held the copyright of *Demetrio e Polibio* and performed in it at the Teatro Carcano, Milan (1813) and in other cities. Castil-Blaze reports that he sang in Florence at over 70 years of age. He was one of the best 'serious' tenors of the Classical period in Italy, perhaps second only to Giacomo Davide: in 1816 he was described by Duke Cesarini Sforza as incomparable 'nelle parti forti e vibrate'. By then his voice was in decline and he turned increasingly to teaching, first in Florence and then in Bologna. An engraving of his profile was printed in about 1790.

ES (R. Celletti); *GSL*; *MGG* ('Gesangskunst', pl.79; H. J. Moser)
J. Rosselli: *The Opera Industry in Italy from Cimarosa to Verdi* (Cambridge, 1984)   ELIZABETH FORBES, COLIN TIMMS

Mombelli, Ester (*b* Bologna, 1794; *d* 1825 or later). Italian mezzo-soprano. A daughter of the tenor Domenico Mombelli, she sang with the family opera company, creating Lisinga in Rossini's *Demetrio e Polibio* at the Teatro Valle, Rome (1812). She also created the title role of Donizetti's *Zoraide di Granata* at the Teatro Argentina, Rome (1822), and Gilda in the same composer's *L'ajo nell'imbarazzo* at the Teatro Valle (1824). In 1825 at the Théâtre Italien, Paris, she sang Madama Cortese in the first performance of Rossini's *Il viaggio a Reims*. A noted exponent of the role of Cenerentola, she sang soprano as well as contralto parts.   ELIZABETH FORBES

Monaco. For discussion of opera in Monaco *see* MONTE CARLO. Monaco is also the German name for MUNICH.

Mona Lisa. Opera in two acts, prologue and epilogue by MAX VON SCHILLINGS to a libretto by Beatrice Dovsky; Stuttgart, Kleines Haus, 26 September 1915.

The central action takes place in Florence at the end of the 15th century but is framed by a prologue and epilogue set in contemporary times. In these the protagonists of the drama are represented as a honeymoon couple, the Stranger (baritone) and the Wife (soprano), who are guided around a Florentine palace by a Lay brother (tenor). The Lay brother begins to narrate the sinister story of Mona Lisa, whose husband and lover experienced a terrible death in that very building. The stage darkens and we are transported back to the 15th century.

The second scene opens at Carnival time. Against a background of riotous singing, Mona Lisa (the Wife in the prologue) returns from confession and retires to her chamber. Disturbed by her cold behaviour towards him, her husband, the jewel merchant Francesco del Gioconda (the Stranger in the prologue), looks at her portrait as painted by Leonardo da Vinci and in a wild outburst determines to solve the puzzle of her enigmatic smile. A new guest, Giovanni del Salviati (the Lay brother in the prologue), appears. He has been instructed by the Pope to obtain a valuable pearl which is kept locked in Francesco's large jewellery cupboard. Francesco opens the cupboard and is ecstatic at the sight of his jewels. Mona Lisa returns and immediately recognizes Giovanni as her former lover. When Francesco and the other guests have left the room, Giovanni implores Mona Lisa to leave her husband and elope with him the next day. Their love duet is interrupted by the sudden reappearance of Francesco. Deeply suspicious, he has locked the gates of the house and has overheard their conversation. Giovanni hides in

Francesco's jewellery cupboard, but Francesco knows he is there and locks the cupboard door, throwing the only set of keys into the Arno. While Giovanni is suffocating, Francesco overpowers the fainting Mona Lisa.

Act 2 opens the next morning as Mona Lisa bemoans that she was unable to save her lover. As her despair rises to a passionate climax, Dionora (soprano), Francesco's daughter from his first marriage, enters with the jewellery cupboard keys which had accidentally fallen into her boat. Mona Lisa impatiently snatches the keys from her. Francesco appears and seeing the keys in his wife's hands angrily rushes towards the cupboard. As he opens it, Mona Lisa pushes him inside and locks the door. Leaving her husband to suffer the same fate as her lover, Mona Lisa breaks out into a triumphant solo that culminates in delirious laughter.

After a short symphonic intermezzo punctuated by ominous timpani rolls, the epilogue begins. The Lay brother has finished his story. Deeply moved by the narrative, the Wife gives him a donation towards a Mass for the spiritual salvation of Mona Lisa. As she and her husband leave the palace, the Wife throws a bunch of irises to the floor. The Lay brother looks at her again and becomes terrified when he sees her enigmatic smile.

Schillings's final and most successful opera marks a notable departure from the composer's earlier works in its absorption of expressionistic elements inherited from Richard Strauss's *Salome* and *Elektra* as well as the potent influence of Italian *verismo*. Although both the scenario and the thematic material of the opera are somewhat insubstantial, its deliberate sensationalism initially attracted much attention and by 1925 the work had received over a thousand performances in theatres throughout Germany and the rest of Europe. Since World War II, however, the opera has been revived very infrequently. ERIK LEVI

Monanni, Angelo [Angiolo] ['Manzoletto'] (*b* *c*1740; *d* after 1796). Italian contralto castrato. His nickname 'Manzoletto' came from the castrato Manzuoli, who was perhaps his teacher and guided the beginnings of his operatic career, which ran from the mid-1750s to the mid-1790s. He was one of the most respected secondi uomi in *opera seria* of his time, while apparently lacking some quality essential for rising to the primo level.

DENNIS LIBBY

Monari, Clemente (*b* Bologna, ?*c*1660; *d* ?Forlì, in or after 1729). Italian composer. He began his career as a violinist in the service of Marquis Guido Rangoni of Modena. By 1692 he was employed by Duke Anton Ulrich at Brunswick, where three of his operas were given. From 1703 to at least 1706 he was *maestro di cappella* of Reggio Emilia cathedral, and he held a similar post at Forlì cathedral from 1713 to 1729. His only surviving opera, *Il Pirro*, generally thought to have been staged in Venice, may instead have been given in Bologna in 1719, along with music by other composers. Of some interest among his oratorios is *Il fasto depresso* (1692), which alludes to the political and dynastic ties of the Este family.

Clemente Monari may have been related to the composer and organist Bartolomeo Monari ('Monarino'; *c*1654–*c*1707), whose only opera *Catone il giovane* (now lost), to a libretto by G. B. Neri, was performed at the Teatro Formagliari, Bologna.

dm – *dramma per musica*

Gl'amori innocenti (pastorale), Brunswick, 1692
La Libussa (dm), Brunswick, 1692
Il Muzio Scevola (dm, N. Minato), Brunswick, 1692
L'Aretusa (op pastorale, P. d'Averara), Milan, 1703
L'amazone corsara (dm, G. C. Corradi), Milan, 1704
Il Teuzzone [Acts 2, 3] (dm, A. Zeno), Milan, 1706 [Act 1 by P. Magni]
L'Atalanta (drama pastorale, Zeno), Modena, carn. 1710
I rivali generosi [Act 1] (dm, 3, Zeno), Reggio Emilia, Pubblico, April 1710 [Act 2 by Pistocchi, Act 3 by Capelli]
Il Pirro [Act 1] (dm, Zeno), Venice or Bologna, 1719, *D-SHsk* [Act 2 by ?Fiorè, Act 3 by ?Caldara]

Arias, some probably from Il Teuzzone, *E-Mn*

SERGIO DURANTE, ELVIDIO SURIAN

Moncayo García, José Pablo (*b* Guadalajara, 29 June 1912; *d* Mexico City, 16 June 1958). Mexican composer. After studying the piano at the Mexico City National Conservatory, he was active as a pianist and a conductor, becoming subdirector of the Orquesta Sinfónica de México in 1945 (until 1949). In 1941 Chávez conducted the première of his lively, folkloric *Huapango*, the orchestral piece on which his worldwide reputation now rests. Moncayo García himself conducted the première of his one-act opera in three scenes, *La mulata de Córdoba*, at the Palacio de Bellas Artes, Mexico City, on 23 October 1948 (vocal score published, Mexico City, 1948). Composed to a libretto by two foremost Mexican playwrights, Xavier Villaurrutia (1903–50) and Agustín Lazo (1898–1971), this is a reworking of the Mexican legend of the black enchantress who, when called before the Inquisition in late colonial times, vanished in a puff of smoke.

See also MULATA DE CÓRDOBA, LA.

E. Olavarría y Ferrari: *Reseña histórica del teatro en México* (Mexico City, 2/1895, 3/1961), v, 3580, 3602–3

ROBERT STEVENSON

Mönchengladbach. Town in western Germany, in North Rhine-Westphalia, which mounts productions jointly with KREFELD.

Monckton, (John) Lionel (Alexander) (*b* London, 18 Dec 1861; *d* London, 15 Feb 1924). English composer. He studied at Oxford, where he did much acting and wrote music for university productions. He took up law as a career and was called to the Bar in 1885. After writing dramatic and musical criticism for the *Pall Mall Gazette* he joined the *Daily Telegraph* as assistant to Clement Scott and Joseph Bennett. A song submitted to the impresario George Edwardes was used in the burlesque *Cinder-Ellen up too Late* (1891), and he continued to contribute numbers to Edwardes's productions, notably for Ivan Caryll's scores for the Gaiety Theatre; it was to Monckton's interpolations that these owed much of their success. The first work predominantly his own was *A Country Girl* (1902), and he went on to write music for the most successful Edwardian musical shows, including *Our Miss Gibbs* (with Caryll, 1909), *The Arcadians* (with Talbot, 1909) and *The Quaker Girl* (1910). Though he sought with some success to emulate Sullivan, it was for his gay and striking melodies that he stood out among the British musical theatre composers of the time. He was married to the soubrette Gertie Millar, for whom he wrote some of his best numbers, including 'Keep off the Grass' (*The Toreador*, 1901), 'Moonstruck' (*Our Miss Gibbs*) and 'Chalk Farm to Camberwell Green' (*Bric-à-brac*, 1915).

stage works all produced in London and published there in vocal
score at time of original production; musical plays unless otherwise
stated

The Shop Girl (musical farce, 2, H. J. W. Dam), Gaiety, 24 Nov
1894, collab. I. Caryll; The Circus Girl (2, J. T. Tanner, W. Pal-
ings [W. Pallant], H. Greenbank and A. Ross), Gaiety, 5 Dec
1896, collab. Caryll; A Runaway Girl (2, S. Hicks, H. Nicholls, A.
Hopwood and H. Greenbank), Gaiety, 21 May 1898, collab.
Caryll; The Messenger Boy (2, Tanner, A. Murray, Ross and P.
Greenbank), Gaiety, 3 Feb 1900, collab. Caryll; The Toreador (2,
Tanner, Nicholls, Ross and P. Greenbank), Gaiety, 17 June 1901,
collab. Caryll; A Country Girl (2, Tanner, Ross and P. Greenbank), Daly's, 18 Jan 1902, collab. P. A. Rubens

The Orchid (2, Tanner, Ross and P. Greenbank), Gaiety, 28 Oct
1903, collab. Caryll; The Cingalee (2, Tanner, Ross and P. Greenbank), Daly's, 5 March 1904, collab. Rubens; The Spring Chicken
(2, G. Grossmith, Ross and P. Greenbank, after A. Jaime and
Duval: Le coquin de printemps), Gaiety, 30 May 1905, collab.
Caryll; The New Aladdin (musical extravaganza, 2, Tanner and
W. H. Risque), Gaiety, 29 Sept 1906, collab. Caryll and F. E.
Tours; The Girls of Gottenberg (2, Grossmith, L. E. Berman, Ross
and B. Hood), Gaiety, 15 May 1907, collab. Caryll

Our Miss Gibbs (2, Tanner, Ross and P. Greenbank), Gaiety, 23 Jan
1909, collab. Caryll; The Arcadians (3, M. Ambient, A. M.
Thompson and A. Wimperis), Shaftesbury, 28 April 1909, collab.
H. Talbot; The Quaker Girl (3, Tanner, Ross and P. Greenbank),
Adelphi, 5 Nov 1910; The Mousmé (3, Thompson, R.
Courtneidge, Wimperis and P. Greenbank), Shaftesbury, 9 Sept
1911, collab. Talbot; The Dancing Mistress (3, Tanner, Ross and
P. Greenbank), Adelphi, 19 Oct 1912; The Boy (musical comedy,
2, F. Thompson, Ross and P. Greenbank, after A. W. Pinero: The
Magistrate), Adelphi, 14 Sept 1917, collab. Talbot

Music for revues Bric-à-brac, 1915; We're all in it, 1916; Airs and
Graces, 1917; and for many other musical shows

*

GänzlBMT
G. Hughes: Composers of Operetta (London, 1962)
R. Traubner: Operetta: a Theatrical History (New York, 1983)
ANDREW LAMB

Moncrieff, Gladys (b Bundaberg, Queensland, 13 April
1892; d Gold Coast, Queensland, 8 Feb 1976).
Australian soprano. She toured as a child performer in
North Queensland before successfully auditioning with
the J. C. Williamson management for professional training and, from 1914, sang principal roles in Gilbert and
Sullivan and other musical comedy works. After a South
African tour with the company she achieved considerable success as Teresa in Harold Fraser-Simson's The
Maid of the Mountains (1921, Melbourne), eventually
playing the role an estimated 2800 times. Contemporary
critics spoke of the purity, richness, power and wide
range of her voice, her conviction of style and clear
enunciation. She had a considerable London success in
Lehár's Die blaue Mazur (1927). Her subsequent
Australian appearances included two Australian
musicals, Collitt's Inn and The Cedar Tree, many
revivals of operettas and musical comedies and concert
tours up to 1959. She became one of the most consistently successful and affectionately regarded
performers in Australia. Her autobiography, My Life of
Song, written with Lillian Palmer, was published in
Adelaide in 1971. ROGER COVELL

Moncrif, François-Augustin Paradis de (b Paris, 1687; d
Paris, 13 Oct 1770). French librettist and historian. He
was elected to the Académie Française in 1733 and
appointed lecteur to Queen Maria Leszczyńska around
1745. He is best known for Les chats (1727), an elegant
and witty history of the cat since ancient Egyptian times.
As a librettist Moncrif worked exclusively on a small
scale, limiting himself to the opéra-ballet, with its
separate entrées, and to the independent acte de ballet.

A taste for exoticism, first explored in his 'contes in-
diens' Les avantures de Zéloïde et d'Amanzarifdine
(1715), is also evident in the librettos. One entrée of
L'empire de l'Amour ('Les génies du feu') inhabits the
enchanted world of Middle Eastern mythology, still a
fairly unusual choice in 1733 but soon to become fashionable; his subsequent librettos, notably Zélindor, roi
des silphes and Les génies tutélaires, mainly adopt
Arabian or Asiatic settings. Most were moderately
successful; Zélindor was revived five times up to 1766
and considered by Marmontel a model of its genre.
Ismène and Almasis were written for Mme de
Pompadour's Théâtre des Petits Cabinets.

L'empire de l'Amour (opéra-ballet), Brassac, 1733; Zélindor, roi des
silphes (acte de ballet), Rebel and Francoeur, 1745; Le trophée
(divertissement), Rebel and Francoeur, 1745; Ismène (pastorale-
héroïque), Rebel and Francoeur, 1747; Almasis (acte de ballet),
Royer, 1748; Les génies tutélaires (divertissement), Rebel and
Francoeur, 1751; La sybille (acte de ballet), Dauvergne, 1753;
Erosine (pastorale-héroïque), P.-M. Berton, 1766

J. F. Marmontel: Le poétique françoise (Paris, 1763)
A. Augustin-Thierry: Trois amuseurs d'autrefois: Paradis de
Moncrif, Carmontelle, Ch. Collé (Paris, 1924)
E. P. Shaw: François-Augustin Paradis de Moncrif, 1687–1770
(New York, 1958) GRAHAM SADLER

*

Mond, Der ('The Moon'). Kleines Welttheater in one
act by CARL ORFF after the fairy-tale by Jacob Ludwig
and Wilhelm Carl GRIMM; Munich, Staatsoper, 5
February 1939.

The stage is divided into three sections: the uppermost
part represents heaven, the lowest part the underworld
and in between there is the earth. The earth is divided
into two countries, each containing an oak tree and a
public house. Between the halves is a pulpit for the
Narrator (high tenor). He recounts a tale about a
country that was once in complete darkness. Four
Rascals (tenor, two baritones and bass) from this dark
country appear and move to the neighbouring country
where the moon hangs above an oak tree. This moon
has been bought by the landlord Schultheiss (spoken
role) for three thalers and its power is maintained by the
use of additional oil. The Rascals decide to steal the
moon and, to the astonishment of the previous owner,
take it back to their own country. Time passes and the
Rascals become old men. Realizing that their lifespan is
at an end, they each request that a part of the moon
should go with them to their graves. The request is
granted and the moon is accordingly cut up into four
quarters. When the last of the men has died, the country
is once again plunged into darkness.

In the underworld, the dead Rascals creep out of their
coffins and glue the parts of the moon together. Soon the
resulting light disturbs the peace of the dead, causing the
inhabitants to behave as if on earth. The noise is so
tumultuous that it extends to heaven, forcing Petrus
(bass) to descend to the underworld to investigate the
proceedings. At first, Petrus is impressed with the power
of the moon and the light it has generated, but eventually he realizes that the normal order of the world is
beginning to disintegrate. He persuades the inhabitants
of the underworld to restore peace. Petrus returns to
heaven and takes with him the moon which now hangs
on the stars. There is peace once again in the underworld, but on earth a new constellation lights up the
sky.

Der Mond was Orff's first staged opera and its
musical language follows the direct and rhythmic style

*'Il mondo della luna':
engraving from Carlo
Goldoni's 'Opere teatrali'
(Venice: Zatta, 1788–95)*

of *Carmina burana*. Although the work enjoyed considerable success during the Nazi era, its message could be interpreted as a veiled attack upon Fascism since it argues that everyone has the right to share the benefits of nature and that they are not simply for the privileged few. ERIK LEVI

Mondo della luna, Il ('The World on the Moon'). Libretto by CARLO GOLDONI, first set by Baldassare Galuppi (1750, Venice).

A false astronomer, Ecclitico, is looking with his students at the moon through a telescope mounted on the balcony of his house. He decides to play a joke on the foolish and gullible Bonafede by telling him that with his powerful telescope he can see not only a world on the moon but can also detect houses, people and women undressing as they go to bed. At the telescope, Bonafede reports seeing a young woman caressing an old man, a husband beating his wife to punish her for infidelity, and a woman being led by the nose by her lover. Pleased that Ecclitico has made it possible for him to see such a world, Bonafede gives him money; but Ecclitico would prefer to have Bonafede's daughter, Clarice, in marriage.

Ernesto loves Bonafede's other daughter, Flaminia; he and his servant Cecco, interested in Bonafede's maid Lisetta, conspire with Ecclitico to take the women away from Bonafede's strict control by marrying them. Clarice and Flaminia are anxious to escape from the stifling atmosphere of their father's home, hoping their future husbands will be too concerned with their own business to care about their wives' social activities.

Ecclitico tells Bonafede that he has been invited to visit the emperor of the moon. Bonafede insists on going with him and drinks a potion which he believes will transport him there; he wakes in a flower-bed in Ecclitico's garden where everything is disguised to give the effect of the lunar environment. Pages bring him special clothes for his encounter with the emperor – Cecco in disguise. Bonafede is delighted: everyone sings,

dances and is happy in this world without jealousy or malice.

Lisetta, brought into the garden blindfolded, is told that she is to marry the emperor; at first incredulous, she soon accepts the idea of marrying into royalty and is crowned in the finale to Act 2. Clarice and Flaminia arrive in a flying machine. Through Cecco's manipulations, Ecclitico and Ernesto each manage to obtain his beloved in marriage, with Bonafede's blessing – until he discovers he has been duped.

Goldoni's text is a clever satire on contemporary human relationships and customs: the gullibility and ignorance of human beings; the institution of marriage; the superiority and arrogance that come with power; and human pretension and falsehood. Its roots are in the *commedia dell'arte*, especially the 1684 *farsa* by Nolant de Fatonville, *Arlecchino, imperatore nella luna*, given by the Italian comedians in Paris.

Goldoni's libretto was set by a number of composers, including Avondano (1765, Lisbon), Astarita (1775, Venice), Haydn (1777, Eszterháza), Neri Bondi (1790, Florence) and Portugal (1791, Lisbon, as *O lunático iludido*). Several of these settings use a revised text by an unknown author, in which the Act 2 finale is extended by the transference of material from Act 3. Paisiello dealt with the topic four times: as *La luna abitata* (1768, Naples), to a text by G. B. Lorenzi including Neapolitan characters; as *Il credulo deluso* (1774, Naples) after Goldoni's libretto; as a one-act *festa teatrale* (1783, Kammeniy Ostrov); and as a shortened two-act version of *Il credulo deluso* (1783, Naples) under the title *Il mondo della luna* with textual alterations by Coltellini.

For a list of settings *see* GOLDONI, CARLO.

GORDANA LAZAREVICH

Mondo della luna, Il (i) ('The World on the Moon'). *Dramma giocoso* in three acts by BALDASSARE GALUPPI to a libretto by CARLO GOLDONI (*see* MONDO DELLA LUNA, IL above); Venice, Teatro S Moisè, 29 January 1750.

Galuppi was the first to set Goldoni's libretto. In many ways *Il mondo della luna* is typical of Galuppi's early *drammi giocosi*, focussed on the deception of an egotistical but naive old man, in this case Bonafede (bass). The music is clear and refined with expressiveness achieved through melodic and textural change rather than harmonic complexity – a brief shift of mode, a short digression to a secondary key area, or an unexpected cadential level are the principal harmonic surprises. The words are allowed to shape the musical form, particularly in the finales to the first two acts. Bonafede's aria (Act 1.iii) describing various lunar wonders is distinctive for its comic virtuosity and characterization: his astonishment at the lunar lifestyle is shown in short, forceful melodic figures and simple, often cadential harmonic support. The role of Ernesto (soprano), in love with Bonafede's daughter Flaminia (soprano), was written for Berenice Penni (it was subsequently sung by castratos as well as women). Bonafede's maid Lisetta is a soprano, his daughter Clarice a contralto; the false astronomer Ecclitico and Ernesto's servant Cecco are both bass roles.   DALE E. MONSON

Mondo della luna, Il (ii) ('The World on the Moon'). *Dramma giocoso* in three acts by JOSEPH HAYDN to a libretto by CARLO GOLDONI (*see* MONDO DELLA LUNA, IL above); Eszterháza, first known performance, 3 August 1777, but possibly July 1777.

Ecclitico *a false astrologer*	tenor
Ernesto *a cavalier*	alto castrato
Buonafede *a protective father*	baritone
Clarice ⎫ *Buonafede's daughters*	soprano
Flaminia ⎭	soprano
Lisetta *Buonafede's maidservant*	contralto
Cecco *Ernesto's servant*	tenor

Pupils of Ecclitico, gentlemen, dancers, pages, servants and soldiers

Setting Italy in the 18th century

Il mondo della luna, the first opera of Haydn's to be staged following the institution of a regular opera season at Eszterháza in 1776, was the last of the three Goldoni librettos that he set. The other two were *Lo speziale* (1768) and *Le pescatrici* (1770). The text of Haydn's opera corresponds to Goldoni's libretto up to the first two lines of Act 2 scene xiv, but beginning with the Act 2 finale it follows that of Astarita's setting (1775, Venice) with the exception of the closing chorus, whose origin is unknown.

Haydn's opera has a complicated genesis; the autograph materials survive in three partial versions. Early fragments show the parts of Ecclitico, Ernesto and Lisetta notated in alto, tenor and soprano clefs, respectively; but Ecclitico's and Ernesto's vocal ranges were later switched, and Lisetta's part was lowered. Ernesto (sung by Pietro Gherardi) is the last castrato role Haydn wrote before his ill-fated *L'anima del filosofo* (1791). Buonafede's role lies in a high baritone range, having been tailored to the voice of Benedetto Bianchi. Catharina Poschwa (or Poschva; Clarice) and Maria Anna Puttler (Flaminia), like Bianchi, had been newly engaged in 1776. Leopold Dichtler (Cecco) sang in some 60 operas at Eszterháza between 1766 and 1788, and occasionally augmented his meagre salary by copying music. The exact date of the first performance is unknown: receipts from the printer of the libretto are dated 28 June 1777; the work was given in honour of the marriage on 3 August 1777 of Prince Nikolaus Esterházy's second son, Count Nikolaus, and Countess Maria Anna Wiessenwolf. According to the libretto, Ecclitico was sung by Guglielmo Jermoli (who also took the role in Astarita's version) and Lisetta by his wife, Maria, but the couple apparently left the prince's service at the end of July. Whether they participated in the wedding performance is unclear. Little is known of other stagings in the 18th century. In the 20th century *Il mondo della luna* has been revived at Schwerin (1932), at the Holland Festival (1959, conducted by Giulini), in London at the Camden Festival (1960) and at Schleswig (1984).

ACT 1.i *A terrace on top of Ecclitico's house* Ecclitico devises a plan to trick Buonafede into allowing Flaminia, Clarice and Lisetta to marry the lovers of their choice: Ernesto, Ecclitico and Cecco, respectively. In a lengthy tripartite intermezzo-recitative-aria sequence, Ecclitico presents three pantomimes representative of life on the moon, which the gullible Buonafede observes through the false astrologer's telescope. Buonafede's longing for the moon is articulated in the tonal ascent from D major to E♭ major, the tonal centre of Ecclitico's aria, 'Un poco di denaro', in which he solicits the help of Ernesto and Cecco in carrying out his scheme.

1.ii *A room in Buonafede's house* Clarice and Flaminia express their desire to marry. Flaminia's coloratura aria in the heroic key of C major, 'Ragion nell'alma siede', in the same *seria* style as Rezia's 'Or vicina a te, mio cuore' (*L'incontro improvviso*, 1775), quickly establishes her as Ernesto's counterpart. The wilful and less obedient daughter, Clarice, openly confronts authority in her first aria sung to Buonafede ('Son fanciulla da marito'). Ecclitico persuades Buonafede to swallow 'an elixir', actually a sleeping potion, which will transport him to the 'world of the moon'. Imaginative accompanied recitative underscores this event. Since Goldoni excluded *seria* characters from the predominantly comic domain of finales, only Clarice and Lisetta witness Buonafede's supposed ascent to the moon, which they interpret as the old man's demise. His hallucinatory journey, depicted in the assonance and alliteration of Goldoni's text ('Vado, vado, volo, volo'), is reflected in Haydn's evocative 'flight' music.

ACT 2 *A delightful garden decorated to look like the world of the moon* On awaking in Ecclitico's garden, Buonafede beholds the moon's many beauties; Haydn depicts its exotic character in several pastoral ballet numbers. Such extended use of instrumental music is found in no other Italian opera by Haydn. Social positions are now reversed: Cecco, disguised as the emperor of the moon, joins Ernesto in teasing Buonafede. Ernesto, pretending to be Hesperus, the evening star, incites Buonafede's curiosity. (In this scene the original Ernesto wore the remodelled costume of Orpheus from the production of Gluck's opera at Eszterháza the previous year.) But the old man remains blissful at being on the moon, as is evident in 'Che mondo amabile', in which he dances and imitates birdcalls.

Lisetta is then brought to the lunar world, followed by Clarice and Flaminia. Now that everyone is assembled, Ecclitico proceeds with his plan. In the finale ('Al comando tuo lunatico') Cecco crowns Lisetta empress. This mock coronation was the only event of Goldoni's Act 2 finale, but the unknown author of Astarita's revisions lengthened the action. The revised text contains frequent comic interjections of nonsense language and several events from Goldoni's Act 3, including the betrothal of Buonafede's daughters and the old man's discovery of the hoax. With this additional action, the second act finale is able to accommodate extended musical development. The serious characters, Flaminia and Ernesto, also participate in the comic action, an advance in finale construction since the mid-century.

ACT 3 *A room in Ecclitico's house* Goldoni's third act is much eviscerated by the additions made to the second act finale. In the end, Buonafede consents to the marriages. Clarice and Ecclitico sing of their love in a beautiful two-tempo duet, 'Un certo ruscelletto', and the opera concludes with a chorus of reconciliation ('Dal mondo della luna').

*   *   *

Il mondo della luna was pillaged for several self-borrowings. The overture circulated widely in an altered version as the first movement of Haydn's Symphony no.63 (*La Roxelane*); the short intermezzo at the beginning of Act 2 scene xi was rearranged as the Andante of *La vera costanza* published by Artaria in a set of six overtures (Vienna, 1782–3); the same intermezzo appeared, along with several other selections from Act 2, in five trios (1784; HIV:6*–8* and 10*–11*); and Ernesto's aria, 'Qualche volta non fa male', with alternating major-minor passages, was adapted as the Benedictus of the 'Mariazell Mass' (1782).

It has often been suggested that harmony and tonality are used to link dramatic events across the opera. The overture opens in C major and closes in G minor, leading to a choral introduction in E♭ major; here the three flats may symbolize the 'triforme dea' ('threefold goddess') addressed by Ecclitico's students in the opening chorus. A similar harmonic path is followed near the end of the first act: as Buonafede contemplates the elixir, an accompanied recitative begins in C major and closes on a G minor chord preceding a move to the finale's key of E♭ major. But it is difficult to assess the significance of such associations given the many revisions and transpositions the music underwent because of cast changes.

CARYL CLARK

Mondonville, Jean-Joseph Cassanéa de (*b* Narbonne, bap. 25 Dec 1711; *d* Belleville, 8 Oct 1772). French composer. Born into an impoverished but aristocratic Languedoc family, Mondonville went to Paris about 1733, when he published the first of five sets of instrumental compositions. He quickly established a reputation as a composer and violinist. This, coupled with a social accomplishment that won him powerful court allies including Mme de Pompadour, helped him secure a succession of posts in the royal chapel, including that of *intendant*. At the Concert Spirituel, of which he eventually became director, many of his compositions became such firm favourites that in popular esteem he was often ranked alongside or even above Rameau.

Mondonville's operatic career began badly with the failure of *Isbé* (1742). By contrast, *Le carnaval du Parnasse*, produced seven years later, was an overwhelming success. Its first run included 37 consecutive performances plus a further 24 during the following 12 months. This triumph doubtless contributed to his being chosen to champion the French cause during the Querelle des Bouffons: *Titon et l'Aurore* (1753), another triumph, scored an important psychological

victory for the supporters of the indigenous style of opera. For *Daphnis et Alcimadure* the following year he provided both music and libretto; this last, as the subtitle 'pastorale languedocienne' suggests, was written in the dialect of his native province. The engraved score supplies a sporadic 'translation' beneath the underlay. The main roles were all taken by singers originating from southern France – Marie Fel, Pierre Jélyotte and La Tour.

In 1765 Mondonville took the unprecedented step of resetting one of Philippe Quinault's librettos: his version of *Thésée* – the original of which had been immortalized in the previous century by Lully, whose setting was still occasionally revived (albeit much modified) – appeared before the court at Fontainebleau. While some of the new music was admired, Mondonville's recitative proved unacceptable as a substitute for Lully's, which many spectators would have known almost by heart. When the work appeared two years later at the Paris Opéra, it was savaged: the composer was humiliated with cries of 'taisez-vous, Mondonville' – a pun on the work's title – and by popular demand his *Thésée* was replaced by Lully's original after only four performances.

At a time of great diversity and change in French musical tastes, Mondonville's popularity derived largely from his ability to please most of the people much of the time. He clearly aimed to divert and entertain more than to move his audience, and with the exception of *Thésée*, he avoided the lofty and demanding *tragédie* in favour of the lighter *pastorale* and *opéra-ballet*. His operas are by no means lacking in scenes of pathos and passion, which benefit from a richly expressive harmonic vocabulary and imaginative orchestration; but such scenes are seldom prolonged and are often contrasted with others of a lighter character. Although his inclination was towards an up-to-date, attractive if sometimes rather empty italianate idiom, he was aware of the need to court his more conservative listeners. Thus brilliant coloratura *ariettes* rub shoulders with popular vaudeville-like melodies; dramatic orchestral movements that would not sound out of place in the latest German symphony are juxtaposed with simple French-style airs that could have been written by Lully's successors 50 years earlier. Yet although his operas seldom exceed the sum of their parts, the parts themselves are always competently written and are seldom dull.

One idiosyncrasy of Mondonville's simple recitative is its avoidance of the customary fluctuating time signatures; instead it is notated almost throughout in simple triple time. As a result, it lacks the flexibility and nuance of traditional French recitative, though it does have a more consistently song-like character.

first performed at the Paris Opéra (Académie Royale de Musique) unless otherwise stated

Isbé (pastorale-héroïque, prol., 5, Marquis H.-F. de La Rivière), 10 April 1742; pubd as op.6 (Paris, c1742)

Bacchus et Erigone (acte de ballet, 1, C.-A. Le Clerc de la Bruère), Versailles, 1747; pubd as part of *Les fêtes de Paphos* (Paris, 1758) of which it then formed part

Le carnaval du Parnasse (ballet-héroïque, prol., 3, L. Fuzelier), 23 Sept 1749; pubd as op.7 (Paris, c1749)

Vénus et Adonis (ballet-héroïque, 1, J. B. Collet de Messine), Bellevue, 27 April 1752; pubd as part of *Les fêtes de Paphos* (Paris, 1758) of which it then formed part; lib. (Paris, c1752)

Titon et l'Aurore (pastorale-héroïque, prol., 3, Abbé de La Marre with addns by C.-H. de F. de Voisenon; prol. by A. H. de Lamotte), 9 Jan 1753; pubd as op.8 (Paris, c1753/R1972)

Daphnis et Alcimadure (pastorale languedocienne, prol. 'Les jeux floraux', Voisenon; 3, Mondonville), Fontainebleau, 29 Oct

431

1754; pubd as op.9 (Paris, 1754/*R c*1981), ed. R. Blanchard (Paris, 1974)

Les fêtes de Paphos (opéra-ballet, 3 entrées: 'Vénus et Adonis', Collet de Messine; 'Bacchus et Erigone', La Bruère; 'L'Amour et Psyché', Voisenon), 9 May 1758; pubd as op.10 (Paris, 1758)

Thésée (tragédie, 5, P. Quinault), Fontainebleau, 7 Nov 1765; lib. (Paris, 1765)

Les projets de l'Amour (opéra-ballet, 3 entrées: 'L'Hymen et l'Amour', 'Jupiter et Calisto', 'Mirzele'; Voisenon), Versailles, 29 May 1771

*

C. Collé: *Journal et mémoires ... sur les hommes de lettres, les ouvrages dramatiques et les événements les plus mémorables du règne de Louis XV, 1748–1772*, ed. H. Bonhomme (Paris, 1868)

M. Tourneux, ed.: *Correspondance littéraire, philosophique et critique par Grimm, Diderot, Raynal, Meister, etc.* (Paris, 1877–82)

E. Borrel: 'L'interprétation de l'ancien récitatif français', *RdM*, xii (1931), 13–21

R. Machard: *Jean-Joseph Cassanéa de Mondonville: virtuose, compositeur et chef d'orchestre* (Béziers, 1980)

GRAHAM SADLER

Monelli, Raffaele (*b* Fermo, 5 March 1782; *d* S Benedetto del Tronto, Adria, 14 Sept 1859). Italian tenor. He studied in Fermo, making his début in 1808. He took part in two Rossini premières: as Duke Bertrando in *L'inganno felice* and as Dorvil in *La scala di seta*, both in 1812 at the Teatro S Moisè, Venice.

His brother Savino Monelli (*b* Fermo, 9 May 1784; *d* Fermo, 5 June 1836) was also a tenor and studied in Fermo. In 1817 he created roles in Rossini's *La gazza ladra* (Giannetto) at La Scala and *Adelaide di Borgogna* (Adelberto) at the Teatro Argentina, Rome. He sang Don Ramiro in the first performance of Donizetti's *Chiara e Serafina* (1822) at La Scala and Enrico at the première of Donizetti's *L'ajo nell'imbarazzo* (1824) at the Teatro Valle, Rome.   ELIZABETH FORBES

Moneta, Giuseppe (*b* Florence, 1754; *d* Florence, 17 Sept 1806). Italian composer. After composing a *farsa* for four voices (its title is unknown), he had, for a young amateur, a remarkable outburst of activity in 1779: his oratorio *Il figliuol prodigo* was given at S Giovannino dei Padri Scolopi on 20 February; his comic opera *I pastori delle Alpi* was produced at the Teatro di Borgo Ognissanti on 1 June; and he directed, from the first harpsichord, Paisiello's *Il tamburo notturno* at the same theatre on 9 September. For the next 20 years he composed a succession of operas, intermezzos and melodramas, as well as sacred and instrumental music. Judging by local reviews, his music was well liked by the Florentines. He won various titles, most importantly *maestro di cappella onorario e compositore* of the courts of Tuscany (1791) and (later) Parma.

Comic genres made up the majority of Moneta's dramatic compositions. He was favoured by the Tuscan court as a composer of ceremonial operas and cantatas, such as *L'Urano*, a cantata for the wedding of Archduke Francesco in 1788. But his most original contribution was to the development in Italy of *melologo* ('melodrama'), a new dramatic form which had been cultivated in France and Germany in the 1770s. Moneta set two such dramas in the 1780s: first *Il Meleagro* (1785), with text by Camillo Federici, who acknowledged his desire to emulate Rousseau's *Pygmalion* of 1770; and second *La vendetta di Medea* (1787).

Like the musical culture of Tuscany in general in his time, Moneta's operas remained largely unknown

beyond the region's borders and the related principalities of northern Italy. The most successful of his comic operas was *Il capitano Tenaglia*, performed in Livorno and Brescia in Carnival 1784, and Geneva in 1786. His composing apparently ceased in 1799, probably because of the French occupation and rule (1799–1814) during which his patron, Grand Duke Ferdinand III, retreated to Vienna. Moneta was among the composers, educators and musicians who formed in 1801 the Collegio di Professori, devoted to raising music in Florence to its 'greatest perfection', promoting the study of music and increasing the number of scholars and 'dilettantes'. In 1806 he was listed among the 'interessati', or financial backers, of the Teatro degl'Intrepidi. Moneta's obituary in the *Gazzetta toscana* (1806, no.40) speaks of the 'universal appreciation and praise' accorded his music.

performed in Florence unless otherwise stated

I pastori delle Alpi (dg, 2, A. Pasquali Valli), Borgo Ognissanti, 1 June 1779

Angelica e Medoro (serenata, 2 pts, P. Metastasio), Porta Rossa, 19 March 1780

La giardiniera accorta (dg, 2), Cocomero, 20 Sept 1781

Il marchese a forza (dg), S Maria, carn. 1783

Il capitan Tenaglia ossia La muta per amore (dg, 2, C. Orcomeno), Livorno, Nuovo Teatro degli Armeni, carn. 1784

Il Meleagro (melodramma, 3, C. Federici), Cocomero, 22 June 1785

Il tutore e la pupilla, ovvero Amor vuol gioventù (int, 2 pts, M. Coltellini), Cocomero, 26 Dec 1785

L'equivoco del nastro (int, 2), Cocomero, carn. 1786

La vendetta di Medea (tragedia lirica, 5, C. Giotti), Intrepidi, 31 Dec 1787

Orfeo negli Elisi (azione teatrale, 1), Intrepidi, 17 May 1788

Il sacrifizio d'Ifigenia (dramma, 1, Giotti), Cocomero, 3 Feb 1789, 1 aria *I-Fm*

La morte di Sansone (tragedia lirica, Giotti), Cocomero, 3 Feb 1789

Le nozze all'inferno (farsa, 2, D. Somigli), Piazza Vecchia, carn. 1791

Il conte Policronio, overo Le bugie hanno le gambe corte (dg, 2, G. Squilloni), Poggio a Caiano, 18 Sept 1791, *Fc*

Le due orfane e i due tutori innamorati (dg, 2), S Maria, 9 July 1792

Oreste (dramma serio in musica, 3, F. Gonella), Pisa, Accademia dei Costanti, spr. 1798, *Fc* (2 copies)

Le varie poi fauste vicende di Flora (azione teatrale, 1, G. de Gamerra), Cocomero, Advent 1799, *Fc*

La poetessa capricciosa amante de' due gemelli (dg, 1), Cocomero, 26 Dec 1799

Revisions of: L. Caruso: La locanda in scompiglio, 1780; G. Sarti: I contratempi, 1781; P. Guglielmi: I due fratelli sciocchi, 1782

M. de Angelis: *La musica del granduca* (Florence, 1978)

R. Zanetti: *La musica italiana nel settecento* (Milan, 1978)

M. de Angelis: *La felicità in Etruria* (Florence, 1990)

——: *Melodramma spettacolo e musica nella Firenze dei Lorena (1750–1800)* (Florence, 1991)

R. L. Weaver and N. W. Weaver: *A Chronology of Music in the Florentine Theater*, ii: *1751–1800* (Warren, MI, 1993)

ROBERT LAMAR WEAVER

Money-Coutts, Francis Burdett (Thomas Nevill) [5th Baron Latymer] (*b* London, 18 Sept 1852; *d* London, 8 June 1923). English poet and librettist. He is best known for his collaboration with the Spanish composer Isaac Albéniz. Born into a family of English bankers, he read law at Cambridge but regarded writing as his career and adopted the pen name 'Mountjoy'. In the early 1890s he became firm friends with Albéniz, then living in London, and offered him a considerable income in exchange for having his librettos set to music. Their first work was the opera *Henry Clifford* (libretto published in Barcelona, 1895, in English and Italian, as *Enrico Clifford*). This success was followed by their most important work, the opera *Pepita Jiménez* (libretto published in Barcelona,

1896, in Italian; Leipzig, 1905, in French), based on the novel by Juan Valera. Money-Coutts's fondest ambition, however, was to create an operatic trilogy based on the *Morte d'Arthur* of Sir Thomas Malory; the libretto for *King Arthur* was published separately (London, 1897), but Albéniz completed only the first opera, *Merlin*; *Lancelot* and *Guenevere* were left incomplete at the composer's death in 1909. Money-Coutts's greatest contribution to music history, however, was his unselfish patronage of Albéniz, which permitted the ailing composer to devote his final years to writing his celebrated work for piano, *Iberia*.

M. Falces Sierra: *Estudio documental de la obra vocal inglesa de Isaac Albéniz: análisis lingüístico-musical de sus canciones de concierto sobre poemas de Francis Money Coutts* (diss., U. of Granada, 1991)
W. A. Clark: *Spanish Music with a Universal Accent: Isaac Albéniz's Opera 'Pepita Jiménez'* (diss., U. of California, Los Angeles, 1992)
——: 'Isaac Albéniz's Faustian Pact: a Study in Patronage', *MQ*, lxxvi/4 (1992)
E. Healey: *Coutts & Co. 1692–1992: the Portrait of a Private Bank* (London, 1992)   WALTER AARON CLARK

Mongini, Pietro (*b* Rome, 29 Oct 1839; *d* Milan, 27 April 1874). Italian tenor. He started his career as a bass, but by 1853 was singing tenor roles at Genoa. In 1855 he made his Paris début at the Théâtre Italien as Edgardo (*Lucia di Lammermoor*), and in 1857 sang at Reggio Emilia in the first performance of Achille Peri's *Vittor Pisani* and in *Anna Bolena*. He first appeared at La Scala in 1858 as Arnold (*Guillaume Tell*), and made his London début in 1859 as Elvino (*La sonnambula*) at Drury Lane, where he also sang Henri in the first London performance of *Les vêpres siciliennes*. In 1860 he sang Manrico at La Scala and Huon (*Oberon*) at Her Majesty's Theatre. He returned to London every year from 1862 to 1873, singing either at Her Majesty's, where his roles included Don Alvaro in the first London performance of *La forza del destino* (1867), or at Covent Garden, where he made his début as Gennaro in *Lucrezia Borgia* (1868). In 1871 he created Radames in *Aida*, at the Cairo Opera House. His heroic voice was not used with much subtlety, but in such roles as Arnold, Manrico and Don Alvaro the sheer brilliance of sound compensated for any lack of artistry.

J. H. Mapleson: *The Mapleson Memoirs* (London, 1888); ed. H. Rosenthal (London, 1966)
C. Gatti: *Il Teatro alla Scala nella storia e nell'arte 1778–1963* (Milan, 1964)   ELIZABETH FORBES

Moniglia, Giovanni Andrea (*b* Florence, 22 March 1624; *d* Florence, 21 Sept 1700). Italian librettist and personal physician to Cardinal Gian Carlo de' Medici. Moniglia, despite lack of appreciation on the part of the academic reformers of the early 18th century, must be reckoned among the most original librettists of the 17th century. His comic librettos, of which the most famous is *Il potestà di Colognole*, better, though incorrectly, known as *La Tancia*, established a genre that continued unbroken into the next century. His own comic operas were frequently revived in Florence as late as 1731 (*La serva nobile*). *Hipermestra* and *Ercole in Tebe* set a standard for the *festa teatrale*. *Il ritorno d'Ulisse* and *Enea in Italia* anticipate in many respects Quinault's librettos for Lully, and the signs of reform are clearly visible in *Il tiranno di Colco*.

His librettos were published under the title *Poesie dramatiche* (3 vols., Florence, 1689–90, 2/1698). The great majority were written for Florence with music by Jacopo Melani and Lorenzo Cattani, but they were also much in demand in Venice and Vienna.

Il potestà di Colognole, J. Melani, 1657 (Buini, 1730); *Scipione in Cartagine*, Melani, 1657; *Il pazzo per forza*, Melani, 1658 (Pagliardi, 1687); *L'Hipermestra* (festa teatrale), Cavalli, 1658; *Il vecchio balordo*, Melani, 1659; *La serva nobile*, Anglesi, 1660; *Ercole in Tebe* (festa teatrale), Melani, 1661 (Boretti, 1670); *Il mondo festeggiante* (balletto a cavallo), Anglesi, 1661; *La Semirami*, Cesti, 1667; *Il ritorno d'Ulisse*, Melani, 1669; *Enea in Italia*, Melani, 1670; *La Semiramide*, Ziani, 1670; *Tacere et amare*, Melani, 1674 (Lucchesini, 1680)
La Giocasta, regina d'Armenia, Grossi, 1677; *Dov'è amore e pietà*, B. Pasquini, 1679; *Amor vuol inganno*, Melani, 1680, as *La vedova, ovvero Amor vuol inganno*; *Quinto Luzio proscritto*, Cattani, 1681; *Il conte di Cutro*, Cattani, 1682; *Ifianassa e Melampo*, Legrenzi, 1685; *Il pellegrino*, Cattani, 1685; *Gneo Marzio Coriolano*, Cattani, 1686; *Il tiranno di Colco*, Pagliardi, 1688; *La pietà di Sabina*, Cattani, comp. before 1690; *Il Germanico al Reno*, comp. before 1690; *L'amor di figlia*, Porta, 1718

A. Ademollo: *I primi fasti del teatro di via della Pergola in Firenze (1657–1661)* (Milan, c1883)
H. Goldschmidt: *Studien zur Geschichte der italienischen Oper im 17. Jahrhundert*, i (Leipzig, 1901)
R. L. Weaver: *Florentine Comic Operas of the 17th Century* (diss., U. of North Carolina, 1958)
R. Weaver and N. Weaver: *A Chronology of Music in the Florentine Theater 1590–1750* (Detroit, 1978)
P. Radicchi: *Giovanni Lorenzo Cattani, musicista carraresi al servizio dei Medici* (Pisa, 1980)   ROBERT LAMAR WEAVER

Moniuszko, Stanisław (*b* Ubiel, nr Minsk, 5 May 1819; *d* Warsaw, 4 June 1872). Polish composer. He was the leading Polish opera composer of the 19th century.

1. LIFE. Born into the Polish middle gentry in Ubiel, a small village in the province of Minsk, he was brought into close contact with music and the other arts early in life. His father, Czesław, at one time an officer in Napoleon's army, was a noted poet and painter, and his mother, Elżbieta, a talented amateur pianist who gave the composer his earliest piano lessons at the age of four. In 1827 the family moved to Warsaw, where Stanisław had lessons with the German-born August Freyer (1803–83), at that time a student of Józef Elsner at the Warsaw Conservatory, where Chopin was a fellow student. In summer 1830 the family returned to Minsk owing to financial pressures, and Moniuszko continued his musical studies with Dominik Stefanowicz, conductor of the local theatre orchestra. He left the gymnasium in Minsk in 1834, ostensibly for health reasons, but probably because his father disliked the growing Russian influence on formal education. This was no doubt why he was sent to Berlin (rather than Moscow or St Petersburg) for further musical studies. Moniuszko enrolled at the Berlin Singakademie in 1837, studying there with F. F. Rungenhagen. His knowledge of opera, which he had already encountered in Vilnius, was naturally widened in Berlin, where Spontini was director of the Königliche Schauspiele and where works by Weber, Marschner and Lortzing were recent additions to the repertory. On completing his studies in 1839, he returned to Vilnius, married Aleksandra Müller and made a meagre living as a piano teacher, organist and occasional conductor of the theatre orchestra.

Moniuszko's earliest music of any significance dates from the Berlin years and includes an operetta *Nocleg w*

Apeninach ('A Night in the Apennines'), given its first performance in Vilnius in 1839. His return to Poland inaugurated a period of intensive composition, including songs – several volumes of his *Śpiewnik domowy* ('Home Songbook') – and 'operettas' composed for the amateur operatic society of Vilnius. The best of these, *Loteria* ('The Lottery'), was composed in 1843, had its first performance in Minsk in that year and was given a Warsaw performance three years later. For Moniuszko the visit to Warsaw in 1846 was an important event. He met there some of the principal figures in Polish artistic circles, including the ethnologist Oskar Kolberg and the poet Włodzimierz Wolski, future librettist of *Halka* and *Hrabina* ('The Countess'). It was the stimulus of this visit which inspired Moniuszko to tackle a 'grand opera', and he began work on *Halka* almost immediately. Its two-act version was given a concert performance in Vilnius in 1848 and a staged production six years later. When it was eventually (and after many difficulties) accepted for production in Warsaw, Moniuszko revised the work and enlarged it to four acts, and this second version was performed to immediate acclaim in January 1858. It remains to this day the most popular of all Polish operas.

The success of *Halka* in Warsaw belatedly launched Moniuszko's career. There had already been a measure of wider recognition during three visits to St Petersburg, but *Halka* made him a national celebrity and he immediately embarked on a European tour, meeting Smetana in Prague and Liszt in Weimar, before spending some time in Paris, where he composed most of his one-act opera *Flis* ('The Raftsman'). On his return to Poland he accepted the post of director of Polish productions at the Wielki Theatre, completed *The Raftsman* and began work on *The Countess*. Both works were performed with great success in Warsaw (1858 and 1860), and Moniuszko began work on another one-act opera, *Verbum nobile*, his first collaboration with Jan Chęciński. *Verbum nobile* was given in 1861, and in the same year Moniuszko and Chęciński began work on *Straszny dwór* ('The Haunted Manor').

While working on *The Haunted Manor*, Moniuszko was inevitably caught up in the growing political ferment which led to the insurrection of 1863. The Wielki Theatre was converted into a barracks, Moniuszko's post was lost and his only source of income was a position (from December 1863) as professor of choral conducting at Apolinary Kątski's newly founded Music Institute (later to become a reconstituted Warsaw Conservatory). In the aftermath of the insurrection, censorship in Warsaw was severe and *The Haunted Manor*, regarded as excessively patriotic in tone, was withdrawn after three performances in 1865. From this point there was a decline in Moniuszko's creative powers and his last major works, the 'Indian' opera *Paria* and the one-act operetta *Beata*, both to librettos by Chęciński, were failures with the Warsaw public on their performances in 1869 and 1872 respectively. Moniuszko died in Warsaw of a heart attack on 4 June 1872.

2. OPERAS. Like Glinka in Russia, Erkel in Hungary and Smetana in the Czech lands, Moniuszko has become associated above all with the concept of a national style in opera, and to some extent he himself fostered this idea. He was very much a product of his time and place. Musical life in Poland following the insurrection of 1830 was uneducated and conservative, with little in the way of sustained institutional development in any of the major cities. The music which responded most directly to the needs of the country during these years was not Chopin's, which so obviously transcended those needs, but Moniuszko's, in the 12 volumes of his *Home Songbook* and in his operas. In the provincial setting of Vilnius and later in Warsaw he fathered a national operatic style of conservative bent, colouring the European styles of an earlier generation with the rhythms of Polish national dances in a manner which was to dictate the musical formulation of 'Polishness' to later composers.

Of his mature operas, only one, *Paria*, does not have a Polish setting. *The Countess*, *Verbum nobile* and *The Haunted Manor* depict the world of the Polish gentry, *The Raftsman* deals with ordinary Polish people, and *Halka* concerns the relation between the two. In all there is a celebration of the social life and customs of Poland, past and present. Moniuszko had great difficulties with the Russian censor in Warsaw, but even with their more overtly patriotic elements removed his operas were bound to be a focus for the nationalist sentiment of a people deprived of political status. The nationalist element would often be heightened in production, moreover, by idealizing the world of an earlier 'grand Poland' as a foil to contemporary discontents. In this context the national dances – polonaise, mazurka and *krakowiak* – which underpin so much of Moniuszko's music carried powerfully symbolic values.

It had been common for early 19th-century vaudevilles or Singspiels by Polish composers to use Polish dances as the basis for arias and ensembles. In Moniuszko's mature works this practice carried a new ideological burden as the chief means of establishing a national operatic idiom. *Halka* set the tone, with choral polonaises and polonaise arias depicting the nobility while mazurka and *krakowiak* arias represent the lower orders. In keeping with its setting, *The Raftsman* employs only mazurka and *krakowiak* elements. *The Countess*, *Verbum nobile* and *The Haunted Manor* again juxtapose movements based on the polonaise and mazurka, with an additional *krakowiak* in Act 1 of *The Haunted Manor* and a sprinkling of polkas (a Czech 'Polish dance') in *The Countess*. Other national elements include the Highlander Dances in Act 3 of *Halka* and the use of folksong for the huntsmen's choruses in *The Countess* and *The Haunted Manor*. Most curious of all are the polonaise and mazurka elements which find their way into the thoroughly Indian setting of *Paria*.

National elements apart, the operas are indebted above all to early 19th-century French models in their overall design. *Halka* and *The Countess* are similar in general layout to French grand opera (Auber's *La muette de Portici* was a particular influence), especially in their extended scenic tableaux, of which Act 3 of *Halka* and Act 2 of *The Countess* are representative. The one-act operas *The Raftsman* and *Verbum nobile* resemble rather some of the one-act operas prepared by Scribe for the Opéra-Comique. *The Haunted Manor* stands somewhat apart, not only in its blend of Opéra-Comique and Italian elements, but also in the role assigned to the chorus, always prominent in Moniuszko, but here of central importance.

Solo vocal writing ranges from simple strophic songs, such as Chorąży's song in Act 1 of *The Countess*, to big, multi-sectional arias such as Halka's aria in Act 2 of *Halka*, Kazimierz's aria in Act 3 of *The Countess* and Stefan's aria in Act 3 of *The Haunted Manor*. It is here above all that Moniuszko comes closest stylistically to Italian vocal lyricism, that of Rossini in particular. In general, however, solo arias are not extensive in the operas, and tend to be outweighed by duets, ensembles and choruses. A major influence on the choral writing and also on the orchestral style of *Halka* and parts of *The Haunted Manor* was Weber. Moniuszko knew *Der Freischütz* well and regarded it as an important model for his own conception of national opera. Moniuszko's particular blend of established European traditions and Polish national dances has ensured his operas a special place in the Polish repertory, though there are as yet few signs that they can be exported with success.

See also HALKA and HAUNTED MANOR, THE.

all printed works published in Warsaw

Biuraliści [The Bureaucrats], 1834 (operetta, 1, I. F. Skarbeck), unperf.

Nocleg w Apeninach [A Night in the Apennines] (operetta, 1, A. Fredro), Vilnius, 1839

Cudowna woda [The Water of Life], c1840 (operetta, 2), lost except ov.

Ideał, czyli Nowa Preciosa [Perfection, or The New Preciosa] (operetta, 2, O. Milewski), Vilnius, 1840

Karmaniol, czyli Francuzi lubią żartować [Carmagnole, or The French Like Joking], 1841 (operetta, Milewski, after Théaulon de Forges and E. Jaime), unperf.

Nowy Don Quichot, czyli Sto szaleństw [The New Don Quixote, or 100 Follies], 1841 (operetta, 3, Fredro, after M. de Cervantes), Lwów, 1849, vs (1927)

Żółta szlafmyca [The Yellow Nightcap], 1841 (operetta, F. Zabłocki), 1 song (Warsaw, 1863)

Pobór rekrutów [Conscription], 1842 (operetta, W. Marcinkiewicz), 1 song in Śpiewnik domowy [Home Songbook], viii (1908)

Loteria [The Lottery] (operetta, 1, Milewski), Minsk, 1843 (1908)

Halka, 1846–7 (2, W. Wolski, after K. Wójcicki: *Stary gawędy i obrazy* [Legends and Pictures]), concert perf., Vilnius, 1848, excerpts, vs (Vilnius, 1850); stage, Vilnius, 18 Feb 1854; rev. (4, Wolski), Warsaw, Wielki, 1 Jan 1858, vs (1858), full score (1861)

Sielanka [Idyll], ?1848 (2, Marcinkiewicz), lost

Cyganie [The Gypsies], 1850 (operetta, F. D. Kniaźnin), Vilnius, 20 May 1852; rev. as Jawnuta, Warsaw, 5 June 1860

Bettly (comic op, 2, E. Scribe and Mélesville [A. H. J. Duveyrier]), Vilnius, 20 May 1852

Flis [The Raftsman] (1, W. Bogusławski), Warsaw, Wielki, 24 Sept 1858, excerpts, vs (1858), ov. (1898), vs (1902)

Rokiczana, 1858–9 (3, J. Korzeniowski), inc., concert perf. (excerpts), 16 Dec 1860, 1 ballad (1913)

Hrabina [The Countess] (4, Wolski, after J. Dierzowski), Warsaw, Wielki, 7 Feb 1860, excerpts, vs (1860), ov. and ballet music (1899), vs (1901)

Verbum nobile (1, J. Chęciński), Warsaw, Wielki, 1 Jan 1861, vs (1861), full score (1953)

Straszny dwór [The Haunted Manor], 1861–4 (4, Chęciński, after Wójcicki: *Stary gawędy i obrazy*), Warsaw, Wielki, 28 Sept 1865, excerpts, vs (1892), vs (1898), full score (1937)

Paria, 1859–69 (prol., 3, Chęciński, after C. Delavigne), Warsaw, Wielki, 11 Dec 1869, ov. (1901), vs (1913)

Beata (operetta, 1, Chęciński), Warsaw, Wielki, 2 Feb 1872, 4 songs (1872)

Trea, 1872 (2, J. Jasiński, after Flemish legend), inc.

Dates unknown: Walka muzyków [The Musician's Struggle] (operetta, Marcinkiewicz); Nowy dziedzic [The New Landlord] (operetta, M. Radziszewski); Sen wieszcza [The Seer's Dream] (W. Syrokomla, after J. B. Rosier and A. de Leuven: *Le songe d'une nuit d'été*), 1 song in Śpiewnik domowy [Home Songbook], vii (1877)

H. von Bülow: 'Stanislas Moniuszko: *Halka*', NZM, xlix (1858), 209–12, 221–3

A. Walicki: *Stanisław Moniuszko* (Warsaw, 1873)

B. Wilczyński: *Stanisław Moniuszko i sztuka muzyczna narodowa* [Moniuszko and National Music] (Warsaw, 1874)

A. Poliński: *Moniuszko* (Kiev, 1914)

Z. Jachimecki: 'S. Moniuszko and Polish Music', *Slavonic Review*, ii (1924), 533–46

——: *Moniuszko* (Warsaw, 1924, enlarged W. Rudziński, Kraków, 1961)

H. Opieński: *S. Moniuszko: życie i dzieła* [Moniuszko: Life and Works] (Lwów, 1924)

Z. Jachimecki: 'Stanislaus Moniuszko', MQ, xiv (1928), 54–62

S. Niewiadomski: *Stanisław Moniuszko* (Warsaw, 1928)

F. Kęcki: *A Catalogue of Musical Works of M. Karłowicz and S. Moniuszko* (Warsaw, 1936)

W. Rudziński and J. Prosnak: *Almanach Moniuszkowski: 1872–1952* (Warsaw, 1952)

W. Rudziński: *Stanisław Moniuszko* (Kraków, 1954, 4/1972)

——: *Stanisław Moniuszko* (Kraków, 1955–61)

J. Prosnak: *Stanisław Moniuszko* (Kraków, 1964, 2/1969)

T. Kaczyński: *Dzieje sceniczne 'Halki' Stanisława Moniuszki* [Performance History of Moniuszko's *Halka*] (Kraków, 1969)

W. Rudziński and M. Stokowska, eds.: *Stanisław Moniuszko: listy zebrane* [Moniuszko: Collected Letters] (Kraków, 1969)

K. Mazur: *Pierwodruki Stanisława Moniuszki* [The First Editions of Moniuszko's works] (Warsaw, 1970)

D. Jasińska: 'Listy Stanisława Moniuszki do Leopolda Matuszyńskiego oraz do Pauliny i Augusta Wilkońskich' [Moniuszko's Letters to Leopold Matuszyński and to August and Paulina Wilkoński], *Muzyka*, xxv/1 (1980), 55–64

L'avant-scène opéra, no.83 (1986) [*The Haunted Manor* issue]

JIM SAMSON

Monjo [de Monjou], **Christel** (*fl* 1720–29). German soprano. She and her sister (also a soprano), whose first name is unknown, sang at the Cöthen court (where their father was a tutor), 1720–22, in Berlin and (possibly in opera) under J. P. Kunzen in Wittenberg; Mattheson reported that 'the younger has a beautiful, clear voice and great mastery of music'. Both sang at the Hamburg Opera, 1722–9. The younger made her début as Maritorne in F. B. Conti's *Don Chisciotte in Sierra Morena* and both sang in Keiser's *Ariadne*, the elder sister as Venus in the prologue, the younger as Phaedra. From 1724 they sang in an extensive repertory, including works by Keiser, Telemann, Handel, Kunzen, Destouches, Gasparini, Caldara, Porta and Porpora. Their wide repertory suggests that they must have been among the leading female singers at the Hamburg Opera during Telemann's tenure as director. Nothing is known of them after 1729.

J. Mattheson: *Critica musica*, i (Hamburg, 1722), 85–6

K. Zelm: 'Die Sänger der Hamburger Gänsemarkt-Oper', HJbMw, iii (1978), 61–4

H. J. Marx: *Johann Mattheson (1681–1764)* (Hamburg, 1982)

HANS JOACHIM MARX

Monleone, Domenico [W. di Stolzing] (*b* Genoa, 4 Jan 1875; *d* Genoa, 15 Jan 1942). Italian composer. He studied in Milan and worked as a conductor in various European cities including Genoa, where he assisted in the artistic direction of the Teatro Carlo Felice. His opera *Cavalleria rusticana* was successfully performed in Amsterdam (1907) and elsewhere but was withdrawn as the result of legal action by Mascagni. Monleone used some of its music for *La giostra dei falchi* (1914), which is set among smugglers in the Swiss mountains. *Arabesca* won the Concorso del Municipio di Roma prize in 1913. Monleone also treated patriotic themes, as in *Alba eroica* (on the political martyrdom of the Bandiera brothers) and *Suona la ritirata*, and composed a comic opera in Genoese dialect (*Scheuggio Campanna*); generally, however, he remained faithful to *verismo* opera (*Il mistero*, *Notte di nozze*), his traditionalist style giving pre-eminence to the melodic element. His operetta *Una novella del Boccaccio* (1909) was presented under the pseudonym W. di Stolzing.

Most of his librettos were by his brother Giovanni, a writer and journalist.

See also CAVALLERIA RUSTICANA (ii).

librettos by Giovanni Monleone unless otherwise stated

Cavalleria rusticana (dramma lirico, prol., 1, after G. Verga), Amsterdam, Paleis voor Volksvlyt, 5 Feb 1907, vs (Milan, 1907)

Una novella del Boccaccio (operetta), Genoa, Politeama Genovese, 1909

Alba eroica (3), Genoa, Carlo Felice, 1910, vs (Milan, 1910)

Arabesca (scene liriche, 1, with B. Montelioi), Rome, Costanzi, 1913, vs (Milan, 1913)

La giostra dei falchi (melodramma, 1), Florence, Verdi, 1914, vs (Milan, 1914)

Suona la ritirata (dramma per musica, 3, after F. A. Beyerlein: *La retraite*), Milan, Lirico, 1916

Il mistero (scene siciliane, 2, after Verga), Venice, Fenice, 1921

Fauvette (3), Genoa, Carlo Felice, 1926, vs (Milan, 1925)

Scheuggio Campanna (comic op, 3, B. Canesi and A. Martinelli), Genoa, Carlo Felice, 1928, vs (Genoa, 1928)

La ronda di notte del Rembrandt (scene fiamminghe, 1), Genoa, Carlo Felice, 1933

Notte di nozze (3, Bonetti), Bergamo, Donizetti, 1940

Sotto il knut, unperf.

*

M. Pedemonte: *Domenico Monleone: il musicista e l'uomo* (Genoa, 1942)
LUCA ZOPPELLI

Monmart, Berthe (*b* *c*1924). French soprano. She made her début in 1951 at the Paris Opéra as Gerhilde (*Die Walküre*) and at the Opéra-Comique as Countess Almaviva; for 20 years she sang in Paris and the French provinces. Her repertory, which ranged from Mozart (Fiordiligi, Donna Anna) to Wagner (Senta, Elsa), and from Verdi (Aida, Desdemona) to Strauss (Ariadne, the Marschallin), included many French works: *Les Indes galantes*, Barraud's *Numance*, *Werther*, Gounod's *Faust*, *La damnation de Faust*, *Béatrice et Bénédict*, *Le roi d'Ys*, *Dialogues des Carmélites* and Fauré's *Pénélope*. As her lyric soprano grew darker in tone, she took more dramatic roles such as Judith (*Bluebeard's Castle*), Marina (*Boris Godunov*), Kabanicha (*Kát'a Kabanová*), the Woman in *Erwartung* and the title role of Milhaud's *Médée*, which she sang in Lisbon in 1971.
ELIZABETH FORBES

Monnaie, La. Theatre in BRUSSELS, built in 1696–9 on the site of the former mint. A new building was opened in 1819; it burnt down in 1855 and was rebuilt in 1856. In 1963 it became the Belgian national opera under the name Théâtre Royal de la Monnaie/Koninklijke Muntschouwburg.

Monnet [Monet], **Jean** (*b* Condrieu, 7 Sept 1703; *d* Paris, 1785). French impresario and writer. Son of a baker, he was orphaned at an early age but benefited from the patronage of the Duchess of Berry until her death in 1719. According to his memoirs (*Supplement au roman comique*, 1772) he led a colourful but dissolute life for some years, was imprisoned briefly in 1741 for publishing scurrilous literature, and thereafter embarked on a series of theatrical enterprises. In 1743 he paid 12 000 livres for the *privilège* of the Opéra-Comique and assembled a talented troupe which included the comedian Pierre-Louis Dubos, *dit* Préville, Charles-Simon Favart as *régisseur*, François Boucher as stage designer, and Dupré as *maître de ballet*, with his pupil, Noverre. (Rameau may also have directed the orchestra: see Sadler.) The troupe enjoyed such success that, in 1745, it was forced by the Opéra (from whom the *privilège* had been acquired) to close.

Later that year Monnet left Paris for Lyons, where he served briefly as director of the Opéra. Productions mounted in Dijon (1746) and London (1749) proved unsuccessful. In December 1751, however, he again secured the *privilège* of the Opéra-Comique and remained its director until 1758. This was an outstanding period in the development of the *opéra comique* and must be attributed in part to Monnet's extraordinary talent for surrounding himself with influential artists. Favart and Noverre contined to work for him, as did Boucher, who designed a new, impressive theatre for the Foire St Laurent in 1752; his friend Vadé wrote the libretto to the historically important work, *Les troqueurs*, set to music by Dauvergne and staged at the fair in July 1753; Michel-Jean Sedaine was encouraged to write his first opera libretto, *Le diable à quatre*, for the fair of 1756; and Egidio Duni composed *Le peintre amoureux de son modèle*, another highly influential work, for the fair of 1757.

Monnet's influence extended even to England, through his 30-year friendship and correspondence with David Garrick (whom he had first met on a visit to London in 1748). He offered much practical advice to Garrick on stage decoration and design, engaged French personnel for his friend's London troupe, and entertained Garrick and his wife on their visits to France. The English actor, in return, ensured the publication of Monnet's memoirs. In a letter to George Colman (27 Jan 1765), Garrick observed that Monnet enjoyed a comfortable lifestyle and that he was 'ye gayest man in Paris … greatly beloved by the Men of Wit & Pleasure'.

Monnet has been credited with some librettos but none can be attributed to him with certainty. His life, however, formed the subject of a vaudeville by Pierre-Yon Barré, Jean-Baptiste Radet and François-Georges Fougues, *dit* Desfontaines (1799).

*

C.-S. Favart: *Mémoires et correspondance littéraires, dramatiques et anecdotiques* (Paris, 1808)

E. Campardon: *Les spectacles de la foire* (Paris, 1877), i, 139–42

A. Heulhard: *Jean Monnet: Vie et aventures d'un entrepreneur de spectacles au XVIIIe siècle* (Paris, 1884)

F. A. Hedgcock: *Un acteur cosmopolite: David Garrick et ses amis français* (Paris, 1911; Eng. trans., 1912)

L. Vallas: *Un siècle de musique et de théâtre à Lyon 1688–1789* (Lyons, 1932), 238–44

D. M. Little and G. M. Kahrl, eds.: *The Letters of David Garrick* (London, 1963)

G. Sadler: 'Rameau, Piron and the Parisian Fair Theatres', *Soundings*, iv (1974), 13–29
ELISABETH COOK

Monodrama. In its narrow meaning, a form of MELODRAMA which features one character, sometimes with chorus, using speech in alternation with short passages of music, or sometimes speaking over music. Simultaneously with melodrama, the initial enthusiasm for monodrama occurred chiefly in Germany during the 1770s and 80s, and the two terms are often used interchangeably, since many of the early melodramas had only one character on stage at a time. The prototypical 'monodrama', Rousseau's *Pygmalion*, actually has two characters, but until the end, when Galatea comes to life and speaks four lines, Pygmalion holds the stage alone. Introduced in Weimar by Goethe in 1772, with music by Anton Schweitzer, *Pygmalion* became the model for several examples of monodrama and DUODRAMA produced in Weimar and Gotha by J. C. Brandes, often as a vehicle for his wife Charlotte, and in Weimar, Dresden, Leipzig and Frankfurt by the Seylers. From 1775 to 1790 over 30 so-called monodramas were performed in Germany, though some of these are actually cantatas with one main character. In Darmstadt, where C. G. Neefe's *Sophonisbe* (1776) and G. F. Vogler's *Lampedo* (1779) were produced, there is now a large collection of monodramas in the Hessische Landes- und Hochschulbibliothek. Other significant monodramas include J. F. Reichardt's *Ino* (1779), Franz Danzi's *Cleopatra* (1780), and Goethe's *Proserpina*, with music by K. S. Seckendorff (1777), a lament perhaps first written for the death of Gluck's niece Marianne and later set within Goethe's parody of melodrama, *Der Triumph der Empfindsamkeit*, and performed in Weimar in 1778. *Proserpina* was revived by Goethe in 1815 with new music by Carl Eberwein.

In modern times, the term monodrama has lost its exclusive association with the combination of speech and music characteristic of melodrama and is most often used as a synonym for a one-character opera, as in Schoenberg's *Erwartung* (1909) and Poulenc's *La voix humaine* (1958); as a non-staged dramatic work for singer and orchestra, as in Poulenc's *La dame de Monte Carlo* (1961), Floyd's *Flower and Hawk* (1972), Rochberg's *Phaedra* (1974), J. E. Ivey's *Testament of Eve* (1976), or Maxwell Davies's *The Medium* (1983); or even as a purely instrumental work, as in Mordecai Seter's *Chamber Music '70* for clarinet and piano (1975), and {H}MWNWDRMH{R}: Monodrama II for viola and piano (1979). In addition, some works are simply entitled 'Monodrama', for example the ballet for orchestra by Karel Husa (1976). In several of the vocal works, some techniques of Sprechstimme are used along with singing (e.g. Maxwell Davies and Floyd), but these are properly seen more as an outgrowth of extended vocal techniques of the 20th century than as a continuation of melodrama techniques of the 18th and early 19th centuries. 20th-century works incorporating speech and music are more often entitled 'monologues' or 'recitations with music' than monodrama.

*

J. C. Brandes: Preface, *Sämtlichen dramatische Schriften*, i (Hamburg, 1790), pp.xxvii–xxxiv

E. Schmidt: 'Goethe's Proserpina', *Vierteljahrschrift für Litteraturgeschichte*, i (1888), 27–52

E. Istel: *Die Entstehung des deutschen Melodrams* (Berlin, 1906)

K. G. Holmstrom: *Monodrama, Attitudes, Tableaux Vivants: Studies on some Trends of Theatrical Fashion, 1770–1815* (Stockholm, 1967)

For further bibliography *see* MELODRAMA.   ANNE DHU SHAPIRO

Monody. A term used particularly of solo vocal music in early 17th-century Italy. It was early used to denote solo pieces of vocal music in ancient Greece, and it was no doubt this association that prompted the occasional use of the term in Italian theoretical writing in the early 17th century to refer to the remarkable flowering of secular vocal music in Italy at that time, in contrast to the hitherto generally prevailing polyphonic music. The vogue for solo song was to some extent inspired by theoretical discussions among groups of scholars, poets and musicians (*see* CAMERATA) persuaded of the wonderful effects of solo song in ancient Greece in making the words intelligible and enhancing their effect. Giovanni Battista Doni, for example, refers to the 'monodic style', which 'is used today on the stage' (*Annotazioni sopra il Compendio de' generi e de' modi della musica*, Rome, 1640).

The term has been widely adopted in modern writings to denote in particular the large number of solo songs, both madrigals and arias, published in Italy in the first third of the 17th century; it can refer to an individual song or to the entire body of such songs. Its use has been extended to embrace solo vocal writing in early Italian operas, by Peri, Caccini, Monteverdi and others: both recitative accompanied only by continuo and more aria-like pieces where melody instruments too may participate. In operatic music, monody can be heard at its most expressive in works by Monteverdi, for example in the recitative of the Messenger scene in Act 2 of *Orfeo* (1607), in the more schematic aria for Orpheus, 'Possente spirto', epitomizing the power of music, in Act 3 of that work, and in the lament of Ariadne which is the only surviving music from *Arianna* (1608). The term is never used of solo music after about the mid-17th century, possibly because such music was so well established by then and because recitative and arias were now so sharply distinguished from each other that there is no need for a single term to embrace them both; nor has it been used of solo pieces in later operas where that distinction is no longer so obvious.

NIGEL FORTUNE

Mono-opera. Term used in the late 20th century for an opera with a cast of one; *see* MONODRAMA.

Monopoli, Giacomo. *See* INSANGUINE, GIACOMO.

Monoyios, Ann (*b* Middletown, CT, 28 Oct 1949). American soprano. She attended Princeton University and studied privately with Oren Brown and Marcy Lindheimer. Her clear, light voice and elegant musicianship immediately marked her as an ideal interpreter of Baroque and Classical music. Her early career included many concert performances with the Folger Consort in Washington, DC, and the Concert Royal, New York, with whom she made her stage début in Rameau's *Les fêtes d'Hébé*. Her European operatic début was in 1987 at the Opéra-Comique as Sangaride in Lully's *Atys*. She has sung leading roles in operas by Handel, Mozart and Rameau in Aix-en-Provence, Frankfurt, Los Angeles, Salzburg and Spoleto.   CORI ELLISON

Monpou, (François Louis) Hippolyte (*b* Paris, 12 Jan 1804; *d* Orléans, 10 Aug 1841). French composer. He was a choirboy at St Germain-l'Auxerrois and Notre Dame in Paris, and at 13 was one of the first students in Choron's Ecole Royale et Spéciale de Chant. He then studied the organ at Tours Cathedral, where in 1819 he became organist, but was recalled to Paris to be master accompanist at the Académie Royale. In 1822 he took harmony lessons with Fétis at Choron's academy and in 1825 taught singing and was *maître de chapelle* at the College of St Louis. He was active as an organist until the Revolution of 1830 closed Choron's school. In 1833 he began writing comic operas. The *Gazette musicale* praised the Opéra-Comique (at the Théâtre des Nouveautés) for staging his *Les deux reines* (6 August 1835), an amusing tale about the queens of Denmark and Sweden travelling incognito, noted for its spirited music; the same magazine also recognized the quality of Dumas *père* and Gérard de Nerval's libretto and Monpou's score of *Piquillo*. Monpou later wrote for Jenny Colon the role of Miss Jenny in *Le planteur*, which was a triumphant success. Deciding that he needed a libretto from Scribe in order to establish his reputation, Monpou succeeded in acquiring Scribe's three-act play *Lambert Simnel*. However, the Opéra-

Comique imposed a penalty of 20 000 francs if the composer could not produce the score by 6 August 1841; he became ill and died before the work was completed.

Monpou, in the judgment of both his contemporaries and his subsequent critics, was an innovator, not an imitator; he was one of the first to set poems by Victor Hugo and Alfred de Musset, his numerous songs showing true originality.

opéras comiques, first performed in Paris, unless otherwise stated; printed works published in Paris

Les deux reines (1, F. Soulié and Arnould [J. Mussot]), 6 Aug 1835, vs (?1840)

Le luthier de Vienne (1, J. H. Vernoy de Saint-Georges and A. de Leuven), 30 June 1836 (1836)

Piquillo (3, A. Dumas *père* and G. de Nerval), 31 Oct 1837, vs (?1845)

Un conte d'autrefois (1, Brunswick [L. Lhérie] and de Leuven), 28 Feb 1838

Perugina la meunière (1, Mélesville [A.-H.-J. Duveyrier]), Renaissance, 20 Dec 1838

Le planteur (2, Saint-Georges), 1 March 1839 (c 1839)

La chaste Suzanne (opéra, 4, P. F. H. Carmouche and F. de Couray), Renaissance, 27 Dec 1839 (c1840)

La reine Jeanne (Brunswick and de Leuven), OC (Favart), 13 Oct 1840, collab. L. Bordèse

Lambert Simnel (3, E. Scribe and Mélesville), OC (Favart), 14 Sept 1843; completed by A. Adam, vs (1843)

L'orfèvre, inc.

*

G. Grand: 'Hippolyte Monpou', *Revue de Paris*, ix (1868), 297–309
H. Bachelin: 'Hippolyte Monpou', *Le ménestrel*, xv (1928), 205, 217
DELBERT R. SIMON

Monsieur. Company based in Paris, known from 1792 as the Théâtre de la rue Feydeau; it amalgamated with the Opéra-Comique in 1801. See PARIS, §4(v).

Monsieur Beaucaire. Romantic opera in three acts by ANDRÉ MESSAGER to a libretto by André Rivoire and Pierre Veber after the novel of the same title by Booth Tarkington; Birmingham, Prince of Wales Theatre, 7 April 1919 (in an English version by Frederick Lonsdale, with lyrics by Adrian Ross; French première, Paris, Théâtre Marigny, 21 November 1925).

The piece is set in 18th-century Bath and concerns the rivalry between the barber Beaucaire (baritone) and the Duke of Winterset (bass) for the affections of Lady Mary Carlisle (soprano). Unable to meet her because of his social position, Beaucaire eventually procures an introduction from Winterset as the price of his silence after Beaucaire has caught the duke cheating at cards. Seeing the success of his rival, Winterset attempts to discredit him, but is outwitted when Beaucaire reveals himself as the exiled Duc d'Orléans. A chorus celebrating the union of England and France concludes the work.

In an interview in 1925 Messager stated that he had begun work on the piece following a visit from the impresario Gilbert Miller in 1916. Jean Messager, the composer's son, noted that most of it was composed at Etretat in summer 1917. However, the 'Air du rossignol' (Act 2, no.13), one of the work's most successful numbers, was supposedly composed in Manchester, between the Birmingham and London premières, and would thus not have been included in the original production. The Parisian première was delayed until 1925, owing to problems of finding a suitable theatre; by this time the film of Tarkington's novel, starring Rudolph Valentino, had already had much success at the Théâtre Mogador. In addition to Messager's use of the waltz, some neo-Classical touches are evident in the overture and in the 'Menuet des roses' in Act 1. At the first performance, the title role was sung by Marion Green, Lady Mary by Maggie Teyte and the Duke of Winterset by Robert Parker.
JOHN WAGSTAFF

M. Choufleuri restera chez lui le ... ('Mr. Choufleuri will be At Home on ...'). *Opérette bouffe* in one act by JACQUES OFFENBACH and 'M. de St Rémy' (Comte de Morny) to an anonymous libretto; private performance, Paris, Présidence du Corps Législatif, Palais Bourbon, 31 May 1861 (public performance, Paris, Théâtre des Bouffes-Parisiens, 14 September 1861).

Seeking entry to Paris society, M. Choufleuri (baritone) has issued invitations to a soirée at which Sontag, Rubini and Tamburini have agreed to sing. However, they fail to turn up. To save face, Choufleuri, his daughter Ernestine (soprano) and her young composer suitor Chrysodule Babylas (tenor) impersonate them, the price being Choufleuri's agreement to the young couple's marriage. The highlight of the operetta is the hilarious mock-Italian trio 'Italia la bella'. The published score names 'St Rémy' and Offenbach as joint composers: Ludovic Halévy, Hector-Jonathan Crémieux and Ernest Lépine (the Comte de Morny's secretary) probably assisted with the libretto.
ANDREW LAMB

Monsigny [Moncigny, Moncini, Monsigni], **Pierre-Alexandre** (*b* Fauquembergues, near Saint-Omer, 17 Oct 1729; *d* Paris, 14 Jan 1817). French composer. He was born into a noble but penniless family; his aristocratic origins were useful to him in his Parisian career, however, and are evident in the fact that all his scores were published anonymously, for it would have been improper for a nobleman to admit to being a musician. He settled in Paris in 1749, intending not to become a composer of operas but, according to Quatremère de Quincy, to 'throw himself into finance'; he did indeed enter the service of the receiver general of the Clergé de France around 1750, and then became *maître d'hôtel* to the Duke of Orléans about 1768. In Paris Monsigny continued the musical studies he had begun in his native province, first with a violin master, then with Pietro Gianotti, an instrumentalist at the Opéra and the author of a didactic work *Le guide du compositeur* (Paris, 1759). His first impressions of *grand opéra* were unfavourable ('I would rather try a different genre', he told his friends), and he therefore naturally found himself drawn to the nascent genre of *opéra comique mêlé d'ariettes*.

His first opera, *Les aveux indiscrets*, was performed in 1759 (the same year as Philidor's first, *Blaise le savetier*), but the preface to the libretto dates its composition four years earlier. *Les aveux indiscrets* is a mixture of elements borrowed from various different genres: the dominant influence is that of the Italian intermezzo, but it also contains characteristics peculiar to the French tradition, such as *petits airs*, a final *divertissement* and dialogue arias. Monsigny's personal touch already shows in the quality of the melodic invention, particularly noticeable in the duet 'L'amour veut du mistère' in the middle of the final *divertissement*. Le *maître en droit* (1760) and *Le cadi dupé* (1761) belong to the hybrid category of the *opéra comique mêlé d'ariettes et de vaudevilles*. Their strong points are the arias expressing an *amoroso* sentiment (this marking appears frequently in Monsigny's work and is generally associated with A or E major); the prototype is Lindor's aria 'Ah, quel tourment' (*Le maître en droit*, 2.i). However, Monsigny also shows an increasing mastery of action ensembles, such as the duet 'Prêtons un peu l'oreille' in *Le maître en droit* (2.vi) and the trio 'Entrez donc' in *Le cadi dupé* (scene vii). It was on hearing the duet 'Je veux former de nouveaux noeuds' (*Le cadi dupé*, scene viii) that the dramatist Sedaine, seeking a musician much as the Cadi was seeking a wife, cried, 'There's my man!' The first result of the collaboration between Sedaine and Monsigny, which proved one of the most fruitful in French opera, was *On ne s'avise jamais de tout* (1761); it was such a success that it was revived at court in December of the same year, an unusual distinction for an opera first performed at the Théâtres de la Foire, and was chosen, with *Blaise le savetier*, for the first performance given by the Comédie-Italienne after its merger with the Opéra Comique, on 3 February 1762.

The comic vein still predominant in *On ne s'avise jamais de tout* gives way, in *Le roi et le fermier*, to a far more complex dramatic conception, not only in the unexpected alternation between comic and serious scenes but also in the use of musical procedures still new to French opera. If Monsigny displays a richer and more ambitious idiom here than in his previous operas, he had the advantage of a libretto well designed to point up the role of the music. It includes, for instance, no less than three narrative arias, the most complex of which, Jenny's tale in Act 1 scene viii, contains recitative passages of great dramatic power. Sedaine himself, in his preface to *Rose et Colas*, drew attention to the possibility in music drama of prolonging a moment of intense emotion by allowing different characters to express contradictory feelings. The scene Sedaine had in mind occurs in the septet in Act 3 scene xiv, in which the King is recognized by the peasants who have welcomed him to their home, while Lurewel and the Courtier try in vain to flatter their sovereign. Another case in point is the first scene of Act 3, in which Betsy, Jenny and their Mother sing different songs in turn before combining their melodies into a continuous sequence in which each character preserves her own individuality. Later, Sedaine and Monsigny reverted to a similar method, making it even more radical, at the end of Act 2 of *Le déserteur* (1769).

With *Rose et Colas* (1764) Sedaine and Monsigny returned to one of the standard themes of *opéra comique*: two young peasants crossed in love. Rather than representing a backward step after the powerful and tormented language of *Le roi et le fermier*, *Rose et Colas* was an attempt to convey the quintessence of traditional *opéra comique* – and perhaps to outdo Favart on his own ground. Sedaine's and Monsigny's liking for experiment is evident again in their one contribution to *grand opéra*, *Aline, reine de Golconde* (1766), considered too close to *opéra comique* by the *Mercure de France* (it includes nine pieces marked *amoroso*), yet condemned by Grimm for conforming too obviously to the conventions of the Académie Royale de Musique. In any case, this ambiguity did *Aline* no harm: the work was performed until 1782, surviving the revolution introduced into the repertory of the Opéra by Gluck and Piccinni.

The bucolic atmosphere of *Aline* and the dark passion of *Le déserteur* clearly show the dangers of drawing too facile a distinction between the Académie Royale and serious opera on the one hand, and the Comédie-Italienne and light opera on the other. *Le déserteur* displays an amazing compendium of procedures all combining to express the purest pathos: the frequent use of minor keys, often intensified by chromaticism; instrumental effects (three pieces call for the use of mutes); dramatic breaks in the discourse; fugal writing; and silence from characters confronted with a fate too cruel to bear. Such concentrated methods had no equivalent in French music of the pre-Classical period, but nonetheless Monsigny struck a deep chord of sympathy in his public, for *Le déserteur* was among the *opéras comiques* most often performed during the last two decades of the *ancien régime*, and had a long history of performance in foreign theatres.

Leaving aside his part in the pasticcio *La rosière de Salency* (1769), Monsigny composed nothing during the two and a half years between *Le déserteur* and *Le faucon* (1771). *La belle Arsène* (1773) occupies a special place in his output, both because the libretto is by Favart and not Sedaine and because the genre of *comédie-féerie* calls for a type of dramaturgy halfway between *opéra comique* and *opéra-ballet*. As usual, Monsigny shows his talent most clearly in the cantabile pieces, such as Alcindor's opening monologue, 'Ah! quel tourment' (in four contrasting sections), in Arsène's *andantino amoroso*, 'Eh quoi, l'amour est-il un bien suprême' (3.vi) and in the moving C minor lament of Alcindor to a still-doubting Arsène (3.ix). The last opera on which Sedaine and Monsigny collaborated, *Félix* (1777), rests on the two dramatic principles characteristic of almost all their work together: social criticism and the exploitation of the sentimental vein. Here Monsigny's music returns to complexity similar to that of *Le déserteur*, although contrasting effects are less systematically employed, yielding to subtler vocal and orchestral writing. The culmination of the opera, which did much for its reputation, is the trio sung by Félix, Morin and Thérèse (3.ix); Monsigny claimed to have thought of the melodic idea for this while looking at Greuze's painting *La bénédiction du père de famille*.

Monsigny wrote no more music after *Félix*. The main reason for this strange silence is the cataract from which he suffered. However another, and not incompatible, reason was suggested by Quatremère de Quincy, to the effect that Monsigny had exhausted his inspiration by identifying too strongly with the passions he set to music. This theory, drawn from Diderot's *Paradoxe sur le comédien*, is corroborated by several contemporary witnesses, who emphasize both Monsigny's remarkable susceptibility to emotion and the slowness, even difficulty, with which he composed – because of this Sedaine decided not to entrust the libretto of *Le magnifique* to him (it was eventually set by Grétry). In any case, his retirement from musical life at the age of 48 did not prevent his operas from continuing their brilliant career at the end of the *ancien régime*, during the Revolutionary period and the first quarter of the 19th century.

See also ALINE, REINE DE GOLCONDE; DÉSERTEUR, LE; ON NE S'AVISE JAMAIS DE TOUT; and ROI ET LE FERMIER, LE.

first performed in Paris and printed works published in Paris unless otherwise stated

Les aveux indiscrets (intermède, 1, Laribadière, after J. de La Fontaine), OC (Foire St Germain), 7 Feb 1759, excerpts *F-Pc*, *Pn*; (1759)

Le maître en droit (opéra bouffon, 2, P.-R. Lemonnier, after La Fontaine: *Le roi Candaule, et le maître en droit*), OC (Foire St

Germain), 13 Feb 1760, excerpts *Pn*; (n.d.)

Le cadi dupé (opéra bouffon, 1, Lemonnier, after *The Thousand and One Nights* and L. Gallet: *Le tour double, ou Le prêté rendu*), OC (Foire St Germain), 4 Feb 1761, excerpts *Pc*, *Pn*; (1761); ed. R. Blanchard (1980)

On ne s'avise jamais de tout (opéra comique mêlé de morceaux de musique, 1, M.-J. Sedaine, after La Fontaine), OC (Foire St Laurent), 14 Sept 1761, excerpts *Pc*, *Pn*, full score (n.d.), vs (1911)

Le roi et le fermier (comédie mêlée de morceaux de musique, 3, Sedaine, after R. Dodsley: *The King and the Miller of Mansfield*), Comédie-Italienne (Bourgogne), 22 Nov 1762, excerpts *Pc*, *Pn*; (1763)

Le nouveau monde, 1763 (divertissement, C.-S. Favart, after S.-J. Pellegrin), unperf.

Rose et Colas (comédie, 1, Sedaine, after F.-G. Desfontaines: *Le van*), Comédie-Italienne (Bourgogne), 8 March 1764, excerpts *Pc*, *Pn*, full score (1764), vs (Berlin, n.d.; Paris, n.d.)

Aline, reine de Golconde [La reine de Golconde] (ballet héroïque, 3, Sedaine, after S.-J. Boufflers: *La reine de Golconde*), Opéra, 15 April 1766, *Po*, excerpts *Pc*, *Pn*; (n.d.)

Philémon et Baucis (1, Sedaine), Bagnolet, 1766, or l'Ile-Adam, 1767 [refused by Opéra, 1785]

L'isle sonnante (oc, 3, Collé, after F. Rabelais: *Le cinquième livre*), Villers-Cotterêts, Aug 1767; rev. (Sedaine), Comédie-Italienne (Bourgogne), 4 Jan 1768; excerpts *Pc*; (n.d.)

Le déserteur (drame en prose mêlée de musique, 3, Sedaine), Comédie-Italienne (Bourgogne), 6 March 1769, excerpts *Pc*, full score (n.d.), vs (Brunswick and New York, n.d.; Paris, n.d.)

La rosière de Salency (ballet pastoral, 3, Favart), Fontainebleau, 25 Oct 1769; Comédie-Italienne (Bourgogne), 14 Dec 1769 (1770), collab. Blaise, E. Duni, Philidor and G. van Swieten

Le faucon (opéra comique en prose mêlée d'ariettes, 1, Sedaine, after La Fontaine), Fontainebleau, 2 Nov 1771; Comédie-Italienne (Bourgogne), 19 March 1772; excerpts *Pc*; (1772)

La belle Arsène (comédie-féerie mêlée d'ariettes, 3, Favart, after Voltaire: *La bégueule*), Fontainebleau, 6 Nov 1773; rev. (4), Comédie-Italienne (Bourgogne), 14 Aug 1775; excerpts *Pc*, *Pn*, full score (1776), vs (1909–11)

Félix, ou L'enfant trouvé (comédie, 3, Sedaine), Fontainebleau, Nov 1777; Comédie-Italienne (Bourgogne), 24 Nov 1777; excerpts *Pc*, *Pn*; (1781)

Pagamin de Monègue (opéra lyri-comique, 1, Sedaine, after La Fontaine: *Le calendrier des vieillards*), unperf. [refused by Opéra, 1785], *Pc**, *Po** (inc.)

Robin et Marion, unperf., *Po**

Music in: Le bouquet de Thalie, 1764

*

P.-J.-B. Nougaret: *De l'art du théâtre* (Paris, 1769)

L. Garcin: *Traité du mélo-drame, ou réflexions sur la musique dramatique* (Paris, 1772)

A.-E.-M. Grétry: *Mémoires, ou Essais sur la musique* (Paris, 1789, 2/1797)

A.-E. Choron and F. J. M. Fayolle: *Dictionnaire historique des musiciens* (Paris, 1810–11)

A.-C. Quatremère de Quincy: *Notice historique sur la vie et les ouvrages de M. de Monsigny* (Paris, 1818)

A. Alexandre: 'Eloge historique de Pierre-Alexandre de Monsigny', *Mémoires de la Société royale d'Arras*, ii (1819), 37–57

P. Hédouin: *Notice historique sur P.-A. de Monsigny* (Paris, 1821); repr. in *Mosaïque* (Paris, 1856), 259–81

'Quelques réflexions inédites de Sedaine sur l'opéra-comique', *Théâtre choisi de G. de Pixérécourt* (Nancy, 1843), iv, 501–16

L.-P. de Ségur: *Mémoires, souvenirs et anecdotes*, ed. F. Barrière (Paris, 1859), 18–20

C. Collé: *Journal et mémoires (1748–1772)* (Paris, 1868)

M. Tourneux, ed.: *Correspondance littéraire, philosophique et critique par Grimm, Diderot, Raynal, Meister, etc.*, (Paris, 1877–82)

A. Font: *Favart, l'opéra comique et la comédie-vaudeville aux XVIIe et XVIIIe siècles* (Paris, 1894)

A. Pougin: *Monsigny et son temps* (Paris, 1908)

C. Collé: *Journal historique inédit pour les années 1761 et 1762* (Paris, 1911), 345–9

G. Cucuel: *Les créateurs de l'opéra-comique français* (Paris, 1914), 135–51

L. de La Laurencie: 'La musique française de Lulli à Gluck (1687–1789)', *EMDC*, I/iii (1931), 1479–81

L. P. Arnoldson: *Sedaine et les musiciens de son temps* (Paris, 1934)

P. Druilhe: *Monsigny* (Paris, 1955)

E. F. Schmid: 'Mozart und Monsigny', *MJb 1957*, 57–62

M. A. Rayner: *The Social and Literary Aspects of Sedaine's Dramatic Work* (diss., U. of London, 1960)

L. Fox: '"La belle Arsène" (1773) by P.-A. Monsigny', *RMFC*, ix (1969), 141–4

K. M. Smith: *Egidio Duni and the Development of the 'Opéra-comique' from 1753 to 1770* (diss., Cornell U., 1980)

D. Heartz: 'The Beginnings of Operatic Romance: Rousseau, Sedaine, and Monsigny', *Eighteenth Century Studies*, xv (1981–2), 149–78

J. B. Kopp: *The 'Drame Lyrique': a Study in the Esthetics of Opéra-comique, 1762–1791* (diss., U. of Pennsylvania, 1982)

D. Charlton: *Grétry and the Growth of Opéra-comique* (Cambridge, 1986)

——: '"L'art dramatico-musical": an essay', *Music and Theatre: Essays in Honour of Winton Dean* (Cambridge, 1987), 229–62

E. A. Cook: *The Operatic Ensemble in France 1673–1775* (diss., U. of East Anglia, 1989)

B. A. Brown: *Gluck and the French Theatre in Vienna* (Oxford, 1991)   MICHEL NOIRAY

Montag aus Licht ('Monday from Light'). Opera in three acts, a greeting and a farewell by KARLHEINZ STOCKHAUSEN to his own libretto; Milan, Teatro alla Scala, 7 May 1988.

Montag is the inaugural opera of Stockhausen's seven-part *LICHT* cycle, though it was the third to be composed (from 1984 to 1988). Monday is 'Eve's Day'; more specifically, in Stockhausen's words, it is 'a musical celebration in honour of the Mother, a festival of the birth and rebirth of Man'. Eve here embodies fertility, regeneration and creativity, as well as eroticism and seduction.

Visually, all three acts are dominated by a huge statue of Eve. At the start of Act 1, 'Eve's First Birth', the statue is seated by the sea, being prepared for birth by 21 attendant midwives. Three sopranos (representing Eve) sing from the transparent larynx of the statue, whose womb then glows and gives birth to 14 strange creatures, seven of them boys already showing signs of senility, and the other seven, boys with animals' heads. Three sailors (tenors) land on the shore, bringing gifts and singing a second 'birth aria' (the Eve-sopranos having sung the first). The newborn are being taken for a pram-ride ('Baby-Buggie-Boogie') when Lucifer (bass/mime) suddenly appears and derides Eve's aberrant progeny. He is buried in the sand by the midwives but re-emerges, imperiously ordering the first-born back to the womb.

At the beginning of Act 2, 'Eve's Second Birth', the sea has frozen over and the women are breaking the ice with axes. Suddenly the stage lights go out and a candle-bearing girls' choir ('Eve's Children') dressed as lily blossoms processes down through the auditorium, singing a hymn of praise in anticipation of the Second Birth. The Eve statue is 'fertilized' by a piano piece (*Klavierstück XIV*, originally written for Pierre Boulez's 60th birthday), her womb glows, and seven boys emerge. Then the heart of the sculpture opens out and Eve (basset-horn) emerges as 'Coeur'. Along with three further 'bassetistes' (one of them actually a singer), she teaches the children the songs of the seven days of the week and then seduces/abducts them.

In Act 3, 'Eve's Magic', the ice has melted. The boys of the second act have become men, and sing in praise of Eve (as basset-hornist), while the women tell of the coming of a miraculous young musician. The flautist Ave (Eva in reverse – her mirror image in male clothing) appears; the two fall in love and intertwine both physically and musically. Some children return, and Ave

'Montag aus Licht'
(Stockhausen): Act 1 (the
arrival of the sailors)
from the original
production at La Scala,
Milan, 7 May 1988

gradually assumes the role of Pied Piper, first inducing the children to mimic her/him musically, and then leading them away into 'higher worlds with green clouds', where their music turns into birdsong. At this, the Eve sculpture loses its overtly human form and reverts to nature: it becomes a mountain, richly overrun by flora and fauna.

Though the general melodic and formal character of *Montag* follows the path established in *Donnerstag*, there are many new features and shifts of emphasis. Perhaps the most striking of these, coming after the hieratic, hard-edged styles of *Donnerstag* and *Samstag*, is a softer, more sensual tone, particularly in Act 3. This has many causes, including the prominence of the major 3rd (Eve's interval, as opposed to Michael's 'heroic' 4th, and Lucifer's 'evil' major 7th), the preponderance of the female voice, often in chorus (recalling Wagner's Rhinemaidens, rather than the Valkyries), and the dominant role of woodwind (basset-horn and flute) as solo instruments. *Montag* calls for six solo instrumentalists, 14 solo voices and an actor.

Apart from the sophisticated microtonal writing and exploration of new timbres for the woodwind soloists, the most notable aspect of the instrumental writing is Stockhausen's replacement of the traditional orchestra with a 'modern orchestra' consisting of three pairs of synthesizers using MIDI facilities, and with programmed timbres created by the composer. On the one hand, this 'modern orchestra' is Stockhausen's latest exploration of the musical potential of current technology; on the other, it presumably signals a final disenchantment with the present-day orchestra, both musically and socially. Although it is always unwise to predict the future course of Stockhausen's music, the 'modern orchestra' seems likely to become a permanent fixture.

The instrumental ensemble having become largely electronic, the function of the music on tape has changed. For *Montag*, Stockhausen has composed a large number of 'sound scenes' which are inserted into the action not as an augmentation of the available forces (as in *Donnerstag*), but almost confrontationally, as *agents provocateurs*.

Although the performance of the *Licht* operas has become almost a 'family affair', in the sense of revolving around a hand-picked group of singers and performers (some of whom are literally members of Stockhausen's family) so as to ensure the highest possible level of performance, *Montag* has also managed, in the passages for children's choir and mixed chorus, to accommodate the skills of gifted and committed amateurs.

RICHARD TOOP

Montagnana, Antonio (*b* Venice; *fl* 1730–50). Italian bass. In 1730 he sang at Rome and in 1731 at Turin in operas by Porpora, who is said to have been his teacher. He was a member of Handel's company at the King's Theatre, 1731–3, and may have made his début as Leo in *Tamerlano*. During the 1731–2 season he sang in revivals of *Poro*, *Admeto*, *Flavio* and *Giulio Cesare*, in first productions of *Ezio* (Varus) and *Sosarme* (Altomaro), and in Ariosti's *Coriolano* and a pasticcio. The following season he was in Leo's *Catone*, revivals of Handel's *Alessandro*, *Tolomeo* and probably *Floridante*, the first production of *Orlando* (Zoroastro) and Handel's first London oratorios. He sang with the Opera of the Nobility throughout its four London seasons (1733–7) in at least 15 operas at Lincoln's Inn Fields and the King's Theatre, including Porpora's *Arianna in Nasso*, *Enea nel Lazio*, *Polifemo*, *Ifigenia in Aulide* and *Mitridate*, Hasse's *Artaserse* and *Siroe*, Veracini's *Adriano* and *La clemenza di Tito*, Giovanni Bononcini's *Astarto* and Handel's *Ottone*. In 1737–8 he was a member of Heidegger's company at the King's, appearing in two pasticcios, Pescetti's *La conquista del vello d'oro*, Veracini's *Partenio* and two new Handel operas, *Faramondo* and *Serse*, as Gustavo and Ariodates. For ten years from 1740 he was attached to the royal chapel at Madrid, where he sang in many operas and cantatas.

When he arrived in London Montagnana was a remarkable singer, a genuine bass with powerful low notes, considerable agility and a compass of more than two octaves (E to f'), as seen in the music composed for him by Handel, who regularly expanded the parts he sang in revivals. But by 1738 his powers were on the wane and in his last two Handel parts his compass had shrunk to G to eb'. Burney singled out his voice's 'depth, power, mellowness and peculiar accuracy of intonation in hitting distant intervals'. In *Orlando* a listener reported that he sang 'with a voice like a Canon' – presumably ballistic rather than clerical.   WINTON DEAN

Montague, Diana (*b* Winchester, 8 April 1953). English mezzo-soprano. She studied in Manchester, then sang in the Glyndebourne chorus, making her solo début in 1977 as Zerlina with the Glyndebourne Touring Opera. While engaged at Covent Garden (1978–83) she sang Kate Pinkerton, Laura (*Luisa Miller*), the Lady Artist (*Lulu*), Annius, Parséis (*Esclarmonde*), Nicklausse and Cherubino, the last a role she has also sung with the ENO and Scottish Opera and at the Salzburg and Aix-en-Provence festivals. She sang Wellgunde and Siegrune at Bayreuth (1983) and has appeared in Lyons, Nancy, Brussels, Lausanne, Frankfurt, Edinburgh and at the Metropolitan, where she made her début in 1987 as Annius. Her repertory includes Proserpine (Monteverdi's *Orfeo*), Purcell's Dido, Idamantes, Dorabella, Isolier (*Le comte Ory*), the Fox (*The Cunning Little Vixen*) and Mélisande. She has a creamy voice, a handsome presence and, adept in the Classical style, excels as Gluck's Orpheus, which she sang at Glyndebourne in 1989, and in the title role of *Iphigénie en Tauride*, which she sang for the WNO in 1992.

ELIZABETH FORBES

Montarsolo, Paolo (*b* Portici, 16 March 1925). Italian bass. He studied in Naples and at the Scuola della Scala, Milan, making his début in 1950 at Bologna as Lunardo in *I quattro rusteghi*. Engagements quickly followed in major Italian centres, notably at the Piccola Scala in 1956 in *Le crescendo* (Cherubini) and at La Scala in 1959 as Gianni Schicchi. The first of his many Glyndebourne appearances was in 1957 as Mustafà (*L'italiana in Algeri*), which he also sang in his American début at Dallas that year. His Metropolitan Opera début was in 1975 as Don Pasquale, and that at Covent Garden with the Scala company in 1976 as Don Magnifico; he did not appear with the Royal Opera until 1988 but was still a wonderfully engaging Mustafà; he returned as Don Pasquale (1990) and Dulcamara (1992). A *basso buffo* specialist, he is a stylish and versatile singer who has been heard in some 185 roles; he has also directed more than 30 opera productions.

NOËL GOODWIN

Monte Carlo. Resort in the principality of Monaco. It was founded in 1858. As Monte Carlo became increasingly fashionable in the 19th century, François Blanc, president of the Société des Bains, owners of the famous casino (built 1862–3), added lyric concerts to the casino's programmes. His widow engaged Charles Garnier, architect of the Paris Opéra, to design an opera house, known today as the Salle Garnier. (It has variously been known as the Grand Théâtre de Monte Carlo, the Théâtre du Casino and the Opéra de Monte Carlo.) Built alongside the casino and sharing its entrance foyer, it seats 524, principally in stalls but with several boxes (see illustration). From its inauguration in 1879 under the direction of Jules Cohen and Camille Blanc, the Monte Carlo Opéra engaged the most famous artists of the day, including Léon Carvalho, Patti, Melba, Nordica, Scalchi, Caron, Faure, Maurel, Plançon, Pandolfini, Devriès and Renaud. The company's celebrity was coupled with that of its most famous director, Raoul Gunsbourg (1893–1951), under whose direction Caruso, Ruffo, Shalyapin (who sang at Monte Carlo for over 30 years), Farrar and Thill were engaged at the earliest stages of their careers and remained faithful performers, together with more established artists such as Tamagno, Litvinne, Journet, Schipa, Gigli, Lauri-Volpi, Lubin, Muzio, Bori, Pons and De Luca. Indeed, Gunsbourg's casts rivalled those of La Scala, the Metropolitan, Covent Garden and the

Interior of the Salle Garnier, Monte Carlo, during a performance of Gounod's 'Faust' on 20 January 1880: engraving from 'L'illustration' (24 January 1880)

Colón, and his company gave guest performances in many capitals. He played an important role in Dyagilev's enterprises, and also presented or commissioned new works for Monte Carlo: *Le jongleur de Notre-Dame*, *Chérubin*, *Thérèse*, *Don Quichotte*, *Roma*, *Cléopâtre* and *Amadis* by Massenet, *Amica* by Mascagni, *Pénélope* by Fauré, *La rondine* by Puccini, *L'aiglon* by Ibert and Honegger, and *L'enfant et les sortilèges* by Ravel, in addition to operas by Saint-Saëns, De Lara and Franck. Many French premières of the works of young Italian composers and of Richard Strauss were also given there. Gunsbourg revived operas by Lully, Rameau, Bizet and Gounod, although he never hesitated to modify works, often profoundly, by cuts, additions and substitutions; he was the first to stage Berlioz's *La damnation de Faust* (1893).

Important conductors of the opera orchestra have included Paul Paray (1928–44) and Louis Frémaux (1956–65). Maurice Besnard (1952–65) continued the casting traditions by employing Corelli, Di Stefano, Bergonzi, Labò, Mödl, Crespin, Tebaldi, Schwarzkopf and Gencer, often quite early in their careers; since Gunsbourg's days, however, financial means have slowly diminished. Succeeding directors have been Louis Ducreux (1966–71); the composer Renzo Rossellini (1972–6), who strove to return to a period of creativity with his own works and those of Menotti, Raffaello de Banfield and Damase; Guy Grinda (1977–84); and, from 1984, John Mordler. The season now runs from January to April and usually consists of three performances of each of four productions, with guest singers, accompanied by the Monte Carlo PO (which also has its own concert season in its own auditorium). The festival Le Printemps des Arts de Monte Carlo is held annually in April and May; it includes lyric recitals and usually one or two performances of a staged opera, generally an 18th-century work.

*

T. J. Walsh: *Monte Carlo Opera, 1879–1909* (Dublin, 1975)

G. Favre: *Etudes musicales monégasques: notes d'histoire (18e–20e siècles)* (Paris, 1976)

T. J. Walsh: *Monte Carlo Opera, 1910–1951* (Kilkenny, 1986)

M. Mari: 'Quarante ans de créations françaises à l'Opéra de Monte Carlo (1945–1985)', *Le théâtre lyrique français 1945–1985*, ed. D. Pistone (Paris, 1987), 339–46   CHARLES PITT

Montéclair, Michel Pignolet [Pinolet] **de** (*b* Andelot, Haute-Marne, bap. 4 Dec 1667; *d* Aumont, 22 Sept 1737). French composer. Shortly after arriving in Paris in 1697, he added 'Montéclair' to his name. A theorist and fine teacher, he is known to have been music master to François Couperin's daughters, and also to Charles-Henri de Lorraine, Prince of Vaudémont and the governor of Milan, whom he accompanied to Italy. As a player of the *basse de violon*, in 1699 he was admitted to the *petit choeur* of the Opéra orchestra; according to Corrette (*Méthode théorique*, 1741) he introduced the double bass into this orchestra, probably for the première of Theobaldo di Gatti's *Scylla* in 1701, and certainly for performances of Campra's *Tancrède* in 1702. His output consists mainly of *airs*, motets and French and Italian cantatas, and he also wrote several musical treatises.

Like Rameau, Montéclair came to opera late in his career; he was 49 when *Les festes de l'été*, an *opéra-ballet* in a prologue and three *entrées* to a libretto by Pellegrin (writing under the pseudonym of Mlle Barbier), had its première at the Opéra on 12 June 1716. The success of this work encouraged him to collaborate with the same librettist in creating one of the most original works of the 18th century, a biblical opera to be produced during Lent (when operatic performances were not usually allowed). *Jephté*, a five-act *tragédie en musique*, given at the Opéra on 28 February 1732, was warmly received and held its place in the repertory until 1761. Both operas were published in Paris, *Les festes* in 1716 and *Jephté* in about 1732.

Despite this small operatic output, Montéclair was nonetheless an important composer of the pre-Ramist period and had a direct influence on Rameau. Many of the features of his style are found in the operas of Campra and Destouches, but there is a new sense of the theatre in *Les festes de l'été* and especially in *Jephté*. The choral writing is varied and imaginative; the third act of *Les festes de l'été*, for example, contains both a double chorus and an *a cappella* one. Moreover, Montéclair had a very precise style of instrumental writing and often sought unusual timbres and combinations. He liked to give his own instrument prominence, as in the prelude for three basses in *Les festes de l'été* (3.i), and his orchestra included *musettes* (already introduced by Marais, Jean-Baptiste Stuck and Jean-Baptiste Matho) and also horns. According to Lemaître, it was not until *Les festes de l'été* (2.iii) that hunting horns featured officially at the Opéra. Montéclair, prudently, wrote no part for these horns, but simply directed that they should play. The care he lavished on instrumental detail was not limited to orchestration; he also gave thought to bowing and fingering (*Méthode facile pour apprendre à jouer du violon*, Paris, 1711–12) and even to notation, particularly in the matter of transposing instruments.

Of the same generation as Campra, Desmarets and Destouches, Montéclair was one of the most original figures of his time, a composer whose aesthetic place was clearly among the next generation.

See also FESTES DE L'ÉTÉ, LES and JEPHTÉ.

*

E. Titon du Tillet: *Le Parnasse françois*, suppl. i (Paris, 1743)

J. A. L. de La Fage: 'Michel Montéclair', *Revue et gazette musicale de Paris* (1857), no.31, pp.250–52, 259–61

J. Carlez: *Un opéra biblique au XVIIIe siècle* (Paris, 1879)

E. Voillard: *Essai sur Montéclair* (Paris, 1879)

E. Borrel: 'Notes sur l'orchestration de l'opéra Jephte de Monteclair (1733) et de la symphonie des Eléments de J. F. Rebel (1737)', *ReM*, no.226 (1955), 105–16

R. Viollier: 'Trois Jephtés, trois styles', *Revue de musicologie*, xliii (1959), 125–6

J. R. Anthony: *French Baroque Music from Beaujoyeulx to Rameau* (London, 1973, 2/1978)

E. Lemaître: *L'orchestre dans le théâtre lyrique français chez les continuateurs de Lully* (thesis, Paris Conservatoire, 1977)

M. Cyr: 'Basses et basse continue in the Orchestra of the Paris Opéra 1700–1764', *EMc*, x (1982), 155–70   JEAN DURON

Montemezzi, Italo (*b* Vigasio, nr Verona, 4 Aug 1875; *d* Vigasio, 15 May 1952). Italian composer. He abandoned engineering for music and entered the Milan Conservatory (at the advanced level) in 1896. His diploma work in 1900 was the lyric scena *Cantico dei cantici*, which was conducted in the same year by Toscanini; he also won a prize for his one-act opera *Bianca*. After teaching harmony at the conservatory he competed (unsuccessfully) for the Sonzogno prize with a one-act version of *Giovanni Gallurese*. The three-act version, conducted by his friend Tullio Serafin, was performed in Turin with financial support from well-wishers in Verona, and won considerable acclaim and the support of the publisher Ricordi. Ricordi introduced him to Luigi Illica and commissioned a new opera,

Héllera, based on Benjamin Constant's *Adolphe*; when performed in 1909, however, it had little success, owing to disagreements between composer and librettist. Montemezzi won lasting fame with *L'amore dei tre re*, performed at La Scala in 1913 (the singers included De Angelis and Galeffi) and at the Metropolitan in the following year. During the war years he wrote *La nave*, adapted by Tito Ricordi from one of D'Annunzio's less successful plays; its first performance coincided with the end of the war, and perhaps the bellicose ideas expressed in the text made it less acceptable in the post-war years. Many critics pointed out that D'Annunzio's text – verbose and rhetorical, and permeated with sensuousness, sadism and imperialist ideology symbolized by the growth of the maritime power of Venice – was not suitable material to provide a sequence of musical events or to identify the psychology of the characters.

Montemezzi continued to compose while engaged mainly in conducting his own works in the most important opera houses, especially in the USA. In 1931 he wrote *La notte di Zoraima*, to a trite libretto with an Inca setting. In 1943 *L'incantesimo*, to a libretto by Sem Benelli with a medieval symbolic subject, was broadcast by NBC; it was not staged until 1952 (in Verona) a few months after the composer's death. From 1939 to 1949 Montemezzi was in the USA, but he returned in his last years to his native Vigasio, where he had composed all his operas.

From *Giovanni Gallurese* on, Montemezzi's style is directed towards the integration of a typically italianate vocal line into a skilfully and densely written orchestral texture, and can thus be considered as continuing the trend, represented above all by Catalani and Franchetti, towards the absorption into the Italian tradition of certain Wagnerian elements. The use of simple thematic references, consisting mainly of rhythmic ostinato figures, is characteristic of his style. In his first operas, especially *L'amore dei tre re*, there are also traces of the influence of Debussy, and in *La nave*, of Richard Strauss. In D'Annunzio's frenzied text, and especially in the hysterical and lascivious central character of Basiliola, who seeks vengeance through seduction, Montemezzi has a chance to create a character reminiscent of Salome and Electra: there are echoes of expressionism in the frequent parlando passages for the chorus and in the animated vocal writing. The later operas add nothing new to Montemezzi's style, and embody a decidedly traditional type of drama; the character of Zoraima, for example, an avenging seductress, is only a pale shadow of Basiliola within an obvious plot and a retrospective musical idiom. An opera based on Edmond Rostand's *La princesse lointaine* was not completed.

See also AMORE DEI TRE RE, L' and GIOVANNI GALLURESE.

autograph MSS in I-Mr
Bianca (1, Z. Strani), unperf.
Giovanni Gallurese (melodramma storico, 3, F. D'Angelantonio), Turin, Vittorio Emanuele, 28 Jan 1905, vs (Milan, 1905)
Héllera (melodramma, 3, L. Illica, after B. Constant: *Adolphe*), Turin, Regio, 17 March 1909, vs (Milan, 1909)
L'amore dei tre re (poema tragico, 3, S. Benelli), Milan, Scala, 10 April 1913, vs (Milan, 1913), full score (Milan, 1925)
La nave (tragedia, prol., 3 episodes, G. D'Annunzio), Milan, Scala, 3 Nov 1918 (Milan, 1919)
La notte di Zoraima (dramma, 1, M. Ghisalberti), Milan, Scala, 31 Jan 1931, vs (Milan, 1931)
L'incantesimo (dramma lirico, 1, Benelli), NBC, 1943; staged, Verona, Arena, 9 Aug 1952

DEUMM (C. Parmentola)
G. Ricordi: 'La nostra musica: Italo Montemezzi', *Musica e musicisti*, lx (1905), 658–9
L. Gilman: 'A Note on Montemezzi', *Nature in Music and Other Studies in the Tone-Poetry of Today* (New York, 1914), 155–66
U. Navarra: *Noterelle critiche sulla tragedia 'La nave'* (Milan, 1918)
G. M. Gatti: 'Gabriele D'Annunzio and the Italian Opera-Composers', *MQ*, x (1924), 263–88
L. Tomelleri: 'La nave (D'Annunzio e Montemezzi)', in L. Tomelleri, I. Pizzetti and others: *Gabriele d'Annunzio e la musica* (Milan, 1939), 40–46; repr. in *RMI*, xliii (1939), 200–06
L. Tretti and L. Fiumi, eds.: *Omaggio a Italo Montemezzi* (Verona, 1952)
T. Serafin: 'Italo Montemezzi', *ON*, xvii/12 (1952–3), 10, 31
M. Morini: 'Carteggi inediti di Montemezzi, Illica e G. Ricordi per *Héllera*', *Ricordiana*, new ser., ii (1956), 229–32
A. Toni: 'Italo Montemezzi', ibid, 233–8
W. B. Rudolph: '*Verismo' and its Influence on 'L'amore dei tre re'* by Italo Montemezzi and *'Francesca da Rimini'* by Riccardo Zandonai (diss., Brigham Young U., 1973)
F. Opice: *Suggestioni dannunziane nel teatro musicale italiano del novecento* (diss., Catholic U., Milan, 1974)
D. Borghi: *'La nave' di G. D'Annunzio, musica di I. Montemezzi* (diss., U. of Bologna, 1976)
LUCA ZOPPELLI

Montepulciano. Town in central Italy, in the province of Siena (Tuscany). It is the headquarters of the Cantiere Internazionale d'Arte, a music festival started in 1976 by Hans Werner Henze. The initial idea of the Comune's administration was to found a festival with special characteristics in a small town where there was little musical activity. In the Cantiere, both young and mature artists are invited from all over the world to take part in works of entertainment, actively cooperating at all levels (administrative, executive, creative) with the residents of the town. The word 'cantiere' (workshop) refers above all to this interchange between professional guests and citizens. The artistic director from 1976 to 1980 and again in 1989 was Henze; in 1981–8 the post was shared by Jan Latham-König and Gianluigi Gelmetti. Performances take place in July and August in the Teatro Poliziano (built in 1795, cap. 400), in churches and in the open air. In addition to operas rarely performed in Italy, like *Il turco in Italia*, *I masnadieri*, *Dido and Aeneas* and the pasticcio *L'ape musicale*, programmes have included first performances of such new works as Thomas Jahn's *Il palazzo zoologico* (1976), Henze's *Pollicino* (1980) and Arturo Annechino's *La notte di gioia*.   ARRIGO QUATTROCCHI

Montero, José Angel (*b* Caracas, 2 Oct 1832; *d* Caracas, 24 Aug 1881). Venezuelan composer. He studied with his father, José María Montero (1781–1869), whom he succeeded as *maestro de capilla* at Caracas cathedral. In addition to writing many sacred works, he collaborated with the leading Venezuelan writers (including Heraclio Martín de la Guardia and Francisco Tosta García) on zarzuelas and 15 extremely well received Spanish-language operettas. His major stage work, *Virginia* (with an Italian text), was the first full-length opera by a native composer performed in the capital. Montero prospered under President Antonio Guzmán Blanco's government; he helped establish the Instituto de Bellas Artes (1877) and in 1881 founded a children's theatre company with Gabriel de Aramburo.

Montero was the most prolific Venezuelan composer of his generation. His zarzuelas show an intimate acquaintance with the music of Arrieta, Barbieri and Gaztambide, and he was equally conversant with the repertory staged by visiting Italian companies at the

Teatro Caracas; *Virginia* may be compared to Verdi's *Attila* or Pacini's *Medea*. It is the consistently high quality of his music rather than any originality of style that places him on a pedestal among his South American contemporaries.

See also VIRGINIA.

all first performed in Caracas

Virginia (tragedia lirica, 3, D. Bancarlari), Teatro Caracas, 27 April 1873

Zarzuelas (selective list): Los alemanes en Italia (4, H. M. de la Guardia), Zarzuela, 22 Sept 1866; Un cortesano en el campo (J. J. de Alcuitta), Zarzuela, 1866; Colegiales sin colegiales (arr. P. Lindaluce), 5 March 1868; Quiero ser ministro (1, M. M. Bermúdez), *c*1870; El charlatan mudo (Aramis [R. Domínguez]), 1873; Doña Irene o La política del hogar (F. Tosta García), Teatro Caracas, 27 Oct 1875; La curiosidad de las mujeres, *c*1876

J. A. Calcaño: *La ciudad y su música: crónica musical de Caracas* (Caracas, 1958, 2/1985)
C. Salas and E. Feo Calcaño: *Sesquicentenario de la ópera en Caracas: relato histórico de ciento cincuenta años de ópera 1808–1958* (Caracas, 1960)
C. Salas: *Historia del teatro en Caracas* (Caracas, 1974)
R. Stevenson: 'National Library Publications in Brazil, Peru, and Venezuela', *Inter-American Music Review*, iii (1980–81), 39–48
A. Calzavara: *Historia de la música en Venezuela: período hispánico con referencias al teatro y la danza* (Caracas, 1987)
M. I. Brito Stelling and S. Daniele: 'Historia del teatro lírico en Caracas: segundo período: del Teatro Caracas al Teatro Guzmán Blanco (1854–1881)', *Revista musical de Venezuela*, ix/24 (1988), 13–45
Diccionario de historia de Venezuela (Caracas, 1988)

ROBERT STEVENSON

Montesanto, Luigi (*b* Palermo, 23 Nov 1887; *d* Milan, 14 June 1954). Italian baritone. He studied in Palermo and made his début there in 1909 as Escamillo. He sang at Buenos Aires from 1910, appearing as John the Baptist in the local première of *Salome*, and sang Rossini's Figaro in the opening season of the Théâtre des Champs-Elysées in Paris (1913). At the Metropolitan he created Michele in *Il tabarro* (1918), thereafter appearing in Chicago during the 1920s. Until 1940 he was successful at the leading Italian houses as Scarpia, Rigoletto, Wolfram and Germont. He appeared in Britain in joint recitals with Toti dal Monte. After his retirement he taught in Milan; Giuseppe di Stefano was among his pupils.

For illustration see TABARRO, IL. DAVID CUMMINGS

Monteux, Pierre (*b* Paris, 4 April 1875; *d* Hancock, ME, 1 July 1964). American conductor of French birth. While still a student at the Paris Conservatoire he was engaged as violist at the Opéra-Comique, where he led his section at the première of *Pelléas et Mélisande*. From 1911 to 1914 he worked for Dyagilev's Ballets Russes (conducting the premières of *Petrushka* and *The Rite of Spring*) and in 1917 was put in charge of French repertory at the Metropolitan Opera for two seasons. In addition to *Faust*, *Carmen*, *Thaïs*, *Samson et Dalila*, *Mireille* and Rabaud's *Mârouf* he conducted the American première of *The Golden Cockerel*. In 1953 he returned to the Metropolitan for a season (which included *Les contes d'Hoffmann* and *Orfeo ed Euridice*) and the following year he conducted Massenet's *Manon* at the San Francisco Opera. Never an ostentatious conductor, Monteux used small but decisive gestures to obtain playing of fine texture, careful detail and powerful effect. He recorded *Manon*, *La traviata* and *Orfeo*. MARTIN COOPER

Monteverdi [Monteverde], **Claudio** (**Zuan** [Giovanni] **Antonio**) (*b* Cremona, bap. 15 May 1567; *d* Venice, 29 Nov 1643). Italian composer. Monteverdi is the earliest composer whose operas are still regularly performed. His *Orfeo* is generally regarded as the first work of genius in the history of opera and, indeed, all his surviving operas are highly regarded for their penetrating exploration of human psychology.

1. Early years. 2. The Mantuan years. 3. The Venetian years. 4. Style.

1. EARLY YEARS. Monteverdi was the eldest child of Maddalena Zignani and Baldassare Monteverdi, a chemist who also practised as a surgeon. He was musically precocious. He published his first volume of compositions in 1582 at the age of 15, and by 1590–91, the years in which he obtained his first employment, he had published no fewer than five volumes of music, including two books of five-part madrigals (1587, 1590). On the title-pages of all these publications he described himself as a pupil of Marc'Antonio Ingegneri, *maestro di cappella* of Cremona Cathedral; presumably he was a private pupil since he does not seem to have been employed at the cathedral in any capacity.

2. THE MANTUAN YEARS. In 1590 or 1591 Monteverdi was appointed 'suonatore di vivuola' at the court of Vincenzo Gonzaga, Duke of Mantua (according to Praetorius, 'vivola' signifies an instrument of the violin family). He also played viols: in the 'Dichiaratione' published in his *Scherzi musicali* of 1607, his brother Giulio Cesare mentioned that he played 'the two *viole bastarde*'; Bertolotti (1890) cites a document in which he is also described as a player of the theorbo [chitarrone]. Monteverdi's appointment at Mantua was part of a more general expansion of the court musical establishment begun by Duke Vincenzo when he succeeded to the duchy in 1587. Among other things, he established at Mantua an ensemble of singers modelled on the *concerto di donne* of Ferrara, who, according to Vincenzo Giustiniani (*c*1628), cultivated a theatrical manner of performance, using gesture and facial expression, as well as musical devices such as rubato, crescendo and diminuendo, to project to an audience the emotions of the texts that they sang. The first impact of this ensemble on Monteverdi's approach to composition can be seen in the dramatically conceived five-part setting *Vattene pur, crudel*, published in his third book of madrigals (1592). This is a setting of three stanzas from Torquato Tasso's epic poem *La Gerusalemme liberata* (xvi. 59–60, 63), in which the sorceress Armida, deserted by the Christian knight Rinaldo whom she loves, first threatens him with vengeance and then laments her loss.

Little is known for certain of Monteverdi's activity during his first ten years at Mantua, although he must have been involved either as instrumentalist or composer in many of the theatrical entertainments – ballets, tournaments and *intermedi* – staged there during these years to celebrate birthdays, weddings and anniversaries, or simply as carnival entertainments (see Parisi 1989). From June to November 1595 he accompanied Duke Vincenzo on a military campaign to Hungary and from June to October 1599 travelled with him to Spa (Flanders). Immediately before departing on this latter journey, on 20 May 1599, he married Claudia Cattaneo, a singer at the Mantuan court.

Following the death of Benedetto Pallavicino on 26 November 1601, Monteverdi successfully petitioned the duke to appoint him court choirmaster, a post which placed him in charge of secular music of all kinds at Mantua. In 1603 and 1605 respectively, he published his fourth and fifth books of madrigals, the music of which belongs entirely to his Mantuan years. In the preface to Book 5 he responded to criticism published in 1603 by Giovanni Maria Artusi of supposed irregularities in his use of dissonance in madrigal settings. In so doing he coined the term *seconda pratica* (the second practice) to describe the musical procedures that he used, which were determined by his response to the text rather than by the purely musical norms of the *prima pratica*. The books include settings which demonstrate that Monteverdi had continued to learn from the experience of writing for virtuoso singers and from the need to devise striking musical images that could easily be appreciated by an audience. They show, too, his growing ability to convey the emotional content of the texts he set and to dramatize the situations they represent. Book 5 includes a number of settings of texts from Guarini's pastoral play *Il pastor fido*, a performance of which had been staged at Mantua in 1598 with *intermedi* by Gastoldi. It also includes six madrigals with obligatory basso continuo accompaniment, a technique also used for the new styles of solo song and opera at Florence; moreover, the first of these, *Ahi, come a un vago sol*, is structured like the refrain choruses of early opera. The styles and techniques of Monteverdi's Mantuan madrigals form an indispensable background to an understanding of his early operatic style. For though in his operas *Orfeo* and *Arianna* he employed the new operatic recitative style of Peri, the individual quality of his writing owes much to his experience as a madrigalist.

The earliest documentary evidence of Monteverdi's involvement in dramatic composition survives in a letter of December 1604 in which he discussed the composition of two *entrate* for a theatrical entertainment, presumably a ballet on the myth of Endymion. This letter, and others like it, in which Monteverdi discusses the composition of music for dramatic entertainments, are valuable not only for the information they provide on works now lost but also because they reveal his keen appreciation of the problems involved in mounting works of this kind, and his ideas on their staging and other aspects of performance.

Monteverdi's first opera, *Orfeo*, to a libretto by the Mantuan court secretary Alessandro Striggio, was first performed on 24 February 1607 in the ducal palace at Mantua. It was commissioned by Francesco Gonzaga, the duke's elder son, as a carnival entertainment to be performed before the Accademia degli Invaghiti. Francesco Gonzaga's interest in opera at this date may have stemmed from a wish to rival the activities of his younger, intellectually gifted, brother Ferdinando, who had been studying law, theology and philosophy at the University of Pisa since 1605. Ferdinando was protector of the Florentine Accademia degli Elevati, whose members included the composers Peri, Caccini and Marco da Gagliano; he wrote the text and music of a ballet performed for the Florentine court at the Pisan carnival of 1606; and for Carnival 1607, the season for which *Orfeo* was commissioned, he wrote a *comedia in musica*. If such rivalry, which also had a larger Florentine–Mantuan dimension, was indeed the motivating force behind the commissioning of *Orfeo*, it might also help to explain why the score of this home-grown Mantuan opera was published, in 1609, while the

apparently more important *Arianna*, which had a Florentine librettist, remained unpublished.

On 10 September 1607 Monteverdi's wife died at his father's house in Cremona. A fortnight later Monteverdi was recalled to Mantua to begin work on the music for the forthcoming marriage of Francesco Gonzaga to Margherita, daughter of Duke Carlo Emanuele of Savoy. His contribution to the festivities was to consist of two large-scale dramatic works, the opera *Arianna* and the ballet *Mascherata dell'ingrate* (as it was called in its 1608 version), both to texts by the Florentine Ottavio Rinuccini, and a prologue for a performance of Guarini's comedy *Idropica*, for which *intermedi* and *licenza* were to be supplied by other composers (the texts were by the Genoese poet Gabriello Chiabrera). All these had to be completed and rehearsed in a short space of time, since it was planned to hold the wedding festivities before the end of Carnival (i.e. by 19 February) 1608. In the event, political considerations caused a postponement of the wedding; the opera *Dafne* by the Florentine Gagliano was staged in February for the entertainment of the guests assembled in Mantua, and the main celebrations took place in May and June. *Arianna* was performed on 28 May in a theatre seating about 5000 people which had been specially constructed for the wedding entertainments (according to Federico Follino, its now famous lament caused all the ladies present to shed tears). *Idropica*, the main theatrical event of the celebrations, was given on 2 June. And the *Mascherata dell'ingrate* was performed on 4 June; the dancers who portrayed the 'ingrate women' included not only eight ladies of the Mantuan aristocracy but also the Duke of Mantua, Prince Francesco and six knights masked and dressed in the same manner as the ladies.

3. THE VENETIAN YEARS. Monteverdi retained the post of court choirmaster at Mantua until 28 July 1612 when, five months after the death of Vincenzo Gonzaga, he was summarily dismissed by the new duke, Francesco. The reasons for his dismissal were partly financial, but he had also incurred the displeasure of Francesco Gonzaga by hinting that he could obtain employment elsewhere (see Parisi 1987). On 19 August 1613 he was appointed choirmaster of the ducal basilica of St Mark's, Venice, a post which effectively made him the city's leading musician. His duties at Venice lay primarily in providing sacred music for St Mark's and in furnishing music for the city's annual round of sacred and civic ritual, the latter including secular music for state banquets. He was also called upon to provide music for state visitors and for those members of the Venetian aristocracy who patronized music. Since the Doge of Venice was a constitutional rather than an absolute ruler, upon whose expenditure from state sources there were severe constraints, and since secular music at Venice was subsidized mainly from the private purses of individuals, there was at first little opportunity there for the composition of opera or other expensive dramatic forms. Monteverdi did, however, continue to receive commissions for such works from outside Venice, and not least from Mantua. During the period up to early 1628 he wrote a number of works for Mantua and began several others, leaving them unfinished as the commissions were cancelled. The ballet *Tirsi e Clori* (1616), the prologue to a sacred play, *La Maddalena* (1617), and the opera *Andromeda* (1620) were completed and performed at Mantua, as was the music for an eclogue by Striggio and an *intermedio* and

licenza for the comedy *Le tre costanti* by Ercole Margliani, which was performed for the celebrations at Mantua following the marriage of Eleonora Gonzaga to the Emperor Ferdinand II in 1622. Monteverdi's subsequent relationship with the imperial court at Vienna seems to have been a close one. In 1628 he revised the text (and possibly the music) of the *Mascherata dell'ingrate* for performance there, and this revised version survives as the *Ballo delle ingrate* in his eighth book of madrigals (*Madrigali guerrieri et amorosi*, 1638), one of the two large-scale collections of music which he dedicated to members of the imperial house towards the end of his life. The same book also includes another ballet, *Volgendo il ciel per l'immortal sentiero*, written probably to celebrate the coronation of the Emperor Ferdinand III in December 1636.

A further commission from outside Venice came in 1627, when Monteverdi was invited by Enzo Bentivoglio to supply music for the wedding celebrations at Parma of Duke Odoardo Farnese. It was originally planned that Odoardo should marry the hunchback Maria Cristina de' Medici (in 1627); in the event, however, he married her younger sister Margherita in 1628. Monteverdi was in Parma in October–November 1627 and again from January to March 1628 working on the music for the wedding; a letter dating from the earlier visit contains an amusing account of his working practices (see Reiner 1964); during the latter visit he wrote a three-part madrigal for a carnival *carro* on the subject of the Argonauts. Monteverdi's contributions to the wedding celebrations were performed in December 1628: they were a prologue, *intermedi* and *licenza* for a performance of Tasso's pastoral play *Aminta* and the music for a tournament on the subject of Mercury and Mars.

Within Venice itself during the 1620s Monteverdi came under the patronage of Girolamo Mocenigo, who, unlike many 17th-century patrons, seems to have had a genuine passion for music. It was for a performance at Mocenigo's apartments in the Palazzo Dandolo (now the Danieli Royal Hotel) that Monteverdi wrote his *Combattimento di Tancredi e Clorinda*, a setting of stanzas from *La Gerusalemme liberata* in which he pioneered his *stile concitato*. The *Combattimento* was presented with stylized staging in Carnival 1624 (possibly 1625) and published as one of the *opuscoli in genere rappresentativo* (little theatrical works) in Monteverdi's eighth book of madrigals. In late 1626 Monteverdi wrote another dramatic work of this kind, *Armida* (now lost), also based on Tasso's poem. He offered this in 1627–8 for performance at Mantua. Another work published under the designation 'opuscolo in genere rappresentativo', the *Lamento della ninfa* (date of composition unknown), was developed as a dramatic work out of a simple strophic text with refrain by Rinuccini.

It was Mocenigo who gave Monteverdi his first opportunity to write a larger-scale dramatic work for Venice. This was the 'favola' *Proserpina rapita*, which Monteverdi composed for the wedding on 16 April 1630 of Mocenigo's daughter Giustiniana to Lorenzo Giustiniani. According to a contemporary description, the performance was given, following a sumptuous wedding banquet in Mocenigo's own apartments, in an upper solar of the Palazzo Dandolo, a part of the palace belonging to the Gritti family. The text was by Giulio Strozzi, who had earlier provided Monteverdi with the text of a comic opera, *La finta pazza Licori*, one of

several aborted projects for Mantua. Several numbers in *Proserpina rapita* were given designations derived from Greek music. One, 'Come dolce hoggi l'auretta', a 'Canzonetta Parthenia cantata da tre ninfe con armonia Lidia, cioè di suono molle', survives in the posthumous *Madrigali e canzonette* (Venice, 1651).

Little is known of Monteverdi's activities during the 1630s, though by mid-1632 he had taken holy orders. He is not known to have been directly involved in the earliest commercial operatic venture at Venice in 1637 – Ferrari and Manelli's *Andromeda* – though singers from the choir of St Mark's took part in the performances. His first contribution to the new commercial opera houses seems to have been a revised version of *Arianna*, given at Venice in 1640, probably at the small Teatro S Moisè. Subsequently, however, he wrote three new operas: *Il ritorno d'Ulisse in patria*, most probably first performed at the Teatro SS Giovanni e Paolo in 1640 and then taken on tour to Bologna, and *Le nozze d'Enea in Lavinia* and *L'incoronazione di Poppea*, both for the Teatro SS Giovanni e Paolo, first performed in 1641 and 1643 respectively. Only a printed scenario for *L'incoronazione* now survives as a record of the first performance (and on its title-page the work is called *La coronatione di Poppea*). The surviving scores date probably from the early 1650s. They seem to have been used by touring companies and probably include music which is not by Monteverdi himself. Curtis (1989) is of the opinion that the finale of Act 3 is by Francesco Sacrati. The text of the renowned final duet, 'Pur ti miro', is taken (possibly with Ferrari's music) from the finale of Benedetto Ferrari's opera *Il pastor regio* in the revised version performed at Bologna in 1641.

Several works once ascribed to Monteverdi are no longer thought to be by him. These are the *Lamento d'Erminia* (I-Vc, Fondo Torrefranca, 'Fucci' MS; see Godt 1979), the *Lamento d'Olimpia* (GB-Lbl, Add. MSS 30491, 31440; ed. W. Osthoff, Milan, 1958; see Bianconi 1982, and Danckwardt 1984), and the opera *Adone* (given at Venice, SS Giovanni e Paolo, 1639–40), the music of which was written by Francesco Manelli.

4. STYLE. The musical setting of *Orfeo* is a remarkable synthesis of elements drawn from the *intermedio* tradition with the new expressive medium of Florentine operatic recitative pioneered by Peri. The *intermedio* tradition is best represented by the first act and the opening of the second act of the opera, in which the action – the celebrations surrounding the marriage of Orpheus and Eurydice – is conveyed mainly through the juxtaposition of choral and instrumental items. The flexibility and expressive power of the new recitative style are fully unleashed only in the second act, in which the messenger Sylvia relates the death of Eurydice. Ex.1 shows Orpheus's reaction to the news, which progresses convincingly from a stunned realization of the finality of death to his angry refusal to accept it. Peri's recitative style, in which rhythm, tessitura and dissonance against the bass combine to convey both the accentuation of the text and its emotional content, is here developed by Monteverdi in a highly sophisticated manner. He repeats lines of the text, emphasizing their meaning and intensifying it through musical repetition and sequence. Moreover, he lends rhetorical and emotional weight to the repetitions of the words 'tu se'' ('you are') by preceding them with long silences. According to one of his contemporaries, Giovanni Battista Doni (a Florentine and thus not an objective commentator) Monteverdi

Ex.1 *Orfeo*, Act 2

['You are dead, my life; and I still breathe? You are parted from me, never more to return, and I remain? No']

Ex.2 *Il ritorno d'Ulisse*, Act 2 scene xii

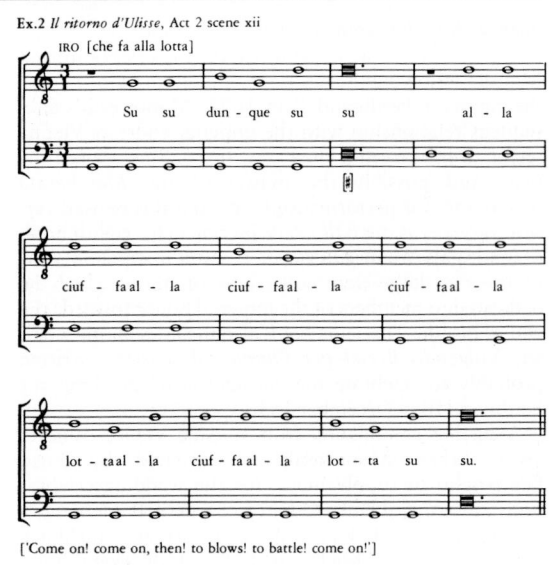

['Come on! come on, then! to blows! to battle! come on!']

and late operas derive from the different demands of court and commercial theatre. For example, the orchestras of the late operas, consisting mainly of strings and continuo instruments, reflect economic considerations in the Venetian public theatres. Their function was mainly to provide ritornellos and sinfonias punctuating the action of the opera: for the most part the voices are accompanied only by continuo instruments in the manner of a sung play. Other changes reflect new directions in dramaturgy and musical style. The librettos of *Ulisse* and *Poppea* move away from the five-act structure of court drama to a three-act form divided into

'received … much aid from Rinuccini' in refining his approach to the setting of poetry. And certainly it is true that in the lament from *Arianna*, dating from 1608, devices such as rhetorical repetition are built into Rinuccini's text: the repetitions of the opening line 'Lasciatemi morire' in part 1 of the lament are a case in point.

Ariadne's lament was widely circulated, in Monteverdi's madrigalian arrangement as well as in manuscript and printed copies of the original, and its success helped to establish laments as a regular feature of later opera. Monteverdi himself included laments in his late Venetian operas, and their style looks back to that of *Orfeo* and *Arianna*; indeed, in the debate over the authorship of *Poppea*, the potency of the writing in a lament such as Octavia's 'A dio Roma' (Act 3) has been cited as indisputable evidence of Monteverdi's authorship. However, Monteverdi's musical legacy to the lament tradition stems rather from his independent *Lamento della ninfa*, which uses a descending four-note ostinato bass. Although Monteverdi was not the first composer to use this device, his stature and his position as one of the founding fathers of Venetian commercial opera may have helped to secure the place of this ostinato as 'an emblem of lament' (Rosand 1979) both in Italian opera and abroad: Dido's lament in Purcell's *Dido and Aeneas*, for example, uses a chromatic form of the same bass.

Some of the differences between Monteverdi's early

Ex.3 *L'incoronazione di Poppea*, Act 3 scene v

['Though lost in you, I shall find myself; in you shall I find myself.']

discrete scenes; and the libretto of *Poppea* was the first to be based on historical rather than mythological characters. Though the late operas still employ choruses – a chorus of Phaeacians in Act 1 of *Ulisse*, for example, and a chorus of Consuls and Tribunes in Act 3 of *Poppea* – the chorus no longer plays a crucial role in articulating the dramatic action of the Venetian operas. As far as musical style is concerned, the late operas combine elements of the older recitative style with styles found in Venetian song- and madrigal-books of the 1620s and 1630s. The first, and least important, of these is Monteverdi's own *stile concitato*. In his original conception it consisted of passages of repeated semiquavers intended to correspond to the pyrrhic measure in poetry, and thus to convey the emotions and sounds of war. In the *Combattimento di Tancredi e Clorinda*, however, he combined this basic conception with other battle-motifs – triadic fanfares, for example, and motifs suggesting the galloping of a horse and the clash of swords. This enlarged conception of the *stile concitato* finds a place in Act 2 scene xii of *Ulisse*, where the comic suitor Irus (whose stutter is also mercilessly guyed by Monteverdi)

offers to fight Ulysses in a passage which, despite its appearance, is intended to be sung rapidly (ex.2). Of more general importance to the musical fabric of Monteverdi's late operas and, indeed, to the growing distinction between recitative and aria in Venetian opera of the 1640s and 1650s, were the aria styles of Venetian songbooks: duple-rhythm arias over basses moving mainly in crotchets of a kind that Monteverdi had anticipated in the aria 'Qual honor di te sia degno' in Act 4 of *Orfeo*, and arias in a suave triple metre. In *Poppea* such triple-time writing becomes almost an emblem of pleasure and sensuality. Nero and Poppaea often sing in this style (ex.3). In delineating the tragic figure of Nero's wife Octavia, however, Monteverdi used triple metre only for a passage in which she speaks scornfully of Nero taking pleasure in Poppaea's arms. For the most part he set her words in the heightened and dignified tones of what was by 1643 the old-fashioned recitative style that he had developed for *Orfeo* and *Arianna*.

See also ARIANNA; INCORONAZIONE DI POPPEA, L'; ORFEO (i); and RITORNO D'ULISSE IN PATRIA, IL.

Editions:	C. Monteverdi: Tutte le opere, ed. G. F. Malipiero (Asolo and Vienna, 1926–42, 2/1954; suppl., 1966) [M] C. Monteverdi: Opera omnia, ed. Fondazione Claudio Monteverdi, IMa, Monumenta, v (1970–) C. Monteverdi: 12 composizioni vocali profane e sacre (inedite), ed. W. Osthoff (Milan, 1958)
Texts:	A. Solerti: Gli albori del melodramma (Milan, 1904/R1969) [SA] ——: Musica, ballo e drammatica alla corte medicea dal 1600 al 1637 (Florence, 1905/R1968 and 1969) [SM] A. Della Corte: Drammi per musica dal Rinuccini allo Zeno (Turin, 1958/R1978) [DC]

title	genre, acts	libretto	first performance	sources, editions and remarks
Orfeo	favola in musica, prol., 5	A. Striggio	Mantua, ducal palace, 24 Feb 1607	lib. (Mantua, 1607 *bis*), score (Venice, 1609/R1927, 1615/R1972); M xi, SA iii, DC i, ed. E. H. Tarr (Paris, 1974)
Arianna	tragedia, 1	O. Rinuccini	Mantua, ducal palace, 28 May 1608	lib. (Mantua, 1608), also in F. Follino: *Compendio delle sontuose feste fatto l'anno M. D.C.VIII nella città di Mantova* (Mantua, 1608), SA ii, DC i; music lost except for 'Lamento d'Arianna' (Venice, 1623), M xi, also pubd in *Il maggio fiorito*, ed. G. B. Rocchigiani (Orvieto, 1623); MS copies of five-section monodic version of lament in *I-MOe* and *Vc*; MS copies of lament, incl. all nine sections of Ariadne's speech, in *GB-Lbl* and *I-Fn* [repr. in SA i]; Monteverdi's five-part arr. of first four sections of lament pubd in his *Il sesto libro de' madrigali* (Venice, 1614), M vi; first four sections of lament also pubd as sacred contrafactum for solo voices, *Pianto della Madonna*, in Monteverdi: *Selva morale e spirituale* (Venice, 1640–41), M xv/3
rev. version			Venice, ?S Moisè, 1640	lib. (Venice, 1640) [according to Ivanovich 1681]
Mascherata dell' In-grate	ballo	Rinuccini	Mantua, ducal palace, 4 June 1608	lib. (Mantua, 1608), also in F. Follino: *Compendio* (Mantua, 1608), SA ii
rev. version			Vienna, imperial court, 1628	text and possibly music rev., pubd as *Ballo delle ingrate* in Monteverdi: *Madrigali guerrieri et amorosi* (Venice, 1638), M viii/2; ed. D. Stevens (London and Mainz, 1960) [incl. 2nd vn pt missing from M viii/2]
Tirsi e Clori	ballo, 1		probably Mantua, ducal palace, carn. 1616	M vii
Le nozze di Tetide	favola marittima	S. Agnelli		known only from Monteverdi's letters; begun Dec 1616 for perf. at Mantua, commission cancelled Jan 1617
Andromeda	favola	E. Margliani [Marigliani]	Mantua, between 1 and 3 March 1620	lib. (Mantua, 1620); music lost
[Apollo]	eclogue ?with ballet	Striggio	Mantua, probably ducal palace, carn. 1620	known only from Monteverdi's letters

title	genre, acts	libretto	first performance	sources, editions and remarks
Combattimento di Tancredi e Clorinda	opuscolo in genere rappresentativo, 1	T. Tasso: *La Gerusalemme liberata* (xii. 52–62, 64–8)	Venice, Palazzo Dandolo (apartments of G. Mocenigo), carn. 1624 [?=1625]	pubd in Monteverdi: *Madrigali guerrieri et amorosi* (Venice, 1638), M viii/1
[Armida]		Tasso: *La Gerusalemme liberata* (xvi. 41ff)		known only from Monteverdi's letters; probably similar in conception to Combattimento, comp. before end of 1626
La finta pazza Licori	comedia/favola, 5	G. Strozzi		known only from Monteverdi's letters (1 May–18 Sept 1627); for perf. at Mantua, lib. completed, but only most of Act 1 of the music; abandoned by 18 Sept 1627
Mercurio e Marte	tornèo regale	C. Achillini	Parma, nel Salone, 21 Dec 1628	text (Parma, 1628), SM; music lost
Proserpina rapita: anatopismo	favola	Strozzi	Venice, Palazzo Dandolo (upper solar), 16 April 1630	lib. (Venice, 1630); music lost except for trio 'Come dolce hoggi l'auretta', pubd in Monteverdi: *Madrigali e canzonette* (Venice, 1651), M ix
Volgendo il ciel per l'immortal sentiero [Movete al mio bel suon]	ballo, 1	Rinuccini	Vienna, imperial palace, ?30 Dec 1636	pubd in Monteverdi: *Madrigali guerrieri et amorosi* (Venice, 1638), M viii/1
Lamento della Ninfa	opuscolo in genere rappresentativo	Rinuccini		pubd in Monteverdi: *Madrigali guerrieri et amorosi* (Venice, 1638), M viii/2; composed before 1 Sept 1638
Il ritorno d'Ulisse in patria	dramma per musica, prol., 3	G. Badoaro, after Homer: *Odyssey*	Venice, probably SS Giovanni e Paolo, 1640	A-Wn (MS 18763); M xii
Vittoria d'Amore	balletto	B. Morando	Piacenza, citadella, 7 Feb 1641	lib. (Piacenza, n.d.); music lost
Le nozze d'Enea in Lavinia	tragedia di lieto fine, prol., 3		Venice, SS Giovanni e Paolo, 1641	music lost
L'incoronazione di Poppea [La coronatione di Poppea; Il Nerone]	opera reggia/dramma musicale, prol., 3	G. F. Busenello, after Tacitus: *Annals*, Suetonius: *The Twelve Caesars*, Dio Cassius: *Roman History*, and pseudo-Seneca: *Octavia*	Venice, SS Giovanni e Paolo, 1643	scenario (Venice, 1643); lib. in DC i; scores *I-Nc*, *Vnm* (*R*1938, 1969), M xiii; ed. A. Curtis (London, 1990)

Other: Two entrate (?for a ballet, Endimione), probably Mantua, ducal palace, carn. 1605, known only from Monteverdi's letter of Dec 1604; Prologue (G. Chiabrera) to a perf. of G. B. Guarini: *Idropica*, Mantua, ducal palace, 2 June 1608, SA iii, music lost; Prologue to La Maddalena (sacra rappresentazione, G. B. Andreini), Mantua, spr. 1617, play (Mantua, 1617), music (Venice, 1617), M xi; Intermedio III [Borea ed Oritia] and licenza [Il trionfo d'Amore] for a perf. of Margliani [Marigliani]: *Le tre costanti*, Mantua, court theatre, 18 Jan 1622, play (Mantua, 1622), music and texts of prol., 4 intermedi and licenza lost, known only from Monteverdi's letters; [Gli argonauti] (carro/mascherata, Achillini), Parma, March 1628, known only from F. Guitti's letter of 3 March 1628 [see Lavin 1964; a three-part madrigal with inst. acc.]; Prologue [Teti e Flora] (Achillini), 4 intermezzi [Il castello di Atlante, Didone ed Enea, Diana ed Endimione, Gli argonauti] and licenza [I quattro continenti] (A. Pio di Savoia), for a perf. of Tasso: *Aminta*, Parma, courtyard of S Pietro Martire (Palazzo della Pilotta), 13 Dec 1628, texts (Parma, 1628, 1629), SM, music lost

LETTERS, RESEARCH SOURCES

D. de' Paoli, ed.: *Claudio Monteverdi: Lettere, dediche e prefazioni* (Rome, 1973)
D. Stevens, ed.: *Claudio Monteverdi: Letters* (London, 1980)
M. Stattkus: *Claudio Monteverdi: Verzeichnis der erhaltenen Werke: kleine Ausgabe* (Bergkamen, 1985)
K. G. Adams and D. Kiel: *Claudio Monteverdi: a Guide to Research* (New York, 1989) [incl. list of modern edns of operas and annotated bibliography to 1986]

DOCUMENTARY STUDIES

F. Caffi: *Storia della musica sacra nella già cappella ducale di San Marco in Venezia dal 1318 al 1797* (Venice, 1854–5); ed. with annotations by E. Surian (Florence, 1987)
P. Canal: *Della musica in Mantova* (Venice, 1881)
S. Davari: *Notizie biografiche del distinto maestro di musica Claudio Monteverdi* (Mantua, 1884)
A. Bertolotti: *Musici alla corte dei Gonzaga in Mantova dal secolo XV al XVIII* (Milan, 1890)
G. Ortolani: 'Venezia al tempo di Monteverdi', *RaM*, ii (1929), 469–82

E. Santoro: *La famiglia e la formazione di Claudio Monteverdi: note biografiche con documenti inediti* (Cremona, 1967)
I. Fenlon: *Music and Patronage in Sixteenth-Century Mantua* (Cambridge, 1980–82)
G. Vio: 'Ultimi ragguagli monteverdiani', *Rassegna veneta di studi musicali*, ii–iii (1986–7), 347–64
S. Parisi: 'Licenza alla Mantovana: Frescobaldi and the Recruitment of Musicians for Mantua, 1612–15', *Frescobaldi Studies*, ed. A. Silbiger (Durham, NC, 1987), 55–91
——: *Ducal Patronage of Music in Mantua, 1587–1627: an Archival Study* (diss., U. of Illinois, 1989)

LIFE AND WORKS

E. Vogel: 'Claudio Monteverdi', *VMw*, iii (1887), 315–450
L. Schneider: *Un précurseur de la musique italienne aux XVIe et XVIIe siècles: Claudio Monteverdi, l'homme et son temps* (Paris, 1921)
H. Prunières: *La vie et l'oeuvre de Claudio Monteverdi* (Paris, 1926, 2/1931; Eng. trans., 1926)
D. de' Paoli: *Claudio Monteverdi* (Milan, 1945, enlarged 2/1979)
H. F. Redlich: *Claudio Monteverdi: Leben und Werk* (Olten, 1949; Eng. trans., rev., 1952)

L. Schrade: *Monteverdi, Creator of Modern Music* (London, 1950)

D. Arnold: *Monteverdi* (London, 1963, rev. T. Carter, 3/1991)

G. Barblan and others: *Claudio Monteverdi nel quarto centenario della nascita* (Turin, 1967)

D. Stevens: *Monteverdi: Sacred, Secular and Occasional Music* (Cranbury, NJ, 1978)

C. Gallico: *Monteverdi: poesia musicale, teatro e musica sacra* (Turin, 1979)

S. Leopold: *Claudio Monteverdi und seine Zeit* (Laaber, 1982; Eng. trans., 1991)

P. Fabbri: *Monteverdi* (Turin, 1985; Eng. trans., forthcoming)

G. Tomlinson: *Monteverdi and the End of the Renaissance* (Berkeley, 1987)

MONTEVERDI'S THEATRICAL WORKS

General Studies and Collections of Essays

G. B. Doni: *Lyra Barberina* [1635] (Florence, 1763) [see particularly Pt II: *Trattato della musica scenica*]

'Notizie: preziose scoperte di autografi di Claudio Monteverdi', *La bibliofilia*, xxxviii (1936), 69–70

A. A. Abert: *Claudio Monteverdi und das musikalische Drama* (Lippstadt, 1954)

D. Arnold and N. Fortune, eds.: *The Monteverdi Companion* (London, 1968), 257–76

N. Pirrotta: 'Scelte poetiche di Monteverdi', *NRMI*, ii (1968), 10–42, 226–54; Eng. trans. in Pirrotta (1984)

Claudio Monteverdi e il suo tempo: Venice 1968 [incl. A. A. Abert: 'Die Opernästhetik Claudio Monteverdis', 35–44; N. Pirrotta: 'Teatro, scene e musica nelle opere di Monteverdi', 45–68; P. Collaer: 'Notes concernant l'instrumentation de l'"Orfeo" de Claudio Monteverdi', 69–74; A. M. Monterosso Vacchelli: 'Elementi stilistici nell'"Euridice" di Jacopo Peri in rapporto all'"Orfeo" di Monteverdi', 117–28; and R. Allorto: 'Il prologo dell'"Orfeo": note sulla formazione del recitativo monteverdiano', 157–70]

N. Pirrotta and E. Povoledo: *Li due Orfei: da Poliziano a Monteverdi* (Turin, 1969, 2/1975; Eng. trans., as *Music and Theatre from Poliziano to Monteverdi*, 1982)

N. Pirrotta: 'Monteverdi e i problemi dell'opera', *Studi sul teatro veneto fra rinascimento ed età barocco*, ed. M. T. Muraro (Florence, 1971), 321–43; Eng. trans. in Pirrotta (1984)

A. Szweykowska: 'Qualche osservazione sulla struttura letteraria del dramma musicale del primo seicento', Quadrivium, xii/2 (1971), 77–88 [Ghisi Festschrift]

H. C. Wolff: 'Ovids *Metamorphosen* und die frühe Oper', ibid, 89–107

N. Pirotta: *Music and Culture in Italy from the Middle Ages to the Baroque: Collected Essays* (Cambridge, MA, 1984)

D. Arnold and N. Fortune, eds.: *The New Monteverdi Companion* (London, 1985)

Claudio Monteverdi: Festschrift Reinhold Hammerstein (Laaber, 1986)

S. McClary: 'Constructions of Gender in Monteverdi's Dramatic Music', *COJ*, i (1989), 202–23

P. Fabbri: *Il secolo cantante: per una storia del libretto d'opera nel seicento* (Bologna, 1990)

N. John, ed.: *The Operas of Monteverdi*, ENO Opera Guide, xlv (London, 1992)

The Mantuan Years

G. Pannain: 'Studi monteverdiani', *RaM*, xxviii (1958), 281–92, xxix (1959), 42–50, 95–105, 234–6, 301–20

M. Murata: 'The Recitative Soliloquy', *JAMS*, xxxii (1979), 45–73

F. W. Sternfeld: 'The Birth of Opera: Ovid, Poliziano, and the *lieto fine*', *AnMc*, no.19 (1979), 30–51

B. R. Hanning: *Of Poetry and Music's Power: Humanism and the Creation of Opera* (Ann Arbor, 1980)

S. Leopold: 'Die Hierarchie Arkadiens: soziale Strukturen in den frühen Pastoralopern und ihre Ausdrucksformen', *Schweizer Jb für Musikwissenschaft*, new ser., i (1981), 71–92

G. Tomlinson: 'Madrigal, Monody, and Monteverdi's "Via naturale alle imitatione"', *JAMS*, xxxiv (1981), 60–108

R. Katz: *Divining the Powers of Music: Aesthetic Theory and the Origins of Opera* (New York, 1986)

Orfeo

A. Heuss: 'Die Instrumental-Stücke des "Orfeo"', *SIMG*, iv (1902–3), 175–224

D. J. Grout: *A Short History of Opera* (New York, 1947, 3/1988 with H. W. Williams) [chap.6]

R. Giazotto: *La musica a Genova nella vita pubblica e privata dal XIII al XVIII secolo* (Genoa, 1951)

N. Fortune: 'Monteverdi', *MR*, xv (1954), 88 [letter]

J. Kerman: *Opera as Drama* (New York, 1956, 2/1988) [chap.2]

D. D. Boyden: 'Monteverdi's *violini piccoli alla francese* and *viole da brazzo*', *AnnM*, vi (1958–63), 387–401

D. J. Grout: 'The Chorus in Early Opera', *Festschrift Friedrich Blume* (Kassel, 1963), 151–61

T. Antonicek: 'Claudio Monteverdi und Österreich', *ÖMz*, xxvi (1971), 266–71

C. Gallico: 'In modo dorico', *Venezia e il melodramma nel seicento: Venice 1972*, 41–50

P. Fabbri: 'Tasso, Guarini e il "divino Claudio": componimenti manieristiche nella poetica di Monteverdi', *Studi musicali*, iii (1974), 233–54

H. Hell: 'Zu Rhythmus und Notierung des "Vi ricorda" in Claudio Monteverdis *Orfeo*', *AnMc*, no.15 (1975), 87–157

L'avant-scène opéra, no.5 (1976) [*L'Orfeo* issue]

T. Carter and D. Butchart: 'The Original Orpheus', *MT*, cxviii (1977), 393 [letter]

H. Seifert: 'Beiträge zur frühgeschichte der Monodie in Österreich', *SMw*, xxxi (1980), 7–33

L. Sirch: '"Violini piccoli alla francese" e "canto alla francese" nell' "Orfeo" e negli Scherzi musicali di Monteverdi', *NRMI*, xv (1980), 50–65

F. W. Sternfeld: 'Aspects of Echo Music in the Renaissance', *Studi musicali*, ix (1980), 45–57

S. Leopold: 'Orpheus in Mantua – und anderswo', *Concerto*, i (1983), 35–42

I. Fenlon: 'Monteverdi's Mantuan *Orfeo*: some New Documentation', *EMc*, xii (1984), 163–72

R. Müller: *Der Stile recitativo in Claudio Monteverdis 'Orfeo': dramatisches Gesang und Instrumentalsatz* (Tutzing, 1984)

W. Osthoff: '*Contro le legge de' Fati*. Polizianos und Monteverdis *Orfeo* als Sinnbild künstlerischen Wettkampfs mit der Natur', *AnMc*, no.22 (1984), 11–68

H. Seifert: *Die Oper am Wiener Kaiserhof im 17. Jahrhundert* (Tutzing, 1985)

J. Whenham, ed.: *Claudio Monteverdi: 'Orfeo'* (Cambridge, 1986)

T. F. Kelly: '*Orfeo da camera*: Estimating Performing Forces in Early Opera', *Historical Performance: the Journal of Early Music America*, i (1988), 3–9

P. Kivy: *Osmin's Rage: Philosophical Reflections on Opera, Drama and Text* (Princeton, 1988) [chap.5]

F. W. Sternfeld: 'Orpheus, Ovid and Opera', *JRMA*, cxiii (1988), 172–202

D. Kimbell: *Italian Opera* (Cambridge, 1991) [chap.4]

Arianna and the 1608 celebrations

J. A. Westrup: 'Monteverdi's "Lamento d'Arianna"', *MR*, i (1940), 144–54

C. Gallico: 'I due pianti di Arianna di Claudio Monteverdi', *Chigiana*, xxiv (1967), 29–42

S. Reiner: 'La vag'Angioletta (and others), Part I', *AnMc*, no.14 (1974), 26–88

U. Michels: 'Das "Lamento d'Arianna" von Claudio Monteverdi', *Festschrift für Hans Heinrich Eggebrecht* (Stuttgart, 1984), 91–109

E. Strainchamps: 'The Life and Death of Caterina Martinelli: New Light on Monteverdi's "Arianna"', *Early Music History*, v (1985), 155–86

Other works

D. Stevens: 'Claudio Unclouded: a Ballet in Five Parts', *MT*, ci (1960), 23

——: 'Monteverdi's Earliest Extant Ballet', *AcM*, xxxvii (1982), 15–24; rev. version, *EMc*, xiv (1986), 358–66

The Venetian Years

C. Ivanovitch: *Minerva al tavolino* (Venice, 1681)

H. Prunières: 'Monteverdi's Venetian Operas', *MQ*, x (1924), 178–92

J. A. Westrup: 'The Originality of Monteverde', *PMA*, lx (1933–4), 1–25

S. T. Worsthorne: *Venetian Opera in the Seventeenth Century* (Oxford, 1954)

W. Osthoff: *Das dramatische Spätwerk Claudio Monteverdis* (Tutzing, 1960)

——: 'Maske und Musik: die Gestaltwerdung der Oper in Venedig', *Castrum Peregrini*, lxv (1964), 10–49; It. trans. as 'Maschera e musica', *NRMI*, i (1967), 16–44

L. Bianconi and T. Walker: 'Dalla "Finta pazza" alla "Veremonda": storie di Febiarmonici', *RIM*, x (1975), 379–454

A. Szweykowska: 'Le due poetiche venete e le ultime opere di Claudio Monteverdi', *Quadrivium*, xx (1977), 149–57

E. Rosand: 'In Defense of the Venetian Libretto', *Studi musicali*, ix (1980), 271–85

A. Szweykowska: 'Sulle analogie fra i melodrammi polacchi e veneziani negli anni quaranta del seicento', *Vita teatrale in Italia e Polonia fra seicento e settecento: Warsaw 1980*, 177–83

B. L. Glixon: *Recitative in Seventeenth-Century Venetian Opera: its Dramatic Function and Musical Language* (diss., Rutgers U., 1985)

E. Rosand: *Opera in Seventeenth-Century Venice: the Creation of a Genre* (Berkeley, 1991)

Il ritorno d'Ulisse in patria

H. Goldschmidt: 'Monteverdis Ritorno d'Ulisse', *SIMG*, iv (1902–3), 671–6

——: 'Claudio Monteverdis Oper: Il ritorno d'Ulisse in patria', *SIMG*, ix (1907–8), 570–92

R. Haas: 'Zur Neuausgabe von Claudio Monteverdis "Il ritorno d'Ulisse in patria"', *SMw*, ix (1922), 3–42

C. van den Borren: '"Il ritorno d'Ulisse in patria" de Claudio Monteverdi', *Revue de l'Université de Bruxelles*, iii (1925), 353–87

W. Osthoff: 'Zu den Quellen von Monteverdis Ritorno d'Ulisse in Patria', *SMw*, xxiii (1956), 67–78

——: 'Zur Bologneser Aufführung von Monteverdis "Ritorno d'Ulisse" im Jahre 1640', *Anzeiger der Österreichischen Akademie der Wissenschaften, philosophisch-historische Klasse*, xcv (1958), 155–60

E. Rosand: 'Iro and the Interpretation of Il ritorno d'Ulisse in Patria', *JM*, vii (1989), 141–64

L'incoronazione di Poppea

H. Kretzschmar: 'Monteverdi's "Incoronazione di Poppea"', *VMw*, x (1894), 483–530

A. Tessier: 'Les deux styles de Monteverde', *ReM*, iii/8 (1922), 223–54

G. Benvenuti: 'Il manoscritto veneziano della "Incoronazione di Poppea"', *RMI*, xli (1937), 176–84

H. F. Redlich: 'Notationsprobleme in Cl. Monteverdis "Incoronazione di Poppea"', *AcM*, x (1938), 129–32

W. Osthoff: 'Die venezianische und neapolitanische Fassung von Monteverdis "Incoronazione di Poppea"', *AcM*, xxvi (1954), 88–113

——: 'Neue Beobachtungen zu Quellen und Geschichte von Monteverdis "Incoronazione di Poppea"', *Mf*, xi (1958), 129–38

D. Arnold: '"L'incoronazione di Poppea" and its Orchestral Requirements', *MT*, civ (1963), 176–8

A. Mondolfo Bossarelli: 'Ancora intorno al codice napoletano della "Incoronazione di Poppea"', *RIM*, ii (1967), 294–313

E. B. Savage: 'Love and Infamy: the Paradox of Monteverdi's L'incoronazione di Poppea', *Comparative Drama*, iv (1970), 197–207

A. Chiarelli: '*L'incoronazione di Poppea o Il Nerone*: problemi di filologia testuale', *RIM*, ix (1974), 117–51

C. Day: 'The Theater of SS Giovanni e Paolo and Monteverdi's L'incoronazione di Poppea', *CMc*, no.25 (1978), 22–38

J. Kowalczyk: 'Le avventure teatrali di Jan Zamoyski "Sobiepan" in Italia', *Vita teatrale in Italia e Polonia fra seicento e settecento: Warsaw 1980*, 43–53

R. Müller: 'Basso ostinato und die "imitatione del parlare" in Monteverdis Incoronazione di Poppea', *AMw*, xl (1983), 1–23

E. Rosand: 'Seneca and the Interpretation of L'incoronazione di Poppea', *JAMS*, xxxviii (1985), 34–71

A. Magini: 'Le monodie di Benedetto Ferrari e L'incoronazione di Poppea: un rilevamento stilistico comparativo', *RIM*, xi (1986), 266–99

A. Curtis: '*La Poppea Impasticciata* or, Who Wrote the Music to L'Incoronazione?', *JAMS*, xlii (1989), 23–54

E. Rosand: 'Monteverdi's Mimetic Art: L'incoronazione di Poppea', *COJ*, i (1989), 113–37

I. Fenlon and P. N. Miller: *The Song of the Soul: Understanding 'Poppea'* (London, 1992)

P. Fabbri: New Sources for "Poppea"', *ML*, lxxiv (1993)

Other works

G. Bertazzolo: *Breve relatione dello sposalitio fatto dalla serenissima Principessa Eleonora Gonzaga con la Sacra Cesarea Maestà di Ferdinando II Imperatore* (Mantua, 1622)

A. Solerti: 'Un ballo musicato da C. Monteverde sconosciuto a' suoi biografi', *RMI*, xi (1904), 24–34

C. Alcari: 'Claudio Monteverdi alla corte di Odoardo Farnese', *Musica d'oggi*, xv (1933), 261–6

I. Lavin: 'Lettres de Parmes (1618, 1627–28) et débuts du théâtre baroque', *Le lieu théâtral à la Renaissance*, ed. J. Jacquot (Paris, 1964), 105–58

S. Reiner: 'Preparations in Parma, 1618, 1627–28', *MR*, xxv (1964), 273–301

D. Arnold: 'Monteverdi and the Art of War', *MT*, cviii (1967), 412–14

R. Strohm: 'Osservazioni su "Tempro la cetra"', *RIM*, ii (1967), 357–64

E. Rosand: 'The Descending Tetrachord: an Emblem of Lament', *MQ*, lxv (1979), 346–59

J. Whenham: *Duet and Dialogue in the Age of Monteverdi* (Ann Arbor, 1982)

D. T. Mace: 'Tasso, "La Gerusalemme liberata" and Monteverdi', *Music and Language*, ed. E. S. Beebe (New York, 1983), 118–56

G. Tomlinson: 'Twice Bitten, Thrice Shy: Monteverdi's "finta" Finta Pazza', *JAMS*, xxxvi (1983), 303–11

A. Rosenthal: 'Monteverdi's "Andromeda": a Lost Libretto Found', *ML*, lxvi (1985), 1–8

L. Zoppelli: 'Il rapto perfettissimo: un'inedita testimonianza sulla "Proserpina" di Monteverdi', *Rassegna veneta di studi musicali*, ii–iii (1986–7), 343–5

M. A. Balsano and T. Walker, eds.: *Tasso, la musica, i musicisti* (Florence, 1988)

I. Mamczarz: *Le Théâtre Farnèse de Parme et le drame musical italien (1618–1732)* (Florence, 1988)

Works of doubtful authenticity

F. Torrefranca: 'Il lamento d'Erminia di Claudio Monteverdi', *Inedito*, ii (1944), 31; suppl., 1

W. Osthoff: 'Monteverdi-Funde', *AMw*, xiv (1957), 253–80

I. Godt: 'A Monteverdi Source Reappears: the Grilanda of F. M. Fucci', *ML*, lx (1979), 428–39

M. Danckwardt: 'Das Lamento d'Olimpia "Voglio voglio morir": eine Komposition Claudio Monteverdis?', *AMw*, xli (1984), 149–75

Performing practice

H. Goldschmidt: 'Die Instrumentalbegleitung der italienischen Musikdramen in der ersten Hälfte des XVII. Jahrhunderts', *MMg*, xxvii (1895), 52–62

J. A. Westrup: 'Monteverdi and the Orchestra', *ML*, xxi (1940), 230–45

P. Collaer: 'L'orchestra di Claudio Monteverdi', *Musica*, ii (Florence, 1943), 51–85

F. Ghisi: 'L'orchestra in Monteverdi', *Karl Gustav Fellerer zum 60. Geburtstag* (Cologne, 1962), 187–92

R. L. Weaver: 'The Orchestra in Early Italian Opera', *JAMS*, xvii (1964), 83–9

E. H. Tarr and T. Walker: '"Bellici carmi, festivo fragor": die Verwendung der Trompete in der italienischen Oper des 17. Jahrhunderts', *HJbMw*, iii (1978), 143–203

P. Fabbri and A. Pompilio, eds.: *Il corago, o vero alcune osservazioni per metter bene in scena le composizioni drammatiche* (Florence, 1983)

N. Harnoncourt: *Der musikalische Dialog: Gedanken zu Monteverdi, Bach und Mozart* (Salzburg, 1984; Eng. trans., 1989)

R. Savage and M. Sansone: '*Il corago* and the Staging of Early Opera: Four Chapters from an Anonymous Treatise circa 1630', *EMc*, xvii (1989), 495–511
JOHN WHENHAM

Monteverdi, Giulio Cesare (*b* Cremona, bap. 31 Jan 1573; *d* Salò, Lake Garda, ?1630 or 1631). Italian composer, younger brother of Claudio Monteverdi. In 1600 he was briefly organist of Mantua Cathedral. In August 1602 he was in the service of the Duke of Mantua. He wrote the music for the fourth *intermedio* (to words by Chiabrera; music lost) in the performance of Guarini's play *L'Idropica* given on 2 June 1608 during the wedding celebrations at the Mantuan court. In 1609 he was appointed *maestro di cappella* to Francesco Gonzaga, then governor of Monferrato, and it was in this capacity that he wrote his opera *Il rapimento di Proserpina* (Ercole Margliani), which was composed for the birthday of Francesco's wife and performed at Casale Monferrato in 1611 (music lost). In 1612 he was dismissed, along with his brother and other artists, from the Gonzaga family's service. He soon became an organist at Castelleone, in the province of Cremona, where he seems to have remained until, on 10 April 1622, he was appointed *maestro di cappella* of Salò Cathedral. He probably died of the plague of 1630–31. The small amount of his music to survive, notably motets, shows to some extent the influence of his brother. More important is his edition of his brother's *Scherzi musicali* (1607), which includes his own explanation of Claudio's ideas and two *scherzi* of his own.

*

A. Solerti: *Gli albori del melodramma* (Milan, 1904), 157–61

DENIS ARNOLD

Montevideo. Capital of Uruguay. Theatre music was derived initially from the Spanish tradition, and the first theatre to be built was the Casa de Comedias, which opened in 1793 with a repertory of *tonadillas escénicas* (musical comedies) and zarzuelas. From 1820 a taste developed for Rossini's operatic music, and in 1830 the first complete Italian opera to be heard in the city, Rossini's *L'inganno felice*, was performed by the Tanni company. When the stage of the Casa de Comedias was found to be too small for important visiting companies, some rebuilding was done and the house was renamed: it became the Coliseo in 1814, the Teatro de Comercio and then the Teatro Nacional in 1843 and the Teatro de S Felipe y Santiago in 1855. Performances were given from April to August each year. Between 1830 and 1860, 60 operas were performed in Montevideo by ten different companies, mostly Italian. They included those of the Tanni brothers (1830–40), Ida Edelvira (1851–2), Justina Piacentini (1849–54), Eliza Biscaccianti (1854) and Sofia Vera Lorini (1855–7). The Teatro de S Felipe y Santiago was demolished in 1879 and another house, the Nuevo Teatro S Felipe, was built on its site in 1880.

The Teatro Solís, with five tiers and 2500 seats, opened on 25 August 1856 with Verdi's *Ernani* and became one of the leading houses in South America. During its first season there were 52 performances of operas by Verdi, Donizetti, Rossini, Bellini and Zanelli (*Luisa Strozzi*). Enrico Tamberlik sang there in 1857, Anna Bishop in 1858 and Carlotta Patti in 1870. From 1882 to the end of the century the singers included Romilda Pantaleoni, Gemma Bellincioni, Elvira Brambilla, Adelina Patti, Hariclea Darclée, Luisa Tetrazzini, Francesco Tamagno, Roberto Stagno, Mattia Battistini, Antonio Scotti and Fernando De Lucia. The Solís's golden age reached its zenith in 1903 when Toscanini brought a 285-strong company from La Scala, including Darclée, Medea Mei, Caruso, De Luca and Giovanni Zenatello. Toscanini returned in 1904 with Rosina Storchio in *Madama Butterfly*, and in 1906 with Salomea Krusceniski singing Wagner. During the first two decades of the 20th century audiences at the Solís heard, in addition to many of the above, Galli-Curci, Boninsegna, Dalla Rizza, Rosa Raisa, Didur, Schipa, Ruffo, Gigli and, later on, Muzio, Dal Monte, Shalyapin and Pertile. José Oxilia, Victor Damiani and José Soler were among the best Uruguayan singers who performed there, and composers such as Puccini, Mascagni, Messager, Strauss and Respighi conducted their own works.

At the beginning of the 20th century other theatres that put on minor opera performances were the S Felipe (opened 1880), the Cibils (1893), the Politeama (1889), the Stella d'Italia (1895) and the Casino. The 3000-seat Teatro Urquiza (1905) was bought by the Uruguayan broadcasting service (SODRE) and functioned as a studio-auditorium from 1930 to 1971, when it burnt down. Both the Urquiza and SODRE put on opera seasons for a few years, but these were never as distinguished as those of the Solís. The Solís continues to function daily as a theatre, but with only brief opera seasons given by national casts and occasional visitors from abroad.

*

L. Ayestarán: *La música en el Uruguay*, i (Montevideo, 1953)
S. Salgado: *Breve historia de la música culta en el Uruguay* (Montevideo, 1971, 2/1980)
——: *The Teatro Solís of Montevideo* (in preparation)

SUSANA SALGADO

Montezuma (i). *Tragedia per musica* in three acts by CARL HEINRICH GRAUN to a libretto drafted in French by FREDERICK II and translated into Italian by GIAMPIETRO TAGLIAZUCCHI; Berlin, Hofoper, 6 January 1755.

Montezuma (castrato) reigns over Mexico in peace and intends to marry Princess Eupaforice (soprano). His general Pilpatoè (castrato) reports on the ferocity and greed of the newly arrived Spaniards. Despite their warlike demeanour, Montezuma feels secure in extending them his hospitality. Cortes [Cortez] (soprano) and his hot-headed captain Navrès (soprano) loathe the Mexican 'heathens'. Cortez determines to bring down Montezuma and wed Eupaforice himself. He seizes the city and arrests the king while his fellow Spaniards set about slaughtering the Mexicans. Cortez offers to spare Montezuma if Eupaforice will forsake her false gods and marry him. She refuses proudly, and as Montezuma is led off to death she stabs herself.

Montezuma was the 24th of Graun's operas for the Berlin court. Frederick, a foe of Christianity, chose this unusual subject largely for ideological reasons. Despite Montezuma's passive streak, the cultural collision furnished Graun with scope for some of his finest dramatic music, especially in Act 3. Frederick had ordered that wherever possible Graun use the cavatina in place of da capo arias (of which only four remain). The concision of the music is nowhere more impressive than in Eupaforice's final aria in B minor, 'Mostro! che sol respiri terrore e crudeltà'. In general, the arias are varied in both style and construction. For important scenes Graun linked elements into imposing larger units (e. g. Montezuma's obbligato recitative and aria with pizzicato accompaniment, and the recitative and duet with Eupaforice at the beginning of Act 3).

Frederick, who supervised the staging during rehearsals, called Graun's score 'un chef-d'oeuvre'. The opera was revived at Berlin in 1771, but apparently was not performed anywhere else until it was given in German at Saarbrücken in 1936.

For illustration *see* BERLIN, fig.1.

THOMAS BAUMAN

Montezuma (ii). Opera in three acts by ROGER SESSIONS to a libretto by Giuseppe Antonio Borgese; West Berlin, Deutsche Oper, 19 April 1964.

Based on the story of Hernán Cortez's conquest of the Aztecs and the colonization of Mexico, *Montezuma* explores themes of cultural juxtaposition, conflict and assimilation, and the ethical ambiguities of military power and state and religious authority. The story is narrated retrospectively by Bernal Diaz (bass), a Spanish conquistador. Bernal comments on Cortez's (baritone) landing and reception by the Aztecs, who believe that he

453

may be the god Quetzalcoatl, and the development of a love relationship between Cortez and Malinche (soprano), an enslaved Indian princess. Act 2 depicts, in tableau scenes, the meeting of Cortez and Montezuma (tenor) and a ritual sacrifice; there follows a complex ensemble in which the principals ponder Christian and Aztec religious sacrifice, the Aztec harvest ritual and the Spaniards' gold lust. While Cortez and Montezuma both argue for cooperation and peace, their subordinates Alvarado (tenor) and Coanhutemoc (baritone) sow discontent in their respective ranks. An auto-da-fé ensues at the beginning of Act 3 which closes with the assassination of Montezuma by a militant Aztec crowd.

Throughout the opera, vocal lines often overlap in a complex phrasing design that consistently reinforces an ironic undercutting of virtually all the ethical and political positions taken by the characters. The entire historical episode is viewed as tragic and absurd in equal parts. While much of the opera's language is complicated and awkward, the drama is psychologically and politically focussed at all times. The music is among Sessions's richest: dense and colourful, gesturally graphic throughout, dramatically motivated and fully integrated at all structural levels. MARTIN BRODY

Montgomery, Kenneth (*b* Belfast, 28 Oct 1943). British conductor. He studied at the RCM, and in Siena with Sergiu Celibidache, and was on the music staff at Glyndebourne from 1964 to 1968. During that period he worked with John Pritchard as assistant chorus master, studied for a season with Hans Schmidt-Isserstedt in Hamburg, and made his Glyndebourne conducting début with *L'elisir d'amore* in 1967. He was a staff conductor with Sadler's Wells Opera (1967–70) in a wide repertory and, while working with the Bournemouth SO and Sinfonietta, appeared at the Wexford Festival in *Il rè pastore* (1971) and *Oberon* (1972). In 1971 his conducting of *Ormindo* with the Netherlands Opera began a long and fruitful association which continued into the 1990s involving a wide range of operas from Cavalli to Janáček and Stravinsky. His Covent Garden début was in 1975 with *Le nozze di Figaro*. He was music director of Glyndebourne Touring Opera, 1975–6, when he conducted *Der Freischütz*, but resigned to become principal conductor of the Netherlands RO and to strengthen his ties with the Netherlands Opera. He has been a guest conductor with the WNO and Canadian Opera, and in 1985 he became artistic director of Opera Northern Ireland in his native city, since when his annual seasons have shown a steady improvement in performance standards and style in a mainstream repertory. ALAN BLYTH, NOËL GOODWIN

Montgomery-Meissner, Kathryn (*b* Canton, OH, 23 Sept 1952). American soprano. In 1979 she won the San Francisco Opera Auditions and created Belle and Martha Cratchit in Musgrave's *A Christmas Carol* at Norfolk, Virginia. During the 1980s she sang in Venice, Brussels, Cologne, Edinburgh, Zürich and Barcelona. She made her début at the Metropolitan Opera in 1984 as Chrysothemis. Her roles include Donna Elvira, Vitellia, Leonore, Elsa, Salome, the Empress (*Die Frau ohne Schatten*) and Aksinya (*Lady Macbeth of the Mtsensk District*), which she sang at the Deutsche Oper, Berlin, in 1988. An effective actress, she has a strong but flexible voice that shows signs of developing into a dramatic soprano. ELIZABETH FORBES

Monti. Italian family of singers and at least one composer, prominent in the 18th century in the development of Neapolitan *opera buffa*.

(1) **Laura Monti** (*b* ?Rome, after 1704; *d* Naples, 1760). Singer. She was a member of comic opera companies at the Teatro Nuovo, Naples, 1726–32, singing second and third comic parts. From 1733 she sang at the royal theatre, S Bartolomeo, in intermezzos between the acts of serious operas, until 1735, when Carlo III replaced intermezzos with ballets. Among her roles was Serpina in the première of Pergolesi's *La serva padrona* (1733); Hasse and Leo also wrote parts for her. In 1738 she took part in the entertainments celebrating Carlo III's marriage, and sang at the newly opened S Carlo in Auletta's expanded intermezzo *La locandiera*, the first and for many years the only comic opera produced in the royal theatre. After appearances at the Teatro Nuovo (1743) and the Fiorentini (1745–6) she seems to have retired. Her sisters Anna Maria Monti (*b* 1704) and Grazia Monti were also singers: Anna Maria made her début at the Fiorentini at the age of 13 in Falco's dialect opera *Lo mbruoglio d'ammore*, in the first regular season of comic opera, and sang there until 1727, chiefly in comic servant roles; Grazia appeared at the Nuovo in Giuseppe de Majo's *La milorda* (1728).

(2) **Marianna Monti** (*b* Naples, 1730; *d* Naples, 1814). Soprano, cousin of (1) Laura Monti. She made her début in Carnival 1746 in Conforto's *La finta vedova* at the Teatro dei Fiorentini and from then until 1759 appeared regularly there and at the Teatro Nuovo, singing comic servant parts. She enjoyed the patronage of the Marchese di Gerace, with whom she was arrested suddenly in 1760 by the theatrical censors, who assumed impropriety; but after petitions and protests both were freed (there were testimonies to her 'honest, philanthropic life, without any scandal' and her regular attendance at church) and after two months she was able to resume singing at the Fiorentini theatre. For almost 20 years Monti was perhaps Naples's most popular *prima buffa*. The best composers of the period created roles for her: Cocchi, Latilla, Logroscino, Jommelli, Traetta, Piccinni, Sacchini, Guglielmi, Paisiello and Cimarosa. Her style almost certainly influenced the development of Neapolitan *opera buffa*. She helped popularize in the south the modern comic opera dramaturgy, with its greater variety of vocal textures and aria forms and longer and more complex finales, developed by Goldoni for Venice and introduced in Naples in the early 1760s, particularly by the librettist Antonio Palomba. Her public career ended with the Palomba-Curcio *farsa*, *Il millantatore* (Carnival 1780), at the newly opened Teatro del Fondo.

(3) **Gaetano Monti** (*b* Naples, *c*1750; *d* ?Naples, ?1816). Composer, younger brother of (2) Marianna Monti. Early reports that he was the brother of the poet and librettist Vincenzo Monti (1754–1828) are unfounded. According to Florimo, he first appeared in public at the age of eight, singing a skirt part in a revival of Piccinni's *Il curioso del suo proprio danno* at the Teatro Nuovo along with his sister who had the lead. This short part (Stellante) was probably written specially for him, since the character did not appear in the original production of 1756 and was in excess of the seven characters then customary for *opere buffe*. After writing one serious opera for Modena in 1775, he confined himself to productions for the comic stage,

usually including a part for his sister until her retirement in 1780. He was also an organist and reportedly composed church music. In 1776 the impresarios of the S Carlo listed him among the 20 best composers then living in Naples. His two most popular operas, *Le donne vendicate* and *Lo studente*, were performed outside Naples as well as revived there; Gerber remarked on the popularity of his music in Germany.

opere buffe unless otherwise stated

L'Adriano in Siria (os, P. Metastasio), Modena, Corte, 31 Jan 1775
Il cicisbeo discacciato, Naples, Nuovo, spr. 1777
La fuga (G. Lorenzi), Naples, Nuovo, sum. 1777, *I-Nc*
Il geloso sincerato (Lorenzi), Naples, Fondo, aut. 1779
La contadina accorta (int), Rome, Capranica, 4 Jan 1781, *D-Dlb*
Le donne vendicate [Il gigante] (G. Palomba), Naples, Nuovo, 17 Oct 1781, *I-Nc*
Il Molaforbice (Palomba), Naples, Nuovo, 26 Dec 1781
Lo sposalizio per dispetto (G. Bertati), Venice, S Moisè, 26 Dec 1781
La viaggiatrice di bell'umore (int), Rome, Capranica, carn. 1782
Lo studente (F. S. Zini), Naples, Nuovo, carn./spr. 1783
La donna fedele (Zini), Naples, Fondo, ?1 Sept 1784

Music in: Tritto: La Scuffiara, 1784; Gazzaniga: La donna soldato, 1793; I tre gobbi (int), *Nc*

*

CroceN; FlorimoN; GerberNL; RosaM
P. Napoli-Signorelli: *Vicende della coltura nelle due Sicilie* (Naples, 1784–6), v, 564ff
M. Scherillo: *L'opera buffa napoletana durante il settecento: storia letteraria* (Naples, 1883, 2/1916)
M. F. Robinson: *Naples and Neapolitan Opera* (Oxford, 1972), 186–7, 209ff   JAMES L. JACKMAN

Monticelli, Angelo Maria (*b* Milan, *c*1712; *d* ?Dresden, ?1758). Italian castrato soprano. He began his career in Venice in 1728, then went to Milan (where he often appeared throughout his career) and Rome (where he sang prima donna roles opposite Caffarelli). He appeared for ten years in secondary roles throughout Italy before being engaged as primo uomo for London (1741–6, returning to Milan for the 1745 carnival). According to Horace Walpole, he was 'infinitely admired' at the King's Theatre, and he sang in two operas by Gluck in 1746. The Viennese court employed him from 1740, although his only confirmed public appearances date from 1748. He sang at the S Carlo in Naples for two years, and then joined Hasse's Dresden troupe as primo uomo (1753–6). His last known performance was in Genoa in October 1756; according to Fürstenau, he died in Dresden in September 1758. Monticelli had a lyric, agile voice and was a great actor, praised by Burney, Walpole and others. He was responsible for much of the popular dispersion of Pergolesi's *L'Olimpiade*, whose arias for Megacles he often sang. He has often been confused with the other singers of the time called Monticelli (particularly Maria Marta).

*

M. Fürstenau: *Zur Geschichte der Musik und Theaters am Hofe zu Dresden* (Dresden, 1861–2)   DALE E. MONSON

Monticelli Novelli, Antonio Felice. *See* NOVELLI, FELICE.

Montpellier. City in southern France with a medieval university and a turbulent history. In the 17th and 18th centuries, before the city had a theatre, opera was already being presented in the houses of the nobility. The first public theatre was built in 1755 by the architect J.-P. Maréschal, under the aegis of the Duke of Richelieu, and opened with the opera *Pyrame et Thisbé* by Francoeur and Rebel. It burnt down in 1785 but was reconstructed and enlarged within the existing walls through public subscription. Again destroyed by fire in 1881, it was replaced by a much larger theatre (1280 seats in stalls, four galleries) on the boulevard Victor Hugo; this new building was designed by Cassien-Bernard, a pupil of Garnier, and inaugurated in 1888 – suitably enough in view of the city's history – with *Les Huguenots*. Successful seasons continued with leading guest artists until World War II, after which the opera declined, especially between 1955 and 1965. Since 1984, under the direction of Henri Maier, the Montpellier opera has gradually regained its place among the provincial companies of France. The season runs from October to May, with some ten productions, each given four or five performances. Records show the progressive augmentation of the opera orchestra, from 18 players in 1755 to 80 in 1989. A new, large concert hall and opera house, the Corum, opened in 1990. The annual festival (July and August), organized by Radio France, gives both staged and concert performances of up to ten operas.

*

A. Gelbseiden: 'Le répertoire lyrique au Théâtre de Montpellier de 1945 à 1985', *Le théâtre lyrique français 1945–1985*, ed. D. Pistone (Paris, 1987), 347–52   CHARLES PITT

Montreal. City in Canada. During the 1780s the Théâtre de Société performed several operas, which included Dibdin's *The Padlock*, Shield's *The Poor Soldier* and Duni's *Les deux chasseurs et la laitière*. In 1790 a local composer, Joseph Quesnel, staged his own *Colas et Colinette*, and two years later Paisiello's *Il barbiere di Siviglia* was given. For most of the 19th century opera was provided by touring companies: in 1841 Arthur Seguin and his wife presented *La sonnambula*, *Fra Diavolo*, *La Cenerentola* and *L'elisir d'amore*; in 1843 a French company gave Auber's *Les diamants de la couronne* and Adam's *Le chalet*; in 1853 a troupe conducted by Luigi Arditi visited Montreal; and in 1874–7 a French company headed by Zulma Bouffar performed several Offenbach operettas. Calixa Lavallée presented Barbier's drama *Jeanne d'Arc*, with incidental music by Gounod, in 1877 and in 1879 conducted *La dame blanche*, both with all-Canadian casts. Emma Albani sang in *Lucia di Lammermoor*, *La traviata*, *Lohengrin* and *Les Huguenots* at the Académie de Musique (1890–92), while the enterprising Opéra Français (1893–6) presented a wide variety of French and Italian operas and operettas that ranged from *Carmen*, *Faust*, *Mireille*, *Martha*, *Guillaume Tell* and *Les Huguenots* to *Norma* and *Lucia di Lammermoor*; as its last production, just before the money ran out, it staged *Le prophète* in the Salle du Monument National.

The Charley Opera from New Orleans and a troupe from Paris visited the city in 1899, introducing such grand operas as *La Juive*, Reyer's *Sigurd*, Gounod's *La reine de Saba*, *Robert le diable* and *L'Africaine*. That year the Metropolitan Opera from New York gave a season at Her Majesty's Theatre; it returned in 1901 to the Montreal Arena, where its productions included Emma Calvé in *Carmen*, *Faust* and *Manon*, and again in 1911 to His Majesty's (as it was now called) bringing *Aida* conducted by Toscanini and *Tannhäuser* with Slezak. Mascagni conducted performances of his *Cavalleria rusticana*, *Zanetto* and *Iris* at the Arena in 1902. The Henry Savage Grand Opera Company brought *Rigoletto*, *Otello* and *Parsifal* to His Majesty's in 1904–5.

The first attempt at founding a permanent opera was made in 1910, when the Montreal Opera Company gave an eight-week season consisting of *Tosca*, *Lakmé*, Giordano's *Fedora*, *Manon*, *Carmen*, *La bohème*, *La traviata*, *Madama Butterfly*, *Thaïs* and *L'amico Fritz*. The company toured to Quebec, Ottawa and Toronto. The second season, 1911–12, was more enterprising, containing Massenet's *Cendrillon*, *Le jongleur de Notre-Dame*, *La Navarraise*, *Werther*, *Louise*, Leroux's *Le chemineau* and Godard's *La vivandière* (most of them Canadian premières), while the third and last, 1912–13, included *Aida*, *Hérodiade* and *Zazà*. The National Opera Company of Canada gave an eight-week season (1913–14) of 14 operas, including *La Gioconda*, *Il segreto di Susanna*, *Samson et Dalila*, *Hérodiade*, *Lohengrin* and *Otello*; this company toured to Ottawa, Toronto and several cities in the USA. During March 1914 the Quinlan English Opera Company presented a Wagner season at His Majesty's, when the first *Ring* cycle heard in Canada as well as *Tannhäuser*, *Lohengrin*, *Der fliegende Holländer* and *Tristan und Isolde* were performed.

The Société Canadienne d'Opérette (1923–33 and 1936–55), which also played in Quebec, included operas (*Martha*, *Le pré aux clercs*, *La fille du régiment*, *Werther*, *Manon*, *Mignon*) in its repertory as well as lighter works. The short-lived Canadian Opera Company (not to be confused with the later company of Toronto) staged one production, of *Roméo et Juliette*, at Loew's Theatre in 1931. The Montreal Festivals first staged an opera, *Pelléas et Mélisande*, in 1940; from 1946 opera was given annually until 1965, and notable productions included *Tristan und Isolde* conducted by Beecham and the Canadian premières of *Ariadne auf Naxos*, Pizzetti's *L'assassinio nella cattedrale* and *L'heure espagnole*, as well as open-air performances of *Carmen*, *Aida* and *Tosca*. In 1942 the Opera Guild of Montreal, founded by Pauline Donalda, staged *Cavalleria rusticana*; until 1968 it presented one opera a year, including *Così fan tutte*, *The Golden Cockerel*, *Fidelio*, *Otello*, *The Consul*, *The Love for Three Oranges*, *Boris Godunov*, *Don Carlos*, *Falstaff* and *Macbeth*. During Expo 67 opera was staged at the Salle Wilfrid-Pelletier (inaugurated in 1963; cap. 3000) by the Royal Opera Stockholm (*Un ballo in maschera*, *Aniara*, *The Rake's Progress*, *Tristan und Isolde*); the Hamburg Staatsoper (*Mathis der Maler*, *Lulu*, *Jenůfa*, *Der Freischütz*); the Bol'shoy (*Boris Godunov*, *The Queen of Spades*, *War and Peace*, *The Legend of the Invisible City of Kitezh*); Montreal Symphony (*Faust*, *Otello*); the Vienna Staatsoper (*Le nozze de Figaro*, *Don Giovanni*, *Der Rosenkavalier*, *Elektra*, *Wozzeck*); La Scala (*Il trovatore*, *I Capuleti*, *La bohème*, *Nabucco*) and the Canadian Opera Company (*Les contes d' Hoffmann*, and *Louis Riel*). The Opéra de Québec (1971–5) staged four operas a season in Montreal; although its repertory was mainly French and Italian, such works as *Salome* and *Tristan und Isolde* were also included. The Opéra de Montréal, which grew out of it, opened in 1980 with *Tosca*. Five or six operas, still predominantly French and Italian, are staged each season; those recently produced have included *Dialogues des Carmélites*, *Le comte Ory*, *Otello*, *Adriana Lecouvreur*, *Un ballo in maschera*, *Der Rosenkavalier*, *Yevgeny Onegin* and André Gagnon's *Nelligan* (1990). Bernard Uzan has been the artistic director since 1989. In addition to the Salle Wilfrid-Pelletier, opera performances are also given in the smaller Théâtre Maisonneuve (cap. 1400), inaugurated in 1967.   ELIZABETH FORBES

Montresor, Beni [Benedetto] (*b* Bussolengo, nr Verona, 11 March 1926). Italian designer and director. He studied art in Venice before going to Rome to study film, and between 1952 and 1959 designed some 20 films, including productions for Fellini and Rossellini. He went to New York in 1960, and his first opera designs were for Menotti's production of *Vanessa* for the 1961 Spoleto Festival. His designs for Carl Ebert's production of *Pelléas et Mélisande* at Glyndebourne (1962) and Menotti's *The Last Savage* at the Metropolitan (1964) launched his international career.

Montresor's productions have travelled regularly from one opera house to another. The tour of the Houston-San Diego joint production of *La fille du régiment* in 1973, with its primary colours and comic-strip scenery, is one example; another is his *Esclarmonde*, a

Beni Montresor's design for Act 3 of Menotti's 'The Last Savage', performed at the Metropolitan Opera, New York, 1964: ink and watercolour (the tigers are orange and the sky bright yellow)

vehicle for Joan Sutherland, first with the San Francisco Opera (1974), then the Metropolitan (1976) and Covent Garden (1983). Montresor's other Metropolitan production was *La Gioconda* in 1966. For Covent Garden he designed a colourful *Benvenuto Cellini* (1966) and *L'elisir d'amore* (1976). He designed his own productions of the first *Madama Butterfly* in the Verona Arena (1978), *Zelmira* and *Falstaff* for the Rome Opera (both 1989) and *Samson et Dalila* for Houston (1990). In 1980 the Italian Government recognized his contribution to the arts with the decoration Grande Cavaliere. Montresor's radiant sense of colour, frequent use of reflective surfaces and preference for painted cloths give a story-book appearance to his productions, which combine a childlike simplicity and directness with a sophisticated visual understanding of the theatre.   DAVID J. HOUGH

Montsalvatge, Xavier (*b* Gerona, 11 March 1912). Spanish composer. He studied at the Barcelona Conservatory with Millet, Morera, Costa and Pahissa (1923–36). In 1942 he began work as a critic, and from 1962 taught at various institutions in Barcelona. Montsalvatge felt it necessary to depart from certain Germanic traditions in Catalan music, and he came nearer to the diverting style of Les Six, besides incorporating the expressive and structural innovations of Stravinsky. At the same time he wanted to acquire Catalan qualities distinct from those implicit in his use of folk music. He also drew on West Indian folk music, itself of Spanish origin, for certàin works, notably the *Canciones negras* (1945–9). Though interested in the plastic arts and the theatre (he wrote some 20 ballets), he wrote only three operas. The magic opera *El gato con botas*, staged at the Barcelona Liceu in 1948, relates to the world of children (as attractive to Montsalvatge as it was to Lorca). Later Monsalvatge's thinking and methods underwent a decisive change. He saw no need to adhere rigidly to new ideas if they invalidated what had gone before; and he affirmed that it was as necessary to re-evaluate the tonal systems as it was to demystify 12-note technique. A new and apparently definitive style was established in the *Cinco invocaciones al Crucificado* (1969), but Montsalvatge's sense of the function of a work and his belief in music as a vehicle for expressive communication led him to take a distinctive point of departure for each composition. Thus in the one-act opera *Una voz en off* (1962), to an Italian text by the composer, his closeness to Puccini resembles that of Menotti. A third opera, *Babel-1948*, in four acts, also to the composer's own libretto, was written in 1968. Whatever the technique, Montsalvatge's music is always structurally firm, imaginatively orchestrated and motivated by an inner core of conviction.

*

M. Valls: *X. Montsalvatge* (Barcelona, 1969)

E. Franco: *Xavier Montsalvatge* (Madrid, 1975)

ENRIQUE FRANCO

Monza, Carlo (*b* Milan, *c*1735; *d* Milan, 19 Dec 1801). Italian composer. He studied with G. A. Fioroni and probably also with G. B. Sammartini, with whom he was closely associated. When Sammartini was promoted to *maestro di cappella* of the ducal court in Milan in 1768 Monza succeeded him as organist, and on Sammartini's death (1775) as *maestro*. By this time he held similar posts at three Milanese churches, and had

established himself as an important church and theatre composer. He was elected a member of the Accademia dei Pugni and the Accademia Filarmonica, Bologna. On 28 December 1787 he was appointed *maestro* of Milan Cathedral; he abandoned his successful opera career and became a remarkably active composer of sacred music. Burney wrote favourably of Monza's sacred music that he heard in Milan and Florence in 1770 and called him, along with Melchiorre Chiesa, the best composer of theatre music in Milan. In the same year Alessandro Verri reported that Monza's opera *Germanico in Germania* was well received in Rome.

Monza wrote *opere serie* almost exclusively; most were traditional 'aria' operas for Milan. As a guest composer elsewhere, he also had opportunities to participate in the Franco-Italian synthesis in opera taking place after the middle of the century; in Turin he set *Oreste* (Verazi's libretto *Ifigenia in Tauride*, originally written for G. F. de Majo at Mannheim), and in Milan he wrote *Ifigenia in Tauride* (based on Coltellini's libretto for Traetta). Both contain such French elements as scene complexes, chorus, pantomime, dance and much orchestrally accompanied recitative. Monza proved himself equal to Verazi's challenging libretto, by providing a dramatic crescendo for the storm at sea and following it with brilliant battle music for pantomime during the programmatic sinfonia. He uses a variety of textures and string effects, solo wind instruments and occasionally a solo cello to enhance the dramatic effect of accompaniments for arias and obbligato recitative. His melodies are more lyric than declamatory. His experience as a church composer helped him to produce unusually complex, contrapuntal textures for Coltellini's choruses, and he wrote an extensive concerted finale in which the principals sing antiphonally, in ensemble and in pairs, with the chorus. These operas also represent early steps towards the restoration of death and tragedy to the operatic stage; in each opera the *lieto fine* is accomplished by the staged death of an unrepentant tyrant. His other two works for Turin, *Cleopatra* and *Erifile*, go even further towards tragic endings, though the deaths do not take place on stage.

Olimpiade (P. Metastasio), Milan, Regio Ducal, May 1758, *P-La* (2 copies)

Sesostri, re d'Egitto (P. Pariati), Milan, Regio Ducal, 26 Dec 1759, *GB-Lbl* (13 arias), *I-Nc*, *P-La* (2 copies)

Achille in Sciro (Metastasio), Milan, Regio Ducal, 4 Feb 1764, *I-Nc*, *P-La* (2 copies)

Temistocle (Metastasio), Milan, Regio Ducal, 1 Jan 1766, *I-Nc*, *P-La* (2 copies)

Oreste (M. Verazi), Turin, Regio, 18 Jan 1766, *I-Tf*, *P-La* (as Ifigenia in Tauride)

Demetrio (Metastasio), Rome, Dame, 3 Jan 1769, *F-Pn*, *I-Bc*, *Rdp*, *P-La*

Adriano in Siria (Metastasio), Naples, S Carlo, 4 Nov 1769, *I-Nc*, *P-La*

Germanico in Germania (N. Coluzzi), Rome, Dame, 7 Jan 1770, *I-Rdp*, *P-La*

Il finto cavalier parigino (intermezzi in musica, 2), Rome, Valle, carn. 1770, *H-Bn*; as Il cavalier parigino (operetta per musica, 2), Milan, Regio Ducal, 3 Sept 1774, string pts *I-Rdp*

Nitteti (Metastasio), Milan, Regio Ducal, 21 Jan 1771; Venice, S Benedetto, carn. 1777, *P-La*

Aristo e Temira (2, L. V. Savioli), Bologna, Comunale, May 1771 (Bologna, 1771) [printed 12 April 1771 together with Gluck's Orfeo ed Euridice]

Antigono (Metastasio), Rome, Argentina, 18 Feb 1772, arias *I-Rc*, *PAc*

Alessandro nell'Indie (Metastasio), Milan, Regio Ducal, 28 Jan 1775, arias *MAc* (dated ?1770), *Gl*

Cleopatra (C. Olivieri), Turin, Regio, 26 Dec 1775, *F-Pn*, *P-La*

Demofoonte (Metastasio), Alessandria, Città, Oct Fair 1776, *I-MAav*

Caio Mario (G. Roccaforte), Venice, S Benedetto, Ascension Fair 1777, sinfonia *BGc*

Attilio Regolo (Metastasio), unperf., *D-Mbs* [according to Leopold Mozart, composed for Munich, carn. 1777–8]

Ifigenia in Tauride (after M. Coltellini), Milan, Scala, Jan 1784, *F-Pc, P-La* (2 copies)

Enea in Cartagine (2, G. M. D'Orengo), Alessandria, Città, Oct. Fair 1784, aria *I-Tn*

Erifile (G. De Gamerra), Turin, Regio, 26 Dec 1785, *P-La*

Music in: La lavandara astuta, 1770, arias *A-Wn*

Misattributed: Berenice, Turin, Regio, 26 Dec 1770 [actually by Ignazio Platania]

Arias in *I-Fc, Gl, Mc, MAav, MAc, Nc, PAc, PEsp, Rc, Rsc, Tf*

*

BurneyFI

E. Greppi and A. Giulini, eds.: *Carteggio di Pietro e di Alessandro Verri*, ii (Milan, 1910), 95; iii (1910), 156; xi (1940), 215

W. A. Bauer and O. E. Deutsch, eds.: *Mozart Briefe und Aufzeichnungen*, i (Kassel, 1962), 322; ii (1962), 113, 212, 230, 299; v (1971), 236, 266, 428, 498

M. Viale Ferrero: *La scenografia del 700 e i fratelli Galliari* (Turin, 1963), 255, 259, 265–6

SVEN HANSELL, KATHLEEN KUZMICK HANSELL,
MARITA P. McCLYMONDS

Monza, Carlo Ignazio [Carlino] (*b* Milan, late 17th century; *d* Vercelli, 9 May 1739). Italian composer. He has often been confused with his namesake Carlo Monza and others, and has also been referred to as Carlo Antonio. There is evidence only for the latter part of his life (from 1735 until his death), when he was *maestro di cappella* at Vercelli Cathedral. His earlier career can be conjectured on the basis of what is known of the places where his operas were performed. In librettos he is always referred to as Milanese. In 1714 he must have been in Naples, in 1716 in Messina, where he probably lived sporadically for some years. In 1722 and 1724 operas and oratorios by him were performed at Ancona, Viterbo and Bologna; in 1724–5 he was in Rome, where his oratorio *S Filippo Neri* was performed in the Arciconfraternità del Ss Crocifisso with the participation of other composers, including P. P. Bencini, G. B. Costanzi, Francesco Gasparini and Alessandro Scarlatti. In 1728 he was in Bologna, where in 1729 he was admitted to the Accademia Filarmonica. On 21 October 1735 he was appointed *Magistrum cantus seu Phonascum* of Vercelli Cathedral and a year later was ordained priest. He remained until his death in Vercelli where he composed a great deal of sacred music.

Of Monza's music for the theatre, some operas were composed entirely by him (*Sidonio*, 1714; *La Floridea regina di Cipro*, 1722), whereas *La principessa fedele* (1716) was written in collaboration with M. A. Gasparini. Numerous arias by Monza (in *GB-Lam*) were inserted into operas by Francesco Gasparini, revived many years after their original performance (*Flavio Anicio Olibrio, Il più fedel fra i vassalli, Sesostri re d'Egitto, Tigrena*), which suggests that Monza knew both the Gasparinis personally and belonged to their circle.

Sidonio (P. Pariati), Naples, Fiorentini, 13 Jan 1714

La principessa fedele, Messina, Munizione, 1716, 18 arias *GB-Lam*; collab. M. A. Gasparini

Carlo in Allemagna, 1719, 3 arias *Lam*

La Floridea regina di Cipro, Ancona, Fenice, carn. 1722

Scipione nelle Spagne, 6 arias *Lam*

Arias in: La Circe in Italia, 1722; F. Gasparini: Flavio Anicio Olibrio, *Lam*; Il più fedel fra i vassalli, *Lam*; Sesostri re d'Egitto, *Lam*; Tigrena, *Lam*

Doubtful: Lucio Vero, Macerata, carn. 1728

*

M. Donà: 'C. Monza, Pergolesi and Stravinsky', préface to C. Monza: *Pièces modernes pour le clavecin* (Milan, 1986)

MARIANGELA DONÀ

Monza, Maria (*fl* 1729–41). Italian soprano. She sang in three operas at Venice in 1729–31 and two at Prague in 1734–5, then for three years at Hamburg, where she was at first very popular, singing in Handel's *Giulio Cesare* and in a number of concerts. Her father Bartolomeo Monza was the last director of the Hamburg Opera (1737–8). Engaged by Handel for London, she made her début at Lincoln's Inn Fields in *Deidamia* (1741), and sang in revivals of the bilingual *Acis and Galatea* and two oratorios. According to Mrs Pendarves, 'her voice is between Cuzzoni's and Strada's – strong, but not harsh, her person *miserably bad*'. Burney dismissed her as below criticism; but Handel, who had written the part of Neraea for a singer of limited capacity, recomposed it for Monza, making heavy demands on her technique and flexibility and extending the compass to two octaves (*b* to *b''*).

WINTON DEAN

Moody [Manners], **Fanny** (*b* Redruth, Cornwall, 23 Nov 1866; *d* Dundrum, Co. Dublin, 21 July 1945). English soprano. She studied with Charlotte Sainton-Dolby, making her début as Arline in *The Bohemian Girl* at Liverpool in 1887 with the Carl Rosa Opera Company, of which she remained the leading soprano until 1898. With her husband, the bass CHARLES MANNERS, she founded the Moody-Manners Company (1898–1916). In 1892 she sang Tatyana in the first English performance of *Yevgeny Onegin* at the Olympic Theatre, London. She created the title role in Pizzi's *Rosalba*, and Militza in McAlpin's *The Cross and the Crescent*, in the Covent Garden seasons that she organized with Manners (1902–3). Her repertory also included Elsa, Gounod's Marguerite and Juliet, Leonora (*Il trovatore*) and Santuzza. Her pleasant light soprano voice and charming stage personality were widely admired.

*

P. Graves: 'The Moody-Manners Partnership', *Opera*, ix (1958), 558–64

HAROLD ROSENTHAL/R

Moody, John (**Percivale**) (*b* Claygate, Surrey, 6 April 1906). English director and translator. With Sadler's Wells Opera, where he was a director from 1945 to 1949, he undertook the first modern revival in Britain of Verdi's *Simon Boccanegra* (1948), and with the WNO the first productions in Britain of Verdi's *Nabucco* (1952) and *La battaglia di Legnano* (as *The Battle*, 1960). He was appointed director of productions at the WNO in 1960, later becoming its artistic director. In partnership with his wife Nell Moody (née Helen Pomfret Burra; *b* 1909) he translated many operas for performance, including *Prince Igor, Guillaume Tell, Carmen, Les pêcheurs de perles* and *Macbeth* (both versions), as well as *Simon Boccanegra* and *La battaglia di Legnano*. His contribution to British operatic life, though attracting only modest publicity, has been substantial.

ARTHUR JACOBS

Moody-Manners Company. English opera company. It was established in 1898 after a successful opera tour in South Africa by the Irish bass Charles Manners and his wife, the soprano Fanny Moody; its aim was to produce grand opera in English. At first it toured the provinces; by 1902 there were two Moody-Manners companies on the road. The principal company, with 175 members, gave seasons that year and in 1903 at Covent Garden, at Drury Lane in 1904 and later at other London theatres. With the Carl Rosa company, it was the principal training ground for British artists in the years before World War I.

Manners encouraged British composers to write for his company, offering prizes for operas. The resulting works included C. McAlpin's *The Cross and the Crescent* (1903, Covent Garden), and Nicholas Gatty's *Greysteel* (1906, Sheffield). In Sheffield Manners sponsored special opera festivals in 1904 and 1906, the profits of which helped to found Sheffield University. A successful season in Glasgow in 1906 led to the creation of the Glasgow Grand Opera Society which, in the interwar years, put on a number of enterprising seasons under Erik Chisholm. The company's music library is now in the Mitchell Library, Glasgow. By 1910 Manners faced financial difficulties and had to disband one of his two companies; his dream of founding a national English opera company centred in London was not realized. After Manners reduced his activities, Joseph O'Mara, a member of the Moody-Manners Company, formed his own group for provincial touring and occasional seasons in the London suburbs. The Moody-Manners Company gave its last performance in May 1916.   HAROLD ROSENTHAL

Moon and Sixpence, The. Opera in three acts, op.32, by JOHN GARDNER to a libretto by Patrick Terry after W. Somerset Maugham's novel; London, Sadler's Wells Theatre, 24 May 1957.

Charles Strickland (bass-baritone) is the artist as egotist, a painter who sacrifices all those around him, and himself, to his work. He leaves his English wife (mezzo-soprano) and moves to Paris, where the devotion of fellow-artist Dirk Stroeve (tenor) and his wife Blanche (dramatic soprano) is rewarded by Strickland's dismissal of Stroeve's talent and exploitation of Blanche as model and mistress. She kills herself when he announces his intention of leaving Paris. He moves to a South Sea island which enriches his painting still further, but he contracts leprosy. His friends include Tiaré Johnson (mezzo-soprano) and Dr Coutras (bass), who attends him, but it is the native girl Ata (soprano, singing actress) who stays with him to the end.

STEPHEN BANFIELD

Moór, Emanuel (*b* Kecskemét, 19 Feb 1863; *d* Mt Pélerin, nr Vevey, 20 Oct 1931). Hungarian composer. Although best known for his invention of the double-keyboard piano with octave couplers (the Emanuel Moór piano), he was a prolific composer of instrumental and vocal music, which was widely performed during his lifetime. After studying music in Prague, Vienna and Budapest he travelled to America in 1885, where he began a career as a concert pianist and conductor. In 1888 he moved to England and subsequently married Anita Burke (1864–1922), who later wrote (with Lolo von Ferro) the libretto of his early opera *La Pompadour*. Moór moved to Switzerland in 1901; both *La Pompadour* and the heroic opera *Andreas Hofer*

were performed at Cologne in 1902. After the composition of *Hochzeitsglocken* in 1908, his later life was taken up with instrumental composition and with the invention of musical instruments.

Moór's first successful opera, *La Pompadour*, captured the lighthearted spirit of the 18th century while using the post-Romantic harmonic vocabulary of his own time. By contrast, *Der Goldschmied von Paris*, based on a story by Balzac set in medieval Paris, combines romantic and heroic characteristics. Though never performed, *Der Goldschmied* provided Moór with valuable experience for the composition of his most substantial opera, *Andreas Hofer*, a historical tragedy mixed with lyrical interludes, which depicts heroic action and patriotic defence against the Napoleonic invasion of Austria in 1809. With his last opera, *Hochzeitsglocken*, Moór returned to the lyricism and smaller scale of his earlier work, although compared with these, the harmonic vocabulary is now surprisingly conservative. As an operatic composer, Moór is perhaps closest to Richard Strauss in style and outlook, but his dramatic works never achieved the stature of those of his great contemporary.

La Pompadour (2, L. von Ferro and A. L. Moór, after A. de Musset), Cologne, Neues, 22 Feb 1902, vs (Leipzig, 1902)
Andreas Hofer (4, von Ferro and E. Moór) Cologne, Neues, 9 Nov 1902, vs (n.p., 1902)
Der Goldschmied von Paris (3, T. Rehbaum, after H. de Balzac), unperf., vs (Leipzig, 1902)
Hochzeitsglocken (2, von Ferro), Kassel, Hof, 24 Aug 1908
Hertha (3, D. Hollins), inc.
The Lord of Fontanelle (B. Harte), lost

*

P. Hiller: 'Andreas Hofer', NZM, xlix (1902), 639–40
M. Pirani: Emanuel Moór (London, 1959)   DOROTHY DeVAL

Moor, Karel (*b* Belgrade, 26 Dec 1873; *d* Prague, 30 March 1945). Czech composer. He studied at the Prague Organ School (1895), took the state examination in singing in Vienna (1896) and went to Trieste for further lessons (1900). Until 1923, when he settled in Prague, he held brief conducting and teaching appointments throughout Czechoslovakia and Yugoslavia, including that of theatre conductor in Brno in 1908. In Prague he held several jobs as a choirmaster or bandmaster. Moor was one of the later generation of Czech Romantics, and his eclectic musical style incorporates both *fin-de-siècle* and pan-Slavonic elements, the latter evident in his use of Russian, Serbian and Slovak themes.

Hjördis, 1899 (4, F. Khol, after H. Ibsen), rev. 1901, Prague, National, 22 Oct 1905
Vij, 1901 (1, Khol, after N. V. Gogol), Prague, National, 14 July 1903; rev. 1910
Pan Profesor v pekle [Mr Professor in Hell] (operetta, 3, A. Rajská-Smolíková, after K. Vaurien [E. Pauk]), Brno, National, 31 March 1908; rev. 1922
Vlkodlak [The Werewolf], 1908 (operetta, M. Žunkovič), unperf.
Výlet pana Broučka do měsíce [Mr Brouček's Excursion to the Moon] (operetta, 3, V. Merhaut and Moor, after S. Čech), Jaroměř, 21 June 1910
Panské právo [Le droit du seigneur], 1914–16 (Žunkovič), unperf.
Satanela (operetta, Brno, Veveři, 16 Jan 1919
Sněška [Sněhurka; Snow-White] (operetta), Sarajevo, 1922
Děti práce [Child's Work] (operetta, J. Balda), Kladno, 1925
Jeho krásná neznámá [His Beautiful Unknown Woman] (operetta, 3, K. Tobis and J. Kohout), Prague, 24 April 1926
Svatební valčík [Bridal Waltz], 1929 (operetta, 3, L. Pohl), Prague, 23 Oct 1931
Vzhůru do pekel [Up to Hell] (operetta-revue, J. L. Novák), Prague, 1929

Pan Amanuensis na venku [Mr Amanuensis in the Country]/
Putování za novelou [In Search of a Novella] (3, Pauk, after F. J.
Rubeš), Prague Radio, 25 March 1930
Poslední akord [The Last Chord]/Episoda z pobytu W. A. Mozarta v
Praze [An Episode from Mozart's Stay in Prague] (1, Pohl),
Prague, 18 June 1930
Noční Prahou [By Night through Prague] (operetta, 3, A.
Přerovský-Caletka), Prague, 24 Feb 1933
W. A. Mozart (3, F. Francl and S. Mann), Prague, Uranie, 24 March
1934

*

O. Sv.: 'Karel Moor', *Ohlas od Nežárky*, i/20 (1920), 2–3
M. Šimáček: 'Karel Moor šedesátníkem' [Moor's 60th Birthday],
Československé divadlo, xvi (1933), 292
H. D.: 'Jubilea' [Birthdays], *Tempo*, xiii (1933–4), 237–8
J. Balda: 'Český muzikant Karel Moor', *Divadlo*, xxix (1943), 106
MILAN KUNA, HELENA HAVLÍKOVÁ

Moore, Charles Garrett Ponsonby. *See* DROGHEDA.

Moore, Douglas S(tuart) (*b* Cutchogue, NY, 10 Aug
1893; *d* Greenport, NY, 25 July 1969). American
composer. Through such works as *The Devil and Daniel
Webster* (1939) and *The Ballad of Baby Doe* (1956) he
did much to define American opera in the middle
decades of the 20th century. The scion of a long-
established and well-connected family, he was educated
at Hotchkiss School and Yale University (BA 1915, BM
1917), where he studied composition with Horatio
Parker. He began to write songs while still at school,
and at Yale he composed songs for social events,
developing a gift for writing melodies in a popular style.
This tendency was reinforced by further songwriting
during his World War I service in the US Navy (from
1917).

After his demobilization in 1919 Moore went to
Paris, where he studied at the Schola Cantorum with
Charles Tournemire (organ) and Vincent d'Indy
(composition). It is the style of d'Indy, rather than that
of Parker, that underlies Moore's mature idiom and is
discernible in his less inspired passages. While in Paris,
Moore's friendship with the writer and poet Stephen
Vincent Benét initiated a collaboration that resulted in
numerous songs and two of the composer's best-known
operas. In 1921 Moore was appointed curator of music
at the Cleveland Museum of Art, a post he held for four
years. In Cleveland he found a more stimulating artistic
environment than he had encountered hitherto: he
studied for a year with Ernest Bloch, whose pupils then
included Roger Sessions, Bernard Rogers and Quincy
Porter. He also gained invaluable experience of practical
stagecraft as an actor in leading roles at the Cleveland
Playhouse. More significant, however, was a chance
meeting in 1923 with the poet Vachel Lindsay
(1879–1931), who befriended Moore and encouraged
him to use Americana as an artistic resource. The
majority of Moore's compositions after 1923 are programme works on archetypal American themes. His
compositional style was now formed, and a final year of
study in Paris with Nadia Boulanger in 1925 proved unnecessary and unproductive.

The following year Moore was appointed to the
faculty of Columbia University, where he became chairman of the music department in 1940, remaining in that
post until his retirement in 1962. He gradually became
one of the most influential figures in American music,
both as a teacher and as a director or board member of
many organizations, including ASCAP and the National
Institute and American Academy of Arts and Letters.

In connection with his acting, Moore had been drawn
to theatrical music from an early age. His first composition for the theatre was incidental music for *Quentin
Durward* (1912) and he wrote music for three other
plays between 1925 and 1927. Later work in this vein
included two 'private entertainments' and three film
scores. This work was closely associated with his youthful songs in popular style, so it is not surprising that his
first attempt at a full-scale theatrical work should have
been a musical, *Oh, Oh, Tennessee* (1925, apparently
never performed). Indeed, Moore only gradually came
to compose real opera. Following the abortive *Jesse
James* (1928) and unsuccessful *White Wings* (1935), his
first 'popular' operas are just that. The two works with
librettos by Benét owe a great deal to operetta and early
Broadway; *The Headless Horseman* (1937), an operetta
for performance by schoolchildren, is more spoken than
sung, with an overture that quotes the melodies of the
principal vocal numbers. Its heavy debt to Gilbert and
Sullivan is exemplified in its third number, which
manages in four lines (the complete text) to echo the
openings of both *Ruddigore* and *Iolanthe*: 'Dear
Katrina, happy bride/When the nuptial knot is tied/We
shall dance and we shall sing/Fol-de-rol-de-rol, O!' The
folk opera *The Devil and Daniel Webster* (1939) also
owes much to *Ruddigore* and is a musical in all but
name; the published score designates its libretto as a
'book'. Both these works, especially the latter, were
highly successful, and were staples at American universities and high schools until late in the 20th century.
The two fairy-tale operas, to texts by Raymond
Abrashkin, *The Emperor's New Clothes* and *Puss in
Boots*, also resemble musicals in structure (as does the
later *Greenfield Christmas Tree*), and it was only with
Giants in the Earth (1949) that Moore came to grips
with the notion of full-length opera, sung throughout.

For most of his career Moore was not thought of
primarily in terms of opera. *The Devil and Daniel
Webster* was greatly admired and is mentioned in all
contemporary accounts of the composer's life, but that
was just one work in an output dominated by orchestral
and chamber music, songs and choruses. It was *The
Ballad of Baby Doe*, composed in 1956 and unquestionably Moore's masterpiece, that made him an
'opera composer'. Immediately and resoundingly
popular, it added an associative lustre to the reputation
of the much weaker *Giants in the Earth*, and to the later
works *The Wings of the Dove* (1961) and *Carry Nation*
(1966). Indeed, for a time it was thought of as the 'great
American opera', and in 1976 (the bicentenary of the
USA) it was given at least five separate professional
productions in the United States alone. Ironically, the
success of *Baby Doe* contributed to the effacement of
Moore's instrumental works, which are now seldom
heard.

The influence of Vachel Lindsay consisted essentially
in Moore's realization that the tuneful, popular style he
had developed was ideally suited to the depiction of
American events. Had he become a writer of popular
songs, as he sometimes wished, his pre-jazz melodic
sense would have led to failure; yet in his chosen métier
these same tunes proved vividly evocative of late 19th-
century America, ever more so as that era receded into
the past. It is when Moore attempted to be 'high-falutin'
that he failed, and his one attempt to treat a contemporary subject in a contemporary way (his opera
Gallantry (1958), a parody of a television soap-opera,
complete with commercials) proved unsuccessful.

Because of its popular roots, his inspiration tends to express itself in static, set-piece 'songs' and choral numbers, so that even *Baby Doe* has more than a whiff of Broadway about it. Some of his famous arias – Baby Doe's 'Willow Song', Webster's 'I've got a ram, Goliath' – lie outside all considerations of character, plot or even musical continuity.

By the same token, Moore's vaunted Americanism is musically both superficial and intermittent. Long stretches of *Baby Doe* are laid out in a blandly functional arioso style in which the influences of d'Indy and Puccini are more clearly evident than any American model. Nonetheless, with the right material Moore hits the target so squarely (as in *Baby Doe*'s superb opening scene) that dullness elsewhere is readily forgotten.

Though he never takes his Americanisms beyond the level of local colour (e.g. contrast *Baby Doe* with Virgil Thomson's *The Mother of us All*), Moore was for many years the most distinctively nationalist composer to find a regular place in America's professional opera seasons. The broadening of the American repertory since 1982 has led to fewer performances of Moore's operas, but *The Ballad of Baby Doe*, at least, will no doubt continue to have a place on the nation's stages and in its heart.

See also BALLAD OF BABY DOE, THE and DEVIL AND DANIEL WEBSTER, THE.

Oh, Oh, Tennessee, 1925 (musical comedy), unperf.
Jesse James, 1928 (J. M. Brown), inc.
White Wings, 1935 (chamber op, 2, P. Barry), Hartford, CT, 9 Feb 1949, sketches US-Wc *
The Headless Horseman (school operetta, 1, S. V. Benét, after W. Irving: *The Legend of Sleepy Hollow*), Bronxville, New York, 4 March 1937, vs (Boston, 1937)
The Devil and Daniel Webster (folk op, 1, Benét, after his own short story), New York, Martin Beck, 18 May 1939, Wc*, vs (New York, 1943)
The Emperor's New Clothes (children's op, 1, R. Abrashkin, after H. C. Andersen), New York, 19 Feb 1949, vs (Boston, 1948); rev. 1956
Giants in the Earth, 1949 (3, A. Sundgaard, after O. E. Rölvaag), New York, Columbia U., 28 March 1951; rev. 1963
Puss in Boots (children's operetta, Abrashkin, after C. Perrault), New York, 18 Nov 1950
The Ballad of Baby Doe (2, J. Latouche), Central City, CO, Opera House, 7 July 1956, Wc*, vs (New York, 1958); rev., New York, 3 April 1958
Gallantry (soap op, 1, Sundgaard), New York, Columbia U., 19 March 1958, vs (New York, 1958)
The Wings of the Dove (1, E. Ayer, after H. James), New York, City Opera, 12 Oct 1961, vs (New York, 1963)
The Greenfield Christmas Tree (Christmas entertainment, 1, Sundgaard), Hartford, Bushnell Memorial Auditorium, 8 Dec 1962, vs (New York, 1963)
Carry Nation (2, W. N. Jayme), Lawrence, U. of Kansas, 28 April 1966, vs (New York, 1968)

*

O. Luening: 'American Composers, XX: Douglas Moore', MM, xx/4 (1942), 248–53
M. Goss: *Modern Music Makers* (New York, 1952)
T. H. Cavendish: *Folk Music in Selected Twentieth Century American Opera* (diss., Florida State U., 1966)
J. Beeson: 'In Memoriam: Douglas Moore (1893–1969): an Appreciation, Written in a Country Churchyard', PNM, viii/1 (1969), 158–60
S. K. Bethea: *Opera for Children: an Analysis of Selected Works* (diss., U. of Kansas, 1971)
J. H. Weitzel: *A Melodic Analysis of Selected Vocal Solos in the Operas of Douglas Moore* (diss., New York U., 1971)
L. J. Hardee: 'The Published Songs and Arias', NATS Bulletin, xxix (1973), 28–31
R. L. Blooding: *Douglas Moore's 'The Ballad of Baby Doe': an Investigation of its Historical Accuracy and the Feasibility of a Historical Production in the Tabor Opera House* (diss., Ohio State U., 1979)

H. Gleason and W. Becker: 'Douglas Moore', *20th-Century American Composers* (Bloomington, 2/1981), 129–37

ANDREW STILLER

Moore, Grace (*b* Nough, TN, 5 Dec 1898; *d* nr Copenhagen, 26 Jan 1947). American soprano. She studied singing with Marafioti in New York and then appeared in revue and operetta. In 1926 she sailed for Europe and after working with Richard Berthélemy at Antibes made her Opéra-Comique début as Mimì in 1928. That year she made her Metropolitan début in the same role, remaining there until the 1931–2 season and returning in several seasons up to 1946, singing such roles as Lauretta, Tosca, Manon, Fiora (*L'amore dei tre re*) and Louise. She appeared at Covent Garden in 1935 as Mimì. Moore died in an aeroplane accident. The most important of her several films was *One Night of Love* (1934). Hers were a glamorous personality, earning the American accolade 'star of stage, screen and radio', and a sensuous, substantial voice, though it lacked technical finish.

*

DAB (W. E. Boswell); G V (R. Celletti; S. Smolian)
O. Thompson: *The American Singer* (New York, 1937), 384ff
G. Moore: *You're Only Human Once* (Garden City, NY, 1944)

MAX DE SCHAUENSEE/R

Moore, Mary (Louise) Carr (*b* Memphis, 6 Aug 1873; *d* Inglewood, CA, 9 Jan 1957). American composer and teacher. She studied composition and singing in San Francisco and in 1894 sang the leading role in the première of her first operetta, *The Oracle*, at Golden Gate Hall. In 1895 she abandoned her singing career and for the rest of her life taught and composed, at first in Lemoore, California, then in Seattle (1901) and San Francisco (1915). Later in Los Angeles she concurrently taught at the Olga Steeb Piano School (1926–43) and was professor of theory and composition at Chapman College (1928–47), where she was awarded an honorary DMus in 1936.

Arthur Farwell's American music movement inspired Moore greatly, and 19th-century German and French models, studied in the populist context of the American West, formed her style and aesthetic approach. She was at her best in opera, where she frequently challenged the limitations of the genteel culture to which she remained bound by inclination and family obligations. Her musical language evolved substantially after *Narcissa* (1909–11). *David Rizzio* (1927–8), whose action takes place during the brief reign of Mary, Queen of Scots, makes much use of the whole tone. *Légende provençale*, a tale of love, faith and sorcery set in the 15th century, has a more expanded post-Romantic harmonic vocabulary. 'Sola, abbandonata' (*Rizzio*) and 'L'étoile du soir' (*Légende*) were often sung independently. Mixed groups of amateurs and professionals, assembled through her own efforts, performed Moore's operas, although she considered *Narcissa*, *David Rizzio*, *Los rubios* and, especially, *Légende provençale* too difficult for amateur singers. All except *The Leper* and *Légende provençale*, which were never produced, had at least limited revivals. Both regional prejudice and sex discrimination probably slowed her artistic development and prevented Moore from receiving the recognition that her achievements warranted.

The Oracle (operetta, 3, Moore), San Francisco, Golden Gate Hall, 19 March 1894; rev. (3), Seattle, 10 Jan 1902, vs US-LAu*
Narcissa, or The Cost of Empire, 1909–11 (grand op, 4, S. P. Carr),

Seattle, Moore Theatre, 22 April 1912, *LAu**, vs (New York, 1912)

The Leper, 1912 (tabloid grand op, 1, D. Burrows), unperf., vs *LAu**

Memories (vaudeville sketch, 1, C. E. Banks), Seattle, Orpheum, 31 Oct 1914, vs *LAu**

Harmony (operetta, 1, various students), San Francisco, Mission High School, 25 May 1917, vs (pts) *LAu**

The Flaming Arrow, or The Shaft of Ku'pish-ta-ya, 1919–20 (operetta, 1, Carr), San Francisco, 27 March 1922, vs (pts) *LAu**

David Rizzio, 1927–8 (2, E. M. Browne), Los Angeles, Shrine Auditorium, 26 May 1932, *LAu**, vs (San Bruno, CA, 1937/ R1981)

Los rubios (3, N. Marquis), Los Angeles, Greek, 10 Sept 1931, *LAu**

Flutes of Jade Happiness, 1932–3 (operetta, 3, L. S. Moore), Los Angeles, Los Angeles High School, 2 March 1934, vs (pts) *LAu**

Légende provençale, 1929–35 (3, E. Flaig), unperf., lost

See also NARCISSA.

*

M. C. Moore: 'Writing and Producing an Opera', *Pacific Coast Musician*, iv/7 (1915), 51

F. H. Martens: *A Thousand and One Nights of Opera* (New York, 1926)

E. E. Hipsher: *American Opera and its Composers* (Philadelphia, c1927, 2/1934)

'Mary Carr Moore – American Composer', *Christian Science Monitor* (16 April 1929)

H. E. Johnson: *Operas on American Subjects* (New York, 1964)

C. P. Smith: Introduction to M. C. Moore: *David Rizzio*, Women Composers, xii (New York, 1981)

C. P. Smith and C. S. Richardson: *Mary Carr Moore, American Composer* (Ann Arbor, 1987)

CYNTHIA S. RICHARDSON, CATHERINE PARSONS SMITH

Moore, Thomas (*b* Dublin, 28 May 1779; *d* nr Calne, Wilts., 25 Feb 1852). Irish poet and musician. He studied at Trinity College, Dublin, and in 1799 went to London as a law student. He made himself popular with his verses and his singing; he also wrote the libretto for Michael Kelly's opera *The Gipsey Prince* (1801), and in 1802–3 wrote the words and often the music of many songs which won instant recognition. When in 1807 a publisher proposed a selection of Irish songs, Moore provided words and tunes; the *Irish Melodies* began serial publication in 1808, eventually reaching ten numbers and a supplement by 1834. Moore drew heavily on the collections by Edward Bunting. This collection clinched Moore's already enormous popularity. In 1811 he wrote the text and (with C. E. Horn) music for an unsuccessful comic opera, *M. P., or The Blue Stocking*. By now rich and famous, he could command an advance of £3000 for *Lalla Rookh* (London, 1817); the first edition sold out in a fortnight, and it was reprinted six times in as many months. Abroad, the enthusiasm for all things Scottish was easily extended to include Moore as their counterpart, with his apparent embodiment of the Irish soul in verse and song: and though the work includes covert references to Irish patriotism, the orientalism of *Lalla Rookh* played expertly on Romantic sensibilities still enraptured by *The Thousand and One Nights* (whose pattern Moore copied). Berlioz found it full of 'splendid images' (*Mémoires*), and set and often quoted it. The story provided material for the librettos of operas by Horn (*Lalla Rookh, or The Cashmerian Minstrel*, 1818), Spontini (*Nurmahal*, 1822), Félicien David (1862) and Anton Rubinstein (*Feramors*, 1863); and the individual poems were the subjects of operas by Eduard Sobolewski (*Der Prophet vom Khorassan*, 1850), Arthur Goring Thomas (*The Light of the Harem*, 1879), and Stanford (*The Veiled Prophet of Khorassan*, 1881).

J. Russell, ed.: *Memoirs, Journals and Correspondence of Thomas Moore* (London, 1853–6)

S. Gwynn: *Thomas Moore* (London, 1905)

W. F. Trench: *Tom Moore* (Dublin, 1934)

S. MacCall: *Thomas Moore* (Dublin, 1936)   JOHN WARRACK

Moorehead [Moorhead], **John** (*b* Ireland, c1760; *d* nr Deal, March 1804). Irish composer. A violinist, he was for several years engaged in the orchestras of various English country theatres before becoming principal viola player at Sadler's Wells Theatre, London, in 1795. From that time he composed music for the entertainments given there, as well as for Covent Garden, whose orchestra he joined in 1798. Moorehead's overtures and songs are unpretentious (and unadventurous), and rely on tonic-dominant harmonic schemes and repetitive melodic patterns. Insanity cut short his career; by 1802 he had been certified and, after a brief term of imprisonment, served in the Navy until his suicide.

all publications are vocal or pf scores, published in London; MS librettos in US-SM

LCG – *London, Covent Garden*   LSW – *London, Sadler's Wells*

The Philosopher's Stone [? = The Philosopher, or The Turns of Fortune (comedy)], LSW, 1795

Birds of a Feather, or Buz and Mum (comic piece, ?J. Moorehead), LSW, 25 July 1796, 2 songs (1796)

The Naval Pillar, or Britannia Triumphant (interlude, T. J. Dibdin), LCG, 7 Oct 1799 (1799), incl. music by Calcott and T. Linley

The Volcano, or Rival Harlequins (pantomime, T. J. Dibdin and C. Farley), LCG, 23 Dec 1799, ov. (c1800)

Boadicea, or The British Amazon (serious pantomime, C. Dibdin), LSW, 14 April 1800

Old Fools, or Love's Stratagem (burletta, C. Dibdin), LSW, 14 April 1800

Il Bondocani, or The Caliph Robber (comic op, T. J. Dibdin), LCG, 15 Nov 1800 (1801), collab. Attwood

Harlequin's Tour, or The Dominion of Fancy (pantomime, T. J. Dibdin), LCG, 22 Dec 1800 (c1800), collab. Attwood

Perouse, or The Desolate Island (pantomime, J. Fawcett), LCG, 28 Feb 1801, ov. (1801), collab. J. Davy

Harlequin Benedick, or Mother Shipton's Ghost (pantomime, C. Dibdin), LSW, 29 June 1801

The Cabinet (comic op, T. J. Dibdin), LCG, 9 Feb 1802 (1802), collab. Reeve, Davy, Corri and Braham

Speed the Plough, or The Return of Peace (musical play, C. Dibdin), LSW, 1 May 1802

Family Quarrels (comic op, T. J. Dibdin), LCG, 18 Dec 1802 (c1802), collab. Braham and Reeve

Harlequin's Habeas, or The Hall of Spectres (pantomime, T. J. Dibdin), LCG, 27 Dec 1802, ov. (1802), collab. Braham and Davy

*

DNB (L. M. Middleton)

T. J. Dibdin: *Reminiscences*, i (London, 1827), 317ff

C. I. M. Dibdin: *Professional & Literary Memoirs of Charles Dibdin the Younger, Dramatist and Upward of Thirty Years Manager of Minor Theatres*, ed. G. Speaight (London, 1956), 42–3

Moral, Pablo del (*fl* 1765–1805). Spanish composer. In 1777 he was violinist at the royal chapel of St Cayetan in Madrid; by then he had also been standing in for more than eight years for violinists attached to the theatrical companies of Madrid. In 1778, after public competition, he was officially named 'violinist of the Madrid theatres', and about the same time began to compose *tonadillas*. In 1790, again after public competition, he was appointed 'composer to the theatres of Madrid', with the responsibility of composing 40 *tonadillas* each year 'as well as everything else needed in the way of music'. In March 1792 he was obliged to abandon the post for reasons of health, but by April 1797 he was able to resume. In 1804 a new post of theatre composer was created, identical with Moral's, and awarded to the Italian G. M. Francesconi, a mediocre but conceited composer, much given to intrigue; Moral, affronted, resigned on 17 April 1805 and disappeared from public life.

In Moral's time the *tonadilla escénica* lost its directness and simplicity, often becoming a miniature comic opera with italianate music. Subirá published one of his *tonadillas*, *La ópera casera* (1799), in which there is some virtuoso vocal writing entirely operatic in character. About 150 of Moral's *tonadillas* survive, as well as the opera *La dama inconstante*, several *sainetes* and other theatre music (*E-Mm*); he also composed sacred music.

*

LaborD
J. Subirá: *La tonadilla escénica* (Madrid, 1928–30)
——: *La tonadilla escénica: sus obras y sus autores* (Barcelona, 1933)   JOSÉ LÓPEZ-CALO

Morales, Melesio (*b* Mexico City, 4 Dec 1838; *d* Mexico City, 12 May 1908). Mexican composer. His teachers included Paniagua y Vasques. At the age of 18 he sketched his first opera, *Romeo e Giulietta* (on Romani's libretto). After revising the orchestration three times he succeeded in getting it performed by the resident Italian company on 27 January 1863. One of the singers, Roncari, advised him to leave Mexico and make a name in Europe. He was unable to leave, however, until spring 1866, and in the meantime his second opera, *Ildegonda*, was produced (27 December 1865) after Maximilian had personally intervened to guarantee the production costs.

Morales spent three years in Europe and shortly before his return saw *Ildegonda* produced at the Teatro Pagliano in Florence (December 1868), where it was received with great acclaim. As predicted, his reputation in Mexico was tremendously enhanced by his European success, and he returned a conquering hero. At the Mexico City Conservatory he organized his own department of composition, 'founded on Neapolitan principles', and numbered among his pupils Campa, Ricardo Castro and Carrillo. Of his later operas two were produced at the Gran Teatro Nacional, Mexico City: *Gino Corsini* (14–15 July 1877) and *Cleopatra* (14–21 November 1891). His last opera, the one-act *Anita*, dealing with the 1867 siege of Puebla, shows *verismo* influence. All his librettos were written in Italian. Despite his apparent propensity for the Italian style, in 1902 he declared Wagner's *Ring* to be 'the best work written during the 19th century'. Nearly a hundred of his works were published, many of them in Italy, including excerpts from *Ildegonda*.

*

I. M. Altamirano: 'Don Melesio Morales', *Revista musical mexicana*, iii (1943), 10–13, 35–8, 63–5, 110–12, 180–82, 206–7, 228–32
O. Mayer-Serra: *Música y músicos de Latinoamérica*, ii (Mexico City, 1947), 660ff
R. Stevenson: *Music in Mexico* (New York, 1952, 2/1971), 197ff
E. de Olavarría y Ferrari: *Reseña histórica del teatro en México* (Mexico City, 1961), i, 670ff, 699; ii, 973–4, 1363–4
H. de Grial: *Músicos mexicanos* (Mexico City, 2/1969)
R. Stevenson: 'Chopin in Mexico', *Inter-American Music Review*, iv/2 (1982), 36–9   ROBERT STEVENSON

Moralt, Rudolf (*b* Munich, 26 Feb 1902; *d* Vienna, 16 Dec 1958). German conductor. He was a nephew of Richard Strauss. After working as a répétiteur at the Staatsoper in Munich under Walter and Knappertsbusch (1919–23), he was conductor at the Kaiserslautern Städtische Oper (1923–38) and music director at the German Theatre, Brno (1932–4). He made a brief return to Kaiserslautern then was appointed to Brunswick in 1934 and to Graz in 1937. That year he also made his Vienna début, where he was chief conductor at the Staatsoper from 1940 until his death. A reliable, unaffected and deeply understanding conductor, he was responsible for a high standard of repertory performances at Vienna for almost 20 years. His stylistic competence and excellent baton technique achieved many notable performances, especially of works by Mozart, Wagner, Pfitzner and Richard Strauss. He appeared at the 1952 Salzburg Festival and as guest conductor in many other European cities and in South America. His records include *Don Giovanni*, *Salome* and the first recording of Lehár's *Giuditta*.
                                            GERHARD BRUNNER

Moran, Robert (Leonard) (*b* Denver, 8 Jan 1937). American composer. A self-confessed 'opera lunatic' from the age of six, he has displayed a strongly dramatic flair in all his compositions; much of his work has taken the form of mixed-media theatre pieces. He first studied privately with Hans-Erich Apostel in Vienna (1957–8). After receiving the BA from San Francisco State College (1961) he studied both drama and composition at Mills College, Oakland (MA 1963), where Berio and Milhaud were his principal teachers. In Vienna in 1963 he studied briefly with Haubenstock-Ramati, who influenced him in the direction of musical graphics and mobile forms. Back in San Francisco, he directed the West Coast Music Ensemble, broadcast contemporary music (KPFA), and taught at the San Francisco Conservatory. Moran spent most of the 1970s in a succession of residencies as composer, pianist and lecturer on contemporary music. In 1978 he moved to New York as a full-time composer, then from 1985 lived in Philadelphia.

Unlike the massive outdoor, multi-media, audience-participation 'city pieces' on which his reputation has been largely based, Moran's theatre-scale dramatic works, including those classifiable as operas, have typically taken a satirical or moralizing tone. The non-operatic *Hitler: Geschichten aus der Zukunft* (1981), a menacing, 'fun-house' environment based on official Nazi-era documents, proved too hot even for modern Germany and was refused performance despite having been commissioned. Its sequel, *Erlösung dem Erlöser* (sarcastically subtitled *Bühnenweihfestspiel*), is a true opera, set within the disordered brain of the dying Wagner.

In 1984 Moran offered to share with Philip Glass a commission for a children's opera. Instead of the proposed pair of works, the collaborative (and entirely adult) *Juniper Tree* resulted. For this work Moran, in a dramatic stylistic departure, adopted a neo-Romantic idiom to balance Glass's minimalism, and he has since continued in this vein, starting with *Leipziger Kerzenspiel*, a celebration of the 1985 Baroque ter- and quatercentenaries. The immense success of *The Juniper Tree* has led Moran into the path of traditional opera, and in 1989 he was commissioned to write *Desert of Roses* for Houston based on the story of Beauty and the Beast. *From the Towers of the Moon*, based on a 3000-year-old Japanese legend, was commissioned by the Minnesota Opera the following year. Both operas, to librettos by Michael John LaChiusa, were first performed in 1992. Like *The Juniper Tree*, they draw remarkably lush sonorities from small casts and orchestras through the use of multiple synthesizers for harmonic reinforcement.

See also JUNIPER TREE, THE.

Let's Build a Nut House (chamber op, 1, R. Moran), San Jose, CA, State College, 19 April 1969
Erlösung dem Erlöser (music drama, 2, Moran), Frankfurt, Turm, ? Oct 1982
Leipziger Kerzenspiel (Spl, 1 or 2, A. Yorinks and Moran), South Hadley, MA, Mount Holyoke College, 15 Feb 1985
The Juniper Tree (prol., 2, Yorinks, after J. L. and W. C. Grimm), Cambridge, MA, American Repertory, 6 Dec 1985, collab. P. Glass
Desert of Roses, 1989–90 (2, M. J. La Chiusa, after the Beauty and the Beast story), Houston, Wortham Centre, 14 Feb 1992
From the Towers of the Moon (1, La Chiusa, after the Kaguyahime legend), St Paul, World, 27 March 1992

*

VintonD
'Events/Comments: Robert Moran', *Source*, iii/2 (1969), 8
'Opera Here and There', *BMI, the Many Worlds of Music* (June 1969), 27
'Conversation with Robert Moran', *Numus-West*, no.3 (1973), 30–36
P. Hoffman: 'An Interview with Robert Moran', *The Composer*, iv/ 2 (1973–4), 46–8
E. R. Anderson: *Contemporary American Composers: a Biographical Dictionary* (Boston, 2/1982)
R. Dyer: 'America: Philip Glass Again', *Opera*, xxxvii (1986), 408–9
A. L. Pincus: 'Opera Everywhere: Cambridge', *HiFi/MusAm*, xxxvi/4 (1986), MA18–19
R. Stoeckl: 'Minimalistenmäander unter dem Machandelbaum', *OW*, xxix/7 (1988), 45–6
R. H. Kornick: *Recent American Opera: a Production Guide* (New York, 1991), 120–22   ANDREW STILLER

Morandi, Pietro (*b* Bologna, 15 April 1745; *d* Senigallia, 8 Dec 1815). Italian composer. He was a pupil of Padre Martini in Bologna and in 1764 was admitted to membership of the Accademia Filarmonica. In 1775 he was appointed *maestro di cappella* at Pergola, near Pesaro, and in 1778 departed for Senigallia. He composed several operas, mostly for small Italian cities. His son Giovanni, an organist and composer, was married to the singer Rosa Morandi.

Il fantasma (int), Bologna, Palazzo Felicini, 1764, *I-Bc*
Il Tobia, Iesi, 1773
La cometa, Fano, 1775
La vara della virtù, Ancona, 1775
Il sogno, Pesaro, 1776
Comala (componimento drammatico, R. Calzabigi), Senigallia, 1780, *F-Pn, I-Nc*
Zemira (3, G. Sertor), Florence, Pergola, carn. 1782, *Fc*
Il premio, Filottrano, 1789
Gli usurpatori delusi, Senigallia, 1791
L'inglese stravagante, Ancona, 1792

Morandi [née Morolli], **Rosa (Paolina)** (*b* Senigallia, 15 July 1782; *d* Milan, 6 April or 4 May 1824). Italian mezzo-soprano. She studied with Giovanni Morandi (son of the composer Pietro Morandi), whom she married in 1804, the year of her début at Vittoria di Montalboddo (now Ostra), and sang at La Scala in 1807 in Simon Mayr's *Nè l'un, nè l'altro* and in *Così fan tutte*. After singing in Rome, she created Fanny in Rossini's *La cambiale di matrimonio* in Venice (1810). At the Théâtre Italien, Paris (1813–17), she sang in Pavesi's *Ser Marcantonio*, and in *Le nozze di Figaro, Il matrimonio segreto, Le cantatrici villane* and *L'italiana in Algeri*. She took part in the first performances of Vaccai's *Malvina* (1816) and Rossini's *Edoardo e Cristina* (1819) at Venice and Donizetti's *Chiara e*

Serafina (1822) at La Scala. Though her repertory included Paer's *Camilla* and *Agnese* and Meyerbeer's *Emma di Resburgo*, her dramatic and flexible voice was best displayed in Rossini: as Matilde di Shabran, Desdemona and Tancredi.   ELIZABETH FORBES

Morani, Lorenzo. *See* MORARI, LORENZO.

Moranzoni, Roberto (*b* Bari, 5 Oct 1880; *d* Desio, Milan, 14 Dec 1959). Italian conductor. He studied at Pesaro with Mascagni and made his début at the Costanzi, Rome, as Mascagni's choice to follow the composer in conducting first-run performances of *Le maschere* (1901). He was music director for Boston Grand Opera, 1910–17, and active in Paris and London; he made his Covent Garden début in the first British production of *L'amore dei tre re* (Montemezzi) in 1914, making a good impression in spite of too little rehearsal. He spent seven seasons at the Metropolitan, beginning in 1917 with *Aida* and including the première of Puccini's complete *Trittico* there the next year. After working at the Chicago Opera, 1924–9, he continued intermittent engagements and returned to Italy in 1947.   NOËL GOODWIN

Morari [Morani], **Lorenzo** (*b* Padua; *fl* 1703). Italian librettist. He is sometimes incorrectly called 'Morani'. He apparently wrote only one libretto, *Farnace*, which Caldara set for the autumn 1703 season at the Teatro S Angelo in Venice. The dedication is signed by the printer Marino Rossetti and dated 15 November, and manuscript newsletters report that the opera opened on 19 November. *Farnace* is loosely based on history. There is no record that it was ever restaged in Italy, but in 1723 it formed the basis for the *Farnace* that Giovanni Bononcini set for the King's Theatre in London. Morari's work should not be confused with two other librettos that share the same title: Lalli's *Farnace* (first set by C. F. Pollarolo for the Teatro S Cassiano in Venice, 1718) and Lucchini's *Farnace* (first set by Vinci for the Teatro Alibert in Rome, 1724). Lucchini's libretto was set many times.

*

AllacciD
G. Bonlini: *Le glorie della poesia e della musica* (Venice, 1730)
A. Groppo: *Catalogo di tutti drammi per musica* (Venice, *c*1745)
W. Dean and J. M. Knapp: *Handel's Operas (1704–1726)* (Oxford, 1987)   HARRIS S. SAUNDERS

Moratelli, Sebastiano (*b* Vicenza, 1640; *d* Heidelberg, 1706). Italian composer. He went to Vienna before 1660 and entered the emperor's service as a chamber musician. He was also music master to the Dowager Empress Eleonore and her daughter Maria Anna Josepha. When the archduchess married the future Elector Palatine Johann Wilhelm he went, at the dowager empress's request, to Düsseldorf, where he remained a member of the Palatine court from 1679 until his death. Correspondence between the elector and the Emperor Leopold I reveals that Moratelli was supplying the court with dramatic music for Carnival by 1681. He was appointed Kapellmeister not later than 1687 and also became court chaplain. Because of ill-health he was increasingly assisted from 1696 by his younger colleague and eventual successor, J. H. von Wilderer. As a musician he was highly esteemed by his contemporaries. Rapparini stated that he composed several operas and serenades and praised him above all for the naturalness and expressive power of his recitatives. Not a note of his music survives. On the basis of extant librettos, all by Rapparini, the following operas can be ascribed to him with certainty: *Erminia ne' boschi* (1687), *Erminia al campo* (Carnival 1688), *Didone* (1688), *I giochi olimpici, ovvero Che fingendo si prova un vero affetto* (1694) and *Il fabbro pittor* (1695). He may also have written the festival opera *La gemma Ceraunia* (Nicolò Minato), performed at Heidelberg in 1687.

G. M. Rapparini: *Le portrait du vrai mérite dans la personne sérénissime de Monseigneur l'Electeur Palatin* (MS, 1709, D-DÜl); ed. H. Kühn-Steinhausen (Düsseldorf, 1958)
F. Walter: *Geschichte des Theaters und der Musik am kurpfälzischen Hofe* (Leipzig, 1898)
A. Einstein: 'Italienische Musiker am Hofe der Neuburger Wittelsbacher, 1614–1716: neue Beiträge zur Geschichte der Musik am Neuburg-Düsseldorfer Hof im 17. Jahrhundert', *SIMG*, ix (1907–8), 336–424
G. Croll: 'Musikgeschichtliches aus Rapparinis Johann-Wilhelm-Manuskript (1709)', *Mf*, xi (1958), 257–64
G. Steffen: *Johann Hugo von Wilderer (1670–1724), Kapellmeister am kurpfälzischen Hofe zu Düsseldorf und Mannheim* (Cologne, 1960)
GERHARD CROLL, SIBYLLE DAHMS

Morawski-Dąbrowa, Eugeniusz (*b* Warsaw, 2 Nov 1876; *d* Warsaw, 23 Oct 1948). Polish composer. He studied at the Warsaw Music Institute with Noskowski; he also studied painting. Exiled by the Russian authorities in 1908, he settled in Paris and continued his music and painting studies. He returned to Poland in 1930 as director of the Poznán Conservatory and in 1932 succeeded Szymanowski as director and professor of composition at the Warsaw Conservatory. His music, distinguished by colourful instrumentation and rich harmony, shows the influence of the late Romantics and Debussy. His output includes five operas (dates of composition unknown): *Aspazja* (after A. Świętochowski), *Lilla Weneda* (after J. Słowacki), *Salammbô* (after Flaubert) and two that remained incomplete, *Dafnis i Chloe* and *Pan Tadeusz*. None of his operas was performed; the scores were all burnt in the Warsaw Uprising. He also composed ballets, symphonic works and chamber music. TERESA CHYLIŃSKA

Mörder, Hoffnung der Frauen ('Murderer, Hope of Women'). Opera in one act, op.12, by PAUL HINDEMITH to a libretto by Oscar Kokoschka; Stuttgart, Landestheater, 4 June 1921.

Hindemith's first operatic work (composed in 1919) uses the words, with a few omissions, of Kokoschka's expressionist play of 1907. Set in antiquity, it depicts a violent erotic encounter (which includes a branding and a stabbing) between a Man (baritone) and a Woman (soprano), observed by two trios of warriors and serving women. It ends with the tower, outside which the action takes place, in flames. The through-composed musical treatment is symphonic rather than episodic, bearing many traces of late Romanticism. GEOFFREY SKELTON

Moreau, Fanchon [Françoise] (*b* 1668; *d* after 1743). French soprano, younger sister of LOUISON MOREAU. Like her sister, Fanchon was a mistress of the dauphin; in fact, as countless anecdotes relate, it was originally she rather than her sister whom the dauphin sought: a letter from Hyacinthe de Gauréault Dumont, co-director of the Paris Opéra, arranging a rendezvous with Fanchon went to the wrong Mlle Moreau (by all accounts, as plain as Fanchon was beautiful), but when he rushed to undo the mistake he found Louison well received by the dauphin. Fanchon was later the mistress of Philippe de Vendôme for 20 years. Although Titon du Tillet (*Le Parnasse françois*, 1732) stated that Fanchon left the stage about 1708, her name disappears from cast lists in 1702; he added that she was still living in 1743.

According to J.-B. Durey de Noinville (*Histoire du théâtre de l'Opéra de l'Académie royale de musique en France*, 1753, 2/1757) Fanchon made her début in 1683 in the prologue of Lully's *Phaéton* (probably as Astraea). From 1683 to 1692 (when Louison left the Opéra) both sisters were entered as 'Mlle Moreau' in cast lists. It is known, however, that it was Fanchon who created the role of Oriane in Lully's *Amadis* (1684) and Sidonie in his *Armide* (1686). Between 1692 and 1702 she appeared in several Lully revivals: as Oriane in *Amadis* (1701), Sangaride in *Atys* (1699), Aegle in *Thésée* (1698), Libya in *Phaéton* (1702) and as Proserpina (1699). She also sang major roles in the first performances at the Paris Opéra of many *préramiste* stage works, among them Charpentier's *Médée*, Campra's *L'Europe galante*, Destouches' *Issé* and operas by Collasse, Desmarets and Gatti. François Couperin's bawdy canon *La femme entre deux draps* names Fanchon as one of the women 'between two sheets'; she was the inspiration for his harpsichord piece 'La tendre Fanchon'. JAMES R. ANTHONY

Moreau, Jean-Baptiste (*b* Angers, 1656; *d* Paris, 24 Aug 1733). French composer. He was educated at the cathedral choir school in Angers. He became *maître de musique* in 1681 at Langres and later at Dijon. By 1687 he was in Paris, where his *Te Deum* was sung on 24 January; after his presentation to Louis XIV, Moreau received royal commissions for the rest of his life. Most of his works were choruses and incidental music for student dramas at St-Louis de St-Cyr, Mme de Maintenon's school for young noblewomen. His music for Racine's biblical plays, *Esther* and *Athalie*, is especially notable (choruses ed. P. Mesnard, *Grands écrivains de France*, Paris, 1873, suppl.). Staged twice, in 1689 and 1690, *Esther* won acclaim from the court as well as from Racine for its simple, syllabic style. A performance in 1691 of *Athalie*, whose plainchant-like music served to re-create the spirit of antiquity, received less attention. Revivals of both works in the 18th and 19th centuries culminated in 1887 with Charles Bordes' restoration of *Esther* with Moreau's music, which entered the repertory at the Comédie Française.

J. Tiersot: 'Les choeurs d'*Esther* et d'*Athalie* de Moreau', *RHCM*, ii (1903), 35–40
M. Garros: 'Madame de Maintenon et la musique', *RdM*, xxv (1943), 8–17
M. Cambrier: *Racine et Madame de Maintenon: 'Esther' et 'Athalie' à St Cyr* (Brussels, 1949)
C. Irwin: *Jean-Baptiste Moreau's Setting of the Racine Play, 'Esther'* (diss., U. of Rochester, 1983)
CAROL O. IRWIN

Moreau, Louison [Louise] (*b* before 1668; *d* after 1692). French soprano. She entered the Paris Opéra in 1680 and in November she created Peace in the prologue of Lully's *Proserpine*. She and her younger sister, FANCHON MOREAU, were among the 'filles de l'Opéra' whose extraordinary amorous episodes were celebrated in many contemporary chansons. For a short time Louison was mistress of the dauphin. Lully dismissed her from the Opéra when her pregnancy (by M. de la Fare) became noticeable; Du Tralage (*Notes et* *documents sur l'histoire des théâtres de Paris au XVIIe siècle*, Paris, 1880) related that her return eight months later caused a 'brouhaha in the theatre which marked the joy of the audience in hearing again one of the most beautiful voices and one of the best actresses at the Opéra'. During the Easter closure of 1692, she finally left. For the period 1683–92, when both sisters sang at the Opéra, it is not always possible to determine which of them is meant by 'Mlle Moreau' in cast lists. Both sang musicians' roles in February 1691 in a court revival of the Molière-Lully *comédie-ballet Le bourgeois gentilhomme*. Occasionally the text of a chanson or a comment in the *Mercure* will indicate which sister (usually Fanchon) sang a particular character: the *Mercure galant* of September 1688, for example, states that Louison sang the role of the Princess Amasie in Paolo Lorenzani's *Orontée* at Chantilly.　　JAMES R. ANTHONY

Moreira, António Leal (*b* Abrantes, 30 June 1758; *d* Lisbon, 26 Nov 1819). Portuguese composer. On 30 June 1766 he entered the Seminário da Patriarcal in Lisbon, where he was a pupil of João de Sousa Carvalho and where he became an assistant teacher in 1775, as well as organist. On 19 May 1777 his *Missa do Espírito Santo* was sung at the acclamation of Queen Maria I, and on 8 August of that year he was admitted as a member of the musicians' union of Lisbon, the Irmandade de S Cecília. Most of his sacred works were composed for the royal chapel, where he was *mestre de capela* from 1787. As a composer of stage works he had a career second only to that of his brother-in-law Marcos António Portugal. From 1782 onwards serenatas by Moreira were performed at the royal palace of Queluz and from 1785 he had stage works performed at the Ajuda Palace and the Castle of S Jorge.

In 1790 he took the post of musical director at the Teatro da Rua dos Condes, where the production of Italian operas was briefly resumed after a 15-year interval. Three years later *Il natale augusto* was performed at the palace of the financier Anselmo José da Cruz Sobral in Lisbon by a cast which included Luísa Todi, who travelled from Madrid for the event, and five singers of the royal chapel. Also in 1793 Moreira became the first musical director of the newly opened Teatro de S Carlos, where some of his own operas and farces on Portuguese texts, including *A vingança da cigana* (1794), were performed. He left the S Carlos in 1799; in the following year his opera *Il disertore francese* was performed at the Teatro Carignano in Turin and at La Scala. From then on he devoted himself almost exclusively to church music. Later he had a brief but distinguished military career during the Peninsular Wars.

In a report written at the time of his death Moreira was praised for the punctuality, probity and interest with which he had performed his duties as a teacher at the Patriarcal for 44 years. Although heavily influenced by Paisiello and Cimarosa, Moreira's stage and sacred works are among the most solidly constructed and technically competent Portuguese masterpieces. After António Teixeira he was the first to compose stage works with Portuguese texts, although the majority of his works are in Italian.

See also VINGANÇA DA CIGANA, A.

first performed in Lisbon, MSS in P-La, unless otherwise stated

dm – dramma per musica

Bireno ed Olimpia (serenata, G. Martinelli), Queluz Palace, 21 Aug 1782

Siface e Sofonisba (dm da cantarsi, 1, Martinelli), Queluz Palace, 5 July 1783
L'imenei in Delfo (drama lírico alegórico, Martinelli), Ajuda Palace, 28 March 1785
Ascanio in Alba (dm da cantarsi, 2, C. N. Stampa), Queluz Palace, 5 July 1785
Artemisia, regina di Caria (dm da cantarsi, 1, Martinelli), Ajuda Palace, 17 Dec 1787
Gli eroi spartani (dm, 1, Martinelli), Ribeira Palace, 21 Aug 1788
Gli affetti del genio lusitano (dm da cantarsi, 2, Martinelli), Real Casa Pia do Castelo de S Jorge, 1 Sept 1789
Il puro omaggio (dm, 3 scenes, Martinelli), Rua dos Condes, 13 May 1791, only lib. extant
Il natale augusto (dm, 2, Martinelli), palace of A. J. da Cruz Sobral, 29 April 1793, only lib. extant
A saloia enamorada, ou O remédio é casar (farsa, 1, D. Caldas Barbosa), S Carlos, 1793, score lost, 1 aria in Lisbon, Instituto Português do Património Cultural, Departamento de Musicologia
A vingança da cigana (drama joco-sério, 1, Caldas Barbosa), S Carlos, 1794, P-Ln
L'eroina lusitana (dm, 2, Martinelli), S Carlos, 21 March 1795
Il disertore francese (ob), Turin, Carignano, carn. 1800, VV (with Port. text)

Arias for Gazzaniga: Il serraglio d'Osmano, VV

*

DBP (E. Vieira)
H. de Campos Ferreira Lima: 'O músico Leal Moreira no Arquivo histórico militar', *História* (Lisbon, 1935)
J. Mazza: 'Dicionário biográfico de músicos portugueses', *Ocidente*, xxv (1945); pubd separately (Lisbon, 1944–5)
L. F. Marques da Gama: 'O compositor António Leal Moreira', *Armas e troféus* (Lisbon, 1975)
J. A. Alegria: *Biblioteca do Palacio Real de Vila Viçosa: catálogo dos fundos musicais* (Lisbon, 1989), 165–6, 168
M. C. de Brito: *Opera in Portugal in the Eighteenth Century* (Cambridge, 1989)
　　MANUEL CARLOS DE BRITO, ROBERT STEVENSON

Morel, Jean (Paul) (*b* Abbeville, 10 Jan 1903; *d* New York, 14 April 1975). French conductor and teacher. He studied in Paris with Gabriel Pierné and Reynaldo Hahn, but apart from engagements in Rio de Janeiro and Mexico his career as an opera conductor was based in the USA. He made his New York City Opera début with *La traviata* in 1944, subsequently conducting *Carmen*, *La bohème*, *Mignon* and *Louise*. From 1956 to 1971 he appeared intermittently at the Metropolitan Opera (début in *La Périchole*) conducting *Madama Butterfly*, *Orfeo ed Euridice* and a number of French operas.　　BERNARD JACOBSON

Morena [Meyer], Berta (*b* Mannheim, 27 Jan 1878; *d* Rottach-Egern, Tegernsee, 7 Oct 1952). German soprano. She studied in Munich with Röhr-Brajnin and Orgeni, and made her début in 1898 at the Munich Hofoper as Agathe (*Der Freischütz*). She remained with the company until her farewell in 1927, being especially admired in Wagner roles. She made her Metropolitan début in 1908 as Sieglinde and later sang Elisabeth, Leonore, Brünnhilde and Santuzza there. When she appeared at Covent Garden in 1914, as Isolde, Sieglinde and Kundry, she was praised more as an actress (she was a woman of great beauty and distinctive stage presence) than as a singer.

*

A. Vogl: *Berta Morena und ihre Kunst* (Munich, 1919)
　　HAROLD ROSENTHAL/R

Moreno [Ponce de León], Benita (*b* La Coruña, 31 Oct 1792; *d* Puente del Arzobispo, Toledo, 29 Jan 1872). Spanish soprano. Daughter of the violinist Francisco-Javier Moreno (1746–*c*1836), who played in theatres in

Madrid, Italy and Lisbon, she probably received her early training in La Coruña. She emigrated to Italy with her family about 1802 and made her début at La Fenice, Venice, in 1808 in the first performance of *La festa della rosa* by Stefano Pavesi, of whose works she became a leading interpreter and promoter. She seems then to have moved to Lisbon and thence to Madrid, where she appeared in concerts with her sister in 1814. She joined the company directed by Eugenio Cristiani, with which she sang (in Spanish) in Rossini's *L'italiana in Algeri* (first performance, 1816), Cimarosa's *Gli Orazi ed i Curiazi*, Pavesi's *Ser Marcantonio*, Spontini's *La vestale* and Paer's *Griselda*, as well as in operas by Guglielmi and Pucitta. After 1820 she sang in various European theatres; she retired in 1845 to her native city, where she taught under her married name, Ponce de León.

Her sister Francisca (*b* 1790; *d* 1820 or later) was also a singer; according to Saldoni, 'her voice had the unusual range of three octaves and was consistent, soft, rich, strong and very agile, and this, together with the elegance of her person, placed her in the front rank'. All that is known of her is that between 1814 and 1820 she often sang with Benita. Benita's two daughters, Angela Moreno and Luisa Santamaria (*b* Valencia, 1827; *d* 1878), were successful sopranos in zarzuela.

L. Cármena y Millán: *Crónica de la opera italiana en Madrid desde el año 1738 hasta nuestros días* (Madrid, 1878)

B. Saldoni: *Diccionario biográfico-bibliográfico de efemérides de músicos españoles* (Madrid, 1880)

E. Cotarelo: *Historia de la zarzuela* (Madrid, 1934)

F. Asenjo Barbieri: *Biografías y documentos sobre música y músicos españoles (Legado Barbieri)*, ed. E. Casares (Madrid, 1986), 349
XOÁN M. CARREIRA

Moreno Torroba, Federico (*b* Madrid, 3 March 1891; *d* Madrid, 12 Sept 1982). Spanish composer, conductor and critic. After early lessons with his father, an organist, he entered the Madrid Conservatory and studied composition with Conrado del Campo. The closure of the Teatro Real, where his first opera had been produced in 1925, caused him to turn his attention to zarzuelas. He became an acknowledged master of the genre, composing over the next 30 years a vast number, mostly distinguished by sensitive workmanship. His greatest success was *Luisa Fernanda* (1932), but he had already made his name with *La Marchenera* (1928). Other well-received works were *La chulapona* (1934), *Maravilla* (1941), *La Caramba* (1942) and *Maria Manuela* (1957). He also made a considerable reputation as a theatre conductor, as a critic for the Madrid daily *Informaciones* (for ten years) and as a composer of guitar music. At the end of his life he returned to opera with *El poeta* (1980), based on an episode in the life of the early 19th-century poet José Ignacio de Espronceda, but despite the presence of Placido Domingo (who had commissioned it) in the title role, the work made little impact, partly because of the weak libretto.

See also LUISA FERNANDA.

La Virgen del Mayo, Madrid, Real, 14 Feb 1925
El poeta (4, J. M. Herrera), Madrid, Zarzuela, 19 June 1980

Zarzuelas: La mesonera de Tordesillas (1, R. de Sepúlveda and J. Manzano), 1925; La pastorela (3, F. Luque and Calonge), Madrid, Novedades, 10 Nov 1926, collab. Luna; El fumadero (Luque and F. de Torres), Madrid, Martín, 1 Dec 1927, collab. Luna; La Marchenera (3, R. González del Toro and Luque), Madrid, Zarzuela, 7 April 1928; La baturra del temple, 1929; Maria la tempranica; Luisa Fernanda (3, F. Romero and G. Fernández Shaw), Madrid, Calderón, 26 March 1932

Azabache, 1933, Una noche en Aravaca, 1933; Xuanón (2, J. R. Martín), 1933; La chulapona (3, Romero and Fernández Shaw), Madrid, Calderón, 31 March 1934; La caravana de Ambrosio, 1934; Paloma Moreno, 1936; Sor Navarra, 1936; Nacimento (3, V. Espinós and J. M. de Arozamena), San Sebastián, Victoria Eugenia, 3 Jan 1938, collab. Guridi; Oro de Ley, 1938; Monte Carmelo, 1939; Cascabeles, 1940

Maravilla (3, A. Quintero and Arozamena), Madrid, Fontalba, 12 April 1941; La Caramba (3, F. Ardavín), 1942; La ilustra moza, 1943; Baile de trajas, 1944; Polonesa (3, A. Torrado and Arozamena), 1944; La canción del organillo, 1945; Orgullo de Jarisco, 1947; La niña del polisón, 1948; El diablo en Sierra Morena, 1952; La boda del Señor Bringas, 1953; Hola Ciqui, 1953; Maria Manuela (3, G. and R. Fernández Shaw), Madrid, Zarzuela, 1957

Dates unknown: La mujer de aquella noche; Lolita Dolores

Luces de Verbena [completion of zar by R. Soutullo] (2, J. Tellaeche and F. Serrano-Anguita), Madrid, Calderón, 2 May 1935, collab. Baudot-Puente
LIONEL SALTER

Morera, Enric [Enrique] (*b* Barcelona, 22 May 1865; *d* Barcelona, 12 March 1942). Spanish (Catalan) composer and conductor. He grew up in Argentina and studied there, in Spain with Pedrell and Albéniz, and at the Brussels Conservatory. After his return to Barcelona Morera's restlessly creative and progressive nature led him into the exhilarating artistic atmosphere of modernism which was transforming cultural life in *fin-de-siècle* Barcelona. He took part in the 'festes modernistes' which his friend the painter Santiago Rusiñol organized in Sitges, where Morera's *La fada* was first performed (1897). In 1900 he conceived the idea of presenting a season of new collaborative works by Catalan dramatists and composers. Thus was born, in early 1901, the Teatre Líric Català company, which performed plays with incidental music, *quadros líric* (short, single-scene operas) and other short pieces of comic music theatre. Morera wrote the music for several of these works, Pedrell and Granados being among the other composers represented. Artistically ambitious but commercially unfeasible, the Teatre Líric ceased after only one season; two attempts at reviving the series were unsuccessful.

Morera moved to Madrid in 1901 to work with Ruperto Chapí, who had offered to help him produce one of his operas there. No opera production ensued and Morera, adapting to the local taste in theatre music, wrote and produced a number of zarzuelas, sometimes collaborating with Chapí or Amadeo Vives. Returning to Barcelona in 1905, he had his greatest operatic success the following year with *Emporium*, given at the Liceo. The work reveals a composer thoroughly at ease with the main compositional trends of the day. Its seamless texture and richly chromatic harmony suggest the influence of Wagner and the Franco-Belgians. There are also passages based on whole-tone scales. The melodic style is occasionally reminiscent of Puccini, though the rhythmic profile is more consistently decisive. There is vigorous choral writing, and the orchestration is robust and colourful. *Emporium* forgoes any reference to Spanish stylistic traditions, but Morera's next important opera, *Bruniselda*, is distinctly imbued with Catalan regional characteristics. Despite Morera's early successes in opera and his copious productivity, he was never able to establish himself in Spain as a composer of opera. His reputation today rests on performances of his more popular choral pieces.

in Catalan, and first performed in Barcelona, unless otherwise stated

La boja, 1895 (3, A. Guimerà), ?unperf.

La fada (1, J. Massó Torrents), Sitges, Prado, sum. 1897

Emporium, 1901 (3, E. Marquina), Liceo, 20 Jan 1906, vs (Madrid, 1907)

Bruniselda (3, J. Puigdolles y Mací and A. Masriera), Liceo, 21 April 1906

Titaina (2, Guimerà), Liceo, 17 Jan 1912

Mar i cel, 1912 (Guimerà), inc.

Tassarba (1, J. Vallmitjana), Liceo, 18 Jan 1916

Don Joan de Serrallonga (3, F. Pujols, after V. Balaguer), Tivoli, 6 Oct 1922

Zarzuelas: El tío Juan (1, C. Fernández Shaw), 1902, collab. Chapí; Su alteza imperial (3, S. Delgado), 14 March 1903, collab. A. Vives; La vuelta de Pierrot (A. Gual), Madrid [in Sp.]; La canción del náufrago (3, C. Arniches and Fernández Shaw), Madrid, Price, Feb 1903 [in Sp.]; Los cortesanos de Farsalia (R. Nogueras Oller), Madrid [in Sp.]; Nit de trons (1, J. Benapres), sum. 1904; La Paula t'e unes mitges [El maco dels encats] (2, L. Planas de Taverne), Victoria, 8 Oct 1924

Quadros líric (all in 1 act; first performed at the Teatre Tivoli unless otherwise stated): L'alegría que passa, 1898 (S. Rusiñol), 12 Jan 1901, vs (Barcelona, 1898); Les caramelles (I. Iglesias), 12 Jan 1901 [in Sp. as Caramellas, Madrid, Apolo, 13 March 1902]; La reina del cor (Iglesias), 15 Jan 1901; La Rosons (A. Mestres), 28 Jan 1901; L'adoració dels pastors (C. Verdaguer), 1 Feb 1901; Cigales i formigues (Rusiñol), 20 Feb 1901; Villa blanca (J. Llopart), 1901; El firaire (J. Orpinell), 1901; Rondalla (A. Capmany), 1901; L'aligot (C. Capdevila), 1901; La barca (Mestres), Principal, 26 Sept 1903; La nit de l'amor (Rusiñol), Intim, 20 Jan 1905

?Unperf.: L'arc de Sant Martí (T. Monegal); L'esparver (Capdevila); Nit de Nadal (J. M. Jordà)

*

DEUMM (M. Alonso Gómez); MGG (M. Querol)

'Homenatge al Mestre Enric Morera', Revista musical catalana, viii (1911), 306–7

F. Curet: El arte dramático en el resurgir de Cataluña (Barcelona, 1917)

I. Iglesias: Enric Morera (Barcelona, 1921)

E. Morera: Moments viscuts (Barcelona, 1936) [autobiography]

J. Pena: Enric Morera (Barcelona, 1937)

J. Llongueras: Evocaciones y recuerdos de mi primera vida musical en Barcelona (Barcelona, 1944)

A. Llopis: 'Enrique Morera, intimo', La vanguardia española (23 May 1965)

F. Curet: Historia del teatre català (Barcelona, 1967)

M. Saperasi: El mestre Enric Morera (Andorra la Vella, 1969)

R. Planes: El mestre Morera i el seu mon (Barcelona, 1972)

——: El modernisme a Sitges (Barcelona, 1979)

X. Aviñoa: La música i el modernisme (Barcelona, 1985)

——: Morera (Barcelona, 1987)   ROLAND J. VÁZQUEZ

Moretti, Ferdinando (d St Petersburg, 1807). Italian librettist. His early librettos for Milan were widely performed during the 1780s and 90s. The first, Idalide, was written for La Scala in 1783 with music by Giuseppe Sarti, composer of a number of the most successful opere serie of the period. Though not among Sarti's most widely performed works, his Idalide received some seven productions in places as far afield as Eszterháza, London and Trieste. Cherubini reset the libretto for Florence in 1784, and Rispoli for Turin in 1786. Moretti's opera for Milan in 1784, Ademira, set by Tarchi and others, was still being performed more than a decade later. His collaboration with Tarchi for Mantua in 1785, Arminio, became his most often reset work, with new music ordered for productions in major houses in Rome (Tritto), Venice (Andreozzi and F. A. de Blasis), Florence (Bianchi), and Naples (Marinelli). His Ariarate became Tarchi's most often produced opera.

Sarti, on his arrival in St Petersburg in 1784, must have recommended Moretti as court poet to follow Coltellini, who had not been replaced after his death in 1777. Even after his arrival in St Petersburg in spring 1786, Moretti continued to supply librettos for La Scala: Il conte di Saldagna (Tarchi, 1787); Ifigenia in Aulide (Zingarelli, 1787); and Antioco (Tarchi, 1788). Shortly after his arrival in St Petersburg he provided Sarti with a libretto for Castore e Polluce, first performed on 22 September 1786, and an opera seria, Zenoclea, which was never performed. For Cimarosa's sojourn in St Petersburg, he reworked his Idalide as La vergine del sole (1789), and produced a new opera seria, Cleopatra, in 1789. Moretti's contract was renewed on 1 September 1790, but he wrote only cantatas and other short pieces during his second term. He also prepared his Opere drammatiche for publication (St Petersburg, 1794). Although his position was terminated in November 1793 he continued to supply the court with short works. In 1797 he was called on to write a great dramatic cantata entitled Il genio della Russia (Sarti), performed in Moscow for the coronation of Paul I. There followed librettos for two new opere serie for Sarti and one for Himmel. In 1799, he provided the ballet Tancrède for Martín y Soler.

Most of Moretti's plots were taken from Greek and Roman sources and many were reworkings of earlier pieces, with a few notable exceptions. His Idalide was the first of a succession of librettos based on Marmontel's Les incas. Perhaps inspired by Verazi's innovatory librettos for the opening of La Scala (1778–9), he moved beyond the opera seria tradition to infuse his operas with spectacle: military displays and battles, scenes with ballet and chorus (Idalide, Ademira, Antioco) and even an earthquake (Idalide). Duets, quartets and trios regularly serve as first- and second-act finales, and there is often a duet in the penultimate scene. None incorporates action. Arminio and Il conte di Saldagna contain early examples of arias with interruptions by others, another Verazi innovation. His Semiramide (1785), which has been mistakenly attributed to Metastasio, is the first of a succession of librettos based on Cesarotti's translation of Voltaire's tragedy Sémiramis. Moretti rewrote the plot to avoid the matricide, which Giovannini not only included but staged in Florence the following year in his libretto La vendetta di Nino with music by Prati, a libretto that has been wrongly attributed to Moretti. (Moretti published his version in his Opere drammatiche.) Moretti's most important libretto, Il conte di Saldagna (1787, Milan), may have been written in St Petersburg. Among the earliest of Romantic or revolutionary operas, it treats a medieval Spanish subject in which an unenlightened king proves capable of the foulest deception. The hero dies of poisoning in the finale amid a rich divertissement of chorus and dance celebrating his pardon. Moretti's Ifigenia in Aulide for Milan a year later proved remarkable only for the staged suicide of Eriphyle, the 'other' Iphigenia. This series of staged deaths, begun in Florence with La vendetta di Nino (1785), abrogated a tradition of more than a century and established a trend in the Italian theatre that would stretch into the next century. Moretti's Castore e Polluce is yet another version of Gentil-Bernard's opera for Rameau. His other operas for St Petersburg incorporate the French elements – solos with chorus, dances, scene complexes, and spectacle – preferred there.

opere serie unless otherwise stated

Idalide [La vergine del sole], Sarti, 1783 (Cherubini, 1784; Rispoli, 1786; Cimarosa, 1788/9); Ademira, Tarchi, 1783 (Lucchesi, 1784; Guglielmi, 1789); Semiramide [La morte di Semiramide], Mortellari, 1784; Alsinda, Zingarelli, 1785; Arminio, Tarchi, 1785 (Tritto, 1786; Andreozzi, 1788; F. A. de Blasis, 1790;

Bianchi, 1790; Marinelli, 1792; Marinelli, 1797, as Germanico); *Ariarate*, Tarchi, 1786 (Giordani, 1788); *Castore e Polluce*, Sarti, 1786; *Zenoclea*, Sarti, comp. 1786; *Ifigenia in Aulide*, Zingarelli, 1787 (Cherubini, 1788); *Il conte di Saldagna* (tragedia), Tarchi, 1787 (Zingarelli, 1794); *Antioco*, Tarchi, 1787; *Cleopatra*, Cimarosa, 1789; *Andromeda*, Sarti, 1798; *Alessandro*, Himmel, 1799; *Enea nel Lazio*, Sarti, 1799

*

*Stieger*O

R.-A. Mooser: *Annales de la musique et des musiciens en Russie au XVIIIme siècle*, ii (Geneva, 1951)

M. McClymonds: 'La morte di Semiramide ossia La vendetta di Nino', *IMSCR, xiv Bologna 1987*, 285–92

——: 'The Venetian Role in the Transformation of Italian Opera Seria during the 1790s', *I vicini di Mozart: Venice 1987*, 221–40

C. Questa: *Semiramide redenta: archetipi, fonti classiche, censure antropologiche nel melodramma* (Urbino, 1989)

MARITA P. McCLYMONDS

Morgan, Beverly (*b* Hanover, NH, 17 March 1952). American soprano. After studying in Boston she took part in the première of Glass's *Satyagraha* at Amsterdam (1980), sang Charlotte in the American première of Zimmermann's *Die Soldaten* (Boston, 1982) and Micaëla in Marius Constant's *La tragédie de Carmen* (after Bizet) in New York in 1983. She sang Dede in Bernstein's *A Quiet Place* at La Scala (1984), at the Vienna Staatsoper (1986) and on record. At Santa Fe she sang Miss Crisp in *The English Cat* (1985) and Benigna in Penderecki's *Die schwarze Maske* (1988), both American premières. She has sung Tatyana and Violetta at Seattle, and Christine (*Intermezzo*) and Lulu (1987) for Scottish Opera. At the Deutsche Oper, Berlin, she sang Fusako from the side of the stage at the première of Henze's *Das verratene Meer* (1990), then played the role at the Teatro Lirico, Milan (1991). A fine musician with a light, flexible voice, she excels in 20th-century music.

ELIZABETH FORBES

Moriani, Napoleone (*b* Florence, 10 March 1806 or 1808; *d* Florence, 4 March 1878). Italian tenor. He made his début at Pavia in 1833 in Pacini's *Gli arabi nelle Gallie*. Between 1840 and 1844 he frequently sang in Vienna and Germany; in 1841 he was made a *Kammersänger* to the Austrian emperor. From 1844 to 1846 he appeared alternately in London and Madrid (where he was awarded the Order of Isabella), and made his Paris début in 1845 at the Théâtre Italien; he also sang at Lisbon and Barcelona, then for two years in Italy. His last important engagements were at the Théâtre Italien (1849–50) and Madrid (1850).

Moriani combined sweetness of tone with great dramatic intensity. With his gaunt good looks he excelled in death scenes: impressed by his performance in *Lucia di Lammermoor* and *Pia de' Tolomei*, composers wrote for him parts portraying the hero in a prolonged death agony, as in Vaccai's *La sposa di Messina* (1839, Venice) and Federico Ricci's *Luigi Rolla* (1841, Florence). He also sang in the premières of Mercadante's *Le due illustri rivali* and Donizetti's *Maria de Rudenz* (both 1838, Venice) and *Linda di Chamounix* (1842, Vienna). For a revival of *Attila* at La Scala in 1847 Verdi wrote an alternative romanza for him, to be inserted in the last act.

*

ES (R. Celletti)

A. Ghislanzoni: 'Il re dei tenori', *Gazzetta musicale di Milano*, xxxiii (1878), 115

L. Neretti: 'Dalle carte di un celebre tenore', *Musica d'oggi*, xvii (1935), 7–11

F. Walker: *The Man Verdi* (London, 1962)   JULIAN BUDDEN

Morichelli [Bosello], **Anna** (*b* ?Bologna or Reggio Emilia, *c*1750–55; *d* Trieste, 30 Oct 1800). Italian soprano. She is sometimes confused with Anna Boselli, a singer of secondary roles, active mainly in Parma in 1757–73. She made her *opera buffa* début at Bologna in autumn 1773, sang in Spain during the period 1774–7 and in Russia in 1779–80. She was by then a star, noted for graceful acting and a beautiful voice. In 1783 she made a successful transition to *opera seria*, singing as prima donna in many leading houses, although not quite so admired in this genre. She spent the 1787–8 season in Vienna, where her creations included Diana in Martín y Soler's *L'arbore di Diana* (a role later taken over by Ferrarese). Between 1788 and 1791 she appeared in both comic and serious parts, thereafter almost exclusively in *opera buffa*. She was in Paris from 1790 to 1792, Spain in 1793 and London from 1793 to 1795. In his memoirs, Da Ponte wrote at length about her time in London, where she and Martín apparently became lovers. She was the *prima buffa* in both his London operas and was probably responsible for their subsequent productions in Italy. Morichelli was still performing up to her death, but through necessity; she was said to be only a shadow of her former self.

DENNIS LIBBY/DOROTHEA LINK

Morigi [Mauriggi, Morici, Muriggi, Morighi], **Pietro Antonio Filippo** (*b* Roccacontrada [now Arcevia], nr Iesi, bap. 31 Jan 1710; *d* ?London, after 1772). Italian soprano castrato. After a modest beginning in his native Marche region and in Rome, in female roles, in 1730 Morigi arrived in Bologna, where he became a member of the Accademia Filarmonica, also receiving the patronage of Count Sicinio Pepoli. Between 1730 and 1734 he took minor roles in various operas by Albinoni, Hasse and Vivaldi in Venice, Verona, Bologna, Florence and Genoa. During the period 1731–5 he was in the service of Philipp of Hessen-Darmstadt, the Imperial Governor of Mantua. In 1733 he was engaged by Empress Anna, though he did not arrive in St Petersburg until summer 1735. He enjoyed remarkable success in operas by Araia and Hasse; castratos were previously almost unheard of in Russia. He returned to Italy at the beginning of 1744, and from 1746 to 1753 he sang in several theatres in northern Italy (occasionally as primo uomo during the period 1749–51), in operas by Hasse, Terradellas, Giuseppe Scarlatti, Bertoni and Latilla. He sang at the Haymarket Theatre in London from 1768, or possibly as early as 1765, until 1772, in less important parts.

The peak of Morigi's career (1735–50) coincided with the rise of Hasse's fame. Like Farinelli he excelled in elaborate coloratura, but the upper limits of his vocal range mostly confined him to 'heroical antagonist' roles. The *buffo* bass Andrea Morigi (active in Venice between 1762 and 1766, and in London from 1766 until at least 1787) was possibly his nephew.

*

O. Penna: *Catalogo degli aggregati della Accademia Filarmonica di Bologna* (MS, *I-Baf*, 1736/R1971) [sometimes attrib. G. B. Martini]

R.-A. Mooser: *Annales de la musique et des musiciens en Russie au XVIIIme siècle* (Geneva, 1948–51)

A. L. Bellina, B. Brizi and M. G. Pensa: 'Il pasticcio Bajazet: la favola del Gran Tamerlano nella messinscena di Vivaldi', *Nuovi studi vivaldiani*, ed. A. Fanna and G. Morelli (Florence, 1988), 185–272

C. Vitali: 'Vivaldi e il conte bolognese Sicinio Pepoli: nuovi documenti sulle stagioni vivaldiane al Filarmonico di Verona', *Informazioni e studi vivaldiani*, x (1989), 25–56

——: 'I fratelli Pepoli contro Vivaldi e Anna Girò: le ragioni di un'assenza', *Informazioni e studi vivaldiani*, xii (1991), 14–33
CARLO VITALI

Morin, Charles. *See* CRABBÉ, ARMAND.

Morin-Labrecque [née Labrecque], **Albertine (Rosalie Odile)** (*b* Montreal, 8 June 1886; *d* Montreal, 25 Sept 1957). Canadian composer. She studied the piano in Montreal and, later, composition and harmony with J. Macaire and singing with Arthur Plamondon in Paris. She appeared in Europe, the USA and Canada as a pianist and dramatic soprano. Her first stage work, *Francine*, was possibly first performed in October 1931 by the students of the Montreal National Conservatory, where she taught from 1922 to 1951; a professional production followed in 1935. She also composed in other genres and published piano methods.

Francine (comic op, 3, B. Lamontagne-Beauregard), Montreal, Her Majesty's, 24 March 1935, C-*On*
Pao-chu, fille de Chine (comic op), *On*
Princesse Nadya (comic op, 4, F. Blanchard and E. Guimond), Montreal, Monument National, 13 Nov 1938, *On*
Mandrini (comic op, 3, A. C. de la Lande), *On*
MIREILLE BARRIÈRE

Morison, Elsie (Jean) (*b* Ballarat, Victoria, 15 Aug 1924). Australian soprano. She studied with Clive Carey both at the Melbourne Conservatory and at the RCM. She made her English concert début at the Albert Hall in *Acis and Galatea* in 1948 and that autumn joined Sadler's Wells Opera, appearing regularly there until 1954. She sang Anne Trulove in the first British staging of *The Rake's Progress* (1953, Edinburgh) and at her Glyndebourne début the following year. After her Covent Garden début (1953) as Mimì, she sang there regularly until 1962. In such roles as Susanna, Pamina, Marzelline, Micaëla, Antonia (*Les contes d'Hoffmann*), Mařenka, and Blanche in the British première of Poulenc's *Dialogues des Carmélites* (1958), she was admired for the touching sincerity of her acting and the lyrical warmth of her voice. In 1955 she created the title role of Arwel Hughes's *Menna* for the WNO. She married the conductor Rafael Kubelík.

HAROLD ROSENTHAL/R

Morlacchi, Francesco (Giuseppe Baldassarre) (*b* Perugia, 14 June 1784; *d* Innsbruck, 28 Oct 1841). Italian composer. He studied with his uncle Giovanni Mazzetti, organist of Perugia Cathedral, and with Luigi Caruso, the choirmaster, and began writing church and instrumental music at an early age. In 1803–4 he studied at Loreto with Zingarelli, but this did not satisfy him and he moved to the school of Stanislao Mattei at Bologna. Here in 1805 he was admitted to the Accademia Filarmonica as master-composer, and he came into contact with the young Rossini.

Morlacchi wrote his first operatic works, a farce and a comic opera, in 1807, but it was an *opera seria*, *Corradino*, first performed at Parma in 1808, that really marked the beginning of a brilliant theatrical career, and he was soon receiving commissions from the leading opera houses of Rome and Milan. His three works for Rome (1809–10) were a comic opera, a farce and an *opera seria*, *Le danaidi*. The success of this last work, whose subject was taken from Metastasio's *Ipermestra*, attracted the attention of the *Allgemeine musikalische Zeitung* in 1810 (v, 412–14), thus making the young composer known to the German public. The anon-ymous author of the article praised Morlacchi as a composer equally at home in both serious and comic works, and stressed the beauty of his expressive and pleasing melodies (only to be expected of an Italian composer), combined with lively and varied harmonic writing. For La Scala he wrote the comic opera *Le avventure d'una giornata*, performed without much success in 1809, but the cantata *Saffo*, performed in the spring of the same year by the famous contralto Marietta Marcolini, had a happier outcome. The singer, who was a relative of Count Camillo Marcolini, minister at the Saxon court, took Morlacchi to Dresden, where in September 1810 he became assistant to Joseph Schuster, Kapellmeister of the Italian Opera. In 1811 he was appointed Kapellmeister for life.

In Dresden Morlacchi's production of operas slowed down considerably: in contrast to the ten from 1807–10, he wrote only 15 during the rest of his life (two unfinished). As Kapellmeister he was required to write a great deal of church music, as well as cantatas for state occasions. His career at Dresden affords one of the last instances of an Italian composer serving abroad, but his situation was very different from that of his many predecessors active at courts throughout Europe, who merely took Italian operatic forms with them. By the time he arrived at Dresden, German opera was well established, and in his early years there he had to expend much effort in order to satisfy the opposing demands of the court and the city audiences. The often harsh criticisms of him in the *Allgemeine musikalische Zeitung* were culturally motivated: to attack him was a way of expressing hostility to the *ancien régime* of the king and those members of the court who opposed the innovations stemming from Romanticism and the birth of German opera. Morlacchi often found himself at odds with Weber, who was the director of the German opera house from 1817 to 1826.

In *Raoul di Crequy*, his first opera for Dresden, Morlacchi did all he could to adapt to local taste. Abandoning Italian conventions, he abolished *secco* recitative and introduced choruses and dances in the manner of Mayr. The tumultuous storm scenes, and the use of a Turkish band on stage, and of hammers and picks in the orchestra to convey the picture of miners working in the bowels of the earth (almost in anticipation of Wagner), created a deliberately Romantic atmosphere, even if the presence of comic elements made it seem old-fashioned.

A few years later Morlacchi did an about-turn and composed comic operas with an 18th-century flavour such as *La capricciosa pentita* (1816), *Il barbiere di Siviglia* (1816) and *La semplicetta di Pirna* (1817). *Il barbiere* was commissioned by the king and reflected the conservative taste of the court, so that while Rossini in Rome was producing his *Barbiere di Siviglia* (also in 1816), with a new, more progressive libretto by Cesare Sterbini, Morlacchi in Dresden was forced to work with the old text by Petrosellini that Paisiello had set in 1782. Even though his use of the orchestra is reminiscent of early Beethoven or Mendelssohn, he followed Paisiello closely, both in the recitatives (some of which he took straight from the old *Barbiere*) and in the structural and tonal articulation of some of the individual numbers. Rosina's fine aria at the end of the second act, 'Giusto ciel che conoscete', marks an advance on those of the general run of lively resourceful girls in 18th-century Italian opera and displays dramatic and melancholy nuances worthy of Donizetti's heroines.

Morlacchi's major works continued to be performed in the leading Italian opera houses, and *Colombo* inaugurated the Teatro Carlo Felice in Genoa (1828). The one which had the most lasting success and the only one of which a complete vocal score was published was *Tebaldo e Isolina*, first given at La Fenice, Venice, in 1822. The audience enjoyed the libretto by Gaetano Rossi (librettist at La Fenice over a long period), but they appreciated Morlacchi's music even more, as well as the masterly performances of the singers, including Gaetano Crivelli and Giovanni Battista Velluti, who was outstanding in the second-act aria 'Caro suono lusinghier'. After the enthusiastic reception of the première, the opera was performed in some 40 cities in Italy and elsewhere over the next ten years, thanks also to Velluti, who made his role in it his own.

In 1823 Morlacchi wrote *La gioventù di Enrico V* for Dresden; coming after the success of *Tebaldo e Isolina* and before his second Venetian commission, *Ilda d'Avenel* (1824), it forms a kind of comic diversion between the two weightier operas, and the music is fluent and fast-moving. While Morlacchi did his utmost in a vain attempt to produce a new type of *opera seria* for Italian theatres, for Dresden he was still writing frivolous comic works clearly deriving from the old Neapolitan school, as his patrons required. One of his last works, the unfinished *Francesca da Rimini*, shows again his interest in a typically Romantic subject drawn from Dante but at the same time the impossibility of bringing it to a successful conclusion. The dilemma that Morlacchi faced was essentially that of choosing between the old Neapolitan style and the new Romantic style. When he attempted to combine the two, the result was often disjointed or ill-defined.

Il poeta disperato (farsa, 1), Florence, Pergola, Feb 1807, *F-Pn**, *I-Fc* (as Il poeta spiantato; No.2, duet*, with words and music different from *F-Pn**)
Il ritratto, o sia La forza dell'astrazione (dg, 2, L. Romanelli), Verona, Filarmonico, sum. 1807, *I-VEc**
Corradino (dramma, 2, A. S. Sografi), Parma, Imperiale, 27 Feb 1808, *D-Dlb* (2 copies), *I-Fc*, *PAc**
Enone e Paride (dramma serio, 2), Livorno, Avvalorati, Oct 1808, lost
Oreste (dg, 2, L. Bottoni), Parma, Imperiale, 26 Dec 1808, *PLcon**
La principessa per ripiego (dg, 2, J. Ferretti, rev. F. S. Zini), Rome, Valle, 15 April 1809, *F-Pn*, *I-Fc*, *Rsc** (recits. not autograph)
Il Simoncino (farsa, 1), Rome, Valle, June 1809, *PEl*, *PESc**
Rinaldo d'Asti, ossia Il tutore deluso (dg, 1, G. Rossena), Parma, private perf., sum. 1809, *BGc**
Le avventure d'una giornata (melodramma buffo, 2, Romanelli), Milan, Scala, 26 Sept 1809, *Mc**
Le danaidi (dramma serio, 2, S. Scatizzi, after P. Metastasio: Ipermestra), Rome, Argentina, 11 Feb 1810, *D-Dlb*, *F-Pn*, *I-Fc*, *Mc*, *PEc**
Raoul di Crequy (dramma semiserio, 3, N. Perotti), Dresden, Hof, April 1811, *D-Dlb* (2 copies), *F-Pn**
La capricciosa pentita (dg, 4, Romanelli), Dresden, Hof, 10 Jan 1816, *D-Dlb*, *I-Fc* (as La nuova capricciosa), *Tco**
Il barbiere di Siviglia (dg, 4, G. Petrosellini), Dresden, Hof, April 1816, *B-Bc**, *D-Dlb*, *Mbs*, *I-Fc* (as Il nuovo barbiere di Siviglia), *Nc*, *PEl*
La semplicetta di Pirna (dramma per musica, 2), Dresden, Hof, Aug 1817, *D-Dlb**, *I-Fc*
Boadicea (dramma per musica, 2, G. B. Bordesi), Naples, S Carlo, 13 Jan 1818, *F-Pn*, *I-Nc**
Gianni di Parigi (melodramma comico, 2, F. Romani), Milan, Scala, 29 May 1818, *D-Dlb*, *F-Pn*, *I-Fc*, *Mc*, *Mr**, *Nc*, *Vt*
Donna Aurora, ossia Il romanzo all'improvviso (melodramma comico, 2, Romanelli), Milan, Scala, aut. 1821, *IE**
Tebaldo e Isolina (melodramma eroico, 2, G. Rossi), Venice, Fenice, 4 Feb 1822, *D-Dlb*, *Mbs* (2 copies), *E-Mm*, *F-Pn*, *I-Bc**, *Fc* (2 copies), *Nc*, *OS*, *PLcon* (Act 1 only), *Vc*, vs (Leipzig, 1823)

La gioventù di Enrico V (opera comica, 2), Pillnitz, nr Dresden, Aug 1823, *D-Dlb*, *GB-Lcm**
Ilda d'Avenel (melodramma eroico, 2, Rossi), Venice, Fenice, 20 Jan 1824, *I-MOe**, *Vt*
I saraceni in Sicilia, ovvero Eufemio di Messina (melodramma serio, 2, Romani), Venice, Fenice, 28 Feb 1828, *Mr**, *Vc*, *Vt*; as Il rinnegato, Dresden, Hof, March 1832, *F-Pn*, *I-PEl**
Colombo (melodramma serio, 2, Romani), Genoa, Carlo Felice, 21 June 1828, *D-Dlb**, *I-Gl**
Don Desiderio, ovvero Il disperato per eccesso di buon cuore (melodramma buffo, 2, B. Morelli), Dresden, Hof, aut. 1829, *Mc**, *PEl*
Francesca da Rimini (melodramma serio, Romani, after Dante: Commedia), inc., *PEl**, ov. (Florence, 1878)
Laurina alla corte, inc. (Introduction only, in Budapest, Kutatóközpont, fondo Nemzeti Zenede*)

*

DEUMM (G. P. Minardi)
A. Mezzanotte: *Catalogo delle opere musicali del celebre maestro Francesco Morlacchi perugino* (Perugia, 1843)
G. B. Rossi-Scotti: *Della vita e delle opere del cav. Francesco Morlacchi* (Perugia, 1860)
G. Ricci des Ferres-Cancani: *Francesco Morlacchi: un maestro italiano alla corte di Dresda (1784–1841)* (Florence, 1958)
W. Becker: *Die deutsche Oper in Dresden unter der Leitung von Carl Maria von Weber, 1817–1826* (Berlin, 1962)
J. Warrack: *Carl Maria von Weber* (London, 1968, 2/1976)
Francesco Morlacchi e la musica del suo tempo (1784–1841): Perugia 1984 [incl. J. Budden: 'German and Italian Elements in Morlacchi's Tebaldo e Isolina', 19–28; S. Franchi: 'Il Barbiere di Siviglia: confronti, suggestioni, linguaggio', 39–52; T. M. Gialdroni: 'Aspetti della vocalità nel Corradino di Morlacchi', 53–60]
B. Brumana: '*La gioventù di Enrico V* von Francesco Morlacchi', *Die italienische Oper in Dresden von Johann Adolf Hasse bis Francesco Morlacchi* (Dresden, 1987), 524–32 [Ger. abridged version], 562–79 [It. orig.]
G. Ciliberti: '*Raoul di Créqui* von Francesco Morlacchi', ibid, 533–41 [Ger. abridged version], 562–79 [It. orig.]
B. Brumana, G. Ciliberti and N. Guidobaldi: *Catalogo delle composizioni musicali di Francesco Morlacchi (1784–1841)* (Florence, 1987)
C. Mori: *Francesco Morlacchi e l'Allgemeine musikalische Zeitung, con una analisi dell'oratorio Isacco figura del Redentore* (diss., U. of Perugia, 1987–8)
G. Ciliberti: '*Il Barbiere di Siviglia* di Francesco Morlacchi: una inutil precauzione tra Paisiello e Rossini' (Terni, 1989) [essay in programme book]   BIANCAMARIA BRUMANA

Morley Opera. A student company emanating from Morley College in Lambeth, London; *see* LONDON, §II, 1.

Moro, Elisabetta (*b* Venice; *fl* 1723–41). Italian contralto. She sang in 15 operas in Venice between 1723 and 1741, including the first performances of Vivaldi's *L'inganno trionfante in amore* (1725), *Cunegonda* and *La fede tradita e vendicata* (both 1726). During Carnival 1727–8 she appeared at Turin, and later she sang in the premières of Vivaldi's *Atenaide* (1728–9, Florence), *Demetrio* (1737, Ferrara) and *Catone in Utica* (1737, Verona), and in a performance of his *L'Adelaide* at Graz in 1739. She specialized in male roles, but Vivaldi gave her female parts in 1725 and 1726 (*Cunegonda*).

*

R. Strohm: 'Vivaldi's Career as an Opera Producer', *Antonio Vivaldi: teatro musicale, cultura e società: Venice 1981*, i, 11–63
S. Mamy: 'La diaspora dei cantanti veneziani nella prima metà del settecento', *Nuovi studi vivaldiani: edizione e cronologia critica delle opere* (Florence, 1988), ii, 591–631   COLIN TIMMS

Morocco. For discussion of opera in Morocco *see* CASABLANCA.

Moroi, Makoto (*b* Tokyo, 17 Dec 1930). Japanese composer, son of the composer Saburō Moroi. He studied with Tomojirō Ikenouchi at the Tokyo National University of Fine Arts and Music, graduating in 1952. The following year he won two international composition prizes. In 1955 he went to Europe, where he worked in the Cologne electronic music studio. He returned to Tokyo after eight months and began work at the NHK electronic studio, for which he wrote a series of dramatic works for radio, combining electronic media with small orchestra: *Pitagorasu no hoshi* ('Stars of Pythagoras') in 1959; *Akai mayu* ('Red Cocoon') in 1960 (Tokyo, Sōgetsu Kaikan Hall, 8 Dec 1960); *Nagai nagai michini sotte* ('The Long, Long Street') in 1961, also broadcast in Italy; and *Hoshi no kurisumasu* ('Christmas for Stars') in 1963. In 1961 *Yamauba* ('The Mountain Witch') was broadcast as part of a short opera trilogy (other parts by Yoshirō Irino and Osamu Shimizu); the work combines electronic media with three vocal solos, ondes martenot, mandolin, celeste, piano, harps and strings. Three years later he wrote another similar, longer work, *Gyosha Paetōn* ('Phaeton the Charioteer'), this time with full orchestra and chorus, which won an Italia Prize. His music is particularly noted for its contrasting sonorities and serialist technique, often requiring virtuoso instrumental playing.

Yamauba [The Mountain Witch]/[Yoruno mukashiko (An Old Tale)] (op-ballad, 1, U. Itoh), broadcast Tokyo, NHK, 26 Nov 1961, as pt 1 of Mittsuno mukashiko [Three Old Tales]; stage Tokyo, Metropolitan Festival Hall, 15 March 1962 [pt 2 by Irino; pt 3 by Shimizu]
Gyosha Paetōn [Phaeton the Charioteer] (music drama, 1), Tokyo, Sankei Hall, 1965   MASAKATA KANAZAWA

Moross, Jerome (*b* Brooklyn, NY, 1 Aug 1913; *d* Miami, FL, 25 July 1983). American composer. Having graduated from New York University in 1932, he initially supported himself by writing ballets and music for the theatre. Gershwin engaged him as assistant conductor and pianist for a West Coast production of *Porgy and Bess*, and Moross began training the principals during the summer following Gershwin's death in 1937. During this period he went to Chicago for a production of his ballet *American Pattern* and began work on one of his most successful works, the ballet *Frankie and Johnny*. When he went to Hollywood in 1940, however, he found that his authentically American vernacular idiom was not understood by producers, so he earned a living as an orchestrator of film scores; only in 1948 did he write his first original film score (*Close-Up*).

During this period Moross produced a substantial number of works, notably the First Symphony (1943) and *Ballet Ballads*, a series of four one-act ballet-operas. Much of Moross's most interesting theatre music was cast in hybrid or experimental forms, such as ballet-opera, or for the semipopular musical stage; he was especially concerned to reconcile elements derived from popular and serious genres. In this he was a forerunner of Stephen Sondheim. The two-act opera *The Golden Apple* (including the song 'Lazy Afternoon') and *Gentlemen, Be Seated!*, a portrait of the Civil War in the form of a minstrel show, belong to this category. American folk and popular idioms form the basis of Moross's style, which is plain and vigorous, diatonically simple, warm and expressive. His best-known work is probably the score he wrote for the film *The Big Country*.

Susanna and the Elders, 1940–41 (ballet-op, 1, J. Latouche)
The Eccentricities of Davy Crockett, 1945 (ballet-op, 1, Latouche)
Willie the Weeper, 1945 (ballet-op, 1, Latouche)
Riding Hood Revisited, 1946 (ballet-op, 1, Latouche)
The Golden Apple, 1948–50 (2, Latouche)
Gentlemen, Be Seated!, 1955–6 (E. Eager), New York, 10 Oct 1963
Sorry, Wrong Number!, 1977 (after L. Fletcher)
CHRISTOPHER PALMER

Morris, James (*b* Baltimore, 10 Jan 1947). American bass-baritone. He studied with Ponselle in Baltimore and Moscona in Philadelphia, making his début with the Baltimore Opera in 1967 as Crespel (*Les contes d'Hoffmann*). In 1970 he joined the Metropolitan Opera, beginning with the King (*Aida*) and similar parts, graduating to Don Giovanni and other principal roles from 1975. He was heard mainly in lyric Italian roles, including Banquo at his British début (1972, Glyndebourne) and Guglielmo at the Salzburg Festival (from 1982; he recorded it under Muti). A suggestion that he should sing Wotan led him to study with Hans Hotter, and he first sang the role in *Walküre* at Baltimore in 1984. He added the *Rheingold* Wotan at San Francisco the next year (when he also first sang the Dutchman at Houston), and sang the three *Ring* Wotans first in Munich in 1987 under Sawallisch. The role brought him conspicuous success also at the Deutsche Oper, Berlin (1987), the Metropolitan Opera (1989) and Covent Garden (*Rheingold*, 1988; *Walküre*, 1989; *Siegfried*, 1990; and the complete cycle, 1991), while he recorded it concurrently under both Haitink and Levine. His imposing presence has a voice to match, notable for line as well as tone, and his dramatic interpretations are supported by clear musical insight.

*

H. Canning: 'James Morris', *Opera*, xxxix (1988), 1177–83
NOËL GOODWIN

Morselli, Adriano (*b* Veneto region; *fl* 1676–91). Italian librettist. He wrote 16 librettos for operas produced in Venice from 1679 to 1692, progressing from minor theatres (S Cassiano and S Angelo) to the more important (S Salvatore and S Giovanni Grisostomo). His *Maurizio*, which enjoyed productions in at least 17 Italian cities between 1687 and 1708, was one of the most widely disseminated operas of the period. His *Tullo Ostilio* and *Teodora augusta* were almost as popular. Alessandro Scarlatti's setting of *Pirro e Demetrio* (1694, Naples, S Bartolomeo) became one of that composer's most widely produced works.

Morselli is described posthumously as 'dottore' on the title-page of *Ibraim sultano*. By 1676 at the latest he had begun to provide occasional poems for the nobility. As house librettist at the Teatro S Giovanni Grisostomo from 1688 until his death, he enjoyed the patronage of the Grimani family who owned it. He wrote a series of sonnets celebrating the accession in 1689 of the Venetian Pietro Ottoboni (1610–91) to the papacy as Alexander VIII. This connection may have contributed to the restaging of several of his works in Rome in the 1690s at theatres under the protection of the pope's nephew Cardinal Pietro Ottoboni (1667–1740).

Although none of his works is entirely lacking in comic elements, Morselli stands out as an early representative of the trend towards librettos on elevated topics, particularly in his works for the Teatro S Giovanni Grisostomo. Bonlini noted that Morselli's *Incoronazione di Serse* (1691), after Pierre Corneille's *Rodogune*, was among the first librettos to be based on

French neo-classical works. Although Vincenzo Grimani had drawn on the subject matter and verse of Corneille's *Horace* for his *Orazio* (1688), Morselli was the first to attempt to incorporate Corneille's concentrated dramatic action and economical plot management into a libretto. Morselli later stated that his new approach was not well received by the audience. *La pace fra Tolomeo e Seleuco* (1691) draws on French drama only superficially, taking only its characters' names from *Rodogune*. *Ibraim sultano* (1692), based on Racine's *Bajazet*, also uses the French playwright's subject without adopting his dramatic style, and Morselli even increased the plot's comic interplay by adding two characters absent in Racine.

dramme per musica or dramme da rappresentarsi in musica

Candaule [Candaule re di Lidia], P. A. Ziani, 1679; Temistocle in bando, Giannettini, 1682; Appio Claudio, G. M. Martini, 1682; L'innocenza risorta, ovvero Etio [Il talamo preservato dalla fedeltà d'Eudossa], P. A. Ziani, 1683 (?A. Scarlatti, 1686, as Etio); Falaride tiranno d'Agrigento, Bassani, 1683; L'incoronazione di Dario [Dario], Freschi, 1684 (Aldrovandini, 1705, later as Li tre rivali al soglio); Tullo Ostilio, M. A. Ziani, 1685 (1686, as Alba soggiogata da' romani; G. Bononcini, 1694; Pescetti, 1729, as I tre difensori della patria); Teodora augusta, D. Gabrielli, 1685 (1689, as Teodora clemente, with addn by Sabadini)
Maurizio [Tiberio in Bisanzio], Gabrielli, 1686; Gordiano, Gabrielli, 1688; Carlo il Grande, Gabrielli, 1688; Amulio e Numitore, G. F. Tosi, 1689 (M. A. Gasparini, 1724, as Il più fedel tra gli amici); Pirro e Demetrio, Tosi, 1690 (A. Scarlatti, 1694; Eng., Scarlatti arr. Haym, 1708, as Pyrrhus and Demetrius; 1700, as La forza dell'amicizia; pasticcio, 1711, as La forza della fedeltà; P. Torri, 1721, as L'amor d'amico vince ogni altro amore); L'incoronazione di Serse, Tosi, 1690; La pace fra Tolomeo e Seleuco [Seleuco], C. F. Pollarolo, 1691; Ibraim sultano, Pollarolo, 1692

*

AllacciD
C. Ivanovich: *Minerva al tavolino* (Venice, 1681, 2/1688)
G. Bonlini: *Le glorie della poesia e della musica* (Venice, 1730)
R. S. Freeman: *Opera without Drama: Currents of Change in Italian Opera, 1675–1725, and the Roles played therein by Zeno, Caldara, and Others* (diss., Princeton U., 1967)
K. Leich: *Girolamo Frigimelica Robertis Libretti (1694–1708): ein Beitrag insbesondere zur Geschichte des Opernlibretto in Venedig* (Munich, 1972)
R. L. Weaver and N. Weaver: *A Chronology of Music in the Florentine Theatre, 1590–1750* (Detroit, 1978)
L. Bianconi and T. Walker: 'Production, Consumption and Political Function of Seventeenth-Century Opera', *Early Music History*, iv (1984), 211–99
H. S. Saunders: *The Repertoire of a Venetian Opera House (1678–1714): the Teatro Grimani di San Giovanni Grisostomo* (diss., Harvard U., 1985)
E. Selfridge-Field: *Pallade veneta: Writings on Music in Venetian Society, 1650–1750* (Venice, 1985)   HARRIS S. SAUNDERS

Mortari, Virgilio (*b* Passirana di Lainate, Milan, 6 Dec 1902). Italian composer. After studying at the Milan Conservatory with C. A. Bossi and Pizzetti, Mortari won the first competition organized by the Società Italiana di Musica Contemporanea (1924). He abandoned a career as a pianist to devote himself to composition and to teaching, first at the Venice Conservatory (1933–40), then at the Conservatorio di S Cecilia in Rome (until 1973). He was artistic director at the Accademia Filarmonica Romana (1944–6) and *sovrintendente* at La Fenice in Venice (1955–9).

As a composer he followed a moderate course in the face of the radical transformation of musical language in the 20th century. His preference for clarity, formal and structural balance and a natural sense of 'cantabilità', influenced in part by Stravinsky, place him among the neo-classical composers. This measured lyricism, together with an element of popular ironic burlesque and an almost childish sense of humour, can be found in his works for the theatre, especially *La figlia del diavolo* (1954), which also contains remarkable choral writing, similar to that of his sacred music.

Secchi e Sberlecchi (opera da camera, 2, A. Beltramelli), Udine, Sociale, 1927
La scuola delle mogli, 1930 (commedia, C. V. Ludovici, after Molière); rev., Milan, Piccola Scala, 17 March 1959
La figlia del diavolo (rappresentazione, 1, C. Pavolini), Milan, Scala, 24 March 1954
Resurrezione e vita (teatro sacro, O. Costa), Venice, Verde, July 1954 [after old Venetian music]
Alfabeto a sorpresa (opera da camera), Como, Villa Olmo, 1959
Il contratto (G. Marotta and B. Randone), RAI, 1962; stage, Rome, Opera, 18 April 1964
Prima di colazione (after E. O'Neill: *Before Breakfast*), Vienna, 1964

*

M. Mila: 'La scuola delle mogli di Mortari', *Cronache musicali 1955–59* (Turin, 1959), 183–5
F. D'Amico: 'Mortari, Peragallo e gli abbonati della Scala', *I casi della musica* (Milan, 1962), 17–18
R. Vlad: *Virgilio Mortari* (Hamburg, 1980)   RAFFAELE POZZI

Morte dell'aria ('Death in the Air'). *Tragedia* in one act by GOFFREDO PETRASSI to a libretto by Toti Scialoja; Rome, Teatro Eliseo, 24 October 1950.

The setting is a European capital city in the early years of the 20th century. On a platform high up on a tower an Inventor (baritone) wearing an elaborate flying device prepares to test his invention by launching himself into the air. Various onlookers voice their feelings about the imminent spectacle: the tower's Custodian (bass) expresses serious misgivings, an official Observer (baritone) spouts grand-sounding platitudes, while four Reporters chatter eagerly in anticipation of some good copy. After a couple of abortive attempts to leap, the Inventor confesses he no longer has any hope of flying successfully, but to be true to his creed he will nevertheless entrust himself to the air. At the third attempt he leaps off the platform, plummeting to his death. The chorus sing a threnody.

The absurdist scenario of caricatured observers and a deeply human – but foolish – protagonist is backed by an unseen female chorus whose commentary and final lament provide, perhaps, the most memorable music. While marking a significant step towards its composer's adoption of serial procedures, *Morte dell'aria* is static as drama and would lose little if presented as a cantata. The scoring is for chamber orchestra without violins.

ALASDAIR JAMIESON

Morte delle maschere, La. Opera by G. F. Malipiero, part 1 of the triptych ORFEIDE, L'.

Morte di Cesare, La ('The Death of Caesar'). *Opera seria* in three acts by FRANCESCO BIANCHI to a libretto by GAETANO SERTOR based on WILLIAM SHAKESPEARE's play *Julius Caesar*; Venice, Teatro S Samuele, 27 December 1788.

Sertor centred the action on the steady progress of the conspirators, led by Cassio [Cassius] (tenor) and Porzia [Portia] (soprano), towards the discrediting and murder of Caesar (soprano castrato); he also built up a tender relationship between Caesar and Calfurnia [Calpurnia] (soprano). In this, the first of several Venetian 'morte' operas, Sertor observed the conventions of taste, and the murder takes place behind closed doors – though

Caesar's body lies on stage for the remainder of the opera. Also innovatory are the two scenes for chorus, soloists and ballet. The second, in the middle of Act 2, uses the entire cast – a septet with chorus in vaudeville form – as Caesar accepts the crown; the scene closes with an aria for Caesar in which the chorus, acting as a character in the drama, interrupts him and engages in dialogue with him between quatrains.

The opera has an unusually large number of emotionally charged ensembles: a quartet closing Act 1 (unprecedented in its tutti opening) and an angry exchange between Bruto [Brutus] (tenor) and Caesar in Act 3 – an early instance both of a duet for two men and of an ensemble serving as cavatina (only Brutus exits). Twice in Act 3 the chorus functions as an active participant in the ensemble: a short trio with chorus for the three conspirators, and a vengeful, three-part finale for Calpurnia, Antonio [Antony] (bass) and chorus.

See also JULIUS CAESAR.

MARITA P. McCLYMONDS

Morte d'Orfeo, La ('The Death of Orpheus'). *Tragicommedia pastorale* in five acts by STEFANO LANDI; ?Veneto region, ?1619.

For declining to invite Bacco [Bacchus] (alto) to his birthday celebrations, against the advice of Mercurio [Mercury] (alto) and Apolline (tenor), Orfeo [Orpheus] (tenor) is slain by the Maenads. In the Underworld, Euridice [Eurydice] (soprano) no longer recognizes him, and Caronte [Charon] (bass) offers him solace from the waters of Lethe with the aria 'Beva, beva securo l'onda'. In the final act Giove [Jupiter] (bass) raises the demigod to the heavens.

This retelling of Greek legend unfolds in five short tableaux, each with a nearly different set of characters in the manner of *intermedi* or the early 17th-century *veglia*. Thus there are 18 'principal' roles, none of them extensive. The dialogue in each act concentrates on presenting a single strong effect, which is summarized by a concluding choral ensemble: Orpheus's heedless enthusiasm is multiplied by a double chorus of satyrs in Act 2; Bacchus's furious resentment makes the shepherds quake in Act 3; and shepherds echo the grief of Calliope (soprano) at her son's death in Act 4.

The origins of the opera are obscure, but Landi's dedication of the printed score (Venice, 1619) from Padua, on 1 June, and the dedicatory sonnets, one to Landi, at the end by a Veronese doctor and dramatist, Francesco Pona, point to a first performance in the Veneto region. In 1939 Vatielli proposed, on the basis of his reading of the dedication, that Landi had been his own librettist. Landi refers to the notion that the Muses spoke or wrote 'musically' and thereby provided a model for reciting by singing, but that seems to be a genealogical metaphor for opera in general, rather than a veiled statement that Landi (like a muse) had created text and music; the librettist remains unknown. Another proposal (Leopold 1976), that the opera might have been part of the celebrations for a Borghese-Orsini wedding (20 October 1619), would apply to a performance after the publication of the score.

MARGARET MURATA

Mortellari, Michele (*b* Palermo, *c*1750; *d* London, 27 March 1807). Italian composer. He moved from Sicily to Naples to study with Piccinni. His career as an opera composer began in Florence and was centred in northern Italy until he moved to London in 1785. Most theatres engaged him to write serious operas, but during a ten-year period, beginning in 1775 with *L'astuzie amorose*, several Venetian theatres commissioned comic operas. These typically begin with an introductory ensemble, each act closing with a finale, and an occasional duet, trio, quartet or quintet is interspersed between the arias. *La fata benefica* is unusual for its many magical scene changes. None of his comic operas achieved complete success, but three serious ones, *Medonte* (*Arsace*), *Armida* and *Antigona*, received two subsequent performances in other cities. In 1785 Mortellari was invited to compose a new version of *Armida* for Florence (*Armida abbandonata*) during a period of intense operatic activity encouraged by Archduke Leopold; this version was repeated in London in 1786.

Mortellari's two successful spectacle operas, *Armida* and *Antigona*, may have earned him the commission to compose *Troia distrutta*, one of Verazi's radical operas for the opening of La Scala in 1778. For the next carnival he wrote a new setting of De Gamerra's *Lucio Silla* for Turin, another theatre with a strong interest in spectacle. In 1784 he returned to Milan to set Moretti's innovatory libretto *Semiramide*, the first in a succession of operas based on Voltaire's *Sémiramis*.

In 1785 Mortellari settled in London, where he composed and taught singing; Mrs Billington is said to have studied with him in 1786 during her first season at Covent Garden. During the same season some of his arias were incorporated into the pasticcio *Didone*, and his opera *Armida* was performed at the King's Theatre. His cantata *Venere e Adone* was first performed at the Hanover Square Rooms on 8 May 1787. Although Mortellari was based in England, he travelled to Italy and Russia in the late 1790s: his *Angelica* (1796, Padua) opens with a storm and disembarkation that harks back to Majo's *Ifigenia in Tauride* (1764) and to Gluck's borrowing for Paris (1779); there are also many ensembles and extensive finales here that are typical of opera in the late 1790s. The trip to Russia in 1798 failed to win the favour of Paul I, newly ascended to the throne, but Mortellari served Count Sheremetyev for some months, before announcing his departure in June 1799.

Burney, having heard Mortellari's *Armida* in London, characterized his taste in singing as being 'of the most refined and exquisite sort' and his music 'less bold, nervous, and spirited, than elegant, graceful, and pleasing'. Mortellari was primarily a melodist with a strong interest in orchestral effects, which he attained through contrasting forces, textural thickening and fast figuration. He used wind instruments liberally, particularly in vocal caesuras and ritornellos, and he frequently wrote for solo instruments. His programmatic orchestrations work well in the finales, and his operas as a whole show evidence of careful tonal planning.

See also TROIA DISTRUTTA.

Didone abbandonata (os, 3, P. Metastasio), Florence, Pergola, 16 Sept 1772

Arsace (os, 3, G. De Gamerra), Padua, Nuovo, June 1775, *I-Pl*

L'astuzie amorose (dg, 3, F. Cerlone), Venice, S Samuele, aut. 1775, *MOe*

Armida (os, 3, after T. Tasso: *Gerusalemme liberata*), Modena, Ducale, carn. 1776, *F-Pn*

Don Salterio Civetta (dg, 3), Venice, S Samuele, carn. 1776

Antigona (os, 3, G. Roccaforte), Venice, S Benedetto, 11 May 1776, *Pn, I-Bc*

Il barone di Lago Nero (dg, 3), Venice, S Cassiano, aut. 1776, *F-Pn* (Act 3)

La governante (int, 2), Rome, Valle, carn. 1777

Ezio (os, 3, Metastasio), Milan, Ducale, Jan 1777, *D-DS, P-La* (Act 2)

Antigono (os, Metastasio), Modena, Ducale, carn. 1778, *F-Pn*

Alessandro nell'Indie (os, 3, Metastasio), Siena, Acccademia degl'Intronati, 22 July 1778, *I-Mc*

Troia [Troja] distrutta (os, 3, M. Verazi), Milan, Scala, 1 Sept 1778, *D-DS, F-Pn, P-La*

Lucio Silla (os, 3, De Gamerra), Turin, Regio, 26 Dec 1778, *F-Pn, I-Tf, P-La*

Il finto pazzo per amore (ob, 2), Venice, S Giovanni Grisostomo, carn. 1779

Medonte (os, De Gamerra), Verona, sum. 1780

I rivali ridicoli (dg, 2, G. Bertati), Venice, S Moisè, aut. 1780

La muta per amore (dg, 2, C. Orcomeno), Venice, S Samuele, carn. 1781

La fata benefica (dg, 2), Venice, S Moisè, carn. 1783

Semiramide (os, 3, F. Moretti), Milan, Scala, 26 Dec 1784, *F-Pn*

Armida abbandonata (os, 3, after Tasso: *Gerusalemme liberata*), Florence, Pergola, aut. 1785, *I-Fc*

L'infanta supposta (os), Modena, Ducale, 1785

Angelica (os, 2, G. Sertor), Padua, Nuovo, June 1796, *Mc, Pl*

*

BurneyH; EitnerQ; FétisB; StiegerO

R.-A. Mooser: *Annales de la musique et des musiciens en Russie au XVIII siècle* (Geneva. 1948)

M. McClymonds: 'Haydn and his Contemporaries: *Armida abbandonata*', *Joseph Haydn: Vienna 1982*, 325–32

——: 'Mattia Verazi and the Opera at Mannheim, Stuttgart, and Ludwigsburg', *Studies in Music* [University of Western Ontario], vii (1982), 99–136

U. Zelaschi: *L'opéra italien jusqu'en 1900* (Brussels, 1982)

M. McClymonds: 'Mozart's *La clemenza di Tito* and Opera Seria in Florence as a Reflection of Leopold II's Musical Taste', *MJb 1984–95*, 61–70

——: 'The Venetian Role in the Transformation of Italian Opera Seria during the 1790s', *I vicini di Mozart: Venice 1987*, i, 221–40

MARITA P. McCLYMONDS

Mortier, Gerard (*b* Ghent, 25 Nov 1943). Belgian administrator. He studied law then journalism at the University of Ghent, and worked as an administrator for the Flanders Festival (1968–72). After a year at the Deutsche Oper in Düsseldorf, he became assistant administrator at the Frankfurt opera, under Christoph von Dohnányi. Positions at the Hamburg Staatsoper (1977) and the Paris Opéra (1979, with Liebermann) led to his appointment as general director of the Théâtre de la Monnaie, Brussels, in 1981. During the following decade Mortier instigated a period of expansion at La Monnaie; he appointed John Pritchard and Sylvain Cambreling as musical directors and Dohnányi as musical adviser, and established the theatre as a centre of operatic excellence with productions noted for their intelligence and thoroughness of preparation. With his judicious casting policies and generous rehearsal schedules he was able to attract a number of leading stage directors and set designers, including Karl-Ernst Herrmann, Luc Bondy, Patrice Chéreau, Peter Stein and Herbert Wernicke, several of whom were previously associated more with spoken theatre than with opera.

Mortier was also involved in commissioning a series of new works, by the Belgian composers Philippe Boesmans (*La passion de Gilles*) and André Laporte (*Das Schloss*), and by Hans Zender (*Stephen Climax*) and John Adams (*The Death of Klinghoffer*). His choice of Peter Sellars as director for the production of Adams's opera provoked a divided response from critics; a succession of such controversial and challenging decisions ensured not only the notoriety but also the popularity of his tenure at La Monnaie. In 1992 he became director of the Salzburg Festival.

S. Lannes and S. Nussac: 'The Bastille's Anti-Star: Part 2', *Opera*, xxxvii (1986), 511–14

R. Christiansen: 'Gerard Mortier', *Opera* (1990), 9–15 [festival issue]

Mosca, Giuseppe (*b* Naples, 1772; *d* Messina, 14 Sept 1839). Italian composer. He studied with Fenaroli at the Conservatory of S Maria di Loreto, Naples; in 1791 his first opera, *Silvia e Nardone*, was performed at the Teatro Nuovo in Rome. For 12 years he composed for various Italian theatres, presenting his operas in Rome, Naples, Venice and elsewhere, usually with much success. In 1803 he went to Paris as *maestro al cembalo* at the Théâtre Italien; he composed additional music when required, but wrote no operas (two operas attributed to him by Florimo were by his brother, Luigi). When Spontini assumed the directorship of the theatre (1810), Mosca returned to Italy.

After the success of Rossini's *La pietra del paragone* (1812), Mosca accused Rossini of having plagiarized his *I pretendenti delusi* (1811), particularly the device of the crescendo, circulating copies of his music as proof. The charge was repeated by critics until Radiciotti discovered that the crescendo had been employed before Mosca's first use of it in *Il foletto* (1797) (by Simon Mayr in *La Lodoiska*, 1796). Mosca's style shows a remarkable similarity to Rossini's in many respects – melodic turns, orchestral melodies under vocal patter, multipartite ensemble structures – but it would be difficult to decide who influenced whom.

In 1817 Mosca went to Palermo as musical director of the Teatro Carolino, but gave up the post after the Revolution of 1820. A return to Milan revived his career; after several years of touring, however, he settled in Messina as director of another theatre (1827). He composed more than 40 operas; all were written by 1826. Fétis described him as a musician without genius, but gifted with stupendous facility.

Silvia e Nardone (int), Rome, Nuovo, Feb 1791

La vedova scaltra (int, 2, L. Ricciuti), Rome, Tordinona, carn. 1796

Il foletto (ob, 2, C. Battimelli), Naples, Nuovo, 1797, *I-Nc*

Chi si contenta gode (ob, B. Sivoli), Rome, Apollo, 29 April 1798, *Mr**

I matrimoni liberi (ob, 2), Milan, Scala, 25 Aug 1798

Ifigenia in Aulide (3, A. Zeno), Rome, Argentina, carn. 1799

La gabbia dei matti (ob, G. Foppa), Ferrara, Civico, sum. 1799 [incl. music from Mayr: Un pazzo fa cento]

L'apparenza inganna (ob, 1, A. Filistri), Venice, S Moisè, aut. 1799

Rinaldo ed Armida (os, F. Gonella, after T. Tasso), Florence, Pergola, 26 Dec 1799

Amore e dovere (farsa, 1, P. Scotes, after G. Bertati), Rome, Dame, 1799

Le gare fra Limella e Valeficco [Le gare fra Velafico e Lomella per servire i loro padroni] (farsa, 1, G. Artusi), Venice, S Luca, sum. 1800

La gastalda ed i lacchè (farsa, 1), Venice, S Samuele, aut. 1800

La vipera ha beccato i ciarlatani (ob), Turin, Regio, aut. 1801

Il sedicente filosofo (ob, Foppa), Milan, Scala, Nov 1801, *F-Pc, Pn, I-Fc*; as Il filosofo, Vicenza, 1819, *F-Pc, I-Fc*

Ginevra di Scozia, ossia Ariodante (G. Rossi), Turin, Regio, carn. 1802

La fortunata combinazione (ob, L. Romanelli), Milan, Scala, 17 Aug 1802

Emira e Conalla (F. Marconi), Genoa, S Agostino, carn. 1803

Sesostri [La feste d'Isida] (3, P. Pariati and Zeno), Turin, Arti, carn. 1803

Chi vuol troppo veder diventa cieco, ossia Mariti gelosi (ob, 2), Milan, Scala, 2 July 1803

Monsieur de Montanciel, ossia L'albergo magico (ob, 2, Marconi), Turin, Carignano, Oct 1810

I pretendenti delusi, ossia Con amore non si scherza (ob, 2, L. Prividali), Milan, Scala, 14 April 1811, *B-Bc, I-Bc, Fc, Mr, Nc*

I tre mariti [La moglie di tre mariti] (farsa, 1, Rossi), Venice, S Moisè, 27 Dec 1811, *GB-Lbl, I-Nc*

Il finto Stanislao re di Polonia (ob, Rossi), Venice, S Moisè, 21 Jan 1812

Romilda (V. Ponticelli), Parma, Ducale, 26 Jan 1812

Gli amori e l'armi (ob, 2, G. Palomba), Naples, Fiorentini, 29 March 1812, Nc

Le bestie in uomini (ob, A. Anelli), Milan, Scala, 17 Aug 1812

La diligenza a Joigni, o sia Il collaterale (ob, 2, Palomba), Naples, Fiorentini, 1813, Nc (?autograph)

Don Gregorio imbarrazzato (ob, 2, A. Tottola), Naples, Fiorentini, 1813, Mc, Nc

Avviso al pubblico, ossia La gazzetta [Il matrimonio per concorso] (ob, Rossi), Milan, Scala, 4 Jan 1814

Il fanatico per l'Olanda (ob), Bologna, Corso, carn. 1814

I viaggiatori, ossia Il negoziante pesarese (ob), Parma, Ducale, 22 Oct 1814

Carlotta ed Enrico (ob, Tottola), Naples, Fiorentini, 1814

Il disperato per eccesso di buon cuore, ossia Don Desiderio (ob, G. Giannetti), Naples, Fiorentini, carn. 1816

La gioventù d'Enrico V (2, F. Romani), Florence, Pergola, 11 Sept 1817, Fc, US-Wc

Attila in Aquileja, ossia Il trionfo del re dei Franchi (2, S. A. Sografi), Palermo, S Cecilia, 1818, I-Mc, Nc

I due fratelli fuorusciti (ob), Bologna, Marsigli Rossi, 26 Sept 1819

Emria, regina d'Egitto (N. Cervelli), Milan, Scala, 6 March 1821

La dama locandiera, ossia L'albergo de' Pitocchi (ob, Romanelli, after C. Goldoni), Milan, Scala, 8 April 1821, Fc; rev. as La poetessa errante (Palomba), Naples, Nuovo, 1822, Nc

La sciocca per astuzia (ob, Romanelli), Milan, Scala, 15 May 1821, duet GB-Lbl

Il Federico II, re di Prussia (2, G. Checcherini), Naples, S Carlo, wint. 1824, I-Nc

L'abbate del épée (ob, 2, L. Ricciuti), Naples, Fondo, 27 June 1826, Nc

I gelosi burlatti (ob, 2), 1 act B-Bc, selections Lc

*

FétisB; FlorimoN; MGG (U. Prota-Giurleo and L. Paduano)

'Verzeichniss sämmtlicher Compositionen des Hrn. Joseph Mosca bis zum Frühjahr 1821 inclusive', AMZ, xxiii (1821), col.477

G. Radiciotti: Gioacchino Rossini, iii (Tivoli, 1927)

O. Tiby: Il Real Teatro Carolino (Palermo, 1957)

MARVIN TARTAK

Mosca, Luigi (b Naples, 1775; d Naples, 13 or 30 Nov 1824). Italian composer. Most early sources state that he was a student at the Turchini conservatory in Naples and also, like his brother Giuseppe, a pupil of Fenaroli. He was for many years maestro al cembalo at the S Carlo opera house. Through the intervention of Paisiello he also became, after 1802, vice-maestro of the royal chamber and chapel. He was considered one of the best singing teachers in Naples, and when Zingarelli became director of the Naples Conservatory in 1813 Mosca was made primo maestro di canto. He was a member of the Naples Accademia di Belle Arti. The first of his 17 operas, L'impresario burlato, was successfully performed at the Teatro Nuovo in 1797. Though he travelled through Italy staging his operas, most were originally written for Naples. He also composed much sacred music.

Luigi Mosca's musical style is more interesting than that of his brother, Giuseppe; Luigi showed a particular aptitude for setting specific dramatic situations and building a scene, and his use of harmony was richer. Whatever the differences between them, neither brother's music lasted, and their works are a dim reflection of those of their contemporary, Rossini.

first performed in Naples unless otherwise stated

L'impresario burlato (ob, 2, F. Signoretti), Nuovo, carn. 1797, B-Bc, F-Pc, I-Fc, Nc

La sposa tra le imposture (ob, Signoretti), Nuovo, carn. 1798

Un imbroglio ne porta un altro (ob, G. Palomba), Nuovo, aut. 1799

Gli sposi in cimento (ob, 2, F. S. Zini), Nuovo, carn. 1800

L'omaggio sincero (G. Pagliuca), Real Palazzo, spr. 1800

Le stravaganze d'amore (ob, 2, Zini), Nuovo, aut. 1800, Nc

Gli amanti volubili (ob, J. Ferretti), Rome, Valle, carn. 1801

L'amore per inganno [L'amoroso inganno; La cantatrice di spirito] (ob, 2, Palomba), Fiorentini, spr. 1801, Nc

Il ritorno impensato (ob, Zini), Fiorentini, carn. 1802

L'impostore, ossia Il Marcotonta (ob, 2, A. Tottola), Nuovo, sum. 1802, Nc

La vendetta feminina (ob), Fiorentini, 1803; as La lezione vendetta, Paris, Italien, 27 March 1806

I finti viaggiatori (ob, 2, N. de Marco), Fiorentini, aut. 1807

L'italiana in Algeri (ob, A. Anelli), Milan, Scala, 16 Aug 1808, Mr*

La sposa a sorte (ob, 2, Palomba), Fiorentini, sum. 1810, Nc

Il salto di Leucade (os, 2, G. Schmidt), S Carlo, 15 Jan 1812, Nc

L'audacia delusa (ob, 2, Palomba), Fiorentini, aut. 1813

Doubtful: La voce misteriosa (F. Romani), Turin, Carignano, 1 Sept 1821

*

FlorimoN; MGG ('Mosca, Giuseppe'; U. Prota-Giurleo and L. Paduano)

MARVIN TARTAK

Moscona, Nicola [Mosconas, Nicolai] (b Athens, 23 Sept 1907; d Philadelphia, 17 Sept 1975). Greek bass. He studied with Elena Theodorini at the Athens conservatory and began singing professionally in 1929. After performing throughout Greece and in Egypt and Italy, he made his Metropolitan Opera début in 1937 as Ramfis in Aida. He spent the next 25 seasons as a principal bass there, singing over 30 different roles, including Pimen, Colline, Raimondo (Lucia di Lammermoor), Sparafucile and Ferrando (Il trovatore). He was a favourite singer of Toscanini, who chose him to participate in his recordings of La bohème, Mefistofele and Rigoletto.

CORI ELLISON

Moscow (Russ. Moskva). Capital of Russia. Founded in the 12th century, it was the capital of the Russian state in the 16th and 17th centuries. When Peter the Great moved the capital to St Petersburg in 1703, Moscow's importance declined; it was reinstated as capital by the Bolshevik government in 1918, and remained the chief city and cultural centre throughout the Soviet period.

1. To 1918. 2. After 1918.

1. To 1918. Moscow was the site of the first true opera performance in Russia: Calandro, a commedia per musica by G. A. Ristori, which was staged in the Kremlin palace by a small troupe of Italians visiting from Dresden on 30 November/11 December 1731. For the coronation in 1742 of the Empress Elizabeth, which took place, according to custom, in Moscow, the old capital, the Russian court opera (established in St Petersburg in 1735) travelled there to perform Hasse's setting of Tito Vespasiano (given as La clemenza di Tito) in a theatre specially constructed for the purpose on the banks of the river Yauza. It was preceded by a prologue, La Russia afflitta e riconsolata, for which Domenico Dall'Oglio and Luigi Madonis, violinists resident in Moscow, composed the music. Opera buffa was first brought to Moscow in 1759 by the impresario G. B. Locatelli.

The first public theatre was opened in Moscow in 1776, at Prince Vorontsov's mansion on Znamenka Street, under the aegis of Prince Pyotr Vasil'yevich Urusov, procurator-general of the city, with day-to-day management in the hands of the English entrepreneur Michael Maddox. Almost all the Russian Singspiels of the late 18th century were performed there, in addition to French and Italian comic operas in Russian translation. Such durable fare as Mel'nik-koldun, obmanshchik i svat ('The Miller who was a Wizard, a Cheat and a Matchmaker') by Alexander Ablesimov and Sokolovsky and Rozana i Lyubim by Nikolay Nikolev and Ivan

Kerzelli were first given at Maddox's 'Theatre on the Znamenka'. In 1780 a big house, known as the Petrovsky after the street (Petrovka) on which it was located, was constructed for the enterprise, by now Maddox's alone, on the site of the present-day Bol'shoy. The other Moscow musical theatres at this time were those on the estates of such ancient families as the Volkonskys, the Yusupovs and the Sheremet'yevs, in which the performers were serfs. The Sheremet'yev theatre gave public performances in Moscow, in which the first Russian diva, Praskov'ya Ivanovna Kovalyova, known as Zhemchugóva, made an extraordinary impression (she married Count Nikolay Sheremet'yev in 1801).

The Petrovsky Theatre burnt down in 1805, and the next year its troupe fell under the jurisdiction of the newly organized Directorate of Imperial Theatres. After a series of temporary homes – Volkonsky House, Pashkov House, Arbat Theatre (the first one called 'Bol'shoy', burnt by the French in 1812), Apraksin House – it moved into the new Bol'shoy (Grand) Theatre, completed in 1825 (the original building burnt down in 1853; the present stone theatre, the work of court architect Alberto Cavos, dates from 1856 and has a seating capacity of 2155). Alexey Verstovsky was named the theatre's director; by 1860 he had risen to the rank of inspector of theatres for the city. As a musician, he made a comparable rise: beginning in the stable of hacks employed to turn out vaudevilles, where he worked as a junior partner to Alexander Alyab'yev, he ended up as a composer of romantic operas, including *Askold's Grave*, first performed at the Bol'shoy in 1835, perhaps the most popular Russian opera of the 19th century. In addition to Verstovsky's operas, the Bol'shoy staged the première of Dargomïzhsky's *Esmeralda* (after Hugo, 1847), which took place while the Russian opera troupe from St Petersburg was in 'exile' in the second city, having been ousted from its theatre in the capital to make room for the Italian troupe of celebrities that had been imported by Tsar Nicholas I. The preference for Italian opera eventually affected Moscow as well. For the inauguration of the restored Bol'shoy Theatre in 1856, which took place amid the festivities attending the coronation of Alexander II, the St Petersburg troupe came down in force, presenting more than 20 performances of eight operas by Bellini, Donizetti and Verdi between 20 August and 27 September. Thus did the Russian Empire, in the mid-19th century, see fit to celebrate its great occasions of state.

Regular Italian subscription seasons began at the Bol'shoy in 1861, and from 1868 to 1873 the theatre became the bailiwick of Eugenio Merelli, son of the venerable Bartolomeo Merelli of La Scala, Milan. Eugenio brought Désirée Artôt to Moscow, where she captured the heart of that unlikeliest of suitors, Tchaikovsky (engaged by Merelli to write recitatives for Auber's *Fra Diavolo*, performed in Italian as Artôt's benefit performance in January 1870). Russian opera performances were to be drastically scaled back until the Italians left in 1882: in 1875 Nikolay Rubinstein, together with two commercial entrepreneurs, petitioned the government for the right to open a private theatre for Russian opera, but this was refused.

From 1866 Moscow had a conservatory, and a great composer in Tchaikovsky, who had come down from St Petersburg to join the new school's faculty. His first assignment from the Imperial Theatres had consisted of couplets for a vaudeville, *Putanitsa* ('A Muddle'),

performed in December 1867. Tchaikovsky's first opera, *Voyevoda* ('The Provincial Governor'), written in collaboration with Ostrovsky, the great Moscow dramatist, was given at the Bol'shoy in 1869. By the mid-1870s he was famous, and his operas mostly went to the capital, where a magnificent theatre, the Mariinsky (later the Kirov), had been built for Russian opera; but *Yevgeny Onegin* (at the conservatory), *Mazepa* and *Cherevichki* had their premières in the composer's home city.

In 1882 the crown monopoly on theatres was finally revoked, and a number of private opera companies sprang up – particularly in Moscow, where merchant patronage was stronger than in the capital. The first and greatest of these enterprises was the Moskovskaya Chastnaya Russkaya Opera (Moscow Private Russian Opera Company), organized in 1885 by the railway tycoon Savva Ivanovich Mamontov (1841–1918). This legendary troupe, which occupied the huge Solodovnikov Theatre (now the State Operetta Theatre), and in which the leading conductors were the composers Ippolitov-Ivanov and (later) Rakhmaninov, gave Shalyapin his start. Mamontov employed leading painters of the so-called neo-nationalist tendency, such as the brothers Vasnetsov, to execute the sets and costumes, and in so doing set a precedent for Dyagilev. Mamontov's company became the main outlet for Rimsky-Korsakov's voluminous late operatic production, from *Sadko* (1897) to *The Tale of Tsar Saltan* (1900), plus *Kashchey the Deathless* (1902) – six works in all. Mamontov's enterprise was succeeded in 1904 by that of Sergey Ivanovich Zimin (1875–1942), who sponsored the posthumous première of Rimsky-Korsakov's last opera, *The Golden Cockerel*, in 1909.

The early 20th century saw a great improvement at the Bol'shoy, beginning with Rakhmaninov's brief tenure (1904–6) as chief conductor, during which time he introduced his own *Miserly Knight* and *Francesca da Rimini* as a double bill. He was succeeded at the helm by Václav Suk and Emil Cooper. During this golden age such outstanding singers as Shalyapin, Nezhdanova, Dmitry Smirnov, Zbruyeva and Sobinov sang at the theatre, and important artists such as Konstantin Korovin and Alexander Golovin (both later engaged by Dyagilev) designed productions.

2. AFTER 1918. After the revolution and the return of the seat of government to Moscow, the city became the dominant artistic centre of the Soviet state, and the Bol'shoy assumed the absolute dominance of Soviet operatic life it enjoyed to the end of the Soviet period. The best singers from every corner of the USSR were routed to the Bol'shoy. Among the most outstanding were Nadezhda Obukhova, Alexander Pirogov, Mark Reyzen, Ivan Kozlovsky and Pavel Lisitsyan. The generation that arose after the 1950s – Galina Vishnevskaya, Irina Arkhipova, Yelena Obraztsova, Yevgeny Nesterenko, Alexander Ognivtsev, Artur Eyzen, Alexander Vedernikov, Vladislav P'yavko, Alexey Maslennikov, Yury Mazurok, Vladimir Atlantov – have made international careers. Chief conductors in Soviet times have included Nikolay Golovanov (1919–28, 1948–53), Václav Suk (1928–32), Samuil Samosud (1936–43), Ary Pazovsky (1943–8), Alexander Melik-Pashayev (1953–62), Gennady Rozhdestvensky (1964–70), Yury Simonov (1970–85), and Alexander Lazarev (from 1987). Boris Pokrovsky's

Interior of the Bol'shoy Theatre, Moscow: engraving from 'L'illustration' (16 February 1861)

eminence as stage director has been internationally recognized.

The theatre's status as the leading house in the USSR was confirmed in a singularly Stalinist way in 1939, with the première of *Ivan Susanin*. This was Glinka's first opera, *A Life for the Tsar*, refurbished with a new, non-tsarist but vehemently patriotic libretto by Sergey Gorodetsky so that the work could continue to function as flagship opera on the Soviet musical stage just as it had done in imperial times (in 1989 the original libretto was restored). In addition, the Bol'shoy became a showcase theatre for regularly organized appearances of troupes from all the union republics. This function was inaugurated in 1930 with the première of the opera *Almast* by Alexander Spendiarov, an Armenian who had studied with Rimsky-Korsakov, in a posthumous redaction by Maximilian Shteynberg, another Rimsky-Korsakov pupil.

The Opernaya Studiya Bol'shogo Teatra (Bol'shoy Theatre Opera Studio) organized under the aegis of the Bol'shoy for Konstantin Stanislavsky in 1918 became an independent musical theatre in 1926 as the Operniy Teatr-Studiya Stanislavskogo (Stanislavsky Opera Theatre Studio). Its production of the original *Boris Godunov* in its earlier (1869) version was much celebrated. Also in 1926, the Muzïkal'naya Studiya Moskovskogo Khudozhestvennogo Teatra (Moscow Art Theatre Music Studio), organized by Vladimir Nemirovich-Danchenko, became an independent theatre, the Muzïkal'nïy Teatr imeni Nemirovicha-Danchenko (Nemirovich-Danchenko Music Theatre). It produced Shostakovich's *Lady Macbeth of the Mtsensk District* in 1934. In 1941 the two theatres were merged into one, providing Moscow with a second major opera house, the Muzïkal'nïy Teatr imeni K. S. Stanislavskogo i V. I. Nemirovicha-Danchenko (Stanislavsky–Nemirovich-Danchenko Music Theatre) on Pushkin Street. Soviet opera in concert was the speciality of the Ansambl' Sovetskoy Operï Vsesoyuznogo Teatral'nogo Obshchestva (Soviet Opera Ensemble of the All-Union Theatrical Society), which gave preliminary hearings to many major works by Soviet composers, including *The Decembrists* (Shaporin) and

War and Peace (Prokofiev), long before their stage premières.

During World War II (called the Great Patriotic War in the USSR) the main musical institutions of Moscow were evacuated to the interior (the Bol'shoy to Kuybïshev [now Samara]), though part of each company remained in the capital to maintain morale. The Bol'shoy put on an opera by Kabalevsky called *V ogne* ('Into the Fire', 1943) depicting the ongoing defence of the city. After the war the Bol'shoy devoted a great deal of its repertory to exhibiting work from the new 'fraternal' republics of the Soviet bloc: *The Bartered Bride* and *Jenůfa* (Czechoslovakia), *Halka* (Poland), *Bánk bán* and *Bluebeard's Castle* (Hungary). This was also the time of gargantuan productions of the Russian classics (the most spectacular being *Boris Godunov*, *Khovanshchina*, *Sadko* and *Prince Igor*), which remained in use into the 1980s. Prokofiev's *War and Peace*, *The Story of a Real Man* and even *The Gambler* received belated productions (1959, 1960, 1974 respectively; the first and last have been successfully exported). In the early 1960s the company gained a second venue in the huge Dvorets S'yezdov (Palace of Congresses) on the Kremlin grounds, originally built for the triumphant 22nd Communist Party Congress in 1961. Its seating capacity of 6000 makes it the largest indoor theatre in the world.

A major event was the 1963 première of *Katerina Izmaylova*, a revision of Shostakovich's long-banned *Lady Macbeth*, at the Stanislavsky–Nemirovich-Danchenko Music Theatre, widely heralded as bellwether of the post-Stalinist thaw. In 1972 the Kamerniy Operniy Teatr (Chamber Opera Theatre) was organized by Pokrovsky in association with the conductor Vladimir Delman for the performance of 18th- and 20th-century Russian works; it made some valuable recordings of both repertories including Pashkevich's *The Miser* and Shostakovich's *Nos* ('The Nose'). The late 1980s witnessed the founding of some cooperative opera companies – for example the peripatetic Teatr Forum (Forum Theatre) – devoted to more challenging contemporary fare by Denisov, Slonimsky and Knaifel, among others.

Bol'shoy Moskovskiy teatr i obozreniye sobïtiy predshestvovavshikh osnovaniyu pravil'nogo russkogo teatra [The Moscow Bol'shoy Theatre and a Survey of the Events leading to the Founding of a True Russian Theatre] (Moscow, 1857)

N. Dmitriyev [pseud. of N. Kashkin]: *Opernaya stsena Moskovskogo imperatorskogo teatra* [The Opera Stage of the Moscow Imperial Theatre] (Moscow, 1897)

V. Yakovlev: 'Moskovskaya opernaya stsena v sorokovïkh godakh' [The Moscow Opera Stage in the 1840s], *Vremennik russkogo teatral'nogo obshchestva* (Moscow, 1924), 91–141

O. Chayanova: *Teatr Maddoksa v Moskve 1776–1825* (Moscow, 1927)

Gosudarstvennaya opernaya studiya-teatr imeni narodnogo artista K. S. Stanislavskogo [The Stanislavsky State Opera Studio-Theatre] (Moscow, 1928)

M. Ippolitov-Ivanov: *50 let russkoy muzïki v moikh vospominaniyakh* [50 Years of Russian Music in my Reminiscences] (Moscow, 1934)

P. Markov: *V. I. Nemirovich-Danchenko i muzïkal'nïy teatr yego imeni* [Nemirovich-Danchenko and the Music Theatre named after Him] (Moscow, 1936)

Chaykovsky na moskovskoy stsene [Tchaikovsky on the Moscow Stage] (Moscow and Leningrad, 1940)

Gosudarstvennïy ordena Lenina akademicheskiy Bol'shoy teatr Soyuza SSR [The Bol'shoy Theatre of the USSR] (Moscow, 1947)

L. Polyakova: *Molodyozh' opernoy stsenï Bol'shogo teatra* [The Young Singers of the Bol'shoy Theatre] (Moscow, 1952)

A. Shaverdyan: *Bol'shoy teatr Soyuza SSR* [The Bol'shoy Theatre of the USSR] (Moscow, 1952)

Bol'shoy teatr: opera, balet (Moscow, 1958)

E. Groshyova: *Bol'shoy teatr v yego proshlom i nastoyashchem* [The Bol'shoy Theatre, Past and Present] (Moscow, 1962)

S. Stepanova: *Muzïkal'naya zhizn' Moskvï v pervïye godï posle Oktyabrya* [Musical Life in Moscow in the Early Years after October] (Moscow, 1972)

'K yubileyu Bol'shogo teatra Soyuza SSR' [On the Jubilee of the Bol'shoy Theatre of the USSR], *SovM* (1976), no.3 [special issue]

V. Borovsky: *Moskovskiy chastnïy opernïy teatr S. I. Zimina* [The Moscow Private Opera Theatre of Zimin] (Moscow, 1977)

B. Pokrovsky and Yu. Grigorovich: *The Bolshoi* (New York, 1979)

A. Skonechnaya: *Moskovskiy Parnas* [Moscow Parnassus] (Moscow, 1983)

V. Rossikhina: *Opernïy teatr S. Mamontova* [The Mamontov Opera Theatre] (Moscow, 1985)   RICHARD TARUSKIN

Mosè in Egitto ('Moses in Egypt'). *Azione tragico-sacra* in three acts by GIOACHINO ROSSINI to a libretto by ANDREA LEONE TOTTOLA after the Old Testament and Francesco Ringhieri's *L'Osiride*; Naples, Teatro S Carlo, 5 March 1818 (revised Act 3, March 1819).

Conceived as a biblical drama suitable for staging during Lent, *Mosè in Egitto* nonetheless grafts on to the Old Testament narrative a love story taken from Ringhieri's drama of 1760. Like Aida and Radames in Verdi's opera, Rossini's heroine, the young Jewish girl Elcia [Anaïs] (soprano), and the Pharaoh's son Osiride [Amenophis] (tenor) fall in love despite the conflict between their two peoples. In its original form, the Neapolitan version of 1818–19, *Mosè in Egitto* is one of the freshest and dramatically most effective of Rossini's *opere serie*, and there is a strong case for preferring this version to the somewhat bloated and more arbitrarily structured revision which Rossini prepared for the Paris Opéra in 1827 under the title MOÏSE ET PHARAON. For its first London performances (1822–3) the opera was given under the title *Pietro l'eremita*.

By deliberate design, *Mosè in Egitto* has no overture, yet the opening is as effective as any created by Rossini. A plague of darkness covers the land of Egypt. After three summoning chords, a semiquaver figure in C minor ushers in the chorus of distraught and bewildered Egyptians. Despairing for his country's plight, Faraone [Pharaoh] (bass) sends for Moses (bass) in an attempt to negotiate the freedom of the Israelites. Moses's brother Aronne [sometimes Elisero; Aaron] (tenor) shrewdly advises caution, recalling earlier acts of deception by Pharaoh, but Moses accepts Pharaoh's word. Moses's magnificent address to the Almighty 'Eterno! immenso! incomprensibil Dio!', accompanied by trumpets, horns and woodwind, recalls the 'Tuba mirum' from Mozart's *Requiem*, just as the brilliant C major transformation which follows – Moses restoring light to Egypt – suggests a debt to one of Rossini's favourite works, Haydn's *The Creation*. News that the Israelites are about to leave Egypt upsets Amenophis. More guileful than the gentle, radiant Anaïs whom he loves, Amenophis plots with the disaffected priest Mambre [Auphis] (tenor) to sow doubts among the Egyptian people who stand to lose much by the Israelites' departure. The first act ends with Pharaoh attempting to go back on his word, whereupon Moses invokes a plague of hail and fire on the land.

In Act 2 Pharaoh once again offers the Israelites their freedom. He also proposes an arranged marriage between his son and an Armenian princess. Amenophis now determines to abduct Anaïs but he is seen by Aaron. Informed of the lovers' intended flight, Moses enlists the help of Amaltea [Sinais] (soprano), wife of Pharaoh but sympathetic to the Jewish cause. In the duet 'Ah! Se puoi così lasciarmi', Amenophis proposes to Anaïs that they abandon the court and live together in the woods but they are discovered by Sinais and Aaron, a confrontation that generates the quartet 'Mi manca la voce'. Pharaoh again attempts to go back on his word but this time Moses threatens that the royal prince and all the first-born of the land will be felled by lightning. Pharaoh pronounces Amenophis co-ruler and demands that he pass sentence of death on the captive Moses. Anaïs reveals her relationship with Amenophis; her 'Porgi la destra amata' is a tender, expiatory aria. But Amenophis, less wise politically than his vacillating father, insolently condemns Moses who strikes Amenophis dead with a lightning shaft. It is a brilliant *coup de théâtre* and its aftermath, Pharaoh's lament for his dead son, draws from the orchestra an eerie *pizzicato strappato*, an effect worthy of Berlioz. Anaïs now becomes febrile, a nascent Lucia di Lammermoor. The breaking up of this superb scene is one of the major aberrations of the 1827 Paris revision.

Act 3 provides a coda to these traumatic events. Having travelled to the edge of the Red Sea, the Israelites can go no further. It is at this point that Moses leads them in the famous prayer, written by Rossini for the 1819 Naples revival of the opera, 'Dal tuo stellato soglio'. The prayer is answered; the waters divide at the touch of Moses's rod, and the pursuing Egyptians, led by Pharaoh and Auphis, are drowned as the waters close about them in the wake of the fleeing Israelites.

RICHARD OSBORNE

Mosel, Ignaz Franz von (*b* Vienna, 1 April 1772; *d* Vienna, 8 April 1844). Austrian composer and writer on music. He conducted the first musical festivals of the Gesellschaft der Musikfreunde in the imperial riding-school in Vienna (1812–16); from 1820 to 1829 he was vice-director of the two court theatres, and from 1829 principal *custos* of the Imperial Library. This work enabled him to write authoritatively about contemporary musical figures and ideas; among his books is *Über das Leben und die Werke des Anton Salieri* (Vienna, 1827). His own operas, however, were forgotten even in his lifetime. He made arrangements for string quartet of

Così and *Don Giovanni*, and of *Médée* and *Les deux journées*.

Die Feuerprobe (Spl, 1, J. Sonnleithner, after A. von Kotzebue), Vienna, Kärntnertor, 28 April 1811, *A-Wn*

Salem (lyrische Tragödie, 3, I. F. Castelli), Vienna, Kärntnertor, 5 March 1813, *Wn*

Cyrus und Astyages (heroische Oper, 3, M. von Collin, after P. Metastasio), Vienna, Kärntnertor, 13 June 1818, *Wn*, ov. (Vienna, 1818)

Music in: Fünf und zwei, 1813

Mosenthal, Salomon Hermann, Ritter von (*b* Kassel, 14 Jan 1821; *d* Vienna, 17 Feb 1877). German librettist and dramatist. In 1842 he broke off his studies in Karlsruhe and moved to Vienna, where he embarked on a career as a writer and dramatist. In 1849 he entered the Austrian civil service, later becoming an official in the Ministry of Culture and Education. In 1868 he became a Knight of the Order of Franz Joseph. He was also appointed to the Gesellschaft der Musikfreunde, where he was instrumental in establishing the drama department.

Mosenthal was the most able and prolific German librettist of his generation, and has with some justice been called 'the German Scribe'. If his plots are usually less complicated than Scribe's, he shared the latter's ability, as Hanslick pointed out, to design effective ensemble scenes and rousing finales and to write verse in which musicality met the composer halfway. After his first great success, the libretto for Nicolai's *Die lustigen Weiber von Windsor* (1849), Mosenthal went on to write for Flotow, Anton Rubinstein, Goldmark and Ignaz Brüll. Other librettists have also drawn on his writings (e.g. John Oxenford on *Der Sonnenwendhof* for Macfarren's *Helvellyn*, 1864; Jaroslav Kvapil on *Debora* for J. B. Foerster's opera, 1893). Hanslick aptly remarked that Mosenthal was 'the poetic foster-father of all hard-pressed composers'.

Die lustigen Weiber von Windsor (komische Oper), Nicolai, 1849; *Ein Abenteuer Carls des Zweiten* (komische Oper), J. Hoven [Johann Vesque von Püttlingen], 1850; *Der lustige Rath* (komische Oper), Hoven, 1852; *Lips Tulipan* (komische Oper), Hoven, inc.; *Albin*, Flotow, 1856 (rev. as Der Müller von Meran, 1860); *Die Kinder der Heide*, Rubinstein, 1861; *Die erste Falte* (komische Oper), Leschetizky, 1867; *Das Landhaus in Meudon* (komische Oper), M. Kässmayer, 1869

Judith, Doppler, 1870; *Die Folkunger* (grand op), E. Kretschmer, 1875; *Die Königin von Saba*, Goldmark, 1875; *Die Maccabäer*, Rubinstein, 1875; *Das goldene Kreuz* (komische Oper), Brüll, 1875; *Der Landfriede*, Brüll, 1877; *Der Ritterschlag* (komische Oper), H. Riedel, 1881; *Wiener Schule* (Spl), R. Weinwurm, 1881; *Antonius and Cleopatra* (grand op), Friedrich Ernst, Count of Sayn-Wittgenstein-Berleburg, 1883; *Fata Morgana* (lyrisch-choreographisches Drama), J. Hellmesberger, 1886; *Moses* (sacred op), Rubinstein, 1892

*

MGG (W. Pfannkuch)

E. Hanslick: *Musikalische Stationen* (Berlin, 1880), 316–18

ALFRED CLAYTON

Moser, Edda (Elisabeth) (*b* Berlin, 27 Oct 1938). Austrian soprano of German birth. She studied at the Berlin Conservatory and made her début at the Städtische Oper in 1962 as Kate Pinkerton, after which she sang for a year in the Würzburg Opera chorus; engagements followed at Hagen and Bielefeld. She has appeared regularly at Vienna, Salzburg (from 1970) and Hamburg; since her Metropolitan début in 1968 as Wellgunde (*Das Rheingold*) her roles there have included Donna Anna, the Queen of Night, Armida in *Rinaldo* and Liù. Equally at home in contemporary music, she sang the title role of Matthus's *Omphale* at Cologne (1979). Her repertory ranges from Konstanze and Aspasia (Mozart's *Mitridate*) to the three heroines of *Les contes d'Hoffmann*, Ariadne, and Marie (*Wozzeck*). Moser's voice is a powerful dramatic coloratura soprano, used with remarkable accuracy and musicianship.

HAROLD ROSENTHAL/R

Moser, Thomas (*b* Richmond, VA, 27 May 1945). American tenor. He studied in Richmond, Philadelphia and California, and made his début in 1975 at Graz. In 1979 he sang Mozart's Titus with the New York City Opera. He has sung in Vienna, Munich, Frankfurt, Geneva, Paris and Rome, at La Scala and Salzburg, where in 1984 he created the Tenor in Berio's *Un re in ascolto*. His repertory includes Don Ottavio, Tamino, Arbaces, Idomeneus, Titus, Lucius Sulla, Gluck's Pylades and Achilles, the title role of Schubert's *Fierrabras*, Florestan, Flamand (*Capriccio*), Paul (Korngold's *Die tote Stadt*) and Franz I (Krenek's *Karl V*). In 1990 he sang Florestan at La Scala. The possessor of a strong, flexible voice, he sings classical and modern music with equal facility.

ELIZABETH FORBES

Moses und Aron ('Moses and Aaron'). Opera in three acts by ARNOLD SCHOENBERG, to his own libretto (Act 3 not composed); *Der Tanz um das goldene Kalb* performed in concert, Darmstadt, 2 July 1951; Acts 1 and 2 performed in concert, Hamburg, Nordwestdeutscher Rundfunk, 12 March 1954; Acts 1 and 2 staged, Zürich, Stadttheater, 6 June 1957.

Moses	speaker (deep voice)
Aron [Aaron] *his brother*	tenor
A Young Girl	soprano
A Young Man	tenor
Another Man	baritone
A Priest	contralto
A Sick Woman	contralto
An Ephraimite	baritone
A Naked Youth	tenor
Another Man	speaker
Four Naked Virgins	sopranos, contraltos
Naked Men	tenors, basses
The Voice from the Burning Bush	semichorus
Twelve Tribal Chieftains	tenors, basses
Beggars	altos, basses
Old Men	tenors
Seventy Elders	basses and silent roles
Six Solo Voices (in the orchestra)	soprano, mezzo-soprano, contralto, tenor baritone, bass

Israelites, dancers, extras of all kinds

The Young Girl is also one of the four Naked Virgins; the Voice from the Burning Bush comprises three to six each of sopranos, trebles, contraltos, tenors, baritones and basses; about a third of the Seventy Elders are sung roles, the rest silent

Setting Egypt, at the time of the Israelites' bondage

From every point of view, whether musical, religious or philosophical, the opera is Schoenberg's most comprehensive masterpiece. The ideas that gave rise to it occupied him for many years before its composition, and their dramatic expression called forth music of immense power and diversity. It is in some respects a sequel to the unfinished oratorio *Die Jakobsleiter*

(1917), for Moses is required to fulfil the prophetic mission laid upon the chosen one in the earlier work, but it is also the product of his deep concern with questions of Jewish politics and religion. About 1922–3 he began planning two works in which conflicting aspects of spiritual revelation were to be symbolized by Moses and Aaron. In the first, the prose drama *Der biblische Weg* (1926–7), which deals with political aspirations in a modern setting, the downfall of the chief protagonist comes about through his attempt to combine the principles of both Moses and Aaron. The second, a cantata to be called *Moses am brennenden Dornbusch*, was expanded to a full-scale oratorio text entitled *Moses und Aron* (1927–8), and transformed into an opera libretto in 1930. The first two acts were composed between 1930 and 1932, but the third hung fire, and although to the end of his life Schoenberg frequently spoke of setting it, he never did so.

In consequence the question of performance did not arise till very late, when he finally accepted that he would probably not be able to complete the work. On 2 July 1951, only 11 days before Schoenberg's death, Scherchen conducted *Der Tanz um das goldene Kalb* at the Darmstadt summer school for new music. It had to be repeated immediately at the same concert, and Schoenberg was told of its great success by telegram. It was another three years before Nordwestdeutscher Rundfunk mounted the first complete performance of the opera, with Hans Herbert Fiedler and Helmut Krebs in the title roles, and Rosbaud conducting at short notice in place of Schmidt-Isserstedt. A recording was made and later issued commercially. In 1957 the opera was staged for the first time in Zürich, without the third act, with the same Moses and conductor but with Helmut Melchert as Aaron. A 1959 production under Scherchen in Berlin, which was seen later in various continental cities, tried the predictably unsuccessful experiment of speaking the third act against a recording of the music of Act 1 scene i. Since then it has become standard practice to omit Act 3 entirely.

ACT 1.i *The calling of Moses* For a brief but unforgettable moment before the curtain rises, *pianissimo* chords sung by Six Solo Voices in the orchestra suggest a spirituality beyond human involvement. Moses is then discovered addressing God in prayer: 'only, eternal, omnipresent, invisible and unimaginable God' (not 'inconceivable' – a common mistranslation). The Voice from the Burning Bush charges him with the task of prophet. It is represented by a six-part speaking chorus which cuts across and intermittently obscures the soloists in the orchestra, so that something of the spiritual quality of the opening music is already lost as God's commands are framed in words. Moses foresees the difficulty of proclaiming the nature of God to his chosen people, and pleads that he lacks eloquence. He is told that Aaron will be his mouthpiece, a dispensation that Schoenberg symbolizes by making Moses a speaking role and Aaron a tenor. At the end of the scene the Six Solo Voices, still dominated by the speaking chorus, sing of God's promise to his chosen people of a spiritual future.

1.ii *Moses meets Aaron in the wilderness* An agile, restless prelude introduces Aaron. Moses does not need to tell him what God demands of them: he already knows, and expresses his understanding of God's purpose in the soaring melodic lines that characterize his music and set the tone of the scene. Moses gives his own, more austere interpretations simultaneously. Although they occasionally seem to unite when echoes from the first scene are heard, Moses knows, for instance, that God cannot be swayed by human actions, whereas Aaron sees him as an arbiter who is susceptible to sacrifices. God is thereby diminished. As Schoenberg said in the words to his chorus op.27 no.2: 'You shall make no image. For an image confines, limits, grasps what should remain limitless and unimaginable. You must believe in the spirit directly, without emotion, selflessly.' Aaron is already setting up images.

1.iii and 1.iv *Moses and Aaron bring God's message to the people* A young girl and two men in a state of religious exaltation have seen Aaron on his way to meet Moses. They believe the new god may help to free the Israelites. Their volatile music infects without convincing the sceptical people. A Priest, the spokesman for law and order, resists it in the stiff accents that mark all his utterances. The people polarize into two groups and end by shouting at each other before preparing to resign themselves again to their servitude. Suddenly Moses and Aaron are seen approaching as though borne along by an unseen power. The people reunite in mounting excitement. Apart from the two brothers, who are God's emissaries, they are the only force in the drama, and a highly inconstant and unpredictable one. Minor characters emerge from among them from time to time to voice varying emotions or opinions, but they do not themselves influence the course of events.

Moses and Aaron arrive. The people promise the new god liberal sacrifices if he can offer them hope. When they are told to fall down and worship an all-powerful but invisible presence they pass from incomprehension to savage derision, each chorus displaying an extraordinarily versatile use of imitation and canon to intensify declamatory power. Moses accepts defeat and blames Aaron, who angrily snatches his staff and turns it into a serpent. This is the first of three miracles by means of which he convinces the people of God's power and their own weakness in allowing themselves to become demoralized in captivity. After each they celebrate their returning courage and new-found belief with a march-like chorus on a cantus firmus. Moses takes hardly any part in the proceedings, but if Aaron's success is based on images it is not entirely without divine sanction: the voices in the orchestra, silent since the first scene, give his actions some support, and their hymn announcing God's promise is taken up by Aaron and the people (to slightly less exalted words) before the final march.

INTERLUDE The Israelites are encamped in the wilderness. Moses has been absent on the mountain for 40 days receiving God's law. A small chorus, in darkness in front of the curtain, partially whispers its fear that he will not return.

ACT 2.i and ii *Aaron and the Seventy Elders before the mountain of revelation* The Priest and the Elders warn Aaron that without laws or intelligible gods the people are growing mutinous. Suddenly there is a sound of tumult and they pour on to the stage threatening to kill their leaders if they do not give them back their old gods. Aaron tells them to bring gold; he will give them the kind of god they long for. Their frustration turns at once to rejoicing.

2.iii and iv *The golden calf and the altar* As the people part to reveal the calf the mountain of revelation becomes visible in the distance. If the cult of the false

'Moses und Aron'
(Schoenberg): Act 2 scene
iii/iv (the golden calf and
the altar) from the first
staged performance at the
Stadttheater, Zürich, 6
June 1957

god leads to an orgy that cannot be presented according to the letter of the stage directions, the music rises to every demand. Offerings of all kinds are brought, including beasts that are slaughtered by butchers who perform a wild dance and throw raw meat to the people. A Sick Woman is cured by touching the calf, and some Old Men kill themselves as a sacrifice. An Ephraimite and Twelve Tribal Chieftains gallop up to pay homage to the calf; they kill a Young Man who denounces their idolatry. A lull ensues during which people exchange gifts till drunken brawling takes over. Four Naked Virgins are sacrificed. Wholesale destruction and suicide break out. Naked Men strip women and carry them off. Gradually the turmoil subsides. Some sleep, others drift away; finally all is still. A voice cries out that Moses is coming down from the mountain. He returns carrying the tables of the law. The golden calf vanishes at his command.

2.v *Moses and Aaron* To music filled with fleeting reminiscences of the first two scenes of the opera Aaron defends himself vigorously against his brother's anger and intransigence. His actions have been prompted, as ever, by Moses's unspoken thoughts. The people respond to the truth when it is presented to them in a comprehensible form; compromise can save them from loss of hope. Even the tables of the law can present only a part of the truth, and hence an image. At this Moses smashes the tables and prays to be relieved of his office. To the hymn of the chosen people, in which Aaron joins, and their march, the Israelites cross the back of the stage following a pillar of fire. Moses is left alone, despairing at their reconversion by yet another image. His idealism too has been no more than an image, for his thoughts cannot and may not be expressed: 'O word, word that I lack'.

*   *   *

The version of the third act libretto that Schoenberg seems in general to have favoured consists of a single brief scene. Aaron has been arrested. Although circumstances have not otherwise changed, Moses is allowed the victory in their debate. Aaron is freed, but falls dead. Moses proclaims a future in which the people will be at one with God. There is also an earlier, slightly longer, version which Schoenberg seems to have remembered as

late as 1950, and a later one (1935) ending with an extraordinary vision of the diaspora. He insisted that the opera was in no way concerned with the artist's role, but he certainly saw that role as prophetic. He once wrote that Beethoven, Bruckner and Mahler had not been permitted to write tenth symphonies because they would have revealed more of the ultimate truth than it was given to man to know. To express in music the unity with God achieved in Act 3 would have been to compose a tenth symphony. Yet it was Schoenberg's prophetic duty never to admit to the impossibility of doing so, or to cease to strive towards its attainment. The first two acts, however, provide a parable of his view of man's religious predicament which is both musically and dramatically complete. At some level he must have been aware of that, and indeed have planned it.
O. W. NEIGHBOUR

Moshinsky, Elijah (*b* Shanghai, 8 Jan 1946). Australian director. He was educated at Melbourne University and at Oxford, and started his career in opera when comparatively young. In 1975 he came to prominence at Covent Garden with a stripped-down, low-budget production of *Peter Grimes* which won enormous popular and critical success and indeed can fairly be said to have gained the opera itself a new lease of life. The production was subsequently recorded and taken across Europe and to the USA on various Royal Opera tours. Moshinsky, currently an associate producer at Covent Garden, has produced there *Lohengrin*, *The Rake's Progress*, *Macbeth*, *Samson et Dalila*, Handel's *Samson*, *Otello*, *Die Entführung* and Verdi's *Attila* and *Simon Boccanegra*. In addition he has worked for all the leading British opera companies (he took charge of the British première of Ligeti's *Le Grand Macabre* for ENO in 1982), at the Metropolitan, New York, and for Australian Opera; more recently he has undertaken the direction of many plays, in the theatre and on television. His operatic stagings are distinguished by their sharp intellectual focus and, at their best, by an undogmatic blend of styles that can shed fresh illumination on a score without going violently against its grain.
MAX LOPPERT

Moskowsky, Moritz. *See* MOSZKOWSKI, MORITZ.

Moskva (Russ.). MOSCOW.

Mosolov, Alexander Vasil'yevich (*b* Kiev, 29 July/11 Aug 1900; *d* Moscow 12 July 1973). Russian composer. He received some lessons from his mother, a singer, and studied at a Moscow high school until 1917. From 1918 to 1920 he fought in the civil war. He attended the Moscow Conservatory (1921–5) as a pupil of Glier, Myaskovsky (composition) and Prokofiev (piano), and in 1925 joined the Association for Contemporary Music. For most of his life Mosolov lived in Moscow. During his early career he occasionally worked as a concert pianist and played his own pieces, but his main activity was composition. At this stage he wrote intensively, his music being marked by drama, a nocturnal urban quality, parody and Musorgskyan intensity; his works were also heard in western Europe. In the late 1920s he wrote his first two operas. The chamber opera *Geroy* ('The Hero', composed 1928) is a tragic farce whose grotesque musical style is characterized by dissonant harmony and rhythmic ostinato. In *Plotina* ('The Dam', 1929–30) Mosolov turned to social themes; a monumental work with cinematographic episodes, the opera combines Russian melodies with a dissonant orchestral setting.

In the period 1927–31 Mosolov's work was severely criticized by the Russian Association of Proletarian Musicians; this caused a long interruption in his creative output and resulted in a change of style. His music became melodically and harmonically simpler, as is evident in the operas *Signal* (1941) and *Maskarad* ('Masquerade', ?1940–44). In the early 1930s he made many expeditions to the Turkmen and Kirghiz republics investigating folk music. He was arrested in 1938 and released a year later. During the 1950s and 60s he collected peasant songs in other regions.

Geroy [The Hero] op.28, 1928 (chamber op, 1, Mosolov), Moscow, Teatr-studiya Kompozitor, 21 Nov 1989
Plotina [The Dam], 1929–30 (5, Y. L. Zadïkhin), unperf., vs (Leningrad, n.d.)
Kreshcheniye Rusi [Baptism of Russia], 1930 (operetta, 3, H. Aduyev), unperf., Acts 2 and 3 lost
Signal, 1941 (1, O. Litovsky), unperf., extracts, vs (Moscow, 1942)
Maskarad [Masquerade], ?1940–44 (1, after M. Yu. Lermontov), unperf., extracts, vs (Moscow, 1944)

*

H. K. Meshko, ed.: *A. V. Mosolov: stat'i i vospominaniya* [Mosolov: Articles and Reminiscences] (Moscow, 1986) [incl. L. Rimsky: 'A. V. Mosolov: biografichesky ocherk' [Mosolov: Biographical Essay], 8–43; I. Barsova: 'Ranneye tvorchestvo Aleksandra Mosolova (dvadtsatïye godi)' [Mosolov's Early Works (of the 1920s)], 44–122; N. Aleksenko: 'O tvorchestve A. Mosolova tridtsatïkh-semidesyatïkh godov' [Mosolov's Works of the 1930s to 70s], 123–72]
I. Barsova: 'Das Frühschaffen Alexander Mossolows: die zwanziger Jahre', *Kunst und Literatur*, v (1987), 676–81 [Russ. orig. in Meshko 1986]
L. Rimsky: 'Aleksandr Mosolov: biographischer Abriss', ibid, 648–9 [Russ. orig. in Meshko 1986]   INNA BARSOVA

Mosonyi, Mihály [Brand, Michael] (*b* Bodogasszonyfalva, Hungary [now Frauenkirchen, Austria], 4 Sept 1815; *d* Pest, 31 Oct 1870). Hungarian composer. Born in western Hungary, near Austria, his mother tongue, both musically and linguistically, was German. About 1832, after spending a few years in Magyaróvár teaching himself the piano, he went to Pozsony (now Bratislava) to train as a teacher. There he studied the piano and music theory with Károly Turányi and from 1835 to 1842 he was music teacher to Count Péter Pejachevich's household in the Slavonian village of Rétfalu. He moved to Pest in 1842 and worked there as a music teacher, composer and writer until his death; his pupils included Ferenc Erkel's sons, Gyula and Sándor Erkel, Kornél Ábrányi, Sándor Bertha and Ödön de Mihalovich.

Until the middle of the 1850s Mosonyi was recognized as a composer of chamber, symphonic and church music. His first opera, *Kaiser Max auf der Martinswand*, was written in 1856–7 to a German libretto in the style of early German Romantics such as Weber and Marschner. Franz Liszt, who intended to give the work its première in Weimar, advised the composer to revise several dramatically rather unconvincing and ineffective passages. Instead of merely revising the work, however, Mosonyi changed his entire concept of composition and the opera was never staged. From 1859 onwards he composed exclusively in the national Hungarian style, and as an outward sign of this change in approach he adopted the Hungarian name of Mosonyi, after Moson, the region of his birth.

Mosonyi composed two operas to Hungarian librettos in the national style: *Szép Ilonka* ('Pretty Helen'), whose 1861 première was conducted by Ferenc Erkel, is a lyric opera showing the influence on the composer of popular folksong and *csárdás* music. Originally in five acts, it was shortened to four before its première, and published as such. *Álmos*, composed in 1862 and given its première in 1934, dramatizes a Hungarian myth involving a struggle between earthly and supernatural powers. Mosonyi applies Wagner's methods to Hungarian musical material and in his attempt to blend Hungarian and European elements shows himself to be a 19th-century precursor of Bartók and Kodály. He wrote extensively on Hungarian music, ceaselessly advocating the national works; his output includes the essay 'A dalmű s a magyar nemzeti színház' ('The Opera and the Hungarian National Theatre', 1860), and an essay on Erkel's opera *Bánk bán* (1861). Liszt composed a fantasy for piano on melodies from *Szép Ilonka* in 1867.

Kaiser Max auf der Martinswand, 1856–7 (3, E. Pasqué), unperf.
Szép Ilonka [Pretty Helen] (4, M. Fekete, after M. Vörösmarty), Pest, National, 19 Dec 1861, vs (Pest, 1862)
Álmos, 1862 (3, E. Szigligeti), Budapest, Magyar Királyi, 6 Dec 1934

*

B. Bartók: 'Two Unpublished Liszt Letters to Mosonyi', *MQ*, vii (1921), 520–6
J. Káldor: *Michael Mosonyi* (Dresden, 1936)
F. Bónis: *Mosonyi Mihály* (Budapest, 1960)
——: 'Die ungarischen Opern Mihály Mosonyis', *SM*, ii (1962), 139–87
——: 'Richard Wagner and his Composer Friend from Pest: Mihály Mosonyi' (Bayreuth, 1978) [festival programme booklet no.6], 21–7
——: 'Liszt- und Wagner-Briefe an Mosonyi in Kodálys wissenschaftlicher Bearbeitung', *Mf*, xxxix (1986), 317–34
——: 'Mosonyiana: a Mosonyi-kutatás új eredményei, 1' [Mosonyiana: New Results of Mosonyi Research, pt 1], *Magyar Zene*, xxx (1989), 155–87, 227–49, 335–77   FERENC BÓNIS

Moszkowski [Moskowsky], **Moritz** (*b* Breslau, 23 Aug 1854; *d* Paris, 4 March 1925). German composer of Polish descent. He studied first at Dresden, then in Berlin, where he settled and taught the piano for many years; he also toured extensively as a pianist. He retired to Paris in 1897 and was elected a member of the Berlin Academy in 1899.

Moszkowski's most popular works were the two books of piano duets, *Spanische Tänze* op.12. He also tried his hand at an opera on a Hispanic-Moorish subject, *Boabdil, der letzte Maurenkönig* (3, C. Wittkowsky), modelled on Meyerbeerian grand opera. The work was first performed in Berlin on 21 April 1892 and given in Prague and New York (in English) the following year, but it was not successful and soon disappeared from the stage. The ballet music, however, similar in style to the earlier *Spanische Tänze*, long remained in concert programmes.

*

A. C. Kalischer: 'Moritz Moszkowski als Opernkomponist', *Nord und Süd*, lxii (1892), 26–43

Motezuma ('Montezuma'). *Opera seria* in three acts by GIAN FRANCESCO DE MAJO to a libretto by VITTORIO AMEDEO CIGNA-SANTI, after Antonio de Solis's *La conquista del Messico*; Turin, Teatro Regio, Carnival 1765.

Cortez (tenor) arrives at the Mexican capital with his Spanish troops and Indian mercenaries led by Teutile (alto castrato). Montezuma (soprano castrato) welcomes the visitors, but they inform him that in order to ensure a peaceful relationship he must renounce his 'false' gods. When Montezuma refuses, the Spaniards capture the palace and take him into custody. Learning that Montezuma's nephew has usurped the throne, Cortez releases his prisoner, who is killed by his own people. Cortez uses the wrongful death of Montezuma as an excuse to destroy the temples and priests, claiming Mexico for Spain. But he soon learns that Montezuma's queen, Guacozinga (soprano), has already set fire to the city to ensure that the treasures Cortez seeks will be destroyed in the flames and ruins.

One of several operas based on an exotic view of the New World, the libretto embellishes a traditional Italian 'aria' opera with the lavish spectacle typical of Turinese opera during the period. The opening set represents a night scene with a temple with smoking altar and a two-headed dragon shooting tongues of fire from the top of the imperial palace. Indians, Mexicans and Spaniards engage in battle pantomimes. Act 3 opens in a seraglio of wild animals and birds and closes with the stage full of smoke. The ballets between acts also follow the Mexican theme and serve to unify the work. Montezuma (first sung by Giuseppe Aprile) had one monologue in obbligato recitative, and Guacozinga (Catterina Pilaia) had two; they sang a duet at the end of Act 2. Majo provided two marches but no programmatic music for the battle pantomimes.

MARITA P. McCLYMONDS

Mother of Us All, The. Opera in two acts by VIRGIL THOMSON to a libretto by GERTRUDE STEIN and a scenario by Maurice Grosser; New York, Columbia University, Brander Matthews Hall, 7 May 1947.

Despite the fame of the first opera on which they collaborated, Virgil Thomson and Gertrude Stein let nearly two decades elapse between *Four Saints in Three Acts* and *The Mother of Us All*. Ruefully, Thomson later explained, 'I am sorry now that I did not write an opera with her every year. It had not occurred to me that both of us would not always be living.' They got together in October 1945 to begin a second project. Thomson, always fascinated by the inflections of American

Susan B. Anthony	dramatic soprano
Gertrude Stein	soprano
Anne *Susan's constant companion*	contralto
Virgil Thomson	baritone
Daniel Webster	bass
Jo the Loiterer	tenor
Chris the Citizen	baritone
Indiana Elliot	contralto
Angel More	light lyric soprano
John Adams	romantic tenor
Thaddeus Stevens	tenor
Constance Fletcher	high mezzo-soprano
Lillian Russell	lyric soprano
Jenny Reefer	mezzo-soprano
Ulysses S. Grant	bass-baritone

Smaller parts, often taken by chorus members or dancers: Henrietta M., Henry B., Anthony Comstock, Gloster Heming, Isabel Wentworth, Anna Hope, Herman Atlan, Donald Gallup, T. T. and A. A. (page boys or postillions; dancers), Andrew Johnson, Negro Woman, Negro Man, Indiana Elliot's Brother

Setting The United States of America 'in the 19th century without too much precision as to decade' (*c* 1870); epilogue 'some years later' in the Halls of Congress, Washington, DC

vernacular speech, felt that the language of American political oratory could form the basis of an opera, and proposed one on political life in the 19th century. Stein, as a feminist, suggested as the central figure Susan B. Anthony (1820–1906), who pioneered political rights for American women. Despite Thomson's fame as chief music critic of the *New York Herald-Tribune* (or because of it), the score was not accepted by either of New York's major opera companies. The première took place at Columbia University, conducted by Otto Luening with Dorothy Dow as Susan B. Anthony. Since then, the score has been widely hailed as the greatest and most enduring of American operas. Although it has not entered the repertory of major opera houses in the United States or Europe, it has been frequently performed by American regional and community companies, especially in the solo-piano and chamber-ensemble reductions made by Thomson. A recording, based on a Santa Fe Opera production and conducted by Raymond Leppard with the miscast mezzo-soprano Mignon Dunn in the leading role, was released on New World Records in 1977.

ACT 1.i *A room in Susan B. Anthony's house, showing the home life of Susan and Anne* Gertrude Stein and Virgil Thomson stand downstage as narrators.

1.ii *A tent political meeting* The politicians, led by Daniel Webster, enter flamboyantly, followed by Jo and Chris, who mock their pomposity. Susan debates with Webster; their words are drawn largely from actual speeches. Jo teases Angel More about a mouse.

1.iii *Village green in front of Susan's house* The scene depicts Andrew Johnson and Thaddeus Stevens as quarrelling politicians, Constance Fletcher and John Adams as tentative lovers, the other characters as sympathetic observers and Jo and Chris as 'satirical philosophers'.

1.iv *Same place* Susan meditates on the difficulties of her mission, seeing, in a dream, potential allies abandon her; she then tries to explain her goals to Jo and Chris.

1.v   Same place: the marriage of Jo and Indiana Elliot   Susan ponders on the solitude of women even when married, yet justifies the institution to Jenny Reefer. As the procession approaches Daniel Webster, who is officiating, there is discussion about the wedding ring, and another love scene between John Adams and Constance Fletcher. Webster interrupts the ceremony to make 'a sentimental address' to Angel More. Susan calls everyone to order. Indiana's brother tries to prevent the wedding. Susan lectures him and everyone on the meaning of marriage for women. All pursue their own (mostly amorous) interests, forgetting the wedding at hand. Finally Webster completes the ceremony, Jo and Indiana kiss and Susan predicts that all their children, women and men, will have the vote.

ACT 2.i   *Susan's drawing-room*   Susan, doing housework, resists the importuning of all that she make a speech. Jo complains that Indiana will not take his name. Susan agrees to deliver the speech.

2.ii   Same place   Susan has been so persuasive that the politicians have inserted the word 'male' into a Constitutional amendment, but Susan remains optimistic. Lillian Russell, a convert to the cause, and others enter. John Adams insists Russell is not as beautiful as Constance Fletcher. Webster reproaches Susan for fixating on unimportant details like women's suffrage. Indiana agrees to change her name to Loiterer if Jo changes his to Elliot. Everyone thanks Susan for her political leadership.

2.iii   Epilogue, some years later, as a statue of Susan is unveiled in the Halls of Congress   Susan enters as a ghost. Virgil Thomson conducts Anne to the speakers' platform; Lillian Russell and General Grant are to dedicate the statue. Everyone becomes tipsy and boisterous. Thomson unveils the statue, to reveal Susan herself, who sings about her life as the women place wreaths around her pedestal. All slowly depart, Jenny Reefer in tears, Anne last. As the stage darkens, Susan continues her song, 'Where is where. In my long life of effort and strife, dear life, life is strife ... But do we want what we have got, has it not gone, what made it live, has it not gone because now it is had ... my long life, my long life', ending on a final consoling chord, 'pp possibile'. Gertrude Stein did not live to see the première, or to hear this, one of the most moving concluding scenes in all opera.

*   *   *

Thomson called *The Mother of Us All* a 'pageant', and as such it abjures linear narration in favour of a kaleidoscopic array of Americana, juxtaposing historical personages from different eras with fictional characters. The dramaturgical method is similar to that of *Four Saints in Three Acts*, with seemingly disconnected phrases and with two characters (Gertrude Stein and Virgil Thomson) acting as 'compère' and 'commère'. But the actual plot is clearer in *The Mother of Us All*, and Thomson's all-American musical idiom – as before a mostly diatonic quilt of marches, waltzes and hymns from his Southern Baptist Missouri heritage – suits the American theme perfectly. In this opera, Thomson's idiom and Stein's greater willingness to reach out to the general public are in surer synchronization, combining to make an opera of truly sophisticated refinement and popular appeal. As Thomson himself said, 'It's foolproof work'.

JOHN ROCKWELL

Motsart i Sal'yeri. Opera by N. A. Rimsky-Korsakov; *see* MOZART AND SALIERI.

Motte, Diether de la (*b* Bonn, 30 March 1928). German composer. He studied at Detmold, and attended classes given by Leibowitz, Krenek, Fortner and Messiaen at the Darmstadt summer courses. He then worked mainly as a teacher, becoming professor of composition and theory at the Hamburg Musikhochschule in 1964, and later settling in Vienna. Following his first opera, *Der Aufsichtsrat*, composed in 1969 (1, R. Schneider; 1970, Hanover), numerous 'visible music' compositions led him to a new conception of the operatic genre in *So oder so*, 1972–4 (5 szenische Variationen, de la Motte; 1975, Hamburg), in which pantomime has an important part. Never attached to a group or school, he has been decisively influenced by 'singing' music – the gamelan and Gregorian chant, Schubert and Berg.

MONIKA LICHTENFELD

Motteux, Peter Anthony (*b* Rouen, 25 Feb 1663; *d* London, 18 Feb 1718). English writer, playwright and opera pasticheur of French birth. A Huguenot refugee, Motteux came to London in 1685 and was naturalized a year later. His literary career began with the publication of *The Gentleman's Journal* (1692–4), a short-lived arts magazine which he edited and partly wrote (with unacknowledged borrowings from the *Mercure de France*). In this periodical Motteux offered the classic *apologia* for SEMI-OPERA: 'Other Nations bestow the name of Opera only on such Plays whereof every word is sung. But experience hath taught us that our English genius will not rellish that perpetual Singing.' Besides plays and miscellaneous entertainments, Motteux wrote the text of the masque *The Loves of Mars & Venus* (1696), actually a miniature comic opera set by John Eccles and Godfrey Finger, and adapted THE ISLAND PRINCESS (1699), the most successful of semi-operas after Purcell.

In spite of his early efforts for the English stage, Motteux was deeply involved in the establishment of Italian opera in London between 1705 and 1709. He probably made the English translation of Tommaso Stanzani's *Arsinoe*, which Thomas Clayton fashioned into the first italianate opera produced in England (1705); Motteux may also have helped with the English singing translation of the London version of Giovanni Bononcini's highly successful *Camilla* (1706). He certainly wrote the libretto of the pasticcio *Thomyris* (1707) which, though damned by the anonymous author of *A Critical Discourse on Opera's and Musick in England* (1709), is a skilful patchwork of English and Italian verse, most of which was added to the previously composed music. The castrato Valentino Urbani paid Motteux the huge sum of 80 guineas for translating Cardinal Pietro Ottoboni's *Love's Triumph* (1708) into English and fitting new words to diverse arias. The early London pasticcios are not musically distinguished, but Motteux's skill in concocting plausible plots from parodied texts was considerable, notwithstanding the occasional mismatch of words and music, of which Joseph Addison complained in *The Spectator* (21 March 1711): 'the finest notes in the air fell upon the most insignificant words in the sentence. I have known the word *and* pursued through the whole gamut, have been entertained with many a melodious *the*'. With the arrival of Handel, Motteux retired from the theatre and became a merchant; he died in a brothel after 'trying a very odd Experiment'.

R. N. Cunningham: *Peter Anthony Motteux* (Oxford, 1933)

R. Fiske: *English Theatre Music in the Eighteenth Century* (London, 1973, 2/1986)

Vice Chamberlain Coke's Theatrical Papers 1706–1715, ed. J. Milhous and R. D. Hume (Carbondale, IL, 1982)

C. A. Price and R. D. Hume: Introduction to P. A. Motteux: *The Island Princess*, MLE, cii (1985)

L. Lindgren: 'Venice, Vivaldi, Vico and Opera in London, 1705–17: Venetian Ingredients in English Pasticci', *Nuovi studi vivaldiani*, ed. A. Fanna and G. Morelli (Florence, 1988), 633–66

CURTIS PRICE

Mottl, Felix (Josef) (*b* Unter-St Veit, nr Vienna, 24 Aug 1856; *d* Munich, 2 July 1911). Austrian conductor, arranger and composer. He entered the Löwenburg Seminary in Vienna as a boy soprano in 1866, and from 1870 studied theory with Bruckner and conducting with the elder Joseph Hellmesberger, as well as composition, at the Vienna Conservatory. He attended many performances of Wagner's operas and, fuelled by Bruckner's enthusiasm for Wagner, was active as choral director of the Wiener Akademie Wagnerverein. In 1876 he was recruited by Hans Richter to assist in the first Bayreuth season, joining the élite 'Nibelungen-Kanzlei', which included Anton Seidl and Herman Zumpe. Mottl's experience of Wagner's interpretations and rehearsals formed an important musical influence, described in his diaries (published in the *Wagner-Forschungen* as 'Bayreuther Erinnerungen'), and he became one of Bayreuth's most dedicated Wagner exponents, conducting the Bayreuth premières of *Tristan* (1886), *Tannhäuser* (1891), *Lohengrin* (1894) and *Der fliegende Holländer* (1901), as well as productions of *Parsifal*, *Die Meistersinger* and the *Ring*.

For a short time in 1878 Mottl was music director at the Ringtheater in Vienna, and for a few months in 1880 he worked with Arthur Nikisch at the Leipzig Opera. From 1881 to 1903 he was music director of the court opera in Karlsruhe, where his exceptional performances of Wagner's dramatic works from *Rienzi* onwards, notably the *Ring* and *Tristan*, earned Karlsruhe the title 'kleine Bayreuth'. He also championed contemporary opera as well as the works of Berlioz; he conducted *Béatrice et Bénédict* (1888, with his own recitatives) and the first complete production of *Les Troyens* (6 and 7 December 1890). Mottl's reorchestration and subsequent performance (1884) of Peter Cornelius's *Der Barbier von Bagdad* established the previously unsuccessful work as a masterpiece of German comic opera. Among the notable German premières he conducted were *Gwendoline* (1889) and *Le roi malgré lui* (1890), both by Chabrier, with whom he enjoyed a close friendship, Handel's *Acis and Galatea* (1888), Grétry's *Raoul Barbe-bleue* (1890), Cherubini's *L'hôtellerie portugaise* (1893) and three of Schubert's stage works – J. N. Fuchs's version of *Alfonso und Estrella* (1881), the melodrama *Die Zauberharfe* (1898) and the world première of *Fierrabras* (1897).

Mottl's own stage works include the three-act opera *Agnes Bernauer*, performed with Liszt's support at Weimar (1880); a 'Festoper', *Eberstein* (1881); *Fürst und Sänger* (1893) and a one-act Festspiel *Ein Kyffhäusertraum* (1896); an opera *Rama* is also attributed to him. His arrangements include vocal scores of Wagner's operas.

Mottl enjoyed a high reputation abroad. Of his Wagner concert on 25 April 1894 in London, Bernard Shaw wrote that 'Mottl is a conductor of the very first rank with immense physical energy and personal influence'. He conducted the *Ring* at Covent Garden in 1898 and 1900, and several operas at the Metropolitan in 1903–4, including *Carmen*, *Siegfried* and new productions of *Die Walküre* and *Die Zauberflöte*. He assisted the conductor Alfred Hertz in the successful American stage première of *Parsifal* (1903), but did not conduct, because of objections by the Wagner family to any production outside Bayreuth.

In 1903 Mottl was appointed Generalmusikdirektor of the Munich Opera, and director of the Akademie der Tonkunst. He again achieved new heights of operatic excellence, especially in the Munich Festival, and performed his own versions of Bellini's *Norma*, Donizetti's *L'elisir d'amore*, Gluck's *Alceste* and Debussy's *Pelléas et Mélisande*. His second marriage was to the soprano Zdenka Fassbender, who sang Isolde in the fateful performance of *Tristan* (his 'musikalische Jugendliebe') during which he collapsed, and died a few days later.

Agnes Bernauer (3, Mottl, after A. Böttger, O. Ludwig and F. Hebbel), Weimar, 28 March 1880

Eberstein (Festoper, 3, G. Pulitz), Karlsruhe, Oct 1881

Fürst und Sänger (1, J. V. Widmann), Karlsruhe, 25 May 1893

Rama, 1894, unperf.

Ein Kyffhäusertraum (Festspiel, 1, A. Herzog), Karlsruhe, 19 Jan 1896

Incomplete: Alfred, 1869; König Heke, 1869; Ekkehard, 1870 (romantic op, 3, Scheffel)

F. Mottl: 'Über eine Stelle im *Fliegenden Holländer*', *Bayreuther Blätter*, x (1887), 331

E. Istel: 'Felix Mottl', *Die Musik*, x (1910–11), 118–19

W. Krienitz: 'Felix Mottls Tagebuchaufzeichnungen aus den Jahren 1873–1876', *Neue Wagner-Forschungen*, i, ed. O. Strobel (Karlsruhe, 1943), 167–234

G. Samazeuilh: 'Felix Mottl', *Musiciens de mon temps: chroniques et souvenirs* (Paris, 1947), 383–5

R. Delage, ed.: 'Correspondance inédite entre Emmanuel Chabrier et Félix Mottl', *RdM*, xlix (1963), 61–107

H. Schonberg: *The Great Conductors* (New York, 1967), 184–8

MALCOLM MILLER

Motto aria (Ger. *Devisenarie*). Term used for the type of aria, during the Baroque period, that begins with a brief and usually emphatic phrase from the singer (the 'motto'), preceding the opening orchestral ritornello. Normally the same phrase will follow the ritornello, beginning the aria proper. The device is used so as to avoid, in a strong dramatic situation, the tautology of a long ritornello before the singer expresses himself or herself. Examples include Eduige's aria 'La farò' from Act 1 of Handel's *Rodelinda* and Oberto's 'Barbara!' from Act 3 of *Alcina*.

Moulinghen [Moulinghem, Moulingzen], **Jean-Baptiste** (*b* Haarlem; *d* Paris, 1812). Dutch composer. It is not known whether he or his brother Louis-Charles Moulinghen wrote the symphonies performed at the Concert Spirituel in 1768 and 1769, but judging by the advertisements for their publication which appeared in 1770 it is likely that they were by the elder brother, Jean-Baptiste, 'of the company of the Comédie-Italienne'. Jean-Baptiste was indeed a cellist in the orchestra of the Comédie-Italienne in 1759 and 1760, and was then among the first violins from 1766 until his retirement in 1809; he also played in the orchestra of the Concert Spirituel until 1790. He composed no operas as such, but arranged the vaudevilles of several *opéras comiques* performed during the 1770s. The first three of these had been produced earlier in the Théâtres de la Foire: *Acajou* in 1744, *La servante justifiée* in 1740 and *Les nymphes de Diane* in 1747. The success of such 'vaudeville operas' indicates the persistence of a taste for this genre long after the establishment of 'pièces à ariettes'. The score of *Acajou* is a valuable illustration of the way in which vaudevilles were performed by the Comédie-Italienne.

Acajou (oc en prose mêlée de vaudevilles, 3, C.-S. Favart, after Duclos), Paris, Comédie-Italienne (Bourgogne), 19 July 1773 (Paris, 1774)
La servante justifiée (oc, 1, Favart and B.-C. Fagan, after J. de La Fontaine), Fontainebleau, 9 Oct 1773
Les nymphes de Diane (Favart, C.-F. Panard and C.-F. Boizard de Pontau, after La Fontaine: *Les lunettes*), Paris, Comédie-Italienne (Bourgogne), 11 Aug 1774
La bonne femme, ou Le phénix (parodie mêlée de vaudevilles, 2, P.-Y. Barré, J.-B.-D. Desprès, P.-A.-A. de Piis and L.-P.-P. Resnier), Paris, Comédie-Italienne (Bourgogne), 7 July 1776 [parody of C. W. Gluck: Alceste]

*
FétisB; StiegerO
E. Gregoir: *Biographie des artistes-musiciens néerlandais des XVIIe et XVIIIe siècles* (Brussels, 1864)
C. D. Brenner: *A Bibliographical List of Plays in the French Language, 1700–1789* (Berkeley, 1947, 2/1979)
B. Brook: *La symphonie française dans la seconde moitié du XVIIIe siècle* (Paris, 1962), ii, 500–03
MICHEL NOIRAY

Moulinghen [Moulinghem, Moulingzen], **Louis-Charles** (*b* Haarlem; *fl* 1768–85). Dutch composer, younger brother of Jean-Baptiste Moulinghen. Only two biographical facts are known about Louis-Charles: he published a *Sinfonia périodique* in Paris in 1768 and he had settled in Paris by 1785, the publication date of the *Tablettes de renommée des musiciens*. According to Fétis he learnt the violin in Amsterdam and then entered the service of Prince Charles de Lorraine in Brussels as *maître de chapelle*. The titles of his operas come from *Les spectacles de Paris* of 1790.

Horisphesme, ou Les bergers (comédie pastorale mêlée d'ariettes et ornée de danses, 2, Montignac), ?Nantes, ?1771
Les amants rivaux (Montignac), Roubaix, 1772
Les talents à la mode, 1772
Le vieillard amoureux (1), 1772
Clarisse, ou Les ruses de l'amour (intermède, 1, Montignac), Bordeaux, 1773
Le mari sylphe, Nantes, 1773
Le mariage malheureux, 1777
Undated: Les deux contrats; Sylvain, collab. Legrand and Davesne

For bibliography see MOULINGHEN, JEAN-BAPTISTE.
MICHEL NOIRAY

Mountain [née Wilkinson], **Rosemond** [Rosoman] (*b* London, *c*1768; *d* Hammersmith, 3 July 1841). English soprano and actress. She sang in a children's company trained by Charles Dibdin and then worked in the provinces before her Covent Garden début in 1786. She was a sweet singer and a handsome woman who was shown to advantage in 'vocal parts of a genteel and sentimental nature' (Oxberry). She married the violinist John Mountain in 1787 and they often worked together. From 1798 to 1800 she studied with Rauzzini while working in Bath and Bristol. On her return to London the *Monthly Mirror* described her as 'clearly the best singer now upon the boards'. When Nancy Storace retired in 1808 Mountain took over her roles; she herself left the stage in 1815.

*
BDA; DNB (L. M. Middleton); LS
'Mrs Mountain', *Thespian Magazine*, i (1792), 139

C. H. Wilson: *The Myrtle and Vine* (London, 1802)
T. Gilliland: *The Dramatic Mirror*, ii (London, 1808)
W. Oxberry: 'Memoir of Mrs Mountain', *Dramatic Biography*, iii (1825), 271–9
W. Robson: *The Old Play-Goer* (London, 1846)
OLIVE BALDWIN, THELMA WILSON

Mountain Sylph, The. Grand opera in two acts by JOHN BARNETT to a libretto by Thomas James Thackeray after Jean Charles Emmanuel Nodier's short story *Trilby, ou Le lutin d'Argail* and Adolphe Nourrit and Jean Schneitzhöffer's ballet *La Sylphide*; London, English Opera House, 25 August 1834.

The opera is set in the Western Isles of Scotland. Eolia (soprano), the mountain sylph, discovers Donald (tenor) sleeping and falls in love with him; she casts a spell on him so that he will return her love. Donald is betrothed to Jessie (soprano), but his rival, the simple-minded Christie (tenor), seeks the aid of Hela, the Wizard of the Glen (baritone), whom Donald has insulted. In revenge Hela gives Donald a magic scarf, claiming that it will bind Eolia to him forever, but immediately the sylphs wrap it around her she finds herself in the power of Astaroth, King of the Underworld (baritone). Protected by Etheria, the Sylphid Queen (soprano), Donald enters the Underworld and rescues Eolia. Jessie, deprived of Donald's love, agrees to marry Christie, and Donald and Eolia (who has forfeited her immortality) are united.

The Mountain Sylph was written for S. J. Arnold's reopened English Opera House and, along with Loder's *Nourjahad*, established English Romantic opera as an authentic genre. The spoken dialogue is minimal. Its importance lies not in the fact of its being largely through-composed (it relies as heavily on spoken dialogue as any Singspiel, and the recitatives are, indeed, quite conventional): what makes it a real opera is its cumulative dramatic effect. The characters have little human reality and no subtlety, yet Barnett's richly scored music succeeds in creating strong emotion and dramatic tension. Inevitably Weber was his chief inspiration: the fairy choruses recall *Oberon* as much as the invocation scene suggests the Wolf's Glen scene in *Der Freischütz*. But Barnett was the only English composer at the time who could master this new and difficult idiom. He abandoned most traditional forms: there are few strophic songs or rondos, no binary or sonata form arias; he created forms according to the demands of the various scenes, though he usually concluded each scene with a conventional cabaletta or stretta. There is rather too much dependence on the diminished 7th and other chromatic chords, but the themes used to evoke the supernatural, many of which recur as motifs at various points in the opera, are distinctly original in style. In the love music the disarming warmth and passion can still move the listener, despite the absurdity of the verses and all the scorn that has been lavished upon sentimental melodrama (the story was satirized in IOLANTHE). The opera's last known revival was at the GSM on 5 July 1906.
NIGEL BURTON, NICHOLAS TEMPERLEY

Mount Edgcumbe, Richard, 2nd Earl [Edgcumbe, Richard] (*b* Plymouth, 13 Sept 1764; *d* Richmond, Surrey, 26 Sept 1839). English critic and amateur composer. A perceptive and sometimes acerbic observer of Italian opera in late 18th-century London, Mount Edgcumbe, like Burney, had the advantage of continental travel to add credibility to his assessments of music and singers. Unlike Burney, he considered Italian opera in decadent decline and, surprisingly from our point of view, looked back to the 1770s and 80s, to works of Sacchini and Anfossi, as a golden age tarnished by the modern works of Mozart and Rossini. His opera criticism was published anonymously in his memoirs, *Musical Reminiscences of an Old Amateur Chiefly Respecting Italian Opera in England for Fifty Years, from 1773 to 1823* (London, 1824), which went through four editions in ten years. Mount Edgcumbe's most useful comments concern the famous singers he had heard. He championed the last great castratos, particularly Gasparo Pacchierotti and Luigi Marchesi, and wrote vivid descriptions of the voices of Gertrud Elisabeth Mara and Brigida Giorgi Banti. He was an unabashed musical snob: when the opera company had to move temporarily to the unglamorous Theatre Royal in the Haymarket after the Pantheon fire in 1792, he cancelled his subscription. Mount Edgcumbe composed an Italian opera, *Zenobia*, for the King's Theatre in 1800, but it sank without trace after one performance.

CURTIS PRICE

Mouret, Jean-Joseph (*b* Avignon, 11 April 1682; *d* Charenton, 20 [not 22] Dec 1738). French composer. The son of an amateur violinist, he may have been trained at the choir school of Notre Dame des Doms in Avignon. The Parfaict brothers indicate that he was employed in Paris as *maître de musique* by the Maréchal de Noailles from 1704, but most later sources follow Titon du Tillet, who believed that Mouret established himself in Paris in 1707. Titon calls attention to Mouret's personal charm and excellent singing voice, assets that enabled him to move with ease in 'the best company'. At the time of his marriage in 1711, Mouret was *ordinaire de la musique* for the Duke of Maine, Louis XIV's son by the Marquise de Montespan, at Sceaux. Later he became *surintendant de la musique* there. Along with Bernier, Marchand, Bourgeois, Colin de Blamont and Courbois, he composed the music for the Duchess of Maine's celebrated 'Grandes Nuits' (1714–15).

Mouret's first opera, *Les fêtes, ou Le triomphe de Thalie*, was given at the Opéra on 19 August 1714 and, according to Titon, had a 'prodigious success'. In the same year, he was appointed director of the orchestra of the Opéra, a post he held until 1718. By 1716 he was composing *divertissements* for Dancourt's comedies at the Comédie-Française; the following year he was appointed composer-director at the Comédie-Italienne (Nouveau Théâtre Italien), where he was to compose some 140 *divertissements* over the next 20 years. Further appointments followed at court and with the Concert Spirituel. After the death of the Duke of Maine in 1736 Mouret was no longer retained at Sceaux, and in 1737 he lost his post at the Comédie-Italienne. He was thus left without employment and dependent on the kindness of such friends as the Prince of Carignan who gave him a pension of 1000 livres. The first signs of his insanity were noted in 1737; by virtue of a royal order on 14 April 1738 he was sent to the Fathers of Charity at Charenton where he died eight months later.

Mouret shared in the innovating spirit that characterized the best in French stage music between Lully and Rameau. His *Le mariage de Ragonde* (1714, Sceaux) is a true lyric comedy composed more than 30 years before Rameau's *Platée*, while for its elevation of comedy over tragedy his *opéra-ballet Les fêtes de Thalie*

caused a minor *succès de scandale* when first staged at the Opéra in 1714. Mouret's melodic gifts, which earned him the posthumous title of 'musicien des grâces', may be seen to better advantage in *Les fêtes de Thalie*, *Les amours de Ragonde* (a second version of *Le mariage de Ragonde* performed in 1742 at the Opéra) and the *divertissements* for the Comédie-Italienne than in his more pretentious, and less successful, *tragédies lyriques* (*Ariane*, 1717; *Pirithous*, 1723) and *ballets-héroïques* (*Les amours des dieux*, 1727; *Le triomphe des sens*, 1732; *Les grâces*, 1735). There is simplicity and naturalness in the music of the first group, which avoids triteness through asymmetrical phrase groupings and rhythmic contrasts. There is also keen observation of the entire spectrum of French stage music resulting from a highly developed sense of musical gesture; in the *divertissement Le procès des théâtres* (1718), for example, Mouret characterizes musically the quarrelsome principals in the battle for supremacy in the Parisian theatrical world. The musical fragments assigned to each 'theatre' are but six or eight bars long and elide imperceptibly with one another without compromising their identities.

See also AMOURS DE RAGONDE, LES and FÊTES DE THALIE, LES.

first performed in Paris unless otherwise stated; all printed works published there

Les fêtes, ou Le triomphe de Thalie (opéra-ballet, prol., 3 entrées: 'La fille', 'La veuve', 'La femme', J. de La Font), Opéra, 19 Aug 1714, reduced score (1714, 2/1720 as Les fêtes de Thalie; 'La critique des fêtes de Thalie' added 9 Oct 1714 (1714), 'La veuve coquette' substituted for 'La veuve', 12 March 1715 (1715), 'La Provençale' added 17 Sept 1722 (1722); *F-Pn*, *Po*

Le mariage de Ragonde et de Colin, ou La veillée de village (comédie lyrique, 3, P. Néricault-Destouches), Sceaux, Dec 1714; rev. as Les amours de Ragonde, ou La soirée de village, Opéra, 30 Jan 1742, reduced score (1742); vocal and inst pts *Po*

Ariane (tragédie lyrique, prol., 5, P.-C. Roy and F.-J. de Lagrange-Chancel), Opéra, 6 April 1717, reduced score (1717)

Pirithous (tragédie lyrique, prol., 5, J.-L.-I. de La Serre), Opéra, 26 Jan 1723, reduced score (1723)

Les amours des dieux (ballet-héroïque, prol., 4 entrées: 'Neptune et Amymone', 'Jupiter et Niob', 'Apollon et Coronis', 'Ariane et Bacchus', L. Fuzelier), Opéra, 16 Sept 1727, reduced score (1727)

Le triomphe des sens (ballet-héroïque, prol., 5 entrées: 'L'odorat', 'Le boucher', 'La vue' (added 8 July), 'Le goût' (added 14 Aug), Roy), Opéra, 29 May 1732, reduced score (1732)

Les grâces (ballet-héroïque, prol., 3 entrées: 'La grâce ingénue', 'La grâce mélancolique', 'La grâce enjouée', Roy), Opéra, 5 May 1735, reduced score (1735)

Le temple de Gnide, ou Le prix de la beauté (divertissement, 1, Bellis and Roy), Opéra, 31 Nov 1741, reduced score (1742)

Recueil des divertissements du Nouveau Théâtre Italien, augmenté de toutes les symphonies, accompagnemens, airs de violons et de flûtes, de hautbois, de musettes, airs italiens et de plusieurs divertissements qui n'ont jamais paru (Paris, *c*1737) [divertissements for 140 plays, contents in Viollier 1950]

Divertissements for comedies performed at the Comédie-Française, music in *Pcf*

*

ES (R. Viollier)

C. Parfaict and F. Parfaict: *Histoire de l'Académie royale de musique depuis son établissement jusqu' à présent* (MS, 1741, *F-Pn*)

E. Titon du Tillet: *Le Parnasse françois* [suppl.] (Paris, 1743)

J.-B. Durey de Noinville: *Histoire du théâtre de l'Académie royale de musique* (Paris, 1757)

L.-F. Beffara: *Dictionnaire de l'Académie royale de musique* (MS, 1783–4, *F-Po*)

A. Pougin: 'Mouret', *Revue et gazette musicale de Paris*, xxvi (1859), 412–19; xxvii (1860), 18–19, 127–8

T. de Lajarte: *Bibliothèque musicale du théâtre de l'Opéra: catalogue historique, chronologique, anecdotique* (Paris, 1878)

L. de La Laurencie: 'La musique française de Lulli à Gluck', *EMDC*, I/iii (1921), 1385–6

P.-M. Masson: 'Le ballet héroïque', *ReM*, ix/7–11 (1928), 132–54

R. Viollier: 'Un opéra-ballet au XVIIIe siècle', *RdM*, xvi (1935), 78–86

C. le Gras: 'Jean-Joseph Mouret, "le musicien des grâces"', *Mémoires de l'Académie de Vaucluse* (Avignon, 1938), 5–20

R. Viollier: 'Les divertissements de Jean-Joseph Mouret pour la "Comédie Italienne" à Paris', *RdM*, xx (1939), 65–71

——: *Jean-Joseph Mouret: le musicien des grâces* (Paris, 1950)

M. Barthélémy: 'Les divertissements de J.-J. Mouret pour les comédies de Dancourt', *RBM*, vii (1953), 47–51

J. Robert: 'Comédiens, musiciens et opéras à Avignon', *Revue de la société d'histoire du théâtre*, xvii (1965), 275–93

J. R. Anthony: *French Baroque Music from Beaujoyeulx to Rameau* (London, 1973, 2/1978; Fr. trans., 1981)

G. le Cost: 'L'expression des affects chez Jean-Joseph Mouret: le "Triomphe des Sens" comme étude de cas', *Jean-Joseph Mouret et le théâtre de son temps* (Aix-en-Provence, 1983), 87–130

R. Fajon: 'Jean-Joseph Mouret, musicien de Marivaux', ibid, 59–86

J. de La Gorce: 'Documents inédits relatifs à la vie de Jean-Joseph Mouret', ibid, 9–37
JAMES R. ANTHONY

Mourning Becomes Electra. Opera in three acts by MARVIN DAVID LEVY to a libretto by Henry Butler after EUGENE O'NEILL's trilogy of plays; New York, Metropolitan Opera, 17 March 1967.

Mourning Becomes Electra was commissioned by the Metropolitan Opera. Eugene O'Neill's trilogy, based loosely on the *Oresteia* of AESCHYLUS, takes some six hours to perform; Butler, the Metropolitan's stage director, had to do some heroic cutting to bring it down to opera-libretto dimensions. The titles of the individual plays, *Homecoming*, *The Hunted* and *The Haunted*, became those of the opera's three acts.

The action takes place in an unidentified New England seaport town in 1865 and the year following. Outside the family home, Christine Mannon (Clytemnestra; soprano) learns from her daughter Lavinia (Electra; soprano) that the men of the family are due to return soon from the Civil War. Lavinia is both jealous and censorious of her mother's relationship with the sea-captain Adam Brant (Aegisthus; baritone), and neither of the lovers can succeed in making her sympathetic to their cause. Feigning resignation, Christine requests a last private moment with Adam, during which he gives her a bottle of poison to be used against her husband Ezra (Agamemnon; bass), who now makes his appearance. That night (Act 1 scene ii) Christine deliberately confesses her affair to Ezra in order to bring on an attack of angina. Instead of his medicine, she gives him the poison, and he dies calling for Lavinia.

The following day (Act 2 scene i) Lavinia's brother Orin (Orestes; baritone) returns home. She draws him aside and reveals her suspicions about the poison. The two follow Christine to a rendezvous with Adam (Act 2 scene ii) aboard his docked ship and hear her describe the murder to him. As Adam sees Christine ashore, Orin and Lavinia enter his cabin; when he returns Orin stabs him in the back. When, outside the house next morning (Act 2 scene iii), Orin tells Christine what he has done, she rushes into the house and shoots herself.

A year later (Act 3 scene i) the brother and sister return from a long voyage, much changed. Lavinia, freed from her obsessive fixation on Adam and Christine, is at last able to return the affection of her suitor Peter Niles (baritone), who has hovered in the background since Act 1 scene i. Orin, however, is consumed by guilt, and is unnaturally possessive of Lavinia. He attempts to give Peter's sister Helen (soprano) a letter in which he confesses the whole sordid family history, but Lavinia intercepts it; Orin locks himself in his study and shoots himself. Lavinia too now loses her reason (Act 3

scene ii). Confusing Peter with Adam Brant she sends him away and shuts herself in the house, to live down the family curse in solitude.

Levy has provided this grim tale with an appropriately expressionist setting, although the opera is not, as has often been declared, atonal. Melodically this 'eased' expressionism takes the form of long, conjunct vocal lines that avoid angularity or extremes of range. The use of leitmotifs resembles that of Berg.
ANDREW STILLER

Moyne, Jean-Baptiste. *See* LEMOYNE, JEAN-BAPTISTE.

Moyzes, Alexander (*b* Klášter pod Znievom, Slovakia, 4 Sept 1906; *d* Bratislava, 20 Nov 1984). Slovak composer. He studied with Novák at the Prague Conservatory, then moved to Bratislava, where he taught at the Academy of Music and Drama. His opera-oratorio *Svätopluk* was written for and broadcast (1935) by Bratislava Radio; the text consists of fragments from Ján Hollý's epic of the same name (written in hexameters) put together by Ľudo Zúbek and the composer. The musical language draws on impressionist and expressionist models (particularly in melody, harmony and instrumentation); in rhythm and form the work is neo-classical, while occasional modal progressions impart an archaic flavour. Its stage version, entitled *Udatný kráľ* ('The Deposed King'), was first performed at the Slovak National Opera in Bratislava on 4 November 1967. Moyzes wrote his own text for this, transforming Hollý's hexameters into free accentual verse. The music grows out of several motivic cells, and uses an extended tonality.

I. Vajda: *Slovenská opera* (Bratislava, 1988), 30–31, 126–9, 232–3
IGOR VAJDA

Mozart, (Johann Chrysostom) Wolfgang Amadeus (*b* Salzburg, 27 Jan 1756; *d* Vienna, 5 Dec 1791). Austrian composer. He was the son of Leopold Mozart, Chamber Composer and Deputy Kapellmeister to the Prince-Archbishop of Salzburg. Mozart is the first composer whose operas have never been out of the repertory. His comprehensive mastery of three genres, *opera seria*, *opera buffa* and Singspiel, is unmatched in operatic history; and although he wrote no operas in French, *opéra comique* is represented in translation by *Bastien und Bastienne* and *tragédie lyrique* by his first masterpiece, *Idomeneo*. This achievement is founded on his genius for assimilation and in the circumstances of his life and early experience of operatic genres.

1. Operatic career. 2. Style.

1. OPERATIC CAREER. Although Mozart's formative experiences in opera lay away from home, the musical life of Salzburg included serenata performances (operatic though not fully staged), plays with music at the University and Gymnasium and *opera buffa* and spoken drama from visiting troupes. Mozart composed three operatic works for Salzburg, as well as his only incidental music to a play.

First, however, Mozart's travels with his family to Vienna, France, England and the Netherlands (1763–6) displayed him as a keyboard prodigy and composer of instrumental music. He quickly became acquainted with opera, which in Austria and Germany was mostly Italian. In Paris the unreformed Opéra, bastion of a tradition particularly disliked by Leopold Mozart, contrasted with the more modern *opéra comique* dominated by Duni, Philidor and Monsigny. In England Mozart met J. C. Bach and imitated his instrumental works; Bach was also at the centre of London's almost entirely Italian operatic culture.

Mozart's early experience of Italian opera is documented in Daines Barrington's report (published 1769) to the Royal Society in London: at nine, the prodigy could already, in improvised recitatives and arias, ape operatic styles suited to anger and tenderness. In London and The Hague Mozart composed his first known arias, including his first settings of Metastasio (K21/19*c* and 23).

Mozart made his dramatic début in Salzburg (1767) with the first act of an oratorio, *Die Schuldigkeit des ersten Gebotes* (K35), and began his lifelong practice of inserting numbers into other composers' operas. His first complete dramatic work was the Latin intermezzo *Apollo et Hyacinthus*. From September 1767 the Mozarts spent 15 months based in Vienna, where they heard Gluck's *Alceste*; its profound impact emerged later, in *Lucio Silla* and especially *Idomeneo* and *Don Giovanni*. Mozart's first real operas, written in Vienna, mark the principal division of his output, between operas in Italian with recitatives and operas in German with spoken dialogue. The *opera buffa La finta semplice*, written with imperial encouragement, was not performed until the return to Salzburg. The Singspiel *Bastien und Bastienne* is said to have been given privately in 1768 at the Vienna home of Dr Franz Anton Mesmer, whose 'magnetism therapy' is pilloried in *Così fan tutte*.

Whereas most of his contemporaries specialized, sometimes writing over a hundred operas, Mozart's mature output is punctuated by gaps which resulted from circumstances rather than inclination. Four serious Italian operas followed between 1770 and 1773, three produced in Milan, then under Austrian rule. The Mozarts were welcomed by the plenipotentiary, Count Firmian, and obtained a commission for Carnival 1771. They travelled widely in Italy; Mozart saw serious operas by Hasse, Guglielmi, Piccinni and, in Naples, Jommelli's late opera *Armida*: 'beautiful, but much too elaborate and old-fashioned for the theatre' (letter of 5 June 1770). The blow is directed at the structure, and particularly the 'pompous' ballets, rather than the music; Mozart had to conform to similar tastes in Milan.

In October he complained that his fingers were aching from writing recitatives. Composition of arias waited until he was in Milan and could discuss them with the singers: referring to the primo uomo Leopold wrote that 'Wolfgang refuses to do the work twice over and prefers to wait for his arrival so as to fit the costume to his figure' (letter of 24 November 1770). Several arias had to be revised, a circumstance that does not seem to have recurred. Yet with *Mitridate re di Ponto* Mozart achieved mastery of *opera seria* in a single stride, a fact recognized by the immediate commission for another *opera seria* two years later.

In the meantime, he gained experience with an oratorio, *La Betulia liberata* (K118/74*c*), intended for Padua, and a serenata, *Ascanio in Alba*, for a royal marriage in Milan. The return to Salzburg in December 1771 just preceded the death of Archbishop Schrattenbach, whose successor, Archbishop Colloredo, was far less generous in allowing leave of absence. But, probably after helping to inaugurate his reign with

another serenata, *Il sogno di Scipione* (originally written for Schrattenbach's anniversary), Mozart obtained leave to present *Lucio Silla* in Milan (Carnival 1773), scoring a triumph on which he was never allowed to capitalize.

Over a year later Count Seeau, theatre Intendant to the Elector of Bavaria, asked Mozart to write another opera, *La finta giardiniera*, performed in Munich early in 1775. It occupies a special place in Mozart's output as his first opera to enter the German repertory, adapted as a Singspiel, and the first whose musical and dramatic qualities have encouraged more than an occasional modern revival. Almost immediately afterwards Mozart set Metastasio's *Il re pastore* as a serenata for a royal visit to Salzburg.

Mozart wrote no more Italian dramatic music (concert arias apart) for five years, the major hiatus of his career. During his traumatic stay in Paris (1777–8) the *opéra comique* repertory provided themes for instrumental variations and Mozart experienced the regenerated repertory of the Opéra; but the 'Querelle des Gluckistes et Piccinnistes' preoccupied the public and the management, and his only theatrical music was a ballet, *Les petits riens*. Yet the period between *Il re pastore* and *Idomeneo* was not entirely wasted for him as a dramatic composer. Affected by his love for Aloysia Weber in Mannheim, he poured out substantial concert arias (their texts usually taken from operas), and he worked out dramatic ideas in his first great concertos. The experience of the Mannheim and Paris orchestras was seminal in the development of the orchestral aspect of his later operas.

Mozart's interest turned to German opera on hearing of Joseph II's establishment of the National Singspiel in Vienna. In 1778 he became interested in melodrama, words spoken to instrumental music: of Benda's *Medea* he wrote 'nothing has ever surprised me so much, for I had always imagined that such a piece would be quite ineffective! … I think that most operatic recitatives should be treated in this way – and only sung occasionally, when the words *can be perfectly expressed by the music*' (letter of 12 November 1778). He may have composed a *Semiramis* (1778) in this form; if so, it is lost. Melodrama is used in the incidental music to Gebler's *Thamos, König in Ägypten* (K345/366*a*), written between 1773 and 1779 when Schikaneder's troupe was in Salzburg, and in his next opera, the unfinished *Zaide*. The neglect of melodrama in later German works may reflect the need to conform to Viennese expectations, or may represent disenchantment with the medium.

Carl Theodor, formerly of Mannheim, became Elector of Bavaria in 1778 and brought singers and his unrivalled orchestra to Munich. Count Seeau may have been induced to commission *Idomeneo* (1781) by musicians who knew Mozart, including the elderly tenor Raaff. It is Mozart's first undoubted masterpiece and marks a watershed in his career. After this close approach to Gluck's development of *tragédie lyrique*, he could never again write so dramatically for chorus, so pictorially for instruments, or provide such an extended ballet; the solo arias and ensembles banish display for its own sake, and have enhanced dramatic impact because they arise directly from the dramatic situations.

The composition of *Idomeneo* gave rise to a fascinating correspondence; this and subsequent letters about *Die Entführung* give us the clearest indication of Mozart's aesthetics, as well as demonstrating his acute dramatic intelligence. Although documentary evidence is lacking (for instance with the Da Ponte operas and

Die Zauberflöte), it seems legitimate to assume that Mozart subsequently took a guiding role in the dramatic construction of his librettos: after *Die Entführung*, only *La clemenza di Tito* was not written specially for him, and even there Metastasio's text was 'turned into a proper opera' by Caterino Mazzolà.

Mozart's absence from Salzburg tested his employer's patience to the limit. Colloredo summoned him to Vienna, where he was happy to go and still happier to stay when dismissed (June 1781). His remaining operas were composed for the capital of the Empire or for the neighbouring capital of Bohemia, Prague. Mozart was quick to make friends, among them Gottlieb Stephanie the younger, director of the National Singspiel. Instead of accepting *Zaide*, however, he offered Mozart a similar libretto, *Die Entführung aus dem Serail*; Mozart's setting was performed two weeks before his marriage, on 4 August 1782, to Constanze Weber. It became popular throughout Germany. Had there been royalties on performances, Mozart's subsequent financial problems would hardly have arisen.

The replacement of the National Singspiel by an Italian troupe was popular with the Viennese, but it led to the last serious break in Mozart's operatic output. He was eager to contribute to the Italian repertory, mostly *opera buffa*, and studied it avidly; he also got to know the performers and was impressed by several of them, notably the *buffo* Francesco Benucci and Nancy Storace, later to be the first Figaro and Susanna.

Paisiello was the most performed opera composer in Vienna during the mid-1780s. The repertory included his *Il barbiere di Siviglia* (1783), and Haydn's *La fedeltà premiata* (1784), an example of the sentimental genre of *La finta giardiniera*. More persistent rivals, whose output was concentrated in Vienna, were Salieri and Martín y Soler, both of whom worked with Lorenzo da Ponte. Martín's operas were particularly successful, but he and Mozart were on amicable terms. Salieri's intrigues against Mozart have probably been exaggerated, but he wielded considerable influence, and Mozart's perception of the situation is clear (letter of 7 May 1783):

[Da Ponte] has promised to write an entirely new libretto for me. But who knows whether he will be able to keep his word – or will want to? For, as you are aware, these Italian gentlemen are very civil to your face. Enough: we know them! If he is in league with Salieri, I shall never get anything out of him.

Mozart honed his skills by working on librettos without commission. He read more than a hundred without finding anything suitable, and in the same letter asks his father to persuade Varesco to write a comedy:

The most essential thing is that on the whole the story should be really *comic*: and, if possible, he ought to introduce *two equally good female parts*, one of these to be *seria*, the other *mezzo carattere* … The third female *character* may be entirely *buffa*, and so may all the male ones.

The prescription for three contrasted female roles is fulfilled in varying degrees in the Da Ponte operas, especially *Don Giovanni*.

Varesco began *L'oca del Cairo*, and Mozart drafted several numbers before abandoning it. A little later he worked on *Lo sposo deluso*, which also remains fragmentary. In 1783 he wrote three arias for Anfossi's *Il curioso indiscreto* (K418–20), two in the two-tempo rondò form which he later put to significant use in his own operas; in 1785 he added two lively comic ensembles to Bianchi's *La villanella rapita* (K479–80). In 1786 *Der Schauspieldirektor* was performed at Schönbrunn alongside Salieri's *Prima la musica*: Mozart's work was buffoonery about German theatre folk, Salieri's a sophisticated consideration of the relation of music and poetry. The contrast might have been galling, but Mozart soon demonstrated his mastery of the Italian genre in *Le nozze di Figaro*.

According to Da Ponte, Mozart himself suggested basing a libretto on Beaumarchais' play, and he again composed much of it before obtaining permission to stage it. Despite an initially good reception *Figaro* was not an unqualified success except in Prague; in Vienna it was soon outstripped by Martín's *Una cosa rara*. *Figaro*, however, marks the last watershed; from now on Mozart was a recognized opera composer and in his remaining five years he produced four major works. The longest interval, between *Don Giovanni* (first performed in Prague in October 1787) and *Così fan tutte* (Vienna, January 1790) was bridged by the Vienna production of the former (1788) and the 1789 revival of *Figaro*, both requiring new music. Adapted as a Singspiel, *Don Giovanni* soon joined *Die Entführung* in the German repertory.

Figaro has lost nothing of its freshness in over 200 years. The preparation for this epiphany in operatic history included, of course, Mozart's previous operas, but also, typically and perhaps more importantly, local conditions including the presence of a large group of expert singers, and Vienna's recent experience of *opera buffa*: Paisiello's *Il barbiere di Siviglia*, a model for 'really *comic*' opera with a fast-moving, realistic plot and precise characterization, and Martín's operas, which display the virtues of a popular, song-like idiom. Memories of *opéra comique*, until recently part of the Viennese operatic scene, may have contributed to the masterly action ensembles, while the long finales are the culmination of an *opera buffa* tradition associated with Goldoni's Venice. Yet Mozart's own genius is needed to account for the radical nature of the transition from the uncompromisingly extended musical developments of *Die Entführung*; from now on, the symbiotic harmony between music and drama is complete.

The last phase of Mozart's career marks a climax in three genres, each transformed by his dramatic insight. *Opera buffa* reached an unsurpassable peak in the three Da Ponte operas, *Figaro*, *Don Giovanni* and *Così fan tutte*. Their length and intensity, although there is no shortage of humour or even farce, make them unique in the literature of 18th-century comedy, and it is no exaggeration to call them the foundation of the modern repertory. Mozart wanted to show his strength in *opera seria* and, contrary to an opinion often expressed, the commission for *La clemenza di Tito* (for the Prague coronation of Leopold II) was far from unwelcome; it enabled him to produce a concise drama which had remarkable success over the next 20 years. His last opera in order of composition, *La clemenza* was performed before *Die Zauberflöte*. Here Mozart transformed the Singspiel into an allegory of his own quasi-religious commitment to Freemasonry, while retaining the popular element appropriate to his only opera since *Bastien und Bastienne* not composed for a court theatre. The loss opera suffered by his early death is incalculable; nevertheless the level and range of his achievement is rivalled only by specialists in the genre such as Verdi and Wagner.

2. STYLE. Mozart's stylistic development in opera parallels that of his instrumental music, but appears less

consistent. Until *Il re pastore* his aims and methods were representative of his time; thereafter he composed individual masterpieces whose qualities have affected operatic composition ever since they became widely known. While the excellence in relation to prevailing standards of all but his earliest operas should be emphasized, the following observations refer mainly to his mature work.

In *opera seria* and Singspiel Mozart's masterpieces stand in direct opposition. The musical riches of *Idomeneo* contrast with the austerity of *La clemenza di Tito*, as does the profuse invention of *Die Entführung*, redolent of court opera, with the demotic *Zauberflöte*. The earlier pair displays the exuberance of invention found in his instrumental works up to about 1785, the Vienna piano concertos and wind serenades, the quartets dedicated to Haydn. The first Da Ponte operas, *Figaro* and *Don Giovanni*, have the riper mastery of the 1786 concertos, the last four symphonies, the string quintets; the style of *Così fan tutte* moves towards the operas of 1791 which share the effortless lucidity, the virtual concealment of what is nevertheless real complexity, of the late instrumental works (the 'Prussian' quartets, the last concertos).

While insisting on the primacy of music in opera, Mozart never lost sight of its dramatic context. He intended his arias to suit both the available voices and the dramatic situation, and fed the appetites and expectations of his audiences rather than defying them; if his greatest works were not an immediate triumph, it was not because their forms or dramatic content were unacceptable, but because of the elaboration of his fundamentally conventional musical language. Mozart explained his priorities in a letter to Leopold (26 September 1781) concerning 'Solche hergelaufne Laffen' (*Die Entführung*):

Osmin's rage is rendered comical by the use of the Turkish music. In working out the aria I have ... allowed Fischer's beautiful deep notes to glow. The passage 'Drum beim Barte des Propheten' is indeed in the same tempo, but with quick notes; and as Osmin's rage gradually increases, there comes (just when the aria seems to be at an end) the Allegro assai, which is in a totally different metre and in a different key; this is bound to be very effective. For just as a man in such a towering rage oversteps all the bounds of order, moderation and propriety and completely forgets himself, so must the music too forget itself. But since passions, whether violent or not, must never be expressed to the point of exciting disgust, and as music, even in the most terrible situations, must never offend the ear, but must please the listener, or in other words must never cease to be *music*, so I have not chosen a key foreign to F major (in which the aria is written) but one related to it – not the nearest, D minor, but the more remote A minor.

Osmin is comical, but represents a threat to the sympathetic characters. To convey this Mozart takes advantage of instrumental possibilities and the capabilities of his singer, and acknowledges the right of expressive exigencies to overrule musical decorum. The resulting blend of serious purpose and comedy is one of his most characteristic dramatic achievements.

Perhaps unwittingly, Mozart followed Gluck's precepts on overtures, even in comedies; as early as *La finta semplice* he joined the last movement to the first scene, and from *Idomeneo* he abandoned the three-movement sinfonia, although a slow central section interrupts the Allegro in *Die Entführung* and three later overtures have slow introductions. Except in the two operas of 1786, the overtures go beyond mere appropriateness to incorporate important musical ideas from the opera. Instrumental expression reaches its zenith in orchestral

recitative (and the melodramas of *Zaide*), enhancing its expressive penetration by harmonic daring and increased use of wind instruments. Conventionally reserved for soliloquy (a notable example is Donna Elvira's 'In quali eccessi' in the Vienna version of *Don Giovanni*), obbligato recitative was used for long dialogues in *Idomeneo* (the sacrifice scene) and *Così*, where it also gives rise to measured music in a recitative context (arioso). Mozart was also imaginative in his use of *recitativo semplice*. Occasionally, but not so often as to become predictable, the bass line has a pertinent shape; a descending scale over a diminished 4th is characteristic of *Idomeneo* (ex.1a: Ilia contrasts the woes of Troy with the gods' defence of Greece; ex.1b: Idamante sings of Arbace's approach bearing evil tidings). Even ostensibly

Ex. 1

(a) Act 1 scene ii

ILIA

Non te - mer. Di - fe - sa di Mi - ner - va è la Gre - cia

['Fear not. Defended by Minerva and Greece']

(b) Act 1 scenes iv-v

IDAMANTE

Ar - ba - ce vie - ne Ma qual pian-to ch'an - nun - zia?

['Arbace approaches. But what complaint does he announce?']

conventional declamation sometimes makes use of shapes related to formal numbers. Before 'Là ci darem' Don Giovanni makes repeated allusions to the pitch-contour A–C♯–F♯ (preceding recitative, bars 1–4, extending F♯–B by bar 7; bar 10; bars 14–16), ending with a direct anticipation of the melody (ex.2); similarly, B♭–D–B♭ in recitative immediately precedes 'Fin ch'an dal vino' (the main motif, *b♭–b♭–b♭–d'–b♭*

Ex.2 Mozart: *Don Giovanni*, Act 1

GIOVANNI

Quel ca - si - net - to è mi - o, so - li sa - re - mo

GIOVANNI

Là ci da - rem la ma - no

['You see that little house there? Well that is my house']

['You'll lay your hand in mine']

repeated, appears at 'voglio divertir'; on *Figaro*, see Drummond 1980, pp.201–22).

Mozart's choice of musical forms was dictated by dramatic requirements, ensuring that the musical numbers emerge from the inner drama of character or the outer drama of action. His ensembles and finales are usually assumed to be more original or significant than the arias, but even in the late comedies solo expression is of paramount importance. Mozart always found a place for arias which explore a character's mental state and contribute to dramatic understanding by changing our perception of the personality; such arias occur even in his fastest-moving comedies, although beside comparable scenes in *opera seria* they gain intensity through their relative brevity and the absence of display.

Writing for a Viennese *buffo* troupe, or for Schikaneder's company, Mozart not only eschewed cadenzas but developed a precision and conciseness of expression which may be gauged by comparing *La finta giardiniera* with *Figaro*, or Belmonte's love song in Eb (*Die Entführung*: 'Ich baue ganz') with Tamino's (*Die Zauberflöte*: 'Dies bildnis'). Yet he can still indulge the voice: Susanna's 'Deh vieni, non tardar' (*Figaro*), Zerlina's arias (*Don Giovanni*) or in a tragic context Pamina's 'Ach ich fühl's' (*Die Zauberflöte*) penetrate to the core of feeling partly because they are so grateful to sing. Virtuosity – the grotesque depths of Osmin, the fireworks of the Queen of Night, the fioriture of Konstanze, Fiordiligi or Sextus – also plays a part in characterization. Shorter arias may be highly dramatic without recourse to structural modulation; often they only briefly visit the dominant before returning to the tonic, a tonal 'flatness' also found in the late chamber music. Mozart prolongs pieces by obsessive repetition (Figaro: 'Aprite un po'), alluring melodic extension (Zerlina: 'Vedrai, carino'), or sensitive play on expectations by cadential postponement, which can be comical and satirical (Don Alfonso's 'Vorrei dir', Dorabella's 'Smanie implacabili'), or project the most intense pathos ('Ach, ich fühl's').

Most arias are composed in close correspondence with the lyrical verse forms (usually two strophes of three or four lines each) supplied by the librettists; but they also take forms peculiar to a situation. In 'Aprite un po' quegl'occhi', Da Ponte provided Figaro with 26 lines. Mozart worked through two quatrains in tonic and dominant sections (to bar 48); then, assisted by changes in verse metre, he ran through the remaining 18 lines in a mere 21 bars (from bar 49), largely on tonic harmony. The first quatrain returns on dominant harmony (bar 71); the incomplete repetition of the remaining text is punctuated by the nagging 'il resto nol

dico'. The whole cadential period (57–70) is repeated exactly, with a mocking coda (85–102). Such a form resists classification, but is unlikely to be experienced as unorthodox, since it combines musical solidity with dramatic directness.

Mozart used all available forms, selecting the simplest (such as the sectional rondo) for single states of mind (Zaide's 'Trostlos schlutzet Philomele'; *Die Entführung*: Blonde's 'Welche Wonne, welche Lust'). Ternary form, descended from the da capo, is appropriate to the controlled fury of Donna Anna's 'Or sai chi l'onore' (*Don Giovanni*). 'Cavatina' implies an aria that is short (*Figaro*: Countess Almaviva's 'Porgi amor') but not always simple in feeling (*Così*: Ferrando's 'Tradito, schernito'). Binary arias, in design resembling sonata form and equivalent to the first section of a full da capo aria, represent a complex of feelings unresolved at the end; this type, prevalent in *Idomeneo* (including Ilia's 'Padre, germani, addio!'), appears also in comedies (*Così*: 'Smanie implacabile'). Additional text may be accommodated in a middle section, sometimes a complete contrast (Titus's 'Se 'all'impero'), sometimes a modulatory section corresponding to a sonata development (Idomeneus's 'Fuor del mar').

Complex feelings which modify in the course of the aria give rise to additive structures. The essential design of the majestic 'rondò' (*Figaro*: Countess Almaviva's 'Dove sono'; *Così*: Fiordiligi's 'Per pietà'; *La clemenza*: Vitellia's 'Non più di fiori') lies in the alternation of tonic areas and episodes, a system which spans both tempos although the mood of the Allegro supersedes that of the preceding slow movement. Less conventionally, Fiordiligi ('Come scoglio') accelerates to a third tempo, her single-mindedness paradoxically demanding such extreme expression; musical coherence resides largely in continuity of key. A similar plan is used in Sextus's 'Parto, parto' (*La clemenza*). Leporello, how-

Autograph score of 'Le nozze di Figaro' (1786): part of the Act 2 trio, showing the upper line (extended to c″) assigned initially to the Countess; as elsewhere in the opera, the upper line may eventually have been taken by the Susanna (Nancy Storace). A German text is written into the score.

ever, proceeds from fast (numerical) to slow (taxonomic) cataloguing of Giovanni's conquests.

Such additive forms commonly occur in ensembles where the final tempo, normally faster, corresponds to the concluding phase in the action which brings the voices together. A simple device of musical form in 'Ah guarda, sorella' (*Così*), this procedure marks Zerlina's complete acquiescence to Don Giovanni in 'Là ci darem la mano'. The slower sections usually contrast tonic and dominant areas, but (unlike the rondò) the faster music is a single section entirely in the tonic, requiring no thematic reprise. The unusual fast-slow pattern is used for the first finale in *La clemenza* (action: despair), and turns from humour to numinous beauty in the quintet (no.5) of *Die Zauberflöte*. Such progressive schemes reach a pitch of complexity in the chain finales, which both in action and musical duration (often over 600 bars) bulk hugely in the comedies.

Mozart's welding of action to musical continuity is usually most appreciated in ensembles and finales, but the action aria can also develop a situation (*Figaro*: 'Non più andrai', 'Venite, inginocchiatevi'; *Don Giovanni*: 'Ho capito', 'Metà di voi quà vadano'). Mozart certainly exploited the necessities of musical language for dramatic ends, but where character and feelings rather than action are concerned careful analysis is required to define what is really happening – or to resist definition, since Mozart's own position frequently appears ambiguous, and allows interpretative scope to the singers and director.

In the often-cited first duet of *Le nozze di Figaro* (ex.3), a marked opposition appears between Figaro's theme and Susanna's gracious melody; he is counting, she admiring her hat. Figaro moves towards the dominant, sufficiently established by the perfect cadence (bar 30) for the music to continue there; instead Susanna enters in the tonic. Figaro resumes counting, and articulates the dominant more decisively (underlining its dominant, bars 45–6). Susanna develops this tonal situation but forgets her melody, resorting to pettish repetition over the pedal A. Figaro sings her tune in the dominant (bar 50), but her insistent 'guarda un pò' (bars 55, 57) suggests that his attention is elsewhere. Susanna leads the music back to the tonic for restatements of her melody, which Figaro now dutifully doubles. These musical processes are usually held to demonstrate Susanna's greater force of personality and intelligence. Yet, conventionally, strength is considered to reside in the establishment of the dominant, here accomplished only by Figaro: Susanna's music twice relaxes to the tonic. Is Figaro, after all, the stronger? Hardly, since Susanna finally seduces him from his work. The rest of the opera tends to support Susanna's claim to superior wit, but the duet itself may be read as striking a balance emblematic of the compromises which make a successful marriage.

Action may be less ambiguously wedded to musical events than character, but even in Mozart's busiest ensembles it does not develop at a rate comparable to recitative. In the *Figaro* sextet, a 24-bar ensemble expands the situation reached at the end of the previous recitative. 16 bars of dialogue follow Susanna's entry, half mingled with further ensemble. Susanna sees Figaro embracing Marcellina and slaps him; this takes 14 bars, reaction to it 20. From bar 74 (reprise of the opening) the misunderstanding is explained (with humorous repetitions); from bar 102 the rest is commentary, embodying contrasted views (Count Almaviva and Don

Ex.3 Mozart: *Le nozze di Figaro*, Act 1

[Figaro: 'Five…ten…twenty…thirty…thirty-six…forty-three… Susanna: 'Now like this I'm happy']

Curzio are angered by what rejoices the others). Commentary exceeds action in a proportion of about 3:2. Often such frozen tableaux, during which the music is extended before the next event or to make a decisive conclusion, are still more prevalent, notably in the closing (and fastest) sections of finales.

The relationship of certain ensembles to sonata form has frequently been described (notably in the trios and sextets of *Figaro* and *Don Giovanni*), and is undoubtedly a remarkable synthesis of styles. But additive designs are also common (*Die Entführung*: quartet-finale; *Così*: sextet). The *Don Giovanni* sextet has been compared in structure to a finale; Rosen (1971) justifies the huge closing section (147 bars entirely in E♭) by the need for tonal resolution of the extreme modulations of the first part. Here sonata form is merely an analogy; unlike the *Figaro* sextet, this has no thematic reprise, and the dramatic effect would be the same if it ended in C rather than E♭ major, a licence the harmonic situation before the Allegro (a dominant of C minor) would certainly permit, exceptional though such a procedure would have been.

Starting from primitive chain finales (*La finta semplice*), Mozart enriched the musical and dramatic content (*La finta giardiniera*); but the action remains slow and the tonal architecture primitive. The realistic *opera buffa* produced swifter action, and Mozart devised appropriate tonal schemes, beginning and ending in the same key and moving between sections by a 5th or 3rd. Landon (1989) postulates influence from the tertial key-changes in Haydn's *La fedeltà premiata*. In *Figaro* and *Don Giovanni* Mozart used this device better, because more sparingly: 5th-progressions are normal and shifts down a 3rd mark a peripeteia (entries of Figaro, Act 2: Bb to G, and the masked trio, *Don Giovanni* Act 1: Eb to C). A more complicated scheme lies behind the first finale of *Così* (see Table 1). It begins with the ladies alone in the garden (*A*). The men rush in, taking poison (*B*); Alfonso and Despina go for the doctor (*C*), leaving the frightened ladies to tend the 'dying' men (*D*). Despina as the doctor cures them (*E*). Feigning to believe they are in paradise, the men plead love to the ladies (*F*), who reject them with renewed energy (*G*).

TABLE 1: *Così fan tutte* Act 1 finale

section	A	B	C	D	E	F	G
key	D	g	Eb	c	G	Bb	D
tempo	Andante	Allegro	(continued)		Allegro	Andante	Allegro
metre	2/4	¢	(continued)		3/4	C	¢

In sections *A* to *E*, all key-changes also involve change of mode; in *E* to *G* the shifts are chromatic. The still more active second-act finale is tonally almost eccentric: at one point the key-sequence is Ab, E, D, Eb. Weaker tonal architecture in comparison with *Figaro* and *Don Giovanni* perhaps reflects the deceptiveness of the dramatic situation.

Mozart's key-schemes can never be completely systematized as signs of character, social class, affect or even musical form. Social structures, however, are more reliably encoded through associations of metre with dance (Allanbrook 1983). The contredanse in the Act 1 finale of *Don Giovanni* is the meeting-point between aristocratic minuet and plebeian waltz. Figaro's 'Se vuol ballare' accelerates from minuet to contredanse; Susanna mocks Count Almaviva by emerging from the closet (Act 2 finale) to a minuet. This system has less applicability in *Così* or *opera seria*, but a parallel hierarchy of musical types (including counterpoint) governs the complex society of *Die Zauberflöte*.

But for each instance of affective key-symbolism a counter-instance can be produced. 'Regal', 'heroic' D major (besides being available for trumpets, it is particularly brilliant on strings) can embody the tenderest feelings (*Così*, opening of the first finale). 'Rustic' G (peasant choruses in *Figaro* and *Don Giovanni*; Papageno) appears in *Idomeneo* for Electra's 'Idol mio' and (in comedy) for arias of Marcellina and Despina, who are far from bucolic. E major is used for gentle breezes in *Zaide*, *Idomeneo* (twice) and the trio in *Così*, but also for deep introspection (*Così*: 'Per pietà') and for a *buffo* duet in a graveyard (*Don Giovanni*). Instrumentation and tempo, harmony, melody and rhythm, contribute more to mood and characterization than tonality or absolute pitch.

It is certainly interesting that 14 Mozart operas begin and end in the same key (the latest exception is *Il re pastore*). Eight are 'in' D and five in another 'trumpet key'. But to relate other keys to this 'tonic' proposes a scheme too vast to be grasped unless fully supported by secondary evidence such as thematic reprise or instrumentation; both can deceive (in the first finale of *Don Giovanni*, music first heard in F recurs in G; in the sextet, the trumpets enter in D, a semitone below the tonic). The claims of affective key symbolism and tonal architecture are virtually irreconcilable, and it is not self-evident that such systematic structures are appropriate to dramatic forms; they are best understood as an aspect of Mozart's musical language. Dramatic criticism is more appropriately founded on the interaction of elements than single cohesive theories.

The statue music in *Don Giovanni*, the folkishness and solemnity of *Die Zauberflöte*, resonated throughout the 19th century; even the gaiety of *Figaro* was occasionally evoked, as in Berlioz's *Béatrice et Bénédict*. But while Mozart's influence was widespread, composers took what they needed – the inspiration of colourful orchestration, an idea like the dance scene in *Don Giovanni* which resurfaces at the opening of *Rigoletto* – rather than imitating his dramatic methods. Mozart's transmutation of the sonata into a vehicle for drama may appear his most radical achievement; yet it was not developed even by Beethoven in *Fidelio* (as distinct from its overtures). The chain finale anticipates 19th-century continuous opera, nowhere more than in *Die Zauberflöte*; the first finale is tonally simple, using only the closest relations to C major, but it includes obbligato recitative building to expressive arioso (Tamino and the Orator), lyrical song (Tamino with the flute), action ensembles and choruses. The second finale incorporates popular and learned styles as well as spectacular scenic effects. Nevertheless the operatic styles engendered by the French Revolution, and the continuity of Italian traditions, played at least as great a role in forming Romantic opera. The musical languages of Rossini and Weber were not sonata-based; Wagner had more immediate models; *Falstaff*, *Der Rosenkavalier* and *The Rake's Progress* are spiritual descendants too remote in time to constitute a tradition.

In every genre Mozart built on existing conventions to point a new way: his Singspiel accommodates heroism and religious quest, as well as a huge musical expansion; *opera seria* is purged of artificiality and humanized; *opera buffa* provides the framework for serious explorations of society and sexuality. His influence on the next century's opera is perhaps the victim of the very perfection of his works. Yet from Goethe and E. T. A. Hoffmann he affected the minds of poets and philosophers as well as musicians; he is the first operatic composer whose work as a whole has never needed to be revived. It is likely to remain the touchstone of operatic achievement.

See also APOLLO ET HYACINTHUS; ASCANIO IN ALBA; BASTIEN UND BASTIENNE; CLEMENZA DI TITO, LA; COSÌ FAN TUTTE; DON GIOVANNI (ii); ENTFÜHRUNG AUS DEM SERAIL, DIE; FINTA GIARDINIERA, LA (ii); FINTA SEMPLICE, LA; IDOMENEO, RE DI CRETA; LUCIO SILLA (i); MITRIDATE, RE DI PONTO; NOZZE DI FIGARO, LE; OCA DEL CAIRO, L'; RE PASTORE, IL; SCHAUSPIELDIREKTOR, DER; SOGNO DI SCIPIONE, IL; SPOSO DELUSO, LO; ZAIDE; and ZAUBERFLÖTE, DIE.

Mozart, Wolfgang Amadeus

Editions: *W. A. Mozarts Werke*, ed. L. von Köchel and others (Leipzig, 1877–83) [MW; nos. shown, e.g. Series (V)/vol.(x)]
W. A. Mozart: Neue Ausgabe sämtlicher Werke, ed. E. F. Schmid, W. Plath and W. Rehm, Internationale Stiftung Mozarteum Salzburg (Kassel, 1955–) [NMA; all operas in Series II, Werkgruppe 5; nos. shown, e.g. Band (x)]

K – *no. in Köchel (1862)*; A: *no. in Anhang (appx)*
K6 – *no. in Köchel (6/1964)*; C: *no. in appx C*
(D) – *date from MS of work (not always clear)*
(V) – *date from Mozart: Verzeichnüss aller meiner Werke (1784–91) in GB-Lbl*

autograph MSS unless otherwise stated; editions published in Mozart's lifetime are noted in the remarks column

K	K6	title	genre, acts	libretto	first performed	remarks; principal sources	MW	NMA
38	38	Apollo et Hyacinthus	Lat. int, 3	R. Widl	Salzburg, Benedictine University, 13 May 1767	perf. with Widl's Lat. play, *Clementia Croesi*; *D-B*	V/ii	i
51	46a	La finta semplice	ob, 3	C. Goldoni, rev. M. Coltellini	Salzburg, Archbishop's Palace, probably 1 May 1769	comp. Vienna, mid-1768; *B* (Act 1); *PL-Kj* (Acts 2 and 3)	V/iv	ii
50	46b	Bastien und Bastienne	Spl, 1	F. W. Weiskern, J. Müller and J. A. Schachtner, after M.-J.-B. Favart and H. de Guerville: *Les amours de Bastien et Bastienne* [*see* Tyler 1990]	Vienna, F. A. Mesmer's house, ?Sept–Oct 1768	*Kj*	V/iii	iii
87	74a	Mitridate, re di Ponto	dramma per musica, 3	V. A. Cigna-Santi, after G. Pavini's It. trans. of J. Racine: *Mithridate*	Milan, Regio Ducal, 26 Dec 1770	main autograph lost, copies in *F-Pn**, *GB-Lbl*, *P-La*	V/v	iv
111	111	Ascanio in Alba	festa teatrale, 2	Parini	Milan, Regio Ducal, 17 Oct 1771	for wedding of Archduke Ferdinand of Austria and Maria Ricciarda Berenice of Modena, with ballet A207/C27.06 (inc.); *D-B*	V/vi	v
126	126	Il sogno di Scipione	azione teatrale, 1	P. Metastasio	? Salzburg, Archbishop's Palace, May 1772	comp. ?April–Aug 1771, ? given as serenata at enthronement of Colloredo as Prince-Archbishop of Salzburg; *B*	V/vii	vi
135	135	Lucio Silla	dramma per musica, 3	G. De Gamerra	Milan, Regio Ducal, 26 Dec 1772	*PL-Kj*	V/viii	vii
196	196	La finta giardiniera	ob, 3	unknown; attrib. ?Petrosellini	Munich, Salvator, 13 Jan 1775	perf. as Spl, Die verstellte Gärtnerin, Augsburg, 1 May 1780; Act 1 lost, *Kj* (Acts 2 and 3), copy *CS-Bm*	V/ix	viii
208	208	Il re pastore	serenata, 2	Metastasio	Salzburg, Archbishop's Palace, 23 April 1775	*PL-Kj*	V/x	ix
344	336b	Zaide [Das Serail]	Spl, 2	Schachtner, after F. J. Sebastiani: *Das Serail*	Frankfurt, 27 Jan 1866 (completed by J. André, addnl text by K. Gollmich)	comp. Salzburg, 1779–80, inc.; *D-B*	V/xi	x
366	366	Idomeneo, re di Creta	dramma per musica, 3	G. B. Varesco, after A. Danchet: *Idoménée*	(i) Munich, Residenz, 29 Jan 1781; (ii) Vienna, Auersperg Palace, 13 March 1786	perf. with ballet, K367, *B*; perf. with K489, 490, both comp. by 10 March 1786 (V); *PL-Kj* (Acts 1 and 2), *D-B* (Act 3), copy *Mbs*	V/xiii	xi
384	384	Die Entführung aus dem Serail	Spl, 3	C. F. Bretzner: *Belmont und Constanze*, rev. G. Stephanie the younger	Vienna, Burg, 16 July 1782	*PL-Kj* (Acts 1 and 3), *D-B* (Act 2), vs (Vienna, 1785)	V/xv	xii

422	422	L'oca del Cairo	ob, 2	Varesco	unperf.	comp. Salzburg and Vienna, late 1783, inc.; 1 trio completed and 6 nos. sketched *B*	XXIV, no.37	xiii
430	424a	Lo sposo deluso	ob, 2	after *Le donne rivali*; attrib. ?Petrosellini [*see* Campana]	unperf.	begun 1783; ov., trio and qt completed, 2 nos. sketched *PL-Kj*	XXIV, no.38	xiv
486	486	Der Schauspiel-direktor	Spl, 1	Stephanie the younger	Schönbrunn Palace, Orangery, 7 Feb 1786	completed Vienna, 3 Feb 1786 (V), perf. with Salieri's *Prima la musica*; *US-NYpm*	V/xvi	xv
492	492	Le nozze di Figaro	ob, 4	L. da Ponte, after P.-A. Beaumarchais: *La folle journée, ou Le mariage de Figaro*	(i) Vienna, Burg, 1 May 1786	completed Vienna, 29 April 1786 (D); *D-Bds* (Acts 1 and 2), *PL-Kj* (Acts 3 and 4)	V/xvii	xvi
					(ii) Vienna, Burg, 29 Aug 1789	with arias K577, 579		
527	527	Il dissoluto punito, ossia Il Don Giovanni	ob, 2	Da Ponte	(i) Prague, National, 29 Oct 1787	Prague, 28 Oct 1787 (V); *F-Pn*	V/xviii	xvii
					(ii) Vienna, Burg, 7 May 1788	perf. with addns K540a, b, c		
588	588	Così fan tutte, ossia La scuola degli amanti	ob, 2	Da Ponte	Vienna, Burg, 26 Jan 1790	Vienna, Jan 1790 (V); *PL-Kj* (Act 1), *D-B* (Act 2), excerpts, vs (Vienna, 1790)	V/xix	xviii
620	620	Die Zauberflöte	Spl, 2	E. Schikaneder	Vienna, Theater auf der Wieden, 30 Sept 1791	vocal nos. begun by July 1791 (V), ov. and march completed 28 Sept 1791 (V); *Bds*, excerpts, vs (Vienna, 1791–2)	V/xx	xix
621	621	La clemenza di Tito	os, 2	Metastasio, rev. C. Mazzolà	Prague, National, 6 Sept 1791	for Prague coronation of Leopold II, completed 5 Sept 1791 (V); simple recits. not by Mozart; *B*	V/xxi	xx

Music in: P. Anfossi: Il curioso indiscreto, Vienna, 1783; F. Bianchi: La villanella rapita, Vienna, 1785; Anfossi: Le gelosie fortunate, Vienna, 1788; Cimarosa: I due baroni, Vienna, 1789; Martín y Soler: Il burbero di buon cuore, Vienna, 1789

CATALOGUES, BIBLIOGRAPHIES, LETTERS, DOCUMENTS, ICONOGRAPHY

L. von Köchel: *Chronologisch-thematisches Verzeichnis sämtlicher Tonwerke Wolfgang Amade Mozarts* (Leipzig, 1862; 2/1905 ed. P. Graf von Waldersee; 3/1937 ed. A. Einstein, with suppl. 3/1947; 6/1964 ed. F. Geigling, A. Weinmann and G. Sievers) [reviews by A. H. King, *Mf*, xviii (1965), 307–13 and B. E. Wilson, *Notes*, xxi (1963–4), 531–40; corrections and suppls. by P. W. van Reijen, *MJb* 1971–2, 342–401]

E. Anderson, ed.: *The Letters of Mozart and his Family* (London, 1938, 3/1985)

O. E. Deutsch: *Mozart: die Dokumente seines Lebens, gesammelt und erläutert* (Kassel, 1961; Eng. trans., 1965, 2/1966; suppl. 1978)

——: *Mozart und seine Welt in zeitgenössischen Bildern* (Kassel, 1961) [in Ger. and Eng.]

O. Schneider and A. Algatzy: *Mozart-Handbuch: Chronik, Werk, Bibliographie* (Vienna, 1962)

W. A. Bauer, O. E. Deutsch and J. H. Eibl, eds.: *Mozart: Briefe und Aufzeichnungen* (Kassel, 1962–75) [complete edn; for later discoveries see G. Croll, *MJb* 1967, 12–17, and R. Angermüller and S. Dahms-Schneider, *MJb* 1968–70, 211–41]

R. Angermüller and O. Schneider: 'Mozart-Bibliographie (bis 1970)', *MJb* 1975

——: *Mozart-Bibliographie 1971–1975 mit Nachträgen bis 1970* (Kassel, 1978)

O. Wessely: 'Ergänzerungen zur Mozart-Bibliographie', *SMw*, xxix (1978), 37–68

B. Hastings: *W. A. Mozart: a Guide to Research* (New York, 1989)

H. C. R. Landon, ed.: *The Mozart Compendium* (London, 1990)

C. Eisen: *New Mozart Documents: a Supplement to O. E. Deutsch's Documentary Biography* (London, 1991)

BIOGRAPHIES, STUDIES OF LIFE AND WORKS

F. Schlichtegroll: 'Johannes Chrysostomus Wolfgang Gottlieb Mozart', *Nekrolog auf das Jahr 1791* (Gotha, 1793), ed. L. Landshoff (Munich, 1924); as *Mozarts Leben* (Graz, 1794) [see also Favier 1976]

F. X. Niemetschek: *Leben des k.k. Kapellmeisters Wolfgang Gottlieb Mozart nach Originalquellen beschrieben* (Prague, 1798, enlarged 2/1808; Eng. trans., 1956) [see also Favier 1976]

F. Rochlitz: 'Verbürgte Anekdoten aus Wolfgang Gottlieb Mozarts Leben: ein Beitrag zur richtigeren Kenntnis dieses Mannes, als Mensch und Künstler', *AMZ*, i (1798–9), cols. 17–24, 49–55, 81–6, 113–17, 145–52, 177–83, 289–91, 480, 854–6; iii (1800–01), cols. 450–52, 493–7, 590–96; Eng. trans. in *Mozart Studies*, ed. C. Eisen (1991), 1–59

G. N. Nissen: *Biographie W. A. Mozarts nach Originalbriefen* (Leipzig, 1828)

A. D. Oulibicheff: *Nouvelle biographie de Mozart* (Moscow, 1843, 2/1890–92)

O. Jahn: *W. A. Mozart* (Leipzig, 1856, 2/1867; ed. H. Deiters, 3/1889–91, 4/1905–7; Eng. trans., 1882) [for later edns. see H. Abert 1919–21]

T. de Wyzewa and G. de Saint-Foix: *Wolfgang Amédée Mozart: sa vie musicale et son oeuvre* (Paris, 1912–46) [iii–v by Saint-Foix alone]

A. Schurig: *Wolfgang Amadeus Mozart: sein Leben und sein Werk* (Leipzig, 1913, 2/1923)

H. Abert: *W. A. Mozart: neu bearbeitete und erweiterte Ausgabe von Otto Jahns 'Mozart'* (Leipzig, 1919–21, 3/1955–66)

L. Schiedermair: *Mozart: sein Leben und seine Werke* (Munich, 1922, enlarged 2/1948)

A. Einstein: *Mozart: his Character, his Work* (Eng. trans., New York, 1945: Ger. orig., 1947, 4/1960)

E. Schenk: *Wolfgang Amadeus Mozart: eine Biographie* (Vienna and Zürich, 1955, 2/1975; Eng. trans., abridged, as *Mozart and his Times*, 1960)

J. Massin and B. Massin: *Wolfgang Amadeus Mozart: biographie, histoire de l'oeuvre* (Paris, 1959, 2/1971)

G. Favier, ed.: *Vie de W. A. Mozart par Franz Xaver Niemetschek précédée du nécrologe de Schlichtegroll* (St Etienne, 1976) [in Ger. and Fr., with introduction and notes]

W. Hildesheimer: *Mozart* (Frankfurt, 1977; Eng. trans., 1982)

S. Sadie: *The New Grove Mozart* (London, 1982)

LIFE AND WORKS: PARTICULAR PERIODS AND ASPECTS

R. Procházka: *Mozart in Prag* (Prague, 1899; rev. and enlarged by P. Nettl as *Mozart in Böhmen*, 1938)

A. H. King: *Mozart in Retrospect: Studies in Criticism and Bibliography* (London, 1955, 3/1970)

A. Ostoja: *Mozart e l'Italia* (Bologna, 1955)

G. Barblan and A. della Corte: *Mozart in Italia* (Milan, 1956)

P. Schaller and H. Kühner, eds.: *Mozart-Aspekte* (Olten and Freiburg, 1956) [symposium]

O. E. Deutsch: 'Mozart in Zinzendorfs Tagebüchern', *SMz*, cii (1962), 211–18

C. Rosen: *The Classical Style: Haydn, Mozart, Beethoven* (London, 1971, 2/1973), 183–325

'Tonartenplan und Motivstruktur (Leitmotivtechnik?) in Mozarts Musik', *MJb 1973–4*, 82–144 [discussions]

V. Braunbehrens: *Mozart in Wien* (Zürich and Munich, 1986; Eng. trans., 1990)

A. Tyson: *Mozart: Studies of the Autograph Scores* (Cambridge, MA, 1987)

H. C. R. Landon: *1791: Mozart's Last Year* (London, 1988)

——: *Mozart: the Golden Years, 1781–1791* (London, 1989)

N. Zaslaw: *Mozart's Symphonies* (London, 1989)

OPERAS
General

I. R. von Seyfried: 'Mozart, der Operncomponist', *Cäcilia*, xx (1839), 178–94

A. D. Oulibicheff: *Mozarts Opern: kritische Erläuterungen* (Leipzig, 1848)

H. Merian: *Mozarts Meisteropern* (Leipzig, 1900)

E. J. Dent: *Mozart's Operas: a Critical Study* (London, 1913, 2/1947, rev. 1991)

H. Cohen: *Die dramatische Idee in Mozarts Operntexten* (Berlin, 1915)

E. Lert: *Mozart auf dem Theater* (Berlin, 1918)

A. Lorenz: 'Das Finale in Mozarts Meisteropern', *Die Musik*, xix (1926–7), 621–32

H. Goerges: *Das Klangsymbol des Todes im dramatischen Werk Mozarts* (Munich, 1937)

L. Conrad: *Mozarts Dramaturgie der Oper* (Würzburg, 1943)

C. Benn: *Mozart on the Stage* (London, 1946, 2/1947)

H. Engel: 'Die Finali der Mozartschen Opern', *MJb 1954*, 113–34

G. Abraham: 'The Operas', *The Mozart Companion*, ed. H. C. R. Landon and D. Mitchell (London, 1956, 2/1965), 283–323

M. Breydert: *Le génie créateur de W. A. Mozart: Essai sur l'instauration musicale des personnages dans 'Les noces de Figaro', 'Don Juan' et 'La flûte enchantée'* (Paris, 1956)

A. Greither: *Die Sieben Grossen Opern Mozarts* (Heidelberg, 1956, enlarged 2/1970, 3/1977)

J. Kerman: *Opera as Drama* (New York, 1956, 2/1989)

L. F. Tagliavini: 'L'opéra italien du jeune Mozart', *Les influences étrangères dans l'oeuvre de Mozart: CNRS Paris 1956*, 125–56

P. C. Hughes: *Famous Mozart Operas* (London, 1957)

M. Levey: 'Aspects of Mozart's Heroines (Pamina and Countess Almaviva)', *Journal of the Warburg and Courtauld Institutes*, xxii (1959), 132–56

J. Liebner: *Mozart a szimpadon* (Budapest, 1961; Eng. trans., 1972, as *Mozart on the Stage*)

B. Szabolcsi: 'Mozart et la comédie populaire', *SM*, i (1961), 65–91

B. Brophy: *Mozart the Dramatist: a New View of Mozart, his Operas and his Age* (London, 1964, 2/1988)

C. Floros: 'Das "Programm" in Mozarts Meisterouvertüren', *SMw*, xxvi (1964), 140–86 [rev. in Floros 1979]

M. Chusid: 'The Significance of D minor in Mozart's Dramatic Music', *MJb 1965–6*, 87–93

A. A. Abert: 'Beiträge zur Motivik von Mozarts Spätopern', *MJb 1967*, 7–11

R. B. Moberly: *Three Mozart Operas: Figaro, Don Giovanni, The Magic Flute* (London, 1967)

S. Döhring: 'Die Arienformen in Mozarts Opern', *MJb 1968–70*, 66–76

W. Osthoff: 'Mozarts Cavatinen und ihre Tradition', *Helmuth Osthoff zu seinem siebzigsten Geburtstag* (Tutzing, 1969), 139–77

A. A. Abert: *Die Opern Mozarts* (Wolfenbüttel, 1970); Eng. trans. in NOHM, vii (1973), 97–172

O. Michtner: *Das alte Burgtheater als Opernbühne von der Einführung des deutschen Singspiele (1778) bis zum Tod Kaiser Leopold II (1792)* (Vienna, 1970)

D. J. Grout: *Mozart in the History of Opera* (Washington DC, 1972)

F. Friebe: 'Idealisierung und skeptischer Realismus bei Mozarts Frauengestalten', *Mf*, xxvi (1973), 180–90

E. Badura-Skoda: 'The Influence of the Viennese Popular Comedy on Haydn and Mozart', *PRMA*, c (1973–4), 185–99

C. Gianturco: *Le opere del giovane Mozart* (Pisa, 1976, enlarged 2/1978, Eng. trans., enlarged, as *Mozart's Early Operas*, 1981)

W. Mann: *The Operas of Mozart* (London, 1977)

F. Noske: *The Signifier and the Signified: Studies in the Operas of Mozart and Verdi* (The Hague, 1977)

I. Singer: *Mozart and Beethoven: the Concept of Love in their Operas* (Baltimore, 1977)

C. Osborne: *The Complete Operas of Mozart* (London, 1978)

C. Höslinger: 'Mozarts Opern in den Sonnleithner-Regesten', *MJb 1978–9*, 149–53

R. Würtz: 'Die Erstaufführungen von Mozarts Bühnenwerken in Mannheim', *MJb 1978–9*, 163–71

C. Floros: *Mozart-Studien*, i: *Zu Mozarts Sinfonik, Opern- und Kirchenmusik* (Wiesbaden, 1979) [incl. 'Stilebenen und Stilsynthese in den Opern Mozarts', 79–129]

R. Stricker: *Mozart et ses opéras: fiction et vérité* (Paris, 1980)

C. Höslinger: 'Mozarts Opern in Wiener Biedermeier', *MJb 1980–83*, 98–104

C. Ballantine: 'Social and Philosophical Outlook in Mozart's Operas', *MQ*, lxvii (1981), 507–26

J. Manika: 'Der Opernkomponist Mozart', *Musik und Gesellschaft*, xxxi (1981), 28–33

'Mozart und die Oper seiner Zeit', *HJbMw*, v (1981), 115–266 [incl. S. Kunze: 'Einführung', 115–20, and 'Mozarts Jugendwerk: Tradition und Originalität', 121–54; C. Floros: 'Stilebenen und Stilsynthese in den Opern Mozarts', 155–68; G. Gruber: 'Gluck und Mozart', 169–86; F. Lippmann: 'Mozart und Cimarosa', 187–202; C.-H. Mahling: 'Mysliveček (1731–1781) und Grétry (1741–1813): Vorbilder Mozarts?', 203–10; H. Lühning: 'Die Rondo-Arie im späten 18. Jahrhundert: dramatischer Gestalt und musikalischer Bau', 219–46]

D. Heartz: 'Mozart's Tragic Muse', *Studies in Music from the University of Western Ontario*, vii (1982), 183–96; repr. in Heartz (1990), 37–63

F. Neumann: 'The Appoggiatura in Mozart's Recitative', *JAMS*, xxxv (1982), 115–37

R. J. Nicolosi: 'The *tempo di minuetto* aria in Mozart's operas', *College Music Symposium*, xxiii/1 (1983), 97–123

R. Stiefel: 'Mozart's Seductions', *CMc*, no.36 (1983), 151–66

J. Kaiser: *Mein Name ist Sarastro: Die Gestalten in Mozarts Meisteropern von Alfonso bis Zerlina* (Munich, 1984)

S. Kunze: *Mozarts Opern* (Stuttgart, 1984)

J. Platoff: *Music and Drama in the Opera Buffa Finale: Mozart and his Contemporaries in Vienna, 1781–1790* (diss., U. of Pennsylvania, 1984)

J. Webster: 'To Understand Verdi and Wagner we must Understand Mozart', *19th Century Music*, xi (1987–8), 175–93

R. Angermüller: *Mozart: die Opern von der Uraufführung bis heute* (Fribourg, 1988; Eng. trans., 1988, as *Mozart's Operas*)

I. Nagel: *Autonomie und Gnade: Ueber Mozarts Opern* (Munich and Vienna, 1988; Eng. trans., 1991, as *Autonomy and Mercy: Reflections on Mozart's Operas*)

W. Crutchfield: 'The Prosodic Appoggiatura in the Music of Mozart and his Contemporaries', *JAMS*, xlii (1989), 229–74

J. Platoff: 'Musical and Dramatic Structure in the Opera Buffa Finale', *JM*, vii (1989), 191–230

C. Abbate and R. Parker: 'Dismembering Mozart', *COJ*, ii (1990), 187–95

D. Heartz: *Mozart's Operas* (Berkeley, 1990) [with T. Bauman]

J. Platoff: 'The Buffa Aria in Mozart's Vienna', *COJ*, ii (1990), 99–120

J. Webster: 'Mozart's Operas and the Myth of Musical Unity', ibid, 197–218

——: 'The Analysis of Mozart's Arias', *Mozart Studies*, ed. C. Eisen (Oxford, 1991), 101–99

W. J. Allanbrook and W. Hilton: 'Dance Rhythms in Mozart's Arias', *EMc*, xx (1992), 142–9

D. Edge: 'Mozart's Viennese Orchestras', ibid, 64–88

J. Platoff: 'How Original was Mozart? Evidence from *opera buffa*', ibid, 105–17

N. Till: *Mozart and the Enlightenment: Truth, Virtue and Beauty in Mozart's Operas* (London, 1992)

Apollo et Hyacinthus

A. Orel: Preface, NMA II:5/i (1959)

La finta semplice

R. Angermüller: 'Ein neuentdecktes Salzburger Libretto (1769) zu Mozarts *La finta semplice*', *Mf*, xxxi (1978), 318–22

——: 'Die vorgesehenen Sänger für die Wiener (1768) und Salzburger (1796) Erstaufführung von Mozarts *La finta semplice*', *Wiener Figaro*, l (Nov 1983), 3

——: Preface, NMA II:5/ii (1983)

Bastien und Bastienne

R. Angermüller: Preface, NMA II:5/iii (1974)

L. Tyler: '*Bastien und Bastienne*: the Libretto, its Derivation, and Mozart's Text-setting', *JM*, viii (1990), 520–52

Mitridate

L. F. Tagliavini: Preface, NMA II:5/iv (1966)

——: 'Quirino Gasparini and Mozart', *New Looks at Italian Opera: Essays in Honor of Donald J. Grout* (Ithaca, NY, 1968), 151–71

A. C. Keys: 'Two Eighteenth-Century Racinian Operas', *ML*, lix (1978), 1–10

L'avant-scène opéra, no.54 (1983) [*Mitridate* issue]

Ascanio in Alba

L. F. Tagliavini: Preface, NMA II:5/v (1956)

W. Plath: 'Der Ballo des "Ascanio" und die Klavierstücke KV Anh. 207', *MJb 1964*, 111–29

K. Hortschansky: 'Mozarts "Ascanio in Alba" und der Typus der Serenata', *AnMc*, no.18 (1978), 148–59

Il sogno di Scipione

J.-H. Lederer: Preface, NMA II:5/vi (1977)

L'avant-scène opéra, no.131 (1990) [*Il re pastore* and *Il sogno di Scipione* issue]

Lucio Silla

W. Senn: 'Mozarts Skizze der Ballettmusik zu "Le Gelosie del serraglio" (KV Anh. 109/135a)', *AcM*, xxxiii (1961), 169–92

G. Croll: 'Bemerkungen zur Ballo Primo (KV Anh. 109/135a) in Mozarts Mailänder *Lucio Silla*', *AnMc*, no.18 (1978), 160–65

E. Warburton: 'Lucio Silla, by Mozart and J. C. Bach', *MT*, cxxvi (1985), 726–30

K. K. Hansell: Preface, NMA II:5/vii (1986)

La finta giardiniera

R. Münster: 'Die verstellte Gärtnerin: neue Quellen zur authentischen Singspielfassung von W. A. Mozarts La finta giardiniera', *Mf*, xviii (1965), 138–60

——: 'Die Singspielfassung von W. A. Mozarts "La finta giardiniera" in den Augsburger Aufführungen von 1780', *Acta Mozartiana*, xiii (1966), 43–8

[R. Münster:] *La finta giardiniera: Mozarts Muenchener Aufenthalt, 1774–5* (Munich, 1975) [catalogue of exhibition at the Bayerische Staatsbibliotek, 1975]

R. Angermüller: 'Wer war der Librettist von *La finta giardiniera*', *MJb 1976–7*, 1–8

R. Angermüller and D. Berke: Preface, NMA II:5/viii (1978)

Il re pastore

K. Hortschansky: '"Il re pastore": zur Rezeption eines Librettos in der Mozart-Zeit', *MJb 1978–9*, 61–70

P. Petrobelli and W. Rehm: Preface, NMA II:5/ix (1985)

L'avant-scène opéra, no.131 (1990) [*Il re pastore* and *Il sogno di Scipione* issue]

Zaide

A. Einstein: 'Die Text-Vorlage zu Mozarts "Zaide"', *AcM*, viii (1936), 30–37

F.-H. Neumann: Preface, NMA II:5/x (1957)

——: 'Zur Vorgeschichte der Zaide', *MJb 1962–3*, 216–47

L. Tyler: '"Zaide" in the Development of Mozart's Operatic Language', *ML*, lxxii (1991), 214–35

Idomeneo

A. Heuss: 'Mozart's "Idomeneo" als Quelle für "Don Giovanni" und "Die Zauberflöte"', *ZMw*, xiii (1930–31), 177–99

B. Szabolcsi: 'Zur Parallele "Idomeneo-Zauberflöte"', *ZMw*, xiii (1930–31), 328–9

H. Keller: 'The Idomeneo Gavotte's Vicissitude', *MR*, xiv (1953), 155–7

K. Böhm: 'Aufführungspraxis der Opera Seria am Beispiel des Idomeneo', *Wissenschaft und Praxis* (Zürich, 1958), 17–21

H. Keller: 'Idomeneo', *MR*, xx (1959), 296–9

D. Heartz: 'The Genesis of Mozart's *Idomeneo*', *MJb 1967*, 150–64; repr. in *MQ*, lv (1969), 1–19 and in Heartz (1990), 15–36

——: Preface, NMA II:5/xi (1972)

D. Cairns: 'Idomeneo', *Responses* (London, 1973), 55–77

R. Angermüller and others: 'Themenkreis "Idomeneo"', *MJb 1973–4*, 7-190, 279–97

D. Heartz: 'Raaff's Last Aria: a Mozartean Idyll in the Spirit of Hasse', *MQ*, lx (1974), 517–43

——: 'Tonality and Motif in Idomeneo', *MT*, cxv (1974), 382–6

J. Hirschberg: 'Formal and Dramatic Aspects of Sonata Form in Mozart's *Idomeneo*', *MR*, xxxviii (1977), 192–210

A. A. Abert: 'Mozarts Italianità in "Idomeneo" und "Titus"', *AnMc*, no.18 (1978), 205–16

W. Gerstenberg: 'Betrachtungen über Mozart "Idomeneo"', *Festschrift Georg von Dadelsen zum 60. Geburtstag* (Stuttgart, 1978), 148–54

D. Heartz: 'Mozart, his Father and "Idomeneo"', *MT*, cxix (1978), 228–31

K. Kramer: 'Giovanni Battista Varesco: Versuch eine Biographie', *Acta Mozartiana*, xxvii (1980), 2–15

D. Heartz: 'The Great Quartet in Mozart's *Idomeneo*', *Music Forum*, v (1980), 233–56

J.-V. Hocquard: *Idomenée* (Paris, 1980)

K. Kramer: 'Antike und christliches Mittelalter in Varescos "Idomeneo", dem Libretto zu Mozarts gleichnamiger Oper', *Mitteilungen der Internationalen Stiftung Mozarteum*, xxviii/1–2 (1980), 6–20

——: 'Frauengestalte in Varescos "Idomeneo"', *Mitteilungen der Internationalen Stiftung Mozarteum*, xxviii/3–4 (1980), 16–24

——: 'Zur Entstehung von Mozarts "Idomeneo"', *Mitteilungen der Internationalen Stiftung Mozarteum*, xxix/3–4 (1981), 23–7

R. Münster, ed.: *Wolfgang Amadeus Mozart: Idomeneo 1781–1981* (Munich, 1981)

E. Valentin: '… Punkte, die die opera betreffen', *Acta Mozartiana*, xxviii (1981), 49–54

R. Münster: 'Neues zum Münchener Idomeneo 1781', *Acta Mozartiana*, xxix (1982), 10–20

D. Neville: 'Idomeneo and La clemenza di Tito: opera seria and "vera opera"', *Studies in Music from the University of Western Ontario*, viii (1983), 107–36

P. Gallarati: 'Mozart e l'opera metastasiana nella "crisi" giovanile dell' "Idomeneo"', *Il centenario della morte di Metastasio: Rome 1983*, 257–75

L'avant-scène opéra, no.89 (1986) [*Idomeneo* issue]

C. Höslinger: 'Die erster Aufführungen des "Idomeneo" in Wien, 1786, 1806', *MJb 1986*, 25–8

A. Csampai and D. Holland, eds.: *W. A. Mozart: Idomeneo: Texte, Materialien, Kommentare* (Hamburg, 1988)

J. Platoff: 'Writing about Influences: *Idomeneo*, a Case Study', *Explorations in Music, the Arts, and Ideas: Essays in Honor of Leonard B. Meyer* (Stuyvesant, NY, 1988), 43–65

J. Rushton: '"La vittima è Idamante": Did Mozart have a Motive?', *COJ*, iii (1991), 1–21

——: *W. A. Mozart: Idomeneo* (Cambridge, 1993)

Die Entführung aus dem Serail

W. Preibisch: 'Quellenstudien zu Mozarts "Entführung aus dem Serail": ein Beitrag zu der Geschichte der Türkenoper', *SIMG*, x (1908–9), 430–76

R. Tenschert: 'Pedrillos Romanze', *AMz*, lxviii (1941), 303 [repr. in *ÖMz*, iii (1948) 301–3]

E. Schenk: 'Zur Entstehungsgeschichte von Mozarts "Entführung aus dem Serail"', *Musik im Kriege*, i (1943–4), 12–13

A. Einstein: 'The First Performance of Mozart's *Entführung* in London', *MR*, vii (1946), 154–60

E. Anderson: 'A Note on Mozart's Bassa Selim', *ML*, xxxv (1954), 120–24

H. Keller: 'The Entführung's "Vaudeville"', *MR*, xvii (1956), 304–13

B. Szabolcsi: 'Die "Exotismen" Mozarts', *Leben und Werk W. A. Mozarts: Prague 1956*, 181–8; Eng. trans., *ML*, xxxvii (1956), 323–32

C. Raeburn: 'Die Entführungsszene aus "Die Entführung aus dem Serail"', *MJb 1964*, 130–37

L. Meierott: 'Der "flauto piccolo" in Mozarts "Entführung aus dem Serail"', *Acta Mozartiana*, xii (1965), 79–84

G. Rech: 'Bretzner contra Mozart', *MJb 1968–70*, 186–205

H. J. Schweizer: 'Bassa Selim', *Sodalitus Florhofiana: Festgabe für Professor Heinz Haffter* (Zürich, 1970), 140–49

C.-H. Mahling: 'Die Gestalt des Osmin in Mozarts "Entführung": vom Typus zur Individualität', *AMw*, xxx (1973), 96–108

R. Angermüller: '"Les époux esclaves ou Bastien et Bastienne à Alger": zur Stoffgeschichte der "Entführung aus dem Serail"', *MJb 1978–9*, 70–88

C. Floros: 'Die Ouvertüre zur *Entführung aus dem Serail*', *Mozart Studien*, i (Wiesbaden, 1979), 40–46

C. Questa: *Il ratto al Seraglio* (Bologna, 1979)

R. Würtz: 'Das Türkische im Singspiel des 18. Jahrhunderts', *Das deutsche Singspiel im 18. Jahrhundert: Amorbach 1979*, 125–37

G. Croll: 'Ein Janitscharen-Marsch zur "Entführung"', *Mitteilungen der Internationalen Stiftung Mozarteum*, xxviii/1–2 (1980), 2–5; xxviii/3–4, p.31

J.-V. Hocquard: *L'enlèvement au sérail (Die Entführung aus dem Serail) précédé de Zaïde* (Paris, 1980)

K. Pahlen, ed.: *Wolfgang Amadeus Mozart: Die Entführung aus dem Serail: Completer Text und Erläuterung zum vollen Verständnis des Werkes* (Munich, 1980)

G. Croll: Preface, NMA II:5/xii (1982)

A. Csampai and D. Holland, eds.: *W. A. Mozart: Die Entführung aus dem Serail: Texte, Materialen, Kommentare* (Hamburg, 1983)

L'avant-scène opéra, no.59 (1984) [*Die Entführung* issue]

T. Bauman: *W. A. Mozart: Die Entführung aus dem Serail* (Cambridge, 1987)

——: 'Coming of Age in Vienna: *Die Entführung aus dem Serail*', in Heartz (1990), 65–87

L'oca del Cairo

H. F. Redlich: '"L'oca del Cairo"', *MR*, ii (1941), 122–31

F.-H. Neumann: Preface, NMA II:5/xiii (1960; suppl., A. Holschneider, 1966)

A. Holschneider: 'Neue Mozartiana in Italien', *Mf*, xv (1962), 227–36

Lo sposo deluso

G. Allroggen: Preface, NMA II:5/xiv (1988)

A. Campana: 'Il libretto de "Lo sposo deluso"', *MJb 1988–9*, 573–88

Der Schauspieldirektor

C. Raeburn: 'An Evening at Schönbrunn', *MR*, xvi (1955), 96–110

G. Croll: Preface, NMA II:5/xv (1958)

C. Raeburn: 'Die textlichen Quellen des "Schauspieldirektor"', *ÖMz*, xiii (1958), 4–10

S. Kunze: 'Mozarts Schauspieldirektor', *MJb 1962–3*, 156–67

L. Tyler: 'Aria as Drama: a Sketch from Mozart's *Der Schauspieldirektor*', *COJ*, ii (1990), 251–67

The Da Ponte operas

W. J. Allanbrook: 'Metric Gesture as a Topic in *Le nozze di Figaro* and *Don Giovanni*', *MQ*, lxvii (1981), 94–112

B. Williams: 'Mozart's Comedies and the Sense of an Ending', *MT*, cxxii (1981), 451–4

S. P. Kiekmann: *Mozart, ein Bürgerlicher Künstler: Studien zu den Libretti 'Le nozze di Figaro', 'Don Giovanni' und 'Così fan tutte'* (Vienna, 1982)

W. J. Allanbrook: *Rhythmic Gesture in Mozart: Le nozze di Figaro and Don Giovanni* (Chicago, 1983)

J. A. Rice: 'Rondò vocali di Salieri e Mozart per Adriana Ferrarese', *I vicini di Mozart: Venice 1987*, 185–209

A. Steptoe: *The Mozart-Da Ponte Operas: the Cultural and Musical Background to 'Le nozze di Figaro', 'Don Giovanni' and 'Così fan tutte'* (Oxford, 1988)

P. Gallarati: 'Music and Masks in Lorenzo da Ponte's Mozartian Librettos', *COJ*, i (1989), 225–47

For further bibliography see DA PONTE, LORENZO.

Le nozze di Figaro

F. Niecks: 'The Second Finale in Mozart's "Le nozze di Figaro"', *MMR*, xlv (1915), 186–8, 217–19

E. Blom: 'The Literary Ancestry of Figaro', *MQ*, xiii (1927), 528–39

A. Einstein: 'Eine unbekannte Arie der Marcelline', *ZMw*, xiii (1930–31), 200–05

S. Anheisser: 'Die unbekannte Urfassung von Mozarts Figaro', *ZMw*, xv (1933), 301–17

E. Schenk: 'Zur Tonsymbolik in Mozarts "Figaro"', *Neues Mozart-Jb*, i (1941), 114–34

S. Levarie: *Mozart's 'Le nozze di Figaro': a Critical Analysis* (Chicago, 1952)

J. A. Westrup: 'Cherubino and the G minor Symphony', *A Fanfare for Ernest Newman* (London, 1955), 181–91

A. Hutchings: 'On Playing Don Curzio', *MR*, xix (1958), 94–104

R. Steglich: 'Bemerkungen zum ersten Duett in "Figaros Hochzeit"', *MJb 1959*, 109–13

H. R. Beard: 'Figaro in England: Productions of Mozart's Opera, and the Early Adaptations of it in England before 1850', *Maske und Kothurn*, x (1964), 498–513

R. Moberly and C. Raeburn: 'Mozart's "Figaro": the Plan of Act III', *ML*, xlvi (1965), 134–6; repr. in *MJb 1965–6*, 161–3

G. Reiss: 'Die Thematik der Komödie in *Le nozze di Figaro*', *MJb 1965–6*, 164–78

K.-H. Köhler: 'Mozarts Kompositionsweise: Beobachtungen am Figaro-Autograph', *MJb 1967*, 31–45

F. Noske: 'Musical Quotation as a Dramatic Device: the Fourth Act of *Le nozze di Figaro*', *MQ*, liv (1968), 185–98; repr. in Noske (1977), 3–17

H. Graf: 'Der 4. Akt des Figaro', *MJb 1968–70*, 95–8

K.-H. Köhler: 'Figaro-Miscellen: einige dramaturgische Mitteilungen zur Quellensituation', *MJb 1968–70*, 119–31

F. Noske: 'Social Tensions in "Le nozze di Figaro"', *ML*, l (1969), 45–62; repr. in Noske (1977), 18–38

B. Brophy: '"Figaro" and the Limitations of Music', *ML*, li (1970), 26–36

A. Livermore: 'Rousseau, Beaumarchais, and Figaro', *MQ*, lvii (1971), 466–90

L. Finscher: Preface, NMA II:5/xvi (1973)

H. Goldschmidt: 'Die Cavatina des Figaro: eine semantische Analyse', *BMw*, xv (1973), 185–207

M. O. Smith: *Beaumarchais et Mozart: Essai d'étude comparée entre 'Le mariage de Figaro' et 'Les noces de Figaro'* (diss., U. of Paris, 1974)

H. L. Scheel: '"Le mariage de Figaro" von Beaumarchais und das Libretto der "Nozze di Figaro" von Lorenzo da Ponte', *Mf*, xxviii (1975), 156–73

W. Ruf: *Die Rezeption von Mozarts 'Le nozze di Figaro' bei den Zeitgenossen* (Wiesbaden, 1977)

G. Schmidgall: *Literature as Opera* (New York, 1977), 67–107

L'avant-scène opéra, no.21 (1979) [*Le nozze di Figaro* issue]

J.-V. Hocquard: *'Le nozze di Figaro' de Mozart* (Paris, 1979)

M. Mila: *Lettura delle 'Nozze di Figaro': Mozart e la ricerca della felicità* (Turin, 1979)

C. Dahlhaus: 'Zur Methode der Opern-Analyse', *Musik und Bildung*, xii (1980), 518–23

J. D. Drummond: *Opera in Perspective* (London, 1980), 193–222

H. Rudiger: 'Muss Mozart verständlich sein? Zu Karl Wolfskehls Übersetzung von Da Pontes Figaro', *Das deutsche Singspiel im 18. Jahrhundert: Amorbach 1979*, 171–89

A. Tyson: 'Le nozze di Figaro: Lessons from the Autograph Score', *MT*, cxxii (1981), 456–61; repr. in Tyson (1987), 114–24

W. J. Allanbrook: 'Pro Marcellina: the Shape of "Figaro", Act IV', *ML*, lxiii (1982), 69–84

A. Csampai and D. Holland, eds.: *W. A. Mozart: Die Hochzeit des Figaros: Texte, Materialien, Kommentare* (Hamburg, 1982)

L. Finscher: 'Verlorengegangene Selbstverständlichkeiten?', *Musica*, xxxvi (1982), 19–23

J. Bernick: *'The Marriage of Figaro*: Genesis of a Dramatic Masterpiece', *OQ*, i/2 (1983), 79–90

S. Dudley: 'Les premières versions françaises du *Mariage de Figaro* de Mozart', *RdM*, lxix (1983), 55–83

N. John, ed.: *The Marriage of Figaro* (London, 1983) [ENO opera guide]

B. A. Brown: 'Beaumarchais, Mozart and the Vaudeville: Two Examples from "The Marriage of Figaro"', *MT*, cxxvii (1986), 261–5

D. Heartz: 'Setting the Stage for Figaro', *MT*, cxxvii (1986), 256–60; repr. in Heartz (1990), 123–31

T. Carter: *W. A. Mozart: Le nozze di Figaro* (Cambridge, 1987)

D. Heartz: 'Constructing *Le nozze di Figaro*', *JRMA*, cxii (1987), 77–98; repr. in Heartz (1990), 133–55

A. Tyson: 'Some Problems in the Text of *Le nozze di Figaro*: Did Mozart Have a Hand in Them?', *JRMA*, cxii (1987), 99–131; repr. in Tyson (1987), 290–327

W. J. Allanbrook: 'Opera Seria Borrowings in *Le nozze di Figaro*: the Count's "Vedrò mentr'io"', *Studies in the History of Music*, ii (New York, 1988), 83–96

M. Schuler: 'Die Aufführung von Mozarts "Le Nozze di Figaro" in Donaueschingen 1787: ein Beitrag zur Rezeptionsgeschichte', *AMw*, xlv (1988), 111–31

A. Tyson: 'The 1786 Prague Version of Mozart's "Le nozze di Figaro"', *ML*, lxix (1988), 321–33

——, ed.: *W. A. Mozart: Le nozze di Figaro: Eight Variant Versions* (Oxford, 1989)

J. Platoff: 'Tonal Organization in "Buffo" Finales and the Act II Finale of "Le nozze di Figaro"', *ML*, lxxii (1991), 387–403

Don Giovanni

K. Engel: *Die Don-Juan Sage auf der Bühne* (Dresden, 1887)

R. von Freisauff: *Mozarts Don Juan* (Salzburg, 1887)

F. Chrysander: 'Die Oper *Don Giovanni* von Gazzaniga und von Mozart', *VMw*, iv (1888), 351–435

C. Gounod: *Le Don Juan de Mozart* (Paris, 1890; Eng. trans., 1895)

V. Maurel: *A propos de la mise en scène de Don Juan: Réflexions et souvenirs* (Paris, 1896)

A. Heuss: 'Das dämonische Element in Mozarts Werken', *ZIMG*, vii (1905–6), 175–86

O. Rank: *Die Don Juan-Gestalt* (Leipzig, 1924; Eng. trans., 1975)

R. Dumesnil: *Le 'Don Juan' de Mozart* (Paris, 1927)

J. Tiersot: *Don Juan de Mozart* (Paris, 1933)

A. Einstein: 'Das erste Libretto des *Don Giovanni*', *AcM*, ix (1937), 149–50; Eng. trans. in Einstein, *Essays on Music* (New York, 1956), 217–20

——: 'Concerning some Recitatives in "Don Giovanni"', *ML*, xix (1938), 417–25; repr. in Einstein (1956), 221–31

P. Stefan: *Don Giovanni: die Opernlegende von Don Juan, dem Versucher und Sucher* (Vienna, 1938)

P. J. Jouve: *Le Don Juan de Mozart* (Fribourg, 1942; Eng. trans., 1957)

E. Wellesz: '"Don Giovanni" and the "dramma giocoso"', *MR*, iv (1943), 121–6

A. Farinelli: *Don Giovanni* (Milan, 1946)

L. Dallapiccola: 'Notes on the Statue Scene in "Don Giovanni"', *Music Survey*, iii (1950), 89–97; repr. in *Dallapiccola on Opera* (London, 1987), 186–211

G. Clive: 'The Demonic in Mozart', *ML*, xxxvii (1956), 1–13

C. Bitter: '*Don Giovanni* in Wien, 1788', *MJb 1959*, 146–64

P. Nettl: 'Die Spanische Seele des Don Giovanni', *MJb 1959*, 262–5

C. Bitter: *Wandlungen in den Inszenierungsformen des 'Don Giovanni' von 1787 bis 1928* (Regensburg, 1961)

A. Livermore: 'The Origins of Don Juan', *ML*, xliv (1963), 257–65

J. Liebner: 'Don Juan et ses ancêtres, ou la métamorphose d'une légende', *SMz*, civ (1964), 237–43

G. Macchia: *Vita, avventure e morte di Don Giovanni* (Bari, 1966)

W. Plath and W. Rehm: Preface, NMA II:5/xvii (1968)

A. Rosenberg: *Don Giovanni* (Munich, 1968)

C. Henning: 'Thematic Metamorphoses in *Don Giovanni*', *MR*, xxx (1969), 22–6

I. M. Schenk: *The Interrelationship of Music and Drama in Mozart's Don Giovanni* (diss., Northwestern U., 1969)

F. W. Müller: 'Zur Genealogie von Leporellos Liste', *Beiträge zur Romanischen Philologie*, ix (1970), 199–228

F. Noske: '*Don Giovanni*: Musical Affinities and Dramatic Structure', *SM*, xii (1970), 167–203; repr. in Noske (1977), 39–75

H. H. Eggebrecht: *Versuch über die Wiener Klassik: die Tanzszene in Mozarts 'Don Giovanni'* (Wiesbaden, 1972)

S. Kunze: *Don Giovanni vor Mozart: die Tradition der Don Giovanni-Opern im italienischen Buffo-Theater des 18. Jahrhunderts* (Munich, 1972)

H. Lagrave: 'Don Juan au siècle des lumières', *Approches des lumières: Mélanges offerts à Jean Fabre* (Paris, 1974), 257–76

H. Kalser: 'Mozarts Don Giovanni und E. T. A. Hoffmann's Don Juan', *Mitteilungen der E. T. A. Hoffmann-Gesellschaft*, xxi (1975), 6–26

P. P. Várnai: '"... è sempre ugual ..."', *NRMI*, ix (1975), 205–18

H. Abert (and O. Jahn): *Mozart's 'Don Giovanni'* (London, 1976) [Eng. trans., from Abert 1919–21]

R. Dammann: 'Die "Register-Arie" in Mozarts *Don Giovanni*', *AMw*, xxxiii (1976), 278–308; xxxiv (1977), 56–80

E. Diet: *Regards sur l'Opéra* (Rouen, 1976)

F. Noske: '*Don Giovanni*: an Interpretation', *Theatre Research/Recherches théâtrales*, xiii (1973–4), 60–74; repr. in Noske (1977), 76–92

J.-V. Hocquard: *Le Don Giovanni de Mozart* (Paris, 1978)

S. Kunze: 'Mozarts Don Giovanni und die Tanzszene im ersten Finale', *AnMc*, no.18 (1978), 166–97

P. Petrobelli: '*Don Giovanni* in Italia: la fortunata dell'opera ed il suo influsso', *AnMc*, no.18 (1978), 30–51

J. Rousset: *Le mythe de Don Juan* (Paris, 1978)

E. Agmon: 'The Descending Fourth and its Symbolic Significance in *Don Giovanni*', *Theory and Practice*, iv/2 (1979), 3–11

L'avant-scène opéra, no.24 (1979) [*Don Giovanni* issue]

F. Goldbeck: 'A travers la partition de Don Giovanni', *ReM*, nos.322–3 (1979), 5–60

D. Heartz: 'Goldoni, Don Giovanni and the dramma giocoso', *MT*, cxx (1979), 993–8; repr. in Heartz (1990), 195–205

C. M. Proctor: *The Singspiel and the Singspiel Adaptation of Mozart's 'Don Giovanni': an Eighteenth-Century Manuscript* (diss., U. of Iowa, 1979)

E. Valentin: '"Don Ottavio balla Minuetto"', *Acta Mozartiana*, xxvi (1979), 66–71

A. Pivara: 'Don Juan et la mort ou la difficulté d'être libertin', *Etudes et recherches sur le XVIIIme siècle* (Marseilles, 1980), 1–56

L. B. Ratner: *Classic Music: Expression, Form and Style* (New York, 1980), 397–411

U. Weisstein: 'So machen's – eben nicht alle! Da Ponte-Mozarts *Don Giovanni* und die vergleichende Erotik', *Elemente der Literatur: Elisabeth Frenzel zum 65. Geburtstag* (Stuttgart, 1980)

K. Werner-Jensen: *Studien zur 'Don Giovanni': Rezeption in 19. Jahrhundert* (Tutzing, 1980)

N. Pirrotta: 'The Traditions of Don Juan Plays and Comic Operas', *PRMA*, cvii (1980–81), 60–70

A. Csampai and D. Holland, eds.: *W. A. Mozart: Don Giovanni: Texte, Materialien, Kommentare* (Hamburg, 1981)

R. Donington: 'Don Giovanni goes to Hell', *MT*, cxxii (1981), 446–8

D. Heartz: '"Che mi sembra di morir": Donna Elvira and the Sextet', *MT*, cxxii (1981), 448–51; repr. in Heartz (1990), 207–15

W. Rehm: 'Zur Dramaturgie von Mozarts *Don Giovanni*: die beiden Fassungen Prag 1787 und Wien 1788 – ein philologisches Problem?', *HJbMw*, v (1981), 247–54

S. Sadie: 'Some Operas of 1787', *MT*, cxxii (1981), 474–7

J. Rushton: *W. A. Mozart: Don Giovanni* (Cambridge, 1981)

M. Staehelin: '"*Ah fuggi il traditor*": Bemerkungen zur zweiten Donna-Elvira-Arie in Mozarts *Don Giovanni*', *Festschrift Heinz Becker zum 60. Geburtstag* (Laaber, 1982), 67–86

N. John, ed.: *Don Giovanni* (London, 1983) [ENO opera guide]

M. Beckerman: 'Mozart's Duel with Don Giovanni', *MJb 1984–5*, 9–14

J. Stone: 'The Making of "Don Giovanni" and its Ethos', *MJb 1984–5*, 130–33

S. Henze-Döhring: *Opera seria, opera buffa, und Mozarts Don Giovanni: zur Gattungskonvergenz in der italienischen Opera des 18. Jahrhunderts*, AnMc, no.24 (1986) [whole issue]

L. Finscher: '"Don Giovanni" 1987', *MJb 1987–8*, 19–27

I. Kristek: *Mozart's Don Giovanni in Prague* (Prague, 1987)

S. Kunze: '[*Don Giovanni*:] Werkbestand und Aufführungsgestalt', *MJb 1987–8*, 205–15

L. Lipperni: *Introduzione al Don Giovanni* (Rome, 1987)

W. Rehm: '"Don Giovanni": nochmals "Prager Original" – "Überarbeitung Wien" – "Mischfassung"', *MJb 1987–8*, 195–203

A. Forti-Lewis: 'Parole o musica? Don Giovanni "illuminato" da Goldoni e Mozart', *Italian Quarterly*, no.117 (1989), 31–42

E. Agmon: 'Dramatic Content in the *Don Giovanni* Overture', *Israel Studies in Musicology*, v (1990), 27–42

J. Miller, ed.: *The Don Giovanni Book: Myths of Seduction and Betrayal* (London, 1990)

J. W. Smeed: *Don Juan: Variations on a Theme* (London and New York, 1990)

A. Tyson: 'Some Features of the Autograph Score of *Don Giovanni*', *Israel Studies in Musicology*, v (1990), 7–26

Così fan tutte

G. de St Foix: 'Quelques observations sur le livret de "Così fan tutte"', *RdM*, xi (1930), 93–7

E. H. Gombrich: 'Così fan tutte (Procris included)', *Journal of the Warburg and Courtauld Institutes*, vii (1954), 372–4

M. Mila: 'Razionalismo di "Così fan tutte"', *Mozart, la vita e le opere*, ed. F. Armani (Milan, 1955), 195

D. J. Keahey: 'Così fan tutte: Parody or Irony?', *Paul A. Pisk: Essays in his Honor* (Austin, 1966), 116–30

G. Reiss: 'Komödie und Musik: Bemerkungen zur musikalischen Komödie Così fan tutte', *Mf*, xx (1967), 8–19

H. Keller: 'Mozart's Wrong Key Signature', *Tempo*, no.98 (1972), 21–7

B. Williams: 'Passion and Cynicism: Remarks on "Così fan tutte"', *MT*, cxiv (1973), 361–4

S. Kunze: 'Über das Verhältnis von musikalisch autonomer Struktur und Textbau in Mozarts Opern: das Terzettino "Soave sia il vento" (No. 10) aus "Così fan tutte"', *MJb 1973–4*, 217–32

H. Meyer: 'Così fan tutte und die Endzeit des ancien régime', *Hans Chemin-Petit: Betrachtungen einer Lebensleitung. Festschrift zum 75. Geburtstag* (Berlin, 1977)

F. Noske: '"Così fan tutte": Dramatic Irony', in Noske (1977), 93–120

L'avant-scène opéra, no.16–17 (1978) [*Così fan tutte* issue]

J.-M. Breque: 'Così fan tutte: l'oeuvre et son livret', *ReM* (1978), no.313, 13–40

J.-V. Hocquard: *Così fan tutte* (Paris, 1978)

B. Porena: 'La parola intonata in *Così fan tutte*', *AnMc*, no.18 (1978), 198–204

S. Vill, ed.: *Così fan tutte: Beiträge zur Wirkungsgeschichte von Mozarts Oper* (Bayreuth, 1978)

C. Kritsch and H. Zeman: 'Das Rätsel eines genialen Opernentwurfs: Da Pontes Libretto zu "Così fan tutte" und das literarische Umfeld des 18. Jahrhunderts', *Die Österreichische Literatur: Ihr Profil an der Wende vom 18. zum 19. Jahrhundert (1750–1830)*, i (Graz, 1979), 355–77

P. Branscombe: 'Così in Context', *MT*, cxxii (1981), 461–4

A. Steptoe: 'The Sources of "Così fan tutte": a Reappraisal', *ML*, lxii (1981), 281–94

G. Brandstetter: 'So machen's alle: die frühen Übersetzungen von Da Pontes und Mozarts "Così fan tutte" für deutsche Bühnen', *Mf*, xxxv (1982), 27–44

N. John, ed.: *Così fan tutte* (London, 1983) [ENO opera guide]

A. Csampai and D. Holland, eds.: *W. A. Mozart: Così fan tutte: Texte, Materialien, Kommentare* (Hamburg, 1984)

A. Tyson: 'Notes on the Composition of *Così fan tutte*', *JAMS*, xxxvii (1984), 356–401; repr. in Tyson (1987), 177–221

A. Steptoe: 'Mozart, Mesmer and *Così fan tutte*', *ML*, lxvii (1986), 248–55

L'avant-scène opéra, no.131–2 (Paris, 1990) [*Così fan tutte* issue]

D. Edge: 'Mozart's Fee for Così fan tutte', *JRMA*, cxvi (1991), 211–35

C. C. Ford: *Così? Sexual Politics in Mozart's Operas* (Manchester, 1991)

B. A. Brown: *W. A. Mozart: 'Così fan tutte'* (Cambridge, forthcoming)

Die Zauberflöte

L. Nohl: *Die Zauberflöte* (Frankfurt, 1862)

E. Komorzynski: *Emanuel Schikaneder: ein Beitrag zur Geschichte des deutschen Theaters* (Vienna, 1901, 2/1951, 3/1955)

E. J. Dent: *The Magic Flute* (Cambridge, 1911)

H. W. von Waltershausen: *Die Zauberflöte: eine operndramaturgische Studie* (Munich, 1920)

P. Nettl: *Mozart und die königliche Kunst: die freimaurerischen Grundlagen der 'Zauberflöte'* (Berlin, 1932, 2/1956)

F. Brukner: *Die Zauberflöte: unbekannte Handschriften und seltene Drucke aus der Frühzeit der Opera* (Vienna, 1934)

P. Stefan: *Die Zauberflöte: Herkunft, Bedeutung, Geheimnis* (Vienna, 1937)

E. Komorzynski: '"Die Zauberflöte": Entstehung und Bedeutung des Kunstwerks', *Neues Mozart-Jb*, i (1941), 147–74

A. H. King: 'The Melodic Sources and Affinities of *Die Zauberflöte*', *MQ*, xxxvi (1950), 241–58; repr. in King (1955), 141–63

G. Friedrich: *Die Humanistische Idee der 'Zauberflöte'* (Dresden, 1954)

E. Schmitz: 'Formgesetze in Mozarts *Zauberflöte*', *Festschrift Max Schneider zum achtzigsten Geburtstage* (Leipzig, 1955), 209–14

R. Hammerstein: 'Der Gesang der geharnischten Männer: eine Studie zu Mozarts Bachbild', *AMw*, xiii (1956), 1–24

P. Nettl: *Mozart and Masonry* (New York, 1957)

E. Werner: 'Leading or Symbolic Formulas in *The Magic Flute*', *MR*, xviii (1957), 286–93

T. Cornelissen: *Die Zauberflöte von W. A. Mozart* (Berlin, 2/1963)

A. Rosenberg: *Die Zauberflöte: Geschichte und Deutung* (Munich, 1964)

P. Branscombe: '"Die Zauberflöte": some Textual and Interpretative Problems', *PRMA*, xcii (1965–6), 45–64

G. Gruber: 'Das Autograph der "Zauberflöte"', *MJb 1967*, 127–49; *MJb 1968–70*, 99–110

J. Chailley: '*La flûte enchantée', opéra maçonnique: essai d'explication du livret et de la musique* (Paris, 1968; Eng. trans., 1972)

E. M. Batley: *A Preface to the Magic Flute* (London, 1969)

G. Gruber and A. Orel: Preface, NMA II:5/xix (1970)

A. Williamson: 'Who was Sarastro?', *Opera*, xxi (1970), 297–305 [see also 695–6]

K. Hammer: 'Zur Allegorisierung und Aktualisierung der "Zauberflöte"', *Acta Mozartiana*, xxi (1974), 60–65

T. Mäkinen: 'Über Mozarts zentrale Motive in der *Zauberflöte*', *IMS: Berlin 1974*, 336–42

G. Gruber: 'Bedeutung und Spontaneität in Mozarts "Zauberflöte"', *Festschrift Walter Senn* (Munich and Salzburg, 1975), 118–30

D. Koenigsberger: 'A New Metaphor for Mozart's *Magic Flute*', *European Studies Review*, v (1975), 229–75

L'avant-scène opéra, no.1 (1976) [*Die Zauberflöte* issue]

G. Fierz: 'Mozarts "Zauberflöte" unter neuen Aspekten: das Libretto Schikaneders im Vergleich mit neueren Übersetzungen', *Acta Mozartiana*, xxiv (1977), 14–24

T. G. Georgiades: 'Der Chor "Triumph, du edles Paar" aus dem 2. Finale der Zauberflöte', *Kleine Schriften* (Tutzing, 1977), 145–55

G. Gruber: '*Die Zauberflöte* (Peroration)', *IMSCR*, xii *Berkeley 1977*, 250–55

K. Thomson: *The Masonic Thread in Mozart* (London, 1977)

H.-K. Metzger and R. Riehn: *Ist die Zauberflöte ein Machwerk?*, Musik-Konzepte, no.3 (1978) [whole issue]

E. Neumann: '"The Magic Flute"', *Quadrant*, ii/wint. (1978), 5–32

J. Starobinski: 'Pouvoir et lumières dans "La flûte enchantée"', *XVIIIe siècle*, x (1978), 435–49

J. A. Eckelmeyer: 'Novus ordo seclorum: Some Political Implications in the Libretto of *The Magic Flute*', *Eighteenth-Century Life*, v/4 (1978–9), 77–89

E. Fuhrich and G. Prossnitz: *Vom Salzburger Hanswurst zum Welterfolg der Zauberflöte* (Salzburg, 1979)

J.-V. Hocquard: *La flûte enchantée* (Paris, 1979)

J. Godwin: 'Layers of Meaning in *The Magic Flute*', *MQ*, lxv (1979), 471–92

H. Zeman: '"Aber ich hörte viel von Pamina, viel von Tamino": Wer kennt den Text der *Zauberflöte*?', *Das deutsche Singspiel im 18. Jahrhundert: Amorbach 1979*, 139–69

J. Eckelmeyer: 'Two Complexes of Recurrent Melodies related to *Die Zauberflöte*', *MR*, xli (1980), 11–25

R. Görner: 'Zu Kierkegaards Verständnis der "Zauberflöte"', *Mitteilungen der Internationalen Stiftung Mozarteum*, xxviii/3–4 (1980), 25–31

N. John, ed.: *The Magic Flute* (London, 1980) [ENO opera guide]

C.-H. Mahling: '"Die Zauberflöte": Mysterienspiel oder Maschinenkomödie?', *Werk und Wiedergabe: Musiktheater exemplarisch interpretiert*, ed. S. Wiesmann (Bayreuth, 1980), 99–108

R. Wangermée: 'Quelques mystères de "La flûte enchantée"', *RBM*, xxxiv–xxxv (1980–81), 147–63

F. Grasberger: 'Zum Inhaltsproblem der Zauberflöte', *Mitteilungen der Kommission für Musikforschung*, xxxii (Vienna, 1981)

A. Csampai and D. Holland, eds.: *W. A. Mozart: Zauberflöte: Texte, Materialien, Kommentare* (Hamburg, 1982)

E. Werner: 'Dualismus und Einheit in Mozarts *Zauberflöte*', *Festschrift Othmar Wessely zum 60. Geburtstag* (Tutzing, 1982), 555–86

D. Heartz: 'La clemenza di Sarastro', *MT*, cxxiv (1983), 152–7; repr. in Heartz (1990), 255–75

C. Peter: *Die Sprache der Musik in Mozarts Zauberflöte* (Stuttgart, 1983)

M. S. Cole: '*The Magic Flute* and the Quatrain', *JM*, iii (1984), 157–76

J. Eckelmeyer: 'Structure as Hermeneutic Guide to *The Magic Flute*', *MQ*, lxxii (1986), 51–73

M. Freyhan: 'Toward the Original Text of Mozart's *Die Zauberflöte*', *JAMS*, xxxix (1986), 355–80

L'avant-scène opéra, no.101 (1987) [*Die Zauberflöte* issue]

N. John: 'Monostatos: Pamina's Incubus', *Opern und Opernfiguren: Festschrift für Joachim Herz* (Anif and Salzburg, 1989), 101–14

T. Bauman: 'At the North Gate: Instrumental Music in *Die Zauberflöte*', in Heartz (1990), 277–97

P. Branscombe: *W. A. Mozart: 'Die Zauberflöte'* (Cambridge, 1991)

R. R. Subotnik: 'Whose *Magic Flute*? Intimations of Reality at the Gates of Enlightenment', *19th Century Music*, xv (1991–2), 132–50

D. J. Buch: 'Fairy-Tale Literature and *Die Zauberflöte*', *AcM*, lxiv (1992), 30–49

J. A. Eckelmeyer: *A Cultural Context of Mozart's 'Magic Flute': Social, Aesthetic, Philosophical* (Lewiston, NY, 1992)

La clemenza di Tito

J. A. Westrup: 'Two First Performances: Monteverdi's "Orfeo" and Mozart's "La clemenza di Tito"', *ML*, xxxix (1958), 327–35

L. T. Volek: 'Über den Ursprung von Mozarts Oper "La clemenza di Tito"', *MJb 1959*, 274–86

F. Giegling: 'Zu den Rezitativen von Mozarts Oper "Titus"', *MJb 1967*, 121–6

——: 'Metastasios Opera "La clemenza di Tito" in der Bearbeitung durch Mazzolà', *MJb 1968–70*, 88–94

B. Brophy: 'Pro Tito', *MT*, cix (1969), 600–07

F. Giegling: Preface, NMA II:5/xx (1970)

R. B. Moberly and C. Raeburn: 'The Mozart Version of *La clemenza di Tito*', *MR*, xxxi (1970), 285–94

H. Lühning: 'Zur Entstehungsgeschichte von Mozarts "Titus"', *Mf*, xxvii (1974), 300–18; see also xxviii (1975), 75–81 [J. H. Eibl], 311–14 [H. Lühning]; xxix (1976), 127–8 [J. H. Eibl]

R. B. Moberly: 'The Influence of French Classical Drama on Mozart's "La clemenza di Tito"', *ML*, lv (1974), 286–98

A. Tyson: '"La clemenza di Tito" and its Chronology', *MT*, cxvi (1975), 221–7; repr. in Tyson (1987), 48–60

J. H. Eibl: '" … una porcheria tedesca"? Zur Uraufführung von Mozarts "La clemenza di Tito"', *ÖMz*, xxxi (1976), 329–34

F. Giegling: '"La clemenza di Tito": Metastasio – Mazzolà – Mozart', *ÖMz*, xxxi (1976), 321–9

D. J. Neville: 'La clemenza di Tito: Metastasio, Mazzolà and Mozart', *Studies in Music from the University of Western Ontario*, i (1976), 124–48

——: 'Idomeneo and La clemenza di Tito: opera seria and "vera opera"', *Studies in Music from the University of Western Ontario*, ii (1977), 138–66; iii (1978), 97–126; v (1980), 99–121; vi (1981), 112–46; viii (1983), 107–36

D. Heartz: 'Mozart's Overture to Titus as Dramatic Argument', *MQ*, lxiv (1978), 29–49; repr. in Heartz (1990), 319–41

W. Dürr: 'Zur Dramaturgie des "Titus": Mozarts Libretto und Metastasio', *MJb 1978–9*, 55–60

D. Heartz: 'Mozart and his Italian Contemporaries: La clemenza di Tito', *MJb 1978–9*, 275–93; repr. in Heartz (1990), 299–317

J. P. Parakilas: *Mozarts "Tito" and the Music of Rhetorical Strategy* (diss., Cornell U., 1979)

W. Pross: 'Neulateinische Tradition und Aufklärung in Mazzolà/ Mozarts "La clemenza di Tito"', *Jb für Österreichische Kulturgeschichte*, vii–ix (1979), 379–401

D. Heartz: 'Mozarts "Titus" und die italienische Oper um 1800', *HJbMw*, v (1981), 255–66

H. Lühning: *Titus-Vertonungen im 18. Jahrhundert: Untersuchungen zur Tradition der Opera seria von Hasse bis Mozart*, *AnMc*, no.20 (1983) [whole issue]

M. P. McClymonds: 'Mozart's "La clemenza di Tito" and opera seria in Florence as a Reflection of Leopold II's Musical Taste', *MJb 1984–5*, 61–70

R. Wiesend: 'Ein "einfaches Sekundanierstück ohne individuelle Züge"? Tradition und Erfindung in der Arie "Torna a Tito a lato"', *MJb 1984–5*, 134–44

D. Neville: *Mozart's 'La clemenza di Tito' and the Metastasian opera seria* (diss., U. of Cambridge, 1986)

L'avant-scène opéra, no.99 (1987) [*La clemenza di Tito* issue]

D. Neville: 'Cartesian Principles in Mozart's *La clemenza di Tito*', *Studies in the History of Music*, ii (New York, 1988), 97–123

J. Rice: *W. A. Mozart: 'La clemenza di Tito'* (Cambridge, 1991)

JULIAN RUSHTON

Mozart and Salieri [*Motsart i Sal'yeri*]. Dramatic scenes by NIKOLAY ANDREYEVICH RIMSKY-KORSAKOV, op.48, to the slightly abridged text of the eponymous 'little tragedy' by ALEXANDER SERGEYEVICH PUSHKIN (1830); Moscow, Solodovnikov Theatre (Savva Mamontov's Private Russian Opera), 25 November/7 December 1898.

Pushkin's terse duodrama, depicting the Romantic legend of Mozart's death at the hands of an envious rival, was another in the same group of tiny verse plays that had furnished the text for *The Stone Guest* of Alexander Dargomïzhsky, to whom the opera is dedicated. The poet used the legend ironically, to proclaim the victory of art – the 'Hellenic' temper, bringer of sweetness and light – over stern Mosaic moralism. The kernel of the play is a pair of despairing monologues for Salieri that frame the opening scene. 'Where is justice', he cries, 'when the holy gift of immortal genius is bestowed not as a reward for fervent love of art, self-sacrificing labour, prayer and zeal, but lights upon the head of a dunce, an idle gadabout?'

Rimsky-Korsakov composed *Mozart and Salieri* in 1897; the première was conducted by Giuseppe Truffi, with Vasily Shkafer as Mozart, Fyodor Shalyapin as Salieri and Sergey Rakhmaninov as pianist behind the scenes. That Rimsky intended his 'dialogue opera' as a homage to Dargomïzhsky's opera – though 'without its

form and modulatory scheme … being quite as much an accident' – would be evident even without his explicit avowal. There are some subtle, half-concealed quotations from *The Stone Guest* in *Mozart and Salieri*, including the poignant orchestral passage that brings the newer work to its close. Rimsky's setting is even more resolutely lyrical than its model, Pushkin's iambic pentameters being for the most part couched not in the neutral common-time of traditional recitative but in a lilting 6/4 metre. Salieri – a juicy role that brought Shalyapin his first fame – is cast as a stormy baritone; Mozart, the lightest (and, one must add, blandest) of lyric tenors, contrasts in every way.

Far more conspicuous than the muted Dargomïzhskian echoes are the Mozartian quotations – *Figaro*, *Don Giovanni* and of course the Requiem – that dot Rimsky's score, along with some able stylistic pastiche (e.g. when the Mozart character 'improvises' at the keyboard). The outwardly sympathetic portrayal of Salieri, artist by dint of noble effort and honest pain, had obvious attractions for Rimsky-Korsakov, who saw himself just that way vis-à-vis his more gifted colleagues Borodin and Musorgsky. That his hard work had indeed won him mastery is evident from the finely wrought texture of the accompaniment (for a reduced 'classical' orchestra with single wind and a pair of horns, plus solo piano where Mozart plays and an ad libitum chorus for the Requiem snatch). The intricate triple counterpoint and motivic inversions nowhere obtrude; indeed, the score is one of the composer's most poetic, quite belying the common contention that he could write for any sort of character except a human one.

The one place where virtuoso counterpoint called attention to itself was in an Intermezzo-Fughetta between the scenes; true to his fabled powers of dispassionate self-criticism, Rimsky excised it before publication. Naturally, it has been reinstated since his death by performers bent on 'authenticity'.

RICHARD TARUSKIN

Mozeen, Mrs. *See* EDWARDS.

Mozzi [Mozzio, Moggi], **Pietro** (*b* ? Florence, Siena or Rome; *fl* 1686–1729). Italian bass. He is first mentioned in 1686, singing Publius in Antonio Sartorio's *Antonino e Pompeiano* in Milan. The libretto designated him a virtuoso of Duke Ferdinando Carlo Gonzaga of Mantua, a title which was made official (or reaffirmed) on 5 June 1688, with a monthly salary and the rent of a house in Mantua. Temperamentally he was unpredictable and troublesome; he tried to shoot the tenor Antonio Ristorini in Bologna in 1696 (failing only because his gun was defective), and this led to his expulsion from the Accademia Filarmonica of Bologna. He performed in most of the main operatic centres in Italy, including Naples in 1707–8, 1710–11 and 1723, and Rome in 1710, 1718–19, 1721 and 1723–4. His name tends to be confused with that of Marcantonio Mozzi, a singer and theorbo player (*b* Florence, 1678; *d* Venice, 4 April 1736).

P. Besutti: *La corte musicale di Ferdinando Carlo Gonzaga ultimo duca di Mantova: musici, cantanti e teatro d'opera tra il 1665 e il 1707* (Mantua, 1989)
PAOLA BESUTTI

Mraczek [Mráček], **Joseph Gustav** (*b* Brno, 12 March 1878; *d* Dresden, 24 Dec 1944). German composer of Czech birth. Son of a cellist and music teacher, he studied at the Musikvereinschule in Brno and later (1894–6) at the Vienna Conservatory with Joseph Hellmesberger and others. He led the German Theatre orchestra in Brno (1897–1902) and taught the violin at the Musikvereinschule (1898–1918) and then composition at the Dresden Conservatory. From 1919 to 1924 he also conducted the Dresden PO. Mraczek composed in many genres besides opera; the work for which he was most popular was the symphonic burlesque *Max und Moritz* (1911, based on Wilhelm Busch's nursery rhymes), a piece brilliantly orchestrated in the Strauss manner.

Der gläserne Pantoffel (3, Mraczek, after A. von Platen), Brno, Stadt, 14 April 1902
Der Traum (3, Mraczek, after F. Grillparzer: *Der Traum ein Leben*), Brno, Stadt, 26 Feb 1909
Kismet (Traumspiel, 5, E. Knoblaack, trans. C. Lindau), Munich, Künstler, 8 June 1912
Aebelö (romantische Oper, 3, A. Nikisch, after S. Michaelis), Breslau, Stadt, 13 Nov 1915
Der Liebesrat (Schäferspiel, G. Glück), Brno, 30 April 1916
Ikdar (3, Glück), Dresden, National, 24 Jan 1921
Herrn Dürers Bild, oder Madonna am Wiesenzaun (3, A. Ostermann, after F. K. Ginzkey), Hanover, 29 Jan 1927
Der arme Tobias (radio op), 1936

*

E. H. Müller: *Joseph Gustav Mraczek* (Dresden, 1917)
EVA HERRMANNOVÁ

Mravina [Mravinskaya], **Yevgeniya Konstantinovna** (*b* St Petersburg, 4/16 Feb 1864; *d* Yalta, 12/25 Oct 1914). Russian soprano. She studied with Pryanishnikov, then with Artôt in Berlin and Mathilde Marchesi in Paris. She made her début at Vittorio Veneto in August 1885 as Gilda. From 1886 to 1897 she sang at the Mariinsky Theatre, where in 1895 she created Oxana in Rimsky-Korsakov's *Christmas Eve*; her repertory also included Antonida (*A Life for the Tsar*), Lyudmila, Tatyana and roles in operas by Gounod, Meyerbeer and Wagner. In 1891–2 she sang in concerts in various Italian cities and in Berlin, and she made further European tours in 1902–3 and 1906. Mravina was outstandingly beautiful, with a voice of exceptional purity and impeccable enunciation, attributes she used with intelligence, to appropriate dramatic and musical ends.

*

E. Stark: *Peterburgskaya opera i eyo mastera, 1890–1910* [St Petersburg opera and its stars] (Leningrad, 1940)
Ye. Alexeyeva: 'Yevgeniya Mravina', *SovM* (1964), no.4, pp.92–7
A. Kollontay: 'Iz vospominaniy' [Reminiscences], ibid, 98–9
Ye. Mravina: 'Stranichka memuarov' [A Page of Memoirs], ibid, 99–100
A. Grigoreva: *Ye. K. Mravina* (Moscow, 1970)

Mshvelidze, Shalva Mikhaylovich (*b* Tbilisi, 15/28 May 1904; *d* Tbilisi, 4 March 1984). Georgian composer. His interest in music began in the Tbilisi Gymnasium choir. Later, after the family had moved to east Georgia, he took part in folk ensembles and, 1920–25, directed student and army choirs, teaching and performing mostly folksongs. He studied at the Tbilisi Conservatory, graduating in 1930, and at the Leningrad Conservatory. His ethnomusicological research, which became an important part of his activities, began with expeditions in 1927. In 1929 he began teaching at the Tbilisi Conservatory, where he became professor in 1942. He held administrative posts, notably as deputy director of the Tbilisi Opera and Ballet Theatre, was on the board of composers' unions and was a deputy to the

Supreme Soviet of the Georgian SSR (1951–6). He received many honours and awards.

Mshvelidze played an important part in the formation and development of 20th-century Georgian music. As in the work of his contemporaries, forms and modes of thought new to Georgian music originated and became established in his music, which shows an organic fusion of national traditions and European music in general. In particular Mshvelidze laid the foundations for Georgian epic symphonism with his symphonic poem *Zviadauri* (1940). As an opera composer, Mshvelidze developed the tradition of the national classics. This is shown with particular force in *Ambavi Tarielisa* ('The Legend of Tariel', 1946), based on *Vepkhis tkaosani* ('The Knight in the Tigerskin') by the 12th-century Georgian poet Shota Rustaveli. The work is in the heroic-epic mould: strongly developed choral scenes occupy an important place in the dramatic structure, and the opera's measured narrative character lends it the quality of an oratorio. Mshvelidze produced a second epic piece in *Didostatis mardzhvena* ('The Hand of a Great Master', 1961), a monumental music drama treating the tragic fate of the architect Arsakidze and his beloved, the clash of powerful human passions against a broad panorama of 11th-century Georgia, and the history of the building of the Svetitskhoveli Temple, a classic of Georgian architecture. Here again the work depends to a great extent on the chorus, and it achieves an expressive combination of archaic folk elements and developed recitative and arioso.

Ambavi Tarielisa [The Legend of Tariel] (4, A. Pagava, after S. Rustaveli: *Vepkhis tkaosani* [The Knight in the Tigerskin]), Tbilisi, 26 Feb 1946 (1947); rev. 1966
Didostatis mardzhvena [The Hand of a Great Master] (4, N. Dzidzishvili, after K. Gamsakhurdia), Tbilisi, 3 June 1961, vs (1966)
Dzhariskatsis kvrivi [Widow of a Soldier], 1967
Aluda Ketelauri, 1972

*

E. Dzidzadze: 'Kartuli sabchota opera' [A Georgian Soviet Opera], *Sabchota khelovneba* (1958), no.3, p.33
G. Ordzhonikidze: 'Opera-epos', *SovM* (1962), no.11, pp.13–18
YEVGENY MACHAVARIANI

Muck, Carl (*b* Darmstadt, 22 Oct 1859; *d* Stuttgart, 3 March 1940). German conductor. After engagements in Zürich, Salzburg, Brno and Graz he was appointed principal Kapellmeister at Angelo Neumann's Deutsches Landestheater in Prague in 1886. Even at that early date he laid the foundations of his reputation as a Wagner conductor with exemplary performances of the *Ring*. In 1892 he became principal Kapellmeister of the Berlin Opera, where he was appointed general music director in 1908. From 1894 to 1911 he directed the Silesian music festivals in Görlitz as guest conductor, Wagnerian performances at Covent Garden and, for almost three decades from 1901, the *Parsifal* performances at Bayreuth. Contemporaries described his conducting as strikingly economical, and praised his sense of form and the strict rhythm of his interpretations. Muck, according to the singer Frida Leider, preferred unusually slow tempos for his Bayreuth *Parsifal* performances and was considered in his time to be the greatest conductor of Wagner's works.

*

H. Schonberg: *The Great Conductors* (New York, 1967), 216ff
HANS CHRISTOPH WORBS

Mudie, Michael (**Winfield**) (*b* Manchester, 3 Dec 1914; *d* Brussels, 27 April 1962). English conductor. He studied at the RCM and was conductor for the Carl Rosa Opera Company from 1935 to 1939. In 1940 he was one of three conductors for a Glyndebourne production of *The Beggar's Opera*, given at Brighton and in London at the Haymarket, and made a recording of its musical numbers. He joined Sadler's Wells Opera in 1946 and became a co-director there in 1948, regularly conducting 50 to 60 performances of a wide range of repertory each season until the early 1950s, when he was affected by ill-health. His work included the first British performance (1948) of *Simon Boccanegra*, from which he recorded several excerpts (sung in English), and Norman Tucker's English version (1951) of *Don Carlos*. His performances were marked by clarity and bold contrasts, sometimes at the expense of polish.   NOËL GOODWIN

Muette de Portici, La ('The Mute Girl of Portici'). *Grand opéra* in five acts by DANIEL-FRANÇOIS-ESPRIT AUBER to a libretto by EUGÈNE SCRIBE and GERMAIN DELAVIGNE; Paris, Opéra, 29 February 1828.

Alphonse *son of the Spanish Viceroy of Naples*	tenor
Elvire *his fiancée*	soprano
Masaniello *a Neapolitan fisherman*	tenor
Fenella *his sister, a mute*	dancer
Pietro	bass
Borella } *Masaniello's companions*	bass
Moreno	bass
Lorenzo *confidant of Alphonse*	tenor
Selva *officer of the Viceroy*	bass
A Lady-in-waiting to Elvire	soprano

Soldiers, fishermen, conspirators, nobles, Spanish women, Neapolitan women, villagers

Setting Naples and Portici in 1647, during the rebellion against the Spanish Viceroy

The first version of the libretto, in three acts, was written by Delavigne in 1825, on a subject of great interest at the time. Entitled *Masaniello, ou la Muette de Portici*, it was submitted to the *comité de lecture* and the censors, who demanded changes. The second version was reworked by Scribe, but was not completed. In this version Scribe not only changed the conception to meet the demands of the censors, suppressing explicitly revolutionary material, but also created a new type of libretto, for a *grand opéra* in five acts. He added a first act introducing the traditional pair of lovers, which inevitably affected the following acts, but this version differed considerably from the final one. The original revolutionary content, and the attempt to provide logical motivation for the actions of the main characters and chorus, gave rise to inconsistencies which could not be corrected in the final five-act version. The introduction of the mute girl Fenella, who participates only in pantomime – an idea indebted to Walter Scott's *Peveril of the Peak* (1822) as well as the *mélodrame* of the boulevard theatres – was part of the original conception; none of the earlier composers who had treated this story (Keiser, Bishop and Carafa) had employed this device. Auber reportedly set the libretto in the space of three months.

ACT 1 *Naples, the gardens of the palace of the Spanish Viceroy* As the chorus rejoices at the forthcoming marriage of Alphonse to the Spanish princess,

1. *Lise Noblet as Fenella in Auber's 'La muette de Portici', the role she created in the original production at the Paris Opéra, 29 February 1828: lithograph by Lemercier after a drawing by Achille Deveria*

Elvire, the bridegroom reveals that he is plagued by a guilty conscience for seducing and abandoning the mute fishermaid Fenella. Elvire approaches with a festive procession; her companions perform two Spanish national dances. The tyrannical Viceroy has had Fenella imprisoned, but she escapes and begs Elvire to protect her from her persecutors. Elvire and her companions enter the church for the wedding ceremony. When it is over, Fenella recognizes Alphonse as her seducer and accuses him in front of Elvire. As the soldiers try to seize Fenella, she manages to escape with the aid of the people.

ACT 2 *The beach at Portici* Masaniello, leader of the revolutionary movement, sings a barcarolle ('Amis la matinée est belle') expressing opposition to the Viceroy. Pietro returns from Naples, having failed to find Fenella. The two friends sing a duet, swearing vengeance on their Spanish oppressors. Fenella rushes in and tells them what has happened to her. The indignant Masaniello swears to be revenged, and urges the fishermen to rebel. They all swear loyalty to him.

ACT 3.i *A room in the palace* Elvire at first rejects Alphonse, but eventually yields to his pleading and they sing of their mutual happiness.

   3.ii *The market-place of Naples* The market is busy; the people dance a tarantella. Selva recognizes Fenella, and his soldiers try to capture her. This is the signal for the rebellion to begin. A soldier who attempts to disarm Masaniello is killed. When the rest of the soldiers have been overpowered the rebels, after praying for divine help, go off to set the palace on fire.

ACT 4 *Masaniello's hut in Portici* Masaniello is horrified by the bloodshed and destruction of the revolution, over which he has lost control. He views

2. 'La muette de Portici' (Auber): design by Pierre-Luc-Charles Ciceri for Act 5 (the entrance of the Viceroy's palace; Vesuvius in the background) for the original production at the Paris Opéra (Salle Le Peletier), 29 February 1828; engraving by Lemaitre

hospitality as a sacred duty, and when Alphonse and Elvire seek shelter from the mob he takes them in, unaware of their identity. Even after learning that Alphonse is both Fenella's seducer and the Viceroy's son, he defends him against his former friends, who demand his execution. Masaniello finally allows the pair to escape. The representatives of the people solemnly ask him to take the keys of the city of Naples. While the people hail him as victor, his former companions threaten to murder him.

ACT 5 *The entrance of the Viceroy's palace; Vesuvius in the background* Pietro reveals that he has poisoned Masaniello. Borella brings the news that Alphonse is approaching the city with a battalion of soldiers. Although Masaniello has gone mad, he is persuaded by Fenella to lead the rebels into battle to prevent the crushing of the revolution. Fenella prays for him. Elvire enters and tells how Masaniello saved her life; because of this he has been murdered by his own men. The people hail Alphonse as the victor. Vesuvius erupts, and Fenella, overcome with grief, flings herself into the lava.

*   *   *

The history of *grand opéra* begins with *La muette de Portici*. The characteristics of the genre include a new degree of magnificence in the sets and sensationally dramatic technical stage effects, the culmination of each act in a large tableau and ingeniously staged crowd scenes. The opera provided new opportunities for the director, librettist, set designer and costume designer to work together, and they made a careful study of the historical background of the Neapolitan revolt. The climax of the final scene with the eruption of Vesuvius was a sensation, and its influence was felt in *grand opéra* from Meyerbeer and his contemporaries to Wagner's *Götterdämmerung*.

On one level, Auber's music is influenced by the *opéra comique* and the popular political song of the time; on another, by the more formal type of operatic aria, ensemble, dance and finale; and on a third (in the

pantomime scenes) by the *mélodrame*. The masterly overture, with its concise themes, is associated in spirit with the world of Fenella and the common people. The mood of unrest in its opening bars recurs a number of times, the tension often enhanced by delayed resolutions. This theme returns again at the beginning of Act 4, at the point when Fenella mimes the devastation brought about by the revolution. A further theme from the overture, one unusually chromatic for Auber, and first appearing before the triumphal march, recurs at the end of the opera at Fenella's suicide. Recent commentary on the opera has drawn attention to the apparent conflict between the character of this march, which not only brings the overture to a stirring end but is also heard again at the end of the fourth act, seeming to imply that the revolution is victorious, and the actual outcome of the opera.

Auber's music is conventional where he is composing for conventional love scenes (which only appear in the five-act version): Elvire's 'Plaisirs du rang suprême' and the duet, 'N'espérez pas me fuir', which follow the cantabile-cabaletta pattern. Masaniello's barcarolle in Act 2, with its concealed challenge to tyrants, became popular throughout Europe. The chorus 'Courons à la vengeance' and the duet for tenor and bass, 'Mieux vaut mourir' by Masaniello and Pietro, dominated by the refrain 'Amour sacré de la patrie', were highly congenial to the revolutionary movements of the 19th century. The suggestive power of the music for Fenella's pantomimes and the dances influenced many other works; for instance, the Allegro vivace in the first part of no.4 is echoed in one of Verdi's rising themes, employed in his overture to *Oberto* (ex.1).

In Masaniello's mad scene Auber employs the commonly encountered device of musical quotation, with the hero repeating themes from the chorus 'Courons à la vengeance' and his barcarolle. Throughout the opera he uses reminiscences to create a network of musico-dramatic relationships supported by deliberate tonal planning. In Act 5, the growing in-

Ex.1
Auber: *La muette*, Act 1, no. 4, bar 54

Verdi: *Oberto*, overture, bar 95

tensity of the finale, where the D minor harmony clearly suggests the Act 2 finale of *Don Giovanni*, is dramatically compelling.

In the vocal score published in England, the Andante of the overture was replaced by the first barcarolle, and the market chorus was inserted after the quotation from the march. In England and the USA, the aria known as 'My Sister Dear', taken from *Le concert à la cour* ('Pourquoi pleurer') to be used as an interlude, was particularly well known and frequently published.

For further illustration *see* DANCE, fig.3 and PRODUCTION, fig.15.

HERBERT SCHNEIDER

Muff, Alfred (*b* Lucerne, 31 May 1949). Swiss bass-baritone. After studying in Lucerne and Berlin, in 1974 he was engaged at Lucerne, making his début as Don Fernando (*Fidelio*). In 1980 he moved to Linz, where he sang Leporello, Don Geronimo and Boris, then in 1984 to Mannheim, where his roles included Philip II, Kecal, Falstaff, the Dutchman and Barak, which he also sang at La Scala (1986). He has appeared at Vienna, Munich and Geneva; his repertory includes Boito's Mephistopheles, John the Baptist and the Speaker (*Die Zauberflöte*), which he sang at Aix-en-Provence in 1989. His fine stage presence and powerful, warm-toned voice were impressive as Wotan in the complete *Ring* cycle at Zürich (1987–9) and as Barak in his American début at San Francisco (1989).　　ELIZABETH FORBES

Muffat, Georg (*b* Mégève, Savoy, bap. 1 June 1653; *d* Passau, 23 Feb 1704). German composer of French birth. He went as a boy to Alsace, then to Paris to study with Lully and others (1663–9); back in Alsace, he was a student first at Sélestat, then in 1671 at Molsheim, where he also worked as an organist. By 1674 he was a law student in Ingolstadt, Bavaria. After periods in Vienna and Prague he went to Salzburg, where in 1678 he became organist and chamber musician to Archbishop Max Gandolf, Count of Kuenberg. His operas *Marina Armena* (5 September 1679) and *Königin Mariamne* (September 1680) were given at the Akademie-Theater there during this time. Muffat's employer granted him leave to visit Italy early in the 1680s, and he studied in Rome with Pasquini. After the archbishop's death in 1687 he continued to work under his successor, and in about 1687 or 1688 his *La fatale felicità di Plutone* (libretto, incomplete, in *A-Wn*) was produced at the university and at the Hoftheater in Salzburg; but eventually he left the city. From 1690 he was Kapellmeister at the court of Johann Philipp of Lamberg, Bishop of Passau.

Muffat was particularly important for his orchestral, chamber and organ music, by which he helped introduce the French and Italian styles into Germany. The music of his three stage works, the only vocal compositions definitely attributable to him, is all lost.

*

L. von Stollbrock: *Die Komponisten Georg und Gottlieb Muffat* (Rostock, 1888)

E. von Werra: 'Georg Muffat (1635 (?)–1704) und Gottlieb Muffat (1690–1770): bio-bibliographische Studie', *KJb*, viii (1893), 42–52

A. Kutscher: *Vom Salzburger Barocktheater zu den Salzburger Festspielen* (Düsseldorf, 1939)　　SUSAN WOLLENBERG

Mugnone, Leopoldo (*b* Naples, 29 Sept 1858; *d* Capodichino, Naples, 22 Dec 1941). Italian conductor and composer. The son of the principal double bass in the S Carlo orchestra, he studied at the Naples Conservatory, composing and producing a comic opera when he was 12. While still in his teens he composed two operettas and a romance which became popular; he made his conducting début in comic opera at La Fenice in Naples. He became conductor at the Teatro Costanzi, Rome, and in 1888 won a contract giving him the musical direction of operas published by Sonzogno and their performances outside Italy. In this capacity he conducted the première of Mascagni's *Cavalleria rusticana* (1890, Rome) and toured abroad, visiting Paris (1889) and London (1905–6), conducting the first Covent Garden production of Giordano's *Andrea Chénier* (1905) and the British première of Giordano's *Fedora* (1906). He encouraged French opera in Italy with productions of Bizet and Massenet, and he conducted the première of *Tosca* (1900, Rome). His relations with Puccini were disrupted by a disagreement over the direction of *Madama Butterfly* at Rome in 1908, but Mugnone later introduced to Italy the only Puccini opera published by Sonzogno, *La rondine*, shortly after its Monte Carlo première (1917). He also conducted the premières of Franchetti's *La figlia di Iorio* (1906, La Scala) and Giordano's *Mese mariano* (1910, Palermo), and took the latter on a South American tour during which he conducted *Götterdämmerung* and Charpentier's *Louise* in addition to Italian works.

Mugnone's interpretations of *Otello* and *Falstaff* were regarded by Boito as particularly notable, and he conducted *Nabucco* at La Scala in 1913 as part of the Verdi centenary celebrations; Beecham considered him the best Italian conductor of his time. Mugnone returned to Covent Garden in 1919, when he gave the British première of Mascagni's *Iris*, and in 1925, when he was summoned to rescue some of the Italian performances that had suffered at other hands. He also conducted symphony concerts at the Augusteo, Rome. He composed two mature operas in the *verismo* style: *Il birichino* (1892, Venice) and *Vita brettone* (1905, Naples). His personal papers, which include correspondence with Verdi, Puccini, Mascagni, Leoncavallo, Massenet and Richard Strauss, were presented to the museum libraries at La Scala, the Rome Opera and the Naples Conservatory.

Il dottor Bartolo Salsapariglia, Naples, 1870/71
Don Bizzarro e le sue figlie (operetta, 1, E. Golisciani), Naples, Nuovo, 20 April 1875
Mamma Angot al serraglio di Costantinopoli (operetta, 3, Golisciani), Naples, Nuovo, 29 July 1875
Il birichino (1, Golisciani), Venice, Malibran, 11 Aug 1892
Vita brettone (3, Golisciani), Naples, S Carlo, 14 March 1905

*

'Leopoldo Mugnone', *Teatro illustrato*, x (1890), 66

T. Ruffo: *La mia parabola artistica* (Milan, 1937), 231ff

P. Panichelli: *Il 'Pretino' di Giacomo Puccini* (Pisa, 1940, 4/1962), 89ff

E. de Leva: 'Leopoldo Mugnone nel dolore e nell'arte', *Corriere di Napoli* (6 Aug 1941)

A. de Angelis: 'Aneddoti su Mugnone', *Voce d'Italia* (23 Nov 1941)

——: 'Leopoldo Mugnone era timido come Verdi', *Giornale d'Italia* (11 April 1958)　　CLAUDIO CASINI

Mula, Avni (*b* Gjakova [now Đakovica], 4 Jan 1926). Albanian composer and baritone. His family settled in Shkodër (1928), where Prenkë Jakova later noticed and encouraged his vocal talents. He studied singing at the Moscow Conservatory (1952–7), then joined the opera company in Tirana, also appearing throughout eastern Europe, Turkey, mainland China, Mongolia, North Korea and Vietnam. His repertory included Rossini's Figaro, Rigoletto, Germont, Iago, Prince Igor, Yevgeny Onegin, Wolfram, Escamillo and Zurga, and he created roles in several contemporary Albanian operas.

As a composer he was self-taught. Of his stage works, *Karnavalet* ('Carnivals'), a scathing satire on bourgeois manners in Korçë during the 1930s, became one of the most popular Albanian operettas on account of its pace, humour and spontaneous flow of appealing and memorable melody. This later became the first Albanian musical comedy to be made into a film. In *Trimat* ('The Valiant'), which deals with the Albanian Resistance during the German occupation of World War II, Mula uses both leitmotifs and 'endless melodies', and numbers (arias and choruses) for dramatic climaxes and finales. The opera reveals the composer's ability to enhance a dramatic situation by harmonic and orchestral means and to differentiate characters through vocal line.

Legjenda kruetane [Legends of Kruja], before 1978 (prol., 3, L. Gurakuqi), extract pubd in Sokoli, 153–64
Karnavalet [Carnivals] (operetta, 2, G. Zheji and Gurakuqi, after S. Çomora: *Karnavalet e Korçës* [Carnivals of Korçë]), Tirana, Opera and Ballet, 5 Feb 1978; film, Tirana, 29 Dec 1980
Borana (3, Zheji), Tirana, Opera and Ballet, 5 April 1984; also known as Kështjellaret [The People of the Castle]
Stuhia [Tempest], 1985 (3, Zheji), inc.
Trimat [The Valiant]/Nënë trimëresh [The Valiant Mother] (2, Zheji), Tirana, Opera and Ballet, 30 Oct 1987

*

R. Sokoli: *Figura e Skënderbeut në muzikë* [The Figure of Scanderbeg in Music] (Tirana, 1978), 57, 153–64
S. Kalemi: *Arritjet e artit tonë muzikor: vepra dhe krijues të muzikës Shqiptaze* [Achievements of our Musical Art: Creations and Creators of Albanian Music] (Tirana, 1982), i/1–6
R. Teqja: 'Un nouveau succès de l'opéra albanais: à propos de l'opéra Borana', *Les lettres albanaises*, no.3 (1984), 189–90
A. Hoxha: *Filmi artistik Shqiptar* [Albanian Art-Films] (Tirana, 1986), 101, 107, 181, 215, 301 GEORGE LEOTSAKOS

Mulata de Córdoba, La ('The Mulatta of Córdoba'). Opera in one act by JOSÉ PABLO MONCAYO GARCÍA to a libretto by Xavier Villaurrutia and Agustín Lazo; Mexico City, Palacio de Bellas Artes, 23 October 1948.

Scene i is set in Córdoba, Veracruz. Accused of being accompanied by an invisible familiar spirit (whom she describes as her 'father'), Soledad (mezzo-soprano) possesses the secret of never growing old. She attracts many suitors, among whom Anselmo (tenor) gains her trust and learns that she cannot love any mortal. Aurelio (baritone), a rejected suitor, tries to kill her and thus liberate Anselmo from her spell, but she disappears from his grasp. In scene ii (set in Mexico City), Soledad is pursued by Aurelio, who accuses her to Inquisition authorities of being a malevolent witch. Again she vanishes. In scene iii the Grand Inquisitor (bass) promises a just investigation, but threatens punishment when she refuses to tell the spirit's name. As she is to be dragged away, Anselmo appears in the guise of a friar, promising to have her write the name on a wall. She pretends willingness to do so, but suddenly flames envelop them both, and they disappear in smoke.

In no sense reminiscent of the jollities of his folkloric orchestral piece *Huapango*, Moncayo's opera is instead composed in a pandiatonic idiom more reminiscent of Chávez's piano preludes; the libretto is set syllabically. At the première Oralia Domínguez sang the title role of Soledad. Almost devoid of melismas, Soledad's melodic lines abound in repeated notes, scale steps and diatonic intervals that only rarely extend to a 6th, and but once to a minor 7th. Rapid repeated notes and passages in running 3rds, contrasted with agitated chords emphasizing 4ths and 5ths, characterize much of her accompaniment.

Originally produced in a triple bill (preceded by Eduardo Hernández Moncada's *Elena* and Sandi's *Carlota*), *La mulata de Córdoba* was revived at the Palacio de Bellas Artes in October 1952, the composer conducting on both occasions. ROBERT STEVENSON

Mulè, Giuseppe (*b* Termini Imerese, nr Palermo, 28 June 1885; *d* Rome, 10 Sept 1951). Italian composer. He studied at the Palermo Conservatory, where he was appointed director in 1922, leaving three years later to take a similar post at the Conservatorio di S Cecilia, Rome, which he held until 1943. His talent for organization was recognized by the fascist government: he became national secretary of the Sindacato dei Musicisti, which he and Lualdi represented in parliament from 1929.

Mulè's music was at first influenced by the *verismo* school, and in particular by Mascagni; but he soon came under the spell of the folksongs and landscape of Sicily, and of the island's ancient Greek heritage. He wrote some of his most characteristic music for Greek plays performed in the open-air theatre at Syracuse. But in his operas, too, the emotion and atmosphere bear the stamp of a racial instinct, evident as much in legendary or mythical drama as in popular comedy. Mulè's harmony, though it never freed itself wholly from derivative elements, is often distinctively rugged, exotic and tritone-obsessed. A first step in this direction is apparent in the immature *La baronessa di Carini*, e.g. in the oddly effective orchestral prelude, with its rasping tritones in the bass (though the piece resolves into pure Mascagni at the end). A far more extreme example of Mulè's individuality is the first half of his last opera, *La zolfara* — particularly the extraordinary 'whiplash' dance, which shows him as a kind of lesser Sicilian counterpart to Bartók. Yet even in this boldest of his operas he lacked the courage to defy conservative taste to the end: the denouement is disappointingly tame and sentimental. Among the intervening operas, which represent intermediate stages in Mulè's evolution, the most celebrated was *Dafni*. Though not his most perfect work (it is uneven, and lacks the concision of the slightly mawkish but evocative *La monacella della fontana*), it contains some of his finest music, particularly in Act 1, which expresses in more complex terms the same archaic, atavistic spirit that pervades the best of the Syracuse scores.

See also DAFNI (ii).

La baronessa di Carini (1, F. P. Mulè), Palermo, Massimo, 16 April 1912
Al lupo! (2, F. P. Mulè), Rome, Nazionale, 13 Nov 1919
La monacella della fontana (1, G. Adami), Trieste, Verdi, 17 Feb 1923
Dafni (3, E. Romagnoli), Rome, Opera, 14 March 1928
Liolà (3, A. Rossato, after L. Pirandello), Naples, S Carlo, 2 Feb 1935
Taormina (1, Adami), San Remo, 4 April 1938
La zolfara (1, Adami), Rome, 1939

M. Labroca: 'Dafni di Giuseppe Mulè', Musica d'oggi, 1st ser., x (1928), 89–92

G. Nataletti: 'La Dafni di Giuseppe Mulè', Italia musicale [Genoa], iv/4–5 (1931), 1

Giuseppe Mulè (Milan, c1930–35) [Ricordi pubn; incl. extracts from press criticism]

M. Saint-Cyr: 'Giuseppe Mulè', Rassegna dorica, v (1933–4), 3–6

A. Gasco: 'La prima rappresentazione di "Dafni" del maestro Mulè al Teatro Reale dell'opera (marzo 1928)', Da Cimarosa a Strawinsky (Rome, 1939), 475–82

J. C. G. Waterhouse: The Emergence of Modern Italian Music (up to 1940) (diss., U. of Oxford, 1968), 533–6

F. Giambrone: 'Palermo: dopo 37 anni torna l'opera Dafni: mito greco e classicismo per riscoprire Mulè', Il giornale della musica, vii/59 (1991), 8 [interview]

ALFREDO CASELLA, JOHN C. G. WATERHOUSE

Mulhouse (Ger. Mülhausen). Town in Haut-Rhin, France. The Théâtre Municipal (stalls and three balconies, 867 seats) was built privately in 1867 and, with a municipal subsidy, housed its own permanent company until 1870. After running into financial trouble it was taken over by the municipality and let to the Strasbourg opera in 1876; performances were then given by the Strasbourg, Besançon and Basle companies. In 1904, when its own opera house was destroyed by fire, the Basle company took over the Mulhouse theatre, which was enlarged in 1911 and 1913. After World War I performances were again given by the Strasbourg and Besançon companies, but from 1922 to 1934 a permanent French company took over until fire destroyed its stage warehouse, and productions were again imported from Strasbourg.

During World War II operas were given by a German troupe, but in 1946 another French company was formed which, under such directors as Roger Lalande, Jean Mercier, Raymond Vogel and Jean-Claude Riber, put on many successful productions, including world premières of operas by Büsser (Roxelane, 1948), Landowski (Le rire de Nils Halerius, 1951) and Tomasi (L'Atlantide, 1954), and French premières of works by Britten, Kodály, Milhaud, Orff and Egk. In 1972 Mulhouse became part of the Opéra du Rhin, each of whose productions is given two or three times there between October and May, accompanied by the Mulhouse SO. A new opera house, seating 1300, was designed by Claude Vasconi as part of a cultural centre to open in 1993.

*

L. J. Brote: 'L'Opéra du Rhin: l'art lyrique régionalise', Le théâtre lyrique français 1945–1985, ed. D. Pistone (Paris, 1987), 383–94.

CHARLES PITT

Müller [Schmid], **Adolf** [Adolph] (b Tolna, Hungary, 7 Oct 1801; d Vienna, 29 July 1886). Austrian composer and Kapellmeister. Orphaned at an early age, he was brought up by an aunt and trained for the stage. After engagements as an actor and singer at Prague, Lemberg (L'viv) and Brünn (Brno) he moved to Vienna in 1823. His Singspiel Wer andern eine Grube gräbt, fällt selbst hinein was given in the Theater in der Josefstadt on 13 December 1825, and in December 1826 he became famous overnight with his music to Die schwarze Frau, Meisl's enormously popular parody of Boieldieu's La dame blanche. In this year Müller was engaged as singer at the Kärntnertortheater, where he rapidly advanced to the position of Kapellmeister and gave up his acting and singing activities. At Beethoven's funeral he sang second tenor in B. A. Weber's Rasch tritt der Tod den Menschen an, after a last rehearsal for Die erste Zusammenkunft, his first Singspiel for the Hofoper, which had its première that night (29 March 1827). In 1828 he became Kapellmeister at the Theater an der Wien under Karl Carl, and until 1847 he was director of music at this theatre or at Carl's other theatre, in the Leopoldstadt suburb. In 1847 he returned to the Theater an der Wien, under new management, and continued as music director until 1878, when he began to write scores for the Ring-Theater. Among his late works are those for some of Ludwig Anzengruber's plays.

Müller's output was prodigious even by the prolific standards of his time. Throughout a long working life he produced new Singspiels and farces at an average of more than one a month, in addition to his activities as arranger, conductor and director. Wurzbach in his incomplete list included about 580 theatre scores for the period up to 1868, including roughly 4500 individual musical numbers; in addition to those listed below, there are dozens of pieces in such genres as Lebensbild and Charakterbild, as well as incidental music. Müller himself made several manuscript copies of many of his scores and arranged some of his most popular numbers for other instruments. Not surprisingly, the bulk of his output proved ephemeral, yet many of his 41 scores to Nestroy's plays are still performed in Vienna, and at his best his music has more than mere melodic charm to commend it. There are innumerable witty, effective couplets, and on occasion extended concerted numbers and large-scale quodlibets; the instrumentation is neat though usually unadventurous. Many of Müller's autograph scores are in the principal Viennese libraries, especially the Stadtbibliothek and Nationalbibliothek. Many songs from his popular theatre scores were brought out in series by Haslinger, Diabelli, Spina and others.

Of his three children, Adolf Müller (b Vienna, 15 Oct 1839; d Vienna, 14 Dec 1901) was also a composer; the best known of his many operettas is Wiener Blut (1899), the first such work to be based on existing music by Johann Strauss.

all first performed in Vienna, at the Theater an der Wien unless otherwise stated

WJ – Theater in der Josefstadt
WK – Kärntnertortheater
WL – Theater in der Leopoldstadt
WR – Ring-Theater
WSB – Sommerarena Braunhirschen

Wer andern eine Grube gräbt, fällt selbst hinein (komische Operette, 1), WJ, 13 Dec 1825; Die schwarze Frau (Parodie, 2, K. Meisl), WJ, 1 Dec 1826; Der Gutsherr und der Schuster (Posse, 2, A. Gleich), WJ, 6 March 1827; Die erste Zusammenkunft (Spl, 1), WK, 29 March 1827; Asträa, die Geisterfürstin, oder Die Reise nach der fliegenden Insel (Zauberspiel, 2, Gleich), 21 Dec 1827; Dreissig Jahre aus dem Leben eines Spielers [Lumpen] (Schauspiel, 3, J. W. Lembert), 21 March 1828; Seraphine, oder Die Kriegsgefangene (romantisch-komische Oper, 3, M. Schmid, after A. von Kotzebue), 21 Oct 1828

Der Barbier von Sievering (Parodie, 2, Meisl), 13 Dec 1828; Othellerl, der Mohr von Wien, oder Die geheilte Eifersucht (Parodie, 3, Meisl), 6 June 1829; Julerl, die Putzmacherin (Parodie, 2, Meisl), WL, 12 Sept 1829; Fortunats Abenteuer zu Wasser und zu Lande (Zauberspiel, 3, Lembert), 16 Oct 1829; Die elegante Bräumeisterin (Posse, 2, J. Schickh), 3 Feb 1830; Cleopatra (Parodie, 2, T. Krones), 26 Feb 1830; Die Walpurgisnacht (Zauberspiel, 4, C. Birch-Pfeiffer), 6 March 1830; Staberl in Floribus, oder Fausts Mantel (Zauberspiel, 3, A. Bäuerle), 13 March 1830

Die Räuber in den Strapazzen, oder Tapperl, der Retter seines Herrn (Parodie, 2, Schickh), 29 July 1830; Tivoli (Posse, 2, G. von Dreger), 31 Dec 1830; Domi, der amerikanische Affe, oder Negerrache (Melodram, 3, F. X. Told), 28 Jan 1831; Der Nimmersatt (Posse, 2, L. Erwin), WL, 1 March 1831, collab. F. Gläser; Vanilli, das redende Stummerl (Parodie, Schickh), 3

March 1831; Der Ritter mit der Sichel, und sein treuer Löwe (Zauberspiel, 3, A. Reidinger), 22 April 1831; Die verhängnisvolle Limonade, oder Liebe und Kabale (Parodie, 2, Schickh), 3 May 1831

Zwölf Mädchen in Uniform (Vaudeville, 1, L. Angely), 30 Aug 1831; Der Gärtner und die Schlange, oder Das Zauberkäppchen (Zauberposse, 3, F. V. Ernst), 30 Sept 1831; Das Zauberrütchen, oder Die Liebhaber als Bettelmusikanten (Zauberposse, 3, K. A. Frey), 2 Dec 1831, vs (Vienna, ?1830); Die Zauberhöhle, oder Der Hausmeister unter den Hottentotten (Posse, 3, J. Krones), 4 Jan 1832; Felix Mauserl, oder Fatalitäten aus gutem Herzen (Posse, 2, Gleich), 25 Jan 1832

Der gefühlvolle Kerkermeister, oder Adelheid, die verfolgte Wittib (Parodie, 3, J. Nestroy), 7 Feb 1832; Nagerl und Handschuh, oder Die Schicksale der Familie Maxenpfutsch (Parodie, 3, Nestroy), 23 March 1832; [Die Verbannung aus dem Zauberreiche, oder] Dreissig Jahre aus dem Leben eines Lumpen (Zauberspiel, 2, Nestroy), 27 April 1832, collab. F. Roser; Schnackerl das Universalerbe, oder Das Weiberduell in Neulerchenfeld (Posse, 3, Frey), 29 May 1832; Zampa der Tagdieb, oder Die Braut von Gips (Parodie, 3, Nestroy), 22 June 1832

Die Brigitten-Aue, oder Die Türken vor Wien im Jahre 1683 (Zeitgemälde, 3, B. Püchler), 14 July 1832; Der konfuse Zauberer, oder Treue und Flatterhaftigkeit (Zauberspiel, 3, Nestroy), 26 Sept 1832; Die Zauberreise in die Ritterzeit, oder Die Übermütigen (Posse, prol., 3, Nestroy), 20 Oct 1832; Der Zaubermund, oder Wolf und Papagei (Zauberspiel, 2, Told), 9 Nov 1832; Der Kampf des Glückes mit dem Neide, oder Der Liebe Zaubermacht (Zauberspiel, 3, Schickh), 7 Dec 1832 [as Der Kampf des Glückes mit dem Verdienst, oder Die Erfindung des Zufalls, WL, 28 Feb 1883]

Der Bergkönig, oder Hopsa, der Retter aus Zauberbanden (Zauberspiel, 2, M. Carl), 29 Dec 1832; Der Sommerfasching auf dem Lande, oder Die bekehrten Verkehrten (Posse, 2), 3 Jan 1833; Der Zauberer Februar, oder Die Überraschungen (Zauberspiel, 2, Nestroy), 12 Feb 1833; Der böse Geist Lumpazivagabundus, oder Das liederliche Kleeblatt (Zauberposse, 3, Nestroy), 11 April 1833, vs (Leipzig, n.d.); Ori, der brasilianische Affe, oder Das Zigeunerweib (Posse, 3, Reidinger), 17 May 1833; Das steinerne Herz (Zauberspiel, 2, J. E. Gulden), 14 June 1833; Robert der Teufel (Parodie, 3, Nestroy), 9 Oct 1833

Goldkönig, Vogelhändler und Pudelscherer (Zauberposse, 2, F. Hopp), 5 Nov 1833; Tritschtratsch (Posse, 1, Nestroy), 20 Nov 1833; Maurerpolier Klucks Reise von Berlin nach Wien (Posse, 1, B. Püchler), 5 Dec 1833; Der Zauberer Sulphurelektrimagnetikophosphoratus und die Fee Walpurgiblocksbergiseptemtrionalis (Zauberposse, 3, Nestroy), 17 Jan 1834; Der Erlkönig, oder Das Gelübde (Melodram, 4), 21 Feb 1834 [with music of Schubert]; Müller, Kohlenbrenner und Sesselträger oder Die Traume von Schale und Kern (Zauberspiel, 3, Nestroy), 4 April 1834

Die Gleichheit der Jahre (Posse, 4, Nestroy), 8 Oct 1834; Die Familien Zwirn, Knieriem und Leim, oder Der Welt-Untergangs-Tag (Zauberspiel, 2, Nestroy), 6 Dec 1834 [continuation of Lumpazivagabundus]; Der Zauberwald, oder Die Brautwerber aus dem Tierreiche (Zauberposse, 2, Told), 12 Dec 1834; Die Entführung vom Maskenball, oder Die ungleichen Nebenbuhler (Posse, 3, Schickh), 8 Jan 1835; Weder Lorbeerbaum noch Bettelstab (Parodie, 3, Nestroy), 13 Feb 1835

Hans Jörgel in Wien, oder Die Überraschung im Floratempel (Posse, 3, Schickh), 31 March 1835; Eulenspiegel, oder Schabernack über Schabernack (Posse, 4, Nestroy), 22 April 1835; Der melancholische Schuster, oder Die Engländer in Wien (Posse, 3), 21 May 1835; Die schöne Holländerin (Posse, 3, Schickh), 3 June 1835; Schnauferl als Toter (Posse, 1, Schickh), 30 July 1835; Entführung über Entführung, oder Der Onkel aus Amerika (Posse, 2, Schickh), 2 Sept 1835; Junker Schnabenschnabel, oder Wer ist der Rechte? (Posse, 3, Clasing), 10 Sept 1835

Die weissen Mohren, oder Der Bräutigam aus Haiti (Posse, 3, Schickh), 17 Sept 1835; Zu ebener Erde und erster Stock, oder Die Launen des Glückes (Posse, 3, Nestroy), 24 Sept 1835; Die Missverständnisse (Posse, 3, E. Ritter), 25 Nov 1835; Die Ballnacht, oder Der Faschingdienstag (Posse, 4, J. K. Waldon, with songtexts by Nestroy), 6 Feb 1836; Prinzessin Gold, oder Die Abenteuer in der Johannisnacht (Zauberspiel, 2, Told), 18 March 1836; Die beiden Nachtwandler, oder Das Notwendige und das Überflüssige (Posse, 2, Nestroy), 6 May 1836; Der Affe und der Bräutigam (Posse, 3, Nestroy), 23 July 1836

Reiseabenteuer zweier Handwerksburschen, oder Armband und Fingerring (Zauberspiel, 2, Told), 10 Sept 1836; Eine Wohnung ist zu vermieten (Posse, 3, Nestroy), 17 Jan 1837; Hutmacher und Strumpfwirker (Posse, 2, Hopp), 7 March 1837 (Vienna, ?1840); Moppels Abenteuer (Posse, 2, Nestroy), 5 May 1837; Maurer und Ziegeldecker als Gymnastiker, oder Die Wette um den Araber (Posse, 2, E. Steinhauser), 27 June 1837; Die Cachucha, oder Er ist Sie und Sie ist Er (Posse, 2, L. Grois), 3 Oct 1837

Das Haus der Temperamente (Posse, 2, Nestroy), 16 Nov 1837; Barbier und Seiler, oder Die Steckbriefe (Posse, 2, K. Haffner), 14 Dec 1837; Die Glücksjäger, oder Die silberne Hochzeit (Zauberspiel, 3, Haffner), 6 Jan 1838; Eine Hand wäscht die andere, oder Der Freier vom Dampfschiff (Posse, 3, Haffner), 14 Feb 1838; Die Fahrt mit der Eisenbahn nach Wagram, oder Der Bräutigam von Ödenburg (Posse, 2, Grois), 2 March 1838; Glück, Missbrauch und Rückkehr, oder Das Geheimnis des grauen Hauses (Posse, 5, Nestroy), 10 March 1838

Der Kobold, oder Staberl im Feendienst (Posse, 4, Nestroy), 19 April 1838; Der Edelstein, oder Die Wiener an der Meeresküste (Posse, 3, A. Reidinger), 4 Sept 1838; Gegen Torheit gibt es keine Mittel (Posse, 3, Nestroy), 3 Nov 1838; Die Theaterwelt, oder Dichter-Schicksale (Posse, 3, F. Kaiser and F. Thalhammer), 12 Dec 1838; Lady Fee und der Holzdieb, oder Die Wette gilt ein Mädchen (Posse, 3, Haffner), WL, 26 Dec 1838, collab. Hebenstreit; Der Bräutigamsspiegel in der Drudenfussgasse, oder Florian Spitzkopf (Posse, 3, F. Hopp), 10 Jan 1839

Der Stock im Eisen, oder Das schwarze Weib im Wienerwalde (Volksmärchen, 4, Haffner), 26 Jan 1839; Die Tischlerherberge, oder Das Scheibenfest zu Schnabelfeld (Posse, 3, Haffner), WL, 1 Feb 1839; Gutsherr und Messerschmied, oder Hilf, was helfen kann (Posse, 3, Kaiser), 15 March 1839; Der dreissigjährige A. B. C.-Schütz (Posse, 3, Hopp), 22 March 1839; Die verhängnisvolle Faschingsnacht (Posse, 3, Nestroy), 13 April 1839; Drei Jahre aus dem Leben eines Wucherers, oder Der Wucherer und sein Erbe (Posse, 3, Scholz), 16 May 1839

Der Malheur-Georgel, oder Glückskind und Unglücksvogel (Posse, 3, Hopp), 12 June 1839; Der Oelerer auf Reisen, oder Geliebte und Schwester in einer Person (Posse, 3, J. E. Gulden), WL, 9 July 1839; Die Bajaderen aus dem Zigeunerwaldl (Posse, 2, Hopp), 28 Aug 1839; Haarlocken statt Dukaten, oder Leichter Sinn, nicht Leichtsinn (Zeitgemälde, 3), 11 Sept 1839; Das Zauberrätsel (Zauberspiel, 4, F. Blum), 5 Oct 1839; Asmodeus, der hinkende Teufel, oder Die Promenade durch das gegenwärtige, das vergangene und das künftige Jahrhundert (Posse, 3, Haffner), 17 Nov 1839

Barnabas, der unglückliche Mädchenhüter (Posse, 3, Haffner), 7 Dec 1839; Der Färber und sein Zwillingsbruder (Posse, 3, Nestroy), 15 Jan 1840; Das unterbrochene Ballfest, oder Die Mädchen in Uniform (Posse, 2, Haffner), 14 Feb 1840; Der Lebensmüde wider Willen (Posse, 3, W. Brabbée), 13 March 1840; Die Räuber bei der Hausunterhaltung, oder Die Gefangenen (Posse, 2, Condorussi), 28 April 1840; Der Erbschleicher (Posse, 4, Nestroy), 21 May 1840; Das Preisstück (Posse, 3, Kaiser), 1 July 1840

Der Menschenfresser, oder Das Mädchen als Ehemann (Posse, 3, Haffner), 25 Aug 1840; Wer wird Amtmann?, oder Des Vaters Grab (Lebensbild, 2, Kaiser), 22 Sept 1840; Die Fee am Schneeberge, oder Fagott und Zither (Zauberspiel, 2), WL, 3 Oct 1840; Der Seiltänzer aus Liebe (Posse, 3, Hopp), 15 Oct 1840; Die Perlenschnur, oder Knecht, Diener, Herr (Drama, 3, K. Holtei), 14 Nov 1840; Der Talisman (Posse, 3, Nestroy), 16 Dec 1840; Käthi, oder 20 Jahre arm, 3 Stunden reich (Posse, 2), WL, 8 Jan 1841

Alle Augenblicke ein Anderer und doch immer Derselbe, oder Die Zauberkorallen (Posse, 2, Schickh), WL, 28 Jan 1841; Die beiden Rauchfangkehrer, oder Welcher ist's? Das ist die Frage (Posse, 3, Schickh), 16 April 1841; Das Marmorherz (Volksmärchen, 3, Haffner), 24 April 1841; Der tote Bär (Schwank, 1, Kaiser), 22 May 1841; Der Mauren Treubruch in Granada (Spektakelstück, 5, Blum), 5 June 1841, collab. P. Fahrbach; Ein Sonderling in Wien (Charakterbild, 4, Bäuerle), 30 Sept 1841; Die Zigeuner in der Steinmetz Werkstatt (Lebensbild, 2, Kaiser), 23 Oct 1841

Hans Jörgel in Wien (Posse, 3, Schickh, after Kringsteiner), WL, 16 Nov 1841; Das Mädl aus der Vorstadt (Posse, 3, Nestroy), 24 Nov 1841; Geld! (Posse, 3, Kaiser), 31 Dec 1841; Die Tränenquelle (Volksmärchen, 3, Haffner), 8 Jan 1842; Einen Jux will er sich machen (Posse, 4, Nestroy), WL, 10 March 1842; Der lustige Chorist, oder Nicht fröhlich und doch fröhlich (Posse, 2, L. Schneider), WL, 14 March 1842; Die Schicksalsstiefeln (Zauberspiel, 3, J. Landner), WL, 2 April 1842; Die Mamsell aus der Stadt (Posse, 3, Scholz), 9 April 1842

Marquis Kappenstiefel, oder Das Mädchen aus dem Thale (Posse, 4, Haffner), 8 July 1842; Die falschen Engländer, oder Die unterbrochene Verlobung (Posse, 2, E. Breier), 14 Oct 1842; Die Papiere des Teufels, oder Der Zufall (Posse, 3, Nestroy), 17 Nov 1842; Chonchon die Savoyardin, oder Die neue Fanchon (vaudeville, 3, F. E. Lyncker), 25 Nov 1842; 24 Stunden Königin (vaudeville, 3, C. W. Koch), 27 Dec 1842; Marie, die Tochter des Regiments (vaudeville, 3, Blum), 11 Feb 1843, collab. others

Der Schneider als Naturdichter, oder Der Herr Vetter aus Steiermark (Posse, 2, Kaiser), WL, 17 Feb 1843; Liebesgeschichten und Heiratssachen (Posse, 3, Nestroy), 23 March 1843; Die Verlobung vor der Trommel, oder Der Mutter Angedenken (vaudeville, 3, Blum), 3 June 1843, collab. others; Kakadu (vaudeville, 3, Blum), WL, 27 June 1843, collab. others; Die Musicantenbraut (Posse, 3, K. Giugno), WL, 7 July 1843; Die gestrengen Herren, oder Tempora mutantur (Posse, 3, Blum), 18 July 1843; Guter und schlechter Ton (Lustspiel, 2, Blum), 29 July 1843

Lisette, oder Borgen macht glücklich (vaudeville, 1, Blum), WL, 15 Aug 1843, collab. others; Der Rastelbinder, oder 10 000 Gulden (Posse, 3, Kaiser), 17 Aug 1843; Serafine, das Blumenmädchen von Paris (vaudeville, 3, Blum, after P. de Kock and Valory), 28 Aug 1843, collab. W. Granfeld; Indienne und Zephirin, oder Die beiden Masken (vaudeville, 2, F. W. Zierrath), 15 Sept 1843; Die Lokalposse im Lerchenfelde (Posse, 3, Blum), WL, 19 Sept 1843

Die Matrosenbraut, oder Die abenteuerliche Wette (Posse, 2, Blum), 7 Oct 1843; Aspasie, der weibliche Figaro (vaudeville, 5, Blum), 14 Oct 1843; Nur Ruhe! (Posse, 3, Nestroy), WL, 17 Nov 1843; Ein Abend, eine Nacht und ein Morgen in Paris (vaudeville, 4, Kaiser), 25 Nov 1843, collab. A. M. Storch; Die Köchin von Baden (Posse, 3, Blum), WL, 27 Jan 1844; Wer wird seine Schulden zahlen?, oder Die seltsame Brautwerbung (Posse, 3, Blum), 18 Feb 1844

Wohlgemuth (vaudeville, 1, Schneider), 24 Feb 1844, collab. F. Gumbert; Die Spiel-Kameraden (Posse, 2, Kaiser), 2 March 1844; Kleine Leiden des menschlichen Lebens (vaudeville, 1, I. Schuselka-Brüning, after Clairville), 12 March 1844; Der Zerrissene (Posse, 3, Nestroy), 9 April 1844; 'S letzte Fensterln (Alpenszene, J. G. Seidl), WL, 3 July 1844; Stadt und Land (Posse, 2, Kaiser), WL, 10 Aug 1844; Viel Lärm um Nichts (vaudeville, 1, Lembert), WL, 3 Sept 1844

Das verhängnisvolle Liebespfand (vaudeville, 2, after J. Bayard), WL, 17 Sept 1844, collab. Gumbert; Hieronymus Klecks (Posse, 2), WL, 24 Sept 1844; Lord und Wirt (Posse, 2, Kaiser), 12 Oct 1844; Sie will zum Theater (vaudeville, 1), 13 Nov 1844; Drei Jahrl'n nach'm letzt'n Fensterln (Alpenszene, V. G. Seidl), WL, 14 Dec 1844; Die beiden Herren Söhne (Posse, 3, Nestroy), 16 Jan 1845; Der Hausherr in der Schindelsdorfergasse (Posse, Hopp), Jan 1845; Das Gewürzkrämerkleeblatt, oder Die unschuldig Schuldigen (Posse, 3, Nestroy), 26 Feb 1845

Die Tänzerin und der Enthusiast (vaudeville, 4, Kaiser), 13 March 1845; Die Schule für Verliebte (vaudeville, 5, Blum), 10 April 1845, collab. others; Die Komödie im Zimmer (Posse, 2, Hopp), WL, 11 April 1845; Unverhofft (Posse, 3, Nestroy), 23 April 1845; Veni, vidi, vici, oder Er geht aufs Land (vaudeville, 3, Blum), WL, 15 July 1845; Red'n S' nur mit 'n Hausmasta (Posse, 1), WL, 16 Nov 1845; Schnepf und Wachtl (Posse, 2, Grois), WL, 18 Nov 1845; Die Figurantin (vaudeville, 3, Blum), WL, 25 Nov 1845

Kein Jux (Posse, 2, Grois), WL, 28 March 1846; Alexander Stradellerl (Parodie, 1, Lödl), WL, 13 April 1846; Der Unbedeutende (Posse, 3, Nestroy), 2 May 1846; Der fliegende Holländer zu Fuss [Zwei ewige Juden für einen] (Burleske, 2, Nestroy), WL, 4 Aug 1846; Das schwarze Blatt (Posse, 3, Blum), WL, 14 Sept 1846; Der Fehlschuss (Alpenszene, Duke Max of Bavaria), WL, 8 Oct 1846; Fanchon, das Leyermädchen (vaudeville, 3, Castelli, after Kotzebue), WL, 3 Nov 1846; Zwei Bräutigame, aber Keiner der Rechte! (Posse, 3, Ehrenhäusel), WL, 31 Dec 1846

Ein Held der modernen Romantik (Posse, 3, J. K. Böhm), WL, 6 Feb 1847; Eine Dorfgeschichte, die in der Stadt endet (Posse, 3, Grois), WL, 23 Feb 1847; Der Schützling (Posse, 4, Nestroy), WL, 9 April 1847; König René's Tochter (lyrisches Drama, 2, J. Bresemann, after Hertz), 5 July 1847; Leni Wind, oder Die Enthusiasten (Scherz, 3, F. Bach and G. Schönstein), WJ, 27 Nov 1847; Die Musketiere der Viertelmeisterin (Parodie, 3, Schickh), 21 Jan 1848

Die Haimons-Bub'n, oder Vier Reiter auf einem Schimmel (Burleske, 2, Haffner), WJ, 3 June 1848; Städtische Krankheit und ländliche Kur (Charakterbild, 3, Kaiser), 24 Sept 1848; Die

Rückkehr ins Vaterland, oder Das ländliche Kirchweihfest (Lokalbild, 2, Böhm), 9 April 1849; Paperl, oder Die Weltreise eines Wiener Kapitalisten (Zauberposse, 3, K. Elmar), 18 April 1849; Bubenstück'ln (Posse, 3, A. Klesheim), 13 Aug 1849; Die Kunst, Frauenherzen zu gewinnen (vaudeville, 4), WL, 10 Feb 1850, collab. Dessauer and Hölzl

Ein Denunziant, oder Lange geborgt ist nicht geschenkt (Lebensbild, 3, Wysber), WSB, 3 Aug 1850; Ein Gefangener in Sibirien (melodrama, 3, J. N. Vogl), WSB, 17 Sept 1850; Schwester Anna, oder Windbeutel und Börsenspekulant (Posse, 4, Haffner), 1 Dec 1850; Die fünf Sinne (Zauberposse, 3, H. Merlin), WSB, 26 June 1851; Da Toni und sein Burgei (Charakter-Gemälde, 3, Prüller), 13 Sept 1851; Ferdinand Raimund (Charakter-Skizze, 3, C. Elmar), 4 Oct 1851; Hanns geht in die Stadt (Posse, 3, E. Liebold), 31 Oct 1851; List und Dummheit (Posse, 3, L. Feldmann), 17 Jan 1852; Der Hauslehrer (Posse, 3, N. J. Kola), 7 Feb 1852; Fledermäuse (Scherz, 1, L. Wysber), 18 Feb 1852

Ein Faschings-Abenteuer (Posse, 1, Wysber), 18 Feb 1852; Das Eckhaus in der Vorstadt (Lokalbild, 3, Böhm), WSB, 13 June 1852; Spatz auf seiner Brautfahrt (Burleske, 3, J. Bauernfeind), WSB, 24 July 1852; Das Mädchen von der Spule (Charakterbild, 3, Elmer), 20 Nov 1852; Ein Abenteuer in Wien (Posse, 5, Kola), 19 Feb 1853; Die Leidenschaften (Märchen, 4, A. Berla), 30 March 1853; Reicher Leute armes Kind (Volksdrama, 4, S. Schlesinger), 14 April 1853; Die Gefopften (Posse, 3, Bittner), WSB, 2 July 1853; Die falsche Pepita (Posse, 2, Böhm), WSB, 13 Aug 1853; Das Ultimatum in der Luft (Schwank, 1, A. Bittner and Grün), 29 Oct 1853

Ein Rappelkopf (Posse, 3, Bittner), 31 Dec 1853; Überlistet! (Posse, 2, J. Doppler), 14 Jan 1854; Der fidele Christl (Posse, 3, Bittner), 25 Feb 1854; Ein alter Deutschmeister (Charakter-Gemälde, 4, Berla), WSB, 5 June 1854; Ein Hausmeister aus der Vorstadt (Posse, 3, A. Langer), WSB, 13 Aug 1854; Der Czikos (Volksstück, 3, E. Szigligeti), 30 Sept 1854, collab. J. Szerdahelyi; Der Karfunkel (Volksstück, 3, W. Faber), 7 Oct 1854; Eine Nacht in Konstantinopel (Posse, 1, Liebold), 22 Oct 1854; Ein Fechter (Parodie, 1, Bittner), 30 Nov 1854

Ein Wiener Freiwilliger (Lokalbild, 2, Langer), 27 Jan 1855; Schwert und Pinsel (Schwank, 2, Juin), 22 Feb 1855; Ausgeliehen (Posse, 2, Doppler), 10 March 1855; Strauss und Lanner (Lokalbild, 3, Langer), 17 March 1855; Paraplui (Posse, 3, Berla), 28 April 1855; Des Glückes und des Unglücks Launen (Posse, 3, Feldmann and F. A. Pann), WSB, 2 June 1855; Dick und Dünn (Schwank, 3, L. Karl), 17 June 1855; Ein deutsches Schullehrer (Lokalbild, 3, J. L. Deinhardstein), WSB, 14 July 1855; Die Ausspielerin (Posse, 3, Langer), 28 July 1855; Warum traut er einem Doktor? (Posse, 3, Feldmann and Pann), 18 Aug 1855; Miss Lydia (Schwank, 3, Böhm), 9 Sept 1855

Die Folgen eines Champagnerdusels (Posse, 2, A. Blank), 19 Sept 1855; Der Gang durch die Vorzeit (Posse, 3, O. F. Berg), 9 Dec 1855; Judas im Frack (Charakter-Gemälde, 4, Langer), 20 Dec 1855, collab. F. Suppé; Er ist unsichtbar (Posse, 1, Stix), 26 Jan 1856; Stadtmamsell und Bäuerin (Posse, 1, Blank), 26 Jan 1856; Eine Schauspielerfamilie (Charakterbild, Blank and Bernhofer), 5 April 1856; Der Aktiengreissler (Posse, 3, Langer), WSB, 12 May 1856; Trau, schau, wem? (Charakter-Gemälde, 3, Gründorf), WSB, 28 July 1856; Der Eine möcht, der Andere nicht (Posse, 2, H. Bauer), 9 Aug 1856; Eine Frau um jeden Preis (Posse, 3, Blank and Bernhofer), 25 Sept 1856

Der Liebezauber, oder Barbier und Pächterin (Spl, 1, A. Bahn), 28 Nov 1856; Das erste Kind (Posse, 3, Langer), 20 Dec 1856; Die Mehlmesser-Pepi (Posse, 3, Langer), 19 March 1857; Die Kartenaufschlägerin von der Siebenbrünnerwissen (Genrebild, 3, Blank and Bernhofer), WSB, 2 June 1857; Ein ehemaliger Trottl (Lokalbild, 3, Langer), WSB, 25 July 1857; Zaunschlupferl (Posse, 4, Berla), WSB, 18 Aug 1857; Die Braut ohne Bräutigam, oder Sie bleibt sitzen (Posse, 3, Turteltaub), 26 Sept 1857, collab. J. Schürer; Alle neune! (Märchen, 4, F. Böck), 12 Nov 1857; Der Wucherer in der Klemme (Schwank, 3, T. Flamm), 28 Nov 1857

Der alte Infanterist und sein Sohn der Husar, (Charakterbild, 4, J. H. Mirani), 9 Jan 1858; Noch ein Wiener Dienstbote (Posse, 3, Juin), WSB, 9 June 1858; Ein Prater Wurstl (Lokalbild, 3, Langer), WSB, 19 Aug 1858; Nur diplomatisch (Posse, 3, T. Megerle), 2 Oct 1858; Die Eisjungfer (Märchen, 3, Elmar), 23 Oct 1858; Ein Wiener Geselle (Posse, 3, Ehrnhäusel), 4 Dec 1858; Drei Kandidaten, oder Dumm, dümmer am dümmsten (Posse, 3, Feldmann), 15 Jan 1859; Ein Faschings-Gugelhupf (Burleske, 3, Langer), 5 March 1859; Der Teufel im Herzen (Lokalbild, 3, Flamm and Wimmer), 18 March 1859

Der Freiheitskampf in Tirol (Volksstück, 4, Berla and W. Tesco), 21

May 1859; Andreas Hofer, der Sandwirt (Volksstück, 3, Böhm), WSB, 3 June 1859; Der Bankier von Wachs (Posse, 3, Langer), WSB, 9 July 1859; Über Land und Meer, oder Abenteuer eines Glücklichen (Zauberstück, 3, Blank), WSB, 21 Aug 1859, collab. Suppé; Ein Wiener Volkssänger (Lokalbild, 3, Fürst), 15 Sept 1859; Salon und Barbierstube, oder Strafe muss sein (Posse, 3, ?Langer), 1 Oct 1859; Fanni, die schieche Nuss (Volksstück, 4, Findeisen), 23 Nov 1859; Eine neue Welt (Charakterbild, 3, Kaiser), 21 Jan 1860

Die Kinder von Aspern (Volksstück, 3, V. Pirzel), WSB, 25 May 1860; Die Weibermühle (Volksmärchen, 3, Morländer), WSB, 9 June 1860; Die Verwahrlosten (Genrebild, 3, Blank), WSB, 23 June 1860; Wiener und Franzos, oder Jäger und Zuave (Lokalbild, 3, Berg), 8 July 1860; Die Wiener auf dem Lande (Posse, 3, Bittner), WSB, 31 Aug 1860; Auf der Bühne und hinter den Coulissen (Schwank, 2, L. Gottsleben), 14 Oct 1860; Der Stern der Liebe (Märchen, 3, Haffner), 10 Nov 1860; Die öffentliche Meinung (Volksstück, 3, J. Findeisen), 19 Jan 1861

Zwei van anno dazumal (Volksstück, 3, Berg), 14 Feb 1861; Auch ein Liberaler (Posse, 1, Berla), 10 May 1861; Die Studenten von Rummelstadt (Posse, 3, Haffner), WS, 15 June 1861; Heillose Confusionen (Posse, 3, Liebold), WSB, 9 July 1861; Versteckt (Posse, 3, Eberhard), WSB, 18 July 1861; Zwei Bürgermeister (Volksstück, 3, J. Konrad), 14 Sept 1861; Ein eiserner Kopf (Posse, 3, Eberhard and Kaiser), 18 Jan 1862; Ein Mann dreier Weiber, oder Ein alter Tarockspieler (Posse, 3, Blank and J. L. Harisch), 22 April 1862; Faustin I., Kaiser von Haiti (Posse, 4, M. Schleich and Feldmann), 3 May 1862

Die Sternenjungfrau (Märchen, 3, Haffner), 13 Sept 1862; Fäustling und Margarethe (Parodie, Juin), 6 Oct 1862; Der Goldonkel (Posse, 3, E. Pohl), 18 Oct 1862, collab. J. Hopp and K. F. Konradin; Der Blitzableiter in der Sylvesternacht (Schwank, 1, Kaiser), 1 Jan 1863; Eine geschlossene Gesellschaft (Genrebild, 3, K. Bruno [Haffner]), 5 Jan 1863; Künstler und Millionär (Posse, 3, Kaiser), 24 Jan 1863; Der Fuchs in der Falle (Schwank, 1, L. Julius), 15 March 1863; Über Land und Meer (Posse, 3, Feldmann), 22 March 1863

Wiener G'schichten (Posse, 3, Blank), 28 March 1863, rev. (1), 1868; Grosses Tanz-Divertissement (Gollinelli), 7 April 1863; Das Abenteuer in der Waldmühle (Posse, 1, Blank), 19 April 1863; Spion von Aspen (Volksstück, 3, J. Megerle), 17 June 1863; Stein und Stahl (Charakterbild, 3 Kaiser), 18 July 1863; Hass und Liebe (Schwank, 1, Blank), 9 Sept 1863; Der Bauernprozess (Posse, 1, Blank), 9 Sept 1863; Bruder Liederlich (Posse, 3, Pohl), 26 Sept 1863; Schafhaxl (Feerie, Strampfer), 7 March 1864

Unsere Nachbarin (Posse, 1, Findeisen), 1 Oct 1864; Rübezahl, oder Peter Nimmersatt und sein Glück (Märchen für Kinder, 3, J. Kurmayer), 15 Oct 1864; Er und sein Weib, oder Die Wiener im Ehestand (Volksstück, 3, Berg), 16 Oct 1864; Eine passende Partie (Charakter-Gemälde, 3, Findeisen), 26 Oct 1864; Dornröschen, oder Der 100-jährige Schlaf (Märchen für Kinder, 3, Kurmayer), 27 Oct 1864; Auf dem Eise und beim Christbaum (Posse, 3, Kaiser), 12 Nov 1864; Der daumenlange Hansel, oder Die verzauberte Prinzessin (Kindermärchen, 3, Kurmayer), 28 Nov 1864

Das Fabriksmädel (Spl, 1, Findeisen), 3 Dec 1864; Das Binsenmännchen und der Binsenmichel (Kinderkomödie, 3, Kurmayer), 4 Dec 1864; Der Weihnachtstraum, oder Der heilige Christabend (Kinderkomödie, 3, Kurmayer), 18 Dec 1864; Der Nörkelkönig, oder Die Kindesliebe (Kinderkomödie, 3, Kurmayer), 12 Jan 1865; Graf und Gräfin (Schwank, 1, Blank), 20 Jan 1865; Der gestiefelte Kater und der Graf von Carabas, oder Die Macht der Zauberei (Kinderkomödie, 5, Kurmayer), 5 Feb 1865; Narr Ciss (Parodistischer Schwank, 1, Berg), 2 March 1865

Die Zwillingsbrüder (Posse, 3, Berg), 4 May 1865; Die Eselshaut (Feerie, 5, Megerle), 25 Aug 1865; Heinrich IV. (Operette, 1), 14 Dec 1865; Die Gärtner-Mali (Posse, 3, Berla), 5 April 1866; Prinzessin Hirschkuh (Ausstattungsstück, 5, Langer), 21 Sept 1866; Eine Schäferin aus der Vorstadt (Posse, 3, Allen), 29 Dec 1866; Wiener Leben, oder Ob schön, ob Regen (Posse, 3, Bittner), 16 Feb 1867; Napoleon, Toulon, Paris, Moskau, Wasserloo (Spektakelstück, Strampfer), 12 Aug 1868; Maria Theresia und ihr Kammerheizer (Volksstück, 3, Mirani), 2 Dec 1868; Die Probiermamsell (Lokalbild, 3, Berg), 26 Feb 1869

Ein Mensch ohne Geld (Posse, 1, Bittner), 19 April 1869; Die Türken vor Wien (Volksstück, 5, Arthur Müller), 10 Aug 1869; An der schönen blauen Donau (Lokalbild, 3, Berg), 21 Aug 1869; Nach Ägypten (Burleske, 3, Bittner), 26 Dec 1869; Das Mädl ohne Geld (Lokalbild, 3, Berg), 1 Feb 1870; Der Pfarrer von Kirchfeld

(Volksstück, 4, L. Anzengruber), 5 Nov 1870; Der verlorene Sohn (Volksstück, 3, Berg), 31 March 1871; Papageno in der Theaterkanzlei (Vorspiel, 1, Berg), 3 May 1871; Die wilden Schwäne (Märchen für Kinder, J. Feld), 8 Oct 1871

Der Meineidbauer (Volksstück, 4, Anzengruber), 9 Dec 1871; Die Kreuzelschreiber (Bauernkomödie, 3, Anzengruber), 12 Oct 1872; König Mammon, oder Peter Winzer's Reiseabenteuer (Märchen für Kinder, 3, Megerle), 13 Oct 1872; Aschenbrödel (Märchen für Kinder, 3, Megerle), Nov 1872; Münchhausen (Märchen für Kinder, 3, Feld), 16 Feb 1873; Die Christfee (Weihnachtsmärchen, Feld), 7 Dec 1873; Der Prinz von Banalien, oder König und Holzbauer (Zauberspiel für Kinder, 3, Kurmayer), 8 Feb 1874; Don Quixote, der Ritter von der traurigen Gestalt (Komödie für Kinder, 3, Kurmayer, after M. de Cervantes), 22 Feb 1874

Der G'wissenswurm (Bauernkomödie, 3, Anzengruber), 19 Sept 1874; Der Geisterfürst, oder Die Prinzessin von Pomare (Zauberposse für Kinder, 3, Kurmayer), 8 Nov 1874; Die Reise um die Erde in 79 Tagen (Ausstattungsstück für Kinder, 5, Feld), 7 March 1875; Doppelselbstmord (Bauernposse, 3, Anzengruber), 1 Feb 1876; Der kleine Heiratsbandler (Schwank, 1, C. Gärtner), 1 April 1876; Ein Flüchtling von anno 1876 (Posse, 5, Flamm), 16 Sept 1876; Der galante Vicomte (Operette, 3, Plank, after Bayard), 30 Nov 1877

Alte Wiener (Volksstück, 4, Anzengruber), WR, 27 Sept 1878; Die Reise durch die Sonnenwelt (Märchen für Kinder, 3, Feld, after J. Verne), WR, 13 Oct 1878; Die Zwiderwurzn (Volksstück, 5, H. T. von Schmid), WR, 16 Oct 1878; Das Weib des Buchbinders, oder Die Österreicher in Bosnien (Volksstück, 3, A. Langer), WR, 27 Oct 1878; Rübezahl, oder Das verkaufte Herz (Märchen für Kinder, 3, Feld, after J. Swift), WR, 15 Nov 1878; Fluidus und Cristalla (Zauberspiel für Kinder, 3, Feld), WR, 1 Dec 1878

Helden von heut! (Posse, 3, L. Krenn and C. Wolff), WR, 7 Dec 1878; Gullivers Reiseabenteuer (Märchen für Kinder, 3, Feld, after Swift), WR, 5 Jan 1879; Teufeleien, oder Die Macht der Liebe (Zauberposse, 3, Feld), WR, 26 Feb 1879; Saat und Ernte (Volksstück, 3, Findeisen), WR, 12 March 1879; Spiritus familiaris (Ausstattungsstück, 5, J. Mühlfeld), WR, 1 Oct 1879; Der Dorflump (Volksstück, 5, E. Toth), WR, 25 Nov 1879; Auf zum Harem! (Posse, 3, M. Oeribauer and B. Zappert), WR, 27 Jan 1880; Adam und Eva (Posse, 1, P. Brand), Fürst, 26 Sept 1884

*

StiegerO; WurzbachL

F. Hadamowsky: *Das Theater in der Wiener Leopoldstadt 1781–1860* (Vienna, 1934)

A. Bauer: *Die Musik Adolph Müllers in den Theaterstücken Johann Nestroys* (diss., U. of Vienna, 1935)

——: *150 Jahre Theater an der Wien* (Zürich, Leipzig and Vienna, 1952)

——: *Opern und Operetten in Wien* (Graz and Cologne, 1955)

——: *Das Theater in der Josefstadt zu Wien* (Vienna and Munich, 1957)

J. Hein and J. Hüttner, eds.: *J. Nestroy: Sämtliche Werke* (Vienna, 1977–)

PETER BRANSCOMBE

Müller [Walther; née Halle], **Carolina Fredrika** (*b* Copenhagen, 5 Feb 1755; *d* Stockholm, 17 Nov 1826). Swedish mezzo-soprano of Danish birth. She studied in Copenhagen and was engaged at the Royal Opera there. She was married to the opera secretary, T. C. Walther, but obtained a divorce on account of his cruelty and in 1780 formed a liaison with C. F. Müller, a leading violinist, with whom she fled to Sweden. She made her début in Stockholm in 1781 in Gluck's *Alceste* and was engaged as a principal singer at the Royal Opera. In late 1782 she and her husband fled to avoid the debtors' prison; her fame as a singer and actress was such that Gustavus III ordered his entire army to capture her. She and her husband were offered a new contract in 1783; she appeared on stage until 1810 and taught at the opera school until 1815. She achieved considerable fame for her expressive acting and a mezzo-soprano voice that was both flexible and dramatic. Her main roles included the principal parts in Gluck's *Alceste* and *Armide*, Christina Gyllenstjerna in *Gustaf Wasa* by Naumann and Queen Dido in Kraus's *Aeneas i Carthago*.

F. Dahlgren: *Anteckningar om Stockholms teatrar* [Notes on Stockholm Theatres] (Stockholm, 1866)

K. Neiendam: 'Caroline Müller', *Gustavian Opera 1770–1809* (Stockholm, 1990)   BERTIL H. VAN BOER

Müller, Christian Friedrich (*b* Brandenburg, 28 Dec 1752; *d* Stockholm, 21 Dec 1827). German composer active in Sweden. A pupil of Johann Peter Salomon, he undertook a concert tour in 1780 as a violinist. In Copenhagen he fell in love with the singer Carolina Walther (née Halle) and eloped with her to Stockholm, where he was engaged as assistant Konzertmeister in 1780 and as Konzertmeister in 1787. He retired in 1817. Müller began writing music for the Stockholm stage as early as 1780, though his earliest surviving dramatic work is his epilogue to Piccinni's *Atys* (epilogue text by A. N. Clewberg-Edelcrantz; Stockholm, Royal Opera, 1 Nov 1784, *S-St*). He also composed much of the music for *Drottning Christina*, a heroic drama with dance and singing (4, J. H. Kellgren, after Gustavus III; Mariefred, Gripsholm, 1785, *S-St*), and for several other productions. His music shows the influences of his colleagues Zander and Kraus.

F. Dahlgren: *Anteckningar om Stockholms teatrar* [Notes on Stockholm Theatres] (Stockholm, 1866)   BERTIL H. VAN BOER

Müller, Gerhard (*b* Saalfeld, 16 Feb 1939). German writer. After working in industry and the press, Müller studied journalism at the Karl Marx University, Leipzig, 1959–63, and was a cultural editor for the state news service in Halle, Leipzig and Berlin until 1980, when he became principal dramatic adviser at the Komische Oper, Berlin. In 1986 he took the doctorate at the Humboldt University, East Berlin, with a dissertation on Heine's views on music.

As well as his musical criticism, musical journalism and satirical pieces for East German radio, the weekly *Sonntag* (*Freitag* from 1990) and the satirical magazine *Eulenspiegel*, Müller has written librettos for the operas *Candide*, after Voltaire, by Reiner Bredemeyer (1986, Halle), *Gastmahl, oder Über die Liebe*, after Plato, by Georg Katzer (1988, Schwetzingen) and *Antigone oder Die Stadt*, after Sophocles, also by Katzer (composed 1989–90). He has also prepared a German text for Joplin's *Treemonisha* (1991). In *Candide* he produced a remarkably effective, condensed version of Voltaire's parable of the Enlightenment, in the form of a journey through life, with certain adaptations typical of life in the German Democratic Republic: for instance, the figure of the radical pessimist is cut, pessimism being as much out of place in a socialist state looking forward to the future as it is under a relentlessly cheerful capitalist system. The libretto for this 'Literaturoper', based on the dialectic spirit of the Enlightenment, is sometimes amusing, sometimes forthright; it would have won the approval of Adorno. His text for Katzer's *Gastmahl* is a witty and grotesque parable, after Plato, Socrates and Aristophanes, in a would-be peaceful domestic setting during the Peloponnesian War.

REINHARD OEHLSCHLÄGEL

Müller, Maria (*b* Theresienstadt [now Terezín, nr Litoměřice], 29 Jan 1898; *d* Bayreuth, 13 March 1958). Czech soprano. She studied in Vienna with Erik Schmedes and made her début as Elsa at Linz in 1919. Engagements followed at the Deutsches Theater in Prague and in Munich, and in 1925 she made her début as Sieglinde at the Metropolitan. She remained there until the 1934–5 season, singing in a number of American premières including Alfano's *Madonna imperia* (1928), Pizzetti's *Fra Gherardo* (1929), *Švanda the Bagpiper* (1931) and *Simon Boccanegra* (1932). She first sang in Berlin at the Städtische Oper as Euryanthe in 1926 and later sang at the Staatsoper until 1943. After World War II she retired to live at Bayreuth, where she had sung regularly from 1930 to 1944 as Senta, Eva, Elisabeth, Elsa and Sieglinde. At Salzburg she appeared as Eurydice (1931), Reiza (1933) and Donna Elvira (1934). She made her Covent Garden début as Eva in 1934 and sang Sieglinde in the 1937 *Ring* cycles. Her large repertory included the title roles in *Die ägyptische Helena*, *Jenůfa* and Gluck's *Iphigénie en Tauride*, Djula in Gotovac's *Ero the Joker*, Pamina, Tosca and Marguerite. Müller possessed a warm, vibrant voice and sang with a rare purity of tone.   HAROLD ROSENTHAL/R

Müller, Therese. *See* MALTEN, THERESE.

Müller, Wenzel (*b* Tyrnau [now Trnava], 26 Sept 1767; *d* Baden, nr Vienna, 3 Aug 1835). Austrian composer. He studied music with the schoolmaster at Kornitz (Koričany), south-east Moravia, and could soon play all the instruments of the orchestra. At the age of 12 he wrote a mass for the ordination of an older brother. He was sent to the Benedictine foundation of Raigern (Rajhrad), near Brünn (Brno), where he concentrated on mastering wind instruments; taught and encouraged by the choirmaster, Maurus Haberbauer, he also composed. When the prelate went to Johannisberg, the seat of the Prince-Bishop of Breslau, he took Müller with him and Dittersdorf became his teacher. In 1782 Müller joined Waizhofer's theatre company at Brno as third violinist and composed a successful Singspiel, *Das verfehlte Rendezvous, oder Die weiblichen Jäger*. Encouraged by the comic actor and singer Anton Baumann, and by the new theatre director Bergopzoomer, Müller made excellent progress. The story that Emperor Joseph II, impressed by Müller, determined to send him to Italy to study must be discounted on grounds of chronology. But in 1786 he was taken on as Kapellmeister by Marinelli at the Theater in der Leopoldstadt in Vienna ('The tenth of May I Wenzel Müller was formally engaged as Kapellmeister', he wrote in his diary – the first definitely authenticated date since his birth).

Müller's first Vienna appearance was on 30 May 1786, when he conducted the Leopoldstadt première of Gassmann's *La contessina*. From then until 1830, except for the period of an engagement in Prague, he served as Kapellmeister to the Leopoldstadt theatre, most of that time in charge of the theatre's musical activities. Not yet 19 at the time of his appointment, he had the task of making the musical side of Marinelli's performances worthy of the actors' skills (these included his friend Baumann, and Johann 'Kasperl' La Roche). Under Müller the orchestra was enlarged and improved, and the appointment of Ferdinand Kauer as second Kapellmeister, and later as head of the theatre's music school, meant that the company was assured of a steady supply of well-trained singers and musicians.

Müller's autograph diary contains a wealth of fascinating information about performances at the theatre as well as its social and economic circumstances. For several years he listed the number of performances he had to conduct and the number of new scores he wrote; in 1794 he was exceptionally busy, conducting on no fewer than 225 evenings, though in this year he wrote a mere seven 'operas' (the title loosely used for Singspiels of some pretension) as opposed to 15 or 20 theatre scores in other years. His first major success as a composer was with *Das Sonnenfest der Braminen* (9 September 1790; text by Hensler), given over 90 times in 15 years and published by at least three German houses. *Das Neusonntagskind*, the first of the Singspiels adapted by Joachim Perinet from originals by Philipp Hafner, was given on 10 October 1793 and heard 162 times in the Leopoldstadt up to 1829. The première was Müller's first benefit night, and as he said in his diary, 'I won my musical renown with this opera; this opera is known in every land'. The 1790s were splendid years for this theatre – the abandonment of the National Singspiel left the field wide open, and the enterprising Marinelli stepped in; the remarkable number of royal and imperial visitors testifies to the theatre's renown. Müller's most popular works of this period include *Kaspar der Fagottist*, *Die Schwestern von Prag*, *Die zwölf schlafenden Jungfrauen*, *Das lustige Beilager* and *Die Teufelsmühle am Wienerberg* (163 performances in the Leopoldstadt up to 1860).

The first few years of the 19th century contained no major success for Müller, which may well account in part for his decision to accept an invitation from the director, Liebich, to become Kapellmeister at the German Opera in Prague, a post he held from March 1807 until May 1813; his daughter Therese (the distinguished soprano Madame Grünbaum, born 24 August 1791) was engaged as a singer at the same time. It is clear from contemporary reports that Müller was not equal to the demands of his Prague contract (even Weber, his successor, was exercised to improve standards); there is, however, a valuable report on Müller as a conductor from J. F. Reichardt, who heard him conduct *Das Neusonntagskind* there in November 1808:

The finale of the second act was performed entirely comically by all the cast, with Italian liveliness. Most of the waltzes and other folk melodies were, however, played and sung much more slowly and gracefully than almost anywhere else, whereby the whole took on a *gemütlich* quality, which obviously pleased all hearers and assuredly has something national about it.

Müller resumed his duties at the Theater in der Leopoldstadt on 15 June 1813; he recovered much of his former fire and enthusiasm, owing at least in part to the successes of his daughter, son-in-law and, later, his grand-daughter Caroline (who made a successful début at the Hofoper in August 1829, aged 15). Müller's numerous popular Singspiels, parodies and *Posse* scores after his return from Prague include *Tankredi, Aline, oder Wien in einem andern Weltteil* (1822; based on Berton's opera), *Der verwunschene Prinz* (1818; based on Seyfried's arrangement of Grétry's *Zémire et Azor*) and his scores for Raimund's *Der Barometermacher auf der Zauberinsel* (1823), *Die gefesselte Phantasie* and *Der Alpenkönig und der Menschenfeind* (both 1828). He continued to compose until the year before his death, though not without meeting charges of self-plagiarism.

Of all the regular composers of music for the Viennese *Volkstheater* Müller was the most popular and the best; some of his scores, especially for Raimund's works, are still regularly performed, and a number of his songs rapidly achieved lasting success in the guise of street songs and *Volkslieder* ('Wer niemals einen Rausch gehabt', 'Lieber kleiner Gott der Liebe', 'So leb denn wohl, du stilles Haus'). Although later in his career he

was seldom as ambitious, a number of his early works fully deserve the description 'opera': the finale to Act 1 of *Die unruhige Nachbarschaft* is so extensive that it was bound as a separate manuscript volume (now in *D-Mbs*); the first finale to *Die Schwestern von Prag*, with its interrupted serenades, beatings and nightwatchman's call, is also a full-scale ensemble. Müller was at his best and most characteristic in simple, unpretentious songs and duets. The famous quintet from *Der Alpenkönig* is nothing more than a plainly harmonized refrain with contrasting solos. His scoring is simple but almost always effective. He experimented eagerly and with success in operatic parody and in melodrama (*Der verwunschene Prinz* includes four melodramas, one of them comic). Müller's most obvious weakness lies in his general inability to develop and combine his ideas to any cumulative effect. Yet in solo song (easily the most important single category in contemporary Viennese theatre) Müller achieved an astonishing number of successes in all types, especially with tender, reflective numbers, but also with gay or satirical and occasionally (*Die Teufelsmühle*) with effectively sinister songs.

See also ALPENKÖNIG UND DER MENSCHENFEIND, DER; BAROMETERMACHER AUF DER ZAUBERINSEL, DER; GEFESSELTE PHANTASIE, DIE; KASPAR DER FAGOTTIST; NEUSONNTAGSKIND, DAS; SONNENFEST DER BRAMINEN, DAS; and TEUFELSMÜHLE AM WIENERBERGE, DIE.

principal sources for MSS and early prints: A-Wgm, Wn, Wst, D-Bds, Mbs

WL – *Vienna, Theater in der Leopoldstadt*
WWD – *Vienna, Freihaus-Theater auf der Wieden*

Das verfehlte Rendezvous, oder Die weiblichen Jäger (heroisch-komisches Spl, L. Zehenmark), Brno, Krautmarkt, 1783

Die Reisenden in Salamanka, oder Das seltene Brüderpaar (Spl, 2, Zehenmark), Brno, Krautmarkt, 1783

Doktor Faust (Parodie), Brno, Krautmarkt, 1784

Die stolze Operistin (Spl), Brno, Krautmarkt, 1784

Der adelige Pächter (Spl), Brno, Krautmarkt, 1785

Gandolin [Gandalin] und Roxane, oder Der Sieg der Liebe (Pantomime, 2, A. Baumann), Brno, Krautmarkt, 1785

Harlekin auf dem Paradebette, oder Nach dem Schlimmen folgt das Gute (Pantomime, 3, Baumann), Brno, Krautmarkt, 1785

Horra und Kloska (Pantomime), Brno

Je grösser der Schelm, je grösser das Glück (Operette), WL, 28 April 1786

Harlekins Neckereien (Pantomime, J. Reisenhuber), WL, 26 Sept 1786

Der lebendige Sack, oder Der gefoppte Dorfbarbier (Spl, 2, K. F. Hensler), WL, 21 Sept 1787

Kaspar, der gefoppte König auf der grünen Wiese, WL, 30 Jan 1788

Die Elektrisiermaschine (Spl, 1, F. Eberl), WL, 13 Nov 1788

Das Sonnenfest der Braminen (heroisch-komisches Original-Spl, 2, Hensler), WL, 9 Sept 1790

Kasperl, der glückliche Vogelkrämer (Zauberoper, 4, Hensler), WL, 3 March 1791

Kaspar der Fagottist [Der Fagottist, oder Die Zauberzither] (Spl, 3, J. Perinet), WL, 8 June 1791

Der Unterthanen Glück ist auch das Glück der Fürsten (Spl, 2, Perinet), WL, 7 Feb 1792

Die Verschwörung der Odalisken, oder Die Löwenjagd (Spl, 3, Hensler), WL, 3 May 1792

Pizichi (Spl, 3, Perinet), WL, 2 Oct 1792 [sequel to Kaspar der Fagottist]

Die Schneider, oder Kaspar, der alte Lehrbub (Spl, 2, Perinet), WL, 6 Feb 1793

Das Neusonntagskind (Spl, 2, Perinet, after P. Hafner: *Der Furchtsame*), WL, 10 Oct 1793

Die Schwestern von Prag (Spl, 2, Perinet, after Hafner), WL, 11 March 1794

Johannes Zauberhorn (Posse, 3, Perinet), WL, 27 Jan 1795

Caro, oder Megärens zweiter Teil (Spl, 2, Perinet, after Hafner), WL, 12 May 1795

Der alte Überall und Nirgends (Schauspiel mit Gesang, 5, Hensler), WL, 10 June 1795; pt 2, 16 Dec 1795

Die Marketänderin (militärisches Spl, 2, Hensler), WL, 13 Oct 1795

Der Lustig-Lebendig (Spl, 2, Perinet, after Hafner), WL, 27 Jan 1796

Nanette (Spl, 2, Perinet, after *Die schöne Wienerin*), WL, 23 July 1796

Österich über alles (Spl, 1, Perinet), WL, 14 Oct 1796

Das Schlangenfest in Sangora (heroisch-komische Oper, 2, Hensler), WL, 15 Dec 1796

Das lustige Beylager (Spl, 2, Perinet, after Hafner: *Der beschäftigte Hausregent*), WL, 14 Feb 1797

Die zwölf schlafenden Jungfrauen (Schauspiel mit Gesang, 4, Hensler), WL, 12 Oct 1797; pt 2, 24 July 1798; pt 3, 27 May 1800

Wer den Schaden hat, darf für den Spott nicht sorgen (komische Oper, 2, Hensler, after Dorvigny), WL, 10 May 1798

Ritter Benno von Ettingen (Schauspiel mit Gesang, 4, Hensler), WL, 27 Sept 1798

Der Sturm, oder Die bezauberte Insel (heroisch-komische Oper, 2, Hensler, after W. Shakespeare: *The Tempest*), WL, 8 Nov 1798

Thaddädl, der dreissigjährige ABC-Schütze (Posse, 3, Hensler), WL, 22 May 1799

Die Teufelsmühle am Wienerberg (Volksmärchen mit Gesang, 4, Hensler and L. Huber), WL, 12 Nov 1799

Die Zigeuner (Spl, 2, J. Richter), WL, 17 Jan 1800

Heroine, oder Die schöne Griechin in Alexandria (militärisches Schauspiel mit Gesang, 3, Hensler), WL, 19 June 1800

Der Bettelstudent (Spl, 3, F. X. Huber), WL, 26 July 1800

Der Teufelsstein bei Mödlingen (historisch-romantisches Volksmärchen mit Gesang, 3, Hensler), WL, 18 Dec 1800

Der [Lustige] Schusterfeierabend (Spl, 3, Hensler), WL, 23 July 1801

Ritter Don Quixote (romantisch-komische Oper, 3, Hensler, after M. de Cervantes), WL, 14 Sept 1802

Die unruhige Nachbarschaft (komische Oper, 2, Hensler, after Huber), WL, 2 March 1803

Das Bergfest (Spl, 2, Hensler), WL, 3 June 1803

Das friedliche Dörfchen (Allegorische Spl, 1, Hensler), WL, 29 Sept 1803

Orions Rückkehr zur friedlichen Insel (Gelegenheitstück, 1, Perinet), WL, 6 Nov 1803

Kasperls neu errichtetes Kaffeehaus, oder Der Hausteufel (komische Oper, 3, Perinet), WL, 10 Dec 1803

Die schwarze Redoute (Spl, 3, Kringsteiner), WL, 16 Jan 1804

Der Bäcker-Aufzug in Wien (Spl, 3, G. Ziegelhauser), WL, 3 April 1804

Die Belagerung von Ypsilon, oder Evakathel und Schnudi (Karrikatur, 2, Perinet, after Hafner), WL, 4 May 1804

Die Bewohner der Türkenschanze (romantisch-komische Oper, 3, J. A. Gleich), WL, 20 Sept 1804

Die Geister im Wäschkasten, oder Der reisende Schneider (Pantomime, 1, P. Hasenhut), WL, 27 Sept 1804

Die Braut in der Klemme (Posse, 1, V. F. Kringsteiner), WL, 7 Nov 1804

Das Mädchen im Spessarter Walde (heroisch-komische Oper, 2), WL, 4 Dec 1804 [based on K. von Steinberg's ballet]

Der Lumpenkrämer (Spl, 2, Kringsteiner), WL, 15 Jan 1805

Die Göttin der Gestirne, oder Der goldene Schlüssel (Zauberoper, 3, Gleich), WL, 31 Jan 1805

Der Desperationsball (komische Oper, 2, Kringsteiner), WL, 21 Feb 1805

Marlborough (Pantomime, 3, J. Kübler), WL, 24 May 1805

Das Sommerlager (ländlich-militärische Oper, 3, Perinet), WL, 28 May 1805

Die Berggeister (Spl, 2, L. Huber), WL, 20 July 1805

Die Hochzeit des Harlekin, oder Die Lustigen Gärtner (Kinderpantomime, 1, M. Fenzl), WL, 11 Dec 1805

Das Körbchen aus der Türkei (Spl, 1), WL, 3 March 1806

Megära (Zauberoper, 3, Perinet, after Hafner), WL, 14 March 1806

Die [travestierte] neue Alzeste (Karrikatur-Oper, 3, Perinet, after Pauersbach and Müller), WL, 12 June 1806

Harlekin auf der Insel Liliput, oder Das Laternenfest der Chinesen (Pantomime, 2, F. Kees), WL, 18 July 1806

Die Mondkönigin, oder Die bezauberte Schneiderwerkstatt (Pantomime, 3, Kees), WL, 28 Oct 1806

Belino und Rosaura (Zauberoper, 3, M. Voll), WL, 9 Jan 1807

Die Windmühle von Trippstrill (Pantomime, 1, Hasenhut), WL, 20 Jan 1807

Der Tanzmeister (Posse, 3, Kringsteiner), WL, 6 Feb 1807, collab. F. Kauer and I. Schuster

Jawina [Laskina] (3), Prague, 21 May 1807

Samson (Melodrama, 3, J. A. Schuster), Prague, 1808

Simon Plattkopf, der Unsichtbare (Spl, 1, K. Costenoble), Prague, 1809

Die Wunderlampe (Zauberoper, 4, Gleich), Prague, 1810

Don Sylvio de Rosalva, oder Der blaue Schmetterling, Prague, 1812

Der Schlossgärtner und der Windmüller (komische Oper, 1, B. J. Koller), WL, 1 July 1813

Der österreichische Grenadier (Spl, 1, Meisl), WL, 9 Sept 1813

Die Jungfrau von Wien (Posse, 2, H. Herzenskron), WL, 29 Oct 1813

Der Kosak in London (Spl, 1, D. Wohl), WL, 14 Dec 1813

Die Kosaken in Wien (Spl, 3, A. Bäuerle), WL, 12 March 1814

Fee Zenobia, oder Die Zauber-Ruinen (Pantomime, 2, K. Hampel), WL, 26 March 1814

Der Riese Molochus, oder Der Mädchenräuber (Pantomime, 2, P. Rainoldi), WL, 14 May 1814

Hans Max Giesprecht von der Humpenburg, oder Die neue Ritterzeit (komische Operette, 1, C. Grünbaum, after A. von Kotzebue), WL, 24 Sept 1814

Die Prinzessin von Kakambo (komische Oper, 2, Perinet, after Kotzebue), WL, 19 Nov 1814

Herr von Schabel, der Senffabrikant aus Krems (Posse, 3, K. Wiedemann), WL, 21 Jan 1815

Die Bekanntschaft vom Leopoldstädter-Theater (Posse, 3, H. Wille), WL, 1 Feb 1815

Maria Stuttgartin (Parodie, 1, Bäuerle), WL, 12 May 1815

Die alte Ordnung kehrt zurück (Posse, 3, K. Meisl), WL, 5 Aug 1815

Der lebendigtote Hausherr (Posse, 3, W. Schmitt), WL, 28 Sept 1815

Die Katze der Frau von Zichory (Parodie, 1, Wiedemann), WL, 2 Nov 1815

Das Badhaus bei Wien (komische Oper, 3, Bäuerle), WL, 16 Dec 1815

Dragon, der Hund des Aubri, oder Der Wienerwald (Parodie, 2, Perinet), WL, 3 Feb 1816

Der Fiaker als Marquis (komische Oper, 3, Bäuerle), WL, 10 Feb 1816

Taddädl auf der Zwergeninsel (Zauberoper, 2, W. Schmitt), WL, 11 May 1816

Die Riesen- und Zwergenfamilie (Pantomime, Rainoldi), WL, 25 May 1816

Die Eipeldauer-Zeitung (Posse, 3, Bäuerle), WL, 8 June 1816

Der Familienschmuck, oder Prellerei über Prellerei (Posse, 1, Wille), WL, 3 July 1816

Die Schmaus Waberl (Posse, 3, Bäuerle), WL, 11 July 1816

Die unvermutete Hochzeit (Spl, 1, K. Schikaneder), WL, 7 Aug 1816

Die Entführung der Prinzessin Europa, oder So geht es im Olymp zu! (Karrikatur, 2, Meisl), WL, 5 Oct 1816

Das Tal der Gnomen (Feen-Spl, 3, Bäuerle), WL, 4 Dec 1816

Die Prellerei in der Narrengasse (Posse, 3, Schikaneder), WL, 14 Dec 1816

Der Tiger im Zaubergebirge (Pantomime, 2, Rainoldi), WL, 20 March 1817

Tankredi (komische Parodie, 2, Bäuerle), WL, 25 April 1817

Mai-Juni-Juli, oder Leopoldstadt, Jägerzeile und Prater (Posse, 3, F. Rosenau), WL, 17 May 1817

Frau Gertrud (Parodie, 2, Meisl), WL, 5 Sept 1817 [parody of F. Grillparzer: *Die Ahnfrau*]

Doktor Fausts Mantel (Zauberspiel mit Gesang, 2, Bäuerle), WL, 11 Dec 1817

Ritter Matthias von Bimsenstein und seine Trudel, oder Die Erlösung des Herrn Vetters und der Frau Mahm (Parodie, 3, Wiedemann), WL, 10 Feb 1818

Der verwunschene Prinz (Parodie, 2, Bäuerle), WL, 3 March 1818 [parody of Grétry: *Zémire et Azor*]

Harlekin als Hund (Pantomime, 2, Rainoldi), WL, 29 April 1818

Die Schlafenden im Walde, oder Die Abenteuer Kilian Wuchtels (Zauberposse, 3, J. Welling), WL, 11 July 1818

Die travestierte Zauberflöte (Posse mit Gesang, 2, Meisl) WL, 13 Aug 1818

Hippogryph, das fliegende Rössel, oder Die Gewalt der Zauberei (Pantomime-Zauberposse, 2, Rainoldi), WL, 1 April 1819

Die Zwillingsbrüder von Krems (Spl, 3, Meisl, after C. Goldoni), WL, 21 April 1819

Der Kurstreit in Baden (Spl, 1, J. S. von Menner), WL, 8 May 1819

Der Bräutigam als Korsar, oder Das Kanonen-Duell (Pantomime, 1, Rainoldi), WL, 11 May 1819

Die alte und die neue Schlagbrücke (Schauspiel mit Gesang, 2, Gleich), WL, 2 July 1819; as Die neue Kettenbrücke an der Donau, WL, 21 Jan 1825

Der Kirchtag in Petersdorf (Posse, 2, Meisl), WL, 21 Aug 1819

Die Brüder Liederlich (Zauberposse, 2, Gleich), WL, 10 March 1820

Bartels Traumbuch, oder Das Schlossgespenst (Posse, 2, Gleich), WL, 5 May 1820

Die Ausspielung des Theaters (Posse, 2, W. Blum), WL, 29 Aug 1820

Überall zu früh, oder Die Reise nach der Erbschaft (Posse, 2, Gleich), WL, 4 Oct 1820

Moderne Wirtschaft und Don Juans Streiche (Posse, 2, Bäuerle), WL, 17 Oct 1821

Die Fee aus Frankreich, oder Liebesqualen eines Hagestolzen (Feenmärchen mit Gesang, 2, Meisl), WL, 23 Nov 1821

Die neue Medea (Posse, 3, Meisl), WL, 17 May 1822

Die Wilden aus Indien (Posse, 2, Gleich), WL, 1 June 1822

Ninna, Nanni, Nannerl und Nannette, oder Das gefoppte Kleeblatt (Posse, 2, Bäuerle), WL, 25 July 1822

Die Affenkomödie (Posse, 2, Gleich), WL, 10 Aug 1822

Apollo und der Dichter, oder Die Fahrt nach der verkehrten Welt (Zauberposse, 2, Herzenskron), WL, 16 Sept 1822

Aline, oder Wien in einem anderen Weltteil (Zauberoper, 3, Bäuerle), WL, 9 Oct 1822 [parody of Berton: Aline, reine de Golconde]

Die Witwe aus Ungarn (Posse, 2, Meisl), WL, 19 Dec 1822

Sechzig Minuten nach zwölf Uhr (Parodie-Posse, 2, Meisl), WL, 17 April 1823

Der Raubritter, oder Harlekin als Pavian (Zauberpantomime, 2, Rainoldi), WL, 3 May 1823

Der Sohn des Waldes (Melodrama, 3, Bäuerle, after Eng. orig.), WL, 23 Oct 1823

Der Barometermacher auf der Zauberinsel (Zauberposse mit Gesang und Tanzen, 2, F. Raimund), WL, 18 Dec 1823

Der Zauberkuckuck, oder Die Probe der Treue (Pantomime, 2, Rainoldi), WL, 29 April 1825

Die musikalische Schneiderfamilie, oder Die Heirat durch Gesang (Posse, 2, Bäuerle), WL, 18 June 1825

Jakob in Wien (Posse, 3, Gleich), WL, 25 July 1825

Thespis, Serapions und Jocus Wanderung in die Leopoldstadt (quodlibet, 2, Meisl), WL, 18 Jan 1826

Jakob in der Heimat (Posse, 3, Gleich), WL, 14 Feb 1826, [sequel to Jakob in Wien]

Der erste Mai im Prater (Pantomime, 2, Rainoldi), WL, 22 April 1826

Herr Josef und Frau Baberl, (Posse mit Gesang, 3, Gleich), WL, 11 May 1826 [rev. version of Der Fleischhauer von Ödenburg]

Fido savant, der Wunderhund (Posse, 2, Gleich), WL, 25 July 1826

Columbinens Glück in Floras Tempel (Pantomime, 1, Rainoldi), WL, 31 July 1826

Harlekin als Taschenspieler (Pantomime, Bäuerle and Rainoldi), WL, 11 Jan 1827

Die schwarzen Frauen (Posse, 2, Gleich), WL, 31 March 1827 [parody of Boieldieu: La dame blanche]

Die Benefizvorstellung (Posse, 2, Meisl), WL, 7 April 1827, collab. J. Drechsler and I. Schuster

Der Hahn im Korbe (Zauberposse, 3, Gleich), WL, 22 Sept 1827

Die gefesselte Phantasie (Zauberspiel, 2, Raimund), WL, 8 Jan 1828

Die Begebenheiten zur Marktzeit (Posse, 2, Gleich), WL, 26 April 1828

Der Alpenkönig und der Menschenfeind (romantisch-komisches Zauberspiel, Raimund), WL, 17 Oct 1828

Die fröhliche Insel (Posse, 1, Korntheuer), WL, 7 Feb 1829

Faschingsleiden (Posse, 2, Gleich), WL, 14 March 1829

Die Drachenhöhle (Posse, 3, Gleich, after J. Kaminsky), WL, 28 March 1829

Die Marokkaner in Dummhausen (Posse, 2, Gleich, after Schikaneder: Die Waldmänner), WL, 1 July 1829

Frau von Drescherl, oder Die verlorene Brieftasche (Posse, 3, Gleich), WL, 30 Dec 1829

Der schwarze Bräutigam, oder Alles à la Mohr (Posse, 2, Meisl), WL, 24 June 1830

Werthers Leiden (Parodie, 2, Meisl, after Kringsteiner), WL, 30 Sept 1830

Die schädlichen Zaubergaben, oder Martin Zwickerls Abenteuer (Posse, 2, Gleich), WL, 30 Oct 1830

Die Bettlerbraut, oder Wer wagt, der gewinnt (Posse, 2, Gleich), WL, 5 Feb 1831

Der Maler und sein Farbenreiber, oder Abenteuer auf einer Fussreise (Posse, 3, Gleich), WL, 11 June 1831

Der Sieg des guten Humors, oder Die Lebenslampen (Zauberspiel mit Gesang, 3, J. K. Schickh), WL, 17 Sept 1831

Bruder Lüftig, oder Faschingsstreiche (Posse, 3, Schickh), WL, 18 Feb 1832

Enzian und Lucie, oder Keine sechs Klafter tief, aber doch fatal (Parodie-Posse, 2, Schickh), WL, 16 June 1832

Das Zauberbuch, oder Die Bräute aus der Waldhütte (Zauberposse, 2, Gleich), WL, 18 Aug 1832

Die Erdgeister und der Brillenhändler (Zauberspiel, 2, K. Schikaneder), WL, 12 March 1883

Der reisende Musikant, oder Die Eifersucht nach dem Tode (Posse, 2, Gleich), WL, 31 Aug 1833

Die dreifache Heirat durch eine Schneelawine (Posse, 2, Gleich), WL, 23 Nov 1833

Die Testamentsklausel (Posse, 2, D. Reiberstorffer), WL, 14 June 1834

Asmodi, oder Das böse Weib und der Satan (Zauberposse, 2, Schick), WL, 10 Nov 1834

Die Familie vom Lande (Posse, 3, ? J. M. R. Lenz), WL, 10 March 1838

Doubtful: Evakathel und Schnudi (Parodie, ? after Hafner), WL, 19 Nov 1790; Das Blumenfest, oder Eis schmilzt durch Wärme (Kinderoper, Kringsteiner), WL, 11 July 1793; Der wohltätige Derwisch, oder Die Schellenkappe (3, Schikaneder), WWD, 10 Sept 1793, collab. Gerl, Henneberg and Schack; Der Friede, oder Die prüfung des Herzens (Spl, 2, J. Weidmann), WWD, 11 May 1797, collab. I. Seyfried and others

*

W. Müller: *Kaiser-königl. priviligirtes Theater in der Leopoldstadt in Wien* (MS, *A-Wst*) [diary of theatre events]

——: *Die von mir Wenzel Müller Kapellmeister ... componirten Opern von 1786 bis 1828* (MS, *A-Wn*) [inc.]

J. F. Reichardt: *Vertraute Briefe geschrieben auf einer Reise nach Wien* (Amsterdam, 1810)

W. Blum: 'Wenzel Müller, der eigentliche Schöpfer echter Volks-Musik', *Allgemeine Theater-Zeitung*, xxviii (1835), nos.161–2

W. A. Riehl: *Musikalische Charakterköpfe: ein kunstgeschichtliches Skizzenbuch* (Stuttgart, 1853–60)

C. von Wurzbach: *Biographisches Lexikon des Kaiserthums Oesterreich*, xix (Vienna, 1868), 407 [incl. list of stage works]

E. von Bauernfeld: *Aus Alt- und Neu-Wien* (Vienna, 1872)

O. Teuber: *Geschichte des Prager Theaters*, ii (Prague, 1885)

W. Krone: *Wenzel Müller: ein Beitrag zur Geschichte der komischen Oper* (Berlin, 1906) [incl. list of stage works]

W. A. Bauer and H. Kraus, eds.: *Raimund-Liederbuch* (Vienna, 1924)

A. Orel, ed.: *F. Raimund: Die Gesänge der Märchendramen, Sämtliche Werke*, vi (Vienna, 1924)

L. Raab: *Wenzel Müller: ein Tonkünstler Altwiens* (Baden, 1928) [incl. list of stage works]

F. Hadamowsky: *Das Theater in der Wiener Leopoldstadt* (Vienna, 1934)

P. Branscombe: 'An Old Viennese Opera Parody and a New Nestroy Manuscript', *German Life & Letters*, xxviii (1975), 210–17

PETER BRANSCOMBE

Mullings, Frank (*b* Walsall, 10 May 1881; *d* Manchester, 19 May 1953). English tenor. He made his début in 1907 at Coventry in *Faust* and in 1913 sang Tristan under Beecham in Birmingham. In 1916 he sang his first Otello in Manchester, and in 1919 made his Covent Garden début in the English première of De Lara's *Naïl*; *Pagliacci* and *Parsifal* followed later that year. As principal dramatic tenor in the British National Opera Company (1922–9), he created Apollo in Boughton's *Alkestis* (1924, Covent Garden) and had such roles as Siegfried, Tannhäuser and Radames in his repertory. Recordings show a strong, heroic voice of distinctive timbre, sometimes uncomfortably produced but beautiful in the middle register. Many considered his Tristan, Otello and Canio the finest heard in England in living memory.

*

J. Fryer and J. B. Richards: 'Frank Mullings', *Record Collector*, vii (1952), 5–19 [with discography]   J. B. STEANE

Mummery, (Joseph) Browning (*b* Melbourne, 12 July 1888; *d* Canberra, 16 March 1974). Australian tenor. He studied singing while working as a mechanic. He made his début as Beppo (*Fra Diavolo*) under the name of Joseph Mummery, and also sang Arturo with the

Frank Rigo company (1919, Melbourne); in the same year he took the title role in Gounod's *Faust* in a special all-Australian performance in English given under the auspices of the Australian Natives Association. Tours of Australia and New Zealand with J. C. Williamson's opera company, and a successful audition with Percy Pitt for the British National Opera Company confirmed his professional transition from mechanic to leading tenor. After further studies in Italy, he sang Rodolfo in Melba's Covent Garden farewell in 1926, appeared as the Italian Singer in *Der Rosenkavalier* conducted by Bruno Walter, returned to Australia with the Melba-Williamson tour of 1928 and, after additional appearances in the USA and London, joined the Australian tour mounted by Benjamin Fuller in 1934–5. Mummery later taught in Melbourne before retiring to Canberra.   ROGER COVELL

Münchheimer, Adam. *See* MINCHEJMER, ADAM.

Munich (Ger. München; It. Monaco). City in southern Germany, capital of the state of Bavaria. Opera as now understood began with courtly musical spectacles on mythological subjects and featuring allegorical characters, performed as acts of homage from about the mid-17th century. Until the later 18th century Italian court opera reigned supreme, but German Singspiel gained an increasingly firm foothold thereafter.

1. To 1726. 2. 1726–1805. 3. From 1806: (i) The Bayerische Hofoper and Staatsoper (ii) Other theatres.

1. TO 1726. The origins of musical and theatrical life in Munich go back to the Middle Ages. From 1253 onwards it was the seat of the Wittelsbach dukes of Bavaria. Duke Albrecht III (1435–60), whose first wife, Agnes Bernauer, took an interest in music and literature, laid the foundations for theatrical development by encouraging the humanist *Schuldrama*. The Jesuits, resident in Munich from 1559 onwards, brought that development to its first flowering even before the introduction of Baroque court opera. The Latin *Schuldramen*, artistically staged as to direction and decor and performed first in the great hall of the Gymnasium, then in the Jesuit College's own theatre, combined subjects from classical antiquity, biblical material and legends of the saints with contemporary music (by Orlande de Lassus, Georg Victorinus and J. C. Pez, among others). Munich reached a cultural peak on the occasion of the famous royal wedding of Duke Wilhelm to Renée of Lorraine in 1568. Contemporary accounts record that an Italian *commedia dell'arte* was presented for the first time with the cooperation of Lassus, who also performed the musical interludes with instrumentalists and singers of the Hofkapelle. The records also state that the Jesuit tragedy *Samson*, by Andrea Fabricius, was performed during the festivities, again with music by Lassus. A dramatization of the Faust story, *Cenedoxus, Doctor von Paris* (1609), by the Jesuit Jakob Bidermann, foreshadowed the Baroque court opera. After a period of stagnation under Duke Wilhelm V 'the Pious' (1579–98), artistic pursuits at court began to revive; Bavaria was raised to the status of an electorate in 1623, and Ferdinand Maria (1651–79) and his highly gifted wife Adelaide of Savoy were responsible for the introduction of Italian opera. A dramatic cantata commissioned by Adelaide, *L'arpa festante*, by the Italian priest and harp virtuoso Giovanni Battista Maccioni, was staged for a visit by Emperor Ferdinand III in 1653; a year later *La ninfa ritrosa*, probably by the court composer Pietro Zambonini, was also performed. The records show that the opera *Oronte* by the court Kapellmeister, J. C. Kerll, was staged in 1657 with scenery by Francesco Santurini (i); it was written in honour of Emperor Leopold. Such works were performed in halls in the ducal residence (usually in the St Georgs-Saal and the Herkulessaal, sometimes in the Schwarzer Saal or the Brunnenhof pavilion). In 1654 the Opernhaus am Salvatorplatz was completed (fig.1); it was not closed until 1799, by when it had fallen into disrepair. Almost all Kerll's operas were performed there,

1. Interior of the opera house in the Salvatorplatz, Munich (completed in 1654), commissioned by Ferdinand Maria from Domenico Mauro and Francesco Santurini: engraving by Michael Wening after Domenico Mauro (note the central elector's box added in 1685)

as well as works by Ercole Bernabei, who succeeded Kerll as court Kapellmeister (the librettos were usually by the court poets Domenico Gisberti and G. G. Alcaini, sometimes by P. P. Bissani and Francesco Sbarra).

Italian opera flourished during the first decade of rule by the artistically inclined Elector Maximilian II Emanuel (1679–1726). Up to four operas and ballets (usually with choreography by M. d'Ardespin) were produced annually, and included works by G. A. Bernabei, Pietro Steffani, Agostino Torri, Albinoni, Porpora, Pistocchi, Vivaldi, Alessandro Scarlatti and Girolamo Tonini (the librettos were mostly by Luigi Orlandi and Ventura Terzago, both of whom were court poets). In addition even at this early date, German operas by Veit Weinberger, Philipp Jakob Seerieder and Franz Simon Schuechbaur were occasionally performed, though German Singspiel could not have offered Italian opera any serious competition. The cultural life of Munich suffered a great blow when Maximilian Emanuel became governor of the Spanish Netherlands in 1691; the entire élite of the court, including the director of the Kammermusik Torri and the Konzertmeister E. F. Dall'Abaco, moved to Brussels with him. Only church and chamber music continued to be regularly performed at the ducal residence in Munich, directed by G. A. Bernabei. Steffani, who wrote five operas in all for Munich before leaving for Hanover, showed the way to the aria opera, which led to *opera seria*. The period between Maximilian Emanuel's re-

turn in 1715 and his death in 1726 restored the musical life of Munich to its former glory; despite French influences, however, Italian opera still predominated.

2. 1726–1805. Although Elector Carl Albert (1726–45, Emperor Carl VII from 1742) also liked magnificence – records mention appearances by the most celebrated singing stars of the time, the castrato Farinelli and the soprano Faustina Bordoni (who first sang at Munich in 1723), in Torri's *Nicomede* (1728) and *Edippo* (1729) – unpropitious political developments (the reoccupation of Bavaria as a result of the War of the Austrian Succession) eventually made it impossible for him to maintain the high cultural standards previously established. Maximilian III Joseph (1745–77), however, raised a new monument to opera when he commissioned the Residenztheater (fig.3; for a plan view *see* THEATRE ARCHITECTURE, fig.3), built by François Cuvilliés (hence, also known as the Cuvilliéstheater). It was ceremonially opened in 1753 with a production of Ferrandini's *Catone in Utica*. Besides Ferrandini, musicians in the service of Maximilian Joseph included Porta, Peli, Aliprandi and Bernasconi. Other operas produced in this period include works by Pietro Pompeo Sales, Antonio Tozzi, Traetta, Sacchini and the elector's sister Maria Antonia Walpurgis, Electress of Saxony, who staged a spectacular production of her opera *Talestri, regina delle amazoni*. Little attention was paid to the performance of Gluck's *Orfeo ed Euridice* given by a

2. Design by Domenico and Gasparo Mauro for the moonlit garden scene in Agostino Steffani's opera 'Servio Tullio', written to celebrate the marriage of Elector Maximilian II Emanuel to Maria Antonia, Archduchess of Austria, in 1686

3. Interior of the Residenztheater (or Cuvilliéstheater), Munich, designed by François Cuvilliés and opened in 1753: watercolour (1867) by Gustav Seeberger

touring company during Carnival 1773, in an adulterated version bringing it closer to the old *opera seria*; the newer, 'reform' opera style was obviously not popular in Munich.

Count Joseph Anton von Seeau contributed to the development of musical drama in the city when he succeeded Count Joseph Ferdinand Maria von Salern in 1756 as Intendant of all the theatres (the Residenztheater, the Opernhaus am Salvatorplatz, the Redoutensaal, the Turnierhaus and the Färberbräu-Saal). While the Residenztheater was reserved for *opera seria* and ballet, middle-class audiences in particular were catered for in the old Opernhaus am Salvatorplatz. Mozart's *La finta giardiniera* had its première there in 1775, while *Idomeneo*, composed for Carnival 1781, was performed in the Residenztheater. Seeau's term of office saw a quantitative increase in productions. During Carnival, German Singspiels, usually translations of *opéra comique* and *opera buffa*, were performed on Sundays in the Salvatorplatz theatre, and court society then attended a ball in the Redoutensaal. Monday was set aside for *opera seria*, concluding with a ballet, Tuesday and Thursday for *opera buffa* (also with a concluding ballet), Wednesday and Friday for plays; only on Saturday was there no theatrical performance.

Now that *opera buffa* in German translation had become well established, from the 1770s onwards the German Singspiel finally made a breakthrough, after over a century of dominance by Italian opera. Singspiel productions in Munich included works by native composers such as Franz Gleissner, Franz Anton Dimmler and Johann Lukas Schubaur. Elector Palatine Carl Theodor, who succeeded Maximilian III Joseph as Duke of Bavaria because there were no direct heirs to the Bavarian Wittelsbach line, moved to Munich with his famous Mannheim Hofkapelle. Christian Cannabich, G. J. Vogler, Peter Winter and Franz Danzi took with them the early Classical style and a high degree of artistic skill. Carl Theodor also brought the Paris-trained Theobald Hilarius Marchand to Munich as director of a theatre company with over 30 members that included Singspiel and ballet in its repertory, and the scene painters Lorenzo Quaglio (i) and Giuseppe Quaglio (succeeding Giuseppe Galli-Bibiena and Paolo Gaspari) were influential as set designers. Marchand introduced the *opéra comique* to Munich, and works by Grétry, Monsigny, Philidor, Dalayrac, Destouches and Gossec met with an enthusiastic reception. For the first time French influence really made itself felt, although it could not yet displace Italian opera (including works by Piccinni, Paisiello, Sacchini, Sarti, Salieri and P. A. Guglielmi). Not until the end of the 1780s can a decline in the popularity of *opera seria* be traced. The genre had one of its last successes with Vogler's carnival opera *Castore e Polluce* (1787); in the same year Carl Theodor issued a decree prohibiting Italian opera. The Hof-National-Schaubühne, which opened that year with Anton Schweitzer's *Alceste*, set the tone. After 45 years in his post, Seeau left the Munich theatres in a state of remarkable mismanagement (the reasons are still obscure because the records have disappeared), and after his death in 1799 it was hard for much progress

4. Maximilian III Joseph (seated) with Count Joseph Anton von Seeau: portrait (1755) by Georges Desmarées

in theatrical affairs to be made under the direction of Josef Marius Babo. The ban on Italian opera was not lifted until 1805, a year before Bavaria became a kingdom.

3. FROM 1806.

(i) The Bayerische Hofoper and Staatsoper. The records indicate that Weber's Singspiel *Abu Hassan*, given its première in 1811 at the Residenztheater, met with a friendly reception. In the same year, however, King Max I laid the foundation stone of a new and larger Königliches Hof- und Nationaltheater (fig.5); built in Max-Joseph-Platz to plans by the architect Carl von Fischer, it opened in 1818 but burnt down on 14 January 1823. Rebuilding began at once, with Leo von Klenze as architect. He made use of Fischer's plans and largely reconstructed the old façade, while adding new touches of his own. By present standards of rebuilding and renovation work, it seems remarkable that the new building could be opened for performance only two years after the fire, in the year of the king's death. The stage was now set for the rise in the fortunes of the Nationaltheater, and of the court opera which was a part of it.

In 1836 Franz Paul Lachner was appointed chief conductor and principal musical director; in practice, he was general musical director of Bavaria. Lachner, a close friend of Schubert until the composer's death, established Munich's reputation as an operatic centre. Initially he produced the works of Beethoven and Mozart, composers then ten and nearly 50 years dead respectively, but soon concentrated on the work of such contemporaries as Spohr, Marschner, Lortzing and Flotow, and also extended the repertory to include French and Italian opera. With the first performance in Munich of *Ernani* in 1848 he began a series of productions of Verdi, who conducted several of the German premières of his own operas in Munich. Lachner had

conducted the first Munich performances of *Tannhäuser* and *Lohengrin* in 1855 and 1858, but he retired when Wagner's connections with Munich became closer after 1864 through his friendship with King Ludwig II, and the city prepared to become a Wagnerian centre, as it were by royal decree.

In 1851 Franz von Dingelstedt became Intendant of the Nationaltheater, where plays had long been performed alongside opera. He paid special attention to spoken drama, and instigated the reopening of the Residenztheater to provide it with a stage of its own. When he left his post in 1858, the court musical director Karl von Perfall took over the direction of the court opera, at first as an interim measure, 11 years later as his main concern. He remained in the post until 1893, and his time in office thus covers the greater period of Wagnerian productions in Munich, coinciding with the reign of Ludwig II up to the time of the king's death in 1886. Hans von Bülow was Hofkapellmeister for part of that time, and he conducted the premières of *Tristan und Isolde* (1865) and *Die Meistersinger* (1868). In 1869 and 1870 Franz Wüllner, as principal musical director, gave the premières of *Das Rheingold* and *Die Walküre*. Perfall had his sights set on continuity. However, Munich could not continue to be so much of a Wagnerian centre, as relations between the composer and the king cooled and Wagner looked to Bayreuth. Perfall founded the Munich Opera Festival, whose origins and traditions constitute a chapter of great importance in operatic history up to the present day. The first summer festival was in 1875, with productions of operas by Mozart and Wagner. Two keystones of the continuing Munich operatic tradition were thus in place (another – Richard Strauss – was added later).

Perfall also tried to achieve continuity of conductors; he had appointed Hermann Levi from Karlsruhe in 1872, and Levi was to stay at Munich until his death in 1900. His influence on the musical life of the city cannot be valued too highly. He greatly increased the importance of the operatic festivals, purged the performance style of arbitrary additions or alterations perpetrated by contemporary taste, continued to promote the works of Mozart, Gluck, Weber and of course Wagner, and also encouraged young composers such as Peter Cornelius, Wilhelm Kienzl and Richard Strauss. While Ernst Possart was director of the Hoftheater (1893–1905) the Prinzregententheater was built, and a separate chapter in the history of opera in Munich began. An important figure at the Nationaltheater, and one who could now style himself general director, was the composer Clemens von Franckenstein (he held the post from 1912 to 1918, and from 1924 to 1934). Meanwhile Herman Zumpe and Felix Mottl had also occupied the post of principal conductor at the Hofoper. Both died in harness as conductors, Mottl in 1911 after his 100th performance of *Tristan*. With great personal commitment, Mottl had prepared the ground in Munich for Richard Strauss and his *Salome* and *Elektra*, thus completing the triumvirate of opera composers which forms the backbone of the Munich repertory, consolidated on 1 February 1911 when Mottl conducted the first performance in Munich of *Der Rosenkavalier*.

There now began a period in which significant occasions connected with particular figures were increasingly important in the history of opera in Munich and thus of Bavarian theatre: Caruso appeared in Munich in 1910;

Karl Erb created the role of Pfitzner's Palestrina; Bruno Walter was principal musical director from 1913 to 1922; new composers whose works were performed included Franz Schreker, Erich Korngold, Max von Schillings, Ermanno Wolf-Ferrari and, repeatedly, Richard Strauss.

Such lists are inevitably incomplete and can serve only as reference points; what is clear is that the greatest period in the history of opera in Munich came in the 20th century. Walter was followed as principal musical director by Hans Knappertsbusch in 1922 (the Hofoper was renamed the Bayerische Staatsoper in that year), and when Franckenstein resigned from his post through pressure of political circumstances in 1934 Knappertsbusch also temporarily took over the general direction of the entire theatre for a year. Knappertsbusch and other conductors, either employed by Munich or performing as guest artists, brought renown to the Staatsoper, and extended the repertory at the Nationaltheater and the Prinzregententheater to include Strauss and Pfitzner.

Knappertsbusch's resignation followed only a little later than Franckenstein's. The fortunes of the Staatsoper rose again from 1937 – when Clemens Krauss became both opera director and general musical director – until the destruction of the Nationaltheater in 1943. As musical interpreter, Krauss consolidated the house's connections with Mozart, Wagner and Strauss, but he also gave strong encouragement to Italian opera and became associated with Carl Orff and Werner Egk. Under him the house again acquired international influence and importance. On stage, his high musical standards found their counterpart in the work of the young director Rudolf Hartmann and the stage designers Emil Preetorius and Ludwig Sievert. The last notable events of this period to win fame internationally were the premières of Strauss's *Friedenstag* (1938) and *Capriccio* (1942), conducted by Krauss.

On the night of 3 October 1943 the Nationaltheater was destroyed during an air raid. Only the outer walls and the entrance façade remained. Operatic performances were sporadic until the end of World War II, when they resumed in the renovated Prinzregententheater (seating 873). The Staatsoper began work again under its new director Georg Hartmann, from whom Rudolf Hartmann took over in 1952. Georg Solti, Rudolf Kempe and Ferenc Fricsay were also general musical directors while the company was in its temporary home; Helmut Jürgens was stage designer and Günther Rennert was director.

It was some time before the Nationaltheater was rebuilt. In the end it was possible to restore the 'famous and beloved house' (to use Rudolf Hartmann's description) only with considerable help from the citizens of Munich and the active participation of the city's artistic society. Deciding to rebuild and getting the reconstruction done took 18 years. The theatre (seating 2100) was reopened on 21 November 1963 with Rudolf Hartmann as Intendant and Joseph Keilberth as general musical director. During its residency in the Prinzregententheater the company had caught up with most of the operatic repertory banned until 1945; now the whole extensive repertory could be developed again in the Nationaltheater, and modern classics could be added.

When Hartmann retired after 14 years as Intendant, Günther Rennert took his place as director of the Staatsoper. Since 1958 the company had also been giving regular performances in the new Residenztheater (seating 523), rebuilt – in the same style as the old theatre – on another site in the Munich Residenz after having been bombed in the war. In 1968 Keilberth died after conducting a performance of *Tristan* at the Nationaltheater; his successor, Wolfgang Sawallisch, was appointed to the post of Bavarian general musical director in 1971. He temporarily directed the opera house after Rennert's departure during the 1976–7 season. August Everding then became its Intendant until 1982, when Sawallisch returned to the post. Peter Jonas and Peter Schneider were appointed Intendant and general musical director respectively, from 1993.

The repertory of the Staatsoper still rests on Mozart, Wagner and Strauss – during the 1980s complete cycles of Strauss and Wagner were performed – but operas from the Italian, Slavonic and Russian repertory are also given, as well as modern works. The season is from September to July, with the festival in July; the première of Penderecki's *Ubu Rex* was given at the 1991 festival.

(ii) *Other theatres*. Between 1812 and 1825 the Isartortheater mounted Singspiels and popular plays. This building, later renovated, was destroyed in World

5. Max-Joseph-Platz, Munich, with the Königliches Hof- und Nationaltheater (centre) and Residenz (left): lithograph

War II. A new theatre was planned in 1864, and the architect Michael Reiffenstuel was commissioned to design an 'Actien-Volkstheater', on the Gärtnerplatz. The Staatstheater am Gärtnerplatz (seating 893) was opened on 5 November 1865 with the festival piece *Was wir wollen*, written by the director Hermann Schmid, with music by Georg Krempelsetzer. Financial difficulties almost led to the closing of the house. In 1870 King Ludwig II managed to avert a threatened auction of the theatre's entire contents, and in 1872 he took it into the royal possession. The theatre saw a rise in its fortunes under the directors Karl von Perfall (1877–9) and Georg Lang (1879–98). Franz Lehár conducted there in 1904. In 1936 the theatre passed into the possession of the Free State of Bavaria, and was used almost exclusively for operetta. After World War II the repertory was broadened again to include comic opera and other kinds of music theatre. In 1969, while Kurt Pscherer was director, the theatre was altered and reopened with Rameau's *Platée* (sung in German).

Hellmuth Matiasek was appointed director of the Staatstheater in 1983. His repertory in Munich's 'other opera house' has included Classical operetta, musicals, German *Spielopern*, 20th-century works of music drama, and ballet. The season runs from September to July.

*

TO 1806

F. J. Lipowsky: *Baierisches Musik-Lexikon* (Munich, 1811)
F. M. Rudhart: *Geschichte der Oper am Hofe zu München*, i: *Die italiänische Oper von 1654–1787* (Freising, 1865)
F. Grandauer: *Chronik des königlichen Hof- und Nationaltheaters in München (1778–1878)* (Munich, 1878)
K. Trautmann: 'Italienische Schauspieler am bayerischen Hofe', *Jb für Münchener Geschichte*, i (Munich, 1887)
K. von Reinhardtstöttner: 'Zur Geschichte des Jesuitendramas in München', *Jb für Münchener Geschichte*, iii (Bamberg, 1889), 53–176
K. Trautmann: 'Archivalische Beiträge zur Schulkomödie in München', *Mitteilungen der Gesellschaft für deutsche Erziehungs- und Schulgeschichte* (Berlin, 1892), 61–8
L. Schiedermair: 'Die Anfänge der Münchner Oper', *SIMG*, v (1903–4), 442–68
P. Legband: 'Münchener Bühne und Litteratur im achtzehnten Jahrhundert', *Oberbayerisches Archiv*, li (1904), 1–546
M. Zenger: *Geschichte der Münchener Oper* (Munich, 1923)
Altes Residenztheater in München, ed. Bayerische Verwaltung der Schlösser und Seen (Munich, 1958)
H. Bolongero-Crevenna: *L'arpa festante: die Münchner Oper 1651–1825* (Munich, 1963)
R. Brockpähler: *Handbuch zur Geschichte der Barockoper in Deutschland* (Emsdetten, 1964)
E. Straub: *Repraesentatio Maiestatis oder churbayerische Freudenfeste: die höfischen Feste in der Münchner Residenz vom 16. bis zum Ende des 18. Jahrhunderts* (Munich, 1969)
R. Münster and H. Schmid, eds.: *Musik in Bayern*, i: *Bayerische Musikgeschichte: Überblick und Einzeldarstellungen* (Tutzing, 1972)
R. Münster: 'Die Musik am Hofe Max Emanuels', *Kurfürst Max Emanuel: Bayern und Europa um 1700*, ed. H. Glaser, i: *Zur Geschichte und Kunstgeschichte der Max-Emanuel-Zeit* (Munich, 1976), 295–316

FROM 1806

O. J. Bierbaum: *Fünfundzwanzig Jahre Münchner Hoftheater-Geschichte* (Munich, 1892)
K. von Perfall: *Ein Beitrag zur Geschichte des königlichen Theaters in München [1867–92]* (Munich, 1894)
P. Busse: *Geschichte des Gärtnerplatztheaters in München* (1924)
P. Beckers: *Die nachwagner'sche Oper bis zum Ausgang des 19. Jahrhunderts im Spiegel der Münchner Presse* (diss., U. of Munich, 1936)
H. Wagner: *Münchner Theaterchronik 1750–1950* (Munich, 1950–60) [with suppl. to 1960]
Magie der Oper: München 1947–51 (Ulm, 1952)

H. Friess: *300 Jahre Münchener Opera* (Munich, 1953)
Die Münchner Theater (Munich, 1957) [pubn of the Freunde des Nationaltheaters]
H. Friess and R. Goldschmidt: *Nationaltheater München: Festschrift der Bayerischen Staatsoper zur Eröffnung des wiederaufgebauten Hauses* (Munich, 1963)
K. Hommel: *Die Separatvorstellungen von König Ludwig II. von Bayern* (Munich, 1963)
W. Panofsky: *Musiker, Mimen und Merkwürdigkeiten im Hof- und Nationaltheater* (Munich, 1963)
P. Schallweg, ed.: *Festliche Oper: Geschichte und Wiederaufbau des Nationaltheaters in München* (Munich, 1964)
100 Jahre Theater am Gärtnerplatz München (Munich, 1965)
Jahrbuch der Bayerischen Staatsoper (Munich, 1978–)
Rendezvous im Rampenlicht: das Gärtnerplatztheater in München (Munich, 1979)
H. E. Valentin and others: *Die Wittelsbacher und ihre Künstler in acht Jahrhunderten* (Munich, 1980)
K. Schultz: *Die Bayerische Staatsoper: 1977/8–1981/2: ein Rückblick* (Munich, 1982)
K. J. Seidel, ed.: *Das Prinzregententheater in München* (Nuremberg, 1984)
——: *Das neue Prinzregententheater: Festschrift zur Wiedereröffnung des Prinzregententheaters in München* (Munich, 1988)
H. Matiasek, ed.: *125 Jahre Gärtnerplatztheater: Vom Actien-Volkstheater zu Münchens anderer Oper* (Burgthann, 1990)
Das Münchner Nationaltheater: vom Königlichen Hoftheater zur Bayerischen Staatsoper (Munich, 1991) [in Ger. and Eng.]
J. Schläder, ed.: *Das Bayerische Nationaltheater – Die Münchner Staatsoper* (Munich, 1992)
JULIA LIEBSCHER (1, 2), KLAUS J. SEIDEL (3)

Munsel, Patrice (Beverly) (*b* Spokane, WA, 14 May 1925). American soprano. She studied in New York and made her début as Philine in *Mignon* at the Metropolitan in 1943. The youngest singer ever to be engaged by the company, she appeared, perhaps too soon and too often, in the principal roles of the coloratura repertory – Lucia, Rosina, Gilda, Olympia and the Queen of Shemakha (*The Golden Cockerel*) – to the detriment of her voice. Rudolf Bing rehabilitated her career by presenting her in soubrette roles including Zerlina, Despina, Strauss's Adele and, particularly, Offenbach's Périchole, in which she was extremely popular. In 1953 she starred in *Melba*, a British film biography of the Australian singer. By 1960 she had virtually retired from opera.

For illustration see GÉRARD, ROLF

*

J. Hines: 'Patrice Munsel', *Great Singers on Great Singing* (Garden City, NY, 1982), 189–92
RICHARD DYER

Münster. City in north-western Germany. Its first theatre was the Comödienhaus of 1775; this had a permanent company supported by a theatre society, but it disbanded in 1782 and performances were thereafter given by touring troupes. Between 1826 and 1833 Lortzing was active in Münster, where his first opera, *Ali Pascha*, had its première (1 February 1828). Financial difficulties led to the closure and demolition of the theatre in 1894, but a new one, the Lortzing-Theater, opened on 30 November 1895 with *Zar und Zimmermann*. The building was destroyed on 9 July 1941, and a new theatre (955 seats) opened on 4 February 1956 with *Die Zauberflöte*. At the time, the *Frankfurter allgemeine Zeitung* described it as 'the most modern theatre in Europe'. Productions have included the première of Milko Kelemen's *Der neue Mieter* (1964), Janáček's *Excursions of Mr Brouček* (1964) and the first performances in Germany of Britten's *Gloriana*

(1968). The company gives some 180 operatic performances a year.

E. Müller: *Albert Lortzing: ein Lebensbild des berühmten Musikers unter besonderer Berücksichtigung seines Wirkens und Schaffens in Münster* (Münster, 1921)   SABINE SONNTAG

Muradeli, Vano Il'ich (*b* Gori, Georgia, 24 March/6 April 1908; *d* Tomsk, 14 Aug 1970). Georgian composer. After graduating from the Tbilisi Conservatory (1931), where he studied composition with Sergey Barkhudaryan, he attended the Moscow Conservatory from 1934 to 1938, studying there with Boris Shekhter and Nikolay Myaskovsky. Muradeli was inspired by propagandist and political themes in his music; he is chiefly remembered as a composer of songs, choruses and patriotic cantatas, many of which entered the popular Communist legacy. From 1939 to 1948 he headed the USSR Music Fund, and during World War II he directed the song ensemble of the Soviet Navy.

Muradeli's niche in operatic history was secured by his first opera, *Velikaya druzhba* ('The Great Friendship'), which was first performed on 28 September 1947 at the Opera and Ballet Theatre in Stalino (now Donets'k). The opera treats historical events of the civil war in the region of the Northern Caucasus. Its hero is modelled on Sergo Ordzhonikidze, Stalin's revolutionary comrade. In the autumn of 1947 many Soviet theatres mounted productions of *The Great Friendship* in honour of the 30th anniversary of the Revolution. But on 10 February 1948, after the opera had been viewed by Party functionaries and a conference of musicians had been convened unexpectedly in January by Stalin's cultural henchman, Andrey Zhdanov, a resolution was issued by the Central Committee of the Communist Party using the public condemnation of Muradeli's opera as the pretext to effect sweeping government repression in the world of Soviet music. Although the resolution was effectively rescinded in May 1958, Muradeli's subsequent revision of his opera (1970) did not meet with success.

In the crisis, Muradeli recanted and helped expand the base of attack. The stigma of his failure did not tarnish his reputation for long. In 1950 his *Pesnya bortsov za mir* ('Song of the Fighters for Peace') took first prize at a competition in Budapest, and in 1951 he was awarded a Stalin Prize for his songs. In 1950 he began work on a second opera, *Oktyabr'* ('October'), but the death of the librettist, V. Lugovskoy, postponed its completion (with the poet Viktor Vinnikov) until 1961, when the composer dedicated it to the 22nd Congress of the Communist Party. It received its première at the Kremlin Palace of Congresses in Moscow on 22 April 1964. Like his first opera, *October* is a deeply patriotic work dealing with historical events during the formation of the Soviet State. It makes extensive use of themes from folk and revolutionary songs. Its most distinctive prerogative, however, is that it marked the first appearance of Lenin in opera as a singing character.

In addition to his two operas, Muradeli composed two operettas, *Devushka s golubïmi glazami* ('The Girl with Blue Eyes') in 1965 and *Moskva – Parizh – Moskva* ('Moscow – Paris – Moscow') in 1968, as well as incidental and film music. From 1959 until his death he was head of the Moscow section of the Union of Composers and was also active in Party politics. He was given many awards and received the titles People's Artist of the Georgian SSR and People's Artist of the USSR in 1968.

See also OKTYABR' *and* VELIKAYA DRUZHBA.

Velikaya druzhba [The Great Friendship] (4, G. D. Mdivani), Stalino, 28 Sept 1947; rev., Ordzhonikidze, 22 April 1970
Oktyabr' [October], 1950–61 (prol., 3, V. Lugovskoy and V. Vinnikov), Moscow, Kremlin Palace of Congress, 22 April 1964
Devushka s golubïmi glazami [The Girl with Blue Eyes] (operetta, 3, Vinnikov and V. Krakht), Moscow, Operetta, 1 May 1966
Moskva – Parizh – Moskva [Moscow – Paris – Moscow] (operetta, 3, Vinnikov and Krakht), Moscow, Operetta, 14 March 1970

N. Slonimsky: *Music Since 1900* (New York, 1937, 4/1971)
A. Werth: *Musical Uproar in Moscow* (London, 1949)
K. Sezhensky: *Vano Muradeli* (Moscow, 1962)
M. Byalik: 'V partiture i na stsene' [In Score and on the Stage], *SovM* (1965), no.3, p.49 [on various stagings of *Oktyabr'*]
D. M. Person, ed.: *V. I. Muradeli: notograficheskiy spravochnik* [Muradeli: Work-list and Bibliography] (Moscow, 1983)
A. D. Skoblionok and I. E. Olinskaya, eds.: *Vano Muradeli: vospominaniya i stat'i* [Vano Muradeli: Reminiscences and Articles] (Moscow, 1983)   LAUREL E. FAY

Muraire, Louis (*b* Avignon; *fl* 1715–27). French *haute-contre*. He joined the Paris Opéra in 1715, initially singing minor roles, but becoming the principal *haute-contre* when Cochereau retired. His voice was a magnificent instrument – sonorous and wide-ranging. He sang Pylades in the famous 1719 revival of Desmarets and Campra's *Iphigénie en Tauride* and took the title roles in revivals of Lully's *Amadis* (1718), *Thésée* (1720), *Phaëton* (1721) and *Persée* (1722). In 1726 he created Ninus in Francoeur and Rebel's *Pirame et Thisbé*. He retired in 1727, after a lengthy illness, returning to a life of piety and devotion in Avignon. Greatly missed by the public, he was replaced by Tribou.   PHILIP WELLER

Muratore, Lucien (*b* Marseilles, 29 Aug 1876; *d* Paris, 16 July 1954). French tenor. He began his career as an actor, then studied singing in Paris, making his début at the Opéra-Comique in 1902 as the King in the première of Hahn's *La Carmélite*. At the Opéra, where he first sang in 1905 as Renaud (Gluck's *Armide*), he created roles in two Massenet operas, Theseus in *Ariane* (1906) and the title role of *Bacchus*, and also Prinzivalle in Février's *Monna Vanna* (1909). At Monte Carlo he created Hercules in Saint-Saëns' *Déjanire* (1911) and Lentulus in Massenet's *Roma* (1912). His roles included Faust, Massenet's Des Grieux, Werther, Romeo, Don José, Wilhelm Meister, Samson, d'Indy's Fervaal, Reyer's Sigurd and Fauré's Ulysses, which he sang in the Paris première of *Pénélope* (Théâtre des Champs-Elysées, 1913). He also sang Walther, Radames, the Duke, Canio and Herod. He appeared in Boston and Chicago (1913–22) and Buenos Aires. In 1931 he sang Ulysses at the Opéra-Comique, where he was manager for a few weeks in 1943. Though his voice was not of great intrinsic beauty, he used it with artistry, intensity of expression and skill, as his recordings demonstrate.

GV (R. Celletti; J. P. Kenyon and R. Vegeto)
K. Neate: 'Lucien Muratore', *Opera*, v (1954), 674–5
                    ALAN BLYTH

Murger [Mürger], Henry [Henri] (*b* Paris, 27 March 1822; *d* Paris, 28 Jan 1861). French novelist. The son of a tailor from Savoy who became a concierge in Paris, he disappointed parental hopes of his making a career in law. He preferred 'une vie de bohème', that is, a life of poverty in an attic on the left bank of the Seine, among witty friends with artistic leanings and pretty girls with loose morals but hearts of gold. The counterpart to the fun was the prospect of dying, from consumption or alcoholism, in the public hospital. All this Murger presented in a series of short stories published between 1845 and 1849 in the satirical magazine *Le corsaire*. In 1849 Théodore Barrière, a popular dramatist, proposed to Murger that they collaborate on a play based on a selection of the tales; *La vie de bohème* was a triumph. Only after this did Murger bring out *Scènes de la vie de bohème*, a reprint of the *Corsaire* material with revisions and additions. The work established Murger's reputation, but his later publications were not particularly well received.

Puccini first took an interest in Murger's stories in 1893, perhaps in part because he had discovered that Leoncavallo was planning to base an opera on them. He invited Giuseppe Giacosa and Luigi Illica to prepare a libretto; they went back to the novel, though it appears that they also consulted the 1849 play. Leoncavallo's *La bohème*, to his own libretto, was a success at its first performance in Venice in 1897, but Puccini's opera, though criticized at its première in Turin a year earlier, has quite eclipsed it.

R. Baldrick: *The First Bohemian: the Life of Henry Murger* (London, 1961)   CHRISTOPHER SMITH

Muro, Bernardo de. *See* DE MURO, BERNARDO.

Murphy, Suzanne (*b* Limerick, 15 Oct 1941). Irish soprano. After singing with a folk group, she studied at the Dublin College of Music and made her début with the Irish National Opera in *La Cenerentola*, later taking other roles. In 1976 she joined the WNO; there she first sang Konstanze, and followed this with more than a dozen leading lyric coloratura roles, having particular success as Norma, Lucia and Elvira (*Ernani*). She has fulfilled regular engagements with the ENO, Scottish Opera and Opera North, and she made her Vienna Staatsoper début in 1987 as Electra (*Idomeneo*). She sang Amelia (*Un ballo in maschera*) and Norma in Munich and with the New York City Opera, and was an admired Alice Ford in Peter Stein's WNO production of *Falstaff*, which was also heard at Covent Garden (1988), New York and Milan (1989). Her vocal agility and warmth of expression are embodied in a generous dramatic character.   NOËL GOODWIN

Murray, Ann (*b* Dublin, 27 Aug 1949). Irish mezzo-soprano. She studied in Manchester and at the London Opera Centre, making her début in 1974 with Scottish Opera at Snape as Alcestis. At Wexford (1974–5) she sang Myrtale (*Thaïs*) and Queen Laodicea (Cavalli's *Eritrea*). She first sang at Covent Garden in 1976 as Cherubino, and later appeared as Siebel, Ascanio, Thibault, Ravel's Child, Octavian, the Composer and Idamantes. In 1979 she made her American début with the New York City Opera as Mozart's Sextus, also the role of her Metropolitan début (1984). She first sang at Salzburg in 1981 as Nicklausse. With the ENO she has sung Rosina, Xerxes, Charlotte and Beatrice. She has appeared at Glyndebourne, Aix-en-Provence and La Scala, and in Cologne, Brussels, Zürich, Hamburg, Munich and Vienna. Her repertory includes Bradamante (*Alcina*), Purcell's Dido, Meg Page (*Falstaff*), Isolier, Cenerentola, Massenet's Prince Charming

and Cendrillon, Dorabella, Donna Elvira, Cecilius (*Lucio Silla*) and Mélisande; her firm, well-focussed voice and youthful appearance make her particularly convincing in travesty roles.

H. Finch: 'Ann Murray', *Opera*, xxxix (1988), 914–19
ELIZABETH FORBES

Murray, William (*b* Schenectady, NY, 13 March 1935). American baritone. Educated at Adelphi University, he won a Fulbright scholarship to Rome and made his début at Spoleto in 1957 as Count Gil (*Il segreto di Susanna*). He sang at Detmold, Brunswick, Munich, Frankfurt, Amsterdam, Salzburg and Berlin, where he became a member of the Deutsche Oper in 1969, remaining for over 20 years. He sang the title role of Dallapiccola's *Ulisse* at La Scala (1970), took part in the première of Nabokov's *Love's Labour's Lost* in Brussels (1973) and sang the General in the first German performance of Henze's *We Come to the River* in Berlin (1976). His wide repertory includes Don Giovanni, Paisiello's King Theodore, Wolfram, Rigoletto, Germont, Luna, Macbeth, Paolo (*Simon Boccanegra*), Don Carlo (*La forza del destino*), Yeletsky (*The Queen of Spades*), Scarpia, Lescaut and Creon (Orff's *Antigonae*). A stylish singer and a fine actor, he excels in dramatic and character roles.   ELIZABETH FORBES

Murska, Ilma di. *See* DI MURSKA, ILMA.

Musgrave, Thea (*b* Barnton, Midlothian, 27 May 1928). Scottish composer, now resident in the USA. After studying at Edinburgh University and privately with Hans Gál she worked under the guidance of Nadia Boulanger in Paris (1950–54). On her return to Britain, she quickly established her reputation with a number of substantial instrumental works and wrote a one-act comic opera, *The Abbot of Drimock* (1955), which owes something to neo-classical Stravinsky in its angular themes and dry humour. Her first full-length opera, *The Decision* (1964–5), was written without a commission at a period when she was making use of serial techniques. The grim and claustral mood of a libretto dealing with a Scottish mine disaster is reflected in a closely worked, contrapuntal, freely chromatic score.

In the late 1960s, Musgrave found a more individual and compelling voice in a series of adventurous instrumental works which made imaginative use of indeterminate notations and exploited the particular skills of virtuoso performers, often introducing an element of music theatre into the concert hall. A similar spirit of adventure and freedom is apparent in the richly romantic *The Voice of Ariadne* (1972–3), in which characterization is sharp and vivid, while the complex web of free-running instrumental strands reflects the rich ambiguities of Henry James's story.

Later operas, all to her own librettos, have revealed an ever widening range of human sympathies and a corresponding broadening and enriching of musical idiom, together with great versatility in setting librettos of very different species. In *Mary, Queen of Scots* she worked on a grand, Verdian scale, weaving together many threads with a fine sense of theatre. *An Occurrence at Owl Creek Bridge* is a true radio opera, evolving its own narrative modes and taking imaginative account of the limitations and potentialities of the medium. *A Christmas Carol*, which is divided into many short scenes and introduces a whole gallery of secondary characters, uses flashbacks and dissolves, enabling action to flow rapidly, without interruption. In *Harriet, the Woman called 'Moses'* the character of a woman inspired by a sense of divine mission is portrayed in music as passionate and intense as any that Musgrave has yet written.

Musgrave is a capable conductor of her own works, and since moving to the USA in the 1970s has been closely involved in the work of the Virginia Opera Company, which her husband Peter Mark directs.

See also CHRISTMAS CAROL, A; DECISION, THE; HARRIET, THE WOMAN CALLED 'MOSES'; MARY, QUEEN OF SCOTS; OCCURRENCE AT OWL CREEK BRIDGE, AN; and VOICE OF ARIADNE, THE.

The Abbott of Drimock, 1955 (comic op, 1, M. Lindsay), London, Morley College, 15 March 1962
Marko the Miser (children's op, 1, Musgrave and F. Samson, after A. N. Afanas'yev), Farnham, Surrey, 1963
The Decision, 1964–5 (3, Lindsay), New Opera Co., London, Sadler's Wells, 30 Nov 1967 (London, 1967)
The Voice of Ariadne (chamber op, 3, A. Elguera, after H. James: The Last of the Valerii), English Opera Group, Snape, Maltings, 11 June 1974, vs (Borough Green, 1977)
Mary, Queen of Scots (3, Musgrave, after Elguera: Moray), Edinburgh, King's, 6 Sept 1977, vs (Borough Green, 1978)
A Christmas Carol (2, Musgrave, after C. Dickens), Norfolk, VA, 7 Dec 1979 (Borough Green, 1981)
An Occurrence at Owl Creek Bridge (radio op, Musgrave, after A. Bierce), BBC, 14 Sept 1982; stage, Bracknell, Wilde, 23 June 1988
Harriet, the Woman called 'Moses' (2, Musgrave), Norfolk, VA, 1 March 1985

T. Musgrave: 'The Decision', MT, cviii (1967), 988–91
S. Walsh: 'Musgrave's "The Voice of Ariadne"', MT, cxv (1974), 465–7
T. Musgrave: 'Mary Queen of Scots', MT, cxviii (1977), 625–7
R. Milnes: 'Dickens into Opera', MT, cxxii (1981), 818–20
H. Cole: 'The Song at the Heart of Scrooge', The Guardian (11 Dec 1981)
R. H. Kornick: Recent American Opera: a Production Guide (New York, 1991), 202–12
HUGO COLE

Mushel', Georgy (*b* Tambov, 16/29 July 1909). Russian composer. He studied at the Tambov Music Technical College (1926–30) and at the Moscow Conservatory. His performance of his First Piano Concerto at the final examination (1936) won Prokofiev's approval, and he was invited to teach composition at the Tashkent Conservatory, where he was later professor. Like other Russian composers in Uzbekistan, he took an active part in creating the first Uzbek works in the major European genres. He worked closely with V. A. Uspensky in studying Uzbek folk music, a collaboration which led to his joining Uspensky and S. Tsveyfeld in revising Uspensky's music drama *Farkhad i Shirin* in 1937. Mushel' and Uspensky later revised the work in 1940 as an opera to a libretto by Sh. Khurshid based on an idea of A. Navoi; the opera was first performed at the Navoi Theatre of Opera and Ballet, Tashkent, on 15 May 1957. With Vasilenko and Ashrafi's *Buran*, this work played an important role in establishing the Uzbek musical theatre. Mushel''s style developed under the influence of the innovations of Debussy, Ravel and Prokofiev, as well as that of specific Uzbek modes and rhythms.
L. M. BUTIR

Musi [Degli Antoni], **Maria Maddalena** ['La Mignatti', 'La Mignatta'] (*b* Bologna, 18 June 1669; *d* Bologna, 2 May 1751). Italian singer. She was the daughter of Antonio Maria Musi and Lucrezia Mignati, from whom she perhaps inherited her equivocal nickname ('the

Leech'), and was one of the most admired and highest-paid female singers of the day. In Reggio Emilia in 1688 she sang Amore in the Prologue to the operatic tableau *Amor non inteso* (composer unknown). She was in the service of Duke Ferdinando Carlo Gonzaga of Mantua for many years; from 24 June 1689 she was assigned an annual salary, the privilege of a passport and the designation 'virtuosa', a title she kept until at least 1702. She performed in many Italian cities and in 1689 sang in *Teodora clemente* (Sabadini's revision of Domenico Gabrielli's *Teodora Augusta*) in Piacenza, in Legrenzi's *Giustino* in Genoa and in G. A. Perti's *Dionisio Siracusano* in Parma. In Naples, where she appeared from 1696 to 1700 and in 1702, she received a salary of 500 Spanish doubloons. In 1703 she married Pietro degli Antoni. Her last public performance was in Ferrara in 1726, in *La fedeltà creduta tradimento* (composer unknown).

G. Cosentino: *La Mignatta: Maria Maddalena Musi cantatrice bolognese famosa, 1669–1751* (Bologna, 1930)
L. Frati: 'Donne musiciste bolognesi', *RMI*, xxxvii (1930), 387–400
S. Durante: 'Il cantante', *SOI*, iv (1987), 347–410
P. Besutti: *La corte musicale di Ferdinando Carlo Gonzaga ultimo duca di Mantova: musici, cantanti e teatro d'opera tra il 1665 e il 1707* (Mantua, 1989)
PAOLA BESUTTI

Musical [musical comedy, musical play]. The major form of popular musical theatre of the 20th century. Consisting of musical numbers integrated into a dramatic framework, its main antecedents are found in comic opera, OPERETTA, Vaudeville (*see* VAUDEVILLE (i)) and BURLESQUE. Using a more direct vocal style than the operatic style on which operetta was based, it has progressively replaced the latter as the predominant form of popular musical theatre. The term 'musical comedy' generally denotes a more lighthearted piece with song and dance numbers linked by a flimsy plot, by contrast with 'musical play', which generally indicates a more serious plot and greater integration of book and music.

1. Before World War II. 2. The 1940s and 50s. 3. Since 1960.

1. BEFORE WORLD WAR II. The term 'musical comedy' had been used in Britain and the USA during the 19th century as a general description of a popular theatrical work that allied music to comedy without obviously falling into a more specific category. In such a loose sense, descriptions such as 'musical farce', 'musical comedy' and 'musical play' were applied in London during the 1890s to works that sought to combine elements of comic opera and burlesque in a more up-to-date, more popular style of work that retained the basic comic opera structure but with contemporary stories and more readily assimilable musical numbers. When this new formula proved immensely popular, the terms came to indicate something more specific.

From today's standpoint, 'musical comedies' such as Sidney Jones's *A Gaiety Girl* (1893, London) and Gustave Kerker's *The Belle of New York* (1897, New York) and the slightly more substantial 'musical plays' such as Jones's *The Geisha* (1896, London), Lionel Monckton and Howard Talbot's *The Arcadians* (1909, London) and Rudolf Friml and Herbert Stothart's *Rose-Marie* (1924, New York) are regarded less as 'musicals' than as part of the European operetta tradition. What can now be seen as stamping the 'musical comedy' as a brand of musical theatre distinct from the operetta was the incorporation of contemporary subjects, everyday characters and essentially American styles of song and voice production with origins in the vaudeville theatre. It was in the extension of vaudeville sketches that one finds, in George M. Cohan's *Little Johnny Jones* (1904), what has been regarded as the first truly American musical comedy. The essence of the work was that it represented a stark contrast to romanticized subjects and extended operatic vocalizing, the aim being to present down-to-earth characters full of popular flag-waving sentiment in songs such as 'I'm a Yankee Doodle Dandy' and 'Give my regards to Broadway'.

In London, too, efforts were made to break away from the more showy operetta style. In 1905 Paul A. Rubens presented his *Mr Popple (of Ippleton)* in an attempt to buck the fashions of the time by creating a more intimate style of production with a consistent story that achieved its effect 'without wanting a string of musical numbers, a large chorus, and scenery and dresses which are so lavish that only a very long run can compensate the management for its lavish expenditure'. The experiment was seen and noted by Jerome Kern, and in 1915 the book was adapted for him as *Nobody Home*, the first of a series of shows at the tiny Princess Theatre in New York.

These various attempts at a more intimate, more modern style of production had, for a long time, to compete with the continuing popularity of operetta-style works that gained added momentum in the wake of the success of Lehár's *Die lustige Witwe* (1905). However, after World War I the popularity of commercial ragtime and jazz-flavoured dance styles swung interest in both the USA and Britain towards American song-and-dance musical comedies. Works such as Kern's *Sally* (1920) and *Sunny* (1925), Vincent Youmans's *No, No, Nanette* (1924, Chicago; 1925, London and New York) and George Gershwin's *Lady, be Good!* (1924) and *Funny Face* (1927) highlighted the trends of the 1920s, being undemanding boy-meets-girl stories concerned more with introducing popular songs that could be promoted outside the theatre than with any firm integration of music and drama.

The work with which the genre truly came of age and which provided a prototype for the modern musical was Kern's *Show Boat* (1927). Here was a work that adhered to the requirements of a show presenting everyday characters in a contemporary American context and containing readily attractive songs; yet at the same time it had a more credible story and stronger characterization. Yet again Kern's lead did not immediately find successors either in his own output or in that of others. For a time it was the traditional song-and-dance musicals such as Gershwin's *Girl Crazy* (1930) and Cole Porter's *Gay Divorce* (1932) and *Anything Goes* (1934) that continued to hold sway. However, the trend towards a more demanding musical and dramatic style, with better integration of book and music, was clearly discernible over the next decade. The book of George and Ira Gershwin's political satire *Of Thee I Sing* (1931) won a Pulitzer Prize for Drama, and their final Broadway show, *Porgy and Bess* (1935), brilliantly succeeded in raising the genre to the level of opera. Moreover, even in more popular vein, there was a clearly discernible interest in developing the scope of the musical during the 1930s. Richard Rodgers and his lyricist Lorenz Hart, especially, employed a range of more demanding subjects and production techniques, as in *On your Toes* (1936), which explored the world of ballet and featured a quasi-jazz ballet sequence, 'Slaughter on Tenth Avenue'.

In developing its higher aspirations during the late 1930s, the American musical theatre was greatly aided by the contributions of various immigrant and other composers with a more serious training. There was the contribution of Kurt Weill, whose *Knickerbocker Holiday* (1938) had a historical subject that drew analogies with Fascist oppression, while his *Lady in the Dark* (1941) dealt with psychoanalysis and most obviously paved the way for developments in the 1940s. While it achieved nothing like the same commercial success, similar influences and aspirations were evident in Vernon Duke's Negro folk musical *Cabin in the Sky* (1940). Meanwhile Marc Blitzstein's left-wing *The Cradle will Rock* fought off an injunction banning it, to achieve production with the composer at the piano in 1937, and Benjamin Britten's *Paul Bunyan* enjoyed a few performances in 1941.

2. THE 1940s AND 50s. It was during the 1940s that the major breakthrough came to a corpus of work combining more demanding musical and dramatic standards and yet producing works that went on to have huge international popular success and, in many cases, acceptance into the opera house. This period of maturity for the American musical began in autumn 1943 with Richard Rodgers and Oscar Hammerstein's *Oklahoma!*. The work was notable for establishing the characteristics that were to dominate the postwar American musical, with musical comedy conventions such as the opening chorus, glamorous chorus line and set numbers firmly abandoned in favour of an integrated structure of dialogue and music that carried the story along in extended vocal and ballet sequences. To the American musical comedy tradition of contemporary characters and popular dance and vocal numbers was added something of mainstream musical traditions in more shapely and demanding vocal lines and more inventive orchestration. Such absorption of the more durable elements of the operetta tradition incidentally helped to kill off much of the remaining devotion to the operetta as an identifiably different style of work.

Rodgers and Hammerstein remained in the forefront of the production of American musicals with a string of successes that included *Carousel* (1945), *South Pacific* (1949), *The King and I* (1951) and *The Sound of Music* (1959). They were also responsible as producers for *Annie get your Gun* (1946), a Wild West musical with a body of enormously popular songs by Irving Berlin, while Cole Porter enjoyed his greatest success with *Kiss me, Kate!* (1948), based on Shakespeare's *The Taming of the Shrew*, which used the idea of a play-within-a-play and had lyrics appropriating some of Shakespeare's lines.

These and other works, such as Burton Lane's *Finian's Rainbow* (1947) and Frederick Loewe's *Brigadoon* (1947), saw the musical ranging far wider in terms of location than the contemporary American subjects of musical comedies between the wars – a trend that also helped to get the musical accepted abroad in translation. Assisted by specialist theatre orchestrators (something from which only Kurt Weill stood apart), composers and producers were increasingly concerned not simply with writing appealing songs but with capturing the flavour of a work's setting and the viewpoint of the characters, even if it seemed to hark back still more obviously to the older operetta. Such was the case, for instance, with Loewe's *My Fair Lady* (1956), an adaptation of George Bernard Shaw's *Pygmalion* which variously evoked the dignity of the Edwardian aristocracy and the bawdiness of the English music hall.

Meanwhile the more essentially American musical comedy style was being brought up to date in various star vehicles such as Jule Styne's *Gentlemen Prefer Blondes* (1949), with its big, brassy production number 'Diamonds are a girl's best friend'. Among Styne's works of the 1950s was *Gypsy* (1959), one of the major successes of the decade along with other shows with thoroughly American subjects such as Richard Adler and Jerry Ross's *The Pajama Game* (1954) and *Damn Yankees* (1955) and Meredith Willson's *The Music Man* (1957).

In Britain, too, the 1950s saw a somewhat belated attempt to abandon more traditional styles in favour of the greater musical and dramatic integration demonstrated by the American musical. This movement culminated in the early 1960s in various works that went on to international success. Most notable was Lionel Bart's *Oliver!* (1960, London; after Dickens's *Oliver Twist*), while another work that achieved lasting popularity also in America was *Stop the World, I Want to get Off* (1961, London) by the songwriting team of Anthony Newley and Leslie Bricusse.

However, during the late 1940s and the 1950s the works of three composers in particular pointed the way to future trends. Weill's innovatory attempts to elevate the Broadway musical culminated in the Broadway opera *Street Scene* (1947) and the tragic *Lost in the Stars* (1949). Frank Loesser's musical eclecticism was moulded to the vernacular phraseology of his own lyrics in the Damon Runyan gangster fable *Guys and Dolls* (1950), the quasi-operatic *The Most Happy Fella* (1956), and the business satire *How to Succeed in Business Without Really Trying* (1961). Finally Leonard Bernstein combined a highly developed musical language, containing both classical and jazz elements, with dynamic book, lyrics, choreography and direction in *On the Town* (1944), *Wonderful Town* (1953), *Candide* (1956; after Voltaire) and *West Side Story* (1957). This last brilliantly transformed Shakespeare's *Romeo and Juliet* into a story of gang warfare in the West Side of New York and was a remarkable fusion of dancing, singing and acting talents.

3. SINCE 1960. The 1960s introduced to the musical a new generation of creators, working in a very different artistic and financial environment. Earlier musical shows had made their profits largely from provincial tours, but the decline of regional theatres, combined with increasing production and touring costs, had since World War II made a long Broadway run of crucial importance. Financial constraints were making producers look at lowering costs by means such as reduced orchestras or the use of electronic instruments. One solution to the financial situation was found in inexpensive 'off-Broadway' productions such as Harvey Schmidt's *The Fantasticks*, which opened at a 149-seat theatre in 1960 and has run ever since.

The advent of rock music also meant that, during the 1960s, the musical was losing its traditional link with current popular taste, and attempts to absorb rock music into the musical achieved mixed success. Stage techniques had changed as well, so that the old musical comedy convention of a subplot for a secondary couple who would sing in front of a backcloth while the main set was being changed was no longer valid. Thus, for

example, when Berlin's *Annie, get your Gun* was revived in 1966, it was without its secondary couple and with substituted songs designed to build up the main story.

Among composers who successfully met these challenges on Broadway during the 1960s and 70s was Charles Strouse, whose *Bye Bye Birdie* (1960) was a spoof of the rock-and-roll cult, while his *Annie* (1977) had a cartoon-strip-character child lead. Cy Coleman composed the exhilarating *Sweet Charity* (1966) and *Barnum* (1980). John Kander evoked Berlin between the wars in *Cabaret* (1966) and 1920s American gangland in *Chicago* (1975). Two considerable international successes that penetrated into the opera house were Mitch Leigh's *Man of La Mancha* (1965; after Cervantes) and Jerry Bock's *Fiddler on the Roof* (1964), which concerned itself with the persecution of Jews in tsarist Russia and incorporated elements of Yiddish folklore. Another major success was Marvin Hamlisch's *A Chorus Line* (1975), an exposé of the selection process of aspirants for a Broadway musical comedy. Song-and-dance traditions were most obviously maintained in the works of Jerry Herman, among them *Hello Dolly!* (1964), *Mame* (1966), *Mack and Mabel* (1974) and *La cage aux folles* (1983).

If Herman catered for the matinée coach-party trade, the composer who largely eschewed commercial success and, in so doing, led the musical in a new direction was Stephen Sondheim. Having made his name as lyricist for Bernstein (*West Side Story*) and Styne (*Gypsy*), he revealed his ability as a composer in *A Funny Thing Happened on the Way to the Forum* (1962) and *Anyone can Whistle* (1964). During the 1970s and 80s he consolidated his reputation with a remarkable series of works covering a wide variety of subjects. Sondheim sought to raise both dramatic and musical standards, and his refusal to compromise on such aspects as orchestral complements has been a significant factor in raising the status of the musical.

If one of the keynotes of Sondheim's works has been experimentation, another has been a cynical attitude to conventional sexuality, notably in *Company* (1970), which explored the subject of marriage. This was followed by *Follies* (1971), which featured former show girls reflecting on their lives; *A Little Night Music* (1973), based on an Ingmar Bergman film (*Smiles of a Summer Night*) and composed entirely in waltz time or derivatives; *Pacific Overtures* (1976), which related the westernization of Japan to the commercialized present; *Sweeney Todd* (1979), a typically uncompromising treatment of a traditional tale of throat-cutting; *Merrily we Roll Along* (1981), which viewed the experiences of college graduates by unfolding the action in reverse; *Sunday in the Park with George* (1984), which sought to represent the painter Georges Seurat's pointillist style in musical terms; and *Into the Woods* (1987), which cleverly varied traditional fairy-tales. Unlike the bulk of musical shows, Sondheim's have introduced melody only for dramatic purposes. If his intellectualism has at times spilt over into pretentiousness (most notably in Act 2 of *Sunday in the Park with George*), his imaginative, scrupulously executed concepts have raised the musical to a level at which it can make the transition into the opera house.

If lack of purely commercial intent has been one of Sondheim's major attributes, it is in marked contrast to his major rival of recent years, the Englishman Andrew Lloyd Webber, who has wasted no opportunity to promote his works and their hit numbers. In their different way, though, these have played a significant part in fusing traditional and popular techniques and thereby raising the artistic standards and sphere of acceptance of the musical. Starting with the religious rock musicals *Jesus Christ Superstar* (1971) and *Joseph and the Amazing Technicolor Dreamcoat* (1968; rev. 1972), Lloyd Webber moved on through *Evita* (1978) to shows allying modern stage conventions to scores of considerable substance and invention in *Cats* (1981; after T. S. Eliot) and *The Phantom of the Opera* (1986), the latter demonstrating an almost Puccinian opulence of sound.

The example of Sondheim and Lloyd Webber has also found expression in other European countries. Germany especially has produced many musicals since World War II, though none has challenged American dominance on an international scale. This situation may have changed with two works by the French composer Claude-Michel Schönberg. *Les misérables* (after Victor Hugo) opened in Paris in 1980 and achieved worldwide acclaim after adaptation for London in 1985. To follow it, *Miss Saigon* (1989), an updating of the *Madama Butterfly* story to the Vietnam War, was tailored specifically for launch in London, in recognition of the worldwide organization needed today to make a musical a big commercial success.

With the works of these three composers the musical has managed not only to survive but to enjoy more serious critical attention. Further interest has also been shown by opera and recording companies in rediscovering and restoring original orchestrations of shows from between the wars. Though financial considerations make the success of any new musical an increasingly speculative matter, the genre remains vigorously alive.

*

GänzlBMT; *GänzlMT*
C. Smith: *Musical Comedy in America* (New York, 1950, 2/1981 rev. G. Litton)
J. Burton: *The Blue Book of Broadway Musicals* (New York, 1952, 2/1969)
D. Ewen: *Complete Book of the American Musical Theater* (New York, 1958, 3/1976)
B. Rust: *London Musical Shows on Record* (London, 1958, 2/1977)
D. Blum: *A Pictorial History of the American Theatre, 1860–1960* (Philadelphia, 1960)
S. Green: *The World of Musical Comedy* (New York, 1960, 4/1980)
D. Ewen: *The Story of America's Musical Theater* (Philadelphia, 1961, 2/1968)
R. Lewine and A. Simon: *Encyclopedia of Theater Music* (New York, 1961)
A. Churchill: *The Great White Way* (New York, 1962)
H. Taubman: *The Making of the American Theater* (New York, 1965, 2/1967)
L. Engel: *The American Musical Theater: a Consideration* (New York, 1967)
D. Ewen: *Composers for the American Musical Theater* (New York, 1968)
A. Laufe: *Broadway's Greatest Musicals* (New York, 1969, 4/1977)
R. Mander and J. Mitchenson: *Musical Comedy: a Story in Pictures* (London, 1969)
B. Atkinson: *Broadway* (New York, 1970)
T. Vallance: *The American Musical* (New York, 1970)
S. Green: *Ring Bells! Sing Songs! Broadway Musicals of the 1930s* (New York, 1971)
L. Engel: *Words with Music* (New York, 1972)
R. Lewine and A. Simon: *Songs of the American Theater* (New York, 1973)
M. Wilk: *They're Playing Our Song: from Jerome Kern to Stephen Sondheim* (New York, 1973)
L. Engel: *Their Words are Music* (New York, 1975)
S. Green: *Encyclopedia of the Musical* (New York, 1976)
E. Mordden: *Better Foot Forward: the History of American Musical Theater* (New York, 1976)
A. Jackson: *The Book of Musicals from 'Show Boat' to 'A Chorus Line'* (London, 1977, 2/1979)
G. Bordman: *The American Musical Theatre: a Chronicle* (New York, 1978, 2/1986)
D. and J. Parker: *The Story and the Song: a Survey of English Musical Plays, 1916–78* (London, 1979)
M. Gottfried: *Broadway Musicals* (New York, 1979)
G. Bordman: *American Operetta* (New York, 1981)
——: *American Musical Comedy* (New York, 1982)
G. Loney, ed.: *Musical Theater in America* (Westport, CT, 1984)
K. Bloom: *American Song: the Complete Musical Theater Companion* (New York, 1985)
A. J. Lerner: *The Musical Theatre: a Celebration* (London, 1986)
G. Mast: *Can't Help Singin': the American Musical on Stage and Screen* (Woodstock, NY, 1987)
S. Morley: *Spread a Little Happiness: the First Hundred Years of the British Musical* (New York, 1987)
R. Simas: *The Musicals No One Came to See: a Guidebook to Four Decades of Musical-Comedy Casualties On Broadway, Off-Broadway and in Out-of-Town Try-Outs, 1943–1983* (New York, 1987)
K. Gänzl: *The Blackwell Guide to the Musical Theatre on Record* (Oxford, 1990)
ANDREW LAMB

Musical comedy. See MUSICAL.

Musical play. See MUSICAL.

Musica nel Chiostro. Opera company and festival founded in 1974 by Adam Pollock, presenting summer seasons in BATIGNANO.

Music [musical] drama. Term used frequently throughout the history of music for a dramatic work with music, and particularly one in which the music plays a primary role 'DRAMMA PER MUSICA' (or 'dramma in musica') is a designation used in Italy from the early 17th century and also in Germany during the 18th; Handel, in 1744, described *Hercules* as a 'musical drama'. The term has been found convenient by composers and others anxious to escape the more specific term 'opera'.

The term is generally used to distinguish Wagner's works from *Das Rheingold* onwards, both from his own earlier operas and from those of other composers, though it was not Wagner's own designation. In his theoretical essays of 1849–51, where the projected new genre is outlined, he used terms such as 'drama', 'drama of the future', 'the complete work of art of the future' ('das vollendete Kunstwerk der Zukunft'), 'the universal drama' ('das *allgemeinsame* Drama') and, of course, GESAMTKUNSTWERK. Wagner himself continued to use various terms: *Tristan* and *Meistersinger* are often called simply 'operas' in his writings (though the former was formally designated 'Handlung', i.e. 'drama'), while the *Ring* and *Parsifal* were called respectively 'Bühnenfestspiel' ('stage festival play') and 'Bühnenweihfestspiel' ('sacred stage festival play'). Wagner further used the expression 'musikalisches Drama', and in the essay *Über die Benennung 'Musikdrama'* (1872) suggested that it was this term that had been corrupted into 'music drama'. The latter, however, he rejected, on the grounds that it attempts to fuse disparate entities: music is an art while drama is an 'artistic act'. Hence the formulation 'acts of music made visible' ('ersichtlich gewordene Taten der Musik') proposed (only semi-seriously) for the new genre. Wagner ended the essay by inviting suggestions for an appropriate designation.
BARRY MILLINGTON

Music for the Living. Opera by G. A. Kancheli; see MUZÏKA DLYA ZHIVÏKH.

Musichetto (It.; diminutive of 'musico'). Term occasionally used for a BREECHES PART, taken by a young singer.

Musico (It.: 'musician'). During the 17th and 18th centuries the term gradually lost its original meaning of a professionally trained musician rather than an amateur (a distinction dating back to the medieval period). It came to be applied first to any professional musician, especially one associated with secular music; then to a musician associated with opera; to an operatic singer; to an operatic singer of mediocre talent; and finally to a castrato. It has usually carried derogatory implications. Pier Francesco Tosi, himself a castrato, referred to singers in his *Opinioni de' cantori antichi, e moderni* (1723) by such respectful terms as 'cantore', 'soprano', 'maestro', and even 'professore'; when he used 'musico', which he did rarely, he implied a mediocre singer. During the 19th century the term – usually PRIMO MUSICO – was inherited by singers, normally contraltos, who specialized in breeches roles, e.g. Benedetta Rosmunda Pisaroni and Marietta Alboni.

Music theatre. A term often used to characterize a kind of opera and opera production in which spectacle and dramatic impact are emphasized over purely musical factors, but first used specifically in the 1960s to describe the small-scale musico-dramatic works by composers of the postwar generations that proliferated in western Europe and North America during that decade.

1. Introduction. 2. The European mainland. 3. Britain. 4. North America.

1. INTRODUCTION. During the early 1960s, the elaborate trappings of the opera house and of 'grand opera' in particular were selfconsciously discarded by a number of progressive composers in favour of a variety of more modest dramatic and musical means, often combining elements of song, dance and mime, which could be tailored to a wide range of performing spaces. The genre came to prominence during the 1960s and early 70s for a combination of aesthetic, economic and political reasons, and though it almost as quickly became unfashionable again the most effective works of the period – especially those by Ligeti, Berio, Henze, Birtwistle and Maxwell Davies – have remained in the repertory and to a large extent have continued to define its parameters.

The advocates of music theatre were quick to cite more remote historical precedents – Schoenberg's *Pierrot lunaire*, Stravinsky's *The Soldier's Tale* and *Renard*, Weill's *Mahagonny* Songspiel, even Monteverdi's *Il combattimento di Tancredi e Clorinda*. In the postwar period, however, it appears to have arisen as a loosely connected tendency, partly dictated by the attempts of a number of composers to come to terms with the prescriptions and proscriptions of total serialism and to reconcile that rigour with their interest in exploring renewed combinations of music and gesture, partly as a political reaction against the conservative musical establishment which traditional opera was perceived as representing, and partly (and perhaps most significantly) as a pragmatic response to the increasing problem of mounting new operas in a period of rapidly increasing production costs.

2. THE EUROPEAN MAINLAND. Even in 1968, when some of the leaders of the postwar avant garde, Nono and Berio in particular, had begun to work within the frame-work of the operatic establishment, and the première of Zimmermann's *Die Soldaten* in 1965 had been hailed as the remaking of an operatic tradition thought broken after Berg's *Lulu*, Boulez was calling for opera houses to be blown up because they were representative of a 'museum culture' antipathetic to the radicalism that composers of his and subsequent generations had espoused. As a composer, Boulez long delayed any reconciliation with the operatic tradition (or indeed with music theatre, which he described in 1992 as 'opera of the poor'), though his career as a conductor has periodically embraced the opera house; but most of his contemporaries have gone on to explore opera in some form and have often used music theatre as the means of first approaching the genre.

As a result of these disparate aims and ideals, 'music theatre' became an umbrella term under which an assortment of highly diverse works was able to shelter. They ranged from those that were in effect chamber operas, demanding traditional vocal techniques and a high degree of virtuosity in performance, to pieces such as Stockhausen's *Herbstmusik* (1974) and *Musik im Bauch* (1975) and many works by Schnebel and Kagel in which the overt musical content was at best minimal. In the case of Ligeti's *Aventures* and *Nouvelles aventures* (1962 and 1962–5) the pieces existed as concert works, albeit ones of a highly individual character, before their theatrical implications occurred to the composer and he concocted (in 1966) a suggested scenario. Kagel's compositions often demanded the description of music theatre even when apparently they were written for conventional genres: in *Match* (composed 1964) for two cellists and percussion, for example, the discourse is more concerned with a theatrical exploration of the relationships between the performers and their struggles to master the technical difficulties of the music than it is with defining itself as a concert piece for three players in any traditional sense. His *Staatstheater* (composed 1967–70), commissioned by the Hamburg Staatsoper, uses all the apparatus of the opera house to explore and question cherished assumptions about the traditions of operatic performance rather than to extend the range of means by which music and gesture might be combined.

If in the work of Kagel and Schnebel, and the Dutch group of experimenters of the 1960s, the political content is implicit, Henze used music theatre as a means of sharpening and focussing an overt political message. He began to explore music theatre only in the late 1960s, when his disaffection with the social trappings of traditional opera had reached a climax, and he sensed that in *The Bassarids* (1966) his own operatic style had reached a stylistic end-point. His increasing politicization during the late 1960s and his espousal of left-wing causes determined both the subject matter and musical language of his theatre pieces, and *El Cimarrón* (1970) in particular, based on the autobiography of a runaway Cuban slave, remains one of Henze's most effective works of that period. His Second Violin Concerto (1971) also contains a strong element of music theatre, and when he returned to the opera house with *We Come to the River* (1976) his musical and dramatic style showed a new directness derived from the experience of these music-theatre pieces, the 'show' *Der langwierige Weg in die Wohnung der Natascha Ungeheuer* (1971) and the 'vaudeville' *La Cubana* (1974).

Nono and Berio had written works for the opera house – *Intolleranza 1960* (1961) and *Passaggio* (1963) respectively – before widening the range of their activities into music theatre. Experimental theatre groups flourished during the 1960s, and both composers incorporated elements from such productions into compositions. Nono's *A floresta e jovem e cheja de vida* (1966) employed part of an anti-Vietnam war play by the Living Theatre, and his large-scale dramatic works, *A gran sole carico d'amore* (1975) and *Prometeo* (1984), forsook the trappings of the opera house altogether.

Berio's *Opera* (1970, revised 1977) used material from the Open Theatre's production *Terminal* as one element in a highly allusive meditation on the nature of opera and the interdependence of music and gesture. But Berio's exploration of music theatre and its possibilities for concert works was already well advanced before *Opera*: there is a clear line of development from the 1961 setting of E. E. Cummings, *Circles*, through *Laborintus II* (1965) to the fully-fledged music theatre of *Recital I (For Cathy)* of 1972. And in his series of solo instrumental *Sequenze* (1958 onwards) there was a gradual drift away from the abstract musical designs of the early pieces towards much more comprehensive studies of performance. Two pieces composed in 1966, *Sequenza III* for female voice and *Sequenza V* for trombone, were particularly influential, and in the instrumental works of Heinz Holliger and Vinko Globokar the dramatic potential of virtuoso performance was used to define a distinct genre for which 'music theatre' seems the most appropriate description.

3. BRITAIN. In Britain, where in the period after 1945 conditions for the encouragement of new opera were arguably more unfavourable than anywhere in western Europe, the composers of the so-called Manchester School – Goehr, Maxwell Davies and Birtwistle – were prominent in efforts to establish a music-theatre repertory, to the extent that their works in that field may be regarded as the most significant achievement of British music in the 1960s and early 1970s. The music-theatre pieces of all three composers represented a much more direct and concentrated fusion of music and gesture than the equivalent works of their continental European contemporaries, perhaps because their aims were less concerned with ideology than with producing a more potent dramatic fusion than traditional opera then appeared to offer.

Thus Goehr's *Triptych* (*Naboth's Vineyard*, *Shadowplay* and *Sonata about Jerusalem*) was composed between 1968 and 1971, immediately after the completion of his first opera, *Arden must Die*. Davies and Birtwistle jointly formed the Pierrot Players (later called The Fires of London) in 1967 with the specific purpose of creating and presenting a repertory of music theatre: for their concerts Davies composed *Eight Songs for a Mad King* (1969) and *Vesalii icones* (1969), in which it was the borderline between concert and theatre piece, rather than that between theatre piece and opera, that was blurred. In *Eight Songs* an actor-singer, using extended vocal techniques, portrays the insane George III, delivering a sequence of songs to his 'caged birds', the six instrumentalists of the ensemble: in *Vesalii icones* a solo cello offers a series of meditations on the stations of the cross while a solo dancer counterpoints against them images and gestures derived from the anatomical drawings of Vesalius.

In both cases the works were consciously designed to be performed in a concert hall. The theatre pieces Birtwistle wrote for the Pierrot Players (including *Monodrama*, 1969) have been withdrawn, but in such works as the 'dramatic pastoral' *Down by the Greenwood Side* (1969) the pared-down instrumentation and skeletal gestures reveal the experience of those explorations. In his *Bow Down*, composed however in 1977, when the music-theatre movement was on the wane across Europe, Birtwistle achieved an unclassifiable fusion of music, text and gesture that was perhaps closer to the music-theatre ideal than anything produced during the movement's heyday ten years earlier.

4. NORTH AMERICA. In the USA and Canada music theatre acquired an entirely distinct and independent pedigree. Its most striking manifestations had their origins in the experimental tradition of the inter-war years, in the multi-media projects of Harry Partch in particular, and from Cage's demonstrations from the 1950s onwards of the open-ended and all-embracing possibilities of any work of art. From Cage's 'happenings' of the 1960s, *HPSCHD* (1967–9, in collaboration with Lejaren Hiller) and *Musicircus* (1967), through *Apartment House 1776* (1976) and the purely electronic *Roaratorio* (1979), he gave demonstrations of the spectacular possibilities of such catholic musical collage, while in *Europeras 1 & 2* (1987) he offered a commentary on the European operatic tradition. (Such works, combined with an increasing awareness of Kagel's significance, also fostered a new phase in British music theatre in the 1970s and 80s, typified by the creations of Trevor Wishart and Michael Nyman.)

In other respects North American music theatre struck out in several directions, often straining the limits of the definition of the term. The works of R. Murray Schafer may be related to developments in the European avant garde of the 1960s, though he has brought to his theatre pieces a far wider range of reference and gesture, while Robert Ashley's explorations of the possibilities of television opera and use of multi-layered technology introduced another ingredient into the experimental mix. And within the broadest sweep of the term, Alvin Lucier's installations and 'sonic environments' offer experiences in which the visual component is certainly intended for consideration alongside the acoustic phenomena, but which take music theatre a very long way from both its origins and its conventional parameters.

ANDREW CLEMENTS

Musorgsky, Modest Petrovich (*b* Karevo, nr Velikiye Luki, Pskov district, 9/21 March 1839; *d* St Petersburg, 16/28 March 1881). Russian composer. Despite his brief career, weak training and failure to complete most of his works, he is regarded by many as the most talented and (posthumously) influential composer of the Russian national school.

1. Background. 2. Early opera projects. 3. *Boris Godunov*. 4. Later operas. 5. Reputation.

1. BACKGROUND. Like most Russian composers of his generation, Musorgsky was born to the leisure class. Following family tradition, he was groomed for a military officer's career. He spent his first decade on his ancestral estate, where from the age of six he was taught the piano by his mother. Within three years he was able to perform a concerto by John Field at a concert arranged by his parents at home. On being sent in 1849 to the élite Peter and Paul School in St Petersburg, Musorgsky continued his piano studies with Anton Herke, a locally celebrated former pupil of Adolf Henselt. He stayed with Herke until 1854, when he was

attending the Cadet School of Guards. There he wrote his earliest surviving composition, *Porte-enseigne Polka* for piano, dedicated to his comrades at the Cadet School and published at his father's expense in 1852 ('to the author's regret', he wrote in 1871). In 1856 he became a member of the Preobrazhensky Guards, since the time of Peter I the tsar's personal regiment. (The regiment, representing its founder, makes an appearance in the fifth scene of *Khovanshchina*.) A project that year for an opera after Victor Hugo's *Han d'Islande* came to nothing ('because nothing could have come of it', the author later wrote).

Later in 1856 Musorgsky met Borodin (whom he impressed as a foppishly elegant young officer with a fluent keyboard technique and a way with the ladies) and Dargomïzhsky, who brought him into contact with Cui and Balakirev, the nucleus of what would become the New Russian School (or 'Mighty Kuchka' ['little heap'], after an 1867 encomium by Vladimir Stasov). He began formal lessons in composition with Balakirev in 1857. By the middle of the next year, Musorgsky was so fired with composerly ambition that he resigned his commission. It proved a fatal step, because with the emancipation of the serfs in 1861 his family would be impoverished and he would have no means of support. He was forced to accept low-grade civil service appointments, the chief one being a clerkship with the forestry department of the Ministry of State Property (1868–80), where he worked copying official documents. (The role of the downtrodden Scrivener in *Khovanshchina* seems an ironic reflection of this unhappy facet of his life.)

Musorgsky's formal début as a composer took place in January 1860, when Anton Rubinstein conducted a Scherzo for orchestra, composed the previous year under Balakirev's guidance, at a concert of the newly founded Russian Musical Society. The next year Konstantin Lyadov, chief conductor of the Russian Opera, directed a performance of a chorus Musorgsky had composed in 1858–9 as incidental music for *Oedipus in Athens*, a neo-classical drama by Vladislav Ozerov (it was not an operatic project).

2. EARLY OPERA PROJECTS. Musorgsky's earliest operatic project to bear some fruit was the ambitious *Salammbô*, based on Flaubert's novel of the Punic Wars, on which he worked from 1863 to 1866 (incorporating the *Oedipus* chorus in the second act), while living with friends in St Petersburg in a communal apartment. Like the song *Tsar' Saul* ('King Saul', 1863) on one side of it, and the chorus *Porazheniye Sennakheriba* ('The Destruction of Sennacherib', 1866–7) on the other, *Salammbô* shows the influence of Alexander Serov's opera *Yudif'* ('Judith', 1863), which Musorgsky disparaged in detail in a letter to Balakirev (who was engaged in a feud with Serov), but which obviously stimulated his imagination greatly. Recollections of Serov's opera cropped up again in both the music and the scenario of *Boris Godunov*, which contains a hallucination for the title character, absent in the literary source but similar to Holofernes' hallucination in *Judith*. The opening of the cell scene (Act 1 scene i) is reminiscent, in its use of an ostinato, of the opening scene in Serov's opera, which Musorgsky quoted in his letter to Balakirev with suggestions ('followed' in *Boris*) for improving it.

The surviving *Salammbô* music – three big scenes and a trio of smaller numbers (partly orchestrated, the rest in vocal score or short score) – shows a flair for choral pageantry on a grandiose scale. The single extended solo scene (for the imprisoned Mâtho) is constructed, like Susanin's monologue in Act 4 of Glinka's *A Life for the Tsar*, around a series of musical reminiscences. Musorgsky drew extensively on *Salammbô* for thematic material (though no complete numbers) in both versions of *Boris Godunov*.

Between scuttling *Salammbô* and embarking on *Boris* Musorgsky set to music several scenes (not, as commonly stated, the whole first act) of Gogol's comedy *Zhenit'ba* ('Marriage'). It is not clear whether he intended to finish setting the whole two-act play in the form of an *opéra dialogué* (recitative opera) or whether this 'experiment in dramatic music in prose', composed in the summer of 1868, was only an exercise in declamation suggested by Dargomïzhsky, who was then at work on a verbatim setting of Pushkin's verse tragedy *The Stone Guest*. Whatever its immediate purpose, *Marriage* (which, like most of *Salammbô*, exists only in the form of a vocal score) is a remarkable essay in life-drawing, the prime musical memento of the extremist realist ferment that seized the Russian arts in the 1860s. 'This is what I would like', Musorgsky wrote to Glinka's sister Lyudmila Shestakova while at work on his setting of *Marriage*:

For my characters to speak on the stage as living people speak, but at the same time in such a way that the manner and intensity of their intonation, supported by an orchestra that acts as the musical canvas for their speech, should hit the bull's-eye – that is, my music must be an artistic reproduction of human speech in all its finest shades, that is, *the sounds of human speech*, as the external manifestation of thought and feeling, must, without exaggeration or strain, become *music* that is truthful, accurate, BUT (read: which means) artistic, highly artistic.

In an autobiographical sketch he prepared in 1880 for Riemann's *Musik-Lexikon*, Musorgsky formulated his artistic goal as 'the reproduction in musical sounds not merely of modes of feeling (*nastroyeniya chuvstv*) but chiefly of modes of human speech (*nastroyeniya rechi chelovecheskoy*)', and cited as authority the German literary historian Georg Gervinus. The reference is to Gervinus's book *Händel und Shakespeare*, which came out in 1868 and which set forth an elaborate mimetic theory, derived from Aristotle, of word-note relations based on the musical realization of what the author called *Gefühlsstimmungen* (compare Musorgsky's 'modes of feeling'). The Russian composer's adaptation of Greek 'imitation' theory via Gervinus was a notable instance of operatic ontogeny recapitulating phylogeny; Musorgsky's operatic 'reform' was an unwitting replay of the Florentine neo-classical ferment out of which, two and a half centuries earlier, opera had first emerged.

Marriage was unveiled before the composer's fellow 'kuchkists' at a gathering at the home of César Cui on 23 September/5 October 1868, with Musorgsky, a skilled baritone, taking the role of Podkolyosin, the reluctant bridegroom, and Dargomïzhsky that of Kochkaryov, his impulsive friend (Nadezhda Purgold, the future Mme Rimsky-Korsakov, accompanied). The reception was cool. Even Dargomïzhsky – 'the great teacher of musical truth', as Musorgsky called him in two separate dedications – felt the composer had compromised the artistic value of his music in his quest for the ultimate in naturalistic declamation. Indeed, *Marriage* is a somewhat cerebral and finicky affair, full of forbiddingly complex rhythmic notations and angularly anti-lyrical melodic lines emphasizing augmented and diminished intervals.

531

Having composed it, however, Musorgsky felt he had 'crossed the Rubicon'. He was now the master of his native musical speech, he thought, and thus equipped to create a truly national music drama. Almost immediately after the run-through at Cui's, Musorgsky shelved *Marriage* and followed the suggestion of his historian friend Vladimir Nikol'sky to turn *Boris Godunov*, Pushkin's celebrated historical tragedy in imitation of Shakespeare, into that drama. It was the only opera he ever completed; in fact he completed it twice.

3. 'BORIS GODUNOV'. The first version was as close as possible in conception to *Marriage*, in that Musorgsky strove to set Pushkin's text directly (i.e. as an *opéra dialogué*), without fashioning a separate libretto. Two whole scenes from the play were set practically verbatim; in the opera they were consecutive and formed the second 'part' (i.e. act; the 'second part' became Act 1, following the prologue, in the revised version). The scene in Pimen's cell was cast by Pushkin in verse; Musorgsky's setting closely resembled Dargomïzhsky's manner in *The Stone Guest* as to declamation. The scene at the inn on the Lithuanian border was, in keeping with the Shakespearean mixture of genres Pushkin deliberately adopted, a comic scene in prose; here Musorgsky's method was modelled closely on his earlier prose-setting experiment in *Marriage*. For the rest, Musorgsky retained and conflated only those scenes from Pushkin in which the title character appeared. They were dominated by his lengthy soliloquies, which Musorgsky cast in a sort of arioso style: melodically heightened recitative over a texture of leitmotifs, the latter drawn to a large extent from *Salammbô*.

The first version of *Boris Godunov* was finished by the end of 1869 and submitted to the selection committee of the Imperial Theatres. During the summer of 1870 Musorgsky briefly embarked on another operatic project, based on a scenario by Stasov that transplanted Friedrich Spielhagen's play *Hans und Grete* to a Russian rural setting. It was to be called *Bobïl'* (roughly translatable as 'The Lonely Old Bachelor'), and Musorgsky actually sketched a divination scene for the superstitious title character (it later turned up in the second act of *Khovanshchina* as Marfa's divination). He otherwise occupied his time, while awaiting news of the fate of *Boris*, with children's songs, later gathered into his *Nursery* cycle; these would be his last essays in the naturalistic vein.

On 10/22 February 1871 the selection committee rejected *Boris Godunov* because it lacked a leading feminine role. This set in train a thorough overhaul of the opera, one that went so far beyond the committee's demands as to suggest a basic aesthetic and ideological change of heart. The stipulated revision was accomplished by supplying the so-called 'Polish act' (Act 3), with its featured role of Marina Mniszek and the love duet in which it culminates. But Musorgsky also completely rewrote the fourth scene of the opera, now designated Act 2 (the second act of Cui's *William Ratcliff*, the one 'kuchkist' opera by then performed, serving as model). The title role was endowed with a fully-fledged aria, based on a lyrical theme salvaged from *Salammbô* and set to a new text by the composer that departed markedly from Pushkin's original, and set off with a wealth of little genre numbers for Boris's children and their nanny (a reflection of Musorgsky's

preoccupation with infantine themes the previous year). The act ended with a new hallucination shaped around an orchestral ostinato, representing a chiming clock, that in its reiterated tritone bass carried ironic resonances from the prologue's coronation bells.

The scene at St Basil's shrine, which contained the searing confrontation between Boris and the Holy Fool (cast in dramatic recitative), was replaced by the so-called 'Kromï Forest' scene at the end of the opera. (Here the public meeting scene in *The Maid of Pskov*, an opera by Rimsky-Korsakov then in progress, served as model; Rimsky and Musorgsky were room-mates at the time.) The new scene, following post-Pushkinian theories of Russian history, depicted the populace in open rebellion against the tsar; it was cast not in choral recitative but in large strophic and da capo numbers, several based on folktunes. The many additions to the opera were compensated by a number of cuts, the net effect of which was a lessened reliance on leitmotifs and the clarification of their significance.

The new *Boris*, completed on 23 June/5 July 1872, was a very different kind of opera from the old: far less naturalistic in its declamation, far more traditional in its structure and its dramaturgical means, and far grander in its scale. It was now unmistakably a tragedy, whereas the earlier version had been cast in a mixed genre whose tone, to the composer's consternation, had been misconstrued by many of its early (private) auditors.

The Polish act and the Inn Scene, representing Musorgsky's newly broadened operatic technique at its two extremes, were performed at the Mariinsky Theatre on 5/17 February 1873, at a benefit performance for Gennady Kondrat'yev, the chief stage director. The public and critical reception was warm, leading to the staging of the whole opera on 27 January/8 February 1874 (excluding the cell scene, to which the censor objected; it was first performed in concert at the Free Music School five years later). Again the reception was generally enthusiastic; the only discordant note was sounded by Cui, Musorgsky's ostensible comrade-in-arms, who was the regular reviewer for an influential St Petersburg daily and was envious of Musorgsky's success. After this, following Balakirev's withdrawal from musical activity in 1872, there could no longer be any talk – save in Stasov's optimistic propaganda – of a unified 'Mighty Kuchka' of Russian nationalist composers.

4. LATER OPERAS. During his last decade Musorgsky worked on three operas, not counting a briefly considered project of 1877 involving Pushkin's *Kapitanskaya dochka* ('The Captain's Daughter'), set amid the peasant revolts led by Pugachyov, for which no music was written. In 1872 he became involved, along with the rest of the Five (less Balakirev), in *Mlada*, a project organized by Stasov at the request of Stepan Gedeonov, the Intendant of the Imperial Theatres, who wanted to stage a colourful opera-ballet on themes from Slavonic mythology. For his contribution to this soon-aborted (and, for him, uncongenial) enterprise Musorgsky again revamped his *Oedipus* chorus, arranged as a choral scene an unperformed tone poem, *Ivanova noch' na Lïsoy gore* ('St John's Eve on Bald Mountain'), and composed a choral market scene. The latter pair eventually found a home in *Sorochinskaya yarmarka* ('The Fair at Sorochintsï').

In 1872, evidently inspired by the festivities commemorating the bicentenary of the birth of Peter the Great, Musorgsky and Stasov began collaborating on

Khovanshchina ('The Khovansky Affair'), a grand historical opera depicting the political convulsions that attended the beginning of Peter's reign. The plot was assembled directly from historical sources and conflated events taking place between 1682 and 1698. Scenes accumulated in vocal score (only two little numbers being orchestrated by the composer) up to his untimely death from alcoholism; when his papers were put in order by Stasov and Rimsky-Korsakov it was found that, although Musorgsky had described the opera as finished, two of its five acts were lacking their endings. Rimsky-Korsakov's performing version (given in 1886) plugged the holes, Süssmayr-fashion, by the use of reprises (Shostakovich did the same in the 1950s). It is doubtful whether the melioristic interpretation thus imposed on the opera's glum action conformed to Musorgsky's intent. What is certain is that the style of *Khovanshchina* continues in the 'new-old' direction inaugurated by the revised *Boris Godunov*. It is a grandiose conception, carried by formally discrete lyric numbers. Naturalistic recitative plays a much subordinated role, confined in the main to incidental and low-born characters.

Even in *The Fair at Sorochintsï*, a peasant comedy after a story by Gogol, on which Musorgsky embarked in 1874 (but mainly composed in 1877–80), recitative is no longer naturalistic but based, like the larger numbers, on Ukrainian folk melodies (here the song-recitatives in Serov's last opera, *Vrazh'ya sila* ('The Power of the Fiend'), may have provided a model). The swing from radical realism to a narrow nationalism in Musorgsky's work mirrors a general tendency in the Russian arts over the period 1860–80. It is a change that is most easily seen in painting, and Stasov was quite right to draw parallels between Musorgsky and the painters of the 'Wanderer' (*Peredvizhnik*) school.

The remains of *The Fair at Sorochintsï* are fragmentary; Rimsky-Korsakov did not attempt to complete the opera, although he did rearrange for orchestra alone the *St John's Eve* music as it finally appeared there, retitling it *A Night on Bald Mountain*. Anatoly Lyadov, a former pupil, undertook the task of completion at Rimsky's suggestion but, notoriously indolent, he never got beyond orchestrating a few numbers. Cui completed the work, possibly as an act of contrition, in 1916. Nikolay Tcherepnin fashioned a pastiche in which the surviving fragments were rounded out by music from other works of Musorgsky. What is now the standard performing version was created in the early 1930s by Pavel Lamm, the editor of Musorgsky's complete works, and the Soviet composer Vissarion Shebalin.

5. REPUTATION. At the time of his death Musorgsky was a composer of local reputation, virtually unknown to the musical world at large. His immortality is due to the selfless labours of Rimsky-Korsakov, his friend and former fellow-'kuchkist', whose posthumous editions of *Boris Godunov* (1896, 1908) restored it to the Russian repertory after the end of its initial run at the Mariinsky, and whose editions of *Khovanshchina* and *Marriage* made them performable. Musorgsky's world fame is due in the first instance to Sergey Dyagilev, whose 1908 Paris production of *Boris Godunov* in Rimsky's second version (augmented for the occasion by the addition of supplementary processional music for the Coronation scene) revealed not only Musorgsky's opera but the histrionic genius of Shalyapin to the West. (*Khovanshchina*, in Rimsky's version supplemented by Ravel and Stravinsky, followed in 1913.) Since that time the 'original' (revised) *Boris* has made a gradual comeback, spurred initially by Parisian modernists who unfairly condemned Rimsky for the editorial tampering that had salvaged Musorgsky's work from oblivion, and marked along the way by compromise versions (that is, orchestrations of Lamm's edition of the original vocal score) by Dmitry Shostakovich and Karol Rathaus.

Musorgsky's impact on his musical contemporaries was virtually nil; his autodidact and non-professional status led to his being patronized as a kind of *idiot savant*. In the 20th century his bluff anti-conventional stance and remarkable powers of psychological penetration have made him a protomodernist icon, profoundly influential on the operatic practice of such composers as Debussy (who called him a 'god'), Ravel (who modelled *L'heure espagnole* on the posthumously published *Marriage*), Janáček, Prokofiev and Shostakovich. Productions of his works, with their critical focus on power relations and their long-masked political pessimism, have always been bellwethers of Russian and Soviet cultural policy; with the coming of *glasnost'* in the 1980s Musorgsky's historical operas became the object of renewed attention and debate on the part of historians, musicologists and producers.

See also BORIS GODUNOV; FAIR AT SOROCHINTSÏ, THE; KHOVANSHCHINA; MARRIAGE; MLADA (i); and SALAMMBÔ (i).

Edition: *M. P. Musorgsky: Polnoye sobraniye sochineniy* [Complete Collection of Works], ed. P. Lamm, with B. V. Asaf'yev (Moscow, 1928–34 (repr. 1969), 1939 [addl vol.viii]) [L]

title	genre, acts	libretto	first performance	sources and remarks	L
Han d'Islande		after V. Hugo		projected 1856	
Salammbô	grand op, 3 scenes, 3 nos.	Musorgsky, after G. Flaubert		comp. 1863–6, inc.	
Zhenit'ba [Marriage]	comic op, 1	N. V. Gogol	private perf., St Petersburg, 23 Sept/5 Oct 1868; stage, St Petersburg, Suvorin Theatre School, 19 March/1 April 1908	comp. 1868	iv/2
Boris Godunov	7 scenes (prol., 4 pts)	Musorgsky, after A. S. Pushkin and N. M. Karamzin	Leningrad, State Academic, 16 Feb 1928	comp. 1868–9	
rev. version	9 scenes (prol. and 4 acts)		St Petersburg, Mariinsky, 27 Jan/8 Feb 1874, cond. E. Nápravník	comp. 1871–2, vs (1874); (London, 1975)	

title	genre, acts	libretto	first performance	sources and remarks	L
Rimsky-Korsakov version (i)			concert perf. St Petersburg, Great Hall of the Conservatory, 28 Nov/10 Dec 1896; stage, Moscow, Solodovnikov, 7/19 Dec 1898	(1896)	
Rimsky-Korsakov version (ii)			Paris, Opéra, 19 May 1908, cond. F. Blumenfeld	(1908); standard version	
Bobïl' [The Lonely Bachelor]		after F. Spielhagen: Hans und Grete		projected 1870	
Mlada	op-ballet, 4	V. A. Krïlov		comp. 1872, unperf., collab. Rimsky-Korsakov, Borodin and Cui	iv/3, vii/1
Khovanshchina	6 scenes (5 acts)	Musorgsky, with V. V. Stasov	St Petersburg, 9/21 Feb 1886, cond. E. Goldshteyn	comp. 1872–80, inc.; completed and orchd Rimsky-Korsakov	ii, vii/2
Sorochinskaya yarmarka [The Fair at Sorochintsï]	3	Musorgsky, with A. Golenishchev-Kutuzov, after Gogol		comp. 1874–81, inc., fragments in concert perf., St Petersburg, 16/29 March 1911; Act 1 excerpts orchd A. Lyadov, Act 2 completed V. G. Karatïgin, St Petersburg, Comedia, 17/30 Dec 1911	
1st version			Moscow, Free, 8/21 Oct 1913, cond. K. Saradzhev	rev. and orchd A. Lyadov and V. G. Karatïgin, incl. Rimsky-Korsakov: Night on Bald Mountain and music by Y. S. Sakhnovsky; completed Sakhnovsky, Moscow, Bol'shoy, 10 Jan 1925, cond. N. Golovanov	
2nd version			St Petersburg, Theatre of Musical Drama, 13/26 Oct 1917, cond. G. Fitelberg	completed and orchd Cui, 1915–16 (1916)	
3rd version	pastiche		Monte Carlo Opera House, 27 March 1923	arr. N. Tcherepnin, incl. items from earlier versions	
4th version			Moscow, Nemirovich-Danchenko, 12 Jan 1932, cond. G. Stolyarov	completed and orchd V. iii Shebalin (1933); rev. of Shebalin version, Leningrad, Malïy, 21 Dec 1931	iii
Pugachyovshchina		after Pushkin: Kapitanskaya dochka		projected 1877	

LIFE AND WORKS

C. Cui: 'M. P. Musorgsky (kriticheskiy etyud)' [A Critical Study; orig. pubd 1881], Izbrannïye stat'i [Selected Articles], ed. Yu. A. Kremlyov (Leningrad, 1952), 286–96

V. V. Stasov: 'Modest Petrovich Musorgsky: biograficheskiy ocherk' [Biographical Essay], Vestnik Yevropï [The European Herald] (1881), no.5, pp.285–316; no.6, pp.506–45; repr. in Izbrannïye sochineniya, ed. E. D. Stasova and others (Moscow, 1952), ii, 161–213

——: 'Perov i Musorgsky' [orig. pubd 1883]; repr. in Izbrannïye sochineniya, ed. E. D. Stasova and others (Moscow, 1952), ii, 133–52

N. Kompaneysky: 'K novïm beregam: M. P. Musorgsky' [Towards New Shores], RMG (1906), nos.11–12, pp.14–18

M. Olenine d'Alheim: Le legs de Moussorgski (Paris, 1908)

MS (1917), nos.5–6 [special issue]

I. Glebov [B. Asaf'yev]: 'M. P. Musorgsky, 1839–1881: opït pereotsenki znacheniya ego tvorchestva' [A Reassessment of the Significance of his Creative Work], Simfonicheskiye etyudï (Petrograd, 1922) [1970 edn., pp.194–221]

——: Musorgsky: opït kharakteristiki [An Evaluation] (Petrograd, 1923)

A. Swan: 'Mussorgsky and Modern Music', MQ, xi (1925), 118–31

I. Glebov [B. Asaf'yev]: 'Die ästhetischen Anschauungen Mussorgskijs', Die Musik, xxi (1929), 561–69

Yu. Keldïsh and V. Yakovlev, eds.: M. P. Musorgsky k pyatidesyatiletiyu so dnya smerti [On the 50th Anniversary of Musorgsky's Death] (Moscow, 1932)

A. N. Rimsky-Korsakov: M. P. Musorgsky: pis'ma i dokumentï [Letters and Documents] (Moscow and Leningrad, 1932)

A. A. Golenishchev-Kutuzov: 'Vospominaniya o M. P. Musorgskom' [Reminiscences about Musorgsky], Muzïkal'noye nasledstvo [Musical Heritage], ed. M. V. Ivanov-Boretsky, i (Moscow, 1935), 13–49

SovM (1939), no.4 [special issue]

M. D. Calvocoressi: Mussorgsky (London, 1946, 2/1974)

J. Leyda and S. Bertensson, eds.: The Musorgsky Reader: a Life of

M. P. Musorgsky in Letters and Documents (New York, 1947) [trans., enlarged, of A. N. Rimsky-Korsakov (1932)]

V. V. Stasov: *Izbrannïye stat'i o M. P. Musorgskom* [Selected Essays about Musorgsky], ed. A. S. Oglevets (Moscow, 1952)

M. D. Calvocoressi: *Modest Musorgsky: his Life and Works* (London, 1956)

A. A. Orlova: *Trudï i dni M. P. Musorgskogo: letopis' zhizni i tvorchestva* (Moscow, 1963; Eng. trans., 1983, as *Musorgsky's Works and Days: a Biography in Documents*)

A. S. Ogolevets: *Vokal'naya dramaturgiya Musorgskogo* [Musorgsky's Vocal Dramaturgy] (Moscow, 1966)

G. Khubov: *Musorgsky* (Moscow, 1969)

A. A. Orlova and M. S. Pekelis, eds.: *M. Musorgsky: Literaturnoye naslediye* [Literary Legacy] (Moscow, 1971–2)

V. Belyayev: *Musorgsky – Skryabin – Stravinsky* (Moscow, 1972)

R. Shirinyan: *Evolyutsiya opernogo tvorchestva Musorgskogo* [The Evolution of Musorgsky's Operatic Works] (Moscow, 1973)

S. I. Shlifshteyn: *Musorgsky: khudozhnik, vremya, sud'ba* [Musorgsky: Artist, Times, Fate] (Moscow, 1975)

E. R. Reilly: *The Music of Musorgsky: a Guide to the Editions* (New York, 1980)

C. Dahlhaus: 'Musorgskij in der Musikgeschichte des 19. Jahrhunderts', *Modest Musorgskij: Aspekte des Opernwerks*, ed. H.-K. Metzger and R. Riehn (Munich, 1981), 7–22

E. Frid: *M. P. Musorgsky: problemï tvorchestva* [Problems of his Works] (Leningrad, 1981)

M. H. Brown, ed.: *Musorgsky: In Memoriam 1881–1981* (Ann Arbor, 1982)

I. Stepanova: 'K teorii muzïkal'nogo yazïka Musorgskogo' [Towards a Theory of Musorgsky's Musical Language], *SovM* (1982), no.3, pp.66–72

E. Gordeyeva, ed.: *M. Musorgsky: Pis'ma* [Letters] (Moscow, 2/1984)

G. Sherikhova and Ye. Pashchenko: 'Modest Musorgsky', *Muzïkal'naya zhizn'* (1984), no.20, pp.15–17

C. Dahlhaus: *Realism in Nineteenth-Century Music* (Cambridge, 1985)

O. Kharitonova: 'Za vekom vek …', *Muzïkal'naya zhizn'* (1985), no.7, pp.18–19

R. Taruskin: 'Serov and Musorgsky', *Slavonic and Western Music: Essays for Gerald Abraham* (Ann Arbor and Oxford, 1985), 139–61

G. Nekrasova: 'Ob odnom tvorcheskom printsipe Musorgskogo' [On a Certain Creative Principle of Musorgsky's], *SovM* (1988), no.3, pp.67–72

E. Gordeyeva, ed.: *M. P. Musorgsky v vospominaniyakh sovremennikov* [Musorgsky in the Reminiscences of his Contemporaries] (Moscow, 1989)

Ye. Levashov, ed.: *Naslediye M. P. Musorgskogo* [Musorgsky's Legacy] (Moscow, 1989) [incl. bibliography of Russ. pubns]

SovM (1989), no.3 [special issue]

D. Logbas: 'God Musorgskogo prodolzhayetsya: v kontekste XX veka' [The Year of Musorgsky Continues: in the Context of the 20th Century], *SovM* (1989), no.11, pp.89–91

G. L. Golovinsky, ed.: *M. P. Musorgsky i muzïka XX veka* [Musorgsky and 20th-Century Music] (Moscow, 1990)

A. Orlova, ed., trans. V. Zaytzeff and F. Morrison: *Musorgsky Remembered* (Bloomington, 1991)

R. Taruskin: *Musorgsky: Eight Essays and an Epilogue* (Princeton, 1992)

M. Rakhmanova: *Operï Musorgskogo: istoki i sud'ba* [Musorgsky's Operas: Sources and Fate] (Moscow, forthcoming)

OPERAS

Salammbô

P. Lamm: Introduction to *M. P. Musorgsky: Polnoye sobraniye sochineniy* [Complete Works], iv/1 (New York, 1939); repr. as vol. xix (New York, 1969), 3–9

G. Abraham: 'The Mediterranean Element in "Boris Godunov"', *Slavonic and Romantic Music* (London, 1968), 188–94

R. Tedeschi: 'Salammbô', *Modest Musorgskij: Aspekte des Opernwerks*, ed. H.-K. Metzger and R. Riehn (Munich, 1981), 23–40

M. Rakhmanova and M. Yermolayev: 'Novaya zhizn' "Salambo"' [A New Life for *Salammbô*], *SovM* (1989), no.9, pp.88–92

Marriage

I. Glebov [B. Asaf'yev]: 'Muzïkal'no-esteticheskiye vozzreniya Musorgskogo' [Musorgsky's Musical and Aesthetic Approach], *M. P. Musorgsky: k pyatidesyatiletiyu so dnya smerti 1881–1931, stat'i i materialï* [On the 50th Anniversary of

Musorgsky's Death, 1881–1931: Articles and Documents], ed. Yu. Keldïsh and V. Yakovlev (Moscow, 1932), 33–49

E. Antipova: 'Dva varianta "Zhenit'bï"', [Two Versions of *Marriage*], *SovM* (1964), no.3, pp.77–85

E. Frid: '"Zhenit'ba"' *M. P. Musorgsky: problemï tvorchestva* [Problems Concerning the Works] (Leningrad, 1981), 48–73

P. Santi: 'Über *Die Heirat*', *Modest Musorgskij: Aspekte des Opernwerks*, ed. H.-K. Metzger and R. Riehn (Munich, 1981), 41–4

R. Taruskin: 'Handel, Shakespeare, and Musorgsky: the Sources and Limits of Russian Musical Realism', *Studies in the History of Music*, i (1983), 247–68

Boris Godunov

C. Cui: 'Tri kartinï iz zabrakovannoy vodevil'nïm komitetom operï Musorgskogo "Boris Godunov"' [Three Scenes from *Boris Godunov*, an Opera rejected by the Selection Committee; orig. pubd 1873], *Izbrannïye stat'i* [Selected Articles], ed. Yu. A. Kremlyov (Leningrad, 1952), 225–34

——: '"Boris Godunov", opera g. Musorgskogo, dvazhdï zabrakovannaya vodevil'nïm komitetom' [Musorgsky's *Boris Godunov*, Twice rejected by the Selection Committee], *Sankt-peterburgskiye vedomosti* (6 Feb 1874)

G. Larosh [H. Laroche]: 'Mïslyashchiy realist v russkoy opere' [A Thinking Realist in Russian Opera], *Golos* (1 Feb 1874)

V. Chernïshyov: 'Pesnya Varlaama' [Varlaam's Song], *Pushkin i yego sovremenniki* [Pushkin and his Contemporaries], ii/5 (1907), 127–8

A. N. Rimsky-Korsakov: '"Boris Godunov" M. P. Musorgskogo', *MS* (1917), nos.5–6, pp.108–67

R. Godet: *En marge de Boris Godounof* (Paris and London, 1926)

E. Braudo and A. Rimsky-Korsakov: '*Boris Godunov*' Musorgskogo (Moscow, 1927)

V. Belaiev, trans. S. W. Pring: *Musorgsky's Boris Godunov and its New Version* (London, 1928)

M. Calvocoressi: *Le vrai Boris Godunov* (Paris, 1928)

P. Lamm: Preface to M. P. Musorgsky: *Polnoye sobraniye sochineniy* [Complete Works] i [vocal score] (Moscow and Vienna, 1928), pp.xv–xxxvi

S. Popov, ed.: *K vosstanovleniyu 'Borisa Godunova'* [On the Restoration of *Boris Godunov*] (Leningrad, 1928)

Yu. Keldïsh and others: *Boris Godunov: stat'i i issledovaniya* [Articles and Research] (Moscow, 1930)

K. Nilsson: *Die Rimskij-Korsakoffsche Bearbeitung des 'Boris Godunoff' von Mussorgskij als Objekt der vergleichenden Musikwissenschaft* (Münster, 1937)

B. Asaf'yev: *Izbrannïye trudï* [Selected Works], ed. T. N. Livanova and others, iii (Moscow, 1954) [incl. 'Muzïkal'no-dramaturgicheskaya kontseptsiya operï "Bori Godunov" Musorgskogo'; orig. pubd 1928] and '"Boris Godunov" Musorgskogo kak muzïkal'nïy spektakl' iz Pushkina [*Boris Godunov* as a Musical Spectacle after Pushkin; orig. pubd 1945]]

I. Zemtsovsky: 'Intonatsionnoye zerno operï "Boris Godunov"' [The Morphological Kernel of *Boris Godunov*], *SovM* (1959), no.3, pp.94–6

N. Isakhanova: 'Put' k sovershenstvu' [The Path to Perfection], *SovM* (1966), no.7, pp.51–60

B. Asaf'yev: '"Boris Godunov" i yego redaktsii [Boris Godunov and its Versions], *Kriticheskiye stat'i, ocherki i retsenzii* [Critical Essays, Articles and Reviews], ed. I. V. Beletsky (Moscow and Leningrad, 1967)

G. Abraham: *Slavonic and Romantic Music* (London, 1968) [incl. 'The Mediterranean Element in *Boris Godunov*', 1942, and 'Musorgsky's "Boris" and Pushkin's', 1945]

Yu. Tyulin and others: 'K izucheniyu naslediya M. P. Musorgskogo: stsena "pod Kromami" v dramaturgii "Borisa Godunova"' [Towards an Understanding of Musorgsky's Legacy: the Scene 'Near Kromï' in the Dramatic Plan of *Boris Godunov*], *SovM* (1970), no.3, pp.90–114

E. Brody: *The Demetrius Legend and its Literary Treatment in the Age of the Baroque* (Rutherford, NJ, 1972)

A. Tsuker: 'Narod pokornïy i narod buntuyushchiy' [The Folk Submissive and the Folk Rebellious], *SovM* (1972), no.3, pp.105–9

A. Gozenpud: *Russkiy opernïy teatr XIX veka* [Russian Operatic Theatre in the 19th Century], iii (Leningrad, 1973), 67–95

G. Fulle: *Modest Mussorgskijs 'Boris Godunov': Geschichte und Werk, Fassungen und Theaterpraxis* (Wiesbaden, 1974)

D. Lloyd-Jones: Critical Commentary to M. Musorgsky: *Boris Godunov: Opera in Four Acts with a Prologue* (Oxford, 1975), ii, 7–79

R. Oldani: *New Perspectives on Mussorgsky's 'Boris Godunov'* (diss., U. of Michigan, 1978) [chaps. pubd as articles: 'Boris Godunov and the Censor', *19th Century Music*, ii (1978–9), 245–53; 'Editions of Boris Godunov', *Musorgsky: In Memoriam 1881–1981*, ed. M. H. Brown (Ann Arbor, 1982), 179–214; 'Mussorgsky's *Boris Godunov* and the Russian Imperial Theaters', *Liberal Arts Review*, vii (1979), 6–24]

M. Schandert: *Das Problem der originalen Instrumentation des 'Boris Godunow'* (Hamburg, 1979)

L'avant-scène opéra, nos.27–8 (1980) [*Boris Godunov* issue]

A. Csampai and D. Holland, eds.: *Modest Mussorgskij: Boris Godunov: Texte, Materialen, Kommentare* (Reinbek bei Hamburg, 1981)

D. Lloyd-Jones: 'Zum Schicksal der "Boris"-Komposition', *Modest Mussorgskij: Aspekte des Opernwerks*, ed. H.-K. Metzger and R. Riehn (Munich, 1981), 45–68

N. John, ed.: *Mussorgsky: Boris Godunov* (London, 1982) [ENO opera guide]

A. Orlova and M. Shneerson: 'After Pushkin and Karamzin: Researching the Sources for the Libretto of Boris Godunov', *Musorgsky: In Memoriam 1881–1981*, ed. M. H. Brown (Ann Arbor, 1982), 249–70

T. Shcherbakova: 'K luchshemu tekstu, kak k idealu ...' [Towards a Better Text, as Towards an Ideal], *SovM* (1982), no.2, pp.85–91 [review of Lloyd-Jones edn, 1975]

Ye. Levashov: 'Drama naroda i drama sovesti v opere "Boris Godunov"' [Drama of the People and Drama of Conscience in *Boris Godunov*], *SovM* (1983), no.5, pp.32–8

A. Men'kov: 'Zhizn' spektak'lya prodolzhayetsya', *SovM* (1983), no.5, pp.39–45

R. Taruskin: '"The Present in the Past": Russian Opera and Russian Historiography, ca. 1870', *Russian and Soviet Music: Essays for Boris Schwarz* (Ann Arbor, 1984), 77–146

——: 'Musorgsky *vs.* Musorgsky: the Versions of *Boris Godunov*', *19th Century Music*, viii (1984–5), 91–118, 245–72

C. Emerson: *Boris Godunov: Transpositions of a Russian Theme* (Bloomington and Indianapolis, 1986)

G. Golovinsky: 'O fol'klornïkh svyazakh "Borisa Godunova"' [On Folklore Associations in *Boris Godunov*], *SovM* (1986), no.3, pp.83–8

E. Nesterenko: 'Operedivshiy vremya' [Ahead of his Time], *SovM* (1989), no.3, pp.40–42

B. Pokrovsky: 'Narod bezmolvstvuyet?', [The People are Silent?] *Literaturnaya gazeta* (22 March 1989)

I. Belenkova: 'Printsipï dialoga v "Borise Godunove" Musorgskogo i ikh razvitiye v sovetskoy opere' [The Principles of the Dialogue in *Boris Godunov* and their Development in Soviet Opera], *M. P. Musorgsky i muzïka XX veka* [Musorgsky and 20th-Century Music], ed. G. L. Golovinsky (Moscow, 1990), 110–36

G. Isakhanov: 'Liki festival'nïkh "Borisov"' [Aspects of the Festival Production of *Boris*], *SovM* (1990), no.12, pp.39–46

A. Kandinsky: 'Tsena podlinnika' [The Worth of the Original], *SovM* (1990), no.8, pp.42–8

S. Korobkov: 'Venchaniye na tsarstvo' [The Coronation], *Muzïkal'naya zhizn'* (1990), no.14, pp.9–10

S. Rumyantsev: 'Podlinnost' istini: yeshchyo raz o "Borise Godunove"' [The Authenticity of Truth: Once More about *Boris Godunov*], *SovM* (1990), no.8, pp.49–52

Khovanshchina

V. Stasov: 'Po povodu postanovki "Khovanshchinï"' (pis'mo k redaktoru)' [Concerning the Production of *Khovanshchina*: a Letter to the Editor: orig. pubd 1886], *Stat'i o muzïke* [Essays on Music], ed. V. Protopov, iii (Moscow, 1977), 277–9

——: [3 short articles on the opera's early performance history], trans. R. Hoops, *Musorgsky: In Memoriam 1881–1981*, ed. M. H. Brown (Ann Arbor, 1982), 321–8

V. Karatïgin: '"Khovanshchina" i yeyo avtorï' [*Khovanshchina* and its Authors], *MS* (1917), nos.5–6, pp.192–218

S. Lopashov and others: *Musorgsky i ego 'Khovanshchina': sbornik statey* [Musorgsky and his *Khovanshchina*: a Collection of Essays] (Moscow, 1928)

B. Asaf'yev: 'V rabote nad "Khovanshchinoy"' [At work on *Khovanshchina*], *Izbrannïye trudï* [Selected Works], ed. T. N. Livanova and others, iii (Moscow, 1954), 160–67

M. Sokol'sky: 'Narod v "Khovanshchine" Musorgskogo' [The People in Musorgsky's *Khovanshchina*], *SovM* (1954), no.12, pp.61–72

B. Asaf'yev: 'Russkiy narod, russkiye lyudi' [Russian Nation, Russian People], *Izbrannïye trudï* [Selected Works], ed. T. N. Livanova and others, iv (Moscow, 1955), 118

A. Gozenpud: 'V bor'be za naslediye Musorgskogo' [In the Struggle for Musorgsky's Legacy], *SovM* (1956), no.3, pp.88–93

V. Gurevich: 'Shostakovich – redaktor "Khovanshchinï"' [Shostakovich as Editor of *Khovanshchina*], *Muzïka i sovremennost'* [Music and the Present Day], vii (Moscow, 1971), 29–68

S. Shlifshteyn: 'Otkuda zhe rassvet?' [Where is the dawn coming from?], *SovM* (1971), no.12, pp.109–13

V. Gurevich: 'Shostakovich v rabote nad "Khovanshchinoy"' [Shostakovich at Work on *Khovanshchina*], *Voprosï teorii i estetiki muzïki* [Questions of Music Theory and Aesthetics], xi (Leningrad, 1972), 84–108

A. Gozenpud: *Russkiy opernïy teatr XIX veka* [Russian Operatic Theatre in the 19th Century], iii (Leningrad, 1973), 96–118

K. Gräwe: 'Die "ungeordnete" Dramaturgie der "Chowanschtschina"', *Jb der Hamburgischen Staatsoper 1974–5*

E. Frid: *Proshedsheye, nastoyashcheye i budushcheye v 'Khovanshchine' Musorgskogo* [The Past, Present and Future in Musorgsky's *Khovanshchina*] (Leningrad, 1974)

G. Bakayeva: '*Khovanshchina*' M. P. Musorgskogo (Kiev, 1976)

A. Andreyev: 'Zametki o soderzhanii "Khovanshchinï"' [Notes on the Content of *Khovanshchina*], *SovM* (1977), no.3, pp.95–103

M. Baroni: 'Chovanščina', *Modest Musorgskij: Aspekte des Opernwerks*, ed. H.-K. Metzger and R. Riehn (Munich, 1981), 69–94

E. Frid: 'Osmïslennaya-opravdannaya melodiya' [Rationally Justified Melody], *M. P. Musorgsky: problemï tvorchestva* [Problems concerning his Works] (Leningrad, 1981), 116–24

R. Threlfall: 'The Stravinsky Version of *Khovanshchina*', *SMA*, xv (1981), 106–15

A. Vul'fson: 'K problemam tekstologii' [On Problems of Textual Criticism], *SovM* (1981), no.3, pp.103–10

G. Norris: 'An Opera Restored: Rimsky-Korsakov, Shostakovich and the Khovansky Business', *MT*, cxxiii (1982), 672–4

L'avant-scène opéra, nos.57–8 (1983) [*Khovanshchina* issue]

M. Rakhmanova: 'K 100-letiyu prem'yerï *Khovanshchinï*' [On the 100th Anniversary of the Première of *Khovanshchina*], *SovM* (1986), no.3, pp.88–96

Ya. Fain: 'Pravo na "Khovanshchinu"' [The Right to *Khovanshchina*], *SovM* (1987), no.8, pp.77–84

C. Emerson: 'Musorgsky's Libretti on Historical Themes: from the Two *Borises* to *Khovanshchina*', *Reading Opera*, ed. A. Groos and R. Parker (Princeton, 1988), 235–67

R. Sturua: '"Khovanshchina" – metafizika istorii?', *SovM* (1989), no.3, p.45

A. Volkov: 'Narod i tolpa: uroki "Khovanshchinï"' [Folk and Crowd: the Lessons of *Khovanshchina*], *Muzïkal'naya zhizn'* (1989), no.23, pp.19–21; no.24, pp.19–21

R. Taruskin: 'The Power of the Black Earth: Notes on *Khovanshchina*' (DG 429 758–2, 1990) [record notes]

I. Vershinina: 'Musorgsky i Stravinsky (o Dyagilevskoy postanovke "Khovanshchinï")' [Musorgsky and Stravinsky: on Dyagilev's Production of *Khovanshchina*], *M. P. Musorgsky i muzïka XX veka* [Musorgsky and 20th-Century Music], ed. G. L. Golovinsky (Moscow, 1990), 192–217

The Fair at Sorochintsï

P. Lamm: Preface to M. P. Musorgsky: *Polnoye sobraniye sochineniy* [Complete Works], iii (Moscow and Vienna, 1933); repr. as vol. v (New York, 1969), pp.v–xxvi [Russ. text repr. in M. Musorgsky: *Sorochinskaya yarmarka* (Moscow, 1970), 213–24]

S. Ginzburg: 'Sorochinskaya yarmarka', opera M. Musorgskogo (Moscow, 1935)

G. Abraham: '"The Fair of Sorochintsy" and Cherepnin's Completion of it', *On Russian Music* (London, 1939), 216–24

G. Tomasi: '*Der Jahrmarkt von Soročincy* und sein Beitrag zur Suche des spezifisch Russischen in der Musik', *Modest Musorgskij: Aspekte des Opernwerks*, ed. H.-K. Metzger and R. Riehn (Munich, 1981), 95–110

RICHARD TARUSKIN

Mussio, Emanuele. See MUZIO, EMANUELE.

Muti, Riccardo (*b* Naples, 28 July 1941). Italian conductor. After childhood music lessons he studied the piano at the Naples conservatory and philosophy at Naples University. At the conservatory his natural aptitude for conducting was discovered almost by chance. He spent the next five years at the Milan Conservatory, studying composition, and receiving tuition in conducting from Antonino Votto. Winning the Guido Cantelli International Conductors' Competition in 1967 at once launched his international career as an orchestral conductor, and his British début with the New Philharmonia led to a long and fruitful relationship with that orchestra, from 1973 as principal conductor and, later, as music director.

Opera began to feature prominently in Muti's work after 1969, when he was appointed principal conductor of the Maggio Musicale in Florence. In 1972 he conducted the first uncut performance of Rossini's *Guillaume Tell* there, and revived Meyerbeer's *L'Africaine* as well as such early Verdi operas as *Attila* and *I masnadieri*. In 1971 he made his début at the Salzburg Festival, and from then on, with the Vienna PO, he was regularly chosen to conduct opera there with the most celebrated international casts; latterly he has made a speciality of Mozart. During the 1970s he appeared in the great opera houses of Vienna, Munich and Paris, and at Covent Garden. He also recorded much opera, and his first recordings of Verdi with the New Philharmonia (later Philharmonia) – *Macbeth*, *Aida* and *Un ballo in maschera* – expanded his international reputation still further, establishing him as a fiery, intense interpreter of Italian opera. Consistently he went back to the original texts and, whether in Rossini, Donizetti, Bellini or Verdi, eliminated traditional performance practices not justified by the score.

As principal conductor and music director of the Philadelphia Orchestra (1980–92) Muti conducted each year much admired concert performances of opera, but when in 1986 he succeeded his rival Claudio Abbado as music director of La Scala, opera conducting became central in his career. He quickly put his mark on the work of that opera house, and continued his intensive series of opera recordings there, notably of Verdi. Though his preference for having performances recorded live often led to indifferent sound quality, the high-voltage electricity was never in doubt. As a conductor he has always been noted as a keen disciplinarian in an age of persuasion; he establishes his dominance with orchestras or singers through his ruthlessly analytical ear, while also drawing on a sharp sense of humour. At a period when Furtwängler's influence was paramount, his work has by contrast reflected the example of Toscanini.   EDWARD GREENFIELD

Muzika dlya zhivïkh ('Music for the Living'). Opera in two acts by GIYA ALEXANDROVICH KANCHELI to a libretto by Robert Sturua; Tbilisi, Paliashvili Theatre of Opera and Ballet, 28 April 1984.

The opera grew from the composer's long and intimate collaboration with the innovatory Georgian director Robert Sturua, for whose productions at the Rustaveli Dramatic Theatre – notably of Shakespeare's *King Lear* and *Richard III* – Kancheli provided the music. On a libretto in Sumerian, English, Italian, French and Georgian they fashioned a work on the essential vulnerability of beauty. Though controversial for its deliberate challenge to the musical and dramatic norms of traditional opera, its powerful message, delivered with stark imagery and ingenuous musical means, achieved a wide resonance.

Music for the Living is an allegorical contemplation of the physical and moral devastation wrought by war and violence. In an imaginary country during a period of bloody war, the young guide (treble) of a blind old man

(tenor) miraculously discovers a violin in a half-destroyed theatre. When the old man begins to play a simple diatonic melody, the boy is transfixed by the music and reverently repeats the melody to isolated Sumerian words and phrases. Other homeless children appear from the shadows and gradually join in the incantation. An officer-conductor (spoken) and a woman with a whip (a dancer) embody the evil antithesis of this scene. The officer attempts to compel an onstage band to play bombastic, military music, unceremoniously eliminating the musicians who fail to satisfy. The quiet, sad sound of the old man's violin proves more powerful than the officer's bullets, but the woman with the whip is able to find willing recruits among the children. To the strains of a grotesque waltz, women are forced to dance for the officer and are whipped into a frenzy. When the dance is over, children and mothers are reunited, but when the woman gives her whip to the young guide, he strikes the violin with all his might.

Much of Act 2 is devoted to 'Love and Duty', a play-within-the-play performed by an Italian opera company visiting an army hospital. Periodic bombardments interrupt the action, terrifying the performers, but they gain courage and resolve as the performance progresses. 'Love and Duty' is a stylized heroic-romantic piece sung primarily in Italian, with some French. Angelo (tenor), an Italian patriot, is dying of love for his sweetheart, Sylvana (soprano), who has married the Marquis de Prudhon (bass), Viceroy of Italy. Angelo's friend Sandro (tenor), a member of the Carbonari, arrives with the news that Sylvana is outside. Angelo threatens to kill her, but his mother, Lucia (soprano), and Sandro plead with him to hear her out. Sylvana arrives and the lovers are reunited; Sylvana reveals that her marriage to the Marquis was a patriotic sacrifice. The Marquis arrives, seeking revenge, but is himself killed by Angelo. Singing the praises of Italy, all the principals die. Only Lucia is left to mourn. As the players accept the applause, a bomb scores a direct hit. In the final section of the opera, sung in Georgian, the old man mourns the dead, who rise as if to continue the performance, speculating on the boundaries between real life and theatre. The officer and the woman with a whip are subdued by the crowd, and the chorus sings a paean to music.   LAUREL E. FAY

Muzio, Claudia [Muzzio, Claudina] (*b* Pavia, 7 Feb 1889; *d* Rome, 24 May 1936). Italian soprano. Her father was a stage director at Covent Garden and the Metropolitan, her mother a chorus singer. Among her teachers was Annetta Casaloni, Verdi's first Maddalena (*Rigoletto*), who probably helped her to obtain engagements at Turin in 1911 and 1914–15. She had made her début at Arezzo on 15 January 1910 in Massenet's *Manon*; her first appearance at La Scala, as Desdemona, was during the 1913–14 season. In the Covent Garden summer season of 1914 she attracted considerable attention in some of her best roles, including Desdemona, Margherita (*Mefistofele*), Tosca and Mimì (the two last with Caruso in the cast), but was never to return to that theatre. In the USA, however, she quickly became a much valued member, first of the Metropolitan company (début as Tosca, 1916), where she remained for seven consecutive seasons and reappeared briefly in 1934, and where she sang Giorgetta (*Il tabarro*) in the première of Puccini's *Trittico*; and subsequently of the Chicago company (début as Aida, 1922), to which she returned for nine seasons with only a single break. During this period she was also much in

Claudia Muzio in the title role of Puccini's 'Tosca'

demand in the principal South American houses; in Italy she made some notable appearances under Toscanini at La Scala in 1926–7 (*La traviata*, *Il trovatore*, *Tosca*), but thereafter sang mostly in Rome.

Muzio's extensive repertory embraced all the leading Verdi and Puccini roles, as well as those of the *verismo* school – which last, however, she interpreted in a more subtle and refined manner than was usual. Nobility and sweetness of voice and aspect, together with intense drama and pathos, were marked features of her style; good judges thought her one of the finest artists of her time. Although she made many recordings, few of them do her full justice. The early groups (1911, 1917–18, 1920–25) are marred by low technical standards; while in many of the technically excellent recordings made in 1934–5 her tone has lost much of its pristine freshness and steadiness. Among this last group, however, there are some unforgettable achievements, notably her infinitely pathetic reading of Germont's letter in the last act of *La traviata*.

For further illustration *see* TABARRO, IL.

GV (R. Celletti; R. Vegeto)
J. B. Richards: 'Claudia Muzio', *Record Collector*, xvii (1967–8), 197–237, 256–63 [with discography by H. M. Barnes]
G. Gualerzi: 'The Divine Claudia', *Opera*, xxxvii (1986), 643–51
DESMOND SHAWE-TAYLOR

Muzio [Mussio], (**Donnino**) **Emanuele** (*b* Zibello, Parma, 24 Aug 1821; *d* Paris, 27 Nov 1890). Italian conductor and composer. He studied literature, and music with Verdi's first teacher, Ferdinando Provesi. In 1844 he moved to Milan to study with Verdi and in 1847 assisted in preparing *Macbeth* for Florence and *I masnadieri* for London. He also made transcriptions and reductions for the publishers Ricordi and Lucca. In 1850 he conducted at the Théâtre du Cirque, Brussels, where his first opera, *Giovanna la pazza*, was performed in 1851. Returning to Italy, he had other works performed, but without great success. In 1858 he conducted at Her Majesty's Theatre, London, then toured in the USA, where in 1861 he introduced *Un ballo in*

maschera and announced a new opera of his own, *La scommessa* (it was never produced). He conducted in Havana in 1862 (and returned there for a season in 1878–9). At the end of 1866 he returned to Europe, having married the singer Lucy Simmons. Late in 1869 and in 1870 he conducted in Egypt and soon afterwards became conductor and adviser at the Théâtre Italien, Paris. He gave the first performances of *Aida* in the USA (1873) and the French première of *La forza del destino* (1876). He was later active as a singing teacher (he composed many songs), as well as a frequent collaborator of Verdi, who named him the executor of his will.

Giovanna la pazza (os, 3, L. Silva), Brussels, Cirque, 8 April 1851, I-Mr*, excerpts (Milan, 1851)
Claudia (dramma lirico, 1, G. Carcano, after G. Sand), Milan, Re, 7 Feb 1853, Mr*, vs (Milan, 1853)
Le due regine (melodramma, 3, G. Peruzzini), Milan, Cannobiana, 17 May 1856, sinfonia, arr. pf (Milan, 1855)
La sorrentina (dramma lirico, 4), Bologna, Comunale, 14 Nov 1857, Mr*, excerpts (Milan, 1858)

G. Ricordi: 'Emanuele Muzio', *Gazzetta musicale di Milano*, xlv (1890), 781
A. Belforti: *Emanuele Muzio, l'unico allievo di Giuseppe Verdi* (Fabriano, 1895)
L. A. Garibaldi: *Giuseppe Verdi nelle lettere di Emanuele Muzio ad Antonio Barezzi* (Milan, 1931)
T. G. Kaufman: 'Emanuele Muzio', *Verdi and his Major Contemporaries* (New York and London, 1990), 109–10
GUSTAVO MARCHESI

Muzio Scevola ('Mucius [Mutius] Scaevola'). Opera in three acts by FILIPPO AMADEI, GIOVANNI BONONCINI and GEORGE FRIDERIC HANDEL to a libretto by PAOLO ANTONIO ROLLI, adapted from SILVIO STAMPIGLIA's libretto as revised for Vienna (1710); London, King's Theatre, 15 April 1721.

Though operas set by a group of composers were not uncommon in Italy in the early 18th century, *Muzio Scevola* is the only example produced in London. It was the sixth opera promoted by the Royal Academy of Music and brings into fascinating juxtaposition the work of its two most important composers – Bononcini and Handel – as well as the slighter but competent Filippo Amadei. The parts of Mucius and Horatius were originally sung by the castratos Senesino and Berselli, Cloelia and Irene by Margherita Durastanti and Anastasia Robinson.

The opera was revived at the King's Theatre on 7 November 1722, with Fidalma's part cut and other changes. There was a production in Hamburg the following year, with a new prologue by Keiser. Handel's act had its first modern performance in Essen in 1928. A concert performance of all three acts was conducted by Denis Arnold at the Holywell Music Room, Oxford, on 23 November 1977. Chrysander's edition of Handel's Act 3 (Acts 1 and 2 remain unpublished) is unfortunately marred by omissions, including Fidalma's 'A chi vive', which gained contemporary popularity. *Muzio Scevola* needs to be performed and published whole.

Rolli's libretto takes certain events of 508 BC related in Livy's *History of Rome* (II.x, xii, xiii), all connected with the attempts of King Lars Porsena of Etruria to restore the expelled emperor Lucius Tarquinius to the Roman throne, and interweaves them with fictional love tangles. In Act 1 (by Amadei), Orazio [Horatius Cocles] (soprano) offers Porsena (bass) a pact on behalf of the Roman Senate provided Tarquinio [Tarquinius] (soprano castrato) remains in exile, but is defied. Porsena has promised his daughter Irene (alto) to

Tarquinius, much against her wishes; she, encouraged by her companion Fidalma (soprano), offers support and affection to Horatius. In Rome Mucius Scaevola (alto castrato) and his lover Clelia [Cloelia] (soprano) prepare for battle and lead an attack on the Tuscan army. Porsena engages in single combat with Cloelia, but refuses to continue the fight when he finds that she is a woman. The Romans are forced to retreat but Horatius holds the Sublicean bridge over the Tiber and escapes into the river as the bridge collapses. In Act 2 (by Bononcini), Mucius goes in disguise into the Tuscan camp in an attempt to kill Porsena, but wounds the wrong man. He puts his hand into the altar flame in punishment for his mistake, earning respect from Porsena and also his liberty. Porsena is further impressed by Cloelia and a troop of female warriors who come to rescue Mucius, and offers a truce to Rome if the women will be hostages for his safety. Handel's Act 3 begins with Porsena taking advantage of his earlier generosity towards Cloelia and Mucius: he asks Cloelia for her hand and compels Mucius to support him. Both men are invited by Cloelia to the banks of the Tiber to bear witness to her Roman valour. She declares she will go to Rome or to death and plunges with her companions into the river. Mucius assures Porsena that he will be welcomed in Rome and that Cloelia will be his. In Rome, Tarquinius attempts to take Irene by force but is prevented by Horatius. At the Capitol Cloelia declares herself honour-bound to marry Porsena but, not to be outdone in generosity, Porsena returns her to Mucius. Tarquinius's flight is reported. Porsena vows hatred to him and his descendants and allows Irene to choose Horatius as her husband.

*   *   *

Each act has its own overture (Amadei's an Italian sinfonia, the others in the French style, Bononcini's being taken from his *Il fiore delle eroine* of 1704). Burney believed that the use of three composers was a 'premeditated plan, to try their several abilities'; whether or not this was so, the music gives the impression that each composer was on his mettle, well aware that comparisons would be made. Amadei's act is weakened by some superficially brilliant arias on common-chord themes, though there is a charming siciliano for Irene and the act ends with an effective accompanied recitative for Horatius as he leaps into the Tiber. In Bononcini's act (not related to his *Muzio Scevola* of 1695 and its later derivatives) are several good arias in his tender style, with a fine F minor lament for Mucius ('Tormento fiero'). But Handel's contribution predictably outshines his rivals', with a parade of arias, duets and accompanied recitatives in his richest vein. The characters of the warrior maiden Cloelia and the more reflective Irene are well brought out in the music, the latter's 'Ah dolce nome' being especially moving. As drama the opera suffers both from the diffuseness and occasional absurdities of Rolli's libretto, and from the ineffectual characterization of Tarquinius (who has no arias), but the listener's interest is consistently held as the quality of the music increases act by act.   ANTHONY HICKS

Myers, Raymond (*b* Sydney, 1 July 1938). Australian baritone. After study in Sydney he made his début in 1963 with the Elizabethan Trust Opera Company (now Australian Opera) as Don Fernando in *Fidelio*, proceeding to further studies with Luigi Ricci in Rome. He sang Napoleon in *War and Peace* with the ENO (1972) and

in the opening production of the Sydney Opera House (1973); he was esteemed as Rigoletto and Amonasro and as a persuasively menacing Dr Miracle. His particularly effective portrayal of Wozzeck, balanced between diligent obtuseness and moments of expressionist frenzy, was unfortunately restricted to Adelaide Festival performances (1976) and an ABC television broadcast. He has made guest appearances in London, New York and Brussels, and at Glyndebourne and La Scala.   ROGER COVELL

Myortvïye dushi ('Dead Souls'). Operatic scenes in three acts by RODION KONSTANTINOVICH SHCHEDRIN to his own libretto after the epic novel by NIKOLAY VASIL'YEVICH GOGOL; Moscow, Bol'shoy Theatre, 7 June 1977.

Pavel Ivanovich Chichikov		baritone
Nozdryov		tenor
Korobochka		mezzo-soprano
Sobakevich	*landowners*	bass
Plyushkin		mezzo-soprano/tenor
Manilov		tenor
Mizhuyev		bass
Selifan *Chichikov's coachman*		tenor in folk style
Peasant with a Goat		bass
Bearded Peasant		bass
Two Female Soloists		mezzo-soprano, contralto in folk style
Lament of the Soldier's Wife		mezzo-soprano
Anna Grigor'yevna *a lady pleasant in all respects*		soprano
Sof'ya Ivanovna *a simply pleasant lady*		soprano
The Governor		bass
The Governor's Wife		contralto
The Governor's Daughter		ballerina
The Procurator		bass-baritone
The Chief of Police		bass-baritone
The Postmaster		tenor
The President of the Chamber of Commerce		tenor
Lizan'ka Manilova		soprano
The Priest		tenor
The Police Captain		bass/bass-baritone
Sïsoy Pafnut'yevich		tenor
MacDonald Karlovich		bass
Pavlushka	*Nozdrev's house serfs*	tenor
Porfiriy		bass
Petrushka *Chichikov's footman*		mime

Landowners, civil servants, guests at the ball, portraits on the walls, footmen, servants, coachmen

Setting Central Russia in the first half of the 19th century

Shchedrin worked on his opera for ten years, completing it in 1976. In adapting Gogol's classic novel-poem, which tells the uniquely Russian story of a man who attempts to gain wealth by purchasing the 'souls' of dead serfs and exploiting a tax loophole, he remained faithful to the original in his portrayal of the principal characters' idiosyncrasies of language and behaviour. Following in the tradition of the Gogol settings of Musorgsky and Shostakovich, Shchedrin attempted in *Dead Souls* to find the inevitable musical interpretation of the spoken intonations and rhythms. Each of the main characters sings a defining 'portrait-aria' and is further identified with a particular instrumental tone colour. The exception is the mysterious hero Chichikov, who adapts himself, chameleon-like, to the characteristics of each companion.

The opera is constructed on two parallel planes: the scenes which develop Chichikov's adventures alternate with episodes conveying the timeless rituals and tragedies of rural peasant life played out against the endlessly unfolding road. The contrast was an attempt by the composer to interpret and amplify the symbolic significance of Gogol's novel. One of the more unusual features of the scoring is the substitution of a small mixed chorus for violins. In 1984 Shchedrin was awarded the Lenin Prize for *Dead Souls*, the choral poem *The Execution of Pugachyov* and the Festive Overture.

ACT 1.i (Introduction) Sung by two female folk soloists and the orchestral chorus with a tragic remoteness, the lament 'Ne belï, belï snegi' ('It is not the white snows') becomes an important element in the musical structure of the opera as well as embodying the virtues of simple peasant life and the boundless expanse of Russia. While the text is traditional, the music is original (indeed, nowhere in the opera does Shchedrin quote from other sources); nevertheless, its folk roots – the lament is specifically modelled on traditional coachmen's songs – are unmistakable.

1.ii ('Lunch at the Procurator's') Having arrived in a provincial city, Chichikov is honoured at a banquet of landowners and civil servants. Between repeated toasts, 'Vivat! Pavel Ivanovich', and protestations of undying affection, the participants ply their guest with prodigious amounts of food and drink, each introducing at the same time the specific manner of singing and accompanying musical colour which will be associated with his character.

1.iii ('The Road') With the folk lament as backdrop, Selifan drives his master to Manilov's estate.

1.iv ('Manilov') Manilov and his wife greet Chichikov with obsequious warmth. Accompanied by a solo flute, Manilov in his portrait-arioso 'O, Pavel Ivanovich' – a sentimental parody of bel canto style – declares in fawning phrases that he would give half his fortune for a few of his guest's virtues. Chichikov steers the conversation to his proposal to purchase dead serfs, which is initially met with incomprehension by his host. Chichikov manages to soothe his misgivings, and in the final trio husband and wife fantasize about ideal friendship as Chichikov adopts a heroic pose. As the scene ends, the portraits of Manilov's relatives apprehensively mutter the phrase 'dead souls'.

1.v ('The Bumpy Road') Chichikov and Selifan are caught in a storm. The roughness of the road is reflected in the music as the master berates his long-suffering coachman, while the folk chorus sings a prayer to Elijah to bear the storm away.

1.vi ('Korobochka') Characterized by a solo bassoon, in her portrait-aria 'Oy, batyushka, beda' ('O sir, misfortune') Korobochka bemoans the bad times and the death of 18 serfs. Assuming a consolatory tone, Chichikov offers to buy them from her; the old woman drives a surprisingly hard bargain in a lively exchange. After Chichikov has departed, Korobochka, resuming the plaintive tone of her portrait-aria, decides to check the going rate for dead souls.

1.vii ('Songs') In an interlude, the folk soloists sing an anguished lament 'Tï, polïn', polïnechka, trava' ('You wormwood plant') interwoven with phrases of two other songs in the chorus.

1.viii ('Nozdryov') Nozdryov is characterized by the french horn, and in his portrait-aria he boasts about his property, gambling losses and drunken feats, concluding boisterously by confessing his affection for Chichikov. Chichikov is drawn reluctantly into a game of draughts as he bargains for his host's dead serfs. Nozdryov is caught cheating, and fighting breaks out. The pandemonium intensifies in the concluding septet as the servants are summoned and the sleeping Mizhuyev wakes. The Police Captain arrests Nozdryov for beating another landowner.

ACT 2.ix ('Sobakevich') Sobakevich's personality is captured by double basses and contrabassoon as well as by the obstinate accompaniment of his portrait-aria, in which he rails against all swindlers. He then demands 100 rubles per 'soul' and proves a stubborn negotiator. When Chichikov reminds him that the serfs are after all, dead, Sobakevich reluctantly accepts a price of two rubles apiece.

2.x ('The Coachman Selifan') Against the familiar backdrop of choral folk singing, Selifan muses on the eternal predicament of the Russian peasantry.

2.xi ('Plyushkin') Projected through the timbre of the oboe and with a monotonous vocal line inflected by wide falsetto leaps, the miserly Plyushkin is reluctant to welcome Chichikov – 'Ya davnen'ko ne vizhu gostey' ('It's a long time since I've seen guests') – until he understands that he will not have to feed him. He complains of all the serfs who have died in the epidemic; out of 'compassion' Chichikov offers to buy them. Taking him for a fool, Plyushkin hastens to complete the deal.

2.xii ('Lament of the Soldier's Wife') Against sustained choral harmonies, a peasant woman bitterly laments the conscription of her son.

2.xiii ('The Governor's Ball') The guests speculate as to Chichikov's reasons for buying so many peasants and make inflated estimates of his merits and wealth. In a triumphal aria, 'Tsel' cheloveka vsyo yeshchyo ne opredelena' ('Man's goal is still not determined'), Chichikov expounds his commercial philosophy. The guests resolve to marry him to the Governor's daughter; the courtship is portrayed in the pantomime 'Love'. Nozdryov bursts in to reveal the true nature of Chichikov's dealings, and Korobochka's request for the going price of dead souls sends the gathering into confusion in the act's concluding ensemble.

ACT 3.xiv ('Chant') The folk soloists repeat 'It is not the white snows'.

3.xv ('Chichikov') Chichikov curses all those who waste their money organizing balls in his aria, 'Chtob vas chyort pobral vsekh' ('May the devil take you all').

3.xvi ('Two Ladies') Anna Grigor'yevna discusses the latest fashions with Sof'ya Ivanovna. When the gossip, against a 'busy' instrumental background, turns inevitably to Chichikov, Anna Grigor'yevna reveals that his real purpose was to abduct the Governor's daughter; both women lambast her character.

3.xvii ('Rumours in the Town') The phrase 'Chto za pritcha' ('What an extraordinary thing') serves as a unifying device in a rhythmic 16-part ensemble as the townspeople try to comprehend the situation. The landowners' stories only confuse the issue. In a pantomime ('Disaster') Chichikov is refused admission to the homes of the town's dignitaries. Speculation about his identity becomes increasingly far-fetched, and panic continues to mount until the Procurator drops dead.

3.xviii ('The Procurator's Funeral') Against the background of traditional funeral chanting, the Governor wonders why the Procurator lived and died, and Chichikov repeats his curse from scene xv.

3.xix ('Scene and Finale') Nozdryov tells Chichikov that the people now take him for a spy or thief and upbraids him for planning to abduct the Governor's daughter. To make his escape, Chichikov calls Selifan. Against a reprise of 'It is not the white snows' the coachman coaxes his horses. Two peasants conclude, after debating the state of the wheels, that the carriage will not take Chichikov far.   LAUREL E. FAY

Mysliveček [Mysliweczek, Mislivecek], **Josef** (*b* Prague, 9 March 1737; *d* Rome, 4 Feb 1781). Czech composer. The son of a prosperous miller (and elder of identical twins), he was apprenticed as a miller a few years after his father's death in 1749, and achieved the rank of master miller in 1761. As a youth, he demonstrated outstanding aptitude in music and mathematics, and his success as a composer of instrumental music in Prague during the early 1760s encouraged him to seek greater prestige as a composer of opera. In 1763 he abandoned the trade of miller and departed for Italy, where he may have received instruction in operatic composition from Pescetti in Venice.

Although it has often been stated that Mysliveček's first opera was performed in Parma, no record of such a work has ever been uncovered; reports of a *Medea* performed there in 1764 are almost certainly false. His earliest opera, it seems, was a *Semiramide* performed in Bergamo in 1765 and Alessandria in 1766. Librettos for these productions confirm that he was already called 'Il boemo' by Italians, who had difficulty pronouncing his name. (There is no evidence that he was referred to as 'Il divino boemo' during his lifetime or that the Italian equivalent of his surname, 'Venatorini', was in common use.)

Mysliveček first achieved great operatic success in 1767, when his *Bellerofonte* was performed at the S Carlo in Naples with a distinguished cast including Anton Raaff and Caterina Gabrielli (*see* BELLEROPHON). Raaff soon became his close friend, but there is no documentation to support reports that he entered into a love affair with Gabrielli or had previously been involved romantically with the singer Lucrezia Aguiari. The success of *Bellerofonte* led to commissions from all the leading operatic centres in Italy, including eight additional productions for S Carlo. Among the honours accorded the composer in Italy was admission to the Accademia Filarmonica in Bologna in 1771, after he had befriended Padre Martini. While in Bologna for a production of his *Nitteti*, in spring 1770, Mysliveček met W. A. Mozart for the first time; from then until 1778 Mysliveček's name is often mentioned in the correspondence of Mozart and his father, and he is known to have met the Mozarts in the course of their three trips to Italy in 1770–73. Besides expressing admiration for his music, the young Mozart made mention in his letters of Mysliveček's cheerful disposition and his reputation for sexual promiscuity.

Outside Italy, Mysliveček is known to have made a triumphant return to Prague in 1768, but attempts to create interest in his works in Vienna in 1772 (when he met Burney) and Munich in 1773 led only to disappointment. In 1777, however, he was invited to return to Munich by the Elector of Bavaria, who sponsored a production of his *Ezio* which was well received. While in Munich, Mysliveček sought treatment for venereal disease that resulted in his nose being burnt off. Mozart visited him in a Munich hospital in the autumn of 1777 and reported to his father that he still retained his dynamic personality ('full of fire, spirit and life') in spite of this ghastly disfigurement. Relations with Mozart appear to have come to an end in 1778 when it became clear that Mysliveček could not fulfil a boastful promise to secure him an operatic commission in Naples. On his return to Italy, Mysliveček was still able to mount successful productions at S Carlo, but a production of *Armida* in Milan during Carnival 1780 was reported by Gerber to have been a disaster. From Milan he travelled to Rome, where he died in squalor, his enormous earnings as a musician long since squandered. The expenses for his burial in the church of S Lorenzo in Lucina were paid by an Englishman named Barry, formerly his pupil.

As a composer of opera, Mysliveček confined himself strictly to *opera seria*. His works are dominated by elaborate da capo arias alternating with simple recitative, but he was capable of writing effective accompanied recitative as well as beautiful choruses and ensembles. His arias, many of which are of fine musical quality, exhibit a wealth of melodic invention, pleasing textural variety and skilful techniques of phrase extension. Besides winning acclaim for his operas, he was an eminent composer of oratorios and instrumental music. The close resemblance of his melodic style to Mozart's has been a source of comment by many scholars, but a full appraisal of the significance of his connection with Mozart and the extent of his participation in the stylistic changes that swept *opera seria* of the 1760s and 70s has yet to be undertaken.

all opere serie

Semiramide (P. Metastasio), Bergamo, Fiera, 1765, *P-La*

Il Bellerofonte (3, G. Bonechi), Naples, S Carlo, 20 Jan 1767, *D-Dlb*, *F-Pn* (dated 1769), *I-Fc*, *P-La*

Farnace (3, A. Zeno), Naples, S Carlo, 4 Nov 1767, *D-Mbs*, *H-Bn*, *I-Nc*, *P-La*

Il trionfo di Clelia (3, Metastasio), Turin, Regio, 26 Dec 1767, *I-Fc*, *Tf* (dated 1768), *P-La*

Il Demofoonte [1st version] (3, Metastasio), Venice, S Benedetto, Jan 1769, *I-Vnm*, *P-La*, *US-Wc*

L'Ipermestra (3, Metastasio), Florence, Pergola, 28 March 1769, *A-Wn*, *I-Fc*, *P-La*

La Nitteti (3, Metastasio), Bologna, Comunale, spr. 1770, *I-Fc*, *P-La*, *RU-SPit*

Motezuma (3, V. A. Cigna-Santi), Florence, Pergola, 23 Jan 1771, *A-Wgm*, *I-Fc*, *P-La* (Acts 2 and 3)

Il gran Tamerlano (3, A. Piovene), Milan, Regio Ducal, 26 Dec 1771, *A-Wn*, *F-Pn*, *I-Fc*, *P-La* (Acts 1 and 3)

Il Demetrio [1st version] (3, Metastasio), Pavia, Nuovo, 25 Jan 1773, *D-Bds*, *I-Fc*, *P-La*

Romolo ed Ersilia (3, Metastasio), Naples, S Carlo, 13 Aug 1773, *A-Wgm*, *I-Fc*, *Nc*, *P-La*

La clemenza di Tito (3, Metastasio), Venice, S Benedetto, 26 Dec 1773, *La*

Erifile, Munich, 1773

Antigona (3, G. Roccaforte), Turin, Regio, carn. 1774, *A-Wn*

Atide (3, T. Stanzani), Padua, Nuovo, June 1774, *Wn*, *I-Pi(l)*

Artaserse (3, Metastasio), Naples, S Carlo, 13 Aug 1774, *I-Fc*, *Nc*

Il Demofoonte [2nd version] (3, Metastasio), Naples, S Carlo, 20 Jan 1775, *A-Wn*, *I-Fc*, *Nc*, *Vsm*, *P-La*

Ezio (3, Metastasio), Naples, S Carlo, 5 June 1775, *A-Wn*, *D-Hs*, *Mbs* (dated 1777), *I-Nc*, *P-La*

Adriano in Siria (3, Metastasio), Florence, Cocomero, aut. 1776, *I-Fc*

La Calliroe (2, M. Verazi), Naples, S Carlo, 30 May 1778, *Nc*, *P-La*

541

L'olimpiade (3, Metastasio), Naples, S Carlo, 4 Nov 1778, *I-Nc*, *P-La*

La Circe (3, D. Perelli), Venice, S Benedetto, May 1779

Il Demetrio [2nd version] (2, Metastasio), Naples, S Carlo, 13 Aug 1779, *D-Bds*, *I-Nc*, *P-La*

Armida (3, G. Migliavacca, after P. Quinault), ? Lucca, Pubblico, 15 Aug 1778; Milan, Scala, 26 Dec 1779, *F-Pn*, *P-La*

Medonte (3, G. De Gamerra), Rome, Argentina, Jan 1780, *F-Pn*, *RU-SPtob*

Antigono (3, Metastasio), Rome, Alibert, April 1780, arias in *I-BGc* and *Rc*, sinfonia *MAav*

Doubtful or spurious: Medea, Parma, Ducale, 1764; Achille in Sciro, Naples, 1775; Merope, Naples, 1775

*

BurneyGN; GerberL; Grove 6 (D. DiChiera)

F. M. Pelcl: *Abbildungen böhmischer und mährischer Gelehrter und Künstler*, iv (Prague, 1782), 189–92

H. Wilkemann: *Joseph Mysliweczek als Opernkomponist* (diss., U. of Vienna, 1915)

A. Hnilička: *Portréty starých českých mistrů hudebních* [Portraits of the Masters of Early Czech Music] (Prague, 1922), 57–63

J. Čeleda: *Josef Myslivecek, tvůrce pražského nářečí hudebního rokoka tereziánského* [Josef Myslivecek, Creator of the Prague Dialect of the Theresian Musical Rococo] (Prague, 1946)

S. Špatová-Ramešová: *Il divino Boemo* (Prague, 1957)

I. Stolařík: *Leningradský rukopis opery Josefa Myslivečka 'Nittetti'* [The Leningrad MS of Mysliveček's Opera *Nitteti*] (Opava, 1963)

M. Shaginian: *Voskreseniye iz myortvïkh* [Resurrection from the Dead] (Moscow, 1964; Cz. trans., 1965)

R. Pečman: 'Zur Leningrader Handschrift der letzten Oper Josef Myslivečeks', *Sborník prací filosofické fakulty brněnské university*, H1 (1966), 121–34

——: *Josef Mysliveček und sein Opernepilog* (Brno, 1970) [with extensive bibliography and list of sources]

——: 'Pietro Metastasio jako libretista Myslivečkových oper', *Otázky divadla a filmu: theatralia et cinematographica*, ii, ed. A. Závodský (Brno, 1970)

M. F. Robinson: *Naples and Neapolitan Opera* (Oxford, 1972)

C. H. Mahling: 'Mysliveček und Grétry – Vorbilder Mozarts?', *Die frühdeutsche Oper und ihre Beziehungen zu Italien, England und Frankreich: Mozart und die Oper seiner Zeit: Hamburg 1978*, 203–9

R. Pečman: *Josef Myslíveček* (Prague, 1981)

D. della Porta: *Josef Myslíveček: profilo biografico-critico* (Rome, 1981)

S. Bohadlo: *Josef Myslíveček v dopisech* [Josef Myslíveček in Letters] (Brno, 1988)

——: 'Josef Myslíveček, Called Il Boemo, in the Light of New Sources', *Music News from Prague*, ii/3 (1988), 4–6

DANIEL FREEMAN (work-list with MARITA P. McCLYMONDS)

Myszuga, Aleksander [Mishuga, Ołeksandr; Myshuga, Olexander] (*b* Nowy Witków, nr Lwów, 7 June 1853; *d* nr Freiburg, 9 March 1922). Polish tenor of Ukrainian descent. After making his début in Moniuszko's *The Haunted Manor* (1880, Lwów), he studied with Bruni in Milan and with Sbriglia in Paris. In Italy he used the stage name 'Filippi'; he also sang in Lwów, at the Wielki Theatre in Warsaw (1884–92), five times in Vienna, and in Prague (1887, 1900), Paris (1892), St Petersburg (1903) and many times in Kiev. His voice, with a register extending to *c″*, was well suited to lyrical parts, but he also sang dramatic roles, notably in *Les Huguenots* and *Aida*, and was highly successful in Moniuszko's *Halka*. Myszuga had been a disciple of Walery Wysocki in Lwów and upheld Wysocki's pedagogical methods as a teacher in Kiev (1905–11) and Warsaw (1911–14); in 1918 he founded a music school in Stockholm.

*

O. Łada: 'Aleksander Myszuga', *Ruch muzyczny*, x/9 (1966), 11–12

M. Golovashchenko, ed.: *Olexander Myshuga: spogady, materialy, lysty* [Memories, Materials, Letters] (Kiev, 1971)

IRENA PONIATOWSKA

N

Nabokov, Nicolas [Nikolay Dmitriyevich] (*b* nr Lubcha, Novogrudok district, 4/17 April 1903; *d* New York, 6 April 1978). American composer of Russian birth. He studied with Rebikov in Yalta and with Paul Juon and Busoni in Berlin before moving to Paris and receiving, thanks in part to Stravinsky's endorsement, an auspicious ballet commission from Dyagilev (*Ode*, 1928). In the USA from 1933 (naturalized 1939), Nabokov held a number of academic and bureaucratic positions (the latter with the American Military Government in Berlin and with the Voice of America) before moving full-time into international artistic promotion and politics, first as secretary-general of the Congress for Cultural Freedom (1951–61), finally as director of the Berlin Music Festival (1963–8) and cultural adviser to the mayor, Willy Brandt. He was responsible for arranging a number of important Stravinsky premières, including that of *The Rake's Progress* in 1951 at the Venice Biennale. His last official position was as composer-in-residence to the Aspen Institute for Humanistic Studies (1970–73).

Nabokov's two operas belong to the later phases of his career. The first, *The Holy Devil*, to a libretto by Stephen Spender, is a heavily romanticized treatment, suggested by Menotti, of the career and the murder of Grigory Rasputin, the Siberian monk who exercised great influence over the Russian royal family in the years immediately preceding the Revolution. Commissioned in 1954 by the Louisville Orchestra, it was performed (in two acts) by the Kentucky Opera Association under Moritz Bomhard on 16 April 1958. Over the next year Nabokov expanded the opera by interpolating an act between the two original ones and reorchestrating the whole; in this form it received its première in Cologne under the title *Der Tod des Grigori Rasputin* on 27 November 1959, Joseph Rosenstock conducting. It was published as *Rasputin's End* (Paris, 1959). The opera is an effective study in Musorgskian dialogue set against a background of traditional and popular musics of the period, including that of the Orthodox liturgy. Its expressionistic tone belies expectations based on the composer's close association with, and many perceptive writings on, the 'neo-classical' Stravinsky.

Love's Labor's Lost, Nabokov's second opera, was commissioned by the Deutsche Oper, Berlin, and composed in 1970–71 to a libretto after Shakespeare's comedy by W. H. Auden and Chester Kallman, the team that had produced the text of *The Rake's Progress*. The music is cast in an eclectic parody style the composer called 'persiflage', sending up *Tristan* and Beethoven's Fifth Symphony in Berowne's love aria, Weill and Eisler in the 'Discourse About Love', American crooning in Moth's songs, Glinka and Musorgsky for the 'Muscovite' masquerade, and catches and madrigals *passim*. The first performance was given by the Deutsche Oper during a visiting tour at the Théâtre de la Monnaie, Brussels, on 7 February 1973 (vocal score, Berlin and Wiesbaden, 1973).

EwenD

N. Nabokov: *Bagázh: Memoirs of a Russian Cosmopolitan* (New York, 1975)

R. H. Kornick: *Recent American Opera: a Production Guide* (New York, 1991), 212–14   RICHARD TARUSKIN

Nabucco [Nabucodonosor]. *Dramma lirico* in four parts by GIUSEPPE VERDI to a libretto by TEMISTOCLE SOLERA after Antonio Cortesi's ballet *Nabuccodonosor* and Auguste Anicet-Bourgeois' and Francis Cornu's play *Nabuchodonosor*; Milan, Teatro alla Scala, 9 March 1842.

Nabucodonosor [Nabucco; Nebuchadnezzar] *King of Babylon*	baritone
Ismaele *nephew of Sedecia, King of Jerusalem*	tenor
Zaccaria *High Priest of the Hebrews*	bass
Abigaille *slave, presumed to be the first daughter of Nabucodonosor*	soprano
Fenena *daughter of Nabucodonosor*	soprano
The High Priest of Baal	bass
Abdallo *elderly officer of the King of Babylon*	tenor
Anna *Zaccaria's sister*	soprano

Babylonian and Hebrew soldiers, Levites, Hebrew virgins, Babylonian women, magi, Lords of the Kingdom of Babylon, populace etc.

Setting Jerusalem and Babylon, 587 BC

The story of *Nabucco* began some 18 months before its first performance, soon after the successful première of Verdi's first opera, *Oberto, conte di San Bonifacio*. A contract was drawn up between Verdi and Bartolomeo Merelli, impresario at La Scala, according to which Verdi would write three further operas. The first of these, the comic work *Un giorno di regno*, was a disastrous failure and (at least according to Verdi's own later memories) the humiliation of public rejection caused the composer to give up his professional calling. However, in the winter of 1840–41, Merelli persuaded Verdi to take on Temistocle Solera's libretto of *Nabucco*, which had been turned down by the young Prussian composer Otto Nicolai.

The background of *Nabucco* (or *Nabucodonosor* as it was originally called) derives from biblical sources, most extensively from *Jeremiah*; and although Nabucco (Nebuchadnezzar) is the only biblical character to appear, the part of the prophet Zaccaria has strong overtones of Jeremiah. Solera's main source was a French play, first performed in 1836, although some of his alterations can be traced to the scenario of a ballet also derived from the play, given at La Scala in 1838. The lack of documentation concerning the genesis of the opera can be put down to a number of factors: Verdi was relatively unknown at the time, and few of his letters were preserved; he and Solera were together in Milan, and had little need of correspondence; and Solera – unlike some of Verdi's future librettists – was an experienced man of the theatre who apparently needed little help in constructing a dramatically convincing text.

After a number of delays, *Nabucco* was first performed at La Scala in March 1842, with a cast that included Prosper Dérivis (Zaccaria), Giuseppina Strepponi (Abigaille) and Giorgio Ronconi (Nabucco). Strepponi was in poor voice (and her final scene was cut after two performances), but the opera was nevertheless a great success. It was revived at La Scala for the autumn season of 1842 and ran for a record 57 performances. For this revival Verdi made a number of small changes to suit the new Abigaille, Teresa De Giuli Borsi, and added some *puntature* to Fenena's preghiera in Part 4. For a Venice revival in the Carnival season 1842–3, he replaced this preghiera with a *romanza* for Fenena. It seems that Verdi wrote ballet music for a revival of *Nabucco* in Brussels in 1848, although no trace of it has survived.

The overture, except for the chorale-like opening, is made up of themes from the opera: the main, recurring idea is from the 'Maledetto' chorus in Part 2; there is also a compound-time, pastoral version of 'Va pensiero' and several more martial inspirations.

PART 1: 'Jerusalem'
Inside the temple of Solomon The Babylonian army has reached Jerusalem and is at the gates of the temple. The Israelites lament their fate, but the prophet Zaccaria rallies them: he has as a hostage Fenena, daughter of Nabucco, the Babylonian king, and God will assist them. The people follow Zaccaria into battle. The two numbers that encompass this action are linked and in many ways comprise a single unit. The opening chorus, 'Gli arredi festivi', is fashioned on a large scale and draws its effect from the juxtaposition of contrasting blocks: a terrified populace, a group of praying Levites, another of supplicant virgins. Zaccaria's response is set in the usual cavatina form of a double aria. The Andante, 'D'Egitto là sui lidi', has an unusual two-stanza structure in which the opening of the second stanza is sustained by unison chorus. The cabaletta, 'Come notte al sol fulgente', also features a unison choral interruption, this time even earlier in the lyric form.

The stage clears, leaving Fenena and Ismaele alone. We learn in recitative that Ismaele and Fenena fell in love while Ismaele was imprisoned in Babylon, and that Fenena has helped him escape to Israel. They are interrupted by Abigaille, who has stolen into the temple at the head of a band of disguised Assyrian warriors. She had also fallen in love with Ismaele during his captivity and now taunts him with her victory. The accompanied recitative that introduces Abigaille immediately fixes her unusual vocal character, which requires power in the lower register, agility above the staff and a forceful dramatic presence throughout. The ensuing terzetto, 'Io t'amava', is a moment of lyrical relaxation graced with much vocal ornamentation, somewhat out of character with the rest of the score.

The finale of Part 1 begins with a pseudo-fugal chorus, 'Lo vedeste?', as the Israelites panic in defeat. Nabucco arrives on horseback to the triumphant strains of a *banda* march, but Zaccaria threatens to kill Fenena if Nabucco profanes the temple. This tableau precipitates the central, static moment of the finale, 'Tremin gl'insani', which is led off by Nabucco and which characterizes by turn the conflicting attitudes of the principals. When the stage action resumes Ismaele, fearful for Fenena, disarms Zaccaria. Nabucco is now free to act and, in a furious stretta, orders the destruction of the temple.

PART 2: 'The Impious One'
2.i *The royal apartments in Babylon* The act opens with a full-scale double aria for Abigaille. After an intense recitative her thoughts turn to Ismaele in the Andante 'Anch'io dischiuso un giorno'. The aria is highly ornamental, with each two-bar phrase rounded by a vocal flourish; but the ornaments, typically for Verdi, are held within a strict periodic structure, giving their proliferation at the climax a compelling energy. The High Priest of Baal arrives with news that Fenena has freed the Israelites; urged on by a warlike chorus, Abigaille decides to assume power herself. Her cabaletta, 'Salgo già del trono aurato', returns to the forceful tone of the recitative and, although in a far more dynamic context, again succeeds in wedding ornamental gestures to a rigorously controlled periodic structure.

2.ii *A room in the palace, giving on to other rooms* Zaccaria's recitativo and preghiera, 'Vieni o Levita', is an oasis of calm in this generally hectic opera, its accompaniment of six solo cellos deployed with great variety of texture. As Zaccaria leaves by one door, Ismaele arrives by another, only to be shunned by the Levites in the chorus 'Il maledetto'. Then follows another grand finale, similar in its opening sections to that of the first part. Abigaille is declared queen and is about to crown herself when Nabucco, who was believed dead, reappears to snatch the crown for himself. This precipitates the centrepiece of the finale, 'S'appressan gl'istanti', a quasi-canonic movement that gains its effect not from individual characterization (each of the principals sings the same melody) but from an inexorable increase in textural complexity and sonic power. Nabucco then faces the crowd and declares himself not only their king but their God. A thunderbolt strikes him down for this blasphemy and the crowd murmurs in shocked response. Italian operatic convention would now suggest a fast concluding movement, but instead Solera and Verdi decided on a mad scene for Nabucco during which his discourse distractedly moves

Autograph manuscript of Verdi's 'Nabucco', showing part of the unaccompanied chorus 'Immenso Jeovha' from Part 4

between fast and slow tempos before he faints. A triumphant cry from Abigaille brings down the curtain.

PART 3: 'The Prophecy'

3.i *The hanging gardens of Babylon* The routinely cheerful opening chorus, complete with *banda* interpolations borrowed from Part 1 ('E l'Assiria una regina'), is in its orchestration perhaps an early Verdian effort at depicting *couleur locale*. It leads to one of the opera's best numbers: the Abigaille-Nabucco duet, in which Abigaille dupes her father into signing Fenena's death sentence. After an opening recitative, the duet unfolds in the traditional four-movement pattern. A fast-paced dialogue movement ('Donna, chi sei?'), in which repeated orchestral motifs supply the continuity, leads to a movement of lyrical repose in which the characters develop their opposing attitudes in greater detail ('Oh di qual'onta aggravasi'). The third movement reimposes the outside world, as offstage trumpets announce the death sentence; and then in the final cabaletta ('Deh perdona') Nabucco and Abigaille restate their fixed positions: he begging her to show mercy, she inflexibly maintaining her dominance.

3.ii *The banks of the Euphrates* The closing scene of Part 3 is entitled 'Coro e Profezia'. The Hebrews' sighs for their lost homeland are violently countered by Zaccaria, who presents a vision of the future in which Babylon will be reduced to ruins. The Hebrews' choral lament ('Va pensiero') is the most famous piece in *Nabucco*, perhaps in all Verdi. It is deliberately simple, almost incantatory in its rhythmic tread, unvaried phrase pattern and primarily unison texture; and by these means it creates that powerful sense of nostalgia which, later in the century, gave the chorus its status as a symbol of Italian national aspirations. In the context of the drama, however, the chorus's attitude is cast aside by Zaccaria, whose two-part minor–major *profezia* ('Del futuro nel buio') takes up rhythmic and melodic strands from 'Va pensiero' and places them in a fresh dynamic context.

PART 4: 'The Broken Idol'

4.i *The royal apartments (as in 2.i)* The scene opens with Nabucco alone on stage, an orchestral prelude representing the king's distraction through scattered recollections of past themes. He hears a funeral march, sees Fenena on her way to execution, but is powerless to help her. As a last resort, he offers a prayer to the God of Israel; sanity returns and he marshals a band of followers to save his daughter. The scene is structured as a double aria for Nabucco, with his prayer ('Dio di Giuda') as the first part. The ensuing cabaletta ('Cadran, cadranno i perfidi') is highly unusual in beginning with a choral statement of a subsidiary theme.

4.ii *The hanging gardens* To an extended version of the funeral march heard fleetingly in the previous number, Fenena and the Israelites are led towards their deaths. Fenena offers a brief but touching preghiera ('Oh dischiuso è il firmamento'), and then, just in time, Nabucco rushes on to save her. He announces his conversion and is restored as king; Abigaille (we learn) has taken poison. All now join in a triumphant hymn to their new God ('Immenso Jeovha'), a grandiose unaccompanied chorus with which, in most 19th-century performances, the opera came to a close. In the score, however, there is a far more restrained ending: the dying Abigaille enters to ask forgiveness, singing a fragmented melody ('Su me ... morente') to the accompaniment of solo cello and english horn.

* * *

There are many ways in which *Nabucco*, as the composer himself said, is the true beginning of Verdi's artistic career, the true emergence of his distinctive voice. It is admittedly an uneven score, with occasional lapses into banality and some unsteady formal experiments that we shall rarely see in future works. But the essential ingredients of Verdi's early style are in place: a new and dynamic use of the chorus, an extraordinary rhythmic vitality and, above all, an acute sense of dramatic pacing. Although, unusually for Verdi, *Nabucco* has no important tenor role, Nabucco and Zaccaria present magnificent opportunities for the baritone and bass, and Abigaille, though always problematic to cast, can prove highly effective for a forceful yet agile soprano. However, as has often been pointed out, the true protagonist of the opera is undoubtedly the chorus, which dominates several of the strongest scenes, and which enters with such stirring effect at climactic points in so many of the solo numbers.   ROGER PARKER

Nachbaur, Franz (Ignaz) (*b* Giessen, nr Friedrichshafen, 25 March 1835; *d* Munich, 21 March 1902). German tenor. After studying in Milan with Lamperti and at Stuttgart with Pischek, he made his début in 1858 at Meiningen. He sang at Prague in *Martha* (1860) and *Faust* (1863), and was engaged at Darmstadt, where he sang Gounod's Romeo (1867). He began a 23-year association with the Hofoper, Munich, in 1867 with Flotow's *Alessandro Stradella*, and sang Walther at the first performance of *Die Meistersinger* (1868), Froh at the première of *Das Rheingold* (1869), the title role in *Rienzi* (1871) and Radames (1877). In 1878 he sang Lohengrin in Rome and in 1882 made his London début as Adolar (*Euryanthe*) at Drury Lane. He also sang in Berlin, Hamburg and Moscow. He made his farewell appearance in Munich in 1890, when he sang Chapelou in Adam's *Le postillon de Lonjumeau*, his 1001st performance there. Although he sang many heavy, dramatic roles, a superb technique preserved the suppleness and lyricism of his voice throughout a long career.

*

E. Newman: *The Life of Richard Wagner* (London, 1933–47)
H. Wagner: *200 Jahre Münchner Theaterchronik 1750–1950* (Munich, 1958)   ELIZABETH FORBES

Nache [née Rodríguez-Nache], **María-Luísa** (*b* La Coruña, 3 Nov 1924; *d* La Coruña, 19 Sept 1985). Spanish soprano. She studied first with Bibiana Pérez in La Coruña and subsequently in Madrid with Angeles Ottein, and in Rome and Milan. She made her début in 1945 at the Teatro Rosalía Castro in La Coruña in *Aida*. Her first performance in Italy was as Desdemona at the Teatro Bellini, Catania, with Francesco Merli as Otello. Subsequently she sang Dirce in a revival of Cherubini's *Médée* at La Scala (1953), with Callas, conducted by Bernstein (a performance captured on record). In Spain she sang in the première of Conrado del Campo's *Lola la piconera* at the Gran Teatro del Liceo, Barcelona (1950). After appearing in the principal theatres of Europe and Latin America and at the Metropolitan, she retired in 1963 for family reasons. Her voice had a wide range (two and a half octaves) and was even over all registers, with absolute precision of attack and control of volume. Her two greatest roles were Aida and Tosca, but her repertory was wide, including, besides Italian operas and Wagner, several Spanish operas (*Amaya* by Guridi, *La llama* and *Mendi mendiyan* by Usandizaga and *Lola la piconera*).

*

R. C. Alvarez: 'Nache, Maria-Luisa', *Gran enciclopedia gallega* (Gijón, 1984)   XOÁN M. CARREIRA

Nacht in Venedig, Eine ('A Night in Venice'). *Komische Oper* in three acts by JOHANN STRAUSS to a libretto by F. ZELL and RICHARD GENÉE after EUGÈNE CORMON and MICHEL CARRÉ's libretto *Château Trompette*; Berlin, Friedrich Wilhelmstädtisches Theater, 3 October 1883.

The action takes place during Carnival celebrations in 18th-century Venice. The elderly Senator Delacqua (baritone), concerned for the virtue of his young wife Barbara (mezzo-soprano), has arranged for her to go by gondola to her aunt at Murano. However, Caramello (tenor *buffo*), personal barber to the Duke of Urbino (tenor), knows of his master's passion for Barbara and arranges to take the gondolier's place. Barbara in turn has her own plans to meet a young naval officer and arranges for her place in the gondola to be taken by the fisher girl Annina (soprano) ('Ich komm' von Chioggia'). All prepare for the evening's fun ('Alle maskiert'), but when Caramello takes the gondola to the Duke's palace ('Komm' in die Gondel') he is unaware that his passenger is Annina, his own girlfriend. In Act 2 Annina arrives at the Duke's palace in trepidation ('Was mir der Zufall gab'). When Caramello discovers his mistake he effects various ruses to prevent the Duke being left alone with Annina, helped by his friend the pastrycook Pappacoda (baritone), whose own girlfriend Ciboletta (soprano) is being wooed by Senator Delacqua. Somehow they succeed in delaying matters until the Duke leaves to attend the midnight carnival in St Mark's Square. There in Act 3 Caramello bemoans the fickleness of women ('Ach, wie so herrlich zu schau'n'). However, as the pigeons flutter around ('Die Tauben von San Marco'), the Duke benevolently restores Annina to him and appoints him his steward.

Eine Nacht in Venedig shows Strauss's descriptive writing at its best, helped by his love of Italy. His depiction of night falling on Venice at the end of Act 1 is especially fine; the quality of the music has enabled the work to survive despite problems with its libretto. From the start, Act 3 was considered weak, and rewriting was needed both before and after the Viennese première on 9 October 1883. The work has since become a paradise for arrangers, all too rarely to its advantage, the most successful and skilful revision being by E. W. Korngold and Ernst Marischka for a production at the Theater an der Wien in October 1923. The structure was tightened and extraneous music added, partly to provide two new solos for Richard Tauber as the Duke ('Sei mir gegrüsst, du holdes Venezia' to music from *Simplicius*, and 'Treu sein, das liegt mir nicht' to music originally given to

Annina as 'Was mir der Zufall gab'). The original Berlin cast included Sigmund Steiner (Duke), Jani Szika (Caramello) and Ottilie Collin (Annina), the Viennese cast Alexander Girardi (Caramello), Caroline Finaly (Annina), Josef Joseffy (Duke) and Felix Schweighofer (Caramello). Strauss's original version was published in full score in 1970.
ANDREW LAMB

Nachtlager in Granada, Das [*Nachtlager von Granada, Das* ('A Night's Shelter in Granada')]. *Romantische Oper* in two acts by CONRADIN KREUTZER to a libretto by Karl Braun, Freiherr von Braunthal after JOHANN FRIEDRICH KIND's play; Vienna, Theater in der Josefstadt, 13 January 1834.

The Prince Regent (baritone), dressed as a simple huntsman and separated from his companions in the chase in 16th-century Granada, falls in with shepherds. He is overwhelmed by the beauty of Gabriele (soprano), but when she tells him that she has been promised to Vasco (bass), despite being in love with Gomez (tenor), he determines to help the young lovers. His own life is endangered by the jealous scheming of Vasco and his accomplices, but Gabriele and Gomez save him, his retinue arrives, and he joins the hands of the lovers, promising them a dowry.

Das Nachtlager, long a favourite in the German repertory and formerly given in most European houses, and some in the USA, is still occasionally revived; it has also been recorded (conducted by Karl Etti). It is now mainly remembered for the Prince Regent's aria, 'Ein Schütz bin ich', and the ensemble that closes the first act, 'Schon die Abendglocken klangen'. Though essentially lyrical rather than dramatic, and deceiving no one with its conventional Spanish local colour, the work is one of the finest products of German opera between *Der Freischütz* and *Der fliegende Holländer*.
PETER BRANSCOMBE

Nafé, Alicia (*b* Buenos Aires, 4 Aug 1947). Argentine mezzo-soprano. She studied in Buenos Aires and then with Teresa Berganza and Luigi Ricci in Europe, making her operatic début as Carmen at Darmstadt in 1975. Engagements followed at La Scala and in Berlin, Paris and other European centres, at the Teatro Colón, Buenos Aires, in San Francisco and with the Chicago Lyric Opera. She was a member of the Hamburg Opera, 1977–80, and made her British début in 1981 with the Cologne Opera at the Edinburgh Festival as Rosina (*Barbiere*), which she also sang for her Covent Garden début in 1985. She sang Charlotte at Parma in 1990. Her dark-toned and flexible coloratura voice has brought her particular success in Rossini and Donizetti and as Carmen.
NOËL GOODWIN

Nagano, Kent (George) (*b* Berkeley, CA, 22 Nov 1951). American conductor. After studying at the University of California at Santa Cruz and at San Francisco State University, he became music director of the Berkeley SO in 1978. In 1981 he made his début with the LSO and in 1983 assisted Seiji Ozawa in the preparation of the première of Messiaen's *St François d'Assise* at the Paris Opéra, returning there to conduct *Wozzeck*, *Elektra* and *Salome*. He made his Boston SO début replacing Ozawa in 1984. Further engagements included his first appearance at La Scala in 1987. In 1989 he joined the Lyons Opéra as music director, developing its policy of mounting works outside the standard repertory, such as the French-language version of Strauss's *Salome*

(recorded in 1990, released 1991) and Martinů's *Les trois souhaits*. In 1991 he conducted the première of John Adams's *The Death of Klinghoffer* in Brussels, with later performances in Lyons, Vienna, Brooklyn, Los Angeles and San Francisco. He became music director of the Hallé in 1992.
NANCY MALITZ

Nagy, János B. (*b* Pocsay, nr Debrecen, 9 July 1940). Hungarian tenor. He studied in Budapest, where he made his début in 1971 as Don José. He has continued to sing with the Hungarian State Opera while also appearing in Düsseldorf, Cologne, Zürich and Berne; among his roles are Pollione, Nemorino, the Duke, Manrico, Riccardo (*Ballo*), Radames, Turiddu, Canio and Maurizio (*Adriana Lecouvreur*). His open voice production and italianate tone make him an ideal interpreter of Puccini's Des Grieux, Calaf, Rodolfo and Cavaradossi.
ELIZABETH FORBES

Nagy, Robert (*b* Lorain, OH, 3 March 1929). American tenor. He studied at the Cleveland Institute of Music and, after local appearances in opera, sang at the Metropolitan from 1957 as Canio, the Emperor (*Die Frau ohne Schatten*), Florestan and Herod. At the Metropolitan and, from 1969, at the New York City Opera he sang in about a thousand performances; he appeared as the Drum Major at the Metropolitan in 1980. Guest appearances in Montreal, San Diego, Seattle and Chicago have included roles in operas by Barber, Wagner, Verdi and Puccini.
DAVID CUMMINGS

Naidenov, Assen (*b* Varna, 12 Sept 1899). Bulgarian conductor. He studied in Vienna and Leipzig, and in 1925 made his début in *Mignon* at the Sofia National Opera. After attending courses with Walter and Krauss at Salzburg in 1930, he returned to the Sofia National Opera, where he was appointed chief conductor in 1944. He made guest appearances with other companies; these included the Berlin Staatsoper (*Khovanshchina*, 1958), the Malïy Theatre, Leningrad (première of Molchanov's *Romeo, Juliet and the Darkness*, 1962–3) and the Bol'shoy Theatre, where in 1963–4 he conducted Verdi's *Don Carlos* in its first Moscow production since 1916. Naidenov's conducting was marked by sure technique and keen feeling for phrase and style. He had a preference for the operas of Mozart, Musorgsky and Verdi, but his repertory included other major operas, Bulgarian operas and many symphonic works.
LADA BRASHOVANOVA

Naïs [*Naïs, opéra pour la Paix* ('Neis, Opera for the Peace')]. *Pastorale-héroïque* in a prologue and three acts by JEAN-PHILIPPE RAMEAU to a libretto by LOUIS DE CAHUSAC; Paris, Opéra, 22 April 1749.

The 'peace' of the subtitle was the Treaty of Aix-la-Chapelle which concluded the War of the Austrian Succession (1740–48). It provides the subject matter of the allegorical prologue, 'L'accord des dieux' ('The Gods' Agreement'), where the war is represented as an attempt by the Titans to storm Olympus. A victorious Jupiter (bass), representing Louis XV, magnanimously shares jurisdiction over the Universe with Pluton [Pluto] (bass) and Neptune (*haute-contre*), the latter popularly viewed as an inept portrayal of France's former enemy, King George II. (Nobody remarked on the incongruity of making Neptune hero of the ensuing drama.)

The opera itself, set on the Isthmus of Corinth, concerns the wooing by Neptune of Naïs [Neis] (soprano), a water-nymph famed both for her beauty and for the outstanding quality of her voice. Cahusac supposes her to have been daughter of the blind soothsayer Tirésie [Tiresias] (bass), who could predict the future by interpreting birdsong. Neptune, who conducts his wooing incognito, eventually wins Neis's hand despite the hostility of two rival suitors, Télénus [Telenus] (bass) and Astérion [Asterion] (*haute-contre*).

As a representative of the lighter genre of *pastorale-héroïque*, *Naïs* contains little of the serious emotional conflict of the *tragédie* and little attempt at characterization. It is nevertheless rich in the kind of spectacle and 'local colour' that were Cahusac's speciality. Moreover, these elements are well integrated, the action being allowed to continue to some extent during the *divertissements*. The first of these, for example, involves the onstage wrestling, boxing and athletics of the Isthmian Games, over which Neis presides. It is here that her emotions are first engaged by the disguised Neptune, and this results in a certain dramatic tension as the nymph attempts to conceal her feelings from the other participants. Tiresias's interpretation of birdsong during the second-act *divertissement* furthers the action in providing the motivation for Neptune's rivals to take up arms against him. In the final act the denouement follows a spectacular sea battle and a sudden transformation to Neptune's underwater palace.

The boldest music is in the prologue. The pungent dissonances and violent syncopations of the overture, a representation of the Titans' storming of the Heavens, continue into the first two choruses to create a long and astoundingly powerful opening sequence. (The idea of allowing the overture to continue into the first scene was one that Gluck's supporters were later to claim as his.) Thereafter the score provides rich contrasts and inventive music. The pastoral music and birdsong of Act 2 are especially fine; so is the music representing the Isthmian Games, comprising a lengthy chaconne full of gestures suggesting athletic movement. The use of piccolos and strummed pizzicatos for the jaunty arrival of Neptune and the Sea Divinities is but one illustration of the work's imaginative orchestration. Since Rameau's day the work was not revived until June 1980, when it was presented at Versailles by the English Bach Festival.

GRAHAM SADLER

Naissance d'Osiris, La [*La naissance d'Osiris, ou La fête Pamilie* ('The Birth of Osiris, or The Pamilian Festival')]. *Acte de ballet* (*ballet allégorique*) by JEAN-PHILIPPE RAMEAU to a libretto by LOUIS DE CAHUSAC; Fontainebleau, 12 October 1754.

Originally conceived as the prologue to a projected *opéra-ballet*, *Les beaux jours de l'Amour* (of which *Anacréon*, *Nélée et Myrthis* and possibly *Zéphyre* were to have formed part), the opera was adapted to mark the birth of the Duke of Berry (the future Louis XVI), who is represented as the god Osiris (*haute-contre*). Jupiter (bass) descends to his temple at Thebes and announces Osiris's birth to Pamilie [Pamyles] (soprano) and the Egyptian shepherds. Much of the music is appropriately pastoral in character.   GRAHAM SADLER

Najac, Comte **Emile de** (*b* Lorient, Dec 1828; *d* Paris, April 1899). French librettist. Throughout the Second Empire and during the first two decades of the Third Republic he regularly supplied the Parisian stage with plays and *opéra comique* librettos, many of them in one act. He had a number of successes. *Divorçons* (1880),

which he wrote in collaboration with Sardou, has a liveliness of plot and dialogue that has made it one of the few French comedies of the period to survive in the repertory to the present day. He also wrote, with Paul Ferrier, the libretto for Lecocq's *La vie mondaine* (1885) and, with Paul Burani, that for Chabrier's *Le roi malgré lui* (1887). However, Najac formed no lasting association with any one librettist or composer, which may explain why he made comparatively little of his talents despite his industriousness.   CHRISTOPHER SMITH

Naldi, Giuseppe (*b* Bologna, 2 Feb 1770; *d* Paris, 14 Dec 1820). Italian bass. He made his début at Milan in 1789 and then sang throughout Italy and in Lisbon. He first appeared in London at the King's Theatre in 1806 in P. C. Guglielmi's *Le due nozze e un sol marito*. During 12 seasons in London he sang in over 35 different operas, among them Mayr's *Che originali*; Paer's *Il principe di Taranto*, *Camilla*, *Griselda* and *Agnese*; Paisiello's *Il barbiere di Siviglia*, *La Molinara* and *Pirro*; Piccinni's *La buona figliuola*, Cimarosa's *Il matrimonio segreto* and Martín y Soler's *Una cosa rara*. He sang Don Alfonso in *Così fan tutte* (1811), Papageno in *Die Zauberflöte* (1811), Figaro in *Le nozze di Figaro* (1812; for illustration *see* CATALANI, ANGELICA) and Leporello in *Don Giovanni* (1817), all first London performances. He also sang Figaro in the first London performance of Rossini's *Il barbiere di Siviglia* (1818). He was killed in an accident at the home of the tenor Manuel García. Although Naldi's critics disagreed on the quality of his voice, they all praised his ability to act and his sense of humour.   ELIZABETH FORBES

Nancy. Town of great architectural distinction in eastern France, formerly the capital of the Dukes of Lorraine. The first theatre was built by Léopold, Grand Duke of Lorraine, in 1708 for his family and court; it opened with Desmarets' *divertissement*, *Le temple d'Astrée*. With the court's departure for Lunéville in 1738 and the building of an opera house in the château there, it fell into disuse. In 1755 the duke ordered his architect Héré to build a second theatre, Le Pavillon de la Comédie, in the beautiful 18th-century Place Stanislas, on the site of the present museum. It was used for opera from 1850 until it burnt down in 1906. A new opera house, the Grand Théâtre (1310 seats), was then built by the architect Hornecher on the opposite side of the square within the outer walls of the Pavillon des Fermes, formerly the bishop's palace. It was inaugurated in 1919 with Reyer's *Sigurd*.

The season runs from October to June, with nine or ten productions of operas and operettas, each performed four or five times. The Opéra has been enterprisingly directed for some years by the producer Antoine Bourseiller, several of whose productions, including Henze's *Boulevard Solitude* and Tippett's *King Priam*, have won critical awards.

L. J. Brote: 'A propos du repertoire lyrique des théâtres français', *Le théâtre lyrique français 1945–1985*, ed. D. Pistone (Paris, 1987), 51–73

A. Bourseiller: 'L'Opéra-Théâtre de Nancy', ibid, 353–4
                    CHARLES PITT

Nannini [Costantini], **Livia Dorotea** (*fl* 1695–1726). Italian soprano. She and her sister, the soprano Lucia Vittoria Nannini, were known collectively as 'Le Polacchine'. There is some confusion about musicians of these names. According to Quadrio there were four singers known as 'Le Polacchine'. The family, which was Bolognese, seems to have consisted of Giovanni Nannini (father), who was associated with the court of Mantua, Margherita (mother and perhaps a singer), Livia, Lucia (the most active of 'Le Polacchine' in the theatre), about whose first names there is some doubt, and a third sister, perhaps called Francesca.

Livia Dorotea Nannini (known after marriage as Costantini), with Lucia Vittoria, was a *virtuosa* of the Duke of Mantua from 20 December 1695. According to the licence, the sisters were noted for the quality of both their singing and their playing. Both were on close terms with the Marchese G. G. Orsi; the poet P. A. Bernardoni was also in their circle. According to Muratori, Livia left the duke's service in November 1699; she formed a professional partnership with the bass Giovanni Battista Cavana that lasted until 1702. Between 1695 and 1706 she sang widely in Italy and Vienna; she first appeared in serious roles but later in *buffa* intermezzo parts. In 1709 she married and moved to Dresden, where she stayed until 1719, singing *buffa* roles from 1717, and where Alessandro Scarlatti wrote for her the part of Vespetta in his intermezzos for Lotti's *Giove in Argo*. She was a member of the Royal Academy company in London in early 1726, playing Matilda in a revival of Handel's *Ottone* and creating Armira in his *Scipione*. The part of Matilda, originally for contralto, was transposed for her, with two new arias. She seems to have been a singer of the second rank; her compass was e' to a''.

Lucia Vittoria Nannini appeared only in serious roles, sometimes in male parts. Damiro, in Alessandro Scarlatti's *Eraclea* (1700, Naples), was written for her; the writing is predominantly syllabic and in pathetic style, with few embellishments.

F. S. Quadrio: *Della storia e della ragione d'ogni poesia* (Bologna, 1739–52)

L. Frati: 'Un impresario teatrale e la sua biblioteca', *RMI*, xviii (1911), 64–84

F. Piperno: 'Buffe e buffi (considerazioni sulla professionalità degli interpreti di scene buffe ed intermezzi)', *RIM*, xviii (1982), 240–84

F. Marri: 'Muratori, la musica e il melodramma negli anni milanesi (1695–1700)', *Muratoriana*, xvi (1988), 19–124

P. Besutti: *La corte musicale di Ferdinando Carlo Gonzaga ultimo duca di Mantova: musici, cantanti e teatro d'opera tra il 1655 e il 1707* (Mantua, 1989)   SERGIO DURANTE, WINTON DEAN

Nannini, Lucia Vittoria. Italian soprano, sister of LIVIA DOROTEA NANNINI.

Nantes. Cathedral city in the west of France on the Loire, one of the two historic capitals of Brittany. In 1687 the troupe of the Sieur d'Aumont visited the city and performed Cambert's *Les peines et les plaisirs de l'amour* and *Pomone*. A permanent company was first established in 1770. The opera house, the Théâtre Graslin, takes its name from the financier and philanthropist who donated the site; the architect Matturin Crucy built it in the neo-classical style and it was inaugurated on 23 March 1788. During a performance of Grétry's *Zémire et Azor* in 1796 the theatre caught fire and only the façade was saved. It lay in ruins until Napoleon's visit to the city in 1808, when he authorized the city council to borrow from the government for its reconstruction. Crucy himself carried out the work, and the new theatre (980 seats) was opened on 3 May 1813. Gas lighting was installed in 1854, and electricity in 1890. Various 19th-century re-

decorations were carried out, but between 1975 and 1978 the theatre was completely restored to its original blue and gold splendour, and the technical installations were thoroughly modernized. The season runs from October to May, with six to eight productions a year, each given three or four performances.

D. Rabreau: 'L'Opéra de Nantes', *Revue de la Caisse nationale de monuments historiques*, no.108 (1980)   CHARLES PITT

Nantier-Didiée, Constance (Betzy Rosabella) (*b* St Denis, Ile de Bourbon [now Ile de la Réunion], 16 Nov 1831; *d* Madrid, 4 Dec 1867). French mezzo-soprano. She studied with Duprez at the Paris Conservatoire and in 1849 won the *premier prix* for opera. In 1850 she made her début at the Teatro Carignano, Turin, as Emilia in Mercadante's *La vestale*. She appeared in *Luisa Miller* at the Théâtre Italien in 1852, and the next year began a three-year engagement at Covent Garden, where she made her début as Gondì in *Maria di Rohan* and sang in the English premières of *Rigoletto* and *Benvenuto Cellini*. In 1854–6 she sang in Spain and North America, then for two years at the Théâtre Italien. On 15 May 1858 she returned to Covent Garden to sing Urbain (*Les Huguenots*) at the gala opening of the present theatre, where she continued to appear until 1864. Meyerbeer and Gounod wrote her additional music for productions there of *Dinorah* (1859) and *Faust* (1863). She was the first Preziosilla in *La forza del destino* (1862, St Petersburg), and had a wide repertory of comic, dramatic and travesty roles.

H. F. Chorley: *Thirty Years' Musical Recollections* (London, 1862, 2/1926)   PHILIP ROBINSON

Napier [Jacobs], Marita (*b* Johannesburg, 16 Feb 1939). South African soprano. She began singing studies in South Africa, continuing in Detmold and Hamburg. Her début, at Bielefeld in 1969 as Venus (*Tannhäuser*), was followed by engagements at several other German centres and as Venus at San Francisco. She joined the chorus at Bayreuth and sang small roles there before a success in 1974 as Sieglinde, a role she also sang for her Covent Garden début the same year. Appearances as Eva (*Meistersinger*) followed at Bayreuth and San Francisco in 1975. She sang Third Norn at the Metropolitan in 1989; her other favoured roles in the dramatic soprano repertory include Abigaille, Donna Anna, Ariadne, Elisabeth de Valois, Elsa, Leonora (*Forza* and *Il trovatore*) and Santuzza.   NOËL GOODWIN

Naples (It. Napoli). City on the south-west coast of Italy, a major centre for the development of opera in the late 17th century and the early 18th.

1. To 1800. 2. From the decade of French rule to the end of the Kingdom of the Two Sicilies. 3. From unification to the present.

1. TO 1800. Music was a regular component of theatrical *comedie* and *festini* at Naples in the early years of the 17th century. It was not until 1640, however, that a work that can properly be described as an opera was performed there. This was *Santa Elisabetta regina di Portogallo*, about which little is known save that it was staged in the viceregal palace. It probably contained features borrowed from the genre of the Spanish *comedia de santos*, familiar because Naples was a Spanish possession, or from the type of sacred opera fashionable in contemporary Rome. A secular opera by

the Roman composer Loreto Vittori, *Galatea*, was performed at the palace of Prince Cariati in February 1644. The real history of opera at Naples however begins during the viceroyalty of Count d'Oñate (1648–53), previously Spanish ambassador to the Holy See. Believing that he could consolidate his political position by promoting performances of opera to entertain his court, D'Oñate first introduced plays with operatic prologues, then in 1650 true operas 'in the Venetian manner'. Among these were *Didone* (1650), *Egisto* and *Il Nerone, overo L'incoronatione di Poppea* (1651), *La finta pazza* and *Veremonda l'amazzone d'Aragona* (1652). All were rearrangements or elaborations of operas earlier heard in Venice (the appearance of Monteverdi's *L'incoronazione di Poppea* on the list, along with operas by Cavalli, is particularly noteworthy).

To stage these operas the viceroy collected together a company called the Febiarmonici, whose members had previously worked in touring opera troupes in north Italy. His support was only partial, for while he permitted them to perform in a pavilion next to the viceregal palace, he did not pay their other expenses, which they had to recoup by charging admission. The Febiarmonici was therefore an organization that depended from the start on the support both of the rulers of Naples and of the aristocratic and moneyed class. Its most elaborate production was *Veremonda l'amazzone d'Aragona* (a reworking of Cavalli's opera seen in Venice earlier the same year, 1652), performed with lavish sets in a new, specially built room in the palace. The association of opera with D'Oñate's political aims is particularly evident here. The plot, concerning the capture of the imaginary Moorish kingdom of Calpe by Alfonso, King of Aragon, was an allegory of the recent capture of Barcelona by the Spaniards from the French. It reinforced the message to Neapolitans that the Spaniards were the legitimate rulers of their city (the Spanish royal house claimed to be successor to the previous Aragonese line of Neapolitan kings) and that the viceroy was therefore justified in suppressing independence movements (notably the Masaniello revolt of 1647–8).

After D'Oñate's departure the Febiarmonici had to leave the palace. In April 1654 the company obtained the leasehold of the city's major public theatre, the S Bartolomeo. Built around 1620, it was owned by the Casa degli Incurabili hospital, and had privileged status in that the Spaniards had granted it a so-called *jus prohibendi*, or right to raise a small tax from other theatres wishing to operate. The move to the S Bartolomeo did not put an end to relationships on a personal level between the Febiarmonici and the city's rulers. Several later viceroys commanded the company to give special performances at the palace of the opera then in current production. Viceroys also began to attend the S Bartolomeo – the first to do so was the Marchese d'Astorga in 1673. This was a significant change of practice which gradually led viceroys to abandon opera performances in the palace itself. One in particular, the Duke of Medinaceli (1696–1702), was a regular theatre-goer. It was he who, on his arrival, concluded that the theatre was too small and asked the Casa degli Incurabili to enlarge it to make it equal to the best opera houses in Italy. To improve the quality of the performances he himself gave large sums for singers and stage architects, and during at least one season (1698–9) personally took charge of the management. His mania

for opera was a major cause of the large debts he incurred, which had not been paid by the time of his departure in 1702.

The viceroy's presence at public performances did much to improve the theatre company's status. But other factors too were tending to enhance its social position, notably the new associations being forged with the viceregal chapel. The musicians of the chapel seem to have shown little interest in opera before 1675, when on the suggestion of the then manageress of the S Bartolomeo, Giulia di Caro, a palace performance of Cesti's *La Dori* was given by her company and the chapel musicians together in honour of the coronation of Charles II of Spain. In the following years the chapel musicians performed several operas of their own in the palace. But their general aloofness from the public performers at the S Bartolomeo could not be sustained after the viceroys began to appoint to the important post of court *maestro di cappella* composers associated with the theatre. The Venetian opera composer P. A. Ziani acquired the post in 1680, and the 23-year-old Alessandro Scarlatti, who had come from Rome to direct the music of the S Bartolomeo in 1683, succeeded Ziani after his death in 1684. Scarlatti's court appointment is not altogether surprising, given that the viceroy, the Marchese del Carpio, had been (like D'Oñate before him) Spanish ambassador at Rome and had come to know of the young composer there. About the time of Scarlatti's appointment several opera singers also acquired places in the chapel. Thenceforth it was common practice to appoint to the court chapel composers and singers who had a high public profile because of their associations with the theatre. The links between chapel and theatre had a beneficial effect on local opera (especially during the 18th century), since the chapel provided stable employment to a pool of excellent operatic composers and singers resident in the city.

Scarlatti staged a large number of his own newly composed operas at the S Bartolomeo, especially during his first period of residence between 1683 and 1702. He thus reversed previous managerial policy, which had promoted operas primarily imported from north Italy. Neapolitan composers had contributed to some of the earliest operas performed in the 1650s at the S Bartolomeo, including Francesco Provenzale, who adapted three Venetian operas for the theatre (his earlier *Il Ciro* may have been performed in the palace in 1653), Francesco Cirillo (who wrote some of the music of *Orontea* in 1654), and Giuseppe Alfiero (whose *Fedeltà trionfante* was performed in 1655). But the number of operas by Neapolitans produced in the theatre during the 1660s and 70s was very small indeed (Provenzale's *Lo schiavo di sua moglie*, performed in 1671, was one of them). Scarlatti's policy of staging his own works had the effect of turning Naples into a centre for locally composed opera and ultimately into an opera centre of world class. It also helped establish his own historical position as a major 'Neapolitan' composer, although he was not Neapolitan by birth.

Another factor contributing to the rise of Neapolitan opera was the musical education provided by the four conservatories of Naples, the S Maria di Loreto, the S Maria della Pietà dei Turchini, the S Onofrio a Capuana and the Poveri di Gesù Cristo. Founded in the 16th century as orphanages providing a religious and classical education, these institutions began in the 17th to concentrate on the teaching of music, which in turn

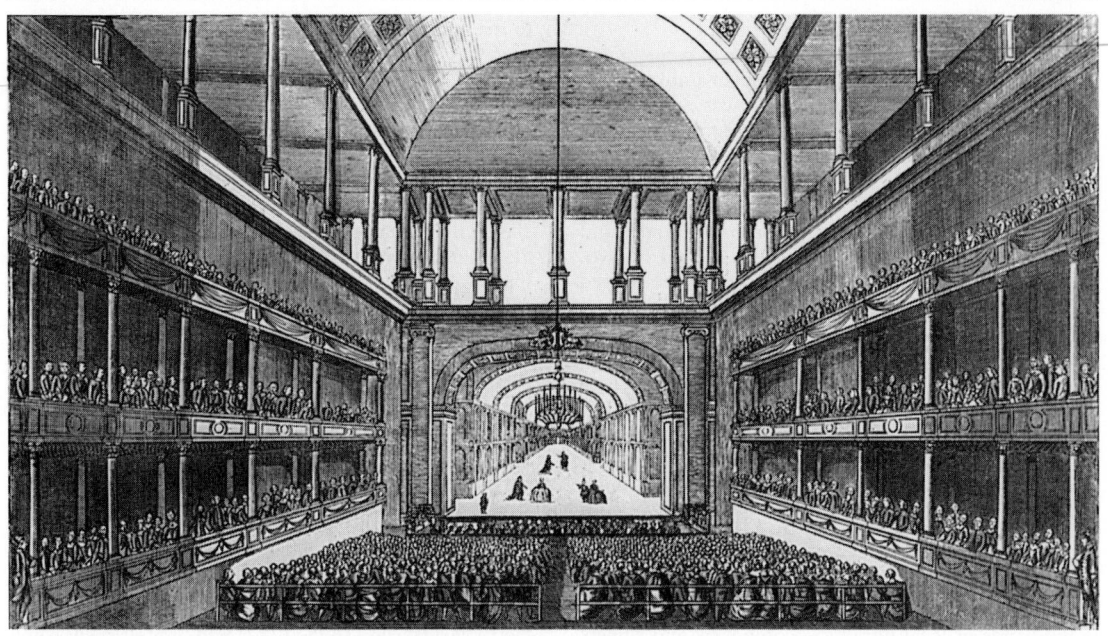

1. Interior of the Teatro S Bartolomeo, Naples: engraving (early 18th century)

attracted fee-paying students who were not orphans and who entered specifically to be trained as musicians. Throughout the 18th century the conservatories continued to serve the dual function of orphanage and music school, and from them graduated large numbers of young composers, later to become famous for their operas. The list includes Francesco Mancini, Domenico Sarro, Nicola Porpora, Leonardo Vinci, Francesco Feo, Leonardo Leo, Nicola Logroscino, G. B. Pergolesi, David Perez, Domingo Terradellas, Nicolò Jommelli, Tomaso Traetta, Pasquale Anfossi, P. A. Guglielmi, Antonio Sacchini, Giovanni Paisiello and Domenico Cimarosa. The decision by one conservatory after another to perform opera, and thus initiate pupils into its various techniques, was taken early on. The earliest conservatory opera on record was *Lo sponsalitio del B. Girolamo Emiani*, composed by the music teacher of the Loreto, Andrea Murino, and performed there by his pupils in autumn 1653. A second opera by him, *Il fido campione, o vero Il B. Caetano*, was staged in 1656. There is no certain record of operas performed by conservatory students in the 1660s, but *L'Onofrio, o Il ritorno d'Onofrio in Padria* was staged by the S Onofrio students in 1671 and Provenzale's *La fenice d'Avila Teresa di Giesù* by the Loreto students the following year. Provenzale, *maestro* at the Loreto between 1663 and 1675 and at the Turchini from 1675 to 1701, seems to have played a major role in establishing the tradition of conservatory operas, the earlier examples of which were always on sacred subjects, underlining the pious objectives of the institutions. Later 18th-century examples, on the other hand, were often comic operas and comic intermezzos. By this time it had become conservatory policy to allow favoured pupils to compose the whole or sections of an opera as a graduation exercise. Leo, Terradellas and Pergolesi were among those who composed sacred operas, and Paisiello among those who wrote comic operas, while they were still students.

The history of comic opera at Naples properly starts with private performances of *La Cilla*, a comic opera in the local dialect with words by Francesco Tullio and music by Michelangelo Faggioli, at the palace of the Prince of Chiusano in December 1707 – January 1708. This was followed by the first public presentation of a comic opera in Neapolitan, *Patrò Calienno de la Costa*, with words by one 'Agasippo Mercotellis' (a pseudonym perhaps for Niccolò Corvo) and music by Antonio Orefice, at the Fiorentini theatre in October 1709. The emergence of comic opera in dialect between 1707 and 1709 is related to the capture of the city in 1707 by the Austrians. Under the new regime, which was less repressive than the Spanish, Neapolitans started to create and use dialect opera as a symbol of a distinctive Neapolitan political identity. The commercial success of *Patrò* paved the way for a succession of such works at the Fiorentini. The management of this theatre, the second theatre of Naples, had abandoned spoken plays in favour of opera in 1706 – clear indication of how opera had become the Neapolitans' preferred form of stage spectacle. The management's decision three years later to promote comic opera in the local dialect may be interpreted both as a piece of opportunism to capitalize on nationalistic feelings and also as a way of avoiding further direct (and financially damaging) competition with the S Bartolomeo. Unlike the operas seen between 1706 and 1709 at the Fiorentini (and during the same period at the S Bartolomeo), which were in Tuscan, with primarily 'heroic' plots enacted by courtly and aristocratic characters drawn from ancient history or classical myth, the new dialect operas presented mainly comic situations of middle- and lower-class life in and around identifiable sectors of contemporary Naples. The differences between these dialect works and the heroic operas staged at the S Bartolomeo created a clearer division of genre, reflecting the tastes of different social classes, than had previously existed. Neapolitan society was not of course rigidly divided in its preferences on class lines. Nonetheless there is some truth in the statement that after 1709 the Austrian viceregal court, the aristocracy and the intelligentsia remained loyal to the heroic operas at the S Bartolomeo, while the bourgeoisie flocked to the comic operas at the Fiorentini.

Naples's position as the leading centre of comic opera – the Fiorentini being the first theatre in Italy to offer regular seasons of works of this type – was enhanced by the opening of two further theatres offering the same thing. The Teatro della Pace, built in 1718, started to present comic opera in 1724, when another house, the Teatro Nuovo, was built and opened for the same purpose. The former was never of great importance and stopped staging opera after about 1751. But the Nuovo, an attractive little theatre with a horseshoe-shaped auditorium on which the auditorium of the much larger Teatro S Carlo was later modelled, became a strong rival of the Fiorentini until well into the 19th century.

Comic opera, as it evolved in Naples, absorbed new international themes and influences that made it less obviously 'Neapolitan' as time went on. But one element remained constant. Although Tuscan infiltrated the librettos more and more, both as a symbol of more refined characterization and as an aid to non-Neapolitans among the singers, a minority of the cast continued to use Neapolitan. This language factor had two important consequences. The first was that the creation of Neapolitan comic opera remained by and large in the hands of local librettists, composers and singers who were dialect speakers. The second was that there was little interchange of opera scores between these Neapolitan theatres and theatres elsewhere in Italy where Neapolitan was not understood. Only in the last quarter of the century in fact were the chief works of the major Neapolitan composers (Paisiello and Cimarosa especially) accepted elsewhere with any regularity, after they had been modified and translated into Tuscan.

In 1734 Charles Bourbon, son of Philip V of Spain and then Duke of Parma and Piacenza, marched on Naples and captured it from the Austrian Habsburgs. Crowned King Charles III of the Two Sicilies, he re-established the state of Naples as a separate monarchy. The new king was no lover of music but, finding opera-going so entrenched in the city, was prepared to support opera in a practical way to suit his political ends. In part because the S Bartolomeo had become rather dilapidated in the last years of Austrian rule and was inconveniently situated in a narrow street, but equally to symbolize the magnificence of his own regime, Charles decided to replace the S Bartolomeo by a sumptuous and larger theatre next to his palace. This was the Teatro S Carlo, erected in 1737 under the supervision of Angelo Carasale (who had previously had a hand in the building and managing of the Nuovo). The first production was Sarro's *Achille in Sciro* in November. The S Bartolomeo was pulled down at the same time by agreement with the Casa degli Incurabili. The Incurabili now lost its *jus prohibendi* privilege, which passed to the S Carlo, but it received a compensatory annual grant.

More is known about the management of the S Carlo than about the other 18th-century theatres of Naples because as a 'royal' theatre its records were strictly maintained and preserved in state archives. Many of these were examined in the late 19th century by Benedetto Croce, whose *I teatri di Napoli* still remains the indispensable study of the subject (enhanced by the fact that some of the documents he relied on were destroyed in World War II). The archives reveal that the court was inconsistent in its delegation of management, sometimes giving artistic and financial control to an impresario and sometimes to a directorate of royal nominees (called either a *giunta* or a *deputazione*). But its requirement as to the number and type of operas was consistent. Whoever was in control was expected to produce three or four heroic operas a year (usually four from 1746–7 to the end of the century), while from 1787 an occasional sacred opera was added in Lent. Operas were produced one at a time. Each was staged for 10–20 nights and then dropped before the next one went into production. This schedule was similar to that adopted in other high-class Italian theatres, such as the Regio in Turin, but unlike that operating abroad, for example at the Paris Opéra or the King's Theatre in London, where managements tended to keep several works in production simultaneously. Because a première at the S Carlo was deemed a political event, opening nights were normally arranged to coincide with birthdays or name-days of the sovereign or his queen or other near relative.

Charles's policy was to attract to the S Carlo the upper-class audiences that had previously attended the S Bartolomeo by offering them still better operas of the kind they were used to. Just how little he thought of the other theatres was demonstrated by the fact that he never personally went inside them. The type of heroic opera presented at the S Carlo has rightly been described as 'Metastasian'. The outstanding librettist of his age, Pietro Metastasio (1698–1782) had himself spent some years in Naples in his youth and there written his first original *dramma per musica*, *Didone abbandonata* (produced at the S Bartolomeo in 1724 with music by Sarro), before going to Rome, Venice and ultimately Vienna, where he settled in 1730. Even from that distance his influence on heroic opera in Naples was profound; it has been estimated that between 1737 and 1776 two-thirds of all operas at the S Carlo were settings of his words. The music of these operas was usually by Neapolitans but by no means always. Hasse, Gluck, J. C. Bach, Galuppi and Mysliveček were among the non-Neapolitans invited to compose music for the theatre. Though Charles tolerated opera of this type, partly because he approved of Metastasio's substantive message (namely, a prince was worthy of his subjects' love if he obeyed the moral code), his real passion was ballet. This explains why, in 1741, he banned the performance of comic intermezzos (such as had been performed as entr'actes to heroic operas at the S Bartolomeo) and insisted that ballets take their place. To ensure that other theatres would not take advantage of the increasing popularity of ballet and promote it themselves, he forbade dancing on stages other than that of his own theatre.

To help management provide lavish, fine productions he granted an annual subsidy, initially set at 3000 ducats (coincidentally, about the same amount the Duke of Medinaceli had annually granted the S Bartolomeo at the end of the previous century). This sum supplemented the income received from the rental and sale of boxes, entry tickets, and other sources such as franchises for particular services (e.g. printing of librettos). The total however was rarely enough to balance expenditure. There is evidence that during both Charles's reign and that of his son, Ferdinand IV (1759–1806; 1815–25), the court was sometimes compelled to provide extra moneys to cancel accrued debts. At the end of the six-year management of the *deputazione* of 'cavalieri' in 1786, for example, the court had to pay an extra 8664.67 ducats to satisfy the theatre's creditors.

The problem was that the court's expectation for the best singing, dancing and stage scenery forced the management to employ artists whose salary demands exceeded what realistically could be afforded. Annual salaries of the two or three top singers were over 2000 ducats each; in exceptional cases they were over 3000. By comparison, composers were rarely paid more than 200 ducats a score. It was only during the 1780s that composers' fees started to rise (in certain cases to 600 ducats by 1786). The need for vast outlays was really because opera, in its totality, was regarded not just as entertainment but as a symbol of the riches and power of the state. S Carlo managements were therefore unable, as a matter of practical politics, to effect economies on too sweeping a scale. Such economies as they could impose affected the musical aspects of a performance above all. The chorus, for example, cost very little, and was customarily obtained by ordering the conservatories to provide their students. The conservatories objected to this practice on the grounds that it disrupted teaching schedules, yet they could not disobey. It fell into disuse only when the number and quality of students at the conservatories started, in about the 1780s, to fall so drastically that they were unable to provide choruses meeting even minimal standards. This helps explain why many operas of the 1780s and 90s lack choral parts altogether.

Two main factors combined to enhance Naples's renown as a music centre among foreigners in the second half of the century. One was the fame of the S Carlo's productions. The other was the increasing reputation of Neapolitan composers abroad. Opera-lovers visiting Naples for the first time, favourably predisposed by what others had told them about the city, rarely found their expectations disappointed within the S Carlo (though some thought the acoustics suffered because the building was too large). But few of them,

hardly surprisingly, were as impressed by performances in the other theatres. One commentator, the Englishman Samuel Sharp, wrote as a result of his visit in the mid-1760s that the dresses, scenery and singers of these theatres 'are much more despicable than one could possibly imagine'. Of course these houses could not challenge the 'royal' theatre on its own ground, having no court subsidy, not being permitted to have dancers on stage, and generally having to operate on a smaller scale. Nonetheless one or two of the most musically perceptive visitors, Charles Burney among them, realized that Neapolitan comic opera had musical and dramatic qualities giving it an intrinsic value of its own. Burney thought the singing and the texts of the comic operas he saw in 1770 bad, but he enjoyed the acting and the music especially. His comments were symptomatic of the growing belief among intellectuals everywhere in Europe that comic opera, although not exactly comparable with heroic, had equal points to commend it.

The social cachet of comic opera in Naples received a particular boost when the young King Ferdinand started to take an interest. Brought up as a Neapolitan and therefore much closer in his sympathies to the ordinary citizenry than his father had been, he decided in 1767 to sample for himself what the smaller theatres were providing and ordered the Nuovo company to give a performance in his palace of their new production of Paisiello's *L'idolo cinese*. Its success led to further palace performances by the Fiorentini and Nuovo companies of other works of the same kind. In 1776 he broke previous taboos and went in person to the Nuovo to see Paisiello's *Dal finto il vero*, thus enhancing the prestige of the theatre and increasing the social acceptability of

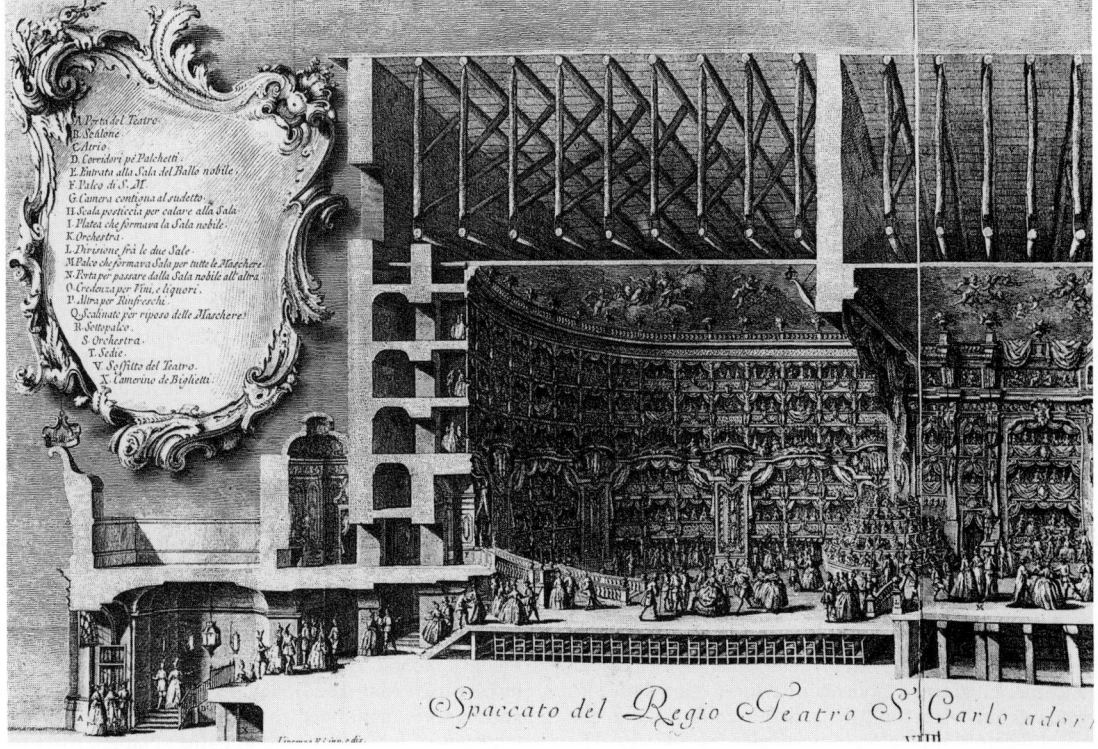

2. Cross-section of the Teatro S Carlo (built by G. A. Medrano, 1737), Naples, decorated for a ball in 1747: engraving by G. Vasi after Vincenzo Re, from 'Narrazione delle solenni reali feste fatte per celebrare in Napoli ... la nascita di ... Filippo Principe delle Due Sicilie' (Naples, 1748)

its offerings – in rather the same way that the Spanish viceroys had enhanced the prestige of the S Bartolomeo when they first went there. In 1779 another theatre for comic opera was opened, the Teatro del Real Fondo di Separazione. Symbolic of the social upgrading of comic opera and in contrast with productions at the older Fiorentini and Nuovo theatres, many of the operas staged at this new theatre were sung in Tuscan only.

2. FROM THE DECADE OF FRENCH RULE TO THE END OF THE KINGDOM OF THE TWO SICILIES. The ten years of French rule on the mainland of the Kingdom of the Two Sicilies began in February 1806 with the flight of Ferdinand to Sicily and the arrival in Naples of Joseph Bonaparte. A wide programme of reform was set in motion, in which musical institutions - schools and theatres - became directly dependent on royal authority. In 1806 Joseph decreed that the two surviving conservatories, those of S Maria di Loreto and of the Pietà dei Turchini, both of which were in a sorry state, were to be combined into a single institute called the Real Collegio di Musica, effectively a new foundation; the merger gave fresh impetus to musical studies and played an important if indirect role in the revival of theatrical activity. In the dramatic years at the turn of the century the royal theatres (S Carlo and Fondo) had deteriorated both in quantity and quality of entertainment and condition of the buildings. The S Carlo received most attention. Its orchestra was overhauled and strengthened, and up to 1835, under the guidance of the leader Giuseppe Festa, had the reputation of being one of the best in Europe. The auditorium was restored and the building enlarged and given a new façade (1811), designed by the neo-classical architect Antonio Niccolini (scenographer, director and superviser of decoration for the royal theatres, 1807–40), who was also later responsible for the efficient restoration of the theatre after a fire that had completely destroyed it on 13 February 1816. It was inaugurated on 12 January 1817 with Mayr's cantata *Il sogno di Partenope*.

The supervision of theatrical activity by the royal authorities was codified by Joachim Murat (who succeeded Joseph Bonaparte in 1808) in a decree of 1811 based on Napoleon's edict to the French theatres of 1806. The Commissione dei Teatri e degli Spettacoli, presided over by a nobleman, was responsible for their orderly activity. Entertainments were also subject to the approval of the ministry of police, which exercised a strict censorship. In 1812 Joachim founded the Regia Scuola di Ballo, directed by Pietro Hus (ordinary courses) and Louis Henry and Ferdinando Taglioni (advanced courses).

The exuberance of theatrical life in Naples under French rule and during the first years of the Bourbon re-storation owed much financially to the practice of gambling in the theatres, which was introduced and then prohibited by Joseph and permitted again by Joachim. From May 1806 the Milanese Domenico Barbaia held the gambling concession; from 1809 until 1840, with a brief interruption in 1834–35, he also managed the royal theatres. The abundant financial means available, the entrepreneurial genius of Barbaia and the enlightened policies of Murat contributed to bring about what could be called a golden age in the royal theatres of Naples, in particular the S Carlo. The number of annual performances increased to over a hundred, and the stage was shared by a double company of singers so that the principal roles could alternate. Its

stars were the soprano Isabella Colbran (from 1811), the tenors Andrea Nozzari (from 1810), Domenico Donzelli, Giovanni Davide (both from 1811), Manuel García (from 1812) and Giovanni Battista Rubini (from 1817) and the basses Michele Benedetti (from 1810) and Filippo Galli (from 1820).

Of the Italian composers who wrote for the S Carlo, the most successful until 1815 was Mayr, whose *Medea in Corinto* (28 November 1813) was performed 33 times and revived in many subsequent seasons. Close to him came the veteran Paisiello (*I pittagorici*, 19 March 1808), and Nicola Manfroce, early in his brief career (*Ecuba*, 13 December 1812). Interest in non-Italian opera, especially French works and those of Mozart, was also keen. The S Carlo staged the Italian premières of Sacchini's *Oedipe à Colone* (14 May 1808), Spontini's *La vestale* (8 September 1811) and Gluck's *Iphigénie en Aulide* (15 August 1812) – all translated into Italian by Giovanni Schmidt, who shared the post of poet to the royal theatres with A. L. Tottola – and *La clemenza di Tito* (14 May 1809). At the Fondo *Don Giovanni*, *Figaro* and *Così fan tutte* were staged between 1812 and 1815, along with many *opere semiserie* by French composers and their imitators, such as Hérold and Paer. There were obvious political reasons for the interest in French theatre: Joseph Bonaparte had summoned a French theatrical company to Naples and it performed at the Fondo throughout the decade, influencing (even if indirectly) the development of opera there. Interest in Mozart's work, apart from Queen Caroline Murat's devotion to it, was further en-couraged by the presence in Naples of Count Gallen-berg, who besides writing much ballet music acted as a courier between Naples and Vienna.

On their restoration in 1815 the Bourbons left intact the structures created by the French administration, adding to them in 1816 the Reale Scuola di Scenografia, directed by Niccolini. Rossini entered a contract with Barbaia in 1815 and found ideal conditions in Naples for widening his horizons and creating more extensive and dramatically weighty operas: *Otello* (4 December 1816, at the Fondo because the S Carlo had burnt down), *Armida* (11 November 1817), *Mosè in Egitto* (5 March 1818), *La donna del lago* (24 September 1819), *Maometto II* (3 December 1820) and *Zelmira* (16 February 1822). Barbaia also entrusted to Rossini the artistic direction of the royal theatres; he was succeeded by Giovanni Pacini in 1825 after the success of his *L'ultimo giorno di Pompei*, and then by Gaetano Donizetti (1828–38). Donizetti's first opera to be seen in Naples was staged at the Teatro Nuovo in the year of Rossini's departure, 1822, and from then on his work practically flooded the theatres of Naples for almost 30 years. Among those written especially for the S Carlo were *Lucia di Lammermoor* (26 September 1835), *Roberto Devereux* (29 October 1837) and *Poliuto* (1838, given posthumously on 30 November 1848), all to librettos by Salvadore Cammarano, who was appointed 'poet and arranger' of the royal theatres in 1834. Other poets active in those years were Domenico Gilardoni and Andrea Passaro. At the S Carlo (where Bellini's second opera, *Bianca e Gernando*, had its pre-mière on 20 May 1826), a galaxy of stars, both singers and dancers, continued to perform, although the new tendency of *ballet blanc* did not affect Naples. After the death of Henry in 1836 the monopoly of choreography remained with Ferdinando Taglioni, who continued the old tradition of heroic and historical ballet.

3. Interior of the Teatro S Carlo, Naples: engraving (after 1816)

At the beginning of the 1830s, although standards remained high, an incipient crisis was evident. Financial resources were diminishing (gambling in the theatre had finally been prohibited in 1820), and censorship increasingly hampered the activity of composers and librettists. Annoyance at the prohibition of his *Poliuto* was one of the reasons for Donizetti's leaving Naples; Verdi, who wrote *Alzira* (1845) and *Luisa Miller* (1849) for the S Carlo, could not have *Il trovatore* or *Un ballo in maschera*, also originally written for Naples, performed in the city, and they were consequently first given in Rome. In the 1840s and 50s the most representative composers connected with the S Carlo were Saverio Mercadante (director of the reorganized conservatory and musical director of the royal theatres) and Giovanni Pacini.

During the first half of the 19th century two more theatres were built, the Fenice (from 1806, in the palace of the dukes of Frizia in Piazza Castello) and the Partenope (from 1828, in Largo delle Pigne, now Piazza Cavour). There were no opera seasons as such, but opera was presented throughout the year, with brief interruptions imposed by church festivals (Holy Week, the two feasts of S Gennaro in April–May and September, and Advent). During the ten years of French rule the S Carlo and the Fondo alternated: the S Carlo opened on 15 August, Napoleon's birthday, and continued until March, and the Fondo covered the period from April to July; with the return of the Bourbons the 18th-century custom was resumed of using the S Carlo from spring until spring. Officially the repertory of the two theatres was strictly separate – *opera seria* and heroic ballet for the major theatre, *opera semiseria* and *buffa* for the minor one. In reality records show that *opera seria* was frequently performed at the Fondo and that the S Carlo sometimes put on comic opera. Of the private theatres, where two performances a day were sometimes given, the Fenice and the Partenope staged both comic and serious opera; the Fiorentini alternated drama with *opera buffa* and *opera semiseria* and at the S Carlino (connected with the opera house because parodies of operas given at the S Carlo were staged there, until its demolition in 1884) *opera buffa* was sometimes performed. But the place where comedy in all its forms (including the *farsa*, generally in one act), remained a speciality was the Teatro Nuovo, as in the 18th century.

Characteristic of Neapolitan comic opera at the beginning of the 19th century was the alternation of song and spoken dialogue instead of traditional recitative, another sign of French influence. On the other hand, a marked accentuation of local features resulted from the choice of subject, the typing of characters (including the mask of Pulcinella from the *commedia dell'arte*) and the use of dialect for the comic parts (in which the basses Gennaro Luzio and Carlo and Raffaele Casaccia excelled). Many such works were produced and they were widely enjoyed. Musicians of all levels contributed to their number (Donizetti, Mercadante, Pacini, Valentino and Vincenzo Fioravanti, Pietro Generali, Carlo Conti, Luigi Ricci, Errico Petrella, Nicola De Giosa, Mario Aspa, Lauro Rossi, Nicola d'Arienzo, Pietro Raimondi and many others), while librettists included Giuseppe Checcherini, Almerindo Spadetta and Marco d'Arienzo. 20th-century music historians have been inclined to condemn the genre, judging it by the yardstick of absolute musical values. But studied as a theatrical phenomenon, this kind of comic opera reveals the mentality, customs and average taste of at least three generations of audiences, and not only of Neapolitans (some of the most successful works were widely performed throughout Italy: Vincenzo Fioravanti's *Il ritorno di Pulcinella dagli studi di Padova*, 1837; Petrella's *Le precauzioni, ossia Il carnevale di Venezia*, 1851; De Giosa's *Don Checco*, 1850; Luigi Ricci's *Il diavolo condannato a prender moglie*, 1826; and *La festa di Piedigrotta*, 1852).

3. FROM UNIFICATION TO THE PRESENT. After the proclamation of the Kingdom of Italy in 1861 the crisis

in the two royal theatres of Naples worsened. From 1862 their management was divided, and for several years there were no musical productions at the Fondo. The S Carlo, deprived of the support of a local court, had to shorten its seasons (October–November and March–April), and to reduce to one (from four in the golden years of Barbaia) the number of compulsory operas written for it. In 1867 the Italian government ceased to finance the activities of the theatres, and in 1874 and 1875 the commune of Naples could not afford to grant a subsidy; the S Carlo had to close. After this interruption the season was shortened once more (seven or eight operas, December–April) and the compulsory opera abandoned. Even operas produced elsewhere arrived with considerable delay, particularly in the case of Wagner (*Lohengrin* in 1881, *Tannhäuser* in 1889, *Die Walküre* in 1895). At the Fondo, renamed in 1871 the Real Teatro Mercadante, there was a lively return to opera while the S Carlo was closed (1874–6); here in 1893–4 the management was undertaken, through an intermediary, by the publisher Edoardo Sonzogno, who made the theatre a bridgehead in the battle with his rival Giulio Ricordi, staging a large number of new works of the 'young Italian school' (Mascagni, Leoncavallo, Giordano), as well as recent French *opéras lyriques*. The Teatro Nuovo had been badly damaged by fire but it was soon restored in 1861 and continued to cultivate the Neapolitan comic vein, which had a final flourish with the success of De Giosa's *Napoli di carnevale* in 1876. But by that time it was a genre already facing extinction and yielding to French operetta (Offenbach and Lecocq). After 1880 plays were increasingly staged at the Nuovo, then revues and variety. It burnt down again in 1935 and was then adapted as a cinema.

The theatrical scene in Naples in the second half of the 19th century was however not one of decline, judging by the increasing number of theatres: the Goldoni (near the cloister of S Tommaso d'Aquino, 1861), the Rossini (Strada fuori Porta Medina, 1861), the Mercadante (Piazza Cavour, 1870, not to be confused with the former Fondo), the Politeama Napolitano (via Monte di Dio, 1871), the Sannazzaro (via Chiaia, 1874), the Filarmonico (Piazza Municipio, 1874) and the Bellini. All offered mixed entertainment – opera, operetta, plays and other forms. Of these theatres the Bellini made the most enduring mark on the later history of opera in Naples, and it is still the only one for which there is any kind of archive. Built in 1864 in Piazza Bellini, it opened with a season of equestrian circus but by the following year was already mounting opera seasons, drawing on both the usual 19th-century Italian repertory and the local comic-opera tradition of Fioravanti, Aspa and others. Destroyed by fire on 17 April 1868, it was rebuilt in via Conte di Ruvo in 1878 in an enlarged and more ambitious form (six tiers of boxes, and holding about 1600). Until 1908 it was used mainly for opera; its seasons had full and interesting programmes of high quality and it was open all year round. On 5 November 1879 it staged the Italian première of *Carmen* with Célestine Galli-Marié, the following year the Neapolitan première of *Der Freischütz*, in 1889 Gluck's *Orfeo ed Euridice* (not seen in Naples since 1774), and the following year Gluck's *Armide*, which was new to Naples. In 1912 the theatre began to show cinema programmes and to give more time to operetta and plays, but until 1940 it continued to have short opera seasons for at least one month a year. It became a cinema in 1950, and in 1988 was restored and used again as a theatre, though not for opera.

There has been little of great interest in the history of the S Carlo since the end of the 19th century. In 1908 Giuseppe Martucci conducted the Neapolitan première of *Tristan und Isolde* and opened the way for the rest of Wagner's works, from that time an annual feature. The S Carlo seasons continued routinely with little in the way of novelty from Italian composers and not much from contemporary Europeans (except Richard Strauss). During World War II, after the Allies had entered Naples, the theatre was requisitioned by the British and its administration entrusted to the 36th British military area. The British command, in agreement with the impresario Pasquale di Costanzo, fostered a rapid and intensive resumption of operatic activity (between 1944 and 1946 there were 88 performances of *Traviata*, 67 of *Rigoletto*, 73 of *Bohème* and 61 of *Il barbiere di Siviglia* among others). It was an unusual period, important in its way: after the convulsions of war and the humiliations inflicted by the dictatorship and defeat, the city rediscovered its historical and cultural identity in its theatre.

Normal activity resumed in the 1947–8 season. Organized as an independent operatic institution and subsidized by the government, the S Carlo had five-month seasons (December to May) for about 20 years, normally with three performances each of 20 productions. A reasonable balance was sought between the traditional repertory, new works both Italian and foreign, and the filling of old gaps. Outstanding among the novelties were the first postwar revival in Italy of *Wozzeck* (1948) and the first Italian performances of Schoenberg's *Von heute auf morgen* (1952), Henze's *Boulevard Solitude* and Hindemith's *Neues vom Tage* (both 1954) and Vaughan Williams's *Riders to the Sea* (1960). More attention was given to Mozart and Gluck, to German Romantic and early 20th-century French opera, and to Rossini's serious works. A regular summer festival, the Estate Musicale Napoletana, also began in 1948, from 1952 to 1967 its performances taking place in the large open-air theatre, the Arena Flegrea, as part of the Mostra d'Oltremare. On 12 November 1954 the Teatro di Corte in the Palazzo Reale was reopened with Paisiello's *Don Chisciotte*. There, from 1958 the Autunno Musicale Napoletano took place, a small festival of 18th-century *opera buffa* organized by the S Carlo in collaboration with RAI; later it was run solely by RAI, which in 1967 transferred the performances to its own auditorium in via Marconi (after 1970 the operas were given only in concert performances).

Decreasing government subsidy led to a progressive contraction of the theatre's activities from the mid-1960s. Seasons were not shortened but there were fewer operatic productions, at first 15 or so and then, in the 1980s, eight or nine (but with more performances of each). The Estate Musicale Napoletana returned to the S Carlo in 1968, but after 1972 closed down completely. In these critical conditions the theatre celebrated its 250th anniversary on 4 November 1987 with an original *festa teatrale* devised by Roberto De Simone, whose study of 17th- and 18th-century popular music injected new life into musical theatre in Naples. He also directed in May 1987 a production of Stravinsky's *Histoire du soldat* which, conducted by Salvatore Accardo, inaugurated the Teatro Mercadante, restored and reopened after 25 years of silence.

CroceN; FlorimoN; RosaM

P. Napoli Signorelli: *Storia critica dei teatri antichi e moderni* (Naples, 1777, 3/1813)

——: *Vicende della coltura nelle Due Sicilie* (Naples, 1784–6, 2/1810–11)

C. Celano: *Noticie del bello, dell'antico e del curioso della città di Napoli*, ed. G. B. Chiarini (Naples, 3/1856–60)

G. Pacini: *Le mie memorie artistiche* (Florence, 1865); ed. F. Magnani (Florence, 1875)

H. M. Schletterer: 'Die Opernhäuser Neapels', *MMg*, xiv (1882), 175–81, 183–9; xv (1883), 12–19

G. Vaccaj: *Vita di Nicola Vaccaj* (Bologna, 1882)

J. Cottrau: *Lettres d'un mélomane pour servir de document à l'histoire musicale de Naples de 1829 à 1847* (Naples, 1885)

S. Di Giacomo: *Storia del Teatro S. Carlino* (Naples, 1891, 6/1967)

S. Procida: 'I teatri', *Napoli d'oggi* (Naples, 1900)

C. de Nicola: *Diario napoletano 1798–1825* (Naples, 1905)

A. Scalera: *Il Teatro dei Fiorentini (dal 1800 al 1860)* (Naples, 1909)

G. Pannain: *Le origini della scuola musicale napoletana* (Naples, 1914)

S. Di Giacomo: *I quattro antichi conservatorii musicali di Napoli* (Palermo, 1924–8)

U. Prota-Giurleo: *La grande orchestra del Teatro di S. Carlo nel settecento (da documenti inediti)* (Naples, 1927)

G. Pannain: 'Saggio sulla musica a Napoli nel secolo XIX da Mercadante a Martucci', *RMI*, xxxv (1928), 198–208, 331–42; xxxvi (1929), 197–210; xxxvii (1930), 231–42; xxxviii (1931), 193–206; xxxix (1932), 51–72; repr. as 'La musica a Napoli dopo Bellini', *Ottocento musicale italiano* (Milan, 1952), 109–72 [without music exx.]

Cento anni di vita del teatro di S. Carlo, 1848–1948 (Naples, 1948)

U. Prota-Giurleo: 'Breve storia del teatro di corte e della musica a Napoli nei secoli XVII–XVIII', *Il teatro di corte del Palazzo reale di Napoli* (Naples, 1952), 19–146

F. Schlitzer: *Mondo teatrale dell'ottocento* (Naples, 1954)

H. Acton: *The Bourbons of Naples* (London, 1956)

E. Cione: *Napoli romantica* (Naples, 1957)

H. Acton: *The Last Bourbons of Naples* (London, 1961)

A. Alberti: *Quarant'anni di storia del Teatro dei Fiorentini in Napoli* (Naples, 1961)

H. Hucke: 'Verfassung und Entwicklung der alten neapolitanischen Konservatorien', *Festschrift Helmuth Osthoff zum 65. Geburtstag* (Tutzing, 1961), 139

F. de Filippis and R. Arnese: *Cronache del Teatro di S. Carlo 1737–1960* (Naples, 1961–)

F. Mancini: *Scenografia napoletana dell'età barocca* (Naples, 1964)

F. de Filippis and N. Mangini: *Il Teatro 'Nuovo' di Napoli* (Naples, 1967)

W. P. Stalnaker: *The Beginning of Opera in Naples* (diss., Princeton U., 1968)

Cronache del Teatro di San Carlo 1948–1968 (Milan, 1969)

F. Lippmann: 'Mozart–Aufführungen des frühen Ottocento in Neapel', *AnMc*, no.7 (1969), 164–79

V. Viviani: *Storia del teatro napoletano* (Naples, 1969)

H.-B. Dietz: 'A Chronology of Maestri and Organisti at the Cappella Reale in Naples, 1745–1800', *JAMS*, xxv (1972), 379–406

M. F. Robinson: 'The Governors' Minutes of the Conservatory S. Maria di Loreto, Naples', *RMARC*, no.10 (1972), 1–97

——: *Naples and Neapolitan Opera* (Oxford, 1972)

L. Bianconi: 'Funktionen des Operntheaters in Neapel bis 1700 und die Rolle Alessandro Scarlattis', *Colloquium Alessandro Scarlatti: Würzburg 1975*, 13–116

L. Bianconi and T. Walker: 'Dalla *Finta pazza* alla *Veremonda*: storie di Febiarmonici', *RIM*, x (1975), 379–454

J. Commons: 'Un contributo ad uno studio su Donizetti e la censura napoletana', *1° convegno internazionale di studi donizettiani: Bergamo 1975*, i, 65–146

R. Bossa: 'Luigi Vanvitelli spettatore teatrale a Napoli', *RIM*, xi (1976), 48–70

F. Degrada: 'L'opera napoletana', *Storia dell'opera*, ed. G. Barblan and A. Basso, i/1 (Turin, 1977), 237–332

F. Mancini: *Scenografia napoletana dell'ottocento: Antonio Niccolini e il neoclassico* (Naples, 1980)

J. Black: *Donizetti's Operas in Naples 1822–1848* (London, 1982)

L. Bianconi and R. Bossa, eds.: *Musica e cultura a Napoli dal XV al XIX secolo: Naples 1982* [incl. D. A. d'Alessandro: 'La musica a Napoli nel secolo XVII attraverso gli *avvisi* e i giornali', 145–64; M. Rak: 'L'opera comica napoletana di primo settecento', 217–24; F. Lippmann: 'Un'opera per onorare le vittime della

repressione borbonica del 1709 e per glorificare Napoleone: *I pittagorici* di Vincenzo Monti e Giovanni Paisiello', 281–306; G. Carli Ballola: 'Presenze e influssi dell'opera francese nella civiltà melodrammatica della Napoli murattiana: il "caso" Manfroce', 307–15; E. Surian: 'Organizzazione, gestione, politica teatrale e repertori operistici a Napoli e in Italia, 1800–1820', 317–67; J. Rosselli: 'Materiali per la storia socio-economica del San Carlo nell'ottocento, 369–81]

D. A. d'Alessandro: 'L'opera in musica a Napoli dal 1650 al 1670', *Seicento napoletano: arte, costume e ambiente*, ed. R. Pane (Milan, 1984)

J. Black: 'Code of Instructions for the Censorship of Theatrical Works, Naples 1849', *Donizetti Society Journal*, v (1984), 147–50

——: *The Italian Romantic Libretto: a Study of Salvadore Cammarano* (Edinburgh, 1984)

B. M. Antolini: 'Ancora sulle prime opere in musica a Napoli', *La musica a Napoli durante il seicento*, ed. D. A. d'Alessandro and A. Ziino (Rome, 1987), 265–349

P. L. Ciapparelli: 'I luoghi del teatro a Napoli nel seicento: le sale private', ibid, 379–412

G. Galasso, ed.: *Napoli* (Bari, 1987)

F. C. Greco, ed.: *Il Teatro di San Carlo* (Naples, 1987)

F. Mancini, A. Ziino and B. Cagli, eds.: *Il Teatro di San Carlo, 1737–1987* (Naples, 1987)

C. Marinelli Roscioni, ed.: *Il Teatro di San Carlo, ii: La cronologia 1737–1987* (Naples, 1987)

T. R. Toscano: 'Gabriele Rossetti e il teatro tra esperienza e memoria: in margine a un'inedita *Memoria* sulla decadenza del melodramma', *Critica letteraria*, xv (1987), 237–86

M. Vajro, ed.: *Il Teatro Bellini 1868–1988* (Naples, 1988)

C. Bruno: *Storia del San Carlo* (Naples, 1989)

T. R. Toscano, ed.: *Il Teatro Mercadante: la storia, il restauro* (Naples, 1989)

M. F. Robinson: 'A Late 18th-Century Account Book of the San Carlo Theatre, Naples', *EMc*, xviii (1990), 73–81

F. Piperno: 'L'opera buffa fra Napoli e Venezia: i cantanti e il repertorio', *Il teatro musicale a Venezia e a Napoli nel settecento*, ed. F. Degrada (Florence, forthcoming)

MICHAEL F. ROBINSON (1), RENATO DI BENEDETTO (2, 3)

Napoli, Jacopo (*b* Naples, 25 Aug 1911). Italian composer. He studied with his father and at the Naples Conservatory. He taught composition at the conservatories of Cagliari and Naples and became director of those of Naples (1954–62), Milan (1962–72) and S Cecilia, Rome (1972–6). He was also artistic director of the Teatro dell'Opera, Rome, and the Teatro S Carlo, Naples.

Napoli followed faithfully the 19th-century Italian operatic tradition in which he was trained, with its emphasis on 'cantabilità', and composed mainly for the theatre. As a traditionalist, his most successful works were comedies, especially when they had an element of Neapolitan local colour, and particularly those written in collaboration with the Neapolitan librettist Vittorio Viviani, for example, *Miseria e nobiltà* (1946) and the comic-grotesque *Il tesoro* (1958).

Il malato immaginario (M. Ghisalberti, after Molière), Naples, S Carlo, 2 Feb 1939

Miseria e nobiltà (V. Viviani, after E. Scarpetta), Naples, S Carlo, 24 March 1946

Un curioso accidente (Ghisalberti, after C. Goldoni), Bergamo, Novità, 19 Sept 1950

Mas'Aniello (Viviani), Milan, Scala, 25 March 1953

I pescatori (Viviani), Naples, S Carlo, 26 March 1954

Il tesoro (Viviani), Rome, Opera, 26 March 1958

Il rosario (Viviani, after F. De Roberto), Brescia, Grande, 5 March 1962

Il povero diavolo (Viviani), Trieste, 23 Nov 1963

Il barone avaro (M. Pasi, after A. S. Pushkin), Naples, 18 March 1970

Dubrowski II (1, Pasi, after Pushkin), Naples, 4 March 1973

Palinuro, 1975 (E. Cetrangolo), Naples, S Carlo, 13 May 1978

A San Francisco (Viviani, after S. Di Giacomo), Naples, S Carlo, 1982

G. Vigolo, '*Il tesoro*', *Mille e una sera all'opera e al concerto* (Florence, 1971), 391–3   RAFFAELE POZZI

Nápravník, Eduard (Frantsevich) (*b* Býšť, nr Hradec Králové, Bohemia, 24 Aug 1839; *d* Petrograd, 10/23 Nov 1916). Russian conductor and composer of Czech birth. The son of a village schoolmaster who also served as precentor in parish churches (first at Býšť, then Dašice), he was originally trained for a career as a church musician. As a child he played the organ at the cathedral church in Pardubice, where his uncle Augustin Svoboda was precentor. Orphaned in 1853, he enrolled the next year at the Prague Organ School, studying the piano at the Maydl Institute, where he taught, 1856–61. Although self-trained as a composer, he did take lessons in orchestration and score-reading from Johann Friedrich Kittl (1806–68), director of the Prague Conservatory.

Nápravník went to Russia in 1861 to conduct the serf orchestra at the St Petersburg residence of Prince Nikolay Yusupov. He also worked as piano teacher and appeared frequently as pianist in chamber concerts. Two years later, Yusupov's orchestra having been disbanded as a result of the Emancipation, Nápravník joined the staff of the recently opened Mariinsky Theatre as the result of a fortunate coincidence. The staff pianist failed to turn up for a performance of Glinka's *Ruslan and Lyudmila*, in the prologue of which the piano plays an indispensable concertante part. The leader spied the young Czech pianist in the audience; Nápravník saved the performance by playing the part at sight, which led to his being hired then and there by the chief conductor of the Russian Opera, Konstantin Lyadov, to assist him as organist and répétiteur. When Lyadov retired, in 1868, Nápravník was named his successor, taking up the reins at the end of the 1868–9 season. In 1869 Nápravník was appointed director of the Russian Musical Society concerts. With these two posts, the 30-year-old immigrant became the most powerful musical executive in the Russian capital.

Nápravník's stewardship of the Musical Society orchestra was stormy and lasted until 1881. The position at the Mariinsky he retained to the end of his life, acting as midwife to virtually the entire Russian 'classical' repertory, which came into being during the decades of his tenure. The following are the most significant of the many Russian operas that had their premières under Nápravník:

1868: *Nizhegorodtsï* (Nápravník)
1869: *William Ratcliff* (Cui)
1871: *The Power of the Fiend* (Serov)
1872: *The Stone Guest* (Dargomïzhsky)
1873: *The Maid of Pskov* (Rimsky-Korsakov)
1874: *Oprichnik* (Tchaikovsky); *Boris Godunov* (Musorgsky)
1875: *The Demon* (Rubinstein)
1876: *Vakula the Smith* (Tchaikovsky); *Angelo* (Cui)
1880: *May Night* (Rimsky-Korsakov)
1881: *The Maid of Orléans* (Tchaikovsky, dedicated to Nápravník)
1882: *The Snow Maiden* (Rimsky-Korsakov)
1883: *The Prisoner in the Caucasus* (Cui)
1884: *Mazepa* (Tchaikovsky)
1890: *The Queen of Spades* (Tchaikovsky)
1892: *Iolanta* (Tchaikovsky); *Mlada* (Rimsky-Korsakov)
1895: *Dubrovsky* (Nápravník); *Christmas Eve* (Rimsky-Korsakov)

The falling-off after the early 1880s reflects the rescinding of the monopoly enjoyed by the Imperial Theatres, after which leadership for new productions passed to the more adventurous private companies. The only important composer to maintain a close relationship with the state-run theatres (and with Nápravník personally) after that point was Tchaikovsky, whose works, operatic as well as balletic, epitomized the so-called Russian Imperial style – also reflected (though far less brilliantly) in Nápravník's own works for the stage.

The Imperial style derived ultimately from the French opera of the First Empire: heroic singing within a traditional numbers format, lavish production values with emphasis on mass scenes and ensemble finales, heavy emphasis on the picturesque and on local colour. To engage even competently in such a creative enterprise required great technical proficiency. Nápravník's utter professionalism may be gauged not only from his sure deployment of all the requisite conventions, but also from such things as his provision of alternative transitional passages to facilitate transpositions of key arias.

More than professionalism, rare and treasurable as that was in the Russia of his day, Nápravník could scarcely claim; his was a Kapellmeisterly gift. His pre-eminent commitment to his conducting career meant, too, that he had relatively little time to compose. His published output in all genres, over the course of a career spanning half a century, totalled 59 works. His operas were few and far between.

The first of them was *Nizhegorodtsï* ('The Nizhniy-Novgoroders'), a historical opera set in the same period as Glinka's *A Life for the Tsar*, depicting the mobilization and triumph of the popular militia under Minin and Pozharsky against the Poles. Its bombastic patriotism was widely read as opportunistic or sycophantic, a bid for the plum position he acquired shortly after the première. A condescending review in the *Sankt-peterburgskiye vedomosti* by the 24-year-old Rimsky-Korsakov (standing in for César Cui, the paper's regular critic, whose *William Ratcliff* was to be produced under Nápravník later the same season) permanently chilled relations between the composer of *Nizhegorodtsï* and the 'Mighty Kuchka'. It was 17 years before Nápravník's second opera *Garol'd* ('Harold') – a grandiose affair set in England at the time of the Norman conquest – was ready. Though a failure (for which composer blamed librettist), it contributed one popular number, a lullaby 'Uspokoysya, dorogoy!' ('Calm thyself, beloved'), to the Russian recital stage. Fyodor Stravinsky created the role of William the Conqueror. *Dubrovsky* (1895), after Pushkin's blood-and-thunder tale, was Nápravník's emblematic score and his one palpable hit. In its way this far from negligible work stands as monument to the golden age of the Imperial Russian opera, testifying to the magnificent company Nápravník assembled and trained and to its distinguished level of routine. A final, fairly modest opera, *Francesca da Rimini* (1902), conceived as a vehicle for Nikolay and Medea Figner, enjoyed little more than a *succès d'estime*. The composer, whose job required that he take meticulous note of royal reaction to his work, recalled in his memoirs the polite praise of Tsar Nicholas II and the Empress Alexandra; but, he went on to reflect, the subject was too lacking in excitement 'to count on prolonged general success'. (Rakhmaninov, to confine matters to the Russian school, disagreed.)

Nápravník was a composer's conductor – cool, conscientious, consummately skilled, not a little pedantic. He inspired little warmth or enthusiasm, though all acknowledged his meritorious contribution to the quality of Russian musical life. Tchaikovsky, his greatest beneficiary, could summon up no greater praise for Nápravník than to aver, 'when the score says C♯ he won't let you play C'. Igor Stravinsky, who as the son of a leading bass of the Mariinsky company knew the conductor well, extolled him in his autobiography of 1936 as a model executant (strictly distinguished in the Stravinskian lexicon of those years from 'interpreter'). Stravinsky expressed a less tendentious opinion in a private communication to Nápravník's son Vladimir (15 November 1932), declining a request for a testimonial to the conductor on account of Eduard Frantsevich's artistic conservatism and his hostility to Musorgsky.

See also DUBROVSKY *and* NIZHEGORODTSÏ.

all given at St Petersburg, Mariinsky Theatre

Nizhegorodtsï [The Nizhniy-Novgoroders] op.15 (5, P. I. Kalashnikov, after M. Zagoskin: *Yury Miloslavsky, ili Russkiye v 1612 godu* [Yury Miloslavsky, or The Russians in 1612]), 27 Dec 1868/8 Jan 1869, vs (Moscow, 1884)
Garol'd [Harold] op.45 (dramatic op, 5, P. I. Veynberg, after E. Wildenbruch), 11/23 Nov 1886, vs (Moscow, 1885)
Dubrovsky op.58 (4, M. I. Tchaikovsky, with J. Paleček, after A. S. Pushkin), 3/15 Jan 1895, vs (Moscow, 1894)
Francesca da Rimini op.71 (4, Ye. P. Ponomaryov, after S. Phillips), 26 Nov/9 Dec 1902, vs (Moscow, 1902)

*

N. Rimsky-Korsakov: '"Nizhegorodtsï" E. F. Napravnika', *Muzïkal'nïye stat'i i zametki (1869–1907)* [Essays and Notes on Music], ed. N. Rimskaya-Korsakova (St Petersburg, 1911), 3–15
V. Val'ter: *Eduard Frantsevich Napravnik: k 50-letiyu artisticheskoy deyatel'nosti 1863–1913* [On the 50th Anniversary of his Artistic Activity] (St Petersburg, 1914)
E. Stark: *Peterburgskaya opera i yeyo mastera 1890–1910* [St Petersburg Opera and its Masters] (Leningrad, 1940)
E. Gordeyeva: *'Dubrovsky' E. F. Napravnika* (Moscow and Leningrad, 1949, 2/1960)
L. Kutateladze, ed.: *E. F. Napravnik: avtobiograficheskiye, tvorcheskiye materialï, dokumentï, pis'ma* [Autobiographical and Creative Material, Documents and Letters] (Leningrad, 1959)
L. Dyachkova: *I. F. Stravinsky: stat'i i materialï* [Essays and Materials] (Moscow, 1973), 491–3
O. Tompakova: '"Nizhegorodtsï" E. Napravnika', *Muzïkal'naya zhizn'* (1982), no.17, pp.20–21
N. Savinov: 'Napravnik i yego vremya' [Nápravník and his Times], *Muzïkal'naya zhizn'* (1983), no.8, pp.6–7
R. Taruskin: 'The Present in the Past: Russian Opera and Russian Historiography, ca. 1870', *Russian and Soviet Music: Essays for Boris Schwarz* (Ann Arbor, 1984), 77–146, esp.104–10
L. Mikheyeva: *Eduard Frantsevich Napravnik* (Moscow, 1985)
M. Malkiel: 'Polveka tvoreniya' [50 Years of Creative Work], *SovM* (1990), no.3, pp.92–8   RICHARD TARUSKIN

Narciso ('Narcissus'). *Dramma boscherrecio* by Domenico Scarlatti (*see* SCARLATTI family, (2)) with additions by Thomas Roseingrave to a libretto by CARLO SIGISMONDO CAPECE, revised by PAOLO ANTONIO ROLLI, after OVID's *Metamorphoses*, books 3 and 7; London, King's Theatre, 30 May 1720.

Three princes, Aristeo [Aristeus] (tenor), Cephalo [Cephalus] (soprano castrato) and Narcissus (soprano), compete to rid Athens of a monstrous boar which has been ravaging the territory, the reward offered being the territory itself and the hand of its ruler, Princess Procris (soprano). Narcissus, disdainful of female beauty and immune to love, is pursued by Echo (soprano), a nymph, who in the disguise of Aura (a breeze) succeeds in arousing the jealousy of Procris. It is Cephalus who kills the boar and is finally united with Procris, but not until Narcissus has fallen in love with a shadow he sees in a fountain and which turns out to be Echo's.

The original opera, with the title *Amor d'un ombra e gelosia d'un aura*, was composed for Queen Maria Casimira's theatre in the Palazzo Zuccari, Rome, and first performed there on 15 January 1714. It was judged to be the best of the carnival operas produced in Rome that year but seems not to have been revived during Scarlatti's lifetime except in the Rolli-Roseingrave version for the first short season of the Royal Academy in London, when it was given five performances. The music is consistently attractive and dramatically effective, giving the lie to the oft repeated (but seldom tested) opinion that Scarlatti's operas were pale imitations of his father Alessandro's.   MALCOLM BOYD

Narcissa [*Narcissa, or The Cost of Empire*]. Grand opera in four acts by MARY CARR MOORE to a libretto by her mother, Sarah Pratt Carr; Seattle, Moore Theatre, 22 April 1912.

Missionary dedication, patriotism and the historical conflict between new settlers and the native peoples of the Oregon Territory, culminating in the 1847 Whitman Massacre, are the central themes of *Narcissa*, which features as its principal characters two missionaries, Marcus Whitman (tenor) and Narcissa Prentiss (soprano). Their duet, 'O longer stay', and Narcissa's 'Ah, another weary day', were often performed separately. Other roles include Dr McLaughlin (bass), the representative of the Hudson's Bay Company, Yellow Serpent (baritone), his son Elijah (tenor) and Elijah's sweetheart Siskadee (contralto), who are friendly Indians, and Delaware Tom (baritone) and the aged Waskema (mezzo-soprano), who are hostile.

Audiences and some critics admired the music, which includes hymns, Indian themes, a French folksong and motifs from 'The Star-Spangled Banner', and were greatly moved by the work's dramatic power. Narcissa Prentiss Whitman is portrayed in her historical role rather than as a typical operatic heroine; the resulting absence of amorous complications led other critics to deny that it was an opera at all. *Narcissa* was revived in 1925 at San Francisco and again in 1945 at Los Angeles. Composed in 1909–11, it was belatedly awarded a David Bispham Memorial Medal in 1930.

CATHERINE PARSONS SMITH

Nash, (William) Heddle (*b* London, 14 June 1894; *d* London, 14 Aug 1961). English tenor. He studied with Giuseppe Borgatti in Milan, where he made his début in 1924 in Rossini's *Il barbiere di Siviglia*. He also sang at Genoa, Bologna and Turin before returning to London in 1925. He was engaged at the Old Vic and at once made his name as the Duke in *Rigoletto*. Tours with the British National Opera Company followed, and in 1929 he appeared at Covent Garden, where his Don Ottavio was considered the finest since McCormack's. He returned regularly to sing this and many other lyrical roles, notably David (*Die Meistersinger*), in both the English and international seasons at that house until 1939; he was again heard there, as Massenet's Des Grieux and as David, in 1947 and 1948. He was a mainstay of the early Glyndebourne seasons, singing every Ferrando, Don Basilio and Pedrillo from 1934 to 1938.

The charm and sweetness of Nash's singing represented a rare natural gift and he had a sure grasp of technical principles. Hardly another tenor of his time sang Mozart with such elegance yet with such a minstrel-like effect of spontaneity. Among the best of his many records are early recordings of solos from *Don Giovanni* and Handel's *Jephtha*, an Act 4 of *La bohème* with Beecham and a complete set of the Glyndebourne *Così fan tutte* with Busch (1935).

J. Jarrett: 'Heddle Nash', *Record Advertiser*, iii/5 (1972–3), 2–11
RICHARD CAPELL, DESMOND SHAWE-TAYLOR

Nasolini, Sebastiano (*b* Piacenza or Venice, ?1768; *d* ?Venice, ? 1798 or 1799). Italian composer. He is said to be a native of Piacenza on the manuscript scores of several of his operas, but some printed librettos refer to him as 'di Venezia' or 'maestro di cappella veneziano'. After musical training during the 1780s, probably in Venice, he was appointed *maestro di cappella* at the Cathedral of S Giusto in Trieste; he became *maestro al cembalo* at the Teatro S Pietro in Trieste before April 1789. According to Choron and Fayolle he died in Venice in 1798; Gervasoni placed his death in 1799. The production of several apparently new operas under his name between 1800 and 1816 has led some scholars (for example Jackman) to suggest that Nasolini may still have been alive in 1816; but a lack of evidence of his activities after 1799 supports the view that he died shortly before 1800. Some of the later operas attributed to him are probably the work of the prolific and long-lived Giuseppe Nicolini. Mount Edgcumbe, writing in the 1820s, remembered Nasolini as 'a young composer of great promise, but who died at an early age' (*Musical Reminiscences*, London, 1824).

Nasolini's early operatic output suggests a devotion to serious opera. His first work, a setting of Metastasio's *Nitteti*, was performed in Trieste during spring 1788. Following its success, he produced a number of other *opere serie*, only occasionally interrupted by comic operas, for the principal theatres of northern Italy (he seems not to have accepted commissions from southern cities, except for some Neapolitan operas of questionable attribution). By the time his *Andromaca* was performed in London in May 1790, the *Public Advertiser* could call him 'the most fashionable composer now extant in Italy'. Only in the late 1790s did he give sustained attention to comic opera, working with Giovanni Bertati among other librettists.

Gli umori contrari (1798), a one-act opera to a libretto by Bertati, was one of the most often performed of Nasolini's comic operas; the relatively large number of surviving manuscripts attests to its popularity. Among his most successful serious operas was *Merope* (1796), a *dramma per musica* written for the soprano Elizabeth Billington, who created the title role in Venice and went on to sing it in Bologna, Bergamo, Livorno and Trieste; she triumphed with it in London in 1802.

dg – *dramma giocoso*
dm – *dramma per musica*

La Nitteti (dm, 3, P. Metastasio), Trieste, S Pietro, 5 April 1788
Il Catone in Utica (dm, 3, Metastasio), Venice, S Samuele, carn. 1789, *GB-Lbl**
Adriano in Siria (dm, 3, Metastasio), Milan, Scala, 26 Dec 1789, *I-Mr*
Andromaca (dm, 3, A. Salvi, after J. Racine), Venice, S Samuele, Feb 1790, *F-Pn*
La morte di Semiramide (dm, S. A. Sografi, after Voltaire: *Semiramis*), Padua, Obizzi, Oct 1790, *Pc, I-Bc, Fc, Gl* (Act 1), *Mr, Nc, Rsc* [also as Semiramide; La morte di Semiramide, ossia La vendetta di Nino; La vendetta di Nino]
Teseo a Stige (dramma tragico per musica, after C. I. Frugoni: *Ippolito ed Aricia*), Florence, Pergola, 28 Dec 1790, *A-Wn, F-Pn, I-Fc*
Ercole al Termodonte, ossia Ippolita regina delle Amazzoni (dramma, Sografi), Trieste, S Pietro, spr. 1791
La morte di Cleopatra (dm, 2, Sografi), Vicenza, Nuovo, 22 June

1791, *D-B, Dlb, F-Pn, I-Fc* [also as La Cleopatra; Cleopatra regina d'Egitto]
La Calliroe (dm, 2, M. Verazi), Florence, Pergola, carn. 1792, *Fc*
Eugenia (dramma, 3, G. Foppa, after P.-A. Beaumarchais), Venice, S Benedetto, aut. 1792
Gl'innamorati [Act 1] (dg, 2, Foppa, after C. Goldoni), Venice, S Benedetto, 4 Feb 1793, *B-Bc* [also as Gli amici; Act 2 by V. Trento]
Tito e Berenice (dm, 2, Foppa), Venice, Fenice, Ascension 1793, *F-Pn*
Amore a vince (dg, Foppa, after Goldoni: *La locandiera*), Venice, S Benedetto, Oct 1793; reduced to 1 act by G. Artusi as La locandiera
Le feste d'Iside (dm, 2, G. Rossi), Florence, Pergola, carn. 1794, *Bc* [also as Sesostri, ossia Le feste d'Iside]
Epponina (dm, P. Giovannini), Bergamo, Riccardi, Aug 1794, aria *I-Gl*, rondo *Mc*, aria *PAc*
I raggiri fortunati (farsa, 1, P. Chiari, after *Il marchese villano*), Venice, S Benedetto, 5 Feb 1795 [also as La contessa di Sarzana, ossia Il maritaggio in contrasto]
Merope (dm, 3, M. Botturini), Venice, S Benedetto, 21 Jan 1796, *D-DS, F-Pn, GB-Lbl, I-Fc, Nc, US-Wc* [also as Merope e Polifonte]
La morte di Mitridate (tragedia per musica, Sografi), Trieste, S Pietro, aut. 1796, *D-Mbs, F-Pc, GB-Lbl, I-Fc, MOe* [also as Vonima e Mitridate; Il Mitridate]
Gl'Indiani (dm, 2, Botturini), Venice, S Benedetto, 9 Dec 1796
Zaira (dm, 2, ?Botturini), Venice, S Benedetto, 22 Feb 1797
Alzira, Bologna, Pubblico, spr. 1797, collab. N. Zingarelli; rev. of Zingarelli's 1794 setting
Il medico di Lucca (dg, 1, G. Bertati), Venice, S Samuele, aut. 1797, *B-Bc, D-Dlb, F-Pc, GB-Lbl* [also as Il medico universale; Il medico dei bagni; Il medico ai bagni]
Timoleone (dramma serio per musica, 2, Sografi), Reggio Emilia, Moderno, 29 April 1798, *I-REm*
Gli umori contrari (dg, 1, Bertati), Venice, S Cassiano, June 1798, *A-Wgm, B-Bc, F-Pc, I-Fc, Nc, Pi(l)*; rev. as Gli opposti caratteri, ossia Olivo e Pasquale (farsa, 1, Foppa and G. Artusi), Venice, S Samuele, 15 Oct 1799 [also as I temperamenti contrari]
Melinda (favola romanzesca in musica, 2, Bertati), Venice, S Benedetto, 12 Sept 1798
Il trionfo di Clelia (dramma, 2, Sografi), Milan, Scala, 26 Dec 1798, *Mc*
Il torto immaginario (farsa giocosa in musica, 1, Foppa), Venice, S Moisè, aut. 1800

Music in: Vasco di Gama, 1792; Pirro, 1793; Ines di Castro, 1795

Works attrib. Nasolini dating from after his supposed death: Gli sposi infatuati (farsa giocosa per musica), 1801; Tersandro in Eleusi (dramma serio per musica), Pergola, 1807; L'Achille (dramma serio per musica), Florence, Pergola, 1811; I riti d'Efeso, 1812; Il ritorno di Serse (dm), Naples, Fondo, 1816; La morte di Patroclo (dramma serio), Milan, Carcano, 1819

Grove6 (J. L. Jackman)
A. E. Choron and F. J. M. Fayolle: *Dictionnaire historique des musiciens* (Paris, 1810–11)
C. Gervasoni: *Nuova teoria di musica* (Parma, 1812)
E. de Giovanni: *Giuseppe Nicolini e Sebastiano Nasolini* (Piacenza, 1927)
J. A. Rice: *Emperor and Impresario: Leopold II and the Transformation of Viennese Musical Theater, 1790–1792* (diss., U. of California, Berkeley, 1987), 269–98 [on *Teseo a Stige*]
JOHN A. RICE

Nast, Minnie (*b* Karlsruhe, 10 Oct 1874; *d* Füssen, 20 June 1956). German soprano. She studied at the Karlsruhe Conservatory and made her début at Aachen in 1897. She sang in Dresden, from 1898 to 1919 and then taught there until the bombing of the city in 1945. She toured the USA and Canada in 1905 and was also heard in Russia, the Netherlands and England, where, at Covent Garden, her principal roles were Aennchen, Marzelline and Eva. This was in the 1907 winter season; its tragic sequel, the shipwreck in which many of the company lost their lives, made her determined never to go overseas again. She sang mostly light and soubrette roles, specializing in Mozart and, in 1911, creating the part of Sophie in *Der Rosenkavalier* (for illustration *see* DRESDEN, fig.8). Her technical accomplishment and clear tone are well preserved in some early solo recordings; she also recorded her original part in the trio from *Der Rosenkavalier* and sang Micaëla in the first recording of *Carmen*. J. B. STEANE

Nastasijević, Svetomir (*b* Gornji Milanovac, 1 April 1902; *d* Belgrade, 17 Aug 1979). Serbian composer. An architect by profession, he played the violin and the viola in various orchestras and chamber ensembles (1920–32) in Belgrade. He also worked as assistant stage manager at the Belgrade Opera (1935–6) and as general secretary of the music programme at Radio Belgrade (1940–41). Nationalistic ideas, in both text and music, are characteristic of his compositions, and he made use of primitive expressive devices. His best operas deal with Serbian national life and history and have librettos by the poet Momčilo Nastasijević, the composer's brother. *Medjuluško blago* ('The Medjulužje Treasure') is based on a Wagnerian motif representing cursed treasure; its main features are its expressive unity of words and music and its sonorous choruses. *Djuradj Branković*, a dramatic portrayal of the tragic destiny of a Serbian emperor, is close in style to Russian historical operas, with melodic recitative, modal diatonic harmony, homophonic textures and leitmotifs; the work contains elements of archaic Serbian folk music and Orthodox chant. *Začarana vodenica* ('The Bewitched Water-Mill') has comic and lyrical elements and uses Serbian folktunes from the Šumadija district. Nastasijević also composed several ballets. His autographs are now held in his place of birth, Gornji Milanovac.

Medjuluško blago, 1927 [The Medjulužje Treasure] (musical drama, 5, M. Nastasijević), concert perf., Belgrade, 4 March 1937
Djuradj Branković, 1938 (musical drama, 5, M. Nastasijević), Belgrade, 12 June 1940
Začarana vodenica, 1946 [The Bewitched Water-Mill] (comic op, 4, V. Goldner, after M. Glišić: *Posle devedeset godina* [Ninety Years After]), Belgrade, 1959
Prvi ustanak, 1953 [The First Uprising] (4, S. Nastasijević), concert perf., Belgrade, 3 Feb 1959
Antigona (musical drama, 4, after Sophocles), unperf.
Nemirne duše [The Restless Souls] (chamber op, 4, S. Nastasijević, after M. Nastasijević: *Nedozvani* [Not Called In]), unperf.
Srećan slučaj [The Lucky Strike] (children's op, 1, S. Nastasijević, after J. Jovanović-Zmaj), unperf.

*

G. Brili: *Svetomir Nastasijević: neimar balkanske muzike* [Svetomir Nastasijević: the Builder of Balkan Music] (Belgrade, 1966)
V. Peričić: *Muzički stvaraoci u Srbiji* [Musical Creators in Serbia] (Belgrade, 1969)
G. Krajačić: *Opere i baleti Svetomira Nastasijevića* [Operas and Ballets by Svetomir Nastasijević] (Belgrade, 1976)
ROKSANDA PEJOVIĆ

Nathan, Isaac (*b* Canterbury, 1790; *d* Sydney, 15 Jan 1864). Australian composer of Polish-Jewish descent and English birth. He was the son of Menehem Mona, a cantor who believed himself to be an illegitimate son of Stanislaus Poniatowski, the last king of Poland. In 1809 Nathan became a singing and composition pupil of Domenico Corri in London, later establishing himself there as a popular singing teacher, catering to the aristocracy. His pupils included Princess Charlotte, daughter of the Prince Regent, who appointed Nathan Royal Music Librarian. In 1812 he eloped with a pupil, the 17-year-old Rosetta Worthington, whose family promptly disowned her. In order to supplement an income overstretched by a growing family, Nathan approached Byron to supply words for ancient Hebrew melodies he claimed to have discovered. Byron supplied, not the requested one or two poems, but 26 collectively titled *The Hebrew Melodies*, the best-known of which is *She walks in beauty like the night*.

At the height of his popularity, Nathan's patron Princess Charlotte died, and Byron's support vanished when he fled from England in 1816. To mend his fortunes Nathan turned to composing operettas: *Sweethearts and Wives* (Theatre Royal, Haymarket, 11 August 1823); *The Alcaid, or Secrets of Office* (Theatre Royal, Haymarket, 10 August 1824); *The Illustrious Stranger, or Married and Buried* (Theatre Royal, Drury Lane, October 1827); and *Triboulet, or The King's Jester* (Sadler's Wells, 1840). These are a mixture of English sentimental light opera styles and elements from bel canto and *opéra comique*.

In 1823 Nathan published *An Essay on the History and Theory of Music, and on the Qualities, Capabilities and Management of the Human Voice* (2/1836 as *Musurgia vocalis*), which achieved a European reputation; he was to publish four further books, including *Memoirs of Madam Malibran de Bériot* (1836). In 1824 Nathan's wife died, leaving two sons and four daughters, and in 1826 he remarried. Again in need of money, Nathan seems to have acted as secret agent to his former patron's father, now George IV. In 1837 his successor, William IV, sent Nathan on a mysterious mission. When Nathan claimed £2000 for this exercise his request went to Lord Melbourne, husband of Lady Caroline Lamb, another of Nathan's early patrons and once Byron's notorious mistress. That Byron's collaborator should send in a questionable bill was taken by Melbourne as an affront and the bill was not honoured. Financially ruined, Nathan emigrated with his family to Australia, arriving at Sydney in April 1841.

In Australia Nathan enjoyed a reputation as a singing teacher and composer and as choirmaster of St Mary's Cathedral, Sydney. Three of his London operettas were revived in Sydney, and he composed two operas. The comedy *Merry Freaks in Troublous Times*, to a libretto by Charles Nagel, was completed on 3 March 1843; part of it was performed on 29 May 1844 at the Royal Hotel, Sydney, and it was claimed to be the first original opera fully composed in Australia. *Don John of Austria*, to a libretto by Jacob L. Montefiore, was performed on 7 May 1847 at the Royal Victoria Theatre, Sydney, conducted by Nathan. The latter work has long been claimed as the first Australian opera to be first performed in full in the country. It is a serious, well-crafted work, bordering on tragedy, and displaying elements of mid-century romantic opera. Nathan was accidentally killed by Sydney's first horse-drawn tram. Sir Charles Mackerras is his great-grandson.

Sweethearts and Wives (comic op, J. Kenney), London, Haymarket, 7 July 1823, vs, excerpts (London, 1823); collab. J. Whitaker, T. S. Cooke and J. Perry
The Alcaid, or Secrets of Office (comic op, 3, Kenney), London, Haymarket, 10 Aug 1824, vs (London, 1824)
The Illustrious Stranger, or Married and Buried (operatic farce, 2, Kenney and J. G. Millingen), London, Drury Lane, Oct 1827, excerpts (London, 1827)
Triboulet, or The King's Jester (drama, Millingen), London, Sadler's Wells, 1840, lost
Merry Freaks in Troublous Times (comic op, 2, C. Nagel), excerpt, Sydney, Royal Hotel, 29 May 1844, vs (Sydney, 1851)

Don John of Austria (3, J. L. Montefiore), Sydney, Royal Victoria, 7 May 1847, vs (Sydney, n.d.)

*

MGG (A. Silbermann)

C. H. Bertie: *Isaac Nathan: Australia's First Composer* (Sydney, 1922)

O. S. Phillips: *Isaac Nathan: Friend of Byron* (London, 1940)

C. B. Mackerras: *The Hebrew Melodist: a Life of Isaac Nathan* (Sydney, 1963)

E. Wood: *Australian Opera, 1842–1970: a History of Australian Opera with Descriptive Catalogues* (diss., U. of Adelaide, 1979)

N. Phelan: *Charles Mackerras: a Musician's Musician* (Melbourne, 1987)
THÉRÈSE RADIC

Natzka, Oscar (*b* Matapara, 15 June 1912; *d* New York, 5 Nov 1951). New Zealand bass. He was at first a blacksmith, but in 1935 won a scholarship to study at Trinity College in London with Albert Garcia. In 1938 he was engaged to sing at Covent Garden, where he made his début as Wagner in *Faust* and later created the leading role of De Fulke in George Lloyd's *The Serf*. He also sang in *Rigoletto* and *Die Meistersinger*. After war service, he returned to sing leading bass roles at Covent Garden in 1947, notably Sarastro; the next year he made his début at the New York City Opera as Sparafucile in *Rigoletto*. Thereafter he sang widely in North America, but in 1951 he was taken ill during a performance of *Die Meistersinger* in New York, and 13 days later he died. Possessor of an outstandingly powerful and resonant bass voice, he made a number of recordings of ballads and operatic arias in the late 1930s and the 1940s.

*

A. Simpson and P. Downes: 'Oscar Natzka', *Southern Voices: International Opera Singers of New Zealand* (Auckland, 1992), 52–63
PETER DOWNES

Nau, Maria(-Dolorès-Bénédicta-Joséphine) (*b* New York, 18 March 1818; *d* Levallois, nr Paris, Jan 1891). American soprano of Spanish parentage. She entered the Paris Conservatoire in 1832 to study with Laure Cinti-Damoreau and made her début in 1836, creating Urbain in *Les Huguenots*. She earned a good reputation in minor roles at the Opéra between 1836 and 1842, numbering Rossini among her mentors. Her career reached its pinnacle in 1840 with Halévy's *Le drapier*. From 1841 she appeared in French provincial opera houses as well. She then embarked on several tours to Belgium, England and the USA, performing in concerts and operas until her retirement in 1856. Charles Hervey (*The Theatres of Paris*, Paris, 1846) praised her voice as 'a high soprano of peculiar sweetness and extraordinary flexibility ... in vocalisation ... surpassed by Mme Persiani alone'. He faulted her acting, however, as 'utterly deficient in animation'.
LAURIE C. SHULMAN

Naudin, Emilio (*b* Parma, 23 Oct 1823; *d* Bologna, 5 May 1890). Italian tenor. He studied in Milan, making his début in 1843 at Cremona in Pacini's *Saffo*. After singing in all the major Italian theatres, in 1858 he made his London début at Drury Lane. From 1863 to 1875 he sang regularly at Covent Garden. His roles there included Ernesto, Nemorino, Edgardo, Pollione, Elvino, Fra Diavolo, Masaniello, Don Ottavio, Robert le diable, Danilowitz (*L'étoile du nord*) and Vasco da Gama, which he had created in *L'Africaine* at the Paris Opéra in 1865. His repertory also included Alfredo, Manrico, the Duke (*Rigoletto*) and the title role of *Don Carlos*, which he sang at the first London performance of Verdi's opera, in 1867. He sang Lohengrin in the English provinces (1875) and Tannhäuser in Moscow (1877).
ELIZABETH FORBES

Naufrageurs, Les. Opera by Ethel Smyth; *see* WRECKERS, THE.

Naumann, Emil (*b* Berlin, 8 Sept 1827; *d* Dresden, 23 June 1888). German composer. He was a grandson of Johann Gottlieb Naumann. He studied with Schnyder von Wartensee and Mendelssohn (1842–4) and received the doctorate from Berlin University in 1867. He was a composer and scholar in Bonn and later in Berlin, where he held the post of Hofkirchen-Musikdirektor from 1850. In 1873 he moved to Dresden, where he lectured on music history at the conservatory and was appointed professor. He published numerous pamphlets on music aesthetics and music history, among them *Musikdrama oder Oper?*(Berlin, 1876), in which he turned against Wagner's Bayreuth productions. His *Illustrierte Musikgeschichte* (Berlin and Stuttgart, 1880–85), which was translated into several languages and had many editions, is his most widely known book. His compositions, reminiscent of the style of Mendelssohn, include three stage works, sacred music and lieder.

Judith (heroische Oper, 3, Naumann), Dresden, 5 Nov 1858

Die Mühlenhexe (Spl, 4), Berlin, Friedrich Wilhelm-Strasse, 3 Jan 1862

Loreley (4, O. Roquette), Berlin, Kgl, 9 April 1889

*

*Stieger*O

C. von Ledebur: *Tonkünstler-Lexicon Berlin's* (Berlin, 1861)
DIETER HÄRTWIG

Naumann, Johann Gottlieb (*b* Blasewitz, Saxony, 17 April 1741; *d* Dresden, 23 Oct 1801). German composer. His earliest musical training was at the Kreuzschule in Dresden, and he probably studied with the court Kapellmeister Hasse. In May 1757 the Swedish violinist Anders Wesström (*c*1720–1781) invited Naumann to travel in Italy with him. During the seven-year journey, he studied with Tartini in Padua and Padre Martini in Bologna. In 1762 he met in Venice with Hasse, who arranged for his début as an opera composer at the Teatro S Samuele with the intermezzo *Il tesoro insidiato*. Two years later an *opera buffa Li creduti spiriti*, which he wrote for the carnival in collaboration with two other composers, prompted Hasse and G. B. Ferrandini to recommend him for the post of second church composer in Dresden. He was promoted to chamber composer in 1765 and then returned to Italy for three years. In 1769 his opera *La clemenza di Tito*, which blended the *buffo* and *seria* styles, had its première in Dresden. A subsequent visit to Italy from 1772 to 1774 established his reputation there as a major composer of opera.

Naumann was appointed Kapellmeister at Dresden in 1776. The following year the Swedish ambassador Count Löwenhjelm persuaded him to travel north to Stockholm to assist King Gustavus III in reforming the Hovkapell and to write operas. His first work for Gustavus, the long one-act *opéra-ballet Amphion*, was performed on 24 January 1778 and its success led to a commission for a large-scale work, *Cora och Alonzo*. Naumann's commitments in Dresden delayed its production in Stockholm until 1782, when it was staged for the inauguration of the Royal Opera House. In 1782 Gustavus III commissioned a Swedish nationalist opera, *Gustaf Wasa*; the work had its première in 1786 and was the most popular opera in Stockholm for over a century, being performed over 250 times. In 1785–6 Naumann was guest opera composer and conductor at the Danish court, and was asked to reorganize the opera for Copenhagen, which he found less advanced than Stockholm. He composed a heavily-revised Danish version of Calzabigi's libretto *Orfeo ed Euridice*, as *Orpheus og Eurydike*, but refused to commit himself to an extended contract and returned to Dresden where he was made Oberkapellmeister. He was invited to Berlin by Friedrich Wilhelm II in 1788–9, and composed the operas *Medea* and *Protesilao* for the royal opera house. In 1792 he married Catarina von Grodtschilling, daughter of a Danish vice-admiral. During the last years of his life he began to talk of a German national opera, drawing on his experiences in Sweden.

Naumann was the most important figure in Dresden's music history between Hasse and Weber, and his operas brought him fame throughout Europe during his lifetime. His earliest operas reflect the prevalent *seria* and *buffo* styles and show the influences of Galuppi, Paisiello, and Naumann's mentor Hasse. Beginning with *La clemenza di Tito* (1769) and *Solimano* (1773), however, his works begin to show more colourful orchestration, a bolder harmonic language and more attention to dramatic elements of the texts. Though his first opera for Sweden (*Amphion*, 1778) still contains a mixed italianate style, the skilful use of chorus and ballet throughout follow French influences, particularly Gluck; his two other Swedish works, *Cora och Alonzo* and *Gustaf Wasa*, are also heavily dependent on Gluckian models. The opera *Osiride* (1781) contains elements in both text and music that anticipate Mozart's *Zauberflöte* of a decade later. The works of his last period in Dresden approach *opera semiseria*, and are characterized by lyrical lines and bold orchestration that presage early Romanticism.

See also AMPHION; ARMIDA (iv); CORA OCH ALONZO; GUSTAF WASA; and ORPHEUS OG EURYDIKE.

DKT – *Dresden, Kleines Kurfürstliches Theater*

Il tesoro insidiato (int, 2), Venice, S Samuele, 28 Dec 1762, *D-Bds, Dlb*

Li creduti spiriti (ob, 3, J. von Kurz and G. Bertati), Venice, S Cassiano, carn. 1764, collab. with 2 other composers

L'Achille in Sciro (os, 3, P. Metastasio), Palermo, S Cecilia, 5 Sept 1767, *Bds, Dlb*

Alesandro nelle Indie (os, 3, Metastasio), 1768

La clemenza di Tito (os, 3, Metastasio), DKT, 1 Feb 1769, *Dlb, F-Pc*

Il villano geloso (ob, 3, Bertati), DKT, 1770, *B-Bc*

L'isola disabitata (azione per musica, 2, Metastasio), Venice, Feb 1773, *D-Dlb*

Solimano (os, 3, G. A. Migliavacca), Venice, S Benedetto, carn. 1773, *Dlb, F-Pc, GB-Lbl*

Armida (dramma per musica, 3, Bertati, after T. Tasso: *Gerusalemme liberata*), Padua, Nuovo, 13 June 1773, *A-Wgm, D-Bds, Dlb* (inc.), ov. (Venice, 1773); Ger. trans. as Armide, Leipzig, Rannstädter Tore, 6 July 1780

La villanella inconstante (ob, 3, Bertati), Venice, S Benedetto, aut. 1773; as Le nozze disturbate, DKT, 1774; *Dlb, H-Bn*

Ipermestra (os, 3, Metastasio), Venice, S Benedetto, 1 Feb 1774, *D-Dlb*

L'ipocondriaco (ob, 3, Bertati), DKT, 16 March 1776, *Dlb, DK-Kk*

Amphion (opéra-ballet, prol., 1, G. G. Adlerbeth, after A. L. Thomas), Stockholm, Bollhus, 24 Jan 1778, *Kk, S-St, Skma*; (Dresden, 1784)

Cora och Alonzo, 1778 (tragédie lyrique, 3, Adlerbeth, after J. F. Marmontel: *Les Incas*), Stockholm, Royal Opera, 30 Sept 1782, *DK-Kk, H-Bn, S-Skma*; full score and vs (Leipzig, 1780)

Elisa (os, 2, C. Mazzolà), DKT, 21 April 1781, *D-Dlb, DK-Kk*; 6 arias (Dresden, 1785)

Osiride (os, 2, Mazzolà), DKT, 27 Oct 1781, *D-Dlb*

Tutto per amore (ob, 2, Mazzolà), DKT, 5 March 1785, *Bds, Dlb*

Gustaf Wasa (tragédie lyrique, 3, J. H. Kellgren), Stockholm, Royal Opera, 19 Jan 1786, *Dlb** (Acts 1 and 3), ~~*Bds** (Act 2), *DK-Kk*~~, *H-Bn, S-Skma, St*; ed. A. Johnson in MMS, xii (1991)

Orpheus og Eurydike (Spl, 3, C. D. Biehl, after R. de' Calzabigi), Copenhagen, Royal Opera, 31 Jan 1786, *DK-Kk*; vs (Hamburg, 1787)

La reggia d'Imeneo (festa teatrale, 1, Migliavacca), DKT, 21 Oct 1787, *D-Dlb*

Medea in Colchide (os, 3, A. Filistri), Berlin, Kgl, 16 Oct 1788, *A-Wgm, D- Bds, Dlb*

Protesilao [Act 2] (os, 2, G. Sertor), Berlin, Kgl, 26 Jan 1789, *Bds, Dlb* [Act 1 by J. F. Reichardt]; rev. version, Berlin, Kgl, 1793

La dama soldato (ob, 2, Mazzolà), DKT, 30 March 1791, *B-Bc, D-Bds, Dlb, LEm* (vs); *SWl*; excerpts, vs (Dresden, n.d.)

Amore giustificato (festa teatrale, 1), DKT, 1792, *Dlb*

Aci e Gallatea, ossia I ciclopi amanti (ob, 2, G. Foppa), DKT, 25 April 1801, *Bds, Dlb*

*

Briefe über Musikwesen besonders Cora in Halle (Quedlinburg, 1781)

A. G. Meissner: *Bruckstücke zu Biographie J. G. Naumanns* (Prague, 1803–4)

F. Mannstein: *Vollständiges Verzeichnis aller Kompositionen des Kurfürstlich Sächsischen Kapellmeisters Naumann* (Dresden, 1841)

M. Fürstenau: *Zur Geschichte der Musik und des Theaters am Hofe zu Dresden* (Dresden, 1861–2)

R. Engländer: *Johann Gottlieb Naumann als Opernkomponist* (Leipzig, 1922)

——: *Joseph Martin Kraus und die Gustavianische Oper* (Uppsala, 1943)

H. Åstrand and others: *Beiträge zur Biographie J. G. Naumanns* (Stockholm, 1991)

B. Stribolt: 'Naumann's *Gustaf Wasa*: Swedish National Opera', *Gustavian Opera 1770–1809* (Stockholm, 1991)

BERTIL H. VAN BOER

Nausicaa. Opera in three acts with a prologue and interludes by PEGGY GLANVILLE-HICKS to a libretto by Robert Graves after his novel *Homer's Daughter*; Athens, Herodes Atticus Theatre, 19 August 1961.

The plot is based on the *Odyssey*, with Homer's Penelope becoming the Princess Nausicaa (soprano) and his Odysseus becoming Aetheon (baritone), a shipwrecked Cretan nobleman. Homer's shooting contest, where Penelope's 50 suitors compete for her, becomes a marriage tournament. The subplot derives from Graves's conceit that the *Odyssey* is the work not of Homer but of Nausicaa.

Glanville-Hicks spent two years researching into Greek folk music in order to find a proper musical base for Graves's libretto; she collaborated with him on the work in 1956 in Mallorca. Greek modes and metres, rather than actual folk material, are combined with 12-note procedure in the score, which draws on idioms from Epirus, the Peleponnese, Crete and the Dodecanese. The opera, structured on a symphonic plan derived from *Wozzeck*, is set in continuous accompanied narrative interspersed with set numbers including arias and ensembles. It was first performed as part of the Athens Festival.

THÉRÈSE RADIC

Navarraise, La ('The Girl from Navarre'). *Episode lyrique* in two acts by JULES MASSENET to a libretto by Jules Claretie and HENRI CAIN after Claretie's short story *La cigarette*; London, Covent Garden, 20 June 1894.

La Navarraise was written in cynical (some would say) response to the enormous popularity with the public of *Cavalleria rusticana*, first given in 1890 (one of Massenet's pupils, Alfred Bruneau, had already written veristic operas in collaboration with Zola). Like its model, *La Navarraise* is set in two short acts with an intermezzo (total running time 50 minutes) and offers violent action in a contemporary setting, in this case the Carlist Wars in Spain in the 1870s. The title role was written for Emma Calvé, a famous Santuzza and Carmen, and Parisian wits soon nicknamed the new work 'Calvélleria española'. The London première, attended by the Prince of Wales, was enough of a success for Queen Victoria to command a special performance at Windsor Castle, after which she remarked to Calvé that performing the title role must be 'very fatiguing'. The work's popularity faded after World War I and performances are rare today, although there have been three complete recordings.

The setting is a village square near Bilbao in 1874, with a rudimentary barricade facing rebel lines. The rebel leader Zuccaraga has recaptured Bilbao and is cursed by General Garrido (baritone). Anita, the eponymous Navarraise (soprano or mezzo-soprano), enters in search of her lover Sergeant Araquil (tenor). He appears, one of the few survivors in his company of a skirmish with the rebels, and is greeted by both Anita and his father Remigio (bass), who disapproves sternly of their liaison: he will consent to their marriage only if the penniless orphan produces a *dot* of 2000 douros. A short, tender love duet ('Mariez donc son coeur') fails to soften the father's resolve. Araquil is promoted to lieutenant for his bravery, which seems to Anita to place him even further beyond her reach. News is brought of further casualties inflicted by Zuccaraga, and Garrido exclaims in anger that he would pay a fortune to anyone ridding him of this troublesome rebel. Anita overhears, and offers to do the job for 2000 douros. Garrido takes her for a lunatic as she hurries away. Araquil returns and, after a gentle soliloquy ('O bien-aimée'), is told that Anita has been seen heading for the Carlist lines asking for Zuccaraga. Fearing that she is a spy, or worse, Araquil hurries after her. After an attractive intermezzo-nocturne, battle is resumed. Anita returns, her arms covered with blood, and demands her reward. Garrido, at first disbelieving, gives her the money. Her triumph is short-lived. Araquil enters mortally wounded, imagining her to be Zuccaraga's mistress; when she produces her *dot*, he assumes she sold herself to him. When news of Zuccaraga's assassination is confirmed, Araquil sees the blood on her hands and dies with a curse on his lips. Anita goes spectacularly mad. The war continues.

*   *   *

Purely technically, *La Navarraise* far outclasses its model. Melodically, orchestrally, dramaturgically, the mature Massenet was an infinitely more resourceful composer than the young Mascagni. The way the action, loaded with folkloric detail and set amidst succulent lyrical outpourings, is contained within the 50-minute timespan denotes the hand of a master. Bugle-calls, dances, regimental songs, an inordinate amount of gunshot, all are woven into the dramatic fabric with great ingenuity; offstage bugles in Bb interrupting a Basque dance in D make a particularly happy effect. But not all Massenet's skill can make the characters anything other than pasteboard, whereas Mascagni's more homespun gifts enhance the status of Verga's principals as genuine archetypes. *La Navarraise* works only at the level of Grand Guignol; as George Bernard Shaw shrewdly wrote after the première, Massenet had not so much composed an opera as 'made up a prescription'.

RODNEY MILNES

Navarrini [Navarini], **Francesco** (*b* Citadella, nr Padua, 1853; *d* Milan, 21 or 23 Feb 1923). Italian bass. He studied in Milan and made his début at Treviso (1878) in *Lucrezia Borgia*. After a season at Malta, he sang in various Italian cities, acquiring a large repertory and making his first appearance at La Scala in 1883 as Alvise in *La Gioconda*. His portrayal there of the Grand Inquisitor in the first Italian presentation of *Don Carlos* was highly praised and he soon took his place as the theatre's principal lyric bass. He sang Lodovico in the première of *Otello* (1887) and was the Pogner of the production under Toscanini of *Die Meistersinger* (1898). Abroad he appeared in London, Paris and Madrid, and from 1894 to 1912 was a favourite in Russia. At Monte Carlo his singing of the Slander Song in *Il barbiere di Siviglia* was a highlight of the 1900 season, and in 1902 he visited the USA as a member of Mascagni's touring company. His virtues as a singer are demonstrated in his dozen or so recordings of 1907: a fine, sonorous voice, evenly produced, and exemplifying the traditional graces of the best Italian school.

J. B. STEANE

Navoigille, Julien [*le cadet*] (*b* Givet, *c*1749; *d* ?Paris, after 1811). French composer. He was known as a violinist in Paris by about 1773 and was active thereafter as teacher, player, director and composer. It is difficult to separate his activities from those of his brother, Guillaume Navoigille *l'aîné*. Julien was apparently deputy leader and later director of the private orchestra of the Count of Provence (later Louis XVIII) from 1789 to 1792. Subsequently he directed at the Théâtre de la Pantomime (later Théâtre de la Cité), for which he wrote *La naissance de la pantomime* and *L'héroïne suisse, ou Amour et courage*. He was in the Netherlands with his brother from 1805 to 1810 but then returned to Paris. As well as stage works, Navoigille composed a substantial body of chamber music.

all first performed at the Théâtre de la Pantomime, Paris; all lost

Les honneurs funèbres, ou Le tombeau des sans-culottes (Ducray-Duminil), 1793

L'orage, ou Quel guignon (oc, 1, J.-G.-A. Cuvelier de Trie), 1793

L'héroïne suisse, ou Amour et courage (Cuvelier de Trie and J.-B.-A. Hapdé), 1798

La naissance de la pantomime (Cuvelier de Trie and Hapdé), 1798

Empire de la folie, ou La mort et l'apothéose de Don Quichotte (pantomime, 3, Cuvelier de Trie), 1799, collab. Baneux

*

MGG (B. S. Brook)

P. Jacob, ed.: *Bibliothèque dramatique de M. de Soleinne* (Paris, 1843); suppl. C. Brunet: *Tables des pièces de théâtre* (Paris, 1919)

JEAN HARDEN

Neate, Kenneth (*b* Cessnock, NSW, 28 July 1914). Australian tenor. He studied at the University of Melbourne and in America with Emilio de Gogorza and Elisabeth Schumann. He appeared in leading roles during the first post-war seasons at Covent Garden: Don José, Tamino, the Duke and Pinkerton. Guest appearances took him to Paris, Bologna, Turin, Palermo and Cairo. At Bayreuth in 1963 he was Loge in the *Ring* cycles conducted by Rudolf Kempe. His last stage appearance was in 1975 at Innsbruck, as Otello. Catalani's *Loreley* is among his recordings.

DAVID CUMMINGS

Neblett, Carol (*b* Modesto, CA, 1 Feb 1946). American soprano. She studied with Lotte Lehmann and Pierre Bernac, making her début in 1969 as Musetta with New York City Opera, where she also sang Marietta/Marie (*Die tote Stadt*), Poppaea, Margherita and Helen of Troy (*Mefistofele*). She sang Thaïs at New Orleans in 1973 and first appeared at Chicago in 1975 as Chrysothemis, returning as Electra (*Idomeneo*), Donna Elvira and Minnie, a role she has also sung at San Francisco, the Vienna Staatsoper (1976) and Covent Garden (1977). She sang Vitellia at Cologne (1978), Salzburg (1989) and in Ponnelle's film. She made her Metropolitan début in 1979 as Senta, returning as Tosca, Amelia (*Un ballo in maschera*), Manon Lescaut and Alice Ford. She sang Leonora (*Il trovatore*) with the Royal Opera in Manchester (1983); the title role of Respighi's *Semirama* at Palermo (1987); Aida at Costa Mesa (1988); Bellini's Alaide (*La straniera*) at Spoleto USA (1989); Madame Lidoine at San Diego and Norma at Miami (1990); and Dido (*Les Troyens*) at Los Angeles (1991). A very attractive woman and a powerful actress with a large, vibrant voice, she excels in roles such as Minnie or Tosca.

JAMES WIERZBICKI / ELIZABETH FORBES

Nebra (Blasco), José (Melchor de) (*b* Calatayud, bap. 6 Jan 1702; *d* Madrid, 11 July 1768). Spanish composer. His date of birth has sometimes been wrongly given as 1688. His first teacher was his father, who was *maestro de capilla* of Cuenca Cathedral from 1729. His two brothers were also musicians. Nebra's earliest music for a Calderón de la Barca *auto sacramental* presented at Madrid is dated 4 June 1723. In May 1724 he became principal organist of the royal chapel and of the Descalzas Reales convent at Madrid; two years later his fame was so widespread that he was considered one of the best Spanish composers of the century.

Although Italian theatre composers enjoyed royal protection, he outdid all others, native as well as foreign, in number of performances during the years 1723–30 and 1737–51; only in the six-year hiatus 1731–6 did the queen's Neapolitan favourites Corradini and Mele oust him. In his active 23 years no fewer than 57 of his stage works were mounted at Madrid and Lisbon: all included spoken dialogue. The longer works with secular subjects are variously classed as 'zarzuela', 'melodrama escénico', 'drama armónico', 'commedia per musica' or 'ópera'; several of those with sacred subjects are settings of *autos sacramentales* by the master of this peculiarly Spanish dramatic genre, Calderón. Whether setting secular or sacred librettos, Nebra followed the national tradition that permitted the free mixing of buffoonery and folkish strains with tragedy. His stage works are usually accompanied by five violins, a single string bass, oboe, bassoon and harpsichord.

Often running for 20 or more days, his stage works enabled him to survive financially at a time when royal chapel payments were often years late; their success carried his fame as far afield as Lima. Summarizing his theatrical achievement, Cotarelo y Mori called Nebra the Lope de Vega of Spanish music 'who for a half-century rose above every would-be competitor, Spanish or Italian'.

When the royal chapel music archive was destroyed by fire in 1734, first Literes and then Nebra were commissioned to compose a substitute repertory: 97 of his religious works survive in the palace library, but only one stage work.

first performed in Madrid unless otherwise stated

Autos sacramentales: La vida es sueño (P. Calderón de la Barca), Príncipe, 4 June 1723; A Dios por razón de Estado, Cruz, 23 June 1724 [Nebra wrote music for only the sainetes]; El año santo en Roma, Príncipe, 8 June 1725; El pintor de su deshonra (Calderón), 8 June 1725; El católico Perseo San Jorje, mártir, Cruz, 18 Oct 1725; Santa Francisca Romana, Cruz, 25 Dec 1725 La venerable Sor María de Jesús de Agreda (M. F. de Armesto), Príncipe, 25 Dec 1725; El pastor fido, Príncipe, 28 June 1726, rev. 21 June 1746; La viña del Señor, Cruz, 28 June 1726; El valle de la zarzuela, Príncipe, 20 June 1727; A cual mejor confesada y confesor S Juan de la Cruz y Sta Teresa de Jesús (J. de Cañizares), Cruz, 22 Oct 1727; El pleito matrimonial, Príncipe, 4 June 1728; La folla armónica, Cruz, 25 July 1728; Santa Brígida (Cañizares), Cruz, 25 Dec 1728; Las proezas de Esplandián y el valor deshace encantos, Cruz, 12 Feb 1729 La semilla y la zizaña, Cruz, 24 June 1729; Música discreta y santa: Santa Matilde (Cañizares), 25 Dec 1729; Santa Catalina, mártir, Oct 1730; El sol de la fe en Marsella y conversión de la Francia: Santa María Magdalena (B. J. Reinoso), 25 Dec 1730; La cura y la enfermedad (Calderón), 1739; La Madre Martina de los Ángeles, 1739; Nuestra Señora del Pilar de Zaragoza, 21 Oct 1743; Santa Inés de Montepoliciano, 26 Dec 1743 Andrómeda y Perseo (Calderón), 12 June 1744; La divina Philotea, 3 July 1745; El nuevo hospicio de pobres, 3 July 1745; La nave del mercader, 9 June 1747; Lo que va del hombre a Dios, 21 June 1748; El laberinto del Mundo, 13 June 1749 [aria by Nebra, rest by A. Guerrero]; Primero y segundo Isaac (Calderón), 13 June 1749; La segunda esposa, triunfar muriendo, Cruz, 7 June 1750; El diablo mudo, Príncipe, 18 June 1751; Lo que va del hombre a Dios (N. González Martínez), Cruz, 29 May 1761 [Nebra added an aria]

Others: De los encantos de amor la música es el mayor (zar, Cañizares), Príncipe, 23 Oct 1725; Buscar la dicha en el riesgo y el espín de Calidonia (zar), Cruz, 10 Feb 1727; Amor aumenta el valor [Act 1], Lisbon, palace of Spanish ambassador, Jan 1728 *E-Mp* [Act 2 by Falconi, Act 3 by Facco]; No siempre el Destino vence, si en su imperio Amor domina (zar, J. Fernández de Bustamante), Nov 1730; Más gloria es triunfar de sí: Adriano en Syria (zar, after P. Metastasio), 30 May 1737

Cumplir con amor y honor, 27 Sept 1737 [in pay accounts called an opera]; Amor, ventura y valor y el invencible Amadís, Cruz, 1739; Viento es la dicha de Amor (A. de Zamora), 28 June 1743, *Mm*; Amor, encanto y fortuna restituyeron a su dueño el cetro (A. Fernández), 4 Feb 1744; No todo indicio es verdad: Alexandro en Asia (N. González Martínez), Cruz, 1744 [in pay accounts called an opera]

Cautelas contra cautelas y el rapto de Ganimedes (zar, Cañizares), Nuevo Coliseo del Príncipe, 5 June 1745 [inauguration, both Petronila Gibaja and José de Parra companies participating]; La colonia de Diana, 7 Sept 1745 [rev. with 3 new arias and added tonadillas, 29 April 1746]; El amante de María, Venerable padre Fray Simón de Rojas, Príncipe, 25 Dec 1745; A falta de hechiceros lo quieren ser los gallegos y asombro de Salamanca, 12 Feb 1746

El venerable padre Fray Simón de Rojas, 2a parte, 29 May 1746; Para obsequio a la deidad nunca es culto la crueldad y Iphigenia en Tracia (González Martínez), Cruz, 15 Jan 1747; No hay perjurio sin castigo (González Martínez), Medinaceli private theatre, 8 May 1747; Amor ni obligación, temor ni amigo logran lo que el enemigo, Comedia, 20 May 1747; El asombro de Salamanca, 3a parte, 30 Nov 1747; Antes que celos y amor la piedad llama al valor y Aquiles en Troya (González Martínez), Príncipe, 1747

La mágica Cibeles, 2a parte, 19 Oct 1748; Hay venganza que es clemencia (González Martínez), 30 Nov 1748; El anillo de Jiges (Cañizares), 24 May 1749; El mágico Apolonio, 6 Nov 1749; No hay mágias ni la invención como la de la diversión y Mágico de tres horas, 21 June 1750; En vano el poder persigue cuando la deidad protege, 25 Dec 1750

*

E. Cotarelo y Mori: *Orígenes y establecimiento de la ópera en España hasta 1800* (Madrid, 1917)

R. Mitjana: 'La musique en Espagne', *EMDC*, I/iv (1920), 1913–2351, esp. 2155–6

E. Cotarelo y Mori: *Historia de la zarzuela* (Madrid, 1934)

N. A. Solar-Quintes: 'El compositor español José de Nebra († 11–VII–1768): nuevas aportaciones para su biografía', *AnM*, ix (1954), 179–206

R. Stevenson: *Renaissance and Baroque Musical Sources in the Americas* (Washington DC, 1970), 91–2, 191, 338

S. Claro: *Antología de la música colonial en América del Sur* (Santiago, 1974), pp.xxix, xc, 134ff
M. Martínez: 'Los Nebra en la Catedral de Cuenca (1711–1748)', *Primer congreso nacional de musicología: Saragossa 1979*, 331–8
ROBERT STEVENSON

Nedbal, Oskar (*b* Tábor, south Bohemia, 26 March 1874; *d* Zagreb, 24 Dec 1930). Czech composer and conductor. He studied with the choirmaster Endler in Tábor and with Bennewitz at the Prague Conservatory (1885–92), where he was also a pupil of Bláha (trumpet and percussion) and Dvořák (composition). He played the viola in the much admired Czech Quartet (1891–1906), in which Suk was the second violinist, and was often heard as the group's pianist. Nedbal was equally successful as a conductor, conducting the Czech PO from 1896 to 1906; with it he toured England (1902), and he also appeared as a guest conductor throughout Europe. Subsequently he settled in Vienna, where he conducted the Tonkünstlerorchester (1906–18). He returned to Prague after the formation of the Czech Republic and conducted the Šak PO (1920–21), before leaving for Bratislava, where he became a leading figure in Slovak musical life: he was head of opera at the newly established Slovak National Theatre, director of the Bratislava radio station and a reader at both the university and the musical academy.

As a composer Nedbal achieved widest renown for his operettas written for Vienna, particularly *Polenblut* (1913). He enlivened his skilled technique with an almost Dvořákian invention and made use of the fresh rhythms of Czech, Polish and Yugoslav folkdance. He also composed chamber and orchestral music and achieved particular note in Czechoslovakia for his ballet-pantomimes, especially *Pohádka o Honzovi* ('The Tale of Johnny'; 1902, Prague), from which the 'Valse triste' has become a popular favourite. It was after conducting a performance of this work at the Zagreb Opera House that he committed suicide by jumping from an upper window.

first performed in Vienna unless otherwise stated
Die keusche Barbara (operetta, 3, R. Bernauer, L. Jacobson), Raimund, 7 Oct 1911; Polenblut (operetta, 3, L. Stein), Carl, 25 Oct 1913; Die Winzerbraut (operetta, 3, Stein and J. Wilhelm), An der Wien, 11 Feb 1916; Die schöne Saskia (operetta, 3, A. M. Willner and H. Reichert), Carl, 16 Nov 1917; Eriwan (romantic operetta, 3, F. Dörmann), Komödienhaus (Colosseum), 29 Nov 1918; Mamsele Napoleon (operetta-revue, 1, E. Golz and A. Golz), Hölle, 21 Jan 1919, rev. Prague, Kleine Bühne, 17 May 1928; Sedlák Jakub [Peasant Jacob] (comic op, 2, L. Novák, after Lope de Vega), Brno, 13 Oct 1922, rev. Bratislava, 15 Dec 1928; Donna Gloria (operetta, 3, V. Léon and Reichert), Carl, 30 Dec 1925

G. Černušák: 'Oskar Nedbal', *Listy hudební matice/Tempo*, x (1930–31), 195–7
L. Novák: *Oskar Nedbal v mých vzpomínkách* [My Memories of Oskar Nedbal] (Prague, 1938)
J. M. Květ: *Oskar Nedbal* (Prague, 1947)
K. Nedbal: *Půl stoleti s českou operou* [Half a Century with Czech Opera] (Prague, 1959)
M. Šulc: *Oskar Nedbal* (Prague, 1959)
A. Buchner: *Oskar Nedbal: život a dílo* [Life and Works] (Prague, 1976)
OLDŘICH PUKL, ANDREW LAMB

Nederlandse Opera. Dutch company formed in 1964 in AMSTERDAM.

Neefe, Christian Gottlob (*b* Chemnitz, 5 Feb 1748; *d* Dessau, 26 Jan 1798). German composer. His early musical education combined local tutelage and independent study, and he began composing when only

12. He matriculated at the University of Leipzig in 1769 as a law student, but on completing his studies in 1771 abandoned law for music. He studied with J. A. Hiller and quickly became his favourite pupil. Hiller asked him to collaborate with him on his comic opera *Der Dorfbalbier* (1771) and on his periodical *Wöchentliche Nachrichten und Anmerkungen die Musik betreffend*. He also promoted Neefe's works with the impresario H. G. Koch (for whom Neefe wrote his first three operas) and the Leipzig publishers Junius and Schwickert. Neefe dedicated his first independent comic opera, *Die Apotheke* (apparently written in competition with J. F. Reichardt, also then Hiller's pupil), to his teacher.

When Hiller resigned after a brief tenure as music director of Abel Seyler's theatrical company in 1776, Neefe agreed to assume his position. The company did not take up any of his earlier works (which are in Hiller's style), and Neefe wrote only one work for their performances in Dresden and Leipzig – the melodrama *Sophonisbe*, composed at Seyler's request for his wife Sophie. After the troupe's removal to the Rhineland in May 1777, Neefe contributed only incidental music (to Shakespeare's *Macbeth* and Möller's *Die Zigeuner*) and a musical prologue.

In 1779 Seyler went bankrupt in Frankfurt. Neefe and his wife left for Bonn, where they joined the troupe of their friend G. F. W. Grossmann. In 1780 Neefe set Grossmann's new libretto, *Adelheit von Veltheim*, a seraglio opera very similar to Bretzner's contemporaneous *Belmont und Constanze*. Neefe's involvement with the troupe declined after his appointment in 1782 as court organist and Grossmann's associations with Bonn ended in 1784. Neefe's last opera, *Der neue Guthsherr*, came to him again by way of Hiller, for whom the librettist Dyck had intended his text. Neefe published his music for only the first two acts in vocal score in 1783–4, and the opera was apparently never produced.

After the death of Elector Max Friedrich in 1784, Neefe worked as a private teacher and as an arranger of vocal scores of Italian and Viennese operas (including all of Mozart's mature operas except *Die Zauberflöte* and *Idomeneo*) for the Bonn publisher Simrock. After the dissolution of the electoral court in 1794 and the French occupation of Bonn he became music director to the Hoftheater in Dessau, but soon after taking up this post late in 1796 he fell ill, and died early in 1798.

Neefe's earliest comic operas, written under Hiller's guidance, show a fine sense of melody (also apparent in the slow movements of his keyboard sonatas) and a keen sense of the low comic. He fully equalled his teacher in musical characterization within the enforced simplicity of the day, and he outdid Hiller in responsiveness to comic situations. Later on, when writing for more accomplished singers, Neefe refused to forsake his commitment to simplicity of means. Instrumental music plays an important part in his later operas, particularly *Adelheit von Veltheim*, which is introduced by a 'Sinfonia turchesa a due orchestre' and includes a vigorous janissary march as an entr'acte. His only melodrama is closely modelled on those of Georg Benda but is more frankly sentimental in tone.

Neefe retained a high respect for French *opéra comique* (which he may have passed on to his pupil Beethoven), and made little effort to follow current trends in *opera buffa*. In 1791 he wrote, 'Modern Italians will have to work with greater effort if they wish to please [music-loving Germany]. As far as music with dialogue and dramatic music as a whole are concerned, preference has generally gone to the French, and with good reason' (Bossler).

See also ADELHEIT VON VELTHEIM.

Der Dorfbalbier (comische Operette, 1, C. F. Weisse, after M.-J. Sedaine: *Blaise le savetier*), Leipzig, Rannstädter Thore, 18 April 1771; rev. version (2), Leipzig, Rannstädter Thore, 1 Aug 1771, vs *B-Bc*, vs (Leipzig, 1771) [10 nos. by Neefe, 13 by J. A. Hiller]

Die Apotheke (comische Oper, 2, J. J. Engel), Berlin, Behrenstrasse, 13 Dec 1771, *Bc*, *D-Bds*, *Dlb*, *SWl*, vs (Leipzig, 1772)

Amors Guckkasten (Operette, 1, J. B. Michaelis), Leipzig, 10 May 1772, *B-Bc*, *D-Mbs*, vs (Leipzig, 1772); ed. G. von Westermann (Munich, 1922)

Der Einspruch (comische Oper, 1, Michaelis), Leipzig, Rannstädter Thore, late 1772; rev. as Die Einsprüche (2), Berlin, Behrenstrasse, 16 Oct 1773, *B-Bc*, *D-B*, *Mbs*, vs (Leipzig, 1773)

Zemire und Azor (komische Oper, 4, M. A. von Thümmel, after J. F. Marmontel), Leipzig (Koberwein company), 5 March 1776; music re-used by G. F. W. Grossmann for Was vermag ein Mädchen nicht!, Frankfurt, 18 May 1787

Heinrich und Lyda (Drama, 1, B. C. d'Arien), Berlin, Döbbelins, 26 March 1776, *A-Wn*, *B-Bc*, *D-Bds*, vs (Naumburg and Zeitz, 1777)

Sophonisbe (musikalisches Drama mit historischen Prolog und Chören, 1, A. G. Meissner), Leipzig, 12 Oct 1776, *A-Wgm*, vs (Leipzig, 1782)

Die Zigeuner (Lustspiel mit Gesang, 5, H. F. Möller, after M. de Cervantes: *Preciosa*), Frankfurt, Nov 1777, *Bds*

Adelheit von Veltheim (Schauspiel mit Gesang, 4, Grossmann), Frankfurt, Junghof, 23 Sept 1780, *Wgm*, *D-Dlb*

Der neue Guthsherr (3, J. G. Dyck [dialogue] and J. F. Jünger [arias], after P. C. de Chamblain de Marivaux: *Le paysan parvenu*), unperf., vs, Acts 1 and 2 (Leipzig, 1783–4)

*

C. G. Neefe: *Beiträge zur Geschichte meines Lebens* (MS, 1775–6) and *Lebenslauf von ihm selbst geschrieben* (MSS, 1782, *D-Bds*, *KIu*) [for edns see Grove6]

H. P. C. Bossler: *Musikalischer Korrespondenz* (Speyer, 1791)

J. Wolter: *Gustav Friedrich Wilhelm Grossmann* (Cologne, 1901)

I. Leux: *Christian Gottlob Neefe, 1748–98: Biographie und Instrumentalkompositionen* (Leipzig, 1925)

A. Becker: *Christian Gottlob Neefe und die Bonner Illuminaten* (Bonn, 1969)

T. Bauman: *North German Opera in the Age of Goethe* (Cambridge, 1985)
THOMAS BAUMAN

Negrea, Marţian (*b* Vorumloc, Sibiu district, 10 Feb 1893; *d* Bucharest, 13 June 1973). Romanian composer. He studied with Timotei Popovici in Sibiu (1910–14), then at the Vienna Academy (1918–21) with Eusebius Mandyczewski and Franz Schmidt. Returning to Romania, he taught at the conservatories in Cluj (1921–41) and Bucharest (1941–63). Although his output was not large, it included music in all genres. His most important work was the two-act opera, *Marin Pescarul* ('Marin the Fisherman'), op.12, to his own libretto, after Mihail Sadoveanu's short story *Boyar Sin* ('A Boyar Custom'). Predominantly a lyrical composer, he drew on Transylvanian folk melodies, and idyllic scenes tend to dominate at the expense of dramatic conflict. The well-crafted vocal writing in the arias has ensured that the opera has remained in the repertory. It was first performed at the Romanian Opera in Cluj on 3 October 1934.

*

O. L. Cosma: *Opera românească* (Bucharest, 1962)
VIOREL COSMA

Negri, Gino (*b* Perledo, nr Como, 25 May 1919; *d* Montevecchia, nr Como, 19 July 1991). Italian composer and critic. He studied at the Milan Conservatory, where his teachers included Renzo Bossi. He taught at the Scuola del Piccolo Teatro in Milan from 1954 to 1959 and later at the Nuova Accademia, Milan. He was music critic of *Panorama* until 1984, and also worked for the RAI. In 1967 he was awarded the Premio Italia for his radio opera *Giovanni Sebastiano*.

Negri composed almost exclusively for the theatre, particularly works for small forces, which he found most congenial. The first, *Divertimenti di Palazzeschi* (composed 1943) for soprano, tenor and eight instruments, from Palazzeschi's *Visita alla contessa* and *Lasciatemi divertire*, exemplifies his surreal and abrasive irony. The characteristic form of Negri's 'chamber theatre' was developed in a series of one-act operas. In *Vieni qui, Carla* (1956) Negri used an idiom based on 12-note technique to treat a morally dubious episode from Alberto Moravia's *Gli indifferenti*. *Massimo* and *Il tè delle tre* (both 1958) tend towards an often bitter social satire and a striking juxtaposition of educated and working-class speech suggestive of Kurt Weill's musical theatre.

librettos by the composer unless otherwise stated

Divertimenti di Palazzeschi, 1943 (due episodi scenici, A. Palazzeschi), Milan, Nuovo, 18 Feb 1948; Evasione, 1945, unperf.; Sei personaggi in cerca di autore, 1950 (after L. Pirandello), unperf.; Vieni qui, Carla (1, after A. Moravia: *Gli indifferenti*), Milan, Piccolo, 21 Nov 1956; Massimo (1), Milan, Gerolamo, 10 June 1958; Il tè delle tre (farsa, 1), Como, Villa Olmo, 12 Sept 1958; L'armonium è utile, 1958 (1), unperf.; Una ragazza arrivò, 1958 (commedia, Negri and D. Buzzati)

Giorno di nozze (1), Milan, Gerolamo, 10 April 1959; Il circo Max (1), Venice, 23 Sept 1959; Costretto dagli eventi, Milan, 1963; Ciao patria, 1965 (commedia), unperf.; Il testimone indesiderato (radio op, Negri and G. Brusa), 1966; Giovanni Sebastiano (radio op), 1967, stage, Turin, 1970; La fine del mondo (television op), 1970; Pubblicità, ninfa gentile, Milan, 1970; Egli mi insegna che, Milan, 1974

Tarantella di Pulcinella (Negri and Luzzati), Milan, 1974; Balera d'amore, Milan, 1976; È l'abito che fa il flauto, 1977 (1), unperf.; Diario dell'assassinata, Milan, 1978; Un labirinto italiano, 1978, unperf.; Messa Maddalena, 1979, unperf.; Abasso Carmelo Bene, Milan, 1982; Storie d'Italia, Asti, 1982; Craxi anno due, Milan, 1985; Dragodstein, 1985, unperf.; Falsariga, ovvero Agguato a Vivaldi, 1985, unperf.; Videopiù, 1985, unperf.

*

M. Mila: 'A scandalous musician', *Score*, no.15 (1956), 31–8

——: 'Le opere impossibili di Gino Negri', *Cronache musicali 1955–1959* (Turin, 1959), 189–96

F. D'Amico: *I casi della musica* (Milan, 1962), 132–4, 267–9, 307–8
RAFFAELE POZZI

Negri, Maria Caterina (*b* Bologna; *fl* 1720–45). Italian contralto. She studied under Pasi and made her first known stage appearance at Modena in 1720 in *Il conte d'Altamura*. She sang in Florence (1721), Livorno (1722), Milan (1722 and 1723), Faenza (1723) and Ferrara (1724). In 1724–7 she was attached to the company of Antonio Denzio at the theatre of Count Sporck in Prague, where she sang Alcina in Antonio Bioni's *Orlando furioso*. She appeared in three operas by Vivaldi in Venice in 1727–8, one at Forlì and one at Livorno in 1729, and two, including Pergolesi's *Lo frate 'nnamorato*, at Naples in 1733. From November 1733 until summer 1737 she was a member of Handel's company in London, singing in 11 of his operas, the serenata *Parnasso in festa* and a number of pasticcios and oratorio revivals. In 1735 she appeared in *Aminta, a Pastoral Opera* in Dublin. After leaving London she sang in Florence (1737–8), Lisbon (1740, 1741), Parma (1743), Rimini and Bologna (1744) and Gorizia (1745). The parts Handel composed for her – Carilda in *Arianna*, Polinesso in *Ariodante*, Bradamante in *Alcina*, Irene in *Atalanta*, Tullius in *Arminio* and Arsace in *Berenice* – suggest a singer of moderate competence, though an occasional aria demands an agile technique. The compass is *a* to *e″*. She often played male roles.

She should not be confused with the singer Caterina Bassi Negri (*fl* 1734–46), known as Caterina Bassi before her marriage to the singer Giovanni Domenico Negri in 1739 or 1740.   WINTON DEAN, DANIEL FREEMAN

Negri, Maria Rosa [Risack, Rosa Negri] (*b* *c*1715; *d* Dresden, 4 Aug 1760). Italian mezzo-soprano. She was engaged for Dresden in 1730 and accompanied her sister Maria Caterina to London in 1733. She sang in four Handel operas, all revivals, in 1733–6. Handel probably wrote the part of Dalinda in *Ariodante* for her, but it was altered for soprano before performance. She was in Dublin with her sister in 1735–6. In Dresden she sang in a series of operas by Hasse, including *Cajo Fabricio* (1734), *La clemenza di Tito* (1738), *Arminio* (1745) and *La spartana generosa* (1747). In 1743 she appeared with her sister at Parma as Rosa Negri Risack. Handel appears to have thought little of her; the parts of Melo in *Sosarme* (1734), Eurilla in *Il pastor fido* (1734) and Morgana in *Alcina* (1736) were much shortened and simplified for her. Their compass is *a* to *f″*; her Hasse parts are more rewarding and call for expressiveness, fluent if limited coloratura and a compass *b* to *g♯″*.

An Anna or Antonia Negri, known as La Mestrina, sang frequently at Venice (1728–42), as well as at Parma, Modena and elsewhere, and married the tenor Pellegrino Tomj. According to Fürstenau she was a sister of Maria Rosa and was engaged for Dresden at the same time, but no parts sung by her at Dresden have been discovered, and there may be confusion with another singer.   WINTON DEAN

Negrini (Villa), Carlo (*b* Piacenza, 24 June 1826; *d* Naples, 14 March 1865). Italian tenor. He studied in Milan, then sang in the La Scala chorus, making his début as a soloist in 1847 as Jacopo (*I due Foscari*). After singing in Como and Constantinople, in 1850 he returned to La Scala as Oronte (*I Lombardi*). In 1852 he sang Pollione and Ernani at Covent Garden. He created Gabriele Adorno in *Simon Boccanegra* (1857) and Glauco in Petrella's *Ione* (1858), both at La Scala, and sang throughout Italy. His roles included Rossini's Otello, Poliuto, John of Leyden, Rodolfo (*Luisa Miller*), Manrico and Riccardo (*Ballo*).   ELIZABETH FORBES

Neher, (Rudolf Ludwig) Caspar (*b* Augsburg, 11 April 1897; *d* Vienna, 30 June 1962). German stage designer and librettist. He was a schoolfellow of Brecht's and studied art in Munich. His first work in opera came with his designs for *Palestrina* at Essen in 1927, although he had worked on *Don Giovanni* in Berlin in 1926 and had created the projections (a medium in which his work was famous) at Baden-Baden in 1927 for the *Mahagonny Songspiel*; other Brecht-Weill designs include *Die Dreigroschenoper* (1928, Berlin; later in New York and London), *Aufstieg und Fall der Stadt Mahagonny* (1930, Leipzig; later in Paris) and the *ballet chanté Die sieben Todsünden* (1933, Paris and London). He worked for the Kroll Opera in Berlin, 1928–31, under Klemperer, where his designs included *Carmen* and *From the House of the Dead*; in 1929 came the first of his seven productions of *Wozzeck*, at Essen. His collaborations with Carl Ebert in Berlin brought him into the operatic mainstream, and their great Verdi productions (*Macbeth*, 1931; *Un ballo in maschera*, 1932; he later designed both at Glyndebourne) did

much to provoke the German revaluation of the composer. Neher worked in Frankfurt from 1934 (*Tannhäuser* with Felsenstein, 1934; Egk's *Die Zaubergeige*, 1935), remaining in Germany during the Hitler years but maintaining his artistic independence, and indeed continuing his 'heterodox and subtly subversive work with Wagner-Régeny' (Drew), with whom he collaborated as librettist in the 1930s and 40s. He worked frequently with O. F. Schuh (beginning with *La traviata*, 1940, Vienna), at the Deutsches Theater in Berlin (from 1937 up to its 1944 closure), and with Noller at Hamburg (including Orff's *Carmina burana*, 1942). He worked much at Zürich in the immediate postwar period and from 1947 with Schuh and von Einem (*Dantons Tod*, 1947, and several Mozart operas). He was principal stage designer at Cologne, with Schuh, from 1959 to 1962.

Neher was an immensely intelligent designer with a true genius for the theatre; his importance within 20th-century stage design has still to be assessed. His work was characterized by minimal elaboration, the telling use of light, rigorously selected painted props and a controlled palette, establishing a stage picture in which the singers existed convincingly in an emotional and historical atmosphere, suggested rather than imposed. There is a collection of his designs in the Österreichische Nationalbibliothek, Vienna.

For illustration *see* DREIGROSCHENOPER, DIE; STAGE DESIGN, fig.22; and WOZZECK, fig.2.

Librettos: *Die Bürgschaft*, Weill, 1932; *Der Günstling*, Wagner-Régeny, 1935; *Die Bürger von Calais*, Wagner-Régeny, 1939; *Johanna Balk*, Wagner-Régeny, 1941; *Persische Episode* [*Der Darmwäscher*] (komische Oper, with B. Brecht), Wagner-Régeny, 1963 (comp. 1940–50)

*

Grove6 (D. Drew)
Caspar Neher: Zeugnisse seiner Zeitgenossen (Cologne, 1960)
G. von Einem and S. Melchinger, eds.: *Caspar Neher* (Hanover, 1966)
R. Wagner-Régeny and C. Neher: *Begegnungen* (East Berlin, 1968)
F. Hadamovsky: *Caspar Nehers szenisches Werk* (Vienna, 1972)
D. Bablet: *Revolutions in Stage Design of the Twentieth Century* (Paris and New York, 1977)
J. Willett: *Caspar Neher: Brecht's Designer* (London, 1986)
MARINA HENDERSON, DAVID J. HOUGH

Neidlinger, Gustav (*b* Mainz, 21 March 1910; *d* Bad Ems, 26 Dec 1991). German bass-baritone. He studied in Frankfurt with Otto Rottsieper and made his début in 1931 at Mainz, where he remained until 1934, taking supporting *buffo* bass roles. After an engagement in Plauen (1934–6) he joined the Hamburg Staatsoper, where his roles included Kecal, Bartolo and van Bett in *Zar und Zimmermann*. In 1950 he moved to the Württembergische Staatsoper, Stuttgart, where his roles included Faninal, Barak and Kaspar in *Der Zaubergeige*. He appeared at Bayreuth from 1952 to 1975 as Alberich, Kurwenal, Klingsor, the Nightwatchman, Hans Sachs and Telramund. He sang with the Stuttgart company at the Festival Hall, London, in 1955 as Pizarro and Kurwenal, and at the 1958 Edinburgh Festival as Lysiart (*Euryanthe*) and Kurwenal. In 1963 he made his Covent Garden début as Telramund. He did not sing in New York until 1973, when he appeared at the Metropolitan as Alberich. He was a guest at most European opera houses during the 1950s and 60s, appearing regularly at the Vienna Staatsoper from 1956. His Alberich, especially, was sung with a smoothness and even beauty of tone quite unusual in the part.

HAROLD ROSENTHAL/R

Nejedlý, Vít (*b* Prague, 22 June 1912; *d* Dukla, 1 Jan 1945). Czech composer and conductor. Son of the musicologist Zdeněk Nejedlý, he studied composition with Otakar Jeremiáš (1929–31) and conducting with Talich. He took the PhD in musicology at Prague University in 1936. He was répétiteur and conductor at the theatre in Olomouc from 1936 to 1938. After the Nazi occupation in 1939 he emigrated illegally to the USSR, where he studied with L. M. Ginzburg (1940–41) and worked as a radio conductor. He joined the Red Army and founded a Czech military ensemble on the Soviet model which still carries his name. He died of typhoid on the Dukla battlefield.

Nejedlý composed in many instrumental and vocal genres. At first he was influenced by contemporary trends, but later he stressed the vocal element, uncomplicated harmony and revolutionary pathos. The content of his works was often dictated by political and social revolutionary convictions. He wrote one opera, *Tkalci* ('The Weavers' op.15, 1940; 3, Nejedlý, after G. Hauptmann), which he left incomplete; the work was finished by Jan Hanuš in 1961 and first performed in Plzeň on 7 May that year. A carefully composed musical drama, it shows expressionist tendencies. Nejedlý also began another opera, *Nelson*, based on the 1934 disaster at the Bohemian coalmine of the same name, to a libretto by Milan Maralík. This was never finished; only a few songs and sketches remain.

*

J. Plavec: *Vzpomínky na Víta Nejedlého* [Memories of Nejedlý] (Prague, 1948)

J. Jiránek: *Vít Nejedlý* (Prague, 1959)

——: 'Vynikající česká moderní opera' [An Excellent Czech Modern Opera], *Divadlo* (1961), no.8, pp.616–30

EVA HERRMANNOVÁ

Nélée et Myrthis ('Neleus and Myrthis'). *Acte de ballet* by JEAN-PHILIPPE RAMEAU to an anonymous libretto; no known date of performance in Rameau's lifetime.

This work was evidently intended for a projected *opéra-ballet*, *Les beaux jours de l'Amour* (*see NAISSANCE D'OSIRIS, LA*). The skeletal action takes place during the Argive Games. Rebuffed by the feigned indifference of the poetess Myrthis (soprano), the athlete Neleus (*haute-contre*) deliberately arouses her jealousy by courting Corinna. But Myrthis's true feelings for Neleus are revealed as she crowns him *victor ludorum*, to the onlookers' delight. The athletics take place during an impressive chaconne (compare Rameau's *Naïs*). While not outstanding, this and the remaining music is well wrought and unfailingly attractive.

GRAHAM SADLER

Nelhybel, Vaclav (*b* Polanka nad Odrou, Czechoslovakia, 24 Sept 1919). American composer of Czech birth. He studied classics and musicology at Prague University and conducting and composition at the Prague Conservatory. In 1942 he went to Fribourg University in Switzerland, where he studied musicology, and from 1947 taught music theory. He has held conducting positions with Radio Prague and the Stadttheater (1939–42), the Czech PO (1945–6), Swiss Radio (1946–50) and Radio Free Europe (1950–7). In 1957 he went to the USA, becoming an American citizen in 1962. He has lectured at schools and colleges throughout the USA and Canada and taught at the University of Lowell, Massachusetts, in 1978–9.

Known primarily for his wind and band compositions, Nelhybel has written three operas, *Legend* (1954), *Everyman* (1974) and *Station* (1978), the last of which received a workshop performance in 1979 at the University of Lowell. Of these, *Everyman* is perhaps the best known. Based on the famous medieval morality play, this one-act work was commissioned by Southwest Missouri State University in Springfield, Missouri, where it was first performed on 24 October 1974. The libretto, by the composer, takes on the shape and demeanour of the original play, focussing on the journey of Everyman as, after being summoned by Death, he gives account of his life in this world. The protagonist tries to persuade his friends, Fellowship, Kindred, Worldly Goods, Beauty and others, to journey with him. Forsaken by all, only Good Deeds remains faithful to him and accompanies him to the grave. Nelhybel sets the work in a musical style that is essentially tonal, with modal colouring to evoke the feeling of the medieval original. The orchestration supports this approach, using winds, brass, chimes, bells, organ and percussion. The harmonic language is chromatic, especially in scenes where the character of Death is important. The voices are given simple diatonic melodies with straightforward rhythms; the voice of God is sung by a men's chorus. One drawback is the text: the attempt to remain faithful to the language of the original results in a stilted libretto that is difficult to understand.

JAMES P. CASSARO

Nelson. Opera in three acts, op.41, by LENNOX BERKELEY to a libretto by Alan Pryce-Jones; London, Sadler's Wells Theatre, 22 September 1954.

Act 1 is set in a drawing-room in the Palazzo Sessa, Naples. Sir William (baritone) and Lady (Emma) Hamilton (soprano) prepare to receive Lord Nelson (tenor), 'the victor of the Nile'. He enters unostentatiously, followed by a fortune-teller who predicts that a stain will 'spread and grow until it covers your whole life'. Left alone, Nelson and Emma tacitly acknowledge their love for each other, before the other guests return to praise Nelson for his naval prowess.

The first scene of Act 2 moves to a drawing-room in London in November 1800. Lady Nelson (mezzo-soprano) finds no comfort in her solitary life. Nelson provokes her sarcasm by mentioning Sir William and Emma, who now enter. Emma is goaded into proclaiming her love for Nelson and leads the powerful final ensemble with the words 'A page has turned. For good or ill we move into the future now'. In the second scene, set in the garden at Merton, outside London, Lord Minto (bass-baritone) demands that Nelson choose between Emma and his career. Nelson and Emma sing a love duet, interrupted by a message from London. With the words 'May the great God whom I adore enable me to fulfil the expectations of my country' Nelson chooses the path of duty.

The first scene of Act 3 is set outside an inn in Portsmouth. Hardy (bass) salutes Nelson for abiding by his duty. Emma has come to see him for one last time, but makes no attempt to dissuade him. The second scene depicts Nelson's death on board the *Victory*, with the Battle of Trafalgar won, before the setting returns to the garden terrace at Merton, where Hardy finishes telling Emma the details of Nelson's death. The opera ends with her exaltedly recalling their love.

If the musical characterization in Act 1 is at times uncertain, Lady Nelson's monologue at the beginning of

Act 2 is a powerful depiction of a woman no longer valued. From here, the music grows in conviction, and Emma's final apostrophe to love is painted in sweeping melodic lines and sumptuous orchestral colouring.

ROGER NICHOLS

Nelson, Havelock (*b* Cork, 25 May 1917). Irish conductor. He was educated in Dublin and was a pupil of Martinon. He joined the BBC in Northern Ireland in 1947, working as conductor, accompanist and broadcaster, as well as directing the Ulster Singers from 1954. During this time he formed and directed the Studio Opera Group with whom he conducted regular Belfast productions of opera in English. He conducted *Hänsel und Gretel* with Sadler's Wells Opera in 1981. His recordings include highlights of various Irish operas. In 1976 he became artistic director of the Trinidad and Tobago Opera Company, later returning to Belfast.

Nelson, John (*b* San José, Costa Rica, 6 Dec 1941). American conductor. He studied in Orlando, Florida, at Wheaton College, Illinois, and with Jean Morel at the Juilliard School, New York, where he won the Irving Berlin Award for conducting. He made his opera début in *Carmen* for New York City Opera in 1972, organized and conducted a complete concert version of *Les Troyens* at Carnegie Hall that year, and made his Metropolitan Opera début in that work in 1973. He subsequently acquired a broad repertory from Monteverdi and Handel to Janáček and Britten, whose *Owen Wingrave* he conducted at Santa Fe in its first American production. In Europe he gained distinction as a Berlioz conductor at Lyons, especially in *Benvenuto Cellini* in 1989. In 1985 he was appointed music director for the Opera Theatre of St Louis, where he has added to the company's reputation with conducting of dramatic flair and musical weight.

MICHAEL WALSH, NOËL GOODWIN

Nelson [née Manes], Judith (*b* Chicago, 10 Sept 1939). American soprano. She studied at St Olaf's College, Minnesota, then sang with various ensembles in Chicago and Berkeley. Her operatic début was as Roberto in Alessandro Scarlatti's *Griselda* at Berkeley in 1976. She has sung with many leading early music specialists including Christopher Hogwood and René Jacobs, and has taken part in revivals of early operas: she sang Drusilla in Monteverdi's *L'incoronazione di Poppea* (1979, Brussels), the title role in Landi's *Sant'Alessio* (1981, Innsbruck) and Martia in Cesti's *Tito* (1983, Innsbruck). She has also appeared at La Fenice, at the Teatro dell'Opera, Rome, at Turin, and at festivals throughout Europe and the USA. Though Nelson's pure, light-textured and warmly expressive voice is particularly suited to Renaissance and Baroque repertory, she has also sung contemporary music. Her recordings include *Poppea*, Cavalli's *Serse* (1985), and Purcell's *Dido and Aeneas* and *The Fairy-Queen*.

NICHOLAS ANDERSON

Németh, Maria (*b* Körmend, 13 March 1897; *d* Vienna, 28 Dec 1967). Hungarian soprano. She studied in Budapest and Naples, and with Giannina Russ in Milan. She made her début in Budapest in 1923 as Sulamith (*Die Königin von Saba*). From 1924 to 1946 she was a member of the Vienna Staatsoper, where her voice and temperament enabled her to sing Puccini, Verdi, Mozart and Wagner with equal success. She was considered a superb Turandot, a role she sang at Covent Garden in 1931. She also appeared in Italy, and as Donna Anna at the Salzburg Festival. Her last appearance was as Santuzza in 1946.

GV (L. Riemens; R. Vegeto)   HAROLD ROSENTHAL/R

Némethy, Ella (*b* Sátoraljauhely, 5 April 1895; *d* Budapest, 14 June 1961). Hungarian mezzo-soprano. She studied at the Liszt Academy of Music, Budapest, and in Milan with Ettore Panizza, making her Budapest Opera House début in 1919 as Delilah. She was the leading mezzo-soprano in the interwar years, above all in Wagnerian roles such as Brünnhilde, Isolde and Kundry. Her interpretations were characterized by vocal amplitude, rich colouring and grand declamation. In the early part of her career she was a splendid Salome, Carmen, Santuzza and Tosca, and later Amneris and Eboli. She made guest appearances in South America, Italy (1929–44) and Barcelona.

PÉTER P. VÁRNAI

Nemirovich-Danchenko, Vladimir Ivanovich (*b* Ozurgeti, Georgia, 11/23 Dec 1858; *d* Moscow, 25 April 1943). Russian director. He began as a drama critic and playwright in Moscow, and supervised the drama course at the Moscow Philharmonic Society, 1891–1901. In 1897 he met KONSTANTIN SERGEYEVICH STANISLAVSKY and they founded the Moscow Art Theatre, where their experiments in naturalist and symbolist theatre were internationally influential. Both directed productions; Nemirovich-Danchenko was primarily responsible for the repertory and its literary quality. He looked for and encouraged new Russian playwrights, including Chekhov, the successful revival of whose *Seagull* was crucial to the dramatist's career.

After the 1917 Revolution the government proposed that the experimental studios set up at the Moscow Art Theatre should be organized for opera. Stanislavsky's Bol'shoy Theatre Opera Studio applied his new ideas of theatrical ensemble and 'Method' acting to opera production. Nemirovich-Danchenko's Moscow Art Theatre Music Studio, founded in 1919, was more avant-garde and revolutionary. While he shared his old colleague's basic concern for rhythm and internal truth in theatrical production, Nemirovich-Danchenko held no brief for psychological realism. He banished all traditional conventions of dramatic and operatic staging. Employing exercises and rehearsal techniques inspired by Jaques-Dalcroze's eurhythmics, he created a stylized performance known as the 'synthetic theatre' and promoted the ideal of the *poyushchiy aktyor* ('singing actor'). Steps and gestures were devised in the strictest synchronization with the music and were executed in abstract, spatial settings devoid of realistic trappings. The company was composed of very young singers. Roles were rotated, and no personality or voice was ever permitted to stand out. The repertory was varied, including both opera and operetta. Nemirovich-Danchenko was particularly eager to stimulate new works; among the group's productions was Shostakovich's *Katerina Izmaylova*, on 24 January 1934, two days after its Leningrad première as *Lady Macbeth of the Mtsensk District*. Productions of standard works were notoriously controversial: librettos were often completely rewritten in the translation process, and scores too were frequently altered. In *Carmen* (1924), for example, the role of Micaëla was eliminated, and in *La traviata* (1934) a new chorus provided a running social commentary on Violetta's tragedy.

Under Isaak Rabinovich's artistic direction, these productions were among the landmarks of Constructivist stage design. They were usually mounted on unit sets consisting of platforms and towers at various levels connected by ramps and stairs. Light was selectively used to define acting areas, as well as to create specific moods. Costumes were characteristically stylized and exceedingly colourful. Both in Russia and abroad on tour these productions were acclaimed for their imaginative daring and high standards of acting and staging. At the same time, critics found the musical standard low and the altered scores intolerable. Although the studio's name was changed in his honour to the Nemirovich-Danchenko Music Theatre in 1926, his influence at home was limited by Stalin's conservative taste. In the West, however, he has proved to be an important contributor to the development of modern opera production. His memoirs, *Iz proshlogo*, were published in Moscow in 1936, and also in an English translation, *My Life in the Russian Theatre* (London, 1936).

*

P. A. Markov: *V. I. Nemirovich-Danchenko i muzïkal'nïy teatr yego imeni* [Nemirovich-Danchenko and the Music Theatre Named after Him] (Moscow, 1936)
——: *Rezhissura V. I. Nemirovich-Danchenko v muzïkal'nom teatre* [The Director Nemirovich-Danchenko in the Music Theatre] (Moscow, 1960)   PAUL SHEREN

Nentwig, Franz Ferdinand (*b* Duisburg, 23 Aug 1929). German baritone. He studied at the Detmold Music Academy and in Hamburg and Essen. Having begun as a concert and recital singer, he joined the Ulm Opera, then sang in Karlsruhe and Hanover, and in 1977 became a member of the Hamburg Staatsoper; in that year he also made his American début in San Francisco. A versatile singer and actor with a bright, forward timbre, he has played the leading Mozart, Strauss and Wagner baritone roles (including Wotan), as well as Wozzeck, Scarpia, Escamillo, Amonasro, Yevgeny Onegin and Boris. His Covent Garden début was in 1985 as the Music-Master (*Ariadne auf Naxos*); he returned as La Roche (*Capriccio*) in 1990 and has sung at other leading European centres as well as at the Metropolitan and the Moscow Bol'shoy.

NOËL GOODWIN

Nepomuceno, Alberto (*b* Fortaleza, 6 July 1864; *d* Rio de Janeiro, 16 Oct 1920). Brazilian composer. His father was his first teacher. His formal education began in Recife and continued, from 1884, in Rio de Janeiro. A trip to Europe, begun in 1888, took him to the most celebrated music schools: the Accademia di S Cecilia in Rome, the Akademische Meisterschule and Stern Conservatory in Berlin, and the Paris Conservatoire. He returned to Rio de Janeiro in 1895 and taught at the National Institute of Music. The next year he took on the directorship of the Sociedade de Concertos Populares, and in 1902 that of the National Institute of Music, but only for a few months. He was again director of the institute from 1906 to 1916.

Nepomuceno's instrumental works, numerous art songs and sacred and secular choral pieces reveal his eclecticism. Although he has been proclaimed the 'father' of Brazilian musical nationalism, he made no attempt to create a national opera. His stage works include the operas *Artémis* (Rio de Janeiro, 14 October 1898) and *Abul*, the incidental music for *Electra* (after Sophocles) and the musical comedy *A cigarra*. *Abul*, which is reminiscent of *Artémis*, was written between 1899 and 1905 and is based on a story by Herbert C. Ward. The action takes place in the ancient city of Ur in Chaldea. Abul and his followers worship an invisible god. Amrafel, King of Ur, orders that the child destined to be offered in sacrifice for the inauguration of the statue of the god Hurki be selected from among Abul's followers. Abul does not oppose the order, but, at the sacrifice, confronts the stone idol and knocks it off its pedestal, so that the people realize that Hurki is not the true god.

See also ARTÉMIS.

*

L. H. Corrêa de Azevedo: *Relação das óperas de autores brasileiros* (Rio de Janeiro, 1938)
B. Kiefer: *História da música brasileira* (Porto Alegre, 2/1977), 110–18
V. Mariz: *A canção brasileira* (Rio de Janeiro, 5/1985)
GERARD BÉHAGUE

Népszínmű (Hung.: 'song-play'). Hungarian genre of the mid-19th century, a local equivalent of the ballad opera and other popular vernacular genres. The setting is normally a Hungarian village or small town, and the music has a folklike quality. Such works were in the repertories of Hungarian travelling opera troupes.

Neri, Giambattista [Giovanni Battista] (*b* Bologna; *d* 11 Aug 1726). Italian librettist. He received a degree in medicine in 1677, but practised for only a short time before turning to writing for a living. He was employed as secretary to Prince Filippo Ercolani, state counsellor to three successive emperors (Leopold I, Joseph I and Charles VI) and imperial ambassador to Venice. After leaving Ercolani's service he had difficulty supporting himself and died in poverty. Neri wrote seven opera librettos, at least seven oratorios and numerous occasional poems. His opera librettos were for either Bologna or Venice, with the exception of his last and most popular work, *L'enigma disciolto*, written for Reggio Emilia. All firmly based in *seicento* style, they do not reflect the tendency towards elevated tone and serious subject matter that characterized Italian libretto writing from the 1690s onwards. His *Gige in Lidia* was the first libretto set by Domenico Gabrielli, and *Catone il giovane* the first by Bartolomeo Monari. In 1696 *Basilio re d'oriente* reopened the Teatro S Cassiano, newly refurbished after being used only sporadically for operas in the preceding three decades. *Clotilde*, which closed the 1696 season there, was used in 1702 (as *Amar per vendetta*) for the reopening of the smaller Teatro S Moisè, which had been closed to opera between 1693 and 1701. Between 1698 and 1723 *L'enigma disciolto*, a small-scale pastorale with five characters, was staged at least 18 times, usually in modest theatres such as the tiny Teatro S Fantino in Venice or in provincial theatres within the Venetian republic, such as those in Treviso, Vicenza, Brescia and Udine.

Gige in Lidia, D. Gabrielli, 1683; *Cleobulo*, Gabrielli, 1683; *Catone il giovane*, B. Monari, 1688; *Basilio re d'oriente*, F. Navara, 1696 (Porpora, 1713); *Clotilde*, Ruggieri, 1696; *Erifile*, Ariosti, 1697; *L'enigma disciolto* (favola pastorale), C. F. Pollarolo, 1698 (comp. unknown, 1712, as L'amor non inteso; A. Cortona, 1726, as L'amor indovino; 1728, as Le vicende amorose)

AllacciD
G. Bonlini: *Le glorie della poesia e della musica* (Venice, 1730)

F. S. Quadrio: *Della storia e della ragione d'ogni poesia* (Bologna, 1739–52)

G. Fantuzzi: *Notizie degli scrittori bolognesi* (Bologna, 1797)

C. Ricci: *I teatri di Bologna* (Bologna, 1888)

E. Selfridge-Field: *Pallade veneta: Writings on Music in Venetian Society, 1650–1750* (Venice, 1985)

C. Sartori: *I libretti italiani a stampa dalle origini al 1800* (Cuneo, 1990–)

HARRIS S. SAUNDERS

Neri, Giulio (*b* Turrita di Siena, 21 May 1909; *d* Rome, 21 April 1958). Italian bass. He studied with Ferraresi in Florence, and at the Rome Conservatory. He made his début at the Teatro delle Quattro Fontane, Rome (1935), and sang major roles at the Rome Opera from 1938; he was widely known in Italy for his powerful performances as the Grand Inquisitor, Alvise (*La Gioconda*), Méphistophélès (Gounod), Sparafucile and Don Basilio. Guest appearances took him to Buenos Aires, Barcelona, Munich and London (Oroveso and Ramfis, 1953). He sang at the 1955 Maggio Musicale, Florence, in a revival of Donizetti's last opera, *Dom Sébastien*.

DAVID CUMMINGS

Neri, Michele Angiolo (*b* Pisa, *c*1755; *d* ?Florence, after 1797). Italian soprano castrato. His first roles were Theagenes in Jommelli's *Achille in Sciro* and Fausta in Anfossi's *Quinto Fabio* at the Teatro delle Dame in Rome during the 1771 Carnival. When the Florentine impresario Giuseppe Compstoff took over at the Dame in 1772, Neri so impressed him that he took him back to Florence to sing in Gluck's *Orfeo ed Euridice* at the Cocomero. Neri sang at the Pergola during the 1772 carnival in Mortellari's *Didone abbandonata* and returned the following year. At this time he also studied in Florence, with Giovanni Manzuoli (Neri is sometimes called 'il Manzuolino'), developing a 'voice of silver', according to a contemporary Florentine critic. He regularly sang in Lenten concerts in Florence (1772–96) and often in unstaged operas, such as Traetta's *Ifigenia in Tauride* (Teatro di Porta Rossa, 1773).

Over the next decade and a half Neri's reputation spread throughout Italy. In 1774 he was at S Benedetto, Venice, in Anfossi's *L'olimpiade*; in 1776 he was the primo uomo in the première in Florence of Myslivecek's *L'Adriano in Siria*; and in 1778 he returned to the Dame in Rome to perform comic operas during carnival. This versatility (surprising in a castrato), as well as his acting ability, is confirmed by his membership of Andrea Patriarchi's prose company in 1787; he undoubtedly sang the incidental music used in their spoken plays. After several seasons of *opera seria* in Venice, in 1790 he was the *primo buffo* in *La villanella rapita* at the King's Theatre, London, together with Nancy Storace, with whom he had sung in Florence.

Neri added 'Angiolo' to his name officially in 1784, to avoid confusion with the Florentine composer Michele Neri Bondi. He joined the paid court musicians of Grand Duke Ferdinando in 1792, becoming elevated to *secondo soprano della Real Camera e Cappella* in 1797. During this time he sang in *opera seria* at the Pergola, but after joining the grand ducal chapel he apparently abandoned the operatic stage. ROBERT LAMAR WEAVER

Neri-Baraldi, Pietro (*b* 1828; *d* 1902). Italian tenor. He sang Fernand (*La favorite*) at the Paris Opéra in 1855. In London (1856–68), first at the Lyceum Theatre then at Covent Garden, he sang a wide variety of roles, including Alfonso (*Zampa*), Giannetto (*La gazza ladra*), Lorenzo (*Fra Diavolo*), Alphonse (*La muette de Portici*),

Elvino (*La sonnambula*), Arturo (*I puritani*), Charlais (*Maria di Rohan*), Danilowitz (*L'étoile du nord*), Raimbaut (*Robert le diable*), Gennaro (*Lucrezia Borgia*), Tonio (*La fille du régiment*) and the Duke (*Rigoletto*). Although essentially a lyric tenor, he also sang Manrico and Florestan. ELIZABETH FORBES

Neri Bondi, Michele (*b* Florence, 16 Oct 1750; *d* Florence, *c*1822). Italian composer. His original name was Michele Neri, but in 1773, owing to the presence in Florence of a singer with the same name, he changed his surname to Neri Bondi while the singer let himself be known as Michele Angiolo Neri. After Ferdinando Rutini, Neri Bondi was the most prolific late 18th-century Florentine composer of comic operas. His most successful, *I matrimoni in cantina*, was heard twice in both Florence and Bologna, and also in Pisa, Lucca, Rome, Ravenna and Palermo; all his other works were composed for and performed only in Florence. His forte was the composition of musical entertainments for those Florentine theatres (the Cocomero, Intrepidi, Piazza Vecchia, S Maria and Borgo Ognissanti) that, following government regulations, performed prose tragedies and comedies as their principal fare. Only one of his comedies, *La locandiera*, was performed at the Teatro di via della Pergola.

Between 1779 and 1790 Neri Bondi was prominent as a music director and first harpsichordist in the small theatres, especially the Intrepidi, directing works by Andreozzi, Borghi, Cimarosa, Moneta and Valentini, as well as his own. Finally, in the carnival of 1790 for the grand reopening of the refurbished Pergola he directed *L'Amleto*, with music by Luigi Caruso, afterwards remaining as music director at that theatre. In 1792 he assumed the role of *maestro dei coristi* there. In the 1793 summer season he became the impresario of the S Maria, directing there in the summer and at the Pergola in the spring and autumn seasons. During carnival he simultaneously directed opera at the Pergola and served as impresario at the S Maria, but he resigned from the latter after one year. He opened a school of music in Fiesole in January 1796 and about the same time became *maestro di cappella* at S Maria de' Candeli, but continued as first harpsichordist at the Pergola until at least autumn 1822, when he was replaced by the second harpsichordist, Luigi Barbieri. His six extant operas have not yet been examined by modern scholars.

all first performed in Florence

Infedeltà delusa (dg, 2, M. Coltellini), Piazza Vecchia, carn. 1783

Le serve in contesa (int, 2, F. Casorri), Intrepidi, aut. 1783

Ogni disgualianza amore aggualiga (int, 1, Casorri), S Maria, carn. 1784, *I-Tf*

Il ripiego improvviso, ovvero Quel che l'occhio non vede, il cor non crede (int, 1, Casorri), S Maria, 26 Dec 1784

L'amor rusticale (int, Casorri), S Maria, carn. 1785

I mietitori, ovvero L'amante dispettosa (int, 1, ?Casorri), S Maria, carn. 1785, *Tf*

I matrimoni in cantina [La finta nobiltà] (dg, 2, G. Bellentani), Intrepidi, 8 Nov 1785, *Tf*

La locandiera, o sia Da ultimo è bel tempo (dg, 2, D. Poggi, after C. Goldoni), Pergola, 2 June 1786

Le spose provenzali (dg, 2), Intrepidi, spr. 1787

Il maestro perseguitato (int, 1), Cocomero, Sept 1787

Tizio, e Sempronio (int, 1, Casorri), S Maria, 26 Dec 1787

La bella incognita, o siano I tre amanti delusi (int, 1, C. Giotti), Intrepidi, carn. 1788

Quello che può accadere (int, 1), S Maria, carn. 1788

L'autunno (int, 1, D. Somigli), Cocomero, 19 Sept 1788

La pianella persa [L'inverno] (farsetta, 2, ? P. Andolfati), Cocomero, 14 March 1789

I vendemmiatori, ovvero I due sindaci (farsetta, 1, ?Andolfati), Cocomero, 18 June 1789, *Fc*

La villa (farsetta, 1, Casorri), Piazza Vecchia, carn. 1790, *Fc*

Il mondo della luna (farsetta, Somigli, after Goldoni), S Maria, 28 Dec 1790; rev. as Il finto astronomo, o sia il mondo della luna (farsa), Piazza Vecchia, 26 Dec 1791, *Fc* [wrongly attrib. G. Moneta], *PAc*

Il vecchio speziale deluso in amore (farsa, Casorri), Piazza Vecchia, 28 Dec 1790

La fata Urgella, o sia Quel che piace alle donne in ogni tempo (farsa, 2, G. Squilloni, after C. S. Favart: *La fée Urgèle ou Ce qui plaît aux dames*), Borgo Ognissanti, 26 Dec 1791

La cameriera raggiratrice, o sia La guerra aperta (int, 2, Somigli), Cocomero, 26 Dec 1793

Il concistoro delle donne, ossia La bizarrie d'amore (int), Piazza Vecchia, 26 Dec 1793

Untitled farsa, Borgo Ognissanti, 26 Dec 1793

Il rivale di se medesimo (dg, 1, after P.-G. Nivelle de la Chausée: *Le rival de lui-même*), Cocomero, 27 Dec 1795

Gli artigiani (ob, 1), Borgo Ognissanti, carn. 1798, *PAc*

La villanella rapita, 1798

*

Indice de' spettacoli teatrali (Milan, 1764–1823)

H. Mendel: 'Bondineri, Michele', *Musikalisches Conversations-Lexikon*, ed. H. Mendel and A. Reissmann (Berlin, 1870–79)

M. de Angelis: *La felicità in Etruria* (Florence, 1990)

R. L. Weaver and N. W. Weaver: *a Chronology of Music in the Florentine Theater, ii: 1751–1800* (Warren, MI, 1992)

ROBERT LAMAR WEAVER

Néron ('Nero'). Opera in four acts by ANTON GRIGOR'YEVICH RUBINSTEIN to a French libretto by JULES BARBIER (adapted by the composer); Hamburg, Theater am Dammtor, 1 November 1879 (in German; Russian première, St Petersburg, Mariinsky Theatre, 29 January/10 February 1884, in Italian, by the resident Italian opera troupe; French première, to original libretto, Rouen, Théâtre des Arts, 14 February 1894).

Rubinstein composed *Néron* on longstanding commission from Émile Perrin, director of the Paris Opéra in the mid-1860s. Barbier's libretto concerns the Roman tyrant Nero (tenor) and his pursuit of Chrysa (soprano), the beautiful daughter of the courtesan Epicharis (contralto), who is loved by Vindex (baritone), Prince of Aquitania, and who, having proclaimed herself a Christian, is martyred by the chorus. This plot provides the thread on which a series of spectacular stage pictures is strung, including an orgy (Act 1), a grandiose temple procession and a ballet (*divertissement*) of circus entertainers (Act 2; the latter was at one time a popular concert piece), the burning of Rome (Act 3), and Nero's suicide, followed by the miraculous apparition of a cross in the sky (Act 4).

By the time Rubinstein finished the opera, Perrin was no longer in charge of the Paris Opéra, and the work was never produced there. One number has survived on the Russian recital stage: Vindex's mock Epithalamium from the Act 1 orgy, 'Poyu tebe, bog Gimeney' ('I sing to thee, divine Hymen!').

RICHARD TARUSKIN

Nerone (i) ('Nero'). *Tragedia per musica* in three acts by GIUSEPPE MARIA ORLANDINI to a libretto by AGOSTIN PIOVENE; Venice, Teatro S Giovanni Grisostomo, Carnival 1721.

The action is centred on the tyrannical power of Nero (tenor), who will use any means in order to crown his favourite, Poppea [Poppaea] (soprano). The fierce opposition of his mother Agrippina (contralto) and the attempted vengeance of Poppaea's husband Ottone [Otho] (tenor) are in vain. Otho's murder attempt is thwarted by Ottavia [Octavia] (soprano), Nero's wife, with the help of Tiridate [Tiridates] (soprano), the Arm-

enian king loyal to the emperor. Octavia's deed, however, serves as a pretext for Nero to repudiate her and send her into exile. The tyrant is thus able to obtain his goal, and also has Agrippina assassinated.

The fame of *Nerone* is chiefly associated with the arrangement of it as *Nero* made by Mattheson for Hamburg, where it was performed many times in 1723 and following years. Mattheson translated the libretto into German, composed new recitatives, added some arias and transposed others; in the Hamburg score all the vocal roles are altered, with the exception of Poppaea and Octavia. Its success is attributable both to the subject of the opera and to the novelty of Orlandini's music (his *Arsace*, another *tragedia per musica*, was also performed in Hamburg during those years). The 'modern' style of this composer, characterized by the prominence of the voice and by a simplification of the orchestral writing, fitted into a new dramatic conception founded on a more precise and coherent definition of characters.

FRANCESCO GIUNTINI

Nerone (ii) ('Nero'). *Tragedia* in four acts by ARRIGO BOITO to his own libretto; Milan, Teatro alla Scala, 1 May 1924.

Nerone occupied Boito for some 60 years and was originally conceived in five acts, ending with Nero playing the role of Orestes on stage as Rome burns around him. It was shortened at Giulio Ricordi's suggestion. The music is rich but episodic, contrasting the diatonicism of the Christian episodes with the strange harmonies and orchestral colour associated with both Nero and Simon the Paraclete. Boito makes considerable use of recurring themes. The score was put in performing shape after Boito's death by Vincenzo Tommasini and Antonio Smareglia, working under Toscanini's direction.

ACT 1 *The Via Appia, Rome, near the catacombs, by moonlight* Nero (tenor) appears, haunted by mysterious voices accusing him of matricide. With him is Simon Mago [Simon Magus] (baritone), a priest of a mysterious cult, who promises to rid Nero of his obsession that he is pursued by the Erinyes. Bearing an urn containing his mother's ashes, Nero hopes to placate her spirit by burying them, and thinks of himself as a new Orestes (aria, 'Queste ad un lido fatal'). Asteria (soprano), in the form of an Erinys, seeks to pursue Nero, not from vengeance but for love. Simon detains her. To the Christian tombs comes Rubria (mezzo-soprano), who kneels and says the Lord's Prayer. Asteria is strangely moved by this, but suddenly she dashes off in pursuit of another god. Fanuèl (baritone), a Christian apostle, enters; Rubria wishes to confess a sin to him but she is interrupted by Simon and leaves. Simon tells Fanuèl of his vision of the Christians triumphing over decadent imperial Rome, and then offers to buy some of this power. Fanuèl curses Simon, and the two declare their enmity. Nero returns with Tigellino [Tigellinus] (bass), who seeks to calm Nero's fears and tells him that he will enter Rome in triumph. The populace hail him as an Apollo.

ACT 2 *Simon's subterranean temple* A crowd of devotees has gathered when a curtain parts to reveal Simon in the sanctuary, surrounded by initiates. He holds a flaming beaker from which issue first blood and then a cloud of steam that obscures him from view. The curtains are drawn and the worshippers express their conviction that Simon has ascended into the sky. When

'Nerone' (Boito), Act 4 scene i (The Oppidium) in the original production at La Scala, Milan, 1 May 1924: from 'L'illustrazione italiana' (4 May 1924)

the crowd disperses Simon sets Asteria upon the altar in preparation for Nero's arrival. Nero enters and, believing Asteria to be a goddess, worships her. He begs forgiveness, confessing his sins, among them the rape of a Vestal virgin. Emboldened, he kisses Asteria and discovers she is no goddess, but a mortal woman. Enraged by this, he starts to smash the deceptive mechanisms of Simon's bogus temple, summons guards to seize Simon and Asteria and declares himself the new divinity of the temple.

ACT 3 *An orchard* Fanuèl recites the Beatitudes to a group of Christians while Rubria and some women weave garlands. Asteria enters, wounded, having escaped from the snake-pit into which Nero had ordered her to be cast. She urges the Christians to escape because Simon has revealed their presence to Nero and his guards. Rubria begs Fanuèl to flee, but he wants to hear her interrupted confession. Disguised as a blind beggar, Simon comes to ask Fanuèl to use his power to assist him; he has been ordered by Nero to give proof of the boast he made that he could fly. When Fanuèl refuses, Simon signals concealed soldiers to arrest him, and Fanuèl bids his followers a moving farewell in the aria 'Vivete in pace'. They accompany their leader to prison, leaving Rubria in torment, alone.

ACT 4.i *The Oppidium* In this antechamber of the Circus Maximus, between the cells and the arena, Gobrias (tenor), Simon's assistant, warns his master that he has arranged a fire in the city to spare Simon from making his 'flight'. Asteria has thought of the fire as a way of sparing the Christians in the resultant confusion. Nero and Tigellinus have also heard of the fire, which the emperor welcomes as a means of redesigning the city. The Christians are forced into the arena, there to enact a sanguinary Greek myth. A veiled Vestal virgin

pleads for the Christians, who are singing a Credo. Nero commands the veil be stripped from the virgin, revealing her to be Rubria, whereupon he orders her to be cast into the arena with her fellow Christians. Simon is hurled from the roof and, failing to fly, crashes to his death. The smoke of the fire envelops the Circus, causing panic.

4.ii *The Spoliarium* To this mortuary beneath the Circus come Fanuèl and Asteria, seeking Rubria's body. Fatally wounded but still alive, she confesses her sin at last: how she had served Vesta, been raped by Nero and become a Christian; but she fears she has not truly served her new faith. Fanuèl pardons her and calls her his betrothed as she dies. He and Asteria flee the burning Circus, but Asteria soon returns, jealous that Rubria had been possessed by Nero. Realizing that Rubria is dead, Asteria drops on her corpse a flower which the girl had given her.

*   *   *

One of the most successful things in the opera is the passacaglia at the beginning of Act 2, with its repeated bass and variations interspersed with brief interludes. Another is Fanuèl's recital of the Beatitudes near the beginning of Act 3. There are, however, a number of passages of empty rhetoric, and others that are merely busy. But in spite of its unevenness, *Nerone* everywhere testifies to Boito's serious, erudite purpose.

WILLIAM ASHBROOK

Nerval, Gérard de [Labrunie, Gérard] (*b* Paris, 22 May 1808; *d* Paris, 26 Jan 1856). French writer and translator. His mother died while he was in his infancy, and his father, an army surgeon, was taken prisoner during Napoleon's Russian campaign and held captive until 1814. To some extent these misfortunes may account for Nerval's chaotic creative personality. He began his literary career with translations of works by contemporary German authors. When his version of the first part of *Faust* appeared in 1828, Goethe praised it, and Berlioz took passages from it for *Huit scènes de Faust* (published in 1829; Berlioz later reissued the work, with additional texts, as *La damnation de Faust*.) Among Nerval's many later works are ten opera librettos (written between 1835 and 1850), including the three-act *opéra-comique Piquillo*, written in collaboration with Alexandre Dumas *père* and set to music by Hippolyte Monpou (1837). His story *Le voyage en Orient* (1853) was the basis of Gounod's opera *La reine de Saba*.

*

R. E. Jones: *Gérard de Nerval* (New York, 1974)
J. Rushton: 'Berlioz's *Huit scènes de Faust*: New Source Material', *MT*, cxv (1974), 471–3
B. L. Knapp: *Gérard de Nerval* (Alabama, 1980)

CHRISTOPHER SMITH

Nessi, Giuseppe (*b* Bergamo, 25 Sept 1887; *d* Milan, 16 Dec 1961). Italian tenor. He studied at the Bergamo Conservatory and made his début at Saluzzo in 1910 as Alfredo. After a short career as a lyric tenor he began to specialize in character roles and became the leading Italian comprimario of his time. From 1921 to 1959 he sang regularly at La Scala, where he created Pong in *Turandot*, Gobrias in Boito's *Nerone*, Dona Pasqua in *Il campiello* and roles in operas by Pizzetti and Malipiero among others. Two of his most notable parts were Bardolph in *Falstaff*, which he sang at Salzburg (1935–9), and Malatestino in *Francesca da Rimini*. He appeared frequently at Covent Garden (1927–37) and was the first London Pong and the first Covent Garden Trabuco (1931). He appeared in most leading Italian opera houses and his repertory included Goro, Spoletta, Missail (*Boris Godunov*) and Vašek. He was a master of make-up and a gifted comic actor. His last appearance was as Pinellino (*Gianni Schicchi*) at La Scala in 1959.

HAROLD ROSENTHAL/R

Nessler, Viktor E(rnst) (*b* Baldenheim bei Schlettstadt, Alsace, 28 Jan 1841; *d* Strasbourg, 28 May 1890). Alsatian composer. The son of a Protestant pastor, he studied theology in Strasbourg. His musical inclinations displeased his university teachers, however, and they expelled him. After the staging of his first opera, *Fleurette*, in Strasbourg (1864), he began musical studies in Leipzig which led to a lifelong connection with that city. There he directed male-voice choirs (for which he wrote many 'volkstümlich' partsongs) before becoming chorus master at the Leipzig Stadttheater; he was later conductor at the Carola-Theater and then director of the Leipzig choral society. Nessler was known for his fairy-tale or saga-derived operas, which were akin to the sentimental poetic romances of J. V. von Scheffel and his imitator Julius Wolff, widely read in mid-19th-century Germany. The particularly successful *Der Rattenfänger von Hameln* (1879) was derived from Wolff. The popularity of Nessler's conservative style, relying on a succession of simple melodies and some recurring motivic material, waned in his lifetime (critics were to scorn his librettos as fake-Gothic or 'Butzenscheiben-romantik'). He nevertheless enjoyed the influential support of the Austrian impresario Angelo Neumann, and *Der Trompeter von Säkkingen* (1884), after Scheffel, achieved startling success in over 900 performances in north Germany; it was translated into five languages,

and inspired Arthur Nikisch to compose an orchestral fantasy on its themes.

See also RATTENFÄNGER VON HAMELN, DER and TROMPETER VON SÄKKINGEN, DER.

Fleurette (komische Oper, 2, E. Feberel), Strasbourg, Municipal, 15 March 1864
Dornröschens Brautfahrt (romantische Oper, 3, R. Bunge), Leipzig, Privat-Theater Thalia, 13 March 1867
Die Hochzeitsreise (Operette), Leipzig, March 1867
Am Alexandertag (komische Oper, 1, L. Julius), Leipzig, Stadt, 17 Dec 1869
Nachtwächter und Student (Operette, 1, E. Engelhand, after T. Körner), Leipzig, Stadt, 10 June 1871
Irmingard (grosse Oper, 5, Bunge), Leipzig, 19 April 1876
Der Rattenfänger von Hameln (grosse Oper, 5, F. Hofmann, after J. Wolff), Leipzig, 19 March 1879
Der wilde Jäger (romantische Oper, 4, Hofmann, after Wolff), Leipzig, 11 Dec 1881
Der Trompeter von Säkkingen (prol., 3, Bunge, after J. V. von Scheffel), Leipzig, 4 May 1884
Otto der Schütz (romantische Oper, Bunge, after G. Kinkel), Leipzig, 15 Nov 1886
Die Rose von Strassburg (4, F. Ehrenburg), Munich, Hof, 2 May 1890

*

MGG (T.-M. Langner); *StiegerO*

PETER FRANKLIN

Nesterenko, Yevgeny (Yevgen'yevich) (*b* Moscow, 8 Jan 1938). Soviet bass. He studied in Leningrad, making his début at the Malïy Theatre in 1962 as Gremin. He sang there and at the Kirov until 1971, when he joined the Bol'shoy; his roles include Dosifey, Khan Konchak, Ruslan, Kutuzov, Salieri and Boris, in which role he made his débuts with the Bol'shoy at La Scala (1973), the Vienna Staatsoper (1974) and the Metropolitan (1975). He made his Covent Garden début in 1978 as Don Basilio, later singing Ivan Khovansky (1982) and Méphistophélès (1983). At La Scala his roles included Massimiliano (*I masnadieri*), Rossini's Moses, Colline, the Grand Inquisitor and Philip II, which he also sang at Munich, San Francisco, Savonlinna and Orange (1990). He sang Zaccaria (*Nabucco*) and Attila at Barcelona (1984) and Bartók's Bluebeard at Budapest (1988), a role he recorded successfully. His voice, full and resonant, has a typically Russian timbre. He colours it expressively and is a competent actor.

ALAN BLYTH

Nestroy, Johann Nepomuk (Eduard Ambrosius) (*b* Vienna, 7 Dec 1801; *d* Graz, 25 May 1862). Austrian playwright, actor and singer. He studied law in Vienna (1817–22), but left without a degree in order to devote himself to singing. On 24 August 1822 he made his début with the court opera as Sarastro at the Kärntnertortheater, and was a member of the company until August 1823, singing ten roles in works by Paer, Rossini, Grétry, Gyrowetz and others, including Don Fernando in *Fidelio*. He then joined the German Theatre in Amsterdam, where in two years he built up his repertory to include Caspar and Ottokar in *Der Freischütz*, Publius (and later Annius) in *La clemenza di Tito*, Masetto (and later Don Giovanni), Papageno, Pizarro, Adam in Schenk's *Der Dorfbarbier*, and numerous Rossini roles. Towards the end of his Dutch engagement comic character parts began to figure prominently, a tendency increasingly marked during his *Wanderjahre* (1825–31) as actor and singer at Brno, Graz, Pressburg, Klagenfurt, Vienna and Lemberg. Throughout his career nearly all his roles included singing, and he occasionally sang Adam until near the end of his life; but he had discovered his métier as a comic

575

actor and tried his hand as a dramatist well before he joined Karl Carl's Theater an der Wien in autumn 1831.

Nestroy was the last and greatest figure in the long line of Viennese popular actor-dramatists; his repertory included both traditional personae from the mid- and late 18th century (Kasperl, and Singspiel comic basses) and Offenbach roles when, late in his career, he helped introduce the Parisian operetta to Vienna. His most characteristic parts, however, are those he wrote for himself. Music played an important part in his plays, which number more than 80, but after 1841 – with the exception of his operatic parodies and his very last stage work, *Häuptling Abendwind* (1862; an adaptation of Gille's *Vent du soir*, given with Offenbach's original music) – he limited song almost entirely to the critical, equivocal *couplets* that he wrote for his own roles, eliminating choruses and ensemble finales.

Nestroy was a brilliant satirist, and among his most successful stage works are parodies of Isouard's *Cendrillon* and Rossini's *Cenerentola* (*Nagerl und Handschuh*, 1832, music by Adolf Müller), Meyerbeer's *Robert le diable* (*Robert der Teufel*, 1833, music by Müller), and *Tannhäuser* (1857, music by Karl Binder); his *Lohengrin* parody (1859) was only moderately successful, and parodies of Hérold's *Zampa* (1832) and Flotow's *Martha* (1848) were failures. During most of his career Nestroy recalled his youthful operatic experiences, incorporating witty allusions and quotations in his quodlibets and often referring in more or less disparaging terms to the world of opera.

Adolf Müller wrote the music for 41 of Nestroy's plays between 1832 and 1847, including *Der böse Geist Lumpazivagabundus* (1833), *Der Talisman* (1840), *Das Mädl aus der Vorstadt* (1841), *Einen Jux will er sich machen* (1842) and *Der Zerrissene* (1844). Michael Hebenstreit wrote the music for ten Nestroy plays (1843–50), including *Die schlimmen Buben in der Schule* (1847) and *Freiheit in Krähwinkel* (1848); Karl Binder for seven (1851–9); C. F. Stenzel for three; Franz Roser for two; and A. Scutta and A. M. Storch for one each. Authorship of some of the lost scores is disputed. For performance outside Austria new scores were sometimes provided, e.g. by Lortzing for *Der Zerrissene*, and songs for *Lumpazivagabundus* and *Einen Jux will er sich machen*. 20th-century operatic adaptations of Nestroy's plays include Sutermeister's *Titus Feuerfuchs* (1958, based on *Der Talisman*) and von Einem's *Der Zerrissene* (1964).

*

WurzbachL
M. Necker: 'Johann Nestroy: eine biographisch-kritische Skizze', *Johann Nestroy's gesammelte Werke*, ed. V. Chiavacci and L. Ganghofer, xii (Stuttgart, 1891), 95–218
M. Bührmann: *J. N. Nestroys Parodien* (diss., U. of Kiel, 1933)
O. Rommel: 'Johann Nestroy, der Satiriker auf der Altwiener Komödienbühne', *J. Nestroy: gesammelte Werke*, ed. O. Rommel, i (Vienna, 1948), 1–193
W. E. Yates: *Nestroy: Satire and Parody in Viennese Popular Comedy* (Cambridge, 1972)
L. V. Harding: *The Dramatic Art of Ferdinand Raimund and Johann Nestroy: a Critical Study* (The Hague, 1974)
J. Hein: *Johann Nestroy* (Stuttgart, 1990)   PETER BRANSCOMBE

Netherlands, The. The present Kingdom of the Netherlands (familiarly but imprecisely called 'Holland') has existed as such since 1830; the region was formerly known as the United Provinces. Only since the late 19th century has there been a strong operatic life there. It is possible that the Musyk Kamer of Jan Hermanszoon Krul, founded in Amsterdam in 1634, may have involved dramatic performances with music, but the beginnings of opera in the area are usually assigned to the later 17th century. Hacquart's *De triomfeerende min* (a pastoral written to celebrate the Peace of Nijmegen and published in 1680), Johannes Schenck's *Bacchus, Ceres en Venus* (1687), Konink's *De vryadje van Cloris en Roosje* (1688) and several operas by Anders (*c*1697) are regarded as the earliest Dutch musical dramatic works; virtually all the music, however, is lost, and no continuous tradition grew from this group of Dutch-language works. For social and religious reasons, the country was slow to develop an operatic tradition, in spite of the fact that Amsterdam was an important commercial centre, with a strong music publishing industry which handled much Italian music. In The Hague, however, the theatre in the Casuaristraat presented French opera as early as 1681, and this continued throughout the 18th century. Amsterdam and other cities, by contrast, were largely dependent on visiting Italian and German companies. An active figure in the late 18th century was Bartholomeus Ruloffs, composer, translator and arranger of many operas, especially from the French *opéra comique* repertory.

While only sporadic attempts were made to establish Dutch opera in the early 19th century, one example being Johannes Bernardus van Bree's *Saffo* (1834), there was keen interest in the latest German developments, and *Tannhäuser* was seen in Amsterdam before it reached Paris or London. The troupe at the Amsterdam Stadsschouwburg under J. E. de Vries undertook tours throughout the country. A number of attempts were made to put Dutch opera, and opera performance in the Netherlands in general, on a more secure and permanent basis with the foundation of institutions such as the Duitse (or Hoogduitse) Opera in Rotterdam (1860, by de Vries, favouring a German repertory) and in particular the Hollandse Opera in Amsterdam (1886, by the composer J. G. de Groot, for giving opera in the vernacular). The first new opera performed by the latter was *Catharina en Lambert*, 1888, by the organization's first conductor, Cornelis van der Linden; works by S. van Milligen, R. Hol, M. Bouman, Dopper, Landré, M. van t'Kruys, K. Mönch, K. Dibbern and A. Loman jr were heard in the ensuing years. The main theatres in the country, at which were performed primarily the central German, French and Italian repertories, were the Amsterdam Stadsschouwburg on the Leidseplein (1894), the Grote Schouwburg in Rotterdam (1887, much modernized a century later) and the Koninklijke Schouwburg in The Hague (renovated 1863): these theatres all still exist. A Wagner Vereeniging was founded in 1883.

After World War I the Concertgebouw Orchestra in Amsterdam played a significant role in operatic life, especially in Wagner productions. Companies from Bremen and Münster often visited the northern provinces; in the south, those of Brussels, Aachen and Liège were close at hand. Dutch opera composers of the inter-war years include Brandts Buys, Wagenaar and Pijper. During the German occupation (1940–44) the Gemeentelijke Theaterbedrijf was founded in Amsterdam and also visited The Hague, Utrecht and Rotterdam. 1946 saw the first company established and financed by national government, the Stichting de Nederlandsche Opera, and the Holland Festival, which fostered national opera as well as presenting foreign companies, was founded two years later. The Zuid-Nederlandse Opera was active in the southern provinces until 1971. Beginning in 1955 Opera Forum, based in Enschede, toured throughout the country. Maurice Huisman's intendancy of the Nederlandse Operastichting (founded 1964) saw the production of several new works; from 1971 to 1986 the company flourished under the direction of Hans de Roo, giving its productions in all the main cities. During those years 11 operas by Dutch composers had their premières, as well as Bruno Maderna's *Satyricon* (1973, The Hague), Viktor Ullmann's *Der Kaiser von Atlantis* (1975, Amsterdam) and Philip Glass's *Satyagraha* (1980, Rotterdam); stagings of Baroque and early Classical operas, sometimes with period instruments, were also a noteworthy feature of the Dutch operatic scene. In 1986 the newly formed Nederlandse Opera opened its first season in the new Muziektheater with Otto Ketting's *Ithaka*. The company, of which Pierre Audi was appointed artistic director in 1988, is not only the focal point of the nation's operatic life but also attracts considerable international attention for the quality of its productions.

For further information on operatic life in the country's principal centres *see* AMSTERDAM; ENSCHEDE; HAGUE, THE; HOLLAND FESTIVAL; and ROTTERDAM.

*

D. J. Balfoort: *Het muziekleven in Nederland in de 17de en 18de eeuw* (Amsterdam, 1938)

E. Reeser: *Een eeuw Nederlandse muziek* (Amsterdam, 1959)

S. A. M. Bottenheim: *Opera in Nederland* (Leiden, 1983)

T. Coleman: *Een noodzakelijke luxe* [A Necessary Luxury] (Zutphen, 1986)
MICHAEL DAVIDSON

Ne tol'ko lyubov' ('Not for Love Alone'). Lyrical opera in three acts and an epilogue by RODION KONSTANTINOVICH SHCHEDRIN to a libretto by V. A. Katanyan after stories by Sergey Antonov; Moscow, Bol'shoy Theatre, 25 December 1961 (revised version with chamber orchestra, Moscow, Chamber Opera Theatre, 18 January 1972).

As a student at the Moscow Conservatory in the 1950s, Shchedrin participated in folklore expeditions to various regions of Russia. It was apparently during that period that he conceived the idea of writing an opera on a contemporary subject relating to rural Russia. The stories of Sergey Antonov provided the inspiration for V. A. Katanyan's composite libretto, which centres on the character of the female chairman of a collective farm, strong and beautiful but unlucky in love. In the music, the fresh and distinctive flavour of popular folk styles, in particular that of the highly colourful *chastushka*, contributed greatly to the appeal and enduring popularity of the opera. *Not for Love Alone* is dedicated to the composer's wife, the dancer Maya Plisetskaya; together with the oratorio *Lenin Lives in the People's Hearts*, it was awarded the USSR State Prize in 1972.

Instead of an overture, women sing a sorrowful *chastushka*, 'Okh, i da skoro sneg rastayet' ('Oh, soon the snow will move on'), which becomes a lyrical refrain throughout Act 1. The setting is springtime. The men of the village play dominoes while the women sing because the rain prevents them from sowing. The tractor drivers bemoan the rain in a four-part fugue that is both melancholy and comic. Volodya Gavrilov (tenor) returns unexpectedly from the city; his cocky behaviour antagonizes the villagers and a fight is broken up by Varvara Vasil'yevna (mezzo-soprano), the overburdened chairman of the collective farm. Alone with

Volodya, she asks what his plans are and a personal interest in his welfare is sparked.

Act 2 takes place on a warm summer evening; the villagers gather for a concert with singing and dancing. Volodya arrives on the arm of his fiancée, Natasha (high lyric soprano), and criticizes the local musicians. Challenged to do better, he sings a song 'V lesu rodilas yolochka' ('In the forest grew a little fir-tree'), full of suggestive allusions, and then joins the women in a more soulful melody. Varvara appears and unexpectedly agrees to dance with Volodya; she becomes visibly more lively and cheerful, while Natasha looks on with tears in her eyes.

Later that evening Varvara, unseen, overhears the tractor driver Fedot Petrovich (bass), who is secretly in love with her, confronting his rival and demanding that he leave the village. Petrovich wants to fight, but Varvara intervenes and sends him away. She and Volodya talk about work. The cattleyard is in need of repair; they make an appointment to meet there the next evening.

Arriving at the cattleyard in Act 3, Varvara discovers the grieving Natasha and sends her on an errand. In the central dramatic scene of the opera, the monologue 'Kak zhit' dal'she bez radosti?' ('How can I go on living without happiness?'), Varvara reflects on her attraction to Volodya and the conflict between love and responsibility. When Volodya appears, singing a carefree song, she makes her decision. Natasha returns, and Varvara sends her to Volodya's side. In the epilogue, Varvara greets the collective farm workers and joins them at work.
LAUREL E. FAY

Netti, Giovanni Cesare (*b* Putignano, nr Bari, ? 4 Sept 1649; *d* Naples, July 1686). Italian composer. He was a member of the clergy. Ricordi gives his date of birth as 1649, but according to Di Giacomo (1924) he was eight years old when, in 1663, he entered the Conservatorio della Pietà dei Turchini at Naples. He studied there until 1667. Netti was later an organist in the royal chapel, Naples. In 1680 he was chosen over Francesco Provenzale as *maestro di cappella* of the Tesoro di S Gennaro at Naples Cathedral. The next year his opera *Adamiro* (B. Pisani; *I-Nc*) was staged at the royal palace. The opera *La Filli* (also *Nc*), given at Casa Capello – probably in Naples, perhaps during Carnival 1682 – may also be by him.

*

RicordiE

S. di Giacomo: *Il Conservatorio di Sant'Onofrio a Capuana e quello di S. M. della Pietà dei Turchini* (Palermo, 1924), 101–2, 222

U. Prota-Giurleo: 'Notizie inedite intorno a Gio. Bonaventura Viviani', *Archivi d'Italia e rassegna internazionale degli archivi*, 2nd ser., xxv (1958), 225–38, esp.230

L. Bianconi: 'Funktionen des Operntheaters in Neapel bis 1700 und die Rolle Alessandro Scarlattis', *Colloquium Alessandro Scarlatti: Würzburg 1975*, 13–116

Neubauer [Neubaur], Franz Christoph (*b* Hořín, nr Prague, *c*1760; *d* Bückeburg, 11 Oct 1795). Bohemian composer. After travelling as a violinist, he worked at Weilburg (1790), Minden and Bückeburg, where he later became Kapellmeister (1795). Though an imaginative and prolific composer of orchestral and chamber music, he wrote only one dramatic work, a *Schauspiel mit Gesang, Fernando und Yariko* (3, K. von Ekhartshausen); it was given in Vienna in 1788 and published in Zürich the same year.

See also FERNANDO UND YARIKO.

F. Schlichtegroll: *Nekrolog auf das Jahr 1795*, ii (Gotha, 1798)
G. J. Dlabacž: *Allgemeines historisches Künstler-Lexikon* (Prague, 1815)   R. D. SJOERDSMA

Neudecker, Monsieur (*b* c1700; *d* after 1733). German singer. Little is known of his origin and training, though he sang (possibly as a tenor) under Telemann at the Hamburg Gänsemarkt (1729–33). His first known appearance was as Malerei ('Painting') in *Die aus der Einsamkeit zurückgekehrte Opera* (10 October 1729) and he subsequently sang four more Telemann roles in 1729–30: Onulfus (*Flavius Bertaridus*), Mercurius (*Die Glückseligkeit des russischen Kaisertums*), Don Carlos (*Margaretha*) and Der Friede (*Das neubeglückte Sachsen*). His next appearances at the Gänsemarkt were as Artamedes in *Der Weiseste in Sidon* (1733) and as the Gott der Künste in the prologue *Als vor einem Rath bey Abdanckung der Opera folgender Prologue* by an unknown composer. Like his colleague, the tenor Möhring, Neudecker may have been a chorister of the Hamburg Kantorei, recruited by the Gänsemarkt for particular performances.

*

K. Zelm: 'Die Sänger der Hamburger Gänsemarkt-Oper', *HJbMw*, iii (1978), 35–73, esp.64   HANS JOACHIM MARX

Neuendorff, Adolph (Heinrich Anton Magnus) (*b* Hamburg, 13 June 1843; *d* New York, 4 Dec 1897). American conductor, impresario and composer of German birth. He went to New York in 1854, and studied the violin and piano; at the age of 16 he became leader of the Stadt Theater orchestra in New York. After a season in Milwaukee (1864–5) he returned to New York as chorus master at the Stadt Theater, where Karl Anschütz was trying to establish a German opera. In 1867 he took over as director for four seasons, during the last of which he brought a troupe from Europe to perform several German works, including *Lohengrin* in its first American production (3 April 1871). In 1872, with Carl Rosa and the tenor Theodor Wachtel, he presented a season of Italian opera at the Academy of Music, and from 1872 to 1874 he was manager of the Germania Theatre. Wachtel returned to the Academy in 1875 with the soprano Eugenie Pappenheim for Neuendorff's season of German opera. Neuendorff attended the opening of the Bayreuth Festspielhaus in 1876 as correspondent for the *New Yorker Staats-Zeitung*, and the next year directed a Wagner Festival at the Academy which included the first American performance of *Die Walküre* (2 April 1877). He conducted the New York Philharmonic Society for a season after Theodore Thomas resigned in 1878.

In 1881 Neuendorff transferred the Germania Theatre company to a new building, but the venture failed and ruined him financially. He moved to Boston, where he conducted the Music Hall Promenade Concerts (1884–9) and the Emma Juch Grand Opera Company (1889–91). In 1892 he conducted English opera in New York, then for the next three years conducted at the Vienna Hofoper, where his wife was a leading singer. He returned to New York in 1896 and succeeded Seidl the following year as conductor of the Metropolitan Opera.

Neuendorff's works include *Der Rattenfänger von Hameln* (1880), *Don Quixote* (1882), *Waldmeisters Brautfahrt* (1887) and *Der Minstrel* (1892), and some orchestral and vocal works.

Kadettenlaunen (operetta), New York
Der Rattenfänger von Hameln (comic op, 4, H. Italiener), New York, 1880, vs (New York, 1881)
Don Quixote (komische Oper, 3, after M. de Cervantes), New York, 1882
Waldmeisters Brautfahrt (3, Italiener), Berlin, Walhalla, 3 Sept 1887
Der Schalk von Aberdeen (operetta, 3, H. Urban), New York, 18 May 1892
Der Minstrel (comic op, 3), New York, Amberg's, 1892

*

DAB (F. H. Martens)
A. Neuendorff: 'Neuendorff, Adolph', *Cyclopedia of Music and Musicians*, ed. J. D. Champlin and W. F. Apthorp (New York, 1888–90)   BRUCE CARR

Neuenfels, Hans (*b* Krefeld, 1941). German director. He first directed an opera in 1974, when he staged *Il trovatore* at Nuremberg. At Frankfurt (1976–80) his controversial productions of two other Verdi operas, *Macbeth* and *Aida*, caused a scandal, but his stagings of two 20th-century works, Schreker's *Die Gezeichneten* (updated from the Renaissance to the present day) and Busoni's *Doktor Faust* (which Neuenfels also designed), aroused enormous interest. Similarly, at the Deutsche Oper, Berlin (1982–6), his productions of *La forza del destino* (transferred to the period of the Spanish Civil War) and *Rigoletto* (part of which took place in a cemetery) displeased critics and audiences, while his staging of Zimmermann's *Die Soldaten* was well received. In 1989 Neuenfels directed the première of Höller's *Der Meister und Margarita* at the Paris Opéra, once more demonstrating his undoubted ability to stage contemporary opera successfully.

For illustration *see* PRODUCTION, fig.25.

*

N. Ely: 'Hans Neuenfels – über die schreckliche Klarheit von Träumen', *Regie heute: Musiktheater in unserer Zeit*, ed. N. Ely and S. Jaeger (Berlin, 1984), 111–34   ELIZABETH FORBES

Neues vom Tage ('News of the Day'). *Lustige Oper* in three parts by PAUL HINDEMITH to a libretto by Marcellus Schiffer; Berlin, Kroll Theater, 8 June 1929 (revised in two acts with the libretto adapted by Hindemith, Naples, Teatro S Carlo, 7 April 1954).

A satire on modern times, with its brittle marital relationships and its sensation-hungry press, this comedy opens with Laura (soprano) and Eduard (baritone) throwing crockery at each other's heads. They decide on a divorce and follow the advice of another married couple with the same intention, Herr and Frau M. (tenor, mezzo-soprano), to engage Hermann, a professional co-respondent (tenor). Eduard, arriving at a museum where a compromising meeting between Laura and Hermann is taking place, is overcome by jealousy and breaks a priceless Venus statue over Hermann's head, an act for which he is imprisoned. Laura, now alone, is surprised in her hotel bath by Hermann, who has fallen in love with her, and they are seen by members of the hotel staff. Both events attract the attention of the press, and Laura and Eduard become 'news of the day'. Publicity managers arrive to exploit their notoriety, and they are engaged to perform their quarrel nightly on the stage. In the process, while still pursuing their divorce plans, they grow used to each other again and wish to resume their married life, but the public, unwilling to lose its entertainment, will not let them go.

Schiffer's frivolous text gave Hindemith plenty of opportunity to poke fun at traditional opera: a divorce duet instead of a love duet; a 'kitsch' duet parodying

Puccini; a soprano singing in her bath of the joys of modern plumbing; and even a parody of German cabaret in the theatre scene at the end. He also satirized features of contemporary life: the bureaucrats at the registry office; typists busy at their machines while dreaming of love; bored tourists being conducted around a museum. The busy music, while including jazz elements, is kept under strict control, and there is a distinct gulf between its subtle wit and the shallow satire of the text.

Conscious in later years of this discrepancy, Hindemith revised the work, on the musical side simplifying florid vocal lines which he had come to consider out of keeping with comedy, and on the dramatic side giving more weight to the pressures of the news hunters. For this he introduced a powerful entrepreneur, Baron d'Houdoux (bass), and a newspaper reporter, Frau Pick (contralto), replacing Herr and Frau M. He also allowed Laura and Eduard to repent their overhasty divorce decision quite early in the story, thus presenting them as victims of, rather than cooperators with, the sensation seekers. He reunited them at the end and took the opportunity of laying an old ghost by removing Laura from the bath (the cause of much unwelcome publicity to himself in previous times) and putting Hermann there instead.

There are a few additions to the music in the revised version, reflecting the new story, but in the main the original score survives intact.   GEOFFREY SKELTON

Neugierigen Frauen, Die. Opera by Ermanno Wolf-Ferrari; *see* DONNE CURIOSE, LE.

Neuhaus, Rudolf (*b* Cologne, 3 Jan 1914; *d* Dresden, 7 March 1990). German conductor. He studied at the Cologne Musikhochschule and with Abendroth, obtaining his first appointment as music director at the Landestheater, Neustrelitz (1934–44). In 1945 he became conductor at the Landestheater, Schwerin, where he was Generalmusikdirektor from 1950. Later he was active in Dresden, conducting at the Staatsoper and teaching at the Hochschule für Musik. He conducted most of the new operas performed at Dresden during his time there, including the premières of Finke's *Der Zauberfisch* (1960), Kunad's *Maître Pathelin* (1969) and works by Cikker, Egk, Khrennikov, Wagner-Régeny and others. A frequent guest conductor in Berlin and Leipzig, he distinguished himself in Wagner and in contemporary operas, including the première of Schwaen's *Leonce und Lena* at the Berlin Staatsoper (1961).

Neukomm, Sigismund Ritter von (*b* Salzburg, 10 July 1778; *d* Paris, 3 April 1858). Austrian composer. His mother, who was related to Michael Haydn, was a singer in the service of the Archbishop of Salzburg. Haydn was responsible for Neukomm's early theoretical studies. In 1796 Neukomm became chorus master at the Salzburg court theatre, and in the following year moved to Vienna to study with Joseph Haydn. There Neukomm gave piano and singing lessons; his pupils included Anna Milder and the young F. X. Mozart. In 1804 he became Kapellmeister at the German Theatre in St Petersburg and he returned to Vienna in 1808. On 7 November 1809 he arrived in Paris, which was to be his principal home for the rest of his life. He soon met such leading musicians as Cherubini, Gossec, Grétry and Monsigny. In 1815 his C minor Requiem was performed at the Congress of Vienna, and he was invested as Chevalier of the Légion d'honneur. Neukomm travelled widely, notably to South America (1816–21) and the British Isles (from 1829), where he conducted many of his works and made his second home. Neukomm wrote some 1300 works, most of which are listed in the thematic catalogue he maintained from 1804 to 1858. The largest number are songs and sacred works.

Neukomm's sister Elisabeth (1789–1816) was a renowned soprano, who 'filled all circles of Vienna with rapture'.

Die Nachtwächter (komisches musikalisches Zwischenspiel, 1, F. Treitschke and F. W. Hunnius), Vienna, 12 Jan 1804
Die neue Oper, oder Der Schauspieldirektor (komische Operette, 1, Hunnius), Vienna, 15 March 1804
Alexander am Indus (Oper, 1, Hunnius), St Petersburg, 15/27 Sept 1804; rev. version, St Petersburg, 30 Jan/11 Feb 1805
Musikalische Malerei (Posse, 1, Neukomm), Moscow, 19 April/1 May 1806
Arkona (melodrama, Kosegarten), Würzburg, 21 Sept 1808
Niobé (tragédie lyrique, 1, F. Rossel), Montbéliard, 28 May 1809

*

G. Pellegrini-Brandacher: 'Sigismund Ritter von Neukomm: ein vergessener Salzburger Musiker', *Mitteilungen der Salzburger Landeskunde*, lxxvi (1936), 1–67
R. Angermüller: *Sigismund Neukomm: Werkverzeichnis, Autobiographie, Beziehung zu seinen Zeitgenossen* (Munich, 1977)
          RUDOLPH ANGERMÜLLER

Neumann, Angelo (*b* Vienna, 18 Aug 1838; *d* Prague, 20 Dec 1910). Austrian impresario. He studied as a baritone with Therese Stilke-Sessi, made his début in 1859 and appeared in Kraków, Pressburg, Prague, Ödenburg (now Sopron) and Danzig. From 1862 to 1876 he sang at the Vienna Hofoper, where he witnessed Wagner's own 1875 productions of *Tannhäuser* and *Lohengrin*. By 1876 he had changed careers and went to Leipzig as director under August Förster. Within six years he had staged all the Wagner operas including, in 1878, the first *Ring* cycle outside Bayreuth. In 1882 Neumann took the *Ring* to London for its first performances there. The conductor at Leipzig was Joseph Sucher, later succeeded by Anton Seidl, but Neumann also introduced the young Arthur Nikisch. In 1882 he left Leipzig to form his own touring company, the Richard Wagner-Theater. Its first tour was to Breslau, Danzig, Magdeburg, Hamburg, Lübeck and Bremen. Here he accepted the post of director, which he held until 1885. The company continued its travels in 1882 throughout Germany, the Netherlands and Belgium, and also to Italy, Austria and Hungary. Neumann contracted Seidl to conduct and engaged most of the leading Wagnerian singers of the day, including Georg Unger, Heinrich and Therese Vogl, Hedwig Reicher-Kindermann and Amalie Materna, but also gave the young Katharina Klafsky her first opportunity. In 1885 Neumann went to the German Theatre in Prague as director, and in 1889 revived his touring company for a *Ring* cycle in Russia under Carl Muck. In 1907 he published his *Erinnerungen an Richard Wagner* (English translation by E. Livermore, 1908).
          CHRISTOPHER FIFIELD

Neumann, František (*b* Přerov, Moravia, 16 June 1874; *d* Brno, 25 Feb 1929). Czech conductor and composer. After an apprenticeship as a meat-smoker and sausage-maker in his father's firm he went to the Leipzig Conservatory, where he studied with Reinecke and Jadassohn and as a répétiteur with Felix Mottl. After completing his studies in 1897 he conducted in Austria,

Germany and the border territories of Bohemia. In 1919 Janáček recommended him as director of opera at the National Theatre, Brno. Neumann was an organizer of great energy and raised the standards of the Brno opera company – in status second to that of Prague – to a remarkable degree. As well as the standard repertory he introduced the works of Richard Strauss, Debussy, Ravel, Stravinsky and Krenek and, perhaps most important, organized several Janáček world premières (*Kát'a Kabanová*, 1921; *The Cunning Little Vixen*, 1924; *The Makropulos Affair*, 1926). At the Brno Conservatory he taught the conductors Chalabala and Bakala. In 1925 he became managing director of the Brno National Theatre.

Of Neumann's operas the most successful was the three-act *Liebelei* (1910), based on Arthur Schnitzler's play. It was performed in various theatres in German- and Czech-speaking countries and was first sung in Czech as *Milkování* in Brno in 1911. *Der Herbststurm* was based on a play by the Yugoslav Ivo Vojnović, and after its première in Berlin (1919) was first performed in Czech as *Ekvinokce* (1920, Brno). *Beatrice Caracci*, to a libretto by the composer based on a novel by Ludwig Hunn, is set in 16th-century Venice. Neumann followed the style of late 19th-century German drama, setting realistic subjects to dramatically effective and rhythmically lively music.

Idalka (1, V. di Dio), concert perf., Berlin, Hof, 5 Nov 1895, lost
Peri, Leipzig, 1896
Assardaï (komische Oper, 2, R. Hartwig), Brunswick, 17 April 1898, lost
Die Brautwerbung (lyrische komische Oper, 3, S. Pohl), Linz, 18 Jan 1901
Marquis (3), Linz, 1901, lost
Liebelei (komische Oper, 3, after A. Schnitzler), Frankfurt, 18 Sept 1910, songs (Mainz, 1910); as Milkování, Brno, 19 Feb 1911
Der Herbststurm (4, I. Schneider, after I. Vojnović), Berlin, Charlottenburg, 9 April 1919; as Ekvinokce [The Equinox], Brno, 23 Jan 1920
Beatrice Caracci (3, Neumann, after L. Hunn), Brno, 29 April 1922, songs (Brno, 1922)

*

V. Helfert: *František Neumann* (Prostějov, 1936)
J. Vratislavský: *Neumannova éra v brněnské opeře* [The Neumann Era in the Brno Opera] (Brno, 1971) JAN TROJAN

Neumann, Horst. *See* LAUBENTHAL, HORST.

Neumann, Václav (*b* Prague, 29 Oct 1920). Czech conductor. He studied at the Prague Conservatory, became a member of the Smetana String Quartet, and made his conducting début in 1948 with the Czech PO. After meeting Felsenstein while at Brno he was invited to work at the Berlin Komische Oper, where his conducting of the celebrated production of Janáček's *The Cunning Little Vixen* in 1956 brought him wide renown and led to his association with that house until 1964, for two seasons as chief conductor. Later he was General-musikdirektor at Leipzig (1964–7) and Stuttgart (1970–73). Thereafter he was engaged mainly in concert work, but he made regular appearances at the Vienna Staatsoper, and in 1985 made his Metropolitan Opera début in *Jenůfa*. In 1990 he conducted Martinů's *Ariane* during the centenary cycle of the composer's operas in Prague. His repertory extends from Mozart and Wagner to Musorgsky and Shostakovich; his performances are distinguished by a grasp of dramatic structure which embraces both the work's emotional and its intellectual aspects. His recordings include Gluck's *Orfeo ed Euridice*, Dvořák's *Rusalka*, Martinů's *Ariane* and

Janáček's *The Cunning Little Vixen* (twice), *The Excursions of Mr Brouček* and *From the House of the Dead*.

*

V. Pospíšil: *Václav Neumann* (Prague, 1981)
ALENA NĚMCOVÁ, NOËL GOODWIN

Neumann, Wolfgang (*b* Waiern, Steiermark, 20 June 1945). Austrian tenor. He studied at Essen and Duisburg, then sang as a baritone in the chorus at Oberhausen. He made his tenor début in 1973 as Max at Bielefeld, moving to Augsburg (1978) and Mannheim (1980). He has appeared at Hamburg, Munich, Vienna, Zürich, Florence, where he sang Tannhäuser (1983), and Dallas, where he made his American début (1984) as Siegfried, the role of his Metropolitan début (1988). His repertory includes Florestan, Rienzi, Erik, Lohengrin, Tristan, Loge, Herod, the Emperor (*Die Frau ohne Schatten*), as well as Canio, Turiddu and Calaf. He has also sung the Drum Major, Schoenberg's Aaron, the Cardinal (*Mathis der Maler*), Edmund (Reimann's *Lear*), Sergey (*Lady Macbeth of the Mtsensk District*) and other 20th-century roles, where his strong, dark-toned and incisive voice is used with particular effectiveness. ELIZABETH FORBES

Neumann-Spallart, Gottfried (*b* Vienna, 29 March 1915; *d* Vienna, 5 May 1983). Austrian stage designer. Before he graduated as an architect with a doctorate in Vienna in 1946, he made his professional début as a designer at the Burgtheater in 1938 and designed his first opera, *Il trovatore*, at the Volksoper in 1941. During his career he designed more than 250 productions. Although he worked in Naples (*Tristan*, 1950; *Parsifal* and *Don Giovanni*, 1955), Rome (*Jenůfa*, 1952), Tokyo (*Figaro*, 1959), Johannesburg (*Tosca*, 1963) and Tel-Aviv (*La Cenerentola*, 1966) and for the Bregenz Festival (1962–7; see illustration), most of his designs were for the Graz Opera and the Theater in der Josefstadt in Vienna, where from 1958 to 1983 he usually designed four productions a season. His principal works for Graz were *Ariadne auf Naxos* (1957), *Boccaccio* (1969), Rudolph Weishappel's *Die Lederköpfe* (1970, première) and *Die Zauberflöte* (1971). Also important were his *Rigoletto* (1953, Vienna, Staatsoper), *The Old Maid and the Thief* (1961, Vienna, Volksoper), *Arabella* (1976, Cologne) and *Zar und Zimmermann* (1981, Bonn).

Neumann-Spallart was a conservative designer in the best sense, with a strong feeling for the realistic. His training as an architect influenced his detailed and authentic three-dimensional approach but he always remained a servant, believing that stage design should be pictorial and illusory, and never seek the limelight. He tended to have long associations with only a few directors, and was happier designing the traditional repertory in his characteristic greys, blues and dark greens. His few attempts at the abstract and the avant garde were unsuccessful.

*

J. Mayerhöfer: *25 Jahre Theaterarbeit Gottfried Neumann-Spallart* (Vienna, 1979) [exhibition catalogue, Österreichisches Theatermuseum]
U. Öttl: *Der Bühnenbildner Gottfried Neumann-Spallart* (diss., U. of Vienna, 1991) DAVID J. HOUGH

Neusonntagskind, Das [*Das neue Sonntagskind* ('Sunday's New Child')]. Singspiel in two acts by WENZEL MÜLLER to a libretto by JOACHIM PERINET after PHILIPP HAFNER's play *Der Furchtsame*; Vienna, Theater in der Leopoldstadt, 10 October 1793.

Set design by Gottfried Neumann-Spallart for a production of Rossini's 'Il turco in Italia' at the Bregenz Festival, 1966

Much of the comedy in *Das Neusonntagskind* results from the fear of ghosts exhibited by the otherwise massive and formidable Hausmeister (the porter and 'Sunday's child' of the title), one blessed by good fortune but also by susceptibility to manifestations of the supernatural. The members of his master Herr von Hasenkopf's family also suffer more or less markedly from his own fear of spirits, his melancholy and superstitions, his obsession that there is no natural explanation for the things that frighten him. The work as a whole is less a typical Viennese farce with scheming servants and disappointed young lovers than a tuneful, witty, yet poignant character-comedy. The first and most successful of the series of six adaptations by Perinet of plays by Hafner, it was performed 162 times in the Leopoldstadt up to 1829. Perinet had the comparatively simple task of building into Hafner's tragicomedy the songs and ensembles that helped ensure the work's popularity; numbers like 'Lieber kleiner Gott der Liebe', and especially the song of the Hausmeister, 'Wer niemals einen Rausch gehabt', attained the status of folksongs. Some of the ensembles are quite ambitious, and Müller noted with pride in his diary, 'I won my musical renown with this opera; this opera is known in every land'. He was guilty of only slight exaggeration: it was widely staged in the Netherlands, France, Hungary, Switzerland, Russia, Poland and throughout German-speaking lands.

PETER BRANSCOMBE

Nevada [Wixom], Emma (*b* Alpha, nr Nevada City, CA, 7 Feb 1859; *d* Liverpool, 20 June 1940). American soprano. A pupil of Mathilde Marchesi, she made her début on 17 May 1880 at Her Majesty's Theatre, London, in *La sonnambula*, an opera that brought some of her greatest successes (her medallion was later placed with those of Pasta and Malibran on Bellini's statue at Naples). She sang to great acclaim in Italy and Paris, where her roles included Lucia and Mignon. On returning to the USA in 1884 she appeared at the New York Academy of Music, and, the following year, on alternate nights with Patti. She made several further tours of the USA and Europe, and sang at Covent Garden in 1887, as Amina and Mireille, her intonation and flexibility being admired but not her free treatment of Gounod's score. Her last appearance on stage was as Rosina (1907, Berlin).

*

W. Armstrong, ed.: 'Reminiscences of Emma Nevada', *New-York Tribune Sunday Magazine* (28 Oct 1906), 7–8
O. Thompson: *The American Singer* (New York, 1937), 190ff

J. B. STEANE

Nevada, Mignon (*b* Paris, 14 Aug 1886; *d* Long Melford, 25 June 1971). English soprano, daughter of Emma Nevada. Taught by her mother, she made her début at the Teatro Costanzi, Rome, in 1908, as Rosina. After appearances in Italy and Portugal, she sang at the opening of Beecham's 1910 winter season at Covent Garden, as Thomas' Ophelia. Other London roles included Olympia, Zerlina and Gounod's Marguerite; her final Covent Garden appearance was in 1922. In 1920 she enjoyed considerable success in Paris at the Opéra-Comique as Lakmé and Mimì; she sang at La Scala in 1923 and at the Opéra in 1932. She was much admired by Beecham, who described her Desdemona as 'the best I have seen on any stage'. Her voice was light and agile, though some (like Beecham himself) considered that her mother had been unwise to train her as a coloratura instead of cultivating her warm mezzo quality. She made a single record in 1938 of a song by her godfather Ambroise Thomas which had been given its first performance by her mother.

J. B. STEANE

Nevada Opera. American company based in RENO.

Nevěsta messinská ('The Bride of Messina'). Tragic opera in three acts, op.18, by ZDENĚK FIBICH to a libretto by OTAKAR HOSTINSKÝ after FRIEDRICH VON SCHILLER's play *Die Braut von Messina*; Prague, National Theatre, 28 March 1884.

Donna Isabella, the reigning Princess of Messina (contralto), succeeds in reconciling her warring sons Don Manuel (baritone) and Don Cesar (tenor). In Act 2 she tells them of the existence of their sister Beatrice (soprano), whom she has secretly hidden in a convent after a dream revealed to her late husband that his daughter would be the cause of his sons' deaths. Both sons now disclose their intention to bring their future wives for Isabella's approval. But the servant Diego (bass), sent to bring back Beatrice, returns with the news that she has been abducted. Act 3 reveals that the culprit is Don Manuel, who, having fallen in love with an unknown girl, has ordered his retinue to take her from the convent for his bride. Unlike his brother, he now realizes who she is, but Don Cesar, who has also seen the girl and fallen in love with her, kills him before Don Manuel can explain that their mutual beloved is also their sister. In remorse Don Cesar kills himself.

Schiller described his play as a 'Trauerspiel mit Chören'. The choruses, technically the retinues of the two brothers, became an important element in the opera, providing the chief means of ensembles in the piece. Apart from a brief trio there are no solo ensembles, and dialogue is conducted in exemplary declamation. This was Fibich's most Wagnerian opera. He wrote it in 1882–3, and it won first prize in 1883 in the competition for a serious opera for the new Prague National Theatre. Despite critical acclaim, its gloomy story, sombre scoring and severe style have restricted its popular appeal.

JOHN TYRRELL

Nevin, Arthur (Finlay) (*b* Edgeworth, PA, 27 April 1871; *d* Sewickley, PA, 10 July 1943). American composer. He studied at the New England Conservatory (1889–93) and in Berlin, where his teachers included Humperdinck. During the summers of 1903 and 1904 he lived among the Blackfoot Indians in Montana, studying their folklore and music. As a result of these studies he wrote the three-act *Poia* (libretto by E. von Huhn, after R. Hartley; full score published Berlin, 1909), which received its first performance, conducted by Muck, at the Berlin Opera on 23 April 1910. From 1911 to 1914 he devoted himself to composition before taking up a post at the University of Kansas, Lawrence, in 1915; later he worked as a conductor in Memphis and travelled in France, returning to the USA in 1926.

Nevin's musical training and output were typical of late 19th-century American composers, with an emphasis on large forms in the Germanic style. His other opera, the one-act *The Daughter of the Forest* (libretto by Hartley; vocal score published Cincinnati, 1917), was first given in the Auditorium, Chicago, on 5 January 1917. Both operas are strongly influenced by naturalist philosophies.

'Explains Berlin's Attack upon *Poia*', *MusAm*, xii/2 (1910), 25 [interview about première of *Poia*]
E. E. Hipsher: *American Opera and its Composers* (Philadelphia, 1934), 337ff

BRUCE CARR

Newark. American city in New Jersey. The New Jersey State Opera was founded in 1965, in Westfield, as the Opera Theatre of Westfield; the name was changed in 1966 to Opera Theatre of New Jersey and in 1974 to New Jersey State Opera. Since 1969 the company has performed chiefly at Symphony Hall, Newark, though it is also heard elsewhere in the state, in particular at Trenton. Under its musical director Alfredo Silpigni its repertory has been predominantly Italian, from Rossini to Puccini and the *verismo* composers; French opera has occasionally been given, notably a *Carmen* (1978) in which Victoria de Los Angeles sang the title role. Other artists have included Birgit Nilsson (her last Turandot in the USA, 1974), Gobbi, Domingo, Gedda and Bumbry. Rarely heard operas of the early 20th century have been staged there (e.g. Leoncavallo's *Zazà* and Mascagni's *Lodoletta*), as well as several new American works, including Kay's *Frederick Douglass* in April 1991. The company usually gives one or two performances a season of each of two or three operas.

New Jersey State Opera: the First Twenty-Five Years (Newark, 1991)

Neway, Patricia (*b* Brooklyn, NY, 30 Sept 1919). American soprano. She made her début as Fiordiligi at the Chautauqua Festival in 1946. Two years later she joined the New York City Opera, singing the Female Chorus in Britten's *The Rape of Lucretia*. In 1950 she created the role of Magda in Menotti's *The Consul*, which she sang for nearly a year on Broadway and subsequently with many companies in Europe and America. In 1952 she was engaged by the Opéra-Comique for two years, and in 1958 she created the Mother in Menotti's *Maria Golovin* at the Brussels World Fair. Her repertory also included Tosca, Marie (*Wozzeck*) and Katiusha (Alfano's *Risurrezione*). Neway's voice, a steely dramatic instrument used with unstinting intensity, declined in the late 1950s, and her later career was devoted to concerts and guest appearances with numerous American companies, mainly in contemporary works.

PETER G. DAVIS

New German School (Ger. *Neudeutsche Schule*). A term coined in June 1859 by Karl Franz Brendel, editor of the Leipzig *Neue Zeitschrift für Musik*, to designate the progressive party in contemporary music under the leadership of Liszt, as opposed to the conservative group of composers who held more closely to the style of Viennese Classicism, exemplified by Mendelssohn and his followers. Brendel adopted the term in preference to the word *Zukunftsmusik* ('Music of the Future'), which he considered had damaged the cause of modernism. The school is further defined by A. W. Ambros in his *Culturhistorische Bilder aus dem Musikleben der Gegenwart* (Leipzig, 1860). In operatic history, the school loosely embraced composers, conductors and critics from the 1850s until the early stage works of Humperdinck and Richard Strauss.

Several important personalities in the history of mid-19th-century opera were intimately associated with Liszt's period at Weimar (1848–61): the composers and writers Joachim Raff and Peter Cornelius, Hans von Bülow (as writer, transcriber and, later, conductor) and pre-eminently Berlioz and Wagner. While Berlioz can hardly be regarded as 'New German', it is significant that his operatic successes were both in Germany: the revised *Benvenuto Cellini* at Weimar and *Béatrice et Bénédict* at Baden and then Weimar. The impetus for *Les Troyens* also came from Weimar and Liszt's companion Princess Sayn-Wittgenstein. Similarly,

Wagner never acknowledged the label 'New German', and had a low regard for Brendel, but Weimar was vital for him in his years of exile from Germany, through Liszt's performances (notably the *Lohengrin* première) and the propaganda for his works in the writings of Liszt, Raff, Cornelius, Bülow, Brendel, Felix Draeseke, Richard Pohl and (another opera composer and critic) Karl Friedrich Weitzmann (1808–80). Other defenders of the cause were Hans von Bronsart (1830–1913), Karl Tausig (1841–71) and Heinrich Porges. The annual festivals of the Allgemeiner Deutscher Musikverein, founded in 1861 by Brendel and Liszt, were the main platform of the movement and often included operatic extracts in concert performances. The ideals of Weimar were carried to the USA by Liszt's pupil, the conductor Leopold Damrosch, and to Russia by Karl Klindworth (1830–1916).

The Wagnerian music drama was the *fons et origo* of the dramatic theories of the New German School. The most significant characteristics of the movement were new boldness in form, harmony and sonority; the abandonment of set operatic numbers; the union of poetry and music; the viewing of music itself as drama; and a preference for heroic myth as subject matter. Another unifying feature of all the figures associated with the school was their literary fecundity. The New German School is mainly of historical interest as a phenomenon of musical criticism and of the party-political musical factionalism of the era. As a term it is frequently met with in the literature of the later 19th century. Yet its boundaries are vague, imprecise and, arguably, meaningless.

The Weimar Opera, however, saw the première of some significant works in the wake of Liszt's conductorship there, as well as some curiosities. His successor as court music director, from 1860 to 1895, Eduard Lassen, himself the composer of three operas, kept the flame of the New German School alight. Works receiving their premières included Cornelius's *Der Cid* (1865) and *Gunlöd* (1891), Saint-Saëns' *Samson et Dalila* (1877), Felix Weingartner's *Sakuntala* (1884), Alex Ritter's *Wem die Krone?* (1890), Humperdinck's *Hänsel und Gretel* (1893) and Richard Strauss's *Guntram* (1894). With these last two figures opera had entered its post-Wagnerian phase. Bülow, Lassen and Ritter all form a direct line, through Weimar, to the career of Strauss. Strauss acknowledged his great indebtedness to Ritter, who was his mentor in progressive musical matters and who was closely concerned with the creation of *Guntram*. Another 'New German' who has been credited with anticipating the Strauss of *Salome* was Joseph Huber (1837–86), with his one-act opera *Irene* (1881, Stuttgart).

The New German School can be said to have come into being in an atmosphere of musical polemicism, although in creating the term Brendel had hoped to reconcile and unify the contending parties in contemporary music. That the polemics of the 20th century had changed emphasis is seen in a pamphlet *Die Konfusion in der Musik* (1906) by the radical New German of half a century before (and the composer of six mythic and heroic operas), Draeseke: it attacks the modernism of Richard Strauss.

*

H. Riemann: *Geschichte der Musik seit Beethoven 1800–1900* (Berlin, 1901)

M. Kalbeck: *Johannes Brahms* (Berlin, 1904–12)

S. Gut, ed.: *Franz Liszt und Richard Wagner* (Munich, 1986)

DEREK WATSON

New Jersey State Opera. American company based in NEWARK.

Newman, Ernest [Roberts, William] (*b* Everton, Lancs., 30 Nov 1868; *d* Tadworth, Surrey, 7 July 1959). English writer on music. He was the most celebrated British music critic in the early 20th century. He received no formal musical education, but taught himself to play the piano 'after a fashion'. While working as a bank clerk he read widely and acquired a knowledge of many subjects, including music, and attained complete or partial mastery of nine foreign languages. By 1889 he was contributing articles on philosophy, literature and music to various periodicals. His approach to the arts was intellectual rather than sensual and, as an apostle of rationalism and champion of progressive ideas, he regarded himself as 'a new man in earnest' and therefore wrote under the pseudonym Ernest Newman.

In 1895 he found a publisher, Bertram Dobell, for his first book, *Gluck and the Opera* (London, 1895), which led Dobell to commission *A Study of Wagner* (London, 1899). Newman gave up banking in 1904 and taught singing and theory at the Midland Institute in Birmingham. A year later he was called to Manchester as music critic of the *Guardian*. Much of his most brilliant and perceptive musical criticism dates from 1906 to 1918, when he was critic of the *Birmingham Daily Post*. During this time he also wrote *Richard Strauss* (London, 1908) and *Wagner as Man and Artist* (London 1914). In 1919 he moved to London, where he was music critic of the Sunday *Observer* and the *Sunday Times*; he remained with that newspaper, apart from a five-month stint in 1923 as guest critic of the *New York Evening Post*, until his retirement in 1958. During these years he also wrote programme notes, more books and from 1930 made weekly broadcasts for BBC radio.

Newman's philosophy of criticism is summed up in his treatise *A Musical Critic's Holiday* (New York, 1925), and his method of analysis is well exemplified in *The Unconscious Beethoven* (London, 1927). His major work was undoubtedly *The Life of Richard Wagner* (London, 1933–47), but he also wrote a valuable series of books, *Opera Nights* (London, 1943), *Wagner Nights* (London, 1949), and *More Opera Nights* (London, 1954) which are widely read. As a critic, Newman aimed for scientific precision in evaluation; his writing is closely argued yet marked by its lively humanity. His major books remain a substantial monument to his long career; but his journalistic occasional writings, as collected in *A Musical Motley* (London, 1919), the volumes *From the World of Music* (London, 1956–8) and *Testament of Music* (London, 1962), as cogently explain his international standing for so many years.

WILLIAM S. MANN

Newmarch [née Jeaffreson], **Rosa** (*b* Leamington, 18 Dec 1857; *d* Worthing, 9 April 1940). English writer on music. In 1897 she made her first visit to Russia, where she worked at the Imperial Public Library of St Petersburg under the supervision of Vladimir Stasov. Her articles on Russian composers in the second edition of *Grove's Dictionary* were to many English musicians the first source of information about the aims and achievements of Russian nationalists, and her libretto translations helped to make their operas accessible. Her last visit to Russia was in 1915; when political events made access difficult she directed her interest to western Slavonic music and enthusiastically took up the cause of emerging Czech composers, including Janáček, who visited England on her initiative in 1926. Newmarch translated several books (from German and French as well as Russian), and wrote a biography of Tchaikovsky (1900), a study of Russian opera (1914) and a volume on Czechoslovak music, published posthusmously in 1942.

New Opera Company. Company founded in Cambridge in 1957 but subsequently based in London; *see* LONDON, §II, 1.

New Orleans. American city in Louisiana. Founded in 1718, it was the capital of French colonial Louisiana until 1762 and then in Spanish possession until 1800. It reverted briefly to French rule before it was granted territorial status as a result of the Louisiana Purchase in 1803. The first known opera performance there was of Grétry's *Silvain* (22 May 1796), at the Théâtre St Pierre, which had opened on 4 October 1792 in the rue St Pierre in the Vieux Carré. Opera, French drama and vaudevilles were given there, and also, during the early 19th century, at the Théâtre St Philippe, opened 1808, and the first Théâtre d'Orléans (721 Orleans Street), which opened on 19 October 1815 but burnt down in summer 1816.

The second Théâtre d'Orléans, built by John Davis, its manager until 1837, opened on 27 November 1819 with Boieldieu's *Jean de Paris* and H.-M. Berton's *Les maris garçons*. It became the city's leading opera house for the next 40 years, with annual seasons usually from October to early spring. Initially the repertory comprised light popular scores by Grétry, Méhul, Isouard and Dalayrac, but it soon expanded to include important works by Paisiello, Cherubini and Rossini.

On 1 January 1824 James Caldwell opened a rival institution, the Camp Street Theatre (cap. 1100), which housed drama, vaudeville and opera. When the 1826–7 season finished Davis's French troupe took its repertory of French drama and opera on tour to north-eastern cities, including Philadelphia, Baltimore and New York, making further tours intermittently until 1845. Though familiar to New Orleans audiences, many of the works were local premières, e.g. Boieldieu's *La dame blanche* (1827, New York), Spontini's *La vestale* (1828, Philadelphia) and Rossini's *La gazza ladra* (1829, Philadelphia).

Caldwell opened the resplendent St Charles Theatre (cap. 4100) on 30 November 1835, intensifying his rivalry with Davis. Caldwell soon imported Italian companies from Havana, staging American premières of Rossini's *Zelmira* and *Semiramide*, Bellini's *Norma* and *I Capuleti e i Montecchi* and Donizetti's *Parisina*, all in 1836–7. Relying on the support of the Creole French population, the Théâtre d'Orléans countered with the latest operas by Adolphe Adam, Auber, Halévy (*La Juive*, 1844) and Meyerbeer, including American premières of *Les Huguenots* (1839), *Le prophète* (1850), *Margherita d'Anjou* (1854), *L'étoile du nord* (1855), *Le pardon de Ploërmel* (1861) and works by Donizetti, Bellini and Verdi.

The original St Charles Theatre was destroyed by fire on 13 March 1842; a replacement, built on a more modest scale, opened on 18 January 1843 and survived until 4 June 1899 when it too burnt down. At the same time Caldwell also managed the American Theatre (opened on 10 November 1840; reopened, after reconstruction following a fire, on 5 October 1842) until 1855. Situated in Poydras Street, it was designed for the presentation of equestrian shows in addition to opera and drama.

Troupes of singers and actors recruited each year in Europe were supplemented by touring artists who made guest appearances at the various theatres. Henriette Sontag appeared in March 1854, and in the same decade Erminia Frezzolini sang in several seasons.

In 1859 a dispute over rental terms for the Théâtre d'Orléans caused the impresario Charles Boudousquié to erect a new theatre, the French Opera House (cap. 1800), in Bourbon Street in the heart of the Vieux Carré. Designed by James Gallier jr, it opened on 1 December 1859 with *Guillaume Tell*. In its second season Adelina Patti appeared as Donizetti's Lucia, the role of her début in New York (aged 16) the previous year; she remained in New Orleans for three months, appearing as Gilda, Rosina, Lady Harriet, Valentine, Dinorah and Leonora (*Il trovatore*).

Theatrical activity declined during the Civil War (1861–5), and the first attempt to establish a resident company following the conflict met with disaster when the ship carrying the singers and musicians to New Orleans was lost in an Atlantic hurricane (1866). By the 1870s, however, regular seasons had been revived, supplemented, as in past years, by visits from travelling opera troupes. Among the many American premières at the French Opera House were Lalo's *Le roi d'Ys* (1890), a number of Massenet works including *Le Cid* (1890), *Hérodiade* (1892), *Esclarmonde* (1893) and *Le portrait de Manon* (1895), the first stage performance of Saint-Saëns' *Samson et Dalila* (1893), Gounod's *La reine de Saba* (1899), Giordano's *Siberia* (1906) and Cilea's *Adriana Lecouvreur* (1907).

During World War I it proved impossible to organize resident troupes recruited from France and Belgium, and the city was visited by only a few touring companies. The French Opera House reopened in November 1919 but it burnt down the following month. Over the next 20 years the city depended on visiting troupes such as Fortune Gallo's San Carlo, Antonio Scotti's Grand Opera and the Metropolitan Opera on its spring tour. In 1922 a Russian troupe staged a week of its native repertory, unfamiliar to New Orleans audiences.

On 11 June 1943 the newly formed New Orleans Opera Association gave its first performance, outdoors, in City Park. By the autumn it had moved to the city's Municipal Auditorium (cap. 2500) and inaugurated a regular autumn and winter season of four to eight works; guest artists, for the leading roles, were supported by local singers and chorus. During its 30 years there, the company gave New Orleans premières of Richard Strauss's more popular works, *Die Entführung*, Verdi's *Attila*, *Macbeth* and *Falstaff*, Puccini's *Manon Lescaut* and *Turandot* and Carlisle Floyd's *Susannah*; in 1966 it gave the world première of Floyd's *Markheim*. In 1973 the association began to perform in the Theatre for Performing Arts (cap. 2317), reviving several 19th-century French works (*La Juive*, *Hérodiade*, *La favorite* and *Les Huguenots*). Contemporary works have not been part of the repertory, but guest companies have staged *Lulu* (Sarah Caldwell, 1967) and *Gloriana* (ENO, 1984).

'New Year' (Tippett): scene from the Glyndebourne première, 1 July 1990 (designed by Alison Chitty)

N. Smither: *A History of the English Theatre in New Orleans* (New York, 1944)

J. S. Kendall: *The Golden Age of the New Orleans Theater* (New York, 1952)

S. Chevalley: 'Le Théâtre d'Orléans en tournée dans les villes du nord 1827–1833', *Comptes rendus de l'Athénée louisianais* (New Orleans, 1955), 27–71

H. A. Kmen: *Singing and Dancing in New Orleans: a Social History of the Birth and Growth of Balls and Opera 1791–1841* (diss., Tulane U., 1961)

R. J. Le Gardeur jr: *The First New Orleans Theatre 1792–1803* (New Orleans, 1963)

H. A. Kmen: *Music in New Orleans: the Formative Years, 1791–1841* (Baton Rouge, LA, 1966)

J. A. Belsom: *Reception of Major Operatic Premières in New Orleans during the Nineteenth Century* (thesis, Louisiana State U., Baton Rouge, LA, 1972)

M. G. Swift: 'The Northern Tours of the Théâtre d'Orléans, 1843 and 1845', *Louisiana History*, xxvi (1985), 155–93

JACK BELSOM

New Orleans Opera Company. French-language travelling troupe based at the Théâtre d'Orléans in New Orleans; under the impresario John Davis it made six tours to cities in the north-eastern USA, 1827–33. *See* TRAVELLING TROUPES, §5(iii).

New Year. Opera in three acts by MICHAEL TIPPETT to his own libretto; Houston, Wortham Theater Center, 27 October 1989.

Tippett composed this opera, his fifth, between 1985 and 1988, to a commission from Houston Grand Opera, Glyndebourne Festival Opera and the BBC. It was originally conceived as a musical rather than as an opera, out of Tippett's desire to communicate with a wide and unstuffy audience. This starting-point was modified during the gestation of the work, though it can still be felt in the wide-ranging use of stylized dancing, set-piece songs and 'skarades' and eclectic popular styles and instrumental sonorities. These elements are transformed in the melting-pot of Tippett's theatrical vision, and the result defies easy categorization: part musical, opera, ballet, masque, pantomime and allegory, the work is an elaborate extension and synthesis of his unique operatic world.

The scenario combines elements of fantasy and reality. Jo Ann (lyric soprano) is a child psychologist who cannot come to terms with the real world, as represented by her anarchic black brother Donny (baritone). Both are orphans, brought up by their sensible foster-mother Nan (dramatic mezzo). This is the world of Somewhere Today. There is also Nowhere Tomorrow – a Utopian world of time travel into the future ruled by the terrifying Regan (dramatic soprano). Their spaceship is piloted by Pelegrin (lyric tenor) and controlled by the computer wizard Merlin (dramatic baritone). The two worlds interact when the computer screen throws up Jo Ann's anguished face. Pelegrin is drawn to her plight, and when the spaceship eventually lands he finds her in the crowd gathered to see in the New Year.

Regan discovers to her horror that the ship has travelled to the past and not the future, and she struggles to reassert her power and, unsuccessfully, to maintain her authority. Pelegrin and Jo Ann have now entered a world of magical communion and ordeal-by-love in which he teaches her to be strong and independent. After he has, inevitably, to leave her, the opera closes as she confidently steps out to face the world, fired by Tippett's universal dream – 'One humanity, one justice'.

The music of *New Year* is often lyrical – long melodic lines of memorable simplicity are woven into a score emphasizing continuity rather than disruption. Though greatly contrasted, the disparate elements cohere: a serene disembodied chorus jostles with a trio of sleazy saxophones supported by electric guitars; an exhilarating rap break-dance is soon followed by a transformed communal rendition of *Auld Lang Syne*; plangent harmonies and coruscating rhythms give way to electronic haze as the space-ship is encountered. Tippett's distinctive voice informs this amalgam, and the result is a theatrically spectacular and musically rejuvenating score which can fairly claim to represent the composer's operatic testament in the form of a vibrant challenge to the future.

GERAINT LEWIS

New York. City in the state of New York, ranked largest in the USA; it is the cultural centre of the country. The heart of the nation's music industry is in New York, and the city is a showcase for individuals and organizations from other parts of the country and abroad. The Metropolitan Opera (familiarly known as 'the Met'), founded in 1883, is one of the world's great companies, and the New York City Opera has established an important presence in the city's musical life.

1. Early history. 2. The Metropolitan Opera. 3. Other companies.

1. EARLY HISTORY. Before 1800 spoken theatre flourished and ballad opera was popular. Opera could be heard at the Nassau Street Theatre from 1750; *The Beggar's Opera* was one of the first performed there. In 1753–4 a troupe from London directed by Lewis Hallam performed operas and plays. David Douglass reorganized it under the name of the American Company (later Old American Company), and it performed at the John Street Theatre and in other coastal cities from 1767 to 1774. During the British occupation (1776–83) plays or ballad operas were occasionally performed, but it was not until 1785 that Lewis Hallam jr and John Henry reopened the Old American Company, which they operated more or less regularly until the turn of the century. The musical repertory consisted largely of pasticcio arrangements of such popular works as *Thomas and Sally*, *Rosina*, *Love in a Village*, *Lionel and Clarissa*, *The Adopted Child*, *The Duenna*, *No Song, No Supper* and *The Flitch of Bacon*. Operas by Grétry (*Zémire et Azor*) and Duni (*Les deux chasseurs*) also served as a basis for local adaptation. For a short time in the 1790s French immigrants performed works such as *Les deux chasseurs*, Audinot's *Le tonnelier* and Rousseau's *Le devin du village* in French.

Native musical theatre came into its own in the last quarter of the 18th century. Among the earliest examples was *May Day in Town* (18 May 1788), with 'music compiled from the most eminent masters'. James Hewitt's *Tammany, or The Indian Chief* (from which only one song survives), the first opera on an American Indian subject, was produced on 3 March 1794; the libretto, by Anna Hatton, succeeded in its intention to arouse Federalist opposition and *Tammany* had only three performances. The pantomime *The Fourth of July, or Temple of American Independence*, with music by Victor Pelissier, had one performance (4 July 1799), as did his *Edwin and Angelina* (19 December 1796). More successful was Benjamin Carr's comic opera *The Archers, or The Mountaineers of Switzerland* (1796), from which only the introductory rondo and a single song survive.

Italian opera first reached New York on 29 November 1825 with a performance at the Park Theatre of Rossini's *Il barbiere di Siviglia* by an Italian company led by Manuel García, the famous Spanish singer and teacher, who took the part of Almaviva. The ensemble of eight singers, four of them Garcías (including the 17-year-old Maria-Felicia, later Maria Malibran), had been recruited in London by a New York vintner, Dominick Lynch. Encouraged by Lorenzo da Ponte, then a professor of Italian at Columbia College, Lynch gave García's troupe to New York for a season of 79 (some sources list 80) performances, accompanied by a local orchestra of 24; the repertory included *Don Giovanni*, Rossini's *Tancredi*, *Otello*, *Il turco in Italia* and *La Cenerentola*, Zingarelli's *Romeo e Giulietta*, and García's own *La figlia dell'aria*. García's performances marked a change from the makeshift adaptations and pasticcios with popular airs inserted in place of difficult arias that had previously characterized opera in the city.

After the Garcías' departure for Mexico late in 1826, a French company from New Orleans gave a brief season of French opera at the Park Theatre, opening on 13 July 1827 with Isouard's *Cendrillon*. The French repertory included at least ten operas, among them Cherubini's *Les deux journées*, Auber's *La dame blanche* and Boieldieu's *Le calife de Bagdad*. The next opera company to appear was led by the tenor Giovanni Montresor in 1832–3; it gave about 50 performances of such works as Bellini's *Il pirata* and Mercadante's *Elisa e Claudio*, in addition to works of Rossini. Another French troupe from New Orleans introduced *Le comte Ory* (Park Theatre, 19 August 1833) and Hérold's *Zampa*.

New York's first opera house, the Italian Opera House at Church and Leonard streets, opened on 18 November 1833 with Rossini's *La gazza ladra*; among its backers were Lynch and Da Ponte. The repertory for the long but not very successful season (80 performances) consisted chiefly of the ever-popular Rossini, but Cimarosa and Pacini were also introduced. A second season was financially disastrous; Italian opera suffered an eclipse, and the house burnt down in 1839. Performances of opera, always a hazardous undertaking, were infrequent until Ferdinand Palmo, a restaurateur, opened Palmo's Opera House on 3 February 1844 with the New York première of *I puritani*. In four seasons Palmo introduced *Beatrice di Tenda*, Donizetti's *Lucrezia Borgia* and *Linda di Chamounix* and Verdi's *I Lombardi*. At other theatres pasticcios of opera in English by Balfe, Rooke and Benedict remained popular. While Palmo's held sway in Chambers Street, 150 wealthy men were raising money for another opera house further uptown, and the Astor Place Opera House opened on 22 November 1847 with Verdi's *Ernani*. The guaranteed support lasted only five years, financial returns were slight and the house closed in 1852. Another early rendezvous for Italian opera, during the summers, was the Castle Garden Theatre, built on an islet by Battery Park with attractive views across the bay on the site of an old fortress (see fig.2); a very large, circular building, it was the scene of Jenny Lind's New York début and, with visiting troupes, drew large audiences at modest prices during the early 1850s and did much to widen the public for opera in the city.

The period between 1847 and the founding of the Metropolitan Opera in 1883 was a turbulent one in the city's operatic history, dominated by colourful impresarios, competitive prima donnas and constantly changing personnel, who appeared in operatic performances in many New York theatres. After the house at Astor Place closed, the only theatre devoted specifically to concerts and opera was the Academy of Music at 14th Street and Irving Place, which opened on 2 October 1854 with a performance of *Norma* starring Giulia Grisi and Giuseppe Mario; it continued to present regular operatic seasons until 1886. When it was built (at a cost of $335 000), the house contained the largest stage in the world (21.5 by 30 m) and had a capacity of 4600. During the first 24 years the management changed every season.

Max Maretzek, who left London in 1848 to conduct at the Astor Place Opera, was among the more prominent impresarios. A frequent lessee and conductor at the Academy of Music, he was associated with the first New York performances of many operas there. Academy audiences heard *Rigoletto* (19 February 1855), *Trovatore* (2 May 1855), *Traviata* (3 December 1856), *L'Africaine* (1 December 1865) and Gounod's *Roméo et Juliette* (15 November 1867), the last two in

1. Jenny Lind portrayed in the title roles of Donizetti's 'La fille du régiment' (top left) and Bellini's 'Norma' (top right): broadside (1850) of Bayard Taylor's 'Greeting to America' which Lind sang at Castle Garden during the first concert of her extended tour of the USA

Italian. The brothers Maurice and Max Strakosch were also among the operatic impresarios active in New York from 1857. Most important was J. H. Mapleson, who went to the Academy of Music in 1878 and directed operatic activities there and abroad until 1886. Many great singers appeared in New York; audiences in 1852, for example, heard Henriette Sontag, Marietta Alboni, Mario, Grisi, Jenny Lind and the nine-year-old Adelina Patti. Later decades saw the appearance of singers such as Christine Nilsson, Lilli Lehmann and Italo Campanini. 39 American singers, among them Clara Kellogg, Minnie Hauk, Annie Louise Cary and Lillian Nordica, sang at the Academy of Music before 1884. Local composers were not so fortunate, although G. F. Bristow's *Rip Van Winkle* ran for four weeks at Niblo's Garden in 1855, and W. H. Fry's *Leonora* was heard in March 1858, 13 years after its première in Philadelphia. The first Wagner opera heard in New York was *Tannhäuser*, given on 4 April 1859 at the Stadt Theater with choruses sung by the Arion Society.

2. THE METROPOLITAN OPERA. The Metropolitan Opera House at Broadway and 39th Street opened with Gounod's *Faust* on 22 October 1883. Originally conceived as a social gesture by a score of millionaires who could not obtain boxes at the Academy of Music, the Metropolitan has transcended its original purpose. It quickly achieved international eminence – virtually every celebrated singer since it opened has sung at the house – and the Metropolitan Opera Association has

the longest continuous existence of any organization of its kind in the USA. In addition to performing in New York, the METROPOLITAN OPERA COMPANY made regular tours to American cities from the company's inception in 1883 until 1986.

Henry Abbey, a well-known theatrical impresario with little operatic experience, directed the first season and incurred a loss of $500 000. The artistic importance of the house dates from the following season, when the board of directors accepted Leopold Damrosch's proposal that he should direct a season of German opera. In the seven years after Damrosch's death in 1885 all Wagner's mature works with the exception of *Parsifal* were introduced by his successor, Anton Seidl. Celebrated European singers including Marianne Brandt, Lilli Lehmann, Amalie Materna and Albert Niemann were members of the company, and in effect the Metropolitan became a German opera house; even *Il trovatore* and *Aida* were given there in German.

The sobriety of the programmes eventually exhausted the patience of the box-holders, and in 1891 Abbey returned as lessee, placing the actual management in the hands of Maurice Grau, a shrewd student of public taste. He built his company around such admirable singers as Emma Eames, the De Reszkes, Emma Albani and Jean Lassalle, at first presenting the repertory exclusively in French and Italian. It was Grau's conviction that audiences attended opera primarily to hear fine singing, a belief he substantiated with some of the most brilliant casts Americans had ever heard. Among them were Nordica, Eames, Zélie de Lussan, Victor Maurel, Edouard de Reszke and Giuseppe Russitano in *Don*

2. The Castle Garden
Theatre, New York:
engraving from
'L'illustration'
(30 August 1851)

3. The Metropolitan
Opera House, New
York, at Broadway
between 39th and 40th
Streets, during a
performance of Wagner's
'Die Meistersinger'

4. The Metropolitan
Opera House, New
York, at Broadway
between 39th and 40th
Streets, opened in
October 1883

Giovanni; Melba, Nordica, Sofia Scalchi, the de Reszkes, Pol Plançon and Maurel in *Les Huguenots*; and Nordica, Brema, the de Reszkes and Giuseppe Kaschmann in *Tristan und Isolde* when the performance of German opera in German was resumed in 1896. In many respects these paralleled the London performances at Covent Garden, where Grau was also the impresario during part of this period. There were no Metropolitan performances in 1892–3 because of a disastrous fire that necessitated extensive reconstruction of the auditorium, or in 1897–8, when Grau reorganized his company. Otherwise a resident company has presented opera continuously at the Metropolitan from 1883. Only 16 Americans sang leading roles there before 1900; these included Hauk, Nordica, Albani, Eames, Olive Fremstad, Emma Nevada and David Bispham.

Grau retired in 1903 and a new administrative group was organized with Heinrich Conried as manager. His theatrical experience as a director of plays in German improved the dramatic aspect of the Metropolitan's productions considerably. Highlights of Conried's tenure included Caruso's début (23 November 1903), a sensational *Salome* with Fremstad (22 January 1907), Shalyapin as an almost nude Méphistophélès (20 November 1907) and Mahler's conducting of *Tristan und Isolde* (1 January 1908).

Giulio Gatti-Casazza, the director of La Scala, was engaged as general manager in 1908. Toscanini went to the Metropolitan with him, making his début in a performance of *Aida* (16 November 1908). With the musical cooperation of Toscanini and the financial assistance of Otto Kahn, Gatti-Casazza established an operatic enterprise of imposing scope and efficiency. Under him the policy of presenting opera in its original language became the rule of the house. Important conductors during his 27-year tenure included Mahler (1908–10), Toscanini (1908–15), Alfred Hertz (1902–15), Artur Bodanzky (1915–39) and Serafin (1924–34). The repertory was expanded to include as many as 48 different works in a 24-week season. Puccini's *La fanciulla del West* and Humperdinck's *Königskinder* had their world premières there in 1910. Gatti-Casazza continued to keep abreast of operatic developments in Italy and elsewhere, at the same time initiating the production of American operas including F. S. Converse's *The Pipe of Desire* (18 March 1910, four years after its Boston première), Horatio Parker's *Mona* (14 March 1912; fig.2) and Deems Taylor's *Peter Ibbetson* (7 February 1931). Although the company prospered under Gatti-Casazza's astute management, the 1929 stock market collapse and ensuing Depression severely depleted a reserve fund, and the season was shortened to 16 and later to 14 weeks. In 1935 Gatti-Casazza retired and was succeeded briefly by the singer Herbert Witherspoon, who died while planning his first season. His successor was the Canadian-born tenor Edward Johnson, who managed the Metropolitan until 1950.

An experiment with a low-priced spring season featuring young American singers sponsored by the Juilliard Foundation lasted only two years (1936–7), but American singers such as Lawrence Tibbett, Eleanor Steber, Rose Bampton, Richard Crooks, Leonard Warren, Dorothy Kirsten and Risë Stevens played an increasingly important role during Johnson's regime. Helen Traubel, Lauritz Melchior and Kirsten Flagstad headed a strong Germanic wing whose Wagner

performances in the late 1930s and early 40s were outstanding. Italian opera continued to dominate the repertory, French works being in the minority. Few modern operas were produced during Johnson's tenure, although the Metropolitan did give Walter Damrosch's *Man without a Country* in 1937, Bernard Rogers's *The Warrior* in 1947 and Britten's *Peter Grimes* in 1948.

For the first part of the Metropolitan's existence its main financial base was a private company, whose members occupied the single tier of socially significant boxes and delegated the production of opera to an independent company. In 1940 the property was sold to the production company, the Metropolitan Opera Association, which raised a million dollars in public appeals to help finance the transaction. Public support for the company has become increasingly important. The Metropolitan Opera Guild, a supporting organization founded in 1935 by Mrs August Belmont, has a national membership of over 100 000 and sponsors an educational programme and special performances for schoolchildren. During the season the guild issues *Opera News*, a periodical with articles, news and details of the Saturday afternoon radio broadcasts of matinée performances (inaugurated in 1931). These, sponsored by Texaco for more than 50 years, and relayed live every Saturday between December and the end of the season, in April, have had a great influence in the popularization of opera across the entire USA, as too, more recently, have the regular television transmissions of performances (often later issued commercially as videos). The Metropolitan Opera Auditions, begun as a radio broadcast in 1936 and sponsored by the National Council of the Metropolitan from 1953, has developed into a showcase for young singers. Early Metropolitan contract winners included Richard Tucker, Martina Arroyo, Robert Merrill and Shirley Verrett. From 1960 to 1976 the Metropolitan Opera Studio, founded by John Gutman, gave young professionals an opportunity to sing repertory and unfamiliar works before school audiences. A short-lived National Company employing young singers toured the country from 1965 to 1967, and currently the Young Artists' Development

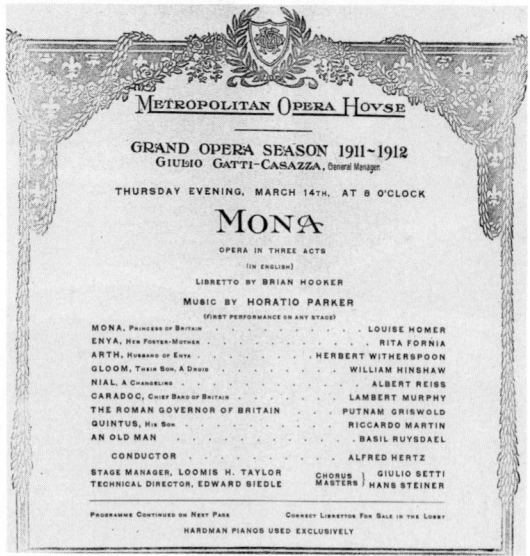

5. Page from the programme for the first performance of Horatio Parker's 'Mona' at the Metropolitan Opera, 14 March 1912

6. *Auditorium of the Metropolitan Opera House at Lincoln Center, New York, opened in September 1966*

7. *Foyer and staircase of the Metropolitan Opera House at Lincoln Center*

Program provides training for new singers.

In 1950 Rudolf Bing, the Viennese impresario who had managed the Glyndebourne and Edinburgh festivals, became general manager of the Metropolitan. His tenure lasted until 1972 and was marked by modernization of stage techniques, an increasingly international cast and the move of the company to new quarters in Lincoln Center. Although the repertory remained basically conservative, Bing introduced several American operas: Barber's *Vanessa* (15 January 1958), Menotti's *Le dernier sauvage* (23 January 1964) and Marvin David Levy's *Mourning Becomes Electra* (17 March 1967); light operas such as *Die Fledermaus* and *La Périchole* were also added to the repertory. Audiences have regularly enjoyed international singers of the calibre of Tebaldi, Nilsson, Sutherland, Corelli and Caballé, as well as American singers such as Leontyne Price, Marilyn Horne and Sherrill Milnes.

The new Metropolitan Opera House at Lincoln Center opened on 16 September 1966 with the world première of Barber's *Antony and Cleopatra*, in which Justino Díaz and Price sang the title roles. Despite, or perhaps because of, an extravagant production designed by Franco Zeffirelli, the work was a spectacular failure; the house, on the other hand, was a success. Although the seating capacity of the new auditorium (3788) is not much larger than the 39th Street building (3625), the inadequate staging facilities of the old house were replaced by a much larger stage and generous backstage quarters. The $46 million required for construction was raised in contributions by Lincoln Center and the Metropolitan Opera Association. In addition to accommodating the regular Metropolitan season of 32 weeks, the house is used by visiting opera and dance companies from the USA and abroad. Bing resigned in 1972 and his successor, the Swedish director Göran Gentele, died before his first season. Since then, the Metropolitan Opera management has undergone several reorganizations, resulting in a gradual separation of the artistic and managerial functions. Artistic control has been increasingly given to the conductor James Levine, appointed music director in 1976. His interests range from the early Mozart operas to the classics of the 20th-century repertory. Notable new productions under his tenure have included *Idomeneo*, *Rinaldo*, *Lulu*, *Wozzeck* and Weill's *Mahagonny*. Management of the company itself has been assumed by a succession of administrators: Schuyler Chapin (1972–5), Anthony Bliss (1975–85, with Levine and John Dexter, 1975–80), Bruce Crawford (1986–9), Hugh Southern (1989–90) and Joseph Volpe (from 1990). The centenary of the company was celebrated during the 1983–4 season with museum exhibitions, a postage stamp (fig.3) and a televised marathon gala on 22 October 1983, in which more than a hundred singers participated. Although the Metropolitan has maintained its international status as a showcase for singers, the repertory remains highly conservative; recent premières for the company have been confined to operas that have already become standard elsewhere, such as *La clemenza di Tito* (1984), *Porgy and Bess* (1985) and *Kát'a Kabanová* (1991). In addition the production style is conservative; value tends to be placed on the artists first rather than on the drama. John Corigliano's *The Ghosts of Versailles*, given its première on 19 December 1991, was the first opera to be commissioned by the Metropolitan company since it opened at Lincoln Center.

8. Postage stamp issued by the United States Postal Service in 1983 to commemorate the centenary of the Metropolitan Opera: design by Ken Davies depicting a combination of features from the original opera house (the proscenium arch appears in the background) and the new building at Lincoln Center (the five-arched entrance is superimposed)

3. OTHER COMPANIES. Although New York has maintained a tradition of both amateur and professional opera performances, only two companies have challenged the hegemony of the Metropolitan on a regular basis. The first, Oscar Hammerstein's Manhattan Opera Company, opened in December 1906 in the Manhattan Opera House on 34th Street; Cleofonte Campanini was artistic director and conductor. Before frustrated guarantors of the Metropolitan bought him out in 1910, Hammerstein had introduced many French works to American audiences, including *Thaïs* (25 November 1907), *Louise* (3 January 1908) and *Pelléas et Mélisande* (19 February 1908), all with Mary Garden. He also presented such celebrated singers as Melba, Calvé, Tetrazzini, Renaud and Dalmorès, in a varied repertory including the American première of Strauss's *Elektra* (1 February 1910).

The New York City Opera was founded as the City Center Opera Company in 1943 and has established itself over the years as a legitimate rival to the Metropolitan. Opening at the City Center Theatre on West 55th Street on 21 February with Dusolina Giannini as Tosca, the company has consistently encouraged participation by younger singers, composers and audiences. Initially seasons were short, a few weeks before and after the Metropolitan's, but the spring and autumn periods were later lengthened to 11 weeks each, with about 175 performances given annually. A succession of conductor-managers – Laszlo Halász (1944–51), Josef Rosenstock (1952–5), Erich Leinsdorf (1956–7) and Julius Rudel (1957–79) – produced an imaginative repertory ranging from *The Love for Three Oranges* (1949), *Wozzeck* (1959), *Giulio Cesare* (1971) and *L'incoronazione di Poppea* (1973) to Gilbert and Sullivan, without neglecting standard works. American opera fared particularly well at the City Opera during its early years; premières included William Grant Still's *Troubled Island* (1949), Copland's *The Tender Land* (1954), Robert Kurka's *The Good Soldier Schweik* (1958), Douglas Moore's *The Wings of the Dove* (1961), Robert Ward's *The Crucible* (1961) and Rorem's *Miss Julie* (1965).

On 22 February 1966 the New York City Opera opened its spring season at its new home, the New York State Theater in Lincoln Center, with a performance of Ginastera's *Don Rodrigo*. The house (cap. 2800) was originally designed for Balanchine's New York City Ballet and has been criticized as acoustically unsound for opera, but a renovation in 1981–2 (cap. 2737) resulted in improved, if not ideal, acoustics for opera performance. The company has always stressed ensemble production in contrast to the international star system, and has produced some fine native singers, among them June Anderson, Patricia Brooks, Ashley Putnam, Samuel Ramey, John Reardon, Beverly Sills, Norman Treigle and Carol Vaness. In 1979 Sills retired from the stage to become director of the City Opera, with Christopher Keene as music director from 1983. She proved a successful manager despite financial problems and a 1985 fire that destroyed many of the company's costumes. Her goals for the company were consistent with those of her predecessors; in addition she encouraged American conductors and operas in English. In 1984 the company was the first in the USA to introduce surtitles. The City Opera has continued to produce new works by American composers, among them Carlisle Floyd's *Of Mice and Men*, Philip Glass's *Akhnaten*, Anthony Davis's *X* and Dominick Argento's *Casanova*. Productions of Bernstein's *Candide* (1982) and Sondheim's *Sweeney Todd* (1984) demonstrated Sills's interest in forging links between opera and musical theatre. In 1984 the company received a gift of $5 million to make possible a regular spring season of musical comedy. The current schedule comprises two seasons, one of such classic musical theatre works as *Carousel*, *Kismet* and *South Pacific* in the spring, and another of more traditional operatic works from midsummer to early autumn. In 1989 Christopher Keene replaced Sills as general director of the company.

Operatic activity in New York has always included occasional performances characterized by departures from the norm, whether unconventional repertory, opera in English or opportunities for new singers and composers. The Amato Opera Theatre, a semiprofessional company founded in 1948 by Anthony Amato, presents 70 fully staged performances each year in its own theatre. Its six annual productions are drawn principally from the standard repertory, but it has also presented the American premières of Boito's *Nerone* and Verdi's *Alzira*. Young American artists are also given exposure in the Bronx Opera Company, founded in 1967 by Michael Spierman. The company's productions juxtapose well-known repertory with lesser-known works such as operas by Schubert and Vaughan Williams; staged performances are given in English. The Opera Orchestra of New York, directed by Eve Queler, carries on a tradition established by the American Opera Society (1951–70) of unusual works given in concert form. Popular staged performances of more familiar operas are given by Vincent La Selva's New York Grand Opera (founded 1973) in the style of the former impresarios Fortune Gallo and Alfredo Salmaggi. Conservatories and schools combine training and performance in contemporary and standard repertory; among the most important are the Juilliard School (whose American Opera Center, begun in 1970 as a forum for young professional singers, presents at least three operas a year), the Manhattan School of Music and the Mannes College of Music. Besides the ensembles already mentioned, over 40 other organizations produce at least one opera in a typical season in New York.

The New York stage has also played host to more popular entertainment throughout its history. Following the success of ballad opera in the 18th century, parody burlesques, minstrel shows and extravaganzas dominated the scene in the mid-19th century. *The Black Crook* (music by Thomas Baker and others, 1866), *Evangeline* (1874) by E. E. Rice, and Charles Hoyt's *A Trip to Chinatown* (1890) were particularly successful productions in a developing vernacular form that eventually fused song, dance and plot into the American musical comedy.

Operettas by Offenbach were popular from the 1860s; but in the two decades after the New York première of *HMS Pinafore* (1879), European light opera by Sullivan, Audran, Millöcker and others had to compete with local operetta by Ivan Caryll, Victor Herbert, Kerker and Reginald DeKoven. Gilbert and Sullivan, Lehár and Strauss still draw enthusiastic audiences both to opera houses and to off-Broadway theatres, especially the Light Opera of Manhattan (founded 1968). The Broadway stage, traditionally the home of the vernacular musical theatre in America, has also been host to a number of works that have later found a permanent home in the opera house, among them Blitzstein's *Regina* (1949) and Menotti's *The Consul* (1950), as well as *Candide* (1956) and *Sweeney Todd* (1979).

*

E. Singleton: 'History of the Opera in New York from 1750 to 1898', *Musical Courier*, xxxvii/23 (1898)

H. E. Krehbiel: *Chapters of Opera* (New York, 1908, 3/1911)

F. Rogers: 'America's First Grand Opera Season', *MQ*, i (1915), 93–101

O. G. T. Sonneck: *Early Opera in America* (New York, 1915)

J. Mattfeld: *A Hundred Years of Grand Opera in New York, 1825–1925* (New York, 1927)

G. C. D. Odell: *Annals of the New York Stage* (New York, 1927–49)

I. Kolodin: *The Metropolitan Opera* (New York, 1936, enlarged 4/1966)

W. H. Seltsam: *Metropolitan Opera Annals* (New York, 1947; suppls., 1957, 1968, 1978)

H. E. Johnson: *Operas on American Subjects* (Boston, 1964)

J. F. Cone: *Oscar Hammerstein's Manhattan Opera House* (Norman, OK, 1966)

M. Nelson: *The First Italian Opera Season in New York City: 1825–1826* (diss., U. of North Carolina, 1976)

C. Bishop: *Opera at the Hippodrome* (Santa Monica, 1979)

M. L. Sokol: *The New York City Opera* (New York, 1981)

J. F. Cone: *First Rival of the Metropolitan Opera* (New York, 1983)

M. Mayer: *The Met: One Hundred Years of Grand Opera* (New York, 1983)

F. P. Fellers: *The Metropolitan Opera on Record: a Discography of the Commercial Recordings* (Westport, CT, 1984)

G. Fitzgerald, ed.: *Annals of the Metropolitan Opera* (Boston and New York, 1989)
SUSAN T. SOMMER

New Zealand. Following European settlement in 1840, Marie Carandini's Australian company first introduced opera to the colony in 1863 through excerpts and linked commentaries. The following year William Lyster's Royal Italian and English Opera Company arrived in Dunedin from Melbourne to inaugurate a 24-night season with 20 different operas including Meyerbeer's *Les Huguenots*. The company aroused such enthusiasm that it toured elsewhere, returning to Dunedin in early 1865 when the repertory extended to *Le prophète*. Lyster's second visit was in 1880, the year of his death. Many of his artists maintained the tradition of the founder of Australian and New Zealand opera in their various ways, so that opera uniquely flourished. Fannie Simonsen Martin, J. C. Williamson and George Musgrove each made many tours, as did companies such as the Cagli and Pompei, and the Majeroni. Only the Pollard Opera Company could claim to be partly indigenous, starting as the Juvenile Lilliputians and, under the direction of Tom Pollard, graduating to light and comic opera. The Pollards endeared themselves to New Zealand audiences from 1881 until 1910. Musgrove's Wagner seasons of 1901 and 1907 proved highlights in the career of an impresario who equalled Lyster in the range and prodigality of his gifts and vision. Notable touring companies of the 20th century have included Sir Benjamin Fuller's Italian Gonsalez (1916–17, 1928), the Williamson of 1920 (with Amy Castles, Strella Wilson and Browning Mummery), the same firm's Imperial Grand Opera Company of 1932, and the 1935 Fuller tour with Florence Austral. In 1940 Isobel Baillie, Gladys Ripley, Heddle Nash and Raymond Beatty performed *Faust* as part of the centennial celebrations; fine companies continued to arrive until 1949, after which the New Zealand Opera Company was formed, in 1954, by Donald Munrow, building on his touring experience in Owen Jensen's Community Arts Service.

Beginning as a spirited chamber opera group, the company gradually encompassed the mainstream repertory, a notable success being a Maori *Porgy and Bess* (1965) with Inia te Wiata. Following *Figaro* and *Aida* (1971) the Arts Council withdrew its subsidy. A period of floundering ensued; the gap was partly filled by the New Opera Company of Wellington, which mounted professional productions in the main centres and toured the provinces, sustained by small Arts Council grants until 1979, when they ceased. The short-lived National Opera of New Zealand (1979–83) was then formed, based in Auckland, until after fine productions of *Aufstieg und Fall der Stadt Mahagonny* and *The Turn of the Screw* (1983) it suffered a similar fate, opera thereafter being deemed a regional responsibility; the bulk of the funds went to Auckland's Mercury Theatre.

Not surprisingly, there have been few New Zealand opera composers. Alfred Hill flourished in the early 20th century, a period of intense activity. Earlier, Luscombe Searelle had his comic opera *The Wreck of the Pinafore* (1880) trounced in 1882 in London, where his *Estrella* (1884) was found to be agreeable by *The Times*. More recently operas and music theatre have been written by David Farquhar, Edwin Carr (*Nastasya*), Jenny McLeod, Gillian Whitehead and Ross Harris.

New Zealand has produced many distinguished soloists, among them the Maori Princess Te Rangi Pai, Princess Iwa, Inia te Wiata and Kiri te Kanawa as well as Rosina Buckman, Frances Alda, Oscar Natzka, Donald McIntyre, Malvina Major and Patricia Payne; it might yet show that a national company in a scattered population of under four million is not an impossibility.

For further information on operatic life in the country's principal centre see WELLINGTON.

*

J. M. Thomson: *A Distant Music: the Life and Times of Alfred Hill 1870–1960* (Auckland, 1980)
——: *European Music in New Zealand 1840–1990* (Auckland, 1990)
A. Simpson and P. Downes: *Southern Voices: International Opera Singers of New Zealand* (Auckland, 1992)
A. Simpson, ed.: *Studies in New Zealand Opera* (in preparation)
J. M. THOMSON

New Zealand Opera Company. New Zealand company formed in 1954, originally based in Wellington. Founded by the baritone Donald Munrow, it first produced small-scale works which could easily be taken on tour. Its high standards attracted regular audiences,

and by 1957 the company was able to mount its first full-scale production, Menotti's *The Consul*. Despite the choice of a modern work, the season was successful and the company became fully professional. In succeeding years a regular touring pattern was established. Performances with piano accompaniment and no chorus were given in small towns all over New Zealand; productions with full orchestra were confined to short tours of the main metropolitan centres.

Despite its often precarious finances the company quickly became a major force in New Zealand music. A landmark in 1962 was the first production of a New Zealand opera: David Farquhar's *A Unicorn for Christmas*, to a libretto by Ngaio Marsh. In the same year, the nucleus of a full-time chorus was built up. The repertory was generally mainstream, although in 1965 an enormous financial success was achieved with the acclaimed all-Maori production of *Porgy and Bess*, which subsequently toured Australia. The company lacked a permanent home until 1968, when a disused Wellington cinema was bought to house a theatre and offices. This move was not particularly successful financially and several years of difficulty followed, although high artistic standards were maintained. However, in 1971, after an abortive attempt to combine the company with the Royal New Zealand Ballet, public funding was withdrawn and the company ceased operating.

Despite its brief existence, the New Zealand Opera Company succeeded in re-establishing opera as a part of the country's cultural life. It gave a platform to New Zealand singers, many of whom (Donald McIntyre, Inia te Wiata, Bryan Drake, Malvina Major, Heather Begg, Kiri te Kanawa) went on to international careers. Its productions set the standards by which later regional companies were judged.
ADRIENNE SIMPSON

Ney [Bürde-Ney], Jenny (*b* Graz, 21 Dec 1824; *d* Dresden, 7 May 1886). Austrian soprano. She made her début in 1845 at Olomouc as Norma. After singing in Prague, Lwów and Vienna, she was engaged at the Dresden Hofoper (1853–67). She made her Covent Garden début in 1855 as Leonore (*Fidelio*), then sang Leonora in the first British performance of *Il trovatore*. She appeared in Berlin, Paris, St Petersburg, Milan and New York. Her roles included Donna Anna, Romeo (*I Capuleti e i Montecchi*), Catherine (*L'étoile du nord*), Valentine (*Les Huguenots*) and Mrs Ford (*Die lustigen Weiber von Windsor*). Though her voice was harsh, she had exceptional technique and was a very dramatic singer, admired by Meyerbeer and Wagner.
ELIZABETH FORBES

Nežádal, Maria (*b* Pardubice, 21 Feb 1897). Czech soprano. She studied at the Prague Conservatory and made her début at Olomouc in 1924. After a season at the Vienna Volksoper and another in Berne, she was engaged by the Staatsoper in Munich, where she sang from 1927 to 1933. In 1935 she married Clemens von Franckenstein, the composer and conductor who was also director of the Staatsoper in Munich during Nežádal's time there. By 1933 she was debarred from pursuing her career in Germany, but she continued to sing elsewhere, making her Covent Garden début in 1935 as Gutrune in *Götterdämmerung* and remaining as the company's regular singer of this part until 1939. Though she was well received, recordings of excerpts made from the stage in those years suggest that her voice had become somewhat unsteady; she is better heard as Woglinde in excerpts from *Das Rheingold* made in 1927, her single season at Bayreuth, in which the voice is clear and firm.   J. B. STEANE

Nezeritis [Neseritis], Andreas (*b* Patras, 30 Nov 1897; *d* Athens, 19 Nov 1980). Greek composer. He studied in Patras and at the Athens Conservatory (1917–22), and also took private lessons (*c*1926–33) in composition and orchestration from Dionyssios Lavrangas. In 1957 he was elected vice-president of the League of Greek Composers and in 1967 he succeeded Mario Varvoglis as president.

Nezeritis composed two operas; the first, *O vassilias Aniliagos* ('King Aniliagos'; 2, I. Polemis), was performed at the National Opera, Athens, on 27 March 1948. The Interlude and Reapers' Dance from this work rank among the most popular items of the Greek symphonic repertory. In *Iro ke Leandros* ('Hero and Leander'; 3, F. Grillparzer: *Des Meeres und der Liebe Wellen*, trans. R. Nezeritis) the dramatic argument is treated in the manner of a symphonic poem; some choral passages and text repetitions weaken the theatrical impact. On the other hand, a profusion of melodic and harmonic procedures and materials is woven together with unobtrusive skill: chromaticism tending towards atonality, whole-tone scales, a rather dense harmonic rhythm, and vague reminiscences of Debussy, Wagner, Puccini, Musorgsky and Prokofiev. The work was composed between 1947 and 1964 and first performed at the National Opera on 12 November 1970. Nezeritis's other compositions include three symphonies, a violin concerto and songs.

*

A. S. Theodoropoulou: 'Synchronoi ellines moussikoi: 3. Andreas Nezeritis' [Contemporary Greek Musicians], *Anglohelleniki epitheorissi*, iii/3 (1947), 87–8
G. Leotsakos: 'Hero and Leander', *Ta nea* (24 Nov 1970)
——: 'Efyge ki o synthetis Andreas Nezeritis', *Theatro*, xi/64–6 (1981), 136 [obituary]   GEORGE LEOTSAKOS

Nezhdanova, Antonina (*b* Krivaya Balka, nr Odessa, 4/16 June 1873; *d* Moscow, 26 June 1950). Russian soprano. She graduated from Umberto Masetti's class at the Moscow Conservatory in 1902; that year she was engaged as a soloist at the Bol'shoy, where she remained for nearly 40 years, singing leading roles in Russian and west European operas opposite Sobinov. In 1912 she sang Gilda at the Paris Opéra with the Monte Carlo company. Her other roles included Lyudmila, Tatyana, Lakmé, the Snow Maiden, Volkhova (*Sadko*), the Queen of Shemakha, Elsa and Rosina. As Glinka's Antonida and Rimsky-Korsakov's Marfa, she achieved a most harmonious musical and dramatic integration.

Nezhdanova was one of the greatest representatives of the Russian school, with a clear, beautiful voice and a coloratura technique of dazzling lightness and brilliance. Her performances were unselfconscious and heartfelt, and she was a subtle, dramatic actress. From 1936 she taught at the Stanislavsky Opera Studio and at the Bol'shoy opera studio, then at the Moscow Conservatory (1943–50).

*

GV [with discography by J. Stratton and R. Vegeto]
M. L'vov: *A. V. Nezhdanova* (Moscow, 1952)
V. Podol'skaya: *A. V. Nezhdanova i eyo ucheniki: zametki kontsertmeystera* [Nezhdanova and her Pupils: Notes of a Solo Performer] (Moscow, 1960)
L. Collingwood: 'Two Famous Russian Singers', *Opera*, xxi (1970), 782–5

G. Polyanovsky: *Antonina Nezhdanova* (Moscow, 1970)
                                               I. M. YAMPOL'SKY

Nibelung's Ring, The. *Bühnenfestspiel* by Richard Wagner; *see* RING DES NIBELUNGEN, DER.

Niccolini, Giuseppe. *See* NICOLINI, GIUSEPPE.

Niccolino. *See* PARIS, NICOLA.

Nice (It. Nizza). Resort city in the south of France. The first theatre, the Teatro Maccarini, built of wood, was opened in 1777 by the Marchese Ali-Maccarini when the town was part of the Italian state of Austro-Sardinia. It became the Théâtre Royal in 1790, and during the Revolutionary period the Théâtre de la Montagne. In 1826 it was acquired by the municipality; it was demolished and replaced with a new opera house designed after the model of the S Carlo in Naples, and was once again named the Théâtre Royal. When Nice was ceded to France in 1860 it became the Théâtre Impérial, and in 1871, under the Republic, the Théâtre Municipal. The first performance in France of *La forza del destino* was given there in 1873. In 1881 the theatre burnt down during a performance of *Lucia di Lammermoor*, causing many deaths. A new theatre, also called the Théâtre Municipal (from 1902 the Opéra), was built on the same site in the rue St François de Paule, in the middle of what is today the picturesque Old Town; it was designed by the architect François Aune, his plans approved and slightly modified by Charles Garnier, and inaugurated with *Aida* in 1885. Originally seating more than 1200 (now 1000), it has three galleries of boxes and an open amphitheatre gallery.

Up to the end of World War II the Opéra had no monopoly in this rich Mediterranean resort: the first performance in France of *Lohengrin* (1881) was given at the Cercle de la Méditerranée, that of *Otello* (1891, with Tamagno and Maurel) at the Casino Municipal, and the world première of Falla's *La vida breve* (1913) at the Casino de la Jetée-Promenade. Most of the great singers of the 19th and early 20th centuries appeared at the Nice Opéra and many important French first performances were given there – *La Gioconda* (1886), *A Life for the Tsar* (1890), Berlioz's *La prise de Troy* (1890), *Yevgeny Onegin* (1895), Leoncavallo's *La bohème* (1899), *Das Rheingold* (1902) and Shostakovich's *Katerina Izmaylova* (1964). Directors have included Raoul Gunsbourg, 1889–91 (later to become famous as the director of the Monte Carlo Opéra), the tenors Thomas Salignac and José Luccioni and, probably the most colourful, Ferdinand Aymé, who from 1950 until his death in 1982 ran the Nice Opéra together with the companies of Nîmes, Montpellier and Toulon and the bullrings of Arles, Nîmes and Fréjus. His casts included Bergonzi, Corelli and the leading Wagner singers of the day, as well as young French singers such as Régine Crespin and Gabriel Bacquier. Since 1982 the Opéra has been under the artistic direction of Pierre Médecin, brother of the ex-mayor. Under his regime the Nice Opéra gave the first uncut staging of *Les Troyens* in France (1988). The municipality provides 80% of the budget.

In 1985 the Acropolis, a vast conference and performing arts centre designed by the architects Buzzi, Baptiste and Bernasconi, was opened. It includes an opera house and concert hall, the Apollon Auditorium, seating 2500;

its stage is the largest in France (1200 sq m). The Opéra now mounts two to four of its productions here each year. In 1987 this rich, well-organized company constructed the Diacosmie, a lyric production centre on the outskirts of the town. It includes two stages identical in all dimensions with the stages of the Opéra and the Apollon where singers can rehearse in the real sets and exact acoustic conditions of performance. In addition, two workshops (each 1600 sq m in area and 7 m high) for the construction of sets adjoin costume workshops and rehearsal rooms for orchestra and ballet. The centre is unique in Europe and has enabled the Nice Opéra to mount co-productions with La Scala and Paris. The season runs from September to June, with up to 80 performances of some 12 operas, together with ballet, recitals and concerts by the town orchestra (110 players). During the summer, operas are often presented in the Roman Arènes de Cimiez.

*

Opéra de Nice 1885–1985: d'un siècle à L'autre (Nice, 1985)
S. Mont Berthon: 'Le théâtre lyrique à Nice', Le théâtre lyrique français, 1945–1985, ed. D. Pistone (Paris, 1987), 355–8
CHARLES PITT

Nicholls, Agnes (b Cheltenham, 14 July 1877; d London, 21 Sept 1959). English soprano. She studied at the RCM with Albert Visetti and in 1895 played Purcell's Dido at the Lyceum Theatre. While still a student, she took part in three private performances before Queen Victoria, and also sang Anne Page in the first English-language production of Falstaff. Her Covent Garden début (1901) was as the Dew Fairy in Hänsel und Gretel; in the 1904–6 seasons she sang with distinction in the great international casts assembled for Don Giovanni and Carmen. In 1906 she also appeared as Venus, the start of a notable series of Wagner roles, including Sieglinde and the Siegfried Brünnhilde in the first English-language Ring productions, under Richter in 1908. She continued to sing at Covent Garden until 1924, and was also a principal of the British National Opera Company, of which she became a director. Her recordings show her purity of tone and soundness of technique, as well as the considerable power of her voice. She was married in 1904 to the conductor Hamilton Harty.
J. B. STEANE

Nicolai, Claudio (b Kiel, 7 March 1929). German baritone. After studying in Vienna, he was engaged in 1954 at the Theater am Gärtnerplatz, Munich, first as a tenor, then as a baritone. In 1964 he moved to Cologne, where he remained for over 25 years; he took part in the première of Die Soldaten (1965) and with the company sang the Secretary in the first London performance of Der junge Lord at Sadler's Wells (1969). His huge and varied repertory includes Almaviva, Guglielmo and Don Alfonso, Rossini's Figaro, Billy Budd, Monteverdi's Ulysses and many operetta roles. In 1979 he sang Count Robinson (Il matrimonio segreto) at Cologne, repeating the part at Edinburgh (1980), Sadler's Wells (1983), Schwetzingen and Washington, DC (1986). A superb character actor, he has a light but serviceable voice.
ELIZABETH FORBES

Nicolai, Elena [Nikolova, Elena Stoianka] (b Cerevo, nr Pazordžik, 24 Jan 1905). Bulgarian mezzo-soprano. She studied at the Milan Conservatory and made her début in Malta, as Maddalena in Rigoletto. Further study led to an Italian début at Naples in 1938. She was successful in Milan and Rome during the war years as Eboli, Orpheus and Ortrud, and in Adriana Lecouvreur and Cavalleria rusticana. Her best roles at the Verona Arena (1946–54) were Amneris and Laura (La Gioconda). At the 1950 Maggio Musicale she was Statira in a revival of Spontini's Olympie and at Naples in 1954 she sang in the première of La figlia di Iorio by Pizzetti. She also appeared in Switzerland, Paris and South America.
DAVID CUMMINGS

Nicolai, (Carl) Otto (Ehrenfried) (b Königsberg [now Kaliningrad], 9 June 1810; d Berlin, 11 May 1849). German composer. As a boy he was subjected to oppressive discipline from his widowed father, a professional musician, who tried to turn him into a child prodigy. At the age of 16 he ran away from home. In Stargard (Pomerania), August Adler, a government official, impressed by the young man's abilities, took him under his wing and furthered his education, sending him to Berlin to study with Carl Friedrich Zelter and Bernhard Klein. Between 1830 and 1833 Nicolai earned his living as a singing teacher and was a member of Zelter's Singakademie; he sang the part of Jesus in Bach's St Matthew Passion in 1831. During this period he became acquainted with the Mendelssohn family. His earliest published compositions, solo songs and part-songs, appeared in 1830.

In 1833 Nicolai accepted the post of organist at the Prussian Embassy in Rome, where he remained for three years. He went often to the Sistine chapel and developed a profound interest in Palestrina and other 16th-century Italian composers; this led him to study counterpoint with Giuseppi Baini, a scholar and ultra-conservative composer who emulated Palestrina's polyphony in his own music. After resigning his post, Nicolai travelled to various Italian cities seeking a commission to write an opera; he failed to get one but accepted a year's contract as an assistant Kapellmeister at the Hoftheater in Vienna beginning on 1 June 1837. Despite his satisfactory performance, his contract there was not renewed and he returned to Italy. Apparently he had ambitions to become a maestro di cappella in Rome, for Fanny Mendelssohn wrote to her brother Felix from there in May 1840 (The Letters of Fanny Hensel to Felix Mendelssohn, trans. and ed. M. J. Citron, Stuyvesant, NY, 1987, p.292).

I hear that Otto Nicolai was planning to become the director of the Papal chapel, and even willing to become a Catholic and a priest – necessary conditions for the position – since it didn't matter to him. But since the plan failed he's thrown himself into the arms of opera and is now in Turin.

Nicolai's first opera, Enrico II, was not particularly successful at its première in Trieste in November 1839; it was given only twice before being withdrawn, and was described by a journalist at the time as 'a fiasco'. The libretto was an old one which, as Rosmonda d'Inghilterra, had been set by Coccia, Luigi Majocchi and Donizetti, while the music had 'nothing special about it and ... was unable to rouse any interest or enthusiasm' (AMZ, xlii, 1840, col. 201–2). However, this failure was followed by the excellent reception of Il templario in Turin less than three months later. Il templario then opened the season in Genoa and was repeated many times; within a year or two it was being widely performed throughout Italy and abroad. One consequence of this success was the immediate offer of commissions. In 1840 Nicolai composed Gildippe ed Odoardo for Genoa and in 1841 Il proscritto for Milan, but these were less successful. (Merelli, the impresario at La Scala, had first offered Nicolai the libretto of *Nabucco*, but when he turned it down it went to Verdi instead, and Nicolai accepted *Il proscritto*, which Verdi had refused.)

In 1841 Nicolai was invited to conduct *Il templario* at the Hofoper in Vienna, where it was 'listened to with rare attention', though a local critic noted rather sourly that it was 'not a classical product either in terms of originality or character, but an effective compilation calculated to win praise and applause' (*AMZ*, xliii, 1841, col.690–91). Its success with the public, however, led to Nicolai's engagement as principal Kapellmeister. He remained in Vienna for the next six years, making a significant impact on the city's musical life. On 28 March 1842 he began a concert series with the Hofoper orchestra that eventually developed into the Philharmonic Concerts, and later he took over the direction of the moribund *concerts spirituels*, considerably raising the standard of performance. Further operatic composition during his years in Vienna was hampered by his failure to find a suitable libretto; he declared that 'eternal raging, bloodletting, insults, beating and murder' were unacceptable to him, and he read widely in an attempt to find the right subject. According to his contract he should have composed a new German opera for the Hofoper in 1845, but when he was unable to decide on a libretto he mounted another production of *Il templario*, this time in a German version as *Der Tempelritter*. In February 1844 he also staged *Il proscritto* as *Die Heimkehr des Verbannten*; but he was taken sharply to task in the press for attempting to palm off his old Italian opera on the Viennese public as a new German one.

By this time, Nicolai had found an opera subject that suited him in Shakespeare's *The Merry Wives of Windsor*, and he began work on setting Hermann Mosenthal's libretto in 1845. When *Die lustigen Weiber von Windsor* was refused at the Hoftheater by the impresario Balochino, however, Nicolai determined to leave Vienna. In 1846 he resigned his post (to be replaced by Conradin Kreutzer) and after giving several numbers from his new opera at a farewell concert in the spring of 1847, he prepared to depart, somewhat uncertain about his future. Three years earlier he had been offered the post of Kapellmeister at the cathedral in Berlin, but had refused it because he could not combine it with the same post at the opera; now he was offered both jobs and eagerly accepted. He began his duties at the Berlin opera on 1 March 1848, where, just over a year later, he conducted the highly successful première of *Die lustigen Weiber von Windsor*. On 11 May 1849, after directing a concert with the cathedral choir, he suffered a fatal stroke.

Nicolai's style was formed by diverse influences. His early studies in Berlin gave him a sound technical knowledge and a self-critical approach to composition which he never lost. As an heir of the Classical tradition of Mozart and Beethoven and the newer German Romantic tradition of Spohr and Weber, he was acutely conscious of the composer's responsibility to his art. This element of Nicolai's creativity, however, was significantly modified by his experience in Italy, where he was attracted both by the purity and beauty of 16th-century church music and by the vivacity of modern Italian opera. He recognized, though, that his German background would not allow him to compose opera entirely in the manner of his Italian contemporaries; he

observed: 'I have more intellect than imagination, and therefore composing is more difficult for me than others. People such as Donizetti … write continuously without self-criticism'. Nonetheless, his earlier operas were attacked by German commentators for being too much in the Italian manner. After the 1841 performance of *Il templario* in Vienna a local critic observed (*AMZ*, xliii, 1841, col.690–91):

> Superficially, the overture appeared to have a somewhat German physiognomy, but decoration and embellishment betrayed the Cisalpine origin, and everything that followed proved that during his stay in Italy, the maestro made the Italian taste his own and learnt to write in that manner which gives the audience what it wants and expects.

Three years later, after the production of *Die Heimkehr des Verbannten*, it was remarked: 'Nicolai loves sensation; he seeks to impress the Italian with German harmony and the German with Italian melody, but in the end neither the one nor the other thanks him for it' (*AMZ*, xlvi, 1844, col.636). With *Die lustigen Weiber von Windsor* he finally found both the libretto and the musical style he had been seeking. Although he did not live to build on his achievement, his last opera continued to hold the stage while his earlier efforts quietly faded into oblivion.

See also Lustigen Weiber von Windsor, Die.

Enrico II, 1836 (melodramma serio, 2, F. Romani: *Rosmonde*), Trieste, Grande, 26 Nov 1839, aria (Milan, *c*1839)
Il templario (melodramma, 3, G. M. Marini, after W. Scott: *Ivanhoe*), Turin, Regio, 11 Feb 1840, vs (Paris, *c*1840); as Der Tempelritter (trans. S. Kapper), Vienna, Kärntnertor, 20 Dec 1845, *A-Wn*
Gildippe ed Odoardo (melodramma, 3, T. Solera, after T. Tasso), Genoa, Carlo Felice, 26 Dec 1840, cavatina (Milan, *c*1841)
Il proscritto (3, G. Rossi), Milan, Scala, 13 March 1841, part pubd (Milan, *c*1841); as Die Heimkehr des Verbannten (tragische Oper, trans. Kapper), Vienna, Kärntnertor, 3 Feb 1844, vs (Vienna, 1844)
Die lustigen Weiber von Windsor (komische-fantastische Oper, 3, S. H. Mosenthal, after W. Shakespeare), Berlin, Kgl, 9 March 1849 (Berlin, 1850)

H. Mendel: *Otto Nicolai* (Berlin, 1866, 2/1868)
B. Schröder, ed.: *Otto Nicolai: Tagebücher nebst biographischen Ergänzungen* (Leipzig, 1892)
E. Hanslick: *Am Ende des Jahrhunderts*, Die moderne Oper, viii (Berlin, 1899), 100ff
K. M. Kolb: *Beiträge zur Geschichte der deutschen komischen Oper* (Berlin, 1903), 87ff
G. R. Kruse: 'Falstaff und die lustigen Weiber', *Die Musik*, vi/4 (1906–7), 63
——: 'Otto Nicolais italienische Opern', *SIMG*, xii (1910–11), 267–96
——: *Otto Nicolai: ein Künstlerleben* (Berlin, 1911)
A. Weissmann: *Berlin als Musikstadt: Geschichte der Oper und des Konzert von 1740–1911* (Berlin and Leipzig, 1911), 201, 203, 245
L. Schiedermaier: *Die deutsche Oper* (Leipzig, 1930)
G. R. Kruse: 'Otto Nicolais "Lustige Weiber" … mit unbekannt gebliebenen Nummern', *Die Musik*, xxviii (1936), 886–94
W. Altmann, ed.: *Otto Nicolais Tagebücher* (Regensburg, 1937)
S. Goslich: *Beiträge zur Geschichte der deutschen romantischen Oper* (Leipzig, 1937)
J. W. Klein: 'Verdi and Nicolai: a Strange Rivalry', *MR*, xxxii (1971), 63–7
T. G. Kaufman: 'Otto Nicolai', *Verdi and his Major Contemporaries: a Selected Chronology of Performances with Casts* (New York and London, 1990), 111–16   CLIVE BROWN

Nicolas, Ernest. *See* Nicolini, Ernest.

Nicolau, Antonio (*b* Barcelona, 8 June 1858; *d* Barcelona, 26 Feb 1933). Spanish composer. He began to study medicine, but soon abandoned this in favour of composition. After living in Paris for eight years, he finally settled in Barcelona in 1886. Belonging to the generation that succeeded Pedrell, he is important not only as a composer but also as one of the outstanding Catalan conductors of the 19th century, and as a leader in the revival of Catalan music. Primarily a composer of choral music, Nicolau also wrote several important operas. The first, the four-act *Constanza*, is deeply rooted in the Romantic tradition. It was first performed at the Liceo on 10 April 1878 but, owing to the unexpected withdrawal of the tenor, the first two acts had to be omitted; it was later performed in its entirety at the Teatro Principal. Another of his dramatic works, *Un rapto*, was performed in Madrid shortly before the opening of the exhibition of 1888, and was acclaimed by both public and critics. His last opera, *El corazón de fuego*, was given its first performance at the Teatro Tivoli in Barcelona in 1895 at the same time as Nicolau was turning to Wagner, whose *Ring* he conducted in March 1896. The *Danza Anakota* from *El corazón* features frequently in concerts in Barcelona.

M. Valls: *La música catalana contemporánea* (Barcelona, 1960)

EMILIO CASARES

Nicolesco [Niculescu], **Mariana** (*b* Gaujani, 28 Nov 1948). Romanian soprano. She trained as a violinist, then studied singing at the Cluj conservatory. A scholarship took her to the Accademia di S Cecilia in Rome, where her teacher was Jolanda Magnoni; she later had lessons from Rodolfo Celletti in Milan and from Elisabeth Schwarzkopf. She made her operatic début in 1972 as Mimì in Cincinnati with Thomas Schippers, who did much to further her career. In 1978 she sang for the first time at the Metropolitan, as Violetta (a role she has sung over 200 times), returning as Gilda and Nedda. She has also appeared at the major European houses, as Donna Elvira, Cinna (*Lucio Silla*), Electra (*Idomeneo*), Marzelline, Desdemona, Liù and Elizabeth (*Roberto Devereux*). She made her début at La Scala when she created Leonora in Berio's *La vera storia* (1982) and has since sung there as Eurydice in a revival of Luigi Rossi's

Orfeo (1985) and as Clymene in a revival of Jommelli's *Fetonte* (1988). An arresting personality with a vibrant voice, she also has the flexibility necessary for such bel canto roles as Donizetti's Anne Boleyn and Mary Stuart.

Nicolini [Grimaldi, Nicolo] (*b* Naples, bap. 5 April 1673; *d* Naples, 1 Jan 1732). Italian alto castrato. He studied under Provenzale, in whose *La Stellidaura vendicata* he made his début in 1685, and sang in the cathedral and the royal chapel as a soprano from 1690. He appeared frequently in opera, at the S Bartolomeo theatre and sometimes in the royal palace, between 1697 and 1724 and was particularly associated with Alessandro Scarlatti, singing in his *La caduta de' Decemviri* (1697), *Il prigioniero fortunato* (1698), *Arminio*, *L'amor generoso* and *Scipione nelle Spagne* (1714), *Tigrane* (1715) and *Cambise* (1719); he also sang in operas by C. F. Pollarolo, Giovanni Bononcini (*Muzio Scevola*), Mancia, Mancini, Lotti, Leo, Porpora, Vinci and others. He sang in Rome and Bologna in 1699 and 1700, Vicenza in 1707–8, Ferrara in 1713, Rome in 1721, Florence in 1725 and 1728, and between 1701 and 1731 appeared many times in Venice, in works by C. F. Pollarolo, Antonio Pollarolo, Gasparini, Caldara, Albinoni, Leo, Orlandini, Vinci, Porpora, Hasse and others.

Nicolini went to London in 1708, promoted by Vanbrugh, and made his début at the Queen's Theatre in Haym's arrangement of Scarlatti's *Pirro e Demetrio*. He enjoyed a great personal triumph and was largely responsible for the increasing popularity of Italian opera in London. In 1709 he signed a three-year contract with Owen Swiney, in which he undertook to arrange operas for the London stage. He sang in all the operas during that period, many of them pasticcios arranged by Haym or himself: *Camilla* (G. Bononcini), *Clotilda* and *Tomiri* in 1709, *Almahide* and Mancini's *Idaspe fedele* (including his notorious scene with a lion) in 1710, Bononcini's *Etearco* and Gasparini's *Antioco* in 1711, *Ambleto* and *Ercole* in 1712. In 1711 he sang the title role in the first performance of Handel's *Rinaldo*. He returned to London in 1715 and created the title role in Handel's *Amadigi*. He continued to sing in pasticcios and revivals

Nicolini with Francesca Cuzzoni: caricature (c1730) by Anton Maria Zanetti

up to 1717. Swiney tried repeatedly to persuade the Royal Academy to re-engage him between 1725 and 1727.

Nicolini was the leading male singer of his age and an outstanding all-round artist. Burney's evaluation, 'this great singer, and still greater actor', was shared by contemporaries such as Steele. Addison called him 'the greatest performer in dramatic Music that is now living or that perhaps ever appeared on a stage'. The two parts Handel composed for him require exceptional agility and breath control, with a compass *a* to *f"*. He never retired, and after singing in Vinci's *Siroe* and Orlandini's *Massimiano* in Venice in 1731 he was engaged for Pergolesi's first opera, *Salustia*, in Naples, but was taken ill and died during rehearsals.

E. Faustini-Fasini: 'Gli astri maggiori del "bel canto" napolitano: il Cav. Nicola Grimaldi detto "Nicolini"', *NA*, xii (1935), 297–316
WINTON DEAN

Nicolini [Nicolas], **Ernest** (*b* St Malo, 23 Feb 1834; *d* Pau, 19 Jan 1898). French tenor. He studied at the Paris Conservatoire and made his début in 1857 at the Opéra-Comique in Halévy's *Les mousquetaires de la reine*. After further study in Italy, he sang at La Scala in *La traviata* (1859), Rossini's *Otello* (as Rodrigo), *I Lombardi* and *La sonnambula* (1860). From 1862 to 1869 he appeared at the Théâtre Italien, Paris, and he made his Covent Garden début (taking the pseudonym Nicolini) in 1866 as Edgardo in *Lucia di Lammermoor*. In 1871 he returned to London to sing in *Faust* and *Robert le diable* at Drury Lane; from 1872 to 1884 he was engaged at Covent Garden. He sang in the first London performances of Gomez's *Il Guarany* (1872), *Lohengrin* (1875), *Aida* (1876) and Jules Cohen's *Estella* (1880), and created Celio in Charles Lenepveu's *Velléda* (1882). His voice had a wide vibrato, but his fine stage presence and intense acting were appreciated in dramatic roles.

H. Klein: *The Reign of Patti* (London, 1920)
H. Rosenthal: *Two Centuries of Opera at Covent Garden* (London, 1958)
ELIZABETH FORBES

Nicolini [Niccolini], **Giuseppe** (*b* Piacenza, 29 Jan 1762; *d* Piacenza, 18 Dec 1842). Italian composer. The sixth of 14 brothers, he first studied music with his father and singing with Filippo Macedone. Then, with a subsidy from Duke Gian Girolamo Sforza Fogliani di Castelnuovo, he studied composition for three years, probably from 1778, at the Conservatorio S Onofrio in Naples, where his teachers were Insanguine and later Cimarosa. After composing an oratorio in Naples and an *azione sacra* for Venice he made his opera début in 1793 with *La famiglia stravagante* for the carnival season of the court theatre in Parma. This first success was followed by about 45 works, produced at the rapid pace imposed by the market. In 1816, when the administration of the Teatro Nuovo of Piacenza (thereafter the Teatro Comunitativo, later Municipale) passed from the Duchess Maria Luisa to the municipality, he was appointed for life to the service of that theatre by a special decree from the duchess, and from that time he wrote little for the stage. In 1819 he was elected *maestro di cappella* of the cathedral; after 1830 he abandoned the theatre to devote himself to sacred music.

Nicolini was one of the last representatives of the old Neapolitan school, which by 1800 was in decline and soon to be engulfed by the strong personality of Rossini. Nicolini imitated Neapolitan models with ability and fluency but reduced them to rather stereotyped formulae. Nevertheless a very large audience, even outside Italy, exalted him to the level of the most celebrated masters. According to Fétis his *Traiano in Dacia* (1807, Rome), starring the castrato Velluti, defeated Cimarosa's much-loved *Gli Orazi e i Curiazi* in a contest for popular favour. Nicolini's care in meeting the demands of bel canto singers was probably the main reason for the success of his works. They were performed by the best virtuosos of the time, including the young Catalani, who sang in *I baccanali di Roma* at La Scala in 1801. Particularly appreciated were his ample and magniloquent castrato arias; one of them, written for Rossini's *Tancredi*, became a favourite virtuoso piece and was published until 1829 in Naples, London and Milan.

From about 1820, as his popularity became obscured by that of Rossini, he assimilated some features of Rossinian style and turned occasionally to more modern subjects, but without success. He died forgotten and in poverty. In 1914 Piacenza named its Liceo Musicale after him.

La famiglia stravagante (dg, 2, G. Petrosellini), Parma, Ducale, Jan 1793
I mulinari (int, 1, G. Foppa), Genoa, S Agostino, spr. 1794; as L'amor mugnaio, ossia I molinari, Florence, Nuovo, 1795; *I-Fc**, *Gl*
Il principe spazzacamino (farsa, 1, ?Foppa), Genoa, S Agostino, spr. 1794, *Gl*
Le nozze campestri (dg, 2, F. Marconi), Milan, Scala, 13 Sept 1794, *Fc*, *Gl*
Artaserse (os, 3, P. Metastasio), Venice, Fenice, 14 Nov 1795, excerpts *B*Ztoggenburg and *PAc*
La donna innamorata (dg, 2, F. Bertati), Venice, S Moisè, 28 Jan 1796; as La donna instabile, Pavia, Condomini, 4 June 1800
Alzira (os, 2, ?G. Rossi, after Voltaire), Genoa, S Agostino, 4 March 1796, *Gl*
La clemenza di Tito (os, 3, Metastasio), Livorno, Avvalorati, sum. 1797, *Fc*
I due fratelli ridicoli [Li fratelli ridicoli] (dg, 2, F. Livigni), Rome, Valle, aut. 1798, *D-Dlb*, *I-Rmassimo*
Bruto (os, 2, G. Marré, after Voltaire), Genoa, S Agostino, 26 Dec 1798, *PAc*
Gli sciti (os, 2, Rossi, after Voltaire), Milan, Scala, Jan 1799; as Indatiro, ossia Gli sciti, Genoa, S Agostino, 1800; *Fc*
Il trionfo del bel sesso, ossia La forza delle donne (dg, 2, L. Romanelli, after Bertati), Milan, Scala, 20 Aug 1799, *Fc*
I baccanali di Roma (os, 2, Romanelli), Milan, Scala, 21 Jan 1801, *Nc*
I Manlii (os, 2, S. A. Sografi), Milan, Scala, 26 Dec 1801, *Nc*; rev. as Il trionfo di Manlio 1822, Piacenza, Comunitativo, 2 March 1833
Fedra, ossia Il ritorno di Teseo (os, 2, M. Prunetti), Rome, Argentina, 26 Dec 1803
La selvaggia nel Messico (os, 2, Prunetti), Rome, Dame, 30 Jan 1804, *D-Dlb*
Il geloso sincerato (farsa, 1, G. B. Lorenzi), Naples, Nuovo, spr. 1804; with lib. rev. L. A. Tottola, Naples, 1808; *I-Nc**, *Rrai*
Peribea e Telamone (os, 2), Naples, S Carlo, 30 May 1804, *Nc*
Gli incostanti nemici delle donne (dg, 2), Naples, Nuovo, aut. 1804
Le nozze inaspettate (op semiseria, 2), Naples, Nuovo, aut. 1805, *Nc*
Abenamet e Zoraide (os, 2, Romanelli), Milan, Scala, 26 Dec 1805, *Mr**
Traiano in Dacia (os, 2, Prunetti), Rome, Argentina, 3 or 7 Feb 1807, *A-Wgm*, *F-Pn*, *GB-Lbl* (inc.), *I-Fc*, *Mr*, *Nc*, *PAc*, *Pl*, *Rsc*, *Rmassimo*, excerpts (Vienna, n.d.; Milan, n.d.)
Le due gemelle (farsa, 1), Rome, Valle, 7 Jan 1808, *B-Bc*, *I-Mr*
Coriolano, ossia L'assedio di Roma (os, 2, Romanelli), Milan, Scala, 26 Dec 1808, *A-Wgm*, *B-Bc*, *I-Fc*, *Mr*, excerpts (Vienna, n.d.; Milan and Turin, 1808)
Dario Istaspe (os, 2, after A. Tana: Fedima), Turin, Imperiale, 20 Jan 1810, excerpts *Mc* and *Tf*, excerpts (Milan, ?1810)
Angelica e Medoro, ossia L'Orlando (os, 2, G. Sertor, after Metastasio), Turin, Imperiale, 26 Dec 1810, *Fc*, *Tco**
Abradate e Dircea (os, 2, Romanelli), Milan, Scala, 29 Jan 1811, *Mr**, excerpts (Milan, ?1811)

Quinto Fabio [Quinto Fabio Rutiliano] (os, 2, Giuseppe [not Gaetano] Rossi), Vienna, Kärntnertor, 24 April 1811, *Fc*
La casa dell'astrologo (dg, 2, Romanelli), Milan, Scala, 11 Aug 1811, *Mc**, excerpts (Milan, ?1811)
Le nozze dei Morlacchi (os, 2), Vienna, Kärntnertor, 1811; as I Morlacchi, *Fc*
La feudataria, ossia Il podestà ridicolo (dg, 2), Piacenza, Nuovo, 18 Jan 1812, excerpts *OS*
Carlo Magno [Vitikingo] (os, 2, A. Peracchi), Piacenza, Nuovo, Feb 1813, *D-Mbs* [Münchener Oper], excerpts (Milan, n.d.)
L'ira di Achille (os, 2, F. Romani), Milan, Scala, 26 Dec 1814, *I-Mr**, excerpts (Milan, 1815)
Adolfo (os, 2, Peracchi), Venice, S Benedetto, 23 June 1815
Balduino duca di Spoleto (os, 2, Peracchi), Venice, S Luca, 15 April 1816, *A-Wn*
Giulio Cesare nelle Gallie (os, 2, Prunetti), Rome, Argentina, 17 Jan 1819, excerpts *I-PAc*; as Il trionfo di Cesare, Palermo, S Cecilia, 8 May 1819
Il conte di Lenosse (os, 2, Gaetano Rossi, after Schiller: *Maria Stuart*), Trieste, Nuovo, spr. 1820, excerpts (Milan, 1823)
La conquista di Granata (os, 2, Romanelli), Venice, Fenice, 26 Dec 1820
L'eroe di Lancastro (os, 2, Rossi), Turin, Regio, 3 Feb 1821, *Tco**, excerpts (Milan, 1821)
Annibale in Bitinia (melodramma eroico, 2, L. Prividali), Padua, Nuovo, June 1821, *Fc, Pl*, excerpts (Milan, ?1821)
Aspasia e Agide (os, 3, Romanelli), Milan, Scala, 8 May 1824, *Mc**
Teuzzone (os, 2, after A. Zeno), Turin, Regio, 22 Jan 1825, excerpts *Gl, PAc*
Ilda d'Avenel, ossia La dama bianca (os, 2, Rossi, after Boieldieu: *La dame blanche*), Bergamo, Riccardi, 14 Aug 1828, excerpts *BGi*, excerpts (Milan, *c*1830)
Malek-Adel (os, 2, Rossi), Verona, Filarmonico, 8 Feb 1830, excerpts (Milan, *c*1830)
I saccenti (farsa), 1 cavatina *Vnm*

Contribs. to: Gli inganni amorosi, 1793; Zelmira e Zamori, 1826

Doubtful: Il medico d'Ischia; La finta erede; Mitridate (? Milan, Re, 1816); Tamerlano

*
FétisB
AMZ, xxii (1820), 287 [on *La feudataria*]; xxvi (1824), 509–10 [on *Aspasia e Agide*]; xxxv (1833), 360–61 [on *Il trionfo di Manlio*]
F. Giarelli: 'Note malnote: Giuseppe Nicolini', *Gazzetta musicale di Milano*, xli (1886), 217–18
E. de Giovanni: *Giuseppe Nicolini e Sebastiano Nasolini* (Piacenza, 1927)
Un maestro di musica piacentino: Giuseppe Nicolini (nel primo centenario della morte) (Piacenza, 1944) [incl. I. Cappa: 'Per Giuseppe Nicolini'; A. Rapetti: 'Vita e opere di Giuseppe Nicolini (1762–1842)'; C. Censi: 'L'arte di Giuseppe Nicolini'; detailed but inaccurate list of works, 117ff]
M. Donà: 'Un'aria di Rossini per un'opera di Nicolini nella Biblioteca Comunale di Civitanova Marche', *AnMc*, no.19 (1979), 320–29 [incl. notes on Nicolini's *Quinto Fabio*]
F. Bussi: *Storia di Piacenza: l'ottocento* (Piacenza, 1980), 749–53
H. Lühning: ' "Titus" – Vertonungen im 18. Jahrhundert', *AnMc*, no.20 (1983) [whole vol.], esp. 77–8, 451–60

ANDREA LANZA

Nicolini, Mariano [Marianino] (*b* ?Brescia; *fl* 1731–58). Italian soprano castrato. He made his operatic début in Rome in Carnival 1731 in a female role, his speciality there up to Carnival 1740; C. De Brosses remarks on the strange effect of the six-foot prima donna in his *Lettres historiques et critiques sur l'Italie* (Paris, 1799). He also sang secondary male roles in Venice (1733) and Naples (1737–8, the inaugural season of the S Carlo) before rising to primo uomo at Venice (autumn 1740 and Carnival 1741). In his penultimate engagement (1756, Verona) he is listed as a singer in the cappella at Padua, in his last (1758, Treviso) as in the service of the Munich court. He was a highly accomplished singer with a brilliant style (range approximately *b* to *b''*), praised by Metastasio, with the caveat that his voice sometimes had a boyish quality.

DENNIS LIBBY

Nicolò [Nicolò de Malte]. *See* ISOUARD, NICOLAS.

Nidecki, Tomasz Napoleon (*b* Studzianka, nr Radom, 2 Jan 1807; *d* Warsaw, 5 June 1852). Polish composer and conductor. He studied composition with Elsner at the Institute of Music and Dramatic Art in Warsaw and in the chief music school (1824–7), before receiving a grant to study in Vienna (1828–31). There, in 1833, he became conductor of the Leopoldstadt theatre orchestra, and composed vaudevilles and musical comedies. In 1838 he returned to Warsaw, where he taught in the singing school attached to the Wielki Theatre; he was appointed deputy conductor of the opera, and in 1840 took over from Karol Kurpiński as director and permanent conductor. He staged a number of first Polish performances of operas – Bellini's *Norma*, Flotow's *Martha*, Moniuszko's *Loteria* and works by Donizetti and Verdi – and translated Adam's opera *Le brasseur de Preston* into Polish.

first performed in Vienna, Theater in der Leopoldstadt, unless otherwise stated
Kathi von Hollabrun (Parodie, 3, K. Meisl), 11 March 1831
Schneider, Schlosser und Tischler, oder Wer das Glück hat, führt die Braut nach Haus (Posse, 3, A. Gleich), 30 July 1831
Der Waldbrand, oder Jupiters Strafe (Zauberspiel, 3, J. E. Gulden), 19 Dec 1833, excerpts, pf score (Vienna, 1835)
Versöhnung, Wohltätigkeit und Liebe (Gelegenheitsstück, 1, Meisl), 11 Feb 1834
Der Schwur bei den Elementen, oder Das Weib als Mann (Zauberspiel, 3, Gulden), 11 Oct 1834; as Przysięga na żywioły, Warsaw, 1845
Der Traum am Tannenbühl, oder 3 Jahre in einer Nacht (Zauberspiel, 2, Gulden), 28 March 1835, *A-Wn*
Die Junggesellen Wirtschaft im Monde (Zauberspiel, 2, Gulden), 13 Aug 1835
Der Temperamentenwechsel (Zauberposse, 2, W. Brabbée), 16 April 1836
Der Geist der düstern Inseln, oder Der Spiegel der Zukunft (Zauberspiel, 3, Gulden), Warsaw, 16 Feb 1837, *Wn, PL-Kj*
Der vierte October (allegorisches Festspiel, 1), unperf., *F-Pn*

*
WurzbachL
F. Hadamowsky: *Das Theater in der Wiener Leopoldstadt 1771–1860* (Vienna, 1934)
Z. Jachimecki: 'Sukcesy kompozytora polskiego w Wiedeńskim Teatrze Muzycznym przed stoma laty: Napoleon Tomasz Nidecki (1807–52)' [The Achievements of Polish Composers at the Vienna Musical Theatre 100 Years Ago: Napoleon Tomasz Nidecki (1807–52)], *Kurier literacko-naukowy*, no.8 (1934), 4
K. Michałowski: *Opery polskie* (Kraków, 1954)
J. K. Elsner: *Sumariusz*, ed. A. Nowak Romanowicz (Kraków, 1957)
T. Błaszczyk: *Dyrygenci polscy i obcy w Polsce działający w XIX i XX wieku* [Polish and Foreign Conductors Active in Poland in the 19th and 20th Centuries] (Kraków, 1964)

IRENA PONIATOWSKA

Niedermeyer, (Abraham) Louis (*b* Nyon, 27 April 1802; *d* Paris, 14 March 1861). Swiss composer. He received his first music lessons from his father, and at the age of 15 went to Vienna to study piano with Moscheles and composition with E. A. Förster. In 1819 he went to Italy to study with Fioravanti in Rome and with Zingarelli in Naples, where he formed a lasting friendship with Rossini. It was on Rossini's recommendation that his first opera, *Il reo per amore*, was produced there in 1820, enjoying some success. The following year he went to Geneva, where he gave piano lessons and began writing songs, some of which immediately became popular. From 1823 he lived in Paris, apart from a period in Brussels (1834–6) when he taught the piano. Soon after he arrived in Paris, and again due to the influence of Rossini, his stage works began to be performed there, but none of them was successful, not even the pasticcio *Robert Bruce*, in which Niedermeyer adapted Rossini's score for *La donna del lago* to a French libretto. After the failure of his last opera, *La fronde*, he devoted himself to sacred compositions. He reopened the school of church music which Alexandre Choron had founded in 1818; as the Ecole Niedermeyer it soon established itself in the forefront of French musical education.

performed in Paris unless otherwise stated; all printed works published in Paris

Il reo per amore, Naples, 1820
La casa nel bosco (comic op, 1), Italien, 15 July 1828 (1877)
Stradella (5, E. Deschamps and E. Pacini), Opéra, 3 March 1837 (1841)
Marie Stuart (5, T. Anne, after F. von Schiller), Opéra, 6 Dec 1844 (1845)
La fronde (5, A. Maquet and J. Lacroix), Opéra, 2 May 1853 (1877)

Music in: Robert Bruce (A. Royer and G. Vaëz), 30 Dec 1846 [rev. of Rossini: La donna del lago]

*

L. A. Niedermeyer: *Louis Niedermeyer, son oeuvre et son école* (Paris, n.d.)
[L. A. Niedermeyer]: *Vie d'un compositeur moderne* (Fontainebleau, 1892, 2/1893 with preface by Saint-Saëns)
GUY FERCHAULT

Niehaus, Manfred (*b* Cologne, 18 Sept 1933). German composer. He studied with Zimmermann in Cologne, where he also read German philology at the university. He worked as a teacher (1962–3), as Dramaturg and director at the Württemberg Landesbühne in Esslingen am Neckar (1963–5), as a freelance composer and director (1965–7), then as an editor for Westdeutsche Rundfunk in Cologne. Since 1989 he has been a freelance composer. In 1966 he received the Förderpreis in music of the city of Cologne. He has become known chiefly for pieces of absurd or surrealist music theatre, often post-modern in musical character, small in scale, flexible in form and designed for studio or workshop theatres.

all music-theatre works

Bartleby, 1961–6 (Kammeroper, Niehaus, after H. Melville), Cologne and Berlin, 1967
Die Pataphysiker (musikalische Farce, after A. Jarry), Kiel, 1969
Maldoror (szenische Komposition, A. Feussner and Niehaus, after Lautréamont), Kiel, 1970
Die Badewanne, 1970 (radiophonisches Lustspiel, J. M. Kamps and Niehaus, after I. Viscocil), Bonn, 1973
It happens (30 aleatorische Wortspiele, Y. Zarai), Bonn, 1973
Sylvester (Kammeroper, 1, G. Wohnmann), Stuttgart, 1973
Tartarin von Tarascon (Kinderoper, after A. Daudet), Hamburg, 1977
Die Komponiermaschine (Kammeroper, 1, Niehaus), Nuremberg, 1980
Das verlorene Gewissen (Kinderoper, 1, after M. Saltykow-Schtschedrin), Gelsenkirchen, July 1981
Das Christbaumbrettl (Kammeroper, 1, after K. Valentin), Bonn and Cologne, 1983
Die Geschichte vom Riesen und dem kleinen Mann im Ohr (Kinderoper, 1, Niehaus), Emmerich, 1984
MONIKA LICHTENFELD

Niehoff, Beatrice (*b* Mannheim, *c*1952). German soprano. After singing in the chorus at Karlsruhe (1977–9), in 1980 she moved to Darmstadt and has since sung in Hamburg, Frankfurt, Zürich, Hanover, Berlin and Vienna; her repertory includes Gluck's Alcestis, Fiordiligi, Countess Almaviva, Pamina, Konstanze, Agathe, Mařenka, Elsa, Eva, Rusalka, Tatyana and Mimì. Her beautiful voice and the musicality of her singing are also advantages in more modern roles: Haitang (Zemlinsky's *Der Kreidekreis*), Regina (*Mathis*

der Maler), the Bride (Fortner's *Die Bluthochzeit*), the title role of Schoeck's *Massimilia Doni* and the Protagonist, which she sang in Düsseldorf in the first German performance of Berio's *Un re in ascolto* (1988).
ELIZABETH FORBES

Niel [Nieil, Nielle], **Jean-Baptiste** (*b* ?1690s; *d* ?1775). French composer. First heard of in 1720, he was a conductor at the Opéra while it was under the direction of Jean-François Berger, but was best known as the composer of the *ballet-héroïque Les romans* and the *opéra-ballet L'école des amants*, and was so listed in the 'Musicien vivant' section of the *Almanach des spectacles* until 1772. *Les romans* was successfully performed at the Opéra in August 1736; subsequently another entrée, 'Le roman merveilleux', was added, and the entire production was staged again the following month. *L'école des amants* was similarly well received in 1744 and expanded the next year. A third ballet, untitled, was rehearsed in 1735 but never publicly performed. Niel also composed some motets, *airs* and keyboard pieces. His success has been attributed to the excellent presentation and performances of his stage works; though charming and at times reminiscent of Rameau, his music is not greatly distinguished.

Les romans (ballet-héroïque, prol., 3, M. de Bonneval), Paris, Opéra, 23 Aug 1736; rev. (prol., 4), Opéra, 23 Sept 1736 (Paris, 1736)
L'école des amants (opéra-ballet, prol., 3, L. Fuzelier), Opéra, 11 June 1744; rev. (prol., 4), Opéra, 27 April 1745 (Paris, 1744)

*

Mercure de France (April, May 1745)
Almanach des spectacles (1754–72)
Y. de Brossard: *Musiciens de Paris (1535–1792)* (Paris, 1965)
N. Dufourcq: 'Nouvelles de la cour et de la ville (1734–8) publiées par le Comte E. Barthélemy en 1879: extraits concernant la vie musicale collationnés par N. Dufourcq', *RMFC*, x (1970), 101–6
VIVIEN LO

Nielsen, Alice (*b* Nashville, TN, 7 June 1876; *d* New York, 8 March 1943). American soprano. She sang first in light opera and musical comedy, becoming a protégée of Victor Herbert. Success in London with his operetta *The Fortune Teller* brought her to the notice of the impresario Henry Russell, who introduced her to Covent Garden audiences in 1904. She was 'a fresh and charming' Zerlina at her début there in *Don Giovanni*, her other roles being Susanna, Gilda, Micaëla and Mimì. She also sang at the S Carlo in Naples before returning in 1905 to New York, where her appearances in *Don Pasquale* at the Casino Theatre failed to impress. In 1909 she joined the newly formed Boston Opera Company and remained with them as principal lyric soprano until 1914. Recognized as a 'gentle and appealing artist', she also enjoyed popularity at the Metropolitan during this time, retiring to teach after a further short spell in operetta in 1917. Her clear, youthful-sounding voice took well to recording, though she lacked the individuality of style and timbre to achieve lasting distinction.
J. B. STEANE

Nielsen, Carl (**August**) (*b* Sortelung, nr Nørre Lyndelse on Funen, 9 June 1865; *d* Copenhagen, 3 Oct 1931). Danish composer. The most important figure in the history of Danish music, he is best known for his six symphonies, while his many songs in simple, folklike idioms continue to be popular in Denmark. His two operas, *Saul og David* (written 1898–1901) and *Maskarade* (1904–6), are widely known from recordings, but productions outside Denmark have been rare, partly owing to problems of translation.

Nielsen's early years are touchingly described in his autobiography, *Min fynske barndom* ('My Childhood on Funen', Copenhagen, 1927; Eng. trans., 1953). His father was a house-painter and village musician, in whose dance bands the young Nielsen played the violin. From 1879 to 1883 he was employed as bugler and alto trombonist in a military band in Odense, and he went on to study at the Copenhagen Conservatory from 1884 to 1886. He continued his composition studies with Orla Rosenhoff and in autumn 1890 received a travel grant to further his knowledge of Wagner's operas in Dresden. His initial enthusiasm for Wagner was soon modified, but he retained a special regard for *Die Meistersinger*, which he found 'more thoroughly healthy than the later operas'.

From 1 September 1889 to May 1905 Nielsen was employed as a second violinist in the orchestra of the Royal Theatre in Copenhagen. Much of the repertory bored him, but he formed a deep attachment to Mozart, which is reflected in his 1906 essay 'Mozart and our Time' (included in *Levende musik*, Copenhagen, 1925; Eng. trans., 1953). In 1908 he succeeded Svendsen as a *kapelmester* at the Royal Theatre; he conducted there until spring 1914. Despite occasional offers of collaboration and serious consideration of a project for Hans Christian Andersen's 125th anniversary in 1930, Nielsen never returned to opera composition after 1906. He continued to supply incidental music for plays, however, including the delightful score for Oehlenschlæger's *Aladdin* (1918–19).

Nielsen's operatic style derives in part from his dissatisfaction with the contemporary Danish Romantic operas and vaudevilles for which he played. He retained something of their external forms but was determined to reinvigorate their largely predictable musical language. It seems likely that he also learnt from the example of Verdi's last operas (*Otello* and *Falstaff* were first produced in Copenhagen on 20 April 1898 and 16 January 1895 respectively). In subject matter and style Nielsen's two operas are poles apart. *Saul og David* is a tragic confrontation of attitudes to divine will; *Maskarade* is a lighthearted comedy with undercurrents of social comment. But they share a fascination with human character, which is also evident in the Second Symphony, 'De fire temperamenter' ('The Four Temperaments', 1901–2), and much of his later work, especially the wind chamber music and concertos.

See also MASKARADE and SAUL OG DAVID.

*

H. Berg: 'Saul og David', *Dansk tidsskrift*, xx (1903), 64–71

H. Hohlenberg: 'Carl Nielsen: Maskarade', *Tilskueren*, xxiii (1906), 1007–11

H. Seligmann: 'Carl Nielsen: Maskarade', *Det ny aarhundrede*, v (1908), 328–36

K. Hjortø: 'Fra Tryllefløjten til Maskarade', *Gads danske magasin*, xix (1925), 297–306

T. Meyer and F. Schandorf Petersen: *Carl Nielsen: kunstneren og mennesket* [Carl Nielsen: the Artist and the Man] (Copenhagen, 1947–8), i, 157–85 [on Saul og David], 224–67 [on Maskarade]

R. Layton: 'Carl Nielsen and the Stage', *The Listener* (7 May 1959)

J. Balzer, ed.: *Carl Nielsen i hundredåret for hans fødsel* [Carl Nielsen Centenary Essays] (Copenhagen, 1965; Eng. trans., 1965), esp. 75–101

G. Colding-Jørgensen: *Carl Nielsens særpræg som dramatisk komponist dokumenteret gennem en analyse af 'Saul og David' og 'Maskarade'* (diss., U. of Copenhagen, 1966)

B. Worn: *Carl Nielsens opera Maskarade* (diss., U. of Copenhagen, 1966)

R. Stevenson: 'Nielsen: Symphonist as Opera Composer', *Denmark: a Quarterly Journal of Anglo-Danish Relations*, clix (1972), 13–15

H. Ottaway: 'Nielsen's Saul and David', *MT*, cxviii (1977), 121–3

M. F. Miller: *Carl Nielsen: a Guide to Research* (New York and London, 1987)

R. Clegg: *The Writing of Carl Nielsen's 'Saul og David'* (diss., U. of Leeds, 1989)
DAVID FANNING

Nielsen, Inga (*b* Holbœke, 2 June 1946). Danish soprano. After studying in Vienna and Stuttgart, she made her début in 1973 at Gelsenkirchen; engagements followed at Münster, Berne and Frankfurt. She sang a flowermaiden at Bayreuth (1979); her roles at this period included Zerlina, Blonde, Ilia, Norina, Nannetta and Aennchen. She sang the Infanta in *Der Zwerg* with the Hamburg Staatsoper at Edinburgh (1983) and created Minette in *The English Cat* at Schwetzingen, repeating the role in Paris and in the American première at Santa Fe (1985). She has sung at Copenhagen, Stuttgart, Düsseldorf and Oslo, in a repertory including Sophie, Violetta, Donna Elvira, Lucia and Mimì. She sang Amenaide (*Tancredi*) at Wexford (1986), Konstanze at Salzburg and for her Covent Garden début (1987), Fiordiligi at Strasbourg (1989) and Christine (*Intermezzo*) at Geneva (1991). A stylish and musical singer, she has a pure-toned voice of great flexibility.

For illustration *see* ENGLISH CAT, THE.   ELIZABETH FORBES

Nielsen, (Carl Henrik) Ludolf (*b* Nørre Tvede, nr Naestved, 29 Jan 1876; *d* Copenhagen, 16 Oct 1939). Danish composer. He studied at the Copenhagen Conservatory (1896–8), then worked as a viola player at the Tivoli, and at the Palaekoncerter, where he was also deputy conductor. Later he played in the Bjørvig Quartet. He conducted the musical society Euphrosyne (1914–20), and during his last years worked for Danish Radio. As a composer Nielsen found it hard to gain recognition at a time when the revolt against Romanticism was paramount in Danish music. He wrote mainly symphonic music, chamber works and songs, but also three operas. Of these, only the one-act *Isbella* op.10 (libretto by P. A. Rosenberg) was performed; composed between 1903 and 1907, it had its première at the Royal Theatre, Copenhagen, on 8 October 1915. *Uhret* op.16 ('The Clock', composed 1908–11, libretto by A. Lind) suffers from a bad libretto. *Lola* op.43 (1916–20, libretto by Rosenberg) is based on Hugo; its style, like that of *Isbella*, is in the Italian *verismo* tradition.

NIELS MARTIN JENSEN

Nielsen, Riccardo (*b* Bologna, 3 March 1908; *d* Ferrara, 30 Jan 1982). Italian composer. He studied with Gatti at the Liceo Musicale G. B. Martini in Bologna until 1931. From 1946 to 1950 he was superintendent at the Teatro Comunale in Bologna and in 1952 was appointed director of the Istituto Musicale G. Frescobaldi in Ferrara. He was awarded the Italia Prize in 1953 for his radio opera *La via di Colombo*.

His early work was influenced by Casella and Stravinsky, but after 1943 his deeper study of Schoenberg's work led him to the 12-note system. His only work for the theatre is the monodrama *L'incubo* (Venice, 11 September 1948), to a libretto by E. Pradella, after a story by Petrus Borle. Based on two characters, simply called 'the Man' and 'the Woman', this expressionist work shows the influence of Schoenberg's *Erwartung*. It consists of seven episodes: Funeral

Sarabande, Madrigal, Toccata, Recitative, Theme with Variations, Nocturne and Funeral March. The radio opera *La via di Colombo* (1953; libretto by A. Piovesan, after a story by Massimo Bontempelli) uses a 12-note technique with tonal implications and seems to return to the more discursive characteristics of his earlier work.

R. Vlad: *Storia della dodecafonia* (Milan, 1958), 223–4
RAFFAELE POZZI

Albert Niemann in the title role of Wagner's 'Tannhäuser'

Niemann, Albert (*b* Erxleben, nr Magdeburg, 15 Jan 1831; *d* Berlin, 13 Jan 1917). German tenor. He made his début in 1849 at Dessau, singing small roles. After studying with Schneider and Nusch, in 1852 he was engaged at Halle. Two years later he moved to Hanover, where the king paid for him to study further with Duprez in Paris. Having already sung Tannhäuser, Lohengrin and Rienzi, he was chosen by Wagner to sing in the first Paris performance of *Tannhäuser* in 1861. After the fiasco of the three performances, Niemann returned to Hanover.

In 1864 he made a guest appearance in Munich, singing Tannhäuser, Lohengrin, Faust and Manrico. From 1866 until his retirement in 1889, he was engaged at the Hofoper, Berlin, where he sang in the first local performances of *Die Meistersinger* (1870), *Aida* (1874) and *Tristan und Isolde* (1876), also taking part in a gala performance of Spontini's *Olympie* (1879). He sang Siegmund in *Die Walküre* during the first complete *Ring* cycle at Bayreuth (1876) and in the first cycle given in London, at Her Majesty's Theatre (1882). It was also as Siegmund that he made his New York début at the

Metropolitan (1886). During his two seasons there he sang in the first New York performances of *Tristan und Isolde* (1886), Spontini's *Fernand Cortez* and *Götterdämmerung* (1888). His last appearance in Berlin was as Florestan (*Fidelio*) in 1888. Of immense physical stature, with a powerful, heroic voice, Niemann was unrivalled as Siegmund and Tristan during his lifetime.

R. Sternfeld: *Albert Niemann* (Berlin, 1904)
A. Neumann: *Erinnerungen an Richard Wagner* (Leipzig, 1907; Eng. trans., 1908)
L. Lehmann: *Mein Weg* (Leipzig, 1913; Eng. trans., 1914)
W. Altmann, ed.: *Richard Wagner und Albert Niemann: Briefe* (Berlin, 1924)
E. Newman: *The Life of Richard Wagner* (London, 1933–47)
J. Kapp: *Geschichte der Staatsoper Berlin* (Berlin, 1937)
W. H. Seltsam: *Metropolitan Opera Annals* (New York, 1949)
H. Fetting: *Die Geschichte der Deutschen Staatsoper* (Berlin, 1955)
G. Skelton: *Wagner at Bayreuth* (London, 1965)
ELIZABETH FORBES

Nienstedt, Gerd (*b* Hanover, 10 July 1932). German bass-baritone. After making his début at Bremerhaven in 1954, he was engaged at Gelsenkirchen, Wiesbaden, Cologne and Frankfurt, and in Vienna (1964–73). At Bayreuth (1961–75) he sang Klingsor, the Herald (*Lohengrin*), Biterolf, Köthner, Donner, Hunding and Gunther. He appeared at La Scala, and in Berlin, Paris, Geneva and Zürich. He made his American début at Chicago in 1968 as John the Baptist, repeating the role at San Francisco in 1970. His repertory ranged from Masetto to the Grand Inquisitor, from Caspar to the Forester (*The Cunning Little Vixen*). A reliable singer, he became manager at Hof and Detmold after leaving the stage. ELIZABETH FORBES

Nieto, Ofelia (*b* Santiago de Compostela, 18 March 1900; *d* Madrid, 21 May 1931). Spanish soprano. She began to study with Lorenzo Simonetti at the age of 12 and made her début in the leading role in *Maruxa* by Amadeo Vives (1914, Madrid) at the composer's request. She sang in other first performances of Spanish works, including *El Avapiés* by Del Campo and Angel Barrios (1919, Madrid) and Vicente Arregui Garay's *Yolanda* (1923). Her début at La Scala was as Agathe in *Der Freischütz*, conducted by Toscanini (6 January 1927). She performed in Florence, Venice, Rome, Barcelona, Buenos Aires, Santiago de Chile, Havana, New York and elsewhere under the direction of Weingartner, Mascagni, Vicenzo Bellezza and Toscanini. She retired to marry in 1929, and died as a result of an overdose of ether administered during an operation after a miscarriage.

Nieto had a strong, rich voice of great extension and flexibility. Her magnificent technique and ability enabled her to sing *lirico spinto* soprano roles with a full and expressive voice, as well as roles requiring greater dramaticism or lyricism. She also showed an extraordinary command of coloratura singing. Her sister was the soprano ANGELES OTTEIN. ANTÓN DE SANTIAGO

Nietzsche, Friedrich (Wilhelm) (*b* Röcken, nr Leipzig, 15 Oct 1844; *d* Weimar, 25 Aug 1900). German philosopher. His aesthetic of opera took its beginnings from an analysis of Greek tragedy and ended in his asserting that he preferred *Carmen* to Wagner. The cause and course of this evolution are easy to trace. Initially, in *Die Geburt der Tragödie* (1872), he maintained that the 'innermost content' of that 'Socratic culture' which had supplanted the true and original Greek tragedy could not be more clearly described than by calling it the 'culture of opera'. In the *stile rappresentativo* and the recitative he saw a 'tendency extraneous to art' that he equated with the rationalizing 'Socratic' drive, which, through Euripides, had disrupted the Apollonian-Dionysian duality on which the evolution of art depended and which had produced Greek tragedy. Opera was a product 'of the theoretical man, of the critical laity, not of the artist: one of the most astonishing facts in the history of any of the arts'. By the time these words were written, however, the Dionysian element in the pre-Socratic Greek drama had risen again in the shape of 'German music as we have principally to understand it in its mighty solar orbit from Bach to Beethoven, from Beethoven to Wagner', and with Wagner this German music had transformed opera into a modern rebirth of tragedy. In *Richard Wagner in Bayreuth*, published in 1876 to coincide with the inauguration of the Bayreuth Festival, he attempted an analysis of Wagner's work and aims; but by 1876 it required an effort of will for him to continue to side with Wagner, and during the festival itself this effort was no longer forthcoming. He left Bayreuth and began work on *Menschliches, Allzumenschliches*, which though it does not mention Wagner by name contains many critical aphorisms on 'the artist' that obviously refer to him. Thereafter Nietzsche maintained a sceptical attitude towards the pretensions of the Wagnerians and an increasingly critical view of Wagnerian music drama, which culminated in *Der Fall Wagner* (1888), a brilliant and ferocious attack that, without diminishing one's sense of Wagner's artistic importance, undercuts his every claim to greatness. This *volte face* was explained by Nietzsche as a consequence of his having recognized that in calling Wagner's music Dionysian he had perpetrated the error of confounding the Dionysian with the Romantic. 'With regard to all aesthetic values', he wrote in *Die fröhliche Wissenschaft* (book 5), 'I now avail myself of this principal distinction: I ask in each individual case: "is it hunger or is it superfluity which had here become creative?".' He explained this distinction:

Every art, every philosophy may be viewed as an aid and remedy in the service of growing and striving life: they always presuppose suffering and sufferers. But there are two kinds of sufferer: first, he who suffers from superabundance of life, who desires a Dionysian art and likewise a tragic view of and insight into life, and then, he who suffers from poverty of life, who seeks in art and knowledge either rest, peace, a smooth sea, delivery from himself, or intoxication, paroxysm, stupefaction, madness. The twofold requirement of the latter corresponds to all Romanticism in art and knowledge; it corresponded ... to Schopenhauer and Richard Wagner, to name the two most famous and emphatic Romantics who were formerly misunderstood by me.

Romantic music is neurotic: 'Wagner's art is sick ... *Wagner est une névrose*' (*Der Fall Wagner*). Nietzsche had now come to believe that the Dionysian in modern music was represented not by Wagner but most completely by *Carmen*.

I heard yesterday – will you believe it? – for the twentieth time Bizet's masterpiece ... How such a work makes perfect! In its presence one becomes almost a 'masterpiece' oneself. [The music of Carmen] approaches lightly, lithely, politely. It is amiable, it does not sweat. 'The good is easy, everything godlike runs on light feet': first proposition of my aesthetics. This music is wicked, cunning, fatalistic: it remains at the same time popular ... It is rich. It is precise. It constructs, organizes, finishes: it is therewith the antithesis of the polyp of music, 'endless melody'. [It dispenses with] the lie of the grand style.

Nietzsche's admiration for the opera may seem unbalanced if one fails to see that it was admiration for specific qualities which he had come to rate extremely highly and which he believed it possessed. 'Here the climate has changed ... there speaks a different sensuality, a different sensibility, a different kind of cheerfulness ... not a French or German cheerfulness. Its cheerfulness is African; a fatality hangs over it, its happiness is brief, sudden, without quarter.' He concluded: '*Il faut méditerraniser la musique*', and demanded a 'return to nature, health, cheerfulness, youth, *virtue*' in music. Finally, in his autobiography *Ecce homo* (1888), he summed up: 'What is it I suffer from when I suffer from the destiny of music? From this: that music has been deprived of its world-transfiguring affirmative character, that it is *décadence*-music and no longer the flute of Dionysus'. The essential point of Nietzsche's encomium of *Carmen* was clearly to assert that its characteristics are those of psychological health; in holding this view he appears to have been a direct precursor of the anti-Romantic reaction against Wagner and against the 'heaviness' of the art of the later 19th century that marked the years following World War I.

Editions: *F. Nietzsche: Werke in drei Bänden*, ed. K. Schlechta (Munich, 1954–6, 6/1969); index (Munich, 1965, 2/1967)
F. Nietzsche: Werke, ed. G. Colli and M. Montinari (Berlin, 1967–82)

Die Geburt der Tragödie aus dem Geiste der Musik (Leipzig, 1872); Eng. trans. in *Basic Writings of Nietzche*, ed. W. Kaufmann (New York, 1968), 3–144
Unzeitgemässe Betrachtungen, iv: *Richard Wagner in Bayreuth* (Schloss-Chemnitz, 1876)
Der Fall Wagner (Leipzig, 1888); Eng. trans. in *Basic Writings of Nietzche*, ed. W. Kaufmann (New York, 1968), 603–53
Nietzsche contra Wagner (Leipzig, 1889)

*

P. Lasserre: *Les idées de Nietzsche sur la musique* (Paris, 1907)
E. Foerster-Nietzsche: *Wagner und Nietzsche zur Zeit ihrer Freundschaft: Erinnerungsgabe zu Friedrich Nietzsches 70. Geburtstag den 15. Oktober 1914* (Munich, 1915; Eng. trans, 1922, as *The Nietzsche-Wagner Correspondence*)
——: 'Wagner and Nietzsche: the Beginning and End of their Friendship', *MQ*, iv (1918), 466–89
K. Hildebrandt: *Wagner und Nietzsche* (Breslau, 1924)
J. W. Klein: 'Nietzsche and Bizet', *MQ*, xi (1925), 482–505
G. Abraham: 'Nietzsche's Attitude to Wagner: a Fresh View', *ML*, xiii (1932), 64–74; repr. in *Slavonic and Romantic Music: Essays and Studies* (London, 1968), 313–22
H. Daffner: *Friedrich Nietzsches Rundglossen zu Bizets Carmen* (Regensburg, 1938)
E. Newman: *The Life of Richard Wagner*, iv (London, 1947)
R. Hollinrake: 'Nietzsche, Wagner and Ernest Newman', *ML*, xli (1960), 245–5
J. W. Klein: 'Nietzsche's Attitude to Bizet', *MR*, xxi (1960), 215–25
F. R. Love: *Young Nietzsche and the Wagnerian Experience* (Chapel Hill, NC, 1963)
M. Vogel: 'Nietzsches Wettkampf mit Wagner', *Beiträge zur Musikanschauung im 19. Jahrhundert*, ed. W. Salmen (Regensburg, 1965), 195–225
J. Galecki: 'Nietzsche und Bizets Carmen', *Wissenschaft und Weltbild*, xxi (1968), 12–29
W. Reichert and K. Schlechta, eds.: *International Nietzsche Bibliography* (Chapel Hill, NC, 1968)
K. Grunder, ed.: *Der Streit um Nietzsches 'Geburt der Tragödie': die Schriften von E. Rohde, R. Wagner und U. von Willamowitz-Möllendorff* (Hildesheim, 1969)
R. Hollinrake: *Nietzsche, Wagner and the Philosophy of Pessimism* (London, 1982)
M. Eger: '*Wenn ich Wagnern den Krieg mache ...*': der Fall Nietzsche und das menschliche Allzumenschliche* (Vienna, 1988)
                                    R. J. HOLLINGDALE

Night at the Chinese Opera, A. Opera in three acts by JUDITH WEIR to her own libretto based in part on Chi

Chun-Hsiang's *The Chao Family Orphan*; Cheltenham, Everyman Theatre, 8 July 1987.

Weir's 'opera within an opera' uses a realization of the Yuan dynasty play as its central act, while the outer acts present a reflection of that drama in the 'real-life' terms of 13th-century China. The 'orphan' is the explorer and canal-builder Chao Lin (baritone), and the story of his exile after the invasion of his city by Kublai Khan and subsequent career is told in a series of swiftly moving scenes. Chao Lin attends a clandestine performance of *The Chao Family Orphan*, but before its final scene it is interrupted by an earthquake, and he then finds events following the course of the play, leading to his capture by the Military Governor (countertenor). After he is led away to be executed for treason, the actors return, to rehearse the final scene of their play, in which the Orphan of Chao finally overcomes the wicked general Tu-an-Ku and is rewarded by the emperor for his deeds.

Though Weir recreates the style and pace of a Chinese opera troupe for the second act, in which music is very much subservient to speech, gesture and high comedy, there is very little anecdotal *chinoiserie* anywhere in her score. The musical influences on the outer acts are Messiaen, Britten and Stravinsky, with clear, uncluttered textures, often ostinato-based, and vocal lines with modal inflections in which directness of expression and verbal clarity seem paramount, while the opera itself preserves an ironic distance from its subject matter.   ANDREW CLEMENTS

Nightingale, The [*Solovey (Rossignol, Le)*]. Lyric tale in three acts (scenes) by IGOR STRAVINSKY to a libretto by STEPAN MITUSOV after the tale by HANS CHRISTIAN ANDERSEN; Paris, Opéra, 26 May 1914.

The Nightingale	soprano
The Cook	soprano
The Fisherman	tenor
The Emperor of China	baritone
The Chamberlain	bass
The Bonze	bass
Death	mezzo-soprano
Three Japanese Envoys	two tenors, bass

Courtiers, Emperor's entourage, spectres (offstage chorus of altos), pages, ladies-in-waiting

Setting China

The first act of this touching little Orphic allegory was begun shortly before the death of Stravinsky's teacher Rimsky-Korsakov in 1908 (Acts 2 and 3 were composed in 1913–14). Both musically and dramaturgically, it continues the line established by Rimsky's late series of fantasy operas culminating in *The Golden Cockerel*, also about a magical bird, with which *The Nightingale* shared a double bill in its first production. The scenario was worked out in March 1908 (old style) at the apartment of Vladimir Bel'sky, Rimsky's librettist, whose influence may be detected in the use of Andersen's Fisherman as a framing character, appearing at the ends of each scene (like the Astrologer in *The Golden Cockerel*).

The musical idiom of the first act adheres closely to what Asaf'yev called the 'modest, rationalized impressionism' of the early 20th-century St Petersburg school. Although the orchestral introduction bears the indubitable imprint of Debussy's *Nuages*, there is little in the exuberantly decorative score that cannot be associated with the idiom of such older Rimsky-Korsakov pupils as Anatoly Lyadov and especially Nikolay Tcherepnin. Stravinsky dedicated the work to its librettist, Mitusov.

When in 1909 Stravinsky began receiving commissions from Sergey Dyagilev, first for some Chopin orchestrations for the ballet *Les sylphides* and then (following Lyadov's and Tcherepnin's refusal) for *The Firebird*, he found himself sidetracked from his operatic project, and eventually turned cold not only to it but (under the influence of Dyagilev and Alexandre Benois) to opera generally. He entitled the first act of *The Nightingale* 'A scene from Andersen's Tale of the Nightingale' and designated it for concert performance. It would have been published as a self-contained tone poem with voices had Stravinsky not been offered an enticing contract by Alexander Sanin (*né* Schoenberg, 1869–1956) to provide an opera for the opening season of a new theatre in Moscow.

Sanin was a leading Russian operatic stage director who had been engaged by Dyagilev for his epochal Paris production of *Boris Godunov* in 1908, and who had become acquainted with Stravinsky in the course of work on the Paris *Khovanshchina* of 1913. As one of the founders of the Moscow Free Theatre, he proposed to Stravinsky that he write a full-length opera for the theatre's first season. 'My greatest dream', he wrote, 'is to show you off to Moscow, to St Petersburg, indeed to all of Russia'. That was also a dream of Stravinsky's, whose three early ballets had made him famous in Western Europe but had not been seen in his homeland. After some hesitation, he decided to complete *The Nightingale* in return for a very high fee, and on the condition that a 45-minute work in three tiny 'acts' could be substituted for the whole evening's entertainment originally requested.

The composer's hesitation had to do not only with his aesthetic estrangement from opera, but with the fact that he had crossed a stylistic Rubicon with *Petrushka* and *The Rite of Spring*, and felt he could no longer return to the gentler impressionistic idiom of the one completed act. He managed to rationalize the resulting stylistic incongruity on the basis of the setting of the second and third acts: the 'artificial' ambience of the Chinese court as opposed to the natural beauty of the opening *paysage*. The music he now composed on commission from Sanin ingeniously exploited interactions between the pentatonic 'Chinese' scale and the maximalistically octatonic idiom of *The Rite of Spring*. The orchestration of the new scenes matched the brash harmonic idiom, exploiting striking colour contrasts in place of the rich and subtly blended sonorities of the first.

The Moscow Free Theatre folded before *The Nightingale* could be staged, and the première went to Dyagilev after all, in a marvellously colourful production designed by Benois and conducted by Pierre Monteux, with the voices of the Nightingale (sung by Aurelia Dobrovol'skaya) and the Fisherman emanating from the pit, turning the opera into a virtual pantomime. At Dyagilev's instigation, Stravinsky extracted a ballet score, *Chant du rossignol*, from the music of the second and third acts. Since its 1919 première under Ansermet it has been so much more successful in the concert hall than in the theatre that in his autobiography the composer falsely claimed to have conceived it as a symphonic poem from the start. The original opera did achieve a Russian production shortly after the revolution (Mariinsky Theatre, May 1918, directed by Vsevolod Meyerhold and conducted by Albert Coates); since then, however, its slender stage career has been mostly a Western one, usually in double or triple bills with ballets.

ACT 1 *The edge of a wood by the seashore* A Fisherman, mending his net, sings of his nightly pleasure in the Nightingale's song. The bird sings its greeting, but is interrupted by the Chamberlain, the Bonze, the Cook and a retinue of courtiers. After first mistaking the Nightingale for a cow and a chorus of frogs, they invite it to sing before the Emperor. The Nightingale willingly accepts, though it prefers to sing in the forest, and declines all compensation, saying its only reward consists of its listeners' tears. As the courtiers leave with the bird, the Fisherman reflects disconsolately on its departure.

ACT 2 *The throne room in the Emperor's porcelain palace* The act opens with a great scurry and bustle (played in silhouette) as the palace is made ready for the Emperor's appearance at a fête. The scrim is lifted on the interior of the porcelain palace, illuminated by countless lanterns and torches. The Emperor is carried in to the strains of the Chinese March. The Nightingale performs its coloratura song, and receives its reward of tears. Three Japanese Envoys present the Emperor with a mechanical nightingale, which is wound up and entrances the court with its whirring air (a travesty of the 'Forest Murmurs' from Wagner's *Siegfried*). The real Nightingale slips away unnoticed. When the Emperor realizes the bird is gone, he banishes it in a fit of pique. The offstage voice of the Fisherman announces the approach of Death.

ACT 3 *A hall in the palace containing the Emperor's bedchamber* The Emperor is ill. Death, wearing the imperial crown and holding the imperial sword and banner, sits at his bedside, while a chorus of spectres sing of the Emperor's misdeeds as he writhes in agony. The Nightingale comes to the rescue: by beguiling Death with a three-stanza song, it redeems the banner, sword and crown one by one. Again it refuses all reward save tears, and flies away. A 'solemn procession' accompanies the slow entrance of the Emperor's retinue as they trudge onstage expecting to collect his corpse. Instead he bids them a hearty good morning. The offstage voice of the Fisherman rounds off the opera with a reprise of the opening invocation to the Nightingale's sunrise song.

* * *

Stravinsky wrote the second and third acts of *The Nightingale* at a time when, influenced by Dyagilev and Benois, he was hostile to opera as a genre. Except for the title character's songs (one in each act) that were, in the event, sung from the pit, they are virtual ballets (or better, pageants) in which the action consists largely of stage processions, and the dominant impression comes from the highly coloured decor (matched by Stravinsky's brilliant orchestration). Later Stravinsky came to more amicable terms with opera and regarded *The Nightingale* as a curiosity. Approached without preconception, it is an entertaining spectacle, if not a very dramatic one.   RICHARD TARUSKIN

Nijazi [Tagi-zade-Hajibeyov, Nijazi Zul'fagarovich] (*b* Tbilisi, 7/20 Aug 1912; *d* Baku, 2 Aug 1984).

Azerbaijani conductor and composer. He studied composition with Mikhail Gnesin and others (1925–30) and at the Baku conservatory (1930–32). He was conductor at the Azerbaijan Opera and Ballet Theatre (1937–51), becoming principal conductor in 1958, and was appointed principal conductor and artistic director of the Azerbaijan State SO in 1948. He played an important role in the development of opera and symphonic music in Soviet Azerbaijan, where he fostered the work of local composers and conducted many premières, including such operas as *Veten* by Hajiyev and Karayev (1945) and Amirov's *Sevil'* (third version, 1959). Nijazi appeared with companies in the USSR, including the Kirov Theatre, Leningrad, and toured in other countries. As a composer Nijazi was important in the early development of distinctively nationalist Azerbaijani music; his works are rich in national character and emotional feeling. His romantic opera *Khosrov i Shirin* (1942) is based on a work by Nizami, the 12th-century Azerbaijani poet and philosopher; it was performed at Kuybïshev (now Samara) in 1962 and in a new version at the Azerbaijan Opera and Ballet Theatre in 1972.

*

L. Karagicheva-Bretanitskaya: *Narodnïy artist Azerbaydzhanskoy SSR kompozitor Niyazi: ocherk tvorchestva kompozitora i dirizhyora* [Nijazi: Essay on the Work of the Composer and Conductor] (Moscow, 1959)
E. Abasova: *Nijazi* (Baku, 1965)   I. M. YAMPOL'SKY

Nikiprowetzky, Tolia (*b* Feodosia, 25 Sept 1916). French composer of Russian descent. He studied at the Marseilles Conservatory and then in Paris with Laloy and Leibowitz. Subsequently he held posts with Radio Morocco (1950–55) and the ORTF (1969–75); he was also active as an ethnomusicologist. He composed two operas. The *conte lyrique Les noces d'ombre* (1, S. Moreux) was first given in a concert performance in Paris on 20 December 1957; it was staged at the Théâtre du Capitole, Toulouse, on 4 May 1974. *La fête et les masques* (2, A. Mouren), commissioned in 1967 (completed 1970), was broadcast by French radio on 26 December 1973. Nikiprowetzky's other works include orchestral and chamber music and songs.

Nikolov, Lazar (*b* Burgas, 26 Aug 1922). Bulgarian composer. He studied composition with Vladigerov and Dimiter Nenov at the State Academy of Music in Sofia. In 1961 he began teaching at the Bulgarian State Conservatory and later served as secretary of the Union of Bulgarian Composers (1965–9). Even in the 1950s, when the state adopted a dogmatic and nationalistic approach to the arts, Nikolov was concerned to free harmony from dependence on tonality and to establish a broader base for Bulgarian music. Predominantly a composer of 'pure' music, Nikolov treats vocal music as part of instrumentation, using the timbre of the human voice to enrich the musical texture. He favours recitative and avoids vocal ensembles. His opera-oratorio *Prikovaniyat Prometey* ('Prometheus Bound', 1969, A. Nichev, after Aeschylus; Ruse, 24 March 1974) and the comic opera *Chichovtsi* ('Uncles', 1974, M. Andonov, after I. Vazov; unperf.) introduced new dimensions to the Bulgarian stage. He has also composed four symphonies and chamber works.

MAGDALENA MANOLOVA

Nilsson [Svennsson], (**Märta**) **Birgit** (*b* Västra Karups, 17 May 1918). Swedish soprano. She studied at the Royal Academy of Music, Stockholm, where her teachers included Joseph Hislop. In 1946 she made her début at the Royal Opera, Stockholm, as Agathe (*Der Freischütz*), later singing Lady Macbeth, the Marschallin, Sieglinde, Donna Anna, Venus, Senta, Aida, Tosca and Lisa (*The Queen of Spades*). In 1951 she sang Electra (*Idomeneo*) at Glyndebourne. During the 1954–5 season she sang her first *Götterdämmerung* Brünnhilde and Salome at Stockholm and made her Munich début as Brünnhilde in the complete *Ring*. Also in 1954 she first appeared in Vienna and, as Elsa, began her long association with Bayreuth, returning (1957–70) as Isolde, Sieglinde and Brünnhilde. She first sang at Covent Garden in the 1957 *Ring*, returning as Isolde, Amelia (*Un ballo in maschera*, with the Royal Swedish Opera in 1960), Strauss's Electra, Turandot and Leonore. She made her American début at San Francisco in 1956, and she first sang at the Metropolitan in 1959 as Isolde. Her only new role in the 1970s was the Dyer's Wife, which she sang at Stockholm in 1975. She retired in 1984.

Nilsson was generally considered the finest Wagnerian soprano of her day. Her voice was even throughout its range, pure in sound and perfect in intonation with a free ringing top; its size was phenomenal. Her dramatic abilities were considerable. Electra was possibly her finest achievement, although the sheer power and opulence of her voice, coupled with a certain coolness, made her an ideal Turandot.

GV
W. Jefferies: 'Birgit Nilsson', *Opera*, xi (1960), 607–12

A. Natan: 'Nilsson, Birgit', *Primadonna: Lob der Stimmen* (Basle, 1962)
W. Weaver: 'The Prima Donna at Work: Die Nilsson and La Nilsson', *HiFi/MusAm*, xv/2 (1965), 48–51, 119
A. Blyth: 'Birgit Nilsson', *Gramophone*, xlvii (1969–70), 1123
J. B. Steane: *The Grand Tradition* (London, 1974), 338ff
J. Young: 'Skanska: Birgit Nilsson on Home Ground', *ON*, xxxix/15 (1974–5), 48–51
B. Nilsson: *Mina minnesbilder* (Stockholm, 1977; Eng. trans., 1981)
S. Wadsworth: 'And Still Champ ... Birgit Nilsson Revisited', *ON*, xliv/13 (1979–80), 8–12, 35   HAROLD ROSENTHAL/R

Nilsson, Christine [Kristina] (*b* Sjöabol, nr Växjö, 20 Aug 1843; *d* Stockholm, 22 Nov 1921). Swedish soprano. She studied with Berwald in Stockholm, then with Wartel, Masset and Delle Sedie in Paris, where she made her début in 1864 as Violetta at the Théâtre Lyrique. She made her London début the same year at Her Majesty's Theatre, again as Violetta, also appearing as Marguerite (*Faust*). At the Opéra she created Ophelia in Thomas' *Hamlet* (1868; see illustration) and sang in the theatre's first performance of *Faust* (1869). She made her Covent Garden début in 1869 in *Lucia di Lammermoor*, and also sang in the first London performance of *Hamlet*. In 1870 she was London's first Mignon at Drury Lane and embarked on a tour of the USA. She sang in the first New York performance of *Mignon* (1871, Academy of Music).

At Drury Lane Nilsson sang Mozart, Meyerbeer, Wagner and Verdi roles and took part in the first performance of Balfe's posthumous opera *Il talismano* (1874). At Her Majesty's Theatre she sang in the first London performance of Boito's *Mefistofele* (1880). She travelled extensively, visiting St Petersburg and Moscow, Brussels, Vienna and Munich. Returning to New York in 1883 for the opening season of the Metropolitan, she sang in the inaugural performance of *Faust* and in the first local performance of Ponchielli's *La Gioconda*; shortly afterwards she retired. Her voice, though not large, was pure and brilliant in timbre, immensely flexible and perfectly even in scale for two and a half octaves.

M. Strakosch: *Souvenirs d'un impresario* (Paris, 1886)
J. H. Mapleson: *The Mapleson Memoirs* (London, 1888); ed. H. Rosenthal (London, 1966)
A. Ehrlich: *Berühmte Sängerinnen der Vergangenheit und Gegenwart* (Leipzig, 1895)
T. Norlind: *Kristina Nilsson* (Stockholm, 1923)
H. Headland: *Christine Nilsson: the Songbird of the North* (Rock Island, IL, 1943)
M. Leche-Löfgren: *Kristina Nilsson* (Stockholm, 1944)
H. Rosenthal: *Two Centuries of Opera at Covent Garden* (London, 1958)   ELIZABETH FORBES

Nilsson, Sven (*b* Gävle, 11 May 1898; *d* Stockholm, 1 March 1970). Swedish bass. He studied in Stockholm and Dresden, making his début in 1930 as the Herald in *Lohengrin* at Stockholm. While engaged at Dresden (1930–43), he sang King Mark at Covent Garden with the Staatsoper (1936), created Peneios in *Daphne* (1938) and took part in the première of Sutermeister's *Romeo und Julia* (1940). Returning to Sweden, he was engaged at the Royal Opera, Stockholm, until 1969, when he made his farewell appearance as Crespel (*Les contes d'Hoffmann*). He made his Metropolitan début in 1950 as Daland. Among his other roles were Sarastro, Osmin, Ochs, Prince Gremin and Padre Guardiano, as well as Pogner and Gurnemanz, the parts for which he was best known.   ELIZABETH FORBES

Birgit Nilsson in the title role of Puccini's 'Turandot'

Christine Nilsson as Ophelia in Thomas' 'Hamlet', the role she created at the Paris Opéra in 1868

Nîmes. Town in the Gard, France. The first theatre there, built by the Comte de Fesc, adjoined the then half-buried Roman arena. Early in the 19th century a new theatre with 1500 seats, designed by M. A. Meusnier, was built by a private syndicate opposite the famous Maison Carrée. This was acquired by the town council in 1819 and the architect Durand added an ionic peristyle (1825–7). During the 19th century and early 20th it was run as a typical provincial theatre, with an impresario, a resident company and guest singers. In 1952, after a dispute with the manager, the Belgian singer Eva Closset set fire to the theatre, only the peristyle being saved. A theatre was then improvised in a neighbouring school of commerce, and when in 1988 it was decided to continue with opera there the architect Jean-Michel Wilmotte was commissioned to redesign it. The resulting Opéra de Nîmes (seating 1038 in stalls and a balcony) is rather like a cinema in internal design.

During the 30 years to 1982, when Ferdinand Aymé was impresario of both the Opéra and the bullfights held in the excavated Roman arena, opera performances were often given in the arena in July, usually of *Mireille* one year and *Carmen* the next (with a real bullfight before the last act). From 1984 these summer performances became somewhat more serious, but in 1989 they were suspended for financial reasons. Opera continues somewhat irregularly from November to May at the Opéra de Nîmes, often with productions from Montpellier and Toulouse. CHARLES PITT

Nimsgern, Siegmund (*b* St Wendel, Saarland, 14 Jan 1940). German baritone. He studied with Sibylle Fuchs

in Saarbrücken, where he made his début in 1967 as Lionel in Tchaikovsky's *The Maid of Orléans* and sang in Enescu's *Oedipe* (1971). He made his London début at Covent Garden in 1973 as Amfortas. He has appeared at La Scala, San Francisco, the Metropolitan, Munich, Vienna and Salzburg, where he sang Telramund at the 1976 Easter Festival. His repertory includes Don Giovanni, William Tell, Caspar, Pizarro, Macbeth, Boccanegra, Amonasro, Iago, and Scarpia, which he first sang in Chicago (1982). He excels in Strauss (Barak, John the Baptist, Kunrad in *Feuersnot*, Mandryka and Altair in *Die ägyptische Helena*), while his Wagner roles include Kurwenal, the Dutchman and Wotan, which he sang at Bayreuth (1983–5). His voice is keenly focussed and well projected, while his fine musicianship makes him an excellent interpreter of Bartok's Bluebeard and Prokofiev's Ruprecht (*The Fiery Angel*). ELIZABETH FORBES

Nina [*Nina, o sia La pazza per amore* ('Nina, or The Love-distressed Maid')]. *Commedia in prosa ed in verso per musica* in one act by GIOVANNI PAISIELLO to a libretto by GIAMBATTISTA LORENZI after GIUSEPPE CARPANI's translation of BENOÎT-JOSEPH MARSOLLIER DES VIVETIÈRES' *Nina, ou La folle par amour*; Caserta, Teatro del Reale Sito di Belvedere, 25 June 1789 (revised version in two acts, Naples, Teatro dei Fiorentini, autumn 1790).

Along with Piccinni's *La buona figliuola*, *Nina* is one of the best examples of 18th-century sentimental comedy. The topic was first treated as an *opéra comique*, *Nina, ou La folle par amour*, with a text by Marsollier des Vivetières and music by Dalayrac (1786, Paris). It was subsequently translated into English for a performance in London as *Nina, or The Love-distressed Maid* (1787), and into German for a performance in Hamburg as *Nina, oder Wahnsinn aus Liebe* (1787). In German-speaking lands the work was presented in the following years with new music by J. G. Naumann, Joseph Schuster and F. A. Hiller.

Carpani translated the text into Italian, and this version, with textual additions by Lorenzi and music by Paisiello, was first presented at the royal palace at Caserta in 1789, in honour of a visit by Queen Maria Carolina of Sicily. The libretto was then enlarged to two acts by Lorenzi, new music was composed by Paisiello, and it was performed as the second opera of the 1790 season at the Teatro dei Fiorentini, Naples. Musical recitatives, probably not by Paisiello, were added for the first time at Parma during Carnival 1793 and later at the Fiorentini, Naples, in 1795.

Anxious for his daughter Nina (soprano) to marry a wealthy man from a noble background, the Count (baritone) initially chooses Lindoro (tenor) as the prospective bridegroom. When a richer bachelor comes along, however, the Count breaks off the engagement and, much to Nina's dismay, starts making new wedding plans. In order to win her back Lindoro fights a duel with his rival and is wounded. Thinking he has been killed, Nina loses her mind in despair. The opera opens with a chorus lamenting her sad fate ('Dormi, o cara'); it is Susanna (soprano), Nina's faithful companion, who recounts events leading up to this in her 'Se il cor gli affetti suoi'. Nina cannot remember anything; imagining that Lindoro is temporarily away, she sits in the countryside, picking flowers and awaiting his return.

The compassionate villagers, all of whom love Nina, praise her good heart, take care of her and pray for her.

In return Nina does good deeds for the whole community, bestowing gifts on the poor. Susanna and the Count's old servant Giorgio (tenor) keep a watchful eye on her. The Count is inconsolable over his daughter's condition and regrets having caused her so much grief. She no longer recognizes him and claims that she has no father. Just when it seems that Nina will not recover, Lindoro is seen approaching the village gate. Relieved and chastened, the Count greets him as his own son and begs forgiveness. Lindoro makes himself known to Nina, who to everyone's jubilation immediately recovers her senses.

The opera's sentimental tone must have appealed to the Romantic spirit; it was given on Italian stages until 1845 and was revived in London in 1825 for Pasta's benefit. It was also sung in German (1793, Mannheim), Czech (1796, Prague), Russian (1796, St Petersburg) and Polish (1809, Warsaw). For its performance in Vienna (1790) Da Ponte augmented the text and converted it into verse for a musical reworking by Joseph Weigl. Eight arias by Weigl were added, but this version, perhaps because of the casting of roles, was a failure: the absence of singers' names indicates a performance by secondary or less popular figures.

Irene Tomeoni in the title role of Paisiello's 'Nina': engraving

Paisiello's melodies have a folklike simplicity and are full of charm. Particularly popular was Nina's aria 'Il mio ben quando verrà'. The original version had no ensembles other than several duets and the finale. Both choruses play an important role: the four-part mixed chorus, 'Dormi, o cara', and the female chorus with Nina's cantilena, 'Lontano da te, Lindoro', a typical Neapolitan folksong with the melodic flattened supertonic. To intensify the Neapolitan flavour further, the two-act version of the opera acquired a shepherd's canzona, 'Già il sol si cela dietro la montagna', to the accompaniment of a zampogna, a variety of Neapolitan bagpipe.   GORDANA LAZAREVICH

Nina, ou La folle par amour ('Nina, or The Love-distressed Woman'). *Comédie mêlée d'ariettes* in one act by NICOLAS-MARIE DALAYRAC to a libretto by BENOÎT-JOSEPH MARSOLLIER DES VIVETIÈRES; Paris, Comédie-Italienne (Salle Favart), 15 May 1786.

Grimm (*Correspondance littéraire*, ed. Tourneux, 1877–82) stated that the source was a true story from several years earlier and had been used by F. T. M. Baculard d'Arnaud in 'La nouvelle Clémentine' in *Délassements de l'homme sensible* (Paris, 1783). Laurence Sterne's figure of Maria de Moulines in *Tristram Shandy* (1760–67) and *A Sentimental Journey* (1768) is probably related. Pre-public performances of *Nina* were said by Grimm to have been tried out at the premises of the Duke of Coigny at Choisy, and at those of Mlle Guimard.

The setting is a garden outside a village. Nina (soprano; the part was written for Dugazon) is sleeping, surrounded by villagers and friends ('Dors, cher enfant'). She has lost her reason, ever since her father, the Count (baritone), dismissed her childhood sweetheart Germeuil (baritone) as a contender for her hand in marriage. After a violent clash between Germeuil and his wealthier rival, the former is supposed dead. In her delirium, Nina goes daily to sit and wait for his return.

Nina appears, dressed in white, walking unsteadily. She sings 'Quand le bien-aimé reviendra', the best-remembered aria of the opera. Then she tries a new song, joining in a *scena* with local women, but becomes distracted. The Count, consumed by remorse, converses with her, but Nina neither recognizes him nor acknowledges his existence. The women try to draw her out by having a shepherd play a familiar *musette*. All leave except the Count, who is informed of Germeuil's return. Germeuil is welcomed as a son, and learns of Nina's condition. In the penultimate ensemble, Nina is prepared for the trauma of seeing Germeuil, and her reason is finally restored.

Nina's subject matter broke new ground in *opéra comique*, though the musical emphasis remained on melodies of sentiment rather than the ensembles of interaction. It was seen in Paris as late as 1852 (according to Loewenberg: *Annals of Opera*, 1943), but the setting by Paisiello (1789) was probably better known outside France.

For illustration *see* DUGAZON, LOUISE-ROSALIE.

DAVID CHARLTON

Nini, Alessandro (*b* Fano, nr Pesaro, 1 Nov 1805; *d* Bergamo, 27 Dec 1880). Italian composer. After studying with the *maestro di cappella* of his native town and undertaking church appointments at Montenovo and Ancona, in 1827 he entered the Liceo Musicale in Bologna, where he completed his musical education. He was director of the school of singing at St Petersburg from 1830 until 1837, then returned to Italy and staged his first opera, *Ida della Torre* (1837, Venice). Six more operas followed; *La marescialla d'Ancre* (1839, Padua) met with particular success and only *Odalisa* (1842, Milan) was a failure. He held appointments at Novara Cathedral (from 1843) and Bergamo (1847–77). He was an excellent composer of church music but his dramatic works, though well written, do not stand out from those of other minor composers of the time. He also wrote chamber music, cantatas and symphonies.

Ida della Torre (dramma tragico, 2, C. Beltrame), Venice, S Benedetto, 11 Nov 1837, *I-Mr**, vs (Milan, 1838)

La marescialla d'Ancre (tragedia lirica, 2, G. Prati, after A. de Vigny), Padua, Nuovo, 23 July 1839, *Mr**, vs (Milan, 1839); rev. for Milan, Cannobiana, *Mr**

Cristina di Svezia (tragedia lirica, 3, G. Sacchèro and S. Cammarano), Genoa, Carlo Felice, 6 June 1840, *Mr**, vs (Milan, ?1840)

Margherita d'Yorck (tragedia lirica, 3, Sacchèro), Venice, Fenice, 21 March 1841, vs (Milan, 1841)

Odalisa (dramma lirico, 2, Sacchèro), Milan, Scala, 19 Feb 1842, *Mr**

Virginia (melodramma, 3, D. Bancalari), Genoa, Carlo Felice, 21 Feb 1843, *Mr**, (Milan, ?1843)

Il corsaro (dramma lirico, 4, Sacchèro), Turin, Carignano, 25 Sept 1847

*

FétisB

A. Cametti: 'Les rossiniens d'Italie', *EMDC*, I/ii (1921), 879–81

GIOVANNI CARLI BALLOLA

Niska [Dice], Maralin (Fae) (*b* San Pedro, CA, 16 Nov 1930). American soprano. Her teachers included Lotte Lehmann. She sang Mimì for the inauguration of the San Diego Opera in May 1965. Later that year she became a principal with the Metropolitan Opera Company, appearing during two years of touring as Carlisle Floyd's Susannah, Violetta, Butterfly, Countess Almaviva and Musetta. In 1967 she joined the New York City Opera, adding Donna Anna and Donna Elvira, Manon Lescaut, Gounod's Marguerite, Tosca, Turandot, Salome, Suor Angelica, the Governess (*The Turn of the Screw*) and Emilia Marty (*The Makropoulos Affair*) to her repertory. Her official Metropolitan début, as Musetta, was in 1973, and she made her Italian début at the 1978 Maggio Musicale as Marie (*Wozzeck*). Her cool, sometimes steely lyric soprano and vivacious stage personality have been assets in a wide variety of roles.

MARTIN BERNHEIMER

Nissen, Hans Hermann (*b* Zippnow, nr Marienwerder [now Kwidzyń], 20 May 1893; *d* Munich, 28 March 1980). German bass-baritone. He studied in Berlin and made his début in 1924 at the Berlin Volksoper. The next year he was engaged by the Staatsoper in Munich, where he remained until 1967. He sang Wotan and Hans Sachs at Covent Garden in 1928 and 1934, and appeared in the Wagnerian repertory at Chicago (1930–32) and the Metropolitan (1938–9). He sang Hans Sachs at Salzburg in 1936–7 and at Bayreuth in 1943, and made guest appearances in Paris, Milan, Vienna, Berlin and elsewhere. In addition to Wagner roles, his repertory included Renato, Amonasro, Barak, Borromeo (*Palestrina*) and Orestes. Although his voice was not large, it was one of the most beautiful of its day, and was used with great artistry and refinement.

HAROLD ROSENTHAL/R

Nitteti ('Nitetis'). Libretto by PIETRO METASTASIO, first set by Nicola Conforto (1756, Madrid).

ACT 1 Aprio, King of Egypt, has surrendered his throne to Amasi, his confidant, in response to the demands of his people. Anxious that his daughter, Nitteti, should some day regain her true royal position, Aprio extracts from Amasi his promise that she will be given in marriage to his son Sammete. While disguised as a shepherd, however, Prince Sammete has met the shepherdess, Beroe, and the two have fallen in love. Beroe, a close friend of Nitteti, confides in her, but soon discovers the true identity of her shepherd and realizes that she is her friend's rival. She tells Sammete that she

'*Nitteti*', Act 2 scene xi (BEROE: '*For pity's sake, my beloved, take me to the temple*'): engraving from the '*Opere*' of Pietro Metastasio (Paris, Hérissant, 1780–82)

knows he must wed Nitteti, but he insists that he is hers alone.

ACT 2 Amasi is embarrassed by Sammete's refusal to marry Nitteti, but she bids him look favourably upon Beroe who has just appraised her of their rival situation. Beroe, however, advises Amasi of her intention to step aside and commit herself to the sacred shrine of Isis. She then encourages Sammete to abandon her for the sake of Egypt, but he responds with defiance.

ACT 3 Amasi declares that his son must marry Nitteti or die. Beroe is thus given further cause to urge his marriage with Nitteti who, for her part, desires the happiness of both Sammete and her friend, and therefore wants to help him escape. Beroe even threatens suicide if Sammete will not save himself and marry Nitteti. In the last scene, it is revealed that Beroe is really Nitteti and that Nitteti is Amestri, daughter of Amasi, long presumed dead. Sammete is united with Beroe/Nitteti and Nitteti/Amestri with a mutual friend, the King of Cyrene.

* * *

The deposition of Apries, King of Egypt, by Amasis, a man of lowly origin, is described in the Herodotus *Historiae* (book 2) and the Diodorus Siculus *Bibliotheca* (book 1). Herodotus (book 3) also outlines a series of events involving an unnamed daughter of Amasis (Metastasio's Amestri), his son Psammenitus (Metastasio's Sammete) and Nitetis, daughter of Apries, at the time of the subjugation of Egypt by Cambyses, King of Persia (and son of Cyrus the Great). The events of this story surface in Madeleine de Scudéry's romance *Le grand Cyrus* (1649–53) and supply the basic action for Marie Desjardins' *Nitétis* (1663), François de

Lagrange-Chancel's *Amasis* (1701) and Antoine Danchet's *Nitétis* (1723). Additional love intrigues are already present in Desjardins' drama, and are significant in the dramas of Lagrange-Chancel and Danchet, where incidents from the MEROPE legend are grafted on to the Nitteti story. Metastasio's *Nitteti* is a twin to his popular L'OLIMPIADE, and, although written over 20 years later, was still set over 30 times. Both dramas deal exclusively with love triangles woven around characters drawn from Herodotus (two men and one woman in *L'olimpiade*, two women and one man in *Nitteti*) in which the two contestants are friends. The resolutions then come about through the discovery of a blood relationship between one of the friends and the character adored, and his/her union with a figure of royalty who has been on hand throughout. In Conforto's setting, *Nitteti* had its première in Madrid under the direction of Carlo Broschi (Farinelli) to celebrate the birthday, in 1756, of Ferdinand VI of Spain, on which occasion Anton Raaff sang the role of Amasi. Giovanni Rutini's appointment as *maestro di cappella* in Modena followed closely upon his successful setting of *Nitteti* for that city in 1770, and Nasolini's career in Trieste began with his setting of this drama in 1788.

For a list of settings *see* METASTASIO, PIETRO.　　　DON NEVILLE

Nitteti (i). *Dramma per musica* in three acts by GIOVANNI PAISIELLO to a libretto by PIETRO METASTASIO (*see* NITTETI above); St Petersburg, Imperial Theatre, *c*17/28 January 1777.

Paisiello's setting of *Nitteti* is noteworthy for including Metastasio's choral scene in Act 1 scene vi, to which a new ballo was added. It uses Metastasio's duet but replaces his trio with a new one, and Act 2 begins with a new 'sorbet' aria for the third-ranking character Bubaste (tenor). Most significant is the new three-scene complex inserted before the last two scenes in Act 2, in which the sacrificial ceremony of Beroe (soprano) leads from an opening chorus and ballo into an obbligato recitative and cavatina. Sammete (soprano castrato) interrupts, and an action ensemble with chorus ensues as the altar is torn down and Beroe is rescued. Amasi (tenor) and the chorus react first in ensemble and then in a cavatina and chorus. The new scene complex was introduced to Italy when Paisiello's *Nitteti* was performed in Florence in 1788. The next year Bianchi set it for Milan and Bertoni for Venice, thus encouraging the use of such constructions in *opera seria* in the 1790s.

Paisiello's score is unusual for including music for the balli as well as programmatic battle music (which the composer of the opera normally did not provide) and for its generous amount of obbligato recitative, occasionally encompassing entire scenes. In his arias Paisiello conventionally uses full orchestra only in ritornellos and caesuras. His string accompaniment textures can still be relatively complex, with the second violins providing rhythmically regular arpeggiation while the firsts contribute motivic commentary over a repeated-note bass, for example. The arias are in through-composed ternary forms, except for the shortened rondos (*ABAB*) of Beroe. Her 'Si sveli il caro oggetto' is a nascent two-tempo rondò, with the change to a fast tempo occurring at the first *B* section.

MARITA P. McCLYMONDS

Nitteti (ii). *Dramma per musica* in three acts by PASQUALE ANFOSSI to a libretto by PIETRO METASTASIO (*see* NITTETI above); Venice, Teatro S Benedetto, 1780.

Anfossi made an earlier setting of this libretto for Naples in 1771. This second version was written a year after his *Cleopatra* (1779, Milan) on a libretto by Verazi, a pioneer of action ensemble finales to *opera seria*. A new ensemble concluding Act 3, called a *finale*, replaces Metastasio's *coro*. It is noteworthy not only because it encompasses three scenes, moving from duo to trio to duo to sextet, but also because, like the finale to Act 1 of Mozart's *Don Giovanni*, it includes a change of stage setting. It apparently established the practice of concluding such a finale with two static sections, the first slow and the second fast. Tonally audacious, Anfossi moves from B♭ to D at the scene change, returning to the original key at the end.

As in many settings of *Nitteti*, Metastasio's chorus in Act 1 is omitted. Many new aria texts replace the original ones, though Metastasio's texts for the duet concluding Act 1 and trio concluding Act 2 remain. Anfossi looks forward to Bianchi's setting (1789, Milan), composing battle and storm music for the pantomime in Act 2. This leads into a new solo scene with a cavatina for Beroe (soprano), set in obbligato style.

MARITA P. McCLYMONDS

Nixon, Marni [McEathron, Margaret Nixon] (*b* Altadena, CA, 22 Feb 1930). American soprano. After studying singing and opera with Carl Ebert, Jan Popper, Boris Goldovsky and Sarah Caldwell, she embarked on a varied career involving television, film and musical comedy, as well as opera and concert. Her operatic repertory includes Zerbinetta, Susanna, Blonde, Konstanze, Violetta, La Périchole and Philine (*Mignon*), performed at Los Angeles, Seattle, San Francisco and Tanglewood. Her light, flexible, wide-ranging soprano and extraordinary accuracy and musicianship have also contributed to her success in works by Webern, Stravinsky, Ives, Hindemith and Goehr.

MARTIN BERNHEIMER

Nixon in China. Opera in two acts by JOHN ADAMS to a libretto by Alice Goodman; Houston, Grand Opera, 22 October 1987.

Conceived in 1982 by Peter Sellars and completed in 1987, *Nixon in China* has as its subject Richard Nixon's visit to China from 21 to 27 February 1972, with the differences between Eastern and Western views of the world as a subtext. The work contains little action; rather, it is divided into six tableaux, within which the characters convey their world views – and sometimes find themselves speaking at cross-purposes – in a series of connected conversations and soliloquies.

The opera begins with the arrival of the presidential aircraft at an airport outside Beijing and includes the expected ceremonial welcome from Chou En-lai (baritone). Nixon (baritone) describes the flight, diplomatically, as smooth, while the music conveys the truth: it was bumpy. Nixon, in his 'News' aria, immediately establishes that the priorities of the journey are symbolic; indeed, he likens his landing in Beijing to that of the Apollo astronauts who landed on the moon, and notes that because it is prime television viewing time in the USA, his arrival will be witnessed by the maximum possible audience. This focus on the superficialities of conveying a public image proves to be Nixon's weakness here. In the second scene, which takes place in Mao Tse-tung's study, Nixon, Mao (tenor), Chou and an oafish caricature of Henry Kissinger (bass) air various

'Nixon in China' (Adams): opening scene from the original production by Houston Grand Opera, 22 October 1987, with Carolann Page as Pat Nixon and James Maddalena as Richard Nixon (set by Adrianne Lobel)

views of history and of the contemporary world, and it becomes clear that the Chinese are operating on a deeper, more philosophical level than the Americans. The first act ends with a banquet scene.

At the start of Act 2, Pat Nixon (soprano) is taken on a tour of a commune and to the Summer Palace, where she sings her central aria, a touching humanitarian vision, 'This is prophetic!'. The next scene brings Nixon, Mao, Chou, Pat and Mao's wife Chiang Ch'ing (soprano) together to watch a contemporary political Chinese ballet, 'The Red Detachment of Women', in which the villainous landlord, Lao Szu, played by Kissinger, is thwarted by the courageous women soldiers of the State. The scene ends with a monologue in which Chiang Ch'ing, the only Chinese character presented unsympathetically, offers her view of the Cultural Revolution and her place in history.

The final scene takes place on the Nixons' last night in Beijing. The Nixons, Mao and Chiang Ch'ing and Chou En-lai occupy individual beds. The two couples reminisce about the beginnings of their personal mythologies in the 1940s: Mao recalls the struggles of the Revolution, while Nixon's war memories revolve around having his own hamburger stand. Chou, in comparatively few words, offers a more sweeping overview of the era, and ties it to the present: 'How much of what we did was good? Everything seems to move beyond our remedy ... Outside this room the chill of grace lies heavy on the morning grass'.

Adams's music is minimalist and eclectic, like many of his chamber and orchestral works of the 1970s and 80s. In the orchestral interludes one hears references, both passing and lingering, to everything from Wagner to Gershwin and Philip Glass. The musical characterizations, however, are often quite striking, and Adams's text settings for Richard Nixon in particular reflect his speech patterns recognizably. ALLAN KOZINN

Nizhegorodtsï ('The Nizhniy-Novgoroders'). Opera in five acts, op.15, by EDUARD NÁPRAVNÍK to a libretto by Pyotr Ivanovich Kalashnikov after Mikhail Zagoskin's historical novel *Yury Miloslavsky, ili Russkiye v 1612 godu* ('Yury Miloslavsky, or The Russians in 1612'); St Petersburg, Mariinsky Theatre, 27 December 1868/ 8 January 1869.

Nápravník's first opera, the successful production of which assured him the post of chief conductor of the Russian Opera in St Petersburg for life, was a patriotic extravaganza modelled both in subject matter and in treatment on Glinka's *A Life for the Tsar*. It concerns the mobilization of a national militia under the Nizhniy-Novgorod merchant Kuz'ma Minin (bass), called Sukhorukiy ('Dry-Hands'), to drive out of Russia the Poles who had accompanied the False Dmitry on his campaign against Boris Godunov (the subject of Musorgsky's opera) and ensure the election of the first Romanov Tsar. The evil boyar Borovskoy (baritone), in league with Vladislav, the Polish pretender, attempts to have Minin killed, but he is saved at the last minute by the Russian loyalist Nevzgoda-Kuratov (tenor), the secret lover of Borovskoy's daughter Olga (soprano). The opera reaches its dramatic and musical height in the fourth act, with its vivid representation of the swearing-in of the militia (impassioned accompanied recitatives from Minin answered by impressive, if monolithic, choral antiphons), followed by a heroic sextet in which the two patriots, Minin and Kuratov, join forces.

Tchaikovsky, who saw the opera in its first Moscow production (1884), praised this act for its dramatic strength and beauty; the young Rimsky-Korsakov, reviewing the St Petersburg première conducted by the composer, singled it out for disparagement on account of its antiquated Meyerbeerian form; he later wrote a pointed kuchkist 'answer' to it in *The Maid of Pskov*.

RICHARD TARUSKIN

Nizhniy Novgorod. City in Russia, on the Volga river. From 1932 to 1991 it was named Gor'kiy (Gorky). The troupe of a local landowner, N. G. Shakhovsky, performed operas as early as 1798 in this, one of the oldest musical centres of imperial Russia. In the 1840s the city was the home of the critic A. D. Ulïbïshev and his salon, which occasionally staged scenes from opera: a volunteer troupe at the Nizhegorodskiy Teatr in 1850 staged *Fra Diavolo* and the first act of Glinka's *A Life for the Tsar*. In 1853 the Shakhovsky theatre (public since 1811) burnt down, and opera was confined to a theatre in a hotel in the central market (designed by N. I. Uzhumetsky-Gritsevich) performed by the troupe of F. K. Smolkov. A new 750-seat stone theatre opened on 1

December 1855 (damaged by fire in 1869, reopened 1871), housing mostly performances by touring companies. Another stone theatre, with four tiers and a capacity of 1800, opened in 1877 on the central square and became known as the Great Market Theatre; P. M. Medvedev's troupe appeared there annually until 1885. A new city theatre (replacing the theatre damaged in 1869) opened on 14 May 1896 with the city's first full-length performance of *A Life for the Tsar*. Both theatres housed touring groups and private enterprises for the next 20 years; after a lull during World War I opera was restricted to private troupes, an opera studio at the conservatory, and an 'opera-concert ensemble'. On 24 October 1935 the 1200-seat Gor'kovskiy Teatr Operï i Baleta opened in the rebuilt Great People's House with a performance of *Prince Igor*. The company early specialized in works based on the writings of Pushkin, after whom the theatre was named the Gor'kovskiy Teatr Operï i Baleta imeni A. S. Pushkina (Pushkin Gor'kiy Theatre of Opera and Ballet) in 1937. Works by local composers are a particular focus of the theatre, which has given premières of operas by Kas'yanov, Kholminov, M. Ia. Magidenko and A. A. Nesterov.

*

ME ('Gor'kiy'; V. A. Kollar)

A. S. Garsusky: *Nizhegorodskiy teatr* (Nizhniy Novgorod, 1867)

V. A. Kollar: 'Ocherk istorii muzïkal'nogo teatra v Nizhnem Novgorode' [A Study of the History of the Musical Theatre in Nizhniy Novgorod], *Iz muzïkal'nogo proshlogo* [From the Musical Past], ed. B. S. Shteynpress, i (Moscow, 1960), 288–370

G. Bernandt: *Slovar' oper vervïye postavlennïkh ili izdannïkh v dorevolyutsionnoy Rossii i v SSSR 1736–1959* [Dictionary of Operas First Performed or Published in Pre-revolutionary Russia and in the USSR 1736–1959] (Moscow, 1962), 536

B. N. Belyakov: *Letopis' Nizhegorodskogo-Gor'kovskogo teatra* [Chronicle of Nizhniy Novgorod-Gor'kiy Theatre] (Gor'kiy, 1967)

B. N. Belyakov, V. G. Blinova and N. D. Bordyug: *Opernaya i kontsertnaya deyatel'nost' v Nizhnem Novgorode-gorode Gor'kom (1798–1980)* [Operatic and Concert Life in Nizhniy Novgorod and in Gor'kiy City (1798–1980)] (Gor'kiy, 1980)

GREGORY SALMON

Nobili, Lila de. *See* DE NOBILI, LILA.

Noble, Dennis (William) (*b* Bristol, 25 Sept 1899; *d* Javea, Alicante, 14 March 1966). English baritone. His freely produced, vigorous voice and good stage presence made him successful in a wide variety of parts, especially in the Italian repertory, at first with English touring companies and later during the international seasons at Covent Garden between 1924 and 1947. His pre-war roles had included the elder Germont with Ponselle in 1931 and leading parts in four new English operas: Goossens's *Judith* and *Don Juan de Mañara*, Albert Coates's *Pickwick* (Sam Weller) and George Lloyd's *The Serf*. He also appeared in New York, Cleveland, Brussels, Rome and elsewhere in Italy.

DESMOND SHAWE-TAYLOR

Noces de Jeannette, Les ('Jeannette's Wedding'). *Opéra comique* in one act by VICTOR MASSÉ to a libretto by JULES BARBIER and MICHEL CARRÉ; Paris, Opéra-Comique (Salle Favart), 4 February 1853.

Jean (baritone) is due to marry his neighbour Jeannette (soprano) but gets cold feet, preferring to go out drinking with his male friends. Jeannette, though, knows the traditional route to a man's heart. She repairs his clothes, cleans and tidies his house and makes him a hearty meal. Returning to a home magically transformed, Jean realizes that marriage is for him after all. Caroline Carvalho was the original Jeannette, who sings the coloratura 'Air du rossignol', the highlight of the opera.

ANDREW LAMB

Noch' pered rozhdestvom. Opera by Nikolay Rimsky-Korsakov; *see* CHRISTMAS EVE.

Nöcker [Nocker], **Hans Günter** (*b* Hagen, 22 Jan 1927). German bass-baritone. He studied with Carl Momberg in Brunswick and in Munich with Hans Hermann Nissen and Willi Domgraf-Fassbänder, making his début in 1952 at Münster as Alfio (*Cavalleria rusticana*). He sang several seasons at Stuttgart and from 1962 at the Staatsoper in Munich, with engagements at other German centres, in Italy, Belgium and at the Edinburgh Festival. He created roles in Egk's *Die Verlobung in San Domingo* (1963, Munich) and Fortner's *Elisabeth Tudor* (1972, Deutsche Oper, Berlin), and his recordings include roles in Orff's *Trionfi* and *Oedipus der Tyrann*. A forceful and accomplished singer of heroic character roles, he also has wide concert experience.

NOËL GOODWIN

Noël, Victoire. *See* STOLTZ, ROSINE.

Nohain. *See* FRANC-NOHAIN.

Nolen, Timothy (*b* Rotan, TX, 9 July 1941). American baritone. He attended the Manhattan School of Music and studied privately with Walter Blazer and Richard Fredericks. In 1968 he made his début as Marcello at the San Francisco Opera. After his European début in 1974, as Pelléas in Rouen, he was a member of the Cologne Opera (1974–8). A lively, vivid actor, committed to American works, he has participated in the premières of Bernstein's *A Quiet Place* and Floyd's *Willie Stark*, established himself in 'crossover' repertory such as Sondheim's *Sweeney Todd*, and starred on Broadway in Lloyd Webber's *Phantom of the Opera*. In the operatic repertory he has chiefly sung Mozart and early 19th-century Italian roles, in centres including Aix, Amsterdam, Chicago, Florence, Geneva, Houston, Miami, New York (City Opera), Philadelphia, San Francisco and Zürich.

For illustration *see* QUIET PLACE, A.   CORI ELLISON

Noni, Alda (*b* Trieste, 30 April 1916). Italian soprano. She studied in Trieste and Vienna, making her operatic début as Rosina at Ljubljana in 1937. After performances at Zagreb, Belgrade and Trieste, she joined the Vienna Staatsoper in 1942 and sang such roles as Despina, Norina, Gilda, Oscar and Zerbinetta. In 1944 she returned to Italy; two years later she made her London début at the Cambridge Theatre as Norina. She appeared at La Scala from 1949 to 1953, making her début as Carolina (*Il matrimonio segreto*) and also singing Armidoro (Piccinni's *La buona figliuola*), Papagena, Zerlina and Nannetta during the 1950 London visit. With Glyndebourne Opera at the 1949 Edinburgh Festival she sang Oscar, and at Glyndebourne itself (1950–54) Blonde, Despina and Clorinda (*La Cenerentola*). She excelled in comic roles and her repertory, which included operas by Cherubini, Auber and Wolf-Ferrari, displayed to advantage her limpid and attractive coloratura soprano.

HAROLD ROSENTHAL/R

Nonne sanglante, La ('The Bleeding Nun'). *Opéra* in five acts by CHARLES-FRANÇOIS GOUNOD to a libretto by EUGÈNE SCRIBE and GERMAIN DELAVIGNE after Matthew Gregory Lewis's novel *The Monk*; Paris, Opéra, 18 October 1854.

Rodolphe (tenor) learns that the hand of his beloved Agnès (soprano) will be given to his brother according to terms of a peace treaty between the Ludorf and the Moldaw families. He persuades Agnès to elope with him disguised as the legendary ghost of the Bleeding Nun. Unfortunately, at the designated midnight rendezvous the ghost herself appears instead of Agnès. Thereafter, Rodolphe is plagued by the Nun's nocturnal visits. He is finally given permission to marry Agnès, but to be rid of the ghost he must kill the man who murdered her while she was a mortal. That man is revealed, at an opulently staged marriage ceremony for Rodolphe and Agnès, to be his own father, Ludorf (bass). As a result, Rodolphe cannot go through with the marriage and the old family feud breaks out again. Moved by his son's turmoil, Ludorf sacrifices himself to Moldaw assassins and the Nun is avenged.

A version of the libretto for *La nonne* was in Berlioz's hands for nearly ten years, and he set portions of the first act. Since the Opéra administration was reluctant to stage a work by Berlioz, it offered the libretto to Félicien David and to Verdi in the late 1840s. Scribe's book passed to Gounod in 1852. Though Gounod's music was well received, the work survived for only 11 performances at the Opéra, partly because of a change of directorship at the house. The libretto, with its unhappy blend of historico-political grand opera and the supernatural, was poorly received by the press. *La nonne* has never been revived. STEVEN HUEBNER

Nono, Luigi (*b* Venice, 29 Jan 1924; *d* Venice, 8 May 1990). Italian composer. Music became a central interest only when he was in his teens, and his subsequent mentors – most notably Gian Francesco Malipiero, Bruno Maderna and Hermann Scherchen – encouraged him to engage directly with the more radical elements of the modernist school rather than passing through traditional conservatory training. (If any other tradition made a strong mark upon him, it was that of Renaissance Italy as expounded by Malipiero and Maderna.) In consequence, his sense of the technical exigencies of post-Webernism was increasingly inflected by a willingness to use sound materials in a disinhibited, almost 'painterly' way in order to further his conception of a socially responsible art that bore witness to the constantly renewed struggle for a more just and coherent society. Although Nono first realized his distinctive mix of artistic and political radicalism in concert works during the 1950s, his two completed theatrical works provided him with the opportunity to apply his aesthetic principles on a large and potent scale.

Nono transferred the range of procedures developed in *Il canto sospeso* (1955–6) directly to his first theatre work, *Intolleranza 1960*, created in some haste for the Venice Biennale of 1961. Whereas the combination of aesthetic and political radicalism central to Nono's vision had few precursors within the concert tradition, it had a vivid and ebullient antecedent in the Russian theatre of the 1920s, in particular in the work of Vsevolod Meyerhold. Meyerhold's use of stylized movement within sets that allowed constructivist artists to explore three-dimensional, architectural space in ways otherwise hypothetical had been explored in a book by Angelo Maria Ripellino which Nono read avidly, subsequently making repeated contacts with the author in order to gain further information. He therefore turned to Ripellino for a libretto, but the result did not suit his purpose: in consequence he substituted a verbal collage of his own, fitted into a narrative whose function was to create exemplary situations rather than to embroil the spectator in a well-turned plot. Another major source of inspiration was the political theatre created by Piscator in the late 1920s (again the fruit of personal contact, since he had met Piscator in 1954 and had borrowed from him his book *Das politische Theater*, previously banned by the Nazis and in consequence not easily available).

What Nono derived from Meyerhold and Piscator was not simply the idea of a hortatory theatre, but of a dynamic one. He was fascinated by Meyerhold's concept of an amphitheatrical space dynamized by multiple acting areas, and by Gropius's designs (commissioned by Piscator but unrealized) for a theatre in the round where acting spaces, projection screens and even part of the seating were mobile. Such ideals only gradually found a convincing corollary in Nono's theatre, but as a step towards them he proposed to incorporate into *Intolleranza 1960* the 'magic lantern' techniques developed in Prague by Josef Svoboda, which coordinated simultaneous slide projections onto moving curtains so that the stage became a mobile collage. Again, collaboration did not run smoothly: Svoboda's proposed materials (slides of architectural details from Prague) hardly accorded with Nono's conception, and Emilio Vedova stepped in at short notice to prepare a more apt mixture of abstract expressionist gesture and verbal slogans. The aural complement was a four-track tape (the second of Nono's incursions into electronic music) played through strategically placed loudspeakers. This incorporation of the audience into a dynamized space became an integral part of Nono's approach to theatre. (In his next completed theatrical project, the electronic music for Peter Weiss's *The Investigation*, he placed one speaker, generating loud, deep sound, beneath the auditorium, so that the audience was physically seized by the vibrations.)

In the mid-1960's Nono put together materials for another theatrical project, based on the work of Pavese. Emphasizing the move away from 'operatic' empathy, he proposed to have the words of the central female character, the prostitute Deola, sung by four sopranos; elements from this unrealized project found a place within his second music-theatre work, *Al gran sole carico d'amore*. Of the original project all that survives is *La fabbrica illuminata* (1964) for soprano and four-track tape.

In 1972 Paolo Grassi commissioned a work on behalf of La Scala, Milan. Nono already had to hand ideas for a work celebrating the Paris Commune, which he had discussed two years previously with Giovanni Pirelli, plus materials from his Pavese project. Prompted by Grassi to clarify from the start who might produce it, and acting purely on reports of his work, which he had never seen, Nono suggested Yury Lyubimov of the Taganka Theatre in Moscow. Lyubimov had never been permitted to work in Western Europe, and the Soviet authorities opposed the project consistently until the head of the Italian Communist party, Enrico Berlinguer, intervened. Then began a process of collaborative synthesis that deliberately flouted the normal progress from libretto through musical setting to staging. Nono, Lyubimov and his scenographer David Borovski, whose articulation of theatrical space through lighting was central to the work of the Taganka, evolved a framework in which gesture, text and music complemented each other. The textural materials thus arrived at were once again a collage, albeit unified by a central theme – the role of women at the heart of revolutionary situations – and by the background presence of two complementary narratives. The musical contribution involved other collaborators: the conductor Claudio Abbado and the technician Marino Zuccheri, responsible for the elaborate 'spatialization' of the auditorium through speakers, by means of which not only electronic sound but also the large chorus who sang from a separate room enveloped and moved among the spectators.

Although the totality of the collective conception was only realized in the two original productions at the Teatro Lirico, Milan (in 1975 and 1978), the text and music that resulted subsequently took on a more conventional autonomy. It is significant, however, that the final version contains no stage directions, so that subsequent productions were able to explore new directions, notably that mounted in a factory in Lyons in which performers were transported by mechanical means and the audience, on foot, moved about with them.

Even while the 1978 version of *Al gran sole* was being staged, Nono was planning with the philosopher Massimo Cacciari a new stage work, *Prometeo*, projecting upon the Aeschylean tragedy a vast associative network of quotation from more recent sources (in effect, an extension of the collage techniques of *Al gran sole*, though into interrogations of inner experience far removed from political exhortation). But it soon became apparent that this work aspired to transcend the concrete image-making of the stage: by the time it was mounted at the deconsecrated church of S Lorenzo in Venice in 1984, it had become instead a purely aural work realized inside a vast wooden shell designed by Renzo Piano that contained both performers and audience within a total acoustic space dynamized and shaped by live electronic sound-projection techniques. Even Cacciari's complex text-collage – essential preparatory reading – becomes dissolved into pure sound: a vast exercise in listening beyond the sense of the words. This conception offers a paradoxical realization of the Gropius-Piscator aspiration towards a totally dynamic theatre in the round: one achieved at the cost not only of the visual dimension, but finally of our submission to the word itself.

See also AL GRAN SOLE CARICO D'AMORE and INTOLLERANZA 1960.

*

L. Nono: 'Appunti per un teatro musicale attuale', *RaM*, xxxi (1961), 418–24

L. Pestalozza: 'Luigi Nono e *Intolleranza 1960*', *La Biennale di Venezia*, xi/43 (1961), 18–34

M. Bortolotto: 'La missione teatrale di Luigi Nono', *Paragone*, xiii/146 (1962), 25–43

L. Nono: 'Alcune precisazioni su *Intolleranza 1960*', *RaM*, xxxii (1962), 277–89

——: 'Possibilità e necessità di un nuovo teatro musicale', *Il verri* [Milan] (1963), new ser., no.9, pp.59–76

E. Vedova: 'Interventi', *Collage* [Palermo] (1966), 93 [on *Intolleranza 1960*]

M. Bortolotto: *Fase seconda* (Turin, 1969), 125ff [on *Intolleranza 1960*]

F. Degrada, ed.: *Al gran sole carico d'amore* (Milan, 1975)

J. Stenzl, ed.: *Luigi Nono: Texte: Studien zu seiner Musik* (Zürich, 1975)

J. Stenzl: '*Azione scenica* und Literaturoper: zu Luigi Nonos Musikdramaturgie', *Musik-Konzepte*, xx (1981), 45–67

H. Vogt: '*Al gran sole* carico d'autocitazione', *Neuland*, v (1984–5), 125–39

P. Albèra, ed.: *Luigi Nono* (Paris, 1987), 122, 132–95

E. Restagno, ed.: *Nono* (Turin, 1987)

G. Manzoni: *Scritti* (Florence, 1991)

DAVID OSMOND-SMITH

Lillian Nordica as Isolde in Wagner's 'Tristan und Isolde'

Nordica [Norton], **Lillian** [Lilian] (*b* Farmington, ME, 12 May 1857; *d* Batavia, Java, 10 May 1914). American soprano. She studied in Milan, where she made her début as Donna Elvira at the Teatro Manzoni in March 1879. She sang in Germany and at St Petersburg and made her début at the Paris Opéra as Gounod's Marguerite (1882), repeating the role for her New York début at the Academy of Music (1883). In 1887 she made her Covent Garden début as Violetta (12 March); later that year she sang at Drury Lane, her roles including Lucia, Donna Elvira, Valentine and Aida. She sang every season at Covent Garden from 1888 to 1893, appearing as Zelica (*The Veiled Prophet*) in 1893. During that period she made her Metropolitan début as Valentine (1891); she sang Elsa there two years later and in the first Bayreuth performance of *Lohengrin* in 1894. It was in Wagnerian roles that she was best known during her years at the Metropolitan (1893–1909). In 1898, 1899 and 1902 she reappeared at Covent Garden, adding Donna Anna, Susanna and Brünnhilde to her repertory. Nordica excelled in dramatic and florid singing and was noted for the purity of her style and the richness and roundness of her upper register, but her acting failed to match her singing.

*

O. Thompson: *The American Singer* (New York, 1937), 159–73
I. Glackens: *Yankee Diva: Lillian Nordica and the Golden Days of Opera* (New York, 1963) [with discography]

Norena, Eidé [Hansen-Eidé (née Hansen), Kaja Andrea Karoline] (*b* Horten, nr Oslo, 26 April 1884; *d* Lausanne, 19 Nov 1968). Norwegian soprano. She studied with Gulbranson in Oslo, where she made her début as Cupid (Gluck's *Orfeo*) in 1907. She sang at the National Theatre in Oslo (1908–18) and then at the Royal Opera, Stockholm; in 1924 she was engaged to sing Gilda at La Scala. She first appeared at Covent Garden in 1924 and was a regular visitor to London, where her Desdemona (1937) was especially distinguished. At the Paris Opéra (1925–37), her roles included the Queen of Shemakha (*The Golden Cockerel*), Marguerite de Valois (*Les Huguenots*), Mathilde (*Guillaume Tell*) and Ophelia (*Hamlet*). Norena sang at the Metropolitan (1933–8), making her début as Mimì, and also in Monte Carlo, Vichy and Amsterdam, where she sang the three heroines of *Les contes d'Hoffmann*. She possessed a beautiful, perfectly trained voice and sang with impeccable taste.

GV (L. Riemens; R. Vegeto)   HAROLD ROSENTHAL/R

Norfolk. American city and port in Virginia. Operatic performances in eastern Virginia before 1975 were either by touring companies or by amateur organizations. In 1974 the Virginia Opera (formerly Virginia Opera Association) was founded by a citizens' group led by Edythe C. Harrison. They engaged professional artists for two performances of *La bohème* in January 1975 in the 1700-seat municipal Center Theater, which has since been the company's home. Four months later Peter Mark, now the General Director, conducted the second production, *La traviata*, the success of which established the company on a firm financial basis. Since 1975–6 it has staged four or five productions a season, chiefly of the standard Italian and French repertory, offering four performances of each in Norfolk, as well as, in recent seasons, two in Richmond and tours to smaller towns in the south-east. Annual budgets increased from $75 000 in 1975 to $2.5 million in 1989–90. The company has mainly employed young American conductors, directors, designers and singers, many of whom, notably Ashley Putnam, Cynthia Haymon, Florence Quivar, John Aler, Rockwell Blake, Jake Gardner and Frederick Burchinal, made their débuts or scored an early success in Norfolk. Virginia Opera's salient achievements have been with works by Thea Musgrave, including the American première of *Mary, Queen of Scots* (March 1978) and world premières of *A Christmas Carol* (December 1979) and *Harriet, the Woman Called Moses* (March 1985). The first two were recorded commercially; in addition, the company's production of *A Christmas Carol*, presented by the Royal Opera in December 1981 at Sadler's Wells, was shown in the UK by Granada Television during the 1982 Christmas season.   CARL DOLMETSCH

Nørgård, Per (*b* Gentofte, 13 July 1932). Danish composer. At 17 he became a composition pupil of Vagn Holmboe and continued to study with him at the Royal Danish Conservatory, where his teachers also included Høffding and Koppel; he later studied in Paris with Boulanger (1956–7), and in 1957 he was awarded the Lili Boulanger Prize. From 1958 to 1962 he was a music critic for the Copenhagen newspaper *Politiken*. He taught at the conservatories in Odense, Copenhagen and Århus (from 1965), and held many administrative posts. He occupied a central position among younger Danish composers as a leader and originator of ideas, and in the 1960s and early 70s his compositions began to be known throughout Europe and the USA.

In his earliest works Nørgård explored a Nordic style deriving from Sibelius, for whom he has always felt a formal affinity, and from Holmboe. However, the 1959 ISCM Festival in Rome provided a turning-point in Nørgård's style; his encounter there with other European avant-garde developments stimulated his awareness of international trends, and caused him to reach out beyond (if not to depart from) his earlier Nordic emphasis. The opera *Labyrinten* (1963), one of the few works by Nørgård to meet with disapproval from the Danish critics, dates from this experimental phase. In the early 1970s Nørgård reached the point of focussing the procedures and concepts with which he had experimented into a stylistic synthesis that employs a variety of modes, including pentatonic, 7-note, 12-note and microtonal scales. The concepts of infinity and 'natural' law have become increasingly important, and are basic in such a work as the opera *Gilgamesh* (1971–2), in which melodic elements are derived from an 'infinite series', rhythmic hierarchies (asymmetry and polarity of pulse) are based on a systematic application of the golden section, and harmonic structures are derived from a theoretical application of the overtone and postulated undertone series. He was awarded the Nordic Music Prize for this work in 1974.

In the mid-1970s Nørgård devoted himself more to opera composition. From 1973 to 1979 he was at work on *Siddharta*, an opera which had been jointly commissioned by the opera houses of Nordic countries. In it the composer emphasized the concept of movement through dance as the plot deals with Prince Siddharta and the fulfilment of the prophecy that he will become ruler of the world. Nørgård's fourth opera, *Det guddommelige tivoli* ('The Divine Circus'), was performed in 1983; based on the life and writings of the schizophrenic Swiss artist, Adolf Wölfli, it uses a complex blend of song, dance and mainly percussive music. Both works have been performed several times and *Det guddommelige tivoli* has gained considerable popularity.

all published in Copenhagen

Labyrinten [The Labyrinth], 1963 (2, B. Nørgård), Copenhagen, Kongelige, 2 Sept 1967
Gilgamesh, 1971–2 ('opera in 6 days and 7 nights', P. Nørgård), Århus, Riiskov Amtsgymnasium, 4 May 1973
Siddharta, 1973–9 (3, P. Nørgård and O. Sarvig), Stockholm, Royal Opera, 18 March 1983
Det guddommelige tivoli [The Divine Circus], 1982 (A. Wölfli), Århus, Gillerupscenen, 5 Jan 1983

*

P. Nørgård: 'Gilgamesh – en 5000-årig aktualitet', *Nutida musik*, xvii/1 (1973–4), 5–7
B. Bjørnum: *Per Nørgårds Kompositioner* (Copenhagen, 1983)
J. Christensen: 'Per Nørgård – Widening the Framework', *Musical Denmark* [Danish Cultural Institute], (1989) no.1, pp.3–5
K. Å. Rasmussen and J. Høm: *Noteworthy Danes: Portraits of 11 Danish Composers* (Copenhagen, 1991), 29–40

WILLIAM H. REYNOLDS

Nørholm, Ib (*b* Copenhagen, 24 Jan 1931). Danish composer. As a boy he studied the piano and organ, and in 1949, while still at school, composed a chamber opera based on Andersen's fairy-tale *Sneglen og rosenhækken* ('The Snail and the Rose Tree'). The next year he entered the Copenhagen Conservatory. He worked as a music critic and organist, and taught at the conservatories in Copenhagen and Odense.

Nørholm's earliest works follow the tonal, lyrical tradition which evolved in Denmark after Nielsen. However, he soon became active in the debate between traditionalists and those who espoused the spirit of 'new internationalism'. He became a member of a group of young Danes who, led by Nørgård, began in 1959 to discuss European modernism in the music of Schoenberg, Webern, Messiaen, Boulez, Stockhausen and others. The work which represents Nørholm's turning-point away from the Danish tradition is the Piano Trio op.22 (1959), his first serial composition. Throughout his career he has experimented with novel procedures and materials in the search for new areas of sound and a broader vocabulary, while striving to compose music with which the listener can identify. One result of this has been the collage technique which appears in his later works, such as the chamber piece *Serenade to Cincinnatus* op.28 (1964); this was a preliminary study for *Invitation til skafottet* ('Invitation to the Scaffold'), a 90-minute opera for Danish Television based on Nabokov's novel, broadcast in 1967.

Nørholm became a leader in the 'new simplicity' movement which emerged in Denmark in the mid-1960s, advocating music in which simplicity – of conception and performance requirements or for the listener – is an important factor, and reacting against the extreme complexity of some avant-garde works. His second opera, *Den unge park* ('The Young Park'), commissioned by the Århus Conservatory and given its first performance there in 1970, is a chamber piece in which leitmotif technique gives rise to an outer form of continuous conversation among six characters in a contrapuntal musical setting. Critics hailed it as an exciting work and praised the interplay between text and music; it was taken on tour and televised, and has become the most widely performed of Nørholm's operas. A chorus opera, *The Garden Wall*, was jointly commissioned by the Copenhagen Conservatory and the RNCM at Manchester, and was performed in both cities and then at Sadler's Wells; it too was given a television production in Denmark, but with less success than *Den unge park*. Nørholm used leitmotif techniques again in *Sandhedens haevn* ('Truth's Revenge'), an opera in an eclectic musical style, based on a marionette comedy by Karen Blixen.

Sneglen og rosenhækken [The Snail and the Rose Tree], 1949 (chamber op)
Invitation til skafottet [Invitation to the Scaffold] op.32 (television op, P. Borum, after V. Nabokov), Danish TV, 10 Oct 1967
Den unge park [The Young Park] op.48 (1, J. Christensen), Århus, Conservatory, 14 Oct 1970
The Garden Wall [Havemuren] op.68 (chorus op, Borum), Manchester, RNCM, 1976; in Danish, Copenhagen, Conservatory, March 1977
Sandhedens haevn [Truth's Revenge] op.95 (prol., 2, J. Heiner, after K. Blixen), Copenhagen, Østre Gasværk, 5 May 1986

*

G. Colding-Jørgensen: 'Den unge park', *Dansk musiktidsskrift*, xlvi (1970), 149–52
——: 'En dansk opera', *Nogle danske komponister* (Copenhagen, 1970–71), 63
M. Andersen: 'Fra opera i TV til TV-opera', *Dansk musiktidsskrift*, lvi (1981–2), 253–5
——: 'Dansk nytidsopera 1940–89', *Dansk musiktidsskrift*, lxiii (1988–9), 226–8
J. Brinker: 'Portrait of Ib Nørholm', *Musical Denmark*, xliv/1 (1991), 5–7
WILLIAM H. REYNOLDS

Noris, Matteo (*b* Venice; *d* Treviso, 6 Oct 1714). Italian librettist. In the course of his career he wrote for all the principal Venetian theatres. His works were dramatically effective, and many were set more than once. In the 1670s and 80s he was closely associated with theatres owned by the Grimani family: the Teatro SS Giovanni e Paolo and their luxury theatre, the Teatro S Giovanni Grisostomo. In 1686, the government castigated those responsible for mounting Pollardo's setting of Noris's *Il demone amante, ovvero Giugurta*, which was deemed offensive on religious grounds and had to be revised. For five years after the scandal, Noris wrote librettos for Florence and Genoa, but none for Venice. In 1692 he began writing principally for the Teatro S Salvatore. He wrote two librettos, *Attilio Regolo* (1693) and *Tito Manlio* (1696), for the Grand Prince Ferdinando de' Medici's theatre at his villa in Pratolino, as well as a *festa teatrale*, *Il greco in Troia*, celebrating the prince's marriage in 1689. It was not until 1697, after the successful restaging of *Tito Manlio* at the S Giovanni Grisostomo, that he began to write once again for the Grimani. By the 1690s, Coronelli included him in a list of poetry instructors, along with Zeno, Silvani and others. He died at an advanced age and was buried in the parish church of S Leonardo in Treviso.

Many of his works of the 1680s, in particular *Il re infante* and *Penelope la casta*, were stupendous affairs requiring elaborate machines, a large cast of principals and many supernumeraries. Noris sought novel subjects and used them imaginatively; he deliberately adopted a cavalier attitude towards historical fact and often referred to his plots as labyrinthine. In his prefaces from the 1690s onward he vigorously attacked the promulgators of imitation, deriding those who borrowed from classical and neo-classical works. The preface to *Flavio, re di Longobardi*, Haym's reworking of *Flavio Cuniberto* for Handel, points to the similarity of one of the subplots to the main plot of Corneille's *Le Cid*, but this may be coincidental. A clearer borrowing is the dependence of *Bassiano, ovvero Il maggior impossibile* on Lope de Vega's *El mayor imposible*. In spirit, Noris's work has much in common with 17th-century Spanish drama.

drammi per musica unless otherwise stated

Zenobia, G. A. Boretti, 1666; Marcello in Siracusa, Boretti, 1670; Semiramide (after G. A. Moniglia), P. A. Ziani, 1670; Attila, Ziani, 1672; Domiziano, Boretti, 1673; Numa Pompilio, Pagliardi, 1674; Diocleziano, C. Pallavicino, 1674 (Franck, 1682, as Diocletianus); Galieno, Pallavicino, 1676; Totila, Legrenzi, 1677 (F. Gasparini, 1696, as Totila in Roma); Astiage (after A. Apolloni [G. F. Apolloni]), Viviani, 1677; I due tiranni al soglio, A. Sartorio, 1679
Dionisio, ovvero La virtù trionfante del vizio, Franceschini and Partenio, 1681; Flavio Cuniberto, Partenio, 1682 (Handel, 1723, as Flavio rè di Longobardi); Bassiano, ovvero Il maggior impossibile, Pallavicino, 1682 (A. Scarlatti, 1694); Carlo re d'Italia, Pallavicino, 1682; Il re infante, Pallavicino, 1683 (Scarlatti, 1688, as Flavio); Licinio imperatore, Pallavicino, 1683; Ricimero re de' vandali, Pallavicino, 1684; Traiano, Tosi, 1684
Penelope la casta, Pallavicino, 1685 (Scarlatti, 1696; comp. unknown, 1705, as Penelope; various, 1721, as Ulysses); Il demone amante, ovvero Giugurta, C. F. Pollarolo, 1686; Amor innamorato, Pallavicino, 1686; Licurgo, ovvero Il cieco di acuta vista, Pollarolo, 1686; Il greco in Troia (festa teatrale), Pagliardi, 1689; Marc'Antonio, Pollarolo, 1692; Furio Camillo, Perti, 1692; Nerone fatto Cesare, Perti, 1693 (Scarlatti, 1695); Attilio Regolo,

Pagliardi, 1693; *Alfonso primo*, Pollarolo, 1694; *L'Amore figlio del Merito*, M. A. Ziani, 1694; *Laodicea e Berenice*, Perti, 1694 (Scarlatti, 1701; Vivaldi ? and others, 1725, as *L'inganno trionfante in amore*); *La finta pazzia di Ulisse*, M. A. Ziani, 1696; *Tito Manlio*, Pollarolo, 1696 (Giannettini, 1701; Vivaldi, 1719; Cocchi, 1761); *I regi equivoci*, Pollarolo, 1697; *Marzio Coriolano*, Pollarolo, 1698; *Il ripudio d'Ottavia*, Pollarolo, 1699; *Il color fa la regina*, Pollarolo, 1700; *Il delirio comune per l'incostanza de' Genii*, Pollarolo, 1700; *Catone Uticense*, Pollarolo, 1701

L'odio e l'amor, Pollarolo, 1702 (Orlandini, 1709; F. Gasparini, 1716, as *Ciro*); *Il giorno di notte*, Pollarolo, 1704; *Virginio consolo*, Giannettini, 1704; *La regina creduta re [Semiramide]*, G. Bononcini, 1706; *Berengario re d'Italia*, Polani, 1710; *Le passioni per troppo amore*, Heinichen, 1713

*

Mercure galant (Aug 1677; April 1679)

Chassebras de Cramailles: *Mercure galant* (March and April 1683)

V. Coronelli: *Guida de' forestieri* (Venice, 1700)

E. A. Cicogna: *Delle inscrizioni veneziane*, vi (Venice, 1853)

H. C. Wolff: *Die venezianische Oper in der zweiten Hälfte des 17. Jahrhunderts: ein Beitrag zur Geschichte der Muzik und des Theaters im Zeitalter des Barocks* (Berlin, 1937)

K. Leich: *Girolamo Frigimelica Robertis Libretti (1694–1708): ein Beitrag insbesondere zur Geschichte des Opernlibrettos in Venedig* (Munich, 1972)

R. S. Freeman: *Opera Without Drama: Currents of Change in Italian Opera, 1675–1725* (Ann Arbor, 1981)

H. S. Saunders: *The Repertoire of a Venetian Opera House (1678–1714): the Teatro Grimani di San Giovanni Grisostomo* (diss., Harvard U., 1985)

E. Rosand: *Opera in Seventeenth-Century Venice: the Creation of a Genre* (Berkeley, 1991) HARRIS S. SAUNDERS

Norma. *Tragedia lirica* in two acts by VINCENZO BELLINI to a libretto by FELICE ROMANI after Alexandre Soumet's verse tragedy *Norma*; Milan, Teatro alla Scala, 26 December 1831.

Oroveso *head of the druids*	bass
Pollione *Roman proconsul in Gaul*	tenor
Flavio *friend to Pollione*	tenor
Norma *druidess, daughter of Oroveso*	soprano
Adalgisa *young priestess at the temple of Irminsul*	soprano
Clotilde *Norma's confidante*	mezzo-soprano
Two Children of Norma and Pollione	mime

Druids, bards, priestesses and Gallic soldiers

Setting The sacred forest and temple of Irminsul, Gaul, during the Roman occupation

Norma was written as the second of two operas planned in summer 1830 for Milan, for which Bellini was paid an unprecedented 12 000 lire. Romani's libretto uses themes from several earlier works: Jouy's libretto *La vestale* (1807, Paris) for Spontini, Chateaubriand's novel *Les martyrs* (Paris, 1808) and Romani's own earlier librettos, *Medea in Corinto* for Mayr (1813, Naples), also treating infanticide, and *La sacerdotessa d'Irminsul* for Pacini (1820, Trieste). Bellini intervened continuously, revising and trimming the libretto (the autograph of which is in *I-Sac*). They did not use Soumet's fifth act, a mad scene where Norma leaps into an abyss, but devised the celebrated final ensemble. The subject was chosen by 23 July 1831 and Romani gave Bellini the text for the *introduzione* on 31 August; the opera went into rehearsal about 5 December. The manuscript evidence affords ample testimony to Bellini's continual revisions (Gossett 1983). He is reputed to have made eight versions of 'Casta diva', and may have discarded an entire sinfonia before composing the present one. There are many sketches of the Act 1 duet between Adalgisa and Pollione (producing melodies developed in 'Mira, o Norma' and 'Già mi pasco' in Act 2). Bellini made changes to the trio at the end of Act 1, possibly for the performances he directed at Bergamo in 1832. Current scores present many problems (Monterosso 1973; Brauner 1976), and the Boosey vocal score (London, 1848) offers alternative readings to Ricordi's.

The demanding role of Norma was written for Giuditta Pasta. Lacking his favourite tenor, Rubini, Bellini had the services of the forceful veteran Domenico Donzelli, whose voice he once described as dark and low; his part rarely rises above *g'*. Adalgisa, now usually given to a mezzo-soprano, was written for the high soprano Giulia Grisi; she later became a famous Norma herself, and also created Elvira in *I puritani* (1835, Paris). Oroveso's role was limited by the insufficiencies of Vincenzo Negrini.

The première was unsuccessful, partly because the first act ends unconventionally with a trio instead of with a more complex ensemble. However, *Norma* quickly became popular; it was staged at Naples, Bergamo and Venice during 1832 and at Rome in 1834 when, because 'norma' was also a liturgical term, performances were given as *La foresta d'Irminsul* with the principals changed to Delia and Galieno. Outside Italy, *Norma* was staged in Vienna (in German) during May 1833, and at the King's Theatre, London, during June of that year, when the cast included Pasta and Donzelli. It was given at the Théâtre Italien, Paris, in 1835, with Grisi, Rubini and Luigi Lablache. Wagner conducted *Norma* at Riga in 1837 and, when in Paris in 1839, wrote an aria which remained unperformed, 'Norma il predisse' (WWV 52), for Lablache to sing as 'Orovisto'. *Norma* reached New York (in English) in 1841; it was the inaugural opera at the Academy of Music in 1854, with Grisi and Giovanni Mario. The first performance at the Metropolitan was in 1890 (in German) with Lilli Lehmann in the title role; Rosa Ponselle sang her first Norma at the Metropolitan in 1927, while Maria Callas, having made her London début as Norma at Covent Garden in 1952, made her American début at Chicago in 1954 and her first appearance at the Metropolitan, in 1956, in the same role.

ACT 1.i *The sacred forest of the Druids* The sinfonia uses themes from Norma's duet with Pollione in Act 2 and a section of the chorus 'Guerra, guerra'. Oroveso, in 'Ite sul colle, o Druidi', instructs the Druids to watch for the first sight of the new moon and then to signal, with three strokes on the bronze shield of Irminsul, the start of the sacred rite over which Norma will preside. The Druids call on Irminsul to inspire Norma with hatred against the Romans in the chorus 'Dell'aura tua profetica'. As they leave, Pollione and Flavio enter the grove. Although Pollione once loved Norma (who has borne him two children), his passion for her has cooled and he now loves Adalgisa, who returns his love. Flavio asks if he does not fear Norma's anger; Pollione trembles at the thought and relates his dream of approaching the altar of Venus in Rome with Adalgisa, only to be confronted with a dreadful phantom while the voice of a demon proclaims Norma's revenge. His cavatina 'Meco all'altar di Venere', more robust than those written for Rubini, is interrupted by the sound of the gong and the voices of the Druids, accompanied by a march, announcing that the moon has risen and commanding that all profaners of the sacred grove be gone. After Pollione's cabaletta on a theme inspired by the march, he and Flavio hurry away.

The Druids file into the grove; in the chorus 'Norma viene: le cinge la chioma' they evoke her appearance, with her hair wreathed in mistletoe and a golden sickle in her hand. Norma arrives surrounded by the priestesses. In her recitative, 'Sediziose voci', she criticizes the Druids' warlike chants; the time is not yet ripe to rise against the Romans, who will be defeated at the appointed hour. Norma cuts a branch of mistletoe from the oak-tree in the centre of the grove; then, raising her arms, she prays to the chaste goddess of the moon in 'Casta diva' (in the autograph MS this cavatina is pitched one tone higher than in Ricordi's printed scores). She asks that there be peace for the present; when the moment arrives to shed the Romans' blood she, Norma, will lead the revolt. The Druids demand that the first victim should be Pollione; Norma realizes that she could not kill him herself, and in the cabaletta, 'Ah! bello, a me ritorna', admits that if he were to return to her, she would defend his life. The melody of this cabaletta is adapted from one used in *Bianca e Fernando* (1828) and *Zaira* (1829) with a new coda added. When the Druids have left the grove, Adalgisa laments her weakness in succumbing to Pollione, then in 'Deh! proteggimi, o dio', prays for strength to resist him. Pollione returns to find her in tears. At first she professes to have overcome her love for him, but in a duet, 'Va, crudele, al dio spietato', he urges her to fly with him to Rome and finally she agrees to renounce her vows.

1.ii *Norma's dwelling* Norma is troubled because Pollione has been recalled to Rome. She asks Clotilde to hide her children as someone is heard outside. It is Adalgisa, who comes to ask Norma for help and counsel. She confesses that while praying in the sacred grove, she saw a man who seemed to be a heavenly vision. In 'Sola, furtiva, al tempio', Adalgisa tells Norma how she continued to see the man in secret and at each meeting fell more deeply in love with him. Her confession is overlaid with Norma's nostalgic recollections of her own love affair. Sympathetically Norma agrees to free Adalgisa from her vows (which are not yet final), so that she can depart with her lover. The two voices unite in 'Ah! sì, fa core e abbracciami', whose cadenza in thirds characterizes their warm friendship throughout the opera. Norma asks who Adalgisa's lover might be; the girl indicates Pollione, who enters at that moment. With 'Oh! di qual sei tu vittima' (adapted from the *Ernani* sketches of 1830), Norma launches into the trio that replaces the usual finale ensemble. She enlightens Adalgisa on her own betrayal by Pollione and vehemently denounces him; he admits his love for Adalgisa and begs her to come away with him, but she refuses, while Norma bursts out with even greater fury in 'Vanne, sì: mi lascia, indegno', dismissing him from her sight.

ACT 2.i *Inside Norma's dwelling* Norma, clutching her dagger, stands regarding her sleeping children and ponders their fate, in one of Bellini's best-known recitatives, 'Dormono entrambi ... non vedran la mano', introduced by a cello melody. Deciding that death while they slept would be preferable to the shame that they would endure alive, she considers their innocence in her arioso, 'Teneri, teneri figli', which re-uses the cello melody. She moves to kill them, then, changing her

'Norma' (Bellini), the final scene in Act 2, with (left to right) Luigi Lablache as Oroveso, Giulia Grisi as Norma and Conti as Pollione (Her Majesty's Theatre, London, 1843): lithograph from a contemporary sheet music cover

mind, embraces them and calls for Clotilde to summon Adalgisa. Norma proposes to the younger priestess that she marry Pollione and accompany him to Rome, on the condition that she take the children with her and care for them after Norma's death. Adalgisa refuses, insisting that she will go to Pollione, but only to persuade him to return to Norma. The expressive duet, 'Mira, o Norma', contains extensive coloratura for both singers and is followed by the brilliant 'Sì, fino all'ore estreme', in which they again sing in thirds as they proclaim their friendship.

2.ii *A lonely place near the Druids' wood* The Gallic warriors discuss Pollione's imminent departure for Rome in 'Non partì? Finora è al campo' (from *Bianca e Fernando* and *Zaira*). Oroveso warns them that freedom is still far away; a more tyrannically oppressive proconsul will certainly replace Pollione, and Norma has given them no guidance. In his aria with chorus, 'Ah! del Tebro al giogo indegno', Oroveso rails against the infamy of the Roman yoke, but bids the Gauls have patience: their chance for revenge will come.

2.iii *The temple of Irminsul* Norma hopes to hear of Pollione's repentance, but Clotilde tells her that he intends to abduct Adalgisa from the temple. Rushing to the altar, Norma strikes the shield of Irminsul three times, the signal for war; the Gauls respond with the ferocious war hymn 'Guerra, guerra! Le galliche selve'. When Oroveso demands to know why Norma does not complete the sacrificial rite, she replies obscurely that the victim is ready. Clotilde brings news that a Roman has been caught in the cloister of the virgin priestesses. It is Pollione, who is brought in under guard. He refuses to answer Oroveso's questions and Norma raises the sacred dagger, but is unable to kill him. She decides to interrogate him alone and the others withdraw. In their duet, 'In mia man alfin tu sei', Norma offers Pollione his life if he will swear to abandon all thoughts of Adalgisa. When he refuses, she threatens to kill not only Pollione but their children as well, and to punish Adalgisa by fire for breaking her vows.

Norma summons back the Gauls and announces that a guilty priestess must die on the sacrificial pyre. When Oroveso and the Druids demand to know the culprit's name, Norma replies 'Son io' – 'It is I'. A huge ensemble builds up, beginning with 'Qual cor tradisti' in which Norma claims that Pollione has not escaped her, for they will die together in the flames; Pollione's love for Norma is reborn in the face of her sublime courage; Oroveso and the Druids, reluctant to believe Norma's confession, gradually accept its truth. In 'Deh! non volerli vittime', Norma beseeches her father to spare her children and to look after them when she is dead. Oroveso at first refuses, then relents, promising to honour Norma's last request. Norma and Pollione are led to the pyre.

*   *   *

Norma has always been revered above other Italian operas of the period (for a contemporary assessment, see Ritorni 1841). Reviews compared *Norma* to Spontini's *La vestale*, whose heroine, Julia, is subjected to similarly overwhelming dramatic pressures; but Donizetti's *Anna Bolena* (1830, Milan) perhaps provides a more immediate musical influence. The title role is one of the most taxing and wide-ranging parts in the entire repertory: a noble character whose tragedy lies in her fatal love for an enemy of her people. The many different aspects of Norma's temperament are marvellously drawn by Bellini, not only in the aria 'Casta diva', but also in the superb duets with Adalgisa and Pollione, and in the ensemble in the finale of Act 2, where Bellini reaches his peak as a musical dramatist.

For further illustration *see* LONDON, fig.9, and PASTA, GIUDITTA; for a page of the autograph score, *see* BELLINI, VINCENZO.

SIMON MAGUIRE, ELIZABETH FORBES

Norman, Jessye (*b* Augusta, GA, 15 Sept 1945). American soprano. She studied at Howard University, the Peabody Conservatory and the University of Michigan (with, among others, Pierre Bernac and Elizabeth Mannion). She won the Munich International Music Competition in 1968 and made her operatic début in 1969 at the Deutsche Oper, Berlin, as Elisabeth (*Tannhäuser*), later appearing there as Countess Almaviva. Further engagements in Europe included Aida at La Scala and Cassandra at Covent Garden, both in 1972. For her American stage début she sang Jocasta in Stravinsky's *Oedipus rex* and Purcell's Dido with the Opera Company of Philadelphia (22 November 1982); she appeared first at the Metropolitan Opera on 26 September 1983, once again as Cassandra. Other roles she has sung include Gluck's Alcestis, the Prima Donna (Strauss's *Ariadne auf Naxos*), Madame Lidoine (*Dialogues des Carmélites*), the Woman (*Erwartung*), Bartók's Judith, and Wagner's Kundry and Sieglinde. Norman has a generous physique and a commanding stage presence; her particular distinction lies in her ability to project drama through her voice. Her opulent and dark-hued soprano is richly vibrant in the lower and middle registers, if less free at the top; although her extraordinary vocal resources are not always perfectly controlled, her singing reveals uncommon refinement of nuance and dynamic variety. Her recordings include

Countess Almaviva, Haydn's Rosina (*La vera costanza*) and Armida, Beethoven's Leonore, Weber's Euryanthe, Verdi's Giulietta (*Un giorno di regno*) and Medora (*Il corsaro*), Bizet's Carmen, and Offenbach's Giulietta and Helen.

*

'Jessye Norman: la vérité du chant', *Harmonie*, no.132 (1977), 46–51
'Jessye Norman Talks to John Greenhalgh', *Music and Musicians*, xxvii/12 (1979), 14–15
E. Southern: *Biographical Dictionary of Afro-American and African Musicians* (Westport, CT, 1982)
M. Mayer: 'Double Header: Jessye Norman in her Met Debut Season', *ON*, xlviii/11 (1983–4), 8–11   MARTIN BERNHEIMER

Noronha, Francisco de Sá (*b* Viana do Castelo, 24 Feb 1820; *d* Rio de Janeiro, 23 Jan 1881). Portuguese composer. He was director of the Teatros S Januário (1852) and Fenix Dramática (1880) in Rio de Janeiro, and also of the Oporto Teatro Baquet (1861, 1875). These appointments resulted in a vast repertory, unknown today, of comic operas, operettas and vaudevilles on Portuguese texts.

Noronha was the first Portuguese composer to write operas based on literary works by national writers. The librettos of *Beatrice di Portogallo* and *L'arco di Sant'Anna*, inspired by Almeida Garrett's works, have many characteristics in common with those of his mid-19th-century Italian contemporaries, but the choice of Pinheiro Chagas's Brazilian novel *A virgem de Guaraciaba* for the libretto of *Tagir* (1876) seems to reflect the influence of Carlos Gomes's *Guarany*. Considered by his contemporaries as a creator of a Portuguese melodic style with authentic folk characteristics, his music is strongly influenced by the Italian operatic tradition, particularly that of Verdi.

A graça de Deus (drama), Rio de Janeiro, 1852
Artur, ou dezasseis anos depois (comedy), Lisbon, 1854
Epitafio e Epitalámio (vaudeville), Lisbon, 1855
Raros mas ainda os há (vaudeville), Oporto, 6 Oct 1858
Santa Iria (sacred drama, 3), Lisbon, 22 March 1862
Um filho famílias (comedy), Lisbon, 1 May 1862
Beatrice di Portogallo (drama lírico, 4, R. C. Montoro, after A. Garrett: *Um auto de Gil Vicente*, It. trans. L. Bianchi), Oporto, S João, 4 March 1863, vs *P-La*
L'arco di Sant'Anna (drama lírico, 4, A. Correia and E. Pinto de Almeida, after Garrett, It. trans. F. Tagliapietra), Oporto, S João, 5 Jan 1867, *Lc*, vs *La*
O fagulha (operetta, Cardoso), Lisbon, Rua dos Condes, 25 Feb 1869
O anel de Prata (operetta, 1), Oporto, Baquet, Aug 1875
Os Boémios (operetta, 1), Oporto, Baquet, Aug 1875
Se eu fosse rei (comic op, 1), Oporto, Baquet, 1875
Tagir (melodrama, 4, L. Botelho, Pinto de Almeida and Noronha, after P. Chagas: *A virgem de Guaraciaba*), Oporto, S João, 25 March 1876
As virgens (operetta), Rio de Janeiro, 1880
O califa da rua do Sabão (comic op), Rio de Janeiro, 1880
Os guardas do Rei de Sião (comic op), Rio de Janeiro, 1880
Os noivos (operetta), Rio de Janeiro, 1880
A princesa dos cajueiros (comic op, 2, A. de Azevedo), Rio de Janeiro, 1880

Undated: A filha do cego (vaudeville); O baiano na corte (vaudeville); Esmeralda (comic op); A família Moreley (comic op); São Gonçalo (sacred drama)

*

A. Moutinho de Sousa, ed.: *Questão Noronha ou colleação de todos os artigos publicados em diversos jornaes* (Oporto, 1856)
H. Carneiro: 'Francisco de Sá Noronha', *O tripeiro*, 1st ser., i/19 (1909), 9–11; i/22 (1909), 21–2
L. Cymbron: *Francisco de Sá Noronha e L'arco di Sant'Anna: para o estudo da ópera em Portugal (1860/1870)* (diss., U. of Lisbon, 1990)   LUISA CYMBRON

Norrington, Roger (Arthur Carver) (*b* Oxford, 16 March 1934). English conductor. He was a choral scholar at Cambridge University, studied conducting with Boult at the RCM and began his musical career as a tenor. His conducting début was with his own Heinrich Schütz Choir in 1962, and from 1969 to 1982 he was music director of Kent Opera, conducting a repertory ranging from Monteverdi to Britten and Tippett. He made his début with Sadler's Wells Opera in 1973 (*Le nozze di Figaro*) and first appeared at Covent Garden in 1986 (Handel's *Samson*), returning there in 1989 for *Albert Herring* and *Peter Grimes*. With his wife, the choreographer Kay Lawrence, he formed in 1984 the Early Opera Project to complement his concert work in period-style performance, beginning with Monteverdi's *Orfeo* at the Maggio Musicale in Florence that year, and touring Britain in 1986; in London he conducted the British stage première of *Les Boréades* at the RAM (1986) and gave concert performances of Beethoven's *Leonore* (1988) and of *Die Zauberflöte* (1989) in a series of exploratory 'experiences' with lecture-demonstrations. He conducted *Rigoletto* in Lyubimov's Florence production, *Ariodante* at the Piccola Scala and at the Edinburgh Festival, and *The Turn of the Screw* at La Fenice, Venice. He was appointed CBE in 1990.

*

A. Blyth: 'Roger Norrington', *Opera*, xl (1989), 552–6
ARTHUR JACOBS, NOËL GOODWIN

Norris, Elizabeth (*fl* 1748–52). English soprano. She made her début as Euphrosyne in Arne's *Comus* at Covent Garden in December 1748 and moved to Drury Lane the following season. There she created leading roles in Boyce's *Chaplet* and *Shepherd's Lottery*, sang the heroine in Burney's *Robin Hood* and played Polly opposite John Beard's Macheath in *The Beggar's Opera*. She left the stage in October 1752, probably on her marriage to Samuel Chitty. In *The Present State of the Stage* she was called 'a sensible, a judicious and elegant Performer'.

*

The Present State of the Stage (London, 1753)
R. Fiske: *English Theatre Music in the Eighteenth Century* (London, 1973, 2/1986)   OLIVE BALDWIN, THELMA WILSON

Norsa, Hannah (*d* London, 1785). English soprano, actress and dancer. The daughter of a Jewish merchant (or tavern keeper) she made her début as Polly in *The Beggar's Opera* at the newly opened Covent Garden Theatre in December 1732, with a run of 20 nights in succession. She played Deidamia in Gay's posthumous *Achilles* and then in a short but successful career built up a large repertory in ballad operas, musical afterpieces and plays. In May 1736 she was taken off the stage by the Earl of Orford, Horace Walpole's brother.

*

BDA; *LS*   OLIVE BALDWIN, THELMA WILSON

Norway (Nor. *Norge*). Until 1814 this sparsely populated country, with no large cities, was a colony of Denmark, with no permanent court or aristocracy. There was no regular opera theatre until the mid-19th century, though the first recorded opera performance took place in 1749 under Gluck, who visited Christiania (now Oslo) with the Danish-Norwegian king, Fredrik V. From 1799 onwards foreign opera companies, Italian, German and Swedish, visited Norway. Operas were also put on by Norwegian theatre societies, a blend of professionals and gifted amateurs. The repertory started

with Danish Singspiele, then introduced Spontini and Cherubini and later embraced Spohr, Weber, Rossini and Mozart. The first Norwegian opera, a Singspiel called *Fjeldeventyret* ('Mountain Adventure') by Waldemar Thrane, had its première in 1825. Folk music was included in it, establishing a pattern that invoked a consciousness of the Norwegian heritage.

Ordinary theatres staged operas, sometimes in collaboration with visiting troupes. French opera was in vogue towards 1850 (Méhul, Boieldieu, Auber, Hérold), but Italian works became increasingly popular after the visit of an Italian company introducing Rossini, Donizetti, Bellini and, later, Verdi. German directors brought more Mozart and Weber, as well as Conradin Kreutzer and Flotow of the newer composers. The first entire Wagner opera to be performed was *Tannhäuser* in 1876. The most popular opera towards the end of the century was *Carmen*.

In the 1870s Edvard Grieg and Bjørnstjerne Bjørnson collaborated in an opera on a national subject, *Olav Trygvason*; the project was never finished, but some of the music is still performed at concerts. In Grieg's home town, Bergen, Den Nationale Scene staged several operas towards the end of the 19th century, and in 1888 a special troupe was formed there composed almost entirely of Norwegian singers. Christiania had by this date become the musical centre of the country; operatic activity quickened at the National Theatre in the early years of the 20th century and later (1918–21) at the Opéra Comique. The Norwegian Opera Company, formed in 1950, became in 1959 the basis for the Norwegian National Opera, now wholly supported by the government. Its main aim is to provide high-quality opera and ballet for the whole country: regular performances in Oslo, tours throughout the various regions, and collaborations with local companies. Several local troupes have also been active.

A number of operas were written by Norwegians around the turn of the century, the composers including Catharinus Elling (*Kosakkena*, 1894) and Ole Olsen at home, while Christian Sinding (*Der heilige Berg*, 1914) and Gerhard Schjelderup had many performances abroad, especially in Germany and Czechoslovakia. There have been fewer new works in later years, but those by A. Bibalo (*Das Lächeln am Fusse der Leiter*, *Frøken Julie*, *Ghosts*) and E. F. Braein (*Anne Pedersdotter*) have enjoyed success abroad.

Norwegian singers who have made an international reputation include Eidé Norena, Kirsten Flagstad, Ivar F. Andrésen, Åse Nordmo Løvberg, Ingrid Bjoner, Ragnar Ulfung, Knut Skram and Anne Gjevang.

For further information on operatic life in the country's principal centre *see* OSLO.

*

H. J. Huitfeldt: *Christiania theaterhistorie* (Copenhagen, 1876)
I. Kindem: *Den norske operas historie* (Oslo, 1941)
G. Brunvoll, ed.: *Operaens verden* (Oslo, 1980)
ARVID VOLLSNES

Norwich. English cathedral city in East Anglia. Early musical theatre performances include what seem to have been the first provincial performances of Purcell's *The Prophetess, or The History of Dioclesian* (January 1700) and the first ever performance in English of *Die Zauberflöte* (1829). From 1757 English ballad opera was given intermittently by visiting companies at the Theatre (called the Theatre Royal from 1768), and may have been a source of inspiration to the young James

Hook. An amateur operatic union gave concert performances of Italian operas in early Victorian times. The Norfolk and Norwich Amateur Operatic Society now concentrates on operetta and musicals; the Norfolk Opera Players (founded 1963) give all forms of opera (and operetta), with works from Mozart to the 20th century. The University Students' Music Society and the more recent Opera Da Camera group have put on many small works. In the 1980s short seasons were presented at the Theatre Royal by companies such as Opera North, Kent Opera and the Glyndebourne Touring Opera.

T. Fawcett: 'The First Undoubted Magic Flute?', *RMARC*, no.12 (1974), 106–14

——: *Music in Eighteenth-Century Norwich and Norfolk* (Norwich, 1979)

Nose, The [*Nos*]. Opera in three acts, op.15, by DMITRY SHOSTAKOVICH to a libretto by the composer, Yevgeny Zamyatin, Georgy Ionin and Alexander Preys after the story by NIKOLAY VASIL'YEVICH GOGOL; Leningrad, Malïy Opera Theatre, 18 January 1930.

Shostakovich began composing *The Nose* in the summer of 1927, at the age of 20. At a time when giant strides were being taken in Soviet visual art, dramatic theatre and film, Soviet opera was comparatively stagnant. Shostakovich's improbable choice of subject – Gogol's absurdist anecdote about a petty bureaucrat who wakes one morning to discover that his nose is missing from its accustomed place and the ludicrous adventures which result – was almost guaranteed to breathe fresh life into Soviet operatic theatre.

Shostakovich completed *The Nose* in the summer of 1928. A suite, op.15a, consisting of seven sections from the opera was successfully performed in Moscow in November 1928, conducted by Nikolay Mal'ko. By the time the opera reached the stage in January 1930 – in a carefully prepared collaboration between the composer, the director Nikolay Smolich, the designer Vladimir Dmitriyev and the conductor Samuil Samosud – the cultural climate had changed for the worse. Self-righteous 'proletarian' critics at the peak of their cultural influence savaged Shostakovich's opera and guaranteed it a short run. By the end of 1930 *The Nose* had been dropped from the repertory. In the 1960s it was performed in a number of Western cities including Florence, Rome, Santa Fe and Berlin. In 1974 the opera was rehabilitated in the Soviet Union, in a production supervised by the composer and directed by Boris Pokrovsky at the Moscow Chamber Opera Theatre.

ACT 1   The introduction opens with a flourish and an angular fugato between trumpet, horn and trombone. A repetitive solo for oboe gives way to comic juxtaposition of pointillist melodic fragments and contrasting tone colours, a style similar to a circus march, that comes to characterize the whole opera. The curtain rises to reveal Ivan Yakovlevich in his barber's shop shaving Kovalyov. The latter remarks that the barber's hands always stink.

1.i *Ivan Yakovlevich's barber's shop* In the morning Ivan Yakovlevich wakes to the enticing smell of Praskov'ya Osipovna's freshly baked bread, and he asks for some warm bread with an onion. As he slices into the bread he discovers, to his horror, a nose embedded there. Praskov'ya Osipovna launches into a breathless stream of shrill scolding, accusing her hus-

Major Platon Kuz'mich Kovalyov *Collegiate Assessor*	baritone
Ivan Yakovlevich *a barber*	bass
Praskov'ya Osipovna *Ivan Yakovlevich's wife*	soprano
District Police Inspector	very high tenor
Ivan *Kovalyov's servant*	tenor
The Nose	tenor
The Countess's Footman	baritone
A Newspaper Clerk	bass
A Traveller	spoken
An Escorting Lady	spoken
An Escorting Gentleman	spoken
A Father	bass
A Mother	soprano
Her Sons	tenor, baritone
Pyotr Fyodorovich	tenor
Ivan Ivanovich	baritone
An Old Countess	contralto
A Pretzel-vendor	soprano
A Doctor	bass
Yarïzhkin	tenor
Pelageya Grigor'yevna Podtochina	mezzo-soprano
Her Daughter	soprano
An Old Man	tenor
Two New Arrivals	tenor, bass
A Con-man	bass
A Distinguished Colonel	tenor
Two Dandies	tenor, bass
An Anonymous Voice	bass
A Respectable Lady	mezzo-soprano
Her Two Sons	basses
Khozrev-Mirza	spoken
Three Acquaintances of Kovalyov	tenor, basses
A Policeman	bass
A Lackey	bass
Porter to the Chief of Police	tenor
A Cabby	bass
A Coachman	bass
An Elderly Lady	silent
A Slender Lady	silent
A Shirtfront Saleslady	silent

Servants, policemen, students, passers-by, dependants, Ivan Yakovlevich's acquaintances, firemen, worshippers, departing passengers, their escorts, residents, eunuchs

Setting St Petersburg in the 1830s

band of drunkenness and other crimes. The perplexed Ivan tries to calm her and buy time for reflection but she, with high-pitched reiterations of 'von' ('shoo'), chases him from the house to get rid of the nose. The stage darkens; an apparition of the District Police Inspector is seen.

1.ii *The embankment* Against a brisk staccato quaver pulse, melodic lines are gradually layered into the texture from lowest registers to highest; the barber rushes along the embankment, in increasing consternation and confronted by acquaintances, unable to dispose of the nose. He flings it into the river, and the tension is broken unexpectedly by an ethereal C major chord and a brass fanfare. The hapless barber is confronted by the Police Inspector, his lofty stature satirically limned by an extremely high tessitura. Ivan's spoken attempts to wheedle out of the situation prove fruitless. He is unable to bribe the inspector who, with a soaring melodic line, demands to know what Ivan was doing. The scene plunges into darkness and an instrumental entr'acte is heard, scored exclusively for unpitched percussion instruments. The interlude has gained fame as one of the earliest examples of Western music for percussion ensemble; it is often performed as a separate piece and forms one of the movements of the op.15a Suite.

1.iii *Kovalyov's bedroom* Accompanied by ingeniously graphic instrumental grunts and groans, Kovalyov wakes gradually. Remembering that the evening before a pimple had appeared on his nose, he calls for a mirror. His listlessness turns to agitation then disbelief when he sees that his nose is no longer on his face. Thinking he must still be asleep, he asks his servant to pinch him, but to no avail. Dressing quickly, he leaves to find the Chief of Police. A shrill piccolo blast introduces the lengthy instrumental interlude, a grotesque galop of frenetic rhythm and differentiated, highly colouristic scoring.

1.iv *Kazan' Cathedral* In a sharp contrast to the preceding grotesque extremes, the musical atmosphere in this scene is more subdued and solemn, the dramatic pace more measured. Against a background of flowing choral prayers with a solo soprano line floating above, the Nose appears, seemingly at its devotions, dressed in the uniform of a State Councillor. Covering the blank spot on his face with a handkerchief, Major Kovalyov enters, recognizes his own nose, and is confused about how to address the appendage garbed in a rank higher than his own. In a nervous staccato he confronts the Nose, who, by contrast, responds throughout the ensuing conversation with utter self-possession and condescension. Kovalyov is unsuccessful in making himself understood; the Nose superciliously rejects any relationship with a man of lower rank. The arrival of two ladies distracts Kovalyov long enough to allow the Nose to escape.

ACT 2 With an introductory trumpet fanfare, Kovalyov appears, seated in a droshky, outside the residence of the Chief of Police, where he learns that the Chief has just left. In frustration he tells his driver to go on to the newspaper dispatch office.

2.v *The newspaper dispatch office* The Countess's Footman is explaining to the Clerk that though he himself would pay nothing for her dog, she offers a hundred rubles for its return, a sum bandied around enthusiastically by the gathered servants. Running in, Kovalyov is impatient to place his advertisement but the Clerk is in no hurry to wait on him and the Footman continues his reflections on dogs. It is not easy to understand Kovalyov's predicament; when he makes it clear that his nose has vanished, the Clerk and servants have a good laugh at his expense. In a plaintive recitative-arioso that leads to tears, 'Ya ne mogu vam skazat'' ('I cannot tell you'), Kovalyov tries to win their sympathy. After some awkwardness, the Clerk replies that he cannot place such a notice, lest the newspaper lose its reputation. He advises Kovalyov to see a doctor. To convince the sceptical Clerk, Kovalyov uncovers his face. Truly amazed, the Clerk now recommends that Kovalyov sell his story as a freak of nature and, in a gesture of friendship, offers him a pinch of snuff. At this final affront, Kovalyov loses his temper. The remaining servants place their advertisements, in an elaborate eight-voice staccato 'hocket' canon that uses a single rhythmic value reinforced by the bass drum and which

leads seamlessly into a lengthy instrumental entr'acte based on fugal entries.

2.vi *Kovalyov's apartment* Compared with the complex contrapuntal texture of the preceding interlude, Ivan's folklike song to a text borrowed from Dostoyevsky's *The Brothers Karamazov*, 'Nepobedimoy siloy priverzhen ya k miloy' ('An invisible force ties me to my beloved') and accompanied by strumming balalaikas, makes a striking contrast. In a foul temper, Kovalyov chases his servant away and lapses into a monologue of self-pity, 'Bozhe moy!' ('My God!').

ACT 3.vii *The outskirts of St Petersburg* An empty coach is seen. The District Police Inspector has orders to capture the Nose, which may be attempting to leave the city, and with slapstick bumbling he attempts to muster and post his recalcitrant men. To rally their spirits they intone, against a steady pulse, a melancholy song, 'Podzhav khvost, kak sobaka' ('With tail between legs, like a dog'), that is capped by the melodic howling of the Inspector.

People due to leave the city start to board the coach. In an increasingly complex ensemble, passengers make their farewells while the police watch for the offender, unsure what he might look like, but convinced that he is the very devil. To the strains of a 'parody' waltz, Ivan Ivanovich exchanges pleasantries with his good friend Pyotr Fyodorovich. On her departure, the old Countess predicts her imminent death, to the earnest protestations of her servants. The momentum picks up as a young lady pretzel-vendor appears, distracting the attention of the police and leading to a scene of mass confusion. At the climax, the coach begins to depart and the Nose runs after it asking for it to stop and thus frightening the horse. The Coachman fires; his passengers jump out and everyone pursues the Nose. They surround it and, with enthusiastic rhythmic ejaculations, beat it mercilessly, which has the effect of returning it to normal size. As the passengers run after the departing coach, the Inspector wraps the nose in a piece of paper and withdraws with his men.

3.viii *Kovalyov's apartment and Podtochina's apartment* The stage is split in two. Triumphantly the District Police Inspector returns the nose to the impatient Kovalyov with much good-natured chatter. At his broad hint, Kovalyov gives him money, but the hint needs to be repeated twice more until the Inspector is satisfied with his reward. To a bassoon solo over an eerie, sustained string texture, Kovalyov tries unsuccessfully to stick the nose back on his face. He calls for the Doctor who, after painful prodding and poking, advises him that trying to re-attach his nose might only make things worse. Kovalyov's entreaties are in vain. In breathless patter, he considers the causes of his affliction: undoubtedly Madame Podtochina, who pressured him to marry her daughter, has used some witchcraft on him. Yarïzhkin advises him to write to her and settle the matter. In Madame Podtochina's apartment, the daughter, a caricature of romantic operatic heroines, tells her fortune with cards. The sighing melodic phrases and arpeggiated chordal accompaniment underscore the parodied sentimental romance. Mother and daughter receive Kovalyov's letter and send a reply, which he in turn receives. Shostakovich sets the reading of both letters simultaneously in a driving staccato quartet.

The polyphonic layering of isolated snippets of gossip, sung *a cappella*, leads to a bustling crowd scene, as the residents of St Petersburg exchange rumours and rush about to catch a glimpse of the elusive Nose. As the pandemonium reaches riot proportions, firemen appear and douse the crowd.

3.ix *Kovalyov's apartment* In the first of the two continuous scenes that form the epilogue, Kovalyov jumps out of bed and dances a polka in joy; his nose is back in its place! Ivan Yakovlevich arrives to shave him and the two exchange their customary pleasantries.

3.x *Nevsky Prospect* The rhythm of the polka continues to dominate as Kovalyov parades along the Prospect, meeting acquaintances and delighting in the return of his nose. He is greeted warmly by Madame Podtochina and her daughter, tells them an anecdote, and is invited to lunch. Flirting with a vendor, he invites her to visit him. The curtain falls to the stroke of a bass drum.

* * *

The Nose was a selfconsciously experimental work, influenced particularly by the productions of the theatre director Vsevolod Meyerhold, but also by the cinematic techniques of Sergey Eisenstein and the music of Stravinsky and Berg, as well as that of music-hall and circus. Though largely non-tonal and non-lyrical in style, it makes extensive use of the parody of familiar genres and the grotesque, highly differentiated juxtaposition of tone colours. The opera's dimensions are almost unwieldy, calling for a minimum of 78 sung roles plus spoken roles and chorus, though the composer indicated that many roles could be doubled and tripled. Shostakovich paid special attention to the nuances of Gogol's language and aimed for an equal balance between music and theatre. LAUREL E. FAY

Noske, Frits (Rudolf) (*b* The Hague, 13 Dec 1920). Dutch musicologist. He studied at the conservatories of Amsterdam and The Hague, at the University of Amsterdam with Karel P. Bernet Kempers and Smits van Waesberghe and at the Sorbonne with Paul-Marie Masson. From 1951 to 1968 he worked at the Music Library at Amsterdam, first as librarian and from 1954 as director. He taught at the University of Leiden from 1965 to 1968, when he took the chair at the University of Amsterdam. His main areas of interest are Italian opera of the late 18th and 19th centuries and the application of structuralism to music analysis. His book *The Signifier and the Signified: Studies in the Operas of Mozart and Verdi* (The Hague, 1977), consisting principally of essays previously published in periodicals, reflects new ways of examining the relationship between character, drama and music.

Noskowski, Zygmunt (*b* Warsaw, 2 May 1846; *d* Warsaw, 23 July 1909). Polish composer. Between 1864 and 1867 he studied composition with Moniuszko at the Music Institute in Warsaw, then was a member of the Wielki Theatre orchestra in Warsaw. In 1872 he went to Berlin to continue composition studies. He returned to Warsaw where, in 1881, he was appointed director of the Music Society, and in 1886 became professor of composition at the Music Institute. He founded a symphony orchestra, and later conducted the Warsaw PO and, from 1907, the opera.

Noskowski wrote in all genres, but his orchestral works are the most important: he is the foremost representative of Polish orchestral music in the second half of the 19th century. Stylistically he retained a certain conservatism: his harmony is less advanced than Wagner's, and despite a greater predilection for contrapuntal techniques, for a long time he showed Moniuszko's influence. Although connected with the theatre (he wrote operettas and incidental music as well as operas), his stage music shows only a limited theatrical sense. He himself considered opera a lesser genre than purely instrumental music, a view he expressed in the essay 'Ideał opery' (1880). According to this, both the older type of Italian opera and that represented by Verdi, as well as Wagner's music dramas, were not appropriate forms for opera: the ideal opera should be a synthesis of symphony and cantata. Noskowski was also opposed to the leitmotif principle. His own operas were written late in life according to these ideas. Orchestral passages, which play an important role, constitute the best moments; the use of contrapuntal techniques under the voices tends to make the texture dense and the words less clear; choruses are rare and more oratorio-like than operatic; dialogues and solo passages with long phrases dominate. Contrary to Noskowski's expressed views, his operas resemble Wagner's in form, although leitmotifs are used in a more limited way. But the musical language is completely different, closer to that of an earlier period, even archaic at times (as in the choruses of *Livia Quintilla* which use modal scales). The operas were not successful; the action is slow, often with distracting subplots. Besides completing three operas, Noskowski also made sketches (lost) for works on the subjects of Coriolanus and Julius Caesar.

Livia Quintilla (prol., 2, L. German, after S. Rzętkowski), Lwów, Count Frederic Skarbek, 15 Feb 1898, vs *PL-Wtm**
Wyrok [The Judgment] (2, Noskowski, after A. Urbański: *Dramat jednej nocy*), Warsaw, Wielki, 15 Nov 1906, vs *Wtm**
Zemsta za mur graniczny [Revenge for the Boundary Wall], 1909 (4, Noskowski, after A. Fredro: *Zemsta*), Warsaw, Wielki, 10 April 1926, vs *Wtm**; left in vs, orchd A. Gużewski, 1911

*

Z. Noskowski: 'Ideał opery', *Echo muzyczne*, iv (1880), 169–71, 186–7, 194–6, 207–8
W. Wroński: *Zygmunt Noskowski* (Kraków, 1960)
ZOFIA CHECHLIŃSKA

No Song, No Supper. Afterpiece dialogue opera in two acts by STEPHEN STORACE to a libretto by PRINCE HOARE; London, Drury Lane, 16 April 1790.

No Song, No Supper was the result of Storace's first collaboration with Prince Hoare in what proved to be a successful five-year partnership in writing short operatic farces. They may have known each other in Italy in the early 1780s; the Storace family certainly became friends with Hoare, who eventually wrote epitaphs for both Stephen and his sister Nancy and was one of Nancy's executors. *No Song, No Supper* was first staged for Michael Kelly's annual benefit night in the same programme as *The Beggar's Opera*. It was immediately adopted into the theatre's regular repertory and became very popular in Storace's lifetime; it continued to be performed at Drury Lane well into the 19th century and was revived in the 20th. At the first performance the main characters were played by Michael Kelly with his usual partner Anna Maria Crouch, Nancy Storace with her partner John Bannister, and Ida Romanzini as the gullible stepmother.

Two sailors, Frederick (tenor) and Robin (baritone), who are shipwrecked on their own coast, return home in the hope of reclaiming their lovers, Louisa (soprano) and Margaretta (soprano). They arrive at the house of

Louisa's father, who is also Robin's brother-in-law. There an avaricious lawyer is trying to seduce Louisa's stepmother into parting with her money. He has already been the cause of both pairs of lovers being separated. Margaretta (disguised as a ballad singer) arrives in search of Robin and witnesses the stepmother entertaining the lawyer, whom she hides when the men return. Margaretta sings a ballad in which she reveals that meat, cake and the lawyer are all concealed in the house. The lawyer is sent packing, peace is made between husband and wife, and the sailors – now rich because they have found a barrel of gold in their wrecked ship – are reunited with their lovers.

A manuscript full score survives (*GB-Lcm*), which is assigned by Roger Fiske (in his edition, 1959) to a date three or four years after the première. He describes the score as an adaptation made for performance at the Little Theatre in the Haymarket, citing a reduction of wind parts from eight to six. The orchestration includes a carillon but is otherwise unexceptional. As usual, Storace adapted some music from other composers. However, these borrowings are unusual in that none is from an Italian opera other than Storace's own. Two are from operas by Grétry, two remain unidentified and one is closely related to the Act 1 finale of Storace's *Gli equivoci*. Storace adapted 'How often thus I'm forced to roam' from 'Ah perché di quel ingrato', which he composed for *Gli equivoci* and then borrowed with its original text for *La cameriera astuta*. *No Song, No Supper* includes twice as many solo songs as ensembles, which is a high proportion for an opera by Storace. The vast majority of the solos are strophic. As a result the opera is full of tuneful and easily memorable melodies which, combined with a lively plot, may have accounted for its immediate success.

JANE GIRDHAM

Noté, Jean (*b* Tournai, 6 May 1859; *d* Brussels, 1 April 1922). Belgian baritone. He studied in Ghent, where he made his concert début in 1883. Early operatic work there and in Lille and Antwerp led to an engagement at La Monnaie, Brussels, in 1887. From 1893 his career centred on the Paris Opéra, where he sang for more than 20 years. At Covent Garden in 1897 his roles included Amonasro, Escamillo, Valentin, Nevers (in *Les Huguenots*), Mercutio and Wolfram; but, despite his ready availability, he had no great success either there or at the Metropolitan in 1908–9. He also appeared in Berlin and Monte Carlo, and was a prolific recording artist, stylistically somewhat rough and uninteresting, but sturdy of tone.

J. B. STEANE

Not for Love Alone. Opera by R. K. Shchedrin; *see* NE TOL'KO LYUBOV'.

Nottara, Constantin C(onstantin) (*b* Bucharest, 13 Oct 1890; *d* Bucharest, 19 Jan 1950). Romanian composer. After studying at the Bucharest Conservatory (1900–07), in Paris (1907–9), where his teachers included Enescu, and in Berlin (1909–13), he made a career as a violinist and conductor. He was also active as a music critic. His compositions include orchestral and chamber works, ballets and four operas. Although his ballets are influenced by Romanian folklore, the operas are written in the *verismo* manner.

Cu dragostea nu se glumeşte [Love is not a Joke], 1933 (comic op, 3, C. Nottara, after A. de Musset), Bucharest, 8 Feb 1941
La drumul mare [On the Highway] (1, Nottara, after A. P. Chekhov), Cluj, Romanian Opera, 3 Oct 1934

Se face ziuă [At Dawn] (1, Nottara, after Z. Bârsan), Bucharest Radio, 1943
Ovidiu [Ovid], 1950 (5, S. Zaleski, after V. Alecsandri); rev. and completed W. Berger, 1960; excerpts Bucharest Radio, 1966

O. L. Cosma: *Opera românească* (Bucharest, 1962)
G. Constantinescu and others: *Ghid de operă* [Opera Guide] (Bucharest, 1971)
VIOREL COSMA

Notte critica, La [*Die unruhige Nacht*] ('The Hazardous Night'). *Opera buffa* in three acts by FLORIAN LEOPOLD GASSMANN to a libretto by CARLO GOLDONI; Vienna, Burgtheater, 5 January 1768.

The libretto is a conventional but amusing exercise in *commedia dell'arte* high-jinks. A wealthy miser, Pandolfo (bass), guards his two daughters jealously; the elder, Cecilia (soprano), is intent on a tryst with her beloved Leandro (tenor), while the younger, Dorina (soprano), threatens to alert her father. The ingenious maid Marinetta (contralto) abets the lovers while coping with the attentions of her two suitors, Carlotto (tenor) and Fabrizio (bass), who spend their time hiding in closets and being mistaken for one another. To a plot laden with physical action, Gassmann's score adds vibrant, rhythmically active accompaniments. Ensembles are few, but the arias and finales are eventful.

JOSHUA KOSMAN

Nottetempo ('Night-time'). *Dramma lirico* in one act by SYLVANO BUSSOTTI to a libretto by the composer and Romano Amidei; Milan, Teatro Lirico, 7 April 1976.

After an introductory chorus sung by martyrs and partisans and based on the motet *Spem in alium* by Thomas Tallis, the stage shows the interior of the Sistine chapel; Michelangelo Buonarroti (tenor) is at work at his frescos when Pope Julius II (baritone) enters. After a discussion with the Pope, Michelangelo falls from the scaffolding and remains injured on the ground. Fantasies of human suffering in other ages are visualized; Michelangelo sees himself as Philoctetes and Pope Julius as Ulysses. The final chorus ('Gloria') glorifies art which came into existence through the suffering of the artists.

Bussotti's score, the first to be called 'Bussottioperaballet', makes use of numerous musical quotations which are transformed by a web of dissonant voices added to the original music. To Tallis's *Spem in alium*, in 40 vocal parts, Bussotti added 40 dissonant instrumental parts, creating a very dense texture of great beauty. He used a technique of composition and decomposition, giving instructions in the score for the adding and taking away of different elements of the orchestral texture, so that passages of chamber-like sound are interspersed with ones of extreme density. Dance plays an important role in this work, as in others by Bussotti from the 1970s, part of the tendency of his theatre towards a 20th-century *Gesamtkunstwerk*. Bussotti's score contains the entire visual material for staging and costumes, the use of which is required for all productions.

JÜRGEN MAEHDER

Nouguès, Jean(-Charles) (*b* Bordeaux, 26 April 1875; *d* Paris, 28 Aug 1932). French composer. Born into a wealthy family, he was able to devote his life to the composition of operas and to obtaining their performance. He was almost entirely self-taught, although he studied for a short time with Gaston Sarreau. *Le roi du Papagey* was written before he was

16. Over 8000 performances of his works took place during his lifetime.

La mort de Tintagiles, a Maeterlinck setting following Debussy's *Pelléas* by only three years, shows little influence of the declamatory style of that opera. Maeterlinck's mistress, Georgette Leblanc, created the important role of Ygraine. *Quo vadis?* was Nouguès's most celebrated work and is a large-scale affair. Despite considerable adverse criticism it was mounted many times and was popular in its day. Set in ancient Rome, it concerns the plight of Christian martyrs and in particular the fate of Lygie (dramatic soprano), whose beauty has attracted the attention of a Roman warrior, Vinicius (tenor). The apostle Peter makes an appearance floating on the water and there are choral scenes of an epic nature as the Christians sing before being thrown to the lions. *La danseuse de Pompéi* is concerned with the destruction of Pompeii. Criticized for its lack of plot, it was Nouguès's last large-scale opera.

Nouguès's musical style is conventional and he attempted to emulate the style of several other composers. He was considered by some to be little more than an amateur who was trying his hand at naturalistic operas, a judgment hardly borne out by his undeniable success at having his works performed.

Yannka [Yannha; Yanuka] (H. Nouguès), Bordeaux, Grand, 1897
Le roy du Papagey des papegais (3), Bordeaux, Grand, 22 March 1901
Rêve de Noël (mystère, 1, J. Nouguès), 1902, vs (1902)
Thamyris (conte lyrique, prol., 4 scenes, J. Sardou and J. Gounouilhou), Bordeaux, Grand, 17 March 1904, vs (1904)
La mort de Tintagiles (drame lyrique, 3, after M. Maeterlinck), Paris, Mathurins, 28 Dec 1905, vs (1907)
Le désir, la chimère de l'amour (pantomime, 1, F. de Croisset), Paris, Mathurins, 6 Feb 1906
Quo vadis? (5, H. Cain, after H. Sienkiewicz), Nice, Opéra Municipal, 10 Feb 1909, vs (Paris, 1908)
Chiquito, le joueur de pelote (4, Cain, after P. Loti), Paris, OC (Favart), 30 Oct 1909, vs (1909); after his Basque (scène-ballet, 1), 1902
L'auberge rouge (nouvelle lyrique, 2, S. Basset, after H. de Balzac), Nice, Casino Municipal, 16 Feb 1910, vs (Paris, 1910)
La vendetta (drame lyrique, 3, R. de Flers and G.-A. de Caillavet, after Loriot-Lecaudey), Marseilles, Opéra, 25 Jan 1911, vs (Paris, 1911)
L'aigle (épopée lyrique, 3, Cain and L. Payen), Rouen, Arts, 1 Feb 1912, vs (Paris, 1912)
La danseuse de Pompéï (opéra-ballet, 5, H. Ferrare and Cain, after J. Bertheroy), Paris, OC (Favart), 29 Oct 1912, vs (1912)
Narkiss (conte-ballet avec chant, 1, J. Brindejant-Offenbach and Mme Mariquita, after J. Lorrain), Deauville, Casino Municipal, 31 July 1913, vs (Paris, 1913)
L'éclaircie (H. de Forge and E. Bertrand), Paris, Antoine, 31 Jan 1914
Le Dante, 1914 (3, J. Nouguès), Bordeaux, Grand, 26 Jan 1930
Le mari trop avisé [L'homme qui vendit son âme au diable] (operetta, P. Weber and S. Weber), Paris, Gaîté-Lyrique, 1926
Jean de France, Paris, Gaîté-Lyrique, 10 May 1931
Le scarabée bleu (operetta, A. Barde), 1931
Une aventure de Villon, 1932 (farce, 1, P. Cleronc, after Villon: Troquez, nippes), unperf.

*

C. d'Ys: 'Le Roy du Papagai', *Le théâtre*, no.64 (1901), 19–24
Brétigny: 'Thamyris au Grand Théâtre de Bordeaux', *Musica*, no.19 (1904), 315
J. Brindejoint-Offenbach: 'Grand Théâtre de Bordeaux: *Thamyris*', *Le théâtre*, no.161 (1905), 12–16
J. Copeau: '*La mort de Tintagiles*', *Le théâtre*, no.172 (1906), 20–24
P. Locard: 'Jean Nouguès, Ch. Silver, André Bloch, Francis Bousquet', *Le théâtre lyrique en France* (Paris, 1937–9), iii, 242–56 [pubn of Poste National/Radio-Paris]
J. Combarieu and R. Dumesnil: 'Réalistes et naturalistes', *Histoire de la musique des origines à nos jours*, iv (Paris, 1958), 84–110
RICHARD LANGHAM SMITH

Nourrit, Adolphe (*b* Montpellier, 3 March 1802; *d* Naples, 8 March 1839). French tenor, son of Louis Nourrit. He studied with the elder García for 18 months, initially against his father's wishes, then made his début at the Opéra in 1821 as Pylades in *Iphigénie en Tauride*. He was coached intensively by Rossini and created the roles of Neocles in *Le siège de Corinthe*, Count Ory, Aménophis in *Moïse et Pharaon* and Arnold in *Guillaume Tell*. Among the other roles he created were Masaniello (*La muette de Portici*), Robert (*Robert le diable*), Eléazar (*La Juive*) and Raoul (*Les Huguenots*). From December 1826, when he succeeded his father as first tenor at the Opéra, until his resignation in October 1836, he created the principal tenor roles in all major new productions, generating an entire repertory for the acting tenor. His success in *Moïse* and *Le siège de Corinthe* was so great that in 1827 he was appointed *professeur de déclamation pour la tragédie lyrique* at the Conservatoire, where his most famous student was the dramatic soprano Cornélie Falcon.

Moïse marked a turning-point in singing at the Opéra, as the singers turned to the more open-voiced, italianate production favoured by Rossini. Here, as in all the scores written for Nourrit, the dynamics and the thickness of the orchestration below his voice part indicate that he could not have been singing in falsetto in his upper register (as has often been stated). He had a mellow, powerful voice that extended to *eb"*; *d"* was the

Adolphe Nourrit's costume for the title role of Meyerbeer's 'Robert le diable' which he created in the original production at the Paris Opéra in 1831: engraving from A. Martinet, 'La petite galerie dramatique', plate 719

highest he ever sang in public. As Nourrit's status at the Opéra increased, so did his influence upon new productions. He wrote the words of Eléazar's aria 'Rachel, quand du Seigneur' and insisted that Meyerbeer rework the love-duet climax of Act 4 of *Les Huguenots* until it met with his approval.

About 1 October 1836, Charles Duponchel engaged Gilbert Duprez as joint first tenor at the Opéra. Nourrit accepted this arrangement in case he should fall ill (among other reasons). He sang *Guillaume Tell* superbly with Duprez in the audience on 5 October. On 10 October, during *La muette de Portici*, with Duprez again in the house, Nourrit suddenly went hoarse. He thought he was being mocked by the claque as they overdid their bravos. After the performance Berlioz and George Osborne walked the tenor up and down the boulevards as he despaired and talked of suicide. On 14 October he resigned; his farewell performance was on 1 April 1837. He immediately set out to perform in the provinces, but a liver condition (possibly the result of alcoholism) and its effects on his singing forced him to cut short his tours. While listening to Duprez at the Opéra, on 22 November 1837, he decided to go to Italy in the hope of succeeding Rubini on his retirement, and left Paris in December 1837.

The following March he began to study in Naples with Donizetti. He worked to eradicate nasal resonance, but as a result lost his head voice. He wanted Donizetti to write the opera for his Naples début, *Poliuto*; when it was forbidden because of its Christian subject matter, Nourrit felt betrayed. His wife, arriving in July 1838, was shocked at the sound of his voice and his thinness; he was being leeched regularly and was constantly hoarse. But his Naples début in Mercadante's *Il giuramento* (14 November 1838) was a success. As his liver disease advanced, his mental health deteriorated and his memory began to fail. On 7 March 1839 he sang at a benefit concert, was disappointed in his performance and upset by the favourable reaction of the audience. The following morning, he jumped to his death from the Hotel Barbaia.

Nourrit's brother, the tenor Auguste Nourrit (1808–53), was for some time theatre director at The Hague, Amsterdam and Brussels, and took over his post at the Conservatoire after his death.

For further illustration *see* COMTE ORY, LE and ROBERT LE DIABLE.

M. L. Quichérat: *Adolphe Nourrit: sa vie* (Paris, 1867)
B. de Monvel: *Adolphe Nourrit* (Paris, 1903)
E. P. Walker: *Adolphe Nourrit* (diss., Peabody Institute, John Hopkins U., 1989)   EVAN WALKER

Nourrit, Louis (*b* Montpellier, 4 Aug 1780; *d* Brunoy, 23 Sept 1831). French tenor, father of Adolphe Nourrit. He entered the Paris Conservatoire in 1802 and began to study with Pierre Garat in the following year. He made his Opéra début on 3 March 1805 as Renaud in Gluck's *Armide*, and later appeared with success as Orpheus. Fétis considered that his engagement marked the beginning of a revival in French singing, his predecessors having been more concerned with generating dramatic excitement than with purity of line. He was a reticent actor at first but later gained assurance, and in 1812 he replaced Etienne Lainez as the Opéra's principal tenor. He sang in the premières of Cherubini's *Les abencérages* (1813) and Spontini's *Olimpie* (1819), and in 1826 appeared opposite his son Adolphe in the

première of Rossini's *Le siège de Corinthe* (9 October). Although his voice was still in good condition, he retired two months later, leaving his son to take over the more florid and demanding new tenor repertory. He lacked ambition as a performer, and throughout his career at the Opéra he also worked as a diamond merchant.

PHILIP ROBINSON

Nouvelles aventures. Music-theatre piece by György Ligeti; *see* AVENTURES, NOUVELLES AVENTURES.

Nova, Vangjo (*b* Korçë, 27 Jan 1927; *d* Tirana, 5 Jan 1992). Albanian composer. He began as a classical guitarist, then worked as assistant chorus master at the Tirana Theatre of Opera and Ballet, 1952–69. From 1969 to 1984 he taught at the Artistic School Jordan Misja, Tirana (founded 1946), which was the first of its kind in Albania and nurtured many pioneers of Albanian music. Nova was self-taught as a composer.

His first opera, *Heroina* ('The Heroine'), received its première in Tirana on 17 June 1967. Set during the war of national liberation (1940–44), it tells of struggle and revolutionary optimism and the music is based on a succession of well-known partisan melodies. His second opera, *Pishtare* ('The Torch of Learning'), was completed in 1989. It deals with events leading to the opening in Korçë in 1886 of the first school in Albania permitted to teach in the Albanian language.

S. Kalemi: *Arritjet e artit tonë muzikor* [The Arrival of our Musical Art] (Tirana, 1982)
J. Emerson: *Albania: the Search for the Eagle's Song* (Studley, Warwicks., 1990)   JUNE EMERSON

Novák, Vítězslav [Viktor Augustin Rudolf] (*b* Kamenice nad Lipou, 5 Dec 1870; *d* Skuteč, 18 July 1949). Czech composer. A southern Bohemian by birth, he had a rebellious and headstrong nature that led him into many unpleasant situations and conflicts but also drove him to realize many of his artistic concepts. He learnt the piano and violin from childhood; after leaving school he went to Prague to study law and then philosophy, but he simultaneously studied harmony and counterpoint at the Prague Conservatory. Eventually he changed to music, joining Dvořák's composition class, and became one of his best pupils along with Josef Suk and Oskar Nedbal. For years Novák made his living by private teaching. In 1909 he was appointed professor of the master school of the Prague Conservatory, where he was one of the most influential teachers until his retirement in 1940. His pupils there included many future opera composers, such as Otakar Jeremiáš, Karel Hába, Boleslav Vomáčka and Ilja Hurník; he was the first to shape the talents of the Slovak composers Ján Cikker, Alexander Moyzes, Eugen Suchoň and others. He was awarded many official prizes and honours, including the title of National Artist in 1945.

Novák was one of the most important promoters of modern Czech music, and he was able to fill the traditional sources of inspiration with new, strong and subjective experience while remaining close to folk music. Besides two pantomimes (*Signorina Gioventù*, 1926–8, and *Nikotina*, 1929) he wrote four operas, all of them during his period of full artistic maturity. However, he had first tried his hand at dramatic techniques in the 1890s: attracted by the period of Charles IV of Bohemia, he composed a symphonic overture based on the drama *Maryša* by the Mrštík brothers (1898). He was also drawn to Stroupežnický's comedy *Zvíkovský rarášek* ('The Imp of Zvíkov Castle'), which he eventually set to music in 1913–14, when in a happy frame of mind around the time of the birth of his son Jaroslav. This one-act piece was intended as a mere 'merry episode from an old Czech nobleman's household'; it follows Stroupežnický's text exactly (in this Novák emulated Ostrčil in *Poupě*, 'The Bud'), consciously using light humour, simple musical expression and declamation.

Novák's opera *Karlštejn* ('Karlštejn Castle') was composed in the war years of 1914–16, which undoubtedly explains his addition of more solemn features and patriotic pathos to Jaroslav Vrchlický's original comedy: the Czech Queen Alžběta (soprano) gains access to her husband Charles IV (bass) and his castle in disguise, despite having been forbidden to do so. Novák uses a musical structure like those of his larger symphonic compositions, and his flexible but weighty orchestral writing overshadows the vocal parts, which are more lyrical and rhythmic. The fast-moving action is enhanced by leitmotifs, composed predominantly as symphonic themes. The fairy-tale idyll *Lucerna* ('The Lantern', 1923), with its mysterious setting in a twilit forest, inspired the composer to delightful imitative effects, as in some of his earlier works. In depicting the Czech landscape Novák was able to draw on the operatic tradition of Smetana and Dvořák, and this is evident in the vocal parts and the characterization. In *Dědův odkaz* ('Grandfather's Legacy', 1926) the symphonic character of Novák's writing grows even stronger; the harmony and sound world of this opera are probably the most sophisticated in all of his work. The plot, however, is much less effective, probably owing to hasty work by the librettist; though the libretto was rewritten in 1943, some of its serious faults remained. Of Novák's operas *The Lantern* has been staged the most often (more than 20 times by 1990). *The Imp of Zvíkov Castle* and *Grandfather's Legacy* appear infrequently, and *Karlstein Castle* very seldom.

See also LUCERNA.

Zvíkovský rarášek [The Imp of Zvíkov Castle] op.49 (comic op, 1, L. Stroupežnický), Prague, National, 10 Oct 1915
Karlštejn [Karlštejn Castle] op.50 (3, O. Fischer, after J. Vrchlický: *Noc na Karlštejně* [A Night at Karlštejn]), Prague, National, 18 Nov 1916
Lucerna [The Lantern] op.56 (musical fairy-tale, 4, H. Jelínek, after A. Jirásek), Prague, National, 13 May 1923
Dědův odkaz [Grandfather's Legacy] op.57 (lyric op with symphonic interludes, 3, A. Klášterský, after A. Heyduk), Brno, National, 16 Jan 1926

*

O. Šourek: 'Novákovo dílo operní' [Novák's Operatic Work], *Národní a stavovské divadlo* (1926–7), no.12, pp.2–3
I. Krejčí: 'Operní dílo V. Nováka' [The Operatic Work of Novák], *Národní divadlo* (1930–31), no.15, p.4
F. Pala: 'Nováková tvorba jevištní' [Novák's Stage Works], *Tempo*, x (1930–31), 123–40
Novák contra Ostrčil (Prague, 1931)
A. Srba, ed.: *Vítězslav Novák: studie a vzpomínky* [Studies and Memories] (Prague, 1932, suppls., 1935, 1940)
J. Hutter and Z. Chalabala, eds.: *České umění dramatické, ii: Zpěvohra* [Czech Dramatic Art: Opera] (Prague, 1941), 268–82
V. Novák: *O sobě a jiných* [On Himself and Others] (Prague, 1946)
M. Skalická: *Tvůrčí rozvoj V. Nováka v létech 1914–25: tvorba operní* [Novák's Creative Development in 1914–25: the Operatic Work] (diss., U. of Prague, 1958)
V. Lébl: *Vítězslav Novák: život a dílo* [Life and Work] (Prague, 1964)

R. Budiš, ed.: *Vítězslav Novák: výběrová bibliografie* [Selective Bibliography] (Prague, 1970)
L. Polyakova: 'Vítězslav Novák i ego opera Karlštejn' [Novák and his Opera *Karlstein Castle*], *SovM* (1970), no.10, pp.129–36
EVA HERRMANNOVÁ

Novelli [Novello; Monticelli Novelli], **(Antonio) Felice** (*b* Venice; *fl* 1717–62). Italian tenor. His career centred on Venice, where he appeared in 21 operas between 1717 and 1749. He also sang in Rome (1720, 1729), Turin (1720–22, 1739–40), Bergamo (*c*1726) and Florence (1728). In 1743 he sang Mathusius in Gluck's *Demofoonte* in Milan, Bologna and Reggio Emilia. He was a 'virtuoso' of the Duke of Massa and Carrara in about 1726, of Princess Henrietta of Hesse-Darmstadt (a native of Modena) in 1749 and of Duke Philip of Parma in 1762; that year he also sang in two *farsette* at Florence. Most of his Venetian appearances were in the less important theatres, especially the tiny S Moisè. He was occasionally primo uomo, but specialized in *buffo* parts after 1747.

*

S. Mamy: 'La diaspora dei cantanti veneziani nella prima metà del settecento', *Nuovi studi vivaldiani: edizione e cronologia critica delle opere* (Florence, 1988), ii, 591–631   COLIN TIMMS

Novello, Ivor [Davies, David Ivor] (*b* Cardiff, 15 Jan 1893; *d* London, 6 March 1951). British composer. His mother was a well-known music teacher and he grew up knowing many prominent musicians. He played the piano, gained a scholarship to Magdalen College School, Oxford, as a treble, and later studied the organ and theory with Herbert Brewer. At 17 he had a song published and performed at the Albert Hall with himself as accompanist, and his song 'Keep the home fires burning' enjoyed enormous popularity during World War I.

Novello composed music for several musical comedies and revues, but from the mid-1920s concentrated on his career as a playwright and as a romantic actor. With *Glamorous Night* (1935) he once more turned to composition with a series of romantic musical plays with himself as non-singing male lead. The most successful was *The Dancing Years* (1939), which ran almost continuously in London or on tour for ten years. He died only a few hours after playing the lead in his *King's Rhapsody*.

selective list; first performed in London unless otherwise stated

Theodore & Co (musical play, 2, H. M. Harwood, G. Grossmith, A. Ross and C. Grey, after P. Gavault), Gaiety, 19 Sept 1916, collab. P. Braham and J. Kern; The Golden Moth (musical play, 3, F. Thompson and P. G. Wodehouse), Adelphi, 5 Oct 1921; Glamorous Night (romantic play with music, 2, Novello and C. Hassall), Drury Lane, 2 May 1935; Careless Rapture (musical play, 2, Novello and Hassall), Drury Lane, 11 Sept 1936; Crest of the Wave (musical play, 2, Novello and Hassall), Drury Lane, 1 Sept 1937
The Dancing Years (musical play, 2, Novello and Hassall), Drury Lane, 23 March 1939; Arc de Triomphe (play with music, 3, Novello and Hassall), Phoenix, 9 Nov 1943; Perchance to Dream (musical romance, 2, Novello and Hassall), Hippodrome, 21 April 1945; King's Rhapsody (musical romance, 2, Novello and Hassall), Manchester, Palace, 24 Aug 1949; Gay's the Word (musical play, 2, Novello and A. Melville), Manchester, Palace, 17 Oct 1950; Valley of Song (musical romance, 3, Novello, Hassall and P. Park); completed by R. Hammer, Blackpool, 1963

*

GänzlBMT
C. N. Davies: *The Life I have Loved* (London, 1940)
P. Noble: *Ivor Novello: Man of the Theatre* (London, 1951)
W. Macqueen-Pope: *Ivor* (London, 1952)
R. Rose: *Perchance to Dream* (London, 1974)
S. Wilson: *Ivor* (London, 1975)

M. Ellis: *Those Dancing Years* (London, 1982)
J. Harding: *Ivor Novello* (London, 1987)   ANDREW LAMB

Noverre, Jean-Georges (*b* Paris, 29 April 1727; *d* St Germain-en-Laye, 19 Oct 1810). French-Swiss choreographer. Son of a Swiss soldier and a Frenchwoman, he rejected a military career for the dance at an early age; by 1740 he was a pupil of the Parisian dancing-master Marcel, and later of Louis Dupré, first dancer of the Paris Opéra. He probably made his début in June 1743 with a troupe directed by Dupré and J.-B. Lany in Monnet's Opéra-Comique at the Foire St Laurent, performing Favart's vaudeville *Le coq du village*; in October he danced at Fontainebleau. His early contacts at the Opéra-Comique with Marie Sallé and with Rameau's music were seminal. In 1744 he joined Lany in Berlin, where he danced in Hasse's *Arminio* (1745) and probably in works by Graun.

Noverre returned to France with Lany about the end of 1747, became ballet-master at Marseilles or at Strasbourg and in 1748 choreographed his first work, *Les fêtes chinoises*. It was probably at Strasbourg in 1749–50 that he met the dancer and actress Marie-Louise Sauveur, whom he married. In April 1750 he became principal dancer at Lyons, partnering Marie Camargo. There, in 1751, he staged *Le jugement de Paris*, his first serious pantomime ballet; it preceded his next similar venture by at least eight years. (Gluck's *Don Juan*, with which Gasparo Angiolini claimed primacy, dates from 1761.) During his engagements at Strasbourg (1753–4) and Paris (1754–5, at the Opéra-Comique) Noverre seems to have been restricted to more conventional entertainments; but with everchanging asymmetrical patterns, carefully coordinated costumes, scenery and lighting and occasional mimed episodes, he considerably altered the effect of traditional entrées. Having failed to gain a post at the Opéra, he arranged with David Garrick to direct a troupe of dancers at Drury Lane Theatre, London, in the 1755–6 and 1756–7 seasons. Unfortunately anti-French sentiment ran high at the time of his visit and his elaborate staging of *Les fêtes chinoises* (8 November 1755) was a failure and provoked infamous riots. But his contact with Garrick produced a positive result: during convalescence after an illness Noverre wrote a book on dancing and the theatre, *Lettres sur la danse*. He put his ideals into practice at the Lyons Opéra, where he collaborated with the composer François Granier in 13 new works between 1757 and 1760, including three of a serious nature (though his lighter, colourful pantomime ballets were the most successful). The dissemination of his works, through former colleagues like V. Saunier, and the enthusiastic Lyons reviews were but a prelude to the renown he gained with the appearance in autumn 1759 of his *Lettres* (with the publication date 1760); esteemed by the literary élite, the treatise was bitterly criticized by Noverre's colleagues. In 1760 he moved to the Württemberg court at Stuttgart, where he worked with the scenographer Servandoni, the costumer Boquet, a large company of dancers (including as guests Gaetano and Angiolo Vestris from Paris) and the musical leadership of Jommelli, Florian Deller and J. J. Rodolphe. Of his 20 new ballets there, *Médée et Jason* (1763) proved his most popular work, and like several of his Stuttgart ballets it was produced all over Europe by other choreographers, most of them his own pupils. He later complained that, when the company dispersed in 1767, 30 dancers became *maîtres de ballet*, 'spread out into Italy, Germany, England, Spain and Portugal ... and rendered only very imperfectly the products of my imagination'.

After negotiations for posts in Warsaw and, through Garrick, in London, Noverre accepted the important position of ballet-master to the imperial family and the two theatres in Vienna. The Viennese, having supported Hilverding's choreographic experiments and the collaborations of his pupil Angiolini with Gluck and Calzabigi, were receptive to Noverre's pantomimes. This was the peak of his career. He staged at least 38 new ballets and revived many earlier ones – as well as choreographing some operas (including Gluck's *Alceste* and *Paride ed Elena*). Under his supervision Starzer (at the Burgtheater) and Aspelmayr (Kärntnertortheater) wrote ballets which, like some of those by Noverre's Stuttgart collaborators, proved to be their best music: these contained, besides conventional closed forms for the set-piece dances, rhapsodic and overtly programmatic sections to accompany mimed episodes, anticipating developments in other instrumental genres. Noverre included in his programme notes for *Les Horaces et les Curiaces* (1774) a 19-page introduction, *Petite réponse aux grandes lettres du Sr. Angiolini*, answering Angiolini's critical *Lettere ... a Monsieur Noverre sopra i balli pantomimi* (Milan, 1773), which initiated a series of polemics that continued for three years.

Having failed to negotiate contracts with Stuttgart or London, Noverre accepted in 1774 an invitation from the Regio Ducal Teatro in Milan. Angiolini replaced him in Vienna. The Milanese had already seen several Noverre ballets in productions by his pupils. His own efforts, however, were poorly received; his notices in printed programmes show his growing bitterness. Angiolini's publications and the barrage of anonymous pamphlets reflect an Italian aesthetic viewpoint put most clearly by the Milanese Count Pietro Verri (letters of 15 March and 3 June 1775), who predicted that Noverre would fail in Paris; he was soon proved right. Noverre left Milan and spent spring and summer 1776 managing a company at the Vienna Kärntnertortheater, then took up the long-sought-after position at the Paris Opéra, always the centre of his ambitions and the chief object of his reformist ideals. He blamed the intrigues against his leadership, instigated by his rivals Gardel and Dauberval, for his failures and eventual resignation; but comments by dispassionate observers were not unlike those voiced at Milan. Apart from a uniquely French disapproval of his insistence on producing independent ballets in preference to dances complementing an opera, criticism centred on the works themselves: his chosen themes were thought unsuited to representation in dance, and his lengthy productions neglecting pure dance for pantomime were often found enigmatic. His pretentious programme notes decrying opposition to his aesthetic ideas aroused hostility. Paris audiences preferred his lighter works, including the revival of *Les petits riens* to music mainly by Mozart (1778); others failed utterly. His employment continued until July 1781, but his resignation had been accepted in November 1779 and he was largely inactive in the interim.

In November 1781, with dancers from Paris, Noverre began a brilliant season's engagement at the King's Theatre, London. He concentrated on splendid revivals of works which had earned him his reputation during his Stuttgart and Vienna days. Even Paris journals reported his triumphs: 'It is not without reason that Garrick called this artist the Shakespeare of the dance'

(Bachaumont, 4 June 1782). He was in retirement from June 1782 until March 1787, when he revived three ballets at Lyons; in London for the 1787–8 and 1788–9 seasons, he again relied mostly on proven successes of earlier years, and the titles of the few new works betray their nature as spectacular *divertissements* of the kind he had long proclaimed to be of secondary importance.

At the Revolution, Noverre escaped to the French countryside at Triel, but financial necessity forced a resumption of his career. He applied unsuccessfully for a court post in Sweden, then spent two seasons as a choreographer in London, where his only important new creation was the successful *Iphigenia in Aulide* (1793); his last known production, fittingly for one whose fortunes had collapsed with the French monarchy, was an allegorical ballet for Paisiello's cantata *La vittoria* (1794) celebrating the English victory over the French. He retired to St Germain-en-Laye and spent his last years revising and amplifying his earlier writings with observations on the rise and decline of pantomime ballet since his *Lettres*; he viewed the current French taste for virtuosity and spectacle with sadness, as a relapse into the infantile state from which he had laboured to raise his art.

In his work and his writings Noverre was most immediately influenced by the theories of Louis de Cahusac (*La danse ancienne et moderne*, 1754) and Denis Diderot (*Troisième entretien sur le fils naturel*, 1757), as well as the programmatic and individualistic dance music of Rameau, the expressive dancing of Marie Sallé, the realistic acting of David Garrick and the dramatic accompanied recitatives in the Italian operas of Hasse and Jommelli. Although Hilverding, Angiolini and others had worked towards the dramatic pantomime ballet, it was Noverre's *Lettres sur la danse* which focussed attention on the function of theatrical dance. In the preface to *Euthyme et Eucharis* (1773), he viewed the *ballet en action* as a union of dance, ballet and pantomime:

Dance is the Art of steps, of graceful movements and of lovely positions. Ballet, which borrows a part of its charms from Dance, is the Art of Design, of forms and of figures. Pantomime is purely that of feeling and of the emotions of the Soul expressed through gestures.

Like the Encyclopedists Noverre proclaimed the 'imitation of nature' and, further, the improvement on it by judicious selection. While he fired composers to create forward-looking descriptive music, he believed that the musician's work could begin only when the choreographer's plans were well advanced, and he detested the practice of fitting choreography to pre-composed music; for Angiolini, who was also a composer, the music dictated to the dance.

Noverre's writings, reprinted many times, have contributed more than his ballets to a distorted view of his importance: he continues to receive credit for reforms put into practice by several other choreographers at the same time. Nevertheless, the elegance and urgency of his prose and his practical, far-seeing approach make his treatise an undisputed landmark. He demanded an end to such repressive traditions as irrelevant and stereotyped, cumbersome costumes, head-dresses and masks, and to the continuing dominance of past musical styles, choreographic routines and all aspects of *le merveilleux*. He also urged aspiring ballet-masters to obtain a knowledge of great paintings, in order to apply the laws of perspective, lighting and colour gradation; of literature

and history, to select interesting subjects for portrayal and to costume them correctly; of contemporary drama, to establish a realistic acting style; of stage machinery and geometry; and of contemporary music, to know what could be expected of composers. The ballet was to be considered as a whole, including the need for diversity, satisfied by the elimination of traditional static, symmetrical groupings, introducing rapidly changing tableaux and using different dancing styles to suit different characters and themes; virtuoso displays had their place only if they did not interfere with dramatic truth. His own productions were so strongly unified that revivals often included not just the original choreography but also the costume designs and musical scores. He saw his work as achieving 'a revolution in dance as striking and as lasting as that achieved by Gluck in music'.

Ballets in: Favart: Cythère assiégée, Paris, 1754; Jommelli: Il trionfo d'Amore, Ludwigsburg, 1763; Gluck: Alceste, Vienna, 1767; Gluck: Paride ed Elena, Vienna, 1770; Gluck: Iphigénie en Aulide, Paris, 1777; Gluck: Armide, Paris, 1777; Piccinni: Roland, Paris, 1778; Gluck: Iphigénie en Tauride, Paris, 1779; Gluck: Echo et Narcisse, Paris, 1779; Floquet: Le seigneur bienfaisant, Paris, 1780; A Masked Ball (?pasticcio), London, 1782; Don Giovanni (pasticcio, music by Gazzaniga and Mozart), London, 1794

J.-G. Noverre: *Lettres sur la danse et sur les ballets* (Lyons and Stuttgart, 1760, 2/1783; Eng. trans., 1783; enlarged 1803 as *Lettres sur la danse*, i)

J. von Sonnenfels: *Briefe über die Wienerische Schaubühne* (Vienna, 1768)

G. Angiolini: *Lettere … a Monsieur Noverre sopra i balli pantomimi* (Milan, 1773)

——: *Riflessioni sopra l'uso dei programmi nei balli pantomimi* (Milan, 1775)

L. Petit de Bachaumont: *Mémoires secrets pour servir à l'histoire de la république des lettres en France* (London, 1777–89)

J.-G. Noverre: *Observations sur la construction d'une nouvelle salle d'opéra* (Amsterdam and Paris, 1781; repr. in *Lettres sur la danse*, iii, St Petersburg, 1804)

——: *Lettres sur la danse, sur les ballets et les arts* (St Petersburg, 1803–4, 2/1807 as *Lettres sur les arts imitateurs en général et sur la danse en particulier*) [incl. histories of theatre and dance, correspondence with Voltaire, comparison of national musical tastes, ballet programmes etc]

M. Tourneux, ed.: *Correspondance littéraire, philosophique et critique par Grimm, Diderot, Raynal, Meister etc.* (Paris, 1877–82)

E. Campardon: *L'Académie royale de musique au XVIIIe siècle* (Paris, 1884), ii, 202ff

J. Sittard: *Zur Geschichte der Musik und des Theaters am Württembergischen Hofe nach Original-Quellen* (Stuttgart, 1891), ii, 59, 94ff, 107, 198ff

H. Abert: 'J. G. Noverre und sein Einfluss auf die dramatische Ballettkomposition', *JbMP 1908*, 29–45

E. Greppi and A. Giulini, eds.: *Carteggio di Pietro e di Alessandro Verri* [Oct 1766–Sept 1782] (Milan, 1923)

R. M. Haas: 'Die Wiener Ballet-Pantomime im 18. Jahrhundert und Glucks Don Juan', *AMw*, x (1923), 6–36

D. Lynham: *The Chevalier Noverre: Father of Modern Ballet* (London, 1950)

P. Tugal: *Jean-Georges Noverre, der grosse Reformator des Tanzes* (Berlin, 1959)

D. Garrick: *Letters*, ed. D. M. Little and G. M. Kahrl (Cambridge, MA, 1963)

M. H. Winter: *The Pre-Romantic Ballet* (London, 1974)

K. K. Hansell: *Opera and Ballet at the Regio Ducal Teatro of Milan, 1771–1776: a Musical and Social History* (diss., U. of California, Berkeley, 1980)

J. Sasportes: 'Noverre in Italia', *La danza italiana*, ii (1985), 39–71

K. K. Hansell: 'Il ballo teatrale e l'opera italiana', *SOI*, v (1988), 197–241

J. Sasportes: 'Due nuove lettere sulla controversia tra Noverre e Angiolini', *La danza italiana*, vii (1989), 51–77

KATHLEEN KUZMICK HANSELL

Novi Sad (Hung. Ujvidék). Town in Serbia (Vojvodina) on the Danube. The Srpsko Narodno Pozorište (Serbian National Theatre) was founded in 1861 when the territory belonged to the Austro-Hungarian empire; its first building was erected in 1885 and operas were introduced into the repertory in 1896. Another theatre, built in 1895 (and burnt down in 1928), was occasionally used by visiting opera troupes performing in German or Hungarian. After World War I the Serbian theatre resumed operations and became especially successful under the direction of Lovro Matačić (1920–22); between 1937 and 1941 the staging of operas was taken over by S. Bombardelli. A modern theatre (937 seats) for both plays and operas was built in 1980. The opera company presents some eight performances a month (almost 90 a year), with each season including two to four premières.

ROKSANDA PEJOVIĆ

Novissimo. Theatre in Venice, opened in 1641 and closed in 1647; see VENICE, §2.

Novosibirsk. City in western Siberia, Russia, known as Novonikolayevsk up to 1925. Although the city was an occasional stop for touring operatic troupes from the later 19th century, local opera was slow to develop. The Gosudarstennaya Opera (State Opera) troupe operated within the Sibirskiy Gosudarstvenniy Teatr (Siberian State Theatre), opening in 1922 with a performance of Dargomïzhsky's *Rusalka* and presenting about 80 operas and other lyric works in an 800-seat hall every year until 1929. A long process of construction, beginning in 1931, finally produced one of the most lavish theatres in the USSR, a building (architect A. Grinberg) housing a 958-seat concert hall and the 2006-seat Novosibirskiy Gosudarstvenniy Akademicheskiy Teatr Operï i Baleta (Novosibirsk State Academic Theatre of Opera and Ballet), which opened on 9 May 1945 – VE Day in the USSR – with a performance of *A Life for the Tsar*. The theatre concentrates on Russian and foreign classics in its ten-month season, but has given premières of more recent works by Kas'yanov, E. L. Lazarev and G. Ivanov; it is noted for imaginative productions under one of its founders, I. A. Zak.

*

ME (M. M. Yakovlev)
G. Bernandt: *Slovar' oper vpervïye postavlennïkh ili izdannïkh v dorevolyutsionnoy Rossii i v SSSR 1736–1959* [Dictionary of Operas First Performed or Published in Pre-revolutionary Russia and in the USSR 1736–1959] (Moscow, 1962), 549
M. Rubina and I. Vershinina: *Novosibirskiy akademicheskiy* (Novosibirsk, 1979)
V. Kaluzhsky: 'Na stsene-russkaya opera' [Russian Opera is on Stage], *Novosibirsk teatral'nïy* (Novosibirsk, 1983), 44–61
Arkhitektura sovetskogo teatra (Moscow, 1986), 148
GREGORY SALMON

Novosielski, Michael (*b* Rome, 1750; *d* Ramsgate, 1795). Italian architect and scene designer. He was in England by 1772 and was first employed at Drury Lane in 1777. He was scene painter and machinist at the King's Theatre between 1781 and 1785, in 1782 reconstructing Vanbrugh's original theatre, converting the auditorium to a horseshoe shape. At the King's he designed scenery for operas, comic operas and ballets mostly by Noverre. He was scenographer for at least 12 composers including Bertoni, Anfossi and Rauzzini, and was also responsible for Cimarosa's *Il pittore parigino* (1785) and Cherubini's *Demetrio* (1785). In 1785–6 he was succeeded by Marinari but, after the fire at the King's in 1789, he was employed on rebuilding the theatre. He returned to the King's as painter and machinist for Paisiello's *L'amor contrastato* (1794), though on the British Library playbill his name is deleted.

*

S. Rosenfeld and E. Croft-Murray: 'A Checklist of Scene Painters Working in Great Britain and Ireland in the 18th Century (4)', *Theatre Notebook*, xix (1964–5), 133–45, esp.138–9
SYBIL ROSENFELD

Novotná, Jarmila (*b* Prague, 23 Sept 1907). Czech soprano. She studied in Prague with Emmy Destinn, and later in Milan, and made her début in Prague in 1925 as Mařenka. In 1928 she sang Gilda at the Verona Arena, and from 1933 to 1938 sang at the Vienna Staatsoper, making regular appearances at Salzburg as Octavian, Eurydice, Countess Almaviva, Pamina and Frasquita (*Der Corregidor*). In Vienna she created the title role in Lehár's *Giuditta* (1934). She made her American début in 1939 as Butterfly at San Francisco, and from 1940 to 1956 she was a valued member of the Metropolitan, where her repertory included Donna Elvira, Mimì, Octavian, Violetta, Freia and Mélisande. She returned to Europe after World War II and sang again at Salzburg, in Paris and in Vienna. She appeared in *The Merry Widow* at San Francisco and in the title role of Korngold's adaptation of *La belle Hélène* on Broadway.

HAROLD ROSENTHAL/R

Nowowiejski, Feliks (*b* Wartenburg [now Barczewo, nr Olsztyn], 7 Feb 1877; *d* Poznań, 18 Jan 1946). Polish composer. He studied at the Stern Conservatory in Berlin and at Regensburg, later returning to Berlin and taking part in Bruch's masterclasses. In addition he had lessons with Dvořák in Prague. He was director of the Kraków music society (1909–14), then taught at conservatories in Berlin (Scharwenka) and in Poznań, where he was professor of church music and organ. Nowowiejski composed in almost all genres. His output is not stylistically uniform, though his style is predominantly late Romantic; much of his music derives from Polish folktunes. Several of his operas were left unfinished or were only sketched, but he often incorporated material from them in operas he did complete. *Legenda Bałtyku* ('Baltic Legend') includes music from the abandoned *Busola* ('Compass', 1903) and *Casteletto* (1905). Constantly revised by the composer (as were his other operas), it became the most popular Polish opera in the period between the two world wars and was produced all over Poland. The influence of Puccini is evident, though there are also archaisms in the choruses, which are treated statically as in an oratorio. *Tatry* ('The Tatra Mountains') is closer to the impressionists in its orchestral colour and treatment of dissonance.

Emigranci [The Emigrants]/*Obieżysasy* op.46, 1917 (3, Z. Kollaren), unperf.
Legenda Bałtyku [Baltic Legend]/*Wineta* op.28 (3, W. Szalay-Groele and K. Jeżewska), Poznań, Wielki, 28 Nov 1924
Malowanki ludowe [Folklore Ornaments] (op-ballet, 1, after folk poetry), Poznań, Wielki, 1 Dec 1928
Tatry [The Tatra Mountains]/*Leluja* op.37 (op-ballet, 4, E. Zegadłowicz, after folk legends), Poznań, Wielki, 27 Feb 1929; later as *Król Wichrów* [King of the Winds]

*

J. Boehm: *Feliks Nowowiejski: zarys biograficzny* [Biographical Outline] (Olsztyn, 1968)

F. M. Nowowiejski and K. Nowowiejski: *Dookoła kompozytora: wspomnienia o ojcu (F. Nowowiejskim)* [On Composers: Recollections of Father] (Poznań, 1968)   ZOFIA CHECHLIŃSKA

Noye's Fludde. 'Chester miracle play' in one act, op.59, by BENJAMIN BRITTEN to his own libretto; Orford Church, Suffolk, 18 June 1958.

This 50-minute work was composed for the Aldeburgh Festival, with the aim of involving young singers and players alongside professionals. After a pre-ludial hymn, 'Lord Jesus think on me', sung by the congregation, the voice of God – spoken, 'tremendous' – instructs Noye (bass-baritone) to build an ark. In a lively ensemble his sons and their wives appear with tools. Mrs Noye (contralto) and her chorus of gossips poke fun, but the work is soon completed. After more quarrelling between Noye and his wife the animals assemble in march time. Noye and his children also embark and Mrs Noye, after some resistance, is carried aboard by her sons – without her gossips. The flood itself is depicted in an extended passacaglia, whose theme gradually assembles all 12 notes, and striking effects of wind and storm are conjured up with minimal resources. At the climax comes the hymn 'Eternal Father, strong to save', the congregation joining in for the last two verses. The storm over, raven and dove bring evidence of dry land. God instructs Noye and his companions to disembark, and after an Alleluia for the animals the work ends with the hymn 'The spacious firmament on high', set to Tallis's Canon. The entire score is a brilliant demonstration of how to combine the relatively elementary instrumental and vocal skills of amateurs with professionals to produce a highly effective piece of music theatre for church performance.

ARNOLD WHITTALL

Nozzari, Andrea (*b* Vertova, Bergamo, 1775; *d* Naples, 12 Dec 1832). Italian tenor. He studied in Bergamo and made his début in 1794 at Pavia. After singing in Rome, Milan, Parma and Bergamo, in 1803 he was engaged at the Théâtre Italien in Paris, appearing in Paer's *Principe di Taranto* and *Griselda*, Paisiello's *Nina* and Cimarosa's *Il matrimonio segreto*. From the 1811–12 season he was engaged in Naples, where he sang in Spontini's *La vestale*, Mayr's *Medea in Corinto* and Gluck's *Iphigénie en Aulide*. At the S Carlo he created roles in eight operas by Rossini: Leicester in *Elisabetta, regina d'Inghilterra* (1815); Rinaldo in *Armida* (1817); Osiride in *Mosè in Egitto* and Agorante in *Ricciardo e Zoraide* (1818); Pyrrhus in *Ermione* and Roderick Dhu in *La donna del lago* (1819); Erisso in *Maometto II* (1820) and Antenore in *Zelmira*, as well as the title role of Donizetti's *Alfredo il grande* (1823). At the Teatro del Fondo he created the title role of Rossini's *Otello* (1816), amazing the public with the force and agility of his singing as well as the nobility of his bearing. He retired in 1825.   ELIZABETH FORBES

Nozze, Le ('The Wedding'). *Dramma giocoso* in three acts by BALDASSARE GALUPPI to a libretto by CARLO GOLDONI; Bologna, Teatro Formagliari, 14 September 1755.

The Count (soprano) and Countess (contralto) are enjoying their favourite diversion, a heated argument, in this case over who should marry their chambermaid, the orphaned Dorina (soprano); the Count supports Titta (tenor), a servant, while the Countess proposes Mingone (tenor), the gardener. Both suitors boast of their

imminent marriage and the influence of their own promoter. Masotto (bass), chief agent of the household, offers a compromise, that he himself marry Dorina, and despite manoeuvring by another servant, Livietta (soprano), he succeeds in convincing his patrons. In the end, a double wedding is held: Masotto to Dorina and Titta to Livietta. The Count and Countess are reconciled, and only Mingone is left 'with a dry mouth'.

This popular comedy, which was given over 15 productions, is conventional in adhering to the model Galuppi and Goldoni created, with lengthy finales and both serious, bi-strophic arias and freely arranged comic ones.   DALE E. MONSON

Nozze di Figaro, Le ('The Marriage of Figaro'). *Opera buffa* in four acts, K492, by WOLFGANG AMADEUS MOZART to a libretto by LORENZO DA PONTE after PIERRE-AUGUSTIN BEAUMARCHAIS' play *La folle journée, ou Le mariage de Figaro* (1784, Paris); Vienna, Burgtheater, 1 May 1786.

Count Almaviva	baritone
Countess Almaviva	soprano
Susanna *her maid, betrothed to Figaro*	soprano
Figaro *valet to Count Almaviva*	bass
Cherubino *the Count's page*	mezzo-soprano
Marcellina *housekeeper to Bartolo*	soprano
Bartolo *a doctor from Seville*	bass
Don Basilio *music master*	tenor
Don Curzio *magistrate*	tenor
Barbarina *daughter of Antonio*	soprano
Antonio *gardener, Susanna's uncle*	bass

Villagers, peasants, servants

Setting Aguasfrescas near Seville, the Almavivas' country house; the action is contemporary with the play and opera

The operatic version of Beaumarchais' *Le mariage de Figaro* may have been a timely notion of Mozart's own. Although the play was banned from the Viennese stage, it was available in print and Paisiello's opera on the earlier play, *Le barbier de Séville*, had triumphed in Vienna in 1783 (and all over Europe). Mozart evidently studied Paisiello's handling of the same personalities and included deliberate references to it (see Heartz 1987; *see also* BARBIERE DI SIVIGLIA, IL (i)). Composition began late in 1785 and the opera may have been drafted in only six weeks. After some opposition attributed to the Italians, and (if Da Ponte is to be believed) after the librettist had overcome the emperor's objections, it was produced in May with an outstanding cast whose character and skills, as well as their performance in Paisiello's *Barbiere*, contributed to its conception: Francesco Benucci (Figaro), Nancy Storace (Susanna), Luisa Laschi (Countess), Stefano Mandini (Count), Dorotea Bussani (Cherubino), Maria Mandini (Marcellina), Francesco Bussani (Bartolo and Antonio), Michael Kelly, who discussed the event in his reminiscences (Basilio and Curzio), and Anna Gottlieb (Barbarina). Mozart may have expected Storace to sing the Countess; he rearranged the Act 2 trio and other passages so that Susanna took the upper line.

Contrary to what is often stated, *Figaro* was generally liked, as is indicated by the emperor's ban on excessive encores (only arias were to be repeated). There were, however, only nine performances in 1786; the Viennese preferred other works, such as Martín y Soler's *Una cosa rara*. *Figaro* was next given in Prague, where according to Mozart's report (letter of 15 January 1787) it created a furore and led to the commission for *Don Giovanni*. The successful Vienna revival (26 performances in 1789) preceded the commission for *Così fan tutte*: Susanna was confirmed as the prima donna's role when Mozart wrote two new arias for Adriana Ferrarese del Bene, Da Ponte's mistress and the first Fiordiligi.

By this time *Figaro* had received isolated performances in Italy (Acts 1 and 2, the rest composed by Angelo Tarchi, Monza, autumn 1787; Florence, spring 1788), and had been translated into German for performances in Prague (June 1787), Donaueschingen (1787), Leipzig, Graz and Frankfurt (1788), followed by other German centres over the next few years. These performances used spoken dialogue, as did the first performance in France (Paris Opéra, 1793, using Beaumarchais). Many productions were given in French-speaking centres during the 19th century. Other premières included Amsterdam (1794, in German); Madrid (1802, in Spanish); Budapest (1812, in German); London (1812, in Italian, following interpolations of numbers into other operas by Storace and Benucci; 1819, in English, reduced to three acts and arranged by Bishop); and New York (1824, in English, and 1858, in Italian). Numerous translations have been used during the 19th and 20th centuries. *Figaro* is now Mozart's most popular opera, displacing *Don Giovanni*. No major company lets many years elapse without presenting it; Glyndebourne opened with it in 1934.

In production, the vein of rococo nostalgia which inspired its epigone, *Der Rosenkavalier*, was displaced by greater realism by Visconti (1963, Rome) and Hall (1973, Glyndebourne); it is now customary to emphasize the socio-political tensions of Beaumarchais which Da Ponte had necessarily suppressed.

In *Il barbiere* Almaviva wooed Bartolo's ward Rosina with the aid of Figaro, now his valet. He has also, despite his Don Juanesque tendencies, abolished the *droit de Seigneur* whereby he had the right to deflower every bride among his feudal dependants.

For the overture Mozart abandoned a planned middle section, leaving an electrifying sonata without development which perfectly sets the scene for the 'Crazy Day'.

ACT 1 *An antechamber* The pacing motif and lyrical response in the opening duet ('Cinque, dieci') belong respectively to Figaro, who is measuring the room, and Susanna, who is trying on a new hat. She finally entices him from his work to admire her, and to sing her motif, suggesting that she may prove to be the stronger personality. Figaro tells her the Count has offered them this room, but she reacts with alarm. In the ensuing duet ('Se a caso madama') she mocks Figaro's imitation of the high and low bells of Count and Countess: the convenience of answering them will also make it easy for the Count to visit Susanna when she is alone. Figaro's confidence is shaken, but if the Count wants to dance, it is he, Figaro, who will call the tune (cavatina, 'Se vuol ballare'), first offering a minuet, then a Presto contredanse.

Figaro has promised to marry Marcellina if he cannot repay money he owes her. By helping her Bartolo will

avenge himself on Figaro (who thwarted his plans to marry Rosina in *Il barbiere*) and rid himself of an embarrassment (Marcellina). His exit aria ('La vendetta') has a full orchestra with trumpets, in the opera's principal key, D major. His vaunted legal knowledge brings formal counterpoint (and a phrase from *Lo sposo deluso*), but his fury also vents itself in comically undignified patter. Susanna finds Marcellina, and hustles her out, the music poised, the exchange of compliments venomous (duettino, 'Via resti servito'). Cherubino confides in Susanna. In a lyrical arch of melody over a sensuously muted accompaniment, he impulsively babbles of his love for all women ('Non so più'), an enchanting musical image of adolescence. The Count is heard; Susanna hides Cherubino behind a chair. Basilio's voice interrupts the Count's amorous proposals; while he too hides behind the chair, Cherubino nips on to it and Susanna covers him with a dress. Basilio's malicious (but accurate) observation that Cherubino adores the Countess rouses the Count. Gruffly, in an ascending line, he demands an explanation (trio, 'Cosa sento!'); Basilio, his motif unctuously descending, disclaims knowledge; Susanna, turning to the minor dominant, threatens to faint. The men officiously come to her aid (a new, ardent motif with a chromatic cadence). The Count describes his discovery of Cherubino in Barbarina's room, hidden under a cloth ... at which he is again revealed, to the Count's self-righteous indignation, Basilio's delight and Susanna's horror. Sonata form perfectly matches the action, the recapitulation fraught with irony (or, from Basilio, sarcasm). Figaro ushers in a rustic chorus praising the Count's magnanimity in renouncing his extra-marital right, but the Count refuses to be trapped into marrying the couple then and there, and banishes Cherubino with an officer's commission. While apparently sending him on his way to a bold march rhythm ('Non più andrai': no more frolicking and flirting; he is off to death or glory), Figaro detains the page for purposes of his own.

ACT 2 *The Countess's chamber* In an achingly tender Larghetto, sharing clarinet-based instrumentation with 'Non so più', the neglected Countess prays to the god of love to restore her husband's affections (cavatina, 'Porgi, Amor'). But she listens eagerly to Susanna and Figaro's plotting (Figaro leaves to a snatch of 'Se vuol ballare'). Cherubino is to be dressed as a girl, take Susanna's place, and compromise the Count. His ardour is formalized, in a song of his own composition, sung to Susanna's 'guitar' accompaniment, but it breaks into recondite modulations before the reprise; Mozart miraculously suggests, but evades, the clumsiness of a tyro (canzona, 'Voi che sapete'). Susanna tries to dress him but he keeps turning his gaze towards the Countess ('Venite, inginocchiatevi': an action aria replaced in 1789 by the strophic 'Un moto di gioia'). Alone with the Countess, Cherubino is close to winning her heart when the Count demands admittance: he has returned precipitately from the hunt because of an anonymous letter (part of Figaro's ill-laid plot). In confusion the Countess thrusts Cherubino into her closet; the Count asks questions; Susanna enters unseen. The Countess says Susanna is in the closet. The Count's jealous fury, his wife's terror and Susanna's anxious assessment of the situation again outline a sonata form, although the action does not advance (trio, 'Susanna, or via sortite'). When the Count leaves (to fetch tools to break down the door), taking the Countess, Susanna thrusts Cherubino through the window (duettino, 'Aprite, presto aprite') and enters the closet.

Mozart's most consummate comic finale begins by resuming the fury and anxiety of the trio (E♭, 'Ecci omai, garzon malnato'). The Countess confesses that Cherubino is in the closet but protests his innocence; the Count is ready to kill. But it is Susanna who emerges, to a simple minuet which mocks the nobles' consternation. Explanations and further confusion occupy an extended Allegro which deploys its thematic wealth with marvellous inventiveness. Although puzzled, the Count has to ask forgiveness. At the single abrupt key-change of the finale (B♭ to G) Figaro enters, again asking for an immediate wedding. Recovering his sang-froid (C major, gavotte tempo), the Count poses questions about the anonymous letter; Figaro prevaricates. Antonio charges in to complain of damage to his garden caused by the page's precipitate exit (Allegro molto, F major). The Count senses more chicanery; Figaro claims it was he who jumped. The tempo slows to Andante (in B♭) and with measured calm the Count questions Figaro about a paper the page has dropped: the music emerges from an harmonic cloud to a shining recapitulation as Figaro (prompted by the women) identifies it as the page's commission, left with him (he claims) to be sealed. The Count is baffled, but revives when Marcellina, Basilio and Bartolo rush in demanding justice (E♭).

ACT 3 *A large room decorated for the marriage-feast* The Countess urges Susanna to make an assignation with the Count; they will exchange cloaks and compromise him with his own wife. Susanna approaches him, explains her previous reticence as delicacy, and offers to meet him that evening. In a rare outburst in the minor (duet, 'Crudel! perchè finora') the Count reproaches her; changing to major, he sings of his coming happiness with exuberant syncopation. She tries to join in but trips over the right replies ('Yes' for 'No', etc.), correcting herself at a melodic high point. Leaving, she encounters Figaro and carelessly shows her satisfaction: 'without a lawyer we've won the case'. The Count is again suspicious and angry (the first obbligato recitative and aria, 'Vedrò, mentre io sospiro'). Must he sigh in vain while a mere servant wins the prize? The martial orchestration and key, even the contrapuntal language, recall Bartolo's aria, but the music snarls with aristocratic jealousy, not pompous self-importance: within the social structure of this opera it is a truly menacing utterance.

At the trial of Marcellina's case Curzio is finding for the plaintiff. Figaro protests that he cannot marry Marcellina without his parents' consent. It emerges that he is the lost son of Marcellina, and Bartolo reluctantly admits paternity. Marcellina embraces Figaro (sextet, 'Riconosci in questo amplesso') and the three express delight while the Count and Curzio mutter their annoyance. Susanna misinterprets the embrace and boxes Figaro's ears. The comical explanation leads to a quartet of satisfaction against which Curzio and the Count fling out a defiant phrase of anger.

The Countess, waiting for Susanna, muses on the past and wonders if there is hope for her marriage. This set piece (obbligato recitative and rondò, 'Dove sono i bei momenti', which, it has been argued, may have been intended to precede the previous scene) shows her as profoundly tender yet impulsive; it reaches a glowing *a″* at the climax. Antonio tells the Count that Cherubino is still in the castle. The Countess dictates a letter from Susanna to the Count confirming their rendezvous (duettino, 'Che soave zeffiretto'), their voices mingling in an expression of the love they feel, each for her own; the honeyed music shows none of the deviousness of their intentions.

During a choral presentation to the Countess, Cherubino is unmasked, but allowed to stay for the wedding as he (and Barbarina) are tempted to make revelations embarrassing to the Count. During the finale, the necessary action is cunningly woven into the sequence of dances. During the march the two couples (Marcellina and Bartolo have decided to regularize their union) are presented to the Count and Countess. The bridesmaids' duet and chorus (contredanse) precede the alluring fandango, during which Susanna slips the letter to the Count, sealed with a pin (to be returned as a sign of agreement); Figaro notices with amusement that the Count has pricked himself.

'Le mariage di Figaro': engraving by J.-P.-J. de Saint-Quentin showing the final denouement, from the first authentic edition of Beaumarchais' 'La folle journée, ou Le mariage de Figaro' (Paris: Kehl, 1785)

ACT 4 *The garden, at night; pavilions on either side* Barbarina, the go-between, has lost the pin (a mock-tragic cavatina, 'L'ho perduta'). Figaro, hearing her tale, concludes that Susanna is unfaithful; an abyss seems to open beneath him. Marcellina is inclined to warn Susanna; she must have a good reason for meeting the Count, and women should stick together ('Il capro e la capretta'). Barbarina is preparing to meet Cherubino in a pavilion. Figaro summons Basilio and Bartolo to witness the betrayal. Basilio moralizes about the wisdom of not resisting one's superiors, adding a tale of his own hot youth ('In quegl'anni'). Figaro's monologue (obbligato recitative and aria, 'Aprite un po' quegl'occhi') uses raw musical gestures to convey the terrors, for a clever but emotionally simple man, of sexual betrayal. Disconnected phrases witness to his anxiety, and horn fanfares mock him without mercy. He overhears but cannot see Susanna, who is disguised as the Countess (obbligato recitative and aria, 'Deh vieni, non tardar'). The floating line and titillating woodwind cadences with which Susanna confides her amorous longing to the night perfectly capture the blended love and mischief with which she deliberately rouses Figaro's passion (in 1789 Mozart replaced the aria with the elaborate rondò, 'Al desio').

From now on all is confusion; the characters mistake identities and blunder into each other in the dark, receiving kisses and blows intended for others, before nearly all of them end up in the pavilions (finale). Cherubino begs Susanna (actually the disguised Countess) for a kiss; Susanna watches anxiously as the Count and Figaro drive the pest away. The Count begins to woo 'Susanna', who responds shyly; Figaro's impotent rage is highlighted in the bass. He contrives a temporary interruption. As the key changes from G to E♭ a serenade-like melody ironically evokes the peace of the night. Seeing the Countess (actually Susanna), Figaro tells her what is going on; then recognizing her by her voice, he pays 'the Countess' passionate court. Enraged, Susanna boxes his ears again, blows which he greets with rapture. This scene unfolds to a frantic allegro, replaced at the reconciliation by pastoral 6/8. Now they enact Figaro pleading passionate love to the Countess; on cue, with a second abrupt key-change (B♭ to G), the Count bursts in on them, calling witnesses, dragging everyone including the false Countess from the pavilion, shouting accusations. The entry of the real Countess (in Susanna's clothes) leaves the company breathless. The humbled Count's prayer for forgiveness, and her loving response, build into a radiant hymn before the brilliant conclusion brings down the curtain on the crazy day.

* * *

Figaro is generally agreed to be the most perfect and least problematic of Mozart's great operas. The libretto, despite its complication (to which any synopsis does scant justice), is founded on a carefully constructed intrigue and Mozart draws musical dividends even from a hat, an anonymous letter and a pin. The advance on the sketched *opere buffe* of the immediately preceding years is astonishing, and must be attributed mainly to the effect on his imagination of the play, ably seconded by Da Ponte's adaptation.

The originality of the ensembles has often and rightly been commented upon. Many of them carry the action forward, not at the 'natural' tempo of recitative but under musical control; this makes such moments as the revelation of Figaro's parents to Susanna (the Act 3 sextet) both touching and funny, and creates palpable tension when the Count comes near to murdering his wife's 'lover' (the Act 2 trio), although we know the unseen Susanna will enable the page to escape. The arias are no less original for their brevity and directness. They convey, economically and unforgettably, the essential characterization of Bartolo, Cherubino ('Non so più'), the Countess and the Count. Figaro and Susanna are presented in ensembles and action arias (his Act 1 cavatina, although it is a kind of soliloquy, and 'Non più andrai'; her 'Venite, inginocchiatevi'). Their central place in the intrigue is confirmed when each has an obbligato recitative (normally a sign of high rank) in the last act; these precede the last arias, soliloquies which deepen Figaro's character (although his cynical denunciation of women is not endearing) and reveal the subtlety and tenderness of Susanna. Mozart's replacement of 'Deh vieni' in 1789 by 'Al desio' is a rare case of his damaging his own work by pandering to a singer.

Modern performances often omit Marcellina's Act 4 aria, a stately minuet and melodious Allegro of deliberately old-fashioned cut (with coloratura and strings-only orchestration), and Basilio's, an elaborate and inventively composed narration in three sections (andante, minuet allegro). Despite their virtues these pieces of moralizing by minor characters create a sequence of four arias inappropriate so near the dénouement, and an excess of minuet tempo.

The only other critical reservation about *Le nozze di Figaro* concerns the episodic structure of the third act. It comes precisely where Da Ponte had to depart decisively from Beaumarchais (omitting the extended trial scene). The reordering of scenes (Moberly and Raeburn 1965) has no documentary foundation, and can be shown not to represent Mozart's original intention (Tyson 1981); but the revised sequence avoids two immediately successive entries for the Countess and works well in the theatre. It would have been unmanageable with the original casting, which doubles Antonio with Bartolo; without the Countess's 'Dove sono' Antonio must enter immediately after the sextet, in which Bartolo sings. The non-sequiturs of Act 3, however, count for little in performance and throw into greater relief the ingenious management of its finale. In the great finales of Acts 2 and 4, Mozart reached a level which he could never surpass; indeed, he was hardly to equal the B♭ Allegro of the second act finale for its mercurial motivic play and the subsequent Andante in 6/8 for the synchronization of dramatic revelation with the demands of musical form.

For a page from the autograph score, *see* MOZART, WOLFGANG AMADEUS. JULIAN RUSHTON

Nozze di Teti e di Peleo, Le ('The Marriage of Thetis and Peleus'). *Opera scenica* or *festa teatrale* in three acts by FRANCESCO CAVALLI to a libretto by Orazio Persiani; Venice, Teatro S Cassiano, 24 January 1639.

Cavalli's first opera, and the first Venetian opera for which a score has survived, takes place at Lepanto, in Greece. It follows the adventures of Thetis (soprano), promised by Giove [Jupiter] (bass) in matrimony to Peleus (tenor), whose father, Eolo [Aeolus] (tenor), wishing to prevent the union because he suspects Jupiter of having seduced Thetis, begs the assistance of Plutone [Pluto] (bass), who agrees to send Discordia [Discord] (contralto) to interrupt the wedding and plant mutual distrust in the hearts of the betrothed couple. After a series of coincidences and deceptions inspired by Discord, whereby Thetis first fears that Peleus has drowned and then that he loves another, and Peleus fears that Thetis has betrayed him, the lovers are united in matrimony by Himeneo [Hymen] (soprano), who banishes Discord.

The rather loosely structured libretto contains a large number of supernatural scenes, situated both above and beneath the earth, which require elaborate scenery and staging. It also calls for a number of choruses (of gods, cavaliers, hunters, Tritons, demons, Bacchantes and nymphs) and ballets, both within and at the ends of the acts. Cavalli's powerful recitative style is illustrated in Thetis's three laments, particularly the one in Act 2 on the presumed death of Peleus. Other musical highlights include a 'sinfonia di viole' invoked by Peleus, and several comic-style strophic arias sung by Momo [Momus], the god of ridicule, and Mercurio [Mercury] (both tenors).

ELLEN ROSAND

Nozze istriane ('An Istrian Wedding'). *Dramma lirico* in three acts by ANTONIO SMAREGLIA to a libretto by LUIGI ILLICA; Trieste, Comunale, 28 March 1895.

The action is set in Dignano, a village in Smareglia's native Istria. Lorenzo (tenor) is in love with Marussa (soprano). The marriage-broker Biagio (baritone) pleads with the girl's father, Menico (bass), for Nicola (baritone), a wealthy young man. Menico, an old miser, is attracted by the prospect. While Lorenzo and Marussa exchange tokens of love they are interrupted by Menico who hastily rejects Lorenzo's marriage proposal. Biagio finds out about the exchange of tokens, retrieves Lorenzo's earring and returns it with the message that Marussa has changed her mind. Consequently, the poor young man hands over the girl's token (a little golden heart) which Biagio takes back to Marussa, making her believe that Lorenzo has left her for another woman. Marussa, in despair, consents to marry Nicola. On the wedding day, a Slavonic woman, Luze (contralto), who had been used as a messenger by Biagio, reveals the broker's intrigues to Marussa. She sends for Lorenzo and they decide that Nicola should be told about their true feelings and how they have all been deceived by Biagio. Nicola, however, is determined to go ahead with the wedding and, in a final confrontation with his rival, he stabs Lorenzo to death.

Nozze istriane is Smareglia's only veristic opera (the text and music were actually written in Dignano). Characters and ambience have a distinct element of authenticity; the music, however, is so far removed from the coarse-grained orchestration and vocal paroxysms of standard *verismo* that the term seems inappropriate to define it. A truly Italian melodic vein pervades the parts of Marussa and Lorenzo, but Smareglia's originality can best be detected in the care and finesse with which he elaborated orchestral details, in the density and expressiveness of the instrumental accompaniment and in the melancholy Slavonic undertones.

MATTEO SANSONE

Nucci, Leo (*b* Castiglione dei Pepoli, Bologna, 16 April 1942). Italian baritone. A pupil of Giuseppe Marchese, he sang Rossini's Figaro at Spoleto in 1967, then sang in the chorus at La Scala during further study and made his fully professional début in 1975 at Venice as Schaunard. He appeared at La Scala in 1976 as Figaro, at Covent Garden in 1978 as Miller (*Luisa Miller*), and as Renato at the Metropolitan in 1980, the Paris Opéra in 1981 and Salzburg in 1989. Nucci has sung throughout Italy and in San Francisco, Chicago, Brussels and Hamburg. His repertory includes Marcello, Lescaut, Sharpless, Belcore, Malatesta, Mamm' Agata (*Le convenienze ed inconvenienze teatrali*), Barnaba (*La Gioconda*), Yevgeny Onegin and Gounod's Mercutio, but his fine voice, strong technique and acting ability are displayed to best advantage in Verdi, in the roles of Germont, Luna, Macbeth, Don Carlo (*La forza del destino*), Posa, Amonasro, Ford and Rigoletto, which he sang at the Metropolitan in 1989.

ELIZABETH FORBES

Nuibo, Augustin [Francisco] (*b* Marseilles, 1 May 1874; *d* Nice, April 1948). French tenor. He studied with Victor Capoul in Paris and made his début there in *Guillaume Tell* (1904). He sang Turiddu at the Metropolitan the same year; he was known as Francisco Nuibo in New York, allegedly because the name Augustin reminded the director of the Metropolitan of a clown. He sang at the Opéra until 1908, his roles including David in *Die Meistersinger* (1906), and later at the Opéra-Comique and the Théâtre des Champs-Elysées in lyric roles. Guest appearances took him to London, Lisbon, San Francisco and Mexico City. He founded a conservatory in the Montmartre district of Paris in 1923.

DAVID CUMMINGS

Nuitter [Truinet], **Charles-Louis-Etienne** (*b* Paris, 24 April 1828; *d* Paris, 23 or 24 Feb 1899). French librettist, writer on music and librarian. His real name was Truinet, of which 'Nuitter' is an anagram. He studied law and by 1849 was practising in Paris. In the 1850s he began writing librettos in his spare time. His first performed work, a vaudeville entitled *L'amour dans un ophicléide* (1852), was followed by more vaudevilles and later by operas, *opéras comiques*, *opéras bouffes*, operettas and ballets. Usually writing with collaborators, in particular Beaumont (Alexandre Beaume), Nérée Desarbres and Etienne Tréfeu, he produced more than 60 works, many of which reveal facility and wit. He wrote for Offenbach, Guiraud, Lecocq and at least 20 other composers. One of the first Frenchmen to appreciate Wagner, he translated *Tannhäuser* (with E. Roche and R. Lindau, 1861), *Rienzi* (with Jules Guillaume, 1869), *Lohengrin* (1870) and *Der fliegende Holländer* (1872). His other translations (most with collaborators) include Weber's *Oberon* (1857) and *Abu Hassan* (1859); Bellini's *I Capuleti e i Montecchi* (1859); Mozart's *Die Zauberflöte* (1865); and Verdi's *Macbeth* (1865), *Aida* (1877), *La forza del destino* (1883) and *Simon Boccanegra* (1883).

In about 1863 Nuitter began to catalogue the Paris Opéra archives and in 1866 he became official archivist there, abandoning his law career. With Théodore Lajarte he reorganized the archives and the library. He rescued many documents from destruction, ensured that the new Opéra (opened in 1875) had adequate facilities for the archives and library and, often at his own expense, acquired for it compositions, autographs, documents and an important collection of journals. He wrote, in a journalistic style, books on opera and the Opéra, including *Le nouvel Opéra* (Paris, 1875), *Histoire et description du nouvel Opéra* (Paris, 1883) and, in collaboration with Ernest Thoinan (A. E. Roquet), *Les origines de l'Opéra français* (Paris, 1886); various articles (notably in *La chronique musicale*) describe little-known works in the Opéra's collection.

Une nuit à Séville (oc, with Beaumont [A. Beaume]), F. Barbier, 1855; *Rose et Narcisse* (oc, with Beaumont), Barbier, 1855; *Le pacha* (opérette), Barbier, 1858; *La fille du golfe* (oc), Delibes, unperf.; *La servante à Nicolas* (opérette, with N. Desarbres), J. Erlanger, 1861; *Les bavards [Bavard et bavarde]* (opéra bouffe), Offenbach, 1863; *Il signor Fagotto* (opérette, with E. Tréfeu), Offenbach, 1863; *L'amour chanteur* (opérette, with E. L'Epine), Offenbach, 1864; *Les fées du Rhin* (opéra), Offenbach, 1864; *Le fifre enchanté* [*Le soldat magicien*] (opérette bouffe, with Tréfeu), Offenbach, 1864; *Jeanne qui pleure et Jean qui rit* (opérette, with Tréfeu), Offenbach, 1864

Le lion de Saint Marc (opéra bouffe, with Beaumont), E. Legouix, 1864; *Coscoletto, ou Le lazzarone* (opéra comique/bouffe, with Tréfeu), Offenbach, 1865; *Une fantasia* (opérette), Hervé, 1865; *Les mémoires de Fanchette* (oc, with Desarbres), N. Gabrielli, 1865; *Le baron de Groschaminet* (opérette), J. L. Duprato, 1866; *Les oreilles de Midas* (opérette, with Desarbres), Barbier, 1866;

Cardillac (?oc, with Beaumont), L. Dautresme, 1867; *Le vengeur* (opéra bouffe, with Beaumont), Legouix, 1868; *Le dernier jour de Pompéi* (opéra, with Beaumont), V. Joncières, 1869; *Les masques* (with Beaumont, after M. M. Marcello: *Tutti in maschera*), C. Pedrotti, 1869

La princesse de Trébizonde (opéra bouffe, with Tréfeu), Offenbach, 1869; *La romance de la rose* (opérette, with J. Prével and Tréfeu), Offenbach, 1869; *Vert-vert* (oc, with H. Meilhac), Offenbach, 1869; *Le Kobold* (oc, with L. Gallet), E. Guiraud, 1870; *Boule de neige* (opéra bouffe, with Tréfeu), Offenbach, 1871; *Le corsaire noir* (opéra comique/bouffe, with Offenbach and Tréfeu), Offenbach, 1872; *Les dernières grisettes* (opérette, with Beaumont), Legouix, 1874; *Whittington* (opéra bouffe-féerie, with Tréfeu), Offenbach, 1874; *Amphitryon* (opérette, with Beaumont), P. Lacome, 1875; *La halte du roi* (opéra), L. Boieldieu, 1875; *Piccolino* (oc, with V. Sardou), Guiraud, 1876; *L'Opoponax* (opérette, with W. Busnach), L. Vasseur, 1877

Maître Péronilla (opéra bouffe, with P. Ferrier), Offenbach, 1878; *Pépita* (oc, with J. L. Delahaye), L. Delahaye, 1878; *Monsieur de Floridor* (oc, with Tréfeu), T. Lajarte, 1880; *Le cœur et la main* (opérette, with Beaumont), C. Lecocq, 1882; *Oscarine* (opérette, with A. Guinon), V. Roger, 1888; *La volière* (opérette, with Beaumont), Lecocq, 1888; *L'Egyptienne* (opérette, with H. C. Chivot and Beaumont), Lecocq, 1890; *Le chat du diable* (opérette-féerie, with Tréfeu), Offenbach, 1893; *Don Quichotte* (with Sardou), A. Renaud, 1895; *Hellé* (opéra, with C. Du Locle), V. A. Duvernoy, 1896; *La gaudriole* (oc, with Tréfeu), A. Vizentini, 1897; *Le tonnelier de Nuremberg* (oc), L. Lacombe, 1897; *Le soleil de minuit* (opérette, with Beaumont), Renaud, 1898

*

ES (F. Lesure); *FétisB*; *LoewenbergA*; *MGG* (A. Ménetrat); *StiegerO*

U. Günther and G. Carrara Verdi, eds.: 'Der Briefwechsel Verdi-Nuitter-Du Locle zur Revision des "Don Carlos"', *AnMc*, no.14 (1974), 414–44; no.15 (1975), 334–401   JEFFREY COOPER

Number opera (Ger. *Nummernoper*; It. *opera a numeri*). Term for an opera consisting of individual sections or 'numbers' which can readily be detached from the whole, as distinct from an opera consisting of continuous music. It is best applied to the various forms of 18th-century opera, including *opera seria*, *opera buffa*, *opéra comique*, ballad opera and Singspiel, as well as to some 19th-century grand operas. Under the influence of Wagner's ideas about the relationship between opera and drama, the number opera became unfashionable, and neither his operas nor those of late Verdi, Puccini and the *verismo* school can strictly be so called although arias can easily be detached (at the point designed to accommodate the applause). In spite of the widespread adherence to Wagner's aesthetic of continuous music drama, some notable 20th-century works can be considered number operas, such as Berg's *Wozzeck* (1925) and Stravinsky's deliberately archaic *The Rake's Progress* (1951).

Numitore ('Numitor'). *Opera seria* in three acts by GIOVANNI PORTA to a libretto by PAOLO ANTONIO ROLLI after Livy's legend of Romulus and Remus; London, King's Theatre (Royal Academy of Music), 2 April 1720.

Romulus (soprano) and Remus (alto), the twins who were cast into the Tiber at birth, restore the kingdom of Alba to the deposed Numitor (tenor). Numitor's daughter Rhea Silvia [Sylvia] (soprano), condemned by the tyrant Amulius (soprano) to be buried alive, is liberated by her unsuspecting son Romulus, while Remus aids the noblewoman Lidia (contralto), in flight from the illicit advances of Amulius. They eventually slay Amulius, and as the rightful king Numitor is about to honour the twins as heirs to his kingdom, Dorilla (soprano), daughter of the deceased shepherd Faustolus

who raised the twins, arrives to reveal their royal identity. Lidia promises to marry Remus. With their tribute Mars (soprano) descends and, in acknowledging his sons, proclaims the founding of Rome.

Numitore is historically significant as the first opera produced by the Royal Academy in London, founded with the intention of promoting Italian opera. It ran for seven performances and was subsequently published as an aria collection by Walsh & Hare. Burney called it 'superior' to any of the preceding operas from Italy, with 'one of the most pleasing Sicilianas'. The music is characteristic of early 18th-century Venetian opera, and it is known that Handel borrowed freely from it, especially for his oratorios, including *Samson*, *Solomon* and *Messiah*. It was also given as *Rhea Silvia* and as *Die heldenmüthige Schäfer Romulus und Remus*.

FAUN TANENBAUM

Nuovo. Theatre in NAPLES, built in 1724 to present comic opera; restored in 1861, it staged plays, then revues and variety, and became a cinema in 1935.

Nuremberg (Ger. Nürnberg). Town in Bavaria, southern Germany. It was of great importance in the Middle Ages and the Renaissance, when the plays of the Meistersinger (such as Hans Sachs) were performed on temporary stages. The first building used as a theatre was the Fechthaus of 1627–8. Johann Löhner and Sigmund Staden were the only Nurembergers to write operas for the city, Staden composing the earliest extant German Singspiel, *Seelewig* (1644). The town did not have a true theatre until 1668, when a warehouse was rebuilt as a Komödienhaus, later called the Opernhaus. In 1685 an opera by J. C. F. Fischer was performed and, in 1697, J. S. Kusser directed two operas there: Bassani's *Alarich* and Giannettini's *Ermione*. However, most of the works staged were by Germans, performed in German by visiting troupes. Nuremberg's operatic life was very modest compared to that of Hamburg or the Italian-dominated court opera in Munich, Dresden and Hanover.

The Stadttheater am Ring, a new building in *art nouveau* style built by the architect Heinrich Seeling, was Nuremberg's first building designed for operatic performances. It opened on 1 October 1905 with a festival piece and the prelude and last scene from *Die Meistersinger*. The first chief conductors were Fritz Stiedry and Robert Heger, and the repertory at that time included some 20 standard operas and operettas as well as the major new works of Strauss, Puccini, Mascagni, Humperdinck, Kienzl and Pfitzner. In 1913 the theatre mounted its first production of *Parsifal*, not previously released for general performance. In 1915 Clemens Krauss, working side by side with Heger, and the baritone Heinrich Schlusnus were engaged. During World War I Max Reinhardt was guest director (productions included *La belle Hélène*), and the *Ring* cycle was produced.

After the war the theatre became municipally owned. Rudolf Hartmann was engaged as director-in-chief in 1927, and he brought new impetus to operatic production. Artistic highlights included the first performances there of Pfitzner's *Palestrina*, Strauss's *Die Frau ohne Schatten* and Hindemith's *Cardillac*. But the economic crisis of 1930 took its toll on the opera.

When the Nazis seized power, Nuremberg became the scene of party rallies and the opera house was drawn into the party programme. Renovated in 1935 by the architect Paul Schultze-Naumburg, it lost all its *art nouveau* features. It was reopened on 10 September 1935 in the presence of Hitler and Winifred Wagner, with *Die Meistersinger* conducted by Wilhelm Furtwängler. Thereafter regular cultural conventions and operatic festivals were held during party rallies.

The opera house was closed in autumn 1944 after a production of *Götterdämmerung*, having been badly damaged in air raids. After World War II, it was requisitioned by the occupying American troops for five years, after which time the company and repertory were quickly built up again. The Woche des Gegenwarttheaters was instituted, during which all the contemporary works in the current season were repeated. There were also many local premières, with productions of *Moses und Aron, Die Soldaten, Elegy for Young Lovers, Lear, Le Grand Macabre, Die wunderbare Schustersfrau, The English Cat, Sturmnacht* and *Über die Dörfer*. Soon after the war a youth theatre was started; it has a special repertory and gives matinée performances.

The repertory of the Nuremberg Opera embraces all areas of music drama. The season, from 1 September to 31 July, comprises about 110 evening performances of opera and 100 of operetta, besides ballet performances. The theatre (cap. 1082) is located in Richard-Wagner-Platz.

*

F. E. Hysel: *Das Theater in Nürnberg von 1612 bis 1683* (Nuremberg, 1863)
T. Hampe: 'Die Entwicklung des Theaterwesens in Nürnberg von der zweiten Hälfte des 15. Jahrhunderts bis 1806', *Mitteilungen des Vereins für Geschichte der Stadt Nürnberg*, xii (1898), 87–306; xiii (1899), 98–237
A. Sandberger: 'Zur Geschichte der Oper in Nürnberg in der zweiten Hälfte des 17. und zu Anfang des 18. Jahrhunderts', *AMw*, i (1918–19), 84–107

KLAUS J. SEIDEL (with HAROLD E. SAMUEL)

Nurmahal, oder Das Rosenfest von Kaschmir ('Nourmahal, or The Feast of Roses of Kashmir'). *Lyrisches Drama* with ballet in two acts by GASPARE SPONTINI, to a libretto by CARL ALEXANDER HERKLOTS after THOMAS MOORE's *Lalla Rookh*; Berlin, Königliches Opernhaus, 27 May 1822.

The plot expands the material in the fourth verse episode of Thomas Moore's oriental romance *Lalla Rookh* with further intrigues. The quarrel between the lovers Nourmahal (soprano) and the Sultan Dsheangir [Jehanguire] (tenor) is the result of jealousy between Nourmahal and her rival Zelia (soprano); in addition, the enmity between Nourmahal's father, Athar (bass), and Jehanguire plunges the heroine into a severe conflict of loyalty. However, Nourmahal succeeds in winning Jehanguire back at the Feast of Roses, using the magic lent to her voice by the enchantress Namuna [Namouna] (soprano).

The modernity of the exotic elements in this, the first operatic version of Moore's story, is diluted from the start by the use of conventional operatic stereotypes, and Spontini's score also inclines towards the classicist *opéra-féerie*. Even the dream scene in Act 2, usually thought to be redolent of German Romanticism, is clearly based on an older French model, and this number, like three others originally composed in 1821 as *tableaux vivants* for the *Festspiel Lalla Rûkh*, is in the spirit of the court *divertissement*. (Spontini revised the introductory march, Nourmahal's song, the geniuses' choir and the ballet music for *Nurmahal*.) There are few moments of dramatic invention of the intensity familiar from Spontini's great Paris operas; one such does occur when the disagreement between the lovers is illustrated by a constantly repeated 7th and the abrupt ending of the ballet music, which is drawn from Spontini's Bacchanale to Salieri's *Les Danaïdes*. There are many choral and ballet scenes, but the characterization of the leading parts remains vague, and the score, composed in great haste with many borrowings from earlier works and a reversion to coloratura arias, resembles pastiche. The work had some success in Berlin, where it was performed with scenery by Schinkel, but it remained entirely unknown outside Prussia.

ANSELM GERHARD

Nurmela, Kari (*b* Viipuri, 26 May 1933; *d* Warsaw, 21 Jan 1984). Finnish baritone. He studied in Helsinki, Vienna and Milan, making his début in 1961 at Helsinki as Luna. After singing at Detmold, Freiburg and Brunswick, from 1976 he sang at larger theatres: Stuttgart, Munich, Hamburg, Frankfurt, Rome, Zürich and Düsseldorf. He sang Enrico Ashton at Buxton (1979), made his Covent Garden début (1980) as Scarpia and sang Macbeth at the Paris Opéra (1982). His repertory included Don Giovanni and the Dutchman, which he sang at Savonlinna in 1983, not long before his early death. He had a powerful voice and personality, best displayed as Scarpia, his favourite role.

ELIZABETH FORBES

Nürnberg (Ger.). NUREMBERG.

Nusch-Nuschi, Das ('The Nusch-Nuschi'). Opera in one act, op.20, by PAUL HINDEMITH to a libretto by Franz Blei; Stuttgart, Landestheater, 4 June 1921.

Though subtitled 'A Play for Burmese Marionettes', this work employs a large cast of live singers and dancers. The 'Nusch-Nuschi', a fabulous beast, half rat, half cayman, plays only a minor role in the story, which concerns the simultaneous seduction of four of the Emperor's wives by the handsome Zatwai (silent role). His astute servant Tum Tum (tenor *buffo*) shifts the blame on to the army chief Kyce Waing (bass), who proves, however, to be physically incapable of having compromised the wives. Hindemith's irreverent quotation of Wagner's words and music (King Mark's monologue directed at Tristan: 'Mir dies? ... echte Art') for the Emperor's reproach to Kyce Waing caused a scandal in Stuttgart. The music is otherwise lively and oriental in flavour.

GEOFFREY SKELTON

Nyman, Michael (Laurence) (*b* London, 23 March 1944). English composer. While at the RAM (1961–5) he studied keyboard and composition (with Alan Bush), and at King's College, London (1964–7), he read musicology with Thurston Dart. As a writer and music critic (1968–78) he was the first to apply the word 'minimalism' in musical description (to a composition by Cornelius Cardew) and wrote the seminal book *Experimental Music: Cage and Beyond* (1974) and the libretto to Birtwistle's 'dramatic pastoral' *Down by the Greenwood Side* (1968–9).

As a composer Nyman draws on a vast bank of musical reference points. Keen to break down the barrier between popular culture and 'serious' composition, he writes, in general, for his own amplified ensemble and uses singers from various vocal traditions. He is widely known for his film music for the British director Peter Greenaway, notably *The Draughtsman's*

Contract (1982), a score based on Purcell; the music frequently leans to the operatic, as in *The Cook, the Thief, his Wife and her Lover* (1989) and *Prospero's Books* (1991). He has completed five operas, of which the principal one is *The Man who Mistook his Wife for a Hat* (1986). Based on the book by Oliver Sacks, it poignantly relates the diagnostic journey by the neurologist Dr S of his patient Dr P, a professional singer, who is suffering from visual agnosia – the inability to recognize or make sense of what he sees. This work amply demonstrates Nyman's musical style in its use of variation and modular form, lyrical vocal lines over restless, chugging, repetitive phrases and doublings of tonal primary-coloured chords within regularly repeated harmonic blocks. Unexpected metrical shifts and harmonic angularities suggest a curious conjunction between Stravinsky and rock and roll.

The Kiss (video-duet), London, Channel 4 TV, 13 Oct 1984

The Man who Mistook his Wife for a Hat (chamber op, C. Rawlence, after O. Sacks), London, Institute of Contemporary Arts, 27 Oct 1986

Vital Statistics (V. Hardie), London, Donmar Warehouse, 3 June 1987, work in progress

Orpheus' Daughter (G. Timmers), Rotterdam, Studio Onafhankelijk Toneel, 13 Dec 1988, withdrawn

La princesse de Milan (dance op, after W. Shakespeare: *The Tempest*), Avignon, 24 July 1991

Letters, Riddles and Writs [Not Mozart] (television op, J. Newson, after L. and W. A. Mozart), BBC TV, 10 Nov 1991; staged London, Shaw, 24 June 1992

4 frags. (after L. Sterne: *Tristram Shandy*)   ANNETTE MORREAU

Obbligato (It.: 'obligatory'). (1) Term used for a prominent instrumental part in an aria (or other number). Early examples are the trumpet arias of a military character in late 17th-century Italian opera, by Alessandro Scarlatti and others; in the arias with flute or recorder in late Baroque opera where the words refer to birdsong, such as Almirena's 'Augelletti' in Handel's *Rinaldo* (1711); and in 'Va tacito' in Handel's *Giulio Cesare* (1724), where a horn has an obbligato part in token of Caesar's reference to being hunted. Examples in Mozart's operas include one for horn in *Mitridate* (1770), one with flute, oboe, violin and cello in *Die Entführung* (1782), one with violin added to *Idomeneo* (K490, 1786), arias with clarinet and bassethorn in *La clemenza di Tito* and with glockenspiel in *Die Zauberflöte*. Obbligato parts become less formal in the 19th century, but prominent obbligato-like writing for flute in particular is not unusual in Romantic opera – for example in the cadenza of the traditional version of the Mad Scene in *Lucia di Lammermoor* (1835) and in the aria for the Italian Tenor in *Der Rosenkavalier* (1911) – and the cello is often assigned an obbligato role in such melancholy contexts as Hermann's aria in the first scene of *The Queen of Spades* (1890) or Cavaradossi's in the last act of *Tosca* (1900).

(2) Term used, in the context *recitativo obbligato* (or *recitativo stromentato*), for 'orchestral recitative', in which the orchestra enhances the sense of the words with expressive or dramatic accompaniments or interjections. (The French counterpart, rarely used, is récitatif obligé.) *See* RECITATIVE.

Oberhausen. German town in northern Rhine-Westphalia. The first opera performed there, on 25 March 1880, was Donizetti's *La fille du régiment*; this began a series of operatic productions by guest companies. A permanent company was founded in 1910; its first production was *Fidelio* (4 January 1911) conducted by Hans Knappertsbusch, who subsequently returned to conduct *Cavalleria rusticana* and *Pagliacci*. The company performed in a variety of halls until 1920, when Oberhausen built its first theatre. The first operatic production there was *Der Freischütz* on 4 December 1923. This theatre was destroyed on 17 April 1943; a new one with 681 seats opened with *Carmen* on 10 September 1949. The Oberhausen company has since concentrated on introducing little-known operas to its audience. Recent productions include Ibert's *Angélique*,

Rossini's *Il Signor Bruschino*, Musorgsky's *Marriage*, Stravinsky's *Mavra* and Lortzing's *Regina*.

SABINE SONNTAG

Oberlin. American town in Ohio. The Oberlin Opera Theater, a programme of the Oberlin College Conservatory, provides training in all aspects of opera. The Opera Laboratory Workshop, begun in 1947 by Daniel A. Harris, professor of singing and formerly a baritone at the Metropolitan, became an accredited course in 1950. Early productions were staged in Finney Chapel and the old Warner Hall, accompanied by piano or by a small orchestral ensemble sometimes conducted by the conservatory dean, David R. Robertson. Productions were soon moved to Hall Auditorium, a well-equipped 500-seat theatre (built 1953). Two or more productions have been presented every year since 1952, the conductors including Robert Baustian (1966–83), Michel Singher (1984–8) and Robert Spano (from 1989). After Harris retired in 1969, the new director, Roy Lazarus, organized the Oberlin Music Theater, which gave summer performances in the early 1970s. Since 1979 Judith Layng has been director. The programme is supported in part by the Louis C. Sudler Opera Fund, and premières have included Walter Aschaffenburg's *Bartleby* (1964), Elaine Barkin's *De amore* (1982) and Conrad Cummings's *Eros and Psyche* (1983).

*

R. D. Skyrm: *Oberlin Conservatory* (diss., U. of Southern California, 1962)
E. B. Chamberlain: *The Music of Oberlin and Some who Made it* (Oberlin, 1968)   JUDITH LAYNG

Oberlin, Russell (Keys) (*b* Akron, OH, 11 Oct 1928). American countertenor. He studied at the Juilliard School of Music. In 1961 he sang Oberon in the first Covent Garden production, and the American première in San Francisco, of Britten's *A Midsummer Night's Dream*. Admired for his sweet tone and subtle phrasing, he appeared with numerous opera companies and in theatrical productions, and was also a leading exponent of early music. In the mid-1960s he turned to teaching.

PATRICK J. SMITH

Oberon [*Oberon, or The Elf King's Oath*]. *Romantische Oper* in three acts, J306, by CARL MARIA VON WEBER to a libretto by JAMES ROBINSON PLANCHÉ after CHRISTOPH MARTIN WIELAND's poem *Oberon*; London, Covent Garden, 12 April 1826.

Oberon *King of the Elves*	tenor
Puck	mezzo-soprano
Reiza *daughter of Haroun al Rachid*	soprano
Sir Huon of Bordeaux *Duke of Guienne*	tenor
Sherasmin *Huon's squire*	baritone
Namouna *Fatima's grandmother*	spoken
Fatima *Reiza's attendant*	mezzo-soprano
Haroun al Rachid *Caliph of Baghdad*	spoken
Babekan *a Saracen prince*	spoken
Abdallah *a corsair*	spoken
Two Mermaids	mezzo-sopranos
Roshana *wife of Almanzor*	spoken
Almanzor *Emir of Tunis*	spoken

Fairies, ladies, knights, slaves, mermaids etc.

Setting Fairyland, the banks of the Tigris, Africa and France in medieval times

On 18 August 1824 Weber received a letter from Charles Kemble in London, inviting him to compose a new opera and to come to England to direct it during the following season, along with performances of *Der Freischütz* and *Preciosa*. He was in an advanced stage of consumption and his doctor warned him that if he went to London he could expect only a few more months, or perhaps weeks, of life. But concern for his family's financial future overrode concern for his own health, and three days later he accepted the commission. Kemble offered him the subjects Faust or Oberon and, having chosen the latter, Weber asked for the libretto to be sent to him as soon as possible. By the beginning of December Planché's libretto had not arrived, and it became clear that the opera would have to be postponed until the 1826 season. Finally, on 30 December, the first act arrived, to be followed by the second on 18 January and the third on 1 February. In order to set the text satisfactorily Weber had already begun an intensive course in English in October 1824 (he took 153 lessons in all), and was thus able to correspond with Planché in English. His letters show his concern over the nature of the libretto, so different from those he was used to; on 19 February he wrote to Planché:

The intermixing of so many principal actors who do not sing, the omission of the music in the most important moments – all these things deprive our *Oberon* the title of an opera, and will make him unfit for all other Theatres in Europe; which is a very bad thing for me, but – *passons la dessus*.

He accepted that, given English taste, there was no alternative; but had he lived he would certainly have revised *Oberon*, adding recitatives, to suit the German stage.

By the time Weber left for England in mid-February 1826 he had completed the bulk of the opera. Travelling via Paris, he reached England on 4 March. Rehearsals began on 9 March, but several of the solo numbers were still lacking. He finished the remaining portions amid an exhausting round of rehearsals, concerts and social engagements. On 23 March he wrote the rondo 'I revel in hope and joy' (no.20) for the immensely popular tenor John Braham, who was cast in the part of Huon; three days later he completed Reiza's cavatina 'Mourn thou, poor heart' (no.19) for Mary Anne Paton and, in another three days, Fatima's 'O Araby' (no.16) for Lucia Elizabeth Vestris. Having rearranged the chorus 'For thee hath beauty' (no.21) for female voices, Weber imagined that the opera, apart from the overture, was complete; but Braham requested a substitute for 'From

boyhood trained' (no.5), which he found too high in tessitura, and Weber grudgingly composed 'Ah! 'tis a glorious sight to see' on 6 April. He finished the splendid overture three days before the première. At the last minute, however, he was obliged to write 'Ruler of this awful hour' (no.12a) for Braham, who wanted another piece to show off a different quality in his voice.

The première on 12 April was a triumph; the overture and all the individual numbers were encored and Weber was loudly called for at the conclusion. By this stage, though, his health was completely shattered, and less than two months later he died, on the night before his planned return to Germany.

Despite the circumstances of its composition, *Oberon* contains some of Weber's most delightful music, which has assured the work a permanent, if peripheral, place in the repertory, even though its overall structure is far from satisfactory. In 1860 Planché produced a revised version in Italian which had recitatives by Weber's pupil Julius Benedict and incorporated some music from *Euryanthe*. There have been many other arrangements, including one with recitative by Franz Wüllner and one

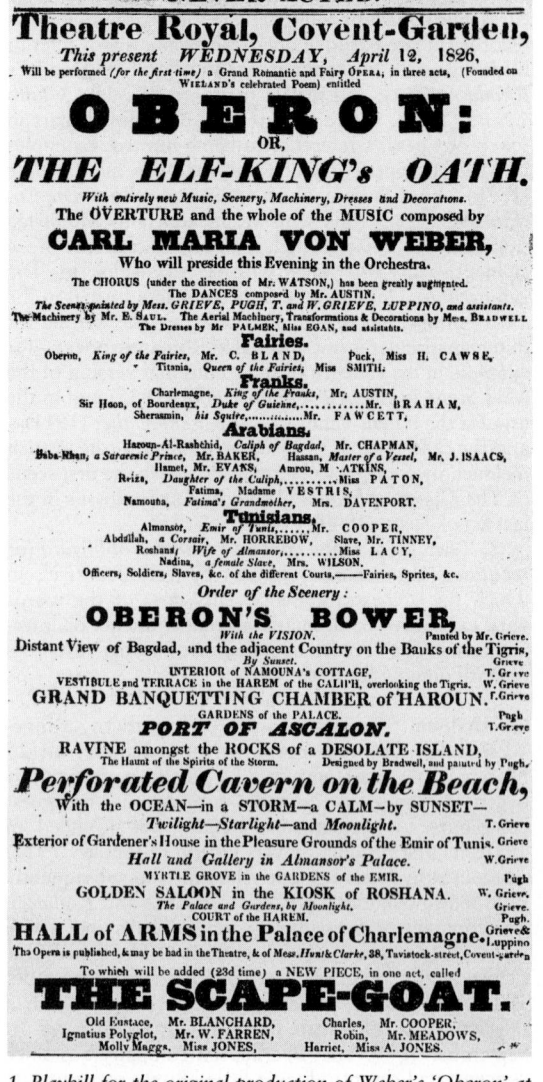

1. Playbill for the original production of Weber's 'Oberon' at Covent Garden, London, 12 April 1826

2. 'Oberon' (Weber): design for a palace garden by a member of the Grieve family for the revival at Covent Garden, 13 March 1843; the design may be based on one for the original 1826 production for which the Grieve family also designed the scenery

by Gustav Brecher with sections of instrumental music by Mahler (based on material from the opera) to accompany the dialogue.

The brilliant overture opens atmospherically with Oberon's horn-call, which acts as a motif throughout the work.

ACT 1 *Oberon's bower* A chorus of fairies keeps guard over the sleeping Oberon (no.1, 'Light as fairy foot can fall'). The number begins with an inversion of the horn-call; syncopation in the voice parts and delicate staccato interjections from wind and strings characterize the chorus. Puck dismisses the fairies and explains that Oberon and Titania have quarrelled over whether man or woman is the more inconstant in love; they have vowed not to be reunited until they find a couple who are constant through adversity. In an impassioned C minor aria, 'Fatal vow' (no.2), in which the horn-call again underlies the melodic invention, Oberon deplores the situation. Puck informs him that Charlemagne has condemned Huon to go to Baghdad, where he must kill the man on the caliph's right hand, then kiss the caliph's daughter and marry her. Puck discloses the sleeping Huon with his squire, Sherasmin. Oberon shows Huon, in a dream, a vision of the caliph's daughter, Reiza, imploring Huon to come to her. Her short guitar song, 'Oh why art thou sleeping' (no.3), also begins with the horn-call. The vision fades, and Oberon wakes them. He pledges his help and gives Huon a fairy horn to call him to his aid. He also gives him a magic goblet which will spontaneously fill with wine but will burn the lips of the impure. (The goblet was excised from Planché's 1860 revision of the text.) Fairies are summoned and in the ensuing ensemble, 'Honour and joy' (no.4), they transport Huon and Sherasmin to Baghdad.

The banks of the Tigris Huon saves Prince Babekan from a lion, but when Babekan drinks from the goblet it burns his lips; he attacks his rescuers but is driven off. Namouna tells them of Reiza's impending marriage to Babekan and of her vision of a knight who is to rescue her from it. (Planché removed the incidents involving Babekan and Namouna in 1860.) Huon reflects that his commitment to knightly honour has

now been joined by the emotion of love. He was originally intended to sing 'From boyhood trained' at this point, but in the première this was replaced by the rather bombastic D major aria, 'Ah! 'tis a glorious sight to see'.

The palace of Haroun al Rachid In the harem Reiza tells Fatima she would rather die than marry Babekan, and anxiously waits for the rescuer she has seen in a vision. In the finale, 'Haste gallant knight', she urges speed on her deliverer, her opening phrase once more recalling the horn motif. Fatima returns with news of Huon's arrival, and then the harem guard is heard approaching, chanting to the accompaniment of an Arabian melody which Weber took from Carsten Niebuhr's *Reisebeschreibung nach Arabien* (1774). The number ends with Reiza anxiously awaiting rescue.

ACT 2 *A magnificent salon in the palace of Haroun al Rachid* The act opens with a B minor chorus of praise, 'Glory to the caliph' (no.7), to which Weber, using bold orchestral unisons, gives an exotic flavour. After Reiza is brought in for her marriage to Babekan, to the accompaniment of woodwind, triangle and tambourine (no.8), Huon and Sherasmin rush in. Babekan confronts Huon, but is killed. Before the slaves can attack, Huon sounds his horn and they are paralysed, allowing Huon and Sherasmin to escape with Reiza and Fatima (no.9a). When Huon has routed the guards in the palace garden, Oberon appears and conjures up the port of Ascalon and a ship to take them to Greece (nos.9b and 9c; in 1860 Planché shortened and rearranged much of the foregoing). Huon and Reiza depart, while Sherasmin woos Fatima; she sings the aria 'A lonely Arab maid' (no.10). Huon returns, urging haste, and they sing of their buoyant hopes in the quartet 'Over the dark blue waters' (no.11), which includes the main *allegro* theme of the overture. In the solo and chorus 'Spirits of air and earth and sea' (no.12) Puck summons the spirits of the four elements to wreck Huon's ship; an extensive orchestral postlude illustrates the storm. After the shipwreck Huon prays for Reiza's recovery (no.12a, 'Ruler of this awful hour'). When she revives, Huon goes in search of help. Reiza, awed by the sea, sings the demanding recitative and aria 'Ocean! thou mighty monster' (no.13), in which orchestral figurations from the storm recur. During the aria a ship comes into sight and she attracts the attention of its crew. However, it is filled with pirates, led by Abdullah, who abduct her, leaving Huon unconscious and bound. Oberon appears, to the sound of the magic horn (no.14); he summons Puck and instructs him to take Huon to the house of the gardener Ibrahim in Tunis in seven days' time. (In Planché's 1860 version Oberon sings 'From boyhood trained' over the unconscious Huon at this point, with the text changed from the first to the third person.) In the finale, 'Oh! 'tis pleasant to float on the sea' (no.15), mermaids and fairies appear and sing irrelevantly, but beautifully, of their joy.

ACT 3 *Outside Ibrahim's house in Tunis* The enslaved Fatima bewails her fate, singing nostalgically 'O Araby!' (no.16). Sherasmin, now married to her, enters and together they sing of their childhood (no.17, 'On the banks of the sweet Garonne'). Puck causes Huon's appearance. Fatima tells him that Reiza has just been brought to Tunis and Sherasmin urges him to disguise himself; they join in the trio 'And must I then dissemble?' (no.18).

Almanzor's palace in Tunis Inside the harem Almanzor welcomes Reiza, but she expresses her sadness in the F minor cavatina 'Mourn thou poor heart' (no.19). Reiza communicates with Huon by means of a bouquet of flowers, and Huon gives utterance to his feelings in the rondo 'I revel in hope and joy' (no.20). Roshana, who is jealous because of her husband Almanzor's passion for Reiza, tries to induce Huon to kill him and marry her; she summons her slaves to help persuade him in the chorus and ballet 'For thee hath beauty' (no.21). He still refuses, and when Almanzor arrives Huon is seized and led away. Meanwhile Sherasmin has found the horn. Just as Huon is about to be burnt at the stake, the horn sounds and the finale, 'Hark! what notes are swelling' (no.22), begins. Weber based the opening section of this number on a *danse turque* from La Borde's *Essai sur la musique*. At first all the slaves begin to dance and then, at a louder blast on the horn, Oberon and Titania appear and the Tunisians flee. Oberon tells the lovers that their trials are at an end, and they are transported to Charlemagne's palace. An extended instrumental march accompanies a procession of king and courtiers. Huon kneels before Charlemagne and explains that he has accomplished his mission. The opera ends with a chorus of praise for Huon and Reiza.

* * *

It is a remarkable testimony to Weber's operatic genius that, notwithstanding the unmitigated awfulness of its libretto, *Oberon* has maintained a toe-hold in the repertory. To a very considerable extent he was able to compensate for triviality and inconsequence in the libretto by skilful musical treatment. The imaginative and expressive quality of his writing for the principals invests them with a depth of characterization far beyond the implications of the text, while his sensitivity to colour and atmosphere in the orchestral and concerted numbers lifts the work above the level of shallow pantomime suggested by its libretto. Above all, however, Weber was able to lend an illusion of coherence to the picaresque farrago of nonsense with which Planché had presented him, by his subtle use of the horn-call as a recurrent musical motif; this technique, which he had already applied in *Der Freischütz* and *Euryanthe*, plays an important part in rescuing *Oberon* from the oblivion to which its libretto so nearly consigned it.

For further illustration *see* COSTUME, fig.9 and VESTRIS, LUCIA ELIZABETH.

CLIVE BROWN

Oberon, König der Elfen ('Oberon, King of the Elves'). *Romantisches Singspiel* in three acts by PAUL WRANITZKY to a libretto by JOHANN GEORG CARL LUDWIG GIESEKE after SOPHIE SEYLER's libretto *Hüon und Amande* (1788), itself based on CHRISTOPH MARTIN WIELAND's epic poem *Oberon* (1780); Vienna, Theater auf der Wieden, 7 November 1789.

The knight Hüon (tenor) has been sent by Charlemagne on an impossible mission to the court of the Sultan of Baghdad. With the aid of Oberon (soprano), however, he is able to fulfil the king's demands and escape with the sultan's daughter Amande (soprano). Oberon and Titania (soprano) follow the fortunes of the lovers with much interest, since their own reconciliation (owing to a rash vow by Oberon) depends on the fidelity of Hüon and Amande, even in the face of death. After a shipwreck the lovers become slaves of Almansor (bass), Pasha of Tunis, and his wife Almansaris (soprano). Attempts by this pair to seduce Hüon and Amande lead to the ultimate test of fidelity. Although threatened with death they refuse to yield, whereupon – their vow fulfilled – Oberon rescues the lovers as they are about to be burnt at the stake.

The popular enthusiasm generated by *Oberon* at Vienna provided an important impulse for the creation of a generation of popular spectacles trading in magic and the exotic. *Die Zauberflöte* in particular shares many features with *Oberon*, musical as well as textual. Sophie Seyler's original libretto had been set first by Karl Hanke for the court theatre at Schleswig, but attracted no attention. Gieseke made major changes in Seyler's texts for the musical numbers to bring the libretto in line with Viennese practice: only six of its 31 numbers were retained; the drama was restructured from five to three acts, the last two with extensive finales; and more musical emphasis was placed on the comic pair. With Wranitzky's music *Oberon* quickly won favour throughout Germany. Wherever it was given, much attention was always lavished on visual effects. In north Germany it was commonly performed with additional music for the part of Almansaris by Carl David Stegmann (1790, Frankfurt).

THOMAS BAUMAN

Oberto, conte di San Bonifacio. *Dramma* in two acts by GIUSEPPE VERDI to a libretto by ANTONIO PIAZZA and TEMISTOCLE SOLERA; Milan, Teatro alla Scala, 17 November 1839.

Verdi's first opera has a chequered history. As we first hear of it in 1836, it was entitled *Rocester*, with a libretto by Antonio Piazza. After unsuccessful attempts to have the work put on in Milan and Parma, and after a lengthy hiatus during which the composer was employed in his home town of Busseto, Verdi – with the help of the librettist Temistocle Solera – revised and renamed the opera for its La Scala première. *Oberto* was moderately successful and was revived a number of times during the next three years, Verdi taking the opportunity to add various new numbers to the score. For Milan (1840) he supplied a new cavatina for Cuniza and a replacement duet for Cuniza and Riccardo, and adapted the role of Oberto for baritone; for Genoa (1841) he wrote a replacement duet for Leonora and Oberto and new music for the chorus 'Fidanzata avventurosa'; and for Barcelona (1841–2) he supplied a new first-act aria for Oberto, the cabaletta of which

('Ma fin che un brando vindice') later became associated with *Ernani*.

The action takes place in Bassano during the 13th century. Act 1 opens as Riccardo (tenor), Count of Salinguerra, is about to be married to Cuniza (mezzo-soprano), the sister of Ezzelino da Romano. Riccardo has previously seduced Leonora (soprano), the daughter of Oberto (bass), Count of San Bonifacio and Ezzelino's defeated enemy. Leonora and Oberto arrive in Bassano and enlist the sympathy of Cuniza. In a grand finale to the act, father and daughter confront Riccardo; Oberto challenges him to a duel. The second act begins as Cuniza resolves to make Riccardo take back Leonora. Oberto, however, continues to swear revenge. After a further confrontation between the four principals, the men withdraw to fight their duel; Riccardo emerges victorious but, guilt-ridden at causing Oberto's death, he departs abroad. Leonora, desolate at her father's death, decides to enter a convent.

Although Verdi was 26 when *Oberto* was first produced, the opera is in some ways an apprentice work, not typical of his early manner. Some of the lyrical pieces have a formal looseness reminiscent of Bellini (clearly, with Rossini, the main stylistic influence), and connecting passages between or within set pieces are often curiously perfunctory or non-existent. On the other hand, there are strong hints of the future: in powerful unison writing for the chorus, in some dramatically striking ensemble pieces and, perhaps most of all, in the brash rhythmic vitality of many episodes. The Adagio movement of the Act 2 quartet, 'La vergogna', probably the last piece to be written, is in many ways the most impressive. Although, as elsewhere in the opera, the daring chromaticism of the opening is rather shakily deployed, the large-scale control of musical rhythm, in particular the dynamic use of triplet figures, offers compelling testimony to what was to be one of the young Verdi's great strengths. However, such successes notwithstanding, it is unlikely that *Oberto* will become anything more than an occasional curiosity in the operatic repertory.
ROGER PARKER

Obey, André(-Alexis) (*b* Douai, 8 May 1892; *d* Montsoreau, 11 April 1975). French dramatist. He studied law and literature at the University of Lille. During World War I he served in the infantry; after demobilization he moved to Paris, where he first made a living as a journalist. Most of his major works, including *Noë* and *Le viol de Lucrèce* (which served as background sources for Britten), both of 1931, are elegant reworkings of familiar material in a highly sophisticated though ostensibly naive theatrical style. They were conceived for performance by the semi-professional Compagnie des Quinze, which had considerable impact both in France and on tour in London. Claude Arrieu's three-act 'imagerie musicale' based on *Noë* dates from 1932–4, though the first performance was given only in 1949. Britten's *Noye's Fludde*, based on a Chester miracle play, owes nothing directly to Obey's *Noë*. At the suggestion of Eric Crozier, impressed by the work of the Compagnie des Quinze, Britten asked Ronald Duncan to devise a libretto for *The Rape of Lucretia* based directly on Obey's *Le viol de Lucrèce*. Duncan, who naturally was also familiar with Shakespeare's poem and added, for instance, the important final section at the composer's last-minute request, did so, but always sought to minimize his obligations to Obey, who was not in fact consulted over the adaptation of his work.

Britten, however, did make the acknowledgment to which Obey was entitled. The Britten opera was first given in 1946, by the English Opera Group, at Glyndebourne.

André Obey: homme de théâtre (Douai, 1968)
R. Duncan: *How to Make Enemies* (London, 1968)
——: *Obsessed* (London, 1977)
C. Clüver: *Thornton Wilder und André Obey: Untersuchungen zum modernen epischen Theater* (Bonn, 1978) CHRISTOPHER SMITH

Obin, Louis-Henri (*b* Asq, nr Lille, 4 Aug 1820; *d* Paris, 1895). French bass. He studied in Lille and Paris, making his début in 1844 as Elmiro in Rossini's *Otello* at the Opéra, where he was engaged for nearly 25 years. In 1850 he sang in the première of Auber's *L'enfant prodigue*. He created Procida in Verdi's *Les vêpres siciliennes* (1855), the High Priest of Brahma in *L'Africaine* (1865) and King Philip in Verdi's *Don Carlos* (1867). His repertory included Don Basilio (*Il barbiere di Siviglia*), Leporello, the title role of *Mosè in Egitto*, Balthazar (*La favorite*) and Bertram (*Robert le diable*), which he sang at Covent Garden in 1863.
ELIZABETH FORBES

Obiols, Mariano (*b* Barcelona, 26 Nov 1809; *d* Barcelona, 10 Dec 1888). Spanish composer. He began his studies in Spain, but went abroad in 1831, becoming a protégé of Mercadante, with whom he toured Europe. His first opera, *Odio e amore* (2, F. Romani), had a successful run at La Scala beginning on 5 September 1837. In the same year Obiols returned to Barcelona to teach at the recently formed Conservatory, becoming its director in 1847, and during the next two decades dedicated himself mostly to teaching, administration and conducting. Not until 1874 did he produce another opera, *Editta di Belcourt* (4, F. Fors de Casamayor), first performed at the Gran Teatro del Liceo on 28 January. Though its italianate features were in harmony with the conservative repertory of the major Spanish theatres, *Editta* represented a compositional path abandoned by many of Obiols's younger contemporaries, such as Bretón and Pedrell. Pedrell's *El último Abencerraje*, in which Moorish and Spanish musical elements are prominent, was produced at the Liceo just a few months after the première of *Editta*.

A. Mestres: *Volves musicals, anecdotes y records* (Barcelona, 1926)
J. Subirá: 'Operas de los maestros catalanes Obiols y Albéniz', *Variadas versiones de libretos operísticos* (Madrid, 1973), 143–51
ROLAND J. VÁZQUEZ

Obraztsova, Yelena (Vasil'yevna) (*b* Leningrad [now St Petersburg], 7 July 1937). Russian mezzo-soprano. While still a student at the Leningrad Conservatory, she appeared with success at the Bol'shoy as Marina; in 1964 she became a soloist there. Her voice, of beautiful, full timbre, is controlled with unusual flexibility and lightness; she is an effective and spontaneous actress, notably in such roles as Marfa (*Khovanshchina*), Konchakovna (*Prince Igor*), Amneris, Eboli, Carmen and Lyubasha (*The Tsar's Bride*). She has also been successful in contemporary opera, particularly as Hélène (*War and Peace*) and Oberon (Britten's *A Midsummer Night's Dream*). Her international appearances have included those at San Francisco, the Metropolitan (during the Bol'shoy company's visit in 1975) and La Scala (as Massenet's Charlotte in 1976). She sang Azucena at Covent Garden in 1985, and made her début as a producer in the Bol'shoy's 1986–7 season with *Werther*. In 1973 she was made a National Artist of the RSFSR, and in 1976 was awarded the Lenin Prize.

I. M. YAMPOL'SKY

O'Brien, Oscar (*b* Ottawa, 7 Sept 1892; *d* Montreal, 20 Sept 1958). Canadian composer and folklorist. He studied the piano and the organ in Ottawa with Amédée Tremblay and piano in Montreal with Alfred Laliberté. From 1915 he collaborated with Charles Marchand on collecting and arranging folksongs, and he was also active as a teacher, orchestral pianist and accompanist. From 1927 to 1930 he took part in the festivals commissioned by the Canadian Pacific Railway and became their joint musical director with Harold E. Key in 1930; it was for these that his ballad operas, based on Canadian folklore and including many folksongs, were written. His operetta *Philippino* was broadcast in 1943. O'Brien became a priest in 1952.

ballad operas unless otherwise stated

Scène des voyageurs (1, L. T. de Montigny, after J.-C. Taché), Quebec, Auditorium, 27 May 1928
Silhouettes canadiennes (1), Quebec, Chateau Frontenac, 16 Oct 1930
Pastorale (1), Quebec, Chateau Frontenac, 16 Oct 1930
Une noce canadienne-française en 1830 (1, A. Bourgeois), Quebec, Chateau Frontenac, 17 Oct 1930
À Saint-Malo (3 scenes), Quebec, Chateau Frontenac, 17 Oct 1930
Philippino, 1931–3 (operetta, 3, G. Valois), Société Radio Canada, 15 March 1943

*

EMC (G. Potvin)
P. Larose: 'Oscar O'Brien', *Le droit* [Ottawa] (1 Dec 1934)
'A Troubadour Turns Monk', *Caecilia*, lxxx (1953), 206–7

MIREILLE BARRIÈRE

Obrucheniye v monastïre. Opera by Sergey Prokofiev; *see* BETROTHAL IN A MONASTERY.

Obukhova, Nadezhda (**Andreyevna**) (*b* Moscow, 22 Feb/6 March 1886; *d* Feodosiya, 15 Aug 1961). Russian mezzo-soprano. She graduated from Umberto Masetti's class at the Moscow Conservatory in 1912, and from 1916 to 1948 sang at the Bol'shoy. Her wide-ranging voice was distinguished by a rare beauty of tone, flexibility and fullness of sound. Her performances were noted for being dramatically true, warm and deeply poetic. She was an exceptional Carmen; among her best roles were Marfa (*Khovanshchina*), the Princess (Rimsky-Korsakov's *Kashchey the Deathless*), Princess Clarice (*The Love for Three Oranges*), Pauline (*The Queen of Spades*), Delilah and Fricka.

I. M. YAMPOL'SKY

Oca del Cairo, L' ('The Goose of Cairo'). *Opera buffa* in two acts, K422, by WOLFGANG AMADEUS MOZART to a libretto by GIOVANNI BATTISTA VARESCO; unfinished.

Mozart requested the libretto from Varesco in May 1783, discussed it in Salzburg during the summer, and by December had composed most of the first act. He abandoned work early in 1784 and in a letter to his father (10 February) he offered sharp criticisms of detail and design. The libretto involves an amorous intrigue on the island of Ripasecca, ruled by Don Pippo (bass); the Cairo goose was to intervene as a mechanical *deus ex machina*.

Full-length musical drafts survive for two duets (one on a text not in the libretto), two arias, a quartet and a finale; another aria survives complete in the hand of J. S. Mayr. Mozart also set one section of continuo recitative, normally composed last. The scenes nearest completion are between *buffo* servants, Aurelia (soprano) and Chichibeo (bass). The richly expressive quartet is for two more serious pairs of lovers, Celidora and Lavina (sopranos), Biondello and Calandrino (tenors). The finale of 461 bars is packed with action and includes a chorus of police preventing an elopement. Various attempts have been made to 'realize' the fragments, among them a scholarly reconstruction by Nicholas Temperley, staged at Urbana-Champaign, Illinois, in 1991.

JULIAN RUSHTON

Occasione fa il ladro, L' ('Opportunity Makes a Thief'). *Burletta per musica* in one act by GIOACHINO ROSSINI to a libretto by Luigi Prividali after EUGÈNE SCRIBE's play *Le prétendu par hasard, ou L'occasion fait le non* (1810); Venice, Teatro S Moisè, 24 November 1812.

While a storm rages over a hostelry near Naples the 'insolvent, egocentric, two-faced, wine-bibbing, womanizing man of the world' Don Parmenione (baritone) and his wily servant, Martino (baritone), encounter Count Alberto (tenor). Alberto is on his way to Naples to take delivery of his bride-to-be, Berenice (soprano), whom he has never met but whose portrait he has been sent by her uncle. When Alberto's comatose servant picks up the wrong luggage, Alberto leaves for Naples with Parmenione's dirty laundry while Parmenione and Alberto are left with Alberto's passport, papers, money and the portrait of Berenice, whom Parmenione resolves to pursue. Meanwhile Berenice has resolved to test her suitor's charms by exchanging clothes with her maid Ernestina (soprano) and observing him from a distance. Alberto in fact treats the disguised Berenice with proper aristocratic condescension, though as he lacks luggage and a passport his credentials are in question, especially when Parmenione arrives posing as the Count. Berenice's lightning cross-examination of Parmenione is very brilliant and has the merit of unmasking the old adventurer; and such is Alberto's attachment to the 'maid' he is more than happy to offer her his hand in marriage. Touched by Alberto's sincerity and angered by all-encircling confusions of identity, Berenice takes decisive steps to accept Alberto and sort things out once and for all. The opera is typical of the substantial one-act works Rossini wrote for the Teatro S Moisè. It has had a number of successful revivals including a Pesaro Festival production directed by Jean-Pierre Ponnelle.

RICHARD OSBORNE

Occurrence at Owl Creek Bridge, An. Radio opera by THEA MUSGRAVE to her own libretto after Ambrose Bierce's story; BBC, 14 September 1982; first stage performance (without background tape) Bracknell, Wilde Theatre, 23 June 1988.

Peyton Farquhar (high baritone), a well-to-do Southern planter living just outside the battle lines at the time of the American Civil War, is caught trying to set fire to a vital bridge on the Yankee line of advance and is condemned to death by hanging. At the moment of execution he imagines himself falling into the river, freeing himself from his bonds, and escaping home to be greeted by his wife.

Musgrave retains the form of the original story, with its 'surprise' ending: the last sentence tells us the escape is purely fantasy. Farquhar's is the only sung role. The narrator is to be played by 'a woman with a soft and beautiful Southern voice', and recordings of natural sounds are incorporated into the score. Musgrave softens the bitterness of the original by identifying the narrator with Farquhar's wife and adding a final sentence: 'The only comfort I know is that when he died his spirit reached out to me and has been with me ever since.'   HUGO COLE

Oceàna. *Commedia fantastica* in three acts by ANTONIO SMAREGLIA to a libretto by Silvio Benco; Milan, Teatro alla Scala, 22 January 1903.

Two sets of characters interact with Nersa (soprano), a restless nomadic girl: fantastic sea creatures with their god Init (tenor) and members of a tribe in ancient Siria headed by the aging Vadar (baritone). Two sea-genii, Ers (baritone) and Uls (bass), are dispatched by Init in search of a suitable bride. They first approach Nersa and henceforth mediate between the fantastic and real figures of the story. Their antics introduce a grotesque humour that justifies Benco's definition of 'fantastic comedy' for his libretto. Nersa is torn between the prospect of a married life with Vadar and the allure of the sea-god who wants to turn her into his queen Oceàna. The magic of the sea wins at first and Nersa leaves the tribe to join Init. Vadar sails with his brother Hareb (bass) to rescue her. A chorus of sirens aroused by Init almost wrecks the ship and drives Hareb to madness. Nersa is moved by Vadar's desperate call and consents to marry him, but, on the wedding day, Init reappears and Nersa surrenders to the charming sea-god. Having realized the true nature of his opponent, Vadar begs Init for the bliss of a quiet retreat so that he may drown despair and loneliness into oblivion. Hareb is brought to his senses and is put in charge of his brother's coveted properties.

The highlight of the opera occurs in the sea-nocturne at the beginning of the second act, in the course of which Init first meets Nersa asleep on a moonlit shore. Vivid music conjures up fantastic sea-spirits emerging from the waves; enraptured melodies for the maiden and the god, brisk fanfares for the tritons, graceful dances of undines and a bewitching chorus of sirens, are built up into a well-proportioned symphonic structure. Benco's text comprises a series of fantastic visions that could only be fully realized by the evocative power of music. It gives full scope to Smareglia's capacity for elaborating large, descriptive and lyrical movements characterized by thematic richness and a lush instrumental palette. Music becomes the prime element of the opera and sets the pace of the action. In *Oceàna* there is no substantial contrast between gods and mortals or fantasy and reality; nor is there any dramatic build-up because of the irrational nature of the events and the psychological tenuousness of the characters. Even Vadar's rescue expedition moves in a dreamlike dimension. Vadar and Nersa aspire to an oneiric state of eternal bliss: the tribal man becomes estranged from his own people and escapes into the unconscious and the irrational; the nomadic girl undergoes a sea change and becomes Oceàna.   MATTEO SANSONE

Ochman, Wiesław (*b* Warsaw, 6 Feb 1937). Polish tenor. He made his début in 1959 as Edgardo (*Lucia di Lammermoor*) at Bytom, where he was engaged until 1963, and then sang in Warsaw, Berlin and Hamburg. In 1968 he made his British début at Glyndebourne as Lensky. He has appeared at Chicago and San Francisco, at Salzburg, where he sang Idomeneus (1973), at the Paris Opéra in *Les vêpres siciliennes* (1974), and in

Vienna, where he sang Alfred in the centenary performance of *Die Fledermaus* at the Theater an der Wien (1975). The plangent tone of his voice is particularly suited to Slavonic music and his repertory includes Grigory (*Boris Godunov*), which he sang at the Metropolitan (1982), Prince Andrey and Golitsïn (*Khovanshchina*), Hermann (*The Queen of Spades*) and Števa (*Jenůfa*). A fine Mozart stylist, as his Don Ottavio and Tamino at Glyndebourne demonstrated, he has also sung Italian roles, including Rossini's Almaviva, Ernesto (*Don Pasquale*), the Duke, Alfredo, Germont and Cavaradossi. He sang the Shepherd in the first American continental performance of Szymanowski's *King Roger* at Buenos Aires (1981). Recent new roles have included Erik, Florestan, Herod and Fritz (Schreker's *Der ferne Klang*), which he sang in Brussels (1988).

ELIZABETH FORBES

Ochs, Siegfried (*b* Frankfurt, 19 April 1858; *d* Berlin, 5 Feb 1929). German composer. He studied at the Berlin Hochschule für Musik and rose to prominence as the founder and conductor of the Berlin Philharmonic Choir in 1882. His activities as a composer had less long-term significance, though his one-act operettas in the style of Offenbach became popular for private social occasions. His three-act comic opera, *Im Namen des Gesetzes*, set in Paris and the Pyrenees, further showed his skills as a pasticheur. It received its première in Hamburg in 1888 (vocal score, Berlin, 1888), but a disastrous performance in Breslau caused it to disappear from the stage. Plans for a further opera in 1889 failed to materialize and Ochs turned to songs and other, folk-based pieces as an alternative outlet for his humorous and unpretentious style.

S. Ochs: *Geschehenes, Gesehenes* (Leipzig, 1922)
K. Singer: *Siegfried Ochs: der Begründer des Philharmonisches Chors* (Berlin, 1933)   AMANDA GLAUERT

Octavia [*Die römische Unruhe, oder Die edelmühtige Octavia* ('The Roman Unrest, or The Noble-Spirited Octavia')]. *Sing-Spiel* in three acts by REINHARD KEISER to a libretto by BARTHOLD FEIND; Hamburg, Theater am Gänsemarkt, 5 August 1705.

Tiridates, King of Armenia (contralto), has been brought to Rome a captive, together with his beautiful wife Ormoena (soprano). Emperor Nero (bass) falls in love with Ormoena and decides to do away with his wife, Octavia (soprano). Ordered to take her own life with a dagger or poison, Octavia is prevented from stabbing herself only by the intervention of the devoted Piso (tenor). Piso then leads a revolution against Nero, causing him to flee the city. At the suggestion of the philosopher Seneca (bass), Octavia appears to Nero posing as her own ghost, and he is stricken with remorse. Rescued by his supporters, who have defeated the rebels, the emperor is overjoyed to learn that Octavia is still alive and pardons Piso because he saved her. Ormoena happily returns to Tiridates, whose crown had previously been restored by Nero.

The opera is particularly noteworthy for two extended and highly expressive dramatic scenes, for Octavia as she faces death in Act 2 (scenes xv–xvi) and for the tormented Nero with Octavia in Act 3 (scenes viii–x). Keiser's orchestration is more lavish than in any of his previous operas: horns appear in four numbers (their first recorded use at the Hamburg Opera), and one aria calls for five bassoons and continuo. The choral arias 'Amor, Amor reitzt zum springen' and 'Hebet und senket' are by Pantaleon Hebenstreit (1667–1750), presumably survivals from a first version of *Octavia* planned for Weissenfels, where Hebenstreit was dancing-master. Handel later borrowed extensively from Keiser's score.   JOHN H. ROBERTS

October. Opera by V. I. Muradeli; *see* OKTYABR'.

Odak, Krsto (*b* Siverić, nr Drniš, 20 March 1888; *d* Zagreb, 4 Nov 1965). Croatian composer. He studied music in Sinj and Šibenik, and later in Munich (1912–13) and in Novák's masterclasses at the Prague Conservatory (1919–22). From 1922 to 1961 he was professor at the Zagreb Academy of Music. In his music he inclined towards polyphonic forms and folk elements. His harmony was enriched with some contemporary developments as well as with ancient modalities, but melody remained his primary expressive means. The lyric opera *Dorica pleše* ('Dorica Dances') is based entirely on folk materials from Medjimurje, and the chorus has an important role, reminiscent of the chorus in an oratorio. According to Andreis, in this work 'he imposed upon himself a task that is almost impossible to solve: that of combining scenes of dramatic tension and intensity with folktunes which lack dramatic quality altogether, or at least possess it to an extent which is totally inadequate'.

Dorica pleše [Dorica Dances] (folk op, Đ. Vilović), Zagreb, 16 June 1934, vs (Zagreb, 1933)
Konac svijeta [Doomsday], 1943 (comic op, M. Fotez), unperf.
Majka Margarita [Mother Margarita] (radio op, V. Rabadan), Zagreb radio, 25 March 1955; stage, Zagreb, 9 Feb 1957

*

K. Kovačević: 'Krsto Odak 1888–1965: in memoriam', *Zvuk*, no.66 (1966), 31–3
J. Andreis: *Music in Croatia* (Zagreb, 1974), 268–71
                KREŠIMIR KOVAČEVIĆ/KORALJKA KOS

Odense. City in Denmark. As the winter residence of the landed gentry of Fyn, the city developed a rich theatrical and musical life from the end of the 18th century. One of the earliest performances of opera was Gluck's *Orfeo ed Euridice*, given in the Odense Klub (founded in 1780). A number of German troupes visited the city in the first half of the 19th century, and many performed operas at the Odense Teater (erected in 1795, renovated in 1840 and 1891). Görbing Franck's company arrived in 1809 and had their greatest success with Kauer's *Das Donauweibchen*. In 1815–16 a troupe from the Kongelige Teater, Copenhagen, performed Méhul's *Le trésor supposé* and later returned (1824–8), offering *Der Freischütz* and other works. Carl Becker's company regularly visited the theatre between 1828 and 1835; the German troupe of Ludwig Huber and Ludwig Delfendahl performed there in 1835–6 with more than 20 operas and Singspiels in their repertory, including *Die Entführung*, *Die Zauberflöte*, *Der Freischütz* and Méhul's *Joseph*. In 1839–40 Karl Friedrich von Hahn's company performed for a season and in 1842 the Huber-Delfendahl company returned with performances of *Fidelio* and *Norma*. Under the director M. W. Brun, operas in Danish were given from 1851 to 1854, including Donizetti's *La fille du régiment* and Auber's *Fra Diavolo*.

Several Singspiels and operettas have been performed at the Odense Teater. A new theatre (designed by N. Jacobsen) opened in 1914, but operas were given regularly only after 1948. In 1953 the Fynske Opera was founded with municipal support and assisted by the Odense City Orchestra. Under the artistic director and conductor Martellius Lundqvist the company flourished until 1964, mounting one new production a year (usually in November) at the Odense Teater. Siegfried Salomon's *Leonora Christina* (1926) was revived there in 1960.

*

K. Schmidt: *Meddelelser om Skuespil og Theaterforhold i Odense i Anledning af Hundredaarsdagen for den første danske Komedies Opførelse paa Odense Theater den 18. November 1896* [Reports on Acting and Theatre Conditions in Odense on the Occasion of the Centenary of the First Danish Comedy's Performance at the Odense Theatre, 18 November 1896] (Odense, 1896)
C. M. K. Petersen: 'Musik og Skuespil fra 1770 til vore Dage' [Music and Acting from 1770 to the Present Day], in H. St. Holbeck and others: *Odense Bys Historie* [Odense City History] (Odense, 1926), ii, 679–783
P. Dreyer, ed.: *Odense Teater 1796–18. November 1946: et tilbageblik paa den fyenske landsdelsscenes virksomhed gennem 150 aar* [Odense Theatre 1796 to 18 November 1946: a Look Back at the Provincial Stage Activity in Fyn During the Last 150 Years] (Odense, 1946)
G. Hansen: *Die Entwicklung des National-Theaters in Odense aus einer deutschen Entreprise: ein Beitrag zur deutsch-dänischen Theatergeschichte*, Die Schaubühne: Quellen und Forschungen zur Theatergeschichte, lix (Emsdetten, 1963)
P. Dreyer, ed.: *Odense Teater 175 år, 1796–1971* [Odense Theatre 175 Years, 1796–1971] (Odense, 1971)
S. Reventlow: *Musik på Fyn blandt kendere og liebhavere* [Music in Fyn Among Connoisseurs and Amateurs] (Copenhagen, 1983)
                CLAUS RØLLUM-LARSEN

Odessa (Ukrainian Odesa). City and port in Ukraine. The Odessa Russian Opera originated in 1809, when the municipal theatre was built. In its early years the theatre featured both drama and opera productions, ballets and vaudevilles, in which Russian, Italian and French companies appeared. In 1873 the theatre burnt to the ground; a new one was built by the Viennese architects Fellner and Helmer in 1884–7. In 1925 fire again damaged the theatre, and the following year it was reopened as the Odes'kyy Akademichnyy Teatr Opery ta Baletu. The next serious reconstruction occurred in 1965–7.

The Odessa Opera was one of the more important musical centres of the tsarist empire. Before the 1917 revolution many illustrious names appeared in a variety of productions. Composer-conductors included Tchaikovsky, Rubinstein, Rimsky-Korsakov, Nápravník, Arensky and Glazunov, and singers included Shalyapin, Krusceniski, Sobinov, Caruso, Battistini, Anselmi and Ruffo; famous dancers and actors appeared there as well. Two of Lysenko's works received their premières in Odessa, *Utoplena* ('The Drowned Maiden', 1885) and *Natalka Poltavka* (1889). By the 1911 season the main diet offered by the theatre was operatic. After the reorganization in 1926, when the company became Ukrainian, it began to produce a number of Ukrainian operas, notably *Rozlom* by Volodymyr Femelidi (1929), *Zolotyy obruch* ('The Golden Ring') by Lyatoshyns'ky and *Karmelyuk* by Valentyn Kostenko (both 1930), and *Taras Bulba* by Lysenko (1971). During the late 1920s and early 30s, until the advent of 'socialist realism', productions were often frankly experimental, borrowing as much from cinema as from the theatrical avant garde. Verykivs'ky's *Sotnyk* ('The Cossack Lieutenant') was given its first performance in 1938. During World War II the company was amalgamated with the Dnipropetrovs'k Theatre of Opera and Ballet and settled in Krasnoyarsk.

In 1944 it returned to Odessa and resumed its former activities. Since 1982 the principal stage director has been A. Pochykovs'ky. Seasons begin in early September and end in August, with more than 30 productions a year.

ME (R. M. Rozenberg; also 'Odesskiy Teatr Operï i Baleta', Yu. S. Yeveleva and S. M. Kogan)

Odes'kyy derzhavnyy teatr opery ta baletu (Odessa, 1929)
Odes'kyy derzhavnyy robitnychyy teatr opery ta baletu, Pyat'rokiv (Odessa, 1932)
V. Hetman, ed.: *Odessa: Teatr operï i baleta* (Odessa, 1957)
L. Rosen and L. Shumakova: *Odesskiy teatr operï i baleta* (Odessa, 1964)
A. Artemov and I. Ignatkin: *Odesskiy opernïy teatr* (Kiev, 1969)

VIRKO BALEY

Odinot, Nicolas-Médard. See AUDINOT, NICOLAS-MÉDARD.

Odyssee, Die ('The Odyssey'). *Musik-Tragödie* in four parts, each in a prologue and three acts, by AUGUST BUNGERT to his own libretto after HOMER; Dresden, Königliches Hoftheater: *Kirke* ('Circe'), 24 January 1898; *Nausikaa* ('Nausicaa'), 20 March 1901; *Odysseus' Heimkehr* ('Odysseus's Homecoming'), 12 December 1896; *Odysseus' Tod* ('Odysseus's Death'), 30 October 1903.

Each opera's overture subsequently acquired its own title: *Polyphemos, Die Syrenen und Odysseus' Strandung, Telemachos Ausfahrt* and *Telegonos Abschied*. The four operas were originally intended to have been preceded by *Die Ilias*, comprising a further two, *Achilleus* and *Klytemnestra*, to form a six-opera cycle entitled *Homerische Welt*.

Odysseus' Heimkehr, the first opera of the cycle to be performed and by far the most successful, is structurally typical of the rest. The staged prologue (introduced by a short, integrated orchestral 'Einleitung') is linked to Act 1 by an orchestral interlude; it introduces the presiding figure of Athene (contralto), and Penelope's suitors, who plot to kill Telemachus (tenor), Odysseus's son. The first act opens with a chorus of naiads, who greet the slowly awakening Odysseus (baritone) on the shore of Ithaca; without revealing his identity, he rescues Telemachus from the sea before being greeted by his blind father, Laertes (bass). Act 2 sets Penelope's grieving faithfulness against the nocturnal bacchanale of her impatient suitors, whose violent intrigues dominate the act before Odysseus enters, disguised as a beggar. Only in Act 3, following the contest with Odysseus's bow, are the suitors vanquished. The hero reveals his identity to Penelope (contralto).

Although Bungert's verse text tends more towards conventional operatic set pieces than does Wagner's *Ring* poem, it incorporates a similar elaborate philosophical conception – the potential mastery of nature (as Gaia and Eros) by ethical consciousness, at its highest in Zeus. In the fourth opera Bungert went beyond Homer; Odysseus is killed by the vengeful Despoina, Penelope's maid.

The musical language of the cycle is much more diatonic than Wagner's. Melodically orientated and orchestrally dominated, the musical discourse falls into large structural units and set-piece choruses but still makes extensive use of leitmotifs, representing characters, motivations and abstract concepts. The 'decorative' tendency noted by some critics manifests itself not only in elaborate scenic requirements (originally realized in the grand manner of Alma-Tadema pain-

tings) but also in Bungert's penchant for large casts (*Odysseus' Heimkehr* includes 18 named roles, with choruses of maidens, suitors, shepherds and naiads).

Bungert signally failed to conquer the Wagnerian high ground in a German musical culture that still lacked accepted criteria for a nationalistic and conservative modernism. His belief that the Bible and Greek literature were the 'nature' from whose soil Germanic culture had grown might nevertheless have accommodated the ideology of subsequent decades (the nature-voice of Gaia is initially given to a chorus of German basses). Rudolf Louis was among those who observed that Bungert's implicit aim of ousting Wagnerism manifested itself in a pseudo-Wagnerism that revealed affinities with the 'Volksoper' tradition of Lortzing and Nessler.

PETER FRANKLIN

Oedipe ('Oedipus'). *Tragédie lyrique* in four acts by GEORGE ENESCU to a libretto by Edmond Fleg, partly after SOPHOCLES' Oedipus plays; Paris, Opéra, 13 March 1936.

The Theban High Priest	bass
A Shepherd	tenor
Créon [Creon] *Jocasta's brother*	baritone
Jocaste [Jocasta] *Queen of Thebes*	mezzo-soprano
Laïos [Laius] *King of Thebes*	tenor
Tirésias [Tiresias] *a blind prophet*	bass
Oedipe [Oedipus] *son of Laius and Jocasta*	bass-baritone
Phorbas *formerly a shepherd, later the Corinthian court messenger*	bass
Mérope [Merope] *Queen of Corinth*	mezzo-soprano
A Watchman	bass
The Sphinx	contralto
Antigone *Oedipus's daughter*	soprano
Thésée [Theseus] *King of Athens*	baritone

Theban people, shepherds, Corinthians, Athenian elders, Furies etc.

Setting Thebes, Corinth and Athens in mythological times

The earliest musical sketches for *Oedipe*, Enescu's masterpiece – and one of the greatest musical works by a Romanian – date from 1910, soon after the composer had been deeply moved by a performance of Sophocles' *Oedipus tyrannus*; yet he did not finish the score until 1931 or 1932. Even Fleg's libretto, though drafted before World War I, matured slowly: by 1921 it had developed (after Enescu had criticized its earlier version) into the most comprehensive of all dramatic treatments of the Oedipus myth, covering the protagonist's life-story from birth to death. Acts 3 and 4 are based (with significant modifications) on Sophocles, but the first two cover events which, though well known in legend, seem never previously to have been presented on stage. Enescu's main period of work on the music (but not the orchestration) extended from summer 1921 until November 1922, when he played the entire opera over to a group of friends. Although the full score took him much longer to complete, two orchestral excerpts were performed separately in 1924 and 1925. The première (with André Pernet in the title role and conducted by Philippe Gaubert) was greeted with enthusiasm, especially by musicians; yet *Oedipe* was dropped from the

Opéra's repertory after 1937 and was not revived anywhere until French radio broadcast it in May 1955 shortly after the composer's death. The first new stage production was in Brussels in 1956. In 1958 the Bucharest Opera Company gave the first performance in Romania (conducted by Silvestri), since when the opera has taken its rightful place in the repertory there. Stage performances outside Romania have remained few, and the work has gained wider recognition mainly through a pioneering Romanian recording (1964) and a French one (1989) conducted by Lawrence Foster with José van Dam as Oedipus.

ACT 1 (Prologue) *A room in Laius's palace* An ominous, tortuously chromatic orchestral prelude introduces several of the work's main motifs, starting with one commonly described as the theme of Fate. There follow the themes of 'parricide' and of 'man's victory' (which have also been identified, respectively, with Laius and Oedipus), as well as a phrase usually associated with Jocasta. Enescu's technique is too flexible, however, for such exact labels to be wholly satisfactory: recurrent themes often change both shape and function, and seemingly distinct motifs can show clear family resemblances.

The curtain rises on the festivities to celebrate the birth of a son to Laius and Jocasta. The first part of the act is pervaded by radiant, modally-inflected music with a strong Romanian folk flavour – not least in the *doina*-like arabesques for flutes and piccolos associated with the shepherds, who lead a dance which brings the celebrations to a climax. But when Jocasta and Laius are about to name the baby, the prophet Tiresias, hitherto grimly silent, suddenly utters a groan of anguish. He predicts that the child, born in defiance of the gods, is destined to kill his father and marry his mother. All joy at once goes out of the festivities, and Laius and Jocasta, in a desperate attempt to flout Tiresias's prophecy, order a shepherd to take the infant to the gorge of Cithaeron and kill him. The stunned desolation of this ending is reflected in broken, dislocated reminiscences of the dance music and of phrases from the prelude.

ACT 2.i *A room in the palace of Polybus, king of Corinth* Ignoring Laius's instructions, the shepherd has given the baby to Phorbas, who has secretly put him in the place of Polybus's and Merope's own infant son who has died while in his care. Oedipus has thus grown up convinced that Polybus and Merope are his parents, and they believe that he is their child. However, after 20 years the young man has been told of his grim destiny by an oracle. He naturally thinks the prediction relates to Polybus and Merope, both of whom he loves dearly; he has therefore become obsessed with leaving Corinth for ever, to prevent the prophecy from coming true. In the present scene Oedipus broods on these thoughts and cannot interest himself in the distant celebrations of Aphrodite and Adonis in which he has been expected to take part. When Merope asks what is troubling him, and assures him that a rumour that he is a foundling is false, he horrifies her by revealing the truth as he understands it, and resolves to leave the city immediately. During this scene, telling contrasts are made between the serenely modal music of the distant festivities and the dark declamatory intensity of Oedipus's own utterances.

2.ii *The meeting point of three roads* The scene is witnessed by the shepherd who disobeyed the order to kill Oedipus as a baby: on his pipe he again plays *doina*-like arabesques of the kind associated with him in Act 1, and these add to the fatalistic atmosphere in which the protagonist's destiny starts to be fulfilled. A storm is approaching as Oedipus enters in a mood of growing fury against the gods, culminating in an impulsive gesture when he raises his club in defiance of Fate. Laius appears in a chariot, with a charioteer and a soldier. They assume that Oedipus is threatening them, and in the fight that ensues they are all killed. Still unaware of the king's identity, Oedipus resumes his journey as the tempest reaches its climax. Throughout this scene, the 'parricide' motif is prominent.

2.iii *Outside the gate of Thebes* From a watchman on the city ramparts Oedipus learns that outside the walls the Sphinx is ravaging the population by challenging passers-by to solve riddles and devouring them when they fail. Whoever succeeds in solving one will cause her to die, thus winning rich rewards as the saviour of the city. At the beginning of the scene, the Sphinx is asleep in the background; her slumber and slow awakening are evoked by the most eerily nightmarish orchestral sounds in the opera. Determined to become the city's saviour, Oedipus confronts her and solves her riddle (which differs significantly from the one in the traditional version of the story): 'Name someone or something that is greater than Fate', to which he replies 'Man!' In her death throes, which culminate in an upward glissando on a musical saw, the Sphinx seems to be half sobbing, half laughing: she leaves Oedipus with the feeling that his victory may, after all, be hollow. But outwardly his triumph is richly rewarded: in the opera's biggest climax of collective jubilation, the Thebans welcome him as their new king and offer him the hand of the recently widowed Jocasta.

ACT 3 *The public square in Thebes* 20 more years have passed, during which Oedipus seems to have proved stronger than Fate: he has been a wise king, Thebes has prospered and Jocasta has borne him several children. Eventually, however, a new calamity has struck the city in the form of a plague which (according to an oracle consulted by Creon) will persist until Laius's murderer, who dwells within the city walls, has been found and punished. Creon has asked Tiresias for his help in identifying the culprit: reluctantly the ancient prophet accuses the king. At first Oedipus believes this to be part of a plot to depose him in favour of Creon; but little by little the facts of his past are revealed with the help of the old shepherd (summoned as the sole surviving witness of Laius's murder) and of Phorbas, who has arrived as a messenger from Corinth. Only now does Oedipus learn the truth. Shattered, Jocasta commits suicide and Oedipus blinds himself. He then leaves the city (the only sure way of freeing it from the plague) and sets out on a life of wandering, accompanied by his favourite daughter, Antigone. Being derived from *Oedipus tyrannus*, this part of the plot closely parallels that of Stravinsky's *Oedipus rex*. But Enescu's version is far more overtly passionate and poignantly human. The act begins with plaintive, exotically inflected funeral choruses; as past events are revealed, musical reminiscences from previous acts are introduced; and the climax is an extraordinary *Sprechgesang* monologue in which the newly blinded Oedipus confesses his guilt and bewails his fate before the assembled Thebans.

ACT 4 (Epilogue) *A sacred grove near Athens* Although basically derived from *Oedipus at Colonus*, the depiction of the protagonist's last hour introduces a quasi-Christian note of redemption – of serenely spiritual liberation from the tyranny of Fate. After years of wandering, the aged Oedipus comes with Antigone to the grove that is the home of the Furies, now transformed into peaceful protectors of Athens and its wise king Theseus (who is in the grove when Oedipus arrives). Creon appears and tries to persuade Oedipus to return to Thebes, which is afflicted by new misfortunes and therefore wants his help. When Oedipus refuses, Creon attempts to force him to come by trying to abduct Antigone; but he is interrupted by the entry of Theseus with some Athenian elders, whereupon he again accuses Oedipus of incest and parricide. Oedipus retorts that he is totally innocent, since his will was never in his crimes. He declares that, in the deeper sense, he has indeed overcome Fate. As if in reply to his last words the Furies are heard in the background calling his name. Oedipus recognizes this as his final call to rest, in a secret place which must be known only to Theseus: his sight restored for his last journey, he leads the Athenian king into the grove. The scenery gradually changes until Oedipus suddenly vanishes in a blaze of light. The Furies have the last word: 'Happy is he whose heart is pure. Peace be upon him!' Despite numerous musical links with earlier parts of the opera (for example, Oedipus's

declaration that he has defeated Fate is set to the 'man's victory' motif), the final act has a hauntingly distinctive atmosphere, beginning and ending in a mood of profound, beatific calm. The evocations of the luxuriantly leafy grove itself reach a high point of orchestral opulence during the final transformation scene; and the moment of Oedipus's death is marked by a climax as powerful (in its different way) as any in Acts 2 or 3. The philosophical and symbolic implications of Fleg's new ending to the story are likely to remain controversial, but at the spiritual level the conclusion is as satisfying and moving as any in 20th-century opera.

JOHN C. G. WATERHOUSE

Oedipe à Colone ('Oedipus at Colonus'). *Tragédie lyrique* in three acts by ANTONIO SACCHINI to a libretto by NICOLAS-FRANÇOIS GUILLARD after SOPHOCLES; Versailles, 4 January 1786.

Oedipe à Colone was written during 1785 and performed for the first time at Versailles. Intrigues against the composer led to the abandonment of a revival at Fontainebleau, but by the time of Sacchini's death in October 1786 a production at the Opéra must have been planned. It was given there on 1 February 1787 and was an immediate and lasting success: it was performed more often – 583 times up to 1830 – than any other operas of its time, including Gluck's.

Polynice [Polynices] (tenor) requests the help of Thésée [Theseus] (bass) against his brother Etéocle [Eteocles], who has usurped his share of the throne of Thebes. Theseus agrees to help, and offers his daughter Eriphile [Eriphyle] (soprano) in marriage. Chorus and ballet celebrate the impending wedding, but when Theseus requests divine assistance Polynices confesses that he has sinned by helping Eteocles drive their father out of Thebes; the old man's whereabouts are unknown. A solemn ritual fails to placate the gods, and the first act ends in confusion.

In a moving scene at the start of Act 2, Polynices, penitent, despairing and banished from Athens, seeks purification from his father's curse at Colonus ('Hélas! d'une si pure flamme'). He sees Oedipe [Oedipus] (bass), blind and aged, his halting footsteps guided by his daughter Antigone (soprano), and leaves to inform Theseus. Oedipus sings angrily of his sons, and is comforted by Antigone. Remembering his own parricide, he suffers a visitation of the Eumenides. The people of Colonus try to eject the accursed man from the sacred grove, and threaten to kill him; Theseus intervenes, proclaiming Oedipus a victim, not a sinner, and the act ends with a trio.

In the third act Polynices and Antigone are united in concern for their father, and Antigone sings the aria 'Dieux! ce n'est pas pour moi que ma voix vous implore'. Polynices is willing to renounce Thebes and Eriphyle (duet with Antigone), and even to win the crown back for Oedipus. At Theseus's request Antigone attempts to reconcile Polynices and her father, who repeats his formal curse. Nevertheless in a long trio, and in a drastic and unconvincing departure from the legend, Oedipus relents; the gods are appeased, and the opera ends happily without reference to the disastrous attack on Thebes.

Guillard planned his adaptation of the Greek tragedy with skill and economy, although too many of the arias engage with secondary feelings (Polynices' flattering of Theseus is emphasized in Act 1 at the expense of his

Costume for Polynices in an early production of Sacchini's 'Oedipe à Colone' by the Académie Royale de Musique in Paris: from 'Costumes et annales des grands théâtres de Paris' (1789)

repentance). He reduced the role of the chorus to provide arias and an unusual profusion of ensembles. Sacchini's forms are characteristically flexible; short ritornellos and avoided final cadences allow measured music to flow into recitative and arioso. Although *Oedipe* is still clearly divided into numbers and is less symphonic than parts of *Renaud*, there is no full close after the overture until after the third number. The sonata-form overture has had an independent life in the concert hall. Sacchini treats the drama intimately, and with melodic finesse. The choral writing is excellent; particularly remarkable are the numerous ensembles, and their development of the action, in which Sacchini goes further than Mozart in his otherwise comparable *La clemenza di Tito*. Ensembles in previous French serious opera tended to leave the dramatic situation unchanged. The second-act duet in *Oedipe* begins with Oedipus suffering the torments of the Eumenides; Antigone soothes him and their voices are united. The trio in the third act ('Où suis-je? Mes enfants!') contains the crucial change in Oedipus, from fighting an inclination to forgive Polynices to the point where he relents.

JULIAN RUSHTON

Oedipus. Music-dance drama in one act by HARRY PARTCH to his own libretto after SOPHOCLES; Oakland, California, Mills College, 14 March 1952 (revised version, Shell Beach, Sausalito, California, 11 September 1954).

Partch originally used *Sophocles' King Oedipus, a Version for the Modern Stage*, by W. B. Yeats, for his libretto, and with this text the work was first heard as *King Oedipus*. Partch had already prepared a musical outline by 1934, and in that year secured the poet's approval in Dublin. The project could not be realized until 1951, however, and after the 1952 performances he found that the Yeats estate would not permit a recording; accordingly, he prepared a new libretto from non-copyright sources, modernizing and Americanizing the language, and revised the score. This version was first performed in 1954. In 1967 Partch further revised the score, modifying the instrumentation.

The action takes place before the palace of King Oedipus (bass) at Thebes. His subjects beg his assistance in overcoming the plagues that have devastated the city, which the oracle of Apollo has declared will subside only when the murderer of Laius, the preceding king, is driven out. The blind prophet Tiresias (bass), with great reluctance, names Oedipus as the murderer and hints that the king is guilty of incest. Oedipus accuses Tiresias of having been suborned to falsehood by Creon, the king's brother-in-law. Creon and Oedipus quarrel and the king's wife Jocasta (low soprano), Laius's widow, tries to intercede. She reveals that an oracle predicted that Laius would be killed by his own son, but the prediction had been forestalled by exposing the infant to the elements; Laius was in fact murdered by strangers at a place where three roads met. Oedipus, who had once killed a man at such an intersection, now begins to suspect part of the truth. After the appearance of an aged Messenger from Corinth and the Herdsman (same actor as Tiresias), who had been sent out to expose Laius's baby son, the truth is plain. The chorus comments in shocked tones and a voice declares that Jocasta has killed herself. The chorus is reduced to wordless syllables of horror. Oedipus re-enters, having blinded himself, and declares his misery antiphonally with the chorus. Wordlessly, Creon assists him on his way out of the city, and the chorus declares that no life can be called fortunate until it is complete.

Unlike his later opera, *Revelation in the Courthouse Park*, *Oedipus* attempts to re-create the musical spirit of Greek drama in fairly strict terms. There is much spoken dialogue (though Partch's unique instruments play almost continuously), and all singing is in the 'intoning voice' that is Partch's equivalent of recitative. The concluding dialogue (after Oedipus's tragic enlightenment) is drastically curtailed and replaced with pantomime and a musical climax of wordless syllables – a characteristic Partchian touch.   ANDREW STILLER

Oedipus rex. Opera-oratorio in two acts by IGOR STRAVINSKY to a libretto by JEAN COCTEAU after SOPHOCLES; Vienna, Staatsoper, 23 February 1928 (previously performed as an oratorio, Paris, Théâtre Sarah Bernhardt, 30 May 1927).

Oedipe [Oedipus]	tenor
Jocaste [Jocasta]	mezzo-soprano
Créon [Creon]	bass-baritone
Tirésias [Tiresias]	bass
A Shepherd	tenor
A Messenger	bass-baritone
'Le Speaker' (narrator)	spoken
Chorus of tenors and basses	

Setting Thebes, mythological time

Stravinsky claimed to have been inspired with the idea of composing a hieratic drama in an archaic sacred language ('not dead but turned to stone') by reading a biography of St Francis of Assisi. Having decided on Sophocles' Oedipus play, he turned to Cocteau, who had been trying to secure his collaboration since 1914, and whose highly compressed *Antigone* he had admired. Jean Daniélou translated the sung portions into Latin. The composer insisted on a conventional numbers format, 'opera' and the music-maiming 'music drama' having become antithetical categories in his mind. It was Cocteau's idea to introduce the opera's six episodes with didactic spoken summaries in the vernacular, though in the event their effect was the opposite of illuminating: they added yet another layer of stiff distancing from the action, which had already been paralysed by Stravinsky's insistence that the main characters behave like statues. (A frieze-like set, drawn by the composer's artist son Théodore, is prescribed in the published score.) While the effect of this procedure has been compared to that of Brecht's 'epic theatre', it seems more likely beholden to older Russian-symbolist notions of art as harbinger of a new mythological age and conveyor of spiritual community. These ideas, it seems hardly necessary to add, were lost on the Ballets Russes audience (and even on Dyagilev, to whom it was presented in token of his 20th anniversary as impresario). Following the première, conducted by Lothar Wallerstein, the opera made its way first in Germany, possibly abetted by the Brechtian resonance. Its very successful production at the Kroll Opera, Berlin (1928, Klemperer conducting), was immortalized by the uncomprehending Schoenberg in a notorious squib.

ACT 1 The Speaker announces that a trap has been laid for Oedipus and that the ensuing drama will display its closing.

'*Oedipus rex*'
(Stravinsky): Théodore
Stravinsky's design for the
set which appears in the
published score, where it
is described by the
composer as presenting
'the advantage of having
no depth. It avoids the
voices becoming lost.
Everything takes place on
the same level.'

Dessin de THÉODORE STRAWINSKY.

Episode i As the action commences the inhabitants of Thebes call upon their king to save them from pestilence; their first invocation of his name is immediately transformed into a famous three-note ostinato that oscillates a baleful minor 3rd on its repetitions (chorus, 'Kaedit nos pestis'). Accompanied by regal dotted rhythms and giving his words proud melismatic emphasis, Oedipus the king promises to save the city from the plague as he had once saved it from the Sphinx (aria, 'Liberi, vos liberabo').

Episode ii Creon, the king's brother-in-law, sent to Delphi to consult the oracle, now returns with the gods' answer, delivered through a peremptory C major arpeggio (aria, 'Respondit deus'): it is revealed that the murderer of the former king Laius is at large in Thebes and must be driven out. Egged on by the crowd, Oedipus vows that he will solve the crime (aria with chorus, 'Non reperias vetus skelus').

Episode iii He calls upon Tiresias the seer, who, knowing that Oedipus is doomed, holds his tongue (aria, 'Dikere non possum'). When Oedipus, enraged, accuses Tiresias of being the murderer himself, the seer intones a clue over a D major cadence that will return when Oedipus finally sees the light: 'the murderer of the king is a king'. For now, however, Oedipus remains blind, (self-)deceptively resolving the harsh truth-cadence to his own dulcet E♭ tonality, in which he floridly accuses Tiresias and Creon of a jealous plot against him (aria, 'Invidia fortunam odit'). The loud argument, which culminates in actual shouting, brings Queen Jocasta to the scene; she is hailed by the populace (chorus, 'Gloria, gloria, gloria!').

ACT 2 *Episode* iv Jocasta upbraids the men for quarrelling at a time of plague (aria, 'Nonne erubeskite, reges, clamare'). Accompanied by an orchestral evocation of aulos and kithara (flute and harp), and insinuating her words seductively in a stereotyped 'oriental' vein, she belittles the oracle. Do they not lie? Had it not been foretold that Laius would be killed by a son of hers, while in fact he had been killed by thieves at a crossroads? At the mention of the word 'crossroads' (*trivium*), reiterated mysteriously by the crowd, now figuratively as well as literally a 'Greek chorus', Oedipus

is seized with fear: accompanied by an ominous timpani tattoo, he recalls that he did once kill an old man at a crossroads (aria with chorus, 'Pavesco subito, Jocasta'). But he remains undeterred in his prideful quest and resolves to send for an old shepherd, the last remaining witness to the crime.

Episode v Now a Messenger (a role often doubled by the singer playing Creon) appears with news of the death of Polybus, King of Corinth, who had raised Oedipus as his son, but who on his deathbed had admitted that Oedipus had been adopted (aria with chorus, 'Mortuus est Polybus'). The Shepherd now gives reluctant testimony: he had seen the finding of the baby Oedipus, abandoned on a mountainside (aria, 'Oportebat takere'). Jocasta senses what is coming and flees, but the crowd jumps excitedly to the conclusion that their king was of divine birth, and Oedipus, swayed willingly to their opinion, exults in a final melismatic cascade (aria with chorus, 'Nonne monstrum rescituri'). But the Messenger and the Shepherd reveal the awful truth before departing: Oedipus was the son of Laius and Jocasta who abandoned him; he was the slayer of Laius who begot him; and now he is the consort of Jocasta who bore him. Oedipus, suddenly shorn of all musical ornateness, sees the light plain, at last confirming the D major cadence he had diverted before (aria, 'Natus sum quo nefastum est … Lux facta est!'). He vanishes.

Episode vi Heralded by pompous fanfares, the Messenger now returns and, with the chorus's help, enunciates what the Speaker calls 'the famous monologue, "Dead is the sacred head of Jocasta"' (aria with chorus, 'Divum Jocastae caput mortuum!'). Three times he pronounces the terrible words, the chorus filling in the details: Jocasta has hanged herself for shame, and Oedipus has put out his eyes with her golden brooch. Oedipus, now literally blinded, reappears, and his former subjects lovingly drive him from Thebes to a reprise of the opening chorus ('Ekke regem Oedipoda … Vale miser Oedipus noster, te amabam').

*   *   *

The music, composed in 1926–7, is the product of Stravinsky's early neo-classic manner at its most extreme: musical materials thought outdated for a century or more – themes formed from arpeggiated triads, diminished 7th chords, formal recitatives – are ostentatiously displayed, and a deliberately offputting *hauteur* is affected. Yet lurking behind the frigid exterior is a very humane conception of the tragedy, centred (the composer's explicit denial notwithstanding) on the person of Oedipus. The character's musical idiom undergoes a wrenching transformation as he is brought low; and the allegorical modulatory scheme, thanks to the composer's extraordinary control, is for once as vivid to the ear as to the score-reading eye (if not so pedantically worked-out as analysts have sometimes maintained).   RICHARD TARUSKIN

Oehman, Carl-Martin (*b* Floda, nr Göteborg, 4 Sept 1887; *d* Stockholm, 26 Dec 1967). Swedish tenor. He studied the piano and the organ at the Stockholm Conservatory, and then, privately, singing in Stockholm and Milan. He appeared first in concerts in 1914, making his operatic début in *Fra Diavolo* at Göteborg three years later. The Stockholm Opera, which became the centre of his career, heard him first in 1919 and last in 1941. He became well known for his singing of the more lyrical Wagnerian roles, yet in his single season at the Metropolitan in 1924 he appeared only as Laca in the American première of *Jenůfa* and as Saint-Saëns' Samson. At Covent Garden in 1928 he sang Tannhäuser and Walther in *Die Meistersinger*: the power of his full voice and the charm of his *mezza voce* were admired. Some of his best work was done in Berlin, where he sang in the local premières of *Don Carlos* and *Simon Boccanegra*. As a teacher he numbered among his pupils Jussi Björling, Martti Talvela and Nicolai Gedda, all of whom paid warm tribute to his musicianship and clarity. On recordings he is somewhat variable, but at best the voice has fine quality and the style remarkable sensitivity.   J. B. STEANE

Oenslager, Donald (*b* Harrisburg, PA, 7 March 1902; *d* Bedford, NY, 20 June 1975). American designer and historian. He began designing while a student at Harvard University, influenced by Professor George Pierce Baker and the emerging stagecraft of Norman Bel Geddes and, in particular, Robert Edmond Jones. He toured Europe in 1923–4 on a Sachs Travelling Fellowship with John Mason Brown (who later became a theatre critic) and began his collection of original designs, now housed in the Museum of the City of New York. He joined the Jones, Kenneth Macgowan and Eugene O'Neill wing of the Provincetown Players. His first production in New York was a dance satire, *Sooner and Later*, for the Neighbourhood Playhouse in 1925. In the same year he joined Baker at the newly-established Yale School of Drama and from that time combined teaching with designing. He served in World War II as a camouflage officer in the US Air Force.

Oenslager designed many musicals, among them Romberg's *The New Moon* (1928), Rodgers and Hart's *America's Sweetheart* (1931), Gershwin's *Girl Crazy* (1930), Cole Porter's *Anything Goes* (1934) and *Red, Hot and Blue!* (1936) and Weill's *Johnny Johnson* (1936). His designs for opera include Milhaud's *Le pauvre matelot* (1937) and Menotti's *Amelia al ballo* (1937). For the Metropolitan he designed *Salome* (1934, described as 'nearer Broadway than the River Jordan'), *Otello* (1937, its first since 1913) and *Die Entführung aus dem Serail* (1947, the first Metropolitan production), and the first telecast of a Metropolitan

Set design by Donald Oenslager for the Tabors' apartment in the original production of Moore's 'The Ballad of Baby Doe' at the Opera House in Central City, Colorado, 7 June 1956

performance, *Otello* (1948). For Central City Opera, Colorado, he designed 18 productions, including *La traviata* (1946), *Fidelio* (1947), *Les contes d'Hoffmann* and *Così fan tutte* (both 1948), Moore's *The Ballad of Baby Doe* (1956; see illustration) and, his last, *Un ballo in maschera* (1967).

Although one of the most prolific designers, with more than 130 major productions to his credit in a variety of styles, Oenslager was probably more influential as a teacher and apostle of continental stage practice than as a designer. 'Give me ideas with resonance' was his exhortation. He published the books *Stage Design* (London, 1975) and *The Theatre of Donald Oenslager* (Middletown, CT, 1978).

DAVID J. HOUGH

Oeser, Fritz (*b* Gera, 18 May 1911). German musicologist and editor. He studied at the Realgymnasium, the university and the conservatory in Leipzig; among his teachers in musicology were Helmuth Schultz and Robert Haas. In 1938 he joined the staff of the Musikwissenschaftlicher Verlag, Leipzig; he became a director in 1948, when the firm became successively the Brucknerverlag, Wiesbaden, and (in 1955) Alkor-Edition, Kassel. He retired in 1971.

Oeser's main areas of study have been Bruckner's music, Czechoslovak music, and Russian and French opera in the 19th century; among his writings, mostly on operatic subjects, is a study of the texts of Bruckner's symphonies, with which he obtained his doctorate at Leipzig University in 1939. He has made a number of German translations of operas and has prepared performing versions of several operas, including Gounod's *Faust* (Kassel, 1972) and Offenbach's *Les contes d'Hoffmann* (Kassel, 1977). The best known is that of Bizet's *Carmen* (Kassel, 1964; see Oeser's article in *Jahrbuch der Komischen Oper Berlin*, iv, 1963–4), in which much music traditionally omitted is restored; his edition has however been criticized for failing to observe Bizet's final intentions (see W. Dean: 'The True Carmen?', *MT*, cvi, 1965, pp.846–55; revised in *Essays on Opera*, Oxford, 1990).

Oestvig, Karl Aagaard (*b* Christiania [now Oslo], 17 May 1889; *d* Oslo, 21 July 1968). Norwegian tenor. He studied at Cologne and made his début in 1914 at Stuttgart, where he sang the Lay-brother and Giovanni in the first performance of Max von Schillings's *Mona Lisa* (1915). Engaged at the Vienna Staatsoper from 1919 to 1927, he created the Emperor in *Die Frau ohne Schatten* (1919); from 1927 to 1930 he sang at the Berlin Städtische Oper. His repertory included Tamino, Lohengrin, Walther, Parsifal, Don José, Paul (Korngold's *Die tote Stadt*), Bacchus and Max (Krenek's *Jonny spielt auf*). A very stylish singer, he brought a lyrical approach even to his heavier, more dramatic roles. He retired in 1932. ELIZABETH FORBES

Offenbach, Jacques [Jacob] (*b* Cologne, 20 June 1819; *d* Paris, 5 Oct 1880). French composer of German origin. He composed some of the most exhilarating and tuneful music ever written; his *Les contes d'Hoffmann* remains one of the most popular of French operas, though his most significant achievements lie in the field of operetta. His *Orphée aux enfers*, *La belle Hélène* and other satirical products of Second Empire Paris remain preeminent in the operetta repertory, and it was through the success of Offenbach's works abroad that the operetta became an established international genre during the late 19th century and the early 20th.

1. LIFE. His father, born Isaac Juda Eberst, left his native Offenbach-am-Main about 1800 for Cologne, where he became known as 'Der Offenbacher' and then simply 'Offenbach'. He earned a living from bookbinding, music teaching and composition, and was later cantor at a synagogue in Cologne. Jacob was the second son and the seventh of ten children, and he was born a short distance from the square in Cologne that today bears his name. He was first taught the violin, but at the age of nine he took up the cello and, with his brother Julius (1815–80) on the violin and sister Isabella (1817–91) at the piano, formed a trio which played in Cologne taverns. He studied at first with Joseph Alexander and then with Bernhard Breuer, to the latter of whom he dedicated his first published composition in 1833. In November of that year Isaac took Julius and Jacob to Paris in search of further tuition. There a place was obtained for Jacob at the Conservatoire, and positions were found for both boys in a synagogue choir before Isaac returned to Cologne.

In Paris the two boys were soon known as Jules and Jacques. The latter left the Conservatoire after a year's study with Vaslin, and after brief periods with two orchestras he found a position in the orchestra of the Opéra-Comique. There he played beside Hippolyte Seligmann, and he received further tuition from Seligmann's own teacher, Louis Norblin. He also met Halévy, who gave him some composition lessons. After leaving the orchestra of the Opéra-Comique in 1838, he made the acquaintance of Flotow, through whom he gained entry to Paris salons, performing with him jointly composed pieces for cello and piano. During the 1840s he continued his career as a cello virtuoso, appearing in Paris in 1841 with Anton Rubinstein and in Cologne in 1843 with Liszt. In August 1844, after becoming a Roman Catholic, he married Herminie d'Alcain. He had met her at the salon of her mother, whose second husband was closely related to a leading London concert agent, John Mitchell. As a result Offenbach visited London in May 1844, performing at concerts of the Musical Union with Joachim and Mendelssohn and at an Ascot Week banquet at Windsor Castle. Meanwhile his attempts to get stage works accepted by the Opéra-Comique were unsuccessful, and he was forced to arrange concerts of his own to have them performed.

In 1850 he was appointed conductor at the Théâtre Français, but he continued to have little success in getting his stage works accepted until the Exhibition year of 1855. Then, no doubt emboldened by the success of Hervé's Folies-Nouvelles, where Offenbach's own *Oyayaie, ou La reine des îles* had been accepted, he rented for the Exhibition season the tiny wooden Salle Lacaze (cap. 300), located in the carré Marigny in the Champs-Élysées. With a hastily compiled programme of short comic pieces the theatre opened as the Bouffes-Parisiens on 5 July. With occasional changes of programme, the entertainments were a big success of the Exhibition season, enabling Offenbach to give up his position at the Théâtre Français and to transfer to winter quarters at the Salle Choiseul (cap. *c*900). The following summer he moved again to the Salle Lacaze, but from the next winter he settled permanently in the Salle Choiseul.

Besides his own works his repertory embraced those of other composers, including Adam, Delibes, Duprato,

653

Gastinel and Jonas as well as adaptations of Mozart's *Der Schauspieldirektor* and Rossini's *Il Signor Bruschino*. In 1856 his competition for young composers attracted 78 entrants, the joint winners being Bizet and Lecocq with their settings of *Le Docteur Miracle*. Initially Offenbach's licence had restricted him to pieces for only two or three stage performers, but the loosening of restrictions gradually enabled him to produce more ambitious works. The two-act *Orphée aux enfers* (1858) was a huge success and the prototype of larger-scale satirical works, but the production of the three-act *Barkouf* at the Opéra-Comique failed to win him greater acceptance in more respectable circles. Although he resigned as director of the Bouffes in January 1862, he continued to compose mainly for that theatre and for the summer theatre at Bad Ems. In 1860 he became a naturalized Frenchman and in August 1861 was appointed a Chevalier of the Légion d'honneur.

The success of the Bouffes had meanwhile persuaded John Mitchell to bring them to London, and Offenbach's works became well established abroad, particularly in Vienna, at first in pirated versions and then under the composer's own direction. His romantic opera *Les fées du Rhin* was performed as *Die Rheinnixen* at the Hofoper in Vienna in 1864, and from the same year dates the period of his greatest Parisian successes with *La belle Hélène*. During the Exhibition year of 1867 *La vie parisienne* (1866) and *La Grande-Duchesse de Gérolstein* (1867) enraptured visitors to the capital, but after the Franco-Prussian War his success began to wane. Popular taste changed, and during the 1870s it was the more escapist works of Lecocq that attracted the French operetta public. On 1 June 1873 Offenbach took over the management of the Théâtre de la Gaîté, where he produced spectacular new versions of *Orphée aux enfers* and *Geneviève de Brabant*. But he was a poor businessman, and losses suffered on the production of his vaudeville *La haine* in 1874 forced him into bankruptcy. He composed music for a Christmas piece, *Whittington* (1874), for the Alhambra in London and also, in an endeavour to make up some of his losses, embarked on a trip to the USA for the World Exhibition of 1876. He gave some 40 concerts in New York and Philadelphia as well as conducting performances of *La vie parisienne* and *La jolie parfumeuse* (1875). On his return he published a volume of his impressions. In his last years he experienced renewed success with *Madame Favart* (1878) and *La fille du tambour-major* (1879) as well as with revivals of earlier works such as *Orphée aux enfers*, with Hervé as Jupiter, for the Exhibition season of 1878. However, from 1877 his major preoccupation was with the score of *Les contes d'Hoffmann*, an *opéra fantastique* by which he set great store. During 1880 he was working on the score at the Pavillon Henri IV in St Germain-en-Laye, but in September worsening health forced him to return to Paris. Rehearsals of *Les contes d'Hoffmann* began, but on 5 October he died, the gout from which he suffered having attacked his heart. At the request of his family, the final shaping of the score of *Les contes d'Hoffmann* was undertaken by Guiraud and the completion of an operetta, *Belle Lurette*, by Delibes.

2. WORKS. As with all stage works of the genre, the success of Offenbach's operettas depended a good deal on the librettists and performers. In this respect Offenbach was both well served and skilful at discovering talent. Like Sullivan, and unlike Johann Strauss, he was consistently blessed with workable subjects and genuinely witty librettos. His chief librettist, Ludovic Halévy, became one of the leading French theatrical writers of the time, having been given his chance at the age of 21 in writing material for the opening night of the Bouffes-Parisiens in 1855. Offenbach's leading lady, Hortense Schneider, who during the 1860s enjoyed immense personal success in *La belle Hélène*, *Barbebleue*, *La Grande-Duchesse de Gérolstein* and *La Périchole*, was also discovered by Offenbach and given a role in *Le violoneux* as early as August 1855.

Offenbach's sound theatrical judgment extended to his part in selecting and shaping the subjects he used. Many of these were satirical treatments of familiar stories, for example mythological (*Orphée aux enfers*, *La belle Hélène*) or well-known French subjects (*Geneviève de Brabant*, *Barbe-bleue*, *Madame Favart*), while others satirized contemporary society and politics (*La vie parisienne*, *La Grande-Duchesse de Gérolstein*). His one-act works include examples such as *M. Choufleuri restera chez lui le ...* which satirized Paris salons and operatic conventions (the latter an especially typical Offenbach trick), while others were slight comic sketches such as the highly successful *Les deux aveugles*. Offenbach satirized particularly the regime of Napoleon III; and it was with the fall of the Second Empire that his own success declined. The humour of his pieces was rarely very subtle in purely musical terms, in keeping with the requirements of his audiences. Effect might be achieved by quoting, or clearly alluding to, familiar music, the satire being not so much in the treatment of the themes themselves as by satirizing the words or by the incongruity of the surroundings. Examples of such allusions are to Meyerbeer's *Les Huguenots* in *Ba-ta-clan*, to Gluck's *Orfeo* ('Che farò') in *Orphée aux enfers*, and to the patriotic trio from Rossini's *Guillaume Tell* in *La belle Hélène*. Other comic devices were the introduction of parts for animals (*Barkouf*) and the setting of gibberish (*Ba-ta-clan*). He further exploited incongruity in *Orphée aux enfers* by providing a cancan for the gods, and in *La belle Hélène* by setting the phrase 'Un vile séducteur' to his most uplifting waltz tune and by building a grandiose operatic ensemble around the banal phrase 'L'homme à la pomme'. He also used the natural flexibility of the French language to comic effect by varying accentuation, while another device was the breaking up of words, as in *La Périchole*:

> Aux maris ré,
> Aux maris cal,
> Aux maris ci,
> Aux maris trants,
> Aux maris récalcitrants.

All this he backed up with simple but effective devices of a purely musical nature. His tunes are very often built upon a rising phrase and in a major key, but he achieved remarkable variety of mood by varying the rhythmic pattern. Noteworthy too is the effect of gradually speeding up the music to the finale of an act to achieve an exciting climax. His vocal writing produced rumbustious comic songs such as the 'Couplets des deux hommes d'armes' (*Geneviève de Brabant*); but it also produced examples of outstanding lyrical writing such as the tenor's 'Au Mont Ida' (*La belle Hélène*) and, in solos written for Hortense Schneider in *La belle Hélène* and *La Périchole*, sensitive shaping of phrases that evokes the work of Berlioz.

In his orchestration Offenbach made effective use of wind instruments, using brass in particular to heighten the impact and excitement of climaxes. However, for much of his work he was restricted in orchestral resources and in any case concerned to ensure that the orchestra did not obscure the words. In fact his own orchestration is not always heard, for the overtures attributed to him are often extended arrangements made for German theatres, with enlarged brass sections. Thus the well-known overture to *Orphée aux enfers* was composed by Carl Binder (1816–60) for the Vienna production of 1860. Through this overture, and more particularly through the famous cancan, *Orphée aux enfers* has remained Offenbach's best-known operetta, though a consensus might prefer *La vie parisienne* for its sparkle, *La Périchole* for its charm and *La belle Hélène* for its all-round brilliance.

During his lifetime Offenbach's success brought a considerable amount of disapproving comment from those who resented the 'naughtiness' of the French stage and the lack of pretence to any elevated form of art, or who considered his use of other composers' music irreverent. Wagner, whom Offenbach parodied in his revue *Le carnaval des revues* (1860), referred to the 'warmth of the dung-heap', though his attitude towards Offenbach later mellowed. The entry in Grove's *Dictionary of Music and Musicians* (1878–9) typified the attitude of more elevated music circles of the time, con-cluding that 'it is melancholy that of all these musical *bouffonneries* little or nothing will remain; since in order to live, a work must possess either style or passion, while these too often display merely a vulgar scepticism, and a determination to be funny even at the cost of propriety and taste'. In the event, their irrepressible gaiety and tunefulness – allied to the genuine wit of their books – would have served to keep his works alive even if it had not been for the success of *Les contes d'Hoffmann*. Here, especially in the Antonia act, Offenbach showed that he could compose music of real passion, and that a musical style that served humorous ends when wedded to incongruous words could appeal no less when presented entirely seriously. The opera's lasting success has undoubtedly been helped by the opportunities for spectacle and the supernatural; but without music of real strength and invention the opera would not have survived incompleteness, posthumous tampering and a reputation for ill-luck to become one of the most popular of all French operas.

See also *BARBE-BLEUE*; *BA-TA-CLAN*; *BELLE HÉLÈNE, LA*; *BRIGANDS, LES*; *CONTES D'HOFFMANN, LES*; *DEUX AVEUGLES, LES*; *FILLE DU TAMBOUR-MAJOR, LA*; *GENEVIÈVE DE BRABANT*; *GRANDE-DUCHESSE DE GÉROLSTEIN, LA*; *MADAME FAVART*; *MARIAGE AUX LANTERNES, LE*; *M. CHOUFLEURI RESTERA CHEZ LUI LE ...*; *ORPHÉE AUX ENFERS*; *PÉRICHOLE, LA*; *PONT DES SOUPIRS, LE*; *ROBINSON CRUSOÉ*; and *VIE PARISIENNE, LA*.

first performed and published in Paris unless otherwise stated
PBP – Bouffes-Parisiens (Salle Choiseul) PBPL – Bouffes-Parisiens (Salle Lacaze, carré Marigny)
POC – Opéra-Comique PV – Théâtre des Variétés
ob – opéra bouffe oc – opéra comique
optte – opérette optteb – opérette bouffe

title	genre, acts	libretto	first performance	sources, publication details; remarks
L'alcóve	oc, 1	P. Pittaud de Forges, A. de Leuven and E.-G. Roche	Ecole Lyrique, 24 April 1847	F-SMcusset*
Blanche	oc, 1	J. H. Vernoy de Saint-Georges	unperf.	D-KNha*; comp. c1847
La Duchesse d'Albe	oc, 3	Saint-Georges	unperf.	KNha*; comp. 1847–8; inc.
Le trésor à Mathurin	tableau villageois, 1	L. Battu	concert perf., Salle Herz, 7 May 1853	
rev. as Le mariage aux lanternes	optte, 1	J. Dubois [M. Carré] and Battu	PBP, 10 Oct 1857	vs (1857)
Pépito	oc, 1	Battu and J. Moinaux	PV, 28 Oct 1853	vs (1854)
Luc et Lucette	oc, 1	Pittaud de Forges and Roche	Salle Herz, 2 May 1854	F-SMcusset*
Le décaméron, ou La grotte d'azur	légende napolitaine, 1	F.-J. Méry	Salle Herz, May 1855	Plambert*
Entrez, messieurs, mesdames	pièce d'occasion, 1	Méry and J. Servières [L. Halévy]	PBPL, 5 July 1855	D-KNha*
Une nuit blanche	oc, 1	E. Plouvier	PBPL, 5 July 1855	vs (1855)
Les deux aveugles	bouffonnerie musicale, 1	Moinaux	PBPL, 5 July 1855	US-KBrobbin*, vs (1855)
Le rêve d'une nuit d'été	saynète, 1	E. Tréfeu	PBPL, 30 July 1855	vs (1855)
Oyayaie, ou La reine des îles	anthropophagie musicale, 1	Moinaux	Folies-Nouvelles, 7 Aug 1855	GB-TWmacnutt*
Le violoneux	légende bretonne, 1	E. Mestépès and E. Chevalet	PBPL, 31 Aug 1855	F-Pn*, vs (1855)
Madame Papillon	optte, 1	Servières [Halévy]	PBPL, 3 Oct 1855	lost
Paimpol et Périnette	saynète, 1	de Lussan [Pittaud de Forges]	PBPL, 29 Oct 1855	D-KNha*
Ba-ta-clan	chinoiserie musicale, 1	Halévy	PBP, 29 Dec 1855	vs (1856)
Un postillon en gage	optte, 1	Plouvier and J. Adenis	PBP, 9 Feb 1856	F-SMcusset*
Tromb-al-ca-zar, ou Les criminels dramatiques	bouffonnerie musicale, 1	C. D. Dupeuty and E. Bourget	PBP, 3 April 1856	vs (1856)
La rose de Saint-Flour	optte, 1	Carré	PBPL, 12 June 1856	vs (1856)
Les dragées du baptême	pièce d'occasion, 1	Dupeuty and Bourget	PBPL, 18 June 1856	lost
Le 66	optte, 1	Pittaud de Forges and M. Laurencin [P. A. Chapelle]	PBPL, 31 July 1856	vs (1856)

title	genre, acts	libretto	first performance	sources, publication details; remarks
Le financier et le savetier	optteb, 1	H.-J. Crémieux and E. About	PBP, 23 Sept 1856	vs (1856)
La bonne d'enfant[s]	optteb, 1	E. Bercioux	PBP, 14 Oct 1856	US-NYpm*, vs (1856)
Les trois baisers du diable	opérette fantastique, 1	Mestépès	PBP, 15 Jan 1857	vs (1857)
Croquefer, ou Le dernier des paladins	optteb, 1	L.-A. Jaime and Tréfeu	PBP, 12 Feb 1857	vs (1857)
Dragonette	ob, 1	Mestépès and Jaime	PBP, 30 April 1857	vs (1857)
Vent du soir, ou L'horrible festin	optteb, 1	P. Gille	PBP, 16 May 1857	vs (1857)
Une demoiselle en loterie	optte, 1	Jaime and Crémieux	PBP, 27 July 1857	vs (1857)
Les deux pêcheurs, ou Le lever du soleil	optteb, 1	Dupeuty and Bourget	PBP, 13 Nov 1857	vs (1857)
Mesdames de la Halle	optteb, 1	A. Lapointe	PBP, 3 March 1858	D-Bbb, vs (1858)
La chatte metamorphosée en femme	optte, 1	E. Scribe and Mélesville	PBP, 19 April 1858	vs (1858)
Orphée aux enfers	opéra bouffon, 2	Crémieux and Halévy	PBP, 21 Oct 1858	vs (1858)
rev. version	opéra-féerie, 4		Gaîté, 7 Feb 1874	vs (1874)
Le mari à la porte	optte, 1	A. Delacour [A. C. Lartigue] and L. Morand	PBP, 22 June 1859	US-STu*, vs (1859)
Les vivandières de la grande-armée	optteb, 1	Jaime and Pittaud de Forges	PBP, 6 July 1859	1 no. (1859)
Geneviève de Brabant	ob, 2	Jaime and Tréfeu	PBP, 19 Nov 1859	vs (1860)
rev. version	3	Tréfeu and Crémieux	Menus-Plaisirs, 26 Dec 1867	vs (1868)
rev. version	5	Tréfeu and Crémieux	Gaîté, 25 Feb 1875	F-SMcusset*, addl nos. (1875)
Le carnaval des revues	revue, 1	E. Grangé, Gille and Halévy	PBP, 10 Feb 1860	4 nos. (1860)
Daphnis et Chloé	optte, 1	Clairville [L. F. Nicolaie] and J. Cordier [E. T. de Vaulabelle]	PBP, 27 March 1860	vs (1860)
Barkouf	ob, 3	Scribe and H. Boisseaux, after Abbé Blanchet	POC (Favart), 24 Dec 1860	SMcusset*, 10 nos. (1861)
rev. as Boule de neige		C.-L.-E. Nuitter and Tréfeu	PBP, 14 Dec 1871	vs (1872)
La chanson de Fortunio	oc, 1	Crémieux and Halévy	PBP, 5 Jan 1861	A-Wn*, vs (1861)
Le pont des soupirs	ob, 2	Crémieux and Halévy	PBP, 23 March 1861	vs (1861)
rev. version	4		PV, 8 May 1868	vs (1868)
M. Choufleuri restera chez lui le ...	optteb, 1	[Halévy, ? with Crémieux and E. de l'Epine]	private perf., Présidence du Corps Legislatif, 31 May 1861; PBP, 14 Sept 1861	vs (1861); collab. Saint-Rémy [Comte de Morny]
Apothicaire et perruquier	optteb, 1	E. Frébault	PBP, 17 Oct 1861	US-NYpm*, vs (1862)
Le roman comique	opéra bouffon, 3	Crémieux and Halévy	PBP, 10 Dec 1861	vs (1862)
Monsieur et Madame Denis	oc, 1	Laurencin [Chapelle] and M. Delaporte	PBP, 11 Jan 1862	vs (1862)
Le voyage de MM. Dunanan père et fils	opéra bouffon, 3	P. Siraudin and Moinaux	PBP, 23 March 1862	D-Bbb*, vs (1862)
Les bavards	ob, 2	Nuitter, after M. de Cervantes: Los habladores	PBP, 20 Feb 1863	vs (1867)
as Bavard et bavarde			Bad Ems, 11 July 1862	
as Die Schwätzerin von Saragossa			Vienna, Kai, 20 Nov 1862	vs (Vienna, 1863)
Jacqueline	optte, 1	P. d'Arcy [Crémieux and Halévy]	PBP, 14 Oct 1862	vs, as Dorothea (Berlin, 1862)
La baguette [Fédia]	oc, 2	H. Meilhac and Halévy	unperf.	F-BOLbrindejoint*; inc.; comp. 1862
La leçon de chant électromagnétique	bouffonnerie musicale, 1	Bourget	Bad Ems, 20 July 1867; Folies Marigny, 17 May 1873	Pcomte-offenbach*, vs (1873); comp. 1862
Il signor Fagotto	optte, 1	Nuitter and Tréfeu	Bad Ems, 11 July 1863; PBP, 13 July 1864	Pbourdon*, vs (1868)
Lischen et Fritzchen	conversation alsacienne, 1	P. Dubois [P. Boisselot]	Bad Ems, 21 July 1863; PBP, 5 Jan 1864	Pcomte-offenbach*, vs (1864)
Fleurette	oc, 1	Pittaud de Forges and Laurencin		comp. ?c1863
as Fleurette, oder Trompeter und Näherin			Vienna, Carl, 12 March 1872	vs (Vienna, 1872; Paris, 1891)
L'amour chanteur	optte, 1	Nuitter and L'Epine	PBP, 5 Jan 1864	SMcusset*, US-NYpm*
Les fées du Rhin	opéra, 3	Nuitter		D-F*, F-Pcomte-offenbach*, vs (Vienna, 1864)
as Die Rheinnixen			Vienna, Hof, 4 Feb 1864	
Les géorgiennes	ob, 3	Moinaux	PBP, 16 March 1864	COGbuckley*, vs (1864)

title	genre, acts	libretto	first performance	sources, publication details; remarks
Le fifre enchanté, ou Le soldat magicien	optteb, 1	Nuitter and Tréfeu	Bad Ems, 12 July 1864; PBP, 30 Sept 1868	vs (1868)
Jeanne qui pleure et Jean qui rit	optte, 1	Nuitter and Tréfeu	Bad Ems, 19 July 1864; PBP, 3 Nov 1865	vs (1865)
La belle Hélène	ob, 3	Meilhac and Halévy	PV, 17 Dec 1864	GB-Lbl*, (1865)
Coscoletto, ou Le lazzarone	oc, 2	Nuitter and Tréfeu	Bad Ems, 11 July 1865; Vienna, Carl, 5 Jan 1866	vs (Berlin, 1868)
Les refrains des bouffes	fantaisie musicale [revue], 1		PBP, 21 Sept 1865	lost
Les bergers	oc, 3	Crémieux and Gille	PBP, 11 Dec 1865	US-NYpm*, vs (1866)
Barbe-bleue	ob, 3	Meilhac and Halévy	PV, 5 Feb 1866	S-Smf*, vs (1866)
La vie parisienne	ob, 5, later 4	Meilhac and Halévy	Palais Royal, 31 Oct 1866	CH-MONbonynge*, vs (1867)
La Grande-Duchesse de Gérolstein	ob, 3	Meilhac and Halévy	PV, 12 April 1867	vs (1867)
La permission de dix heures	oc, 1	Mélesville, P. F. A. Carmouche and ?Nuitter	Bad Ems, July 1867	
as Urlaub nach dem Zapfenstreich			Vienna, Carl, 13 Feb 1868	vs (Berlin, 1868)
rev. version			Renaissance, 4 Sept 1873	US-NYpm*, vs (1873)
Robinson Crusoé	oc, 3	E. Cormon and Crémieux, after D. Defoe	POC (Favart), 23 Nov 1867	NYpm*, vs (1867)
Le château à Toto	ob, 3	Meilhac and Halévy	Palais Royal, 6 May 1868	vs (1868)
L'île de Tulipatan	ob, 1	H. Chivot and A. Duru	PBP, 30 Sept 1868	CH-MONbonynge*, vs (1868)
La Périchole	ob, 2	Meilhac and Halévy, after P. Mérimée: La carrosse du Saint Sacrement	PV, 6 Oct 1868	F-COGbuckley*, vs (1868)
rev. version	3		PV, 25 April 1874	vs (1874)
Vert-Vert	oc, 3	Meilhac and Nuitter, after de Leuven and Pittaud de Forges	POC (Favart), 10 March 1869	vs (1869)
La diva	ob, 3	Meilhac and Halévy	PBP, 22 March 1869	vs (1869)
La princesse de Trébizonde	ob, 2	Nuitter and Tréfeu	Baden-Baden, 31 July 1869	
rev. version	3		PBP, 7 Dec 1869	vs (1870)
Les brigands	ob, 3	Meilhac and Halévy	PV, 10 Dec 1869	SMcusset*, vs (1870)
La romance de la rose	optte, 1	Tréfeu, J. Prével and Nuitter	PBP, 11 Dec 1869	SMcusset*, vs (1870)
[Mam'zelle] Moucheron	optteb, 1	E. Leterrier and A. Vanloo	Renaissance, 10 May 1881	comp. 1870
rev. Delibes				vs (1881)
Le roi Carotte	opéra bouffe-féerie, 4	V. Sardou, after E. T. A. Hoffmann: Die Königsbraut	Gaîté, 15 Jan 1872	CH-Zschmitt*, vs (1872)
Fantasio	oc, 3	P. de Musset, after A. de Musset	POC (Favart), 18 Jan 1872	GB-Lbl*, vs (1872)
Le corsaire noir	oc, 3	Nuitter, Tréfeu and Offenbach		
as Der schwarze Corsar			Vienna, An der Wien, 21 Sept 1872	S-Smf*
Les braconniers	ob, 3	Chivot and Duru	PV, 29 Jan 1873	vs (1873)
Pomme d'api	optte, 1	Halévy and W. Busnach	Renaissance, 4 Sept 1873	vs (1873)
La jolie parfumeuse	oc, 3	Crémieux and E. Blum	Renaissance, 29 Nov 1873	vs (1875)
Bagatelle	oc, 1	Crémieux and Blum	PBP, 21 May 1874	vs (1874)
Madame l'archiduc	ob, 3	A. Millaud, Meilhac and Halévy	PBP, 31 Oct 1874	vs (1874)
Whittington	opéra bouffe-féerie, 3	Nuitter and Tréfeu	London, Alhambra, 26 Dec 1874	vs (London, 1875)
as Le chat du diable			Châtelet, 9 Oct 1893	
Les hannetons	revue, 3	Grangé and Millaud	PBP, 22 April 1875	
La boulangère a des écus	ob, 3	Meilhac and Halévy	PV, 19 Oct 1875	vs (1875, rev. 1876)
Le voyage dans la lune	opéra-féerie, 4	Leterrier, Vanloo and A. Mortier	Gaîté, 26 Oct 1875	A-Wn*, vs (1875)
La créole	oc, 3	Millaud and Meilhac	PBP, 3 Nov 1875	vs (1875)
Tarte à la crème	valse, 1	Millaud	PBP, 14 Dec 1875	F-Pcomte-offenbach*
Pierrette et Jacquot	optte, 1	J. Noriac and Gille	PBP, 13 Oct 1876	vs (1876)
La boîte au lait	ob, 4	Grangé and Noriac	PBP, 3 Nov 1876	vs (1876)
Le docteur Ox	ob, 3	Mortier and Gille, after J. Verne	PV, 26 Jan 1877	S-Smf*, vs (1877)
La foire Saint-Laurent	ob, 3	Crémieux and A. de Saint-Albin	Folies-Dramatiques, 10 Feb 1877	vs (1877)
Maître Péronilla	ob, 3	Nuitter, P. Ferrier and Offenbach	PBP, 13 March 1878	vs (1878)
Madame Favart	oc, 3	Duru and Chivot	Folies-Dramatiques, 28 Dec 1878	vs (1878)
La marocaine	ob, 3	Ferrier and Halévy	PBP, 13 Jan 1879	vs (1879)
La fille du tambour-major	oc, 3	Duru and Chivot	Folies-Dramatiques, 13 Dec 1879	vs (1880)
Belle Lurette	oc, 3	Blum, E. Blau and R. Toché	Renaissance, 30 Oct 1880	vs (1880); completed Delibes

title	genre, acts	libretto	first performance	sources, publication details; remarks
Les contes d'Hoffmann	opéra fantastique, 5	J. Barbier, after Barbier and Carré's play based on Hoffmann: *Die Gesellschaft im Keller, Der Sandmann, Die Abenteuer der Sylvester-Nacht, Rath Krespel, Klein Zaches genannt Zinnober*	POC (Favart), 10 Feb 1881	vs (1881); completed Guiraud

Contribs to: Elodie, ou Le forfait nocturne, 1856; Les petits prodiges, 1857; Bruschino, 1857; Les musiciens de l'orchestre, 1861; La chatte blanche, 1875

Grove1 (G. Chouquet)

L. Halévy: *La belle Hélène: Epître à mon ami Paul Duport* (Paris, 1865)

E. de Mirecourt [C.-J.-B. Jacquot]: *Auber, Offenbach* (Paris, 1869)

Richard Wagner und Jacob Offenbach: ein Wort im Harnisch von einem Freunde der Tonkunst (Altona, 1871)

Argus [P. Gille]: *Célébrités dramatiques: Jacques Offenbach* (Paris, 1872)

Monsieur de l'Orchestre [A. Mortier]: *Promenade autour d'Orphée aux enfers* (Paris, 1874)

J. Offenbach: *Offenbach en Amérique: notes d'un musicien en voyage* (Paris, 1877; Eng. trans., as *Orpheus in America*, 1958)

A. Jullien: 'M. Offenbach, critique: sa profession de foi musicale', *Airs variés* (Paris, 1877), 347–58

E. Pirazzi: *Bilder und Geschichten aus Offenbachs Vergangenheit* (Offenbach-am-Main, 1879)

A. Wolff: 'Jacques Offenbach', *La gloire à Paris* (Paris, 1886)

A. Martinet: *Offenbach: sa vie et son oeuvre* (Paris, 1887)

C. Bellaigue: *Etudes musicales et nouvelles silhouettes de musiciens* (Paris, 1898)

P. Bekker: *Jacques Offenbach* (Berlin, 1909)

L. Schmidt: *J. Offenbach* (Berlin, 1912)

R. Northcott: *Jacques Offenbach: a Sketch of his Life and a Record of his Operas* (London, 1917)

E. Rieger: *Offenbach und seine Wiener Schule* (Vienna, 1920)

O. Bie: *Die schöne Helena* (Berlin, 1923)

L. Schneider: *Offenbach* (Paris, 1923)

K. Soldan, ed.: *Jacques Offenbach: Beiträge zu seinem Leben und seinen Werken* (Berlin, 1924)

J. Brindejont-Offenbach: 'L'opérette', *Cinquante ans de musique française de 1874 à 1925*, ed. L. Rohozinski (Paris, 1925), 199–322

R. Brancour: *Offenbach* (Paris, 1929)

L. Schneider: *Une heure de musique avec Offenbach* (Paris, 1930)

A. Henseler: *Der Aufstieg des Kölners Jacques Offenbach: ein Musikerleben in Bildern* (Berlin, 1931)

S. Kracauer: *Jacques Offenbach und das Paris seiner Zeit* (Amsterdam, 1937, 2/1962; Eng. trans., 1937)

J. Brindejont-Offenbach: *Offenbach, mon grand-père* (Paris, 1940)

R. Lyon and L. Saguer: *Les Contes d'Hoffmann* (Paris, 1948)

Le siècle d'Offenbach (Paris, 1958)

A. Decaux: *Offenbach, roi du Second Empire* (Paris, 1958, 3/1975)

G. Hughes: *Composers of Operetta* (London, 1962)

I. I. Sollertinsky: *Offenbach* (Moscow, 1962)

O. E. Deutsch: 'Offenbach, Kraus und die anderen', *ÖMz*, xviii (1963), 408–12

O. Schneidereit: *Jacques Offenbach* (Leipzig, 1966, 2/1970)

P. W. Jacob: *Jacques Offenbach in Selbstzeugnissen und Bilddokumenten* (Hamburg, 1969, 2/1980)

A. Lamb: 'How Offenbach Conquered London', *Opera*, xx (1969), 932–8

R. Budis: *Nápad monsieura Offenbacha: Vyprávení o cestách svetové operety s prislusnou zastávkou v Praze* (Prague, 1970)

J. Hüttner: 'Baugeschichte und Spielplan des Theaters am Franz Josef Kai', *Jahrbuch der Gesellschaft für Wiener Theaterforschung*, xvii (1970), 87–161

R. L. Folstein: 'A Bibliography on Jacques Offenbach', *CMc*, xii (1971), 116–28

R. Pourvoyeur: 'Verne et Offenbach', *Bulletin de la Société Jules Verne*, no.20 (1971), 87; no.21 (1972), 112

F. Mailer: 'Jacques Offenbach – ein Pariser in Wien', *ÖMz*, xxvii (1972), 246–62

C. Casini: *Les contes d'Hoffmann* (Turin, 1973)

F. Bruyas: *Histoire de l'opérette en France* (Lyons, 1974)

R. Pourvoyeur: *Jacques Offenbach: Essay in Toengepaste Muziek-en Toneelsociologie* (Brussels, 1977; rev. as *Offenbach: Idillio e parodia*, 1980)

M. Šulc: *Papá Offenbach* (Prague, 1977)

O. Schneidereit: *Tödlicher Cancan* (Leipzig, 1978)

G. Hauger: 'Offenbach in English: a Checklist', *Theatre Notebook*, xxxiv (1979–80), 9–14; xxxv (1980–81), 87–8; xxxvi (1981–2), 34; xxxvii (1982–3), 31–2

A. Faris: *Jacques Offenbach* (London, 1980)

P. Gammond: *Offenbach: his Life and Times* (Tunbridge Wells, 1980, 2/1981)

J. Harding: *Jacques Offenbach: a Biography* (London, 1980)

A. Lamb, G. Hauger and H. Macdonald: 'Jacques Offenbach, 1819–1880', *MT*, cxxi (1980), 615–21

H.-K. Metzger and R. Riehn, eds.: *Jacques Offenbach* (Munich, 1980)

K. Pahlen, ed.: *Hoffmanns Erzählungen* (Munich, 1980, 2/1982)

D. Rissin: *Offenbach, ou Le rire en musique* (Paris, 1980)

L'avant-scène opéra, no.25 (1980) [*Les contes d'Hoffmann* issue]

Offenbach 1819–1880: a Tribute (London, 1980)

F. Oeser: *Jacques Offenbach: Hoffmanns Erzählungen: Quellenkritische Neuausgabe: Vorlagenbericht* (Kassel, 1981)

L'avant-scène opéra, no.66 (1984) [*La Périchole* issue]

G. Brandstetter, ed.: *Jacques Offenbachs Hoffmanns Erzählungen* (Laaber, 1988)

L'avant-scène opéra, no.125 (1989) [*La belle Hélène* issue]

A. Lamb: 'Tales of a Monte Carlo Hoffmann', *Opera*, xxxxii (1991), 634–7

A. de Almeida: *Jacques Offenbach: a Thematic Catalogue of his Works* (Oxford, forthcoming)

ANDREW LAMB

Offers, Maartje (*b* Koudekerke, 27 Feb 1892; *d* Island of Tholen, 28 Jan 1944). Dutch contralto. She studied at The Hague and in Rotterdam, making her début in concert at Leiden. Her career in opera began in 1917 when she sang Delilah in Saint-Saëns' *Samson et Dalila* at The Hague. Appearances in Paris and Milan established her for a while as one of the leading contraltos of the day; she made a special impression as Erde and as Fricka, and, in 1925, repeated her Delilah at La Scala under Toscanini. Other operatic roles included Orpheus, Azucena and Amneris. Her recordings of Bach suggest that shortness of breath must have been a limitation. During the latter part of her career she sang mostly in concerts.

J. B. STEANE

O'Gallagher, Eamonn [Ó Gallchobhair, Éamonn] (*b* Dundalk, 30 Sept 1906; *d* ?Rome, 27 Dec 1982). Irish composer. He studied at the Leinster School of Music, Dublin, and at the Royal Irish Academy of Music (1927–35). His compositions, which draw mainly on the resources of conventional triadic harmony and of traditional Irish music, include five operas, all with texts in Gaelic.

Nocturne sa Chearnóg [Nocturne in the Square], 1942
Traghadh na Taoíde [The Ebb Tide], Dublin, Gaiety, 1950
Ioc-shláinte an Ghra [The Balm of Love], 1954
An Mhaighdean Mhara [The Mermaid], Dublin, Mansion House, 1960
An Tinncéir agus an tSidheog [The Tinker and the Fairy], Dublin, Abbey, 1963

E. Deale, ed.: *Catalogue of Contemporary Irish Composers* (Dublin, 1968, 2/1973)

B. Harrison: *Catalogue of Contemporary Irish Music* (Dublin, 1982)   SEÓIRSE BODLEY

Ogiński, Michał Kazimierz (*b* Warsaw, 1728; *d* Warsaw, 31 May 1800). Polish prince, Grand Hetman of Lithuania and composer. In his youth he spent seven years in France; he was taught the violin by G. B. Viotti and also learnt the clarinet and harp. From 1771 he maintained an opera company with ballet and orchestra at his residence at Słonim, Lithuania; it had a large repertory of Polish, Italian, French and German operas. His second theatre was at Siedlce, near Lublin.

Ogiński's compositions include six operas and a ballet. It is likely that he used some of his extant songs in his Singspiels. Several of these songs reveal affinities with the melodic shape of the Polish folksong and the rhythms of the mazurka and polonaise.

all Singspiels; librettos by the composer, first performed at Słonim, unless otherwise stated

Filozof zmieniony [The Transformed Philosopher], 1771, lib. *PL-Wn*

Opuszczone dzieci [The Forsaken Children], 1771, lib. *WRol*

Kondycje stanów [The Social Position of the Classes], 1781, lib. *Wn*

Pola Elizejskie [The Elysian Fields], 1781, lib. *Wn*

Cyganie [The Gypsies] (F. D. Kniaźnin), Siedlce, 1786

Mocy Świata [The Powers of the World], before 1788, lib. *Wn*

R. Haas: 'Ein polnischer Werther', *MJb 1959*, 95–8

A. Ciechanowiecki: *Michał Kazimierz Ogiński und sein Musenhof zu Słonim* (Cologne, 1961)

A. Nowak-Romanowicz: 'Muzyka polskiego os wiecenia i wcresuego romantyzmu' [Polish Music in the Age of the Enlightenment and Early Romanticism], *Z dziejów polskiej kultury muzycznej* [Historical Survey of Polish Musical Culture], ii (Kraków, 1966)   ALINA NOWAK-ROMANOWICZ

Ognennïy angel. Opera by Sergey Prokofiev; *see* FIERY ANGEL, THE.

Ognivtsev, Alexander Pavlovich (*b* Petrovskoye, Lugansk region, 27 Aug 1920). Russian bass. In 1949 he graduated at the Kishineu conservatory and was engaged as a soloist by the Bol'shoy. His début as Dosifey (*Khovanshchina*) and his performances as Boris soon afterwards brought him immediate recognition as a singer of unusual dramatic accomplishment and authority, with a strong, beautiful voice of velvety timbre, and an imposing stage presence. A versatile actor, he has taken with equal success roles in high tragedy, complex psychological drama and comedy: his repertory includes Ivan the Terrible (*The Maid of Pskov*), Prince Gremin (*Yevgeny Onegin*) and René (*Iolanta*), Gounod's Méphistophélès, Rossini's Don Basilio, Philip II, and the General (Prokofiev's *Gambler*), which he sang on the Bol'shoy visit to the Metropolitan in 1975. He created Nicholas I in Shaporin's *The Decembrists* (1953) and the Leader in Kholminov's *Optimisticheskaya tragediya* ('An Optimistic Tragedy', 1964), and sang Theseus in the first performances in the USSR of Britten's *A Midsummer Night's Dream* (1965). His film appearances include Aleko (in Rakhmaninov's opera, 1954). In 1965 he was made People's Artist of the USSR.

I. M. YAMPOL'SKY

Ohana, Maurice (*b* Casablanca, 12 June 1914). Composer of Spanish descent. His father was a Gibraltarian of Andalusian origin, his mother was of Andalusian and Castilian lineage. Cosmopolitan in upbringing, Ohana spent his youth in Morocco, Spain and the Basque country. After musical studies in Casablanca and at the Bayonne Conservatoire, he moved to Paris in 1932 to study architecture but took piano lessons with Lazare Lévy and Frank Marshall. From 1937 to 1940 he studied at the Schola Cantorum with Daniel-Lesur, the ensuing studies in counterpoint, plainsong and the medieval and Renaissance repertory having a lasting influence on his musical language and vocal style. Towards the end of his war service in the British Army, he enrolled in Alfredo Casella's class at the Accademia di S Cecilia in Rome in 1944. On being demobilized in 1946 he settled permanently in Paris.

As founder of Groupe Zodiaque (1947–50), Ohana established a fierce independence from the 'new serialism' of his contemporaries, developing a musical language based on plainsong and techniques of early counterpoint, combined with rhythmic processes from African folk music and some melodic features of the *cante hondo*. Seeking to translate the spontaneity of improvisation into composed music, Ohana incorporates sections of aleatory counterpoint into his closed forms, and makes extensive use of third-tone micro-intervals in both melodic and harmonic instrumental and vocal writing. A colouristic view of harmony as timbre, or sound-mass, owes much to Debussy and has parallels with Varèse, just as his contrapuntal layering of ostinatos owes much to Stravinsky and has parallels with Lutosławski.

A prolific composer for the voice, Ohana has developed a vocal style designed to extend the technical capabilities of the performer, in a manner similar to Berio and Ligeti, while still being based on more traditional techniques of vocal production. Fond of setting a variety of languages, often in a polyglot context, he also disintegrates text into onomatopoeic phonemes. His opera *La Célestine* is based on the 15th-century 'dialogue-novel' by Fernando de Rojas and was first performed at the Opéra in 1988. Ohana has also written three chamber operas: *Syllabaire pour Phèdre* (1968), an adaptation of Euripides with scenic references to the Japanese noh play; *Autodafé* (1973), a series of allegorical tragicomic historical episodes set against a background of the Spanish Inquisition; and *Le mariage sous la mer* (1991), an early score (1961) originally conceived as incidental music and later revised and expanded into a lighthearted chamber opera for children, based on a Celtic legend from Camilo José Cela's collection *Petit retable de Don Christobal*. Other dramatic vocal works are of a music-theatre type, the most important being *Trois contes de l'honorable fleur* (Avignon, 15 July 1978), a setting of three fairy-tales by the composer for soprano and chamber ensemble, and *Office des oracles* (Sainte Baume, 9 August 1974) for three choruses and orchestra. Ohana has written two oratorios, one of which, the *oratorio scénique Récit de l'an zéro* (Paris, 11 April 1959), is intended for dramatic performance.

See also CÉLESTINE, LA.

Syllabaire pour Phèdre (chamber op, 6 episodes, R. Cluzel and M. Ohana, after Euripides), Paris, Musique, 5 Feb 1968

Autodafé (chamber op, 10 tableaux, Ohana), Lyons, Opéra, 23 May 1973

La Célestine (lyric tragicomedy, 2, Ohana and O. Marcel, after F. de Rojas), Paris, Opéra, 13 June 1988

Le mariage sous la mer (children's chamber op, 3, A. Trutat, after

C. J. Cela), Boulogne-Billancourt, National Conservatory, 18 April 1991

*

M. Cadieu: 'A l'Opéra de Lyon: Autodafé de Maurice Ohana', *Lettres françaises* (8 June 1972)

M. Ohana: 'La marionette à l'Opéra', *ReM*, no.351–2 (1982), 75

F. Bayer: 'Sous le signe de l'imaginaire: autour du langage musical de Maurice Ohana', *L'esprit*, no.99 (1985), 43–57

R. Cluzel: 'Syllabaire pour Phèdre: pour et sur la musique de Maurice Ohana', *ReM*, no.391–3 (1986), 171–5

O. Marcel: 'L'usage de la parole: musique et théâtre dans l'oeuvre de Maurice Ohana', ibid, 87–105

C. Prost: 'Catalogue raisonné', ibid, 183–225

G. Reibel: 'La musique vocale et chorale de Maurice Ohana', ibid, 71–85

M. Cadieu: 'La Célestine de Maurice Ohana: une tragi-comédie de moeurs', *Opéra international* (1988), June, 24–5

C. A. Rae: 'La Célestine: Maurice Ohanas Oper in Paris', *NZM*, cxlix/10 (1988), 35–6

——: *The Music of Maurice Ohana* (diss., U. of Oxford, 1989)

——: 'Le symbolisme et l'archétype du mythe européen dans l'oeuvre de Maurice Ohana', *Cahiers du C.I.R.E.M.*, no.24–5 (forthcoming)

——: 'L'improvisation dans l'oeuvre de Maurice Ohana', *L'improvisation musicale: Rouen 1992* (forthcoming)

CAROLINE A. RAE

Ohanesian, David (*b* Bucharest, 6 Jan 1927). Romanian baritone. He studied in Bucharest, and with Dinu Bădescu in Cluj. He made his début in *Pagliacci* at the Romanian Opera House in Cluj on 4 December 1950. In 1958 he moved to the Romanian Opera House in Bucharest, performing there until 1977. His repertory included roles in *Aida, Otello, Rigoletto, Il trovatore, Tosca, Margherita d'Anjou, Carmen, Boris Godunov, Lohengrin, Mazeppa, Il barbiere di Siviglia, Yevgeny Onegin* and many other operas; his performance of the title role in Enescu's *Oedipe* helped to make him famous more widely. He performed on most of the great European stages, with full seasons at the Hamburg Staatsoper and at the Bol'shoy Opera in Moscow. A dramatic baritone with a peculiarly dark timbre and an impressively large voice, he was also a good actor with faultless diction.

*

D. Ohanesian and I. Sava: *Iatima muzicii* [Passion of Music] (Bucharest, 1986)

VIOREL COSMA

Ohio Light Opera. American company founded in 1979 in WOOSTER.

Ohms, Elisabeth (*b* Arnhem, 17 May 1888; *d* Marquartstein, Bavaria, 16 Oct 1974). Dutch soprano. After study in Amsterdam and Frankfurt, she made her début at Mainz in 1921, and in 1923 joined the Munich Opera, where she spent the greater part of her career; she was appointed *Kammersängerin*, and married the Munich stage designer Leo Pasetti. Her many notable performances as Brünnhilde and Isolde during the Munich summer festivals made her name familiar to a wider public, and she began to make guest appearances elsewhere, notably at La Scala, in 1927 and 1928, under Toscanini in *Fidelio* and *Parsifal*, at Bayreuth in 1931 in *Parsifal* (again with Toscanini), and at Covent Garden during three seasons in Wagnerian roles and as Strauss's Marschallin. At the Metropolitan during three consecutive seasons (from January 1930) she appeared in all the heavier Wagner roles. She had a dark-coloured, heroic voice.

DESMOND SHAWE-TAYLOR

O'Keeffe [O'Keefe], **John** (*b* Dublin, 24 June 1747; *d* Southampton, 4 Feb 1833). Irish librettist. He wrote his first play at the age of 15 and acted on the Irish stage before settling in London in 1781. He was a prolific comic dramatist for the Haymarket and Covent Garden theatres, although an accident when he was 27 led to deteriorating sight and he had to dictate all his works from 1781. His most successful pieces were librettos for pasticcio operas with music composed, selected and arranged by Samuel Arnold or William Shield. He carefully designed parts for his singers, such as the 'broken English' role for Giovanna Sestini in *The Castle of Andalusia* and Patrick in *The Poor Soldier* for the Irish contralto Margaret Kennedy. He provided Shield with tunes for this opera by singing to him 'the fine Irish airs' of the harper Carolan. 'The Ploughboy', Shield's most famous song, is from his short opera *The Farmer*. Kelly remembered O'Keeffe in 1793 as 'broken down, and almost blind; but still full of pleasantry and anecdote'.

aft – *afterpiece* pan – *pantomime*

The Shamrock, or The Anniversary of St Patrick (comic op aft), W. Shield, 1777 (1783, as The Poor Soldier); *The Son in Law* (aft), S. Arnold, 1779; *The Dead Alive* (comic op aft), Arnold, 1781; *The Agreeable Surprise* (aft), Arnold, 1781; *The Banditti, or Love's Labyrinth* (comic op), Arnold, 1781 (1782, as The Castle of Andalusia); *The Positive Man* (aft farce), with incidental music by Arnold, M. Arne and Shield, 1782; *Harlequin Teague, or The Giant's Causeway* (pan aft, with G. Colman (i)), Arnold, 1782; *The Birthday, or The Prince of Arragon* (aft), Arnold, 1783; *Gretna Green* (aft, with C. Stuart), Arnold, 1783

Peeping Tom (aft), Arnold, 1784; *Fontainbleau, or Our Way in France* (comic op), Shield, 1784; *A Beggar on Horseback* (aft farce), with incidental music by Arnold, 1785; *Love in a Camp, or Patrick in Prussia* (musical farce), Shield, 1786; *The Siege of Curzola* (comic op), Arnold, 1786; *The Farmer* (musical farce), Shield, 1787; *The Constant Maid* (entertainment), C. T. Carter, 1788; *The Gnome, or Harlequin Underground* (pan aft, with R. Wewitzer and Invill), Arnold, 1788; *The Highland Reel* (comic op), Shield, 1788; *Aladin, or The Wonderful Lamp* (pan aft), Shield and others, 1788; *The Czar* (comic op), Shield, 1790 (1790, as The Fugitive)

The Basket Maker (comic op aft), Arnold, 1790; *Sprigs of Laurel* (comic op aft), Shield, 1793 (1797, as The Rival Soldiers); *The Irish Mimic, or Blunders at Brighton* (musical farce), Shield, 1795; *Merry Sherwood, or Harlequin Forester* (pan aft, with W. Pearce), Reeve, 1795; *The Lad of the Hills, or The Wicklow Gold Mine* (comic op), Shield, 1796 (1796, as The Wicklow Mountains); *Olympus in an Uproar, or The Descent of the Deities* (aft, partly based on K. O'Hara: The Golden Pippin), Reeve, 1796; *Britain's Brave Tars! or All for St Paul's* (musical farce), Attwood, 1797

*

DNB (W. FitzPatrick); *LS*

The Dramatic Works of John O'Keeffe (London, 1798)

Recollections in the Life of John O'Keeffe, written by himself (London, 1826)

M. Kelly: *Reminiscences* (London, 1826, 2/1826); ed. R. Fiske (London, 1975)

A. O'Keeffe: *O'Keeffe's Legacy to his Daughter* (London, 1834)

R. Fiske: *English Theatre Music in the Eighteenth Century* (London, 1973, 2/1986)

OLIVE BALDWIN, THELMA WILSON

Oktyabr' ('October'). Folk-heroic opera in a prologue and three acts by VANO IL'ICH MURADELI to a libretto by V. Lugovskoy and Viktor Vinnikov; Moscow, Kremlin Palace of Congresses, 22 April 1964.

After the devastating criticism of his first opera, *Velikaya druzhba* ('The Great Friendship') in 1948, Muradeli might have been expected to avoid the genre altogether. Nevertheless, in 1950 he began to collaborate with the poet Lugovskoy on a new project dealing with events leading up to the Bolshevik Revolution in 1917. Work on the opera was interrupted by Lugovskoy's death. Muradeli returned to it in 1961, dedicating it to the 22nd Congress of the Communist

Party of the Soviet Union; the poet Viktor Vinnikov was responsible for the final version of the libretto. A work imbued with the legacy of Russian revolutionary songs and folksongs and most noteworthy for its choral writing, *October* – specifically Act 2.iii – marked the first time that Lenin was portrayed on the operatic stage as a singing character.

The action takes place between 3 April and 25 October 1917 in Petrograd. In the prologue, the long-standing revolutionary Ivan Timofeyevich (low bass) reminisces about the revolutionary events of 1905 and tells a growing audience about the fight for freedom and happiness being led by Lenin (lyric bass). Returning from the front in April 1917, the nurse Marina (dramatic soprano) meets a childhood friend, Boris Masal'sky (dramatic tenor), an officer of the tsarist death battalion. Among a crowd of workers and soldiers singing a revolutionary song and hurrying to Finland Station to greet Lenin, she recognizes the soldier Andrey (high bass or dramatic baritone), whose life she saved at the front. She introduces him to Boris. At Finland Station, Andrey makes an impassioned speech to the assembly before Ivan Timofeyevich announces, 'Comrades, Lenin has arrived!' Lenin delivers a speech about peace and the coming Bolshevik revolution. In a sharply contrasting scene, all the aristocrats of Petrograd attend a ball given by the Countess (mezzo-soprano). Boris brings Marina, who is horrified by the decadence. She does not know that Boris is in league with counter-revolutionary forces, who gather and debate how to rid themselves of Lenin. Boris volunteers to assassinate him. When Marina guesses that Boris is a conspirator, she breaks with him.

Marina meets Andrey and tells him about the ball and the conspiracy. He tells her about his inspirational meeting with Lenin. The two become closer. Boris has followed them, however, and after Andrey leaves he tries to persuade Marina to leave Russia. She refuses. Sought by the police, Lenin is hiding at Ivan Timofeyevich's home, a fact disguised by the sham wedding festivities for Ivan's daughter. Warned by Marina, Andrey arrives to escort Lenin to a safer hiding place. As the young people dance, police and secret agents arrive, headed by Boris. But Lenin has already escaped and the police leave in hot pursuit. Lenin takes refuge in a cabin by the lakeside. While they wait for the arrival of other Bolsheviks, Andrey and the fishermen listen to Lenin. In the distance they hear the Volga barge haulers' song 'Kamushka', a simple tune which is taken up and continued, without vocal elaboration, by Lenin.

At the battleship *Aurora*, Andrey wants to persuade the sailors to give the signal for revolution. Boris tries to convince them to support the Provisional Government, but they drive him away. On the evening of 25 October, workers, soldiers and sailors gather at Smolny, preparing to storm the Winter Palace. Marina is happy to be with her beloved Andrey. Boris arrives to assassinate Lenin, but Marina exposes him. When, in his frustration, Boris fires at Andrey, Marina shields him with her body and is killed instead. The salvo from the *Aurora* is heard and Lenin emerges to launch the revolution. He and the crowd triumphantly sing the *Internationale*.

LAUREL E. FAY

Ölander, Per [Pehr] **August** (*b* Linköping, 8 Jan 1824; *d* Stockholm, 3 Aug 1886). Swedish composer. He was largely self-taught as a composer, but took lessons with J. E. Nordblom while a student at the University of Uppsala. Although his main employment was as a civil servant, he was active as a music critic and as a violinist. He composed his first opera, *Blenda* (4, L. Josephson and E. Wallmark; *S-Skma**), for a competition organized by King Oscar II. It was staged at the Royal Opera, Stockholm, in 1876 but remained in the repertory only until 1879. The work met with some criticism, owing to its poor libretto (based on Schiller's *Die Jungfrau von Orleans*) and its lack of originality. However, the composer's lyric and melodic gifts as well as the dramatic power of certain scenes were much acclaimed. The opera deals with the conflict between rising Christianity and the old Aesir cult. Despite the Wagnerian overtones of the plot, Ölander skilfully sets the most dramatic scenes with precision, colourful orchestration and a sense of the musical drama. His lyricism and intensity are often reminiscent of Bellini. Notable scenes in the opera include Blenda's dream scene in the first act, her monologue in the third and Sverker's funeral speech in the last: all have a lyrical flow and dramatic power unique in Swedish 19th-century opera. Ölander's other dramatic work, the operetta *Mäster Placide* (T. Merula, Stockholm, New Theatre, 1879, lost; ov. in *Skma*), was rather more successful than *Blenda*, perhaps owing to its lightness and comic verve – both rare in Swedish theatre.

*

F. J. Huss: 'Pehr August Ölander', *Svensk musiktidning*, vi (1886), 105–6

T. Norlind: 'Ölander, Per August', *Allmänt musiklexikon*, ii (Stockholm, 1916, 2/1928)
ANDERS WIKLUND

Oldenburg. City in northern Germany, in Niedersachsen. It acquired a permanent theatre in 1833 with performances given by the Bremen theatrical company. From 1834 it was known as the Grossherzogliches Hoftheater. A new house was built in 1881, but it burnt down in 1891 and was replaced in 1893 by a new theatre in the late classical style. In 1922 the city took control of it, and in 1925 the theatre was described in a new contract as 'a civic enterprise' and was renamed the Oldenburger Landestheater. In 1938 it became the Oldenburgisches Staatstheater when the state assumed control. After renovation in 1961 and extensive alterations in 1972–4 the theatre acquired its present form, with seating for 861.

Although the theatre opened in 1833 with the Bremen production of Auber's *La neige* (as *Der Schnee*), no independent opera company was set up until 1921. Its first major production, *Die Meistersinger*, was given on 25 September that year. The Oldenburg opera is noted for its new production of *Wozzeck* in March 1929, the first German one since the work's première and the one which fostered its popularity by demonstrating that it was within the capabilities of provincial houses. Hans Häckermann was appointed Intendant in 1985, Knut Mahlke general musical director in 1986.

*

H. Schmidt, ed.: *Hoftheater, Landestheater, Staatstheater: Beiträge zur Geschichte des oldenburgischen Theaters 1833–1983* (Oldenburg, 1983)
IMRE FABIAN

Old Maid and the Thief, The. Radio opera in one act by GIAN CARLO MENOTTI to his own libretto; NBC, 22 April 1939 (staged, Philadelphia, 11 February 1941).

While Miss Todd (contralto) is serving tea to Miss Pinkerton (soprano), a beggar, Bob (baritone), comes to the back door. After Miss Pinkerton leaves, he is let in by Miss Todd's servant Laetitia (soprano). Desperate for male company, the women persuade him to stay indefinitely and they lavish food and comforts on him. Later Miss Todd learns of an escaped thief whose description fits Bob, but she continues to shelter him. The women even rob a liquor store in order to bring him gin. When Miss Todd tells him of this he says that she, not he, is the one who should be in gaol. Enraged by his ingratitude she threatens to go to the police and leaves as if to do so, but does not. While she is gone Bob and Laetitia decide to elope, stealing her car and other items. Miss Todd returns to her empty house; she rants and faints.

The great success of Menotti's *Amelia al ballo* brought a commission from NBC for an opera for radio. The work is in 14 short scenes, one being just a brief recitative and aria. A short spoken narrative before each scene, called 'Announcements', is used only in radio broadcasts. The action is more compact and the texture thinner than in *Amelia*, but the same conservative tonal language prevails. BRUCE ARCHIBALD

Oldmixon, Lady [Mrs]. *See* GEORGE, GEORGINA.

Old Vic. London theatre built in 1817–18 as the Royal Coburg Theatre, and renamed the Royal Victoria Theatre in 1833; *see* LONDON, §II, 2.

Olimpiade, L' ('The Olympiad'). Libretto by PIETRO METASTASIO, first set by Antonio Caldara (1733, Vienna).

ACT 1 Megacle [Megacles] arrives in Sicyon just in time to enter the Olympic Games under the name of Licida [Lycidas], a friend who once saved his life. Unknown to Megacles, Lycidas is in love with Aristea [Aristaea], whose hand is to be offered to the winner of the games by her father, King Clistene [Cleisthenes]. Lycidas, once betrothed to Princess Argene of Crete, is unaware that Megacles and Aristaea already love each other, and he subsequently tells his friend of the prize. Aristaea and Megacles greet each other fondly, but Megacles now feels bound by his promise to compete as Lycidas. Meanwhile Argene arrives in Olympia disguised as a shepherdess, to win back Lycidas.

ACT 2 Megacles wins the games, confesses the truth to Aristaea and departs, broken-hearted. When Lycidas comes to claim her, Aristaea reproaches him, as does the disguised Argene, much to his dismay. Aminta [Amyntas], tutor to Lycidas, reports that Megacles has drowned himself, and King Cleisthenes, apprised of the deception, banishes Lycidas.

ACT 3 Argene prevents the desperate Aristaea from suicide, Megacles is rescued by a fisherman, and Lycidas contemplates the assassination of the king. Aristaea pleads mercy for Lycidas and Argene offers herself in his place; as proof that she is a princess, she shows Cleisthenes a chain given her by Lycidas. He recognizes it as belonging to his son, abandoned in infancy to forestall the prophecy that he would kill his father. Lycidas, reinstated, accepts Argene, leaving his sister to Megacles.

*   *   *

A philosophical and historical account of the Olympic Games is provided in the Comes, *Mythologiae* (book 5), and other references are scattered throughout the Pausanias *Graeciae*. Metastasio's plot, however, draws upon the narrative of 'The Trial of the Suitors' provided in the Herodotus *Historiae* (book 6), and the drama, as set by Caldara, served to celebrate the birthday in 1733

'*L'olimpiade*', Act 2 scene x (MEGACLES: '*Whatever will she say when she regains consciousness?*'): engraving from the '*Opere*' of Pietro Metastasio (Paris: Hérissant, 1780–82)

of Empress Elisabeth Christine, consort of the Austrian emperor, Charles VI. Metastasio commented to Saverio Mattei that *L'olimpiade* had been 'performed and repeated in all the theatres of Europe'. Indeed, it ranks with *Demofoonte* and *Didone abbandonata*, dramas excelled in popularity only by *Artaserse* and *Alessandro nell'Indie*. The popularity of *L'olimpiade* may subsequently have prompted Metastasio's NITTETI, a twin drama in several respects.

Although Pergolesi's initial setting for Rome (1735) was not immediately successful, the number of subsequent stagings and extant manuscripts have particularly associated his name with this drama. Settings of *L'olimpiade* are regarded as Galuppi's most successful serious opera (1747, Milan) and as Mysliveček's finest dramatic work (1778, Naples). Sacchini's setting for Padua (1763) also proved popular, and Weber was to praise Poissl's rendition of 1815 when it was revived in Dresden in 1820. Vivaldi's *L'olimpiade* (1734, Venice) provides one of several examples of his use of obbligato instruments (in this case, a horn); revivals of Leo's setting and that of his *Ciro riconosciuto* are credited with introducing the chorus to Naples in 1742–3; and Cimarosa's opera (1784, Vicenza) contains his first use of an ensemble finale in a work of the *seria* type. Gluck would have preferred to set *L'olimpiade* rather than the newly written *Il trionfo di Clelia* for the opening of the Teatro Comunale in Bologna in 1763.

For a list of settings *see* METASTASIO, PIETRO. DON NEVILLE

Olimpiade, L' (i) ('The Olympiad'). *Dramma per musica* in three acts by ANTONIO CALDARA to a libretto by PIETRO METASTASIO (*see* OLIMPIADE, L' above), with ballet music by Nicola Matteis; Vienna, Teatro della Favorita (outdoors), 30 August 1733.

Written for the birthday celebrations of the Habsburg empress Elisabeth Christine, Caldara's *L'olimpiade* initiated a long sequence of settings. The pastoral-heroic plot is dominated by two women, Aristea [Aristaea] and Argene (both sopranos), who, without weighty moralizing but through force of character and, of course, virtue, triumph to claim their rightful lovers. It was an appropriate subject for the occasion, just as the grandiose settings were best accommodated in an outdoor performance.

Emphasis on the spectacular is apparent in the massed choral numbers. Seldom did Caldara integrate the chorus so completely into the overall fabric and provide music for so many diverse groups – nymphs and shepherds, athletes, pagan priests and the inevitable 'populace'. He provided obvious contrasts, such as that between the rustic minuet 'O care selve' (1.iv) and the astringent minor-key triumphal march of the athletes (2.vi). These are reinforced by varied structures and textures: the recurring minuet frames solo passages for Argene in an extended rondo; sections for full chorus and semichorus delineate the da capo march.

Caldara usually included only one accompanied recitative in his ceremonial operas; in *L'olimpiade* there are three. The mental collapse of Licida [Lycidas] (alto) in 'Ah perché tremi' (2.xv) is finely drawn. Other exceptional features include the accompaniment for double string orchestra to Aristaea's 'Grandi è ver' (2.iii), the through-composed 'Se cerca, se dice' (2.x) for the departure of the grief-stricken Megacle [Megacles] (soprano) and the successive arias of fury and revenge for Aristaea and Argene (2.xi and xii), which create the opera's central dramatic point. Pictorialisms, in accompaniments rather than vocal lines, abound in a number of arias; in others Caldara's concern is for the interpretation of mood. Occasionally, as in Argene's 'Fiamma ignota' (3.iv), he combines both illustrative intentions.

BRIAN W. PRITCHARD

Olimpiade, L' (ii) ('The Olympiad'). *Opera seria* in three acts by GIOVANNI BATTISTA PERGOLESI to a libretto by PIETRO METASTASIO (*see* OLIMPIADE, L' above); Rome, Teatro Tordinona, ?2 January 1735.

Pergolesi's setting of *L'olimpiade* was the most popular version before Galuppi's (1747, Milan), attested by the unusually large transmission of over 20 complete manuscript copies. Following Roman practice, the text was performed largely uncut, except for the choruses, which were omitted, and a few lines of recitative were added in Act 3 scene vi. The fact that several arias were borrowed from Pergolesi's *Adriano in Siria* (1734, Naples) suggests that *L'olimpiade* was probably prepared in a rush. Of these, only 'Torbido in volto e nero', a bravura aria with divided orchestra, was repeated unaltered; others were more heavily adapted. *L'olimpiade*, along with *La serva padrona* and the *Stabat mater*, established Pergolesi's reputation throughout Europe. It was praised for its lyric beauty and passionate expression; the *parlante* aria 'Se cerca, se dice' for Megacle [Megacles], the dramatic climax of the opera, was called the 'classic aria' by Rousseau. Burney thought that although the text 'has often been set since to a more elaborate and artificial Music, ... [it] has never been so truly dramatic; all other compositions to those words are languid on the stage, and leave the actor in

too tranquil a state for his situation'. Its poignant, sighing melodic line, reinforced by an orchestral *agitato* accompaniment, was imitated in other settings.

Over the next ten years Pergolesi's music all but monopolized *L'olimpiade* pasticcios throughout Europe. At least four productions were based directly on his original setting: Perugia (Pavone, 1738), Cortona (Accademia, 1738), Siena (Accademia Inconsiderati at the Teatro Grande, 1741) and London (King's, 1742). A Venetian version at S Giovanni Grisostomo (1738), widely attributed to Pergolesi (but not in the libretto), is actually based on Vivaldi's setting (1734), although it may contain some of Pergolesi's music. Angelo Maria Monticelli, a castrato who learnt of the work while in Naples in 1735, sang the primo uomo role in an anonymous Florentine pasticcio (1737, probably also containing Pergolesi's music), in the Venetian production (1738) and finally in London, where his rendition of Pergolesi's music brought widespread accolades.

DALE E. MONSON

Olimpiade, L' (iii) ('The Olympiad'). *Dramma per musica* in three acts by LEONARDO LEO to a libretto by PIETRO METASTASIO (*see* OLIMPIADE, L' above); Naples, Teatro S Carlo, 19 December 1737.

Leo's setting of *L'olimpiade* was only the second opera to be staged at the S Carlo. The performance was given in honour of the birthday of Philip V of Spain; the work was dedicated, however, to his son Charles III, King of the Two Sicilies.

The libretto set by Leo was very close to Metastasio's original; a few cuts were made and a few arias added. Leo's musical style is generally more complex and his textures thicker than those of his contemporaries. Even by comparison with his own *Catone in Utica*, one detects an increasingly periodic phrase structure, slower harmonic rhythm and more sophisticated orchestration typical of the period. Basso continuo arias are absent; full da capo arias, though common, are evenly matched with the modified da capo type. A greater interest in dramatic strength is indicated by the presence of an accompanied recitative, several agitated arias that begin immediately with the voice, and the occasional chorus. As in *Andromaca*, Leo employed 16 of his students from the conservatory of S Maria della Pietà dei Turchini to sing the simple choruses, unusual in Neapolitan opera. The scenery was created by Pietro Righini, the dances by Francesco Aquilanti. Singers in the original production were the tenor Angelo Amorevoli (Clistene [Cleisthenes]), the soprano Anna Peruzzi (Aristea [Aristaea]), the soprano Agata Elmi (Argene), the soprano castrato Mariano Nicolini (Licida [Lycidas]), the soprano Vittoria Tesi (Megacle [Megacles]), the tenor Christofano Rossi (Aminta [Amyntas]) and the soprano castrato Giovanni Manzuoli (Alcandro [Alcander]). The opera was revived at the S Carlo in 1743.

STEPHEN SHEARON

Olimpiade, L' (iv) ('The Olympiad'). *Dramma per musica* in three acts by BALDASSARE GALUPPI to a libretto by PIETRO METASTASIO (*see* OLIMPIADE, L' above); Milan, Regio Ducal Teatro, 26 December 1747.

Galuppi set this famous libretto only once, although at least eight restagings and pasticcios followed. Metastasio's choruses were all eliminated except for the final tutti; five arias were replaced and two new ones added for Alcandro [Alcander] (alto): the fact that Metastasio assigned only a single aria to Alcander often

663

'Olimpie' (Spontini): design by Pierre-Luc-Charles Ciceri for Act 1 in the original production at the Paris Opéra (Théâtre National de la rue de la Loi), 22 December 1819

gave rise to this change. Much recitative was eliminated, most (though not all) of the omissions being indicated by *virgole* in the libretto. The arias of Megacle [Megacles] (soprano castrato, sung by the primo uomo Angelo Maria Monticelli) are virtuoso and expressive, particularly the *agitato* 'Se cerca, se dice', modelled (as were many settings) on the Pergolesi setting of 12 years earlier. The famous tenor Ottavio Albuzio sang Clistene [Cleisthenes], the king; his attest to his virtuosity. Other roles included Aristea [Aristaea], Argene and Licida [Lycidas] (all sopranos) and Aminta [Amyntas] (tenor).

DALE E. MONSON

Olimpiade, L' (v) ('The Olympiad'). *Opera seria* in three acts by NICCOLÒ JOMMELLI to a libretto by PIETRO METASTASIO (*see* OLIMPIADE, L' above); Stuttgart, Herzogliches Theater, 11 February 1761.

Metastasio's libretto received nearly a complete setting by Jommelli, though Licida [Lycidas] (soprano castrato), Aminta [Amyntas] (soprano castrato) and Argene (alto) each lose one aria. All the choruses are set completely, except that the chorus in Act 2 includes new parts for soloists, and marches introduce the choruses in Acts 2 and 3. Jommelli replaces the return of the chorus 'I tuoi strali' in Act 3 with a beautiful trio for Megacle [Megacles] (soprano castrato), Clistene [Cleisthenes] (tenor) and Lycidas, 'Dolce amico'. The duet at the close of Act 1 is Metastasio's text. This opera also marks Jommelli's move from the da capo to the dal segno aria, with the sign occurring within the *A'* section or second statement of the first strophe of text, rather than at the initial entry of the vocal part. A bridge passage following the *B* section effected a smooth transition to this interior return.

MARITA P. McCLYMONDS

Olimpie ('Olympia'). *Tragédie lyrique* in three acts by GASPARE SPONTINI to a libretto by Joseph Marie Dieulafoy and Charles Brifaut after VOLTAIRE's *Olympie*; Paris, Opéra, 22 December 1819.

In Ephesus, the enemy kings Cassandre [Cassander] (tenor) and Antigone [Antigonus] (bass) have made peace. When the Hiérophante (bass) is about to give Aménaïs (soprano), whom Antigonus loves, to Cassander as his wife, Alexander's widow, Statira (mezzo-soprano), recognizes Cassander as her husband's murderer. Cassander asks her pardon and reveals the identity of Aménaïs, who is really Statira's daughter Olympia. He is taken prisoner by Antigonus, but manages to escape and overthrow his rival. Fearing the vengeance of Cassander, Statira stabs herself, and Olympia too escapes Cassander, whom she still loves, by committing suicide. The tragic ending is transfigured by the apotheosis of Statira, Olympia and Alexander.

In his third grand opera, begun in 1815, Spontini combined the psychologically exact character-drawing of *La vestale* with the massive choral style of his *Fernand Cortez*, and wrote a work stripped of spectacular effects. In its grandiose conception, it appears the musical equivalent of neo-classical architecture. The aim was to revive *tragédie lyrique*, using means which anticipate the idea of opera as a *Gesamtkunstwerk*; the recitatives are scored with unusual elaboration, often merging into arioso and aria or ensemble, while the big choral scenes are often based on the symphonic working of orchestral figures. But the work failed in its purpose; mixed reviews caused Spontini to withdraw it after seven performances to revise the finale. After the closing of the Opéra in February 1820, this second version, in which Antigonus becomes the real murderer of

Alexander, was performed in E. T. A. Hoffmann's German translation (Berlin, Königliches Opernhaus, 14 May 1821). The composer, who was always revising his work, retained the happy ending for a new French version performed at the Paris Opéra on 28 February 1826. Despite its initial success in Berlin, however, the backward-looking tone of the opera meant that it could not compete with Weber's triumphs there, or with Rossini's in Paris.   ANSELM GERHARD

Olin, Elisabeth (*b* Stockholm, 8 Dec 1740; *d* Stockholm, 26 March 1828). Swedish soprano. The daughter of the organist Peter Lillström (1714–77) and an actress, she made her début at the age of seven in the first *opéra comique* in Swedish, *Syrinx, eller Then uti Wass förvandlade Wattennymph* ('Syrinx, or The Water Nymph Transformed from Reeds'). She was employed at the Royal Opera from 1773 to 1803 and was famous for her roles in Uttini's *Thetis och Pelée*, Handel's *Acis and Galatea* and Gluck's operas. Critics considered her the best opera singer in Stockholm during the Gustavian period. Her voice was characterized as light and expressive, her acting as realistic and her textual declamation as lively. She was elected a member of the Royal Academy of Music in 1783.

*

F. Dahlgren: *Anteckningar om Stockholms teatrar* [Notes on Stockholm's Theatres] (Stockholm, 1866)
J. Flodmark: *Stenborgska skådebanorne* [Stenborg's Theatres] (Stockholm, 1893)
——: *Elisabeth Olin och Carl Stenborg* (Stockholm, 1903)
                      BERTIL H. VAN BOER

Olitzka, Rosa (*b* Berlin, 6 Sept 1873; *d* Chicago, 29 Sept 1949). German contralto. She studied in Berlin and Paris, making her début in 1892 at Brno. From 1893 to 1907 she sang regularly at Covent Garden, where she made her début as Erda (*Siegfried*). Her roles included Urbain (*Les Huguenots*), Ortrud, Emilia (*Otello*), Fricka, Maddalena (*Rigoletto*), Marthe (*Faust*), Amneris, Ulrica, Magdalene (*Die Meistersinger*) and Carmen. She was engaged at the Metropolitan from 1895 to 1901, making her début as Siébel. She also sang in Germany, Chicago and Boston. Her nephew, Walter Olitzki (*b* Hamburg-Altona, 17 March 1899; *d* New York, 2 Aug 1949), was a baritone who, after a ten-year contract in Königsberg, East Prussia, moved to New York and was engaged at the Metropolitan (1939–47). He made his début as Beckmesser and also sang Alberich and Klingsor.   ELIZABETH FORBES

Oliva, Francesco [Auliva; Ciccio Viola] (*b* ? Naples, 1671; *d* ? Naples, 1736). Italian librettist. During the early 18th century he was a prominent literary figure and a member of the Arcadian Academy with the pastoral name Acantede Antegnano. It is likely that he was educated at the Seminario Arcivescovile, entering the priesthood in 1695. The absence of Oliva's name from the title-pages of his Neapolitan comic operas (authenticated only through references in the address 'a chi vo lejere') indicates a reluctance towards publicity compatible with the priestly calling. Oliva demonstrated strong concern for the value of the Neapolitan dialect both in his writings (see his translation of Tasso's *Aminta* and his treatise on grammar) and his theatrical works, where he exploited the linguistic distinction between social strata (the 'perzone cevile' and the 'perzone prebbeje'). The popularity of Oliva's comedies

is attested by the revivals of both *Lo castiello saccheato* and *La mpeca scoperta*.

Lo Funnaco revotato, before 1722 (lost); *Lo castiello saccheato* [*sacchejato*] (commeddea), Falco and Vinci, 1720 (comp. unknown, 1732, as 'commeddeja ammascherata pe mmuseca'; M. Capranica, 1747, as L'Emilia, with addns by P. Trinchera); *La noce de Veneviento* (commeddia pe' mmuseca), 1722; *La mpeca scoperta* (commeddia pe' mmuseca), Leo, 1723 (comp. unknown, 1732, as La mbroglia scoperta, with addns by E. M. Orenghi); *L'ammore fedele* (favola sarvateca), Leo, 1724

Doubtful: *Lo passo apposta* (commedia per musica), Leo, 1724; *Li duje figlie a no ventre* (commeddea Napolitana pe mmuseca), D. Galasso, 1725

*

F. Oliva: *Grammatica della lingua napolitana* (Naples, 1728); repr. in *Ferdinando Galiani. Del dialetto napoletano*, ed. E. Malato (Rome, 1970), 211–327
M. Scherillo: *L'opera buffa napoletana durante il settecento: storia letteraria* (Naples, 1883, enlarged 2/1916), 177–94
U. Prota-Giurleo: 'Francesco Oliva', *Nicola Logroscino, 'il dio dell' opera buffa'* (Naples, 1927), 79
E. Malato, ed.: *La poesia dialettale napoletana*, i (Naples, 1960)
C. Perrone, ed.: *Francesco Oliva: opere napoletane* (Rome, 1977)
P. Simonelli: 'Lingua e dialetto nel teatro musicale napoletano del '700', *Musica e cultura a Napoli dal XV al XIX secolo* (Florence, 1983), 232–4   GRAHAM HARDIE

Oliver, Stephen (*b* Chester, 10 March 1950; *d* London, 29 April 1992). English composer. He took a BA and BMus at Oxford, studying with Kenneth Leighton and Robert Sherlaw Johnson. For two years he taught composition at the Huddersfield School of Music, but from 1974 worked as a freelance composer. Three of his operas, *All the Tea in China*, *Slippery Soules* and *A Phoenix too Frequent*, had been performed while he was an undergraduate, before the three-act *Duchess of Malfi* (1971), given by the Oxford University Opera Club, attracted wider attention as the work of a composer of fluent and versatile technique, possessing a keen sense of characterization, dramatic pace and theatrical effect. Oliver, who had written his own libretto for *The Duchess of Malfi*, also played the part of the villain, Bosola. His later stage works include ten full-length operas, 18 one-act operas of several types, operas for children and the musical *Blondel* (with lyrics by Tim Rice). He continued to write most of his own librettos and to concern himself with every aspect of opera production, and was adventurous in choice of subject, treatment, and the use of unconventional forces. Many pieces were been commissioned for small groups or for particular places, for instance those for Musica nel Chiostro (*Il giardino*, *La bella e la bestia*, *Mario ed il mago* and *L'oca del Cairo*), performed in the cloisters of the monastery at Batignano; *The Girl and the Unicorn* was written for performance in the church of St James Norland, London W11, by the children of the W.11 Opera Group; the witty *Waiter's Revenge* was written for the Purcell Consort; *Tom Jones* (1976) was commissioned by the English Music Theatre Company; and the ENO commissioned *Timon of Athens* (1991).

Oliver wrote with special sympathy for the voice, and was a skilled orchestrator and a fluent master of many styles and idioms. He also wrote a symphony, a recorder concerto, several cantatas, a series of chamber works called *Ricercare*, and music for more than 80 plays, films and television documentaries (including the Royal Shakespeare Company's *Nicholas Nickleby* and a 26-part radio adaptation of *The Lord of the Rings*); he translated operas, and prepared English librettos for

Sallinen's *The Red Line* (vocal score, Borough Green, 1982) and *The King Goes forth to France* (vocal score, Borough Green, 1986).

librettos by the composer unless otherwise stated

Elymas, 1962 (1), unperf.
The Warden of the Tower, 1964 (1, L. du Garde Peach), unperf.
Thespis, 1966 (2, W. S. Gilbert), unperf.
Dr Faustus, 1967 (2, C. Marlowe), unperf.
Comus, 1968 (1, J. Milton), unperf.
All the Tea in China (1, W. Harvey), Oxford, Clarendon Press Institute, Oct 1969
Slippery Souls (4 pts), Oxford, Wychwood School, Dec 1969; rev. 1976; rev., London, St Paul's Girls' School, 12 Dec 1988
A Phoenix too Frequent (1, C. Fry), Oxford, Holywell Music Rooms, June 1970
The Enchanted Shirt, 1970 (1, C. Girdlestone), unperf.
The Duchess of Malfi (3, after J. Webster), Oxford, Playhouse, 23 Nov 1971; rev., Santa Fe, 5 Aug 1978
The Dissolute Punished (4 one-act operas), Edinburgh, St Mary's Hall, Aug 1972
  A Dialogue Between Jupiter and Cupid (after T. Heywood)
  The Blind (after M. Maeterlinck)
  The Fall of Miss Moss (after K. Mansfield)
  Il dissoluto punito
The Three Wise Monkeys (1, D. Pountney), 1972
The Donkey (1, Pountney), Stirling, MacRobert Centre, 20 Sept 1973
A Furcoat for Summer, 1973 (4), unperf.
Sufficient Beauty, 1973 (3 one-act operas), unperf.
  The Burrow (after F. Kafka)
  The Kiss (after A. P. Chekhov)
  The Professor
Three Instant Operas (children's operas), London, 1973 (Borough Green, 1976)
  Paid Off
  Time Flies
  Old Haunts
Past Tense (2 one-act operas), Huddersfield, School of Music, 5 June 1974
  Old Times
  Come and Go (S. Beckett)
Perseverance, 1974 (4, after a mystery play and C. Dickens), unperf.
Bad Times (1), London, Eltham Palace, 24 June 1975
Tom Jones (3, after H. Fielding), Snape, 6 April 1976
The Great McPorridge Disaster (1), Bath, May 1976
The Waiter's Revenge (1), Nottingham, 15 June 1976
Il giardino (1), Batignano, 27 July 1977; as The Garden, London, Wigmore Hall, 17 April 1980; vs (Borough Green, 1985)
A Stable Home (1), Canada, Dec 1977, vs (Borough Green, 1980)
The Girl and the Unicorn (children's op, 3 pts), London, St James Norland, 9 Dec 1978, vs (Borough Green, 1984)
The Dreaming of the Bones, 1979 (1, W. B. Yeats), unperf.
Jacko's Play (children's operetta, 1, after R. Smith), book and record (London, 1980)
A Man of Feeling (1, after A. Schnitzler: *Der Empfindsame*), London, Islington, King's Head Theatre Club, 17 Nov 1980, vs (Borough Green, 1983)
Euridice (3), London, Riverside Studios, 4 March 1981 [after Peri]
Sasha (3, after A. N. Ostrovsky: *Artists and Admirers*), Banff, 7 April 1983
Blondel (musical, 2, T. Rice), Bath, Royal, 5 Sept 1983
Britannia Preserv'd (1, A. N. Wilson), Hampton Court, 30 May 1984
The Ring (1, after television serial: *Coronation Street*), Manchester, Free Trade Hall, 31 May 1984
La bella e la bestia (2, after Mme Le Prince de Beaumont), Batignano, 26 July 1984; as Beauty and the Beast, London, St John's Smith Square, 21 June 1985; vs (Borough Green, 1987)
Exposition of a Picture (1), London, Royal Academy of Arts, 24 June 1986
Commuting, 1986 (1), unperf.
Waiting (1), Buxton, June 1987
Mario ed il mago (1, after T. Mann), Batignano, 5 Aug 1988; as Mario and the Magician, Milwaukee, 3 May 1989
Table's Meet (1), London, Royal Festival Hall, Review Restaurant, 20 May 1990
Timon of Athens (2, after W. Shakespeare), London, Coliseum, 17 May 1991
L'oca del Cairo (2), Batignano, 28 July 1991 [after Mozart]

J. Glover: 'Stephen Oliver', *MT*, cxv (1974), 1042–4
P. Griffiths: 'Stephen Oliver', *New Sounds, New Personalities* (London, 1985), 140–47
J. Glover: Obituary, *The Independent* (1 May 1992)
A. Pollock: 'A Handful of Operas', *Opera*, xliii (1992), 789–95
G. Vick: 'Stephen Oliver, 1950–1992', ibid, 787–8   HUGO COLE

Oliveri, Cesare. *See* OLIVIERI, CESARE.

Olivero, Magda [Maria Maddalena] (*b* Saluzzo, nr Turin, 25 March 1912). Italian soprano. She studied in Turin and made her début there in 1933 as Lauretta. Her early roles included Manon Lescaut, Mimì, Elsa, Liù, Violetta (Reggio Emilia and Parma) and Butterfly (Modena and Naples). During the 1939–40 season she sang Adriana Lecouvreur in Rome, Naples, Venice and Florence, becoming Cilea's preferred interpreter of the role. She added the title roles in *Francesca da Rimini* and *Suor Angelica* and Zandonai's Giulietta to her repertory. In 1941 she married and retired, but at Cilea's urging she made her reappearance in 1951 as Adriana Lecouvreur at Brescia.

During the next 20 years Olivero became specially identified with Fedora, Tosca, Minnie and Mascagni's Iris. She made her London début in 1952 at the Stoll Theatre as Mimì and in 1963 sang Adriana Lecouvreur at the Edinburgh Festival. She sang in the USA at Dallas in 1967 as Medea, in New York in 1970 in *La voix humaine* and at the Metropolitan in 1975, when she was over 60, as Tosca. By no means a perfect vocalist, she was an artist who by her magnetic personality could rouse an audience to the heights of enthusiasm.

GV (R. Celletti; R. Vegeto)
M. Olivero: 'Cilea and "Adriana Lecouvreur"', *Opera*, xiv (1963), 523–8
R. Celletti: 'Magda Olivero, ieri, oggi, domani', *Discoteca*, no.87 (1969), 21–5 [with discography]
R. M. Connolly: 'The (Re)discovery of Magda Olivero', *Stereo Review*, xxiii (1969), Nov, 70–73
M. Morini: 'Magda Olivero: l'artista, le scelte, il personaggio', *Discoteca*, no.87 (1969), 16–20   HAROLD ROSENTHAL/R

Olivieri [de Massimi], **Angelo** (*fl* Rome, *c*1678–91). Italian composer. He was a member of the household of Maffeo Barberini, Prince of Palestrina, from an unknown time until the prince's death in 1685. The significance of his alias is not known. He composed three secular cantatas and some dramatic works of which only six or seven arias survive, in Barberini manuscripts. A single complete opera score remains, *Dalla padella alla bragia* (D. Contini, *I-Rvat*; also known as *Da Scille in Cariddi*). It was first performed in Palestrina in 1681 for the wedding festivities of Costanza Barberini and G. F. Caetani, Duke of San Marco, and restaged a few weeks later at the Collegio Clementino in Rome for Queen Christina of Sweden. It has five characters involved in a romantic comedy of short scenes; quick dialogue is laced with mostly syllabic arias and duets. The arias often have long, elaborate ritornellos and motto openings, and are mostly strophic. Each of the three acts closes with dancing. In many ways it resembles the early operas of Alessandro Scarlatti.

  MARGARET MURATA

Olivieri [Oliveri], **Cesare** (*fl* Turin, 1776–92). Italian poet. He wrote librettos for the Teatro Regio, Turin, between 1776 and 1792, though his principal occupations were that of lawyer and public official. He is credited with only five works, but he may have been the author of a number of unattributed librettos for operas produced in Turin during the late 18th century. In *Cleopatra*, he avoided a staged double suicide: Mark Antony's body is discovered on stage, and Cleopatra departs to die during the final scene. His exotic libretto *Sicotencal*, set in Yucatan, enjoyed some success in Italy both in the original three-act version, which Colla set for Pavia in 1776, and in a two-act version entitled *Zulima*, produced in Florence in 1777 with Rutini's music and reset by Bianchi for Naples in 1782. This opera, together with Cigna-Santi's *Alcina e Ruggiero* (1775), initiated a trend in Turin towards operas with chorus, sizable ensemble finales, shorter third acts, more elaborate accompanying ballets and less emphasis on military battles and display. The two *feste teatrali Il trionfo della pace* and *Bacco ed Arianna*, as well as the *opera seria Atalanta*, involve supernatural interventions and contain some French-inspired machine spectacle.

Cleopatra (os), C. Monza, 1776; *Sicotencal* (os), Rutini, 1776 (Colla, 1776; Rutini, 1777, as Zulima; Bianchi, 1782, as Zulima); *Il trionfo della pace* (festa teatrale), Bianchi, 1782 (Sarti, 1783); *Bacco ed Arianna* (festa teatrale), Tarchi, 1784; *Atalanta* (os), G. Giordani, 1791

A. Basso, ed.: *Storia del Teatro Regio di Torino*, i: M.-T. Bouquet: *Il teatro di corte dalle origini al 1788* (Turin, 1976)

MARITA P. McCLYMONDS

Olivo e Pasquale ('Olivo and Pasquale'). *Melodramma giocoso* in two acts by GAETANO DONIZETTI to a libretto by JACOPO FERRETTI after SIMEONE ANTONIO SOGRAFI's comedy *Olivo e Pasquale*; Rome, Teatro Valle, 7 January 1827.

Olivo e Pasquale is a romantic comedy of character, contrasting the two brothers of the title: the former choleric, the latter gentle. The action centres on the marriage of Isabella (soprano), the daughter of Olivo (baritone). Her father wants her to marry a wealthy merchant from Cádiz, Le Bross (tenor), but she loves a young apprentice, Camillo (mezzo-soprano, later revised as a tenor role). Le Bross becomes her active ally but Olivo remains adamant. Isabella swears that unless he relent before five o'clock, she and Camillo will kill themselves. The clock strikes; shots are heard. Pasquale (tenor) faints and Olivo announces that to avoid seeing his daughter dead he would rather see her married to the man of her choice, at which the smiling couple appear to receive everyone's congratulations. WILLIAM ASHBROOK

Ollendorf, Fritz (*b* Darmstadt, 24 March 1912; *d* Zürich, 29 March 1977). German bass. He studied in Salzburg and Milan, making his début in 1937 as Leporello at Basle, where he was engaged until 1951. He then went to Düsseldorf and, in 1957, to Stuttgart. At Glyndebourne (1953–4) he sang Osmin, Truffaldino (*Ariadne auf Naxos*) and Dr Bombasto (Busoni's *Arlecchino*). He created the Mayor in Egk's *Der Revisor* at Schwetzingen (1957) and sang in Amsterdam and Vienna and at La Scala. His repertory included Don Alfonso, Count Robinson (*Il matrimonio segreto*), Don Pasquale, Mustafà (*L'italiana in Algeri*) and Swallow (*Peter Grimes*). An effective comic actor, he had a strong, flexible voice. ELIZABETH FORBES

Ollmann, Kurt (*b* Racine, WI, 19 Jan 1957). American baritone. His principal teachers were Yolanda Marculescu, Gérard Souzay and Marlena Malas. After a period as resident baritone at the Milwaukee Skylight Opera, 1979–82, he appeared in Brussels, Milan, St Louis, Santa Fe, Seattle and Washington, DC, in roles including Mercutio (Gounod), Papageno and Pelléas. In 1987 he sang the title role in Peter Sellars's production of *Don Giovanni* at the Pepsico Summerfare in New York. A protégé of Bernstein, he appeared in the local première of *A Quiet Place* at the Vienna Staatsoper in 1986 and recorded *Candide* and *West Side Story* under him. Ollmann's clear, lyric voice and musical suavity have also distinguished him as a recitalist.

CORI ELLISON

Ollone, Max(imilien-Paul-Marie-Félix) d' (*b* Besançon, 13 June 1875; *d* Paris, 15 May or 9 Sept 1959). French composer. A pupil of Massenet at the Paris Conservatoire, he won the Prix de Rome in 1897. He was successively director of music in Angers, director of the Fontainebleau conservatory, professor at the Paris Conservatoire and director of the Opéra-Comique. His operas show the influence of Massenet and Wagner and range from the biblical quasi-oratorio *La samaritaine* to *L'arlequin*, a comedy of intrigue. *Jean*, his first operatic venture, uses massive quasi-religious choral effects to accompany the tale of a mother who places her son in a monastery for protection during the French Revolution. *Le retour*, a melodramatic love story set on a wild island, shows the influence of Maeterlinck and Ibsen; it is Ollone's most serious work and contains finely orchestrated passages depicting the sea and storms. For *Les uns et les autres* the composer used pastiche Baroque music to complement Verlaine's Watteauesque *Fêtes galantes*, and in *George Dandin* he carried further this interest in period intrigue. Ollone also worked as a critic and writer; his book *Le théâtre et le public*, published in 1955 (Paris and Geneva), advocated a popularist view of music.

printed works are vocal scores, unless otherwise stated, published in Paris

Jean, 1900–05 (drame lyrique, prol., 5 tableaux, Ollone), ?unperf. (1908)
Le retour (drame lyrique, 2, Ollone), Angers, 13 Feb 1913 (1911)
L'étrangère (1, Ollone), Paris, Concerts Colonne, 1913
Les amants de Rimini (4, Ollone), partial perf., Paris, Opéra, 2 March 1916
Les uns et les autres (comédie lyrique, 1, P. Verlaine: Fêtes galantes), Paris, OC (Favart), 6 Nov 1922 (1922)
L'arlequin (comédie lyrique, 5 [6 tableaux], J. Sarment), Paris, Opéra, 22 Dec 1924, full score (1925)
George Dandin, ou Le mari confondu (oc, 3, M. Belvianes, after Molière), Paris, OC (Favart), 19 March 1930 (1930)
La samaritaine (3, E. Rostand), Paris, Opéra, 23 June 1937

P. Landormy: 'Henri Rabaud, Max d'Ollone, Roger Ducasse', *Le théâtre lyrique en France* (Paris, 1937–9) [pubn of Poste National/Radio-Paris], iii, 154–8 RICHARD LANGHAM SMITH

Olomouc (Ger. Olmütz). Town in Moravia. Its theatrical tradition can be traced from the 16th century. Opera was performed in German following the opening in 1830 of the civic theatre. Originally built by the architect Kornhäusel, the theatre has since been rebuilt in 1920 and 1976, and has a seating capacity of 522. Mahler conducted there in 1882–3, and Gustav Brecher in 1903; Maria Jeritza made her début as Elsa in *Tannhäuser* in 1910.

The high standards achieved at the civic theatre posed a challenge to the Czech theatre tradition that was developing at the time and which remained on an amateur basis until the end of World War I. Only after

667

independence in 1918 did the Czech professional theatre come into being, performing in the civic theatre from 1920, when Smetana's *Libuše* opened the new season. Under the guidance of Karel Nedbal (1921–8) and Adolf Heller (1932–8) the Czech opera company soon attained a remarkable level of performance; any suggestion of provincialism was offset by the wide repertory that included works by Strauss, Wagner and Verdi, Monteverdi's *Orfeo*, the première of Roussel's *Le testament de la tante Caroline* and the Czech première of Shostakovich's *Lady Macbeth of the Mtsensk District* (both in 1935–6). The Czech opera also undertook many tours including regular visits to Opava and Liberec; the company also appeared in Prague in 1923 and Vienna the following year in a cycle of Smetana's operas.

After 1945 the civic theatre's identity was firmly established, with opera performances predominating. In 1948 responsibility for the theatre was transferred from the town to the National Regional Committee, which confirmed the company's obligation to tour. In 1958 the theatre was renamed the Divadlo Oldřicha Stibora (Oldřich Stibor Theatre). The remarkable era of Iša Krejčí (1945–58) saw productions of almost 50 operas by Czech composers, as well as many works by Mozart, Verdi and Russian composers, including Musorgsky, whose *Boris Godunov* was given in the original version. Under Zdeněk Košler (1958–63) the opera company reached a peak of artistic achievement.

*

E. Ambros and J. Čičatka: *Dvacet let české opery v Olomouci 1920–1940* [Twenty Years of the Czech Opera in Olomouc] (Přerov, 1942)
Olomoucké divadlo v desetiletí 1945–1955 [The Theatre of Olomouc in the Decade 1945–1955] (Olomouc, 1957)
K. Nedbal: *Půl století s českou operou* [Half a Century with the Czech Opera] (Prague, 1959)
V. Hudec: 'Olomoucká operní dramaturgie Iši Krejčího' [Iša Krejčí's Olomouc Opera Dramaturgy], *O divadle na Moravě* (Prague, 1974), 137–44
Státní divadlo Oldřicha Stibora v Olomouci 1965–75 [The Oldřich Stibor State Theatre in Olomouc] (Olomouc, 1975)

EVA HERRMANNOVÁ

Olsen, Ole (*b* Hammerfest, 4 July 1850; *d* Oslo, 9 Nov 1927). Norwegian composer. He studied in Trondheim (1865–9), and in Leipzig (1870–74) with Reinecke and others. From 1874 he worked as a music teacher and conductor in Oslo. In 1884 he was appointed music director of the Akershus 2nd Brigade, for which he composed marches, many of them based on Norwegian folktunes that he had had a hand in collecting. His concert and stage works are also representative of the nationalist tradition; some of them enjoyed great popularity. His operas show the influence of Wagner's ideas.

Stig Hvide, 1872–6 (O. Olsen)
Lajla, 1893 (Olsen), Christiania, 8 Oct 1908
Stallo, 1902 (Olsen)
Klippeøerne, 1904–10 (Olsen)

*

A. C. Dahl: *Ole Olsen* (Oslo, 1910)

KARI MICHELSEN

Olszewska [Olczewska], **Maria** [Berchtenbreitner, Marie] (*b* Ludwigsschwaige, nr Donauwörth, 12 Aug 1892; *d* Klagenfurt, 17 May 1969). German mezzo-contralto. She studied in Munich and made her début as a Page in *Tannhäuser* at Krefeld in 1915. After an engagement at Leipzig she sang at the Hamburg Staatsoper, where she took part in the joint première

(with Cologne) of Korngold's *Die tote Stadt* (1920). She sang regularly in Vienna (1921–30). She also appeared frequently at the Staatsoper in Munich, and at Covent Garden (1924–32), where her performances in such roles as Fricka, Ortrud, Brangäne and Herodias (*Salome*) drew the highest critical acclaim. Her Carmen and Amneris were less successful, but her Octavian and Orlofsky (*Die Fledermaus*) were highly regarded. She sang in Chicago (1928–32) and at the Metropolitan (1933–5). Olszewska possessed a rich, beautiful voice and great dramatic temperament. She married the baritone Emil Schipper.

*

H. M. Barnes: 'Maria Olczewska Discography', *British Institute of Recorded Sound Bulletin*, no.6 (1957), 17–20

HAROLD ROSENTHAL/R

Oltrabella, Augusta (*b* Savona, 27 Dec 1897; *d* Milan, 4 June 1981). Italian soprano. She studied in Milan and made her début in 1917 at Mondovi in *Il trovatore*. Singing mostly lyric roles, of which her most famous was Suor Angelica, she appeared throughout Italy in the 1920s, with a brief spell in the winter of 1929 in New York at the Metropolitan, where her roles were Musetta and Liù (also Butterfly on tour). Her début at La Scala in 1931 in Humperdinck's *Königskinder* marked the turning-point of her career. She remained there until 1940, taking part in the premières of two operas by Lodovico Rocca, *Il Dibuk* (1934) and *La morte di Frine* (1937). At Salzburg she sang in *Falstaff*, as Nannetta under Toscanini and later as Mrs Ford under Gui. Her appearances at Covent Garden were limited to an under-rehearsed production of *Manon Lescaut* under Constant Lambert in the winter season of 1936. She became an admired Salome in Italy, and at Florence sang in the first Italian performance of Busoni's *Doktor Faust* (1942). She retired in 1960. A lively responsive style and a clear voice can be heard in her recordings.

*

L. Rasponi: *The Last Prima Donnas* (London, 1984)

J. B. STEANE

Olympians, The. Opera in three acts by ARTHUR BLISS to a libretto by J. B. Priestley; London, Covent Garden, 29 September 1949.

Set in a Provençal village in 1836, the action concerns the legend that the dispossessed classical deities forever travel the roads of Europe as a troupe of strolling players. Priestley has them regain their divine powers for a few hours on Midsummer Night, once every hundred years.

The players, stranded penniless at an inn, are hired to entertain the guests of the wealthy but mean Lavatte (bass), at a party celebrating the engagement of his daughter Madeleine (lyric soprano) to an elderly nobleman. She, however, falls in love at first sight with the young poet Hector de Florac (lyric tenor) who is also staying there. In Act 2, set outside Lavatte's house, the gods (Jupiter, baritone; Diana, dramatic soprano; Venus, mime; Bacchus, tenor; Mars, bass-baritone; and Mercury, dancer) resume their powers and one by one lead the guests a corybantic dance. In a mock exorcism staged by the Curé (tenor) in Act 3, Lavatte is reduced to giving away gold and granting the young lovers' betrothal.

Adverse conditions dogged the opera's Covent Garden production, since when it has never been professionally staged. Amateur and concert performances reveal a romantic work too prodigal of musical wealth and major roles but radiant and exciting in the masque-like tableaux of Act 2.

STEPHEN BANFIELD

Olympia Theatre. Theatre in Athens, inaugurated in 1916, the home of the Ethniki Lyriki Skini (National Opera) since its inception in 1940; *see* ATHENS.

Omaha. American city, in Nebraska. It promoted opera in the late 19th century by constructing several theatres: in 1871, Redick's Opera House (16th Street and Farnam); in 1881, Boyd's Opera House (15th and Farnam), with a seating capacity of 1700, renamed the Farnam Street Theatre and destroyed by fire in 1893; in 1887, Grand Opera House (15th and Capitol), seating more than 2500, which burnt down in 1895; and in 1891, Boyd's New Theatre (17th and Harney), also seating more than 2500, which closed in 1920. The most durable theatre, the Creighton Orpheum (1895; 16th and Howard), was elegantly restored in 1974 and placed on the National Register of Historic Places; it is the home of Opera Omaha. Founded in 1958, Opera Omaha has combined local talent, national stars, enthusiastic volunteers and outstanding musical and financial direction to become an important regional opera company with a growing national reputation. Since 1973 it has presented seasonally three major productions, with at least two performances each, featuring traditional operas as well as less familiar ones. The company's growing sophistication is apparent from its sponsoring of the 1988 American première of Handel's *Partenope*.

KAREN M. DYER

Oman, Julia Trevelyan (*b* London, 11 July 1930). British designer. After studying with distinction at the Royal College of Art with Hugh Casson, she joined the BBC in 1955 as a television designer, remaining until 1967. She designed a number of distinguished theatre, ballet and opera productions between 1967 and 1988, including *Yevgeny Onegin* (1971), *La bohème* (1974; for illustration *see* COSTUME, fig.21) and *Die Fledermaus* (1977) for Covent Garden, and *Arabella* (1984) for Glyndebourne. International productions include *Un ballo in maschera* for the Hamburg Staatsoper (1973), *Otello* for the Royal Opera, Stockholm (1982), *Die Csárdásfürstin* for Kassel Opera (1983) and *The Consul* for Connecticut Opera (1985).

Oman is much admired by critics and audiences for the social and historical accuracy of her designs. Her costumes appear as real clothes worn by real people, and her sets as places where people actually live, work and play. She stylishly and inventively combines the visually appealing with a particular care for detail that always serves the dramatic needs of the work at hand. She was elected a Royal Designer for Industry (1977) and was made a CBE in 1986.

DAVID J. HOUGH

O'Mara, Joseph (*b* Limerick, 16 July 1861; *d* Dublin, 5 Aug 1927). Irish tenor. He studied in Milan with Moretti and made his début at the Royal English Opera House, London in 1891 as Sullivan's Ivanhoe. After further study he was engaged by Augustus Harris for a tour of the British Isles, singing Lohengrin, Walther, Don José and other roles. In 1896 he created Mike in *Shamus O'Brien* at the Opera Comique, London. From 1902 to 1908 he was the leading tenor of the Moody-Manners Company, and in 1910 he joined Beecham's company at Covent Garden. In 1912 he founded the O'Mara Grand Opera Company, appearing with it until 1924. O'Mara had a repertory of nearly 70 roles, of which Eléazar (*La Juive*) was his most successful.

E. O'Mara Carton: 'Joseph O'Mara', *Record Collector*, xix (1970–71), 33–42 [with discography]

HAROLD ROSENTHAL/R

Ombra scene. A scene set in Hades, or one involving a ghost or shade (*ombra*). These scenes were included in 17th-century Italian opera and the French *tragédie en musique*, and remained a feature of 18th-century operas, particularly those based on the Orpheus, Iphigenia and Alcestis themes. 19th-century operas on Shakespeare's plays (*Macbeth*, *Hamlet*) give rise to some notable *ombra* scenes; Berlioz's *Les Troyens* and Britten's *The Turn of the Screw* contain other remarkable examples.

See also SOMMEIL.

Oncina, Juan (*b* Barcelona, 15 April 1925). Spanish tenor. He studied in Oran (Algeria) and in Barcelona with Mercedes Capsir, opposite whom he made his début as Massenet's Des Grieux at the Gran Teatro del Liceo, Barcelona, in 1946. Later that year he made his Italian début at Bologna as Almaviva and quickly established himself as a leading exponent of the Rossini-Donizetti repertory. He appeared at Glyndebourne from 1952 to 1961 as Don Ramiro, Count Ory, Almaviva, Lindoro, Ferrando, Don Ottavio and Fenton, and as Scaramuccio in the first British stage performance (1954) of *Arlecchino*. In 1963 he began to sing heavier roles, including Maurizio in *Adriana Lecouvreur* at the Edinburgh Festival, Rodolfo, Cavaradossi, Pinkerton, Boito's Faust and Don José. He returned to Glyndebourne in 1965 as Percy (*Anna Bolena*) and sang Leicester in *Maria Stuarda* at Naples (1968) and Rome (1970) as well as Monteverdi's Nero in Vienna (1969). He was less successful in the dramatic repertory than in Rossini and Mozart, in which his charm and wit compensated to a great extent for a voice inclined to whiteness. He retired in 1974.

HAROLD ROSENTHAL/R

Onegin [Onégin; née Hoffmann], (**Elisabeth Elfriede Emilie**) **Sigrid** [Lilly] (*b* Stockholm, 1 June 1889; *d* Magliaso, Switzerland, 16 June 1943). Franco-German contralto and mezzo-soprano. Though often described as Swedish, she was in fact the daughter of a French father and a German mother. She sang first as Lilly Hoffmann; after her marriage to Baron Eugene Borisovitch Lvov Onégin (1883–1919) – a Russian émigré, pianist and composer who had adopted the surname of Pushkin's celebrated hero – she used the name Lilly Hoffmann-Onégin, but soon adopted the professional name by which she was to become famous. She studied in Munich and Milan, and later had lessons or advice from Lilli Lehmann and Margarete Siems. She was first engaged by the Stuttgart Opera in 1912; but from 1919 to 1922, after her husband's early death, she was a member of the Munich Opera, and in 1920 married Dr Fritz Penzoldt. She had two Metropolitan Opera seasons (1922–4) and one at Covent Garden (1927), in both houses singing only Amneris and Wagner roles; she also sang at Salzburg (Gluck's Orpheus, 1931–2) and at Bayreuth (1933–4). Her greatest successes were in concerts. She had the finest and most highly trained voice of its kind since Schumann-Heink, whose repertory and manner of singing she emulated without approaching the older singer's fire and communicative power. Notwithstanding her rich tone and astonishing technique, her recordings suggest also something marmoreal in their smoothness and coldness of style.

*

F. Penzoldt: *Alt-Rhapsodie: Sigrid Onégin – Leben und Werk* (Magdeburg, 1939, 3/1953)

J. Dennis: 'Sigrid Onegin', *Record Collector*, v (1950), 225–31 [with discography], 280–81; xii (1958–60), 200

DESMOND SHAWE-TAYLOR

O'Neill, Dennis (*b* Pontardulais, 25 Feb 1948). Welsh tenor. He studied at Sheffield University and the RNCM, and after solo appearances with Scottish Opera's 'Opera for All' (1971) he joined the Glyndebourne chorus (1974) and sang at the Wexford Festival. During two seasons as principal tenor with South Australian Opera, he created a role in Sitsky's *Fiery Tales* (1976). Thereafter he sang lyric roles with Scottish Opera and the WNO, then studied further in Italy with Ettore Campogalliani and Luigi Ricci. His débuts at Covent Garden in 1979 as Flavio (*Norma*) and at Glyndebourne in 1980 as the Italian Tenor (*Der Rosenkavalier*) were followed by leading roles in both theatres and with the ENO. In 1983 he made débuts in the USA at Dallas as Edgardo (*Lucia*) and at the Vienna Staatsoper as Alfredo, a role he also sang with the Metropolitan Opera on tour in 1986 before singing Rodolfo with them in New York the next year. In 1990 he sang Gabriele Adorno in Cologne and Foresto (*Attila*) at Covent Garden. O'Neill combines a fine-spun tone with a musical perception of style and character.

NOËL GOODWIN

O'Neill, Eugene (Gladstone) (*b* New York, 16 Oct 1888; *d* Boston, 27 Nov 1953). American playwright. Initially influenced by Ibsen and Strindberg, he found his distinctive voice in the expressionist tragedy *The Emperor Jones*, about the rise and fall of a West Indian tyrant, and *Anna Christie*, a sympathetic portrayal of a prostitute's fortunes on the New York waterfront. O'Neill's experiments in stage technique revolutionized American theatre in the 1920s, and he was awarded the Nobel prize for literature in 1936. It was apropos his trilogy *Mourning Becomes Electra* that he declared his need of 'a speech that is dramatic and not just conversation. I'm so strait-jacketed by writing in terms of talk'. But this did not dispose O'Neill to an interest in opera, and he declined to write the libretto for Louis Gruenberg's opera *The Emperor Jones*. The rhetorical intensity he sought is most fully realized, in its weaknesses as well as its strengths, in *A Long Day's Journey into Night* (1940–41). Musical interest in his plays, particularly from American composers, was especially strong in the decade or so after his death.

Before Breakfast (play, 1916): E. Chisholm, 1952, as Dark Sonnet; V. Mortari, 1964, as Prima di colazione
Ile (play, 1917): B. Laufer, 1958
The Moon of the Caribbees (play, 1918): A. Lualdi, 1953, as La luna dei Caraibi
The Rope (play, 1918): L. Mennini, 1955
Beyond the Horizon (play, 1920): N. Flagello, 1983
The Emperor Jones (play, 1920): L. Gruenberg, 1933; S. Fuga, 1976, as L'imperatore Jones
Anna Christie (play, 1921): G. Abbott and B. Merrill, 1957, as New Girl in Town
Mourning Becomes Electra (trilogy, 1931): M. D. Levy, 1967
Ah! Wilderness (play, 1933): B. Merrill, 1959, as Take Me Along

ANTHONY PARR

One Man Show. Comic opera in two acts by NICHOLAS MAW to a libretto by ARTHUR JACOBS after Saki's story 'The Background' (*Chronicles of Love*); London, Jeannetta Cochrane Theatre, 12 November 1964.

A man's tattooed back is pronounced a valuable work of art, and is bought – with the man, Joe (baritone) – by a fashionable art collector, Maggie Dempster (mezzo-soprano), who develops more than artistic admiration for her purchase, but who is resisted. Sold to the 'British State Gallery', the design (in fact, the man's name inverted) is read correctly by the gallery director, Sir Horace Stringfellow (tenor), who likes to stand on his head for the sake of his health. The opera is notable for its sprightly and lyrical word-setting, though it is possibly of more taste than character. Commissioned for the opening of the Jeannetta Cochrane Theatre at the Central School of Art and Design, Holborn, it was produced again at Morley College in 1969 and at the Carnegie-Mellon University Opera Workshop, Pittsburgh, in 1975.

NOËL GOODWIN

Ongarelli, Rosa. See UNGARELLI, ROSA.

On ne s'avise jamais de tout ('You Can't Think of Everything'). *Opéra comique* in one act by PIERRE-ALEXANDRE MONSIGNY to a libretto by MICHEL-JEAN SEDAINE after Jean de La Fontaine's tale *On ne s'avise jamais de tout*; Paris, Opéra-Comique (Foire St Laurent), 14 September 1761.

La Fontaine's plot, derived from *Cent nouvelles nouvelles* (1455), concerns a young man who takes a married woman into his home after having previously thrown a 'basket of rubbish' over her from his balcony; since the fair theatres were at that time in search of greater respectability, Sedaine changed the character of the jealous husband into that of an old doctor, M. Tue (tenor), obsessed with the virtue of his ward, Lise (soprano). Tue is about to marry the girl, and engages a chaperon, Margarita (soprano), to spy on her. The opera's main character, Dorval (tenor), appears in various disguises (as a stammering footman, a beggar and an old woman) and finally succeeds in obtaining Lise's hand, aided in his designs by a particularly enlightened Commissar (bass). The work's originality lies not in its plot (which is one of many antecedents of Beaumarchais' *Le barbier de Séville*), but in the skill with which no fewer than 17 musical numbers were distributed within a one-act opera. Dorval's first aria, for example, which is sung immediately following the overture, is sufficient to affirm the sentimental nature of the work, even though the following four numbers are completely comic in character. The middle scenes (vii–ix) are notable for their two *romances* (for Lise and for Dorval), and for the lyrical quality of Dorval's main aria, 'Amour, achève ton ouvrage'. The final section, in which comedy reasserts itself, includes two ensembles which in their way are as varied as the preceding solo arias: the quartet in scene xv is intended as a joyful uproar, while the splendid quintet in scene xviii shows Monsigny's ambition – and ability – to rival Philidor in structural and harmonic complexity.

MICHEL NOIRAY

Onslow, (André) Georges (Louis) (*b* Clermont-Ferrand, 27 July 1784; *d* Clermont-Ferrand, 3 Oct 1853). French composer of English descent. He received a nobleman's education, which included the study of music, travel, horsemanship and hunting. He spent his youth in London, where he studied the piano, acquiring some facility but showing no marked aptitude for music. After his return to the Auvergne his friendship with musical amateurs aroused his interest in chamber music, and led him to study the cello; later, during two years spent in Germany and Austria, he started composing. He began studies with Reicha in Paris in 1808. Onslow kept his early contacts in England and in 1830 was elected the second honorary member of the Philharmonic Society of London (Mendelssohn being the first, in 1829). In 1842 he succeeded Cherubini to the chair of the Institut de France; his rivals for election included Auber and Berlioz.

Onslow wrote a number of songs and piano variations that satisfied the current taste for sentiment and piety. His three operas are conservative for their time, reflecting the influence of Cherubini and Méhul, not that of the advanced Auber nor even of the relatively conservative Boieldieu. His vocal lines seldom show much individuality, and this results in weak characterization, especially in ensembles. His orchestration is conventionally good but he often repeats a pattern monotonously; only the overture to *Le colporteur* achieved brief success as a concert piece. His symphonies were quickly forgotten, but his chamber works and the larger works for piano (e.g. the piano duo op.22) are superior, and show a performer's idiomatic ease.

L'alcade de la vega (drame lyrique, Bujac), Paris, OC (Feydeau), 10 Aug 1824, vs (Paris, 1824)
Le colporteur, ou L'enfant du bûcheron (oc, E. Planard), Paris, OC (Feydeau), 22 Nov 1827, vs (Bonn, ?1827)
Guise, ou Les états de Blois (Planard and J.-H. Vernoy de Saint-Georges), Paris, 8 Sept 1837, vs (Paris, ?1837)

*

C. E. Vulliamy: *The Onslow Family* (London, 1953)

BENEDICT SARNAKER

Opava (Ger. Troppau). Town in Czech Silesia. The first theatre to be built in this former provincial capital was the Theater unter dem Stadtturm in 1750; it burnt down in 1763 and was rebuilt in 1774. Opera was performed there from 1790. The German civic theatre was built in 1805, enlarged in 1883, and rebuilt in 1909, 1948 and again in 1990. Besides plays and operettas, an extensive opera repertory was performed until 1944, encompassing all Wagner's works, operas by Smetana, Dvořák and Janáček and many modern works. Distinguished visitors included Marie Gutheil-Schoder and Leo Slezak; Hans Hotter began his career there in 1931. Between 1919 and 1938 Czech opera was also performed by companies from Ostrava and Olomouc.

A professional Czech theatre company was founded in the badly damaged town in 1945, with specialized groups for plays, operas and operettas, and ballet. At first the theatre was under civic administration and was known as the Slezské Národní Divadlo (Silesia National Theatre); from 1949 it was a regional theatre making numerous tours throughout Silesia. From 1957 to 1990 it was called the Slezské Divadlo Zdeňka Nejedlého (Silesian Theatre of Zdeněk Nejedlý), and in 1990 became the Slezské Divadlo Opava (Silesian Theatre of Opava). The opera company, led by experienced conductors such as František Preisler (1946–53), has performed Czech and foreign operas from the modern and standard repertories.

*

O. Wenzelides: *Das Troppauer Theater* (Nordmährerland, 1943)
K. Boženek and M. Weimann: *50 let českých profesionálních divadelních představení v Opavě* [50 Years of Czech Professional Theatre Performances in Opava] (Opava, 1969)

25 let Slezského divadlo Zdeňka Nejedlého v Opavě 1945–1970 [25 Years of the Silesian Zdeněk Nejedlý Theatre in Opava] (Opava, 1970)
K. Boženek: *Historický vývoj opery v opavském Slezsku* [The Historical Development of Opera in Opava's Silesia] (MS, 1970)
——: *Opavská německá opera* [Opava's German Opera] (MS, 1974)

EVA HERRMANNOVÁ

Opera (It., from Lat. *opera*, plural of *opus*, 'work'; Fr. *opéra*; Ger. Oper).

I. 'Opera'. II. The origins of opera. III. The nature of opera.

I. 'Opera'. Most narrowly conceived, the word 'opera' signifies a drama in which the actors and actresses sing throughout. There are, however, so many exceptions among the operatic works of the West – so many works popularly called operas in which some parts are spoken or mimed – that the word should be more generically defined as a drama in which the actors and actresses sing some or all of their parts. Numerous sub-genres, such as *opera seria, opera buffa, tragédie en musique* and the like, have grown up in the history of opera; information about these sub-genres will be found in separate entries. Some of the sub-genres mix spoken and sung drama in conventional ways. Thus, in operetta, Singspiel, *opéra comique* and musical comedy the dialogue is normally spoken and musical numbers interrupt the action from time to time. The history of opera is inextricably intertwined with the history of spoken drama. Moreover, since all operatic works combine music, drama and spectacle, though in varying degrees, all three principal elements should be taken into account in any comprehensive study of the genre, even though music has traditionally played the dominant role in the conception and realization of individual works.

Questions of the role of music in the theatre came to the fore in Italy in the 16th century. Musical-dramatic genres in other countries, such as the *ballet de cour* in France and the courtly masque in England, played no role in the development of the genre. The central importance of Italian musicians and poets in the development and early history of opera is suggested by the fact that the word 'opera' means simply 'work' in Italian and as such was applied to various categories of written or improvised plays in the 16th and early 17th centuries. To cite but one example arbitrarily, Francesco Andreini's play *L'ingannata Proserpina* (1611) – according to its dedication intended either to be recited or sung depending on the wishes of its producers – was called an *opera rappresentativa, e scenica*. The earliest operas either had no generic subtitle (like Ottavio Rinuccini's *Dafne* of 1598 and his *Euridice* of 1600) or else adopted one or another ad hoc definition: *favola, opera scenica, tragedia musicale, opera tragicomica musicale, dramma musicale* or the like (see Rosand 1991). It has been suggested (by Grout and Pirrotta) that either the term *opera scenica* or the term *opera regia* (the latter meaning a drama with royal protagonists and a happy ending, a term applied to various *commedia dell'arte* scenarios as well as to Monteverdi's *L'incoronazione di Poppea* of 1642) might be the origin of the usage that defines 'opera' as a specifically musico-dramatic work. In the second third of the 17th century, however, *dramma per musica* became the more normal term for opera, although it has been pointed out that to English speakers as early as the 1650s the word was used to mean a dramatic work set to music

(Strahle; John Evelyn used the term in 1644). Nevertheless, the use of the word 'opera' with this meaning seems to have developed only gradually; it became widespread only much later than the invention and early development of the genre.

II. The origins of opera

1. Background, precursors. 2. Immediate origins.

1. BACKGROUND, PRECURSORS.   Music was inserted into plays as early as ancient Greek times. Choral songs, performed on occasion to the accompaniment of mimetic dancing, served to divide the play into sections and commented on the action in ancient Greek tragedy and comedy. During the 16th century, when Greek drama came to serve as a model for certain aspects of musical theatre, scholars debated the possibility that the plays were sung from beginning to end, a speculation long since abandoned, although it seems probable that some portions of Greek plays other than the choral interludes may also have been sung or at least declaimed musically, by soloists or ensembles of singers. The tradition of including music as an integral part of theatrical activities continued and even expanded in Roman times. With the destruction of the Roman theatres in the 6th century, however, all trace of official theatrical activity, musical or otherwise, disappeared from the archival records. Fragmentary evidence of various kinds, however, suggests that professional entertainers – *mimi*, *histriones*, *joculatores* and the like – continued to perform plays and skits which combined music with acting during the early Middle Ages.

A vast corpus of medieval drama with music survives. It can be roughly divided into two kinds: so-called liturgical drama, and vernacular plays with incidental music. Some parts of the sacred service came to be dramatized in order to make the events depicted – and especially the Resurrection of Christ, his Nativity, and the events leading up to it – more vivid and immediate. These liturgical and para-liturgical dramas, whether performed in church as part of a service or somewhere else, were sung in chant from beginning to end. It is for this reason that they have been called the first music dramas, though it should be stressed that the various repertories of religious dialogues, ceremonies and plays from the Middle Ages are far from having common origins or a single continuous history.

Similarly diverse in origin, destination and nature are the various sorts of plays in the vernacular that survive most copiously from the 15th and 16th centuries. On the one hand, vast medieval mystery and morality plays that often lasted several days were organized by towns for the purposes of both religious celebration and commercial gain. On the other hand, during the 15th and 16th centuries, troupes of professional actors, members of various guilds, and even amateurs performed a more modest repertory of comedies and short plays for a variety of occasions in many countries of western Europe. Both the gigantic religious plays and the shorter comedies made use of music as an incidental part of the action. Indeed, this use of music is one of the few things both kinds of plays have in common. Only rarely did music play a larger role in vernacular drama. Adam de la Halle's *Jeu de Robin et Marion*, for example, written during the 1280s, is an exception in incorporating so many melodies (most of them presumably pre-existent) into its action; it can be classified as a *pastourelle* with an unusually large amount of

music, but account should be taken of its unique nature with regard to the amount and kind of music it required.

None of these early musical-dramatic activities seems to have been connected historically. No single grand narrative can be written to link medieval drama to the history of 16th-century Italian comedy and tragedy, let alone to the events that led to the invention of opera in the early 17th century. The history of Italian upper-class theatre in the Renaissance should probably begin with the series of classical plays performed at the Ferrarese court in the late 15th and early 16th centuries, and especially the performances of comedies by Plautus and Terence that became models for many of the erudite written comedies during the century. These courtly performances of classical plays were commissioned by the duke and acted by the courtiers themselves. Later in the century, erudite neo-classical comedies came to be performed by amateurs, by members of the learned academies that flourished during the century, or even by those professional troupes of actors who were better known for their ability to improvise comedies, the so-called *commedie dell'arte*.

Learned comedy was, of course, not the only genre cultivated in Italy during the 15th and 16th centuries. *Sacre rappresentazioni*, church pageants enlivened with music (much of it related to *laude*), flourished; they may even have had an important influence on the establishment of the pastoral as a genre, or on the idea of vernacular drama with music, but those connections have yet to be solidly established. A repertory of rustic plays featuring peasants and other members of the lower classes also came to be written and performed. Eventually, too, the genre of tragedy was cultivated.

In the late 15th and early 16th centuries, there were also some exceptional plays that did not fit comfortably within any of the principal genres. Angelo Poliziano's *Orfeo*, performed at the court in Mantua about 1480, was such an exception. Poliziano called it a *favola*. Music played a central part. None of it survives, probably because it was not 'learned' written music but belonged rather to the tradition of improvised or semi-improvised music cultivated by Italian poet-musicians in the 15th century. One such poet-musician, Baccio Ugolini, played the role of Orpheus and accompanied himself on the *lira*, almost certainly the *lira da braccio*. In addition to Ugolini's solo sections, there were several choruses. It has been argued persuasively that there is some connection between Ugolini's performance and the philosopher Marsilio Ficino's Orphic singing to the lyre, if not between Ficino's ideas and Poliziano's play (Tomlinson 1988). In any case, Poliziano's *Orfeo* was an important landmark in the pre-history of opera, not so much for its form or its influence as for its symbolic significance as a highly musical play outside the Aristotelian genres (it was neither tragedy nor comedy) that dealt with the power of music in a classical setting.

2. IMMEDIATE ORIGINS.   The traditional view of the origins of opera – that it developed directly from discussions in the 1570s led by Count Giovanni de' Bardi of Florence and his group of friends who constituted an informal academy known as the Camerata, and from later discussions in the circle around Jacopo Corsi – continues to offer the best narrative of the events leading directly to the first operas: Rinuccini's *Dafne* of 1598 with music by Jacopo Peri and Jacopo Corsi, Rinuccini's *Euridice* of 1600, set by Peri and by Giulio Caccini, and Gabriello Chiabrera's *Il rapimento di Cefalo* of 1600,

set by Caccini. (Emilio de' Cavalieri's *Rappresentatione di Anima, et di Corpo* of 1600 should also doubtless be included in this group of early dramatic works, even though it was performed in Rome and is regarded as the first example of oratorio.) Among the many things discussed by Bardi and his friends, music occupied an important place, and specifically the nature of ancient Greek music and the source of its emotive power. Moreover, various experiments in writing an appropriately dramatic music were made in Florence at the end of the century, most notably Vincenzo Galilei's lost settings of the Lamentations for Holy Week and a scene from Dante, and Laura Guidiccioni's three pastorals set to music, also lost, by Emilio de' Cavalieri.

Nevertheless, a full account of how opera came into existence and how it came to take precisely the form it did needs to consider a number of other 16th-century developments, among them: (1) the history of music in erudite comedy, and especially the nature and role of the *intermedi*, the musical compositions, sometimes sung to the accompaniment of stage action or dancing, that closed each act; (2) the nature of music in 16th-century tragedies, and especially the choruses that divided the scenes; (3) the debate about genres that engrossed literary circles in 16th-century Italy, and especially the debate about the nature of the pastoral, since pastoral eclogues served as a principal model (perhaps the principal model) for the earliest operas; and (4) the nature of the other kinds of music written for staged or semi-staged presentation at courts, academies, civic celebrations and the like – shorter staged scenes and dialogues that have no agreed-upon generic designation, although they were widespread in 16th-century Italy. In addition, in considering the origins of opera and its early history, we should take into account not only the activities of court musicians and singers, and those employed as musicians to members of the highest reaches of society, but also *commedia dell'arte* players who fulfilled an important though not as yet completely understood function in the history of Italian musical theatre.

Aside from the few songs introduced naturalistically into the plots of various plays, music in 16th-century erudite comedy consisted mainly of madrigals (or in some cases instrumental music), which closed each act. At some performances the musicians were hidden behind the stage, but more often they appeared on stage to sing (and sometimes to dance). In many cases, these *intermedi* did nothing more than mark the passing of time, as in Verdelot's madrigals used as *intermedi* for Machiavelli's *La Mandragola* and *La Clizia*, one of the very few sets of normal madrigalesque *intermedi* to survive (some of the same music served for both plays). In many cases, the madrigals used as *intermedi* may not have been written specifically for that purpose (or at least not for particular plays or performances); it sufficed that the texts dealt with approximately the right subject matter. There seems not to have been a particular theatrical style that distinguished these madrigals from others, but it is difficult to be precise about the nature of the music for plays, since so little music survives for the texts that appear in many play books.

For great occasions, and especially weddings within the Medici family in Florence, more elaborate *intermedi* were staged between the acts of a play. In these courtly *intermedi*, several musical compositions were performed between the acts, and they were accompanied by stage action, including elaborate machines and dancing. Detailed descriptions of some of these grand occasions were published, and at least two sets of partbooks include the music composed especially for the events: those commemorating the wedding in 1539 of Cosimo I de' Medici with Eleonora of Toledo, and those commemorating the wedding in 1589 of Ferdinando I de' Medici with Christine of Lorraine. Courtly *intermedi* did not have plots, but many of them were centred on a common theme, often pastoral or mythological in character. Grand courtly *intermedi* were the most impressive examples of musical theatre of the 16th century.

The most famous and probably the most elaborate *intermedi* of the entire century were those organized for the Medici wedding of 1589, originally performed between the acts of Girolamo Bargagli's *La pellegrina*. They were devised by Count Bardi around the theme of the power of music in the ancient world (the subject of many discussions of the Camerata), directed by Cavalieri, and composed by Peri, Caccini, Marenzio and various other composers of the Medici circle. The 1589 performance was a seminal event for the history of musical theatre, even though the music itself did not differ in character very much from regular madrigals or lighter Italian secular forms. The music of 1589 does not represent any advance towards an operatic style, that is, a kind of music appropriate for setting dramatic dialogue.

Whereas the *intermedi* have been well studied and performed, music for 16th-century tragedies is much less well known, at least partly because so little of it survives, and partly because the surviving music, notably Andrea Gabrieli's music for *Edipo tiranno* (Orsatto Giustiniani's adaptation of the *Oedipus* of Sophocles), which opened the Teatro Olimpico in Vicenza in 1585, seems so unimpressive. Virtually every 16th-century tragedy includes long choruses to divide the action, and 16th-century commentators seem to make a distinction between these sorts of choruses and *intermedi*. To judge from Gabrieli's example, choruses for tragedies were set to a music simple enough to allow the words to be heard easily by the audience. Doubtless, however, producers and composers devised various solutions to the problem of an appropriate music for tragedy, and in many cases may have organized music indistinguishable from that appropriate for *intermedi*.

The role of music in tragedy, comedy and pastoral (the three principal dramatic genres of the late 16th century) was discussed by a number of writers on dramatic theory and practice in the 16th and 17th centuries, notably Leone de' Sommi (1556), Angelo Ingegneri (1598), the anonymous author of *Il corago* (1628–37) and Giovanni Battista Doni (c1633–5). Sommi and Ingegneri write mostly about *intermedi* and tragic choruses with some consideration of incidental music, *Il corago* and Doni about operatic works. Whereas the author of *Il corago* wished to offer advice about how best to compose and produce opera, Doni, as an antiquarian concerned about the nature of music in ancient Greek and Roman theatre, criticized the new genre on the grounds (among other things) of monotony and lack of verisimilitude and advocated instead a judicious mixture of speech and song, the song reserved chiefly for monologues and choruses.

Such discussions of dramatic practice took place against a longstanding literary debate about genres, and especially about the propriety of the new mixed genres of tragicomedy and pastoral, unknown to Aristotle and hence suspect in the eyes of 16th-century intellectuals, debates chronicled in Weinberg's magisterial study of literary criticism in the Italian Renaissance. The new pastoral drama, including such famous literary landmarks as Agostino Beccari's *Il sacrificio: favola pastorale* (1555), Tasso's *Aminta: favola boscareccia* (1573) and Guarini's *Il pastor fido: tragicomedia pastorale* (written *c*1580–85), made use of an unusually large amount of music. *Il sacrificio*, for example, included a scene in which priests chanted in a kind of recitative and were answered by a chorus (only the vocal part of a fragment of the music by Alfonso dalla Viola survives); and *Il pastor fido* included a famous blind-man's-buff scene (the so-called 'Giuoco della cieca') with singing and dancing.

These plays are important precursors of opera, since discussions about them overlapped and intersected with the discussions that led to the first operas. It is no exaggeration to say that the first operas came about partly as a result of debate about the kind of music most appropriate for the pastoral genre. The pastoral plays like those listed above did not however serve as models for the earliest operatic librettos. The first operas, instead, seem to have been modelled on the much shorter pastoral eclogues, of 500–700 verses, which put into dramatic (and usually amorous) conflict shepherds and shepherdesses, nymphs and satyrs and gods and goddesses. Most eclogues are quite static dramatically and evidently derive from the long tradition of courtly entertainment. In truth, though, the study of the literary climate in Italy in the late 16th century, and of genres and debates about genre, has hardly been exhausted, especially as these questions relate to music and musicians. We still need to know much more about the way in which various literary debates impinged on the ideas of those who shaped opera as a genre.

The staged entertainments that had enlivened court life (and also academic and civic life) for centuries provided yet another contributing element to the diverse mixture of traditions and genres that established the character of early opera. *Mascherate* and *moresche* already had a venerable history by the second half of the 16th century. Entertainments in which masked singers and dancers interrupted a banquet or a ball are described by various chroniclers from at least the 14th century on. In the late 16th century, short tableaux were sometimes offered as entertainment in upper-class society. They are called by a variety of names (including *morescha* and *mascherata* but also *favola pastorale*, *favola*, *ballo* or simply *festa*, among other things); there is no generic descriptive term for such entertainments. Madrigal comedies, for example, surely belong in this category, especially since it has been shown (by Farahat 1991) that some of these cycles of polyphonic madrigals, canzonettas and villanelle were actually staged in private rooms. (Many madrigal comedies include characters and dramatic situations derived from *commedia dell'arte*; most of them were written for performance in academies.) More squarely in the tradition of courtly entertainments, though, were the three scenes by Laura Guidiccioni, including the blind-man's-buff scene from *Il pastor fido*, set to music, now lost, by Cavalieri, performed in Florence in the 1590s; or the shorter dramatic works of Monteverdi like *Il ballo delle ingrate*, *Tirsi e Clori* and the *Combattimento di Tancredi e Clorinda*.

Opera can thus be seen as a genre that grew out of literary discussion in high society. But we should not exclude from our considerations another tradition that went into making opera, that of the *commedia dell'arte* (as Pirrotta has pointed out). During the second half of the 16th century several professional acting troupes toured Italy, performing not only their own special repertory of improvised or semi-improvised plays with stock characters but also written comedies and other kinds of plays. Although scholars have been inclined to characterize *commedia dell'arte* players as only semi-literate artisans, the truth is that many of the actors and actresses were highly educated, highly literate and highly musical. Isabella Andreini, for example, the leading lady of the troupe called I Gelosi, was a poet, author of a pastoral eclogue, member of an academy and an accomplished linguist and musician; and Monteverdi's first Ariadne in his mostly lost opera *L'Arianna* (1608) was an actress. Moreover, *commedia dell'arte* plays influenced the form and style of some opera librettos towards the middle of the 17th century (Bianconi and Walker 1975), and troupes of professional actors and actresses sometimes performed opera. In short, scholars should investigate much more closely the musical orientation of the *commedia dell'arte* players in general and their connection with opera in particular.

There was a vast amount of dramatic music heard in Italy in the 16th century, and a large literature of debate and discussion about it. All this activity contributed to musicians' ideas of what an appropriate music for the theatre should be. The crucial change from courtly entertainment to opera came about when a kind of music appropriate for dramatic dialogue was invented, by Caccini, Cavalieri, Vincenzo Galilei or Peri (all of them claimed credit). The overall shape of the earliest operas, *Dafne* and the two *Euridice* settings (as well as Monteverdi's *Orfeo*), was deeply influenced by earlier traditions, at least in that scene divisions were closed off by large *intermedi* choruses; and their subject matter was determined after extensive literary debate about genre, ancient history and the nature of music's power.

*

L. de' Sommi: *Quattro dialoghi in materia di rappresentazioni sceniche* (MS, 1556); ed. F. Marotti (Milan, 1968)

A. Ingegneri: *Della poesia rappresentativa e del modo di rappresentare le favole sceniche* (MS, 1598); ed. M. L. Doglio (Modena, 1989)

Il corago o vero Alcune osservazioni per metter bene in scena le composizioni dramatiche (MS, *c*1628–37); ed. P. Fabbri and A. Pompilio (Florence, 1983)

G. B. Doni: *Trattato della musica scenica*, in *Lyra Barberina ampichordos* [1633–5]; ed. A. F. Gori and G. B. Passeri (Florence, 1763), ii

A. Solerti: *Le origini del melodramma* (Turin, 1903)

——: *Gli albori del melodramma* (Naples, 1904)

——: *Musica, ballo e drammatica alla corte medicea dal 1600 al 1637* (Florence, 1905)

F. Ghisi: *Feste musicali della Firenze Medicea (1480–1589)* (Florence, 1930)

D. J. Grout: *A Short History of Opera* (New York and London, 1947, rev. H. W. Williams, 3/1988)

C. V. Palisca: *Girolamo Mei (1519–1594): Letters on Ancient and Modern Music to Vincenzo Galilei and Giovanni Bardi*, MSD, iii (1960, 2/1977)

——: 'Vincenzo Galilei and some Links between "Pseudo-Monody" and Monody', *MQ*, xlvi (1960), 344–60

L. Schrade: *La représentation d'Edipo Tiranno au Teatro Olimpico (Vicence 1585)* (Paris, 1960)

B. Weinberg: *A History of Literary Criticism in the Italian Renaissance* (Chicago, 1961)

D. P. Walker, F. Ghisi and J. Jacquot, eds.: *Musique des intermèdes de 'La Pellegrina'* (Paris, 1963)

A. M. Nagler: *Theatre Festivals of the Medici: 1539–1637* (New Haven and London, 1964)

Scenarios of the Commedia dell'Arte: Flaminio Scala's Il Teatro delle favole rappresentative, trans. H. F. Salerno (New York, 1967)

A. C. Minor and B. Mitchell: *A Renaissance Entertainment: Festivities for the Marriage of Cosimo I, Duke of Florence, in 1539* (Columbia, MO, 1968)

C. V. Palisca: 'The Alterati of Florence, Pioneers in the Theory of Dramatic Music', *New Looks at Italian Opera: Essays in Honor of Donald J. Grout* (Ithaca, NY, 1968), 9–38

N. Pirrotta and E. Povoledo: *Li due Orfei: da Poliziano a Monteverdi* (Turin, 1969, 2/1975; Eng. trans., 1982, as *Music and Theatre from Poliziano to Monteverdi*)

H. M. Brown: 'How Opera Began: an Introduction to Jacopo Peri's *Euridice* (1600)', *The Late Italian Renaissance 1525–1630*, ed. E. Cochrane (London, 1970), 401–43

W. Kirkendale: *L'Aria di Fiorenza id est Il Ballo del Gran Duca* (Florence, 1972)

C. V. Palisca: 'The "Camerata Fiorentina": a Reappraisal', *Studi musicali*, i (1972), 203–36

H. M. Brown: *Sixteenth-Century Instrumentation: the Music for the Florentine Intermedii*, MSD, xxx (1973)

L. Bianconi and T. Walker: 'Dalla *Finta Pazza* alla *Veremonda*: storie di Febiarmonici', *RIM*, x (1975), 379–44

C. V. Palisca: 'The Musical Humanism of Giovanni Bardi', *Poesia e musica nell'estetica del xvi e xvii secolo*, ed. H. Meyvalian (Florence, 1979), 45–72

M. Murata: *Operas for the Papal Court 1631–1668* (Ann Arbor, 1981)

C. V. Palisca: 'Peri and the Theory of Recitative', *SMA*, xv (1981), 51–61

N. Pirrotta: *Music and Culture in Italy from the Middle Ages to the Baroque: a Collection of Essays* (Cambridge, MA, 1984)

G. Tomlinson: *Monteverdi and the End of the Renaissance* (Berkeley, 1987)

——: 'The Historian, the Performer, and Authentic Meaning in Music', *Authenticity and Early Music: a Symposium*, ed. N. Kenyon (Oxford, 1988), 115–36

T. Carter: *Jacopo Peri 1561–1633: his Life and Works* (New York and London, 1989)

L. G. Clubb: *Italian Drama in Shakespeare's Time* (New Haven and London, 1989)

C. V. Palisca: *The Florentine Camerata: Documentary Studies and Translations* (New Haven and London, 1989)

K. Richards and L. Richards: *The Commedia dell'Arte: a Documentary History* (Oxford, 1990)

M. Farahat: 'On the Staging of Madrigal Comedies', *Early Music History*, x (1991), 123–43

E. Rosand: *Opera in Seventeenth-Century Venice: the Creation of a Genre* (Berkeley, 1991)

G. Strahle: *Early Music Dictionary drawn from English Lexicographic Sources c1440–1740* (forthcoming)

III. The nature of opera

1. Definitions and borderlines. 2. Words, music, drama. 3. Time, expression and the inner world. 4. Performance and repetition.

1. DEFINITIONS AND BORDERLINES. Opera is by definition staged sung drama, but that leaves many questions unresolved, some simply verbal, but others interesting for the nature of the form. 'Staged' represents a significant requirement. Operas can of course be given concert performances, and these are sometimes 'semi-staged', under conventions that allow some token costume, decor and movement. But works not intended at all for costumed theatrical presentation do not count. Sunk in financial disaster from his efforts with Italian opera in London, Handel turned to the oratorio, and the resulting works are not seen as a form of opera, because they were not designed for a theatrical style of presentation (though they do contain a number of what might be called stage directions). However, this example itself shows that, from a musical or stylistic point of view, less may turn on these classifications than one might assume. It has often been remarked that Handel's English oratorios can be intensely dramatic in their effect –

sometimes more so than the examples of *opera seria* to which he had devoted his efforts in the theatre.

The main stylistic point that underlies the distinction between opera and oratorio tends to be the role of the chorus, which in oratorio is a constant presence and a major structural feature. But, besides operas in which the chorus has an important part, such as *Fidelio* and *Boris Godunov*, there are others in which it provides a framework and commentary (a recent example is Goehr's *Behold the Sun*). There are other works that are sometimes presented in theatrical form and sometimes not, the most famous perhaps being Stravinsky's *Oedipus rex*, which, having been first performed, in 1927, as an oratorio and in the following year produced as an opera, has subsequently moved in and out of the theatre. In this particular case, the ambiguity marked by this history is central to the work, which by a variety of devices, including a Latin text, aims at a monumental neo-classical effect.

The requirement that opera be sung is unbreakable, though there are styles that question the distinction between speech and song, in particular the device of *Sprechgesang* developed by Schoenberg and his pupils. A more wide-ranging question concerns the amount or proportion of song that an opera should contain. *Recitativo secco* is at once heightened speech and a form of song. Controversy about its use, as contrasted with opera that is *durchkomponiert*, has played an important part in the history of changing conceptions of opera, but the conventions of recitative do not call in question the identity of opera as song. The role of spoken dialogue, on the other hand, raises issues of genre that connect in curiously complex ways with matters of nationality, content, audience and performance style.

No-one denies that the German tradition of Singspiel has produced not only operas but at least two of the greatest operas there are, *Die Zauberflöte* and *Fidelio*. A descendant of this tradition, however, also German-speaking but more associated with Vienna, is segregated under the separate name of 'operetta', presumably a diminutive of contempt for works that have a stereotyped type of frivolous plot and are often musically very thin. However, pieces in this style have regularly been performed by some leading opera singers, and there are at least two outstanding examples, *Die Fledermaus* and *Die lustige Witwe*, that have established themselves in the international repertory of opera houses. In Vienna itself, there were two different houses, and the convention was that operetta did not appear at the Staatsoper; in Paris there were similar distinctions, between the Opéra at the Palais Garnier, the Opéra-Comique at the Salle Favart and the Bouffes-Parisiens, though the relation between the content of a given piece and the house in which it was produced was not altogether straightforward. In the French tradition, it was not the presence of spoken dialogue that made the difference between opera and operetta, any more than it did in the German case: perhaps the greatest of French operas, *Carmen*, has spoken dialogue in its original version (Guiraud's recitatives, written for a production in Vienna in 1875, have by no means gained general acceptance). It seems a question rather of musical ambition and dramatic content. Not much French operetta has made its way into the international repertory; the one work of Offenbach's to hold a steady place there is *Les contes d'Hoffmann*, and that was called by him an opera ('opéra fantastique').

With works originally written in English, the situation

is different. At various periods, virtually no work with English spoken dialogue was regularly produced in an opera house. Of the five stage works with dialogue for which Purcell wrote the music, and which were later called 'semi-operas', only one, *King Arthur*, was specially written to be performed with music, the others being adaptations of existing plays. They all stand in the tradition of the masque, and demand discouragingly elaborate staging. (Purcell's *Dido and Aeneas* is sung throughout and is a genuine opera; at the time it was written, it was not a 'public' work and therefore had no influence.) In the first half of the 18th century many ballad operas with dialogue appeared. The most famous of them, *The Beggar's Opera*, has been popular ever since, with the exception of a period in the 19th century, and is sometimes produced in opera houses. The ballads, arranged by Pepusch, originally existed only as melodic line and bass. The music has been arranged by several composers, including Benjamin Britten (Weill's *Die Dreigroschenoper* is derived from it, but musically is a different work).

The English counterpart to Offenbach is to be found in the works of Gilbert and Sullivan. They have borne a peculiar relation to the operatic tradition, in part because of the historical accident that for decades a monopoly was exercised over them by the D'Oyly Carte Opera Company, which imposed not only a stereotyped manner of production but also, and more significantly, a particular style of singing. Many of the performers were G & S specialists, who did not appear in the operatic repertory. Now that the copyright has lapsed, some of the pieces have been successfully staged by operatic companies.

The most significant fact, however, about the English-speaking tradition is not the absence of partly spoken works which might be operas, but the immense success of a type of work with dialogue which is quite clearly not an opera, the musical. In English-speaking countries, it is the musical that has played the role in popular taste which, earlier, was played in Vienna by operetta and in Italy by Italian opera itself. To deny that the musical is opera is not simply a stipulation. It originated in part from English 19th-century burlesque, and in part from operetta, in particular from the emigration of German composers to the USA, but it has developed in such a way that, at least as things now stand, the styles of dramatic performance and singing appropriate to it are different from those needed for most kinds of opera. The point has been sharply illustrated by opera companies' occasional attempts to perform musicals (*Kiss Me Kate* is an example), which are almost always unsuccessful, and also by the unsatisfactory casting of operatic artists in a recording of Bernstein's *West Side Story*, a work that tries to stand on the boundary between the two traditions.

In the 1980s there were signs of some convergence between a broadening taste for opera (associated with the immense success in various media of certain singers, notably Luciano Pavarotti) and popular musical theatre. However, this has not yet been translated into any worthwhile new forms. Several shows have tried to combine the form and appeal of the musical, compositional tricks taken from Puccini, and theatrical effects on a Meyerbeerian scale, and financially have been very successful, but in terms of anything except spectacle they fall below their sources.

The relations between opera and the other forms that are contrasted with it are thus complex, and the distinctions (in particular, that between opera and operetta) are to some degree arbitrary. The present position is that 'opera' is to some extent an evaluative term, used to refer to sung drama which is either 'serious' enough, or traditional enough in form and technique, to be staged in an opera house. (These criteria can of course themselves diverge: some bel canto works which are canonical examples of opera have virtually no serious dramatic content.) Moreover, history has had different effects on various national traditions. After Wagner's achievement, and the failure of his unnecessary attempt to distinguish his works from opera by calling them 'music dramas', it has come about that new operas almost inevitably have pretensions to being serious and often difficult works of art. The Italian tradition was most resistant to this modernist development, but its capacity to produce highly popular new works in what was indisputably an operatic tradition did not survive the death of Puccini. (It is tempting to speculate that the reasons why he was unable to write the love duet at the end of *Turandot*, his last work, were not just depth-psychological, as Mosco Carner well argued, but cultural: the Princess of Death, with her orchestral complexities, had claimed the popular tradition as well as her previous suitors.)

The entrenched division between opera as art-work and other kinds of musical theatre such as the musical, is now expressed in differences of vocal and performance style. However, this in itself should not be insuperable: what is by general agreement opera already accommodates a wide variety of vocal styles. The problem is cultural rather than merely stylistic. The fear is often expressed that opera has become a museum category, under which a restricted (and in fact quite small) repertory of works by dead composers is supplemented only by a few difficult new works, of which virtually none survive their first production. This last point is nothing new. At various times in which opera has flourished, such as in the 19th-century heyday of Italian opera, hundreds of works have been staged and never revived. The difference is that, as is generally the case with popular forms in which most works are expected to be disposable, the investment of resources was relatively low compared with what is now involved in staging a new opera. Above all, the composer's investment of effort in any one work was less. The Wagnerian model of the heroic composer creating a unique and challenging masterpiece will work only on the rare occasions that this is indeed what is created, and it cannot sustain a practice or tradition. A few 20th-century composers have tried to deal with this problem, but their experiments have not had continuing results. Weill, in his collaboration with Brecht, worked in music theatre outside the opera house. Benjamin Britten, who was comparatively prolific among 20th-century opera composers, deliberately aimed in some of his works at an effect simpler than that of his first (and still most successful) opera, the very traditional *Peter Grimes*, and in the 'church parables' looked both to Japanese traditions and to a staging that would avoid the theatre.

The fact that the operatic repertory is small, old and not expanding, does not mean that this repertory has only a small or 'élitist' audience; that complaint is also made, but it is to an increasing extent untrue. The opera house may be a museum, but museums are popular. The problem is not so much that the tradition of opera is cut off from popular appreciation, as that new pieces of musical theatre which are unselfconsciously enjoyed by many people are cut off from the tradition of opera, and so from what makes opera uniquely interesting, the achievement of intense dramatic expression by essentially musical means. Cultural critics such as Adorno saw this development as a historical inevitability, but despair over the future of interesting musical theatre is uncalled for. There will perhaps be new works that will cut through current anxieties and make these definitional complexities out of date. What they will be cannot of course be foreseen, except by someone who will write one.

2. WORDS, MUSIC, DRAMA. The relations of speech and song are a problem only for some operas, but all opera has to find an accommodation between words and music. Burney wrote in the 1780s:

As the British government consists of three estates: King, Lords, and Commons, so an opera in its first institution consisted of Poetry, Music, and Machinery: but as politicians have observed, that the ballance of power is frequently disturbed by some one of the three estates encroaching upon the other two, so one of these three constituent parts of a musical drama generally preponderates, at the expence of the other two. In the first operas POETRY seems to have been the most important personage; but about the middle of the last century MACHINERY and DECORATION seemed to take the lead ... But as the art of singing and dramatic composition improved, MUSIC took the lead ...

Burney's words are carefully chosen to avoid the false idea that the balance of power between music and words is the same thing as a balance between music and *drama*. It is a fallacy to argue that since, in a musical drama, the music obviously provides the music, so the words must provide the drama. As anyone knows who has ever enjoyed an opera, music and words both provide the drama. In the terms of Burney's political analogy, the drama is the government itself, rather than one of the estates. Yet it has proved easy to forget this, particularly on the various occasions when it has been thought that through some imbalance opera had become undramatic and stood in need of reform.

Dr Johnson's celebrated description of opera as 'an exotic and irrational entertainment' was directed to the Italian opera of his time, above all to *opera seria* with its lengthy da capo arias, which imposed an elaborate musical structure, were not intended to secure any dramatic development in the course of the song itself, and greatly emphasized musical decorations which gave singers an opportunity for technical display. As well as implying certain musical and dramatic forms, *opera seria* also involved a set of rigid theatrical conventions, under which, for instance, a singer expected to exit at the end of his or her aria.

Opera seria was so effectively ridiculed (notably in *The Beggar's Opera*), so eloquently criticized, and so creatively replaced, that it has stood for almost two centuries as a paradigm of ways in which an operatic style may fail to realize the potentialities of sung drama. The lack of performances mirrors the reputation: no true *opera seria* holds the stage, even though Handel's, in particular, contain much outstanding music. (Neither *Idomeneo* nor *La clemenza di Tito* follows the strict conventions of the form.) The seeming finality of this historical judgment on *opera seria* has perhaps discouraged discussion of what exactly was wrong with it. The standard criticism is that it is 'static' or 'undramatic', but such terms do no more than register what needs to be explained. *Opera seria* did not, as the criticisms may imply, simply ignore the relations of music and words to drama; it approached them, rather, in a

special way, and if, having taken that way, it seems now to lie in irreversible coma, it is instructive to ask why that should be.

Burney (in a different work) used his preferred terms of the division of labour to describe the war between the tradition of *opera seria* and Gluck's 'reform' operas:

Party runs as high among poets, musicians and their adherents, at Vienna as elsewhere. Metastasio and Hasse, may be said, to be at the head of one of the principal sects; and Calsabigi and Gluck of another. The first, regarding all innovations as quackery, adhere to the ancient form of the musical drama, in which the poet and the musician claim equal attention from the audience; the bard in the recitatives and the narrative parts; and the composer in the airs, duos, and chorusses. The second party depend more on theatrical effects, propriety of character, simplicity of diction, and of musical execution, than on, what *they* style, flowery descriptions, superfluous similes, sententious and cold morality, on one side, with tiresome symphonies, and long divisions, on the other.

Calzabigi, who as librettist and propagandist was a prime mover of the reform associated with *Orfeo* and other later works of Gluck, himself wrote of the new style:

All is nature here, all is passion; there are no sententious reflections, no philosophy or politics, no paragons of virtue ... [The plot is] reduced to the dimensions of Greek tragedy, and therefore has the unique advantage of exciting terror and compassion in the same way as spoken tragedy ... The music has no other function than to express what arises from the words, which are therefore neither smothered by notes nor used to lengthen the spectacle unduly, because it is ridiculous to prolong the sentence 'I love you' (for instance) with a hundred notes when nature has restricted it to three.

Each of these texts may give the impression that the reform party's aim was to redress the balance in favour of words as against music; and since the reformers may be understood now as urging in their own time a message about musical drama that is rather the same as Wagner's or Verdi's in the next century, we may well ourselves see the reform in those same terms. But it is not an adequate account of what the reformers themselves wanted, and even less so of what modern taste may find lacking in *opera seria*. The da capo aria was not emotionally inexpressive, and the emotions it expressed (at its best, very effectively) were relevant to the action. Moreover, it cannot be an objection to those arias or to the other conventions of this style that the music is not evenly directed to the onward movement of the action. That is true in some way of almost all operas, and in an opera that contains self-contained arias it is standard that they should not move the action forward in time but deepen it psychologically.

The peculiarity of the da capo arias lay, rather, in the fact that, by a well-established rhetorical decorum, each aria standardly expressed only one emotion. In addition, the words, having established what the emotion was, could be used decoratively for musical, or at least vocal, purposes, with the repetitions and the elongations of syllables about which Calzabigi complained. To a later taste, the very idea of identifying and labelling the emotions in the way that this tradition required is likely to seem schematic and unsatisfactory. Later Italian opera, particularly in the hands of Verdi, can of course wonderfully express very simple emotions, but then the means of expression themselves are, or seem, very direct. In *opera seria*, what are labelled as very simple feelings receive an elaborate musical expression; the complexity of the musical means is not matched by any complication of feeling or psychological development. The power of the music, though it can be considerable, is, so to speak, earthed by the simplicity of the dramatic content and the determined labelling effected by the text.

The difficulties with *opera seria* cannot be captured in terms of the relative importance of words and music; nor by the charge – which is in good part untrue – that the form was emotionally inexpressive. The reformers themselves spoke in praise of the simple and the natural as contrasted with the complex and artificial. In part, this merely represented the Rousseau-esque fashion of the time, and certainly the lesson could not be drawn that the way for opera to succeed where *opera seria* had failed was just by being simpler – the technical innocence of Gluck was not in itself the signpost pointing towards Mozart. The basic point was rather that the elaboration of means in *opera seria* was not well related to its emotional and dramatic content. The music was too complex for the content, but equally the content was too simple for the music. Above all, the style did not adequately acknowledge the power of music to express feeling that cannot be adequately captured in words, a power which underlies the special opportunities that opera possesses as a form of drama. Those possibilities are not, of course, a more recent discovery, but are exploited by some of the earliest operas, notably Monteverdi's.

Some of its limitations were implicit in *opera seria*'s forms, but it was also true that it suffered from having ceded (not for the last time in the history of opera) too much control to the performers, whose demands could impede both the composer and the librettist. Wagner shrewdly said that Gluck's reforms did not really advance the dramatist in relation to the composer, but the composer in relation to the singers, a remark which itself implies that if the older form was undramatic, it was not because the music was emphasized at the expense of the words.

The innovations that Wagner himself preached in his writings claimed to reassert a balance between the elements of opera, but some of the terms that he used do not express very satisfactorily what was most radical in his practice (or, rather, his constantly developing practice) in the works from *Das Rheingold* on. He sometimes expressed his aspirations in terms of the *Gesamtkunstwerk*, a drama that would bind into a total unity music, words, acting and stage spectacle. As critics have pointed out, this conception in itself determines very little. Every opera puts these elements together in one way or another, and indeed a kind of opera that Wagner peculiarly despised, the French grand opera of Scribe and Meyerbeer (of which he memorably said that it consisted of effects without causes), could claim in one sense to offer a more 'total' work of art than his, since it standardly included ballet, which his typically did not. The theory of the *Gesamtkunstwerk* did not in itself fully reveal how the relations of words, music and the visual were to be adapted to what Wagner really wanted, which was a new conception not just of opera but of drama.

Wagner regarded French opera as bombastically empty, distinguished neither for its words nor for its music. Rossini, the master of Italian opera, he saw as a counter-revolutionary, comparing him to a reactionary statesman: 'As Metternich, with perfect logic on his side, could not conceive the state under any form but that of absolute monarchy, so Rossini, with no less force of argument, could conceive the opera under no other form than that of absolute melody'. In this context, and granted also that he thought that the genius of Mozart

had been poured into inadequate texts (and, in the case of *Così fan tutte*, a deplorable subject), Wagner particularly emphasized the importance of the words – which, for all his operas, were of course his own. In developing his later style, he at first tended to assert the primacy of words, and *Das Rheingold*, in particular, is to some extent an expression of this ideal. However, as the music of the *Ring* developed, and in the light of his experience with *Tristan* and *Die Meistersinger*, he gave up this emphasis. The words were always of course important; he invested them with a complex philosophical content, removed almost all repetitions, and did his best to make the text heard over the music, placing the orchestra in the Festspielhaus at Bayreuth under the stage (though he chose this arrangement also because he wanted there to be an uninterrupted view of the stage picture). But while the force of the words was essential, he moved to a view that if anything was primary, it was the music: in a later essay, he described his dramas as 'deeds of music made manifest'. The sheer cumulative progression of the work almost inevitably meant that the music should become more complex as the drama went on, and in addition to that, the technical developments in his style during the period in which he broke off from the cycle produced an alteration in the music, in particular a symphonic flexibility in the use of the motifs, which is very evident at the beginning of the third act of *Siegfried*, the point at which he took it up again.

3. TIME, EXPRESSION AND THE INNER WORLD. Perhaps the single most powerful resource of opera as a dramatic form is its capacity to use musical means not only to advance the action in time, but to deepen it. It implies a complex relation between real and dramatic time; while time passes in the theatre, a sequence is unfolded by the orchestra and singers which does not represent a sequence at all, or at least not a sequence of events, but some other dimension of the action, often a state of mind, a mood or a motivation. The arias in *opera seria*, it has already been suggested, were a device for exploring the emotional implications of the action, but it was not entirely successful, partly because of a restrictive rhetoric of the emotions, partly because the parts in which the action was advanced were schematic and compressed and often without musical interest.

In Mozart's and Da Ponte's comedies, the resource is developed in many different and very subtle ways. It is used to distinguish the characters from one another; moreover, it is deployed differently in the various operas, and this contributes significantly to their distinctive atmospheres. In *Le nozze di Figaro*, each principal character has at least one self-revelatory aria, and these arias differ not only in what they say and in their musical character but also in their occasion. Both Figaro and the Count burst into declaration of their feelings in the face of immediate events, but the Countess needs no special occasion, and when we first see her, she is overflowing with nostalgia and regret. In *Don Giovanni* it is important that, while other characters sing about themselves, Giovanni never does. He is all action, and the lack of any piece that reveals anything more about him leaves us with a very appropriate sense that there is nothing to be revealed; his significance lies in such things as the vitality that he, in his music, communicates to everyone else. *Così fan tutte* uses to contrasting effect declarations made by the same characters at different stages of the action. It creates the remarkable impression that the elaborate conventional arias in the first act are public performances, occurring in real time, while the expressions of feeling later in the work, particularly from Fiordiligi, come from an inner world; just for this reason, when the tenor interrupts her most affecting piece, 'Fra gli amplessi', the sense is given that he has broken not just into her song but into her life.

In Wagner's work, the resources of psychological exploration became the essence of musical drama. This was not altogether his intention. He wanted his works to constitute a new kind of myth, a modern analogue to Aeschylean tragedy. To some extent, he succeeded, but it was perhaps inevitable that in the 19th century these aims should be shaped by explorations of the subjective individual consciousness. Particularly in the *Ring*, mythic, symbolic and political themes are arranged in a structure of personal motivation which in itself could well figure in a more naturalistic style of drama. The means that Wagner invented to make this possible are to be found in a text and a musical texture that make it very easy to move between the inner and the outer world: exchanges between characters, first-personal declarations made by one character to another, and music or words that express a welling up of the characters' conscious or unconscious thoughts, merge into one another in a fluent and natural way. At the same time, the flow of these materials is controlled by a powerful sense of theatrical pace. Critics of Wagner's works (who include some who hate them, with an intensity probably unique in operatic taste) are disposed to say that they are too long, but this is the consequence of dislike, not its ground: since the works are long, those who hate them naturally find them too long. Some passages can be recognized even by enthusiasts as unnecessary (though it is not easy to get agreement on which they are), but none of the mature works is seriously too long for what it is trying to do, and in all of them, well performed, there is a steady pulse against which the developments of both the inner and the outer life unfold.

The contrasts in almost all respects between Wagner and Verdi are so sharp that in general there is not much to be learnt from them about the aesthetics of opera. The fact that two musical geniuses, born in the same year, should produce works so totally different in their aims and methods is, certainly, revealing about two national cultures. Verdi took up a popular tradition of opera and insisted that he remained within it as he developed works of increasing complexity and technical sophistication. It is entirely fitting that at his funeral the large crowd should have spontaneously started to sing 'Va pensiero', the famous patriotic chorus from *Nabucco*, his first masterpiece, written nearly 60 years before. Verdi was a national hero, and he was popular in the straightforward sense that his tunes could be taken up by the town band, the café trio or the barrel organ. The contrast with Wagner's artistic relations to nationalism, and with his conception of 'a people', could not be more striking. Wagner wanted to give the German people a German art. This implied both that they did not yet have such a thing, and that a creative individual was needed to bring it into being. Moreover, this creative act was to occur at the frontiers of expressive innovation. The work that more than any other Wagner acknowledged as his inspiration was Beethoven's Ninth Symphony, and his ambitions were defined in terms of the selfconsciously progressive artwork. Verdi merely ignored any such ideas for most of his career, and treated them with great suspicion when in his later years they were pressed on him by Boito.

Granted these vast differences, comparisons between the two composers are often uninteresting. In the handling of dramatic time, however, the diametrical differences between them are instructive. Verdi was always concerned to achieve pace, constantly urging his librettists to cut and condense, and his works are marked by a powerful forward movement, very characteristic of him and not simply of the Italian tradition (there is a marked contrast with Bellini). The pace is that of external events; his characters are almost always doing something, and their psychology is expressed typically in action rather than in reflection. Some of his operas, above all *Rigoletto*, achieve a perfect dramatic pace in these terms: rapid developments are rapidly unfolded, with no sense of theatrical strain. He had other ways, as well, of handling dramatic pace. *Falstaff* sustains a very fast pace adjusted to comic developments, and does it by using a radically original and fluent musical idiom. *Don Carlos* is slower and more reflective, and leaves greater space for the exploration of motive; but it is typical of Verdi that, reworking the opera in 1882, he rewrote the duet between Philip and Posa so as to 'strip everything that is purely musical, keeping only what is necessary for the action'.

There are Verdi operas in which the effect of his brisk dealings with time is questionable, and they include some which in other respects are among his finest. Just because the inner life of his characters is given very largely through the events presented, there is a danger that as the presentation of the events speeds up, so, seemingly, does their inner life: we may be left with no sense of a space beside or among the happenings, in which we can locate their thoughts or feelings. There is a problem of this kind in the second act of *La traviata*, where the narration is so briskly compressed that both the hero and the heroine seem to be acting in a state of frantic haste. There is not much to encourage the thought that this effect is intended, and the impression can be distinctly like that of watching an old film.

A similar difficulty, at a deeper level, affects *Otello*. Boito is often complimented for having eliminated the first act of Shakespeare's play, but that act in fact lays the basis of the relations between the main characters, and its removal, together with the compression of time in which Otello's feelings change, moves his character sharply towards the pathological. In addition, within the tight boundaries set by the compression, Boito could find no room for the already difficult matter of Iago's motivation, and tried to condense it into one self-revelatory monologue, the famous 'Credo', which produced a magnificent aria but also contributed to making the situation less humanly credible. In the case of *Otello*, considerations of speed, more than anything else, serve to turn a tragedy into a melodrama.

The extraordinary success of Wagner's manipulation of the relations between outer action and inner feeling had its own cost. Because every aspect of the characters' experience is expressed and nourished by the unified flow of musical material, which in each work has its own distinctive quality, there is a danger that the characters will seem to merge – at the limit, that the whole may seem to belong to one experience. If this goes too far, the spectator's sense of the drama may take on the quality of being inside the composer's head: it is related to the feeling of being consumed or absorbed which is a well-known reaction to Wagner's work, and which is notoriously feared and resented by many who experience it. It is a kind of reaction inconceivable in the case of Mozart or of Verdi, where there is no tendency for the power and individuality of the style to threaten the seeming autonomy of the characters.

Debussy had this kind of difficulty in mind in setting out to write a post-Wagnerian opera. It was not merely what he called the 'American opulence' of Wagner's textures that he wanted to escape. Harmonically *Pelléas et Mélisande* owes a good deal to the experiments of *Parsifal*, but it conceives the relations of music and drama in terms very different from Wagner's. 'I do not feel tempted to imitate what I admire in Wagner', Debussy wrote; 'my conception of dramatic art is different. According to mine, music begins where speech fails. Music is intended to convey the inexpressible ... I would have her always discreet.' This in itself might seem to fit a traditional view of *Pelléas*, that it achieves its great refinement at the cost of an enervated passivity, an image of it which is encouraged if one is too impressed by Debussy's admiration for Poe. But Debussy also said that what he wanted for librettos were 'poems that will provide me with changing scenes, varied as regards place and atmosphere, in which the characters will not argue, but live their lives and work out their destinies'. Joseph Kerman has described *Pelléas* as a 'sung play', and this arrives at the same point, from the opposite direction, as Mallarmé's remark about Maeterlinck's drama when it first appeared, that it was an opera without music. The music does not cancel its character as a drama or impose passivity on it. What it emphasizes, rather, is the imperfection of action, and human beings' indeterminate understanding of what they are doing. 'Nous ne voyons jamais que l'envers des destinées', the aged Arkel remarks, 'l'envers même de la nôtre': the back, or reverse side, of our lives. We do see something, but it is the wrong way round and fragmentary, gaining a sense only from another point of view. Debussy presents this compelling picture of the mental world in a way uniquely successful in opera. He laid aside every convention by which opera had traditionally been assumed to express the inner life of its characters explicitly, totally and on the authority of the composer.

Pelléas is particularly difficult to produce; it is hard to embody its basic sense of the indeterminacy of human relations, and of there simply being no truth of the kind that the jealous Golaud seeks. Pressed in one direction, it dissolves into a faintly Symbolist vagueness, while in the other it offers a rather nasty but underdescribed domestic disaster. But its difficulties also measure its achievement, as being one of the few operas to have engaged with the typically 20th-century idea that reality is not merely given, but both demands interpretation and can defeat it. Some works of Richard Strauss flirt with such ideas – *Ariadne auf Naxos*, perhaps, or *Capriccio* – but none is committed to developing them. Stravinsky, in *The Rake's Progress*, characteristically changed the subject, and selfconsciously addressed the technical problems of a less selfconscious operatic tradition.

The one composer besides Debussy whose operas successfully took up typically modern problems of psychological opacity and the dramatist's narrative authority was Berg. He is a descendant of Wagner not just in technical terms of the history of atonality, but as one who created a new kind of musical drama from demandingly avant-garde materials. He resembles Wagner, too, in an insistent (in his case, obsessional)

compositorial presence, but he avoided the problem that Wagner had left, of reconciling that presence with the characters' autonomy, by cultivating a dramatic effect in which any appearance of that autonomy has disappeared. His characters lack effective action, or an inner life, or both. The protagonists of the two operas are victims, and almost every other character (with the exceptions of Marie in *Wozzeck* and Countess Geschwitz in *Lulu*) is a grotesque and empty construct of behaviour. The conventional name of this style, 'Expressionism', may well have been applied to it by an imperfect analogy with painting, but it has its logic in the history of music. An operatic technique that restricts characters to depersonalized aspects of a compelling and disturbing musical development is directly descended, through Schoenberg's experiments, from Wagner's design of expressing the rich inner life of his characters by making it immediately accessible to their musical environment. This design contains the possibility, which is already present in *Tristan* and is most obvious in Amfortas's music in *Parsifal*, that the expression will itself become the environment. The distinctions dissolve between the characters' inner life and the whole world of the opera, and that part of Wagner's project which consisted in finding new musical means to represent individual psychological character (in itself, a traditional aim) falls away.

4. PERFORMANCE AND REPETITION. There are a few plays that are constantly revived, and they are almost all masterpieces, frequently performed because they are thought to reward repeated reinterpretation. There are many pieces of music of which the same is true, but there are more that do not make the same claim to inexhaustible depth, but are frequently performed simply because people wish to hear them, or to hear a particular artist perform them. In this respect, musical drama is music rather than drama. Some of the works in the repertory do fall into the class of inexhaustible masterpieces, but more do not, and they are repeatedly performed because of an interest in performance rather than in dramatic reinterpretation.

The interest in performance is in the first place an interest in singers, and there are some people whose concern with opera is primarily directed to singers' talents and achievements. This is a traditional phenomenon: in the history of opera, an interest in singers is older than an interest in composers. As well as discriminating connoisseurs, there are devoted and enthusiastic fans who attach themselves to leading artists. Their popularity can give these artists great power in the opera house, and the demands, tantrums and absurdities of some performers in the past are legendary. The tyranny of artists now usually takes subtler forms, and there are probably no singers left who insist, as some used to do, on wearing their own costume in a given role whatever the production might be. Gluck, Verdi and others opposed the excesses in their time, and in the last 50 years, particularly under Wagnerian influence, the dramatic demands of opera have to a great extent prevailed against the tastes and habits of more traditional performers and their supporters. The development has brought about a great improvement in operatic acting, and it has also yielded many radically new and interesting productions.

It is true that the idiosyncrasies of singers have to some extent been replaced by those of directors, and most seasoned operagoers have seen in the 1970s or

1980s some production of a well-known work in which only the music revealed what opera it was. This is not only a matter of a fashionable trend; it also involves a shift in what is meant by the repetition of operas. When the emphasis moves to dramatic realization, a new staging of an opera cannot count as simply a new series of performances but is an invitation to a reinterpretation. However, since many operas that are worth performing offer few rewards to dramatic rediscovery, attempts to find new significance in their drama can be very strained. In an extreme case, the enterprise may be thought to be based on a misunderstanding, a confusion between an exploration of a work and, simply, a performance of it. However, there is no easy road back from this point. A merely conventional production may well be disappointing unless the performance is very good indeed, and the growing popularity of opera, which means more performances, joins, rather paradoxically, with increasing dramatic demands on the works performed, with the effect that the already small repertory becomes even more restricted. The next demand on directors' ingenuity may be to invent ways in which dramatically less interesting operas can be merely performed.

The historical conflicts between the dramatic and the performance aspects of opera have been concerned with the power of singers. They do not call in question the power of singing, which is at the heart of all opera. The enjoyment of opera, particularly of Italian opera, immediately involves the enjoyment of a technique. At a fine operatic performance, the audience is conscious of the singers' achievement and the presence of physical style and vitality; a feeling of performance and of the performers' artistry is more constantly at the front of the mind than it is with other dramatic arts. It is because of this that outbreaks of applause may be appropriate, though the granting of encores is a lot less common than it once was. These practices may sometimes get in the way of the drama, but the sense of performance in itself does not; it is allied with musical intensity in reinforcing the drama. There are interesting comparisons in these respects with ballet, where the sense of performance and technique is paramount, but which (in Western culture at least) is less committed to being a dramatic art, and has closer relations with both the decorative and the athletic. At the same time, the demands on opera singers, even more than on other musical performers, are not altogether unlike those on athletes, and high-risk aspects of physical performance uniquely combine in the case of opera with possibilities of dramatic expression to make it an exceptionally difficult enterprise, and all the more powerful when it goes well.

W. H. Auden said 'in a sense, there can be no tragic opera', because singing in itself too evidently seems a free and enjoyable activity: 'the singer may be playing the role of a deserted bride who is about to kill herself, but we feel quite certain as we listen that not only we, but also she, is having a wonderful time'. The judgment about tragedy might be disputed, but Auden's remark contains an important truth about the aesthetics of opera. Particularly in the Italian style, it presents its audience immediately with musical artistry and achievement, and so, more generally, with an obvious artifice – conventions of musical form and performance that are not transparent, as blank verse can sometimes be, but constantly manifest. Because of this, there is a particular technique available to the operatic composer, which is that of securing an effect through the audience's con-

sciousness that this is what is happening. A theatrical device is made to work, not by concealing it, but by securing the audience's complicity in it. This technique is not peculiar to opera, but it is specially important to it, and its importance is connected to the point that operas do not have to have dramatic or musical depth in order to be worth seeing over and over again. When one sees an effective opera again, not because it is the kind of work that one might understand more deeply on further experience of it, but just because one wants to see a good performance of it, the enjoyment of it at the level of drama is often increased by this sense of familiarity, of seeing the wheels of artifice turn.

The master of this technique is Puccini. He is an outstandingly popular opera composer, and his works are staged by every opera house. He had remarkable melodic gifts and was a notably inventive orchestrator. The librettos of his operas (several by Giacosa and Illica) are ingeniously constructed. Yet his critical reputation is not as unqualified as his success, and many, while acknowledging his achievement, find it hard to dismiss a distinct sense of the cynical and the manipulative about it. All his major works are sentimental or melodramatic or both, and while 'melodrama', etymologically speaking, is what all opera must be, the term in fact carries a limiting sense which, in Puccini's case, is compounded by the fact that the melodrama is not at all innocent. His consciousness that he came at the end of a long tradition, together with the taste for cruelty which he himself called his 'Neronian instinct', mean that *Tosca* or *Madama Butterfly* is a very long way from *Un ballo in maschera*. It is hard to think of a parallel in any other art to enduring works that are at once as effective and as dubious as these. The secret of their working so well is that their skill and their very selfconsciousness play into the audience's experience of opera as performance. In enjoying these familiar works, part of the pleasure lies in the sense of seeing Puccini do the trick again. In relying so ingeniously on this sense, he was exploiting something that is inherent to some degree in the performance of any opera, and that is why his talent, suspect as it is, is true to the nature of the form.

The case of Puccini, and the relation of his achievements to opera as performance, are important for the aesthetics of opera. In his path-breaking work of opera criticism, *Opera as Drama*, Joseph Kerman was particularly and quotably scathing about *Tosca*, as he was also about *Der Rosenkavalier*. It is certainly important for the critic to mark off these triumphant examples of, respectively, sensationalism and *kitsch* from such works as *Le nozze di Figaro* or *Tristan* or *Don Carlos*. Yet it is probable that *Tosca* and *Der Rosenkavalier* will be popular with opera-lovers as long as there are opera-lovers, and rightly so. If they are not unqualified masterpieces, they are masterpieces of opera. It is very characteristic of opera that this should be possible. Because opera is musical drama, some of its works can bring these resources together to achieve a power unsurpassed in the dramatic arts. At the same time, opera is musical performance, and this does not merely have its consequences for the practice of operagoing, for the loyalties of its audience, and for the kinds of interest that enthusiasts can appropriately take in it. It has its own implications for the opportunities that opera can offer its creators.

For the definition and discussion of sub-genres and related genres *see* AFTERPIECE; AZIONE TEATRALE; BALLAD OPERA; BALLET DE COUR;

BALLET-HÉROÏQUE; BURLESQUE; BURLETTA; CHAMBER OPERA; CHILDREN'S OPERA; COMÉDIE-BALLET; COMÉDIE MÊLÉE D'ARIETTES; DIVERTISSEMENT; DRAME LYRIQUE; DRAMMA GIOCOSO; DRAMMA PER MUSICA; DUODRAMA; ENTRÉE; EXTRAVAGANZA; FARSA; FAVOLA IN MUSICA; FESTA TEATRALE; GRAND OPÉRA; INTERMÈDE; INTERMEDIO; INTERMEZZO; JAZZ OPERA; JESUIT DRAMA; LEHRSTÜCK; LIEDERSPIEL; LITERATUROPER; MADRIGAL COMEDY; MAINPIECE; MÄRCHENOPER; MASQUE; MELODRAMA; MELODRAMMA; MONODRAMA; MUSICAL; MUSIC DRAMA; MUSIC THEATRE; NÉPSZÍNMŰ; NUMBER OPERA; OPÉRA-BALLET; OPÉRA BOUFFE; OPÉRA BOUFFON; OPERA BUFFA; OPÉRA COMIQUE; OPÉRA FÉERIE; OPERA SEMISERIA; OPERA SERIA; OPERA-TORNEO; OPERETTA; PANTOMIME; PARADE; PASTICCIO; PASTORAL; PASTORALE-HÉROÏQUE; POSSE; PUPPET OPERA; RAPPRESENTAZIONE SACRA; RESCUE OPERA; ROCK OPERA; SACRED OPERA; SAINETE; SCHULDRAMA; SCHULOPER; SEMI-OPERA; SEPOLCRO; SERENATA; SINGSPIEL; TONADILLA; TRAGÉDIE EN MUSIQUE; VAUDEVILLE (i); ZARZUELA (i); ZAUBEROPER; and ZEITOPER.

*

THE NATURE OF OPERA

BurneyH; BurneyFI; BurneyGN

R. M. Haas: 'Geschichtliche Opernbezeichnungen', *Festschrift Hermann Kretzschmar zum 70. Geburtstag* (Leipzig, 1918), 43–5

E. J. Dent: 'The Nomenclature of Opera', *ML*, xxv (1944), 132–40, 213–26

J. Kerman: *Opera as Drama* (New York, 1956, 2/1988)

W. H. Auden: 'Notes on Music and Opera', *The Dyer's Hand* (London, 1963), 465–74

——: 'The World of Opera', *Secondary Worlds* (London, 1968), 85–116

P. H. Lang: *The Experience of Opera* (New York, 1973)

F. Noske: *The Signifier and the Signified: Studies in the Operas of Mozart and Verdi* (The Hague, 1977)

J. Drummond: *Opera in Perspective* (London, 1980)

H. Lindenberger: *Opera: the Extravagant Art* (Ithaca, NY, 1984)

P. Robinson: *Opera and Ideas: from Mozart to Strauss* (New York, 1985)

M. Poizat: *L'opéra ou le cri de l'ange: Essai sur la jouissance de l'amateur d'opéra* (Paris, 1986; Eng. trans., 1992)

P. Conrad: *A Song of Love and Death: the Meaning of Opera* (London, 1987)

E. T. Cone: 'The World of Opera and its Inhabitants', *Music: a View from Delft* (Chicago, 1988), 125–38

P. Kivy: *Osmin's Rage: Philosophical Reflections on Opera, Drama and Text* (Princeton, 1988)

C. Abbate and R. Parker, eds.: *Analyzing Opera: Verdi and Wagner* (Berkeley, 1989)

R. Parker and A. Groos, eds.: *Reading Opera* (Princeton, 1989)

C. Abbate: *Unsung Voices: Opera and Musical Narrative in the Nineteenth Century* (Princeton, 1991)

R. Donington: *Opera and its Symbols: the Unity of Words, Music and the Myth* (New Haven, CT, 1991)

GENERAL HISTORIES

H. S. Edwards: *History of the Opera from Monteverdi to Donizetti* (London, 1862, 2/1862)

H. M. Schletterer: *Die Entstehung der Oper* (Nördlingen, 1873)

R. A. Streatfeild: *The Opera* (London, 1897, enlarged 2/1902, rev. E. J. Dent, 5/1925)

W. F. Apthorp: *The Opera Past and Present* (New York, 1901)

J. Goddard: *The Rise and Development of Opera* (London, 1912)

O. Bie: *Die Oper* (Berlin, 1913, 10/1923)

K. M. Klob: *Die Oper von Gluck bis Wagner* (Ulm, 1913)

H. Kretzschmar: *Geschichte der Oper* (Leipzig, 1919)

H. Abert: *Grundprobleme der Operngeschichte* (Leipzig, 1926)

E. Rabich: *Die Entwicklung der Oper* (Langensalza, 1926)

E. J. Dent: *Opera* (Harmondsworth, 1940, 5/1949)

W. Brockway and H. Weinstock: *The Opera: a History of its Creation and Performance, 1600–1941* (New York, 1941, 2/1962)

J. Gregor: *Kulturgeschichte der Oper: ihre Verbindung mit dem Leben, den Werken des Geistes und der Politik* (Vienna, 1941, 3/1950)

D. J. Grout: *A Short History of Opera* (New York and London, 1947, rev. W. H. Williams, 3/1988)

A. A. Abert: *Die Oper von den Anfängen bis zum Beginn des 19. Jahrhunderts* (Cologne, 1953; Eng. trans., 1962)

J. Kerman: *Opera as Drama* (New York, 1956, 2/1988)

R. Leibowitz: *Histoire de l'opéra* (Paris, 1957)

G. R. Marek: *Opera as Theater* (New York, 1962)

K. Pahlen: *Oper der Welt* (Zürich, 1963)

C. Hamm: *Opera* (Boston, 1966)

R. Hofmann: *Histoire de l'opéra* (Paris, 1967)

L. Orrey: *Opera: a Concise History* (London, 1972, rev. R. Milnes, 2/1987)

A. Basso and G. Barblan, eds.: *Storia dell'opera* (Turin, 1977)

R. Donington: *The Opera* (London, 1978)

P.-J. Salazar: *Idéologies de l'opéra* (Paris, 1980)

C. Headington, R. Westbrook and T. Barfoot: *Opera: a History* (London, 1987)

S. Sadie, ed.: *History of Opera* (London, 1989)

For further bibliography *see* LIBRETTO (ii).

HOWARD MAYER BROWN (I, II), BERNARD WILLIAMS (III)

Opera ('Works'). Opera in three acts by LUCIANO BERIO, to a text by the composer after Furio Colombo, Umberto Eco, Alessandro Striggio, and Susan Yankowitz with the Open Theatre of New York; Santa Fe, 12 August 1970 (revised version, Florence, Teatro Comunale, 28 May 1977).

The title, to be understood as the plural of *opus*, can be taken in at least two ways: *Opera* incorporates a number of self-contained pieces that may be performed independently, but it also consists of three radically dissimilar types of dramaturgical material. Alternation among these constitutes the nucleus of the work. Two fragments from Striggio's libretto for Monteverdi's *Orfeo*, translated into English, are set once in each act as Air and Memoria. This evocation of opera's origins contrasts with materials that Berio had preserved from an unrealized project with Umberto Eco and Furio Colombo in 1956 on the sinking of the *Titanic* – an ironic, quasi-Brechtian parable on the incautious fetishization of technical achievement. As a third strand, Berio incorporates materials from the Open Theatre of New York's *Terminal*, an indictment of the treatment of the terminally ill. Momentary congruences allow him to pass from one layer to another, thus creating a sort of theatrical mobile around the theme of death.

Intended as a vehicle for the freewheeling theatrical invention of Jo Chakin, the work suffered badly when Berio was forced to withdraw from directing it: its first performance at Santa Fe ended in a fiasco. Seven years later Berio revised it for the Maggio Musicale (1977, Florence), giving this essentially 'open' theatrical experiment a perhaps alien but nonetheless effective sense of ending. Two children are hunted down by a spotlight: the originally separate works Agnus and *E vò* are incorporated as a telling threnody.   DAVID OSMOND-SMITH

Opéra (i) (Fr.). The French word for 'opera' carries meanings beyond those of its counterparts in Italian or English. It usually signifies a French lyric stage work sung throughout (if composed for the Académie Royale de Musique and its successors) or with spoken dialogue (if composed for the Comédie-Italienne, the Opéra-Comique and other theatres). Modern scholars sometimes restrict the term to the former, preferring to call the latter *opéra comique*. In the Baroque period *opéra* was also the French translation for 'opus' (it was gradually replaced in the later 18th century by 'oeuvre').

In the context of stage works *opéra* entered the French language as a translation of the Italian 'opera' in the mid-17th century. In the 18th century it had two primary meanings. First, it was 'a dramatic and lyric spectacle in which the goal was to unite all the charms of the fine arts by depicting a passionate action' (Rousseau); its component parts were the libretto ('poëme'), the music, the choreography and the sets (see also Brossard and Diderot). Second, on a more restricted level, *opéra* was a synonym for libretto; poets wrote *opéras*, and composers set them to music. The latter usage was the more prevalent.

Throughout the *ancien régime* authors preferred in general more specific terms for genres (*tragédie lyrique, pastorale, comédie lyrique, comédie-ballet, divertissement* and the like for works at the Académie Royale and *opéra comique en vaudevilles, comédie-parade* and *comédie mêlée d'ariettes* for works at the Comédie-Italienne and fair theatres). *Opéra* is occasionally found as a more neutral term for works that did not fit easily into standard categories (such as Rameau's *Naïs* to a libretto by Cahusac written to celebrate the Peace of Aix-la-Chapelle, 1749). With the diversification of the repertory at the Comédie-Italienne/Opéra-Comique during the reign of Lous XVI and the Revolution and the ambitious works performed at the Théâtre Feydeau, the terminology for operas with spoken dialogue expanded: *drame lyrique, comédie lyrique, fait historique* and sometimes even *tragédie lyrique* (as in Le Sueur's *Télémaque*, libretto by P. Dercy, 1796). *Opéra* appeared frequently for works serious in tone, such as Grétry's *Callias, ou Nature et patrie* (libretto by F.-B. Hoffman, 1794), and Cherubini's *Médée* (libretto also by Hoffman, 1797).

By the 19th century *opéra* became the standard term for works sung throughout – from Spontini to Rossini, Meyerbeer, Verdi, Gounod and beyond (*see* GRAND OPÉRA and DRAME LYRIQUE). Serious works for the Opéra-Comique were also termed *opéra* (e.g. Méhul's *Valentine de Milan*, to a libretto by Bouilly, finished after the composer's death by his nephew, Daussoigne-Méhul, 1822), but with the swing to a preference there for comedy (only), *opéra comique* in the modern sense became the usual designation (as in the works of Boieldieu and Auber). The *opéra/opéra comique* division remains generally valid for the 20th century as well, but occasionally there are others in keeping with the French tradition of more specific terminology reflecting the literary and dramatic type (for example in the works of Honegger, Milhaud and Poulenc).

*

S. Brossard: *Dictionaire de musique, contenant une explication des termes grecs, latins, italiens, & françois les plus usitez dans la musique* (Paris, 1703)

D. Diderot: 'Opéra', *Encyclopédie, ou Dictionnaire raisonné des sciences, des arts et des métiers*, ed. D. Diderot and others (Paris, 1751–80)

J.-J. Rousseau: *Dictionnaire de musique* (Paris, 1768)

Castil-Blaze [F. H. J. Blaze]: *De l'opéra en France* (Paris, 1820)

L. Lalo: 'L'Opéra', *Cinquante ans de musique française de 1874 à 1925*, ed. L. Rohozinski, i (Paris, 1925), 1–117

M. N. Rio and M. Rostain: *L'opéra mort ou vif* (Paris, 1982)

M. ELIZABETH C. BARTLET

Opéra (ii). The name commonly used by the Académie Royale de Musique, Paris; *see* PARIS, §§2(i), 3(i), 4(ii), 5(ii) and 6(i, ii).

Opera America. A non-profit-making organization based in Washington, DC. Founded in 1970, the 'Opera Producers Entity for Related Activity' offers a wide range of services and information to professional companies in North America and those affiliated outside the country, as well as to performers and administrators, the media, funding bodies and the public. Its publications include regular reports and surveys on the practical and financial aspects of performance, production and management, a directory of sets and costumes, a guide to competitions and artist-in-residence programmes, and various educational materials. Opera

America maintains an information service, originally established by the CENTRAL OPERA SERVICE, which collects and disseminates data on performances and productions, catalogues available sets, costumes, translations and editions, and keeps various fiscal and operational records. It awards grants to take new works and innovative productions to under-served areas, to fund the training of promising singers and to provide training in arts administration; it also offers legal advice, runs a consultancy programme covering all aspects of marketing and public relations, and organizes an annual conference as well as a number of seminars and workshops.

MARTHA PERRY

Opéra-ballet (Fr.). A French genre of the early and middle 18th century. *Opéras-ballets* usually consisted of a prologue and three or four acts, written for the Académie Royale de Musique, combining elements of both opera and ballet. At the time, the term 'ballet' was generally used, but modern scholars, reversing Framery's order, prefer *opéra-ballet* to distinguish the type from the later *ballet d'action* or ballet pantomime. The *opéra-ballet* drew on 17th-century antecedents in the *ballet de cour, divertissement* and *tragédie en musique*, but from their examples a different type of theatrical work developed.

The genre was characterized by a separate plot or subject for each act (or *entrée*), though usually with some unifying idea, and an emphasis on *divertissements* that included vocal music as well as dance (and were generally placed at the climax of the act). Cahusac (1754) compared the aesthetics of *opéra-ballet* with Watteau's in contrast to those of the *tragédie en musique* whose artistic parallel was to be found in the work of Raphael and Michelangelo. The goal in *opéra-ballet* was to amuse and please the sometimes fickle audiences of the early 18th century – both at court and in public performance – through a variety of dances, *airs, ariettes* and *choeurs dansés*, as well as colourful tableaux with often elaborate costumes; dramatic continuity and force were not of primary concern, while fantasy was an important ingredient. The only unity was a common theme, broadly treated, whose component parts were contrasting.

During the first two decades approximately, contemporary characters and comic intrigues (or tender love stories) frequently give *opéra-ballet* a tone markedly different from that of the *tragédie en musique* with its austere gods and heroes and its emphasis on grand subjects such as honour. Generally tragedy was absent (or restricted to a single entrée, as in Campra's *Les muses*, 1703). The overall mood was light and festive. From then to the end of the reign of Louis XV the *ballet-héroïque* type on classical or exotic subjects was preferred. During the late *ancien régime* even the desire for a unifying theme gradually disappeared; an evening's programme might be made up of 'fragments', that is, several one-act works (entrées from longer *opéras-ballets* already in repertory, *actes de ballet* in similar style newly written or old favourites, *opéras*, pastorals and so on). The popularity of the *ballet d'action* led to the virtual disappearance of the *opéra-ballet* by the time of the Revolution. In the 19th century the term came occasionally to be applied to operas in which ballet had a more extensive role than usual and whose unified plots were classical and whose tone was often festive. In form and style, however, these owe more to contemporary opera than its 18th-century predecessor.

In spite of a few antecedents during the previous decade, Campra's frequently performed *L'Europe galante* (libretto by A. H. de Lamotte, 1697) so impressed Cahusac and his contemporaries that they credited him with creating the genre; it is certainly true that this work was an important model (for illustration see *EUROPE GALANTE, L'*). In the prologue Venus predicts Love's triumph over Discord, and the four entrées depict the contrasting approach to love in France, Spain, Italy and Turkey. (In the third, two *airs* added in 1699 with Italian texts and musical style, though not virtuoso, and a *forlana* add local colour.) In keeping with the dramatically slight intrigue, *récitatif* has a reduced role; indeed, occasionally the action is conveyed by gesture during dance (as in the incident during a masked ball which arouses the Italian's jealousy). Short *airs*, choruses and a variety of set dances, pleasing to the eye and ear, form the bulk of the score.

During the first half of the 18th century innovations in lyric theatre often occurred in the *opéra-ballet* and *ballet-héroïque*: the simplification in string textures, the greater use of wind instruments for expressive purposes, the introduction of new dances (such as the tambourin) and showy *ariettes*, the development of a light and gracious musical style and a sense of 'spectacle' that no longer relied so heavily on the 'merveilleux'. Destouches made a major contribution, and several of his works remained in the repertory for decades. Rameau was a master in the genre, as was established by his first essay in it, *Les Indes galantes* (1735). In *Les fêtes d'Hébé* (called a 'ballet', 1739) he continued the multi-story format, but the tone has changed: comic scenes are few and touching ones many. The prologue announces that Hebe, the goddess of Youth, will be entertained on the banks of the Seine by a ballet with tales illustrating by analogy the Lyric Talents (Poetry, Music and Dance) at Love's command. Pseudo-history, fable and *pastorale-héroïque* are the sources for the episodes chosen; the last, with its mixture of gods and mortals celebrating the art of Terpsichore, is significantly placed last. In the score the composer made brilliant use of the forms he inherited, but compared with works of a few decades earlier the *divertissements* are more substantial, regularly placed at the ends of acts and concluding with impressive *choeurs chantés*; the vocal style is more strongly contrasting, as italianate *ariettes* (like 'L'objet qui règne dans mon âme', third entrée) highlight the singer's virtuosity and contrast sharply with *airs* in the French tradition (including *airs tendres*); and dances conveying the dramatic action in pantomime have a much more substantial role.

In spite of the hostility of Rousseau (1768), who termed the genre 'bizarre' and criticized its lack of dramatic continuity, *opéras-ballets* were still performed during the reign of Louis XVI. Representative of this period is Gossec's *Fragments nouveaux* of 1775: the first entrée, 'Alexis et Daphné', is an Arcadian tale of unjustified jealousy easily dissipated; the second, 'Philémon et Baucis', a classical myth of hospitality rewarded. They were most often given with Rameau's 'La musique' from *Les fêtes d'Hébé*. Gossec's score still includes *choeurs dansés*, *ariettes* and favourite dances inherited from the Rameau generation, but the orchestration, harmonic language and melodic style reflect more recent developments.

The rare 19th-century *opéra-ballet* was most often a *pièce de circonstance*, for in these works set dances seemed a dramatically appropriate representation for celebration (see, for example, *Les dieux rivaux* by Spontini, Louis-Luc Loiseau de Persuis, Henri-Montan Berton and Rodolphe Kreutzer, written in honour of the Duke of Berry's marriage, 1816). Significantly, Cherubini's *Anacréon* (1803), which had no political overtones and makes even more extensive use of gesture (in the manner of the contemporary ballet pantomime), was a failure: the score, one of the composer's richest, could not compensate for a dramatic action virtually non-existent in contemporary opinion. (*La tentation* by Fromental Halévy and Casimir Gide, 1832, called a *ballet-opéra*, is an experiment in ballet pantomime to which some solo music and more frequently choruses have been added.)

*

L. Bordelon: *Diversitez curieuses pour servir à la récréation de l'esprit* (Amsterdam, 1699–1710)

R. de Saint-Mard: *Réflexions sur l'opéra* (Paris, 1741)

L. de Cahusac: 'Ballet', *Encyclopédie, ou Dictionnaire raisonné des sciences, des arts et des métiers*, ed. D. Diderot and others (Paris, 1751–80)

——: *La danse ancienne et moderne, ou Traité historique de la danse* (The Hague, 1754)

L. C. de La Baume Le Blanc, Duc de la Vallière: *Ballets, opéra et autres ouvrages lyriques* (Paris, 1760)

J.-J. Rousseau: *Dictionnaire de musique* (Paris, 1768)

N. Framery: 'Ballet-opéra', and P. L. Ginguené: 'Ballet', *Encyclopédie méthodique: Musique*, i, ed. N. Framery and P. L. Ginguené (Paris, 1791)

P. M. Masson: 'Le ballet héroïque', *ReM*, ix/8 (1927–8), 132–54

J. R. Anthony: 'The French opéra-ballet in the Early Eighteenth Century: Problems of Definition and Classification', *JAMS*, xviii (1965), 197–206

——: 'Some Uses of Dance in the French opéra-ballet', *RMFC*, ix (1969), 75–90

——: *French Baroque Music from Beaujoyeulx to Rameau* (London, 1973, 2/1978; Fr. trans., 1981)

M. Barthélemy: 'Opéra-ballet', *Dictionnaire de la musique: Science de la musique*, ed. M. Honegger (Paris, 1976)

W. Hilton: *Dance and Music of Court and Theatre: the French Noble Style, 1690–1725* (Princeton, 1980)

R. Fajon: *L'Opéra à Paris du Roi-Soleil à Louis le Bien-Aimé* (Geneva and Paris, 1984)   M. ELIZABETH C. BARTLET

Opera ballo (It.: 'opera dance'). Term used for the Italian variant of French *grand opéra*, of which Verdi's *Aida* is the prime example.

Opéra Bastille. The complex occupied by the Paris Opéra since 1990; *see* PARIS, §6(ii).

Opéra bouffe (Fr.). A mid- to late-19th-century French comic opera in which a witty spoken dialogue and sparkling, light music combine in a genre designed to entertain. Its period of greatest popularity coincides with the reign of Napoleon III. It takes its name from the theatre directed by Offenbach where many were first performed, the Théâtre des Bouffes-Parisiens (opened in 1855; *see* OPERETTA, fig.1). It differs from *opéra comique* of the same period in its more frankly humorous tone, often bordering on farce, and its use of parody and satire (literary, musical, social and sometimes political). The earliest is Offenbach's own *Orphée aux enfers* (1858), in which he amused his audience with a familiar story retold with characterizations of the principals very different from those in the legend. Even Orpheus's stature as a musician comes in for satirical treatment; his violin playing clearly bores his wife. Jupiter's undecorous transformation as a fly and his buzzing in the duet with Eurydice is a fine example of the broad comedy typical of the genre. For over two decades Offenbach continued to write *opéras bouffes*, some of which, like *La belle Hélène* (1864) and *La vie parisienne* (1866), have long outlasted the society whose foibles were their targets. Among the most successful and prolific of Offenbach's contemporaries and successors were Hervé (also a singer and theatre director) and Charles Lecocq, whose *La fille de Madame Angot* (1872) and several other works remain in the French light opera repertory.

*

J. Bruhr: *L'opérette* (Paris, 1962, 2/1974)
F. Bruyas: *Histoire de l'opérette en France* (Lyons, 1974)
C. Dufresne: *Histoire de l'opérette* (Paris, 1981)

M. ELIZABETH C. BARTLET

Opéra bouffon (Fr.). In 18th-century France the customary designation for Italian *opera buffa* performed in the original language or in French translation (for example, Paisiello's *Le roi Théodore à Venise*, a 1786 parody of *Il re Teodoro in Venezia*). It was also occasionally applied to *opéras comiques* whose plots were indebted to Italian or Spanish prototypes for characterizations or dramatic construction and, more broadly, to those in which the comedy approached farce (as in Philidor's *Blaise le savetier* of 1759 and Grétry's *Les deux avares* of 1770). A few contemporary writers, notably Contant d'Orville, used *opéra bouffon* as a synonym for *opéra comique*.

*

A. G. Contant d'Orville: *Histoire de l'opéra bouffon* (Amsterdam and Paris, 1768)
A. C. Quatremère de Quincy: 'Dissertation sur les opéras bouffons italiens', *Mercure de France* (March 1789), 124–48 [also pubd separately]
N. Framery: *De l'organisation des spectacles de Paris* (Paris, 1790)
L. Péricaud: *Théâtre de Monsieur* (Paris, 1908)
M. Robinson: '*Opera buffa* into *opéra comique*: French Adaptations of Italian Opera, 1775–1792', *Music and the French Revolution*, ed. M. Boyd (Cambridge, 1992), 37–56
M. Noiray: 'L'opera italiana in Francia nel XVIII secolo', *SOI*, ii (forthcoming)

M. ELIZABETH C. BARTLET

Opera buffa (It.: 'comic opera'). The term 'opera buffa' was first applied to the genre of comic opera as it rose to popularity in Italy and abroad over the course of the 18th century. At first, 'opera buffa' did not appear as a designation in the librettos. Like 'opera seria', it was used in informal writings (letters, memoirs etc.) and in ordinary conversation, with reference to the spectacle as a whole. Librettists, even in the lowlier comic genre, had literary pretensions and accordingly entitled their work in ways that emphasized its status as literature. 'Dramma giocoso' occurs as early as 1695 (in G. C. Villifranchi's preface to his *L'ipocondriaco*, composer unknown, performed at the Medici villa, Pratolino) and recurs sporadically thereafter, alternating from about 1740 with 'dramma bernesco', 'dramma comico', 'divertimento giocoso', 'commedia per musica' etc. The last-named survived on an equal footing with 'dramma giocoso' from about 1760. The early Neapolitan-dialect librettos favoured 'commedeia pe' museca'. No special significance can be attached to any of these designations.

1. Comic opera before the 18th century. 2. Neapolitan opera buffa to c1730. 3. The north to c1750. 4. The later 18th century. 5. The 19th century.

1. COMIC OPERA BEFORE THE 18TH CENTURY. A small number of comic operas were produced in the 17th century, although no great need for them can have been felt at a time when 'serious' operas were liberally inter-laced with comic episodes. Comic opera had no conventions of its own at this time but on the whole tended to be modelled on the (spoken) *commedia erudita*. Both Villifranchi and his rather more famous predecessor at the Medici court, G. A. Moniglia, pointed to Terence as their model. Florence, indeed, could be said to have been the 'centre' of this 'erudite' type of comic opera: the inaugural work at the Teatro della Pergola in 1657 had been Moniglia's *dramma civile rusticale*, *Il potestà di Colognole*, set to music by Jacopo Melani. It was followed, at irregular intervals and at different public or Medici theatres, by a dozen more such works up to 1699, when there occurred a hiatus of nearly 20 years before the next comic production.

Rome had pioneered in this field with Giulio Rospigliosi's *Chi soffre speri* (1637 as *Il falcone*) and *Dal male il bene* (1653), the former based on a Boccaccio *novella*, the latter on a Spanish *comedia*, and so both, quite clearly, in the 'erudite' tradition. Bologna, too, witnessed some comic operas in the 17th century, several of them imported from Florence. Here the Inquisition inhibited the free growth of what might otherwise have been a truly popular genre: eight different indigenous *scherzi giocosi* are listed by Ricci for the period 1669–98, after which, as at Florence, no more comic operas were seen for some 20 years. It is perhaps no coincidence that Rome, Florence and Bologna were to become important stations in the spread of the 18th-century *opera buffa*, a more 'modern' genre whose true birthplace was Naples.

2. NEAPOLITAN OPERA BUFFA TO *c*1730. It was at Naples that a new type of comic opera had its beginnings, patronized at first by eminent and, it would seem, enlightened members of the legal profession and aristocracy. The earliest known example is *La Cilla* (music by Michelangelo Faggioli, a lawyer, text by F. A. Tullio, later a prolific librettist), first performed in 1706, presumably at the home of the Neapolitan minister of justice to whom it was dedicated, then revived at the palace of the Prince of Chiusiano in 1707 and 1708. Only the libretto survives (no score from earlier than 1717 has been preserved, and no complete score earlier than 1722), but it, at least, is the very prototype of the kind of spectacle that was soon to thrive in the 'little theatres' of Naples: the setting is a district of the city itself, and the characters all speak in the local dialect. This lends an air of unadorned reality to what would otherwise have simply been the conventional characters and plot of an 'erudite' comedy. The *innamorati*, true to convention, are serious roles; but as they express themselves in the everyday dialect, their sentiments sound natural rather than stylized. Later Neapolitan comic operas often feature two pairs of lovers (the male lovers often portrayed by female sopranos) and the plot hinges on their fate. Surrounding them one finds such stock comedy figures as the old man, the old woman (a tenor role), the swaggering captain (bass), the saucy shop boy (soprano) etc. The local dialect and setting transmute all these traditional types from the caricatures they had been in earlier, Baroque comedy (both written and improvised) into more believable characters. Thus from the very beginning Neapolitan *opera buffa* reflects a new perception of everyday life; and from the very beginning it deals with both serious and comic characters and situations. These traits remained characteristic of the genre even after it was divested of the local setting and dialect, and became cosmopolitan.

The Teatro dei Fiorentini, a century-old playhouse, became the earliest public theatre to house Neapolitan *opera buffa*. Its first offering, in October 1709, was *Patrò Calienno de la Costa*, with music by Antonio Orefice, words by 'Mercotellis' (a pen-name); this was soon followed by another dialect opera, *Lo spellecchia*, with music by Tomaso de Mauro, words by C. de Petris. According to one witness, a northern nobleman, Neapolitans now began to abandon the S Bartolomeo theatre, home of *opera seria*, preferring to fill 'the Teatro de' Fiorentini, which is presenting real trash [*una vera porcheria*], unworthy of being seen, in the Neapolitan language' (see Croce 4/1947, p.140). Other theatres, the Nuovo and the Pace, opened their doors to *opera buffa* in 1724, by which time the new genre was a Neapolitan fixture attracting some of the best *opera seria* composers (Alessandro Scarlatti had tried his hand at it in 1718 with *Il trionfo dell'onore* at the Fiorentini, an unusual work in that the text was in Italian rather than Neapolitan, and the lovers were aristocrats). The new generation of composers – among them Vinci, Hasse and Pergolesi – were equally at home in both the serious and the comic genres.

The earliest singers were for the most part local and not professionally trained. Their music is accordingly relatively free of bravura passages but in other respects not unlike that of the contemporary *opera seria* (the arias are nearly all in da capo form). Like *opera seria*, these works are in three acts; Acts 1 and 2 often end with a short brawl for three or four of the cast, the germ of what later, in the north, was to become the extended *opera buffa* finale. The overtures, three-movement *sinfonie*, are indistinguishable from those of *opera seria*.

3. THE NORTH TO *c*1750. From Naples, *opera buffa* spread to Rome. Bernardo Saddumene, one of the leading Naples librettists, arrived there with some *buffo* singers and a composer (Giovanni Fischietti) in January 1729. Having recruited local castrato singers to play the female roles (women were not allowed on stage in Rome), he produced his *Li zite* (performed at Naples in 1722 to Vinci's music) under a new name, *La Costanza*, and with new music (by Fischietti). The serious roles were sung in Italian, the comic ones in the original dialect (a scheme that Saddumene later introduced to Naples, where it remained standard for the rest of the century). This and his *La somiglianza* (produced in February) appear to have been the earliest Neapolitan comic operas performed in Rome. The time was evidently ripe for the new genre to spread north. During the 1730s Rome became a centre of *opera buffa*; italianized Neapolitan operas as well as original Italian ones were produced there, principally at the Teatro Valle. Among the former, Gaetano Latilla's *La finta cameriera* (1738, known in Naples as *Il Gismondo*, 1737), among the latter Latilla's *Madama Ciana*(1738) and Rinaldo di Capua's *La commedia in commedia* (1738) and *La libertà nociva* (1740) formed the nucleus of Roman operas that soon began travelling north (one G. Barlocci is credited with having written or adapted their librettos). The composers, it should be noted, were at first all Neapolitans, while the singers tended to be native, often with previous experience as intermezzo specialists.

La finta cameriera travelled by the following route: Naples, 1737; Rome, 1738; Faenza and Modena, 1741; Siena, Florence, Genoa, 1742; Bologna, Venice, Vicenza, 1743; Milan, 1745; Turin, Mantua, Verona, Parma, 1747; and meanwhile, Graz, Leipzig, Hamburg, 1745 (carried there from Venice by the Mingotti troupe). The work's progress reflects fairly exactly the northward progress of the new *opera buffa*. There were early excursions outside Italy, and by the 1750s *opera buffa* was spreading to most of Europe.

4. THE LATER 18TH CENTURY. Venice quickly capitulated to the new genre. After the Teatro S Angelo produced *La finta cameriera* in May 1743, the S Moisé and S Cassiano theatres threw their doors open to *opera buffa*, remaining its chief purveyors until 1748, when other theatres joined in. The earliest composers were Latilla, Pietro Auletta, Rinaldo di Capua, Antonio Palella and Giuseppe Avossa, all Neapolitan. But in January 1745 they were joined by the Venetian Baldassare Galuppi, whose first *opera buffa*, *La forza d'amore*, was produced at the S Cassiano. Other northerners, Giuseppe Scolari and Ferdinando Bertoni, followed the next year; and yet another, Vincenzo Ciampi, made his Venetian *opera buffa* début in autumn 1748, having enlisted the aid of the then relatively unknown Carlo Goldoni. The Ciampi-Goldoni collaboration extended to two more works, but meanwhile Galuppi and Goldoni produced their first joint effort, *L'Arcadia in Brenta* (S Angelo, 14 May 1749), thereby initiating a new epoch in the history of the genre.

In a series of highly successful works, Galuppi and Goldoni established a model for the *opera buffa* just as it was beginning to rival the *opera seria* in popularity. It was a propitious moment, and several of the brilliant actor-singers at their disposal (e.g. Francesco Baglioni, Francesco Carattoli, Filippo Laschi, Serafina Penni) were to carry the new repertory far and wide, repeating their Venetian successes in other cities and countries. Notable among the new operas were *Il mondo della luna* (S Moisé, 1750), *La calamità de' cuori* (S Samuele, 1752), *Il filosofo di campagna* (S Samuele, 1754) and *La diavolessa* (S Samuele, 1755), all of which, but especially *Il filosofo di campagna*, were to enjoy European fame (see Loewenberg). Goldoni's spoken comedies were then in the ascendant, and his librettos were merely lucrative by-products; yet they are cleverly wrought, treat a wide variety of subjects from the realistic to the fanciful and (unlike his plays) are always rich in scenic effects. How much their musical component reflects Galuppi's wishes it is impossible to say, but the composer is given splendid opportunities with such standard features as opening ensembles, metrically varied arias (often departing from the da capo convention), a comic vocabulary designed for musical reiteration and, above all, 'chain' finales, of which, according to Gozzi, Goldoni was 'the first inventor'. A forerunner of this highly important innovation is already present in their *L'Arcadia in Brenta*; Act 2 ends with a play within the play, most of it set to music. In succeeding librettos, the finales to the first two acts, growing out of the plots themselves, become increasingly long and eventful, and Galuppi set them as a series of separate sections contrasted in key and tempo, assigning to the orchestra the task of continuing the music amid the hectic comings and goings of the actors onstage. The importance of this new feature, which was hugely enjoyed by the public, lies in the fact that here, for the first time in opera, action, not just sentiment, was being set to music. This trend was to gain in importance in later years, affecting even *opera seria*. Act 3 normally closes with a simpler

'Il filosofo di campagna': engraving from Carlo Goldoni's 'Opere teatrali' (Venice: Zatta, 1788–95)

ensemble or chorus, but in the penultimate scene Goldoni introduces yet another convention: the duet of reconciliation between the two principals, patently a legacy from the now obsolescent intermezzo.

As early as 1749 (in *Il conte Caramella*, another Galuppi opera) Goldoni listed his characters under the headings 'seri', 'buffi' and 'mezzi caratteri', the last denoting something between 'serious' and 'comical'. He was not blazing new trails but merely codifying what doubtless was already theatrical jargon: the same categories would have been applicable to the earliest Neapolitan comic operas. And when he wrote *La buona figliuola* for the court of Parma in 1757 (the composer was Duni), he dispensed with those headings altogether. Yet the latter libretto, as reset in 1760 by Piccinni in Rome, is widely quoted by historians as marking a turning-point in the history of *opera buffa* because of its mixture of comedy with a sentimental, 'larmoyant' element. However, the opera's resounding success in Rome and throughout Europe cannot be ascribed to a formula that was in itself not at all new. Here again, a conjunction of work, place and time must be considered responsible: Piccinni undoubtedly struck just the right note in portraying the sufferings of Cecchina, the innocent heroine (played in Rome of course by a castrato); and Europe must have been ready just then to take such a heroine to its heart, having already embraced the heroines in novels (notably Richardson's *Pamela*, Cecchina's model) and in the French *comédie larmoyante*.

Despite the great success of *La buona figliuola*, Italian *opera buffa* did not develop farther along the lines of sentimentality. The sly observation of human foibles within the context of contemporary society was and remained its main business; and, precisely because of its success in this, *opera buffa* now became the dominant form, greatly reducing the role of *opera seria* everywhere. It successfully reflected the Zeitgeist and thus exerted a widespread influence, infusing with its spirit the new instrumental genres of the Classical period as well as the comedies of contemporary authors such as Goldsmith, Sheridan and Beaumarchais. Not the least of its effects was the stimulus it provided for the development of new, national forms of opera in countries other than Italy (e.g. *opéra comique*, Singspiel, zarzuela etc.).

With the rise in prestige of *opera buffa*, its history in the later 18th century becomes virtually that of opera in general and its composers. In Italy, the new composers were Anfossi, Francesco Bianchi, Cimarosa, Giuseppe Gazzaniga, P. A. Guglielmi, Paisiello and Sarti among countless others; the new librettists Giovanni Bertati, G. B. Lorenzi, Pasquale Mililotti, Giuseppe Palomba, Giuseppe Petrosellini and others, among whom Bertati stands out as a talented innovative man of the theatre. Some of the most important operas of this period were first performed in foreign capitals; for example *Il barbiere di Siviglia* (librettist unknown; 1782, St Petersburg) and *Il re Teodoro in Venezia* (G. B. Casti; 1784, Vienna); and Cimarosa's *Il matrimonio segreto* (Bertati; 1792, Vienna). Non-Italian composers, from Gassmann to Martín y Soler, became adept practitioners. It was left to one of them to crown the development of *opera buffa* in the 18th century with three enduring masterpieces. Mozart's *Le nozze di Figaro* (1786, Vienna), *Don Giovanni* (1787, Prague) and *Così fan tutte* (1790, Vienna), to librettos by Da Ponte (who, like Casti and some others, never wrote for Italy), may in some respects be regarded as characteristic of their time: their one-movement overture form and two- or four-act division, the proliferation in them of action set to music in numbers other than the finales proper, and the variety of aria forms (including the nascent cantabile-cabaletta type) were not recent inventions. In their psychological depth, dramatic timing and technical mastery, however, Mozart's Italian comic operas stand alone, dwarfing their predecessors and reducing the prior history of the genre, in the perspective of later generations, to a period of preparation for his coming.

5. THE 19TH CENTURY. In the Romantic age the importance of *opera buffa* became vastly diminished.

Here the forms are generally freer and less extended than in the serious genre and the set numbers are linked by *recitativo secco*, except in the solitary case of Donizetti's *Don Pasquale* (1843). With Rossini a standard distribution of four characters is reached: a prima donna soubrette (soprano or mezzo); a light, amorous tenor; a *basso cantante* or baritone capable of lyrical, mostly ironical expression; and a *basso buffo* whose vocal skills, largely confined to clear articulation and the ability to 'patter', must also extend to the baritone for the purposes of comic duets. The classic *opera buffa* of the early 19th century is Rossini's *Il barbiere di Siviglia* (1816, Rome), that of the Romantic age Donizetti's *L'elisir d'amore* (1832), in which the hero's silliness is tinged with pathos. Sometimes there is a second *basso buffo* and even a sub-heroine, as in Verdi's *Un giorno di regno* (1840). The last example of the genre to survive is Luigi and Federico Ricci's *Crispino e la comare* (1850), a morality which breaks with the Italian tradition by admitting an element of the supernatural (hence its description as 'opera comico-fantastica'). After 1860 *recitative secco* was dropped from comic opera and with it the title of *opera buffa*, to be replaced by *dramma comico*.

*

CroceN; LoewenbergA

M. Scherillo: *L'opera buffa napoletana durante il settecento: storia letteraria* (Naples, 1883, 2/1916)

C. Ricci: *I teatri di Bologna nei secoli XVII e XVIII: storia aneddotica* (Bologna, 1888)

T. Wiel: *I teatri musicali veneziani del settecento: catalogo delle opere in musica rappresentate nel secolo XVIII in Venezia* (Venice, 1897)

G. Ortolani and N. Mangini, eds.: *Opere complete di Carlo Goldoni edite dal Municipio di Venezia nel II centenario della nascita* (Venice, 1907–71), i, xxvii–xxxi, xxxvi–xxxvii

A. Zardo, ed.: *Gasparo Gozzi: La 'Gazzetta Veneta' per la prima volta riprodotta nella sua letteraria integrità* (Florence, 1915)

A. Della Corte: *L'opera comica italiana nel '700: studi ed appunti* (Bari, 1923)

G. Ortolani, ed.: *Tutte le opere di Carlo Goldoni* (Milan, 1935–56), i, x–xii

M. F. Robinson: *Naples and Neapolitan Opera* (Oxford, 1972)

R. L. Weaver and N. W. Weaver: *A Chronology of Music in the Florentine Theater, 1590–1750* (Detroit, 1978)

R. Strohm: *Die italienische Oper im 18. Jahrhundert* (Wilhelmshaven, 1979)

M. Murata: *Operas for the Papal Court* (Ann Arbor, 1981)

P. Weiss: 'Ancora sulle origini dell'opera comica: il linguaggio', *Studi pergolesiani/Pergolesi Studies*, i (1986), 124–48

——: 'La diffusione del repertorio operistico nell'Italia del settecento: il caso dell'opera buffa', *Civiltà teatrale e Settecento emiliano*, ed. S. Davoli (Bologna, 1986), 241–56

M. Hunter: 'Some Representations of *opera seria* in *opera buffa*', *COJ*, iii (1991), 89–108

PIERO WEISS (1–4), JULIAN BUDDEN (5)

Opera Colorado. American company founded in 1981 in DENVER.

Opera Comique. London theatre, opened in 1870 and closed in 1899; *see* LONDON, §II, 2.

Opéra-Comique. Opera company formed in Paris in 1714 through the amalgamation of various fairground troupes. It operated seasonally at the Foires St Germain and St Laurent until 1762, when it merged with the Comédie-Italienne and moved to that company's base at the Hôtel de Bourgogne. It then moved to the Salle Favart, merging again in 1801 with a rival company at the Théâtre Feydeau. It had various homes during the 19th century but was predominantly at the Favart. It

was administratively merged with the Opéra in 1939 and closed in 1972 but partly reconstituted as the Opéra-Studio. *See* PARIS, §§2(iii), 3(i), 4(iii), 5(iii) and 6(i, ii).

To distinguish between the genre (see below) and the institution, it is customary (and the practice in this dictionary) to use initial capital letters and a hyphen for the latter.

Opéra comique (Fr.). Term for a French stage work of the 18th, 19th or 20th centuries with vocal and instrumental music and spoken dialogue (though it may also include recitative). Its origins are found in the 18th-century Parisian Fair Theatres (known from about 1715 as the Opéra-Comique) and also the Comédie-Italienne (*see* PARIS, §2(iii)). The essentially popular appeal of these repertories formed the antithesis of the stately *tragédie mise en musique* and allied works at the Académie Royale de Musique (the Opéra). Soon, however, a broad range of subjects and styles was developed: *drame* and other literary and dramatic models became important. The word 'comique' should thus be broadly construed, in the spirit of Balzac's term 'la comédie humaine', or perhaps that of Shakespeare's comedies.

1. Terminology. 2. 18th-century antecedents and models. 3. From the Querelle des Bouffons to the end of the *ancien régime*. 4. From the Revolution to the Restoration (1789–1830). 5. 1830–70. 6. 1870–1918. 7. Epilogue.

1. TERMINOLOGY. The term first appears in current usage in the 18th century when, in the phrase 'opéra-comique en vaudevilles' (or similar expression), it designated stage works using pre-existing tunes and usually spoken dialogue (as in C.-S. Favart's *L'amour au village*, 1745). Sometimes modified, for example by 'en ariettes et en vaudevilles', it was extended to those works using a mixture of *timbres* (or traditional ditties) and newly composed *airs* (e.g. *La fausse aventurière*, libretto by Anseaume and Marcouville, with additional music by Laruette, 1757). At this time it rarely designated *opéras comiques* in the modern sense. (Most of the exceptions are works whose subject matter is in similar taste and style to *vaudevilles* or lighthearted *divertissements*, such as Grétry's *suite*, the third act of the *drame Le comte d'Albert*, 1786.)

In spite of inconsistencies in terminology among some theorists, critics and authors during the 1750s and 60s, the phrase COMÉDIE MÊLÉE D'ARIETTES soon became the generally accepted designation during the *ancien régime* for the majority of what are now called *opéras comiques* (there are numerous examples in the output of Duni, Monsigny, Philidor, Grétry and their contemporaries). 'Comédie' attests to the significance of certain literary norms in part judged by the standards of French spoken theatre, and 'mêlée d'ariettes' to the unique quality of the genre in which specially written music (mostly, though not exclusively, lighter *airs* for soloists was implied) had an increasingly significant role.

Other words or phrases also appear either on the title-pages of librettos and scores or in contemporary descriptions. Some point to additional literary models (as the *drame* was for the *drame lyrique*); others, to subject matter ('féerie' for fairy stories, 'chevaleresque' for knightly or pseudo-medieval tales); still others, to style or tone dominating the text and sometimes matched by the music (e.g. 'larmoyant' for sentimental comedies, made popular by Denis Diderot and Nivelle de la

Chaussée in plays, and soon adopted in lyric works). M.-J. Sedaine (1764) was not alone in protesting that 'ariettes' could not effectively describe the range of music in the new genre: 'mêlée de musique' or 'mise en musique' became alternatives.

By the Revolution, 'comédie mêlée d'ariettes' declined in usage and was restricted, in the main, to lighter, old-fashioned works. 'Opéra comique' still almost always meant 'vaudeville'. Many librettists and composers sought greater precision: they continued to borrow from spoken theatre (as in 'comédie héroïque'), modifying the phrases with 'mise en musique' or 'lyrique', as had been occasionally found before. More works were called *drames lyriques*, and the rise in the number of operas based on recent historical events resulted in a huge increase in the designation *fait historique* (particularly in 1793–4). More frequently, authors opted for the comparatively neutral 'opéra' for their works in a serious tone. Frankly comic operas, especially those influenced by *opera buffa* models, were termed *opéras bouffons*, as custom dictated.

Only with the Empire and the Restoration does 'opéra comique' appear in its modern sense – French operas with spoken dialogue – with any frequency, and even then authors were loath to apply it to their works where comic elements were less important than dramatic or melodramatic ones (for example, Méhul's *Joseph* is called an *opéra* or *drame mêlé de chants*). Castil-Blaze (1821), among others, agreed with librettists and composers and argued that the repertory of the Opéra-Comique was too varied to fall into a single category and that the term was entirely misapplied to many items performed there. Authors' continuing commitment to accurate labelling remained a feature into the 20th century, and often newly invented terms or unusual ones appear: 'roman musical', 'complainte', 'fantaisie lyrique', to cite but a few. Monsigny's *Le déserteur* (1769), Cherubini's *Médée* (1797), Gounod's *Faust* (1859), Bizet's *Carmen* (1875), Massenet's *Manon* (1884), Milhaud's *Le pauvre matelot* (1927) and many others were not called 'opéras comiques' by their librettists and composers; indeed, the use (or misuse) of the term to cover all French operas with spoken dialogue, at least those given at the Opéra-Comique, seems to date from the late 19th century (it so appears in the writings of Pougin, Clément and Larousse, and the first edition of Grove's *Dictionary*).

Finally, the French 'comédie' and 'comique', when used by librettists, composers and their contemporaries, have no precise equivalents in other languages: European traditions differ, at times substantially. Marmontel (*Encyclopédie*) defined *comédie* as 'staged mores' designed to portray the human condition and human frailties while entertaining (sentiments in part echoed in Balzac's phrase 'la comédie humaine'). Marmontel divided *comédie* into three distinct categories – 'bas', 'bourgeois' and 'noble' (or 'haut') – based not just on the rank and social position of the leading characters, but also on the tone (from the pathetic or even tear-jerker to the lighthearted) and type of humour (or absence thereof). Even so, he oversimplified the then current situation, as his own qualifications (for example, his exclusion of satire and the 'comique grossier' of the *comédie-parade*) here and in other articles in the same work indicate, and a survey of theatrical productions including works using music would support.

Furthermore, French playwrights drew on a rich heritage, sometimes centuries old. That words like 'rabelaisien' (from Rabelais, the satirical and licentious 16th-century poet) and 'marivaudage' (from Marivaux, the witty early 18th-century playwright noted for sparkling bourgeois dialogues) entered standard vocabulary, still used today – not to denote principally their own works, but rather others in similar style, or indeed situations reminiscent, however vaguely, of ones they described or might have described today – should serve as ample warning. (There are also terms for the most important figures; applied more restrictively, e.g. 'molièresque' for Molière, whom Marmontel and others took as the model for *comédie* and revered in a way similar to the English view of Shakespeare.) It is impossible to define Gallic humour in a few words. Marmontel mentioned 'malice naturelle', certainly a component, but repartee, word-play and other elements contribute as well.

Rather than the blind labelling of all French lyric works with spoken dialogue as 'opéras-comiques', a more fruitful approach to individual works is to heed the terminology of the authors and their contemporaries and, with that as a guide, to place them in appropriate theatrical, musical, literary and aesthetic traditions. In any case, 'opéra comique', as currently used, is not so much a genre (with many sub-genres) as an indication of procedure: the mixing of spoken and sung elements.

2. 18TH-CENTURY ANTECEDENTS AND MODELS. Mid-18th-century *opéra comique* drew on a rich theatrical heritage. The Fair Theatres of St Germain and St Laurent (the Opéra-Comique) offered passers-by numerous *vaudevilles* in which earthy humour and social and sometimes political critique were often intermingled. Nor were the official, prestigious theatres (the Opéra and the Comédie-Française) spared biting satirical treatment in parodies. The mixture of well-known *airs*, the audience's interpretation of the couplets (in part informed by the recollection of the original words and an appreciation of the irony resulting from a comparison with the new) and, in the spoken dialogue, witty repartee among the actors (in which improvisation had a significant role) – all contributed to the popularity of the genre. It is little wonder that many of the early librettists of *opéra comique* had extensive experience in the *vaudeville* (Favart is an excellent example), and the tradition continued well into the 19th century (in the works of Eugène Scribe and his contemporaries). Occasionally an *opéra comique en vaudevilles* was reset as a *comédie mêlée d'ariettes* (e.g. J.-P.-E. Martini's *Annette et Lubin* of 1789, based on Favart's 1762 work). A.-F. Quétant (1765) and others felt that the *vaudeville* was the major source of the *opéra comique*. But the Fair Theatres and the Comédie-Italienne provided other models in their *comédies-parades* with stock characters drawn from the *commedia dell'arte* tradition, but now with a distinctive Gallic accent (Colombine, Arlequin and company): nonetheless, slapstick remained an important ingredient.

Other successful theatrical entertainments, too, showed the way for later 18th-century authors. *Divertissements* were a frequent and popular feature of the Comédie-Italienne play repertory, though little of the music survives (except in Mouret's work). Dance forms and rhythms permeated many *vaudevilles* and *ariettes*. Molière's *comédies-ballets* often lampooned middle-class stereotypes in a way that had a lasting appeal; they not only combined vocal music, dance and dialogue effectively but also proved that verbal finesse and comedy could coexist. In fact, to separate 'opera' and 'play' into neat categories does a disservice to French theatre of the 18th century. Marivaux, the most famous Comédie-Italienne playwright of the first half of the century, provided enduring *bourgeois* characters and situations in sparkling dialogue exploited by librettists for more than 100 years. The tighter dramatic structure, the 'better' tone and other features distinguishing his works from the *vaudevilles* and *comédies-parades* influenced, among others, Favart, whom Voltaire credited with the creation of *opéras comiques* suitable for polite society (unlike the offerings of the Fair Theatres). Finally, authors at the Opéra-Comique and the Comédie-Italienne (which absorbed its Fair rival in 1762) were sensitive to the elements that contributed to favourable reactions to the repertory at the Académie Royale de Musique, particularly certain *opéras-ballets*. Though the staging and costumes could not compare with those at the *premier théâtre lyrique*, the taste for the fanciful and exotic, for an idealized *villageois* and for a display to please the eye as well as the ear was common to both.

No single genre provided the unique source for *opéra comique*. Authors drew from different parts of the French heritage in varying degrees and sometimes added to it elements from foreign theatrical traditions in plays (such as the English) and in operas (particularly the Italian *opera buffa*). But the result was truly French, and the best works had continuing popularity in Paris and a wider, European appeal.

3. FROM THE QUERELLE DES BOUFFONS TO THE END OF THE ANCIEN RÉGIME. *Opera buffa* and intermezzos had made occasional appearances in France before the mid-18th century without arousing much interest or controversy. But in 1752–4 a visiting Italian troupe's performances of Pergolesi's *La serva padrona* and other works at the Académie Royale de Musique initiated the Querelle des Bouffons, during which the merits of Italian (comic) opera and French (serious) opera were hotly debated. An ardent italophile, Rousseau nevertheless produced a charming *intermède*, *Le devin du village* (1752), French in spirit though using some *buffo* forms. In it he sought to capture village innocence in naive melodies: his strengths lie in a sensitivity to declamation, and even his lack of interest in complex harmonies and orchestral textures becomes an asset for the unsophisticated tale. Sung throughout and in the repertory of the Académie Royale, this work as well as the *opere buffe* served as a model for *comédies mêlées d'ariettes*.

The entrepreneurs of the Fair Theatres and the *sociétaires* of the Comédie-Italienne soon capitalized on the public curiosity and fondness for these works. During the 1750s *opere buffe* in French translation and sometimes with additional pieces appeared, and other works with new plots and dialogue parodied Italian models for the music. *La servante maîtresse*, Baurans' translation of Pergolesi's masterpiece at the Comédie-Italienne (1754), proved a favourite. Sedaine's *Le diable à quatre* at the Opéra-Comique (1756; for illustration *see* PARIS, fig.8) drew on pieces by several composers, including Galuppi and Duni. Newly composed scores in similar vein soon appeared. Dauvergne's *Les troqueurs* (libretto by J.-J. Vadé, Opéra-Comique, 1753), at first falsely announced as an Italian-based work for publicity purposes, is the earliest example.

By the 1760s, *comédies mêlées d'ariettes* were more than mere *opere buffe* in French. Lively spoken dialogue and constructions of scenes and acts in accordance with *comédie* principles reflected the native heritage. Audiences required excellence in acting as well as singing. From the *vaudeville* and the *divertissement*, composers inherited strophic and other simple forms for their *airs* and a vocal style often close to popular songs. Librettists (who were often also playwrights) ensured that the texts presented a variety of theatrical entertainment and kept up with the latest trends. But *opera buffa* did provide important models for more florid *airs* (generally assigned to the heroine), for conversational duets and for an occasional extended ensemble.

Three composers merit special mention. Duni, an Italian who arrived in Paris in 1757, immediately achieved a stunning success with *Le peintre amoureux de son modèle* (Opéra-Comique, libretto by Anseaume), in which he showed his assimilation of French features within a light and lyrical style. Other influential works at the Comédie-Italienne soon followed, such as the 'villageois' *Les deux chasseurs et la laitière* (Anseaume, 1763) and the 'féerie' *La fée Urgèle* (Favart, 1765). Philidor, from a long line of French musicians, also had English experience, and in *Tom Jones* (Poinsinet, 1765), based on Fielding's novel, he sought to exploit a growing anglophile trend. In it he handled duets and ensembles with dramatic and musical flair. In collaboration with Sedaine, Monsigny contributed to the variety of types – from the lighthearted *On ne s'avise jamais de tout* (Opéra-Comique, 1761) to another English-based work, *Le roi et le fermier* (Opéra-Comique, 1762), in which a benevolent monarch appears as a central character, and to the *drame lyrique*, *Le déserteur* (Comédie-Italienne, 1769), in which comedy and pathos are adroitly juxtaposed in the libretto and supported by an appropriate musical translation.

The works of Grétry at the Comédie-Italienne best represent the achievements in *comédie mêlée d'ariettes* and other operatic types of the *ancien régime*. He combined a gift for lyricism matching the declamation of the words with a fine dramatic sense and an ability to depict individual characterization musically. He experimented in matching musical forms to scenic requirements, and particularly in his later works sought more extended structures.

Marmontel's librettos often reflect a moralizing sentimental tone and exploit currently fashionable themes: the noble savage in *Le huron* (1768; Grétry's first success), intrinsic merit as more important than birth (*Lucile*, 1769), conjugal love in adversity (*Silvain*, 1770), and so on. The most popular of their collaborations was *Zémire et Azor* (1771), an ambitious *opéra féerie* in four acts. The composer responded with scores dominated by touching *airs*, but ones in which duets and ensembles played an increasingly important role in defining characters and translating their emotional states (in *Zémire* the trio of the heroine's grieving family shown to her in a magic picture is an excellent example of Grétry's artistry; see fig.1). He also continued to set more frankly comic works reminiscent of the Fair Theatres' repertory: the *comédie-parade Le tableau parlant* (Anseaume, 1769), with its witty dialogue and light *airs*, proved an enduring opera.

With the mid-1770s and 1780s came some works in a consistently serious vein, although comedies remained the core of the Comédie-Italienne's repertory. The librettist B. F. de Rosoi led the way with his patriotic

1. 'Zémire et Azor' (Grétry), Act 3 (trio in which the heroine's grieving family are shown to her in a magic 'picture'): engraving by Pierre-Charles Ingouf after a gouache by François-Robert Ingouf (c1771)

Henri IV (set by J.-P.-E. Martini, who used a military and heroic musical style to good effect, 1774) and his classical *drame*, *Les mariages samnites* (set by Grétry, 1776); significantly, neither was a popular success. A much better man of the theatre, Sedaine provided Grétry with a series of challenges in 'chevaleresque', pseudo-historical and *drame* or *drame*-influenced works, including *Aucassin et Nicolette* (1779), their masterpiece *Richard Coeur-de-lion* (1784), *Le comte d'Albert* (1786) and *Raoul Barbe-bleue* (1789). Grétry responded with scores in which some attention was given to aspects of 'local colour' or music's contribution to definition of a specific setting (such as Blondel's 'Une fièvre brûlante', in which Grétry re-created, though did not precisely imitate, a medieval tune and used it symbolically in recurring fashion at strategic moments: it even becomes the means by which the imprisoned king recognizes his faithful minstrel and makes his presence known to him). *Barbe-bleue* especially is remarkable for its time for the freedom and continuity of musical forms to underline the dramatic situations. A newcomer, Dalayrac, also made notable additions to the repertory in *Nina* (1786), on a *larmoyante* subject, and in the 'chevaleresque' *Sargines* (1788). Both composers made effective use of expansion of resources at the theatre in terms of personnel (a greater number of soloists, a newly formed chorus and a slightly larger orchestra) and of staging (with an increase in spectacle, particularly in 'chevaleresque' works). While *air*-dominated operas, true *comédies mêlées d'ariettes*, remained very popular, these works pointed the way to the next decade.

By the eve of the Revolution, operas with spoken dialogue on a wide range of subjects and in a variety of styles were the most important part of the Comédie-Italienne's repertory, so much so that Italian plays were dropped in 1780 and the proportion of new *vaudevilles* and French plays declined. The troupe enjoyed increasing aristocratic and royal patronage (particularly that of Queen Marie Antoinette) during the final two decades of the *ancien régime*. The move to a new theatre building in a better quarter (1783) was one sign that it had become accepted by polite and fashionable society: its Fair origins were scarcely mentioned. Furthermore, the export of the operatic successes to the provinces (Lyons and Bordeaux, for example) and to other European centres (Vienna and St Petersburg among them) is a measure of their extraordinary popularity.

4. FROM THE REVOLUTION TO THE RESTORATION (1789–1830). To be sure, genuinely comic or light-hearted 'villageois' works did not disappear altogether from the stage during the 1790s. Popular items from the *ancien régime* repertory (such as Grétry's *Le tableau parlant* and Monsigny's *Rose et Colas*) were still performed in Paris and elsewhere. New works relying on tested formulae, like J.-P. Solié's *Le secret* (libretto by F.-B. Hoffman, 1796), with its plot turning on mistaken identities and unfounded jealousy, were successfully given. But more often comedy was combined with and subordinated to dramatic twists and melodramatic elements, as in Le Sueur's *La caverne* (libretto by Dercy, 1793).

Still, 1789 and the early years of the Revolution brought major changes to the Comédie-Italienne (from 1793, the year French plays were dropped, called the Opéra-Comique). First, its monopoly on operas with spoken dialogue was challenged and soon disappeared. In the Théâtre de Monsieur (from 1791 the Théâtre Feydeau), founded to produce *opera buffa* in Italian and in French translation, it gained a powerful rival. This theatre introduced Parisians to major works by a later generation of Italian composers (such as Paisiello and Cimarosa), had an orchestra renowned for its precision and featured singers known for their virtuosity. For a time Cherubini was music director there and wrote additional music for several works by other composers. Noting that works with French texts proved the more popular, its directors occasionally had newly composed *comédies lyriques* and similar French works staged (such as Champein's *Le nouveau Don Quichotte*, 1789), falsely claiming them as adaptations to avoid legal prosecution. With the decree of the 'liberty of the theatres' (1791), such subterfuge was no longer necessary, and the Feydeau repertory became predominantly French. Other theatres sprang up and many put on *vaudevilles* and shorter operas. The Opéra-Comique had to compete for audiences and for authors – the more so since court patronage, of course, disappeared and some of the other rich patrons suffered (although both it and the Feydeau remained out of the reach of all but the better-off). The 1790s saw a huge increase in the number of lyric works; but few achieved lasting success. In 1801 the Feydeau and Opéra-Comique, both beset by financial troubles, merged, and in 1807 Napoleon again extended a measure of official protection by regulating the repertories of other theatres and suppressing several.

The Revolution brought changes to the repertory. 'Royalist' works (such as Grétry's *Pierre le Grand*, 1790, and his *Richard Coeur-de-lion*) disappeared after 1792 and the declaration of the Republic, and 'aristocratic' ones (such as Dalayrac's *Raoul, sire de Créqui*, 1789) were subject to revision or suppression. Topical references to recent events or political and social questions were frequent. Indeed, *faits historiques*, hurriedly written and staged, were little more than dramatic re-enactments fleshed out with appropriate additional details created by the authors; the rhetoric often mirrors that of government leaders and influential journalists. While most of these ephemeral works were by minor librettists and composers, occasionally recognized authors contributed, as did Grétry in *Callias* (libretto by Hoffman, Opéra-Comique, 1794) and Méhul in *Le pont de Lody* (libretto by E.-J.-B. Delrieu, Feydeau, 1797).

More significant musically and theatrically are sub-stantial works without such obvious propagandist in-tentions (though less direct reflections of current ideals are not infrequent). In several exceptional compositions, so far have the composers moved from the models of their predecessors one may detect in them a new spirit and even the development of style and procedures important for Romanticism (as Dean, 1967–8, and Dent, 1976, have done). Among this group, best represented in the works of Méhul, Le Sueur and Cherubini, the *comédie mêlée d'ariettes* has virtually disappeared in fact as well as in terminology. *Drame lyrique*, *comédie lyrique* and *opéra* become the most frequent designations: they were not merely semantic choices, but proof of their authors' intentions to point to aesthetic principles of French dramaturgy and the importance of models from serious *opéra* (though the heritage of the Comédie-Italienne persisted in the romances and the increasingly few comic pieces). Hitherto forbidden subjects on these stages were tackled, from classical tragedy (Cherubini's *Médée*, 1797) to incest (Méhul's *Mélidore et Phrosine*, 1794). And the general tone was heroic, at times violent.

Individual numbers, even most of the *airs*, are more substantial and have greater musical weight than those of the previous generation. Méhul's *Stratonice* (libretto by Hoffman, Comédie-Italienne, 1792), with only six pieces in one act, takes longer to perform than his pre-decessors' scores with double that number. Principles of symphonic development were exploited in often complex textures, as in the quartet from the same opera. Here and elsewhere, the orchestra is more than mere accompaniment to tuneful vocal lines: it becomes the main means of cohesion and of articulation of form. Distinctive timbres and orchestral effects are used for expressive purposes. Much of the dramatic action takes place in huge ensembles, as in Cherubini's *Lodoïska* (Fillette-Loraux, Feydeau, 1791), Le Sueur's *La caverne* and Méhul's *Ariodant* (Hoffman, Opéra-Comique, 1799). More extended harmonic vocabularies and sometimes remote modulations, too, set the works of all three apart from 1780 norms. Musical contrast (as in Grétry) becomes at times striking musical confronta-tion: contemporaries considered Méhul's jealousy duet from *Euphrosine* (Hoffman, Comédie-Italienne, 1790) particularly impressive. The chorus, often representing a picturesque group (brigands, Savoyards, monks, sailors) or even two opposing groups in conflict, take on major roles. Romantic aspects in the libretto prompted often descriptive musical responses: a violent storm in Le Sueur's *Paul et Virginie* (Dubreuil, Feydeau, 1794) and an avalanche in Cherubini's *Elisa* (Saint-Cyr, 1794). Against a more symphonic orchestral part, composers could write emotionally heightened parts for the voice where beauty of melody took second place to theatrical truth: the Countess in Méhul's *Euphrosine*, Calypso in Le Sueur's *Télémaque* (Dercy, Feydeau, 1796) and the title character in Cherubini's *Médée* are examples. All three composers experimented in making opera with

spoken dialogue a more continuous and integrated form. Among the techniques found in varying degrees were the reduction of spoken dialogue, effective employ-ment of *mélodrame*, linking of pieces, overall tonal structures to scenes, acts and sometimes entire operas, and sophisticated orchestral use of reminiscence motifs as much more than melodic tags. Cherubini's *Médée* and Le Sueur's *Télémaque*, both on librettos intended for the Opéra, reflect concern for unity, but probably the most remarkable work from this point of view is Méhul's *Mélidore et Phrosine* (A.-V. Arnault, Opéra-Comique, 1794), particularly for its third act.

Of the three, Cherubini, trained in Italian *opera seria*, *opera buffa* and church music before going to France (where he absorbed much from the Académie Royale repertory of Gluck, Sacchini and others), was technic-ally the most polished. His music, admired by Beethoven and others, has the clearest ties to these earlier tradi-tions. Le Sueur, interested in theories of imitation and Greek metres, consciously tried to put some of his principles into practice (as in his rhythmic experiments in *Télémaque*); interesting musical passages sometimes result but, lacking musical extension and development, they occasionally seem more bizarre than convincing. His new ideas fail to sustain a whole score. In his other two works, he showed greater affinity for the style and forms of the genre as defined by Grétry and his con-temporaries than his confrères. Méhul was the boldest innovator. Indebted primarily to the Gluckian tradition for his training (though not a student of Gluck), he exceeded its models even in his first opera. He invented memorable figures, matched dramatic shocks with musical ones and, in *Mélidore* and *Ariodant*, found novel formal designs and scenic constructions. But in places his scores are flawed and cliché-ridden. Some scholars, echoing Weber, see Cherubini as the leader; the chronology of composition and the individuality of approach (though with some goals and procedures in common) argue against this. All three, and some of their contemporaries (particularly Dalayrac, who continued to produce popular and influential works, such as *Léon*, libretto by Hoffman, Opéra-Comique, 1798), provided a rich heritage for later French composers and German Romantics.

Beginning with the Thermidorian reaction and more pronounced during the Consulate and Empire, audiences favoured lighter, less moralizing and dramatic fare. *Comédies-parades* again became popular (for example Méhul's *L'irato*, dedicated to that musical italophile Napoleon Bonaparte; libretto by B.-J. Marsollier des Vivetières, 1801). The Maltese composer Isouard excelled in ensemble writing in *buffo* tone and style (*Les rendez-vous bourgeois*, Hoffman, 1807, and other works). Successes among the *drame*-influenced works again included comic figures and situations with greater frequency, as in Cherubini's *Les deux journées* (J.-N. Bouilly, Feydeau, 1800). Entirely serious works, such as Méhul's biblical opera *Joseph* (A. Duval, Opéra-Comique, 1807), were more admired than popular in Paris. Boieldieu's *La dame blanche* (Scribe, after Scott, 1825), whose plot combined in a mildly Romantic brew a long lost hero, a haunted castle and buried treasure, had a tuneful score with touches of 'local colour' (such as the citation of 'Robin Adair' in the last act) and proved a long-lasting crowd pleaser. The achievements of Revolutionary opera (in orchestra-tion and structure) were not forgotten entirely (Méhul continued to experiment with the sombre middle range

2. 'La dame blanche'
(Boieldieu): Act 1 scene
vii (Dickson receives a
letter from the White
Lady) of the original
production at the Opéra-
Comique (Salle Feydeau),
Paris, 10 December 1825,
with (left to right) Jenny
(sung by Mme
Boulanger), Dickson
(sung by M. Fériol) and
George Brown (sung by
M. Ponchard)

of the orchestra, going so far as to replace the violins with violas for his Ossianic *Uthal*; J. M. B. B. de Saint-Victor, 1806), but the spirit in the majority of works – and nearly all those that stayed in the repertory – ranged from sentimental to comic: in short, more in keeping with the aesthetics of the generation of Grétry (many of whose works were revived at this time), though without a return to forms of that period.

5. 1830–70. Between the July Revolution and the Franco-Prussian war, the Opéra-Comique offered Parisians numerous new works appealing to their desire for diversion. Generally eschewing the low humour of the boulevard theatres and the often farcical or satirical situations of the *opéra bouffe*, *opéra comique* authors provided romantic tales allowing for the exploitation of 'local colour' and with happy endings – a welcome alternative to *grand opéra* – as well as 'chevaleresque' works and comedies relying on traditional situations and character types. Several composers were influenced by Rossini and demanded vocal virtuosity in the Italian style, particularly for the soprano and tenor, but these *grands airs* contrasted with sentimental romances and comic strophic songs, the French heritage. Auber (in collaboration with Scribe) was one of the most prolific and popular: *Fra Diavolo* (1830), a whimsical bandit tale, and *Le domino noir* (1837), whose setting prompted the use of Spanish dance rhythms, remained repertory items into the 20th century. Indeed, the decade of the 1830s was in some respects the golden years of 19th-century *opéra comique*. The contributions of Hérold, such as *Zampa* (Mélesville, 1831) and *Le pré aux Clercs* (Planard, 1832), and of Adam, such as *Le chalet* (Mélesville and Scribe, 1834) and *Le postillon de Lonjumeau* (de Leuven and Brunswick, 1836), held the stage in Paris and elsewhere for over 50 years.

Foreigners, too, tried their hand at *opéra comique*: the most successful example was Donizetti's *La fille du régiment* (Saint-Georges and Bayard, 1840), which remains close to *opera buffa* in forms and styles.

Meyerbeer's works for the Opéra-Comique are richer orchestrally and scenically than the norm: his *L'étoile du nord* (Scribe, 1854), a pseudo-historical drama set in the Russia of Peter the Great, demonstrates most clearly the influence of *grand opéra*, of which the composer was the acknowledged master.

Specifically French in flavour and almost an *opéra bouffe*, Massé's *Les noces de Jeannette* (Barbier and Carré, 1853) proved with its over 1500 performances in Paris alone the continuing vitality of well-known plot formulae (in this case the 'correction' of a loutish man by a practical and virtuous young woman). Better known for his operas and ballets for the Opéra, Halévy wrote also for the Opéra-Comique: among his popular works for it, *Les mousquetaires de la reine* (Saint-Georges, 1846) is a fine example of the 'chevaleresque' and sentimental. The increasing interest in the exotic is perhaps best exemplified in David's *Lalla-Roukh* (Lucas and Carré, 1862), set in Kashmir, re-created through imaginative orchestral writing. Finally, towards the end of this period there was in a few works a shift to a dominantly serious tone. In Thomas' *Mignon* (Carré and Barbier, 1866) melodic grace and gentle, chromatic harmonies match the sweet melancholy of the libretto. (Significantly, however, the original ending was still a happy one; in Germany a tragic conclusion, more faithful to Goethe, was substituted.)

The Opéra-Comique was not the only major Parisian theatre to put on opera with spoken dialogue. Though generally presenting a more conservative and traditional repertory (including revivals of Grétry and Méhul) and introducing the public to foreign works in translation and adaptation (including operas by Verdi), the Opéra-National (founded in 1847 and from 1852 called the Théâtre Lyrique) provided opportunities for French virtual operatic newcomers, such as David in *La perle du Brésil* (Gabriel and Saint-Etienne, 1851) and Bizet in *Les pêcheurs de perles* (Carré and Cormon, 1863). Furthermore, composers were allowed to experiment in more intense, almost psychological, dramas, avoiding the grandiose favoured at the Opéra and the sometimes facile humour and resolutions of the plot preferred at the Opéra-Comique. The best example is surely the original version of Gounod's *Faust* (Barbier and Carré, 1859), still among the most admired of 19th-century French works in the repertory.

In short, there was at the Opéra-Comique and the Théâtre Lyrique a wide range of subjects, an eclecticism in musical styles and forms and a willingness to adopt and adapt from other genres. Tradition dictated that acting and stage presence remained important. The costume and set designs and *mise-en-scène*, now often more elaborate than in previous generations and newly prepared for each work, were exported with the scores: all were considered essential for a faithful rendition of the authors' intentions and for the audience's satisfaction.

In 1856, Offenbach published an extensive guide to the traditions of *opéra comique* as he saw them, sending a copy to potential entrants to a competition for a one-act operetta. He saw it as a particularly French creation, distinguishable from the Italian *opera buffa*, on which it had originally been modelled, by its love of wit and mischief. He lamented the hybrid forms, leaning more towards the traditions of *grand opéra*, which had seduced several composers away from the pure traditions of *opéra comique*, which he regarded as a stream that had turned into a river and subsequently burst its banks.

Nonetheless, certain features can be considered to distinguish *opéra comique* traditions from those of *grand opéra*, apart from its convention of spoken dialogue rather than recitative. First, there was a tendency for grand spectacle at the Opéra, only rarely matched (such as in Meyerbeer's *Le pardon de Ploërmel*, staged with a real waterfall in 1859) by the Opéra-Comique. The tendency, around 1860, for the theatre to become 'a branch of the Opéra' did not pass unnoticed among the critics. Secondly, while ballet was *de rigueur* at the Opéra, it was not at the Opéra-Comique. Instead, crowd scenes involving choral writing rather than ballet leant more towards the traditions of *opéra comique*.

There were also unwritten conventions in the distribution of roles. While large-scale works at the Opéra tended to have two prominent female roles, the Opéra-Comique tended towards a lighter leading soprano role, the *soprano à roulades* rather than the *soprano falcon* (named after Cornélie Falcon, who made her début in the leading female role in *Robert le diable*). The second female role in *opéra comique* was often the *soprano dugazon* (named after the 18th-century singer Louise-Rosalie Dugazon). Light in character, but neither virtuoso nor dramatic, this voice became the norm for many a composer writing the strophic pieces with refrains (often *couplets* or *romances*) that, again, were a hallmark of *opéra comique*.

A similar preference for a lighter type of voice production was also present in the male roles, for the *ténor léger* and the *basse chantante*. These voices customarily took high notes with a lighter head voice. It was not until 1871 that a *fort-ténor* was employed at the Opéra-Comique, when a high C was sung with chest voice (an *ut de poitrine*) in Hérold's *Le pré aux Clercs*.

These four decades saw the premières of some of the most popular operas ever produced, and they remained in virtually continuous repertory in Paris and throughout the world wherever French opera was staged until World War II. Many had more than 1000 performances

at the Opéra-Comique alone and were the staples of regional theatres in Germany and Austria as well as francophone countries.

6. 1870–1918. The Théâtre Lyrique did not long survive the Franco-Prussian War. The Opéra-Comique took over part of its repertory and, to a greater extent than before, included recent foreign works (by Mascagni and Puccini, for example). The most memorable of the new operas by Frenchmen departed from the conventional mould for this theatre. In all of them comedy is minimal or entirely absent, and there were several works that included no spoken dialogue. Of these Gounod's *Roméo et Juliette* was the first, followed by Massenet's *Werther* and *La Navarraise* and Bizet's *Les pêcheurs de perles* as well as operas by Bruneau. Works performed at the Opéra-Comique were less and less frequently characterized by their composers as *opéras comiques*, and there was a return to the practice of naming each work appropriately. Thus titles such as *comédie lyrique*, *roman musical* and *conte lyrique* were used, and once and for all the link between genre and theatre was broken.

3. Poster by Prudent Leray for Bizet's 'Carmen' (showing the final scene in Act 4) printed for Choudens at the time of the original production at the Opéra-Comique (Salle Favart), Paris, in 1875

The tendency towards the seriousness of plots seemingly more suited to the Opéra had also been demonstrated with increasing frequency in the second half of the century. Bizet's *Carmen* (Meilhac and L. Halévy, 1875) caused a scandal with its 'immoral' heroine, frank sexuality and tragic conclusion when she is murdered on stage (see fig.3). Not successful at first, it soon became the best known of all French operas. The composer's effective use of *mélodrame*, memorable pieces and vivid musical characterization did more than match the drama: they created it musically. Offenbach in *Les contes d'Hoffmann* (Barbier, 1881) produced an episodic fantasy but, particularly in the Antonia act, one of great poignancy. Massenet's *Manon* (Meilhac and Gille, 1884) presents another strong and unconventional heroine who dies at the end; the score is among the most nuanced and, while the set numbers are clearly marked off, Massenet incorporated them into a more fluid whole. In *Louise*, a *roman musical* (1900), Charpentier sought social realism in a working-class setting. Debussy's *Pelléas et Mélisande* (Maeterlinck, abridged by the composer, 1902) finally demonstrated that the Opéra-Comique could rival the Opéra in terms of seriousness. Debussy wrote a complex and subtle work in which the natural quality in the setting of conversation contributes to an often ambiguous and suggestive impression. Yet its lightness of touch, fairy-tale setting and unspecific historical place perhaps accorded with the best traditions of the house and with the essential definition of *opéra comique* as a play turned into opera.

7. EPILOGUE. After World War I the Opéra-Comique remained committed to producing new works for its audience, but the genre of *opéra comique*, and its related forms of *opéra bouffe*, took on a new lease of life with the lighter touch exemplified by the neo-classicists and Les Six. Although none of Milhaud's works is named as an *opéra comique* several have a *buffo* element and *Esther de Carpentras* is categorized as an *opéra bouffe*. These trends were continued by Jacques Ibert, whose light style matched that of Milhaud and whose *Le roi d'Yvetot* he called an *opéra comique* (and it was given at the Opéra Comique).

Situation comedies and operas with a 'kitchen-sink' setting, as well as parodies of classical myths and *commedia dell'arte* subjects, also became prime material for *opéra comique* or *opéra bouffe*. Into these categories fall Roussel's *Le testament de la tante Caroline*, Barraud's *Lavinia* and Bloch's *Guignol*, along with many of the operas for which Nino wrote the librettos. Works by younger composers such as Claude Arrieu have continued these trends.

The Opéra-Comique also mounted premières of operas written for other theatres, such as Stravinsky's *The Rake's Progress* (Auden and Kallman, 1951; 1953) and Britten's *The Rape of Lucretia* (Duncan, 1946; 1971) and a few world premières of works by French composers. Among the most significant were Milhaud's *Le pauvre matelot* (Cocteau, 1927), a *complainte* set in a melodically direct style, and two works by Poulenc: *Les mamelles de Tirésias* (after Apollinaire, 1947), an *opéra bouffe* whose mordant wit caused an uproar at its première, and *La voix humaine* (Cocteau, 1959), a *tragédie lyrique* for solo soprano depicting with psychological depth a modern relationship gone sour.

But the Opéra-Comique was no longer the leader: theatres in Monte Carlo, Brussels and Geneva rivalled or surpassed it in the performance of new works (as sometimes benefited Honegger, among others). Dramatic composers preferred to write operas sung throughout or to explore new areas, such as film music or works for radio. Furthermore, the Opéra-Comique's audience dwindled for the recent operas, whatever their critical reception, to the extent that none of the post-World War I works entered the standard repertory as had those by earlier composers from Grétry to Massenet; only warhorses, such as *Mignon*, *Carmen* and *Manon*, could draw the public consistently. The dissolving of the resident troupe in 1972 marked the end of a distinguished tradition, which for over two centuries had given Paris and other cities some of the most endearing and enduring examples of music theatre. The procedures for mixing music and speech, character types, situations, stage presentations and other features developed here set important models for *opéra bouffe*, operetta and even musical comedy. The spirit of *opéra comique* (or opera with spoken dialogue) and some of the masterpieces live to this day.

*

M.-J. Sedaine: 'L'auteur au lecteur', *Rose et Colas* (Paris, 1764), [ii–iv]

A.-F. Quétant: 'Essai sur l'opéra-comique', *Le serrurier* (Paris, 1765)

A.-G. Contant d'Orville: *Histoire de l'opéra bouffon* (Amsterdam and Paris, 1768)

P.-J.-B. Nougaret: *De l'art du théâtre en général* (Paris, 1769)

Desboulmiers [J.-A. Julien]: *Histoire du Théâtre de l'Opéra Comique* (Paris, 1770)

A.-J.-B. d'Origny: *Annales du Théâtre Italien* (Paris, 1788)

J.-B. Colson: *Manuel dramatique, ou Détails essentiels sur deux cent quarante opéras comiques* (Bordeaux, 1817)

Castil-Blaze [F.-H.-J. Blaze]: 'Opéra', *Dictionnaire de musique moderne* (Paris, 1821, 2/1825)

——: *Histoire de l'Opéra Comique* (F-Po Rés. 660, autograph *c*1856)

T. Gautier: *Histoire de l'art dramatique en France* (Paris, 1858–9)

A. Thurner: *Les transformations de l'opéra-comique* (Paris, 1865)

G. Chouquet: *Histoire de la musique dramatique en France* (Paris, 1873)

F. Clément and P. Larousse: *Dictionnaire des opéras (dictionnaire lyrique)* (Paris, 1881, rev. A. Pougin, 2/1905)

A. Soubies and C. Malherbe: *Précis de l'histoire de l'Opéra-Comique* (Paris, 1887)

A. Pougin: *L'Opéra-Comique pendant la Révolution de 1788 à 1801* (Paris, 1891)

A. Soubies and C. Malherbe: *Histoire de l'Opéra-Comique: la seconde Salle Favart (1840–1887)* (Paris, 1892–3)

M. Dietz: *Geschichte des musikalischen Dramas in Frankreich während der Revolution bis zum Directorium (1787 bis 1795)* (Leipzig, 2/1893)

A. Font: *Favart, l'opéra-comique et la comédie vaudeville au XVIIe et XVIIIe siècles* (Paris, 1894)

A. Soubies: *Histoire du Théâtre-Lyrique, 1851–1870* (Paris, 1899)

G. Cucuel: *Les créateurs de l'opéra-comique français* (Paris, 1914)

E. Genest: *L'Opéra-Comique connu et inconnu* (Paris, 1925)

H. Malherbe: 'L'Opéra-Comique', *Cinquante ans de musique française de 1874 à 1925*, ed. L. Rohozinski, i (Paris, 1925), 119–97

'L'Opéra-Comique au XIXe siècle', *ReM*, no.140 (1933) [special issue with articles by H. Prunières, H. de Curzon, J. Tiersot, R. Duhamel, M. d'Ollone]

L. P. Arnoldson: *Sedaine et les musiciens de son temps* (Paris, 1934)

D. J. Grout: *The Origin of the Opéra-comique* (diss., Harvard U., 1939)

M. Cooper: *Opéra comique* (London, 1949)

——: *French Music from the Death of Berlioz to the Death of Fauré* (London, 1951)

S. Wolff: *Un demi-siècle d'Opéra-Comique (1900–1950)* (Paris, 1953)

C. D. Brenner: *The Théâtre Italien, its Repertory, 1716–1793* (Berkeley and Los Angeles, 1961)

N. Wild: 'Aspects de la musique sous la Régence: les foires [et] la naissance de l'opéra-comique', *RMFC*, v (1965), 129–41

W. Dean: 'Opera under the French Revolution', *PRMA*, xciv (1967–8), 77–96; repr. in *Essays on Opera* (Oxford, 1990), 106–22

E. Dent: *The Rise of Romantic Opera*, ed. W. Dean (Cambridge, 1976) [lectures given in 1937–8]

H. Schneider: 'Zur Gattungsgeschichte der frühen Opéra-comique', *Bayreuth 1981*, 107–16

T. J. Walsh: *Second Empire Opera: the Théâtre Lyrique, Paris, 1851–1870* (London and New York, 1981)

J. Gourret: *Histoire de l'Opéra-Comique* (Paris, 1983)

J. B. Kopp: *The 'Drame Lyrique': a Study in the Esthetics of Opéra-*

comique, 1762–1791 (diss., U. of Pennsylvania, 1982)

M. E. C. Bartlet: 'Archival sources for the Opéra-Comique and its Registres at the Bibliothèque de l'Opéra', *19th Century Music*, v (1982–3), 119–29

D. Charlton: 'Orchestra and Chorus at the Comédie-Italienne (Opéra-Comique), 1755–1789', *Slavonic and Western Music: Essays for Gerald Abraham* (Ann Arbor and Oxford, 1985), 87–108

J. Mongrédien: *La musique en France des Lumières au Romantisme, 1730–1830* (Paris, 1986)

A. Spies: *French Opera during the Belle Epoque: a Study in the Social History of Ideas* (diss., U. of North Carolina, 1986)

D. Charlton: '"L'art dramatico-musical": an Essay', *Music and Theatre: Essays in Honour of Winton Dean* (Cambridge, 1987), 229–62

D. Pistone, ed.: *Le théâtre lyrique français, 1945–1985* (Paris, 1987)

E. A. Cook: *The Operatic Ensemble in France, 1673–1775* (diss., U. of East Anglia, 1989)

S. Sadie, ed.: *History of Opera* (London, 1989) [contributions by M. Cooper, D. Charlton, W. Dean, R. Crichton]

P. Vendrix, ed.: *Grétry et l'Europe de l'opéra-comique* (Liège, 1992)

D. Charlton: 'Kein Ende der Gegensätze: Operntheorien und *opéra comique*', *Musik und Literatur: zur Theorie ihrer wechselseitigen Beziehungen*, ed. M. Walter (forthcoming)

M. ELIZABETH C. BARTLET (5–7, with RICHARD LANGHAM SMITH)

Opera Delaware. American company founded in 1945 in WILMINGTON.

Opéra du Nord. Opera association active in LILLE, Roubaix and TOURCOING, 1981–5.

Opéra du Rhin. Opera association formed in 1972 between COLMAR, MULHOUSE and STRASBOURG.

Opera Factory. Company founded by David Freeman in 1973 and resident in London from 1981; *see* LONDON, §II, 1.

Opéra féerie (Fr.). A type of French opera or *opéra-ballet* which has a plot drawn from fairy-tales and/or makes extensive use of elements of magic and the *merveilleux*. In his *ballet-héroïque Les fêtes de Polymnie* (1745), Rameau ranked the 'féerie' with history and fable as a resource for the lyric stage. A huge corpus of *opéras* (such as Monsigny's *La belle Arsène*, 1773), *opéras-ballets* (such as *Zélindor, roi des silphes* by Francoeur and Rebel, 1745) and *opéras comiques* (such as Duni's *La fée Urgèle*, 1765, and Grétry's *Zémire et Azor*, 1771) of the late Baroque and Classical periods in France attests to its popularity. While the term *opéra féerie* was uncommon in the 18th century (although it did exist, e.g. Dezède's *Alcindor*, 1787), and entered the current vocabulary only after 1800, modern scholars use it with justice to refer to these earlier works. Some early 19th-century examples employ the term (e.g. Isouard's *Cendrillon*, 1810, Catel's *Zirphile et Fleur de Myrte*, 1818, and Carafa's *La belle au bois dormant*, 1825). After this period the *féerie* survived in ballet. (For the German 19th-century fairy-tale opera, *see* MÄRCHENOPER.)

*

D. Diderot: 'Féerie', 'Merveilleux', *Encyclopédie, ou Dictionnaire raisonné des sciences, des arts et des métiers*, ed. D. Diderot and others (Paris, 1751–80)

'Fée, féerie', *Annales dramatiques, ou Dictionnaire général des théâtres*, ed. Babault (Paris, 1809)

D. J. Buch: 'Fairy-tale Literature and *Die Zauberflöte*', *AcM*, lxiv (1992), 30–49   M. ELIZABETH C. BARTLET

Opera for All. A small company formed in 1949 by the Arts Council of Great Britain to take opera to small towns and villages throughout the country which other-wise would have no opportunity of seeing live opera. It gave its first performance in September 1949 at Blaenau-Ffestiniog; initially the group consisted of four soloists, a pianist and a compère who also acted as stage manager. In its first season it visited 69 different centres, each for one night only. By 1952 it had expanded enough to give a modest stage performance of *Così fan tutte*, accompanied by a piano. By the 1966–7 season there were three Opera for All groups, each comprising 12 members; one was based at the London Opera Centre, one at Scottish Opera and one at the WNO. The increased touring commitments of the last two companies, and expanded touring by the English Opera Group and Phoenix Opera, resulted in the two regional groups being absorbed into the larger Scottish and Welsh companies as small touring ensembles with chamber orchestra. The London-based group retained the original name. Although works like *La Cenerentola*, *Le comte Ory*, *Le nozze di Figaro*, *Così fan tutte*, *La fille du régiment*, *Les contes d'Hoffmann* and *La bohème*, all tailored to the requirements of a small group touring without an orchestra and sung in English, were the mainstays of the three groups, lesser-known works, including *La jolie fille de Perth*, *Die lustigen Weiber von Windsor*, *Il turco in Italia* and *Fra Diavolo*, were included in the repertory, as well as more ambitious, large-scale operas such as *Lucia di Lammermoor*, *Faust*, *Un ballo in maschera* and *Yevgeny Onegin*. Among the artists who gained their early experience with Opera for All were Josephine Barstow, Patricia Kern, Josephine Veasey, Keith Erwen, William McAlpine and Richard Van Allan. In 1979 the company ceased to exist and was succeeded by OPERA 80, a group with similar aims but having its own orchestra.   HAROLD ROSENTHAL

Opera glasses (Fr. *jumelles (de théâtre)*, *lorgnette*; Ger. *Opernglas*; It. *binocolo*, *occhialino (da teatro)*). A small telescope with a narrow field of view, binocular from the second quarter of the 19th century, for the use of the audience in the theatre. The earliest reference to the term given in the *Oxford English Dictionary* is to Robert Smith's *Optics* (1738), where a somewhat different instrument from the one known today is described: 'There is an instrument sold in the shops which some call an Opera-glass, others a diagonal

1. Monocular opera glass: drawing (c1780) by Thomas Rowlandson

2. Binocular opera glasses in a box at the Paris Opéra: lithograph after Eugène Lami from Jules Janin, 'L'été à Paris' (Paris, 1843)

perspective; it is properly a reflecting perspective, so contrived for viewing a person in a publick place that no one can distinguish who it is you look at, even though they know the design of the instrument'. A comparable instrument, seeming 'to look to the right, yet to see partly on the right and partly on the left side', is referred to in a letter from Florence on 23 October 1721 by a writer who had seen an 'occhialino da teatro' at the home of an Englishman and was ordering it from London.

An early illustration of the use of a true opera glass in the theatre is a drawing by Thomas Rowlandson of about 1780 (Huntington Collection, *US-SM*), which shows a lady seated in a box using a single glass (fig.1). In 1784 the speaker of the epilogue of a play enters carrying a spyglass; and in 1787 Fanny Burney refers to being scrutinized through a glass by the king and queen at a performance of Thomas Holcroft's *Seduction*. Only single glasses were in use at this period, and other Rowlandson drawings depict members of the audience holding them.

That the term 'Opera Glass' was in common use early in the 19th century is shown by its adoption in 1808 as the title of Edmund Waters's exposé of 'all the curious proceedings of the King's Theatre' and between 1826 and 1848 as the title of no fewer than four theatrical and musical periodicals.

Interest in the binocular telescope, invented in 1608, was revived in the 1820s, initially in Vienna and then in Paris. In January 1833 an advertisement for the availability of opera glasses in the theatre is found in a Covent Garden playbill: glasses were 'lent in the theatre, by Mr. Hudson'. In 1843 a lady holding binoculars is depicted by Eugène Lami in his view of the interior of a box at the Paris Opéra (fig.2). From the 1860s many London theatres announced that opera glasses could be hired from the attendants, usually for one or two shil-

lings for the evening. A subsequent and widespread custom was for the glasses to be fixed to the backs of the seats, releasable by the insertion of a coin in a slot – a practice that is now becoming less common.

*

LS, v, ccxii–xix
R. Smith: *Optics* (London, 1738), 377ff
L. Lindgren: 'Musicians and Librettists in the Correspondence of Gio. Giacomo Zamboni', *RMARC*, no.24 (1991) [whole issue], esp. 39
RICHARD MACNUTT

Opera Iowa. Touring company founded in 1987 as a subsidiary of the Des Moines Metro Opera; *see* INDIANOLA.

Opera North. British company based in LEEDS, founded in 1977 as English National Opera North and renamed in 1981.

Opera of the Nobility. The name sometimes given to the London opera company active, in rivalry to Handel's company, from 1733 to 1737, initially at Lincoln's Inn Fields Theatre, later at the King's Theatre; *see* LONDON, §§I, 5 and II, 1.

Opera Pacific. American company, in COSTA MESA, California.

Opera Restor'd. English touring company. It was formed in 1985 from members of the Holme Pierrepont Opera Trust, based in Nottingham, which from 1979 mounted productions of early English operas at Holme Pierrepont Hall (Blow's *Venus and Adonis*, 1980; Pepusch's *The Death of Dido* and Arne's *Thomas and Sally*, 1981; Arne's *Comus*, 1983; Greene's *Phoebe*, 1984; *Dido and Aeneas*, Lampe's *Pyramus and Thisbe*, 1985). Under the artistic direction of Jack Edwards, and using mainly young singers, the company has taken its versatile 'pocket' presentations throughout Britain; from 1988 it gave its larger productions, including *La serva padrona* (Pergolesi) and *The Ephesian Matron* (Dibdin) at the South Bank, London, and elsewhere. The harpsichordist Peter Holman is musical director and Robin Linklater design director. In 1989 the company, which had no direct grant or sponsorship, began to receive the assets of the former company Opera da Camera (*see* LONDON, §II, 1).

Opera semiseria (It.: 'half-serious opera'). An intermediate genre first identified during the early 19th century. The term was originally applied mainly to Italian equivalents of the French post-revolutionary 'pièce de sauvetage' such as Paer's *Camilla* (1799) or Simon Mayr's *Le due giornate* (1801), sometimes labelled 'drammi eroicocomici'. Later it was extended to comedies, akin to the French *comédie larmoyante*, that contain a strong element of pathos, such as Rossini's *La Cenerentola* (1817). The range of characters is generally wider than in *opera buffa*, but the same types prevail, the *basso buffo* being often more dangerous than his purely comic counterpart (as in *La gazza ladra*, 1817). During the Romantic period *opera semiseria* usually has a pastoral setting, its heroine being a village maiden whose innocence, at first called into question, is finally vindicated amid general rejoicing. A classic instance is Donizetti's *Linda di Chamounix* (1842). To the same category belongs *Il furioso all'isola di San Domingo* (1832), whose hero is restored to sanity by the reappearance of the woman whom he believed to have deserted him. Bellini's *La sonnambula* (1831) has all the attributes of the genre except the *basso buffo*; hence its description as a 'melodramma' *tout court*. Opera *semiseria* shares with *opera buffa* the tradition of 'recitativo secco'. A late example is Mercadante's *Violetta* (1853). Thereafter the term lapses, but it is noteworthy that in 19th-century Italian revivals Mozart's *Don Giovanni* (1787) was frequently described as an *opera semiseria*.

*

E. Masi: 'Giovanni de Gamerra e i drammi lagrimosi', *Sulla storia del teatro nel secolo XVIII* (Florence, 1891), 28–354
M. Ruhnke: 'Opera semiseria und dramma eroicomico', *AnMc*, no.21 (1982), 263–74　　　　　　　　　　JULIAN BUDDEN

Opera seria (It: 'serious opera'). A term used to signify Italian opera on a heroic or tragic subject during the 18th and 19th centuries. It was rarely used at the time. It can sometimes be found on manuscript scores, particularly in the last quarter of the 18th century, but 'dramma per musica' is the usual genre description on most 18th-century and many early 19th-century printed librettos. 'Opera seria' begins to appear on librettos late in the century, but infrequently, for example for Prati's *Armida abbandonata* (1785, Munich). Only as serious opera of this period came to be viewed historically was the term 'opera seria' applied exclusively to it (particularly to that part of it in which the librettos of Metastasio dominated the stage). So completely had the literary, dramatic and musical principles of Metastasian opera been rejected, forgotten or misunderstood by that time, the late 19th century, that the distinguishing attributes tended to be set forth in a negative way: *opera seria* was static and entirely predictable, dramatically and musically; its only interest had lain in music, not in drama; both dramaturgy and musical style had remained virtually the same from generation to generation; during the 18th century *opera buffa* had overtaken it in public interest, frequency of performance and prestige; Gluck's 'reform' had redeemed it from its deficiencies; and Mozart and other non-Italians had regressed whenever they approached it.

1. Dramaturgy. 2. 1720–40. 3. 1740–70. 4. 1770–1800.

1 DRAMATURGY. 1.　The characteristics of *opera seria* took shape during the first two decades of the 18th century as part of a literary reform led by the Arcadian Academy of Rome established in 1690. Responding to French criticism of Italian poetry and drama, the reformers looked with particular disfavour on the undisciplined, irrational and often licentious opera librettos then in use. They took steps to bring the libretto into accord with the principles of classical Greek drama as set forth in Aristotle's *Poetics* and as exemplified in the 17th-century French neo-classical dramatists, JEAN RACINE and PIERRE CORNEILLE.

To what extent the Aristotelian UNITIES of action, time and place needed to apply continued as a matter for debate, but by the end of the first decade of the 18th century a number of practices had been established as desirable. The action should be limited to a single, central argument involving no more than eight characters, whose entrances and exits were strictly regulated so that the stage was never empty except during set changes and between acts. The action should take place within a short period of time, preferably 24 hours, and in locations of close proximity.

The rules of verisimilitude and good taste rejected the tragic endings of classical literature as unworthy of the civilized state now enjoyed. Poets were expected to portray what, according to an orderly moral system, should have happened rather than what actually did happen. Death, if unavoidable, should be handled with dignity, and preferably off stage. Suicides and deaths in battle could be tolerated but murder could not. Subject matter taken from ancient history was to be preferred to fables or myths. Spectacle should be confined to natural phenomena and human activity. Resolutions should occur through natural means, not through supernatural intervention (in contrast with French opera). Trips to the underworld were to be banished, along with all but an occasional ceremonial chorus. Ballet and the coarse, unseemly behaviour endemic to comic scenes were to be relegated to entr'actes (or intermezzos) unrelated to the serious drama.

Poets were admonished to strive for simplicity, naturalness, verisimilitude and dignity, and to instruct as well as to entertain. The end result should be of high enough literary quality to be enjoyed as literature. No attempt was made to alter the established theatrical format. The action moved forward in *versi sciolti* (freely alternating, unrhymed seven- and eleven-syllable lines) to be realized in spare, continuo-accompanied recitative, broken from time to time with moments of reflection, reaction or summation, in strophic verse, to be realized in da capo arias accompanied by strings, possibly with horns and oboes (occasionally flutes). The reform produced librettos with a greatly expanded number of *versi sciolti* and a decrease in the number of arias to no more than 30. Theatres, in turn, persistently reduced the amount of recitative to a minimum, indicating cuts in the *versi sciolti* by enclosing them in *virgole* or quotation marks in the printed libretto: the original text might thus be read in full, though only those lines essential to the understanding of the plot might survive in the setting. Operas in three acts persisted, unaffected by attempts to follow the French pattern of five acts, each closing with a chorus. Ensembles were restricted to one per opera, usually a duet for the principal couple, and only an occasional ceremonial chorus might supplement the traditional closing tutti (*coro*) for all the characters at the end of Act 3.

By the end of the first decade of the 18th century the 'exit aria' had become firmly established as the norm. This meant that arias were always placed at the ends of scenes, after which the singer would leave the stage. Occasionally a cavatina (a short aria without exit) would appear at the beginning or in the course of a scene in which the same singer would later perform a full-length exit aria. In an *opera seria* libretto the scene as a block of text with a stable number of characters on stage was strictly observed. As soon as someone arrived or left, a new scene began. There were two common deviations from this procedure: the 'poi' construction and the 'vuol partire'. In the 'poi' construction ('Cleonice, e poi Barsene'), a new character (Barsene) joins those already on stage (Cleonice) early in the scene. In the 'vuol partire' construction, a character starts to leave following an aria but is prevented from doing so. As the century went on and arias became longer and fewer, one or more characters (usually those playing secondary roles) might exit without an aria or leave with a character who had just completed one.

At the next level of organization in an *opera seria* libretto, a set of scenes is terminated either by a change of stage setting or by the end of an act. There is normally one set change in the middle of each act. The number of characters on stage tends to increase towards the centre of each set of scenes and then to decrease to the point where one character is left on stage to sing a monologue and aria. Only Act 3 ends with everyone on stage, to celebrate the happy conclusion. The second stage setting in each act tends to be a public scene with many extras and perhaps some spectacle – often a public ceremony or a military procession. By about 1750 the emphasis began to shift from the middle to the end of each act, which then becomes the province of the principals, whether in solo, duet or trio.

Librettists usually served as poets for a specific court or theatre, where they often remained for their entire careers; their duties included the revising of existing librettos and the writing of new ones to suit local requirements. Composers took similar permanent positions as *maestro di cappella* for a theatre or court; their duties included making revivals of their own operas and those of others as well as composing new operas, always designed to enhance the strengths and to conceal the weaknesses of the singers assembled for the season. They directed performances while providing continuo realizations from the harpsichord. Haydn's operatic activities at Eszterháza conformed to just such a position. Many composers depended on church-affiliated posts for their livelihood and contracted with individual theatres to compose one or more operas per year; such composers were expected to travel to each theatre in time to become acquainted with the singers and to write their arias and ensembles (recitatives might be written in advance of arrival; the opening sinfonia was often the last component to be written). Whereas the same setting of an *opera buffa* might be performed at 20 different theatres, an *opera seria* setting was usually performed only once; for subsequent performances, the libretto was usually heavily revised, and would either be set afresh or would acquire new or borrowed arias, thus moving towards a PASTICCIO. Such borrowed arias were often the favourites of the singers, who carried them from theatre to theatre. In most theatres, pasticcios were used to round out the season, though in theatres of modest means, and in London, they predominated.

By the middle of the century the concentration of musical interest in the aria and the practice of tailoring roles to suit individual performers gave extraordinary power and control to singers. A complex set of rules maintained a strict hierarchy of rank, regulated the distribution of arias and determined their characteristics. At the pinnacle of the profession were to be found the best of the castratos – an aberration inherited from the previous century and fostered in order to maintain the treble voice in both ecclesiastic and secular situations where women were prohibited from participating: in Rome and Lisbon, for example, male singers and dancers specialized in impersonating women in the theatre. A castrato played the leading man (primo uomo or primo musico); he and the first woman (prima donna), male or female, usually formed the principal romantic couple. The number of arias per opera had been further reduced to about 20; the principal couple would have four or five each. Duets were virtually the exclusive province of this pair. The tenor, usually a patriarchal or ruling figure, might be either first or second ranking; he might join the principal couple in a trio. The second ranking couple had three or four arias each. Advisers and confidants, characters of third rank,

would have no more than one or two each. Existing librettos were often revised to ensure that the least of this group sang the 'sorbet' aria (*aria di sorbetto*), at the beginning of Act 2, when sorbet was served and the clinking of spoons on glass is said to have obscured what was happening on stage. As the total number of arias decreased, the number assigned to individuals of each rank decreased proportionally. Ensembles might be counted as arias, as might sizable monologues. Each role required arias in a variety of affections or styles (*aria cantabile, aria d'affetto, aria di bravura, aria di mezzo carattere*). A character with a dominant musical personality would have at least one aria in contrasting style. Arias in the same style or key could not follow one another. The loose textual relationship between an aria and the preceding scene made it easy for a singer to substitute a favoured aria or aria text as long as the affection was appropriate.

Meeting both the strict literary requirements and the unyielding theatrical conventions presented the librettist with a formidable task. Often little remains of a historical plot once the librettist has altered events to avoid offence while at the same time inventing enough political and amorous intrigue to provide excuses for 25 arias, properly distributed among six singers, and placed strategically in the plot to allow each character reasonable exits. Critics agreed that the two who came closest to realizing the ideal were Apostolo Zeno and Pietro Trapassi, known as Metastasio.

Zeno, greatest of the first generation 'reform' librettists, took little interest in how his librettos were translated into musical productions. An appointment to the Vienna court late in his career afforded him at last the luxury of writing librettos without the love interest and intrigue that theatres and patrons required in Italy. Metastasio, on the other hand, inherited the reform libretto much as it was to remain for the rest of the century. The remarkable success of his librettos resulted from a number of factors. First and foremost they embodied Enlightenment ideals, portraying characters able to overcome selfish human desires in order to achieve greatness in thought and deed in a world where monarch and subject alike must adhere to the highest of moral principles. In their universality his messages remained apolitical and so posed no threat to the nobility who supported the theatre in most Italian centres. Secondly, Metastasio was greatly admired for his rational approach to the libretto, for the purity, elegance, clarity and dignity of his texts, and for the skill and artistry with which he was able to breathe realism and drama into the confining form that he had inherited and went on to perfect. A third and equally important aspect of Metastasio's librettos was their supreme suitability for musical setting. Metastasio had begun his career under the tutelage of the venerable soprano Marianna Benti-Bugarelli, called 'La Romanina', and during his early career had worked closely with the young composer Vinci, whom 18th-century critics and historians consistently cited as among the originators of the modern or *galant* style in opera. The librettos Metastasio wrote for Vinci during the 1720s endured for 75 years, were set and reset by composers of several generations, and became the ideal against which all subsequent works were measured. The association ended with the death of Vinci and the appointment of Metastasio to replace Zeno in Vienna, where he remained. Though Metastasio continued to experiment in his own librettos, by the middle of the century his

Artaserse of 1730 had become a rigid model that theatre poets followed in reworking librettos (Metastasio's as well as others') for local presentation. Thus the genre and the dramaturgy it represents came to be called, rightly or wrongly, Metastasian.

The format of the reform libretto endured in no small part because it produced an evening of entertainment that served the social functions of the theatre. The opera house in 18th-century Italy was an important social meeting place. The fashionable part of the audience, who customarily owned boxes or rented them by the season, attended night after night. Since the season consisted of a few works, each given a continuous run of up to several dozen performances, the audience could scarcely have been expected to take a close interest in the stage action after the first few; and since the literate part of it knew Metastasio's dramas virtually by heart, they could dip in and out at will, interrupting the flow of social intercourse to attend to the most affecting scenes or the favourite arias of the leading singers. From this resulted the audience's noisiness and inattention, so often remarked by foreign visitors.

2. 1720–40. Although *opera seria* acquired its definitive literary and dramatic form only during the 1720s, many of its musical characteristics were present earlier. Alessandro Scarlatti had led in the development of aria forms and by simplifying his accompaniments, thus placing greater emphasis on the melodic line. But he continued to intermix many arias in the older style. The transition is evident from a comparison between *Ciro* (1712) and *Griselda* (1721). In the former, minor-mode arias with rapidly changing harmonies predominate, and the binary key scheme that was to underlie the *A* sections of the later da capo aria still had only a weak hold in the major-mode arias (*see* ARIA). In the latter, the old style co-exists with a newer type characterized by static bass lines and slower harmonic change.

Excluding Handel, whose operas, written for London, lie outside the Italian tradition and had little or no influence, the dominating figures of the first age were Vinci, Leo, Porpora, Hasse and Pergolesi, who followed Scarlatti (if indeed the older of them did not teach him) in pursuing the new, more clearly articulated melodic style. Their style was perceived as a departure, at the time and long afterwards; its success carried their music not only all over Italy but also throughout Europe. Vinci was credited with a major role in forming the new style, especially as regards periodic melody, with balanced (often three-bar) phrases. His settings of Metastasio for Naples, from *Didone abbandonata* for Carnival 1726 to *Artaserse*, completed shortly before his death in 1730, proved epoch-making. The dimensions of his arias were modest, compared with what came later, and in perfect harmony with Metastasio's mellifluous verses. Algarotti praised the last act of *Didone* for its wealth of obbligato (or orchestrally accompanied) recitative including the final lament, and recommended it as worthy of emulation (*see* RECITATIVE).

Hasse, who set *Artaserse* for Venice during the 1730 Carnival, when Vinci's was composed for Rome, invites comparison with Vinci. Hasse was then the more adventurous, in his use of ritornellos, his fondness for subdominant harmonies and his accompaniments, which struck contemporary listeners as richer (though he rarely departed from the prevailing three-part texture). Although best known for his limpid cantabile, Hasse was also a born dramatist. His inserted scene for

Artabanus to end Act 2 of *Artaserse* raised the expressiveness of orchestral commentary to new potency in the obbligato recitative.

Pergolesi's setting of Metastasio's *L'olimpiade* (1735) is the Arcadian opera *par excellence*. The passionate aria 'Se cerca, se dice', which also illustrates his mastery of periodic phrase structure, long remained popular, while the degree of lyric intensity that Pergolesi attained in the love duet at the end of Act 1 was as consequential for its genre as his much better-known successes in the comic style. Dent, contrasting Leo's *L'olimpiade* (1737) with Pergolesi's, found Leo's textures more solid and old-fashioned and his melodies, while well constructed and remarkably free of *fioritura*, lacking the tuneful charm and theatrical sense of Pergolesi's.

For these composers, the primary problem in putting together an opera of 25 or more arias was that of contrast. Metastasio's fine control and subtle variety of moods helped solve it. Departures on the composer's part, such as the omission of a ritornello, as well as the singer's improvised decorations, accomplished still more. Instrumental colour remained fairly uniform and minimal. Metric variety was limited. Expressive harmonic nuance was used sparingly and restricted to Neapolitan 6ths, augmented 6ths, diminished 7ths, deceptive moves, modulation and modal contrast. Tonal planning consisted of the choosing of keys to suit the affections of the arias. The recitative that connected them moved towards the flat side or into the minor mode for tender emotions or 'negative' events and towards the sharp side for 'positive' events or aggressive actions. The keys used rarely went beyond three accidentals. As a result several arias were likely to share the more popular ones (such as D major for bravura, D minor for rage, Eb for pathetic affects, G minor for lyrical yearning, G major for pastoral tone, A major for amorous sentiment, etc.). D major remained the overwhelming favourite for the opening sinfonia and the closing *coro*. Characters tended to acquire either a sharp- or flat-dominated personality and even occasionally a predominant tonal reference, but always with one aria in a contrasting tonality. In observing the rules dictating that affections must alternate between successive arias, composers often wrote arias alternately in sharp and flat keys; some composers also seem concerned with establishing close key relationships among arias within a set of scenes or at major articulations, such as the beginning and ending of an act or a group of scenes. Symbolic relationships of a tritone or a semitone may be found, and the composer may also set up moves in one direction or the other (towards the sharp or flat side) within groups of scenes or acts. Last-minute revisions, transpositions and substitutions may obscure such planning, which also tends to disappear in later revivals, especially when additions and substitutions are made. In spite of whatever tonal planning the composer might have had in mind, the stark stylistic contrast between aria and recitative tends to produce the impression of a loose stringing together of individual numbers rather than an organic unity; efforts in achieving the latter were made only slowly and fitfully.

3. 1740–70. The second age of *opera seria* was dominated by Hasse, Jommelli, Galuppi, Traetta, G. F. de Majo, Perez, Terradellas and J. C. Bach, most of them Neapolitan or Neapolitan-orientated. The careers of Gluck and Graun ran parallel with it. Several of the most important composers worked outside Italy, and

1. *Interior of the Teatro Regio, Turin, during a performance of Feo's opera seria 'Arsace': painting (1740) by Pietro Domenico Olivero*

this period was marked by the diffusion of *opera seria* and its associated styles throughout Europe. Hasse carried the perfected form to Germany in the 1730s and was long *maestro di cappella* at Dresden. In 1737 the great castrato Farinelli, Metastasio's adopted brother, entered the employment of the Spanish court in Madrid, where he directed Italian *opera seria* until his retirement in 1759. In 1749 Jommelli and Galuppi, at turning-points in their careers, were called to Vienna; Majo and Traetta were later called to both Vienna and Mannheim. Perez moved to Lisbon in 1752 and Jommelli began his long reign at Stuttgart in 1754. During the 1760s in Mannheim, the Italian librettist Mattia Verazi provided innovatory librettos for a succession of guest composers. In France, at the middle of the century, an Italian *buffo* troupe inspired the QUERELLE DES BOUFFONS and paved the way for the eventual arrival in Paris of Gluck, Piccinni and others, who established an international style in the French *tragédie lyrique* during the 1770s and 80s.

Metastasian librettos quickly gained popularity and dominated the Italian repertory during the 1750s. Thereafter the works of younger librettists, reworkings of earlier librettos, and a growing interest in comic opera gradually eroded this monopoly. Opera continued to consist of a succession of simple or continuo-accompanied recitatives and orchestrally accompanied arias. The action moved forward in *recitativo semplice* (simple recitative), composed in a spare, narrow-ranging, declamatory style with a basso continuo made up of a harpsichord, cello and violone providing one or two harmonies per bar. Usually no more than one or two select solo scenes or speeches leading to an aria or ensemble would be set in *recitativo obbligato* (obbligato recitative), where strings enhance the drama by provi-

ding expressive ritornellos and obbligato motivic commentary in vocal caesuras. To heighten the effect of solemn pronouncements, the strings might play sustained harmonies, a style known as *accompagnato* or accompanied recitative. Occasionally a composer provided recitative with a measured accompaniment in aria style. Jommelli, a commanding figure in *opera seria* at the middle of the century, was among the first to exploit the heightened dramatic intensity inherent in orchestrally accompanied recitative. As early as the 1740s, before his foreign visits, he was transforming *opera seria* through the use of such recitative and through the introduction of declamatory elements into the arias, the exploration of orchestral sonorities (including four-part textures) and the development of the crescendo and other dynamic contrasts.

Ensembles became more frequent, contributing to a decrease in the number of arias; they might replace the last few scenes and arias in an act, where the characters were reflecting on the action, singing arias and leaving one at a time. When Galuppi, perhaps the only composer of this period as gifted, as prolific and as widely recognized as Hasse and Jommelli, set *Artaserse* for Vienna (1749), the last five scenes of Act 1 were collapsed into a single quartet, a dramatic action piece in F minor, the first of a new breed; in the 1760s only Jommelli in Stuttgart and Galuppi in Venice regularly concluded Act 1 and Act 2 with ensembles, a duet and a trio (occasionally a quartet). When *Artaserse* was given at the opening of the new opera house at Padua in 1751, Galuppi scrapped his quartet and restored the arias. He may have been unwilling to chance such a departure with the Italian public; more probably, the singers would not tolerate an ensemble in place of their arias. The well-regulated and varied operatic theatre that

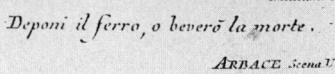

2. 'Artaserse': opening of Act 3 scene i from the 'Opere' of Pietro Metastasio (Venice: Zatta, 1781–3) with (left) an engraving of the final scene

Algarotti sought to promote was much more likely to be realized, as he noted, in the great authoritarian capitals – the court-sponsored theatres of Berlin, Dresden, Vienna, Paris and St Petersburg – than in the mainly civic enterprises of the Italian towns or London.

Efforts began in 1755, with Jommelli and Verazi's French-inspired *Enea nel Lazio* and *Pelope*, for Stuttgart, to escape from the rigidity of the Arcadian reform libretto, by blurring the lines between recitative and aria (with obbligato recitative and the infusion of the aria with declamatory elements and action), by circumventing the exit-aria convention with cavatinas and by reintroducing to opera long-banished spectacular elements. These works, based on mythological subject matter involving deities, superimpose supernatural appearances, machine spectacle, chorus and pantomime on an italianate format. In 1759 Traetta, in Parma, became involved in quite another approach, that of setting Italian translations by C. I. Frugoni of two reworked French operas by Rameau, as *Ippolito ed Aricia* and *I Tindaridi*. Despite the much-heralded breakthrough they supposedly represented, the results were similar: Italian aria opera on mythological subject matter with choruses, programmatic orchestral music and spectacle. *Ippolito ed Aricia* (possibly adjusted by Holzbauer) was performed in Mannheim the same year. In 1762 Traetta was invited to collaborate with Verazi on *Sofonisba*. Here can be found the earliest of his efforts to challenge Italian formal and dramaturgical conventions: the tragic ending (Sophonisba dies after drinking from a poisoned cup) is a flagrant departure from the laws of verisimilitude; pantomime ballet invades the programmatic overture as well as the opera itself; extensive obbligato recitative and declamatory elements in the arias blur the normally stark demarca-

tions between the two. Finally, Verazi invented for Traetta a trio of diminishing forces which, like the ending of an *opera seria* act, closes with a single character on stage.

In Vienna, the francophile Count Durazzo had engaged Gluck to produce French comic operas in the Italian taste in 1758. As early as 1760, Hasse's *festa teatrale Alcide al bivio*, showed some French influence. Traetta was invited to Vienna in 1761 to write a short, French-inspired serious piece, *Armida*, which closely follows Quinault's libretto for Lully (1686). An *azione teatrale* in 20 scenes, it carries the *divertissements* for chorus, dance and pantomime found in the original. Gluck's celebrated *Orfeo*, a similar piece, followed in 1762. Spectacular elements as well as the suspension of the exit aria convention are not uncommon in the *azione teatrale* and do not constitute the same deviation from conventional practice that they would if appearing in a full-length *opera seria*. In 1763 Traetta wrote the first such opera for Vienna on a text by Coltellini, *Ifigenia in Tauride*. Coltellini's libretto is based on classical subject matter and focusses on a single action, but the work still largely adheres to the formal and musical conventions of *opera seria*. Its principal departures take the form of several scene complexes (single scenes encompassing a multiplicity of set pieces, usually cavatinas, choruses and dance, without the disruption of an exit aria), a duet with chorus and a duet for Iphigenia and her confidante. The French-inspired scene complex stands at odds with Italian practice, which dictated that exits must follow all ensembles and most arias, and that choruses and ensembles must be kept to a minimum. Furthermore, composers frequently set scene complexes in orchestrally accompanied recitative, whereas in Italian opera before 1790 orchestrally accompanied recitative was still invariably reserved for emotional solo scenes and seldom accompanied action. In Mannheim, Verazi responded with his own *Ifigenia in Tauride* libretto the following year. Here the emphasis is on spectacle – shipwrecks, battles, gladiatorial games, magnificent ceremonies and processions. (Guillard borrowed his programmatic sinfonia for Gluck's Paris opera on the same subject.) Formally, Verazi too builds great scene complexes; but most challenging to Italian formal tradition are the multiple ensembles – a quartet, two duets and two trios that slim down to duets and then solos. Majo responded with through-composed arias and ensembles, elaborate choruses and programmatic orchestral music. Gluck's *Alceste* had its première in Vienna in 1767, and in Stuttgart the next year Verazi and Jommelli produced their most radical collaboration, *Fetonte*. In *Fetonte* the multiple ensembles of diminishing personnel, the choruses and the great scene complexes cut the exit arias to less than half the usual number. As in *Alceste*, neither the exit aria nor the simple continuo-accompanied recitative has entirely disappeared, but the restoration of death and tragedy, chorus, ensemble and pantomime to the stage as well as the formal innovations look forward 20 years.

Gluck's unique contribution in *Orfeo* and the principal implications inherent in his reform efforts as they impinge on the history of *opera seria* lie in his attempts to erase the harsh lines of demarcation between action (recitative) and reflection (aria) and to create a musical and dramatic unity from diverse components of chorus, air, ballet, ensemble – a 'scene complex' that encompasses the entire work. Secondly, he maintained a heightened dramatic intensity by confining the action to a single central argument taken from classical Greek sources. Calzabigi's libretto for Gluck's *Alceste* is *sui generis*: it is neither a translation of a French opera nor an Italian opera with French elements. There are no secondary characters, and there is no attempt to provide scenes with arias for the third-ranking ones (except for Ismene's sorbet aria at the beginning of Act 2). As a result the number of arias is greatly reduced, and various choruses step to the forefront, becoming characters in the drama and bringing the first and third acts to a close. The classical subject matter and the superimposed, divinely achieved happy ending betray its French origins and the remnants of simple recitative and the occasional exit aria point to two of the strongest and most persistent of Italian practices. The fluidity of its scene complexes and its great stretches of orchestrally accompanied recitative remain a bold challenge to formal and musical conventions in *opera seria* for the rest of the century.

4. 1770–1800. About 1770 a stylistic break was apparent on several levels, one that condemned most of the mid-century composers to rapid oblivion. The last works of Hasse and Jommelli, composed for Italy in the early 1770s, were not particularly successful, and Galuppi wrote his last serious opera in 1772, 12 years before he died. Traetta spent most of his years after

3. Design by Galli-Bibiena (probably Giuseppe) for Act 1 of a production of 'Didone abbandonata', possibly Berlin, 1753

4. Design by Fabrizio Galliari for the final scene of Act 3 in the original production of Giuseppe Colla's 'Didone' at the Teatro Regio, Turin, Carnival 1773

1770 in St Petersburg. The major figures replacing them were Piccinni, Sarti, Sacchini, Anfossi, Salieri, Paisiello and Cimarosa, and among non-Italians J. G. Naumann, Haydn and Mozart. There was some overlapping of generations: Piccinni managed to modify his style and to stay active into the last decade of the century, including a successful sojourn in Paris, where he was placed in competition with Gluck. Near the end of his life he made yet a second transition to the new Venetian style in his *Ercole al Termedonte* (1793, Naples). These composers were melodists in a more modern style, using a greater variety of aria forms including a new popular favourite, the expressive RONDÒ (a two-tempo aria, slow–fast). Paisiello appears to have been a leading figure in the establishment of the new style. His broad, simple melodic lines and longer periods took centre stage, while accompaniment styles carried over entire sections with little change and seldom stepped out of the role of beat-keeping repeated notes or arpeggiation except to insert brief obbligato motif 'comments' during vocal caesuras. Orchestras had become larger, making the contrast between segments for full orchestra and the thin string accompaniments maintained during the vocal sections even greater than before. Great crescendos of thickening texture and quickening rhythmic motion combined with expansive displays of vocal *fioritura* to articulate major sections.

During the 1770s da capo and dal segno aria forms quickly disappeared in favour of various types of through-composed ternary, binary and rondo forms that shared characteristics with instrumental sonata and concerto forms. By the 1780s, most operas showed a combination of very long arias, some based on three strophes of poetry, with very short ones often based on only one strophe. The climactic arias for the principal roles usually took the form of the rondò. Only the newly fashionable minuet retained the da capo form. The number of arias per opera continued to decline, from about 15 during the 1780s to fewer than ten in the 1790s. The third act often had only one or two scenes and sometimes disappeared completely. Ensembles took

the place of the solo scenes and arias at the ends of Acts 1 and 2. Ceasing to take the prevailing aria forms, these were through-composed, usually with one or more tempo changes moving from slow to fast. During the 1780s, the final *coro* began to expand to include soloists. These as well as the ensemble finale gradually began to fluctuate in personnel and to incorporate action. After 1785, finales that function in the same way as those of comic opera appeared in *opera seria* in all the major musical centres. The extensive action finales in Paisiello's *Pirro* (De Gamerra; 1787) were neither the first (they had earlier appeared in operas to libretto by Verazi) nor the only ones to be composed that year, though they were certainly new to the Italian operatic mainstream, as De Gamerra claimed in his preface. Paisiello's espousal of the form undoubtedly contributed to its increased appearance in the last years of the decade. In the mid-1790s action ensembles moved to the interiors of acts when the scene complex became the preferred closing construction. During the 1780s scenes realized in obbligato recitative became more common and covered longer spans of time. They also became quite elaborate, involving wind instruments, and combining obbligato commentary during vocal caesuras with *accompagnato* chords or tremolo during the vocal declamation, and occasionally moving into measured style or cavatina; often they were the ravings of a character insane with fear and dreadful imaginings. They remained introspective solo scenes for the principals until the late 1780s, when they began to encompass action.

Metastasio's librettos still provided a substantial proportion of the repertory, enduring the usual cuts in recitatives and arias, the substitution of new texts, the addition of a scene for the sorbet aria, the condensing of act endings into ensembles, the omission of choruses, and the combining of the second and third acts into one. As the number of arias shrank, the number of exits without aria increased, giving rise to many compound exits at the conclusion of an aria and the practice of having the remaining character deliver a short speech before an aria-less exit. Among the steady supply of new librettos, a goodly number originated in French librettos and plays. The several dozen 'Armida' librettos of the 1770s and 80s, however, divide into two groups, one from French sources and the other from Italian. The French-inspired group originated from operas either by Migliavacca for Traetta (1761, Venice) or Coltellini for Giuseppe Scarlatti (1766, Vienna), both based on Quinault's libretto for Lully. The Italian, from which Haydn took the libretto for his *opera seria*, represented a composite of two operas of 1770 – Jommelli's *Armida abbandonata* (De Rogatis) for Naples and Manfredini's *Armida* (Durandi) for Turin; both contain additional extracts from Tasso's *Gerusalemme liberata*. Those after Migliavacca or Coltellini carry the hallmarks of French-inspired italianate opera – ballet, chorus and scene complexes – while the Italian group produced traditional *opera seria* with a lavish overlay of spectacle and a multiplicity of approaches to the problems of an evil enchantress as heroine and the consequent unhappy ending.

In 1778 Verazi was called back to Italy from Mannheim to produce four spectacle operas for the opening of La Scala, Milan. The goals that led him to the development of his *drammi in azioni*, as articulated in the prefaces to these librettos, differ little from those set forth by Calzabigi and Gluck in their preface (1769) to *Alceste*. Verazi advocates the use of instruments in the recitative to interpret the words and to blur the sharp lines between recitative and aria; the tightening of the action by eliminating long, sententious and moralizing speeches; the use of the overture as dramatic argument; and 'heartfelt language, strong passions, interesting situations and endlessly varied spectacle'. His approach shares some means with that of Gluck and Calzabigi – spectacle, ballet, chorus and scene complexes connected by obbligato recitative. But the differences are pronounced. In Verazi's librettos the secondary characters and complex intrigues remain. Rather than attempt to re-create an aura of antique tragedy with a French-inspired *deus ex machina* to soften the unhappy ending, Verazi amplifies the spectacular, the terrifying and the horrific in his plots and ignores the laws that proscribed death on stage and unhappy endings. Verazi's innovations, unlike Calzabigi's, had had no exposure outside Germany. The first of the new La Scala works, Salieri's *Europa riconosciuta*, inspired a storm of outraged protest. In the last two operas Verazi was forced to relinquish all spectacular elements, chorus and dance, and to restore the exit aria without disruptive dramatic action. Apparently the Italians were willing to tolerate the multiple ensembles, the introductions and finales, and in Anfossi's *Cleopatra* the unhappy ending with two staged deaths. After 1785 these and other of his innovations gradually gained acceptance – single sex duets, arias and ensembles with interjections from others (*pertichini*) in solo, ensemble or chorus (possibly yet another borrowing from French opera), the integration of chorus and dance into the action, multiple scene complexes, and the abrogation of many of the rules pertaining to the hierarchy of singers, including a suspension of the exit-aria convention.

The 1780s were a decade of experimentation and innovation. Actual change in the make-up of the theatrical repertory came gradually, and most operas remained solidly based in traditional practices and precepts that harked back to the Arcadian reform. These did not truly begin to give way until the 1790s. Not surprisingly, among the most widely performed operas of the decade were settings of *Medonte*, to the innovatory librettist De Gamerra's most conservative libretto, and of Giovannini's *Giulio Sabino*, which was performed more widely and more frequently than any other *opera seria* setting in the history of the genre (see fig.5). Sarti's masterly settings of these librettos undoubtedly contributed greatly to their success. His *Giulio Sabino* (1781, Venice) shows how composers and librettists, when writing for the Italian public, continued to rely mainly on the aria and on principles originating in the Arcadian reform. There is no chorus; ensembles are restricted to a duet at the end of Act 1, a trio at the end of Act 2 and the traditional *coro* of soloists to end the opera. Most of the dialogue remains in simple recitative, although Sarti makes good use of obbligato recitative. Each singer has one full aria in Act 1 and one in Act 2; the keys do not go beyond three accidentals, and little large-scale tonal planning is evident. Most of the arias are in binary form and some are quite short. Multi-tempo arias with a stringendo effect occur several times, following the fashionable rondò; as was usual, Sarti allows rondòs only for the primary characters, here the prima donna and primo uomo, reserving the primo uomo's for the penultimate scene, where it forms the dramatic and musical climax and turns into a short *presto* duet.

Verazi's radical innovations were not the only factors pushing Italian theatres towards change. Coltellini's French-inspired librettos received new settings for Italian theatres in the 1780s and Bertoni reset Calzabigi's *Orfeo* for Venice. Gluck's *Alceste* was performed without the usual revisions and substitutions, as an integral unit. Their multiple scene complexes, ballets and choruses remain anomalies until the 1790s, though the increasing attraction of the 'merveilleux' of French-style subjects was evident even in conservative Naples in such works as Cimarosa's *Oreste* (1783) and Paisiello's *Fedra* (1788). Turin, close neighbour to Stuttgart and Mannheim, borrowed the man- and nature-inspired spectacle but not the attendant dramaturgical innovations, a tendency observed throughout the repertory of the 1780s. Paisiello returned from St Petersburg to compose *opere serie* incorporating action ensemble finales (*Pirro*) and French spectacle (*Fedra*). He also brought a Metastasian text infused with scene complexes (*Nitteti*), which was quickly adopted by others. Marmontel's *Les Incas* offered the exotic Peruvian setting for Moretti's *Idalide* and Foppa's *Alonso e Cora*. Voltaire's tragedy *Sémiramis*, Noverre's bloodstained ballets and Alfieri's equally bloody tragedies impelled the Italians towards the restoration of tragedy and death to the stage.

Several composers working with innovatory librettists in the 1780s escaped the notice of contemporary critics and commentators. Among this number is Bianchi, who became associated with Sertor, the earliest of the innovatory Venetian librettists. When most composers were producing large quantities of *opera buffa* and only an occasional *opera seria*, Bianchi specialized in *opera seria* and was the first to set several of Sertor's librettos. Among them was the first of a number of 'morte' operas, *La morte di Giulio Cesare* (1788), a work also distinctive for the active role of the chorus as a participant in the drama. Bianchi's *Alonso e Cora* (1786), also a pioneering work, was the product of a collaboration with Foppa, another innovatory Venetian librettist probably ten years younger than Sertor. Here

5. 'Giulio Sabino'
(Giuseppe Sarti): Act 2
scene x, from the first
edition of the full score
(Vienna, c1781)

the extensive opening chorus, the many cavatinas of one, two and even three strophes, and the scene complexes incorporating cavatinas, ensembles, chorus and dance that conclude Act 1 and Act 3 served to reduce the number of exit arias from about 14 or 15 to only 11. Angelo Tarchi worked with the innovatory Milanese librettist Moretti before the latter was called to St Petersburg. Their landmark opera *Il conte di Saldagna* (1787) treats a subject from medieval history in which the hero dies by design of an unrepentant ruler on stage during a celebration of his marriage. In applying French-inspired elements to plots based on human affairs rather than mythology, this opera and Bianchi's *Alonso* took a giant step beyond the innovators of the past and opened the door to Romantic opera of the 19th century. Prati's setting of Giovannini's libretto *La vendetta di Nino* (1786, Florence) contained the first staging of a parricide in more than a hundred years and initiated a vogue for ghost scenes. Prati was called to Munich in 1785 to set Sertor's relatively conservative *Armida* – another French-inspired *opera seria* there, in the tradition of Mozart's *Idomeneo* (1781) and Holzbauer's *Tancredi* (1783). He later travelled to Vienna to remount *Nino* as part of Leopold II's efforts to reintroduce *opera seria* to audiences there in the 1790s.

Thus the way was paved for a group of Venetian librettists led by Sertor, Foppa and Sografi to break away from singer-dominated Arcadian reform dramaturgy and to begin providing operas with a rich variety of newly available dramatic and spectacular options. Their activities may account for the increase in the output of *opera seria* in the 1790s, especially in Venice where production nearly doubled. Choruses, ballet, introductions, finales, ensembles (including single-sex duets, trios and quartets), cavatinas and scene complexes reduced the number of to arias below ten. Arias, ensembles and obbligato recitatives increasingly carried the action. Arias often included interjections by other characters or incorporated chorus, and ensembles frequently fluctuated in personnel. Action ensembles began appearing within acts when divertimento-like scene complexes became the favoured act ending.

Divertimentos within the opera itself succeeded in absorbing the ballet, which as entr'actes had threatened to engulf the parent genre a decade earlier. Sografi led the way towards the development of an entirely new concept of operatic dramaturgy moving freely among textual options in such fluid constructions that by the mid-1790s most operas no longer fitted the traditional definition of *opera seria*. At the same time subject matter came increasingly from more recent history and from contemporary literature. The plot for Andreozzi's and Giordani's *Ines de Castro* (1793, Florence and Venice, respectively) was taken from medieval Portuguese history, and Trento's *Bianca de' Rossi* (1797, Venice) was a contemporary tragedy in which Bianca buries herself in her dead husband's tomb. These developments coincided with the social and political turmoil caused in Italy by the French Revolution, culminating in the French invasion of 1796 and engendering an egalitarian climate in which Arcadian idealism and the dramaturgy it spawned seemed increasingly obsolete. Under these conditions the most persistent of all the *opera seria* conventions – the exit aria and the hierarchy of singers – gave way, hastening the demise of 'aria' opera and its attendant excesses. In the newly established Italian republics, rulers were no longer free of vice nor immune to violent ends. In the conclusion of Nasolini's *Merope* (Zeno's libretto reworked by Botturini, 1796, Venice), the dead monarch, victim of his own son's treachery, lies unnoticed during the victory celebrations. At the same time the principal composers of the preceding period – Cimarosa, Sarti, Paisiello and Guglielmi – were replaced by a group of new composers, including Nasolini, Zingarelli, Mayr, Paer, Portugal and Generali.

*

BurneyH; *CroceN*; *FlorimoN*

B. Marcello: *Il teatro alla moda* (Venice, c1720; abridged Eng. trans. in O. Strunk, ed.: *Source Readings in Music History*, New York, 1950)

P. F. Tosi: *Opinioni de' cantori antichi e moderni* (Bologna, 1723; Eng. trans., 1742, 2/1743, as *Observations on the Florid Song*)

L. Riccoboni: *Réflexions historiques et critiques sur les différens théâtres de l'Europe* (Paris, 1738; Eng. trans., 1741)

F. S. Quadrio: *Della storia e della ragione d'ogni poesia* (Bologna and Milan, 1739–52)

F. Algarotti: *Saggio sopra l'opera in musica* (Bologna, 1755; Eng. trans., 1767)

Lettre sur le méchanisme de l'opéra italien (Naples and Paris, 1756)

G. Ortes: *Riflessioni sopra i drammi per musica* (Venice, 1757)

A. Planelli: *Dell'opera in musica* (Naples, 1772)

A. Eximeno y Pujades: *Dell'origine e delle regole della musica* (Rome, 1774)

A. Goudar: *Le brigandage de la musique italienne* (Venice, 1777)

A. M. Beloselsky: *De la musique en Italie* (The Hague, 1778)

S. Arteaga: *Le rivoluzioni del teatro musicale italiano dalla sua origine fino al presente* (Bologna, 1783–8, enlarged 2/1785)

C. Goldoni: *Mémoires* (Paris, 1787; Eng. trans., 1814)

J. Brown: *Letters upon the Poetry and Music of the Italian Opera* (London, 1789, 2/1791)

C. Burney: *Memoirs of the Life and Writings of the Abate Metastasio* (London, 1796)

C. de Brosses: *Lettres historiques et critiques sur l'Italie* (Paris, 1799) [written 1739–40]

Stendhal: *Lettres … sur le célèbre compositeur Haydn: suivies d'une vie de Mozart et considérations sur Métastase* (Paris, 1814, 2/1817, as *Vies de Haydn, de Mozart et de Métastase*; Eng. trans., 1972)

V. Lee [V. Paget]: *Studies of the Eighteenth Century in Italy* (London, 1880, 2/1907)

T. Wiel: *I teatri musicali veneziani del settecento* (Venice, 1897)

E. J. Dent: *Alessandro Scarlatti: his Life and Works* (London, 1905, rev. F. Walker, 2/1960)

H. Abert: *Niccolo Jommelli als Opernkomponist* (Halle, 1908)

E. J. Dent: 'Ensembles and Finales in 18th Century Italian Opera', *SIMG*, xi (1909–10), 543–9, xii (1910–11) 112–38

——: 'Italian Opera in the Eighteenth Century, and its Influence on the Music of the Classical Period', *SIMG*, xiv (1912–13), 500

E. Bücken: *Der heroische Stil in der Oper* (Leipzig, 1924)

R. Gerber: *Der Operntypus Johann Adolf Hasses und seine textlichen Grundlage* (Leipzig, 1925)

R. Giazotto: *Poesia melodrammatica e pensiero critico nel settecento* (Milan, 1952)

A. Yorke-Long: *Music at Court: Four Eighteenth-Century Studies* (London, 1954)

N. Burt: 'Opera in Arcadia', *MQ*, xli (1955), 145–70

E. O. D. Downes: 'The Neapolitan Tradition in Opera', *IMSCR, viii New York 1961*, i, 277–84

H. Hucke: 'Die Neapolitanische Tradition in der Oper', *IMSCR, viii New York 1961*, i, 253–77

M. F. Robinson: 'The Aria in Opera Seria, 1725–1780', *PRMA*, lxxxviii (1961–2), 31–43

W. Binni: *L'Arcadia e il Metastasio* (Florence, 1963)

W. Vetter: 'Italienische Opernkomponisten um Georg Christoph Wagenseil', *Festschrift Friedrich Blume* (Kassel, 1963), 363–74

D. Heartz: 'Opera and the Periodization of 18th-century Music', *IMSCR, x Ljubljana 1967*, 160–68

W. Dean: *Handel and the Opera Seria* (Berkeley, 1969)

L. Bianconi: 'Die pastorale Szene in Metastasios "Olimpiade"', *GfMKB, Bonn 1970*, 185–91

E. Surian: *A Checklist of Writings on 18th Century French and Italian Opera (excluding Mozart)* (Hackensack, NJ, 1970)

J. Rushton: 'The Theory and Practice of Piccinnisme', *PRMA*, xcviii (1971–2), 31–46

M. F. Robinson: *Naples and Neapolitan Opera* (Oxford, 1972)

D. Heartz: 'Hasse, Galuppi and Metastasio', *Venezia e il melodramma nel settecento: Venice 1973*, 309–39

R. Strohm: *Italienische Opernarien des frühen Settecento*, *AnMc*, no.16 (1976) [whole issue]

F. Degrada: *L'opera a Napoli nel settecento* (Turin, 1977)

R. Strohm: *Die italienische Oper im 18. Jahrhundert* (Wilhelms-haven, 1979)

M. P. McClymonds: *Niccolò Jommelli: the Last Years* (Ann Arbor, 1980)

——: 'Haydn and his Italian Contemporaries: *Armida abbandonata*', *Joseph Haydn: Vienna 1982*, 325–32

D. Neville, ed.: 'Crosscurrents and the Mainstream of Italian Serious Opera, 1730–1790: a Symposium', *Studies in Music from the University of Western Ontario*, vii (1982) [incl. D. Heartz: 'Traetta in Vienna: *Armida* (1761) and *Ifigenia in Tauride* (1763)', 65–88; M. P. McClymonds: 'Mattia Verazi and the Opera at Mannheim, Stuttgart and Ludwigsburg', 99–136; M. F. Robinson: 'The Ancient and the Modern: a Comparison of Metastasio and Calzabigi', 137–47]

E. Weimer: *Opera Seria and the Evolution of Classical Style* (Ann Arbor, 1984)

R. Wiesend: *Studien zur Opera Seria von Baldassare Galuppi* (Tutzing, 1984)

M. P. McClymonds: 'Mozart's *La clemenza di Tito* and Opera Seria in Florence in the 1780s as a Reflection of Leopold II's Musical Taste', *MJb 1984–5*, 61–70

T. Bauman: 'Alessandro Pepoli's Renewal of the Tragedia per Musica', *I vicini di Mozart: Venice 1987*, 211–20

M. P. McClymonds: 'The Venetian Role in the Transformation of Italian Opera Seria during the 1790s', *I vicini di Mozart: Venice 1987*, 221–40

——: '*La morte di Semiramide, ossia La vendetta di Nino* and the Restoration of Death and Tragedy to the Italian Operatic Stage in the 1780s and 90s', *IMSCR, xiv Bologna 1987*, iii, 285–92

C. Questa: *Semiramide redenta* (Urbino, 1989)

D. Heartz: *Mozart Operas*, ed. T. Bauman (Berkeley, 1990)

J. Joly: *Dagli Elisi all'inferno* (Florence, 1990)

MARITA P. McCLYMONDS (with DANIEL HEARTZ)

Opera South. American company, in JACKSON, Mississippi.

Opera-torneo [*torneamento*] (It.: 'opera-tourney'; Fr. *tournoi*; Ger. *T(o)urnierspiel*). A tournament with music in an operatic style. Derived from the *abbattimento* and other Renaissance spectacles, it was cultivated mainly in the 17th century at the ducal courts of northern Italy and in Paris, Vienna and Munich. It was usually presented by squadrons of horsemen, but some tourneys were performed by individuals and some on foot. No real combat was involved, but there was normally a plot and a stylized contest between such allegorical or symbolical characters as the seasons (*La gara delle quattro stagioni*, 1652, Modena), the elements (A. Bertali and J. H. Schmelzer's *La contesa dell'aria e dell'acqua*, 1667, Vienna) or Childhood, Adolescence and Youth (*I trionfi di virtuosa bellezza*, 1668, Munich). The introduction and conclusion to the spectacle were sung to music in an operatic style, while the contest itself and any preliminary or closing parade or display were accompanied by dance music, often on trumpets and drums; little of the music appears to survive.

Such entertainments were frequently prompted by royal birthdays or weddings and were occasions for lavish pageantry and feasting. The emphasis on spectacle and stylization increased as the century progressed, heightening the similarities between the tourney and the equestrian ballet ('balletto a cavallo') and carousel ('carosello').

COLIN TIMMS

Opera 80. Opera company, founded by the Arts Council of Great Britain in 1980; it succeeded OPERA FOR ALL. One of the most active touring companies in the country, Opera 80 has undertaken two national tours each year, visiting 25 theatres over a period of 18 weeks. All productions are in English and are fully staged with an orchestra of 30 players. Independent performances have been given at Sadler's Wells, Bath Festival and in France. In addition, the company works in a wide range of settings, including schools and hospices. Repertory has included operas by Mozart, Verdi and Britten. In June 1992 the company adopted a new name, English Touring Opera.

Operetta (It. diminutive of 'opera'; Fr. *opérette*; Ger. *Operette*; Sp. *opereta*). A light opera with spoken dialogue, songs and dances. Emphasizing music rich in melody and based on 19th-century operatic styles, the form flourished during the second half of the 19th century and the first half of the 20th. During the 20th century it evolved into, and was largely superseded by, the MUSICAL. The term 'operetta' has also commonly been applied in a more general way to describe other works that are short, or otherwise less ambitious, derivatives of opera.

1. Nature and development. 2. France. 3. Central Europe. 4. Britain and the USA. 5. The modern scene.

1. NATURE AND DEVELOPMENT. As a specific artistic form, what we now regard as operetta evolved in Paris in the 1850s as an antidote to the increasingly serious and ambitious pretensions of the *opéra comique* and *vaudeville*. It was to fill this gap that various attempts were made to establish a home for short, lighthearted operatic-style works. The particular success of Jacques Offenbach and his company at the Théâtre des Bouffes-Parisiens, offering programmes of two or three satirical one-act sketches, was such that it led to the extension of the format into works of a whole evening's duration and to the establishment of *opéra bouffe* as a separately identifiable form of full-length entertainment.

The success of Offenbach's works was not confined to France, and indeed their popularity in other countries led to the development of national styles. In keeping with historical precedent, the term *opérette* had been used by Offenbach only for his one-act works, his full-length works customarily being *opéras bouffes*. It was with the evolution of the *Operette* in Vienna during the 1870s that the term first became applied to full-length works. When English-language works were produced, the terms customarily used were 'comic opera' or 'comedy opera'; it is only in retrospect that the term 'operetta' has come to be applied to all national schools.

In Austria the importation of the 'Waltz King' Johann Strauss into the theatre from the ballroom provided Viennese operetta with a composer to rival Offenbach. Strauss also provided the particular Austrian style – romantic rather than satirical and with a strong dependence on dance rhythms, especially the waltz. Meanwhile a counterpart had emerged in Spain with the revival of the ZARZUELA (i), at first owing much to that country's Italian operatic traditions but later developing an essentially Spanish national style. The English-language counterpart, most notably the 'comic operas' of Gilbert and Sullivan, owed much to the British theatrical traditions of ballad opera and burlesque and even something to the Victorian choral tradition.

As a popular form of entertainment, the operetta reflected contemporary taste in the nature of its plots and moral attitudes as well as in topical references. As the predominant form of popular musical theatre of its time, it attracted composers, librettists, performers, managers, directors and designers. The importance of its dialogue made it even more dependent than opera upon a strong libretto. Some of its major successes involved recognized comic playwrights such as Henri Meilhac and Ludovic Halévy in France and W. S. Gilbert in Britain. Many of the most successful and enduring of 19th-century Viennese operettas also had librettos adapted from French originals, which again were often by Meilhac and Halévy. Specialist performers developed who could combine singing with acting (and perhaps dancing) ability. Although composers such as Bizet, Chabrier and Delibes tried their hand at operetta in its early years, the most successful were generally specialists in such lighter forms.

By the 1880s and 90s the expansion of the form from its one-act origins had brought it to a point where it occupied much the same position as the *opéra comique* of 40 or 50 years earlier. With the passing of many of the major practitioners of operetta and the periodic quest for change that typifies the popular musical theatre, the 1890s saw an interest in bringing the genre up to date. Elements of the contemporary variety theatre were increasingly incorporated, a trend that evolved particularly in London under the designation 'musical comedy' or 'musical play' and in Berlin with the 'revue-operetta'. Where previously the logical development of the story had been of particular importance, the significance of displays of female glamour, fashionable dress and elaborately staged routines became greater. At the same time, Spain was developing along a more nationalistic path with the evolution of the *género chico*, celebrating Madrid low-life.

At least until World War I the operetta, along with the early musical comedies, retained much of its traditional grounding in 19th-century light operatic styles. Indeed it enjoyed a powerful renaissance as a new school of more sensuous Viennese operettas, exemplified by Lehár's *Die lustige Witwe* (1905), gave the genre its most glittering international success. Lehár himself continued to maintain high standards of musicianship, rooted in a European classical musical training, so that he could aspire to write for the opera house while Puccini (in *La rondine*) aimed to write operetta in the manner of Lehár.

Yet after World War I, and increasingly during the 1920s, the works of Messager, Hahn and Lehár that conspicuously sought to maintain classical operetta standards were becoming the exceptions in a popular theatrical scene increasingly dominated by song-and-dance musical comedy based on American vaudeville and dance-band song styles, seeking relief from the escapist, Ruritanian operetta world of dukes and princesses. As more substantial American musicals became fashionable in the wake of *Show Boat* (1927), they embraced many of the musical traditions of operetta, but the nature of their plots and their integration of words and music were very different. To all intents and purposes the era of the classical operetta ended before World War II, though in Europe the term has continued to be attached to works that evoke European traditions.

There remains no clearly defined and universally agreed dividing line between operetta and the musical, and different lines of demarcation are drawn depending upon nationality, individual taste and prejudice. Such works as *South Pacific*, *My Fair Lady*, *West Side Story*, *Fiddler on the Roof* and *Sweeney Todd* have been seen as a modern continuation of operetta (Bordman 1981). However, for all the undoubted operetta characteristics to be found in them, they are more precisely musicals, and their structures, production techniques and audience appeal are significantly different from those of the classical operetta.

2. FRANCE. Although it was not until the mid-1850s that what is now regarded as operetta began to emerge as a separately identifiable genre, works that would today be classified as such were already in existence. Adolphe Adam's *Le chalet* (1834) and *La poupée de Nuremberg* (1852), Massé's *Les noces de Jeannette* (1853) and Offenbach's *Pépito* (1853) had scores far more operatic in form than the collections of songs provided for

1. *Interior of the Théâtre des Bouffes-Parisiens, Paris, during a performance of Offenbach's 'Le mari à la porte': cover of a piano arrangement of the overture (Paris: Heugel, 1859)*

vaudevilles but were nonetheless lighter and more modest than the works increasingly being accepted by the Théâtre de l'Opéra-Comique.

Adam himself had opened an Opéra-National in 1847, though the venture proved short-lived. More successful was Hervé's Théâtre des Folies-Nouvelles, opened in 1854 as the Théâtre des Folies-Concertantes. However, it was with the opening of Offenbach's Théâtre des Bouffes-Parisiens during the Paris Exhibition year of 1855 that these foundations were firmly built upon (see fig.1). The works of Offenbach's repertory were initially little more than satirical sketches with just a few musical numbers, as in *Les deux aveugles* (1855). However, the improbable plots and the wit and sparkle of the productions, composed not always by Offenbach himself but also by such men as Adam, Emile Jonas and Delibes, made them the rage of Paris. Within a couple of years Offenbach was able to tour not only in France but abroad.

With a small theatre licensed initially for only three or four stage performers, Offenbach's early *opéras bouffes* or *opérettes* remained for some time necessarily modest one-act pieces, satirical or farcical in tone, used musical scores of up to eight numbers (solos, duets, trios and quartets) and were accompanied by an orchestra of up to 16 players. The relaxation of restrictions on the number of stage performers permitted him, in 1858, to put on his first two-act *opéra bouffe*, the mythological satire *Orphée aux enfers*, which added enormously to his reputation at home and abroad and provided operetta with its first enduring masterpiece.

Although Offenbach continued to produce one-act works, the pattern for the future was set by the sequence of longer works that included, most particularly, *La belle Hélène* (1864), *Barbe-bleue* (1866), *La vie parisienne* (1866), *La Grande-Duchesse de Gérolstein* (1867; see fig.2) and *La Périchole* (1868). All had light-hearted and witty books by Meilhac and Halévy, satirizing the Paris of Napoléon III. They call for a full cast, chorus, orchestra of up to 30 musicians, and scores comprising some 20 to 30 musical numbers including fully developed opening numbers and finales. By the end of the 1860s the French *opéra bouffe* had grown into a fully fledged genre with characteristics that firmly distinguished it not only from contemporary vaudeville but also, in its satirical wit and popular appeal, from *opéra comique*.

After the civil war of 1869–70 and the demise of the Second Empire, Offenbach's popularity began to wane. The French public came to prefer a more romantic form of entertainment and they found it in such works as Charles Lecocq's *La fille de Madame Angot* (1872), Robert Planquette's *Les cloches de Corneville* (1877), Louis Varney's *Les mousquetaires au couvent* (1880) and Edmond Audran's *La mascotte* (1880). Other successful composers of the time were Léon Vasseur, Paul Lacome and Gaston Serpette, while Hervé, having been Offenbach's principal competitor during the 1860s, finally achieved his most lasting success with *Mam'zelle Nitouche* (1883).

A trend towards a more fragile kind of musical score was exemplified by the *opérettes-vaudevilles* of Victor Roger, for example in his *Les vingt-huit jours de Clairette* (1892). Grace and refinement allied to classical musical standards were brought to French operetta by André Messager. His *Véronique* (1898), together with Louis Ganne's rousing *Les saltimbanques* (1899), ensured that at the turn of the century French operetta could still be ranked as a worthy successor to the old *opéra comique*.

2. *'La Grande-Duchesse de Gérolstein' (Offenbach), scene from Act 1 of the original production at the Théâtre des Variétés, Paris, 12 April 1867: engraving from 'L'univers illustré' (27 April 1867)*

During the 20th century French operetta progressively lost ground in international terms to Anglo-American musical plays on the one hand and Viennese operetta on the other. Messager continued to uphold French musical standards as late as 1928 in *Coups de roulis*, and another cultured musician who combined a more modern style with traditional *opéra comique* standards was Reynaldo Hahn in *Ciboulette* (1923). Increasingly, however, French operetta could be typified by such works as Henri Christiné's *Phi-Phi* (1918) and Maurice Yvain's *Ta bouche* (1922), which owed more to the French music-hall *chanson* than to operatic traditions. Since World War II the name of operetta has been kept alive by the *opérette à grand spectacle* exemplified by Vincent Scotto's *Violettes impériales* (1948) and a series of works by Francis Lopez that began with *La belle de Cadix* (1945); these have retained the operetta's taste for escapist stories, exotic locations, spectacle and effects, but any substantial contact with the operatic format of the classical operetta is scarcely to be found.

3. CENTRAL EUROPE. During the late 1850s Viennese theatres began staging Offenbach's *opéras bouffes*, at times in pirated versions, but often under the composer's own direction. These in turn inspired one-act comic and satirical operettas in similar style from locally active composers, of whom the most notable was Franz von Suppé, whose *Das Pensionat* (1860) is generally reckoned the first Viennese operetta, and his mythological satire *Die schöne Galathee* (1865) the most successful of its one-act successors.

Offenbach's virtual monopoly of larger-scale productions remained unchallenged in Vienna until Johann Strauss was recruited from the dance hall. In 1871 the Theater an der Wien staged his first operetta, the three-act *Indigo und die vierzig Räuber*, which introduced the distinctively Viennese operetta style, with more exotic settings, romantic rather than satirical stories, and scores built around dance forms, especially the waltz. Strauss's *Die Fledermaus* (1874), based on a play by Meilhac and Halévy, became the most widely celebrated of all operettas. His gift for melody and atmospheric writing was also well demonstrated by *Eine Nacht in Venedig* (1883), though he lacked the greater theatrical flair of Suppé and Carl Millöcker. Suppé's greatest full-length successes came with *Fatinitza* (1876) and *Boccaccio* (1879) and Millöcker's with *Der Bettelstudent* (1882) and *Gasparone* (1884). All five of these successes of the years 1877–84 had librettos by F. Zell and Richard Genée, in some cases based on French sources.

Thereafter Johann Strauss demonstrated ambitions to move towards full-scale opera, most notably in *Der Zigeunerbaron* (1885). The major operetta successes of the 1890s came from composers who favoured a more relaxed, more charming and insinuating style – especially Carl Zeller (*Der Vogelhändler*, 1891, and *Der Obersteiger*, 1894) and Richard Heuberger (*Der Opernball*, 1898). In the early 20th century, Viennese taste showed signs of succumbing to the musical-comedy style. However, the classical operetta found a new lease of life when Franz Lehár perfected his technically assured, sensuous musical style in *Die lustige Witwe* (1905). It achieved the most wide-ranging contemporary success of any operetta and was followed by a string of similar works, including Lehár's own *Der Graf von Luxemburg* (1909), Oscar Straus's *Ein Walzertraum* (1907) and Leo Fall's *Die Dollarprinzessin* (1907).

Before World War I temporarily restricted the central European international currency of operetta, these three composers had been joined in the forefront of the Viennese school by Emmerich Kálmán, who fused the Viennese waltz style with an intensely rhythmic Hungarian sound, most notably in *Die Csárdásfürstin* (1915). Kálmán's contribution highlighted an extension of operetta's field of play, for he had begun his career in a burgeoning Hungarian school of operetta that embraced essentially nationalistic works such as Pongrác Kacsóh's *János vitéz* (1904) as well as Viennese-style works such as Viktor Jacobi's *Sybill* (1914). The taste for Lehár also struck an especial chord in Italy, later inspiring native Italian works such as Virgilio Ranzato's *I paesi dei campanelli* (1923).

After the war Vienna saw other notable premières, including Kálmán's *Gräfin Mariza* (1924) and Edmund Eysler's *Die gold'ne Meisterin* (1927). However, shifts in the political and popular musical balance had by now moved the centre of German operetta to Berlin.

Since the 1860s Germany had produced its own operetta composers in such men as August Conradi, Rudolf Dellinger and Herman Zumpe, but it was with works such as Paul Lincke's one-act 'spectacular burlesque-fantasy operetta' *Frau Luna* (1899) that a recognizably different Berlin school of operetta emerged. During the early years of the 20th century the Berlin revue-operetta continued to flourish through the works of Lincke, Victor Holländer and Walter Kollo. Jean Gilbert's *Die keusche Susanne* (1910) conformed more to the currently popular 'musical play' style, while Léon Jessel's *Schwarzwaldmädel* (1917) was a score of considerable substance and appeal that conformed more to older operetta standards.

The considerable international success of *Der Vetter aus Dingsda* (1921) then helped to establish Eduard Künneke as the leading German composer of the 1920s and 30s. The shift of the centre of German-language operetta production in the 1920s also saw Berlin witness the premières of works of Viennese composers, such as Fall's *Madame Pompadour* (1922), a major success for Fritzi Massary, and Lehár's *Der Zarewitsch* (1927) and *Das Land des Lächelns* (1929), with Richard Tauber. By now the German operetta formula provided less for an integrated set of characters than a series of operatic-style solos and duets for the leading soprano and tenor, interspersed with comic duets for a *buffo* and soubrette and supported by choral contribution. Moreover, in Lehár's works the often zany plots of 50 or 60 years earlier were now sometimes replaced by stories with unhappy endings.

If such features were an indication of the decline of the classical operetta, signs could be found also in Berlin in the raiding of melodies by the classical masters for 'new' works, as with Johann Strauss for *Casanova* (1928) and Carl Millöcker for *Die Dubarry* (1931). At the same time composers such as Nico Dostal and Rudolf Kattnigg were seeking to perpetuate the Lehár formula, while other works such as Paul Abraham's *Viktoria und ihr Husar* and Ralph Benatzky's *Im weissen Rössl* (both 1930) sought to combine the traditional romance of operetta with modern stories and dance styles. Musical comedy elements were even more dominant in works such as Friedrich Schröder's *Hochzeitsnacht im Paradies* (1942) and Paul Burkhard's *Feuerwerk* (1949).

4. BRITAIN AND THE USA. In London, too, English versions of Offenbach's *opéras bouffes* began to appear during the 1860s, and it was directly under the influence of Offenbach's *Les deux aveugles* that Arthur Sullivan composed *Cox and Box* (1866). The series of works on which Sullivan collaborated with W. S. Gilbert between 1871 and 1896, including *HMS Pinafore* (1878; see fig.3), *The Mikado* (1885), *The Yeomen of the Guard* (1888) and *The Gondoliers* (1889), swept the stages of the English-speaking world, though success in translation was limited by the distinctively British nature of both humour and music. Other British examples came from Frederic Clay, Alfred Cellier, Edward Solomon and the immigrant Edward Jakobowski. Jakobowski's *Erminie* (1885) proved a huge hit in America, while Cellier's *Dorothy* (1886) ran in London for longer than any of the Gilbert and Sullivan works.

It was especially in London, during the 1890s, that a trend emerged that was to have fundamental significance for the development of operetta and the popular musical theatre. At a time when imported French operettas and the native comic operas of Gilbert and Sullivan were losing their immediate appeal, the London public took readily to the style of show loosely termed 'musical comedy' or 'musical play'. While retaining the basic framework of the operetta, these shows were concerned less with the integrity of the libretto than with a more immediate appeal, with an emphasis on contemporary fashion, glamorous male and female chorus lines, catchy interpolated numbers, and specially staged song-and-dance numbers.

These elements were particularly noticeable in a string of shows with 'girl' titles, such as *The Shop Girl* (1894) with music by Ivan Caryll and additional numbers by Lionel Monckton. Despite the historical significance of such shows as the first 'musical comedies', their scores were still closer to 19th-century comic opera than the song-and-dance musical comedies of the 1920s. Sidney Jones's *The Geisha* (1896), especially, retained much of the comic opera tradition of Sullivan and proved a phenomenal contemporary success not only throughout the British Empire but around the world, receiving more performances in Germany than any contemporary native work.

By the end of the century the fashion for the musical comedy or musical play had been confirmed through other highly successful works such as Leslie Stuart's *Florodora* (1899). This was just one British work to be welcomed in the USA, where a significant body of native works had also begun to emerge in the 1890s. Among those that owed allegiance to the example of Gilbert and Sullivan were Reginald De Koven's *Robin Hood* (1890) and John Philip Sousa's *El capitan* (1896), while Victor Herbert's *The Fortune Teller* (1898) and Gustave Kerker's *The Belle of New York* (1897) demonstrated the trend towards melodically more ingratiating works.

Sullivan's acknowledged comic opera successor was Edward German, with *Merrie England* (1902) and *Tom Jones* (1907). In commercial terms, however, it was the Edwardian 'musical plays' that captured the public fancy with their light songs and dances, elaborate chorus routines and fashionable dress. Through them

3. Poster by Alfred Concanon for Gilbert and Sullivan's 'HMS Pinafore', printed at about the time of the original production at the Opera Comique, London, in 1878

the British musical theatre product was, for a few years at the beginning of the century, the most readily exported school of operetta.

The Edwardian musical play reached its zenith in such works as Paul Rubens's *Miss Hook of Holland* (1907), Monckton and Howard Talbot's *The Arcadians* (1909) and Monckton's *The Quaker Girl* (1910). Thereafter the genre faded rapidly in favour of, first, the Viennese operettas of Lehár, Straus and Fall, and then ragtime-inspired revue and song-and-dance musical comedy from America. Only in the special conditions of wartime did the glamorous Edwardian-style musical show enjoy a brief revival of fortune, in *The Maid of the Mountains* (1916), with a score by Harold Fraser-Simson and additional numbers by James W. Tate, and the 'spectacular musical tale of the east' *Chu Chin Chow* (1916), with music by Frederic Norton. Later isolated attempts at 'light opera' as opposed to 'musical comedy' or 'musical play' were made by Montague Phillips in *The Rebel Maid* (1921) and Walter Leigh in *The Pride of the Regiment* (1932).

During the 1920s British taste readily embraced American musical comedy, but the lingering taste for works in the older European operetta traditions was still catered for in the USA by works such as Sigmund Romberg's *The Student Prince in Heidelberg* (1924) and Rudolf Friml and Herbert Stothart's *Rose-Marie* (1924), and in Britain by Noël Coward's *Bitter Sweet* (1929), George Posford and Bernard Grun's *Balalaïka* (1936), Ivor Novello's *The Dancing Years* (1939) and Vivian Ellis's *Bless the Bride* (1947).

5. THE MODERN SCENE. Since World War II the decline in significance of operetta as a contemporary phenomenon has continued. By 1964 the staging of the première of Robert Stolz's *Frühjahrsparade* at the Volksoper in Vienna was already a throwback to former times, being a nostalgic reworking of a pre-war film musical. Today operetta is scarcely to be found in the commercial theatre and, apart from a few works that have been accepted into the operatic repertory, it has become increasingly of interest only to a specialist audience. Whereas French and Austrian radio would, until the late 1960s, broadcast regular full-scale operetta productions, that exposure has not been replicated in the television age.

The revival of classic operettas itself raises difficult questions. For popular consumption, librettos are deemed to need modernizing to remove references unintelligible to a present-day audience. For a more intellectual audience, however, those dated contemporary references constitute much of the essence of a work. Absorption of operetta into operatic repertories also raises other questions of style, since operetta performance requires a range of talents not to be found in the typical opera performer, including an ability to put across words in both song and dialogue and to scale down the grand-opera style of projection.

Ready availability of material is another important determinant of what can be revived. Much original material is lost. Often it is in versions rewritten between the wars that works such as Johann Strauss's *Eine Nacht in Venedig* and Millöcker's *Gasparone* are revived, though the relevance of perpetuating a 1920s or 30s view of works from the 1880s is difficult to see.

Fidelity to the original has been affected by other factors, notably the desire of opera singers for vocal challenge and greater vocal contrasts, which has influenced the public conception of the voices for which roles were conceived. By pushing up a voice trained in a lower register, a more brilliant effect can be achieved than would be the case with music written for a more restricted voice range. This has led to the taste for giving soubrette roles to a mezzo-soprano or tenor *buffo* roles to a baritone. The preferences of individual singers have accentuated the matter. The point is vividly made by considering just three of the many enduring songs written for parts created by the Viennese tenor *buffo* Alexander Girardi: 'Ach wie so herrlich zu schau'n' (Caramello in Johann Strauss's *Eine Nacht in Venedig*),

'Ja das Schreiben und das Lesen' (Zsupán in Strauss's *Der Zigeunerbaron*) and 'Sei nicht bös' (Martin in Zeller's *Der Obersteiger*). Today they are associated with a range of voices, from soprano to bass-baritone.

If striking a balance between authenticity and tradition thus poses particular problems, operetta nevertheless continues to enjoy its small specialist niche. In Germany, Austria and other central European countries, classic operettas continue to be staged professionally as lighter fare in the repertory of subsidized opera companies. The Volksoper in Vienna remains above all as the standard-bearer of the Viennese operetta tradition, with a repertory of operettas supplemented by the lighter operatic fare. Operetta productions at summer festivals in spa towns such as Bad Ischl or Baden bei Wien help perpetuate the tradition. Likewise, in France, productions of classical French and foreign works enjoy weekend productions in major towns, as well as in the summer festival at the spa town of Lamalou-les-Bains.

That a substantially different situation has developed in English-speaking countries is due to two particular factors. The first is the overwhelming success of the Savoy operas, which have long eclipsed other works from before World War I. Works such as Monckton's *The Arcadians* and *The Quaker Girl* at least enjoy occasional amateur productions, but Jones's *The Geisha*, despite surviving into modern times in the operetta repertory in continental countries, has virtually disappeared from the British scene. The second factor is the growth of a strong native-language successor in the form of the American musical, which has largely superseded earlier traditions. The D'Oyly Carte Opera Company, for so long able to tour continuously with an unrelieved diet of Gilbert and Sullivan, finally expired from a static repertory, declining audiences and increased costs, though it has since been revived for limited seasons with commercial sponsorship.

Increasingly the international survival of the major operettas has been achieved through their establishing a place in the repertory of opera companies – a tradition that dates back to the production of *Die Fledermaus* under Mahler at Hamburg in 1894. In Britain a rediscovery effort was made during the 1960s by Sadler's Wells Opera, beyond which the most significant revival of classical operettas in London has been by student companies and by the privately financed John Lewis Music Society, whose operetta productions have covered Chabrier, Lecocq, Messager, Planquette, Suppé and Millöcker. In the USA, meanwhile, productions of Herbert, Lehár and Romberg at the New York City Opera have been more liberally supplemented by revivals of Sousa, Lecocq, Offenbach, Kálmán and Johann Strauss at festivals at Wooster, Ohio, and elsewhere.

Thus has operetta found its own somewhat ill-defined place in the modern musical repertory, with an uncertain balance between tradition and authenticity and with a dependence on operatic productions that ensure a high quality of singing but not necessarily the lightness of touch that is the essence of the genre.

*

GänzlBMT; *GänzlMT*; *StiegerO*

J. Scholtze: *Vollständige Operettenführer* (Berlin, 1906)
C. Preiss: *Beiträge zur Geschichte der Operette* (n.p., 1908)
L. Melitz: *Führer durch die Operetten* (Berlin, 1911, rev. 2/1933 by R. Kastner)
E. Rieger: *Offenbach und seine Wiener Schule* (Vienna, 1920)
——: *Die gute alte Zeit der Wiener Operette* (Vienna, 1921)
A. Orel: 'Wiener Tanzmusik und Operette', *Handbuch der Musikgeschichte*, ed. G. Adler (Frankfurt, 1924, 2/1930)
J. Brindejont-Offenbach: 'Cinquante ans de l'opérette', *Cinquante ans de musique française de 1874 à 1925*, ed. L. Rohozinski (Paris, 1925), i, 199–322
O. Keller: *Die Operette in ihrer geschichtlichen Entwicklung* (Leipzig, 1926)
M. S. Mackinlay: *The Origin and Development of Light Opera* (London, 1927)
K. Westermeyer: *Die Operette im Wandel des Zeitgeistes* (Munich, 1931)
C. Altmann: *Der französische Einfluss auf die Textbücher der klassischen Wiener Operette* (diss., U. of Vienna, 1935)
S. Czech: *Das Operettenbuch* (Dresden, 1938, 4/1960)
'Histoire de l'opérette française au XIXe siècle', *Le théâtre lyrique en France*, ii (Paris, c1938), 265–325
F. Hadamovsky and H. Otte: *Die Wiener Operette* (Vienna, 1947)
A. M. Rabenalt: '*Operette als Aufgabe*' vom sein im Schein (Berlin, 1950)
R. Holzer: *Die Wiener Vorstadtbühnen: Alexander Girardi und das Theater an der Wien* (Vienna, 1951)
A. Bauer: *150 Jahre Theater an der Wien* (Vienna, 1952)
A. Würz: *Reclams Operettenführer* (Stuttgart, 1953, 19/1988)
A. Bauer: *Opern und Operetten in Wien* (Graz, 1955)
H. Kaubisch: *Operette* (Berlin, 1955)
P. E. M[arkus]: *Und der Himmel hängt voller Geigen* (Berlin, 1955)
O. Schneidereit: *Operettenbuch* (Berlin, 1955)
H. Steger and K. Howe: *Operettenführer* (Frankfurt, 1958)
O. S. Gál and V. Somogyi: *Operettek könyve* (Budapest, 1959)
B. Grun: *Kulturgeschichte der Operette* (Munich, 1961, 2/1967)
O. Schumann: *Ich weiss mehr über die Operette und das Musical* (Stuttgart, 1961)
J. Bruyr: *L'opérette* (Paris, 1962)
D. Ewen: *European Light Opera* (New York, 1962)
G. Hughes: *Composers of Operetta* (London, 1962)
M. Lubbock and D. Ewen: *The Complete Book of Light Opera* (London, 1962)
O. Schneidereit: *Operette von Abraham bis Ziehrer* (Berlin, 1966)
A. Witeschnik: *Dort wird champagnisiert: Anekdoten und Geschichten zur Geschichte der Operette* (Vienna, 1971, 2/1980)
F. Bruyas: *Histoire de l'opérette en France, 1855–1965* (Lyons, 1974)
O. Schneidereit: *Berlin wie es weint und lacht* (Berlin, 1976)
G. Bordman: *American Musical Theatre* (New York, 1978, 2/1986)
A. Hyman: *Sullivan and his Satellites: a Survey of English Operettas, 1860–1914* (London, 1978)
J. Harding: *Folies de Paris: the Rise and Fall of French Operetta* (London, 1979)
V. Klotz: *Bürgerliches Lachtheater* (Munich, 1980, 2/1987)
G. Bordman: *American Operetta from 'HMS Pinafore' to 'Sweeney Todd'* (New York, 1981)
C. Dufresne: *Histoire de l'opérette* (Paris, 1981)
R. Traubner: *Operetta: a Theatrical History* (New York, 1983)
L. Garinei and M. Giovannini: *Quarant'anni di teatro musicale all'italiana* (Milan, 1985)
E. Oppicelli: *L'operetta: da Hervé al musical* (Genoa, 1985)
D. Zöchling: *Operette: Meisterwerke der leichten Muse* (Vienna, 1985)
A. Jacobs: 'Wooster: Operetta Restored', *Opera* (1989), festival issue, 123–5
V. Klotz: *Operette: Porträt und Handbuch einer unerhörten Kunst* (Munich, 1992)
A. Lamb, ed.: *Light Music from Austria: Reminiscences and Writings of Max Schönherr* (New York, 1992)   ANDREW LAMB

Opernball, Der ('The Opera Ball'). Operetta in three acts by RICHARD HEUBERGER to a libretto by VICTOR LÉON and Heinrich von Waldberg after Alfred Delacour and Alfred Hennequin's comedy *Les dominos roses*; Vienna, Theater an der Wien, 5 January 1898.

At carnival time in Paris, Angèle Aubier (soprano) and Marguerite Duménil (soprano) seek to put to the test the fidelity of their husbands Paul (tenor) and Georges (tenor *buffo*) by having their maid Hortense (soubrette) send them anonymous invitations to an assignation at the Opéra ball. Each will recognize his partner by her pink domino. However, unknown to the wives, Hortense sends her own similar invitation to the young sea-cadet Henri (mezzo-soprano). The consequent unexpected presence of three pink dominoes causes so much confusion that, in the subsequent inquests, all concerned decide that discretion is the best solution. In various ways a palpable imitation of *Die Fledermaus*, the operetta is celebrated for Hortense's invitation to Henri at the ball ('Geh'n wir ins Chambre séparée') and has only a minimal chorus part that is frequently omitted, making it an economical work to stage. Annie Dirkens created the role of Hortense.

ANDREW LAMB

Ophelia of the Nine Mile Beach. Comic opera in one act by JAMES PENBERTHY to his own libretto; Hobart, Tasmania, Theatre Royal, July 1965.

Ophelia (soprano), married to Harold (tenor), is infatuated with the poet who lives next door to their home on the beach. The chorus of neighbours is critical of the poet's laziness, but his wife Hannah (contralto) defends his genius. Harold chides Ophelia for staring at the poet over the fence, and offering him gifts. Ophelia tries to seduce the sleeping poet in his garden. When he fails to respond she throws herself into the surf and cries for help. A team of surf lifesavers appears and proceeds to act out its rituals. When Harold rushes in and takes over the rescue Ophelia is angered by his interference. After Ophelia has tried a few more antics Hannah appears, strikes her, and tells the neighbours to go home and mind their own business. Written in a light romantic style, the music makes appropriate use of parody to reinforce the richly vernacular text.

MICHAEL HANNAN

Opie, Alan (*b* Redruth, Cornwall, 22 March 1945). English baritone. He studied in London, making his début in 1969 at the Coliseum as Papageno with Sadler's Wells Opera. Since then he has sung a wide variety of roles, including Rossini's Figaro, Guglielmo, Valentin, Massenet's Lescaut, Germont, Zurga, Marcello, Junius (*Rape of Lucretia*), Cecil (*Gloriana*), Oblonsky in the première of Hamilton's *Anna Karenina* (1981) and Busoni's Faust (1990). He made his Covent Garden début in 1971 as an Officer (*Il barbiere*), returning for Ping, Hector (*King Priam*), Mangus (*The Knot Garden*), Dr Falke and The traveller in *Death in Venice* (1992), which he repeated at Glyndebourne. He sang János Háry at Buxton (1982) and Sid (*Albert Herring*) at Glyndebourne (1985). He has sung with Scottish Opera (Baron de Goldmarck in *La vie parisienne* and Robert Storch in *Intermezzo*), in Chicago, Santa Fe, Paris, Cologne and Amsterdam. An excellent actor with a strong voice and very good diction, he scored a major success as Beckmesser with the ENO (1984) and at Bayreuth (1987).

*

A. Blyth: 'Alan Opie', *Opera*, xlii (1991), 150–56

ELIZABETH FORBES

Opitz, Martin (*b* Bunzlau [now Bolesławiec], 23 Dec 1597; *d* Danzig [now Gdańsk], 20 Aug 1639). German poet. He outlined German poetics in his treatise *Buch von der deutschen Poeterey*, providing poetic examples of these rules in his *Teutsche Poemata* (both 1624), and is widely regarded as the father of modern German poetry. The prime musical interest of his texts lies in the insistence on a correspondence between natural word stress and metrical stress, which produced poetry that was natural, graceful and readily set to music. His poems were set by many 17th-century composers, in-

cluding Heinrich Schütz, for whom he provided the libretto of *Dafne* (Breslau, 1627), a German paraphrase of Rinuccini's work set by Jacopo Peri. Performed at a Saxon court festival on 13/23 April 1627, *Dafne* is widely regarded as the first opera in the German language; the music is no longer extant. Opitz's libretto may have served as a model for another *Dafne*, by M. G. Peranda and G. A. Bontempi, which was performed at the Dresden court in 1671.

Opitz's *Judith* (Breslau, 1635), a reworking of Andrea Salvadori's Italian text for Marco da Gagliano, has frequently been associated with Schütz's name, since Opitz undertook the translation after the collaboration on *Dafne*; however, Schütz never set this three-act libretto. In 1646 another version of Opitz's *Judith* was published in Rostock, expanded to five acts by Andreas Tscherning with its choruses set to music by Matthias Apelles von Löwenstern, Kapellmeister to the Duke of Oels. In *Dansktalende Judith* (1666), Mogens Skeel translated Opitz's *Judith* into Danish in connection with a court performance in Copenhagen; it is not known if this version was performed with music.

A hunting song, 'Auff Ihr Jäger auff! Es tagt', with text by Opitz, was inserted into Johann Lauremberg's *Wie die Harpyiæ ... verjaget ... wird* (Act 1. iv), the second of a pair of musical dramas published as *Zwo Comoedien* and performed during the Danish royal wedding celebrations of 1634.

*

H. M. Schletterer: *Das deutsche Singspiel* (Augsburg, 1863)

O. Taubert: 'Dafne, das erste deutsche Operntextbuch', *Programmheft des Gymnasiums zu Torgau* (Torgau, 1879)

H. H. Borcherdt: 'Beiträge zur Geschichte der Oper und des Schauspiels in Schlesien bis zum Jahre 1740', *Zeitschrift des Vereins für Geschichte Schlesiens*, xliii (1909), 217–42

A. Mayer: 'Zu Opitz' Dafne', *Euphorion*, xviii (1911), 754–60

H. H. Borcherdt: *Andreas Tscherning* (Munich, 1912)

A. Mayer: 'Quelle und Entstehung von Opitzens *Judith*', *Euphorion*, xx (1913), 39–53

G. Dünnhaupt: *Bibliographisches Handbuch der Barockliteratur* (Stuttgart, 1980–81)

M. R. Wade: 'The Reception of Opitz's *Judith* during the Baroque', *Daphnis*, xvi (1987), 147–65

M. R. Wade and K. H. Ober: 'Martin Opitz's *Judith* and Mogens Skeel's *Dansktalende Judith*', *Scandinavian Studies*, lxi (1989), 1–11

G. Gillespie: 'Humanist Aspects of the Early Baroque Opera Libretto after the Italian Fashion (Opitz, Harsdörffer, Anton Ulrich)', *Beiträge zur Aufnahme der italienischen und spanischen Literatur in Deutschland im 16. und 17. Jahrhundert*, ed. A. Martino, Chloe: Beihefte zum Daphnis, ix (Amsterdam, 1990), 151–70

M. R. Wade: 'Geist- und weltliche Dramata, Hecuba, Dafne, Judith, Antigone: the Dramatic Works and Heroines of Martin Opitz', *Opitz und seine Welt: Festschrift für George Schulz-Behrend zum 12. Februar 1988*, ed. B. Becker-Cantarino and J.-U. Fechner, Chloe: Beihefte zum Daphis, x (Amsterdam, 1990), 541–59

——: *The German Baroque Pastoral Singspiel* (Berne, 1990)

MARA R. WADE

Oporto (Port. Porto). City in north-west Portugal. Its operatic history begins in 1760, when a former stable was transformed into the Teatro do Corpo da Guarda, to present Italian operas performed by Nicolà Setaro's travelling company as part of the wedding festivities of Prince Pedro and his niece, the future Queen Maria I. The theatre was later placed under the protection of the military governor and presented Italian opera irregularly, along with spoken drama, until the inauguration of the Teatro S João in 1798. The new theatre, built through public subscription, was usually rented to an impresario who mounted the whole season and directed the companies, which consisted almost exclusively of Italian singers. The repertory generally followed contemporary Italian trends closely, the most popular composers being Rossini, Donizetti and Verdi. Portuguese operas were rarely performed, one exception being a performance in 1874 of *Eurico* by the Oporto composer Miguel Ângelo Pereira. In the Palácio de Cristal (built in 1865, modelled on the Crystal Palace in London) an Italian opera company also performed during the 1869–70 season. The fire which destroyed the S João theatre in 1908 ended a century-old tradition revived only partly and irregularly in recent years by the Círculo Portuense de Ópera. In the latter part of the 19th century comic operas and zarzuelas were presented at the D. Afonso and Carlos Alberto theatres, inaugurated in 1885 and 1887 respectively.

*

DBP

T. Braga: *Historia do theatro portuguez*, iii: *A baixa comedia e a opera no seculo XVIII* (Oporto, 1871)

A. Sousa Bastos: *Diccionário do theatro portuguez* (Lisbon, 1908)

J. de Freitas Branco: *História da música portuguesa* (Lisbon, 1959)

J. López-Calo: 'Portogallo', *Storia dell'opera*, ed. G. Barblan and A. Basso, ii (Turin, 1977), 65–77

M. C. de Brito: *Opera in Portugal in the Eighteenth Century* (Cambridge, 1989)

M. C. de Brito and D. Cranmer: *Crónicas da vida musical portuguesa na primeira metade do século XIX* (Lisbon, 1990)

M. C. de Brito: 'La penisola iberica', *SOI*, ii (1991) [covers only the 18th century]   MANUEL CARLOS DE BRITO

Oprichnik ('The Oprichnik'). Opera in four acts by PYOTR IL'YICH TCHAIKOVSKY to his own libretto after Ivan Lazhechnikov's tragedy (1834); St Petersburg, Mariinsky Theatre, 12/24 April 1874.

The title character, Andrey Morozov (tenor), is a boyar's son who joins the *oprichniki* (the tsar's mercenary retinue, set up to assert his power against the boyars) in order to avenge his family's honour against the depredations of Prince Zhemchuzhnïy (bass), with whose daughter Natal'ya (soprano) he is in love – and she with him, though plighted to another. He is disowned and cursed by the boyarïnya Morozova (contralto), his widowed mother, which catastrophic event prompts him to seek release from his vows. The tsar (an offstage presence in the opera by reason of the censorship but represented by a spokesman, Vyazminsky, baritone) ostensibly grants Andrey's request and also approves his marriage to Natal'ya; but then by trickery Tsar Ivan gets Andrey to break his vows just before their expiration, providing a pretext to have him executed before his mother's eyes, thus killing her as well. The opera is dedicated to the Grand Duke Konstantin Nikolayevich; Eduard Nápravník conducted the première, with Ivan Mel'nikov as Vyazminsky.

Tchaikovsky's libretto skilfully rearranges the melodramatic events of Lazhechnikov's play into a classic grand-opera format in the manner of Scribe (hence the opera's reputation as 'Meyerbeer translated into Russian'). Act 3, to pick the most arresting example, is constructed, apart from an introductory chorus, as a steady accumulation of characters – Morozova alone, then Natal'ya, then Zhemchuznïy, then Andrey, his companion Basmanov (a contralto trouser role), and the *oprichniki* – culminating in a monumental *morceau d'ensemble avec choeurs* of really harrowing power to fix the moment of the curse, the drama's fatal turning-point. Neo- and post-kuchkist opinion notwithstanding, *Oprichnik* is well worthy of occasional revival.

The main dramaturgical obstacle is Act 1, consisting mainly of material salvaged from *Voyevoda*, Tchaikovsky's withdrawn maiden opera. It is short on characterization and gives little inkling of the scale of what is to follow, relying instead on folkish charm, for which reason it is predictably overestimated by those Western critics for whom the sole measure of worth in Russian music is its 'Russianness'. A less hackneyed Russianism is found in Act 2 scene ii, where the assembled *oprichniki* sing choruses of mock-ecclesiastical cast. The virtuosically orchestrated dances in Act 4, based on five Russian folksongs previously published as such in the composer's popular piano four-hand collection, are eminently detachable for concert purposes.

As a matter of record it should be noted that the entr'acte before Act 2 was composed not by Tchaikovsky but by his pupil Vladimir Shilovsky (1852–93), brother of the co-librettist of *Yevgeny Onegin*.   RICHARD TARUSKIN

Optimisticheskaya tragediya ('An Optimistic Tragedy'). Opera in three acts by ALEXANDER NIKOLAYEVICH KHOLMINOV to a libretto by A. Mashistov and the composer after Vsyevolod Vishnevsky's play; Frunze (now Bishkek), Kirghiz Theatre of Opera and Ballet, 20 November 1965.

Kholminov worked on his first opera from 1959 to 1964, composing three versions as the dramatic conception crystallized. Romanticizing the revolutionary struggle of the Bolsheviks, the composer emphasized mass choral scenes and monumental images over individual characterization in a tuneful idiom infused with motifs from folksongs and the popular revolutionary legacy. After its successful première *An Optimistic Tragedy* was staged in Moscow, Leningrad and many other cities of the Eastern bloc. For a production at the Bol'shoy Theatre to commemorate the 50th anniversary of the October Revolution, Kholminov made a special edition of the opera, reinforcing the choral parts and rewriting several episodes. In 1969 he was awarded the State Prize of the RSFSR for *An Optimistic Tragedy* and his *Pesnya o Lenine* ('Song of Lenin').

The action of the opera is divided between the Baltic fleet and the front line during the Civil War. In Act 1, a group of anarchists has disarmed the crew and seized command of one of the Baltic ships. Their Leader (bass), with his sidekick Husky (tenor), subdues all attempts to restore order. The sailor Alexey (tenor) warns that the Bolsheviks are sending a Commissar, who, to everyone's surprise, turns out to be a woman (mezzo-soprano). The anarchists react with menace to this humiliation. As they amuse themselves at her expense, the Commissar shoots a sailor about to molest her. She reprimands the crew in the name of the Revolution and finds some support among them. The Leader realizes that he is losing power over his men and, using Alexey as scapegoat, hastens to smooth things over with the Commissar. She appoints a new commander, Bering (spoken), who announces the reorganization of the regiment and its imminent departure for the front.

In Act 2, at the regimental camp, the Commissar weans the popular Alexey from the anarchist Leader's pernicious influence; Alexey declares his love for her and commits his fate to her. The Finnish-communist sailor Vaynonen (tenor) informs the Commissar that the Leader has arrested Bering and the Boatswain (bass), has condemned them to death for treachery to the

715

Revolution and is sending the death warrant for her signature. When the Leader orders the execution of two wounded German officers, Alexey stands up in their defence. The Commissar, supported by the majority, turns the tables on the insubordinate Leader, substituting his name in the death warrant. Alexey carries out the execution.

In Act 3 the Commissar impatiently awaits her rendezvous with Bering. Husky arrives, ostensibly to relieve Vaynonen from guard duty, but when Vaynonen is distracted he kills him, opening the way to a crushing enemy attack. The Commissar, Alexey and the surviving sailors are imprisoned. Husky betrays the Commissar to a White Guard officer (baritone). Shots announce the arrival of Bering and his men; the imprisoned sailors break down the doors and fell the sentries. Alexey kills Husky. The mortally wounded Commissar, with her last breath, asks for her report to be carried to the Revolutionary Council. A wordless chorus joins the orchestra in a stirring peroration.   LAUREL E. FAY

Orange. Ancient town in southern France with fine Roman ruins. The 2000-year-old amphitheatre is the only one in France to have conserved its rear wall – 103 metres long and 37 high. The 55 rows of stepped seats can accommodate up to 9000 spectators. The stage is of impressive dimensions, 65 metres wide (although generally only 45 are used), and 16 deep; it suits broad gestures and big voices, although the natural acoustics are good. The Mistral wind can, however, be a problem. In July and August the famous Chorégies d'Orange take place, a festival comprising one or two performances of three popular operas on the grand scale. The festival dates back to 1869, when Méhul's *Joseph* was performed with Vaccai's *Giulietta e Romeo*. Massenet's *Hérodiade* and Saint-Saëns' *Samson et Dalila*, two works ideally suited to the antique setting, were given in 1902 and have since been repeated several times. In 1905, Raoul Gunsbourg, then the director, organized a whole festival of operas on antique themes: *Mefistofele* (with Shalyapin) and Berlioz's *Les Troyens*. Gluck's works made their first appearance in 1900 with *Iphigénie en Tauride* (repeated in 1922, 1931 and 1947), followed in 1903 by *Orphée* (repeated seven times until 1951, with Alice Raveau in 1911, 1926 and 1927). *Alceste* followed in 1912 with Litvinne, repeated in 1928, 1929 and 1938 (with Lubin) and in 1948. These performances made Gluck the most frequently heard composer of the festival, although his works have not been given since 1951. *Aida* was first presented in 1937 and has been repeated five times. Eight other Verdi operas have been given; so have *Tosca* and *Turandot*. Gounod's *Faust* (six performances between 1936 and 1969) and *Mireille* (six performances between 1930 and 1970) were favourites. Strangely, *Carmen* was not performed until 1961 (repeated in 1962 and 1984). Wagner first appeared in 1930, when Jacques Rouché was director of the festival (at the same time director of the Paris Opéra), with *Tannhäuser* (repeated in the 1930s, and in 1958 and 1986), *Die Walküre* (1932, repeated in 1937, 1950 and 1975), *Tristan* (1934, repeated in 1973 with Nilsson and Vickers), *Lohengrin* (1955 and 1976), *Parsifal* (1979) and *Der fliegende Holländer* (1980 and 1987). The complete *Ring* under Marek Janowski was performed in 1988. Mozart has been represented only by *Die Zauberflöte* (1981 and 1989). *Les Troyens* was given in an abridged version in 1931 with a spectacular wooden horse, and *La damna-*

tion de Faust five times (in 1935 with Ninon Vallin, Georges Thill and André Pernet, conducted by Paul Paray). Although the vast stage would be ideal for many Russian works, only *Boris Godunov* has proved popular enough to fill the 9000-seat theatre. It was staged in 1985 in a production by J.-C. Auvray with Martti Talvela, in an audacious set by Bernard Arnould.

CHARLES PITT

Oranienbaum [now Lomonosov]. Town in Russia, on the Finnish gulf near St Petersburg. Formerly a royal summer residence and fashionable aristocratic resort, it contains a complex of palaces and gardens built for the Empress Elizabeth. Two opera premières took place there in the mid-18th century: *Amor prigioniero*, a one-act *dialogo per musica* by Francesco Araia to a libretto by Metastasio (16/27 June 1755); and *Semiramide riconosciuta*, a three-act *dramma per musica* by Vincenzo Manfredini (his first opera), also to a Metastasio libretto (summer of 1760). Stravinsky happened to be born at Oranienbaum during his parents' vacation there in 1882.   RICHARD TARUSKIN

Oratorio (from Lat. *orare*, 'to pray', and It. *oratorio*, 'prayer hall', 'oratory'). An extended musical setting of a religious text made up of dramatic, narrative and contemplative elements. The religious content apart, oratorio differs from opera mainly in the greater narrative and contemplative qualities of its text, its characteristic concert manner of performance – without scenery, costumes or actions – and, throughout much of its history, its greater emphasis on the chorus. In exceptional cases, however, only a thin line divides oratorio from opera.

The earliest known use of 'oratorio' to designate a musical composition dates from 1640, when the Roman Pietro Della Valle wrote that he had composed an 'Oratorio della Purificatione' for the Roman Oratory of the Congregazione dell'Oratorio, the prayer hall from which the genre took its name. This brief work (about 12 minutes) includes a narrative role for Poeta, dialogue among three personages and a choral conclusion. 20 years earlier, however, works similar to Della Valle's in text, music and social function are included in G. F. Anerio's *Teatro armonico spirituale di madrigali* (Rome, 1619).

Also composed for the Roman Oratory, Emilio de' Cavalieri's *Rappresentatione di Anima, et di Corpo* (Rome, 1600) was apparently first called an oratorio by Burney in his *General History*, presumably because it has a sacred, dramatic text and is music for an oratory. An imposing work about an hour and a half long, the *Rappresentatione* is sung in dialogue throughout, without a narrator's role, and was intended to be presented with scenery, costumes, acting and dancing. Others have occasionally used Burney's term for the work, but 20th-century scholars (Alaleona, 106; Schering, 40; Pasquetti, 130; Palisca, 114; Smither 1977, i, p.89) have questioned this designation. That the 17th century considered oratorio an unstaged genre is clear from the use of 'oratorio' on title-pages of the period and in writings about the genre (Spagna, G. M. Crescimbeni). Rather than the first example of a new genre, Cavalieri's work is better understood as a late example of an old one, the *rappresentazione sacra* (a term that takes the composer at his word). It is a work that figures significantly in the early history of opera and is an important antecedent of oratorio. Another piece with a sacred dramatic text, Stefano Landi's *Sant'Alessio*, first performed at the Barberini Palace in 1631 or 1632, also bears a close relationship to both the *rappresentazione sacra* and opera, but could hardly have been considered an oratorio in its time. Its social function and elaborate staging distinguish it from oratorio, with its devotional function and simple presentation.

Throughout their history, serious opera and oratorio have been close relatives in both libretto and music. As opera changed, so did oratorio. The libretto of the 17th- and 18th-century Italian oratorio parallels that of opera in versification, aria types, poetic images and minimal use of chorus (Carissimi's oratorios are exceptions). Oratorio librettos differ from opera librettos, however, in their consistently religious subjects, typical two-part structures (in an oratory the parts framed a sermon) and often in their greater emphasis on contemplative and narrative elements. The role of the narrator (*Historia*, *Testo* or *Poeta*), superfluous in opera, was characteristic of the 17th-century oratorio but abandoned in the early 18th. The same librettists often wrote both oratorios and operas, as did Zeno and Metastasio, whose oratorios were important models for 18th-century librettists. Both followed the Arcadian Academy in aiming to classicize the oratorio and to abolish offences to the sacred spirit of the genre. Oratorios in German, English and French, which began to appear in the 18th century, use the Italian oratorio as a point of departure. The librettos for most of Handel's English oratorios are dramatic, but *Israel in Egypt* (1738) and *Messiah* (1741) initiate a new type of libretto in which the words are all selected from the Bible.

In the 17th and 18th centuries, the music of an Italian oratorio differs little from that of an opera. As in opera, the flexible mixture of recitative, arioso and aria styles in early oratorio gives way to a clearer distinction between recitative and aria, and by 1700 most arias are in da capo form. In the 18th century, changing styles in *opera seria* are reflected in oratorio. Choruses, usually brief and perfunctory in Italian oratorios, are more significant in German ones and particularly elaborate in the English oratorios of Handel.

As an essentially unstaged genre, oratorio differs from opera more in manner of presentation than in any other way. Exceptionally, however, a work called 'oratorio' (or one of its synonyms, such as *azione sacra*) is staged as an opera, and when that happens the line between the genres grows thin. Isolated examples of oratorios given as operas begin at the end of the 17th century. Early instances are Pietro Torri's six oratorios composed between 1692 and 1734 for Maximilian II, Elector of Bavaria. In 1736 Giuseppe Terradellas set a modified version of Metastasio's oratorio *Giuseppe riconosciuto* to be acted at the Naples Oratory, and in 1759 Giuseppe Bonno's setting of Metastasio's *Isacco figura del Redentore* was acted in Vienna at the palace of the Prince of Saxe-Hildburghausen. A few other examples could be mentioned. Handel might have established the English oratorio as a religious form of opera had not the Bishop of London prevented his performing *Esther* in a theatre with staging and action in 1732. In the Naples theatres, staged oratorios were presented in about half of the Lenten seasons between 1786 and 1810, after which the practice waned. The pasticcio *Il convito di Balsassarre: oratorio* (1786) was the first of these, and the next year Giuseppe Giordano's *Distruzione di Gerusalemme: azione sacra* was seen by Goethe, who noted that 'Here,

during Lent, they perform sacred operas [*geistliche Opern*]. The only difference between them and profane operas is that they have no ballets between the acts; otherwise, they are as gay [*bunt*] as possible'. The most important work in this tradition is Rossini's *Mosè in Egitto*, which was announced as an 'oratorio' by a Naples newspaper but termed *azione tragico-sacra* in its printed libretto (Naples, 1818). Reflecting the practice of staging Italian oratorios, Pietro Lichtenthal's definition of 'oratorio' in his dictionary of 1826 first defines the genre as a religious drama with singers and orchestra, adding that it may be performed 'either in a church, or in a hall, or indeed on a theatrical stage – in this last case one means *Opera sacra* and it bears the mark of the usual *Opere in musica*, having the same form and conduct'.

Close relationships between opera and oratorio continued in the 19th and 20th centuries. Librettos began to follow the scene structure of operas, musical settings used new operatic techniques including the leitmotif (Liszt's *Die Legende von der heiligen Elisabeth* and Elgar's *Dream of Gerontius*, among others), and sporadic staging of oratorios continued. In 1833, for instance, Mendelssohn performed Handel's *Israel in Egypt* with *tableaux vivants* in Düsseldorf, where Mendelssohn's *St Paul* was staged in 1870; and in 1881, Liszt's *Elisabeth* was staged in Weimar to celebrate the composer's 70th birthday. Some works originally intended to be staged became better known in oratorio-like versions, among them the sacred operas of Anton Rubinstein, Debussy's music for *Le martyre de St Sébastien* (1911) and Honegger's *Le roi David* (1921, 1924). Stravinsky acknowledged a blurring of genres in his *Oedipus rex*, described as an 'opera-oratorio' (1927).

The 20th-century tradition of staging Handel's oratorios began in Germany, where *Saul* was staged in 1923, and continued in Cambridge in the 1920s (*Jephtha*, *Susanna*, *Saul* and *Solomon*, among others) and elsewhere in Britain. Founded in 1955, the Handel Opera Society (later called Handel Opera) continued the tradition of staging Handel's oratorios. Problematic in staging German and Handelian English oratorios are the sometimes long and contrapuntally complex choruses that are calculated for concert performance rather than dramatic effect, the entrances and exits of a chorus that was originally intended to be 'on stage' for the entire performance, and the integration of the chorus into the stage action. These problems are less acute with the staging of Italian oratorio from the 17th century to the early 19th, however, which characteristically makes little use of the chorus.

*

G. Pasquetti: *L'oratorio musicale in Italia* (Florence, 1906, 2/1914)

D. Alaleona: *Studi su la storia dell'oratorio musicale in Italia* (Turin, 1908, 2/1945 as *Storia … Italia*)

A. Schering: *Geschichte des Oratoriums* (Leipzig, 1911)

W. Dean: *Handel's Dramatic Oratorios and Masques* (London, 1959)

C. V. Palisca: *Baroque Music* (Englewood Cliffs, NJ, 1968)

H. E. Smither: *A History of the Oratorio* (Chapel Hill, NC, 1977–)

——: 'Oratorio and Sacred Opera, 1700–1825: Terminology and Genre Distinction', *PRMA*, cvi (1979–80), 88–104

HOWARD E. SMITHER

Orazi ed i Curiazi, Gli ('The Horatii and the Curiatii'). *Tragedia per musica* in three acts by DOMENICO CIMAROSA to a libretto by SIMEONE ANTONIO SOGRAFI

717

after PIERRE CORNEILLE's tragedy *Horace*; Venice, Teatro La Fenice, 26 December 1796.

Publio Orazio [Publius Horatius]	tenor
Marco Orazio [Marcus Horatius] *his son*	tenor
Orazia [Horatia] *Publius Horatius's daughter*	contralto
Curiazio [Curiatius] *Horatia's bridegroom*	soprano castrato
Sabina *Curiatius's sister and Marcus Horatius's wife*	soprano
Licinio [Licinius] *friend of the Horatii*	soprano castrato
High Priest	bass
The Chief Augur	bass
Tullio Ostilio [Tullus Hostilius] *King of Rome*	silent
Mario Suffezio [Marius Suffetius] *dictator of Alba*	silent
Oracle	bass

Roman senators, citizens of Alba, the populace

Setting Rome in the 7th century BC

This opera is based on Corneille's tragedy (1640); the main difference is in Horatius's role. In Corneille's play Horatius is the protagonist, and Curiatius is a secondary character. According to operatic conventions Curiatius, as the partner of the prima donna, had to be sung by the primo uomo (a soprano castrato), while Horatius, as the tenor role, was relegated to a secondary position.

At its première the opera featured an illustrious cast, including Matteo Babbini (Marcus Horatius), Josephina Grassini (Horatia), Girolamo Crescentini (Curiatius) and Carolina Maranesi (Sabina). At the age of 17 Crescentini had appeared in the Rome première of Cimarosa's *L'italiana in Londra*; his singing partner, Grassini, appeared in this opera over a period of 20 years. The piece was popular on the European stage for several decades; in Venice alone it had more than 130 performances in six years. Over the years it was considerably altered, and its three acts were compressed to two. For the 1798 performance at La Fenice it was revised by Marcos António Portugal. In 1802 it was published in Paris with a French text by Imbault. A pasticcio based on its music appeared in Naples in 1804 as a *tragedia sacra*, arranged by Niccolò Zingarelli.

ACT 1 Rome and Alba are embarking upon a truce after a period of war. The Horatii and the Curiatii, two families of the enemy cities, are opponents, as well as friends through intermarriage: Curiatius's sister Sabina is married to Marcus Horatius, whose own sister Horatia is preparing to marry Curiatius. After the overture (one movement, in binary form), scored for a large orchestra of trumpets, horns, flutes, oboes, clarinets, bassoons and strings, the opera opens in the exterior atrium of the temple of Janus. Sabina, surrounded by the Roman populace, prays to the gods for peace and a long life of glory for the majestic city of Rome: 'Odi o ciel i nostri lai' is a through-composed, continuous scene in which the choral numbers are interspersed with recitatives and solos.

Throngs of people assemble outside the palace of the Horatii, including Roman senators with the Horatii family and Alban citizens with the Curiatii. The chorus extols Roman honour and heroes, particularly Marcus Horatius ('Germe d'illustri eroi'). General happiness is expressed at the safe return of Curiatius and Horatius from the war, notably in the trio 'Oh dolce e caro istante'. In the following cavatina, 'Quelle pupille tenere', Curiatius declares his love for Horatia, imploring her to remember his eternal affection should his duty to Alba ever demand that he leave her. Following a simple *ABAC* structure, the vocal part, which alternates with solo wind instruments, is particularly demanding.

In the interior atrium of the Horatii palace, Marcus Horatius's aria 'Se alla patria ognor donai' alternates with choral passages. He declares that he is prepared to lay down his life for the glory and honour of his city. The following scene combines spectacle and pantomime: a magnificent portico in the palace, leading to a family temple, is adorned with garlands for the wedding of Horatia and Curiatius. The orchestral music accompanying this nuptial scene, 'Scopransi i vaghi rai', an Andante con moto, has beautiful oboe and clarinet solos, and is followed by an Andantino *a tempo di marcia*. The proceedings are interrupted by the news that three warriors from each family have been chosen to go to war against each other. The scene, which began happily with nuptial music, ends darkly, without a wedding.

ACT 2 The two armies, led by Marius Suffetius, dictator of Alba, and Tullus Hostilius, King of Rome, are facing each other across the Campo Marzio. They work themselves into a warlike frenzy to the accompaniment of an orchestral march. Before the battle begins, however, they ask the Oracle's opinion on the advisability of the fight. Located in a deep, dark cave, the Oracle pronounces, amid the rumbling sounds of an earthquake, that they must fight.

ACT 3 A huge square in Rome is filled with people celebrating Marcus Horatius's triumphant entry into the city. The body of Curiatius is among the spoils of war. Horatia, horror-stricken, realizes that Marcus Horatius has killed her bridegroom, and her brother then murders her for lamenting the death of an enemy instead of praising the honour of Rome. The opera ends with the chorus commenting on the tragedy.

*   *   *

This post-Metastasian *opera seria* is imbued with revolutionary fervour. Written in the wake of the French Revolution, it emphasizes pomp, spectacle and massed battle scenes, as well as the notion that honour and duty override personal feelings. It exalts the republican virtues of ancient Rome within the context of the developments of the French Revolution. The tender love duets between Horatia and Curiatius, which anticipate the spirit of early 19th-century Romanticism, contrast starkly with the essentially artificial embodiment of such ideals as duty and honour. The chorus assumes a dominant position, akin to that in a Greek tragedy, and the music expresses inner unity through the integration of scenes that are frequently continuous dramatic blocks rather than sequences of closed musical numbers.

GORDANA LAZAREVICH

Orazio. Libretto by ANTONIO PALOMBA, first set by Pietro Auletta (1737, Naples).

The main characters are the lovers Orazio and Ginevra, who eloped from Genoa in defiance of their parents, were captured by Moorish pirates, and were separated when only Ginevra was rescued. The action begins seven years later with Orazio's arrival, under the name of Leandro, at the residence of Lamberto, a

Venetian singing teacher. Ginevra (now known as Giacomina), a pupil of Lamberto's, is reluctantly to make her Naples début. She recognizes Leandro, but the two do not make themselves known to each other immediately. Orazio hatches an elaborate plot to free Ginevra from her Neapolitan engagement and, after the usual deceits, diversions and misunderstandings, the lovers are reunited. A subplot involves Lamberto, who is in love with Lauretta, another of his pupils: he contrives to keep her with him by declaring that her training is only half-finished, but she is discovered by the Neapolitan impresario Colagianni; after much scheming on both sides, Lamberto prevails.

Frank Walker ('Orazio: the History of a Pasticcio', *MQ*, xxxviii, 1952, pp.369–83) recorded 21 revivals of *Orazio*, all over Europe, for the period 1740–58. Auletta's music slowly disappeared as the opera travelled, six numbers surviving with some consistency. Additions included numbers by Pergolesi, Jommelli, Leo, Alessandro Maccari, Michele Fini and others. The subplot involving Lamberto, Colagianni and Lauretta was presented separately as *Il maestro di musica* (1752, Paris). Shortly afterwards, Boivin published a score under Pergolesi's name (Paris, 1753), which led to the assumption that *Orazio* was an expanded version of *Il maestro di musica*, a myth Walker laid to rest ('Two Centuries of Pergolesi Forgeries and Misattributions', *ML*, xxx, 1949, pp.297–320). In 1755 a French parody appeared (Paris, Comédie-Italienne; revised 1757), and Chevardière published a score. An even more condensed version was presented in Florence in 1760, as *La scolara alla moda*, without specific attribution. *Orazio* was also set by F. J. Deller as *Il maestro di cappella* (1771, Vienna).

BRYAN MARTIN

Orchard, (William) Arundell (*b* London, 13 April 1867; *d* at sea, 7 April 1961). Australian composer of English birth. He took the BMus at Durham in 1893 and then worked in Perth and Hobart as an organist and choral conductor. After teaching in schools in England and New Zealand he moved permanently to Australia in 1903. There he was admired as a choral and orchestral conductor and wrote three works for the stage, all to librettos by W. J. Curtis. His two operettas were first performed at the Palace Theatre, Sydney: *The Coquette* in 1905, and *The Emperor* the following year. In his autobiography, *A Distant View* (1948), he described *The Coquette*, his most successful stage work, as a light opera in the style of Gilbert and Sullivan; it tells the story of a suicide club. His only serious opera, *Dorian Gray* (after Oscar Wilde's novel), had its première at the New South Wales State Conservatorium on 11 September 1919. Orchard took the DMus at Durham in 1928 and was appointed OBE in 1936.

Orchestra (It.; Fr. *orchestre*; Ger. *Orchester*). The word 'orchestra', which in ancient Greece referred to the place in the theatre where the chorus sang and danced, was applied in about the early 17th century to the space immediately in front of the stage reserved for the instrumentalists. By the late 17th century the meaning of the word had been extended to refer to the instrumentalists themselves and their identity as an ensemble (Staehelin, *HMT*). The history of the opera orchestra from the 17th century to the present involves the consideration of how many and what kinds of instruments this ensemble comprised, how these instruments were used in individual works, the relation of instruments to voices and the role of the orchestra in the drama.

1. Before opera. 2. Early opera. 3. 17th century. 4. French opera to 1763. 5. 18th century. 6. 19th century. 7. 20th century.

1. BEFORE OPERA. The instrumental ensemble of early opera developed out of ensembles for *intermedi* and similar entertainments at 16th-century courts in Italy and France. These ensembles might include a variety of instruments – lutes, viols, violins, flutes, trombones, trumpets, cornetts, keyboards – assembled and deployed variously according to the occasion. The principal role of the instruments seems to have been to double the voices in polyphonic songs. When a singer sang alone, the instruments filled in the remaining parts of the polyphonic texture. Occasionally the instruments played without the voices in sinfonias or other interludes. Published descriptions of the Florentine *intermedi* of 1539, 1565 and 1589 provide examples of this sort of instrumentation (Brown 1973). A similar French practice can be seen in the *Balet comique de la Royne* of 1581. The instrumentalists for these entertainments were not placed in front of the stage: either they were hidden offstage or they appeared onstage in costume (fig.1). In the Florentine *intermedio* of 1565, for example, Alessandro Striggio's madrigal *Fuggi speme mia* was sung to the accompaniment of four bass viols concealed 'with singular ingenuity' behind four snakes, with a lirone and four trombones playing offstage (Sonneck 1921).

The scoring for these instrumental ensembles in the 16th-century theatre has been characterized as 'programmatic' (Weaver 1961). Instruments were chosen for each number in accordance with established stereotypes. Thus in the Florentine *intermedi* of 1586 the Virtues (*I beni*) are accompanied by an 'Olympian' ensemble of lutes, viols, flutes and harps. On the other hand, Evils (*I mali*) are accompanied by an 'infernal' ensemble of trombones and bass viols. Shepherds and shepherdesses are accompanied by a 'pastoral' ensemble which includes bagpipes, recorders, cornetts, violins and *dolzaina* (Brown 1973). There was no notion of a single, standard ensemble accompanying the entire work; instead, a variety of instrumentalists participated directly in the drama, both through their appearance in costume on the stage and through the symbolic associations of their ensembles.

2. EARLY OPERA. In the operas of the very early 17th century – works associated with the Florentine Camerata and written in the new 'reciting' style – the role of instruments was more limited than in the *intermedio* tradition. In Caccini's *Euridice* (1600, performed in Florence in 1602), for example, the only instrumental part is a figured bass line, which accompanies the voices throughout. There are no sinfonias or dances. Caccini did not say which instruments should realize the basso continuo, but Peri, in the preface to his contemporaneous *Euridice* (1600, Florence), noted that the instrumentalists at the first performance played the *gravicembalo* (harpsichord), chitarrone (large, long-necked lute), *lira grande* (large bowed fiddle) and *liuto grosso* (archlute). He also said that the instruments were placed offstage ('dentro della scena'). Like Caccini, Peri wrote out the instrumental part as a single line of figured bass. In several places marked 'ritornello' the bass line continues without the voice, implying that one or more instruments played a refrain. Cavalieri's *Rappresentatione di Anima, et di Corpo* (1600, Rome) gives the in-

1. 'Olympian' ensemble in a Florentine intermedio: 'The Descent of Rhythm and Harmony', the sixth intermedio in the 1589 performance of 'La pellegrina' in Florence: engraving by F. Succhielli after Bernardo Buontalenti's design

strumental ensemble a role somewhat larger than it occupied in Florentine operas: there are five-part sinfonias between the acts; there are short ritornellos between vocal numbers; and the layout of the score suggests that the instruments doubled the voices in the choruses. In the introduction to the printed edition Cavalieri wrote that the instrumental ensemble might include *lira doppia*, harpsichord, chitarrone and organ, and that it should be augmented or reduced according to the size of the room where the work is performed; the instruments should be placed behind the scenery and should play loudly and without adding improvised ornamentation. Marco da Gagliano, in the preface to his *Dafne* (1608, Mantua), distinguished between instruments that accompany solo singing, which should be placed where the players can see the singers, and the off-stage instruments, which accompany the choruses and play sinfonias and ritornellos. He even called for a special instrumental effect: Apollo, on stage, strums his lyre, but what the audience hears is an ensemble of four viols playing behind the scenery.

Monteverdi's *Orfeo* (1607, Mantua) represents a combination of the *intermedio* tradition of programmatic instrumentation with the basso continuo tradition of the Camerata. The opera calls for a large and diverse ensemble including harpsichords, organs, chitarroni, *viole da brazzo* (violins, violas and cellos), cornetts, trombones, *flautini* (sopranino recorders) and others, totalling over 30 instruments. In the printed score Monteverdi lists the instruments next to the *dramatis personae*, implying that the instrumental ensemble is a vital part of the opera. Indeed, *Orfeo* does contain a striking amount of instrumental music. There is an opening Toccata and a closing Moresca. When the scenery is changed or when characters enter or leave the stage, the instruments play sinfonias; before and after songs and between verses, they play ritornellos. In the choruses the instruments double the voices. Solo songs are accompanied by basso continuo, and in two passages Monteverdi accompanies the solo voice with melody instruments as well, notably in 'Possente spirto', where Orpheus appeals for Eurydice's release first to the accompaniment of two violins (*see* ORFEO (i), fig.2),

then a pair of cornetts, then a harp and finally a trio of two violins and large cello (*basso da brazzo*). The use of instruments for sinfonias, ritornellos and choruses was already established in opera, as was the basso continuo, but the obbligato accompaniment of solo song was new. The instrumental ensemble for *Orfeo* seems to have been placed in two areas, some instrumentalists playing from behind the scenes, others from the sides of the act-ing stage (Kelly 1988). Twice during the opera Monteverdi calls for the backstage instruments to come out and join the visible ensemble in a sinfonia.

Instruments play a dramatic role in *Orfeo* in two ways. First, Monteverdi continued the *intermedio* tradition of programmatic instrumentation. The choir in the first act sings and dances to an 'Olympian' ensemble of violin consort, chitarrone, two harpsichords, harp, double bass and recorder. The shepherds in Act 2 are accompanied by a 'pastoral' ensemble of violins and recorders. In Act 3 the underworld scenes are accompanied by 'infernal' ensembles of cornetts, trom-bones and reed organ. Secondly, Monteverdi used in-strumental colour in a new, expressive way to highlight crucial moments in the drama. For example, when the messenger enters with the news that Eurydice is dead, the scoring of the continuo is specified as chitarrone and flue-pipe organ, giving a soft, plaintive sound.

Monteverdi did not call his *Orfeo* ensemble an orchestra, and indeed it was not an orchestra, at least in the later sense of the term (Zaslaw 1988): the core of the ensemble was keyboards and plucked strings; the bowed strings played one-to-a-part; the ensemble was split into onstage and offstage bands; and it was deployed in accordance with programmatic stereotypes. In its merger of *intermedio* and Camerata traditions, in the importance of purely instrumental music, in the accompaniment of solo song by melody instruments and in the use of instrumental colour for dramatic effect, *Orfeo* was innovatory and potentially influential. Yet the example was not soon followed.

3. 17TH CENTURY. Several changes took place during the 17th century that transformed the instrumental en-semble of the early operas into what is now understood

as an opera orchestra. First, the ensemble moved from onstage or backstage into a designated space in the 'orchestra' of the theatre. Secondly, the programmatic instrumental groupings of the *intermedio* tradition were consolidated into a single, more or less standard ensemble, based on bowed strings of the violin family. Thirdly, the instrumental ensemble was integrated into the musical texture of the opera. These changes were driven to some extent by technical improvements in violin-family instruments that increased volume and carrying power. Also important was the rise of public opera, beginning with the opening in Venice of the S Cassiano theatre in 1637. The new violin-based ensembles required fewer players and were thus less costly than the diverse *intermedio* ensembles. Also, the standardization of the ensemble allowed operas to travel easily from city to city. The shift to this violin-based, 'monochrome' orchestra can also be attributed to a change in the aesthetic ideals of opera, whereby meanings were communicated less by symbols and stereotypes and more by melodic and harmonic expression (Weaver 1964).

17th-century Italian opera orchestras in public theatres were comparatively small – smaller than the ensembles for the *intermedi* had been, and smaller than the ensembles for such other contemporary genres as oratorio, serenata and concerto. Information from scores, payrolls and pictures suggests that the typical orchestra for Italian opera during the period 1640 to 1690 consisted of two to four violins, two violas (alto or tenor), two bass instruments (8' or 16' bass), one or two archlutes or theorbos and one or two harpsichords. Oboes, trumpets and flutes were added in isolated numbers, often in accordance with their traditional symbolic functions. Cornetts, trombones, harps and organs more or less disappeared. Depending on the size of the hall, the instrumentalists available and the character of the music, the bowed strings might be scored in three, four or five parts; scorings sometimes varied within an opera. Cavalli's *Antioco* (1659, Venice), scored for five-part strings and continuo, was performed with the strings one-to-a-part and the continuo played by two harpsichords and two theorbos (Glover 1978, p.108). The frontispiece of a Venetian libretto from 1690 (fig.2) depicts an orchestra of 13 instruments, including six bowed strings, two oboes, two trumpets and a theorbo. An engraving of the S Giovanni Grisostomo theatre in Venice in 1709 (fig.3) shows 12 instruments: harpsichord, lute and trumpet, and various

3. *Orchestra at the Teatro S Giovanni Grisostomo, Venice, c1709: detail of the engraving reproduced in* VENICE, *fig.2*

violin-family instruments that cannot be made out clearly. Reports of larger orchestras in the Venetian public theatre should be regarded with caution (Selfridge-Field 1985). Opera at the courts of princes and emperors, on the other hand, often used large ensembles. Reports and pictures from Naples, Turin, Dresden, Vienna and Paris attest to regular ensembles of 30 to 40. The orchestra was expanded by doubling the parts to form string bands suitable for stately overtures and dance music. By the early 18th century court opera sometimes assembled truly impressive instrumental resources, especially for so-called 'festival' operas given at royal weddings and coronations. Quantz gives the startling figure of 200 instrumentalists assembled in Prague for Fux's *Costanza e Fortezza* at the coronation of Emperor Charles VI as King of Bohemia in 1723 (Nettl 1951). A contemporary engraving of the event shows at least 90 musicians, playing violins, cellos or basses, harpsichord, theorbo, horns, oboes, flutes and other instruments (fig.4). Festival opera preserved and extended the tradition of *intermedio* orchestration; for example, in Cesti's *Il pomo d'oro* (1668, Vienna), performed for Emperor Leopold I's wedding, infernal scenes are accompanied by ensembles of cornetts and trombones.

In operas of the first half of the 17th century the musical role of the instrumental ensemble was limited. The basic rule was that, when someone was singing, only keyboards and plucked instruments should play. Bowed strings joined in the sinfonias, dances and ritornellos between arias or between verses of an aria. But from about the middle of the century – and connected with the separation of aria from recitative – the instrumental ensemble, particularly the violins, began increasingly to encroach on the preserve of the voice. At first the instruments were restricted to echo-like tags at the ends of vocal phrases, reinforcing the meaning of the text without unnatural word repetition (Rosand 1983). But soon the violins began to overlap more and more with the voice, playing along with the last few beats of the vocal phrase, then with the last few bars, and finally accompanying whole sections of the aria. The ensemble did not accompany every aria in this fashion; the procedure was used mainly to accompany in arias that called for heightened effect or special attention. The remaining arias continued to be accompanied only by basso continuo, though by 1680 cello or bass was usually added to the continuo group. By the end of the 17th century the instrumental ensemble in Italian opera had assumed the function of differentiating between levels of discourse and dramatic significance: accompaniment in recitative by harpsichord or theorbo signified ordinary discourse; accompaniment by harpsichord or theorbo

2. *Venetian opera orchestra, c1690: engraving from an edition of D. F. Contini's libretto for 'Gli equivoci nel sembiante' (Venice, 1690), set by Alessandro Scarlatti in 1679*

and a bowed bass instrument in so-called 'continuo' arias signified heightened discourse; aria accompaniment by the full ensemble signified a further heightening of discourse and greater weight in the drama.

4. FRENCH OPERA TO 1763. Opera was introduced into France by Cardinal Mazarin, who imported productions of seven operas from Italy between 1645 and 1662 (Zaslaw 1989). These presentations most often consisted of Italian vocal music grafted on to French ballet music, a hybrid arrangement that subsequently proved viable in many parts of Europe. They seem to have made use of the large instrumental forces already assembled at the French court. For example, Luigi Rossi's *Orfeo* (1647, Paris) opened with a sinfonia played by 20 violins and violas of varying sizes, four *violini* (over-sized cellos), four harpsichords, four theorbos, two lutes and two *chitarri*; the curtain went up to a fanfare of four trumpets with drums. Soon after the introduction of Italian opera, French composers began to compose works to French librettos in imitation of Mazarin's imports. In the earliest surviving example, Robert Cambert and Pierre Perrin's *Pastorale à musique* (1659, Issy; later known as *Pastorale d'Issy*), the four-part instrumental accompaniment was apparently realized by a string band assisted by oboes, bassoons and recorders.

The synthesis that proved defining for French opera was the work of the Florentine-born Giovanni Battista Lulli, who, naturalized as Jean-Baptiste Lully, eventually controlled both the Paris Opéra and the music at the French court. The court already maintained two large instrumental ensembles: the 24 violons du roi, a string band, and the Grande Ecurie, an ensemble of oboes and bassoons. To these Lully added the Petits violons du roi, a select ensemble of about 18 string players, to which could be added singers, lutenists and harpsichordists from the king's *musiciens de la chambre*. In his court ballets, beginning with *Alcidiane* (1658), and later in performances of his operas at court, Lully used these ensembles in various combinations, particularly in overtures and dance music, where he displayed the full splendour of his instrumental resources and which became models for instrumental music throughout Europe.

Lully created a style of vocal declamation based upon Italian recitative modified to suit the French language. Like Italian recitative, French recitative was accompanied by one or several chordal and melodic continuo instruments: at a revival of Lully's *Le triomphe de l'amour* in 1681, for instance, there were two harpsichordists and seven players of large lutes and cellos or bass violas da gamba (La Gorce 1989). To his newly-minted recitative Lully added songs derived in style from the *air de cour*, already well established in French secular music. The *air de cour* was a simple, usually strophic song for one or several voices, which could be accompanied by basso continuo and occasionally by one or two obbligato instruments. In general Lully did not use the string or wind ensembles to accompany *airs*, although the full ensemble played occasional *ritournelles*. It was in the *ouvertures*, 'sinfonies' (instrumental interludes) and in the dance music found in every act of his operas that Lully's orchestra came into its own. Here he wrote in a style specifically conceived for large ensemble, with full scoring, homophonic textures, strongly marked rhythms and contrasts of timbre. Unlike most Italian opera of the 17th and 18th centuries, French opera often gave an important role to the chorus, which was always accompanied by the orchestra.

Lully's instrumental ensembles were internationally admired for their unanimity of attack, bowing and ornamentation. His orchestra was not 'monochrome' but 'bichrome', consisting of the string band, the wind band or the two bands combined. The strings were usually set in five-part texture but occasionally in a trio texture of divided violins with cellos. The winds were scored in the much-imitated 'trio' of two oboes and bassoon, usually doubled or tripled, or in a four-part texture of soprano, alto and tenor oboes with bassoon (Harris-Warrick 1990). When string and wind bands played together, they usually doubled one another's parts. It seems almost certain that the lutes and harpsichords of the continuo group played only during vocal music, not in overtures, 'sinfonies' or dances (Sadler 1980).

At court opera and ballet productions (see fig.5) the 24 violons du roi were distributed approximately into seven violins, ten violas in three sizes, and eight *basses*

4. Fux's 'Costanza e Fortezza', Prague, 1723: detail of the engraving by Birckart after Giuseppe Galli-Bibiena (fully reproduced in PRAGUE, fig.1) showing the orchestra

5. *Orchestra for a performance of Lully's 'Alceste' in the Cour de Marbre, Versailles, 1674: details of the engraving by Jean Le Pautre (fully reproduced in* ALCESTE (i))

de violon (over-sized cellos), making five parts in all. When the Petits violons were used, they were divided approximately into seven violins, seven violas in three sizes, and four *basses de violon*. The wind band probably consisted of eight to ten players of oboes and bassoons, who doubled on flutes and recorders. The Paris Opéra had its own orchestra, the precise make-up of which before the beginning of the 18th century is not known. There were no double basses or other 16' instruments at court or at the Opéra until the first decade of the 18th century, when composers began to use them for special effects such as thunder and earthquakes.

In 1704 an administrative reform at the Paris Opéra set the orchestra's size at 44, and from at least 1719 to 1756 it hovered around 45–7, a number that could be accommodated in the Palais Royal, which housed the Opéra from 1673 until 1763. This was therefore the orchestra for the operas of Marais, Campra and Rameau, among others, as well as for numerous revivals of Lully's operas (see fig.6). During this period the string texture was altered, under growing Italian influence. In a continuing series of experiments, Lully's five-part texture was supplanted, first by another five-part scoring, in which the violins were divided and second and third violas combined, then by the modern four-part texture (two violins, viola, cello plus double bass). The use of these textures overlapped considerably during the first half of the 18th century. Rameau, for example, in *Hippolyte et Aricie* (1733) writes for strings in three-, four-, five- and even seven-part textures. The role of the orchestra in the *récits* and *airs* remained modest, but to the already considerable use of the orchestra in dance music, entr'actes and descriptive 'sinfonies', orchestrally accompanied arias were added in imitation of the early 18th-century Italian style. These were known, illogically, as 'ariettes'. Fine examples of *ariettes* with important orchestral participation are found in each of Rameau's operas, for instance 'Brillez, brillez' from the last act of *Castor et Pollux* (1737). Rameau had a refined sensibility for combinations of orchestral instruments, which he no longer restricted to the role of string or wind bands. He introduced the horn and the clarinet into the French opera orchestra, and his operas are filled with strikingly original orchestration.

5. 18TH CENTURY. By about 1720 the orchestra had become a standard and indispensable feature of opera throughout Europe. The word 'orchestra' and its cognates had come to refer to the instrumental ensemble as a distinct corporate entity. Instrumental ensembles had come to resemble one another in composition and proportions from one theatre to the next and from one country to another. And the orchestra had established for itself a secure and well understood role, serving formal and dramatic functions in both comic and serious opera. The opera orchestra did change somewhat during the 18th century – it grew larger, new instruments were added and old instruments were used in new ways. But for the most part the century was a period of stability. In its essentials the orchestra of Handel was the same as the orchestra of Pergolesi, of Rameau, of Gluck and of Mozart.

Copious data are available on the size and composition of opera orchestras in the 18th century. Figures for representative orchestras are given in Table 1. These figures are based on court rosters, payrolls, travellers' reports and similar documents. It is important to recognize that such figures do not represent the ensemble for any given production, where the instrumental forces might be reduced by absences or enlarged by supernumeraries. In addition, players often doubled on two or more instruments. In French and Italian orchestras, flute and oboe, and sometimes horn and trumpet, were played by the same personnel at least until the last quarter of the century. A note appended to the Paris Opéra roster for 1780 explains that all the violinists can play the viola if needed, that one of the oboists can play the clarinet, that the horn players can play either the trumpet or the trombone, and that one of the bassoonists can play the drum (*Almanach*, 1781).

Table 1 shows that 18th-century opera orchestras varied considerably in size. Haydn produced his operas and those of other composers at Eszterháza in the 1780s with orchestras of only 20 to 25. Gluck's *Orphée* (1774), *Alceste* (1776) and *Iphigénie en Tauride* (1779), on the other hand, were introduced at the Paris Opéra with orchestras of 60–70 players. Mozart wrote his operas for orchestras of varying size: 57 players for *Lucio Silla* (1772) in Milan; about 35 plus a stage band for *Idomeneo* (1781), drawn from the 83 instrumentalists on the payroll at the Munich court; 39 at the Burgtheater in Vienna for *Die Entführung aus dem Serail* (1782); and an ensemble of 30 or fewer at the Estates Theatre in Prague for *Don Giovanni* (1787). When a series of yearly figures is available for a given orchestra, the pattern that emerges in almost every case is one of steady growth over the course of the 18th century. The Paris Opéra grew from 43 players in 1704

6. Orchestra for a performance of Rameau's comédie-ballet 'La princesse de Navarre' at Versailles, 1745: watercolour by Charles-Nicolas Cochin fils (for an engraving showing the interior of the Grande Écurie during this performance see PARIS, fig.3)

to 52 in 1764 to 68 in 1793, the S Carlo orchestra in Naples from 45 in 1737 to 59 or 60 in 1786, and the court orchestra in Berlin from 28 in 1712 to 40 in 1754 to 64 in 1802. Although orchestras grew larger, the proportions of instruments tended to stay roughly the same. In the Berlin orchestra, for example, the number of violins approximately doubled from 1754 to 1788, but the viola, cello and bass sections also doubled. And the proportion of strings to wind in the Berlin orchestra hovered around 2 to 1 for most of the century. Proportions were similarly stable within the other orchestras noted in Table 1. On the other hand, proportions could vary significantly between orchestras, particularly those in different countries. Italian orchestras used comparatively more violins and double basses, fewer violas, cellos and wind instruments. German orchestras tended to use more wind than Italian or French orchestras, as contemporary listeners often noted (Zaslaw 1989).

The instruments used in opera remained relatively stable during the 18th century. The clarinet, invented during the first quarter of the century, was the only really new instrument to be introduced in the opera orchestra. Marc'Antonio Ziani called for a chalumeau, an early clarinet, in his opera *Caio Popilio* (1704, Vienna), as did other Viennese composers. (Emperor Joseph I contributed an ornate chalumeau obbligato to Ziani's *Chilonida*, 1709.) Rameau introduced a clarinet in *Zoroastre* (1749, Paris); however, Gluck still used the chalumeau in *Orfeo* (1762) and *Alceste* (1767). Clarinettists first appeared on the regular roster of the Paris Opéra in 1771, in Munich in 1774, in Naples in 1786 and in Stuttgart not before 1803. Horns (natural, valveless horns) were present in many German and Italian orchestras by the 1720s; they were not much used in French opera until the 1760s. All opera orchestras contained at least one harpsichord, and many had two. The *maestro* or the composer sat at the first harpsichord (house left) with the first violinist nearby; the second harpsichordist was placed at the other side of the orchestra. 18th-century sources do not explain the purpose of the two-harpsichord system and its function remains unclear (Libby 1992). Perhaps the main purpose was acoustical: when both instruments played, they distributed the harmonies and the beat throughout

the orchestra. It has been suggested that, when two singers were on stage, the first harpsichord accompanied one, the second the other (Chrysander 1877); or possibly recitatives were accompanied by the first harpsichord alone, arias and instrumental pieces by both. The only instruments to disappear from opera orchestras during the course of the century were the theorbo, a survivor from the days when plucked strings had constituted the core of the orchestra, and the recorder, which was replaced by the transverse flute. Trumpets and timpani were present (or at least available) for the entire period, although the players often did not appear in orchestra rosters as they were from the military establishment.

The ways that the orchestra was used in opera – that is, the scoring practices of composers – also remained relatively stable during the 18th century. Overtures, sinfonias and dances were played by the whole ensemble. A speciality of French opera were the 'descriptive symphonies', instrumental set pieces depicting events on the stage, for example a battle or a sea voyage or a storm (Masson 1930). Recitative was accompanied by harpsichord and one or more cellos and/or basses. At emotional moments in the drama, the composer might accompany the recitative with full strings, a technique used already in the 17th century by Cavalli and Cesti. For arias, instrumental accompaniment throughout by strings had become standard, with selected wind instruments often added as well. The orchestra played opening, intermediate and closing ritornellos and furnished a rhythmic and harmonic underlay for the vocal line, reinforcing the voice as necessary, providing contrast through idiomatic instrumental figuration or answering phrases, and unifying the aria with motivic repetition and instrumental texture.

The strings were usually scored in four parts, although the old five-part textures persisted in the form of *divisi* viola parts, which turn up in French, German and Italian operas throughout the 18th century. On the other hand, first and second violins were often scored in unison to give a three-part or (when violas doubled the bass) two-part texture. Cellos and basses usually played from the same part, the basses sounding an octave lower and omitting notes in rapid passages. In arias the en-

7. Orchestra for a performance of Feo's 'Arsace' at the Teatro Regio, Turin, 1740: detail from a painting by Pietro Domenico Olivero (fully reproduced in OPERA SERIA, fig.1)

8. Orchestra for Hilverding and Starzer's ballet-pantomime 'Le Turc généreux' at the Burgtheater, Vienna, in 1758: engraving by Bernardo Bellotto

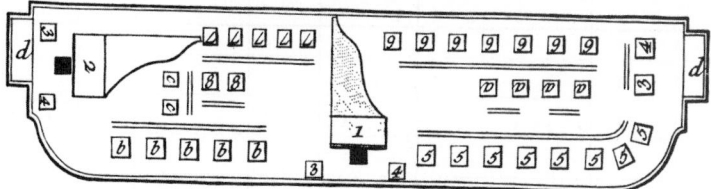

Renvois des Chiffres.

1. Clavecin du Maître de Chapelle.

2. Clavecin d'accompagnement.

3. Violoncelles.

4. Contre-basses.

5. Premiers Violons.

6. Seconds Violons, ayant le dos tourné vers le Théâtre.

7. Hautbois, de même.

8. Flutes, de même.

a. Tailles, de même.

b. Bassons.

c. Cors de Chasse.

d. Une Tribune de chaque côté pour les Tymballes et Trompettes.

9. Seating plan for the orchestra of the Dresden court opera under Hasse in 1754: from J.-J. Rousseau's 'Dictionnaire de musique', Paris, 1768

TABLE 1

City, institution	Date	STRINGS				WOODWIND				BRASS		OTHER			Total	Source
		violins	violas	cellos	double basses	flutes	oboes	clarinets	bassoons	horns	trumpets	drums	harpsichords			
Berlin, court opera	1712	11	2	5 (cellos+d.b.)		3	4		3				?		28	
	1754	12	3	4	2	4	3		4	2		2	2	1 theorbo, 1 violas da gamba	40	Mahling 1971
	1772	12	4	5	2	4	4		4	2			2	1 harp	40	BurneyGN
	1788	20	6	8	4	2	4	2	4	4	2	1	?	1 harp, 3 trombones	61	Mahling 1971
Dresden	1709	4	3+2	2	1	2	2+2		2	2	2	1		2 theorbos	27	
	1719	9	6	3	3	1	4		3	2	[2]	[1]	2	2 violas da gamba, 2 theorbos	40	Landmann 1989
	1733	10	4	6	2	3	6		4	2	[2]	[1]	2	1 theorbo	43	
	1756	19	4	3	2	3	5		6	3	[2]	[1]	1		49	
	1771	16	4	4	3	3	4		4	3	[2]	[1]	[1]		45	Mahling 1971
	1789	20	6	4	5	2	4		4	4	[2]	[1]	[1]		53	
Eszterháza	1776	4 (vlns+vlas)		1	1		3		3	5	2		[1]		20	
	1777	6 (vlns+vlas)		1	1	1	3		4	5	2		[1]		24	Bartha and Somfai 1960
	1782	9 (vlns+vlas)		2	1	1	2		4	5			[1]		25	
	1788	8 (vlns+vlas)		2	1	2	2		3	5			[1]		24	
London Queen's Theatre	1708	11	2	7 (cellos+d.b.)			2		3		1		1		27	Milhous and Hume 1982
	1710	9	2	6	1		2		3		1		1		25	
Royal Academy	1720	16	2	3	2		4		3		1		[1]	1 theorbo	33	Burrows 1985
Drury Lane Theatre	1775	9	3	3	1	2 (fl+ob)			2	2			1		23	Fiske 2/1986
Little Theatre in the Haymarket	1790	15	4	4	3	2	2	2	2	2					36	LS, v
Naples, Teatro S Carlo	1737	24	6	3	3		2		3		2		2		45	
	1740	38	8	2	4		6		4		6		2		70	Prota-Giurleo 1927
	1759	28	4	3	4		4		?		4		2		49	
	1786	27	4	4	8	2	2	4	2	2	2	1	2		60	
	1786	30	4	3	7		4	2	2	?	4		2	1 tromba spezzata	59	Robinson 1990

semble might be reduced while the singer was singing, then expanded to full orchestra for the ritornellos, a practice analogous to the alternation of concertino and ripieno groups in the concerto. Composers or copyists sometimes wrote 'solo' and 'tutti' in the score to indicate reduced and expanded forces, but the principle may also have applied where not indicated. When separate parts were not supplied, the bassoons usually doubled the cellos and basses. Oboe parts sometimes doubled the violins in the same fashion, usually with both oboes on the first violin part. In overtures, sinfonias and dances the wind instruments were more often used as a section, reinforcing the harmony with sustained chords or alternating en bloc with the strings. In arias, separate parts for wind were usually obbligato accompaniments: a single instrument or a pair of instruments accompanied the voice throughout, matching the singer's passage-work and often joining the voice in a double cadenza at the end (Spitzer 1988). Examples of such obbligato accompaniments are 'Con tromba guerriera' for alto with obbligato trumpet in Handel's *Silla* (1713, London), 'La fauvette avec ses petits' for soprano and flute in Grétry's *Zémire et Azor* (1771, Paris) and 'Parto, parto' for soprano with clarinet obbligato in Mozart's

City, institution	Date	STRINGS				WOODWIND				BRASS		OTHER			Total	Source
		violins	violas	cellos	double basses	flutes	oboes	clarinets	bassoons	horns	trumpets	drums	harpsichords			
Paris, Opéra	1704	11/12	3+3+2	9/10	0/1	4/5	4/5		3/4		0/1		1	2 theorbos, 2 basses de viole	44	La Gorce 1990
	1713	14	3+2+2	10		6			4				1	2 theorbos, 2 basses de viole	46	
	1738	16	3+3	11		5			5				1		44	
	1758	14	7	12		6			4	1	1	1			46	
	1764	17	6	12		5			5	2	1	2	1	1 musette	52	Almanach des spectacles de Paris
	1774	20	3	8	7	7	2		8	2	1	2	1		61	
	1776	28	4	12	5	8	2		8	2	2	1	1		73	
	1779	24	6	9	4	7	2		5	4	?	2			63	
	1787	24	6	12	5	2	4	2	4	2	3	4		2 piccolos, 1 harp	71	
	1793	24	5	10	5	2	4	2	5	4	4	1		2 serpents	68	Zaslaw 1976–7
Turin	1725	7	4	2			2+3		2				[1]	1 theorbo	22	Bouquet 1968
	1742	17	4	9		3			2	2		2			39	Bouquet 1976
	1755	16	5	10		3			2	4		2			42	
	1773	28	5	10		6			4	4	2	1	2		62	
	1780	26	4	3	6	4		2	3	4	2	1	2		57	
	1790	23	7	5	7	5		2	3	4	2	1	2		61	Galeazzi 1791
(Mozart operas) (Lucio Silla) Milan	1772	28	6	2	6	4			2	4	2	1	2		57	Zaslaw 1989
(Idomeneo) Munich	1781	12	2	2	2	3	2	2	2	4	2	1	1	offstage wind band	35	Zaslaw 1991
(Die Entführung aus dem Serail) Vienna	1782	12	4	3	3	3	2	2	2	4	[2]	[1]	[1]		39	Edge 1992
(Le nozze di Figaro) Vienna	1786	12	3	3	3	2	2	2	2	2	2	[1]	[1]		35	
(Don Giovanni) Prague	1787	8	2	1	2	2	2	2	2	2	2	1	[1]		27	Jahrbuch 1796

Note: Figures in square brackets are not shown in primary sources but are based on other firm evidence.

La clemenza di Tito (1791). Towards the end of the 18th century this tradition was supplanted by a more flexible style in which various wind instruments take momentary solos, then return to the general orchestral texture. This kaleidoscopic wind writing is common in the operas of Mozart and Rossini, and it had a great influence on symphonic style in the late 18th and early 19th centuries.

The orchestra in an 18th-century opera house was placed in front of the stage at floor level and separated from the audience by a rail. In the most common seating plan two long rows of violinists faced one another across double-sided desks which held the music (see fig. 7). Oboes, flutes and violas were distributed among the violins, whose parts they often doubled. To the sides were the harpsichords, each surrounded by a group of cellos, basses and bassoons, some of whom played from the same parts as the keyboard players. Brass instruments and drums were further to the sides. Contemporary paintings, engravings and diagrams show many variations of this plan (figs.8 and 9). French opera used a fundamentally different seating scheme, with all the players facing the stage, arranged in semicircles around the *batteur de mesure*, who stood at centre stage in front of the apron (figs.6 and 10). Outside France orchestras did not use a time beater (*see* CONDUCTOR,

§1); to some extent the orchestra was led by the player of the first harpsichord, who was often the composer himself, otherwise the *maestro* (Kapellmeister). But the orchestra was also led by the first violinist (Konzertmeister), who was sometimes placed on a raised platform so that the other players could see him and follow his lead. Recitatives were the responsibility of the harpsichordist, dance music of the violinist. Arias could be disputed ground. Contemporary sources give amusing accounts of performances in which the two would-be leaders struggled for control (Spitzer and Zaslaw 1986). Many of the players faced the stage in any case and could follow the singers directly.

6. 19TH CENTURY. Around the beginning of the 19th century the opera orchestra entered another period of change. The physical layout was altered, first with new seating patterns, and later by lowering the entire orchestra into an orchestra pit. Many new instruments were introduced, particularly in the brass section, and

many old ones were redesigned. Also, as the distinction between aria and recitative was attenuated, the entire orchestra began to play during more and more of the opera, leading to changes in the orchestra's dramatic role. Finally, the keyboard continuo disappeared, and the direction was taken over by a baton conductor, who directed not just the instrumentalists but the singers as well.

Seating plans of 19th-century opera orchestras have been studied in detail (Koury 1986). During the first quarter of the century orchestras abandoned the pattern of facing rows and began to sit in pairs facing the centre and reading from stands rather than desks. The 18th-century system of arranging the instruments according to musical function was replaced by a system of seating in sections by type of instrument. Typical arrangements from the first half of the century placed strings on one side, wind on the other (fig.11); later it became common to split the first violins from the seconds and the woodwind from the brass (fig.12). To help keep the beat, the

10. Plan of the stage and orchestra at the Grand Théâtre, Versailles, in 1773, giving the names of the instrumentalists, the chorus (disposed around the stage at the sides of the orchestra), and some of the principal singers at that time (centre stage): watercolour by J. B. Métoyen; note the position of the interchangeable scenery flats, and benches for the audience on either side of the orchestra.

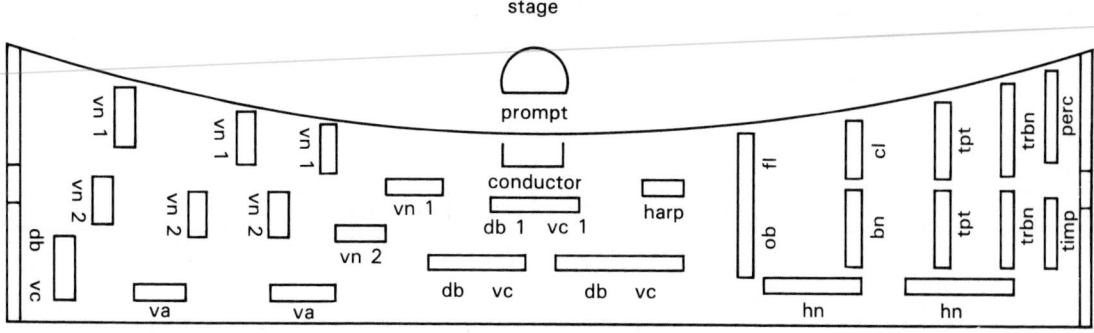

11. Seating plan of the orchestra of the Dresden court opera, c1840: after F. Gassner, 'Dirigent und Ripienist' (Karlsruhe, 1844)

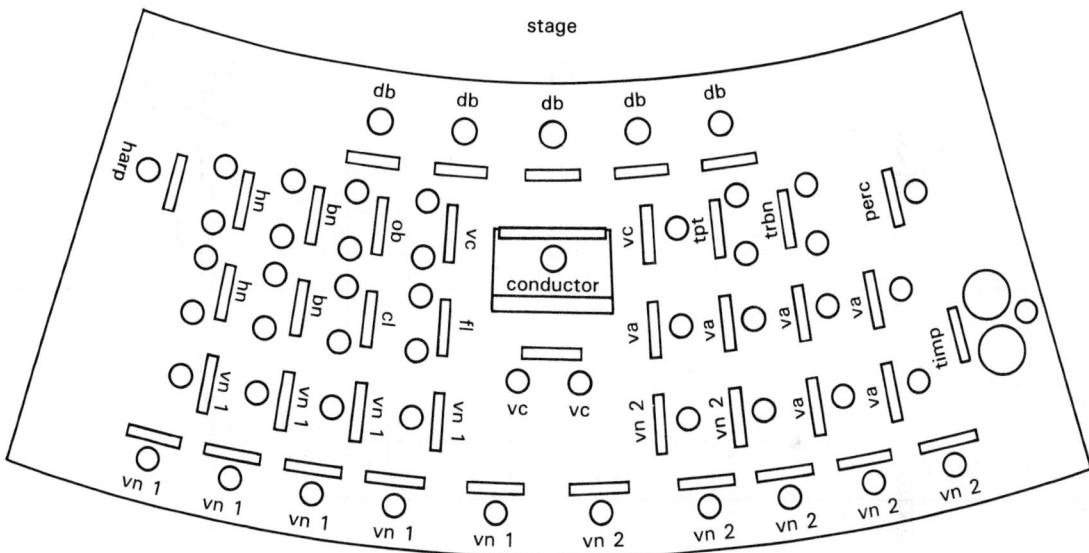

12. Seating plan of the orchestra of the Vienna court opera, c1890: after H. Kling, 'Der vollkommene Musik-Dirigent' (Hanover, 1890)

double basses were often placed in a row stretching across the orchestra, a practice about which Verdi repeatedly complained, saying that it ruined the sonority of the section (Harwood 1986–7).

During most of the 19th century, the orchestra remained at the level of the theatre floor. A theatre built by Ledoux at Besançon in 1784 had a sunken pit for the orchestra, as did Schinkel's Schauspielhaus am Gendarmenmarkt in Berlin (1821). It was Wagner's Festspielhaus at Bayreuth (inaugurated 1876), however, with its placing of the orchestra in a *mystischer Abgrund* ('mystic chasm') between stage and audience (see figs.13 and 14), that made the orchestra pit a standard feature in opera. Most new opera houses in the late 19th century adopted modified versions of Wagner's innovation. Instrumentalists also appeared on the stage and in costume, particularly in Italian and French operas, as a 'banda sul palco' (or 'musique de scène'). Early instances of this practice, as in the Act 1 finale of *Don Giovanni* (1787, Prague), used instruments and players drawn from the orchestra. In the 19th century the *banda* tended to consist of military band instruments – clarinets, cornets, keyed bugles, ophicleides etc. – with players sometimes borrowed from the local garrison. The *banda* accompanied processions and military events on stage, sometimes exchanging phrases with the

orchestra in the pit (e.g. Verdi, Act 2 of *I Lombardi*, 1843, Milan; Meyerbeer, Act 4 of *Le prophète*, 1849, Paris).

The piano replaced the harpsichord in the opera orchestra about the end of the 18th century, but it did not serve the same function of supplying the harmonies and guiding the ensemble. Even accompaniment of simple recitative was taken over for the most part by the cello. The piano remained in the orchestra as a place where the composer or chorus master could sit and supervise the performance. Beethoven, for example, pre-

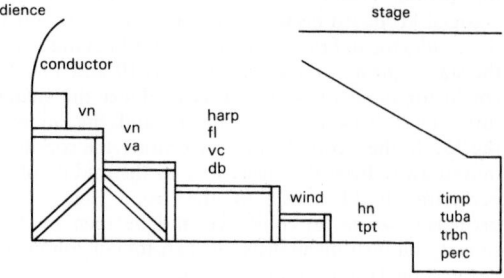

13. Cross-section of the orchestra pit at Bayreuth, c1900: after A. Lavignac, 'The Music Dramas of Wagner and his Festival Theatre in Bayreuth' (New York, 1902)

TABLE 2

City, institution	Date	STRINGS				WOODWIND				BRASS			OTHER		Total	Source
		violins	violas	cellos	double basses	flutes	oboes	clarinets	bassoons	horns	trumpets	trombones	drums			
Berlin	1802	25	4	9	4	3	5	3	4	4	[2]		[1]		64	Mahling 1971
	1821	24	7	9	5	4	6	5	5	8	2	2	1		78	
	1843	28	8	10	8	4	4	4	4	[8]	4	[3]	2	2 harps	89	Koury 1986; Mahling 1971
	1865	32	8	11	7	5	5	5	5	8	3	4	1	1 harp	95	Mahling 1971
	1890	22	8	8	8	8	2	2	2	4	2	2	1	1 harp, 1 piano	71	Koury 1986
Dresden	1804	20	4	4	4	3	3	2	4	4	[2]		[1]		51	Mahling 1971
	1832	16	4	6	4	5	4	4	5	5	3		2		58	Carse 1948
	1850	18	5	5	5	4	4	4	4	5	4	3	1	1 harp	63	
	1863	18	5	6	3	5	4	4	4	6	[4]	3	2		64	
	1884	19	7	5	5	5	4	5	4	6	[5]	3	3	2 harps	73	Mahling 1971
	1896	26	9	7	5	3	5	4	4	6	[4]	3	3	2 harps	81	
London King's Theatre	1818	19	4	4	5	2	2	2	2	2	2	1	1		46	
	1832	20	6	6	6	2	2	2	2	4	2	2	1		55	
Her Majesty's Theatre	1839	28	8	8	8	2	2	2	2	4	3	3	4	1 harp, 1 ophicleide	76	Carse 1948
Covent Garden	1847	28	10	10	9	2	2	2	2	4	2	3	3	1 harp, 1 ophicleide	79	
Paris, Opéra	1810	24	8	12	6	2	4	2	4	4	4	3	2	1 contrabassoon	76	Koury 1986
	1826	24	8	10	8	3	3	3	4	4	2	3	1	1 harp	74	
	1839	24	8	10	8	3	2	2	4	4	2	3	2	1 cor anglais, 2 cornets, 1 keyed bugle, 1 ophicleide, 2 harps	79	Carse 1948
	1855	22	8	10	8	3	3	2	4	5	4	4	5	2 harps	80	Koury 1986
	1890	23	8	10	8	4	2	2	4	6	2	3	1	2 cornets, 1 tuba, 1 harp	77	

sided at the piano for the first performance of *Fidelio* (1805, Vienna), Rossini for the performances of his operas at the King's Theatre in London in 1824. As baton conducting became established in opera during the period 1790–1865 (*see* CONDUCTOR, §1), this vestigial keyboard disappeared. The usual position for the conductor in France, Germany and England was at the stage apron in the centre (see figs.10 and 11). The conductor faced the stage so as to direct the singers, turning his back to the orchestra and the audience (fig.15). In the second half of the century the conductor moved away from the stage, first to the middle of the orchestra (fig.12), then to the front edge of the orchestra, where he could see and be seen by both singers and instrumentalists (fig.13); Italian conductors had occupied this position all along.

The number of players in opera orchestras tended to rise during the 19th century, continuing the earlier trend. This increase was due both to the multiplication of instruments and also to the introduction of new ones. Table 2 gives statistics for representative orchestras. As in Table 1, most of the figures are based on personnel rosters, not on the orchestras for given productions. The table shows an overall trend towards strengthening the strings in relation to the woodwind. It also shows a growing tendency towards international uniformity, particularly with the bolstering of the viola and cello sections in Italian orchestras after mid-century. The most significant new instruments were in the brass section. Trombones, which had been available in a few German theatres during the 18th century, became standard throughout Europe. The ophicleide and *cimbasso* were added from the 1820s to give the brass family a bass voice; they were gradually replaced by the tuba from the 1830s. Just as important were modifications in old instruments: the addition of valves to horns and trumpets allowed them to play melodies in their low and middle registers and to modulate freely. For some

City, institution	Date	Composition of typical 19th-century opera orchestras													Total	Source
		STRINGS				WOODWIND				BRASS			OTHER			
		violins	violas	cellos	double basses	flutes	oboes	clarinets	bassoons	horns	trumpets	trombones	drums			
Verdi operas (*Ernani*) Venice	1844	24	5	3	10	2	2	2	2	4	2	3	6	1 harp, 1 cimbasso, 1 bass clarinet, stage band	68	Gallico 1985
(*I masnadieri*) London	1847	28	8	8	8	2	2	2	2	4	3	3	[1]	1 harp	72	Harwood 1986–7
(*Jérusalem*) Paris	1847	24	8	9	8	3	3	3	4	6	4	3	[2]	2 harps, 2 cornets, 1 ophicleide, stage band	82	Carse 1948
(*Rigoletto*) Venice	1851	24	6	3	9	2	2	2	2	4	2	3	6	1 harp, 1 cimbasso, stage band	67	Chusid 1983
(*Il trovatore*) Rome	1853	18	2	2	4	2	[2]	2	2	3	2	3	1	1 harp, 1 cimbasso	45	
(*La traviata*) Venice	1853	24	6	3	8	2	2	2	2	4	2	3	2	1 bombardon, stage band	61	Harwood 1986–7
(*Les vêpres siciliennes*) Paris	1855	22	8	10	8	3	3	3	4	5	4	4	2	1 harp	77	
(*Otello*) Milan	1887	30	10	11	11	2	2	2	4	4	2	3	5	2 harps, 1 piccolo, 1 cor anglais, 1 bass clarinet, 2 cornets, stage band	93	Koury 1986 (figures for 1890)

Note: Figures in square brackets are not shown in primary sources but are based on other firm evidence.

time old and new instruments played side by side in the same orchestras. For example, Wagner in *Rienzi* (1842, Dresden) called for two natural trumpets along with two valved cornets, two natural horns along with two valved horns, and both serpent and ophicleide. Many percussion instruments were also added – bass drum, snare drum, cymbals, bells, anvil – and increased numbers of percussionists were engaged to play them. Keywork added to the woodwind during the first half of the century enabled these instruments to play in any key rapidly and in tune.

These technological developments meant the end of the 'monochrome' orchestra in opera. Bowed strings no longer provided the standard orchestral sonority. Now woodwind and brass sonorities could be equally satisfactory, and with judicious combinations a composer could achieve a myriad of orchestral colours and effects. Fétis (1828) criticized 18th-century scoring practices and extolled these new colouristic possibilities, which he observed harked back to the earliest days of opera:

What a source of monotony is this obstinate adherence to the constant reproduction of the same sounds, the same accents, the same associations! With such an increase of means, why not imitate the happy idea of Monteverdi, by imparting to each piece a particular character, by employing the variety of sound afforded by different instruments?

This technique of colouring each segment of the opera with uniquely appropriate instrumental combinations was being developed at the time of Fétis's essay by such composers as Spontini and Weber; it was soon to be extended by Berlioz, Meyerbeer and Wagner.

The role of the orchestra in the musical drama also changed significantly during the course of the 19th century. In 18th-century opera the orchestra had differentiated between levels of discourse by distinguishing simple recitative from accompanied recitative, and from aria. During the last quarter of the century, however, accompanied recitative became increasingly prevalent, breaking down these distinctions. The introduction into opera of episodes of melodrama – spoken dialogue with instrumental accompaniment – as in the dungeon scene of Beethoven's *Fidelio* (1805 and 1814, Vienna) or the Wolf's Glen scene in Weber's *Der Freischütz* (1821, Berlin), had a similar effect. When such composers as Rossini (*Maometto II*, 1820, Naples) and Weber (*Euryanthe*, 1823, Vienna) set longer and longer sections of the drama in continuous musical units with orchestral accompaniment, the distinctions between levels of discourse were blurred still further. These tendencies culminated in Wagner's notion of 'unendliche Melodie', where the discourse shifts seamlessly from one level to another without formal markers. Freed from its structural functions and endowed with new colouristic possibilities, the orchestra of 19th-century opera assumed the roles of depiction and narration. Orchestration became as important as stage design in establishing the setting of the drama, particularly in operas with exotic locales, for example Bizet's *Carmen* (1875, Paris) or Delibes' *Lakmé* (1883, Paris). The

14. *The orchestra pit at the Bayreuth Festspielhaus, 1955 (conductor Joseph Keilberth)*

15. *Conductor standing immediately in front of the stage, with his back to the orchestra, at the Royal Italian Opera, Covent Garden: engraving showing the 'late Royal Italian Opera' (it had burnt down on 5 March 1856), from 'The Illustrated London News' (6 December 1856)*

orchestra could also be used to depict the personalities and inner states of the characters, a technique used to great effect by Verdi from *Rigoletto* (1851, Venice) onwards. With the LEITMOTIF technique, developed by Wagner but used by many other composers, the orchestra could help tell the story or probe into the thoughts and emotions of the characters. Thus, in the operas of the late 19th century the orchestra functions as a central element in the drama: as the medium in which the story unfolds, as a commentator on the dramatic action and sometimes as an actor in its own right.

7. 20TH CENTURY. Because the operatic stage in the 20th century has been dominated by 19th-century repertory, the 20th-century opera orchestra has remained frozen to a considerable extent in the 19th-century mould. Consequently, 20th-century composers of opera have tended to use the orchestra in very much the same manner as their 19th-century predecessors.

In size, composition, proportions and seating patterns, the orchestras of modern opera houses resemble the orchestras of the late 19th century (fig.16). The only section to be much expanded has been the percussion, with the addition of bells, gongs, xylophones, vibraphones and marimbas, and any number of non-Western instruments. The size and composition of the ensemble usually varies according to the repertory being performed. *Die Meistersinger* is performed with a larger orchestra than *Norma*; a keyboard instrument is added for the recitative in operas by Mozart or Rossini. Still older repertory – Handel, Cavalli or Monteverdi – has become largely the province of early music specialists playing period instruments.

Most 20th-century opera composers, whatever their musical idiom, have contented themselves with the ensemble they have found in the orchestra pit. Debussy, Strauss, Puccini, Berg, Janáček, Prokofiev, Poulenc and Adams have all written for this traditional orchestra, and they all use it in traditional ways. Typically the orchestra plays throughout, both along with the singers and in orchestral interludes. Instruments are combined freely for dramatic, rhetorical and colouristic effects. If anything, the pick-and-choose principles of 19th-century orchestration have been extended, so that at a given moment only a handful of instruments may be playing. This is particularly useful when the orchestra accompanies a solo singer. Examples of sparse scoring may be found in operas by Strauss (*Intermezzo*, 1924, Dresden), Berg (*Wozzeck*, 1925, Berlin) and Britten (*Death in Venice*, 1973, Snape), as well as many other 20th-century composers.

Related to this trend is the emergence of 'chamber opera' as a distinct genre in the 20th century, with relatively small casts, modest staging requirements, and small orchestras. In *Ariadne auf Naxos* (1912, Stuttgart; 1916, Vienna), for example, Strauss specifies an orchestra of only six violins, four violas, four cellos and two basses, along with pairs of woodwind and horns, trumpet, piano and two harps. Milhaud, in *Les malheurs d'Orphée* (1926, Brussels), asks for single wind and strings one-to-a-part. Hindemith's *Hin und zurück* (1927, Baden-Baden) uses an ensemble of only nine wind instruments with two pianos and harmonium. Britten's chamber operas, among them *The Rape of Lucretia* (1946, Glyndebourne), *Albert Herring* (1947, Glyndebourne) and *The Turn of the Screw* (1954, Venice), call for small string sections, single wind and piano along with harp and percussion. In some operas

16. *Orchestra pit at the Royal Opera House, Covent Garden, London, during a performance of Puccini's 'Manon Lescaut', conducted by Giuseppe Sinopoli in 1983*

the reduced orchestra is associated with a return to the aesthetics and the operatic techniques of the 18th century. In *The Rape of Lucretia*, for example, recitative is accompanied by the conductor playing a 'continuo' part on the piano. Stravinsky, in *The Rake's Progress* (1951, Venice), makes selfconscious use of orchestral conventions of 18th-century opera for an 18th-century plot: aria versus recitative, harpsichord continuo, orchestral ritornellos, woodwind obbligatos.

Comparatively few 20th-century operas call for orchestras that are radically different from the orchestras of the past. In *Die Dreigroschenoper* (1928, Berlin) Kurt Weill uses what is essentially a jazz band: tenor and alto saxophones, two trumpets, trombone, banjo, drum set and piano, with several of the players doubling on other instruments. Other jazz-influenced operas, such as Weill's *Aufstieg und Fall der Stadt Mahagonny* (1930, Leipzig) or Krenek's *Jonny spielt auf* (1927, Leipzig), use a standard orchestra with jazz instruments added for occasional colour. Carl Orff, in *Antigonae* (1949, Salzburg) and *Prometheus* (1968, Stuttgart), experimented with an orchestra based on multiple pianos and percussion, with string basses added for sustained passages and wind choirs for special effects. Harry Partch's musical dance-dramas (*Oedipus*, 1952, Oakland; *Revelation in the Courthouse Park*, 1961, Urbana; and *Delusion of the Fury*, 1969, Los Angeles) use a unique set of specially constructed string and percussion instruments tuned to scales based on just intonation. Other composers use a standard orchestra but ask for novel playing techniques, as in Penderecki's *The Devils of Loudun* (1969, Hamburg), which uses tone clusters and strings playing glissando, molto vibrato and behind the bridge. Stockhausen in his *Licht* series returns to the Renaissance notion of symbolic ensembles participating in the action onstage. In the 'Lucifer's Dance' scene from *Samstag aus Licht* (1984, Milan), for example, a wind band is arranged on risers in the form of a giant human face (see fig.17).

Electronic instruments have been used sparingly in 20th-century opera. Messiaen uses three ondes martenots as part of an otherwise standard orchestra in *Saint François d'Assise* (1983, Paris). Blomdahl's *Aniara* (1959, Stockholm) features pre-recorded taped segments, as does Penderecki's *The Devils of Loudun*. Adams makes use of electric piano and synthesizer in

Nixon in China (1987, Houston). Electronics are more integral to the instrumental textures in the operas of Philip Glass, particularly *Einstein on the Beach* (1976, New York), where three electronic organs play alone for long stretches. An example of an almost entirely electronic opera is *Valis* (1987, Paris), by Tod Machover, in which piano and percussion are transformed by real-time computer electronics and occasionally combined with pre-recorded taped material (see fig.18 overleaf).

For further illustration of 18th-century orchestras *see* DRESDEN, fig.2; MILAN, fig.2; SEATING, fig.1; and SOCIOLOGY OF OPERA, fig.1.

17. *Wind band arranged in the form of a human face, on stage in the 'Lucifer's Dance' scene from Stockhausen's 'Samstag aus Licht' (Palazzo dello Sport, Milan, 1984; La Scala production)*

18. The 'orchestra' for 'Valis' by Tod Machover (Centre Pompidou, Paris, 1987)

GENERAL

HMT ('Orchester'; M. Staehelin)
O. Schreiber: Orchester und Orchesterpraxis in Deutschland zwischen 1780 und 1850 (Berlin, 1938)
D. J. Grout: A Short History of Opera (New York, 1947, 3/1988)
H. C. Wolff: Oper: Szene und Darstellung von 1600 bis 1900, Musikgeschichte in Bildern, iv (Leipzig, 1968)
M. Forsyth: Buildings for Music (Cambridge, 1985)
N. Zaslaw: 'When is an Orchestra not an Orchestra?', EMc, xvi (1988), 483–95

BEFORE OPERA

O. Sonneck: 'A Description of Alessandro Striggio and Francesco Corteccia's Intermedi "Psyche and Amor"', Miscellaneous Studies in the History of Music (New York, 1921), 269–86
R. L. Weaver: 'Sixteenth-Century Instrumentation', MQ, xlvii (1961), 363–78
H. M. Brown: Sixteenth-Century Instrumentation: the Music for the Florentine Intermedii, MSD, xxx (1973)

EARLY OPERA

A. Solerti: Le origini del melodrama (Turin, 1903)
T. F. Kelly: '"Orfeo da Camera" – Estimating Performing Forces in Early Opera', Historical Performance, i (1988), 3–9

17TH CENTURY

H. Goldschmidt: 'Die Instrumentalbegleitung der italienischen Musikdramen in der ersten Hälfte des XVII. Jahrhunderts', Monatshefte für Musikgeschichte, xxvii (1895), 52–62
R. L. Weaver: 'The Orchestra in Early Italian Opera', JAMS, xvii (1964), 83–9
R. Leppard: 'Cavalli's Operas', PRMA, xciii (1966–7), 67–76
E. Selfridge-Field: Venetian Instrumental Music from Gabrieli to Vivaldi (Oxford, 1975)
J. Glover: Cavalli (London, 1978)
E. Rosand, ed.: A. Aureli and A. Sartorio: L'Orfeo, DMV, vi (Milan, 1983)
E. Selfridge-Field: Pallade Veneta: Writings on Music in Venetian Society, 1650–1750 (Venice, 1985)
J. Spitzer: 'The Birth of the Orchestra in Rome – an Iconographic Study', EMc, xix (1991), 9–27
P. Holman: Four and Twenty Fiddlers: the Violin at the English Court, 1540–1690 (Oxford, forthcoming)

FRENCH OPERA TO 1763

J. Eppelsheim: Das Orchester in den Werken Jean-Baptiste Lullys (Tutzing, 1961)
J. de La Gorce: 'L'Académie royale de musique en 1704', RdM, lxv (1979), 160–91
G. Sadler: 'The Role of the Keyboard Continuo in French Opera 1673–1776', EMc, viii (1980), 148–57
——: 'Rameau and the Orchestra', PRMA, cviii (1981–2), 47–68
——: 'Rameau's Singers and Players: a Little-known Inventory of 1738', EMc, xi (1983), 453–67
N. Zaslaw: 'Lully's Orchestra': Lully: Heidelberg and St Germain-en-Laye 1987, 539–79

——: 'The First Opera in Paris: a Study in the Politics of Art', Jean-Baptiste Lully and the Music of the French Baroque: Essays in Honour of James R. Anthony (Cambridge, 1989), 7–23
J. de La Gorce: 'Some Notes on Lully's Orchestra', ibid, 99–112
——: 'L'orchestre de l'Opéra et son évolution de Campra à Rameau', RdM, lxxvi (1990), 23–43
R. Harris-Warrick: 'A few Thoughts on Lully's hautbois', EMc, xviii (1990), 97–106

18TH CENTURY

BurneyFI; BurneyGN; LS
Almanach des spectacles de Paris (1752–94)
F. Galeazzi: Elementi teorico-pratici di musica (Rome, 1791–6)
Jahrbuch der Tonkunst von Wien und Prag (Vienna, 1796)
F. Chrysander: 'Zwei Claviere bei Händel Cembalo-Partituren', AMZ, xii (1877), 175–80; xiii (1878), 193–7
H. Goldschmidt: Studien zur Geschichte der italienischen Oper im 17. Jahrhundert, i (Leipzig, 1901)
U. Prota-Giurleo: La grande orchestra del R. Teatro San Carlo nel settecento (Naples, 1927)
P.-M. Masson: L'opéra de Rameau (Paris, 1930)
A. Carse: The Orchestra in the Eighteenth Century (Cambridge, 1940)
P. Nettl: Forgotten Musicians (New York, 1951)
E. Borrel: 'L'orchestre du Concert Spirituel et celui de l'Opéra de Paris, de 1751 à 1800, d'après les Spectacles de Paris', Mélanges d'histoire et d'esthétique musicales offerts à Paul-Marie Masson (Paris, 1955), ii, 9–15
D. Bartha and L. Somfai: Haydn als Opernkapellmeister (Budapest, 1960)
M.-T. Bouquet: Musique et Musiciens à Turin de 1648 à 1775 (Turin, 1968)
C. H. Mahling: Orchester und Orchestermusik in Deutschland von 1750 bis 1850 (Habilitationsschrift, Saarbrücken U., 1971)
R. Fiske: English Theatre Music in the Eighteenth Century (London, 1973, 2/1986)
M.-T. Bouquet: Il Teatro di Corte dalle origini al 1788 (Turin, 1976)
N. Zaslaw: 'Toward the Revival of the Classical Orchestra', PRMA, ciii (1976–7), 158–87
J. Milhous and R. D. Hume: Vice-Chamberlain Coke's Theatrical Papers 1706–1715 (Carbondale, IL, 1982)
D. Burrows: 'Handel's London Theatre Orchestra', EMc, xiii (1985), 349–57
D. Charlton: 'Orchestra and Chorus at the Comédie-Italienne (Opéra-Comique), 1755–1799', Slavonic and Romantic Music: Essays for Gerald Abraham (Oxford, 1985), 87–108
J. Spitzer and N. Zaslaw, 'Improvised Ornamentation in 18th-Century Orchestras', JAMS, xxxix (1986), 524–77
J. Spitzer: 'Improvised Ornamentation in a Handel Aria with Obbligato Wind Accompaniment', EMc, xvi (1988), 514–22
O. Landmann: 'The Dresden Hofkapelle during the Lifetime of Johann Sebastian Bach', EMc, xvii (1989), 17–31
N. Zaslaw: Mozart's Symphonies (Oxford, 1989)

M. F. Robinson: 'A Late 18th-Century Account Book of the San Carlo Theatre, Naples', *EMc*, xviii (1990), 73–81

N. Zaslaw: 'Mozart's orchestra for *Idomeneo*', *Mozart: Tokyo 1991* (forthcoming)

D. Edge: 'Mozart's Viennese Orchestras', *EMc*, xx (1992), 64–88

D. Libby: Introduction to G. B. Pergolesi: *Salustia* (New York, 1992)

19TH CENTURY

F.-J. Fétis: 'On the Revolutions of the Orchestra', *Harmonicon*, vi (1828), 194–7

E. O. Sachs: *Modern Opera Houses and Theatres* (London, 1896–8)

A. Carse: *The Orchestra from Beethoven to Berlioz* (Cambridge, 1948)

F. I. Travis: *Verdi's Orchestration* (Zürich, 1956)

R. M. Longyear: 'The *banda sul palco* in 19th-Century Opera', *Journal of Band Research*, xiii/2 (1978), 25–40

G. Reinäcker: 'Zu einigen Besonderheiten der Orchesterdramaturgie in Wagners Opern', *Musik und Gesellschaft*, xxviii (1978), 149–56

M. Chusid: Introduction to G. Verdi: *Rigoletto* (Chicago, 1983)

C. Gallico: Introduction to G. Verdi: *Ernani* (Chicago, 1985)

J. Maehder: '"Banda sul Palco" – Variable Besetzungen in der Bühnenmusik der italienischen Oper des 19. Jahrhunderts', *GfMKB, Stuttgart 1985*, 293–310

D. Koury: *Orchestral Performance Practices in the Nineteenth Century – Size, Proportions, and Seating* (Ann Arbor, 1986)

G. W. Harwood: 'Verdi's Reform of the Italian Opera Orchestra', *19th Century Music*, x (1986–7), 108–34

JOHN SPITZER, NEAL ZASLAW

Orchestral recitative. Term for recitative in which the orchestra enhances the sense of the words with dramatic or expressive accompaniments or interjections. It is sometimes known as *recitativo obbligato* or *recitativo stromentato*; the term *recitativo accompagnato* ('accompanied recitative') is generally taken to signify a more passive, sustained, manner of orchestral accompaniment. *See* RECITATIVE.

Ordonez [Ordoñez, Ordonitz, Ordonetz], **Carlo d'** [Karl von] (*b* Vienna, 19 April 1734; *d* Vienna, 6 Sept 1786). Austrian composer. According to Count Karl von Zinzendorf, he was the 'fils naturel de Mr. de Buquoy'; his surname (never apparently spelt with a tilde in 18th-century documents) is probably from his adoptive family, whose Viennese origins may have begun with the reign of Charles VI as Imperial ruler. He worked as an official in the Lower Austrian administration, and was a violinist and a founder-member of the Tonkünstler-Sozietät of Vienna.

As a composer, Ordonez was active from the 1750s, especially in orchestral and chamber music. He wrote two stage works. *Alceste*, a marionette parody of Gluck's opera, to a text by J. K. von Pauersbach (score *H-Bn*), had its first performance on 30 August 1775, conducted by Haydn at Eszterháza. The work was given at Schönbrunn in 1777 and staged 49 times from 1783 to 1795 at the theatre in the Leopoldstadt. In this popular work Ordonez not only quoted directly from Gluck's model but also adopted the unadorned melodic style and refrain concept of Gluck's reform operas. *Alceste* was parodied as *Die neue Alzeste* by Wenzel Müller in 1806; this parody continued in the Leopoldstadt repertory until 1821. On 22 April 1778 the première of Ordonez's 'Originalsingspiel' *Diesmal hat der Mann den Willen!* (1, J. F. Schmidt, after Lemonnier; abbreviated version of score *A-Wn*, complete pubd lib. *Wn*, *US-NYp*, *Wc*) opened the second season of the National Singspiel at the Burgtheater, Vienna. Mentioned by nearly every contemporary source on the composer, it reached the stage of the Berlin Hoftheater in 1783; it too was a parody, this time based on

Monsigny's *Le maître en droit*. There are no records of Ordonez's musical activities after 1780.

MGG (H. C. R. Landon); *WurzbachL*

K. von Zinzendorf: *Diaries* (MS, *c*1761–1813, Haus-, Hof- und Staatsarchiv, Vienna)

J. N. Forkel: *Musikalischer Almanach 1783* (Leipzig, 1782), 54; *1784* (Leipzig, 1783), 108; *1789* (Leipzig, 1788), 86

H. C. R. Landon: 'Haydn's Marionette Theatre at Esterház Castle', *HayJb*, i (1962), 111–97

O. Michtner: *Das alte Burgtheater als Opernbühne* (Vienna, 1970)

T. L. Bankston: *A Transcription and Translation of 'Musica dalla parodie d'Alceste' by Carlos d'Ordoñez* (diss., North Texas State U., 1972)

A. P. Brown: 'An Introduction to the Life and Works of Carlos d'Ordoñez', *Music East and West: Essays in Honor of Walter Kaufman* (New York, 1980), 243–59

D. Young: 'Karl von Ordonez (1734–1786): a Biographical Study', *RMARC*, no.19 (1983–5), 31–56   A. PETER BROWN

Ordonneau, Maurice (*b* Saintes, Charente-Maritime, 18 June 1854; *d* ?Paris, ?1916). French librettist. Like his contemporaries Clairville, Chivot and Duru, Ordonneau was a prolific collaborator on librettos for many light-opera composers, including Audran, Planquette, Serpette and Roger. Among over 40 stage works his outstanding libretto is that for Louis Ganne's *Les saltimbanques* (1899), which despite many changes in fashion has held its place in the French repertory, partly because of the charm of Ordonneau's tale of travelling players and their adventures. Later in his career he wrote texts for operettas by Edy Toulouche and Henri Goublier and two works for London, *Babette* and *The Royal Star*; his libretto for Audran's *La poupée* (1896) owes something to the setting of Hoffmann's Coppelius story, but has a young woman substitute herself for the automaton.

selective list

Les diamants de Florinette (opérette, with E. Hamm), L. C. Désormes, 1875; La Princesse Colombine (oc, with E. André), R. Planquette, 1886; La financée des Verts-Poteaux (opéra-bouffe, with André), E. Audran, 1887; L'oncle Célestin (opérette, with H. Kéroul), Audran, 1891; Cousin-Cousine (opérette, with Kéroul), G. Serpette, 1893; Au premier hussard (opérette), L. Vasseur, 1896; Les saltimbanques (oc), L. Ganne, 1899; Le jockey malgré lui (opérette, with P. Gavault), V. Roger, 1902; La marquise de Chicago (opérette, with F. Beissier and P. Bérel), E. Toulouche, 1911; La cocarde de Mimi Pinson (opérette, with F. Gally), H. Goublier, 1915

StiegerO

R. Traubner: *Operetta: a Theatrical History* (New York, 1983)
                                        PATRICK O'CONNOR

Orefice [Arefece, Orefici], **Antonio** (*fl* 1708–34). Italian composer. According to most sources he was trained as a lawyer; but his success as a composer suggests he also received expert instruction in music. He began his career as a composer with *Il Maurizio*, a heroic opera, produced at S Bartolomeo, Naples, in December 1708. His next opera, *Patrò Calienno de la Costa*, was presented at the Fiorentini, Naples, on 1 October 1709, and is historically important as the first comic opera in Neapolitan dialect performed on a public stage. Its popularity led the Fiorentini management to promote further operas of this type, some of which were set by Orefice, and the success of these in turn made dialect comic opera as a genre the established form of popular entertainment at the Fiorentini and some other small theatres in Naples. Only one of Orefice's comic operas, *Il gemino amore* (1718), is without roles in dialect.

Given his reputation, which can be gauged from the number of operas he wrote, it is surprising that so little of his music survives. His largest remaining work is the first half of *Engelberta*, a heroic opera first performed at the Neapolitan royal palace on 4 November 1709. This was therefore presented just 34 days after the première of *Patrò Calienno de la Costa*; the closeness of the dates may explain why Orefice did not compose the whole work but only the first half of it. The manuscript score attributes the remainder of the music to Francesco Mancini; the three comic intermezzos, for the characters Vespetta and Pimpinone, are by a third composer, Tomaso Albinoni. Orefice's music in *Engelberta* seems to be modelled on that of leading contemporary Neapolitans, including Alessandro Scarlatti. It compares well with Mancini's contribution from the point of view of technical competence and expressive quality, though Orefice's style is a little less forceful than Mancini's. The other remaining operatic music by Orefice is a group of seven arias from *Le fente zingare* of 1717. This is the earliest surviving music from any comic opera in Neapolitan dialect and is invaluable as a guide to the development of the musical style adopted by the Neapolitans Vinci and Leo in their dialect operas of the 1720s. An undated cantata by Orefice, *Sopra un verde colle*, survives (*I-Nc*).

According to Prota-Giurleo and Paduano, Anastasio Orefice, perhaps a son or brother of Antonio, had his own opera *La Limpia* performed at the Teatro Nuovo, Naples, at Carnival 1727; during the same season he was responsible for a revival of Vinci's *Lo cecato fauzo* in the Teatro dei Fiorentini. *La Limpia* was revived as *La zingara* at the Teatro dei Fiorentini during Carnival 1728. Anastasio also, according to Gatti and Basso (*La Musica*), wrote a comic opera, *La Milla o puro Chi è la primmo vence*, performed in Naples in 1726.

all first performed in Naples
NFI – *Naples, Teatro dei Fiorentini*

Il Maurizio (dramma per musica, N. Minato, addns Abbé Papis), S Bartolomeo, 27 Dec 1708
Patrò Calienno de la Costa (ob, A. Mercotellis [N. Corvo]), NFI, 1 Oct 1709
Engelberta, ossia La forza dell'innocenza [Act 1 and part of Act 2] (dramma per musica, 3, A. Zeno and P. Pariati), Palazzo Reale, 4 Nov 1709, *A-Wn*, (listed as Pimpinone), perf. with ints Pimpinone by T. Albinoni [Act 3 and part of Act 2 by F. Mancini]
La pastorella al soglio (dramma per musica, G. C. Corradi), S Bartolomeo, 4 Nov 1710
La Camilla (ob), NFI, 1710
Circe delusa (drama, G. A. Falier), NFI, 1713
La Caligola delirante (dramma per musica), NFI, 1714
Lo finto Armenio (ob, F. A. Tullio), NFI, spr. 1717
Le fente zingare (ob, Tullio), NFI, aut. 1717, 7 arias *I-MC*, 1 in Pastore
La fenta pazza co la fenta malata (ob, Tullio), NFI, carn. 1718
Il gemino amore (ob, Tullio), NFI, aut. 1718
Chi la dura la vince (ob), NFI, aut. 1721
La Locinca (traggecommeddeja, Tullio), NFI, aut. 1723; rev. as La Rosilla, Nuovo, aut. 1733, collab. L. Leo
Lo Simmele (ob, B. Saddumene), Nuovo, 15 Oct 1724, collab. Leo
L'onnore resarciuto (ob, N. Gianni), NFI, 1727
La vecchia trammera (ob, Tullio), Nuovo, 1732, collab. Leo
La finta pellegrina (ob, Tullio), Nuovo, carn. 1734, collab. D. Sarro

CroceN; LaMusicaD; MGG (U. Prota-Giurleo and L. Paduano)
M. Scherillo: *L'opera buffa napoletana* (Naples, 2/1916)
G. A. Pastore: 'Le "arielle co'wioline" di Antonicco Arefece', *Studi Salentini*, xx (1965), 249–62   MICHAEL F. ROBINSON

Orefice, Giacomo (*b* Vicenza, 27 Aug 1865; *d* Milan, 22 Dec 1922). Italian composer and critic. He studied composition with Mancinelli and the piano with Busi at the Liceo Musicale in Bologna, where he took his diploma in 1885, presenting the short opera *L'oasi* as his final exercise. He was at first active as a pianist, but from the late 1890s he turned increasingly to the stage. In 1896 he was placed third in the Steiner competition in Vienna with the one-act *Il gladiatore*; in 1901 the opera *Chopin*, loosely based on Chopin's life and through composed with quotations from his works, aroused some interest despite the conflicting opinions of critics. It was revived successfully in Warsaw (1904) and Paris (1905). In February 1905 his most highly regarded opera, *Mosè*, was performed in Genoa, followed in 1907 by the one-act *Il pane altrui* at La Fenice. Meanwhile he was taking an active part in the musical life of Milan, where in 1904 he founded the Società degli Amici della Musica and from 1909 until his death taught composition at the conservatory; among his pupils were Nino Rota, Victor de Sabata and Lodovico Rocca. He was also a music critic, mostly for the *Rivista musicale italiana* and from 1920 for *Il secolo* (Milan), and contributed to the early music revival with transcriptions of Monteverdi's *Orfeo* (1909, Milan) and Rameau's *Platée*.

Orefice composed 12 operas, along with several fine piano pieces, songs, chamber music and orchestral works. As an opera composer he was influenced by the *verismo* tendencies of late 19th-century Italian theatre and late 19th-century literature. He first assimilated *verismo* through the vivid historical settings of the dramas of Pietro Cossa, the author who inspired Mascagni's *Nerone*. Later, in his most mature and refined works, *Il pane altrui* and *Radda*, he found literary bases in the social realism of Turgenev's and Gorky's stories, which he interpreted as dramas of passion. *Chopin*, his most famous if not his best opera, was a case apart, in essence a kitsch contribution to the last vestiges of late 19th-century romanticized bohemianism and to the Italian 'scapigliatura'.

See also CHOPIN.

all printed works published in vocal score in Milan

L'oasi (4 scenes, G. Dal Monte), Bologna, Liceo Musicale, 1885 (1886)
Mariska (3, G. Orefice), Turin, Carignano, 19 Nov 1889 (1889)
Consuelo (commedia lirica, 3, Orefice, after G. Sand), Bologna, Comunale, 27 Nov 1895 (1895)
Il gladiatore (1, after P. Cossa: *Messalina*), Madrid, Real, 20 March 1898 (1898)
Chopin (4, A. Orvieto), Milan, Lirico, 25 Nov 1901 (1901)
Cecilia (4, after Cossa), Vicenza, Verdi, 16 Aug 1902
Mosè (4, Orvieto), Genoa, Carlo Felice, 18 Feb 1905 (1905)
Il pane altrui (1, Orvieto, after I. S. Turgenev: *Chuzhoy Khleb*), Venice, Fenice, 12 Jan 1907 (1907)
Marcello Spada, 1909 (3), unperf.
Radda (3, C. Vallini, after M. Gorky: *Makar Chudra*), Milan, Lirico, 25 Oct 1912 (1912)
Ugo e Parisina, 1915 (3, C. Raimondo, after Byron: *Parisina*), unperf.
Il castello del sogno, 1921 (3, R. Simonini, after E. A. Butti), unperf.

'Pan.': 'Giacomo Orefice', *Musica d'oggi*, v (1923), 10–11
A. Bassi: *Giacomo Orefice: tradizione e avanguardia nel melodramma del primo '900* (Padua, 1987)   ANDREA LANZA

O'Reilly, Robert Bray (*fl* 1789–93). Irish impresario. Of obscure origin, he reputedly trained as a law clerk in London in the mid-1780s and was employed by a lawyer representing Giovanni Gallini in his struggle to acquire control of the King's Theatre in the Haymarket. After the fire that destroyed the theatre on 17 June 1789, Gallini was issued a licence to mount a season of

Italian opera at the Little Haymarket Theatre, and in early September he sent O'Reilly to Italy to recruit singers. With the help of Gallini's contact in Florence, Lord Cowper, O'Reilly assembled a fine company which included the castrato Luigi Marchesi, Anna Storace as *prima buffa* and Gertrud Elisabeth Mara as *prima donna seria*.

In early 1790 two competing schemes were launched to re-establish an Italian opera house in London. WILLIAM TAYLOR and Michael Novosielski started to rebuild on the site of the old King's Theatre. In the meantime, the Earl of Salisbury and the Duke of Bedford, with the approbation of the Prince of Wales, planned a grand opera house in Leicester Square. Because Salisbury was also Lord Chamberlain and thus controlled the licensing of public theatres, a front-man had to be found to conceal his conflict of interest. For reasons that remain unknown, O'Reilly was the ostensible proprietor. Borrowing ideas from the French theatre architect Victor Louis and consulting Sir John Soane in London, he designed a lavish opera house for Leicester Square. When the Lord Chancellor refused him a royal patent on the grounds that natural justice favoured creditors of the old Haymarket theatre, O'Reilly leased the Pantheon in Oxford Street in summer 1790 and executed Bedford and Salisbury's instructions to convert it into an opera house. As manager of the new company, O'Reilly engaged Pacchiarotti, Mara and Dauberval as the principal performers and, probably at the behest of the Prince of Wales, invited first Mozart and then Paisiello to become house composers. Mozart apparently did not respond, but Paisiello composed *La locanda* for the Pantheon, though he never came to London.

In spite of huge subsidies from Bedford and Salisbury, the Pantheon quickly went into the red. By Easter 1791 the noble backers had already decided to transfer their interest to Taylor's new Haymarket theatre and O'Reilly was cynically sacrificed, being legally responsible for the Pantheon's debts. He fled penniless to Paris in late 1791 to avoid arrest. The Pantheon was burnt to the ground on 14 January 1792. O'Reilly rightly suspected arson, but he was ruined and powerless. His attempt to redirect the course of opera in London, although it came to a dismal end, is notable as the one real effort to rescue the opera from the debts and the artistic inflexibility of the old establishment at the King's Theatre, Haymarket.

F. H. W. Sheppard, ed.: *Survey of London*, xxix (London, 1960)

C. Price: 'Italian Opera and Arson in Late Eighteenth-Century London', *JAMS*, xlii (1989), 55–107

C. Price, J. Milhous and R. D. Hume: 'A Royal Opera House in Leicester Square (1790)', *COJ*, ii (1990), 1–28   CURTIS PRICE

Oreli [Orelia], **Diana Margherita.** *See* AURELI, DIANA MARGHERITA.

Oreste ('Orestes'). Opera in three acts by GEORGE FRIDERIC HANDEL to a libretto anonymously adapted from Giangualberto Barlocci's *L'Oreste* (1723, Rome), after EURIPIDES' *Iphigeneia in Tauris*; London, Covent Garden Theatre, 18 December 1734.

Oreste is the first of the three pasticcio operas which Handel himself created from his own works (the others being *Alessandro Severo* and *Giove in Argo*). The overture, sinfonias, arias, duet and final *coro* are taken (with verbal and a few musical changes) from earlier operas or cantatas; only the recitatives and some of the dances appended to each act are entirely new. (The dance sequences were included for Marie Sallé and her company, who appeared in all Handel's productions in his first Covent Garden season of 1734–5.) The story, like that of Gluck's *Iphigénie en Tauride*, is based on Euripides' play, though with additional characters, and tells of the reunion of Ifigenia [Iphigenia], daughter of King Agamemnon of Greece, with her brother Oreste [Orestes] after the ending of the Trojan War. Iphigenia (soprano), miraculously saved from sacrifice at Aulis, serves as high priestess of Diana in the remote land of the Taurians (traditionally assumed to be the Crimea); there she has to operate the harsh laws of King Toante [Thoas] (bass), which require all strangers to be sacrificed. Orestes (mezzo-soprano castrato), driven mad by remorse for murdering his mother Clytemnestra, has been guided by an oracle to seek relief in Taurian lands. In Act 1 his arrival is discovered by Iphigenia, who, though not recognizing him, is prompted to save him from sacrifice. She engages the cooperation of Thoas's captain Filotete [Philoctetes] (contralto), who is in love with her. Orestes' wife Ermione [Hermione] (soprano) and his friend Pilade [Pylades] (tenor) come in search of Orestes and are arrested and condemned to death. Philoctetes mentions that Thoas believes Orestes is his mortal enemy. Thoas, captivated by Hermione's beauty, offers to spare her if she will become his queen. In Act 2 Orestes comes out of hiding to meet Pylades and is arrested; he is released by Iphigenia and reunited with Hermione. The couple are discovered together by Thoas; unaware of their relationship, he condemns Hermione for wanton behaviour and has both rearrested. In Act 3 Iphigenia is ordered to sacrifice Orestes. Pylades tries to save him by claiming to be Orestes himself; Hermione, though threatened with death, refuses to point out the true Orestes. Iphigenia reveals herself as Orestes' sister and with Philoctetes' help inspires the Taurians to overthrow Thoas and restore peace.

Oreste is a well-crafted compilation, the arias and other numbers being carefully matched to their new contexts. Act 2 has an especially powerful close, with Hermione and Orestes bidding each other a moving farewell in a minor-key duet written for a similar context in *Floridante*. The original cast was led by the castrato Giovanni Carestini in the title role (in 1723 he had sung Pylades in Benedetto Micheli's setting of Barlocci's libretto); the other singers were Cecilia Young (Iphigenia), Anna Maria Strada del Pò (Hermione), John Beard (Pylades), the contralto Maria Caterina Negri (Philoctetes) and Gustavus Waltz (Thoas). Handel performed *Oreste* only three times. It was first revived (without the dances) on 4 June 1988 by the company of the Landestheater Halle in the Goethe-Theater at Bad Lauchstädt.   ANTHONY HICKS

Oresteya ('The Oresteia'). 'Musical trilogy in three parts' by SERGEY IVANOVICH TANEYEV to a libretto by Alexey Alexeyevich Venkstern after AESCHYLUS; St Petersburg, Mariinsky Theatre, 17/29 October 1895.

More pageant than opera, Taneyev's single dramatic composition, written during the period 1887–94 and dedicated to the memory of Anton Rubinstein, was the work of a musical idealist who fairly despised the musical stage. Though necessarily a longish work with an actual running time over three hours, the action is exceedingly compressed, schematic, indeed minimal.

The result, although by choice of subject something of an anomaly among the Russian operas of its time, belongs nonetheless to an identifiable (and identifiably) Russian operatic genre: a series of loosely connected individual scenes from a well-known, well-loved literary source (compare *Ruslan and Lyudmila*, *Yevgeny Onegin* or *War and Peace*).

Part 1 *Agamemnon*
   i Agamemnon's victory in Troy is celebrated; Aegisthus (baritone) and Clytemnestra (contralto) plan his murder.
   ii Agamemnon (bass) enters Argos with Cassandra (soprano), who prophesies Agamemnon's death and her own; the murders are carried out.
Part 2 *Choephorae* ('The Libation Bearers')
   i Clytemnestra, haunted by Agamemnon's ghost, bids Electra (soprano) placate the gods with a sacrifice.
   ii Orestes (tenor) reveals himself to Electra.
   iii Orestes, assisted by Electra, murders Aegisthus and Clytemnestra.
Part 3 *Eumenides* ('The Furies')
   i Orestes, pursued by the Furies, resolves to seek Apollo's forgiveness at Delphi.
   ii Apollo (baritone) restrains the Furies and orders Orestes back to Athens to await judgment.
   iii The court of Areopagites renders a split verdict which is tipped in Orestes' favour by the goddess Athena (soprano), releasing him from guilt.

None of the gory events that constitute the famous story takes place on stage. The drama proceeds through narratives, psychological monologues (some, like Clytemnestra's in 2.i, not in Aeschylus) and leitmotif-laden entr'actes. Two of the latter – Agamemnon's Meyerbeerian march before 1.ii and the representation of Apollo's temple at Delphi before 3.ii – have achieved repertory status in Russia as concert pieces, as has Taneyev's concert overture *Oresteya*, op.6. The latter, though composed during the long period of the opera's gestation and based on the opera's thematic material (the chief leitmotif in both bearing a striking resemblance to the 'fate' motif in *Carmen*: see TANEYEV, SERGEY IVANOVICH, ex.1), is not a part of the opera, which begins with its own brief prelude.

Oresteya contains some very impressive music of a monumental character, nor is it wholly deficient in traditional operatic values. Orestes is one of the few heroic tenor roles in Russian opera. The extended, intricately contrapuntal quartet before the murders in 2.iii is followed by an extraordinary dramatic stroke: Clytemnestra's protracted stare, in which she recognizes her son and fated killer, is accompanied by a unison crescendo in the orchestra anticipating the famous pair in the last act of *Wozzeck*. At the beginning of Part 3 the Furies, declaiming their lines in a unison monotone, are effectively cast as implicit participants in an interior dialogue of conscience within the maddened Orestes' mind.

The opera has had an unhappy stage history. Eduard Nápravník, musical director of the Mariinsky Theatre, who refused to conduct the work, nevertheless demanded merciless cuts as the price of production. The première was conducted by Eduard Krushevsky, with Mariya Slavina as Clytemnestra and Ivan Yershov as Orestes. Taneyev withdrew the 'mutilated' opera after eight performances, and he never saw it again. It was revived at the Mariinsky shortly after his death in 1915 (Albert Coates conducting); two years later it was staged in Moscow on the eve of the Revolution. The only staging the opera received during the Soviet period was in Minsk (Belorussian State Opera and Ballet Theatre under Tat'yana Kolomiytseva), in the 1960s; a

recording of this production was made in 1966. Full and vocal scores were published by Belyayev (Leipzig, 1900).

                             RICHARD TARUSKIN

Orfeide, L' ('The Orpheid'). Triptych of one-act operas by GIAN FRANCESCO MALIPIERO, consisting of *La morte delle maschere* ('The Death of the Maskers'), *Sette canzoni* ('Seven Songs') and *Orfeo, ovvero L'ottava canzone* ('Orpheus, or The Eighth Song'), to librettos by the composer, using old Italian poems by Angelo Poliziano and others; Paris, Opéra, 10 July 1920 (*Sette canzoni* alone); Düsseldorf, Stadttheater, 5 November 1925 (whole triptych).

Although Malipiero repeatedly declared that '*L'Orfeide* is not a cycle of three one-act operas but a single opera in three parts', there is evidence that *Sette canzoni* – which was composed in 1918–19 and performed before the other two panels of the triptych – was originally conceived as a self-contained work. Moreover, it has understandably had far more performances on its own than as an integral part of the trilogy, which, for all its wild inventiveness, has a somewhat heterogeneous air when viewed as a whole.

Whereas *Pantea*, Malipiero's other important theatrical experiment completed in 1919, cannot be regarded as an opera in however wide a sense, owing to its lack of onstage voices and even (for the most part) of sung words, *Sette canzoni* does have a sung text of a sort, although mute characters outnumber singing ones. The work plays continuously, with orchestral interludes linking the seven little dramatic episodes. But each episode has its own separate cast; each is based (rather freely) on a personal experience of the composer's; and each has some kind of song as its musical nucleus (hence the confusing title). The action that surrounds these songs is carried on mainly in mime, with no recourse to recitative-like declamation; but there is also a chorus, which, as in *Pantea*, mostly performs offstage.

At the fundamental level, each episode in *Sette canzoni* depicts a stark contrast between a 'positive' and a 'negative' principle, reduced to the tersest possible terms. In the first episode a ballad-singer (baritone) tempts a girl to leave her blind companion, who does not realize he has been left helpless until too late (love versus desertion); in the second, a bereaved woman, fervently (though mutely) praying, is rudely interrupted by a monk who wants to lock the church (religious fervour versus mundane practicality); in the third a mother (soprano), driven to distraction by her son's absence at the war, is haunted by memories of his childhood and sings lullabies, nursery ditties etc. – but when he returns unexpectedly, she appears not to recognize him and her last link with sanity snaps (motherly love versus madness). The fourth, fifth and sixth episodes similarly juxtapose love and drunkenness, love and mourning, mortal danger and indifferent frivolity; and the seventh reduces the process to symbolic terms: early on Ash Wednesday some clowns left over from the end of the Carnival celebrations are put to flight by a figure 'horrible to behold', which rises from the traditional Chariot-of-Death procession that happens to be passing by – yet this does not deter one of the bolder clowns from returning and picking up a girl when the 'penitents' have gone.

Malipiero's decision to draw the texts of his songs largely from old Italian poetry (in apparently perverse contrast to the present-day origins of the plots) seems basically to have arisen from musical needs: he evidently wanted a certain kind of sound in the language to match the 'archaic' component that was increasingly emerging in his music (although *Sette Canzoni* is less extreme in this respect than the slightly later *San Francesco d'Assisi*). Alongside the archaisms, *Sette canzoni* contains elements stemming from Debussy, from early Stravinsky (up to and including *The Rite of Spring*) and even occasionally – despite intentions to the contrary – from Puccini. Yet the resultant synthesis is remarkably unified and intensely personal. When sympathetically produced, with adequate foreknowledge in the spectator of what to expect, *Sette canzoni* can make a profound impact in the theatre.

The wilful disparity, in *Sette canzoni*, between the old Italian poems and their dramatic contexts gives parts of the work a distinctly surreal character which is an important part of its fascination. In this, however, it is decisively surpassed by the altogether wilder eccentricities of the extraordinary one-act pieces that Malipiero designed (ostensibly at least) to stand on either side of it. In *La morte delle maschere* (composed in 1921–2 and designed to be performed as the first item in the triptych) a series of *commedia dell'arte* characters present themselves in turn before a mute impresario, each introducing himself in characteristic style – until Orpheus (tenor) suddenly enters dressed in red and wearing a hideous mask, drives the impresario out with a whip and locks the *commedia dell'arte* figures away in a cupboard. Only then does he remove his disguise to reveal his true identity, lyre and all. Such seemingly anarchic shock tactics were typical of Malipiero's response to some of the more subversive artistic trends of the time.

In *Orfeo, ovvero L'ottava canzone* (the third item in the triptych), composed in 1919–20, Orpheus again appears, this time interrupting a sadistic performance, on a small, raised 'stage upon the stage', by a singer (baritone) representing Nero and made up to look like a marionette: some of the subsidiary mute parts are to be played by real marionettes. The small stage is surrounded, on three of its sides, by contrasted audiences who react each in their own way: one audience, consisting entirely of children, greets Nero's atrocities with wild enthusiasm; another, of aged pedants, is horrified and protests violently; a third, of 18th-century aristocrats, remains sleepily indifferent.

Such frankly grotesque extravaganzas obviously have little real affinity of spirit with *Sette canzoni* and seem like irrelevant afterthoughts. Nevertheless, *La morte delle maschere* and *Orfeo* have a fascination of their own: a varied series of divertingly inventive vocal solos is carried forward on a stream of kaleidoscopic orchestral textures, whose irrepressible vitality amply justifies concert performances, even if as stage pieces these outer panels of the triptych may be little more than amiably provocative freaks.

See also ORPHEUS.   JOHN C. G. WATERHOUSE

Orfeo (i) [*L'Orfeo*] ('Orpheus'). *Favola in musica* in a prologue and five acts by CLAUDIO MONTEVERDI to a libretto by ALESSANDRO STRIGGIO based mainly on the ORPHEUS myth as told in OVID's *Metamorphoses*, though drawing also on the account in VIRGIL's *Georgics*; Mantua, ducal palace, 24 February 1607.

Unlike Peri's *Euridice* (1600), on which it is modelled, Monteverdi's *Orfeo* was not written for dynastic celebrations, but simply as an entertainment for the

La Musica [Music] *the prologue*	soprano
Orfeo [Orpheus]	tenor
Euridice [Eurydice]	soprano
Silvia [Sylvia] *the messenger*	soprano
Speranza [Hope]	soprano
Caronte [Charon]	bass
Proserpina	soprano
Plutone [Pluto]	bass
Apollo†	tenor

Nymphs and shepherds, infernal spirits and Bacchantes‡

Setting The fields of Thrace (Prologue, Acts 1, 2, 5); the underworld (Acts 3, 4)

† the role of Apollo occurs in the published score but not in the libretto for the 1607 Mantua performances

‡ this last chorus occurs in the librettos for the 1607 Mantua performances but not in the published score

1607 carnival season at the Mantuan court. It was prepared under the auspices of Francesco Gonzaga, elder son of the Duke of Mantua, for performance before the Accademia degli Invaghiti. It is possible that *Orfeo* owes its existence to nothing more than sibling rivalry between Francesco Gonzaga and his brother Ferdinando, who from 1605 had studied at the university of Pisa and had become closely involved in musical and theatrical activity at Pisa and Florence. On 5 January 1607 Francesco wrote to Ferdinando mentioning the new opera and asking him to request the loan of a castrato in the service of the Grand Duke of Tuscany. The singer whom Ferdinando selected, the young castrato Giovanni Gualberto Magli, who did not arrive at Mantua until 15 February, was at first expected to sing the prologue and one other unspecified role (possibly that of Speranza); later, he was also allotted the role of Proserpina. The other members of the cast, insofar as they can be identified, were the singer-composer Francesco Rasi (presumably in the title role) and 'a little priest' (possibly Girolamo Bacchini) who sang Eurydice. It seems likely, then, that most, if not all, the principal female roles of the opera were sung by castratos. The instrumentalists and chorus were probably drawn from the court musical establishment. The apparently large and diverse instrumental ensemble required (related to the rich ensembles of *intermedi*) can, in fact, be managed by a small group of players.

Orfeo was first performed in the ducal palace at Mantua in a room (apparently restricted in space) in the apartments occupied by the duke's sister Margherita Gonzaga d'Este. Tradition has it that this was the Rivers Room, but the location is, in fact, uncertain. The duke ordered a second performance on 1 March. Two printings of the libretto survive from 1607 and presumably correspond to these two performances. A third performance was projected for the proposed visit to Mantua in 1607 of the Duke of Savoy, but the visit was cancelled, and the performance seems not to have taken place. The score of the opera was published at Venice in 1609, and a second edition appeared in 1615.

It has been suggested that *Orfeo* was presented at various venues outside Mantua soon after its first performance: at Florence (1607), Cremona (1607), Florence (1609), Milan (*c*1610) and Turin (1610). None of these suggestions is based on sound evidence. A *dramma pastorale* with the title *Orfeo* was given at

Salzburg in 1614, and another *Orfeo* was given there in 1619; these may have been performances of Monteverdi's work. A revival at Genoa before 1646 appears more securely documented. Thereafter, *Orfeo* seems to have remained unperformed until the early years of this century. The score was examined and discussed by the two 18th-century music historians Burney and Hawkins, and an abridged modern edition was published in 1881 by Robert Eitner. The first edition to have been given in a modern performance, however, was that published by Vincent d'Indy in 1905. D'Indy had directed concert performances of this edition, which omits Acts 1 and 5, at the Schola Cantorum, Paris, on 25 February and 2 March 1904, and it was later used for the first modern stage performance, a charity matinée given under Marcel Labey at the Théâtre Réjane, Paris, on 2 May 1911, with Robert Le Lubez as Orpheus, and Claire Croiza in the role of the messenger.

Modern editions of *Orfeo* (and their associated performances) have been, broadly speaking, of two kinds. The first is the free adaptation or modern arrangement of the original. In this area, composers have been particularly active. Besides d'Indy, Orff (1923, first performance 1925), Respighi (Milan, 1935), Frazzi (Cremona, 1943), Bucchi (Milan, 1967), Maderna (Amsterdam, 1967) and Berio (Florence, 1984) all responded to the opera by making arrangements of their own; and editors like Giacomo Orefice (Milan, 1909, and elsewhere), Hanns Erdmann-Guckel (Breslau, 1913) and Giacomo Benvenuti (Rome, 1934) also prepared versions in which the original musical text was much adapted. The second kind of edition and performance is the one informed by research into the performance conventions of Monteverdi's own time. Two composers – G. F. Malipiero and Hindemith – are represented here; and Malipiero's edition of 1930, a faithful transcription of the 1609 edition, remains valuable today. For the most part, though, this area has been the province of the scholar and scholar-performer, from Jack Westrup, whose Oxford University Opera Club performance of 1925 was revived at the Scala Theatre, London, in 1929, through August Wenzinger (Hitzacker, Saxony, 1955; a recording was issued in the same year), Raymond Leppard (London, 1965), Denis Stevens (edition published 1967) and Nikolaus Harnoncourt (recording issued 1969) to Jane Glover (Oxford, 1975), Roger Norrington (Kent Opera, 1976, and Florence, 1984) and John Eliot Gardiner (London, 1981). Although recent performances have all sought an authentic presentation of the musical aspects of Monteverdi's work, approaches to production and design have varied between attempts to capture the spirit rather than the letter of the period (Gardiner-Freeman 1981) and the more authentic style of Norrington-Lawrence (1984).

Although *Orfeo* is divided into a prologue and five acts, a division which relates it to classical tragedy, it was almost certainly played without breaks between the acts, the scene changes between Acts 2 and 3, and Acts 4 and 5 taking place in front of the audience.

TOCCATA. The opera is preceded by a toccata (=tucket) 'to be played three times ... before the raising of the curtain'.

PROLOGUE *The fields of Thrace* The curtain rises to reveal a wood by the banks of a stream before which the personification of music sings five stanzas – 'Dal mio Permesso amato' – set as variations over a repeated bass (strophic variations). She pays compliments to the audience, the Gonzaga family in particular, and introduces herself as the power which can soothe troubled hearts or arouse the coolest minds to love or anger, a reference to the affective power of music mentioned by Greek philosophers and a concept very much in the minds of the creators of early opera. In stanza 4 she introduces the protagonist of the opera, Orpheus, and refers to the mythical power of his singing, which 'drew the wild beasts and made a servant of the Inferno'. Finally, she bids silence for the action which is to follow. The stanzas of the prologue are introduced and punctuated by a five-part ritornello for strings which will be heard again at the end of Act 2 and at the beginning of Act 5, where it can be seen as an emblem of music's power.

ACT 1 *The fields of Thrace* Orpheus and Eurydice enter in the company of a chorus of nymphs and shepherds, who, as in classical drama, introduce and comment on the action, both as individuals and as a group. One of the shepherds reveals that this is the wedding day of Orpheus and Eurydice and urges his companions to celebrate it in song. They do so first in a solemn invocation to Hymen, god of marriage, and then, after a brief introduction by one of the nymphs, with a lively choral and instrumental dance. A shepherd invites Orpheus to sing of his love; he responds with a passionate arioso, 'Rosa del ciel', in which he addresses first the sun (Apollo, his father) and then Eurydice, expressing his happiness that she has at last accepted him. She responds, pledging her heart to him, and the chorus round off this first action symmetrically with a shortened repeat of their dance and invocation. A shepherd reminds the company that they should go to give thanks at the temple, and Orpheus, Eurydice and most of their companions exit to the sound of a processional ritornello for strings.

A small ensemble is left on stage to sing a chorus in which they reflect that no-one should abandon himself to despair since after darkness 'the sun displays its bright rays all the more clearly'. The chorus is set as strophic variations for two and three voices separated by restatements of the processional ritornello, and it serves to suggest the passage of time while the nuptials of Orpheus and Eurydice are celebrated at the temple. The concluding lines of the act as they appear in the libretto – 'Orfeo di cui pur dianzi' – are changed in the score to 'Ecco Orfeo cui pur dianzi' and sung by five voices, implying that Orpheus and some of his companions (but not Eurydice) return at this point, rather than at the nominal beginning of Act 2. The sinfonia which follows, and which precedes the rubric 'Atto Secondo', is clearly the introduction to the arioso sung by Orpheus at the beginning of Act 2. The implication is that there should be no break between the acts.

ACT 2 *The fields of Thrace* Orpheus responds to the chorus with the words 'Ecco pur ch'a voi ritorno, care selve e piaggie amate' and initiates a sequence of music in which he and his companions celebrate the pleasures of the day. They do this in a series of strophic arias: first, three arias sung by the nymphs and shepherds and introduced and separated by ritornellos for which Monteverdi gives precise instrumentation; then Orpheus himself sings an aria of four stanzas, 'Vi ricorda, o boschi ombrosi', telling of the sorrow that he suffered before Eurydice accepted him. This sequence of

1. Monteverdi's 'Orfeo': a scene from Act 1, with Guy de Mey as Orpheus, in the Early Music Project staging first produced in Florence, 1984 (London revival, 1986)

music conveys a sense of unaffected joy before the sudden reversal of Orpheus's fortune. Following Orpheus's aria, one of the shepherds urges him to continue in the same vein, but before he can do so, a chromatic change in the bass line marks the entrance of the messenger, Sylvia, and words which are to become a refrain during the remainder of the act: 'Ahi caso acerbo, ahi fato empio e crudele!'.

In the exchanges which follow, the import of these words is not immediately understood by the chorus, and Monteverdi suggests the two levels of awareness by using cadence centres chiefly of A and E for the messenger and C for the chorus. Only as Orpheus becomes disturbed by the messenger's distress does he sing a line, 'D'onde vieni? Ove vai? Ninfa che porti?', in which he moves to her cadence centre of E. She attempts to give her news, but at the mention of Eurydice's name, Orpheus interrupts in anguish with a line which completely disrupts the prevailing tonality. The messenger, now resolute, forces the tonality back to the prevailing level and announces Eurydice's death. Orpheus utters only the word 'Alas' before falling silent 'like a mute stone, so grieved that he cannot express his grief'. The messenger paints a vivid picture of Eurydice's death. She describes the way in which Eurydice, gathering flowers to make a garland for her hair, was bitten by a snake; she tells how she and her companions made vain efforts to revive Eurydice; and, as her narration rises to a climax, she repeats Eurydice's dying invocation of Orpheus's name. As she finishes, a shepherd takes up the cry 'Ahi, caso acerbo', initiating a sequence of reactions to the news. Orpheus rouses himself, and in a brief but poignant lament mourns Eurydice's death and resolves to bring her back from the underworld.

He exits, and the chorus is left to mourn, singing first 'Ahi, caso acerbo' and then turning to reflect upon the transience of human happiness. Sylvia, having acted as messenger, and consumed by self-loathing, banishes herself from human company, and the chorus conclude the act with duet laments punctuated by the refrain 'Ahi, caso acerbo'. As they leave, Music's ritornello is heard once more, as if to bring comfort and hope, and the scene changes as the first of the underworld sinfonias is heard. In contrast to the instrumental music for the upper world, which has been scored mainly for strings, with occasional use of recorders, this sinfonia is scored for cornetts and trombones with continuo played on a regal (reed organ).

ACT 3 *The underworld* Orpheus enters, accompanied by Hope, who has guided him to the underworld and now describes the scene in images drawn from Virgil's *Aeneid* and Dante's *Inferno*. She can accompany him no further, for inscribed on a rock at the entrance to Pluto's kingdom are the words (from Dante) 'Abandon all hope, you who enter'. She leaves, and Orpheus is confronted by the awesome figure of Charon, ferryman of the River Styx. He, remembering 'ancient outrages' (the attempted abduction of Proserpina by Theseus and Pirithous, and the theft of Cerberus by Hercules), forbids Orpheus entry to Pluto's domains. Orpheus responds with an aria, 'Possente spirto', cast in the form of strophic variations, in which he employs all his arts as a singer to persuade Charon to ferry him across the Styx (see fig.2). The importance of this aria is reinforced by its placing almost exactly at the centre of the five-act structure. The aria is preceded by a sinfonia which represents Orpheus playing his lyre and should be scored for strings and organ with wood pipes as Monteverdi indicates when it is repeated later in the act. In the first four stanzas of his aria, Orpheus attempts to impress Pluto by displaying his ability as a virtuoso singer. For these stanzas Monteverdi provided two versions of the vocal line, one which the performer could ornament himself and one which provides a model of the complex ornamentation that he had in mind for a demonstration of Orpheus's power. The stanzas are punctuated by phrases for the three main classes of late Renaissance instruments: bowed strings, wind, and plucked string instruments. In the fifth stanza, as Orpheus's thoughts turn to Eurydice, Monteverdi abandons variations in favour of a simpler, more passionate style of declamation. The variation bass returns, however, for the final stanza, and here Monteverdi surrounds the voice with a halo of strings.

Charon, singing substantially the same music as before, declares himself flattered, but unmoved, and his obduracy provokes a final passionate outburst from Orpheus, culminating in the words 'Rendetemi il mio ben, Tartarei numi'. He plays his lyre, and though his singing has failed, his playing succeeds in lulling Charon to sleep. Seizing his opportunity, Orpheus steals

2. Opening of Orpheus's aria 'Possente spirto' from Act 3 of Monteverdi's 'Orfeo', from the first printed edition (Venice: Amadino, 1609)

Charon's boat, and as he crosses the Styx he sings again 'Rendetemi il mio ben, Tartarei numi'. He enters Pluto's kingdom. The sinfonia heard at the beginning of the act is repeated twice, and between the playings a chorus of infernal spirits reflect that no enterprise undertaken by man is undertaken in vain.

ACT 4 *The underworld* Pluto and Proserpina enter. Although Orpheus's singing failed to move Charon, it has profoundly affected Proserpina, and she pleads with her consort for Eurydice's release. He is moved by her entreaties and sends one of the spirits to announce that he will allow Orpheus to lead Eurydice back to the upper world provided that he does not turn to look upon her until they have left the abyss. The spirit departs, and another reflects that Orpheus will only lead his bride to freedom if he is able to let reason rule his youthful passion. While Orpheus and Eurydice are being informed of Pluto's decision, Proserpina and Pluto play out a short love scene in which Proserpina blesses the day that she was herself stolen away from the earth by Pluto and brought to the underworld. Orpheus enters, leading Eurydice. As they begin their progress from the underworld he sings a lively aria, 'Qual honor di te fia degno', another set of strophic variations, though this time over a 'walking bass' in crotchets, in which he praises the power of his lyre in subjugating the will of Tartarus. After three stanzas, however, doubts assail him. How can he be sure that Eurydice is following him? Is it simply envy that makes Pluto forbid him to look at her? Why should he hesitate to turn? – for what Pluto forbids Cupid demands.

After each of these questions he pauses to listen, and on the last occasion there is a great noise off stage. Imagining that the Furies are carrying off Eurydice, Orpheus turns, and for a few moments looks upon her before the vision is abruptly cut off and a spirit tells him that he has broken the law and is unworthy of grace. Eurydice is heard lamenting his losing her 'for too much love' before she is ordered back to the realms of the dead, nevermore to see the stars (an echo of Dante). Orpheus tries to follow her but is drawn back to the upper world by a force invisible to him. The chorus of spirits sing that only he who can conquer his passions is worthy of eternal glory. A final 'underworld' sinfonia is heard. The scene changes back to the fields of Thrace, and Music's ritornello is heard again as the last act begins.

ACT 5 *The fields of Thrace* Orpheus is alone, lamenting the loss of Eurydice. He looks at the familiar scenes which comforted his suffering before Eurydice accepted him. Now, however, there is no hope of regaining her, and he will join the hills and rocks in their grief. As he laments, an echo gives back the final syllables of each phrase, subtly changing their meaning so that it supplies words of sympathy. Lamentation gives way to praise of Eurydice's beauty, and in the final paragraph of his soliloquy Orpheus resolves to reject all other women. At this point the ending of the opera found in the 1607 librettos diverges from that of the 1609 score. In the librettos, which we must assume represent the original ending, Orpheus sees the Bacchantes approaching and withdraws as they erupt on to the stage. They threaten to take revenge on Orpheus for rejecting them and perform an extended finale, with solos and choral refrain, in praise of Bacchus. This finale is close in spirit to the ending of the Orpheus story given by Ovid and Virgil and would certainly have been practicable in the constricted space in which we suppose that *Orfeo* was first performed. The 1609 score substitutes a more spectacular ending, based on Hyginus's *Astronomia*, which allowed for the use of a cloud machine. In this, Apollo descends to Orpheus and chides him for being a slave to his emotions. He invites Orpheus to join him in the heavens, from where he can look upon Eurydice's semblance in the stars. The two ascend to the heavens singing a virtuoso duet, and nymphs and shepherds sing a very brief chorus concluding with a moral drawn from Psalm 126 (Vulgate 125): 'he who sows in tears shall reap the fruit of grace'. The opera closes with a *moresca* (a 'Moorish' dance) performed by shepherds.

Various theories have been advanced to explain the changed ending. It has been suggested that the ending found in the score was the original version, altered when it was found that the opera was to be played in a room too small to accommodate a cloud machine. On the whole, though, it seems more likely that the Bacchanalian finale was the original version. This being the case, opinions differ as to whether the more spectacular, but more perfunctory, ending was written in anticipation of the projected performance at Mantua for the Duke of Savoy, or whether the original version was thought by Monteverdi and/or others to be too nearly tragic to provide a suitable ending for an opera. In either case the authorship of the literary text for the 1609 ending is uncertain.

*   *   *

Monteverdi's *Orfeo* is generally regarded as the first work of genius in the history of opera. It presents a rich blend of Greek myth with 16th-century dramatic conventions, and of the varied instrumental and vocal groupings of the *intermedio* and madrigal traditions with the newer expressive recitative style of the Florentines. Though it stands somewhat apart from the mainstream by virtue of its being a court opera, it is not simply a courtly entertainment but a work which addresses with economy and passion the most profoundly felt of human emotions.   JOHN WHENHAM

Orfeo (ii) [*L'Orfeo*] ('Orpheus'). *Tragicommedia* in a prologue and three acts by LUIGI ROSSI to a libretto by FRANCESCO BUTI; Paris, Palais Royal, 2 March 1647.

From January 1647, after most of the Italian singers had joined the composer in Paris, the Queen Regent, the Prince of Wales and other courtiers heard Rossi's compositions in several chamber performances. They were especially charmed by the singing of two young castratos from Rome, Marc'Antonio Sportonio and Domenico Dal Pane, both protégés of Rinaldo d'Este, the new Cardinal Protector of France. In *Orfeo*, the favoured Sportonio was given the roles of Himeneo [Hymen], Sospetto [Suspicion], one of the three Graces and one of the three Fates. Dal Pane sang a Grace, a Fate and Proserpina. The queen also heard the leading soprano castratos: Marc'Antonio Pasqualini (in the service of Cardinal Antonio Barberini) and Atto Melani (in the service of Prince Mattias de' Medici); they would play Aristeo [Aristaeus] and Orpheus, rivals for the affections of Euridice [Eurydice] (soprano). Venantio Leopardi, a tenor who performed the role of Caronte [Charon], reported that he sang a quartet with Melani and the two boys for the queen. These chamber soirées found reflection in the extraordinary number of ensembles in the opera: six duets (including three love duets between Orpheus and Eurydice, Anna Francesca Costa) and 12 trios.

In a prologue, the French army, represented by 24 soldiers singing in three four-part choruses, assaults an enemy fortress; when the walls fall, Vittoria [Victory] (soprano) emerges to praise the queen and the young Louis XIV. A brief epilogue, sung by Mercurio [Mercury] (alto), promises immortality to the house of France.

In the woods, Orpheus and Eurydice with Eurydice's Nurse (soprano) and her father Endimione [Endymion] (tenor), consult a group of Augurs to witness omens of their impending marriage. Two doves are attacked by vultures, but the lovers reaffirm their vows. Aristaeus (soprano), a shepherd son of Bacco [Bacchus] (soprano), is tormented by Eurydice's rejection of him. A mocking Satiro [Satyr] (baritone) and Venere [Venus] (soprano), accompanied by Amore [Cupid] (soprano) and the three Graces, cannot dissuade or calm him. Finally Venus offers to disguise herself as an old woman and to attempt to ingratiate the shepherd with Eurydice. Hymen, Giunone [Juno] (sopranos) and Phoebus Apollo (alto) attend a wedding banquet for the lovers. The cynically comic comments of Momo [Momus] (tenor) do not dampen the festivities, but when the torches suddenly blow out, all address an eight-part, heartfelt plea to the gods to avert misfortune.

Act 2 slowly brings about the catastrophe. As promised, an old woman (alto) tries to persuade Eurydice that to change the bad omens she need only change her betrothed and suggests Aristaeus. Eurydice remains steadfast, singing 'Mio ben teco il tormento' over a descending, chromatic ostinato bass line. Annoyed, the Satyr offers to abduct her during a dance at the temple. Meanwhile Juno and Apollo attempt to dissuade Cupid from making Orpheus fall in love with someone else. Juno also dissuades Endymion and the Augur (baritone) from making a sacrifice to Venus. When Cupid tells Orpheus about the plot against him, Venus is enraged, upbraids her errant son, and determines to have immediate revenge. Indeed, as Eurydice dances at the temple, the Satyr rushes at her. Fleeing, she is bitten by a viper and, refusing help from Aristaeus, she dies. Aristaeus, Apollo and the nymphs mourn her death.

Wandering the wastelands, the grieving Orpheus asks the Fates where he can find Eurydice. They tell him he must seek her in Pluto's realm. Her shade, however, persecutes Aristaeus and causes him to go mad. He mistakes the Satyr for Eurydice and Momus for his old nurse, and thinks himself the python (slain by Apollo). Juno, in full battle with a gloating Venus, sends Gelosia [Jealousy] (alto) and Suspicion (soprano) to hell in order to persuade Proserpina that it is in her best interests to remove Eurydice from Pluto's sight. Proserpina sees that Orpheus is allowed to sing his plea in the three quatrains of 'Io che lasciato fui senz'alma in vita'. Plutone [Pluto] (bass) grants him his wish. But during the festive dance of the monsters of hell, Charon (tenor) reports that Orpheus has lost his bride by breaking his promise. Back above ground, Venus urges Bacchus and his Bacchantes to revenge themselves on Orpheus for the death of Aristaeus. Giove [Jupiter] (tenor) in turn makes the musician immortal and places his lyre among the constellations.

Rossi controlled the somewhat sprawling story by creating complexes of 'closed' but connected ensemble pieces within groups of scenes. In scenes i and ii of Act 1, the first aria and a trio are in G minor, as are the central love duet and the quartet that closes scene ii. The complex also includes a six-part chorus of Augurs, a song for Orpheus and dialogue between him and Eurydice with numerous ariosos that leads to the love duet, and an aria for Endymion that leads to the short closing quartet. Scenes iii and iv similarly form a group, centring on B♭, with two solos for Aristaeus, two for a satyr friend, trios and a solo for the Graces, and a duet for Venus and Cupid. G minor, F major and D minor serve as related keys. The finale to Act 1 also encompasses a number of closed pieces. Eurydice sings a happy *canzone* and a *sarabanda* treated like a chaconne, the two airs separated by a choral lullaby for six singers. 24 dancing dryads make the *sarabanda* festive, but Eurydice is bitten by a viper. After a lengthy, dissonant dialogue between her, the Nurse and Aristaeus, she expires. Her death is immediately lamented by a chorus and by Apollo, who descends in a flaming chariot, illuminating the walks and avenues in the surrounding gardens.

Orpheus has two expressive set pieces in the last act with surprisingly little recitative. In the first he laments the loss of Eurydice in a soliloquy with the recitative refrain 'Lagrime, dove sete' that frames two strophes in aria style. Then, in alternation with the Fates, he sings two more strophes of another aria. The whole exchange takes on the solemn tone of a tragic Greek *kommos*, emphasized by the constant return to G minor cadences by Orpheus and to G major by the Fates, until their closing declaration to G minor. More than Rossi's *Il palazzo incantato* (1642), *Orfeo* is a musical carousel, whose short, rhythmically delightful arias and lively imitative ensembles are better held together by a stronger narrative line and scenic breadth, one musical indication of which is harmonic structuring by similarity of key.

Rossi's music was in little danger of being overshadowed by the sumptuous sets of parks, a palace, gardens, caverns and a scene in hell, or by the flying figures of Victory, Apollo or Cupid. His opera has songs, ensembles and choruses in abundance, all with shapely lyric phrasing and more than a hint of French musical style in some of the dance music and arias. The opera follows the three principals to their tragic ends, but lightens the fate of Eurydice by leaving her in the Elysian Fields (possibly with a brief ballet), and that of Orpheus by granting him a place among the immortals. The two comic characters, the Satyr and Momus, both mock the earnestness of the three lovers; the Satyr symbolizes uncivil, opportunistic desire (the lack of which fills Aristaeus with frustration) and Momus speaks like a misogynist and misanthrope. The two trios of boys, the Graces and the Fates, bear a remarkable similarity of presence and function to the Three Boys in Mozart's *Die Zauberflöte*.

See also ORPHEUS.   MARGARET MURATA

Orfeo (iii) [*L'Orfeo*] ('Orpheus'). *Dramma per musica* in three acts by ANTONIO SARTORIO to a libretto by AURELIO AURELI; Venice, Teatro S Salvatore, 14 December 1672.

The plot combines details of the ORPHEUS myth as told by Ovid and Virgil with inventions based on contemporary Venetian practice. Euridice [Eurydice] (soprano), married to Orpheus (soprano castrato), and loved by his brother Aristeo [Aristaeus] (soprano castrato), whom she rejects, dies of a snake-bite. Orpheus, whose jealousy provoked the snake-bite, is convinced by the ghost of Eurydice (singing a memorable lament, accompanied by strings) to seek her in Hades. His appeal to Plutone [Pluto] (bass) is successful in restoring Eurydice to earth; but he loses her again, permanently, when he insists on looking back at her as she follows him. Meanwhile, Aristaeus's wife Autonoe (soprano), disguised as a gypsy, labours successfully to regain her husband's affections. To this basic framework is appended an irrelevant subplot involving another of Orpheus's brothers, Esculapio [Aesculapius] (bass), the Trojan hero Achille [Achilles] (alto castrato) and Ercole [Hercules] (tenor), all pupils of the centaur Chirone [Chiron] (bass). Two comic servants, Erinda (tenor), a nurse, and Orillo (soprano castrato), a page, Achilles' mother Tetide [Thetis] (soprano) and Bacco [Bacchus] (bass) round out the cast. The extra characters, subplots and conventional operatic scenes (an invocation scene, a singing scene, a sleep scene), combined with the portrayal of Orpheus as an anti-hero, transform the mythological story into a typically Venetian drama of jealousy and intrigue. The opera contains more than 50 brief arias, averaging 30 bars in length, about half of them strophic with refrains, and almost evenly divided between da capo and bipartite refrain form, depending on the dramatic situation. Strings are added to the standard continuo accompaniment in fewer than a third of them and in only two passages of recitative, which otherwise is of the simple type.   ELLEN ROSAND

Orfeo, ovvero L'ottava canzone. Opera by G. F. Malipiero, part 3 of the triptych ORFEIDE, L'.

Orfeo ed Euridice (i) [*Orphée et Eurydice* ('Orpheus and Eurydice')].

Italian version: *Azione teatrale* in three acts by CHRISTOPH WILLIBALD GLUCK to a libretto by RANIERI DE' CALZABIGI; Vienna, Burgtheater, 5 October 1762.

French version: *Tragédie opéra* in three acts by Gluck to a libretto by PIERRE LOUIS MOLINE after Calzabigi; Paris, Opéra, 2 August 1774.

ITALIAN VERSION

Orfeo [Orpheus]	alto castrato
Euridice [Eurydice] *his wife*	soprano
Amore [Cupid]	soprano

Shepherds, nymphs, Furies and spectres from Hades, heroes and heroines in Elysium, followers of Orpheus

Setting Classical Thrace

FRENCH VERSION

Orphée [Orpheus]	tenor
Eurydice *his wife*	soprano
Amour [Cupid]	soprano

Shepherds, shepherdesses, nymphs, demons, Furies, happy spirits, heroes and heroines

Setting Classical Thrace

Orfeo ed Euridice was the first of Gluck's three so-called reform operas written with Ranieri de' Calzabigi (the other two were *Alceste* and *Paride ed Elena*) in which a 'noble simplicity' in the action and the music was intended to replace the complicated plots and florid musical style of *opera seria*. Calzabigi had gone in 1761 to Vienna where he was encouraged to collaborate with Gluck by Count Durazzo, the Intendant of Viennese theatres; a further important collaborator was the influential choreographer GASPARO ANGIOLINI. *Orfeo ed Euridice* was first performed on the name-day of Emperor Francis I, when it was a great success; it went on to become the most popular of Gluck's works, as it has remained. The principals in the first performance were Gaetano Guadagni (Orpheus), Marianna Bianchi (Eurydice) and Lucia Clavarau (Cupid).

The 1762 production of *Orfeo ed Euridice* was revived in Vienna the following year, but the work was not then performed until 1769, when Gluck himself conducted it in Parma as part of a triple bill, *Le feste d'Apollo*. This consisted of a prologue and three acts: an *Atto di Bauci e Filemone* ('Philemon and Baucis'), an *Atto d'Aristeo* ('Aristaeus') and an *Atto d'Orfeo*. For this, *Orfeo ed Euridice* was given without an interval and with the alto castrato part originally written for Guadagni transposed up for the soprano castrato Giuseppe Millico. Then, in 1774, Gluck revised the opera for performances at the Académie Royale de Musique (the Opéra), transposing and adapting the role of Orpheus for an *haute-contre*, the type of voice usually used for heroic or amatory roles in French opera rather than the castrato, which had virtually no place in French music and was something of an object of ridicule. Gluck also altered the orchestration of the opera to suit the

TABLE 1: Italian and French versions of *Orfeo ed Euridice* (i)

N – new to 1774 version; R – revision of number in 1762 version; items in 1774 version neither N nor R are in effect direct transcriptions; italic numerals represent 1774 version

Orfeo ed Euridice, 1762		*Orphée et Eurydice*, 1774	
	ACT 1		**ACT 1**
1	Sinfonia, C	*1*	Ouverture, C
Scene i		*Scene i*	
2	Coro: Ah, se intorno, c	*2*	Choeur: Ah! dans ce bois, c
3	Recit. (Orfeo): Basta, basta	*3*	Récit (Orphée): Vos plaintes (*R*3)
4	Ballo, E♭	*4*	Pantomime, E♭
5*a*)	Coro: Ah, se intorno, c	*5*	Choeur: Ah! dans ce bois, c (*R*5a)
b)	Ballo (ritornello), c		
		6	Récit (Orphée): Eloignez-vous! (*N*)
		7	Ritournelle, c (=5*b*)
		Scene ii	
6*a*)	Aria (Orfeo): Chiamo il mio ben così, F	*8a*)	Air (Orphée): Objet de mon amour, C
b)	Recit. (Orfeo): Euridice, Euridice!, f	*b*)	Récit (Orphée): Eurydice! Eurydice!, c
c)	Aria (Orfeo): Cerco il mio ben, F	*c*)	Air (Orphée): Accablé de regrets, C
d)	Recit. (Orfeo): Euridice, Euridice!, F	*d*)	Récit (Orphée): Eurydice! Eurydice!, C
e)	Aria (Orfeo): Piango il mio ben, F	*e*)	Air (Orphée): Plein de troubles, C
7	Recit. (Orfeo): Numi! barbari Numi	*9*	Récit (Orphée): Divinités de l'Achéron (*R*7)
Scene ii		*Scene iii*	
8	Recit. (Amore, Orfeo): T'assiste Amore	*10*	Récit (Amour): L'Amour vient au secours
		11	Air (Amour): Si les doux accords, F (*N*)
		12	Récit (Orphée, Amour): Dieux! Je la reverrais! (*R*8)
9	Aria (Amore): Gli sguardi trattieni, G	*13*	Air (Amour): Soumis au silence, G
		Scene iv	
10	Recit. (Orfeo): Che disse?	*14*	Récit (Orphée): Impitoyables Dieux! (*R*10)
		15	Ariette (Orphée): L'espoir renaît, B♭ (*N*)
11	Orchestral coda, D		
	ACT 2		**ACT 2**
Scene i		*Scene i*	
12	Ballo, E♭	*16*	Maestoso, E♭
13	Introduction, c	*17*	Prélude, d
14	Coro: Chi mai dell'Erebo, c	*18*	Choeur: Quel est l'audacieux, d
15	Ballo, c	*19*	Air de Furie, d
16	Coro: Chi mai dell'Erebo, c	*20*	Choeur: Quel est l'audacieux, d
17	Ballo (=12), E♭		
18	Orfeo, Coro: Deh placatevi, E♭	*21*	Orphée, Choeur: Laissez-vous toucher, B♭ (*R*18)
19	Coro: Misero giovane, E♭	*22*	Choeur: Qui t'amène, B♭
20	Aria (Orfeo): Mille pene, c	*23*	Air (Orphée): Ah! La flamme, c
21	Coro: Ah, quale incognito affetto, c	*24*	Choeur: Par quels puissants remords, g
22	Aria (Orfeo): Men tiranno, c	*25*	Air (Orphée): La tendresse, g
23	Coro: Ah, quale incognito affetto, f	*26*	Choeur: Quels chants doux, f
		27	Air de Furies, d (*N*)
Scene ii		*Scene ii*	
		28	Ballet des Ombres heureuses
24	Ballo, F	*a*)	Lent très doux, F
		b)	Même mouvement, d (*N*)
		c)	28a, F (*N*)
		d)	Air, C (*N*)
		29	Air (Eurydice, Choeur): Cet asile, F (*N*)
		30	Ritournelle, F (*N*)
		Scene iii	
25	Aria (Orfeo, Coro): Che puro ciel, C	*31*	Air (Orphée): Quel nouveau ciel, C (*R*25)
26	Coro: Vieni a' regni, F	*32*	Choeur: Viens dans ce séjour, F
27	Ballo, B♭	*33*	Lent, B♭
28	Recit. (Orfeo): Anime avventurose	*34*	Récit (Orphée): O vous, ombres
29	Coro: Torna, o bella, F	*35*	Choeur: Près du tendre objet, F
	ACT 3		**ACT 3**
Scene i		*Scene i*	
30	Recit. (Orfeo, Euridice): Vieni, segui i miei passi	*36*	Récit (Orphée, Eurydice): Viens, viens, Eurydice (*R*30)
31	Duetto (Orfeo, Euridice): Vieni, appaga il tuo consorte, G	*37*	Duo (Orphée, Eurydice): Viens, suis un époux, F (*R*31)
32	Recit. (Euridice): Qual vita	*38*	Récit (Eurydice): Mais d'où vient (*R*32)
33	Aria (Euridice): Che fiero momento, c	*39a*)	Air (Eurydice): Fortune ennemie, c
		b)	Duo (Eurydice, Orphée): Je goûtais les charmes, E♭ (*R*33, part)
		c)	Air (Eurydice): Fortune ennemie, c

34	Recit. (Orfeo, Euridice): Ecco un nuovo tormento		40	Récit (Orphée, Eurydice): Quelle épreuve cruelle (*R*34)
35	Aria (Orfeo): Che farò senza Euridice, C		41	Air (Orphée): J'ai perdu mon Eurydice, F (*R*35)
36	Recit. (Orfeo): Ah finisca e per sempre		42	Récit (Orphée): Ah! puisse ma douleur (*R*36)

Scene ii

| 37 | Recit. (Amore, Orfeo, Euridice): Orfeo, che fai? |

Scene ii

| 43 | Récit (Amour, Orphée, Eurydice): Arrête, Orphée! (*R*37) |
| 44 | Trio (Eurydice, Orphée, Amour): Tendre Amour, e (*N*) |

Scene iii

| 38 | Maestoso, D |

*Scene iii**

| 45 | Orphée, Amour, Eurydice, Choeur: L'Amour triomphe, A–D (*R*43) |

Ballo

| 39 | Grazioso, A |
| 40 | Allegro, a |

Ballet

46	Gracieux, A (=39)
47	Gavotte, a (*R*40)
48	Air vif, C (*N*)
49	Menuet, C (*N*)
50	Maestoso, A (*R*38)

| 41 | Andante, D |

| 51 | Très lentement, D (*R*41) |
| 52 | Chaconne, D (*N*) |

| 42 | Allegro, D |
| 43 | Orfeo, Amore, Euridice, Coro: Trionfi Amore, D |

*in original conducting score, items appear in the order: 50, 46, 47, 48, 49, 45, 51, 52; between 48 and 49 is a Lent et gracieux, G (Collected Edition, appx, pp.324–5), and 49 is followed by 2 bars of modulation (Collected Edition, appx, p.310)

different forces of the Opéra, and added vocal and instrumental pieces to make the opera much larger, longer and grander (see Table 1 above for a comparison of the two versions). This work, *Orphée et Eurydice*, had a new French text by the young French poet Moline, based on Calzabigi's libretto but with additions. The principals were Joseph Legros (Orpheus), Sophie Arnould (Eurydice) and Rosalie Levasseur (Cupid). The work's success surpassed even that of Gluck's first Paris opera, *Iphigénie en Aulide*, earlier in 1774, and it continued to feature prominently in the repertory of the Opéra.

Performances abroad began with the production of the Italian version at the King's Theatre in London in 1770, but although Guadagni again sang the title role only seven numbers of Gluck's original remained and the opera was lengthened with words by Giovanni Bottarelli and music by J. C. Bach. Productions were soon given at many opera houses throughout Europe, usually of the Italian version, including one conducted by Haydn at Eszterháza in 1776. In the first part of the 19th century the tenor Adolphe Nourrit was celebrated for his portrayals of Orpheus at the Paris Opéra; and in 1854 Liszt conducted the opera at Weimar, writing his symphonic poem *Orpheus* to replace the overture and adding some closing music on the same themes.

The first appearance of a female singer in the role of Orpheus was one Demoiselle Fabre in Milan in 1813, but the most famous female interpreter of the role in the 19th century was the contralto Pauline Viardot, for whom Berlioz made his edition of the opera in 1859. For this, Berlioz re-adopted the original vocal register of the Italian Orpheus and combined what he considered to be the best of Gluck's Italian and French versions. Basically, he followed the 1774 French score, rearranging it in four acts, and reverting to the Italian original only where he thought it musically or dramatically superior. In the process he cut several numbers from the French score, including the third verse of Orpheus's first-act lament 'Objet de mon amour', the Act 3 trio and the whole of the final *divertissement*, and replaced the final chorus with that of *Echo et Narcisse*, 'Le Dieu de Paphos et de Gnide'. He also made adjustments to Moline's French text and restored much of the key

scheme and some of the original, more subtle orchestration of the Italian version.

During the 19th century the part of Orpheus was sung nearly as often by a tenor as by a contralto; Berlioz's edition is just one of many composite versions of the opera, albeit the most famous and most distinguished. However, the versions of the opera most frequently given since the 1870s are adaptations of Berlioz's version back into Italian, in three acts, still with a contralto as Orpheus, and incorporating music that Berlioz omitted from Gluck's 1774 French score. The most popular of these hybrid Italian versions was published by Ricordi in 1889. Gluck's opera has even been transposed down for a baritone; Dietrich Fischer-Dieskau and Hermann Prey have both sung the role in Germany. It only remains for a soprano to sing the Parma version, which has not been performed in modern times.

Toscanini was a great champion of *Orfeo ed Euridice*, and conducted it regularly during his seasons at La Scala, Milan. There is a recording of him conducting Act 2 in a concert performance with Nan Merriman and Barbara Gibson and the NBC Symphony Orchestra. Clara Butt sang Orpheus in 1920 at Covent Garden, under Sir Thomas Beecham; Kathleen Ferrier took the role at Glyndebourne in 1947 and Covent Garden in 1953. Other notable postwar female interpreters of Orpheus have included Rita Gorr at the Opéra-Comique in Paris in 1959 and Marilyn Horne at the Metropolitan in 1972; she also made a distinguished recording of the opera with Sir Georg Solti conducting. Another, conducted by Renato Fasano, was made in 1965 by Shirley Verrett, who sang the role at Covent Garden in 1972. Janet Baker was also an admired Orpheus, and chose the opera for her Glyndebourne farewell in 1982 conducted by Raymond Leppard; this version too was recorded.

The recordings and most of the performances mentioned above are of a composite version in Italian. Despite its fame, even the Berlioz edition has been little performed this century, an omission which has been rectified by Anne-Sofie von Otter, who recorded a modification of it (changing it back into three acts and restoring the third-act trio) conducted by John Eliot

'Orfeo ed Euridice' (Gluck), Act 3 scene i: painting by Pehr Hilleström showing a production by the Swedish Royal Opera in 1773

Gardiner in 1989. Recently several countertenors have sung the original Italian version with great success, among them John Angelo Messana, René Jacobs and Derek Lee Ragin; Jacobs made a fine recording of the 1762 version with La Petite Bande under Sigiswald Kuijken in 1982. The 1774 French version has made lamentably few appearances this century either on the stage or in the record catalogues, partly because of the difficulty of finding adequate high tenors. Two of its most distinguished interpreters, however, made recordings: Nicolai Gedda, who sang the role at the Paris Opéra as late as 1973, recorded it in his prime in 1955 under Louis de Froment; and, finest of all, Léopold Simoneau recorded it in 1956 under Hans Rosbaud.

In the synopsis that follows, '*I*' stands for the Italian version, '*F*' for the French version; see Table 1 (pages 745–6) for a comparison of the two versions.

ACT 1.i (*I*), i–ii (*F*) *A pleasant but solitary grove with the tomb of Eurydice in the middle of an avenue of laurel and cypress trees* After a lively overture, nymphs and shepherds enter to a sombre orchestral introduction with garlands of myrtle and antique vases as part of the funeral rites for Eurydice, some burning incense and scattering flowers. The chorus sings a mourning hymn, whose solemnity is intensified by the low pitch of the soprano line and the use of three cornetts (in *Orfeo*; three trombones in *Orphée*). Orpheus, who lies prostrate on a rock, interrupts them three times with an anguished cry of 'Euridice!'/'Eurydice!'. He tells them to perform the last rites and strew Eurydice's grave with flowers; this they do to a dance, full of chromatic inflections, after which the chorus is repeated, the orchestral introduction now serving as postlude. (The French version has a brief recitative for Orpheus before this post lude, or 'ritournelle', breaking the palindromic symmetry of the original.)

Left alone, Orpheus calls to Eurydice in the aria 'Chiamo il mio ben così'/'Objet de mon amour': this lament is in three verses, separated by two increasingly impassioned recitatives, each beginning with Orpheus's cries of 'Euridice!', akin to those heard during the opening chorus. The echo effects of the opening chorus are also extended here with a second, offstage orchestra of chalumeaux and strings (there were no chalumeaux in Paris, where Gluck replaced them with an oboe). Each verse has different solo instruments: respectively flute, horns and english horns in *Orfeo*, and two flutes, one horn and two clarinets in *Orphée* (again Gluck had to replace an unusual and distinctive timbre with one much less so). After the third strophe Orpheus rages against the cruelty of the gods and determines to wrest Eurydice from them and bring her back to the land of the living.

1.ii (*I*), iii–iv (*F*) Cupid appears and tells Orpheus that Jove has taken pity and will allow him to descend into Hades; if he can appease the Furies with his singing he can bring Eurydice back. This is all told in recitative in *Orfeo*; for *Orphée*, Gluck shortened it, adding an air ('Si les doux accords de ta lyre') for Cupid that covers similar ground to the second part of the original recitative. Orpheus is delighted, but Cupid warns him that if he looks at Eurydice before he has brought her back to earth he will lose her for ever; neither is he allowed to explain this curious behaviour to his wife. Cupid leaves him, singing a little aria in which he warns Orpheus to be silent and control his desire ('Gli sguardi trattieni'/'Soumis au silence'; the livelier sections increase the agony and the irony, with their simple 3/8 rhythm, rather like a serenade).

Orpheus imagines Eurydice's anxiety and distress at his behaviour at their reunion; but he must bow to the will of the gods. Thunder and lightning are heard as he leaves for Hades. In *Orfeo* this is set as recitative, with a brief orchestral coda; for *Orphée* Gluck cut the recitative substantially, removing the simulated encounter between Orpheus and Eurydice, and gave Orpheus a long, heroic bravura aria, a display piece for Legros ('L'espoir renaît dans mon âme'). This virtuoso italianate aria, complete with provision for a cadenza, has provoked much criticism partly because it is inconsistent with Gluck's declared reform principles (although it was very popular in the 18th century). It has not been established for certain whether its music is in fact by Gluck or by Ferdinando Bertoni, who claimed to have composed it, although Gluck had used it twice before, in his opera *Il Parnasso confuso* (1765) and in the *Atto d'Aristeo*, one of the companion operas to the 1769 Parma production of *Orfeo ed Euridice*. Lasting over five minutes, the aria is by far the longest piece in Act 1 of *Orphée*; although its length and its style may seem at odds with the music of the rest of the opera, there is no denying that it brings the act to a spectacular conclusion.

ACT 2.i *A terrifying grotto beyond the river Cocytus, hidden in the distance by thick smoke billowing out of the grotto* An 'orribile sinfonia' (Calzabigi's description) is heard, a short, terrifying dance with jerky rhythms, chromatic harmony and open-ended phrases (Gluck replaced the two horns of *Orfeo* with a solo trumpet in *Orphée*). Gluck again uses a double orchestra: harp and pizzicato strings accompany Orpheus and represent his lyre, with the rest of the orchestra for the Furies. A brief prelude for the harp indicates that Orpheus is on his way, and immediately the Furies and demons of the underworld threaten him in a chorus whose relentless repeated rhythms, homophonic writing and stark octave lines heighten the tension. The music hurries on into another short dance for the Furies, full of rushing scales, which leads to a repeat of the opening chorus, extended now to portray the barking of the multi-headed guard dog Cerberus with quick string glissandos. In *Orfeo* there is a repeat of the opening sinfonia; in *Orphée*, Orpheus actually interrupts the chorus of Furies here with his first attempt to placate them.

'Be moved by my tears', he pleads, to be answered by the Furies' angry cries of 'No!'/'Non!' (Orpheus's wide-ranging line is more ornate in the French revision). The Furies ask Orpheus why he is there: 'Misero giovane, che vuoi, che mediti?'/'Qui t'amène en ces lieux?'. (The Furies sing quietly at first, but the obsessive rhythms of the first chorus continue.) Orpheus interrupts, and his brief arias are followed by continuations of the chorus, which however gradually become less fierce until the Furies, finally moved by Orpheus's singing, make way for him to move on into Elysium. The Furies' music dies away and comes to rest (on their first perfect cadence in the act, the surprise of which is increased and strengthened by the major-key ending).

In *Orfeo*, at this point the second scene begins; but when he revised the opera Gluck added an 'Air de Furies', a substantial dance of terror drawn from his ballet *Don Juan* (1761), which also seems to have been the melodic and harmonic inspiration for the five choruses of Furies in the first scene of *Orfeo* the following year. The inclusion of this dance in *Orphée* gives an extra purpose and dimension to the preceding choruses.

2.ii (*I*), ii–iii (*F*) *The Elysian Fields; flowery arbours, groves and fountains and grassy areas on which groups of Blessed Spirits are resting* As the scene changes from Hades to the Elysian Fields, so the music, which has been predominantly in the minor mode, turns to the radiance of F major, the traditional pastoral key, for the opening Dance of the Blessed Spirits. In *Orphée*, Gluck expanded this celebrated piece for two flutes and strings, surely the most other-worldly minuet ever written, and indeed made it nearly three times its original length by adding a central section with a solo flute (the D minor piece generally known simply as 'Dance of the Blessed Spirits'), followed by a reprise of the opening; a further extra dance follows, and an *air* for Eurydice and the chorus ('Cet asile aimable et tranquille'), another pastoral piece, in F major and a flowing 6/8 metre, repeated in instrumental form as a dance for the heroes and heroines.

Then follows one of Gluck's most original arias as Orpheus marvels at the beauty of the scene in which he finds himself ('Che puro ciel'/'Quel nouveau ciel'). Its orchestration in *Orfeo* is the most complex that Gluck ever wrote: an oboe melody, with a softly rippling triplet accompaniment from the strings, solo cello and solo flute, with supporting parts provided by solo bassoon, horn and continuo. Gluck simplified the solo flute and cello parts when he revised *Orfeo* for Parma in 1769, and retained this less demanding version in Paris in 1774: a great loss, as is Orpheus's brief dialogue with the Blessed Spirits at the end of the aria when they tell him that Eurydice is coming. 'Quel nouveau ciel' has no chorus and ends with Orpheus's words to Eurydice: 'Your attractive glances and gentle smile are the only blessings that I want'. The Blessed Spirits continue with a chorus, 'Vieni a' regni del riposo'/'Viens dans ce séjour paisible', after which there is a slow dance for flutes and strings.

Orpheus, mildly impatient, begs the Spirits to restore Eurydice to him as soon as possible, which they do during a reprise of the previous chorus with different words; the act ends as Orpheus leads Eurydice away, without looking at her.

ACT 3.i *A dark labyrinthine grotto surrounded by rocks, thickets and wild plants* The scenes built around choruses, solo voices and dances of the two previous acts are replaced in this act by the encounter between Orpheus and Eurydice alone. And unlike the other two acts this one begins, after a few bars of agitated strings, with recitative, as Orpheus urges Eurydice to hurry up and follow him. She is naturally suspicious of his strange and impatient behaviour which, no matter how much she questions him, he cannot explain. Their exchanges culminate in a duet ('Vieni, appaga il tuo consorte'/'Viens, suis un époux'): here is no sweet, submissive Eurydice but a passionate and jealous wife, as she shows in her following aria, 'Che fiero momento'/'Fortune ennemie'. When Gluck revised this number for *Orphée* he recast its central slower section as a dramatic duet to press the action forward. In the next recitative, inevitably, Eurydice faints, and as Orpheus turns to look at her she dies (the Paris version is particularly moving here as the two voices unite for one last note). Orpheus gives vent to his desperation first in impassioned recitative, and then in an apparently controlled aria, a lament in the major key ('Che farò senza Euridice?'/'J'ai perdu mon Eurydice'). Gluck added an orchestral postlude to this famous aria when he revised it, greatly intensifying its noble tragedy. Its three verses balance 'Chiamo il mio ben così'/'Objet de mon amour' in Act 1; the two subsidiary sections begin with Orpheus's cries, 'Euridice!', as do the two recitatives that separate the strophes of the first-act aria.

3.ii Orpheus is about to kill himself when Cupid reappears, says that Orpheus has given proof enough of his fidelity and restores Eurydice to life, telling them to enjoy the pleasures of love. Gluck added a trio when he revised the opera, initially a rather sombre piece with its minor key, repeated syncopated rhythms and dark orchestration (low strings with bassoons), but brightening to a faster, major-key ending as the three principals celebrate the power of love.

3.iii *The magnificent temple of Cupid* Orpheus, Eurydice, Cupid and shepherds and shepherdesses celebrate. The symmetry characteristic of the opera is maintained even in the concluding ballet of *Orfeo*, which begins with an instrumental version of the final chorus and, after four dances, ends with a reprise of the chorus. *Orphée*, on the other hand, has a lengthy final *divertissement* which is apt to seem rather overextended (and is often cut altogether) when it is performed, as in the collected edition, after the final chorus.

The engraved score of *Orphée* published in 1774 after the first performances places the Act 3 trio in the middle of the final *divertissement*, between the Menuet and the Maestoso; but in the Gluck collected edition (1967) it is restored to its original position before the final chorus, as in the 1774 libretto. Recent research on the conducting scores used for the first Paris performances shows that the original order of the Act 3 *divertissement* was different from that in the printed score (see footnote to Table 1).

*　　*　　*

Orfeo ed Euridice is a milestone both in Gluck's work and in the history of opera. It is in effect the first of Gluck's so-called reform operas, although it was not until the publication of the Italian *Alceste* of 1767 that his and Calzabigi's reformist principles and aims were presented, in a manifesto, as a preface (for a translation and discussion, *see* GLUCK, CHRISTOPH WILLIBALD, §6). *Orfeo*, although an *azione teatrale* with roots in the dramatic pastoral tradition, embodies all his reforms except for that of the overture, which instead of apprising the audience of the nature of the opera is a jolly, high-spirited sinfonia in one movement which could well have served as curtain-raiser to a comic opera. But gone are the coloratura and the da capo arias of Italian *opera seria*, together with the regular and restrictive alternation of recitative and aria and the *recitativo secco* accompanied only by the continuo. Instead, in *Orfeo*, the chorus assumes a role of much greater importance than was usual in Italian opera, sometimes rivalling that of the protagonist, as at the beginnings of the first two acts. The recitative is very varied and fluid, and often impassioned and colourful, partly because it is orchestrated throughout and partly because it is so attentive to the words and their sense; and the arias themselves are placed at telling dramatic points – each is vital to the drama, the structure and the characterization.

Orfeo owes much to French opera and drama in spite of the fact that it is in Italian. Calzabigi had spent much time in Paris; his experience of French theatre and opera are evident throughout the libretto. Gluck generously declared that he was indebted to Calzabigi for the invention of the new form of Italian opera, but he himself was certainly familiar with both *tragédie lyrique* and *opéra comique*, and the influences of both are manifest in

Orfeo. The opening *tombeau* is reminiscent of Act 1 of Rameau's *Castor et Pollux*, and even a lament as profound as Orpheus's 'Chiamo il mio ben così' is related to the three-verse French *romance* of the kind found in *opéras comiques*. Gluck's revision for the Paris performances of 1774 brought the work even closer to the French tradition. However, the transposition and adaptation of the role of Orpheus from alto castrato to *haute-contre* resulted not only in the loss of much of the formal balance and the satisfying tonal sequence (compare in Table 1 the key relationships of the two versions in Act 1 and especially Act 2) but also the change of emphasis in the role of Orpheus from the elegiac, disembodied beauty of the castrato to the much more heroic high tenor.

But there were undoubtedly gains as well as losses in the transformation and expansion of the short, intimate court chamber opera into a full-scale work for a large public opera house. When Gluck made the French revision, some 12 years after the Italian original, he was a much more experienced composer and man of the theatre, and the revision has an added sweep and grandeur; the addition of Eurydice's aria and the ballets in the second act and the trio in the third act are undoubted gains. It is ironic that the versions of the opera best known and most widely performed today are based on Berlioz's hybrid edition and in consequence, since the 19th century, Orpheus has nearly always been sung by women 'en travesti'. Nowadays, however, the original Italian role can be sung by a countertenor, and although there are few high tenors who can negotiate the consistently dizzy heights of the French version, the score could be transposed down a tone to correspond with what we believe 18th-century French pitch to have been. Such means would bring us as close as possible to Gluck's originals.

See also ORPHEUS. For a page from the autograph score of the French revision *see* GLUCK, CHRISTOPH WILLIBALD, fig.2.　　　JEREMY HAYES

Orfeo ed Euridice (ii) ('Orpheus and Eurydice'). *Dramma per musica* in three acts by FERDINANDO BERTONI to a libretto by RANIERI DE' CALZABIGI; Venice, Teatro S Benedetto, 3 January 1776.

Performed after Bertoni's one-act *Aristo e Temira*, this setting of Calzabigi's 'reform' libretto, previously used by Gluck (1762) and Antonio Tozzi (1775), was a farewell vehicle for the castrato Gaetano Guadagni who had sung Orpheus in both earlier settings. Eurydice (soprano) was sung by Camilla Passi Sarti; Calzabigi's character Amore was changed to Imene [Hymen] (tenor), and sung by Giacomo Davide. According to the libretto, a chorus of 16 men and six women was employed. The 'extraordinary success of my Orfeo' resulted in Emperor Joseph II commissioning the printing of the full score (letters to Padre Martini, 24 February and 30 March 1776, 26 April 1777 in *I-Bc*). Gluck's partisans in Paris later accused Bertoni of having plagiarized Gluck's *Orfeo*, but this was perhaps a reaction to the revelation in the *Journal de Paris* (27 July 1779) that Gluck had appropriated a bravura aria, 'Sò che dal ciel discende', from Bertoni's *Tancredi* (1767) for the end of Act 1 of his French version of *Orfeo* (1774). In a preface to the second edition of the printed score (1783), Bertoni acknowledged his indebtedness to Gluck, stating that he had a copy of Gluck's score to guide him in the absence of the poet's assistance, but he noted: 'Gli uomini per altro di giusto e fino discernamento potranno ben conoscere la diversità nel rimante'. His music, as Berlioz noted in 1862, does show some obvious rhythmic similarities to Gluck's setting, especially in the Infernal Scene (2.i) and in the homophonic, syllabic choral settings. Bertoni also employs Calzabigi and Algarotti's idea of *recitativo accompagnato* throughout, adding an oboe to the strings. The orchestration, however, is dissimilar to that of Gluck in view of the limited resources of the Venetian opera orchestra (two oboes, two horns, strings and basso continuo). Bertoni does follow Gluck in adding a harp to Act 2, but it is doubled by violins in case of unavailability.

Bertoni's aria settings, however, demonstrate his independence from Gluck's model. In Orpheus's first solo song he omits the verse 'Chiamo il mio ben così', and begins with recitative leading to the cavatina 'Cerco il mio ben così' in C major. The second verse of the cavatina, 'Piango il mio ben così', is in D major after the recitative. Orpheus's Act 3 lament after losing Eurydice for the second time ('Che farò senza Euridice') is accompanied by oboes and horns in addition to the strings, which double the melodic line in typical 18th-century Italian fashion. The autograph score (*I-OS*) contains a different version of 'Che farò' which, according to a note in the margin, was used in later performances. It also contains a duet, 'Ah mio ben, in questo amplesso', which may be that described by Michael Kelly in his *Reminiscences* as 'the most exquisite treat I ever received'. Bertoni's *Orfeo ed Euridice* was staged throughout Europe during the last quarter of the century; Reichardt added new music for the Berlin production of 1788, and that same year Haydn adapted the work for Eszterháza.

See also ORPHEUS.   GEORGE TRUETT HOLLIS

Orff, Carl (*b* Munich, 10 July 1895; *d* Munich, 29 March 1982). German composer and educationist.

From the age of five he learnt the piano, organ and cello, and he studied at the Munich Academy of Music with Beer-Walbrunn and Zilcher, graduating in 1914. He was Kapellmeister at the Munich Kammerspiele (1915–17) and from the 1918–19 season occupied a similar position at the Nationaltheater, Mannheim, and the Landestheater, Darmstadt. The following season he returned to Munich where he took further lessons in composition with Heinrich Kaminski. During the 1920s he began teaching, and in 1924, together with Dorothee Günther, he founded the Güntherschule for gymnastics, music and dance in Munich with the intention of exploring the relationships between movement and music. From 1930 to 1933 he conducted the Munich Bach Society, presenting many stimulating arrangements of early music including a stage version of the *St Luke Passion* formerly attributed to Bach. His real breakthrough came in 1937 with the première of *Carmina burana*, staged at Frankfurt during the final Allgemeine Deutsche Musik Verein Festival. Orff remained in Germany during World War II and secured an international reputation after 1945 with a series of stage works based mostly on classical and metaphysical subjects; these were first performed at the Salzburg Festival or the Stuttgart Staatstheater. From 1950 to 1960 he directed a masterclass in composition at the Staatliche Hochschule für Musik, Munich, and received honorary doctorates from the universities of Tübingen (1955) and Munich (1960), and membership of the Bavarian Academy of Fine Arts.

Orff's interest in music theatre was stimulated from an early age. Profoundly influenced by hearing and studying Debussy's *Pelléas et Mélisande*, he completed in 1913 a music drama, *Gisei, das Opfer*, based on a play with a Japanese theme, *Terakoya*. *Gisei*, which never reached the stage, displays features that anticipate his mature style: the preponderance of recitative-like writing for the voice, the massive orchestration which includes unusual instruments such as a wind machine and a glass harmonica, and an interest in exotic effects.

Scene from the original production of Carl Orff's 'Prometheus' at the Württembergisches Staatstheater in Stuttgart, 24 March 1968 (designed by Teo Otto)

While Debussy's influence was to be superseded in the following years by those of the German late Romantics, Orff was to share with the French master a subtle approach to instrumental colour.

Another equally significant influence was the music of Monteverdi. During the 1920s Orff was engaged in adapting *Lamento d'Arianna*, *Orfeo* and *Il ballo delle ingrate* for the German stage. These arrangements would be regarded nowadays as anachronistic; in *Orfeo*, for example, Orff removed the original allegorical figure of La Musica. In place of La Musica's prologue, the Narrator declaims the Old High German Orpheus Story (*c*1000) by Notker Labeo, after Boethius; Orff even altered the order of certain scenes. At the same time, however, the process of immersing himself in the conventions of early Italian Baroque opera led him to re-examine the whole nature of music theatre in a post-Wagnerian age: Orff's subsequent stage compositions manifested a more direct and forceful language, discarded anything dramatically superfluous and highlighted the words in the sharpest relief.

Yet Orff went beyond mere imitation of 17th-century stylistic features. From *Carmina burana* onwards, his main concern was to realize a *Gesamtkunstwerk* in which music, words and movement combine to produce a ritualized spectacle. Believing that Western music was open to no further development, he rejected the subjectivism and isolation of the individual in favour of a stringent and universally valid collective experience. Consequently, he deliberately cultivated a musical language of primordial simplicity which aimed to achieve the maximum theatrical intensity through the minimum of means. Although Orff drew upon a wide variety of sources for his stage works – from the parable-like fairy-tales of *Der Mond* and *Die Kluge*, and the fundamental themes of love, the joy of living and the wheel of fortune in the *Trionfi*, to episodes in Bavarian peasant life in *Die Bernauerin* and *Astutuli*, and the conflict between gods, men and fate in the Greek trilogy of *Antigonae*, *Oedipus der Tyrann* and *Prometheus* – this musical language remained strikingly consistent throughout his career. Its characteristics include an almost elemental rhythmic insistence (somewhat influenced by Stravinsky's *The Wedding*), a consciously restricted melodic structure which incorporates both plainsong and folktunes as well as melismatic arioso, a virtual absence of counterpoint, and an orchestral accompaniment of drones and repetitive ostinatos often using a vast array of percussion instruments. In his later compositions these elements are presented in even starker terms. *Prometheus*, which sets the original Greek of Aeschylus, and the apocalyptic *De temporum fine comoedia* rely heavily upon incantation and both spoken and sung declamation. Indeed, the musical substance in these scores is reduced to the barest of essentials.

Apart from *Carmina burana*, which is better known in the concert hall, and the early operas *Der Mond* and *Die Kluge*, the reception of Orff's other stage works has been mixed outside Germany and Austria. He has been criticized for his reliance upon simple, even banal formulae which seem at odds with the generally sophisticated musical language of the 20th century. However, it is debatable whether his brand of primitivism remains as isolated from more recent developments in music theatre as his detractors would suggest. Certainly, the minimalist musical materials employed in the operas of Philip Glass owe much to his example.

See also ANTIGONAE; CARMINA BURANA; CATULLI CARMINA; KLUGE, DIE; MOND, DER; and TRIONFO DI AFRODITE.

scores published in Mainz

Gisei, das Opfer (music drama, after K. Florenz: *Terakoya*), 1913, unperf.

Der Mond (kleines Welttheater, 1, Orff, after J. L. Grimm and W. C. Grimm), Munich, National, 5 Feb 1939, vs (1939), rev. 1970, full score (1970)

Die Kluge (12 scenes, Orff, after J. L. Grimm and W. C. Grimm), Frankfurt, Städtische Bühnen, 20 Feb 1943, vs (1942), full score (1957)

Die Bernauerin (bairisches Stück, 7 scenes, Orff), Stuttgart, Württembergisches Staats, 15 June 1947, vs (1946), rev. 1956, full score (1974)

Antigonae (5, Sophocles, trans. F. Hölderlin), Salzburg, Felsenreitschule, 9 Aug 1949, vs (1949), full score (1959)

Trionfi (trittico teatrale), Milan, Scala, 13 Feb 1953
    Carmina burana (cantiones profanae, 3 scenes, medieval Lat. lyrics), Frankfurt, Städtische Bühnen, 8 June 1937, vs (1937), full score (1953)
    Catulli carmina (ludi scaenici, 3 acts and Exordium, partly by Catullus), Leipzig, Städtische Bühnen, 6 Nov 1943, vs (1943), full score (1955)
    Trionfo di Afrodite (concerto scenico, 7 scenes, Catullus, Sappho and Euripides), Milan, Scala, 13 Feb 1953 (1952)

Astutuli (bairische Komödie, 1, Orff), Munich, Kammerspiele, 20 Oct 1953 (1953)

Comoedia de Christi resurrectione (Osterspiel, Orff), TV perf.; Bayerischer Rundfunk, Munich, 31 March 1956; stage, Stuttgart, Württembergisches Staats, 21 April 1957, vs (1957)

Lamenti (trittico teatrale, after Monteverdi), Schwetzingen, Schloss, 15 May 1958, vs (1958)
    Orpheus (3, A. Striggio), Mannheim, National, 17 April 1925; rev., Munich, Kammeroper, 13 Oct 1929; rev., Dresden, Staatsoper, 4 Oct 1940
    Klage der Ariadne (O. Rinuccini), Karlsruhe, Staats, 28 Dec 1925; rev., Gera, Reuss, 30 Nov 1940
    Tanz der Spröden (Rinuccini), Karlsruhe, Staats, 28 Dec 1925; rev., Gera, Reuss, 30 Nov 1940

Oedipus der Tyrann (Trauerspiel, Sophocles, trans. Hölderlin), Stuttgart, Württembergisches Staats, 11 Dec 1959, vs (1959), full score (1965)

Ludus de nato infante mirificus (Weihnachtsspiel, Orff), Stuttgart, Württembergisches Staats, 11 Dec 1960 (1962)

Prometheus (1, Orff, after Aeschylus), Stuttgart, Württembergisches Staats, 24 March 1968, reduced score (1967), full score (1973)

De temporum fine comoedia (Bühnenspiel, 3 pts, Orff), Salzburg, Festspiel, 20 Aug 1973 (1973), rev. 1979

*

C. Sachs and O. Lang: *Einführung in der Neugestaltung von Orfeo* (Mainz, 1925)

H. Schmidt-Garre: 'Neue Formen der Musikbühne zu Carl Orff', *SMz*, lxxix (1939), 226–9

W. Zentner: 'Carl Orffs Der Mond', *ZfM*, cvi (1939), 276–8

C. Niessen: *Die deutsche Oper der Gegenwart* (Regensburg, 1944)

O. Oster: 'Carl Orff und das musikalische Theater', *Theateralmanach Desch* (Munich, 1947)

W. Keller: *Carl Orffs Antigonae* (Mainz, 1950)

W. Riezler: 'Neue Horizonte: Bemerkungen zu Carl Orffs Antigonae', *Gestalt und Gedanke Jahrbuch der Bayerischen Akademie der Schönen Künste* (Munich, 1951)

H. Staeps: 'Das Phänomen Carl Orff oder Magie und Manier', *ÖMz*, vi (1951), 119–24

B. Stäblein: 'Schöpferische Tonalität zum Grossaufbau von Carl Orffs Antigonae', *Musica*, vi (1952), 145–8

E. Helm: 'Carl Orff', *MQ*, xli (1955), 285–304

A. Liess: *Carl Orff: Idee und Werk* (Zürich, 1955, 3/1980; Eng. trans., 1966, 2/1971)

——: 'Zum Verständnis des Orffschen Theaters', *SMz*, xcv (1955), 185–7

K. H. Ruppel, G. R. Sellner and W. Thomas: *Carl Orff, ein Bericht in Wort und Bild* (Mainz, 1955, 2/1960; Eng. trans., 1960)

W. Wagner and W. E. Schäfer: *Carl Orff* (Bayreuth, 1955)

I. Kiekert: *Die musikalische Form in den Werken Carl Orffs* (Regensburg, 1957)

K. H. Ruppel: 'Carl Orffs "Trionfi"', *ÖMz*, xii (1957), 54–8

E. Doflein: 'Über Carl Orff und seine "Bernauerin"', *SMz*, xcviii (1958), 104–7

U. Klement: *Vom Wesen der Alten in den Bühnenwerken Carl Orffs* (Leipzig, 1958)

W. Zillig: 'Carl Orff: der Erneuerer des Musiktheaters', *Musica*, xiii (1959), 153–8

H. Kaufmann: 'Carl Orff als Schauspieler', *Forum*, vii (1960), 107–9

R. U. Klaus: 'Hymen, Kypris und die Hymenaien. Zu mythologischen Quellen von Orffs "Trionfo di Afrodite" ', *Maske und Kothurn*, vi (1960), 1–16

H. Löhmüller: 'In Orffs "Oedipus" wird Musik zum mythischen Urgrund', *Melos*, xxvii (1960), 14–16

W. Schadewaldt: *Carl Orff* (Zürich, 1960)

W. Thomas: 'Raum und Figur im Musiktheater Carl Orffs', *NZM*, Jg.121 (1960), 231–3

H. Kemnitz: *Die Kluge von Carl Orff* (Berlin-Lichterfelde, 1961)

K. Schumann: 'Magie und Kalkül: Über die Form in der Musik Carl Orffs', *NZM*, Jg.122 (1961), 95–9

A. Liess: 'I "Trionfi" di Carl Orff', *RaM*, xxxii (1962), 256–63

H. J. Moser: 'Carl Orff und das Musiktheater der Gegenwart', *Universitas*, xvii (1962), 1095–102

U. Dibelius: 'Die Gegenwart der Antike im Musiktheater', *NZM*, Jg.126 (1965), 277–81

K. Honolka: 'Welttheater auf dem Urgrund Musik', *OW*, vi/7 (1965), 20–22

A. Liess: 'Carl Orff und das musikalische Theater', *Musica*, xix (1965), 192–4

K. H. Ruppel: 'Orffs grosses Welttheater', *Melos*, xxxii (1965), 196–200

K. Schumann: 'Orffs Ein-Mann Theater', *Melos*, xxxii (1965), 201–4

K. H. Wörner: 'Carl Orff und die Problematik des Musiktheaters', *Das Opernjournal*, ix (1967–8), 11–13

G. Hausswald: 'Antikes Welttheater: Uraufführung', *Musica*, xxii (1968), 214–16

S. Melchinger: ' "Prometheus" ', *NZM*, Jg.129 (1968), 322–30

F. Willnauer, ed.: *Prometheus: Mythos, Drama, Musik: Beiträge zu Carl Orffs Musikdrama nach Aischylos* (Tübingen, 1968)

W. Thomas: 'Orff – Bühne und Theatrum Emblematicum: Zur Deutung der Szene in Orffs "Trionfi" ', *Jb des Orff-Institut*, iii (1969), 144–66

R. Münster, ed.: *Carl Orff, das Bühnenwerk* (Munich, 1970)

W. Weifert: ' "… auf dem Geist kommt es an": Carl Orff zum 75. Geburtstag – Kommentar und Gespräch', *NZM*, Jg.131 (1970), 370–77

H. W. Schmidt, ed.: *Carl Orff: sein Leben und sein Werk in Wort, Bild und Noten* (Cologne, 1971)

H. H. Stuckenschmidt: 'Carl Orff und das Musiktheater der Gegenwart', *Universitas*, xxvii (1972), 1031–8

H. Kaufmann: 'Carl Orffs Musik heute: an Beispielen aus "Prometheus" ', *NZM*, Jg.134 (1973), 421–6

A. Liess: 'Carl Orffs De temporum fine comoedia: Zu Entstehung und Werk', *Wissenschaft und Weltbild*, xxvi (1973), 305–13

R. Raffalt: 'Orffs "De temporum fine comoedia": Einführungsvortrag der Uraufführung', *NZM*, Jg.134 (1973), 640–43

W. Thomas: *Carl Orff: De temporum fine comoedia … eine Interpretation* (Tutzing, 1973)

J. C. Sloop: 'Der Mond' Opera by Carl Orff: a Translation and Notes for an American Performance (diss., U. of Rochester, 1974)

W. E. von Lewinski: 'Carl Orff: er schuf eine neue Dimension des musikalischen Theaters', *Musik und Medizin*, i/7 (1975), 45–50

Carl Orff und sein Werk: Dokumentation (Tutzing, 1975–83)

W. Seifert: 'Der grosse Unzeitgemässe: Carl Orff zum 80. Geburtstag', *Melos/NZM*, i (1975), 259–63

T. Georgiades: 'Zur Antigonae-Interpretation von Carl Orff', *Kleine Schriften* (Tutzing, 1977)

J. Häusler: 'Carl Orff und sein Werk für das Musiktheater der Gegenwart', *Universitas*, xxxiv (1979), 343–9

W. Thomas: 'Carl Orffs "Antigonae". Wieder-Gabe einer antiken Tragödie', *Werk und Wiedergabe: Musiktheater exemplarisch interpretiert*, ed. S. Wiesmann (Bayreuth, 1980), 349–67

L. Gersdorf, ed.: *Carl Orff in Selbstzeugnissen und Bilddokumenten* (Reinbek bei Hamburg, 1981)

A. Liess: *Zwei Essays zu Carl Orff: De temporum fine comoedia* (Vienna, Cologne and Graz, 1981)

U. Klement: *Das Musiktheater Carl Orffs* (Leipzig, 1982)

C. Orff: 'Antigonae: ein Trauerspiel des Sophokles von Friedrich Hölderlin', *NZM*, Jg. 143, no. 5 (1982), 19–22

W. Seifert: 'Die humanistische Botschaft eines zeitgemässen Unzeitgemässen: kleines und grosses Welttheater. Das Vermächtnis

des Carl Orff (10. Juli 1895–29. März 1982)', *NZM*, Jg. 143, no. 5 (1982), 4–15

H. Leuchtmann, ed.: *Carl Orff: ein Gedenkbuch* (Tutzing, 1985)

ERIK LEVI

Orgeni, Aglaja [Görger St Jörgen, Anna Maria von] (*b* Rimászombat, Galicia [now Rimavská Sobota, Slovakia], 17 Dec 1841; *d* Vienna, 15 March 1926). Hungarian soprano. She studied with Pauline Viardot at Baden-Baden, and made her début in 1865 at the Hofoper, Berlin, as Amina in *La sonnambula*. In 1866 she sang at Covent Garden in *La traviata*, *Lucia di Lammermoor* and *Martha*. Leaving Berlin, she sang in Leipzig, Dresden, Hanover and other cities. In 1872 she appeared in Vienna and the following year in Munich, where she sang Leonora (*Il trovatore*), Amina, and Valentine (*Les Huguenots*). Her repertory also included Agathe (*Der Freischütz*) and Marguerite (*Faust*). She had style and great technical proficiency, especially in coloratura.

A. Ehrlich: *Berühmte Sängerinnen der Vergangenheit und Gegenwart* (Leipzig, 1895)

E. Brand: *Aglaja Orgeni* (Munich, 1931)

ELIZABETH FORBES

Orgiani, Teofilo (*b* Vicenza; *d* Vicenza, 1725). Italian composer. He was appointed *maestro di cappella* of Udine Cathedral on 14 July 1690; before this he was a minor ecclesiastic at Aquileia Cathedral. He was briefly called to the imperial court at Vienna in the summer of 1696, and in 1704 he was criticized for not fulfilling his duties at Udine. He left on 14 December 1711 to become *maestro di cappella* of Vicenza Cathedral. All his operas are lost.

Il vitio depresso e la virtù coronata (A. Aureli), Venice, S Angelo, 24 Nov 1686

Il Dioclete (A. Rossini), Venice, S Angelo, 18 Jan 1687

Le gare dell'Inganno e dell'Amore (P. E. Badi), Venice, S Moisè, 1689

Il tiranno deluso (G. B. Bottalino), Vicenza, Novissimo di Piazza, 1691 [rev. of Il Roderico, Pavia, 1684; only new arias by Orgiani]

Li amori e incanti d'Armida con Rinaldo, Treviso, aut. 1698 [presumably a new setting of A. Chiochiolo: L'Armida, Rovigo, 1694]; as Li avenimenti di Rinaldo con Armida, Udine, Mantica, 18 Dec 1698; probably the same as L'honor al cimento (G. Colatelli), Venice, S Fantin, 1703; as Armida regina di Damasco, Verona, 1711

La maga trionfante, Este, 1 Oct 1700 (pubd Venice) [possibly identical with Li amori e incanti d'Armida con Rinaldo]

La fedeltà nell'amore, Vicenza, 1707 [possibly identical with Li amori e incanti d'Armida con Rinaldo]

Le vicende d'Amore, Brescia, 1707 [mentioned by Guerrini, possibly identical with Li amori e incanti d'Armida con Rinaldo]

Euridice (D. Lalli), Padua, Obizzi, 1712

*

AllacciD

T. Wiel: *I teatri musicali veneziani del settecento* (Venice, 1897)

P. Guerrini: 'Per la storia della musica a Brescia', *Note d'archivio per la storia musicale*, xi (1934), 1–28

U. Manferrari: *Dizionario universale delle opere melodrammatiche* (Florence, 1954–5)

G. Mantese: *Storia musicale vicentina* (Vicenza, 1956)

THOMAS WALKER

Orgitano, Raffaele (*b* Naples, *c*1770; *d* ?Paris, 1812). Italian composer, son of Vincenzo Orgitano. After studying with Sala at the Conservatorio della Pietà dei Turchini in Naples, he held supernumerary positions at the Tesoro di S Gennaro (1790) and the royal chapel (1791). In 1800 he was in Palermo, and during the following years composed several highly successful comic operas for Venice, Rome and Naples. He then moved to Paris, but was unable to establish himself as an opera composer there. Two of his operas, *Non credere alle apparenze* (1801, Venice) and *Amore ed interesse* (1802, Naples), remained popular for over a decade and were staged by various theatres throughout Italy.

Non credere alle apparenze, ossia L'amore intraprendente (farsa, G. Foppa), Venice, S Moisè, 10 Oct 1801, *GB-Lam, I-Fc, Mr, Vnm*

Adelaide e Tebaldo (ob, G. Rossi), Venice, S Benedetto, 27 Dec 1801

Gli amanti al cimento (dg, M. Prunetti), Rome, Valle, carn. 1802, lib. *Bc*

Amore ed interesse, ossia L'infermo ad arte (farsa, G. Palomba), Naples, Fiorentini, aut. 1802, *A-Wn* (Act 1), *I-Fc, Nc, PAc*

Arsinoe (op teatrale), Naples, *Nc*

Miscellaneous opera excerpts: *A-Wn, I-Bc, Fc, Mc, Nc, Vnm*

*

FlorimoN; StiegerO

O. Tiby: *Il Real Teatro Carolino e l'ottocento musicale palermitano* (Florence, 1957), 115–16, 381

H.-B. Dietz: 'A Chronology of Maestri and Organisti at the Capella Reale in Naples, 1745–1800', *JAMS*, xxv (1972), 402

HANNS-BERTOLD DIETZ

Orgitano, Vincenzo (*b* c1735; *d* Naples, ?1807). Italian composer. He started his career as a composer of comic operas, writing the *opera buffa Il finto pastorello* on a libretto by Antonio Palomba for Naples (Nuovo, spring 1759) and the *farsa Le pazzie per amore* for Rome (Argentina, carnival 1761; 1 duet in *US-AUS*). By about 1779 he was engaged at the court of Ferdinand IV of Naples and Sicily as music master of the princesses Maria Teresa (the future empress of Austria) and Maria Louisa. From 1787 until his death he served as *primo maestro* of the royal chapel. He became a prolific composer of instrumental music, especially of accompanied piano sonatas.

*

BurneyH; FlorimoN; StiegerO

H.-B. Dietz: 'A Chronology of Maestri and Organisti at the Capella Reale in Naples, 1745–1800', *JAMS*, xxv (1972), 398, 400–401

HANNS-BERTOLD DIETZ

Orione [*Orione, o sia Diana vendicata* ('Orion, or Diana Reveng'd')]. *Opera seria* in three acts by JOHANN CHRISTIAN BACH to a libretto by GIOVANNI GUALBERTO BOTTARELLI; London, King's Theatre in the Haymarket, 19 February 1763.

The arrogant behaviour of Orion (mezzo-soprano castrato), son of the god Mercurio [Mercury] (tenor) and Retrea (soprano), Queen of Thebes, has offended the goddess Diana (soprano). Orion is in love with Candiope (soprano), daughter of Enopione [Oenopion] (tenor), King of Arcadia. The oracle of Diana (tenor) promises Orion glory and death on the battlefield but forbids his union with Candiope on earth. Orion bids farewell to Candiope and leaves to fulfil his destiny. He is victorious in battle but is then slain (offstage) by one of Diana's arrows, to the extreme anguish of his mother. However, Orion is loved by the gods and they place him in the firmament, to inspire among all mankind 'piety to the gods, and justice towards men'.

One contemporary commentator noted that Bach adapted his style in his first opera for the King's Theatre to accommodate the fondness of the London audience for choral music and for the music of Handel. Burney, however, commented on the connoisseurs' awareness of 'the emanations of genius throughout the whole performance; but were chiefly struck with the richness of the harmony, the ingenious texture of the parts, and,

above all, with the new and happy use [Bach] had made of wind instruments'; he added that the arias, apart from those for Anna Lucia de Amicis, who was making her début in serious opera, were 'indifferently sung'. Bach used not only clarinets (in just the overture and two arias) but also 'tallies' (*tailles*, alto oboes in F). The extended opening scene, at the Temple of Diana, is notable for its use of accompanied recitative and thematic links to articulate its structure and sense. *Orione* was revived, in a revised version, with the part of Diana eliminated and Orion dying on stage, at the King's Theatre in 1777.

ERNEST WARBURTON

Oristeo. *Drama per musica* in a prologue and three acts by FRANCESCO CAVALLI to a libretto by GIOVANNI FAUSTINI; Venice, Teatro S Apollinare, 1651.

Diomeda (soprano), Princess of Caonia, had been betrothed to Oristeo (baritone or bass), King of Epirus. While she travelled to meet her bridegroom, her army became involved in an accidental battle with Oristeo's forces. In the mêlée her father was killed, and to avenge his death Diomeda vowed a lifetime of celibacy. Since those unhappy events, Diomeda and Trasimede (tenor), Prince of Achaea, have met and fallen in love. Trasimede hopes to marry Diomeda but finds her distressed by indecision. They sing a plaintive recitative and duet, 'Campion di tua beltà … E quando mai l'havrò?' Meanwhile, Oristeo has come to Caonia and, disguised as a gardener, works in the royal gardens alongside the also disguised Corinta (soprano), Princess of Locri and the former betrothed of Trasimede. While the two pairs of lovers attempt to restore their tattered emotions, the army of Oristeo's son, Eurialo (soprano), lays siege to the palace and captures Trasimede as he attempts to flee. Corinta, begging for his release, discloses her identity. Oristeo also reveals his identity and is forgiven by Diomeda; Trasimede and Corinta find that they still love each other as the opera ends.

Although *Oristeo* is concise, it contains poignant and original arias. In Act 2 scene xiii Oristeo expresses pride in his son's valour and fear for the safety of Diomeda in a nervous recitative, followed by an impassioned aria, 'Colei, che rea tu credi'. Corinta's 'Udite amanti' (1.vi [=vii]) is one of the earliest examples of a da capo aria, identified with this instruction written in the composer's hand. The middle section, as is often the case in Cavalli's da capo arias, provides a shift in metre as well as mood. Major episodes of the pseudo-historical plot alternate with interludes in which such allegorical characters as the Three Graces, Beauty and Virtue comment on the loss of Love, here portrayed as the son of Poverty and Wealth. The customary Prologue, as presented by the two sides of Oristeo's personality, Genio cattivo [Evil Genius] and Genio buono [Good Genius], is extended throughout the opera as a thread linking the various scenes into a concise whole.

MARTHA NOVAK CLINKSCALE

Orlandi, Chiara (*b* Mantua; *fl* 1717–35). Italian soprano. She took part in 22 operas in Venice between 1717 and 1732. Her earliest appearances there were at the Teatro S Moisè, where she was known as 'la Manto[v]anina', but in 1721–5 she performed regularly at the Teatro S Angelo. In 1720, when she was in the service of the Duke of Massa and Carrara, she sang at Vicenza in Vivaldi's *Gli inganni per vendetta*. Her last known appearance was in 1735 in Brno, in a production of *Orlando furioso* with music mostly by Vivaldi.

Although she had sung the title role in Albinoni's *Laodice* (1724), she normally played secondary parts. According to Strohm, she was conservatively trained, with a limited compass, and typical of the Mantuan and Bolognese singers active in Venice at the time.

R. Strohm: 'Vivaldi's Career as an Opera Producer', *Antonio Vivaldi: teatro musicale, cultura e società: Venice 1981*, i, 11–63
COLIN TIMMS

Orlandi, Elisa (*b* Macerata, 1811; *d* Rovigo, 1834). Italian mezzo-soprano. She made her début in 1829 and the following year sang in Donizetti's *Olivo e Pasquale* at the Teatro della Cannobiana, Milan. She created Jane Seymour in *Anna Bolena* (1830) at the Teatro Carcano, Milan, and also sang in Donizetti's *Gianni di Calais* there. In 1833 she created Eleonora in *Il furioso all'isola di San Domingo* at the Teatro Valle, Rome. She collapsed and died during a performance of *Norma* at Rovigo, in which she was to sing Adalgisa.
ELIZABETH FORBES

Orlandi [Orland, Orlando], **Ferdinando** (*b* Parma, 7 Oct 1774; *d* Parma, 5 Jan 1848). Italian composer. His teachers included Paer and, at the Conservatorio della Pietà dei Turchini in Naples, Sala and Tritto. In 1800 he held a post in the ducal chapel at Parma and in the same year produced his first opera, *La pupilla scozzese*, at the Teatro Ducale. Between 1806 and 1822 he taught in Milan, then in Munich (1822–3) and Stuttgart (1823–8). He later lived in Parma as honorary *maestro di cappella* at the court and director of the school of singing of the Teatro Ducale. Orlandi composed 25 operas between 1800 and 1820, which show him as a facile melodist and imitator of the typical forms of 18th-century opera.

La pupilla scozzese, Parma, Ducale, carn. 1801
Il podestà di Chioggia (dg, 2, A. Anelli), Milan, Scala, 12 March 1801
Azemiro e Cimene (G. Rossi), Florence, Pergola, Oct 1801
L'avaro (dg, G. Bertati), Bologna, Marsigli-Rossi, 1801
Il deputato di Rocca, Venice, 1801
I furbi alle nozze (2), Rome, Valle, carn. 1802
L'amor stravagante (G. Greppi), Milan, Scala, May 1802
L'amore deluso, Florence, 1802
Il fiore, ossia Il matrimonio per svenimento (farsa giocosa, 2, G. M. Foppa), Venice, S Benedetto, 20 Sept 1803
La sposa contrastata (2, S. Zini), Rome, Valle, carn. 1804
Le lettere o Il sarto declamatore (commedia, Anelli), Milan, Carcano, April 1804
Nino (2, I. Zanella), Brescia, Grande, 21 July 1804
Nozze chimeriche (A. Locrence), Milan, Carcano, 27 Nov 1804
Corrado (2), Turin, Imperiale, 26 Dec 1805
La villanelle fortunata (2), Turin, Carignano, 1805
I raggiri amorosi (2), Milan, Scala, 30 May 1806
Pandolfo e Baloardo, ossia Le nozze per l'armi antiche [Baloardo] (farsa giocosa, 1, Foppa), Venice, S Moisè, carn. 1807
L'amico dell'uomo (farsa giocosa, 1, Foppa), Novara, Nuovo, carn. 1808
L'uomo benefico (commedia di sentimento, 2, Foppa), Turin, Carignano, sum. 1808
La donna [dama] soldato (ob, 2, C. Mazzolà), Milan, Scala, 20 Sept 1808, 1 aria (Munich, ?1810)
Il cicisbeo burlato (dg, Anelli), Milan, Scala, 2 May 1812
Amore intraprendente, ossia Non credere alle apparenze (farsa, Foppa), Parma, Nuovo, 8 Aug 1812
Il quid pro quo (melodramma comico, Rossi), Milan, S Radegonda, 1812
Rodrigo di Valenza (melodramma serio, F. Romani), Turin, Regio, Jan 1820
Fedra (melodramma serio, L. Romanelli), Padua, Nuovo, 10 June 1820

DEUMM; StiegerO
GIOVANNI CARLI BALLOLA

Orlandi, Santi (*d* Mantua, 1619). Italian composer. After holding an ecclesiastical post in Florence he became *maestro di cappella* in the household of Prince Ferdinando Gonzaga there. In 1608, when Ferdinando was created a cardinal, he followed him to Rome, continuing in his service after Ferdinando became Duke of Mantua (1612). Besides madrigals, he composed an opera, *Gli amori di Aci e Galatea*, which was performed at Mantua in 1615 and was repeated two years later with *intermedi* as part of the festivities celebrating Duke Ferdinando's marriage to Caterina de' Medici. The libretto was by Chiabrera; the music is lost. Severo Bonini (*Discorsi e regole sopra la musica*) placed Orlandi's madrigals on a level with Monteverdi's and recommended his works as models.

A. Bertolotti: *Musici alla corte dei Gonzaga in Mantova dal secolo XV al XVIII* (Milan, 1890)
L. Galleni Luisi: *Discorsi e regole sopra la musica di Severo Bonini* (Cremona, 1975), 119
S. Parisi: *Ducal Patronage of Music in Mantua, 1587–1627: an Archival Study* (diss., U. of Illinois, Urbana-Champaign, 1989)
IAIN FENLON

Orlandi Malaspina, Rita (*b* Bologna, 28 Dec 1937). Italian soprano. She studied in Milan, making her début there in 1963 at the Teatro Nuovo in *Giovanna d'Arco*. She became a Verdi specialist, in 1967 alone singing Lucrezia (*I due Foscari*) at Bologna, Elisabeth de Valois at Brescia, Leonora (*Il trovatore*) at Philadelphia, Vienna, La Scala and Montreal, Amelia (*Simon Boccanegra*) at Genoa, Amelia (*Ballo*) at Turin, Aida in Munich and Elvira (*Ernani*) in Venice. She made her Metropolitan début (1968) in *Simon Boccanegra* and her Covent Garden début (1969) in *Un ballo in maschera*. She also sang Odabella, Luisa Miller, Abigaille, Hélène (*Les vêpres siciliennes*) and Desdemona. She had a robust, exciting voice, but little dramatic involvement in her roles.
ELIZABETH FORBES

Orlandini, Giuseppe Maria (*b* Florence, 4 April 1676; *d* Florence, 24 Oct 1760). Italian composer. His previously accepted birth date, 19 March 1675, based on a baptism record in the archive of S Maria del Fiore, Florence, probably refers to a brother who died before the composer was born. Orlandini's work as an opera composer began in the first years of the 18th century under the patronage of Prince Ferdinando de' Medici. From 1711 he styled himself *maestro di cappella* to Gian Gastone (Prince and, from 1723, Grand Duke of Tuscany), but it is unlikely that he served continuously at court. In fact he soon moved to Bologna, where he married the singer Maria Maddalena Buonavia and, in 1719, became a member of the Accademia Filarmonica. His residence in Bologna is documented from 1717 to 1731. Performances of some of his operas in Venice brought him much acclaim. Two of these, *Antigona* (1718) and *Nerone* (1721), became known throughout Europe, as did *Arsace*, composed in 1715 (as *Amore e maestà*) for performance in Florence. Evidence of his celebrity at this time is the reference to him on the frontispiece of Benedetto Marcello's *Il teatro alla moda*. Orlandini returned to Florence in 1732, when he was appointed *maestro di cappella* at S Maria del Fiore and to the Medici court. The post was confirmed by the Lorraine successors to Gian Gastone (1737). These new duties did not interrupt the production of operas, which he regularly provided for the Florentine theatres La Pergola and Il Cocomero. In the 1740s Orlandini, who had previously composed some successful intermezzos, among them *Il marito giocatore e la moglie bacchettona*, also tried his hand at *commedia per musica*.

His importance as a composer in the context of 18th-century opera is confirmed by the widespread success of his operas and intermezzos and by the opinions of writers such as Quadrio, La Borde and Burney. To Burney his compositions seemed 'more dramatic and elegant than those of any master in the Italian school, anterior to Hasse and Vinci'. More recently Orlandini has been considered, with Vivaldi, Porta and others, one of the principal creators of the new style that dominated opera from the second decade of the century. In his arias there are *galant* features such as the predominance of the vocal line, often strengthened by *colla parte* instrumentation, simple accompaniments based on repeated figures, a slower and more regular harmonic rhythm, and frequent use of sequences.

See also Marito giocatore e la moglie bacchettona, Il *and* Nerone (i).

drammi per musica, in 3 acts, unless otherwise stated

Artaserse (P. Pariati ?and A. Zeno), Livorno, S Sebastiano, 1706; Naples, S Bartolomeo, 2 July 1708, addl music by F. Mancini

L'amor generoso (Zeno), Florence, Cocomero, aut. 1708, collab. R. Ceruti

L'odio e l'amore (M. Noris), Genoa, S Agostino, 1709

La fede tradita e vendicata (F. Silvani), Genoa, S Agostino, aut. 1709; Bologna, Marsigli-Rossi, 15 Aug 1712, addl music by F. Gasparini

Ataulfo re de' Goti, ovvero La forza della virtù (after D. David), Rome, Capranica, carn. 1712

Teuzzone (Zeno), Ferrara, Bonacossi, spr. 1712, with addl music

Madama Dulcinea e il cuoco del Marchese del Bosco (int, Marchese Trotti), Rome, Capranica, carn. 1712; as La preziosa ridicola, Naples, S Bartolomeo, carn. 1716; *A-Wn*

L'innocenza difesa (Silvani), ? Ferrara, Bonacossi, spr. 1712; as Carlo re d'Alemagna, Bologna, Formagliari, 28 Oct 1713; as L'innocenza giustificata, Fano, Fortuna, sum. 1731

L'amor tirannico (D. Lalli), Rome, Capranica, carn. 1713; as Il Farasmane (5), Bologna, Formagliari, 20 Oct 1720; Pesaro, Pubblico, carn. 1722, addl music by A. Tinazzoli

Lisetta e Delfo (int), Rome, Capranica, carn. 1713

Bacocco [Bajocco] e Serpilla (int, A. Salvi), Verona, May 1715; as Il marito giocatore e la moglie bacchettona, Venice, S Angelo, carn. 1719; as The Gamester, London, King's, 1 Jan 1737; as Serpilla e Bacocco, Venice, S Angelo, 1741; with addl music as Il giocatore, Paris, Opéra, 22 Aug 1752, Les ariettes du Joueur (Paris, *c*1752) [attrib. Doletti]; *A-Wn*, *B-Bc* (both R1984: IOB, lxviii), *D-MÜs*, *ROu*, *W* (2 copies, one attrib. Vinci); *F-Pc*, *I-Fc*, *S-Skma*

Amore e maestà (tragedia per musica, Salvi), Florence, Cocomero, 30 June 1715; as Arsace (rev. P. A. Rolli), London, King's, 1 Feb 1721, addl music by F. Amadei; as Der ehrsüchtige Arsaces, Hamburg, 18 May 1722, arr. J. Mattheson, *D-B*; rev., Florence, Pergola, carn. 1739, *A-Wn*, Act 2 *GB-Lbl*

La pastorella al soglio (G. C. Corradi), Mantua, Arciducale, carn. 1717

La virtù al cimento (Zeno), Mantua, Arciducale, carn. 1717; as La costanza trionfante, Recanati, fair and carn. 1720, addl music by Tinazzoli; rev. as Griselda, Venice, S Samuele, May 1720, arias *A-Wn*

La Merope (Zeno), Bologna, Formagliari, 24 Oct 1717

Lucio Papirio (Salvi), Naples, S Bartolomeo, Dec 1717, arias and buffo scenes by Feo, doubtful (by ? F. Gasparini; see Strohm); Pesaro, Pubblico, carn. 1721, addl music by Tinazzoli

Antigona (tragedia, 5, B. Pasqualigo), Venice, S Cassiano, carn. 1718; Pesaro, Pubblico, carn. 1723, addl music by Tinazzoli; as La fedeltà coronata, Bologna, Malvezzi, 2 June 1727, *GB-Lbl*; as Antigona vendicata, Breslau, 1 Oct 1728

Le amazoni vinte da Ercole (Salvi), Reggio Emilia, Pubblico, spr. 1718

Ifigenia in Tauride (tragedia, 5, Pasqualigo, after P. J. Martello), Venice, S Giovanni Grisostomo, carn. 1719, arias *D-ROu* and *SHs*

Il carceriero di se stesso (Salvi), Turin, Carignano, carn. 1720

Paride (5, F. Muazzo), Venice, S Giovanni Grisostomo, carn. 1720, arias *SHs*

Melinda e Tiburzio (int), Venice, S Angelo, carn. 1721; as La donna nobile, Venice, S Cassiano, carn. 1730

Nerone (tragedia per musica, A. Piovene), Venice, S Giovanni Grisostomo, carn. 1721, arias *Mbs*; as Nero, Hamburg, 17 Nov 1723, arr. Mattheson, *B*

Nino (I. Zanella), Rome, Capranica, 7 Jan 1722, arias *F-Pc*; as Semiramide, Turin, Carignano, 1722; as Nino, Pesaro, Pubblico, carn. 1723, addl music by Tinazzoli

Ormisda (Zeno), Bologna, Malvezzi, 16 May 1722; as Artenice, Turin, Regio, carn. 1723, addl music by A. Giai and others

L'artigiano gentiluomo [Larinda e Vanesio] (int, Salvi, after Molière: *Le bourgeois gentilhomme*), Florence, 1722; as Le bourgeois gentilhomme, Florence, Pergola, carn. 1725; London, King's, 1737

Alessandro Severo (Zeno), Milan, Regio Ducal, carn. 1723, *GB-Lbl*

L'Oronta (C. N. Stampa), Milan, Regio Ducal, carn. 1724

Berenice (Pasqualigo, after J. Racine), Venice, S Giovanni Grisostomo, carn. 1725, *B-Bc*, arias *I-Vnm*

Il malato immaginario [Erighetta e Don Chilone] (int, Salvi, after Molière: *Le malade imaginaire*), Florence, Pergola, carn. 1725

Un vecchio innamorato (int, D. Marchi), Florence, Pergola, carn. 1725

Monsieur di Porsugnacchi [Grilletta e Porsugnacco] (int, after Molière: *Monsieur de Pourceaugnac*), Milan, Regio Ducal, carn. 1727; as Pourceaugnac and Grilletta, London, King's, 1737

Berenice (A. M. Lucchini: *Farnace*), Milan, Regio Ducal, carn. 1728

Adelaide (Salvi), Venice, S Cassiano, carn. 1729, *GB-Lam*, arias *I-Vqs*

L'impresario dell'isole Canarie [Dorina e Nibbio] (int, Metastasio), ? Venice, S Cassiano, 1729

Massimiano (G. Boldoni, after Pariati ?and Zeno: *Constantino*), Venice, S Giovanni Grisostomo, carn. 1731, *B-Bc*

Grullo e Moschetta (int), Venice, S Angelo, carn. 1732; London, King's, 1737

Ifigenia in Aulide (Zeno), Florence, Pergola, carn. 1732

Il marito geloso [Giletta e Ombrone] (int), St Petersburg, 1734

Il Temistocle (P. Metastasio), Florence, Pergola, 3 Feb 1737

L'olimpiade (Metastasio), Florence, Pergola, sum. 1737

Le nozze di Perseo e d'Andromeda (azione drammatica, 2, Marchi), Florence, Pergola, 9 April 1738, *A-Wgm*, *Wn*

Balbo e Dalisa (int, Salvi), Rome, Capranica, carn. 1740, doubtful

La Fiammetta (commedia per musica), Florence, Cocomero, 29 Sept 1743

Lo scialacquatore (commedia per musica, Borghesi), Florence, Cocomero, 14 Sept 1744; as Lo scialacquatore alla fiera, Venice, S Cassiano, aut. 1745, with addl music

Probably arr. Orlandini: Arianna e Teseo (Pariati), Florence, Pergola, carn. 1739; Venceslao (Zeno), Florence, Pergola, 27 Dec 1741; Vologeso re de' Parti (after Zeno), Florence, Pergola, Jan 1742

Arias in *A-Wgm*, *Wn*; *B-Bc*, *Lc*; *D-B*, *Bds*, *Dlb*, *SWl*; *F-Pc*, *Pn*; *GB-Lbl*, *Lgc*, *Mp*, *T*; *I-Bc*, *BGi*, *Fc*, *Mc*, *Rc*; *US-BE*, *FAlewis*, *Wc*

*

BurneyH

F. Quadrio: *Della storia e della ragione d'ogni poesia* (Bologna and Milan, 1739–52)

G. B. Martini: 'Serie cronologica de' principi dell'Accademia de' Filarmonici di Bologna', *Diario bolognese* (1776)

J.-B. de La Borde: *Essai sur la musique ancienne et moderne*, iii (Paris, 1780)

O. G. Sonneck: 'Il giocatore', *MA*, iv (1912–13), 160–74

G. Lazarevich: *The Role of the Neapolitan Intermezzo in the Evolution of Eighteenth-Century Musical Style: Literary, Symphonic and Dramatic Aspects* (diss., Columbia U., 1970)

I. Mamczarz: *Les intermèdes comiques italiens au XVIIIe siècle en France et en Italie* (Paris, 1972)

R. Strohm: 'Italienische Opernarien des frühen Settecento (1720–1730)', *AnMc*, no.16 (1976) [whole issue]

G. Lazarevich: 'Eighteenth-Century Pasticcio: the Historian's Gordian Knot', *AnMc*, no.17 (1976), 121–45

R. L. Weaver and N. W. Weaver: *A Chronology of Music in the Florentine Theater 1590–1750* (Detroit, 1978)

C. E. Troy: *The Comic Intermezzo: a Study in the History of Eighteenth-Century Italian Opera* (Ann Arbor, 1979)

R. Strohm: 'Die Tragedia per Musica als Repertoirestück: zwei Hamburger Opern von Giuseppe Maria Orlandini', *HJbMw*, v (1981), 37–54

W. C. Holmes: 'An Impresario at the Teatro La Pergola in Florence: Letters of 1735–1736,' *Music and Civilization: Essays in Honor of Paul Henry Lang* (New York, 1984), 127–40

F. Piperno: 'Note sulla diffusione degli intermezzi di J. A. Hasse (1726–1741)', *AnMc*, no.25 (1987), 267–86

F. Giuntini: 'Giuseppe Maria Orlandini e la commedia per musica a Firenze agli inizi della dominazione lorenese', *Inaugural Conference for the Ricasoli Collection: Patrons, Politics, Music, and Art in Italy 1738–1859: Louisville 1989*

FRANCESCO GIUNTINI

Orlando. American city, in east-central Florida. Its first opera company, founded in 1958, was the Opera Gala, a subsidiary of the Florida SO. Since March 1979 the Orlando Opera Company has been an independent professional corporation. In 1984 it became a member of Opera America. The company performs four or five operas a year in the Bob Carr Performing Arts Auditorium (2600 seats). Its season runs from November to June. The 1990–91 season included *Les contes d'Hoffmann, Tosca, Hänsel und Gretel* and *The Mikado*. Normally, each opera is performed three times. In addition to its regular season, the company provides educational programmes and a lecture series for over 40 000 people each year. In July 1990 Robert Swedberg became the general director. The company went on tour to France in 1991 under the sponsorship of the Florida Department of State.

BRUCE A. WHISLER

Orlando (i) [*Orlando furioso*]. *Drama per musica* in three acts, RV728, by ANTONIO VIVALDI to a libretto by GRAZIO BRACCIOLI after LUDOVICO ARIOSTO; Venice, Teatro S Angelo, autumn 1727.

Vivaldi's only surviving complete setting of Braccioli's libretto *Orlando furioso* received its *fede* (i.e. permission from the censors) on 5 November 1727, and it bore the short title *Orlando*. This was not, however, Vivaldi's first contact with Braccioli's text. In autumn 1713 the libretto was set for the S Angelo by G. A. Ristori; Vivaldi was probably the impresario at that time and may well even have contributed some of the music (he had just made his operatic début in Vicenza). He certainly provided many new numbers when the work was revived the following autumn to replace his own *Orlando finto pazzo*, again to a text by Braccioli, which had proved less successful. The manuscript score of Acts 1 and 2 of this composite work survives in Turin. The next production of *Orlando furioso* with which Vivaldi was directly connected was at the same theatre in 1727. For this he reset much of the text, though a few sections of the 1714 version – notably the closing sequence of Act 2 – were reworked. As usual with a Vivaldi revival, many new aria texts were provided, in some cases to facilitate the re-use of arias from his earlier operas. Presumably the opera was successful, since Vivaldi borrowed ten arias for *L'Atenaide*, which was produced in Florence two years later.

The story of *Orlando* draws on several episodes from Ariosto's epic. The knight Orlando (contralto) is in pursuit of Angelica (soprano), with whom he has fallen hopelessly in love. She, however, is seeking her lover Medoro (contralto); in Act 2 they are married and, in celebration, carve their names on trees. When Orlando discovers this he is driven mad with jealousy, and his sanity is restored only with magical help from his cousin Astolfo (bass). Ruggiero (contralto) has been enchanted by the evil sorceress Alcina (contralto) but is eventually saved by his fiancée Bradamante (contralto), who disguises herself as a man with the help of a magic ring. At the end of the opera the furious Alcina is defeated and Orlando gives his blessing to Angelica and Medoro.

The libretto mixes magic, heroic and comic elements and provides opportunities for spectacular scenic effects. Vivaldi set an unusually high proportion of the text as accompanied recitative or arioso, partly because of the re-use of material from the 1714 version. Orlando's madness is portrayed by the rapid juxtaposition of unrelated ideas, notably in the extraordinary closing passage of Act 2. The style of the music is very varied; some arias reflect the latest fashions associated with the younger generation of Neapolitan composers, while others are more traditional. Although most arias are scored for strings and continuo, Ruggiero's fine Act 2 aria 'Sol da te mio dolce amore' includes a florid obbligato part for transverse flute accompanied by muted violins and a bass line for '1 Violone con Arco/Violette e Bassi/Pizzicatti/Senza Cembali'.

See also ANGELICA E MEDORO. ERIC CROSS

Orlando (ii). Opera in three acts by GEORGE FRIDERIC HANDEL to an anonymous libretto adapted from CARLO SIGISMONDO CAPECE's *L'Orlando* (1711, Rome), after LUDOVICO ARIOSTO's *Orlando furioso*; London, King's Theatre, 27 January 1733.

Orlando *a knight*	alto castrato
Angelica *Queen of Cathay, in love with Medoro*	soprano
Medoro *an African prince, in love with Angelica*	alto
Dorinda *a shepherdess*	soprano
Zoroastro *a magician*	bass
Isabella *a princess*	silent

Orlando was the only new opera of Handel's season of 1732–3. He wrote it during the first weeks of the season (which opened on 4 November with an adaptation of Leo's *Catone in Utica*) and completed the score on 20 November. The libretto is considerably changed from Capece's original, most notably in the introduction of the character of the magician Zoroastro, who becomes the presiding genius of the opera; the role was created for the distinguished bass Antonio Montagnana. There are only four other singing roles, originally taken by the alto castrato Senesino (Orlando), Anna Maria Strada del Pò (Angelica), the contralto Francesca Bertolli (Medoro) and Celeste Gismondi (Dorinda) – the last probably identical with the Neapolitan *buffa* soprano Celeste Resse. The princess Isabella, important in Capece's libretto, appears briefly in Act 1 of the opera as a silent role. *Orlando* is the first of the three Handel operas with a text deriving from Ariosto's epic poem (the others being *Ariodante* and *Alcina*) and, despite the extensive variations, remains closest to the spirit of the original. There are a number of fleeting references to other characters and incidents in the poem and its predecessor, Boiardo's *Orlando innamorato*, but as they mostly appear in Orlando's ravings it does not matter if they are not recognized. (*See also* ANGELICA E MEDORO.)

The opera achieved ten performances, six before a Lenten run of oratorios and four afterwards. Further performances were reported to have been deferred because of the indisposition of a singer. It seems likely that this was a hint of Handel's breach with Senesino, which came to a head in June 1733 with the defection of that singer and most of Handel's company to the newly formed 'Opera of the Nobility'. Sir John Clerk of

Penicuik (a wealthy Scottish landowner who was also a skilled amateur musician) saw the last performance of *Orlando* on 5 May and recorded the contrast between the excellence of the opera and the poor attendance, the latter no doubt depleted by hostile machinations against Handel:

I never in all my life heard a better piece of musick nor better perform'd – the famous Castrato, Senesino made the principal Actor the rest were all Italians who sung with very good grace and action, however, the Audience was very thin so that I believe they get not enough to pay the Instruments of the Orchestra ... One Signior Montagnania sung the bass with a noise like a Canon ... amongst the violins were 2 brothers of the name Castrucci who play'd with great dexterity.

Handel never revived the opera and it remained unheard until the production at Halle on 28 May 1922, in an arrangement by H. J. Moser. The first British revival was at the Unicorn Theatre, Abingdon, on 6 May 1959, in which year it was also given in Florence; it has had numerous revivals since, particularly in the 1980s, when it was heard in Britain, Germany and the Low Countries and in Venice, Paris, Chicago and San Francisco.

ACT 1   The time and place of the action are undefined, the scenes ranging from conventional pastoral landscapes to symbolic tableaux created by Zoroastro's magic. (In Ariosto Orlando is attached to the court of Charlemagne, implying a period around AD 800.) The opening scene is the countryside at night, with a view of a mountain on which Atlas is seen supporting the heavens. Zoroastro contemplates the constellations, obscure in meaning to ordinary mortals, but which tell him that Orlando will one day return to noble deeds. Orlando himself appears, torn between conflicting desires for love and glory. Zoroastro rebukes him for his devotion to love, and illustrates the dangers of that emotion by causing the distant mountain to change to the Palace of Love, where heroes of antiquity appear asleep at Cupid's feet. He urges Orlando to follow Mars, the god of war. Orlando, at first shamed by the vision, decides that glory can be obtained in pursuit of love.

The scene changes to a wood with shepherds' huts, Dorinda's domain. Her thoughts, troubled by love, are interrupted as Orlando rushes past with a princess (later identified as Isabella), whom he has rescued. Angelica appears: despite Orlando's attentions to her she has fallen for Medoro, whose wounds she healed while he was being looked after by Dorinda. Medoro overhears and enters with a declaration of his love for Angelica. Dorinda returns; it is clear that she loves Medoro. To avoid hurting her he pretends that Angelica is a relation of his; Dorinda knows he is lying but his words still enchant her. Zoroastro tells Angelica he knows of her love for Medoro, and warns her of Orlando's likely revenge. When Orlando appears, Angelica cannot tell him what has happened but pretends to be jealous and taunts him about the princess he has rescued. Zoroastro prevents Medoro's untimely approach by causing him to be concealed by a fountain as the scene is transformed into a garden. Angelica tells Orlando he must prove his faith by never seeing the princess again. Orlando agrees; he will fight the most terrible monsters to show his love. Medoro asks Angelica who she has been talking to; she tells him and persuades him not to fight such a rival. Their embrace is seen by Dorinda, who forces Angelica to explain that Medoro is her betrothed. Angelica thanks Dorinda for her kindness and gives her a piece of jewellery, but Dorinda would sooner have had a gift

from Medoro. He begs her to forgive him, but she says she has been hurt and remains inconsolable.

ACT 2   In a wood, Dorinda's melancholy reflections on the song of the nightingale are interrupted by Orlando, who learns of Angelica's love for Medoro. Dorinda shows him the jewel, saying it came from Medoro. Orlando recognizes it as a bracelet he once gave to Angelica. Believing himself betrayed, he threatens to kill himself and pursue Angelica into hell.

In a grove of laurels, near a grotto, Zoroastro rebukes Angelica and Medoro for arousing Orlando's anger; mortal minds wander in darkness when led by the blind god of love. Medoro carves his name and Angelica's on the laurel trees to declare their love, and Angelica resolves to return with him to Cathay. Orlando, entering, is enraged at the sight of the names on the trees and rushes into the grotto in pursuit of Angelica. She, however, appears from the opposite side and bids a sad farewell to the trees and the streams. Orlando emerges and pursues her, Medoro following. Zoroastro's magic now intervenes: Angelica is engulfed by a large cloud which bears her away in the company of four genii. Orlando loses his reason. He believes that shades from the underworld have taken Angelica from him; he will follow them, becoming a shade himself, and imagines himself crossing the Styx in Charon's boat and entering Pluto's kingdom. There he sees a Fury in the form of Medoro, who runs into the arms of Proserpina; her weeping rouses his pity, but finally his heart is hardened. As he runs back into the grotto it bursts open to reveal Zoroastro on his chariot. The magician gathers Orlando up in his arms and flies off with him.

ACT 3   Medoro explains to Dorinda that Angelica has sent him to her for refuge; she is glad he is no longer deceiving her. Orlando appears and declares his love for Dorinda. She is at first flattered, but as Orlando becomes more ardent and addresses her as Venus it becomes obvious he is still raving; and in a fit of delusion he squares up for unarmed combat with an imagined enemy and leaves. Dorinda, telling Angelica of Orlando's madness, delivers her thoughts on love as a wind that sets the brain spinning, bringing as much pain as joy. Zoroastro appears and orders his genii to change the scene to a dark cavern; he promises to restore Orlando's former glory. Dorinda tells Angelica that Orlando has destroyed her house and buried Medoro in the ruins. Orlando appears, addresses Angelica as the sorceress Falerina and threatens to kill her; grief-stricken at the news of Medoro's death, she defies him. As Orlando throws her into the cavern, it changes into a beautiful temple of Mars. Orlando claims he has rid the world of its monsters; sleep overcomes him. Zoroastro declares that the time has come to restore Orlando's senses. He pours liquid over the face of Orlando, who awakens, his senses restored. Dorinda tells him he has murdered Medoro in his frenzy. Full of remorse, he decides to kill himself, but Angelica begs him to live on. Medoro was saved by Zoroastro, who now implores Orlando to accept the lovers' betrothal. A statue of Mars, with fire burning on an altar, rises as Orlando proclaims victory over himself. He wishes joy to Angelica and Medoro, who promise to be true to each other. Dorinda, inviting them to her cottage, says she will forget her sorrows. All join in praise of love and glory.

*   *   *

Though *Orlando* shares characteristics with both earlier and later Handel operas involving supernatural effects, it is unique in its mix of characters and in its flouting of Baroque operatic conventions to depict the deranged state of the hero's mind. Angelica and Medoro are on the whole conventional lovers, their best music being in their slower numbers (notably Medoro's exquisite 'Verdi allori') and in the moving trio at the close of Act 1 when they vainly try to console the distraught Dorinda. The shepherdess herself never becomes the comic role that her status might have suggested, despite the quirky rhythms of her arias. The gentle pathos of her unrequited love is always present, and there is a slightly manic ring to her solo in the final ensemble as she invites the company to the home she previously declared to be destroyed. Zoroastro, a striking figure, has three magnificent arias, of which the last ('Sorge infausta una procella') is well known (and long held a place in 19th-century versions of *Israel in Egypt* as 'Wave on wave congeal'd with wonder'). Orlando is a highly original creation, and a role which makes few concessions to the expectations of an operatic primo uomo. (Its unusual features – notably the limited opportunities for improvised display – may have contributed to Senesino's break with the composer.) There are only three regular da capo arias, two in Act 1 and the impassioned 'Cielo! se tu il consenti' in Act 2. Irregular forms then predominate, including the astonishing Mad Scene ('Ah! stigie larve') at the close of Act 2, in which a mixture of accompanied recitative and measured passages in various tempos depict Orlando's imaginary journey to the underworld, taking in a lament over a chromatic ground bass and ending with a haunting rondo in gavotte rhythm. In this scene occur the notorious bars of 5/8 time, but they appeal only briefly between sections of unmeasured recitative and their impact on the ear is slight. Orlando's final aria of slumber ('Già l'ebro mio ciglio'), through-composed and accompanied by the veiled tones of two solo *violette marine* over a pizzicato bass, is both moving and mysterious. *Orlando* makes a special appeal to modern sensibility with its concentration on the psychological states of characters in a fantasy world lending itself to reinterpretation; it is also a splendid exemplar of what the Baroque theatre could achieve in allying stage-craft to drama expressed through music. ANTHONY HICKS

Orlando, Ferdinando. *See* ORLANDI, FERDINANDO.

Orlando paladino ('The Paladin Orlando'). *Dramma eroicomico* in three acts by JOSEPH HAYDN to a libretto by NUNZIATO PORTA after LUDOVICO ARIOSTO's *Orlando furioso*; Eszterháza, 6 December 1782.

Haydn's opera, combining comic, tragic, magic and pastoral elements, joins a long history of works that recount the story of the knight-errant in Ariosto's *Orlando furioso*. Porta, resident poet at Eszterháza after July 1781, adapted C. F. Badini's libretto (set by Guglielmi as *Le pazzie d'Orlando*, 1771) and his own earlier librettos for Prague (1775) and Vienna (1777); he replaced all the aria texts for the Leporello-like squire Pasquale, revised many of Angelica's lines and lengthened the finale texts. That madness itself is an ambiguous state, capable of evoking laughter and pity, derision and sympathy, is not lost on either the poet or the composer, who in the spirit of Ariosto exaggerate the emotional responses not only of the deluded knight but

Angelica *Queen of Cathay*	soprano
Rodomonte *King of Barbaria*	bass
Orlando *Paladin of France*	tenor
Medoro *in love with Angelica*	tenor
Licone *a shepherd*	tenor
Eurilla *a shepherdess*	soprano
Pasquale *Orlando's squire*	baritone
Alcina *a sorceress*	soprano
Caronte [Charon] *ferryman of the underworld*	bass

Shepherds, shepherdesses, spectres, savages and Saracens

Setting An island in the Indian Ocean

also of his squire and his proud and boastful rival, Rodomonte.

In a letter to Artaria, in July 1782, Haydn reports that he is writing a new Italian opera for the impending visit of the Russian Grand Duke and Duchess to Eszterháza; but the visit never materialized, and *Orlando paladino* was first performed in honour of Prince Nikolaus's name-day. Seven of the cast members had performed in the revival of *La fedeltà premiata* (1782): Matilde Bologna (Angelica), Costanza Valdesturla (Alcina), Maria Antonia Specioli (Eurilla) and her husband Antonio Specioli (Orlando), Vincenzo Moratti (Pasquale), Domenico Negri (Rodomonte) and Leopold Dichtler, who displayed his exceptional vocal range in two secondary roles (Licone and Charon). Prospero Braghetti (Medoro) was new to the troupe. By the end of the century *Orlando paladino* had been staged throughout central Europe, including Pressburg (1786), Prague (1791), Vienna (1791–2), Budapest (1792), Dresden (1792), Mannheim (1792, for which Haydn corrected the score of Act 1), Frankfurt (1793), Cologne (1793), Berlin (1798), Leipzig (1800) and Munich (1800). In 1982 it was performed at the Theater an der Wien in Vienna as part of the celebrations in honour of the 250th anniversary of the composer's birth, and the following year at the Stadttheater, Basle.

ACT 1.i *A snow-covered, mountainous landscape* Rodomonte, in search of Orlando, threatens to harm Eurilla and Licone if they do not help him. The shepherd and shepherdess tell the impatient knight that Angelica and Medoro have sought refuge from Orlando's wrath in a nearby castle. Rodomonte, who is infatuated with Angelica, sets off to find her.

1.ii *The foot of a tower* Angelica, alone and anxious, laments her fate. She summons Alcina, who promises to protect her. The sorceress describes the extent of her powers in a commanding C major aria, 'Ad un guardo, a un cenno solo'. Medoro, arriving with the news that Orlando and his squire are near, expresses his indecision about whether or not to escape, in a Metastasian-style text ('Parto, ma ...').

1.iii *A grove* Unlucky in love and without food, Pasquale meets Rodomonte, who challenges him to fight. But when Eurilla reports that Orlando is searching for Rodomonte, the braggart knight quickly runs away. In a patter-style catalogue aria riddled with innuendo, 'Ho viaggiato in Francia, in Spagna', Pasquale begs Eurilla for sustenance, periodically interrupting news of his extensive forays with descriptions of his hunger for food and love.

'Orlando paladino'
(Joseph Haydn): stage
design by Pietro Travaglia
for Act 1 scene i (a snow-
covered, mountainous
landscape) of the original
production at Eszterháza,
6 December 1782

1.iv *A delightful garden with a fountain*
Medoro expresses his desire to leave Angelica so as
not to endanger her further. Angelica's impassioned
plea that her lover should not leave ('Non partir, mia
bella face') is a demanding two-tempo aria with
pronounced *seria* overtones. While Medoro dithers,
Orlando arrives. The hero sings a lengthy accompanied
recitative and aria, during which he smashes the
fountain and surrounding trees and shouts the names of
the lovers.

1.v *A grove* Rodomonte and Orlando narrowly miss meeting one another. Orlando quizzes Eurilla about Angelica and Medoro's whereabouts,
threatening to kill his rival.

1.vi *A garden as before* In an *ombra* scene,
replete with 'premonition' flat-6th chords, Angelica en-
visions the spectre of her beloved. The dramatic tempo
of the finale begins to escalate as the characters, all
afraid except for the vainglorious Rodomonte, assemble
and contemplate the deranged hero's impending arrival.
Brandishing a sword, Orlando swaggers in; his disjointed sputtering and heightened emotional state are
expressed through accompanied recitative, a musical
feature usually absent from finales. Alcina imprisons
Orlando in an iron cage, a symbol of insanity in the 18th
century.

ACT 2.i *A grove* Eurilla breaks up a fight between
Orlando and Rodomonte with the news that Angelica
and Medoro are fleeing.

2.ii *A vast plain by the sea* Medoro, having
escaped to this desolate place, confides in Eurilla. In
another Metastasian-style text, 'Dille che un infelice',
the wretch utters his parting words for the shepherdess
to convey to Angelica. He then hides in a grotto.
Pasquale's shouts of victory are tempered by Eurilla,
who coyly invites the squire to follow her to a castle, in a
flirtatious duet, 'Quel tuo visetto amabile'.

Angelica expresses her suffering in a two-tempo
rondò ('Aure chete') with demanding coloratura
passages enhanced by solo oboe. Alcina, speaking

directly to the audience, promises that Angelica will find
her beloved and not hurl herself into the sea. Having
been reunited, the lovers sing a tender duet ('Qual contento'), one of Haydn's last contributions to the score.
Orlando blocks the lovers' escape, but Alcina's magic
curtails his desire to follow them. A highly effective
accompanied recitative, preceding the aria 'Cosa vedo!
cosa sento!', portrays the hero's mental deterioration.

2.iii *A room in the castle* Pasquale brags to
Eurilla about his ability to charm women with music in
the virtuoso aria 'Ecco spiano', in which he
demonstrates many difficult vocal techniques, including
a castrato imitation in the upper register. Alcina invites
Rodomonte to join her and the others in her cavern.

2.iv *Alcina's enchanted grotto* Orlando comes
in search of Alcina, a nervous Pasquale at his side. During a long passage of recitative within the finale,
Orlando continues to insult the sorceress, who turns
him into stone. In broken, incoherent phrases Pasquale
attempts to tell the others, who are venturing deeper
into the cave, about Orlando's fate. Alcina restores
Orlando to life, only to have him entombed in her
grotto.

ACT 3.i *A view of the river Lethe with the Elysian
Fields in the distance* Alcina commands Charon to
wash away Orlando's madness. Orlando awakens and
conveys his confused thoughts in his third and final aria
('Miei pensieri, dove siete?').

3.ii *A room in the castle* Eurilla and Pasquale
are discussing their marriage when Orlando, restored to
health, returns to solicit his squire's aid.

3.iii *A forest* Medoro rescues Angelica from
the wild savages, but is seriously wounded in the fray.
Orlando and Rodomonte duel.

3.iv *A courtyard* Believing that Medoro has
perished, a delirious Angelica seeks repose in death. But
Alcina comes to her rescue with news that Medoro's
wounds are healed, and they are reunited in front of an
acquiescent, though somewhat bewildered, Orlando. All
join in a closing vaudeville chorus (Haydn later used its

melodic structure for a chorus and duet in the second act of *L'anima del filosofo, ossia Orfeo ed Euridice*, 1791).

*   *   *

The character Orlando represents a mixture of comic and serious elements as befits the opera's designation. Both poet and composer challenge traditional textual and musical forms (especially in the finales) to portray the hero's journey into madness. Pasquale, one of Haydn's more fully developed *buffo* characters, along with Rodomonte and Eurilla provide the necessary comic relief, although their repetitive and predictable actions occasionally become redundant. Characterization of the *seria* roles is less successful, that of the vacillating and emasculated Medoro being the weakest of all. The widespread popularity of the Orlando story contributed to the opera's success, and helps to explain its broad circulation throughout German-speaking lands during the composer's lifetime. Pasquale and Eurilla's duet in Act 2 scene ii was inserted into the revival of Martín y Soler's *Il burbero di buon core* (first performed in Vienna in 1786), at the King's Theatre, London (1794), with Anna Morichelli and Giovanni Morelli singing a new text by Da Ponte; in 1795 Haydn's original duet was performed at his benefit concert in London.

See also ANGELICA E MEDORO.   CARYL CLARK

Orleanskaya deva. Opera by P. I. Tchaikovsky; *see* MAID OF ORLÉANS, THE.

Ormeville, Carlo d'. *See* D'ORMEVILLE, CARLO.

Ormindo. *Favola regia per musica* in three acts by FRANCESCO CAVALLI to a libretto by GIOVANNI FAUSTINI; Venice, Teatro S Cassiano, 1644.

Ormindo, the third collaboration between Cavalli and Faustini, follows the adventures of two pairs of lovers through deceit, disguise and feigned death to the requisite happy ending. Prince Ormindo (tenor) has fallen in love with Erisbe (soprano), who is married to the elderly Hariadeno (bass), King of Mauritania, Morocco and Fessa, and Ormindo's long-lost father; Amida (alto), Prince of Trasimede, who has travelled to Hariadeno's kingdom with his page, Nerillo (soprano), has likewise fallen in love with Erisbe, forgetting his former beloved, Princess Sicle (soprano), whom he has left behind in Susio. Sicle, disguised as an Egyptian and accompanied by her nurse Erice (tenor) and lady-in-waiting Melide (soprano), arrives to reclaim her beloved. She manages to convince Erisbe that Amida already has a beloved, and, by means of a feigned seance, inspires Amida with intense guilt, causing him to love her once again.

Now that Erisbe has committed herself to Ormindo alone, the two plan to flee Hariadeno's kingdom by boat but are prevented from doing so by a storm, which is caused by Fortune (mezzo-soprano) and the winds under orders from Destiny (tenor). They are captured, and the jealous Hariadeno orders his captain, Osman (tenor), to poison them. Their death scene, in prison, comprises a lengthy, powerful dialogue aria on a descending tetrachord ostinato bass, which is the musical peak of the score – untypically, Cavalli used it again, for another prison scene, in *Erismena* (1655). As the lovers prepare to die, Hariadeno relents, and regrets the murder, though it is apparently too late. Fortunately, however, urged on by Mirinda (soprano),

Erisbe's confidante, Osman had substituted a sleeping draught for the poison and the lovers are saved. Learning that Ormindo is his long-lost son, Hariadeno fulfils the role of magnanimous king and father by renouncing his claims on his youthful bride.

Ormindo is one of Cavalli's most attractive operas. In addition to the prison scene, a number of musical moments stand out, for instance the tripartite duet between Erisbe and Mirinda that opens Act 2 ('Aure, trecce'). Cavalli uses lyricism as a means of characterization. Thus the initially fickle Erisbe expresses herself frequently in arias, while Sicle, a more passionate character, sings primarily in recitative interrupted by arioso refrains. All the comic characters have extended solo scenes that comprise multiple sections of recitative and aria, most of them involving refrains of some kind. Erice's first scene (1.vi), for example, begins with nine lines of recitative leading to an aria of three strophes ('Mai volsi ch'il mio core'), each terminating in a comic punch-line. Nerillo's solo scene (2.v) is even more complex. It opens and closes with a three-line refrain ('Che città, che città') which is set lyrically, in a jaunty duple metre, and recurs within the scene as well; and the refrain encloses a triple-metre, three-strophe aria ('Mille perigli, e mille') with its own recurrent refrain.

Somewhat surprisingly, given the quality of its text and music, *Ormindo* does not seem to have been revived outside Venice during the 17th century. But it was the first of Cavalli's operas to enjoy popularity in the 20th century, thanks to the realization by Raymond Leppard.

ELLEN ROSAND

Ornamentation. The present article is concerned with the improvised embellishments added by singers (as opposed to notated ornaments indicated by the composer, or instrumental improvisation in opera). It is scarcely surprising that evidence about improvisation should be sparse and often imprecise. Writers were often more concerned to criticize what they considered excessive or tasteless embellishment than to give positive advice as to what was appropriate. For much of the repertory conclusions have to be based on inference and hypothesis, one source of which is the tendency of what was once improvised embellishment to graduate into notated melodic decoration. The paucity of documentary evidence does not necessarily imply that singers of certain repertories eschewed ornamentation. The (relatively) ephemeral nature of opera combined with the professional status of the singers meant that precision of notation was not a priority. As in all aspects of performing practice, the evidence that does survive must be interpreted carefully: with what body of music was the writer concerned? what were the circumstances surrounding the genesis of a document? for which singer were particular embellishments intended? Even if answers are not immediately forthcoming, the questions themselves at least emphasize the often provisional nature of present knowledge.

For the use of appoggiaturas, *see* APPOGGIATURA; for the insertion of cadenzas and lead-ins, and the elaboration of fermatas, *see* CADENZA.

1. Up to 1750. 2. 1750–1825. 3. Since 1825.

1. UP TO 1750. From its earliest years, opera was associated with the art of embellishment. One of the seeds from which opera grew was the series of discussions and experiments conducted by singers and composers in the Camerata in late 16th-century

Florence. In his two printed volumes of monodies, *Le nuove musiche* (Florence, 1601/2) and *Nuove musiche e nuova maniera di scriverle* (Florence, 1614), Giulio Caccini left not only examples of his own ornamentation but also his views on the subject. Indeed, one reason he gave for publishing the 1602 collection was that his compositions had been decorated to excess:

I see ill-used those single and double vocal roulades – rather, those redoubled and intertwined with each other – developed by me to avoid that old style of *passaggi* formerly in common use (one more suited to wind and stringed instruments than to the voice); and I see vocal crescendos-and-decrescendos, *esclamazioni*, tremolos and trills, and other such embellishments of good singing style used indiscriminately.

Caccini wished to demonstrate how, through greater sensitivity to the text, a composer could mirror the poetic structure and at the same time intensify the expression of the words. The idea of embellishment was not in itself new: 16th-century theorists had been guiding singers in the application of diminutions for several decades. Caccini claimed that the novelty of his compositions lay in their observance of the neo-Platonic aesthetic ideals of the Camerata, with their emphasis on the primacy of the text. His claim is sometimes borne out by the music itself, as in the opening phrases of 'Queste lagrim'amare' (ex.1), in which the light

Ex.1 Caccini: *Le nuove musiche* (1602), 'Queste lagrim'amare', bars 1–9

['These bitter tears, this anguished weeping,']

embellishments on 'amare' (bitter) and 'pianto' (weeping) make effective use of dissonance (as well as Caccini's favoured dotted rhythms) to heighten the expression of the words. (In their unembellished forms, bars 4 and 8 would consist of semibreves on *f'* and *g'* respectively.) Although Caccini deprecated the introduction of *passaggi* merely 'as a kind of tickling of the ears', he employed them himself as a means of underlining a stressed syllable (especially the penultimate one in a line of verse); and he admitted that he occasionally introduced short *passaggi* 'as a bit of decoration'.

A link with Caccini's operas is provided by the extracts from *Il rapimento di Cefalo* included in *Le nuove musiche*, and Caccini's headings confirm that melodic decoration featured in the performance of the opera, although not always in the printed form: 'Muove si dolce' was sung 'with the *passaggi* as given, by Melchior Palontrotti [sic]'; 'Caduca fiamma' was sung 'with different *passaggi*, according to his own style, by

Jacopo Peri'; and 'Qual trascorrendo' was sung 'with some of the *passaggi* as given and some according to his own taste, by the famous Francesco Rasi'.

Not only the title but also the preface of Caccini's 1614 collection draws attention to the one undeniably novel feature of both publications: the removal of responsibility for ornamentation from the performer and its assumption by the composer. Caccini states in the preface that the songs are ornamented precisely as he himself sang them; he also clarifies his concept of *sprezzatura*, the 'noble negligence of song' that finds expression in the freedom with which he treats dissonance.

In the preface to *Euridice* (Florence, 1600), Peri praises the embellishments introduced in his music by Vittoria Archilei: she has 'always made my compositions worthy of her singing, adorning them not only with those ornaments and those long turns of the voice, simple and double … but also with those pretty and graceful [things] which cannot be written, and if written, cannot be learned from writings'. The ambivalent attitude to diminutions in the early 17th century is summed up by Della Valle's comment on Archilei, who 'ornamented the written monody with long flourishes and turns which disfigured it but were very popular'.

The printed score (Venice, 1609) of Monteverdi's *Orfeo*, first performed on 24 February 1607 at Mantua, contains both a plain and an embellished version of the aria 'Possente spirto', sung by Orpheus to Charon in his attempt to gain entry to the underworld. The aria, both the musical centrepiece of the opera and its dramatic turning-point, epitomizes the theme of the opera: the divine power of music. It is not known what was sung at the first performance, but it was surely not the plain version, which would cut a sorry figure in the dramatic context and can only have been intended for the convenience of a singer who wished to invent his own embellishments. Monteverdi's printed ornamentation demands exceptional virtuosity, but the figuration (ex.2) is always organic, never mechanical; most telling of all, the absence of ornate decoration in the last two stanzas demonstrates the potency of pure, lyrical melody.

For much of the 17th century the extant evidence on styles of ornamentation consists merely of isolated clues and sheds little light on the practice of such composers as Cavalli, Cesti or Legrenzi. In a letter of 18 December 1627 to Alessandro Striggio, Monteverdi made it plain that one of his criteria in judging singers was their ability to perform ornaments and *trilli*. A comparison of the Venice and Naples scores of *L'incoronazione di Poppea* (1643) reveals instances where one source (usually the Venice score) has an ornamented version of the other, but the embellishments are rarely extended and in any case the question of priority remains open. G. B. Doni, in his *Trattato della musica scenica* (1633–5), explicitly states that the most suitable place for embellishment is the theatre, where 'one tries, with costumes and with perfection of gesture and of speech and consequently also in the music, to show how far human artifice can go'. He has advice on the nature and execution of the ornamentation, and on maintaining a proper sense of proportion: 'composers and singers should remember, nevertheless, that those [passages], if they are so long that they interrupt the syllable too much and impede the understanding of the words, can never be pleasing to men of good sense and judgment'. A

Ex.2 Monteverdi: *L'Orfeo* (1607), 'Possente spirto', bars 70–77

['(for wherever) such beauty (is found), is paradise itself.']

strophic aria from an early opera of Alessandro Scarlatti, *Statira* (1690), contains discreet embellishments in its setting of the second stanza ('Deh, sospendi il ferro acuto': no.79 in the Holmes edition). The sparseness of the evidence does not indicate that the art was moribund; the luxuriant manifestation in the 18th-century da capo aria could hardly have grown from nothing.

Italian musical culture dominated the rest of Europe throughout the 17th century, and might have been expected to have sown the seeds for national schools of operatic ornamentation; but this seems not to have happened. In Germany, Italian diminution practices were propagated by such theorists as Praetorius, Herbst, Bernhard and Crüger, but there is no evidence that they were adopted later in the century during the modest flowering of German opera, in which vocal display seems to have held little interest. The most gifted German operatic composer, Keiser, made less conspicuous use of the da capo aria than did his Italian contemporaries. In England, Robert Dowland's anthology *A Musicall Banquet* (1610) included four Italian songs, two of them by Caccini. About 50 English songs of the period exist in florid versions (see Duckles 1957); a few of these set verses from contemporary plays. John Playford published an anonymous (and inaccurate) translation of the preface to Caccini's *Le nuove musiche* in *An Introduction to the Skill of Musick* (London, 1655). Whether improvised embellishment featured in the two true English operas, Blow's *Venus and Adonis* and Purcell's *Dido and Aeneas*, is not known; it has been noted that in his vocal writing Purcell usually incorporated melodic decoration with more completeness than in his instrumental writing.

The French became acquainted with the singing not only of Caccini (he visited Paris in 1604–5) but also of Leonora Baroni, who was invited to Paris by Mazarin (an Italian by birth) in 1644, and they heard Italian operas performed by visiting Italian musicians between 1645 and 1662. French opera was late in establishing a firm foothold, and when it did its progenitor, Lully, did

not tolerate additional embellishment of his carefully notated melody. Experiments with more elaborate decoration were conducted in the context of the *air de cour*; examples are cited by Mersenne (*Harmonie universelle*) and Millet (*L'art de bien chanter*). In chapter 13 of his important treatise *Remarques curieuses sur l'art de bien chanter* (1668) Bacilly strenuously rebuts the prevalent criticisms of *passages* and *diminutions*. He gives no music examples, but his references too are to *airs de cour*. Later treatises likewise make no mention of opera; indeed Montéclair (*Principes de musique*, 1736) recalled: 'the incomparable Lully … preferred melody, beautiful modulation, pleasing harmony, truthfulness of expression, naturalness and finally noble simplicity to the ridiculousness of the *doubles* and the heteroclite melodies whose supposed merit consists only in deviations, in twisted modulations, in the harshness of the chords, in noise and confusion'. Quantz (1752) confirmed the self-sufficiency of French musical notation in general and the lack of added decoration in their vocal performance in particular.

The da capo aria represents the apogee of vocal embellishment in the Baroque era. An important source of information is Tosi's treatise *Opinioni de' cantori antichi e moderni, o sieno Osservazioni sopra il canto figurato* (Bologna, 1723), which acquired an influential status through its partial translation into Dutch (1731) and its complete translations into English (1742) and German (1757). Unfortunately the treatise contains no music examples (Galliard added a few in the English translation), no references to compositions, and only a few references to singers (Faustina Bordoni and Francesca Cuzzoni are alluded to but not named) and composers (Agostini, Stradella, Pistocchi). Writing as a representative of an older generation (born in about 1653), Tosi was deeply critical of many aspects of 'modern' music, including the extravagant embellishments with which singers often disfigured the melody:

The Presumption of some Singers is not to be borne with, who expect that an whole *Orchestre* should stop in the midst of a well-

Ex.3 Vignati: *Ambleto* (1719), 'Sciolta dal lido', bars 40–51

['Set adrift from the shore by a treacherous wind, the boat heads towards the rock']

regulated Movement, to wait for their ill-grounded Caprices, learned by Heart, carried from one Theatre to another, and perhaps stolen from some applauded female Singer, who had better Luck than Skill, and whose errors were excused in regard to her Sex.

Tosi sanctions ornamentation in all three parts of the da capo aria, but to varying extents:

In the first they [the airs] require nothing but the simplest Ornaments …; in the second they expect, that to this Purity some artful Graces be added, by which the Judicious may hear, that the Ability of the Singer is greater; and, in repeating the *Air*, he that does not vary it for the better, is no great Master.

Even allowing for his conservative taste and the often vitriolic tone of his writing, Tosi's advice on ornamentation is sensible: care should be taken to avoid errors with the accompanying instruments; private practice should precede public performance; at a first rehearsal only the most natural ornaments should be introduced, the more ornate ones to follow later; ornamentation should not destroy the pulse of the music; and it should not be mechanically applied but should reflect the sense of the words and the nature of the particular aria.

Several musical sources provide actual examples of ornamentation. Some of these are instrumental arrangements, and do not necessarily reflect vocal practice. In particular the harpsichord arrangements by William Babell of arias from Handel's operas *Rinaldo*, *Il pastor fido* and *Teseo* are not idiomatic for the voice. A recently discovered early source of the same composer's *Amadigi* (Dean 1991) contains instrumental arrangements of arias; the trills and some of the *passaggi* are more instrumental than vocal in conception, but other aspects of the ornamentation may reflect contemporary vocal practice. There is also an arrangement for

harpsichord of the aria 'Sventurato' from *Floridante*, ornamented by the composer himself (Best 1969). Further keyboard arrangements with ornamentation survive in manuscript copies (Dean and Knapp 1987). More valuable are those sources in which ornamentation is applied to the original vocal versions of arias. Two of these have embellishments attributed to Faustina Bordoni, wife of Hasse and one of Handel's *prime donne* in London. 'Sciolta dal lido' from Vignati's opera *Ambleto* (1719, Milan; see Buelow 1977 and Brown 1984) demonstrates Bordoni's tasteful artistry (ex.3). Similar qualities are apparent in the later example, 'Digli ch'io son fedele', sung by the eponymous heroine in Hasse's *Cleofide* (1731, Dresden; see Wolff 1972). In contrast, the embellishments of Frederick the Great for the same aria (also in Wolff) seem extravagant and at odds with Tosi's injunction that singers should be 'a little more Friends to the *Pathetick* and the *Expressive*, and a little less to the *Divisions*'. Two of the arias in a presentation volume (*A-Wn*, 19111) containing music sung by Farinelli (Carlo Broschi) incorporate his 'molti cambiamenti ne' passaggi': 'Quell'usignolo' from Giacomelli's *Merope* (1734, Venice; see Donington 1982 and Brown 1984) and 'Son qual nave', which Farinelli performed in Giai's *Mitridate* (1730, Venice), and Hasse's *Demetrio* (1734, Venice) and *Artaserse* (1734, London; see Schmitz 1955 and Freeman 1974).

Two arias from Handel's *Amadigi* (1715) exist in decorated forms. The light embellishments added to 'S'estinto è l'idol mio' in one source (in the Malmesbury collection), though not in the composer's hand and probably intended for an amateur singer, successfully intensify Oriana's resigned grief (ex.4). Handel's auto-

Ex.4 Handel: *Amadigi* (1715), 'S'estinto è l'idol mio', bars 18–22

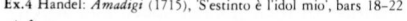

['If my beloved is dead, I too wish to die']

Ex.5 Handel: *Ottone*, 'Affanni del pensier', bars 39–43

che os - ti - na - ti la pa - - - - - - - - - - - - ce a

me_____ tur - ba - - te.

[omitting parts for two violins and viola]

['that you, unceasing (sorrows), disturb my peace.']

graph copy of 'O caro mio tesor' (*GB-Cfm*; Dean 1970) cannot strictly be called an embellished version; it is recomposed (probably from memory), with slight but significant differences of musical substance, and ends with the instruction 'Da Capo', implying the addition of ornamentation to what is written. Nonetheless, Handel's recomposed vocal line incorporates ornamental figures that illuminate his views on embellishment.

Most valuable of all, three arias from Handel's *Ottone* (1723), transcribed by J. C. Smith (*GB-Ob*, MS Don.c.69), have vocal ornaments added by the composer for the da capo and – in two cases – for the middle section (Dean 1976 and Wolff 1972). Handel's priorities in vocal ornamentation were to embellish but not obliterate the original line, to leave crucial pitches untouched (invariably the first and last notes of phrases and also other significant points in the melodic contour), and to employ ornamentation not merely to demonstrate a singer's virtuosity but also to intensify the expression. The range of the original is exceeded only once, and only by a tone at the top; upward transposition by an octave is unknown. The last two phrases of the middle section of 'Affanni del pensier' illustrate Handel's style (ex.5).

2. 1750–1825. Instructional and theoretical works come, through their sheer quantity, to assume a new importance to the student of ornamentation as the Classical period began and music publishing flourished. Some 20 comprehensive vocal methods or critical studies appeared in the period between 1763 and 1825 (after which the Rossinian revolution begins to be reflected). Many contain extensive notated examples, and these are of especial value in a period both of operatic reform and of virtuoso vocalism. The latter was cultivated with care, ambition and respect, though its extreme manifestations found cogent and persuasive detractors. Most writers on the subject discuss questions of taste and judgment, balancing the claims of composer and virtuoso; there is much thoughtful argument, and subtle differences of emphasis are found between writers. But without matching such accounts to detailed, notated examples it is impossible to determine what might have sounded restrained and what daring, still

more to establish what were considered the idiomatic ways of carrying out standard ornamental procedures.

Domenico Corri is probably the most valuable single theorist as far as the provision of practical examples is concerned: he printed details of execution that were normally left unwritten, over a wide range of music; he was reporter more than advocate; and he was respected by his contemporaries. Other important writers were Mancini, Hiller, Lasser, Pellegrini Celoni, J. F. Schubert, Lanza, Garaudé, Ferrari, J. B. Rocourt, Nathan and Bacon. Annotated performance materials are plentiful but not readily accessible for study; in London, following Corri's lead, publishers began to issue arias with embellishments and nuances indicated by small noteheads, and there and in Paris arias were published showing a particular performer's 'realizations' on a separate staff.

Little or no ornamentation is advised for plain recitative; Hiller (1780) stated that ornaments should be confined to occasional mordents and *Pralltriller*, though he accepted the need for more in scenas in accompanied recitative. J. F. Schubert advocated 'appropriate free embellishment' for fermatas but cautioned that this should be avoided where the word to which it would be sung made it inappropriate. In slow arias, or the slower sections of two-part rondò arias, the use of portamento was advocated by Corri, with *messa di voce* on longer notes, and the line might be highly graced, with appoggiaturas (single or compound) and acciaccaturas as the most common ornaments; little running passages might bridge leaps or fill out long notes, and syncopation, echo effects and division-like passages might be used. The surviving examples embellished by Mozart show the use of such devices (ex.6). Allegro arias or sections were less subject to decorative ornament, largely because of their greater speed and stricter tempo. Passing notes, appoggiaturas and the like are found but in less profusion, and unmeasured flurries of quick notes are rare. Staccato and syncopation are sometimes used as ornamental devices and running passages of semiquavers may be constructed on the outlines of melodies in longer note values. Hiller (1780) explained the distinction: 'in slow and pathetic arias, slurred and drawn-out ornaments are the most appropriate, just as thrusting ones belong more to the Allegro'. In both

Ex.6 J. C. Bach: 'Cara, la dolce fiamma' from *Adriano in Siria* with embellished versions by Mozart

['You are the dear flame of my soul, and in my affections I shall always be faithful']

styles, ornamentation generally involves adding notes of quicker rhythmic denomination rather than rerouting existing semiquavers into another region of the voice or simply recomposing the melodies (a practice often followed in modern revivals). Some degree of thematic variation, however, was expected in the case of an aria with a recurring theme as it reappeared.

they decried ornamentation that overwhelmed the original. At least eight examples were published of the decorations sung by Angelica Catalani, which were also extremely florid. Mozart's preferred style of ornamentation, ascertainable from ex.6 and from his elaboration of an aria from his *Lucio Silla* (1772), show a number of features: (*a*) the use of passing notes and other small

Ex.7

['Darling, my desire fulfils itself in your eyes.']

Many complete arias survive with ornamentation attributable to specific composers or singers. The Czech composer Václav Pichl noted, in Milan in 1792, the variants sung by Luigi Marchesi in different performances of Zingarelli's *Pirro* (ex.7); its opening line gives some indication of what theorists meant when

ornaments in the first statement, increased in the repeat; (*b*) the standard use of appoggiaturas on feminine line endings (and often elsewhere; the speed of their resolution should be noted); (*c*) the variety of pace in the passage-work, with the prevailing semiquavers often enlivened by a burst of demisemiquavers or uneven groups of quick notes; (d) the tendency to use embellishment to increase the complexity and speed of figuration (as opposed to altering melodic shape or tessitura: the idea of adding 'excitement' through high notes seems to play no part); (e) the use of syncopation and phrasing to vary the line; and (f) the increase in elaboration as cadences are approached. In the *Lucio Silla* aria it is worth noting, additionally, that the wide leaps in long notes are left unornamented.

Several theorists stress the importance of exactitude and curtailment of liberties when two or more voices are singing together. Pellegrini Celoni wrote:

Duets, trios, quartets etc. must be sung as they are written, and though it is permissible to vary this or that in the solos, in the remainder it is necessary to proceed with unanimity, and to pay close attention to *forte, piano* and *pianissimo*; to smooth out, connect and separate … in concerted pieces, … appoggiaturas, trills and mordents are still permitted, but always with moderation.

Others emphasize that cadenzas for two voices or for voice with obbligato instrument (which was expected when the accompaniment featured one) must be prepared in advance and are often written out by composers. Many examples survive, among them several for the duet for Susanna and Countess Almaviva in *Le nozze di Figaro* and for 'Ah perdona' from *La clemenza di Tito*.

Most of the foregoing discussion applies primarily to Italian music. Outside the Italian sphere, the application of italianate style decreased in proportion to the distance of the music itself from Italian models. Germans noted approvingly (and Italians complainingly) that sophisticated German accompaniments made vocal freedom and ornamentation less appropriate. J. F. Schubert admonishes that the 'compositions of Mozart, Haydn, Cherubini and Winter will bear fewer embellishments than those of Salieri, Cimarosa, Martín and Paisiello'. French singers seem to have carried from earlier generations some of their system of well-defined and differentiated ornaments, which they preferred to the bolder manifestations of italianate passage-work, and to have applied them quite liberally to the *ariettes* and the strophic songs in their operas. In one kind of English song, where the voice moves predominantly in octaves with the bass, it is implied by Corri that the voice did not normally break the unison to add ornamentation; the basic shape of the vocal melody is retained, but passing notes and other smaller graces might be added. These, along with the *gruppetto* or turn and portamento, seem to have been regarded more as a part of tasteful execution than as ornamentation.

3. SINCE 1825. Pedagogical sources of the Romantic period tend to concentrate more on technical and physiological matters than on questions of performing practice; but the increasing publication of vocal scores provides a rich surviving body of annotated performance material. By the end of the period a far more specific and illuminating type of evidence is available in the form of sound recordings. The most informative vocal methods are those of Lanza, Garaudé (the revised 1825 edition in particular), Ferrari, Bacon, Winter, Nathan, Marx, Crivelli, Lablache (with a brief, intelligent overview of ornamental practices), Duprez (for the new dramatic style and cadenzas), Garcia (the most comprehensive), Faure (valuable for the distinction between French and Italian practices) and Delle Sedie. The books of Sieber, Lemaire and Lavoix, and Bach also

contain valuable stylistic information with special emphasis on practices in Germany, France and England respectively, while such authors as Ella and Castil-Blaze provide important accounts of performing practices with music examples. There also survive, published and in manuscript, arias 'realized' or annotated by Rossini and Donizetti and by (or after) many of the leading singers of the time, as well as isolated ornaments by Verdi and various singers. Some clues may additionally be obtained from instrumental adaptations or fantasias.

In orchestrally accompanied recitative, cantabile, arioso elements and ornamental vocalization continued to be important; composers increasingly wrote the ornaments into the score. Ex.8 shows part of Tancredi's opening recitative, as scored and then as realized by Rossini for a singer. Examination of this, along with recitative realizations by Rubini, Garcia and others, shows that the greater floridity and greater variety of long and short note values observed in the recitatives of Verdi (especially the soprano recitatives up to the mid-1850s) reflect an increase not so much in elaborateness of recitative style as in the specificity of notating it; indeed, the actual elaboration of execution probably decreased somewhat, in contrast to the notational practice.

The 'aria cantabile' continued to be the principal locus for melodic embellishment. Garcia, who is more explicit even than Corri, gives details of phrasing, dynamics and expression as well; ex.9 shows a section from one of his examples. The most basic units of ornamentation are passing notes, scales, *gruppetti* and elaborations thereof. A decrease in density of figuration across the first half of the century is easy to discern; extending the examples backwards to, say, Catalani, at the beginning of the century, and forward to the artists heard on early recordings, would show this to be a steady, continuous process.

The cabaletta, the fast final section of the aria from the time of Rossini until the dissolution of standard aria structures into the more flexible forms of the mature Verdi, consisted of a strophe, a ritornello, an exact repeat (occasionally abbreviated) and a coda whose length and complexity varied considerably. Rossini wrote to Clara Novello that 'The repeat is made expressly that each singer may vary it, so as best to display his or her peculiar capacities'. The transitional passage from the slow section (sometimes in recitative) often concluded with a vocal flourish, which could recur between the strophes. These flourishes most often expressed a simple, unresolved dominant 7th. Surviving examples include variants by Pauline Viardot (for a pupil) for the lead-in to 'Sempre libera' (*La traviata*) and one in the role-book for Azucena used to launch 'Deh! rallentate, o barbari' in the French version of *Il trovatore* in Paris (1857).

Ornamentation in the cabaletta itself is of three kinds: elaboration of fermatas, most often at the end of each strophe or during the coda; variation of the basic stanza on repetition; and elaboration of the coda's stock cadential sequences, whose similarity from piece to piece facilitated free improvisation. In contrast to the usual gracings of cantabile, cabaletta repeats took the form of genuine variations, freely altering the melodic shape at times. Orchestral doublings of the melodic line were often removed to facilitate ornamentation, as can be seen from numerous sets of 19th-century parts, including those used by Verdi for the première of *I*

Ex.8 Rossini: *Tancredi*

['Oh homeland! sweet and undeserving homeland! At last I return to you my greeting. O dear land of my forefathers I kiss you. And on this happy day for me my heart starts to beat again in my breast']

['A new being. I feel reborn']

Ex.9 Cimarosa: *Il matrimonio segreto*

['Before the sunrise begins to show in the sky, softly and with a slow pace']

Ex.10 Bellini: *Norma*

['Ah lovely, return to me mischievous first love, and protected by you against the whole world']

masnadieri with Jenny Lind. Ex.10 shows a concordance of five Pasta-related sources for part of Norma's 'Ah! bello, a me ritorna'. Only the brief excerpt cited by Garcia is described as offering Pasta's own variants, but the similarity of approach and Pasta's renowned association with the role suggest that her influence on the subsequent traditions of performing it was strong. Many other examples of cabaletta variation survive; Rossini's for several of his own cabalettas, and one each by Bellini and Nicolini, were published (with imperfect but decent fidelity) by Ricci.

In Rossini, Bellini and Donizetti, the coda is based on the same chord sequence observed at the end of the cantabile, but this time in tempo and usually with accelerating harmonic rhythm, as (for example) in ex.11, this portion was elaborately and freely varied. Garcia, Lanza and others give tables showing the multiple possibilities, and examples by Rossini and many singers exist. Cabalettas continued to be embellished in early Verdi (Giulia Grisi's variations for *I due Foscari*

survive in Rome). By the time he stopped writing them – his last orthodox solo cabaletta is in the 1863 version of *La forza del destino*; *Un ballo in maschera* (1859) is his first opera to have none at all – the repeat was commonly omitted in performance. It seems likely that cabalettas were ornamented as long as they were repeated.

The end of the coda is a problematic moment; up to, and probably throughout, Rossini's time, it seems to have been taken without rallentando and with a burst of florid virtuosity, often concluded in the low register. But as the excitement of the held top note gradually assumed a greater role in vocal expression, it became customary to add one to the end of the cabaletta while the orchestra pauses or sustains, just before the final note. This is sometimes found in Verdi's scores, and was occasionally applied earlier, though it became a universal practice only later. Increasingly, towards the end of the century, much or all of the coda was omitted; the singer proceeded from the final fermata of the strophe

Ex.11

(a) Rossini: *La donna del lago* 'O quante lagrime'

[mer-]cè, gra - ta mer - cè, gra - ta mer -

(b) Rossini: *Il barbiere di Siviglia*, 'Una voce poco fa'

[gio-]car, e cen-to trap-po-le fa - rò gio-car, e___ cen-to trap-po-le fa - rò gio-

(c) Rossini: variants for (b)

[gio-]car, e cen-to trap-po-le fa - rò gio - car,___ cen-to trap-po-le fa - rò gio-

- cè, gra - ta mer - cè, gra - ta mer - cè

- car, fa - rò gio - car, fa - rò gio - car,

- car, fa - rò gio - car,___ fa-rò gio-car,

car, fa - rò gio - car,

(a) ['gracious pity']
(b) ['then a hundred traps will I set in action']

Ex.12

(a) Rossini: *Torvaldo e Dorliska*, 'Ferma constante immobile'

original

(non) dà, no, no, non dà, no, no, non dà,___ no,___ no, non dà

Naldi

(b) Verdi: *La traviata*, 'Sempre libera'

original

(pen-)sier, _____ il mio___ pen - sier

Viardot

directly to the last few bars of coda or to the postlude. The conclusions in ex.11 clearly envisage an ending in tempo. Ex.12 shows two more cabaletta conclusions: one by Naldi, clearly ending in tempo, and one by Viardot from about 1880, showing a hold before the final note, now taken in the high register. Many sets of cabaletta variants break off at this point, suggesting a conclusion more or less as in the score or with conventionalized elaboration, and many sources that are specific about accompaniment practice (above all Garcia) show the conclusions of their cabalettas with no hint that the tempo was to be retarded. The practice of

dropping out for several bars of the coda to save strength for a final annihilating top note is strictly a 20th-century innovation, dating from after World War I.

It is clear from Rossini's revisions of his Italian music for Paris that the norm there was less florid than in Italy (despite the fact that the Paris operas were still liberally embellished, as we know from Cinti-Damoreau and numerous other sources). The strong penetration of the Italian repertory in the 1840s and 50s by translated versions of Meyerbeer and Auber (to be followed by Gounod, Thomas and Massenet) led the way towards a

Ex.13

(a) Bellini: *La sonnambula*

['that it lasted only a day, ah just a day it lasted . . . my grief could bring new vigour']

(b) Verdi: *La traviata*

['to that love is the heart-beat of the entire universe']

(c) Verdi: *Otello*

['this is the end']

simpler style of impassioned lyricism in Italian singing (G. M. Mario, regularly described as less brilliant than his predecessors in *fioritura*, was a leading figure). Nevertheless, it was the French who maintained the old Italian skills of florid singing rigorously to the end of the century, while their Italian contemporaries had long simplified Rossini's *Otello* and were beginning to do the same to the less demanding *Barbiere*.

In Germany and eastern Europe, a tension between the dominance of Italians and emerging native styles was felt throughout the century, with the Italians essentially ranged on the side of more freedom for the soloist. By the middle of the century in Germany, and by its end throughout Europe, schools of singers had emerged as specialists in national repertory (eventually in Wagner) – and in these singers the roots of what we know as 20th-century style are found.

Recordings provide valuable evidence on ornamentation. The first opera singer known to have made a surviving record is Peter Schram (1819–95), who in 1889 sang two excerpts from the role of Leporello into a cylinder machine; they show a very free rhythmic treatment, with appoggiaturas and ornaments that correspond closely to practices observable in Mozart's own day. This record provides interesting testimony to the transmission of Classical music but has little bearing on the performance of Romantic music. Seven singers born in the 1830s, and 24 born in the 1840s, also recorded, as did several dozen born in the 1850s and 60s.

This body of evidence brings the priceless opportunity to observe many aspects of vocal technique. Ornamentation was still practised, mostly by Italian singers but also by foreigners who made their careers in Italy or who became part of the budding 'international' scene in New York and London, and by some of the more old-fashioned artists based in France and Germany. Ex.13 gives examples of passages recorded by singers born between 1843 and 1860, with transcriptions of ornaments, dynamics, portamento and rubato (necessarily 'impressionistic') set against the original notation. Ex.13*b* attempts to show the displacements and tempo modifications in two lines from *La traviata* as sung by Gemma Bellincioni, whom Verdi admired in the role. The ornaments are simpler and fewer than those in use earlier in the century. Most however were staples of ornamental practice going back at least to the Classical period: *gruppetti* of four or six notes, acciaccaturas, two-note slides, and the accented reiteration of the antepenultimate note of a cadence that Garcia traces back to the castratos and that was popularized by Rubini. For the music of Puccini and the *verismo* school, only the acciaccatura remained prominent as an improvised addition, though *gruppetti* were occasionally used by older singers.

These ornaments were all started on the main note, even the acciaccatura: though notated with a single 'small note' above the main note, it was uniformly executed as what we would now call an inverted mordent (unless approached by step from below, in which case it was sometimes sung in the 'modern' one-note fashion). The only prominent ornament not found in earlier sources, and that seems to have developed in the second half of the century, is the extended acciaccatura figure (ex.11*c*); this was widely used in Verdi. French singers – less often Germans, almost never Italians – still introduced trills and executed the written ones with great clarity and elegant resolutions.

On early records, the preoccupation with interpolated high notes had not reached its later peaks; singers with good high notes often added them, but many recordings of the *Pagliacci* prologue, 'Largo al factotum', 'Sempre libera', 'La donna è mobile' and other favourite arias lack the familiar extra high notes. These, like the 'standard' coloratura variations of 'Una voce poco fa' and the *Lucia* Mad Scene, are mostly products of the 1920s and 30s, when Italian conductors and coaches set about the task of establishing more or less fixed texts for surviving Italian operas from the period of improvisation.

*

BurneyH; GroveI ('Cadenza', E. Badura-Skoda; 'Improvisation', §1, I. Horsley and others); Grove6 ('Tosi, Pier Francesco', M. Boyd)

J. Peri: Preface, *Euridice* (Florence, 1600/*R*1981 with Eng. trans., RRMBE, xxxvi–xxxvii)

G. Caccini: *Le nuove musiche* (Florence, 1601/2); ed. H. W. Hitchcock, RRMBE, ix (1970)

——: *Nuove musiche e nuova maniera di scriverle* (Florence, 1614); ed. H. W. Hitchcock, RRMBE, xxviii (1978)

G. B. Doni: *Trattato della musica scenica* (MS, 1633–5); extracts in A. Solerti, *Le origini della melodramma* (Turin, 1903), 195–228

M. Mersenne: *Harmonie universelle* (Paris, 1636–7)

C. Bernhard: *Von der Singe-Kunst, oder Maniera* (MS, *c*1649); trans. W. Hilse in 'The Treatises of Christoph Bernhard', *Music Forum*, iii (1973), 1–196

J. Millet: *La belle méthode, ou L'art de bien chanter* (Besançon, 1666)

B. de Bacilly: *Remarques curieuses sur l'art de bien chanter* (Paris, 1668, 4/1681); ed. A. B. Caswell as *A Commentary upon the Art of Proper Singing* (New York, 1968)

W. C. Printz: *Compendium musicae signatoriae et modulatoriae vocalis* (Dresden, 1689, 2/1714)

F. Raguenet: *Paralèle des italiens et des françois, en ce qui regarde la musique et les opéra* (Paris, 1702); excerpts trans. in O. Strunk, *Source Readings in Music History* (New York, 1950)

B. Marcello: *Il teatro alla moda* (Venice, 1720); excerpts trans. in O. Strunk, *Source Readings in Music History* (New York, 1950)

P. F. Tosi: *Opinioni de' cantori antichi e moderni, o sieno Osservazioni sopra il canto figurato* (Bologna, 1723); Eng. trans. J. E. Galliard as *Observations on the Florid Song; or Sentiments on the Ancient and Modern Singers* (London, 1742, 2/1743)

G. P. Telemann: Preface, *Harmonischer Gottes-Dienst* (Hamburg, 1725–6)

M. P. de Montéclair: *Principes de musique* (Paris, 1736)

J. J. Quantz: *Versuch einer Anweisung die Flöte traversiere zu spielen* (Berlin, 1752; Eng. trans., 1966, 2/1985)

J. F. Agricola: *Anleitung zur Singekunst* (Berlin, 1757) [Ger. trans., with addl notes and comments, of Tosi's *Opinioni de' cantori antiche e moderni*, 1723]

F. W. Marpurg: *Anleitung zur Musik überhaupt und zur Singkunst besonders mit Uebungsexampeln erläutert* (Berlin, 1763)

J. A. Hiller: *Anweisung zum musikalischrichtigen Gesange* (Leipzig, 1774, enlarged 2/1798)

——: *Exempelbuch der Anweisung zum Singen* (Leipzig, 1774)

G. Mancini: *Pensieri, e riflessioni pratiche sopra il canto figurato* (Vienna, 1774, 3/1777; Eng. trans., 1967)

J. A. Hiller: *Anweisung zum musikalisch-zierlichen Gesang* (Leipzig, 1780; Eng. trans., 1980)

J. B. Lasser: *Vollständige Anleitung zur Singkunst* (Munich, 1798, 2/1811)

J. F. Schubert: *Neue Sing-Schule oder gründliche und vollständige Anweisung zur Singkunst* (Leipzig, 1804)

A. de Garaudé: *Méthode de chant* (Paris, 1809, 2/1825)

G. Lanza: *The Elements of Singing* (London, 1809–13)

D. Corri: *The Singer's Preceptor* (London, 1810)

A. M. Pellegrini Celoni: *Grammatica o siano regole di ben cantare* (Rome, 1810, 2/1817)

G. Ferrari: *Breve trattato di canto italiano* (London, 1818; Eng. trans., 1818)

J. B. Roucourt: *Essai sur la théorie du chant* (Brussels, 1821)

I. Nathan: *An Essay on the History and Theory of Music and on the Qualities, Capabilities and Management of the Human Voice* (London, 1823, 2/1836 as *Musurgia vocalis*)

R. M. Bacon: *Elements of Vocal Science* (London, 1824)

P. von Winter: *Vollständige Singschule* (Mainz, 1825, 2/1874)

M. Garcia: *Traité complet de l'art du chant* (Paris, 1840, 3/1851)

L. Lablache: *Méthode de chant* (Paris, *c*1840; Eng. trans., 1840)

D. Crivelli: *L'arte del canto, ossia Corso completo d'insegnamento sulla coltivazione della voce* (London, 1841, Eng. trans., ?1843, 2/1844)

G. Duprez: *L'art du chant* (Paris, 1845, Eng. trans., 1847)

Castil-Blaze: *L'opéra italien de 1548 à 1856* (Paris, 1856)

F. Sieber: *Vollständiges Lehrbuch der Gesangkunst* (Magdeburg, 1858, 2/1878; Eng. trans., 1872)

J. Ella: *Musical Sketches* (London, 1869, 3/1878)

J.-B. Faure: *La voix et le chant* (Paris, 1870)

E. Delle Sedie: *Arte e fisiologia di canto* (Milan, 1876)

T. Lemaire and H. Lavoix: *Le chant, ses principes et son histoire* (Paris, 1881)

A. B. Bach: *On Musical Education and Voice Culture* (Edinburgh, 1883, 5/1898)

E. Delle Sedie: *Estetica del canto e dell'arte melodrammatico* (Livorno, 1885)

H. Goldschmidt: *Die italienische Gesangsmethode des XVII. Jahrhunderts und ihre Bedeutung für die Gegenwart nach Quellen jener Zeit* (Breslau, 1890, 2/1892)

M. Kuhn: *Die Verziehrungs-Kunst in der Gesangs-Musik des 16.–17. Jahrhunderts (1535–1650)* (Leipzig, 1902)

H. Goldschmidt: *Die Lehre von der vokalen Ornamentik* (Berlin, 1907)

A. Beyschlag: *Die Ornamentik der Musik* (Leipzig, 1908)

F. Haböck: *Die Gesangskunst der Kastraten: erster Notenband* (Vienna, 1923)

——: *Die Kastraten und ihre Gesangskunst* (Stuttgart, 1927)

R. Haas: *Aufführungspraxis der Musik* (Potsdam, 1931)

L. Ricci: *Variazioni, cadenze, tradizioni per canto* (Milan, 1937)

H. C. Wolff: *Die venezianische Oper in der zweiten Hälfte des 17. Jahrhunderts: ein Beitrag zur Geschichte der Musik und des Theaters im Zeitalter des Barock* (Berlin, 1937)

E. T. Ferand: *Die Improvisation in der Musik* (Zürich, 1938)

N. Fortune: 'Italian 17th-Century Singing', *ML*, xxxv (1954), 206–19

E. T. Ferand: *Die Improvisation in Beispielen aus neun Jahrhunderten abendländischer Musik*, Mw, xii (1955, Eng. trans., 1961)

H.-P. Schmitz: *Die Kunst der Verzierung im 18. Jahrhundert* (Kassel, 1955, 2/1965)

V. Duckles: 'Florid Embellishment in English Song of the Late 16th and Early 17th Centuries', *AnnM*, v (1957), 329–45

W. Georgh: *Die Verzierungen in der Musik: Theorie und Praxis* (Zürich and Freiburg, 1957)

J. S. Hall and M. V. Hall: 'Handel's Graces', *HJb*, ix (1957), 25–43

E. T. Ferand: 'Embellished "Parody Cantatas" in the Early 18th Century', *MQ*, xliv (1958), 40–64

H. C. Wolff: 'Orientalischen Einflüsse in den Improvisationen des 16. und 17. Jahrhunderts', *IMSCR vii: Cologne 1958*, 308–15

R. Donington: 'Performing Purcell's Music Today', *Henry Purcell (1659–95): Essays on his Music*, ed. I. Holst (London, 1959), 74–98

I. Spink: 'Playford's "Directions for Singing after the Italian Manner"', *MMR*, lxxxix (1959), 130–35

H. C. Wolff: 'Vom Wesen des alten Belcanto', *Händel: Halle 1959*, 95–9

R. Donington: *The Interpretation of Early Music* (London, 1963, 2/1974), chaps. 7–12

G. Frotscher: *Aufführungspraxis alter Musik* (Wilhelmshaven, 1963; Eng. trans., 1981)

A. B. Caswell: *The Development of Seventeenth-Century French Vocal Ornamentation and its Influence upon the Late Baroque Ornamentation Practice* (diss., U. of Minnesota, 1964)

G. Rose: 'Agazzari and the Improvising Orchestra', *JAMS*, xviii (1965), 382–93

W. Dürr and U. Siegele: 'Cantar d'affetto: zum Vortrag monodischer Musik', *GfMkB: Leipzig 1966*, 208–14

A. B. Caswell: 'Remarques curieuses sur l'art de bien chanter', *JAMS*, xx (1967), 116–20

T. Best: 'An Example of Handel Embellishment', *MT*, cx (1969), 933

A. Cohen: '*L'art de bien chanter* (1666) of Jean Millet', *MQ*, lv (1969), 170–79

M. Cyr: 'A Seventeenth-Century Source of Ornamentation for Voice and Viol: British Museum MS. Egerton 2971', *RMARC*, no.9 (1970), 53–72

W. Dean: 'Vocal Embellishment in a Handel Aria', *Studies in Eighteenth-Century Music: a Tribute to Karl Geiringer on his Seventieth Birthday* (London, 1970), 151–9; rev. in W. Dean, *Essays on Opera* (Oxford, 1990), 22–9

H. W. Hitchcock: 'Vocal Ornamentation in Caccini's *Nuove Musiche*', *MQ*, lvi (1970), 389–404

H. C. Wolff: *Originale Gesangsimprovisationen des 16. bis 18. Jahrhunderts*, Mw, xli (1972, Eng. trans., 1972)

R. Freeman: 'Farinello and his Repertory', *Studies in Renaissance and Baroque Music in Honor of Arthur Mendel* (Kassel, 1974), 301–30

D. H. Till: *English Vocal Ornamentation, 1600–1660* (diss., U. of Oxford, 1975)

H. M. Brown: *Embellishing 16th-Century Music* (London, 1976)

W. Dean, ed.: *G. F. Handel: Three Ornamented Arias* (Oxford, 1976)

G. J. Buelow: 'A Lesson in Operatic Performance Practice by Madame Faustina Bordoni', *A Musical Offering: Essays in Honor of Martin Bernstein* (New York, 1977), 79–96

E. Sąsiadek: 'O technice wokalnej i realizacji ozdobników w utworach Monteverdiego' [On Vocal Technique and the Execution of Mordents in Monteverdi's Works], *Ruch muzyczny*, xxi/14 (1977), 6–7

F. Neumann: *Ornamentation in Baroque and Post-Baroque Music with Special Emphasis on J. S. Bach* (Princeton, 1978)

M. Cyr: 'Eighteenth-Century French and Italian Singing: Rameau's Writing for the Voice', *ML*, lxi (1980), 318–37

R. Donington: *Baroque Music: Style and Performance* (London, 1982)

H. Krones and R. Schollum: *Vokale und allgemeine Aufführungspraxis* (Vienna, 1983)

W. V. Porter: 'A Central Source of Early Monody: Brussels, Conservatory 704 (I)', *Studi musicali*, xii (1983), 239–79

S. Willier: 'Rhythmic Variants in Early Manuscript Versions of Caccini's Monodies', *JAMS*, xxxvi (1983), 481–97

W. Crutchfield: 'Vocal Ornamentation in Verdi: the Phonographic Evidence', *19th Century Music*, vii (1983–4), 3–54

H. M. Brown: 'Embellishing Eighteenth-Century Arias: on Cadenzas', *Opera and Vivaldi*, ed. M. Collins and E. K. Kirk (Austin, 1984), 258–76

T. Carter: 'On the Composition and Performance of Caccini's *Le nuove musiche* (1602)', *EMc*, xii (1984), 208–17

F. Neumann: *Ornamentation and Improvisation in Mozart* (Princeton, 1986)

W. Dean and J. M. Knapp: *Handel's Operas: 1704–1726* (Oxford, 1987)

R. Jackson: *Performance Practice, Medieval to Contemporary: a Bibliographic Guide* (New York and London, 1988)

S. Carter: 'Francesco Rognoni's *Selva de varii passaggi* (1620): Fresh Details concerning Early-Baroque Vocal Ornamentation', *Performance Practice Review*, ii (1989), 5–33

A. B. Caswell, ed.: *Embellished Opera Arias*, Recent Researches in Music of the Nineteenth and Early Twentieth Century, vii–viii (1989)

W. Crutchfield: 'Voices', *Performance Practice: Music after 1600*, ed. H. M. Brown and S. Sadie (London, 1989), 292–319, 424–58

D. Fuller: 'Ornamentation', ibid, 124–30

E. T. Harris: 'Voices', ibid, 97–116

D. Fuller: 'Ornamentation', *Companion to Baroque Music*, ed. J. A. Sadie (London, 1991), 417–34

N. Rogers: 'Voices', ibid, 351–65

W. Dean: 'A New Source for Handel's "Amadigi"', *ML*, lxxii (1991), 27–37

For further bibliography *see* SINGING: A BIBLIOGRAPHY.

ANDREW V. JONES (1), WILL CRUTCHFIELD (2, 3)

Orontea. *Dramma musicale* in a prologue and three acts by ANTONIO CESTI to a libretto by GIACINTO ANDREA CICOGNINI revised by GIOVANNI FILIPPO APOLLONI; Innsbruck, Teatro di Sala, 19 February 1656.

Filosofia [Philosophy]	soprano
Amore [Cupid]	soprano
Orontea *Queen of Egypt*	soprano
Creonte *court philosopher*	baritone
Tibrino *a young page*	soprano
Aristea *supposed mother of Alidoro*	contralto
Alidoro (Floridano) *a young painter*	tenor
Gelone *a drunken servant*	bass
Corindo *a young courtier*	alto
Silandra *a lady of the court, loved by Corindo*	soprano
Giacinta (Ismero) *a former lady of the court, disguised as a boy*	soprano

Setting Ancient Egypt

Cristoforo Ivanovich (*Minerva al tavolino*, 1681) reported that Cesti composed *Orontea* for performance at the Teatro di SS Apostoli, Venice, in 1649. A letter of 30 January 1666 from P. A. Ziani to the impresario Marco Faustini (in *I-Vas*), however, indicates that Francesco Lucio composed the music for this performance. Cesti almost certainly wrote his music for performances in Innsbruck during 1656. Extant scores of Cesti's version follow the Innsbruck libretto closely, and most contain music for G. F. Apolloni's Innsbruck prologue involving Philosophy and Cupid rather than Cicognini's Venetian prologue featuring two Tritons, a Siren and Cupid. Moreover, Cesti's music for *Alessandro vincitor di se stesso* (1651) is stylistically earlier than that for *Orontea*.

PROLOGUE In a typical mid-17th-century prologue, Philosophy and Cupid argue the merits of the mind versus the senses, engaging in increasingly heated debate. The latter declares that he will make Queen Orontea fall in love; the former rejoins that the philosopher Creonte has better sense than to approve Orontea's choice. Cupid, undeterred, flies off to Egypt to set the wheels in motion. Cesti's use of a ritornello four times (the last a 5th higher) adds cohesion to a section built on recitative interspersed with brief arioso passages and two other ritornellos.

ACT 1 Orontea proclaims herself impervious to love, is chided by Creonte for rejecting every suitor, is surprised by Tibrino who, sword in hand, has just saved a stranger accosted by a thief, and is filled with self doubt at having taken pity on the stranger Alidoro, who is accompanied by his supposed mother, Aristea. Feelings of love for Alidoro torment Orontea. The drunken servant Gelone worships his god, wine; Cesti's excellent accompanied arias for Gelone underscore the opera's comic nature. Gelone is joined by Corindo, who extols the virtue of love, and by Silandra, who expresses her love for Corindo. Some of the music in scene vii is used again in scene viii, and in both, music from the arias reappears in the subsequent ritornellos. Arias predominate here; recitative is used sparingly. Orontea and Alidoro return and are attracted to each other. After Orontea leaves, Silandra enters and confesses to Alidoro her love at first sight for him. Cesti intertwines her amorous advances with Alidoro's cautious responses in a 3/2 strophic-variation aria, in which the principals sing alternate strophes punctuated by a three-voice ritornello. The act ends with hilarity when Gelone, imagining himself on a foundering ship, is discovered by Tibrino, who tells him that Queen Orontea awaits him. Gelone entertains the audience with his drunken philosophy.

ACT 2 Scenes i–v are framed by Orontea's confession of love for Alidoro. Giacinta appears disguised as the boy Ismero and tells of her encounter with and wounding of Alidoro, which sends the queen into a rage that even Creonte has difficulty calming. Orontea's initial profession of love ('Adorirsi sempre') is an aria with obbligato accompaniment, perhaps intended for violin. The remaining text is predominantly set as recitative. Aristea fans the flames of her infatuation with Ismero, who is not responsive. Silandra bids farewell to her love for Corindo in favour of that for Alidoro, but Corindo appears and receives the rejection in person. Cesti sets the two five-line strophes of Silandra's solo scene (not present in Cicognini's original Venetian libretto) to different music. Strophe 1 ('Addio, Corindo, addio') is a duple metre introduction to strophe 2 ('Vieni, Alidoro, vieni'), a fully-fledged accompanied ostinato aria on a descending tetrachord bass. Corindo expresses amazement at the sudden change of affection, set by Cesti as brief, alternating sections of 3/2 arioso and recitative. Alidoro, painting Silandra's portrait, is discovered by Orontea. The encounter overwhelms Alidoro, who faints and is found by Gelone. When Gelone departs, Orontea sings her famous aria 'Intorno all'idol mio' over Alidoro's prostrate body, and, professing her love anew, leaves him her crown and sceptre and a note. Some of the finest music occurs in this solo scene. As the act concludes Alidoro awakes, discovers the objects left by Orontea and reads the note, in which she proclaims that he, a commoner, will be her husband and the King of Egypt.

ACT 3 Silandra makes another attempt to woo Alidoro, but is rejected. A comic interlude follows in which Gelone and Tibrino suggest that Orontea has abandoned caution and that the city is alive with rumour. Creonte tries to persuade Orontea to banish the unworthy Alidoro. When Alidoro, accompanied by

Silandra, encounters Orontea he is asked to produce the note and is then rebuffed. He implores Silandra to take him back, but is rebuffed again. Gelone is enlisted to reunite Silandra and Corindo and he idly threatens to kill Alidoro. He is overheard by Tibrino, who threatens to kill Gelone if he harms Alidoro. Scenes x–xiii are largely concerned with misunderstandings over identities and a golden medallion presented first by Aristea to Giacinta, then by Giacinta to Alidoro, who is accused of its theft by Gelone. Meanwhile Alidoro has challenged Corindo to a duel. Act 3 has so far included six arias – fewer than in the first two acts – but from the beginning of the denouement in scene xiii, no further arias interrupt the action. Scenes xiv–xix are extremely brief and prepare for the final resolution in scene xx. Corindo and Orontea discuss the forthcoming duel, which Orontea decides to prevent by making Alidoro a nobleman against Creonte's wish; Silandra agrees with Creonte, and Orontea demands to know why Alidoro is being accused of theft; Gelone reports having seen Alidoro with the medallion; Alidoro appears in chains with Tibrino, claiming that Ismero (Giacinta) gave it to him; and Giacinta explains the original act of piracy. In the final scene it is established that the medallion is one of three struck for the Egyptian King Tolomeo, who kept one and gave the others to Creonte and the infant prince of Phoenicia. Alidoro is revealed to be Prince Floridano of Phoenicia, whom Orontea may marry owing to his royal ancestry. Delighted, Orontea unites Silandra and Corindo, completing the *lieto fine*.

* * *

Orontea's success is primarily due to the human characters in the drama, the plausible nature of the plot, the lack of complicated stage machinery, the excellent comic writing by Cicognini as set by Cesti and the fine music. Although the denouement is contrived and the uniting of Corindo and Silandra hasty, the opera deals with people, not gods or immortals who possess extraordinary powers. Orontea is a dominant figure, human in her emotions, yet torn between these emotions and her sense of duty. Her reactions to Creonte's counselling are far more reserved and reasonable than Poppaea's are towards Seneca in Monteverdi's and Busenello's *L'incoronazione di Poppea*. Alidoro is an opportunist whose affection changes according to the situation, and Gelone, reminiscent of earlier *commedia dell'arte* figures like Zanni because of perpetual inebriation, is one of the first comic characters allowed to participate in the actual plot of a music drama. Cesti's skilfully composed arias are fluid in motion, and his rapid recitative exchanges are often inventive, rather than merely fillers. *Orontea*, a brilliant and successful combination of poetry and music, was revived many times, making it one of the most important mid-17th-century Italian operas, along with Cavalli's *Giasone* and Cesti's *Dori*. *Orontea* helped point the way for Italian opera in the later 1650s and 60s.

CARL B. SCHMIDT

Orphée aux enfers ('Orpheus in the Underworld'). *Opéra bouffon* in two acts by JACQUES OFFENBACH to a libretto by HECTOR-JONATHAN CRÉMIEUX and LUDOVIC HALÉVY after classical mythology; Paris, Théâtre des Bouffes-Parisiens (Salle Choiseul), 21 October 1858 (revised version, as an *opéra-féerie* in four acts, Paris, Théâtre de la Gaîté, 7 February 1874).

Orphée aux enfers marked a significant advance for Offenbach in 1858. From being restricted by the terms of his licence to producing short works for just a few

Pluton [Pluto] *god of the underworld, disguised
as Aristée [Aristaeus], a farmer*   tenor
Jupiter *father of the gods*   baritone
John Styx *servant of Pluto, formerly King of
Bœotia*   tenor
Mercure [Mercury] *Jupiter's messenger*   tenor
Orphée [Orpheus] *a musician*   tenor
Bacchus *god of wine*   spoken
Mars *god of war*   baritone
Cerbère [Cerberus] *three-headed watchdog
of the underworld*   barked
Morphée [Morpheus] *god of sleep*   baritone
Eurydice *wife of Orpheus*   soprano
Cupidon [Cupid] *god of love, son of
Venus*   mezzo-soprano
Diane [Diana] *goddess of chastity*   soprano
L'Opinion Publique [Public Opinion]   mezzo-soprano
Junon [Juno] *wife of Jupiter*   soprano
Vénus [Venus] *goddess of beauty*   soprano
Minerve [Minerva] *goddess of wisdom*   soprano

Gods, goddesses, shepherds, shepherdesses, lictors, infernal spirits

Setting The countryside near Thebes; Mount Olympus; the underworld

performers, he was now permitted to use larger casts and chorus and to offer his audiences a full-length work for the first time. Though the idea of parodying Greek mythology (*see* ORPHEUS) was not new, the vehemence with which Offenbach did so, not least by turning a stately minuet into a cancan, caused a good deal of critical comment. However, this merely served to increase interest in the work and ensure its overwhelming success in Paris. In turn this led to international celebrity on an enlarged scale and substantially accelerated the pace of acceptance of his works abroad. *Orphée* was produced in Breslau and Prague in 1859 and, in a new German version by Johann Nestroy, at the Carltheater, Vienna, on 17 March 1860. It was for this version that Carl Binder (1816–60) arranged the familiar overture, which has helped to maintain the work's place as the most widely known of all Offenbach's *opéras bouffes*. During the 1860s it continued to attract worldwide productions, and in 1874 Offenbach expanded the four scenes into four separate acts for a spectacular production at the Théâtre de la Gaîté (for an illustration of the poster, *see* PLAYBILL, fig.4). This opened with a new overture ('Promenade autour d'Orphée') and introduced new characters, two ballets and several new vocal numbers, among them (in Act 3) Mercury's saltarello 'Eh hop! eh hop! place à Mercure' and a Policemen's chorus 'Nez au vent, œil au guet'. Subsequent productions have generally made selective pickings from the 1874 additions.

The original 1858 production (with the cast listed above) featured Lise Tautin as Eurydice, and Tayau as an Orpheus who genuinely played the violin. A revival of the Théâtre de la Gaîté production in 1878 featured Offenbach's compositional rival Hervé in the role of Jupiter. The satire of the piece consists largely of portraying the revered figures of antiquity in farcical and incongruous situations, the only direct musical satire being a quotation of Gluck's 'J'ai perdu mon Eurydice'. Berlioz's version of Gluck's opera appeared the year after *Orphée aux enfers*.

ACT 1 *The countryside near Thebes, with the house of Orpheus* Public Opinion righteously parades herself as guardian of public virtue ('Qui suis-je? du Théâtre Antique'), after which Eurydice arrives, singing of her lover, the farmer Aristaeus ('La femme dont le cœur rêve'). Her husband, Orpheus, then enters. Alas, the two can't stand each other, and above all Eurydice can't abide Orpheus's violin playing. Orpheus therefore deliberately taunts her by playing part of his latest violin concerto ('Ah! c'est ainsi'). He goes on to inform her that he has laid a trap for her lover Aristaeus by filling the cornfields with snakes. Aristaeus appears ('Moi, je suis Aristée'), and Eurydice tries to warn him, but he simply encourages her to walk through the field. Of course she is bitten, whereupon Aristaeus reveals himself as Pluto, god of the underworld, which for Eurydice makes the prospect of death much brighter ('La mort m'apparaît souriante'). He duly sets off with Eurydice to his realm, leaving Orpheus to contemplate joyful freedom. However, Orpheus's joy is cut short by Public Opinion, who insists that, for the sake of public decency, he must go to the underworld and bring back his wife.

ACT 2 *Mount Olympus in the clouds at dawn* The gods are still sound asleep ('Dormons, dormons que notre somme') when Venus, Cupid and Mars return from their amorous nocturnal pursuits ('Je suis Vénus!'). No sooner have they settled down than a blast on Diana's hunting horn tells them it is time to get up ('Quand Diane descend dans la plaine'). To their chagrin, Jupiter reprimands them for ungodly behaviour. As they disperse to their duties, Mercury enters, having been sent by Jupiter to summon Pluto to appear before the father of the gods; when Pluto then arrives, Jupiter berates him for having kidnapped a mortal woman. They are interrupted by a revolt of the gods, who have finally had enough of Jupiter's hypocrisy and parade his own amorous adventures ('Aux armes, dieux et demi-dieux!'). Just then Public Opinion arrives with Orpheus, reluctantly reclaiming his wife. Jupiter tells Pluto to return Eurydice, and all the gods decide to go with him to the underworld to ensure that the order is carried out.

ACT 3 *Pluto's boudoir, in Hades* Eurydice is bored. Her only company is Pluto's servant John Styx, who tells of his sad life since he was King of the Bœotians ('Quand j'étais roi de Béotie'). He has been charged with keeping Eurydice under lock and key, and he hastily returns her to her room at the sound of Pluto returning with Jupiter. Cupid tells them that Eurydice is a prisoner in the next room. Jupiter is understandably anxious to verify this, which he can finally do when Cupid enables him to get through the keyhole by transforming him into a fly. Eurydice is sufficiently bored to welcome even a fly, which she playfully chases ('Bel insecte à l'aile dorée'). Finally allowing himself to be caught, Jupiter identifies himself and suggests that, in the confusion created by Pluto's forthcoming party, Eurydice should flee with him to Olympus.

ACT 4 *Hades and the River Styx* An extravagant party is in full swing, and the gods sing the praises of wine ('Vive le vin! vive Pluton!'). Eurydice is there, disguised as a Bacchante ('J'ai vu le Dieu Bacchus'), and everyone thoroughly enjoys a dance that turns from a stately minuet into an infernal galop or cancan ('Ce bal est original'). Jupiter tries to sneak off with her, but Pluto bars the way and points out that Orpheus is on his

The Bacchanal from Act 4 of Offenbach's 'Orphée aux enfers': drawing by Gustave Doré, who designed some of the costumes for the original production at the Théâtre des Bouffes-Parisiens, Paris, in 1858

way with Public Opinion. Jupiter is momentarily put out until Cupid thinks of a plan. When Orpheus arrives and demands the return of his wife, Jupiter agrees on condition that, on his exit from Hades, Orpheus leads the way and does not look round. The procession duly starts but, by hurling a thunderbolt just behind Orpheus, Jupiter shocks him into turning round. To the delight of everyone except Public Opinion, he thus forfeits his right to Eurydice, and Jupiter transforms her into a priestess of Bacchus.   ANDREW LAMB

Orphée et Eurydice. Opera by C. W. Gluck; *see ORFEO ED EURIDICE* (i).

Orpheus. Libretto subject used in many periods.

On the surface, the myth of Orpheus seems tailor-made for opera: a tale of faithful love beyond the grave and the magical power of music. In reality the well-known story has impressed the Western mind more as a symbol of a superhuman protagonist who conquers death, and who is at various times perceived as a prophet, a sage, a 'shaman' or an allegorical depiction of Christ, Apollo, Dionysus or Osiris. The Orpheus plot looms large in the history of the stage from Aeschylus to Tennessee Williams and in the history of stage music from Renaissance *intermedi* to Stravinsky and Birtwistle. The ubiquitous myth appears not only in operas and ballets (and films) that bear the names of Orpheus or Eurydice (or their spelling variants) in the titles, but also as important episodes, for instance in a play by Seneca or an opera by Cavalli (*Egisto*, 1643). (In the list of operas and the bibliography below, reference is made solely to works where the myth is of central rather than of passing importance.)

The plot surfaces often in the literature of ancient Greece and Rome, from the 6th century BC on. 'Allegorization' – that is, seeing in Orpheus more than a faithful lover and a successful musician – already appears in antiquity. The basic tale is told, fairly coherently, from the 3rd century BC (Phanocles) to the 2nd century AD (Hyginus); the most widely read accounts were those of Virgil (*Georgics*) and Ovid (*Metamorphoses*), though certain details transmitted by Hyginus (*Astronomica*) proved important for a number of composers from Monteverdi to Stravinsky.

The raw material for any Orpheus libretto or scenario is predominantly tragic. Eurydice is lost once, regained and lost again, and Orpheus is torn to pieces by the Bacchantes. In a poetic coda, his severed head and his lyre, floating in the water, still sing and sound; but these features tend to be revived only in non-operatic works (for example those by Berlioz, Carter and Tippett) rather than in operas because they are difficult to represent on the stage. On the other hand, the *lieto fine* ('happy ending') that seems to rule in the history of opera almost without exception from Peri and Monteverdi to Gluck and Beethoven can be achieved in two other ways. In either case the plot is radically altered, with Orpheus and Eurydice reunited at the end of the opera. Rinuccini (1600) was the first poet to perceive the advantages of this. Fux, Wagenseil and Gluck were among the composers who profited from his innovation. Another modification of the Orpheus plot was not so much radical alteration, but shift of emphasis: the finale of the opera stresses the immortality of Orpheus's music, and of music altogether as victorious over the ravages of time, by returning to the tales of ancient astronomy (Manilius, Hyginus). Orpheus and his lyre (or only his lyre) are transposed to the heavens. This 'apotheosis', as Stravinsky calls it, or 'stellification' is found in the operas of Monteverdi, Landi, Rossi and Keiser, and in Stravinsky's ballet of 1948, probably the most successful musical representation of the myth on the 20th-century stage (the operas of Krenek, Milhaud and Birtwistle notwithstanding). Debussy's *Orphée-Roi* remained unfortunately a mere project, as did Rameau's *Orphée aux enfers*.

In Peri's opera the librettist Rinuccini achieves his happy ending quite plausibly, not by the sudden intervention of a *deus ex machina*: there is no interdict against Orpheus's looking back, no second loss of Eurydice, no spurning of womanhood, no death of Orpheus. This 'reasonable' plot appealed to humanists, Aristotelians and other literary critics. Indeed Rinuccini's libretto remained well known and was copied in dramatic method as well as drawn on for individual lines throughout the next two centuries; it was still discussed and praised by Arteaga and Burney. Striggio's libretto for Monteverdi, on the other hand, concludes the action with a bacchanale of the spurned followers of Bacchus, a sound classical procedure but evidently not to the liking of Monteverdi, whose 1609 score ends with the ascent of Orpheus and Apollo to heaven. This score was studied by a few composers of the 17th century but does not seem to have been very popular with the public or impresarios: there are no recorded performances between 1607 and d'Indy's revival of 1904.

In Orpheus's pleading with Charon and the underworld in general (Monteverdi), in his intercession with the Furies (Gluck) and in his dealing with Hades and the Bacchantes (Stravinsky), the divine singer is represented by harp and soft strings opposed by a tutti, coloured by trombones, cornetts or both. The idea of the victory of music over opposing forces, represented by solo instruments with a characteristic sonority, was bequeathed largely by Gluck to subsequent composers. Recent research (Sternfeld 1988) has ventilated an Egyptian dimension to the Orpheus tradition which would create an analogy between the trials and tribulations of Tamino (using a magic flute) and of Orpheus. When speaking of influences Gluck is more to the point than Monteverdi because only his opera stayed continuously in the repertory from the staging of the Paris revision in 1774, and because his score was generally known long before the 20th-century revival of early opera.

The element of courtly or aristocratic entertainment was never far away from the Orpheus operas between Peri and Gluck; neither was the dimension of allegory and symbolism. Perhaps this latter was best expressed by Stravinsky when he played the final apotheosis of his ballet to Nicolas Nabokov (1947): 'Here in the Epilogue it sounds like a kind of ... compulsion, like something unable to stop ... Orpheus is dead, the song is gone, but the accompaniment goes on'.

For musicians, poets and philosophers the translation to the heavens of Orpheus's lyre, which provides the indispensable accompaniment to his song, stands for high matters, associated with the divine singer. It seems not too fanciful to speculate that the fascination of this myth for composers from the 17th century to the present was that it symbolized a belief in the miraculous continuity of that 'accompaniment' on the harp (or lyre). It is, of course, no mere accompaniment; rather it is the spirit of music itself which conquers time and death.

See also ANIMA DEL FILOSOFO, L' [Haydn]; CARNAVAL DE VENISE, LE [Campra]; EURIDICE (i) [Peri]; EURIDICE (ii) [Caccini]; FAVOLA DI ORFEO, LA [Casella]; MALHEURS D'ORPHÉE, LES [Milhaud]; MASK OF ORPHEUS, THE [Birtwistle]; MORTE D'ORFEO, LA [Landi]; ORFEIDE, L' [Malipiero]; ORFEO (i) [Monteverdi]; ORFEO (ii) [Rossi]; ORFEO (iii) [Sartorio]; ORFEO ED EURIDICE (i) [Gluck]; ORFEO ED EURIDICE (ii) [Bertoni]; ORPHÉE AUX ENFERS [Offenbach]; ORPHEUS [Benda]; ORPHEUS OG EURYDIKE [Naumann]; and ORPHEUS UND EURYDIKE [Krenek].

operas based on the Orpheus myth; anonymous versions and pasticcios are not included

J. Peri (1600, as Euridice); G. Caccini (1602, as Euridice); C. Monteverdi (1607); Belli (1616); Landi (1619, as La morte d'Orfeo); L. Rossi (1647); C. d'Aquino (1654); J. J. Löwe von Eisenach (1659, as Orpheus aus Thracien); A. Sartorio (1672); Locke (1673); G. di Dia (1676); F. della Torre (1677); J. P. Krieger (1683, as Orpheus und Euridice); Draghi (1683, as La lira d'Orfeo); M.-A. Charpentier (c1685, as La descente d'Orphée aux enfers)

Sabadini (1689, as Amor spesso inganna); L. Lully (1690); W. Goodson (1697); R. Keiser (1698, rev. 1699, 1709); Campra (1699, as Orfeo nell'Inferni: Act 3 of Le carnaval de Venise); Weldon (c1701, as Orpheus and Eurydice); Fux (1715, as Orfeo ed Euridice); Telemann (1726); Lampe (1740, as Orpheus and Eurydice); Rameau (c1740, as Orphée aux enfers, projected); Ristori (1749, as I lamenti di Orfeo); Wagenseil (1750, as Euridice); Graun (1752)

Gluck (1762, as Orfeo ed Euridice); Barthélemon (1767); Tozzi (1775, as Orfeo ed Euridice); Bertoni (1776, as Orfeo ed Euridice); L. Torelli (1781); F. Benda (1785); J. G. Naumann (1786, as Orpheus og Eurydike); Dittersdorf (1788, as Orpheus der Zweyte); Reichardt (1788, rev. of Bertoni, 1776); Trento (1789, as Orfeo negli Elisi); Haydn (comp. 1791, as L'anima del filosofo, ossia Orfeo ed Euridice, unperf.); Paer (1791, as Orphée et Euridice)

Winter (1792, as La mort d'Orphée et d'Euridice); Deshayes (1793, as Le petit Orphée, parody of Gluck); L. Lamberti (1796); F. Morolin (1796, as Orfeo ed Euridice); Dauvergne (before 1797, as La mort d'Orphée, unperf.); G. Bachmann (1798, as Der Tod des Orpheus); Carl Cannabich (1802); Kanne (1807); Kauer (1813, as Orpheus und Euridice); L. Sampieri (1814); Offenbach (1858, as Orphée aux enfers); G. Michaelis (1860, as Orpheus auf der Oberwelt)

K. F. Konradin (1867, as Orpheus im Dorfe); Godard (1887); Sélim (1902, as Orphée et Pierrot); F. de Azevedo e Silva (1907, as A morte d'Orpheus); Debussy (1907–16, as Orphée-roi, projected); Roger-Ducasse (1913, as Orphée); G. F. Malipiero (1925, pt 3 of the triptych L'Orfeide); Milhaud (1925, as Les malheurs d'Orphée); Krenek (1926, as Orpheus und Eurydike); Casella (1932, as La favola d'Orfeo); Birtwistle (1986, as The Mask of Orpheus)

*

H. C. Wolff: 'Orpheus als Opernthema', *Musica*, xv (1961), 423–5

N. Pirrotta: *Li due Orfei: da Poliziano a Monteverdi* (Turin, 1969, 2/1975; Eng. trans., as *Music and Theatre from Poliziano to Monteverdi*, 1982)

H. Knoch: *Orpheus und Eurydike: Der antike Sagenstoff in den Opern von Darius Milhaud und Ernst Krenek* (Regensburg, 1977)

R. Myers: 'The Opera that Never Was: Debussy's Collaboration with Victor Segalen in the Preparation of *Orphée*', *MQ*, lxiv (1978), 495–506

F. W. Sternfeld: 'The First Printed Opera Libretto', *ML*, lix (1978), 121–38

——: 'The Birth of Opera: Ovid, Poliziano and the *lieto fine*', *AnMc*, no.19 (1979), 30–51

B. R. Hanning: *Of Poetry and Music's Power: Humanism and the Creation of Opera* (Ann Arbor, 1980)

E. Rosand: 'L'Orfeo: the Metamorphosis of a Musical Myth', *Israel Studies in Musicology*, ii (1980), 101–20

S. Leopold: 'Haydn und die Tradition der Orpheus-Opern', *Musica*, xxxvi (1982), 131–5

E. Rosand: 'L'Ovidio trasformato', introduction to A. Aureli-A. Sartorio: *L'Orfeo*, DMV, vi (1983)

W. Osthoff: 'Contro le legge de' Fati: Polizianos und Monteverdis Orfeo als Sinnbild Künstlerischen Weltkampfs mit der Natur', *AnMc*, no.21 (1984), 11–68

C. A. Price: 'Orpheus in Britannia', *Music and Context: Essays for John Ward* (Cambridge, MA, 1985), 264–77

S. Leopold: 'Lyra Orphei', *Festschrift Reinhold Hammerstein* (Laaber, 1986), 337–45

J. Whenham, ed.: *Claudio Monteverdi: 'Orfeo'* (Cambridge, 1986)

S. Harris: 'The Significance of Ovid's *Metamorphoses* in Early Seventeenth-Century Opera', *MR*, xl (1988), 12–20

F. W. Sternfeld: 'Orpheus, Ovid and Opera', *JRMA*, cxiii (1988), 172–202   FREDERICK W. STERNFELD

Orpheus. Singspiel in three acts by Friedrich Benda (*see* BENDA family, (2)) to a libretto by Gottfried Ferdinand von Lindemann; Berlin, Corsika'scher Saal, 16 January 1785 (concert performance).

Unlike Calzabigi's, Lindemann's libretto retains Eurydice's rival Hersilia from the ORPHEUS legend. Spurned by Orpheus (tenor) as he grieves for his lost wife, Hersilia (soprano) leads a band of Bacchantes bent on his destruction, but he is restored to Eurydice (soprano) on Olympus. Benda's score is the most progressive and successful of the through-composed German serious operas of the mid-1780s. Many of its finest features bespeak Gluck's inspiration: a central role for the chorus (six different groups are called for), architectonic re-use of choral numbers, and simple cavatinas, rather than extensive arias, that flow into succeeding numbers. In Berlin the opera proved popular among those opposed to the Italian musical establishment at the Prussian court.   THOMAS BAUMAN

Orpheus og Eurydike ('Orpheus and Eurydice'). Singspiel in three acts by JOHANN GOTTLIEB NAUMANN to a libretto by Charlotte Dorothea Biehl after RANIERI DE' CALZABIGI; Copenhagen, Royal Opera, 31 January 1786.

At the Temple of Apollo the High Priest (bass) encourages Orpheus (tenor) as he prepares for the journey to Hades. A companion of Eurydice, Hersilia (soprano), comments on Eurydice's tragic death and on her own hopes of becoming Orpheus's new love. In Hades Orpheus pleads his case before Pluto (baritone) and Proserpina (soprano), and the latter persuades her husband to give up Eurydice, warning Orpheus not to look at Eurydice until they reach the upper world. Eurydice (soprano) and another shade (soprano) sing of the delights of the real world. Orpheus looks back at Eurydice as they leave Hades, and thus loses her; Hersilia tries to comfort him, but she and her Bacchante followers are rejected. As they are about to stab Orpheus, the high priest reappears and drives the Bacchantes away. At Apollo's command, Eurydice is restored.

Orpheus was intended to test Naumann's abilities before King Christian VII offered him an official appointment at the Danish court. The music was praised for its colourful harmonies and sensitive orchestration; Naumann uses Gluckian accompanied recitative throughout, while the choruses and arias range from expressive through-composed scenas to short, perfunctory lied forms. The orchestra consisted of 40 players at the première and included trombones, for which the theatre had to be enlarged. *Orpheus* remained on the stage in Copenhagen until December 1791, and, in addition to a vocal score in German translation (Hamburg, 1787), excerpts appeared in the catalogues of Dresden publishers until 1800.

See also ORPHEUS.   BERTIL H. VAN BOER

Orpheus und Eurydike ('Orpheus and Eurydice'). *Schauspiel* in three acts, op.21, by ERNST KRENEK after Oskar Kokoschka's play; Kassel, Staatstheater, 27 November 1926.

Kokoschka's expressionistic rendering of the Orpheus myth concerns the fate of creativity following the breakdown of the relationships between man, God and nature, and between the sexes. In his interpretation, the psycho-sexual crisis provoked by the 'love' of Orpheus (tenor) and Eurydice (soprano) is the product of their human fallibility and manipulation by a supernatural power. Death on various levels is the focal point of the text, which bears the wounds of Kokoschka's World War I experiences and his love affair with Alma Mahler. Eurydice's physical 'death' and her impregnation by the spirit of Hades in the underworld brings jealousy into the idealized sentiments of the lovers; her loss, through Orpheus's hatred, induces his psychic 'death' – the paralysis of his creative powers. Amor [Cupid] (silent role) and Psyche (soprano) function as archetypes of redemptive romantic love to which Kokoschka poses an alternative concept of regeneration through madness. Krenek's atonal musical setting of 1923 unifies and underpins the text by means of motifs (intervallic and, particularly, fourth chords), rhythmic ostinatos and pedal points, which enhance the play's symbolism and serve to reinforce the narrative framework. This framework is tightened by Krenek's adaptation of the spirit of Hades (who never actually appears or speaks in the original play) in the personae of a fool (baritone), drunk (bass), soldier (baritone) and sailor (tenor). Krenek's use of extremes in dynamics and colouration is as much a product of *fin-de-siècle* Vienna as is Kokoschka's psychoanalytically-saturated text.

See also ORPHEUS.   CHARLOTTE PURKIS

Orr, Robin [Robert] (**Kemsley**) (*b* Brechin, Angus, 2 June 1909). Scottish composer and teacher. He studied at the RCM, at Cambridge University and with Casella and Boulanger. He joined the music faculty at Cambridge in 1938, became professor of music at Glasgow University in 1956, then professor at Cambridge (1965–76). He was chairman of Scottish Opera from 1962 to 1976 and director of the WNO, 1977–83.

He wrote his one-act opera *Full Circle* for Scottish Opera as a companion piece to Stravinsky's *Histoire du Soldat*, and scored it for the same instruments plus viola. The libretto by Sydney Goodsir Smith, written in the Scottish vernacular, tells the story of a Clydesider, unemployed during the depression of the 1930s, who is driven by desperation to steal and ends up by being arrested for killing a policeman.

The libretto of *Hermiston*, by Bill Bryden, is based on R. L. Stevenson's unfinished novel *Weir of Hermiston*, and was also commissioned by Scottish Opera. Archie Weir (baritone), son of Lord Hermiston (bass), a famous 'hanging judge', witnesses a hanging. When he protests at the harshness of his father's judgments he is banished to the remote family estate. There he learns that his false friend Frank (tenor) has raped Christina (soprano), the girl he loves, and in his turn Archie is led to murder and to death on the gallows.

On the Razzle is based at two removes on the Nestroy comedy from which the musical *Hello Dolly!* derives. It was composed for student performance, with roles of varying weight and importance for a cast of more than 20 and with substantial choruses. The grocer Zangler (bass) visits Vienna to attend the annual parade of the Grocers' Company, taking his niece Marie (soprano) to keep her away from her lover Sonders (tenor); all make their way to Vienna, finding themselves continually at cross-purposes as the comedy of intrigue and mistaken identity develops.

In all three operas action is carried forward mainly in recitative and arioso, with few set pieces, the orchestral commentary providing continuity. In *Full Circle* and *Hermiston*, key motifs are closely worked, those associated with the main characters undergoing many transformations. *On the Razzle*, less tightly organized, pays tribute to the spirit of the Viennese waltz; Orr's score is clear and telling, his fine sense of dramatic pacing evident particularly in the scenes of vigorous action.

Full Circle (1, S. G. Smith), Perth, 10 April 1968
Hermiston (3, B. Bryden, after R. L. Stevenson), Edinburgh, King's, 27 Aug 1975
On the Razzle (3, Orr, after T. Stoppard's adaptation of J. N. Nestroy: *Einen Jux will er sich machen*), Glasgow, New Athenaeum, 27 June 1988

R. Orr: 'Full Circle', *MT*, cix (1968), 321–3
——: 'Hermiston', *MT*, cxvi (1975), 700–02   HUGO COLE

Orrego-Salas, Juan (Antonio) (*b* Santiago, 18 Jan 1919). Chilean composer. His initial musical training in Chile (1936–43) led to Guggenheim and Rockefeller grants for studies in the USA with Thompson and Copland (composition), Paul Henry Lang and George Herzog (musicology). Besides composing and writing, he was the founder and director of the Instituto de Extensión Musical at the Catholic University in Santiago, and of the Latin American Music Center at Indiana University (1961–88). Between 1943 and 1966, he wrote many vocal and choral works reflecting a neo-classical nationalism. His opera-oratorio of 1952, *El retablo del rey pobre*, to his own libretto after an *ensaladilla* by J. de Valdivielso (first given on 10 November 1990 at Indiana University, Bloomington), is a mystery play sung throughout, with dance and mime underlining the dramatic action. Orrego-Salas abandoned his second three-act opera, *El callejon de los ausentes*, as being too circumstantial in content (the Chilean coup of 1973), but he found a perfect symbolic allegory for his abstract musical ideas in Ariel Dorfmann's novel *Widows*. In Orrego-Salas's opera of the same name (composed 1990), set in a village in a Third World country a year after a military coup has deposed its democratically elected government, physical horror and death are juxtaposed with spiritual love and renewal as the six main characters and their representative sonorities enact the theme of memory.

V. Salas Viú: *La creación musical en Chile (1900–1951)* (Santiago, 1951)
G. R. Benjamin and J. E. Druesedow, jr: *The Music of Juan Orrego-Salas, 1936–1967* (Bloomington, IN, 1967)
L. Merino: 'Visión del compositor Juan Orrego-Salas', *Revista musical chilena*, nos.142–4 (1978)   GERALD R. BENJAMIN

Orrey, (Gilbert) Leslie (*b* West Hartlepool, 11 Sept 1908; *d* Bath, 20 Sept 1981). English writer on music. He studied at the RCM, London, and lectured at Morley College (1934–9) before being appointed head of the music department of Goldsmiths' College, London in 1945; he retired in 1969. He wrote a sympathetic study of Bellini in the Master Musicians series (London, 1969) and a *Concise History of Opera* (London, 1972) as well as editing *The Encyclopedia of Opera* (London, 1976).

Orrigoni, Marc'Antonio (*b* Milan; *fl* 1677–94). Italian soprano castrato. He first appeared in Milan in 1677 in

P. A. Ziani's *Attila* and Legrenzi's *Germanico sul Reno*. In the following year he sang in Carlo Pallavicino's *Vespasiano* at the Teatro S Giovanni Grisostomo in Venice. Thereafter until 1694 he was in Reggio Emilia, Modena, Bologna, Florence, Parma and Milan. By 1684 he was a virtuoso of the Duke of Modena. The peak of his career was probably between 1685 and 1690 when he appeared in the title roles of Perti's *Oreste in Argo* (Modena) and *L'incoronazione di Dario* (Bologna), and M. A. Ziani's *Alcibiade* (Modena); he also took part in the festivities in Parma for the marriage of Ranuccio II and Dorothea of Neuburg.

J. Rosselli: 'From Princely Service to the Open Market: Singers of Italian Opera and their Patrons, 1600–1850', *COJ*, i (1988), 1–32
      SERGIO DURANTE

Orsini [Orsino], Flavio (*b* Rome, 4 March 1620; *d* Rome, 5 April 1698). Italian librettist. From one of Rome's leading and wealthiest families (they vied only with the Colonnas), he became Duke of Bracciano on his father's death. Apparently a spendthrift, he was forced to sell almost all the Orsini property. He was especially interested in poetry, oratory, music and mathematics and in ancient stone inscriptions, of which he had a rare collection. In 1675 he received the Order of Santo Spirito from the French, but when he fell out with them in 1688 he turned to the Spanish, who gave him the Toson d'Oro. His first wife was Ippolita Ludovisi (widow of Prince Giorgio Aldobrandini); on her death he married Anna de la Trémouille (widow of Adriano Blasio di Talleyrand, Prince of Chalais). No children resulted from either marriage. Orsini's poetry was praised by Balducci, and he was also made a member of the Arcadian Academy (as Clearco Simbolico: he also used the anagram Filosinavoro). His libretti were all *opere regie*; one prologue for music is extant. Stradella and Alessandro Scarlatti are the only composers known to have set his texts to music, and all his works were probably performed privately. Flavio's brother, Lelio, wrote librettos mainly for oratorios.

Opere regie (arranged according to Mandosi ?in chronological order): *La gelosia*; *L'Adalinda*; *Ermenegilda finta schiava*; *Gli eventi d'amore*; *Il geloso ingannato*; *La Doriclea*, ?A. Stradella; *Le sventure di Lindauro*; *Il disperato amante*; *Il moro per amore*, Stradella, 1681; *La guerriera costante*, A. Scarlatti, 1683
Prologue: *Reggetemi, non posso più*, Stradella, ?1668

F. Balducci: 'Per don Flavio Orsino, figliuolo di don Ferdinando', *Rime* (Venice, 1663), 169
P. Mandosi: *Bibliotheca Romana seu Romanorum scriptorum centuriae*, ii (Rome, 1692), 108–10
Cesennio Issunteo [C. Doni]: 'Flavio Orsini', *Notizie istoriche degli arcadi morti*, iii (Rome, 1721), 172–4
P. Litta: *Famiglie celebri italiane*, fasc.lxii/118, 'Orsini di Roma, parte V ed ultima' (Milan, 1848), tavola xxix
C. Gianturco: *The Operas of Alessandro Stradella* (diss., U. of Oxford, 1970), 102–5
——: 'Sources for Stradella's *Moro per amore*', *Memorie e contributi alla musica dal medioevo all'età moderna*, ii (Bologna, 1971), 129–40
P. Fabbri: 'Questioni drammaturgiche del teatro di Stradella', *Chigiana*, xxxix (1988), 91–108   CAROLYN GIANTURCO

Ortega, Sergio (*b* Antofagasta, 2 Feb 1938). Chilean composer. He studied at the conservatory of the University of Chile, under G. B. Schmidt and Roberto Falabella, and became a professor there in 1969, taking over the artistic direction of the university television station the following year. In 1973 he left Chile to settle in France, where he was appointed head of the Ecole

Nationale de Musique at Pantin. His chamber opera *Un roi sans soleil* was given by the Atelier Lyrique (the opera workshop of the Opéra du Rhin) in 1974. He is a prolific composer of chamber works and songs (notably settings of Neruda), many of which have been heard at festivals of contemporary music, in Germany, Italy, Greece and elsewhere; he has also composed cantatas, 'contes musicales', film music and much incidental music for the theatre, many works of the 1960s being written for the Young Theatre of the University of Chile. A number of his works touch on social issues arising from his experiences in Chile. Several of his operas (some of which treat French Revolution themes, on the bicentenary) make use of children's voices; some are on a chamber music scale. An opera *Popol Vuh* (to a text by Adamante and Destal) was planned in commemoration of the quincentenary in 1992 of the discovery of America and another, *Pedro Páramo* (after the novel by Juan Rulfo), for Mexico Opera.

La dama del canasto (musical comedy, I. Aguirre), Santiago de Chile, 1965
Un roi sans soleil (chamber op, M. Rio), Colmar, 1974
La trace de tes mains (chamber op, C. Pöppelreiter, after P. Neruda), Berlin, 1980
Messidor (Adamante, G. Destal and S. Ortega), Argenteuil, 1988
Le Louis perdu (J. Gaucheron), Pantin, 1989
Les contes de la Révolution à Aubervilliers (F. Combes), Aubervilliers, 1989
Le dernier domineur (C. Monet), Chalon-sur-Saône, 1990

Ortega del Villar, Aniceto (*b* Tulancingo, Hidalgo, 1825; *d* Mexico City, 17 Nov 1875). Mexican composer. His father was the literary figure and statesman Francisco Ortega Martínez (1793–1849). He studied medicine in Mexico City, graduating in 1845. From 1849 to 1851 and again in 1869 he continued his medical studies in various European centres. An avid concert-goer, he became a founder member of the Sociedad Filarmónica Mexicana in 1866; the same year he was appointed director of the maternity hospital in Mexico City. His one-act opera, *Guatimotzín*, was first performed at the Gran Teatro Nacional on 13 September 1871, with Angela Peralta and Enrico Tamberlik in the leading roles. To a libretto by the Mexican novelist, dramatist and diplomat José Tomás de Cuéllar (1830–94), it concerns the defence of Mexico by the last Aztec ruler, Cuauhtémoc. The story departs from history by making Cuauhtémoc (Tamberlik) die when Cortés stabs him (he was in fact hanged after leading a conspiracy in Honduras). Local colour is supplied in the music for Cortés's Tlaxcalan allies, cast in the rhythm of a Huastecan *tzotzopizahuac*. The success of this first nationalist opera caused the composer to be hailed as the Mexican Glinka. A copy of the unpublished score is in the library of the Conservatorio Nacional de Música, Mexico City. Ortega also wrote a nationalistic *Marcha Zaragoza* (1867) and several piano pieces including *Invocación a Beethoven* (1867), a work which helped establish a vogue that culminated in the first Beethoven Festival in Mexico City in 1871.

ROBERT STEVENSON

Ortiz de Zárate, Eleodoro (*b* 29 Dec 1865; *d* Valparaíso, 1952). Chilean composer of Spanish and Italian descent. He studied at the National Conservatory in Santiago and in 1885 was awarded a scholarship to study at the Milan Conservatory (1887–9); he graduated with his opera *Juana la loca*. Back in Chile he intended to compete with Italian opera, which at that time was favoured by the Chilean public to the exclusion of all other music. *La florista de Lugano*, composed in about 1890 to his own Italian libretto, was the first Chilean opera to be staged in complete form. The plot concerns Osvaldo, a famous tenor, and his fiancée Blanca (soprano), a countess; he, however, loves a florist, Laura (soprano), who is betrothed to the fisherman Fabio (baritone). Osvaldo and Laura decide to escape in Fabio's boat, but Chinchilla (bass), in love with Blanca, betrays them and they drown. In the meantime Blanca's palace is burnt down by Chinchilla, and he and Blanca perish in the flames. The opera was first performed in Santiago in 1895, with moderate success. The music includes duets, arias, cavatinas, sentimental interludes, a tempest and a final apotheosis, but one can find 'no other traces than a decadent operatic Romanticism' (Salas).

Ortiz de Zárate's next opera, *Lautaro (la conquista) Chile: 1553–1558* (1899), was dedicated to the president of the Republic; it was performed in Santiago in 1902. It is the first part of a trilogy called *La araucana: Chile, 1553–1818*, based on the 16th-century poem *La araucana* by Alonso de Ercilla. *La Quintrala* and *Manuel Rodríguez* form the second and third parts, and both remain unperformed. In the first part, an Indian prince becomes the leader of the Araucanians and puts the Spanish conquest in peril. He is assassinated by an Indian-Spanish captain, who loves the prince's mistress.

During a stay in Europe (1905–13) Ortiz de Zárate composed the opera *Tasso y Leonora* and five symphonies. He also composed one other opera, *Mozart y María Antonieta*, and some chamber music. He was never recognized by his contemporaries, and his music has not been performed for more than half a century.

Juana la loca, 1889, Milan, Conservatory, perf. date unknown, lost
La florista de Lugano, c1890 (2, E. Ortiz de Zárate), Santiago, Municipal, 2 Nov 1895
La araucana: Chile, 1553–1818 (trilogy, after A. de Ercilla)
    Lautaro (la conquista) Chile: 1553–1558, comp. 1899 (3), Santiago, Municipal, 12 Aug 1902
    La Quintrala, unperf.
    Manuel Rodríguez, unperf.
Tasso y Leonora, 1905–13, ?unperf.
Mozart y María Antonieta, ?unperf.

V. Salas: *La creación musical en Chile, 1900–1951* (Santiago, 1951)
E. Pereira: *Historia de la música en Chile (1850–1900)* (Santiago, 1957)
M. Cánepa: *La opera en Chile (1839–1930)* (Santiago, 1976)
SAMUEL CLARO-VALDÉS

Orvieto. Italian city, in Umbria. The earliest known operatic performance was of *Rinaldo prigioniero* (text by F. Miedelchini) in August 1629. It was followed in autumn 1633 by *Il pianto di Rodomonte* (score in *I-Bc*) by A. M. Abbatini, *maestro di cappella* at the cathedral. In 1680 a group of 45 local nobles founded the Accademia della Città, also called the Accademia del Pubblico Teatro, or dei Misti, under the protection of Queen Christina of Sweden. In May of the same year the architect F. Sforzini rebuilt the communal theatre that had been erected in 1672, and provided four tiers of boxes. Musical and dramatic performances took place there from 1683 to 1792; among the most notable operas were Sacchini's *La contadina in corte* (Carnival 1778), Sarti's *Le gelosie villane* (Carnival 1788), Caruso's *Il poeta di villa* and Bernardini's *Le donne bisbetiche* (both Carnival 1791), and Cimarosa's *L'impresario in angustie* and *L'italiana in Londra* and Anfossi's *La maga Circe* (Carnival 1792). After a break in 1814 the academy was revived as the Accademia del Teatro della Fenice and it put on operas almost exclusively. From 1824 to 1841 at least 35 were performed, including works by Rossini, Bellini, Donizetti, Verdi, Luigi Ricci and Vincenzo Fioravanti. The academy ceased to function in 1851, lacking funds to renovate the theatre. In 1863 the architect V. Vespignani succeeded in building a new theatre; in 1921 it was named after Luigi Mancinelli, who was born in the city.

DEUMM (M. Pascale)

T. Piccolomini: *Il nuovo teatro di Orvieto* (Orvieto, 1866)

——: *Regolamento per il corpo musicale di Orvieto* (Orvieto, 1872)

——: *Il Teatro comunale di Orvieto e le pitture di C. Fracassini descritto e illustrato* (Orvieto, 1879)

R. Bonelli and L. Conti: 'L'Accademia del Teatro in Orvieto', *Bollettino della deputazione di storia patria per l'Umbria* (Perugia, 1946), 119–35

C. Ferri: 'Accademia "Nuova Fenice" di Orvieto', ibid, 136–41

——: 'L'archivio del Teatro Mancinelli', *Bollettino dell'Istituto storico artistico orvietano*, iii/1 (1947), 12–13

G. Ciliberti: *Antonio Maria Abbatini e la musica del suo tempo (1595–1679): documenti per una ricostruzione bio-bibliografica* (Perugia, 1986), 47–103   GALLIANO CILIBERTI

Osborne, Adrienne. *See* KRAUS-OSBORNE, ADRIENNE VON.

Osborne, Charles (Thomas) (*b* Brisbane, 24 Nov 1927). British writer on music and critic. He studied the piano, composition and singing privately in Brisbane and Melbourne, and moved to England in 1953. He was assistant editor of the *London Magazine* from 1958 before being appointed assistant literature director of the Arts Council in 1966 and director in 1971. Besides his writings on literary topics Osborne has written mainly on vocal music, particularly 19th-century opera, including a useful descriptive survey of Verdi's operas; he is also known as a critic and broadcaster.

The Complete Operas of Verdi (London, 1971)

ed. and trans.: *The Letters of Giuseppe Verdi* (London, 1971)

ed. and trans.: *Richard Wagner: Stories and Essays* (London, 1973)

Richard Wagner and his World (London, 1977)

The Complete Operas of Mozart (London, 1978)

The Complete Operas of Puccini (London, 1981)

The Dictionary of Opera (London, 1983)

Verdi: a Life in the Theatre (London, 1987)

The Complete Operas of Richard Wagner (London, 1990)   DAVID SCOTT

Osborne, Conrad L(eon) (*b* Lincoln, NE, 22 July 1934). American music critic. He was educated at Columbia University and also studied singing with Cornelius Reid and acting with Frank Corsaro. He has acted in the theatre and on TV and has sung baritone roles with various musical organizations in the New York area. As a writer, he was chief vocal critic and contributing editor of *High Fidelity* (1959–69), and New York music critic of the London *Financial Times* (1962–9). In 1970 he was appointed advisory editor of the *Musical Newsletter*.

Osborne has contributed numerous articles to publications in the USA and England, including detailed critical discographies of the operas of Verdi (1963), Mozart (1965), Wagner (1966–7) and Russian composers (1974–5) for *High Fidelity*, and articles and reviews for *Opus* (1984–). His chief interest is opera, and his background as a performer has strongly influenced his critical writing on the subject. Since the early 1970s he has devoted more of his time and interest to private singing teaching than to journalism. Osborne is widely regarded as one of the most discriminating vocal critics in the USA.   PATRICK J. SMITH

Osborne, Nigel (*b* Manchester, 23 June 1948). English composer. He studied with Leighton and Wellesz at Oxford, where he was musical director of several theatre companies. Although he was awarded the Radio Suisse Romande opera prize for his dramatic cantata *Seven Words* (1969–71), he did not complete a work for the stage until 1985. *Hell's Angels* (1986), the first work commissioned by Opera Factory, received much publicity and, because of the sensational nature of its subject matter, no little notoriety. Freeman's libretto interleaves an adaptation of Oskar Panizza's play *Das Liebeskonzil* – a fanciful account of divine retribution by syphilis inflicted on the court of the Borgia Pope Alexander VI in 1494 – with his own allegory of punishment by AIDS in a parallel situation of corruption today. The vocal line is basically a free arioso which occasionally proliferates into a short ensemble and only rarely develops into a shape as lyrical as that uttered by the first AIDS victim at the end of the work. More often it reverts to plain speech or to a partially notated parlando. An atmospheric background is provided by taped electronic sounds in the introduction and interludes, and by colouristic orchestral scoring, a prominent feature of which (in a central scene of papal debauchery) is a prolonged and unsophisticated percussion passage.

In spite of the lyrical illumination which occasionally emerges in solos and ensembles, *Hell's Angels* offers less convincing evidence of Osborne's skill as an opera composer than the two-act *The Electrification of the Soviet Union* (1987), which was commissioned jointly by Glyndebourne and the BBC. Essentially his compositional method is similar. Beginning with a suggestive taped background, layers of more precise meaning (i.e. colouristic instrumental textures, material associated with certain characters or ideas, and words spoken or sung in a more or less developed melodic line) are added or are periodically removed to reveal the background again. In *The Electrification*, however, the instrumental writing is much more sophisticated and elaborate, the spoken word restricted to an effectively empty-sounding epilogue and the melodic line wrought into a pleasingly regular series of songs of emotional significance for all the major characters. Though the literary quality of the text does not, paradoxically, ensure consistent verbal coherence when the words are set to music, Craig Raine's libretto is one of the most intelligent examples of its kind in recent British opera and has inspired a score of like-minded poetry and similar technical distinction.

Terrible Mouth, based on the life and work of Francisco Goya, takes place in a war hospital set up in a house belonging to a count of the *ancien régime*. In this work Osborne explores the relationship between singing and speaking: Goya the actor heightens speech to a point where it meets the speech-like singing of Goya the singer; the chorus, three actors and three singers provide an aural landscape for the protagonists, exploring in several dimensions the continuum of speaking to singing.

See also ELECTRIFICATION OF THE SOVIET UNION, THE.

Hell's Angels (2, D. Freeman, after O. Panizza: *Das Liebeskonzil*), London, Royal Court, 6 Jan 1986

The Electrification of the Soviet Union (2, C. Raine), Glyndebourne, 5 Oct 1987

Terrible Mouth (1, H. Barker), London, Almeida, 10 July 1992
GERALD LARNER

Osborn-Hannah, Jane (*b* Wilmington, OH, 8 July 1873; *d* New York, 13 Aug 1943). American soprano. She studied with Mathilde Marchesi in Paris and Rosa Sucher in Berlin, making her début at Leipzig in 1904 as Elisabeth (*Tannhäuser*). After appearances at Dresden, Berlin and Munich, in 1908 she sang Eva (*Die Meistersinger*) at Covent Garden. She made her Metropolitan début in 1910 as Elisabeth, and first sang at Chicago the same year as Nedda (*Pagliacci*). Her repertory included Elsa, Sieglinde, Gutrune, Desdemona, Butterfly, and Barbara in Victor Herbert's *Natoma*. She retired in 1914. Her voice, a lyric soprano, was not large, but pure-toned and managed with secure technique.

*

E. C. Moore: *Forty Years of Opera in Chicago* (New York, 1930)
R. Davis: *Opera in Chicago: a Social and Cultural History 1850–1965* (New York, 1966)   ELIZABETH FORBES

Osijek (Ger. Esseg). Town in Croatia. The name Osijek is documented from the 11th century; the German name, connected mainly with the period of the Austrian Empire, was not used after 1918. From the mid-18th century theatre performances took place in the old building in Tvrota (the Roman fortress) and from 1866 in the new building in the town. From the middle of the 19th century German companies brought opera and operetta to Osijek. The Hrvatsko narodno kazalište (Croatian National Theatre) company, founded in 1907 in the same building, toured locally with performances of *The Bartered Bride* and *Der Freischütz* in its first season, besides drama and operetta. The first works produced in the company's own theatre were operettas; the opera repertory was gradually extended thanks to the efforts of the conductors and directors Mirko Polič (1914–23) and Lav Mirski (1924–8, 1934–41, 1947–56). However, productions of opera went into abeyance between 1928 and 1937 because of financial difficulties, and the theatre's musical activity was restricted to operetta, always popular with the general public. Directors and conductors have included Vlado Kobler (1956–61), Dragutin Savin (1961–70), Antun Petrušić (1962–89) and Željko Miler (1970–90), and besides the standard works of the opera and operetta repertories, there have been productions of works by many Croatian composers.

The Annals of Chamber Opera and Ballet (founded in 1970 by Savin), a festival mainly of Croatian premières of contemporary repertory, is an important part of the city's operatic life; operas by Monteverdi, Mozart, Pergolesi and Salieri have been given, as well as works by Richard Rodney Bennett, Bjelinski, Britten, Bruči, Egk, Dallapiccola, Menotti, Papandopulo and Savin. The opera company of the National Theatre has often gone on tour, and has been a major cultural influence in Slavonia.

*

Spomen-knjiga o pedesetoj godišnjici narodnog kazališta u Osijeku 1907–1957 (Osijek, 1957) [commemorative volume celebrating the 50th anniversary of the founding of the National Theatre in Osijek]
M. Malbaša: 'Glazbeni život u Osijeku' [Musical Life in Osijek], *Osječki zbornik*, ix–x (1965), 137–87
D. Mucić: *Hrvatsko kazalište u Osijeku 1907* [The Croatian Theatre in Osijek 1907] (Osijek, 1967)
A. Petrušić: 'Analiza muzičkog repertoara Osječkog narodnog kazališta 1907–1967' [Analysis of the Musical Repertory of the Osijek National Theatre 1907–1967], *Kazalište*, iii/5 (1967), 52–4 [jubilee issue]
G. Gojković: 'Muzički teatar na Osječkoj pozornici u drugoj polovini 19. stoljeća' [Musical Theatre on the Osijek Stage in the Second Half of the 19th Century], *Četvrti znanstveni sabor Slavonije i Baranje, zbornik radova*, i (Osijek, 1984), 233–60 [lists operetta repertory 1859–1900 and opera repertory 1867–1900]
Kazališne tradicije grada Osijeka; HNK 1907–1982 [The Theatrical Traditions of the City of Osijek; the Croatian National Theatre 1907–1982] (Osijek-Novi Sad, 1984) [includes the complete repertory 1907–83]   KORALJKA KOS

Oslo. Capital of Norway. The city was founded about 1050 and officially known as Oslo until 1624, when it was renamed Christiania. From 1877 it was known as Kristiania, and in 1925 became Oslo again. Although many foreign performers made visits, including Mingotti's opera company in the mid-18th century, the first local dramatic society was not formed until 1764. The better-known Dramatiske Selskab, which gave entertainments and Singspiels, was established in 1780, reorganized in 1799 and disbanded in 1838; in 1825 it presented the first Norwegian Singspiel, Waldemar Thrane's *Fjeldeventyret*, at the Musikalske Lyceum (founded 1810).

Oslo began to replace Trondheim and Bergen as Norway's musical centre in the early 19th century. From 1827 there were occasional light opera performances at the Christiania Theatre. French works at first predominated, but Italian singers and musicians (including the conductor Paolo Sperati) were soon taken on, and there was a shift towards the Italian repertory, besides Mozart and Weber. From about 1860 this theatre (from 1899 the National Theatre) produced one new opera a year; operetta performances ('Offenbachiades') were given to finance the main productions. The first performance of a Wagner opera (*Tannhäuser*) occurred in 1876. Between 1899 and 1919, while under the directorship of Bjørn Bjørnson and the baton of Johan Halvorsen, the National Theatre mounted some 40 premières.

Between 1918 and 1921 the city had a permanent stage for opera, the Opéra Comique, but it was plagued by economic difficulties. In the 1920s and 30s, several German and Italian troupes visited Oslo; one German company brought Schjelderup's *Sturmvögel*. In 1950, the Norwegian Opera Company was formed. It gave frequent performances, and eventually the Norwegian National Opera opened in 1959 under the direction of Kirsten Flagstad. Sven Eliasson was appointed its General Director in 1990. The company is now wholly funded by the government, and gives about 75 opera performances a year as well as ballets.

The festival Oslo Sommeropera (founded 1983) gave the Norwegian premières of *Ariadne auf Naxos*, *La clemenza di Tito*, *La finta giardiniera* and *A Midsummer Night's Dream*; from 1990 it concentrated on the earlier repertory, under the title 'Monteverdi to Mozart'.

*

H. J. Huitfeldt: *Christiania theaterhistorie* (Copenhagen, 1876)
I. E. Kindem: *Den norske operas historie* (Oslo, 1941)
G. Brunvoll, ed.: *Operaens verden* [The World of Opera] (Oslo, 1980)   KARI MICHELSEN, ARVID VOLLSNES

Osnabrück. Town in Lower Saxony, northern Germany. In 1771 a section of the famous Seyler company played in the Marstall. The Theater an der Gildewart was built by 1800, and performances were given there from 1819 until 1909. Albert Lortzing worked in Osnabrück for six years from 1827. It was not until 1871 that a theatre for regular use was built; it was a small one, run by the Aktientheater Osnabrück company and taken over by the city in 1882. The Grosses Haus on the Domhof was begun in 1908 and opened on 29 September 1909. The *art nouveau* building was badly damaged in 1942 and destroyed in March 1945. Musical drama moved to the Blumenhalle, but economic difficulties led to its closure in 1949. After the currency reform and with the rebuilding of the theatre, local interest revived, and the theatre was reconstructed in its original form (639 seats); it opened on 9 September 1950. Among the artists who have worked in Osnabrück are Oscar Fritz Schuh and Kurt Pscherer.

SABINE SONNTAG

Osorio, José María (1803–52). Venezuelan composer, whose *El maestro Rufo zapatero* (1847), an opera with spoken interludes, has been reckoned the first opera by a Venezuelan composer. The score was printed in Osorio's shop in Mérida in 1845, but only fragments survive, and the circumstances of its first performance are uncertain. For further information *see* CARACAS.

Ossi, Giovanni (*fl* 1716–34). Italian mezzo-soprano castrato. He was one of the most active pupils of Francesco Gasparini, whose works he sang in Rome between 1716 (*Ciro*) and 1720. He sang for Prince Ruspoli and was a virtuoso of Prince Borghese (1718–32) and a member of the Confraternity of S Cecilia, of which he was warden in 1735–6. According to Luigi Nerici (*Storia della musica in Lucca*, 1879) he was a member of the papal chapel. His career was spent mainly in Rome, but he also sang in Naples and Venice. He had a low voice for a castrato, from *b*♭ to *g″*, a compass particularly attractive to Leonardo Vinci, who wrote the part of Megabyzus in his *Artaserse* for Ossi, and to Vivaldi, who cast Ossi in the works he wrote for the Teatro Capranica in Rome (*Ercole su'l Termodonte*, *Giustino* and *La virtù trionfante dell'amore, e dell'odio*). Ossi's range and voice quality were similar to those of Vivaldi's pupil Anna Girò.

*

F. Piperno: 'F. Gasparini, le sue abitazioni romane, i suoi allievi coabitanti', *Esercizi: arte, musica, spettacolo*, iv (1981), 104–15
R. Strohm: 'Vivaldi's Career as an Opera Producer', *Antonio Vivaldi: teatro musicale, cultura e società: Venice 1981*, 11–66
F. Della Seta: 'I Borghese: la musica di una generazione', *NA*, new ser., i (1983), 139–208
D. E. Monson: 'The Trail of Vivaldi's Singers: Vivaldi in Rome', *Nuovi studi vivaldiani: edizione e cronologia critica delle opere*, ed. A. Fanna and G. Morelli (Florence, 1988), 563–89

FRANCO PIPERNO

Ossiach. Small town in Carinthia, southern Austria. It is the home of the Carinthian Summer festival, held annually from June to August. On 25 June 1969 the pianist Wilhelm Backhaus gave a recital in the Stiftskirche in Ossiach, signalling the start of a new musical tradition in southern Austria. Under the guidance of Helmut Wobisch, further performances soon crystallized into a festival at the highest international level. Celebrated performers make regular appearances and the informal rural atmosphere allows direct contact between artists and audience. Since Wobisch's death in 1980 Dr Gerda Fröhlich has managed the festival and developed its ideas. The chief venue is the splendid Baroque Stiftskirche, and adjoining Benedictine monastery, now a hotel, and the pro-

gramme focusses on works of a solemn or sacred nature. With the building in 1974 of the Kongresshaus (1042 seats) in the nearby town of Villach orchestral concerts and performances by visiting opera ensembles, such as the Warsaw Chamber Opera and Moscow Chamber Opera, began to take place.

A permanent feature since 1974 has been the continuance of church opera productions in the Stiftskirche, in particular the church parables of Britten. In addition, theatrical works by Handel, Vivaldi, P. A. Ziani and Mysliveček have been performed. Among Austrian works written specially for Ossiach are Cesar Bresgen's *Das Spiel vom Menschen* (1982), Herbert Lauermann's *Simon* (1984), Karl Heinz Füssl's *Kain* (1986) and Dieter Kaufmann's *Bruder Boleslaw* (1989).

HARALD GOERTZ

Ossian, ou Les bardes ('Ossian, or The Bards'). *Opéra* in five acts by JEAN-FRANÇOIS LE SUEUR to a libretto by Palat (known as P. Dercy) and Jacques-Marie Deschamps after James Macpherson's Ossianic epic; Paris, Opéra, 10 July 1804.

It is still sometimes claimed that the subject of *Ossian* was suggested to Le Sueur by Napoleon, an enthusiastic reader of the Scottish bard, but this is inaccurate: the idea had first come to Le Sueur in the final years of the 18th century, before he knew Napoleon personally. The vogue for Ossianic poetry in late 18th-century Europe is well known; it was particularly popular in France, where Macpherson's text had been popularized by Le Tourneur's translation of 1777. However, no opera had been composed on the subject before 1800, and Le Sueur had the privilege of introducing Celtic and Scandinavian mythology to the French operatic stage. He and his librettist Dercy thought briefly of offering it to the Théâtre Feydeau, because of the difficulties in getting his work performed at the Opéra. Finally, after a struggle lasting at least five years, *Ossian* had its première at the Opéra, exactly two months after the Empire was proclaimed in May 1804. This work, which with Spontini's *La vestale* was the Opéra's greatest theatrical success between 1804 and 1815, brought its composer fame. Le Sueur had recently been appointed by Napoleon to be musical director of the Tuileries Chapel; he now became the most prominent composer of the new regime.

Dercy and, after his death, Deschamps, who revised the work thoroughly, adapted the libretto freely from the Ossianic epic; they endeavoured to retain its sombre and fantastic colouring, but though the framework remained indisputably Ossianic, the plot, almost all of it newly invented, had very little to do with Le Tourneur's French translation. The basic theme is the rivalry between the Caledonians and the Scandinavians. The latter, led by their chieftain Duntalmo (bass), have invaded and conquered Caledonia (Scotland). The Caledonian bards and their chieftain Hydala (countertenor) are thus prisoners of the Scandinavian invaders on their own soil. The heroine Rosmala (soprano), daughter of the old bard Rozmor (bass) and betrothed to Ossian (tenor), is a prisoner of the Scandinavians and of Duntalmo, who intends to marry her against her will to his son Mornal (tenor). The main part of the plot thus centres on the conquest of Caledonia and Ossian's rescue of his imprisoned fiancée. The opera ends with the reconciliation of the two warring tribes, and there is a concluding *chaconne*, in the purest 18th-century tradi-

Costume designs by Jean-Simon Barthélémy for the original production of Le Sueur's 'Ossian, ou Les bardes' at the Paris Opéra, 10 July 1804; on the right is one of the designs for Ossian himself

tion, in which the antagonistic themes of the Caledonians and Scandinavians are briefly superimposed.

Compared to Le Sueur's previous operas, *Ossian* represents a break with traditional forms; the difference between recitative and aria is often blurred in favour of a kind of arioso style. The recitative is punctuated by frequent changes of metre and tempo which reinforce its expressivity and give it greater dramatic significance. The arias, on the other hand, tend to be less developed than in the earlier operas, and are often very free in structure: there are no more grand arias constructed as two-part Allegros (as, earlier, in *La caverne*). The choruses are of great importance throughout the opera, with a double chorus frequently employed, and the orchestration is often original. The harp, the Ossianic instrument *par excellence*, features prominently in the orchestra; indeed, Le Sueur used 12 harps (much of their music being written in two parts) to accompany the singing of the bards.

Among those passages which incontestably make *Ossian* a pre-Romantic opera are the remarkable Prophecy of the bards against Duntalmo (Act 3 scene viii) and the famous scene of the Dream of Ossian in Act 4, for which Le Sueur and his librettist had no model in the Ossianic epic. Ossian, alone in his prison and condemned to death, falls asleep. In his dream, he sees the walls of his dungeon open up and his soul rise to the abode of his ancestors, where the dead heroes of his race are being ministered to by young women who prefigure the Valkyries of the Wagnerian Valhalla. This fine choral passage, tinged with mysticism and esotericism, was set off by some remarkable scenery that delighted all Le Sueur's contemporaries and probably served Ingres as the model for his famous canvas *Le songe d'Ossian*. The phantasms of the dream, embodied on stage, marked the opening of a new chapter in the history of French sensibility.

The score of *Ossian* shows strokes of brilliance, although it also contains passages that are musically rather flat and will no doubt preclude any idea of reviving the work as a whole. Many excerpts are nonetheless deserving of closer study, while historically the work constitutes an essential link in a chain leading gradually from Classical to Romantic opera.   JEAN MONGRÉDIEN

Osten, Eva von der (*b* Heligoland, 19 Aug 1881; *d* Dresden, 5 May 1936). German soprano. She studied in Dresden, where she made her début at the Hofoper in 1902 as Urbain (*Les Huguenots*). She remained a member of the company until her farewell performance in 1927 as Brünnhilde (*Die Walküre*). Her most notable creation there was Octavian (for illustration *see* DRESDEN, fig.8), and she was also the first Dresden Ariadne, Dyer's Wife, Kundry, Tatyana and Maliella (*I gioielli della Madonna*). She was the first Covent Garden Octavian (1913) and Kundry (1914); she also appeared as Ariadne at His Majesty's Theatre in 1913. She toured the USA with the German Opera Company (1922–4), as Isolde and Sieglinde. Her large repertory also included Senta, Carmen, Louise, Tosca and Zazà. Osten's acting and beauty were much admired, as was her fine dramatic soprano voice. She was married to the bass-baritone Friedrich Plaschke.   HAROLD ROSENTHAL/R

Osterc, Slavko (*b* Veržej, 17 June 1895; *d* Ljubljana, 23 May 1941). Slovene composer. After lessons with Beran, a pupil of Janáček, he studied with Novák and Hába at the Prague Conservatory (1925–7). He then taught at both the conservatory and the academy in Ljubljana, establishing himself as a leader of Slovene musical life; he was particularly active in the ISCM. Osterc used a wide range of techniques, many of which are reflected in his operas. *Krst pri Savici* ('Baptism at the Savica Waterfall', composed 1921) is a through-composed, richly orchestrated tonal work in three acts. In direct contrast to this his next opera, *Iz komične opere* ('From the Comic Opera', 1928), in one act, is performed by an ensemble of five musicians, employs *Sprechstimme* and is atonally and polytonally linear. A similar, yet more homophonic and arioso approach is apparent in *Krog s kredo* ('The Chalk Circle', composed 1928–9). With his last three operas Osterc introduced into Slovene music the 'opéra minute' – a type of opera composed slightly earlier by Milhaud, with conciseness of libretto and musical treatment; behind their expressiveness lies an intellectual rigour.

Krst pri Savici [Baptism at the Savica Waterfall], 1921 (3, S. Osterc and G. Šilih, after Prešeren), radio broadcast, 3 Jan 1961
Iz komične opere [From the Comic Opera] (comic op, 1, Osterc, after H. Murger), Ljubljana, 9 Nov 1928

Krog s kredo [The Chalk Circle], 1928–9 (5, M. Skrbinšek, after
  Klabund), unperf.
Salome, 1919–30 (operatic parody, 1, Osterc), unperf.
Medea, 1930 (1, Osterc, after Euripides), Ljubljana, 27 Feb 1932
Dandin v vicah [Dandin in Purgatory] (grotesque op, 1, Osterc, after
  Molière and H. Sachs), Ljubljana, 27 Feb 1932

*

DEUMM (P. Derossi)
S. Osterc: 'Minutna opera', Nova muzika, ii (1929–30)

ANDREJ RIJAVEC

Osthoff, Wolfgang (b Würzburg, 17 March 1927). German musicologist. He studied at Frankfurt, where his father Helmut Osthoff was among his teachers, and at Heidelberg, where he took the doctorate; his dissertation (1954) was published as *Das dramatische Spätwerk Claudio Monteverdis* (Tutzing, 1960). After research in Italy he taught in Munich, where he completed his *Habilitation* in 1965 with a study, later published, *Theatergesang und darstellende Musik in der italienischen Renaissance* (Tutzing, 1969). He became professor at Würzburg in 1968. A central figure in German operatic studies, his work has ranged unusually widely, his publications treating areas from Monteverdi, Cesti and Venetian opera of the 17th century generally and Alessandro Scarlatti, through Metastasian drama and Mozart, to Verdi and Wagner; he has written extensively on Pfitzner and contributed to the discussion of opera production techniques.

Östman, Arnold (b Malmö, 24 Dec 1939). Swedish conductor. He studied first art history, then music, in Paris and in Stockholm, where later he taught at the Musikhögskölan. He was music director at the academy at Vadstena in southern Sweden, 1970–82, where he fostered the study and performance of Baroque opera, notably works by Monteverdi and Stradella, and in 1979 became music director of the Drottningholm court theatre near Stockholm, where he remained until 1991. There he directed many performances, in particular of Mozart's operas but also of works by Gluck, Kraus and others, on period instruments. A production of Cimarosa's *Il matrimonio segreto* that he conducted in 1983 at Cologne, also seen in Washington, DC, and London, won much praise for its spirit and style. The next year he made his Covent Garden début, in *Don Giovanni*, since when he has conducted widely in Europe, chiefly in a Classical repertory but also in operas by Rossini, notably a *Cenerentola* at Dresden in 1991. He conducted *Lucio Silla* at the Vienna Staatsoper in 1990. Östman's recordings of the three Da Ponte-Mozart operas, made in the late 1980s, set new standards in period-style performance of these works and did much to enhance general awareness of the advantages of light instrumental textures, lively tempos, stylish ornamentation and observation of the obligatory appoggiaturas. *Così fan tutte*, the first to appear, attracted criticism for its tempos (often substantially faster than traditional ones), as have many of his performances; but some mild moderation of his approach, coupled with an increasing public sympathy with his artistic aims, led to the two other recordings receiving critical and general praise as well as winning a number of awards.

STANLEY SADIE

Ostrava (Ger. Ostrau, later Mährisch Ostrau). City in northern Moravia. Only at the end of the 19th century was Czech theatre music first performed in this industrial town. Theatre companies, which also presented operas and operettas, were allowed to play in the Národní dům (National House) between 1894 and 1918. The town theatre was built in 1906–7 by Alexander Graf; enlarged in 1942, 1955, and in 1971 (by Ivo Klimeš), it now has 874 seats. Originally it served as a German theatre. In 1919–20 performances in Czech and German alternated and it was called the Národní divadlo moravsko-slezské (National Moravian-Silesian Theatre). From 1920 performances were given in Czech, except between 1938 and 1945 when they were given in German only. After World War II the name of the theatre changed to Zemské divadlo v Ostravě (Provincial Theatre in Ostrava); it opened in 1946 with Smetana's *Libuše*. In 1948 the theatre was nationalized as the Státní divadlo Zdeňka Nejedlého (Zdeněk Nejedlý State Theatre) and presented only opera and ballet. Since 1990 this theatre has been known as the Divadlo Antonína Dvořáka (Antonín Dvořák Theatre). Plays and operettas were staged in a second, smaller house, Lidové divadlo (People's Theatre – since 1954 the Divadlo Jiřího Myrona).

Under Emanuel Bastl (1918–27) a Czech opera ensemble was created. It had a remarkable repertory (the first Smetana cycle was staged in 1924), giving special attention to contemporary works, above all Janáček. Soon the conductor Jaroslav Vogel (1927–44) brought the company to the forefront of Czech musical culture, with a notable repertory of German and Russian operas (Wagner, Strauss, Musorgsky, Rimsky-Korsakov), and modern Czech works, again focussing on Janáček. After 1945, such conductors as Zdeněk Chalabala (1945–7), Rudolf Vašata (1949–56), Bohumil Gregor (1958–62) and Zdeněk Košler (1962–6), and singers including Ivo Žídek (1945–8) and Ludmila Dvořáková (1949–54), performed a wide selection of classical and modern works. The première of the children's opera *Kolotoč* ('Merry-go-round') by Václav Trojan was given in 1960, and Václav Kašlík's *Krakatit* in 1961.

*

F. M. Hradil: 'Ostravsko v hudbě a zpěvu' [The Ostrava Region in Music and Singing], *Od Ostravice k Radhošti* (Ostrava, 1941)
60 let Státního divadla v Ostravě 1919–1979 [60 Years of the State Theatre in Ostrava] (Ostrava, 1979)   EVA HERRMANNOVÁ

Ostrčil, Otakar (b Prague, 25 Feb 1879; d Prague, 20 Aug 1935). Czech composer, conductor and musical director. He studied composition privately with Fibich from 1895, helping the latter with the orchestration of some of his works as well as in preparing the vocal score of the opera *Bukovín*. Although he worked initially as a professor of Czech and German in Prague (1903–19), from 1909 he appeared as a guest conductor at the National Theatre, and between 1914 and 1919 was musical director at the Vinohrady Theatre. He then joined the staff of the National Theatre as Dramaturg and succeeded Kovařovic as musical director in 1920; remaining there until his own death, he contributed to the theatre's most fruitful period of opera production. In addition he taught conducting at the Prague Conservatory (1926–9) and founded the Opera Studio there.

A constant feature of every aspect of Ostrčil's artistic activity was a concern for the development of modern music; he introduced works such as Foerster's *Debora* and Zich's *Malířský nápad* ('A Painter's Whim') to the Vinohrady Theatre. However, his principal achievements were at the National Theatre, where he built up an exemplary basic repertory extending from Gluck through Mozart, Beethoven, Verdi and Bizet to Wagner

785

and Strauss. In the sphere of Czech music he revived the classics and included cycles of operas by Smetana (1924, 1927 and 1934), Dvořák (1929 and 1934), Fibich (1925 and 1932), Foerster (1929) and Novák (1930). He conducted a new production of *Jenůfa* in 1926, gave the première of *The Excursions of Mr Brouček* and introduced all Janáček's postwar operas to Prague immediately after their first performances in Brno. Among other Czech stage works whose premières he conducted were Zich's *Vina* ('The Sin', 1922) and *Preciézky* ('Les précieuses', 1926), Rudolf Karel's *Ilseino srdce* ('Ilsa's Heart', 1924), E. F. Burian's *Před slunce východem* ('Before Sunrise', 1925), Jeremiáš's *Bratři Karamazovi* ('The Brothers Karamazov', 1928) and Karel Hába's *Jánošík* (1934). He also gave the first performances in Czechoslovakia of important foreign works, including *Pelléas et Mélisande* (1921), Max Brand's *Maschinist Hopkins* (1930) and Szymanowski's *King Roger* (1932). For his conducting of *Wozzeck* in 1926 he was awarded the Czech State Prize for the following year, although conservative factions incited a demonstration in the theatre and unleashed a lengthy controversy in the daily and specialist press.

Ostrčil's approach to conducting was rational: he calculated everything down to the smallest detail, producing measured performances devoid of impulsive outbursts. He was largely responsible for establishing the modern performing practice for Smetana's operas, and recorded *The Bartered Bride* for HMV in 1933. Besides presenting works of the standard operatic repertory and of contemporary Czech composers, he helped to guide the leading Czech opera singers of his time, including Ada Nordenová, Emil Burian, Otakar Mařák, Vilém Zítek and Emil Pollert, and brought the orchestra to an extremely high standard; he worked regularly with the stage manager Ferdinand Pujman and the scene-painter František Kysela. Thus he shaped a whole era in the development of the National Theatre.

Ostrčil's compositions show a development in style from late Romanticism to the expressionism of the interwar years. Together with Janáček, Novák, Suk and Foerster, he helped Czech music evolve from nationalism to the avant garde. He had a special flair for instrumentation, and orchestral pieces predominate in his modest output. A self-critical composer in whom the rational takes precedence over the emotional – just as in his conducting – he left only 25 compositions with opus numbers. In addition to the early *Jan Zhořelecký*, with its libretto drawn from 14th-century Czech history, and two uncompleted projects (*Rybáři*, 'The Fishers', 1893; *Cymbeline*, 1899), he wrote five operas. *Vlasty skon* ('The Death of Vlasta', 1904) is a work of genuine Czech Romanticism and shows an indebtedness to Fibich, especially in Ostrčil's use of a Czech mythological theme – it tells the story of the 'maidens' war' from the end of Fibich's *Šárka*. *Kunálovy oči* ('Kunála's Eyes', 1908) and *Legenda z Erinu* ('The Legend of Erin', 1921) both have texts by the Czech symbolist Julius Zeyer. It was not simply the exotic themes of ancient India or of Irish mythology that attracted Ostrčil: he concentrated above all on expressing in dramatic form the ethical aspects and emotional richness of the texts, especially where they concern the fundamental questions of guilt and forgiveness. He followed the spirit of Mahler rather than of Richard Strauss, but the structures of both *Kunálovy oči* and *Legenda z Erinu* are still based on the principles of Wagner and Smetana.

Between these two philosophical dramas Ostrčil wrote the one-act opera *Poupě* ('The Bud', 1911), a direct setting of a Svoboda play, whose entertaining story from everyday life concerns the amorous whims of a teenage girl; the music underlines the lightness of the small talk and good-natured humour and follows sensitively each subtle change of mood. *The Bud* is among the most original 20th-century Czech compositions for the stage. *Honzovo království* ('Johnny's Kingdom', 1934) lacks the complex and altered harmony of the earlier works, and makes much use of folksongs. The simple Tolstoyan theme of faith in the victory of good over evil symbolizes in legendary guise the conditions in Europe on the eve of World War II, and the work embodies Ostrčil's personal belief in democracy and humanism.

See also HONZOVO KRÁLOVSTVÍ.

Rybáři [The Fishers], 1893 (J. Prušák), inc.
Jan Zhořelecký, 1896–8 (3, A. Šetelík), extracts, Prague, Smetana Museum, 7 March 1939
Cymbeline, 1899 (F. Zákrejs, after W. Shakespeare), inc.
Vlasty skon [The Death of Vlasta] op.5 (3, K. Pippich), Prague, National, 14 Dec 1904
Kunálovy oči [Kunála's Eyes] op.11 (3, K. Mašek, after J. Zeyer), Prague, National, 25 Nov 1908
Poupě [The Bud] op.12 (comic op, 1, F. X. Svoboda), Prague, National, 25 Jan 1911
Legenda z Erinu [The Legend of Erin] op.19 (4, Zeyer), Brno, National, 16 June 1921
Honzovo království [Johnny's Kingdom] op.25, 1928–33 (prol., 7 scenes, J. Mařánek, after L. N. Tolstoy), Brno, National, 26 May 1934

*

O. Zich: 'Kunálovy oči', *HR*, i (1908), 465–77
O. Payer: *Ottokar Ostrčil und die tschechische Opernbühne unserer Tage* (Prague, 1912)
J. Hutter: *Legenda z Erinu* (Prague, 1923)
Památce Otakara Ostrčila [In Memory of Otakar Ostrčil] (Prague, 1935)
J. Bartoš: *Otakar Ostrčil* (Prague, 1936)
Rok po premiéře Honzova království [A Year After the Première of *Johnny's Kingdom*] (Prague, 1936)
A. Rektorys: 'Repertoir Otakara Ostrčila na Národním divadle v roku 1919–1935' [The Ostrčil Repertory at the National Theatre, 1919–35], *Smetana*, i (1936–7), 124–8
J. Hutter and Z. Chalabala, eds.: *České umění dramatické*, ii: *Zpěvohra* [Czech Dramatic Art: Opera] (Prague, 1941), 291–300
A. Rektorys: *Korespondence L. Janáčka s O. Ostrčilem* (Prague, 1948)
——: *Korespondence Otakara Ostrčila s Vilémem Zítkem* (Prague, 1951)
J. Válek: *Vznik a význam Honzova království* [The Origin and Significance of *Johnny's Kingdom*] (Prague, 1952)
A. Rektorys: 'Otakar Ostrčil a Leoš Janáček', *HRo*, vi (1953), 620–21
V. Lébl: 'Dramatická tvorba Otakara Ostrčila a její jevištní osudy' [Ostrčil's Dramatic Work and its Fate on the Stage], *Divadlo*, x (1959), 294–302, 333–9
F. Pala and V. Pospíšil: *Opera Národního divadla v období Otakara Ostrčila* [The National Theatre Opera in Ostrčil's Time] (Prague, 1962–89)
J. Válek: 'Technické prostředky hudební mluvy Otakara Ostrčila' [The Technical Devices of Ostrčil's Musical Language], *HV*, ii (1965), 594–615; iii (1966), 74–87, 292–303
Bibliografie Otakara Ostrčila (Prague, 1971)
OLDŘICH PUKL, EVA HERRMANNOVÁ

Ostrobothnians, The. Opera by Leevi Madetoja; *see* POHJALAISIA.

Ostrovsky, Alexander Nikolayevich (*b* Moscow, 31 March/12 April 1823; *d* Shchelïkovo, Kostroma province, 2/14 June 1886). Russian dramatist. While his plays cover a very wide range of style and subject matter, from historical costume dramas in verse to fairy-tales, he is chiefly associated with the realist tendency, and in particular with the portrayal of life among the Moscow merchant class, the social environment in which he was brought up. A great connoisseur of Russian folklore, he participated (along with the composer Konstantin Vil'boa) in a collecting expedition along the Volga (1856), and studded his dramas liberally with Russian folk verses, sometimes even specifying the tunes to be sung, thus providing prospective composers with many stimulating cues.

Ostrovsky's interest in professional music was primarily focussed on Italian opera and bel canto singing, of which he was also an acknowledged connoisseur as well as an amateur practitioner. This made for a peculiar situation in which he was eager to collaborate with musicians, but got along poorly with the more progressive ones – precisely those most inclined to seek him out. His most successful joint venture was with Vladimir Kashperov, an Italian-trained imitator of Donizetti. His least successful was with Alexander Serov, ending in a veritable scandal over changes the composer insisted on making, not only in the libretto, but in the actual plot of the play on which the libretto was based (*Live Not the Way you'd Like, but as God Commands*, 1855). Of the five acts in Serov's finished opera *Vrazh'ya sila* ('The Power of the Fiend'), only the first three were by Ostrovsky; the fourth and fifth were by hacks commissioned by the composer against the wishes of the author, who under existing Russian law had no right to prevent the adaptation. A contretemps also marred Ostrovsky's working relationship with the young Tchaikovsky, who lost the libretto Ostrovsky had kindly made him gratis from his play *Voyevoda* ('The Provincial Governor', 1865), and who therefore had to write the text of the second and third acts of his first opera himself.

Ostrovsky's most famous play, *The Storm* (1859), has served as subject for a number of operas besides Kashperov's, the best known being Janáček's *Kát'a Kabanová*. It is less widely known that one of the play's crucial scenes, Katerina Kabanova's farewell and oath to her departing husband, was interpolated by Shostakovich and his librettist Alexander Preys into the scenario of *Lady Macbeth of the Mtsensk District*, otherwise ostensibly derived from a novella by Nikolay Leskov, as part of a general effort to soften Leskov's grim portrayal of the murderess Katerina Izmaylova, and to cast her, like Ostrovsky's Katerina, in the role of a victim.

In addition to adapting his own plays for his musical acquaintances, Ostrovsky also acted as librettist for Mikhail Ippolitov-Ivanov, supplementing Alexey Tolstoy's text for the biblical opera *Ruth* (1887).

all plays

Bednost' ne porok [Poverty is no Vice] (1854): N. N. Tcherepnin, 1937, as Svat [The Matchmaker]
Ne tak zhivi kak khochetsya, a tak kak bog velit [Live Not the Way you'd Like, but as God Commands] (1855): Serov, 1871, as Vrazh'ya sila [The Power of the Fiend]
Groza [The Storm] (1859): V. N. Kashperov, 1867; Janáček, 1921, as Kát'a Kabanová; B. V. Asaf'yev, comp. 1939–40; V. N. Trambitsky, 1941; L. Rocca, 1952, as L'uragano; I. I. Dzerzhinsky, 1956; V. V. Pushkov, 1972
Voyevoda/Son na Volge [The Provincial Governor/A Volga Dream] (1865): Tchaikovsky, 1869, as Voyevoda; Arensky, 1890, as Son na Volge
Tushino (1867): P. I. Blaramberg, 1895, as Tushintsï [Inhabitants of Tushino]

Les [The Forest] (1871): N. S. Kogan, 1954; R. Liebermann, 1987, as La forêt
Komik XVII stoletiya [A Comedian of the 17th Century] (1872): Blaramberg, 1908, as Skomorokh [The Minstrel]
Snegurochka: vesennyaya skazka-feyeriya [The Snow Maiden: a Springtime Fairy-Tale] (1873): Rimsky-Korsakov, 1882; V. M. Orlov, 1895, as Snegurka
Bespridannitsa [The Bride without a Dowry] (1879): A. P. Novikov, comp. 1941–5; D. G. Frenkel, 1959
Talantï i poklonniki [Artists and Admirers] (1882): S. Oliver, 1983, as Sasha

*

V. Yakovlev: 'Ostrovsky i muzïkal'naya stikhiya' [Ostrovsky and the Musical Element], *Ostrovsky 1823–1923* (Moscow, 1923)
M. Ippolitov-Ivanov: *50 let russkoy muzïki v moikh vospominaniyakh* [50 Years of Russian Music in my Reminiscences] (Moscow, 1934)
E. Kolosova and V. Filippov, eds.: *A. N. Ostrovsky i russkiye kompozitorï* (Moscow and Leningrad, 1937) [incl. correspondence with K. Vil'boa, N. Rubinstein, A. Dyubyuk, Kashperov, Serov, Tchaikovsky, Rimsky-Korsakov]
G. Ivanov: *A. N. Ostrovsky v muzïke: spravochnik* [Ostrovsky in Music: a Reference Guide] (Moscow, 1976)
R. Taruskin: 'The Opera and the Dictator', *New Republic* (20 March 1989), 34–40   RICHARD TARUSKIN

Osud ('Fate'; 'Destiny'). 'Three novelesque scenes' by LEOŠ JANÁČEK to a libretto by Janáček and Fedora Bartošová; Brno, National Theatre, 25 October 1958 (arranged Václav Nosek; original version, České Budějovice, South Bohemian Theatre, 7 April 1978).

Živný *a composer*	tenor
Míla Válková	soprano
Míla's Mother	contralto
Dr Suda *a lawyer*	tenor
Lhotský *a painter*	bass
Konečný	baritone
Miss Stuhlá *a schoolteacher*	soprano
Poet	tenor
First Lady	soprano
Second Lady	soprano
Old Slovak Woman	contralto
Councillor's Wife	contralto
Major's Wife	soprano
Miss Pacovská (Fanča)	soprano
First Guest	tenor
Second Guest	baritone
Waiter	tenor
Young Widow	contralto
Engineer	tenor
First Young Gentleman	baritone
Second Young Gentleman	baritone
Student	tenor
Doubek *Živný and Míla's son*	
(*as a* child)	boy soprano
(*as a* student)	tenor
Hrazda ⎫	tenor
Verva ⎪ *students at the Conservatory*	baritone
Součková ⎬	soprano
Kosinská ⎭	contralto
Žán ('Jean') ⎫ *servants*	
Nána ⎭	silent

Women teachers, students and young girls, visitors at the spa, conservatory students

Setting A spa promenade about 1890 (Act 1); Živný's study, four years later (Act 2); Živný's class at the Conservatory, 11 years later (Act 3)

The spa town of Luhačovice, Moravia, where Janáček's 'Osud' is set: photograph from a guide book owned by the composer

Janáček began writing his fourth opera after a visit to the spa of Luhačovice, Moravia, in August 1903. There he met Mrs Kamila Urválková, who claimed that Ludvík Čelanský's opera *Kamila* (1897) had portrayed her in an unsympathetic light and it was Janáček's chivalrous duty to clear her name with another opera. The original motivation became obscured in the complicated genesis of the piece, so that by the end it took on a more autobiographical aspect. Janáček wrote the scenario himself (October to 8 December 1903) and sent it in instalments to Fedora Bartošová, a young schoolteacher and a friend of Janáček's daughter Olga. Her brief was to turn it into a verse libretto. She finished her task by Christmas 1903, though extensive changes, particularly affecting Act 2, were made on Janáček's instructions in April 1904 and beyond. Act 1 of Janáček's score was composed between 8 December 1903 and 12 April 1904; the whole opera was completed by 12 June 1905. Janáček, however, did not submit the opera to the Brno Theatre until a year later, by which time he had extensively revised the opera introducing, for instance, the crucial figure of Míla's mother. Brno Theatre agreed to Janáček's terms on 11 December 1906 and early the next year Janáček was in consultation with a designer and producer.

However, Janáček was persuaded by a Prague friend to submit the opera to the new Vinohrady Theatre in Prague in May 1907, a move which entailed yet another far-reaching revision. This was completed by 19 November 1907, when the final version of the score was sent to the Vinohrady Theatre. It was accepted there, contracted but never performed, even after a court case initiated by Janáček (and dropped, in exchange for more promises). Although Brno Theatre remained keen to produce the opera, and planned to do so in autumn 1914, the outbreak of World War I put an end to this hope. Janáček thought of revising the opera in 1917–18 but no literary expert that he consulted was able to help him. The work was first heard after his death in broad-cast performances by Brno Radio (13 March 1934, excerpts, and 18 September 1934, complete) but the first stage performance took place only in 1958, and even then in a version adapted by Václav Nosek in which Acts 1 and 2 were inserted as a flashback within Act 3. However, an intelligent and committed production of Janáček's original, such as David Pountney's for the ENO in 1984, showed itself able to overcome the opera's odd dramaturgy and often impenetrable verbiage and bring into the repertory some of Janáček's most incandescently lyrical music.

ACT 1 *The spa promenade [at Luhačovice], early morning* Janáček's declared aim was to present a 'completely realistic' scene 'drawn from life at a spa'. The opera opens, without an overture, on the company enjoying the sunshine and singing their delight in an elaborate ensemble of chorus and soloists built on a waltz – an evocation of a spa orchestra. The chief soloists are then portrayed against this background: the dapper solicitor Dr Suda, the painter Lhotský, and in particular Míla Válková and the composer Živný. Introductions are made, but it seems that Živný and Míla know each other already: 'have you come for your son?', she asks him when they are alone. Their conversation is interrupted by the schoolteacher Miss Stuhlá, who attempts to rehearse a party of women teachers in a partsong (to the mirth of the other spa guests). Then Dr Suda sings a slightly risqué three-verse ballad, 'Ty zlatá naše sluníčko' ('You, our dear little sun'), joined by the chorus, which then follows him out on an impromptu excursion. Left alone, Živný and Míla muse over the past in what is the extended lyrical heart of the act: they had been lovers, but her Mother had enforced a separation to ensure a more advantageous match for her. It is growing dark, and as the excursionists return Živný and Míla decide to run off together. Their departure is viewed with the gravest apprehension by Míla's Mother, who arrives too late to stop them.

ACT 2 *Živný's study on a winter's day, four years later* Živný and Míla are married, living with the son born to them out of wedlock and with Míla's Mother, now deranged and guarded by servants. Her voice is occasionally heard from offstage, butting into a rather one-sided conversation between Živný and Míla (originally a monologue for Živný) as he ruminates about the opera that he has written about their relationship. In a fit of remorse he begins to tear up the score in which he has portrayed Míla's 'shame'. They are interrupted by their young son Doubek, who asks what love is and gives the answer himself. Míla's Mother now breaks into the room, mockingly singing the love song from Živný's opera and flourishing her jewel-box. She runs off. Míla attempts to restrain her; offstage both topple to their deaths over a balcony. Živný believes even more that fate is against him.

ACT 3 *The great hall in the Conservatory, 11 years later (the present)* Students are trying out a passage (a storm scene) from the new opera written by their professor Živný. After they make a high-spirited storm of their own, the student Verva enters and provides more information about the work. It is autobiographical and though complete it is 'without the last act'. He sings through one of the solo scenes (between Míla and Doubek, asking what love is), to the embarrassment of Doubek, now a student at the Conservatory. Suddenly Živný enters, to an awkward silence. The students ask him to say something about the opera. In one of the lyrical highlights of the work he begins describing its chief character Lenský and how he fell in love. But the pent-up autobiographical emotion of the work is too much for Živný. Against a storm rising outside he thinks he hears the sighs of his dead wife and sees visions of her and collapses in a faint. The arrival of the lawyer Dr Suda (though a medical doctor was called for) brings the opera to an ambiguous conclusion.   JOHN TYRRELL

O'Sullivan, Denis (*b* San Francisco, 25 April 1868; *d* Columbus, OH, 1 Feb 1908). Irish-American baritone. He made his début with the Carl Rosa Company in Dublin on 25 August 1895 as Ferrando (*Il trovatore*) and sang on tour as Prince John (Sullivan's *Ivanhoe*), the Mayor (*Die Heimkehr aus der Fremde*), Lothario (*Mignon*) and, at five hours' notice without rehearsal, the Dutchman (*Der fliegende Holländer*). In 1896 he sang at Daly's Theatre in London with the Carl Rosa Opera Company as Biterolf (*Tannhäuser*) and Alfio (*Cavalleria rusticana*). On 2 March he created the title role in Stanford's *Shamus O'Brien* at the Opéra Comique Theatre, London. Between 1897 and 1899 he divided his time between England and the USA, singing in New York on 19 September 1898 as the Marquis of Saint-André in Ludwig Englander's *The Little Corporal*. He was noted for the excellence of his phrasing and enunciation.

O'Sullivan, John (*b* Cork, 1878; *d* Paris, 28 April 1955). Irish tenor. He studied in Paris and made his début in 1910 at Toulouse. From 1914 to 1922 he was engaged at the Paris Opéra (usually billed as Sullivan), where he sang Raoul (*Les Huguenots*), Arnold (*Guillaume Tell*), Reyer's Sigurd, Fernand (*La favorite*), Romeo, Nicias (*Thaïs*), Don Gomez (*Henry VIII*), Manrico, the Duke (*Rigoletto*), Radames, Samson, Dick Johnson, Faust (Gounod and Berlioz), Aeneas (*Les Troyens*), John the Baptist (*Hérodiade*) and Dmitry (*Boris Godunov*). He

sang in Chicago (1918–20), at La Scala, where he took the title role of Verdi's *Otello* (1924), and at Covent Garden (1927). Returning to the Opéra (1929–33), he sang Lohengrin, Tannhäuser and Eléazar (*La Juive*).
                                    ELIZABETH FORBES

Otava, Zdeněk (*b* Vítějeves, nr Polička, Bohemia, 11 March 1902; *d* Prague, 4 Dec 1980). Czech baritone. As a choirboy he impressed Janáček; subsequently he studied the piano and violin with Martinů. After singing lessons in Prague, he studied in Rome (with Riccardo Stracciari), Milan and Vienna. He made his début in Bratislava as Iago (1925), and a year later was engaged by the Brno Opera with which he sang Baron Prus in the première of Janáček's *The Makropulos Affair* and the title role in Krenek's *Jonny spielt auf*. From 1929 to 1972 he worked at the National Theatre in Prague, singing more than 160 roles; he also toured widely abroad. Otava's voice had a very wide range and a marked intensity, and while light, was extremely varied in colour, with an even tone, free of vibrato; his diction was absolutely clear. With his striking stage presence, he gave characteristic portrayals of Figaro, Germont, Yevgeny Onegin and Telramund, and masterly projections of such villains and conspirators as Pizarro, Scarpia and Iago. He was no less versatile and successful in the Czech repertory, and learnt a large number of contemporary roles.

ČSHS
Jen ve zpěvu [Only in Song] (Prague, 1947)
A. Rektorys: *Naši operní pěvci* [Our Opera Singers] (Prague, 1958), 70–76
L. Šíp: *Pěvci před mikrofonem* [Singers before the Microphone] (Prague, 1960), 59–62
R. Fikerle: *Portréty* [Portraits] (Prague, 1967), 17–28
E. Kopecký and V. Pospíšil: *Slavní pěvci Národního divadla* [Famous Singers of the National Theatre] (Prague, 1968), 172–82
V. Procházka, ed.: *Národní divadlo a jeho předchůdci* [The National Theatre and its Predecessors] (Prague, 1988), 350–52
                                    ALENA NĚMCOVÁ

Otello (i) [*Otello, ossia Il moro di Venezia* ('Othello, or The Moor of Venice')]. *Dramma* in three acts by GIOACHINO ROSSINI to a libretto by Francesco Berio di Salsa after WILLIAM SHAKESPEARE's play *Othello, or The Moor of Venice*; Naples, Teatro del Fondo, 4 December 1816.

The libretto, by a Neapolitan literary dilettante, follows the broad outline of Shakespeare's play; only in the opera's third act (Acts 4.iii and 5 of the play) does the libretto follow Shakespeare at all closely.

Otello (tenor), captain of the Venetian fleet, is received with acclaim by the people after his victory over the Turks. The Doge (tenor) confers Venetian citizenship on him, but Otello is preoccupied with thoughts about Desdemona (soprano) whom he has been forced to marry secretly because of the opposition of her father, the influential senator Elmiro (bass). The celebrations are not shared either by Iago (tenor), Otello's lieutenant and a man increasingly jealous of his political power, or the Doge's son Rodrigo (tenor), who is in love with Desdemona himself. In a hurried private consultation, Rodrigo learns from Elmiro that Desdemona seems oppressed with some secret sorrow. Rodrigo fears that this is because a decision has been made to give Desdemona to the Moor in marriage, but Iago, who has been eavesdropping on the conversation, assures Rodrigo that Otello cannot thrive. Without telling Rodrigo what he intends to do with it, Iago produces

789

a letter he has obtained in Desdemona's own handwriting. Meanwhile, Desdemona is distraught that the letter has gone astray. She expresses her several fears in a *scena* and *duettino*, 'Vorrei che il tuo pensiero', with her confidante, Emilia (soprano). Elmiro now decides that a marriage between his daughter and Rodrigo would be a political bolster against Otello's rising power. Desdemona is called to a secret ceremony only to find herself told before the whole court that she is to be married to Rodrigo. Otello enters and is startled into confessing that he is bound to Desdemona by a solemn oath. Elmiro curses his daughter, and the first act ends with Otello and Rodrigo angrily challenging one another.

Rodrigo now pleads his love to Desdemona. But the revelation that she and Otello are legally married drives him into a paroxysm of anger and jealousy. Otello is also jealous, fearful that Desdemona may love Rodrigo, a jealousy that Iago fans with guileful use of the stolen letter. In a virulent trio, Otello and Rodrigo confront one another, watched by the helpless Desdemona. Repulsed by Otello, she is revived by Emilia but though the subsequent duel passes off without bloodshed she now has to face the wrath of her father, who demands new acts of expiation.

The third act is set in Desdemona's bedchamber. As she begins to tell Emilia about her sufferings a gondolier's song is heard across the water:

> There is no greater sorrow
> Than to remember happiness
> In time of grief.

Desdemona is reminded of the sad fate of her friend Isaure and tries to assuage her sadness by singing the mournful Willow Song, 'Assisa a piè d'un salice'. As a storm begins to gather, Desdemona dismisses Emilia, and prays ('Deh calma, o Ciel, nel sonno'). Otello enters the bedchamber but cannot bring himself to kill his wife. She is awakened by the storm and bravely argues her innocence; but Otello is only maddened further and, after telling her that he has ordered Iago to murder Rodrigo, he kills her. An officer (tenor) arrives to report that Iago, mortally wounded by Rodrigo, has confessed to his foul deceptions; he is followed by Rodrigo and Elmiro, both now determined to forgive Otello his clandestine marriage. But it is too late: he shows them Desdemona's dead body and stabs himself to death.

*   *   *

Rossini's choice of Shakespeare's *Othello*, complete with its tragic denouement, was a bold and original one at the time, however much the opera's ending was subsequently censored and bowdlerized. By comparison with the later Verdi setting, it is an obviously compromised work. In the first two acts Shakespeare's plotting and characterization are reduced by Berio di Salsa to mere schematic banality and the abundance of tenors in Barbaia's Naples company gives the musical texture a persistently brilliant colour, though there is high drama to be had in Rodrigo's Act 2 aria 'Ah, come mai non senti', with its difficult, high-lying cabaletta, and in the Act 2 confrontation between Rodrigo and Otello, 'Non m'inganno; al mio rivale'. What redeems Rossini's *Otello* is the original and highly sympathetic portrait of Desdemona and the superb third act, which is dominated by her and unforgettably coloured by the offstage gondolier, whose fleeting contribution was added at Rossini's own suggestion. Interestingly, Desdemona is given no formal entrance aria in Act 1,

nor is there a love duet, yet the character leaves an indelible impression. In the 19th century the opera's huge popularity owed much to the final act. Meyerbeer wrote: 'The third act of *Otello* established its reputation so firmly that a thousand errors could not shake it. This third act is really godlike, and what is so extraordinary is that its beauties are quite un-Rossini-like. First-rate declamation, continuously impassioned recitative, mysterious accompaniments full of local colour, and, in particular, the style of the old romances brought to highest perfection'.   RICHARD OSBORNE

Otello (ii) ('Othello'). *Dramma lirico* in four acts by GIUSEPPE VERDI to a libretto by ARRIGO BOITO after WILLIAM SHAKESPEARE's play *Othello, or The Moor of Venice*; Milan, Teatro alla Scala, 5 February 1887.

Otello *a Moor, general of the Venetian army*	tenor
Iago *an ensign*	baritone
Cassio *a platoon leader*	tenor
Roderigo *a Venetian gentleman*	tenor
Lodovico *an ambassador of the Venetian Republic*	bass
Montano *Otello's predecessor as Governor of Cyprus*	bass
A Herald	bass
Desdemona *Otello's wife*	soprano
Emilia *Iago's wife*	mezzo-soprano

Soldiers and sailors of the Venetian Republic, Venetian ladies and gentlemen, Cypriot populace of both sexes, Greek, Dalmatian and Albanian men-at-arms, island children, an innkeeper, four servants at the inn, common sailors

Setting A maritime city on the island of Cyprus, at the end of the 15th century

As the 1870s progressed, Verdi seemed increasingly isolated from current trends in Italian music, in particular by the tendency of both public and composers to look outside Italy (to France and, later, even more to Germany) for new ideas and aesthetic attitudes. It is against this background that we should examine his reluctance to write new works after the Requiem of 1874: Verdi was a composer who, after being at the forefront of Italian musical taste for two decades, suddenly found himself accused of being distinctly old-fashioned, out of touch with the times; and indeed he probably felt so too. Those who sought to lure him out of self-imposed retirement, among whom the prime mover was the young director of the Ricordi publishing house, Giulio Ricordi, had to tread carefully. Ricordi eventually teamed up with Arrigo Boito, the librettist and composer, who in the 1860s had been one of the most visible of the Italian avant garde, but whose respect for the old maestro was growing with the years. In June 1879 Ricordi and Boito mentioned to Verdi the possibility of his composing a version of Shakespeare's *Othello*; surely a canny choice given Verdi's lifelong veneration for the English playwright and his attempts after *Macbeth* to tackle further Shakespearean topics (notably *King Lear*). Verdi showed cautious enthusiasm for the new project, and by the end of the year Boito had produced a draft libretto, one full of ingenious new rhythmic devices but with an extremely firm dramatic thread.

Although Verdi eventually agreed – with a characteristic show of reluctance – to collaborate with Boito on *Otello*, the project was long in the making. First came two other tasks, the revisions to *Simon Boccanegra* (effected with Boito's help) and to *Don Carlos*, both of which can be seen in retrospect as trial runs for the new type of opera Verdi felt he must create in the changed Italian artistic climate. Verdi also bombarded Boito with alterations to the libretto draft of *Otello*, especially to the Act 3 finale, which he felt must furnish occasion for a grand concertato finale in the traditional manner. The opera was then composed in a series of intensive bursts, the comparative speed suggesting that Verdi had previously sketched the music rather thoroughly. The première at La Scala was conducted by Franco Faccio, the cast including Francesco Tamagno (Otello; for illustration *see* TAMAGNO, FRANCESCO), Victor Maurel (Iago) and Romilda Pantaleoni (Desdemona), all of whom had been carefully selected and intensively coached by Verdi himself. The *prima* was a predictable, indeed a well-nigh inevitable success, although some critics of course lamented the sophistication and lack of immediacy they found in Verdi's new manner. The opera was soon given in the major European capitals and became an important element of the operatic repertory. Though it has never reached the level of popularity of the middle-period masterpieces – something hardly surprising considering the severe vocal and orchestral demands made by the score – *Otello* remains one of the most universally respected of Verdi's operas, often admired even by those who find almost all his earlier works unappealing.

For the Paris première at the Théâtre de l'Opéra in 1894 Verdi added a ballet score to the third act and also made some significant revisions to the same act's concertato finale, reducing the musical detail in an effort to bring out the embedded conversations. These revisions were not incorporated into the Italian version and are rarely heard today.

ACT 1 *Outside the castle* A sudden burst of orchestral dissonance begins the opera with an immediacy Verdi had never before attempted: a clear sign that this work will engage a more realistic notion of musical drama. A violent storm is raging, and the on-lookers from the shore, among them Iago, Cassio and Montano, comment on the fortunes of their leader Otello's ship. The crowd's reaction momentarily coalesces into 'Dio, fulgor della bufera', a desperate prayer to save the ship, but then all is again confusion until, to cries of 'È salvo!', Otello safely arrives. He greets his followers with a ringing salute, 'Esultate!', proudly announcing that the Turks have been beaten. The chorus then closes this opening 'storm' scene with a triumphant victory chorus, 'Vittoria! Sterminio!'

As the crowd goes about its work, Iago and Roderigo come to the fore. In a texture alternating simple recitative with arioso, Iago assures his friend that Desdemona will soon tire of her new husband, Otello, and thus become available to the besotted Roderigo. Iago then reveals his hatred for Cassio, whom he thinks has unjustly overtaken him in rank. Their conversation is followed by the fireside chorus 'Fuoco di gioia!', a series of contrasting sections tied together by brilliant orchestral effects imitating the crackling flames. As the fire dies down, Iago encourages Cassio to drink, eventually breaking into the brindisi 'Inaffia l'ugola', a three-stanza song with choral refrain, by the end of which

1. *Design by Alfredo Edel for Desdemona's costume in Act 4 of the original production of Verdi's 'Otello' at La Scala, Milan, 5 February 1887*

Cassio is far the worse for wine. Roderigo provokes him to a fight, which is interrupted by Montano, who himself becomes embroiled with Cassio. Iago skilfully stage-manages the confusion by ordering Roderigo to call the alarm; soon there is general panic. At the height of the disturbance, Otello enters, sword in hand, and with an imperious gesture, 'Abbasso le spade!' ('Lower your swords!'), restores calm. His inquiry finds Cassio guilty and he dismisses him from service (to a stifled cry of triumph from Iago). Desdemona has by now appeared, and Otello dismisses the crowd, to be left alone with his new bride.

The ensuing love duet, although it bears a certain distant relationship to earlier 19th-century practices, is really *sui generis*, the form's tendency towards a series of short, contrasting sections all but obliterating vestiges of any larger, multi-movement structure. After a brief orchestral transition as the stage clears, a choir of solo cellos heralds the opening exchange, 'Già nella notte densa'; Otello evokes the nocturnal ambience before Desdemona turns to the past, and in the largest lyrical section, 'Quando narravi l'esule tua vita', recalls with Otello the manner in which his narrations of past exploits first won her over. At the close of this episode the lovers sing a patterned alternation, 'E tu m'amavi per le mie sventure', a paraphrase of Shakespeare's 'She lov'd me for the dangers I had passed, And I lov'd her that she did pity them'. In a *Poco più mosso*, Otello wishes for death at this moment of ecstasy, but soon their mutual feelings spread forth into a final gesture of intimacy: a thrice-repeated kiss ('Un bacio ... ancora un bacio') whose intensity is reflected in the appoggiatura-laden violin melody that underpins the stage action. With a final gesture towards the night, 'Vien ... Venere splende', Otello leads Desdemona back into the castle. The solo cellos return to effect a tender close.

ACT 2 *A room on the ground floor of the castle*
After an orchestral introduction suggesting Iago's busy energy, the villain is revealed, assuring Cassio that with help from Desdemona he will regain his place in Otello's estimation. Iago sends Cassio off to attend her and comes forward to deliver his famous soliloquy, 'Credo in un Dio crudel', a kind of evil Credo in which he plays to the hilt his demonic character. As befits Iago's slippery energy, this dynamic Credo hovers between arioso and aria, its devious harmonic and formal twists continuing to the last. Iago now notices Desdemona and Emilia in the garden and offers a *sotto voce* commentary as Cassio approaches them with his suit. Then, seeing Otello approach, he positions himself for the crucial confrontation.

The Otello-Iago duet continues to the end of the act, although interrupted by a series of set pieces and dialogues that become increasingly caught up in the central action. The first phase of the duet, and its most fragmentary, involves the initial testing of Otello: Iago's teasing questions and repetitions, Otello's angry confusion, and then Iago's first mention of 'jealousy', to a sliding chromatic figure of great harmonic audacity. And the first set-piece interruption is a jarring one: Desdemona is seen again in the garden, and distant voices serenade her in a simple chorus, 'Dove guardi splendono raggi', a piece whose musical atmosphere recalls the choral evocations of Act 1 in both style and tonality. As the chorus ends, Desdemona approaches Otello to intercede on Cassio's behalf. But Otello's response is disturbed: so much so that Desdemona gently asks for pardon in a second set piece, the quartet 'Dammi la dolce e lieta parola', in which Otello bemoans his supposed loss while Iago extracts from Emilia a handkerchief of Desdemona's that has been cast aside in the preceding dialogue. As the quartet comes to a close, Otello dismisses Desdemona and Emilia, and is again left alone with Iago. This time the emotional temperature is near boiling point, and a few comments from Iago are enough to precipitate the aria 'Ora e per sempre addio', in which Otello bids farewell to his past life in a closed form that, appropriately given the dramatic situation, has strong hints of the younger Verdi's lyrical style. The aria disintegrates into furious orchestral figures as Otello demands proof of his wife's infidelity, eventually grabbing Iago by the throat and hurling him to the ground. Iago now takes over and gradually leads the atmosphere into those calmer waters where he can begin his *racconto*, 'Era la notte', in which – to a musical structure as complex and surprising as Otello's was simple and direct – he offers as 'proof' words he has overheard Cassio mumble in his sleep. From there to the end of the act, all is gathering dramatic energy. Iago produces Desdemona's handkerchief as a final, visible proof, and Otello unleashes the cabaletta, 'Sì, pel ciel', in which he and then Iago swear to exact a terrible vengeance.

2. 'Otello' (Verdi), the handkerchief scene from Act 3, set in the great hall of the castle (designed by Carlo Ferrario):
(a) engraving showing the original production at La Scala, Milan, 5 February 1887, from 'Il teatro illustrato' (February 1887)

Jago profitterà di questa mossa di **Cassio**, per guardare rapidamente dalla parte di **Otello**: poi si rivolge a **Cassio**, e gli dice ad alta voce: *L'hai teco?* **Cassio** estrae dal giustacuore il fazzoletto di **Desdemona** (1), ed avvicinandosi a **Jago**, esclama: *Guarda.*

Jago prendendo il fazzoletto, in modo che si spieghi, lo osserva e dice, con ammirazione: *Qual meraviglia!* **Cassio**, rimane pensieroso, perchè ignora a chi appartenga il fazzoletto, **Jago** guarderà nuovamente dalla parte di **Otello**, che sarà sempre più agitato:

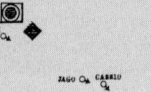

e col pretesto d'inchinarsi scherzosamente a **Cassio**, nel dirgli: *Bel cavaliere*, indietreggia di due passi, e mentre colla sinistra fa un cenno di scherzoso rallegramento a **Cassio**, mette la destra, col fazzoletto, dietro la schiena, perchè **Otello** lo possa osservare, e così trovasi fra **Cassio** ed **Otello**, in modo che il primo non veda il secondo.

Otello s'avvicina con molta cautela a due o tre passi dietro le spalle di **Jago**, osserva il fazzoletto, e con urlo represso esclama: *È quello! è quello!*

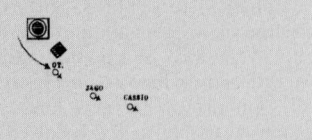

(1) Questo fazzoletto dev'essere lo stesso che portava Desdemona nel 2.° Atto, e che raccolto da terra da Emilia, fu carpito poi da Jago: è quindi necessario che presenti qualche cosa di strano, di rimarchevole: dovrà essere fatto con un tessuto bianco sottilissimo, sia garza di seta, o battista assai fine: avrà tutt'intorno un ricamo a fili d'oro e seta rossa e verde, formante un ornato a fiori, di stile moresco: in un angolo una grandissima cifra in lettere arabe, ricamata in oro e nero: dimensioni, 45 centimetri circa, quadrati.

(b) *corresponding page from the disposizione scenica (production book) of the same production, compiled by Giulio Ricordi: Otello advances (bottom diagram) to identify the handkerchief which Iago (centre) covertly reveals to him*

ACT 3 *The great hall of the castle* An orchestral introduction derived from Iago's Act 2 description of jealousy shows that his machinations are still working. A herald announces the imminent arrival of Venetian ambassadors and Iago directs Otello to conceal himself and await the arrival of Cassio and further 'proof'. As Iago retires, Desdemona appears for the second of her extended duets with Otello; like the first, it is loosely structured around contrasting sections, with a prominent thematic reminiscence to aid the sense of closure. First comes 'Dio ti giocondi, o sposo', in which the semblance of lyrical normality (a patterned alternation of the voices, and periodic phrasing) soon gives way to agitated, fragmentary music as Desdemona mentions the plight of Cassio. Otello describes with repressed intensity the magical nature of the handkerchief Desdemona has mislaid, his anger rising further as she again attempts to deflect him into talk of Cassio. Finally he hurls out a brutal accusation of infidelity. Desdemona is crushed and at first can only murmur confusedly; but then, with 'io prego il cielo per te', her melody flows into the lyrical centre of the duet as she prays for Otello and bids him look at the first tears she has shed through grief. Otello at first seems calmed by this outburst, but soon his accusations return with added fury. As a cruel parting gesture, he recalls the calmer opening music of the duet, only to break it off with a gross insult and push Desdemona from the room.

Otello returns to centre stage for his most extended solo of the opera, the self-pitying soliloquy 'Dio! mi potevi scagliar', which begins in barely coherent fragments, rises gradually to a controlled lyricism, and again collapses, this time into furious invective. Iago appears and quickly takes charge, leading Otello aside where he can observe and listen to Cassio talking of Desdemona, and then involving Cassio in discussion of his dalliance with the courtesan Bianca. The terzetto 'Essa t'avvince coi vaghi rai', set in the form of a scherzo and trio, skilfully counterposes Iago's and Cassio's comic exchange with Otello's anguished commentary. Cassio even produces Desdemona's handkerchief (hidden in his lodgings by Iago), and Iago's elaborate description of this item forms a hectic stretta to the terzetto.

Offstage trumpets announce the arrival of the Venetian ambassadors. As the ceremonial sounds approach, Otello hurriedly discusses with Iago the method of Desdemona's death, which they agree should be strangulation in her bed. As Iago slips off to fetch Desdemona the dignitaries appear, welcomed by a choral salute. Lodovico gives Otello a letter from the Doge, but is disturbed by the violent interruptions Otello makes to his ensuing conversation with Desdemona, especially to her wish that Cassio be reinstated. Otello reports that the letter calls him back to Venice, with Cassio left in his place. During this speech, Otello directs a series of angry asides to Desdemona and at its close seizes his wife with such violence that she falls to the ground. The general amazement precipitates the Largo concertato, 'A terra! ... sì ... nel livido fango', led off by an unusually long and thematically developed solo from Desdemona, much of it later repeated by the ensemble. As the Largo unfolds, Iago works furiously in the musical background, assuring Otello that he will deal with Cassio and delegating Roderigo for the task. As the movement comes to a close, Otello wildly dismisses everyone, unleashing on Desdemona a final, terrible curse. Left alone with Iago, he can only mutter incoherently before fainting. Iago gestures triumphantly

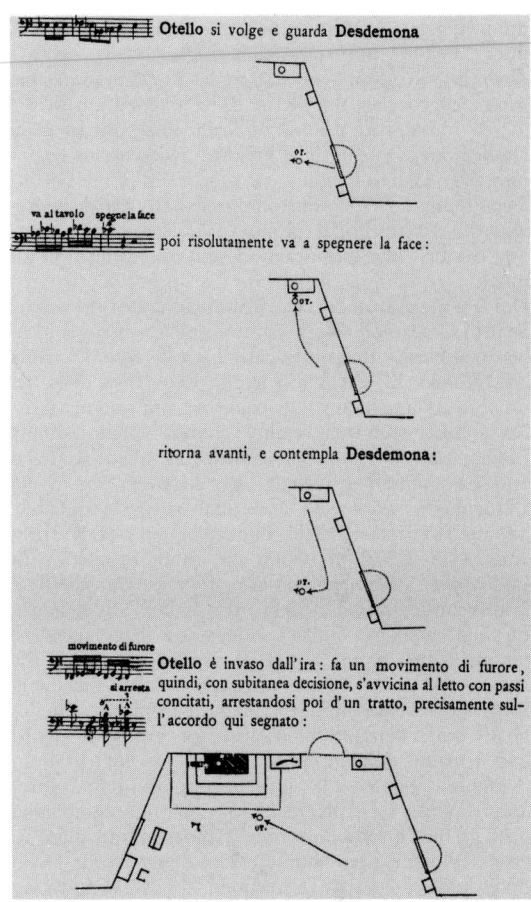

3. *Page from the disposizione scenica (production book) for the original production of Verdi's 'Otello' (La Scala, Milan, 1887), showing part of the instrumental prelude to the final scene of Act 4: the music examples (rare in disposizioni sceniche) are included because of the absence of sung text. The suggestion of an elaborate series of mimed gestures to specific phrases in the music may be surprising for those accustomed to modern, 'naturalistic' operatic acting. Phrase 1: Otello turns and looks at Desdemona. Phrase 2: he goes to the table and puts out the torch; he returns to front stage and contemplates Desdemona. Phrase 3: consumed by anger, Otello makes a movement of fury after which, with sudden decisiveness, he approaches the bed with agitated steps; he stops, at a distance, precisely on the chord indicated.*

at the body and, with offstage voices still hailing Otello as the 'Lion of Venice', brings down the curtain with a derisive shout of 'Ecco il Leone!' ('Here is the Lion!').

ACT 4 *Desdemona's bedroom* A mournful english horn solo with fragmentary phrases sets the tone of this final act. Desdemona discusses with Emilia the present state of her husband and then, with presentiments of death upon her, sings the famous Willow Song, 'Piangea cantando', whose three stanzas with refrain poignantly tell of a young girl abandoned by her lover. After a final, passionate farewell to Emilia, Desdemona kneels to offer an 'Ave Maria', softly intoned over a gentle string accompaniment before flowering into 'Prega per chi adorando', Desdemona's personal entreaty for divine assistance. Accompanied by high strings of the utmost delicacy, Desdemona settles in her bed.

A mysterious, double bass solo introduces Otello to

the bedchamber. Miming to an instrumental recitative punctuated by motivic fragments (see fig.3), he lays down his sword, puts out the torch that illuminates the room, approaches the bed and, to a repetition of the 'bacio' music from the end of Act 1, kisses the sleeping Desdemona. On the third kiss she awakens, so beginning the final and in many ways the freest of the Otello-Desdemona duets, a confrontation that even dispenses with the clear sectional form of earlier examples, reflecting through the proliferation and intensification of motivic repetitions an inexorable progress towards Desdemona's death. At the brutal climax of the scene, deaf to Desdemona's protestations of innocence and to her final pleas, Otello suffocates his wife with a terrible cry of 'È tardi!' ('It is too late!'). Only then does the orchestral surge finally flow back and attain some stasis. To a succession of weighty chords, Otello admits Emilia, who tells him that Cassio has killed Roderigo and has himself survived. She discovers the dying Desdemona, who with her final gasps desperately attempts to protect Otello. But Emilia guesses the truth and raises the alarm. Soon the room is filled with Lodovico, Cassio, Iago and armed men. Again the free, arioso musical texture takes over as Iago's plot is unravelled, first by Emilia's admission that Iago had obtained the handkerchief from her, then by the appearance of Lodovico, who reports that the dying Roderigo revealed his part in the conspiracy. Otello, finally understanding his tragic error, grabs his sword and, to slow, solemn chords, begins his final oration, 'Niun mi tema'. He reflects on his past glory, apostrophizes Desdemona in an unaccompanied passage that briefly flowers into lyricism and then, to general horror, stabs himself. His dying words as he drags himself towards Desdemona's body call forth yet another repetition of the 'bacio' music from Act 1.

* * *

The chronological position of *Otello* in Verdi's long list of tragic operas – the last work, separated from all the others by a considerable time gap – has inevitably made it seem a special case; indeed, for many earlier in the century, perhaps even for some today, it is his only serious opera to merit sustained critical attention. Recent critics have sometimes reacted against this by stressing the many traditional aspects of the score: its reliance, especially in Act 1, on 'characteristic' numbers such as the storm scene, victory chorus and brindisi; the clear remnants of traditional forms in the 'cabaletta substitutes' such as 'Sì, pel ciel'; and of course its most unequivocal gesture to traditional form, the great concertato finale that closes Act 3. Some have gone even further, and suggested for example that passages such as the Act 1 love duet should be regarded as further manipulations of the standard four-movement duet, and that there is in effect an unbroken tradition with Verdi's earlier works.

This last position may swing too far towards the claims of tradition. It is more profitable to regard *Otello* as an opera that attempts a break with the past in an effort to produce a new, more modern conception of musical drama. There may well be gestures towards the traditional, normative structures of earlier in the century – given the patterned alternation of action and reflection within these structures it would be difficult to imagine how any opera could completely avoid them. But for the most part the opera strives for a different, more fluid type of musical drama: one that is closer to prose drama in its willingness to admit a swift succession of emotional attitudes during a series of dramatic confrontations. Of course, no value judgments should be attached to this greater fluidity: musical drama is endlessly protean in the manner and the forms in which it may be expressed, and there is nothing intrinsically superior in a type of opera that approaches the rhythms of the spoken theatre. We should, however, preserve a sense of distance between *Otello* and Verdi's earlier operas, a fact that renders even more remarkable Verdi's creative energy and capacity for self-renewal during the last years of his life.

ROGER PARKER

Otescu, Ion Nonna (*b* Bucharest, 15 Dec 1888; *d* Bucharest, 25 March 1940). Romanian composer. He studied composition at the Bucharest Conservatory, 1903–7, then in Paris at the Schola Cantorum, 1908–11 (with d'Indy), and the Conservatoire, 1911–12. Subsequently he worked as a professor and director at the Bucharest Conservatory and as a conductor at the Bucharest Opera (1921–39). After composing ballets and several symphonic poems, he demonstrated his originality with *De la Matei citire* ('From the Writings of St Matthew'), 1938, an *opera buffa* in three acts (to his own libretto), which was revised and completed by Aurel Stroe, and performed posthumously at the Romanian Opera in Cluj (27 December 1966). A delicate orchestrator and a disciple of the French impressionist movement, Otescu wrote a new type of Romanian music, adapting instrumental folk music to Classical orchestral instrumentation.

*

O. L. Cosma: *Opera românească* [Romanian Opera] (Bucharest, 1962)
VIOREL COSMA

Ots, Charles (*b* Brussels, 13 May 1776; *d* Brussels, 1845). South Netherlands composer. He probably received his musical education in Brussels, and settled in Ghent at the end of the 18th century. His *opéra comique La ruse villageoise* was performed in the municipal theatre there in 1796. Later he was active there as a music teacher and was a member of the Société des Beaux-Arts et de la Littérature. His second opera, *Le nouveau marié, ou Les imposteurs*, was performed in Brussels in 1808. Between 1816 and 1818 he devoted himself chiefly to opera, writing two more works for Ghent. Of these, *David Teniers* was particularly successful, and he became conductor at the Ghent theatre for the 1819–20 season. He was extremely active in this post, but intrigues and rivalries caused him to resign. Disappointed, he abandoned opera and turned to composing sacred music. In form his operas were similar to Dalayrac's, in one act and with arias of the *romance* type. Ots chose subjects popular at the time of the French Revolution and under the Empire – historical portraits, battle scenes and the glorification of the nation – contributing to the importation of French operatic trends into the Low Countries.

His daughter Emilie (*b* 24 April 1808) studied singing with him and embarked on a career that took her to the Opéra-Comique in Paris in 1827.

opéras comiques in one act

La ruse villageoise, Ghent, 2 Jan 1796
Le nouveau marié, ou Les imposteurs (J. F. Cailhava), Brussels, Monnaie, June 1808
Jean Second, ou Charles V dans les murs de Gand, Ghent, 18 Dec 1816
David Teniers, Ghent, 28 Oct 1818

*

BNB (E. Beeckman)
PHILIPPE VENDRIX

Ots, Georg (Karlovich) (*b* Petrograd [now St Petersburg], 21 March 1920; *d* Tallinn, 4 Nov 1975). Soviet baritone. The son of the Estonian opera singer Karl Ots, he graduated from the Tallinn Conservatory in 1951. In 1945 he had joined the chorus of the Estonia Opera, Tallinn, and in 1951 became a soloist there. A talented actor and singer, Ots worked in opera and operetta with equal success. His voice, superbly cultivated in all registers, had a beautiful soft tone, and his performances were dramatically well balanced. Among his best roles were Yevgeny Onegin, Rubinstein's Demon, Oleg (Meytus's *Moloda hvardiya*, 'The Young Guard'), Toomas and Petrov (Ernesaks's *Käsi käes*, 'Hand in Hand', and *Tormide rand*, 'The Shore of Storms').

I. M. YAMPOL'SKY

Ottani, Bernardo (*b* Bologna, 8 Sept 1736; *d* Turin, 26 April 1827). Italian composer. In the early literature he is often confused with his elder brother Gaetano. He studied with Padre Martini, who remained a lifelong friend; the letters to his master, described by Tagliavini, survive in the Bologna Conservatory. His earliest composition to be performed was reportedly a cantata in 1760 in Bologna. In 1765 he was elected to the Accademia Filarmonica. He was in Genoa by February 1766 to write an opera (of which the only known record is a letter from him to Martini), and that autumn he went to Venice to provide new music and revisions for a popular Piccinni opera. This work earned him a commission from the Teatro S Moisè to set a new comic opera, *L'amore senza malizia*, for the following year's carnival season, and early in 1768 he wrote to his teacher of its clamorous success. It was immediately taken on tour throughout northern Italy and central Germany. Ottani may have gone with the company to Germany, for the comedy was performed in Dresden that same year, and he wrote two further comic operas for the court there.

By late 1769 Ottani was a *maestro di cappella* in Bologna, and as his reputation grew he started to travel again on opera commissions: in 1776 to Turin, where he became a friend of Quirino Gasparini; in autumn and winter 1777–8 to Naples and Rome; and for those seasons the following year to Venice, Florence and again Turin. In spring 1778 he was *primo cembalo* at the Teatro Pubblico, Bologna, in the production of Gluck's *Alceste*, and in 1779 his serious opera *Fatima*, written for Turin, resulted in an appointment as *maestro di cappella* at the cathedral there. He wrote at least three serious operas for Turin, but devoted most of his attention to church music.

Although Ottani exerted no great historical influence, his music was admired by his contemporaries, and his career is of interest because it is unusually well documented for the period. His music was progressive in the early Classical style, and in his comic operas his melodic invention was easy and graceful. But compared with those of more brilliant contemporaries his music now appears conservative in conception and without notable originality.

L'amore senza malizia (dg, P. Chiari), Venice, S Moisè, carn. 1768, *D-Dlb, Rtt?**, *H-Bn, I-MOe* (score and pts), *P-La*
Le virtuose ridicole (dg, C. Goldoni), Dresden, Piccolo, carn. 1769, *D-Dlb*
L'amore industrioso (dg, G. Casori), Dresden, Piccolo, 21 Nov 1769, *Dlb, I-Tf*
La semplicità in amore (dg), Udine, carn. 1771
Calipso [L'isola di Calipso] (os, Donzel), Turin, Regio, 26 Dec 1776, *D-Bds, P-La*

Catone in Utica (os, P. Metastasio), Naples, Reale, Nov 1777, *I-Nc, P-La*
La sprezzante abbandonata, ovvero La finta sprezzante (dg), Rome, Dame, carn. 1778
Le industrie amorose (dg, G. Bertati), Venice, S Moisè, aut. 1778
Le nozze della Bita (dg, N. Tassì), Florence, Cocomero, aut. 1778, *B-Bc*
Fatima (os), Turin, Regio, carn. 1779, *I-Mc, P-La*
La Didone (os, Metastasio), Forlì, Pubblico, spr. 1779, *I-Tf*
Arminio (os, Coluzzi), Turin, Reggio, carn. 1781, *D-Dlb, P-La*
Amaionne (os, F. S. Gambino), Turin, Regio, carn. 1784, *La*
La clemenza di Tito (os, Metastasio), Turin, Regio, carn. 1798, duet *I-Mc*

Several arias and a duet for Piccinni's Il fumo villano (orig. title Il cavaliere per amore), Venice, S Moisè, aut. 1766; new pieces for Traetta's opera (?Le serve rivali), Venice, aut. 1767

Doubtful: Adriano, Mantua, 1765, arias *I-MAav*, duet *Vc*; Il maestro (ob), Munich, Hof, carn. 1770; Le Amazzoni (Bertati), Turin, Carignano, carn. 1784

Individual arias and ensembles in *A-Wgm, CH-Zz, D-Bds, Dlb, DS, SWl, W, F-Lm, Pc, I-Fc, Gl, Mc, MAav* (Ciro aria), *Pca, Vmc* and in contemporary anthologies

*

BurneyFI; ES (L. F. Tagliavini)
C. Ricci: *I teatri di Bologna nei secoli XVII e XVIII: storia aneddotica* (Bologna, 1888), pp.xix, 486, 654
G. Sacerdote: *Teatro regio di Torino: cenni storici … dal 1662 al 1890* (Turin, 1892), esp. 59
M.-T. Bouquet and A. Basso: *Storia del Teatro regio di Torino* (Turin, 1976–)
JAMES L. JACKMAN (work-list with MARITA P. McCLYMONDS)

Ottani, Gaetano [Bernardino] (*b* ?Bologna, before 1736; *d* Turin, 1808). Italian tenor, brother of Bernardo Ottani. His first known performance was in Bologna in 1747; he then sang in Lucca (1748) and Turin (1750), and from 1754 until 1768 was a leading singer at the Turin court opera. He also sang in Milan in 1752, and again in 1770 when the Mozarts heard him in the convent of S Marco. Burney, who met him in July 1770 in Turin, thought him 'a master in his profession', possessing an 'excellent voice', and performing 'with taste and in a pleasing manner'. Gaetano was also a landscape painter of some repute (to Burney's eye, in the style of Claude Lorrain), and occasionally received royal commissions. He is sometimes confused with his more famous brother.

For bibliography *see* OTTANI, BERNARDO.   JAMES L. JACKMAN

Ottawa. Capital of Canada. Early performances of opera were given by touring companies in the Grand Opera House (built 1874; burnt down in 1913); visiting troupes then used the Russell Theatre (opened in 1897) which burnt down in 1928. In 1949 the Grand Opera Company was formed; for 15 years it performed works such as *The Bartered Bride*, *La bohème*, *Carmen*, *Faust*, *Samson et Dalila*, *La Gioconda*, *La traviata* and *Il trovatore* in Ottawa Technical High School Auditorium. The National Arts Centre (NAC), a theatre and auditorium complex including the Opera Theatre (2300 seats), was inaugurated in 1969. The Canada Council commissioned Gabriel Charpentier's *Orphée* to open the Studio Theatre in the same complex. From 1971 to 1983 Festival Canada (later Festival Ottawa) sponsored three or four operas each summer at the NAC. *Rinaldo*, *Idomeneo*, *Die Zauberflöte*, *Die Entführung aus dem Serail*, *Cendrillon*, *Thérèse* (Canadian première), *La fille du régiment*, *Pelléas et Mélisande*, *A Midsummer Night's Dream*, *Rigoletto*, *The Queen of Spades*, *Yevgeny Onegin* and *La Cenerentola* were included in the repertory. Opera Lyra, founded in 1986, stages one or two productions a year of works such as *Il barbiere di Siviglia*, *Werther*, *L'elisir d'amore* and *Carmen*. Opera returned to the NAC in 1988 with *Le nozze di Figaro*, followed by *Don Giovanni* (1989) and *Così fan tutte* (1990).

ELIZABETH FORBES

Ottein [Nieto], **Angeles** (*b* Santiago de Compostela, 24 June 1895; *d* Madrid, 9 March 1981). Spanish soprano. The sister of the soprano Ofelia Nieto, she added another 't' to her surname and inverted it. She studied with Lorenzo Simonetti from 1912 and made her début in May 1914, replacing her sister in the title role of Vives's *Maruxa* at the Teatro Calderón, Valladolid. She sang in the first performance of Del Campo's *Fantochines* (1924), which was written for her. After World War I she was active in Italy, her roles including Lucia, Rosina, Gilda, Violetta, Lakmé, the Queen of Night, Ophelia (in Thomas' *Hamlet*), Elvira (*I puritani*) and Amina. She sang extensively in Europe (in Denmark she was known as the 'Spanish Nightingale') and then in the Americas as *prima assoluta*. In 1941 she made a farewell tour of Spain.

Ottein set up a private school and then taught at the Royal Conservatory in Madrid and also (1960–71) at the Puerto Rico Conservatory. Her pupils included Pilar Lorengar and María-Luísa Nache. Lauri-Volpi wrote that she 'electrified audiences', producing echo effects from the middle to the high register, terminating with delicate and brilliant high notes 'like rockets flying into space'.

G. Lauri-Volpi: *Voci parallele* (Milan, 1955)

ANTÓN DE SANTIAGO

Otter, Anne-Sofie von (*b* Stockholm, 9 May 1955). Swedish mezzo-soprano. She studied in Stockholm and London. Engaged at Basle (1983–5), she made her début as Alcina (Haydn's *Orlando paladino*) and sang Cherubino, Hänsel, Orpheus and Clairon (*Capriccio*). She sang Ramiro (*La finta giardiniera*) at Aix-en-Provence (1984) and made her Covent Garden (1985) and Metropolitan (1988) débuts as Cherubino. She has sung at Berlin, Munich, Rome and La Scala, and her roles include Dorabella, Mozart's Sextus, Ismene (*Alceste*), Octavian, the Composer and the title role of *Tancredi*, which she sang at Geneva (1990). A stylish singer with an even, creamy voice, she is specially effective in trouser roles.

A. Clark: 'Anne Sofie von Otter', *Opera*, xlii (1991), 627–34

ELIZABETH FORBES

Otto, Lisa (*b* Dresden, 14 Nov 1919). German soprano. Daughter of the singer Karl Otto, she studied in Dresden, making her début in 1941 as Sophie at Beuthen; she remained there until 1944. She was engaged at Nuremberg (1945–6) and Dresden (1946–51) and joined the Berlin Städtische (later Deutsche) Oper in 1952. She also appeared at Salzburg from 1953, and as Blonde at Glyndebourne in 1956. She created Frau Hasentreffer in Henze's *Der junge Lord* (1965, Berlin). Vocally a light engaging soubrette, she excelled as Sophie, Marzelline, Blonde and Despina (recorded under Karajan).

ALAN BLYTH

Otto [née Alvsleben], **Melitta** (*b* Dresden, 16 Dec 1842; *d* Dresden, 13 Jan 1893). German soprano. She studied with Theile in Dresden, where she was engaged at the

Hofoper from 1860 to 1873, at first for light coloratura parts, later for more dramatic roles. In 1875 she was engaged at the Hamburg Stadttheater. In 1877 she returned to Dresden and sang there until her retirement in 1883. Her roles included Anna in Marschner's *Hans Heiling*, Rowena in the same composer's *Der Templer und die Jüdin*, the Queen of Night, Alice (*Robert le diable*) and Eva in *Die Meistersinger*, which she sang at the first Dresden performance (1869).

A. Ehrlich: *Berühmte Sängerinnen der Vergangenheit und Gegenwart* (Leipzig, 1895)

ELIZABETH FORBES

Otto, Teo (*b* Remscheid, 4 Feb 1904; *d* Frankfurt, 9 June 1968). Swiss painter, set and costume designer of German origin. He trained and worked as a mechanic before studying painting at the Kassel Academy with Ewald Dülberg, whose assistant he became at the Bauhaus, Weimar, and then at the Berlin Staatsoper, succeeding him there as chief scenographer in 1928. At the same time he was also working as a regular designer for Klemperer's Kroll Opera. He exhibited with the Berlin Sezession in 1929 and 1930. In 1931 he was appointed chief designer at the Berlin Staatsoper but in 1933 emigrated to Switzerland where, for over 20 years, he designed up to 30 plays a year for the Zürich Schauspielhaus. He worked at all the leading German theatres after World War II, succeeding Neher as principal designer for the Cologne theatres in 1962. Parallel with his career in the theatre was his involvement with opera; he collaborated with Ebert from 1931 to the onset of World War II, and from the 1950s contributed to all the principal German houses, most frequently in productions by Rennert and Schuh. For a short time before his death he taught stage design in Düsseldorf.

Otto's style typified the postwar German school; deeply influenced by Neher, he unfailingly provided an unobtrusive yet highly theatrical framework constructed from a few essential elements (*Mavra*, 1960, Frankfurt and Edinburgh); he favoured a minimalist decorative or symbolic vocabulary (*Le nozze di Figaro*, 1956, Frankfurt, and 1963, Covent Garden), and used light, picking out painted highlights and reflecting off carefully chosen materials, as an integral part of his designs (*Tristan und Isolde*, 1959, Metropolitan). Designs by him are in the theatre collection of Cologne University and the Österreichische Nationalbibliothek, Vienna.

For illustration *see* ORFF, CARL.

ES (H. Grosse)
A. R. Mohr: *Zauberwelt: Bühnenbildentwurf der Frankfurter Oper aus zwei Jahrhunderten* (Nördlingen, 1986)

MARINA HENDERSON

Ottoboni, Pietro (*b* Venice, 2 July 1667; *d* Rome, 28 Feb 1740). Italian patron and librettist. In November 1689, a month after his great-uncle was elected Pope Alexander VIII, he was made a cardinal and given a lifetime appointment as Vice-Chancellor of the Church. During the next 50 years, his annual income exceeded the staggering sum of 50 000 scudi, and he spent much of it subsidizing performances and employing musicians and dramatists including Andrea Adami, Arcangelo Corelli, Alessandro Scarlatti and Arcangelo Spagna. According to Blainville (writing in 1707), he held weekly 'a kind of Academy of Music' at his residence, the Palazzo della Cancelleria, 'maintaining, at his own

Charge, some of the finest Voices and Instrument Players in all Italy'. Alessandro Scarlatti's setting of Ottoboni's first libretto, *La Statira*, reopened the Teatro di Tordinona, which had been closed for 15 years, and within a year Ottoboni had written and produced three more three-act librettos. The Pope's death temporarily halted this proliferation of rather mediocre texts. His next four works, produced in 1694–8, were influenced by his membership and protectorship of the Arcadian Academy, in which his pastoral name was Crateo Pradelini. A papal ban on operas prevented him from producing any between 1698 and 1710, when he wrote the first of four heroic librettos for his new theatre designed by Juvarra. All of them were regarded as marvels, especially in scenic terms.

In addition to his opera librettos, Ottoboni wrote at least 12 oratorio librettos, most of which were set by Alessandro Scarlatti; some attributions are uncertain and should perhaps be made to his father Antonio (1646–1720), who was among the 14 founders of Arcadia and who wrote texts for at least two operas, four oratorios and 21 serenatas. Pietro was an inveterate reviser of his own works: revivals thus required much new music from the composers who served him. The new productions, revivals and concerts given in his palace throughout his career kept him at the centre of Roman musical life from 1690 until the 1730s.

L'amante del suo nemico (dramma per musica), 1688, F. C. Lanciani, unperf.; *La Statira*, A. Scarlatti, 1690; *Il martirio di S Eustachio* (oratorio), Lanciani, 1690; *Amore e gratitudine* (dramma pastorale), Lanciani, 1690; *Il Colombo, overo L'India scoperta* (dramma per musica), Pasquini, 1690; *La Santa Rosalia* [*La costanza nell'amor divino, overo La Santa Rosalia; L'amante del cielo*] (dramma per musica), De Luca, F. Gasparini and Lanciani, 1696; *L'amore eroico fra pastori* (favola pastorale per puppets), G. Bononcini, Cesarini and Lulier, 1696 (arr. A. Scarlatti, 1705, as *La pastorella*; Eng., arr. Urbani, 1708, as *Love's Triumph*]; *Il console tutore* [*Il console in Egitto*] (dramma per musica), ?Lanciani, 1698; *Il Costantino pio* (dramma), C. F. Pollarolo, 1710; *Teodosio il giovane* (dramma), F. Amadei, 1711; *Il Ciro* (dramma), A. Scarlatti, 1712; *Carlo Magno* (festa teatrale), G. Costanzi, 1729

Doubtful: *La Santa Genuinda, overo L'innocenza difesa dall'inganno* (dramma sacro), Lulier, C. F. Pollarolo and A. Scarlatti, 1694

J. de Blainville: *Travels through Holland, Germany, Switzerland and Other Parts of Europe, but Especially Italy*, trans. G. Turnbull and W. Guthrie (London, 1743–5), ii, 391–4; iii, 70–71

A. Cametti: *Il Teatro di Tordinona poi di Apollo* (Tivoli, 1938), ii, 342–9

H. J. Marx: 'Ein neuer Fund zur römischen Operngeschichte des ausgehenden Seicento [*Amore e Gratitudine*]', *AnMc*, no.3 (1966), 43–8

——: 'Die Musik am Hofe Pietro Kardinal Ottobonis unter A. Corelli', *AnMc*, no.5 (1968), 104–77

M. Viale Ferrero: 'Antonio e Pietro Ottoboni e alcuni melodrammi da loro ideati o promossi a Roma', *Venezia e il melodramma nel settecento: Venice 1973*, i, 271–94

G. G. Jones: 'Alessandro Scarlattis *Il Ciro*', *HJbMw*, iii (1978), 225–37

T. E. Griffin: *The Late Baroque Serenata in Rome and Naples: a Documentary Study with Emphasis on Alessandro Scarlatti* (Ann Arbor, 1983)

W. C. Holmes: *La Statira by Pietro Ottoboni and Alessandro Scarlatti: the Textual Sources, with a Documentary Postscript* (New York, 1983)

F. Piperno: 'Crateo, Olinto, Archimede e L'Arcadia: rime per alcuni spettacoli operistici romani (1710–11)', *Händel e gli Scarlatti a Roma: convegno internazionale di studi: Rome 1985*, 349–65

M. Talbot and C. Timms: 'Music and the Poetry of Antonio Ottoboni (1646–1710)', ibid, 367–438

S. Franchi: *Drammaturgia romana: repertorio bibliografico cronologico dei testi drammatici pubblicati a Roma e nel Lazio, secolo xvii* (Rome, 1988)

M. L. Volpicelli: 'Il teatro del Cardinale Pietro Ottoboni al Palazzo della Cancelleria', *Il teatro a Roma nel settecento*, iii (Rome, 1989), 681–782   LOWELL LINDGREN

Ottone [*Ottone, re di Germania* ('Ottone, King of Germany')]. Opera in three acts by GEORGE FRIDERIC HANDEL to a libretto adapted by NICOLA FRANCESCO HAYM from STEFANO BENEDETTO PALLAVICINO's *Teofane* (1719, Dresden); London, King's Theatre, 12 January 1723.

Ottone was the first new opera in the Royal Academy of Music's fourth London season; in it the soprano Francesca Cuzzoni made her London début, as Teofane. The castratos Senesino and Berenstadt sang Ottone and Adalberto, and the cast was completed by Margherita Durastanti (Gismonda), Anastasia Robinson (Matilda) and Giuseppe Boschi (Emireno).

Handel's first post-performance revision appeared on Cuzzoni's benefit night (26 March 1723, during the initial run) when three new arias (including 'Spera, sì', known as 'The Pigeon's Song') were added for Teofane and another for Adalberto. This version was probably repeated in the revival opening on 11 December the same year and it formed the basis of a concert version performed at Paris in 1724, in which four London singers (but not Handel) took part. The score was substantially revised for a further revival on 8 February 1726, when Gismonda became a contralto and Matilda a soprano; the alterations strengthen the character of Ottone but generally are disadvantageous. There was another revival of two performances only in 1727, and a final one by Handel on 13 November 1733, originally intended for the previous season. A heavily altered version, with Farinelli in the role of Adalberto, was produced at the King's Theatre by the Opera of the Nobility in December 1734. There were productions at Brunswick in 1723 and 1725, and at Hamburg (in Telemann's adaptation) in 1726, 1727 and 1729.

The production of Oskar Hagen's heavily arranged version under the title *Otto und Theophano* at Göttingen on 5 July 1921 was the first revival of a Handel opera in the 20th century, and was frequently repeated. The first revival outside Germany was by the Handel Opera Society at Sadler's Wells Theatre, London, on 19 October 1971. Chrysander's edition is one of his most confused and incomplete scores, but most of Handel's versions of the opera can be accurately reconstructed from the surviving word-books and manuscript sources.

The libretto is based on historical events connected with both Otho I and Otho II of Germany, but primarily the latter's marriage to Theophano, Princess of the Eastern Empire, at Rome in April 972. (Antonio Lotti's setting of Pallavicino's original text was produced at Dresden in 1719 to celebrate the marriage of the Electoral Prince of Saxony to the Archduchess of Austria; Handel almost certainly attended performances.) The action is set in and around Rome. Ottone, king of Germany (alto castrato), is on his way to the city to marry Teofane (soprano), but has been delayed by a sea engagement with the pirate Emireno (bass). Gismonda (soprano), widow of the Italian usurper Berengar, and her son Adalberto (alto) take advantage of the delay. Adalberto greets Teofane as if he were Ottone, knowing that she has never previously seen either of them. Ottone reaches Rome with Emireno as his prisoner. He learns from his cousin Matilda (alto), betrothed to Adalberto, that Gismonda has proclaimed Adalberto king of Italy. Gismonda summons Adalberto to deal with Ottone just as he is about to marry Teofane, leaving the latter baffled. Ottone takes Adalberto prisoner. Teofane, misunderstanding part of an overheard conversation between Ottone and Matilda, jealously rejects Ottone when he finally meets her. Gismonda and Matilda help Adalberto escape with Emireno, not knowing that the men are taking Teofane with them. Emireno is pleased to learn from Teofane that the usurper keeping her brother from the throne of the Eastern Empire has been deposed. He returns to Ottone with Adalberto as his prisoner. Ottone, joyfully reunited with Teofane, spares Adalberto at her pleading. Emireno is revealed as Teofane's brother Basil, rightful heir to the Eastern Empire. Gismonda is pacified, Adalberto swears loyalty to both Ottone and Matilda, and all look forward to the return of peace.

* * *

Haym's clumsy condensation of Pallavicino's libretto, subjected to further heavy revision while Handel was setting it, turned the opera into a series of disjunct episodes lacking sustained dramatic tension, though, as in most *opera seria*, this is not too serious a consideration in a well-sung performance and is offset by the melodic grace of much of the music. Several of the arias (and the gavotte of the overture) gained immediate popularity. Gismonda and Matilda emerge strongly in their music, Gismonda's 'Vieni, o figlio' being one of Handel's greatest E major arias, full of passionate yearning. Ottone's arias tend to be lyrical or pathetic at points where heroic resolution is called for, and the role of Teofane lacks the brilliance that might have been expected in a Cuzzoni role, though it begins to acquire it in later versions.   ANTHONY HICKS

Ottone in villa ('Otho at his Villa'). *Drama per musica* in three acts, RV729, by ANTONIO VIVALDI to a libretto by DOMENICO LALLI after Francesco Maria Piccioli's *Messalina*; Vicenza, Teatro delle Garzerie, May 1713.

Ottone in villa was Vivaldi's first opera, performed not in his native Venice but in Vicenza, where there was a tradition of late spring opera productions by Venetian casts. Vivaldi had received a month's leave from his post at the Ospedale della Pietà on 30 April 1713 'in order to employ his skill' ('al impiego delle sue vertuose applicattioni'); as well as *Ottone*, which was put on in competition with the newly opened Teatro delle Grazie, Vivaldi's oratorio *La vittoria navale* received its première in Vicenza on 8 June. The opera's librettist, Domenico Lalli, was also just beginning his career, and Vivaldi was to collaborate with him again. The production was probably devised with a limited budget in mind: the opera requires no special effects; it probably used stock scenery from the theatre; there are only five singers in the cast; and the orchestra calls for just a pair of oboes and recorders (doubtless using the same players) in addition to strings and continuo.

Piccioli's source for Lalli's lightweight libretto was set to music by Carlo Pallavicino in 1680. The story, in Lalli's version, tells of the Emperor Otho (contralto), who is staying at his country villa close to Rome. He is besotted with the flirtatious Cleonilla (soprano), despite the disapproval of his faithful adviser Decio (tenor); she, however, is in love with Caio Silio [Caius Silius] (soprano), a handsome young Roman who was formerly engaged to Tullia (soprano). Tullia has followed her betrothed and, disguising herself under the name Ostilio

[Ostilius], has become Cleonilla's page. Cleonilla is attracted by 'Ostilius' and rejects Caius, who becomes so jealous of his new rival that he tries to kill him. Cleonilla and Otho intervene, however; Caius bitterly accuses 'Ostilius' of treachery, and Tullia is forced to reveal her true identity. She is then reunited with Caius, and Otho, gullibly believing Cleonilla's claim that she knew Ostilius was a woman all along, forgives his lover.

Many features of Vivaldi's early operatic style can be seen in the arias: contrapuntal interest in the orchestral parts; light accompanimental textures in two or three parts; omission of the bass during vocal sections; unexpected melodic intervals such as the diminished 3rd and augmented 2nd; and changes of tempo. Two arias are of particular interest: Otho's 'Come l'onda' (Act 2 scene i) presents a typically Vivaldian picture of a storm at sea, while 'L'ombre, l'aure, e ancora il rio' (2.iii), a traditional echo aria in which Caius's words are repeated by the unseen Tullia, uses trilling pairs of onstage violins and recorders.

The opera was revived at the Teatro Dolfin, Treviso, in October 1729; nine arias and much recitative were cut, and there were 15 new aria texts.   ERIC CROSS

Oudin, Eugène (Espérance) (*b* New York, 24 Feb 1858; *d* London, 4 Nov 1894). American baritone of French descent. He studied with Moderati in New York, where he made his début in 1886 at Wallack's Theatre with the M'Caul Opéra-Comique Company as Montosol in an English version of Roger's *Joséphine vendue par ses soeurs*. He was engaged by Sullivan to create the part of the Templar in *Ivanhoe* at the Royal English Opera House, London, in 1891. He sang the title role in the English première of *Yevgeny Onegin* (1892) at the Olympic Theatre, and in 1893 he sang the High Priest in the first performance in England (a concert version) of *Samson et Dalila*, in his own translation. Oudin sang with notable success in 1893 and 1894 at St Petersburg as Wolfram, Telramund and Albert (*Werther*).

HAROLD ROSENTHAL/R

Oudinot, Nicolas-Médard. See AUDINOT, NICOLAS-MÉDARD.

Oudrid (y Segura), Cristóbal (Domingo) (*b* Badajoz, 7 Feb 1825; *d* Madrid, 12 March 1877). Spanish composer. He was taught the rudiments of music and of several wind instruments by his father and, as a boy, was able to transcribe classical pieces for various wind combinations. He also studied the piano and in 1842 moved to Madrid to continue his studies with Pedro Albéniz. In 1844 he gained the protection of the Semanario Pintoresco Español, founded in 1836 by the writer Ramón de Mesonero Romanos, and he became known for his operatic arrangements for various music societies. In 1847 he began to make his mark in the musical theatre with the production of his first zarzuelas, *La venta del puerto, ó Juanillo el contrabandista* and (in collaboration with Iradier and Cepeda) *La pradera del Canal*. During the following years he composed many such pieces, sharing with the likes of Barbieri, Gaztambide and Hernando the credit for the rejuvenation of the genre as a popular entertainment. His own greatest successes were *El postillón de la Rioja* (1856) and *El molinero de Subiza* (1870), the latter achieving 300 performances within a year. Both contained a *jota* that enjoyed wide popular success, as did the tango from *El último mono* (1859) and his music for *El sitio de Zaragoza*, a play by Lombia. Oudrid delighted in stressing his lack of formal training, the naturalness of his inspiration, and his adherence to national forms rather than the italianisms prevalent at the time. In all he composed about a hundred stage scores, among them those of *1866 y 1867* (with L. Arche), a year-end revue. He also became musical director at the Teatro de la Zarzuela and the Teatro Real, where he died during rehearsals for a production of Ambroise Thomas' *Mignon*.

zarzuelas, first performed in Madrid, unless otherwise stated; most published in Madrid in vocal score at about the time of production

MDC – *Madrid, Teatro del Circo*
MDZ – *Madrid, Teatro de la Zarzuela*

La venta del puerto, ó Juanillo el contrabandista (1, M. Fernández), Príncipe, 16 Jan 1847; La pradera del Canal (1, Azcona), Cruz, 1847, collab. Iradier and Cepeda; Las sacerdotisas del sol (1, J. del Peral), Instituto, 24 Dec 1848, collab. Hernando; Misterios de bastidores (1, Montemar), Instituto, 15 March 1849; La paga de Navidad (1, Montemar), Instituto, 5 July 1849; El alma en pena (1, Montemar), Circo de Paul, 2 Aug 1849; Pero-Grullo (2, Larrea and Lozano), Variedades, 14 Nov 1850

Escenas en Chamberí (1, J. Olona), Variedades, 19 Nov 1850, collab. Hernando, Gaztambide and Barbieri; Misterios de bastidores (2nd part) (1, Montemar), MDC, Jan 1851; Todos son raptos (1, Larra), MDC, 28 May 1851; El castillo encantado (3, E. Bravo), MDC, 18 Dec 1851; Por seguir á una mujer (4, L. Olona), MDC, 24 Dec 1851, collab. Hernando, Gaztambide, Barbieri and Inzenga; Un embuste y una boda (1, L. M. de Larra), MDC, 1851; Mateo y Matea (1, R. Maiquez), MDC, 12 Feb 1852; Buenas noches, Sr Don Simón (1, L. Olona), MDC, 16 April 1852; De este mundo al otro (1, L. Olona), MDC, 13 May 1852; El violino del diablo (1, García), MDC, 25 Nov 1852; Las dos venturas (1, García), Príncipe, 24 Dec 1852, collab. L. Arche; Salvador y Salvadora (1, García), Príncipe, 24 Dec 1852, collab. Arche; D. Ruperto Culebrin (2, L. Olona), MDC, 24 Dec 1852; El alcalde de Tronchon (1, C. Boldum), MDC, 28 May 1853; El hijo de familia (3, L. Olona), MDC, 24 Dec 1853, collab. Gaztambide

Un dia de reinado (3, G. Gutierrez and L. Olona), MDC, 11 Feb 1854, collab. Gaztambide, Barbieri and Inzenga; Moreto (3, Azcona), MDC, 20 May 1854; Pablitu (1, L. Olona), MDC, 24 Dec 1854; La cola del diablo (2, L. Olona), MDC, 24 Dec 1854, collab. Allú and Barbieri; Amor y misterio (1, L. Olona), MDC, 1 May 1855; Estebanillo (3, V. de la Vega), MDC, 5 Oct 1855, collab. Gaztambide; Alumbra á este caballero (1, J. Olona), MDC, 1 Dec 1855; El conde de Castralla (3, A. Lopez de Ayala), MDC, 20 Feb 1856

El postillón de la Rioja (2, L. Olona), MDC, 7 June 1856; La flor de la Serranía (1, J. Gutierrez de Alba), Verano, 2 Aug 1856; Un viaje al vapor (1, J. Olona), MDC, 24 Dec 1856; ¡Concha! (1, J. Olona), MDC, 15 June 1857; El hijo del regimiento (1, V. Tamayo), MDC, 22 Aug 1857; Don Sisenando (1, Puerta Vizcaino), MDC, 4 April 1858; Beltran el aventurero (3, F. Camprodón), MDZ, 1 Sept 1858; El jóven Virginio (3, M. Pina), MDZ, 30 Nov 1858

¡Un disparate! (1, R. de Velasco), MDZ, 14 May 1859; El último mono (1, Narciso Serra), MDZ, 30 May 1859; El Zuavo (1, P. N. Sobrado), MDZ, 28 June 1859; Enlace y desenlace (1, Pina), MDZ, 27 Sept 1859; Un viaje acrostático (1, Pina), MDZ, 14 Dec 1859, collab. Gaztambide; Tetuan por España (1, Pina), MDZ, 8 Feb 1860, collab. others; Memorías de un estudiante (3, J. Picon), MDZ, 5 May 1860; Nadie se muere hasta que Dios quiere (1, Serra), MDZ, 19 Sept 1860

Doña Mariquita (1, Frontaura), MDZ, 13 Nov 1860; A rey muerto (1, L. Rivera), MDZ, 17 Nov 1860; El gran bandido (2, Camprodón), MDZ, 23 Dec 1860, collab. M. F. Caballero; Las piernas azules (3, V. de la Vega), MDZ, 9 Feb 1861, collab. M. Vázquez; El caballo blanco (1, Frontaura), MDZ, 12 June 1861, collab. Caballero; Llegar y besar el Santo (1, E. Inza), MDZ, 15 June 1861, collab. Caballero; Un concierto casero (1, Picon), MDZ, 3 Dec 1861; Un viaje al rededor de mi suegro (3, Rivera), MDZ, 24 Dec 1861, collab. Vázquez

Roquelaure (3, J. Belza), MDZ, 17 March 1862, collab. Caballero and Rogel; Por sorpresa (2, F. Ruiz del Cerro), MDZ, 20 April 1862, collab. Vázquez and Rogel; Equilibrios del amor (1, F. Martinez Pedrosa), MDZ, 20 April 1862, collab. Caballero; La isla de San Balandran (1, Picon), MDZ, 12 June 1862; Juegos de azár (2, Pina), MDZ, 30 Oct 1862, collab. Caballero; El galan incógnito (3, R. de la Vega), MDZ, 1 Nov 1862; Matilde y Malek-Adel (3, Frontaura), MDZ, 7 March 1863, collab. Gaztambide

Walter, ó la huérfana de Bruselas (3, F. Ossorio), MDZ, 5 April 1863, collab. Javier Gaztambide; Por amor al prójimo (1, Belza), MDZ, 10 April 1863; Influencias políticas (1, Pina), MDZ, 24 April 1863; Julio César (1, Rivera), MDZ, 5 June 1863; La voluntad de la niña (1, E. Alvarez), MDZ, 17 June 1863, collab. Carreras; Un marido de lance (1, R. Caltañazor), MDZ, 6 June 1864; La córte del rey Reuma (1, E. Blasco), MDZ, c1864, collab. Rogel

La paloma azul (3, R. M. Liern), Novedades, 25 Feb 1865; 1866 y 1867 (2, Gutierrez de Alba), MDC, 24 Dec 1866, collab. Arche; La espada de Satanás (4, Liern), Novedades, 23 Feb 1867; Bazar de novias (1, Pina), Variedades, 9 March 1867; El camisolin de Paco (2, J. Catalina), MDC, 29 Oct 1867, collab. Vázquez; Un estudiante de Salamanca (3, Rivera), MDZ, 4 Dec 1867; Café-teatro y restaurant cantante (1, Alvarez), Circo de Paul, 11 July 1868

La reina de los aires (1, R. G. Santisteban), MDC, Feb 1869; La gata de Mari-Ramos (2, Pina), MDZ, 27 Jan 1870; El paciente Job (1, R. de la Vega), MDZ, 13 May 1870; El molinero de Subiza (3, L. Eguilaz), MDZ, 21 Dec 1870; Los encantos de Brijan (3, Eguilaz), 1870; Justos por pecadores (3, Larra), MDZ, 25 Oct 1871, collab. P. M. Marqués; Miró y Compañia, ó los cómicos de Alcorcon (1, García Vivanco), Barcelona, 8 Aug 1872; Ildara (3, R. Puente y Brañas), MDZ, 5 Jan 1874; El demonio de los bufos (1, Puente y Brañas), MDZ, 24 June 1874

El testamento azul (3, L. Amalfi [Liern]), Jardín del Retiro, 20 July 1874, collab. Barbieri and Aceves; El señor de Cascarrabias (1, Amalfi), Jardín del Retiro, 17 Aug 1874; Compuesto y sin novia (1, Pina), Variedades, 5 Dec 1875; La paz (1, Puente y Brañas), Comedia, 20 March 1876; Los pajes del rey (2, Larra), MDZ, 20 Oct 1876; Blancos y azules (3, Liern and Nogués), Apolo, 22 Dec 1876, collab. Caballero and Caseres; El consejo de los diez (1, Nogués), Apolo, May 1884

Other works: Yo y mi tia (1, I. Fernández); Don Isidro en San Isidro (1, Fernández); Los polvos de la madre Celestina (3, Hartzenbusch); La pata de cabra (3, Grimaldi)

*

A. Peña y Goñi: *La ópera española y la música dramática en España en el siglo XIX* (Madrid, 1881), 348–76

'Oudrid y Segura (Cristóbal)', *Enciclopedia universal ilustrada europeo-americana* (Barcelona, 1907–), xl

E. Cotarelo y Mori: *Historia de la zarzuela, o sea el drama lírico* (Madrid, 1934)

R. Alier and others: *El libro de la zarzuela* (Barcelona, 1982, 2/1986 as *Diccionario de la zarzuela*)
ANDREW LAMB

Our Man in Havana. Opera in three acts by MALCOLM WILLIAMSON to a libretto by Sidney Gilliatt after Graham Greene's novel; London, Sadler's Wells Theatre, 2 July 1963.

Set in pre-revolutionary Havana, the opera follows Greene's novel in highlighting violent comedy in an uneasy society in which the simple materialistic ambitions of a not-very-successful dealer in vacuum cleaners, Bramble (Greene's Wormold; tenor), on behalf of his spoilt, pretty, horse-riding daughter Milly (soprano), can exploit the gullibility of official espionage. Recruited as a British agent, Bramble invents journeys, agents and information for his expense accounts and submits the working drawings of a vacuum cleaner as the plan of a military installation. His private comedy of incompetence blundering into prosperity brings him an admirer in Beatrice (soprano), a London-dispatched assistant (whose sensational *f'''* ends Act 2) and a puzzled adversary in Milly's Cuban policeman admirer, Captain Segura (baritone); however, it has fatal consequences for his best friend, the elderly German doctor Hasselbacher (bass), and brings disaster to the namesakes of his imaginary agents. The opera inevitably loses the throwaway humour of the novel but offers in compensation a lively musical representation of Cuban local colour in the orchestral writing (there are two versions: the smaller mostly uses single wind) and through extensive chorus and small solo parts. Set pieces for Milly (characterized by waltz tunes), Bramble, Beatrice and the chorus, and a long and effective dying scene for Hasselbacher help give shape to a melodious, rhythmically resourceful and occasionally surprisingly dissonant score in which intricately subdivided arioso and recitative passages and some difficult solos and ensembles in irregular metres exist beside racy or pious simplicities with ancestry in contemporary musicals.

ROGER COVELL

Overton, Hall (*b* Bangor, MI, 23 Feb 1920; *d* New York, 24 Nov 1972). American composer. He studied counterpoint with Gustav Dunkelberger (1940–42) and composition with Persichetti at the Juilliard School (1947–51); later he took private lessons with Riegger and Milhaud. Serving overseas in the US Army (1942–5), he developed remarkable skill in jazz improvisation. He taught at the Juilliard School (1960–71), the New School, New York (1962–6), and the Yale School of Music (1970–71). His music was deeply influenced by jazz. The text of his opera *Huckleberry Finn* abandons the simple nature of the character and treats him as one concerned with issues of conscience.

The Enchanted Pear Tree (ob, 4 scenes, J. Thompson, after Boccaccio: *Decameron*), New York, Juilliard School of Music, 7 Feb 1950
Pietro's Petard (chamber op, 1, R. DeMaria), New York, After Dinner Opera Company, June 1963
Huckleberry Finn (2, Overton and J. Stampfer, after M. Twain), New York, Juilliard American Opera Center, 20 May 1971

*

D. Cohen: 'The Music of Hall Overton', *American Composers Alliance Bulletin*, x/4 (1962), 8–12   OLIVER DANIEL

Overture (Fr. *ouverture*; Ger. *Ouvertüre*; It. *sinfonia*). A short or medium-length instrumental number, usually for orchestra, most often in several sections in different tempos, serving to introduce a theatrical work; also a similar composition intended for concert use. *See also* FRENCH OVERTURE; ITALIAN OVERTURE; MEDLEY OVERTURE; PRELUDE; REPRISE OVERTURE; SINFONIA; and SINFONIA AVANTI L'OPERA.

1. Terminology. 2. To 1750. 3. 1750–1800. 4. After 1800.

1. TERMINOLOGY. The word 'overture' derives from the French *ouverture*, 'opening', which in its musical sense originally (in the 17th century) applied to an instrumental piece used to open a ballet, opera or oratorio. 18th-century writers sometimes use the term 'ouverture' to refer specifically to the French overture in contrast to the Italian overture, to which the term 'sinfonia' was applied. (Such terms as 'intrada', 'sonata' and 'apertura' were also used.) Only around 1800 did the terms 'overture' and 'symphony' become consistently applied on the basis of size and function in the various European languages. Besides the theatrical overture discussed here, the term 'overture' could also refer to the Baroque suite (originally 'ouverture avec suite'), the concert symphony and the concert overture of the 19th century and after. Some composers have used the terms 'prelude' or 'introduction' for pieces fulfilling the function of an overture, often to designate a fairly short piece in one tempo or – particularly in the case of German composers – simply to avoid using a word of French origin.

The history of the operatic overture can best be understood as part of the history of the opera, participating in the same aesthetic and stylistic trends as any other component. Though it was often the last part of an opera to be composed and was necessarily subordinate in function to the vocal portions of the work, at certain times and places the overture was treated as one of the primary components of the musical drama. From modest beginnings, the operatic overture gradually developed to a peak in the decades around 1800, then declined and nearly disappeared from the more serious types of opera in the late 19th century.

2. TO 1750. Threefold fanfares often announced the beginning of a Renaissance entertainment. The little toccata that opens Monteverdi's *Orfeo* (1607) is unusual merely as a particularly memorable instance of the type and one that can be identified with a specific performance. On other occasions composers might simply indicate, as Gagliano did for his *Dafne* (1608), 'per render attenti gli uditori, suonisi una Sinfonia composta di diversi istrumenti' ('to gain the attention of the audience, a sinfonia with several instruments is played'), leaving it to be chosen from whatever pieces were available.

With the appearance of opera houses and the emergence of the opera orchestra around 1640, it became common for operas to begin with an orchestral number written for that particular work. These were called by the same term, 'sinfonia', used for most sorts of instrumental number in these operas other than ritornellos or functional dances and marches, sometimes with the added distinction 'avanti l'opera' or 'avanti il prologo', and at first they were not necessarily longer or more significant than the sinfonias preceding the later acts or those within the acts themselves. Generally they comprised several sections in different tempos and metres, one common pattern being a slow section in duple metre followed by a fast section in triple, not altogether unlike a pair of dances (e.g. Cavalli's *Scipione affricano*, 1664).

Later in the century overtures, like other types of operatic number, became larger and more specialized in function as well as more standardized in style and form. The French overture was established by Lully in the slow–fast pattern just described. The term 'ouverture' itself had already been in use for the processional entrée of a ballet, or of an act of a ballet, at least from 1640 (the *Ballet de Mademoiselle*; printed in Prunières). The movements were normally homophonic and in binary form but with the second in a faster tempo and a different metre from the first, though they were not necessarily longer than the other movements of the work. Lully, perhaps referring to Italian models, expanded this form, added contrapuntal interest, and sharpened the contrast between the two sections. The opening was now march-like, while the lively second section was usually in triple or compound metre and made at least some use of imitation; the two sections were longer, and the material or at least the tempo of the first might return at the end. The first fully characteristic French overture is that to Lully's ballet *Alcidiane* of 1658, and the first use of the type in opera came in an overture he composed for a performance of Cavalli's *Xerse* two years later. Lully's overtures were still short enough to be performed both before the prologue and before the first act of the opera proper, a practice retained in French opera until the time of Rameau.

Lully's adherence to the type in his later works led to its establishment not only in France but also in other parts of Europe subject to French cultural influence, including Germany, Britain and at times even Italy.

The other important late 17th-century type of overture was the Italian overture. Like its predecessors, it consisted of several homophonic movements with a dance-like finale, which was most often in triple or compound metre. But the outer movements and later the slow movements grew much larger than the sections of earlier overtures. The Italian overture most often assumed a fast–slow–fast pattern. But other possibilities existed: these include a two-movement type, fast–slow, in which the number following the curtain functioned as the finale of the overture (Fux, *Elisa*, 1719), and the reprise overture (Caldara, *Don Chisciotte in corte della duchessa*, 1727), in which the concluding section used the same material as the opening one. Alessandro Scarlatti employed the characteristic fast–slow–fast Italian overture as early as 1681 (*Tutto il mal non vien per nuocere*), but it was only in the 1690s that he and others began to use the design regularly. While French overtures could be in either mode, Italian ones were nearly always in the major. In accordance with their tendencies concerning texture and mode French overtures were normally scored for strings and woodwind, but with the wind confined to doublings and possibly trio episodes in the fast sections; by contrast, Italian overtures often employed trumpets.

After 1700 the Italian overture gradually replaced the French design as the predominant type of operatic overture in one country after another. Thus when Keiser composed his *Croesus* for Hamburg in 1711, he gave it a French overture, notated for strings only; for a revival in 1730, he provided a new overture in the Italian style, a reprise overture scored with *zuffolo* (a wind instrument), three trumpets and timpani (both are printed in DDT, xxxvii–xxxviii, 1912). Later French overtures often show hybrid features – an indication that operatic composers were mingling French and Italian elements – and by the middle of the century even the French and the conservative English were composing Italian overtures. An indication of the increasing prominence of the overture is the amount of debate this change occasioned, with such writers as Quantz (*Versuch einer Anweisung die Flöte traversiere zu Spielen*, Berlin, 1752) and d'Alembert ('De la liberté de la musique', *Mélanges de littérature*, Paris, 2/1759) expressing regret, but Scheibe (*Der critische Musikus*, Leipzig, 1745) and Rousseau (*Dictionnaire de musique*, Paris, 1768), among others, revealing enthusiasm for the simpler Italian style.

Within the general outlines of the style already described, the Italian overture underwent changes in the first half of the 18th century, and was an important focus for the development of the emerging Classical orchestral style (as Hell, in particular, has documented). The wind, particularly the brass, came to play a greater role; the key structure was simplified but the thematic material and the orchestral writing became more differentiated, with fanfare passages in the first movements and lyrical accompanied melodies in the slow movements and secondary thematic material. The outer movements of three-movement overtures began to resemble sonata-form designs without development sections, and the outer sections of reprise overtures came to resemble sonata expositions and recapitulations.

3. 1750–1800. Perhaps the most common fault found with the overture in 18th-century writings was the absence of any specific relationship between most operatic overtures and the works they introduced (among others see d'Alembert; Algarotti, *Saggio sopra l'opera in musica*, 1755; Planelli, *Dell'opera in musica*, 1772). It should hardly be surprising that this was so in an era when operas tended to consist of chains of set numbers, such as da capo arias, linked only by simple recitative and in which neither performers nor audiences showed much concern for dramatic and musical unity. In the operatic reform of the late 18th century, the form and role of the overture were redefined in the same way as those of every other component of the genre, making the overture much more a part of the whole than it had formerly been.

An operatic overture may be linked to the rest of the work in a number of ways. It may be structurally incorporated into an opening complex. It may establish the principal key of the opening scene or even the central key of the entire work. A programmatic overture may set the mood for the work or for the opening scene, summarize the entire drama, or depict the events that lead up to the opening situation. The overture may also introduce thematic ideas to be heard again later. While these possibilities had been employed before, from the middle of the 18th century composers began to use them more systematically than had their predecessors. Their change in attitude also led them to experiment with different formal designs more appropriate to the new function of the overture.

Like the da capo aria, the three-movement Italian overture, which predominated in operas about 1760, had nearly disappeared by 1790 in favour of less static formal patterns – Haydn, in fact, abandoned it after 1762. The reprise overture was used by, among many others, Piccinni (*La finta baronessa*, 1767), Paisiello (*Socrate immaginario*, 1775) and Grétry (*L'amitié à l'épreuve*, 1770). The two-movement Italian overture flourished in the works of such varied composers as Hasse (*Adriano in Siria*, 1752), Traetta (*Sofonisba*, 1762), Monsigny (*Le roy et le fermier*, 1762) and Haydn (*Philemon und Baucis*, 1773). Single-movement overtures corresponding to the first movement of the Italian type also occur in the period, but composers generally preferred forms using several tempos. (The familiar overture to Mozart's *Le nozze di Figaro*, 1786, was planned as a reprise overture, which explains its lack of a development section: an anomaly in a work by an Austrian.) Slow introductions, marked either by an actual change of tempo or a change of note values, appeared once in a while with three-movement overtures (Hasse, *Alcide al bivio*, 1760), reprise overtures (Paisiello, *Socrate*), or two-movement overtures (Haydn, *Der Götterrat*, 1773), but they were particularly common in the one-movement type (Gluck, *Alceste*, 1767; *Iphigénie en Aulide*, 1774). Though programmatic overtures with no set formal pattern (such as some of Rameau's later ones) and medley overtures also began to appear in the late 18th century, it was the one-movement type with slow introduction that became the standard by the 1790s.

As composers grew more accustomed to linking operatic numbers into larger units, they began to incorporate their overtures into opening complexes. Two-movement overtures often functioned in this way, but one-movement overtures and even reprise overtures could also be used as building blocks of larger structures. That to Rameau's *Naïs* (1749) is an important early example: the overture runs into the opening chorus of the prologue, to which it is thematically linked, much like the more famous opening of Gluck's *Iphigénie en Aulide* a quarter-century later. Where the overture is a musically closed unit, it may still set the key of the opening scene, as in Gluck's *Alceste*. Salieri's *La fiera di Venezia* (1772) and Mozart's *Die Entführung aus dem Serail* (1782) and *Don Giovanni* (1787), have particularly noteworthy opening complexes.

Mozart was particularly concerned with the role of the overture in the tonal structure of the entire opera; his mature operas (from *Idomeneo* onwards) invariably end in the key of the overture. Other composers were less consistent; oddly enough, Haydn and Beethoven both observed the practice early in their operatic careers but abandoned it later, with *L'incontro improvviso* (1775) and the 1814 version of *Fidelio* respectively.

In the preface to *Alceste*, Gluck says, 'Ho imaginato che la Sinfonia debba prevenir gli Spettatori dell'azione' ('I planned that the sinfonia would forewarn the audience of the drama'). Though his overture probably serves more to establish the sombre mood of the opening scene than to foreshadow the unfolding of the drama, Gluck's calling attention to the relationship is a significant indication that attitudes on the matter were changing. Rameau had already taken the lead in such works as *Naïs*, in which the overture represents the conflict of the Titans and giants against the Olympian gods. Later overtures with detailed programmes include those to Salieri's *Armida* (1771) and Grétry's *Le jugement de Midas* (1778). Operas set in exotic locales received suitably flavoured overtures, such as the 'Chinese' overture Gluck composed for *Le cinesi* (1754); the 'Turkish' one he provided for *La rencontre imprévue* (1764) belongs to a lineage that includes the overtures to Haydn's *L'incontro improvviso* and Mozart's *Die Entführung*. The storm scene has always been a popular topic of programmatic overtures. Early examples include Draghi's *L'albero del ramo d'oro* (1681) and Marais' *Alcione* (1706). Gluck essayed one in *L'île de Merlin* (1758) and Haydn several, beginning with *Philemon*. It had become a convention to begin an opera on the subject of Iphigenia in Tauris with a storm overture, as in the settings by G. F. Majo (1764), Galuppi (1768) and Jommelli (1771; this overture also includes a battle scene); curiously, Gluck's opera (1779) has no overture, using a reworking of the *Merlin* overture with chorus as an opening scene, and the overture to Piccinni's (1781) is not programmatic.

Thematic anticipations of later numbers became common in overtures from the late 18th century. Rameau used them regularly in his later operas. Some genuine medley overtures exist from the period (Dibdin, *The Touchstone*, 1779). More often quotations appear in subsidiary sections of overtures in one of the standard designs mentioned earlier, such as the slow movement of a two-movement overture (Traetta, *Sofonisba*), the finale of a three-movement overture (Naumann, *Cora och Alonzo*, 1782), the middle section of a reprise overture (Mozart, *Die Entführung*; Haydn, *Armida*, 1784) or the introduction of a one-movement overture (Gluck, *Iphigénie en Aulide*; Mozart, *Don Giovanni*). The quotation may be from the opening scene (*Iphigénie*, *Die Entführung*) or it may be from a climactic moment later in the work (*Sofonisba*; *Cora*; *Don Giovanni*; *Armida* – in this last work several quotations are juxtaposed). The latter possibility, of course, was made possible only by the fact that operas now had musico-dramatic climaxes, in itself an important feature of the reform.

4. AFTER 1800. Though the early 19th century produced many fine overtures – those of Cherubini, Weber and Rossini, for example – the pace of innovation was slower than in the preceding decades. 19th-century overtures on the whole showed yet greater concern for thematic relationships between the overture and the rest of the work than had earlier ones, perhaps as a reflection of the role of such relationships in 19th-century thought about musical form in general. The medley overture became increasingly popular; now such works often revealed at least enough concern for musical structure to end with a substantial quick section (Reichardt's *Die Geisterinsel*, 1798, provides an early example). Composers showed great ingenuity in working material from various sections of an opera into sonata-form overtures, the most spectacular examples being Beethoven's overtures for the 1805 and 1806 versions of *Fidelio* ('Leonore overtures' nos.2 and 3) and the overtures of Weber. The type of material being used in operas had changed to a point where composers could now find many of the components of an overture ready for assembly, as Spontini demonstrated in *La vestale* (1807) and Rossini did with considerably greater art in works like *La gazza ladra* (1817).

It is significant that the first two overtures Beethoven wrote for *Fidelio* ('Leonore' nos. 2 and 3) are rarely used to preface the opera; the shorter, less dramatic work we call the *Fidelio* overture is more effective in the theatre even though it has no thematic relationship to the rest of the opera and is in the 'wrong' key. The real descendants of works like 'Leonore no.3' are the concert overtures and similar works ('symphonic poems', 'tone poems' and the like) that began to flourish in the early 19th century. As the musical language became more grandiose, operatic composers found it more appropriate to write medley overtures, as Verdi occasionally did (*La forza del destino*, 1862) or, as Wagner often did, to use less elaborate structures than a fully developed Romantic sonata form. To an increasing extent later in the century they virtually abandoned the overture altogether, perhaps because the pacing and musical continuity of opera had changed to the point where a separate, or separable, orchestral number at the beginning would have been out of place; a few bars of orchestral texture to establish the atmosphere for the opening scene normally sufficed (the three grim chords that introduce Puccini's *Tosca* (1900), representing Scarpia, carry this to an extreme).

The most significant survival of the operatic overture into the 20th century has been in the operetta and the musical. These works often have medley overtures, but a few are sufficiently well-written to merit serious attention (Bernstein, *Candide*, 1956). In a sense the fanfare that opens Stravinsky's *The Rake's Progress* represents a return to the beginnings of opera, being similar as a gesture to the one that precedes Monteverdi's *Orfeo*.

*

H. Prunières: 'Notes sur les origines de l'ouverture française', *SIMG*, xii (1910–11), 565–85

H. Botstiber: *Geschichte der Ouvertüre und der freien Orchesterformen* (Leipzig, 1913)

H. Livingston: *The Italian Overture from A. Scarlatti to Mozart* (diss., U. of North Carolina, 1952)

H. Hell: *Die neapolitanische Opernsinfonie in der ersten Hälfte des 18. Jahrhunderts* (Tutzing, 1971)

B. Deane: 'The French Operatic Overture from Grétry to Berlioz', *PRMA*, xcix (1972–3), 67–80

J. R. Anthony: *French Baroque Music from Beaujoyeulx to Rameau* (London, 1973, 2/1978; Fr. trans., 1981)

R. Fiske: *English Theatre Music in the Eighteenth Century* (London, 1973, 2/1986)

S. Steinbeck: *Die Ouvertüre in der Zeit von Beethoven bis Wagner: Probleme und Lösungen* (Munich, 1973)

S. C. Fisher: *Haydn's Overtures and their Adaptations as Concert Orchestral Works* (diss., U. of Pennsylvania, 1985)

STEPHEN C. FISHER

Ovid [Publius Ovidius Naso] (*b* Sulmo, 43 BC; *d* Tomis, AD 17). Roman poet. The scion of an equestrian family, he studied rhetoric, held minor public posts, but made his reputation as a poet with the *Amores* (*c*20 BC). He was exiled to the Black Sea by the emperor Augustus in AD 8; there he wrote the *Tristia* and *Epistulae ex Ponto* ('Letters from the Black Sea').

At Rome he had completed a tragedy, *Medea*, now lost; but the most influential of his Roman works, in his lifetime, for European literature (from the 12th century), and eventually opera, were the *Heroides* and *Metamorphoses*. The *Heroides* took the form of fictional letters from heroines of antiquity to their absent husbands and lovers. The epistles of Phaedra to Hippolytus, Dido to Aeneas, Ariadne to Theseus, Medea to Jason, and Helen to Paris were absorbed by many opera librettists. In medieval and Renaissance Europe the *Metamorphoses* were a main source for plots based on Greek and Roman mythology. Operas treating such characters as Acis and Galatea, Apollo and Hyacinth, Ariadne, Daphne, Echo and Narcissus, Hercules, Medea, Orpheus and Eurydice, Pygmalion, Venus and Adonis, are greatly indebted to them. In Rinuccini's libretto *Dafne*, set by Peri and Corsi (Carnival 1598), Gagliano (1608) and (in translation) Schütz (1627), Ovid actually delivers the prologue. Gregor's libretto for Strauss's *Daphne* (1938) owes Ovid a similar debt.   ROBERT ANDERSON

Owen Wingrave. Opera in two acts, op.85, by BENJAMIN BRITTEN to a libretto by MYFANWY PIPER after HENRY JAMES's short story; BBC television, 16 May 1971 (London, Covent Garden, 10 May 1973).

Owen Wingrave *the last of the Wingraves*	baritone
Spencer Coyle *who runs a military cramming establishment*	bass-baritone
Lechmere *a young student with Owen at Coyle's establishment*	tenor
Miss Wingrave *Owen's aunt*	dramatic soprano
Mrs Coyle	soprano
Mrs Julian *a widow and dependant at Paramore*	soprano
Kate *her daughter*	mezzo-soprano
General Sir Philip Wingrave *Owen's grandfather*	tenor
Narrator *a ballad singer*	tenor

Distant chorus of treble voices

Setting London and at Paramore, the Wingrave family seat, in the late 19th century

BBC television commissioned an opera from Britten in 1966, and in 1968 he and Myfanwy Piper began to sketch the scenario of *Owen Wingrave*, a story Britten had known since at least the time of his earlier Henry James opera, *The Turn of the Screw*. The composition, whose style reflects Britten's later interest in aspects of 12-note technique, was sketched between the summer of 1969 and February 1970; the full score was completed by August. The television recording was made at Snape Maltings in November 1970, and a month later a gramophone recording was made with the original cast, including Peter Pears, Janet Baker and John Shirley-Quirk with Benjamin Luxon in the title role. Britten thought of the work as a chamber opera, although it requires an orchestra of 46. He intended it for the stage as well as television, but it has been seen relatively infrequently in either medium.

ACT 1   During the Prelude, a succession of portraits of military ancestors is seen at Paramore. At the end Owen himself is seen, bearing a marked resemblance to the last portrait, that of his late father.

1.i   *The study of Spencer Coyle's military crammer*   Coyle is completing a lesson on tactics for his students Lechmere and Owen Wingrave. Wingrave's distaste for violence is already evident in his response to Lechmere's naive enthusiasm for warfare, and he explains to Coyle that he feels unable to pursue the family tradition. After Owen has left, Coyle expresses his perplexity at Owen's decision.

1.ii   *Hyde Park*   Owen reflects on the horrors of war, relieved that he has told Coyle of his feelings. This *scena* is intercut with the dialogue between Coyle and Owen's aunt at her residence. Miss Wingrave is enraged at her nephew's refusal to do his family duty.

1.iii   *At the Coyles'*   Mrs Coyle joins her husband and Lechmere in a last attempt to persuade Owen to change his mind, but without success. As they drink to Owen's future, Coyle gives him his aunt's instructions to go home to the country at once.

1.iv–vii   *Paramore*   Scene iv introduces Kate Julian and her widowed mother, family friends. Both are worried by the news of Owen's disgrace and when Owen arrives he is dismayed at their evident hostility. His aunt and his grandfather, General Sir Philip Wingrave, are no more welcoming. Scene v comprises an extended ensemble: 'a week passes during which Owen is under constant attack'. In scene vi the Coyles and Lechmere arrive, all three sympathetic to Owen but still unable to understand his rejection of all they stand for. The family has ordered Coyle 'to make one last appeal', and he and Owen recognize that the qualities of a fighter underlie Owen's refusal to conform. In scene vii, family and guests assemble for dinner. The atmosphere is tense, and when Coyle encourages him to recall his military past Sir Philip launches a new attack on Owen, in which the Julians and Miss Wingrave join. Owen is driven to assert that he would make declaring and waging war a criminal offence, and his grandfather walks out. The others follow, leaving Owen alone.

ACT 2   In the Prologue a narrator sings a ballad relating how once a young Wingrave who shamed the family through cowardice was taken to his room and accidentally killed by a blow from his father. Later the father was found dead in the same room 'without a wound', and thereafter the ghosts of father and son have haunted Paramore.

2.i   *Paramore*   Owen explains to Coyle how real this story remains to him, while Mrs Coyle attempts unsuccessfully to persuade Kate that she is being too harsh with Owen. Sir Philip appears, and summons Owen to his room. The others remain in the hall and comment variously as Sir Philip is heard telling his grandson that he 'must obey'. Owen's replies cannot be heard, but in the end the General exclaims that he must 'never return'. As Owen explains when he emerges, 'I'm disinherited'. Mrs Julian's reaction, to Kate's intense embarrassment, is to bewail the loss of her daughter's prospects as Owen's possible bride. Lechmere and the Coyles are more sympathetic, though Lechmere takes his chance to flirt with Kate, and she encourages him. After Miss Wingrave announces that Sir Philip is too upset to reappear that night, the guests disperse, leaving Owen alone. To music recalling the well-nigh atonal material of the Act 1 Prelude, he addresses the family portraits; then, in the opera's most sustained lyrical and diatonic music, affirms that 'in peace I have found my image, I have found myself'. The Wingrave ghosts appear, and when Owen tells them that he is no longer afraid they disappear into the locked room. Kate returns, expressing her sorrow at Owen's resistance to family traditions. He joins her in voicing regret for what they will lose. However, any prospect of reconciliation is dashed when she taunts him with Lechmere's declaration that he would be willing to sleep in the haunted room for her. Furious at the accusation of cowardice, Owen decides to take up the challenge.

2.ii The Coyles discuss their unease, and Lechmere, having overheard the outcome of Owen's scene with Kate, tells Coyle of his worries. As they go to see what has happened, they hear Kate cry out. She has entered the haunted room and found Owen dead. As everyone freezes in horror the first stanza of the ballad is heard again, its repeated refrain, 'Paramore shall welcome woe!', fading away to end the opera.

*　　*　　*

Owen Wingrave is a less compelling dramatic expression of Britten's pacifist convictions than *Billy Budd*: the story itself has fewer subtleties, and the need to aim for televisual effectiveness may have encouraged the abandonment of that gradual establishment of character in all its aspects on which his best operas depend. As the church operas which precede it and *Death in Venice* which follows it prove, Britten's work in the last 15 years of his life was at its best when the strongest constraints were imposed on it. *Owen Wingrave* is not as sheerly concentrated as the church operas, yet its forms are often severely foreshortened. Even so, it has considerable musical strengths: the sinisterly simple ballad, Owen's unaffected moment of vision and, overall, the pervasive shadow of threatening martial music.

ARNOLD WHITTALL

Oxenbould, Moffatt (*b* Sydney, 18 November 1943). Australian administrator and director. He studied production at the National Institute for Dramatic Art and then worked as a stage manager with the Elizabethan Trust Opera (now the Australian Opera) from 1963 to 1965, the Sutherland-Williamson touring company (1965) and at Sadler's Wells (1966–7). As planning coordinator for the Elizabethan Trust Opera and the Australian Opera (1967–73) he developed a tireless and meticulous command of administrative and artistic detail. His appointment as personal assistant to the general manager (1973–4) was followed by a decade (1974–84) as artistic administrator, working closely with Richard Bonynge, the company's musical director for most of those years. His own productions include

The Rape of Lucretia (1972) and *Il trittico* (1974, revived in 1982). Oxenbould succeeded Bonynge as artistic director of the company in 1984.

ROGER COVELL

Oxenford, John (*b* Camberwell, London, 12 Aug 1812; *d* Southwark, London, 21 Feb 1877). English dramatist, librettist and critic. He was almost entirely self-educated. Besides translating works of German, Italian, French and Spanish literature, he translated or adapted librettos to operas by Hérold, Massé, Maillart and Cagnoni. He also wrote original librettos for G. A. Macfarren and Edward Loder, and collaborated with Dion Boucicault on *The Lily of Killarney* for Benedict. Oxenford was unquestionably the best-read English librettist of his day, though his scholastic stance sometimes detracted from the dramatic force of his stage pieces. Nevertheless he succeeded in raising the literary qualities of British opera to a level which greatly narrowed the gap between native and continental products. He was aided in this by the highly professional attitude of Macfarren, for whom he wrote eight librettos, 1834–64; in *Robin Hood* (1860) the two men created so thoroughly nationalist a work that the way lay open for composers such as Stanford and Ethel Smyth. For more than 30 years Oxenford was dramatic critic of *The Times*, but in this role his 'excessive kindliness of disposition induced such leniency of judgment as was fatal to the value of his verdict' (*Athenaeum*, 24 February 1877). His fine essay 'Iconoclasm in German Philosophy' (*Westminster Review*, new ser., iii, 1853, pp.388–407), which remains one of the most lucid introductions to Schopenhauer ever written, helped to advance the cause of Wagner in Britain.

I and my Double (farce), Macfarren, 1835; *The Dice of Death* (musical drama), Loder, 1835; *Allan of Aberfeldy*, Macfarren, comp. *c*1850; *The Sleeper Awakened* (op), Macfarren, 1850; *Aminta, or A Match for a Magistrate* (comic op), W. H. Glover, 1852; *Robin Hood*, Macfarren, 1860; *The Lily of Killarney* (with D. Boucicault), J. Benedict, 1862; *Freya's Gift* (ballet), Macfarren, 1863; *Jessy Lea* (opera di camera), Macfarren, 1863; *The Soldier's Legacy, or The Old Corporal's Story* (drama), Macfarren, 1864; *Helvellyn*, Macfarren, 1864

*

DNB (R. H. Legge); *NicollH*
Men of the Time (London, 9/1875), 779
Obituaries: *The Times* (23 and 26 Feb 1877); *The Athenaeum* (24 Feb 1877); *The Academy* (3 March 1877); *The Era* (4 March 1877)
'John Oxenford's Dramatic Works', *Musical World*, lv (1877), 172 [incl. list of works; see also pp.196, 231 for addenda]
E. W. White: *A Register of First Performances of English Operas and Semi-Operas* (London, 1983)　　NIGEL BURTON

Oxford. English university city. Operatic events were haphazard until the present century. The beginning of a consistent tradition in the university was established with a production of Monteverdi's *Orfeo* in 1925, after which the Oxford University Opera Club (OUOC) was formally constituted. Since then it has put on, in a variety of theatres and halls, a remarkable series of productions as an adventurous amateur group, sometimes employing young professional soloists. In addition there have been regular visits of touring companies, especially the WNO but also Glyndebourne Touring Company, occasional festival productions, and special performances such as Delius's *Irmelin* on its 60th anniversary under Sir Thomas Beecham (1953).

The OUOC has continued to adhere to its founding aim of reviving 'neglected works of historical importance'. Its own history (summarized to 1970 by White, and in more detail to 1950 by Ponsonby and Kent) is studded with important first revivals in England. The 1925 *Orfeo* shows characteristic features: a British première, involving scholarly effort (Westrup edited it from the 1615 score in the Bodleian Library) and translation into English. A peak period, under Westrup's conductorship during his tenure of the Heather Professorship, was from 1947 to 1962, when a wide range of operas was given in translations by Westrup from Slavonic and other languages, as well as the première of Wellesz's *Incognita* (1951) and the British première of Alan Bush's *Men of Blackmoor* (1961). The OUOC has pioneered early opera (including Monteverdi's *L'incoronazione di Poppea*, 1927; Alessandro Scarlatti's *Il Mitridate Eupatore*, 1961; and Cavalli's *Rosinda*, 1973). It has given works by major composers not primarily known for their operas, such as Haydn and Schubert. It has put on English stage premières of 19th- and 20th-century works including Dvořák's *The Devil and Kate*, 1932; Marschner's *Hans Heiling*, 1953; *L'enfant et les sortilèges* and *Oedipus Rex*, 1958; and it has commissioned new operas from Oxford composers (Wellesz's *Incognita*; Robert Sherlaw Johnson's *The Lambton Worm*, 1978). In addition it has put on student operas (including Stephen Oliver's *The Duchess of Malfi*, 1971) and such rarities as Mendelssohn's *Die Hochzeit des Camacho*, with text restored from material in the Bodleian Library (1987).

*

R. Ponsonby and R. Kent: *The Oxford University Opera Club: a Short History (1925–1950)* (Oxford, 1950)

E. W. White: 'A Note on Opera at Oxford', *Essays on Opera and English Music in Honour of Sir Jack Westrup* (Oxford, 1975), 168–76   SUSAN WOLLENBERG

Oxilia, José (Giuseppe) (*b* Montevideo, 1861; *d* Montevideo, 18 May 1919). Uruguayan tenor. The son of Italian parents, he went to Italy when 16 years old to study medicine but switched to singing lessons. He made his début in Barcelona and sang in Madrid, Turin, Naples, Milan and South America. His great triumph was singing Otello in the second production of Verdi's opera, under Faccio, at Brescia (1887) and repeating it at La Scala (1889); Verdi himself commented on Oxilia's success in a letter to Faccio. He had a wide range and a heroic voice, with forceful top notes and a tender, warm *mezza voce*, and was a convincing actor. Even if his war-horse role was Otello, he sang with great success Radames, Fernand (*La favorite*), Faust (*Mefistofele*), Turiddu and Gennaro (*Lucrezia Borgia*).

SUSANA SALGADO

Ozawa, Seiji (*b* Fenytien [now Shenyang], China, 1 Sept 1935). American conductor of Japanese descent. He studied at the Toho School, Tokyo. In 1959 he won the International Conductors' Competition at Besançon. At Tanglewood the next year he won the Koussevitzky Award and a scholarship to work with Karajan in Berlin, after which Bernstein engaged him for the New York PO. He became music director of the Boston SO in 1973. His operatic début was in *Così fan tutte* at the 1969 Salzburg Festival. He first appeared at Covent Garden in 1974 with *Yevgeny Onegin* and at the Paris Opéra in 1979 with a double bill of *Oedipus rex* and *L'enfant et les sortilèges*. In 1983 in Paris he conducted the première of Messiaen's *Saint François d'Assise*, which he also recorded. His début at the Vienna Staatsoper was with *Onegin* in 1988. His opera performances are notable for fluency of line and lyricism, but possibly stronger in the expression of sentiment rather than character. His recordings include a praised *Elektra* with Behrens (1988) and a less successful *Carmen* with Jessye Norman (1989).

MICHAEL STEINBERG, NOËL GOODWIN

P

Paalen, Bella [Pollack, Izabella] (*b* Pásztó, N. Hungary, 9 July 1881; *d* New York, 28 July 1964). Hungarian mezzo-soprano. She studied with Rosa Papier and Johannes Ress in Vienna. Her début was at Düsseldorf as Fidès in *Le prophète* in 1904, and the following year she was engaged at the Graz Opera. Mahler heard her sing in his Third Symphony and engaged her for the Vienna Hofoper, where she appeared until 1937 in operas by Puccini, Verdi and Wagner. She sang Fricka in *Die Walküre* at Covent Garden in 1925, and other guest engagements took her to Salzburg (1934–7), the Netherlands, Poland, Spain and Czechoslovakia. With the rise of the Nazis she moved to America.   DAVID CUMMINGS

Pablo, Luís de (*b* Bilbao, 28 Jan 1930). Spanish composer. Self-taught in composition, he studied law at Madrid University and held several civil service and political posts; later he became a professor at the Madrid Conservatory. He has written two operas, both first performed at the Teatro de la Zarzuela, Madrid: *Kiú*, in two acts, to his own libretto after Alfonso Vallejo's *El cero trasparente* (16 April 1983), and *El viajero indiscreto*, in a prologue, two acts and epilogue, to a libretto by Vicente Molina Foix (12 March 1990). Pablo has expressed reservations about opera as a genre, and has aimed to find an idiom related to modern Spanish, drawing on its rhythms and pitch inflections to develop an ornamental vocal style. Critical opinion however has been sharply divided as to his success. The action of *Kiú* takes place in a railway carriage with the singers seated and singing within the confined space, their voices directed to the opposite wall; *El viajero indiscreto* deals with the adventures, past and future, of a time-traveller. The musical language of both operas is highly eclectic, using a multiplicity of vocal, orchestral and syntactical elements.

Paccagnini, Angelo (*b* Castano Primo, Milan, 17 Oct 1930). Italian composer. He studied with Bettinelli at the Milan Conservatory (1949–53), and in the fifties frequented the RAI's Studio di Fonologia in Milan, making contact with Berio and Maderna and directing that studio from 1968 to 1970. He taught electronic music at the Milan Conservatory (1969–80) and was director of the Mantua and Verona conservatories. Paccagnini's compositions of the fifties place him in a post-Webern structuralist vein, and his first opera, *Le sue ragioni* (1959), is an attempt to bring Webern-like stylistic elements to the stage. His interest in vocal characteristics and his electro-acoustic explorations emerge as dominant traits in his works of the sixties and are reflected in his music theatre which, having surpassed its Webern-influenced beginnings, develops a more open musical search in the evolving context of contemporary post-structuralist experience. The radio opera *Il dio di oro* won the Italia Prize in 1964.

Le sue ragioni (1, Paccagnini and E. Pagliarani), Bergamo, 1959
Mosè (radio op), 1963
Il dio di oro (radio op), 1964
Tutti la vogliono, tutti la spogliano (3, Paccagnini), Venice, 1966
Un uomo da salvare, Milan, 30 March 1969
Partner (pezzo elettronico scenico), Turin, 1969
E l'ora (radio op, J. Arias), 1970
La misura, il mistero (racconto poetica, Paccagnini, L. Piccioni and G. Ungaretti), Milan, 1970
C'era una volta un re (television op), 1974
Olivo Verdevivo (television op), 1977

*

L. Pestalozza: 'Compositori milanesi del dopoguerra', *RaM*, xxvii (1957), 27–43   RAFFAELE POZZI

Pacchierotti [Pacchiarotti], **Gasparo** [Gaspare] (*b* Fabriano, nr Ancona, bap. 21 May 1740; *d* Padua, 28 Oct 1821). Italian soprano castrato. Trained at either Forlì Cathedral, or St Mark's, Venice (where he was principal soloist 1765–8), he remained in Venice until 1770, taking a minor operatic role at the Teatro S Giovanni Grisostomo (1766) and singing in Galuppi's *Il re pastore* in 1769. After an appointment as primo uomo at Palermo he sang in Naples as the partner of Anna de Amicis, beginning in 1771 with Jommelli's *Ifigenia in Tauride* and performing frequently at S Carlo up to Carnival 1776. He also sang in Bologna in Carnival 1773 (Bertoni's *Olimpiade*) and at the Naples court theatre in Carnival 1774 (Gluck's *Orfeo*), and for Carnival 1775 he was engaged at the Regio Ducal Teatro, Milan.

In 1776 he left Naples permanently, passing through Rome, Florence and Forlì (where his singing in Bertoni's *Artaserse* provoked the famous incident reported by Stendhal – the orchestra were unable to continue for the tears in their eyes), then Milan, Genoa, Lucca, Turin and Padua, at each singing in an opera by Bertoni. For two years (1778–80) he sang regularly at the King's Theatre in London, where Bertoni was resident composer. He then left for Italy, singing at Lucca in Bertoni's *Quinto Fabio* (1780); at the Teatro S Benedetto, Venice, in the première of Bertoni's *Armida abbandonata* (Carnival 1780–81); and at Mantua, in Luigi Gatti's *Olimpiade* (1781). Persuaded by William Beckford, an English admirer and patron, he returned to the King's Theatre, where Bertoni was again composer, singing there with consistent success (1781–4); the London *Public Advertiser* called him 'superior to any Singer heard in this country since Farinelli'.

Pacchierotti then appeared as primo uomo nearly every season at the Teatro S Benedetto, Venice, and sang at Trieste (1785), Genoa and Crema (1788), and Padua and Bergamo (1789), faithfully promoting Bertoni's operas each season and remaining in Italy until his last London visit, in 1791, where he sang at many concerts as well as in opera. The inauguration and first Carnival season of the Teatro La Fenice, Venice (1792–3), were his last operatic appearances.

By all accounts the greatest of the late 18th-century castratos, Pacchierotti was last in the line of the finest male sopranos. Both Mount Edgcumbe ('the most perfect singer it ever fell to my lot to hear') and Burney devoted more space to describing his genius than they accorded any other performer of the era. He was able to sing with facility from Bb to *c'''*, had a command of many different styles, was a considerable actor and moved even casual listeners by his rendition of pathetic airs. He was the principal author of the anachronistic vocal treatise *Modi generali del canto premessi alle maniere parziali onde adornare o rifiorire le nude o semplici melodie o cantilene giusta il metodo di Gasparo Pacchiarotti* (Milan, 1836), published under the name of his friend Antonio Calegari.

BurneyH; *ES* (R. Celletti); *FétisB*

C. F. Cramer, ed.: *Magazin der Musik*, ii (Hamburg, 1784), 568

Lord Mount Edgcumbe: *Musical Reminiscences* (London, 1834)

G. Cecchini Pacchiarotti: *Cenni biografici intorno a G. P.* (Padua, 1844)

L. Melville: *The Life and Letters of William Beckford of Fonthill* (London, 1910)

E. Greppi and A. Giulini, eds.: *Carteggio di Pietro e di Alessandro Verri* (Milan, 1923), viii, 237, 243; x, 42, 70 [correspondence Oct 1766–Sept 1782]

G. Chapman, ed.: *The Travel Diaries of William Beckford of Fonthill* (Cambridge, 1928)

R. Sassi: *Un celebre musico fabrianese: Gaspare Pacchiarotti (col testamento)* (Fabriano, 1935)   KATHLEEN KUZMICK HANSELL

Pace. Theatre in Rome, opened in 1694. *See* ROME, §§2 and 3(i).

Pacetti, Iva (*b* Prato, 13 Dec 1898; *d* Rome, 19 Jan 1981). Italian soprano. After study in Florence she made her début at Prato as Aida. She arrived at La Scala, Milan, in 1922, and sang Helen of Troy in *Mefistofele* under Toscanini, with whom she also worked in Dukas' *Ariane et Barbe-bleue*. She was the first Rome Turandot (1926) and gave her farewell performance there in the same role 21 years later. Abroad her greatest success was in South America, though she also sang at Chicago and throughout Europe. At Covent Garden she appeared in 1930, 1931 and 1938, as Desdemona, Leonora in *La forza del destino* and, most frequently, Tosca. Her pianissimo singing was admired, but *The Times* observed in 1930 that she lacked the ringing quality required, and the *Liverpool Post* nominated her 'wobbler of the season'. Her large repertory included such varied parts as the Dyer's Wife in *Die Frau ohne Schatten*, Norma and Leonore in *Fidelio*. Her best-known recording is of *Pagliacci* made in 1934 with Beniamino Gigli, though the role of Nedda is one she never sang on stage.

L. Rasponi: *The Last Prima Donnas* (London, 1984)

J. B. STEANE

Pacini, Andrea ['Il Lucchesino'] (*b* Lucca, *c*1690; *d* Lucca, March 1764). Italian alto castrato and composer. He sang in Venice (12 operas: 1708, début in Albinoni's *Astarto*, 1714–16, 1726), Florence (1709–10, 1720, 1725–6, 1731–2), Rome (1711, 1721), Lucca (1711, 1714–15, 1724), Ferrara (1713), Naples (ten operas at the S Bartolomeo and the royal palace, 1713–14, 1722–3), Livorno (1717–18), Bologna (1719–20, 1722), Turin (1719), Milan (1720), Genoa (1720, 1728) and Parma (1724, 1729). He was engaged by the Royal Academy, London, as second man to Senesino for 1724–5, making his début in the title role of Handel's *Tamerlano* and scoring a success: Lady Bristol told her husband that 'the new man takes extremely'. He sang Ptolemy in Handel's *Giulio Cesare* (Handel wrote a new aria for him) and Unulfo in *Rodelinda*, and in Ariosti's *Artaserse* and *Dario* and the Vinci-Orlandini *Elpidia*. The parts Handel wrote for him demand a good technique but limited range (compass *a* to *e''*). In later life he became a priest.

WINTON DEAN

Pacini, Giovanni (*b* Catania, 17 Feb 1796; *d* Pescia, 6 Dec 1867). Italian composer. He was one of the leading composers of Italian operas from the late 1820s to the 1840s.

1. LIFE. Pacini began his musical studies with his father, a well-known tenor (later a *buffo* bass), who intended him to have a career in church music and sent him at the age of 12 to Bologna to study singing with Luigi Marchesi. Manifesting an interest in composition at an early age, Pacini studied counterpoint for a short time while in Bologna and composition in Venice, 1809–12. He composed his first opera, *Don Pomponio* (not performed), in 1813. Later that year he had his first work staged, the *farsa Annetta e Lucindo*, in Milan. His earliest success, the *opera semiseria Adelaide e Comingio* (1817, also Milan) followed productions of more than a dozen other light works. The next year his *Il barone di Dolsheim*, which marked his début at La Scala and ran for 47 nights, brought him to the forefront of the Italian operatic scene.

In 1821 Pacini established himself in Lucca with an appointment as *maestro di cappella* to the Duchess Marie-Louise de Bourbon, and in 1822 he had a house built in Viareggio, where he resided throughout most of his operatic career. The tremendous success of two serious operas – *Alessandro nelle Indie* (1824) and *L'ultimo giorno di Pompei* (1825) – at the Teatro S Carlo in Naples gained him a position as the leading Italian composer of the late 1820s and began a productive relationship with the impresario Domenico Barbaia, who gave him a nine-year contract as musical director of the Neapolitan theatres, a post vacated by Rossini in 1822. Pacini's contract required him to compose two operas each year, which were eventually divided between Naples and Milan when Barbaia became director of La Scala in 1826. Barbaia also took Pacini to Vienna in 1827 to oversee productions of four of his operas at the Kärntnertortheater.

Pacini's popularity declined in the early 1830s, partly because of competition from Bellini, Donizetti and, to a lesser extent, Mercadante. The failure of three successive operas in Naples in 1833, which Pacini himself described in deprecating terms, followed by the disastrous première of *Carlo di Borgogna* in Venice (1835), led him to retire from the operatic scene for almost five years. During this period he devoted his time to the Liceo Musicale which he had established in Viareggio in 1834, and he had a substantial opera theatre built there for performances by his students. His appointment as *maestro di cappella* to the archducal court of Lucca in 1837 also spurred his production of liturgical works, an interest left dormant from his student years. Pacini's status as a teacher was affirmed in 1842 through his appointment as director of a new music school in Parma, which united all the music schools in the duchy and which bore his name from his death until 1924.

After considerable soul-searching – and with Bellini gone, Donizetti's Italian career in decline and Mercadante left as his principal rival – Pacini returned to the operatic stage in 1839, determined to write in a more innovative, thoughtful and overtly dramatic style. In his memoirs (cited by Gossett 1986, *Saffo*) he recalled that during his period of retirement he

had meditated on new developments, on the changing taste of the audience, and on what should be the path to follow … If my compositions were to have any hope for long life, I had to develop that aesthetic sense that I had previously sought but rarely achieved. I set to work, with the firm intention of putting aside the procedures that I had followed in my earlier career, and I looked for characteristic ideas from the diverse melodies of different peoples, drawing them from traditional sources, so that I could inform my works with that truth so difficult to achieve in our art.

After experimenting with his new approach in *Furio Camillo* (1839, Rome), he achieved enormous success with *Saffo* (1840, Naples), which to the present day has been regarded as his masterpiece. Over the next few years he continued to produce forward-looking works, most notably *La fidanzata corsa* (1842, Naples) and *Maria, regina d'Inghilterra* and *Medea* (both 1843, Palermo), and maintained his popularity throughout the 1840s, despite the rivalry of the ascending Verdi. However, Pacini himself noted that as early as 1846, in *La regina di Cipro*, he began to retreat from the more modern style seen in *Saffo* and fell back on earlier habits. After moving to Pescia in 1855, he increasingly focussed his activities on teaching and on writing instrumental music. His last major success was *Il saltimbanco* (1858, Rome).

Pacini married three times, outliving Adelaide Castelli (*d* 1828) and the singer Marietta Albini (*d* 1849) and spending his final years with Marianna Scoti. He was survived by five of his nine children. He had ill-disguised liaisons with Napoleon's sister, the Princess Pauline Borghese (begun during his year in Rome, 1821), from which a hasty marriage to his first wife eventually provided the only escape, and with the notorious Russian countess Giulia Samoylov (in Milan, apparently from about 1828 to 1831). Both women played important roles in nurturing his social and professional status in those musical centres.

2. STYLE. An extraordinarily prolific composer even by the standards of his own time, Pacini composed over 80 operas, in addition to many instrumental compositions and sacred vocal works, and authored numerous historical, theoretical and didactic writings. His operatic career mirrored the contemporary trend from comedy to tragedy that reached a turning-point around 1820: before 1817 he composed only comic operas; during the years 1817–20 he produced an even mix of serious, semi-serious and comic types; and from 1821 on he wrote primarily serious works.

Pacini's comic operas, particularly his early ones, show clearly the influence of their forebears, displaying such elements as 'Rossinian' instrumental crescendos, fast vocal parlandos and driving, often repetitive rhythms in fast movements. Such *opere semiserie* as *Il barone di Dolsheim* are also typical of the period in mixing complex, virtuoso music for the hero and heroine that in some cases verges on the style of *opera seria* with simpler, folklike melodies or comic parlando for other characters. In these operas more than in his *opere serie* Pacini often curtailed the standard forms of lyric numbers and wrote shorter individual movements, in particular the reflective movements in ensembles.

Pacini's serious operas provide the best opportunity, however, to examine the development of his style across his career. He set a cross-section of 19th-century libretto types, from operas with antique settings derived from 18th-century *opera seria* (*Alessandro nelle Indie*), to horror stories rooted in turn-of-the-century French opera (*Medea*) and Bellinian Romantic *melodrammi* (*Saffo*). In their treatments of these subjects his librettos display a number of shifts of focus that characterized the first part of the 19th century: from ancient settings and noble heroes to more modern settings populated by non-traditional types of characters (pirates, outlaws and gypsies), from cities and metropolitan palaces to small provincial towns or castles of petty princes, from intrigues and moral issues to painful amorous entanglements which result in murder, suicide or insanity, and from general, idealized characterizations to more personal ones.

Although Pacini admired many of his Italian predecessors – among them Paisiello, Cimarosa, Mayr, Paer, Generali and Pavesi – as well as such foreigners as Gluck, Haydn and Mozart, the works of his first period (before his temporary retirement in 1835) were influenced most clearly by the operas of Rossini, a debt that he readily acknowledged. Like Rossini, Pacini maintained the traditional separation of recitative and lyrical styles. Although in some cases he decorated the vocal lines of his obbligato recitatives with florid ornamentation, he rarely incorporated aria-like sections, and his lyric numbers seldom include the impulsive melodic phrases or emotionally frank declamatory interpolations of Bellini's. The music of Pacini's first period, much like Rossini's, remains largely within the tradition of ideal expressiveness and avoids direct representation of the actions or emotions of his characters.

Early in his career Pacini was known to contemporary audiences primarily as a fecund melodist who, in his own words, carefully 'tailored' his vocal lines to the strengths of individual singers. Reflecting Rossini's influence, his arias incorporate a broad range of melodic types. Although he claimed to have set aside the earlier composer's florid style, his early slow movements often display a proliferation of embellishments and adopt the relatively free, additive phrase structures usually associated with Rossini's melodies. At the other end of the spectrum, the themes of his fast cabalettas normally come closer to the mid-century lyric form $AA'BA'$, although the ends of phrases are still normally punctuated with *gruppetti*. These lively tunes, marked by disjunct contours, abrupt rhythmic motifs, frequent syncopation and a sometimes martial, sometimes playful or even trivial quality, made the composer famous in his day as the 'maestro delle cabalette'. Between these two extremes, Pacini also began to develop simpler, more fluid cantabile melodies like those that were to be the hallmark of Bellini's style.

In his memoirs Pacini later disparaged his orchestral writing during this period:

My instrumentation was never careful enough, and if it was sometimes beautiful or brilliant, this resulted not from reflection but rather from that natural taste God granted me. I frequently slighted the string section, nor did I take pains about the effects that might be drawn from other instrumental families.

While interesting exceptions to this self-deprecating evaluation do exist – the exotically flavoured overtures to *Il barone di Dolsheim* and *Gli arabi nelle Gallie* are two numbers in which he exploited instrumentation to convey a special atmosphere – during his first period Pacini mostly provided his melodies with minimal accompaniments that have little dramatic impact. And although he claimed to have tried to create new forms for his set pieces – notably in *L'ultimo giorno di Pompei* – and often expanded their designs from within by writing longer solos, or truncated traditional forms by eliminating unnecessary movements (a technique also seen in Donizetti's operas), he normally adhered to the conventional practices of Rossini and his other contemporaries. Most of his arias follow the common two- or three-movement formats that had become popular by the end of Rossini's career. His most complex duets, like Rossini's, contain four movements: an opening active movement, a contemplative slow one, an interactive *tempo di mezzo* and a reflective cabaletta (usually of the Bellinian type, which presents the main theme three times, the last with the voices together). Similarly, his larger ensembles and finales habitually have the Rossinian duet-like core of four long sections.

The innovations seen in the operas of Pacini's second period – beginning with *Furio Camillo* and especially *Saffo* – parallel many of those pioneered by Bellini and Donizetti as those composers also broke from norms established by Rossini. In his lyric melodies, Pacini virtually abandoned Rossinian *fioriture* (at least in his earliest works from this period) and adopted an almost exaggerated version of Bellini's frankly expressive style. He moved closer to the typical mid-century lyric form in his slow melodies, although he treated its phrase structure even more freely than Bellini and Donizetti had, normally separating the opening thematic block *AA'* from the remainder of the melody with a decisive articulation and providing a more extensive central section of short, quasi-declamatory phrases before returning to the opening ideas. He also smoothed out the melodic and rhythmic contours of his cabaletta themes – sometimes introducing Bellinian triplet rhythms – and, like Donizetti, occasionally cast them in a slow tempo.

Beginning with *Saffo*, Pacini began more consistently to obscure traditional distinctions between recitatives and lyric numbers, skilfully matching different styles of text-setting to individual events or reactions. His efforts at coaxing new expressive and atmospheric effects from the orchestra are apparent throughout his scores from this period. He also diverged from the relatively diatonic harmonic language of his first period by experimenting

with sudden modulations and non-tonic openings to heighten the expressive impact of his lyrical melodies, with juxtapositions of distantly related keys in active sections to underscore shocking events, and (like his contemporaries) with open-ended tonal plans for his lyric numbers, reflecting the mobility of his characters' situations and relationships.

In his memoirs Pacini stated flatly that operatic design was the province of his librettists. Perhaps as a consequence of this attitude, the operas of his second period do not display the same degree of innovation in the sectional forms of their individual scenes as that which characterizes Mercadante's operas. Even in *Saffo*, all the lyric numbers – except for the Part 1 duet for Sappho and Faone, which omits the traditional slow movement – conform to the standard three- and four-movement models for arias and ensembles. Yet unconventional structures do appear occasionally in his latest works (see, for example, the introductions to Acts 1 and 2 of *Il saltimbanco*), and individual movements may incorporate such mid-century variations as the replacement of the matched solo statements characteristic of Rossini and Bellini with free dialogue or contrasting solos in the first movements of duets. The active movements of lyric numbers of Pacini's second period are noteworthy for their great length and complexity (as in Sappho's aria finale in Part 3 or the trio of the same part). Many of his operas are forward-looking in the decisive dominance of ensembles over solo numbers and in a consistent inclusion of secondary characters in arias. For example, *Saffo* allots only one aria to each of its principals – neither Sappho nor Faone has a cavatina, and both characters must wait until Part 3 for their arias – and incorporates chorus or other soloists in all of them.

Unlike Bellini and Donizetti, and despite his self-conscious attempt to correct the defects that he perceived in his early style and to find a more up-to-date approach, Pacini never gained a significant following outside Italy. His operas met with mixed reviews in Vienna in the late 1820s, Fétis wrote a scathing criticism of his music in 1830, and Berlioz and Mendelssohn were completely unsympathetic. Yet his failure to gain international renown hardly diminishes his importance as a principal player in the Italian scene from 1820 to 1850. And while his role in the development of opera after Rossini was secondary to those of Bellini and Donizetti, both his operas and his memoirs provide a fascinating glimpse into the efforts of Italian composers to adapt Rossini's approach to the new musico-dramatic climate of the 1830s and 40s.

See also ALESSANDRO NELLE INDIE; MEDEA (ii); SAFFO; and ULTIMO GIORNO DI POMPEI, L'.

FP – *Florence, Teatro della Pergola* MR – *Milan, Teatro Re*
MSC – *Milan, Teatro alla Scala* NC – *Naples, Teatro S Carlo*
VF – *Venice, Teatro La Fenice*

f – *farsa* dg – *dramma giocoso*
os – *opera seria* oss – *opera semiseria*
tl – *tragedia lirica*

Don Pomponio, 1813 (opera buffa, G. Paganini), unperf.
Annetta e Lucindo (f, 2, F. Marconi), Milan, S Radegonda, 17 Oct 1813, *I-Bc, Fc, Mr*
La ballerina raggiratrice (opera buffa, 2, G. Palomba), FP, spr. 1814
L'ambizione delusa (opera buffa, 2, Palomba), FP, spr. 1814, *Mr*, PEA*
L'escavazione del tesoro (f, 1, Marconi), Pisa, Ravvivati, 18 Dec 1814, *PEA*
Gli sponsali de' silfi (commedia, 2, Marconi), Milan, Filodrammatici, carn. 1814–15, *PEA*, Mr*

Bettina vedova [Il seguito di Ser Mercantonio] (dg, 2, A. Anelli), Venice, S Moisè, spr. 1815

La Rosina (f, 1, Palomba), FP, sum. 1815, *PEA**

L'ingenua (f, 1, Marconi), Venice, S Benedetto, 4 May 1816, *PEA**

Il matrimonio per procura (dg, 1, G. Scannamusa [Anelli]), MR, 2 Jan 1817, *Mr**

Dalla beffa il disinganno, ossia La poetessa (f, 1, G. Scopabirba [Anelli]), MR, carn. 1816–17, *Mr** [suppressed after 3 perf.]; rev. with new text as Il carnevale di Milano (dg, 1, P. Latanzio [Anelli]), MR, 23 Feb 1817, *Mr*

Piglia il mondo come viene (dg, 2, Anelli), MR, 28 May 1817, *Mr*

Adelaide e Comingio (oss, 2, G. Rossi), MR, 30 Dec 1817, *Mr**, *Fc*, *Os*, excerpts (Milan, 1818); also as Isabella e Florange, Il comingio, Comingio pittore

Atala (os, 3, A. Peracchi), Padua, Nuovo, June 1818

Gl'illinesi, 1818 (os, F. Romani), unperf.

Il barone di Dolsheim (oss, 2, Romani), MSC, 23 Sept 1818, *Mc*, *Mr*, *Nc*, *Vt*, Catania (Biblioteca Chisari), vs (Milan, 1831); also as Federico II re di Prussia, Il barone di Felcheim, La colpa emendata dal valore

La sposa fedele (oss, 2, Rossi), Venice, S Benedetto, 14 Jan 1819; rev. version, MSC, 1819; *Bc*, *Fc*, *Mc*, *Mr**, *Nc*, *US-Bp*, excerpts (Milan, 1820–22)

Il falegname di Livonia (dg, 2, Romani), MSC, 12 April 1819; rev. version, FP, 1823; *Mr*, *I-Nc**, *Rsc*, duet (Milan, n.d.), trio (Milan, 1819)

Vallace, o L'eroe scozzese (os, 2, Romani), MSC, 14 Feb 1820, *Mc*, *Mr*, excerpts (Milan, 1820); also as Odoardo I re d'Inghilterra, *PEA*

La sacerdotessa d'Irminsul (eroico, 2, Romani), Trieste, Grande, 11 May 1820, *Fc* [not the same text as Bellini's Norma], *PEA**

La schiava in Bagdad, ossia Il papucciaio (dg, 2, V. Pezzi), Turin, Carignano, 28 Oct 1820, *Mt*, *Nc*, *PEA*, *Vt*, cavatina (Milan, 1827)

La gioventù di Enrico V (dg, 2, G. Tarducci or J. Ferretti, partly after W. Shakespeare), Rome, Valle, 26 Dec 1820, *FC*, *Mr*, *Nc*, *PEA**, *Rsc*; also as La bella tavernara, ossia Le avventure d'una notte

Cesare in Egitto (eroico, 2, Ferretti), Rome, Argentina, 26 Dec 1821, *PEA**

La vestale (os, 2, L. Romanelli), MSC, 6 Feb 1823, *Mc*, *Mr**, *Vt*, vs (Milan, 1830 or 1831)

Temistocle (os, 3, P. Anguillesi, after P. Metastasio), Lucca, Giglio, 23 Aug 1823, *B-Bc*, *I-Mr*, *PEA*, *Rsc*, excerpts (Milan, 1824)

Isabella ed Enrico (oss, 2, Romanelli), MSC, 12 June 1824, *Mr**, excerpts (Milan, 1824)

Alessandro nelle Indie (os, 2, G. Schmidt, after Metastasio), NC, 29 Sept 1824, *Mr*, *Nc*, *PEA*, excerpts (Milan, 1825–7)

Amazilia (os, 1, Schmidt), NC, 6 July 1825; rev. version (2), Vienna, 1827; *Fc*, *Mc*, *Mr*, *Nc*, *PEA**, *Rsc*, vs (Milan, 1830 or 1831)

L'ultimo giorno di Pompei (os, 2, A. L. Tottola [not after Bulwer-Lytton]), NC, 19 Nov 1825, *Mr*, *Nc**, *Vt*, vs (Milan, 1830 or 1831)

La gelosia corretta (oss, 3, Romanelli), MSC, 27 March 1826, *Mc*, *Mr**, excerpts (Milan, 1826)

Niobe (os, 2, Tottola), NC, 19 Nov 1826, *Mr*, *Nc**, *PEA*, excerpts (Milan, 1827)

Gli arabi nelle Gallie, ossia Il trionfo della fede (os, 2, Romanelli, after C. V. P. d'Arlincourt: *Le renégat*), MSC, 8 March 1827, *Bc*, *Mr*, *PEA**, vs (Milan, 1828); rev. with 7 new nos. as L'ultimo dei clodovei, Paris, Italien, 1855

Margherita regina d'Inghilterra (os, 2, Tottola), NC, 19 Nov 1827, *Mr*, excerpts (Milan, 1828); also as Margherita d'Anjou

I cavalieri da Valenza (tragico, 2, Rossi), MSC, 11 June 1828, *Mc**, *Mr*, vs (Milan, ?1833)

I crociati a Tolemaide, ossia Malek-Adel (os, 2, C. Bassi), Trieste, Grande, 13 Nov 1828, *Mr**, *PEA*, excerpts (Milan, 1830); also as La morte di Malek-Adel

Il talismano, ovvero La terza crociata in Palestina (opera storica, 3, G. Barbieri, after W. Scott), MSC, 10 June 1829, *Mc**, *Mr*, *PEA*, vs (Milan, 1830 or 1831)

I fidanzati, ossia Il contestabile di Chester (romantico, 3, D. Gilardoni, after Scott), NC, 19 Nov 1829, *Mc*, *Mr*, *Nc**, *Vt*, vs (Milan, ?1830)

Giovanna d'Arco (os, 2, Barbieri, after F. von Schiller), MSC, 14 March 1830, *Mc**, *Mr*, *PEA*, excerpts (Milan, 1830)

Il corsaro (romantico, 3, Ferretti, after Byron), Rome, Apollo, 15 Jan 1831, *Mc**, *Mr*, vs (Milan, 1831)

Il rinnegato portoghese [Gusmano d'Almeida], 1831 (os, Romanelli), for VF, unperf. [replaced by Ivanhoe]

Ivanhoe (os, 2, Rossi, after Scott), VF, 19 March 1832, *Mc*, *Mr**,

Nc, *PEA*, *Vt*, vs (Milan, 1832) [no connection with Rossini pasticcio, arr. A. Pacini]

Don Giovanni Tenorio, o Il convitato di pietra (f, 2, G. Bertati), Viareggio, Casa Belluomini [private theatre], spr. 1832

Gli elvezi, ovvero Corrado di Tochemburgo (os, 2, Rossi), NC, 12 Jan 1833, *Mr**, *Nc*, excerpts (Milan, n.d.)

Fernando duca di Valenza (os, ?1, P. Pola), NC, 30 May 1833, *Mr**

Irene, o L'assedio di Messina (os, 3, 'Cirino da Palermo' [Rossi], NC, 30 Nov 1833, *Mr*, *Nc**, excerpts (Milan, 1834)

Carlo di Borgogna (romantico, 3, Rossi), VF, 21 Feb 1835, *PEA*, *Vt*

Bellezza e cuor di ferro (dg, 2), Viareggio, Casa Belluomini, carn. 1835–6 [? revival of Rossini's Matilde Shabran, ossia Bellezza e cuor di ferro, for which Pacini wrote 3 nos.]

La foresta d'Hermanstadt (ob), private perf., Viareggio, 1839 [existence uncertain]

Furio Camillo (tragico, 3, Ferretti), Rome, Apollo, 26 Dec 1839, *Nc*, excerpts (Milan, 1841)

Saffo (tl, 3, S. Cammarano, after P. Beltrame), NC, 29 Nov 1840, *CATc*, *Mc*, *Mr*, *Nc**, excerpts (Milan, 1841)

L'uomo del mistero (oss, 2, D. Andreotti, after Scott), Naples, Nuovo, 9 Nov 1841, *Mr*, *Nc**, vs (Naples, n.d.), excerpts (Milan, n.d.)

Il duca d'Alba (tl, 2, G. Peruzzini and F. M. Piave), VF, 26 Feb 1842, *Mr**, *Nc*, *Vt*, vs (Milan, 1842); also as Adolfo di Werbel

La fidanzata corsa (tragico, 3, Cammarano, after P. Mérimée: Colomba), NC, 10 Dec 1842, *Mc*, *Mr*, *Nc**, vs (Milan, 1843)

Maria, regina d'Inghilterra (tl, 3, L. Tarantini, after V. Hugo: *Marie Tudor*), Palermo, Carolino, 11 Feb 1843, *Mc*, *Mr*, *Nc**, vs (Milan, ?1843)

Medea (melodramma tragico, 3, B. Castiglia), Palermo, Carolino, 28 Nov 1843; rev. version, Vicenza, 1845, *Mr**, *Nc*, vs (Milan, n.d.)

Luisetta, ossia La cantatrice del molo [di Napoli] (commedia, 2, Tarantini), Naples, Nuovo, 13 Dec 1843, *Mr*, *Nc*, *PEA*, excerpts (Milan, n.d.), vs (Naples, 1844) also as Luisella

L'ebrea (os, 3, G. Sacchèro), MSC, 27 Feb 1844, *Mc*, *Mr**, *PEA*, vs (Naples, 1844), excerpts (Milan, 1844)

Lorenzino de' Medici (tl, 4, Piave), VF, 4 March 1845, *Nc*, *Vt*, vs (Naples, 1865); rev. as Rolandino di Torresmondo, NC, 1858; also perf. as Elisa Valasco

Bondelmonte (tl, 3, Cammarano, after Voltaire), FP, 18 June 1845, *Mc*, *PEA*, vs (Milan, n.d.)

Stella di Napoli (dramma lirico, 3, Cammarano), NC, 11 Dec 1845, *Bc*, *Nc*, *Mr**, vs (Milan, 1846)

La regina di Cipro (dramma lirico, 4, F. Guidi), Turin, Regio, 7 Feb 1846, *Mr**, vs (Milan, 1846)

Merope (tl, 3, Cammarano, after Voltaire), NC, 25 Nov 1847, *Mr**, *Nc*, vs (Naples, 1848), excerpts (Milan, 1848)

Ester d'Engaddi (os, 3, Guidi), Turin, Regio, 1 Feb 1848

Allan Cameron (os, 4, Piave), VF, 28 March 1848, *Mr**, *Vt*, excerpts (Milan, n.d.)

L'orfana svizzera (oss, 3, F. Rubino), Naples, Fondo, spr. 1848

Alfrida (os, Bertolozzi), unperf. [existence uncertain]

Zaffira, o La riconciliazione (oss, 3, A. de Lauzières), Naples, Nuovo, 15 Nov 1851, *Nc*

Malvina di Scozia (tl, 3, Cammarano), NC, 27 Dec 1851, *Mr*, *Nc*, vs (Naples, 1852)

L'assedio di Leida [Elnava] ?1852, (os, Piave), unperf.

Rodrigo di Valenza (os), for Palermo, Carolino, carn. 1852–3, unperf.

Il Cid (os, 2, de Lauzières), MSC, 12 March 1853, *Mc**

Lidia di Brabante (os, Gaetano [surname illegible]), Palermo, Carolino, spr. 1853 [given thus by Pacini in an MS list, 1859; probably the orig. version of Lidia di Bruxelles, 1858]

Romilda di Provenza (os, 3, G. Miccio), NC, 8 Dec 1853, *Nc**, *PEA*

La donna delle isole (os, Piave), for VF, carn. 1853–4, unperf. [replaced by La punizione]

La punizione (os, 3, G. Cencetti, ? rev. C. Perini), VF, 8 March 1854, *Vt* [apparently the same subject as Lidia di Brabante, 1853]

Margherita Pusterla (os, 2, D. Bolognese), NC, 25 Feb 1856, *Nc*, *PEA*, excerpts (Rome, n.d.)

I portoghesi nel Brasile (os, 2, de Lauzières), ? Rio de Janeiro, Italiano, 1856

Niccolò de' Lapi (melodramma tragico, 3, Pacini, after Cencetti: *La punizione*, 1854), announced in Rio de Janeiro, 1857, possibly not perf. there, *BR-Rn*; 1st known perf. Florence, Pagliano, 29 Oct 1873; Act 1 *I-PLcon** (with orig. title, Lidia di Brusselle, deleted), complete copy *Fc*

Il saltimbanco (dramma lirico, 3, G. Checchetelli), Rome, Argentina, 24 May 1858, *Mr**, *Nc*, *PEA*, *Rsc*, vs (Milan, n.d.), vs

(Naples, 1859)

Lidia di Bruxelles (os, 3, ? Cencetti), Bologna, Comunale, 21 Oct 1858, Act 1 PLcon* (with title amended to Niccolò de' Lapi) [probably comp. earlier as rev. of Lidia di Brabante, 1853]

Gianni di Nisida (os, 4, Checchetelli), Rome, Argentina, 29 Oct 1860, PEA*

Il mulattiere di Toledo (commedia lirica, 5, Cencetti), Rome, Apollo, 25 May 1861

Belfagor (oss, 3, A. Lanari, after N. Machiavelli), FP, 1 Dec 1861, PEA* [probably comp. 1851]

Carmelita, 1863 (os, Piave, after A. Dumas père: Don Juan de Marana), for MSC, unperf.

Don Diego di Mendoza (opera fantastica, 3, Piave), VF, 12 Jan 1867, PEA, Vt*, excerpts (Milan, n.d.)

Berta di Varnol (os, 3, Piave), NC, 6 April 1867 [partly comp. 1859]

Doubtful: La chiarina (f, 1, Anelli), Venice, S Moisè, carn. 1815–16 [? a confusion with G. Farinelli's setting]; I virtuosi di teatro (f, 1, Rossi), MR, 1817 [? by S Mayr]; La bottega di caffè (opera buffa, G. Foppa, after C. Goldoni), MR, 1817 [? F. Gardi]

*

G. Pacini: Le mie memorie artistiche (Florence, 1865); ed. F. Magnani (Florence, 1875) [incl. posth. new material and work-list]

L. Lianovosani [G. Salvioli]: 'Serie cronologica delle opere teatrali, cantate ed oratori del maestro Giovanni Comm. Pacini', Gazzetta musicale di Milano, xxxi (1876), 215–418 passim

A. Ghislanzoni: 'Giovanni Pacini', Libro serio (Milan, 1879), 49

O. Chilesotti: 'Giovanni Pacini', I nostri maestri del passato (Milan, 1882)

J. Carlez: Pacini et l'opéra italien (Caen, 1888)

M. Davini: Il maestro Giovanni Pacini (Palermo, 1927)

F. Lippmann: 'Giovanni Pacini: Bemerkungen zum Stil seiner Opern', Chigiana, xxiv (1967), 111–24

R. Profeta: 'Giovanni Pacini e la Saffo', L'opera (Milan, 1967), no.6, pp.31–6

G. Ugolini: 'Pacini alle origini del melodramma ottocentesco', L'opera (1967), no.6, pp.22–9

G. Kessler: 'Giovanni Pacini "Sappho"', OW, ix (July 1968), 40–41

F. Lippmann: Vincenzo Bellini, und die italienische Opera Seria seiner Zeit, AnMc, no.6 (1969), esp. 317–28

M. Rose: 'A Note on Giovanni Pacini', MT, cxxiv (1983), 163–4

P. Gossett: Introduction to G. Pacini: Saffo and excerpts from Furio Camillo, IOG, xxxvi (1986)

——: Introduction to G. Pacini: L'ultimo giorno di Pompei and excerpts from Niobe, IOG, xxxii (1986)

J. Commons: 'Giovanni Pacini and "Maria Tudor"', Donizetti Society Journal, vi (1988), 57–92

J. Black: 'The Eruption of Vesuvius in Pacini's L'ultimo giorno di Pompei', ibid, 93–104

T. G. Kaufman: 'Giovanni Pacini', Verdi and his Major Contemporaries (New York and London, 1990), 117–54

SCOTT L. BALTHAZAR (text, bibliography)
MICHAEL ROSE/SCOTT L. BALTHAZAR (work-list)

Pacini, Regina (b Lisbon, 6 Jan 1871; d Buenos Aires, 18 Sept 1965). Portuguese soprano. She came from a family of musicians, her father, José Pacini (who was also her first teacher), being a well-known baritone and director of the S Carlos at Lisbon, where Regina made her début in 1888 as the heroine of La sonnambula. The following year she appeared in Milan and Palermo and in James Mapleson's last season at Her Majesty's in London. She quickly became a favourite in Spain, singing also in the 1890s in Russia, Poland and South America. In 1902 she reappeared in London, singing at Covent Garden with Caruso in L'elisir and Lucia, and was praised by the Musical Times for 'vocal agility such as this generation seldom hears'. She was again Caruso's partner at Monte Carlo in 1904, and in 1905 sang there in I puritani and Il barbiere with Bonci. At the height of her career in 1907 she retired and married Marcelo de Alvear (later president of Argentina), which enabled her to exercise an influence on the musical life of the country. Her recordings are rarely without some flaw of voice or style, but she is impressively fluent; the upper part of her voice is particularly lovely.   J. B. STEANE

Paciorkiewicz, Tadeusz (b Sierpc, 17 Oct 1916). Polish composer. He studied the organ in Warsaw (1936–43) and after the war became a composition pupil of Kazimierz Sikorski at the Łódź State College of Music. Teaching appointments followed at the conservatories of Łódź (1949–59) and Warsaw (from 1959). He has also been active as an organist and choral conductor. His largest-scale opera, Romans gdański, set in 17th-century Gdańsk, plays on patriotic themes, dealing with Poland's longstanding connections with the sea. Paciorkiewicz has also written two radio operas. His works are characterized by lyrical melodiousness and harmonic simplicity; the best of them have a late Romantic, rhapsodic expansiveness.

Ushiko (radio op, 1, Z. Kopalko, after ancient Jap. subject), Polish Radio, 9 May 1963

Ligea (radio op, 1, Kopalko, after Herodotus and Archilochus), Polish Radio, 4 Oct 1967

Romans gdański (4, W. Brégy, after J. Łuszczewska: Panienka z okienka [The Maid from a Window]), Łódź, Wielki, 30 Nov 1968

K. Mazur: 'O utworach Tadeusza Paciorkiewicza', Ruch muzyczny, vi/1 (1962), 14

M. Hanuszewska and B. Schaeffer: Almanach polskich kompozytorów współczesnych [Almanac of Contemporary Polish Composers] (Kraków, 1982)

MIECZYSŁAWA HANUSZEWSKA, JIM SAMSON

Pacius, Fredrik [Friedrich] (b Hamburg, 19 March 1809; d Helsinki, 8 Jan 1891). Finnish composer of German birth. His teachers were Spohr (violin) and Hauptmann (composition) at Kassel. From 1828 to 1834 he was a violinist in the court orchestra in Stockholm, but in 1835 he settled in Helsinki as lecturer in music at the university, and became professor in 1860.

Pacius became the central figure in Finland's musical life and is regarded as the father of Finnish music. He organized symphony concerts and founded choirs, which he conducted. His compositions follow the German Romantic school of Mendelssohn and Spohr, but are influenced by Finnish folk music. His operas Kung Karls jakt ('The Hunt of King Charles', 1852) and Die Loreley (1887) were composed to Swedish texts; he also wrote a fairy opera, Prinsessan av Cypern (1860), and a vinterstycke ('winter-piece'), Veteranens jul ('The Veteran's Christmas', 1859). His non-operatic works include several cantatas, orchestral pieces, partsongs and solo songs.

Kung Karls jakt [The Hunt of King Charles] (3, Z. Topelius), Helsinki, 24 March 1852

Veteranens jul [The Veteran's Christmas] (winter-piece, 1, Topelius), Helsinki, 4 Feb 1859

Prinsessan av Cypern (fairy op, 4, Topelius), Helsinki, 28 Nov 1860

Die Loreley (2, E. Geibel), Helsinki, 28 April 1887

M. Colan-Beaurain: Fredrik Pacius (Helsinki, 1921)

O. Andersson: Den unge Pacius och musiklivet i Helsingfors på 1830-talet [The Young Pacius and Musical Life in Helsinki in the 1830s] (Helsinki, 1938) [also in Finnish]

J. Rosas: Fredrik Pacius som tonsättare (Turku, 1949)

K. Maasalo: 'Fredrik Pacius', Suomalaisia sävellyksiä, ii (Borgå, 1969), 71–88

Paderewski, Ignacy Jan (b Kuryłówka, Podolia, 18 Nov 1860; d New York, 29 June 1941). Polish composer. Born in provincial Poland, he studied at the Warsaw Music Institute, in Berlin and in Vienna with the celebrated piano teacher Leschetizky. By the turn of the century he was Poland's most famous virtuoso pianist and composer, giving concert tours throughout the world. After World War I he devoted himself to politics and became Prime Minister and Minister of Foreign Affairs in a newly independent Poland. He resumed his concert career in 1922.

His one opera, *Manru* (described as a 'lyric drama'), to a libretto by Alfred Nossig after J. I. Kraszewski's novel *Chata za wsią* ('A Cabin Outside the Village'), is set in the Tatra mountains in the 19th century. The hero, Manru (tenor), is a young gypsy who marries a Polish peasant girl, but he resists assimilation into her world, in the end returning to his tribe. For all the promise of the subject, the libretto lacks dramatic coherence and the music is indebted variously to Italian composers, Wagner and Bizet. The successful première took place in Dresden on 29 May 1901.   JIM SAMSON

Padilla, José (*b* Almería, 28 May 1889; *d* Madrid, 25 Oct 1960). Spanish composer. He was educated in his native town by his family, including an uncle who was the local bandmaster. Later he studied at the Madrid Conservatory with Rivera and Ramón Nicolás Fontanilla, and then in Italy with Pacini. At the age of 17 he substituted as conductor in a zarzuela company, later conducting at the Teatro de la Comedia in Buenos Aires. He composed many stage works, but achieved worldwide success with individual songs such as *Princesita* (1917), derived from *La corte del amor* (1916) and popularized by Tito Schipa, as well as *El relicario* (1918) and *La violetera* (1918). During the 1920s, numbers from his zarzuelas *La bien amada* (1925) and *La mayorala* (1926) were adapted for Paris into the hit songs *Valencia* and *Ça ... c'est Paris* respectively. Besides being active in revue in Paris in the 1920s, he worked in Italy from 1930 to 1934. Padilla is reckoned to have composed music for some 60 zarzuelas as well as some 400 songs.

selective list; zarzuelas unless otherwise stated

Mala hembra (1, V. de la Vega), Madrid, Barbieri, 24 March 1906; Copla gitana (1, J. Tavares), Madrid, Barbieri, 8 Jan 1909, collab. Quislant; La presidaria (1, Vega), Madrid, Barbieri, 19 Nov 1909; De los barrios bajos (1), Madrid, 1909, collab. Franco; Los hombres de empuje (1), Madrid, Benevento, June 1910; Mirando a la Alhambra (1), Madrid, 1911; Pajaritos y flores (1, M. Mihura and R. González de Toro), Madrid, Apolo, 28 Sept 1910; El divino juguete (1, Q. Pastor), Madrid, Novedades, Dec 1911; De España al cielo (1), Barcelona, Feb 1914, collab. Jiménez; La corte del amor (M. Fernández Palomero), Buenos Aires, Comedia, 24 June 1916; La oración de la vida (1, Palomero), Madrid, Martín, June 1916; El secreto de la paz (1, J. R. Franquet), Barcelona, Cómico, 30 March 1918; Reyes, la Jerezana (1, F. Pérez Capo), Madrid, Martín, 30 Jan 1919

Sol de Sevilla (3, J. A. de la Prada), Barcelona, Tívoli, 18 March 1924; La bien amada (3, Prada), Barcelona, Tívoli, 1924; La mayorala (3, Prada), Barcelona, Tívoli, ?1924/5; Mucho cuidado con la Lola (musical comedy, 3, T. Borrás, after J. Vaszary), Barcelona, Comedia, 11 March 1935; La giralda (3, S. and J. Álvarez Quintero), Barcelona, Victoria, 22 Sept 1939; La faraona (op, J. Mantilla de los Ríos), ?Italy, 1930s; Scala 1946 (revue, Druisberg), Barcelona, Calderón, 7 April 1946; Symphonie Portugaise (operetta, M. Cab and R. Vincy), Paris, Gaîté Lyrique, ?27 Oct 1949; La hechicera en Palacio (musical comedy, 2, Rigel and A. Ramos de Castro), Madrid, Alcázar, 23 Nov 1950; La chacha, Rodríguez y su padre (musical comedy, 2, J. Muñoz Román), Madrid, Martín, 19 Oct 1956; Norga, o El sol de medianoche (3, L. Fernández Ardavín), ?unperf.

*

StiegerO

Enciclopedia universal ilustrada europeo-americana (Barcelona, 1907–30), appx viii (1933), 5–6; suppl. 1959–60 (Madrid, 1964), 302

A. Fernández-Cid: *Cien años de teatro musical en España (1875–1975)* (Madrid, 1975)   ANDREW LAMB

Padlock, The. Afterpiece opera in two acts by CHARLES DIBDIN to a libretto by ISAAC BICKERSTAFF after MIGUEL DE CERVANTES's story *El celoso extremeno*; London, Drury Lane, 3 October 1768.

The Padlock was the third work on which Bickerstaff and Dibdin collaborated, and the first dialogue opera for which Dibdin composed all the music. Cervantes's story had been translated into English (as *The Jealous Estremaduran*) and edited by Samuel Croxall in 1720. The opera was an outstanding success. In its opening season it commanded 54 performances, and it had more than a hundred in its first three years. Its popularity as an afterpiece carried it well into the 19th century. It was also popular abroad, receiving performances during the 18th century in New York, Montego Bay, Kingston, Madras, Calcutta and St Petersburg.

The story concerns a wealthy man, Don Diego (bass), who hopes to marry his ward, Leonora (soprano). Leaving his house one evening he places a large padlock on the front door. Nevertheless, a young scholar, Leander (tenor), climbs over the garden wall, bribes the servants and woos Leonora. Don Diego returns unexpectedly and catches the two lovers, but accepts that he is too old and that Leonora should wed Leander.

Part of the initial success of *The Padlock* was due to Dibdin's excellent portrayal of Mungo, Don Diego's black servant (tenor; for illustration *see* DIBDIN, CHARLES). The part was one of the first written in 'coon' English. Mungo's first song, 'Dear heart, what a terrible life am I led' (Act 1 scene vi), contains a line which quickly became a catch-phrase: 'Mungo here, Mungo dere, Mungo everywhere'. The part of Mungo was originally designed for John Moody, who had visited the West Indies and was familiar with Negro dialect. However, Dibdin deliberately made the songs too difficult for Moody so that he himself eventually landed the part. The other singers at the first performance were Elizabeth Arne (wife of Michael Arne) as Leonora, Joseph Vernon as Leander, Charles Bannister as Don Diego and Elizabeth Young (Mrs Dorman) as Ursula (soprano).

IRENA CHOLIJ

Padmâvatî ['Padmāvatī']. Opéra-ballet in two acts, op.18, by ALBERT ROUSSEL to a libretto by LOUIS LALOY; Paris, Opéra, 1 June 1923.

Roussel's attraction to the idea of a hybrid form embracing dance as well as solo and choral singing dates from before his oriental travels. He expressed this after attending a performance of Lalo's ballet *Namouna* but it was not until his visit to the ruins at Chitor (now Chittaurgarh), Rajasthan, the following year that he found a suitable theme, commissioning a libretto from Laloy.

ACT 1 *Outside the royal palace* The work is based on the true story of Padmâvatî, Queen of Chitor, who reigned around 1300. The moghul Sultan Aladdin enters the city on the pretext of signing a peace treaty, but surrounds the town with troops. He is provided with extensive entertainment which draws from Roussel exotic, quasi-oriental ballet music orchestrated with the utmost subtlety. A Brahmin who accompanies him testifies to his conversion thus allowing him to witness a dance by the women of the palace, but he desires more, asking to see Padmâvatî herself: a woman renowned for her breathtaking beauty. Reluctantly Ratan-Sen, the King, agrees and Padmâvatî lifts her veil. Overcome by

Padmâvatî *Queen of Chitor*	contralto
Ratan-Sen *her husband, King of Chitor*	tenor
Alaouddin [Aladdin] *Sultan of the Moghuls*	baritone
The Brahmin	tenor
Gora *administrator of the palace*	baritone
Badal *Ratan-Sen's envoy*	tenor
Nakamti *a young woman from Chitor*	mezzo-soprano
The Watchman	tenor
A Priest	bass
First Woman of the Palace	soprano
Second Woman of the Palace	contralto
Two Women from the Crowd	sopranos
A Warrior	tenor
A Merchant	tenor
An Artisan	baritone

Warriors, priests, women of the palace, men and women
from the crowd

Dancers: two women of the palace, a slave, a warrior,
Kali, Dourga, Prithivi, Parvati, Ouma, Gaouri, women
of the palace, female slaves, warriors

Setting Chitor, about 1300

---

her beauty, Aladdin withdraws from the city without
having signed the treaty. A message is sent by Aladdin:
unless Padmâvatî is surrendered to him, the city will be
mercilessly destroyed. The crowd murder the Brahmin
and the act ends as Padmâvatî fears that the gods will
abandon her in view of this sacrilegious deed.

ACT 2 *In the temple* Padmâvatî has abandoned the
palace while Ratan-Sen attempts a final defence. Chanting by the priests punctuates Padmâvatî's lamenting and
a funeral pyre has been prepared. 'There will be more

than one sacrifice', warn the priests. Ratan-Sen enters,
wounded, and entreats Padmâvatî to deliver herself up
to Aladdin so that the people of the city might be spared.
Outraged at this suggestion she stabs him: she would
rather see him dead than guilty of betraying their union.
As he dies she promises him that they will eventually be
united in death.

After a processional scene where the priests carry off
the body, Padmâvatî's women begin to prepare her for
death. Grooming her and decking her with her jewels as
her husband's funeral pyre is lit, the priests sing of a
ritual death in incantatory style. The smoke clearing
from the pyre provides a pretext for ballet: first four
vampire-like creatures enact a macabre dance; then, as
more powder is thrown on to the fire, a female dancer,
Kali, enacts a dance where she moves like a snake, but
brandishing a trident. As another dancer joins her, they
gradually encircle Padmâvatî. The funeral ceremony
follows. Roussel is here at his most oriental: quasi-
Indian modes, an incantation from the priests and a
haunting soprano vocalise accompany the *cortège* where
the brazier is carried towards the log funeral pyre. The
tension rises and all the voices, now in seven-part
harmony, adopt wordless singing or ritualistic chanting
syllables. At the end of the opera, expressed purely in
balletic terms, Aladdin appears at the temple doors, only
to see Padmâvatî consumed by the flames of her husband's funeral pyre.

* * *

Roussel's conception of the spectacle is closer to ballet
than to opera and the way the plot is handled (the
characters are treated as cardboard puppets with minimal psychological development) owes more than a little
to oriental forms of music theatre. With the element of
dance dominant over the unfolding of the drama, some
commentators have criticized what appear to be tenuous

'Padmâvatî' (Roussel): designs by Valdo-Barbey for the costumes of Kali (left) and Padmâvatî in the original production at the
Paris Opéra (Salle Garnier), 1 June 1923

Interior of the Teatro Verdi, Padua, during the inaugural performance of Verdi's 'Aida' in 1884: engraving from 'Il teatro illustrato' (July 1884)

links between the balletic and the operatic elements. But seen in the light of a collaboration between a librettist and a composer, both deeply interested in renewing Western music through an adoption of oriental means of expression, the work appears in a clearer perspective.

The powerful score is deeply rather than superficially inspired by oriental musical techniques; indeed it has few precursors which draw impetus from oriental music at so many levels. On a melodic level, decorative arabesques, such as were used by Debussy, occur frequently in the orchestra and many of the melodies and their resultant harmonies have their basis in synthetic or oriental modes. Several of the dance interludes, with their hypnotic rhythms underlined by eastern-sounding gongs, pay more than lip-service to the sound world of oriental instrumental groupings.

Most original, and creating a striking musical effect, is the extensive use of choral writing, often wordless, incantatory, or intoning mantras in their original language. Many commentators have remarked upon Roussel's debt to Stravinsky, not only with regard to *Padmâvatî*. But even if Roussel followed Stravinsky in certain musical techniques as well as in the use of hybrid forms of song and dance, the sound-world he creates is ultimately totally different and in *Padmâvatî* no less striking.   RICHARD LANGHAM SMITH

Padova (It.). PADUA.

Padovanis [Padovas], **Domenicos** [Kyriakos] (*b* Corfu, 14 July 1817; *d* Corfu, 21 March 1892). Greek composer. A distinguished disciple of Mantzaros, he trained in Rome, possibly at the Accademia di S Cecilia, before returning to Corfu to study organ with Giovanni Ponzetta. From 1839 he was organist at the Catholic cathedral. He was one of the earliest members of the Corfu Philharmonic Society and taught from 1841; after Mantzaros's death (1872) he was elected president of the musical department of the Society.

Padovanis is one of the few composers of the earlier

Ionian School whose operas have not been lost. Possessing a refined technique based on his Italian training, he belonged to the bel canto school of Bellini and Donizetti. In his two operas, *Dirce, figlia di Aristodemo* (*tragedia lirica* in three acts to a libretto by S. Fogacci, after V. Monti's *Aristodemo*; Corfu, Teatro Comunale, 12 February 1857; vocal score and full score of Sinfonia published Corfu, 1857) and *Il ciarlatano preso per principe* (*farsa* in one act to a libretto by S. Fogacci; Corfu, Teatro Comunale, ?1857), his melodic eloquence is matched by his capacity to create a 'theatrical', if not dramatic, atmosphere through simple musical means. *Dirce*, which has an unusual subject for an Ionian composer of that time, for the mere savagery of the plot, adheres to the bel canto ethos, where dramatic, even bloody events are rendered through the euphoria of the major mode. In *Il ciarlatano* Padovanis showed the melodic spontaneity and rhythmical verve associated with Rossini.

F. di Mento: *Elogio funebre, letto dopo le esequie ... del compianto Cav. Domenico Padovani ... maestro compositore ed organista della cattedrale cattolica di Corfù, il giorno 10/22 Marzo 1892* (Corfu, 1892)

S. Motsenigos: *Neoelliniki moussiki, symvoli is tin istorian tis* [Modern Greek Music: a Contribution to its History] (Athens, 1958), 189, 226

G. Leotsakos: 'Padovanis, Domenicos', *Pangosmio viografiko lexico*, viii (Athens, 1988)   GEORGE LEOTSAKOS

Padua (It. Padova). City in north-east Italy. Its operatic activity was conditioned by its proximity to Venice (it was part of the Venetian Republic until 1797) and by its position as the seat of the only university in the republic. The history of opera in Padua began with the production in 1636 under the aegis of Pio Enea degli Obizzi of a tourney with a 'dramatic introduction', *L'Ermiona*, to a libretto by Obizzi with music by G. F. Sances (for illustration *see* RIVAROLA, ALFONSO); the performers, who had come from Rome and Venice, later took part in the first public performance of opera in Venice,

Francesco Manelli's *Andromeda* (1637). In Padua, however, apart from a *favola boschereccia*, *La Cidippe*, performed in 1670, there was no real opera until 1691 when Domenico Gabrielli's *Maurizio* was performed in the renovated Teatro dello Stallone. The Teatro degli Obizzi, inaugurated in 1652, was used for opera only from Carnival 1693 (*Isifile*); the theatre's archives, which survive, are not accessible.

Operatic activity early in the 18th century either was sporadic or is undocumented. For several years from 1743 the soprano castrato Mariano Nicolini was active as impresario; opera centred on the summer season and the Fiera del Santo (St Anthony), which attracted many visitors. *Dramma giocoso* was performed towards the middle of the century in the form of pasticcios or revivals. The Teatro Nuovo, a new and larger theatre controlled not by a single proprietor but by an association of nobles, was inaugurated in 1751 with a new setting of Metastasio's *Artaserse* by Galuppi. This began the most splendid period of operatic activity in Padua, often in direct competition with Venice. Among many operas composed for the Teatro Nuovo were Bertoni's *Il trionfo di Clelia* (1769), Naumann's *Armida* (1773), Mysliveček's *Atide* (1774), Anfossi's *Adriano in Siria* (1777), Joseph Schuster's *Ruggero e Bradamante* (1779), Gaetano Andreozzi's *Amleto* (1792) and Paer's *Cinna* (1795). From the 1770s the theatre kept scores of all the works commissioned for it; the resulting collection is held at the conservatory. Between 1779 and 1791 the Teatrino del Prato della Valle staged *opera buffa*, as did the Teatro degli Obizzi in the autumn season, which included the Fiera di S Giustina. Towards the end of the 1780s there was fierce rivalry between the two larger theatres; from 1792 they divided the seasons between them, the Nuovo being allotted the fairs of St Anthony and S Giustina and the Obizzi the spring and carnival seasons. Giuseppe Ximenes d'Aragona, a nobleman formerly attached to the Viennese court who had commissioned, among other works, Mozart's oratorio *La Betulia liberata*, arranged the first performance in Italy of Gluck's *Alceste* (1777), at a private academy in the city.

The final years of the Venetian republic were characterized by stagnation in Paduan theatres and a growing dependence on the principal Italian ones; the last important premières in Padua were Meyerbeer's *Romilda e Costanza* (1817, Nuovo) and Temistocle Solera's *Genio e sventura* (1843, Nuovo). The works of Rossini, Bellini, Donizetti and Verdi were as successful in Padua as in the rest of Italy and in instrumental arrangements, as entr'actes in spoken drama; appreciation of Wagner, however, was late and restricted. In 1884 the Teatro Nuovo was renovated and given the name Teatro Verdi, which it still bears (see illustration); in the 20th century it has staged predominantly travelling productions. When after World War II a bill was passed regulating operatic activity in Italy, Padua failed to achieve the denomination of 'teatro di tradizione' which would have guaranteed the survival of opera seasons in the city, and today the local opera public goes to theatres in Venice, Verona, Treviso and Rovigo. There is, however, a Centro Lirico in Padua which organizes concerts of operatic repertory.

*

A. Pallerotti [A. Pittarello]: *Spettacoli melodrammatici e coreografici rappresentati in Padova nei teatri Obizzi Nuovo e del Prato della Valle dal 1751 al 1892* (Padua, 1892)

B. Brunelli: *I teatri di Padova* (Padua, 1921)

P. Petrobelli: 'L' "Ermiona" di Pio Enea degli Obizzi e i primi spettacoli d'opera veneziani', *QRaM*, iii (1965), 125–41

M. N. Massaro: 'Il ballo pantomimo al Teatro Nuovo di Padova', *AcM*, lvii (1985), 215–74

P. Cattelan: 'L' "Accademia" nei dintorni del Santo (1762–1785)', *Storia della musica al Santo di Padova*, ed. S. Durante and P. Petrobelli (Vicenza, 1990)   SERGIO DURANTE

Paer, Ferdinando (*b* Parma, 1 June 1771; *d* Paris, 3 May 1839). Italian composer. He was one of the central figures in the development of *opera semiseria* during the first decade of the 19th century.

1. LIFE. Paer received his first musical instruction from his father Giulio, a horn player in the Parma court theatre orchestra after 1778, and later studied with the court *maestro di cappella* Gian Francesco Fortunati. Paer's first known stage work was *Orphée et Euridice* (1791, Parma), on a French text with spoken dialogue, and his earliest Italian opera was *Circe* (1792, Venice). On the strength of these initial accomplishments he was appointed honorary *maestro di cappella* to the Parma court, a post which allowed him to compose numerous comic operas, many for other cities (among them *L'intrigo amoroso* for Venice in 1795 which as *Saed, ossia Gli intrighi del serraglio* was his first opera to make a mark outside Parma), and three *opere serie* (*L'Idomeneo, Ero e Leandro* and *Il Cinna*). In 1797 he was promoted to *direttore musicale di tutti i regi servizi* in Parma, a position which called for him to substitute for the two regular *maestri di cappella* when they were ill or absent.

Later that same year Paer moved to Vienna to become musical director of the Kärntnertortheater and thus, like many other Italian composers of his day, began a series of foreign appointments that was to lead him to achieve his greatest success outside Italy. In 1798 he married the soprano Francesca Riccardi (*b* Parma, 1774; *d* Bologna, 1845), whom he had known in Parma and for whom he later created the roles of Briseis in *Achille*, Isabella in *I fuorusciti di Firenze*, Sofia in *Sargino* and Leonora in *Leonora, ossia L'amore conjugale*. The first two of Paer's operas in the *semiseria* style that made him famous were produced during his tenure in Vienna – *Griselda* (1798, Parma), on a famous Boccaccio tale of feminine virtue, set by many other Italian composers, and *Camilla, ossia Il sotterraneo* (1799, Vienna), a macabre 'rescue opera' whose libretto was based on that used for Dalayrac's opera *Camille*; his very successful though rather old-fashioned *opera seria Achille* was also given there in 1801. While in Vienna, Paer met Beethoven and encountered a broad spectrum of musical styles, which probably enriched his already skilful treatment of the orchestra.

After a short time in Prague in 1801, Paer accepted the post of court Kapellmeister in Dresden, where for the court theatre he wrote in successive years three of his most important works: *I fuorusciti* (1802), *Sargino* (1803) and *Leonora* (1804), the last based on a story that Mayr and Beethoven used in operas staged the following year. In Dresden he came to the attention of Napoleon, who is said to have particularly admired *Achille*. Paer followed Napoleon to Posen (now Poznań) and Warsaw in 1806, became his *maître de chapelle* in Paris in 1807 and eventually director of the Opéra-Comique and, after Spontini's dismissal, music director of the Théâtre Italien in 1812. After Napoleon's abdication in 1814 he retained only the last of these positions (until 1818, serving again in 1819–24 and 1826–7), but through connections made previously was able to support himself handsomely as a singing-master and composition teacher to members of the upper classes (Liszt studied composition with him in the 1820s). Apart from *L'oriflamme* (1814, written in collaboration with Méhul, Berton and Kreutzer), Paer's operas written in Paris were exclusively Italian (including *Agnese* for Parma, 1809) until 1816. Then, perhaps to regain some of the popularity he had lost to Rossini and to such new stars as Boieldieu, he began with *Le maître de chapelle, ou Le souper imprévu* (1821) an intermittent series of French works which ended with the *opéra comique Un caprice de femme* (1834). His last opera, *Olinde et Sophronie*, was never completed.

From 1824 to 1826 Paer yielded his directorship of the Théâtre Italien to Rossini, who agreed to assume the position only if his older colleague were not displaced. Rossini's solicitude seems surprising, since Paer had for years been accused publicly of intriguing against Rossini's operas in Paris – a charge that Paer himself felt obliged to rebut in a pamphlet printed after his dismissal as director in 1826. He received the cross of the Légion d'honneur in 1828 and in 1831 succeeded Catel as a member of the Académie des Beaux-Arts; in 1832 he became director of chamber music and *maître de chapelle* to Louis-Philippe. From 1837 until his death he taught composition at the Conservatoire, where he had been superintendent since 1834.

2. STYLE. Paer was a prolific composer, producing at least 55 operas, most of them during the 25-year span from 1791 to 1816. Although he wrote many traditional *opere serie* and *opere buffe*, his historical contribution centres on his operas of mixed genre, the Italian counterparts (with sung recitatives) of the hybrid French *opéras comiques* of the post-Revolutionary period. The balance between comic and serious elements in these works varies considerably. Paer's *dramma eroicomico*, *Sargino* has a mock-heroic flavour, emphasizing comic elements over serious ones and giving *buffo* characters roles at least as weighty as those of the hero and heroine. His *opere semiserie*, on the other hand, are essentially serious operas with happy endings. For example, *Camilla*, *I fuorusciti* and *Leonora* are 'rescue operas' after the model of Cherubini, set in the lonely, ominous settings of Gothic romances – ruined castles, threatening forests and dank underground vaults; *Agnese* even incorporates a mad scene. Yet the tension of these situations is relieved regularly by the intrusion of cowardly servants and pairs of rustic lovers, who provide comic relief and express nostalgic or folklike sentiments.

Paer's operas of *mezzo carattere*, like those of his contemporaries, have expansive multi-sectional arias alternating with ones of more modest size; they range through the entire gamut of vocal styles from comic parlando to elaborate, highly ornamented melody; and, like comic operas, they incorporate a high proportion of elaborate, freely constructed action ensembles (this is especially true of *Leonora*). Operas of this type – and Paer's in particular, because they were relatively well known – played an influential role in the infusion of comic elements such as continuous action, formal flexibility and complexity, and dramatic and musical continuity into serious opera later in the century. Moreover, in their situations and settings they constitute early examples of the infusion of northern Romanticism into Italian opera.

Paer's particular contribution to these intermediate genres extends to many aspects of style. Perhaps more successfully than his contemporaries he managed to integrate the attributes of comic and serious opera (notably in *Agnese*), characterizing his heroes and heroines more realistically and giving his intermediate characters greater vocal weight by making their roles more florid and technically demanding, while not eliminating entirely the traditional distinctions between different types of character. He made use of orchestration to evoke the gloomy atmosphere of many of his scenes, particularly in their pantomime preludes, and he expanded the role of orchestrally accompanied recitative, using tonal and rhythmic tension and instrumental colour to exploit more fully its psychological and expressive potential.

In his vocal writing Paer provided a link between late 18th-century composers (Cimarosa and Paisiello) and Rossini and his followers. Like his predecessors', Paer's works overflow with sweet, luminous italianate melodies organized in elegant phrases and supported by transparent harmonies. Yet he led the move away from casting sopranos – women and castratos – as the male love interest, and towards adapting the tenor voice for this purpose, raising its tessitura to bring it closer to the brilliant clarity of traditional soprano heroes and separating it from the other tenor roles (compare, for example, the parts of Florestano and Pizzarro in *Leonora*). Moreover, in contrast to Mayr, who shared with 18th-century composers a taste for long vocal melismas, Paer anticipated Rossini's techniques of scattering relatively short ornaments throughout his melodies, ending phrases with *gruppetti*, and writing in a semi-syllabic style (in which two or three notes are given to each syllable). Paer had a talent for inventing vocal filigree – his *fioriture* constitute a primary source of aesthetic and dramatic effect in many of his melodies – and the patterns that he devised show striking similarities to Rossini's repertory of ornaments.

As a person Paer was disliked – apparently with some justification – by many of his contemporaries, particularly by envious native composers at courts where he was Kapellmeister. He showed no compunction about using his power at the Théâtre Italien against such rivals as Spontini and Rossini, and he was said to have led a dissolute life. Yet he won over contemporary audiences with his engaging music. His skill at achieving virtually immediate success in several operatic centres of contrasting character – Parma and other Italian cities, Vienna, Dresden and Paris – demonstrates his ability to adapt his style to varying tastes. And although Stendhal (letter, 1824, in Minardi 1987) criticized his *canto spianato* for its lack of passion, Berlioz judged his instrumentation (in *Agnese*) to be 'sober and sensible', and Carpani praised him, with Mayr, Zingarelli and others, for exploring the expressive possibilities of the orchestra without overpowering his melodies – in short, for defending 'good music'. Paer's late *opéra comique Le maître de chapelle* was his only work to survive as part of the 19th-century repertory (and to a lesser extent that of the 20th century); moreover, it is usually performed in a severely truncated and dramatically inconclusive version which emphasizes its most conservative traits (although Barnabé's self-congratulatory aria and Gertrude's singing-lesson are certainly charming), thus constituting an inadequate and unrepresentative legacy for a composer who, with Mayr, dominated the Italian operatic scene at the turn of the century.

See also ACHILLE; AGNESE; CAMILLA, OSSIA IL SOTTERRANEO; FUORUSCITI DI FIRENZE, I; LEONORA; and MAÎTRE DE CHAPELLE, LE.

PMD – *Parma, Teatro Ducale* VM – *Venice, Teatro S Moisè*
WK – *Vienna, Kärntnertortheater*

Orphée et Euridice (prose op [play with songs], 1, Duplessis), Parma, Court, 1791

Circe (op, 3, D. Perelli), Venice, S Samuele, carn. 1792; also perf. as Calypso, *I-Fc**, *B-Bc*

Le astuzie amorose, o Il tempo fa giustizia a tutti (dg, 2, A. Brambilla), PMD, aut. 1792, *F-Pc*, *I-Bc*, *Mr*, *PAc*; also perf. as La locanda dei vagabondi, *D-MÜs*, *I-Fc*, *US-Bp*, *Wc*

I portenti del magnetismo (ob, 2), VM, carn. 1793

Icilio e Virginia (2, G. Foppa), Padua, Nuovo, June 1793

Laodicea (3, Foppa), Padua, Nuovo, June 1793, duet *I-PAc*; as Tegene e Laodicea, Florence, 1799, *Fc*

I pretendenti burlati (dg, 2, G. C. Grossardi), Medesano, Teatrino Privato Grossardi, sum. 1793, *PAc*

L'oro fa tutto (dg, 2, A. Anelli), Milan, Scala, Aug 1793, *D-Dlb*, *I-Fc*, *Mr*, *PAc*; as Geld ist die Lösung, Dresden, 1795

Il nuovo Figaro (dg, 4, L. da Ponte), PMD, Jan 1794, *Fc* [as Il matrimonio di Figaro]

Il matrimonio improvviso (farsa, 1, Foppa), VM, 22 Feb 1794; as I due sordi, Parma, 1801

I molinari (farsa, 1, Foppa), VM, 22 Feb 1794, *D-Dlb*, *F-Pc*, *US-Bp*

Il fornaro (farsa, 1), VM, carn. 1794

L'Idomeneo (dramma serio, 2, G. Sertor), Florence, Palla a Corda, spr. 1794, *I-PAc*

Ero e Leandro (dramma, 2), Naples, S Carlo, 13 Aug 1794, *Fc*, *Nc*, *PAc*

L'inganno in trionfo (int, 1), Florence, Palla a Corda, 1794

Una in bene e una in male (dg, 2, Foppa), Rome, Valle, 1794, *B-Bc*, *I-Fc*, *Mr*, *PAcc*, *US-Bp*, vs, lacking recit. (Paris, ?1810); as Le astuzie di Patacca, Dresden, 1802

La Rossana (melodramma serio, 3, A. Aureli), Milan, Scala, carn. 1795, *I-Mr**, *PAc*

Il Cinna (melodramma serio, 2, Anelli), Padua, Nuovo, 13 June 1795, *Fc*, *PAc* [2 copies]

Anna (ob, 2), Padua, Nuovo, June 1795

L'intrigo amoroso (dg, 2, G. Bertati), VM, 4 Dec 1795, *D-Dlb*, *I-Fc*; as Saed, ossia Gl'intrighi del serraglio, Venice, 1795, *Fc*; as Il male vien dal buco, Bologna, 1797, *US-Bp*

L'orfana riconosciuta (dg), Florence, Pergola, 2 April 1796, *I-Fc*

L'amante servitore (commedia in musica, 2, A. Sografi), VM, 26 Dec 1796, *Fc*

Il principe di Taranto (dg, 2, F. Livigni), PMD, 11 Feb 1797, *B-Bc*, *D-Dlb*, *I-Bc*, *Fc*, *Mr*, *PAc* [2 copies], *US-Bp*; rev. as La contadina fortunata (A. L. Tottola), 1807

Il fanatico in Berlina, WK, 1797

Griselda, ossia La virtù al cimento (dramma semiserio, 2, Anelli), PMD, Jan 1798, *A-Wgm*, *B-Bc*, *D-Dlb*, *DS*, *F-Pc*, *GB-Lbl*, *I-Fc* [2 copies, titled La virtù al cimento], *Mr*, *PAc* [2 copies], *US-Bp*, *CA*, *Wc*, vs (Bonn, ?1815)

Camilla, ossia Il sotterraneo (dramma semiserio, 3, G. Carpani, after B.-J. Marsollier des Vivetières), WK, 28 Feb 1799, *A-Wgm*, *Wn*, *B-Bc*, *D-Bds*, *DS*, *Mbs*, *F-Pc*, *I-Fc* [2 copies], *Mc*, *Mr*, *Nc*, *Pca*, *PAc* [5 copies], Bottini collection, Pisa, *US-Bp*, *Wc*, vs (Bonn, 1799; Paris, n.d.)

Il maestro di ballo (farsa, 1, Foppa), VM, carn. 1799

Il morto vivo (ob, 2, C. P. Defranceschi), WK, 12 July 1799, *B-Bc*, *D-Bds*, *Ds*, *I-Fc*, *US-Bp*

La testa riscaldata (farsa, 1, Foppa), Venice, S Benedetto, 20 Jan 1800, *D-Dlb*, *I-Fc*, *US-Bp*, vs (Mainz, n.d.)

La sonnambula (farsa, 1, Foppa), Venice, S Benedetto, 15 Feb 1800, *I-Mr**, *Fc*, *US-Bp*

Ginevra degli Almieri (op tragicomica, 4, Foppa), WK, 2 Sept 1800, *A-Wgm*, *B-Bc*, *D-DS*, *I-Bc*, *Fc* [2 copies], *Mr*, *PAc*, *US-Bp*

Poche ma buone, ossia Le donne cambiate (ob, 2, Foppa), WK, 18 Dec 1800, *I-Fc* [1 act]; in Ger. as Der lustige Schuster, *D-Bds*, *Ds*, ov. (Offenbach, *c*1800), excerpts, vs (Leipzig, *c*1890)

Achille (melodramma eroico, 2, G. De Gamerra, after Homer), WK, 6 June 1801, *B-Bc*, *D-Bds*, *Dlb*, *DS*, *F-Pc*, *GB-Lbl*, *I-Bc*, *Fc*, *Mr*, *Nc*, *PAc*, *US-Bp*, vs (Bonn, n.d.; Hamburg, n.d.; Paris, n.d.)

I fuorusciti di Firenze (op semiseria, 2, Anelli), Dresden, Hof, 27 Nov 1802, *D-Bds*, *Dlb*, *F-Pc*, *GB-Lbl*, *Lcm*, *I-Fc* [2 copies], *Mr*, *PAc*, *US-Bp*, Ger. vs (Leipzig, *c*1805)

Sargino, ossia L'allievo dell'amore (dramma eroicomico, 2, Foppa), Dresden, Hof, 26 May 1803, *B-Bc* [Ger.], *D-Bds*, *Dlb*, *Ds*, *DS*, *I-Fc*, *Mr*, *Nc*, *PAc* [2 copies], *US-Bp*, vs (Leipzig, ?1803; Bonn, n.d.; Brunswick, n.d.)

Lodoiska (dramma eroico, 3, F. Gonella), Bologna, Comunale, sum. 1804

Leonora, ossia L'amore conjugale (dramma semiserio, 2, G. Schmidt, after J. N. Bouilly), Dresden, Hof, 3 Oct 1804, *B-Bc*, *D-Bds* [Ger.], *Dlb* [Ger.], *DS*, *I-Fc* [2 copies], *Mr*, *US-Bp*, excerpts, vs (Leipzig, ?1805)

Sofonisba (dramma serio, 2, Schmidt), Bologna, Corso, 19 May 1805, *I-Mr**, *A-Wgm*, *B-Bc*, *D-DS*, *MÜs*, *I-Fc*, *Nc*, *US-Bp*, vs (Bonn, ?1808)

Il maniscalco (dg), Florence, Palla a Corda, sum. 1805, *I-Mr*, *PAc*

Numa Pompilio (dramma serio, 3, M. Noris), Paris, Tuileries, carn. 1808, *B-Bc*, *D-Dlb*, *I-Fc*, vs, lacking recit. (London, n.d.)

Cleopatra, Paris, 1808

Diana e Endimione, ossia Il ritardo (int, S. Vestris), Paris, Tuileries, aut. 1809, *Fc*, vs (Leipzig, ?1811)

Agnese (dramma semiserio, 2, L. Buonavoglia, after F. Casari), Parma, Villa Douglas-Scotti, Ponte d'Attaro, Oct 1809, *B-Bc*, *D-Bds*, *Mbs*, *I-Bc*, *Fc*, *Gl*, *Mc*, *Mr*, *Nc* [2 copies], *PAc* [2 copies], *Pca*, *US-Su* [Act 1], *Wc*, vs (Paris, ?1811)

La Didone (melodramma serio, 2, P. Metastasio), Paris, Tuileries, 1810, *D-Dlb*, *I-Fc*, *MOe*, *PAc* [2 copies], vs (London, 1814)

Un pazzo ne fa cento (ob, 2), Florence, Pergola, aut. 1812

I Baccanti (os, 2, G. Rossi), Paris, Tuileries, 7 Jan 1813, excerpts, *A-Wn**

Poche ma buone, ossia La moglie ravveduta (farsa comica, 1, De Gamerra), Rome, Valle, sum. 1813

L'oriflamme (opéra, 1, C.-G. Etienne and L. P.-M.-F. Baour-Lormian), Paris, Opéra, 1 Feb 1814, collab. E.-N. Méhul, H.-M. Berton, R. Kreutzer; *F-Pn*, *Po*, *I-PAc*; (Paris, 1814)

Oro non compra amore (ob, 2), Pavia, Quattro Signori, 1814

L'eroismo in amore (melodramma serio, 2, L. Romanelli), Milan, Scala, 26 Dec 1815, *Mr**, *Fc*

La primavera felice (op giocosa, 1, L. Balocchi), Paris, Italien, 5 July 1816, *Fc*, excerpts (Paris, n.d.)

Lo sprezzatore schernito (musical joke), Florence, Pergola, 22 Nov 1816; pasticcio of G. Pacini, N. Paganini, [?P. C.] Guglielmi, Sampieri, P. Generali, M. A. Portugal, G. Farinelli

Le maître de chapelle, ou Le souper imprévu (oc, 2, S. Gay, after A. Duval), Paris, Feydeau, 29 March 1821 (Paris, ?1821), vs (Paris, ?1854)

Blanche de Provence, ou La cour des fées (opéra, 1, M. E. G. M. Théaulon and de Rancé), Paris, Tuileries, 1 May 1821, *F-Po*, collab. Berton, A. Boieldieu, Cherubini, Kreutzer

Olinde et Sophronie (after T. Tasso), intended for the Opéra, ?1824, inc., *US-Wc**

La marquise de Brinvilliers (oc, 3, E. Scribe and Castil-Blaze), Paris, OC (Ventadour), 31 Oct 1831 (Paris, 1831), collab. Auber, Batton, Berton, Blangini, Boieldieu, Carafa, Cherubini and Hérold

Un caprice de femme (oc, 1, J. P. F. Lesguillon), Paris, OC (Bourse), 23 July 1834 (Paris, 1834)

*

DEUMM (G. P. Minardi); *Grove*6 (J. Budden)

G. Carpani: *Le rossiniane ossia Lettere musico-teatrali* (Padua, 1824)

L. Schiedermair: 'Über Beethovens "Leonore"', *ZIMG*, viii (1906–7), 115–26

——: *Beiträge zur Geschichte der Oper um die Wende des 18. und 19. Jahrhunderts* (Leipzig, 1907–10)

A. Della Corte: *L'opera comica italiana nel '700* (Bari, 1923)

R. Engländer: 'Ferdinando Paer als sächsischer Hofkapellmeister', *Neues Archiv für sächsische Geschichte und Alterthumskunde*, l (1929), 204–24

——: 'Paers "Leonora" und Beethovens "Fidelio"', *NBJb*, iv (1930), 118–32

M. Carner: 'Simone Mayr and his "L'amor coniugale" ', *ML*, lii (1971), 239–58; repr. in M. Carner: *Major and Minor* (New York, 1980), 148–71

R. Celletti: 'La "Leonora" e lo stile vocale die Paër', *RIM*, vii (1972), 214–29

D. Heartz: 'Mozarts "Titus" und die italienische Oper um 1800', *HJbMw*, v (1981), 255–66

M. Ruhnke: 'Opera semiseria und dramma eroicomico', *AnMc*, xxi (1982), 263–75

G. P. Minardi: 'Paër semiserio', *I vicini di Mozart: Florence 1987*, 343–58

R. L. Weaver and N. W. Weaver: *A Chronology of Music in the Florentine Theater, 1751–1800* (Warren, MI, 1992)

SCOTT L. BALTHAZAR (text, bibliography), JULIAN BUDDEN (work-list)

Paganelli, Giuseppe [Gioseffo] **Antonio** (*b* Padua, 6 March 1710; *d* ?Madrid, *c*1763). Italian composer. His membership of the Accademia dei Geniali in Padua (which in 1731–2 performed his oratorio *Il figliuol prodigo* and his cantatas *Narciso al fonte* and *L'apoteosi di Alcide*) has been taken as evidence that his family was respectable and his education good; this is consistent with contemporary description of him as a 'virtuoso dilettante di Padova'. He made his début as an opera composer at Venice in 1732 with *La caduta di Leone, imperator d'Oriente*. Five more operas by him were staged there up to 1743. Meanwhile, he travelled widely; in 1733 he appeared as a harpsichordist with A. M. Peruzzi's troupe in Augsburg, and he supplied the last opera, *La pastorella regnante* (1735), directed by Antonio Denzio at the Sporck Theatre in Prague. His life was subsequently dominated by instrumental composition, although in 1752 he took a minor singing part in Galuppi's *Alessandro nell'Indie* in Munich. Title-pages of librettos and instrumental collections mention many court appointments held by him (Bayreuth, Brunswick, Lisbon and Madrid), though no firm details are known.

La caduta di Leone, imperator d'Oriente (dramma per musica, 3, C. Pagani Cesa), Venice, S Angelo, aut. 1732
L'asilo d'amore (festa teatrale, 1, Metastasio), Brunswick, 1732
Ginestra e Lichetto (int, L. Giusti), Venice, S Angelo, carn. 1733
Tigrane (dramma per musica, 3, B. Vitturi), Venice, S Angelo, carn. 1733
La pastorella regnante (azione musicale drammatica, 2), Prague, Sporck, spr. 1735
Artaserse (dramma per musica, 3, P. Metastasio), Brunswick, 1737
Tirsi (pastorale, 3, F. de Lemene), Wolfenbüttel, 1737
Farnace (dramma per musica, 3, A. M. Lucchini), Brunswick, 1738
Barsina (dramma per musica, 3, F. Silvani, after J. Pradon: *Statira*), Venice, S Cassiano, aut. 1742
Engelberta (dramma per musica, 5, A. Zeno and P. Pariati), Venice, S Cassiano, carn. 1743
La forza del sangue (pastorale, 2, Vitturi), Venice, S Cassiano, carn. 1743

Arias in: *D-KA*, *ROu*, *Sl*; *S-Uu*

*

E. Schenk: *Giuseppe Antonio Paganelli* (Salzburg, 1928)

MICHAEL TALBOT

Paganini. *Operette* in three acts by FRANZ LEHÁR to a libretto by Paul Knepler and BÉLA JENBACH; Vienna, Johann Strauss Theater, 30 October 1925.

Paganini was the first of Lehár's operettas composed with Richard Tauber in mind, though Tauber took up the leading role, with Vera Schwarz as Maria Anna Elisa, only at the Berlin première, on 30 January 1926. In Vienna the leading singers were Carl Clewing and Emmi Kosáry. The work was the first of two that Lehár wrote with Tauber cast as a historical character (the second being Goethe in *Friederike*), and it also provided an opportunity for some important solo violin writing.

Paganini (tenor) has a concert in Lucca ('Schönes Italien'). It is sold out, but the ruling Prince has banned it because of the violinist's dissolute reputation. Paganini chances upon the Prince's wife, Princess Maria Anna Elisa (soprano), sister of Napoleon, and she soon falls under his spell. By threatening to disclose her husband's affair with the dancer Bella Giretti (soprano), she persuades her husband to allow the concert to take place. By Act 2, Paganini has been detained in Lucca for a whole six months by the Princess's charms. However, he has lost his violin in a bet with the court chamberlain Pimpinelli (*buffo*), who will return it only in exchange for lessons from Paganini on the art of wooing ('Gern hab' ich die Frau'n geküsst'). Pimpinelli tries out

Paganini's technique on Bella with some success ('Einmal möcht' ich was Närrisches tun'). By now the Princess and Paganini are deeply infatuated with each other ('Niemand liebt dich so wie ich'), and she reacts emotionally when he is ordered out of town to end the scandal of their affair ('Liebe, du Himmel auf Erden'). However, his inability to resist any attractive woman almost proves his downfall, when he presents Bella with a love song ('Deinen süssen Rosenmund') written for the Princess. The latter nevertheless helps him to escape, and in Act 3 she follows him to an inn on the border of Lucca, where she and Bella both realize that music is his true mistress.

ANDREW LAMB

Paganini, Maria Angiola [Angiola, Maria Angiosa] (*b* Florence, *fl* 1742–73). Italian soprano. An excellent singer of comic opera, she performed mainly in Florence, Venice and cities connected with them, and was a leading performer at a time when *opera buffa* was at the height of its expansion and success (1743–50). Her repertory included the most highly acclaimed works by Latilla, Auletta, Galuppi, P. A. Guglielmi, Cocchi and others, in which she performed in all the principal theatres of northern Italy. In London she achieved great success and was admired by Burney. She performed in *opera seria*, preferring Metastasian works, she sang the title role in Giuseppe Scarlatti's *Artaserse* (1747) and was active in that repertory in Palermo towards the end of her career (1772–3).

*

BurneyH
P. Weiss: 'La diffusione del repertorio operistico nell'Italia del settecento: il caso dell'opera buffa', *Civiltà teatrale e settecento emiliano*, ed. S. Davoli (Bologna, 1986), 241–56

FRANCO PIPERNO

Pagliacci ('Players'). *Dramma* in a prologue and two acts by RUGGERO LEONCAVALLO to his own libretto, based on a newspaper crime report; Milan, Teatro Dal Verme, 21 May 1892.

Canio (in the play, Pagliaccio) *leader of the players*	tenor
Nedda (in the play, Colombina [Colombine]) *Canio's wife*	soprano
Tonio (in the play, Taddeo) *a clown*	baritone
Beppe (in the play, Arlecchino [Harlequin])	tenor
Silvio *a villager*	baritone
Two Villagers	tenor, baritone

Villagers, peasants

Setting Near Montalto, in Calabria, between 1865 and 1870 on the Feast of the Assumption

The success of Mascagni's *Cavalleria rusticana* encouraged the music publisher Sonzogno to look for other subjects with strong emotional appeal, and when Leoncavallo offered him the libretto of a story of love and jealousy in a company of wandering players he was sure that it would be successful. Leoncavallo tried first to follow Mascagni's example faithfully by making it a one-act opera, but apart from the larger dimensions of the work he found it dramatically necessary to use the curtain to make clear the distinction between the 'real life' first part of the opera, and the second part in which the play is performed. The triumph of *Pagliacci* was helped by the excellent cast: Victor Maurel (Verdi's Iago and future Falstaff) created Tonio and recited the

Prologue, which the composer added to the original plan specially for him. Nedda was Adelina Stehle, Canio Fiorello Giraud, and the Dal Verme orchestra was conducted by the young Arturo Toscanini. The opera was soon widely performed, and in the first two years alone it was translated into all the European languages, including Swedish and Serbo-Croat (also into Hebrew for the Tel-Aviv production in 1924), and the role of Canio was the prerogative of the great tenors from Caruso and De Lucia to the present day. The pairing of *Pagliacci* and *Cavalleria* on the stage – in spite of the individuality of each – is clear evidence of the common purpose of the two composers, and rescues from neglect the only masterpieces produced in the circle of the GIOVANE SCUOLA.

The plot can be easily summarized. Before the curtain rises, the hunchback actor Tonio announces that the story is about real people. Canio is the leader of the travelling troupe who are to perform that evening. Someone suggests that Tonio would like to make love to Canio's wife, Nedda, and Canio replies that he would not hesitate to knife Tonio. Tonio tries in vain to kiss Nedda, but she drives him away. In revenge, Tonio fetches Canio while Nedda is talking to her real lover, the villager Silvio, but Canio does not arrive in time to kill his rival, who runs off. The play begins, and Canio has to re-live on stage the situation that exists in real life: Beppe/Harlequin is making love to Nedda/Colombine when Canio/Pagliaccio returns unexpectedly. Overwhelmed, he stabs his wife, who refuses to name her lover, and also kills Silvio who runs to help her.

When the author Catulle Mendès read Leoncavallo's libretto he at once decided to sue him for plagiarism, claiming that Leoncavallo had made unacknowledged use of his *La femme du tabarin* (1887), and Manuel Tamayo y Baus could have made the same claim for his *Un drama nuevo* (1899). It was at this point that Leoncavallo explained in *Le Figaro* of 9 June 1899 that his point of departure had been an incident that had occurred in Montalto, a village in Calabria, and that it had been his father Vincenzo, then a magistrate at Cosenza, who had delivered judgment. In fact, though Leoncavallo was aware of both dramas (as well as others on similar themes presented in the Parisian drama theatres) and could certainly have had them in mind, it is more relevant that plots based on jealousy with violent results were fashionable in both plays and operas at the time, from *Carmen* to *Otello* and *Cavalleria*, to mention only the masterpieces. The other notable feature of the opera, the play-within-a-play, also had plenty of precedents and parallels, constituting almost a genre in themselves. But Leoncavallo's undeniable originality lies in the way he was able to combine news item and play in a tragedy of unusually disturbing violence by making 'stage' and 'life' identical. This successful combination of *dramma buffo* and 'reality' was the model for other experiments, from Strauss's elegant *Ariadne auf Naxos* to Mascagni's disastrous *Le maschere*.

Apart from the original practical incentive of Maurel's participation, the Prologue presents a problem of interpretation. The actor who appears in front of the curtain to announce the author's intentions anticipates the subsequent break in the theatrical illusion; when Tonio (as the Prologue) gives the order for the show to begin the audience knows that a drama is already being enacted. The 'reality' poetically established by this beginning is more real than the verisimilitude of an event in the action of the opera, to which the play gives another dimension, and the double murder takes us back to the earlier one. Canio's 'La commedia è finita' closes the circle opened by Tonio's 'Incominciate' (Canio's phrase was originally also assigned to Tonio, but was appropriated by Caruso when singing Canio and has since remained in the role); and the acknowledged fiction announced in the words of the prologue gives further assurance to the *verismo* of *Pagliacci*, established by the actors' claim to be real human beings with ordinary feelings.

Pagliacci was intentionally directed at the same audience as *Cavalleria*, and the similarity between them is evident not only in the basis of the story (the jealousy and the setting in the south of Italy), but also in the structure of the work. First, there is the division into two parts separated by an intermezzo, with similar proportions between them (the first being longer and setting the scene for the drama). Then there is the initial gesture of breaking the theatrical illusion, with a Sicilian dialect being used by Mascagni (in conformance with 19th-century tradition), while a still greater separation is achieved by Leoncavallo's Prologue, in spite of its clear reference to the *commedia dell'arte*.

The two works are further apart in the details of structure. Mascagni used traditional 'number opera' technique (although his treatment is original), while Leoncavallo treated each scene as a unity in which the numbers are cleverly used, sometimes as traditional structures (especially in character-pieces such as the Bell Chorus and Nedda's ballade in Act 1 scene ii, sometimes incorporating melodic references and leitmotifs, and sometimes combining both possibilities). The melody of Canio's famous aria, 'Ridi pagliaccio', is heard in the prologue and returns (in the low strings) soon after, transformed into an outline of intervals and rhythm, when the crowd sees the company of actors approaching and comments on the sad life of the actors for whom life is performance. But in general the weaving of themes in the prologue is aimed at preparing the audience to react emotionally to the drama through the words of the singer. Apart from Canio's melody, at the centre of the brief instrumental introduction between the exposition and reprise of a gay and lively theme, a poetic melody is associated with the furtive love of Nedda and Silvio, while Tonio's aria 'Un nido di memorie', a shrewd reference to a world of popular images, is evoked by a melancholy melody.

If the initial appearance of the chorus (introduced by a discordant fanfare of trumpets, spoilt by too many progressions) is conventional, the character of Canio's arioso announcing 'un gran spettacolo a ventitrè ore' (scene i), is striking, particularly in the mocking trills and the textual alliteration. A sparkling theme in the violins introduces the tenor cantabile which follows, and the sudden change to gravity in his words ('Un tal gioco'), at first restrained and ironic and then in the central section an almost sarcastic melody – which re-appears later, in the play – is followed by a short chromatic passage in which there is no longer any pretence ('Ma se Nedda sul serio sorprendessi') and which anticipates what happens soon afterwards. The return of the cantabile followed by the *scherzoso* theme concludes an arc-shaped form (the proportions of the ABCB'A' structure are not perfectly symmetrical) which serves the development of the drama, with the violent expression of the leading character's jealousy at the centre of its

Scenes from the original production of Leoncavallo's 'Pagliacci' at the Teatro Dal Verme, Milan, 21 May 1892: engraving from 'Il teatro illustrato' (June 1892)

structure. Leoncavallo thus cleverly succeeds in confirming the causes of the action through the music, although it is followed by the banal Bell Chorus 'Din, don, dan' which is unwittingly reminiscent of Verdi's 'Rataplàn' chorus and Chabrier's orchestral work *España*.

Nedda is introduced in scene ii by a character passage inspired by the sound of birds, a metaphor for freedom in which Leoncavallo displays his ability for imitative orchestration, followed by a passage of *verismo* in the cracking of the whip and the scornful words with which she drives away the lustful Tonio. Here too there is the mingling of stage and life, with Nedda referring to the script of the play that they are to perform in the evening.

The love duet between Nedda and Silvio (scene iii), a long episode necessary for the development of the action which temporarily absorbs the tensions that have preceded it, provides the only really lyrical interlude in the opera. Divided into three parts, all in slow tempos (*Andante amoroso*, *Andante appassionato* and *Largo assai*), and dominated by long cantabile phrases, it ends with a romantic recapitulation of the love theme on the cello accompanying the lovers' kiss.

The influence of Verdi's *Otello* is apparent when a solo for double basses and a sinister melodic tritone introduces the unexpected arrival of the jealous husband accompanied by Tonio (scene iv), whose words are underlined by muted brass. Prevented by Beppe from stabbing Nedda, Canio sings the celebrated arioso 'Vesti la giubba'. The intermezzo which follows contains the most significant semantic references of the opera. The sad melody of the preceding arioso returns – altered and depending on diminished 7th chords – and the chromatic progressions lead to the melody of the prologue 'Un nido di memorie', another reminiscence implying the unity of life and art, as is the reworking of Canio's first cantabile 'Un tal gioco' which follows.

The curtain goes up for the second act almost exactly as it does in the first, with the same festive music suggestive of a wind band attracting the chattering crowd to the entertainment (scene i). This time Leoncavallo uses Verdi's device of gaiety to emphasize tragedy, although this is hardly necessary as the action on the stage repeats what has just been happening among the actors. The play (scene ii) begins with a *minuet* with a reprise framing Harlequin's famous serenade accompanied by solo flute and oboe; then comes the comic *scena* with Tonio and the duet *a tempo di gavotta* between Harlequin and Colombine. These numbers precede the *scena e duetto finale* with Canio/Pagliaccio, which conclude both the play and the opera itself. Canio comes on stage to hear the same words and the same music which his wife had used to her lover in the previous act. His repeated fierce demands to know the name of his rival are also accompanied by musical reminiscence. He no longer tries to act and is indifferent to the laughter of the crowd, who gradually realize that the scene is no longer realistic acting. Nedda tries in vain to continue the performance, which ends with the double murder and Canio's terse comment 'La commedia è finita', completing the combination of reality and pretence.

* * *

Pagliacci takes the technique of *verismo* to its limits. Leoncavallo's patient reconstruction of his subject is necessarily less immediate than Mascagni's, but he gained from his study of precedents a refinement of detail, a more significant and shrewd use of orchestration, and a more original and expressive harmony. Hanslick rightly defined Leoncavallo as a less original but better musician than Mascagni. A continuity with the late works of Verdi can be found in the transformation of a peaceful strolling player into a truculent and violent man. The difference lies in the moral perspective: Otello degrades himself by murder, but Canio recovers his dignity. Leoncavallo understood the connection between social values and the market for entertainment. While its effect is perhaps obvious and at times overemphatic, it is a necessary and original feature of the opera, whose vitality is still applauded by audiences all over the world.   MICHELE GIRARDI

Pagliardi, Giovanni Maria (*b* Genoa, 1637; *d* Florence, 3 Dec 1702). Italian composer. He seems to have begun his career as a church musician at Genoa. The libretto of his first opera (1672) gave him the title of *maestro di cappella* to the Grand Duke of Tuscany; he therefore may have succeeded Cesti, who died in that post in 1669. A document cited by Fabbri (1959) indicates that in 1679 he was serving the Grand Duchess of Tuscany. Later (in 1701) it is revealed that he had been *maestro di cappella* of S Lorenzo, Florence, a position that normally carried with it a benefice established by the Medici family that over the years had been awarded to the most important composers of the city, provided they were priests, as was Pagliardi. From 1681, when his name appears in the pay records of the Tuscan court, until his death he remained the musical director and principal composer of the operas produced at Prince Ferdinando's villa at Pratolino and at the Palazzo Pitti, Florence; in 1701 he also became *maestro di cappella* of Florence Cathedral.

Pagliardi was best known as a composer of operas. His most successful, *Caligula delirante*, was revived at least 14 times, playing in five cities in 1675 alone. Its music is notable for its impassioned, even bizarre, chromaticism, a trait shared by other Florentine opera composers of the time.

Caligula delirante (melodramma, 3, D. Gioberti), Venice, SS
  Giovanni e Paolo, 18 Dec 1672, *D-MÜs*, *I-Vnm*
Lisimaco (dramma per musica, 3, C. Ivanovich), Venice, SS
  Giovanni e Paolo, 10 Dec 1673, *MOe*, *Vnm*
Il Numa Pompilio (dramma per musica, 3, M. Noris), Venice, SS
  Giovanni e Paolo, 11 Jan 1674, and Vienna, Hof, 1674, *A-Wn*, *I-Vnm*
Il tiranno di Colco (dramma musicale, G. A. Moniglia), Florence,
  Pratolino, 2 Aug 1687
Il pazzo per forza (dramma musicale, A. Moniglia), Florence,
  Pratolino, 26 Aug or 16 Sept 1687
Il Greco in Troia (festa teatrale, Noris), Florence, Pergola, 29 Jan
  1689

Attilio Regolo (dramma per musica, Noris), Florence, Pratolino, 6
  Sept 1693

*

ES (P. M. Capponi)
C. Ivanovich: *Poesie* (Venice, 1675), 372–4 [incl. letter of Pagliardi;
  letter transcribed in H. Becker, ed.: *Quellentexte zur Konzeption
  der europäischen Oper im 17. Jahrhundert* (Kassel, 1981)]
M. Fabbri: 'Due musicisti genovesi alla corte granducale medicea:
  Giovanni Maria Pagliardi e Mar[t]ino Bitti', *Musicisti piemontesi
  e liguri*, Chigiana, xvi (1959), 79–94   JOHN WALTER HILL

Pagliuca, Giuseppe (*fl* 1775–1805). Italian librettist. He was described in contemporary sources as being 'of the counts of Manupello', a title that connects him with the Orsini family. He wrote librettos for three *opere serie*, a comic opera, and a number of occasional pieces dedicated to Ferdinand IV of Naples. His considerable cultivation of the *componimento drammatico* after the suppression of the short-lived Neapolitan republic in 1799 attests to the reactionary nature of the Bourbon monarchy; his recourse to the *licenza* in his last two *opere serie* suggests a similar ideological framework – an attempt to stem the revolutionary tide by royalist propaganda. His first *opera seria* libretto, *Creso in Media*, is constructed almost entirely of exit arias, with only single examples of duet, trio and chorus. This typical 18th-century pattern gave way in both *Laconte* and *Ifigenia in Aulide* to a more flexible form, in which the ensemble plays a larger part. The ensembles in *Ifigenia* are longer and more varied than those in *Laconte* and show a greater interaction of chorus and principal characters, thus confirming Pagliuca's prefatory statement that the libretto conformed with the modern Italian taste for *melodramma*, as epitomized in works of Paisiello, Paer and Piccinni.

Creso in Media (dramma per musica), J. Schuster, 1779; *Laconte*
  (dramma per musica), P. A. Guglielmi, 1787; *Gl'inganni fortunati*
  (ob), Valentino Fioravanti, 1788; *Ifigenia in Aulide* (dramma per
  musica), Trento, 1804   STEPHEN McCLATCHIE

Pagliughi, Lina (*b* Brooklyn, New York, 27 May 1907; *d* Rubicone, 1 Oct 1980). Italian soprano. Born in New York of Italian parents, she studied in San Francisco with Brescia and in Milan with Manlio Bavagnoli. She made her début at the Teatro Nazionale, Milan (1927), as Gilda. Between 1931 and 1949 she appeared at Monte Carlo, the S Carlo in Naples, La Scala (as Sinais in *Mosè in Egitto*), Covent Garden (Gilda), the Florence Maggio Musicale (Queen of Night) and the Rome Opera as Elvira (*I puritani*). She retired from the stage in 1957. Her vocal and stylistic gifts – sweet, pure tone, smooth, flexible technique, perfect legato and delicacy of expression – made her the leading Italian light soprano after Toti dal Monte. Her unimpressive stage presence was a hindrance to her theatrical career, but she made many successful records.

*

L. di Cave: 'Lina Pagliughi', *Record Collector*, xxi (1973), 101–25
  [with discography]   RODOLFO CELLETTI

Pahissa, Jaime (*b* Barcelona, 7 Oct 1880; *d* Buenos Aires, 27 Oct 1969). Spanish composer. He abandoned a career in architecture and studied composition with Enric Morera in Barcelona. By 1906, through the success of his incidental music for Gual's *La presó de Lleida*, he was already considered an important young composer. Some of his works, especially the operas, are influenced by Pedrell and the Catalan Wagnerian tradition, but he was equally open to the most advanced movements of his day. He was one of the first Spaniards to explore expressionism and the 12-note scale, which he considered a continuation and culmination of Wagnerism and polyphonic experimentation.

Gala Placidia received its first complete performance in 1913. Because the opera was written at two different periods, the first act (1906) is relatively simple while the other two are in a complex style with intricate polyphony, strong dissonances and rich and vigorous orchestration. The opera was well received in spite of the novelty of the music. Pahissa's second opera was La morisca (1919). It is more symbolic and less passionate, with one dominant character, Mari Cruz. Its single act is divided into ten scenes but avoids both the picturesque music that the theme invites and also the complex texture of Gala Placidia; melody predominates, making it probably the composer's most accessible work, with recitative, semicantados (recitatives similar to Sprechgesang) and more conventional harmonic writing. Marianela, similar in its emphasis on melody, followed in 1923. La princesa Margarida, described as a romantic Catalan opera, was first performed in 1928; based on the youthful work La presó de Lleida, it retains some numbers of the original. It contains much descriptive writing, especially in the intense third act, and shows a new tendency to elaborate harmony.

In 1937, as a result of the civil war, Pahissa, like Falla and Julián Bautista, went to Argentina. There he composed two more operas, Don Gil de las calzas verdes (1955) and, a year later, Tragicomedia de Calisto y Melibea.

Gala Placidia (3, A. Guimerá), Barcelona, Liceu, 15 Jan 1913
La morisca (1, E. Marquina), Barcelona, Liceu, 15 Feb 1919
Marianela (3, S. and J. Alvarez Quintero, after B. Pérez Galdós), 1923
La princesa Margarida (3, A. Gual), Barcelona, Liceu, 8 Feb 1928
Don Gil de las calzas verdes, Montevideo, 1955
Tragicomedia de Calisto y Melibea, Buenos Aires, 1956

*

R. Villar: Músicos españoles (Madrid, 1918–27)
M. Valls: La música catalana contemporània (Barcelona, 1960)

EMILIO CASARES

Paine, John Knowles (b Portland, ME, 9 Jan 1839; d Cambridge, MA, 25 April 1906). American composer. As a youth in Portland he studied with the local German 'professor', Hermann Kotzschmar. On a visit to Boston he met the Beethoven scholar Alexander Wheelock Thayer, under whose guidance he went to Berlin in 1858 to complete his musical education. On returning to the USA in 1861 Paine was recognized as one of the country's finest organists, and in 1862 was appointed organist at Harvard University – the only musical position on the staff. Gradually he expanded his activities there, establishing a music department in 1871; among his composition students was Frederick S. Converse. In 1867 he joined the faculty of the newly founded New England Conservatory of Music in Boston, becoming at the same time professor of music at the closely associated Boston University. He came to be the first broadly successful American composer of orchestral works, and he established a lasting academic career pattern for composers in the USA.

Paine was a highly conservative, strongly Germanic composer. His most characteristic works fall within the limits of the Viennese Classical style, with contrapuntal elements derived from Bach. His later works gradually became more chromatic, however, and his three-act grand opera Azara (composed 1883–98) represents a major late turning-point in his career. His only previous operatic work had been the pastiche Il pesceballo ('The One Fishball'; F. J. Child and J. R. Lowell, libretto published Cambridge, MA, 1862), which he had assembled for a Civil War benefit in 1862; the music, consisting mainly of arrangements of Mozart, Rossini, Bellini and Donizetti, is now lost. Under the influence of Wagner (whom he had severely denigrated in earlier decades), Paine wrote his own libretto for Azara, based on the 13th-century chante-fable Aucassin et Nicolette, and scored the work for a considerably larger orchestra than he had employed hitherto, with wind in threes and fours, extra brass and much percussion. Also Wagnerian is the opera's extensive and elaborate chromaticism, as well as its continuous musical structure in which, however, the outlines of individual numbers can readily be discerned. Azara's several recurring musical themes have been called leitmotifs, but they are not; thematic transformation is not employed. A certain 'naivety' in the use of word-painting, used with similar literalness in the works of Heinrich and Gottschalk, may be seen as an American trait.

Interest in Azara was expressed by Emma Eames (for whom the title role was conceived) and others; yet though Breitkopf & Härtel published the vocal score (Leipzig, 1901), no performance was ever staged. (This contrasted with the success of his incidental music for Sophocles' Oedipus tyrannus, 1881, and Aristophanes' The Birds, 1901.) All Paine's accumulated influence and goodwill proved inadequate to overcome the Metropolitan Opera's prejudice against American works, which stood until 1910 – by which time Paine was dead. The opera did receive incomplete concert performances with piano accompaniment (1903, 1905), and an abridged concert performance with orchestral accompaniment in 1907 (to favourable reviews); the composer's widow published the full score and parts at her own expense in 1908.

*

W. S. B. Mathews, ed.: A Hundred Years of Music in America (Chicago, 1889), 675–9
C. Thaxter: Letters (Cambridge, MA, 1895)
E. Eames: Some Memories and Reflections (New York, 1927)
G. T. Edwards: Music and Musicians of Maine (Portland, ME, 1928)
M. A. D. Howe: 'John Knowles Paine', MQ, xxv (1939), 257–67
E. Fisk, ed.: The Letters of John Fiske (New York, 1940)
J. C. Huxford: John Knowles Paine: Life and Works (diss., Florida State U., 1968)
J. A. Mussulman: Music in the Cultured Generation: a Social History of Music in America, 1870–1900 (Evanston, IL, 1971)
J. C. Schmidt: The Life and Works of John Knowles Paine (Ann Arbor, 1980)

ANDREW STILLER

Paisiello, Giovanni (b Roccaforzata, nr Taranto, 9 May 1740; d Naples, 5 June 1816). Italian composer. He was one of the most successful and influential opera composers of the late 18th century.

1. LIFE. Paisiello received his education first at the Jesuit school in Taranto and then, between 1754 and 1763, at the Conservatorio di S Onofrio, Naples. According to his autobiographical sketch (published in Choron and Fayolle), he composed his first short opera, a comic intermezzo, while still a conservatory student. At about the time he left the S Onofrio he attracted the attention of a young nobleman, Giuseppe Carafa, who appointed him musical director of the small opera company he was forming at the time. It was due to Carafa that Paisiello acquired his first commissions to write works for the Teatro Marsigli-Rossi, Bologna, in 1764. The second of these, I francesi brillanti, failed at

823

its first performance but was more successful when it was transferred to Modena two weeks later. This led to a commission from Modena for some new music for an opera originally by Guglielmi, *La donna di tutti i caratteri*. Paisiello's revision, *Madama l'umorista*, contained much new music; its success led in turn to requests for new operas for other north Italian theatres.

Paisiello regarded himself as Neapolitan, and he preferred living and working in Naples to anywhere else. In 1766 he returned to Naples; as freelance composer his chief activity was setting comic operas for the Nuovo and Fiorentini theatres, where his chief rival was Piccinni. But he was also happy to accept commissions for serious operas at the S Carlo. Signs that the court, and in particular the King of Naples, Ferdinand IV, approved of his music are the three operas (*Lucio Papirio dittatore*, *Olimpia* and the so-called *Festa teatrale in musica*) staged at the S Carlo between June 1767 and May 1768. Thereafter however the royal approval seems to have been withdrawn, possibly because of Paisiello's unusual behaviour over his marriage to a widow, Cecilia Pallini. In the summer of 1768 he contracted to marry her but then tried to withdraw from the bargain, using various excuses. Pallini appealed, perhaps to the Queen of Naples, and Paisiello was confined in prison until the marriage was solemnized on 15 September. He received no further recognition from the court until 1774, when his short *Il divertimento de' numi* was performed at the royal palace, and no further commission came from the S Carlo until mid-1776.

Paisiello was unable to fulfil this commission because in 1776 he received and accepted an invitation from Catherine II of Russia to become her *maestro di cappella* in St Petersburg for three years at an annual salary of 3000 roubles. He left Naples for Russia on 29 July. His duties in St Petersburg included composing all the theatrical pieces ordered by the court and directing the court's orchestra and opera company. His new patroness maintained her small Italian opera company less out of personal affection for opera than with an eye to its political prestige value. Her relative indifference to music explains perhaps why Paisiello composed fewer stage works in Russia than he had done in a comparable period of time in Naples. Fortunately for him the empress liked him enough to renew his contract in September 1779 for another three years at an increased salary of 4000 roubles. And in 1781 she offered him a further four-year contract from September 1782, the date when his existing contract was due to expire. Paisiello accepted this latest offer, although he was starting to have second thoughts about staying in Russia much longer. His relationship with the court became strained in November 1783 after he had quarrelled with the newly formed committee of court theatres. Using his wife's ill-health as an excuse, he asked to be granted permission to return to Italy. Rather than lose her *maestro* altogether, Catherine granted him paid leave for a year. Once out of Russia, however, he made no attempt to return.

One reason why Paisiello did not go back to St Petersburg was his nomination by King Ferdinand of Naples on 9 December 1783 as *compositore della musica de' drammi* of the Neapolitan court. This was the result of a determined campaign by Paisiello to persuade the king, through the intercession of friends and intermediaries, to give him an official court position. During this campaign Paisiello sent his latest scores to Ferdinand

through the diplomatic mail. His nomination was announced 17 days after *Il barbiere di Siviglia* (one of the operas he had sent from Russia) was performed at the Palace of Caserta in the king's presence on 22 November 1783.

As the king's *compositore* Paisiello had no regular duties at court and no regular salary. Perhaps for this reason he did not reach Naples until October or November 1784, spending the summer of that year in Vienna, where he composed *Il re Teodoro in Venezia* (performed at the Burgtheater on 23 August). His first offering to the Neapolitan court after his return was *Antigono*, first given at the S Carlo on 12 January 1785. Shortly after its successful première, on 7 March the king granted him a pension, the conditions of which were published in the *Gazetta civica napoletana* of 18 March: Paisiello was in future obliged to write an annual opera for the S Carlo and other occasional music as needed; in return he was to receive 1200 ducats annually, half from the treasury and half from the S Carlo (in effect payment for his annual opera); he was forbidden to leave Naples to compose music for anywhere else without royal permission; lastly, he was to receive the pension 'even if he could no longer compose in the service of His Majesty'. Paisiello faithfully obeyed these conditions for the next five years, and wrote no operas for theatres outside Naples during that period. On 29 October 1787 the king also appointed him *maestro della real camera* with an annual salary of 240 ducats. This appointment put Paisiello in charge of all secular music at court. His positions as court composer and *maestro della real camera*, with their large pension and salary, made him the most favoured musician in the city.

In 1790 Paisiello seems to have suffered some kind of physical or mental breakdown. He had contracted to write three operas for different Neapolitan theatres during the autumn and winter season of 1789–90 when Ferdinand gave him the extra task of composing *Nina, o sia La pazza per amore* (performed outside Caserta on 25 June 1789). This put him behind schedule with the other works. He was able to finish the first, *I zingari in fiera*, basically on time for the Fondo theatre in the autumn. But the other two, for the Fiorentini and the S Carlo theatres, both of which should have been staged the following carnival, did not appear until later in the year. The late completion of *Zenobia in Palmira* brought him into dispute with the impresario of the S Carlo, who maintained that he had failed to fulfil his annual contract. Paisiello petitioned the king to be relieved of all further duties to the theatre and once more gained his wish. On 30 October 1790 Ferdinand ordained that he should in future receive his full pension without being obliged to write music for the S Carlo. This left him free to write operas for theatres outside Naples if he wished, and in fact he wrote three such works for Padua, London and Venice during the 1791–2 period. After 1792 his output of new operas slowed down; by 1800 it had virtually ceased, and he subsequently wrote only two complete stage works.

The wars and unsettled political conditions in Italy at the end of the century had considerable effect on Paisiello's later career. In January 1799 republican forces gained control of Naples and established there the so-called Parthenopaean Republic. The king and his court fled to Sicily, but Paisiello stayed behind. On 4 May he was made *maestro di cappella nazionale* to the republic, although he later claimed he had not wanted

Design by Innocente Colomba for the original production of Paisiello's 'Annibale in Torino' at the Teatro Regio, Turin, 16 January 1771

this appointment. After royalist forces recaptured Naples at the end of June 1799 his part in the affairs of the republic was officially investigated, and he was suspended from all court duties. Not until 7 July 1801 was he pardoned and reinstated in his former posts.

One of the greatest admirers of his music by this time was Napoleon Bonaparte, First Consul of France. Towards the end of 1801 Napoleon negotiated with Ferdinand for Paisiello's temporary release for a visit to Paris. These negotiations must have been completed by 19 January 1802, when Paisiello requested the Naples court to pay his monthly salary to his lawyer during his French visit. He arrived in Paris in April and was offered a monthly salary of 1000 francs, free housing and a free carriage, to direct the music of the consular chapel and to compose two operas a year and a military march each month. Paisiello took on the duty of *maître de chapelle*, but basically ignored the other tasks. During the two years in France he wrote only one opera, *Proserpine*; this failed when it was produced in March 1803. Newspaper reports early the following year stated that he was considering composing a new stage work on the subject of the Orestes by Euripides. But he was probably not serious about this project. In fact by this time he was determined to return to Naples once more, and obtained his release from his chapel post (though not immediately from Napoleon's service altogether) around 10 April 1804. He left Paris for Naples on 29 August and had probably arrived by the end of September.

In 1806 Joseph Bonaparte, brother of Napoleon, ousted Ferdinand IV and installed himself as King of Naples. Paisiello, already a favourite with the Bonaparte family, was now appointed director of all sacred and secular music at Joseph's court. Joseph's successor, Joachim Murat (king, 1808–15), confirmed these posts. It is not true, as Florimo maintained, that when Murat lost control of Naples and King Ferdinand returned to power in 1815 Paisiello lost all his royal appointments except the directorship of the court chapel. In fact, as a result of a general amnesty declared in Naples on 23 May 1815, the composer retained all his previous positions until the time of his death.

2. WORKS. The precise number of operas Paisiello wrote is unclear, but over 80 works can be safely attributed to him. During the earlier part of his creative life he was most in demand as a composer of comic operas, for which his naturally effervescent and graceful music was particularly suitable. During his first Neapolitan period (1766–76) he showed shrewdness in choosing to work with Giambattista Lorenzi, the finest Neapolitan librettist of the century. Lorenzi provided him with texts containing plenty of humour and well-coordinated plots. The first of their collaborations, *L'idolo cinese* (1767), was also Paisiello's first great success in Naples. His music was marked by simple harmonies, constant use of traditional cadence formulae, a felicitous mixture of staccato and legato phrases and frequent repetition of short figures in the accompaniment. He was the first Neapolitan to discard the second and third movements of the opera overture.

During his Russian period (1776–84) Paisiello had to write in a more concentrated manner, as Catherine decided, probably in 1778, that operas at her court should not last longer than an hour and a half. Composing Italian operas for a court in which Italian was not the normal spoken language, he had to make his music good enough to compensate for any lack of understanding of the libretto. As a result, his powers of musical characterization sharpened, his orchestration became more colourful and his melodies acquired greater warmth. At this time there appeared in his melodic style turns of phrase reminiscent of Mozart; Mozart himself, after hearing *Il re Teodoro in Venezia* in Vienna in 1784 and perhaps also *Il barbiere di Siviglia*, first produced there in 1783, displayed discernible traces of Paisiello's style in *Le nozze di Figaro* and *Don Giovanni*.

After Paisiello returned to Naples in 1784 his melodies tended to become simpler and more popular in their appeal. Some of his songs of this time became great favourites with the public, the most successful of all perhaps being 'Nel cor più non mi sento' from *L'amor contrastato* (1788; later better known as *La molinara*). Many composers, including Beethoven, used this song as basis for variations or free fantasias. The opera in which Paisiello's tendency towards simple tunes is most apparent is *Nina* (1789), a work that is important because of the exceptional acclaim it received during his lifetime and because it is a locus classicus of 18th-century sentimental comedy in music.

Paisiello's heroic or tragic operas have not been highly regarded in recent times, partly because his music has been considered too light and frivolous for the sober nature of the genre. Yet he took their composition seriously, and the fact that all but one of his full-length operas written after 1792 have heroic or tragic texts suggests that he retained an affection for this genre longer than for comic opera. He greatly admired Metastasio, whose librettos he extolled to his pupils, and he did not follow the example of Gluck in taking radical steps to cure the chief fault of heroic opera, which was that it permitted singers too many chances for virtuoso display at inappropriate moments in the drama. He did, however, do much to limit singers' abuses. His attitude to the subject became defined during his Russian period. About his setting of Metastasio's *Alcide al bivio* (1780, St Petersburg), he wrote: 'I have worked very hard at it, since I wanted to get away from the inconveniences created in Italian theatres, and have completely excluded vocalizations, cadenzas and ritornellos, and set nearly all the recitatives with orchestral accompaniment'. After his return to Naples in 1784 he was no longer able to work towards a comprehensive reform of heroic opera because of the necessity of pleasing local taste, which was conservative. Nonetheless, several of his later operas lack vocalizations and pauses for cadenzas, and a few contain interesting experimental features. *Pirro* (1787) uses ensemble finales of a type till then reserved for comic opera, during which the dramatic action continues to progress. *Elfrida* (1792, the first of two operas with texts written for him by Calzabigi) is unusual in allocating all solo songs to the principal characters. *Proserpine* (1803), Paisiello's only French opera, has orchestral accompaniment for all recitatives, as was usual in French grand opera of the period. This feature was so rare in contemporary Italian opera that it is worth noting that the Italian version, called *Proserpina* (adapted c1806–8 but never performed), also has orchestral accompaniment throughout.

Paisiello's popularity was at its height during the last 20 years or so of the 18th century. At that time his works were as much in demand outside Italy as they were inside it. In Vienna, for example, the Italian opera company installed by Joseph II performed more works by Paisiello during the 1780s than by any other composer. London was another city where operagoers showed particular partiality for his music in the late years of the century. The decline in the demand for his music, which became noticeable everywhere after 1800, was a sign that taste had changed. The works that retained their popularity longest were his best comic operas, *Il barbiere di Siviglia*, *L'amor contrastato* and *Nina*, but even these went out of the repertory by around the 1820s. His compositions are therefore a gauge of what the public of the late 18th century regarded as excellent. Coincidentally, they also are a source of comparison with the operas of Mozart, who knew that the standards set by Paisiello were those he had to beat to win the heart of the operagoing public.

See also BARBIERE DI SIVIGLIA, IL (i); DUE CONTESSE, LE; ELFRIDA; FEDRA (i); FILOSOFI IMMAGINARI, I; FRASCATANA, LA (ii); GIUOCHI D'AGRIGENTO, I; MODISTA RAGGIRATRICE, LA; MOLINARA, LA; NINA; NITTETI (i); PIRRO; RE TEODORO IN VENEZIA, IL; and SISMANO NEL MOGOL.

NC – *Naples, Teatro di S Carlo*
NFI – *Naples, Teatro dei Fiorentini*
NN – *Naples, Teatro Nuovo*

cm – *commedia per musica*   dg – *dramma giocoso*
dm – *dramma per musica*   int – *intermezzo per musica*

variants are MSS that include musical alterations by other composers

Il ciarlone (dg, 3, A. Palomba), Bologna, Marsigli-Rossi, 12 May 1764

I francesi brillanti (dg, 3, P. Mililotti), Bologna, Marsigli-Rossi, c24 June 1764, *D-Wa*

Madama l'umorista (dg, 3, after A. Palomba), Modena, Rangoni, 26 Feb 1765 [rev. of P. A. Guglielmi: La donna di tutti i caratteri, 1762]

L'amore in ballo (dg, 3, A. Bianchi), Venice, S Moisè, carn. 1765, *E-Mp*, *I-Nc**, *P-La*

Le virtuose ridicole (dg, 3, C. Goldoni), Parma, Ducale, 1765, *US-Eu* (Act 2)

Le nozze disturbate (dg, 3, G. Martinelli), Venice, S Moisè, carn. 1766, *I-Nc**, *P-La*

Le finte contesse (int, 2, after P. Chiari: Il marchese Villano), Rome, Valle, Feb 1766, *F-Pn*, *I-Nc* (2 copies, 1 autograph); variants *B-Bc*, *I-Vnm*

La vedova di bel genio (cm, 3, Mililotti), NN, spr. 1766, *Nc**

Le 'mbroglie de le Bajasse (cm, 3, Mililotti), NFI, carn. 1767; rev. as La serva fatta padrona, NFI, sum. 1769, *E-Mp*, *I-Nc**

L'idolo cinese (cm, 3, G. Lorenzi), NN, spr. 1767, *A-Wn*, *E-Mp*, *F-Pn* (2 copies), *GB-Lbl*, *I-Mc* (Acts 2 and 3), *Nc* (2 copies, 1 autograph); variants *B-Bc*, *F-Po*, *US-Bp*, *Wc*

Lucio Papirio dittatore (dm, 3, A. Zeno), NC, c30 June 1767, *I-Nc**, *P-La*

Il furbo malaccorto (cm, 3, Lorenzi), NN, wint. 1767, *E-Mp*, *I-Nc**

Olimpia (dm, 3, A. Trabucco), NC, 20 Jan 1768, *Nc**, *P-La* (2 copies)

Festa teatrale in musica [Peleo; Le nozze di Peleo e Tetide] (2, G. B. Basso Bassi), NC, 25 or 31 May 1768, *I-Nc**, *S-St*

La luna abitata (cm, 3, Lorenzi), NN, sum, 1768, *E-Mp*, *I-Nc**, *S-St*

La finta maga per vendetta (cm, 3, Lorenzi), NFI, aut. 1768, *I-Nc**

L'osteria di Marechiaro (cm, 2, F. Cerlone), NFI, ?carn. 1769, *E-Mp*, *I-Nc** [perf. with a separate Act 3, La Claudia vendicata, *Nc**]

Don Chisciotte della Mancia (cm, 3, Lorenzi, after M. de Cervantes), NFI, sum. 1769, *A-Wn* (variant), *E-Mp*, *F-Pn*, *I-Nc**; vs (Milan, 1963)

L'arabo cortese (cm, 3, Mililotti), NN, wint. 1769, *E-Mp*, *F-Pn*, *I-Nc* (2 copies, 1 inc. autograph), *US-Wc* (Acts 1 and 2)

La Zelmira (cm, 3, Cerlone), NN, sum. 1770, *F-Pn*, *I-Nc**

Le trame per amore (cm, 3, Cerlone), NN, 7 Oct 1770, *B-Bc*, *F-Pn*, *I-Nc**

Demetrio [1st version] (dm, 3, P. Metastasio), Modena, Corte, carn. 1771, *F-Pn*, *I-Mc*, *Nc**

Annibale in Torino (dm, 3, J. Durandi), Turin, Regio, 16 Jan 1771, *Nc**, *Tf*, *P-La*

La somiglianza de' nomi (cm, 3, Mililotti), NN, spr. 1771, *E-Mp* (frag.), *F-Pn*, *I-Nc**

I scherzi di amore e di fortuna (cm, 3, Cerlone), NN, sum. 1771, *Nc**; rev. (int), *Nc*

Artaserse (dm, 3, Metastasio), Modena, Corte, 26 Dec 1771, *Nc**

La Semiramide in villa (int, 2), Rome, Capranica, carn. 1772, *Nc**

Motezuma (dm, 3, V. A. Cigna-Santi), Rome, Dame, Jan 1772, *Nc**

La Dardané (cm, 3, Cerlone), NN, sum. 1772, *E-Mp*, *I-Nc**

Gli amanti comici (cm, 3, Lorenzi), NN, aut. 1772, *E-Mp* (Acts 2 and 3), *F-Pn*, *I-Nc**, *OS*; rev. as Don Anchise Campanone, Venice, S Samuele, aut. 1773, *E-Mp* (Acts 1 and 2), *H-Bn* (variant, Act 1), *I-Vnm*

L'innocente fortunata (dg, 3, F. Livigni), Venice, S Moisè, carn. 1773, *Fc*, *Vnm*; variants *H-Bn*, *RU-SPtob*; rev. as La semplice fortunata, NN, sum. 1773, *I-Nc**

Sismano nel Mogol (dm, 3, G. De Gamerra), Milan, Regio Ducal, 30 Jan 1773, *Nc**, *Vnm* (variant), *P-La* (2 copies inc.)

Il tamburo (cm, 3, Lorenzi, after J. Addison: The Drummer), NN, spr. 1773, *A-Wn* (variant), *E-Mp*, *I-Nc* (2 copies, 1 autograph); rev. as Il tamburo notturno, Venice, S Moisè, aut. 1773, *Nc**, *Vnm*, *RU-SPtob*

Alessandro nell'Indie (dramma serio, 3, Metastasio), Modena, Corte, 26 Dec 1773, *I-Nc* (inc. autograph)

Andromeda (dm, 3, Cigna-Santi), Milan, Regio Ducal, carn. 1774, *F-Pn*, *I-Nc**, *P-La* (Acts 2 and 3)

Il duello (cm, 1, Lorenzi), NN, spr. 1774, *E-Mp*, *F-Pn*, *I-Mc* (2 copies), *US-Bp*; rev. as Il duello comico, Tsarskoye Selo, 1782, *I-Nc**, *RU-SPtob*, vs (Rome, 1944); rev. as Le duel comique (P.-L. Moline), Paris, Comédie-Italienne (Bourgogne), 16 Oct 1776 (Paris, 1777)

Il credulo deluso (cm, 3, after Goldoni: *Il mondo della luna*), NN, Sept 1774, *F-Pn*, *I-Nc* (2 copies, 1 autograph), *OS*; rev. as Orgon dans la lune (M. J. Mattieu de Lépidor), *F-Pn*, *R(m)*

La frascatana (dg, 3, Livigni), Venice, S Samuele, aut. 1774, *B-Bc*, *D-Wa*, *I-Bc*, *Mc*, *Nc**, *PAc*, *Rsc*, *Vnm*, *P-La*, *S-Skma*, *US-R*, *Wc*; variants *A-Wn* (2 copies), *D-B* (2 copies, 1 in Ger.), *Hs*, *DK-Kk* (in Dan.), *F-Pn* (2 copies), *GB-Lbl* (2 copies inc.), *I-Bc*, *Vnm*, *US-Bp*, *NYp*; rev. as L'infante de Zamora (N. E. Framery), Strasbourg, 1779, and Versailles, 1781 (Paris, n.d.)

Il divertimento de' numi (scherzo rappresentativo per musica, 1, Lorenzi), Naples, Reale, 4 Dec 1774, *I-Fc* (inc.), *Nc**

Demofoonte (dm, 3, Metastasio), Venice, S Benedetto, carn. 1775, *F-Pn*, *I-Mc*, *P-La*

La discordia fortunata (dg, 3), Venice, S Samuele, carn. 1775, *I-Fc*, *P-La*; variants *A-Wn*, *D-Dlb*, *Wa*, *H-Bn* (Act 1)

Le astuzie amorose (cm, 3, Cerlone), NN, spr. 1775, *E-Mp*, *I-Nc**, *Tf* (variant)

Socrate immaginario (cm, 3, Lorenzi and Galiani), NN, Oct 1775, *A-Wgm* (inc.), *D-B*, *F-Pn*, *GB-Ob*, *H-Bn* (Acts 1 and 2), *I-Nc* (2 copies, 1 autograph with later alterations), *PAc*, *Rsc* (Act 1), *RU-SPsc*, *S-St*, *US-Wc*; variants *GB-Lbl* (Act 1), *I-Bc*, *P-La* (Acts 1 and 2); vs (Florence, 1931)

Il gran Cid (dm, 3, ? after G. G. Bottarelli), Florence, Pergola, aut. 1775, *I-Fc*, *Nc**, *US-Wc*

Le due contesse (int, 2, G. Petrosellini), Rome, Valle, 3 Jan 1776, *E-Mp* (2 copies), *F-Pn* (4 copies), *GB-Lbl* (2 copies), *H-Bn*, *I-MOe*, *Nc**, *Vnm*, *S-St*, *US-NYp*, *Wc*; variants *A-Wn* (2 copies), *RU-SPtob*; rev. as Les deux comtesses (Framery), Versailles and Strasbourg, 1781 (Paris, n.d.)

La disfatta di Dario (dm, 3, Duke of S Angelo Morbilli), Rome, Argentina, carn. 1776, *B-Bc* (Acts 1 and 2), *D-Hs*, *GB-Lbl*, *I-Bc*, *Nc**, *Vnm*, *S-St*, *US-Wc*; variants *F-Pn*, *I-Nc*, *P-La*

Dal finto il vero (cm, 3, F. S. Zini), NN, spr. 1776, *F-Pn*, *I-Nc* (2 copies, 1 autograph), *OS*, *US-Wc*; variants *D-Dlb*, *I-Vnm*, *RU-SPtob*

Nitteti (dm, 3, Metastasio), St Petersburg, Imperial, *c*17/28 Jan 1777, *D-B*, *F-Pn* (2 copies), *GB-Ob*, *I-Mc*, *Nc**, *RU-Mcm*, *SPtob*

Lucinda ed Armidoro (azione teatrale, 2, M. Coltellini), St Petersburg, aut. 1777, *D-B*, *F-Pn* (Act 1), *GB-Lbl*, *Ob*, *I-Nc**, *RU-SPtob*, *Wc*

Achille in Sciro (dm, 3, Metastasio), St Petersburg, 26 Jan/6 Feb 1778, *D-B*, *F-Pn*, *GB-Lbl*, *Ob*, *RU-Mcm* (Acts 1 and 3), *SPtob*, *US-Wc*

Lo sposo burlato (dg, 2, G. B. Casti), Peterhof, 13/24 July 1778, *RU-SPtob* [pasticcio assembled by Paisiello, incl. music by him and other composers]

I filosofi immaginari [Gli astrologi immaginari] (dg, 2, G. Bertati), St Petersburg, Hermitage, 3/14 Feb 1779, *A-Wn**, *B-Bc*, *DK-Kk*, *F-Pn* (2 copies), *GB-Ob*, *H-Bn*, *I-Fc*, *RU-SPtob*, *S-Skma*; variants *D-Wa*, *DK-Kk* (2 copies, 1 inc. in Dan.), *I-Pc*, *Vnm*, *US-Bp*, *Wc*; as Le philosophe imaginaire (P. U. Du Buisson), Paris, Tuileries, 1780 (Paris, n.d.); as Die eingebildeten Philosophen, *A-M*, *Sca*, *Wn*, *D-B*, *Hs*, *DK-Kk*, *RU-SPtob*; as I visionari, Dresden, 1793

Demetrio [2nd version] (dm, 2, Metastasio), Tsarskoye Selo, 13/24 June 1779, *GB-Lcm*, *Ob* (Act 1), *I-Nc**, *RU-SPtob*

Il matrimonio inaspettato (dg, 1 [some MSS in 2 pts], after Chiari: *Il marchese Villano*), Kammenïy Ostrov, St Petersburg, 21 Oct/1 Nov 1779, *F-Pn* (2 copies), *I-Mc*, *Nc**, *RU-SPtob*; variants *B-Bc*, *E-Mp*, *GB-Cfm*, *Lbl*, *I-Vnm*, *RU-SPtob* (in Russ.), *S-St* (in Swed.); as La contadina di spirito o sia Il matrimonio inaspettato, *A-Wn*, *H-Bn*, *I-MOe*; as Le marquis Tulipano (C. J. A. Gourbillon), Paris, Monsieur, 28 Jan 1789, *F-R(m)* (Paris, n.d.)

La finta amante (ob, 2, ?Casti), Moghilev, Poland, 25 May/5 June 1780, *A-Wn* (2 copies), *B-Bc*, *D-B*, *F-Pn* (3 copies), *GB-Lbl*, *I-MOe*, *Nc* (2 inc. copies, 1 autograph), *Vnm*, *RU-SPtob* (2 copies, 1 shortened)

Alcide al bivio (festa teatrale, 1, Metastasio), St Petersburg, Hermitage, 25 Nov/6 Dec 1780, *B-Bc*, *GB-Lcm*, *Ob*, *I-Nc**, *RU-SPit* (inc.)

La serva padrona (int, 2, G. A. Federico), Tsarskoye Selo, 30 Aug/10 Sept 1781, *A-Wn*, *B-Bc*, *D-MÜs* (inc.), *F-Pn* (4 copies), *GB-Lbl*, *I-Bc*, *Mc* (2 copies), *MC*, *Nc* (3 copies), *PAc* (variant), *PESc*, *Rsc*, *Rvat*, *Vnm*, *RU-SPsc*, *SPtob* (3 copies, 1 in Fr., 1 in Russ.), *S-Skma*, *US-Bp*, *NYp*, *SFsc*, *Wc* (Paris, n.d.)

Il barbiere di Siviglia, ovvero La precauzione inutile (dg, 4, ? G. Petrosellini, after P.-A. Beaumarchais: *Le barbier de Séville*), St Petersburg, Hermitage, 15/26 Sept 1782, *A-Wn*, *C-Lu*, *CH-Zz*, *D-Hs*, *Wa*, *E-Mc*, *F-Pn* (2 copies), *GB-Lbl*, *Lcm*, *Ob*, *H-Bn*, *I-Bc*, *Mc* (2 copies), *MOe*, *OS*, *Pc*, *PAc* (2 copies), *PESc*, *Rsc*, *Rvat*, *Vc*, *Vnm*, *P-La*, *RU-SPsc*, *S-Skma*; rev. (3), NFI, spr. 1787, *I-Nc* (2 copies, 1 autograph); variants *A-Wn*, *B-Bc*, *D-B* (in Ger.), *Hs*, *I* copies, 1 in Ger.), *I-PAc*, *S-St* (in Swed.), *US-CA*; as Le barbier de Séville (Framery), Versailles, 14 Sept 1784, *F-Pn* (Paris, ?1784); as Le barbier de Séville (Moline), ? Paris, 1787 (Paris, 1787); ed. G. Guidi (Florence, 1868)

Il mondo della luna (festa teatrale comica, 1, after Goldoni), Kammenïy Ostrov, St Petersburg, 24 Sept/5 Oct 1783, *A-Wn*, *I-Nc**, *RU-SPtob*, *US-Wc*; variants *A-Wn*, *E-Mp*, *F-Pn*, *I-Fc*

Il re Teodoro in Venezia (dramma eroi-comico, 2, Casti), Vienna, Burg, 23 Aug 1784, *A-Wgm* (2 copies), *Wn* (3 copies, 1 in Ger.), *B-Bc*, *CH-Zz*, *D-B* (2 copies in Ger.), *HR*, *Mbs* (inc.), *DK-Kk* (2 copies, 1 in Dan.), *F-Pn* (3 copies), *Po*, *GB-Lbl*, *H-Bn* (inc.), *I-Bc* (variant), *Gl*, *Mc*, *Nc**, *OS*, *Pc*, *PAc* (2 copies), *Rvat*, *Vnm* (2 copies), *RU-SPtob*, *US-Bp* (Act 1 in Ger.), *CA*, *Wc*; as Le roi Théodore à Venise (Du Buisson), Fontainebleau, 28 Oct 1786 (Paris, n.d.); as Le roi Théodore à Venise (Moline), Paris, Opéra, 11 Sept 1787, *F-Po* (Paris, n.d.); ? as Gli avventurieri (Mazzolà), Dresden, Elettorale, 1791

Antigono (dm, 3, Metastasio), NC, 12 Jan 1785, *B-Bc*, *D-Mbs*, *I-Nc**, *P-La*, *US-Wc*

L'amore ingegnoso (int, 2), Rome, Valle, carn. 1785, *F-Pn*, *I-Nc**, *Vnm*

La grotta di Trofonio (cm, 2, G. Palomba, after Casti), NFI, aut. 1785, *A-Wn*, *D-Mbs*, *Wa*, *E-Mp* (as Amor mon a' riguardi), *F-Pn* (2 copies), *GB-Ob*, *I-Nc**, *RU-SPsc*, *US-R* (Act 1); variants *A-Wgm*, *Wn* (in Ger., as Die Trofonius Höhle), *F-Pn* (2 copies), *I-Gl*, *Vnm*

Olimpiade (dm, 3, Metastasio), NC, 20 Jan 1786, *D-Mbs*, *I-Nc*, *P-La*, short score, arias, duet, terzet (Naples, 1786); rev. NC, 30 May 1793, *F-Pn*, *GB-Ob*, *I-Nc**

Le gare generose (cm, 2, G. Palomba), NFI, spr. 1786, *A-Wn*, *D-Wa*, *E-Mp*, *F-Pn* (2 copies), *I-Gl*, *Nc**, *Tf*, *Vnm*; variants *A-Wn*, *B-Bc* (Act 2), *F-Pn*, *H-Bn*, *RU-SPtob*, *US-Wc*; as Gli schiavi per amore, London, King's, 24 April 1787, *GB-Lbl*, vs of Act 1 (London, n.d.); as Le bon maître, ou L'esclave par amour (Gourbillon and P. G. Parisau), Paris, Monsieur, March 1790, *F-R(m)* (shortened) (Paris, 1790)

Pirro (dm, 3, De Gamerra), NC, 12 Jan 1787, *A-Wn*, *B-Bc*, *F-Pn* (4 copies), *GB-Cpl*, *I-Bc*, *Nc**, *PAc*, *Rc*, *Vnm*, *P-La*, *S-Skma*, *US-Bp*; variant, Tuileries, Paris, 24 Jan 1811, *F-Pn*

Giunone Lucina (componimento drammatico, 1, C. Sernicola), NC, 8 Sept 1787, *D-Mbs*, *GB-Lbl*, *I-Nc**

La modista raggiratrice (cm, 3, Lorenzi, after G. A. Federico: *Il Filippo*), NFI, aut. 1787, *GB-Ob*, *I-Nc* (2 copies, 1 autograph), *Pc*, *Rsc*, *Vc*, *Vnm*; variants *A-Wn*, *Ob*, *Dlb*, *F-Pn* (2 copies), *GB-Lbl*, *I-PAc*, *Rsc*, *Tf*, *P-La*, *RU-SPtob*, *US-Bp*; as La scuffiara raggiratrice, Florence, 1788; as La scuffiara amante, o sia Il maestro de scuola napolitano, Rome, 1788; as La cuffiara, Monza, 1789

Fedra (dm, 3, L. B. Salvioni, after C. I. Frugoni), NC, 1 Jan 1788, *A-Wn*, *D-B*, *F-Pn*, *GB-Lbl*, *Ob*, *I-Nc**, *P-La*

L'amor contrastato [La molinara] (cm, 3, G. Palomba), NFI, aut. 1788, *D-Mbs* (2 copies), *E-Mp*, *F-Pn* (2 copies), *GB-Lbl*, *I-Mc*, *Nc**, *US-SFsc* (in Ger.), *A-Wgm*, *Wn* (3 copies, 2 in Ger.), *B-Bc*, *CH-Zz* (in Ger.), *D-B* (2 copies, 1 in Ger.), *NEhz* (in Ger.), *DK-Kmk*, *F-Pn* (2 copies), *I-OS*, *PAc*, *Vnm*, *P-La*, *RU-SPit*, *SPsc*, *SPtob* (4 copies, 1 in Ger.), *US-Bp*, *BE* (inc.), *Wc* (2 copies); Acts 1 and 2 (Florence, 1962), vs (Berlin, n.d.), vs in Ger. (Leipzig, n.d.)

Catone in Utica (dm, 3, Metastasio), NC, 5 Feb 1789, *F-Pn*, *GB-Lcm*, *Ob*, *I-Gl* (variant), *Nc**, *P-La*

Nina, o sia La pazza per amore (commedia in prosa ed in verso per musica, 1, G. Carpani, after B.-J. Marsollier des Vivetières, with addns by Lorenzi), S Leucio, Belvedere, 25 June 1789, *A-Wn*, *D-Mbs*, *GB-Lbl*; rev. (2), NFI, aut. 1790, *D-B*, *Hs*, *Mbs*, *DK-Kk* (2 copies), *E-Mc*, *EIRE-Dtc*, *F-Pn*, *GB-Lbl*, *Lcm*, *Ob*, *I-Bc*, *Mc*, *Nc* (3 copies, 1 autograph), *OS*, *Rsc*, *Vc*, *S-Skma*, *St*, *US-Bp*, *Wc*; variants *A-Wn*, *B-Bc*, *Br*, *D-Hs* (Act 2), *DK-Kk*, *F-Pn*, *R(m)* (in Fr.), *GB-Lcm* (Act 1), *I-Mc* (2 copies), *Mr*, *PAc* (2 copies), *Tf*, *Vc*

(2 copies), *Vnm* (2 copies), *RU-SPit*, *SPsc* (in Russ.), *US-NYp*; vs ed. Gatti (Milan, 1940)

I zingari in fiera (dm, 2, G. Palomba), Naples, Fondo, 21 Nov 1789, *B-Bc*, *D-B*, *Hs* (2 copies), *E-Mp*, *F-Pn*, *GB-Lbl* (2 copies), *Ob*, *I-Mc*, *MOe*, *Nc**, *P-La*, *S-Skma*; variants *A-Wgm*, *Wn*, *I-Pc*, *PAc*, *Rsc*, *Vnm*, *RU-SPtob* (in Russ.)

Le vane gelosie (cm, 3, Lorenzi), NFI, spr. or early sum. 1790, *E-Mp*, *I-Nc**, *P-La*; as La discordia conjugale, *GB-Lcm* (Act 1); collab. S. Palma

Zenobia in Palmira (dm, 2, G. Sertor), NC, 30 May 1790, *GB-Lcm*, *I-Nc**, *US-Bp*

Ipermestra (dm, 3, Metastasio), Padua, Nuovo, June 1791, *GB-Lcm* (variant), *I-Pc*, *Vnm* [incl. music by Bertoni, Fabrizi and Tarchi]

La locanda (dg, 2, G. Tonioli, after Bertati), London, Pantheon, 16 June 1791, *I-Nc**; rev. as Il fanatico in Berlina (3), NFI, carn. 1792, *A-Wn*, *E-Mp*, *EIRE-Dtc*, *GB-Lbl* (Acts 1 and 2), *I-Mc*, *Pc* (Acts 1 and 2), *PAc*, *PESc*, *Vnm*, *P-La* (Act 1), *US-Bp*; variants *A-Wn*, *D-B*, *I-OS*, *RU-SPtob*

I giuochi d'Agrigento (dm, 3, A. Pepoli), Venice, Fenice, 16 May 1792, *A-Wgm*, *D-Mbs*, *F-Pn* (2 copies), *GB-Lcm* (2 copies), *Ob*, *I-Nc* (2 copies), *PAc*, *Vlevi*, *Vnm*, *RU-SPit*, *SPtob*, *US-Bp* (variant), *Wc* (inc.)

Elfrida (tragedia per musica, 2, R. de Calzabigi), NC, 4 Nov 1792, *B-Bc*, *F-Pn*, *GB-Lbl*, *Ob*, *I-Nc**, *PAc*, *Rmassimo*, *Rsc*, *Vnm*, *S-St*, *US-Bp*; variants *A-Wgm*, *RU-SPtob*, *US-NYp*

Elvira (tragedia per musica, 3, Calzabigi), NC, 12 Jan 1794, *B-Bc*, *F-Pn*, *I-Nc**, *PAc*, *Vnm*, *US-Bp*

Didone abbandonata (dm, 2, Metastasio), NC, 4 Nov 1794, *A-Wgm*, *D-B*, *F-Pn*, *GB-Lbl*, *I-Nc**, *Rsc*, *Vnm*, *US-Bp*

La Daunia felice (festa teatrale, 1, F. P. Massari), Foggia, Palazzo Dogana, 25 June 1797, *I-Nc**

Andromaca (dm, 2), NC, 18 Nov 1797, *A-Wn*, *F-Pn*, *I-Nc**, *RU-SPsc*, *SPtob*, *US-Bp*; variants *I-Pc*, *Vnm*

L'inganno felice (cm, 2, G. Palomba), Naples, Fondo, wint. 1798, *GB-Ob*, *I-Mc* (2 copies), *Nc**, *Rsc*, *Vnm*, *US-Bp*; variants *B-Br*, *RU-SPtob* (as L'ingiusta gelosia)

Proserpine (tragédie lyrique, 3, N.-F. Guillard, after P. Quinault), Paris, Opéra, 29 March 1803, *F-Pn*, *Po* (2 copies) (Paris, 1803); rev. as Proserpina (G. Sanseverino), *I-Bc*, *Bsf*, *Nc*

Epilogue for S. Mayr: Elisa (farsa, 1, ?Nicolini), NC, 19 March 1807, *F-Pn**

I pittagorici (dramma, 1, V. Monti), NC, 19 March 1808, *D-Mbs*, *F-Pn*

Doubtful [operas mentioned in Paisiello's autobiographical sketch (see Choron and Fayolle 1811) and for which no other evidence has been found; comp. ?before 1776]: Il mondo alla rovescia, Bologna; I bagni d'Albano, Parma; Le pescatrici, Venice; Il giocatore, Florence; Il finto principe, Bologna; Il negligente, Parma

*

FlorimoN; *RosaM*

A.-E. Choron and F. J. M. Fayolle: 'Paisiello', *Dictionnaire historique des musiciens*, ii (Paris, 1811) [incl. autobiographical sketch]

L. Cassitto: 'Elogio storico', *Onori funebri renduti alla memoria di Giovanni Paisiello*, ed. G. B. Gagliardo (Naples, 1816), 11–35

G. de Dominicis: *Saggio su la vita del Cavalier Don Giovanni Paisiello* (Moscow, 1818)

F. Schizzi: *Della vita e degli studi di Giovanni Paisiello* (Milan, 1833)

H. Abert: 'Paisiellos Buffokunst und ihre Beziehung zu Mozart', *AMw*, i (1918–19), 402–21

A. Della Corte: *Paisiello* (Turin, 1922)

——: *L'opera comica italiana nel settecento* (Bari, 1923)

U. Prota-Giurleo: *Paisiello ed i suoi primi trionfi a Napoli* (Naples, 1925)

N. Cortese: 'Un' autobiografia inedita di Giovanni Paisiello', *RaM*, iii (1930), 123–35

E. Faustini-Fasini: 'Documenti paisielliani inediti', *NA*, xiii (1936), 105–27

H. V. E. Somerset: 'Giovanni Paisiello: 1740–1816', *ML*, xviii (1937), 20–35

A. Loewenberg: 'Paisiello's and Rossini's "Barbiere di Siviglia"', *ML*, xx (1939), 157–67

E. Faustini-Fasini: *Opere teatrali, oratori e cantate di Giovanni Paisiello* (Bari, 1940)

U. Rolandi: 'Contributi alla bibliografia di Giovanni Paisiello', *Rinascenza salentina* (Lecce, 1940)

R.-A. Mooser: *Annales de la musique et des musiciens en Russie au XVIIIme siècle*, ii (Geneva, 1951)

G. Pannain: '"Don Chisciotte de la Mancia" di G. B. Lorenzi e Giovanni Paisiello', *RMI*, lvi (1954), 342–5

A. Einstein: 'A "King Theodore" Opera', *Essays on Music*, ed. P. H. Lang (New York, 1956, 2/1958), 191–6

I. Samson: 'Paisiello – "La bella Molinara"', *NZM*, Jg.120 (1959), 368–71

A. Della Corte: 'Un'opera di Paisiello per Caterina II di Pietroburgo: *Gli astrologi immaginari* (1779)', *Chigiana*, xxiii (1966), 135–47

A. Ghislanzoni: *Giovanni Paisiello: valutazioni critiche rettificate* (Rome, 1969)

M. F. Robinson: *Naples and Neapolitan Opera* (Oxford, 1972)

G. C. Ballola: 'L'ultimo Calzabigi, Paisiello e l'*Elfrida*', *Chigiana*, xxix–xxx (1975), 357–68

J. L. Hunt: *Giovanni Paisiello: his Life as an Opera Composer* (New York, 1975)

F. Lippmann: 'Un'opera per onorare le vittime della repressione borbonica del 1799 e per glorificare Napoleone: *I pittagorici* di Vincenzo Monti e Giovanni Paisiello', *Musica e cultura a Napoli dal XV al XIX secolo: Florence 1983*, 281–306

F. Blanchetti: 'Tipologica musicale dei concertati nell'opera buffa di Giovanni Paisiello', *RIM*, xix (1984), 234–60

M. F. Robinson: *Giovanni Paisiello: a Thematic Catalogue of his Works*, i (Stuyvesant, NY, 1991)   MICHAEL F. ROBINSON

Paita, Giovanni (*b* ?Genoa; *fl* 1708–29). Italian tenor. His operatic career ran from 1708 (début at Vicenza) until Carnival 1729, and he was one of the leading tenors of that period, especially admired by Metastasio and praised by Mancini, both for his singing and his acting. He was very active in Venice in 1709–14, was later in the service of the Duke of Parma and visited Munich in 1725. According to Gerber he also taught singing in Genoa. His voice was rather low (approximately *c* to *g'*) but very flexible, as demonstrated by his brilliant coloratura. He was a highly finished singer with mastery of a wide range of vocal genres.   DENNIS LIBBY

Palace Theatre. London theatre opened in 1891 and known as the Royal English Opera House until 1911; *see* LONDON, §II, 2.

Paladilhe, Emile (*b* Hérault, nr Montpellier, 3 June 1844; *d* Paris, 8 Jan 1926). French composer. He was a child prodigy who entered the Paris Conservatoire at nine, studying composition, the piano and organ (with Halévy, Marmontel and Benoist respectively); he won the Prix de Rome in 1860 with barely 16. Apparently during his Rome period he wrote what was to become his most popular piece, the song *La Mandolinata*. It was included in his first staged opera, *Le passant* (1872), but neither that nor the colourful singing of his mistress Galli-Marié could save the work from closing after only three performances by the Opéra-Comique. *L'amour africain* (1875) fared little better, but the graceful, attractive score of his third work for the company, *Suzanne* (1878), received an honourable 30 performances.

Although the *opéra comique Diana* (1885) failed, with the grand opera *Patrie!* (1886) Paladilhe, no longer a prodigy, finally achieved true success. He had matched Sardou and Gallet's fine libretto with a score of power and range (from the delicate and touching to the noble and vast). The work was revived and given at the Opéra to the end of World War I, and was staged elsewhere in Europe as well. Even here, however, critics noted resemblances to Meyerbeer and Gounod, for Paladilhe lacked a truly original musical personality, despite elegant ideas, a sense of form and great skill in orchestration. Paladilhe did not repeat his long-sought success in opera; instead, the most important large-scale works in the years after *Patrie!* are his sacred choral

'Les Paladins' (Rameau): model of the set for Act 3 scene ii (a Chinese palace) for the original production at the Paris Opéra (Palais-Royal), 12 February 1760

pieces. He was elected to the Institut Français to succeed Guiraud in 1892, and became an Officier of the Légion d'honneur in 1897.

first performed in Paris unless otherwise stated

Le chevalier Bernard (oc, 1), Salle Herz, 16 Feb 1859, excerpts perf.
La reine Mathilde (oc, 3), Salle Herz, 28 Feb 1860, excerpts perf.
La fiancée d'Abydos, 1864 (opéra, 3, J. Adenis), unperf.
La coupe du roi de Thulé, 1868–9 (opéra, 3, L. Gallet and E. Blau), unperf.
Le passant (opéra en vers, 1, F. Coppée), OC (Favart), 24 April 1872, aria 'La Mandolinata' *F-Pc**; vs (Paris, 1872)
L'amour africain (oc, 2, E. Legouvé, after P. Mérimée: *Le théâtre de Clara Gazul*), OC (Favart), 8 May 1875, vs (Paris, 1875)
Suzanne (oc, 3, Lockroy [J.-P. Simon] and E. Cormon), OC (Favart), 30 Dec 1878, vs (Paris, 1879)
Diana (oc, 3, J. Normand and H. Régnier), OC (Favart), 23 Feb 1885, vs (Paris, 1885)
Patrie! (grand opéra, 5, V. Sardou and Gallet), Opéra, 20 Dec 1886, *Po**; vs (Paris, 1886)
Dalila, ?1896–7 (opéra, 4), unperf.
Toute la France (à-propos lyrique, 6 tableaux, Sardou, Sully-Prudhomme, de Bornier and Hérédia), Palais Bourbon, 1900, collab. Reyer, Massenet, T. Dubois and Lenepveu
Vanina (opéra, 3), unperf.

Inc.: Untitled work, 1862–3 (oc), *Pc**

*

FétisBS; *MGG* (M. Frémiot)
F. Clément and P. Larousse: *Dictionnaire lyrique* (Paris, 1867–81; 2/1897, 3/1905 ed. A. Pougin as *Dictionnaire des opéras*)
A. Pougin: 'Patrie!', *Le ménestrel*, liii/4 (1887), 26–9
H. Q.: 'Paladilhe', *La grande encyclopédie* (Paris, 1887–1901)
G. Vapereau: *Dictionnaire universel des contemporains* (Paris, 6/1893)
A. Jullien: *Musiciens d'aujourd'hui*, 2nd ser. (Paris, 1894), 383–406
C. Le Senne: 'Période contemporaine: Paladilhe', *EMDC*, I/iii (1921), 1769–72
H. Büsser: 'Emile Paladilhe', *Le ménestrel*, lxxxviii/3 (1926), 32
P. Landormy and J. Loisel: 'Institut de France: Paladilhe', *EMDC*, II/vi (1931), 3548–9
M. Curtiss: *Bizet and his World* (New York, 1958)
G. Favre: *Compositeurs méconnus* (Paris, 1983), 61–99

LESLEY A. WRIGHT

Paladins, Les ('The Paladins'). *Comédie lyrique* in three acts by JEAN-PHILIPPE RAMEAU to a libretto attributed to, among others, Duplat de Monticourt; Paris, Opéra, 12 February 1760.

Of all Rameau's major works, *Les Paladins* was the least successful: after 15 performances at the Opéra it was taken off and it was never revived. Though scarcely the worst that Rameau set, the libretto, after La Fontaine's *Le petit chien qui secoue de l'argent et des pierreries* (in turn based on canto xviii of Ariosto's *Orlando furioso*), was generally considered inept. It contained an uneasy mixture of comic and serious (or at least non-comic) elements, a combination which the French found distasteful. From about halfway through, comedy is largely displaced by the transformations, magical events and reversals of fortune that were the stock-in-trade of *la féerie*, a genre explored by Rameau in such works as *Zaïs*.

Set in medieval Venetia, the opera concerns the love between Atis (*haute-contre*), a young Paladin or knight-errant, and Argie (soprano), an Italian girl. Argie is kept under the surveillance of a cowardly gaoler Orcan (bass) on the orders of her absent guardian, the aged senator Anselme (bass), who wishes to marry her. By various means, including disguises and some help from the fairy Manto (*haute-contre*), Atis outwits the jealous Anselme to win Argie's hand.

In changing La Fontaine's Anselme from husband to guardian of Argie, the librettist altered the theme from cuckoldry to rivalry between an old and a young suitor. Given the plot's uncertainty of purpose, there is little opportunity for characters to transcend their stereotypes. Only the gaoler Orcan emerges as a genuinely comic creation, engaging sympathy despite his craven behaviour.

Rameau's score is astonishingly lively for a composer well into his 70s (it may possibly have been begun by 1756). Most immediately striking is the sheer colour of its orchestration, and in particular the brilliant use of piccolos, horns, and bassoons at the top of their range. Humour comes largely from the many parodies of 'serious' operatic conventions or from such on-omatopoeic effects as the pizzicatos that imitate the clinking of Orcan's keys. The first modern revival took place in June 1967 as part of the Lyons Festival.

GRAHAM SADLER

Palais Garnier. Theatre designed by Charles Garnier and occupied by the Paris Opéra from 1875 to 1987; see PARIS, §§5(ii) and 6(i, ii).

Palais Royal. Theatre used by the Paris Opéra from 1673 to 1763, reconstructed on the same site in 1770 for use by the company until 1781; see PARIS, §§2(i) and 3(i).

Palay, Elliot (*b* Milwaukee, 18 Dec 1948). American tenor. He studied with Charles Kullman at Indiana University, Bloomington. After singing Matteo (*Arabella*) at Lübeck in 1972, he appeared in the Heldentenor repertory (Tristan, Walther and the Emperor in *Die Frau ohne Schatten*) in Munich, Stuttgart and Frankfurt. He returned to the USA to sing at the New York City Opera and performed Siegfried in the *Ring* cycles mounted in Seattle in 1983 and 1984. In the latter year he sang the Drum Major (*Wozzeck*) in Dresden and appeared in *Mahagonny* at the Munich Festival. Other repertory includes Boris (*Kát'a Kabanová*), Siegmund, Siegfried, Radames and Ismaele (*Nabucco*).

DAVID CUMMINGS

Palazzi, Giovanni (*fl* 1718–49). Italian librettist. He is described as a Venetian in librettos. Of his five *drammi per musica* for the Venetian stage the most interesting are his first two, *Armida al campo d'Egitto* and *La verità in cimento*, both of which were set by Vivaldi. His collaborator on the second, Domenico Lalli, later dedicated a sonnet to him in his *Rime* (Venice, 1732). Less well known than the *drammi* are his librettos for two comic intermezzos, *Pasquale gastaldo* and *Lisetta e Caicanturco*, performed at S Salvatore in 1734.

Palazzi's opera librettos, light and fanciful, were ideally suited to Vivaldi's taste and talents. Significantly, he is the only librettist to whom allusion is made (through the phrase 'il palazzo d'Orlando') on the title-page of Benedetto Marcello's satire *Il teatro alla moda*.

drammi per musica unless otherwise stated

Armida al campo d'Egitto, Vivaldi, 1718; *La verità in cimento* (with D. Lalli), Vivaldi, 1720; *Medea e Giasone*, F. Brusa, 1726; *Rosilena ed Oronta*, Vivaldi, 1728; *Pasquale gastaldo* (comic int), 1734; *Lisetta e Caicanturco* (comic int), 1734; *Il vello d'oro*, Scolari, 1749   MICHAEL TALBOT

Palazzi, Matilde (*b* Montecarotto, 1 March 1802; *d* Barcelona, 3 July 1842). Italian soprano. She studied in Pesaro and made her début in Dresden in the title role of Rossini's *Zelmira* (1824). She sang in Dresden until 1833 as a member of the Italian Opera, notably in operas by Rossini, Morlacchi, Donizetti and Mercadante, and as Mozart's Countess Almaviva and Donna Elvira. She was successful at La Scala and elsewhere in Italy. She appeared as Leonora in Verdi's *Oberto* at Barcelona in 1841, but died soon after at the height of her career.   DAVID CUMMINGS

Palazzo incantato, Il [*Il palazzo incantato, ovvero La guerriera amante* ('The Enchanted Palace, or The Warrior Lover')]. *Attione in musica* in a prologue and three acts by LUIGI ROSSI to a libretto by GIULIO ROSPIGLIOSI after LUDOVICO ARIOSTO's *Orlando furioso*; Rome, Palazzo Barberini alle Quattro Fontane, 22 February 1642.

Alternative titles for the opera were *Lealtà con valore* and *Il palazzo d'Atlante*. In the prologue, Pitture [Painting], Poesia [Poetry], Musica [Music] and Magia [Magic] (all sopranos) argue over who is the most powerful; the question will be decided by the story of Ruggiero's valour.

The sorcerer Atlante (alto) has created an enchanted palace in the woods, on the French side of the English Channel, to which he has lured both Christian and pagan knights and ladies in search of lost lovers and friends. He has made them all prisoners in its endless, empty corridors, stairways and balconies. He lures Orlando (tenor) by abducting Angelica (soprano) disguised as a giant, Gigante (bass). The warrior maiden Bradamante (soprano) arrives with Marfisa (soprano), hoping to free her lover, Ruggiero. The saracen Ferraù (tenor) and Circassian Sacripante (bass) seek Angelica in rivalry with Orlando. The knight Ruggiero (tenor), hoping to find Bradamante, meets Angelica instead. Bradamante, overhearing their encounter, is filled with jealousy and disappointment. She gives Ruggiero no opening to defend himself. The lords and ladies wander in and out, sighing and searching, while an octet of phantoms in two choruses dances and comments on the deceptions of love.

Ruggiero collapses from helplessness and frustration, and Bradamante nearly slays him out of spite and jealousy; he revives in time to declare his constancy, but cannot convince her. Finally, after a letter from him, she decides to confront Angelica, who in the meantime has received a portrait of Medoro from Atlante. Bradamante's presumed rival allays her suspicions. The unexpected arrival of the English Duke Astolfo (tenor), who is uninterested in women and love, forces Atlante to rescue his plans: he makes everyone in the palace see Astolfo as a dangerous enemy, and all attack him. When at last Bradamante and Ruggiero seem reconciled, a false Ruggiero (tenor) – in fact Atlante transformed – appears. The true Ruggiero decides the two men must duel; when he draws his sword, Atlante takes on his real form and admits defeat. The power of love causes the sorcerer to lose his powers as the prisoners find and greet one another. The palace vanishes.

The story, filled with well-known characters from Ariosto's epic *Orlando furioso*, enabled Rossi to write scenes for 16 fine soloists in all voice ranges, as well as including six-, eight- and ten-part writing in double-chorus formation, and one 12-part, triple-chorus finale. Each soloist has at least one aria or duet; some sing additional recitative monologues. Ariosto's crusaders sing tenor-bass and bass-bass duets, Angelica sings in three trios, and choruses of imprisoned ladies, nymphs, hunters and spectres enliven five scenes in Acts 1 and 2, in addition to their closing finales. The proliferation of separated lovers made for a long opera, with little inter-action or musical connection between scenes not involving the three principals. Perhaps there were too many unhappy lovers: the earliest reports deemed the opera 'long and lachrymose', 'too serious and lacking in plot' though well sung. (Notably, a number of strophes were cut from arias and duets.)

The instrumental scoring is expansive, consisting of two treble staves for the violins and four inner parts notated in soprano, alto and tenor C clefs, and sometimes a bass line in addition to the continuo ensemble line. The exact instrumentation is unknown (in a Barberini opera of 1635 the strings consisted of three violins, three *violoni*, a *lira*, two lutes, a theorbo and a guitar). One of Cardinal Antonio Barberini's main preoccupations was not the music but the stage machinery (the sets were designed by Andrea Sacchi). Duke Astolfo entered on a hippogriff, Angelica disappeared with the aid of a magic ring, Atlante transformed himself once into a giant and once into Ruggiero, and the enchanted palace itself vanished in Act 3, signifying the power of love over sorcery and deception.   MARGARET MURATA

Palella, Antonio (*b* S Giovanni a Teduccio, Naples, 8 Oct 1692; *d* Naples, 7 March 1761). Italian composer. He is known only from his works; early biographers did not mention him. His librettos describe him as 'maestro di cappella napoletano'. From the opening of the new Teatro S Carlo on 11 October 1737 he was second harpsichordist, with the additional duties of adapting foreign operas for production there; one of these was the revival in autumn 1745 of Hasse's *Tigrane*, for which Palella rewrote about half the music. Despite his personal obscurity he occupies a clear place in the history of *opera buffa*: at the time he was writing his three comedies for the Teatro Nuovo the genre was moving in several new directions, and his music may be supposed to have helped popularize them. The most immediately noticeable of these novelties is elimination of Neapolitan dialect: in all three works, the characters speak Tuscan. This allowed export of the works to northern Italy. Second, in all three the subject matter leans even more heavily than formerly on literary romance (the plot of *Origille* self-confessedly paraphrases an incident in Ariosto's *Orlando furioso*), with consequent increased emphasis on *parti serie* and *semiserie*, and less time spent on below-stairs antics of servant characters. Musically this widened the range of emotional expression in comic opera. In addition, as a result of their plots, all three works require more elaborate mounting, with such special effects as a jousting scene. These features combined to improve the literary and social respectability of *opera buffa*; economically they imply higher production budgets.

Palella's setting of a libretto by Pietro Trinchera, *L'incanti per amore* (1741), incorporates the new decade's principal morphological development: fewer musical 'numbers' at the expense of ensembles and short ariettas; here, Trinchera retained only Act 1's opening duettino and the finales, leaving a total of 25 numbers compared with the previous decade's average of 30–37. The result is an increased emphasis on solo arias, an increased proportion of recitative to arias, and, in the best works, more attention to tight, straightforward plot construction. (*L'incanti* is also an example of that special sub-species of *opera buffa*, the 'magic' opera, an intermittently popular type that was to culminate in *Die Zauberflöte*; here the leading lady is a sorceress). *Origille* deserves particular mention because it was one of the southern works soon to be introduced to north Italy (Mantua and Venice, summer and autumn 1744) and to start the vogue there for *opera buffa*, even if the exported version was considerably cut to suit local tastes and retained only a few of its original numbers.

Palella's arias are early Classical in style, showing symmetrical periodization of phrasing and a firm sense of structure based on the tonic–dominant relationship. In the second half of an aria's first section, where the text is repeated, melodic material is closely derived from the first half, but varied with extensions of phrases and intensification of harmonic detail (for example, the first half's cadence progression of dominant of V–V–I could become augmented 6th–V–I). Second sections remain tonally close to the tonic key and usually contain motivic references to the aria's opening. Palella possessed a pleasant, if not especially striking, lyric talent, and was particularly fond of the 'Scotch snap' rhythmic device in melodic scale passages.

all first performed in Naples

L'Origille (ob, A. Palomba), Nuovo, 8 Dec 1740
L'incanti per amore (ob, P. Trinchera), Nuovo, 2 Oct 1741
Il trionfo del valore (Palomba, commedia per musica), Nuovo, wint. 1741, collab. G. Signorille, Porpora and G. di Domenico
Il chimico (ob, Palomba), Nuovo, wint. 1742
Tigrane (os, F. Silvani), S Carlo, 4 Nov 1745 [rev. of Hasse's work of 1725; of the orig., only recit of Act 3 scene xi, a duet and 13 of 26 arias remained; Palella wrote a new sinfonia, new recit, 13 arias, and a coro finale for Act 3]
Il geloso (ob, D. Macchi), Fiorentini, sum. 1751, 4 arias *GB-Lbl*, *Lcm*

*

U. Prota-Giurleo: *La grande orchestra del R. Teatro San Carlo nel settecento* (Naples, 1928), 8, 17
G. Hardie: 'Neapolitan Comic Opera, 1707–1750: Some Addenda and Corrigenda for *The New Grove*', *JAMS*, xxxvi (1983), 127
          JAMES L. JACKMAN

Palentrotti [Palantrotti, Palontrotti], **Melchior** (*b* Venafro, nr Naples; *d* in or before 1618). Italian bass. He was employed in the choir of S Luigi de' Francesi, Rome (1588–9, 1612–14), and at the Este court in Ferrara (1589–97) and entered the Cappella Sistina on 14 July 1597. Palentrotti was one of a generation of bass singers praised by Vincenzo Giustiniani for their range and virtuoso technique. In Rome, he was closely associated with the distinguished patron Cardinal Montalto (Alessandro Perretti), from whom he received lodging, and later a salary. Montalto had close links with Florence, and Palentrotti took part in Peri's *Euridice* (as Pluto) and Caccini's *Il rapimento di Cefalo* at the festivities for the wedding of Maria de' Medici and Henri IV of France (October 1600). He sang in Paolo Quagliati's *Carro di Fedeltà d'Amore* (1606, Rome) and returned to Florence for the marriage of Prince Cosimo de' Medici and Maria Magdalena of Austria in 1608. His last known appearance was as Jupiter in Giacomo Cicognini's *L'amor pudico* (with music by G. B. Nanino, C. Marotta and others) sponsored by Montalto in 1614.

*

S. Reiner: 'Preparations in Parma – 1618, 1627–28', *MR*, xxv (1964), 273–301, esp. 277
G. Caccini: *Le nuove musiche (1602)*, ed. H. W. Hitchcock, RRMBE, ix (Madison, 1970)
C. MacClintock, trans.: *Hercole Bottrigari, 'Il Desiderio'; Vincenzo Giustiniani, 'Discorso sopra la musica'*, MSD, ix (1972)
J. Chater: 'Music and Patronage in Rome at the Turn of the Seventeenth Century: the Case of Cardinal Montalto', *Studi musicali*, xvi (1987), 179–227   TIM CARTER

Palermo. Italian city, capital of Sicily. Opera was late to arrive but quick to take root. Marcantonio Sportonio, who arrived in Palermo in 1653, sang in Cavalli's *Giasone* produced by the Musici Accademici Sconcertati in 1655. The libretto of another work by Cavalli, *Xerse*, was printed in 1658 'as performed in the city of Palermo ... at the insistence of the Accademia delli Musici of that city'. In 1679 Michelangelo Falvetti founded the 'Unione dei Musici', named after St Cecilia; this institution was probably responsible for the construction in 1692 of the Teatro S Cecilia, which for over a century eclipsed the small theatres that had earlier staged opera productions such as the Teatro della Corte del Pretore (later S Lucia) and the Teatro della Misericordia (constructed from storehouses of the convent of that name). From 1681 a distinctive place of entertainment, giving serenatas and *dialoghi* rather than *melodrammi*, was the Teatro Marittimo, designed and built by Paolo Amato at the centre of the seaside promenade and popular in the summer evenings.

While the first opera productions originated in Naples and Venice, Sportonio's development as a composer of opera (*Elena*, 1661) marked a step towards Palermo's operatic independence. He set a libretto by a local author, Antonio Salamone, as *La Fiordispina* in 1678. Works by other local poets and musicians were introduced, including several in genres close to opera. In 1690 the best singers came together for Alessandro Scarlatti's *Pompeo*. Ignazio Pulici's *L'innocenza penitente*, which inaugurated the Teatro S Cecilia in October 1693, must have been a kind of *dialogo sacro* with scenic components; a production of Scarlatti's *Penelope la casta* (?1694) was probably the first true opera performance there. From that time the S Cecilia was dominated by his works; this continued into the 18th century. Francesco Gasparini's *Totila in Roma* had its première there in 1696; he was musical director for the 1699 season.

There was an intensification of musical activity at the beginning of the reign of Philip V of Spain, whose accession in 1700 was celebrated with great pomp in the gallery of the royal palace with a serenata for 32 voices and 160 instruments. The worldly Cardinal Viceroy Del Giudice encouraged opera, but the War of the Spanish Succession brought a temporary lull. In 1713 the S Cecilia reopened to celebrate the coronation of Vittorio Amedeo of Savoy as King of Sicily. Although Savoy rule brought an unwelcome austerity, musical activity continued. Despite the wars, the aristocrats of Palermo had acquired the habits of theatre-going and of including female singers in their dissipations: a diarist writes of scandals meriting divine punishment in the form of the earthquake of 1726. Following these disruptions there was almost a decade of inactivity in the public theatres, after which the reopened S Cecilia had as rival the S Lucia, enlarged from the old Teatro della Corte del Pretore, owned by the Valguarnera di Santa Lucia family and also known as the Teatro Valguarnera. This venue, which had originally been restricted to the minor Neapolitan *buffo* repertory, grew in importance during the 18th century. It was renamed Carolino in 1809 in gratitude for the patronage of the Queen of Naples who had taken refuge in Sicily.

In the late 18th century the S Cecilia attempted to stave off the opposition by inviting to Palermo famous singers – Caterina Gabrielli (on a three-year engagement), Marina Balducci and Gasparo Pacchierotti – as well as established composers (Naumann) and promising young ones (Spontini). But the 19th century belonged to the Teatro Carolino, with directors such as Natale Bertini (1813–17, 1820–22), Giuseppe Mosca (1817–20), Pietro Generali (1823–5), Pietro Raimondi (1833–52) and the young Donizetti, who composed

Alahor in Granata for the theatre during his season there (1825–6). Public taste had moved away from the traditional Neapolitan repertory towards more recent operas, including works by Donizetti, Bellini, Pacini and eventually Verdi, often with the text mutilated by obtuse Bourbon censorship and the music diminished by third-rate execution. It was usually considered most important to engage famous leading singers while economizing otherwise, which had at least the merit of acquainting the audiences of the Carolino with great singers, among them Domenico Donzelli, G. B. Rubini, Karoline Unger, Francilla Pixis, Emilie Hallez, Marietta Gazzaniga and Teresa Stolz. The theatre was renamed the Bellini during the revolutionary period of 1848 and definitively in 1860 after the fall of the Bourbon monarchy.

It was only after the unification of Italy that Palermo acquired an opera house of European standing, with the Politeama Garibaldi, designed by Damiani Almeyda and inaugurated in 1874, and with the Teatro Massimo, designed by G. F. Basile and opened in 1897 after political disagreements. Under the energetic impresario Carlo Emanuele di Giorgi, the Politeama had already staged new works such as *La Gioconda*, *Mefistofele*, *Otello*, *Carmen* and *Lohengrin*. The International Exhibition of 1891–2 brought fresh artistic advances with Leopoldo Mugnone and Federico Nicolao conducting and singers including Francesco Tamagno, Victor Maurel, Nellie Melba, Mattia Battistini, Francesco Viñas and Teresa Arkel. The 1892–3 season was directed by the young but already well-established Arturo Toscanini. On 24 April 1896 Puccini's *La bohème*, conducted by Mugnone and sung by Stehle and Garbin, had its most successful performance (its première in Turin had been coolly received). Meanwhile the lesser theatres, the Bellini, the S Cecilia, the S Ferdinando (later Principe Umberto and then Umberto I), the little Garibaldi, the Nazionale, the Biondo and the Anfiteatro Mangano, continued to be active.

The Teatro Massimo is the third largest European opera house (covering 7730 square metres, 1280 occupied by the stage), after those of Vienna and Paris. From its opening, and in spite of political dissension (including the closure in 1974 for restoration, which was still incomplete in 1992), the administrators tried to ensure that the theatre's activity matched its capacity. Although some would have preferred 'una grandiosa opera-ballo' for the inauguration, the choice fell on *Falstaff* (16 May 1897, conducted by Mugnone, with Arturo Pessina in the title role). The other works performed during the first season, *Gioconda* with Enrico Caruso at the start of his career, and a revival of *Bohème*, now a certain success, ensured public acceptance without lapsing into the obvious. During those years Palermo was attracting discriminating tourists and the theatre was gaining European renown. The architectural activity of Ernesto Basile (son of the theatre's designer) and the engagement of promising young singers was largely dependent on private contributions, especially from the Florio family of industrialists and shipowners, one of whom, Ignazio (manager, 1905–19), saw in the prestige of the Teatro Massimo a possible symbol of his own: he spent a great deal of money bringing many artistic benefits to the house before he ruined himself. Works by Mascagni, Pizzetti, Tosatti and Zandonai were presented there, and Savagnone's *Millesima seconda* had its première in Palermo in 1949, but in general the years after World War II were characterized by traditional repertory and the occasional return of great singers. A more courageous line was taken by Simone Cuccia, superintendent from 1953, with the revival of rarities from the past alternating with the better-known masterpieces, while a further updating of taste was introduced by Baron Leopoldo de Simone and F. E. Raccuglia with 20th-century works not previously heard at the Massimo. Another Savagnone première, of *Né tempo, né luogo*, took place in 1961, while Musco's *Il gattopardo* had its première in 1967. More recently Ubaldo Mirabelli and Girolamo Arrigo rediscovered and revived important Italian operas of the early 20th century, ignored by other theatres. Less attention has been paid to avant-garde productions, though recent works were seen in the Settimane Internazionali di Nuova Musica (1960–68), with the première of Egisto Macchi's *Anno Domini* at the Biondo in 1965. Other premières have included Rota's *La visita meravigliosa* (1970) and Malipiero's *Merlino mastro d'organi* (1972). In 1987 Respighi's *Semirâma* was revived in honour of his 50th anniversary. Seasons of 18th-century *opera buffa* are given in the summer.

*

F. M. Emanuele di Villabianca: *De teatri antichi e moderni della città di Palermo* (MS, 18th century, *I-PLcom*, Qq D 107); ed. in R. Pagano: 'Teatri palermitani, musica e "campo del diavolo" negli scritti del Villabianca', *Le arti in Sicilia nel settecento: studi in memoria di Maria Accascina* (Palermo, 1986)

G. Pitré: *La vita in Palermo cento e più anni fa* (Palermo, 1904)

L. M. Majorca Mortillaro: *Il Real Teatro S Cecilia e le sue vicende* (Palermo, 1909)

G. Sorge: *I teatri di Palermo nei secoli XVI, XVII, XVIII* (Palermo, 1926)

I. Ciotti: *La vita artistica del Teatro Massimo di Palermo, 1897–1937* (Palermo, 1938)

I. Ciotti and O. Tiby: *I cinquant'anni del Teatro Massimo* (Palermo, 1947)

O. Tiby: *Il Real Teatro Carolino e l'ottocento musicale palermitano* (Florence, 1957)

R. Pagano: 'La vita musicale a Palermo e nella Sicilia del seicento', *NRMI*, iii (1969), 439–66

J. Freeman: 'Donizetti in Palermo and *Alahor in Granata*', *JAMS*, xxv (1972), 240–50

A. M. Fundarò: *Il concorso per il Teatro Massimo di Palermo* (Palermo, 1974)

R. Pagano: 'Le origini ed il primo statuto dell'Unione dei Musici intitolata a Santa Cecilia in Palermo', *RIM*, x (1975), 545–63

G. Isgrò: *Festa Teatro Rito nella storia di Sicilia* (Palermo, 1981)

R. Pagano: 'Le attività musicali nella Sicilia del settecento', *La Sicilia del settecento: Messina 1981*, 859–99

L. Maniscalco Basile: *Storia del Teatro Massimo di Palermo* (Florence, 1984)

M. S. Maraventano: *Le attività culturali a Palermo negli ultimi venti anni, 1945–65: i periodici, la musica, il teatro* (Rome, 1984)

G. Pirrone: *Il Teatro Massimo di G. B. Filippo Basile a Palermo 1867/97* (Rome, 1984)

R. Pagano: *Scarlatti, Alessandro e Domenico: due vite in una* (Milan, 1985)

U. D'Arpa: *Vincenzo Amato: Sacri concerti a 2, 3, 4, 5 voci con una messa a 3 o 4: Palermo 1652* (diss., U. of Pavia, 1987)

G. Leone: *L'opera a Palermo dal 1653 al 1987* (Palermo, 1988)

R. Pagano: 'Giasone in Oreto: considerazioni sull'introduzione del melodramma a Palermo', *Musica ed attività musicali in Sicilia nei secoli XVII e XVIII*, I quaderni del conservatorio, i (Palermo, 1988), 11–18

S. Giacobello: 'Il sistema produttivo nel Teatro Santa Cecilia di Palermo sul finire del XVIII secolo', ibid, 75–89

——: *Una stagione operistica (1793–94) al Teatro Santa Cecilia di Palermo* (Palermo, 1990)

A. Tedesco: *Il Teatro Santa Cecilia e il seicento musicale palermitano* (Palermo, 1992)   ROBERTO PAGANO

Palester, Roman (*b* Śniatyń, 28 Dec 1907; *d* Paris, 25 Aug 1989). Polish composer. He studied the piano at the Lwów Conservatory, composition (from 1925) at the Warsaw Conservatory and then art history at Warsaw University. He became a leading figure in Polish musical life during the 1930s and also achieved successes abroad. After World War II he taught at the Kraków Conservatory and in 1949 moved to Paris; he lived in Munich, 1952–72. His opera *Żywe kamienie* ('The Living Stones', in three acts, after W. Berent) dates from 1944 but was left incomplete. In 1962 he won a prize in the Italian section of the ISCM for his one-act opera, written between 1959 and 1961, *La mort de Don Juan* (after Oscar Milosz); it was performed on Brussels Radio on 6 March 1965, but not staged until 19 September 1991, when it was given in Kraków. The work, in seven symmetrically constructed scenes, is relatively traditional in scenes iii and iv but elsewhere uses *Sprechgesang* and declamation; the musical style is influenced by the Second Viennese School, in particular Berg.   TERESA CHYLIŃSKA

Palestrina. *Musikalische Legende* in three acts by HANS PFITZNER to his own libretto; Munich, Prinzregententheater, 12 June 1917.

Pope Pius IV		bass
Giovanni Morone	*cardinal legates*	baritone
Bernardo Novagerio	*of the Pope*	tenor
Cardinal Christoph Madruscht		
[Madruzzo] *Prince Bishop of Trent*		bass
Carlo Borromeo *a Roman cardinal*		baritone
The Cardinal of Lorraine		bass
Abdisu, Patriarch of Assyria		tenor
Anton Brus of Müglitz *Archbishop of Prague*		bass
Count Luna *ambassador of the King of Spain*		baritone
Bishop of Budoja [Budua]	*Italian bishops*	tenor
Theophilus, Bishop of Imola		tenor
Avosmediano, Bishop of Cadiz *Spanish bishop*		bass-baritone
Giovanni Pierluigi da Palestrina *maestro di cappella at S Maria Maggiore, Rome*		tenor
Ighino *his son, aged 15*		soprano
Silla *his pupil, aged 17*		mezzo-soprano
Bishop Ercole Severolus, *Master of Ceremonies to the Council of Trent*		bass-baritone
Five Choristers of S Maria Maggiore		2 tenors, 3 basses
Apparitions:		
Lucrezia *Palestrina's deceased wife*		alto
Nine Dead Masters of the Art of Music		3 tenors, 3 baritones, 3 basses
Voices of Three Angels		high sopranos
Two Papal Nuncios		silent
Lainez	*Jesuit generals*	silent
Salmeron		silent
Massarelli, Bishop of Telese *secretary to the Council*		silent
Giuseppe *Palestrina's old servant*		silent

Choristers from the papal chapel; archbishops, bishops, abbots, heads of orders, ambassadors, procurators for princes spiritual and temporal, theologians, doctors of all Christian nations; servants; soldiers of the city guard; street-folk; angels (apparitions)

Setting Rome (Acts 1 and 3) and Trent (Act 2) in November and December 1563, the year in which the Council of Trent concluded; between Acts 1 and 2 about eight days elapse, between Acts 2 and 3 approximately two weeks

'Palestrina' (Pfitzner): the angels' scene from Act 1 of the original production at the Prinzregententheater, Munich, 12 June 1917, with Karl Erb as Palestrina; set by Adolf Linnebach

First performed in Munich, while World War I was in progress, *Palestrina* established itself as Pfitzner's masterpiece, not least for its high moral and philosophical seriousness. Its first conductor, Bruno Walter, regarded the première as one of the major events of his life (the title role was sung by Karl Erb). In November 1917 he took the Munich production on what he was to describe as a 'propaganda tour' of neutral Switzerland (Basle, Berne and Zürich), to demonstrate the continuing quality of wartime German musical culture. Vienna and Berlin productions followed in 1919, and the work continued to be performed regularly in Germany until World War II. A fine recording under Rafael Kubelik was made in 1973, with Nicolai Gedda (Palestrina) and Dietrich Fischer-Dieskau (Borromeo).

Among the work's many admirers, mention must be made of the Munich-based novelist Thomas Mann, whose enthusiasm led to his involvement in 1918, with Walter and others, in founding a Hans Pfitzner-Verein für Deutsche Tonkunst. Mann also included a long and searching discussion of *Palestrina* in his *Betrachtungen eines Unpolitischen* of 1918 (in chap. 6, 'On Virtue'). This book, completed during the war, was an extended and complex apologia for Germany and German culture and its anti-democratic, idealistic nature. It became a significant focus of postwar debate, not least in the light of Mann's subsequent shift towards democratic republicanism. Pfitzner, by contrast, remained steadfast in the nationalistic, idealistic conservatism of the *Palestrina* period and to the epigraph from Schopenhauer's *Die Welt als Wille und Vorstellung* which prefaces the score and libretto. In it, Schopenhauer set the intellectual life of the individual against the corporate life of mankind and concluded: 'alongside world history there goes, guiltless and unstained by blood, the history of philosophy, science and the arts'. For all its impressive and carefully researched historical atmosphere, Pfitzner thus significantly located *Palestrina*'s debate about modernism and conservatism in musical style within the timely, if troubled, intellectual and political context which gave birth to

Mann's novel *Der Zauberberg*, published in 1924 but begun in 1914.

ACT 1 *A room in Palestrina's house* Pfitzner's musico-dramatic technique in *Palestrina* is such as to allow no extractable episodes beyond the preludes to each of the three acts, sometimes performed as an orchestral suite. The D minor Prelude to Act 1 begins with music associated with the central character's introspective nostalgia for a time in which personal happiness was linked with creative fluency in the widely cherished manner of 16th-century sacred polyphony. Although the opera requires a large orchestra, the opening of the prelude, scored for four flutes and four solo violins, is characteristic of the work as a whole, in its chamber-textured evocation of 16th-century contrapuntal manners and cadential formulae (although Pfitzner adopted a pragmatic disregard for strict stylistic mimicry). The manner is predominantly restrained and halting.

The curtain rises on a gloomy and frugal chamber containing Palestrina's work-table, portative organ and a hanging portrait of his deceased wife, Lucrezia. A single large window affords a distant view of Rome; it is late afternoon (night falls during the course of the act). Beside the window sits Palestrina's pupil Silla, musing on his planned departure for Florence as he accompanies himself on a viol in a love song of his own composition. The song is in the manner of the Florentine innovators with whom Silla wishes to study. Rome, whose leitmotif (ex.1) includes a phrase that will be

Ex.1

repeatedly associated with the rhythm of Palestrina's first name, now seems to him the venerable guardian of restrictive tradition from which he longs to escape in search of the 'wonderful current of freedom which flows through our time'. Silla represents Pfitzner's most sympathetic portrayal of a musical 'modernist' (his main motif is boyishly Straussian), whose nevertheless respectful affection for his master manifests itself in the tactful restraint he shows to his friend, the composer's son Ighino (the other travesty role) who soon enters, troubled by his father's current mood of sad resignation.

Palestrina himself arrives with Cardinal Borromeo, who is critical of the 'cacophonous' song which Silla had begun to perform for Ighino. Palestrina excuses his pupil's modernist inclinations after he has sent the boys off to bed. Borromeo recommends a firm hand, but Palestrina suggests that what seems right to their generation might, after all, give way to 'new sounds'. This humility provides Borromeo with a suitable pretext for explaining the threat to polyphonic music posed by the Council of Trent's deliberations, which the Pope requires to be concluded after 18 years of debate. The final session will deal with ritual and the Mass itself, which the purists would have had sung in future to plainsong. All polyphonic compositions would be destroyed. The Emperor Ferdinand, however, has declared his opposition to the purists, enabling Borromeo to persuade the Pope to permit the question to be decided by an exemplary demonstration mass, reconciling conflict in the 'miraculous play of interweaving sounds'. Palestrina, he ceremoniously announces, should accept the task of composing this mass.

Pleading age and declining power, Palestrina incites Borromeo to accuse him of blasphemy before the latter storms out. Palestrina is left alone to ponder his sense of loss and meaninglessness and to recall the inspiring presence of his wife. Mysterious apparitions of former masters now gather around him (they include Josquin and Enrico Tedesco and are dressed in a variety of historical and national costumes). In stylized and statuesque music they counter Palestrina's nihilistic despair with the assurance that he is required to add the final gem or 'last stone' (ex.2) to the jewelled necklace of

Ex.2
Sehr ruhig

the ages. They disappear, leaving Palestrina in total darkness. Fearfully, he calls out in prayer. Unnoticed by him, a shining angel has appeared who sings the initial motif of the Kyrie of the *Missa Papae Marcelli*, regarded in legend as the work which decided the Council in favour of polyphony. Mechanically, Palestrina begins to write. Other fragments of the mass are sung by a gathering throng of angels, although their music develops into an original polyphonic texture featuring only the opening 'Kyrie' motif of the historical original. Palestrina fills page after page as he senses a mysterious new power

within him. The apparition of his wife joins the angels, who fill the entire stage as the back wall and ceiling disappear to reveal 'a full glory of angels and heaven' (see illustration). The chorus concludes in a triumphant C major that is enriched by deep offstage bells, reinforced by two large tam-tams. Representing the dawn bells of Rome, they ring out in a processional crescendo towards a climactic, full orchestral statement of the 'Pierluigi' figure. In a brief epilogue to the act, Silla and Ighino enter the room, now filled with morning sunlight, to find Palestrina sleeping soundly at his desk. They pick up the strewn sheets. Ighino is filled with joy at what he sees. Eight bars of the renewed dawn processional conclude the hour-and-a-half-long act in a mighty crescendo of tolling bells.

ACT 2 *The great hall of Cardinal Madruscht's palace in Trent* After a prelude of driving energy and ceremonial brilliance (the Straussian orchestra includes six horns, four trumpets and four trombones), the Master of Ceremonies to the Council of Trent is found preparing for the session, keeping a diplomatic eye on the seating of national groups. The gradually assembling participants include Borromeo, who is anxious for news of the visit to the Emperor Ferdinand by Cardinal Morone (historical 'saviour of the Council'). He is also embarrassed that Palestrina had refused to compose the demonstration mass, for which disloyalty he has had him imprisoned. Amid growing tension between the Spaniards and the Italians, the splendidly assembled Council goes into session. Morone delivers his message from the emperor, who is anxious for unity among Catholic nations. The ensuing discussion about music and the Mass nevertheless degenerates into risibly chaotic factionalism, and the session is adjourned. The members withdraw, leaving their servants to turn their masters' verbal antagonism into physical threats. A crowd of street-folk pour into the hall and join in a violent brawl, which is only brought to an end by Cardinal Madruscht, 'German' host to the Council, who enters with soldiers whom he orders to shoot into the mob. He threatens torture as people fall in the gunfire.

ACT 3 *The room in Palestrina's house* A meditative prelude introduces the shortest of the three acts, in which artistic inwardness once again prevails over the turmoil of public affairs. It is evening, and Palestrina sits with Ighino and members of his choir. During his imprisonment his mass had been forcibly removed from the house. It is now being performed before the Pope, although Palestrina seems dazed by his suffering. Cries of 'Evviva Palestrina!' shortly herald the arrival of papal singers to congratulate the 'saviour of music'; his mass has so impressed the Pope that he briefly appears to compliment the composer in person and invite him into his service in the Sistine Chapel. Ighino rejoices, and Borromeo, contrite, makes his peace with his friend. Palestrina, left alone as night falls, goes to his portative organ and prays 'Now forge *me*, the last stone on one of your thousand rings, oh Lord, and I will be of good heart and at peace'. Outside, the cries die away, and the opera concludes with the 'last stone' motif. From the final D minor chord, a single soft D from Palestrina's organ improvisation is held as the curtain falls.

*   *   *

Palestrina represents an important, if often ponderously discursive, late application of the techniques of Wagnerian music-drama in Germany. Pfitzner himself interestingly regarded it as an autumnal and even valedictory reflection upon *Die Meistersinger*. Some of its musical innovations, particularly the bony linearity of its contrapuntal and harmonic texture and an expanded range of orchestral coloration, are pre-Wagnerian as much as post-Wagnerian in nature and intention. The reversion to historical drama is matched by an idiosyncratic affection of 16th-century mannerisms (the anachronistic treatment of quotations from the *Missa Papae Marcelli* is striking). Pfitzner's purpose could be construed as a deliberately 'Germanizing' one: musically reconstructing Palestrina as a north European master. The opera certainly seems to present Cardinal Madruscht as a specifically German *alter ego* of the conservative composer in Act 2, thus heightening the documentary interest of Pfitzner's complex verse-libretto. Nevertheless the character of Palestrina himself, particularly in his solo scenes in Acts 1 and 3, draws from Pfitzner his finest music, which achieves passages of elevated and moving pathos.

PETER FRANKLIN

Paliashvili, Zakhary Petrovich (*b* Kutaisi, 4/16 Aug 1871; *d* Tbilisi, 6 Oct 1933). Georgian composer. He received his early musical education in the Catholic church at Kutaisi. In 1887 he became a church organist in Tbilisi; his first serious encounter with Georgian music came that year when he joined Agniashvili's Georgian folk choir. In 1891 he began formal studies at Tbilisi Music College with Mosko (horn) and Klenovsky (theory and composition), graduating in 1899. The next year he entered Moscow Conservatory and studied composition with Taneyev. After graduating in 1903 he returned to Georgia, where he worked as teacher and choirmaster. In 1905 he helped to set up the Georgian Philharmonic Society, and in 1906 he co-founded the Fraternity for the Creation of Opera in the Georgian Language. He made several expeditions within Georgia to collect and record folksongs, later publishing them along with his own arrangements. When Georgia became a Soviet republic (1921) he was made Rector of the Tbilisi Conservatory, where he continued to teach until his death.

Given the course of his work, it was inevitable that Paliashvili would eventually try his hand at a national opera. In 1909 he began to write *Abesalom da Eteri* ('Absalom and Etery') to a libretto by P. Mirianashvili based on the ancient Georgian legend *Eteriani*, in which his understanding of indigenous folk styles, his appreciation of 19th-century Russian operatic techniques (encouraged by Taneyev) and even his experience as a church musician all bore fruit. The first performance of *Absalom* (Tbilisi, 21 February 1919) was an outstanding success, and the four-act opera remains Paliashvili's most celebrated work. In the 'lyric-dramatic' *Daisi* ('Twilight', 3, V. Guniya, after Sh. Rustaveli, N. Baratashvili, A. Tsereteli and V. Pshaveli), the themes of love and rivalry are interwoven with the story of the nation's struggle against foreign aggression; the work was first performed in Tbilisi on 19 December 1923. Like *Absalom*, *Daisi* successfully blends national elements with traditional number structures. His third and last opera, *Latavra*, begun in 1925 and first performed in Tbilisi on 16 March 1928, also deals with national themes.

The influence of these works, particularly *Absalom*, on Georgian music has been considerable. Paliashvili has even been dubbed 'the Georgian Glinka'. He was made a People's Artist of the Georgian SSR in 1925, and at his death the opera house in Tbilisi was named after him.

See also ABESALOM DA ETERI and *DAISI*.

YEVGENY MACHAVARIANI

Palla a Corda. Theatre in Florence, properly the Regio Teatro degl'Intrepidi detto della Palla a Corda, used for opera from the 1780s; *see* FLORENCE, §6.

Pallacorda. Theatre in Rome, properly the Pallacorda di Firenze, built in 1714 opposite the Palazzo Firenze; *see* ROME, §3(i).

Pallavicini [Pallavicino], **Giovanni Domenico** (*b* Brescia; *fl* 1702–23). Italian librettist. His connections with the Düsseldorf court were apparently brought about through Cosimo III de' Medici, father-in-law of the Elector Palatine Johann Wilhelm. Pallavicini served as the elector's secretary; in 1707 Johann Wilhelm recommended him as secretary to his younger brother Karl Philipp, who was in Innsbruck acting as governor of the Tyrol and in 1716 succeeded Johann Wilhelm as elector. Pallavicini was in Mannheim in 1723, still serving Karl Philipp. He should not be confused with the more prolific Stefano Benedetto Pallavicino, who also served as secretary to Johann Wilhelm.

The preface to the Venetian libretto of *Tiberio imperatore d'Oriente* (set by Francesco Gasparini, 1702) states that the author was not involved in the production. The staging was modest; the work involved only six characters, all of them historical. Within a year Alessandro Scarlatti wrote a new setting of it for Naples; S. B. Pallavicino is credited with revising the work for Düsseldorf in 1703, and it was given in Venice (1710) as *Le vicende d'amor e di fortuna*. Pallavicini's *festa teatrale L'allegrezza dell'Eno* (set by Jakob Greber, overture by G. Finger) was performed in honour of Elisabeth Christina of Brunswick-Wolfenbüttel, who passed through Innsbruck in 1708. It was staged in the courtyard of the old castle, which was transformed into an Alpine landscape for the occasion.

*

F. S. Quadrio: *Della storia e della ragione d'ogni poesia*, iii, pt 2 (Milan, 1744), 485–6

F. Walter: *Geschichte des Theaters und der Musik am kurpfälzischen Hofe* (Leipzig, 1898)

A. Einstein: 'Italienische Musiker am Hofe der Neuburger Wittelsbacher (1614–1716): neue Beiträge zur Geschichte der Musik am Neuburg-Düsseldorfer Hof im 17. Jahrhundert', *SIMG*, ix (1907–8), 336–424, esp. 412

W. Senn: *Musik und Theater am Hof zu Innsbruck: Geschichte der Hofkapelle vom 15. Jahrhundert bis zu deren Auflösung im Jahre 1748* (Innsbruck, 1954)

G. Croll: 'Musikgeschichtliches aus Rapparinis Johann-Wilhelm-Manuskript (1709)', *Mf*, xi (1958), 257–64, esp. 263

HARRIS S. SAUNDERS

Pallavicini, Vincenzo (*b* Brescia; *d* after 1756). Italian composer. Gerber's suggestion that he may have been a son of the more illustrious composer Carlo Pallavicino (*d* 1688) seems unlikely on both temporal and stylistic grounds. A serious opera of his, *Il Demetrio*, was performed at Brescia during Carnival 1751. His principal claim to historical notice derives from the fact that he set the first act of Goldoni's libretto *Lo speziale* (Domenico Fischietti set Acts 2 and 3), first performed in Venice at the Teatro di S Samuele on 26 December 1754 (MSS in *A-Wn* and *B-Bc*). This work was a critical and a popular success, achieving performances throughout north Italy as well as in Dresden and Vienna (sometimes under the title *Il botanico novellista* or in German as *Der Apotheker*). The libretto, according to its preface, had been written three years earlier; Ortolani suggested that Pallavicini might at that time have been commissioned to write the whole opera but left it unfinished, and that completion was left to Fischietti.

See also SPEZIALE, LO (i).

FétisB; GerberL

G. Ortolani, ed.: *Tutte le opere di Carlo Goldoni* (Milan, 1935–56), xi, 1277   JAMES L. JACKMAN

Pallavicino [Pallavicini], **Carlo** (*b* Salò, *c*1640; *d* Dresden, 29 Jan 1688). Italian composer. He dominated Venetian opera in the 1670s and 1680s, writing 21 operas for four Venetian opera houses. At the end of his life he was also briefly involved with opera at the Saxon electoral court in Dresden. His ties to Dresden are analogous to those of Antonio Sartorio to Brunswick-Wolfenbüttel, another German court that had military connections with the Venetian republic.

By 1665, Pallavicino was organist at the Basilica of S Antonio in Padua. Towards the end of 1666 he moved to Dresden, where he served under Johann Georg II, Elector of Saxony, as vice-Kapellmeister, replacing Heinrich Schütz on his death in 1672 as Kapellmeister. From June 1673, he again served as organist at the Basilica in Padua, but moved to Venice one year later, where he served as *maestro di coro* (1674–85) at the Ospedale degli Incurabili. During Carnival 1685, Johann Georg III, the son of Pallavicino's earlier employer, visited Venice and offered him the position of *camerae ac teatralis musicae praefectus*. Sources indicate that Pallavicino did not leave for Dresden until the beginning of 1687. In August and September of that year, he again visited Venice and then returned to Dresden; he was reportedly about to return to Venice, to supervise the Ospedale degli Incurabili, when he died.

Pallavicino's first operatic productions in Venice, *Demetrio* and *Aureliano*, were for the small Teatro S Moisè in 1666, before his first departure for Dresden. His association with theatres owned by the Grimani brothers began with his third opera, *Il tiranno humiliato d'amore*, written for the Teatro SS Giovanni e Paolo and produced in his absence in 1667. After his return in 1673, he contributed to this theatre on a regular basis, and in 1678, when the Grimanis opened the Teatro S Giovanni Grisostomo, the most luxurious Venetian opera house of their day, Pallavicino received the commission for the inaugural opera, *Vespasiano*, an emblematic choice since Vespasian, the founder of the Colosseum, was a touchstone for regal theatricality. During the next two decades, *Vespasiano* was often restaged for the opening of theatres; Pallavicino may have supervised the Genoese production at the Teatro Falcone in 1680, since he signed the dedication of the libretto. In 1679 Pallavicino's *Le amazoni nell'isole fortunate* inaugurated the private theatre of the Procurator Marco Contarini in Piazzola, where Domenico Freschi later became house composer; the *Mercure galant* (December 1679 and February 1680) provides a description and an engraving of this work. For Carnival 1680 he also provided an opera, *Messalina*, for the Teatro S Salvatore, where Sartorio was house composer.

After becoming the house composer of the S Giovanni Grisostomo, Pallavicino monopolized seven seasons and provided ten scores during the first ten years. He also continued to write for the SS Giovanni e Paolo. His operas focus on the rapid interaction of characters engaged in lively stage action, and several involve a great deal of spectacle, particularly those for the S Giovanni Grisostomo. Along with Legrenzi and Sartorio, Pallavicino created a style that responded to the audience's insatiable desire for tunefully ingratiating pieces. Their operas are packed with many short arias and recitative is minimal. The arias usually comprise two strophes in da capo form: settings often establish a constant rhythmic and motivic background against which Pallavicino highlighted certain details with word-painting or melismas in order to illuminate the affect of the particular piece. The declamatory pattern of the voice and the accompaniment is usually the same. Motto arias are frequent. Recitatives and the vast majority of arias are supported by continuo alone. Upper melodic instruments are used in a strictly compartmentalized manner in arias, mostly in homorhythmic ritornellos after the singer has concluded, thereby prolonging the mood of the aria and covering the singer's exit. Less often, ritornellos precede rather than follow the aria. When upper melodic instruments actually accompany an aria they nearly always alternate with the voice, anticipating and echoing vocal phrases and joining the voice only to add weight to the closing vocal phrase. The use of instruments simultaneously with the voice is limited to certain well-defined situations that invoke a shadowy atmosphere, such as oncoming sleep, foreboding, night and incantation. Pallavicino usually called for five-part strings (two violins, two *violette* and cello) with basso continuo (at least two harpsichords, as well as lutes and several theorbos). Certain scores call for one or two trumpets.

See also AMAZONE CORSARA, L'.

drammi per musica in three acts, first performed in Venice, unless otherwise stated

VGG – *S Giovanni Grisostomo*   VGP – *SS Giovanni e Paolo*

Demetrio (G. dall'Angelo), S Moisè, ded. 1 Jan 1666, *I-Vnm*
Aureliano (prol., 3, dall'Angelo), S Moisè, ded. 25 Feb 1666
Il tiranno humiliato d'amore, ovvero Il Meraspe (prol., 3, G. Faustini, rev. N. Beregan), VGP, 12 Dec 1667
Diocleziano (M. Noris), VGP, ded. 10 Dec 1674, *MOe*, *Vnm*, arias *Vqs*
Enea in Italia (G. F. Bussani), VGP, carn. 1675, *Vnm*, arias *Nc*
Galieno (Noris), VGP, ded. 23 Dec 1675, *A-Wn* (?autograph), *I-Nc*, *Vnm*, arias *Vqs*
Vespasiano (G. C. Corradi), VGG, carn. 1678, *MOe*; carn. 1680, *Vnm*, arias *B-Bc*, *I-MOe*, *Rvat* and *Vqs*
Nerone (Corradi), VGG, carn. 1679, arias, *GB-Ob*, *I-MOe*, *Rvat*, *Vqs* and *Mercure galant* (April 1679)
Le amazoni nell'isole fortunate (prol., 3, F. M. Piccioli), Piazzola sul Brenta, Contarini, 1679, *Vnm*
Messalina (Piccioli), S Salvatore, ded. 28 Dec 1679, *I-Vnm* (Rforthcoming: DMV, viii), arias *MOe*, *Tn* and *Vqs*
Bassiano, ovvero Il maggior impossibile (Noris), VGP, carn. 1682, *MOe*, arias *Tn* and *Vqs*
Carlo re d'Italia (Noris), VGG, carn. 1682, arias *Tn* and *Vqs*
Il re infante (Noris), VGG, 10 Jan 1683, arias *B-Bc*, *F-Pn*, *GB-Lbl*, *I-Vqs* and *Mercure galant* (April 1683)
Licinio imperatore (Noris), VGG, 18–25 Dec 1683
Ricimero re de' vandali (Noris), VGG, carn. 1684
Massimo Puppieno (Aureli), VGP, 6 Jan 1685, *Nc*, *PESc*
Penelope la casta (Noris), VGG, ded. 28 Jan 1685
Amore inamorato (Noris), VGG, 19 Jan 1686, arias *MOe*
Didone delirante (A. Franceschi), VGP, carn. 1686
L'amazone corsara, ovvero L'Avilda regina de' Goti (Corradi), VGP, *c*1 Feb 1686; carn. 1688, *D-Mbs* (R1978: IOB, xiii), *I-Nc*, arias *GB-Lbl* and *I-MOe*

Elmiro re di Corinto (V. Grimani and G. Frisari), VGG, 26 Dec 1686, arias *GB-Lbl*, *Ob* and *Pallade veneta* (Jan 1687)

La Gierusalemme liberata (Corradi, after T. Tasso), VGP, 4 Jan 1687; as Armida (Ger. trans. G. Fiedler, retains Pallavicino's arias), Hamburg, Gänsemarkt, 1695, *B-Bc* (19th-century copy), *D-Dlb*, *F-Pn* (19th-century copy), *US-LAu*, ed. in DDT, lv (1916/*R*1959), arias *F-Pn*, *I-Rvat* and *Pallade veneta* (Jan 1687)

Antiope (S. B. Pallavicino), Dresden, Hof, 14 Feb 1689, Acts 1 and 2 *D-Dlb* [completed by N. A. Strungk]

*

Mercure galant (April 1679, Dec 1679, Feb 1680, March 1683, April 1683)

M. Fürstenau: *Zur Geschichte der Musik und des Theaters am Hofe zu Dresden* (Dresden, 1861–2)

H. C. Wolff: *Die Venezianische Oper in der zweiten Hälfte des 17. Jahrhunderts* (Berlin, 1937)

S. T. Worsthorne: *Venetian Opera in the Seventeenth Century* (Oxford, 1954)

R. Brockpähler: *Handbuch zur Geschichte der Barockoper in Deutschland* (Emsdetten, 1964)

J. Smith: 'Carlo Pallavicino', *PRMA*, xcvi (1969–70), 57–71

H. C. Wolff: 'Italian Opera from the Later Monteverdi to Scarlatti', *NOHM*, v (London, 1975), 1–72, esp. 42–4

L. Bianconi: *Storia della musica*, iv: *Il seicento* (Turin, 1982); Eng. trans., rev., as *Music in the Seventeenth Century* (Cambridge, 1987)

E. Selfridge-Field: 'One Hundred Venetian Arias of the Late Seicento in the Bodleian Library', *Notes*, xl (1983–4), 503–9

H. S. Saunders: *The Repertoire of a Venetian Opera House (1678–1714): the Teatro Grimani di San Giovanni Grisostomo* (diss., Harvard U., 1985)

B. Glixon: *Recitative in Seventeenth-Century Venetian Opera: its Dramatic Function and Musical Language* (diss., Rutgers U., 1985)

E. Selfridge-Field: *Pallade veneta: Writings on Music in Venetian Society, 1650–1750* (Venice, 1985)

R. M. McKee: *A Critical Edition of Carlo Pallavicino's 'Il Vespasiano'* (diss., U. of North Carolina, Chapel Hill, 1989)

E. Rosand: *Opera in Seventeenth-Century Venice: the Creation of a Genre* (Berkeley and Los Angeles, 1991)   HARRIS S. SAUNDERS

Pallavicino [Pallavicini], **Stefano Benedetto** (*b* Padua, 21 March 1672; *d* Dresden, 16 April 1742). Italian librettist and poet, son of Carlo Pallavicino. After completing his studies at the college of the Padri Somaschi at Salò he went early in 1687 with his father to Dresden, where in 1688, at the age of only 16, he was employed as court poet. From 1695 to 1716 he was court poet and private secretary to the Elector Palatine Johann Wilhelm at Düsseldorf. On the elector's death he returned via Kassel to Dresden, where he again entered the service of the Saxon electoral court. He remained there until his death. From 1701 he was a member of the Arcadian Society. A prolific author of opera, oratorio and cantata texts, he was one of the leading reformers of the opera libretto at the beginning of the 18th century. At the age of 15 he wrote a libretto, *Antiope*, for his father, who died before completing the score (it was finished by Strungk). Several other composers set his opera librettos, among them Lotti, Steffani, Wilderer and above all Hasse, who also set three oratorio texts by him. A four-volume edition of Pallavicino's works was issued by Francesco Algarotti two years after his death.

Antiope (dramma per musica), C. Pallavicino and Strungk, 1689; *Giocasta*, Wilderer, 1696; *Telegono* (tragedia in musica), C. L. P. Grua, 1697; *Teofane* (os), Lotti, 1719 (Handel, 1723, as Ottone, re di Germania); *Calandro* (dg), Ristori, 1726; *Un pazzo ne fà cento, ovvero Don Chisciotte* (dg), Ristori, 1727; *Arianna*, Ristori, 1736; *Le fate*, Ristori, 1736; *Asteria* (favola pastorale), Hasse, 1737; *Atalanta* (os), Hasse, 1737; *Senocrita* (os), Hasse, 1737; *Alfonso* (os), Hasse, 1738; *Irene* (os), Hasse, 1738; *Numa Pompilio* (os), Hasse, 1741

*

F. Algarotti: Biographical introduction to S. B. Pallavicino: *Opere* (Venice, 1744)

M. Fürstenau: *Zur Geschichte der Musik und des Theaters am Hofe zu Dresden*, i (Dresden, 1861)

——: 'Die Oper "Antiope" und die Bestallungen des kurfürstlich sächsischen Vice-Kapellmeisters Nicolaus Adam Strunck und des Hofpoeten Stefano Pallavicini', *MMg*, xiii (1881), 1–6

I. Becker-Glauch: *Die Bedeutung der Musik für die Dresdener Hoffeste bis in die Zeit Augusts der Starken* (Kassel, 1951)

H. Riemenschneider: 'Tanz und Hofoper in der Residenz Düsseldorf', *Die Tanzarchiv-Reihe*, xiii–xiv (1972)

L. Bianconi and G. La Face Bianconi, eds.: *I libretti italiani di Georg Friedrich Händel e le loro fonti*, i (Florence, 1992)

SIBYLLE DAHMS

Palló, Imre (*b* Matisfalva, 23 Oct 1891; *d* Budapest, 25 Jan 1978). Hungarian baritone. He studied at the Budapest Academy of Music under Georg Anthes, and later in Italy with Sammarco. He made his Budapest Opera début in 1917, as Alfio, and was soon its leading interpreter of lyric baritone roles. He sang with refined diction and velvety tone, his voice showing good balance in all registers, and he also possessed an imposing stage presence; all these qualities were notably displayed in his Verdi roles, especially Posa, Luna, Falstaff (the first in Hungary) and Simon Boccanegra. His peasant origins were advantageous in Kodály – he created the title role in *Háry János* (1926) and the Suitor in *Székely fonó* ('The Spinning Room', 1932). In 1935 he took part in Rocca's *Il dibuk* in Rome. From 1957 to 1959 he was Intendant of the Budapest Opera. His son, Imre Palló jr (*b* Budapest, 15 May 1941), conducted the New York City Opera (1977–87) before becoming guest conductor at the Frankfurt Opera (1989).

*

A. Németh: *Palló Imre* (Budapest, 1970)   PÉTER P. VÁRNAI

Palma [De Palma, Di Palma], **Silvestro** (*b* Barano d'Ischia, 15 March 1754; *d* Naples, 8 Aug 1834). Italian composer. According to Villarosa's *Memorie*, he owed his initial musical education to a patroness, Carlotta di Sangro, daughter of the Prince of Sansevero, and entered the Conservatorio S Maria di Loreto in Naples at the age of 16. In the late 1780s he studied with Paisiello, whose music he took as a model; contemporary documents often refer to him as 'pupil of Paisiello'. He became well known as a composer of opera, especially comic opera, because of his talent for witty, effervescent and lightly textured music; one of his most successful stage works was *La pietra simpatica* (1795). The Naples *Monitore* (2 May 1810) praised his opera *Lo scavamento* for the naturalness and simplicity of its music and for its avoidance of the contemporary fault of too many notes and too prominent accompaniment. He was, it says, the 'support of the good Neapolitan school', a reference to the close affinity between his music and that of the previous generation of Neapolitan composers. After 1813 his operas disappeared from the repertory. This may have been caused by changing tastes among Neapolitan audiences; Villarosa provided another explanation in saying that Palma fell ill, which forced him to cancel contracts for new music and wrecked his chances of a more prosperous livelihood.

commedie per musica, first performed in Naples, Teatro dei Fiorentini, unless otherwise stated

La finta matta (2, D. Piccinni), 1789

Gli amanti della dote (dg, 2, S. Zini), Florence, Risoluti, sum. 1791

Le nozze in villa (int, 2), Rome, Valle, carn. 1792

Chi mal fa, mal aspetti, ovvero Lo scroccatore smascherato (dramma tragicomico, 2), Venice, S Moisè, aut. 1792

L'ingaggiatore di campagna (int), Florence, Palla a Corda, 1792, *I-Fc*

La pietra simpatica (2, G. Lorenzi), aut. 1795; 5 excerpts, A-Wgm, I-Fc, Nc; as L'anello incantato (farsetta per musica), Rome, Valle, carn. 1796

Gli amanti ridicoli (2, Lorenzi), aut. 1797, Nc

Il pallone aerostatico (2, G. Palomba), spr. 1802, Nc

Le seguaci di Diana (2, Lorenzi), sum. 1805; also as Le ninfe di Diana, Nc

L'erede senza eredità (2, Palomba), 29 Sept 1808, Nc

Lo scavamento (2, Palomba), 29 April 1810, Nc

I furbi amanti (2, Palomba), aut. 1810, Nc

Il palazzo delle fate (2, Palomba), aut. 1812, Nc

I vampiri (2, Palomba), Naples, Nuovo, 1812, Nc

Le miniere di Polonia (melodramma, 3, G. Giannetti), wint. 1813, Nc

8 arias in G. Paisiello's Le vane gelosie (3, Lorenzi), spr. 1790, Nc

Doubtful: La schiava fortunata, 1801; Il geloso di sè stesso, 1814

FlorimoN; RosaM   MICHAEL F. ROBINSON

Palma de Mallorca. Principal city of Mallorca, a Mediterranean island off the south-east coast of Spain. In the first half of the 18th century there was considerable musical activity of a theatrical nature in Palma Cathedral, whose musicians performed the melodrama *Venus y Adonis* by Carlos Julián in 1739 and the music drama *Píramo y Tisbe* by Salvador de Lorenzo in 1748. The earliest known performance of Italian opera was in 1767–8, when Francisco Creus presented Traetta's *Buovo de Antona* and Jommelli's *Andromaca*, Galuppi's *Demofoonte*, Piccinni's *Artaserse*, Florian Gassmann's *Gli uccellatori* (in Spanish as *Los cazadores*) and G. M. Rutini's *L'olandese in Italia*. Chief among the patrons was the Conde de Ayamans, proprietor of the Casa de las Comedias, which he gave to the city on the sole condition that there be a place permanently reserved for him. The opera company appeared the following year at the theatre in Cartagena, Spain. The theatre was enlarged in 1799–1800 by 800 seats, and alterations resulting in an italianate neo-classical design were carried out in 1824, 1839 and 1842. The building was destroyed in 1854.

From the beginning of the 19th century the Casa de las Comedias played an important role in musical life which is only partially recorded, although it seems that by the late 1860s, as in most Spanish theatres, Italian opera was being supplanted in public favour by the Spanish zarzuela. Between 1854 and 1858 the present Teatro Principal was built, but it burnt down a few months after its inauguration. After rebuilding it was opened in 1860 by Isabel II. In recent years there have been short but good seasons of opera through the initiative of the Asociación de Amigos de la Opera.

B. Saldoni: *Diccionario biográfico-bibliográfico de efemérides de músicos españoles* (Madrid, 1868–81)

E. Cotarelo y Mori: *Orígenes y establecimiento de la ópera en Espana hasta 1800* (Madrid, 1917)

C. Cantarellas: *La arquitectura mallorquina desde la ilustración a la restauración* (Parma, 1981)   XOÁN M. CARREIRA

Palm Beach. American town in Florida. The Palm Beach Opera began as the Grand Opera Company of Palm Beach County in 1961. It was later known as the Civic Opera of the Palm Beaches before adopting its present name. The original company was founded by a group of local women including Isabel Chatfield, Charlotte Miller, Rosita Franks, Princess Jane Obolensky (the first president), Octavia Gould, Alberta Grant and Thelma Miller. Several years later Arthur Silvester was named president and established the Opera's reputation by bringing in the soprano Licia Albanese. The Opera has continued to grow and attract many stars, performing the works of Verdi, Mozart, Puccini, Bellini and Offenbach as well as Lehár and Menotti. Paul Csonka was the first music director; the artistic director and principal conductor from 1983 was Anton Guadagno. The Palm Beach Opera stages three works each season, normally in December, January and March. Notable adjuncts are an education programme taking 'mini-operas' to children in schools and a scholarship programme for the encouragement of promising young music students.

RAYMOND A. BARR

Palmer, Felicity (Joan) (*b* Cheltenham, 6 April 1944). English soprano, later mezzo-soprano. She studied at the GSM in London (1962–7) and then for a year with Marianne Schech at the Musikhochschule, Munich. In 1970 she won a Kathleen Ferrier Scholarship and made her Queen Elizabeth Hall début in Purcell's *Dioclesian*. Her operatic début was as Dido with Kent Opera (1971), with whom she later sang Handel's Agrippina (1982). She has sung Pamina, Donna Elvira, Adriano (*Rienzi*) and Katisha (*Mikado*, 1986) for the ENO, Elvira and Fricka (*Das Rheingold*, 1989) for Scottish Opera and Gluck's Armida at the 1982 Spitalfields festival (also recorded). Her American début was as Mozart's Countess, at Houston, in November 1983, and she has also performed in Hong Kong and Australia. She later turned to mezzo roles, doubling the Mother and Witch in *Hänsel und Gretel* (1987, ENO) and singing Kabanicha (*Kat'a Kabanová*) and Mistress Quickly at Glyndebourne in 1988 and Gertrude (Thomas' *Hamlet*) at Chicago in 1990. In Madrid she took the title role in the 1992 first staged performance of Gerhard's *The Duenna*; for Opera North she has been a notable interpreter of Handel's Tamerlane and Gluck's Orpheus. She has a magnetic presence and a powerful musical command in shaping phrases and projecting words, such that in her portrayals there is ample compensation for tone occasionally edgy or metallic and moments of strain in high-lying passages.

MAX LOPPERT

Palmerini, Giovanni Battista (*fl* 1722–8). Italian bass. He was a member of the Elector Palatine's chapel at Düsseldorf in 1723, and was probably the Palmerini from Mantua who sang in Pietro Torri's *Adelaide* at Munich in 1722. In 1726 he was at the Hamburg Opera. He sang at the King's Theatre, London, during the last two seasons of the Royal Academy (1727–8). Handel wrote small parts for him in *Admeto* (Meraspes, in which he made his début), *Riccardo Primo* (Berardo) and *Siroe* (Arasse); he also sang in revivals and in Ariosti's *Teuzzone*. He was said to have been an aging singer whose powers were on the decline. The arias Handel composed for him indicate a baritone with a high tessitura and a compass from G to *f'*. Another bass singer of this name, Andrea Palmerini of Genoa, sang at the festival of S Croce at Lucca in 1741.   WINTON DEAN

Palmgren, Selim (*b* Pori, 16 Feb 1878; *d* Helsinki, 13 Dec 1951). Finnish composer. He studied at Helsinki, then in Germany and Italy with Busoni among others. He was a virtuoso pianist, and most of his music was written for the piano. Much of his work is impressionistic, although his musical outlook stemmed from Chopin, Schumann and Liszt. His single opera *Daniel Hjort* (in three acts, to his own libretto after J. J.

Wecksell; Turku, 15 April 1910, revised in 1938) was based on a historical drama concerning events in 16th-century Finland. The plot, dealing with power struggles, treason, love and jealousy, is gothic in its complexity. The music is lyrically romantic and skilfully crafted, though lacking dramatic tension. However, with Oskar Merikanto's *Pohjan neiti* ('The Maid of the North') and Melartin's *Aino*, *Daniel Hjort* was one of the first steps in the development of Finnish opera.   ERKKI ARNI

Palmira, regina di Persia ('Palmira, Queen of Persia'). *Dramma eroicomico* in two acts by ANTONIO SALIERI to a libretto by GIOVANNI DE GAMERRA; Vienna, Kärntnertortheater, 14 October 1795.

A monster has been terrorizing Persia. The High Priest (bass) makes an oracular pronouncement: one of the kings who seek the hand of Princess Palmira (soprano) in marriage will kill the monster and thereby win her. Three kings arrive: the timid Egyptian Alderano (bass), the boastful Scythian Oronte (bass) and the brave Indian Alcidoro (tenor) are welcomed by King Dario [Darius] of Persia (bass). Alcidoro and Palmira are already secret lovers; they express their passion in the duet 'O del cor speme gradita'. After Alderano's cowardice is made known and Oronte fails to kill the monster, Alcidoro triumphs; the opera ends with joyful celebration of his impending marriage to Palmira.

The competition for the honour of first fighting the monster takes up much of the opera: Alderano arrives on a camel, Oronte on an elephant and Alcidoro on a horse, each singing an aria as he presents gifts. The unaccompanied quartet in Act 2 for King Darius and the three suitors, 'Silenzio facciasi', is one of the first *a cappella* ensembles in an opera. In setting the work in an exotic, Middle-Eastern court, mixing comic and serious elements, and calling for large choral forces and spectacular scenic effects, Salieri and De Gamerra came close to recapturing the popularity of Salieri's *Axur, re d'Ormus* (1788, Vienna). *Palmira* was performed 39 times in the Viennese court theatres between 1795 and 1798 and was given in German translation throughout Germany into the early 19th century.   JOHN A. RICE

Palomba, Antonio (*b* Naples, 20 Dec 1705; *d* Naples, 1769). Italian librettist, uncle of Giuseppe Palomba. A lawyer by profession, he wrote more than 50 comic librettos in Neapolitan dialect. His earliest known libretto, *L'amor costante* (1734), was a minor success; in 1737 his career took off with the immensely popular *Orazio*, which soon joined the legion of works falsely attributed to Pergolesi. In 1749 he was *maestro al cembalo* at the Teatro della Pace. From 1756 to 1761 his new works were presented with some frequency outside Naples (although to music by composers associated with that city). Critical assessment of Palomba's work has been harsh. Scherillo dismissed him as a scribbler – 'his comedies are colourless, inconsequential, improbable and completely artificial' – and only Cimaglia has offered enthusiastic praise. He is remembered chiefly for his association with such composers as Jommelli, Piccinni and Paisiello.

See also ORAZIO.

comic operas unless otherwise stated

L'amor costante, Auletta, 1734 (Logroscino, 1741, as La violante); *Lo creduto infedele*, Logroscino, 1735; *Carlo*, M. Capranica, 1736; *Orazio*, Auletta, 1737 (pasticcio, as Il

maestro di musica, 1752; pasticcio, as La scolara alla moda, 1760; F. J. Deller, 1771, as Il maestro di capella); *L'errore amoroso*, Jommelli, 1737; *La Camilla*, I. Prota, 1737; *Il Marchese Sgrana*, Auletta, 1738; *I travestimenti amorosi*, Perez, 1740; *L'Origille*, Palella, 1740 (N. Piccinni, 1760); *Il trionfo del valore*, Palella, Porpora, G. Signorille and Domenico, 1741

Le due zingare simili, Abos, 1742; *Il chimico*, Palella, 1742 (Scolari, 1750); *Il geloso*, Abos, 1743; *Li dispiette d'ammore*, Comes, 1744 (Logroscino and Calandra, 1748); *L'Elisa*, Cocchi, 1744; *Don Saverio*, Avossa, 1744; *L'amore ingegnoso*, V. Ciampi, 1745; *Il Demetrio*, M. Valentini, 1745; *L'Eugenia*, Capranica, 1745; *Il barone di Vignalunga*, Latilla, 1747; *La costanza*, Logroscino, 1747 (Traetta, 1752); *La Faustina*, Girolamo [?Geronimo] Cordella, 1747; *La maestra*, Cocchi, 1747 (pasticcio, as La scaltra governatrice, 1753)

La moglie traduta, Calandra, 1747; *L'amore in maschera*, Jommelli, 1748; *Lo chiacchiarone*, Comes, 1748; *La villana nobile*, Valentini, 1748; *La Celia*, Latilla, 1749; *Il finto turco*, Cocchi, 1749 (Cocchi and Errichelli, 1753); *La serva bacchetona*, Cocchi, 1749; *Monsieur Petitone*, A. Corbisiero, 1749 (Piccinni, 1758, as Madama Arrighetta); *L'amor comico*, Sellitto, 1750; *La Gismonda*, Cocchi, 1750; *Il gioco de' matti*, Latilla, 1750; *Amore figlio del piacere*, Logroscino and Ventura, 1751

La Griselda, Logroscino, 1752 (Valentino Fioravanti, 1800); *La schiava amante*, Capranica, 1753; *Olindo*, N. Conti and Capranica, 1753; *La commediante*, Conforto, 1754; *Le donne dispettose*, Piccinni, 1754; *La Rosmonda*, Logroscino, Traetta, Comes and Cecere, 1755; *Il finto pastorella* [sic], Sciroli, 1755 (V. Orgitano, 1759); *L'amore alla moda*, Sellitto, 1755; *Il curioso del suo proprio danno*, Piccinni, ?1755–6 (Piccinni and Sacchini, 1761, as Il curioso imprudente); *La fante furba*, Traetta, 1756; *La fante di buon gusto*, Logroscino, ?1758

La scaltra letterata, Piccinni, 1758; *La ricca locandiera* (int), P. A. Guglielmi, 1759; *I due soldati*, Guglielmi, 1760; *Il cavalier parigino*, Piccinni ? and Sacchini, 1762; *La donna di tutti i caratteri*, Guglielmi, 1762 (Paisiello, 1765, as Madama l'umorista o Gli stravaganti); *La pupilla*, Avossa, 1763 (Paisiello, 1764, as Il ciarlone; Scolari, 1765); *Lo sposo di tre e marito di nessuna*, Anfossi and Guglielmi, 1763 (Gnecco, 1793); *La donna vana*, Piccinni, 1764; *La giocatrice bizzarra*, Gabellone and Insanguine, 1764; *L'incostante* (int), Piccinni, 1766

Doubtful or spurious: *La Matilde*, Cocchi, 1739; *Gl'intrichi delle cantarine*, 1740; *Gli incanti per amore* [actually by P. Trinchera], Palella, 1741; *La fedeltà odiata*, Leo, 1744; *La moglie gelosa*, Abos, 1745; *Il vecchio deluso* [possibly confused with G. Palomba: *I vecchi delusi*], Arena, 1746; *La serva astuta*, 1753, ? Cocchi and Errichelli; *La finta cameriera*, 1762; *Le quattro malmaritate* [actually by G. Palomba], Insanguine, 1766; *Le Magie*; *Bernardone e Carmosina*; *L'incostante finta matta* [the last 3 attrib. to A. Palomba by Napoli-Signorelli]

CroceN; ES (A. Mondolfi); *FlorimoN*

P. Napoli-Signorelli: *Vicende della coltura nelle due Sicilie* (Naples, 1784–6)

V. M. Cimaglia: *Saggi teatrali analitici* (Naples, 1817)

——: *Saggi di diverse rappresentazioni musicali* (Naples, 1817)

P. Napoli-Signorelli: 'Ricerche sul sistema melodrammatico lette da Pietro Napoli-Signorelli ai Soci Pontaniani nel nov. e dic. del 1812', *Atti della Società Pontaniana*, iv (1847), 59ff

G. Méry: *Quadro cronologico dal 1200 sino a' giorni nostri degli scrittori in dialeto napoletano* (Naples, 1879)

M. Scherillo: *L'opera buffa napoletana durante il settecento: storia letteraria*, (Naples, 1883)

U. Rolandi: *Il libretto per musica* (Rome, 1951)

U. Prota-Giurleo: *Breve storia del teatro di corte e della musica a Napoli nei secoli xvii–xviii* (Naples, 1952)

F. Walker: 'Orazio: the History of a Pasticcio', *MQ*, xxxviii (1952), 369–83

G. Tintori: *L'opera napoletana* (Milan, 1958)

M. F. Robinson: *Naples and Neapolitan Opera* (Oxford, 1972)

G. Hardie: 'Neapolitan Comic Opera, 1707–1750: some Addenda and Corrigenda for *The New Grove*', *JAMS*, xxxvi (1983), 124–7
                    BRYAN MARTIN

Palomba, Giuseppe (*fl* 1765–1825). Italian librettist. Almost nothing is known about his life, except that he was the nephew of the librettist Antonio Palomba. Written during the period 1765–1825, his many librettos are all comic, apart from *Admeto* (set by P. A.

Guglielmi, 1794). They were set by some of the most prominent composers of the time, including Cimarosa, Paisiello, Piccinni, Raimondi and Spontini. Palomba's work has been repeatedly criticized as confused and awkward, his characters as flat and one-dimensional. Almost all of his librettos were set only once. His extraordinary popularity may have resulted to some extent from his reliance on local tradition: during the period when dialect comedies were giving way to purely Italian texts, his best librettos retained sections in Neapolitan dialect. For example, *Le cantatrici villane*, written for Valentino Fioravanti in 1799, contains passages in dialect and other references to the Neapolitan area, but was popular enough to receive productions in Milan (1802, 1810, 1833), Florence (1803, 1804) and Turin (1806, 1830). It features little profound characterization, and relationships among the characters are portrayed unconvincingly, but it is fast-paced and offers ample opportunity to a composer with comic gifts. Although Palomba's librettos continue an 18th-century tradition of Neapolitan *opera buffa*, they continued to be performed in Italy after his death. Several of Paisiello's settings were translated into German and performed in Dresden and Hamburg.

comic operas unless otherwise stated

Il corsaro algerino, Astarita, 1765; *La vedova capricciosa*, Insanguine, 1765; *Le quattro malmaritate*, Insanguine, 1766; *I ladri di spirito*, V. Curcio, 1769; *Il maritato fra le disgrazie*, Latilla, 1774; *Il matrimonio in contrasto*, P. A. Guglielmi, 1776; *Armida immaginaria*, Cimarosa, 1777; *Il fanatico per gli antichi Romani*, Cimarosa, 1777; *I matrimoni per inganno*, G. M. Curcio, 1779; *Il raggiratore di poca fortuna*, Guglielmi, 1779; *La dama avventuriera*, Guglielmi, 1780; *Il faligname* [*Il falegname*], Cimarosa, 1780; *I finti nobili*, Cimarosa, 1780

Il millantatore, Curcio, 1780; *L'amante combattuto dalle donne di punto*, Cimarosa, 1780; *Le donne vendicate*, G. Monti, 1781; *La fiera di Brindisi*, Giordani, 1781; *Il Molaforbici*, Monti, 1781; *Le nozze in commedia*, Guglielmi, 1781 (Caruso, 1781, as Il matrimonio in commedia; Astarita, 1792, as Il medico parigino, o sia L'ammalato per amore); *La ballerina amante* (commedia per musica), Cimarosa, 1782; *Il convito*, Giordani, 1782; *La semplice ad arte*, Guglielmi, 1782; *Don Papirio*, Tritto, 1782; *La quakera spiritosa*, Guglielmi, 1782/3; *Chi dell'altrui si veste presto si spoglia*, Cimarosa, 1783

La donna amante di tutti, e fedele a nessuno, Guglielmi, 1783; *I due baroni di Rocca Azzurra*, Cimarosa, 1783; *L'intrigo delle mogli*, Gazzaniga, 1783; *La villana riconosciuta*, Cimarosa, 1783; *La scuola degli amanti*, Tritto, 1783; *Puntigli e gelosie tra moglie e marito*, Caruso, 1784; *Le quattro stagioni*, Caruso, 1784; *La donna sempre al suo peggior s'appiglia*, Cimarosa, 1785; *La grotta di Trofonio*, Paisiello, 1785; *Le tre fanatiche*, Andreozzi, 1785

L'astuzie villane, Guglielmi, 1786; *Le gare generose*, Paisiello, 1786; *L'inganno amoroso*, Guglielmi, 1786; *Gli amanti trappolieri*, Fabrizi, 1787; *Amor non ha riguardi*, L. Platone, 1787 (F. Rutini, 1789); *Le convulsioni*, G. M. Curcio, 1787; *La scaltra avventuriera*, Tritto, 1788; *L'amor contrastato*, Cimarosa, 1788 (Paisiello, 1788, also as La Molinara); *Gl'inganni delusi*, Guglielmi, 1789; *La pruova reciproca*, Tritto, 1789; *I zingari in fiera*, Paisiello, 1789

Gli accidenti inaspettati, Marinelli, 1790; *La bizzarra contadina in amore*, Marinelli, 1790; *I due fratelli perseguitati*, G. Coppola, 1790; *L'equivoco curioso*, D. Cercià, 1790; *La serva innamorata*, Guglielmi, 1790; *La dispettosa in amore*, A. Marcori, 1791; *Le false apparenze*, Guglielmi, 1791; *Le false magie per amore*, Cercià, 1791; *Amor tra le vendemmie*, Guglielmi, 1792; *Lo sposo a forza*, Marinelli, 1792; *I traci amante*, Cimarosa, 1793; *Le trame spiritose*, Tritto, 1792; *Le donne dispettose*, Gabriele Prota, 1793

Le furberie deluse, Prota, 1793; *I traci amante*, Cimarosa, 1793; *Le trame in maschera*, Luigi Piccinni, 1793; *I vecchi delusi*, Marinelli, 1793; *Admeto* (dramma per musica), Guglielmi, 1794; *Le astuzie femminili* (after Bertati: Amor vende sagace), Cimarosa, 1794; *L'astuta in amore, ossia Il furbo malaccorta*, Valentino Fioravanti, 1795; *I commedianti*, Cercià, 1795;

L'uomo indolente, G. Farinelli, 1795 (Gnecco, 1797, as L'indolente); *I raggiri amorosi*, Rutini, 1796 (P. C. Guglielmi, 1799)

I studenti, Gabriele Prota, 1796; *Il barone in angustie*, Tritto, 1797; *Le nozze a dispetto*, G. M. Curcio, 1797; *L'amore a dispetto*, Fioravanti, 1798; *L'inganno felice*, Paisiello, 1798; *Le cantatrici villane*, Fioravanti, 1799; *Lo sposo senza moglie*, Fioravanti, 1799; *Un imbroglio ne porta un altro*, L. Mosca, 1799; *Gli amanti in cimento*, Guglielmi, 1800; *La fuga in maschera*, Spontini, 1800; *L'ambizione punita*, Fioravanti, 1800; *L'amore per inganno*, Mosca, 1801; *La fiera*, Guglielmi, 1801

Quanti casi in un sol giorno, ossia Gli assassini, Trento, 1801; *Lo sposo in periglio*, F. A. de Blasis, 1801; *Amore ed interesse, ossia L'inferno ad arte*, R. Orgitano, 1802; *Il pallone aerostatico*, S. Palma, 1802; *La serva bizzarra*, Guglielmi, 1803; *Il servo furbo*, Giovanni Prota, 1803; *L'inganno non dura*, Farinelli, 1804; *Il naufragio fortunato*, Guglielmi, 1804; *Amor tutto vince*, Guglielmi, 1805; *Bref il sordo*, Capotorti, 1805; *L'equivoco delli sposi*, Guglielmi, 1805; *La sposa de Tirolo*, Guglielmi, 1806; *I strani accidenti d'amore*, Naples, 1806

Amore e gelosie tra congiunti, Guglielmi, 1807; *I furbi burlati*, F. Grazioli, 1807; *L'erede senza eredità*, Palma, 1808; *L'idolo cinese* (after Lorenzi), Generali, 1808; *I raggiri ciarlataneschi*, Fioravanti, 1808; *Lo sposo che più accomoda*, Fioravanti, 1808; *La bella carbonara*, Fioravanti, 1809; *Le due compari*, F. Catugno, 1809; *L'ambizione punita*, Fioravanti, 1810; *I furbi amanti*, Palma, 1810; *Lo scavamento*, Palma, 1810; *La sposa a sorte*, Mosca, 1810

Le due simili in una, Guglielmi, 1811; *Il fanatico deluso*, Raimondi, 1811; *Le nozze in campagna*, Guglielmi, 1811; *Gli amori e l'armi*, G. Mosca, 1812; *Il palazzo delle fate*, Palma, 1812; *Lo sposo agitato*, Raimondi, 1812; *I vampiri*, Palma, 1812; *L'audacia delusa* (after Lorenzi: Il furbo malaccorto), L. Mosca, 1813; *La diligenza di Joigny, ossia Il collaterale*, G. Mosca, 1813; *L'ambizione delusa*, G. Pacini, 1814; *L'avaro*, Cordella, 1814; *La ballerina raggiratrice*, Pacini, 1814

Inganni ed amori, Fioravanti, 1814; *Da un disordine ne nasce un ordine*, R. Russo, 1815; *La Rosina*, Pacini, 1815; *La gazzetta*, Rossini, 1816; *Lo scaltro millantatore*, Cordella, 1819; *La caccia di Enrico IV*, Raimondi, 1822; *La poetessa errante*, Mosca, 1822; *L'ombre notturna*, C. Assenzio, 1825

Doubtful or spurious: *I fuorusciti*, P. A. Guglielmi, 1777; *Il matrimonio per industria*, ?Cimarosa, ?1778; *Narcisso*, Guglielmi, 1779; *Il vecchio burlato*, Caruso, 1783; *Le confusioni*, Caruso, 1787; *Li matrimoni per sorpresa* [? *La serva innamorata*], Platone, 1788; *L'inganno fortunato* [?alternative title of La pruova reciproca], Tritto, 1789; *Non v'è matrimonio senza disturbo*, A. Buccelli, 1808; *La procidana*, ? Giuseppe Latilla, 1809; *I finti sdegni*, Latilla, 1811

*

ES (A. Mondolfi)

O. Sonneck: *Catalogue of Opera Librettos Printed before 1800*, iii (New York, 1914), 1360–62
R. Zanetti: *La musica italiana nel settecento*, iii (Milan, 1978), 1351

MARY ANN PARKER (text, bibliography),
BRYAN MARTIN (work-list)

Palomino, José (*b* Madrid, 1755; *d* Las Palmas, 9 April 1810). Spanish composer. His skill as a violinist earned him a place in the Spanish royal chapel as a youth. A pupil of Antonio Rodríguez de Hita, he had early success in composing *tonadillas*, including the popular *El canapé* (1767). In 1774 Palomino emigrated to Lisbon, where he became a member of the S Cecilia brotherhood on 21 March, and by 1785 he was named 'virtuoso instrumentalist of the royal chapel' in the court of Maria I. On 15 June 1785 his *serenata Il ritorno di Astrea in terra*, celebrating the double marriages of the Portuguese and Spanish *infantes*, was produced at the Spanish embassy under the auspices of the ambassador, Count Fernán Nuñez, grandee of Spain. It so delighted the audience that he was given an elegant box containing 4000 duros as well as special pensions. His intermezzos and Portuguese *entremeses* were produced in the theatres for national music, the Teatro do Salitre and the Teatro da Rua dos Condes. Despite the insanity of

Maria I in 1792, Palomino remained at the court, petitioning for Portuguese citizenship after '28 years of service'. According to contemporaries, he played in one of the best court orchestras in Europe; but in addition he served as orchestral leader at both theatres for national music. He left Lisbon in about 1807–8, when the royal family fled the Napoleonic invasion, and accepted a post as *maestro de capilla* in Las Palmas.

Palomino's vocal writing is characterized by a melodic focus with little polyphony. Frequently, melodies are strung together by small rhythmic motifs. There are prominent ensemble sets, possibly influenced by his comic works such as the popular *Os amantes astutós* (*P-Ln*) and *O enganno aparente* (both 1793, for the Salitre theatre). Another *entremés* (for the Rua dos Condes), *As Regatieras zelozas* (1801; *Ln*), featured a fashionable Brazilian *modinha* (a sentimental art song).

The most significant surviving work is *Il ritorno di Astrea in terra* (*Ln, La*), which deals with the return of the goddess of a golden age who retired to the stars in face of earthly disharmony and who now returns to see Portugal and Spain reunited. The singers at the première were Antonio Puzzi (Jupiter, bass), Gioacchimo d'Olviera (Mercury, tenor), Giovanni Gelati (Genio Ibero), Arnanzo Ferracuti (Genio Lusitano) and Fidele Venturi (Astraea) – the last three being castratos. Although the vocal parts differ in character, all have written-in ornamentation, except for trill and appoggiatura signs. Astraea's part includes wide leaps and sustained notes (with dynamics carefully marked), suggesting the need for a powerful castrato voice. The orchestra provides a sinfonia of three parts and an accompaniment of Italian-style doubling for the bass instruments, but includes duos for flutes and oboes and even bassoon solos; there are important parts for second violins and bowing is carefully marked. Palomino was able to delineate character and provide a more lively orchestral support in accompanied recitatives and arias than was current in the fashionable Italian style.

DPB (E. Vieira)

J. Subirá: *La tonadilla escénica* (Madrid, 1928–30), iii/4, pp.41–67; iii/5, pp.37–41, 153–5

——: *La tonadilla escénica: sus obras y sus autores* (Barcelona, 1933), 51, 122–4

M. C. de Brito: *Opera in Portugal in the Eighteenth Century* (Cambridge, 1989), 72, 159
ELEANOR RUSSELL

Paluselli, Stefan [Johann Anton] (*b* Kurtatsch, South Tyrol, 9 Jan 1748; *d* Stams, Oberinntal, 27 Feb 1805). Austrian composer. From around 1760 he was a boarder at the St Nikolaihaus in Innsbruck and attended the Innsbruck Gymnasium; in 1768 he probably studied philosophy at the University of Innsbruck. At his departure in 1770 his Singspiel *Das alte teutsche Wörtlein Thut* was performed at the Gymnasium theatre. In the same year he entered the Cistercian abbey of Stams, notable for its cultivation of music, and in 1774 he was ordained a priest. From 1785 he was violin teacher and from 1791 choirmaster at the abbey school.

Paluselli's secular dramatic music shows a more individual modern style than his church music. His best works are distinguished by a melodic inventiveness which at times approaches the character of folksong.

all Singspiels; all MSS in A-ST

Das alte teutsche Wörtlein Thut, Innsbruck, Gymnasium, 1770
Operetta der Zoll, Stams, 1778
Opfer der Gärtner, Stams, 1780
Die Weintraube in der Torkel, Stams, 1781
Die Hirtenfeyer, Stams, 1789
Diana und Ursus, Stams, 1802
WALTER SENN

Pampani [Pampino, Pampini], **Antonio Gaetano** (*b* Modena, *c*1705; *d* Urbino, Dec 1775). Italian composer. Until the late 1730s librettos and other sources often identified him as Pampino or Pampini. While Eitner's belief that these spellings designate two composers is probably incorrect, the existence of an older Antonio Pampini might explain the appearance of a Pampini in Fermo as late as 1748 (according to Paolucci) when the composer under consideration was already engaged at the Poveri Derelitti (also known as the Ospedaletto) in Venice. On the other hand, Fétis's statement that Pampani died in Venice in 1769 is without foundation. That his birthplace was Florence (Paolucci) or Romagna (La Borde) may be rejected; printed librettos of several Venetian works indicate Modena.

The earliest reference to Pampani relates that when elected *maestro di cappella* of Fano Cathedral in 1726 he was unable to assume duties promptly because engaged at the opera in Urbino. Some time after coming to Fano, he began directing the orchestra of the Teatro del Sole in Pesaro and providing occasional arias (e.g. for Bononcini's *Crispo*, 1730) as well as intermezzos (*Delbo mal maritato*, 1730). After his resignation from the cathedral in 1734, he conducted in Pesaro at least until autumn 1737 and composed two operas for Venice (1735, 1737). Between 1740 and 1746 he apparently stopped composing.

Pampani's acceptance as member of the Accademia Filarmonica of Bologna in 1746 marked a turning-point in his career. A considerable number of major works appeared during the ensuing decade. For the opera houses of Venice and major theatres of Rome, Milan and Turin he wrote an *opera seria* annually. The libretto for a revival in 1765 of his oratorio *L'innocenza rispettata* in Venice still identifies Pampani as *maestro* of the Ospedaletto, but in the following year Traetta directed an oratorio as the institution's new *maestro*. On 27 December 1767 Pampani was named *maestro di cappella* of Urbino Cathedral but was excused from duties until 1 July 1768 in order to supervise the production in May of *Demetrio*, his last opera for Venice. Gazzaniga assumed his position at Urbino in late December 1775, shortly after Pampani's death.

Almost nothing is known about Pampani's personal life. A certain Teresa Fortunata Pampino, who appeared in his first opera for Venice (*Anagilda*, 1735), may prove to be a relative, perhaps his wife.

opere serie unless otherwise stated

Delbo mal maritato (int), Pesaro, Sole, 1730
Anagilda (A. Zaniboni), Venice, S Cassiano, carn. 1735, *D-Wa*
Artaserse Longimani (P. Metastasio: *Temistocle*), Venice, S Angelo, carn. 1737
Siroe (?Metastasio), Ferrara, 1738 [?pasticcio]
La caduta d' Amulio (C. Gandini), Venice, S Angelo, carn. 1747
La clemenza di Tito (Metastasio), Venice, S Cassiano, carn. 1748, arias *F-Pn*
Artaserse (Metastasio), Venice, S Giovanni Grisostomo, carn. 1750, arias in *GB-Lbl, I-Vc* and *MAav*
Adriano in Siria (Metastasio), Milan, Regio Ducal, 26 Dec 1750
Venceslao (A. Zeno), Venice, S Cassiano, carn. 1752
Andromaca (os, A. Salvi), Rome, Argentina, carn. 1753, arias *GB-Lbl*, pasticcio, collab. Aurisicchio
Madama Dulcinea, o Tiberio cuoco del maestro del bosco (int), Pesaro, Sole, carn. 1753
Eurione (A. Papi), Rome, Capranica, 8 Jan 1754, arias *Lbl*
Astianatte (Salvi), Venice, S Moisè, carn. 1755, aria *I-MOe*

Artaserse (Metastasio), Venice, S Benedetto, carn. 1756
Antigono (Metastasio), Turin, Regio, 26 Dec 1756
Demofoonte (Metastasio), Rome, Dame, carn. 1757, *P-La*
L'olimpiade [Act 2] (Metastasio), Venice, S Benedetto, 26 Dec 1766, *P-La* [Act 1 by P. A. Guglielmi, Act 3 by Brusa]
Demetrio (Metastasio), Venice, S Benedetto, Ascension 1768, *La*

Insertion aria in Vivaldi's Rosmira fedele, Venice, 1738, *I-Tn*
Arias from unidentified operas in *D-B, Dlb, DS, Mbs, SWl; F-Pn; GB-Lbl, Lcm; I-A, Fc, MAav, MOe, Nc, Vc*

*

EitnerQ; FétisB
G. B. Martini: 'Serie cronologica dei principi dell'Accademia dei Filarmonici di Bologna', *Diario bolognese* (Bologna, 1776), 31
J.-B. de La Borde: *Essai sur la musique ancienne et moderne* (Paris, 1780), iii, 211
C. Baccili: *Il teatro di Fermo* (Recanati, 2/1886), 36
C. Cinelli: *Memorie cronistoriche del teatro di Pesaro* (Pesaro, 1898), 51, 53, 56
R. Paolucci: 'La cappella musicale del Duomo di Fano', *NA*, iii (1926), 130–31
SVEN HANSELL

Pampanini, Rosetta (*b* Milan, 2 Sept 1896; *d* Corbola, 2 Aug 1973). Italian soprano. A pupil of Emma Molajoli, she made her début in 1920 at the Teatro Nazionale, Rome, as Micaëla. She was then heard at the S Carlo, Naples (1923), at the Comunale, Bologna (1923–4), and at La Scala (1925) in *Madama Butterfly* under Toscanini; she sang there until 1930 and in 1934–7. She appeared at leading Italian theatres until 1943, at the Colón, Buenos Aires (1926), at Covent Garden (1928) in *Butterfly* and *Pagliacci* and as Liù (returning in 1929 and 1933), at the Berlin Städtische Oper (1929) and at the Paris Opéra (1935). Pampanini's pure, natural voice was warm and brilliant, with a strong, resonant top register; she was considered one of the world's leading Puccini sopranos between 1925 and 1940, partly because of the variety of colour and inflection she brought to Mimì, Butterfly and Manon, partly because of the grace and simplicity of her bearing. She was also admired in *Andrea Chénier*, *Iris* and *Tosca*.

*

GV (R. Celletti; R. Vegeto)   RODOLFO CELLETTI

Pamphili, Benedetto (*b* Rome, 25 April 1653; *d* Rome, 22 March 1730). Italian patron. His immense wealth was derived from a pension granted by his great-uncle, Pope Innocent X, and from the income produced by his election in 1678 as Roman Grand Prior of the Knights of Malta and in 1681 as a cardinal. Unlike Cardinal Ottoboni, he did not write any opera librettos or participate in public theatrical endeavours; his main contribution to opera was through his generous patronage of opera composers and performers. His academies featured the best musicians and the newest sacred and secular music in Rome, including works by Alessandro Scarlatti, Bernardo Pasquini, Carlo Francesco Cesarini and Handel. His musical performances were managed by Alessandro Melani from about 1676 to 1680, by G. L. Lulier from 1685 to 1690 and by C. F. Cesarini from 1690 onwards. Pamphili served from 1689 to 1730 as the Cardinal Protector of the Collegio Clementino, where two dramatic works (often spoken rather than sung and usually moralistic in nature) were produced during each carnival season. In the 1690s he also served as Cardinal Protector of the Oratorio del Santissimo Crocifisso di S Marcello, where oratorios in Latin were performed regularly during Lent. He wrote texts for at least two oratorios and presumably for many of the cantatas performed at his academies.

L. Zambarelli: *Il nobile pontificio Collegio Clementino di Roma* (Rome, 1936)
L. Montalto: *Un mecenate in Roma barocca: il Cardinale Benedetto Pamphili (1653–1730)* (Florence, 1955)
C. Annibaldi: 'L'archivio musicale Doria Pamphili: saggio sulla cultura aristocratica a Roma fra 16° e 19° secolo', *Studi musicali*, xi (1982), 91–120, 277–344
H. J. Marx: 'Die "Giustificazioni della Casa Pamphili" als musikgeschichtliche Quelle', *Studi musicali*, xii (1983), 145–61
LOWELL LINDGREN

Pandolfini, Angelica (*b* Spoleto, 21 Aug 1871; *d* Lenno, Como, 15 July 1959). Italian soprano. As the daughter of Francesco Pandolfini, she was brought up with a singing career in view, though she first studied the piano in Paris. She trained as a singer under Jules Massart and made her début in *Faust* at Modena in 1894. Later that year in Malta she became associated with the new *verismo* operas, and was soon known throughout Italy as an outstanding Mimì. 1897 brought her début at La Scala where, in 1902, she created the title role in Cilea's *Adriana Lecouvreur*. Her repertory also included Eva in *Die Meistersinger* (sung in Italian), Desdemona and the heroines of *La traviata* and *Aida*, both of which revealed weaknesses and presaged her early retirement in 1909. She made only five records, all extremely rare in their original form. Among them is Adriana's first aria, sung with tenderness and some endearing personal touches.

J. B. STEANE

Pandolfini, Francesco (*b* Termini Imerese, Palermo, 22 Nov 1833; *d* Milan, 15 Feb 1916). Italian baritone. He studied in Florence with Ronconi and made his début in 1859 at Pisa as the Count of Vergy in Donizetti's *Gemma di Vergy*. After singing in Genoa, Turin and Rome, in 1871 he was engaged at La Scala, where he sang Don Carlo (*La forza del destino*) and, in 1872, Amonasro in the first Italian performance of *Aida*. He created Arnoldo in Ponchielli's *I lituani* (1874). At Covent Garden in 1877 he sang Rigoletto, Antonio (*Linda di Chamounix*) and Ford (*Die lustigen Weiber von Windsor*), returning in 1882 for Nélusko and Amonasro. He sang at Monte Carlo (1884) as Alphonse (*La favorite*) and Valentin (*Faust*). In 1887 he was engaged at the S Carlo. His repertory included Severo (*Poliuto*), Alfonso (*Lucrezia Borgia*), Riccardo (*I puritani*), Thomas' Hamlet, Macbeth, Don Carlo (*Ernani*) and Alfio (*Cavalleria rusticana*), which he sang at his farewell in Rome (1890).   ELIZABETH FORBES

Panerai, Rolando (*b* Campi Bisenzio, nr Florence, 17 Oct 1924). Italian baritone. He studied in Florence and Milan, making his début in 1946 in Florence as Enrico Ashton (*Lucia di Lammermoor*). At Naples (1947–8) he sang Pharaoh (*Mosè in Egitto*), Luna, Germont and Rossini's Figaro. In 1951 he made his La Scala début as the High Priest (*Samson et Dalila*), returning as Enrico Ashton, Apollo (*Alceste*), the Husband (*Amelia al ballo*) and in the title role of *Mathis der Maler* (Italian première, 1957). In 1955 he created Ruprecht in the stage première of *The Fiery Angel* in Venice and sang Mozart's Figaro in Aix-en-Provence. He made his Salzburg début in 1957 as Ford, then sang Masetto, Paolo (*Boccanegra*) and Guglielmo. At San Francisco (1958) he sang both Figaros and Marcello. In 1962 he created the title role of Turchi's *Il buon soldato Svejk* (Milan). He has sung all over Italy, in Vienna, Munich, Paris and at the Metropolitan. His many recordings include Amfortas in a broadcast of *Parsifal* from Rome

(1950). Having made his Covent Garden début in 1960 as Rossini's Figaro, he returned in the 1980s as Don Alfonso, Don Pasquale, Falstaff and Dulcamara. He has a dark-toned, vibrant voice and incisive diction, and acts with panache. ALAN BLYTH

Paniagua y Vasques, Cenobio (*b* Tlalpujahua, Michoacán, 30 Oct 1821; *d* Córdoba, Veracruz, 2 Nov 1882). Mexican composer. After an early career as an orchestral violinist, he became the first Mexican to have an opera produced in the capital; he prided himself on having mastered his craft by studying an Italian translation of Reicha's *Cours de composition musicale*, sent to him from Paris in 1847. He had already, in 1845, completed two of the three acts of what was to be his passport to fame, *Catalina di Guisa*, to a libretto by Felice Romani. After improvements, he had a triumphant success with the opera, sung in Italian by a visiting company at the Teatro Principal, Mexico City, on 29 September 1859, the birthday of the president of Mexico, Miguel Miramón. The opera is set in France during the Huguenot wars and involves Catalina's supposed infidelity to her husband, the Duke of Guise. He kills her suspected lover, the Count of Megrino, lured to her chambers by a letter that she was forced to write by her jealous consort. At a later performance (10 November 1859) Paniagua's one-act comic skit in Spanish, *Una riña de aguadores*, was also performed. *Catalina* was repeated in the Teatro Principal on 27 June 1861 by a visiting troupe under Max Maretzek, and again as late as 18 November 1862. Maretzek warmly praised the opera and recalled it as late as 1890 as an example of excellence that composers in the USA could not duplicate.

Paniagua's second opera, *Pietro d'Albano*, to a libretto by Antonio Boni, had its première at the Teatro Principal on 5 May 1863 (the first anniversary of the defeat of the French invaders at Puebla) but was withdrawn after one performance. It was given by Paniagua's own opera company, founded in 1861 and composed exclusively of Mexican singers. The plot deals with a 14th-century Italian necromancer (sung at the première by Francisco Pineda) who, after recovering his daughter from her lover, is tortured to death for supposed dealings in the black arts. *Pietro d'Albano* was less successful than *Catalina* for two reasons: first, Paniagua gave his daughter Mariana, a less than first-rate soprano, one of the chief roles (Luisa); secondly, the French sympathizers in the capital who were opera patrons disliked the political implications of the première date.

Paniagua and members of his opera company left Mexico City and remained at Veracruz from June 1865 to November 1868. Thereafter the composer lived nearby at Córdoba, devoting himself chiefly to religious works. Always a partisan of Donizetti, he found *Aida* sung by Angela Peralta's company in the capital (which he revisited in 1877) admirable and sublime but too scientific for his own taste (see Revilla, p.234).

Before 1908, the autograph vocal scores of his two operas were held by the diplomat and art historian Manuel G. Revilla (1863–1924). *Catalina di Guisa* has had more performances in Mexico than any subsequent opera by a Mexican composer.

Inspired by their teacher's success, five of Paniagua's pupils each wrote an opera, four to Italian librettos and one to a Spanish libretto. Although only Antonio Valle and Melesio Morales succeeded in having their operas produced, Paniagua nevertheless established a school of Mexican opera composers.

M. Maretzek: *Sharps and Flats* (New York, 1890), 53–4
E. de Olavarria y Ferrari: *Reseña histórica del teatro en México* (Mexico City, 1895, 3/1961)
M. G. Revilla: '[Don] Cenobio Paniagua', *Revista musical mexicana*, ii (1942), 178–252
R. Stevenson: *Music in Mexico: a Historical Survey* (New York, 1952, 2/1971), 196–7 ROBERT STEVENSON

Panizza, Héctor [Ettore] (*b* Buenos Aires, 12 Aug 1875; *d* Milan, 27 Nov 1967). Argentine conductor and composer. The son of Giovanni Grazioso Panizza (1851–1903), an Italian cellist and composer who settled in Argentina, he began his musical studies with his father and continued them in Italy, at the Milan Conservatory (1887–91, 1895–8), graduating as a pianist and composer. While still a student he composed a dramatic sketch *Il fidanzato del mare*, which he conducted at the conservatory and later had performed in Buenos Aires under Mascheroni (1897). His next lyrical work, *Medioevo latino*, a triptych to a libretto by Luigi Illica, was given in Genoa in 1900 and 1905, and in Buenos Aires in 1901, conducted by Toscanini. By the time he had completed *Aurora* (1907), a dramatic story on a heroic national theme, his work as a composer had become secondary to his conducting activities. He had first conducted French operettas at the Teatro Odeón in Buenos Aires in about 1892. As a student in Milan he conducted the conservatory orchestra, and in 1898 he was substitute conductor at the Teatro Costanzi in Rome for Mascheroni, whom he subsequently replaced. From this followed a gradually but continuously increasing career as conductor, which took him to all the important opera houses in Italy, Europe and America. His first appearance at Covent Garden was in 1907, and he conducted there for eight seasons. At La Scala in 1916 his conducting was greatly admired by Toscanini, who engaged him as assistant between 1921 and 1931. In 1933 he succeeded Serafin in charge of the Italian repertory at the Metropolitan Opera, where he remained until 1941. Meanwhile, in Buenos Aires in 1939 he conducted the first performance of his opera *Bizancio*, a mature work based on a four-act opera composed between 1901 and 1904 and reworked in 1937–8. The story is set in the capital of the Eastern empire during the years of its decline, the libretto being based on the novel *Théodore et Bizance* by Auguste Bailly. An autobiographical essay by Panizza, *Medio siglo de via musical*, was published in 1952.

See also AURORA.

Il fidanzato del mare (R. Carugati), Milan, Conservatory, 1897
Medioevo latino (triptych, L. Illica), Genoa, Politeama Genovese, 1900
Aurora (3, H. Quesada and Illica), Buenos Aires, Colón, 1908, vs in Sp. (Buenos Aires, 1945)
Bizancio (3 with int, G. Macchi, after A. Bailly), Buenos Aires, Colón, 1939

E. de la Guardia and R. Herrera: *El arte lírico en el Teatro Colón: con motivo de las Bodas de Plata (1908–1933)* (Buenos Aires, 1933)
C. J. Luten: 'The Impassioned Argentine', *ON*, xxxviii/14 (1973–4), 26–7 CARLOS SUFFERN

Pannain, Guido (*b* Naples, 17 Nov 1891; *d* Naples, 6 Sept 1977). Italian musicologist and composer. He was taught the piano by his father Edoardo and counterpoint by his grandfather Antonio, finishing his studies at the Naples Conservatory under Camillo de Nardis. He graduated in arts at Naples University (1914) and taught at the Naples Conservatory (1915–47). He contributed to various daily newspapers and to numerous specialized periodicals. His activity as a music critic was influenced by Crocean aesthetic ideas, expressing conservative convictions. His output for the theatre includes *L'intrusa* (1926), an early experimental work; in contrast, the operas *Beatrice Cenci* (1942) and *Madame Bovary* (1955) look to the Italian tradition of the late 19th century, essentially reiterating the forms and melodies of realist opera.

L'intrusa, 1926 (1, R. Giani, after M. Maeterlinck), Genoa, Carlo Felice, 15 Feb 1940; rev. version, Milan, 1940
Capri, 1930–31 (mimodramma), unperf.
Il sogno di Agnese, 1935 (mimodramma, R. Forges Davanzati), unperf.
Beatrice Cenci (3, V. Viviani), Naples, S Carlo, 21 Feb 1942
Madame Bovary (3, Pannain and Viviani, after G. Flaubert), Naples, S Carlo, 17 April 1955

WRITINGS
Da Monteverdi a Wagner (Milan, 1955)
L'opera e le opere (Milan, 1958)
Giuseppe Verdi (Turin, 1964)
Richard Wagner: vita di un artista (Milan, 1964)
Saggi wagneriani (Venice, 1968)
Introduzione al teatro di Riccardo Wagner (Venice, 1971)

RAFFAELE POZZI

Pannell, Raymond (*b* London, Ont., 25 Jan 1935). Canadian composer and pianist. He studied the piano with Edward Steuermann and composition with Bernard Wagenaar and Vittorio Giannini at the Juilliard School of Music, then returned to Canada to teach at the Royal Conservatory of Music of Toronto in 1959. From 1966 he directed an opera workshop at the Stratford Festival, Ontario. In 1968 he was appointed assistant director and resident conductor of the Atlanta Municipal Theater, and in 1969 he became director of the Youth Experimental Opera Workshop, which was chosen to represent the USA in the simultaneous television broadcast celebrating the 25th anniversary of UNICEF. He returned to Canada in 1970, and in 1975 was co-founder and general director of the Co-Opera Theatre in Toronto. He received the Governor General's Jubilee Medal in 1977.

Music for the stage makes up the bulk of Pannell's output. As well as operas he has written incidental music for several Stratford Festival productions, in a variety of styles ranging from serial procedures through sparse atonality to lush chromaticism and use of electronic means. The influence of American composers such as Bernstein, Copland and Roy Harris is reflected in *The Luck of Ginger Coffey* (1967), commissioned by the Canadian Opera Company for the country's centenary celebrations. *Exiles* (1973) is an experimental work without conductor, combining instrumental and electronic music, improvisation, poetry and photography. *Aberfan*, commissioned for CBC Television, won the Salzburg Television Opera Prize in 1977; it was commended for its economy of means (both in production and in composition) and for the impact of its emotional intensity. Pannell's juxtaposition of different styles within one opera is deliberate, reflecting his view that 'our lives are not musically seen in one palette'. *Push* (1976), produced by the Co-Opera Theatre, is an improvisatory work in which the singers create their own lines and intercut the characters of Osip Mandelstam and Ezra Pound.

librettos by the composer unless otherwise stated

Aria da Capo (1, E. St Vincent Millay), Hart House, U. of Toronto, 5 April 1963
The Luck of Ginger Coffey (3, R. Hambleton, after B. Moore), Toronto, O'Keefe Centre, 15 Sept 1967
Exiles (1, with B. Pannell), Stratford, Ont., 15 Aug 1973
Go (children's op, 1), 1975
Midway, 1975
Push (developmental op, 1, after O. E. Mandelstam and E. Pound), Toronto, St Lawrence Hall, 31 March 1976
Circe (masque, 1, M. Atwood), Toronto, Co-Opera, 9 April 1977
Aberfan (video op, 1, with B. Pannell), CBC, 1977
N-E-U-S (radio op, 1), 1977
Souvenirs (1, B. Pannell), Toronto, Toronto Free, 24 April 1979
Refugees (vaudeville op, 2), Toronto, Co-Opera, 25 Oct 1979; rev. as As Long as a Child Remembers (music-theatre work, 2), Little Rock, AR, Arkansas Opera, 10 April 1986
The Downsview Anniversary Song-Spectacle Celebration Pageant, Toronto, Downsview School, 1979
Harvest (television op, 1), CBC, 1980
The Forbidden Christmas (musical, 2, with Atwood), completed 1990

*

R. Pannell: 'Aria da Capo', *OC*, iv/1 (1963), 5–6
B. Marshall: 'Raymond Pannell', *OC*, v/4 (1964), 17–18
M. Shulman: 'Opera goes Co-op with Raymond Pannell', *Canadian Composer*, no.105 (1975), 25–6

GAYNOR G. JONES

Panofka, Heinrich (*b* Breslau, 3 Oct 1807; *d* Florence, 18 Nov 1887). Silesian singing teacher, violinist, composer and critic. He studied singing with the Kantors Strauch and Förster, and learnt the violin with Joseph Mayseder. His initial career was as a violinist. About 1834 he settled in Paris, as a performer, critic and composer, and editor of and contributor to the new *Gazette et revue musicale*; he was also a correspondent for the *Neue Zeitschrift für Musik*. He was a prolific composer for the violin and of solo songs. After 1840 Panofka's interest turned towards the art and techniques of the great singers he heard in Paris. He studied the methods of Marco Bordogni, and went to London in 1847 and directed the chorus of the Italian Opera under Lumley. He met Jenny Lind there and studied her vocal techniques, as well as those of Lablache, Fraschini and Staudigl. In London he was esteemed more as a singing teacher than as a violinist. His first didactic work, the *Practical Singing Tutor* (London, 1852), was published shortly before he returned to Paris, and his *L'art de chanter* op.81 (Paris, 1854) brought him fame which he could never have achieved as a violinist or a composer. His *Abécédaire vocal* (Paris, 1858), intended for beginners, was equally successful and innovatory, by-passing the interminable *solfège* exercises found in other singing tutors of the time. The *Voix et chanteurs* (Paris, c1870), which includes biographical notices of famous contemporary singers, is the product of Panofka's stay in Florence in the late 1860s. Panofka's vocal studies were enormously influential in Europe and America during the second half of the 19th century. They still provide useful practice material; the *Vademecum du chanteur* (the second part of *L'art de chanter*) and two sets of vocalises (opp.85–6) are available in modern editions.

*

ADB (R. Eitner); *DEUMM* (P. Mioli)
F. Pazdírek: *Universal-Handbuch der Musikliteratur* (Vienna, 1904–10) [with list of published works]

ALBERT MELL/R

Panseron, Auguste (Mathieu) (*b* Paris, 26 April 1796; *d* Paris, 29 July 1859). French composer and singing teacher. He studied at the Paris Conservatoire with Berton and Gossec, and won the Prix de Rome in 1813.

After travels throughout Europe he returned to Paris, where he became an accompanist at the Opéra-Comique. His three *opéras comiques* were successful at the time, but Panseron is best remembered as the author of several collections of vocal exercises, which remained in use throughout the 19th century.

La grille du parc (oc, 1, M. J. Pain, J. Ancelot and Audebert), Paris, OC (Feydeau), 9 Sept 1820 (Paris, ?1820)

Le mariage difficile, ou Les deux cousines (oc, 1, Rousseau and Ménard), Paris, OC (Feydeau), 19 Feb 1823

L'école de Rome (oc, 1, Lassagne, Rochefort and A. Vulpian), Paris, Odéon, 4 Nov 1826

Pantaleoni, Adriano (*b* Sebenico [now Šibenik, Croatia], 7 Oct 1837; *d* Udine, 18 Dec 1908). Italian baritone, brother of Romilda Pantaleoni. He studied at Udine and Milan. In 1869 he was engaged at the Teatro Apollo, Rome, the following season in Genoa. From 1871 he sang regularly at La Scala. His repertory of over 50 roles included Donizetti's Belisarius, Marin Faliero, Alphonse (*La favorite*) and Enrico Ashton (*Lucia di Lammermoor*), as well as Verdi's Rigoletto, Don Carlo (*La forza del destino*), Germont and Amonasro. He was also a notable Escamillo.   ELIZABETH FORBES

Pantaleoni, Romilda (*b* Udine, 1847; *d* Milan, 20 May 1917). Italian soprano. She studied in Milan, making her début there in 1868 at the Teatro Carcano in Foroni's *Margherita*. After singing in Rome, Genoa, Modena, Naples, Turin, Vienna and Brescia, in 1883 she made her début at La Scala as La Gioconda. She sang Anna in the first Milan performance of Puccini's *Le villi* (1884) and created the title role in Ponchielli's *Marion Delorme* (1885). She sang Desdemona in the first performance of Verdi's *Otello* (1887) and created Tigrana in Puccini's *Edgar*. Her repertory included Mathilde (*Guillaume Tell*), Paolina (*Poliuto*), Valentine (*Les Huguenots*), Sélika (*L'Africaine*), Marguerite (*Faust*) and Margherita (*Mefistofele*), as well as many Verdi roles: Leonora (*Il trovatore* and *La forza del destino*), Amelia (*Un ballo in maschera*), Elisabeth de Valois (*Don Carlos*) and Aida. She also sang Santuzza and Elsa. A magnificent singing actress, she retired in 1891 after the death of the conductor Franco Faccio, with whom she had a liaison.   ELIZABETH FORBES

Pantheon. London exhibition hall, built in 1772 and converted into an opera house in 1790–91; *see* LONDON, §§I, 7 and II, 2.

Pantomime (from Gk. *pantomimos*: 'one who does everything by imitation'). The Latin *pantomimus* originally referred to a Roman actor who specialized in dumb show, supported by instrumental music and chorus; by extension the word denotes a dramatic representation in dumb show. Normal modern English usage is confined to a theatrical entertainment, usually presented in the Christmas season, which, while no longer in dumb show, continues to use music and other spectacular elements to support a children's tale that is often no more than a flimsy backcloth for buffoonery, dancing, topical songs and allusions and, until comparatively recent times, a harlequinade.

Pantomime was made fashionable in Rome in 22 BC by Pylades of Cilicia and Bathyllus of Alexandria. According to Macrobius (*Saturnalia*, ii, 7), Pylades introduced instruments and chorus; Bathyllus seems to have specialized in light, satyric themes while Pylades

was in style closer to tragedy. Pantomime usually took its subject matter from mythology, history and the themes of tragic drama; unlike straight mime, it was not coarse. The performance took place in public or private. The *pantomimus*, sometimes supported by a speaking actor, wore a graceful silk costume and a fine mask with closed lips; chorus and instrumentalists stood behind him. He sometimes appeared in as many as five roles in turn. There are tributes to the eloquence and directness of a dancer who could undertake to retell a whole tale with several parts and to the expressiveness of a performer whose powers of mime, Lucian wrote, were rich enough to overcome the language barrier for a foreign visitor (a similar tribute was paid to 'Kasperl' Laroche – himself originally a dancer – in Vienna at the beginning of the 19th century, by a Turkish minister who, largely ignorant of German, claimed to understand what Laroche was saying; see *Ueberblick des Ueberblicks des neuesten Zustandes der Literatur des Theaters und des Geschmacks in Wien*, by C** X**, 1802, p.78).

The use of steps, posture and especially gesture was aided by conventions not unlike those of modern ballet. The role of the songs seems to have been minor. Pantomime became a highly popular entertainment, important in its effects on morality (especially after females began to appear) and even politically – the historian Zosimus attributed the moral decline of Rome to the popularity of the *pantomimi*.

The renewal of interest in ancient forms of drama during the Renaissance led to the birth of various kinds of pantomime. The traditional British pantomime has its origins in the *commedia dell'arte*, in modified forms that became established north of the Alps, above all in Paris. From the beginning of the 18th century, when the earliest known pantomimes appeared on the London stage, until the early 20th, the genre developed along fairly consistent lines. More recently, changes in taste and the influence of modern forms of mass entertainment banished the harlequinade from the pantomime, leaving vestiges of its old character in the acrobatic antics of comic actors, but little else beyond its traditional name.

The English pantomime was a mixed-medium entertainment, not unlike the contemporary intermezzos performed between the acts of serious operas. The same composers and singers were employed for pantomimes as for operas. Between the sung numbers were short instrumental pieces ('comic turns') during which the action was mimed. Dialogue was not introduced until late in the 18th century. The subjects were usually mythological or based on exotic legends; extravagant stage effects were an important element. Whether or not one accepts John Weaver's claim that his *The Tavern Bilkers* (1702, Drury Lane) or his *The Loves of Mars and Venus* (1717, Drury Lane) was the first pantomime, the genre was slow to take root. It was John Rich who established it; he managed the Lincoln's Inn Fields theatre, and regularly performed the part of Harlequin. When David Garrick took over Drury Lane, he tried to suppress pantomime; however, he enjoyed great success with the pantomimes staged for him by his Harlequin, Henry Woodward, and even persuaded the ballet-master Noverre to come from Paris with his ensemble to take part in *Les fêtes chinoises* (8 November 1755). Noverre was sufficiently impressed by Garrick and by the miming of his London company to adopt English stylistic features in his *ballet d'action*.

In time, the pantomime changed in character, becoming a more fully integrated comic play, the characters and action of which were close to the stock elements of the Italian comedy, with young lovers and their resourceful servants outwitting jealous parents and guardians, often with supernatural assistance. Vocal music dominated, and some of the leading composers provided scores (J. E. Galliard and Pepusch in the early years; later the Arnes, Boyce, the elder Thomas Linley, Shield, Dibdin and others). Instrumental music accompanied the elaborate transformation scenes, though as the emphasis shifted towards the spectacular elements of the age of the British melodrama, reputable musicians more rarely wrote pantomime scores. In the 20th century, popular songs of the moment are introduced without relevance or apology; under the influence of the music hall and variety turn little remains but the name and the framework of a moral fairytale.

On the Continent too the pantomime was popular in the 18th and 19th centuries, though it varied widely between different centres and periods. In France, where Noverre demonstrated the virtues of Garrick's realistic approach to stage characterization, it tended to be a dignified danced entertainment. Rousseau's *Dictionnaire de la musique* (1768) defines it as an 'Air to which two or more dancers execute an action (which is itself also known under the same term). The pantomime airs ... speak, as it were, and form images, in the situations in which the dancer is to put on a particular expression'. The French tradition of pantomimic scenes and characters in the lyric theatre lived on in the famous mute title role of Auber's *La muette de Portici* (or *Masaniello*; 1828); and though Wagner (who greatly admired *La muette*) had completed the second act of *Rienzi* before he moved to Paris in autumn 1839 the ballet sequence in that act is often referred to as a pantomime, because of the thematic and even dramatic relevance of the dances to the story. Adam's *La poupée de Nuremberg* (1852) and the Olympia act of Offenbach's *Les contes d'Hoffmann* (1881) contain important pantomimic elements. Wagner may be held to have written the most successful of all pantomimic scenes in opera, in Act 3 of *Die Meistersinger von Nürnberg*, where Beckmesser, painfully reminded of his beating of the night before, finds and misappropriates Walther's Prize Song when he visits Sachs's temporarily deserted workshop.

There was a strong pantomime tradition in 18th-century Vienna, where the presence of a vital popular theatre (including native elements, above all the characters of Hanswurst and Bernardon, and elements derived from the *commedia dell'arte*, such as Harlequin, Pantaloon and Columbine) was combined with a marked south German tendency to use music in the theatre. The appellation 'Pantomime' was used in Vienna at least as early as the 1720s. Among authors of pantomime scenarios Kurz-Bernardon is the most important, and Haydn's lost music for Kurz's *Der neue krumme Teufel* (*c*1758) includes a pantomime, *Arlequin der neue Abgott Ram in America*. Mozart gave a pantomime of his own composition (K446/416*d*; only a fragment survives) at a public rout during Carnival 1783 (see his letter to his father, 12 March 1783). The pantomime tradition continued strongly in Vienna roughly until the advent of the operetta; elements of its more elevated aspect live on in the Kessler-Richard Strauss collaboration *Josephs-Legende* (1912).

J. Weaver: *The History of the Mimes and Pantomimes* (London, 1728)

C. Cibber: *An Apology for the Life of Mr Colley Cibber* (London, 1740)

[J. C. Strodtmann]: *Abhandlung von den Pantomimen* (Hamburg, 1749)

R. M. Haas: 'Die Wiener Ballet-Pantomime im 18. Jahrhundert und Glucks *Don Juan*', *SMw*, x (1923), 3–36

W. Beare: 'Pantomimus', *The Oxford Classical Dictionary* (Oxford, 1949, 2/1970)

P. Hartnoll, ed.: *The Oxford Companion to the Theatre* (London, 1951), 598ff

A. Nicoll: *Early Eighteenth Century Drama* (London, 1955)

——: *The World of Harlequin* (Cambridge, 1963)

R. J. Broadbent: *A History of Pantomime* (New York, 1964)

E. Stadler: 'Das abendländische Theater im Altertum und im Mittelalter', *Das Atlantisbuch des Theaters*, ed. M. Hürlimann (Zürich and Freiburg, 1966), esp. 512ff

A. M. Heiss: *Die Pantomime im Alt-Wiener Volkstheater* (diss., U. of Vienna, 1969)

R. Fiske: *English Theatre Music in the Eighteenth Century* (London, 1973, 2/1986)

H. Lagrave: 'La pantomime à la Foire, au Théâtre-Italien et aux Boulevards (1700–1789)', *Romanistische Zeitung für Literaturgeschichte*, lxxix (1980), 408–30   PETER BRANSCOMBE

Pantomime ballet. *See* BALLET D'ACTION.

Pan Voyevoda. Opera in four acts by NIKOLAY ANDREYEVICH RIMSKY-KORSAKOV to a libretto by Il'ya Fyodorovich Tyumenev; St Petersburg Conservatory (Prince Alexey Akakiyevich Tsereteli's New Opera troupe), 3/16 October 1904.

This unfortunate opera stands as a cautionary example of what happens when the decorative tail is allowed to wag the dramatic dog. In his autobiography Rimsky-Korsakov attributed his impulse to write it to a wish to pay tribute to Chopin and to use some Polish melodies that had haunted him ever since childhood. He commissioned a libretto from a former pupil who had become a travel writer, specifying that it be set in 16th- or 17th-century Poland (where local authority rested with military commanders called *voyevodas*), that it not have 'political colouring' (Poland being a touchy subject to the Russian censorship) and that the fantastic element be soft-pedalled or eliminated. Tyumenev came up with a trite amalgam of thwarted love, petty tyranny o'erthrown, poison and revenge. The poison, intended for a romantic rival and supplied by an evil wizard, was a leftover from Tyumenev's own contribution to the *Tsar's Bride* libretto.

Rimsky's music, the product of a fatigued imagination temporarily fallen back on well-practised routine and cliché, was well matched to the libretto. The première was conducted by Václav Suk, with Mariya Insarova in the *ingénue* role of Mariya. The opera had three productions in the first year of its stage career (the second in Warsaw, the third at the Moscow Bol'shoy under Rakhmaninov); together they reached 18 performances. It has since been mounted only in Soviet provincial houses and conservatory opera workshops. A concert suite op.59 consists of the opera's introduction, a Nocturne and three dances, which resemble Glinka far more than they do Chopin. The heroine's Song of the Dying Swan (Act 3) is occasionally revived.

RICHARD TARUSKIN

Pan y toros ('Bread and Bulls'). Zarzuela in three acts by FRANCISCO ASENJO BARBIERI to a libretto by José Picon; Madrid, Teatro de la Zarzuela, 22 December 1864.

The somewhat involved action, in which various historical characters – including Goya (bass) – appear, takes place among the Madrid lower classes and bullfighters, during the political intrigues of the reign of Carlos IV. His prime minister, Godoy, has concealed from him the news of his army's reverses in countering the French Revolution (reference to which is immediately made by the quotation of the *Marseillaise* in the overture). The liberal Princess de Luzán (soprano), a patroness of the arts, is anxious to open the King's eyes to the situation, but a group of Godoy's supporters is intent on discrediting and silencing her. Her thoughts of entering a convent, abandoned on falling in love with a young captain wounded in the war (baritone), are renewed – to the delight of the conspirators – when he is believed to have been killed by an assassin they had hired to keep his dispatches from reaching the King. The victim, however, was in fact a beggar to whom the captain had generously given his cloak; so the princess and he are happily reunited, and the King, on learning the true state of affairs, dismisses the hated Godoy. The chief musical numbers are the seguidillas 'Aunque soy de la Mancha' and the soprano romance 'Este santo escapulario'. LIONEL SALTER

Panzacchi [Pansacchi], **Domenico** (*b* Bologna, *c*1730; *d* Bologna, 1805). Italian tenor. He is said to have been a pupil of Bernacchi and sang in *opera seria* from 1746, in 1748–9 in Vienna, where he first worked with Raaff, who was to overshadow him in parts of his later career. In 1751–7 he was at Madrid (Raaff arriving at a higher salary in 1755) and from 1760 until his pensioning in 1782 in the service of the Munich court (which Raaff joined after 1778), with occasional operatic engagements in Italy. He is remembered for creating Arbaces in *Idomeneo* (1781), Mozart finding his singing and acting still worthy of respect in spite of his age. DENNIS LIBBY

Paoli, Antonio [Marcano, Antonio Emilio Paoli] (*b* Ponce, 14 April 1871; *d* San Juan, 24 Aug 1946). Puerto Rican tenor. Encouraged by his elder sister Amalia, a singer active in Spain, he studied in Madrid and Milan. During his early career (and while studying singing in Milan), he adopted the name Ermogene Imleghi Bascarán. He made his début in Paris as Arnold in *Guillaume Tell* (1899) and developed a career as a dramatic tenor in the tradition of Tamagno. Paoli toured with a company headed by Mascagni in 1902, singing in Chicago and New York. Following his début as Otello in Madrid (1905), he sang that role some 570 times; he had also given, by the end of his career, 425 performances of Manrico. Other important appearances were at the new Teatro Colón, Buenos Aires, in 1908, and at La Scala as Samson in 1909–10. His many recordings include excerpts from *Pagliacci*, under the direction of Leoncavallo (1907). He occasionally performed in Puerto Rico during his tours of North and South America, and retired there in the early 1920s; his last public appearances were in San Juan in 1928 as Manrico and Otello with a visiting New York company. In such roles as Samson, Canio and Otello he contributed to the development of a true dramatic tenor style of characterization as distinct from that of the 'elevated baritone'.

GV (R.Celletti; R. Vegeto)
J. López, E. Arnosi and L. Alvarado: 'Antonio Paoli', *Record Collector*, xxii (1974–5), 5 [with discography by J. Dennis]
DONALD THOMPSON

Paolis, Alessio de. *See* DE PAOLIS, ALESSIO.

Papandopulo, Boris (*b* Honnef, Germany, 25 Feb 1906; *d* Zagreb, 16 Oct 1991). Croatian composer. He studied composition with Bersa at the Zagreb Academy of Music and conducting in Vienna. Afterwards he made his career as an opera and choral conductor in Zagreb, Rijeka (where he was director of the Opera from 1953 to 1959), Sarajevo and Split. When he started composing he declared himself to be a follower of the national style, but he was one of the first Yugoslav composers to take an interest in neo-classicism. However, he quickly found a means of synthesizing such techniques with the rhythms and melodies of folksong. Papandopulo employed different styles almost concurrently. A prolific composer, he wrote important works for the stage: among his operas, the musical drama *Rona* portrays an impressive true story of the lives of beggars; the vocal expression is concentrated in flexible declamation, and comments on the drama are suggested by the varied symphonic orchestration. His dramatic output also includes musical comedies, ballets, melodramas, incidental music and music for children's plays.

Amfitrion, 1936 (comic op, M. Štimac and E. Golisciani, after Molière), Zagreb, 17 Feb 1940
Sunčanica [The Sun Girl], 1934–5 (romantic op, 3, M. Šoljačić, after J. Gundulić), Zagreb, 13 June 1942
Rona, 1955 (3, F. Delak, after A. Leskovac), Rijeka, 25 May 1955
Marulova pisan [Marul's Song] (solemn musical play, V. Rabadan), Split, 15 Aug 1970
Madame Buffault, 1971 (fantastic op, P. Strunck), unperf.
Kentervilski duh [The Canterville Ghost] (comic op, N. Turkalj, after O. Wilde), Osijek, 5 June 1979
Požar u operi [Fire in the Opera] (comic op, F. Hadžić), Zagreb, 12 April 1983

*

K. Kovačević: *Hrvatski kompozitori i njihova djela* [Croatian Composers and their Works] (Zagreb, 1960), 358–81
I. Supičić: 'Estetski pogledi u novijoj hrvatskoj muzici: pregled temeljnih gledanja četrnaestorice kompozitora' [Aesthetic Approaches in Contemporary Croatian Music: a Survey of the Views of 14 Composers], *Arti musices*, i (1969), 23–61
J. Andreis: *Music in Croatia* (Zagreb, 1974), 326–9
A. Petrušić: 'Boris Papandopulo kao operni kompozitor s posebnom analizom opere *Kentervilski duh*' [Boris Papandopulo as Opera Composer, with Particular Analysis of *Kentervilski duh*], *Zvuk* (1980), no.4, pp.56–63
KREŠIMIR KOVAČEVIĆ/KORALJKA KOS

Papavoine [first name unknown] (*b* ?Normandy, *c*1720; *d* ?Marseilles, 1793). French composer. His first names may have been Louis-Auguste. He is first mentioned early in 1752 as a violinist of the Académie de Musique, Rouen, though he apparently lived in Paris. About 1754 he married Mlle Pellecier, a musician and composer. From 1760 to 1762 he was chief of the second violins in the orchestra of the Comédie-Italienne, for which he composed the *comédie mêlée d'ariettes Barbacole* and the *opéra comique Le vieux coquet*. About 1767 he joined N.-M. Audinot in forming the Théâtre de l'Ambigu-Comique, devoted primarily to marionette and pantomime productions with music. He was attached to that theatre as late as 1789. In the *Almanach des spectacles* for 1790 he is listed among the living composers, and according to Gerber he was in that year orchestra director and first violinist at the Marseilles Opera.

Most of Papavoine's compositions are lost; they included music for many plays and pantomimes performed at the Ambigu-Comique, symphonies and chamber works.

all performed in Paris; music unpublished and lost

Barbacole, ou Le manuscrit volé (cmda, 1, A.-J. Labbet de Morambert, J. de Lagrange and A.-F. Sticotti), Comédie-Italienne (Hôtel de Bourgogne), 15 Sept 1760, lib. *F-Pn*

Le vieux coquet, ou Les deux amies (oc, 3, A. Bret, after W. Shakespeare: *The Merry Wives of Windsor*), Comédie-Italienne (Hôtel de Bourgogne), 7 Sept 1761; also known as Les deux amies, ou Le vieux garçon

Le répertoire (comédie, 1, J.-F. Mussot [Arnould]), Ambigu-Comique, 1771

Zélie (pièce mêlée de musique), Ambigu-Comique, 1775

Also music for a large number of plays and pantomimes at Ambigu-Comique, incl. Alceste, ou La force de l'amour et l'amitié, Les filets de Vulcain, Le fort pris d'assaut, La curiosité punie, Le magicien de village, ou L'âne perdu et retrouvé

*

Almanach des spectacles (Paris, 1791)

E. G. J. Gregoir: *Documents historiques relatifs à l'art musical et aux artistes-musiciens*, i–iv (Brussels, 1872–6)

——: *Panthéon musical populaire*, iii (Brussels, 1876–7), 60

——: *Souvenirs artistiques*, i–iii (Brussels, 1888–9)

BARRY S. BROOK, RICHARD VIANO

Papi, Gennaro (*b* Naples, 11 Dec 1886; *d* New York, 29 Nov 1941). American conductor. A child prodigy, he studied the piano, organ, violin and theory at the Naples Conservatory. He was engaged as a chorus master at San Severo (1906), Warsaw (1909–10), Turin and Covent Garden (1911), and conducted his first opera, *La traviata*, at Milan in 1910. He was Toscanini's assistant, first on a tour of Argentina (1912), then at the Metropolitan (1913–15), and conducted *Rigoletto* on tour in Atlanta in 1915. Between 1916 and 1931 he appeared regularly at the Ravinia Park festivals in Chicago. After leaving the Metropolitan in 1932, he conducted in St Louis, San Francisco and Mexico, with the touring Scotti Opera, and with the reorganized Chicago Opera in 1934. The Metropolitan again engaged him in 1935. His conducting was sometimes criticized as lethargic; like Toscanini he always conducted from memory.

CHARLES JAHANT

Papillon de la Ferté, Denis Pierre Jean (*b* Châlons-sur-Marne, 18 Feb 1725; *d* Paris, 7 July 1794). French administrator. He was the son of Pierre Papillon, president-treasurer of France 'de la généralité de Champagne' at Châlons-sur-Marne. In the mid-1740s Papillon moved to Paris, where he completed his law studies. He bought the three official positions of *intendant-contrôler de l'argenterie* (1756), *menus-plaisirs* (1762) and *affaires de la chambre du roi* (1762). Until 1760 the *intendant* had no control over the two Comédies, but Papillon obtained management of the Comédie-Italienne in 1760 and of the Comédie-Française in 1762. In 1773 he was appointed *intendant de l'Ordre royal et militaire de St Louis*. At the king's request Papillon assisted in the reorganization of the Opéra in 1776. Although this position lasted only one year, his efforts were so successful that he obtained the supervisory direction of the Opéra (1780–90), as well as direction of the Ecole Royale de Chant (the forerunner of the Paris Conservatoire) from its establishment in 1784 until 1790.

The Opéra was at this time in financial trouble, and further difficulties arose from the discontented artists. In 1790 they demanded reforms in a pamphlet, to which Papillon published a reply. As *intendant des menus-plaisirs*, Papillon was responsible for all royal ceremonies including the coronation of Louis XVI; his journal covering the years 1756–80 was published in Paris in 1887 (ed. E. Boysse) and offers valuable insights into the court's operatic life. Papillon was, for example, in frequent conflict with Marie Antoinette over the cost of meeting her extravagant tastes, and in particular her generous payments to singers and musicians which he felt encouraged an over-familiarity. She, in turn, rebuked him on one occasion for his manners towards the librettist Sedaine. During the Revolution Papillon was guillotined; his autobiographical note written in prison on the eve of his death is reproduced in Jullien (1876).

*

A. Jullien: *Un potentat musical: Papillon de la Ferté: son règne à l'Opéra de 1780 à 1790* (Paris, 1876)

J. G. Prod'homme and E. de Crauzat: *Les Menus plaisirs du roi* (Paris, 1929)

M. Barthélemy: 'Les règlements de 1776 et l'Académie royale de musique', *RMFC*, iv (1964), 239–48

ETHYL L. WILL/ELISABETH COOK

Pappenheim, Marie (*b* Pressburg [now Bratislava], 1882; *d* Vienna, 1966). Austro-Hungarian writer and librettist. She came from a prosperous Jewish family and studied medicine, qualifying as a specialist in skin diseases in 1910. She married a psychiatrist, Hermann Frischauf. A convinced socialist by 1930, she joined the outlawed Austrian communist party but emigrated to Paris before the Anschluss and escaped to Mexico in 1940. In 1947 she returned to Vienna, where she continued to practise medicine until 1952.

As early as 1906 Pappenheim had published verses in Karl Kraus's journal *Die Fackel*. Her importance in music is as the librettist of Schoenberg's monodrama *Erwartung* (1909). After this collaboration she remained in touch with Schoenberg's circle. She published a novel (1946) and a volume of poetry (1962).

*

E. Weissweiler: '"Schreiben Sie mir doch einen Operntext, Fräulein!": Marie Pappenheims Text zu Arnold Schönbergs "Erwartung"', *NZM*, Jg.145 (1984), no.6, pp.4–8

O. W. NEIGHBOUR

Parać, Ivo (*b* Split, 24 June 1890; *d* Split, 4 Dec 1954). Croatian composer. As a child he acquired a love for Italian art and culture, which was strengthened during his studies in Florence, Rome and Pesaro between 1909 and 1923. He also studied privately with Pizzetti and Alaleona. After returning to Split he taught briefly in Belgrade; from 1925 until his death (which occurred on the day of the Split première of his only opera) he lived in Split, conducting and teaching (from 1948) at the music school. Parać's post-Romantic, lyrical musical language grew out of the Italian tradition, although he never used the typical Italian bel canto style. After 1924 his work underwent a change: he discovered the national Croatian tradition and tried to include elements of it in his own musical idiom. His artistic interest was nevertheless always focussed on vocal forms. His opera, *Adelova pjesma* ('Adel's Song'; 3, epilogue, V. Desnica, after L. Botić; Zagreb, 7 June 1941; revised 1951), composed on the same subject as Hatze's *Adel i Mara*, is a romantic lyrical tragedy. Its musical language shows an individual use of Wagnerian technique, with leitmotifs in the orchestral texture and predominantly declamatory vocal writing; it thus occupies an exceptional position among Croatian operas of the time. Parać was also a gifted and prolific poet.

J. Andreis: *Music in Croatia* (Zagreb, 1974)
———: 'Ivo Parać: život i djela' [Ivo Parać: Life and Works], *Rad JAZU*, no.377 (1978), 5–127
———: 'Luka Botić dva puta na opernoj pozornici' [Luka Botić Twice on the Operatic Stage], *Zvuk* (1979), no.3, pp.5–18

KORALJKA KOS

Parade (Fr.). Type of French street entertainment. Its origins date from the Renaissance. The practice of singers, dancers, jugglers and other performers to accompany parades (in the English sense of the word) and to entertain spectators during halts gave its name to improvised comedy on the balconies of fair and boulevard theatres used to attract audiences. The characters were drawn from the *commedia dell'arte* tradition (Harlequin, Cassandre and company), and the humour was of the crudest sort, relying on sexual innuendos or even explicit remarks and actions, obscene gestures and references to defecation and other bodily functions. The COMÉDIE-PARADE draws heavily on this tradition (though usually in a slightly politer style – at least in public theatres).

For illustration *see* PARIS, fig.5.

L. de Tressan: 'Parade', *Encyclopédie, ou Dictionnaire raisonné des sciences, des arts et des métiers*, ed. D. Diderot and others (Paris, 1751–80)
G. d'Heylli, ed.: *Théâtres des boulevards* (Paris, 1881)
H. d'Alméras and H. Quentin [P. d'Estrée]: *Les théâtres libertins aux XVIIIe siècle* (Paris, 1905)
J. L. Brown: 'Contribution à l'histoire du mot parade', *Le français moderne*, xxvii (1959), 111–24
R. M. Isherwood: *Farce and Fantasy: Popular Entertainment in Eighteenth-Century Paris* (New York and Oxford, 1986)

M. ELIZABETH C. BARTLET

Paradies [Paradisi], **(Pietro) Domenico** (*b* Naples, 1707; *d* Venice, 25 Aug 1791). Italian composer. He is supposed to have been a pupil of Porpora. Neither his opera *Alessandro in Persia*, written for Lucca in 1738, nor a serenata for Venice in 1740 proved successful. He emigrated to London about 1746–7, but his attempt to woo the English public with *Fetonte* at the King's Theatre (17 January 1747) was equally abortive. Burney (in his *General History*) attributed the failure partly to Paradies's lack of experience as an opera composer, and partly to a lack of '*estro* or grace' in any of the songs. Six arias, however, which were published by Walsh, were frequently sung by Signora Galli.

From 1753 to 1756 Paradies, together with Francesco Vanneschi, held the licence for the King's Theatre in the Haymarket and supplied arias for insertion in the pasticcio productions there. His greatest success in England, however, was as a singing teacher and harpsichord master, and his harpsichord sonatas were reprinted many times. One of his early pupils was Cassandra Frederick ('Miss Frederica'), a favourite of Handel's, and he also taught Gertrud Schmeling (later famous as the singer Mme Mara) and the elder Thomas Linley. About 1770, possibly because of financial difficulties, he appears to have parted with a number of his manuscript scores to Richard (later Viscount) Fitzwilliam. Towards the end of his life he returned to Italy. Among Paradies's operas *Fetonte* is of interest because of the unusual abundance of ballet music for chorus. His musical style is natural and fluent but of limited breadth of expression.

Alessandro in Persia (F. Vanneschi), Lucca, 1738, *A-Wgm**
Fetonte (Vanneschi), London, King's, 17 Jan 1747, *GB-Cfm**, Favourite Songs (London, 1747)

La forza d'amore (pasticcio), London, Little Theatre in the Haymarket, 19 Jan 1751, *Cfm**, *Lbl*, Favourite Songs (London, 1751)
Antioco, ? not perf., frags. *Cfm**

CHARLES CUDWORTH, CHRISTOPHER HOGWOOD

Paradis [Paradies], **Maria Theresia von** (*b* Vienna, 15 May 1759; *d* Vienna, 1 Feb 1824). Austrian composer. Blinded as a child, she received a broad education from Leopold Kozeluch (piano), Vincenzo Righini (singing), Salieri (singing, dramatic composition), Abbé Vogler (dramatic composition) and Karl Frieberth (theory). She performed extensively in Vienna, where Mozart wrote a piano concerto (K456) for her. Between 1783 and 1786 she toured in the company of her mother and Johann Riedinger, her librettist, appearing in Paris (as both pianist and singer), London and elsewhere. Later she lived mainly in Vienna and in 1808 founded an institute for music education.

Paradis apparently had exceptionally accurate hearing, as well as ready comprehension and a good memory; when composing she used a composition board invented by Riedinger. Her music for the stage comprises the melodrama *Ariadne und Bacchus* (1, J. Riedinger; Laxenburg, Schloss, 20 June 1791); the 'ländliches Singspiel' *Der Schulkandidat* (3, ?Riedinger; Vienna, 5 December 1792); and the comic opera *Rinaldo und Alcina* (also known as *Die Insel der Verführung*; 3, L. von Baczko; Prague, Estates, 30 June 1797). Only the second of these survives (*A-LIm*). Her stage works owe much to Viennese Singspiel; she also composed cantatas, songs and piano works.

H. Ullrich: 'Maria Theresia Paradis: Werkverzeichnis', *BMw*, v (1963), 117–54
———: 'Maria Theresia Paradis' zweite Reise nach Prag 1797: die Uraufführung von "Rinaldo und Alcina"', *Mf*, xix (1966), 152–63

RUDOLPH ANGERMÜLLER

Paraguay. For discussion of opera in Paraguay *see* ASUNCIÓN.

Pardon de Ploërmel, Le. Opera by Giacomo Meyerbeer; *see* DINORAH.

Parenti, Paolo Francesco (*b* Naples, 15 Sept 1764; *d* Paris, 1821). Italian composer. He studied with Sala and others in Naples and, in Villarosa's description, took Traetta's music as his guide. According to Gervasoni and the *Biografia* he composed four serious operas and three comic ones; oddly, except for *Nitteti*, no production records are known for these, although Florimo said that *La vendemmia* was his first opera, written for Naples, and Villarosa reported that *Il matrimonio per fanatismo* was greatly applauded in Rome.

In 1790 Parenti went to Paris, where, according to Fétis, he was first employed by the Opéra-Comique to add pieces to a revival of Gluck's *La rencontre imprévue*, given in translation as *I pazzi di Medina* on 1 May; however, Loewenberg maintained that the new musical arrangement was by J. P. Solié. Parenti subsequently wrote four comic works for that company. Villarosa claimed that Parenti served as director of the Italian comic opera in Paris for the year 1802, though this fact has not been substantiated. Otherwise, he supported himself as a singing teacher of the Italian style, for which he had a high reputation.

La vendemmia (ob), Naples, ? before 1783, aria *B-Bc*
La Nitteti (os, P. Metastasio), Florence, Pergola, carn. 1783

Il matrimonio per fanatismo (ob), Rome, ? before 1790
Les deux portraits (oc, C.-J. L. d'Avrigny), Paris, OC (Favart), 19 Aug 1790
Les cordonnières (oc, d'Avrigny), Paris, OC (Favart), spr. 1792
L'homme et le malheur (oc, d'Avrigny), Paris, OC (Favart), 22 Oct 1793
Le cri de la patrie (oc, d'Avrigny), Paris, OC (Favart), spr. 1794

?Unperf.: I viaggiatori felici (ob); Antigono (os), *F-Pn**; Il re pastore (os, ?Metastasio), 1810, *Pn**; Artaserse (os, ?Metastasio); Pezzi siolti, *Pn**; Philomedia, ou L'art de chanter, *Pn* (possibly autograph); Pimmalione, *Pn*

*

FétisB; FlorimoN; LoewenbergA; RosaM
C. Gervasoni: *Nuovo teoria di musica* (Parma, 1812), 227
[A. Mazarella, ed.:] *Biografia degli uomini illustri del Regno di Napoli ... che contiene gli elogj dei maestri di cappella, cantori, e cantanti più celebri ... compilato da diversi letterati nazionali* (Naples, 1816), 52   JAMES L. JACKMAN

Parepa(-Rosa) [Parepa de Boyescu], **Euphrosyne** (*b* Edinburgh, 7 May 1836; *d* London, 21 Jan 1874). Scottish soprano. She studied with her mother, the soprano Elizabeth Seguin, and made her début in Malta (under the name of Euphrosyne Parepa) in 1855 as Amina in *La sonnambula*. After appearances in Italy, Spain and Portugal she was engaged for the 1857 season of the Royal Italian Opera at the Lyceum (Covent Garden having burnt down the previous year), where she made her début as Elvira in *I puritani*. Between 1859 and 1865 she sang at both Covent Garden and Her Majesty's. In 1867 she and her husband Carl Rosa formed the Parepa-Rosa Grand English Opera company (*see* CARL ROSA OPERA COMPANY), which toured in the USA and Britain, 1867–71, and in which she sang leading roles. In 1872 she appeared in New York in Italian opera and then returned to Covent Garden as Donna Anna and Norma. Her voice combined power and sweetness, and had a compass of two and a half octaves, extending to *d″*.   HAROLD ROSENTHAL/R

Pareto, Graziella [Graciela] (*b* Barcelona, 15 May 1889; *d* Rome, 1 Sept 1973). Spanish soprano. She studied with Vidal in Milan, and made her début as Amina in *La sonnambula* at Madrid in 1908, a role she repeated in Parma. For two seasons from 1909 she appeared at the Colón in Buenos Aires, as Gilda, Adina, Rosina and Ophelia in Thomas' *Hamlet*, parts she sang there again in 1926. In Italy she sang at Rome, Naples, as Marguerite de Valois at Turin (1912) and reached La Scala in 1914, as Gilda. At Covent Garden in 1920 she sang Norina, Violetta, and Leïla (*Les pêcheurs de perles*) under Beecham, who considered her the best light soprano of her day. She appeared at Chicago (1923–5), and sang Carolina (*Il matrimonio segreto*) at Salzburg (1931). Her records, which include extracts from her leading roles, offer proof of a pure, limpid soprano, capable of considerable pathos.

*

GV (R. Celletti; J. P. Kenyon)
G. Fraser: 'Graziella Pareto', *Record Collector*, xvii (1966–8), 77–89   ALAN BLYTH

Parfaict, François (*b* Paris, 10 May 1698; *d* Paris, 25 Oct 1753). French theatre historian. He and his brother Claude (*b* Paris, 1705; *d* Paris, 26 June 1777) came from an upper middle-class family. François was closely associated with the theatre and in 1724 collaborated with Marivaux on comedies. His most important works, written in collaboration with Claude, deal with the history of French theatre. The *Dictionnaire des théâtres de Paris* treats alphabetically all plays (including operas) performed in Paris since 1552. Cast lists, revival dates, cross-references to the *Mercure de France* and the *Recueil général des opéra*, and anecdotes concerning authors, composers, actors and actresses, dancers and stage designers make this a valuable source. Equally important is the manuscript *Histoire de l'Académie royale de musique*, a chronological discussion of important events in French opera from 1645 (*La finta pazza*) to 1741. Its descriptions are striking. The singer Du Mény, for example, 'never knew his music and often sang out of tune. Added to this he was extremely addicted to drink'. Lully is described as having a 'lively and strange countenance, without nobility, dark complexioned, with small eyes, protruding nose and large mouth'. After François' death, Claude prepared a second edition of the *Dictionnaire des théâtres* and began a *Dramaturgie générale*.

Histoire générale du théâtre françois depuis son origine jusqu'à présent (Paris, 1734, 3/1745–9)
Agendas historiques et chronologiques des théâtres de Paris (Paris, 1735–7; repr. as *Agendas des théâtres de Paris, 1735, 1736 et 1737*, 1876)
Histoire de l'Académie royale de musique depuis son établissement jusqu'à présent (MS, 1741, *F-Pn* nouv. acq. fr.6532; 1835 copy with annotations by Beffara, *Pn* fr.12.355)
Mémoires pour servir à l'histoire des spectacles de la Foire, par un acteur forain (Paris, 1743)
Histoire de l'ancien théâtre italien, depuis son origine en France, jusqu'à sa suppression en l'année 1697 (Paris, 1753, 2/1767)
Dictionnaire des théâtres de Paris, contenant toutes les pièces qui ont été representées jusqu'à présent sur les differens théâtres françois, et sur celui de l'Académie royale de musique (Paris, 1756, 2/1767–70, with G. d'Abguerbe)

*

ES (M. Spaziani) [with complete list of writings]
J. G. Prod'homme: 'Les frères Parfaict, historiens de l'Opéra', *ReM* (1930), no.101, pp.110–18
P. Mélèse: *Répertoire analytique des documents contemporains ... concernant les théâtres sous Louis XIV* (Paris, 1934)
H. Finke: *Les frères Parfaict: ein Beitrag zur Kenntnis des literarischen Geschmacks in der ersten Hälfte des xviii Jahrhunderts* (diss., U. of Dresden, 1936)   JAMES R. ANTHONY

Pariati, Pietro (*b* Reggio Emilia, 27 March 1665; *d* Vienna, 14 Oct 1733). Italian poet and librettist. Secretary to Rinaldo, Duke of Modena, he was in Madrid in 1695 and after his return to Italy spent three years in prison. He then lived in Venice from the end of 1699 until summer 1714, when he was appointed to work as court poet in Vienna by Charles VI, for whom he had already written laudatory theatrical works staged in Barcelona.

In Venice Pariati started to work as a librettist with Apostolo Zeno, contributing to the versification and drafting of his librettos. The extent of their collaboration is not as great as has been thought, however; Pariati alone was responsible for *Artaserse*, *Anfitrione*, *La Svanvita*, *Il falso Tiberino*, *Sesostri re di Egitto* and *Costantino* (for an alternative view, *see* ZENO, APOSTOLO). He began by revising 'in the modern style' 17th-century works such as *Sidonio* and turning into *dramma musicale* form recent tragedies such as Giulio Agosti's *Artaserse*. Very soon he began to turn out prose works on his own account for the Milan and Bologna stages – in 1707 *Il Cajo Marzio Coriolano* and *La casta Penelope*. Established at the same time in Venetian theatrical circles, where he met composers including Albinoni and Gasparini and the *buffo* singers Giovanni Battista Cavana and Santa Marchesini, he devoted himself to writing comic scenes, *tragicommedie*

851

(*Anfitrione*) and intermezzos, particularly for the S Cassiano theatre. The celebrity he acquired in this field was to be repeated 50 years later by Goldoni. Drawing on Plautus, Molière and Cervantes, together with a wide theatrical experience, he refined the features that became characteristic of his comic style – rapid pace, brightness of dialogue and a taste for lexical extremes.

In Vienna, where he was joined by Zeno in 1718 and replaced by Metastasio in 1729, Pariati wrote oratorios (13), cantatas and chamber works (15), pastoral dramas and theatrical pieces (14) for the festive celebrations of the imperial family. The most famous such piece was the *festa teatrale Costanza e Fortezza*, set by Fux in 1723. For the court theatre he revived earlier works – his own, Pietro d'Averara's and Zeno's – wrote two new librettos and continued to collaborate with Zeno. But now his stylistic confidence and encounter with F. B. Conti (a musician well versed in comedy), together with the Viennese tradition that allowed for lighter works in the season, made him heir to a form perfectly suited to his love of caricature and the grotesque – the fantasy inter-mezzo and comic scene. The result was mastery of a new expressive freedom in which comedy is not only a source of laughter and entertainment, but an instrument with which to provoke, deride and debunk. Between 1716 and 1724 Pariati wrote alone four intermezzos and four *tragicommedie*; with *Don Chisciotte in Sierra Morena* and *Alessandro in Sidone* he even involved Zeno in his chosen field, dragging him beyond the confines of serious works into the territory of literary parody and social criticism. He exploited his favourite devices fully, varying and intertwining them: dual identity in *Il finto Policare* and *Penelope*, the philosopher's ironic situation in *Alessandro in Sidone* and in *Creso*, mental imbalance in *Don Chisciotte* and *Archelao*. Avoiding generic forms, Pariati flung his darts at ever diverse targets, in-cluding personal enemies and court intrigue, the very foundations of *opera seria*. He thus effected a twofold distortion: corrosive parody undermines the drama's heroic virtue and progressively erodes credibility, while an explosive stylistic mixture gives rise to the transformation into tragicomedy.

See also SESOSTRI, RE DI EGITTO.

dm – *dramma per musica*   int – *intermezzo*

Artaserse (dm, after G. Agosti), Giannettini, 1705 (Orlandini, 1706; Sandoni, 1709; Ariosti, 1724); *Antioco* (dm, with A. Zeno), F. Gasparini, 1705; *Ambleto* (dm, with Zeno), Gasparini, 1706 (Carcani, 1742); *Statira* (dm, with Zeno), Gasparini, 1706 (Albinoni, 1726); *Sidonio* (dm), Lotti, 1706; *Florinetta e Frappolone* (int), ?Gasparini, 1706; *Anfitrione* (tragicommedia), Gasparini, 1707; *La svanvita* (dm), A. Fiorè, 1707 (Schürmann, 1715, as Regnero)

Flavio Anicio Olibrio (dm, with Zeno), Gasparini, 1708 (Porpora, 1711; G. Porta, 1726, as Il trionfo di Flavio Olibrio; Vinci, 1728; E. Duni, 1736, as La tirannide debellata; Jommelli, 1740, as Ricimero re dei Goti); *L'Engelberta* (dm, with Zeno), Fiorè, 1708; *Astarto* (dm, with Zeno), Albinoni, 1708 (F. Conti, 1718; Caldara, 1725); *Zenobia in Palmira* (dm, with Zeno), ?Chelleri, 1709 (Leo, 1725; Brusa, 1725, as L'amore eroico); *Pollastrella e Parpagnacco* (int), Gasparini, 1708; *Vespetta e Pimpinone* (int), Albinoni, 1708 (Conti, 1717, as Grilletta e Pimpinone)

Il falso Tiberino (dm), C. F. Pollarolo, 1709; *Brunetta e Burlotto* (int), 1709; *Ciro* (dm), Albinoni, 1710 (Conti, 1715); *Sesostri re d'Egitto* (dm), Gasparini, 1710 (A. M. Bononcini, 1716; Conti, 1717; Fiorè, 1717; Sellitto, 1742; Terradellas, 1751; Cocchi, 1752; Bertoni, 1754; Sarti, 1755; Galuppi, 1757; Sciroli, 1759; C. Monza, 1760; P. Guglielmi, 1766); *Bertolda e Volpone* (int), 1710; *Galantina e Tulipano* (int), ?Albinoni, 1710; *Il Giustino* (dm, after N. Beregan), Albinoni, 1711 (Vivaldi, 1724; Handel, 1737)

Costantino (dm), Gasparini, 1711 (Lotti and Caldara, 1716; Orlandini, 1731, as Massimiano); *Dorimena e Tuberone* (int), Conti, 1714; *Teseo in Creta* (dm), Porpora, 1714, as Arianna e Teseo (Conti, 1715; Leo and others, 1721, as Arianna e Teseo; Porpora, 1727, as Arianna e Teseo; Broschi, 1732, as Arianna e Teseo; Handel, 1734, as Arianna in Creta; Lampugnani, 1737, as Arianna e Teseo; P. Chiarini, 1739, as Arianna e Teseo; G. de Majo, 1747, as Arianna e Teseo; Abos, 1748, as Arianna e Teseo; Pescetti, 1750, as Arianna e Teseo; Sarti, 1756, as Arianna e Teseo; Mazzoni, 1758, as Arianna e Teseo; Carcani, 1759, as Arianna e Teseo; Ponzo, 1762, as Arianna e Teseo; Galuppi, 1763, as Arianna e Teseo; Insanguine, 1773, as Arianna e Teseo; Fischietti, 1777, as Arianna e Teseo; Winter, 1792, as I sacrifizi di Creta)

Bagatella, Mamalucca e Pattatocco (int), Conti, 1715; *Galantina e Pampalugo* (int), Conti, 1715; *Il finto Policare* (tragicommedia), Conti, 1716; *Cajo Marzio Coriolano* (dm), Caldara, 1717; *Farfalletta, Lirone e Terremoto* (int), Conti, 1718; *Don Chisciotte in Sierra Morena* (tragicommedia, with Zeno), Conti, 1719; *Alessandro in Sidone* (tragicommedia, with Zeno), Conti, 1721; *Archelao re di Cappadocia* (tragicommedia), Conti, 1722; *Costanza e Fortezza* (festa teatrale), Fux, 1723; *Creso* (tragicommedia), Conti, 1723; *Penelope* (tragicommedia), Conti, 1724

Doubtful: comic scenes for *Alba Cornelia*, 1704 (Conti, 1714) [lib. also attrib. S. Stampiglia]; *Erighetta e Don Chilone* (int), ? Gasparini, 1707 [lib. also attrib. A. Salvi]

A. Zeno: *Poesie drammatiche*, ed. G. Gozzi (Venice, 1744)

N. Campanini: *Un precursore del Metastasio* (Reggio Emilia, 1889, 2/1904)

O. Wessely: *Pietro Pariatis Libretto zu Johann Joseph Fuxens 'Costanza e fortezza'* (Graz, 1969)

G. Gronda: 'Per una ricognizione dei libretti di Pietro Pariati', *Civiltà teatrale e settecento emiliano* (Bologna, 1986), 115–36

E. Kanduth: 'Das Libretto im Zeichen der Arcadia, Para-digmatisches in den Musikdramen Zenos (Pariatis) und Metastasios', *Opern als Text: Romanistische Beiträge zur Libretto-Forschung*, ed. A. Gier (Heidelberg, 1986), 33–53

G. Gronda: *La carriera di un librettista: Pietro Pariati da Reggio di Lombardia* (Bologna, 1990) [incl. essays by B. Dooley, H. Seifert and R. Strohm]

L. Bianconi and G. La Face Bianconi, eds.: *I libretti italiani di Georg Friedrich Händel e le loro fonti* (Florence, 1992–)

GIOVANNA GRONDA

*

Paride ed Elena ('Paris and Helen'). *Dramma per musica* in five acts by CHRISTOPH WILLIBALD GLUCK to a libretto by RANIERI DE' CALZABIGI; Vienna, Burgtheater, 3 November 1770.

Paris *son of King Priam of Troy*	soprano castrato
Helen *Queen of Sparta*	soprano
Amore [Cupid] *under the name of Erasto, Helen's confidant*	soprano
Pallas Athene (Minerva) *goddess, daughter of Jupiter*	soprano
A Trojan	soprano

Trojans, Spartans and Pallas's retinue

Setting Sparta just before the Trojan War

Paride ed Elena was the third and last of Gluck's so-called Italian reform operas, written for Vienna in collaboration with Calzabigi as a reaction against the stylization, the complicated plots and the florid music of Italian *opera seria*. It was first performed before the Viennese imperial court, and had a mixed reception; it was destined to be Gluck's last Italian opera, for after it he turned his attentions to Paris and composed for the French stage. The principals in the first performance were Giuseppe Millico (Paris), Katherina Schindler (Helen), Teresa Kurtz (Cupid) and Gabriella Tagliaferri (Pallas Athene).

Performances of *Paride ed Elena* have been few since its première, even in the 18th century. There were only 25 in Vienna before 1800 as opposed to more than 100 of *Orfeo ed Euridice* and more than 70 of *Alceste*. *Paride ed Elena* was given in Naples in 1777 but no other productions have been traced until 1901, when it was revived in Prague, and 1905, when it was produced in Hamburg (in German, in a cut version in two acts). There have been a few concert performances since, and one in 1983 was followed by a recording. The opera was staged at the Drottningholm Theatre in 1987.

Like Gluck's second Italian reform opera, *Alceste*, *Paride ed Elena* was published with a dedicatory preface outlining the composer's and librettist's intentions, the relevant portion of which may be translated as follows:

The drama of Paris and Helen did not require from the composer's fancy those strong passions, those majestic images and those tragic situations which shook the audience in *Alceste*; neither did it necessitate so many grandiose harmonic effects. Thus the same forceful and energetic music will surely not be expected … There is no question of a wife about to lose her husband, who, in order to save him, has the courage to evoke the eternal gods in a terrible forest in the blackest shades of night; who in the extreme agonies of death still trembles for the fate of her sons, and has to tear herself from a husband she adores. Here a young lover is presented in contrast with the waywardness of a lovely and honest woman; he at last triumphs by all the stratagems of consuming passion. I was obliged to exert myself in order to find some variety of colour, seeking it in the different characters of the two nations, Phrygia and Sparta, by contrasting the rude and savage nature of the one with all that is delicate and soft in the other. I believed, seeing that song in an opera is nothing else than a substitute for declamation, that I ought to imitate in Helen the native ruggedness of her country, and I thought that my having preserved that character in the music would not earn me any reproach for having sometimes stooped so low as to become trivial.

The overture to *Paride ed Elena*, like that to *Alceste*, and following Gluck's principles as set out in the *Alceste* preface (*see* GLUCK, CHRISTOPH WILLIBALD, §6), anticipates the events of the drama; but unlike the *Alceste* overture it uses music heard later in the opera. Its first section is a martial Allegro whose second part is built on an arpeggio phrase in the bass to be heard when Pallas Athene appears in Act 5 scene iii; its second provides a foretaste of the lyricism of much of Paris's music and its sighing phrases return in Act 5 scene iv; and its final section, transforming the opening march into a joyful dance, returns in the duet for Paris and Helen in the penultimate scene.

ACT 1 *A seashore, with a view of the nearby city of Sparta; ships are visible in the distance and small boats on the shore; the Trojans' tents are on the beach, and in the centre is a statue of Venus under a bower of roses shaped like a small temple* Paris, with his followers and Trojan sailors, is wearing a garland of flowers, and offering a sacrifice to the goddess. The Trojans sing and dance. The opening chorus is a hymn praying for Venus's help for Paris in his desire for Helen; it is followed by his first passionate avowal, 'O del mio dolce ardor' (notable for its minor key, the restless semiquavers in the lower registers of the strings and the plaintive echoing oboe). Paris's second aria, 'Spiagge amate', follows after a dance, but it is interrupted by a Trojan who tells Paris that a messenger from Sparta is on his way.

Cupid, disguised as Erasto, enters with a group of Spartans; the music changes character, with angular octaves contrasting with the indolent lyricism of the Trojans' music (and anticipating that of the barbarians in Gluck's Iphigenia operas). Erasto has been sent by Helen to discover the identity and intentions of the newly arrived strangers. Paris tells Erasto that Zeus chose Paris to judge who was the most beautiful woman: Juno, Minerva (Pallas Athene) or Venus. Paris chose Venus, but has heard that Helen is even lovelier and has come to see for himself. Erasto accuses him of being in love; in the ensuing duet, Paris questions him ('Ma, chi sei?'), and begs him not to divulge to Helen the purpose of his visit. Left alone, Erasto reveals that he is there to help Paris win Helen (aria, 'Nell'idea ch'ei volge'). The act ends with a five-movement ballet in which the angular and lively music of the Spartans alternates with two gentle and lyrical dances for the Trojans.

ACT 2 *A hall in the royal palace of Sparta with a throne at one side* Erasto is extolling to Helen the virtues of Paris. Paris enters with his retinue bearing gifts for Helen. Their first meeting is conducted in recitative as each is struck by the other's beauty; Paris declares that Helen is indeed as beautiful as Venus, and she invites him to remain in Sparta as her guest. There follows a trio, virtually an aria for Helen with interjections from Paris and Erasto ('Forse più d'una beltà'); she sings of the women who may be missing Paris, who is puzzled and disturbed by her remarks.

Paris, left alone, gives expression to his fears of losing Helen in a minor-key aria with restless, syncopated string accompaniment ('Le belle immagini').

ACT 3 *The great courtyard of the royal palace of Sparta, surrounded by colonnades and galleries used for athletic games; on one side is a raised platform for the throne* A procession of Spartans, Trojans, guards, athletes and other contenders in the games enter to a short, warlike march. Helen explains to Paris that he must join her in judging the games and competitions with which the Spartans will celebrate his presence; he tells her that his eyes are only for her. The games begin with a chorus of athletes (with angular lines, bare octaves and often unpredictable harmony: 'Dalla reggia riluscente scendi a noi'). A tenor leads the people in a hymn in praise of great warriors ('Negli strali, nell'arco possente'), followed by a dance for the athletes with dotted rhythms and furious scales. Helen announces that Paris will award the prizes; and after a repeat of the chorus in praise of warriors she admits he may find the Spartans' songs harsh and rough and asks him to sing something more melodious. Accompanying himself on his lyre (a harp in the orchestra), Paris sings an impassioned aria in praise of Helen's beauty ('Quegli occhi belli'); she exclaims at his audacity after each verse and, indignant and embarrassed, interrupts as he is beginning the fourth, breaking into his aria in distraught recitative. Gluck conveys their tension in breathless, offbeat rhythms, both in the recitative and the ensuing duet, 'Ah ferma! … Ah senti!', which Paris launches by declaring that he adores her and has come to Sparta to win her; Helen replies that loyalty and virtue rule her heart, and orders him to leave her. She goes; Paris says he has been betrayed by the gods and his only consolation is death. The music, ironically, turns from C minor to C major for a bright, celebratory march for the returning athletes after their tournament, and the act ends with an extended chaconne.

ACT 4 *A room in the royal palace with a writing table* Helen is reading a letter from Paris, saying that the gods promised her to him and begging her to leave her poor, barren country and return with him to Troy. She angrily replies that he has abused the laws and customs and she cannot love him because she is betrothed; he should go and find another lover. Helen asks Erasto to deliver her letter when Paris appears, and Erasto hands it to him: in a trio ('Ah lo veggo') Helen imagines that Paris plans to deceive her with flattery, he is devastated by the contents of her letter and Erasto declares that Helen cannot resist the power of the gods.

Paris now begs Helen to kill him and put an end to his torments. She tells him that she is betrothed to another man whom it is her duty to love, and beseeches him to leave Sparta if he truly loves her. Paris protests that he would rather die ('Di te scordarmi, e vivere!': a predominantly *adagio* aria, characterized by falling, sighing phrases, chromatic harmony and a heroic vocal line). Helen is torn between the claims of love and duty (aria, 'Lo potrò! … Ma frattando, oh infelice', where her indecision is portrayed by syncopated strings, sharp accents and racing semiquavers).

ACT 5.i *The gardens of the royal palace of Sparta* As Paris is preparing to leave, Erasto must act quickly. Soon his new plan is revealed. When Helen enters, Erasto feigns sadness, pretending to love Paris and to be lamenting his imminent departure. Helen, angry with Paris, whom she thinks has deceived her, warns all women of men's insincerity (aria, 'Donzelle semplici': a heroic C major piece in the style of much of the Spartan music, made more so by the high horns, trumpets and timpani). Then Helen swears vengeance on Paris and is about to order her navy to pursue him and burn his ships when he enters, presumably to bid her farewell. Erasto immediately tells Paris that Helen loves him. Helen dismisses Erasto from her service, and only then does he reveal his true identity, as Cupid. Paris thanks Venus, Cupid's mother, for her help in winning Helen. But as Helen tells Paris that she is his, thunder is heard, Pallas Athene appears on a cloud and her attendants rush in as Paris and Helen flee to opposite sides of the stage. To music based on part of the overture, the enraged goddess tells the unhappy pair that her wrath will fall on them soon. Then Pallas predicts the terrible war to come, telling Paris and Helen to go to Troy but warning them that their joy will soon turn to sorrow (aria with chorus, 'Va coll'amata in seno'). She disappears, and after a brief shocked interlude Paris and Helen lament their fate; to music from the start of the scene they question whether they should leave one another, but their love is too great and, as the music moves to the bright C major of the overture's final section, they swear that they will not be deterred no matter how terrible their destiny (duet, 'L'amo! L'adoro!'). Cupid reassures them: Pallas's anger is in vain and he, Cupid, will accompany them to Troy and protect them. The end of his recitative concludes a succession of open-ended numbers (recitative, aria with chorus, recitative, duet and recitative), continuous since Pallas's appearance. Paris and Helen now swear eternal fidelity in the only love duet in the opera; Cupid joins them and the three of them praise the eternal flame of love (trio, 'Sempre a te sarò fedele!').

5.ii *A bay close to the royal palace of Sparta; Paris's Trojan ships can be seen illuminated, and there are various small boats by the shore and Trojan tents on the beach; it is night* After 'a cheerful sinfonia' with piccolos and tambourine, during which Trojan sailors and servants of Paris and Helen dance in, all prepare to embark. The opera ends, as it began, with one of Gluck's great choral tableaux: a jubilant, optimistic chorus, 'Vieni al mar', is heard three times, with two short arias for Cupid, the second of which leads to a brief duet for Paris and Helen (a repeat of that in Act 5 scene i).

* * *

Paride ed Elena has always been one of the most unjustly neglected among Gluck's operas. It lacks the direct emotional appeal of its predecessors *Orfeo ed Euridice* and the Italian *Alceste*, or of his only other mature opera that deals with sexual passion, *Armide*. In comparison with *Armide*, the treatment in *Paride ed Elena* is somewhat cool and detached; this has its roots in Calzabigi's libretto and in Gluck's characterization and his effective differentiation between the two peoples. The Phrygians or Trojans, and their leader Paris, have predominantly lyrical music, while the Spartans and their queen are portrayed by angular lines and strong rhythms, often sounding modal and with a preponderance of unisons and octaves ('rude and savage', Gluck called it). In adhering strongly to this as a principle, Gluck made rather a rod for his own back, especially in his assigning to Helen music typical of the Spartans. As a result, as Rousseau pertinently observed, Helen's music has a certain austerity, even when she is expressing her love for Paris; and this makes her one of Gluck's less sympathetic heroines. Her recitatives are certainly austere by comparison with Paris's, and she has only two arias. Yet the national contrasts are often incorporated in a most inspired way into the many ensembles.

Another unusual feature is the prominence of Cupid/Erasto, whose presence throughout the opera, urging on both Paris and Helen, gives a new slant to the *deus ex machina* tradition, as does the appearance of Pallas Athene in Act 5. *Paride ed Elena* is a late example of the operatic tradition that shows the mortals as virtually the playthings of the gods. Instead of putting all to rights like a conventional *deus ex machina*, Pallas is with her threats and terrible warnings a kind of anti-*deus ex machina* who casts a shadow over the *lieto fine*.

The performance of *Paride ed Elena* poses a problem unique among Gluck's major operas. The role of Paris, for a soprano castrato, lies too high for it to be taken by a countertenor. The alternatives are to assign it to a soprano, which would result in a cast exclusively of sopranos, or (the one usually adopted) to transpose it down an octave for a tenor – a compromise, but one that could be made in the knowledge that Gluck arranged the leading male roles in *Orfeo ed Euridice* and the Italian *Alceste* both upwards and downwards to suit other types of voice, and that, had he made a French version of *Paride ed Elena*, he would have given the role of Paris to the high tenor Joseph Legros.   JEREMY HAYES

Parigi, Giulio (*b* Florence, 6 April 1571; *d* Florence, 13 July 1635). Italian architect, engineer and scene designer. After initial training from his father, the architect Alfonso Parigi (the elder), he entered the service of Bernardo Buontalenti in 1589, succeeding him in 1608 as architect and engineer to the Medici court, though he was already on the payroll from 1599. He oversaw all the works and surveying in the grand duchy, including the festive and dynastic displays, and so captured the interest of the Medici princes. His innovatory mastery of scene design soon acquired a European scope and reputation, thanks to contact with Inigo Jones, Joseph Furttenbach, Cosimo Lotti and

Alfonso Parigi's design for the final scene ('Scena di tutto cielo') of 'Le nozze degli dei' performed in the courtyard of the Palazzo Pitti, Florence, for the marriage of Ferdinando II de' Medici and Vittoria della Rovere, 8 July 1637: the dancers have formed themselves into the shapes of abbreviations of the names Ferdinando (FO) and Vittoria (VA); engraving by Stefano della Bella

Jacques Callot. In addition to designing displays, spectacles and entertainments in Florence, Parigi was also involved in operatic design, providing machines and 'cloud' for Rinuccini's *Festa dell'Agnolo Gabriello* (1620). He was responsible for the machines and scenic perspectives for Marco da Gagliano's *La regina Sant'Orsola* (1624). He restored and enlarged the imperial Villa di Poggio, which was the setting for Caccini's entertainment *La liberazione di Ruggero dall'isola di Alcina* (1625). Parigi expressed the scenic magnificence of court life in his designs of theatres and spaces for any type of performance. He witnessed the birth of opera, providing it with cosmic and mythological themes, ingenious machines, refined costumes and scenic variety. On stage he depicted cities, mythological places, gardens, inferno, the palace of Fame, mountains, the sea and Vulcan's cave, with a single perspective axis linking the stage to the prince's box.

His son, the younger Alfonso Parigi (*b* Florence, 1606; *d* Florence, 17 Oct 1656), succeeded his father as architect and engineer at the Medici court. His most famous works were the stage designs for Marco da Gagliano's *La Flora* (1628) and for *Le nozze degli dei*, a *dramma per musica* by several composers to a libretto by C. Coppola, performed in Florence in 1637 (see illustration). He also engraved some of his father's scenes, notably for *La liberazione di Ruggero* and *La regina Sant'Orsola*.

For further illustration *see* FLORENCE, fig. 1; INTERMEDIO; and PRODUCTION, fig.3.

*

ES (E. Povoledo)
C. Molinari: *Le nozze degli dei* (Rome, 1968)
M. Fossi: *Il taccuino dei Parigi* (Florence, 1975)
A. R. Blumenthal: 'Giulio Parigi and Baroque Stage Design', *La scenografia barocca*, ed. A. Schnapper (Bologna, 1982), 19–34
——: *Giulio Parigi's Stage Designs: Florence and the Early Baroque Spectacle* (New York, 1986)   MARINELLA PIGOZZI

Paris. Capital of France. Its operatic traditions were shaped initially by the city's role as the seat of a strong, centralized monarchy. In the 17th and 18th centuries many operas were first staged at court; public theatres received subsidies from the crown but were subject to royal regulation. The dominant musical theatre was the Académie Royale de Musique (the Opéra), whose hegemony was only gradually lessened during the second half of the 18th century by the growth of the Opéra-Comique. Laws passed during the Revolution revoked the monopolies held by the established theatres, the resulting profusion of companies and operatic ventures from the early 19th century onwards giving rise to much confusion of nomenclature. Since the construction of the new Opéra in the 1870s, productions have largely centred on this celebrated institution. But although the Opéra can claim the credit for the creation of major 20th-century French operas, various other enterprises (such as the Opéra-Comique) have rivalled the Opéra in adventurous commissions.

1. To 1669. 2. 1669–1725: (i) The Académie Royale de Musique (Opéra) (ii) The court theatres (iii) The Fair Theatres and the Comédie-Italienne. 3. 1725–89: (i) The public theatres (ii) The court. 4. 1789–1870: (i) Background (ii) The Opéra (iii) The Opéra-Comique (iv) The Théâtre Feydeau (v) The Théâtre Italien (vi) The Théâtre Lyrique (vii) Other companies. 5. 1870–1902: (i) Background (ii) The Opéra (iii) The Opéra-Comique (iv) Other theatres. 6. 20th century: (i) To 1939 (ii) Since 1939.

1. TO 1669. Before the creation in 1669 of the Académie d'Opéra (later known as the Académie Royale de Musique), the court was the centre for most musical theatre, which consisted primarily of *ballets de cour*. No single theatrical space was used, and ballets were staged in many venues, both indoors and out, depending on the location of the still peripatetic court, the season, the nature of the work and the demands it made for sets and scenery. The Grande Salle of the Louvre, the Grand Salon of the Tuileries Palace, the Hôtel de Ville in Paris and royal chateaux at Compiègne, Fontainebleau, Chantilly, Vincennes, St Germain-en-Laye and Chambord are among the places where ballets by Jean-Baptiste Lully and his predecessors were presented. Many of these spaces were large, rectangular rooms in which temporary stages could be constructed. The same ad hoc conditions prevailed at outdoor performances such as the magnificent productions in the gardens of Versailles in 1668 and 1674. During this period, the

court also had at its disposition various fixed theatres. The Salle du Petit Bourbon, located between the Louvre and the church of St Germain-l'Auxerrois, was not originally constructed as a theatre, but underwent substantial modifications by the Italian stage designer Torelli in 1645. Even before its transformation, the hall had served for productions such as the *Balet comique de la royne* (1581) and the *Ballet de Madame* (1621). After the renovated theatre was inaugurated with *La finta pazza* in 1645, it served both for court productions such as the *Ballet de la nuit* (1653) and for public theatrical performances. The hall was torn down in 1660 to permit construction of the colonnade of the Louvre. That year Louis XIV hired Gaspare Vigarani to build a huge theatre in the Tuileries Palace (estimates of its capacity range from 6000 to 8000) that could accommodate elaborate stage machinery. The Salle des Machines (see fig.6a below) opened with a production of Cavalli's *Ercole amante* in 1662, but despite the hall's visual magnificence, its poor acoustics condemned it to very little use. By far the most important theatre was that built by Richelieu as part of his residence, the Palais Royal, located away from the Seine near the Louvre. Designed by Le Mercier and opened in 1641, this theatre was later to become the home of the Académie Royale de Musique (fig.1). Lully's ballets *Les arts* (1663) and *Les amours déguisés* (1664) were among the court ballets performed there. Audiences consisted of members of the court and visiting dignitaries; their numbers varied enormously depending on available space in the different venues. Those present received a published libretto that described each entrée in the ballet including the names of the singers and dancers. The musicians were members of the royal musical establishment (the *grands* and *petits violons* often played), but the dancers included both courtiers and professionals.

Although performances of court ballets were not open to the general public, there were several public theatres in mid-17th-century Paris, and each of the few troupes permitted to operate within the city had a clearly defined repertory. Actors located in the Hôtel de Bourgogne (where 29 rue Etienne-Marcel now stands) performed primarily tragedy, while the troupe in the Théâtre du Marais (now 90 rue Vieille-du-Temple) specialized in plays with elaborate machinery. Molière's troupe, after travelling in the provinces for several years, established itself in Paris in 1658 and was allowed to share the Petit Bourbon with an Italian *commedia dell'arte* troupe that had recently taken up residence in France. The two troupes played on alternate days and shared expenses, and after the Petit Bourbon was torn down in 1660 they moved to the Palais Royal. Both employed musicians and incorporated music and dance into their productions. Molière's collaboration with Lully resulted in a brilliant series of *comédies-ballets* during the 1660s. Initially the Italians performed exclusively in their native language, but during the 1680s they began performing much of their repertory in French and developed new roles that appealed to French audiences. In addition to their public performances, both the Italian and the French comedians received subsidies from the royal treasury, and thus performed frequently at court.

During the minority of Louis XIV the Italian-born prime minister Mazarin made several attempts to introduce Italian opera into France. As with the *ballet de cour*, these works were private entertainments for members of the court. The first such, performed modestly on 28 February 1645 at the Palais Royal

(probably Marazzoli's allegorical *Il giuditio della Ragione tra la Beltà e l'Affetto*: see Zaslaw 1989), was followed by a fully staged production of Sacrati's *La finta pazza* in December of the same year at the Petit Bourbon (for illustration *see FINTA PAZZA, LA*). For these and the five subsequent operas – Cavalli's *Egisto* (1646, Palais Royal), Luigi Rossi's *Orfeo* (1647, Palais Royal), Caproli's *Le nozze di Peleo e di Theti* (1654, Petit Bourbon), Cavalli's *Xerse* (1660, Grande Galerie of the Louvre) and his *Ercole amante* (1662, Salle des Machines of the Tuileries Palace) – Mazarin imported Italian singers, instrumentalists and stage designers who returned to Italy after the performances. However, unlike Italian comedy, Italian opera did not take root in France; French audiences preferred the ballets that Lully and others inserted between the acts, and the importation of Italian opera ended in 1662 with the last performance Mazarin had organized before his death. Nonetheless, these performances helped pave the way for the development of a native French opera.

2. 1669–1725.

(i) The Académie Royale de Musique (Opéra). On 28 June 1669 the poet Pierre Perrin received a 12-year privilege to set up an Académie d'Opéra for the performance of operas in French. Perrin transformed the Bouteille tennis court, which extended from the rue de Seine (where no.43 now stands) to the rue des Fossés-de-Nesles (now 42 rue Mazarine), opposite the rue Guénégaud, into a rectangular theatre accommodating approximately 1200 spectators with provisions for machinery and changes of scenery. His first opera, *Pomone*, with music by Robert Cambert, opened on 3 March 1671 and ran for 146 performances. Despite the initial success of the Académie (a second work, *Les peines et les plaisirs de l'amour* by Cambert and his librettist Gabriel Gilbert, was performed in early 1672), a series of financial difficulties led Perrin to a debtors' prison. Lully, *surintendant* of the king's music, acquired the privilege on 13 March 1672. The new letters-patent from the king gave Lully's company, now renamed the Académie Royale de Musique (known familiarly as the Opéra), a monopoly on public operatic performances in Paris. One month later Lully moved to limit his competition further by obtaining from the king an ordinance that reduced the number of musicians employed by the French and Italian comedians from six singers to two and from 12 instrumentalists to six. Until his death in 1687, Lully was the only composer whose work appeared on the stage of the Opéra, and his operas continued to form the core of its repertory well into the 18th century.

Because of legal entanglements with the previous occupants, Lully did not take over Perrin's theatre but had Carlo Vigarani construct a new one at the Bel Air tennis court on the rue de Vaugirard (now between the Odéon theatre and the Luxembourg gardens). His first production, *Les fêtes de l'Amour et de Bacchus*, opened there in November 1672, followed by his first *tragédie lyrique*, *Cadmus et Hermione*, on 27 April 1673. Although the theatre was equipped with stage machinery, Lully regarded it as a temporary expedient, and after Molière's death in 1673 he persuaded the king to grant him the Palais Royal rent-free. (Molière's troupe subsequently merged with that of the Théâtre Guénégaud, using the theatre that had housed Perrin's Académie d'Opéra. This troupe merged again in 1680 with players from the Hôtel de Bourgogne to form the

1. Cardinal Richelieu's theatre in the Palais Royal during the performance of a play in 1643: engraving (1643) by M. van Lochun; seated (left to right) are Richelieu, Louis XIII, Anne of Austria and the dauphin, the future Louis XIV (note the musicians playing in the upper right gallery)

Comédie-Française, the Italian players thereafter acquiring exclusive use of the Hôtel de Bourgogne.) The Palais Royal was to house the Opéra until it burnt down in 1763. Built in 1641 (see fig.1), it had undergone modifications in 1660 and again in 1671. The last major renovations were made by Vigarani in 1674 at Lully's instigation; later changes were purely cosmetic. The theatre was much longer than it was wide; it had a parterre in which approximately 600 people could stand, a nine-row amphitheatre seating approximately 120 and three rows of boxes (to the first of which two balconies were attached) seating around 550, making a total of 1270. The stage measured 17 metres deep by 9.4 across the front, and the area in front of the stage for the orchestral musicians 3 metres by 7.6. Contemporary plans do not show the arrangements for the stage machinery, but numerous drawings and engravings evoke the visual magnificence of which the theatre was capable.

The Opéra functioned all year round, closing only for three weeks during the Easter season, for other religious holidays or for periods of official mourning. Performances were given on Tuesday, Friday and Sunday, and also on Thursday when premières of new works or of revivals were staged. As at the other Parisian theatres, performances began at the end of the afternoon; in 1714 their start was fixed at 5.15 p.m. Lully's practice was to compose one new opera every year, relying on revivals of one or two of his earlier works to fill out the season. During his lifetime new works were generally given at court during the carnival season and transferred to the Palais Royal after Easter. Following Lully's death in 1687, the number of productions mounted at the Palais Royal each year increased from two or three to between three and six, as Lully's successors – among them Collasse, Desmarets, Campra, A. C. Destouches and Marais – had more difficulty sustaining public enthusiasm for an individual work. The most notable success of the period was Campra's

opéra-ballet L'Europe galante (1697), the first work in this new genre (often called simply 'ballet') to be performed on the operatic stage. Lully's works were relied upon to draw the public into the theatre if a new work failed to please, and most seasons included at least one Lully revival. Unlike in Italy, where composers often provided new settings of familiar librettos, French composers set newly written librettos that had first been approved by the directorate of the Opéra; not until the 1760s was the Italian practice, initially controversial, adopted in Paris.

The earliest surviving administrative records for the Opéra date from the post-Lullian period. Royal ordinances of 1713 and 1714 (in Durey de Noinville, i, 108–46) describe the workings of the Opéra and define the positions and salaries of its employees. Singers were governed by official regulations and sanctions were available which permitted, for example, the imprisonment of Mlle Lemaure for wilfully quitting in mid-performance in 1735. Salaries were graded according to rank; promotions were possible, and one-off payments or specially negotiated salaries were not uncommon. The principal singers often held their posts for years, and the long-term stability of the company was remarkable. Among the solo singers there were six female sopranos, three hautes-contre, two tenors and three basses. The chorus numbered 36, including 12 women (all of whom sang soprano), 2 boys and 22 men (two of whom apparently sang soprano: see Rosow 1987, the rest divided between haute-contre, tenor and bass); there were 22 dancers (12 men and 10 women). The orchestra had nearly 50 members: the petit choeur consisted of 2 violins, 2 transverse flutes (who also played oboe), 2 basses de violon, 1 bass viol, 2 theorbos and a harpsichord; the grand choeur contained 12 violins, 7 violas (3 hautes-contre, 2 tailles, 2 quintes), 8 basses de violon, 8 woodwind players (oboes, flutes or bassoons), 1 kettledrum and a batteur de mesure who directed the orchestra. Given that this list does not account for all of

2. 'Persée' (Lully), Act 5 scene v: engraving by Dolivar after Jean Berain's design, probably for the original production at the Paris Opéra (Académie Royale de Musique), 18 April 1682

the instruments found in operatic scores (e.g. trumpets), extra musicians were probably hired when needed.

(ii) The court theatres. During the early years of the Opéra's existence many works were staged at court. Between 1673 and 1682 five premières and several revivals took place at the royal chateau of St Germain-en-Laye, where the Salle de Ballet in the west wing had been equipped to permit changes of scenery and the use of stage machinery. The newly enlarged chateau of Versailles, into which Louis XIV officially moved his court and the seat of his government in 1682, contained no permanent theatre capable of accommodating elaborate operatic performances. Although work on such a theatre was begun in 1685, the project was abandoned (the opera house still standing in the chateau dates from 1770), and court performances of Lully's operas took place in a variety of spaces. As had been the case for the *ballets de cour*, some performances were held out of doors, either in temporary theatres constructed in the gardens or in the Cour de Marbre (*Alceste*, 1674; see ALCESTE (i), fig.2). Others took place in the covered riding arena of the Grande Ecurie. (Engravings depicting the performance there of Rameau's *La princesse de Navarre* in 1745 reveal how elaborate such temporary theatres could be; see fig.3) The tiny Salle de Comédie, located within the chateau, between the marble courtyard and the south wing, was used primarily by the French and Italian troupes of actors, although Lalande's *Le ballet de la jeunesse* was performed there in 1686. It was constructed between 1681 and 1685; its stage measured approximately 5 metres by 8, and it held approximately 250 spectators. A small, short-lived theatre in the Grand Trianon (torn

down in 1703) was occasionally used for scaled-down operatic performances, and the salon in the main pavilion at Marly served for little ballets and masquerades. Outside Versailles the largest number of theatrical performances took place at the royal chateau at Fontainebleau, where the court spent several weeks each autumn. These included operas by Lully and his successors, and the French and Italian comedians who regularly performed during these voyages were sometimes obliged to close their theatres in Paris while present at this more distant chateau. As at Versailles, many spaces within the chateau and its gardens served as performance venues, but in 1682 Louis XIV converted the Salle de la Belle Cheminée into a theatre. As the aging king's interest in theatrical entertainments declined, however, fewer operas were put on at court, and even these tended to be done in concert versions, often in the intimacy of the royal apartments.

Towards the end of Louis XIV's reign the centre for entertainment began to shift away from Versailles. Members of the extended royal family and the aristocracy sponsored elaborate musical entertainments in their private residences, sometimes relying upon their own musical establishments, sometimes hiring for the occasion musicians and dancers from the court or from the Opéra. The Duchesse du Maine put on a particularly brilliant series of 16 *divertissements* at her chateau at Sceaux in 1714 and 1715; the 'Grandes Nuits de Sceaux', well documented thanks to an adulatory book written by one of the participants (Genest 1712), featured cantatas, *comédies lyriques*, plays with musical *intermèdes* and an early example of what was to be called the *ballet d'action*. Much of the music was composed by the young Jean-Joseph Mouret. In addition to these private entertainments, educational institutions training aristocratic youth staged dramatic *divertissements* of various types. Each year the principal Jesuit school in Paris, the Collège de Clermont (renamed the Collège Louis-le-Grand in 1683), performed sacred dramas such as M.-A. Charpentier's *David et Jonathas* (1688) and ballets with allegorical subjects (e.g. *L'empire du soleil* of 1673). Pierre Beauchamps, choreographer at the Opéra under Lully, was but one of the eminent artists who created works for the Jesuit theatres. At St Louis de St Cyr, the school for young gentlewomen founded by Mme de Maintenon in 1686, two tragedies by Racine with incidental music by Jean-Baptiste Moreau, *Esther* (1689) and *Athalie* (1691), were performed by students.

(iii) The Fair Theatres and the Comédie-Italienne. Since the Middle Ages annual fairs held in Paris had included popular entertainments such as farces and acrobatic displays. During the 17th century entertainers at the Foire St Germain (which occupied a large site near the church of St Germain-des-Prés and ran from 3 February to Palm Sunday) and the Foire St Laurent (located where the Gare de l'Est now stands, and generally running from July to the end of September) attracted large audiences from all levels of society to their makeshift stages. When Louis XIV expelled the Italian comedians from France in 1697 for the licentiousness of their performances, the *forains* were quick to adopt the Italians' repertory. The widening of their theatrical horizons necessitated more suitable structures for performances, and the different groups of players were obliged either to build theatres, some of which were quite substantial despite their wooden construction, or to convert tennis courts near

3. Performance of Rameau's 'La princesse de Navarre' in the theatre of the Grande Ecurie, Versailles, on 23 February 1745 to celebrate the marriage of the dauphin Louis to Maria Teresa of Spain: engraving by Charles-Nicholas Cochin fils (for a detail showing the stage and orchestra pit, see ORCHESTRA, fig.6)

4. Section of the court theatre at the Château of Fontainebleau, 1725: drawing, probably by Sébastien-Antoine Slodtz who was responsible for the interior remodelling that year. Rousseau's 'Le devin du village' received its première at this theatre in 1752; two years later Ange-Jacques Gabriel (architect of the Versailles Opéra, 1768–70) reconstructed the interior of the theatre to increase the seating capacity, improve the sightlines and extend the length of the perspective stage

the fair grounds to their purposes. However, the use of music on the one hand and of spoken theatre on the other provoked strong reactions from both the Opéra and the Comédie-Française, who saw the Fair Theatres as a threat to their own livelihood. A series of repressive measures aimed at preventing performers from singing or speaking on stage forced the *forains* into imaginative expedients for getting around the restrictions. In 1714, however, the Fair Theatres made a new series of agreements with the Opéra by which they paid an annual fee for the right to put on plays mixed with music and dance and to call themselves the 'Opéra-Comique'. The first work to bear the new appellation was *Télémaque* (A.-R. Lesage, 1715), a parody of Destouches' opera; with D'Orneval and Fuzelier, Lesage provided the texts for many early *opéras comiques*. Composers, such as Jean-Claude Gillier, who worked at the fairs served primarily as arrangers of the vaudevilles and parodied operatic airs that formed the core of the repertory, although as time went on the amount of original music they composed increased. The number of singers, dancers and instrumentalists employed at the Fair Theatres varied considerably, largely depending on the degree to which the restrictions imposed by the established theatres were enforced; the 15 instrumentalists who played in *Télémaque* seem to represent a large ensemble for this period. The troupes also made use of those regular members who could sing, dance or play.

The competition among the theatres increased in 1716 when the Duc d'Orléans, regent during the minority of Louis XV, recalled a new troupe of Italian comedians to replace the one expelled in 1697. They returned to the Hôtel de Bourgogne and became known as the Comédie-Italienne (or the Théâtre Italien). Although initially performing in their own language,

they began playing more frequently in French to texts by French playwrights; their first such production was Autreau's *Le naufrage au port à l'anglais* (1718), each of whose three acts included a *divertissement* by Mouret, the troupe's newly appointed official composer. The subsidy the new troupe received from the royal treasury made it less vulnerable to attack by the Opéra and the Comédie-Française than the Fair Theatres; nonetheless, the rivalries gave birth to such topical plays as *La désolation des deux comédies* and *La querelle des théâtres*, staged in 1718 at the Comédie-Italienne and the Foire St Laurent respectively. The same year the Comédie-Française succeeded in forcing the closure of the Fair Theatres for two years, excepting only marionettes and acrobats. The Opéra-Comique returned briefly in 1721, only to be banned again until 1724; the Comédie-Italienne took advantage of its absence to play at the Foire St Laurent.

3. 1725–89.

(i) The public theatres. By 1725 an uneasy equilibrium prevailed among the four public theatrical establishments in Paris. The Opéra, with its status as an academy, occupied the top rung of the hierarchy, followed by the Comédie-Française, which was also subsidized by the king and whose members held the title of *comédiens ordinaires du roi*. Upon the death of the regent in 1723 this title was also granted to the Italian players; they, however, as foreigners and more recent arrivals, had less security than their French counterparts. The bottom of the hierarchy was occupied by the Fair Theatres, whose livelihood depended entirely on box-office receipts and whose activities were restricted by the various conditions placed upon them by the official theatres. To a considerable degree all the theatres

5. Crowd watching a 'parade' outside Nicolet's theatre at the Foire St Laurent: watercolour (c1786)

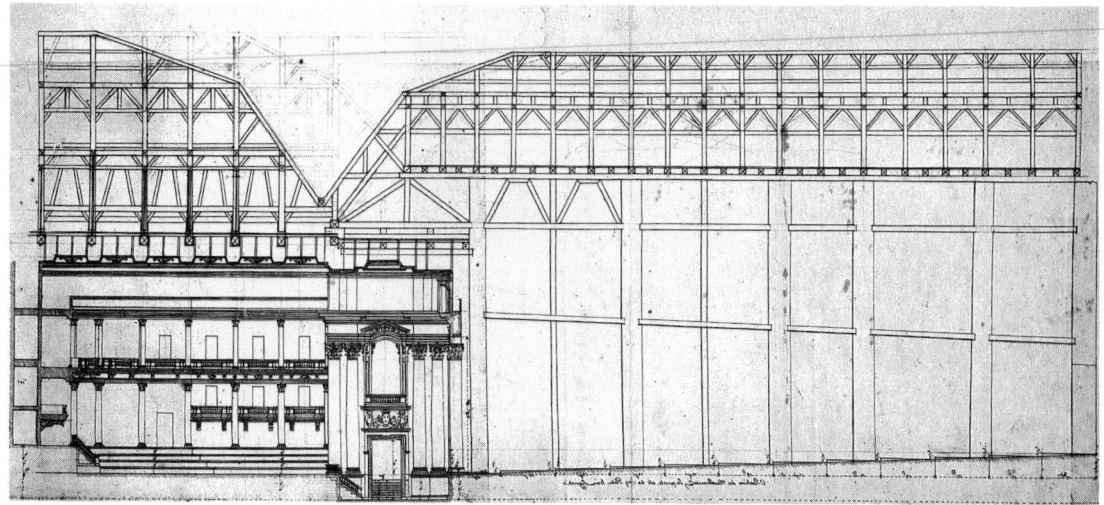

6. (a) The Salle des Machines in the Tuileries Palace: interior side elevation (c1750) of the auditorium (left) and stage

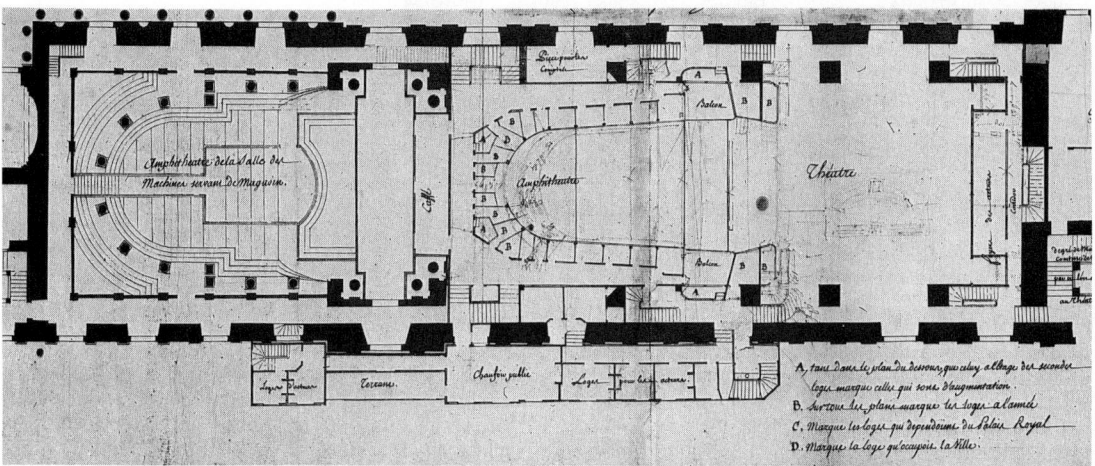

6. (b) Plan of the Salle des Machines as remodelled by J.-G. Soufflot and A.-J. Gabriel (1763) by converting the original stage into a new stage and auditorium

seem to have competed for the same audience, a phenomenon that helps account for the bitter disputes that recurred among them. Although the commercial success of each theatre varied over the years, this state of affairs prevailed until the merger in 1762 of the Opéra-Comique and the Comédie-Italienne. Around the same time a new group of popular theatres began to appear.

The Opéra offered a repertory of both new works and revivals. One Lully opera was usually performed each season, although these were increasingly modified as the century progressed to bring them into line with changing tastes; they left the stage in 1779. The ascendancy of Jean-Philippe Rameau, whose first tragédie lyrique, Hippolyte et Aricie, was performed at the Opéra in 1733, set off public debate between Lullistes, the upholders of tradition, and Ramistes, partisans of the modern style. Yet Rameau's operas became classics in their turn, and stayed in the repertory for two decades after the composer's death in 1764, along with newer works by composers such as Mondonville, Monsigny, Gossec and Grétry. A breach in French resistance to the importation of Italian opera occurred in 1752 when the management of the Opéra arranged for an Italian troupe to perform Pergolesi's La serva padrona and other comic intermezzos. Their performances led to another

paper war, the Querelle des Bouffons, pitting those who claimed the superiority of Italian opera, most notably the philosopher Jean-Jacques Rousseau, against the partisans of French taste. Although the Parisian public evinced enough enthusiasm for the novel operatic style to keep Bambini's troupe in the city for 20 months, Italian opera was not to return to the stage of the Opéra for another 24 years. However by its next brief appearance during the 1778 season, when several three-act opere buffe were performed, a foreign composer – Gluck – had finally succeeded in making an impact upon the native tragédie lyrique, starting with Iphigénie en Aulide in 1774. These foreign influences were accompanied by yet another pamphlet war, and although pure Italian opera failed once again to sustain audience interest, Italian composers such as Piccinni, Sacchini and Salieri had a series of notable successes at the Opéra during the 1780s by setting French librettos and adapting their styles to French taste. Another innovation in the Opéra's performing tradition occurred in 1782, when Colinette à la cour, the first in a series of lyric comedies by Grétry, was given at the Opéra.

The large role of dance in Rameau's operas, even more substantial than in those of Lully, reflected a shift in the repertory as a whole from domination by the

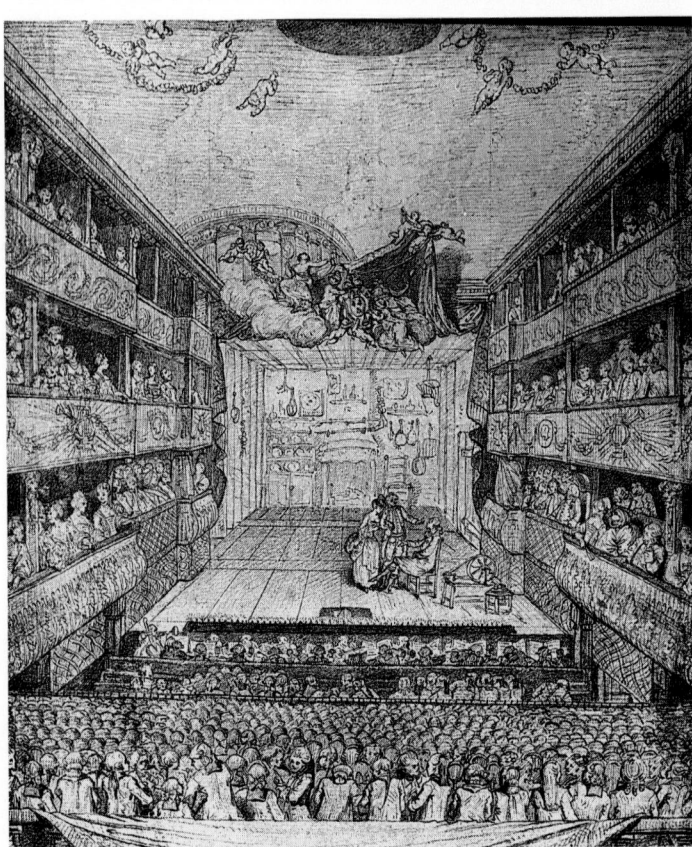

7. Interior of the Hôtel de Bourgogne, Paris: drawing (1767) by P. A. Wille (the younger)

tragédie lyrique, which had made up about three-quarters of the repertory at the beginning of the century, to lighter, more dance-orientated genres such as the *opéra-ballet*, the *pastorale-héroïque* and the *ballet-héroïque*. By the mid-1770s the proportion of *tragédies lyriques* to other genres had been completely reversed. In 1776 the ballet pantomime was introduced at the Opéra with Gaetano Vestris's staging of Noverre's *Médée et Jason* (first performed in Stuttgart in 1763). This genre, for which the music was entirely instrumental, was to occupy a significant proportion of the Opéra's repertory as the Revolution approached. The greater emphasis on dance led to an enormous increase in the number of dancers employed at the Opéra: from 22 members in 1714 the dance troupe increased to 91 in 1770, of whom 19 were soloists. The growth in the musical forces was less dramatic: in 1770 there were 8 female and 10 male solo singers, with a chorus of 50 (16 women and 34 men) and an orchestra of 68.

In 1763 fire destroyed the theatre in the Palais Royal. The Opéra moved to the Salle des Machines of the Tuileries Palace after renovations by Soufflot had reduced its enormous size by placing both auditorium and stage in the space formerly occupied by the stage alone (see fig.6); its dimensions and seating capacity were modelled on those of the Palais Royal. In 1770 a magnificent new theatre, designed by Pierre-Louis Moreau on Italian models and constructed on an enlarged Palais Royal site, opened with a revival of Rameau's *Zoroastre*. The stage was somewhat larger than that of the old theatre, and, as before, scene changes were carried out in full view of the 2000 spectators. Despite precautions designed to protect the new building against fire, it burnt down on 8 June 1781. By

27 October of the same year a new theatre had been constructed near the Porte-St-Martin, work having been carried on around the clock in order for the architect, Samson-Nicolas Lenoir, to meet his contracted deadline. During the brief interim, the Opéra made use of the small Salle des Menus-Plaisirs, then belonging to the crown and used for rehearsals for court spectacles, but formerly one of the theatres of the Foire St Laurent. The stage of the Porte-St-Martin theatre had approximately the same dimensions as the newer Palais Royal theatre and could accommodate around 2000 spectators in its parterre, amphitheatre and four rows of boxes. As in the earlier theatres, the least expensive tickets were for the parterre where the spectators, all of them male, stood throughout the performances. The Opéra remained at the Porte-St-Martin until 1794.

The Hôtel de Bourgogne, which from 1716 housed the Comédie-Italienne, was the oldest theatre in Paris, having been constructed in the late 16th century. Since it had stood empty during the Italians' absence, renovation was required before it could be put into use again. It could hold about 1500 spectators in the parterre and three rows of boxes, and had an orchestra pit for the approximately 14 instrumentalists who performed for the productions. The theatre was in use throughout the year except during the Easter season and for a few weeks in autumn when the troupe was in residence at Fontainebleau. The repertory, unlike that of the Opéra, relied primarily on new pieces: Italian farces, French plays by writers such as Pierre Marivaux, *comédies à vaudevilles* and *parodies* similar to those appearing on the stages of the Fair Theatres, for example *Arlequin Tancrède* (1729) or Mouret's *Les Indes chantantes* (1735), a parody of Rameau's *Les Indes galantes*. A number of librettists and composers, among them Favart and Mouret, wrote for both the Comédie-Italienne and the Opéra-Comique.

In the first half of the 18th century performances by the Opéra-Comique were seasonal, depending on the opening of the fairs. As the fair troupes became more established, they built larger semi-permanent structures, similar in design and seating capacity to the established theatres, that permitted them to make scene changes and use machinery. The theatres were situated just outside the fair grounds, a location which sometimes enabled them to extend their seasons after the fairs had closed for the year. Initially, facilities were better at the Foire St Germain, where a theatre recalling the one in the chateau of Fontainebleau was built in 1735 by the director of the Opéra-Comique, Boizard de Ponteau; his successor, Jean Monnet, renovated the theatre at the Foire St Laurent in 1743, then built an entirely new one there in 1752 (see fig.15 below). Constructed in only 37 days, the new theatre was praised for its comfort, the quality of its acoustics and the beauty of the decorations designed by the painter Boucher.

In the early years of the Opéra-Comique's existence, the role of the librettist was much greater than that of the composer. For over four decades starting in 1732 the most important librettist at the Opéra-Comique was Charles-Simon Favart, who provided both original plays and operatic parodies for the troupe; his first major success was *La chercheuse d'esprit* (1741). Composers associated with the Opéra-Comique included Gillier, Mouret, Dornel, Corrette and, early in his career, Rameau. Although the agreement by which the Opéra-Comique paid a substantial annual fee to the Opéra for the privilege of using music in its productions protected it from attacks from one quarter, continued pressure from the Comédie-Française forced the Fair Theatres to close periodically or to restrict their offerings to acrobatics or marionette shows; the longest forced closure lasted from 1745 until 1752. The popularity of the intermezzos performed at the Opéra by the visiting

Bouffon troupe between 1752 and 1754 led the Comédie-Italienne and the recently reopened Opéra-Comique to incorporate the Italians' music into their own repertories. Several arias from these intermezzos were immediately parodied, and *La serva padrona* was translated into French and performed at the Comédie-Italienne as *La servante maîtresse* (1754). Favart's *Ninette à la cour*, performed at the same theatre in 1755, reaped an enormous success by setting Italian music, primarily borrowed from Ciampi's intermezzo *Bertoldo in corte*, to an entirely new French text. More important, French composers began to write new works in the Italian style; the first of these, passed off at its première in 1753 by the Opéra-Comique as a translation of an Italian work, was *Les troqueurs*, with music by Dauvergne. The new style, which granted a much more substantial role to music, opened the way for the *opéras comiques* of composers such as Duni, Monsigny, F.-A. D. Philidor and Grétry, working in conjunction with the librettists Favart, Sedaine and Marmontel.

In 1762 the Opéra-Comique merged with the Comédie-Italienne and moved into the Hôtel de Bourgogne. In so doing it lost some of its independence but gained in respectability, acquiring for its members the desirable title of *comédiens du roi* which allowed them to perform at Versailles before the king. It also became possible for the troupe to perform throughout the year in a permanent theatre, and audiences that had begun to dwindle at the Hôtel de Bourgogne in recent years arrived in greater numbers. The repertory of the combined company included semi-improvised Italian comedies, French plays, *opéras comiques* (often called *comédies mêlées d'ariettes*) and ballets. Regulations forbade the company from mounting opera in Italian and using recitative in their productions. Despite the domination of the repertory by the Opéra-Comique and an edict by the king in 1780 renaming the theatre the Opéra-Comique, the appellation of Comédie-Italienne or Théâtre Italien still adhered to the company in the minds of the public and the press. In 1783 the company moved to a new theatre, the Salle Favart, the first of three by that name on the site where the Opéra-Comique still stands. The names of the adjoining streets – boulevard des Italiens, rue Marivaux, rue Favart, rue Grétry and place Boieldieu – bear witness to the history of the troupe. After certain design faults by the original architect J. F. Heurtier were corrected by C. de Wailly in 1784, the sumptuous new theatre could hold 1282 spectators. The orchestra pit was designed to accommodate the growing group of instrumentalists attached to the company, who by then numbered around 30.

For most of the 18th century the Comédie-Française occupied a remodelled tennis court in the rue des Fossés-St-Germain-des-Prés (now rue de l'Ancienne Comédie) to which it had moved in 1688. The theatre held about 1500 spectators and had a small semicircular area in front of the stage for the musicians who played before the performances and in the intervals. The troupe alternated performances of tragedy and comedy; approximately a third of its repertory consisted of revivals of works from the 17th and early 18th centuries, including some of the *comédies-ballets* of Molière with music by Lully and Charpentier. Although regulations imposed at Lully's instigation in 1672 still officially limited the number of instrumentalists to six and of singers to two, the Comédie-Française generally managed to ignore these restrictions. From 1770 to 1782 the troupe occupied the theatre in the Tuileries

8. Scene from M.-J. Sedaine's 'Le diable à quatre' (1756), one of the longest-lived comic operas created for the Parisian Fair Theatres

Palace before moving into a newly constructed theatre now known as the Odéon.

A number of popular theatres emerged from 1759 onwards, primarily along the boulevard du Temple, presenting farces, pantomimes, parodies, marionette plays, acrobatic shows and sometimes *opéras comiques*. Their rapid growth occurred during a time when the fairs were in decline: some of the troupes on the boulevards moved there directly from the fairs. Like the more established theatres, the boulevard theatres employed instrumental ensembles to provide the music that was an essential part of their spectacle; in 1785 the Comédie-Française accused one of them, the troupe headed by J. B. Nicolet, of having in its employ 30 actors, 20 musicians and 60 dancers. Like the Fair Theatres during the first half of the century, the pre-Revolution boulevard theatres provided vigorous competition for the official theatrical establishments.

(ii) The court. During the reigns of Louis XV (1715–74) and Louis XVI (1774–92) the court continued its annual sojourn at Fontainebleau, where theatrical performances by the three official troupes contributed to the entertainment. Major renovations were made to the theatre in 1725 and again in 1753–4; the later ones permitted greater use of machinery and special effects, but the theatre was never as capable of elaborate sta-

gings as those in Paris. During the early part of Louis XV's reign opera was performed primarily in concert versions, but from 1745, when several operas and ballets were performed in the Grande Ecurie at Versailles to celebrate the wedding of the dauphin, interest in staged opera revived and a number of works had their premières at Fontainebleau, including Rousseau's *Le devin du village* (1752), Rameau's *Anacréon* (1754), Grétry's *Zémire et Azor* (1771) and Piccinni's *Didon* (1783). The extent of theatrical entertainment at Fontainebleau varied considerably depending upon political events and the state of the royal treasury; under Louis XVI such spectacles declined dramatically and visits to Fontainebleau ceased entirely in 1786. In 1768 construction finally began at Versailles on the large and fully equipped permanent theatre that the chateau had previously lacked. Designed by the architect A.-J. Gabriel (fig.10), it was completed in 1770 for the wedding of the dauphin (the future Louis XVI) to Marie Antoinette and opened with a performance of Lully's *Persée*. The theatre was used not only for performances by the Opéra, the Comédie-Française and the Comédie-Italienne but also for balls, since removable flooring could extend the surface of the stage over the parterre. Ironically, however, court spectacles entered a state of decline shortly afterwards. Louis XVI had little interest in theatre, and the deteriorating political situation in

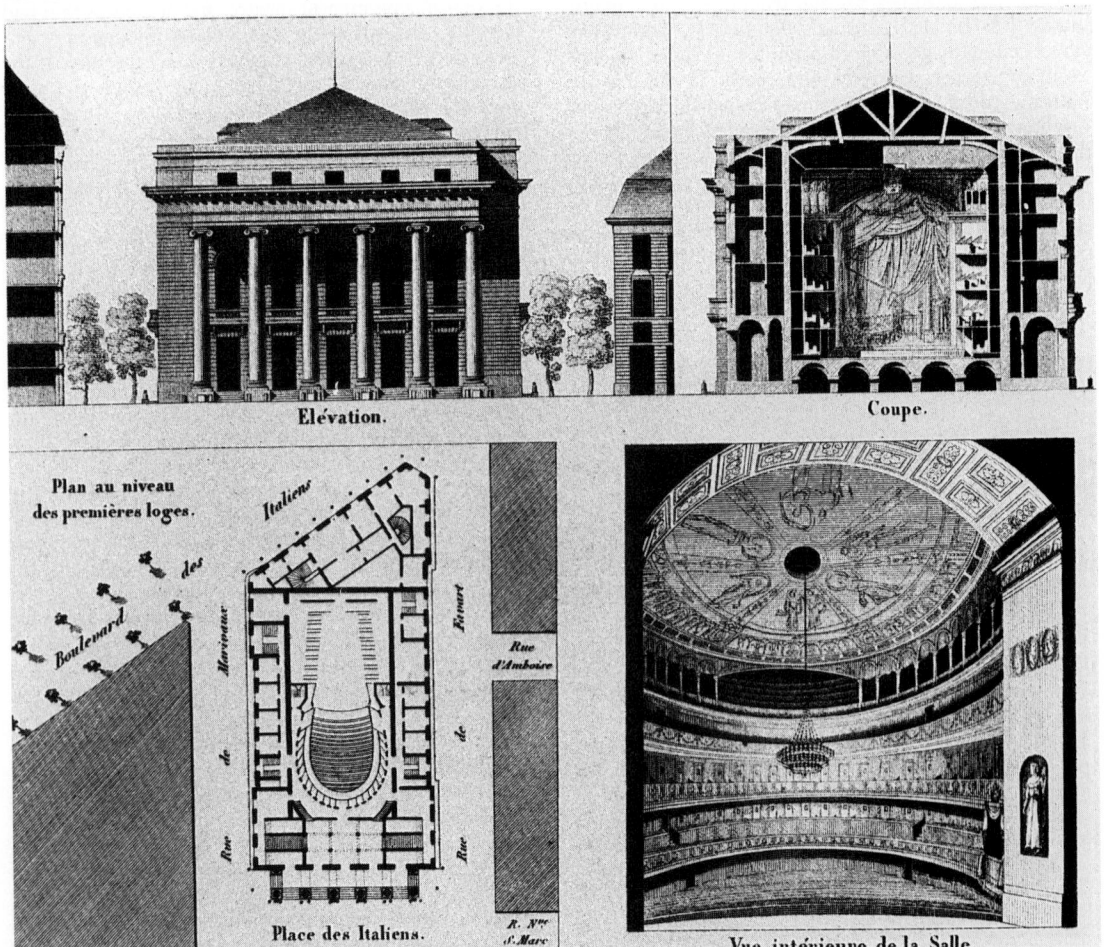

9. *Plan, sections and elevation of the first Salle Favart, built for the Comédie-Italienne and opened in 1783: engraving from A. Donnet, 'Architectonographie des théâtres de Paris' (Paris, 1837–40)*

10. Auditorium of the Opéra, Versailles (designed by A.-J. Gabriel, 1768–70), during the celebrations to mark the wedding of the dauphin and Marie Antoinette in 1770: pen and ink drawing, with wash, by Jean-Michel Moreau

France further limited expensive productions.

In 1747 Louis XV's mistress, Mme de Pompadour, had a tiny portable theatre built inside the royal apartments at Versailles, the Théâtre des Petits Cabinets, where she and other courtiers performed plays, operas, *opéras-ballets* and ballet pantomimes before small, select audiences. The solo roles, both sung and danced, were filled by Mme de Pompadour and other courtiers, who also accounted for about a third of the 28-member orchestra. Members of the king's musical establishment supplied the rest as well as the chorus, which at its largest numbered 26. The *corps de ballet* consisted of children between the ages of nine and 12 who were found places in the professional dance troupes of Paris when their engagements at Versailles concluded. Mme de Pompadour's most ambitious productions included Campra's *Tancrède* and Lully's *Acis et Galatée* (see fig.11). Public outcry against the expense obliged her to move these theatricals to her own chateau of Bellevue in 1751, where they lasted for two more years. A short-lived and small-scale revival in court theatricals was instigated by Marie Antoinette who, like Mme de Pompadour, enjoying singing and acting. An exquisite theatre, still standing in the grounds of the Petit Trianon, was constructed by the architect Richard Mique in 1779; for the next five years the queen and her troupe put on plays and *opéras comiques*, including *Le devin du village* in which the queen sang the role of Colette. The theatre closed its doors in 1785 with a performance of Beaumarchais' *Le barbier de Séville*, with the queen as Rosine.

4. 1789–1870.

(i) Background. Laws passed in 1791 made it possible for anyone to open a public theatre. Opera and theatre life during this period became complex because of the proliferation of companies before 1807 and their regular growth in number after 1820. There are also complexities in the way companies and theatres were named. A building might be known by the name of a previous patron or company; theatres quite often burnt down and were rebuilt elsewhere, to be christened with the name of an old or new company, or an old or new patron. Only the more important of the Parisian institutions are discussed (see also Table 1). The new legislation abolished the prevailing hierarchy that placed the Opéra at the top. No longer did other theatres have to pay dues to it, or restrict their repertory to works they did not 'own'. The resulting abundance of new spectacles included *opéra comique*, melodrama, pantomime and vaudeville. Napoleon took an early interest in the public situation of theatres, supporting the return of Italian opera. In 1806 and 1807, however, he passed three decrees which ended the automatic right to open a theatre, defined the limits of repertory of each company and reduced the total number to eight (four primary and four secondary). The primary theatres were the Opéra, Théâtre Français, Opéra-Comique and Théâtre de l'Impératrice (Théâtre Italien). The secondary theatres were the Vaudeville, Variétés, Gaîté and Ambigu-Comique. The primacy of the Opéra was thus reestablished. In 1810 the Théâtre de la Porte-St-Martin obtained permission to reopen (as the Jeux Gymniques) and in 1820 the Gymnase-Dramatique did likewise. Under the monarchy of Louis-Philippe (1830–48) there was continuing pressure from several quarters for a third French-language opera house of prestige to be established beside the Opéra and Opéra-Comique, particularly for the benefit of younger composers beginning their career. There were repeated initiatives involving a range of theatres (see §4(vii) below) but nothing permanent happened until 1847 when the Opéra-National was opened on the boulevard du Temple, the traditional area for Parisian popular entertainment.

11. The Théâtre des Petits Cabinets, Versailles, with Mme de Pompadour taking part in a performance of Lully's 'Acis et Galatée' in 1749: engraving after Charles-Nicolas Cochin fils

12. The Opéra on the rue Le Peletier (Salle Le Peletier), Paris, designed by François Debret and inaugurated in 1821: lithograph by Rousseau and Courvoisin

Ruined by the 1848 Revolution, it later became the celebrated Théâtre Lyrique (see §4(vi) below). In 1855 Offenbach opened his Théâtre des Bouffes-Parisiens (see OPERETTA, fig.1). Napoleon III passed further legislation in 1864 that finally abolished the theatrical hierarchy, again allowing anyone to open a theatre and present any type of dramatic work on their stage. However, these laws did nothing to remove existing censorship.

(ii) The Opéra. The principal opera company of Paris underwent several changes of title as the result of political events. The main ones are recorded in Table 1; for a full list see Wild (1989). The company also occupied several theatres, the most permanent of which were the Théâtre National de la rue de la Loi (cap. 2800), created by Marguerite Brunet ('La Montansier'), and the Salle Le Peletier (cap. 1900), built specially for the company and designed by François Debret (see figs.12 and 13; see also CATEL, CHARLES-SIMON for an illustration of the inaugural performance).

The Opéra traditionally gave performances on Mondays, Wednesdays and Fridays and the season lasted for most of the year. It also held regular balls and benefit performances. Administered by the City of Paris

during much of the 1790s, it was taken over directly by Napoleon in 1802. He retained the right to determine expenses for new works and exercised influence over the repertory, suggesting certain subjects in order to maintain it as the state's showpiece. In 1811 he imposed dues payable to the Opéra by other theatres (as under the *ancien régime*); this persisted until 1830. The main conductors were Jean-Baptiste Rey (to 1810), Rodolphe Kreutzer (to 1824), François-Antoine Habeneck (to 1846), Narcisse Girard (to 1860) and George Hainl (to 1873). The orchestra was large, with an average of 85 players, and maintained a high standard, owing its great fame not least to soloists such as the violinist Baillot, the oboist Vogt and the horn player Dauprat. Conversely, the traditional French style of singing often continued to be censured. Gradually the impact of Italian vocal training became irresistible, and when Rossini went to live in Paris he began the process of revolutionizing standards. Meyerbeer, who was frequently in Paris from 1825, also had great influence on the development of solo singers. Of female singers at the Opéra the most celebrated were Branchu, Alexandrine Gavaudan, Dorus-Gras, Viardot and Cinti-Damoreau; famous male singers included Lays, Adolphe and Louis Nourrit, Henri-Etienne and

TABLE 1: Principal Paris theatres, 1789–1870

company	theatre
Opéra [Théâtre des Arts, Théâtre de la République et des Arts, Académie Impériale de Musique, Académie Royale de Musique and others]	Théâtre de la Porte-St-Martin (until Aug 1794) Théâtre National de la rue de la Loi (7 Aug 1794–13 Feb 1820) Salle Favart (i) (19 April 1820-11 May 1821) Salle Louvois (15 May–15 June 1821) Salle Le Peletier (16 Aug 1821 onwards)
Opéra-Comique [Comédie-Italienne, Théâtre Italien, Théâtre Favart, Théâtre National de l'Opéra-Comique, Théâtre Impérial de l'Opéra-Comique]	Salle Favart (i) (until 20 July 1801) Salle Feydeau (16 Sept 1801–22 July 1804) Salle Favart (i) (23 July 1804–4 July 1805, except 3–23 Oct 1804 at the Salle Olympique) Salle Feydeau (2 Sept 1805–12 April 1829) Salle Ventadour (20 April 1829–22 March 1832) Salle de la Bourse (24 Sept 1832–30 April 1840) Salle Favart (ii) (16 May 1840 onwards)
Théâtre (de la rue) Feydeau [Théâtre de Monsieur, Opéra-Comique Français and others]	Salle des Machines, Palais des Tuileries (26 Jan–22 Dec 1789) Ancienne Salle des Variétés, Foire St Germain (10 Jan–31 Dec 1790) Salle Feydeau (6 Jan 1791 onwards; merges with Opéra-Comique in 1801)
Théâtre Italien [Opera Buffa, Opera Seria e Buffa, Théâtre Royal Italien, Théâtre Royal Italien et Anglais, Théâtre Impérial Italien; popularly: 'Bouffons', 'Théâtre des Italiens']	Salle Olympique (31 May 1801–13 Jan 1802) Salle Favart (i) (17 Jan 1802–19 May 1804) Salle Louvois (9 July 1804–4 Aug 1808) Salle de l'Odéon (ii) (16 June 1808–30 Sept 1815) Salle Favart (i) (2 Oct 1815–20 April 1818) Salle Louvois (20 March 1819–8 Nov 1825) Salle Favart (i) (12 Nov 1825–14 Jan 1838) Salle Ventadour (30 Jan–31 March 1838) Salle de l'Odéon (iii) (Oct 1838–31 March 1841) Salle Ventadour (2 Oct 1841 onwards)
Théâtre Lyrique [Opéra-National]	Salle du Théâtre Historique (27 Sept 1851–June 1862) Salle du Théâtre Lyrique (30 Oct 1862–31 May 1870)

Prosper Dérivis, Etienne Lainez, and later Lafont, Duprez and Faure.

Under the Revolution the Opéra fell behind other theatres in importance; recovery was made with works such as Catel's *Sémiramis* (1802), Spontini's *La vestale* (1807), his *Fernand Cortez* (1809, rev. 1817) and Rodolphe Kreutzer's *Abel* (1810). Earlier works were constantly revived, for example Gluck's *Orphée* (1800), his *Alceste* (1803) and Rousseau's *Le devin du village* (1810). Famous works were increasingly imported from elsewhere, whereas this had previously been very much the exception. Mozart's *Figaro* was seen in 1793, *Die Zauberflöte* (as *Les mystères d'Isis*) in 1801 and *Don Giovanni* in 1805, although all three were in mutilated form. Rossini appeared with *Le siège de Corinthe* in 1826 and *Moïse* the next year, both revised from earlier works. His only original composition for the Paris Opéra was *Guillaume Tell* (1829), a long-popular work which, with Auber's *La muette de Portici* (1828), completed the path to Romantic grand opera. This path required the creation of a new staging committee (in 1827) and the post of stage manager. Productions thenceforth were meticulously planned to respond to the needs of music and scenery in order to produce a totality of effect. They involved complex sets for each act with both painted flats and practicable scenery in three dimensions, high standards of scene painting and lighting and sumptuous costumes designed with respect for historical accuracy. Some works were famous for their use of spectacular stage machines, for example the erupting volcano in *La muette de Portici* and the holocaust ending Meyerbeer's *Le prophète* (1849), the first work staged at the Opéra to use electric lighting.

Gas lighting had previously been introduced in 1822 with Isouard and Benincori's *Aladin*. Production books were published for every new opera and their information and diagrams ensured that provincial or foreign performances reproduced the Paris Opéra original as far as possible.

Under the directorship of Louis Véron (1831–5) came the first operas fully benefiting from such types of artistic investment: Meyerbeer's *Robert le diable* (1831), Auber's *Gustave III* (1833) and Fromental Halévy's *La Juive* (1835). All these works had librettos by Eugène Scribe, who had established the ground rules of *grand opéra* with Auber in *La muette*. The directorships of Charles Duponchel (1835–40) and Léon Pillet (1840–47) saw the continuation of the line with Meyerbeer's most enduring and popular grand opera, *Les Huguenots* (1836), Halévy's *La reine de Chypre* (1841) and his *Charles VI* (1843). Berlioz's *Benvenuto Cellini* (1838) is not a conventional work in this context, though the casting of Cellini's statue in the final act reflects the grand machines of its contemporaries. Infinitely more popular with the public was Donizetti's *La favorite*, conceived for the Théâtre de la Renaissance but completed for the Opéra in 1840. In 1841 the Opéra commissioned recitatives by Berlioz for Weber's *Freischütz*, since spoken dialogue was forbidden on its stage.

The early part of the Second Empire and the directorships of Nestor Rocqueplan (1849–54), François-Louis Crosnier (1854–6) and Alphonse Royer (1856–62) were mixed rather than eventful. Meyerbeer's position as the leading figure was confirmed with *Le prophète*, and he exerted a palpable influence on Verdi's first commission

13. Interior of the Paris Opéra (Salle Le Peletier) during a performance of Meyerbeer's 'Le prophète' (1849): engraving by G. Janet

14. Playbill for the première of Meyerbeer's 'Robert le diable' at the Paris Opéra (Salle Le Peletier), by the Académie Royale de Musique on 21 November 1831

for the Opéra, *Les vêpres siciliennes* (1855). Gounod's *Sapho* (1851) reacted strongly against *grand opéra* (it had only three acts, a classical theme, private rather than public conflicts and a lyrical, not rhetorical, musical style). It paid the price and was not a popular success. The first work by Wagner staged at the Opéra was *Tannhäuser*, for which the composer wrote the Venusberg music (1861); elements of the public forced it off the stage after three nights, causing a scandal that has never been forgotten. No further Wagner work was seen at the Opéra until *Lohengrin* in 1891. Meyerbeer's reputation was reaffirmed in the year after his death by *L'Africaine*, edited for its first performance in 1865 by his friend, the historian Fétis. Verdi's second commission, *Don Carlos*, came in 1867, and the new age of literature-based work, smaller in conception than the older historical dramas, was confirmed with Ambroise Thomas' *Hamlet* (1868) and the recitative version of Gounod's *Faust* (Opéra, 1869).

Ballets were at least as popular as operas and were normally worked into operatic evenings. The principal landmarks were Hérold's *La fille mal gardée* (1828), Adolphe Adam's second ballet, *Giselle* (1841), and Delibes' *Coppélia* (1870), the last important work given in the Salle Le Peletier before it burnt down on 29 October 1873.

(iii) The Opéra-Comique (Comédie-Italienne). This well-established company continued in its home since 1783, the Salle Favart. It was self-governing through its shareholding actor-members and gave performances every night of the week throughout the year, except for major festivals. In 1793 its name was finally confirmed as Opéra Comique National. It continued to present *opéras comiques* by older and newer composers: H.-M. Berton (*Les rigueurs du cloître, Le délire, Montano et Stéphanie*), Dalayrac (the most prolific *opéra comique* composer of the 1790s), Grétry (*Pierre le Grand, Guillaume Tell, Lisbeth, Elisca*), Rodolphe Kreutzer (*Paul et Virginie* and many others) and the young Boieldieu (*Le calife de Bagdad*). The most experimental composer, however, was Méhul, whose reputation

based on works created at this theatre reached into Germany and beyond, since with the temporary decline of the Opéra and the death of Mozart, Méhul's operas (with those of Cherubini at the Théâtre Feydeau) constituted the world's avant garde.

Competition from other theatres during the Revolution, especially from the Feydeau company, caused difficulties. The Opéra-Comique orchestra and chorus had both gained in size and thus expense. In spite of successes by Berton, Dalayrac and others, the company closed its doors on 20 July 1801 and merged with the Théâtre Feydeau on 16 September 1801 to become the new Opéra-Comique.

This new company, formally created by act of government, occupied the Salle Feydeau until 1804 and the Salle Favart until 1805, returning to the Salle Feydeau until 1829. At that point a series of financial crises and disaseers interrupted the company's history. It moved briefly into the Salle Ventadour, rue Neuve-Ventadour (cap. 1106, rising in 1841 to 1294), which had been built specially for it, but finally attained security in the Salle de la Bourse at the Théâtre des Nouveautés, rue Vivienne (built 1827, cap. 1200–1300), which it occupied from 1832 until 1840. Meanwhile the original Salle Favart had burnt down in January 1838, to be replaced by a second one on the same site (cap. c2000). The Opéra-Comique moved into this new building in 1840 and stayed there until it too was destroyed by fire in 1887. Performances, at least in the first part of the century, took place on most evenings of the week throughout the year except for major festivals or state occasions. There were boxes for hire for up to a year at a time, and the clientele was in many cases wealthy;

before 1848 as many as a third of the subscribers were of the aristocracy. It remained essentially a middle-class theatre after 1848. The company maintained a good orchestra of around 55 players, and sometimes held balls.

The Opéra-Comique remained second only to the Opéra in status and achievement, and was recognized in Napoleon's reforms of 1806–7. Until further legislation in 1864, its repertory was bound by legal statute to comprise spoken dialogue linking the musical numbers. Occasional works with recitative instead of dialogue began to be seen in the 1870s. In the early 19th century the repertory established a mainly light tone. Spontini's first French works were presented there, but the staple repertory consisted of operas by many now forgotten names, as well as those by Boieldieu (*Jean de Paris*, *Les voitures versées*, *La dame blanche*), Isouard (*Cendrillon*), Rodolphe Kreutzer and Méhul (*Joseph* and *Uthal* being in stark contrast to the generality of works seen). The next generation produced Hérold, whose best works, *Zampa* and *Le pré aux clercs*, came in the 1830s. The repertory as a whole stood as a bulwark against the italianate invasion of Rossini, but by 1830 not even *opéra comique* could avoid the influence of italianate lyricism and vocal techniques. Thus many works composed by the new generation contained more robust virtuosity. It was a great age of gaiety and wit, in which librettos by Scribe, Saint-Georges, de Leuven, Brunswick and Thomas Sauvage were set by Auber, Adolphe Adam, Fromental Halévy, Ambroise Thomas, Monpou, Grisar, Bazin, Massé and Clapisson. After 1848 Emile Perrin, the new impresario of the company, dedicated himself to renewing the repertory.

15. *The different theatres of the Opéra-Comique: engraving marking the centenary (28 April 1883) of the first Salle Favart. (1) Salle de la Foire St Laurent; (2) Hôtel de Bourgogne; (3) Salle Favart (i); (4) Salle Feydeau; (5) Salle Ventadour; (6) Salle de la Bourse; (7) Salle Favart (ii)*

Public taste changed and, in a sense, became split between a more literary and ambitious sort of dialogue opera, and a simpler, more farcical entertainment. Works by Thomas (*Mignon*), Meyerbeer (*Dinorah*, *L'étoile du nord*) and Auber (*Manon Lescaut*) belong to the first category and were in competition with the nascent repertory of the new Théâtre Lyrique (see §4(vi) below), where Gounod, Bizet, Halévy and Félicien David now chose to put on operas. The second category, closer in style to operetta, was prompted partly by the successes at Offenbach's company, the Bouffes-Parisiens (see §4(vii) below); they included Adam's *Si j'étais roi* and, particularly, Massé's *Les noces de Jeannette*.

(iv) The Théâtre Feydeau. The Feydeau, inaugurated on 26 January 1789, had been founded by L.-A. Autié and the composer G. B. Viotti under the patronage of the king's brother, Monsieur, Comte de Provence (later Louis XVIII), and was originally known as the Théâtre de Monsieur. Performances in 1789 were in the Tuileries, in 1790 in the Salle des Variétés at the Foire St Germain, and from 6 January 1791 in a custom-built theatre on the rue Feydeau (cap. 1700–1900) designed in neoclassical style by Jacques Legrand and Jacques Molinos. At first, Italian opera (by Pergolesi, Sarti and Paisiello among others) and French plays and vaudevilles were given. Cherubini was the musical director and composed new arias and ensembles for works by others. The first important French dialogue opera to be staged was Cherubini's *Lodoïska* (1791), famed for its final conflagration scene; this established the Feydeau as an innovative company, having a particular reputation for realistic scenery and effects. Its orchestra was acknowledged the best in Paris. After 1792 Italian opera was dropped in favour of a mixture of French works. Important ones included Le Sueur's *Paul et Virginie*, Devienne's *Les visitandines*, Gaveaux's *Léonore, ou L'amour conjugal* (the model for *Fidelio*) and Cherubini's *Médée* and *Les deux journées*. For much of the time opera was given on alternate nights with spoken drama, given by a separate company of actors. Composers tended to work exclusively for either the Feydeau or the Opéra-Comique, with Dalayrac the main floater between them.

As an opera company the Feydeau's musical distinction was embodied in the partnership between Mme Scio and Pierre Gaveaux. Gaveaux (a notable composer) was known for agile singing, but Scio was a legendary artist endowed with a superb voice and acting skill. Scio was Médée to Gaveaux's Jason, Léonore to his Florestan, Eliza to his Florindo, and Constance to his Armand. She also excelled in comedy and in *travesti* roles. Under the directorship of Sageret (1795–9) the Feydeau was also famed for its gala orchestral concerts; but gradually he was overwhelmed by the complexities of operating different companies and theatre buildings simultaneously (including the République and the Odéon). After periods of temporary closure the Feydeau shut on 12 April 1801, and was merged with the Opéra-Comique as a new company later the same year (see §4(iii) above).

(v) The Théâtre Italien. Founded by Marguerite Brunet ('La Montansier') in 1801, this company (known officially as the Opera Buffa, and familiarly as the Bouffons) was granted exclusive rights to the performance of Italian opera in Paris in 1807. It gave original-language productions in various theatres under a succession of mostly state-supervised entrepreneurial managements

until 1878. Seasons opened in April and continued throughout the year with two or three performances each week. In 1829 an annual closure from April to October was instituted (partly owing to exchange agreements with the King's Theatre, London, and to diminishing government support). Housed originally at the Salle Olympique, rue Chantereine (now rue de la Victoire), the company was moved by Napoleon to the Salle Favart (1802), then to the Salle Louvois (1804) and the Salle de l'Odéon (1808). It was run by Louis Picard until 1807, from 1804 together with the Théâtre de l'Impératrice (by which name the buildings became known). The 'Italiens' drew at first upon the repertory of the earlier Théâtre de Monsieur (see §4(iv) above), performing works by Cimarosa and Paisiello; they then introduced those by Paer and Mayr and in 1807 commissioned Valentino Fioravanti's *I virtuosi ambulanti*. Operas by Mozart received their first performances in France in Italian: *Figaro* (1807), *Così* (1809) and *Don Giovanni* (1811). Spontini's musical direction (1810–12) added *opere serie* by Zingarelli and others to the theatre's repertory. The expansion that this entailed, the fall of the Empire, and Angelica Catalani's mismanagement of the Salle Favart (the company's home from 1815 to 1818) led the theatre to ruin, though it at first prospered under the musical direction of Paer (1812–18). His initial productions of the works of Rossini, beginning in 1817 with *L'italiana in Algeri*, however, gained him an apparently justified reputation for attempting to sabotage Rossini's reception in Paris.

The company (from 1818 to 1848 officially the Théâtre Royal Italien) was consequently placed under the administration of the Opéra (from 1818 to 1827, as part of an expanded 'Académie Royale de Musique' itself answerable directly to the Maison du Roi) and moved to the nearby Salle Louvois. Paer served again as musical director from 1819 to 1824 and in 1826–7. With productions thus bolstered by the Opéra's resources, the company soon outgrew its quarters (built in 1791 to accommodate 1100 spectators). Between 1821 and 1824, premières of Rossini's *La gazza ladra*, *Elisabetta, regina d'Inghilterra*, *Mosè in Egitto* and *La donna del lago* were given at the Opéra's Salle Le Peletier, and in 1825 the company returned to the Salle Favart. (Its dated elliptical space, built for the Comédie-Italienne in 1783, had in the meantime been made circular.) Members of the troupe's orchestra, famed for its discretion in accompanying singers, gained positions at the Opéra.

The Théâtre Italien was the point of entry in Paris for Rossini, who staged *Semiramide* and *Zelmira* and revived eight earlier works including *Barbiere* and *Tancredi* during his directorship, which interrupted that of Paer from 1824 to 1826. His last Italian opera, *Il viaggio a Reims* (1825), was composed for the troupe which then included Giuditta Pasta, Laure Cinti-Damoreau, Ester Mombelli, Nicholas Levasseur, Zucchelli, Donzelli, Felice Pellegrini and Vincenzo Graziani. That same year, Rossini launched Meyerbeer's Parisian career with a production of *Il crociato in Egitto*. After the management reverted to entrepreneurs in 1827, he assisted with the recruitment of singers such as Malibran, Sontag, Pisaroni, Filippo Galli, Lablache, Tamburini, Giovanni Battista Rubini and Giulia Grisi, and the commissioning of operas, including Bellini's *I puritani* and Donizetti's *Marino Faliero* (both given in 1835) and Mercadante's *I briganti* (1836). Productions of more than a dozen of Donizetti's works (including

16. Performance by the Théâtre Italien at the Salle Ventadour, Paris: lithograph by C. Mottram after Eugène Lami, from Jules Janin's 'Un hiver à Paris' (1843)

Sonnambula and *Anna Bolena* in 1831, *Norma* in 1835, *Lucia* in 1837) led to the commissioning, in 1843, of *Don Pasquale*; this première took place at the Salle Ventadour, the company's new home following the destruction of the Salle Favart in 1838. Revivals, particularly of Rossini, thenceforth sustained the theatre through frequent changes of management and competition from the Théâtre Lyrique and the Opéra, where Italian opera was also staged. However, 15 works by Verdi, beginning with *Nabucco* (1845) and *Ernani* (1846), including such singers as Giorgio Ronconi, Borghi-Mamo and Fraschini, infused the repertory with new life. Verdi preferred this theatre to other Parisian ones and conducted *Aida* and his Requiem there in 1876. From 1852 to 1870 the company was known as the Théâtre Impérial Italien. It was abandoned in 1878 and the house was converted to offices, currently owned by the Banque de France.

(vi) The Théâtre Lyrique. The composer Adolphe Adam, backed by the impresario F.-L. Crosnier, opened the Opéra-National in 1847. It occupied 66 boulevard du Temple, using the newly converted Cirque Olympique building (cap. 2400). Its inspirations had been the common desire to see a third opera house dedicated to French music, the desire to revive *opéra comique* of an earlier period and the perceived need to open opera up to a wider clientele. Owing to the revolutionary events of 1848 the theatre closed in March that year. Subsequently the project resumed at 72 boulevard du Temple, in the Théâtre Historique (cap. 1500–1700). It opened on 27 September 1851, and was renamed the Théâtre Lyrique on 12 April 1852. A new building was erected for the company, the Salle du Théâtre Lyrique, situated on the place du Châtelet opposite the Châtelet theatre (fig.17 overleaf), and inaugurated in October 1862 (cap. 1800). It was burnt down during the Commune, on 25 May 1871. After that, there was a brief period at the Théâtre de l'Athénée (17 rue Scribe; cap. 760–900). The company ceased to exist in 1872.

The Théâtre Lyrique became the most important rival to the Opéra and the Opéra-Comique during its two decades of existence. It was permitted by statute to give all types of opera, including two non-French works per year. At first it was run by Edmond Seveste, then by his brother Jules (1852–4). In 1856 the directorship went to the 30-year-old Léon Carvalho, himself a professional singer, who went on to direct the Opéra-Comique from 1876. Carvalho was a flamboyant and inventive spirit, and was assisted by his wife Marie Caroline, a considerable singer. He remained in charge until 1868 (except for the years 1860–62), after which Jules Pasdeloup succeeded him. The repertory, which was large, can be divided into four categories: earlier French *opéra comique*, including Grétry (with modernized orchestration), Boieldieu and Hérold; contemporary French opera; 19th-century opera from Germany and Italy given in translation; and finally the work of young, untried composers. In the second category Carvalho attracted new works of major importance: Gounod's *Le médecin malgré lui*, *Faust*, *Mireille* and *Roméo et Juliette*; Bizet's *Les pêcheurs de perles* and *La jolie fille de Perth*; Halévy's *Jaguarita l'indienne*; Félicien David's *La perle du Brésil*; and, in 1863, the last three acts of Berlioz's *Les Troyens*, as *Les Troyens à Carthage*. New operas by Reyer, Adam, Delibes and others were also seen. Berlioz's *Mémoires* bear witness to Carvalho's tendency to alter at will the works that he presented. Major non-French works at the Théâtre Lyrique included operas by Mozart, Beethoven, Weber, Bellini, Donizetti, Verdi and Wagner (*Rienzi* in 1869). These performances played an influential role in popularizing the mainstream repertory, and it is hard not to see connections between runs of, for example, *Oberon* or *Traviata* and the development of Bizet's style. Works by many young composers were staged, their names forgotten today. (For a complete list see Walsh 1981, pp. 323–30).

(vii) Other companies.
Théâtre de l'Ambigu-Comique. This company went back to the later 18th century. In 1786 a new theatre was made for it on the boulevard du Temple (cap. 1500–1600), and after this burnt down in 1827 the company moved to a new building of slightly greater capacity at 2 boulevard Saint-Martin. Even before the Revolution of 1789 it gave vaudevilles, melodramas and small-scale *opéras comiques*, and continued these, with ballet pantomimes, until 1815, when it was required to limit itself to melodrama, pantomime and one-act

17. *Interior of the Salle du Théâtre Lyrique (place du Châtelet), during the original production of Ernst Boulanger's 'Don Quichotte', 10 May 1869: engraving from 'Le journal illustré' (May 1869)*

spoken comedies. This situation obtained until 1847. It also maintained a *corps de ballet* and an orchestra of about 25. After 1847 its repertory was limited to spoken theatre.

Théâtre des Bouffes-Parisiens. This opened in 1855 on the Champs-Elysées, carré Marigny, moving in December the same year to the Salle Choiseul (*see* OPERETTA, fig.1), still standing at 4 rue Monsigny (cap. 840–940). Here Jacques Offenbach established his own company, giving *opéra bouffe* and operetta, including his masterpiece *Orphée aux enfers* (1858). In 1866 Offenbach quarrelled with his partners and withdrew his works. The theatre continued with light opera until 1879.

Cirque Olympique. Famous for its equestrian shows and similar spectacles, the company, after 1830, gave pantomimes and spectacular historical dramas with music. It was on the boulevard du Temple and had a capacity of about 2250.

Théâtre de la Gaîté. This company made its name before the 1789 Revolution under J.-B. Nicolet, giving harlequin plays, marionette plays and various acrobatic shows. After the reforms of 1807 it continued with pantomime, harlequin plays and, later, melodramas. Situated at 58 boulevard du Temple, the theatre housed just over 1800 spectators. The director was the famous dramatist R. C. G. de Pixérécourt (1825–35) and the musical director was Louis Alexandre Piccinni (1818–31). It was demolished in 1862 when the Temple area was modernized. A new theatre was then constructed, with the same capacity, on the square des Arts

et Métiers; a mixture of musical entertainment and opera was given, under various company names.

Gymnase-Dramatique. The company began in 1820 in a new theatre at 38 boulevard Bonne-Nouvelle (cap. 1000–1300). From 1824 to 1830 it took the name of Madame, Duchesse de Berry. It gave smaller *opéras comiques* and vaudevilles, many being by Scribe. The orchestra was some 24 strong.

Théâtre des Nouveautés. Two separate ventures used this name. The first, in the Salle de la Bourse, rue Vivienne (cap. 1250), existed from 1827 to 1831 and gave *opéras comiques* and other musical pieces, especially non-French works in the French language (e.g. *Le barbier de Séville*) for which Castil-Blaze often acted as arranger. The chorus at one period included Berlioz. The second venture, on the Faubourg St-Martin (cap. 400), existed from 1866 to 1873, giving a range of light opera and vaudeville.

Théâtre de l'Odéon. Inaugurated in September 1819, this theatre stood on the place de l'Odéon on the same site as its predecessor (occupied from 1808 to 1815 by the Théâtre Italien), which had burnt down in 1818. Its new capacity was around 1600. From 1823 to 1828 the company maintained an opera troupe and an orchestra of up to 50. It gave 18th- and 19th-century *opéras comiques* and works by Winter, Mozart, Beethoven and Weber (in Castil-Blaze's mutilated French versions). Meyerbeer's *Marguérite d'Anjou*, adapted from the Milanese original (1820), had a successful run in 1826. Some light opera was given from time to time in later years, especially in 1849–50.

Porte-St-Martin. This theatre building was erected in

1781 on the boulevard St-Martin (where it still stands, in its second incarnation) as a home for the Opéra. It became a theatre company in its own right in 1802, specializing in pantomime, melodrama and spectacular entertainments. Napoleon closed it in 1807 but in 1810 it reopened under the name Jeux-Gymniques, which it held until 1812. Its fame as a ballet company then began, with pieces such as *Les chevaliers de la table ronde* (1811), complete with horses, and *Lise et Colin dans leur ménage* (1812). Piqued by these, the Opéra successfully applied for an injunction on the grounds that the company had infringed its right to ballets of 'noble and gracious style, such as those whose subjects derive from mythology or history'. The Porte-St-Martin reopened under its original name late in 1814 with a licence to give ballet, which it did with great success.

Théâtre de la Renaissance. This name was used by various enterprises. The first existed from 1838 to 1841 in the Salle Ventadour (built in 1829 for the Opéra-Comique) and gave both *opéra comique* and Italian opera. Donizetti's *La favorite* originated as a commission for this company, under the title *L'ange de Nisida*. In 1868, in the same building, Carvalho (having just resigned from the Théâtre Lyrique) put on works by Gounod and Clapisson. A third enterprise began in 1873, and still exists. Its theatre was on the boulevard St-Martin (inaugurated 1873; cap. 750). In the 19th century it gave a range of *opéra comique*, operetta and opera.

Théâtre des Variétés. Opened in 1790 in the small theatre in the Palais-Royal used by the Théâtre Beaujolais, the Variétés presented *opéra comique*, vaudeville and comedies until 1806. It survived Napoleon's decrees and in 1807 moved to the boulevard Montmartre (cap. *c*1240), where its repertory was limited to vaudevilles, parodies and small *opéras comiques* like Blangini's *Le chanteur des romances*. After the liberalization of 1864 it gave operetta and *opéra bouffe* by Offenbach, Lecocq, Hervé and Audran among others.

Théâtre du Vaudeville. Founded on 12 January 1792, this became one of the four secondary theatres established by imperial decree in 1807. Until 1838 it occupied a ballroom designed by Nicolas Lenoir (cap. 1257) situated on the corner of the rue de Chartres and the rue de St-Thomas-du-Louvre. When this building was destroyed by fire, the company moved briefly to the boulevard Bonne-Nouvelle before taking over the Salle de la Bourse, vacated by the Opéra-Comique, on 16 May 1840. It remained there until 1869. Pierre-Yon Barré directed the Vaudeville from 1792 to 1815; few subsequent directors remained in post for more than one or two years. The repertory was light in tone, consisting almost exclusively of vaudevilles and *parodies*. Only after 1860 did legislation enable more substantial plays with original music to be presented, such as Daudet's *L'Arlésienne* in 1872, with Bizet's score. The orchestra varied in size between 22 and 32 players.

Many other theatres staged lighter works, including the Théâtre de la Galerie Vivienne (for 18th-century *opéra comique*), the Salle des Menus-Plaisirs, the Théâtre Beaumarchais and the Théâtre du Châtelet. From around 1820 a number of theatres were constructed in the suburbs and their names indicate the areas they served: Batignolles, Belleville, Grenelle, Mont-

martre, Montparnasse and Ranelagh (at the Barrière du Roule).

5. 1870–1902.

(i) Background. The last 30 years of the 19th century present a relatively simple picture of two main opera houses in co-existence, each contributing to the development of opera in France in its own way. There is, however, a somewhat confusing picture caused by the destruction of the Opéra-Comique building (the second Salle Favart) on 25 May 1887, after which performances were moved to other locations; and by operatic ventures where confusion can still arise between the name of a company and that of the theatre in which they operated (see Table 2). While the construction of the new Paris Opéra naturally stole the lion's share of public attention, the Opéra-Comique continued to play an important role, especially in staging the works of contemporary French composers. Only a few other theatres contributed to the development of French opera during this period, and none of them substantially. Of these the most important was the Opéra National Lyrique which produced new operas by French composers, such as Joncières' *Dimitri*, Massé's *Paul et Virginie* and Saint-Saëns' *Le timbre d'argent*. The Eden-Théâtre (1883–94) secured itself a place in French operatic history by mounting, against considerable public opposition, the first Paris performance of *Lohengrin*. Also deserving mention are the activities of the Théâtre de l'Odéon, particularly noted for its production of plays with incidental music, a practice it continued well into the 20th century. In 1885 Daudet's *L'Arlésienne* was produced with Bizet's music (originally 1872), and three years later Fauré composed music for Dumas' *Caligula*.

(ii) The Opéra. The year 1860 marked the conception of a new building for the Paris Opéra. A decree dated 29 September indicated the approximate borders of a newly planned opera house between the boulevard des Capucines, the rue de la Chaussée-d'Antin, the rue Neuve-des-Mathurins and the passage Sandrié. On 29 December these boundaries were prescribed as preconditions for a competition inviting architects to submit proposals within a time-limit of only one month. During that time 171 proposals were received, reduced at once to 43, then to 16 and finally to 7. Each architect submitted a motto, most often in Latin or French, in some way pertinent to his plans for the building and its subsequent use. The winner, announced on 29 May 1861, was Charles Garnier, who had christened the building in Italian: 'Bramo assai, poco spero'. Work on the foundations began without delay, the first problem being to drain the sodden site of water. From 2 March to 13 October 1861 eight steam engines pumped 24 hours a day and by 21 May 1862 the upright supports were in place. Little did Garnier realize that this scrupulous preparation would make the building ideal for storing provisions, a fate to which it succumbed during the Commune in 1869–70. It finally achieved its intended use in 1875.

Many features merit description: the numerous statues of composers and mythical figures that provided the themes for so much of the repertory; the latest-style gas lighting with an 'organ' of distribution pipes to simulate night or day at the pull of a lever (*see* LIGHTING, fig.3); the immense reservoirs of water for use in case of fire; the entirely separate inner corridors to lead

TABLE 2: Principal Paris theatres, 1870–1902

company names in italics duplicate the name of the theatre

company	theatre
Opéra [Théâtre National de l'Opéra]	Salle Le Peletier (until 28 Oct 1873) Salle Ventadour (19 Jan–Dec 1874) Palais Garnier (5 Jan 1875 onwards)
Opéra-Comique [Théâtre National de l'Opéra-Comique]	Salle Favart (until 25 May 1887) Théâtre Lyrique (15 Oct 1887–30 June 1898) Théâtre du Château-d'Eau (26 Oct–30 Nov 1898) Salle Favart (iii) (8 Dec 1898 onwards)
Opéra National Lyrique [Théâtre National Lyrique, Théâtre Lyrique National]	Théâtre de la Gaîté (5 May 1876–2 Jan 1878)
Opéra Populaire (i)	Théâtre du Châtelet (13 Nov–13 Dec 1874)
Opéra Populaire (ii)	Théâtre de la Gaîté (27 Oct 1879–Feb 1880)
Opéra Populaire (iii) and (iv)	Théâtre du Château-d'Eau (summer seasons, 1879–82; 8 May 1883–29 Nov 1884; 27 Nov 1900–11 March 1901)
Théâtre Lyrique (i)	Salle de l'Athénée (11 Sept 1871–31 May 1872)
Théâtre Lyrique (ii)	Théâtre du Château-d'Eau (13 Oct 1888–5 March 1889)
Théâtre Lyrique (iii)	Théâtre de la Renaissance (Jan–March 1893; March 1899–March 1900)
Théâtre du Château-d'Eau	Théâtre du Château-d'Eau (11 Dec 1869–1888; 3 Aug 1889–25 May 1890; 9 Oct 1891–13 July 1893; March 1901–1903; summer festivals including opera, 1879–1902)
Eden-Théâtre	Eden-Théâtre (17 Jan 1883–1894)
Théâtre de la Gaîté	Théâtre de la Gaîté (1 June 1873–1 July 1875; Jan 1878–27 Oct 1879; Feb 1880 onwards); see also above, Opéra National Lyrique and Opéra Populaire (i)
Nouveau-Lyrique	Théâtre Taitbout (Oct–Nov 1879)

the head of state to his box. But nothing rivalled the celebrated staircase that justifiably became a talking-point for many years (fig.19): even Debussy mentioned it in a criticism of 1902. Staircases were a speciality of Garnier, whose architectural philosophy anticipated modern thought with its stress on the use of a building, while at the same time borrowing ideas from Italian art. Garnier explained his principles:

On each floor, the spectators leaning on the balconies garnish the walls, rendering them alive, as it were, while those going up and down the stairs themselves added to this impression. In adding

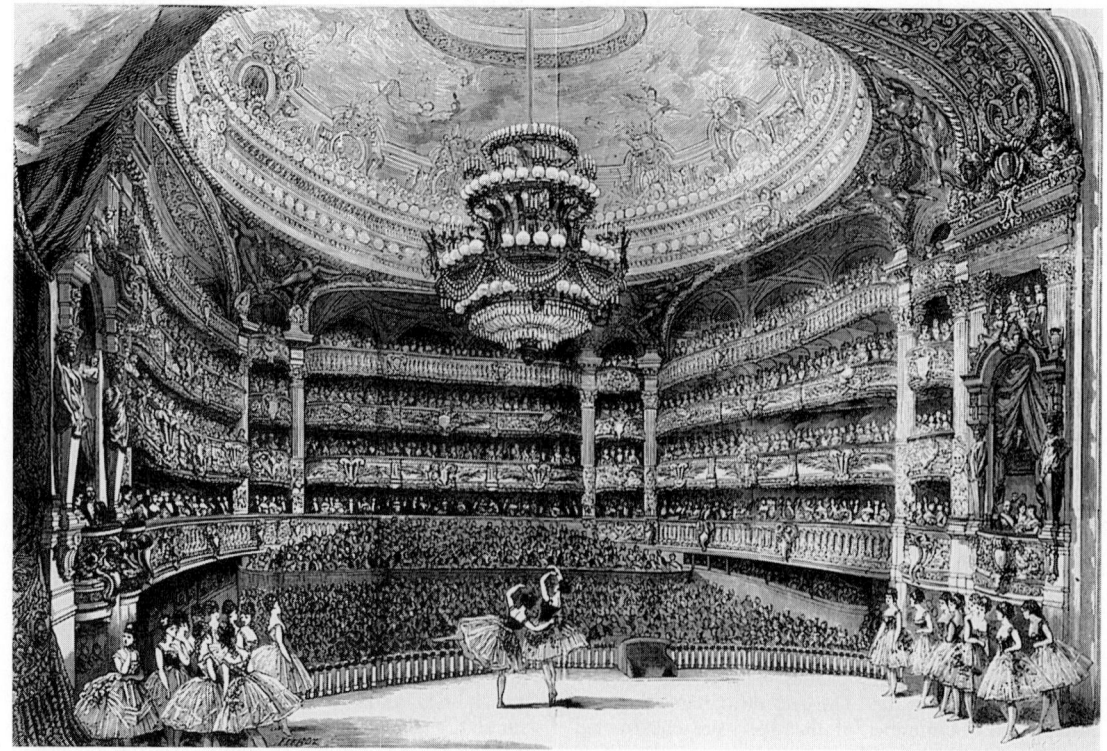

18. *Auditorium of the Théâtre National de l'Opéra (Palais Garnier): engraving from 'L'illustration' (16 January 1875)*

19. Staircase of the Théâtre National de l'Opéra (Palais Garnier) during the opening ceremony on 5 January 1875: painting by Edouard Detaille

materials and hanging draperies, chandeliers and candelabra, and with the marble adorned with flowers, a sumptuous and brilliant composition will result, recalling in real life one of those scenes which Veronese captured on canvas.

Clearly, in Garnier's vision of the building, art and the *tableau vivant* were not to be restricted to the opera stage (*see* THEATRE ARCHITECTURE, fig.4).

The opening performance of the newly designated Théâtre National de l'Opéra, given before the president of the Republic and other national and international notables (including the Lord Mayor of London), took place on 5 January 1875. Even this was beset by last-minute changes common in the opera's previous homes. One of the main female singers was unable to sing, and thus an act of *Faust* and one of *Hamlet* (by Ambroise Thomas) were cancelled, leaving only extracts from *La Juive*, *Les Huguenots* and *La source*, a ballet by Delibes. The first director, Hyacinthe Halanzier (also known as Halanzier-Dufrénoy or Dufresnoy), profited from public interest in the novelty of the building but made few significant musical inaugurations, and during ten years of directing operas produced not one foreign work. So healthy were the receipts during his incumbency (until 1879) that he was called before members of the grant-awarding national assembly to discuss reduction of their support. However, after he underlined the precariousness of the political future and the sudden downturn in

attendances that might easily befall the opera house, the level of subsidy was sustained. During the first year no new works were given. 1876 saw the creation of the now forgotten *Jeanne d'Arc* by Mermet, and Delibes' ballet *Sylvia*. In 1877 the Opéra produced its first Massenet première, *Le roi de Lahore*, which ran to 57 performances. Gounod's *Polyeucte* was created the following year, and Joncières' *La reine Berthe*, which ran to only five performances, was the last new opera given during Halanzier's directorship.

The next landmark in the history of the building was the installation of electric lighting in 1881 (*see* LIGHTING, fig.5), by which time Auguste Vaucorbeil was director. A man from the ministry, he had been known for his campaign to have Lalo's *Le roi d'Ys* staged at the Opéra, but immediately after his appointment he rejected the work, which was instead taken up by the Opéra-Comique. Vaucorbeil's directorship was cut short in 1884 by his untimely death. He is perhaps best remembered for a remarkable experiment in 1881 when *Les Huguenots* was transmitted to an audience in the scenery store by means of a *théâtrephone*, preceding radio transmission by some 50 years. Vaucorbeil's replacement was Pierre Gailhard, a man of great character who returned to the directorship or co-directorship of the house several times. Trained as a singer, Gailhard on one occasion sang the part from the

20. Riot outside the Palais Garnier that followed the first production there of Wagner's 'Lohengrin' on 16 September 1891: engraving from 'Le journal illustré' (27 September 1891)

wings for a miming singer who had lost his voice. Among his other bequests was the inauguration of matinées; he was much criticized for this and accused of attracting children and old people whose behaviour was incompatible with the solemnity of the place. One of Gailhard's main achievements was his introduction of staged performances of Wagner, previously (though fairly frequently) heard only in concert extracts. In 1891 he mounted *Lohengrin*, the first Wagner production at the Opéra since 1861, to an audience some of whom were armed with stink-bombs. So unruly was the crowd that strong police intervention was required (see fig.20): the 'Marseillaise' was raucously played outside the building, and the arrested spent the night in the basement of the opera building, having wrecked the German-owned Brasserie de Hanovre. A report on these events in the *Univers illustré* sardonically pointed out that while the majority of the 'inferior races' present had acclaimed the work, one person had asked Lamoureux to play the 'Marseillaise'. Such events were not unexpected: of the ten performances of the same work announced by the Eden-Théâtre in 1887 only two took place, on account of street disturbances.

Eugène Bertrand took over the directorship of the house in 1892, and in April 1893 Gailhard reappeared as co-director. 1892 was an important year not only for the Opéra's première of Saint-Saëns' *Samson et Dalila* (which has since run to over a thousand performances), but also for a concert performance of Charpentier's symphony-drama *La vie du poète*, indicating the inroads this realist composer had made into an institution largely affiliated to grand operas on classical or historical themes. That year Chabrier's *Gwendoline*, previously given elsewhere in Europe, was staged. Most important, perhaps, was the sudden advance made on the Wagner front: *Rheingold* was given in a piano version and *Walküre* was at last staged following performances in New York, Brussels and London. The event passed relatively calmly, though by now the French had seen the opportunity for parody, with several operettas and novels satirizing *Lohengrin* and *Walküre* (*La Valkyrigole*, for example) being produced. Serious questioning about the right of the French to perform Wagner was to be muted, at least until after World War I.

Italian opera had not been neglected amid the furore of Wagner disputes, and there was a steady if unambitious programming of new works. Rossini was treated to yet another revival of *Guillaume Tell* (first mounted by the house in 1829) and the systematic introduction of Verdi's operas was begun, *Aida* and *Rigoletto* having been staged in the new building in 1880 and 1885 respectively, following performances elsewhere in Paris. *Otello* was given in 1894. That year a serious fire in the scenery store resulted in the cancellation of several planned revivals although some of the scenery was rebuilt. The short run of Lefebvre's *Djelma* was overshadowed by the première of Massenet's *Thaïs*, a production whose fashionable mix of the erotic and the ascetic led to several successful revivals. 1895 saw the premières of two works that quickly fell into oblivion: Holmès's *La montagne noir* and Guiraud's *Frédégonde*, completed by Dukas and Saint-Saëns. These were followed in 1896 by Duvernoy's *Hellé*, during a performance of which one of the counterweights to the grand chandelier fell into the auditorium, killing a member of the audience and injuring two others.

1897 was a more fortunate year, with Bruneau's half-fantastic, half-*vériste Messidor* receiving its première, marking a substantial departure from the Opéra's conservative policy with regard to subject matter in an era when the librettist's name almost always preceded that of the composer. The same year saw a concert performance of Berlioz's *La damnation de Faust*, as well as the Paris première of *Meistersinger*, previously given in Lyons. Samuel Rousseau's *La cloche du Rhin* and Vidal's *La Burgonde* marked an uneventful 1898 and at the end of the year the directorship reverted to Gailhard as sole incumbent, a post he was to hold unchallenged until the 1906–7 season.

1899 was a year of considerable interest with the Garnier première of Méhul's *Joseph* (first given in Paris in 1807 and during the 1860s but not revived again until 1946), the first act of Chabrier's incomplete *Briséïs* some six years after its successful introduction in a concert performance, and the first part of Berlioz's *Les Troyens* given under the title *La prise de Troie*. In 1900 Joncières' *Lancelot* had its première, one of the less successful operas on the fashionable Arthurian themes, and a gala performance included the second act of *Carmen*, hitherto the exclusive property of the Opéra-Comique. While this was a year of revivals and centenaries, the following year broke all records for the number of new productions: four operas and a new ballet. Leroux's *Astarté*, Hüe's *Le roi de Paris*, and Saint-Saëns' *Les barbares* and *Siegfried* were all mounted for the first time. 1902 saw the première of the Hillemachers' opera *Orsola* and the Opéra's first production of Leoncavallo's *Pagliacci*, known in France as *Paillasse*.

(iii) The Opéra-Comique. During the period of construction of the new Opéra, the activities of the Opéra-Comique carried on without interruption until the second Salle Favart was destroyed by fire in 1887. The Salle Ventadour was also affiliated to the Opéra-Comique until December 1878. A third Salle Favart, occupying the same site as the second in the place Boieldieu, was in operation from 1898. In the interim (15 October 1887–30 June 1898) the company had played in the Salle du Théâtre Lyrique in the place du Châtelet, subsequently known as the Théâtre Sarah Bernhardt and still in use today under the name Théâtre de la Ville.

From January 1874 to March 1876 the director was Camille Du Locle, who had co-directed from July 1870. With hindsight there can be no doubt that his greatest achievement was his championing of Bizet: he was dedicatee of both the words and music of *Djamileh* and it was he who mounted *Carmen*, although he appears to have loathed both music and libretto. Little did he realize that it was to become one of the most successful pieces created by the house, having notched up 1000 performances by 1904 and 2000 by 1930. Apart from newly staged works, the Opéra-Comique continued to revive the operas it had made its own during the first half of the century, including Adam's *Le chalet*, Auber's *Fra Diavolo* and *Le domino noir*, Thomas' *Mignon* and *Le caïd*, Hérold's *Zampa* and Méhul's *Joseph*. Boieldieu's *La dame blanche* received over 1600 performances before the end of the century and Massé's *Les noces de Jeannette* ran to over 1800. Grétry's *Richard Coeur-de-lion* was another popular piece revived regularly throughout the century. One of Du Locle's preferred composers was Gounod, as is reflected by the yearly revivals he mounted of operas first performed at the Théâtre Lyrique in the 1860s: *Le médecin malgré lui* (1872), *Roméo et Juliette* (1873), *Mireille* (1874) and *Philémon et Baucis* (1876). It was in 1876 that financial problems at the Opéra-Comique

came to a head, and in May that year Du Locle declared bankruptcy. He was succeeded in August by the energetic Léon Carvalho, previously the incumbent at the Théâtre Lyrique and stage director at the Opéra who, knowing that Gounod could be trusted to produce a further opera within a prescribed time, commissioned *Cinq Mars*, created by the house in 1877.

After the 1872 performance of his *Don César de Bazan*, Massenet's career at the Opéra-Comique had continued with a highly successful revival of his *drame sacré Marie-Magdeleine*, previously given at the Odéon. From then until the end of the century, eight of his operas were given at the Opéra-Comique: *Manon* (1884), *Esclarmonde* (1889), *Werther* (1893), *Le portrait de Manon* (1894), *La navarraise* (1895), *Sapho* (1897), *Cendrillon* (1899) and *Grisélidis* (1901). If no other composer could claim so many Opéra-Comique successes as Massenet, others contributed no less important works to the house repertory. Offenbach's final stage work, *Les contes d'Hoffmann*, was created there in 1881; Saint-Saëns' *La princesse jaune* (1872), *Proserpine* (1887) and *Phryné* (1893) were performed by the company, as were Delibes' *Le roi l'a dit* (1873),

21. *Poster by François Flameng for Massenet's 'Grisélidis' printed by Bourgerie at the time of the original production at the Opéra-Comique in 1901*

22. The fire that engulfed the second Salle Favart of the Opéra-Comique on 25 May 1887: engraving

Jean de Nivelle (1880), Lakmé (1883) and Kassya (1893). Lakmé was Delibes' most lasting opera – reminiscences of early performances invariably mention the wealth of fresh flowers used in the production – and had run to 1000 performances by 1931. Lalo's Le roi d'Ys became a successful repertory piece of the Opéra-Comique after rejection by the Opéra, and mention must also be made of the company's support for Chabrier, whose Le roi malgré lui was given in 1887.

Some of the repertory of the period has rightly or wrongly fallen into obscurity: pieces such as Maréchal's Les amoureux de Cathérine (1876) had received over a hundred performances by the end of the century. 1895 saw productions of Dubois' Xavière and Godard's La vivandière, and the new century brought Camille Erlanger's Le Juif polonais and Hahn's La Carmélite. Imported opera also played its part with both revivals and creations. Figaro and Zauberflöte had several revivals, as did Donizetti's La fille du régiment. Verdi made some headway with Traviata (1886), which had achieved over a hundred performances by the end of the century. Falstaff followed in 1894, and the French première of Puccini's La bohème in 1898 was successful.

Carvalho remained as director until 25 May 1887, when more than 400 people were asphyxiated by a fire that destroyed the building and forced the company to find other locations for its performances. Carvalho resigned but was acquitted of blame, resuming directorship of the house from 1 January 1891 to 31 December 1897. In the interim, Jules Barbier (May–December 1887) and Paravey (January 1888–91) occupied the post.

Towards the end of the century the Opéra-Comique transferred to the musical stage the aesthetic pioneered by André Antoine at his Théâtre Antoine, namely the cultivation of staged works in the naturalist tradition of Zola. Operatically the two most important composers to ally themselves to this movement were Bruneau and Charpentier. Gallet's first libretto after Zola was for Bruneau's Le rêve, produced in 1891; this was followed by L'attaque du moulin (1893) and by Zola's own L'ouragan (1901). Although the Opéra had mounted Messidor in 1897, the Opéra-Comique can claim to have championed the realist cause more than did the Opéra.

From 16 January 1898 Albert Carré assumed the role of director, marking a new phase of adventurousness in the company's history. His reign was to last until December 1913, and it was he who inaugurated the third Salle Favart on 8 December 1898 with an entirely new production of Carmen. The decor was by L. Jusseaume, whose detailed and evocative sets were to become the visual hallmark of productions for some years. The culmination of Carré's achievements was yet to come. First was Charpentier's highly successful roman musical Louise, created by the Opéra-Comique in 1900, which continued the realist traditions already established with the productions of Bruneau. Louise was many times revived at the new Salle Favart, having run to over 900 performances when it was memorably revived in 1950 with sets by the Montmartre painter Maurice Utrillo. Diametrically opposite in terms of its aesthetic was Carré's second success of the new century, Debussy's Pelléas et Mélisande. Here, for the first time, the contrary voice of symbolism, as yet relatively undeveloped in terms of theatre and dominated during the 1890s by the Belgian playwright Maurice Maeterlinck, was for the first time successfully transferred to the operatic stage.

(iv) Other companies. Paris continued to play host to a great deal of theatrical activity during the closing decades of the 19th century. Companies specializing in either opera or *opéra comique*, in addition to the Eden-Théâtre and the Opéra National Lyrique mentioned above, included several ventures using the name of Opéra Populaire, performing at the Châtelet, the Gaîté and the Château-d'Eau mainly during the 1870s and 1880s (see Table 2). The Théâtre Lyrique, likewise an appellation for different theatrical enterprises (see Table 2) – as well as a building in its own right – offered a similar repertory, as did the Théâtre de la Gaîté, directed during the 1870s by Offenbach and performing mainly Italian opera, the Théâtre du Château-d'Eau, which closed on 9 April 1903, and the Nouveau Lyrique.

Companies specializing in lighter forms, particularly operetta and vaudeville, and operating from their own theatres, included the Beaumarchais (1884–92), Capucines, Déjazet (from 1880), Folies-Dramatiques (1863–99) and Menus-Plaisirs (until 1874; 1877–8; 1882–97). The Théâtre des Menus-Plaisirs was also used by companies such as the Théâtre des Arts (1874–6; 1879–80), the Opéra-Bouffe (1876) and the Comédie Parisienne (1881–2), while the Théâtre des Fantaisies-Parisiennes used the Beaumarchais (1878–84) and the Théâtre des Folies-Nouvelles the Déjazet (1871–2; 1880). The Théâtre de la République played for several years at the Château-d'Eau (1893–1900).

23. *Poster by Georges Rochegrosse for Gustave Charpentier's 'Louise', printed by E. Delanchy at the time of the original production at the Opéra-Comique in 1900*

6. 20TH CENTURY.

(i) To 1939. In 1900, Gailhard's contract as director of the Opéra was renewed for a further six years. Melba and Jean de Reszke were added to a company that already included Ackté, Bréval, Calvé, Noté and Renaud, but Gailhard's commissioning policy was cautious and the principal French composers were obliged to stage premières in the provinces or at La Monnaie, Brussels. The Opéra mounted well-known works suitable for gala performances for visiting royalty, of which there were many. In 1915 Jacques Rouché became director and during the next 30 years he created a disciplined, mainly French troupe of singers who sang almost exclusively at the Opéra, their appearances elsewhere being frowned upon. He commissioned new works from established composers like Bruneau, Mariotte, d'Indy, Widor, Canteloube and Hüe; other notable premières included Roussel's *Padmâvatî* (1923) and Milhaud's *Maximilien* (1932). There were revivals of operas by Lully and Rameau, and works by Wagner were also staged, but the repertory was mostly French post-romantic. It was a period of 'déclamation lyrique' rather than bel canto, and only about a dozen Italian works were performed during Rouché's regime, five of them by Verdi. Ballet continued as an essential feature of the repertory.

Carré continued as director of the Opéra-Comique, with Messager as musical director from 1898 to 1904. As the distinction between opera and *opéra comique* faded, the two theatres became rivals, each with their own orchestra and company, although some singers sang at both. The Opéra-Comique, however, produced more audacious contemporary works, including, in addition to *Louise* and *Pelléas*, *Ariane et Barbe-bleue* and Leroux' *Le chemineau* (both 1907), *L'heure espagnole* (1911) and works by Puccini, Mascagni, Leoncavallo and Falla. Several other theatres had operatic seasons; some, like the Trianon-Lyrique (1887–1934), received subsidies from the Paris city council. A further eight theatres – the Apollo, Bobino, Casino, Casino de Paris, Empire, Montparnasse, Européen and Mogador – were almost entirely devoted to operetta, and others held short seasons featuring lyric works and ballet. In 1905 a season of Italian opera with Enrico Caruso, Titta Ruffo, Angelo Masini, Amadeo Bassi, Lina Cavalieri and Amalia Pinto was held at the Théâtre des Nations (today the Théâtre de la Ville). The Théâtre du Châtelet's programmes included *Salome* with Destinn, conducted by Strauss, in 1907, Dyagilev's Ballets Russes with Shalyapin, Litvinne and Lipkowska giving scenes from *Prince Igor*, *Ruslan and Lyudmila* and other operas in 1909, and, in 1910, a season of Italian opera by the Metropolitan under Toscanini, when *Aida*, *Cavalleria rusticana* and *Pagliacci*, *Otello*, *Falstaff* and *Manon Lescaut* were performed by Bori, Destinn, Fremstad, Alda, Caruso, Pasquale Amato, Slezak and Jadlowker.

The Théâtre des Champs-Elysées in the Avenue Montaigne opened in 1913, after an inaugural concert, with *Benvenuto Cellini*, conducted by Weingartner. The first theatre to be built of reinforced concrete, designed by Auguste Perret, it housed three theatres, the principal one seating 2100. (The two smaller theatres are used mainly as playhouses.) The initial season continued with *Freischütz* (conducted by Weingartner), *Lucia* and *Barbiere* (Barrientos), *Khovanshchina* and *Boris* (both with Shalyapin and conducted by Emil Cooper; *Boris* was also given in French under Inghelbrecht with Eugenio Giraldoni in the title role), and the Paris première of *Pénélope* with Bréval and Muratore. This sumptuous season also included Dyagilev's Ballets Russes giving the première of *The Rite of Spring*. In spring 1914 various Italian companies, whose soloists included Melba, Claudia Muzio, Giovanni Martinelli and Vanni-Marcoux, presented several works, most notably the French première of *L'amore dei tre re*. Performances of *Tristan*, *Meistersinger* and *Parsifal* under Arthur Nikisch, Weingartner and Albert Coates followed, all for the first time in their original language. This all led to bankruptcy, and opera was not presented again until 1922, although the high standards set by the director, Gabriel Astruc, were never entirely forgotten. In 1922 Serafin conducted a season of Wagner operas in Italian with Pertile and Bassi, and in 1924 two Mozart cycles were given, one of *Don Giovanni*, *Entführung* and *Figaro* by the Vienna Staatsoper under Schalk, the other by a French troupe under Walther Staram who had become director of the theatre. In 1928 *Figaro*, *Don Giovanni* and *Così* were given under Bruno Walter, and Krenek's *Jonny spielt auf* was given its French première. The Opéra Russe de Monte Carlo and the Opéra Russe de Paris appeared at the Champs-Elysées during the 1920s and at the Châtelet during the 1930s, with Shalyapin and Dmitry Smirnov giving French premières of *Sadko*, *Tsar Saltan* and *The Snow Maiden* among others. In 1929 the first *Ring* in German was given at the Champs-Elysées by the Bayreuth ensemble with Melchior, Larsen-Todsen, Onegin and Margarete Klose. In 1937 a visit of the Berlin Staatsoper included *Ariadne auf Naxos* and *Rosenkavalier* (conducted by Clemens Krauss), *Tristan* (Furtwängler) and *Walküre* (Elmendorff).

(ii) Since 1939. In 1940, after the Opéra and the Opéra-Comique had merged to become the Réunion des Théâtres Lyriques Nationaux, Rouché was confirmed as administrator by the Vichy government; he continued until the liberation in 1945, when he was forcibly retired at the age of 82. During the years of occupation many German companies appeared at the Opéra. *Walküre*

was given by the Mannheim Opera under Elmendorff in 1941; the Berlin Staatsoper performed *Entführung* with Erna Berger and Rosvaenge, and *Fledermaus* with Schwarzkopf, the same year; also in 1941 *Tristan* was performed by the Bayreuth Festival, conducted by Karajan with Lubin as Isolde; in 1942 *Der fliegende Holländer* was staged by the Cologne Opera; and in 1943 *Walküre* was given again, by artists from Cologne and Vienna. The Opéra, in addition to its normal repertory, gave the first French performance of Pfitzner's *Palestrina* (1942). Rouché's successors – Maurice Lehmann (1945–6), Georges Hirsch (1946–56), Jacques Ibert (1956), A. M. Julien (1959–62), Georges Auric (1962–8), René Nicoly (1969–71) and Daniel-Lesur and Bernard Lefort (1971–2) – basically continued his system of a repertory and a fixed troupe, albeit with more guest artists, although from the mid-fifties works were given more often in their original language. (*Rigoletto* and *Traviata*, two of the mainstays of the repertory, continued to be given in French until 1969.) Works like *Les Indes galantes*, *Oberon*, *Carmen*, *Turandot* and *Don Carlos* were staged sumptuously; *Norma*, *Tristan*, *Aida*, *Tosca* and *Falstaff* were given with superb casts. Important creations like *Wozzeck* (1963) were added to the repertory, but these exceptions could not hide the low routine level to which the Opéra had generally sunk, with few new competent French singers coming forward. With morale in the institution falling, strikes became a constant and serious problem. The Opéra-Comique, which was now run as a secondary branch of the Opéra, became little more than a musical museum.

The dormant state of both repertories contrasted with works given from 1956 at the annual festival begun in 1954 as the Festival de Paris and known as the Théâtre des Nations between 1957 and 1963 (housed initially at the Théâtre Sarah Bernhardt – now the Théâtre de la Ville – and later at the Champs-Elysées and the Odéon). Much opera new to Paris was played by famous foreign companies, including the Berlin Komische Oper (*The Cunning Little Vixen*), the English Opera Group (*A*

24. Exterior of the Opéra Bastille, Paris, designed by Carlos Ott and opened in 1990

25. Scene from P. L. Pizzi's production of Berlioz's 'Les Troyens', performed at the Opéra Bastille, Paris, 17 March 1990

Midsummer Night's Dream, The Turn of the Screw), Sadler's Wells (The Mines of Sulphur), the Glyndebourne Festival Opera and various Italian companies. Additionally, the Berlin Staatsoper and the operas of Stuttgart, Frankfurt, Belgrade and Zagreb gave many French or Parisian premières: Berg's Lulu, Blacher's Abstrakte Oper, Egk's Der Revisor, Dessau's Die Verurteilung des Lukullus, Fortner's Die Bluthochzeit, Schoenberg's Moses und Aron, and Janáček's Kát'a Kabanová and The Makropulos Affair.

In the early 1970s important reforms were made by the government. The Opéra-Comique was closed in 1972 (though the building continued to be used by visiting companies) and its orchestra transformed, with some changes, into the Orchestre de l'Ile de France. The budget of the Opéra-Comique was added to that of the Opéra, where the permanent company system was abandoned and Rolf Liebermann appointed general administrator (1973–80). He had at his disposal a budget raised to a hitherto unheard-of level. With, initially, Solti as music adviser, Liebermann totally transformed the Opéra, introducing the stagione system, and employing eminent conductors, singers, directors and designers. Most productions were highly successful, although his Ring project ended with Walküre. Liebermann commissioned new operas, but few were considered suitable for production; those that were were generally given at the Opéra-Comique after its reopening in 1976. Messiaen's Saint François d'Assise was completed and available only for Liebermann's successors. The most famous world première of this period was therefore the complete Lulu (the third act was orchestrated by Friedrich Cerha) on 24 February 1979 in a production by Patrice Chéreau conducted by Boulez, with Stratas, Minton, Blankenheim, Tear, Mazura and Riegel.

The Opéra-Comique was reconstituted as the Opéra-Studio under Louis Erlo (1973–6) and was afterwards used by Liebermann for small-scale productions with those French singers excluded from the Opéra. Liebermann's successors – Bernard Lefort (1980–82), Massimo Bogianckino (1983–5) and Jean-Louis Martinoty (1986–7) – were transitory, struggling to maintain Liebermann's achievement with only modest success. Bogianckino's short period was marked by

revivals of some of the former glories of the Opéra's repertory like Robert le diable, Alceste and the Paris version of Macbeth, together with the world première of Boehmer's Dr Faustus (1985). In 1982 President Mitterrand announced his plan to build a new opera house, the Opéra Bastille; opera performances at the old house, the Palais Garnier, ceased in 1987 and it is now used mainly for ballet.

Carlos Ott was chosen as the architect for the new Opéra Bastille (fig.24), which was virtually completed for its inaugural operatic concert on 13 July 1990. It had cost over £210 million. A short operatic season had already opened on 17 March 1990 with P. L. Pizzi's production of Les Troyens (fig.25). There are four theatres in the complex, equipped to the highest technical levels. The Grande Salle, seating 2700 (1450 stalls and two balconies with 625 seats each), is equipped with ten side stages on two levels, each as large as the central stage. The Salle Modulable (due to open in 1994), for Baroque and contemporary works, has an adaptable stage and seating (cap. 600–1500). The Amphitheatre, a classical Greek arena (cap. 500), has a small stage; the Studio seats 240. From the beginning the Opéra Bastille has been treated as a political football. Daniel Barenboim, appointed artistic director in 1987, was dismissed in 1989 by the newly appointed president of the board, Pierre Bergé, who took overall artistic control, appointing Myung-Whun Chung as his musical director. Many problems, both financial and practical, remain to be solved. The Grande Salle was designed to give 250 performances a year of 20 works.

In 1980 the Châtelet, which had become devoted to spectacular operetta productions, was taken over by the Paris municipal council, renovated, and reopened as the Théâtre Musical de Paris. Four to six operas are staged each year, as well as up to ten concert performances of operas; the theatre is often used for recitals. In 1990 the running of the Opéra-Comique was taken over by Thierry Fouquet, with a small state subsidy supplemented by such sponsorship as he could arrange. The Théâtre des Champs-Elysées continued to invite guest companies including those of Moscow and St Petersburg, and the WNO. Such organizations as the Festival Estival de Paris, the Festival du Marais, the Festival de Montmartre and the Festival d'Automne present operas in various Paris theatres; in 1987 the Festival d'Automne gave the French première of Nono's *Prometeo* at the Palais de Chaillot. The Péniche Opera, founded in 1982, is a unique company that performs on a barge moored in the Canal St Martin. Its stage is probably the smallest in France but is also one of the liveliest. 20 productions of chamber opera and music theatre have been given, to over 350 000 spectators. The Palais des Congrès, built in 1975 for the Orchestre de Paris but rapidly abandoned by it because of the poor acoustics, has been used for visits by the Berlin Staatsoper, the Warsaw Opera and other companies, but the performances have needed acoustic enhancement. The Opéra has used the Palais des Sports for large-scale productions, and since its completion in 1983 the Palais Omnisports de Bercy, seating 13 000, has also presented 'spectaculars' that have required electronic amplification; the 20 or so performances of *Aida* (1984), *Turandot* (1985), *Nabucco* (1987), *Carmen* (1989) and *Faust* (1991) each attracted an audience of over a quarter of a million, more than the total audience for a season at the Opéra.

In the suburbs, where there is a well-established tradition of independent operatic activity, there are about 20 independent cultural centres that buy in performances from such companies as the Opéra Ile de France, the Atelier Lyrique de Tourcoing, the Atelier de Recherche et de Création pour l'Art Lyrique and the Teatro Lirico Arturo Toscanini, Milan. The Théâtre des Amandiers at Nanterre, directed by Patrice Chéreau, has received productions from La Monnaie, and that at Bobigny, Peter Sellars's Mozart productions.

The Théâtre Gabriel at Versailles, renovated during the 19th century and used during the 1870s as the seat of the Senate and the Third Republic, was restored to its 18th-century glory in 1957 for special performances, often by the Opéra or the Opéra-Comique. A gala for Queen Elizabeth II in 1957 included the flower act ('Les fleurs') of Rameau's *Les Indes galantes*. Liebermann's regime as director of the Opéra was inaugurated there on 30 March 1973 with Strehler's production of *Figaro* conducted by Solti. The Versailles May Festival uses the theatre each May or June for its opera productions, usually of 18th-century works such as Pergolesi's *Il Flaminio* (1983) and Vivaldi's *Giustino* (1985). An unsuccessful attempt was made in 1989 to mount a large-scale opera festival in the park using a floating stage on the lake. 1988 saw the creation, under the artistic direction of Philippe Beaussant, of the Centre de Musique Baroque de Versailles, which includes a studio opera directed by René Jacobs. In 1992 the Ministry of Culture inaugurated a new festival at Versailles to include performances of Baroque opera.

*

ES (D. Bernet)

C. Genest: *Les divertissements de Sceaux* (Paris, 1712)

C. Parfaict and F. Parfaict: *Mémoires pour servir à l'histoire des spectacles de la foire* (Paris, 1743)

——: *Histoire du théâtre français* (Paris, 1745–9)

Almanach des spectacles de Paris (1751–94)

J.-B. Durey de Noinville: *Histoire du Théâtre de l'opéra en France depuis l'établissement de l'Académie royale de musique, jusqu'à présent* (Paris, 1753, 2/1757)

C. Parfaict and F. Parfaict: *Histoire de l'ancien Théâtre italien* (Paris, 1753, 2/1767)

[——]: *Dictionnaire des théâtres de Paris* (Paris, 1756, 2/1767–70)

[L. C. de Lavallière]: *Ballets, opéra, et autres ouvrages lyriques, par ordre chronologique depuis leur origine* (Paris, 1760)

J. A. J. Desboulmiers: *Histoire anecdotique et raisonnée du Théâtre italien, depuis son rétablissement en France jusqu'à l'année 1769* (Paris, 1769)

[——]: *Histoire du théâtre de l'Opéra-Comique* (Paris, 1770)

A. d'Origny: *Annales du Théâtre italien depuis son origine jusqu'à ce jour* (Paris, 1788)

Castil-Blaze: *Théâtres lyriques de Paris: l'Académie impériale de musique de 1645 à 1855* (Paris, 1855)

——: *L'opéra-italien de 1548 à 1856* (Paris, 1856)

A.-L. Malliot: *La musique au théâtre* (Paris, 1863)

J. Bonnassies: *Les spectacles forains et la Comédie française* (Paris, 1875)

A. de Lasalle: *Les treize salles de l'Opéra* (Paris, 1875)

C. Nuitter: *Le nouvel Opéra* (Paris, 1875)

A. Jullien: *Les grandes nuits de Sceaux* (Paris, 1876)

E. d'Auriac: *Le Théâtre de la foire* (Paris, 1878)

A. Heulhard: *La Foire St Laurent: son histoire et ses spectacles* (Paris, 1878)

T. de Lajarte: *Bibliothèque musicale du théâtre de l'Opéra* (Paris, 1878)

L. Dussieux: *Le château de Versailles: histoire et description* (Versailles, 1881)

O. Fouque: *Histoire du Théâtre Ventadour, 1829–1879: Opéra-Comique, Théâtre de la Renaissance, Théâtre-Italien* (Paris, 1881)

E. Despois: *Le théâtre français sous Louis XIV* (Paris, 1882)

E. Campardon: *L'Académie royale de musique au XVIIIe siècle* (Paris, 1884)

C. Nuitter and E. Thoinan: *Les origines de l'opéra français* (Paris, 1886)

A. Font: *Favart, l'opéra-comique et la comédie-vaudeville aux XVIIe et XVIIIe siècles* (Paris, 1894)

M. Albert: *Les Théâtres de la foire (1660–1789)* (Paris, 1900)

C. Malherbe: Preface to J. P. Rameau: *Oeuvres complètes*, vi (Paris, 1900)

N. M. Bernardin: *La Comédie italienne en France et les Théâtres de la foire et du boulevard (1570–1791)* (Paris, 1902)

F. Jourdain: 'Charles Garnier et son oeuvre', *Musica*, xxiv (1904), 389–401

H. Lecomte: *Histoire des théâtres de Paris* (Paris, 1905–12)

G. Cucuel: 'Sources et documents pour servir à l'histoire de l'Opéra-Comique en France', *L'année musicale*, iii (1913), 247–82

H. Prunières: *L'opéra italien en France avant Lully* (Paris, 1913)

A. Soubies: *Le Théâtre-Italien de 1801 à 1913* (Paris, 1913)

G. Cucuel: 'Notes sur la Comédie italienne de 1717 à 1789', *SIMG*, xv (1913–14), 154–66

E. Genest: *L'opéra-comique connu et inconnu* (Paris, 1925)

J.-G. Prod'homme: *L'Opéra (1669–1925)* (Paris, 1925)

L. Rohozinski, ed.: *Cinquante ans de musique française de 1874 à 1925*, i (Paris, 1925)

P. Mélèse: *Le théâtre et le public sous Louis XIV* (Paris, 1934)

D. J. Grout: *The Origins of the Opéra-Comique* (diss., Harvard U., 1939)

——: 'The Music of the Italian Theatre at Paris, 1682–1697', *PAMS 1941*, 158–70

——: 'Seventeenth-Century Parodies of French Opera', *MQ*, xxvii (1941), 211–19, 514–26

R. Viollier: *Jean-Joseph Mouret* (Paris, 1950)

A. Marie: 'La salle du théâtre du château de Fontainebleau d'Henri IV à Louis-Philippe', *Revue d'histoire du théâtre*, iii (1951), 237–47

S. Wolff: *Un demi-siècle d'opéra-comique (1900–1950)* (Paris, 1953)

M. Barthélemy: 'La musique dramatique à Versailles de 1660 à 1715', *XVIIe siècle*, no.34 (1957), 7–18

J. Lough: *Paris Theatre Audiences in the 17th and 18th Centuries* (London, 1957)

P. Mélèse: *Le théâtre en France au XVIIe siècle* (Paris, 1957)

C. Brenner: *The Théâtre Italien* (Berkeley and Los Angeles, 1961)

P. Daval: *La musique en France au XVIIIe siècle* (Paris, 1961)

S. Wolff: *L'Opéra au Palais Garnier (1875–1962)* (Paris, 1962, 2/1982)

C. Barnes: *The 'Théâtre de la Foire' (Paris 1697–1762): its Music and Composers* (diss., U. of Southern California, 1965); extracts in *RMFC*, v (1965), 142–68, and viii (1968), 141–60

M. Spaziani: *Il Teatro della Foire* (Rome, 1965)

N. Wild: 'Aspects de la musique sous la Régence: les foires, naissance de l'Opéra-Comique', *RMFC*, v (1965), 129–41

A. Ducrot: 'Les représentations de l'Académie royale de musique à Paris au temps de Louis XIV (1671–1715)', *RMFC*, x (1970), 19–55

H. Lagrave: *Le théâtre et le public à Paris de 1715 à 1750* (Paris, 1972)

F. Lesure: *L'opéra classique français* (Geneva, 1972)

J. R. Anthony: *French Baroque Music from Beaujoyeulx to Rameau* (London, 1973, 2/1978)

N. Dufourcq: 'Les fêtes de Versailles: la musique', *XVIIe siècle*, nos. 98–9 (1973), 67–75

R. M. Isherwood: *Music in the Service of the King: France in the Seventeenth Century* (Ithaca, NY, and London, 1973)

M. H. Winter: *The Pre-Romantic Ballet* (London, 1974)

O. Merlin: *L'Opéra de Paris* (Paris, 1975)

I. Guest: *Le ballet de l'Opéra de Paris* (Paris, 1976)

E. Giuliani: 'Le public de l'Opéra de Paris de 1750 à 1760: mesure et définition', *IRASM*, viii (1977), 159–81

J. Gourret: *Histoire de l'Opéra de Paris (1669–1971): portraits de chanteurs* (Paris, 1977)

B. Labat-Poussin: *Archives du Théâtre national de l'opéra: inventaire* (Paris, 1977)

R. M. Isherwood: 'Popular Musical Entertainment in Eighteenth-Century Paris', *IRASM*, ix (1978), 295–310

J. de La Gorce: 'L'Académie royale de musique en 1704', *RdM*, lxv (1979), 160–91

J. Gourret: *Le miracle Liebermann: sept saisons à l'Opéra de Paris (1973–1980)* (Paris, 1980)

R. Liebermann: *Actes et entractes* (Paris, 1980)

J. Gourret and J. Giraudeau: *Encyclopédie des cantatrices de l'Opéra de Paris* (Paris, 1981)

J. de La Gorce: 'L'opéra et son public au temps de Louis XIV', *Bulletin de la Société de l'histoire de Paris et de l'Ile de France* (1981), 27

H. Schneider: 'Dokumente zur französischen Oper von 1659 bis 1699', *Quellentexte zur Konzeption der europäischen Oper im 17. Jahrhundert* (Kassel, 1981)

T. J. Walsh: *Second Empire Opera: the Théâtre lyrique, Paris 1851–1870* (London, 1981)

J. Gourret: *Dictionnaire des chanteurs de l'Opéra de Paris* (Paris, 1982)

T.-G. Boucher: 'Rameau et les théâtres de la cour (1745–1764)', *Jean-Philippe Rameau: Dijon 1983*, 565–77

J. Gheusi: 'Histoire du Théâtre des Italiens de Paris', *L'avant-scène opéra*, no.55 (1983), 143–9; no.56 (1983), 149–53; nos.57–8 (1983), 205–11; no.60 (1984), 147–53; no.61 (1984), 129–37; no.62 (1984), 129–37; nos. 63–4 (1984), 239–49; no.65 (1984), 85–107

J. Gourret: *Histoire de l'Opéra-Comique* (Paris, 1983)

M. Kahane and N. Wild: *Wagner et la France* (Paris, 1983)

J. de La Gorce: 'L'opéra français à la cour de Louis XIV', *Revue d'histoire du théâtre*, xxxv (1983), 387–401

S. Pitou: *The Paris Opera: an Encyclopedia of Operas, Ballets, Composers and Performers* (Westport, CT, and London, 1983)

G. Sadler: 'The Paris Opéra Dancers in Rameau's Day: a Little-Known Inventory of 1738', *Jean-Philippe Rameau: Dijon 1983*, 519–31

——: 'Rameau's Singers and Players at the Paris Opéra: a Little-Known Inventory of 1738', *EMc*, xi (1983), 453–67

M. E. C. Bartlet: 'Archival Sources for the Opéra-Comique and its *Registres* at the Bibliothèque de l'Opéra', *19th Century Music*, vii (1983–4), 119–29

C. Dupechez: *Histoire de l'Opéra de Paris: un siècle au Palais Garnier 1875–1980* (Paris, 1984)

J. Gourret: *Ces hommes qui ont fait l'Opéra* (Paris, 1984)

——: *Histoire des salles de l'Opéra de Paris* (Paris, 1985)

D. Charlton: *Grétry and the Growth of Opéra-Comique* (Cambridge, 1986)

R. M. Isherwood: *Farce and Fantasy: Popular Entertainment in Eighteenth-Century Paris* (New York, 1986)

D. Pistone, ed.: *Le théâtre lyrique français 1945–1985* (Paris, 1987)

L. Rosow: 'From Destouches to Berton: Editorial Responsibility at the Paris Opéra', *JAMS*, xl (1987), 285–309

J. Johnson: *The Théâtre Italien and Opera and Theatrical Life in Restoration Paris, 1818–1827* (diss., U. of Chicago, 1988)

C. Laulhère-Vigneau, ed.: *Opéras d'Europe* (Paris, 1989)

J. Mongrédien: 'Paris: the End of the Ancien Régime', *The Classical Era*, ed. N. Zaslaw (London, 1989), 61–98

P. F. Rice: *The Performing Arts at Fontainebleau from Louis XIV to Louis XVI* (Ann Arbor, 1989)

N. Wild: *Dictionnaire des théâtres parisiens au XIXe siècle* (Paris, 1989)

N. Zaslaw: 'The First Opera in Paris: a Study in the Politics of Art', *Jean-Baptiste Lully and the Music of the French Baroque: Essays in Honor of James R. Anthony* (Cambridge, 1989), 7–23

B. Coeyman: 'Theatres for Opera and Ballet during the Reigns of Louis XIV and Louis XV', *EMc*, xviii (1990), 22–37

L. Mason: *Singing the French Revolution: Popular Songs and Revolutionary Politics in Paris* (diss., Princeton U., 1990)

M. de Saint Pulgent: *Le syndrome de l'Opéra* (Paris, 1991)

REBECCA HARRIS-WARRICK (1–3), DAVID CHARLTON (4, i–iii, v, vi), JANET JOHNSON (4, iv), RICHARD LANGHAM SMITH (5), CHARLES PITT (6)

Paris, Guillaume-Alexis [Alexandre] (*b* Liège, ?1756; *d* St Petersburg, 18/30 Jan 1840). South Netherlands composer. In 1776 he was on the staff of the theatre at Maastricht. He directed the orchestra of the Théâtre de la Monnaie in Brussels from 1780, was musical director and conductor of a theatre at Ghent in 1782–3, was in Lyons in 1784 and by 1786 was conducting in a Liège theatre, where his opera *Le nouveau sorcier* (libretto by Paul Dubuisson) was given on 9 January that year. In 1787–8 he conducted French operas in Amsterdam, and from 1790 to at least 1792 he did the same at La Monnaie. It was there that his *scène lyrique Les lois et les rois* was performed on 15 April 1793. When the French invaded Brussels in 1794 Paris and his company fled to Hamburg, where he encountered C.-F.-H. Duquesnoy, with whom he probably collaborated in mounting French operas for émigrés. In 1799 he was engaged to direct the French theatre at the St Petersburg court, where he began a remarkable career as a conductor and a composer of operas and ballets; he was succeeded in 1804 by Boieldieu. His vaudeville *Les amants protées*, first performed in Moscow (January 1806), was given at St Petersburg (1808) in Russian, under the title *Le revirement, ou Les disputes jusqu'au larmes*. At least four ballets also date from this period. In addition to his theatrical post he conducted the Sankt-Peterburgskoye Filarmonicheskoye Obshchestvo (St Petersburg Philharmonic Society, founded 1802) for 20 years.

R.-A. Mooser: 'Un musicien belge en Russie au début du XIXe siècle: Guillaume-Alexis Paris (1756–1840)', *RBM*, i (1946–7), 21–6

——: *Annales de la musique et des musiciens en Russie au XVIIIe siècle*, iii (Geneva, 1951)

——: *L'opéra-comique français en Russie au XVIIIe siècle* (Geneva, 1954)

PHILIPPE MERCIER

Paris, Nicola [Niccolò; Niccolino; 'Brunsvic'] (*b* ?Naples; *fl* 1645–1721). Italian soprano castrato. He is mentioned for the first time in 1645, among the performers of an unspecified *festa in musica* in Florence, and in 1685 he took part in Legrenzi's opera *Ifianassa e Melampo*, also in Florence. In 1688 and 1694 he is mentioned as a musician of the Elector Ernst August of Brunswick-Lüneburg. From around 1696 until 1699 he was in the service of the Margrave of Brandenburg-Ansbach, and from 1699 in that of the viceroy of Naples.

Paris was admired as an interpreter of Alessandro Scarlatti, Albinoni and Porpora, and acquired epithets such as 'the famous swan'. He also sang in Genoa, Venice, Piacenza, Bologna, Milan and Turin, and was still active in Rome in 1721, when he took part in Porpora's *Eumene*.

PAOLA BESUTTI

Pâris, Pierre-Adrien (*b* Besançon, 25 Oct 1745; *d* Besançon, 1 Aug 1819). French stage designer. His father, who was Intendant des Bâtiments to the Prince-Bishop of Basle, sent him in 1760 to study architecture in Paris, where he was taught by L.-F. Trouard and J.-F. Blondel and studied painting with Carpentier. Despite failing to obtain the Grand Prix, he went, under royal patronage, to Rome, where he spent five years studying ancient and Renaissance monuments. On his return to Paris in 1774 he was encouraged by the Académie d'Architecture and, supported by the Duc d'Aumont, he rapidly pursued a brilliant career. In 1778, after the death of M.-A. Challe, he obtained the post of Dessinateur du Cabinet du Roi, and in 1784, after a brief stay in Italy, that of Architecte des Menus-Plaisirs. His tasks were onerous: he was responsible for the court festivities, for the decorations for all the royal spectacles (at Versailles, Marly, Fontainebleau and Choisy), and for the sets at the Paris Opéra, where he was principal designer until his retirement in 1792. Faithful to the monarchy, he left the capital in 1792 and retired first to Doubs, then to Normandy. After a stay in Rome (1806–17), where he divided his time between his archaeological work and the temporary direction of the Académie de France (in 1807), he returned to Besançon. He left his large collection of drawings to his native town.

Pâris, who was influenced by the school of Piranesi, had a fertile imagination but was still one of the first stage designers to set store by historical accuracy. Ten years after he left the Opéra, its director, Morel, was still regretting his loss: 'This famous artist was profoundly erudite. The day after reading a text upon which he was to work, he would deliver a design uniting the ideas of its authors with everything that was appropriate as to period, scene, customs and characters. From this design, the painters could easily tell the colours that were to be used and the perspective which would bring out its effect'.

For illustration *see* STAGE DESIGN, fig.9.

*

C. Weiss: *Catalogue de la bibliothèque de Pâris* (Besançon, 1821)

E. de Ganay: 'Pierre-Adrien Pâris, architecte du roi (1745–1819)', *Revue de l'art ancien et moderne*, xlvi (1924), 249–64

L. Hautecoeur: *Histoire de l'architecture classique en France* (Paris, 1950–53), iv, 309–14

A. C. Gruber: 'L'oeuvre de P.-A. Pâris à la cour de France, 1779–1791', *Bulletin de la Société de l'histoire de l'art français* (1973), 213–27

NICOLE WILD

Parisina (i). *Melodramma* in three acts by GAETANO DONIZETTI to a libretto by FELICE ROMANI after BYRON; Florence, Teatro alla Pergola, 17 March 1833.

The plot, set in the early 15th century, deals with the fatal love between Parisina (soprano; at the première Karoline Unger), wife of Azzo, Duke of Ferrara (baritone; Domenico Cosselli), and Ugo (tenor; Gilbert Duprez), who is eventually revealed to be Azzo's son by his first wife. Believing himself the son of a minister at the court, Ernesto (bass), Ugo returns without permission from exile to participate in a tourney, which he wins, receiving the victor's crown from Parisina's hands. That night Azzo overhears Parisina murmur Ugo's name in her sleep and believes his jealous suspicions confirmed; furious, he goads her into confessing their love. Determined to avenge his honour, Azzo is not stayed from having Ugo killed by Ernesto's revelation of the lad's true paternity. Parisina swoons at the sight of Ugo's corpse.

The score of *Parisina* testifies to Donizetti's efforts to deal more flexibly with conventional forms. Evidence is found in the canonic quartet in Act 1, in the *romanza* for Parisina at the opening of Act 2, where the chorus and

extended ritornello form a novel compound structure, and in the powerful duet for Parisina and Azzo in which he impels her confession. Her final cabaletta, 'Ugo è spento!', conveys vividly her hysteria at the sight of her lover's corpse.

WILLIAM ASHBROOK

Parisina (ii). *Tragedia lirica* in four acts by PIETRO MASCAGNI to a libretto by GABRIELE D'ANNUNZIO; Milan, Teatro alla Scala, 15 December 1913.

Offered first to Puccini and then to Franchetti, D'Annunzio's *Parisina* was intended as the successor to *Francesca da Rimini* in a trilogy on the Malatesta family, and it became Mascagni's second *Literaturoper*. He cut 330 of the original 1400 lines, with the poet's approval, and the whole of the fourth act after the première at La Scala; the opera was revived by Gavazzeni in 1952.

In the d'Este villa on the Po, Ugo (tenor) explains his dilemma to his friend Aldobrandino (bass). His mother Stella de' Tolomei (mezzo-soprano) arrives, having been repudiated by his father, Niccolò d'Este (baritone). She incites Ugo against Parisina Malatesta (soprano), his father's new wife, and insults her publicly. In a fury Ugo leaves the palace, but during a pilgrimage to Loreto, after having led a victorious battle against pirates, he throws himself at the feet of his stepmother Parisina and they fall violently in love. Niccolò discovers them together and condemns them to death, which they accept serenely as the only possible outcome of their union.

Mascagni's music follows closely the precise 'musical' directions given by D'Annunzio, creating more than usually complex structures without entirely mastering them. The effort of making himself equal to D'Annunzio's decadent aestheticism results in an impressive work, especially in the second act; but his use of musical declamation, though marking his point of closest contact with European theatre, often becomes monotonous, while in the most highly charged moments his *verismo* and generally agitated tone still predominate.

MICHELE GIRARDI

Parker, Horatio (William) (*b* Auburndale, MA, 15 Sept 1863; *d* Cedarhurst, NY, 18 Dec 1919). American composer. After early piano and organ lessons he studied composition with George Chadwick and then, from 1882 to 1885, at Chadwick's instigation, in Munich with Rheinberger. There he wrote his first extensive works, including the cantata *King Trojan*, which already revealed a dramatic flair. He also considered writing a comic opera. From 1894 until his death he taught at Yale University, where the School of Music gained a national reputation under his guidance.

Much of Parker's time was devoted to playing the organ and directing the choirs of important churches in New York and Boston. Given the prejudice against the theatre among clerics and churchgoers at the time, opera would seem an unlikely interest, but Parker continued to compose concert works in a dramatic vein. By 1898 he had written *The Legend of Saint Christopher*, a dramatic oratorio in the fully developed leitmotif technique that he was to adopt in his two operas. He went on to compose incidental music for two plays, *The Eternal Feminine* (1904) and *The Prince of India* (1906).

When in 1908 the Metropolitan Opera announced a competition for an American opera, Parker and the dramatist Brian Hooker set to work on *Mona*. The judges unanimously chose it as the winner; in three acts, it was produced at the Metropolitan on 14 March 1912 (for illustration *see* NEW YORK, fig.5) and had four performances before passing into oblivion.

Although it was generally agreed that *Mona* was not designed for easy popularity, there were many who felt that it was something more than a worthy first effort. The story, reminiscent of Bellini's *Norma*, is set in England during the Roman occupation. Mona (soprano or mezzo-soprano), a Princess of Britain and last in the line of Boadicea, has been pledged to Gwynn (tenor) who, unknown to her, is the son of the Roman governor. Ultimately she must choose between love and her mission to free the Britons from Roman rule. Parker was determined to have a 'poetic' libretto, but Hooker's decision to use complex, old-fashioned English made the plot difficult to follow. The unremittingly gloomy character of the story affected the orchestral colours, which were criticized as monotonous. Although *Mona* was regarded as an important step in the production of an American opera, many critics claimed that it lacked melodic interest. In the mid-1930s however several writers recalled it with considerable warmth, expressing the hope that a new generation might discover its strengths.

With his second opera, *Fairyland*, also in three acts and to a libretto by Hooker, Parker sought to write a more overtly entertaining work, with more 'tuneful' music; the result was astonishingly different from *Mona*. He aimed at elements regarded as typically American, claiming that *Fairyland* would be 'cheerful, buoyant, and confident'. Certainly little else about it could be described as American; as the title itself indicates, it avoids any confrontation with the kind of reality that was the great strength of American literature and painting at the time. Set in the 13th century, *Fairyland* tells the story of a struggle over the monarchy and the heroine's search for a fairy lover; the sudden denouement, however, leaves important plot elements dangling. The wide variety of musical numbers includes extensive choral writing, of which Parker was a master.

Most of the critics at the première in Los Angeles (Clune's Auditorium, 1 July 1915) regarded *Fairyland* as a great musical event and an important cultural step for the city. Certainly its richness and aim at popular appeal were appropriate for a festival opera; yet, despite the reaction of the first audiences, *Fairyland* dropped out of sight as quickly as *Mona*. Parker was tarred with the brush of academicism. His failing health prevented him from attempting in a third opera to fuse the lessons already learnt into a work of lasting success.

M. Andrews: 'Operatic Debut of Dr. Parker', *Musical World* (April 1912), 4

J. van Broekhoven: '*Mona*: a Thematic Analysis', *Musical Observer*, vi/4 (1912), 22–8

E. E. Hipsher: *American Opera and its Composers* (Philadelphia, 1927)

P. Rosenfeld: *An Hour with American Music* (Philadelphia, 1929)

'Mephisto's Musings', *MusAm*, liv/5 (1934), 9 [on *Mona*]

H. E. Johnson: 'In the World of Music', *New Haven Evening Register* (19 March 1935) [on *Mona*]

I. Parker Semler: *Horatio Parker: a Memoir for his Grandchildren* (New York, 1942)

W. K. Kearns: *Horatio Parker, 1863–1919: his Life, Music, and Ideas* (Metuchen, NJ, and London, 1990)   STEVEN LEDBETTER

Parker, Roger (Leslie) (*b* London, 2 Aug 1951). English writer. He studied at London University under Margaret Bent and Pierluigi Petrobelli, completing his doctoral studies with a dissertation (later published) on early

Verdi. He became a professor at Cornell University in 1982; in 1988 he was appointed coordinating editor of the critical edition of Donizetti and the next year became founding co-editor of the *Cambridge Opera Journal*. His edition of *Nabucco* (1987) inaugurated the new critical edition of Verdi's operas. Parker's central interests lie in Italian opera of the 19th century, in which area his work has led to the re-examination of traditional assumptions and entrenched attitudes; but his knowledge and perceptions extend to many other areas, as his writing on analytical topics and his enterprising editing have demonstrated.

with A. Groos: *Giacomo Puccini: La bohème* (Cambridge, 1986)
Studies in Early Verdi (New York, 1989)
with C. Abbate: *Analyzing Opera: Verdi and Wagner* (Berkeley, 1989)
with A. Groos: *Reading Opera* (Princeton, 1989)

Parlamagni, Antonio (*b* 1759; *d* Florence, 9 Oct 1838). Italian bass. Having made his début about 1788, he sang very successfully as a *basso buffo* in Rome, Florence and Venice, and at La Scala, where in 1812 he created Macrobio in Rossini's *La pietra del paragone*. In 1821 he sang Isidoro in the first performance of Rossini's *Matilde di Shabran* at the Teatro Apollo, Rome; his daughter Annetta Parlamagni sang the contralto role of Edoardo and was also a fine Rosina (*Barbiere*), a role she sang in Siena (1835).   ELIZABETH FORBES

Parlando (It.: 'speaking'). A term used to denote a style of singing akin to ordinary speech with diminished vocalization; it is occasionally used as a direction, requiring the singer to use a manner approximating to speech.

Parlante (It.: 'spoken'). A 19th-century term to describe a passage consisting of an orchestral melody over which the voices engage in dialogue, sometimes doubling the melodic line ('parlante melodico'), sometimes adding a rudimentary counterpoint ('parlante armonico'). During the first half of the century *parlanti* frequently form the basis of the 'tempo d'attacco' and 'tempo di mezzo' sections of a central finale. Such melodies are mostly short and self-perpetuating either through sequential development or repetition in related keys. Typical examples can be found in *Il barbiere di Siviglia* (Rossini, 1816), *La sonnambula* (Bellini, 1831) and *Lucia di Lammermoor* (Donizetti, 1835). Instances also occur in the course of isolated ensembles. The entire duettino 'Signor! ... Va, non ho niente' (*Rigoletto*, Verdi, 1851) is conceived as a *parlante*. As operas became more continuous and recitative declined, this procedure was increasingly used as a bridging device by the more conservative composers, such as Petrella, Ponchielli and Gomes. The 'giovane scuola', however, beginning with Catalani, avoided it altogether in favour of the motif.   JULIAN BUDDEN

Parly, Ticho [Christiansen, Frederick] (*b* Copenhagen, 16 July 1928). American tenor of Danish birth. He studied in Paris, at Bloomington, Indiana, where he took part in the première of Dello Joio's *The Ruby* (1955), and New York, making his début in 1958 at New Orleans as Pong (*Turandot*). Engaged at Aachen in 1959 he sang Radames. At San Francisco (1960) he sang the Emperor (*Die Frau ohne Schatten*), the Drum Major and Rinuccio. At Wuppertal (1961) his roles included Busoni's Mephistopheles and Peter Grimes. In 1963 he sang Leandro (Henze's *Il re cervo*, the revised version of

König Hirsch) at Kassel and made his Bayreuth début as Vogelgesang (*Die Meistersinger*), returning as Siegmund (1966) and Siegfried (1968). In 1966 he made his débuts at Covent Garden as Siegfried, at the Paris Opéra as Tannhäuser, and at the Metropolitan and the Colón as Tristan. He sang Herod at La Scala (1967), returning as the Drum Major. For Scottish Opera he sang Siegfried (1971) and Peter Grimes (1973). He sang Loge at San Diego (1974) and at Seattle (1975–7). He appeared frequently at Copenhagen in Wagner roles and also as Florestan, Shuysky and Otello, which he sang in 1988 as a last-minute replacement. He created a sense of youthful exuberance on stage to second a strong, rather baritonal voice.

ALAN BLYTH

Parma. City in northern Italy. With the creation of the duchy by Pope Paul III in 1545 for his son Pier Luigi Farnese, the first signs of theatrical life developed. The new duke at once founded the ducal chapel, and the association with it of Claudio Merulo and Cipriano de Rore indicates the importance of music at court. The first appearance of music for the theatre was the four *intermedi* inserted between the acts of Niccolò Secchi's comedy *Gli inganni*, which was performed by the Accademia degli Amorevoli on 22 February 1569. In 1583 there was a performance of *La danza di Venere*, a pastoral drama with choruses and dances by Angelo Ingegneri, a member of the Accademia degli Innominati. It seems likely that such performances were frequent at the Farnese court.

In 1618 the Gran Teatro dei Farnese (designed by Giovanni Battista Aleotti, see fig.1; *see also* THEATRE ARCHITECTURE fig.1) was built in the huge Palazzo della Pilotta on the order of Ranuccio Farnese, to honour a proposed visit to Parma of Cosimo II de' Medici (the visit did not in fact take place). It was inaugurated in 1628 on the marriage of Odoardo Farnese and Margherita de' Medici. The festivities were divided between the Teatro 'inferiore', in the courtyard of S Pietro Martire, where on 13 December Tasso's *Aminta* was performed with a prologue *Teti e Flora* and five *intermedi* with texts by Claudio Achillini and Ascanio Pio di Savoia and music by Monteverdi, and the Gran Teatro, where Achillini's 'royal spectacle' *Mercurio e Marte* with a *torneo* by Monteverdi was performed (all the music for the occasion is lost). Other works staged in the Gran Teatro were *Le vicende del tempo* (1652), a 'dramma fantastico musicale' by the Genoese poet Bernardo Morando with music by Francesco Manelli, who served the Farnese court; Francesco Berni's *La Filo, overo Giunone repacificata con Ercole*, also with music by Manelli (1660); and another 'dramma fantastico musicale', *Il favore degli dei* (1690; for illustration *see* MAURO), by Aurelio Aureli with music by Bernardo Sabadini, for the marriage of Odoardo, son of Ranuccio II, to Dorothea Sophia of Neuburg-Pfalz. Performances in the 18th century included two 'caroselli', *Le nozze di Nettuno* (1728) and *La venuta d'Ascanio in Italia* (1732), both with texts by C. I. Frugoni.

Other musical entertainment of various kinds was provided by the Teatro di S Caterina, built in 1656 in the grounds of the Collegio dei Nobili; the ducal Teatro della Racchetta, built in 1673 and in use until 1832; and the Teatro Ducale, designed by Stefano Lolli for Ranuccio II in 1688 in the Palazzo della Riserva. The Teatro Ducale became the centre of theatrical activity and remained in use until 1829, when it was replaced by the Nuovo Teatro Ducale, now the Teatro Regio.

The history of musical productions in these theatres in the 17th and 18th centuries is not complete, but it is known that operatic performances gradually increased in importance. Productions included Francesco

1. *Proscenium of the Gran Teatro dei Farnese, Parma, designed by Giovanni Battista Aleotti, and built in 1618*

Manelli's *La Licasta* (1664) and G. B. Policci's *Amalassunta in Italia* (1681) at the Teatro del Collegio dei Nobili; F. M. Bassani's *Ottone in Italia* (1679) and Marco Uccellini's *Gli eventi di Filandro ad Edessa* (1685) at the Teatro di S Caterina; and *Teseo in Atene* (1688; libretto by Aureli, music attributed to Sabadini) and Aureli and Sabadini's *Amor spesso inganna* (1689; the first comic opera to be staged in Parma) at the Teatro Ducale. Other musicians associated with Parma included Geminiano Giacomelli, Giovanni Maria Capelli and Francesco Zilioli Poncini, indicating a continued connection with the prominent personalities of Italian opera.

An important landmark in the history of theatre occurred after 1749, when the duchy passed to Philip Bourbon, second son of Elisabetta Farnese. In his time Parma gained a reputation throughout Europe that justified its name of 'Aurea Parma'. This was largely the work of Guillaume du Tillot, the administrator of the royal household. He was responsible for what came to be seen as a reform in the theatre, in keeping with the wider debate on opera then exercising intellectual Europe. Francesco Algarotti described this reform in a well-known letter to Voltaire as 'opera in a new style which combines French spectacle with Italian music'. It was a change that du Tillot achieved gradually, from the performance of French plays translated by Frugoni (the court poet) to Italian productions on similar lines, entrusted to Frugoni and Tommaso Traetta. Their collaboration resulted in *Ippolito ed Aricia* (1759), *I Tindaridi* (1760) and *Le feste d'Imeneo* (1760) – the last written to celebrate the marriage of the Infanta Isabella to the Archduke and future Emperor of Austria, Joseph II, which put an end to any dispute about the 'reform'.

The late 18th century saw some interesting works: *Le feste d'Apollo* (1769), a theatrical triptych which included a shortened form of Gluck's *Orfeo ed Euridice* (the first work of his to be seen in Italy), for the marriage of Maria Amalia, daughter of Maria Theresa of Austria, to Ferdinand of Bourbon; and Giuseppe Sarti's *Alessandro e Timoteo* (1782). Paer, who was born and educated in Parma, produced his first work, *Orphée et Euridice*, there in 1791; he returned in 1809 for the première of his *Agnese* in the Villa Douglas-Scotti.

In the 19th century musical activity in Parma (as elsewhere in Italy) centred on opera, and the theatre became a focal point. From 1816 Marie Louise of Austria, wife of Napoleon and Duchess of Parma, ensured an enlightened administration of the city for 30 years, during which a music school was founded, a far-sighted reform of the ducal orchestra was entrusted to Paganini, and the Nuovo Teatro Ducale was built (designed by Nicola Bettoli) and inaugurated in 1829 with Bellini's *Zaira*. The programmes and posters of the seasons that followed (the theatre was renamed Teatro Regio in 1849) give an accurate picture of developments in Italian opera, from Rossini to Bellini, Donizetti, Mercadante and Pacini. Most of Verdi's operas were performed there relatively early. Verdi himself had little connection with the city until after the performance of *Aida* (the second in Italy) on 20 April 1872, but thereafter he was a dominant figure in its musical life. Several smaller theatres contributed to the musical life of the city, especially the Teatro Reinach (given to the municipality in 1869 by the German banker Oscar Reinach), which was frequently used as an alternative to the Teatro Regio for opera. In 1880 Cleofonte Campanini made his début as conductor there at the age

2. *Poster for the Verdi Centenary at the Teatro Regio, Parma, in 1913*

of 20, and in 1913 he bought it, intending to create a centre for experimental works by young composers and singers, but this was not a success.

In 1944 bombs destroyed the Farnese theatre; it has since been rebuilt, on its original model. In 1963 Parma became the home of the Istituto di Studi Verdiani, founded on the initiative of Mario Medici, its director until 1980; he was succeeded by Pierluigi Petrobelli. Since 1989 a Verdi Festival has been held annually in September and October.

*

G. Negri: *Cronologia del Nuovo teatro ducale di Parma* (Parma, 1839)

P. Bettoli: *I nostri fasti musicali, dizionario biografico* (Parma, 1875)

P. E. Ferrari: *spettacoli drammatico-musicali e coreografici in Parma dal 1628 al 1883* (Parma, 1884)

L. Balestrieri: *Feste e spettacoli alla corte dei Farnesi: contributo alla storia del melodramma* (Parma, 1909)

G. Lombardi: *Il Teatro farnesiano in Parma: note e appunti con documenti* (Parma, 1909)

E. Bocchia: *La drammatica a Parma (1400–1900)* (Parma, 1913)

C. Alcari: *Cinquant'anni di vita del Teatro Reinach di Parma (1871–1921)* (Parma, 1921)

——: *Il Teatro regio di Parma nella sua storia dal 1883 al 1929* (Parma, 1929)

——: *Parma nella musica* (Parma, 1931)

N. Pelicelli: 'Musicisti in Parma nel secolo xvii', *NA*, viii (1931), 196–215; ix (1932), 112–29, 217–46; x (1933), 32–43, 233–48, 314–25; '…nel secolo xviii', xi (1934), 29–57, 248–81; xii

(1935), 27–42, 82–92; '...dal 1800 al 1860', 213–22, 317–42; xiii (1936), 180–97

A. de Angelis: 'Il Teatro Farnese di Parma', *RMI*, xliii (1939), 364

M. Ferrarini: *Parma musicale ottocentesca* (Parma, 1946)

A. Yorke-Long: 'The Duchy of Parma', *Music at Court* (London, 1954), 3–40

M. Corradi Cervi: *Cronologia del Teatro regio di Parma (1928–1948)* (Parma, 1955)

S. Reiner: 'Collaboration in "Chi soffre speri"', *MR*, xxii (1961), 265–82

——: 'Preparations in Parma – 1618, 1627–8', *MR*, xxv (1964), 273–301

D. Heartz: 'Operatic Reform at Parma: *Ippolito ed Aricia*', *Convegno sul settecento parmense nel 2° centenario della morte de C. I. Frugoni: Parma 1968*, 271–300

I. Allodi, ed.: *I teatri di Parma dal Farnese al Regio* (Milan, 1969)

R. Campari: *Lettura comparata di 'Castor et Pollux' di G. Bernard - J. P. Rameau e di 'I Tindaridi' di C. I. Frugoni - T. Traetta* (diss., U. of Parma, 1978)

Omaggio al Regio nel 150 anniversario dell'apertura (Parma, 1979)

V. Cervetti, C. del Monte and V. Segreto, eds.: *Teatro regio: cronologia degli spettacoli lirici* (Parma, 1979–82)

M. G. Borazzo: *Musica, scenotecnica, illusione nel grande apparato farnesiano dal 1628 a Parma* (diss., U. of Parma, 1982)

N. Albarosa and R. Di Benedetto, eds.: *Musica e spettacolo a Parma nel settecento* (Parma, 1984)

C. Gallico: *Le capitali della musica, Parma* (Milan, 1985)

L. Allegri and R. Di Benedetto, eds.: *La Parma in festa: spettacolarità e teatro nel ducato di Parma nel settecento* (Modena, 1987)

G. Cirillo and G. Godi: *Il trionfo del barocco a Parma* (Parma, 1989)
                                                    GIAN PAOLO MINARDI

Parma, Ildebrando da. *See* PIZZETTI, ILDEBRANDO.

Parma, Viktor (*b* Trieste, 20 Feb 1858; *d* Maribor, Slovenia, 25 Dec 1924). Slovene composer of Italian descent. He studied composition while a law student in Vienna, and attended Anton Bruckner's lectures. After World War I he became honorary Kapellmeister of the National Theatre in Maribor. At the end of the 19th century and the beginning of the 20th, Parma was the most prolific and popular operatic composer of Slovenia. Although cosmopolitan by inclination – his principal model was Verdi in his early and middle creative periods, and he also followed the *verismo* trend to some extent – he was devoted to the national Slovene cause. As well as several operettas, he composed four operas, of which *Urh, grof celjski* ('Ulrich, Count of Cilli') was the first all-sung Slovene opera. *Zlatorog* ('The Goat with the Golden Horns') is his best opera in terms of musical technique and artistic achievement.

first performed in Ljubljana unless otherwise stated

Urh, grof celjski [Ulrich, Count of Cilli] (3, A. Funtek), 15 Feb 1895

Ksenija (1, F. Göstl and Funtek), 5 Jan 1897

Stara pesem [The Old Song] (dramatic romance, 1, G. Menasci, after H. Heine), Zagreb, 24 March 1898

Caričine Amazonke [The Empress's Amazons] (operetta, A. D. Borum), 24 March 1903

Nečak [The Nephew] (operetta, F. A. Hirsch), Zagreb, 18 Sept 1907

Venerin hram [The Temple of Venus] (operetta, R. Felden and B. Swowsky), Zagreb, 27 March 1909, as Apolonov Hram

Zaručnik v škripcih [The Fiancé in a Fix], 1917 (operetta, A. Grund)

Zlatorog [The Goat with the Golden Horns] (prol., 3, R. Brauer, after R. Baumbach), 17 March 1921   MANICA ŠPENDAL

Parmeggiani, Ettore (*b* Rimini, 15 Aug 1895; *d* Milan, 28 Jan 1960). Italian tenor. He studied in Milan, making his début there in 1922 at the Teatro dal Verme as Cavaradossi. From 1926 to 1942 he sang regularly at La Scala, where he took part in the first performances of Mascagni's *Nerone* (1935) and Respighi's *Lucrezia* (1937), as well as in the first Milan performance of Rimsky-Korsakov's *Sadko* (1938). At Genoa he sang in the première of Malipiero's *Giulio Cesare*. His roles included Huon (*Oberon*), Max (*Der Freischütz*), Siegmund, Lohengrin and Parsifal, as well as Pinkerton and Folco (Mascagni's *Isabeau*). After retiring from the stage he taught in Milan and then became the leader of the claque at La Scala.   ELIZABETH FORBES

Parodi, Teresa (*b* Genoa, 27 Aug 1827; *d* after 1878). Italian soprano. She showed early promise and entered the musical institute in Genoa at the age of 12. In 1844 she studied with Felice Ronconi in Milan, where she was heard by Pasta, who was so impressed that she accepted Parodi as a student and adopted her. Parodi's début was in Bergamo (1845, in *Gemma di Vergy*) and from there she went to Verona, La Spezia, Florence and Rome; her success throughout Italy was immediate. Her London début, as Norma, was at Her Majesty's Theatre (1849). She was engaged by Max Maretzek as the prima donna for his Astor Place Opera Company in 1850–51; with that troupe she appeared to great acclaim in New York, Philadelphia and Boston. At the conclusion of her engagement, she and Maurice Strakosch organized a concert troupe and embarked on an extended tour of the eastern USA. Parodi subsequently performed again with the Astor Place company (1851–2), toured with Strakosch (1852, 1855 and 1856) and sang with the Paris Opéra (1853–4). In the late 1850s she returned to the USA and (again with Strakosch) organized the Parodi Opera Company, with which she appeared all over the American South and Mid-west (1859–60); she was one of many European and American prima donnas to tour the country successfully with her own opera troupe. The extent of Parodi's activities after 1860 is unknown, but as late as 1878 she appeared with James Henry Mapleson's company at the Academy of Music in New York; her vocal powers at the time apparently were undiminished, for her voice was described as 'rich, sweet, clear and sympathetic ... [with] a fine, strong, firm vibration and inexhaustible strength'.

M. Maretzek: *Crotchets and Quavers* (New York, 1855)

——: *Sharps and Flats* (New York, 1890)

G. E. Schiavo: *Italian-American History*, i: *Italian Music and Musicians in America* (New York, 1947)

H. Rosenthal: *Two Centuries of Opera at Covent Garden* (London, 1958)

K. K. Preston: *Travelling Opera Troupes in the United States, 1825–1860* (diss., CUNY, 1989)   KATHERINE K. PRESTON

Parody. The term is used in opera to signify a number of devices which have in common that they make reference to pre-existing material, and thereby make some specific effect through the relationship with the parodied model. The word can thus stand, for example, for an entire work based in some way (by drawing on the music, the characters or the text) on an existing one, or for one that alludes to aspects of an existing one, or for such devices as the quotation of themes that are familiar in themselves or evocative of a different milieu. The objective is to create a special effect, humorous, ironic or satirical; it may often involve ridiculing either the work that is drawn upon (or parodied) or some element within the work that itself embodies the parody.

Elements of parody appear in early Venetian opera through the juxtaposition of comic scenes with ones where serious characters express themselves in elevated fashion; they serve to ridicule those who take themselves over-seriously. This tradition persisted into the comic intermezzos of the early 18th century where, very often, their plots ran in parallel in some way with those of the parent, serious opera within which they were performed. Their characters, closely linked with those of the *commedia dell'arte*, had parallels in France, where parody flourished particularly, because of the rigorous monarchical controls exercised over musical theatre in general, at both courtly and popular levels. The Comédie-Italienne and the fair theatres presented, throughout the first half of the 18th century, parodies of the *tragédies en musique* of Lully and his followers; leading figures among the librettists, who were the prime movers, were A.-R. Lesage, Louis Fuzelier and C.-S. Favart. English parodists include, besides John Gay (writer of *The Beggar's Opera*) such composers as Henry Carey and J. F. Lampe.

The set conventions of Metastasian *opera seria* – for example the imagery of the simile aria and bravura singing – invited parodistic treatment in the comic genres, equally for the purpose of mocking the exalted genre and for making points about characters within the comic work. An *opera buffa* composer could make characters seem absurd by putting *opera seria* phraseology into their mouths; the best-known examples are the first-act arias for the sisters in Mozart's *Così fan tutte* (1790). In France, the nature of parody altered after the middle of the century with the appropriation of Italian musical material, in works called *parodies*, to help establish a style for the developing *opéra comique*; for example, Pergolesi's *La serva padrona* was adapted to French words by P. Baurans as *La servante maîtresse* (the recitative becoming spoken dialogue), and Vincenzo Ciampi's *Bertoldo, Bertoldino e Cacasenno* was revised as *Bertholde à la ville*. In England similar methods were used but the heavy prevalence of pasticcio obscures parody as such. In all countries, successful works naturally attracted parody in one form or another: a prime example is Gluck's *Orfeo* and his *Iphigénie* operas, and another is Mozart's *Die Zauberflöte*, much parodied in the Viennese popular theatre of the early 19th century.

Later in the century J. N. Nestroy's parodies of Rossini, Meyerbeer, Wagner and others were particularly successful in Vienna, with their disparaging allusions to the world of opera. In the 19th century, parody chiefly found its outlet in the specialist operetta theatre, notably in the works of Offenbach, who introduced allusion to works by Gluck, Donizetti, Meyerbeer and others in incongruous contexts to satirical effect, also providing a cancan for the gods in *Orphée aux enfers* and an ingratiating waltz for 'Un vile séducteur' in *La belle Hélène*. Sullivan's operettas make frequent use of the serious devices of contemporary opera (Donizetti, Verdi, French opera) to parodistic effect, for example in the large-scale ensemble finales (notably in Act 1 of *The Yeomen of the Guard*) and in the use of recitative and melodrama. In the 20th century parody is less able to focus because of the lack of established stylistic convention; Britten was able to use it effectively in the 'Pyramus and Thisbe' playlet in *A Midsummer Night's Dream*, where a high-flown Italian operatic idiom hints at the pretensions of the rustics, and Stravinsky's use of Mozartian and Bellinian idioms in *The Rake's Progress* helps catch the highly stylized nature of the Hogarthian subject matter. *Carmen Jones* may be regarded as a parody of *Carmen* and *Die Dreigroschenoper* as one of *The Beggar's Opera*.

*

C. Sallier: 'Discours sur l'origine et sur le caractère de la parodie', *Histoire de l'Académie royale des inscriptions et belles lettres*, vii (Paris, 1730), 398–410

A. Font: *Favart, l'opéra-comique et la comédie-vaudeville aux XVIIe et XVIIIe siècles* (Paris, 1894)

A. Arnheim: 'Le devin du village von Jean-Jacques Rousseau und die Parodie *Les amours de Bastien et Bastienne*', *SIMG*, iv (1902–3), 686–727

G. Calmus: *Zwei Opernburlesken aus der Rokokozeit* (Berlin, 1912)

P. A. Merbach: 'Parodien und Nachwirkungen von Webers "Freischütz" ', *ZMw*, ii (1919–20), 642–55

G. Cucuel: 'Les opéras de Gluck dans les parodies du XVIIIe siècle', *ReM*, iii (1922), no.5, pp.201–21; no.6, pp.51–68

R. Haas: 'Wiener deutsche Parodie-Opern um 1730', *ZMw*, viii (1925–6), 201–25

M. Chat: *Studien zur Technik der Parodie und des Komischen an Parodien Favarts* (diss., U. of Vienna, 1930)

V. B. Grannis: *Dramatic Parody in 18th-Century France* (New York, 1931)

M. Bührmann: *J. N. Nestroys Parodien* (diss., U. of Kiel, 1933)

R. Rüschka: *Wiener literarische Parodien von den Anfängen bis auf Nestroy* (diss., U. of Vienna, 1935)

F. Brukner: 'Die Alt-Wiener Parodie', *Jb deutscher Bibliophilen und Literaturfreunde*, xxi-xxii (1937)

D. J. Grout: 'Seventeenth-Century Parodies of French Opera', *MQ*, xxvii (1941), 211–19, 514–26

L. Frank: *Dramatic Parody by Marionettes in 18th-Century Paris* (New York, 1946)

O. Rommel: 'Johann Nestroy, der Satiriker auf der Altwiener Komödienbühne', *J. Nestroy: Gesammelte Werke*, i (Vienna, 1948), 1–193

S. Dörffelt: *Die musikalische Parodie bei Offenbach* (diss., U. of Frankfurt, 1954)

F. W. Sternfeld: *Goethe and Music: a List of Parodies and Goethe's Relationship to Music* (New York, 1954)

K. Hortschansky: *Parodie und Entlehnung im Schaffen Chr. W. Glucks* (diss., U. of Kiel, 1966)

D. Keahey: 'Così fan tutte: Parody or Irony?', *Paul A. Pisk: Essays in his Honor* (Austin, TX, 1966), 116–30

M. See: 'Opernparodie und Parodieoper', *NZM*, Jg.127 (1966), 372–88

W. E. Yates: *Satire and Parody in Viennese Popular Comedy* (Cambridge, 1972)

R. Fiske: *English Theatre Music in the Eighteenth Century* (London, 1973, 2/1986)

M. Noiray: 'Hippolyte et Castor travestis: Rameau à l'Opéra-Comique', *Rameau: Dijon 1983*, 109–25

R. M. Isherwood: *Farce and Fantasy: Popular Entertainment in Eighteenth-Century Paris* (New York and Oxford, 1986)

F. Moureau: 'Lully en visite chez l'Arlequin: parodies italiennes avant 1697', *Lully: Heidelberg and St Germain-en-Laye 1987*, 235–50

M. Harley: 'Technika komedii w "Falstaffie" G. Verdiego', *Muzyka*, xxxvi/3 (1991), 3–25

M. Hunter: 'Some Representations of *opera seria* in *opera buffa*', *COJ*, iii (1991), 89–108   ELISABETH COOK, STANLEY SADIE

Paroisse-Pougin, Arthur. *See* POUGIN, ARTHUR.

Parrott, (Horace) Ian (*b* London, 5 March 1916). English composer. He was educated at Harrow (1929–32), the RCM (1932–4) and New College, Oxford (1934–7), taking the Oxford DMus in 1940. During World War II he served in the Middle East and North Africa and in 1943 his opera *The Sergeant-Major's Daughter* was produced in Cairo.

He taught at the University of Birmingham (1947–50), and in 1950 was given the Gregynog Chair at the University College of Wales, Aberystwyth, since when his music has been coloured by a practical interest in the Welsh language and Welsh culture. He has written widely on Welsh music, and among his most ambitious compositions is a folk opera, *The Black Ram* (1957), which incorporates traditional Welsh melodies. *Once Upon a Time*, a comedy for three voices and piano, was first performed in Christchurch, New Zealand, when Parrott was visiting the country and has had several subsequent productions, including one to mark European Music Year in 1985. He retired in 1983.

The Sergeant-Major's Daughter (burlesque, 3, K. Wormersley), Cairo, Sharia Maarouf, 20 July 1943
The Black Ram, 1951–3 (H. Idris Bell), BBC, 28 Feb 1957 (concert perf., in Welsh), staged Aberystwyth, King's Hall, 9 March 1966, in Eng.
Once Upon a Time (C. J. Price, after Russ. story), Christchurch, U. of Canterbury, 3 Dec 1960
The Lady of Flowers (chamber op), Colchester, U. of Essex, 17 Sept 1982

*

H. F. Redlich: 'A New Welsh Folk Opera', *ML*, xxxvii (1956), 101–6   MALCOLM BOYD

Parruchiera, La. *See* PERUZZI, ANNA.

Parry, Sir (**Charles**) **Hubert** (**Hastings**) (*b* Bournemouth, 27 Feb 1848; *d* Rustington, Sussex, 7 Oct 1918). English composer and teacher. Educated at Oxford, he later held the chair of music there (1900–08), but his main work was done at the RCM. He joined the staff on its opening in 1883 and succeeded Grove as director in 1894, holding the position until his death. Gentleman by birth, democrat by nature, Parry has always been viewed as a regenerative, even moral force in British musical history, rescuing it from Victorian complacency without entirely freeing it from Victorian inhibitions. Accordingly, his choral compositions, songs and early chamber and instrumental music hold greatest claim to attention, for, unlike his colleague Stanford, he had little propensity for opera, which he tended to disparage; on the other hand, it should not be forgotten that he wrote successful scores for five Greek plays at Oxford and Cambridge. His only opera, *Guenever*, in four acts, to a libretto by Una Taylor (1884–6; *GB-Lcm*, unpublished), although hailed by Dannreuther as 'the real English opera for which we have waited so long' (Graves, i, 266), was rejected by Carl Rosa, remained unorchestrated and has never been performed.

*

C. L. Graves: *Hubert Parry* (London, 1926)
J. Dibble: *Hubert Parry: a Life and Works* (forthcoming)
                                STEPHEN BANFIELD

Parry, John (*b* Denbigh, 18 Feb 1776; *d* London, 8 April 1851). Welsh composer. After studying the harp and the clarinet he joined the band of the Denbighshire militia in 1793 and became master of it in 1795. In this position he became proficient on a large number of instruments, and he exhibited his talents at Covent Garden in 1805. He settled in London in 1807, and in 1809 was engaged to provide some music for Vauxhall Gardens; in 1814 he began composing and arranging music for various operatic farces and other stage productions. In several cases he was responsible for the libretto as well as the music. At least five dramatizations of Scott's *Ivanhoe* were presented in London in 1820: the one at Covent Garden was the most successful, partly because of Parry's song 'The Lullaby'. He was particularly skilled at composing ballads with a Celtic flavour, which he often sang himself.

Parry was an assiduous collector and arranger of Welsh melodies, and he also wrote several books on musical subjects. From 1834 to 1849 he was music critic of the *Morning Post*.

music lost; librettos by the composer unless otherwise stated
LCG – *London, Covent Garden*   LDL – *London, Drury Lane*

Fair Cheating, or The Wise Ones Outwitted (operatic farce), LDL, 15 June 1814, vs pubd
Harlequin Hoax, or A Pantomime Proposed (extravaganza, T. Dibdin), Lyceum, 16 Aug 1814, vs pubd
Oberon's Oath, or The Paladin and the Princess (musical drama, B. Thompson), LDL, 21 May 1816
High Notions, or A Trip to Exmouth (operatic farce), LCG, 11 Feb 1819, 2 songs pubd
Helpless Animals, or Bachelor's Fare (operatic farce), LCG, 17 Nov 1819, vs pubd
Ivanhoe, or The Knight Templar (musical drama, S. Beazley, after W. Scott), LCG, 2 March 1820, ov. pubd
Two Wives, or A Hint to Husbands (operatic farce), LDL, 2 June 1824
My Uncle Gabriel (operatic farce), LDL, 10 Dec 1824, 2 songs pubd
A Trip to Wales (operatic farce), LDL, 11 Nov 1826
Caswallon, or The Briton Chief (tragedy, C. E. Walker), LDL, 12 Jan 1829
The Sham Prince (burletta), St James's, 29 Sept 1836

Music in: The Merry Wives of Windsor (1824)
                    PETER CROSSLEY-HOLLAND, NICHOLAS TEMPERLEY

Parry, Joseph ['Pencerdd America'] (*b* Merthyr Tydfil, 21 May 1841; *d* Penarth, 17 Feb 1903). Welsh composer. In 1854 he emigrated with his family to Pennsylvania, but he returned to Britain to study at the RAM, 1868–71, also taking the Cambridge MusB in 1871. After another short period in Pennsylvania, he was appointed professor of music at University College, Aberystwyth (1874–80), and in 1878 took the MusD at Cambridge. He then ran his own music school in Swansea until 1888, and from then until his death lectured at University College, Cardiff. In 1878 Parry composed the first Welsh opera, *Blodwen*, a tale of romance and chivalry set in 14th-century Wales. The historical setting, together with some tuneful music indebted to early Verdi and quoting traditional Welsh airs, ensured the work's popularity; Parry himself claimed in 1896 that it had by then received over 500 performances. Of his other operas, only *Arianwen*, a story of rural courtship in 18th-century Wales, found some success.

Blodwen (3, R. Davies), concert perf., Aberystwyth, 1878; stage, Swansea, 20 June 1878 (Aberystwyth, 1878)
Virginia (E. R. Jones), Swansea, Royal, 1883, lost
Arianwen (3, D. Rowlands and J. Parry), Cardiff, Royal, 5 June 1890 (Cardiff, 1890)
Sylvia (3, D. M. Parry), Cardiff, Royal, 12 Aug 1895 (Cardiff, 1895)
Cap and Gown (operetta, 1, I. B. John), Cardiff, South Wales School of Music, 1898
King Arthur, 1896–9 (3, H. E. Lewis), ?unperf.
His Worship the Mayor, 1895–1900 (3, A. Mee), unperf.
Ceridwen (1, E. Rees), concert perf., Liverpool, 1900 (London, 1900)
Y ferch o'r scer, 1900–02 (3, ? J. Parry), unperf.
The Maid of Cefn Ydfa (3, J. Bennett), Cardiff, Grand, Dec 1902

*

E. K. Evans, ed.: *Cofiant Dr. Joseph Parry* (Cardiff and London, 1921)
O. T. Edwards: *Joseph Parry, 1841–1903* (Cardiff, 1970)
D. Rhys: 'Yng nghwmni *Blodwen*', *Welsh Music*, v/9 (1978), 37–45
——: *Joseph Parry: ei fywyd a'i waith* (diss., U. of Wales, Bangor, 1986)   MALCOLM BOYD

Parsifal. *Bühnenweihfestspiel* in three acts by Richard Wagner (*see* WAGNER family, (1)) to his own libretto; Bayreuth, Festspielhaus, 26 July 1882.

Wagner acquainted himself with the relevant source material for his final opera as early as the summer of 1845, when he read Wolfram von Eschenbach's Parzivâl and Titurel poems, in versions by Simrock and San-Marte. The first prose sketch (now lost) was made in

Amfortas *ruler of the Kingdom of the Grail*	baritone
Titurel *his father*	bass
Gurnemanz *a veteran Knight of the Grail*	bass
Parsifal	tenor
Klingsor *a magician*	bass
Kundry	mezzo-soprano
First and Second Knights of the Grail	tenor, bass
Four Esquires	sopranos, tenors
Voice from Above	contralto
Klingsor's Flowermaidens	6 sopranos

Knights of the Grail, youths and boys, flowermaidens

Setting The Grail castle 'Monsalvat' and its environs, the northern mountains of Gothic Spain, in mythological times

1857 – not, however, on Good Friday as Wagner poetically recollected in subsequent years (see Millington 1984). The first prose draft did not follow until 1865, and the second (written mostly in dialogue form) not until 1877. The poem was written between 14 March and 19 April 1877 and the music between August 1877 and April 1879 (Wagner alternating, in his now customary fashion, between two drafts). He orchestrated the prelude (first version, with concert ending) in autumn 1878 and made his full score of the rest between August 1879 and January 1882.

The first performances were given at Bayreuth on 26 and 28 July 1882 for members of the Society of Patrons, followed by 14 further performances in July and August. Wagner's intention of consecrating the Festspielhaus with *Parsifal* is indicated by the term *Bühnenweihfestspiel*, which may be translated 'festival play for the consecration of a stage'. In spite of the 30-year embargo placed on performances outside Bayreuth, *Parsifal* was occasionally given elsewhere in those years: Ludwig II had it put on privately in Munich in the years after Wagner's death; it was seen by members of the Wagner Society in Amsterdam in 1905, and again in 1906 and 1908; and in the face of bitter hostility from Bayreuth it was mounted by the Metropolitan in 1903 under Alfred Hertz. Various concert performances were given in Europe during the period of the embargo, including two under Joseph Barnby in London in 1884. The first stage performance in Britain was at Covent Garden in 1914, under Artur Bodanzky.

At the first Bayreuth performances, Parsifal was sung by Hermann Winkelmann, Heinrich Gudehus and Ferdinand Jäger; Gurnemanz by Emil Scaria and Gustav Siehr; Kundry by Amalie Materna, Marianne Brandt and Therese Malten; and Amfortas by Theodor Reichmann. The conductor was Hermann Levi. Parsifal has also been sung by Melchior, Vinay, Jess Thomas, Vickers, René Kollo, Brilioth, Jung, Peter Hofmann and Jerusalem; Gurnemanz by Kipnis, Ludwig Weber, Hotter, Frick, Theo Adam, Talvela, Mazura, Moll, Sotin and Robert Lloyd; Kundry by Nordica, Fremstad, Leider, Flagstad, Varnay, Traubel, Mödl, Crespin, Rysanek, Ludwig, Meier and Minton; and Amfortas by Van Rooy, Whitehill, Janssen, Schorr, Hotter, London, Fischer-Dieskau, McIntyre, Weikl and Estes. Notable conductors of the work have included Mottl, Seidl, Muck, Weingartner, Knappertsbusch, Furtwängler, Kempe, Boulez, Goodall, Jochum, Solti, Karajan, Levine and Barenboim.

In as far as it addressed the 'meaning' of *Parsifal* at all, much of the literature on the opera up to World War II dealt with the question of whether or not it could be regarded as a religious work (for a summary, see Beckett 1981). An equally strong claim, based on Wagner's acknowledged sympathies, could be made for a Schopenhauerian/Buddhist interpretation, taking the concept of *Mitleid* ('compassion') as the ethical centre of the work. Darker undercurrents of racial supremacy and anti-semitism have been revealed (Gutman 1968; Zelinsky 1978), but the notion that the concepts of racial purity and regeneration formulated by Wagner in his last years were woven into the ideological fabric of *Parsifal* (Millington 1984; Rose 1992) was less readily embraced by directors in the 1980s than the theme of sexuality. Progressive stage interpretations in recent years have attempted to rehabilitate Kundry and womankind generally, allowing them a more prominent role in the final act of redemption (see Millington 1988).

The prelude begins with a broadly phrased theme (ex.1),

Ex.1

containing three elements of significance, of which (*y*) is generally associated with suffering, and (*z*) with the spear. A shimmering background is built up, against which a trumpet (with oboes and violins) reiterates ex.1, establishing the tonality of Ab major. The whole process is then repeated in C minor, before two new themes, those associated with the Grail (the 'Dresden Amen': ex.2) and with faith (ex.3) are announced. After some

Ex.2

Ex.3

chromatic intensification, especially of ex.1, the curtain rises.

ACT 1.i–ii *A forest glade* Gurnemanz rouses two of the esquires from sleep and together they kneel and pray (ex.3, as extended in the prelude, followed by ex.2). Gurnemanz bids them prepare the bath for Amfortas, approaching on his sickbed (ex.4 makes its first

Ex.4

appearance in the bass here). But first the 'wild woman' Kundry rushes in, her arrival signalled by agitation in the orchestra; she is bringing balsam from Arabia for the sick guardian of the Grail. Amfortas's entrance on his litter is accompanied by ex.4, which eventually in-

'Parsifal' (Wagner): Paul von Joukowsky's diorama for the Transformation Music in Acts 1 and 3 of the original production at the Festspielhaus, Bayreuth, 26 July 1882. The continuously moving painted backcloth (above), situated a few metres from the front of the stage, is wound to the right during the Transformation Music for Act 1 as Gurnemanz leads Parsifal to the Grail hall (centre), and during the Transformation Music for Act 3 the backcloth (below) is wound to the left as Gurnemanz leads Parsifal and Kundry to the Grail hall (see also MACHINERY, §5; and for the Grail scene at the end of Act 3 see SACRED OPERA); this diorama remained in use until the early 1930s.

troduces a paragraph in which he looks forward to his relief from pain ('Nach wilder Schmerzensnacht'). The sustained dominant pedal suggests a cadence on Bb, but the ultimate resolution is on to an evasive Gb, hinting that the hope of relief is illusory. Amfortas intones the formula of the 'pure fool made wise by suffering' ('durch Mitleid wissend, der reine Thor'), whom he has been promised as a saviour. He is carried away again to the grieving strains of ex.4.

Gurnemanz reprimands the esquires for their harsh words about Kundry; she is perhaps atoning with good deeds for a past sin, he says. Their taunt that she should be sent in quest of the missing spear draws from Gurnemanz an emotional recollection of how Amfortas was seduced and dealt his terrible wound, losing possession of the sacred spear to the magician Klingsor ('O, wunden-wundervoller heiliger Speer!': ex.1y and z). The esquires enquire how Gurnemanz knew Klingsor, and he begins his Narration proper ('Titurel, der fromme Held'). The sacred relics of the cup used at the Last Supper and the spear that pierced Christ's side on the Cross had been given into the care of Titurel, then guardian of the Grail. Ex.1 and a new theme, evolved from ex.3, are developed here in a mystical atmosphere conjured partly by the long, flowing phrases and partly by the radiantly translucent scoring. The brotherhood of the Grail, assembled by Titurel to guard the relics, was closed to Klingsor (his motif, ex.5, is now heard) on

Ex.5

account of some unnamed sin. Desperate to quell his raging passions, Klingsor even castrated himself, but was still rebuffed. To avenge himself, he turned to magic and created a garden of delights, where he lies in wait for errant knights, seducing them with 'devilish lovely women' (intimations of the Act 2 flowermaidens' music are heard here). The aging Titurel sent his son Amfortas to defeat Klingsor, with the consequences already described. Gurnemanz ends his narrative with a recollection of the divine prophecy concerning a 'pure fool', echoed homophonically by the esquires.

A flurry of activity is initiated by the opening figure of Parsifal's motif, ex.6. Parsifal has shot down a swan on

Ex.6

the holy ground and is dragged in by the knights. Gurnemanz's rebuke fills him with remorse and he breaks his bow. To Gurnemanz's questions about his name and origins, however, he professes ignorance. The two are left alone with Kundry, and Parsifal tells what he knows about himself: his mother's name was Herzeleide (Heart's Sorrow), he had strayed from home in search of adventure and had made his own arms for protection. When Kundry, who clearly knows more about him than he does himself, announces that his mother is dead, Parsifal attacks her and has to be restrained.

In the distance, the knights and esquires are seen bearing Amfortas back to the Grail castle. As the processional music starts, Gurnemanz offers to lead Parsifal there. The change of scene, from forest to castle, is

effected during the Transformation Music, which builds the dissonances associated with Amfortas's suffering (ex.7) to an immense climax. Bells ring out with the

Ex.7

four-note motif of the procession.

1.iii *The castle of the guardians of the Grail* Gurnemanz and Parsifal enter the Grail hall and the chorus of knights, 'Zum letzen Liebesmahle', firmly establishes C major as the second primary key of the act. A chorus of youths is heard from mid-height and then one of boys' voices from the top of the dome. Amfortas has been borne in, and the Grail, still covered, placed on a marble table.

Amfortas, reluctant to accede to Titurel's request for him to uncover the Grail, breaks into his monologue of torment, 'Wehvolles Erbe'. He seeks atonement for his sin and the motif of his suffering (ex.7) is prominent along with ex.1. His passionate cry for forgiveness ('Erbarmen!') is answered by the chorus repeating the prophecy. At Titurel's insistence, the cover is removed from the golden shrine and the crystal Grail chalice taken from it. Ex.1 returns, as in the prelude, first in Ab major and then in C minor, as the voices from above repeat Christ's words offering his body and blood: 'Nehmet hin meinen Leib, nehmet hin mein Blut'. Amfortas consecrates the bread and wine and they are distributed to the knights, who take up a sturdy new theme in Eb started by the boys and youths from above. Exx.2 and 3 are heard and then the processional music and ex.7 as Amfortas is borne out again, his wound gaping anew. Parsifal, who had convulsively clutched his heart at Amfortas's cry of agony, is unable to tell Gurnemanz what he has seen and is roughly shepherded out. A voice from above (contralto solo) repeats the prophecy, answered by ex.2 from other voices in the dome.

ACT 2 *Klingsor's magic castle, on the southern slopes of the mountains facing Moorish Spain* The act opens with a sinister chromatic transmutation of ex.1, introducing a disruptive tritone, followed by Klingsor's theme (ex.5). Klingsor, surrounded by magical and necromantic apparatus, watches over his domains from a tower. Seeing Parsifal approach, he summons Kundry, whose monosyllabic groans are accompanied by unprepared dissonances. Attempting to resist Klingsor's instructions to seduce Parsifal, she taunts her master with his self-enforced chastity. Parsifal's motif (ex.6) announces that he has reached the battlements; Klingsor watches as he fells one guard after another. The tower suddenly sinks and in its place appears a luxuriant magic garden.

Flowermaidens rush in from all sides, their excited questions accompanied by a playful, dotted variant of ex.1 and by a continuous triplet figure in the strings. As Parsifal appears, they squabble over him, but join forces for their alluring, triple-time 'Komm, komm, holder

Knabe!'. A number of striking parallels between this scene and the Act 3 finale of Meyerbeer's *Robert le diable* suggest that Wagner may have intended to demonstrate here the superiority of the music drama over conventional opera (see Keller 1971). The flowermaidens caress Parsifal insistently; a series of modulations recalls the love music of *Tristan und Isolde* and the 'Tristan' chord' itself is heard. Just as he manages to free himself from their attentions, he is stopped in his tracks by the sound of his long-forgotten name. It is Kundry, now transformed into an enchanting beauty, who calls, her voice emerging seductively out of the orchestral texture. At Kundry's command the flowermaidens reluctantly disperse.

She tells, in a flowing, compound-time narrative, how she saw him as a baby on his mother's breast: 'Ich sah das Kind'. His mother watched over him lovingly, but one day he broke her heart by not returning and she died of grief. Parsifal's distress at the news is reflected in the chromatic intensification both of his line and of the orchestral texture. Kundry consoles him, urging him to show her the love he owed his mother. As she kisses him, the 'Tristan' chord' (at pitch, as ever) is outlined by stopped horns and cello. By a clever twist of its tail, the theme associated with sorcery gradually reveals part of the chaste opening theme of the work (ex.8). Parsifal

Ex.8

leaps up, clutching his heart. His cry 'Amfortas! Die Wunde!' indicates his first real identification with Amfortas's suffering, and his first step on the road to self-knowledge. Falling into a trance, he hears Christ the Redeemer himself call on him to save him from 'guilt-tainted hands' and cleanse the polluted sanctuary. The flowermaidens' blandishments are chromatically enhanced as Parsifal realizes that it was caresses such as Kundry is conferring on him now that brought about Amfortas's downfall.

He repels her, but she appeals to him to use his redemptive powers to save her: for her blasphemous mockery of Christ she has wandered the world for centuries. One hour with him would bring her release, she says. But Parsifal, recognizing that salvation for them both depends on his withstanding her allurements, resists. She attempts to block his way to Amfortas and calls to Klingsor. The magician appears and hurls his spear at Parsifal (an upward glissando on a harp). Parsifal seizes the spear and as he makes the sign of the Cross with it, the castle collapses and the magic garden disappears.

ACT 3 The years of anguish and wandering that intervene between the second and third acts are depicted by the heightened chromaticism of the prelude. The curtain rises on an open spring landscape in the domains of the Grail. Gurnemanz, grown very old and dressed as a hermit, emerges from his hut and uncovers Kundry, whose groans, as she lies stiff and apparently lifeless in the undergrowth, he has heard. He revives her, but receives no thanks, just two words: she wants only to serve ('Dienen ... Dienen!'). A man approaches in a suit of armour and bearing a spear. A sober variant, in the minor, of Parsifal's motif (ex.6) tells us both the stranger's identity and that he is a changed man.

Gurnemanz welcomes him but bids him divest himself of his weapons: it is Good Friday and this is holy ground. As Parsifal does so, Gurnemanz recognizes the man whom he once roughly turned away.

He also recognizes the spear (ex.1 is recalled), but his outburst of joy is undercut by the music associated with Amfortas's suffering (ex.7). Throughout his troubled wandering, Parsifal tells him, he has guarded the spear safely. Gurnemanz hails its return with an impassioned outburst that again recalls each of the elements of ex.1: 'O Gnade! Höchstes Heil!'. The mystical elaboration of ex.3 from Gurnemanz's Act 1 narrative is now recalled. Gurnemanz tells Parsifal that his return with the healing spear is timely. Amfortas, longing for death, has refused to reveal the Grail, the brotherhood has degenerated, and Titurel has died. The elegiac music of the Act 3 prelude, and its original key of Bb minor, accompanies his words.

Parsifal is almost overcome with remorse. His feet are bathed by Kundry, and Gurnemanz sprinkles water from the spring on his head, asking that he be blessed ('Gesegnet sei'). Kundry then anoints his feet and dries them with her hair. The hesitant reminiscence of the flowermaidens' music suggests that Parsifal may now be aware of Kundry's alter ego. To a grandiose statement of Parsifal's theme, ex.6, in B major, Gurnemanz anoints his head. After an unusually emphatic cadence (twice confirmed) in this key, and before the Good Friday Music begins 27 bars later also in B major, there occurs the incident of Kundry's baptism by Parsifal. The inner significance for Wagner of this act – as an expression of a Schopenhauerian pacification of the will, but also, probably, as a symbol of the liberation of the world from impure racial elements (see Millington 1987) – is intimated by the divorcing of this passage from the immediate tonal context.

Gazing on the beautiful meadows, Parsifal says that on Good Friday every living thing should only sigh and sorrow. As the Good Friday Music modulates from B to D major (asserting itself, along with D minor, as a primary tonality of the work) Gurnemanz replies that on this day repentant sinners rejoice at the Redeemer's act of self-sacrifice and nature herself is transfigured. In a transformation scene similar to that in the first act (but in the reverse direction), and underpinned by a processional ostinato rhythm, Gurnemanz now leads Parsifal and Kundry to the Grail hall. There one group of knights bears Titurel in his coffin, while a second group carries Amfortas on a litter. When Titurel's coffin is opened, all break into a cry of woe. The cry establishes D minor for Amfortas's final monologue: 'Mein Vater!'. He refuses to uncover the Grail, and when the knights become threateningly insistent, he merely invites them to plunge their swords into his heart.

Parsifal has meanwhile appeared unobserved; he holds out his spear and with its point touches Amfortas's wound: 'Nur eine Waffe taugt'. Amfortas is miraculously healed and his theme (ex.4) gives way to Parsifal's (ex.6), now in a triumphant D major, as he yields his office as lord of the Grail to the new redeemer. D major turns to D minor before a momentous modulation to the final tonality of Ab major, on the words 'öffnet den Schrein!' ('open the shrine!'). Here the work's central polarity of Ab/D (major and minor) is resolved by an integration of the two, as of two complementary spheres. Parsifal takes the Grail from the shrine and it shines softly, then radiantly as light falls from above. Kundry sinks lifeless to the ground, redeemed at last. As the motifs of faith (ex.3) and the Grail (ex.2) make their final, luminously scored appearance, Parsifal waves the Grail in blessing over the worshipping knights. A white dove descends to hover above his head.

* * *

Parsifal is the most enigmatic and elusive work in the Wagnerian canon. No attempt to elucidate its mysteries can afford to ignore any of its elements, whether its Christian, pagan, Buddhist or Schopenhauerian ideas, or its concepts of racial purity and regeneration. The only one of Wagner's music dramas written with direct experience of the Bayreuth Festspielhaus, the text of *Parsifal* is set to a diaphanous score of unearthly beauty and refinement. The score offers frequent clues to an understanding of the text, but Wagner's characteristically ambivalent treatment of consonance and dissonance, as of pleasure and pain, and his interweaving of diatonicism and chromaticism, resists any over-simplified interpretation. The juxtaposition of sublimity with richly ambivalent symbolism and an underlying ideology disturbing in its implications creates a work of unique expressive power and endless fascination.

BARRY MILLINGTON

Partch, Harry (*b* Oakland, CA, 24 June 1901; *d* San Diego, 3 Sept 1974). American composer. One of the finest American composers of dramatic music, and certainly one of the most influential, he remains relatively little known because of the difficulties involved in producing and disseminating his major works.

1. Life and works. 2. Philosophy and influence.

1. LIFE AND WORKS. Partch's childhood was spent in southern Arizona, then still a frontier territory; his parents encouraged his musical ability and he learnt to play a wide variety of wind and string instruments as well as the piano. His initial conception of music theatre was formed from an encounter with Beijing Opera in San Francisco's Chinatown when he was 13; the following year he began to compose. Between 1923 and 1925 he developed the aesthetic and theoretical foundations of his mature style, and began to employ microtonal just intonation. He completed the first draft (1927–8) of *Genesis of a Music* and in 1928 began work on a viola designed to accommodate his compositional techniques; on its completion in 1930 he burnt everything he had composed until then. In its austere early form, his theory allowed for only solo voice with solo accompaniment, as his earliest surviving works attest.

In 1934 Partch received a grant to study the history of intonation at the British Museum. Returning to the USA during the Great Depression, he was unable to find more than temporary employment and travelled as a hobo for eight years; his chief artistic activities during this period were the making of experimental instruments and the maintenance of a journal, *Bitter Music*. A Guggenheim Fellowship in 1943 enabled him to complete *The Wayward*, a series of cantata-like compositions; its performance brought the composer his first significant recognition (1944). Partch held a research fellowship, 1944–7, at the University of Wisconsin, Madison, where he created two chromelodeons (modified reed-organs) and four pitched idiophones (1949–51); these and the eight instruments he already had formed the basis of an ensemble to which he continued adding for the rest of his life. In 1954–5 he rescored most of his earlier works to include the new instruments.

The core of Partch's output is a group of five full-length music-theatre pieces, all composed after the age of 50. Each was created and first performed in connection with a university as the result of a commission or as the end product of a research residency: *Oedipus* (1951) at Mills College, Oakland, California; *The Bewitched* (1955), *Revelation in the Courthouse Park* (1960) and *Water! Water!* (1961) at the University of Illinois, Urbana-Champaign; and *Delusion of the Fury* (1966) at the University of California, Los Angeles.

In Urbana in 1956 Partch met the percussionist and conductor Danlee Mitchell, thereafter his close associate and *de facto* manager. Under Mitchell's direction, a retrospective concert of Partch's work was mounted in New York in 1968, and the première of *Delusion of the Fury* in Los Angeles the following year received concentrated critical attention. Commercial recordings followed, and Partch's music at last entered the mainstream. Partch spent his final years in Encinitas, near San Diego, where Mitchell was a music professor. All subsequent performances of Partch's music have involved Mitchell's cooperation and supervision. Among the most important were the European première of *The Bewitched* (1980, Berlin and Cologne) and a fully professional production of *Revelation in the Courthouse Park* (1987, Philadelphia).

2. PHILOSOPHY AND INFLUENCE. The cornerstone of Partch's aesthetics is the concept of 'corporeality' – that is, 'physicality', or better, 'bodiliness'. Music as a human emanation is intimately tied to the actions of the human body, to dance, mime, speech and song. Music-making should ideally express an almost biological *joie-de-vivre*: 'I believe in musicians who are total constituents of the moment, irreplaceable, who may sing, shout, whistle, stamp their feet; in costume always, or perhaps half naked, and I do not care which half'. This applies to instrumentalists as well as singers, and instrumental performers in Partch's theatre works participate in the action or at least appear prominently on stage. The instruments themselves are unique works of art, to be appreciated as much for their visual and tactile values as for their sound; that is why Partch discouraged their duplication. He did not totally reject abstract music, but regarded it as a subsidiary and inferior mode of expression. His one extended essay in abstraction was a study for *Delusion of the Fury*.

For the theoretical elaboration of corporeality Partch turned to the ancient Greeks, and seems at first to have duplicated much of the work of the Florentine Camerata. His initial concept of 'monophony' – 'One Voice' accompanied by one instrument and hewing as closely as musically possible to speech – is almost indistinguishable from Caccinian monody, though its musical expression is very different. As fully elaborated, his system became far broader and more flexible, and not monophonic in any conventional sense. His equivalent of recitative is the 'intoning voice' – speech-like tone and delivery applied to precisely notated pitches laid out in detailed realistic speech contours, based on his microtonal scale. His scale uses 43 unequal tones to the octave, tuned to precise harmonic ratios derived from partials up to the 11th; the system, whose fundamental note is G, allows for limited modulation to related keys (though modulations are regarded as illusory). Because of the system's radical acoustic unity, Partch came to view any musical expression of it as monophonic, even when that expression involved full harmonization or even counterpoint; by the same token, the composer himself was seen as supplying a central 'One Voice' even for the most elaborate ensembles.

Of Partch's five big theatrical works, *Oedipus*, *Revelation* and *Water! Water!* are operas by any definition. The other two are not; they contain much singing, but most of it is wordless. *Delusion* has only a few lines of dialogue, while *The Bewitched* contains but a single word: 'Bah!'. To draw such generic distinctions does violence to the composer's conception, however: all five works are 'music-dance dramas' with the weight and balance of two-act operas, though only *Delusion* and *Water! Water!* are so divided. All are musically continuous, though individual scenes and numbers are identified by intriguingly whimsical titles. Partch projected *Oedipus* as early as 1934, but did not feel ready for so large a project until much later. *U.S. Highball* (1943), the 25-minute capstone of *The Wayward*, was conceived as a kind of prototype or trial run for his music-theatre ideas; with its counterpoint of 'objective' and 'subjective' voices, it is clearly intended for the theatre of the mind, though it has been successfully staged.

For someone so isolated from the normal avenues of musical and theatrical performance, Partch has been enormously influential. Among his disciples may be counted all American composers who employ just intonation and most of those who use microtones. He also affected the development of multi-media 'music theatre' – especially in its more spectacular manifestations – and of minimalism, mostly through Terry Riley. Outside the realm of music, Partch is considered the founder of American sound-sculpture, and is one of the lesser patriarchs of 'green' political philosophy: his unneurotic approach to sex, his proto-feminism (*Bewitched*, *Revelation*), environmentalism (*Water! Water!*) and unselfconscious use of salty language (*The Wayward*) seem prescient because the characteristic California blend of pioneer, oriental and Amerindian values which he displays has become widespread since the 1960s. Long dismissed as an eccentric, Partch belongs, alongside Heinrich, Ives, Cowell and Cage, to that tradition of idealistic individualism in which the American musical spirit finds its clearest voice. As the key operatic exponent of that tradition, he is essential to any understanding of what American opera is or can be.

See also OEDIPUS and REVELATION IN THE COURTHOUSE PARK.

librettos by the composer

King Oedipus (music-dance drama, 1, after W. B. Yeats: *Sophocles' King Oedipus, a Version for the Modern Stage*), Oakland, CA, Mills College, 14 March 1952; rev. as Oedipus, 11 Sept 1954; rev., 1967
The Bewitched (dance satire, 1), Urbana, IL, U. of Illinois, 26 March 1957
Revelation in the Courthouse Park (music-dance drama, 1, after Euripides: *The Bacchae*), Urbana, U. of Illinois, 11 April 1961
Water! Water! (intermission with prologues and epilogues, 2), Urbana, U. of Illinois, 9 March 1962
Delusion of the Fury, 1966 (ritual of dream and delusion, 2), Los Angeles, UCLA, 9 Jan 1969

*

EwenD; VintonD
N. Heath Taylor: 'Monophony: Looking into the Future', *Pacific Coast Musician*, xxviii/16 (1939), 2
H. Partch: *Genesis of a Music* (Madison, WI, 1949, enlarged 2/1974) [incl. annotated work-list, bibliography, discography, filmography]
R. H. Hagan: 'The Mills College Production of "King Oedipus"', *San Francisco Chronicle* (9 March 1952)

W. Leach: 'Music for Words Perhaps', *Theatre Arts*, xxxvii/1 (1953), 65–8
P. Yates: 'Music: Revelation in Illinois', *Arts & Architecture*, lxxviii/8 (1961), 4–6, 28–9
W. Mellers: 'An American Aboriginal', *Tempo*, new ser., no.64 (1963), 2–6
P. Earls: 'Harry Partch: Verses in Preparation for "Delusion of the Fury"', *Inter-American Institute for Musical Research: Yearbook*, iii (1967), 1–32
A. Woodbury: 'Harry Partch: Corporeality and Monophony', *Source*, i/2 (1967), 91–113
G. Chase: 'Toward a Total Musical Theatre', *Arts in Society*, vi/1 (1969), 26–37
E. Paul: 'Delusion of the Fury', *Delusion of the Fury, a Ritual of Dream and Delusion* (Columbia M2 30576, 1971) [notes]
B. Johnston: 'The Corporealism of Harry Partch', *PNM*, xiii/2 (1975), 85–97
W. Zimmerman: *Desert Plants: Conversations with 23 American Musicians* (Vancouver, 1976), 350–65
D. S. Augustine: *Four Theories of Music in the United States, 1900–1950: Cowell, Yasser, Partch, Schillinger* (diss., U. of Texas, 1979)
M. L. Blankenburg and K. Gaburo: 'The Bewitched Goes to Europe', *Interval*, ii/1 (1979), 27–32
H. Henck: 'Literatur zu Harry Partch', *Neuland Ansätze zur Musik der Gegenwart*, ii (1981–2), 252–4, 269 [bibliography, discography, filmography]
P. Garland: *Americas: Essays on American Musicians and Culture, 1973–80* (Santa Fe, 1982), 56–63, 267–90
B. Johnston: 'Beyond Harry Partch', *PNM*, xxii/1–2 (1983–4), 223–32
W. Salmon: 'The Influence of Noh on Harry Partch's *Delusion of the Fury*', *PNM*, xxii/1–2 (1983–4), 233–45
K. Gaburo: 'In Search of Partch's "Bewitched": Concerning Physicality', *Percussive Notes Research Edition*, xxiii/3 (1985), 54–84
A. Stiller: 'Rethinking Harry Partch: a "Revelation" for the '90s', *MusAm*, cx/5 (1990), 90–92   ANDREW STILLER

Partenio [Partenico], **Gian** [Giovanni] **Domenico** (*b* Spilimberg, Friuli, before 1650; *d* Venice, 1701). Italian composer. He rose through the musical ranks at St Mark's, Venice, beginning as a tenor in February 1666. In July 1685 he succeeded Legrenzi as vice-*maestro di cappella* and in May 1692 succeeded Volpe as *maestro di cappella*, having acted in this capacity since the previous December. He was also *maestro di coro* at the Ospedale dei Mendicanti from 12 August 1685 until 1689; however, the death of Legrenzi in 1690 seems to have redirected his attention entirely towards music at St Mark's.

Although perhaps more important in his own day for his church music, Partenio is now remembered chiefly as an opera composer. His operatic activities enjoyed the sporadic patronage of the Duchess Benedetta of Brunswick (in 1669), Count Giovanni Antonio Mesmes (in 1673), Count Carlo Vicenzo Giovanelli (in 1682) and Prince Eugenio of Savoy (in 1687). The two operas he composed entirely by himself, *La costanza trionfante* (1673) and *Flavio Cuniberto* (1682), do not survive intact. The latter was revised for a production at S Giovanni Grisostomo in February 1687 and performed in Modena and Fontanelli the following year. The performance of Catterina Ducrò as Teodata is noted in the February issue of *Pallade veneta*. *Flavio Cuniberto* followed the example of Pallavicino's *Vespasiano* (1678) and his subsequent works in providing a *basso buffo* role.

all performed in Venice

Generico (melodrama, 3, N. Beregan), SS Giovanni e Paolo, ded. 31 Jan 1669, *I-Vnm* [some music by A. Cesti]
Iphide greca [Act 1] (drama per musica, 3, N. Minato), I Saloni, spr. 1671, *Vnm* [Act 2 by D. Freschi, Act 3 by A. Sartorio]

La costanza trionfante (drama per musica, C. Ivanovich), S Moisè, 1673

Dionisio, overo La virtù trionfante del vitio [Acts 2 and 3] (drama per musica, 3, M. Noris), SS Giovanni e Paolo, ded. 12 Jan 1681, *Vc*, arias *Vqs* [Act 1 by P. Franceschini]

Flavio Cuniberto (drama per musica, 3, Noris), S Giovanni Grisostomo, 1682, arias and duets *Vqs*

*

G. Ellero, J. Scarpa and M. C. Paolucci, eds.: *Arte e musica all'ospedaletto: schede d'archivio sull'attività musicale degli ospedali dei Derelitti e dei Mendicanti di Venezia* (Venice, 1978)

E. Selfridge-Field: *Pallade veneta: Writings about Music in Venetian Society, 1650–1750* (Venice, 1985)

ELEANOR SELFRIDGE-FIELD

Partenope. Opera in three acts by GEORGE FRIDERIC HANDEL to a libretto anonymously adapted from SILVIO STAMPIGLIA's *Partenope* (1699, Naples) as revised for Venice (1708); London, King's Theatre, 24 February 1730.

Handel wrote *Partenope* as the second new opera of his first season at the King's Theatre following the collapse of the Royal Academy of Music, completing the score on 12 February 1730. Stampiglia's popular libretto, set by several composers, is an amusing fictional romance set in the court of Queen Partenope (or Parthenope), the legendary founder of Naples. The other characters are Partenope's three princely lovers, Arsace, Armindo and Emilio; Rosmira, Princess of Cyprus, Arsace's abandoned fiancée; and Ormonte, the captain of Partenope's guard. *Partenope* seems to have been first considered for an Academy production in 1726 with Cuzzoni and Faustina in the leading female roles – a letter of Owen Swiney's suggests as much – but the directors, perhaps influenced by Swiney's prudish view that it was 'the very worst book (excepting one)' that he had ever read, did not pursue the idea. Handel's choice of the libretto for his first season free from directorial rule, together with the serious *Lotario*, signalled an intention to explore a wider range of operatic taste than the Academy had been prepared to accommodate.

The original cast consisted of Anna Maria Strada del Pò (Partenope), the castrato Antonio Maria Bernacchi (Arsace), Francesca Bertolli (Armindo), Annibale Pio Fabri (Emilio), Antonia Margherita Merighi (Rosmira) and Johann Gottfried Riemschneider (Ormonte). The initial run of seven performances suggests only moderate public success, but Handel revived the opera in his next season for a further seven performances beginning on 29 December 1730, making some cuts and adding a new aria in the final scene for Senesino, who took over the role of Arsace. There were several German productions between 1733 and 1736, beginning with those at Brunswick in February 1733 and at Hamburg (in a version prepared by Keiser) on 28 October 1733. Handel revived the opera for the last time at Covent Garden on 29 January 1737, when the mezzo-soprano castrato Domenico Annibali sang Arsace, Bertolli sang Rosmira, and the roles of Armindo and Ormonte were adapted for the soprano castrato Gioacchino Conti ('Gizziello') and the contralto Maria Caterina Negri. The opera was not heard again until the production at Göttingen on 23 June 1935, in a version by Fritz Lehmann. The first modern British revival was by Unicorn Opera at Abingdon on 4 May 1961. Chrysander's edition largely follows the original 1730 version and includes features of later versions (including the additional aria of December 1730), but several minor cuts made in 1737 are silently adopted in the main text.

ACT 1 In the presence of Prince Arsace of Corinth (alto) and Prince Armindo of Rhodes (alto), Partenope (soprano) invokes Apollo's blessing on her new-founded city of Naples. Rosmira (alto), dressed in male Armenian habit, introduces herself as Prince Eurimene, the sole survivor of a shipwreck. She and Arsace recognize each other but, before they can meet, Ormonte (bass) announces the approach of Prince Emilio of Cuma (tenor), whose troops are threatening Partenope's lands; she goes to meet him. Rosmira learns that Armindo loves Partenope, but will never reveal it as Partenope has sworn fidelity to Arsace. Arsace claims he still loves Rosmira; she will not forgive his abandoning her but, to test his faith, makes him swear he will never reveal who she is or that she is a woman. Armindo, pressed by Partenope to explain his sorrow, admits that Arsace is his rival in love. As Partenope and Arsace renew their vows, Rosmira (as Eurimene) intervenes and claims also to be in love with Partenope. Emilio appears as yet another suitor and asks Partenope to be his queen, saying his troops are merely to honour her; when she refuses him he declares war. Partenope appoints Arsace as her general, but this causes jealousy among the princes and she herself takes supreme command. Armindo feels betrayed by 'Eurimene', apparently an additional rival, but Rosmira assures him that she is in pursuit of another prey.

ACT 2 The troops of Emilio and Partenope confront each other. Armindo saves Partenope from a fatal attack. Arsace and his soldiers rescue Rosmira as she is about to be overcome by Emilio, whom they capture. Partenope returns in triumph. Rosmira reminds her that she owes Armindo her life and claims that Emilio is her captive. Emilio contradicts her, but Rosmira persists and demands single combat with Arsace to prove her honour. Arsace, able neither to accept the challenge nor to reveal why, tries to pacify her. Partenope remains faithful to him and puts a guard on 'Eurimene', but the others think him cowardly. Rosmira nevertheless defends Arsace to Armindo and Emilio; she is torn between love and jealousy. Partenope, after questioning Arsace, orders the release of 'Eurimene' provided 'he' never again approaches her. Armindo finally declares his love for her; she begins to weigh his merits against those of Arsace. Rosmira sends Armindo to tell the queen that 'Eurimene' has a secret to impart which will help Armindo's cause; but Rosmira remains cold to the despairing Arsace.

ACT 3 Partenope and her suitors await Rosmira's revelation. She says her desire to fight Arsace is really to avenge his treatment of Princess Rosmira of Cyprus, whom he abandoned in favour of Partenope. Arsace meekly admits to the accusation; Partenope disowns him and turns to Armindo. Emilio offers to be Arsace's supporter in the forthcoming duel and Rosmira chooses Armindo as hers. In deep despair, Arsace lies down to sleep. Rosmira wakens him, aware that Partenope is watching. Arsace addresses her as Rosmira and offers her his sword; Partenope asks why he calls on the woman he has betrayed. Both women scorn him, and he rails against the tyranny of love. On the field of combat, Ormonte reads the challenge and Rosmira and Arsace take their swords. Arsace, reluctant to fight, is mocked by Rosmira; but he turns the tables by demanding that they fight bare-chested. The company agree and Arsace taunts the discomforted Rosmira with echoes of her previous mockery. She admits her identity, confessing that

Arsace has proved his love by keeping the vow of silence. Partenope takes Armindo as her husband, presents Rosmira to Arsace and allows Emilio to reign once more in Cuma as her ally.

* * *

One of Handel's most delightful operas, *Partenope* is essentially a comedy clothed in the musical richness and formal dignity of the *opera seria* form, and sometimes touching unexpected emotional depths. The usual quota of da capo arias is varied by several ensembles, including a quartet and a trio in Act 3 and a sequence of jaunty military music to begin Act 2. Both the lofty Partenope and the vivacious Rosmira are memorable creations (the latter an exceptionally rewarding role for a mezzo-soprano), so that Arsace's initial inability to choose between them does not seem mere fickleness. As Rosmira heaps humiliation on him, Arsace's music expresses a growing sense of heartbreak; his arias 'Furibondo spira il vento' (ending Act 2) and 'Fatto è Amor un dio d'inferno' (Act 3) are especially powerful outbursts. Armindo is sensitively portrayed as the humbly devoted lover who eventually gets his reward, and Emilio appears as a passionate but honourable soldier. A pair of horns makes a striking contribution to Rosmira's aria 'Io seguo sol fiero' at the close of Act 1, illustrating the hunting metaphor; flutes and a trumpet give further colour to a score full of lively invention.

ANTHONY HICKS

Pasatieri, Thomas (*b* New York, 20 Oct 1945). American composer. A prolific composer by the age of 15, he studied with Nadia Boulanger before entering the Juilliard School of Music, where he studied composition with Vittorio Giannini. At 19 he received the first doctorate in composition awarded by the school. He composed two operas in 1964, *The Trysting Place* and *Flowers of Ice*, but his first opera to be staged was *The Women* (1965), at Aspen, Colorado, where he was a pupil of Milhaud. Its success convinced him that opera was his natural medium. His next two operas, *La Divina*, a comedy about the last performance of an aging coloratura soprano, and *Padrevia*, a gothic horror story based on Boccaccio, were given their premières in college opera theatres in New York. In 1971–2, six of Pasatieri's operas were produced in Seattle, including *Calvary*, based on the play by W. B. Yeats, and *Black Widow*, his first full-length opera, staged by Lotfi Mansouri in 1972. Derived from Miguel de Unamuno's novella *Dos madres*, the opera presents in stark tableaux the tragic situations caused by a barren woman obsessed with motherhood.

Pasatieri's operas characteristically deal with highly emotional characters in strong theatrical situations. *The Trial of Mary Lincoln*, with a libretto by the television writer Anne Howard Bailey, is a moving portrait of the tragic first lady in her later years during the court trial that judged her insane. A work tailored for the intimacy of television, the opera uses flashbacks, dissolves and voice-overs.

The Seagull, Pasatieri's most successful opera, is based on Chekhov's play of 1896. To make it more effective as musical theatre, Pasatieri and his librettist, Kenward Elmslie, concentrated the action of the story, heightening the personal and dramatic relationships. They added an aria to expand the role of Masha; an overtly incestuous duet between Madam Arkadina and Konstantin; and a dramatic final aria that coincides with Konstantin's offstage suicide. Its lush, romantic score,

excellent cast and creative production by the Houston Grand Opera afforded *The Seagull* a favourable critical reception. His *Three Sisters*, composed in 1979, was given its première by Opera Columbus in 1986 and is the first of his operas to have been recorded complete. It was performed in Russian at the Moscow Musical Theatre in October 1988.

Pasatieri has taught at the Juilliard School, the Manhattan School of Music and the Cincinnati College-Conservatory of Music; he was also the director of the Atlanta Opera, 1980–84. Early in 1984 he moved to California to work in films and television. With the exception of a somewhat more dissonant score for *Before Breakfast* (1980), Pasatieri's style has evolved little over the years. His music is conservative and melodic, with dramatic, soaring lines in the manner of Puccini and Strauss. The lyrical, singable nature of his music has attracted many fine singers to take part in premières of his operas, including Evelyn Lear, Frederica von Stade, Richard Stilwell, John Reardon, Lili Chookasian, James Morris, Jennie Tourel and Theodor Uppman.

The Trysting Place, 1964 (1, Pasatieri, after B. Tarkington), unperf.
Flowers of Ice, 1964 (2, R. Rogers), unperf.
The Women (chamber op, 1, Pasatieri), Aspen, CO, 20 Aug 1965
La Divina (comic op, 1, Pasatieri), New York, Juilliard School, 16 March 1966; Baltimore, 23 Jan 1985
Padrevia (1, Pasatieri, after G. Boccaccio), New York, Brooklyn College, 18 Nov 1967
The Penitentes, 1967 (3, A. H. Bailey), Aspen, CO, 3 Aug 1974
Calvary (chamber op, 1, after W. B. Yeats), Seattle, St Thomas Episcopal Church, 7 April 1971
The Trial of Mary Lincoln (television op, 17 scenes, Bailey), Boston, NET, 14 Feb 1972
Black Widow (3, Pasatieri, after M. de Unamuno: *Dos madres*), Seattle, 2 March 1972 (Melville, NY, 1977)
The Seagull (3, K. Elmslie, after A. P. Chekhov), Houston, 5 March 1974
Signor Deluso (comic op, 1, Pasatieri, after Molière: *Sganarelle, ou Le cocu imaginaire*), Wolf Trap, VA, 27 July 1974
Ines de Castro (3, B. Stambler), Baltimore, 30 March 1976
Washington Square (chamber op, 2, Elmslie, after H. James), Detroit, 1 Oct 1976 (Melville, NY, 1977)
Three Sisters, 1979 (1, Elmslie, after Chekhov), Columbus, OH, 13 March 1986
Before Breakfast (1, F. Corsaro, after E. O'Neill), New York, City Opera, 9 Oct 1980
The Goose Girl (children's op, 1, Pasatieri, after J. L. and W. C. Grimm), Fort Worth, TX, 15 Feb 1981
Maria Elena (1, Pasatieri), Tucson, AZ, 6 April 1983

*

R. Jacobson: 'Thomas Pasatieri: Opera is the Plural of Opus', *After Dark*, vi/11 (1974), 45–9
S. Fleming: 'Pasatieri's *The Seagull*', *HiFi/MusAm*, xxiv/6 (1974), 32–3
H. Saal: 'Chekhov from the Heart', *Newsweek* (18 March 1974), 75
G. Stockholm: 'The Seagull – an Opera Composer Emerges', *Cincinnati Enquirer* (9 March 1974)
H. C. Schonberg: 'Ines de Castro in Baltimore', *New York Times* (1 April 1976)
A. Hughes: 'Pasatieri's *Washington Square* Opera States its Case', *New York Times* (15 Oct 1977)
J. Rockwell: 'Baltimore Opera's Three Portraits of Women', *New York Times* (3 Feb 1985)
R. H. Kornick: *Recent American Opera: a Production Guide* (New York, 1991), 222–32
ELISE K. KIRK

Pasero, Tancredi (*b* Turin, 11 Jan 1893; *d* Milan, 17 Feb 1983). Italian bass. He studied with Arturo Pessina and made his début at Vicenza as Rodolfo (*La sonnambula*) in 1919. In 1924 he appeared at the Teatro Costanzi, Rome, and at the Colón, Buenos Aires, where he appeared until 1930. In 1926 he made his La Scala début (*Don Carlos*), and sang there almost continuously until 1952. He was engaged at the Metropolitan (1929–30, 1932–3), at Covent Garden (Padre Guardiano in *La forza del destino*, 1931) and at the Paris Opéra (1935). He retired in 1953. His voice was not exceptionally beautiful, but was full, mellow and very extensive (his repertory ranged from Sarastro to Escamillo), and he showed fine stylistic and interpretative qualities. His other notable roles were in *Norma*, *Simon Boccanegra*, *Mefistofele* and, later, *Boris Godunov*.

S. Winstanley: 'Tancredi Pasero', *Record Advertiser*, iii/4 (1973–4), 2 [with discography]
RODOLFO CELLETTI

Pashchenko, Andrey Filippovich (*b* Rostov-na-Donu, 3/15 Aug 1885; *d* Moscow, 16 Nov 1972). Russian composer. As a child he sang in a church choir, received violin lessons, studied at a charitable music school and took correspondence courses. He directed amateur choirs and wrote reviews for Moscow periodicals, and from 1911 to 1931 was librarian of the St Petersburg Court Orchestra (later the Leningrad PO). He received his formal compositional training as a mature student at the St Petersburg Conservatory (1914–17). With Glazunov and others he founded the Society for the Propagation of Contemporary Russian Music (1923) and he became a member of the artistic council of the Leningrad PO (1926) and of the State Academic Theatre for Opera and Ballet (1928). In 1962 he settled in Moscow.

Pashchenko's output is extensive. In the choral music his epic, monumental style is most evident, its objective tone conveying mass feelings and impulses. He displayed a deep understanding of Russian peasant singing and polyphony and employed a diversity of techniques, often to illustrative effect. It is the broadly presented choral music that distinguishes his opera *Orliniy bunt* ('The Eagle Revolt', 1925), concerning the Pugachyov uprising. This work played an important part in shaping Soviet music drama, although Pashchenko's reputation as an opera composer was established by later comic-satiric works. *Tsar' Maximilian* (1929) is a 'buffoon action' based on ideas from folktales and linked with Rimsky-Korsakov's *The Golden Cockerel* and traditional Russian farce; it has the sharpness of a political pamphlet. The opera *Pompaduri* ('The Pompadours', 1939) was taken from works by the Russian satirical writer M. E. Saltïkov-Shchedrin; this strong satirical spirit is also present in *Svad'ba Krechinskogo* ('The Krechinsky Wedding', 1949), where the composer depicts everyday life and gives a psychological portrait. Pashchenko's earlier music is tonally simple and lapidary, with a somewhat rough energy, winning straightforwardness and resoluteness of expression. In later years he explored more impressionistic and dissonant harmonies.

Orliniy bunt [The Eagle Revolt]/Pugachyovshchina [Pugachyov's Domain] (S. Spassky), Leningrad, State Academy Theatre, 7 Nov 1925
Tsar' Maximilian, 1926–9 (A. Remizov), concert perf., Leningrad, 6 Oct 1929
Chyorniy yar [The Black Ravine] (L. Seyfullina), Leningrad, 12 June 1931
Pompaduri [The Pompadours], 1936 (A. Ivanovsky and V. Rozhdestvensky, after M. E. Saltïkov-Shchedrin), Leningrad, Maliy, 20 Oct 1939
Svad'ba Krechinskogo, 1947 [The Krechinsky Wedding] (Spassky, after A. Sukhovo-Kobïlin), Leningrad, Maliy, 10 June 1949; rev., as Igrok [The Gambler], Leningrad, 1955
Shut Balakirev [The Buffoon Balakirev], 1949 (A. Mariengof)

Goryachiye serdtsa [Passionate Hearts], 1952 (N. Tokunovy)
Kapriznaya nevesta [The Stubborn Bride], 1953
Radda i Loyko (after M. Gorky: *Makar Chudra*), 1957; rev. 1966
Nila Snishko (after A. D. Salinsky), 1961
Al'piyskaya ballada [Alpen Ballad], 1963–6 (V. V. Bïkov)
Velikiy soblaznitel' [The Great Seducer], 1963–6 (after A. K. Tolstoy)
Afrikanskaya lyubov' [African Love], 1966
Zhenshchina, eto d'yavol [Woman, She is the Devil], 1966
Kon' v senate [The Horse in the Senate], 1967
Portret (after N. V. Gogol), 1968
Master i Margarita (after M. A. Bulgakov), 1971

Yu. V. Kremlyov: 'A. F. Pashchenko: ocherk tvorchestva' [Pashchenko: an Essay on his Works], *Ocherki po istorii i teorii muzïki* [Essays on the History and Theory of Music] (Leningrad, 1939)
E. Meylikh: *A. F. Pashchenko* (Leningrad, 1960)
GENRIKH ORLOV

Pashkevich, Vasily Alexeyevich (*b* c1742; *d* St Petersburg, 9/20 March 1797). Composer and singer, possibly of Russian birth (the name is Polish). He probably received his training from Vincenzo Manfredini, the chief composer in the early 1760s at the court of Peter III and later at that of Catherine II. From 1763 he is listed as a member of the court orchestra, and he presumably also sang in the court chapel choir. In 1773–4 he taught singing at the Academy of Fine Arts. His first musical comedy, *Neschast'ye ot kareti*('Misfortune from a Coach'), was produced at the Hermitage in 1779, Pashkevich himself appearing in one of the roles. The next year he was among those entrusted with the preparation of a grandiose 'theatrical festival' in honour of the empress's name-day, the others all being Italians (none of the music survives). After the success of his early operas in a privately owned enterprise, Pashkevich was re-employed by the court (1783) as a violinist in the 'first' orchestra; six years later he was put in charge of music for the royal balls, and was leader of the orchestra. At the same time he held the rank of soloist (*bol'shoy pevchiy*) in the chapel choir. Catherine II put him to work setting her own librettos and in 1790, after *Nachal'noye upravleniye Olega* ('The Early Reign of Oleg'), made him an award of 1600 rubles 'for divers composing of music and efforts beyond his obligation'. By the end of his career Pashkevich had attained the salary rank of Collegiate Assessor, the civilian equivalent of colonel (only Giuseppe Sarti equalled his standing, and not until the reign of Tsar Paul). His closeness to Catherine cost him dearly in the end, for on the accession of her son Paul he was dismissed without pension; he died shortly thereafter.

Pashkevich and Fomin were the most important native composers of opera in 18th-century Russia. Pashkevich's output can be divided into two groups. The earlier consists of five comedies (of which three survive) that formed the core repertory of Karl Knipper's 'free' (public) theatre on Tsaritsin Lug (Queen's Meadow), where Pashkevich directed the music for the duration of its existence as a private enterprise (1779–83). This was primarily a dramatic theatre, and all of the musical plays written for it, though called comic operas, were of the type known in France as *comédie mêlée d'ariettes*, a spoken comedy interspersed with modest musical numbers (songs, simple ensembles and occasionally choruses) that could be performed by actors with the ordinary ability to carry a tune. The genre had been imported by a French troupe that toured St Petersburg in 1764–8, presenting works of Favart, Sedaine and others. The first Russian specimen, *Anyuta* (1772; text by the court actor Mikhail Popov, music lost) has been attributed to Pashkevich; but while he may have taken part in the performance (at the Tsarskoye Selo palace, by members of the court chapel choir), it is more likely that *Anyuta*, like many of its French prototypes, was made up of contrafacta to folk and popular tunes.

The libretto of *Misfortune from a Coach*, like that of *Skupoy* ('The Miser', 1781), Pashkevich's second opera, was by Knyazhnin, an outstanding neo-classical poet and playwright. One of the classics of 18th-century Russian drama, it is a typical satirical tale of rustic wit. Firyulin (tenor), a maniacally francophile squire, having taken a fancy to a brand new Parisian coach, decides to sell one of his serfs, Luk'yan, into military service in order to afford it. Acting on the advice of Klimenty (tenor), the squire's house jester, Luk'yan and his beloved (soprano, named Anyuta, like all peasant heroines) affect Gallic mannerisms and so arouse their master's sympathy. Though it seems an indictment of serfdom (and has been much touted as such by Soviet scholarship), it was not regarded so by contemporary audiences (indeed, the play was a great favourite of Catherine II). Pashkevich's music, in keeping with the literary style of the libretto, is devoid of the popular tone one might expect in an opera with peasant characters. Instead, the music sung by the peasant couple, especially in the duet in Act 2 through which they make their appeal to their master, is couched in a parodistically sentimental idiom, full of exaggerated appoggiaturas and *soupirs* (quaver rests). By contrast, Pashkevich's third surviving opera, *Sanktpeterburgskiy gostinnïy dvor* ('The St Petersburg Bazaar', 1782), to a libretto by Mikhail Matinsky, is a bench-mark of the emergent Russian national style. The music to a second libretto by Matinsky, *Tunisskiy pasha* ('The Pasha of Tunis', 1782), has not survived.

Three works to librettos by the Empress Catherine (written with the help of her literary secretary, Alexander Khrapovitsky) make up the second group of Pashkevich's operas. These were lavish court productions, in up to five acts, with choruses, ballets, large instrumental forces and singers capable of a decorative vocal idiom. Nevertheless, they all remained true to the simple conception of a play with musical numbers. Only the music of the first of them, *Fevey* (1786), was wholly by Pashkevich. The title character of this work – which is based on a fairy-tale that Catherine had written to entertain and instruct her grandsons (they included two future tsars) – is a Siberian prince (tenor), a paragon of virtue who pursues a dream vision of a beautiful princess to the ends of the earth. Curiously foreshadowing the technique of certain 19th-century Russian masters, Pashkevich based his score on the contrast between a selfconsciously Russian idiom and an 'oriental' one, in this case an imaginary Mongol style. His 'Kalmyk chorus', a concoction of Lombard rhythms and drone 5ths, attracted a great deal of favourable attention, many spectators (including Louis XVI's ambassador, who wrote about it in a letter) taking it as authentic. What was authentic was the 'Russian' music ('from ancient local tunes', in the ambassador's words), much of it founded on the strains of the famous wedding song *Iz-pod kamushka* ('From beneath a Stone'). One of the secondary characters (Ledmer, tenor) sings a song consisting of ostinato variations on a folklike tune, often cited by historians of Russian music as the earliest ancestor of Glinka's epochal orchestral work

Kamarinskaya. Pashkevich's contribution to the other operas with texts by Catherine – *The Early Reign of Oleg* (mainly by Sarti) and the one-act *Fedul s det'mi* ('Fedul and his Children'; mainly by Martín y Soler) – was (apart from the attractive overture to *Fedul*) largely confined to interludes of local colour in the form of choral harmonizations of Russian folksongs. The wedding scene in Act 3 of *The Early Reign of Oleg*, with its three finely wrought choruses, a refinement on the bride's party in *The St Petersburg Bazaar*, is perhaps Pashkevich's most elegant and characteristic achievement in the national vein.

See also MISER, THE and SANKTPETERBURGSKIY GOSTINNÏY DVOR.

all first performed in St Petersburg; all extant MSS in RU-SPtob

Neschast'ye ot kareti [Misfortune from a Coach] (comic op, 2, Ya. B. Knyazhnin), Hermitage, 7/18 Nov 1779, excerpt in Ginzburg

Skupoy [The Miser] (comic op, 1, Knyazhnin, after Molière and A. Sumarkov), Knipper's, sum. 1781; ed. Ye. Levashov (Moscow, 1973); excerpt in Ginzburg

Lzhets [The Liar] (Knyazhnin), 1 no. pubd (1781), music otherwise lost

Tunisskiy pasha [The Pasha of Tunis] (comic op, 2, M. A. Matinsky), Knipper's, 22 June/3 July 1782

Sanktpeterburgskiy gostinnïy dvor [The St Petersburg Bazaar] (comic op, 3, Matinsky), Knipper's, aut. 1782; rev. as Kak pozhivyosh', tak i proslïvyosh [You'll be Known by the Way you Live], Bol'shoy, 2/13 Feb 1792; ed. Ye. Levashov (Moscow, 1980); excerpts in Ginzburg

Fevey (comic op, 4, Catherine II), Bol'shoy, 19/30 April 1786; vs arr. I. Pratsch (St Petersburg, 1789); excerpt in Ginzburg

Nachal'noye upravleniye Olega [The Early Reign of Oleg] (5, Catherine II), Hermitage, 15/26 Oct 1790 (St Petersburg, 1791), collab. G. Sarti and C. Canobbio

Fedul s det'mi [Fedul and his Children] (play with music, 1, Catherine II and A. V. Khrapovitsky), Hermitage, 16/27 Jan 1791; vs (Moscow, 1895); collab. V. Martín y Soler

*

J. Grot, ed.: *Lettres de Grimm à l'impératrice Catherine II* (St Petersburg, 2/1866)

V. A. Prokof'yev: 'Mikhail Matinsky i ego opera "Sankt-Peterburgskiy gostinïy dvor"', *Muzïka i muzïkal'nïy bït staroy Rossii* [Music and Musical Life in Old Russia], i (Leningrad, 1927), 58–69

A. S. Rabinovich: *Russkaya opera do Glinki* [Russian Opera Before Glinka] (Moscow, 1948)

R.-A. Mooser: *Annales de la musique et des musiciens en Russie au XVIIIme siècle*, ii (Geneva, 1951)

D. Lehmann: *Russlands Oper und Singspiel in der zweiten Hälfte des 18. Jahrhunderts* (Leipzig, 1958)

M. Whaples: 'Eighteenth-Century Russian Opera in the Light of Soviet Scholarship', *Indiana Slavic Studies*, ii (1958), 113–34

Yu. V. Keldïsh: 'Nachalo russkoye operï: V. Pashkevich, Ye. Fomin' [The Origins of Russian Opera: Pashkevich, Fomin], *Russkaya muzïka XVIII veka* (Moscow, 1965), 244–380

S. L. Ginzburg: IRMO, i

O. Levashova: *Russkaya vokal'naya lirika XVIII veka*, Pamyatniki russkogo muzïkal'nogo iskusstva [Monuments of Russian Art Music], i (Moscow, 1972)

Ye. Levashov: 'Sushchestvoval li kompozitor Matinskiy?' [Did the Composer Matinsky Exist?], *SovM* (1973), no.5, pp.81–8

——: Commentary to *Skupoy*, Pamyatniki russkogo muzïkal'nogo iskusstva [Monuments of Russian Art Music], iv (Moscow, 1973)

——: Commentary to *Sankt Peterburgskiy gostinïy dvor*, Pamyatniki russkogo muzïkal'nogo iskusstva [Monuments of Russian Art Music], viii (Moscow, 1980)

S. Karlinsky: *Russian Drama from its Beginnings to the Age of Pushkin* (Berkeley and Los Angeles, 1985), chap. 5

Ye. Levashov: 'V. A. Pashkevich', *Istoriya russkoy muzïki v desyati tomakh* [The History of Russian Music in Ten Volumes], ed. Yu. V. Keldïsh, iii (Moscow, 1985), 46–83   RICHARD TARUSKIN

Pasi, Antonio (*b* Bologna, *fl* 1704–32). Italian mezzo-soprano castrato. He is said to have been a pupil of Pistocchi and is first found in opera in 1704–8 in Venice, Modena and Florence. He then disappeared from the Italian stage until 1716, at least part of the interim having been spent in the service of the Elector Palatine, presumably at Düsseldorf. He then sang regularly in Italian theatres until 1728; in Carnival 1729 he was at Brussels, and he ended his stage career with engagements in Venice in 1730 and Florence in 1732. From at least 1724 he was in the service of the Duke of Parma. Mancini (*Pensieri*, 1774) called his singing style 'individual and arresting', particularly because of his highly personal use of ornamental nuances. His range, at least late in his career, seldom exceeded *e'* to *f''*.

DENNIS LIBBY

Pasini, Laura (*b* Gallarate, nr Varese, 28 Jan 1894; *d* Rome, 6 Sept 1942). Italian soprano. She studied at the Accademia di S Cecilia, Rome, and made her début in 1921 at the Teatro Eden, Milan, as Zerlina in *Fra Diavolo*. She sang at La Scala from 1923, making her début there as the Queen of Night, and in 1926 appeared in the title role in the local première of Stravinsky's *The Nightingale*, conducted by the composer. Her coloratura was admired in revivals of Rossini's *L'italiana in Algeri* and *La Cenerentola*, in which she sang with Conchita Supervia. At the 1931 Salzburg Festival she was heard as Elisetta in *Il matrimonio segreto*. She taught in Rome and Cagliari from 1934.

DAVID CUMMINGS

Pasini-Vitale [née Pasini], **Lina** [Carolina] (*b* Rome, 8 Nov 1872; *d* Rome, 23 Nov 1959). Italian soprano. After study in Rome she made her début at the Teatro Dal Verme, Milan, as Cecilia in *La tilda* by Cilea (1892). Early in her career she was successful at La Scala and in Rome and Turin as Mascagni's Iris and Suzel (*L'amico Fritz*), Micaëla, Mimì and Gretel. In 1897 she married the conductor Edoardo Vitale. From 1914 she was widely known in operas by Wagner, singing Kundry in the South American première of *Parsifal* at Buenos Aires, and appearing as Brünnhilde at Rome in 1926. She retired in 1928, after singing Kundry at Naples.

Pasini-Vitale's sister Camilla (1875–1935), whose married name was Muzii, made her début in Rome as Inès and went on to create Musetta in *La bohème*. She sang at La Scala in 1897 and again in 1904 after touring in South America.

DAVID CUMMINGS

Paskalis, Kostas (*b* Levadia, Boeotia, 1 Sept 1929). Greek baritone. He studied in Athens, making his début there in 1951 as Rigoletto. In 1958 he sang Renato in Vienna, where he was a member of the Staatsoper for 20 years. He made his British début in 1964 as Macbeth at Glyndebourne, where he also sang Don Giovanni (1967), and his Metropolitan début in 1965 as Don Carlo (*La forza*), returning as Ford. At Salzburg he created Pentheus in Henze's *The Bassarids* in 1966 and at La Scala sang Valentin (1967). He made his Covent Garden début in 1969 as Macbeth, returning for Iago, Scarpia and Rigoletto. He sang in Rome, Florence, Berlin, Munich, Dallas, Houston and San Francisco. His repertory included William Tell, Barnaba (*La Gioconda*), Yevgeny Onegin and Harlequin (*Ariadne auf Naxos*), but it was in Verdi that he excelled, as Posa, Amonasro, Boccanegra, Luna, Germont, Nabucco and, his finest roles, Iago and Macbeth. He was an arresting actor and had a warm, resonant voice with a wide range.

ALAN BLYTH

Pasqua, Giuseppina (*b* Perugia, 19 March 1855; *d* Pieve di Budrio, Bologna, 24 Feb 1930). Italian soprano and mezzo-soprano. Trained first in Perugia, she made her soprano début in Bologna as Oscar in *Un ballo in maschera* and continued training with Piccolomini in Palermo, where she sang Marguerite de Valois in *Les Huguenots*. She then studied as a mezzo-soprano with Luigia Abbadia; she sang Amneris at La Scala in 1878. Her fame in Europe was such that Verdi wanted her as Mistress Quickly for the première of *Falstaff* at La Scala (1893). Her repertory was very wide, but she was particularly successful in *Mignon*, *La favorite*, *La Gioconda*, *Il trovatore*, *Lohengrin* and *Saffo*.

*

A. Lupattelli: *Giuseppina Pasqua* (Perugia, 1880)

GALLIANO CILIBERTI

Pasquali [née James], **Bernice de** (*b* Boston, 1880; *d* Omaha, NE, 3 April 1925). American soprano. After instruction in New York with Oscar Saenger she studied in Milan, where she made her début in 1900. She went on to sing in major Italian cities, as well as in Berlin, London and Paris. Her Metropolitan Opera début was in 1909 as Susanna, and she remained a company member until 1917; her roles included Adina, Lucia, Rosina and Violetta. In 1924 she became the first American woman to become a member of the Accademia Filarmonica in Rome. She died of pneumonia during a vaudeville tour undertaken against the advice of her physician.

CORI ELLISON

Pasqualigo, Benedetto [Fesanio, Merindo] (*b* Venice, *fl* 1706–34). Italian librettist. He was a Venetian nobleman and a member of the Venetian colony of the Arcadian Academy, the Accademia degli Animosi, in which he used the name Merindo Fesanio. His seven opera librettos were written for various Venetian theatres between 1718 and 1725 (Allacci and Ricci's references to a Bolognese production of *Berenice* in 1706 are probably mistaken) and adhere to the elevated principles of the academy. Most are in five acts and labelled *tragedia* or, in the case of *Il pastor fido*, *tragicommedia*. Pasqualigo's broad knowledge of classical tragedy is clear from his verse translations of Euripides' *Hippolytus* and Seneca's *Hippolytus*, *Oedipus*, *Medea* and *Troades*, which were published in Venice in 1730. *Cimene* is based on Corneille's *Le Cid*, and *Mitridate re di Ponto vincitore di se stesso* on Racine's *Mithridate*. Two of his librettos had unusually successful careers in Venice: *Antigona* enjoyed three productions in two theatres within six years; *Ifigenia in Tauride*, which draws on Pier Jacopo Martelli's work, was produced at the Teatro S Giovanni Grisostomo in two settings within six years. Several of the arias from *Ifigenia* (1725) and *Berenice* found their way, with their musical settings, into Handel's first pasticcio, *Elpidia* (London, King's, 1725).

Antigona [*La fedeltà coronata*] (tragedia), Orlandini, 1718 (with addl music by A. Tinazzoli, 1723); *Ifigenia in Tauride* (tragedia), Orlandini, 1719 (Vinci, 1725); *Il pastor fido* (tragicommedia), C. L. P. Grua, 1721; *Cimene* (tragedia), Girolamo Bassani and M. Zucchini, 1721; *Giulio Flavio Crispo* (tragedia), G. M. Capelli, 1722; *Mitridate re di Ponto vincitore di se stesso*, Capelli, 1723; *Berenice*, Orlandini, 1725

*

AllacciD

G. Bonlini: *Le glorie della poesia e della musica* (Venice, 1730)

A. Groppo: *Catalogo di tutti i drammi per musica recitati ne' teatri di Venezia* (Venice, 1745)

N. Haym: *Biblioteca italiana*, i (Milan, 1803)

C. Ricci: *I teatri di Bologna* (Bologna, 1888)

C. Sartori: *I libretti italiani a stampa dalle origini al 1800* (Cuneo, 1990–)

HARRIS S. SAUNDERS

Marc'Antonio Pasqualini Crowned by Apollo: portrait by Andrea Sacchi (1599–1661)

Pasqualini, Marc'Antonio ['Malagigi'] (*b* Rome, bap. 25 April 1614; *d* Rome, 3 July 1691). Italian soprano castrato. The fourth son of a barber from Imola, he boarded and studied with Vincenzo Ugolini while employed as a boy soprano at S Luigi dei Francesi in Rome from 1623. In Parma, where he would have sung in Monteverdi's *intermedi* and *torneo* of 1628, Monteverdi described the 14-year-old Pasqualini's voice as agreeable and flexible (with 'qualche gorgietta' and 'qualche trillo') though produced with some opacity ('alquanto ottusa'). In 1629, on the recommendation of Paolo Aringhi, Pasqualini became a protégé of the younger Cardinal Antonio Barberini, who paid 200 scudi to release him from his contract with Ugolini. He sang in the Sistine Chapel choir from 1631 and continued to fill in even after his retirement in 1659.

Pasqualini performed in at least ten seasons of court opera, with leading soprano roles in five Barberini operas as well as in *Il ratto di Proserpina* given by Pompeo Colonna in 1645. He first sang for the French in *La sincerità trionfante* (text by Ottaviano Castelli, music by Cecchini), presented by the French ambassador in Rome in the 1638–9 season, and then in Luigi Rossi's *Orfeo*, given in Paris in 1647. A portrait by Andrea Sacchi (Metropolitan Museum, New York; see illustration) celebrated his prowess as a singer in the Barberini orbit, and his ability was noted by foreigners such as John Evelyn and Jean-Jacques Bouchard (who in 1632 called him a 'soprano maraviglioso e bello'), and in the *Gazette de France*, as well as by his colleagues in the papal chapel. He characteristically played choice roles portraying lamenting females with great expressiveness (see letter of 1642 from Castelli in A. Ghislanzoni, *Luigi Rossi*, Rome, 1954, p.188). In Rossi's *Orfeo*, his Paris triumph, he played a similar male character, Aristaeus, whose love is spurned by Eurydice.

Pasqualini was also a prolific composer of vocal chamber music. Many of his works show stylistic similarities to the music of the roles he played, but it is also possible that his operatic parts reflect to some extent his own vocal style. An amended section to one of his arias in Rossi's *Il palazzo incantato* is in his own script.

E. Vogel: 'C. Monteverdi', *VMw*, iii (1897), 435, 437

A. Cametti: 'Musicisti celebri del seicento in Roma: M. A. Pasqualini', *Musica d'oggi*, iii (1921), 69–71, 97–9

H. Prunières: 'Les musiciens du Cardinal Antonio Barberini', *Mélanges de musicologie offerts à M. Lionel de la Laurencie* (Paris, 1933), 119–22

M. Murata: 'Further Remarks on Pasqualini and the Music of *MAP*', *AnMc*, no.19 (1979), 125–45

——: *Operas for the Papal Court, 1631–1668* (Ann Arbor, 1981)

T. Ford: 'Andrea Sacchi's "Apollo Crowning the Singer M. A. Pasqualini"', *EMc*, xii (1984), 79–84

F. Hammond: 'More on Music in Casa Barberini', *Studi musicali*, xiv (1985), footnote 12

J. Lionnet: *La musique à Saint-Louis des français de Rome au XVIIe siècle* (Venice, 1985), i, 57–8; ii, 53–4, 71–2

F. T. Camiz: 'The Castrato Singer: from Informal to Formal Portraiture', *Artibus et historie*, no.18 (1988), 171–86

MARGARET MURATA

Pasquini, Bernardo (*b* Massa Valdinievole [now Massa e Cozzile, Pistoia], 7 Dec 1637; *d* Rome, 22 Nov 1710). Italian composer. His known dramatic works include 17 operas and 14 oratorios. He was first employed in Rome as an organist: in 1661–3 at the Chiesa Nuova and at S Luigi dei Francesi, in February 1664–1710 at S Maria in Aracoeli (with the title 'organist of the Senate and Roman people'), in March 1664–85 for oratorios at S Marcello and in 1673–5 for a second time at S Luigi dei Francesi. As a harpsichordist, he played for Louis XIV in 1664 (while in the entourage of the papal legate, Cardinal Flavio Chigi) and with Arcangelo Corelli and others at chamber concerts and operas. He was also a renowned harpsichord teacher: his pupils included Francesco Gasparini, J. P. Krieger and Georg Muffat. From about 1669 until his death he served Prince Giambattista Borghese and resided at the Palazzo Borghese. He took the name Protico Azetiano in the Arcadian Academy on 26 April 1706, when he, Corelli and Alessandro Scarlatti were enrolled as the first musicians in the group.

Pasquini is termed the harmonic standard-bearer for the century in the dedication of *La donna ancora è fedele* (1676); and he was the composer without equal in Rome, according to the preface in *Dov'è amore, è pietà* (1679), which he wrote 'in the space of a few days … in the modern fashion, with bizarre and spirited ariettas'. Scores for 12 of his operas survive, and they manifest the gradual transformation of the aria from a lyrical effusion, which does not disrupt the continuity, to an action-halting focal point, which is usually followed by the exit of the singer. The da capo form is the basis for many of the brief arias in his works, but it is often less prominent than ostinato basses or strophic texts, and through-composed structures are common for ensembles. At least two-thirds of the arias in a work are accompanied only by the continuo, and moderate coloratura passages are common in the vocal line. Pasquini's early operas are mainly comedies, with pastoral or 'neighbourhood' characters rather than heroic or historical ones. His last four works include a *festa teatrale* for the wedding of Carlos II of Spain and Mariana, Countess Palatine, that was probably the most extravagant operatic production in Rome during

Pasquini's career, and a work about Christopher Columbus of which the text, by the pope's nephew, was mercilessly ridiculed at the time.

Pasquini was the leading dramatic composer in Rome during the 1670s. During the next decade, he shared this honour with Alessandro Scarlatti (*b* 1660), who had his first opera produced in Rome in 1679. After 1690 Pasquini received only one more commission, perhaps because many composers born around 1670 wrote music that seemed much more expressive. Indeed, his lack of 'dramatic genius' seems to be the main point of a news report dated 2 January 1692: 'Since Bernardo, *maestro di cappella*, was not asked to compose and play for either of the theatres [i.e. the Tordinona or Capranica], he worked diligently, so that his musical *comedia* [*Eudossia*], which they will perform in the Seminario Romano, would be successful; and he has truly made a fine composition, but more out of pique than genius' (Cametti, 351).

See also IDALMA. *For illustration see* FONTANA, GIROLAMO.

first performed in Rome unless otherwise stated

dm – *dramma per musica*

La sincerità con la sincerità, overo Il Tirinto (favola drammatica per musica, G. F. Apolloni and other Accademici Sfaccendati), Ariccia, Palazzo Chigi, 20 Oct 1672, *I-MOe*

La forza d'amore (componimento drammatico rusticale, Apolloni), ?1672, *B-Bc*, *GB-Cfm*, *Lcm*, *I-Fc*

L'Amor per vendetta, overo L'Alcasta (dm, Apolloni), Tordinona, 27 Jan 1673, *D-MÜs*, *I-MOe*, arias in *Nc*

La donna ancora è fedele (dm, D. F. Contini), Palazzo Colonna, carn. 1676, *MOe*, arias in *Bc*, *Nc* and *Rvat*

[Il Trespolo tutore balordo] (commedia per musica, G. C. Villifranchi, rev. Bertucci), Palazzo Colonna, 10 Feb 1677, *F-Pn*

Dov'è amore, è pietà (drama musicale, C. Ivanovich, after G. A. Moniglia: *Ipermestra*), Palazzo Capranica, 6 Jan 1679, 1 aria in *I-MOe*

L'Idalma, overo Chi la dura la vince (commedia per musica, G. D. De Totis), Palazzo Capranica, 6 Feb 1680, *F-Pn* (R1977: IOB, ii), arias in *Pc*, *I-Fbecherini*, Folschki (see Bonaventura 1906–8) and *Vnm*

Il Lisimaco (dm, 'Comagio Baldosini' [Giacomo Sinibaldi]), ? Palazzo Riario, carn. 1681, formerly *D-Hs*, *WD*, arias in *I-Bsp* and *US-Su*

La Tessalonica (dm, N. Minato), Palazzo Colonna, 31 Jan 1683, *A-Wgm*, arias *D-MÜs*, *F-Pc*, *GB-Lbl*, *I-Nc*, *Rc*, *Rsc*, *Rvat*, *Vnm*

La vita e un sogno di notte (commedia, 3, J. Cicognini), Palazzo Pamphili, 12 Feb 1684

L'Arianna (dm), Palazzo Colonna, 3 Feb 1685, arias in *GB-Lbl*, *Ob*, *I-Bc* and *Rvat*

Il silentio d'Arpocrate (dm, Minato), Palazzo Colonna, 26 Jan 1686, arias in *F-Pn* and *I-Rvat*

Santa Dimna, figlia del re d'Irlanda [Act 2] (sacred op, 3, B. Pamphili), Palazzo Pamphili, carn. 1687 [Act 1 by Alessandro Melani, Act 3 by A. Scarlatti], arias in *Gb-Lbl*, *I-Rvat*

I giochi Troiani (dm, C. S. Capece), Palazzo Colonna, Feb 1688, 2 arias *Rvat*, 1 aria *Bc*

La caduta del regno dell'Amazzoni (festa teatrale, De Totis), Palazzo Colonna, before 15 Jan 1690, *GB-Lbl*, *F-Pc* (inc.), arias in *I-Fc*, *MOe*, *Rli* and *Rvat*

Alessio, Seminario Romano, 1690

Il Colombo, overo L'India scoperta (dm, P. Ottoboni), Tordinona, 28 Dec 1690, *GB-Lbl*, arias in *D-MÜs*, *I-Bc*, *Rli* and *Rvat*

Eudossia (A. Pollioni), Seminario Romano, 6 Feb 1692, arias in *D-MÜs* and *I-Rsc*

S. M. Barlettani Attavanti: 'Bernardo Pasquini', *Notizie istoriche degli Arcadi morti*, ed. G. M. Crescimbeni, ii (Rome, 1720), 330–34

G. O. Pitoni: *Notitia de contrapuntisti e de compositori di musica* (MS, c1725), ed. C. Ruini (Florence, 1988), 342–3

A. Bonaventura: 'Di un codice musicale del secolo XVII', *La bibliofilia*, viii (1906–7), 321–35; ix (1907–8), 327–9

——: *Bernardo Pasquini* (Ascoli Piceno, 1923)

G. Roncaglia: 'Il Tirinto di B. Pasquini e i suoi intermezzi', *RaM*, iv (1931), 331–9

A. Cametti: *Il teatro di Tordinona poi di Apollo* (Tivoli, 1938)

G. Roncaglia: 'Di un autore e di un'opera ignorati (P. P. Cappellini: *La forza d'amore*)', *Rivista nazionale di musica*, xix (1938), 4255–9

V. Golzio: *Documenti artistici sul seicento nell'archivio Chigi* (Rome, 1939)

G. F. Crain jr: *The Operas of Bernardo Pasquini* (diss., Yale U., 1965)

C. Gianturco: 'A Possible Date for Stradella's *Il Trespolo tutore*', *ML*, liv (1973), 25–37

——: '*Il Trespolo tutore* di Stradella e di Pasquini: due diversi concezioni dell'opera comica', *Venezia e il melodramma del settecento: Venice 1973*, i, 185–98

——: 'Evidence for a Late Roman School of Opera', *ML*, lvi (1975), 4–17

L. E. Lindgren and C. B. Schmidt: 'A Collection of 137 Broadsides Concerning Theatre in Late Seventeenth-Century Italy: an Annotated Catalogue', *Harvard Library Bulletin*, xxviii (1980), 185–233

T. Griffin: 'Nuove fonti per la storia della musica a Napoli durante il regno del marchese del Carpio (1683–7)', *RIM*, xvi (1981), 207–28

G. Morelli: 'L'Apolloni librettista di Cesti, Stradella e Pasquini', *Chigiana*, xxxix (1982), 211–64

H. J. Marx: 'Die "Giustificazioni della casa Pamphili" als Musikgeschichtliche Quelle', *Studi musicali*, xii (1983), 121–87

R. Lefevre: '*Il Tirinto* di Bernardo Pasquini all'Ariccia (1672)', *Lunario romano, 1986: musica e musicisti nel Lazio* (Rome, 1985), 237–68

S. Franchi: *Drammaturgia romana: repertorio bibliografico cronologico dei testi drammatici pubblicati a Roma e nel Lazio, secolo XVII* (Rome, 1988)

R. Lefevre: 'La rappresentazione all'Ariccia nel 1673 dell'*Adalinda* di P. S. Agostini', *Strenna dei Romanisti*, l (1989), 239–58

LOWELL LINDGREN

Pasquini, Giovanni Claudio (*b* Siena, 1695; *d* Siena, Nov 1763). Italian librettist and poet. His Arcadian name was Trigenio Migontidio. Initially aided by Zeno, he was tutor to the Habsburg archduchesses Maria Theresa and Maria Anna Eleonora from 1726, court poet at Vienna from 1733 and imperial court poet from 1739.

Though losing Zeno's favour, he enjoyed a warm friendship with Metastasio: their enlightening correspondence flourished until Pasquini's death. After the death of Emperor Charles VI in 1740 Pasquini left Vienna for Mannheim, where in January 1742 his libretto *Meride* for the wedding of Carl Theodor inaugurated the newly constructed Hoftheater. But he soon moved to Dresden as poet to the Saxon court, succeeding S. B. Pallavicino. He resigned in 1749 to return to Siena, where he preached and taught. In addition to his librettos for full-length operas, *feste teatrali* and serenatas, he wrote about 30 *feste di camera* and other smaller-scale dramatic works, many of which were set to music by Reutter. Some of his sacred librettos were published as *Azioni sacre per musica* in Vienna in 1728; ten of them appeared as *Opere di Pasquini* (Arezzo, 1751).

Spartaco (dramma per musica), Porsile, 1726; Issicratea (festa teatrale), F. B. Conti, 1726; Il tempio di Giano, chiuso da Cesare Augusto (componimento per musica di camera), Porsile, 1726; Il contrasto della bellezza e del tempo (componimento per musica di camera), F. B. Conti, 1726; Archidamia (festa teatrale), G. Reutter, 1727; Don Chisciotte in corte della duchessa (opera serioridicola), Caldara, 1727; La forza dell'amicizia in Oreste e Pilade, ovvero Pilade ed Oreste (dramma per musica), Reutter (Act 1) and Caldara (Acts 2 and 3), 1728

Pieria (festa teatrale), I. M. Conti, 1728; Telesilla (festa teatrale), Porsile, 1728; Il natale di Minerva (serenata), ?Caldara, 1729 (Caldara, 1735); I disingannati (componimento per musica di camera), Caldara, 1729; Plotina (festa teatrale), Reutter, 1730; Livia (festa teatrale), Caldara, 1731; Zenobia (festa teatrale),

Reutter, 1732; *Clelia* (festa teatrale), I. M. Conti, 1733; *Sancio Pansa, governatore dell'isola Barrataria* (componimento per musica di camera), Caldara, 1733
Dafne (festa teatrale), Reutter, 1734; *Diana vindicata* (festa teatrale), Reutter, 1736 (Ristori, 1746); *La speranza assicurata* (serenata), Reutter, 1736; *La gara del genio con Giunone* (serenata), Bonno, 1737; *La generosità di Artaserse* (serenata), Bonno, 1737; *L'alloro illustrato* (festa teatrale), Reutter, 1738; *Gli auguri spiegati* (serenata), L. A. Predieri, 1738; *Meride* (dramma per musica), C. P. Grua, 1742; *Arminio* (dramma per musica), Hasse, 1745; *Leucippo* (favola pastorale), Hasse, 1747

DEUMM; ES (W. Bollert); *SchmidlDS; StiegerO*
M. Fürstenau: *Zur Geschichte der Musik und des Theaters am Hofe der Kurfürsten von Sachsen*, ii (Dresden, 1862), 239
B. Brunelli, ed.: *Tutte le opere di Pietro Metastasio*, ii–iii (Milan, 1951–4)
G. Natali: *Il settecento*, ii (Milan, 4/1955), 780–81, 842
R. Gerber: Preface to *J. A. Hasse: Arminio*, EDM, 1st ser., xxvii–xxviii (1957)   SVEN HANSELL

Passacaglia (It.; Fr. *passecaille*). A term used in the Baroque period, originally for a type of ritornello in a song, later for a phrase serving as a constructional unit, normally four bars in 3/4 metre, in a continuous variation movement akin to a CHACONNE, or for a movement so derived. The term is unusual in opera, 'chaconne' being preferred in the French repertory and its derivatives. The term has however been used occasionally in 20th-century opera, for example for the scene in Act 1 of Berg's *Wozzeck* (1925) for the Doctor and Wozzeck and for the interlude portraying a manhunt in Act 2 of Britten's *Peter Grimes* (1945); both are constructed on a repeated bass figure and both are in 4/4 metre.

JULIAN BUDDEN

Passaggio (It.: 'passage', 'transit'). The singing voice is generally recognized as comprising three 'registers', the high, middle and low; the 'passaggio' is the point at which two of them meet. It is often at the crucial point in the 'passaggio' that a singer may be most conscious of a dilemma concerning method of production. For the tenor, for instance, $f\sharp'$ is a note that he may be tempted to sing with open tone but which it would probably be wiser (and more musical if less exciting in effect) to cover. For the dramatic soprano a similar problem may occur lower in the voice where the chest register gives way to the middle: here the abuse of the 'passaggio' may be particularly harmful, as the break, or change of tone, is obvious to the listener, resulting in a kind of yodelling effect, and the notes just above the break may be seriously weakened.

The term is also used for a transition section or for an improvised ornamental passage in Baroque music.

J. B. STEANE

Passaggio ('Passage'). *Messa in scena* in one act by LUCIANO BERIO to a libretto by Edoardo Sanguineti; Milan, Piccola Scala, 6 May 1963.

The punning description *messa in scena* raises liturgical expectations that are only obliquely fulfilled. It indicates something 'put on stage', but also 'a mass on stage'. Indeed, Sanguineti entitles each of the six sections of the work a 'station', after the Stations of the Cross, and appends a quotation, often ironically apt, from the Vulgate. But the 'Passion' acted out between the single female protagonist on stage and commentators in the audience is a purely secular one. The protagonist (soprano) is described simply as She. Tracing her 'passage' from station to station, she anxiously pursues a jumble of intimate recollections, in the main oblivious

to external circumstance. Yet from visual clues, and the vivid reactions of singing and speaking choruses, one infers a story of arrest, interrogation, torture and release into a squalid bedsit where She vainly awaits an unknown person and searches for an unknown object. In the final station, the soprano leaves off acting, acknowledges the skeletal plot as she prepares to go home and finally, in a gesture borrowed from Genet's *Le balcon*, turns on the members of the audience and screams at them to get out.

The eight-part singing chorus shares the pit with a large instrumental ensemble, for the most part reacting with empathy to the protagonist's sufferings. However, the speaking chorus, split into five groups scattered through the auditorium, gives imprudently explicit voice to the darker thoughts that might lurk in the spectator's mind: in a polyglot, exclamatory counterpoint the speakers abuse and lust after the protagonist, chant 'kein Ende' as she is tortured, place bids as this 'perfectly domesticated woman' is auctioned, and babble lists of consumer durables that metamorphose into armaments. The authors' provocative intent was rewarded on the first night with a famous furore. But spectators unwise enough to voice their discontent found themselves incorporated into the action: the speaking groups simply echoed and elaborated on their protests.

DAVID OSMOND-SMITH

Passarini [Passerini], **Francesco** (*b* Verona; *fl* 1696–1731). Italian librettist. Although he did most of his work for theatres in and around Venice, his first libretto, *Briseide*, was for Hanover; he revised it for his Venetian début. He usually wrote for small theatres, and most of his works therefore have modest staging requirements, several calling for only five singers. Few of his works are heroic. Between 1703 and 1712 he wrote five librettos for autumn productions in Rovigo, which were usually pastorals in keeping with the season of *villeggiatura*. In 1703, his first production for Rovigo boasted a well-known singer, Nicola Grimaldi, who sang the same role in 1704 in Naples. Two of his Rovigo works, *La costanza nell'onore* and *Le pazzie degli amanti*, were restaged at the Teatro S Fantino, a tiny Venetian theatre that specialized in small-scale works and provided a stage for beginning singers. Between 1717 and 1720 Passarini wrote four original librettos for that theatre, including the last opera presented there. Several of them are set in everyday contexts and involve characters who use Venetian dialect. *Amor e fortuna*, as set to music by Giovanni Porta for Naples, proved to be Passarini's most frequently performed work.

Briseide, Torri, 1696 (Boniventi, 1702, as La vittoria nella costanza); *La costanza nell'onore*, 1703 (Polani, 1704, as La vendetta disarmata dall'amore); *Ergisto* (dramma pastorale), C. F. Pollarolo, 1708; *L'amante alla moda* (dramma pastorale), 1709; *Le pazzie degli amanti*, Pollarolo, ?1701, 1711; *Gli equivoci del caso* (favola boschereccia), Baseggio, 1712; *Amor e fortuna*, Baseggio, 1712 (Porpora, 1723, as Amare per regnare; Porta, 1725; B. Galuppi, 1748, as Clotilde); *Chi la fà l'aspetta* (dramma comico), Polani, 1717; *Bertoldo* (dramma tragicomico), Girolamo Bassani, 1718; *Il vecchio deluso* (dramma comico), various, Venice, 1718; *La figlia che canta* (divertimento comico), various, Venice, 1720; *Gli stratagemi amorosi*, Albinoni, 1730 (pasticcio, 1742, as L'odio vinto dall'amore); *Gli sponsali d'Enea*, Cordans or M. Fino, 1731

AllacciD
G. Bonlini: *Le glorie della poesia e della musica* (Venice, 1730)
A. Groppo: *Catalogo di tutti i drammi per musica recitati ne' teatri di Venezia* (Venice, 1745)

C. Sartori: *I libretti italiani a stampa dalle origini al 1800* (Cuneo, 1990–)
HARRIS S. SAUNDERS

Passaro, Andrea (*fl* 1829–50). Italian librettist. Between 1829 and 1850 he wrote prolifically for the Neapolitan opera houses; over 30 texts were for the Teatro Nuovo, where he was 'poeta e concertatore'. He may well have been the Andrea Passaro who wrote a libretto for the Teatro Argentina in Rome in 1815. He had a remarkable facility for witty and sharply pointed verse, and his plots are well articulated. He was an obvious partner for Vincenzo Fioravanti: their imperishable *Il ritorno di Pulcinella dagli studi di Padova* was one of the very few Pulcinella comedies to have a success beyond Naples.

Il trionfo di Alessandro Magno (dramma per musica), Andreozzi, 1815; *Il pacchetto a vapore*, 1829; *Una notte di carnevale* (melodramma), F. Sparano, 1829; *Il vecchio della selva di Ardenna* (melodramma semiserio), G. Festa, 1831; *La villana contessa* (melodramma buffo), Lauro Rossi, 1831; *Il nascondiglio*, 1831; *Il pittore e la suonatrice* (melodramma buffo), P. Maranesi, 1831; *La bella ostessa del granatello* (melodramma), N. Carparelli, 1831; *L'eredità di Pulcinella* (commedia buffa), G. Moretti, 1831; *Il nemico degli ammogliati*, P. Raimondi, 1832; *La verdummara de Puorto Andromaco*, Raimondi, 1832; *La fidanzata del parrucchiere* (dg), Raimondi, 1832 (D'Arienzio, 1860, as *Monzù Gnazio*); *La vedova di un vivo*, P. Fabrizi, 1832; *Il marito disperato* (commedia giocosa), Cordella, 1833

Il biglietto del lotto stornato (commedia buffa), Raimondi, 1833; *La bella pirata*, 1833; *La festa di Carditiello* (commedia buffa), Fabrizi, 1833; *Il sarto ed i tabarri* (melodramma), Curci, 1834; *Il supposto sposo* (commedia buffa), Vincenzo Fioravanti, 1834; *Amore e scompiglio* (commedia per musica), F. Raejntroph, 1834; *Una moglie per 24 ore*, Lillo, 1834; *L'equivoco delle lettere* (commedia buffa), Moretti, 1835; *I due furbi* (commedia giocosa), Cordella, 1835; *L'orfana russa* (azione romantica), Raimondi, 1835 (E. Elia, 1850, as *L'orfana di Smolensko*); *La gelosia alimentata da false apparenze* (commedia), L. Andreatini, 1835; *La lettera perduta* (commedia), N. Gabrielli, 1836; *La giornata critica di D. Taddeo* (commedia buffa), G. Cajano, 1836; *La parola di matrimonio* (ob), Gabrielli, 1837

Palmetella maritata (commedia buffa), Raimondi, 1837; *Il ritorno di Pulcinella dagli studi di Padova* (commedia), Fioravanti, 1837 (rev. Cambiaggio, as *Il ritorno di Columella*); *L'americano in fiera* (opera per musica), Gabrielli, 1837; *I due pedanti*, Agnelli, 1838; *Un matrimonio in prigione*, Fioravanti, 1838; *Matilde di Lanchefort* (melodramma storico), Cordella, 1838; *Un curioso stratagemma* (commedia), Moretti and others, 1838; *Il previdente disgraziato* (commedia), Raimondi, 1838; *Il barone di Trocchia*, Cajano, 1838; *Buggie e verità* (commedia), Curci, 1838; *Il padre della debuttante* (commedia buffa), Gabrielli, 1839; *Le disgraziate nozze di Pulcinella* [I panduri] (commedia), A. Brancaccio, 1839; *Il fuorbandito di Montalbore* (melodramma), A. Traversari, 1839; *La sentinella notturna*, Agnelli, 1840

La dama ed il zoccolajo (commedia buffa), Fioravanti, 1840; *La lettera di raccomandazione* (commedia), Traversari, 1840; *Il finto feudatorio* (commedia buffa), A. Pistilli, 1840; *Il bugiardo veritiero* (ob), Gabrielli, 1841; *Pulcinella servo di quattro padroni*, P. Pagliuolo, 1841; *Il condannato di Saragozza* (melodramma), Gabrielli, 1842; *La casa di tre artisti* (commedia buffa), De Giosa, 1842; *Sofia di Valenza* (melodramma), L. Lanzetta, 1842; *Le sante calabresse*, Brancaccio, 1843; *I pirati di Baratteria* (melodramma semiserio), F. Altavilla, 1846; *Le nozze di un principe* (melodramma giocoso), Altavilla, 1846; *L'arrivo del signor zio* (ob), De Giosa, 1846; *Don Procopio* (commedia buffa), G. Grassi, 1848; *I pretendenti* (commedia buffa), P. Spada, 1850; *Il marito di un'ora* (commedia), Delfico [M. de Filippis], 1850

*

F. de Filippis and M. Mangini: *Il teatro nuovo di Napoli* (Naples, 1967)
JOHN BLACK

Passau. Cathedral city in Bavaria, southern Germany. The Fürstbischöfliche Opernhaus, converted by the architect Johann Georg Hagenauer from an existing ballroom into a theatre combining boxes with tiers of seats, was built in 1783. It was the only early classical theatre building in Bavaria. Its ceremonial opening took place on 1 November 1783, with Anton Schweitzer's *Alceste*. The house came into state ownership in 1803, and was known first as the Kurfürstliches and then as the Königliches Theater. Throughout the 19th century it was threatened with closure because of dilapidation and inadequate funds. Opera performances were suspended in 1853. The city acquired the building in 1883 and set up a permanent company, which continued until 1914. From 1914 to 1946 the theatre had performances by touring companies, and from 1946 to 1949 there was an annual series of chamber operas. *Die Walküre*, in 1933, was the only Wagner production given in Passau. In 1952 the Südostbayerisches Stadttheater was founded, combining the companies of Passau, Landshut and Straubing; its musical department is in Passau. The building, which seats 350, was completely renovated in 1960–61. The season runs from mid-September to the end of June, and the repertory consists of both operas and operettas.
KLAUS J. SEIDEL

Passerini, Christina (*b* Bologna; *fl* 1750–76). Italian soprano. After meeting Handel on the recommendation of Telemann at The Hague in 1750, she and her husband, Giuseppe Passerini, a violinist, conductor and composer, went to Scotland. They moved to London about 1752 and were engaged in operas at the King's Theatre in 1753–4. Christina sang Thrasymedes in *Admeto* (1754), the last revival of a Handel opera for more than a century. Handel engaged her for his 1754 and 1755 oratorio seasons. In 1755 she sang in J. C. Smith's *The Fairies* at Drury Lane. She rejoined the opera company at the King's Theatre for the closing weeks of the 1757 season. The Passerinis were very active in promoting performances of Handel's oratorios in the provinces. About 1762 they settled in Dublin where Christina sang in Purcell's *King Arthur* (1763) at Crow Street Music Hall and as Arbaces in the first Dublin production of Arne's *Artaxerxes* at Smock Alley (1765). Their son, Francis (*d* 1809), also a singer, appeared with his mother in *King Arthur* and in operas by Giordani (1766) and Arne, Gazzaniga, Piccinni (*La buona figliuola*), Paisiello and Anfossi at Smock Alley (1776–8).
WINTON DEAN

Passion selon Sade, La ('The Passion according to Sade'). *Mystère de chambre* in one act by SYLVANO BUSSOTTI to his own libretto after Louise Labé; Stockholm, Kungliga Teatern (Rotunda), 1 November 1968 (partial perf., Palermo, Teatro Biondo, 5 September 1965).

Bussotti's first stage work belongs to the genre of experimental music theatre; its title, which suggests a text by the Marquis de Sade as a basis for the vocal parts, is deliberately misleading as the entire work is in fact based on a sonnet by Louise Labé (1555). The mezzo-soprano represents Justine and Juliette at the same time; the role was written for Cathy Berberian and requires an excellent actress. The stage is filled with various fragments of sets for *Traviata*, *Otello*, *Turandot*, *Manon Lescaut* and other works from a mostly Italian repertory. Bussotti's score is one of the most important examples of graphic notation in the realm of music theatre; it leaves a considerable amount of freedom to the performers, but meticulously prescribes effects of lighting and staging. The action on stage is sometimes interrupted by purely musical sections and by a 'happening' which completely interrupts the work for an indefinite time.

Bussotti's score renounces the idea of representing continuous action; instead, the inherent erotic potential of musical instruments and of the act of music-making is represented on stage.   JÜRGEN MAEHDER

Pasta, Carlo Enrico (*b* Milan, 17 Nov 1817; *d* Milan, 31 Aug 1898). Italian composer. He studied at the Milan Conservatory and in Paris. Claiming to be a nephew of Giuditta Pasta, he succeeded in having his first opera, *I tredici*, produced at Turin in 1851. He went to Lima in November 1855, announcing himself as having been the Sardinian king's director of military bands for several years. In 1857 he joined the Lima fraternity of S Cecilia. The première of his zarzuela *La cola del diablo* at the Teatro Principal on 3 October 1865 was so successful that the work was repeated several times and his female pupils gave him a large gold medal inscribed 'Al eminente compositor Enrique Pasta, sus discípulas'. On 11 April 1867 Pasta directed the première of his one-act zarzuela *Rafael Sanzio*, the first of his works to a libretto by Juan Cossio (1833–81). In 1871 his four-act *La Fronda* was advertised as the first opera composed in independent Peru. After further stage successes, in 1873 he returned to Italy, where he composed the opera *Atahualpa* (first performed at Genoa in 1875). In 1876 he was back in Lima, where *Atahualpa* was produced to great acclaim on 11 January 1877; the first opera on an Inca subject to be presented there, it received eight more performances. He was rewarded by the dedicatee, the banker Dionisio Derteano, and on his final departure from Lima, newspapers announced (February 1877) that his total profit from *Atahualpa* (including sales of the vocal score published by the composer, 1875) exceeded 5000 soles. *Atahualpa* was also performed in Milan at the Teatro dal Verme in September 1877.

one-act zarzuelas sung in Spanish at the Teatro Principal, Lima, unless otherwise stated

I tredici (4, G. Giachetti), Turin, Sutera, 14 Jan 1851
El loco de la guardilla, 13 Feb 1863
La cola del diablo, Lima, 3 Oct 1865
Rafael Sanzio (J. Cossio), 11 Apr 1867, *US-Wc*
Placeres y dolores (Cossio), 1867
El pobre indio (Cossio and J. Vicente Camacho), 8 March 1868
Por un inglés, 5 May 1870
La Fronda (4), 5 Sept 1871
Una taza de thé, 4 Sept 1872
Atahualpa (4, A. Ghislanzoni), Genoa, Paganini, 23 Nov 1875, vs
  BE

*   *

StiegerO
R. Barbacci: 'Apuntes para un diccionario biográfico musical peruano', *Fénix*, vi (1949), 414–510, esp.483–4
A. Tauro: *Enciclopedia ilustrada del Perú* (Lima, 1987), ii, 595; iv, 1563   ROBERT STEVENSON

Pasta [née Negri], Giuditta (Angiola Maria Costanza) (*b* Saronno, nr Milan, 26 Oct 1797; *d* Como, 1 April 1865). Italian soprano. She studied in Milan with Giuseppe Scappa and Davide Banderali and later with Crescentini and Paer among others. In 1816 she made her début at the Teatro degli Accademici Filodrammatici, Milan, in the première of Scappa's *Le tre Eleonore*; soon after, she appeared in Paris at the Théâtre Italien as Donna Elvira, Giulietta in Zingarelli's *Giulietta e Romeo* and in two operas by Paer. Her London début at the King's Theatre in 1817 was as Telemachus in Cimarosa's *Penelope*. She also sang Cherubino and Despina.

Giuditta Pasta in the title role of Bellini's 'Norma' which she created at La Scala, Milan, in 1831: portrait (painted between 1831 and 1835) by François Gérard

After singing in all the main Italian centres from 1818 (her roles included Rossini's Cenerentola and Cimarosa's Curiazio), she achieved her first great triumph singing Rossini's Desdemona at the Théâtre Italien, Paris, in 1821, subsequently appearing there as Tancredi and Queen Elizabeth. In the following decade she established herself as Europe's greatest soprano, exerting a major influence on the styles of Bellini and Donizetti and becoming one of Rossini's favourite singers. Her great roles included Zingarelli's Romeo, Mayr's Medea and Paisiello's Nina. She made a triumphant return to London in 1824 as Desdemona and also sang Zerlina and Semiramide (one of her greatest interpretations). For the next few years she alternated between London and Paris, adding roles by Meyerbeer and Rossini (she created Corinna in *Il viaggio a Reims* in 1825) to her repertory. In 1826–7 she sang in Naples, creating the title role of Pacini's *Niobe* at the S Carlo.

Her first Bellini role was Imogene in *Il pirata* (1830, Vienna). Subsequently she created Amina in *La sonnambula* (1831, Teatro Carcano, Milan) and the title roles in *Norma* (her début at La Scala in 1831) and *Beatrice di Tenda* (1833, La Fenice). For Donizetti she created the title role in *Anna Bolena* (1830, Teatro Carcano) and Bianca in *Ugo, conte di Parigi* (1832). After 1835, when she retired from the stage, Pasta's appearances were infrequent, though she performed in London in 1837 and Berlin and Russia in 1840–41. Her voice had begun to show signs of wear and she lost the desire to compete with the legend she had created.

Pasta's greatness lay in her naturalness, truth of expression and individual timbre, which enabled her, within a phrase, to achieve soul-stirring emotion. She could execute intricate *fioritura* but channelled her bravura to illuminate the drama, though she was often criticized for faulty intonation. An accomplished actress, her deportment and portrayal of dignity were without peer.

For illustration *see* Anna bolena; Medea in corinto; and Sonnambula, la, fig.1.

*

Stendhal: 'Madame Pasta', *Vie de Rossini* (Paris, 1824; Eng. trans., 1956, 3/1971)

J. Ebers: *Seven Years of the King's Theatre* (London, 1828)

H. S. Edwards: *The Prima Donna: her History and Surroundings from the Seventeenth to the Nineteenth Century* (London, 1888)

M. Ferranti-Giulini: *Giuditta Pasta e i suoi tempi* (Milan, 1935)

L. Cambi, ed.: *Vincenzo Bellini: Epistolario*, (Verona, 1943)

F. Pastura: *Bellini secondo la storia* (Modena, 1959)

K. Stern: 'The Theatre of Bel Canto', ON, xl/16 (1975–6), 10–16

V. Pini: *Giuditta Pasta – i suoi tempi e Saronno* (Milan, 1977)

K. Stern: 'Giuditta Pasta', ON, xlvi/12 (1981–2), 8–11

——: *Giuditta Pasta: a Documentary Biography* (diss., City U., New York, 1983)
KENNETH STERN

Pasterz. Opera by Karol Szymanowski; *see* King roger.

Pasticcio (It.: 'jumble', 'hotch-potch', 'pudding'; Fr. *pastiche*). An opera made up of various pieces from different composers or sources and adapted to a new or existing libretto. The practice began in the late 17th century but the term came into general use only after about 1730 to describe an *opera seria* or *buffa*, typically based on popular librettos of Metastasio or Goldoni. Arias were selected mainly by the singers in a given production, the recitatives and ensembles being supplied by the house composer, music director or even the theatre manager.

1. Definition. 2. Origins. 3. The early London pasticcios. 4. The composer as pasticheur. 5. The later pasticcio.

1. Definition. As applied to opera, the term was at first somewhat pejorative. J. J. Quantz, during a visit to Florence in 1725 (though writing in 1755), heard several operas 'patched together with arias of various masters, which is called "pastry" by the Italians, "un pasticcio"'. The verb form was used more loosely to describe the process of revision. In 1735, when Vivaldi asked Goldoni to fit aria texts into an existing libretto, the poet said he had to 'accommodate or cook up the drama' to the composer's taste, 'for better or worse' ('accomodare o impasticciare il Dramma a suo gusto, per mettervi bene o male le Arie'). During the second half of the 18th century the pasticcio acquired a degree of respectability. In 1742 Horace Walpole wrote: 'Our operas begin tomorrow with a pasticcio, full of most of my favourite songs'. Later, the designation appears without stigma on the title-pages of librettos and in composers' contracts. Most first-rank opera composers – including Vivaldi, Bononcini, Handel, Hasse, Gluck, Mozart and Haydn – arranged or at least willingly contributed to pasticcios. Nevertheless, 18th-century critics and modern historians have tended to dismiss such pieces as inartistic medleys. This attitude is unjustified, but no discussion should skirt the issues of originality and authorial integrity.

The term 'pasticcio' has been applied to several different kinds of work:

(*i*) Revival with substitutions: arias by various composers are substituted for pieces thought unsuitable for the available singers;

ii) True pasticcio:

   (*a*) a patchwork in which singers, librettist or impresario fill out an existing libretto entirely with *arie di bagaglio* ('suitcase' arias), or

   (*b*) a composite original, in which diverse arias by several composers are fashioned into a new plot;

(*iii*) a composer patchwork: a composer incorporates his own arias, old or new, into another's score; and

(*iv*) a self-pastiche: an amalgam of a composer's own arias in a new context.

There is considerable overlapping among these various types. Parody, defined here as the adding of new words to old music, is a process common to those pasticcios in which care has been taken to fit the borrowed arias into the new dramatic context. Related to the pasticcio is the collaborative medley, a fairly rare type, in which two or more composers divide the labour of setting a new or specially adapted libretto, usually act by act. Examples are *Muzio Scevola* (1721, London: Act 1 by F. Amadei, Act 2 by G. Bononcini, Act 3 by Handel) and *La virtù trionfante* (1724, Rome: Act 1 by B. Micheli, Act 2 by Vivaldi, Act 3 by N. Romaldo). Though usually called a pasticcio, Haydn's *La Circe, ossia l'isola incantata* (1789, Eszterháza), which incorporates parts of J. G. Naumann's *L'ipocondriaco* and an anonymous opera based on the Circe story, as well as large chunks of original music by Haydn, would be more accurately described as a 'collaborative medley' or a 'composer patchwork', type (*iii*).

2. Origins. The pasticcio arose from practical exigency. The opening of many new public and court theatres at Venice and then throughout Italy in the 1640s and 50s increased the demand for opera and caused companies to become ever more dependent on revivals. Because operas were almost always composed for specific singers and adapted to local conditions, revivals with new singers in different theatres required extensive changes; even a perennial favourite such as Cavalli's *Giasone* was revised from production to production. In works of this period, recitative, aria and ensemble are closely bound together; revisions accordingly tended not to be of the piecemeal kind characteristic of the later pasticcio. But when, by about 1670, the aria had acquired greater musical weight and detached itself from the recitative, it became easier for an impresario to allow singers to substitute arias they already knew than to hire someone to adjust the original music to suit new voices and characters.

Almost all revivals of Italian operas in the last 20 years of the 17th century were subjected to the pasticcio process, in that they comprised diverse arias by more than one composer. The practice seems to have had only one major drawback, apart from the inevitable disturbance of the work's original integrity (assuming it had any): without the composer or an enlightened impresario to guide them, singers might make substitutions which were inappropriate to the dramatic context or might overlook the need for variety and contrast between arias.

Few 17th-century operas are of type (*ii*), that is, works assembled entirely from existing arias to old or new librettos. An exception is the Milan production of *Arione* (1694), the libretto of which lists 27 different local composers whose arias were assembled in a deliberate patchwork. When Italian opera was exported to northern European courts and cities in the early years of the 18th century, local companies without experienced or capable *opera seria* composers had to turn to the pasticcio. Such works were common in Hamburg, Brunswick, Brussels and especially London.

3. THE EARLY LONDON PASTICCIOS. The first extended discussion of the pasticcio appears in the English translation of François Raguenet's *Paralèle des italiens et des français, en ce qui regarde la musique et les opéra* (*A Comparison between the French and Italian Musick and Opera's*, 1709). Raguenet opined provocatively that Italian operas are 'poor, incoherent Rapsodies without any Connexion or Design ... patch'd up with thin, insipid Scraps'. In a footnote the English translator qualified this sweeping remark, explaining that Raguenet meant revivals, in which for 'Convenience or Necessity ... Airs are alter'd or omitted, according to the Fancy or Ability of the Singers, without the Approbation or Knowledge of the Composer'. Appended to the translation of Raguenet is the anonymous 'Critical Discourse on Opera's and Musick in England', an account of the London opera scene during 1705–9 which centres on the pasticcio (called here 'a patchwork' or 'medley'), the dominant kind of Italian opera heard in London before Handel arrived in 1710. Included is the following satirical recipe, which nevertheless describes how several of the London pasticcios were actually concocted:

Pick out about an hundred *Italian* Airs from several Authors, good, or bad, it signifies nothing. Among these, make use of fifty five, or fifty six, of such as please your Fancy best, and Marshall 'em in the manner you think most convenient. When this is done, you must employ a Poet to write some *English* Words, the Airs of which are to be adapted to the *Italian* Musick. In the next place you must agree with some Composer to provide the Recitative ... When this is done, you must make a Bargain with some Mungril *Italian* Poet to Translate the Part of the *English* that is to be Perform'd in *Italian*; and then deliver it into the Hands of some Amanuensis, that understands Musick better than your self, to Transcribe the Score, and the Parts.

The principal target of this paragraph is *Thomyris, Queen of Scythia* (1707), produced by J. J. Heidegger, who helped choose the arias by Alessandro Scarlatti, Dieupart, Francesco Gasparini, Albinoni and Giovanni Bononcini. J. C. Pepusch arranged the music, composed fresh recitatives and directed from the harpsichord, while P. A. Motteux provided the libretto *post facto*. The castrato Valentino Urbani sang in Italian, the rest of the cast in English.

The author of the 'Critical Discourse' did not condemn the pasticcio *per se*; rather, he claimed that there was no Italian opera which 'will go down here without some Alterations'. Moreover, he praised the pasticcio version of Scarlatti's *Pyrrhus and Demetrius* (1708) in which the arranger Nicola Haym 'first consider'd what Places of Necessity required new Airs' and composed them himself according to 'the Taste of the *English*'. Perhaps with some knowledge of Handel's imminent arrival, the author concluded that no Italian operas ought to be produced in London that were not 'intire, and of one Author, or at least prepar'd by a Person that is capable of uniting different Styles so artfully as to make 'em pass for one'. The implied distinction between good and bad pasticcios resurfaces in criticism throughout the 18th century.

4. THE COMPOSER AS PASTICHEUR. During the heyday of *opera seria*, the pasticcio became a genre in its own right, no longer simply the unwelcome by-product of a hasty revival or the last resort of an opera company without a resident composer. Even Handel and Vivaldi, who exceptionally for the time were their own impresarios, produced significant numbers of pasticcios. These works were generally mounted either early in the season, before a new opera was ready, or near the end to fill out the repertory or to appease certain star singers. Though a pasticcio required much less labour than an original opera, the composer-arranger could claim it as his own and be paid accordingly.

Elpidia (1725, London) will serve as an example of Handel's procedure. He took the dramatic skeleton from a 1697 libretto by Zeno, retaining only the text of two duets and some recitative. Eschewing the first setting by M. A. Ziani, he then selected most of the arias from recent works – Vinci's *Ifigenia* and *Rosmira fede* and Orlandini's *Berenice* – while composing himself only the *secco* recitative and perhaps the duets. The arias were chosen with reference to his singers (Cuzzoni, Senesino, Francesco Borosini and others), some of the pieces being already in their repertories. Naturally, the result is stylistically removed from Handel, but it is not less dramatic or coherent than many of his own operas; and (as Strohm has observed) the pasticcios allowed Handel to test the *galant* tastes of the fickle London audience more radically than he dared to do in his own operas.

Handel's *Oreste* (1734, London), consisting, of arias borrowed from his own works with only the recitatives and ballet music newly composed (type (*iv*)), presents an aesthetic dilemma. Since most Italian operas contained significant amounts of previously composed music (the proportion increased with each revival), and since Handel was anyway a prodigious borrower and adapter of his own and others' music, there is only a fine line of distinction between this self-pastiche and, say, *Rinaldo* (1711), his first London opera and the supposed vanquisher of the despised polyglot pasticcios. Ironically, *Rinaldo* was constructed much like a pasticcio: several arias were taken with little change from earlier works; some were given parodied texts; a few were borrowed from other composers. As with *Oreste*, the only part of *Rinaldo* which is entirely new is the *secco* recitative.

5. THE LATER PASTICCIO. London did not of course have a monopoly on pasticcios; all Italian opera houses indulged in the practice to some extent. But the King's Theatre continued to be the largest consumer till the end of the century. After Handel abandoned opera for oratorio in the 1730s, the Haymarket opera house, which was run as a commercial venture without government subvention, was left with no first-rank composer and tended to pander to the fickle tastes of the audience. Vast sums were spent on singers, while virtually the entire repertory was imported. Later, even with reputable house composers such as J. C. Bach (1762–72), Sacchini (1772–81) and Anfossi (1782–6), the King's Theatre still relied on revivals and pasticcios for the bulk of its repertory.

Charles Burney, who chronicled this era from direct experience in his *General History of Music*, did not belittle the pasticcio; with its infinite capacity for substitution, it was an ideal showcase for the latest Italian music and singers. Neither did he make much distinction between the dramatic quality of one-composer operas and pasticcios. One of Burney's rare criticisms of the pasticcio as drama is directed at the popular 1770 revival of Gluck's *Orfeo*, to which J. C. Bach had added recitatives and arias as well as some pieces by P. A. Guglielmi, while the Haymarket house poet Giovanni Bottarelli made the necessary adjustments to Calzabigi's original libretto: 'the unity, simplicity, and dramatic

Playbill for the original production of Arne's pasticcio 'Love in a Village' at Covent Garden, London, 8 December 1762

excellence of this opera, which had gained the composer so much credit on the Continent, were greatly diminished here by the heterogeneous mixture of Music, of other composers, in a quite different style'. Burney expected less of true pasticcios (type (ii)), such as the 1786 *Didone abbandonata*, for which he complimented the prima donna Gertrud Mara on her choice of songs.

Other English critics identified 'a general defect of all pasticcios', namely, 'the want of proper light and shade in the disposition of the songs'. A reviewer of Antonio Andrei's 1784 *Silla* (music selected from Anfossi, Gluck, Alessandri, Martini, Sarti and Tommaso Giordani) elucidated this defect: 'the sole objection which can be urged against this opera, with regard to the music, lies in its superlative excellence ... a feast, where the viands were entirely of sugar ... where the singers, regardless of the necessary imposition of the shades, the chiaroscuro, have no other aim but to elevate and surprize'.

Opera seria, still essentially a succession of self-contained virtuoso arias, was better suited for pastiche treatment than *opera buffa*, with its much longer and more complicated librettos and greater reliance on *secco* recitative and through-composed finales. But, while serious pasticcios constitute the vast majority, comic opera was subjected to the same process. Even the early intermezzos, such as Alessandro Scarlatti's *Lesbina e Milo* (1701, Naples), were liable to be transformed by patchwork revivals. Full length *buffa* pasticcios had become well established by mid-century, both reworkings of Goldoni classics (type (iia)) and those with new plots fashioned from diverse pieces (type (iib)). An

example of the latter is *La donna di spirito* (1775, London), which includes arias and duets by 12 different composers; interestingly, the borrowed pieces are found only in the first few scenes of each act, the much longer finales being newly composed, presumably by the anonymous pasticheur.

By the third quarter of the century 'pasticcio' had lost its pejorative connotation. Two *drammi giocosi* (1759, Venice, and 1791, Udine) were actually titled 'Il Pasticcio', the latter being an adaptation of various works by Da Ponte and Vicente Martín y Soler. The adapter of the former explained in a preface that, with apologies to all composers concerned, he had selected the most popular arias from recent Goldoni operas and devised a plot ('una comica azione') to link them together. A further sign of acceptance if not respectability is Joseph Mazzinghi's contract as house composer at the King's Theatre, London, in 1790–92: he agreed to 'compose and select all such new Music' as required and to 'arrange all the Pasticcios'.

Related to the various types of Italian pasticcio are ballad opera, English comic opera, *opéra comique* and Singspiel – all of which incorporated diverse, existing music into a framework of spoken dialogue, or mixed traditional or popular tunes with newly composed ones. Among the various types of national quasi-opera, perhaps the closest to the spirit of the Italian pasticcio is the late 18th-century English melodrama, such as Stephen Storace's *The Siege of Belgrade* (1791, London). Music of various composers (both vocal and instrumental – all but Mozart's 'Rondo alla turca' being clearly identified in the published score) has been fitted with parodied texts, rescored, arranged and abridged. Storace's pastiche technique resembles Grétry's plan (not implemented) to produce an *opéra comique* by selecting certain symphonic movements of Haydn, working out a vocal line from the texture and, finally, adding suitable words.

It is difficult to say exactly when the Italian pasticcio died out. In the 1790s few operas were so billed, but Da Ponte and Martín y Soler, both employees of the King's Theatre at the time, provided parodies, arrangements and substitute arias for works which are pasticcios in all but name. A growing awareness of the complexity and unity of contemporary opera, together with the establishment of the operatic canon, gradually rendered the pasticcio obsolete. In 1828 John Ebers, a former manager of the King's Theatre, acknowledged the existence of the canon, but also confirmed the late survival of the pasticcio in London: 'Experience sufficiently proves to us, that the operas imported from the continent are, both in music and poetry, such as to render nugatory here [in London] the employment either of a poet, or a composer (other than as a conductor and arranger)'.

*

BurneyH; *Grove6* (R. Strohm)
'A Critical Discourse on Opera's and Musick in England', in F. Raguenet: *A Comparison between the French and Italian Musick and Opera's Translated from the French* (London, 1709)
J. Ebers: *Seven Years of the King's Theatre* (London, 1828)
O. G. Sonneck: 'Ciampi's *Bertoldo, Bertoldino e Cacasenno* and Favart's *Ninette à la cour*: a Contribution to the History of Pasticcio', *SIMG*, xii (1910–11), 525–64
'The Life of Herr J. J. Quantz as Sketched by Himself', in P. Nettl: *Forgotten Musicians* (New York, 1951), 280–319
F. Walker: '*Orazio*: the History of a Pasticcio', *MQ*, xxxviii (1952), 369–83
W. S. Lewis and others, eds.: *Horace Walpole's Correspondence with Horace Mann* (New Haven, 1954)

G. Ortolani, ed.: *C. Goldoni: Tutte le opere*, i (Verona, 4/1959)

K. Hortschansky: 'Gluck und Lampugnani in Italien: zum Pasticcio *Arsace*', *AnMc*, no.3 (1966), 49–64

——: '*Arianna* – ein Pasticcio von Gluck', *Mf*, xxiv (1971), 407–11

H. Becker: 'Opern-Pasticcio und Parodie-Oper', *Musicae scientiae collectanea: Festschrift Karl Gustav Fellerer* (Cologne, 1973), 40–46

R. Strohm: 'Händels Pasticci', *AnMc*, no.14 (1974), 209–67; Eng. version in *Essays on Handel and Italian Opera* (Cambridge, 1985), 164–211

G. Lazarevich: 'Eighteenth-Century Pasticcio: the Historian's Gordian Knot', *AnMc*, no.17 (1976), 121–45

R. Strohm: 'Italienische Opernarien des frühen Settecento', *AnMc*, no.16 (1976) [whole issue; incl. sources for 61 pasticcios and similar works, c1715–40]

F. L. Millner: *The Operas of Johann Adolf Hasse* (Ann Arbor, 1979)

F. C. Petty: *Italian Opera in London 1760–1800* (Ann Arbor, 1980)

C. Price: 'Italian Opera and Arson in Late Eighteenth-Century London', *JAMS*, xl (1989), 55–107   CURTIS PRICE

Pastoral [pastorale] (Fr.; It. *pastorale*; Ger. *Hirtenstück, Hirtenspiel, Schäferspiel* etc.). A work that depicts aspects of 'simple' (generally rural) life, usually in opposition to that of the court or city, or that is expressive of its atmosphere or values. Such works are attested in many different media and genres, among which opera occupies a particularly important place.

1. General. 2. Antiquity and Middle Ages. 3. Renaissance to the 17th century. 4. 18th century. 5. 19th century. 6. 20th century.

1. GENERAL. Pastoral opera, like pastoral in other media and genres, depends upon the projection of a philosophical opposition, generally one between art and nature or between country and city. In the classicizing Renaissance tradition, this is done through the personification of country and city by shepherds and courtiers respectively; and in pastoral music, the opposition between art and nature is generally reinforced by the use of distinctive styles, with the 'natural' style falling appreciably short of the complexity of the conventional style of the day. The philosophical oppositions traditional in pastoral have been a preoccupation of the secondary literature, especially in English, since Empson (1935; see in particular Kermode 5/1954), and encourage very general definitions of pastoral that often transcend the traditional limitations of subject matter as well as those of genre or medium.

Even when pastoral appears to deal purely with rural life, its implied audience is almost invariably a knowing one; for such an audience, the confrontation with 'natural' values traditionally represents a moral challenge. Accordingly, pastoral is often associated with political and religious allegories, and indeed most Renaissance and Baroque courtly operas and other musical entertainments seeking to celebrate the status of a ruler drew on pastoral.

The form and character of pastoral works are often influenced by notions of rhetorical persuasiveness, particularly when they invoke the myth of the shepherd naturally talented at poetry and music (e.g. Orpheus). In consequence, the history of pastoral is often understood as a parallel to the history of rhetoric; it is often assumed that classically derived pastoral was extinguished after the 18th century in parallel to the disappearance of formal rhetoric, and that later pastoralists had necessarily to choose between using pastoral elements purely decoratively or inventing pastoral completely *ab initio*. (The account below replaces this model with one depending more on gradual evolutionary change.) However this occurred, new attitudes to the rhetorical force of pastoral took root in the 18th century, and they have been associated (Halperin 1983) with the critical attitude crystallized in Schiller's essay *Über naive und sentimentalische Dichtung* (1800). Here the category of the idyll was defined for the first time as an *Empfindungsweise* – a 'mode of experience' – in terms of its psychological and expressive value rather than its subject matter; and indeed pastoral is today often defined as a 'mode' rather than a genre or style (see Loughrey 1984).

Other useful concepts have emerged from the 20th-century theoretical literature. A distinction can be drawn between 'hard' and 'soft' pastoral, following the definitions of hard and soft primitivism (Lovejoy and Boas 1935): these reflect the ease or lack of ease presupposed by the pastoral model, and the parodies of pastoral so important in its history usually arise from the substitution of hard for soft pastoral or vice versa. Furthermore, the term 'pastoral oasis' has been used (Poggioli 1975) for a section featuring pastoral characteristics within a longer, non-pastoral work, and been shown to be subject to different constraints from those governing a work which is completely pastoral.

2. ANTIQUITY AND MIDDLE AGES. The prestige and authority of pastoral drama in the Renaissance and later derive principally from the literary verse idylls of the 3rd-century BC Alexandrian Greek court poet Theocritus, set as a literary fiction in his birthplace, Sicily, and the analogous Latin eclogues of Virgil, set in an equally fictitious Greek 'Arcadia'. Although semi-dramatic public performances of the latter are known to have taken place in late antiquity, the closest equivalent to pastoral drama in antiquity was the satyr play: an example making use of pastoral subject matter is the *Cyclops* of Euripides, particularly in the first choral ode. Ancient dramatic theory (Aristotle, Horace etc.) takes no account of pastoral, however, and there is no contemporary account of the music used in satyr plays (see Brommer 1944). This circumstance embarrassed some later 'neo-classical' pastoralists – those who sought to conform to ancient precedent – for the use of traditional pastoral, in opera or elsewhere, is itself virtually a statement of loyalty to classical ideals.

In the Middle Ages the social criticism underlying Virgil's eclogues was occasionally taken up in political verse allegory, criticizing corruption in high places through the use of pastoral conventions borrowed from antiquity; yet the application of these conventions to drama was generally resisted until the late Middle Ages. The *mise-en-scène* of the medieval pastourelle (itself basically narrative in conception) was, however, extended to quasi-dramatic structures in the so-called *bergerie* dramas of which the earliest secular example is the 13th-century *Jeu de Robin et Marion* ascribed to Adam de la Halle. From the 14th century, similar treatment was accorded to ecclesiastical dramas including shepherds and low-life characters.

3. RENAISSANCE TO THE 17TH CENTURY. From the late 15th century, dramatic pastorals became increasingly popular in Italian aristocratic courts and academies, and strongly influenced early opera. Renaissance pastoral drama, especially in its influential Italian manifestation, adheres remarkably uniformly to subject matter from the traditional reconciliation of Catholic theology and Platonic love doctrine originally found in the vernacular poetry of Dante and Petrarch and exemplified in the final speech in Castiglione's *Il libro del cortegiano* (1528; see Cody 1969). Dramatic and, later, musical

1. Scene from Act 2 of Torquato Tasso's 'Aminta': woodcut from an edition published in Venice (1583)

pastorals drawing on this tradition generally took the form of elegant courtly entertainments with a classical veneer, especially for festivities such as weddings.

This conception of pastoral underlies the most influential pastoral dramas of the Renaissance, namely *Aminta* of Torquato Tasso (1581) and *Il pastor fido* of Battista Guarini (1585), the latter of which raised a storm of theoretical controversy even before its publication; in his subsequent *Compendio* (1601), Guarini defended pastoral drama as 'tragicomedy'. These works were produced in north Italian courts such as Mantua and Ferrara, from which emerged also many other musical versions of pastoral, with fewer contemporary theoretical pretensions – the *intermedi* and similar 'celebratory' occasional pieces, a flood of semi-dramatic polyphonic madrigals setting Guarini and other poets, and the earliest operas, notably Monteverdi's *Orfeo* (1607). Cavalieri's sacred allegorical pastoral *Rappresentatione di Anima et di Corpo* (1600, Rome) is also comparable to this repertory. (On the relationship between Tasso, Guarini and the opera, see Abert 1970.)

With the rise of the commercial opera in Italy, pastoral was often channelled into occasional pieces such as serenatas. Otherwise it was generally restricted to pastoral 'oases', supplying a distinctive, affective colouring for the sake of variety; these became part of the opera composer's stock-in-trade for centuries to come, first in *opera seria* (for an example, see Bianconi 1970) and later in grand opera. At the end of the 17th century, however, literati patronized by Queen Christina of Sweden and other aristocrats in Rome, and who formed the nucleus of the later Arcadian Academy, together with composers such as Alessandro Scarlatti, sought to reconstruct Italian literary culture according to the traditional Christian classical pattern of Petrarch. Pastoral operas as such once more took their place in the repertory of this circle (see Dent 1951 for an example); the suggestion (Harris 1980) that certain simplified musical forms are by definition typical of these Italian pastorals has not won universal acceptance.

Of the countries in which pastoral drama and prose were cultivated in the Renaissance, Spain was also influential; a well-known early example of Spanish dramatic pastoral was the *Diana* of Jorge de Montemayor (c1560), and the Spanish pastoral romance was burlesqued in Cervantes's *Don Quixote* (1605–15). The most characteristic pastoral genre of the 17th century in Spanish musical theatre was the zarzuela, with spoken dialogue and songs; the earliest such piece sung throughout was Lope de Vega's *La selva sin amor* (1627). This repertory persisted until the introduction of Italian opera to Spain in the early 18th century.

Aminta was translated into French in 1584 and *Il pastor fido* in 1595; French pastoral dramas drawing on these and Spanish precedents, with music, choruses, dancing and machines, appeared first in the late 16th century. Although the pastoral drama retreated in France in the 17th century in the face of French classical tragedy, pastoral theory was formulated at that time in classic texts by Rapin (loyal to classicizing ideals) and Fontenelle (opposed to them), which formed the basis for much subsequent theorizing on the subject in France, England and elsewhere (see Congleton 1952). The first pastoral to be sung throughout in France was *Le triomphe de l'amour* of Charles de Bey and Michel de La Guerre (first performed 1655), and subsequent pastorals included the famous *Pastorale d'Issy* of Cambert and Perrin (1659), establishing the opera in France. From the generation of Lully, a – perhaps paradoxical – subgenre of 'pastorale-héroïque' is found: Mattheson later distinguished between pastorals which were 'tragique, heroisch' and those which were 'comique, Landmässig', emphasizing the simplicity (*Einfalt, naïveté*) of musical (and especially melodic) style that should characterize both varieties (*Der vollkommene Capellmeister*, pp.218–19); P. J. B. Nougaret still later defined the 'pastorale-héroïque' as a 'drama whose subject is more serious than simple and whose denouement is sometimes tragic' (*De l'art du théâtre*, 1769).

Italian pastoral opera was performed as early as 1618 in the Steintheater at Hellbrunn (Salzburg) and also in other places in central Europe (including Bohemia and Poland) in the early 17th century. The earliest German operas were also chiefly indebted to the pastoral opera of the Italian courts (for example Rinuccini's *Dafne*, in a German adaptation by Martin Opitz set by Schütz, 1627, now lost, and Harsdörffer's sacred pastoral *Seelewig*, set by Staden, published 1644). Pastorals remained popular in German- and Slavonic-speaking areas, largely because musical institutions were centred on local aristocratic courts; later examples include J. S. Kusser's *Erindo* (1694).

2. 'La Representacion de la Opera Pastoral': engraving (c1780) showing characters conventionally associated with pastoral opera

Italianate pastoral drama was established in England first by Lyly (for example, *Endimion*, 1579, printed 1591) and others (Shakespeare, *As you Like it*, 1600; Fletcher, *The Faithful Shepherdess*, c1610), decades before Fanshawe's translation of Guarini was published (1647); these traditions, together with court masques, which reached their peak in the early 17th century, and pastoral entertainments such as Henry Lawes's setting of Milton's *Comus* (1634), represented the chief manifestations of dramatic pastoral in England before pastoral operas such as Blow's *Venus and Adonis* (c1683) and, perhaps, Purcell's *Dido and Aeneas* (1689; see Harris 1980). However, the traditional pastoral opera was never strongly established in England during the Baroque or later.

4. 18TH CENTURY. During the 18th century traditional pastoral opera retained its usefulness as a vehicle for graceful entertainments before noble patrons, especially in France and Germany; examples range from Fux's *Orfeo ed Euridice* (1715) and Caldara's *Dafne* (1719) to Haydn's 'dramma pastorale giocoso' *La fedeltà premiata* (1780). The expression of the polarity of 'art' and 'nature' continued to develop, however, in accordance with the evolution of the conception of 'naturalness'. In the early 18th century, German composers could allude to pastoral by means of simple, 'folklike' aria structures, often with vernacular texts, probably first found in pastorellas and other non-operatic genres. One such is 'Mein Kätchen ist ein Mädchen' from Keiser's *Croesus* (1711). Similar pastoral touches occur also, for example, in Bumbalka's Czech aria 'Já jsem plná veselosti' from the vernacular intermezzos to František Antonín Míča's opera *L'origine di Jaromeriz in Moravia* (1730; see Helfert 1925). They are of great importance for the later creation of national styles in central European and German opera.

In Germany and elsewhere, this simple pastoral style contributed to the rise of the ballad opera, and (particularly in theatres subject to commercial pressures) to the pastoral parody, a wide variety of which was manifested in the 18th and 19th centuries; this at first often presupposed a fairly sophisticated understanding of the pastoral tradition. Among the most inventive parodies of the early 18th century are those of Augustan England, as exemplified in the so-called Scriblerus Club (Swift, Pope, Gay and others), who met in 1714 and collaborated with the aim of ridiculing 'all the false tastes in learning'. Gay's absurd versions of pastoral include – at Swift's suggestion that a Newgate pastoral 'might make an odd pretty sort of thing' – the enormously successful *Beggar's Opera* (1728). Another, rather different product was Gay's pastoral 'serenata' *Acis and Galatea*, set by Handel (1718); here the parodistic element is absent, and the work perhaps stands as a manifesto of contemporary English neo-classical pastoral. Of later 18th-century parodies, this time of the traditional Italian Platonic love pastoral, Lorenzo da Ponte's libretto for Mozart's opera *Così fan tutte* (1790) particularly deserves mention, though Mozart's setting is scarcely pastoral in any distinctive sense.

The French equivalents to the simple melodies of German and English ballad operas were the vaudevilles (popular melodies to which new texts were added), from which so-called vaudeville comedies were constructed in the first half of the 18th century. These became the basis of a tradition of soft pastoral, of which J.-J. Rousseau's *Le devin du village* (1752) is an early example: this comprises *opéras comiques* in rural settings, often with deliberately simplified music, whose plots reflect a mythical, idealized view of the peasantry along the lines of Rousseau's own thought. Analogous works were also produced in England (for example the pasticcio *Love in a Village*, 1762); the Singspiels composed by J. A. Hiller in Leipzig in the second half of the century (for example *Die Jagd*, 1770) also represented adaptations of French librettos of this type. All such works reflect a simplified musical style which was regarded as the 'natural' pastoral style of the period – a natural style comparable, perhaps, to the soft pastoral of Marie Antoinette's milkmaid disguise.

5. 19TH CENTURY. The eclectic approach of composers such as Meyerbeer ensured the survival of pastoral 'oases' among other means of creating local colour in French grand opera and elsewhere; among the most original of these should be counted the shepherd's 'alte

Weise' in Act 3 of Wagner's *Tristan und Isolde* (1865). Otherwise, in the French repertory as in the Italian, pastoral traits are not very evident, even with subject matter that would in earlier times have virtually demanded their use (for example Mascagni's *Cavalleria rusticana*, 1890).

The 'folk-based' pastoral style in 18th-century opera became the basis, however, for many new developments in national opera repertories. Since the common conception of 'nature' at this period comprised landscape, often a specifically national landscape, the Singspiel pastoral idiom acquired powerful new ideological and psychological content. From the early 19th century it was able to symbolize national aspirations, both in German Romantic operas such as Weber's *Der Freischütz* (1821) and later (through the rediscovery of equivalent idioms: see especially Nejedlý 1929, iii) in works of the Czech nationalist school, of which the most prominent example is Smetana's *The Bartered Bride* (1866).

Pastoral parody, normally comic, also continued throughout the century, principally in French operettas and their offshoots elsewhere; to an unexpected extent these returned to Renaissance and Baroque pastorals for their basic subject matter or style (for example, Offenbach's *Orphée aux enfers*, 1858, and Sullivan's *Iolanthe*, 1882). In addition a new form of pastoral, the 'pastoral of childhood' (see Empson 1935) may be discerned later in the century in *Märchenopern* ('fairy-tale operas') such as Humperdinck's *Hänsel und Gretel* (1893).

6. 20TH CENTURY. The new soft Mediterranean pastoral idiom which had been developed from the late 19th century in French orchestral music and ballet, as in Debussy's *Prélude à l'après-midi d'un faune* (1892–4) and Ravel's *Daphnis et Chloé* (1912, suggested by Longus's pastoral novel), in turn suggested hard equivalents in the early 20th century, as in Stravinsky's *The Rite of Spring* (1913) and *The Wedding* (1923), or later in the crude primitivism of Carl Orff (*Der Mond*, 1939; *Die Kluge*, 1943). Other deliberately 'simple' and by that token pastoral styles, when used in opera or other 'classical' genres, were developed from various styles of commercial popular music, often drawn from jazz, either direct or via the Broadway or Hollywood American musical (for example, in Milhaud's ballet *La création du monde*, 1923; Krenek's *Jonny spielt auf*, 1927; Gershwin's *Porgy and Bess*, 1935, among many others); these form an obvious hard counterpart to the soft pastoral both of the continuing folksong tradition, exemplified in Vaughan Williams's *Hugh the Drover* (1924), and of the musical-comedy tradition itself (e.g. Rodgers and Hammerstein's *Oklahoma!*, 1943). Another source of 'simple' music has been found in the styles of past ages, as in a number of the works of Stravinsky.

In some works composers did not merely cultivate 'simple' idioms but also rejected 19th-century notions of realism in opera, at the same time succeeding in returning to a more profound, moral version of pastoral. With Brecht and Weill, the use of a 'hard' cabaret idiom at odds with conventional expectations of opera very effectively reinforces the moral imperative of the 'Newgate pastoral', in *Die Dreigroschenoper* (1928) as in *Aufstieg und Fall der Stadt Mahagonny* (1930), whether or not the audience may feel 'alienated' by it. Stravinsky's *The Rake's Progress* (1951) appears to represent a different, religious conception of pastoral.

Here both libretto and music, ostensibly set in the 18th century, set up a pastoral opposition between country and city against which the spiritual progress of the hero can be measured; it suggests that his final state (madness) represents his achievement of faith, in an apotheosis of the 'pastoral à la Theocritus' specified by Auden, the librettist, for the opening scene, rather than a descent into tragedy (on his conception of the dramatic force of madness, see Auden 1949). In both these examples, the pastoral mode supplies the essential dynamic which permits an appropriate moral assessment of the dramatic action.

*

G. B. Guarini: 'Compendio della poesia tragicomica' [1601], ed. A. Timermani, *Opere* (Verona, 1737)

R. Rapin: *Dissertatio de carmine pastorali* (Paris, 1659; Eng. trans., 1684)

B. le Bovier de Fontenelle: *Poésies pastorales … avec un traité sur la nature de l'églogue et une digression sur les anciens et les modernes* (Paris, 1688; Eng. trans., 1695)

F. von Schiller: 'Über naive und sentimentalische Dichtung', *Kleinere prosaische Schriften*, iii (Leipzig, 1800), 3–216 [earlier version in *Die Horen*, iv (Tübingen, 1795), 43–76; v (1796), 1–55]

A. Arnheim: 'Le devin du village von Jean-Jacques Rousseau und die Parodie *Les amours de Bastien et Bastienne*', *SIMG*, iv (1902–3), 686–727

J. Marsan: *La pastorale dramatique en France à la fin du XVIe et au commencement du XVIIe siècle* (Paris, 1905)

W. W. Greg: *Pastoral Poetry and Pastoral Drama* (London, 1906)

E. Carrara: *La poesia pastorale* (Milan, 1909)

L. de La Laurencie: 'Les pastorales en musique au XVIIe siècle en France avant Lully et leur influence sur l'opéra', *IMusSCR, iv London 1912*, 139–45

V. Helfert: *Hudba na jaroměřickém zámku* [Music at the Castle of Jaroměřice] (Prague, 1925)

Z. Nejedlý: *Bedřich Smetana*, iii: *Praha a venku* [Prague and the Countryside] (Prague, 1929)

W. Empson: *Some Versions of Pastoral* (London, 1935)

A. O. Lovejoy and G. Boas: *Primitivism and Related Ideas in Antiquity* (Baltimore, 1935)

F. Brommer: *Satyrspiele* (Berlin, 1944, 2/1959)

W. H. Auden: 'The Ironic Hero', *Horizon*, xx (1949), 86–94

E. J. Dent: 'A Pastoral Opera by Alessandro Scarlatti', *MR*, xii (1951), 7–14 [*La fede riconosciuta*, 1710]

J. E. Congleton: *Theories of Pastoral Poetry in England 1684–1798* (Gainesville, FL, 1952)

F. Kermode: *English Pastoral Poetry* (London, 1952)

A. Hartmann: 'Battista Guarini and *Il pastor fido*', *MQ*, xxxix (1953), 415–25

F. Kermode: *Introduction to W. Shakespeare: The Tempest* (London, 5/1954, 6/1958)

N. Burt: 'Opera in Arcadia', *MQ*, xli (1955), 145–70

R. Cody: *The Landscape of the Mind: Pastoralism and Platonic Theory* (Oxford, 1969)

N. Pirrotta: *Li due Orfei: da Poliziano a Monteverdi* (Turin, 1969, 2/1975; Eng. trans., 1982 as *Music and Theatre from Poliziano to Monteverdi*)

T. G. Rosenmeyer: *The Green Cabinet: Theocritus and the European Pastoral Lyric* (Berkeley, 1969)

A. A. Abert: 'Tasso, Guarini e l'opera', *NRMI*, iv (1970), 827–40

L. Bianconi: 'Die pastorale Szene in Metastasios *Olimpiade*', *GfMKB: Bonn 1970*, 185–91

P. V. Marinelli: *Pastoral* (London, 1971)

R. Poggioli: *The Oaten Flute: Essays on Pastoral Poetry and the Pastoral Ideal* (Cambridge, MA, 1975)

H. Cooper: *Pastoral: Mediaeval into Renaissance* (Ipswich, 1977)

E. T. Harris: *Handel and the Pastoral Tradition* (London, 1980)

H. Jung: *Die Pastorale: Studien zur Geschichte eines musikalischen Topos* (Berne and Munich, 1980)

D. M. Halperin: *Before Pastoral* (New Haven, 1983)

G. Chew: 'Handel as Shepherd', *MT*, cxxv (1984), 498–500

B. Loughrey, ed.: *The Pastoral Mode* (London, 1984)

A. Patterson: *Pastoral and Ideology: Virgil to Valéry* (Berkeley and Los Angeles, 1987)

M. R. Wade: *The German Baroque Pastoral 'Singspiel'* (Berne, 1990)

GEOFFREY CHEW

Pastorale-héroïque (Fr.). A type of BALLET-HÉROÏQUE whose plot often turns on the loves of nobles or gods (or goddesses), usually in disguise, for shepherdesses (or shepherds) in Arcadian-like settings. The tone is sentimental, rather than comic. It could be in several acts (e.g. Rameau's *Acante et Céphise* of 1751) or a single entrée or act in a larger work (e.g. Floquet's 'La cour d'amour' in *L'union de l'Amour et des arts* of 1773).

*

D. M. Powers: *The 'Pastorale Héroïque': Origins and Development of a Genre of French Opera in the 17th and 18th Centuries* (diss., U. of Chicago, 1988)

Pastorella nobile, La ('The Noble Shepherdess'). *Commedia per musica* in two acts by Pietro Alessandro Guglielmi (*see* GUGLIELMI family, (1)) to a libretto by FRANCESCO SAVERIO ZINI; Naples, Teatro del Fondo, 15 or 19 April 1788.

In the village of Belprato, in the Kingdom of Naples, the shepherdess Eurilla (soprano) attracts the amorous Marchese Astolfo (tenor), but she avoids his advances. Astolfo is engaged to Donna Florida (soprano), who arrives for the wedding, accompanied by her brother Don Astianatte (tenor). Don Polibio (bass), the pompous mayor, provides much broad humour as he argues with his impudent son Don Calloandro (baritone). The opera ends with the discovery that the rustic heroine is of noble birth; Eurilla and Don Calloandro express their surprise and delight, and their love for one another.

One of the strengths of the opera is the vividness of the musical characterization. The title role, like that of Guglielmi's *La bella pescatrice*, was created by the great *buffa* soprano Irene Tomeoni. Eurilla's music, in arias such as 'Quel visino a me volgete', reflects Tomeoni's talents: it is simple and sweet, yet hints at the delicate combination of innocence and sexuality with which Tomeoni charmed audiences. In Don Calloandro Guglielmi created a fine portrait of an attractive rascal.

La pastorella nobile was one of Guglielmi's most popular works, and one of the most widely performed late 18th-century comic operas. It was heard in most of Italy's operatic centres and in Vienna (where it was performed more often than any other opera during the years 1790–92), London, Paris, Madrid, Dresden, Prague and elsewhere; it was presented also as *L'erede di Belprato* and in Germany often under the titles *Die Schöne auf dem Lande*, *Die adelische Schäferin* and *Das adelige Landmädchen*.   JOHN A. RICE

Pastor fido, Il ('The Faithful Shepherd'). Opera in three acts by GEORGE FRIDERIC HANDEL to a libretto by GIACOMO ROSSI after the play by BATTISTA GUARINI; London, Queen's Theatre, 22 November 1712 (second version, with added choruses, London, King's Theatre, 18 May 1734; third version, with prologue *Terpsicore* and added dances, London, Covent Garden Theatre, 9 November 1734).

Rossi's libretto is a drastic condensation of Guarini's famous pastoral play of 1585, most of the background to the story and its final resolution remaining unexplained though some material is added. (Eurilla corresponds to Corisca in the play.) Handel made further cuts by omitting several lines printed in the wordbook, but the recitatives still contain just enough information to set the context for each aria. The roles of Mirtillo and Silvio were originally sung by castratos (Valeriano Pellegrini and Valentino Urbani). *Il pastor*

fido was Handel's second opera for London, and, coming after the brilliant *Rinaldo*, was a disappointment to contemporary audiences; a diarist commented that 'the scene represented only the Country of Arcadia; the Habits [costumes] were old – the Opera short'. After six performances it was replaced with a pasticcio (*Dorinda*) using the same sets, and there was just one more performance, on 21 February 1713.

In the spring of 1734, when facing the rivalry of the productions of the 'Opera of the Nobility' at Lincoln's Inn Fields, Handel revived *Il pastor fido* in a much changed version, preserving the outlines of the story but retaining only seven of the original arias; the rest (except for a new setting of Mirtillo's opening cavatina) were taken from cantatas or earlier operas, with the significant addition of choruses taken from the serenata *Parnasso in Festa* (performed two months earlier for the wedding of the Princess Royal). The role of Mirtillo was taken by the mezzo-soprano castrato Giovanni Carestini. The production proved popular and received 13 performances. This version was the basis of yet another revision which opened Handel's first season at John Rich's new theatre in Covent Garden on 9 November 1734. There were two new arias (one for Carestini as Mirtillo and one for the tenor John Beard, who took over Silvio's part), but the main changes were prompted by Rich's engagement of a dance troupe led by Marie Sallé. For her benefit Handel added a new prologue, *Terpsicore*, a mixture of vocal solos, choruses and orchestral dance movements (some taken from earlier works) in which Terpsichore, the Muse of Dance (played by Sallé), is encouraged by Erato (soprano) and Apollo (mezzo-soprano) to demonstrate her talents. (Handel seems to have used the prologue to Collin de Blamont's *Les festes grecques et romaines* of 1723 as a model.) Newly composed dances were also added at the end of each act of the opera. There were five performances. Though this version is almost a pasticcio, modern revivals have shown that it works surprisingly well on the stage.

A version of *Il pastor fido* with *Terpsicore* was given in Göttingen on 20 June 1948. On 14 September 1971 the 1712 version received its first modern revival, at the Unicorn Theatre, Abingdon. The first British revival of the November 1734 version (without *Terpsicore*) was on 3 September 1974 at the King's Theatre, Edinburgh (a production by the Royal Opera, Stockholm, first given at the Drottningholm Court Theatre, Stockholm, on 4 September 1969). Chrysander's edition of the 1712 version is generally reliable except for matters of detail (though it does not indicate that the aria 'Ho un non so che nel cor' for Dorinda in Act 3 is an addition – surely an unhappy one – probably made during the 1712 run). His treatment of the 1734 versions is extremely confused, however, though both versions can be reconstructed with accuracy by reference to the original wordbooks and other source material.

The action is set in a mythical Arcadia. The country is oppressed by the displeasure of the goddess Diana, who can be placated only by the joining of 'two of heavenly race'. The Arcadians believe that the shepherdess Amarilli (soprano) and the young huntsman Silvio (alto), being of divine ancestry, are alone capable of meeting this requirement, and the couple have been betrothed against their wills: Amarilli secretly loves the shepherd Mirtillo (soprano), while Silvio is interested only in the hunt and devotion to Diana. Mirtillo laments that he cannot gain the love of Amarilli. She, too, is in torment, being in love with Mirtillo but unable to admit it. Mirtillo decides on suicide, but is interrupted by Eurilla (soprano), who tells him that Amarilli loves him. Eurilla is in love with Mirtillo herself, however, and is actually plotting to get rid of Amarilli. Another shepherdess, Dorinda (alto), is deeply in love with Silvio, but he is as indifferent to her as to Amarilli. Eurilla puts her plans into action by attaching a garland to Mirtillo while he is asleep: it bears the message 'Mi fian cari i tuoi voti, e là t'attendo' ('Thy vows are become dear to me, and I await thee'). On waking and finding the garland Mirtillo believes it comes from Amarilli and is overjoyed; but Amarilli overhears part of his soliloquy and, misunderstanding, assumes he loves someone else. Eurilla confirms to Mirtillo that the garland was from Amarilli and tells him she is waiting for him in the nearby cave of Erycina. She then tells Amarilli that Mirtillo does love someone else and that she will see for herself if she hides in the cave. When the two lovers have entered the cave Eurilla arranges for them to be found together by the priests: the stern laws of Arcadia condemn to death a woman who betrays her vows. Silvio, out hunting, sees a movement in the bushes and throws his dart; but it is Dorinda that he wounds. Her devotion to him, despite her wound, remains steadfast, and Silvio, deeply moved, now responds to her love. In the temple of Diana, prepared for a sacrifice, Amarilli openly declares her love for Mirtillo. He interrupts the ceremony and demands to die in her place. The impasse is resolved by the intervention of Tirenio (bass), the high priest of Diana: he declares that Mirtillo is of heavenly race and that his marriage to Amarilli will meet the conditions for placating Diana. Dorinda and Silvio share the joy of the newly united couple and Eurilla is forgiven.

*   *   *

The initial cool reaction to Il pastor fido, though understandable, was unfair. The pastoral atmosphere, tinged with melancholy, is aptly evoked by the restrained scoring (oboes, flutes, bassoons and strings), and a sympathetic performance (especially of the recitatives, which preserve some of Guarini's exquisite language) allows the opera to exercise a tender charm. Mirtillo, Amarilli and Dorinda remain serious characters throughout, but there is a lightening touch of caricature in the roles of the gleefully mischievous Eurilla and the boyish Silvio. Dorinda's 'Mi lasci, mi fuggi' is a happy example of Handel's ability to plumb emotional depth with music of great simplicity. The extended, very fine overture, in six movements, may originally have been written as an independent orchestral suite.

ANTHONY HICKS

Pászthory, Casimir von (b Budapest, 1 April 1886; d Salzburg, 18 Feb 1966). Austrian composer of Hungarian origin. He studied in Vienna, Paris and Brussels; he taught the cello in Vienna, 1927–34, then lived as a freelance composer. His first public success came with the melodrama Die Weise von Liebe und Tod des Cornets Christoph Rilke (1914, Linz), which received particular praise from Rilke himself; his chamber opera Die drei gerechten Kammacher was performed in Graz in 1932. His works are in an original style that avoids the extremes of rigid traditionalism and avant-garde experiment.

Die drei gerechten Kammacher (Pászthory, after G. Keller), Graz, 6 Feb 1932

Die Prinzessin und der Schweinehirt (Pászthory, after H. C. Andersen), Weimar, 1937
Tilman Riemenschneider (D. von Pászthory, after L. G. Bachmann), Basle, 1957
JOSEPH CLARK

Pataky, Kálmán [Koloman von] (b Alsólendva, 14 Nov 1896; d Los Angeles, 3 March 1964). Hungarian tenor. After little serious study, he made his début at the Budapest Opera in 1922, as the Duke, which led to an invitation to sing under Schalk at the Vienna Staatsoper in 1926. Until the Nazi invasion of Austria, Vienna remained his base, although he often sang in Budapest and abroad (sometimes as Koloman von Pataky), notably at the Paris Opéra (1928), Glyndebourne (1936), La Scala (1940), Stockholm and, frequently, at the Colón. He sang Florestan under Toscanini at Salzburg in 1936. He spent the war in Hungary, returning to the Colón for a few performances in 1946. Pataky was not an accomplished actor, but his classically beautiful voice and thorough understanding of style (developed largely during his years in Vienna), his wide cultural background and gift for musical characterization made him one of the leading Mozart tenors; he was an outstanding Don Ottavio, Belmonte and Tamino. Other roles included Rodolfo, Puccini's Des Grieux and (though he was perhaps less well suited to these heroic roles) Radames, Cavaradossi and Turiddu. His recordings include Don Ottavio in Busch's Glyndebourne Don Giovanni.

GV (with discography by T. Kaufmann and R. Vegeto)
V. Somogyi and I. Molnár: Pataky Kálmán (Budapest, 1968)
A. Blyth: 'Koloman von Pataky and Walter Widdop', Opera, xl (1989), 288–95
PÉTER P. VÁRNAI

Patanè, Giuseppe (b Naples, 1 Jan 1932; d Munich, 29 May 1989). Italian conductor, son of the conductor Franco Patanè (1908–68). He studied at the Naples Conservatory and made his début at the Teatro Mercadante there in 1951 conducting La traviata from memory (he later claimed to know over 200 operas note-for-note). He was engaged as répétiteur and assistant conductor at the Teatro S Carlo until 1956, and was later based at Linz (1961–2), then as resident conductor for Italian repertory at the Deutsche Oper, West Berlin (1962–8). His American début was at the San Francisco Opera in 1967, his British at Covent Garden in 1973 with La forza del destino. After La Gioconda at the Metropolitan in 1975 he appeared regularly there until 1982. Patanè was last heard at Covent Garden in 1987 in La bohème, the first performance screened simultaneously in the outdoor piazza. He was then working mainly in charge of Italian repertory at Munich, where he suffered a fatal heart attack while conducting Il barbiere di Siviglia. His recordings include Madama Butterfly (1971), Samson et Dalila (1973), Andrea Chénier (1987), Massenet's Iris (1988), a distinctive Il barbiere di Siviglia with an all-Italian cast (1989) and Boito's Mefistofele (which he also conducted at Geneva in 1988). His performances were marked by an innate feeling for melodic line and careful balance between voices and orchestra, as well as rhythmic verve. BERNARD JACOBSON, NOËL GOODWIN

Pate, John (d Hampstead [now in London], bur. 14 Jan 1704). English countertenor. Evelyn described him as 'reputed the most excellent singer, ever England had'. His first recorded appearance was in Purcell's The Fairy-Queen (1692), when he sang the shepherdess

Mopsa 'in woman's habit'. He had Jacobite sympathies and visited Italy at least once. From March 1698 he sang in dramatic operas and masques at Drury Lane, including *The Island Princess*, where the librettist Motteux praised his performance for giving 'life to the whole Entertainment'. In 1700 he was in Daniel Purcell's opera *The Grove* and his 'Secular Masque' in *The Pilgrim*. That September he was reported held in the Bastille, condemned to death on the wheel for 'killing a man', but he was back in England by December 1701.

BDA; LS

O. Baldwin and T. Wilson: 'Alfred Deller, John Freeman and Mr. Pate', *ML*, l (1969), 103–10

OLIVE BALDWIN, THELMA WILSON

Patience [*Patience; or, Bunthorne's Bride!*]. Operetta in two acts by ARTHUR SULLIVAN to a libretto by W. S. GILBERT; London, Opéra Comique, 23 April 1881.

The poets Bunthorne and Grosvenor (baritones) compete for the affections of the aesthetic maidens and of Patience (soprano), the milkmaid. When the manly attractions of Colonel Calverley (baritone) and his dragoons fail to interest the ladies, desperation leads the officers to adopt the aesthetic manner. In the end, however, Grosvenor and the maidens discard sham aestheticism, leaving Bunthorne alone.

The libretto originated in one of Gilbert's *Bab Ballads*, 'The Rival Curates'. The substitution of poets for clerics, made after much of the play had been written, enabled him to lampoon the *poseurs* of the fashionable aesthetic movement, of which Oscar Wilde was a noted disciple. The contrast between the languid music of the maidens and the dragoons' robust strains is as striking as the visual foil the groups create. Sullivan also deftly characterized the patter songs for the Colonel ('If you want a receipt') and Bunthorne ('If you're anxious for to shine'). 'I cannot tell what this love may be' is a sparkling soprano showpiece, other outstanding numbers being the effervescent 'If Saphir I choose to marry' and 'Silver'd is the raven hair', in which Sullivan's setting of the unkind lyric evokes sympathy for the aging Lady Jane (contralto). The duet 'Prithee, pretty maiden' is an enchanting folksong burlesque, but the quasi-religious sextet 'I hear the soft note' (at the heart of the excellent Act 1 finale) was probably sincerely intended. Sullivan's pupil Eugen d'Albert arranged the overture. Despite Gilbert's fears, *Patience* has outlived the fashion that inspired it.

DAVID RUSSELL HULME

Paton, Mary Anne. *See* WOOD, MARY ANNE.

Patorzhinsky, Ivan (Sergeyevich) (*b* Petro-Svistunovo, Zaporozhskiy province, 20 Feb/3 March 1896; *d* Kiev, 22 Feb 1960). Ukrainian bass. He graduated from the Yekaterinoslav Conservatory in 1922, and was a soloist at the Kharkiv Opera (1925–35) and at the Kiev Opera from 1935. He was the most distinguished Ukrainian singer of his time, with a rich, powerful voice, a commanding stage presence, a keen awareness of national style and an individual sense of humour. His roles included Boris, Konchak, Galitsky, Gounod's Méphistophélès and Don Basilio; in classical Ukrainian operas he was Lysenko's Taras Bulba and Ivan Karas' in Gulak-Artemovsky's *Zaporozhets za Dunayem* ('A Cossack beyond the Danube'); he created Gavrila in Dan'kevych's *Bohdan Khmel'nyts'ky* and Val'ko in Meytus's *Moloda hvardiya* ('The Young Guard').

M. Stefanovich: *I. S. Patorzhinsky* (Moscow, 1960)

I. M. YAMPOL'SKY

Patras. Greek city, capital of the Peloponnesus. Theatrical archives are scarce. The local press and other archive sources report music theatre performances in a café as early as 1829; in 1843 and 1844 two Greek texts, probably opera librettos, were printed there: *I doxa tis Lefkados* ('The Glory of Leucadia'), a two-act 'melodrama' by Spyridon Ioannou Kavvadas, and *Dimitrios Kallerghis*, a three-act 'lyric drama' by Nikitas Soliotis. Visiting Italian companies are reported from 1850; by 1856 they seem to have become usual, their performances ending at two o'clock in the morning (librettos of *Lucia di Lammermoor* and of *Lucrezia Borgia*, the latter in Greek, were printed in 1850 and 1851 respectively). In 1861 Pavlos Carrer acted as impresario for the première of his *Marcos Botsaris*, despite the efforts of conservative elements to prevent performances. Years later Carrer described the Patras theatre at that time as 'a shabby wooden construction'. The Apollo theatre (three tiers of boxes, *c*700 seats) was completed in 1872. Until the end of the century it presented the standard French and Italian repertory (24 operas are known to have been given including Bizet, Gounod, Donizetti, Verdi, Mascagni and lesser-known Italians). The theatre's records are incomplete, however; characteristically in 1878–9, 100 performances of 11 different operas were given. Between 1900 and 1921 operetta became more popular, and Greek companies began to outnumber by far Italian ones. A 'Summer' (open-air) theatre opened in 1900 (subsequently designated 'Spring' or 'Paradissos'). After 1940 the Ethniki Lyriki Skini (National Opera), based in Athens, occasionally visited Patras. The Apollo is now used for prose dramas. The International Patras Festival, founded in 1986 and until 1990 directed by the composer Thanos Mikroutsikos, is held every year in July and August but offers only limited possibilities for opera; its events take place predominantly in open-air premises such as the ancient Roman Hodheion (2nd century AD), with a capacity of about 2200.

D. Conomos, ed.: 'Anekdota apomnimonevmata tou Pavlou Carrer' [The Unpublished Memoirs of Pavlos Carrer], *Filologiki protohronia*, xix (1962), 239–78

K. N. Triandafyllou: 'Theatra', *Istorikon lexikon ton Patron* [Historical Dictionary of Patras] (Patras, 1980), 156–9

N. A. Bakounakis: *I ipodochi tis operas stin Ellada: to lyriko repertorio tou Dimotikou Theatrou ton Patron, 'Apollon', 1871–1900* [The Reception of Opera in Greece: the Lyrical Repertory of the Patras Municipal Theatre, 'Apollo', 1871–1900] (Patras, 1986)

——: *To fantasma tis Norma: i ipodochi tis operas stin Ellada ston 19on eona* [Norma's Phantom: the Reception of Opera in Greece in the 19th Century] (Athens, 1991)

GEORGE LEOTSAKOS

Patria. Collective title for a cycle of music-theatre works by R. MURRAY SCHAFER to texts by the composer; 12 were planned up to 1991.

The works in this cycle share certain features of Schafer's innovatory 'theatre of confluence', a fusion of music, theatre, dance and other arts. Texts are generally multi-lingual. All involve elements of ritual and mythology (most prominently the legends of Ariadne and the Minotaur and of Beauty and the Beast). Many demand highly unorthodox times, places or durations of performance, often involving audience participation. 'The big revolutions in musical history', Schafer has asserted, 'are changes of context more than changes of style.'

Though interrelated by both narrative and musical themes, these works are to be performed independently, and Schafer does not expect consecutive presentation as of Wagner's *Ring* cycle; yet each gains in depth from a knowledge of the others. After the creation myth depicted in the Prologue, *Patria 1* and *2* portray, respectively, the hero Wolf (known also as D. P. or Beast) in a hostile social environment, and a heroine, Ariadne, in an asylum for the insane. The hero and heroine then magically disappear at the beginning of *Patria 3*, a process that Schafer likens to a Jungian alchemical transmutation of elements. Remaining segments depict ritual attempts to reconstitute the hero and heroine anew, the conclusion returning to the wilderness setting of the Prologue. The works are listed here in numerical sequence, not in order of composition.

Prologue: *The Princess of the Stars*; Heart Lake, Ontario, 26 September 1981.

This enactment of an 'Indian' creation myth (invented by Schafer) takes place around the perimeter and on the surface (in canoes) of a lake in deep wilderness, where the audience has gathered in the darkness before dawn. The actors and singers interact with the echoes and awakening birds, while the piece, which is meant to begin exactly 52 minutes before dawn, reaches its climax with sunrise.

Patria 1: Wolfman (formerly *The Characteristics Man*); Toronto, Shaw Festival, 21 November 1987.

Presented in a conventional theatre, *Patria 1* follows the frustration of D. P., i.e. 'Displaced Person' (silent role), an immigrant antihero who tries in vain to find acceptance in his adopted country, a place projected through images of grotesque violence. In desperation he seizes a young girl, Ariadne (mezzo-soprano), at knifepoint, but finally turns the weapon against himself.

Patria 2: Requiems for the Party Girl; Stratford (Ontario) Festival, 23 August 1972.

The action depicts the fantasies and hallucinations of Ariadne, a schizophrenic patient in an asylum for the insane. Surrounded by threatening and incomprehensible figures – Ariadne being one of the few characters to speak intelligibly in the language of the audience – she ultimately shoots herself in the head.

Patria 3: The Greatest Show; Peterborough (Ontario) Festival of the Arts, 6 August 1987.

This is a theatre piece presented in the form of a small town carnival. The audience assembles at a main stage (the 'Odditorium') where magicians make the hero and heroine vanish. The spectators then disperse, free to explore the countless exhibits and games, or be accosted by strolling players; if ingenious, they may win tickets into special performances in one of three sideshows. All are summoned at last to the Odditorium stage, where the magicians attempt to restore the hero and heroine but fail, with unexpected results.

Patria 4: The Black Theatre of Hermes Trismegistos; Liège Festival, 9 March 1989.

The audience is transported to an unknown location (Schafer suggests an abandoned mine-shaft or factory) for a performance that begins at midnight. There they witness the Alchemical Brotherhood ritually transmuting base metals into silver and gold, symbolizing the eventual perfection of the heroine and hero, respectively, in the cycle's conclusion.

Patria 6: RA; Toronto, Science Center, Comus Music Theatre, 4 May 1983.

A dramatization of Egyptian underworld mythology, *RA* begins at sunset. The audience, robed as initiates, witnesses and participates in the ten-hour ritual that follows the sun god through the perils of the underworld to sunrise the following morning. The hero, incarnated as the jackal-god Anubis, acts as a guide for the initiates.

Six further works have not yet been fully realized. *Patria 5: The Crown of Ariadne* tells the Ariadne legend largely through dance. *Patria 7: Asterion* conducts its audience members individually through the Cretan labyrinth. Additional outdoor works (*Patria [8]: The Enchanted Forest*; *Patria [9]: The Spirit Garden*; and *Patria [10]: The Palace of the Cinnabar Phoenix*) are projected. The conclusion, *And Wolf Shall Inherit the Moon*, takes the form of a seven-day event in the wilderness, where the participants learn to prepare a final ritual which is enacted on the final day to reunite the cycle's hero and heroine.

STEPHEN J. ADAMS (WITH KIRK MACKENZIE)

Patronage. For discussion of the patronage of opera, *see* SOCIOLOGY OF OPERA. The patronage of opera is also discussed in individual entries on patrons and on cities.

Patterson, Franklin Peale (*b* Philadelphia, 5 Jan 1871; *d* New Rochelle, NY, 6 July 1966). American composer and journalist. He studied at the University of Pennsylvania and the Akademie der Tonkunst in Munich. He founded the Pasadena Orchestra and Choral Society in California, where he was also programme annotator for the Los Angeles SO. In New York he joined the staff of the *Musical Courier* and helped organize the American section of the ISCM, serving as chairman of its music committee. He wrote both comic and serious operas. His tragedy *A Little Girl at Play* was rejected by the Metropolitan Opera because of its gruesome libretto. Retitled *Beggar's Love*, it was given its New York première at the Matinee Musicale in January 1930. *Mountain Blood*, composed in 1925, is based on a work of the same name by the composer Hergesheimer, who also wrote his own libretto. *The Echo*, which uses four soloists, chorus and ballet, received the David Bispham Medal and, in 1925, a major award from the National Federation of Music Clubs. While its style is conservative with emphasis on vocal line and melody, its libretto shows the influence of Wagner, especially in its mythological characters and theme of love's redemptive powers.

The Titlomaniacs, 1897 (comic op, 2, H. H. Hertzberg), *US-Wc*
Through the Narrow Gate, c1913 (grand op, 3, Patterson), * *Wc*
The Echo, 1918 (chamber op, 1, Patterson), Portland, OR, Conference of the National Federation of Music Clubs, 9 June 1925, vs (New York, 1922)
A Little Girl at Play: a Tragedy of the Slums (chamber op, 1, T. Gray and Patterson), Los Angeles, 1918; as Beggar's Love, New York, Jan 1930, vs (Boston, c1930)
Mountain Blood, 1925 (grand op, 3, Patterson, after Hergesheimer), lib. *Wc*
The Forest Dwellers (chamber op, 1, Patterson)
Caprice (grand op, 3, Patterson)

E. E. Hipsher: *American Opera and its Composers* (Philadelphia, 1927, 2/1934), 355–8   ELISE K. KIRK

Patter song. A comic song in which the humour derives from having the greatest number of words uttered in the shortest possible time. The technique was foreshadowed by such composers as Alessandro Scarlatti (the duet 'Non ti voglio' from *Tiberio imperatore d'Oriente*, 1702) but was not in common use until the second half of the 18th century, when composers often introduced the idea into *buffo* solos (e.g. Bartolo's aria 'La vendetta' in Act 1 scene iii of Mozart's *Le nozze di Figaro*). Other examples are found in the works of Logroscino, Piccinni, Paisiello, Haydn, Rossini (notably the 'confusion' ensemble in the Act 1 finale of *Il barbiere di Siviglia*), Donizetti and Sullivan (whose patter song in *Ruddigore* includes the lines: 'this particularly rapid, unintelligible patter isn't generally heard and if it is it doesn't matter').

Patti, Adelina [Adela] (**Juana Maria**) (*b* Madrid, 19 Feb 1843; *d* Craig-y-Nos Castle, nr Brecon, Wales, 27 Sept 1919). Italian soprano, daughter of Salvatore Patti and Caterina Barilli-Patti. She studied with her half-brother, Ettore Barilli, in New York, where she made her début in 1859 at the Academy of Music in *Lucia di Lammermoor*, which she had studied with the conductor Emmanuele Muzio. She made her European début at Covent Garden in 1861, as Amina in *La sonnambula*, then sang in Berlin, Brussels and Amsterdam. She made her Paris début at the Théâtre Italien in 1862 and her first appearance in Vienna at the Carltheater in 1863, on both occasions as Amina. Later that year she sang Gounod's Marguerite for the first time, at Hamburg. In the winter of 1865–6 she visited Italy, singing at Florence, Bologna, Rome and Turin; she spent the winter of 1868–9 in St Petersburg and Moscow.

Patti was London's first Aida (1876) and she made her début at La Scala as Violetta (1877). Returning to New York after an absence of over 20 years, she was engaged by Mapleson for his operatic tour of the USA. In 1885, her 25th consecutive season at Covent Garden, she sang Carmen, one of the few misjudgments of her career. The following year she again made a tour of the USA, ending with six farewell performances at the Metropolitan (1887). After singing in Madrid and Lisbon, in 1888 she appeared in Buenos Aires and Montevideo. She also sang in *Roméo et Juliette* at the Paris Opéra, with Gounod conducting. In 1895 she gave six farewell performances at Covent Garden, two each of Violetta, Zerlina and Rosina. In 1897 she sang at Monte Carlo and at Nice, where she created the title role of André Pollonnais' *Dolorès*. Her amazing purity of tone and flexibility of voice were retained for more than half a century.

For illustration see *ROMÉO ET JULIETTE* (ii).

*

M. Strakosch: *Souvenirs d'un impresario* (Paris, 1886, 2/1887)
J. H. Mapleson: *The Mapleson Memoirs* (London, 1888); ed. H. Rosenthal (London, 1966)
M. Maretzek: *Sharps and Flats* (New York, 1890)
L. Arditi: *My Reminiscences* (London, 1896)
H. Klein: *The Reign of Patti* (London, 1920)
H. Rosenthal: *Two Centuries of Opera at Covent Garden* (London, 1958)
ELIZABETH FORBES

Patti, Salvatore (*b* Catania, 1800; *d* Paris, 21 Aug 1869). Italian tenor. Engaged as second tenor at the Teatro Carolino, Palermo, for the 1825–6 season, which was directed by Donizetti, he sang Pipetto in *L'ajo nell'imbarazzo* and Ismaele in the first performance of *Alahor in Granata*. For the next decade he appeared at other theatres in Sicily and Italy, then in 1836 at the Teatro Valle, Rome, he sang Ugo (*Parisina*) and Tamas (*Gemma di Vergy*), repeating the latter role in Naples the following year. His career as a singer continued in Italy and Spain until 1844, when he went to New York to manage seasons of Italian opera, first at Palmo's, then at the Astor Place Opera House.

Salvatore's wife was the soprano Caterina Chiesa Barilli-Patti (*b* Rome; *d* Rome, 6 Sept 1870), whom he married after her first husband had died. She sang in Naples, both at the S Carlo, where she created Eleanor in *L'assedio di Calais* (1836), and at the Teatro Fondo, where she sang the title role of *Gemma di Vergy* (1837). Other roles included Elvira (*I puritani*) and Norma, which she is reputed to have sung at Madrid in 1843, the night before the birth of her youngest daughter, Adelina Patti. The baritone Ettore Barilli, one of four children by her first marriage, was the first to sing Rigoletto in the USA (1855, New York).

ELIZABETH FORBES

Pattiera, Tino (*b* Cavtat, nr Dubrovnik, 27 June 1890; *d* Cavtat, 24 April 1966). Croatian tenor. He studied in Vienna and after gaining experience in operetta made his début at the Dresden Opera in 1914 as Manrico in *Il trovatore*. His fine voice was matched by good looks, and he became the most popular tenor in Dresden, especially when paired in the 1920s with the soprano Meta Seinemeyer. With her, and under Fritz Busch, he sang in some notable productions, including *La forza del destino*, *Don Carlos*, *The Queen of Spades* and *Andrea Chénier*. Although he specialized in the Italian repertory, he also sang Tannhäuser, and Bacchus in *Ariadne auf Naxos*. He joined the Chicago Opera Company in the 1921–2 season, and was a guest artist in Berlin, Vienna, Budapest and Belgrade. He gave his last concert at Dresden in 1953 and taught for some years in Vienna. Although a highly gifted singer, he lacked the secure technique and stylistic discipline to make the best use of his voice. Recordings preserve its distinctive timbre, and his duets with Seinemeyer make it understandable that Dresdeners are said to have compared their performances together to the Melba-and-Caruso evenings at Covent Garden.

*

A. Vincenti and J. Dennis: 'Tino Pattiera', *Record Collector*, xvii (1966–8), 268–85
J. B. STEANE

Patzak, Julius (*b* Vienna, 9 April 1898; *d* Rottach-Egern, Bavaria, 26 Jan 1974). Austrian tenor. After studying music and conducting, he took up singing in earnest but was entirely self-taught. Provincial engagements led to an invitation to join the Munich Opera in 1928, where he stayed until he joined the Vienna company in 1945, participating during this period in the premières of Pfitzner's *Das Herz* (1931), Strauss's *Friedenstag* (1938, in which he created the role of the Rifleman) and Orff's *Der Mond* (1939). For more than three decades he was much in demand, particularly for Mozart roles, and as his voice grew larger he became an incomparable Florestan and Palestrina. His extensive repertory ranged from Singspiel and operetta through the lighter Wagner roles and Richard Strauss to Verdi, Puccini and Musorgsky. He appeared at Covent Garden as Tamino in 1938, and as Florestan and Herod during the 1947 Vienna Staatsoper season; he returned to sing

Julius Patzak as Florestan in Beethoven's 'Fidelio'

Florestan and Hoffmann with the resident company. He also made notable appearances at the Salzburg Festival, where he created Desmoulins in von Einem's *Dantons Tod* (1947). Although Patzak's voice was generally considered small, it was so finely projected and allied to such intelligent phrasing, meticulous enunciation and effective stage deportment that it seldom failed to make its mark. His slightly nasal timbre was immediately recognizable and he was able to sing with no loss of impact when well into his fifties. He was a notable concert singer, and much sought after as the Evangelist. Though there are only 'unofficial' complete recordings of his grandest roles, he has left a legacy of memorable records of operatic excerpts.

*

P. Branscombe: 'Julius Patzak', *Opera*, v (1954), 403–7
J. Dennis: 'Julius Patzak', *Record Collector*, xix (1970–71), 195–222 [with discography by D. Brew]   PETER BRANSCOMBE

Pauer, Jiří (*b* Libušín, nr Kladno, 22 Feb 1919). Czech composer and impresario. He studied composition with Alois Hába at the Prague Conservatory (1943–6) and with Bořkovec at the Academy of Musical Arts (1946–50). He was appointed to many leading posts, including head of opera at the Prague National Theatre (1951, 1953–5, 1965–7), director of the Czech PO (1958–79) and director of the National Theatre (1979–89); he was also professor of composition at the academy (1965–89).

Pauer's composition technique developed directly in line with the Czech national classical music of Smetana and Dvořák. His music tends to be tonal, with expressive melodies and rhythms, brilliant instrumenta-

tion and a characteristic concision, and displays an energetic temperament, spontaneity and jovial pithiness. His choice of subjects for his operas demonstrates his sense of theatre. The chamber opera *Žvanivý slimejš* ('Prattling Slug'), composed during his student years, is a good example of his interest in children's opera. The libretto by M. Mellanová, a specialist in children's theatre, interweaves oriental fairy-tales about a talkative slug and a rejuvenating spring. Pauer's setting, which lasts one hour, is dynamic and witty; the bragging slug is characterized in ariosos, and the aging wife in a lament, while mischievous monkeys are portrayed with ironic giggling, and a wailing coloratura when one of them is caught. Although the opera waited eight years for its première, it became the most frequently performed postwar opera in Czechoslovakia. The libretto of *Červená Karkulka* ('Red Riding Hood'), based on the fairy-tales 'Red Riding Hood' and 'The Goat and her Kids' and also by Mellanová, was intended to combine with *Prattling Slug* to make a full-length opera. Composed for small children, it uses communicative and witty imitative and illustrative effects to portray animal sounds, and has many extensive sections of ballet and pantomime.

Pauer's traditionalism meanwhile enabled him to follow the socialist aesthetic tendencies of the 1950s, and he composed a national historical opera in the style of Smetana, *Zuzana Vojířová* (1958). His optimism can be seen in *Manželské kontrapunkty* ('Matrimonial Counterpoints', 1962, 1966), consisting of five separate ten-minute grotesques which depict conflicts in everyday family life: 'Řízek' ('The Steak'), a couple having lunch at a restaurant; 'Vyletí ptáček' ('Cheese!'), taking pictures of a child; 'Tragédie s návštěvou' ('The Tragedy with the Guests'), hypocritical hosts having guests; 'V úzkém rodinném' ('In the Family Circle'), a tense Easter idyll; and 'Spisovatel Babský' ('The Writer Babský'), the solicitude of a wife and mother-in-law. Satirical elements are also used in *Zdravý nemocný* ('The Hypochondriac'; 1970, after Molière's *Le malade imaginaire*), in which hypochondriacs, quacks, misers and reactionaries are held up to ridicule. The shortened story adapts traditional *buffo* procedures and features a resolute maid, a girl in love, a rude hypochondriac and a doctor's clumsy son. The monodrama *Labutí píseň* ('Swan-song', 1974) shows a lonely, aging actor whose nostalgic resignation results in the glorification of art and man's creativity; the work stands on the borderline between opera and concert music.

See also Zuzana Vojířová.

Žvanivý slimejš [Prattling Slug], 1949–50 (children's op, 1, M. Mellanová, after J. Hloucha), Prague, Academy of Musical Arts, 5 April 1958; 2 ovs. comp. 1984
Zuzana Vojířová (5, Pauer, after J. Bor), Prague, National, 30 Dec 1958; rev. 1978
Červená Karkulka [Red Riding Hood] (fairy-tale for children, 1, Mellanová), Olomouc, Stibor, 22 Oct 1960
Manželské kontrapunkty [Matrimonial Counterpoints], 1960–61, 1965 (5 operatic grotesques, Pauer, after S. Grodzieńská), Ostrava, Nejedlý, 27 Feb 1962 (partial perf.), Liberec, Šaldy, 26 March 1966
Zdravý nemocný [The Hypochondriac], 1965–8 (comic op, 3, Pauer, after Molière: *Le malade imaginaire*), Prague, Tyl, 22 May 1970; rev., Prague, National, 13 Oct 1988
Labutí píseň [Swan-song] (monodrama, 1, Pauer, after A. P. Chekhov), Prague, Dvořák Hall, 23 March 1974

ČSHS

*

J. Brožovská: 'O současné opeře dvakrát' [Twice about a Contemporary Opera], *Kultura*, iii/3 (1959), 5

J. Hach: 'Dvě operní novinky' [Two New Operas], *Divadlo*, x (1959), 222–5

B. Karásek: 'Pauerova opera o Zuzaně Vojířové', *HRo*, xii (1959), 72–6

V. Pospíšil: 'Pohádkové operní aktovky J. Pauera' [Pauer's One-act Fairy-tale Operas], *HRo*, xiii (1960), 945

I. Jirko: 'Pauer a Ravel v divadle J. K. Tyla' [Pauer and Ravel at the Tyl Theatre], *HRo*, xiv (1961), 116

V. Pospíšil: 'Nad skladatelským dílem J. Pauera' [J. Pauer's Compositional Work], *HRo*, xvi (1963), 704–7, 751–5

B. Karásek: 'Orff a Pauer v Liberci' [Orff and Pauer in Liberec], *HRo*, xix (1966), 270

M. Černohorská: 'Pauer s Raráškem v Plzni' [Pauer with The Imp in Plzeň], *Divadelní noviny*, xii/8 (1969), 8

J. Bajer: 'Dobré herecké představení' [Well-acted Performance], *HRo*, xxiii (1970), 388–90

——: 'Ještě k Pauerově nové opeře' [Yet Another New Opera by Pauer], *HRo*, xxiv (1971), 17

V. Pospíšil: 'Jak inscenovat operu' [How to Stage an Opera], *HRo*, xxiv (1971), 205–6

——: 'Návrat Zuzany Vojířové' [The Return of *Zuzana Vojířová*], *HRo*, xxxiii (1980), 131–2

E. Herrmannová: 'Zuzana Vojířová po dvaceti letech' [*Zuzana Vojířová* After 20 Years], *Tvorba* (1981), no.13, p.18

V. Pospíšil: 'Zuzana Vojířová', *HRo*, xxxiv (1981), 360–61

L. Šíp: *Česká opera a její tvůrci* [Czech Opera and its Composers] (Prague, 1983), 299–309

J. Brožovská: 'První opera na Nové scéné' [The First Opera on the New Stage], *Scéna*, ix/7 (1984), 4

V. Pospíšil: 'Žvanivý slimejš v Laterně magice' [*Prattling Slug* at the Magic Lantern], *HRo*, xxxvii (1984), 376–7

HELENA HAVLÍKOVÁ

Paul Bunyan. Operetta in a prologue and two acts by BENJAMIN BRITTEN to a libretto by W. H. AUDEN; New York, Columbia University, Brander Mathews Hall, 5 May 1941 (revised version, Snape, Maltings, 4 June 1976; previously broadcast, BBC, 1 February 1976).

This work is about the emergence of American civilization from what Auden termed 'the struggle between Man and Nature'. The prologue describes 'the virgin forest that is America before man tames it'. Then Bunyan (spoken) is born, a gentle giant who, as Auden emphasized, 'has no magical powers', is not seen, and does not sing. In speech he emerges as the fount of wisdom, the great enabler. In Act 1 he organizes a group of lumberjacks to clear the forest and a quartet of Swedes to cook for the workers. A more bookish character, Johnny Inkslinger (tenor), is persuaded to run the community's finances. An early crisis over food is resolved by the arrival of a 'good cook', Slim (tenor). Inkslinger reports the community's various discontents to Bunyan, who promises that things will improve and wishes them a benign goodnight. In Act 2 Bunyan suggests that the men volunteer to work as farmers. He knocks out one of the more obstreperous workers, Hel Helson (baritone), who then becomes a willing helper. At a Christmas party, Inkslinger announces that Slim 'has been put in charge of a very large hotel in mid-Manhattan', while Helson goes to Washington 'to join the Administration'. Bunyan, his work complete, bids everyone a sad farewell.

The opera's subject lends itself perfectly to the mixture of lyricism and satire special to Auden's verse, and Britten's music is also suitably fresh, evoking Broadway and popular idioms yet able to expand convincingly into a more serious, lyrical vein. Although Britten had no desire to revive the work after its first performances – on the whole not well received – he recognized its worth near the end of his life. Excerpts were performed at the 1974 Aldeburgh Festival, and Britten made various revisions before its first complete British performance (a BBC broadcast in 1976). It was staged at the Aldeburgh

Festival later that year. A gramophone recording, conducted by Philip Brunelle, was issued in 1988.

ARNOLD WHITTALL

Paul et Virginie [*Paul et Virginie, ou Le temple de la vertu* ('Paul and Virginia, or The Temple of Virtue')]. *Opéra comique* in three acts by JEAN-FRANÇOIS LE SUEUR to a libretto by Alphonse du Congé Dubreuil after Bernardin de Saint-Pierre's novella; Paris, Opéra-Comique (Théâtre Feydeau), 13 January 1794.

Bernardin de Saint-Pierre's *Paul et Virginie*, published in 1788, was extraordinarily successful during the French Revolution, and composers and librettists immediately seized upon it as a fashionable subject. On the very evening of the opera's première at the Théâtre Feydeau, the rival Opéra-Comique company at the Théâtre Favart also staged a version of *Paul et Virginie*, a collaboration by Rodolphe Kreutzer and Edmond de Favières. These two *opéras comiques* mark the appearance of exoticism in French musical drama: in its artless pursuit of dramatic truth and local colour, it claimed to be entirely different from the conventional, decorative exoticism of the middle of the century, seen for instance in the works of Rameau. Later settings include a popular one by Victor Massé (1876).

The plot differs somewhat from that of Saint-Pierre's work. The idyll between Paul (tenor) and Virginie (soprano) unwinds beneath the gazes of Herminie (soprano), the mother of Virginie, and Saint-Albe (bass), Paul's father. In contrast to the novella, the opera has a happy ending: the Indian savages prevent Virginie from embarking for Europe and assassinate the captain of the ship who has come to take her back to France on the orders of the king.

Le Sueur's score is the only work in his dramatic output which, despite a certain tendency to dramatize effects (as in Paul's grand aria in the third act, 'Du bord escarpé de ce rivage'), really belongs in the tradition of the contemporary *opéra comique*, one to which Le Sueur's fiery and epic genius must have had some difficulty in bowing. The opening chorus of Indian savages praying to the rising sun is remarkable: constructed entirely on a basis of common chords, mostly in root position, it perfectly illustrates Grétry's remark in his *Mémoires*: 'Pure melody is for simple souls, the practice of dissonance for corrupt peoples'. This chorus, which certainly constitutes the best musical illustration we have of the literary theme of the noble savage, was unanimously praised by contemporaries, and at a later date Berlioz himself admired it. Despite a favourable reception, the music of *Paul et Virginie* was not given again during the 19th century.

JEAN MONGRÉDIEN

Pauline. Opera in four acts by FREDERICK HYMEN COWEN to a libretto by Henry Hersee after EDWARD BULWER-LYTTON's drama *The Lady of Lyons, or Love and Pride*; London, Lyceum Theatre, 22 November 1876.

Claude Melnotte (baritone), poor but honest, having been rebuffed by the proud beauty Pauline Deschapelles, 'The Lady of Lyons' (soprano), is tempted by his morally dubious friends Beausant (baritone) and Glavis (tenor), whom she had also rejected, into winning her hand under the pretence of being a nobleman. Having married Claude, Pauline falls in love with him and refuses to desert him when the truth is revealed. After further vicissitudes Claude enlists for military service overseas, where he distinguishes himself by his bravery.

His honour thus restored, he is forgiven by all concerned and the opera ends happily.

Pauline exemplifies Cowen's lightest stylistic vein, in which mild French chromaticisms support italianate melodic lines. It was the first British opera to be commissioned by Carl Rosa, and although only partially successful during its initial run it merits revival as an exquisite period piece.   NIGEL BURTON

Paulus, Stephen (Harrison) (*b* Summit, NJ, 24 Aug 1949). American composer. He studied composition with Paul Fetler and Dominick Argento at the University of Minnesota. From 1973 to 1984 he was one of the managing composers of the Minnesota Composers' Forum, which he co-founded to perform and support works by American composers. Paulus was awarded fellowships by the Guggenheim Foundation and the National Endowment for the Arts. In 1988 he received a Kennedy Center Friedheim prize for his Violin Concerto and became composer-in-residence with the Atlanta Symphony Orchestra.

Paulus has written four operas, three of them commissioned and first performed by the Opera Theatre of St Louis, whose stage director, Colin Graham, wrote two of the librettos. They are about ordinary people in small towns who are involved in intense, dramatic situations. *The Village Singer* is set in New England (1900), *The Postman Always Rings Twice* on the California coast (1934), and *The Woodlanders* in a hamlet in England (1870), where its inhabitants are, according to the librettist, 'as deep-rooted as the trees themselves'.

The Village Singer is based on a short story written in 1891 by the Vermont author Mary Wilkins Freeman. It melds humour and pathos in its story of an elderly church singer, involuntarily retired, who competes with her replacement by singing from her house next to the church. *The Postman Always Rings Twice*, drawn from the novel by James M. Cain, is a tragedy about two people who have little sense of good or evil and become aware of their true natures only when they are ultimately doomed. *The Postman* was the first American opera to be staged at the Edinburgh International Festival (September 1983); subsequent productions (Fort Worth Opera, Greater Miami Opera, Washington Opera and others) have omitted the original Black Comedy scene, or foiled murder attempt, in Act 1. Paulus's one-act opera *Harmoonia* (1991), to an original libretto by M. D. Browne, was written specifically for family audiences.

Paulus composes with a clear sense of musical characterization, dramatic intensity and lyric expressivity. His orchestration is skilful, varied and transparent, especially in *The Village Singer*, written for six woodwind, horn, two percussion instruments, harp, organ, piano and 11 strings. In this opera, the use of traditional hymns layered and juxtaposed with dissonance provides a whimsical, almost Ivesian, touch. While polytonal and polyrhythmic inflections often characterize Paulus's style, his use of harmonic tension and tonal ambiguity underpins the powerful dramatic situations within his operas.

The Village Singer (1, M. D. Browne, after M. W. Freeman), St Louis, Opera Theatre, 9 June 1979
The Postman Always Rings Twice (2, C. Graham, after J. M. Cain), St Louis, Opera Theatre, 17 June 1982
The Woodlanders (3, Graham, after T. Hardy), St Louis, Opera Theatre, 13 June 1985

Harmoonia (1, Browne), Muscatine, IA, Central Middle Auditorium, 23 Feb 1991

A. Porter: 'Musical Events', *New Yorker* (25 June 1979)
M. A. Feldman: 'Triple Header', *ON*, xlix/17 (1984–5), 24–6
P. Dienhart: 'Making Music', *University of Minnesota Update*, xii/2 (1985), 8
B. Cartland: 'Stephen Paulus and his "Postman"', *Opera Monthly*, i/10 (1989), 24–32
R. H. Kornick: *Recent American Opera: a Production Guide* (New York, 1991), 232–7   ELISE K. KIRK

Pauly [Pauly-Dresden; née Pollak], **Rose** (*b* Eperjes, 15 March 1894; *d* Kfar Shmaryahn, nr Tel-Aviv, 14 Dec 1975). Hungarian soprano. She studied in Vienna with Rosa Papier-Paumgartner, making her début during the 1917–18 season at Hamburg in a minor role in *Martha*. After singing at Gera and Karlsruhe, she went to Cologne, where she sang the title role in the German première of *Kát'a Kabanová* in 1922. She made her first appearance at the Vienna Staatsoper in 1923, singing Sieglinde, the Empress (*Frau ohne Schatten*) and Rachel (*La Juive*); in 1931 she created Agave in Wellesz's *Die Bakchantinnen*. Engaged at the Kroll Oper, Berlin (1927–31), she sang Leonore at the opening performance of *Fidelio* as well as Donna Anna, Senta, Carmen and Maria in Krenek's *Der Diktator*. At the Berlin Staatsoper she sang Marie (*Wozzeck*), Jenůfa and Electra. She appeared at Salzburg as the Dyer's Wife (1933) and as Electra (1934–7), the role of her débuts in 1938 at Covent Garden, where she also sang Leonore, and at the Metropolitan, where she later sang Venus and Ortrud. She made her final appearances in 1943 at Buenos Aires. A most versatile singer, with a rich, powerful voice, she excelled as Strauss's Electra, Salome and the Dyer's Wife, as well as Marie in *Wozzeck*, all roles where her intensity of characterization was of particular benefit.

GV (L. Riemens; J. P. Kenyon and R. Vegeto)
                    LEO RIEMENS/ELIZABETH FORBES

Paumgartner, Bernhard (*b* Vienna, 14 Nov 1887; *d* Salzburg, 27 July 1971). Austrian musicologist. He first studied law, and later musicology with Adler; his first professional appointment was as répétiteur at the Vienna Opera (1911–12). He was subsequently director of the Salzburg Mozarteum (1917–38, 1945–59), where he ran the conducting department and was professor of theory and history. He was closely connected with the Salzburg Festival from its first year (1920) and a major influence on its character; he became president in 1960. Paumgartner's *Mozart* (Berlin, 1927) was translated into many languages and substantially expanded in its sixth edition (1967). Many of his 140 published articles concern historical performing practice (a list of his writings by R. Angermüller is included in G. Croll, ed.: *Bernhard Paumgartner*, Salzburg and Munich, 1971). His adaptation of Mozart's *Idomeneo* was given at the 1956 Salzburg Festival, and his version of Cavalieri's *Rappresentatione di Anima, et di Corpo* was heard in a series of festival performances from 1968. His own compositions include the opera *Die Höhle von Salamanca* (libretto after Cervantes: *La cueva de Salamanca*; Dresden, 1923) and the comic opera *Rossini in Neapel* (libretto by Hans Adler; Zürich, 1935).

Pauvre matelot, Le ('The Poor Sailor'). *Complainte* in three acts, op.92, by DARIUS MILHAUD to a libretto by

JEAN COCTEAU; Paris, Opéra-Comique, 16 December 1927.

A Wife (soprano) has been without news of her husband, a Sailor (tenor), for several years. In spite of the efforts of her Father (bass) to persuade her to remarry, she persistently refuses. The Sailor, returning unexpectedly, goes first to a Neighbour (baritone) who tells him of his wife's virtuous behaviour. Hoping 'to see his happiness from the outside' the Sailor passes himself off to his wife as a friend of her husband, who, he tells her, is still a prisoner, destitute and in poor health. He confides that he himself has been more fortunate, has money, and would like to spend the night in her house. She agrees, then kills him in order to rescue her husband with his money. The curtain falls before she realizes her mistake.

Despite a disastrous first performance, *Le pauvre matelot* became Milhaud's most widely performed opera, its four singers, plain, modern costumes, lack of scene changes and comparative brevity (40 minutes) making it easy to produce. Its theme, a recurrent one in folklore and actuality, may also contribute to its appeal, as may its accessible musical language – predominantly lyrical and liberally spiced with the folk and popular elements that Milhaud always handled with individuality, and, in this case, with some irony. Milhaud's original scoring was for symphony orchestra, but he made an alternative version for 13 instruments at Hermann Scherchen's request when the latter wanted to programme *Le pauvre matelot* and Stravinsky's *Histoire du soldat* together. CHRISTOPHER PALMER

Pauwels, Jean-Englebert (*b* Brussels, 24, 26 or 29 Nov 1768; *d* Brussels, 3 or 4 June 1804). South Netherlands composer. He was a chorister at the royal chapel by the end of 1780; there he studied the violin with van Maldere and composition with Ignaz Vitzthumb. In 1788 he went to Paris and studied composition with Le Sueur. He played the violin in the Théâtre Feydeau orchestra, and in 1790 became orchestra director in the Strasbourg theatre. By 1791 or 1792 he was playing first violin in the Brussels Théâtre de la Monnaie; he became director of the orchestra (1794), and all his stage works received their first performances there. Pauwels's contemporaries evidently thought highly of both his instrumental music and his stage works. However, Fétis commented that, in spite of many strong sections and good musical organization, Pauwels's operas are hindered by their weak librettos.

all first performed at Brussels, Théâtre de la Monnaie

La maisonnette dans les bois (oc, 1), 3 Aug 1796
L'auteur malgré lui (oc, 1, Claparède), 2 Nov 1801
L'arrivée du héros (scène lyrique, A. Verteuil) (Brussels, c1803)
Léontine et Fonrose (oc, 4, Verteuil), 13 April 1804, ov. (Brussels, n.d.)

*

FétisB
A. Choron and F. Fayolle: *Dictionnaire historique des musiciens* (Paris, 1810–11)
E. Fétis: *Les musiciens belges*, ii (Brussels, 1849, 2/1854), 169–73
F. Faber: *Histoire du théâtre français en Belgique*, ii (Brussels, 1879), 194, 197; iv (1880), 148, 287, 335
E. Gregoir: *Les artistes-musiciens belges au XVIIIme et au XIXme siècle* (Brussels, 1885)
J. Isnardon: *Le Théâtre de la Monnaie* (Brussels, 1890), 101, 107, 109 PHILIPPE MERCIER

Pavarotti, Luciano (*b* Modena, 12 Oct 1935). Italian tenor. He studied in Modena with Pola and in Mantua with Campogalliani, making his début in 1961 at Reggio Emilia as Rodolfo and quickly making an impression for his eloquent lyrical singing. In 1963 he sang Edgardo (*Lucia*) in Amsterdam and made his Covent Garden début as Rodolfo, returning as Alfredo, Elvino, Tonio (*Fille du régiment*), Riccardo, Cavaradossi, Rodolfo (*Luisa Miller*), Radames and Nemorino (1990). In 1964 he sang Idamantes at Glyndebourne; in 1965 he made his American début at Miami, toured Australia with the Sutherland-Williams company, as Edgardo, and made his La Scala début as Rodolfo, returning for the Duke, Bellini's Tebaldo and Massenet's Des Grieux. He first sang at San Francisco in 1967 as Rodolfo; later roles there included Nemorino, Riccardo, Calaf and Enzo.

Pavarotti made his Metropolitan début in 1968, again as Rodolfo, later singing Manrico, Fernand (*La favorite*), Ernani, Idomeneus, Arturo (*I puritani*), Radames, Rodolfo (*Luisa Miller*, 1991) and the Italian Singer (*Der Rosenkavalier*). He has appeared in Vienna, Philadelphia, Chicago and Rome, where he sang Oronte (*I Lombardi*) in 1969. He sang Otello, a role that extended his dramatic powers, in a concert performance with the Chicago Symphony under Solti in 1991. He has recorded extensively, not only his stage roles but also Arnold (*Guillaume Tell*), Orombello (*Beatrice di Tenda*) and the title role in *L'amico Fritz*. His bright-toned, incisive voice is full and vibrant throughout its range, with penetrating high notes. In 1989 he directed *La favorite* at La Fenice.

During the 1980s and early 90s he achieved almost the status of a pop star through his frequent appearances at recitals in huge arenas and through television programmes devoted to his larger-than-life personality. His genial, eupeptic looks and generous figure, added to his natural gift of communication, enabled him to extend his fame well beyond the comparatively confined area of opera. The familiar white handkerchief held on an outstretched hand while the voice beguiled his enraptured audiences with yet another Neapolitan song exalted him into a being of popular acclaim; and his beautiful and impassioned singing of 'Nessun dorma' in association with the football World Cup of 1990 brought him fame and affection beyond that achieved by any other opera singer of the past. At the same time he pursued the more serious side of his career diligently, his voice losing little of its colour or vibrancy even when he was well past 50.

*

G. Gualerzi: 'Luciano Pavarotti', *Opera*, xxxii (1981), 118–24
L. Pavarotti: *My Own Story* (London, 1981)
M. Mayer: *Grandissimo Pavarotti* (Garden City, NY, 1986)
ALAN BLYTH, STANLEY SADIE

Pavesi, Stefano (*b* Casaletto Vaprio, nr Crema, 22 Jan 1779; *d* Crema, 28 July 1850). Italian composer. From 1795 to 1797 he studied with Piccinni in Naples. In 1797 he entered the Conservatorio di S Onofrio, and studied there until 1799 under Fenaroli. Expelled in that year of revolution for political reasons, he was deported to France, where he took part in the Italian campaign. He left the army at Crema and completed his musical studies under Gazzaniga, *maestro di cappella* of the cathedral there. In 1803 in Venice, thanks to the protection of Gazzaniga, he staged his opera *Un avvertimento ai gelosi*. Nearly 70 more operas, both *serie* and *buffe*, followed in the next 20 years. In 1818, on the death of Gazzaniga, he succeeded him at Crema and held the post until his death. From 1826 to 1830 he spent half of each year as music director of the Hofoper in Vienna, succeeding Salieri.

Among the many opera composers who flourished in Italy in the period following the last great masters of the 18th century and before the advent of Rossini, Pavesi stands out for his strikingly individual musical personality. He had an original and lively melodic invention, supported by a mastery of the orchestra and polished craftsmanship that were perhaps learnt from Gazzaniga, who had formed his own style from a complex variety of European sources. Pavesi's opera *Ser Marcantonio* (1810), similar in subject to Donizetti's *Don Pasquale*, had 54 successive performances at La Scala and was taken up by the principal opera houses of Italy. *La fiera* (1804, Florence) and *La festa della rosa* (1808, Venice) also enjoyed great success, as did his last opera, *Fenella* (1831, Venice). His output also included sacred works and six keyboard sonatas.

f – farsa

La pace (G. Bertati), Livorno, Avvalorati, carn. 1801
Un avvertimento ai gelosi (f, 1, G. Foppa), Venice, S Benedetto, 7 Aug 1803
L'amante anonimo (f, 1, Foppa), Venice, S Moisè, aut. 1803
I castelli in aria, ossia Gli amanti per accidenti (f, 1, Foppa), Verona, Filarmonico, aut. 1803
La forza dei simpatici, ossia Lo stratagemma per amore (f, 1, Foppa), Verona, Filarmonico, 26 Dec 1803
Andromaco (os, G. Artusi), Genoa, S Agostino, carn. 1804
La fiera (comic op. 2, G. Palomba), Florence, Pergola, 2 April 1804; as La fiera di Brindisi, Modena, Via Emilia, 26 Dec 1814
L'amore prodotto dall'odio (f, Foppa), Padua, Nuovo, 7 May 1804
L'accortezza materna (f, Foppa), Venice, S Moisè, 12 May 1804
La vendetta di Medea, 1804, unperf.
Trionfo d'Emilia (1, G. Rossi), Milan, Scala, 9 Feb 1805
Fingallo e Camala (os, L. Fidanza), Venice, Fenice, carn. 1805
Amare e non voler essere amante (f, Foppa), Venice, Fenice, 25 April 1805; as L'incognito, o l'abitatore del bosco, Milan, Scala, 27 Sept 1805
Il giuocatore (2), Rome, Valle, carn. 1806 [? = Le donne fuggitive]
Le donne fuggitive (2), Rome, Valle, carn. 1806
I Baccanali di Roma (os, L. Buonavoglia), Livorno, Carlo Lodovico, spr. 1806
Ines de Castro (A. Gasparini), Naples, S Carlo, 11 Oct 1806, collab. G. Farinelli and N. A. Zingarelli [based on Zingarelli work, 1798]
Amore vince l'inganno (Foppa), Venice, S Moisè, aut. 1806
La sorpresa, ossia Il deputato di grosso latino (f, Foppa), Venice, S Moisè, aut. 1806
I cherusci (os, Rossi), Venice, Fenice, carn. 1807; as Gli antichi cherusci, Milan, Re, sum. 1818
Sapersi scegliere un degno sposo, ossia Amor vero e amor interessato (f, Foppa), Venice, Fenice, April 1807
Aristodemo (os, 2, Rossi, after his Argene), Naples, S Carlo, 15 Aug 1807
Il maldicente, ovvero La bottega del caffè (comic op, 2, G. Gasparri, after C. Goldoni), ? Florence, Infuocati, aut. 1807
L'amor perfetto, ovvero Il servo padrone (comic op, C. Mazzolà), Bologna, Marsigli-Rossi, carn. 1808
La festa della rosa (2, Rossi), Venice, Fenice, 21 May 1808, I-Mr*
Ser Marcantonio (comic op, A. Anelli), Milan, Scala, 26 Sept 1810
Il trionfo delle belle, ovvero Corradino Cuor di Ferro (f, Rossi), Venice, S Moisè, 3 Feb 1809
Ippolita, regina delle amazzoni (os, 2, Rossi), Venice, Riccardi, sum. 1809
Elisabetta regina d'Inghilterra (os, 2, G. Schmidt), Turin, Regio, 26 Dec 1809
Arminia (os, M. Landi [pseud. of Anelli]), Milan, Scala, 3 Feb 1810
I gauri (Rossi), Venice, Fenice, carn. 1810
Odoardo e Cristina (os, Schmidt), Naples, S Carlo, 1 Dec 1810
L'alloggio militare, Naples, Fondo, spr. 1811
La giardiniera abruzzese, ovvero Il signorino e l'ajo (comic op, 2), Naples, Fondo, spr. 1811
Il monastero (comic op), Naples, Nuovo, spr. 1811
Il trionfo dell'amore, ovvero Irene e Filandro (2), Naples, Nuovo, spr. 1811
Nitteti (3, after P. Metastasio), Turin, Regio, 26 Dec 1811

Tancredi (os, L. Romanelli, after T. Tasso), Milan, Scala, 18 Jan 1812
Amore e generosità (Foppa), Venice, S Moisè, 22 Sept 1812
Aspasia e Cleomene, Florence, Pergola, Oct 1812
L'Ostregaro (f, 1), Venice, S Moisè, aut. 1812
Teodoro (os, Rossi), Venice, Fenice, 26 Dec 1812
Una giornata pericolosa (f, L. Prividali), Venice, S Moisè, 20 Feb 1813
Agatina, ovvero La virtù premiata (comic op, ? F. Romani), Milan, Scala, 10 April 1814
Celanira (os, 3, Rossi), Venice, S Benedetto, 27 May 1815
La villanella fortunata (?Bertati), Urbino, Pascolini, carn. 1816
Le Danaide romane (os, 2, A. Sografi), Venice, Fenice, carn. 1816
La gioventù di Cesare (Romani), Milan, Scala, 7 April 1817
I pitocchi fortunati (comic op, Foppa), Venice, S Benedetto, 11 Feb 1819
Gli esiliati da Firenze, Paris, Italien, spr. 1819
Don Gusmano (comic op), Venice, S Benedetto, 1 June 1819
Il gran naso (comic op), Naples, Nuovo, carn. 1820
Eugenia degli Astolfi (A. L. Tottola), Naples, Nuovo, aut. 1820
Arminio, ovvero L'eroe germano (?Tottola, after G. Kreglianovich [pseud. D. Tindario]), Venice, Fenice, Jan 1821
Antigona e Lauso (Romanelli), Milan, Scala, 26 Jan 1822
Sandrina, Trieste, Grande, carn. 1822
Anco Marzio (Schmidt), Naples, S Carlo, spr. 1822
Ines di Almeida (2, Tottola), Naples, S Carlo, aut. 1822
I cavalieri del nodo (1, Schmidt), Naples, S Carlo, 12 Jan 1823
Egilda di Provenza (Romani), Venice, Fenice, 26 Dec 1823
Ardano e Dartula (P. Pola), Naples, S Carlo, 5 March 1825
Il solitario ed Elodia (2, Tottola), Naples, S Carlo, 19 April 1826
Gli Arabi nelle Gallie (Romanelli), Naples, S Carlo, 4 Oct 1827
La donna bianca di Avenello (3, Rossi), Milan, Canobbiana, 13 Nov 1830
Fenella, (3, Rossi, after E. Scribe), Venice, Fenice, 5 Feb 1831, Mr*
La testa riscaldata, unperf.

ES (M. Morini); *FlorimoN*
AMZ, xxii (1820), cols. 446–7
F. Sanseverino: *Notizie intorno alla vita e alle opere del Maestro S. Pavesi* (Milan, 1851)   GIOVANNI CARLI BALLOLA

Pavilion Opera. British opera company. It was founded in 1981 by Freddie Stockdale to perform *Così fan tutte* in a pavilion in the grounds of his country house in Lincolnshire. Over the following decade the company increased its activity, giving some 125 performances each year in the great halls of castles and palaces like Blenheim and Chatsworth and in clubs and embassies. It has performed in Algiers, Moscow, Karachi, the USA, Tokyo, Hong Kong, Australia and France, with a repertory of standard classics (*Don Giovanni*, *Don Pasquale*, *Lucia di Lammermoor*, *La traviata*, *Die Fledermaus*) performed in the round with piano accompaniment.   CHARLES PITT

Pavlovsk. Resort town in Russia, 25 km south of St Petersburg. A palace was built there in 1777–8 by the Empress Catherine the Great for her estranged son Paul (later tsar). The railway station boasts a large theatre-pavilion, which was a popular site for outdoor concerts and theatrical presentations in the 19th century and the early 20th. Two comic operas by Bortnyansky were presented at the palace during the composer's period of personal service to the crown prince: *La fête du seigneur*, a 'comédie mêlée d'aires et des balets' to a libretto adapted from Favart's *Annette et Lubin*, performed in the summer of 1786 on the prince's name-day; and *Le fils-rival, ou La moderne Stratonice*, a three-act *opéra comique* to a libretto after Boccaccio via Sedaine by Paul's secretary and tutor François-Hermann Lafermière (11/22 October 1787). Much later, on 19 June/2 July 1912, a three-act 'medieval legend' entitled *Beatrisa* by Alexey Avgustovich Davïdov (1867–1923), to a libretto by the ballet critic Valerian Yakovlevich

Svetlov (né Ivchenko) after Maeterlinck's *Soeur Beatrice*, was performed at the railway station to benefit orphans of railway workers.   RICHARD TARUSKIN

Pavlovskaya [née Berman], **Emiliya Karlovna** (*b* St Petersburg, 28 July/9 Aug 1853; *d* Moscow, 23 March 1935). Russian soprano. She studied at the St Petersburg Conservatory, graduating in 1873. In 1873–4 she sang in western Europe, principally in Italy, and from 1876 in theatres in Kiev, Odessa, Tbilisi and Kharkiv. From 1876 until her retirement she alternated between the Bol'shoy in Moscow and the Mariinsky, creating a Tchaikovsky role at each: Mariya (*Mazepa*, 1884) and the title role in *The Enchantress* (1887) respectively. From 1895 she taught at the Bol'shoy; Dmitry Smirnov was one of her pupils.   BORIS SEMEONOFF

Payne, Patricia (*b* Dunedin, 8 March 1942). New Zealand mezzo-soprano or contralto. In 1971 she sang Joacim in Handel's oratorio *Susannah* for the Handel Opera Society at Sadler's Wells. She made her Covent Garden début in 1974 as Schwertleite (*Die Walküre*) and during the next decade sang Erda, Filippyevna, Mrs Sedley, Grandmother Buryjovka, Geneviève, Mother Goose, Marcellina and Mother Jeanne (*Dialogues des Carmélites*), as well as her most successful role, Ulrica. She has sung Ulrica at San Francisco, the Metropolitan, Chicago, Buenos Aires, La Scala, Bonn and for the WNO, with which her roles, between 1976 and 1986, also included Florence Pike (*Albert Herring*), Azucena, the Nurse (*Die Frau ohne Schatten*), Fricka and Waltraute (*Götterdämmerung*). At Bayreuth (1977) she sang Schwertleite and the First Norn. She has appeared at Geneva, Verona and Orange as La Cieca; in Florence, Barcelona and Turin; and with the ENO (most recently as Herodias, 1991), Opera North and Scottish Opera. Her rich, mellow-toned voice and the dramatic intensity of her singing have been specially valuable in the Verdi and Wagner roles of her repertory.   ELIZABETH FORBES

Pazovsky, Ary Moiseyevich (*b* Perm', 21 Jan/2 Feb 1887; *d* Moscow, 6 Jan 1953). Russian conductor. After studying at the St Petersburg Conservatory he began his career as a violinist. He turned to conducting in 1905, first with provincial opera companies, then with Sergey Zimin's opera company in Moscow (1908–10), and successively at Kharkiv, Odessa and Kiev until 1916. He became musical director of the Petrograd People's Opera (1916–18), conducted at the Bol'shoy Theatre (1923–4, 1925–8), and from 1926 to 1936 was musical director of the opera houses at Baku, Sverdlovsk, Kharkiv and Kiev. He was artistic director at the Kirov Theatre, Leningrad (1936–43), when he conducted the premières of Oles' Chishko's *Bronenosets 'Potyomkin'* ('The Battleship Potyomkin') in 1937 and also Marian Koval''s *Yemel'yan Pugachyov* (1942, Perm'), as well as memorable productions of operas by Bizet, Glinka, Rimsky-Korsakov and Tchaikovsky. In 1943 he took a similar post at the Bol'shoy, but became seriously ill and was forced to give up conducting in 1948. Pazovsky was an outstanding conductor whose attention to detail and painstaking rehearsals were the key to his success, and whose greatest performances were characterized by artistic restraint, a careful balance between music and production and a deeply personal interpretation based on precise concern for the score. His *Zapiski dirizhyora* ('Notes of a Conductor'; Moscow, 1966) includes a

detailed study of opera conducting. He was made People's Artist of the USSR in 1940.   I. M. YAMPOL'SKY

Peacock, Lucy (*b* Jacksonville, FL, 21 June 1947). American soprano. She studied at Northwestern University and in Berlin, where in 1969 she made her début as the Milliner (*Rosenkavalier*) with the Deutsche Oper. During her 20-year engagement with the company, she has also appeared in Vienna, Munich, Hamburg, Geneva and Paris and at La Scala. In 1985 she sang Freia, Gerhilde and Wellgunde at Bayreuth. Her repertory includes Cavalli's Callisto, Pamina, Countess Almaviva, Vitellia, Rosina, Lady Harriet (*Martha*), Micaëla, Nedda and Musetta. A lyric soprano with a secure coloratura technique, she is a fine actress and made a good Lucy in Britten's version of *The Beggar's Opera*.   ELIZABETH FORBES

Pearl Tree, The. 'Opera phantasy' in two acts by EDGAR BAINTON to a libretto by Robert Trevelyan; Sydney, Conservatorium Opera School, 20 May 1944.

The opera is based on a Hindu legend in which the God Krishna (tenor), then a young village herdsboy, reveals his magic power to make a pearl, borrowed from his mother Yashoda (contralto), grow into a magnificent tree. Krishna's love for the village girl Rahda (soprano), who had refused to lend him a pearl and who had scorned both Krishna and the story of his exploit, is fulfilled at the end of the opera.

Although composed in England in 1927 the opera was not performed until 1944, when it was staged by the Sydney Conservatorium Opera School conducted by the composer. In his glowing review (*Sydney Morning Herald*, 22 May 1944), Neville Cardus was particularly struck by the beauty of the orchestration into which vocal melody and recitative are superbly fused. Its harmonic style is not unlike that of Delius's music, although the vocal line tends to be less chromatic. There are also moments of exotic modality appropriate to the libretto subject.   DAVID TUNLEY

Pears, Sir Peter (**Neville Luard**) (*b* Farnham, 22 June 1910; *d* Aldeburgh, 3 April 1986). English tenor. He studied with Elena Gerhardt and Dawson Freer in London, and in the USA, where he had accompanied Britten in 1939. Returning to London in 1942 he made his début at the Strand Theatre as Hoffmann. In 1943 he joined Sadler's Wells, singing Almaviva, Rodolfo, the Duke, Tamino, Ferrando and Vašek, and creating the title role of *Peter Grimes* (1945). Co-founder of the English Opera Group, he created the Male Chorus in *The Rape of Lucretia* (1946) and the title role of *Albert Herring* (1947) for them at Glyndebourne. He created Captain Vere in *Billy Budd* (1951) and Essex in *Gloriana* (1953) at Covent Garden; Quint in *The Turn of the Screw* (1954) at Venice; Flute in *A Midsummer Night's Dream* (1960), the Madwoman in *Curlew River* (1964), Nebuchadnezzar in *The Burning Fiery Furnace* (1966), the Tempter in *The Prodigal Son* (1968) and Aschenbach in *Death in Venice* (1973), all at Aldeburgh; and Sir Philip Wingrave in *Owen Wingrave* (1971, BBC television). At Covent Garden he created Pandarus in *Troilus and Cressida* (1954), and sang Tamino, Vašek and David (*Die Meistersinger*). With the English Opera Group he created Boaz in Berkeley's *Ruth* (1956) and sang Macheath (in Britten's version of *The Beggar's Opera*), Satyavān (*Sāvitri*) and Idomeneus. In 1974 he sang Aschenbach at the Metropolitan. He recorded all his Britten roles, which were composed with his voice – clear, reedy, flexible and of great expressive power – in mind. Made a CBE in 1957, he was knighted in 1978.

For illustration *see* ALBERT HERRING; BRITTEN, BENJAMIN; DANCE, fig.5; LONDON, fig.11; and TURN OF THE SCREW, THE.

*
H. Keller: 'Peter Pears', *Opera*, ii (1950–51), 287–92
A. Blyth: 'Peter Pears Talks', *The Gramophone*, xlvi (1968–9), 331–2
T. Heinitz: 'The Art of Peter Pears', *Records and Recording*, xvi/9 (1972–3), 16–22 [with discography by D. McLachlan]
J. B. Steane: *The Grand Tradition* (London, 1974), 506ff
'Sir Peter Pears 1910–1986: Three Tributes', *Opera*, xxxvii (1986), 624–30   ALAN BLYTH

Pease, James (*b* Indianapolis, IN, 9 Jan 1916; *d* New York, 26 April 1967). American bass-baritone. He studied at the Curtis Institute, making his début with the Philadelphia Opera Company as Méphistophélès in Gounod's *Faust* (1941). He sang with the New York City Opera, 1946–53, where his repertory included Escamillo, Wozzeck, Ochs, Hans Sachs and Mozart's Figaro. At the Berkshire Music Festival, between 1946 and 1949, he sang in the American premières of *Peter Grimes* (Captain Balstrode) and *Albert Herring* (Mr Gedge). He was engaged by the Hamburg Staatsoper (1953–8), making his début there as Orestes, and later singing Falstaff, Mandryka, Count Almaviva, Briano (*Aroldo*), Wotan, and Socrates in the première of Krenek's *Pallas Athene weint* (1955). He sang Don Giovanni at Glyndebourne in 1954, and made his Covent Garden début as Wotan the following year, continuing to sing there until 1961. His roles included Boris, which he sang at Graz in 1966. Pease's performances, if not profound, were pleasing and well conceived. Although his voice was light by Wagnerian standards, it was well focussed and he made a good Wotan and Hans Sachs; perhaps his finest role was Captain Balstrode.   CHARLES JAHANT, ELIZABETH FORBES

Pêcheurs, Les ('The Fishermen'). *Opéra comique* in one act by FRANÇOIS-JOSEPH GOSSEC to a libretto by A. N. Piédefer, Marquis de La Salle d'Offémont; Paris, Comédie-Italienne (Hôtel de Bourgogne), 23 April 1766 (revised 7 June 1766).

A fisherman, Jacques (bass), would like to see his daughter Suzette (soprano) married to the young fisherman Bernard (tenor), but his wife Simone (contralto) is determined that Suzette should marry the 60-year-old Bailli (tenor). Simone mistrusts Bernard, a newcomer to the village and of unknown origin. Suzette hates Bailli, however, and asks her father to support her in her love for Bernard. Jacques promises to help if she can resolve the mystery of Bernard's identity. The wicked Bailli announces his marriage plans, disclosing his decrepitude in a fit of coughing. Suzette is finally relieved of his attentions by Bernard. After Bailli has left, issuing threats, Bernard reveals that he had to flee from the neighbouring village after a brawl. Ambroise (bass), Jacques' brother-in-law, recognizes Bernard: he reveals that Bernard's real name is Lubin and that he has inherited a farm. Simone is nevertheless unwilling to let Suzette marry Bernard, but when Bailli threatens to ruin the family if his wishes are not met she agrees to Suzette's marriage with Bernard.

Gossec scored the opera for flutes, oboes, bassoons, horns and strings, taking care to achieve the greatest possible instrumental variety by notating the wind parts separately, in order to facilitate free imitation between groups of instruments. An agreeable flow is enlivened by devices of ornamentation and purposeful dynamics. Gossec's tuneful, well-structured melodies closely follow the rhythm of the text, but he portrayed the characters' emotions only to a limited extent, rendering the most dramatic scenes as dialogues. Perhaps the best characterization is in Bailli's coughing *ariette*; the quartet near the end, however, barely serves to unmask his wickedness. According to Grimm, the opera was first performed in April 1766, but an unfavourable response led Gossec to revise it substantially. All commentators have observed that the weak plot unfolds rather slowly; but Grimm nevertheless praised Gossec for his 'many *airs* which could be compared with the best of this genre in France'. *Les pêcheurs* was given in Paris every year up to 1790 and in Brussels as late as 1815. It marked Gossec's greatest success as an opera composer.

MICHAEL FEND

Pêcheurs de perles, Les ('The Pearl Fishers'). *Opéra* in three acts by GEORGES BIZET to a libretto by EUGÈNE CORMON and MICHEL CARRÉ; Paris, Théâtre Lyrique, 30 September 1863.

Zurga *head fisherman*		baritone
Nadir *fisherman*		tenor
Leïla *priestess of Brahma*		soprano
Nourabad *high priest of Brahma*		bass

Fishermen, Indians, Brahmins

Setting Ceylon in ancient times

Les pêcheurs de perles, which Bizet composed very rapidly in the summer of 1863 when he was 24, was his second opera to be staged but probably the sixth he had composed. It was commissioned by Carvalho for the Théâtre Lyrique, and the contract was signed in early April 1863. The librettists, Cormon and Carré, had recently written a somewhat similar libretto, *Les pêcheurs de Catane*, for an opera by Maillart staged in 1860. The original setting for the new libretto was Mexico, later changed to Ceylon, and the original title was *Leïla*. The central dilemma of Act 2, a priestess torn between love and her sacred vows, was based, as was observed from the beginning, on Spontini's *La vestale*, Bellini's *Norma* and other operas. The problem of how to resolve the drama remained a point of contention right up to the 1863 performances and has continued to cause misunderstanding through the variants found in corrupt posthumous scores.

Bizet wrote the music as an *opéra comique* with spoken dialogues, which were replaced by recitative shortly before the work opened. The original date planned for the opening, 15 September, was postponed for two weeks owing to the soprano's illness. Leïla was sung by Léontine de Maësen, Nadir by François Morini, and Zurga by Jean-Vital Ismaël. This was not a strong cast, but the work was enthusiastically received by the audience and played 18 times during the autumn of 1863. The opera was nonetheless poorly treated by the press, who had little ear for Bizet's talent and no patience with his personal appearance for a curtain call. Berlioz, writing his last feuilleton for the *Journal des débats*, was almost the only critic to study the work seriously and treat Bizet with respect.

The opera was not played again in Bizet's lifetime. In 1886–9, following the belated success of *Carmen*, it was played in a dozen cities outside France, and there was a performance in Paris in Italian in 1889. This led to its revival by the Opéra-Comique in 1893 with Carvalho again directing, 30 years after the première. Its success has grown steadily to the point where it has become almost a repertory work in the last 30 years, an interest stimulated by the appearance of an authentic vocal score in 1975 to replace the many corrupt editions issued by Choudens since 1886. Since the autograph manuscript has disappeared, some passages of the 1863 version survive in vocal score only.

Interpreters have included Calvé, Tetrazzini and Eda-Pierre in the role of Leïla, and Caruso, Tagliavini, Kraus and Gedda in the role of Nadir. At Covent Garden in 1887 the baritone role of Zurga was sung by Lhérie, the original Don José in *Carmen*.

Poster by Prudent Leray for Bizet's 'Les pêcheurs de perles' printed for Choudens at the time of the original production at the Théâtre Lyrique, Paris, in 1863

ACT 1 *A wild seashore on the island of Ceylon* The curtain rises after a short, serene prelude. Some fishermen are working on their nets; others are drinking, dancing or playing Hindu instruments. The ruins of an old Hindu temple are seen. The opening chorus ('Sur la grève en feu'), with its beautiful middle section for men's voices alone, is one of the most striking numbers in the opera, fully characteristic of Bizet's lyrical style. Zurga reminds the fishermen that they have to choose a leader. Their immediate choice is Zurga himself, whom they beg to become their king. Next arrives Nadir, a young fisherman who has been wandering in the forest. Zurga welcomes his former friend, and a resumption of the dancing closes the scene.

Left alone, Zurga and Nadir recall their days together. 'Have you been faithful to your vow?', Zurga asks. Their duet ('Au fond du temple saint') recalls the beautiful girl they both once set eyes on in Candy; both were simultaneously enslaved by her beauty, and both then swore to renounce her and to remain friends for ever. This duet is the best-known piece in the opera. It is a noble melody accompanied with bald root-position triads and scored, on its first appearance, for flute and harp, always a symbol of sanctity in French opera of that time. The correct version of the duet ends with a section in 3/4 ('Amitié sainte'), replaced in all the corrupt versions by a reprise of the main melody for 'Oui, c'est elle, c'est la déesse!'.

A boat arrives carrying a veiled woman. She has been chosen to pray for the fishermen on their annual pearl-fishing expedition and to ward off evil spirits. This is Leïla, who is accompanied by Nourabad, the high priest of Brahma. The music which accompanies her entrance has already been heard as the prelude. 'C'est elle!', the chorus murmur, while the orchestra tells us what we have already guessed: 'C'est la déesse'. Neither Nadir nor Zurga is yet aware of this. The chorus offer her flowers ('Sois la bienvenue'), and from Zurga, who does not recognize her, she takes an oath of obedience. Nadir however does recognize her and cries out; she too recognizes Nadir. But in response to Zurga's questioning she reaffirms her vows, and a solemn hymn to Brahma rings out.

Leïla and Nourabad enter the temple; Zurga and the chorus go off. Nadir, alone, confesses that he has long dreamt of Leïla and has followed her here (*romance*, 'Je crois entendre encore'). He falls asleep. To the distant sound of fishermen's voices Nourabad leads Leïla in. Her incantation to Siva, full of *fioriture*, is interrupted by Nadir's voice. She briefly draws aside her veil and the hymn is transformed into a declaration of love.

ACT 2 *The ruins of an Indian temple at night* An off-stage chorus, with a piquant accompaniment for two piccolos, greets the night. Nourabad leaves Leïla to watch out the night. She tells him in a dramatic recitative how she once saved a stranger's life, protecting him from capture. He gave her a necklace and begged her to wear it for ever. Nourabad goes out and the offstage chorus briefly concludes the scene.

Leïla sings a cavatina ('Comme autrefois dans la nuit sombre'), full of joy that her admirer is near. A 'guzla' is heard (solo oboe recalling Nadir's *romance*) and then Nadir's voice approaching. The lovers are reunited in a breathless Allegro leading to a broad duet ('Ton coeur n'a pas compris le mien') in which Bizet's melodic gift is in full flood. In a recitative Nadir promises to return the next night, and slips away. A shot is heard. Nourabad summons the guards and rushes off in pursuit of the intruder. The people, though agitated, sing a magnificent brief chorus of distress and prayer. Nadir is led in. In a ferocious finale he and Leïla are about to be put to death by the angry crowd when Zurga intervenes. With his new authority as their king he orders their lives to be spared and whispers to them to leave at once. But Nourabad tears aside Leïla's veil, forcing Zurga to recognize her. His mercy now turns to rage, and he condemns them both to death. As they are led away, both captors and captives invoke Brahma's aid.

ACT 3.i *Zurga's tent* Zurga, alone, sings tenderly of his agony, having ordered his friend to his death ('O Nadir, tendre ami de mon jeune âge'). Leïla appears, under guard. She has begged to see him. At first they sing together, both deploring their own distress. She then begs for Nadir's life, saying he is innocent. But when Zurga realizes that she loves Nadir, his jealousy is inflamed against them both. Nourabad and the fishermen come to lead away their victims. Leïla hands her necklace to a young fisherman and asks him to take it to her mother. Zurga snatches the necklace as the curtain falls.

3.ii A pyre has been erected beneath a statue of Brahma. The chorus are singing, dancing and drinking in bloodthirsty anticipation, while Nadir prays that he may save Leïla. She is led in by Nourabad and some fakirs. She and Nadir sing a hymn-like duet in the face of death. As the dawn finally arrives Nourabad and the men raise their daggers and are about to strike when Zurga intervenes and stops them. Flames from their burning camp have deceived them that it was already dawn. All rush off to save the camp while Zurga frees the captives. He tells them that he set the camp on fire and shows Leïla the necklace. They all embrace. Zurga urges them to escape while he watches Nourabad and the Indians fleeing from the flames.

* * *

Various alternative endings for the opera were current before the original was restored. One version had Zurga dying in a grand conflagration, another had him stabbed in the back by an Indian as he calls 'Je t'aimais' after the departing Leïla; the lovers appear on a distant rock singing the melody of 'Oui, c'est elle, c'est la déesse'. The melody has entered the consciousness of millions, yet it would be unfair to credit the opera's success to that melody alone. It is, in any case, deliberately exotic in its orchestration and harmony. Bizet was still happy to rely on the strength of his melodic gift, even though there is abundant evidence in this opera of his growing subtlety with harmonic and tonal colouring. The drama is inevitably weakened by its dependence on two separate vows pledged many years before, and the potential for conflict between jealousy and brotherly feeling is not given full scope, partly because space had to be found for the conventional apparatus of priests, dancing and incantation. The action strains credulity at times. Yet the three principal roles are some of the best in French opera of its time, and the opera's success is now assured.

HUGH MACDONALD

Pechner, Gerhard (*b* Berlin, 15 April 1903; *d* New York, 21 Oct 1969). German baritone. He sang at the Charlottenburg opera house, Berlin, from 1924, notably as Don Pasquale, with Maria Ivogün and Karl Erb. He was obliged to leave Germany in 1933 and sang first at the German Opera, Prague, and then in Buenos Aires. He made his American début at San Francisco in 1940 as Mozart's Bartolo and the following year joined the Metropolitan, appearing as Alberich, Beckmesser, Klingsor and Melitone. He taught in New York after his retirement in 1966. DAVID CUMMINGS

Pécour [Pécourt], **Louis Guillaume** (*b* Paris, 10 Aug 1653; *d* Paris, 22 April 1729). French dancer and choreographer. He first appeared in 1674 at St Germain-en-Laye in Lully's *Cadmus et Hermione* and at the Paris Opéra in *Alceste*. He danced leading roles in the premières of Lully's *Thésée* (1675), *Atys* (1676), *Isis* (1677), *Bellérophon* (1679), *Proserpine* (1680), *Persée* (1682), *Amadis* (1684), *Roland* (1685), *Armide* (1686) and the ballet *Le triomphe de l'Amour* (1681). In 1687

he succeeded his teacher Pierre Beauchamps as balletmaster at the Opéra, making his choreographic début in Lully and Collasse's *Achille et Polyxène* (1687). He choreographed revivals of Lully's ballets as well as dances for operas by Destouches and Philidor, and Louis XIV appointed him dancing-master to the Duchess of Burgundy. Choreography and music for his elegant *pas de deux* were notated in a number of dancing-manuals (notably the *Recüeils de dances* published in Paris, 1700–12, and Pierre Rameau's *Abregé de la nouvelle méthode*, Paris, 1725), which are important sources for 18th-century social and theatrical dance practices.

A. Witherell: *Louis Pécour's 1700 Recüeil de dances* (Ann Arbor, 1983) MAUREEN NEEDHAM COSTONIS

Pécs. Town in Hungary. A permanent theatre, built in 1839 and demolished in 1886, was used by touring opera companies, including A. Bogyó's company which performed 12 operas (mainly by Verdi, Erkel, Donizetti and Rossini) in 1881–2. The present theatre, Pécs National Theatre, was opened in 1895 (cap. 630), and staged opera performances with soloists generally from Budapest. In 1935–6, *Rigoletto*, *La traviata*, *Faust* (with Dezső Ernster, who was born in Pécs) and *La bohème* were performed. A permanent opera company was founded in 1959; its conductors included Elemér Paulusz, Tamás Breitner and János Sándor. In the same theatre Imre Eck founded the Ballet Sopianae in 1960, which has had success at home and abroad. The opera company gives between 50 and 60 performances annually from September until June; its varied repertory has included Menotti's *The Medium* (1963), Shostakovich's *Lady Macbeth* (1964), Janáček's *Jenůfa* (1966), Handel's *Giulio Cesare* (1966) and Hindemith's *The Long Christmas Dinner* (1977).

E. Kardos: *A pécsi német sajtó és színészet története* [History of the German Press and Stage-playing in Pécs] (Pécs, 1932)
T. Nádor: *A Pécsi Nemzeti Színház operatársulatának 25 éve* [25 Years of the Opera Company of Pécs National Theatre] (Pécs, 1984)
P. Szkladányi: 'Színházi zene Pécsett a 19. század első felében' [Music Theatre in Pécs in the First Half of the 19th Century], *Baranyai levéltári füzetek*, lxx (Pécs, 1985), 391–412
DEZSŐ LEGÁNY

Pederzini, Gianna (*b* Vo di Avio, Trento, 10 Feb 1900; *d* Rome, 12 March 1988). Italian mezzo-soprano. She studied in Naples with De Lucia, making her début in 1923 at Messina as La Cieca (*La Gioconda*) and then singing Preziosilla (1924). She first sang in Rome in 1928, in Mascagni's *Zanetto*, and was engaged at La Scala from 1930 (as Nancy in *Martha*) to 1943. She appeared at Covent Garden (1931) and the Paris Opéra (1935). Her early repertory included many travesty parts: Cherubino, Isolier, Urbain, Maffio Orsini, Hänsel and Octavian, as well as Rossini roles such as Rosina, Cenerentola and Isabella. Later she sang heavier roles, among them Santuzza, Mignon, Charlotte, Adalgisa, Delilah, Bloch's Lady Macbeth, Mistress Quickly and the Old Prioress, which she created in *Dialogues des Carmélites* at La Scala (1957). Her last appearance was in Menotti's *The Medium* (1960, Rome). Her voice was rich and warm-toned. ELIZABETH FORBES

Pederzuoli [Pederzoli, Pedezzuoli], **Giovanni Battista** (*d* in or after 1692). Italian composer partly resident in Austria. He was a *maestro di cappella* at Bergamo in

1664–5. In 1677 he became organist at the court of the Dowager Empress Eleanora in Vienna and in 1682 succeeded Antonio Draghi as her Kapellmeister, a position he retained until her death in 1686. During his service in Vienna, music at the Habsburg court was almost entirely dominated by Draghi, but Pederzuoli composed more sacred dramatic works than any other late 17th-century Habsburg musician except Draghi. His operas and oratorios, like Draghi's, are in the rather conservative middle Baroque style favoured by the Emperor Leopold I. His sinfonias show both French and Venetian influence. In his arias he occasionally called for some unusual instrumental colour, but in general he scored for voice and continuo only. His ensemble numbers are usually simpler than Draghi's, as are his recitatives, which contain no florid arioso. His melodies include occasional expressive chromatic writing reminiscent of the early 17th century. Among Pederzuoli's other works are occasional dramatic pieces and cantatas. Minato was his chief librettist.

MSS in A-Wn unless otherwise stated

I presagi della sorte (festa musicale), Vienna, 6 Jan 1677, lost
Vienna festeggiante (serenata), Vienna, 1679
Il giudice di villa (intermedio), Vienna, 1681, perf. with A. Scarlatti: Gli equivoci nel sembiante
Il monte Chimera (trattenimento musicale, N. Minato), Vienna, Augarten, 9 July 1682
Le fonti della Boezia, 1682 (festa musicale, Minato), unperf., lost
Didone costante, Vienna, Hofburg, carn. 1685, lost
Musica, pittura e poesia (trattenimento musicale, Minato), Vienna, Bellaria, 24 July 1685

*

A. von Weilen: *Zur Wiener Theatergeschichte* (Vienna, 1901)
E. Wellesz: 'Die Opern und Oratorien in Wien von 1660–1708', *SMw*, vi (1919), 5–138
P. Nettl: 'Zur Geschichte der kaiserlichen Hofmusikkapelle von 1636–1680', *SMw*, xix (1932), 33–40
A. Bauer: *Opern und Operetten in Wien* (Vienna, 1955)
F. Hadamowsky: 'Barocktheater am Wiener Kaiserhof', *Jb der Gesellschaft für Wiener Theaterforschung 1951–52* (1955), 7–117
O. E. Deutsch: 'Das Repertoire der höfischen Oper, der Hof- und der Staatsoper in Wien: chronologischer Teil', *ÖMz*, xxiv (1969), 369–421
LAWRENCE E. BENNETT

Pedrazzi, Francesco (*b* Bologna, *c*1802; *d* after 1850). Italian tenor. He studied with Giuseppe Tadolini and made his début in 1828 at Pisa. After singing in Parma, in 1832 he sang Tebaldo in Bellini's *I Capuleti e i Montecchi* at Bologna. He was then engaged at La Scala, where he created Gennaro in *Lucrezia Borgia* (1833) and Viscardo in Mercadante's *Il giuramento* (1837). He also sang Justinian in *Belisario* (1836). At S Carlo he sang Leicester in the first performance of Donizetti's *Maria Stuarda* (1834), given under the title of *Buondelmonte* because of censorship problems. He retired in 1850.
ELIZABETH FORBES

Pedrell, Carlos (*b* Minas, 16 Oct 1878; *d* Montrouge, nr Paris, 3 March 1941). Uruguayan composer of Spanish origin, nephew of Felipe Pedrell. He studied with his uncle in Madrid, then in Barcelona (1898–1900), and at the Schola Cantorum, Paris, under d'Indy and Bréville. From 1906 he taught in South America, but returned to Paris in 1921. His works are largely in a French style, but much influenced by the rhythms of Hispanic music. He wrote three operas: *Ardid de amor* (in one act; 1917, Buenos Aires), *La guitare* (1924, Madrid), and *Cuento de abril*.

*

R. Petit: 'Carlos Pedrell', *ReM*, no.116 (1931), pp.46–50

Pedrell, Felipe (*b* Tortosa, 9 Feb 1841; *d* Barcelona, 9 Aug 1922). Spanish (Catalan) composer. He began his musical studies at the age of seven as a chorister at Tortosa Cathedral. Otherwise he was largely self-taught. The chief impetus for his career as an opera composer was provided by a visit in 1859 to Barcelona, where he saw *Lucia di Lammermoor* and *I puritani*. His later enthusiasm for Wagner found expression in his article 'La música del porvenir' in the *Almanaque de La España musical* (1868). In 1873 he moved to Barcelona as assistant director of an operetta company. His activities in this post coincided with a tremendous outpouring of light theatrical works, including the two-act Catalan zarzuela *Lluch-Llach*. The following year a revision of his first opera, *El último Abencerraje*, was successfully performed in Italian at the Gran Teatro del Liceo in Barcelona; his second opera, *Quasimodo*, was given in 1875 at the same theatre under his own direction. He spent a year in Rome, then went to Paris, where he conceived his opera *Cléopâtre*; he completed it in Spain in 1878 and submitted it, without success, to an opera competition in Frankfurt. It was in this work that Pedrell first systematically applied Wagnerian principles of continuous melody and leitmotif.

For the next ten years Pedrell concerned himself increasingly with musicological work; his operatic activities resumed with *Eda* (1887), *Little Carmen* (1888) and *Mara* (1889), all commissioned by a friend in New York. In 1890 he began composition of *Els Pireneus*, a monumental work inspired by Wagner and incorporating Pedrell's ideas on the use of folklore in opera. *Els Pireneus* consists of a prologue and three acts: 'Anima mare', 'Lo comte de Foix', 'Raig de Lluna' and 'La jornada de Panissars'. The action (to a Catalan libretto by Víctor Balaguer) takes place in Aragon and Catalonia between 1218 and 1285 and consists of a series of historical episodes dealing with the liberation of Catalonia. Troubadour melodies and references to Spanish Renaissance music are blended with 19th-century harmonic language and Wagnerian techniques. It is a sprawling work requiring large orchestral forces. In conjunction with its completion, Pedrell published the book *Por nuestra música* (Barcelona, 1891), in which he set forth his philosophy regarding Spanish musical nationalism in opera. *Els Pireneus* had to wait until 1902 for its première, at the Liceo, where it was well received. In 1910 it was successfully staged (in Spanish) at the Teatro Colón in Buenos Aires.

Pedrell spent the years 1894 to 1904 in Madrid, where he continued to compose, write and teach. His next opera, *La Celestina*, with its 15th-century Salamanca setting, exhibits the same stylistic features as *Els Pireneus*, including the use of a large orchestra; it was never performed in full. *Els Pireneus* and *La Celestina* were intended as the first two parts of a projected trilogy on Patria, Amor and Fides, the motto of Catalonia. The third part, an opera dedicated to Ramon Llull, was never composed; according to Bonastre, however, the trilogy was completed with *Visió de Randa* (1905), for soloists, chorus and orchestra. *El Comte Arnau* (1904) is designated a 'festival lirich-popular en dues partes', which Pedrell stipulated could be realized in any of three ways – as a concert work, a lyric drama with costumes and staging, or an outdoor piece in the manner of classical Greek theatre. It is full of references to folksong, much of it later used in his own *Cancionero musical popular español* (Valls, 1918–22, 2/1936), and quotes from Renaissance liturgical music.

The work thus constitutes the supreme example of the combination of Pedrell's activities as composer and musicologist, but it has never been performed.

Pedrell's operas have found no permanent place in the repertory. Nevertheless, through his writings and teaching (Albéniz, Granados and Falla were his pupils) as well as through his compositions, Pedrell made an inestimable contribution to the musical culture of his homeland, especially in the field of musical theatre.

El último Abencerraje, 1868 (4, J. B. Altés), unperf.; rev. as L'ultimo Abenzeraggio, 1870 (F. Fors de Casamayor), destroyed 1894; rev., with new nos., Barcelona, Liceo, 14 April 1874, excerpts (Barcelona, 1874); rev., Barcelona, Liceo, 6 Oct 1889, *E-Bc**
Les aventures de Cocardy, 1873 (ob, Gelée-Bertal), unperf.
Quasimodo (4, J. Barret, after V. Hugo), Barcelona, Liceo, 20 April 1875, in *Bc**
Le roi Lear, 1877 (5, A. Baralle), unperf., vs *Bc**
Mazeppa, 1878 (poema lírico, A. de Lauzières de Thémines), unperf., vs *Bc**
Il Tasso a Ferrara (poema lírico, 1, Lauzières de Thémines), Madrid, Apolo, 1881, *Bc**
Cléopâtre, 1878 (4, Lauzières de Thémines), unperf., *Bc**
Eda, 1887 (ópera cómica), unperf.
Little Carmen, 1888 (ópera, 3), inc., 6 nos. in *Bc**
Mara, 1889 (ópera cómica, 4), unperf., vs unpubd
Els Pireneus [Los Pirineos], 1891 (prol., 3, V. Balaguer), Barcelona, Liceo, 4 Jan 1902, *Bc**, vs (Barcelona, 1893) [pt 1 of trilogy]
La Celestina: tragi-comedia lírica de Calisto y Melibea, 1902 (4, Pedrell, after F. de Rojas), excerpts, concert perf., Barcelona, 1921, *Bc**, vs (Barcelona, 1903) [pt 2 of trilogy]
El Comte Arnau, 1904 ('festival lirich-popular', 2 pts, J. Maragall), *Bc**, vs (Leipzig, 1911)

Zarzuelas: Lluch-Llach, 1873 (2, A. Ferrer i Codina) [orig. El diplomático (ob)]; Ells i Elles, 1873 (1, J. Riera i Bertrán); Lo rei tranquil, 1873 (Riera); La veritat i la mentida, 1873 (3, C. Colomer); La guardiola, 1873 (3, E. Vidal i Valenciano); Los secuestradores, 1889 (zarzuelita, 3 nos.)

*

R. Mitjana: *La música contemporánea en España y Felipe Pedrell* (Madrid, 1901)
H. de Curzon: *Felipe Pedrell et 'Les Pyrénées'* (Paris, 1902)
N. Otaño, ed.: *Al maestro Pedrell: escritos heortásticos* (Tortosa, 1911)
H. Anglès: *Catàleg dels manuscrits musicals de la Collecció Pedrell* (Barcelona, 1921)
J. Barberà: 'Els fonaments de l'obra musical del mestre Pedrell', *Revista musical catalana*, xix (1922), 103–7
E. Istel: 'Felipe Pedrell', *MQ*, xi (1925), 164–91
J. A. Ribó: 'Felipe Pedrell', *Música*, i/5 (1938), 61–9
A. de Larrea: 'Sobre *La Celestina* (ópera de Pedrell)', *Arbor*, lvi/213 (1963), 135–6
M. de Falla: *Escritos sobra música y músicos* (Madrid, 1972; Eng. trans., 1979)
M. Jover: 'Felipe Pedrell (1841–1922): biografía', *AnM*, xxvii (1972), 5–20
——: *Felipe Pedrell (1841–1922): vida y obra* (Tortosa, 1972)
M. Querol: 'i: Felipe Pedrell, compositor; ii: El Comte Arnau', *AnM*, xxvii (1972) 21–38
J. Subirá: 'Felipe Pedrell y el teatro musical español', ibid, 61–76
A. Fernández-Cid: *Cien años de teatro musical en España (1875–1975)* (Madrid, 1975), 460–63
F. Bonastre: *Felipe Pedrell: acotaciones a una idea* (Tarragona, 1977)
J. T. Snow: '*La Celestina* of Felipe Pedrell', *Celestinesca*, i/3 (1979), 19–32
C. Gómez Amat: *Historia de la música española*, v: *Siglo XIX* (Madrid, 1984), 273–85
A. Gallego: 'Nuevas obras de Falla en América: el canto a la Estrella, de *Los Pirineos* de Pedrell', *Inter-American Music Review*, xi/2 (1991), 85–102   WALTER AARON CLARK

Pedrollo, Arrigo (*b* Montebello Vicentino, 5 Dec 1878; *d* Vicenza, 23 Dec 1964). Italian composer. He studied first with his father Luigi, an organist and band conductor, and later at the Milan Conservatory with Gaetano Coronaro, Amintore Galli and Luigi Mapelli,

earning a diploma in composition in 1897; his graduation composition, a symphony, was first conducted by Toscanini (June 1900). After a short career as a pianist, he began a successful career as an opera composer: between 1908 and 1936 he had eight operas performed, some several times, in Italy and abroad. In 1912 his *Juana* won the Sonzogno competition. He was also active as a conductor and founded the Milan and Turin radio symphony orchestras (1928–34). He taught composition at the conservatories in Milan (1930–41) and Vicenza. From 1941 to 1959 he was director of the Liceo Musicale Cesare Pollini, Padua. His pupils included Gianandrea Gavazzeni, Alceo Galliera, Bruno Maderna, Claudio Scimone and Nello Santi.

The dramatic conception and musical language of Pedrollo's operas are strongly reminiscent of 19th-century ideals, and his debt to the Italian tradition, as well as to Wagner and Strauss, and to Berlioz and Debussy, is equally evident. The originality of his work lies mainly in the subtleties of his harmonic language and especially in the wonderful palette of his orchestration, but the dramatic tension of his operas is not consistently sustained.

Terra promessa (quadro lirico, C. Zangarini), Cremona, Ponchielli, 18 Feb 1908; rev., (poema drammatico, 3 pts), after 1913 [pt 2 'La morte di Mosè' corresponds, with variants, to version of 1908]
Juana (3, C. De Carli), Vicenza, Eretenio, 3 Feb 1914
La veglia (1, C. Linati, after J. M. Synge: *The Shadow of the Glen*), Milan, Filodrammatici, 2 Jan 1920; rev. 1921
L'uomo che ride (3, A. Lega, after V. Hugo: *L'homme qui rit*), Rome, Costanzi, 6 March 1920
Rosmunda, c1920 (4, L. Siciliani), unperf.
Maria di Magdala (3, A. Rossato), Milan, Dal Verme, 11 Sept 1924
Delitto e castigo (3, G. Forzano, after F. M. Dostoyevsky: *Crime and Punishment*), Milan, Scala, 16 Nov 1926
Primavera fiorentina (1, M. Ghisalberti, after G. Boccaccio), Milan, Scala, 28 Feb 1932
L'amante in trappola (1, G. Franceschini), Vicenza, Verdi, 22 Sept 1936
La regina di Cirta [Sofonisba], 1943–4 (3, Lega), unperf.
Il giglio di Alì, 1948 (3, E. Romagnoli), unperf.

*

P. Petrobelli: 'Arrigo Pedrollo: una figura d'artista', *Musica d'oggi*, viii (1965), 82–3
F. Grassi, ed.: *Arrigo Pedrollo nel centenario della nascita (1878–1978)* (Padua, 1979)   PIERLUIGI PETROBELLI

Pedro Malasarte ['Pedro Malazarte']. Comic opera in one act by CAMARGO GUARNIERI to a libretto by Mário de Andrade; Rio de Janeiro, Teatro Municipal, May 1952.

This popular opera, composed in 1932, depicts in a simple manner some of the characteristic traits of typical Brazilian figures, in one of the rare attempts in the 20th century to create a distinctly 'Brazilian' opera. The story is set in the state of Santa Catarina at the beginning of the 20th century and involves three characters: Pedro Malasarte (baritone), a roguish Brazilian *caboclo* (mestizo, i.e. of mixed blood), Baiana (soprano, a 'typical Brazilian woman from Bahia'), and Alamão (tenor, a 'characteristically Teutonic-Brazilian figure'), Baiana's husband. While preparing dinner, Baiana looks at the clock and constantly goes to the window. Malasarte arrives, elegantly dressed, bringing a portfolio and pulling a cat by a rope. Baiana says quite happily that her husband has gone to the city until the following week, and Malasarte enquires about dinner. They hug, and Malasarte explains that his father has just died and left him some money and the portfolio, which he wants to sell. As soon as they begin to eat, Alamão arrives home. Malasarte hides under cotton bundles in the roof while Alamão explains that he returned early because he was able to sell his tea for a good price. He asks why the table is set for two and Baiana answers unconvincingly. Malasarte then falls from his hiding-place and, while dancing an *embolada* (folk dance), gives a very confusing explanation for his presence which nevertheless satisfies Alamão. Malasarte then displays his cat's extraordinary feats, including its alleged speech. Impressed with Malasarte's ability, Alamão gradually gets drunk and falls asleep. Malasarte decides to leave. Baiana wants to go with him but he tries to dissuade her by extolling Alamão's good qualities. Unable to convince her, he manages to wake up her husband who, still intoxicated, offers Malasarte all his tea earnings in exchange for the marvellous cat. Malasarte reduces the price to half the original amount and, after a long farewell, leaves the house.

The means used to convey this amusing situation are effective in their simplicity. The musical style is sober and pictorial, without the grandiloquence usually associated with opera. In addition to the *embolada* dance, Guarnieri used melodic and rhythmic elements with instrumental colouring reminiscent of Brazilian popular music.

GERARD BÉHAGUE

Pedrotti, Carlo (*b* Verona, 12 Nov 1817; *d* Verona, 16 Oct 1893). Italian composer and conductor. He studied with Domenico Foroni. His first two attempts at opera were not performed but the third, *Lina*, was successfully given at the Teatro Filarmonico in Verona in 1840, followed by *Clara di Mailand*. In 1841 he was appointed conductor at the Italian opera in Amsterdam, where he stayed for four seasons, gaining practical experience and producing his own *Matilde* and *La figlia dell'arciere*.

Pedrotti was back in Verona from 1845 until 1868, teaching and later doubling the posts of opera coach and conductor at the Teatro Filarmonico and the Teatro Nuovo. This was his main period as a composer: the ten operas he produced during this time, especially those in the *buffa* or *semiseria* style, established his reputation throughout Italy; his first major success, *Fiorina* (1851), took it outside Italy as well, and in 1856 his best work, *Tutti in maschera*, was quickly recognized as a minor masterpiece, reaching Vienna in 1865 and Paris in 1869. Another important success came with *Guerra in quattro* in 1861.

In 1868 Pedrotti was appointed director of the Liceo Musicale and director and conductor of the Teatro Regio in Turin. He threw himself into the musical life of the city, making radical improvements in the quality of the performances at the opera, and founding in 1872 an influential series of weekly Concerti Popolari at the Teatro Vittorio Emanuele. In 1876 Giovanni Depanis, an admirer of Wagner, was appointed impresario of the Teatro Regio, and his first season included a performance of *Lohengrin* (before which Pedrotti went to Munich to meet the composer). Following its successful Italian première, conducted by Angelo Mariani (1871, Bologna), the opera proved a spectacular failure in Milan in 1873, but the Turin production was a success and gave a new impetus to Wagner performances in Italy. Pedrotti was also responsible for a number of Italian 'firsts' at the Teatro Regio, as well as the third Italian production of *Carmen* – which had to be cancelled after two disastrous performances, only to return in triumph at the end of the same season.

Pedrotti's 14 seasons put the Teatro Regio on a level rivalling La Scala itself, and placed Turin beside Milan as one of the chief musical centres of Italy. But in the process the composer Pedrotti was extinguished: in 1870 he produced *Il favorito*, the only one of his own operas given in Turin during his directorship, and two years later his last opera, *Olema la schiava*, at Modena. In 1882 he left Turin for Pesaro, to become first director of the Liceo Musicale established there in accordance with the terms of Rossini's will. He spent ten years building up the new institution and in 1892 organized the celebrations for the centenary of Rossini's birth; but in the following year ill health forced him to resign. Returning to his family home at Verona, he suffered from acute nervous depression and committed suicide by throwing himself into the river Adige.

As a composer, Pedrotti was highly regarded in his day. Technically accomplished and an exceptional orchestrator, he was at his best in *opera buffa* where his cultured eclecticism, rhythmic vitality and lightness of touch made an immediate appeal. His masterpiece, *Tutti in maschera*, is full of happy invention and tuneful ensemble writing, but even here (and more so in his serious operas) he was the representative of a dying style. His influence as an orchestral director was more significant: he was probably the first Italian conductor in the modern sense of the word, the eldest of an important group of conductor-composers that included Bottesini, Mariani, Faccio, Mancinelli, Mugnone and Mascheroni. It was his hand that prepared the orchestra and public that gave Toscanini his first sustained success at Turin in 1895–8.

See also TUTTI IN MASCHERA.

Antigone (os, M. M. Marcello), unperf.
La sposa del villaggio (op semiseria, Marcello), unperf.
Lina (op semiseria, 2, Marcello), Verona, Filarmonico, 2 May 1840, excerpts (Milan, 1840)
Clara di Mailand (os, 3), Verona, Filarmonico, 1840
Matilde (os, 3), Amsterdam, Italiano, spr. 1841
La figlia dell'arciere (op semiseria, 2, F. Romani), Amsterdam, Italiano, 29 Feb 1844
Romea di Montfort (os, 3, G. Rossi), Verona, Filarmonico, 19 Feb 1846, *I-Mr**, vs (Milan, 1846)
Fiorina, o La fanciulla di Glaris (op semiseria, 2, L. Serenelli Honorati), Verona, Nuovo, 22 Nov 1851, *Mr**, vs (Milan, 1852)
Il parrucchiere della reggenza (op comica, 3, Rossi), Verona, Nuovo, 5 May 1852, *Mr**, vs (Milan, 1852)
Gelmina, o Col fuoco non si scherza (op semiseria, 3, G. Peruzzini), Milan, Scala, 3 Nov 1853
Genoveffa del Brabante (os, 3, Rossi), Milan, Scala, 20 March 1854, excerpts (Milan, 1854)
Tutti in maschera (commedia lirica, 3, Marcello, after C. Goldoni: L'impresario delle Smirne), Verona, Nuovo, 4 Nov 1856, *Mr**, vs (Milan, 1857); in Fr. as Les masques (C.-L.-E. Nuitter and Beaumont [A. Beaume]), Paris, 1869
Isabella d'Aragona (os, prol, 2, Marcello), Turin, Vittorio Emanuele, 7 Feb 1859, *Mr**, vs (Milan, n.d.)
Guerra in quattro (ob, 3, Marcello), Milan, Canobbiana, 25 May 1861; rev. Trieste, 22 Feb 1862, *Mr**, vs (Milan, 1862)
Mazeppa (tragica, 4, A. de Lauzières de Thémines), Bologna, Comunale, 3 Dec 1861, *Mr**, vs (Milan, 1861)
Marion de Lorme (os, 3, Marcello, after V. Hugo), Trieste, Comunale, 16 Nov 1865
La vergine di Kermo (os, 3, F. Guidi), Cremona, Concordia, 16 Feb 1870 [incl. music by Cagnoni, Ricci, Ponchielli, Pacini and others]
Il favorito (tragedia lirica, 3, G. Bercanovich), Turin, Regio, 15 March 1870, excerpts (Milan, n.d.)
Olema la schiava (os, 4, F. M. Piave), Modena, Municipale, 4 May 1872, *Mr**, vs (Milan, n.d.)

E. Hanslick: 'Opern und Theater in Italien', *Musikalische Stationen* (Berlin, 1880)

I. Valetta: 'Carlo Pedrotti', *Nuova antologia*, no.131 (1893), 251–68

T. Mantovani: *Carlo Pedrotti* (Pesaro, 1894)

L. Torchi: 'Carlo Pedrotti', *RMI*, i (1894), 137–41

G. Depanis: *I concerti popolari ed il T. regio di Torino* (Turin, 1914)

C. Bianchi: 'Carlo Pedrotti a Torino', *Musicalbrandé* (Dec 1962), 10–11

V. Mazzonis, ed.: *Il Teatro regio di Torino* (Turin, 1970)

T. G. Kaufman: *Verdi and his Major Contemporaries* (New York, 1990), 155–68

MICHAEL ROSE

Peduzzi, Richard (*b* Argentan, 28 Jan 1943). French stage designer. He studied sculpture at the Académie de Dessin in Paris, but preferred painting and scenic design. In 1967 he met the director Patrice Chéreau; since 1969 he has designed all Chéreau's productions, beginning with *L'italiana in Algeri* (1969) for the Spoleto Festival. They collaborated on *Les contes d'Hoffmann* in 1974 and *Lulu* in 1979, both for the Paris Opéra. *Lulu* was transposed from the late 19th century to the 1920s, and Peduzzi's split set was an effective metaphor for the femme fatale's physical and moral journey. Their last opera was *Lucio Silla* in 1984–5 for La Scala, the Théâtre des Amandiers in Nanterre and the Théâtre de la Monnaie. Their most famous, and controversial, production was the 1976 'industrial revolution' Bayreuth *Ring*. Greeted at first with a storm of protest, it then generated much scholarly criticism. By 1980 outrage had been replaced by a more enlightened appreciation of its creative merit. From 1982 until April 1989, Peduzzi shared with Chéreau the artistic directorship of the Théâtre des Amandiers. He has also worked in the spoken theatre and in films (with Chéreau), and has designed a number of exhibitions, including Degas at the Grand Palais (1988) and the history of the Louvre (1989). He has completed a number of murals for the museum of the Paris Opéra.

For illustration *see* PRODUCTION, fig.24.   DAVID J. HOUGH

Peellaert, Auguste [Augustin] (**-Philippe-Marie-Ghislain**), Baron de (*b* Bruges, 12 March 1793; *d* Saint Josse-ten-Noode, Brussels, 10 April 1876). Belgian composer. The son of one of Napoleon's chamberlains, he spent his youth in Paris and studied the piano and harmony with J.-J. de Momigny. In 1813 his family returned to Bruges, where he intended to pursue an artistic career, but in 1815, when his father became bankrupt, he decided to join the army, eventually reaching the rank of lieutenant-colonel. Peellaert was a prolific composer who devoted himself chiefly to vocal music. Claiming musical kinship with Rossini, whose friend he became in 1860, he concentrated on *opéra comique*, often writing his own librettos. His sense of local colour and dramatic expression also induced him to try his hand at grand opera. Although several of his works were well received at La Monnaie, the simplicity of their melodies ensuring them a certain success, they were never staged in Paris. Some fragments of his operatic works were published in Brussels. After 1850 he confined himself to unpretentious operettas, and at the end of his life he wrote, in disillusionment: 'I have done a little of everything without succeeding at anything'.

first performed at Brussels, Théâtre de la Monnaie, unless otherwise stated

L'heure du rendez-vous (oc, 1, Peellaert), Ghent, 16 March 1819, *B-Bc**

Le sorcier par hasard [Le souper magique] (oc, 1, Peellaert), Courtrai, 16 May 1820, *Bc**

Agnès Sorel (oc, 3, J. N. Bouilly and E. Dupaty), 3 Aug 1824, *Bc**

Le barmécide, ou Les ruines de Babylon (opéra, 3, G. de Pixérécourt), 5 July 1825, *Bc**

Teniers, ou La noce flamande (oc, 1, Bouilly and M. J. Pain), 9 March 1826, *Bc**

L'exilé (oc, 2, T. Anne, A. Dartois and A. Tully, after W. Scott: *Old Mortality*), 25 Sept 1827, *Bc**

Faust (drame lyrique, 3, E. Théaulon), 19 Feb 1834, *Bc**

Le coup de pistolet (oc, 1, Léon), 22 March 1836

Louis de Male (grand opéra, 4, J. Vanderbelen), 14 Nov 1838, *Bc**

Le Barigel (oc, 1, G. Oppelt), 3 Nov 1842, *Bc**

Monsieur et Madame Putiphar (opérette comique, 1, Peellaert), Brussels, Château des Fleurs, 19 Aug 1857, *Bc**

Unperf.: L'amant troubadour, 1819 (oc, 1, Peellaert); Songe et réalité, 1829 (3); Les trois clefs, 1858 (opérette de salon, Peellaert); Castor et Pollux (grand opéra, 3); Drack, ou Le château d'Ernestal (grand opéra, 4, C. Lavry), music based on Faust (1834); Le mariage par testament (oc, 1); Myrrha la bohémienne (2, Peellaert), inc.; Régilde (grand opéra, 2); Sans dot (opérette, 1, Peellaert); La sirène (opérette, 1); Thécla (opérette, 1, Peellaert); Trois contre un (1, Peellaert)

*

A. de Peellaert: *Cinquante ans de souvenirs recueillis en 1866* (Brussels, 1867)
          HENRI VANHULST

Peerce, Jan [Perelmuth, Jacob Pincus] (*b* New York, 3 June 1904; *d* New York, 15 Dec 1984). American tenor. He studied with Giuseppe Boghetti and was chosen by Toscanini to sing in his broadcasts and recordings of *La bohème*, *La traviata*, *Fidelio*, *Ballo* and the last act of *Rigoletto*. He made his stage début in Philadelphia as the Duke on 14 May 1938 and joined the Metropolitan in 1941, making his first appearance as Alfredo; he stayed with that company until 1968. He toured abroad with many ensembles, specializing in the Italian and French *spinto* repertories, and in 1956 he became the first American to sing with the Bol'shoy since the war. In 1971 he made his Broadway début as Tevye in *Fiddler on the Roof*, but in later years he was plagued by physical infirmities and failing eyesight. In his prime Peerce was most admired for a remarkably even scale, a strong technique, and a voice with a dark vibrancy in the middle register and a metallic ring at the top. Though his diminutive size precluded an ideal romantic illusion, he was an actor of restraint and dignity.

*

GV (G. Gualerzi; S. Smolian)

A. Levy: *The Bluebird of Happiness: the Memoirs of Jan Peerce* (New York, 1976)

J. Hines: 'Jan Peerce', *Great Singers on Great Singing* (Garden City, NY, 1982), 224–30

Obituary, *New York Times* (17 Dec 1984)

MARTIN BERNHEIMER

Peer Gynt. Opera in a prelude and three acts by WERNER EGK to his own libretto after HENRIK IBSEN's dramatic poem; Berlin, Staatsoper, 24 November 1938.

The action takes place in the middle of the 19th century. Peer Gynt (baritone), a good-for-nothing and an outsider, longs for a more fulfilled life. He dreams of becoming emperor of the world, claiming that as far as he is concerned he will behave as he pleases. He disrupts the wedding between Ingrid (soprano) and the fool Mads (tenor) and elopes with the bride. Pursued by the wedding party he escapes to a mountain slope where he encounters an old man who is the King of the Trolls (tenor) and his Red-headed Daughter (soprano). Peer then rejects Ingrid and seduces the Red-headed Daughter whom he follows into the hall of the mountain king. Peer appears before the trolls and requests that he should become their emperor. When he refuses to submit to their tests and denounces them, they in turn swear to seek revenge for his behaviour. Peer disappears to a cottage in the mountains. Solveig (soprano), his lover, follows him, but her entry into the cottage is barred by the Red-headed Daughter. Peer decides that he must leave for ever.

Act 2 opens at the quay of a Central American harbour. 15 years have elapsed and Peer, now elegantly dressed, reminisces about his rise to fortune. He owns a steamer laden with a thousand cases of gold, but the President of the Republic (bass) informs him that the ship cannot leave the harbour unless an ancient law is changed. Meanwhile, three Merchants (tenor, baritone and bass) secretly occupy the ship and attempt to weigh anchor. The ship and its goods are totally destroyed after a boiler overheats just at the moment when Peer learns that the law has been changed and he can take his merchandise with him. The scene changes to a bar, where Peer encounters the landlord and a dancer, who closely resemble the King of the Trolls and his Red-headed Daughter. After the dancer rebuffs Peer's cynical advances, he has a nightmarish dream of her taming five grotesque *commedia dell'arte* figures.

In Act 3 Peer returns home, but when he tries to make his way to the cottage, his path is blocked by a Stranger (baritone) dressed in a black cloak. The Stranger drags Peer down to the bowels of the earth where he is to be crowned emperor of the trolls. In order to assure the mountain king that the claim to the throne is justified, a series of witnesses including Mads and Ingrid are called to attest to Peer's character. They denounce him, and Peer bemoans his fortune. Only Solveig's selfless love can release him from his torment.

Peer Gynt, Egk's third opera, was commissioned by the Berlin Staatsoper in 1936. The work aroused hostility from the Nazi press, who accused the composer of plagiarizing *Die Dreigroschenoper* and resorting to grotesque harmonies and orchestrations in certain passages. This opinion was dramatically reversed when Adolf Hitler attended the opera and personally congratulated the composer on his achievement. Nevertheless, after 1940 the opera was not performed in Nazi Germany and had to wait until the early 1950s for further revivals.

For illustration *see* EGK, WERNER.   ERIK LEVI

Peines et les plaisirs de l'amour, Les ('The Pains and Pleasures of Love'). *Pastorale-héroïque* in a prologue and five acts by ROBERT CAMBERT to a libretto by Gabriel Gilbert; Paris, Jeu de Paume de la Bouteille, February or March 1672.

The plot concerns the pains and joys of love, notably the sadness and grief of Apollon [Apollo] (*haute-contre*) at the death of his lover, the nymph Climène [Clymene] (soprano), and, after she is brought back to life, the couple's happiness when reunited.

Written and rehearsed while *Pomone* was in performance, *Les peines et les plaisirs* was Cambert's second true opera. It was poised to become an even greater success than *Pomone*, but, because the theatre was closed by royal decree on 1 April 1672, it ran for only a few weeks. 15 years later the work was performed in Nantes by the troupe of the Sieur d'Aumont. The prologue to Louis XIV, which was on a very grand scale, and the scene at Clymene's tomb were much admired. Only the overture, prologue and Act 1 survive.   CHRISTINA BASHFORD

Peintre amoureux de son modèle, Le ('The Painter in Love with his Model'). *Opéra comique* in two acts by EGIDIO DUNI to a libretto by LOUIS ANSEAUME; Paris, Foire St Laurent, 26 July 1757.

Le peintre amoureux stands as a landmark in the history of the *opéra comique* in that Anseaume's text was set almost entirely to original music. The printed score (Paris, ?1757) is the first of its kind. *Opéras comiques* written before that date had relied on popular *vaudevilles* or on *ariettes* parodied (i.e. borrowed) from existing sources for their musical content, and had contained little or no new material. Duni's work acted as a spur to native composers in demonstrating that the French language, though declamatory in style and therefore more suited to the style of the *tragédie en musique*, could successfully form the basis for a lighter style of musical comedy.

Jean Monnet, director of the Opéra-Comique at the time when *Le peintre amoureux* was first staged, was doubtful whether a work in French by an unknown foreign composer would prove successful. He therefore publicized it as a parody of an Italian intermezzo entitled *Il pittore innamorato* (in much the same way that he had earlier disguised the authorship of *Les troqueurs*). The plot is indeed reminiscent of the intermezzos heard in Paris during the Bouffon season of 1752–4: an elderly painter (Alberti, tenor) and his young apprentice (Zerbin, tenor) both fall in love with a young *ingénue* (Laurette, soprano) and compete for her hand. Alberti was played by the popular singer-actor Jean-Louis Laruette, Zerbin by M. Bouret and Laurette by Mlle Rosaline, with Mlle Deschamps as the elderly governess Jacinte (soprano).

The immediate success of *Le peintre amoureux* prompted Monnet to engage Duni on a full-time basis. The composer settled in Paris and substantially revised the work for further performances at the Foire St Germain in February 1758. It remained in the repertory of the Opéra-Comique until the Revolution and was performed widely in Europe, both in the original French version and in translation. In 1758 Jean-Benjamin de La Borde produced a parody, *Gilles, garçon peintre, z'amoureux-t-et-rival*.

Le peintre amoureux is notable for its charming melodies which faithfully observe the rhythmic metre of the French language. The work also contains some fine vocal ensembles, in particular the quartet closing the first act which depicts a violent argument and results in one of the earliest examples of an ensemble of perplexity in the *opéra comique*.   ELISABETH COOK

Peking [Beijing]. For an account of operatic activity in the city *see* CHINA.

Pelemans, Willem (*b* Antwerp, 8 April 1901; *d* Berchem-Sainte-Agathe, Brussels, 28 Oct 1991). Belgian composer. Essentially self-taught, he composed four operas, three ballets, music for a radio play and many other works, most of them instrumental. His early music was sober, direct and little ornamented, though later works have a more lyrical character. Pelemans also worked all his life as a music critic.

La rose de Bakawali, 1938 (chamber op, A. Lepage, from Hindustani)
Le combat de la vierge et du diable, 1949 (chamber op, J. Weterings)
De mannen van Smeerop, 1952 (M. Kröjer, after C. de Coster), Antwerp, 1963

De nozem en de nimf (chamber op, L. Bruylants), Radio Brussels,
1961   CORNEEL MERTENS/R

Peleus and Thetis. Masque by WILLIAM BOYCE to a
libretto by George Granville, Lord Landsdowne;
London, by 1740.

No evidence has yet been identified to support the
tradition of a first performance by the Philharmonic
Society at the Crown and Anchor Tavern in 1734. However, the inclusion of the libretto in a collective wordbook published by the Apollo Academy in 1740
suggests a performance at the academy by that date.

Peleus (tenor), a mortal, consults the God Prometheus
(countertenor), who can see into the future, on his forbidden love for the nymph Thetis (soprano). Jupiter
(bass), who also courts Thetis, intervenes, but is
persuaded by Prometheus to relinquish her in favour of
Peleus, since he is warned that union with Thetis may
produce a son who would dethrone him. Granville's
somewhat vapid text of 1701 (written as part of his play
The Jew of Venice, an adaptation of Shakespeare's *The
Merchant of Venice*) was modified for Boyce in order to
facilitate the inclusion of additional da capo arias and to
improve the weak ending. Boyce's work displays an unusual balance between solo airs and ensembles, and
shows deft and pointedly contrasted musical
characterization – in particular, the contrapuntally
motivated air in C minor for Jupiter, 'The fatal blessing I
resign', which gives weight to the dignity and
magnanimity of his renunciation; there is an impressive
final section in which both the passion and the
exuberance ultimately felt by the lovers are vividly
communicated. *Peleus and Thetis* has been successfully
revived by Opera da Camera in London (1970) and by
Opera Restor'd in Edinburgh (1988).   IAN BARTLETT

Pélissier [Pellissier], **Marie** (*b* 1706 or 1707; *d* Paris, 21
March 1749). French singer. Soon after her début in
1722 at the Paris Opéra, she married the impresario
Pélissier and sang at his theatre in Rouen. After her husband's bankruptcy, she returned to Paris and appeared
at the Opéra in a revival of Collasse's *Thétis et Pélée* on
16 May 1726 to considerable acclaim. Later that year
she attracted even greater applause for her creation of
Thisbe in Rebel and Francoeur's *Pyrame et Thisbé*.
Sensing danger, Cathérine-Nicole Le Maure returned in
December from one of her 'retirements', and a fierce
rivalry developed between the two singers and between
their respective supporters, the 'mauriens' and
'pélissiens'. On 15 February 1734 Pélissier was dismissed after a scandal involving her lover Dulis. She fled
to London, but returned to sing at the Opéra on 19
April 1735, remaining there until her retirement
in October 1741. Among the many roles she created
were five in operas of Rameau: Aricia in *Hippolyte et
Aricie*, Emilie in *Les Indes galantes*, Telaira in *Castor
et Pollux*, and Iphise in both *Les fêtes d'Hébé* and *Dardanus*.

Pélissier's voice was small and, initially at least, somewhat forced. She was nevertheless regarded as an heir to
the famous Marthe Le Rochois in the emotional power
of her declamation and the eloquence of her gestures
and facial expressions, though she never equalled Le
Rochois' stature.

*

F. Parfaict and C. Parfaict: *Histoire de l'Académie royale de
musique depuis son établissement jusqu'à présent* (MS, 1741, F-
Pn)

C.-E. Aissé: *Lettres de Mlle Aissé à Madame C*** (1725–33)* (Paris,
1787)
E. J. F. Barbier: *Chronique de la régence et du règne de Louis XV*
(Paris, 1857)
M. Marais: *Journal et mémoires ... sur la régence et le règne de
Louis XV (1715–1737)* (Paris, 1863–8)
A. Jullien: *Amours d'opéra au XVIIIe siècle* (Paris, 1907), 59–88
G. Sadler: 'Rameau's Singers and Players at the Paris Opéra: a
Little-Known Inventory of 1738', *EMc*, xi (1983), 453–67
                                              GRAHAM SADLER

Pelissier [Pelesier, Pelliser, Pellisier], **Victor** (*b* ?Paris,
*c*1740–50; *d* ?New Jersey, *c*1820). French composer
and arranger active in the USA. A virtuoso horn player,
he played in Philadelphia in 1792. In 1793 he joined the
orchestra of the old American Company in New York,
becoming one of its principal composers and arrangers.
Besides two operas, he wrote five melodramas and, now
mostly lost, 14 pantomimes. From 1811 to 1814 he was
back in Philadelphia, where he issued, in 12 instalments,
Pelissier's Columbian Melodies (1811–12), consisting of
songs, dances and instrumental pieces arranged for
piano, many of them originally for New York and
Philadelphia theatres.

Pelissier's American career saw a change in theatrical
music from an emphasis on historical spectacle,
pantomime and comic opera to an age of sentimental
melodrama. His *Ariadne Abandoned by Theseus in the
Isle of Naxos* (1797) was one of the earliest and most influential melodramas composed in America, though a
more complete idea of his style may be had from the incidental music to William Dunlap's play *The Voice of
Nature* (1803, *US-NYp*) and from the *Ode on the Passions ... Every Stanza expressing a Different Passion*, included in the *Columbian Melodies*. Pelissier was a
prolific composer who displayed 'variety of thought and
readiness of invention, with the full knowledge of all the
powers of an orchestra' (Parker). He was honoured in
1814 and 1817 with benefit concerts given by New
York musicians.

Collection: *Pelissier's Columbian Melodies*, i–xii (Philadelphia,
1811–12); ed. K. Kroeger, RRAM, xiii–xiv (1984) [PCM]

melodramas unless otherwise stated
Edwin and Angelina, or The Banditti (opera, 3, E. H. Smith, after O.
Goldsmith), New York, 19 Dec 1796, 2 songs in PCM, i, vi
Ariadne Abandoned by Theseus in the Isle of Naxos, New York,
1797
Sterne's Maria, or The Vintage (opera, 2, W. Dunlap), New York,
14 Jan 1799, 3 songs in PCM, xi
A Tale of Mystery (3, T. Holcroft), New York, 16 March 1803,
collab. J. Hewitt, 2 dances in PCM, i
Valentine and Orson, New York, 1805, song in PCM, xii
The Lady of the Lake, Philadelphia, 1 Jan 1812, songs in PCM, iii, iv
The Bridal Ring, Philadelphia, 10 Feb 1812, ov., dances, 2 marches
in PCM, iii–vii

*

EitnerQ
J. R. Parker: 'Musical Reminiscences: Pelliser', *The Euterpeiad*, iii/3
(1822–3), 18
W. Dunlap: *History of the American Theatre* (New York, 1832)
C. Durang: 'The Philadelphia Stage', *Philadelphia Sunday Dispatch*
(1854, 1856, 1860) [series of articles; compiled by T. Westcott as
*History of the Philadelphia Stage, between the Years 1749 and
1855* (MS, 1868, *US-PHu*); similar compilations as *The
Philadelphia Stage* in PHlc and *History of the Philadelphia Stage*
in PHhs]
O. G. T. Sonneck: *Early Opera in America* (New York, 1915)
J. T. Howard: *Our American Music* (New York, 1931, 4/1965)
J. Mates: *The American Musical Stage before 1800* (New Bruns-
wick, NJ, 1962)
A. D. Shapiro: 'Action Music', *American Music*, ii (1984), 49–71
                                          ANNE DHU SHAPIRO

Pelléas et Mélisande ('Pelléas and Mélisande'). Opera in five acts by CLAUDE DEBUSSY after MAURICE MAETERLINCK's play; Paris, Opéra-Comique (Salle Favart), 30 April 1902.

Arkel *King of Allemonde*		bass
Geneviève *mother of Pelléas and Golaud*		contralto
Pelléas	} *grandsons of Arkel*	baritone ('Martin')
Golaud		baritone
Mélisande		soprano
Yniold *Golaud's son from a former liaison*		boy treble or soprano
The Doctor		baritone
The Shepherd		baritone

Unseen chorus of sailors (male voices); serving-women, paupers (silent)

Setting The kingdom of Allemonde and its surroundings; the time unspecified but presumably medieval

Maeterlinck established his reputation as a leading exponent of symbolist theatre in the early 1890s; his launch on to the Paris literary scene came with his play *La princesse Maleine* (1890). Debussy had considered setting this play, the first in a series of symbolist works set loosely in medieval times and praised by *Le Figaro* as 'superior in beauty to what is most beautiful in Shakespeare'.

Published in May 1892, Maeterlinck's *Pelléas* was first performed at the Théâtre des Bouffes-Parisiens on 17 May 1893. Debussy attended the single matinée but had already read the work, as he recounted in a short article, 'Pourquoi j'ai écrit *Pelléas*', in 1902. In this article he also explained his attraction to the play, revealing his confirmed allegiance to the tenets of symbolism:

The drama of *Pelléas* which, despite its dream-like atmosphere, contains far more humanity than those so-called 'real-life documents', seemed to suit my intentions admirably. In it there is an evocative language whose sensitivity could be extended into music and into the orchestral backcloth ['décor orchestral'].

Debussy had obtained Maeterlinck's permission to use the play in August 1893, and the following month he began work on the opera, starting, curiously, with the climactic love scene between Pelléas and Mélisande in Act 4 scene iv. The initial process of composition, when he worked mainly on one act at a time, lasted until August 1895.

It was probably relatively early on that Debussy decided to cut four scenes from the play, a procedure endorsed by Maeterlinck. The opening, with its perhaps over-obvious symbolism of the serving-women trying to open the door of the castle and wash an indelible stain from the entrance, is difficult to imagine as the opening of an opera. The other cut scenes cause some detail to be lost but do not affect the essence of the drama. Perhaps the most notable effect of the transition from play to opera is the reduction of the serving-women to one silent appearance in the last act.

In addition to the excised scenes, Debussy made many cuts in Maeterlinck's text, several times eliminating repeated phrases, and also reducing the descriptive details that Maeterlinck intentionally incorporated into the dialogue rather than into the almost non-existent stage directions; in Act 1 scene ii of the opera, for example, Geneviève's description of Mélisande as 'always dressed like a princess, even though her clothes were torn by brambles' is removed, although it is clearly

the sort of detail that stage designers can incorporate into the visual aspect of a production.

Throughout the early period of intense composition Debussy revealed to several correspondents the difficulties he found in portraying the mysterious and elusive nature of Maeterlinck's characters. To Ernest Chausson, he wrote of the difficulty of capturing the 'nothingness' ('de ce "rien"') he found in Mélisande's character, and the 'beyond-the-grave' ('outre-tombe') impression made by Arkel (originally spelt Arkël), as well as his 'gentleness', which is 'of those who are going to die'. Such ideas clearly reveal Debussy's deep response to the text; they also reflect Maeterlinck's ideas as expressed in his essays, which first appeared while Debussy was working on the opera and were later published in the collection *Le trésor des humbles*. Other letters from the period of composition reflect Debussy's personal identification with the characters. He saved Act 2 until last. Here he found new challenges, more to do with communicating the impending sense of mystery and catastrophe than with characterization. On 17 August 1895 he could claim to have finished the opera.

In accordance with his normal method of working, he had written the initial text in short score with ideas for orchestration indicated, often in coloured inks. It was not until its acceptance at the Opéra-Comique in 1898 that Debussy was spurred on to produce the vocal score necessary for rehearsal purposes and the full score. In these he continued to make revisions, on occasion adding and subtracting the appearances of principal motifs.

More radical revisions became necessary when the work went into rehearsal. It emerged that several of Debussy's original interludes were too short for the stage to be reorganized between scenes. Under pressure, and with some reluctance, Debussy hastily extended several of them. The original interludes are preserved in the first vocal score, in French only, published by Fromont in 1902, while the full score and the French-English vocal score give the newer, longer interludes. Also from the rehearsal period date several cuts, notably an exchange in Act 3 scene iv where Golaud asks Yniold, who is spying on Pelléas and Mélisande, if the couple are near the bed. Despite the publication in 1905–6 of a full score, Debussy continued to refine the orchestration. Some alterations were incorporated into a second published edition (the study score in 1950 and the full score in 1966), but further alterations are preserved only in Debussy's personal copy.

At the première, Mary Garden sang the role of Mélisande and Jean Périer that of Pelléas (originally a baritone role but later adapted for tenor). André Messager conducted and Albert Carré was the producer. The realistic, detailed sets were by Lucien Jusseaume and Eugène Ronsin. At the dress rehearsal a brochure satirizing the plot was distributed and this caused much levity during the performance. Mary Garden claimed that Maeterlinck himself, angered by Debussy's refusal to allow his mistress Georgette Leblanc to sing the role of Mélisande, was responsible.

Critical reaction to the première was divided. One critic found the music 'sickly' and 'lifeless'. Others criticized the 'impressionism' of the work. Among the most perceptive reactions were those of Dukas and d'Indy. Dukas found that 'each bar exactly corresponded to the scene it portrayed ... and to the feelings it expressed'; while d'Indy elaborated on Debussy's own comments on his work, finding in it 'simply felt and expressed *human* feelings and *human* suffering in *human* terms, despite the outward appearance the characters give of living in a mysterious dream'.

Until 1914, *Pelléas* was revived almost every year at the Opéra-Comique. The casts included, from 1908, Maggie Teyte as Mélisande. Owing to the difficulty of finding a boy treble for Yniold, a precedent was soon established (contrary to Debussy's wishes) of giving the part to a woman. The first performances outside France took place in Brussels and Frankfurt in 1907. The following year the work was given in New York (with the Paris cast), at La Scala under Toscanini, in Prague, Munich and Berlin, and at Covent Garden. After 1918 the work was many times revived, but it hardly accorded with the anti-symbolist Cocteau-esque aesthetics of the interwar era. In the 1930s Valdo-Barbey produced a new, less realistic set, merely suggesting where Jusseaume had defined. Possibly drawing his inspiration from Maeterlinck himself, his décors paved the way for many future productions in laying stress on the symbolic significance of everyday or natural objects: windows, doors and trees.

A significant event in the opera's history was the 1942 performance under Roger Désormière, captured in the classic recording that many consider unsurpassed. Irène Joachim sang the part of Mélisande and Jacques Jansen Pelléas. Postwar productions have often treated Maeterlinck's setting with considerable freedom, transferring the setting to the present day or, as in the 1985 Lyons Opéra production, to the Edwardian era (with a short-haired Mélisande).

The performances and recording under Pierre Boulez were the first consciously to break with the accepted, somewhat muted approach to the score. Rhythms were tightened up, contrasts enhanced. Since the 1960s, several conductors – for better or worse – have revived the original shorter interludes, among them two ENO productions conducted by Mark Elder. In 1985 John Eliot Gardiner incorporated some of the changes in Debussy's manuscript full score into the Lyons Opéra performances.

ACT 1.i *A forest* The orchestral prelude outlines three principal themes: the first – modal and ecclesiastical with its bare 5ths and plainsong-like outline – is allied not to a character but rather to the sense of timelessness, or perhaps the forest itself (for illustration *see* DEBUSSY, CLAUDE). Mainly confined to the first act, it contrasts with the following two, which are clear character motifs pervading the whole opera: that of Golaud, with its distinctive dotted rhythm, and that of Mélisande, a pentatonically curved phrase. Rhythmic and harmonic transformations mirror the actions and symbolic development of the play.

Golaud has been out hunting but has lost his hounds and the boar he was pursuing. He lights upon a maiden weeping by a well. She is nervous and rebuffs Golaud's approaches ('Ne me touchez pas! Ne me touchez pas!'). Debussy captures the scene with the three motifs of the prelude, submitting them to harmonic and rhythmic variants appropriate to the detailed emotions and symbols of the text. Golaud's energy for hunting is captured in the dotted rhythm which marks his motif, while the loss of his quarry is reflected in the motif's loss of its dotted-rhythm element (ex.1). The sadness and fragility of Mélisande are suggested by the harmonizing of her essentially pentatonic motif with half-diminished ('Tristan') chords (ex.2). The awakening of Golaud's desire is represented by more conventional added-note

Ex.1

['and my dogs can no longer find me . . . I'll retrace my steps']

Ex.2

Ex.3

[Golaud: 'Oh how beautiful you are' Mélisande: 'Don't touch me!']

harmony (ex.3). It is more through the questions that are posed than by the answers given that Mélisande's character is developed: we learn that someone has done her wrong ('Tous! Tous!') but we never learn who it was, nor where Mélisande has come ('Je me suis enfuie! enfuie! enfuie!'). Here Debussy's attention to pacing becomes evident. To underline important dialogue, he could stretch the declamation towards arioso, while leaving more mundane remarks to be quickly declaimed. He uses whole-tone chords in predominantly tonal surroundings to convey her sense of being lost or confused.

Maeterlinck stresses the contrast between Mélisande's youth and Golaud's age: Golaud is taken with Mélisande's eyes, which never close, while she is repelled by his grey hair and giant-like quality. Her oblique answers to his questions increase her air of mystery: 'Quel âge avez-vous?', ('How old are you?') he asks. 'Je commence à avoir froid' ('I'm beginning to feel cold'). The orchestra, too, contributes to the feeling of mystery, with an inverted pedal note high in the strings. Golaud bids Mélisande accompany him; she agrees only reluctantly, after a comment whose significance – like many such remarks about the weather – clearly goes deeper than its literal meaning: 'La nuit sera très noire et très froide' ('The night will be very dark and very cold'). Debussy throws this into relief with a ritardando and tenuto singing. The scene ends with Golaud's admission that he too is lost, and his motif is for the first time imbued with the white-note modality of the opening one: the strongest forces are not those of the characters but in some power above and beyond, contained perhaps within the dark forest itself.

In the first interlude, highlighted on a trumpet, comes a motif hinted at only once before, when Golaud announced that he was Arkel's grandson. Its importance is evident, but it extends beyond the idea of a mere character-motif, demonstrating how Debussy could extend Maeterlinck's theatre of implication rather than direct expression by adding recurrent motifs intentionally unspecific in their frame of reference (ex.4).

Ex.4

1.ii *A room in the castle*

Geneviève reads Arkel a letter from Golaud to Pelléas, telling him that he has married Mélisande. In depicting her character he adds to her mystery: 'some great terror has evidently befallen her', he writes, going on to recount how she will 'suddenly burst into tears like a child'. Debussy sets the scene with utter simplicity, using Locrian and Phrygian modes on E. Arkel, the silent sage, listens without interrupting. At the end of the letter, as Mélisande's motif is heard, Golaud expresses his anxiety about Arkel's acceptance of her. If Arkel accepts, a lamp must be lit.

Emphasizing the character's inner strength, Debussy prepares for Arkel's first statement with the trumpet motif of the interlude, now played in the cellos 'avec une grande expression' and harmonized with a half-diminished chord at once linking Arkel's musical language with Mélisande's (ex.5). His response to

Ex.5

Geneviève's question 'Qu'en dîtes-vous?' ('What do you say about this?') at the end of the letter clearly marks him as a man who is passive when faced with the force of destiny. The E modes have now opened out to a clear E major and Debussy literally underscores the import of Arkel's utterances with held pedal notes: 'Je n'en dis rien' ('I have nothing to say') is his response, and he goes on to point out that human beings can only ever see 'the underside of fate'.

Pelléas enters and Arkel, emphasizing his paradoxical blindness (since metaphorically he sees more than most),

asks who has come in. Geneviève explains that it is Pelléas, remarking that 'he too has been in tears', linking him in our minds with Mélisande. Initiating a symbolic framework that will become increasingly important, Arkel asks Pelléas to 'move into the light'. The final phrase of the scene forms a link between the external events of the play and a more symbolic level: 'Aie soin d'allumer la lampe dès ce soir' ('Take care to light the lamp before this evening'), Geneviève reminds Pelléas, alluding to the prearranged signal to indicate Arkel's acceptance of Golaud's new wife. But we surmise from Debussy's setting that the remark has a deeper significance.

1.iii *Outside the castle*

Prefaced in the interlude by appearances of Mélisande's motif, a different level of response is required. Almost nothing happens. Instead there is a dialogue about darkness and light, seeing and half-seeing, with objects appearing as mists clear or disappearing as night falls. The gardens and forests are dark, and are portrayed with the key of C major, while the coast where Geneviève and Mélisande have been seeking more light is portrayed with its diametrical opposite, F♯ major. A ship passes, with a chorus of sailors, but cannot be seen clearly in the mist. Mélisande sees a guiding beacon out to sea. It grows dark, and she fears a shipwreck. Geneviève leaves Pelléas and Mélisande alone for the first time: they see more guiding beacons, but the wind rises and they have to leave. As we learn that they have a steep path to descend, and that Pelléas must support Mélisande by the arm, we may again suspect a symbolic significance. The act cadences, as yet tentatively in F♯ major, as Mélisande perhaps flirtatiously expresses her hopes that Pelléas will not go away. The key is significant. It has formed a link between the 'light' and the growing bond between Pelléas and Mélisande.

ACT 2.i *By a well in the park*

The well's magic powers are remarked upon by Pelléas: 'it used to cure the blind', he observes, extending the symbolism of 'seeing' initiated in the first act. Mélisande leans over from the cold marble beside the well, and her hair, longer than herself, dangles into the water. Pelléas notices, and it seems to awaken a desire in him to know about Golaud's first meeting with her. Did Golaud try to kiss her, he asks, and did she want him to? She answers with a simple 'Non'. Suddenly distracted, she plays with her wedding ring above the water. As inevitably it falls in, a harp arpeggio is heard, outlining a half-diminished chord on A♯. It is the chord that had introduced the weeping Mélisande in Act 1. By using it here, Debussy subtly indicates that a chapter in her life has been closed. 'The ring is lost', she remarks, 'nought but a circle of water remains'. Pelléas innocently remarks that if it cannot be recovered they can get another one. Mélisande persuades herself that she lost it 'in spite of herself', 'throwing it up too high into the sunlight'. Pelléas remarks that it was striking noon as it fell; to Mélisande's question as to what they should tell Golaud he replies 'the truth'. In an interlude, Golaud's motif interrupts the flowing semiquavers which have permeated the scene.

2.ii *A room in the castle*

Golaud is wounded (as the dislocation of his dotted rhythm portrays: as noon struck, his horse inexplicably bolted, ending up on top of him. He felt his 'heart had been torn in two'). Debussy introduces chiming discords perfectly capturing both the bells and Golaud's stifling pain (ex.6).

Ex.6

['I thought the whole forest had fallen on my chest. I thought my heart had been torn in two.']

Mélisande is tender to Golaud, offering him water and a change of pillow. Suddenly, as the music continues with the plaintive oboe phrases and half-diminished harmonies of her first-act weeping, Mélisande dissolves into tears. By no means the cardboard villain, Golaud is sensitive and compassionate, understanding Mélisande's complaint about the darkness and antiquity of the castle. But suddenly the mood is broken as he notices that her ring is missing. He erupts, demanding that she go and find it at once. He adds that she should take someone – Pelléas – with her. She leaves, weeping.

2.iii *Outside a grotto* Pelléas and Mélisande enter the grotto, and the music, in contrast to the scene by the well, moves to the 'dark' areas of C and F, with minor-key A♭s. The triplets that oscillated diatonically in the outdoors in Act 2 scene i are now filled with an eerie tension: chords of C major are uneasily juxtaposed with chords of D♯ minor. But as the moonlight floods into the cavern, a luxuriously orchestrated burst of the 'light' key of F♯ is heard (notated as G♭). Its beauty is, however, short-lived, giving way to stark 5ths reminiscent of *Nuages* from the *Nocturnes*. Three paupers can be discerned in the moonlight, and this time, as they leave, Mélisande rejects Pelléas's offer of a helping hand.

ACT 3.i *One of the towers of the castle* After a grooming-song reminiscent of a trouvère chanson, Mélisande lets her hair down from the tower. She has opened the window to let in the warm night air. Pelléas has never seen so many stars. Noticing her hair, he tells her that he finds her beautiful, for the first time addressing her with the familiar 'tu'. He wants to kiss her hand, since he has to leave the next day. A fleeting symbol appears, a rose: Mélisande sees it, but Pelléas cannot. As her hair cascades over him, Debussy gives us the nearest we have had to an aria, but the melody is in the orchestra. The vocal lines curve more lyrically than before, more like an expressive *mélodie* than a real aria. At the end of the scene Mélisande notices that her doves have flown away. Pelléas must leave her, she remarks, 'or else they will never come back'. A long pedal note C (the tonic of the 'dark' key) heralds their disturbance by Golaud. It is nearly midnight, he points out, underlining the contrast with their previous midday meeting. Angrily he warns them to stop behaving like children.

3.ii–iii *The castle vaults* The key of C forewarns of the symbolic darkness of the scene (which Debussy considered particularly original). Golaud leads Pelléas down to the stagnant water where he may 'smell the stench of death'. Encapsulating, for the second time, the 'dark-light' contrast in immediate juxtaposition, the interlude directly portrays his escape into the sea air: 'Je respire enfin'. As he remarks that the gardens have been watered, the music moves into F♯ major. But Golaud now warns Pelléas that he suspects there may be something between him and Mélisande and tells him to avoid her.

1. 'Pelléas et Mélisande' (Debussy), Act 4 scene ii (a room in the castle, designed by M. Ronsin), with Hector Dufranne (Golaud), Mary Garden (Mélisande) and Félix Vieille (Arkel) in the original production at the Opéra-Comique (Salle Favart), Paris, 30 April 1902: photograph from 'Le théâtre' (June 1902)

3.iv *Outside the castle* Yniold is introduced for the first time. Considerable dramatic tension is built up as Golaud gradually increases his physical and emotional pressure on the child to tell him what he knows of Pelléas and Mélisande's activities together. As he becomes increasingly frustrated by Yniold's innocently uninformative answers, the music rises to a feverish pitch, mirroring the dramatic irony of the situation. At its climax, Golaud remarks that 'he is like a blind man searching for treasure on the ocean bed'. He recovers, and begins to interrogate Yniold afresh. He asks him whether he has seen Pelléas and Mélisande kissing. Yniold replies that he has, and shows Golaud how with a peck on the mouth, but recoiling at the prickliness of his beard as Mélisande had done when she first met Golaud. Finally, employing a sinister ruse, 'Veux-tu voir petite mère?', he gets Yniold to spy into the room where Pelléas and Mélisande are gazing silently at the light.

ACT 4.i *A room in the castle* To the sound of the semiquavers that had accompanied the 'hair' scene (3.i), but now with more foreboding harmonies, Pelléas and Mélisande make an assignation to meet again by the well. 'It will be [our] last night', Pelléas remarks ominously.

4.ii *The same* Arkel enters with Mélisande, his music clearly in E major. He foresees the return of joy and light to the kingdom and remarks that Mélisande will be the agency of renewal. However, he has been watching her, and explains that he has pitied her, for she has seemed like 'someone waiting for some dreadful doom in the sunlight of a beautiful garden'. In a scene of great poignancy he explains the need of an old man 'to touch the brow of a maid or the cheeks of a child': 'one has a need for beauty alongside death'. The rich added-note chords, in unusual orchestration, are the closest to conventional cadences of operatic love music thus far in the opera.

Again, Maeterlinck used the poignancy of the scene to contrast with the violence of what happens next. Golaud enters, at once angry with Mélisande, whom he will not have touch him. He takes his sword from the prayer stool, inspecting the blade as the music nervously hints at motifs without any real continuity, jumping from feigned calm to outbursts of violence. He looks into Mélisande's eyes, remarking, with heavy irony, upon their innocence: 'You would think that the angels of heaven were bathing there'. He bursts out that her flesh disgusts him and seizes her by her hair, forcing her to her knees. As he regains his composure, he tells Mélisande that she may do as she pleases: he will not play the spy. Arkel, in a line weightily set by Debussy, remarks 'If I were God, I would have pity on the hearts of men'. His utterance resonates into an interlude of extended power, full of double-accented passing notes and middle-register brass.

4.iii *By a well in the park* Again in direct contrast, this scene is a symbolic one, with Yniold playing. Debussy responds with a lightly scored, playful, off-beat rhythm to unify it. Two symbols are introduced: first, Yniold's golden ball is trapped and he cannot move it – a hopeless struggle against destiny, perhaps; secondly, a flock of sheep passes. The shepherd remarks that they are not on their way to the stable. 'Where will they sleep for the night?', asks Yniold pathetically.

4.iv *The same* In this, the final love scene, Pelléas, suddenly eloquent in his imagery, realizes 'I have been playing and dreaming with the snares of destiny round about me'. As he remarks that he has not yet really looked at Mélisande, her motif is heard for the first time. If he does not look, it will be like 'fetching water in a muslin bag'. Several times, perfectly capturing the nervous intensity of their tryst, Debussy withdraws the orchestra: they meet, as it were, in total silence. Immediately the dialogue returns to questions of light and dark. The couple hesitate, not knowing whether to seek the light and shun the dark or vice versa. It is Pelléas who first declares his love: a moment where again Debussy refrains from any orchestral accompaniment. 'We have broken the ice with red-hot irons', he exclaims. With a new motif characterized by a quintuplet figure, Debussy again introduces a quasi-aria, clearly in the 'light' key of F♯ major. But ominous shadows threaten, and the sound of the drawbridge closing is heard. Debussy's portrayal of the contrary emotions experienced by the couple is masterly: 'All is lost! All is won!', says Pelléas, 'How beautiful it is here in the darkness'. The two embrace passionately; but then Golaud falls on Pelléas with his sword and kills him.

ACT 5 *A bedroom in the castle* The act begins at once with a new sound. The harmony is bare, using diminished intervals and plangent wind, and hinting at the octatonic scale. Mélisande is dying and the doctor is in attendance. He raises hopes of her recovery but Arkel knows better, sensing that those in the room are quiet in spite of themselves. Golaud is full of remorse, persuading himself that the love between Pelléas and Mélisande was like that 'of little children'. As Mélisande asks for the window to be opened, a triplet motif from the opening of the act is heard, floating in on the curious harmonic basis of an unprepared second-inversion chord. 'Which window?', asks Arkel. Mélisande replies, significantly, that she means 'la grande fenêtre'. The 'light-dark' imagery is now to be resolved, since the sun she and Pelléas sought is now to set. United with Arkel, 'she knows, but she does not know what she knows'. Golaud is again doubting and, soon after she realizes his presence, his desire to interrogate her again overcomes him and he asks Arkel and the doctor to leave. His first intense question – 'do you pity me as I pity you?' – is again highlighted by silence in the orchestra. He asks whether she loved Pelléas. 'Mais oui', she replies, innocently asking whether Pelléas is there. Golaud has learnt nothing, and Arkel and the doctor return. Mélisande is cold and asks if the winter is coming. She has recently given birth to a little girl and Arkel asks her to hold her daughter. Suddenly the serving-women enter in silence, not answering when Golaud demands to know why they have come. Mélisande speaks no more; her eyes, too, are full of tears. Golaud still wants to speak to her, but Arkel, accompanied by the final appearance of his motif (ex.4) has his last utterance (see ex.7). The serving-women fall to their knees. 'They are

Ex.7 Lent et grave

['You do not know what the soul is . . .']

2. 'Pelléas et Mélisande'
(Debussy), Act 5 (a
bedroom in the castle,
designed by Lucien
Jusseaume), the death of
Mélisande, in the original
production at the Opéra-
Comique (Salle Favart),
Paris, 30 April 1902:
photograph from 'Le
théâtre' (June 1902)

right, they know', says the doctor. Golaud sobs, and
Arkel remarks that it is now the turn of the little child.
Finally, as the curtain falls, the music moves into the key
of C♯ major – sharper still than the F♯ major associated
with light and love. The slow four-beat rhythm of the
opening completes the tragic circle of life, love and
destiny as the curtain falls.

*   *   *

However it is produced or performed, the external
events that form the plot of Pelléas are only part of the
point of the play. Maeterlinck's symbolism, couched in
seemingly insignificant dialogue, demands a response far
removed from that required for conventional 19th-
century opera. A more central question is the opera's
debt to Wagner. Whatever Debussy claimed, there are
strongly Wagnerian elements in Pelléas, notably in the
harmony, which reflects procedures found in Tristan
and Parsifal, and in the system of leitmotifs portraying
characters, themes and symbols. In an article in Le
théâtre in 1902, Debussy himself wrote out motifs,
identifying one of them as the 'thème initiale de
Mélisande', and in a rare technical comment about his
opera, he interestingly referred to his conscious treatment of Mélisande's motif to emphasize the view he held
of her character:

Notice that the motif which accompanies Mélisande is never altered.
It comes back in the fifth act unchanged in every respect because in
fact Mélisande always remains the same and dies without anyone –
only old Arkel, perhaps – ever having understood her.

RICHARD LANGHAM SMITH

Pellegrin, Abbé **Simon-Joseph** [La Roque, Sieur de; La
Serre; Pellegrin, Chevalier] (b Marseilles, 1663; d Paris,
1745). French poet, playwright and librettist. The son of
a judge in Marseilles, he was intended for the church,
entered the novitiate of the Servites at Moûtiers and
then became a naval chaplain. He went to Paris in 1703,
and in 1704 won a poetry prize at the Académie
Française for a work entitled Epitre sur le glorieux
succès des armes de Sa Majesté. As he had also entered
an Ode au Roy for this prize, and the other votes went
to this ode, the incident caused a great stir, and Pellegrin, as his own rival, immediately acquired a certain degree of fame as well as the goodwill of Mme de Maintenon. In 1701 he had published collections of
Cantiques spirituels and Noëls nouveaux, new texts to
old melodies whose success led Mme de Maintenon to
commission similar works from him, probably for Saint
Cyr; these cantiques spirituels were fitted to the tunes of
well-known vaudevilles or arias from fashionable
operas.

Thanks to the support of Mme de Maintenon, Pellegrin obtained permission to leave his original order and
join the Cluniacs without any obligation to lead a
monastic life. Having no means of subsistence now but
his fees for saying Mass, he was obliged to make a living
by opening a business selling epigrams, madrigals and
complimentary verses, which caused a certain amount
of amusement at his expense: so well known was he
throughout the 18th century for his facility in writing
that in 1801 a vaudeville play appeared entitled L'abbé
Pellegrin, ou La manufacture de vers.

Pellegrin wrote two unsuccessful tragedies for the
theatre and a play for the Théâtre de la Foire St Laurent,
before trying his hand at opera librettos, his first known
attempt being Médée et Jason (1713). Because of an
interdict of the Cardinal de Noailles, Archbishop of
Paris, he was forced to write subsequent works under
pseudonyms, sometimes adopting the name of another
librettist and in one case using that of his brother, the
Chevalier Pellegrin. The name 'Mlle Barbier' however,
once held to have been Pellegrin's pseudonym, is now
thought to refer to the dramatist MARIE-ANNE BARBIER,
who may have collaborated with him on a number of
librettos.

Pellegrin, diffident by nature and a modest poet,
would willingly revise his works in response to criticism.
This facility to adapt, the familiarity with opera shown
in his Cantiques spirituels, and his talent for lyric verse
naturally brought him opportunities to collaborate with
composers of the first rank, among them Montéclair and
Rameau; his style, however, was often criticized, as in
Le Mercure for March 1761: 'We will say only that the
author [Pellegrin], whose talents were greater than

supposed, was well able to reconcile the wisdom of the laws of drama with those freedoms allowed, and even demanded, by the operatic genre'.

Jephté, set by Montéclair and first performed in 1732, was one of the greatest successes of the century, but Pellegrin was cautious in publishing the libretto, writing in the preface: 'I had to fight against prejudice, and prejudice does not take the trouble to reason'. It was probably the acclaim that greeted *Jephté* that persuaded Rameau to choose him as the librettist for *Hippolyte et Aricie*. They collaborated again on *Les fêtes d'Hébé* (1739), when Pellegrin revised part of A. G. de Montdorges' libretto.

Médée et Jason (tragédie, after Ovid: *Metamorphoses*), J.-F. Salomon, 1713; *Télémaque et Calypso* (tragédie), A. C. Destouches, 1714; *Théonoé* (tragédie, as 'Sieur de La Roque'), Salomon, 1715; *Les fêtes de l'été* (opéra-ballet, with M.-A. Barbier), Montéclair, 1716; *Le jugement de Pâris* (pastorale-héroïque, with Barbier), Bertin de la Doué, 1718; *Les plaisirs de la campagne* (opéra-ballet, with Barbier), Bertin de la Doué, 1719; *Polidore* (as 'La Serre'), J.-B. Stuck, 1720; *Renaud, ou La suite d'Armide* (tragédie, after T. Tasso: *Gerusalemme liberata*), Desmarets, 1722; *Le nouveau monde* (comédie), J.-B.-M. Quinault, 1722; *Le divorce de l'amour et la raison* (comédie), Quinault, 1723; *Télégone*, L. de Lacoste, 1725; *La princesse d'Elide* (ballet-héroïque), A. de Villeneuve, 1728; *Orion* (tragédie), Lacoste, 1728; *Jephté*, Montéclair, 1732; *Hippolyte et Aricie* (tragédie, as 'Chevalier Pellegrin'), Rameau, 1733; *Les caractères de l'amour* (ballet-héroïque), Collin de Blamont, 1738; *Alphée et Aréthuse*, 1752

E. de Briqueville: *Deux abbés d'opéra au siècle dernier* (Amiens, 1889)
C. M. Girdlestone: *Jean-Philippe Rameau: his Life and Work* (London, 1957, 2/1969)
M. Hoefer, ed.: *Nouvelle biographie générale* (Copenhagen, 1968)
C. M. Girdlestone: *La tragédie en musique (1673–1750) considérée comme genre littéraire* (Paris, 1972)   JEAN DURON

Pellegrini, Valeriano (*b* Verona, ?*c*1663; *d* Rome, 18 Jan 1746). Italian soprano castrato. He sang in the Oratorian Church and the Sistine Chapel choir in Rome, at Cardinal Ottoboni's private concerts and in Bononcini's *La fede publica* in Vienna (1699). From 1705 to 1716 he was in the service of the Elector Palatine at Düsseldorf, where he created the difficult role of Gheroldo (requiring a range of c' to b'') in Steffani's *Tassilone* (1709) and was knighted. During this period he also appeared at Venice (as Nero in Handel's *Agrippina*, 26 December 1709) and, in 1712–13, in London, where Handel composed for him Mirtillo in *Il pastor fido*, the title role in *Teseo* and probably Lepidus in *Silla*. He seems to have been a technically proficient rather than a glamorous singer. By 1728 he had lost his voice and become a priest. In his last years in Rome he was dependent on charity. A caricature of Pellegrini (with an extended caption) by Pierleone Ghezzi survives (*I-Rvat* Cod. Ottob. Lat.3116 c.162).

WINTON DEAN, JOHN ROSSELLI

Pelletier, Wilfrid (*b* Montreal, 20 June 1896; *d* New York, 9 April 1982). American conductor of Canadian birth. He studied in Paris with Samuel-Rousseau (harmony), Camille Bellaigue (opera repertory) and Charles-Marie Widor (composition) before moving to New York in 1917. On the recommendation of Pierre Monteux, Pelletier was engaged by Gatti-Casazza as a répétiteur and assistant conductor at the Metropolitan Opera. He was made conductor of the Metropolitan's Sunday Night Opera Concerts in 1932, and under Edward Johnson's administration he became director of the company's French repertory, a post he filled until the arrival of Rudolf Bing. In 1936 Pelletier initiated not only the Metropolitan Auditions of the Air but also a summer season of events in Montreal that later became the Montreal Festivals. His conducting of the Canadian première of *Pelléas et Mélisande* in 1940 was the first of many Canadian operatic premières at the festivals. In the early 1940s Pelletier founded the Conservatoire de Musique du Québec, of which he was director until 1961. He worked for the Quebec government until his retirement in 1970, after which he wrote an autobiography, *Une symphonie inachevée* (Quebec, 1972). In 1937 he married the soprano Rose Bampton.

ERIC McLEAN

Pellizari, Antonia ['La Tonina'] (*b* Venice; *fl* 1710–27). Italian soprano. In 1710 she sang in the anonymous *Erginia immascherata* at the Teatro S Fantino in Venice, alongside Annetta Pellizari, who presumably was related to her. She appeared in three operas at the Teatro S Angelo in 1716–17, including Vivaldi's *Arsilda regina di Ponto* and *L'incoronazione di Dario*. During the carnivals of 1718–19 and 1725–6 she performed in four operas in Florence, and in 1719 she sang in Bologna. Between 1719 and 1722 she appeared in six further productions in Venice and in 1726–7 in four in Naples. She specialized as terzo uomo, singing, according to Strohm, 'male roles of a youthful character'.

R. Strohm: 'Vivaldi's Career as an Opera Producer', *Antonio Vivaldi: teatro musicale, cultura e società: Venice 1981*, i, 11–63
S. Mamy: 'La diaspora dei cantanti veneziani nella prima metà del settecento', *Nuovi studi vivaldiani: edizione e cronologia critica delle opere* (Florence, 1988), ii, 591–631
G. Vio: 'Una satira sul teatro veneziano di Sant'Angelo datata "febbraio 1717"', *Informazioni e studi vivaldiani*, x (1989), 103–30   COLIN TIMMS

Peñaflorida, Count of [Munibe e Idiaquez, Xavier María] (*b* Azcoitia, Guipúzcoa, 23 Oct 1729; *d* Vergara, Guipúzcoa, 12 Jan 1785). Basque composer. Of noble birth, he was educated at the Jesuit school in Toulouse. One of the principal figures behind the introduction of Enlightenment thinking to the Basque country, in 1764 he founded the Real Sociedad Bascongada de los Amigos del País, the first of the Spanish economic societies whose concerns included music, especially musical theatre as exemplified by French comic opera. His works were written to his own librettos, and privately performed. His comic opera *El borracho burlado*, performed in Azcoitia in 1764, consisted of 35 scenes divided into two acts; it was the first opera in which the text was sung in Basque, though the spoken parts were in Spanish. In 1781 he wrote *El amo querido*, a comic opera for the students at the Real Seminario Patriótico Bascongado in Vergara. He died while he was composing *La paz*, another comic opera for the same school. All his operas are lost.

JON BAGÜÉS

Penberthy, James (*b* Melbourne, 3 May 1917). Australian composer. A prolific writer of stage and concert music, he had his first successes with ballet scores when he was musical director of the Australian National Ballet (1947–50). He studied in Europe for two years but was drawn back to Australia in 1952 for compositional inspiration, and he settled in Perth.

Penberthy's musical style is eclectic, especially in his operas. At heart he is a mystical romanticist, but he draws on modernist, experimental, period and ethnic styles and influences as appropriate to reinforce the theatrical intentions of his works. In a number of his operas he has drawn heavily on personal experience, Aboriginal culture and social issues. These include the tragic operas *Larry*, *The Earth Mother* and *Dalgerie*, all of which are concerned with problems arising from white interaction with blacks. In *Larry* a young half-caste dies in gaol. The tragedy of *The Earth Mother* (in which two Aborigines marry, only to discover that they have the same mother) arises from the early policy of forcibly removing half-caste babies from their black mothers. In *Dalgerie* a genuine love relationship between an Aboriginal woman and her white boss is doomed because of its conflict with tribal laws. Other operas are also based on Australian themes. *Ophelia of the Nine Mile Beach* is a comedy drawing on Australian attitudes and ways of life; *The Bullock Driver* is a fantasy exploiting the myth of the superhuman abilities of bush pioneers; and the street opera *Swy* explores the celebratory practice of illegal gambling (two-up) on the national day of remembrance for the victims of war. A space opera, *Stations*, is potentially the most spectacular of Penberthy's stage works. Documenting the social attitudes of the 1960s and 70s in a space-time warp, *Stations* employs innumerable technical innovations from contemporary theatre and music. *Henry Lawson*, based on Lawson's Bourke stories and poems, is typical of Penberthy's approach to theatre. It is rich with exuberant crowd scenes, action, comedy and romance.

See also DALGERIE and OPHELIA OF THE NINE MILE BEACH.

The Whip, 1952 (3, J. Hanson), unperf.
Larry, 1955 (tragic op, 1, Penberthy), unperf.
Ophelia of the Nine Mile Beach, 1955 (comic op, 1, Penberthy), Hobart, Theatre Royal, July 1965
The Earth Mother, 1957–8 (tragic op, 3, Penberthy and D. Stuart), unperf.
The Bullock Driver, 1958 (fantasy op, 1, Penberthy, after L. Skuthorpe: *The Champion Bullock Driver*), unperf.
Dalgerie (tragic op, 1, M. Durack, after her novel: *Keep him my Country*), Perth, Somerville Auditorium, 22 Jan 1959
The Miracle (television op, 1, Penberthy), stage, Perth, Winthrop Hall, 28 March 1964
The Town Planner, 1965 (comic op, 1, Penberthy), unperf., withdrawn
Swy (street op, 1, D. Kevans), Canberra, Parliament House Lawn, March 1975
Stations, 1975 (space op, 3, G. Harwood), unperf.
Henry Lawson, 1989 (3, Penberthy, after stories and poems by H. Lawson), unperf.
The Creation of the World, 1990 (comic op, 1, Harwood), unperf.

J. Meyer: 'James Penberthy', *Australian Composition in the Twentieth Century*, ed. F. Callaway and D. Tunley (Melbourne, 1978), 81–7
MICHAEL HANNAN

Penderecki, Krzysztof (*b* Debica, 23 Nov 1933). Polish composer. He was one of the first composers from his country to develop a distinctive profile after the decade of near-isolation after World War II.

1. LIFE. Penderecki studied composition privately with Franciszek Skolyszewski and then (1955–8) with Artur Malawski and Stanisław Wiechowicz at the Kraków Conservatory. He himself later taught there and was appointed rector in 1972. His reputation was established in 1959 when he won three first prizes in a national competition. In the early 1960s Penderecki seemed to personify the Polish avant garde, with his brutist instrumental sonorities. His reputation quickly spread abroad, notably through performances of such works as *Anaklasis* (1960), *Threnody for the Victims of Hiroshima* (1960) and the *St Luke Passion* (1963–6). For a work of such complexity, this last won an exceptionally wide audience and led, with other successful compositions to numerous commissions from both Europe and the USA. He taught composition in Essen, 1966–8, and in 1972 began to appear as conductor of his own compositions. He has been a member of the faculty of Yale University and has taught at Aspen, Colorado.

Almost from the first, Penderecki has been able to write music of wide and direct appeal, using advanced vocal and instrumental effects and placing no long-term reliance on tonality. His success may be ascribed in part to his treatment of momentous subject matter, whether religious or secular: tearing conflicts, drama, mourning and victory are his strong points. Yet his music contains the most subtle shades of sound alongside shattering blocks, delicacy as well as vehemence. His qualities as a composer do not depend solely on his handling of great themes; in all his works he has shown himself a highly skilled exploiter and developer of the sonic resources opened up by the music of Stockhausen, Boulez and Xenakis. His use of disparate musical languages and sources as well as his fascination with grand gesture and design undoubtedly led him not only to the long series of compositions with sacred or religious connections but also to the four substantial stage works.

2. OPERAS. All four of Penderecki's principal stage works take existing literature as the basis for their librettos – plays for *The Devils of Loudun* (composed 1968–9), *Die schwarze Maske* ('The Black Mask', 1984–6) and *Ubu Rex* (1990–91), and John Milton's epic poem for *Paradise Lost* (1975–8), although Penderecki first came across this last subject in a film screenplay. Characteristically, Penderecki and his co-librettists fashioned the texts into a succession of short scenes, ranging from ten in *Ubu Rex* to over 40 in *Paradise Lost*; in *Die schwarze Maske* the frenzied pace leads to a more through-composed score. While the first two operas explore in dramatic form the humanitarian and religious concerns that are also to be found in Penderecki's concurrent choral music (he called *Paradise Lost* a *sacra rappresentazione*), the two more recent operas seem to be deliberately located in a secular Polish context. Penderecki has never been afraid to express his views on the state of Poland and, with a Polish setting in *Die schwarze Maske* (as with *The Devils of Loudun*, the action takes place in the 17th century) and the scatological surrealism of Jarry's Polish fantasy in *Ubu Rex*, Penderecki has pulled no punches in parodying what he sees as the failings of Polish society past and present.

The four operas are united by Penderecki's fascination with the grotesque and with the confrontation of good and evil. *The Devils of Loudun* is a 'factional' interpretation of an actual event, but the interest lies not so much in the story (which is straightforward) as in Penderecki's emphasis on the sins of the flesh, on torture and on intrigue and inquisition; goodness is given short shrift. If this makes the plot one-sided, the succeeding *rappresentazione* attempts to redress the balance. *Paradise Lost* is cast in the mould of Renaissance Florentine entertainments, incorporating elaborate contrasts of scene, gods and devils, and frequent dances. Penderecki drew on all these components in his attempt to convey the magnificence of Milton's vision. Crucial moments are given over to dance (the creation of Adam and Eve, their courtship and marriage and Eve's revelations on eating the apple), while the chorus plays a significant role, joining the invented figure of Milton himself as commentators on the action. The voice of God is given not just to a speaker but also to male voices from the chorus, with their Middle-Eastern intonations (Penderecki was to return to such a duality for the Tsar in *Ubu Rex*).

If *Paradise Lost* falls short, it is largely because the musical language is severely restricted by Penderecki's obvious reliance on sequences of semitones and tritones (as is also the case in *Die schwarze Maske*). But when the same material tends to smother both Paradise and Hell, dramatic verity is hindered. There are surprises, however: the passacaglia structure towards the end of Act 2, with the four visions of death, pestilence, war and flood, provides a strong culminating force, only to be dissipated by the composer's not unfamiliar use of a final D major triad. Penderecki's orchestration is often imaginative and linked to characters (e.g. the Adagietto added to Act 2 in 1979 or the telling use of the clarinet as a solo instrument, a feature that may also be observed in the other operas); sometimes, however, it just glisters. In his subsequent operas, he has tended to paint his orchestral colours in broad sweeps, emphasizing the darker end of the range in *Die schwarze Maske*, while being exuberantly idiosyncratic in *Ubu Rex*, where the complement of instruments includes a musical saw.

Penderecki's use of pastiche or quotation (in *Paradise Lost* this includes a chorale from Bach's *St John Passion*, the 'Dies irae' motif and a truncated snatch from Wagner's *Lohengrin* at the passing mention of a swan) can seem gratuitous and unintegrated. In *Die schwarze Maske* he referred more subtly to his own music, while the quixotic nature of *Ubu Rex* enabled him effectively to incorporate mock-Wagnerian choruses (shades of *Der fliegende Holländer*), polonaises, waltzes and marches that smack not a little of Weill. In fact, with *Ubu Rex* Penderecki's musical language has shed its overbearing intervallic obsessions and, in keeping with the madcap nature of Jarry's drama, has become more jocular and tonal (swathes of major tonalities), akin to the modern musical. Like *Die schwarze Maske*, *Ubu Rex* is an ensemble opera, with strong character definition, particularly in the female roles (Ma Ubu, like Benigna in *Die schwarze Maske*, is given most of the musical fireworks). As in all Penderecki's operas, his concern seems to be to provide a vivid theatrical experience that is perhaps closer to straight drama with incidental music or to the world of the cinema than to opera; his compositional language is geared to this end, being immediate in its impact in the *verismo* tradition, but to some ears lacking in profound and sustained musical insights.

See also DEVILS OF LOUDUN, THE, and SCHWARZE MASKE, DIE.

Najdzielniejszy z rycerzy [The Most Valiant of Knights] (children's op, 3, Penderecki, after E. Szelburg-Zarembina; collab. M. Stachowski), Poznań, Teatr Lalki i Aktora 'Marcinek', 15 May 1965
The Devils of Loudun (3, Penderecki, after A. Huxley), Hamburg, Staatsoper, 20 June 1969 (Mainz, 1969)
Paradise Lost (sacra rappresentazione, 2, C. Fry, after J. Milton), Chicago, Lyric Opera, 29 Nov 1978 (Mainz, 1978)
Die schwarze Maske (3, H. Kupfer and Penderecki, after G. Hauptmann), Salzburg, 15 Aug 1986 (Mainz, 1986)

Ubu Rex (ob, 2, J. Jarocki and Penderecki, after A. Jarry), Munich, Bayerische Staatsoper, 6 July 1991 (Mainz, 1991)

*

L. Erhardt: *Spotkania z Krzystofem Pendereckim* [A Meeting with Krzysztof Penderecki] (Kraków, 1975)
S. Jahnke: 'Musikdramatischer Exorzismus in Penderecki's Oper "Die Teufel von Loudun"', *Musik und Bildung*, xii (1975), 615–17
L. Erhardt: 'Chicago: 29 listopada 1978: Bóg, Szatan i Człowiek' [Chicago, 29 November 1978: God, Devil and Man], *Ruch muzyczny* (1979), no.1, pp.3–5; no.2, pp.14–15; no.3, pp.12–13
W. Schwinger: *Penderecki: Begegnungen, Lebensdaten, Werkkommentare* (Stuttgart, 1979; Eng. trans., 1989, as *Krzysztof Penderecki: his Life and Work*)
R. Chłopicka and K. Szwajgier, eds.: *Współczesność i tradycja w muzyce Krzysztofa Pendereckiego* [Modernity and Tradition in the Music of Krzysztof Penderecki] (Kraków, 1983)
K. Penderecki and I. Grzenkowicz: 'O "Czarnej masce" bez maski', *Ruch muzyczny* (1986), no.24, pp.3–4
J. Ekiert: 'Czarna maska Krzysztofa Pendereckiego', *Ruch muzyczny* (1987), no.20, pp.14–15
J. Warnaby: 'Penderecki's Ubu Rex', *Tempo*, no. 179 (1991), 56–8
ADRIAN THOMAS

Penella (Moreno), Manuel (*b* Valencia, 31 July 1880; *d* Cuernavaca, Mexico, 24 Jan 1939). Spanish composer. He first studied music with his father, the composer Manuel Penella Raga, who was director of the Valencia Conservatory, where he later studied with Salvador Giner. He achieved a considerable technique as a violinist under Andrés Goñi, but was forced by an accident to give up the instrument. He was briefly organist at the church of S Nicolás, but was soon attracted by the theatre. He travelled widely in Spain and South America, as a conductor in Ecuador, and with a company in Mexico during the Spanish civil war. Between 1894 and his death he composed some 80 zarzuelas, musical comedies and revues. Of these, *Las musas latinas* (1913), *El gato montés* (1916) and, above all, the three-act *Don Gil de Alcalá* (1932) achieved enduring success, the pasodoble from the second of these becoming universally familiar as the epitome of Spanish bullfight music.

selective list, zarzuelas unless otherwise stated

El queso de boda (E. de C. Bonet), Valencia, Apolo, 1893; Sidi-Guariach (Bonet), Valencia, Apolo, 1893; La fiesta del puebla (Algarra and Diaz), Valencia, Ruzafa, Dec 1899; Un anticuario (J. Guzman Guallar), Valencia, Ruzafa, 1899; Don Canuti (J. Fambuno), Valencia, Ruzafa, 1899; Sacristán y cantinera (1, Bonet), Valencia, Ruzafa, 1899; Gracia e justicia, Madrid, Martín, April 1910; La niña mimada (3), Barcelona, Cómico, June 1910; La reina de los tintos (1), Madrid, Dec 1910
Los romanas aprichosas, Madrid, 1910; La niña de los besos (1), Madrid, 1911; Las musas latinas (M. Moncayo), 1913; Galope de amor (2), Madrid, Gran, Jan 1914; La muñeca del amor (2), Madrid, March 1914; La isla de los placeres, Madrid, April 1914; El gato montés (opera, 3, Penella), Valencia, Principál, 1916; Bohémia dorada (operetta, 3), Madrid, Eslava, Oct 1918; La sucursal de la gloria, Mexico City, Arben, Oct 1920; El hermano lobo, 1930; Don Gil de Alcalá (opera, 3, Penella), Barcelona, Novedades, 1932; La malquerida (opera), 1930s

Full details unknown: Amor ciego; Día de reyes; La perra chica; Corpus Christi; El viaje de la vida; Las gafas negras; La España de pandereta; La cara del ministro; El amor de los amores; La última españolada; El teniente Florisel; Frivolina

*

StiegerO
Enciclopedia universal ilustrada europeo-americana, ed. J. Espasa and others (Barcelona, 1907–30)
R. Mindlin: *Die Zarzuela* (Zürich, 1965)
A. Fernández-Cid: *Cien años de teatro musical en España (1875–1975)* (Madrid, 1975)
ANDREW LAMB

Penelope. *Dramma per musica* in two acts by DOMENICO CIMAROSA to a libretto by GIUSEPPE MARIA DIODATI; Naples, Teatro del Fondo, 26 December 1794.

Ulisse [Ulysses] (tenor), King of Ithaca, hands over the rule of his country and custody of his son Telemaco [Telemachus] (soprano castrato) to his wife Penelope (contralto) when he joins the Trojan wars. After a considerable length of time during which there has been no news from Ulysses, Penelope is urged to remarry, but she remains faithful to her husband. Evenore (bass), King of Lesbos, arrives in Ithaca intending to marry Penelope and proclaim himself king. Evenore's daughter Arsinoe (soprano) has fallen in love with Telemachus, who has also gone to war. Soon, however, a triumphant Telemachus returns with Ulysses, who upon seeing Evenore in Ithaca becomes suspicious that his wife has been unfaithful.

Ulysses learns that in fact his wife has been faithful, but that Perimede (soprano castrato) is plotting with Evenore to kill him in order to claim Arsinoe's hand in marriage. Ulysses is imprisoned, facing death. Telemachus, however, manages to free his father and to imprison Evenore and Perimede. In his aria 'Ah non vivrai mio ben' Telemachus sings of the conflict between his love for Arsinoe and his filial obligation to kill his father's enemy Evenore (her father). In a magnanimous gesture Ulysses forgives Evenore and accepts his friendship, allowing Arsinoe to marry Telemachus.

The opera stresses the themes of conjugal faithfulness, constancy, filial love, courage and magnanimity. Cimarosa combined the operatic conventions of the day with an expressive sentimentalism in the bel canto arias. The music of Telemachus, originally sung by the castrato Girolamo Braura, has some demanding passages.
GORDANA LAZAREVICH

Pénélope ('Penelope'). *Poème lyrique* in three acts by GABRIEL FAURÉ to a libretto by René Fauchois; Monte Carlo, Opéra, 4 March 1913.

Pénélope [Penelope] *Queen of Ithaca*		soprano
Ulysse [Ulysses] *King of Ithaca*		tenor
Euryclée [Eurycleia] *Ulysses' nurse*		mezzo-soprano
Eumée [Eumaeus] *an old shepherd*		baritone
Antinous		tenor
Eurymaque [Eurymachus]		baritone
Léodès [Laertes]	*Penelope's*	tenor
Ctésippe [Ctesippos]	*suitors*	baritone
Pisandre [Peisander]		baritone
A Shepherd		tenor

Attendants, servants, dancers, flautists, shepherds, people of Ithaca

Setting The island of Ithaca after the Trojan war

When Fauré, with some theatrical but no specifically operatic experience, was searching for a libretto, the singer Lucienne Bréval recommended a text by René Fauchois on the subject of Penelope and Ulysses. Fauré started work in 1907. His directorship of the Paris Conservatoire meant that composing was virtually restricted to the summer break: it took him five years to complete the opera. The shaping of the libretto is competent if conventional; the language tends to be stiff. Fauré's progress is fully documented in letters to his wife (see *Lettres intimes*, ed. P. Fauré-Fremiet, Paris, 1951).

ACT 1 *In the palace* While they spin, Penelope's attendants discuss their mistress's determination to await the long-delayed return of her husband Ulysses from the war. For more than ten years the palace has been infested with suitors clamouring in vain for her hand. Eurymachus, Antinous and the other three suitors burst in to renew the pressure. The nurse Eurycleia rebukes them. Penelope appears, scorning their pleas, convinced that Ulysses will return. She has undertaken to marry one of the suitors when the shroud she is weaving is finished. Wine and dancing-girls are summoned. As Penelope appeals to the absent Ulysses to save her, a voice is heard outside. A vagrant in rags begs for hospitality. To the disgust of the suitors Penelope, moved by sudden compassion, welcomes him. While Eurycleia washes his feet she recognizes a scar; the stranger (Ulysses disguised) pledges her to silence. She leads him out to give him food. Penelope, seated at her loom, unravels the day's work but is observed by the suitors and forced to promise to make her choice next day. The stranger consoles her with the thought of her husband's return. Penelope and Eurycleia prepare for their evening walk to keep watch over the sea. The stranger follows them.

ACT 2 *A moonlit night on a hill-top above the sea with a tall column* Penelope recalls how she and Ulysses used to come here after dark to take the air. Now, every evening, knowing that it can be seen from the sea, she garlands the column with roses. The faithful Eumaeus prays that he may be spared to see his master again. Penelope gently questions the stranger, who reveals that Ulysses on his wanderings sought shelter in his home in Crete. As evidence he describes Ulysses' royal cloak and tunic. When Penelope confesses to misgivings about Ulysses' fidelity, the stranger reassures her. He suggests a stratagem – only a suitor who can bend the great bow of Ulysses may win her hand. The women return to the palace. Ulysses reveals his identity to Eumaeus and the shepherds, and calls for their help on the morrow.

ACT 3 *The great hall of the palace* Ulysses has spent the night reconnoitring the building. Among his old weapons he has chosen a sword, which he hides under the throne. Eumaeus informs him that the suitors have ordered sheep and cattle to be brought for sacrifice – so the shepherds are armed with knives. The suitors call for preparations to be made for the wedding feast. They summon Penelope, who announces her one condition: only he who can bend the great bow may claim her hand. The suitors are filled with consternation. Three of them try, with humiliating results. The stranger slyly offers to try in his turn. The suitors are scornful, but when he succeeds and shoots an arrow, they are terrified. The second arrow is aimed at Eurymachus. Ulysses declares himself, the suitors are slaughtered and Penelope is finally convinced. The reunited couple sing of their happiness and there is general rejoicing and praise to Zeus, in which the people of Ithaca join.

* * *

Pénélope is a carefully constructed score. Fauré used leitmotifs of striking quality (those connected with Penelope and Ulysses are fully treated in the fine prelude, sometimes heard as a separate piece), but Wagnerian influence is more evident in pages of quiet intensity than at climaxes, where the lean, cutting texture is quite un-Wagnerian. Fauré called on a young musician, Fernand Pécoud, to orchestrate (for final revi-

'Pénélope' (Fauré): scene from Act 3 of the original production at the Opéra, Monte Carlo, 4 March 1913, with Lucienne Bréval in the title role (left)

sion by himself) much of the second act and part of the finale. Although Fauré professed to abhor illustrative music he was remarkably successful in suggesting such incidents as the weaving (and unravelling) of the shroud and the stranger's description of Ulysses' royal garments. The elliptical style of *Pénélope* is related to the piano music (e.g. the nine Préludes op.103) of the same period. Many solo passages for voice resemble Fauré's later songs rather than recitative and arioso in the French operatic manner, but they are *mélodies* with contours moulded to dramatic ends. It is typical that the heroine's cry in Act 1 'J'ai tant d'amour à lui donner encore ...' should be marked 'sans ralentir'. In the opera as elsewhere in his music, interpreters should beware of confusing sentiment with sentimentality. The character of Penelope – proud, loyal, passionate, merciless to the suitors, a woman (as her entrances in Acts 1 and 3 show) of formidable presence – is strongly drawn. Ulysses' music, sinewy with a suggestion of ruthlessness, overcomes the inherent improbability of Penelope's having no more than a lurking suspicion of his real identity. The dances in the outer acts, delightful in themselves, are adroitly woven into the fabric. Here as in the general layout one may detect the influence of *Samson et Dalila*. In a letter to his wife (1 October 1909) Fauré complained that the public were moved only by 'the excessive if always justifiable polyphony of Wagner, the *chiaroscuro* of Debussy, or Massenet's contemptibly passionate squirmings', but were indifferent to the 'clear and *straightforward*' music of Saint-Saëns, to which he himself felt closest – 'All that gives me shivers down the spine!'.

Although he admired the conductor, Léon Jehin, Fauré regarded the Monte Carlo première (with Bréval in the title role) as a try-out for the Paris production two

months later (Champs-Elysées), again with Bréval but with Louis Hasselmans conducting; this started well but was overshadowed by a Dyagilev season with the premières of Debussy's *Jeux* and Stravinsky's *The Rite of Spring*. When, in 1919, *Pénélope* reached the Opéra-Comique, it was no longer, by Parisian standards, an interesting novelty. Notable interpreters of the title role have included Lubin, Croiza, Balguerie and Crespin. Like another major opera of the period, Dukas' *Ariane et Barbe-bleue*, *Pénélope* has won high regard among musicians, but has not entered the repertory. Outwardly unsensational and unspectacular, concerned not with doomed love but with a marriage lasting and happy in spite of the strain of external events, composed in a bare, economical, pared-down musical style in which Fauré clothes feelings running at high tension below the surface, *Pénélope* does not try to seduce the wider operatic public.   RONALD CRICHTON

Penherski, Zbigniew (*b* Warsaw, 26 Jan 1935). Polish composer. He studied with Szeligowski (1956–9) at the Warsaw Conservatory. Though he has been overshadowed by contemporaries such as Górecki and Penderecki, he shares their interest in new compositional techniques, albeit tempered by a milder musical personality, and has been one of the most prolific composers of opera in postwar Poland. *Sąd nad Samsonem* ('The Judgment of Samson', 1969) is one of a number of operas of the period to take advantage of the facilities of Polish Radio, and its reliance on Pendereckian techniques of repetition and layering is evident. Of the stage operas *Zmierzch Peryna* ('The Twilight of Peryn', 1974) has achieved the greatest success; although its use of a prehistorical setting and closed musical forms suggests an almost self-denying discipline, Penherski used the withering of the Holy Tree (Peryn) as a more immediate and personal symbol for the relationship of the individual with society and for the processes of death and regeneration.

Dziewczęta zza muru [Girls from Behind the Wall], 1961 (1, L. E. Stefański)

Mały książę [The Little Prince], 1962 (1, Penherski, after A. de Saint-Exupéry)

Sąd nad Samsonem [The Judgment of Samson] (radio op, J. Prutkowski and Penherski), Warsaw, 23 Sept 1969

Zmierzch Peryna [The Twilight of Peryn] (3, K. Meissner, after J. I. Kraszewski: *Stara baśń*, Poznań, Grand, 6 Oct 1974; orig. title Historii dzień pierwszy [The First Day of History]

Edgar, syn Wałpora [Edgar, Son of Walpor], 1982 (3, Penherski, after S. I. Witkiewicz: *Kurka wodna*); orig. title Alicja, księżna of Nevermore [Alice, Princess of Nevermore]

*

T. Marek: 'A New Polish Opera "The First Day of History" by Zbigniew Penherski/Eine neue polnische Oper "Der Geschichte erster Tag" von Zbigniew Penherski', *Polish Music* (1973), no.2, pp.28–31
ADRIAN THOMAS

Pennarini [Federler], **Aloys** (*b* Neudorf, nr Vienna, 21 June 1870; *d* Ustí nad Labem, 23 May 1927). Austrian tenor. He studied in Vienna, making his début in 1893 at Bratislava as Turiddu, and his Bayreuth début in 1899, in *Parsifal* and *Die Meistersinger*. After engagements at Olomouc, Elberfeld, Graz and Hamburg (1900–13), he became director of the Nuremberg Opera, where he continued to sing until 1920. He made his Covent Garden début in 1902 as Lohengrin, also singing Walther, Siegmund and Siegfried, and Heinrich in the British première of Ethel Smyth's *Der Wald*. In 1904 he toured the USA with the Savage Opera Company as Parsifal. Renowned as an excellent interpreter of Wagner, he had a powerful, well-managed but hard-toned voice.
ELIZABETH FORBES

Penni [Penna], **Serafina** (*b* ?Siena; *fl* 1743–64). Italian singer. Her place of birth is suggested by the librettos of two of the four operas in which she performed in Naples in 1743–7 where she is described as 'la Senesina' and 'Sanesina'. The bulk of her career appears to have been centred on Venice, where she sang in over 20 operas in 1749–53 (various theatres), 1755–6 (S Samuele), 1759–60 (S Moisè) and 1764 (S Cassiano). She specialized in comic roles, some of them male, and was presumably related to the Berenice Penni who sang at Venice in 1749–51 and at Naples in 1767.
COLIN TIMMS

Pennisi, Francesco (*b* Acireale, 11 Feb 1934). Italian composer. A descendant of an aristocratic Sicilian family, he developed an idiosyncratic talent in both music and the visual arts. An analogous sensibility governs both the spare, clear, exquisitely detailed compositional style of his instrumental pieces from the 1960s and his fastidiously executed drawings and paintings. He first combined his talents in *Sylvia Simplex* (1971–2), which he described as an 'ornitoscopia' (ornithoscopy). Written for the Venice Festival of 1972, this witty venture at the margins of music theatre combines a lecture on birds (illustrated with his own drawings) with a solo soprano and a chamber orchestra. Ten years later he was drawn by another piece of natural history into a more developed theatrical venture, a one-act 'scene in seven pictures', *Descrizione dell'Isola Ferdinandea* (1982); it was performed on 19 October 1983 alongside Haydn's *L'isola disabitata* at the Teatro Olimpico, Rome (for which he also designed a single set,

serving both works). The work was inspired by the appearance in 1831 of a volcanic island off the Sicilian coast, near Sciacca; hastily named after the King of the Two Sicilies, Ferdinand II, who had hoped to make of it a hunting reserve, the island sank without trace a few months later. Pennisi's polished libretto, incorporating material from Baudelaire and F. Gravina di Palagonia, sheds a metaphysical perspective on the ironies of a royal bureaucracy attempting to come to grips with an unexpected and unstable addition to the kingdom.

For the 1991 'Orestiadi', the summer festival held in Gibellina in western Sicily, Pennisi wrote a further theatre work, *L'esequie della luna*, on a libretto by Roberto Andò after the Sicilian poet Lucio Piccolo. It was first performed on 23 July 1991 in the Case di Lorenzo, Gibellina. In a series of fantastic images, organized in four 'movements', it charts the melancholic consequences of the falling of the moon (an image derived from Leopardi) but also celebrates the last rites of a rich, Mediterranean civilization nearing extinction.
DAVID OSMOND-SMITH

Pennsylvania Opera Theatre. American opera company, established in 1975 and based in PHILADELPHIA.

Penny for a Song, A. Opera in two acts by RICHARD RODNEY BENNETT to a libretto by COLIN GRAHAM after John Whiting's play; London, Sadler's Wells, 31 October 1967.

The action takes place in a Dorset garden in summer 1804. Sir Timothy Bellboys (tenor) is obsessed by England's lack of preparation against invasion, and his brother Lamprett (baritone) by a fear of fire. When the local home guard is mistaken for an invading force, much comic confusion ensues. The cast is completed by a further six adult male characters (including two speaking parts) and three female, plus a boy (silent).

The opera, composed in 1966, is lightly scored, marked by an imaginative use of chamber-sized ensembles drawn from the full orchestra.
SUSAN BRADSHAW

Penthesilea. Opera in one act, op.39, by OTHMAR SCHOECK to his own libretto after the tragedy by HEINRICH VON KLEIST; Dresden, Staatsoper, 8 January 1927.

In a battlefield near Troy, the Amazons – female warriors who may give themselves in love only to a man they have defeated in battle – are fighting against the Greeks in the Trojan War under their queen and leader Penthesilea. Schoeck shortened and rearranged Kleist's tragedy of 1808 but added nothing. The opera begins at the play's ninth scene.

A fight is in progress offstage. The High Priestess of Diana (soprano) awaits the outcome. One of Penthesilea's companions-in-arms, Meroe (soprano), tells how Achilles, leader of the Greeks, has unhorsed his opponent. The Queen (mezzo-soprano) staggers in, wounded, supported by Prothoe (soprano). She is in a confused state, apparently believing she is the victor, Achilles the vanquished. Achilles (baritone) follows, unarmed, in pursuit of her, and is struck by her beauty as she lies unconscious. To win her love he must allow her to believe herself the victor. With friendly courtesy he behaves as if this were the case. She garlands him with roses. They plight their love. When Achilles gently reveals the true situation, she is appalled. News is brought that the Amazons are rallying. But when

Achilles, in imminent danger of capture by the Amazons, hurriedly leaves, Penthesilea forbids them to touch him. The High Priestess bitterly accuses her of treachery. A herald brings a message from Achilles inviting Penthesilea to single combat. In scorn and fury and on the verge of madness the Amazon queen, with her followers, rushes to do battle. Achilles reappears, throws away his armour, pursued by Penthesilea with drawn bow, greets her unavailingly as his bride and disappears from sight as she takes aim. Meroe describes how the now raving Penthesilea joins her hounds in savaging what is now a corpse. Attendants bring on the hero's remains hidden under a purple cloth. Slowly, in a state of shock, Penthesilea returns, convinced until she sees the bier that she is in Elysium. The truth begins to dawn as the High Priestess explains that Achilles had faced her, unarmed, not in war but in love. She kneels and kisses him, kills herself with a dagger and sinks down on the body.

'Schoeck wrote neither an opera nor a music-drama – he wrote Kleist's *Penthesilea*' (Hans Corrodi). Well aware of the difficulty of Kleist's language, Schoeck, while maintaining that the usual slowing-down imposed by music on the spoken word helped rather than hindered understanding, took great pains to keep the text audible, blending song, melodrama and spoken word. The composition of the large orchestra is unusual: there are ten clarinets at various pitches, the 'voice-devouring' violins are reduced to four solo players, much use is made of two pianos, for atmospheric effects recalling *Peter Grimes*, and of offstage war cries and dissonant trumpet calls. The sound of Schoeck's orchestra in this work was likened by Corrodi to bronze, but it may equally well be compared to the rough, lurid surface of much expressionist painting. At its most intense the language of *Penthesilea* surpasses in ferocity Strauss's *Elektra* (a work with which it invites comparison). Curiously enough Schoeck's opera came in time halfway between *Elektra* and *Peter Grimes*. After the première the composer decided to relieve the continuous high tension by extending the lyrical scene between Penthesilea and Achilles.　　RONALD CRICHTON

People's Friendship, The. Opera by V. I. Muradeli; *see* VELIKAYA DRUZHBA.

Pepita Jiménez. Lyric comedy in one act by ISAAC ALBÉNIZ to a libretto by FRANCIS BURDETT MONEY-COUTTS after Juan Valera's novel; Barcelona, Gran Teatro del Liceo, 5 January 1896.

Set in a village in Andalusia in the mid-19th century, the story takes place on a day in May celebrating the feast of the Infant Saviour. At 16, Pepita Jiménez (soprano) married her 80-year-old uncle Don Gumersindo, a rich money-lender. On his death three years later, she is left a wealthy widow with many suitors, including Don Pedro de Vargas (baritone), a prominent member of the community and prosperous farmer, and Count Genazahar (baritone), who still has not repaid money borrowed from her deceased husband. While the handsome young Don Luis (tenor), Don Pedro's son and seminarian, is visiting his father, Pepita falls in love with him. She confesses this to the Vicar (bass), who admonishes her to renounce Don Luis so that he can pursue his higher calling. Antoñona (mezzo-soprano), Pepita's faithful but contentious servant, knowing of her mistress's affection for Don Luis, explains the situation to Don Pedro, while reprimanding

him for his son's irresponsible actions. Though at first surprised by the news, Don Pedro decides to foster the romance with Antoñona's help. For his own part, Don Luis, realizing his strong feelings for Pepita, resolves to resist temptation; he bids Pepita farewell, and she in turn bids him follow his vocation. But Antoñona intercedes and reproaches Don Luis, making him promise to see Pepita once more to console her. Don Luis overhears Count Genazahar making insulting remarks about Pepita (who has refused his advances) to two officers (tenor and bass). Enraged, he challenges the count to a duel and wounds him. When Don Luis again sees Pepita, she cannot restrain her true emotions. Desperate, she tells him that her life will be sacrificed for his calling, and she locks herself in her room. Fearing her suicide, Don Luis breaks open the door, and the two lovers embrace to the joy of Antoñona.

To depict the feast day, Albéniz used a chorus as well as a children's chorus, and incorporated a dance. The opera's striking rhythmic profile and decorative chromatic melodic figures effectively evoke the Andalusian milieu; its appealing vocal lines slip in and out of a full orchestral texture that continually animates the work. The first Pepita was to have been the Romanian soprano Hariclea Darclée, but probably because of production delays the role was created by Emma Zilli. The original English libretto was translated into Italian by Angelo Bignotti for the first production, but Albéniz subsequently revised the score. It was performed in its final two-act form at the Théâtre de la Monnaie in Brussels on 3 January 1905. More recently it was revised by the composer and conductor Pablo Sorozábal into a three-act opera with Pepita's suicide concluding the drama. Sorozábal's version was performed at the Teatro de la Zarzuela in Madrid on 6 June 1964, with Pilar Lorengar as Pepita and Alfredo Kraus as Don Luis.

　　FRANCES BARULICH

Pepoli, Alessandro (*b* Venice, 1 Oct 1757; *d* Florence, 12 Dec 1796). Italian playwright and librettist. His *Lettera ad un uomo ragionevole sul melodramma detto serio*, published in 1789 as a preface to *Meleagro*, is an outspoken essay of some 50 pages criticizing the state of Italian *opera seria*. By linking a reformist tract with a sample libretto Pepoli imitated Algarotti, who had published an illustrative *Ifigenia in Aulide* along with his *Saggio sopra l'opera in musica* of 1755. Pepoli blamed the defects of *opera seria* on the pervasive and pernicious influence of Metastasio, and argued for a restoration to the genre of the grandeur and nobility of ancient Greek drama by integrating the ballets and choruses and omitting secondary characters and amorous intrigues. He cited Calzabigi's librettos as worthy examples, calling his *Alceste* equal if not superior to Euripides' play.

Three years after publishing the essay Pepoli was commissioned, with Paisiello, to produce the inaugural opera for the new Teatro La Fenice in Venice (Ascension 1792). *I giuochi d'Agrigento* reflects Pepoli's ideas in its abundance of choruses, which often interrupt or frame vocal solos, its large-scale scene complexes and its spectacular scenic effects. The plot, nevertheless, reflects Metastasio's for *Olimpiade* and *Demofoonte*; Pepoli's use of exit arias alternating with dialogue in blank verse also recalls Metastasio.

Meleagro (tragedia per musica, pubd 1789); *Ati e Cibele* (favola per musica), Cimador, 1789; *La morte d'Ercole* (tragedia per musica); *Cefalo e Procri* (favola per musica), Capuzzi, 1792; *I giuochi d'Agrigento* (dramma per musica), Paisiello, 1792;

Piramo e Tisbe (favola per musica), Giuseppe Rossi, 1792; *Apollo esule, ossia L'amore alla prova* (favola per musica), Gardi, 1793; *Il cinese in Italia* (dramma giocoso per musica), F. Bianchi, 1793; *Virginia* (dramma per musica), Alessandri, 1793; *Belisa, ossia La fedeltà riconosciuta* (dramma tragicomico), Winter, 1794; *Tancredi* (tragedia), Gardi, 1795

*

G. Bustico: 'Alessandro Pepoli', *R. deputazione di storia patria: nuovo archivio veneto*, xxv (1913), 199–229
P. Müller: *Alessandro Pepoli als Gegenspieler Vittorio Alfieris: ein literarischer Weltstreit im Settecento* (Munich, 1974)
T. Bauman: 'The Society of La Fenice and its First Impresarios', *JAMS*, xxxix (1986), 332–54
——: 'Alessandro Pepoli's Renewal of the Tragedia per Musica', *I vicini di Mozart: Venice 1987*, 211–20
D. Libby: 'Italy: Two Opera Centres', *The Classical Era*, ed. N. Zaslaw (London, 1989), 15–60
JOHN A. RICE

Pepoli, Carlo (*b* Bologna, 22 July 1796; *d* Bologna, 7 Dec 1881). Italian poet and librettist. Born of a noble Bolognese family, as a young man he was a leader in the city's intellectual life and a friend of Leopardi, who addressed a verse epistle to him. A patriot, he took an active part in the unsuccessful revolution of 1831 in central Italy. Captured and imprisoned by the Austrians, he was subsequently exiled to France. In Paris he met Bellini and wrote for him the libretto of *I puritani* (1835). Though Bellini complained of Pepoli's lack of theatrical experience and dramatic sense, he complicated the librettist's task by shifting the position of various numbers in the opera. Despite the libretto's consequent dramatic flaws the opera was a great success. In 1836 Pepoli wrote the libretto of *Giovanna Gray* for Vaccai, and in 1837 *Malek Adel* for Michael Costa. In 1837 he moved to London where he taught Italian literature, and in 1848 he returned briefly to Italy, but was again forced into exile the following year. He went back to Bologna in 1859. He served as a member of parliament of united Italy.

*

C. Albicini: *Carlo Pepoli, saggio storico* (Bologna, 1888)
WILLIAM WEAVER

Pepoli, Count Sicinio (Ignazio Gaspare Melchiorre Baldassarre) (*b* Bologna, 17 June 1684; *d* Bologna, 11 Nov 1750). Italian patron. The second son of Count Cornelio and Maria Caterina Bentivoglio, he was married to Princess Eleonora Colonna of Rome. In 1740 he was appointed privy councillor to the German emperor Karl VI. With his fine taste, considerable wealth and personal or family connections he had a far-reaching influence on European theatrical life, not only in Bologna (where he led the management committee of the Malvezzi theatre), but also in Venice, Florence, Rome, Vienna, London and in various German cities. His correspondence during 1717–50 (*I-Bas*), includes many letters from his protégés, most importantly Farinelli, in whose career and personal affairs he took an interest from an early stage. Among composers, he favoured Leo, Hasse, Sandoni, G. M. Orlandini and L. A. Predieri, often providing them with commissions for new operas or court employments; but not Vivaldi, whom he apparently disliked. Among prima donnas, he sponsored Tesi, Bordoni, Cuzzoni, Turcotti and Anna Maria Peruzzi ('La Parrucchiera'); as for male singers, he showed a predilection for such representatives of the modern school as (besides Farinelli) the castrato Giuseppe Appiani and the tenors Fabri and Babbi.

*

S. Durante: 'Alcune considerazioni sui cantanti di teatro del primo

settecento e la loro formazione', *Antonio Vivaldi, teatro musicale, cultura e società: Venice 1981*, 460–69
P. Guidotti: 'Lettere da Vienna (1738–1741) di Luca Antonio Predieri al conte Sicinio Pepoli', *Strenna storica bolognese*, xxxviii (1988), 219–46
C. Vitali: 'Vivaldi e il conte bolognese Sicinio Pepoli: nuovi documenti sulle stagioni vivaldiane al Filarmonico di Verona', *Informazioni e studi vivaldiani*, x (1989), 25–56
F. Boris and G. Cammarota: 'La collezione di Carlo Broschi detto Farinelli', *Accademia clementina: atti e memorie*, xxvii (1990), 183–237
C. Vitali: 'Una fonte inedita per la biografia di Farinelli: il carteggio Pepoli presso l'Archivio di Stato di Bologna', ibid, 239–50
——: 'I fratelli Pepoli contro Vivaldi e Anna Girò: le ragioni di un'assenza', *Informazioni e studi vivaldiani*, xii (1991), 14–33
CARLO VITALI

Pepsico Summerfare. American festival held in PURCHASE, New York, from 1980 to 1989.

Pepusch, Johann Christoph (*b* Berlin, 1667; *d* London, 20 July 1752). German composer and theatre musician. Little is known of his early career in Germany. He arrived in London some time after September 1697 and joined the Drury Lane band; in his first ten years in London he rose to an important position there and, after January 1708, at the Queen's Theatre (later the King's Theatre), Haymarket. By 1705 he was well known as a prolific composer of instrumental music, and as a performer in and organizer of public and private concerts, but he wrote surprisingly little vocal music for the stage before 1714. In fact only one work was intended as a theatrical production, the pasticcio *Thomyris, Queen of Scythia* (1707), and that was largely an arrangement of other composers' music.

When Colley Cibber and his fellow actor-managers at Drury Lane decided to reintroduce musical entertainments for the 1714–15 season they sought out Pepusch for their musical director. Pepusch revitalized the small and inept company of singers and instrumentalists already at the theatre, and augmented their number with better artists including the opera-house soprano Françoise Marguerite de l'Epine (whom he married some time between 1719 and 1724). The period 1714–16 saw an attempt, led by Pepusch, to revive the English masque. To fresh revivals of old masques, Pepusch added four new ones of his own, beginning late in the season with *Venus and Adonis* (1715). The next season saw the production of his pastoral *Myrtillo and Laura* and the masques of *Apollo and Daphne* and *The Death of Dido*.

As dramas, the masques – *Venus and Adonis* and the two works of 1716 – are a logical extension of the Restoration masque, employing mythological characters in a classical setting. They differ from the Restoration model in that they were intended as independent afterpieces, with plots that are completely self-contained, interpolate no real element of comedy, and have a tragic denouement. Pepusch's music is intentionally italianate, with da capo arias, *secco* recitatives and typical Italian instrumentation using strings and woodwind. Each masque employs only three or four characters, and the principal male role is sung as a travesty part. There is hardly any use of chorus or dances. These masques, in particular the longest and most successful, *Venus and Adonis*, are virtually italianate operatic presentations in miniature. The four works for Drury Lane, though unpretentious, did initiate a fashion for English masques 'after the Italian manner' which led to Galliard's *Pan and Syrinx* (1718), and found its justification and immortality in Handel's *Acis and Galatea* (1718). Pepusch was at Drury Lane for only two seasons, but the period was the most productive, though the shortest, of his whole career as a theatre musician. Indeed, it was the only period in which he composed dramatic works of sufficient substance and regularity for him to be regarded as a composer of theatre music, rather than merely of entr'acte pieces.

It appears that Pepusch transferred to Lincoln's Inn Fields in autumn 1716. While he played an important role there as musical director for about 15 years, he composed nothing of dramatic significance for that theatre. His concurrent duties as musical director for the Duke of Chandos at Cannons (*c*1716–32), along with his life-long scholarly interests (he helped found the Academy of Ancient Music and was later its director), probably allowed him little time to compose for the theatre. He did, however, continue to conduct the theatre band through the pantomime vogue of the 1720s and was almost certainly in charge for the opening night of Gay's famous satire *The Beggar's Opera* on 29 January 1728. Though Pepusch probably composed the overture, there is no firm evidence to support the claim that he arranged the airs, nor do the bass lines reflect his elegance and his technical skill. For several years, he took part fitfully in the stream of ballad operas which followed *The Beggar's Opera*. It is perhaps unfortunate that Pepusch's reputation as a composer rests almost exclusively on his accidental involvement in ballad opera, a genre which afforded no scope for the full exercise of his abilities, and which appears hardly to have interested him at all. It seems likely that he retired from the theatre at the end of the 1732–3 season. From 1737 until his death he was resident organist at the Charterhouse, and he was elected to the Royal Society in 1745.

See also BEGGAR'S OPERA, THE; DEATH OF DIDO, THE; POLLY; and VENUS AND ADONIS (ii).

all performed in London; all printed works published in London

Thomyris, Queen of Scythia (pasticcio, P. A. Motteux), Drury Lane, 1 April 1707, recits., ?arrs. by Pepusch, songs (*c*1719)

Venus and Adonis (masque, C. Cibber, after Ovid: *Metamorphoses*), Drury Lane, 12 March 1715, score and parts *GB-Lcm*, songs (1715)

Myrtillo (pastoral masque, Cibber), Drury Lane, 5 Nov 1715, *Lam*, frag. *Cfm*

Apollo and Daphne (masque, J. Hughes), Drury Lane, 12 Jan 1716, *Lam*

The Death of Dido (masque, B. Booth, after Virgil: *Aeneid*), Drury Lane, 17 April 1716, *Lam*

The Union of the Three Sister Arts (musical entertainment, ?Walsh), Lincoln's Inn Fields, 22 Nov 1723, frag. *Ckc*

The Prophetess, or The History of Dioclesian (op with spoken dialogue, T. Betterton and J. Dryden, after J. Fletcher and P. Massinger), Lincoln's Inn Fields, 28 Nov 1724

BALLAD OPERAS

The Beggar's Opera (J. Gay), Lincoln's Inn Fields, 28 Jan 1728 (1728; facs. edn 1922), ?airs arr. Pepusch, ?ov. by Pepusch

The Wedding (E. Hawker), Lincoln's Inn Fields, 6 May 1729, ov. by Pepusch (1729)

Polly (3, Gay), Little Theatre, Haymarket, 19 June 1777 (1729), ?by Pepusch

Doubtful: Music in Marsaniello, or a Fisherman Prince, Lincoln's Inn Fields, 29 March 1725, prelude, songs *Lam* [revival of D'Urfey: The History of the Rise and Fall of Marsaniello]

C. Cibber: *An Apology for the Life of Mr Colley Cibber* (London, 1740; ed. B. R. S. Fone (Ann Arbor, 1968)

C. W. Hughes: 'John Christopher Pepusch', *MQ*, xxxi (1945), 54–70

A. J. E. Lello: 'Dr. Pepusch (1667–1752)', *MT*, xciii (1952), 209–10

R. Fiske: *English Theatre Music in the Eighteenth Century* (London, 1973, 2/1986)

D. F. Cook: *The Life and Works of Johann Christoph Pepusch, 1667–1752* (diss., U. of London, 1982)   D. F. COOK

Peragallo, Mario (*b* Rome, 25 March 1910). Italian composer. He studied composition with Vincenzo di Donato and Casella, and was attracted to the musical theatre from the beginning of his career. His first work, the *melodramma Ginevra degli Almieri*, written between 1931 and 1934 and set in 14th-century Florence, adheres to realist forms, with influences ranging from Zandonai to Puccini's *Gianni Schicchi*. His next opera, *Lo stendardo di San Giorgio* (1941), follows the same stylistic line; here the plot revolves around an imaginary Genoese navigator, Rainaldo Arcanto, who after various adventures defeats the pirates of Massilia. After an uncompleted attempt to compose an opera to his own libretto after Hawthorne's *The Scarlet Letter*, Peragallo wrote the *madrigale scenico La collina* (1947). Arranged in seven solo episodes with an introduction for chorus and orchestra, it marks a shift in his musico-dramatic direction, which until then had followed the path of realist theatre. In *La gita in campagna* (1954) Peragallo, adopting 12-note technique in a free and personal way, made a final stylistic turn that was reflected in subsequent orchestral works. Later operas continued this development – although Peragallo openly retained such elements of traditional *melodramma* as closed forms and strophic structures – and include the *rondò scenico La parrucca dell'imperatore* (1959), which reveals the composer's more extrovert vein.

See also GITA IN CAMPAGNA, LA.

Ginevra degli Almieri, 1931–4 (melodramma, 3, G. Forzano), Rome, Opera, 12 Feb 1937, vs (Milan, 1937)

Lo stendardo di San Giorgio (melodramma, 3, Forzano), Genoa, Carlo Felice, 9 March 1941

La collina (madrigale scenico, after E. L. Masters: *Spoon River*), Venice, La Fenice, 27 Sept 1947, vs (Vienna, 1950)

La gita in campagna (1, A. Moravia: *Andare verso il popolo*), Milan, Scala, 24 March 1954, vs (Vienna, 1956)

La parrucca dell'imperatore (rondò scenico, G. Maselli), Spoleto, Festival, 12 June 1959

*

H. Fleischer: 'La collina di Mario Peragallo', *Il diapason* (1951), nos.3–4

M. Mila: *Cronache musicali 1955–1959* (Turin, 1959), 217–18

F. d'Amico: *I casi della musica* (Milan, 1962), 18–20

RAFFAELE POZZI

Peralta, Angela (*b* Puebla, 6 July 1845; *d* Mazatlán, 30 Aug 1883). Mexican soprano. She made her début at the Gran Teatro Nacional in 1860 as Leonora (*Il trovatore*) and went in January 1861 to Milan, where she studied with Francesco Lamperti. In 1862 she first appeared at La Scala as Lucia and, with equal success, in Turin as Amina (*La sonnambula*). Between 1862 and 1865 she toured Europe, where she was hailed as 'the Mexican nightingale'. After returning to Mexico in November 1865 she triumphed at the Teatro Imperial as Amina, and in January 1866 she began an international tour that took her to Havana, New York, Spain and Italy. Upon returning to Mexico in 1871 she toured the country with her own company, singing 166 times in *Lucia*, 122 times in *La sonnambula*, and in *La traviata*, *Dinorah*, *I puritani*, *Norma* and other operas. Peralta also appeared in Melesio Morales's *Ildegonda* (1866) and *Gino Corsini* (1877) and in Aniceto Ortega del Villar's Aztec opera, *Guatimotzín* (1871). Her last appearance was in *Trovatore* at Mazatlán on 23 August

1883, a week before her premature death of yellow fever.

E. Olavarría y Ferrari: *Reseña histórica del teatro en México* (Mexico City, 1895), ii, 337, 373–4, 380–81; iii, 106–14
R. Stevenson: *Music in Mexico: a Historical Survey* (New York, 1952), 201–3, 206, 210   ROBERT STEVENSON

Peranda [Perandi, Perande], **Marco Gioseppe** (*b* Rome or Macerata, *c*1625; *d* Dresden, 12 Jan 1675). Italian composer and singer. Possibly a pupil of Carissimi in Rome, he seems to have been first employed as an alto singer in the chapel of the heir to the electorate in Dresden; in 1656 this chapel was absorbed into the court chapel, in which he continued to sing. He became vice-Kapellmeister in 1661, and joint Kapellmeister in 1663; from the death of Schütz in 1672 until his own death he was first Hofkapellmeister.

With G. A. Bontempi and Vincenzo Albrici, Peranda was one of the chief members of the newer Italian school in Dresden. His many sacred concertos, together with his other sacred music and his stage and instrumental works, were far more representative of the repertory of the court in the period from about 1660 to 1680 than the music of Schütz, with whom he worked closely for some 20 years. In both his operas he collaborated with Bontempi, who also wrote the librettos. That of *Dafne* (1671; one of the earliest German operas surviving in full score) is modelled on Martin Opitz's *Dafne* (after O. Rinuccini), which was set by Heinrich Schütz in 1627.

Dafne (5, G. A. Bontempi), Dresden, 3 Sept 1671, *D-Dlb*, copies *B-Bc* (score, 1863) and *D-Mbs* (score, *c*1870); collab. Bontempi
Jupiter und Io (Bontempi or C. C. Dedekind), Dresden, 16 Jan 1673, collab. Bontempi

MGG (I. Becker-Glauch)
M. Fürstenau: *Zur Geschichte der Musik und des Theaters am Hofe zu Dresden* (Dresden, 1861–2)
R. Engländer: 'Zur Frage der "Dafne" (1671) von G. A. Bontempi und M. G. Peranda', *AcM*, xiii (1941), 59–77
          WOLFRAM STEUDE

Percier, Charles (*b* Paris, 22 Aug 1764; *d* Paris, 5 Sept 1838). French architect and stage designer. He worked in collaboration with PIERRE-FRANÇOIS-LÉONARD FONTAINE.

Peretti, Niccolò (*fl* 1762–82). Italian contralto castrato. He made his English début in the title role of Arne's *Artaxerxes* (February 1762) and continued to sing at Covent Garden until the 1763–4 season, when he also appeared with the Italian opera company at the King's Theatre. For the next two seasons he sang in Dublin in Italian operas and the Irish premières of *Artaxerxes* and *The Royal Shepherd*. He taught singing in Dublin until at least 1782. One of his pupils was Michael Kelly, who appeared with him in Italian comic operas at Fishamble Street in 1777–8 and wrote of him: 'He had a fine contre alto voice, and possessed the true portamento so little known in the present day'.

BDA; LS
M. Kelly: *Reminiscences of the King's Theatre* (London, 1826, 2/1826); ed. R. Fiske (London, 1975)
T. J. Walsh: *Opera in Dublin, 1705–1797* (Dublin, 1973)
          OLIVE BALDWIN, THELMA WILSON

Perez, David [Davide] (*b* Naples, 1711; *d* Lisbon, 30 Oct 1778). Italian composer. While essentially a transitional figure in 18th-century opera, he was nevertheless one of the great composers of *opera seria*.

1. LIFE. Perez's parents were Neapolitans of Spanish descent, but his training and early experience were exclusively Italian. At the age of 11 he became a pupil at the Conservatorio di S Maria di Loreto in Naples, where he remained until 1733. The violin was his principal instrument and his operas abound in virtuoso string passages; in later years he was renowned for his singing, a talent perhaps reflected in the graceful melodic profile of his arias.

On completion of his studies, Perez immediately established himself as a composer of merit. He composed *La nemica amante* in 1735 for the Teatro S Bartolomeo in Naples (though it was first performed at the Palazzo Reale), and continued his activity there for the next five years; he also served as vice-*maestro di cappella* of the royal chapel in Palermo (1738–9). On his return to Naples he firmly established himself as a mature composer with an *opera buffa*, *Li travestimenti amorosi*, and an *opera seria*, *Il Siroe*; Caffarelli and Manzuoli sang in the latter. He was recalled to Palermo as *maestro di cappella*, and his operas were performed in Genoa, Florence and Naples. He ultimately obtained leave of absence and never returned to Palermo, though he continued to receive half his Palermo salary until his death. He then set out on the cosmopolitan existence of the typical Neapolitan. In 1749 his patron, the Princess di Belmonte of Naples, introduced him to Metastasio, who thought his setting of *Vologeso* for Vienna promised 'a glorious future'.

In 1752 José I, King of Portugal, invited Perez to become *mestre de capela* and music master to the royal princesses, a position he occupied until his death. He soon became intimate with the royal family, and the king made him a Cavalier of the Order of Christ. The annual stipend of 50 000 francs, coupled with the excellent musical and theatrical resources of the Portuguese court, undoubtedly influenced his decision to remain in Lisbon. Italian opera had been firmly entrenched there since 1735. Sumptuous scenic treatment was the rule, and Perez's operas were mounted by such famous designers as Berardi, Dorneau and Bouteux. G. C. S. Galli-Bibiena's amazing sets for *Alessandro nell'Indie* in 1755 (described by Burney) and those for *La clemenza di Tito* are typical examples (for illustration *see* GALLI-BIBIENA, fig.3 and LISBON, fig.1). Equally important were the great singers who appeared at the Portuguese court, including Raaff, Elisi, Manzuoli, Gizziello and Caffarelli.

Perez wrote *Lucio Vero* for Verona in 1754 and travelled to London in 1755 for a performance of *Ezio*. After that he rarely left Lisbon and executed few commissions elsewhere, so that his international acclaim declined. Still, Gerber noted that by 1766 Perez's compositions were 'known and in demand in Germany', and J. C. Krause named Hasse, Perez and Paisiello as satisfactory models. In later years Perez became blind, but he continued to compose.

2. OPERAS. Perez's fame rests almost entirely on more than 35 dramatic works composed between 1735 and 1777. Excerpts from *Arminio*, *La Didone abbandonata*, *Ezio*, *Farnace*, *Solimano* and *Vologeso* were published in London by John Walsh, and at least 26 works exist in manuscript. He composed nearly 30 of his stage works between 1740 and 1757, his most significant period of composition in terms of quality and influence.

In the *opere serie* written before 1752 Perez was often bound by the formality of Baroque conventions. *Il Siroe*, *Andromaca* and *Alessandro nell'Indie* (1744 version) are prime examples: 20 or more full da capo arias (more than half accompanied by strings alone) are consistently used, with between one and four accompanied recitatives, usually a single duet, a perfunctory three-movement sinfonia and a simple choral finale for the principals. The arias are usually written in the Baroque concerto idiom, with extravagant word-painting in the orchestra and extensive vocal bravura passages. Adhering to Metastasio's prescription of character definition as the sum of a pattern of dramatic reversals, each aria usually depicts a single affect. Even in these operas exceptions to the predominant formalism of contemporary *opera seria* occurs: *Artaserse* (1748) and *Alessandro* each contain a scene complex of related arias and accompanied recitatives.

With *Demofoonte* in 1752, as Perez began his lengthy residence in Lisbon, the monumental idiom declined and the *galant* style gained increasing prominence, with a resultant clarity of texture, greater symmetry of phrase, frequent *buffa* motifs and an emphasis on the pathetic. In accordance with parallel changes in mid-century philosophical thought, texts which stress the inner feelings of the characters take precedence over abstract ones, and sometimes introduce *Empfindsamkeit* and *Sturm und Drang* idioms. Formal modifications include the frequent absence of ritornellos, truncated da capo arias, sectional arias, between five and nine accompanied recitatives and several small ensembles. Perez's operas of the 1750s frequently display an orchestral mastery superior to that of the contemporary Italian opera school. The strings are in three to five parts, the wind are often used for solo passages, and there is less doubling of the vocal part and an increase in concertante passages. Among the better examples of this later manner are *Olimpiade*, *Lucio Vero* (both contain significant choral sections), *Demofoonte*, *Ipermestra* and *Alessandro nell'Indie* (1755 version).

In *Solimano* (1757; rev. 1768) and *Demetrio* (1766) emphasis on dramatic situation and plasticity of form largely replaced the concept of affect as a guiding force. *Demetrio* represents a transitional aesthetic, in which Perez combined a modified Baroque dramaturgy with a more up-to-date musical style: he eliminated 14 Metastasio aria texts, used eight accompanied recitatives and two duets for moments of personal reflection, and gave the da capo aria more musical and dramatic coherence. *Solimano* is his acknowledged masterpiece. The 1757 MS contains 14 *dal segno* arias, one cavatina and six accompanied recitatives, the scope and procedures of which are exceptional; several times the individual numbers are integrated into large-scale scene complexes. The flexibility of form, dramatic contrasts and musical vitality of *Solimano* are due in large part to the juxtaposition of *buffa* and *seria* idioms and to an interchange of compositional techniques between aria and accompanied recitative. Kretzschmar (1919) claimed that *Solimano* 'belongs under the heading of masterworks … richness of invention and of feeling, originality of means and of form, everything is therein, which makes an art great'.

Several of Perez's works written after 1757 reflect French influence. *Creusa in Delfo* contains prominent chorus and ballet scenes and accompanied recitatives for two to five characters. Many of the 11 arias lack the convincing musical content of the earlier operas. In the final scenes of *Creusa* Perez achieved a continuous musical fabric, beginning with a lengthy accompanied recitative for three characters, followed by a concertante trio, which in turn leads into the final scene for all the principal characters in which declamatory recitative, arioso phrases of great expressiveness and brief arias intermingle, until a full-scale trio develops. For the most part, however, his operas of the 1760s and 70s do not appear to be the equal of some earlier works. The mixture of styles in his one-act *componimento drammatico La pace* (1777, Lisbon) and *L'isola disabitata* indicates that he drew on earlier operas to complete the necessary quota of arias. Evidently the *opera seria* no longer occupied a dominant position in his thoughts; it was his sacred works which were gaining favour.

18th-century critics often ranked Perez with Hasse and Jommelli. Burney found 'an original spirit and elegance in all his production', and when Jommelli's *Vologeso* and *Enea nel Lazio* alternated with Perez's *Demetrio* and *Solimano* in Lisbon, he noted that Jommelli was chiefly admired for the 'ingenious and learned texture of the instrumental parts' and Perez for 'the elegance and grace of his melodies, and expression of the words'. 19th- and 20th-century commentary, based for the most part on a few earlier operas, has generally downgraded this judgment. A more complete examination of his operas affirms the stature his contemporaries assigned to him.

See also SOLIMANO.

drammi per musica in three acts unless otherwise stated

La nemica amante, Naples, Palazzo Reale, 4 Nov 1735

Li travestimenti amorosi (ob, A. Palomba), Naples, Palazzo Reale, 10 July 1740, *I-Mc, US-Wc*

Il Siroe (P. Metastasio), Naples, S Carlo, 4 Nov 1740; rev. Lisbon, 1752; *D-Hs, I-Nc* (Act 1), *Vnm, P-La*, S-Skma*

Demetrio [1st version] (Metastasio), Palermo, 13 June 1741, *B-Bc, F-Pn, P-La**

L'eroismo di Scipione, Palermo, 1741

Astartea, Palermo, 1743

Alessandro nell'Indie [1st version] (Metastasio), Genoa, Falcone, carn. 1744, *A-Wn, GB-Lbl, I-Vnm, P-La, S-Skma, US-BE*

Merope (A. Zeno), Genoa, Falcone, carn. 1744, *F-Pn, P-La*

Leucippo, Palermo, S Cecilia, 1744, *F-Pn*

Medea, Palermo, 1744

L'isola incantata, Palermo, 1746

Artaserse (Metastasio), Florence, Pergola, aut. 1748, *D-Hs, GB-Lcm, I-Nc, Vnm, P-La, US-Wc*

La clemenza di Tito (Metastasio), Naples, S Carlo, 1749

Andromaca, Vienna, Imperial, 1750, *A-Wn, US-Wc*

Il Farnace (Zeno, rev. ?Lucchini), Rome, Dame, 1750, *F-Pn** (Act 1), *P-La*; Favourite Songs (London)

Semiramide (Metastasio), Rome, Dame, 1750, *GB-Lbl, P-La*, arias *I-Fc, Gl, MOe, Nc*

Vologeso (Zeno), Vienna, Imperial, 1750, *A-Wn*; Favourite Songs (London)

Ezio (Metastasio), Milan, Ducale, carn. 1751, *F-Pn*; Favourite Songs (London, 1755)

La Zenobia (Metastasio), Milan, Ducale, aut. 1751, *P-La*, arias *I-MAav, Nc, PLcon*

La Didone abbandonata (Metastasio), Genoa, 1751, *GB-Lbl, Vnm, P-La*, S-Skma, US-Wc*; Favourite Songs (London, 1761)

Adriano in Siria (Metastasio), Lisbon, Corte, 1752, *D-Hs, GB-Lbl, Lcm, I-Vnm, P-La, S-Skma, US-BE*

Demofoonte (Metastasio), Lisbon, Corte, 1752, *D-Hs, GB-Ob, I-Vnm, P-La*, S-Skma*

L'eroe cinese (Metastasio), Lisbon, Corte, 6 June 1753, *P-La**, arias *GB-Lbl, Lcm, I-Vnm, US-BE*

Olimpiade (Metastasio), Lisbon, Corte, aut. 1753, *B-Bc, D-Hs, GB-Lbl, I-Nc, Vnm, P-La*, S-Skma, US-Wc*

Andromeda, Lisbon, 1753, *GB-Lbl, I-Nc*

L'Ipermestra (Metastasio), Lisbon, 1754, *D-Hs, GB-Lbl, Lcm, I-Vnm, P-La, S-Skma, US-Wc*

Lucio Vero (Zeno), Verona, 1754, arias *I-Nc, MOe, P-La*

Alessandro nell'Indie [2nd version] (Metastasio), Lisbon, Opera, 31 March 1755, *GB-Lbl*, *P-La*
Solimano (G. Migliavacca), Lisbon, Ajuda, carn. 1757; ? rev. 1768; *F-Pn*, *GB-Lbl* (R1978: IOB, xlv), *Lcm*, *I-Nc*, *P-La*, *US-Wc*; Favourite Songs (London)
Enea in Italia, Lisbon, Salvaterra, 1759
Arminio (Salvi), London, King's, 1760, Favourite Songs (London)
La Berenice, Verona, Nuovo, carn. 1762
Giulio Cesare, Lisbon, 1762
Demetrio [2nd version] (Metastasio), Lisbon, Salvaterra, 1766, *D-Hs*, *F-Pn*, *GB-Lcm*, *I-Nc*, *US-Wc*
L'isola disabitata (pastorale, Metastasio, rev. Perez), Lisbon, Queluz, 1767, *F-Pn*, *GB-Lcm*, *I-Nc*, *P-La*
Il cinese (Metastasio), Lisbon, Quelez, 1769
Creusa in Delfo (2, G. Martinelli), Lisbon, Salvaterra, carn. 1774, *P-La*
Il ritorno di Ulisse in Itaca (1, B. Mortelli), Lisbon, Queluz, 1774, *F-Pn*

*

BurneyH; *EitnerQ*; *FlorimoN*
H. Kretzschmar: 'Aus Deutschlands italienischer Zeit', *JbMP*, viii (1901), 45
H. Abert: *Niccolò Jommelli als Opernkomponist* (Halle, 1908)
H. Kretzschmar: *Geschichte der Oper* (Leipzig, 1919)
U. Prota-Giurleo: *Musicisti napoletani alla corte di Portogallo* (Naples, 1923)
W. Vetter: 'Gluck und seine italienischen Zeitgenossen', *ZMw*, vii (1924–5), 609–46
E. Soares: *David Perez: subsidios para a biografia do célébre mestre de musica de camera de D. José* (Lisbon, 1935)
P. J. Jackson: *The Operas of David Perez* (diss., Stanford U., 1967)
G. Allroggen: 'Piccinnis Origille', *AnMc*, no.15 (1975), 258–97
A. McCredie: 'La riforma operatistica prima di Gluck e il teatro musicale eroico tedesco dello Sturm und Drang', *Ricerche musicali*, v (1981), 86–108
M. C. de Brito: *Opera in Portugal in the Eighteenth Century* (Cambridge, 1989)
PAUL J. JACKSON

Pérez Soriano, Agustín (*b* Valtierra, Navarra, 28 Aug 1846; *d* Madrid, 27 Feb 1907). Spanish composer. He studied first with his father, and abandoned ecclesiastical studies in Pamplona to enter the Madrid Conservatory. Settling in Saragossa, he developed the musical life by organizing concerts and music societies; he also helped found the Saragossa music school and published studies of folk music. His compositions include chamber and orchestral music, but his speciality lay in the popular field. The zarzuela *El guitarrico* (1900) achieved a notable success and is remembered for its striking serenade, which has been recorded by many singers, including Carreras and Domingo.

all zarzuelas
Atila, 1895; Pepita Melaza, 1895; Los bárbaros, 1897; El Bohemio (1, Pinedo), Barcelona, May 1897; Al compás de la jota (1, C. Navarro), Saragossa, May 1897; La panadera (L. Ballesteros), Barcelona, 8 May 1899; El guitarrico (M. Fernández de la Puente and L. P. Frutos), Madrid, Zarzuela, 9 Oct 1900; El rosario de coral (J. C. de Arpe), Madrid, 1 Jan 1905

StiegerO
'Pérez Soriano (Agustín)', *Enciclopedia universal ilustrada europeo-americana* (Barcelona, 1907–30)
ANDREW LAMB

Perfall, Karl Freiherr **von** (*b* Munich, 29 Jan 1824; *d* Munich, 14 Jan 1907). German administrator and composer. After studying law, he was briefly a civil servant before becoming a pupil of Moritz Hauptmann in Leipzig (1848–9). Moving back to Munich, he directed the Liedertafel from 1850 and founded the Oratorienverein in 1854; he was appointed court Intendant by Ludwig II in 1864. He took over direction of the Nationaltheater, at first provisionally, but in 1869 he became Intendant there and in 1872 general Intendant. An energetic and practical administrator, he greatly improved the theatre itself (installing electric

lighting as early as 1882) and the scope and standard of the performances. He took up Wagner's cause with what seems to have been genuine and independent enthusiasm, and in the face of dictatorial hostility from the composer, who even tried to enforce his suspension upon the king. *Die Meistersinger* (1868), *Das Rheingold* (1869) and *Die Walküre* (1870) were all first performed during his intendancy, and over 700 Wagner performances were given in 25 years. In 1878 he proposed to the king that the Munich Opera, having benefited so greatly from Wagner's music, should pay the composer a 10% royalty until the discharge of the deficit that had accumulated after the Bayreuth Festival of 1876; this was a crucial step in saving Bayreuth. Wagner and his early champions give a prejudiced view of Perfall, but Bülow found him both artistically and administratively very competent. The Munich Opera Festival, which began in the summer of 1875, was founded by him. He retired in 1893 and published two books on theatre history, *Ein Beitrag zur Geschichte des königlichen Theaters in München* (Munich, 1894) and *Die Entwicklung des modernen Theaters* (Munich, 1899). His own operas were performed in Munich with moderate success.

all performed at Munich, Hoftheater
Sakuntala (grosse Oper, 3, Teichert), 10 April 1853
Das Konterfei (komische Oper, 3, M. Schleich), 20 Dec 1863
Raimondin (5, H. Schmid), 27 March 1881 (Leipzig, 1882); rev. as Melusine, 1885
Junker Heinz (3, F. Grandauer), 9 April 1886; rev. as Jung Heinrich, 1902

*

StiegerO
S. Roeckl: *Ludwig II und Richard Wagner* (Munich, 1920)
A. von Mensi-Klarbach: *Alt-Münchener Theater-Erinnerungen* (Munich, 1923)
E. Stemplinger: *Richard Wagner in München* (Munich, 1933)
E. Newman: *The Life of Richard Wagner*, iv (London, 1947)
G. Oexle: *Generalintendant Karl von Perfall* (diss., U. of Munich, 1954)
JOHN WARRACK

Perfect Fool, The. Opera in one act, op.39, by GUSTAV HOLST to his own libretto; London, Covent Garden, 14 May 1923.

The opera begins with a ballet of the Spirits of Earth, Water and Fire, summoned by the Wizard (baritone). Conceived in part as a parody of *Parsifal*, the action concerns the efforts of the Mother (contralto) to marry off her son, the Fool (spoken role). The Wizard intends to drink a magic potion which will cause the Princess (soprano) to fall in love with him; but the Mother gives the potion to her son. A Troubadour (tenor) and a Traveller (bass) – rather heavy-handed parodies of Verdi and Wagner respectively – unsuccessfully woo the Princess, who is captivated by the Fool. In spite of the Wizard's efforts a wedding is arranged for the Princess and the Fool, but the latter is so apathetic that he falls asleep as he is about to be crowned.

The Perfect Fool is a naive and dramatically inept curiosity, whose libretto is only occasionally saved by the quality of the score, particularly the opening ballet music.
COLIN MATTHEWS

Pergola. Theatre in FLORENCE, in the via della Pergola, opened in 1657 and reconstructed in 1718; it became an 'imperial theatre' in 1810.

Pergolesi, Giovanni Battista (*b* Iesi, Marche, 4 Jan 1710; *d* Pozzuoli, nr Naples, 16 March 1736). Italian composer. He was a leading figure in the rise of Italian comic opera in the 18th century.

1. Life. 2. Posthumous fame. 3. Works.

1. LIFE. His grandfather, Cruciano Draghi, was a shoemaker, a son of Maestro Francesco from Pergola; he married a woman from Iesi in that town on 1 January 1663. The family was known as 'Pergolesi' from the town of their origin (although the composer's elder brother and sister were entered in the baptismal register under the name 'Draghi'). In the files of the conservatory where he studied, Giovanni Battista is entered under the name 'Jesi', although he called himself 'Pergolesi'; in contemporary records the form 'Pergolese' is also used.

The composer's father, Francesco Andrea Draghi-Pergolesi, was a surveyor, and in that capacity formed links with the nobility of Iesi. One such nobleman was the godfather of Giovanni Battista, the third child; another defended his interests in a dispute over the will after his father's death on 27 May 1732 (his mother had died in 1727). The composer's two brothers and one sister died in infancy, and even as a child Giovanni Battista seems to have been sickly: it is significant that he was confirmed as early as 27 May 1711. The Roman caricaturist Leone Ghezzi depicted him (probably in 1735) with a deformed leg and remarked that Pergolesi limped and had a serious deformity; it has been suggested that he also suffered from a tubercular disease.

According to later tradition, Pergolesi received his elementary musical training from the *maestro di cappella* at Iesi, Francesco Santi, and was instructed on the violin by Francesco Mondini, the public music master. Through the Marquis Cardolo Maria Pianetti, of Iesi, he was sent to study at the Conservatorio dei Poveri di Gesù Cristo in Naples at some time between 1720 and 1724, probably in the late summer of 1722 or 1723. Gaetano Greco, *maestro di cappella* of the conservatory until his death in 1728, was Pergolesi's instructor in composition; Greco was succeeded for a few months by Leonardo Vinci and then, from October 1728, by Francesco Durante. Pergolesi did not have to pay maintenance or tuition expenses at the conservatory because he took part in musical performances, first as a choirboy, later as a violinist and as *capoparanza* (the leading violinist of one of the groups of instrumentalists made available by the conservatory for performances in Naples and the surrounding area).

Pergolesi must have left the conservatory in the late summer of 1731. He received his first opera commission in 1731, which suggests that he enjoyed influential patronage. The libretto chosen was *Alessandro Severo*, written by Zeno for Venice in 1716 and now revised as *Salustia*. It would seem, from the fact that the author of the text for the intermezzo (Domenico Caracajus) himself set the recitatives of the second part to music, that Pergolesi had to compose the music in haste. The most famous member of the cast for *Salustia*, Nicolini, died on 1 January 1732; Gioacchino Conti was brought from Rome to replace him, and Pergolesi had to make last-minute alterations. Accordingly, the opera was not staged until the second half of January 1732, and apparently it had little success; the second opera of the season, *Alessandro nelle Indie* by the court *maestro di cappella* Francesco Mancini, followed as early as 2 February.

In 1732 Pergolesi became *maestro di cappella* to Prince Ferdinando Colonna Stigliano, equerry to the Viceroy of Naples. *Lo frate 'nnamorato*, his first *commedia musicale*, was performed at the Teatro dei Fiorentini in Naples on 27 September 1732; the libretto was by G. A. Federico, a lawyer and the leading Neapolitan comedy writer of the time. *Lo frate 'nnamorato* met with unusual success. The performances may have continued into 1733, and for Carnival 1734 Pergolesi had to revise the work for a new cast. When there was a new production of the opera in 1748, at the Teatro Nuovo, the work was said to have been recited and sung in the city streets for the previous 20 years.

There were earthquakes in Naples in late November and early December 1732; during Carnival 1733 the theatres of Naples remained closed as a sign of atonement. For the empress's birthday (28 August 1733) Pergolesi was commissioned to write an opera, *Il prigioniero superbo* (after Silvani's libretto *La fede tradita e vendicata*). The impresario had engaged an unusual and small cast: there was no primo uomo and the prima donna was an alto. The text of the intermezzo, *La serva padrona*, was written by Federico. For some reason the first performance did not take place until 5 September 1733; there were further performances continuing into October. On 23 February 1734, presumably because of his services during the festivities in honour of St Emidius, Pergolesi was appointed deputy to the *maestro di cappella* of the city, Domenico Sarro, with the right to succeed him.

In March 1734 the claimant to the Neapolitan throne, Charles Bourbon, approached the city with Spanish troops. The Austrians, who had ruled Naples since 1707 through a viceroy, retreated into the citadel and remained there until the beginning of May; on 10 May Charles celebrated his solemn entry into the city and reinstated the Kingdom of Naples. Pergolesi's patron, the Prince of Stigliano, had withdrawn to Rome. Another Neapolitan nobleman, Marzio Domenico IV Carafa, Duke of Maddaloni, ordered a performance of a mass by Pergolesi in the church of S Lorenzo in Lucina, Rome, on the festival of St John Nepomuk (16 May 1734); this was the Mass in F, which aroused great interest, if only because the Neapolitan 'number' mass was unusual in Rome.

It may have been in connection with the performance that Pergolesi entered the Duke of Maddaloni's service as *maestro di cappella*. He probably returned to Naples in the duke's entourage in June 1734. The duke's uncle and guardian, Lelio Carafa, Marquis d'Arienzo, was among the closest friends of King Charles, and in September 1734 was entrusted with the supervision of the opera house. Pergolesi was commissioned to write an opera for the birthday of the king's mother on 25 October 1734. The libretto chosen was Metastasio's *Adriano in Siria*; the text of the intermezzo (now known as *Livietta e Tracollo*) was supplied by Tommaso Mariani. One of the most famous singers of the 18th century, Caffarelli, who had been admitted into King Charles's musical establishment, was engaged as primo uomo. In setting the libretto Pergolesi had to take note of Caffarelli's wishes, and Metastasio's text was considerably rewritten. This was Pergolesi's last opera for Naples. In a statement by the impresario of the Teatro S Bartolomeo to the Marquis d'Arienzo in 1735, Pergolesi is no longer mentioned among the composers who could be called on, and in a second document it is stated that he was esteemed as a musician but that his last opera had failed to please.

It must accordingly have come as some compensation to Pergolesi that his mass in S Lorenzo in Lucina had aroused the interest of the Roman public; he was commissioned to set Metastasio's *L'olimpiade* for the Teatro Tordinona in Rome for Carnival 1735. Metastasio, who had reports sent to him in Vienna about the preparations for the première, became indignant: the chorus which he required had been omitted, and the cast was mediocre. Nevertheless Pergolesi (who apparently wrote most of the opera in Naples) had to make further alterations for the singers; he composed one new aria, and in four others drew on *Adriano in Siria*. The performances began in January. After a few days they were interrupted when the Rome theatres were closed because of the death of Maria Clementina Stuart-Sobieski, wife of the pretender to the English throne. Performances were resumed on 23 January, but the theatres were again closed on 1 and 2 February for the Candlemas festival; by 5 February the next opera, Ciampi's *Demofoonte*, was in production. Grétry's report, which depends on Duni for its evidence, states that *L'olimpiade* was a failure and that a member of the audience threw an orange which struck Pergolesi on the head (one of the many traditional stories about him). It must be admitted that initially *L'olimpiade* did not apparently enjoy any special success; but it lived on in a manner unusual for an *opera seria* of the time. It was staged in Perugia for Carnival 1738, and again in Cortona that year. It was also heard in numerous pasticcio versions throughout Europe, including the one given on 20 April 1742 at the King's Theatre, London, as *Meraspe*. An extensive manuscript tradition attests the fact that *L'olimpiade* was still highly esteemed by connoisseurs and operagoers in the second half of the century.

Pergolesi's health seems to have deteriorated in the summer of 1735 (De Brosses said that he died of tuberculosis). He had his last theatrical success with *Flaminio*, a comedy on a text by Federico produced in the Teatro Nuovo in Naples in autumn 1735; the libretto refers to Pergolesi as organist of the royal chapel. The comedy was performed again in winter 1737 at the Teatro dei Fiorentini, and for Carnival 1743 it was given in Siena as a *divertimento giocoso*; it was also staged with a new production of *Lo frate 'nnamorato* in the Teatro Nuovo in Naples in 1748 and 1749. Pergolesi was commissioned to write a serenata (*Il tempo felice*) for the wedding of Raimondo di Sangro, Prince of Sansevero, at Torremaggiore in December 1735. According to the libretto, dated 9 November 1735, the second part was set by Nicola Sabatino because Pergolesi was in poor health.

Early in 1736 Pergolesi moved into the Franciscan monastery in Pozzuoli founded by the ancestors of his patron, the Duke of Maddaloni. His aunt, Cecilia Giorgi, from Iesi, who had been his housekeeper, remained in Naples; he is said to have handed his possessions over to her, which suggests that he did not expect to recover. According to Boyer, during his final illness Pergolesi composed the cantata *Orfeo*, the *Stabat mater* and (his last work) the *Salve regina* in C minor for soprano and strings (the cantata was in fact written before *Flaminio*). Villarosa, however, said that Pergolesi's last work was the *Stabat mater*, written for the noble fraternity in the church of S Maria dei Sette Dolori in Naples as a replacement for Alessandro Scarlatti's *Stabat mater*. Pergolesi, aged 26, died in Pozzuoli and was buried in the common pit next to the cathedral. The Marquis Domenico Corigliano di Rignano, who then owned the *Stabat mater* manuscript and was a friend of the first Pergolesi biographer, Villarosa, had a memorial tablet for him set up in the cathedral at Pozzuoli; the inscription on it was by Villarosa. In September 1890 a side-chapel of the cathedral was prepared as Pergolesi's burial chapel and the memorial tablet was transferred there.

2. POSTHUMOUS FAME. Pergolesi enjoyed only limited success during his lifetime, but the almost universal fame he attained posthumously represented a new phenomenon in music history. Shortly after his death a collection of four of his cantatas was published: this was the first time that cantatas had been printed in Naples, and as early as 1738 a second edition appeared. Queen Maria Amalia of Naples ordered in 1738 that *La serva padrona* and *Livietta e Tracollo* be performed, and added: 'Questo autore è difonto, ma fu uomo grande'. President De Brosses called Pergolesi 'mon auteur d'affection' as early as 1739. Pergolesi's fame was spread by performances of *Lo frate 'nnamorato*, *Flaminio*, *L'olimpiade* and his church music, but above all by travelling troupes of players who took his comedies, particularly *La serva padrona*, into their repertory. The work received at least 24 new productions in its first ten years, including Rome, Spoleto, Parma, Milan, Fermo, Graz, Lucca, Venice, Munich, Dresden, Modena, Siena and Hamburg. It was given on 1 August 1752 in Paris, where it had first been heard in 1746. This second series of performances met with a tremendous response and was the cause of the Querelle des Bouffons, the pamphlet war between the supporters of traditional French opera and the proponents of Italian *opera buffa*; Pergolesi's name came to symbolize the aesthetics of J.-J. Rousseau and the 'progressive' party. Two printings of *La serva padrona* appeared in Paris in 1752; these were followed by two editions of a French adaptation under the title *La servante maîtresse* by Baurans, and in 1759 by the appearance of *The Favourite Songs in the Burletta La serva padrona* in London.

Livietta e Tracollo, the *Salve regina* and above all the *Stabat mater* achieved equally widespread fame. The vogue for Pergolesi caused many works to be wrongly attributed to him, creating a confusion that has long persisted and is reflected in the *Opera omnia* (1939–42). Among the most important misattributions are an intermezzo, *Il maestro di musica* (based largely on a work by Auletta).

3. WORKS. Pergolesi had the good fortune to be able to apply himself at an unusually early age to what was then the most important musical genre, the *opera seria*. All his *opere serie* were written under unfavourable circumstances. *Salustia* has conservative features not to be found in his later works; this may be connected with the choice of libretto and with the fact that the intended primo uomo, Nicolini, was at the end of his career (and died before it was performed). No other of Pergolesi's operatic characters has the grandeur and pathos of Marziano, intended for Nicolini: it is like an echo of the music of the high Baroque era. The notable influence of the *buffo* melody in some of the arias is a new and significant departure for Pergolesi. The style, so disjointed in *Salustia*, is more polished in *Il prigioniero superbo*. Pathos is replaced by sentimentality and gallantry, and formal accompanying figures become more prominent in the orchestral writing. Because of the

unusual cast there are none of the splendid soprano arias that normally highlight an *opera seria*. This makes the opera a strangely colourless work, for Pergolesi was not yet able to turn the performers' lack of virtuosity to account so as to increase the dramatic intensity.

Adriano in Siria is an excellent example of the extent to which the composition of an *opera seria* could be influenced by the demands of a single singer. The alterations to Metastasio's libretto affected not only the part of Pharnaspes (composed for Caffarelli) but also the relationship of his arias to those of the other performers, which in turn affected their number, position and character. Of Metastasio's 27 aria texts, only ten were retained: eight were omitted, nine replaced by different texts; one additional new aria was inserted, making ten new arias altogether. Caffarelli's three arias are extended beyond anything else in Pergolesi's music up to that date; they are veritable concert pieces and the focal points of the opera. Each of these expresses a different 'affection', but the expression is subordinated to the need for allowing Caffarelli the opportunity to shine vocally; this is done differently each time and with new effects. The unusual care and precision which Pergolesi lavished on the arias of the supporting cast is still more remarkable. In *L'olimpiade*, composed for Rome, the special requirements which Pergolesi had to fulfil were comparatively modest. As with *Il prigioniero superbo*, the cast was relatively undistinguished, but the result was quite different. The fact that in *L'olimpiade* Pergolesi used arias from no opera older than *Adriano in Siria* might be taken to suggest that he was conscious of his recent development as an artist. *L'olimpiade* is characterized by idyllic and delicate tone-colours, smooth, expressive melodies which exclude virtuosity, free treatment of the text (for example with verbal repetitions of the kind used in *opera buffa*) and a greater intensity of feeling. To some extent the arias have a new function, for instead of summing up the content of a scene and rounding it off, they bring the action to a climax, in the manner of the *commedia musicale*. In the well-known aria 'Se cerca, se dice' this causes the da capo form to be broken.

Of Pergolesi's two *commedie musicali* the earlier, *Lo frate 'nnamorato*, is his first completely independent work and also the most important extant example of the genre. It is in Neapolitan dialect, and a local note is prominent in its music. Folksong-like pieces, *seria* arias, *seria* parodies and *buffo* numbers are juxtaposed with great assurance. Federico's text for *Flaminio* is less fortunate; it testifies to the decline of the Neapolitan comedy under the influence of Metastasian opera. Federico tried to link comedy motifs according to *opera seria* convention, and adopted the hierarchy of roles characteristic of that form: the *buffo* elements were compressed into individual scenes, and the plot became sentimental. Pergolesi's music seems to be full of allusions and quotations, only a few of which can be deciphered. In *Flaminio*, unlike *Lo frate 'nnamorato*, the *parti serie* and *parti buffe* are clearly differentiated, and what were later to be known as *parti caricate* are introduced; using a wide stylistic repertory, Pergolesi endowed these roles with unusually personal and individual traits.

La serva padrona, the intermezzo to *Il prigioniero superbo*, is a work of true genius. Pergolesi's basic method of portrayal is the gesture-like *buffo* style, which he developed to an unsurpassed vitality and effectiveness. As Federico's libretto provided him not only with effective *buffo* scenes but also with a plot which develops logically between credibly drawn characters, it was possible both for the characters to express themselves naturally within the idiom of the music and for the music to make clear the characters' motivation. On the other hand, Mariani's libretto for *Livietta e Tracollo*, the intermezzo to *Adriano in Siria*, offered no more than buoyant situation comedy and robust scenes on which Pergolesi's music could not impose unity. His *buffo* style is still more concentrated and cryptic than in *La serva padrona*, but the individual numbers are not part of a plot which develops in a credible way; instead they appear as single pieces (including some of a characteristically melancholy and tender tone for Livietta).

See also ADRIANO IN SIRIA (ii); FLAMINIO; FRATE 'NNAMORATO, LO; LIVIETTA E TRACOLLO; OLIMPIADE, L' (ii); PRIGIONIERO SUPERBO, IL; and SERVA PADRONA, LA.

Editions: G. B. Pergolesi: Opera omnia, ed. F. Caffarelli (Rome, 1939–42) [C]
[Of the 148 works in this edition, 69 are misattributed, 49 are questionable and only 30 may be considered genuine. A large number of works attributed to Pergolesi, some of which may be authentic, were omitted. For further information see Paymer (1977)]
G. B. Pergolesi: The Complete Works, ed. B. S. Brook and others (New York and Milan, 1986–) [B]
[for complete contents see Brook (1986)]

title	genre, acts	libretto	first performance	sources, edn; remarks
Salustia	os, 3	?S. Morelli, after A. Zeno: *Alessandro Severo*	Naples, S Bartolomeo, Jan 1732	*I-Mc, Nc*; C ix; B i
[Nibbio e Nerina]	int, 2	?D. Caracajus	Naples, S Bartolomeo, Jan 1732	perf. with Salustia; music lost; recit in pt 2 set by Caracajus
Lo frate 'nnamorato	commedia musicale, 3	G. A. Federico	Naples, Fiorentini, 27 Sept 1732; rev. Naples, carn. 1734	*B-Bc, GB-Lbl, I-Mc, Nc*; C ii; B vii
[Capetà Cola, Spaviento e Giulietta]	introduction, balli		Naples, Fiorentini, 27 Sept 1732	perf. with Lo frate 'nnamorato; music lost
Il prigioniero superbo	os, 3	after F. Silvani: *La fede tradita e vendicata*	Naples, S Bartolomeo, 5 Sept 1733	*Nc*; C xx; B ii

title	genre, acts	libretto	first performance	sources, edn; remarks
La serva padrona [characters: Serpina, Umberto]	int, 2	Federico	Naples, S Bartolomeo, 5 Sept 1733	perf. with Il prigioniero superbo; *A-Wgm, Wn, B-Bc, Br, D-Dlb, W, F-Pn, I-Bc, BGc, Fc, Gl, Mc, Nc, PAc, PESc, Rsc, Tf, Vc*; C xi/l, sinfonia spurious, probably Viennese; B v
Adriano in Siria	os, 3	P. Metastasio	Naples, S Bartolomeo, 25 Oct 1734	*GB-Lbl, I-Nc*; C xiv; B iii
[Livietta e Tracollo/La contadina astuta]	int, 2	T. Mariani	Naples, S Bartolomeo, 25 Oct 1734	perf. with Adriano in Siria; *B-Bc, Br, GB-Lbl, I-Bc, Fc, Mc, Nc, PESc, Rsc, Tf*; C xi/3; B vi
L'olimpiade	os, 3	Metastasio	Rome, Tordinona, ?2 Jan 1735	*A-Wn, B-Bc, Br, D-Dlb, F-Pn, I-BGc, Mc, MOe, Nc, Rsc*; C xxiv; B iv
Il Flaminio	commedia musicale, 3	Federico	Naples, Nuovo, aut. 1735	*B-Bc, I-Nc* [Act 3*]; C xii; B viii

Works based on or related to Livietta e Tracollo: Il ladro finto pazzo, Milan, Regio, 1739; Il finto pazzo (addns C. Goldoni), Venice, S Samuele, May 1741, addl arias by P. Chiarini, rev. Goldoni and Chiarini as Amor fa l'uomo cieco, Venice, 1742; Il Tracollo, Venice, S Moisè, aut. 1744; Livietta, Venice, S Moisè, carn. 1746; La finta polacca, Rome, 2 Feb 1748; Il ladro convertito per amore, Venice, 1750; Tracollo, medico ignorante, Paris, 1753; Le charlatan

Spurious works: Ricimero, 1732 [probably an alternative title for Il prigioniero superbo]; Il geloso schernito, C iii [probably pasticcio by P. Chiarini, sinfonia by B. Galuppi]; La contadina astuta [characters: Tabarano, Scintilla], C xi/2 [pasticcio (B. Saddumene) based on 2 ints by J. A. Hasse: La contadina and Il tutore, and 1 duet from Pergolesi's Il Flaminio; also known as Il Tabarano]; Il maestro di musica, Paris, Opéra, 19 Sept 1752, C xxv [pasticcio based largely on P. Auletta: Orazio, but incl. 2 authentic arias – 'Son timida fanciulla', C xxv, 67, and 'Non vo' più dargli ascotto', C xxv, 45, and 1 authentic duet – 'Venite, deh siate gentile', C xxv, 51; also perf. as Le maître de musique, Paris, Comédie-Italienne (Bourgogne), 31 May 1755]

BurneyH; *FlorimoN*

J.-J. Rousseau: *Lettre de MM. du coin du roi à MM. du coin de la reine sur la nouvelle pièce intitulée La servante maîtresse* (Paris, 1754)

C. Boyer: 'Notices sur la vie et les ouvrages de Pergolèse', *Mercure de France* (July 1772)

C. de Rosa, Marquis of Villarosa: *Lettera biografica intorno alla patria ed alla vita di Gio: Battista Pergolese celebre compositore di musica* (Naples, 1831, enlarged 2/1843)

C. de Brosses: *L'Italie il y a cent ans, ou Lettres écrites d'Italie à quelques amis en 1739 et 1740* (Paris, 2/1836)

G. Annibaldi: *Alcune delle notizie più importanti intorno al Pergolesi recentemente scoperte: il Pergolesi in Pozzuoli: vita intima* (Iesi, 1890)

E. J. Dent: 'Ensembles and Finales in 18th-century Italian Opera', *SIMG*, xi (1909–10), 543–69; xii (1910–11), 112–38

G. Radiciotti: *G. B. Pergolesi: vita, opere ed influenza su l'arte* (Rome, 1910, 2/1935)

E. J. Dent: 'Italian Opera in the Eighteenth Century and its Influence on the Music of the Classical Period', *SIMG*, xiv (1912–13), 500–09

A. della Corte: *G. B. Pergolesi* (Turin, 1936)

F. Schlitzer: *G. B. Pergolesi* (Turin, c1940)

S. A. Luciani, ed.: *G. B. Pergolesi (1710–1736): note e documenti*, Chigiana, iv (1942)

F. Walker: 'Two Centuries of Pergolesi Forgeries and Misattributions', *ML*, xxx (1949), 297–320

——: 'Goldoni and Pergolesi', *MMR*, lxxx (1950), 200–05

——: 'Pergolesiana', *ML*, xxxii (1951), 295–6

U. Prota-Giurleo: 'Breve storia del Teatro di corte e della musica a Napoli nei secoli XVII–XVIII', *Il Teatro di corte del Palazzo reale di Napoli* (Naples, 1952)

F. Walker: 'Orazio: the History of a Pasticcio', *MQ*, xxxviii (1952), 369–83

——: 'Pergolesi Legends', *MMR*, lxxxii (1952), 144–8, 180–83

A.-E. Cherbuliez: *G. B. Pergolesi: Leben und Werk* (Zürich and Stuttgart, 1954) [based on Radiciotti]

H. Hucke: 'Die neapolitanische Tradition in der Oper', *IMSCR, viii New York 1961*, i, 253–76

F. Degrada: 'Falsi pergolesiani: dagli apocrifi ai ritratti', *Convegno musicale*, i (1964), 133–42

——: 'Linee d'una storia della critica pergolesiana', *Convegno musicale*, ii (1965), 13–43

——: 'Alcuni falsi autografi pergolesiani', *RIM*, i (1966), 32–48

——: 'Uno sconosciuto intermezzo di Giovanni Battista Pergolesi', *CHM*, iv (1966), 79–91

H. Hucke: 'Die musikalischen Vorlagen zu Igor Strawinskys Pulcinella', *Helmuth Osthoff zu seinem siebzigsten Geburtstag* (Tutzing, 1969), 241–50

H. Hell: *Die neapolitanische Opernsinfonie in der ersten Hälfte des 18. Jahrhunderts* (Tutzing, 1971)

B. S. Brook: 'Piracy and Panacea in the Dissemination of Music in the Late Eighteenth Century', *PRMA*, cii (1975–6), 13–36

M. E. Paymer: *G. B. Pergolesi: a Thematic Catalogue of the Opera Omnia with an Appendix Listing Omitted Compositions* (New York, 1977)

O. Ferrari: 'Considerazioni sulle vicende artistiche a Napoli durante il viceregno austriaco (1707–1734)', *Storia dell'arte*, xxxv (1979), 11–27

H. Hucke: 'Pergolesi: Probleme eines Werkverzeichnisses', *AcM*, lii (1980), 195–224

B. Brook and M. E. Paymer: 'The Pergolesi Hand: a Calligraphic Study', *Notes*, xxxviii (1981–2), 550–78

D. E. Monson: *Recitativo semplice in the Opere Serie of G. B. Pergolesi and his Contemporaries* (diss., Columbia U., 1982)

H. E. Beckwith: *Giovanni Battista Pergolesi and the Chamber Cantata* (diss., U. of Maryland, 1983)

Studi pergolesiani, i (1986), 3–217 [incl. J. A. Rice: 'Pergolesi's *Ricimero* reconsidered', 80–88; D. E. Monson: 'The Last Word: the Cadence in *recitativo semplice* of Italian Opera Seria, 89–105'; H. E. Beckwith: 'Text and Harmony in Pergolesi's Recitatives for Stage and Chamber', 116–23; P. Weiss: 'Ancora sulle origini dell'opera comica: il linguaggio', 124–48; G. Lazarevich: 'From Naples to Paris: Transformations of Pergolesi's Intermezzo *Livietta e Tracollo* by Contemporary Buffo Singers', 149–65; F. Piperno: 'Gli interpreti buffi di Pergolesi: note sulla diffusione de *La serva padrona*', 166–77]

J. Blume: 'Sempre in contrasti: Heiterkeit und Empfindsamkeit bei Pergolesi', *NZM*, Jg.147 (1986), no.2, pp.4–7

B. Brook: 'Pergolesi: Vindication after 250 Years', *MT*, cxxvii (1986), 141–5

D. E. Monson: Preface to *Adriano in Siria*, The Complete Works of Giovanni Battista Pergolesi, ed. B. S. Brook and others (New York and Milan, 1986–)

G. Rotondella: 'Giovanni Battista Pergolesi: fra leggenda e realtà', *Rassegna musicale curci*, xxxix/2 (1986), 17–19

Studi pergolesiani, ii (1988), 3–238 [incl. D. E. Monson: 'Evidence for Pergolesi's Compositional Method for the Stage: the *Flaminio* Autograph', 49–66; M. E. Paymer: 'The Pergolesi Overtures: Problems and Perplexities', 78–88; D. Libby: 'The Relation of the Score to Performance in Pergolesi's *opere serie* based on a Study of his *Salustia*', 103–9; G. Lazarevich: 'Pergolesi and the "Guerre des Bouffons"', 195–203; E. Owens: '*La serva padrona* in London, 1750–1783', 204–21]

H. Weber: 'Der Serva-padrona-Topos in der Oper: Komik als Spiel mit musikalischen und sozialen Normen', *AMw*, xlv (1988), 87–110   HELMUT HUCKE, DALE E. MONSON

Peri, Achille (*b* Reggio Emilia, 20 Dec 1812; *d* Reggio Emilia, 28 March 1880). Italian composer. He studied the piano and composition with local teachers and then spent several years in Paris studying with Carafa. He assembled an opera company in Paris and toured the provinces, putting on his first stage work, *Una visita a Bedlam*, in Marseilles in 1839. Economic difficulties forced him to return to Italy where the first of his serious operas, *Il solitario*, was performed in 1841. Several of those that followed had considerable success, particularly *Dirce* (1843), *Tancreda* (1847) and his best work, the biblical drama *Giuditta*, which, after a disastrous première at La Scala in 1860, was revived there two years later with great success. His last two operas, performed at La Scala in 1861 and 1862, were complete failures, causing him to give up writing for the stage. Peri was also *maestro di cappella* of Reggio Cathedral, for which he composed a large amount of church music of slight value, and was conductor at the opera there. As an opera composer he was an imitator of Donizetti and Mercadante.

Una visita a Bedlam (operetta), Marseilles, 1839, 1 duet, vs (Paris, n.d.)
Il solitario (os, 2, G. Bassi), Reggio Emilia, Comunale, 29 May 1841
Ester d'Engaddi (dramma tragico, 3, S. Cammarano), Parma, Reggio, 19 Feb 1843, *I-Mr**, vs (Milan, n.d.)
Dirce (tragedia lirica, 3, P. Martini), Reggio Emilia, Comunale, May 1843
Tancreda (dramma lirico, 3, F. Guidi), Genoa, Carlo Felice, 26 Dec 1847, vs, excerpts (Milan, n.d.)
Orfano e diavolo (melodramma comico, 3), Reggio Emilia, Comunale, 26 Dec 1854
I fidanzati (melodramma, 3, F. M. Piave), Genoa, Carlo Felice, 7 Feb 1856, *Mr**, vs (Milan, 1856)
Vittore Pisani (melodramma, 3, Piave), Reggio Emilia, Comunitativo, 21 April 1857, *Mr**, vs (Milan, ?1857)
Giuditta (melodramma biblico, 3, M. M. Marcello), Milan, Scala, 26 March 1860, *Mr**, vs (Milan, 1861)
L'espiazione (os, 3, T. Solera), Milan, Scala, 7 Feb 1861, *Mr**, vs (1861)
Rienzi (os, 3, Piave), Milan, Scala, 26 Dec 1862, *Mr**, excerpts, pf acc. (Milan, ?1863)

*

T. G. Kaufman: 'Achille Peri', *Verdi and his Major Contemporaries* (New York, 1990), 169–78   GIOVANNI CARLI BALLOLA

Peri, Jacopo ['Zazzerino'] (*b* Rome or Florence, 20 Aug 1561; *d* Florence, on or before 12 Aug 1633). Italian composer. He was a central figure in the development of opera. His contributions to *Dafne* (Carnival 1597–8) and *Euridice* (1600), the earliest operas for which complete music survives, were crucial in establishing the musical styles of the new genre in the early 17th century.

There is some doubt about the place of his birth, but at an early age he was in Florence. As early as 1573 he was engaged by the convent of Ss Annunziata (where he may have been a student) to sing *laude* to the organ. Peri studied music with Cristofano Malvezzi, *maestro di cappella* of the cathedral and one of the most prominent musicians in Florence, and from him Peri presumably gained a solid grounding in counterpoint and composi-

tion. Malvezzi had enough confidence in the ability of his pupil to include two of Peri's compositions (a ricercare and a madrigal) in his own publications. Before his 18th birthday, in 1579, Peri had been appointed organist at the Badia and a few years later, in 1586, he served as a singer in the Florentine Baptistery (S Giovanni Battista).

By 1588, Peri had been engaged at the Medici court as a musician, but his association with courtly circles certainly predated his appointment, for as early as 1583, along with Malvezzi, Alessandro Striggio and others, he had contributed music (now lost) for the *intermedi* to Giovanni Fedini's comedy *Le due persilie*. During the 1580s, Peri may also have frequented the house of Count Giovanni de' Bardi, whose informal discussions with a group of intellectual friends and followers on literary and musical questions, such as the nature of ancient Greek music, the form that new music should take, and various other subjects were important in shaping the character of music in Florence during the late 16th and early 17th centuries (*see* CAMERATA). Bardi's influence on artistic events in Florence was never greater than in 1589 when he devised *intermedi*, all of them dealing with the power of music, for Girolamo Bargagli's comedy *La pellegrina*, performed at the wedding of Grand Duke Ferdinando de' Medici to Christine of Lorraine. Peri took part in the performance, singing to great acclaim his aria 'Dunque fra torbid'onde' while accompanying himself on the chitarrone.

Once established, Peri maintained his relationship with the Medici court for the rest of his life. At various times during his career as a court musician, Peri accompanied the *concerto de' castrati*, played the organ for sacred services, composed music for various theatrical entertainments, and sang his own and other people's music (he was a tenor). Throughout most of his career at court, Peri was seen to be in opposition to his greatest rival Giulio Caccini. It may have been this rivalry, Peri's fragile health, or his sense of social position – he described himself as a member of the nobility – that made him slightly diffident both as courtier and as composer. Relatively little of his music survives, the great bulk of it concentrated in the music for *Euridice*, performed in 1600 and published the same year, and in his collection of music for one or more voices and continuo, *Le varie musiche* of 1609 (republished with some changes in 1619). *Le varie musiche* appeared in print just at the time when Peri enjoyed his greatest successes at the Florentine court, when Caccini was out of favour and the faction led by Marco da Gagliano and Peri was in the ascendancy. Aside from his opera and the one anthology of monodies, only fragments of Peri's music have come down to us, a circumstance explained partly by the fact that much of Peri's work consisted of occasional music, written for particular celebrations and thus presumably not saved, but also partly by his apparent lack of interest in preserving a record of his own achievements. This paucity of material makes an accurate assessment of Peri's achievements precarious, although *Euridice* assures him a place in operatic history.

To describe the musical atmosphere of Florence in the last two decades of the 16th century and the first decade of the 17th as a battle between Peri and Gagliano on the one side and Giulio Caccini and his entourage on the other is over-simple, for there were a good many tensions and rivalries among the other musicians at the

Medici court, involving Bardi, Jacopo Corsi (Bardi's successor as the chief musical patron in the city), Emilio de' Cavalieri, Vincenzo Galilei and others. Among other things, the various actors in this drama argued over who wrote the first completely sung drama and created a music wholly responsive to the needs of the theatre, a series of events that should in any case be evaluated against the background of the strong traditions in the late 16th century of theatrical courtly entertainments. Whatever the real course of events, our present state of knowledge suggests that Galilei first wrote some sample monodies intended to exemplify the aesthetic possibilities of a new kind of music and Cavalieri set completely sung episodes from Guarini's *Il pastor fido* for performance at the Florentine court, and he has some claim to have established an alternative style of musical theatre with his setting of the *Rappresentatione di Anima, et di Corpo*, performed in Rome in 1600.

It is Ottavio Rinuccini's pastoral eclogue *Dafne*, however, that should be regarded as the first genuine opera. A result of discussions between Corsi and Rinuccini and based on a subject already partially treated in the 1589 *intermedi*, *Dafne* was an experiment intended to explore the ways in which a brief pastoral drama might be sung from beginning to end. Only six fragments survive: two choruses preserved in versions for solo voice and continuo, three strophic songs and a single recitative. It is not clear which pieces were composed by Corsi and which by Peri, although one chorus is attributed to Corsi, and Peri (who had been called in to help only after Corsi had already composed some *arie bellissime*, a fair description of the choruses and songs) presumably wrote the recitative. The musical style of the choruses derives from 16th-century dancing songs and *canzonette*. The strophic songs resemble 16th-century arias; they continue the Italian tradition of declaiming narrative or lyric poetry over musical formulae. Only in the single recitative, 'Qual' nova meraviglia', setting the report of the messenger describing Daphne's transformation into a laurel tree, has the composer fully confronted the problem of how to write speech-like song, a kind of music fully responsive to the demands of theatrical dialogue.

Rinuccini's *Euridice*, a pastoral drama enriched by formal and stylistic elements of tragedy, was performed as a part of the entertainment provided to celebrate the wedding between Maria de' Medici and King Henri IV of France in 1600. As usual, tensions were high and rivalries intense among the musicians at court. The grand climax to the wedding celebrations was provided by Giulio Caccini, whose *Il rapimento di Cefalo* has survived only in some fragments published in his *Le nuove musiche* of 1602. It appears to have been a set of glorified *intermedi*, with elaborate scenic effects and an extremely large cast. The much smaller *Euridice*,

sponsored by Jacopo Corsi and given in Don Antonio de' Medici's rooms in the Pitti Palace, was given much less attention and it was not very well received. The scenery was not quite finished, the music was dismissed by critics as similar to the chanting of the Passion, and some of the roles were taken by members of Caccini's entourage, who sang his music while most of the cast sang that written by Peri (who took the title role). Moreover, after the celebrations Caccini quickly set the entire libretto and published his version before Peri could get his own ready for the press. Thus neither Peri's score nor Caccini's reflects what was actually sung at the first performance.

Euridice was a more ambitious effort than *Dafne* to explore the ways a drama could be sung from beginning to end. Nevertheless it maintained many points of contact with earlier traditions. Each of the five scenes ends with a strophic chorus in a simple, more or less homophonic style reminiscent of earlier dance songs; the final elaborately choreographed tableau has much in common with the finale of the 1589 *intermedi*; there is a traditional scene in hell; and much of the work consists of set pieces. *Euridice* is a moving work, but its solutions to aesthetic problems are very special. As Carter (1989, p.204) has said, 'in a very real sense it is a work that could only have been composed once'.

In spite of the fact that Peri spent the largest part of his career writing music for courtly entertainments, not much of his theatrical music has survived beyond *Euridice* and the fragments of *Dafne*: only the recitatives for the part of Chloris in Marco da Gagliano's opera *La flora* (1628) and a few songs, choruses and laments. Some of the surviving compositions re-use music previously composed for some other purpose. Thus *Le varie musiche* includes a set of strophic variations beginning 'Se tu parti da me' originally written to serve as the final chorus to Act 3 of Michelangelo Buonarroti's *Il giudizio di Paride* (1608), beginning 'Poiche la notte con l'oscure piume'. And some of the surviving compositions seem to be modelled on existing music. Thus, Peri's lament 'Uccidimi, dolore' (no.32 in the 1985 edition by Carter), probably intended for Antonio Salvadori's *Iole ed Ercole* (planned for the Florentine court in 1628 but never performed), was almost certainly modelled on Monteverdi's *Lamento d'Arianna*. These and the other surviving fragments of theatrical music by Peri (all published in Carter 1985) suggest that the composer was not ambitious to write great quantities of new music (or at least not to take pains to collect it as a written record of his achievements), and that his music did not change much once he had established suitable components for an operatic style in his masterwork *Euridice*.

See also EURIDICE (i).

Edition: J. Peri: *Le varie musiche and Other Songs*, ed. T. Carter (Madison, WI, 1985) [C]

first performed in Florence unless otherwise stated

title	librettist	first performance	remarks; sources
Dafne	O. Rinuccini	Palazzo Corsi, carn. 1597–8	collab. J. Corsi; rev. 1598–1600; frags. *B-Bc, I-Fn*, see Porter (1965) and Carter (1989)
Euridice	Rinuccini	Palazzo Pitti, 6 Oct 1600	5 scenes; collab. G. Caccini; (Florence, 1600, repr. 1607), ed. in Brown (1981)

title	librettist	first performance	remarks; sources
Le nozze di Peleo e Tetide	F. Cini	unperf.	planned for Mantua, 1608
Adone	J. Cicognini	unperf.	comp. 1611, planned for Mantua, 1620
Lo sposalizio di Medoro et Angelica	A. Salvadori, after L. Ariosto	Palazzo Pitti, 25 Sept 1619	collab. M. da Gagliano; rev. c1622
Iole ed Ercole	Salvadori	unperf.	planned for Florence, 1628; ? frag. 'Uccidimi, dolore' in Cs-Pnm and I-Bc, ed. in C
La Flora, o vero Il natal de' fiori	Salvadori	Palazzo Pitti, 14 Oct 1628	collab. M. da Gagliano, only Chloris's music by Peri; (Florence, 1628)

Sacre rappresentationi (all collab. G. B. da Gagliano): Le beneditione di Jacob (G. M. Cecchi, rev. Cicognini), 1622; Il gran natale di Christo salvator nostro (Cicognini), 1622; La celeste guida, o vero L'arcangelo Raffaello (Cicognini), 1623

Other: Intermedio I in G. Fedini: Le due persilie, 1583; Intermedio V in G. Bargagli: La pellegrina (Rinuccini), 1589, *RISM* 1591[7]; [Torneo] (M. Buonarroti), Pisa, 1605, ed. in C; Chorus in Il giudizio di Paride (Buonarroti), 1608, ed. in C; Mascherate di ninfe di Senna (Rinuccini), 1611, collab. M. da Gagliano and others, ed. in C; [?Torneo] (G. Villifranchi), 1613, collab. M. da Gagliano and others, ed. in C; [Marte e Amore] (F. Saracinelli), 1614; Intermedi to Veglia delle grazie (G. Chiabrera), 1615; Guerra d'Amore (festa a cavallo, Salvadori), 1616, collab. P. Grazi and G. B. Signorini; [Ballo] (Saracinelli), collab. L. Allegri; Guerra di bellezza (festa a cavallo, Salvadori), 1616, collab. Grazi; [Ballo] (? A. Striggio ii), Mantua, 1620; La precedenza delle dame (Salvadori), 1625

Doubtful: Ballo della cortesia (Buonarroti), 1614 [collab. A. Brunelli or by F. Caccini]; La liberazione di Tirreno ed Arnea (Salvadori), 1617 [? by M. da Gagliano]

G. O. Corazzini: *Jacopo Peri e la sua famiglia* (Florence, 1895)

A. Solerti: *Le origini del melodramma* (Turin, 1903)

——: *Gli albori del melodramma* (Milan, 1904)

——: *Musica, ballo e drammatica alla corte medicea dall 1600 al 1637* (Florence, 1905)

O. G. Sonneck: ' "Dafne", the First Opera: a Chronological Study', *SIMG*, xv (1913–14), 102–110

M. Mila: 'Jacopo Peri', *RaM*, vi (1933), 219

F. Ghisi: *Feste musicali della Firenze medicea* (Florence, 1939)

——: *Alle fonti della monodia: due nuove brani della 'Dafne'* (Milan, 1940)

——: 'An Early Seventeenth Century Ms. with Unpublished Italian Monodic Music by Peri, Giulio Romano and Marco da Gagliano', *AcM*, xx (1948), 46–60

——: 'Ballet Entertainments in Pitti Palace, Florence, 1608–1625', *MQ*, xxxix (1949), 421–36

N. Fortune: 'A Florentine Manuscript and its place in Italian Song', *AcM*, xxiii (1951), 124–36

N. Pirrotta: 'Temperamenti e tendenze nella Camerata fiorentina', *Le manifestazioni culturali dell'Accademia nazionale di Santa Cecilia* (Rome, 1953); Eng. trans. in *MQ*, xl (1954), 169–89

N. Fortune: *Italian Secular Song from 1600 to 1635: the Origins and Development of Accompanied Monody* (diss., U. of Cambridge, 1954)

M. Mila: 'La nascita del melodramma', *RMI*, lvi (1954), 307–25

A. M. Nagler: *Theatre Festivals of the Medici, 1539–1637* (New Haven, CT, 1964)

C. V. Palisca: 'The First Performance of "Euridice" ', *Queens College Department of Music Twenty-fifth Anniversary Festschrift (1937–1962)* (New York, 1964), 1–23

W. V. Porter: 'Peri and Corsi's *Dafne*: Some New Discoveries and Observations', *JAMS*, xviii (1965), 170–96

A. M. Monterosso Vacchelli: 'Elementi stilistici nell' "Euridice" di J. Peri in rapporto all' "Orfeo" di Monteverdi', *Monteverdi e il suo tempo: Venice, Mantua and Cremona 1968*, 117–27

N. Pirrotta: 'Early Opera and Aria', *New Looks at Italian Opera: Essays in Honor of Donald J. Grout* (Ithaca, 1968), 39–107

B. R. Hanning: *The Influence of Humanistic Thought and Italian Renaissance Poetry on the Formation of Opera* (diss., Yale U., 1969)

N. Pirrotta: *Li due Orfei: da Poliziano a Monteverdi* (Turin, 1969, enlarged 2/1975; Eng. trans., 1982)

H. M. Brown: 'How Opera Began: an Introduction to Jacopo Peri's *Euridice* (1600)', in E. Cochrane: *The Late Italian Renaissance, 1525–1630* (New York, 1970), 401–43

F. W. Sternfeld: 'The First Printed Opera Libretto', *ML*, lix (1978), 121–38

T. Carter: 'Jacopo Peri (1561–1633): Aspects of His Life and Works', *PRMA*, cv (1978–9), 50–62

——: 'Jacopo Peri', *ML*, lxi (1980), 121–35

H. M. Brown, ed.: Introduction to J. Peri: *Euridice: an Opera in One Act, Five Scenes* (Madison, WI, 1981)

T. Carter: 'Jacopo Peri's *Euridice* (1600): a Contextual Study', *MR*, xliii (1982), 83–103

——: 'A Florentine Wedding of 1608', *AcM*, lv (1983), 89–107

N. Pirrotta: *Music and Culture in Italy from the Middle Ages to the Baroque* (Cambridge, MA, 1984)

T. Carter: *Jacopo Peri (1561–1633): his Life and Works* (New York, 1989)   HOWARD MAYER BROWN

Périchole, La. *Opéra bouffe* in two acts by JACQUES OFFENBACH to a libretto by HENRI MEILHAC and LUDOVIC HALÉVY after PROSPER MÉRIMÉE'S comedy *Le carrosse du Saint-Sacrement*; Paris, Théâtre des Variétés, 6 October 1868 (revised in three acts, 25 April 1874).

First performed (in both 1868 and 1874) with Hortense Schneider as La Périchole, José Dupuis as Piquillo and Grenier as the Viceroy, *La Périchole* is in Offenbach's most charming, rather than satirical, vein and is one of his richest and most delightful works.

In the main square of Lima, Peru, the crowds are celebrating the Viceroy's birthday. The Viceroy, Don Andrès del Ribeira (baritone), is there himself – supposedly incognito ('Sans en rien souffler à personne'), though everyone recognizes him. A pair of impoverished and hungry street-singers, La Périchole (soprano) and Piquillo (tenor), sing a lively song of a Spaniard and a young Indian girl ('Il grandira, car il est espagnol'), and the Viceroy takes a particular fancy to La Périchole. When Piquillo leaves, the Viceroy offers La Périchole a position as lady-in-waiting at the palace. Reluctant as she is to accept, hunger proves the determining factor, and in slow waltz tempo she writes a farewell love letter to Piquillo ('O mon cher amant, je te jure'). On his return, Piquillo is driven to consider suicide. However, it is necessary for the Viceroy's favourites to be married and, for the sake of a hot meal, Piquillo takes up an offer from the court chamberlain Comte Miguel de Panatellas (baritone) to marry the latest 'favourite' – not knowing that she is La Périchole. Well fed and wined, they reappear for the marriage, with La Périchole thoroughly tipsy ('Ah, quel dîner!') and Piquillo too drunk to realize the identity of his bride. Only in Act 2, when he and his wife are presented to the Viceroy, does he grasp the situation. He accuses La Périchole of treachery, sparking a spirited retort ('Que veulent dire ces colères?') and securing his own condemnation to the cell reserved for recalcitrant husbands ('Aux maris ré, aux maris cal, aux maris ci, aux maris trants'). The Viceroy is finally persuaded to give them their freedom, though only (in Act 3 of the 1874 version) after further complications in Piquillo's prison cell, in which La Périchole further testifies to her love for Piquillo in the gloriously sensuous 'Tu n'es pas beau', Offenbach's last major song for Hortense Schneider.

ANDREW LAMB

Périer, Jean (Alexis) (*b* Paris, 2 Feb 1869; *d* Paris, ?3 Nov 1954). French baritone. He made his début on 16 December 1892 as Monostatos (*Die Zauberflöte*) at the Opéra-Comique, where he remained (except from 1894 to 1900) until 1920. His repertory lay chiefly in operetta – he took leading roles in the premières of Messager's *Véronique* (1898), and *Fortunio* (1907) – but he also sang Don Giovanni, Lescaut (*Manon*) and Scarpia, and was the first Pelléas (1902) and Don Ramiro (*L'heure espagnole*, 1911). He sang Pelléas at the Manhattan Opera in 1908 and appeared at Monte Carlo. He acted in several films between 1900 and 1938. His was essentially a declamatory art, and even with limited gifts as a singer he created convincing characters through his clear diction and acting ability. He made seven recordings about 1905.

HAROLD BARNES

Perinet, Joachim (*b* Vienna, 20 Oct 1763; *d* Vienna, 4 Feb 1816). Austrian dramatist and actor. Born into a wealthy merchant family, as a young man he received a poor education, frequented Vienna's taverns, and on his father's death squandered an inheritance of 6000 gulden in six weeks. He became an actor, first at the Leopoldstadt theatre, then with Schikaneder. Many of his countless texts for Vienna's suburban stages are adaptations or travesties of popular comedies and operas. Perinet is also the author of the poetic pamphlet *Mozart und Schikaneder: ein theatralisches Gespräch* (Vienna, 1801).

Kaspars Zögling, oder Der Sieg der Bescheidenheit auf der Insel des Vergnügens (Original-Spl), Kauer, 1791; *Kaspar der Fagotist, oder Die Zauberzither* (Spl), W. Müller, 1791; *Der Unterthanen Glück ist auch das Glück der Fürsten* (Spl), Müller, 1792; *Pizichi* (Original-Spl [sequel to Kaspar]), Müller, 1792; *Die Schneider, oder Kaspar, der alte Lehrbub* (Spl), Müller, 1793; *Das Neusonntagskind* (komisches Spl), Müller, 1793; *Merkur der Heiratsstifter, oder Der Geiz im Geldkasten*, Wranitzky, 1793; *Die Schwestern von Prag* (Spl), Müller, 1794; *Das Fest der Lazaronen* (Operette), Wranitzky, 1794; *Rübezahl, oder Liebe stärker als Zauber* (Zauberoper), 1794
Johannes Zauberhorn (Posse), Müller, 1795; *Caro, oder Megärens zweiter Theil* (komische Oper), Müller, 1795; *Der lustig Lebendig* (Spl), Müller, 1796; *Nannette* (Spl), Müller, 1796; *Oesterreich über alles* (kleine vaterländische Szene mit Chören), Müller, 1796; *Idoly* (Spl), Weigl, 1796; *Das lustige Beilager* (Spl), Müller, 1797; *Orion, oder Der Fürst und sein Hofnarr* (Hofgemälde), Seyfried, 1798; *Liebe macht kurzen Prozess, oder Die Heyrath auf gewisse Art* (Oper), pasticcio, 1798; *Die Schneiderhochzeit* (Lustspiel mit Gesang), Seyfried and Stegmayer, 1798
Der Kopf ohne Mann (grosse heroisch-komische Zauberoper), Wölfl, 1798; *Astaroth der Verführer, oder Der Gürtel und die Harfe* (Ritter- und Feenmärchen in 2 pts: Ritter und Harfner, Der Kampf mit dem Fürsten der Finsternis), Haibel (pt 1) and Lickl (pt 2), 1799; *Rinaldo Rinaldini, der Räuberhauptmann* (romantisches Schauspiel), Seyfried and Stegmayer, 1799; *Der Kirchtag zu Messbrunn* (ländliches Lustspiel), Seyfried, 1799; *Roxelane, oder Die drei Sultaninnen* (Spl), Seyfried, 1799; *Das Jahr 1803, oder Der Wirt von der blauen Maise* (Lustspiel), Seyfried, 1802
Der lustige Schusterfeyerabend (Spl), 1802; *Alle neun und 's Centrum* (Posse), Haibel, 1803; *Kasperls neu errichtetes Kaffeehaus, oder Der Hausteufel* (komische Oper), Müller, 1803; *Orions Rückkehr zur friedlichen Insel* (Gelegenheitsstück),

Müller, 1803; *Ariadne auf Naxos* (musikalisches Quodlibet), Satzenhofen, 1803; *Das Scheibenschiessen, oder Die ausgespielten Bräute* (Lustspiel), Haibel, 1804; *Der kleine Cäsar, oder Die Familie auf dem Gebirge* (Schauspiel mit Gesang), Haibel, 1804; *Das Loch in der Mauer* (komische Oper), Kauer, 1804
Evakathel und Schnudi, oder Die Belagerung von Ypsilon (Karrikatur), Müller, 1804; *Baron Baarfuss, oder Der Wechselthaler* (Zauberoper), Schuster, 1804; *Der travestirte Telemach* (Karrikatur mit Gesang), Kauer, 1805; *Antiope und Telemach* (Travestie [sequel to the preceding]), Kauer, 1805; *Das Sommerlager* (ländliche militärische Oper), Müller, 1805; *Megära, die fürchterliche Hexe* (Zauberoper), Müller, 1806; *Die neue Alceste* (Karrikatur-Oper), Müller, 1806; *Das Fest der Liebe und Freude* (Lustspiel mit Gesang), M. Umlauf, 1806
Die neue Semiramis (heroisch-komische Travestie-Oper), Tuček, 1808; *Hamlet Prinz von Tandelmarkt* (Karrikatur), Schuster, 1807; *Idas und Marpissa* (travestirte Decorations-Oper), Tuček, 1807; *Der Feldtrompeter, oder Wurst wider Wurst* (Spl), Kauer, 1808; *Pumphia und Kulikan* (Karrikatur-Oper), Teyber, 1808; *Das Laternenfest* (Oper), Tuček, 1809; *Der Geisterseher* (Schauspiel mit Chören und Tänzen), Volkert, 1810; *August und Gustawina, oder Der Kopf von Erz* (Schauspiel mit Chören und Tänzen), Volkert, 1810
Johann Faust, der Erfinder der Buchdruckerkunst (Schauspiel), Volkert, 1811; *Dankmar von Sachsen* (Schauspiel), Volkert, 1811; *Aschenschlägel* (grosse travestirte Oper), F. X. Gebel, 1812; *Die Zauberin aus Liebe* (komische Zauberoper), Kauer, 1812; *Der Baum der Diana* (travestirte Oper), Schuster, 1812; *Kora die Sonnenjungfrau* (Karrikatur-Oper), Schuster, 1812; *Erich von Lilienstein, oder Der Geisterkampf* (Schauspiel), Volkert, 1812; *Isaak* (historische Melodrama), Fusz, 1812; *Die travestirte Palmira* (Oper), Gebel, 1813
Diamantino, der Ritter im Zauberlande, oder Der Schutzgeist (Zauberstück), Gebel, 1813; *Der travestirte Fridolin* (Karrikatur-Oper), Schuster, 1813; *Die travestirte Medea* (Travestie), Volkert, 1813; *Der Narrenthurm* (komisches Spl), Kauer, 1814; *Die Prinzessin von Kakambo* (grosse komische Oper), Müller, 1814; *Das Linzer Schiff* (Oper), Volkert, 1814; *Der Nachfasching, oder Der närrische Schmaus* (Quodlibet), Volkert, 1815; *Dragon der Hund des Aubri, oder Der Wienerwald* (historisch-romantisch-komisches Drama mit Musik), Müller, 1816

THOMAS BAUMAN

Perini, Flora (*b* Rome, 20 Nov 1887; *d* Rome, Sept 1975). Italian mezzo-soprano. She studied at the Accademia di S Cecilia in Rome and made her début at La Scala in 1908 as Anacoana in Franchetti's *Cristoforo Colombo*. She made her début at the Metropolitan Opera as Lola in *Cavalleria rusticana* in 1915; there she also sang roles including Amneris and Maddalena, as well as creating Pepa in *Goyescas* (1916) and the Princess in *Suor Angelica* (1918). She remained at the Metropolitan until 1924, after which she sang for one season in Chicago. While in the USA she made some recordings for Victor, including the classic *Rigoletto* Quartet with Galli-Curci, Caruso and De Luca in 1917. She returned to Italy in 1925, where she sang principally at the Teatro Costanzi in Rome.

CORI ELLISON

Periodicals. Periodicals are publications appearing usually at regular (though sometimes irregular) intervals and, normally, furnished with serial numbers indicating volumes (usually annual) or issue numbers, or both; they primarily contain such material as essays, reports, critiques and news items. In addition to their periodical mode of publication they have in common with newspapers an intention of continuance, an approach determined by publisher or editor, and an objective of variety of content and, to some extent, contemporary relevance. In music, the concept of the periodical also includes yearbooks, annual reports and the proceedings of institutions, almanacs on music and similar publications. Works published in fascicles (part-works, serials etc.) are to be distinguished from periodicals proper.

This article provides an account of the history of periodicals devoted entirely or in large part to opera. These include early general periodicals and music journals containing operatic materials, serial publications containing operatic excerpts, theatre and general arts periodicals of particular importance in the history of opera, and specialist operatic journals. Dates given normally represent first and last volumes or, in certain cases, issues; dates given with an oblique stroke (e.g. 1971/2) refer to a volume beginning in one year and ending in another. Fuller information on title changes, breaks in a periodical's run, and similar kinds of publication information will be found in the list of opera-related periodicals at the end of the discussion. (For a comprehensive list of music periodicals up to c1978, see *The New Grove*.)

I. History. II. List.

I. History

1. Antecedents. 2. The 18th century. 3. The 19th century. 4. The 20th century.

1. ANTECEDENTS. In the late 17th century publishers of cultural and scholarly periodicals began to offer commentaries on theatrical productions of the day, including opera. One of these journals, the *Mercure galant* (Paris, 1672–1832), founded by the writer Donneau de Visé and known after 1724 as the *Mercure de France*, was principally literary and political in content but contained a good deal of information on French serious opera and *opéra comique*. In Germany the *Historische Remarques der neuesten Sachen in Europa des 1699ten Jahrs* (Hamburg, 1699–1700) reported in particular on Venetian opera.

Moral weeklies, which were primarily journals of instruction, occasionally contained references to opera. In 1710 Joseph Addison published three satirical and critical essays in the *Spectator* on Italian opera in England. One issue of *Der Vernünfftler* (Hamburg, 1713/14), the first publication of this kind in Germany, contained Johann Mattheson's article 'Theatralische Remarques' on Johann Philipp Förtsch's *Thalestris* and Reinhard Keiser's *Julius Cäsar* and *Iphigenie*. *Der Patriot* (Hamburg, 1724–8), as the organ of the Teutsch-übende Gesellschaft, a society devoted to the promotion of the German language and to works written in it, at first contained articles on audience conduct during opera performances but later included essays on stage sets and machinery, performers and dance; no.25 of the first volume was devoted exclusively to opera in Hamburg and took a rationalist attitude towards illusionism in Baroque opera. In his moral weekly *Vernünfftige Tadlerinnen* (Leipzig, 1725) Gottsched too tried to influence his readers with opinions and verdicts on various opera-related topics.

Periodicals consisting exclusively of musical pieces appeared in France and England from the 1690s onwards, and serial publications like *Mercurius Musicus, or The Monthly Collection of New Teaching Songs compos'd for the Theatres and Other Occasions* (London, 1699–1702) show a clear relationship between these publications and the music currently being performed in local theatres. The Dutch publisher of French origin Estienne Roger greatly expanded his periodical collection *Les airs sérieux et à boire* (Amsterdam, 1701–23) by including 'some of the finest passages from opera'. In a somewhat later periodical, *Der getreue Music-Meister* (1728), Telemann published operatic arias from his own works. The *Journal hebdomadaire* (Paris, 1764–1808) offered arias mainly by French and Italian masters, and Carl Friedrich Cramer opened his twice-yearly publication *Polyhymnia* with Salieri's *Armida* (Leipzig, 1783). After 1780 the growing number of operas in the stage repertory and the lively public interest in such works led to the appearance of an increasing number of excerpts arranged for piano or for the voice with instrumental accompaniment (piano, harp or guitar) in serial publications. Selections appeared in periodicals published purely for the purpose of entertainment (such as the successors of the *divertissement* collections of the 18th century), in specialized theatre journals (e.g. the *Musikalsk theater-journal*, published in Copenhagen, 1817/18–1839/41) and in serial collections tailored to the repertory of particular opera houses (e.g. the *Musikalisches Wochenblatt*, published in Vienna, 1806/7–1810/12, which contained selections from the repertory of the Vienna Hofoper).

2. THE 18TH CENTURY. The first journals in Germany devoted entirely to music all contained essays on opera. In a section of *Critica musica* (Hamburg, 1722/3–1725) entitled 'Neues von musicalischen Sachen und Personen', Mattheson published commentaries on the music and performance of operas currently being mounted in various European cities, such as Telemann's *Gensericus* in Hamburg, Keiser's *Ulysses* in Copenhagen and *Ariadne* in Hamburg, Francesco Brusa's *L'amore eroico* in Venice and Handel's *Tamerlano* in London; Mattheson also expounded the differences between French and Italian opera and other music. He was even more forceful and anxious to convey his views to a wide circle in his second journal, *Der musicalische Patriot* (Hamburg, 1728), in which he included a list of all the operas produced in Hamburg since 1678. Although L. C. Mizler's publication *Neu eröffnete musikalische Bibliothek* (Leipzig, 1736/8–1754) was devoted more to acoustical and physiological aspects of music, it also contains various essays on the merits and significance of opera, such as Gottsched's 'Gedanken von den Vorzügen der Oper vor den Tragödien und Comödien' and Johann Friedrich Uffenbach's article 'Von der Würde der Singgedichte oder Vertheidigung der Oper'. Johann Adolph Scheibe's *Critischer Musicus* (Hamburg, 1737/8–1739/40; rev., enlarged, Leipzig, 2/1745) contains several critical commentaries on contemporary operas and operatic style. Friedrich Wilhelm Marpurg's *Historisch-kritische Beyträge zur Aufnahme der Musik* (Berlin, 1754/5–1760/78) was devoted to the state of opera in Berlin and Paris at the time and includes a defence of the entire genre. Marpurg also published discussions of operas and pastorales, and particular mention should be made of such features as a chronological catalogue of operas performed in Paris from 1645 to 1752, essays on the lives of various French composers, running commentaries on both the Berlin Hoftheater and sacred and secular opera in England, and a catalogue of operas performed in Venice. The journal *Wöchentliche Nachrichten und Anmerkungen die Musik betreffend* (Leipzig, 1766/7–1770), published by J. A. Hiller, contains commentaries on productions of operas and Singspiels in Dresden, Vienna and other European cities (e.g. the Singspiel *Talestris, Königinn der Amazonen* in Gotha). J. F. Reichardt's periodical *Musikalisches Kunstmagazin* (Berlin, 1782, 1791) offers analyses of arias from Gluck's operas. The almanac

Musik (Copenhagen, 1789), edited by C. F. Cramer, contains among other things a history of the Berlin Opera, with a commentary on Salieri's *Les Danaïdes*. Johann Ferdinand von Schönfeld's *Jahrbuch der Tonkunst von Wien und Prag* (Prague, 1796) printed accounts of opera orchestras in the national theatres of Vienna and Prague as well as articles on operas by Salieri, F. X. Partsch, Ignaz Umlauf, Süssmayr and Joseph Weigl. Mention should also be made of two long-running almanacs, the Parisian journal *Calendrier historique des théâtres, de l'opéra, et des comédies françoise et italienne et des foires* (Paris, 1751–1793/4, 1800–01, 1815) and the *Indice de' teatrali spettacoli* (Milan and elsewhere, 1764–1823), which cover Italian theatres and Italian opera on foreign stages and give complete lists of singers, composers, librettists and titles of works performed in various Italian opera houses.

3. THE 19TH CENTURY. Music journals of a general nature in the 19th century continued to include discussion of opera. The *Allgemeine musikalische Zeitung* (Leipzig, 1798/9–1848), which treats both opera and church music as two of the most popular musical genres, contains articles on the history and aesthetics of opera (including Singspiel) and offers suggestions for improvement. With the development of national styles came publications reflecting those repertories. The journal *Tygodnik muzyczny* (Warsaw, 1820–21), edited by Karol Kurpiński, devoted much space to singing and Polish national opera. In an 1827 issue of the *Berlinische allgemeine musikalische Zeitung* (Berlin, 1824–30), the publisher Adolf Bernhard Marx wrote an essay on the state of German opera, taking as his points of reference Spontini's *Nurmahal* and Weber's *Oberon*; this article also appeared in the fourth volume of the journal *Cäcilia* (Mainz, Brussels and Antwerp, 1824–39, 1842–8), which was devoted principally to contemporary German, French and Italian opera and contains three essays on the operas of Mozart as well. The *Gazzetta musicale di Milano* (Milan, 1842–8, 1850–62, 1866–1912), in which particular attention is given to the progress of Italian opera, deserves special mention for its chronological lists of productions at La Scala and La Fenice. In his *Neue Wiener Musik-Zeitung* (Vienna, 1852–60) Franz Glöggl gave a weekly account of the Kaiserlich Königliche Hofoperntheater in Vienna. The journal *Zenészeti lapok* ('Musical Papers'; Budapest, 1860–76, with some interruptions), founded by Kornél Ábrányi, contains extensive discussion of opera productions in Budapest.

Towards the middle of the century, discourses on the styles of particular composers became prominent. Ludwig Rellstab's journal *Iris im Gebiete der Tonkunst* (Berlin, 1830–41) was hostile to Spontini and his operas. Robert Schumann began publication of the *Neue Zeitschrift für Musik* (Leipzig, 1834–1928; Regensburg, 1929–43, 1950–55; Mainz, 1955–74, 1979–) at a time when, according to its introduction, Rossini still dominated the stage. In later issues, under the editorship of Franz Brendel, articles defended the operas of Wagner in particular; Schumann's own essay on a production of *Tannhäuser* appeared in 1852. Meyerbeer's operas were prominently featured in the *Revue et gazette musicale de Paris*, the name given to Maurice Schlesinger's *Gazette musicale de Paris* (founded 1834) after it merged with F.-J. Fétis's *Revue musicale* (Paris, 1827–35) in 1835; the *Revue*, however, included wider-ranging surveys of opera in Europe as

well. *La France musicale* (Paris, 1837/8–1870) defended Rossini and the Italian school. The journal *Le guide musical* (Brussels, 1855–89; Brussels and Paris, 1889–1914, 1917/18) became in the last 12 years of the century a forum for argument about the Wagnerian *Gesamtkunstwerk*.

Many music periodicals presented a broader view of opera. The journal *Signale für die musikalische Welt* (Leipzig, 1843–1907; Berlin and Leipzig, 1907–19; Berlin, 1920–41) contains news and detailed accounts of major operatic productions at home and abroad, including operas by Meyerbeer, Wagner, Flotow, Nicolai, Balfe and, later, Tchaikovsky and Smetana. Johann Christian Lobe announced in his *Fliegende Blätter für Musik* (Leipzig, 1855–7) that coverage was to include technical aspects of dramatic aesthetics, with particular regard to opera librettos. The *Musikalisches Wochenblatt* (Leipzig, 1870–1910) includes articles on specific productions and engagements of guest singers. From the 1870s the monthly founded by Alfred Novello in 1844, *The Musical Times and Singing Class Circular*, now *The Musical Times* (London, 1844/5–), also covered opera, with articles on operatic organizations, English opera houses, individual operas from all over Europe (with perhaps less attention to those of Wagner), ballet and melodrama.

Apart from the music journals intended for general interest and for certain local centres, it was the theatre journals that dealt with individual opera houses or the theatres of particular cities. An important source for information about opera in the 19th century is the *Wiener Hof-Theater-Almanach* (Vienna, 1804–16), called from 1805 the *Wiener Hof-Theater-Taschenbuch* and edited by H. J. Collin and I. F. Castelli. The *Annuaire dramatique* (Paris, 1805–1821/2) is of similar significance for Paris, giving names and addresses of the directors, actors, musicians and other employees of all the Parisian theatres, while the *Annuaire dramatique de la Belgique* (Brussels, 1839–47) covers all the theatres in Belgium. (The *Covent Garden Theatrical Gazette* (London, 1816–17), however, though devoted to a single theatre, deals mainly with plays, as opera was not given there at the time.)

An example of a journal type initially popular in Vienna dealing with theatre, music and fashion is the short-lived *Wiener Journal für Theater, Musik und Mode* (Vienna, 1806). Ten years later appeared the *Wiener Moden-Zeitung* (Vienna, 1816–48), known after 1817 as the *Wiener Zeitschrift für Kunst, Literatur, Theater und Mode*, which must be regarded, together with Bäuerle's *Wiener Theater-Zeitung* (published with many title changes in Vienna and Trieste, 1806; Vienna, 1807–8, 1811–60), as the leading periodicals in this genre. The *Zeitschrift* contains reviews of operatic productions in Vienna (including works by Auber, Bellini, Boieldieu, Donizetti, Conradin Kreutzer, Meyerbeer, Mozart, Rossini and Weber) and essays on music for Singspiels, melodramas, plays and ballet, particularly by contemporary Austrian composers. Journals of a similar nature were published in other European capitals, for example *Omnibus: journal mensuel de la littérature, des anecdotes, des faits politiques, des théâtres, de la musique et des modes* (The Hague, 1835–6), and *L'écho musical* (Paris, 1839–40), known in 1840 by its subtitle *Revue des théâtres, des concerts et des modes*. Nor should the directory *Deutsches Bühnen-Jahrbuch* (Hamburg, 1889–), published from 1890 to 1914 as *Neuer Theater Almanach*, be overlooked; it continues to list many addresses of opera houses and singers.

One of the first periodicals to contain a specific reference to opera in its title was poet August von Kotzebue's *Opern-Almanach* (Leipzig, 1815, 1817), which contains nothing but his own librettos. The late 19th-century journal *Opernstatistik für das Jahr 1894 der in Deutschland und auf den deutschen Bühnen Oesterreichs, der Schweiz und Russlands aufgeführten Opern*, compiled by Max Friedlaender (Leipzig, 1895), is an important source of information about the operatic repertory. Some other journals alluding to opera in the title but to be regarded more as general cultural periodicals in which opera does not play a major part are *The Opera Box* (London, 1849–51), *The Opera Goer, or Studies of the Town* (head-title, *The Lorgnette*; London, 1852), *L'opéra: musique, littérature, sport* (Bordeaux, 1882–4) and *Opera Glass* (New York, 1886–?).

In line with further specialization, journals and yearbooks devoted entirely to an individual opera composer, notably Wagner, began to appear in the second half of the century. The first of these was the *Bayreuther Blätter* (Chemnitz [Karl-Marx-Stadt], 1878; Bayreuth, 1879–1938), although the *Anregungen für Kunst, Leben und Wissenschaft* (Leipzig, 1856–61), which concentrated principally on Wagner and the 'Kunstwerk der Zukunft', may be regarded as a precursor. These journals were followed by *La renaissance musicale* (Paris, 1881–3), *Parsifal: Halbmonatsschrift zum Zwecke der Erreichung der Richard-Wagnerschen Kunstideale* (Vienna and Leipzig, 1884–8), the *Revue wagnérienne* (Paris, 1885/6–1887/8), the *Richard Wagner-Jahrbuch* (Stuttgart, 1886), the *Maandblad voor muziek* (Amsterdam, 1888/9–1893/4), *The Meister* (London, 1888–95), the *Cronaca wagneriana* (Bologna, 1893–5) and the *Richard Wagner-Jahrbuch* (Leipzig, 1906; Berlin, 1907–8, 1912–13). Another periodical that should be mentioned in this context is the *Gluck-Jahrbuch* (Berlin and elsewhere, 1913, 1915, 1917–18), edited by Hermann Abert for the Gluck-Gesellschaft.

4. THE 20TH CENTURY. After World War I a whole range of journals specifically devoted to opera began to appear. Various European opera houses started to publish annuals, beginning with the *Jahrbuch des Deutschen Opernhauses in Charlottenburg* (Berlin, 1919/20–1922/3), its successor the *Jahrbuch der Städtischen Oper Berlin* (Berlin, 1925/6) and *Die Oper: Blätter des Königsberger Opernhauses* (Königsberg, 1930/31–1933/4). In the 1936–7 season the Metropolitan Opera Guild began to publish *Opera News* (New York, 1936/7–), which contains news of the Metropolitan Opera and the Guild, and is regarded today as a leading organ both of the Metropolitan and of the international operatic scene.

A number of periodicals produced in the first half of the century were intended for music lovers and often aficionados of ballet as well. These include *Opera: a Magazine for Music Lovers*, which changed its title in 1924 to *Opera and the Ballet* (London, 1923–4), and *L'opéra-comique*, published by the Association des Amis de l'Opéra-Comique (Paris, 1929–32). Next to appear were journals representing the interests of operatic societies, such as the *Operatic Association Gazette*, later entitled the *National Operatic and Dramatic Association Yearbook* (London, 1930–). The San Francisco Opera Association published *Opera, Concert*

and Symphony, known as *Counterpoint* after 1935 (San Francisco, 1934–53).

Since the 1950s, specialist opera journals have appeared in increasing number. In 1950 the Earl of Harewood founded the journal *Opera* (London, 1950–), which he edited for the first three years, his intention being to include items on all subjects of interest to the intelligent operagoer. With Harold Rosenthal as editor, *Opera* continued to develop into the highly regarded journal it is today, covering opera in Britain and elsewhere, including festivals; it also encourages British composers to write operas and devotes much space to new works. The yearbook *Opera Annual* (London, 1954/5–1961/2), also edited by Rosenthal, contained accounts of the previous season's productions in various opera houses, with details of singers, conductors and repertories. In the same year that *Opera* first appeared, the Académie Nationale de Musique et de Danse began publication of *L'Opéra de Paris* (Paris, 1950–67), the official organ of the Théâtres Lyriques Nationaux. Other specialist journals include *Der Opernfreund* (Vienna, 1956–64), which deals primarily with contemporary issues in the music drama of Vienna; *Oper und Tanz* (Lechenich, nr Cologne, later Erftstadt, 1957–), a kind of union journal published by the Vereinigung Deutscher Opernchöre und Bühnentänzer of the German trades union association in Cologne; and Canada's leading opera journal, *Opera in Canada* (later *Opera Canada*; Toronto, 1960–), published by the Canadian Opera Guild.

A number of German publications from the second half of the 20th century deserve mention. *Opernwelt* (Velber, Hanover, later Zürich, 1960–) and its annual *Oper* (1966–) cover the international operatic scene. The *Jahrbuch der Komischen Oper* (E. Berlin, 1960/61–1971/2) and its successor *Musikbühne* (1974–7) are devoted to an exploration of Walter Felsenstein's ideas of realistic music drama in East Germany; these were succeeded by *Oper heute: ein Almanach der Musikbühne* (E. Berlin, 1978–88), which was more international and comprehensive in its approach. *Oper und Konzert* (Munich, 1963–) concentrates on operatic activities in Germany and its neighbours, and the informative arts bulletin *Orpheus* (W. Berlin, 1973–) has since its inception included a section on international operatic repertories. More recently, the *Jahrbuch für Opernforschung* (Frankfurt, 1985–) can be viewed as a forum for studies in the literary and social history of operatic production, with essays on music, literature and drama (particularly librettos) and reports on productions of rarely heard operas and unusual productions of the established repertory. *Musik und Theater* (W. Berlin, 1987–) is a comprehensive international artistic journal concerned with opera, ballet, dance and music drama, including articles on works for children and their composers.

A French publication of note is *Opéra international* (Paris, 1977–), which had commenced publication in 1961 as the journal *Opéra 61* (later appearing with title changes to reflect the year); in Italy there is the quarterly *L'opera* (Milan, 1966–). The English yearbook *Opera*, edited by Charles Osborne (London, 1966), aroused great expectations but lasted only a year. *Opera Review* (Washington, DC, 1977), which aimed to be a general but scholarly organ, and *The World of Opera* (New York, 1978/9), a journal of information, analysis and opinion, were similarly short-lived. *The Opera Quarterly* (Chapel Hill, 1983–) is a scholarly periodical devoted to all aspects of opera. The *Cambridge Opera Journal* (Cambridge, 1989–) is devoted to the study of opera in its various musicological, literary and dramatic aspects as well as from anthropological, historical and philosophical viewpoints. *Opera Now* (1989–), lavishly illustrated, reflects the genre's more glamorous aspects.

Since the 1950s, journals devoted to individual opera composers have concentrated principally on Rossini, Donizetti, Verdi, Wagner and Richard Strauss. Among these are the two separate series of the *Bollettino del Centro rossiniano di studi* (Pesaro, 1955/6–) and the *Donizetti Society Journal* (London, 1974–). Verdi's operas are the focus of *Verdiana: bollettino di notizie* (Milan, 1950–51), the *Bollettino quadrimestrale dell'Istituto di studi verdiani* (Parma, 1958–), retitled *Verdi* in 1960, and the *AIVS Newsletter* (New York, 1976–), published by the American Institute for Verdi Studies and renamed the *Verdi Newsletter* in 1977; this last biannual has offered a selective bibliography of publications on the composer since 1974. Chief among journals devoted to Wagner are the *Nachrichtenblatt* of the Österreichische Richard Wagner-Gesellschaft, Landesstelle Steiermark (Graz, 1959–1984/7), its successor *Richard Wagner Nachrichten* (Graz, 1989–) and *Richard Wagner Blätter* (Bayreuth, later Tutzing, 1977–). For Strauss there are the *Richard Strauss Jahrbuch* (Bonn, 1954, 1959/60), the *Mitteilungen* of the Internationale Richard-Strauss-Gesellschaft (W. Berlin, 1952–69), and its successor *Richard Strauss-Blätter* (Vienna, 1971/2–1978; new ser., 1979–), each number of which is devoted to one of the composer's principal works.

More periodicals connected with individual opera houses appeared after 1960, beginning in Germany with the *Opern Journal* of the Deutsche Oper (W. Berlin, 1961/2–1971/2) and its successors, *Deutsche Oper Berlin* (1972/3–1980/81, a programme-notes series) and *Deutsche Oper Berlin aktuell* (1981/2–). Thereafter followed the *Frankfurter Opernhefte* (Frankfurt, 1972/3–1976/7), the *Jahrbuch der Bayerischen Staatsoper* (Munich, 1978–), *Das Opernglas* (Pinneberg, later Hamburg, 1980–), which focusses on Hamburg but contains reports from Berlin, Bonn, Cologne, New York and Salzburg, and, in Italy, *Opera: annuario EDT dell'opera lirica in Italia* (Turin, 1987–), devoted mainly to the Teatro Regio in Turin. Among the newest publications is the *Leipziger Operngucker* (Leipzig, 1990/91–), the organ of the Leipzig opera house, which has articles on productions and on members of the ensemble.

*

Grove6 (I. Fellinger)

W. Freystätter: *Die musikalischen Zeitschriften seit ihrer Entstehung bis zur Gegenwart: chronologisches Verzeichniss der periodischen Schriften über Musik* (Munich, 1884)

T. Haas: 'Die Wiener Musikzeitschriften', *Der Merker*, x (1919), 735

M. (Bruckner-)Bigenwald: *Die Anfänge der Leipziger 'Allgemeinen musikalischen Zeitung'* (Hermannstadt [Sibiu], 1938)

K. Dolinski: *Die Anfänge der musikalischen Fachpresse in Deutschland* (Berlin, 1940)

P. A. Scholes: 'Music in the Theatre', 'Singers and Songs', *The Mirror of Music 1844–1944: a Century of Musical Life in Britain as Reflected in the Pages of the 'Musical Times'* (London, 1947), i, 229–73, 275–98

I. Fellinger: *Verzeichnis der Musikzeitschriften des 19. Jahrhunderts* (Regensburg, 1968); suppls. in *FAM*, xvii (1970), 7–8; xviii (1971), 59–62; xix (1972), 41–4; xx (1973), 108–11; xxi (1974), 36–8; xxiii (1976), 62–6

H. G. Otto: 'Wissenschaft und Theater: einige Anmerkungen zu den "Jahrbüchern der Komischen Oper"', *Musik und Gesellschaft*, xxi (1971), 319–23

R. Vogler: *Die Musikzeitschrift 'Signale für die musikalische Welt' 1843–1900* (Regensburg, 1975)

K. Höslinger: *Musik-Index zur 'Wiener Zeitschrift für Kunst, Literatur, Theater und Mode' 1816–1848* (Munich and Salzburg, 1980)

I. Fellinger: 'Mattheson als Begründer der ersten Musikzeitschrift (*Critica musica*)', *New Mattheson Studies*, ed. G. J. Buelow and H. J. Marx (Cambridge, 1983), 179–97

J. A. Deaville: 'Anregungen für Kunst, Leben und Wissenschaft: an Introduction and Index', *Periodica musica*, ii (1984), 1–5

R. Verti: 'The "Indice de' teatrali spettacoli", Milan, Venice, Rome 1764–1923: Preliminary Research on a Source for the History of Italian Opera', *Periodica musica*, iii (1985), 1–7

I. Fellinger: 'Historischer Überblick', *Periodica musicalia (1789–1830)* (Regensburg, 1986), pp.xi–xxxv

K. Szerző: 'The Most Important Hungarian Music Periodical of the 19th Century: "Zenészeti lapok" [Musical Papers] (1860–1876)', *Periodica musica*, iv (1986), 1–5

I. Fellinger: 'Musik aus italienischen Opern in europäischen Musik-Periodica aus der Zeit von 1800–1830', *Periodica musica*, vii (1989), 1–4; summary in *IMSCR*, xiv Bologna 1987, ii, 11–12

D. Knapp: 'Opera', 'Opera News' and 'Opernwelt', *International Music Periodicals*, ed. L. M. Fidler and R. S. James (New York, 1990), 327–33

II. List

1. Preface. 2. List.

1. PREFACE. The list that follows provides information on music periodicals devoted exclusively to opera and to those published by opera companies and related organizations. Though intended as comprehensive it is not claimed as complete. Extensive references to opera can be found in many other music periodicals and journals devoted to the arts in general (see the article 'Periodicals' in *The New Grove*). Excluded from the present list are modern almanacs, directories, congress reports, periodical Festschriften, monograph series, series containing collections of essays, publicity and sale sheets from music publishers, concert guides and programmes, annual reports of opera houses, and periodical publications consisting solely of music. Journals are numbered chronologically within each country of publication according to the date of first issue; countries are defined by modern boundaries.

Each entry is based on the following scheme:

Title. Each periodical is given under its full original title, normally according to the title-page of the first volume. Subsequent title changes, as well as details of incorporations, combinations etc. with other periodicals are given in chronological order after the first title when the numbering system is continuous. Title variations are shown, with their dates, in parentheses; the word or words within the parentheses replace the single word immediately preceding (e.g. 'Sadler's Wells (from 1969 Wells Opera) Magazine' indicates that the *Sadler's Wells Magazine* was published from 1969 onwards as the *Sadler's Wells Opera Magazine*). Subtitles are given only when the main title is not fully self-explanatory unless expanded (e.g. *La Scala: rivista dell'opera*). If the journal's contents are not sufficiently clear from the title information, an annotation is supplied in brackets. Titles in less familiar languages are translated.

Sponsoring organization. Any sponsoring organization is named; later variations are given in parentheses.

Editors, publishers. Founding editors' names are given where they are particularly significant. Publishers are named if of special importance and if not identical with the sponsoring organization or founding editor.

Places and dates of publication. Places of publication and their significant changes are noted, with the dates of the publication, in parentheses. Actual places of publication are named; these may not necessarily correspond with title-page imprints. Dates given with an oblique stroke (e.g. 1931/2) indicate that the journal's publication year, or volume arrangement, does not correspond with a single calendar year; lacunae in publication are normally indicated. Dates of yearbooks etc., if different from publication years, are given in angled brackets (e.g. Boston, then Chicago, <1883/4–1892/3> 1884–94) and are used in preference to publication dates as the basis for chronology. Information that is partly conjectural or dependent on secondary sources is preceded by a question mark. '1950–' indicates that a journal is still being published, '1950–?' that it ceased publication at an unknown date; '?1950–…' or '…–?1970' indicates that the first or last volume available belongs to the date given.

Volume arrangement. When a journal is defunct, the number of volumes and/or issues it comprised is indicated if available. When a journal is untraceable after a certain date the number of volumes and/or issues published to that date is given if available. Continuous numeration as a coordinating system to the volume numbering is shown as '68 nos. in 2 vols.'.

Frequency of publication. The periodicity is indicated as follows: D–daily, W–weekly, F–fortnightly, S–semimonthly, M–monthly, B–bi-monthly, Q–quarterly, H–half-yearly, Y–yearly, O–occasionally or irregularly. A formula such as '4 nos. Y' signifies the publication of four numbers at irregular intervals over a publishing year.

Additional information. Other features of a journal are indicated as follows: music – regular single music supplements; bibl. – regular bibliographical material, including book-lists, but not lists of publications received; c.i. – cumulative indexes, with dates of coverage if less than the complete run; suppl(s). – general supplement(s), with title, dates and frequency if different from the periodical itself.

Language. Journals are presumed to be published in the language(s) of the country of publication; exceptions to that rule are noted. Languages are also cited for bilingual and multilingual journals where the contents are in more than one language (e.g. '[in Eng. and Fr.]').

Relationships between periodicals. Relationships between periodicals – continuation, incorporation and combination – are shown by reference to the numbers of the periodicals concerned, using the abbreviations 'contd' and 'incorp.' (e.g. in the Great Britain list, 7 '*The Gilbert and Sullivan Journal* … [contd as 26]' and '26 *Gilbert and Sullivan News* … [contd from 7]').

2. LIST.

ARGENTINA

1 *Ayer y hoy de la opera* (Buenos Aires, 1977–) H

AUSTRALIA

1 *Sydney Opera House Diary*, Sydney Opera House Trust (Sydney, 1973–) B
2 *Opera Australia* (Sydney, 1974–) 5 nos. Y, from 1975 O, from 1978 M; c.i. 1981–5

AUSTRIA
(published in Vienna unless otherwise stated)

1 *Wiener Hof-Theater-Almanach* (from 1805 *Hof-Theater-Taschenbuch*) (1804–16) 13 vols., Y
2 *Theater-Journal: enthaltend das Verzeichniss aller in dem landschaftlichen Theater in Grätz aufgeführten Trauer-, Schau-, Lustspiele, Singspiele, Opern, Ballette und Pantomimen*, from 1838 *Grätzer Theateralmanach* (Graz, 1811–1917) 107 vols., Y
3 *Chronologisches Verzeichniss aller auf den fünf Theatern Wien's gegebenen Vorstellungen* (1826–7) 2 vols., Y
4 *Almanah* [sic] *für das K.[aiserlich] k.[önigliche] Hofoperntheater nächst dem Cärntnerthore* (1845–8) 3 vols., Y
5 *Jahrbuch des K.[aiserlich] k.[öniglichen] Hofoperntheaters in Wien* (1863–1906) Y
6 *Jahres-Bericht des Wiener akademischen Wagner-Vereines* (<1873–1917/18> 1874–1919) 46 vols., Y
7 *Parsifal: Halbmonatsschrift zum Zwecke der Erreichung der Richard-Wagnerschen Kunstideale*, from 1886 *Leipziger Musik- und Kunst-Zeitung*, ed. E. Kastner (Vienna and Leipzig, 1884–8) 5 vols., S; suppl.: *Wiener* (from 1885 (no.13) *Leipziger*) *musikalische Blätter*, 1884–5, 2 vols. [incorp. into *Der Kunstwart*]
8 *Ausschuss-Bericht Verein 'Nicolai'*, Kranken-Cassa der Mitglieder des K. K. Hofopern-Orchesters (1886/7–1919/20) 34 vols., Y
9 *Richard Wagner: illustrierte Blätter für wagner'sche Musik, Kunst und Literatur* (1908/9) 24 nos., S
10 *Richard Wagner-Kalender* (1913–18) 6 vols., Y
11 *Blätter des Operntheaters*, ed. R. Strauss and F. Schalk (1919/20) 11 nos., M
12 *Der Merker*, Verein Opernfreunde (1956–88) 33 vols., M, mimeographed [contd as 19]
13 *Der Opernfreund* (1956–64) 86 nos. in 9 vols., mainly M
14 *Österreichische Richard Wagner-Gesellschaft, Landesstelle Steiermark: Nachrichtenblatt*, 1981/3 *Festschrift: Österreicher um Richard Wagner*, 1984/7 *Richard Wagner-Jahrbuch 1988* (Graz, 1959–1984/7) Y, from 1981/3 O [contd as 21]
15 *Richard Strauss-Blätter*, Internationale Richard Strauss-Gesellschaft (1971/2–1978) 12 nos., O [contd from Germany 35; contd as Austria 16]
16 *Richard Strauss-Blätter*, new ser., Internationale Richard Strauss-Gesellschaft (1979–) H [contd from 15]
17 *Verein der Freunde der Wiener Staatsoper: Mitteilungen* (1981/2–?)
18 *Wiener Staatsoper aktuell* (1986–?90)
19 *Der neue Merker: Berichte aus der Welt der Oper und des Konzerts*, from 1989 (no.2) *Mitteilungen der Opernfreunde* (1989–) [contd from 12]
20 *Opern-Tagebuch*, Freunde der Wiener Staatsoper (1989–90) 13 nos.
21 *Richard Wagner Nachrichten*, Österreichische Richard Wagner Gesellschaft (Graz, 1989–) [contd from 14]
22 *Die Wiener Staatsoper/Vienna State Opera*, Freunde der Wiener Staatsoper (1989/90–) [in Eng. and Ger.]
23 *Die Fledermaus: Mitteilungen*, Wiener Institut für Strauss-Forschung (1990–)
24 *Linzer Musiktheater: Mitteilungen*, Freunde des Linzer Musiktheaters (Linz, 1990/91–)

BELGIUM

1 *Annuaire dramatique de la Belgique: contenant pour chaque jour de l'année des éphémérides des auteurs, musiciens, artistes morts ou vivans*, ed. F. Delhasse (Brussels, 1839–47) 9 vols., Y
2 *De operagids*, Koninklijke Vlaamsche Opera (Antwerp, 1932/3–1934/5) 3 vols., W
3 *Onze opera*, Vrienden van de Vlaamsche Opera (Ghent, 1937/8–1938/9) 2 vols., M
4 *Le courrier du Théâtre royal de la Monnaie* (Brussels, 1954/5–1958/9) 5 vols., S [contd as 6]
5 *Opéra et bel canto*, Les Amis de l'Art Lyrique (Liège, 1956–65) 97 nos. in 10 vols., M
6 *Opéra ballet*, Théâtre Royal de la Monnaie (Brussels, 1959–65) 70 nos. in 7 vols. [contd from 4]
7 *Prologue: magazine mensuel pour la diffusion et la promotion de l'art lyrique*, Opéra de Wallonie (Liège, 1967–) M
8 *Opera Magazine*, Opéra National (Brussels, 1981–)
9 *Info opera: maandelijks informatieblad*, Opera voor Vlaanderen (Antwerp, 1982/3–) M except July–Aug

BRAZIL

1 *Opera* (Rio de Janeiro, 1962–)

CANADA
(all published in Toronto)
See also: Germany 10, 60; Italy 23, 25, 27

1 *Opera in Canada*, from July 1963 *Opera Canada*, Canadian Opera Guild, 1967–76 Canadian Opera Association (1960–) 6, in 1975 5 nos. Y, from 1976 Q [mainly in Eng., occasionally in Fr.]
2 *Guild News*, Canadian Opera Guild (1968–76, 1978–82) 8 vols., Q, from 1978 O, unnumbered [contd as 6; see also 3]
3 *COC Overtures*, from Dec 1977 *Overtures*, Canadian Opera Co. (1975–82) Q [absorbed the function of 2 in 1977, 1983–8; contd as 5]
4 *Canadian Opera Company Souvenir Programme* (1980/81–1990/91), 11 unnumbered issues, Y [contd as 7]
5 *COC News*, Canadian Opera Co. (1982–) 3 nos. Y [contd from 3]
6 *Friends Newsletter*, Canadian Opera Guild (1989–) Y [contd from 2]
7 *COC Season Guide*, Canadian Opera Co. (1991/2–) Y, unnumbered [contd from 4]

CZECH AND SLOVAK REPUBLICS

1 *Oesterreichisches Theater- und Musik-Album zur Förderung dramaturgischer und musikalischer Interessen* (Prague, 1847–8) 2 vols.
2 *Le théâtre en Tchécoslovaquie: opéra, ballet, théâtre musical* (Prague, 1966/7–)

DENMARK

1 *Ascolta*, Operaens Venner (Vaerløse, 1982–) 8 nos. Y

FRANCE
(published in Paris unless otherwise stated)
See also: Canada 1; Germany 60; Italy 25; USA 24

1 *Calendrier historique des théâtres, de l'opéra, et des comédies françoise et italienne et des foires*, from 1752 *Almanach historique et chronologique de tous les spectacles*, from 1753 *Calendrier historique des théâtres de l'opéra et des comédies françoise et italienne et des foires*, from 1754 *Les spectacles de Paris, ou Suite du calendrier historique et chronologique des théâtres*, from 1800 *Almanach des spectacles de Paris* (1751–1793/4, 1800–01, 1815) 46 vols., Y [contd as 5]
2 *Annuaire dramatique, contenant les noms et demeures de tous les directeurs, acteurs, musiciens et employés de tous les théâtres de Paris* (1805–1821/2) 18 years in 17 vols., Y
3 *Annuaire de la Société des auteurs et compositeurs dramatiques*, ed. M. Lockroy (<1866/7–1871/2> 1867–72) 6 vols., Y [contd as 4]
4 *Bulletin de la Société des auteurs et compositeurs dramatiques* (1872/3–1878/9) 7 vols. [contd from 3; contd as 6]
5 *Almanach des spectacles*, ed. P. Milliet and A. Soubies (1874–1913) 43 vols., Y [contd from 1]
6 *Annuaire de la Société des auteurs et compositeurs dramatiques* (1879/80–1928/9) 10 vols., Y [contd from 4]
7 *Revue wagnérienne*, ed. E. Dujardin (1885/6–1887/8) 3 vols.
8 *La question Wagner* (1891) 1 no.
9 *Société des artistes et des amis de l'Opéra … rapport du Comité* (1904–10) 7 vols.
10 *Le guide du concert* (later *concert et des théâtres lyriques*, from 1966 (no.490) *concert et du disque*, from 1970 (no.560) *concert, du disque, de la musique et du son*), from 1970 (no.573) *Le guide musical du concert, du disque, de la musique et du son*, incorp. 16 in 1973 to form *Le guide musical – Opéra*, from Sept 1974 *Le guide musical* (1910/11–1938/9, 1945–) W during concert season, later F, from 1973 M; suppls.: *Guide musical*, 1928–39, 12 vols., contd as *Information musicale*, 1940–42, 79 nos. [incorp. *Musique* in 1930; incorp. 15 as numbered col. or suppl. 1955–60]
11 *L'Union des artistes dramatiques et lyriques des théâtres français* (1918–?) M
12 *Lyrica: revue mensuelle illustrée de l'art lyrique et de tous les arts* (1922/3–1939/40) 158 nos. in 18 vols., mainly M
13 *L'opéra–comique*, Association des Amis de l'Opéra-Comique, ed. M. Cauchie (1929–32) 4 vols., B
14 *L'Opéra de Paris*, Académie Nationale de Musique et de Danse, later Théâtres Lyriques Nationaux (1950–67) 25 nos.
15 *L'entr'acte: la revue des théâtres lyriques*, subtitle varies (1955–71) 394 nos., from 1960 20 nos. Y during theatre season [nos.8–179 part of 10]
16 *Opéra 61: la revue de l'art lyrique*, from 1974 (no.98) *Opéra: théâtre musical, danse, disques, variétés* (1961–77) 121 nos., M; suppl. [incorp. into 10 from March 1973 to Aug 1974; contd as 19]

17 *Lyrica: revue française de l'art lyrique* (Boulogne, 1973/4–) M except July–Aug
18 *L'avant-scène opéra* (title varies) (1976–) 6–9 nos. Y, from 1983 M
19 *Opéra international: le magazine de l'art lyrique* (1977–) 10, later 11 nos. Y [contd from 16]
20 *La maison: bulletin intérieur du Théâtre national de l'opéra de Paris* (1978/9) Q

GERMANY
See also: Austria 7; Italy 18, 23, 25, 27; USA 3, 24

1 *Theater-Journal derjenigen Schauspiele und Opern, welche in Augsburg von der Karl Ritter von Steinsbergischen Gesellschaft deutscher Schauspieler aufgeführt wurden* (Augsburg, 1799–1800) 2 vols.
2 *Theater-Journal, enthaltend alle in den königlichen Hoftheatern aufgeführten Stücke und Opern* (Stuttgart, 1810) 1 vol.
3 *Taschenbuch* (from 1816 *Theaterkalender*, from 1829 *Taschenbuch*) *für die Freunde des hiesigen Hoftheaters* (from 1820 *Hofoperntheaters*, from 1824 *Hof-Opern-Theaters*) (Darmstadt, 1812–25, 1828–30) 17 vols., Y
4 *Opern-Almanach*, ed. A. von Kotzebue (Leipzig, 1815, 1817) 2 vols., Y
5 *Gesang und Oper*, pubd Heinrichshofen (Magdeburg, 1861–2) 7 nos., O
6 *Jahres-Bericht des Akademischen Richard Wagner-Vereins zu Leipzig* (Leipzig, 1865/6–1909/10) 46 vols., Y
7 *Theatralia: allgemeines Interessenorgan für Bühnenvorstände und Mitglieder, dramatische Autoren und die mit dem Theater verbundenen Geschäftszweige* (Berlin, 1876) 1 vol.
8 *Bayreuther Blätter*, Bayreuther Patronatsverein, from 1884 Allgemeiner Richard-Wagner-Verein, ed. H. von Wolzogen (Chemnitz [Karl-Marx-Stadt], 1878; Bayreuth, 1879–1938) 61 vols., M, from 1883 Q; c.i. 1878–1927, 1928–32, 1933–7
9 *Richard Wagner-Jahrbuch*, ed. J. Kürschner (Stuttgart, 1886) 1 vol., Y
10 *Bayreuth-Album* (Berlin, 1889–91; Elberfeld [Wuppertal], 1892–6) Y [parallel texts in Eng. and Ger.]
11 *Opernstatistik für das Jahr 1894 … der in Deutschland und auf den deutschen Bühnen Oesterreichs, der Schweiz und Russlands aufgeführten Opern*, ed. M. Friedlaender (Leipzig, 1895) 1 vol. Y [contd as *Deutscher Bühnen-Spielplan*, 1896/7–1937/8]
12 *Bericht über die Tätigkeit der Anstalt*, Hochschule für Musik in Mannheim, zugleich Opern- und Schauspielschule (Mannheim, 1899/1900–1903/4) 5 vols. Y
13 *Jahres-Bericht des Konservatoriums der Musik, Opern- und Schauspielschule Klindworth-Scharwenka* (Berlin, 1904/5–1927/8) 24 vols., Y
14 *Tempelkunst*, Richard Wagner-Gesellschaft (Berlin, 1904) 1 vol.
15 *Die Operette: eine Bühnen-Zeitschrift* (Leipzig, 1906) 1 vol.
16 *Richard Wagner-Jahrbuch*, ed. L. Frankenstein (Leipzig, 1906; Berlin, 1907–8, 1912–13) 5 vols., Y
17 *Frankfurter Theater-Almanach für Opernhaus und Schauspielhaus* (Frankfurt, 1907–?1950/51) Y
18 *Wagner-Kalender* (Berlin and Leipzig, 1908) 1 vol.
19 *Gluck-Jahrbuch*, Gluck-Gesellschaft, ed. H. Abert, pubd Breitkopf & Härtel (Berlin and elsewhere, 1913, 1915, 1917–18) 4 vols., Y
20 *Jahrbuch des Deutschen Opernhauses in Charlottenburg* (Berlin, 1919/20–1922/3) 3 vols., Y [contd as 26]
21 *Almanach für Opernhaus, Schauspielhaus, Neues Theater* (Frankfurt, 1920/21–?) Y
22 *Blätter der Staatsoper*, Intendanz der Staatsoper, Berlin, ed. J. Kapp (Berlin, 1920/21–1942/3) O
23 *Jahrbuch des Reussischen Theaters*, ed. Heinrich XLV Reuss (Leipzig, 1923/4–1930/31) 4 vols., Y
24 *Ausblick: Blätter der Dresdner Staatstheater: Opernhaus*, W. and B. von Baensch-Stiftung (Dresden, 1924–6) 3 vols. [contd as 28]
25 *Almanach*, Staatsoper Berlin, ed. J. Kapp (Berlin, 1925; Leipzig, 1939) 2 vols.
26 *Jahrbuch der Städtischen Oper Berlin* (Berlin, 1925/6) 1 vol., Y [contd from 20]
27 *Die Oper: Blätter des Breslauer Stadttheaters* (later *Opernhauses*) (Breslau, 1926/7–1930/31) 5 vols.
28 *Blätter der Staatsoper* (Dresden, 1927/8–1938/9) 12 vols., O [contd from 24]
29 *Die geistige Wiedergeburt*, Richard-Wagner-Gemeinschaft (Freiburg, 1930–31) 2 vols.

30 *Die Oper: Blätter des Königsberger Opernhauses* (Königsberg, 1930/31–1933/4) 4 vols., M

31 *Mitteilungsblatt für die Opern- und Schauspielgemeinde der deutschen Bühne*, Ortsgruppe Breslau Deutsche Bühne (Breslau, 1933–?)

32 *Gestaltung und Gestalten: dramaturgische Blätter*, Staatstheater Dresden, ed. G. Hausswald (Dresden, 1945/6–1950/51; E. Berlin, 1951/2; Dresden, 1952/3–1958/61) 12 vols., Y

33 *Blätter der Bayerischen Staatsoper* (Munich, 1948/9–) O

34 *Bayreuther Musikbriefe* (Weiden, 1950–54) 5 vols., Q

35 *Internationale Richard-Strauss-Gesellschaft: Mitteilungen* (W. Berlin, 1952–69) 63 nos., O, from 1957 4 nos. Y [contd as Austria 15]

36 *Richard Strauss Jahrbuch*, ed. W. Schuh, pubd Boosey & Hawkes (Bonn, 1954, 1959/60) 2 vols., O

37 *Bayreuth: Richard-Wagner-Festspiele*, Festspielleitung (Bayreuth, 1955–) Y

38 *Operette*, Staatliches Operettentheater Dresden (Dresden, 1955–?)

39 *Der Operettendramaturg*, Dramaturgie des Metropol-Theaters (E. Berlin, 1957–9) 3 vols., 6, from 1958 3, nos. Y, mimeographed

40 *Oper und Tanz*, Vereinigung Deutscher Opernchöre und Bühnentänzer in der DAG, Köln (Lechenich, nr Cologne, later Erftstadt, 1957–) 4–6 nos. Y

41 *Jahrbuch der Komischen Oper Berlin*, Dramaturgische Abteilung der Komischen Oper Berlin, ed. H. Seeger and M. Vogler, pubd Henschel (E. Berlin, 1960/61–1971/2) 12 vols., Y [contd as 51]

42 *Opernwelt* (Velber, nr Hanover, 1960–74; Seelze, 1975–81; Zürich, 1981–) M; incl. *Oper*, 1966–, Y

43 *Opern Journal*, Deutsche Oper Berlin (W. Berlin, 1961/2–1971/2) 9–10 nos. Y [contd as the programme-notes ser. *Deutsche Oper Berlin* and later as 57]

44 *Deutsche Staatsoper Berlin im Bild*, from 1965 *Oper im Bild* (E. Berlin, 1963–?75) 13 vols.

45 *Die Welt der Oper: Informationsblatt der Komischen Oper Berlin*, Dramaturgische Abteilung der Komischen Oper, ed. H. Seeger and M. Vogler (E. Berlin, 1963–) 10, 1965–6 5 nos. Y

46 *Dramatiker und Komponisten auf den Bühnen der Deutschen Demokratischen Republik*, Akademie der Künste (E. Berlin, <1964/5–1971/2>, 1966–72)

47 *Die Leipziger Bühne: Blätter der Städtischen Theater Leipzig*, subtitle varies (Leipzig, 1965/6–1969/70) 15 nos.

48 *Der Opern- und Konzertfreund: ein Auswahlverzeichnis zu Hamburger Opern- und Konzertprogrammen* (Hamburg, 1965/6–1972/3)

49 *Frankfurter Opernhefte*, Frankfurter Oper (Frankfurt, 1972/3–1976/7) 5 vols., M

50 *Rundbrief* [opera broadcasts], ed. R. and M. Bauer (Viernheim, 1972–81), mimeographed [contd as 59]

51 *Musikbühne*, ed. H. Seeger (E. Berlin, 1974–7) 4 vols., Y [contd from 41; contd as 55]

52 *Almanach für Theaterfreunde*, Deutsche Oper am Rhein, Düsseldorf (Duisburg, 1975/6) Y

53 *Richard Wagner Blätter*, Aktionskreis für das Werk Richard Wagners (Bayreuth, later Tutzing, 1977–) 4 nos. Y

54 *Jahrbuch der Bayerischen Staatsoper*, Gesellschaft zur Förderung der Münchner Opernfestspiele und Intendanz der Bayerischen Staatsoper (Munich, 1978–86, 1987/8–) Y

55 *Oper heute: ein Almanach der Musikbühne*, ed. H. Seeger (E. Berlin, 1978–88), 11 vols., Y [contd from 51]

56 *Das Opernglas* (Pinneberg, later Hamburg, 1980–) 11 nos. Y

57 *Deutsche Oper Berlin aktuell* (W. Berlin, 1981/2–) 11 nos. [contd from the programme-notes ser. *Deutsche Oper Berlin* and earlier from 43]

58 *Oper in Hamburg*, Intendanz der Hamburgischen Staatsoper (Hamburg, 1981/2–) Y [contd from *Spielzeit*]

59 *Der Opernfreund* (Munich, 1982–) 6–9 nos. Y [contd from 50]

60 *Jahrbuch für Opernforschung* (Frankfurt and elsewhere, 1985–) Y [in Eng., Fr. and Ger.]

61 *Leipziger Operngucker* (Leipzig, 1990/91–) 5–6 nos. Y in season

GREAT BRITAIN

(*published in London unless otherwise stated*)

See also: Germany 10, 60; Italy 23, 25, 27

1 *Opera Glass* (Glasgow, 1829–?48)

2 *The Opera-Glass: a Weekly Musical and Theatrical Miscellany* (Edinburgh, 1840–41) 2 vols., W

3 *The* (from 6 July *The Westminster and*) *Covent Garden Journal* (1861) 1 vol.

4 *The Meister*, London Branch of the Wagner Society, ed. W. A. Ellis, pubd Redway, from 1890 Kegan Paul, Trench & Trübner (1888–95) 8 vols., Q

5 *Covent Garden Musical Annual* (<1898/9> 1898) 1 vol., Y

6 *Opera: a Magazine for Music Lovers*, from 1924 (no.5) *Opera and the Ballet* (1923–4) 2 vols., M

7 *The Gilbert and Sullivan Journal*, Gilbert and Sullivan Society (Sawbridgeworth, Cambridgeshire, 1925/6–1981) 3 nos. Y; bibl. [contd as 26]

8 *Operatic Association Gazette*, later *National Operatic and Dramatic Association Yearbook* (1930–) Y

9 *Ballet*, from 1948 *Ballet and Opera*, from 1950 *Ballet* (1939, 1946–52) 12 vols.; c.i. 1939–48 [in 1950 partly contd as 10]

10 *Opera*, ed. Earl of Harewood (1950–) 6 nos. Y, later M [contd from 9]

11 *Opera Annual*, ed. H. Rosenthal (1954/5–1961/2) 8 vols., Y

12 *About the House*, Friends of Covent Garden (1962/5–) 3–4, from 1970 3, nos. Y; c.i. 1962–7

13 *Scottish Opera News* (Glasgow, 1964–9) M [contd as 18]

14 *Sadler's Wells* (from 1969 *Wells Opera*) *Magazine*, Sadler's Wells Opera (1965/8–1969), 2 vols., 3–5 nos. Y

15 *The Wagner Society Newsletter*, from Nov 1971 *Wagner: the Magazine of the Wagner Society* (1965–80) [contd as 24 and 25]

16 *Wagner Society Review* (1965) 1 no.

17 *Opera*, ed. C. Osborne (1966) Y

18 *Scottish Opera Magazine*, Scottish Opera (Glasgow, 1970–75) 3 unnumbered issues Y [contd from 13; contd as 22]

19 *Donizetti Society Newsletter* (1973–) H; bibl.

20 *Donizetti* (from 1975 *The Donizetti*) *Society Journal* (1974–) Y, from 1975 O

21 *Opera North* (Newcastle upon Tyne, 1974–9) 20 nos., 2–4 nos. Y

22 *Scottish Opera News*, Scottish Opera (Glasgow, 1976–) M [contd from 18]

23 *Welsh National Opera News* (Cardiff, 1978–85) Q [contd as 28]

24 *Wagner*, Wagner Society (1980–) Q, from 1991 3 nos. Y [Jan 1982 to April 1984 also called nos. 90–99 of old ser.; contd from 15]

25 *Wagner News*, Wagner Society (1980–) 8 nos. Y [contd from 15]

26 *Gilbert and Sullivan News* (Orpington, Kent, 1982–) [contd from 7]

27 *The Opera Enthusiast* (London, 1984–)

28 *Friends of Welsh National Opera Newsletter* (Cardiff, 1985–) Q [contd from 23]

29 *Amici di Verdi: Newsletter* (London, 1987–) Q

30 *Cambridge Opera Journal* (Cambridge, 1989–) 3 nos. Y

31 *Opera Now* (1989/90–) M

ISRAEL

1 *The Israel Opera* (Tel-Aviv, 1949–50) 2 vols. [in Heb.]

ITALY

See also: Great Britain 29; USA 14, 20, 24

1 *Indice de' teatrali spettacoli* (Milan and elsewhere, 1764–1823)

2 *Rossini e la musica, ossia Amena biografia musicale: almanacco* (Milan, 1827) 1 vol., Y

3 *Rossini: giornale artistico teatrale* (Naples, 1862–6) 5 vols.

4 *Rivista teatrale melodrammatica* (Milan, 1863–1934) 72 vols.

5 *Il Gioacchino Rossini* (Bologna, 1868/9) 1 vol.

6 *Bellini* (Florence, 1872/3–1898) 13 vols.

7 *Cronaca wagneriana*, Sezione Bolognese della Associazione Universale R. Wagner (Bologna, 1893–) S

8 *Il Falstaff melodrammatico: giornale dell'Agenzia teatrale Angelo Villa* (Milan, 1896–7) 2 vols.

9 *La rassegna melodrammatica* (Milan, 1899–1917, 1919–34, 1946–) S

10 *L'arte melodrammatica* (Milan, 1904/5–1914) 10 vols., Q

11 *L'opera comica: giornale d'operette*, from 1918 *Nuova opera comica* (Milan, 1907–?29)

12 *Rassegna wagneriana* (Rome, 1909) 1 vol.

13 *La gazzetta musicale drammatica e il Signor Pubblico* (Milan and Rome, 1915–16) 2 vols.

14 *L'argante operettistico* (Milan, 1923–8) 6 vols.

15 *Verdi: pubblicazione delle Commemorazioni nel 1926*, Comitato di Busseto (Bologna, 1926) M

16 *Annuario del teatro lirico italiano* (Milan, 1940–) 1 vol.
17 *Corriere del teatro*, later with subtitle *mensile d'opera* (Milan, 1949–81) S, from 1963 10 nos. Y
18 *La Scala: rivista dell'opera* (Milan, 1949–63) 161 nos., M; c.i. 1949–59 in no.121 [also Ger. edn]
19 *Verdiana: bollettino di notizie*, Comitato Nazionale per le Onoranze a Giuseppe Verdi (Milan, 1950–51) 12 nos., M, later B
20 *Melodramma: quindicinale del teatro di musica* (Venice, 1954) 1 vol., S
21 *Bollettino del Centro rossiniano di studi* (Pesaro, 1955/6–1959/60, 1967–), B, then 1–3 nos. Y [1967–70 as new ser.; in 1988 resumes orig. numeration, as anno xxviii]
22 *Il melodramma italiano: periodico d'informazione sull'attività lirica* (Rome, 1956–8) 3 vols.
23 *Bollettino quadrimestrale dell'Istituto di studi verdiani*, from 1960 *Verdi*, Istituto di Studi Verdiani (Parma, 1958–) 3 nos. Y, later O [in Eng., Ger. and It.]
24 *Corriere internazionale del teatro* (Milan, 1960–?) 20–23 nos. Y
25 *L'opera: rassegna internazionale del teatro lirico* (Milan, 1966–) Q [mainly in It., some articles in Eng., Fr., Ger., Sp., and Russ.]
26 *Lirica nel mondo* (Rome, 1971/2–) 4 nos. Y
27 *Studi verdiani*, Istituto di Studi Verdiani (Parma, 1982–) Y [in Eng., Ger. and It.]
28 *Stagione d'opera e balletto*, Teatro alla Scala (Milan, 1983/4–)
29 *Opera: annuario EDT dell'opera lirica in Italia* (Turin, 1987–) Y
30 *OperaOggi* (Milan, 1987–) B

NETHERLANDS

(all published in Amsterdam)

1 *Maandblad voor muziek*, Wagner-Vereeniging te Amsterdam, ed. H. Viotta, pubd van Munster (1888/9–1893/4) 5 vols., M [contd as *Weekblad voor muziek*, not pubd by the Wagner-Vereeniging]
2 *Opera: periodiek voor muziekdramatische kunst*, Nederlandse Opera Stichting (1960/61–1971/2) 12 vols. [contd as 3]
3 *Opera journaal*, Nederlandse Opera-Stichting (1972/3–) [contd from 2]
4 *Opera jaarboek*, Nederlandse Operastichting (1980–85) Y

NORWAY

1 *Opera og ballet* (Oslo, 1951–2) 2 vols.
2 *Da capo: tidsskrift for den norske opera* (Oslo, 1971/2–1978/9) 31 nos., 4 nos. Y

POLAND

(all published in Warsaw)

1 *Lirnik: kalendarz operetkowy* [The Lyre Player: Calendar of Operettas] (1898–9) 2 vols., Y
2 *Biuletyn muzyczny Towarzystwa przyjaciół muzyki i opery narodowej* [Musical Bulletin of the Society of Friends of Music and the National Opera] (1933–4) 2 vols.
3 *Opera viva*, Państwowa Opera w Warszawie (1961–3) 6 nos., O

PORTUGAL

1 *Opera* (Lisbon, 1969/70–1970/71) 2 vols.

SPAIN

See also: Italy 25

1 *La opera española* (Madrid, 1875/6–1876/7) 2 vols., M

SWEDEN

(all published in Stockholm)

1 *Operaboken*, Kungl.[iga] Teatern Stockholm (1939/40–1941/2) 3 vols.
2 *Vår opera* [also ballet], Kungl.[iga] Teatern (1964–78) 4–5 nos. Y [contd as 3]
3 *På operan* [also ballet], Kungl.[iga] Teatern (1978/9–) 2–4 nos. Y [contd from 2]

SWITZERLAND

See also: Germany 42

1 *Richard Wagner-Blätter*, Schweizerischer Richard Wagner-Bund (Zürich, 1949–50) 2 vols.
2 *Annuaire de l'opéra* (Geneva, 1961/2) 1 vol., Y
3 *Oper* (Zürich, 1966–) Y

USA

See also: Germany 10, 60; Italy 23, 25, 27

1 *Theatrical Censor and Musical Review* (Philadelphia, 1828) 28 nos., D, from no.4 3 nos. W
2 *The Lorgnette, or Studies of the Town, by an Opera Goer* (New York, 1850) 24 nos.
3 *Bühnen-Almanach des St. Louis-Opern Hauses* (St Louis, 1861) 1 vol., Y
4 *Opera* (New York, 1893–?5) 68 nos. in 2 vols., B
5 *Opera* (Chicago, 1894–5) 2 vols., W, in 1895 F
6 *Opera Glass: a Musical and Dramatic Magazine* (Boston, 1894–8) 5 vols., M
7 *Opera News* (Philadelphia and New York, 1909/10–1920) 11 vols., W aut.–spr. [contd as 11]
8 *Century Opera Weekly*, from no.8 *Opera* (New York, 1913) 13 nos. in 1 vol., W
9 *International Music and Drama*, Bertrand De Berny's Opera and Oratorio Society (New York, 1914/15–1915/16) 4 vols., W
10 *Opera Magazine* (New York, 1914–16) 3 vols., M
11 *Music Record and Opera News* (New York, 1921–) [contd from 7]
12 *Opera, Concert and Symphony*, from 1935 *Counterpoint*, 1947–51 *Opera and Concert*, San Francisco Opera Association (San Francisco, 1934–53) 18 vols.
13 *Opera News*, Metropolitan Opera Guild (New York, 1936/7–) W in opera season, from 1939/40 also F in aut. and spr., from 1972/3 W in opera broadcast season and M otherwise; c.i., *All-Time Index to Opera News, 1936–1981*, 1982
14 *International Lyric Courier* [It. opera and musicians] (New York, 1946–) Q [in Eng. and It.]
15 *Chicago* (from vol.ii *Lyric*) *Opera News*, Lyric Opera of Chicago (Chicago, 1954/5–) 2–4 nos. Y, from 1981 2 nos. Y [spr. issue is an annual report]
16 *Central Opera Service Bulletin*, Metropolitan Opera National Council, Central Opera Service (New York, 1960/61–1989/90) 30 vols., 5–7 mimeographed nos. Y, from 1965/6 (no.3) B, from 1971/2 (no.4) Q; bibl.
17 *Opera Cues*, Houston Grand Opera Guild (Houston, 1960/61–) 3–5 nos. Y
18 *Opera Journal*, U. of Mississippi and the National Opera Association (University, MS, later Columbia, MS, 1968–) Q
19 *Intercompany Announcements*, Opera America (Washington DC, 1972–) 10 nos. Y
20 *AIVS* (from 1977 (no.3) *Verdi*) *Newsletter*, American Institute for Verdi Studies, Dept of Music, New York U., ed. A. Porter, from 1981–2 M. Chusid and A. Porter (New York, 1976–) O [in Eng. and It.]
21 *NOA Newsletter*, National Opera Association (Norfolk, VA, then Commerce, TX, 1977–) Q
22 *Opera Review* (Washington DC, 1977) 2 nos., B
23 *Dallas Civic Opera Magazine*, from 1981 *The Dallas Opera Magazine*, Dallas Civic Opera (Dallas, 1978–) 4 nos. Y
24 *The Opera Companion*, San Francisco Opera (San Francisco, 1978–) 15, from May 1986 14, nos. Y [summaries in Fr., Ger. and It.]
25 *Opera Journal Newsletter*, National Opera Association (Columbia, MS, 1978–?84) 7 vols., 4 nos. Y
26 *The World of Opera*, ed. I. Kolodin (New York, 1978/9) 6 nos. in 1 vol., B
27 *Opera Digest* (New York, 1980–) 6–10 nos. Y
28 *The Opera Quarterly* (Chapel Hill, later Durham, NC, 1983–) Q; bibl.
29 *Opera Annual U.S.* (Englewood, NJ, 1984/5–) Y
30 *Opera Fanatic*, Bel Canto Society (New York, 1986–), mainly Y
31 *Opera Monthly* (New York, 1988/9–) M

IMOGEN FELLINGER (list with JULIE WOODWARD, JOHN SHEPARD)

Perlea, Jonel (*b* Ograda, Romania, 13 Dec 1900; *d* New York, 29 July 1970). Romanian conductor. He studied in Munich and Leipzig and, except for a year at Rostock (1924–5), conducted mostly in Bucharest, at the Opera where he became Intendant (1929–30; 1934–6). He spent the last year of the war in a German internment camp. Afterwards, he conducted in Italy, and went to the Metropolitan, New York, in 1949, making his début with *Tristan und Isolde*. The urgency, clarity and beautiful orchestral sonority of that performance were remarkable, and he made an equally strong impression that season in *Carmen*, *La traviata* and *Rigoletto*. But he became the victim of internal intrigues and stayed at the Metropolitan for only one season (the new general manager in 1950 offered him only *Die Fledermaus*).

Perlea continued to conduct opera in Italy, but his American career was unsuccessful. Weakened by a heart attack in 1957, then crippled by a stroke, he learnt to conduct with his left arm alone. In his last years he taught and conducted at the Manhattan School of Music, was musical director of the Connecticut SO and once more made a stirring impression with his performances of *Tosca* for Sarah Caldwell's American National Opera Company in 1967.

MICHAEL STEINBERG

Perli, Lisa. *See* LABBETTE, DORA.

Perm'. City in western central Russia, on the western slope of the Urals. From 1940 to 1957 it was known as Molotov. Occasional operatic appearances were made in the city by the St Petersburg dramatic troupe of P. A. Sokolov from 1843, the first locals performing in an 1870 production of *A Life for the Tsar* by A. D. Kheruvimov's troupe. A new stone theatre built in 1878 housed Perm''s first opera season in 1879, in which operas staged by P. M. Medvedev's company alternated with straight dramas. A standing opera company existed from 1894 to 1904, at first under Medvedev but later under the theatre directorship and various entrepreneurs; an unusual special event was A. D. Gordotsov's production of *A Life for the Tsar* by peasants from 1911 to 1913, in 1913 performed 'in natural surroundings' in 84 locations in and around the city. Regular operatic activity was resumed in 1920, with the company renamed the Vtoraya Gosudarstvennaya Opera Urala (Second State Theatre of the Urals; after Sverdlovsk [now Yekaterinburg]) in 1931, the Permskiy Oblastnoy Operniy Teatr (Perm' Regional Opera Theatre) in 1938, and finally the Permskiy Teatr Operï i Baleta in 1939. During World War II the city and theatre housed the evacuated Leningrad Opera and Ballet Theatre. The theatre has since given premières of operas by Koval', L. B. Stepanov, Spadavecchia, D. A. Tolstoy and Slonimsky, but its particular dedication to the works of Tchaikovsky led to its being renamed after that composer in 1965; in 1969 it became the Permskiy Gosudarstvenniy Akademicheskiy Teatr Operï i Baleta imeni P. I. Tchaikovskogo (Tchaikovsky Perm' State Academic Theatre of Opera and Ballet).

*
ME (E. V. Mayburova and M. M. Yakovlev; also 'Permskiy teatr operï i baleta', L. N. Demeneva)

A. Shvarts: 'Put' teatra' [The Theatre's Path], *Prikam'ye* (1947), no.10

Iu. Kurochkin: *Iz teatral'nogo proshlogo Urala* [From the Urals' Theatrical Past] (Sverdlovsk, 1957)

E. V. Mayburova: 'Muzïkal'naya zhizn' dorevolyutsionnoy Permi' [Musical Life in Pre-revolutionary Perm'], *Iz muzïkal'nogo proshlogo* [From the Musical Past], ed. B. S. Shteynpress, i (Moscow, 1960), 72–124

G. Bernandt: *Slovar' oper vpervïye postavlennïkh ili izdannïkh v dorevolyutsionnoy Rossii i v SSSR 1736–1959* [Dictionary of Operas First Performed or Published in Pre-revolutionary Russia and in the USSR 1736–1959] (Moscow, 1962), 549

S. Korobkov: 'Spektakli i sud'bï' [Shows and Fortunes], *SovM* (1987), no.5, pp.58–66

M. Raku: 'Chetïre vechera v Permi' [Four Evenings in Perm'], ibid, 52–8

GREGORY SALMON

Per Massimiliano Robespierre ('For Maximilien Robespierre'). Opera in a prologue, two acts and a

critical intermezzo by GIACOMO MANZONI to a libretto by the composer and Virginio Puecher, from texts by Robespierre and others; Bologna, Teatro Comunale, 12 April 1975.

With *Per Massimiliano Robespierre* Manzoni developed to the full his conception of musical theatre as an arena for thoughtful debate, rather than narrative. An attempt to confront seriously the aspirations of Robespierre, as well as the mythology surrounding him, the work is structured as an alternation between five 'percorsi' (routes) presenting elements of Robespierre's thought, and four scenes evoking specific aspects of his impact upon those around him. Percorso C, at the end of Act 1, assembles historical judgments on Robespierre, thus allowing the director, where appropriate, to stage a 'critical intermezzo' that will open out into a debate among the audience during the interval. Robespierre is not impersonated on stage; his words are divided between a quartet of singers and various speakers.

Manzoni's score gives a sense of large-scale shape by cutting between strongly differentiated types of sound-mass, including materials from the Revolutionary period: at one striking point Gossec's *Hymne à l'être suprême* is cut into a complex assemblage of materials evoking the Festival of the Supreme Being. The work ends with an impassioned valediction from Charlotte, Robespierre's sister, accompanied by string quartet.

DAVID OSMOND-SMITH

Pernerstorfer, Alois (*b* Vienna, 3 June 1912; *d* Vienna, 12 May 1978). Austrian bass-baritone. He studied in Vienna with Josef Krips and made his début at Graz in 1936, as Biterolf in *Tannhäuser*. He sang at the Vienna Volksoper during the war and later sang Mozart's Figaro under Krips at the Staatsoper. At the Salzburg Festival he appeared from 1948 in *Elektra*, Barber's *Vanessa*, *La finta semplice*, *Die Zauberflöte*, *Macbeth* and *Der Rosenkavalier*. He sang Alberich in the *Ring* performances conducted by Furtwängler at La Scala in 1950, and the following season was heard as Mozart's Figaro and Leporello at Glyndebourne. Among his other roles were Pogner, Kecal (*The Bartered Bride*) and Hunding.

DAVID CUMMINGS

Pernet, André (*b* Rambervillers, Vosges, 6 Jan 1894; *d* Paris, 23 June 1966). French bass. He studied at the Paris Conservatoire with Gresse and made his début at Nice in 1921. After seven years in the French provinces he was engaged in 1928 by the Paris Opéra and became its leading bass; from 1931 he also sang at the Opéra-Comique. At the Opéra he was much admired as Boris, Don Quichotte, Méphistophélès and Don Giovanni. He created, among other parts, the title roles in Milhaud's *Maximilien* (1932) and Enescu's *Oedipe* (1936) and Shylock in Hahn's *Le marchand de Venise* (1935). He made guest appearances throughout Europe and appeared in the film version of Charpentier's *Louise*. He had a beautiful, supple voice of ample range with a great feeling for words.

HAROLD ROSENTHAL/R

Perosio, Ettore (*b* Genoa, 10 May 1868; *d* Genoa, 14 Feb 1919). Italian composer. His father, Giuseppe Perosio (1844–1922), was an art critic and amateur musician and a friend of Verdi. Ettore studied at the Nicola Paganini Institute in Genoa, then pursued a career as a conductor in many large Italian cities, as well as in Spain, Portugal and America. Two of his operas were first performed in Genoa: *Adriana Lecouvreur*, to a libretto by his father, at the Teatro Paganini on 13 January 1889 and *Per l'amore* (I. Rasi) at the Teatro Politeama on 27 May 1893. His other stage works, *Furio* (L. Orsini), *Scacco al re* (E. Ducati) and *Morosina*, seem not to have been performed. In 1900 he married the soprano Giuseppina Falconis della Perla (*née* Battaglia).

*

F. Beltrame: *Ricordo di Ettore Perosio* (Genoa, 1969)

M. Conati: 'Le lettere di Giuseppe e Giuseppina Verdi a Giuseppe Perosio', *Nuova rassegna di studi musicali*, i (1977), 47–67

PATRICK O'CONNOR

Perotti, Giovanni Domenico (*b* Vercelli, 20 Jan 1761; *d* Vercelli, 24 March 1825). Italian composer. He studied in Milan before 1779, and with Martini and Mattei in Bologna in late 1780 and early 1781. In March 1781 he was admitted to the Accademia Filarmonica there and from about this time until his death was *maestro di cappella* at Vercelli Cathedral. Despite this rather insular career he had two operas performed at important theatres: *Agesilao re di Sparta* at the Teatro Argentina, Rome (1789), and *La vittima della propria vendetta* at La Fenice, Venice (1808). Two other opera scores survive (in *D-Dlb*): *Zemira e Gandarte* (1787, Alessandria) and *Bianca di Melfi*. Perotti was the first teacher of his more famous younger brother, Giovanni Agostino Perotti (1769–1855), whose one-act comic opera *La contadina nobile* was performed in Pisa in 1795.

*

C. Gervasoni: *Nuova teoria di musica* (Parma, 1812), 227–8

C. Dionisotti: *Notizie biografiche dei vercellesi* (Biella, 1862)

HOWARD BROFSKY

Perra [Perras], **Margarita** [Margherita] (*b* Monastir [now Bitola, Macedonia] or Salonica, 15 Jan 1908; *d* Zürich, 2 Feb 1984). Greek soprano. She studied at the Salonica State Conservatory and then at the Berlin Hochschule für Musik; there, in 1927 as Norina, she caught the attention of Bruno Walter, who engaged her for the Städtische Oper. She appeared as Nuri in d'Albert's *Tiefland* and as Cupid in Gluck's *Orfeo ed Euridice* (1927) and sang the title role in the Berlin première of Paul Graener's *Hanneles Himmelfahrt* (1928). She later moved to the Berlin Staatsoper, having toured in Spain, Argentina and Brazil. In 1935 she was engaged by the Vienna Staatsoper and was highly praised as Mozart's Konstanze under Felix Weingartner. She repeated the role in Salzburg (1935) and at Glyndebourne (1937), and had further successes as the Queen of Night, Susanna, Pamina and other Mozart roles. In 1936 she sang Gilda at Covent Garden. Having married in 1937, she settled in Zürich and until 1944 appeared only in recitals, but returned to the operatic stage for a season in Vienna (1946–7). Her firm, highly trained voice possessed a gently glowing tone colour.

*

Obituary, *Opera*, xxxv (1984), 376–7

G. Leotsakos: *Ellinikó Lyrikó Théatro, 100 chronia, 1888–1988* (YP 4–6, A/A 14564–6, 1988), 148–51 [record notes]

GEORGE LEOTSAKOS

Perrin, Pierre (*b* Lyons, *c*1620; *d* Paris, bur. 26 April 1675). French poet, librettist and co-founder of French opera. He arrived in Paris in about 1645 and, having secured publication of some early poetry (including a translation of the *Aeneid*), became attached to the court of Gaston d'Orléans (1648). In January 1653 he married Mme La Barroire, a wealthy 61-year-old widow who incurred vast debts to obtain for Perrin the post of *Introducteur des ambassadeurs* at Gaston's court. Although the marriage was annulled and La Barroire died shortly afterwards, Perrin became legally responsible for the debts. Unable to pay them, he spent the rest of his life in and out of a debtors' prison.

From about 1655 Perrin began to turn to lyric poetry and in 1659 collaborated with the composer ROBERT CAMBERT on the *Pastorale*, a simple, five-act stage piece for seven singers, with minimal dramatic action. Described by Perrin as the 'première comédie françoise en musique', it was performed at the house of M. de la Haye at Issy in April 1659. People thronged to see it and there was a special performance for the king, queen and Cardinal Mazarin at Vincennes. Perrin, in gaol at the time, recounted the events and essayed his theories on French opera alongside criticisms of Italian opera in a letter to the Cardinal della Rovere (1659; trans. in Auld), whom he had met at Gaston's court. At Mazarin's suggestion a second *pastorale* followed: *Ariane, ou Le mariage de Bacchus*, a *comédie en musique*, the libretto for which Perrin fashioned to the wedding of Louis XIV and the Infanta of Spain. Again, Cambert wrote the music. Public rehearsals took place in Paris (*c*1660–61), but the work was abandoned after the large-scale Italian operas that had also been commissioned for the celebrations overshadowed the enterprise, and the deaths of Gaston (1660) and Mazarin (1661) left Perrin without a protector. A third libretto for a *tragédie en musique*, *La mort d'Adonis*, was written at the same period. It was set to music by J.-B. Boesset but never performed.

In about 1666 Perrin sent Colbert, the king's chief minister, a large manuscript collection of his lyric works (*Recueil de paroles de musique*, now in *F-Pn*) in the hope of securing the performance of some of them. In the preface he exposed his operatic theories and suggested that the king set up an academy of poetry and music to encourage the development of a national opera. His audacity was rewarded and on 28 June 1669 Louis XIV accorded him a 12-year privilege to establish 'Académies d'Opéra' in France. Perrin and Cambert renewed their association, engaged singers and began to rehearse *Ariane* once more. In December 1669 Perrin took on as business managers the Marquis de SOURDÉAC, an extravagant nobleman and famous machinist, and the Sieur de Champeron, a rich financier; Pierre Beauchamps was appointed dancing-master. By spring 1670 new singers had been recruited from Languedoc and *Ariane* had been replaced by a new collaboration, *Pomone*. A theatre was erected in the rue de Vaugirard, but the company was forced to transfer to another site (the Jeu de Paume de la Bouteille in the rue des Fossez-de-Nesle) in October 1670. *Pomone* finally inaugurated the Académies on 3 March 1671. Later considered the first true French opera, it was on a larger scale than the earlier *pastorales* and involved ballet, pageantry and machines. Although admission to performances was costly, *Pomone* was a great success and would have made a healthy profit for the company but for the actions of Sourdéac and Champeron, who pocketed most of the takings and refused to pay Perrin, Cambert or the performers. This left Perrin, in whose name the licence was held, with a string of debts he could not pay. He began legal proceedings against his managers but in June 1671 found himself again in prison for insolvency and resorted to selling off parts of his privilege.

By 1672 most of the rights had been sold to the

composer Jean Sablières and his librettist Henry Guichard; even so, Sourdéac and Champeron managed to produce, in February or March, Cambert's second opera, *Les peines et les plaisirs de l'amour* (to a libretto by Gabriel Gilbert), which was even more successful than *Pomone*. There were also plans for a third opera, most probably a revised version by Perrin of *Ariane*, later taken by Cambert to London and staged there in 1674 (for illustration *see* ARIANE (i)). Lully, presumably aware of the musical-financial potential at stake, visited Perrin in gaol on 13 March 1672 and persuaded him to resell the privilege. Squabbling as to who rightfully owned it broke out immediately, but Lully was able, through his connections with the king, to seize control of the monopoly. This freed Perrin from prison but put an end to his theatrical career. After his death, his landlord discovered four unset opera librettos, which he tried unsuccessfully to pass to Lully. Three are lost (*Diasne amoureuse, ou La vengeance d'amour, La reyne du Parnasse, ou La muse d'amour* and *La nopce* [sic] *de Venus*); the fourth, *Ariane, ou Le mariage de Bacchus*, may well have been the text for the revised version that was staged in London.

In its day, Perrin's poetry was harshly criticized, even ridiculed. Passages in *Pomone*, in particular, attracted adverse comment, causing Perrin to defend his style in a preface to the published score (Paris, 1671). Comic episodes and his characteristic use of facile rhymes, earthy – at times vulgar – language, and realistic visual imagery (sausages, truffles, mushrooms) may have led to such judgments as that of Saint-Evremond, who reported that 'people listened to the music with delight, the words with disgust'.

Perrin's conception of opera was strongly linked to the pastoral play and in contrast with Italian opera relied on a simple plot, being more concerned with communicating emotions through the union of words and music than with developing dramatic intrigues. In true French tradition, he allowed space for ballet and spectacle and provided panegyrical prologues in honour of Louis XIV. The incorporation of elaborate machine effects into *Pomone* and the revised *Ariane* was essential, for if the Académies d'Opéra were to flourish they had to compete successfully with the popular machine plays in the Marais. Although Perrin's poor judgment of character and lack of business acumen led to his ultimate downfall, his belief that a French form of opera should be created was sincerely held.

*

C. de Saint-Evremond: 'Les opera: comedie', *Oeuvres meslées*, xi (Paris, 1684; Eng. trans., 1728)

A. de Boislisle: *Les débuts de l'opéra français* (Paris, 1875)

A. Pougin: *Les vrais créateurs de l'opéra français* (Paris, 1881)

C. Nuitter and E. Thoinan: *Les origines de l'opéra français* (Paris, 1886)

H. Prunières: 'Lully and the Académie de musique et de danse', *MQ*, xi (1925), 528–46

R. Isherwood: *Music in the Service of the King: France in the Seventeenth Century* (Ithaca, NY, 1973)

S. Pitou: *The Paris Opéra: an Encyclopedia of Operas, Ballets, Composers, and Performers*, i: *Genesis and Glory, 1671–1715* (Westport, CT, 1983)

P. Danchin: 'The Foundation of the Royal Academy of Music in 1674 and Pierre Perrin's *Ariane*', *Theatre Survey*, xxv/1 (1984), 53–67

L. E. Auld: *The Lyric Art of Pierre Perrin, Founder of French Opera* (Henryville, PA, 1986)

C. Bashford: 'Perrin and Cambert's "Ariane, ou Le Mariage de Bacchus" Re-examined', *ML*, lxxii (1991), 1–26

CHRISTINA BASHFORD

Perron [Pergamenter], **Karl** (*b* Frankenthal, Pfalz, 3 June 1858; *d* Dresden, 15 July 1928). German bass-baritone. He studied with Julius Hey in Berlin and Julius von Stockhausen in Frankfurt, making his début in 1884 at Leipzig as Wolfram. In 1892 he moved to Dresden, where he was engaged at the Hofoper until 1913. There he created John the Baptist in *Salome* (1905), Orestes in *Elektra* (1909) and Ochs in *Der Rosenkavalier* (1911). In addition to his Strauss roles he sang Don Giovanni, Count Almaviva (*Le nozze di Figaro*), Hans Heiling, Nélusko (*L'Africaine*), Thomas' Hamlet, Escamillo and Yevgeny Onegin. At Bayreuth between 1889 and 1904 he sang Amfortas, Wotan, King Mark and Daland. A powerful actor, he sang with great authority.

For illustration *see* DRESDEN, fig.8.   ELIZABETH FORBES

Perry, Janet (*b* Minneapolis, 27 Dec 1947). Swiss soprano of American birth. She studied at the Curtis Institute with Eufemia Giannini-Gregory and made her début in Linz as Zerlina in 1969. Since then, her career has been primarily in Europe. She has specialized in coloratura and soubrette roles such as Adèle (*Le comte Ory*), Musetta, Nannetta, Olympia, Oscar and Zerbinetta, as well as many Mozart and *bel canto* heroines, which she has sung in Aix, Cologne, Frankfurt, Munich, Vienna and elsewhere. In 1977 she sang Aminta in *Die schweigsame Frau* at Glyndebourne. She has made several recordings.   CORI ELLISON

Perry, Julia (**Amanda**) (*b* Lexington, KY, 25 March 1924; *d* Akron, OH, 24 April 1979). American composer. Her principal composition teachers were Henry Switten, Nadia Boulanger and Luigi Dallapiccola. Among her honours were two Guggenheim fellowships, an award from the National Institute of Arts and Letters and a Boulanger Grand Prix. She composed two one-act operas based on Edgar Allan Poe's *The Cask of Amontillado*: the first, *The Bottle*, was written (to her own libretto) in 1953 but was never performed; the second, *The Cask of Amontillado* (libretto by herself and V. Card), was staged at Columbia University, New York, on 20 November 1954; both works were published in New York (1953, 1954). She also wrote a three-act opera-ballet, *The Selfish Giant*, after the short story by Oscar Wilde, which, though unperformed, was published in New York in 1964. Her eclectic music reflects wide cultural interests; her style is neo-classical, with richly dissonant harmonies, contrapuntal textures, an intense lyricism, and frequent reference to black folk idioms.

*

SouthernB

M. Green: *Black Women Composers: a Genesis* (Boston, 1983)

EILEEN SOUTHERN

Persée ('Perseus'). *Tragédie en musique* in a prologue and five acts by Jean-Baptiste Lully (*see* LULLY family, (1)) to a libretto by PHILIPPE QUINAULT after OVID's *Metamorphoses*; Paris, Opéra, 17 or 18 April 1682.

Andromède [Andromeda] (soprano) and Perseus (*haute-contre*) love each other, but Andromeda is betrothed to Phinée [Phineus] (baritone); Mérope [Merope] (soprano), who loves Perseus, sides with Phineus. This human drama is resolved only through Perseus's triumph over supernatural obstacles. In a series of elaborate spectacles he is supplied by the gods with armour and weapons, he slays the Gorgon Méduse [Medusa] (tenor), and monsters are born of Medusa's blood, all in full view of the audience; Perseus's rescue of Andromeda is described by the chorus. *Persée* was the first of Lully's operas to make extensive use of orchestral accompaniment for solo voices. In addition to the normal Paris revivals (up to 1746), a reworked version was performed at the marriage celebrations of Louis XVI and Marie Antoinette (1770).

See also ANDROMEDA; for illustration *see* PARIS, fig.2.

LOIS ROSOW

Perséphone ('Persephone'). Melodrama in three scenes by IGOR STRAVINSKY to a text by André Gide; Paris, Opéra, 30 April 1934.

Stravinsky included this neo-classical extravaganza in a discussion of 'three operas' in *Memories and Commentaries* (1960), although the title role, commissioned and first performed by the famous mime Ida Rubinstein, is spoken rather than sung. Gide's original conception was of a 'symphonic ballet' consisting of recitation, dances and choral song. Later, at the composer's suggestion, he added the tenor role, created by René Maison, of the priest Eumolpus, who narrates the myth of the daughter of the earth goddess Demeter, seduced and raped by Pluto, whose yearly peregrinations between surface world and underworld give rise to the seasons. In Gide's version Persephone goes to Hades willingly, out of compassion for the Shades, thus turning the myth into a Christian parable. The three scenes – The Abduction of Persephone, Persephone in the Underworld, Persephone Reborn – correspond to the seasonal round. Since the composer made the suggestion in *Dialogues and a Diary* (1963), the title role is often split between two performers, a dancer or mime and a reciter.

RICHARD TARUSKIN

Persiani, Fanny. *See* TACCHINARDI-PERSIANI, FANNY.

Persiani, Giuseppe (*b* Recanati, *c*1799–1805; *d* Paris, 13 Aug 1869). Italian composer. He was taught the violin by his father, but was left an orphan in 1814. He played in the Teatro Valle orchestra in Rome and from 1820 at the S Carlo in Naples, where he also studied at the conservatory under Zingarelli and Tritto. He was *maestro di cappella* in Cerignola, but by late 1824 he had settled in Rome, where he composed oratorios. The first of his 11 operas, *Piglia il mondo come viene* (1825, Florence), was an instant success; his subsequent stage works, in the Bellinian mould, were sought by impresarios at home and abroad. All but three were produced between 1825 and 1829. He owed much of his subsequent fame to the soprano Fanny Tacchinardi, whom he married in 1830. She sang in many of his operas, but Persiani's most famous opera, *Ines de Castro* (1835, Naples), was a vehicle for Malibran. His last opera, *L'orfana savoiarda* (1846, Madrid), was a fiasco. In 1847 he was named impresario of the Teatro Italiano in Covent Garden, London, but because of competition with Verdi's *I masnadieri* at the Haymarket, his season was a failure. The couple moved to Paris; he ended his career as a singing teacher.

The style of *Ines de Castro* resembles that of Donizetti; the limited rhythmic accompaniment supports a vocal line spiced with appoggiaturas. The arias are in the standard four-part form popularized by Bellini and Donizetti and the harmonic language is simple. *Ines*, like many of its contemporaries, ends with a mad scene and death.

See also INES DE CASTRO (ii).

Piglia il mondo come viene (ob, 2, A. Anelli), Florence, Pergola, 26 Dec 1825
L'inimico generoso (2), Florence, Pergola, 17 Oct 1826
Attila in Aquileja (A. Sografi), Parma, Ducale, 31 Jan 1827
Danao re d'Argo (2, F. Romani), Florence, Pergola, 16 June 1827
Gastone de Foix (Romani), Venice, Fenice, 26 Dec 1827, *I-Vt*
Il solitario (C. Bassi), Milan, Scala, 20 April 1829
Eufemio di Messina, ossia La distruzione di Catania (Romani), Lucca, del Giglio, 20 Sept 1829; as I saraceni in Catania, Padua, 29 July 1832; as Il rinnegato, Naples, 1837
Costantino in Arles (3, P. Pola), Venice, Fenice, 26 Dec 1829, *Vt*
Ines de Castro (tragedia lirica, 3, S. Cammarano), Naples, S Carlo, 28 Jan 1835, *Mc*, *US-Bp*
Il fantasma (3, Romani), Paris, Italien, 14 Dec 1843
L'orfana savoiarda (3), Madrid, Circo, 25 July 1846

G. Radiciotti: *Teatro, musica e musicisti in Recanati* (Recanati, 1905), 109–60
G. Tebaldini: 'Giuseppe Persiani e Fanny Tacchinardi', *RMI*, xii (1905), 579–91
A. Pougin: *Marie Malibran; histoire d'une cantatrice* (Paris, 1911); Eng. trans. (London, 1911), 193–7
H. Bushnell: *Maria Malibran: a Biography of the Singer* (University Park, PA, 1979), 181–4
R. Giazotto: *Maria Malibran* (Turin, 1986), 294–5, 297–8
T. G. Kaufman: 'Giuseppe and Fanny Persiani', *Donizetti Society Journal*, vi (1988), 123–51
MARVIN TARTAK

Persichetti, Vincent (*b* Philadelphia, 6 June 1915; *d* Philadelphia, 15 Aug 1987). American composer. He studied the piano with Olga Samaroff and composition with Paul Nordoff at the Philadelphia Conservatory, and conducting with Fritz Reiner at the Curtis Institute. In 1941 he was appointed to teach at the Philadelphia Conservatory, and in 1947 joined the faculty of the Juilliard School. From 1952 he also served as director of publications for Elkan-Vogel.

Persichetti's one-act opera *The Sibyl* op. 135, composed in 1976 to his own libretto, was commissioned by the Pennsylvania Opera Theater, which first produced it in Philadelphia on 13 April 1985. Subtitled 'Parable XX', it uses as a point of departure the fable of Chicken Little who is convinced the sky is falling, and focusses on the darker aspects of the story. The work's musical language is essentially atonal. Vocal lines contain awkward leaps, and the complex rhythmic patterns often break words apart, compromising proper text declamation. Most effective are the colourful orchestration and the choral writing, making the work more suitable for presentation as a cantata than as a staged dramatic work. Unfortunately, because of hollow characterization and a lack of dramatic tension in both text and music, the work met with little success after its initial performance.

R. Baxter: 'Our Critics Abroad: Philadelphia', *Opera*, xxxvi (1985), 1293–4
W. Crutchfield: 'Opera: Premiere of Persichetti Work', *New York Times* (21 April 1985)
JAMES P. CASSARO

Persico, Mario (*b* Naples, 1 Dec 1892; *d* Naples, 17 Dec 1977). Italian composer. He studied harmony and counterpoint with A. Savasta, then composition at the S Pietro Conservatory in Naples. In 1922 his first opera, *Morenita*, won second place in the national competition for lyric art in Italy. His most successful work for the stage was *La bisbetica domata*, a setting of Shakespeare's *The Taming of the Shrew* first performed in 1931; when this was revived in Naples in 1962, Lord Harewood described it as 'one of the most honest and most successful adaptations since Verdi'. Persico's third opera, *La locandiera*, after Goldoni's play, was admired for its first-act aria 'Mirandolina mia disperazione' and the second-act duet 'L'amore è un soave tormento'.

Morenita (L. Sbraglia), Naples, S Carlo, 19 April 1923
La bisbetica domata (A. Rossato, after W. Shakespeare: *The Taming of the Shrew*), Rome, Reale dell'Opera, 12 Feb 1931
La locandiera (M. Ghisalberti, after C. Goldoni), Rome, Reale dell'Opera, 17 March 1941   PATRICK O'CONNOR

Persuis, Louis-Luc Loiseau de (*b* Metz, 4 July 1769; *d* Paris, 20 Dec 1819). French composer and conductor. He spent his early childhood in the provinces, where he was educated by his father, himself a composer and choirmaster at the cathedrals of Angers and Metz. As a young man Louis-Luc was a violinist in the Metz orchestra and then tried his luck in Paris, arriving there in 1787 on the eve of the Revolution. He played in theatre orchestras, first at the Montansier and then at the Opéra. In 1805 he became chorus master, stage director and, in 1810, conductor of the Opéra; at the same time he was principal assistant conductor in the Emperor's orchestra. He had also been appointed professor of singing at the Conservatoire when it was founded in 1795, but he left in 1802 when reform measures involved the abolition of a number of posts.

Persuis' works were almost exclusively for the stage and included operas, *opéras comiques*, ballets and occasional dramatic works. He often wrote in collaboration with other composers; with Jean-François Le Sueur he composed a one-act occasional work *L'inauguration du temple de la Victoire* and a three-act *tragédie lyrique Le triomphe de Trajan* (both 1807). The latter, a propagandist piece written to glorify Napoleon, was well attuned to the neo-classical tastes of contemporary audiences and was a huge success. Two of his other music dramas are notable examples of their time: *Fanny Morna, ou L'écossaise*, with its setting of landscaped gardens and weeping willows, marks a unique point in the history of the pre-Romantic sensibility; and *La Jérusalem délivrée* exemplifies the tendency of contemporary French opera to look back to medieval subjects. The work is weak in itself but opens with a remarkable overture which was to feature prominently in anthologies of French symphonic music under the Empire; it displays a force and originality for which the rest of Persuis' compositions does not prepare us.

first performed in Paris unless otherwise stated
PO – Opéra

La nuit espagnole (oc, J. Fiévée), Feydeau, 14 June 1791
Estelle (oc, 3, Villebrune), National, 17 Dec 1793
Phanor et Angéla (oc, 3, Faur), Feydeau, July 1798
Léonidas, ou Les Spartiates (opéra, R. C. G. de Pixérécourt), PO, 15 Aug 1799, *F-Po*, collab. A.-F. Gresnick
Fanny Morna, ou L'écossaise (drame lyrique, 3, E. Favières), OC (Favart), 22 Aug 1799
Le fruit défendu (opéra, 1, E. Gosse), OC (Favart), 7 March 1800
Marcel, ou L'héritier supposé (oc, 1, Pixérécourt), OC (Favart), 12 Feb 1801
Le triomphe de Trajan (tragédie lyrique, 3, J. Esménard), PO, 23 Oct 1807, *Po*, collab. J.-F. Le Sueur
La Jérusalem délivrée (tragédie lyrique, 5, P.-M. Baour-Lormian, after T. Tasso: *Gerusalemme liberata*), PO, 15 Sept 1812
L'heureux retour (opéra-ballet, 1, Milon), PO, 25 July 1815, collab. H.-M. Berton and R. Kreutzer
Les dieux rivaux, ou Les fêtes de Cythère (opéra-ballet, 1, M. Dieulafoy and C. Briffaut), PO, 21 June 1816, *Po*, collab. Berton, Kreutzer and G. Spontini
Other works, mentioned by Fétis

EitnerQ; *FétisB*; *MGG* (B. Bardet)
A. Choron and F. Fayolle: *Dictionnaire historique des musiciens* (Paris, 1810–11)

C. E. Poisot: *Histoire de la musique en France depuis les temps les plus reculés jusqu'à nos jours* (Paris, 1860)
G. Chouquet: *Histoire de la musique dramatique en France* (Paris, 1873)
C. Pierre: *Histoire du Concert Spirituel 1725–1790* (Paris, 1975)
JEAN MONGRÉDIEN

Perth. Capital of Western Australia. The city's size (pop. about 750 000) and its great distance from other centres in Australia have made it particularly difficult for opera to take root. With the exception of the Melba-Williamson company of 1928, touring companies that took opera to the rest of the country made very few visits there. The newly formed Australian Opera Company gave its inaugural all-Mozart season there in 1956, but has made only occasional appearances since then. It was not until 1967 that the Western Australian Opera Company was established, with the composer James Penberthy as artistic director. Its first production, *Carmen*, was in His Majesty's Theatre (opened in 1904, renovated 1980). Besides touring, the company has presented three operas a year in Perth. From 1976 to 1984 a small amateur group, Opera Viva, provided more adventurous programming. An annual festival, taking place in February and March, was established in 1953 and includes opera productions.   A. I. GYGER

Perti, Giacomo Antonio (*b* Bologna, 6 June 1661; *d* Bologna, 10 April 1756). Italian composer. He was born into a well-to-do family, of Crevalcore, near Bologna; after early musical studies with an uncle and with the organist Rocco Laurenti, he learnt counterpoint with Petronio Franceschini. His first compositions date from the 1670s, both sacred (an eight-voice *Magnificat*, 1678, and an oratorio, *I due gigli*, 1679) and secular (Act 3 of *Atide*, 1679). He was admitted as a composer to the Accademia Filarmonica in 1681, and at the end of that year he went to Parma to complete his study of counterpoint with Giuseppe Corsi, known as Il Celano. He was balloted *principe* of the Accademia five times between 1687 and 1719, when he was made definitor for life. In 1689 he was turned down for the post of vice-*maestro di cappella* at the basilica of S Petronio – according to Vitali because of objections from G. P. Colonna, whom he had opposed in a controversy over Corelli's use of consecutive 5ths. The following year he became *maestro di cappella* of the cathedral, S Pietro, under his uncle Lorenzo. After Colonna's death, in 1696 he took up the post of *maestro di cappella* at S Petronio, a post he held until his own death, rarely leaving Bologna. (The only journeys he is known to have made are to Rome and Naples in 1703 and to Rome in 1747.)

During his 60 years of activity at S Petronio and other important musical institutions in Bologna (the oratory of S Maria di Galliera, 1706–50; S Domenico, 1704–55, but replaced by G. M. Alberti after 1734), Perti gained wide renown and came to be considered an authority on every kind of composition, teaching many generations of Bolognese musicians, including Torelli, Domenico Gabrielli, Pistocchi, Aldrovandini, P. P. Laurenti, Giuseppe Jacchini, Uttini, Francesco Manfredini and Martini. He was honoured by rulers including Ferdinando III de' Medici (who commissioned several operas from him for the theatre of his villa at Pratolino), the emperors Leopold I and Charles VI, and the Bolognese Pope Benedict XIV. According to Penna, Leopold offered him a post, but there is no documentary confirmation of this.

In spite of his long and illustrious career and the

wealth of surviving documentary material, including important correspondence, Perti is still perhaps the least-studied composer of his generation, and a critical evaluation of his operas is hampered by the fact that few have survived. His career as an opera composer proper began with *Marzio Coriolano* (1683, Venice) and embraced both late 17th-century experiments with subjects based mainly on love intrigues (with the intervention of *buffo* parts) and the new Arcadian and French types of plot. The decade during which he worked for Ferdinando, collaborating with the librettist Antonio Salvi and coinciding with Alessandro Scarlatti and Handel, was of great importance. The subject of *Rodelinda* (1710), like others written by Salvi for the Pratolino theatre, derives from Corneille and, like *Astianatte* (1701), belongs to a series based on imitation of French classics; it was used also by Handel and Giovanni Bononcini in London in 1725 and 1727. It is representative of a purified type of libretto far removed from those most likely to please audiences in the public theatres, such as the successful *Rosaura*, written for Venice. Later Perti abandoned the theatre, although some of his stage works were eventually revived.

In spite of the varied dramatic language of his librettists, Perti's music was always elegant, simple and intelligible, homophonic or semi-imitative, refined in detail and closely attentive to the relationship of music and text. The instrumental writing, in up to five parts following the regional practice of the time, is developed most fully in the principal ritornellos and in shorter passages between the vocal sections. However, Perti also used more modern orchestration, with fewer parts and with violins in unison where dramatically desirable (e.g. the aria 'Chi vanta un lieto core' in *Nerone fatto cesare*); in 1687 he had introduced the 'concertino and concerto grosso all'usanza di Roma' into oratorio, and he did the same in his operas, with instrumental groups divided between the orchestra and the stage. He made discriminating use of the whole available range of musical devices and forms, from the aria with continuo to the use of particular instrumental combinations ('Chi trionfò' in *Nerone* requires cellos and trumpet, and elsewhere in the same opera oboes are called for). Traces of probable French influence are seen in the use of dance forms (bourrée and rigaudon) and in frequent recourse to *inégalité* ('Esca aggiungi alla mia face' and 'Parto, ma lascio il core' also in *Nerone*). Neither the structure nor the orchestration of the arias is tied to fixed forms, but both are adapted stylistically to characterization and to the dramatic situation. The intermezzos that survive (in *I-Rsc*), of uncertain authorship but of assured comic effect, require on the stage 'Thisbe with a troop of old women who have taken Cupid prisoner' and refer to the text of *Nerone*.

Evidence of Perti's fame and esteem as an opera composer is provided by, among others, G. O. Pitoni, who in his *Guida armonica* quoted vocal and instrumental passages from *Laodicea e Berenice* and *Penelope la casta*. Perti also revised the following works by others for performance in Bologna: Alessandro Scarlatti's *L'eroe innocente* (1679), Domenico Gabrielli's *Teodora Augusta* and Freschi's *Pompeo Magno in Cilicia* (both 1687), Carlo Pallavicino's *Il re infante* (1694) and, in part, C. F. Pollarolo's *Faramondo* (1710). Vitali (*DEUMM*) also attributed to him the opera *Foca* (or *Foca superbo*), given in Munich (date unknown).

See also ROSAURA.

---

dm – *dramma per musica*

Atide [Act 3] (dm, 3, T. Stanzani), Bologna, Formagliari, 23 June 1679, lib. (Bologna, 1679) [Act 1 by G. F. Tosi, Act 2 by P. degli Antoni]
Marzio Coriolano (dm, 3, F. Silvani), Venice, SS Giovanni e Paolo, 20 Jan 1683
Oreste in Argo (drama [per musica], 3, G. A. Bergamori), Modena, Spelta, carn. 1685, *I-MOe*
L'incoronazione di Dario (dm, A. Morselli, rev. G. M. Rapparini), Bologna, Malvezzi, 13 Jan 1686
La Flavia (dm, 3, Rapparini), Bologna, Malvezzi, 16 Feb 1686, *MOe*
La Rosaura (dm, 3, A. Arcoleo), Venice, S Angelo, carn. 1689, *D-SWl, I-MOe*
Dionisio Siracusano (dm, A. Salvi), Parma, Ducale, carn. 1689
Brenno in Efeso (dm, 3, Arcoleo), Venice, S Salvatore, 1690
Il Pompeo (dm, N. Minato), Genoa, Falcone, carn. 1691
L'inganno scoperto per vendetta (dm, Silvani), Genoa, Falcone, 1691, *MOe*
Furio Camillo (dm, 3, M. Noris), Venice, S Salvatore, carn. 1692, *D-Bds*
Nerone fatto cesare [Nerone infante] (dm, 3, Noris), Venice, S Salvatore, 1693, *SWl, I-Rsc* (inc.); sinfonia by Giuseppe Torelli
La forza della virtù (dm, 3, D. David, with alterations), Bologna, Malvezzi, 25 May 1694
Laodicea e Berenice (dm, Noris), Venice, S Salvatore, 26 Dec 1694; rev. as L'inganno trionfante in amore
Penelope la casta (dm, Noris), Rome, Tordinona, 25 Jan 1696
Fausta restituita all'impero (dm, 3, N. Bonis), Rome, Tordinona, 19 Jan 1697
Perseo (P. J. Martello), Bologna, 1697, collab. other composers
Rosinda ed Emireno (Arcoleo) ? Florence, Cocomero, 1697, [according to *StiegerO*], *A-Wn*
Apollo geloso (Martello), Bologna, Formagliari, 16 Aug 1698
La prosperità di Elio Sejano (drama musicale, Minato), Milan, Ducale, carn. 1699, collab. A. F. Martinenghi and A. Vanelli
Ariovisto [Act 1] (drama musicale, 3, P. d'Averara), Milan, Ducale, Sept 1699, collab. F. Ballarotti and P. Magni
Lucio Vero [Acts 2 and 3] (dm, 3, A. Zeno), Florence, Pratolino, 1700
Astianatte (dm, Salvi, after J. Racine: *Andromaque*), Florence, Pratolino, 1701; sinfonia by Giuseppe Torelli
Dionisio rè di Portogallo (dm, Salvi), Florence, Pratolino, Sept 1707
Il Venceslao, ossia Il fratricida innocente (dm, Zeno), Bologna, Malvezzi, 19 May 1708
Ginevra principessa di Scozia (dm, Salvi, after L. Ariosto: *Orlando furioso*), Florence, Pratolino, aut. 1708
Berenice regina d'Egitto (dm, Salvi), Florence, Pratolino, Sept 1709
Il riso nato tra il pianto (drama da rappresentarsi, ?A. Aureli), Bologna, 11 Feb 1710, collab. other composers
Rodelinda regina de' Longobardi (dm, Salvi, after P. Corneille: *Pertharite, roi des Lombards*), Florence, Pratolino, aut. 1710
Il più fedele tra i vassalli (dm, Silvani), Bologna, 1710, collab. others

DEUMM (C. Vitali); *StiegerO*
*
G. C. Bonlini: *Le glorie della poesia e della musica contenute nell'estatta notizia de' teatri della città di Venezia* (Venice, 1730)
C. Ricci: *I teatri di Bologna nei secoli XVII e XVIII* (Bologna, 1888)
G. Vecchi: 'Il "Nerone fatto cesare" di G. A. Perti a Venezia', *Venezia e il melodramma nel seicento: Venice 1972*, 299–318
M. de Angelis: 'Il teatro di Pratolino tra Scarlatti e Perti: il carteggio di G. A. Perti con il principe Ferdinando de' Medici (1705–1719)', *NRMI*, xxi (1987), 606–40   SERGIO DURANTE

Pertichini (It.). Small interventions by other singers into an aria sung by a principal, sometimes conferring on it the character of a duet or trio. 'Arie con pertichini' include 'Ah! chi mi dice mai' (*Don Giovanni*, Mozart, 1787), 'Ah! rimiro il bel sembiante' (*Maria Stuarda*, Donizetti, 1834, as *Buondelmonte*) and 'Vidi dovunque gemere' (*Stiffelio*, Verdi, 1850). Librettists and composers frequently took advantage of the dramatic opportunities offered by *pertichini*, particularly by planning an intervention after the cantabile of a two-section number, thus providing motivation for the cabaletta. A familiar example comes at the end of Part 3 of *Il trovatore*, when after the duet for Leonora and Manrico news arrives of Azucena's capture and Manrico bursts into 'Di quella pira'.

973

Pertici, Caterina Brogi. *See* BROGI, CATERINA.

Pertici, Pietro (*b* Florence, *c*1700; *d* ? Florence, early Dec 1768). Italian tenor and bass. He began his career as early as 1723 in Foligno, singing minor roles in *opere serie* and intermezzos, and from 1730 specialized in comic roles in *commedie per musica* at the Teatro del Cocomero in Florence. From 1742 he performed in a number of *opere buffe* (including *La finta cameriera*, *Libertà nociva*, *Madama Ciana*, *Il giramondo* and *La Fiammetta*) in the area bounded by Florence, Venice, Genoa and Milan. In 1748–9 he was a member of a *buffo* company under G. F. Crosa, performing in London and Brussels. He entered the service of the court of Parma (1749). As a comic singer and actor he was praised by Burney, Garrick, Walpole, Casanova and Goldoni, who called him 'the greatest actor in the world' (preface to *Il cavaliere e la dama*, 1749–50). From 1750 Pertici directed, with Domenico Umiliano Guagni, a Tuscan national theatre in Florence based on the Cocomero. In this context, he worked as a translator and librettist, adjusting existing texts and possibly writing *Il prepotente* (1758). He was married to the soprano Caterina Brogi.

R. L. Weaver and N. W. Weaver: *A Chronology of Music in the Florentine Theater, 1590–1750* (Detroit, 1978)
P. Weiss: 'La diffusione del repertorio operistico nell'Italia del settecento: il caso dell'opera buffa', *Civiltà teatrale e settecento emiliano*, ed. S. Davoli (Bologna, 1986), 241–56
R. L. Weaver and N. W. Weaver: *A Chronology of Music in the Florentine Theater, 1751–1800* (Warren, MI, 1993)
R. G. King and S. Willaert: 'Giovanni Francesco Crosa and the First Italian Comic Operas in London, Brussels and Amsterdam', *JRMA* (forthcoming)
RICHARD G. KING, FRANCO PIPERNO, SASKIA WILLAERT

Pertile, Aureliano (*b* Montagnana, 9 Nov 1885; *d* Milan, 11 Jan 1952). Italian tenor. A pupil of Orefice and Fugazzola, he made his début at Vicenza in *Martha* in 1911. He began to attract notice in 1914 at the S Carlo, Naples, in *Madama Butterfly* and *Carmen*, and then at La Scala (1916) and at the Colón, Buenos Aires (1918). He achieved fame in 1922 in *Mefistofele* at La Scala under Toscanini, whose favourite tenor he then became. At La Scala, where he appeared regularly until 1937, he scored notable successes as Lohengrin, Puccini's Des Grieux, Edgardo, Chénier, Canio, Radames, Riccardo, Don Alvaro and Manrico, and took the title roles in the premières of Boito's *Nerone* (1924) and Mascagni's *Nerone* (1935). He sang until 1946, in the later years frequently as Otello. His voice was not particularly powerful and the tone, rather thick in the middle register, took on nasal and guttural inflections. It became smooth and mellifluous, however, in lyrical moments as well as vibrant and incisive in dramatic ones. Musically and stylistically extremely gifted, Pertile stood out for his fine enunciation, variety of expression and sensitive acting. At his best (1922–32) he was widely held, in Italy and Argentina, the equal of the most famous tenors of the period. Though less fortunate in the USA (he sang at the Metropolitan only during the 1921–2 season), he was very popular at Covent Garden (1927–31), especially as Manrico, Radames and Canio.

D. Silvestrini: *Aureliano Pertile e il suo metodo di canto* (Bologna, 1932)
P. Morby: 'Aureliano Pertile', *Record Collector*, vii (1952), 245–60, 267–74 [with discography by H. M. Barnes and V. Girard]
R. Celletti: 'Pertile: il tenore che a furia di studio trasformò una voce

modesta in uno strumento eccellente', *Musica e dischi*, no.109 (1955), 35 [with discography by R. Vegeto]
J. B. Steane: *The Grand Tradition* (London, 1974), 156–7
B. Tosi: *Pertile, una voce, un mito* (Venice, 1985)
RODOLFO CELLETTI

Peru. For discussion of opera in Peru *see* LIMA.

Perucci, Anna (Maria). *See* PERUZZI, ANNA.

Perugia. City in northern Italy, capital of Umbria. It was founded in ancient times and has one of the oldest universities. In the 17th century, theatrical entertainments took place in the Sala del Malconsiglio in the Palazzo Comunale and in the salons of the palaces of the nobility, some of which were subsequently equipped as theatres (Teatro dell'Aquila in the Palazzo Vincioli, Teatro del Leon d'Oro in the Palazzo Graziani). The Teatro della Nobile Accademia del Casino, also called the Teatro del Pavone, open only to the nobility, was completed on 25 May 1723. It was built of wood on a square plan with four tiers of boxes. In 1765 it was rebuilt in brick on a horseshoe plan with 82 boxes in four tiers. In 1781 the larger Teatro Civico del Verzaro was built by the city's bourgeoisie, on a horseshoe plan with 135 boxes in five tiers, and it was opened in September 1781 with *Didone abbandonata* by Francesco Zannetti and *Artaserse* by Giacomo Rust, both composed for the occasion. In 1874, on the occasion of the reopening after a restoration, Verdi's *Aida* was given (the third production in Italy, after those of Milan and Ancona), and the theatre was named after the Perugian musician Francesco Morlacchi. In 1942 it became the Teatro Comunale Morlacchi; since 1946, the year of the founding of the Sagra Musicale Umbra, it has occasionally been used by that institution for important first performances of melodramas given as oratorios. In 1891 the Teatro Turreno, built mainly to present spectacles for the less affluent social classes, was inaugurated with Pedrotti's *Tutti in maschera*.

B. Orsini: *Le scene del nuovo teatro del Verzaro di Perugia ragionate dall'autore delle medesime* (Perugia, 1785)
F. Guardabassi: *Appunti storici sull'accademia civica del teatro Morlacchi di Perugia* (Perugia, 1927)
G. Pascucci: *La nobile accademia del Pavone e il suo teatro* (Perugia, 1927)
A. Iraci: 'Il teatro Morlacchi di Perugia', *Augusta Perusia*, no.13 (1954), 5–33
B. Brumana and M. Pascale: 'Il teatro musicale a Perugia nel settecento: una cronologia dai libretti', *Esercizi: arte, musica, spettacolo*, vi (1983), 71–134
M. M. R. Ventura: *Teatro Francesco Morlacchi: archivio storico, inventario* (Perugia, 1983)
B. Brumana: *Il fondo musicale dell'Archivio di San Pietro a Perugia: Catalogo* (Perugia, 1986)
BIANCAMARIA BRUMANA

Perusso, Mario (*b* Buenos Aires, 16 Sept 1936). Argentine conductor and composer. As a deputy conductor at the Teatro Colón in Buenos Aires he has long been associated with opera in Argentina. Between 1966 and 1968 he wrote a one-act opera in Spanish, *La voz del silencio*, based on an idea of his own with a libretto by Leónidas Barrera Oro. Without being set at any particular time or place, the work deals with the conflict within a group of people in the aftermath of an apocalyptic catastrophe, such as a nuclear explosion. It was first performed at the Colón on 27 November 1969 and was recorded in 1971. Musically it belongs to the avant garde of the 1960s, with free atonality and no adherence to conventional forms. The orchestra plays the most important part and generates considerable dramatic tension.

Perusso's second opera is the one-act *Escorial*, completed in 1987 (though the first sketches date back to 1973). He wrote his own libretto (in Spanish), an adaptation of the play of the same name by Michel de Ghelderode set in the Escorial palace in Spain and dealing with a role-change between the king and his clown. Also atonal, it includes some elements drawn from Renaissance music. Its first performance was at the Colón in December 1989, conducted by Perusso himself.

In 1991 Perusso began work on an opera based on the play by Octavio Paz *Sor Juana Inés de la Cruz*.

JUAN MARÍA VENIARD

Peruzzi [Perucci], Anna (Maria) ['La Parruchierra'] (*b* ?Bologna; *fl* 1728–56). Italian soprano. Her nickname means 'wig dresser'. She made her début at Bologna at Carnival 1728, singing as seconda donna until 1733, then as prima donna in leading houses, including the S Carlo, Naples, in its inaugural season (1737–8). From 1739 she was in Farinelli's company in Spain. After returning to Italy in 1753, she tried to re-establish her career there, but engagements at Parma in 1754 and Bologna in 1756 only are documented. She is said to have had a large voice of fine quality and commanded a brilliant singing style (range approximately *e'* to *c'''*).

DENNIS LIBBY, JOHN ROSSELLI

Peruzzini, Giovanni (*b* Venice, 6 June 1815; *d* Venice, 16 May 1869). Italian librettist. He published accomplished verse at an early age. His literary sympathies were wide, and he translated Uhland and Heine, among others, into Italian. He turned to writing librettos in the early 1840s, but ill-health prevented him from completing his first text (*Il duca d'Alba*, for Giovanni Pacini) and the third act was written by Piave. He became Poet and Director of Productions at La Fenice in Venice but was exiled in 1848, turning up in Milan where, after a short spell as editor of a music journal, he was appointed Poet at La Scala. He returned to Venice in 1859, as secretary to the prefecture. He produced librettos for many of the second-ranking composers of the time, his best-known being *Jone* for Petrella (1858). Peruzzini clearly modelled his verse on that of Felice Romani, but while it has the essential simplicity of the latter's, his style and elegance are absent. Peruzzini's librettos are dramatically effective but lacking in invention and tension.

Pietro Candiano IV (dramma lirico), G. B. Ferrari, 1842 (M. Röder, 1878); *Il duca d'Alba* [Adolfo di Warbel] (tragedia lirica, with F. M. Piave), G. Pacini, 1842; *Ultimi giorni di Suli* (azione lirica), Ferrari, 1843; *Giuditta* (tragedia lirica), S. Levi, 1844; *Il borgomastro di Schiedam* (melodramma buffo), Lauro Rossi, 1844; *Luisa Strozzi* (tragedia lirica), L. A. Ronzi, 1844; *Cellini a Parigi* (melodramma semiserio), Rossi, 1845; *La sposa d'Abido* (tragedia lirica), G. Poniatowski, 1846 (F. Sandoni, 1858, as La fidanzata d'Abido); *Amleto* (tragedia lirica), A. Buzzolla, 1848 (L. Moroni, 1860); *I gladitori* (tragedia lirica), G. J. Foroni, 1851; *Le sabine* (melodramma), Rossi, 1852; *Don Cesare di Bazan* (melodramma), A. Traversari, 1853; *Gelmina* (melodramma semiserio), C. Pedrotti, 1853

Ottavia (melodramma tragico), G. Sanelli, 1854; *Gusmano il buono* [Gusmano il prode] (melodramma tragico), Sanelli, 1855; *La sirena* (melodramma giocoso), Rossi, 1855; *Le due regine* (melodramma tragico), E. Muzio, 1856; *L'orfana svizzera* (melodramma), F. Pollini, 1856; *Il diavolo* (melodramma), Traversari, 1857; *L'ultimo abenceraggio* (dramma lirico), F. Tessarin, 1858 (G. Setaccioli, 1893, as L'ultimo degli abenceragi);

Jone (dramma lirico), E. Petrella, 1858; *Veronica Cybo* (melodramma, with M. M. Marcello), A. Graffigna, 1858 (G. B. Meiners, 1866); *Il duca di Scilla* (dramma lirico, with L. Fortis), Petrella, 1859; *La contessa d'Amalfi* (dramma lirico), Petrella, 1864; *Il paggio* (melodramma tragico), R. Gandolfi, 1865; *Imelda* (melodramma tragico), G. Cottrau, 1891 (also as La lega lombarda)

G. Mazzoni: *Storia letteraria d'Italia: l'ottocento* (Milan, 1913)
L. Miragoli: *Il melodramma italiano nell'ottocento* (Rome, 1934)

JOHN BLACK

Pesaro. Italian city in the Marche region. During Carnival 1637 the Teatro del Sole, established by a group of local nobles, opened in the Piazza del Trebbio (now Lazzarini). It was equipped with elaborate scenographic and stage machinery designed by Niccolò Sabatini but it had a relatively small stage (about 8 square metres). Opera was performed there occasionally from 1639 onwards and more regularly from 1677 until 1695, when the municipality replaced it with a new theatre: designed by Pietro Mauro with three tiers (each containing 17 boxes) and a gallery, it opened on 7 February 1696 and remained in use until its demolition in 1816 to make way for another new theatre. During the ensuing period of construction the Teatrino della Pallacorda (in via Zongo) housed productions and continued to be used until the end of the century.

The Teatro Nuovo, designed by Pietro Ghinelli on a truncated oval plan with 99 boxes in four tiers and a gallery, opened on 10 June 1818 with a revival of Rossini's *La gazza ladra*. Rossini, a native of Pesaro, conducted the first of the 24 performances and made several alterations to the score for the occasion; his operas became the most frequently performed there and, after renovations in 1854–5, the theatre was renamed the Teatro Rossini. Opera seasons were arranged primarily for Carnival, though in the 1830s a second autumn season for the S Terenzio fair was introduced, and in the second half of the century there were occasional summer performances to coincide with the institution of seaside holidays.

In 1864 a series of performances, the Feste Rossiniane, was arranged for the unveiling of a Rossini monument; similarly, in August 1869, after Rossini's death, the 'Pompe Funebri Rossiniane' included productions of *Guillaume Tell* (in Italian, conducted by Angelo Mariani), *Semiramide* and *Otello*. *Guillaume Tell* and *Il barbiere di Siviglia* were staged in 1892 to celebrate the centenary of the composer's birth. In accordance with Rossini's will, a Liceo Musicale was founded in Pesaro in 1882. It is now the home of the Museo Rossiniano which houses autographs of some of Rossini's operas. Pietro Mascagni, principal of the Liceo from 1895 to 1902, conducted *Cavalleria rusticana* for Carnival 1896, and on 2 March of that year his *Zanetto* was first performed in the Salone Pedrotti (part of the conservatory).

The Teatro Nuovo closed in 1966 for complete restoration and reopened in 1980. Together with the Salone Pedrotti, it is now the most important venue for productions of the Rossini Opera Festival. Founded in 1980 by Bruno Cagli, director of the Fondazione Rossini, the festival is held annually during August and September and has concentrated principally on revivals of the *opere serie* of Rossini's so-called Naples period. Distinguished Rossini specialists are invited to contribute and, with the research involved in these productions and the use of the critical editions of the scores produced by the Fondazione, the festival provides a notable example of collaboration between musicology and live theatre.

DEUMM (F. Piperno); Grove6 (E. Surian)
C. Cinelli: 'Memorie cronistoriche del teatro di Pesaro (1637–1897)', *Cronaca musicale*, ii (1897), 149ff; iii (1898), 8ff
G. Romagnoli: 'Gioacchino Rossini: Giulio Perticari e *La gazza ladra*', *Vita italiana*, iii (1897), 106–9
G. Ugolini: *Nozze Mochi-Daffanà: notizie di vari autori e documenti relativi alla fondazione e ai restauri del Civico teatro di Pesaro* (Pesaro, 1925)
A. Zedda: Preface to G. Rossini: *La gazza ladra* (Pesaro, 1979)
A. Brancati: *Vicende architettoniche e strutturali del Teatro Rossini di Pesaro* (Pesaro, 1980)   PAOLO FABBRI

Pescatrici, Le ('The Fisherwomen'). Libretto by CARLO GOLDONI, first set by Ferdinando Bertoni (1751, Venice).

Nerina and Lesbina are two fisherwomen, betrothed to each others' brothers, the fishermen Burlotto and Frisellino. Old Mastricco also belongs to this community, but his presumed daughter, Eurilda, has never felt comfortable there. The fishermen's routine is interrupted one day by the arrival of Lindoro, Prince of Sorrento, and his entourage of noblemen. The prince asks the villagers to help in finding the object of his search: the lost heiress of Benevento.

Nerina and Lesbina, attracted to the stranger, are prepared to abandon their bridegrooms to marry into a higher social rank; each feigns royal blood and proclaims herself the lost princess. Lindoro's confusion is heightened by Burlotto and Frisellino, each of whom names his sister as the woman that Lindoro seeks. To arrive at the truth Lindoro offers jewellery to the villagers. Everyone reaches out for the gold except for Eurilda, who unwittingly takes the dagger with which her father was killed. Lindoro recognizes her as the object of his search. Mastricco reveals that she is not his daughter but was given into his custody as a baby by a man who had saved her from her father's murderer; she is now free to marry Lindoro.

To test their brides' fidelity, Burlotto and Frisellino disguise themselves as noblemen from Lindoro's entourage and propose marriage to Nerina and Lesbina if they will return with them to Lindoro's home town. The women accept, to the men's dismay; the men's unmasking and their admonitions are followed by a happy ending.

The libretto deals not so much with the topic of actual fishing as with the idyllic concept of pretty women fishing for men's hearts, as displayed in the literary genre of the 'ecloghe pescatorie'. Typical of Goldoni's theatre, the satire is directed at those who aspire to a higher social rank, in the process assuming a pretentious and haughty attitude. The libretto was subsequently set to music in 1754 by Rocco Gioanetti (a musician active in Turin), in 1770 by Haydn and in 1771 by Gassmann for the Viennese court. Although based on Goldoni's text, the version of the libretto used by Haydn for the Eszterháza performance was revised (possibly by Carl Friberth) to include five new arias and a rearranged ending.   GORDANA LAZAREVICH

Pescatrici, Le (i) ('The Fisherwomen'). *Dramma giocoso* in three acts by FERDINANDO BERTONI to a libretto by CARLO GOLDONI; Venice, Teatro S Samuele, 26 December 1751.

Bertoni's most successful comic opera was the first of three Goldoni librettos set by the 26-year-old composer. The seven roles mix *parti buffe* (fisherwomen and fishermen) and *parti serie* (a prince and a noblewoman believed to be the daughter of a fisherman). The music includes a mixture of aria types, all without *passaggi*, including four bipartite arias (*AA'* or *AB*) which could be called cavatinas, although Bertoni did not use that term for similar arias until *La moda* (1754). Of the four MS copies (*D-B*, *Dlb*, *F-Pc* and *P-La*) only the last contains the recitatives; it also includes *buffa* finales for Acts 1 and 2, music for the chorus within the acts and a final scene in Act 3 with added trumpet. *Favourite Songs* (London, *c*1761) contains the aria 'Un pescatore me l'ha fatta brutta' ('constantly encored' according to Burney), sung by Maria Angiola Paganini as Lesbina (contralto), one of the *pescatrici*. She and Carlo Paganini, the old fisherman Mastricco (tenor), also sang in the Venetian production (1746) of Bertoni's first opera *La vedova accorta*. *Le pescatrici* was staged widely in Europe during the 1750s and 60s.

See also PESCATRICI, LE above.   GEORGE TRUETT HOLLIS

Pescatrici, Le (ii) [*Die Fischerinnen*] ('The Fisherwomen'). *Dramma giocoso* in three acts by JOSEPH HAYDN to a libretto by CARLO GOLDONI possibly revised by CARL FRIBERTH; Eszterháza, 16 September 1770.

The libretto is the first one set by Haydn that contains both comic and serious characters. (Although *Lo speziale*, performed in 1768, is called a *dramma giocoso*, Goldoni's *seria* roles were excised in Haydn's setting.) Of the seven characters, two are *parti serie*: the noble-born Eurilda (contralto), raised as the daughter of a fisherman; and Lindoro (bass), Prince of Sorrento. The remaining five are all fishing-folk who live on the shores of Taranto: two pairs of brothers and sisters, Nerina (soprano) and Frisellino (tenor), and Lesbina (soprano) and Burlotto (tenor); and the old fisherman Mastricco (bass), foster parent of Eurilda.

The plot concerns Prince Lindoro's desire to discover who among the fisherwomen is the heiress of Benevento. Some 15 years earlier the princess was brought to this remote place to escape the wrath of her father's usurper and murderer. Nerina and Lesbina, each claiming to be the lost princess Lindoro wishes to marry and restore to her throne, assume aristocratic airs and spurn their lovers, Burlotto and Frisellino respectively. Wishing to get even with Nerina and to win Lindoro's promised reward of gold and jewels, Burlotto informs the prince that Lesbina is the lost heiress. Immediately afterwards Frisellino, desiring the same reward and seeking revenge against Lesbina, contends that Nerina is the one Lindoro seeks. Then Mastricco informs Lindoro that Eurilda is of noble birth. As the others claim treasures from among the gold and jewels brought on shore by Lindoro's attendants, Eurilda is seized with terror when she recognizes the jewel-studded dagger used to murder her father and thus reveals herself as the princess. Burlotto and Frisellino disguise themselves as cavaliers who wish to take Nerina and Lesbina away with them on Lindoro's ship. As in *Così fan tutte*, the women fall for the deception, only to be deflated when the suitors reveal their true identities. All is forgiven and the couples are re-united as Lindoro and Eurilda, accompanied by Mastricco, sail away.

The opera's main theme – that those that are high-born are noble, dignified and honest – made the work especially appropriate for the marriage celebrations in honour of Countess Lamberg, Prince Nikolaus Esterházy's niece, and Count Poggi. Although the opera was completed in 1769, its première was reserved for the couple's wedding day. Identical descriptions of the wedding festivities in the *Pressburger Zeitung* and *Wiener Diarium* affirm that the opera was repeated two days later 'to no less generous applause than at the first performance'. To show his appreciation, Prince Nikolaus gave presents of cash to Haydn and members of the cast after the second performance.

Among the libretto changes presumably made at Eszterháza are three new aria texts for Lesbina. Here Maddalena Friberth, who created this role, moved a step closer to the independence of the role of Vespina, her tour de force in Haydn's *L'infedeltà delusa* (1773). One of several arias only partly preserved in the score, Lindoro's 'Varca il mar', to a text borrowed from Metastasio's *Galatea* (1722), is a stormy piece in D minor containing difficult vocal leaps, as befits his noble rank. Eurilda's only complete aria, 'Questa mano e questa cuore' in Act 3, is a tender love song in which she reveals the depth of her character. The many vocal ensembles – the opening 'Coro di pescatori' in D major, 'Bell'ombra gradita' in E♭ major, Lindoro's feisty and fast solo with chorus 'Fiera strage dell'indegno', the opening chorus in Act 3 'Nume, che al mare' in C major, and the tranquil 'Soavi zeffiri' in E major among them – all survive intact. Since the comic characters and their actions are overshadowed by Lindoro's noble presence and the gradual revelation of Eurilda's tragic past, the opera's two finales, which exclude the *seria* characters, are devoid of action. Each divides into four sections and features a prominent return of the opening theme in its original key.

Approximately a quarter of Haydn's autograph is missing, with only the third act surviving in its entirety. Since the vocal and orchestral parts were apparently destroyed in the fire at the opera house in 1779, modern revivals have opted for either a complete musical performance based on H. C. Robbins Landon's reconstruction for the Holland and Edinburgh festivals in 1965, or an incomplete musical production, like the one staged in Budapest in 1982, based on Dénes Bartha's edition for the Haydn-Institut's complete works of Haydn. In the latter case, lines for which no music survives (including the dagger recognition scene in Act 2) are recited.

See also PESCATRICI, LE above.

CARYL CLARK

Pescetti, Giovanni Battista (*b* Venice, *c*1704; *d* Venice, 20 March 1766). Italian composer, grandson of C. F. Pollarolo. He studied with Antonio Lotti, opera composer and organist at St Mark's, Venice. During the first part of his career, Pescetti worked almost exclusively in Venice, writing and revising operas, often in collaboration with his colleague Baldassare Galuppi. In April 1736 Pescetti appeared in London, and in the 1736–7 season he replaced Porpora as director of the Opera of the Nobility, thereby initiating a rivalry with Handel. He enjoyed some success with his first London opera, *Demetrio* (1737), produced in competition with Handel's *Giustino* and featuring the castrato Farinelli; it received 14 performances during the season. Burney, writing about *Demetrio*, was guarded: 'This composer ... though he never had much fire or fertility of invention was a very elegant and judicious writer for the voice. His

melodies are extremely simple and graceful'. After the production of Pescetti's *La conquista del velo d'oro* (1738) he was forced to remove his company to the smaller New Theatre in the Haymarket; salaries were reduced and extravagant productions ceased. His opera, *Busiri, ovvero Il trionfo d'amore*, received only four performances there. After this his activities in London were confined to arranging pasticcios. Around 1745 he left London and returned to Venice, where for 15 years he wrote and arranged operas. Following the première of *Zenobia* (1761) he was appointed second organist at St Mark's on 16 May 1762. His reputation in London was revived, however, in 1764 by the production there of the pasticcio *Ezio* for the castrato Giovanni Manzuoli, who greatly favoured Pescetti's music.

Melodic facility best describes Pescetti's vocal style. Burney wrote that 'his style was then too meagre and simple for our ears ... Pescetti condescended not only to adhere to simplicity in his melodies, but to simplify and thin the accompaniments'. During his lifetime, his reputation was based not so much on the intrinsic value of his music as on his association with Galuppi in Venice, his rivalry with Handel and, above all, the patronage of such famous singers as Farinelli and Manzuoli.

Nerone detronato (G. Pimbaloni), Venice, S Salvatore, carn. 1725, arias *GB-Lbl*; Favourite Songs (London, 1740)
Il prototipo (D. Lalli), Venice, S Samuele, aut. 1726
La cantatrice (Lalli), Venice, S Samuele, Ascension 1727
Gli odii delusi dal sangue [Act 2] (A. M. Lucchini), Venice, S Angelo, 1728, Acts 1 and 3 by Galuppi
Dorinda (pastorale, Lalli), Venice, S Samuele, Ascension 1729, collab. Galuppi
I tre difensori della patria (A. Morselli), Venice, S Angelo, aut. 1729; as Tullio Ostilio, wint. 1740
Costantino Pio, Rome, palace of Cardinal Ottoboni, 1730, for the birth of the dauphin, *F-Pn*
Siroe re di Persia (P. Metastasio), Venice, 1731, collab. Galuppi [rev. of Vinci]
Alessandro nelle Indie (Metastasio), Venice, S Angelo, carn. 1732, arias *I-Bas*
Demetrio (Metastasio), Florence, Pergola, carn. 1732; rev., London, King's, 12 Feb 1737; Favourite Songs (London, 1737)
La conquista del velo d'oro (A. M. Cori), London, King's, 28 Jan 1738, *GB-Lbl*; arias in Le delizie dell'opere, ii (London, 1740)
L'asilo d'amore (int, Metastasio), London, King's, spr. 1738
Diana e Endimione (serenata, Metastasio), London, New, 1 Dec 1739, arias in Le delizie dell'opere, ii (London, 1740), Favourite Songs (London, *c*1740)
Busiri, ovvero Il trionfo d'amore (P. Rolli), London, New, 10 May 1740
Ezio (Metastasio), Venice, Grimani, carn. 1747
Farnace (A. Lucchini), Florence, Pergola, carn. 1749
Fra i due litiganti il terzo gode (ob, G. Lorenzi), Venice, S Cassiano, spr. 1749, aria *I-Vc*
Arianna e Teseo (P. Pariati), Florence, Pergola, carn. 1750
Il Farnaspe (Metastasio), Siena, Rinnovati, 1750; as Adriano in Siria, Reggio Emilia, Moderno, 1750
Artaserse (Metastasio), Milan, Regio, 26 Dec 1751, *Fc*
Tamerlano (A. Piovene), Venice, S Samuele, carn. 1754, collab. Cocchi
Solimano (G. A. Migliavacca), Reggio Emilia, Moderno, 1756, arias in Favorite Songs (London, 1765)
Zenobia (Metastasio), Padua, Nuovo, June 1761, *P-La*
Andimione, *D-Hs*

Contribs. to: Arsaces, 1737; Sabrina, 1737; Angelica e Medoro, 1739; Merode e Olympia, 1740; Alessandro in Persia, 1741; Aristodemo, tiranno di Cuma, 1744; Ezio, 1764; Lionel and Clarissa (London, n.d.)

Doubtful: Olimpia in Ebuda (Rolli, after L. Ariosto: *Orlando furioso*), London, King's, 15 March 1740 [formerly attrib. J. A. Hasse]

BurneyH; *Grove6* (J. W. Hill)

S. Dalla Libera: 'Cronologia musicale della basilica di San Marco in Venezia', *Musica sacra* (Milan, 1961), 143

M. Fabbri: 'Giovanni Battista Pescetti e un concorso per maestro di cappella a Firenze', *RIM*, i (1966), 120–26

F. Petty: *Italian Opera in London, 1760–1800* (Ann Arbor, 1980)

FREDERICK PETTY

Peskó, Zoltán (*b* Budapest, 15 Feb 1937). Hungarian conductor. He studied at the Liszt Academy, Budapest, and began conducting for Hungarian radio and television in 1960. After further study in Rome with Petrassi and Ferrara, and with Boulez in Basle, he was engaged as assistant to Maazel at the Deutsche Oper, West Berlin (1969–73), while also teaching at the Hochschule für Musik. He made his début at La Scala in 1970, and became principal conductor at the Teatro Comunale, Bologna, in 1974 and at La Fenice, Venice, in 1976, presenting a repertory ranging from Mozart and Bizet to *The Fiery Angel* and *Billy Budd*. He was later active in other centres, conducting the *Ring* at Turin (1986–9), the first performance of a German version of Liebermann's *La forêt* at Schwetzingen in 1988, the Ruth Berghaus production of *Tristan und Isolde* in Hamburg the same year, his own orchestration of Musorgsky's *Salammbô* for Netherlands Opera in 1989 and the première of Azio Corghi's *Blimunda* at the Teatro Lirico, Milan, in 1990. He is admired for his passionate, subtly coloured performances, and has a keen ear for contemporary music.

PÉTER P. VÁRNAI, NOËL GOODWIN

Pessard, Emile (Louis Fortuné) (*b* Paris, 29 May 1843; *d* Paris, 10 Feb 1917). French composer. He studied with Bazin, Carafa and others at the Paris Conservatoire, winning the Prix de Rome in 1866. In 1878 he was appointed inspector of vocal teaching in the Paris municipal schools and later he became director of musical studies at the establishment of the Légion d'honneur at St Denis. From 1881 he was a professor at the Conservatoire, where his pupils included Ravel. He composed several operas, among which *Les folies amoureuses* was particularly successful, as well as choral, orchestral, chamber and piano works and arrangements of opera excerpts. His songs were highly regarded during his lifetime, but none of his rather conventional operas ever entered the standard repertory.

all printed works published in Paris; all first performed in Paris

La cruche cassée (oc, 1, H. Lucas and E. Abraham), OC (Favart), Feb 1870, vs (1872)

Don Quichotte (opérette-bouffe, 1, A. Deschamps, after M. de Cervantes), Salle Erard, 13 Feb 1874 (1873)

Le char (oc, 1, P. Arène and A. Daudet), OC (Favart), 18 Jan 1878, vs (1878)

Le Capitaine Fracasse (oc, 3, C. Mendès, after T. Gautier), Lyrique, 2 July 1878, vs (1878)

Tabarin (opéra, 2, P. Ferrier), Opéra, 12 Jan 1885, vs (1885)

Les folies amoureuses (oc, 3, A. Lénéka and E. Matrat, after J. F. Régnard), OC (Lyrique), 15 April 1891, vs (1891)

Mam'zelle Carabin (operetta, 3, F. Carré), Bouffes-Parisiens, 3 Nov 1893

Une nuit de Noël, Théâtre de l'Ambigu, 1893

La dame de trèfle (oc, 3, C. Clairville and M. Froyez), Bouffes-Parisiens, 13 May 1898

L'armée de vierges (operetta, 3, E. Depré and L. Héral), Bouffes-Parisiens, 15 Oct 1902

L'épave (operetta, 1, Depré), Bouffes-Parisiens, 17 Feb 1903

JOHN TREVITT, ROBERT ORLEDGE

Pest. Hungarian town, united in 1873 with Buda and Óbuda to form BUDAPEST.

Peter Grimes. Opera in a prologue and three acts, op.33, by BENJAMIN BRITTEN to a libretto by MONTAGU SLATER after GEORGE CRABBE's poem *The Borough*; London, Sadler's Wells, 7 June 1945.

Peter Grimes	*a fisherman*	tenor
Boy (John)	*his apprentice*	silent
Ellen Orford	*a widow, schoolmistress*	soprano
Captain Balstrode	*retired merchant skipper*	baritone
Auntie	*landlady of 'The Boar'*	contralto
Niece 1	} *main attractions of 'The Boar'*	soprano
Niece 2		soprano
Bob Boles	*fisherman and Methodist*	tenor
Swallow	*a lawyer*	bass
Mrs Sedley	*a widow*	mezzo-soprano
Rev. Horace Adams	*the rector*	tenor
Ned Keene	*apothecary and quack*	baritone
Dr Thorp [Crabbe in some sources]		silent
Hobson	*carrier*	bass

Townspeople, fisherfolk

Setting The Borough, a small fishing town on the east coast of England, about 1830

Despite the difficulties attending the composition and production of *Paul Bunyan* (1941), his first fully musical work for the stage, Britten was soon contemplating a more ambitious operatic project. In the summer of 1941, while visiting California with Britten, Peter Pears bought a copy of George Crabbe's *Works*; singer and composer had already read E. M. Forster's article in *The Listener* (29 May 1941), 'George Crabbe: the Poet and the Man', with its evocation of Aldeburgh and the English east coast. Pears and Britten began to sketch out a scenario before they left America in March 1942, and more drafting took place during the voyage itself. As Pears later put it, 'by the time we came back to London, the whole story of *Peter Grimes* as set in the opera was already shaped, and it simply remained to call in a librettist to write the words'. That process of drafting had already transformed Crabbe's essentially evil Grimes into a character who is as much the victim of an uncomprehending society as of his own weaknesses and contradictions. Above all, Britten's Grimes is unstable, swinging unpredictably between the visionary and the violent.

Montagu Slater agreed to provide a libretto, Christopher Isherwood having declined, and a complete draft was ready around the end of 1942. Britten did not begin to compose the music until January 1944, and it was then that various changes to the libretto were initiated. The complete full score, dated 10 February 1945, shows several striking differences from the definitive vocal score published later in 1945, and the full score published in 1963 includes further minor revisions. The 'Four Sea Interludes' were published separately with the descriptive titles 'Dawn', 'Sunday Morning', 'Moonlight' and 'Storm'. At a fairly early stage of the compositional process the Sadler's Wells Opera Company, where Eric Crozier was Stage Director and Pears had been singing various leading roles, decided to re-open their theatre in north London with *Peter Grimes* at the end of the war in Europe. The première was conducted by Reginald Goodall, and the cast was headed by Peter Pears as Grimes (for illustration *see* LONDON, fig.11) and Joan Cross as Ellen Orford.

In terms of productions and performances, *Peter Grimes* is one of the most successful of 20th-century operas after those by Puccini and Richard Strauss. For at least 20 years, performances in English were dominated by the voice and personality of Peter Pears. Pears led the cast in a fine complete recording under Britten's direction (1959), and the only alternative on disc is a version with the heavier, less subtle Jon Vickers in the title role, conducted by Colin Davis (1978). Within three years of its première the opera had been staged at Covent Garden and in many European and Scandinavian countries. Serge Koussevitzky, who commissioned it, and to whom it is dedicated, relinquished the American première to Leonard Bernstein: this took place at Tanglewood in 1946. After a relatively fallow period in the 1950s the opera gained new popularity, and there were productions in the Soviet Union and South America. It was filmed for BBC television in 1969.

PROLOGUE *Interior of the Moot Hall arranged as for a coroner's inquest* This plunges into the action without preliminaries and establishes the essence of the opera's dramatic and musical tension. The main body of the scene is bound together by recurrences and developments of the brusque initial idea representing the Borough's collective impatience with the likes of Grimes, and there is the clearest contrast – rhythmic as well as harmonic – between this material and Grimes's own more lyrical music. The inquest concerns the death at sea of Grimes's boy apprentice. Despite the evident hostility of virtually everyone present to the fisherman, who is obsessed with his work to the point where he is cruelly neglectful, the Coroner Swallow rules that the boy died accidentally, accepting Grimes's explanation that his boat was blown off course as he tried to sail for London, and that the boy died of exhaustion. Swallow acknowledges that Grimes had earlier saved the boy from drowning, but he tells the fisherman not to hire another young apprentice. Grimes reacts angrily, but only Ellen Orford shows any sympathy, and their brief but highly charged duet first intensifies the Prologue's pervasive dissonances (most basically, the conflicting tonal centres of Bb and A), then resolves them, though only precariously, since the arching phrase that they sing in octaves is itself too chromatic to express more than a temporary repose. The Prologue is through-composed, with clear evidence of that arioso style that is an important aspect of Britten's operatic technique, alongside more formal aria and ensemble, and it demonstrates his instinctive ability to devise pithy, memorable ideas that serve both dramatic and purely musical purposes.

ACT 1.i *A street by the sea* The Prologue is linked to Act 1 by the first of the orchestral interludes that encapsulate so much of the opera's atmosphere. This 'dawn' music provides the background to a chorus describing and accompanying the early-morning work of the fisherfolk, and within the chorus various characters, many of whom have already been heard briefly in the Prologue, are introduced again: the placid landlady ('Auntie') of 'The Boar' inn, the tippling Methodist local preacher, the Rector, the drably respectable but vulnerable widow Mrs Sedley and the retired sea-captain Balstrode.

After this chorus the main part of the scene falls into five distinct but linked sections: first a vigorous ensemble in which, after initial reluctance, the men help Grimes to haul his boat on to land; second, the short gruff song in which Hobson, the carter, refuses to fetch Grimes's new apprentice (an arrangement made by Ned Keene) from the workhouse; third, another short but expansively lyrical aria (interrupting the carter's song) in which Ellen Orford underlines her willingness to help Grimes ('Let her among you without fault Cast the first stone'); fourth, a large-scale fugal ensemble and chorus responding to the approaching storm; and fifth, the extended dialogue between Grimes and Balstrode in which the irreconcilable conflicts in Grimes's character between the visionary and the conventional, between his desire to earn a place in society and his absolute determination to behave as he thinks fit, are fully evident for the first time. The process traced in the music of this fifth section, from Peter's anguished narration of the events culminating in the death of the apprentice ('Picture what that day was like') through his agitated explanation of how he intends to win over the Borough ('They listen to money') to the uninhibited eloquence of his final self-analysis ('What harbour shelters peace?') shows Britten's music at its most powerful: instantly expressive and evocative, the depiction of wind and waves never banal, yet bringing genuine depth to the tensions inherent in the opera's central character. The music has a spontaneity and sense of purpose that generously compensate for the drawbacks of what is at many points a rather laborious, selfconsciously poetic libretto. Britten skilfully balanced the presence of distinct sections or 'numbers' against pervasive motivic reminiscences and larger-scale tonal recurrences. For a first opera (as distinct from the operetta *Paul Bunyan*) and despite the occasionally strong associations with other works – notably Gershwin's *Porgy and Bess* – *Peter Grimes* is a remarkably personal and convincing music drama.

1.ii *Interior of 'The Boar' inn* The scenes are linked by a brilliantly resourceful and hectic interlude, and a storm continues to rumble in the background throughout the scene, which is built from a mixture of short solos. These are linked by passages of recitative-like dialogue in which the dramatic tension is never allowed to slacken; there is one extended contrapuntal ensemble in the later stages. As the regulars brave the storm to assemble in 'The Boar', there are straightforward but splendidly pointed strophic songs for Auntie and Balstrode, the latter with a refrain ('We live and let live, and look, We keep our hands to ourselves') that is ironic to the extent that the tolerance it apparently preaches (genuine in Balstrode's case) is in truth a mask for indifference and incomprehension of Grimes-like nonconformity. As the atmosphere becomes more convivial Grimes bursts in, expecting to collect his new apprentice. In the shocked silence that ensues he sings the aria 'Now the Great Bear and Pleiades' which, despite its brevity, magically conveys the opposing poles of his visionary yet violent personality. The descending E major scale of his last line ('Who can turn skies back and begin again?') has a directness and poignancy that only the greatest masters of opera can achieve. A substantial ensemble now builds up as the people become increasingly hostile to Grimes. Auntie calls for a song to defuse the tension, and Ned Keene launches the round 'Old Joe has gone fishing', whose seven-beat metre quickly generates a powerful tension of its own. When Grimes tries to join in he breaks the unanimity of the round apart, and at this moment of maximum instability Hobson, Ellen and the new apprentice arrive, drenched by the storm. With no greeting to those who

"PETER GRIMES" - *Benjamin Britten. Sadlers Wells 1945*　　　Act 1. sc 2. The Boar interior.

'Peter Grimes' (Britten): Kenneth Green's design for Act 1 scene ii (interior of 'The Boar' inn) of the original production at Sadler's Wells, London, 7 June 1945; ink and watercolour

have done him this favour, Grimes hustles the boy away, as the all too transparent irony of Ellen's last line 'Peter will take you home' is derisively taken up by the chorus; the storm music gives the act its emphatic final cadence.

ACT 2.i   *A street by the sea; a fine sunny morning, some weeks later*   The orchestra evokes a bright Sunday morning, with resonating bells. At first Ellen's mood is tranquil. She sits with John, the new apprentice, knitting, while the church service proceeds offstage. But her mood soon changes when she notices a tear in the boy's coat, and a bruise on his neck. Her gloom-laden advice to the boy, ending 'After the storm will come a sleep, Like oceans deep', is ironically counterpointed with the worshippers' *Gloria*, and the irony is intensified when Grimes enters and the *Benedicite* interacts with his ruthless determination to exploit the apprentice, because only through hard work will he win the respect of society. As they quarrel Ellen's music grows more measured and resigned, Peter's more jagged and aggressive, culminating, as he strikes her, in his mocking echo of the church service: 'So be it – and God have mercy upon me!'.

As Grimes rushes off with the apprentice, leaving Ellen distraught, the Borough assemble, and an extended chorus and ensemble is built around the sardonic refrain 'Grimes is at his exercise!', set to one of the work's most pervasive motifs, emphasizing a descending octave with prominent central tritone (Bb–E–Bb). Boles turns the crowd's thoughts towards retribution, and a new refrain emerges: 'The Borough keeps its standards up!'. Ellen, still eloquent and restrained, attempts to explain Grimes's motives, but no longer to justify them, and the rest mock her words (and her music). Fearing for the apprentice's safety, the men decide to march to Grimes's hut, and they set off to an extravagantly bloodthirsty chant, whose text may seem unconvincing but is set by Britten to music of chilling force. As the procession recedes the four remaining women – Auntie, Ellen and the Nieces – sing a haunting ensemble of tender regret, a brief three-part structure

with refrain, whose expressive intensity results primarily from the modal ambivalence of its underlying harmony. This promotes a luminous texture in which dissonance seems more significant than the resolving consonance. In this way Britten uses a basic technical feature to link the scene's extreme contrasts: Ellen's eloquence, Grimes's vehemence, the crowd's aggression, the women's reflectiveness.

2.ii   *Grimes's hut (an upturned boat on the cliff edge)*   The interlude between the scenes of Act 2 is a passacaglia built on the 'Grimes is at his exercise' motif and progressing from the quiet despair of the women's quartet to the unrestrained fury with which Grimes enters in scene ii. The scene is an extended scena for Grimes himself with an epilogue for the town representatives who enter his hut. The scena is in three main sections. In the first, whose music in part relates to the 'They listen to money' material in Act 1 scene i, Peter's own confusion, his conflicting impulses of violence and tenderness towards the boy, are vividly displayed. The central section, itself essentially a three-part form, contains Peter's most sustained expression of his vision of happiness with Ellen. But the more he dwells on this the more insistent its impossibility becomes. Peter is haunted, not only by the memory of his dead apprentice, but also by the knowledge that he can never achieve the kind of stability and social acceptability for which he yearns. In a masterly transition the serene dream music curdles and dissolves into the sinister march of the approaching men. In the final part of the scena Peter accuses the apprentice of lying to Ellen about him. Despite the move from singing to Sprechgesang, Britten avoids excessive melodrama, and there is genuine horror in the process whereby, in adopting the threatening music of the march himself, the fisherman drives the apprentice to his death. The boy falls down the cliff as Grimes, in his haste to avoid the crowd, urges him out of the door. (The stage directions are clear: Grimes does not actually push him.) In the eerie, understated final section of the scene, the Rector and Swallow, finding the hut empty but apparently neat and tidy, decide that all is well. Only Balstrode, looking down the cliff face, knows better, and the act ends with the recall of the viola solo that began the passacaglia.

ACT 3.i *A street by the sea; a summer evening a few days later* The orchestral introduction is one of Britten's most subtle nature scenes, a night-piece shot through with luminous shafts of moonlight. Like both scenes of Act 2, this scene counterpoints onstage and offstage events, the various dances heard from the Moot Hall providing an almost surreal background to the sinister events seen enacted. (It is this scene that offers the closest parallel to a scene in Berg's *Wozzeck*, Act 3 scene iii, though there the dance music is played on stage.) The first half of the scene employs subsidiary characters only: Swallow flirting with the Nieces, Mrs Sedley telling Keene of her belief that Grimes has murdered his new apprentice; the creeping chromatics of her 'Murder most foul it is' are a telling blend of grotesque humour and doom-laden menace. A second stanza of the song follows the cheerful exchanges between the Rector and other burgesses, and Mrs Sedley then overhears Ellen and Balstrode in conversation. Grimes's boat has returned, though Peter himself cannot be found. Balstrode has also discovered the boy's jersey, and Ellen, in a short but ornate aria, remembers embroidering the anchor on it. They decide that, although Peter cannot be saved, they can still help him: what this means becomes clear in the next scene.

Meanwhile Mrs Sedley arouses the populace with the news that Peter's boat is back. After a third stanza of her song there is another violent chorus and ensemble, vowing vengeance and reaching a climax as the crowd shout the name of their prey, 'Peter Grimes!'. The music here achieves an uninhibited ferocity rare in Britten's work.

3.ii *The same, some hours later* The final orchestral interlude rapidly establishes a complete change of mood, though the scene itself is unchanged. The only sounds are a distant fog-horn and the distant cries of the chorus. Grimes's final scene is an extended arioso that periodically flowers into more lyrical phrases and reminiscences of earlier moments in the opera. The basic material grows from the two-note fog-horn motif and, in keeping with Grimes's disturbed mentality, there are rapid changes of mood, as when a memory of Ellen (at one stage in the opera's evolution she was heard calling to Peter at this point) turns rapidly to a contemptuous dismissal of both friendship and gossip. At the climax of the scene the choral shouts reach the same octave B♭s used at the end of the previous scene, and Grimes's delirious response, rapid repetitions of his own name, gradually sinks into a hopeless silence.

Ellen and Balstrode appear. Ellen seeks to take Peter home, but Balstrode – in speech, not song – tells him in as many words to take his own life. This, after Grimes's movingly restrained recapitulation of 'What harbour shelters peace?', accompanied only by distant choral reiterations of Grimes's name, may seem a harsh effect, and a harsh judgment: but as cold reality, both are appropriate.

The 'dawn' music returns, the orchestra heard for the first time since Act 3 scene i, and there are three further stanzas of the choral song that began Act 1; the only remarks of the various subsidiary characters who assemble are that a boat, seen sinking out at sea, is no longer visible. 'One of these rumours', says Auntie. After the final choral stanza the work's purely harmonic resolution is not in doubt, but the texture darkens as if to underline the fact that, despite its apparent ability to carry on as usual, the Borough has experienced a tragedy from which it ought never to recover.

*   *   *

The more determinedly commentators seek to emphasize *Peter Grimes*'s weaknesses, particularly in the libretto, the more memorable its musical ideas and the more resilient its formal design appear to be. By comparison with *Kát'a Kabanová*, or *Wozzeck*, *Grimes* may seem conventional in structure, conservative in style. Yet the ambivalence of its subject matter – in particular, the way the audience is left to decide whether or not Grimes is to be pitied rather than blamed – and the remarkable vitality of the music, come together to create an experience that rarely fails to grip in the theatre. Britten has always been praised for his ability to set a scene in orchestral preludes and interludes, but his skill at embodying character in an at times florid vocal style is even more memorable, and never more effective than in *Grimes*. The work can now be seen as expressing Britten's early and abiding doubts about the viability of 'grand opera' as powerfully as it expresses doubts about the motivation and personality of the principal character. It is therefore no cliché to assert that it laid the technical and expressive foundations for Britten's entire operatic career.

ARNOLD WHITTALL

Peterhof [now Petrodvorets]. Town in Russia, on the Finnish gulf near St Petersburg. The site of Peter the Great's summer residence, it contains a dazzling complex of palaces, gardens, statuary and fountains. From 1757 to 1763 G. B. Locatelli's *opera buffa* troupe entertained the empresses Elizabeth and Catherine there during the summer. An *opera seria*, Hermann Raupach's *Al'tsesta* ('Alceste'), to a libretto by Elizabeth's court poet Alexander Sumarokov, was performed there on 28 June/9 July 1758. The other Peterhof première was that of *Abderkan*, an *opéra comique* by Boieldieu to a libretto by Dégligny, performed by the court French opera troupe before Tsar Alexander I on 26 July/7 August 1805.

RICHARD TARUSKIN

Peter I. Opera by Andrey Petrov; *see* PYOTR I.

Peters, Roberta (*b* New York, 4 May 1930). American soprano. She studied with William Hermann and was engaged by the Metropolitan at 19, without previous stage experience. She made her début in November 1950 as Zerlina, a last-minute replacement for Nadine Conner; her official début was to have been as the Queen of Night, two months later. By her 25th anniversary with the company she had given 303 performances of 20 roles in 19 operas, notably Gilda, Despina, Norma, Rosina, Oscar and Lucia. Later she attempted to broaden her repertory in lyric soprano roles, playing Violetta, Mimì and Massenet's Manon outside New York and performing in musical comedy. She performed at Covent Garden (*The Bohemian Girl* under Beecham, 1951), in Salzburg (*Die Zauberflöte*, 1963), Vienna (1963), Munich (1964) and Berlin (1971), and with the Kirov and Bol'shoy companies (1972). A singer of considerable charm and flute-like accuracy, she maintained the Pons and Galli-Curci tradition of coloratura singing at a time when the more dramatic attitudes of Callas and, later, Sutherland were in vogue.

*

M. de Schauensee: 'Coloratura', *ON*, xxix/9 (1964–5), 27
R. Peters and L. Biancolli: *A Debut at the Met* (New York, 1967)

J. Gruen: 'Lucky Star: Roberta Peters', *ON*, xl/6 (1975–6), 16
J. Hines: 'Roberta Peters', *Great Singers on Great Singing* (Garden City, NY, 1982), 231–9
MARTIN BERNHEIMER

Peter Schmoll und seine Nachbarn ('Peter Schmoll and his Neighbours'). Opera in two acts, J8, by CARL MARIA VON WEBER to a libretto by Joseph Türk (or Türke) after Carl Gottlob Cramer's novel; Augsburg, ?March 1803.

Peter Schmoll und seine Nachbarn was composed in 1801–2 in Salzburg while Weber was receiving his second period of instruction from Michael Haydn. The plot deals with an episode in the lives of people uprooted by the French Revolution. Weber's score consists of 20 musical numbers; the dialogue is lost. Michael Haydn, under whose supervision it seems to have been written, declared that it was 'composed according to the true rules of counterpoint, with much fire and delicacy, and appropriately to the text'. It was staged at Lübeck in 1927 with dialogue by Karl Eggert, and there have been infrequent revivals in more recent years.
CLIVE BROWN

Petersen, David (*b* Lübeck, *c*1650–51; *d* ? shortly before 5 May 1737). Netherlands composer of German birth. Probably not a professional musician but more a wealthy dilettante, he settled in Amsterdam in about 1675. He composed violin sonatas and numerous Dutch continuo song settings. He may have provided music for Abraham Alewijn's play *Amarillis* (1693). He certainly did so for Frans Ryk's translation of Corneille's *Andromeda* (first published 1690), when it was performed at the Amsterdam Stadsschouwburg in 1730–31.
RUDOLF A. RASCH

Peterson-Berger, Wilhelm (*b* Ullånger, Ångermanland, 27 Feb 1867; *d* Östersund, 3 Dec 1942). Swedish composer and writer. He studied at the Stockholm Conservatory (1886–9) and at Dresden (1889–90). In 1895 he settled in Stockholm, where he was music critic of the *Dagens nyheter* from 1896 to 1930, except for a period when he was stage manager at the Stockholm Opera (1908–10) and when he visited Italy in 1920–21. Peterson-Berger made a major contribution to the Swedish national-romantic movement. His Wagnerian aesthetic standpoint was expressed in a series of music dramas, for which he wrote the texts, creating a Swedish *Gesamtkunstwerk*. *Arnljot*, based on the story of the warrior Arnljot Gelline from Sturlasson's *Saga of St Olav*, has often been viewed as the Swedish national opera. Each summer from 1936 it has been performed, as a spoken drama with incidental music, at Fröson, where the composer had a villa. The comedy *Domedagsprofeterna* ('The Doomsday Prophets'), concerning a wager on the date of the Last Judgment, makes a charming blend of lyrical freshness with textual and musical 17th-century pastiche. *Adils och Elisiv* ('Adils and Elisiv') combines the restraint of a saga with a yearning for peace and reconciliation determined by the period in which it was composed (after World War I); there are melodic features of Italian opera.

Peterson-Berger's material progress was hindered by the many enemies he made through his writings as a critic; he attacked showy virtuosity and dry academicism with satire, but also with strict conscientiousness (his selected criticism, *P.-B. recensioner*, was published in Stockholm, 1923). His writings also include articles on Wagner and *Richard Wagner som kulturföreteelse*

(Stockholm, 1913; Ger. trans., 1917); his translations into Swedish include *Tristan und Isolde* (Stockholm, 1908), Quinault's *Armide* (1907–8, unpublished) and Wagner's writings (Stockholm, 1901). His large musical output includes five symphonies, vocal works and chamber music.

first performed at Stockholm, Royal Opera; publication dates are for texts, all by Peterson-Berger and published in Stockholm

Ran, 1899–1900, 20 May 1903 (1898)
Lyckan [The Happiness], 27 March 1903 (1903)
Arnljot (after Sturlasson), 13 April 1910 (1906, rev. 2/1910, 3/1956; Ger. trans. 2/1914)
Domedagsprofeterna [The Doomsday Prophets], 1912–17, 21 Feb 1919 (1912)
Adils och Elisiv [Adils and Elisiv], 1921–4, 27 Feb 1927 (1919)

*

B. Carlberg: *Wilhelm Peterson-Berger* (Stockholm, 1950)
S. Beite: *Wilhelm Peterson-Berger: en känd och okänd tondiktare* (Östersund, 1965) [incl. bibliography and discography]
F. Bohlin: 'P.-B. och operan', *Vår opera* (1967), no.1, p.4
G. Percy: 'Five Swedish National Romantics', *Tradition and Progress in Swedish Music* (Stockholm, 1973), 92
——: 'Peterson-Bergers Storsjöopera', *Konsertnytt* (1973), no.12, p.3
L. Sjöberg: 'Nittiotalisterna och musikdramat – Stenhammar och Peterson-Berger', *Operan 200 år: jubelboken* (Stockholm, 1973), 120
F. Abenius: 'Arnljot för mig, då och i dag', *Musikrevy* (1979), 26
J. Kask: 'Domedag i repris', *MusikDramatik* (1984), no.1, p.24
W. Peterson-Berger: *Arnljot: handling i tre akter* (Östersund, 1984)
ROLF HAGLUND

Petipa, (Joseph) Lucien (*b* Marseilles, 22 Dec 1815; *d* Versailles, 7 July 1898). French choreographer, brother of Marius Petipa. He was one of the finest male dancers of his time, renowned for the nobility of his style. He made his début at the Paris Opéra in 1839, and in 1841 created his most celebrated role, Albrecht in *Giselle*. As well as independent works, he created the ballets for a number of operas. Specially important was his collaboration with Verdi in the Opéra's offerings for the first and second Universal Exhibitions in Paris. For *Les vêpres siciliennes* (1855) he arranged a long ballet, 'Les Quatre Saisons', skilfully integrated into the action. *Don Carlos* (1867) contained an important ballet, 'La Pérégrina', with a theme of its own. Less successful was Petipa's Venusberg Scene for the Paris production of *Tannhäuser* in 1860; the uproar the opera caused was one of the great scandals of operatic history, but the opposition was less a matter of musical taste than a chauvinistic outcry against a German composer and an objection to the placement of the obligatory ballet too early in the opera. Petipa also arranged a charming ballet for Thomas' *Hamlet* (1868).

*

I. Guest: *The Romantic Ballet in Paris* (London, 1972)
——: *The Ballet of the Second Empire* (London, 1974)
IVOR GUEST

Petipa, (Victor) Marius (Alphonse) [Marius Ivanovich] (*b* Marseilles, 11 March 1818; *d* Gurzuf, Crimea, 2/15 July 1910). French (later naturalized Russian) choreographer, brother of Lucien Petipa. Born into a theatrical family, he first staged opera dances at Nantes at the age of 16 (possibly 19, as he falsified the year of his birth in his memoirs). Later he travelled to Spain, America and, in 1847, to St Petersburg. Together with his work in opera, he created or revived 75 independent ballets for Russia, an achievement reckoned among the greatest in the history of ballet.

Petipa's career as an opera choreographer in the Imperial Theatres began in 1849, when he staged the dances for Flotow's *Alessandro Stradella* in Moscow, and continued for more than 50 years. An accurate list of productions on which he worked is difficult to establish: those before 1862, when he was promoted to ballet-master, were subsumed under his duties as a dancer, and in any production he might have collaborated with another choreographer. *Marius Petipa: materialï, vospominaniya, stat'i* lists 27 opera productions omitted from his memoirs, while the memoirs cite nine others not confirmed there; he may have contributed to 68 in all.

Petipa excelled at opera dances with subjects similar to those of his independent ballets. Stylized French dances of earlier times, prominent in ballets like his *Camargo* and *Ruses d'amour*, have operatic counterparts in *Manon* and the *intermède* in *The Queen of Spades*, while stories set in Mediterranean lands and India – the basis of *ballets à grand spectacle* such as *Pharaoh's Daughter* and *La bayadère* – find echoes in Félicien David's *Lalla-Roukh*, Delibes' *Lakmé* and Rubinstein's *Néron*. Petipa specially favoured Spanish dances, which he had mastered while touring Spain; his ballet in Act 4 of *Carmen*, with additional music from *La jolie fille de Perth*, survived well into the Soviet era. He mounted Russian dances infrequently, often deferring to native choreographers; thus for *Yevgeny Onegin* he composed the waltz and polonaise but assigned the *khorovod* in Act 1 to Lev Ivanov. His opera dances of the 1880s – a period of reform and administrative restructuring in ballet proper – were distinctive for their splendour, though some were in works now largely forgotten (Gounod's *Philémon et Baucis*, Gaston Salvayre's *Richard III*).

*

L. Moore, ed.: *Russian Ballet Master: the Memoirs of Marius Petipa* (London, 1958)

A. Nekhendzi, ed.: *Marius Petipa: materialï, vospominaniya, stat'i* [Marius Petipa: Materials, Recollections, Articles] (Leningrad, 1971)   ROLAND J. WILEY

Petitpas, Mlle (*d* Paris, 24 Oct 1739). French soprano. She made her début with the Paris Opéra in January 1727 in the last three performances of the opening run of Francoeur and Rebel's *Pirame et Thisbé* and was well received. She created Ismene to Pélissier's Polyxena in J.-N.-P. Royer's *Pyrrhus* (1730). In the première of Rameau's *Hippolyte et Aricie* (1733) she sang four parts, and was the only singer named and praised by the *Mercure* for her 'nightingale's cantilena' (*ramage de rossignol*). Her light, supple voice had a coloratura quality and great flexibility: according to La Borde, 'Elle avait autant de talent pour chanter les ariettes que la Pélissier pour déclamer le récitatif', though he considered Lemière even greater in florid singing. Immediately after these performances she disappeared surreptitiously to England for an assignation, returning in April 1734. She sang Electra in the 1734 revival of Desmarets and Campra's *Iphigénie en Tauride*, and created roles in Rameau's *Les Indes galantes* (1735) and *Castor et Pollux* (1737). Her career was short and she died young.

*

J.-B. de La Borde: *Essai sur la musique ancienne et moderne* (Paris, 1780), 493, 526

A. Pougin: *Un ténor de l'Opéra au XVIIIe siècle: Pierre Jélyotte et les chanteurs de son temps* (Paris, 1905), 74ff   PHILIP WELLER

Petits Cabinets. Private theatrical company founded by Mme de Pompadour and based in the royal apartments at Versailles from 1747; *see* PARIS, §3(ii).

Petkov, Dimiter (*b* Sofia, 5 March 1938). Bulgarian bass. He studied in Sofia, making his début there in 1964 as the King in *Aida*. In 1968 he sang Osmin at Glyndebourne, returning in 1970 as Gremin. He has appeared at principal theatres throughout Europe, including the S Carlo, where he sang the High Priest in the first staged performance of Musorgsky's *Salammbô* (1983). Among his other Russian roles are Pimen, Varlaam and Boris, Prince Andrey Khovansky, the General (*The Gambler*) and Sobakin (*The Tsar's Bride*); he also sings Henry VIII (*Anna Bolena*), Oroveso, Fiesco, Zaccaria, Silva and Gounod's Méphistophélès. He has a resonant voice which is particularly strong in the lowest register, and an imposing presence.   ELIZABETH FORBES

Petrassi, Goffredo (*b* Zagarolo, nr Palestrina, 16 July 1904). Italian composer. From the age of seven he was brought up in Rome; he was educated at the Schola Cantorum of S Salvatore in Lauro and (after nine years working in a music shop) at the Conservatorio di S Cecilia (1928–33), where he gained diplomas in composition and organ playing. Between 1937 and 1940 he was Superintendent of the Teatro La Fenice, Venice. On his return to Rome he began a teaching career which continued until his retirement in 1978.

Although a late starter by conventional standards, Petrassi gained rapid national and international recognition with his *Partita* (1932) – a work revealing a formidable orchestral technique combining clarity and rhythmic drive inherited from Hindemith and Casella, though by 1940 Stravinsky had become the principal stylistic influence. The onset of World War II and the collapse of Fascism provoked a period of profound self-examination; this is reflected in Petrassi's compositions from the 1940s, which include his two operas. *Il cordovano* (1, E. Montale), based on Cervantes's *Entremes del viejo celoso*, was first performed at La Scala on 12 May 1949; a revised version was given at the Piccola Scala on 18 February 1959. *Morte dell'aria* (*tragedia*, 1, T. Scialoja) had its première at the Eliseo in Rome on 24 October 1950. All his stage works to some degree represent in their central characters the composer's disorientation during this decade: in the ballets the madness of Orlando (*La follia di Orlando*, 1942–3) and the delusions of Don Quixote (*Ritratto di Don Chisciotte*, 1945), and in the operas the insane jealousy of Cannizares in *Il cordovano* (which was begun in 1944) and the absurdity of the Inventor in *Morte dell'aria*.

Stylistically, both operas maintain a neo-classically inspired elegance of sound despite the music's many chromatic threads. Scattered hints of serial procedures may be discerned, foreshadowing the partially dodecaphonic concertos for orchestra (nos.2–6) from the 1950s. In other ways the two operas are antitheses of each other: *Il cordovano* is a comedy with mainly female principals and a male chorus, presented in bright, brittle timbres at breakneck speed; whereas *Morte dell'aria* is a tragedy with male principals and a female chorus, set forth in suitably sombre music. The impressive choral writing in the latter work shows affinities with Petrassi's choral-symphonic masterpieces; one of these, *Noche oscura* (1950–51), was a kind of mystical pendant to *Morte dell'aria*. Among the projects that Petrassi began to

983

explore but abandoned were operas based on Camus' *Les justes* and Giraudoux's *La folle de Chaillot*.

See also CORDOVANO, IL and MORTE DELL'ARIA.

*

F. D'Amico: 'Astrattismo puro del secondo Petrassi', *L'Italia domani*, ii/10 (1959), 14

——: 'Petrassi operista', *Teatro alla Scala: la stagione lirica 1970–71* (Milan, 1971), 533

G. Petrassi: 'Esperienze teatrali', *Cinquant'anni del Teatro dell'Opera* (Rome, 1979), 199–213

C. Annibaldi and M. Monna: *Bibliografia e catalogo delle opere di Goffredo Petrassi* (Milan, 1980)

L. Lombardi: *Conversazioni con Petrassi* (Milan, 1980)

E. Restagno, ed.: *Petrassi* (Turin, 1986)   ALASDAIR JAMIESON

Petrauskas, Kipras (*b* Ceikiniai, Lithuania, 18 Nov 1885; *d* Vilnius, 17 Jan 1968). Lithuanian tenor. He trained first as an organist and then, after appearing in his brother Mikas's opera *Birute* in 1906, as a singer in St Petersburg. In 1911 he made his professional début at the Bol'shoy in Gounod's *Roméo et Juliette*, and was at the Mariinsky in St Petersburg until 1920, singing such lyrical roles as Almaviva, Alfredo, Des Grieux and Levko in Rimsky-Korsakov's *May Night*. Returning to Lithuania, he helped to found the opera at Kaunas; this moved in 1948 to Vilnius, where Petrauskas made his final appearance in 1958 as Don José in *Carmen*. His light voice gained weight, so that by 1930 he was to be heard as Hermann, Lohengrin and Radames, and in 1938 he sang a greatly admired Otello. He travelled widely in North and South America, Spain and Germany, sang also in Paris and Stockholm, and in 1934 appeared at La Scala as Grishka in Rimsky-Korsakov's *The Legend of the Invisible City of Kitezh*. In the last 20 years of his life he taught in Vilnius. Recordings show a sensitive style and a voice of remarkable sweetness and lyric grace.   J. B. STEANE

Petrella, Clara (*b* Greco Milanese, 28 March 1914; *d* Milan, 19 Nov 1987). Italian soprano. She studied with Giannina Russ in Milan, where she made her début as Liù at the Teatro Puccini in 1939. After wartime engagements in the Italian provinces she sang Giorgetta (*Il tabarro*) at La Scala in 1947. For the next 20 years she was a regular performer there, creating roles in operas by Pizzetti, Rocca, Bianchi and others, and singing Magda Sorel in the Italian première of *The Consul* (1951). She also took part in important revivals of *L'incoronazione di Poppea*, *I gioielli della Madonna*, *L'amore dei tre re* and *Adriana Lecouvreur*. At Naples she created Mila in Pizzetti's *La figlia di Iorio* (1954), the title role in Pannain's *Madame Bovary* (1955) and Anna in Rossellini's *Il vortice* (1958). Her voice was not naturally beautiful, but her dramatic abilities and vivid stage presence were particularly suited to the *verismo* repertory. Her career was based almost entirely in Italy, but she made guest appearances in Switzerland and South America.   HAROLD ROSENTHAL/R

Petrella, Errico (*b* Palermo, 10 Dec 1813; *d* Genoa, 7 April 1877). Italian composer. He studied at the Naples Conservatory first with Bellini and later with the director, Zingarelli. While still only 15 he was invited by the impresario Sangiorgi to write an opera for the local Teatro della Fenice. It is said that up to this time he had never seen an opera performed in public, yet, in spite of the disapproval of his teachers, he accepted, and in July 1829 produced *Il diavolo color di rosa* with considerable success. For this audacity he was expelled from the Conservatory before completing the full course, though he continued to study privately. During the next nine years another four comedies followed at the more important Teatro Nuovo, though his first attempt at a serious subject was turned down by the Teatro S Carlo in 1835. His success at the Nuovo was cut short, however, in 1839; as the result of a quarrel over fees he stopped composing altogether (at least for Neapolitan theatres) and for the next 12 years studied and supported himself by giving singing lessons.

This period ended with his appointment as musical director at the Teatro Nuovo, and in 1851 he made a brilliant return to composition with the *opera buffa Il carnevale di Venezia, ossia Le precauzioni*, which received 40 performances. A year later, at the Teatro del Fondo, the *melodramma semiseria Elena di Tolosa* met with such enthusiasm that it was transferred after nine days to the S Carlo, and in 1854, at the same theatre, Petrella produced his first operatic tragedy, *Marco Visconti* – with a success that rivalled even that of *Il trovatore* at the beginning of the same season.

Marco Visconti carried Petrella's name all over Italy: a commission followed from La Scala, Milan (*L'assedio di Leida, o Elnava*, 1856), and in 1858 he produced there the best known of all his serious operas, *Jone*. It was at this time that Petrella was taken up by the Milanese publisher Lucca, who saw in him a potential competitor for Verdi (published by the rival firm of Ricordi). Though not in the long run to his advantage, the resulting publicity tickled his personal vanity and from then on he concentrated almost entirely on serious works, among which the most interesting are *La contessa d'Amalfi* (1864), *Caterina Howard* (1866) and *Giovanna di Napoli* (1869) – the last to a text by Ghislanzoni, the librettist of *Aida*. Later in 1869, with the same collaborator, he produced *I promessi sposi*, which was performed at Lecco, where the action of Manzoni's novel is set: the publicity was carefully prepared, and although it seems unlikely that Manzoni was actually present at the première (as was widely believed at the time), Petrella was called before the curtain 28 times and the work obtained a notoriety that had little to do with (and ultimately tended to obscure) the merits of the music. Two more operas in Naples concluded his public career, and he ended his life in poverty in Genoa, where he died of diabetes.

Petrella was one of the last composers of the old Neapolitan tradition. His first works, mainly in the *buffo* style, earned him comparisons with Cimarosa and Paisiello – to the indignation of Verdi, who wrote in 1871: 'Let's have the honest truth … Petrella doesn't know music; his masterpiece, *Le precauzioni*, may please the amateurs with its brilliant violin figures, but as a work of art it can't stand up, not only to the great works, but even to operas like [Ricci's] *Crispino*, *Follia in Roma*, etc' (Luzio, 1935). This view was not universally shared, and *Le precauzioni* has more generally been accepted as a spirited, if not very refined example of a dying style. But in his assessment of Petrella's musical understanding Verdi was certainly right. An instinctive, wholly unintellectual composer, whose training was interrupted by early success, Petrella worked vigorously but unevenly: the primitive vitality which stood him in good stead in the animated 'parlanti' passages of his comedies was not sufficient for his serious works, where the poverty of melodic resource is unable to sustain the passion that his subjects demand. He imitated the Verdian model without Verdi's deep seriousness, and in the face of the formal problems of dramatic music was too easily content with the commonplace solution.

Nevertheless, there is an advance in dramatic consistency from *Marco Visconti* to *Jone* and, side by side with curious ineptitudes, there are moments of beauty in the operas of his middle period. The works of his last years show some refinement in style: in *I promessi sposi* there is more imagination in the accompaniments, and the theme of simple life is treated with a sensitivity that is unusual amid the thunder of contemporary Italian opera, recalling rather the older lyrical manner of Bellini. *Manfredo* too has moments of subtler lyrical quality.

See also CARNEVALE DI VENEZIA, IL; JONE; and PROMESSI SPOSI, I (ii).

mels – *melodramma serio*
melss – *melodramma semiserio*
melt – *melodramma tragico*

Il diavolo color di rosa (ob, 2, A. L. Tottola), Naples, Fenice, July 1829, *I-Nc*
Il giorno delle nozze, ovvero Pulcinella marito e non marito (commedia, 2, Tottola), Naples, Nuovo, carn. 1830, *Nc*
Lo scroccone (commedia, 2, ? G. Peruzzini), Naples, Nuovo, spr. 1834 [? first perf. 1831]
La Cimodocea (mels), comp. for Naples, S Carlo, 1835, unperf.
I pirati [I pirati spagnuoli] (melss, 2, G. E. Bidera), Naples, Nuovo, 13 May 1838; rev., Nuovo, 16 July 1856; *Mr, Nc,* vs excerpts (Milan, n.d.)
Le miniere di Freinbergh (melss, 2, Bidera), Naples, Nuovo, 16 Feb 1843; *Mr, Nc,* vs excerpts (Milan, n.d.)
Galeotto Manfredi, Modena, carn. 1843, attrib. doubtful
Il carnevale di Venezia, ossia Le precauzioni (ob, 3, M. D'Arienzo), Naples, Nuovo, 20 May 1851; rev., Milan, 16 Feb 1858; *Mr, Nc,* vs (Milan, n.d.)
Elena di Tolosa (melss, 3, D. Bolognese), Naples, Fondo, 12 Aug 1852, *Mr, Nc,* vs (Rome, ?1852; Milan, n.d.)
Marco Visconti (melt, 3, Bolognese), Naples, S Carlo, 9 Feb 1854, *Mr*, Nc,* vs (Milan, 1855)
L'assedio di Leida, o Elnava (melt, prol., 3, Bolognese), Milan, Scala, 4 March 1856; *Mr*, Nc,* vs (Milan, 1856; Naples, ?1856)
Jone, o L'ultimo giorno di Pompei (dramma lirico, 4, Peruzzini, after E. Bulwer-Lytton), Milan, Scala, 26 Jan 1858, *Mr*, Nc,* vs (Milan, ?1863; Naples, n.d.)
Il duca di Scilla (mels, 4, Peruzzini and L. Fortis), Milan, Scala, 24 March 1859, *Mr*, Nc,* vs (Milan, ?1859; Naples, ?1859)
Morosina, ovvero L'ultimo de' Falieri (melt, 3, Bolognese), Naples, S Carlo, 6 Jan 1860, *Mr, Nc,* vs (Milan, ?1859; Naples, ?1859)
Il folletto di Gresy (commedia lirica, 3, Bolognese), Naples, Fondo, 28 Aug 1860, *Mr*, Nc,* vs (Milan, ?1860)
Virginia (melt, 3, Bolognese), Naples, S Carlo, 23 July 1861, *Mr, Nc,* vs excerpts (Milan, n.d.)
La contessa d'Amalfi (mels, 4, Peruzzini, after O. Feuillet: *Dalila*), Turin, Regio, 8 March 1864, *Nc,* vs (Turin, 1864)
Celinda (melt, 3, Bolognese), Naples, S Carlo, 11 March 1865, *Nc,* vs (Turin, 1865)
Caterina Howard (melt, 4, G. Cencetti), Rome, Apollo, 7 Feb 1866, vs (Milan, 1866; Turin, n.d.)
Giovanna [II] di Napoli (dramma lirico, prol., 3, A. Ghislanzoni), Naples, S Carlo, 27 Feb 1869, *Mr*, Nc,* vs (Milan, 1869)
I promessi sposi (melss, 4, Ghislanzoni, after A. Manzoni), Lecco, Sociale, 2 Oct 1869, *Mr*,* vs (Milan, 1870)
Manfredo (mels, prol., 3, G. T. Cimino, after Byron), Naples, S Carlo, 24 March 1872, *Mr*,* vs (Milan, 1872)
Bianca Orsini (mels, 4, Cimino), Naples, S Carlo, 4 April 1874, *Mr*,* vs (Milan, 1874)
Diana, o La fata di Pozzuoli, 1876 (ob, R. d'Ambra), unperf., *Mr*,* vs (Milan, 1878)
Salammbô (opera-ballo, Ghislanzoni), inc.
Solima (mels), *Mr**

*

FétisB; FlorimoN
G. Carotti: *Cenni biografici e ritratto di Errico Petrella* (Turin, 1877)
G. Masutto: *I maestri di musica italiani del secolo XIX* (Venice, 1882)
A. Colombani: *L'opera italiana nel sec. XIX* (Milan, 1900)
F. Guardione: *Di Errico Petrella e della traslazione della salma da Genova a Palermo* (Palermo, 1908)
G. Cosenza: *Vita e opere di Errico Petrella* (Rome, 1909)
S. Farina: 'Errico Petrella', *Lettura* (Nov 1913)
G. Siciliano: *Di Errico Petrella musicista palermitano* (Palermo, 1913)
A. Luzio: *Carteggi verdiani,* i (Rome, 1935), 128
F. Schlitzer: 'Opere e operisti in un carteggio di Giovannina Lucca', *Mondo teatrale dell'ottocento* (Naples, 1954), 183–212
A. Camurri: 'I promessi sposi di Petrella', *La Scala* (Aug–Sept 1959), 32–5
M. Morini: 'Antonio Ghislanzoni: librettista di Verdi', *Musica d'oggi,* new ser., iv (1961), 56–64, 98–112
T. G. Kaufman: 'Errico Petrella', *Verdi and his Major Contemporaries* (New York, 1990), 179–220
MICHAEL ROSE

Petrenko, Yelizaveta Fyodorovna (*b* Akhtirka, 23 Nov/5 Dec 1880; *d* Moscow, 28 Oct 1951). Ukrainian mezzo-soprano. She entered the St Petersburg Conservatory in 1902 and studied singing with Natal'ya Iretskaya and ballet with Fokin. She made her début at the Mariinsky as Delilah in 1905 while still a student; at her graduation recital the following year her rendering of Arsace's aria from *Semiramide* created a sensation. She continued at the Mariinsky until 1915 and thereafter sang elsewhere in Petrograd and in Moscow, retiring in 1922 to take up teaching. Between 1907 and 1915 she made frequent appearances in the West: in 1913 and 1914 she participated in the Russian seasons in Paris and London with Dyagilev and Beecham, creating the role of Death in Stravinsky's *The Nightingale*. She was equally at home in mezzo-soprano and contralto parts, her enormous repertory including Amneris, Carmen, Fricka, Stéphano (Gounod's *Roméo et Juliette*), Ratmir (*Ruslan and Lyudmila*), Bonny Spring (*Snow Maiden*) and Paulina and the Countess (*Queen of Spades*). She sang with nearly all the great Russian singers of her day, including Shalyapin, Yershov and Smirnov. Her recordings show a voice with a warm, caressing quality, equally effective in opera and in the Tchaikovsky songs for which she became famous.
BORIS SEMEONOFF

Petrobelli [Pietrobelli], Francesco (*b* Vicenza; *d* Padua, 31 March 1695). Italian composer. A member of the clergy, he was *maestro di cappella* of Padua Cathedral, 1647–84. He composed chiefly concerted church music. His one surviving opera, *Il Teseo in Creta* ('A. P. D.'; 1672, Padua, *I-Vnm*), is old-fashioned by Venetian standards and its melodic writing often rambling and dull. *Teseo*'s libretto ascribes to Petrobelli an opera called 'Angelica'; this was possibly *Angelica in India* (P. P. Bissari; 1656, Vicenza), whose authorship is uncertain and whose music is lost.

*

EitnerQ; VogelB; WaltherML
G. Mantese: *Storia musicale vicentina* (Vicenza, 1956)
THOMAS WALKER

Petrobelli, Pierluigi (*b* Padua, 18 Oct 1932). Italian musicologist. He studied composition with Arrigo Pedrollo at the Liceo Musicale of Padua and took a *laurea* at the University of Rome (1957), where he wrote a dissertation on Tartini. Later he studied at Princeton, and spent a year at the University of California at Berkeley. He worked at the Istituto di Studi Verdiani in Parma, becoming its director in 1980, and has held posts at the universities of Parma (1970–72), London (1973–80), Perugia (1980–83) and Rome (from 1983). A member of several international boards and committees, including that of the complete Verdi edition, he has written extensively on Verdi (particularly his creative processes), and also on Bellini, Gluck, Haydn, Mozart, Rossini and Vivaldi, and on 17th-century Venetian opera.

'Dal "Mosè" di Rossini al "Nabucco" di Verdi', *Associazione amici della Scala: Milan 1967*, 15–47 [title incorrectly printed as 'Nabucco di Verdi']
'The Italian Years of Anton Raaff', *MJb 1973–4*, 233–73
with M. Di Gregorio Casati and C. M. Mossa, eds.: *Carteggio Verdi-Ricordi 1880–1881* (Parma, 1988)
Music in the Theatre: Essays on Verdi and other Composers (Princeton, 1991)   CAROLYN GIANTURCO

Petrodvorets. PETERHOF.

Petrograd. ST PETERSBURG.

Petrosellini, Giuseppe (*b* 29 Nov 1727; *d* after 1797). Italian librettist. He worked in Rome, where he was secretary to Prince Giustiniani and a member of several Arcadian academies. As a librettist he worked with the most illustrious composers of *opera buffa* in the late 18th century – Piccinni, Galuppi, Anfossi, Guglielmi, Salieri and Cimarosa, among others. He wrote *opere buffe* almost exclusively, and was responsible for some of the most successful texts of the period: *L'incognita perseguitata* (Piccinni, 1764; Anfossi, 1773), *Il pittore parigino* (Cimarosa, 1781) and – though some doubt has been cast on his authorship because it was initially anonymous – *Il barbiere di Siviglia* (Paisiello, 1782). He was one of the post-Goldonian generation of *opera buffa* librettists along with such figures as Giovanni Bertati, who worked primarily in Venice, Caterino Mazzolà in Dresden and Vienna, and Lorenzo da Ponte in Vienna. Like them, Petrosellini was primarily interested in expanding the scope of the Goldonian plot, while reducing the number of arias, increasing the number of ensembles and expanding the finales. In keeping with current practice, most of his librettos have two acts. He tended to write comedies of disguise and intrigue rather than sentimental comedies; *L'incognita perseguitata* was, however, one of the best-known sentimental pieces of the time. More typical is *Le due contesse* (Paisiello, 1776), in which a servant girl impersonates her noble mistress who is away at her country estate; much of the libretto is taken up with untangling the ensuing confusion. Petrosellini has not fared well at the hands of 20th-century commentators; though not a great poet, he had considerable skill in constructing scaffolding for effective moments of dramatic and musical entertainment.

Le vicende della sorte (int), N. Piccinni, 1761; *Il cavaliere per amore* (int), Piccinni, 1762 or 1763; *Le contadine bizzarre* (farsetta), Piccinni, 1763; *L'incognita perseguitata* (dg), Piccinni, 1764 (Anfossi, 1773); *Il barone di Rocca Antica* (int), C. Franchi and Anfossi, 1771 (Salieri, 1772); *Le finte gemelle*, Piccinni, 1771; *Gli intrighi amorosi* (dg), Galuppi, 1772; *L'astratto, ovvero Il giocator fortunato* (dg), Piccinni, 1772; *Telemaco* (componimento drammatico), Guglielmi, 1775; *Le due contesse* (int), Paisiello, 1776

Gli amanti comici, o sia La familia in scompiglio (dg), Cimarosa, 1778 (Valentino Fioravanti, 1792, as La famiglia stravagante, ovvero Gli amanti comici); *La partenza inaspettata* (int), Salieri, 1779; *La dama pastorella*, Salieri, 1780; *L'italiana in Londra* (dg), Cimarosa, 1779; *Il pittore parigino* (dg), Cimarosa, 1781; *Il barbiere di Siviglia, ovvero La precauzione inutile* (dg), Paisiello, 1782; *Il regno delle Amazzoni* (dg), Accorimboni, 1783; *L'amore in villa* (componimento per musica), Guglielmi, 1797

Doubtful: *La finta giardiniera* (dg), Anfossi, 1774 (Mozart, 1775); *Il curioso indiscreto* (dg), Anfossi, 1777 [attrib. by Angermüller, 1987]; *I tre amanti* (int), Cimarosa, 1777; *Il controgenio, ovvero Le speranze deluse* (int), Anfossi, 1778; *Il ritorno di Don

Calandrino (int), Cimarosa, 1778; *Le donne rivali* (int), Cimarosa, 1780; *La nuova Giannetta*, F. Robuschi, 1787; *I nemici generosi* (farsa), Cimarosa, 1796

*

ES (A. Mondolfi)
A. Della Corte: *L'opera comica nel '700* (Bari, 1923)
W. Bollert: 'Giuseppe Petrosellini quale librettista d'opera', *RMI*, xliii (1939), 531–8
U. Rolandi: *Il libretto per musica attraverso i tempi* (Rome, 1951)
R. Angermüller: 'Wer war der Librettist von *La finta giardiniera*?', *MJb 1976–7*, 1–8
D. Goldin: 'Il barbiere di Siviglia da Beaumarchais all'opera buffa', *La vera Fenice: librettisti e libretti tra sette e ottocento* (Turin, 1985), 164–89
R. Angermüller: 'Die Wiener Fassung von Pasquale Anfossis "Il curioso indiscreto" ', *I vicini di Mozart: Florence 1987*, 35–98
                                                                    MARY HUNTER

Petrov, Andrey Pavlovich (*b* Leningrad [now St Petersburg], 2 Sept 1930). Russian composer. He studied composition at the Leningrad Conservatory with Orest Evlakhov, 1949–54. After graduation he worked as an editor at the Muzgiz publishing house and taught at the Leningrad Conservatory from 1961 to 1963. He has served in the influential position of Chairman of the Leningrad Composers' Union (from 1964) as well as in other government posts, and has won numerous awards, including USSR state prizes.

Though best known for his film scores and popular songs Petrov gained his first success as a composer of ballet music, establishing a fruitful relationship with the Kirov Opera and Ballet Theatre, Leningrad, where all his ballets and operas up to 1990 have been staged. He also made a point of synthesizing aspects of light music and jazz with modern compositional techniques and stylization into an eclectic mix in his theatrical works. His first opera, *Pyotr I* ('Peter I', 3; Leningrad, Kirov, 14 June 1975), more precisely labelled 'musical-dramatic frescoes', highlights the triumphs and tragedies of the legendary Russian leader and founder of St Petersburg in a sweeping historical pageant. Collaborating with the same librettists, Natal'ya Kasatkina and Vladimir Vasil'yov, Petrov continued his exploration of famous Russian figures in the ballet *Pushkin: razmïshleniya o poete* ('Pushkin: Reflections on the Poet', 1978). Dealing with a poet of radically different sensibilities, the 'poet of the Revolution', Petrov's *Mayakovsky nachinaetsya* ('Mayakovsky Begins', 1983), a fantasy opera in two acts, completed his trilogy of works on Russian figures progressing through three centuries. The predictably eclectic score, to a libretto by M. Rozovsky, attempts to capture the scope and spirit of the early post-revolutionary 'events' into a kind of fantastic poetic theatre, where historical episodes alternate with the poet's imagined exchanges with Hamlet, Dostoyevsky's Raskolnikov and Don Quixote. The opera received its première at the Kirov Theatre on 13 April 1983.

See also PYOTR I.

*

L. Entelis: 'Opera o Petre Pervom' [An Opera about Peter I], *Muzikal'naya panorama Leningrada*, ed. A. G. Yusfin (Leningrad and Moscow, 1977), 6–13
V. Rubtsova: 'Opera rozhdena dlya stsenï: "Pyotr Pervïy" A. Petrova' [An Opera Born for the Stage: Petrov's *Peter I*], *Muzïka Rossii*, ed. E. Grosheva, ii (Moscow, 1978), 145–71
E. Ruch'evskaya: ' "Pyotr Perviy", muzikal'no-dramaticheskie freski' [Peter I, Musical-dramatic Frescoes], *Andrey Petrov: sbornik statey* [Petrov: Collected Essays], ed. M. Druskin (Leningrad, 1981), 10–47
L. Dan'ko: 'Mayakovsky – nash sovremennik' [Mayakovsky – our Contemporary], *SovM* (1986), no.2, pp.73–6

A. Petrov: *Vremya, muzïka, muzïkantï: razmïshleniya i besedï* [Time, Music, Musicians: Reflections and Conversations] (Leningrad, 1987)

LAUREL E. FAY

Petrov, Ivan (Ivanovich) [Krause, Hans] (*b* Irkutsk, 29 Feb 1920). Russian bass. His father was of German extraction. He studied with A. Mineyev (in his time a famous Bol'shoy artist) and in 1939 joined Ivan Kozlovsky's opera group, performing minor roles. In 1943 he joined the Bol'shoy. An outstanding representative of his generation of Soviet opera singers and a cultivated musician, he had a powerful voice of rich timbre, expressive in both declamatory and sustained singing, which, combined with his dramatic talent, gave him great authority. Thanks to an unusually wide range he easily performed roles such as Ruslan, which was regarded as his finest part. His other main roles were Boris and Dosifey, Kochubey (*Mazepa*), Yeryomka in Serov's *Vrazh'ya sila* ('The Power of the Fiend'), Gounod's Méphistophélès and Rossini's Don Basilio. In 1954 he was made an honorary member of the Opéra, and in 1959 People's Artist of the USSR.

I. M. YAMPOL'SKY

Osip Afanas'yevich Petrov as Ivan Susanin in Glinka's 'A Life for the Tsar', the role he created in the original production at the Bol'shoy Theatre, St Petersburg, in 1836

Petrov, Osip Afanas'yevich (*b* Yelizavetgrad [Kirovograd], 3/15 Nov 1806 or 1807; *d* St Petersburg, 28 Feb/ 12 March 1878). Russian bass. His date of death is often given incorrectly as 27 February/11 March or 2/14 March, the latter being the date of his burial. He made his début in Yelizavetgrad in 1826 in Cavos's *The Cossack Poet*; in 1830 he made his St Petersburg début as Sarastro. At the première of *A Life for the Tsar* (1836) he set a tradition for the interpretation of Ivan

Susanin with a performance of overwhelming dramatic power. Other roles written for and created by Petrov include Ruslan (1842), which he shared after the première with Gulak-Artemovsky, the Miller in Dargomïzhsky's *Rusalka* (1856), Oziya in Serov's *Judith* (1863), Vladimir in Serov's *Rogneda* (1865), Leporello in *The Stone Guest* (1872), Ivan the Terrible in *The Maid of Pskov* (1873), Varlaam in *Boris Godunov* (1874), Prince Gudal in *The Demon* (1875) and the Mayor in *Vakula the Smith* (1876). In April 1876 at the Mariinsky Theatre, to mark his 50th anniversary on the stage, he was presented with a gold medal by the tsar and a gold, diamond-studded wreath on whose leaves were engraved the names of the 100 operas in which he had sung.

Petrov's voice, which ranged from *B* to *f♯'*, from a rich bass to a flexible baritone, was admired for its warmth, depth and evenness; and his vivid personality and generous perception made him specially successful as a character actor. His non-Russian roles included Rossini's Figaro, Meyerbeer's Bertram and Weber's Caspar. But his embodiment of essential Russian types in a voice of peculiarly Russian character provided many composers with an example and an inspiration. He was married to the contralto Anna Yakovlevna Vorob'yova-Petrova.

*

E. Lastochkina: *Osip Petrov* (Moscow and Leningrad, 1950)
V. M. Bogdanov-Berezovsky, ed.: *M. Glinka: zapiski* [Memoirs] (Leningrad, 1953; Eng. trans., 1963)
P. Markov, ed.: *Teatral'naya entsiklopediya* (Moscow, 1965)

JOHN WARRACK

Petrov, Vasily (*b* Moscow, 28 Feb/12 March 1879; *d* Moscow, 4 Sept 1937). Russian bass. He studied in Moscow, where he was engaged at the Bol'shoy from 1904 until his retirement in 1936. His vast repertory contained many Russian roles, such as Ivan Susanin, Ruslan, Khan Konchak, Prince Gremin and King Dodon, which he sang in 1914 at the Paris Opéra and Drury Lane, London, in the French and British premières of *The Golden Cockerel*. His powerful, dark-coloured voice was also heard to advantage in Italian, German and French roles, including Don Basilio, Sarastro, Marcel (*Les Huguenots*), Nilakantha (*Lakmé*) and Gounod's Méphistophélès.

ELIZABETH FORBES

Petrova, Anna Yakovlevna (Vorob'yova-) (*b* St Petersburg, 2/14 Feb 1817; *d* St Petersburg, 13/26 April 1901). Russian contralto. Her mother, Avdot'ya Vorob'yova (*d* 1836), and her mother's former husband, Yakov Stepanovich Vorob'yov (1766–1809), were leading singers of their day. Trained originally for ballet, she studied singing with Glinka, among others, and identified closely with that composer's musical outlook. After her début as Pippo in Rossini's *La gazza ladra* in 1833, she created the part of Vanya in *A Life for the Tsar* (1836) and later Ratmir in *Ruslan and Lyudmila* (1842). She and her husband Osip Petrov were recognized as pioneers of the Russian nationalist school of music, notably by the critic and musicologist Stasov, who described her voice as 'one of the most exceptional and astonishing in all Europe: size, beauty, strength, gentleness'. Petrova also excelled in the bel canto operas of Rossini and Bellini, in which her singing was compared to that of Albani and Viardot. Her reminiscences were published in *Russkaya starina*, xxvii (1880), 611–17.

BORIS SEMEONOFF

Petrovics, Emil (*b* Nagybecskerek [now Zrenjanin, Vojvodina], 9 Feb 1930). Hungarian composer. He studied with Ferenc Farkas at the Budapest Academy of Music (1952–7). From 1960 to 1964 he was director of the Petőfi Theatre, Budapest, from 1964 professor at the academy of dramatic art, and from 1969 professor at the Budapest Academy of Music. From 1986 to 1990 he was director of the Budapest State Opera. Awards made to him have included the Erkel Prize (1960 and 1963) and the Kossuth Prize (1969).

Petrovics's first instrumental pieces show the influences of Falla, Prokofiev and Ravel as well as the Hungarian tradition. Although these pieces gained some attention, it was the one-act opera *C'est la guerre*, on a libretto by Miklós Hubay, that quickly established his reputation. Broadcast by the Hungarian Broadcasting Corporation on 27 August 1961, the work was staged at the Budapest Opera in the following year (11 March) and enthusiastically received; further productions were put on in Oberhausen, Nice and Sarajevo. The opera is Puccinian in its dramaturgy, but the declamatory style looks back to *Wozzeck*, and its free 12-note technique is a further link with Berg. Nonetheless, the work has an individual musical character and a striking dramatic power. It was followed by a comic opera, *Lysistrate* (1, G. Devecseri, after Aristophanes), written in 1962 for concert performance and staged on 3 November 1971.

After developing his style in instrumental works, Petrovics produced the large-scale oratorio *Jónás könyve* ('The Book of Jonah', 1966), which displays his lyrical vein. He returned to composition for the stage with a full-length, three-act opera, *Bűn és bűnhődés* ('Crime and Punishment'; libretto by Gyula Maár; Budapest, 26 October 1969), based on Dostoyevsky; it was produced in Helsinki in 1970 and Wuppertal in 1971. Although much of the novel had to be omitted, the opera is distinguished by Petrovics's gift for underlining dramatic situations and, above all, by his handling of Hungarian prose. Here again the music is freely atonal with more or less serial episodes; the polyphonic textures owe much to the Second Viennese School, but the vocal style is fully in accord with the Magyar language. Dramatic moments and sections of closed musical form are skilfully balanced.

See also C'EST LA GUERRE.

*

I. Fábián: 'Two Opera Composers', *Tempo*, no.88 (1969), 15
I. Földes: *Harmincasok* (Budapest, 1969), 125–46

JÁNOS KÁRPÁTI

Petrucci, Brizio (*b* Massalombarda, nr Ferrara, 12 Jan 1737; *d* Ferrara, 15 June 1828). Italian composer. Trained in both music and the law, he served at the cathedral in Ferrara, becoming *maestro di cappella* in 1784. His early career reflects an interest in dramatic music, his first known work being choruses for a tragedy, *Giovanni di Giscala* (1760, Ferrara). Two *opere serie* were staged at Ferrara in 1765; in the second, *Demofoonte*, his pupil, the celebrated Lucrezia Aguiari, made one of her early appearances. He also served as *maestro al cembalo* at the Bonacossi and Scroffa theatres and produced a comic opera in 1770. Later he concentrated on sacred music.

Ciro riconosciuto (os, P. Metastasio), Ferrara, Bonacossi, carn. 1765, *I-FEd*
Demofoonte (os, Metastasio), Ferrara, Bonacossi, 26 Dec 1765, arias *Gl* (Lucca, 1765), *PAc*
Nitteti (dramma per musica, Metastasio), Mantua, Vecchio, carn. 1766

I pazzi improvvisati (ob), Ferrara, Bonacossi, carn. 1770, *FEd*

Petruccio. Opera in one act by ALICK MACLEAN to a libretto by Sheridan Ross; London, Covent Garden, 29 June 1895.

The action takes place on an island in the Gulf of Mexico to which an Italian Mother (mezzo-soprano) has emigrated with her three children. The daughter, Elvira (soprano), has eloped in former years, and her lover (tenor) has killed her angry father; in the New World she marries Petruccio, a well-to-do Creole (bass). Elvira's elder brother kills the lover out of revenge, and she does not long survive him. Petruccio justifies his eponymity by introducing the plot in a 'proem' which takes place years later. The music is efficiently eclectic and includes an intermezzo along the lines of *Cavalleria rusticana*.

STEPHEN BANFIELD

Petrusenko [Borodavkina], **Oxana Andriïvna** (*b* Balaklia, nr Kharkiv, 5/17 Feb 1900; *d* Kiev, 15 July 1940). Ukrainian soprano. She studied with P. Saksahans'ky and began to appear with touring troupes in 1916; from 1927 she sang with companies in Kazan', Samara and Sverdlovsk (now Yekaterinburg), and in 1934 she joined the Kiev Shevchenko Academic Theatre. She typified the Ukrainian vocal school with her bright, silvery timbre of unusual beauty and was noted for the dramatic conviction of her singing. Her roles included Oxana (Gulak-Artemovsky's *Zaporozhets za Dunayem*), Violetta and Gilda, Zemfira (*Aleko*) and Yaroslavna.

*

V. Chahovets': *Oxana Petrusenko* (Kiev, 1949)
Oxana Petrusenko: spohady pro vydatnu ukraïns'ku spivachku [Recollections of a Famous Ukrainian Singer] (Kiev, 1964)
M. Kaharlyts'ky: *Oxana Petrusenko* (Kiev, 1973)
M. Kaharlyts'ky and H. Filipenko, eds.: *Oxana Petrusenko: spohady, lysty, materialy* [Recollections, Correspondence, Documents] (Kiev, 1980)

VIRKO BALEY

Petyrek, Felix (*b* Brno, 14 May 1892; *d* Vienna, 1 Dec 1951). Austrian composer. He studied in Vienna with Schreker and others. As a piano teacher, he held posts in Salzburg, Berlin, Athens, Stuttgart, Leipzig and finally Vienna. His works for the stage are among his most important compositions. In addition to two pantomimes and a 'Nachtstück' *Der Schatten*, with text by the Swiss writer Hans Reinhart, he wrote two operas, also to librettos by Reinhart: *Die arme Mutter und der Tod* (after H. C. Andersen: *The Story of a Mother*; Winterthur, 9 January 1923) and a *dramatische Rhapsodie*, *Der Garten des Paradieses* (Leipzig, 1 November 1942). His music shows strong ties with late Romanticism, the influence of Mahler being particularly clear in the use of extreme chromaticism and the tendency towards parody. Petyrek's choice of dramatic or lyric subjects, in which he was motivated by Reinhart, also recalls Mahler in its preoccupation with folktale situations and exotic atmosphere. He was progressive in his employment of Sprechgesang and modality, and his assimilation of eastern European folk music.

CHARLOTTE ERWIN

Pez [Petz], **Johann Christoph** (*b* Munich, 9 Sept 1664; *d* Stuttgart, 25 Sept 1716). German composer. He attended the Jesuit school at Munich, where he sang, played the viol and lute and took part in the annual school plays. He sang tenor at the church of St Peter but moved in 1688 to the Munich court as a chamber musician. The Elector Max Emanuel believed in sending promising composers abroad to study, so Pez spent the years 1689–92 in Rome. From 1694 to 1701 he served in the musical establishment of Joseph Clemens, Archbishop-Elector of Cologne, at Bonn, from 1696 as Kapellmeister; in 1701 the outbreak of the War of the Spanish Succession caused him to return to Munich, where, however, music was almost non-existent. Finally, in 1706, he moved to Stuttgart as Kapellmeister to the Württemberg court.

Pez's music shows strong Italian influence, the result not only of his visit to Italy but also of his contacts with other Italian-trained musicians, especially J. C. Kerll. Pez's only surviving stage work is his *drama musicale* in three acts, *Trajano, imperator romano*, given in Bonn in 1696 (Bonn, 1699; ed. in DTB, Jg.xxvii–xxviii, 1928); his works also include a *festa da camera*, *Il giudizio di Marforio*, 1695; a *serenata teatrale*, *Il riso d'Apolline*, 1701; and seven Latin school dramas, 1684–1706.

B. A. Wallner: Introduction to *J. C. Pez: Ausgewählte Werke*, DTB, xxxv, Jg. xxvii–xxviii (1928)   ELIZABETH ROCHE

Pezzo concertato (It.: 'concerted piece'). A large ensemble of soloists and chorus generally to be found as the second movement of a central finale, to which it forms the lyrical climax. It is sometimes called simply 'concertato', or 'largo concertato' (if in *largo* tempo). With rare exceptions it was a constant feature of Italian opera throughout the 19th century, sometimes cast as a 'falso canone' or CANON, e.g. 'Freddo e immobile' (*Il barbiere di Siviglia*, Rossini, 1816) or 'S'appressan gli istanti' (*Nabucco*, Verdi, 1842), sometimes led by a single voice, e.g. 'Chiuse al dì per te le ciglia' (*Maria di Rudenz*, Donizetti, 1838) or 'Di sprezzo degno' (*La traviata*, Verdi, 1853), or more rarely by two, e.g. 'Chi mi frena in tal momento' (*Lucia di Lammermoor*, Donizetti, 1835), and sometimes choral from the start, e.g. 'Schiudi, inferno, la bocca ed inghiotti' (*Macbeth*, Verdi, 1847). *Pezzi concertati* can also occasionally be found elsewhere in the course of the action – during a *prologo*, e.g. 'Maffio Orsini, signora, son io' (*Lucrezia Borgia*, Donizetti, 1833), or in the middle of an act, e.g. 'Su noi prostrati e supplici' (*La forza del destino*, Verdi, 1862). Such pieces are normally slow and contemplative, the characters advancing to the footlights and losing all count of time. A livelier type of concertato ensemble is 'È scherzo od è follia' (*Un ballo in maschera*, Verdi, 1859). Indeed in his later operas Verdi attempted, not always successfully, to give his *pezzi concertati* a sense of movement. The problem was triumphantly solved by Puccini in the roll-call of the prostitutes that concludes Act 3 of *Manon Lescaut* (1893). Thereafter the static *pezzo concertato* became obsolete.

JULIAN BUDDEN

Pezzo di baule (It.). SUITCASE ARIA.

Pfauenfest, Das ['The Feast of the Peacock']. Singspiel in two acts by JOHANN RUDOLF ZUMSTEEG to a libretto by F. A. C. Werthes; Stuttgart, Hoftheater, 24 February 1801.

Through the evil slander of the fairy Morgana, Lenore has lost the love of the knight Karados and has been banished from the court of King Arthur. A guardian spirit brings her wool, which he has woven into a gown. Arthur orders her to be brought back to court to witness the betrothal of Karados to his niece on the occasion of the Feast of the Peacock. Lenore's guardian spirit, a harpist, arrives with the gown, which he tells the men will fit only one who has never been unfaithful. The women are told that the gown will fit only the most beautiful among them. Queen Ginevra, much to the knights' dismay, insists on trying it on first. The gown flies in the air, as it does for each of the others except Lenore. Similarly, a drinking-horn which only a true knight can empty brings all the men to grief except Karados.

THOMAS BAUMAN

Pfeiffer, Georges Jean (*b* Versailles, 12 Dec 1835; *d* Paris, 14 Feb 1908). French composer. His father was a partner in the piano firm of Pleyel, Wolff & Cie, and his mother, Clara Pfeiffer, a renowned pianist, was his first teacher. After a successful début in 1862 Pfeiffer was regularly in demand as a pianist. His compositions had contemporary favour: his Third Piano Concerto was performed several times in Paris. *Le légataire universel* (1901), after the comedy by Regnard (1708), was regarded as his best opera, with 'light, improvised fantasy … enriched by very elegant and sentimental artistic touches' (*RHCM*, i, 1901, p.287).

Le Capitaine Roche op.19 (opérette, G. d'Onquaire [J. H. A. Galoppe]), private perf., Paris, 23 Feb 1862
L'enclume (oc, 1, P. Barbier), OC (Favart), 23 June 1884 (Paris, 1884)
Le baron Frick (opérette, 1, E. Depré and Clairville), Paris, Cercle Artistique et Littéraire, 19 Dec 1885, collab. E. Guiraud, V. Joncières, F. Thomé and others [incl. spoken dialogue]
Le légataire universel (opéra bouffe [with spoken dialogue], 3, J. Adenis and L. Bonnemère, after J. F. Regnard), Paris, OC (Favart), 6 July 1901 (Paris, 1897)

Posthumous: Les Truands (J. Richepin), Jeanne de Naples, Kénilworth

Le ménestrel, xxix (2 March 1862), 110–11
A. Pougin: Obituary, ibid, lxxiv (22 Feb 1908), 64

DAVID CHARLTON

Pfitzner, Hans (Erich) (*b* Moscow, 23 April/5 May 1869; *d* Salzburg, 22 May 1949). German composer and conductor. He gained some of his earliest musical experience in the theatre, as a spectator in the orchestra pit of the Frankfurt Stadttheater, where his violinist father was music director. He received his formal musical education at the Hoch Conservatory, Frankfurt, whose Brahmsian director, Bernhard Scholz, condemned a student cello concerto by him for its inclusion of three trombones and some harmonic irregularities. These Scholz pessimistically diagnosed as signs of Wagnerism.

The rebuke signals a continuing strain of wayward harmonic and contrapuntal experimentation in Pfitzner's works and proves interesting in the light of his later public stance as an anti-modernist adherent of traditional Classical and Romantic values. Indeed, one reason why his operas are important, even though they are outnumbered by his works in other genres, is that they provide invaluable documentation of the way in which pre-1914 Wagnerian modernism was convertible into nationalistic conservatism during the period leading up to World War II. In Germany this was marked by the increasing politicization of a musical culture riven by factional controversy, in which Pfitzner played a prominent part. His essays 'Futuristengefahr' (1917) and 'Die neue Aesthetik der musikalischen Impotenz' (1920) occasioned heated debate and were to be quoted approvingly in publications of the Nazi years. Pfitzner himself, however, grew judiciously silent after 1933 and angrily suffered de-Nazification after the war, not long before his death.

Pfitzner's career as a teacher and conductor began in Mainz, where his *Tannhäuser-* and *Lohengrin-*orientated *Der arme Heinrich* was first performed in 1895; in the same year Ibsen's play *Gildet på Solhaug* was given as *Das Fest auf Solhaug* with Pfitzner's incidental music. These theatrical successes carried him forward to a teaching post at the Stern Conservatory, Berlin. His ten years in Berlin saw the consolidation of his reputation and included the première of his second opera, *Die Rose vom Liebesgarten* (1901). This was an elaborate pageant in which *Parsifal* was revisited in a spirit of Rosicrucian mysticism, the characters including ethereal Germanic nobles, woodland folk, fairies, a primitive bog-dweller, dwarfs and giants. The opera was given an important production in Vienna by Mahler and Roller in 1905, the year in which Kleist's *Das Kätchen von Heilbronn* was performed in Berlin with music by Pfitzner. More incidental music followed in 1906, composed for the fairy-tale play *Das Christelflein* by Pfitzner's friend Ilse von Stach; Pfitzner turned this into a *Spieloper*, *Das Christelflein*, in 1917. Where in *Die Rose vom Liebesgarten* Pfitzner's Wagnerian idealism found its way logically into the realm of *fin-de-siècle* symbolism, the sentimental children's-story morality of *Das Christelflein* seems to anticipate preoccupations of the *Blut und Boden* school of the National Socialist period and occasioned a significant retreat into diatonic tunefulness.

In 1907 Pfitzner became head of the conservatory at Strasbourg, where he briefly directed the Opéra from 1911, reviving Marschner's *Der Templer und die Jüdin* in a new version of his own in 1912. German Romantic opera was a continuing interest of his; he was responsible for the first publication in vocal score of E. T. A. Hoffmann's *Undine* (1908) and also produced a new edition of Marschner's *Der Vampyr*, which was staged at Stuttgart in 1924. In 1911 he completed the libretto of his masterpiece, *Palestrina* (1917). This was the most moving and coherent of all his expressions of idealistic, 'inspiration'-orientated musical conservatism and brought him into contact with Thomas Mann, who was fascinated by the work, though he found Pfitzner personally difficult ('not born to feel at ease'). Their later creative and intellectual divergence was symbolically marked by the inclusion of Pfitzner's signature on the public letter of April 1933 in the *Münchner Neueste Nachrichten* condemning Mann's supposedly un-German lecture for the 50th anniversary of Wagner's death ('Leiden und Grösse Richard Wagners').

Pfitzner was at that time growing increasingly isolated from the wider intellectual life of Europe, which he considered decadent, and from all but conservative sympathy within Germany itself. The death of his first wife in 1926 had come as a severe blow at a time when he had begun to gain public attention in anticipation of his 60th birthday celebrations in 1929. In that year he completed his book *Werk und Wiedergabe*; it formed the third volume of his *Gesammelte Schriften* (Augsburg, 1926–9), of which a large proportion is devoted to opera: there are essays on *Der Freischütz*, *Undine*, *Der Vampyr* and *Parsifal*, as well as discussions of his own operas and writings on general issues concerning opera. In his last opera, *Das Herz*, Pfitzner paid final homage to the spirit of Hoffmann. Although given simultaneously under Knappertsbusch (Munich) and Furtwängler

(Berlin) in 1931, the critical failure of this work seems to have led Pfitzner increasingly to assume the manner of the composer in the final act of *Palestrina*. His marriage to Mali Stoll in 1939 brought some comfort, but the trials of the war years (his Munich house received a direct bomb hit) and their aftermath accumulated into a sad final chapter to the career of one of the most significant opponents of trans-national progressive 'modernism' in 20th-century European music.

See also ARME HEINRICH, DER; CHRISTELFLEIN, DAS; HERZ, DAS; PALESTRINA; and ROSE VOM LIEBESGARTEN, DIE.

Der arme Heinrich, 1891–3 (Musikdrama, 3, J. Grun and Pfitzner, after H. von Aue), Mainz, Stadt, 2 April 1895, vs (Frankfurt, 1896), full score (Leipzig, 1901)

Die Rose vom Liebesgarten, 1897–1900 (romantische Oper, prol., 2, epilogue, Grun), Elberfeld, Stadt, 9 Nov 1901, vs (Stuttgart, 1901), full score (Leipzig, 1905)

Das Christelflein op.20 (incidental music, I. von Stach), Munich, 11 Dec 1906, vs (Berlin, 1906); rev. (Spieloper, 2, Pfitzner, after Stach), Dresden, 11 Dec 1917, vs (Berlin, 1918)

Palestrina, 1911–15 (musikalische Legende, 3, Pfitzner), Munich, Prinzregent, 12 June 1917 (Berlin, 1916), *A-Wgm*

Das Herz op.39 (Drama für Musik, 3, H. Mahner-Mons), Berlin, Staatsoper, and Munich, National, 12 Nov 1931 (Berlin, 1931), *Wn*

*

R. Louis: *Hans Pfitzners 'Rose vom Liebesgarten'* (Munich, 1904)

H. Pfitzner: 'Der Boycott meiner Werke am Münchner Hoftheater', *Süddeutsche Monatshefte*, vii/8 (1910)

——: 'Die Rose vom Liebesgarten in Wien', *Gustav Mahler: ein Bild seiner Persönlichkeit in Widmungen*, ed. P. Stefan (Munich, 1910), 40–41

E. Mehler: *Die Rose vom Liebesgarten: vollständiges Regiebuch nach der Inszenierung und Spielleitung des Komponisten* (Leipzig, 1917)

W. Reizler: *Hans Pfitzner und die deutsche Bühne* (Munich, 1917)

O. Erhardt: *Die Inszenierung von Hans Pfitzners musikalische Legende Palestrina: vollständiges Regiebuch in Übereinstimmung mit der Spielleitung des Dichterkomponisten* (Berlin, 1922)

K. Halusa: *Pfitzners musikdramatisches Schaffen* (diss., U. of Vienna, 1929)

F. Hirtler: *Hans Pfitzners 'Armer Heinrich'* (diss., U. of Freiburg, 1939)

W. Schwartz: 'Die Bedeutung des Religiösen im musikdramatischen Schaffen Hans Pfitzners', *Festgabe für Joseph Müller-Blattau* (Saarbrücken, 1960), 95–111

R. Kriss: *Die Darstellung des Konzils von Trient in Hans Pfitzners Musikalische Legende 'Palestrina'* (Munich, 1962)

H. Rectanus: 'Pfitzner als Dramatiker', *Beiträge der Geschichte der Oper*, ed. H. Becker (Regensburg, 1969), 139–45

J. Newsom: 'Hans Pfitzner, Thomas Mann and "The Magic Mountain"', *ML*, lv (1974), 136–50

W. Osthoff: 'Pfitzner – Goethe – Italien: die Wurzeln des Silla-Liedchens im Palestrina', *AnMc*, no.17 (1976), 194–211

M. Carner: 'Pfitzner v. Berg or Inspiration v. Analysis', *MT*, cxvii (1977), 379–80

W. Osthoff: 'Eine neue Quelle zu Palestrinazitat und Palestrinasatz in Pfitzners Musikalische Legende', *Renaissance-Studien: Helmuth Osthoff zum 80. Geburtstage* (Tutzing, 1979), 185–209

B. Adamy: *Hans Pfitzner: Literatur, Philosophie und Zeitgeschehen in seinem Weltbild und Werk* (Tutzing, 1980)

U. Skouenborg: *Von Wagner zu Pfitzner: Stoff und Form der Musik* (Tutzing, 1983)

G. Winkler: 'Hans Sachs und Palestrina: Hans Pfitzner's "Zurücknahme" der Meistersinger', *Richard Wagner 1883–1983: die Rezeption im 19. und 20. Jahrhundert*, ed. U. Müller, H. Hundsnurscher and C. Sommer (Stuttgart, 1984), 107–30

P. Franklin: 'Palestrina and the Dangerous Futurists', *The Idea of Music: Schoenberg and Others* (London, 1985), 117–38

R. Ermen: *Musik als Einfall: Hans Pfitzners Position im ästhetischen Diskurs nach Wagner* (Aachen, 1986)

W. Osthoff: 'Hans Pfitzners "Rose vom Liebesgarten", Gustav Mahler und die Wiener Schule', *Festschrift Martin Ruhnke zum 65. Geburtstag* (Stuttgart, 1986), 265–93

J. Williamson: 'Pfitzner and Ibsen', *ML*, lxvii (1986), 127–46

W. Osthoff: 'Palestrina e la legenda musicale di Pfitzner', *Studi Palestriniani: Palestrina 1991*, 529–68
J. Williamson: *The Music of Hans Pfitzner* (Oxford, 1992)
PETER FRANKLIN

Pforzheim. City in south-western Germany. Its theatre traditions date back to the time of Johannes Reuchlin (1455–1522) and his celebrated school dramas. Later, visiting companies offered a mixture of drama and opera performances, with *Don Giovanni* and *Die Zauberflöte* receiving their local premières in 1810 at the Komödienhaus, a barnlike building with a capacity of 200. In the mid-19th century the company of the nearby Heilbronner Aktien-Theater gave occasional guest performances of operas; later they were succeeded by the Landestheater Karlsruhe, which performed at the Saalbau (opened in 1900), where Richard Strauss conducted his *Ariadne auf Naxos* in 1923. The private Victoria-Theater (established 1904) was granted official Stadttheater status in 1935, and from then on the city had its own company for opera and operetta. Closed in 1944, the theatre was bombed in February 1945. Two former school gymnasiums were rebuilt as a substitute theatre with seating for 394 and a makeshift stage. Opened in 1948, this building housed the Stadttheater for 40 years with its drama, opera, operetta and ballet companies; a new theatre was opened in September 1990. In addition to four or five opera productions a season, regular operetta, musical and ballet performances are given. Operatic rarities of recent seasons include Wagner-Régeny's *Der Günstling*, Musorgsky's *The Fair at Sorochintsï*, Wolf-Ferrari's *Il campiello* and Egk's *Der Revisor*. Manfred Berben was appointed Intendant in 1974 and Klaus Eisenmann became Generalmusikdirektor in 1977.

HORST KOEGLER

Phaëton ('Phaethon'). *Tragédie en musique* in a prologue and five acts by Jean-Baptiste Lully (*see* LULLY family, (1)) to a libretto by PHILIPPE QUINAULT after OVID's *Metamorphoses*; Versailles, 6 January 1683.

Phaethon (*haute-contre*), son of Climène [Clymene] (soprano) and Le Soleil [The Sun] (*haute-contre*), is filled with excessive ambition and pride. He abandons his beloved, Théone (soprano), and requests the hand of the king's daughter Libie [Libya] (soprano); then, goaded by the taunts of his rival, Epaphus (baritone), he rides recklessly across the sky in his father's chariot (a famous machine by Jean Berain). According to Le Cerf de la Viéville, *Phaëton* was called 'the people's opera'; Parfaict attributed the nickname to the success of the public première (Paris, Opéra, 27 April 1683), citing in particular the magnificent scenery. One famous episode, the attempt by Protée [Proteus] (baritone) to evade Triton (*haute-contre*) by successive metamorphoses (1.vii), uses orchestral imagery to reflect visual spectacle: 'in vain he goes from *symphonie* to *symphonie* as if from hiding place to hiding place' (La Laurencie: *Lully*, 1911). The end is spectacular: Jupiter (*basse-taille*) uses a thunderbolt to stop Phaethon's wild ride, and Phaethon crashes to earth; an ensemble and chorus provide a sorrowful denouement.

For illustration *see* MACHINERY, fig.8, and TRAGÉDIE EN MUSIQUE, fig.2.
LOIS ROSOW

Philadelphia. American city, in Pennsylvania. Founded in 1682 by William Penn as the chief town in the Pennsylvania colony, it became the cultural capital of the American colonies and was the official capital of the USA from 1776 to 1800. Although the original settlers were English Quakers who had little interest in music, Penn's hospitality to other religious groups ensured the growth of musical activities.

The earliest recorded performance of a musical drama in Philadelphia was *Flora, or Hob in the Well*, a ballad opera given by an English company in 1754. For 75 years the resident theatrical troupes usually performed a musical piece (ballad opera, comic opera or ballet) in addition to a play. The American Company of David Douglass opened the Southwark Theatre in 1766 with Arne's *Thomas and Sally*, and in the following years the comic operas of Attwood, Arne, Arnold, Dibdin, Shield and Storace were frequently performed, often soon after their creation in London. In 1767 the first American ballad opera was announced, *The Disappointment*, a satire on Philadelphia social life by Andrew Barton (a pseudonym; his identity is unknown), but it was cancelled at the last moment 'as it contained personal reflections ... unfit for the stage' and was not performed until 1976 (two editions of the libretto were published in the 18th century). The New Company, which was also active in Baltimore, gave light operas during the 1790s and early 1800s; one of the partners in this enterprise was Reinagle. An exception to the English character of nearly all the operas presented was the series of performances of a troupe of French refugees from Santo Domingo in 1796–7. In 1827 the impresario John Davis brought his French company from New Orleans for several weeks; it enjoyed such success that the troupe made eight visits over a period of 16 years, introducing a wide variety of operas in French by both French and Italian composers. Nearly all these works – by Auber, Boieldieu, Grétry, Halévy, Hérold, Méhul and Meyerbeer as well as lesser-known composers – and those of Donizetti, Rossini and Spontini were new to Philadelphia.

Lorenzo da Ponte, a familiar figure in Philadelphia in his later years, was instrumental in bringing the first Italian companies to the city and in igniting an enthusiasm for Italian opera that has been maintained ever since by its large Italian population. Rossini and Bellini were the most frequently performed composers by both the Montressor troupe and the Rivafinoli company in 1833–4, which performed in the Chestnut Street Theatre, also known as the New Theatre and renamed the Italian Opera House. Bellini's *La sonnambula* was immensely popular (61 performances in three years) and dealt the death-blow to English opera, though a few of the more popular works continued to have occasional performances. 1845 saw the première of the first publicly performed American grand opera, *Leonora* by William Henry Fry, based on Edward Bulwer-Lytton's *The Lady of Lyons*. The Havana Opera Company brought Verdi's music to Philadelphia in 1847. The success of Balfe's *The Enchantress*, performed 32 times in ten weeks in 1846, proved an exception to the long series of Italian operas.

With the erection of the American Academy of Music in 1857, the city acquired the finest opera house in the country. Built by Napoleon Le Brun on the model of La Scala, the house has three balconies and 2900 seats. The impressive interior and fine acoustics are still enjoyed by more than half a million people a year; the Academy (which never was a teaching institution) is also the home of the Philadelphia Orchestra.

Many first American performances were given in the

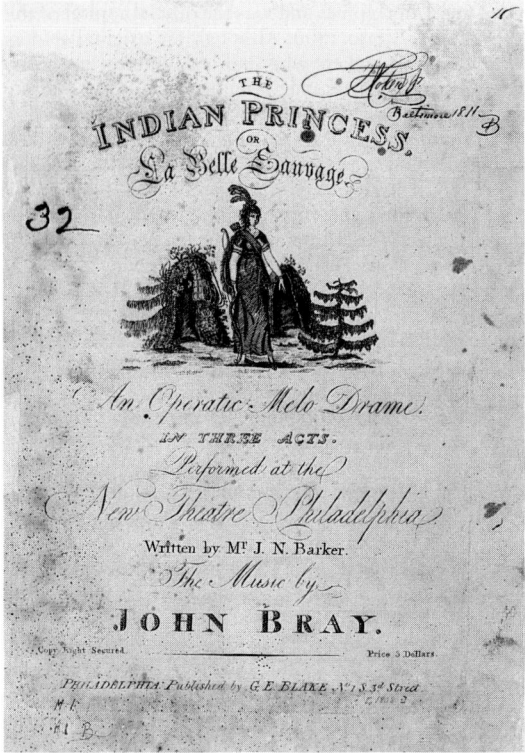

Title-page of the vocal score of John Bray's 'The Indian Princess, or La belle sauvage', first performed at the New Theatre, Chestnut Street, Philadelphia, 6 April 1808; Bray was a member of Warren and Reinagle's New Company from 1805

Academy of Music (as it was later called), including Gounod's *Faust* (in German, 1863) and *Mireille* (1864), Nicolai's *Die lustigen Weiber von Windsor* (1863), Spohr's *Jessonda* (1864), and *Der fliegende Holländer* (in Italian, 1876). In the second half of the 19th century many visiting companies brought famous European singers to Philadelphia, under the management of Max Maretzek, Maurice Strakosch, Maurice Grau, Gustav Hinrichs and James Henry Mapleson. Two more theatres, the Chestnut Street Opera House (1885) and the Grand Opera House (1888), offered additional facilities for opera. Among the American premières given by Hinrichs were Mascagni's *Cavalleria rusticana* (1891) and *L'amico Fritz* (1892), Bizet's *Les pêcheurs de perles* (1893), Puccini's *Manon Lescaut* (1894) and the première of Hinrichs's own opera, *Onti-Ora* (1890).

The Metropolitan Opera of New York first appeared in Philadelphia in 1885, and in 1889 gave the first complete performance in the city of the *Ring* cycle, under Anton Seidl. From that time until 1968 (when production costs became prohibitive) the company presented an annual season in Philadelphia, ranging from six to 25 performances a year. Oscar Hammerstein I, challenging the supremacy of the Metropolitan, built a new theatre in Philadelphia to seat 4000; this was one of the largest opera houses in the world. It opened in 1908 as the Philadelphia Opera House but was sold to the Metropolitan in 1910, renamed the Metropolitan Opera House and used for some years for the performances of that company. The new house was far from the centre of the city and after 1931 was seldom used for opera; its

impressive interior was destroyed by fire in 1948. Hammerstein, in his two seasons in Philadelphia, gave the first local performances of *Pelléas et Mélisande*, *Salome* and *Elektra*, and his reorganized company, the Philadelphia-Chicago Opera Company, gave the première of Victor Herbert's *Natoma* in 1911.

Since the end of World War I there have been many local opera companies. The Philadelphia Civic Opera Company (1924–30) under the musical direction of Alexander Smallens announced 'professional performances but not for profit' and was subsidized for a short time by the city. Among the operas given their first American performance by the company were Strauss's *Ariadne auf Naxos* and *Feuersnot* and Korngold's *Der Ring des Polykrates*. The Philadelphia Grand Opera Company (1926–43) gave the first American performance of *Wozzeck* in 1931, conducted by Stokowski with the Philadelphia Orchestra. The Pennsylvania Grand Opera Company, founded in 1927, presented the American première of Musorgsky's *Khovanshchina* in 1928. This company was later reformed as the Philadelphia-La Scala Company and in 1954 merged with the Civic Grand Opera Company; this and the Lyric Grand Opera Company were the major local companies. They performed the popular Italian repertory, with only an occasional sortie into French or German opera. In 1976 the two companies merged to form the Opera Company of Philadelphia. The principal singers are generally brought from France and Italy; directors have included Frank Corsaro and Menotti. The Pennsylvania Opera Theatre, established in 1975 with Barbara Silverstein as conductor, has specialized in little-known works of the past and in contemporary music; in 1985 it gave the première of Persichetti's *The Sibyl*.

Stokowski's interest in contemporary opera continued with the American première of Schoenberg's *Die glückliche Hand* (1930) and the first staged performance in the USA of Stravinsky's *Oedipus rex* (1931). In 1934–5 the Philadelphia Orchestra gave a series of operatic performances under Smallens and Fritz Reiner, which included first American performances of Stravinsky's *Mavra* and Gluck's *Iphigénie en Aulide*, and a performance of Shostakovich's *Lady Macbeth of the Mtsensk District*. The season was an artistic success but a financial disaster. The first performances of Menotti's *Amelia al ballo* (1937) and *The Consul* (1950) were both given in Philadelphia, the first at the Curtis Institute. The première of *William Penn*, an opera by Romeo Cascarino, a local composer, was given in 1982 with the support of a private foundation to mark the 300th anniversary of the establishment of the city. Several American premières have been given as part of the American Music Theatre Festival (which began in 1984 and runs from March to June each year), including Nyman's *The Man who Mistook his Wife for a Hat* (1987) and Glass's *1000 Airplanes on the Roof* (1989); Bolcom's *Casino Paradise* received its world première during the festival of 1990.

*

C. Durang: 'The Philadelphia Stage', *Philadelphia Sunday Despatch* (1854, 1856, 1860) [series of articles; compiled by T. Westcott as *History of the Philadelphia Stage, between the Years 1749 and 1855*, *US-PHu*, 1868; similar compilations as *The Philadelphia Stage* in PHlc, and *History of the Philadelphia Stage* in PHhs]

W. G. Armstrong: *Record of the Opera in Philadelphia* (Philadelphia, 1884)

J. Curtis: *One Hundred Years of Grand Opera in Philadelphia* (MS, 1920, PHf, PHhs)

R. D. James: *Old Drury of Philadelphia: a History of the Philadelphia Stage, 1800–1835* (Philadelphia, 1932)

T. C. Pollock: *The Philadelphia Theater in the 18th Century* (Philadelphia, 1933)

O. E. Albrecht: 'Opera in Philadelphia, 1800–1830', *JAMS*, xxxii (1979), 499–515

OTTO E. ALBRECHT (with NINA DAVIS-MILLIS)

Philémon et Baucis ('Philemon and Baucis'). *Opéra* in three acts by CHARLES-FRANÇOIS GOUNOD to a libretto by JULES BARBIER and MICHEL CARRÉ after Jean de La Fontaine's fable; Paris, Théâtre Lyrique, 18 February 1860.

The gods Jupiter (baritone) and Vulcain [Vulcan] (bass) are warmly received by the aging couple Philemon (tenor) and Baucis (soprano) after having been turned away by other Phrygians. Jupiter punishes the decadent neighbours by engulfing their temple in fire and rewards Philemon and Baucis by restoring youth to them. But much to Philemon's chagrin, the god falls in love with the rejuvenated Baucis. She contrives to make Jupiter lose interest in her by requesting that he restore old age to the couple. Vocal highlights include Vulcan's Act 1 *couplets* 'Au bruit des lourds marteaux', Baucis's Act 2 *romance* 'Ah! si je redevenais belle!' and the Act 3 *air* 'O riante nature', the last a late rehearsal addition made to highlight the soprano, Caroline Carvalho. At the suggestion of Léon Carvalho, director of the Théâtre Lyrique, Gounod expanded his original two-act frame into three by adding a middle act that depicts the orgiastic celebrations of the townspeople in Jupiter's temple. The addition of a tableau unconnected to the main story and containing no dramatic development accentuated the libretto's overall lack of momentum. There is little in Gounod's score that is dramatic: most of the numbers are purely decorative accretions to the spoken dialogue. For the 1876 revival at the Opéra-Comique which established *Philémon* in the repertory of that house until World War II, Gounod reduced the work to two acts.

STEVEN HUEBNER

Philemon und Baucis [*Philemon und Baucis, oder Jupiters Reise auf die Erde* ('Philemon and Baucis, or Jupiter's Journey to the Earth')]. Singspiel marionette opera by JOSEPH HAYDN to a libretto by Gottlieb Konrad Pfeffel; Eszterháza, 2 September 1773.

Preceded by a Vorspiel, *Der Götterrath* ('The Council of the Gods'), of which only the sinfonia and a brief orchestral movement survive, the 'little play with music' ('ein kleines Schauspiel mit Gesang') tells the story of Jupiter (spoken) and Mercury (spoken) finding shelter on earth with the poor couple Philemon (tenor) and Baucis (soprano), who mourn the deaths of their son Aret (tenor) and his betrothed, Narcissa (soprano), both struck by a thunderbolt. After they have told their story to their disguised visitors, Jupiter brings the young lovers back to life. He and Mercury reveal themselves, transform the hut into a temple and Philemon and Baucis into priests, admonish the other, inhospitable villagers and ascend to the heavens in a chariot. The text alone survives for a final scene apotheosizing the house of Habsburg – the work was first given during Maria Theresa's historic visit to Eszterháza; it was revived, with some revisions, in 1776.

The opera consists of a crisp overture in D minor and F major, two choruses, two arias for Philemon, one each for Baucis and Aret, and a duet for the re-animated young couple. The fiery D minor storm-chorus that follows the overture, succeeded by a brief major-key song of praise as storm gives way to a calm sunset, provides a dramatic opening. But because Jupiter and Mercury are spoken roles, and Philemon sings consecutive arias in moderate tempos, followed by three further solo numbers all in slow tempos, the piece remains fairly static. The elegance of the melodies, tonal contrast and enrichment of the string textures (with oboes, horns and, in one number, trumpets and timpani) provide considerable variety. The opera was recorded by Vox in 1951 under Meinhard von Zallinger.

PETER BRANSCOMBE

Philidor, François-André Danican (*b* Dreux, 7 Sept 1726; *d* London, 31 Aug 1795). French composer. He was the youngest child of André Danican Philidor *l'aîné* (*c*1647–1730), best known as the organizer and chief copyist of the Philidor Collection. His father died when François-André was four; but as a member of one of France's principal musical dynasties, which had long enjoyed royal favour, the child did not suffer from lack of patronage. At the age of six he entered the royal chapel at Versailles, where his musical education was entrusted to André Campra. Philidor soon displayed his gifts by outplaying his seniors at chess and by having a motet performed at Versailles when he was only 12. Another motet was given in 1743 at the Concert Spirituel in Paris. Philidor's early music is lost, but was presumably modelled on that of his master.

From 1740 Philidor lived in Paris, performing, teaching and, in the family tradition, copying music. He also assisted Rousseau, in an unknown manner, with *Les muses galantes*. His skill at chess marked him out earlier than his musical gifts. At the Café de la Régence he came into contact with many of the brightest minds of the time, including Diderot who was to call him, in *Le neveu de Rameau*, 'Philidor le subtil'. He soon became France's strongest chess-player, and when other means failed he could depend on his mastery of the game for support. He was obliged to do so when a concert tour to the Netherlands in 1745 collapsed, one of his colleagues having died. Philidor was helped by a group of English officers, and shortly afterwards travelled to England, beginning an association which was to last until his death. In 1749 the Duke of Cumberland helped him to publish his *L'analyze des échecs* (later revised as *Analyse du jeu des échecs*). Frequently translated and reprinted, it soon became the standard work on the subject. Philidor remained in England until 1754, returning in 1771 and 1773, then annually for a season from 1775 until 1792, giving lectures and demonstrations subscribed by the St James Club and moving in the same circles as Dr Johnson and Dr Burney.

Philidor's return to Paris in 1754 was encouraged by friends such as Diderot, but his efforts to establish himself as a composer met with mixed fortunes. A trial motet for a post at Versailles was deemed too Italian (unfortunately none of Philidor's sacred music survives). During his travels he had encountered the newest Italian music, including the Neapolitan style which had made such an impression in France during his absence abroad. Appearing in the aftermath of the Querelle des Bouffons, Philidor's early operas show the unmistakable imprint of Pergolesi.

Philidor probably intended no affront to ingrained French traditions, but he was undoubtedly of use to those who did, such as the *philosophes* and his librettist A. A. H. Poinsinet. Philidor's personality seems to have been engaging and somewhat naive. As a composer he was not lacking in self-criticism, as the four versions of *Ernelinde* testify; but he allowed free rein to a natural fluency supported by too good a memory, of obvious value in chess but dangerous for a composer. The problem of what Burney called Philidor's 'Italian plunder', which led to charges of deliberate plagiarism, is especially acute in *Ernelinde*. The likeliest explanation is that he read, heard and subconsciously assimilated to such effect that he was unaware of the extended near-quotations that appear in some of his scores.

He soon tried to enter the hallowed arena of the Académie Royale de Musique; according to Ginguené, the Opéra director Rebel objected to Philidor's italian-ism and wanted nothing to do with 'airs dans les scènes', by which he meant substantial arias occurring in dia-logues rather than confined to the *divertissements* (the traditional '*ariettes*' of *tragédie lyrique*). At the fair theatres, however, Philidor's triumphs began with his arrangement of vaudevilles and composition of addi-tional numbers in M.-J. Sedaine's *Le diable à quatre* (1756). His first fully original score, *Blaise le savetier* (1759, also to a text by Sedaine) began a series of comic masterpieces whose lightness of touch and brilliance in characterization and handling of ensembles still come delightfully to life on the stage. Several were published in score (sometimes reduced score) and orchestral parts.

Besides occasional collaboration with such leading authors as Favart and Sedaine, Philidor worked with Louis Anseaume in *Le soldat magicien*, and with A. F. Quétant in the brilliantly successful *Le maréchal ferrant*. But Philidor's literary sense was relatively undeveloped. His chief collaborator was Poinsinet, whom the memoirs of Jean Monnet and Grimm's *Correspondance littéraire* present as possessed of little poetic ability, but of a monumental conceit and gullibility which made him the butt of innumerable practical jokes. Nevertheless, after *Sancho Pança* Poinsinet wrote the three works with which Philidor's career reached its apogee, *Le sorcier*, *Tom Jones* and *Ernelinde*.

The success of *Le sorcier* led to Philidor's being the first French composer to be applauded in person, on stage, after the première. Written shortly after he had helped with the publication of Gluck's *Orfeo ed Euri-dice*, *Le sorcier* contains one clear (if unintentional) plagiarism: Bastien's 'Nous étions dans cet âge' is based on the first and last phrases of 'Chiamo il mio ben così'. Nevertheless, this is a well-structured opera in which the music is otherwise all new: Philidor and Poinsinet dis-pensed with the traditional *timbres*. *Tom Jones* failed at first, but succeeded on its revival in 1766. With *Ernelinde* Philidor became the centre of a typical Parisian musical controversy, although the prospectus and two pamphlets, and the writing of journalists and memorialists, are slight beside the literature of the imminent Gluck-Piccinni rivalry.

The success of Monsigny and Grétry in *opéra comique* ended Philidor's supremacy, which he never regained, although several of his works continued in the repertory of the Comédie-Italienne (which by then had merged with the Opéra-Comique). Given a good libretto like *Les femmes vengées* (1775), he could still write a successful comedy. His *Carmen saeculare* (1779), an extended cantata to words by Horace, achieved con-siderable success both in London, where it was written on the suggestion of Giuseppe Baretti, and in Paris. Neither of the serious operas that followed *Ernelinde* achieved a comparable *succès d'estime* and neither is as dramatically effective. *Persée* was one of the few

tragédies lyriques of this period not to be published; but there is distinguished solo and choral music in this reset-ting of Quinault, especially when Philidor evokes an older French style (as in the opening chorus and the sleep scene). The reconciliation scene in *Thémistocle*, using a melody from the overture, is touching, its surroundings comparatively uninspired.

Philidor pursued two careers for much of his working life, yet his operatic output is considerable, with a high proportion of effective works, and even his failures in-clude fine numbers. But his musical productivity declined with his popularity, and he did little to main-tain the impetus he gave to stylistic change in comic and serious genres. The need to support a family explains Philidor's increasing preoccupation with chess. After the Revolution, war between France and England left him stranded in London. Despite his eagerness to return home he was placed on the list of émigrés and died in London on 31 August 1795.

Philidor was the first French composer successfully to use a modern Italian style in the major theatres. He was preceded by Duni in *opéra comique*, but *Ernelinde* was a pioneering attempt to modernize the dramatic and musical character of the Paris Opéra. He soon developed a more ornate melodic style than was usual in *comédie mêlée d'ariettes*, and applied the Italian style to French forms at the Opéra well before Gluck. He was superior to his early rivals in his instrumentation, which though seldom elaborate is always telling, in the solid but undeniable virtues of his harmony and, if not in melodic invention, then in the power to characterize through melody.

Philidor's early comedies subject the mixture of social classes and human foibles, like gullibility and greed, to scrutiny under the guise of farce. *Blaise le savetier* deals with such mundane matters as evading the rent by compromising the landlord. Simple domestic farce (*Blaise* and *Le soldat magicien*) developed into sophisticated comedy (*Tom Jones* and *Les femmes vengées*); rustic dramas in which the dialogue is spiced with *patois* (*Le maréchal ferrant* and *Le bûcheron*) culminate in *Le sorcier*.

Parody of serious genres appears in the simile aria 'Je suis comme une pauvre boule', which marks the height of Sancho Panza's difficulties in governing his 'island'. In *Le bûcheron* the aria for the woodcutter, its chopping motif already heard in the overture, breaks off for the draught of wine that gives him enough strength for a roulade. Mercury then offers him three wishes, singing accompanied recitative ('sostenuto' in the score). The reference to *tragédie lyrique* was doubtless appreciated at Versailles, where it was given two weeks after its pre-mière. Another such parody is Julien's conjuration in *Le sorcier*.

Philidor's inventive use of onomatopoeia often marks an *air* dealing with a *métier*: the woodcutter; blacksmith and coachman (*Le maréchal ferrant*); Blaise the wine-maker (*Le sorcier*); and hunters (*Tom Jones*). It is part of an affection for making the commonplace musical; the first number in *Le soldat magicien* is a game of back-gammon. *Le bûcheron* and *Le sorcier* demand male singers capable of grotesque falsetto to *d″*. Another favourite comic genre is the sung invoice, in *Le soldat magicien*, *Le bûcheron* and *Le maréchal ferrant*.

In ensemble writing Philidor pioneered the simultan-eous use of compound and simple metres in *Le maréchal ferrant*, *Tom Jones* and the battle music of *Ernelinde*. In the quartets and quintets of *Blaise le savetier* and *Le soldat magicien* Philidor manages to convey the utmost confusion while remaining musically transparent; among the best of these ensembles is the septet in *Le bûcheron*. Poinsinet did not take full advantage of Philidor's abilities in *Sancho Pança* and *Le sorcier*, but another masterly septet ends the second act of *Tom Jones*.

See also BLAISE LE SAVETIER; ERNELINDE, PRINCESSE DE NORVÈGE; MARÉCHAL FERRANT, LE; and TOM JONES (i).

opéras comiques, first performed in Paris, unless otherwise stated; all printed works published in Paris

OC – *Opéra-Comique*
PCI – *Comédie-Italienne*   PSL – *Théâtre de la Foire St Laurent*

Le diable à quatre, ou J. de La double métamorphose (3, M.-J. Sedaine), OC (PSL), 19 Aug 1756; pastiche with some new music by Baurans, J.-L. Laruette and Philidor (1757)
Blaise le savetier (1, Sedaine, after La Fontaine), OC (Foire St Germain), 9 March 1759 (1759)
L'huître et les plaideurs, ou Le tribunal de la chicane (1, Sedaine), OC (PSL), 17 Sept 1759
Le quiproquo, ou Le volage fixé (1, Moustou), PCI (Bourgogne), 6 March 1760, excerpts (n.d.)
Le soldat magicien (1, L. Anseaume), OC (PSL), 14 Aug 1760 (?1760)
Le jardinier et son seigneur (1, Sedaine), OC (Foire St Germain), 18 Feb 1761 (1761)
Le maréchal ferrant (2, A. F. Quétant), OC (PSL), 22 Aug 1761 (?1761)
Sancho Pança dans son isle (1, A. A. H. Poinsinet, after M. de Cervantes: *Don Quixote*), PCI (Bourgogne), 8 July 1762 (?1762)
Le bûcheron, ou Les trois souhaits (1, Guichard and N. Castet), PCI (Bourgogne), 28 Feb 1763 (?1763)
La bagarre (1, J. F. Guichard and Poinsinet), PCI (Bourgogne), 4 July 1763, collab. P. van Maldere
Les fêtes de la paix (1, C.-S. Favart), PCI (Bourgogne), 4 July 1763, excerpts pubd with lib.
Le sorcier (2, Poinsinet), PCI (Bourgogne), 2 Jan 1764 (?1764)
Tom Jones (3, Poinsinet, after H. Fielding), PCI (Bourgogne), 27 Feb 1765; rev. (3, Sedaine), 30 Jan 1766 (1766); vs ed. N. McGegan (London, 1980)
Le tonnelier (oc, 1, N.-M. Audinot and A.-F. Quétant, after La Fontaine: *Le cuvier*), PCI (Bourgogne), 16 March 1765 (c1765); collab. Alexandre, Ciapalanti, Gossec, Kohaut, J. Schobert and J.-C. Trial
Ernelinde, princesse de Norvège (tragédie lyrique, 3, Poinsinet, after F. Silvani: *La fede tradita, e vendicata*), Opéra, 24 Nov 1767; rev. as Sandomir, prince de Dannemarck, Opéra, 24 Jan 1769 (1769); rev. as Ernelinde (5, Sedaine), Versailles, 11 Dec 1773; rev., Opéra, 8 July 1777; vs (5 acts) ed. A. Pougin and C. Franck (1883)
Le jardinier de Sidon (2, R. T. R. de Pleinchesne, after P. Metastasio: *Il rè pastore*), PCI (Bourgogne), 18 July 1768 (1768)
L'amant déguisé, ou Le jardinier supposé (1, Favart and C.-H. de Voisenon), PCI (Bourgogne), 2 Sept 1769 (1770)
La rosière de Salency (3, Favart), Fontainebleau, 25 Oct 1769, excerpts with lib. (1769), collab. Blaise, Duni, Monsigny, van Swieten
La nouvelle école des femmes (3, A. Mouslier de Moissy), PCI (Bourgogne), 22 Jan 1770, *F-Pn*
Le bon fils (1, F. A. Devaux [G. A. Lemonnier]), PCI (Bourgogne), 11 Jan 1773, excerpts (n. d.)
Zémire et Mélide [Mélide, ou Le navigateur] (2, C.G. Fenouillet de Falbaire), Fontainebleau, 30 Oct 1773 (1774), MS in 3 acts, intended for Opéra, *Po*
Berthe (3, Pleinchesne), Brussels, Monnaie, 18 Jan 1775, collab. H. Botson, Gossec, I. Vitzthumb
Les femmes vengées, ou Les feintes infidélités (1, Sedaine), PCI (Bourgogne), 20 March 1775 (1775)
Persée (tragédie lyrique, 3, J. F. Marmontel, after P. Quinault), Opéra, 27 Oct 1780, *Po*, excerpts pubd separately
Thémistocle (tragédie lyrique, 3, E. Morel de Chédeville), Fontainebleau, 13 Oct 1785 (1786)
L'amitié au village (3, Desforges [P.-J.-B. Choudard]), Fontainebleau, 18 Oct 1785, excerpts *Pn*
La belle esclave, ou Valcour et Zéila (1, A. J. Dumaniant), Théâtre du Comte de Beaujolais, 18 Sept 1787 (?1787)
Le mari comme il les faudrait tous, ou La nouvelle école des maris (1, de Senne), Théâtre du Comte de Beaujolais, 12 Nov 1788
Bélisaire [Acts 1 and 2] (3, A.-L. Bertin d'Antilly, after Marmontel), OC (Favart), 3 Oct 1796 [Act 3 by H.-M. Berton]

Contribs. to: M. A. Charpentier: Le retour du printemps, perf. privately, Dec 1756; J. C. Gillier: Les pèlerins de la Mecque, PSL, 1758; J.-B.-M. Quinault: Le triomphe du temps, Versailles, 10 Dec 1761; Au Dieu qui vous enchaine, ariette in 1763 edn of J.-J. Rousseau: Le devin du village
Inc.: Protogène (Sedaine), 1779
Spurious: Le rendez-vous (P. Légier), 1763; Les puits d'amour, ou Les amours de Pierre de Long et de Blanche Bazu (Landrin), 1779; Le dormeur éveillé (Marmontel), 1783 [music by N. Piccinni]

*
Prospectus [for the pubn of Ernelinde] (Paris, 1768)
Lettre à M. le Chevalier de *** à l'occasion du nouvel opéra [Ernelinde] (Paris, 1768)
Réflexions sur un prospectus où l'on propose par souscription la partition complète d'Ernelinde … par M. T *** (Paris, 1768)
L. Petit de Bachaumont and others: *Mémoires secrets pour servir à l'histoire de la république* (London, 1777–89)
A. E. M. Grétry: *Mémoires, ou Essais sur la musique* (Paris, 1789, enlarged 2/1797)
P. L. Ginguené: 'France', *Encyclopédie méthodique: musique*, i (Paris, 1791)
A. Choron and F. Fayolle: *Dictionnaire historique des musiciens* (Paris, 1810–11)
F. M. von Grimm: *Correspondance littéraire* (Paris, 1812–14); ed. M. Tourneaux (Paris, 1877–82)
J. Lardin: *Philidor peint par lui-même* (Paris, 1847); extract in *Le Palamède*, 2nd ser., vii (1847), 2–3
G. Allen: *The Life of Philidor, Musician and Chessplayer* (New York, 1858, enlarged 2/1863, 3/1865)
A. Pougin: 'Philidor', *Revue et gazette musicale de Paris*, xxvi (1859), 303–5, 318–20, 327–9
——: 'André Philidor', *Chronique musicale*, iv (1874), 241–8; v (1874), 74–82, 203–8; vi (1874), 22–32, 105–12, 200–07; vii (1875), 10–16, 111–19, 215–23; viii (1875), 20–26, 118–25, 264–75
C. Piot: 'Particularités inédites concernant les oeuvres musicales de Gossec et de Philidor', *Bulletin de l'Académie royale des sciences, des lettres et des beaux-arts de Belgique*, 2nd ser., xl (1875), 624–54
A. Pougin: Introduction to vocal score of *F.-A. Philidor: Ernelinde* (Paris, 1883)
H. Quittard: 'Le bûcheron, opéra-comique de Philidor', *RHCM*, vii (1907), 421–4
——: 'Ernelinde de Philidor', *RHCM*, vii (1907), 469–74
——: 'Le sorcier, opéra-comique de Philidor', *RHCM*, vii (1907), 537–41
G. Cucuel: *Les créateurs de l'opéra-comique français* (Paris, 1914)
G.-E. Bonnet: 'La naissance de l'opéra-comique en France', *ReM*, ii/6–8 (1921), 231–43
——: 'L'oeuvre de Philidor', *ReM*, ii/9–11 (1921), 223–50
——: *Philidor et l'évolution de la musique française au XVIIIe siècle* (Paris, 1921)
M. Pincherle: 'Ernelinde et Jomelli', *ReM*, iv/7 (1923), 67–72
E. Blom: ' "Tom Jones" on the French Stage', *Stepchildren of Music* (London, 1925)
C. M. Carroll: *François-André Danican-Philidor: his Life and Dramatic Art* (diss., Florida State U., 1960)
——: 'The History of "Berthe" – a Comedy of Errors', *ML*, xliv (1963), 228–39
J. G. Rushton: *Music and Drama at the Académie Royale de Musique, Paris, 1774–1789* (diss., U. of Oxford, 1970)
J. F. Magee: *A. D. Philidor: his Life in Pictures and Stories: a Scrapbook of Portraits, Letters, Clippings* (MS, US-NYp)
J. G. Rushton: 'Philidor and the Tragédie Lyrique', *MT*, cxvii (1976), 734–7
E. A. Cook: *The Operatic Ensemble in France, 1673–1775* (diss., U. of East Anglia, 1989)
M. Couvreur: 'Diderot et Philidor: le philosophe au chevet d'Ernelinde', *Recherches sur Diderot et l'Encyclopédie*, xi (1991), 83–107
J. G. Rushton: Introduction to *F.-A. Philidor: Ernelinde*, FO, lvi (1992)

JULIAN RUSHTON

Philippe de Bourbon [Philippe II] (*b* St Cloud, 4 Aug 1674; *d* Versailles, 2 Dec 1723). French patron. He was

Duke of Chartres (until the death of his father in 1701) and then Duke of Orléans, Regent of France, 1715–23. As a nephew of Louis XIV, he grew up in Paris at the Palais Royal, where the Académie Royale de Musique made its home, and became an ardent lover of opera, partly as an escape from his enforced marriage to Louis XIV's illegitimate daughter Mlle de Blois. When in Paris he regularly attended performances, and many of his mistresses came from the corps of actresses and dancers. As a young man, he was tutored in music first by Etienne Loulié and then by Charpentier, with whom he collaborated on an opera, *Philomèle*, which was performed at the Palais Royal in 1694; he is said to have collaborated later with his *maître de musique* C.-H. Gervais on *Penthée* (1705), *Suite d'Armide, ou La Jérusalem délivrée* (1712, Fontainebleau) and *Hypermnestre* (1716). His circle of friends included the dauphin and the Princess of Conti, the Duke of Burgundy, the Elector of Bavaria and the financier Pierre Crozat, all well known for their patronage of French opera and Italian music. The duke employed both French and Italian musicians, some of whom (for example J.-B. Stuck) had *tragédies lyriques* performed, and patronized others, like Campra and Collin de Blamont, who were experimenting with new operatic genres (*opéra-ballet* and *ballet-héroïque*), and the writers Fontenelle, Lamotte and J.-B. Rousseau.

Philippe's italophilia was undoubtedly fuelled by his visit to Venice in 1706 while commanding the French army in Italy; he spoke Italian, among several languages. As regent he patronized the Opéra-Comique at the Foire St Laurent and the re-established Comédie Italienne, and he allowed the Nouveau Théâtre Italien (under the musical directorship of J.-J. Mouret) to perform at the Palais Royal when there was no opera. In 1720 he spared no expense in remodelling the Tuileries theatre (the Salle des Machines). He must have authorized the passports for Giovanni Bononcini, Cuzzoni, Durastanti, Senesino, Berenstadt and Boschi to travel from London in 1723.

*

E.-J.-F. Barbier: *Chronique de la régence et du règne de Louis XV, 1718–63* (Paris, 1857)

R. Viollier: *Jean-Joseph Mouret: le musicien des grâces* (Paris, 1950)

C. Masson: 'Journal du marquis de Dangeau', *RMFC*, ii (1961–2), 197–223

L. Norton, ed. and trans.: *Historical Memoirs of the Duc de Saint-Simon* (London, 1968)

J. R. Anthony: *French Baroque Music from Beaujoyeulx to Rameau* (New York, 2/1978)

J. H. Shennan: *Philippe, Duke of Orléans: Regent of France 1715–1723* (London, 1979)

R. Fajon: *L'Opéra à Paris du Roi Soleil à Louis le Bien-Aimé* (Geneva, 1984), 280–88

B. Coeyman: 'Theatres for Opera and Ballet during the Reigns of Louis XIV and Louis XV', *EMc*, xviii (1990), 22–37

JULIE ANNE SADIE

Philippines. For discussion of opera in the Philippines *see* MANILA.

Phillips, Anna Maria. *See* CROUCH, ANNA MARIA.

Phillips, Montague F(awcett) (*b* London, 13 Nov 1885; *d* Esher, 4 Jan 1969). English composer. He was educated at the RAM, where he won the Henry Smart and Macfarren scholarships and other awards. He first made a name with popular ballads composed for his wife, the soprano Clara Butterworth, who also starred in the work to which his fame was mainly due. This was the romantic light opera *The Rebel Maid* (3, A. M. Thompson and G. Dodson; London, Empire, 12 March 1921), a skilfully crafted and melodic work, noteworthy for the soprano aria 'Sail my ships' and, especially, the baritone's 'The fishermen of England'. Phillips also composed a further light opera, *The Golden Triangle*, which was never performed, and much orchestral music. He was for many years professor of harmony and composition at the RAM.

ANDREW LAMB

Philomèle ('Philomela'). *Tragédie en musique* in a prologue and five acts by LOUIS DE LACOSTE to a libretto by PIERRE-CHARLES ROY; Paris, Opéra, 20 October 1705.

Philomèle was the only one of Lacoste's operas to enjoy a certain success; it was revived in 1709 and again in 1723, when it was also parodied at the Comédie-Italienne. On its first performance, the observer Raimond praised the librettist for handling the subject from Ovid's *Metamorphoses* 'with fire' and for 'providing infinite variety in the spectacle'. The composer also received praise: his recitative was considered 'a model', and the scene between Philomela (soprano) and Térée [Tereus] (baritone) in the first act, 'one of the finest in the lyric theatre', was described as 'a perfect piece'. Moreover, the audience was greatly impressed by the appearance from hell of Jalousie [Jealousy] (tenor) accompanied by the Furies, one of 'the most frightening' to be seen at the Opéra.

JÉRÔME DE LA GORCE

Phoebe. Pastoral opera in three acts by MAURICE GREENE to a libretto by John Hoadly; first known performance, London, Mr Ogle's Great Room, Dean Street, 16 January 1755.

Phoebe was apparently composed in 1747, though the date on the only edition of the libretto ever printed is 1748. There is no evidence, however, of the opera ever having been staged, and, like *FLORIMEL, OR LOVE'S REVENGE* (1734), it was probably intended as a private entertainment for the delight of Bishop Hoadly and his family at Farnham Castle, the episcopal seat. Like that work too, it is an entirely artificial affair, very much in the manner of Handel's *Acis and Galatea* (1718), but that to an 18th-century audience was undoubtedly part of its charm. The setting is 'A Champain Country', and there are four characters: Phoebe (soprano), a shepherdess in love with Amyntas, but disguised as 'Sylvio' for most of the opera; Amyntas (mezzo-soprano), her shepherd swain; Celia (soprano), sister of Amyntas, in love with 'Sylvio'; and Linco (bass), a comically boorish peasant, in love with Celia. The plot, such as it is, is said to have been copied from Gay's *Dione* (1720), but it may also owe something to Guarini, whose classic *Il pastor fido* (1589) was still popular with 18th-century readers of Italian. Though the music is mostly of high quality and the balance of dramatic incident much better managed than is the case with *Florimel*, only one contemporary performance is recorded: a benefit for John Robinson, organist of Westminster Abbey, in Dean Street, Soho, in 1755. Its first modern performance was at Holme Pierrepont Hall, Nottingham, on 28 September 1984.

H. DIACK JOHNSTONE

Phoenix. American city, capital of Arizona. Since 1972 the Arizona Opera Company has presented four productions each year in the Symphony Hall (2400 seats), with three performances of each production. The company also performs in Tucson and is based in both cities. The Lyric Opera Theatre, which is affiliated with Arizona State University at Tempe (a few miles outside Phoenix), performs in Phoenix itself as well as in the university's College of Fine Arts Music Theatre (500 seats).

Phoenix Opera. English touring company. It was founded in 1965, 'to take a varied repertory of opera and operetta sung in English to those regional audiences which have few or no opportunities of seeing live performances'. The original group sprang from the National School of Opera Ltd and the Young Performers Fund which, in collaboration with the London County Council, had been responsible for the production in November 1964 of Nicholas Maw's *One Man Show*.

Phoenix began operations in the spring of 1966, when, under the general management of Anne Wood, and with Joan Cross, William Chappell, Ralph Koltai and Vilem Tausky as artistic directors, it gave a series of performances of *Così fan tutte*, culminating in performances conducted by Yehudi Menuhin at the Bath Festival. It was also responsible for the Bath Festival production of *Die Entführung aus dem Serail* (later recorded), *Le nozze di Figaro* at the 1969 York Festival and *La vie parisienne* at the 1974 Brighton Festival. In 1975, under the auspices of the British Council, Phoenix Opera toured Austria and Yugoslavia, appearing at the Dubrovnik and Ljubljana festivals, and presenting a new production of John Frederick Lampe's *Pyramus and Thisbe* in a double bill with Purcell's *Dido and Aeneas*, as well as giving performances of *The Beggar's Opera*. The repertory also included *Don Pasquale*, *Martha* and *Albert Herring*. Artists who performed with the company include Teresa Cahill, Ava June, Lillian Watson, Kenneth Bowen, Alan Opie and John Wakefield.

Although initially supported by the Arts Council, Phoenix Opera became the victim of the economic situation, of the competition resulting from the establishment of the English Music Theatre Company (1975) and of the overall Arts Council plans for regional opera. With the loss in 1975 of its public grant it ended its regular seasons, but continued to give occasional performances until the end of the decade.   HAROLD ROSENTHAL

Phonograph. For a discussion of recorded opera and its performers, *see* RECORDING.

Piacenza. City in Emilia Romagna in northern Italy. Opera was one of the entertainments given at the Farnese court: in 1644, to celebrate the peace with France and the papacy, Sacrati's *La finta pazza* was performed by the Accademici Febiarmonici in the Palazzo Comunale – probably the site of the Teatro di Piazza (or di Palazzo Gotico), designed by Cristoforo Rangoni (known as Ficcarelli), with four rows of boxes. At first this theatre staged exclusive court productions (including Olivo's *Il ratto di Elena*, 1646) but it was re-arranged in 1669 for Cavalli's *Coriolano*. A larger theatre seems to have been built in 1687: the dedication of Sabadini's *Didio Giuliano* suggests that the performance inaugurated a 'Nuovo Teatro Ducale', possibly the Cittadella (adjacent to the Palazzo Farnese, with 62 boxes in five tiers and usually attributed to the early 17th century), which staged almost all entertain-

ments at the end of the century, often jointly with Parma.

In the first decade of the 18th century the most active theatre was the 'Teatro Ducale Piccolo', probably the Teatro di Piazza, where activity continued into the 1720s. Public management probably began when an opera season was combined with the spring fair: a celebratory eclogue was performed in 1730, but the connection was formalized only in 1751 in service contracts for the Regio Ducal Teatro della Cittadella. Comic opera was soon performed there, but by the end of the century that repertory was the preserve of the Teatro delle Saline (in what is now via Cavour). The Saline, in use since 1593, had from 1768 – with P. A. Guglielmi's *Il ratto della sposa* – staged *opera buffa* in secondary Carnival seasons.

After a fire at the Cittadella in 1797 a new theatre, the Comunitativo (later Municipale, designed by Lotario Tomba with 114 boxes in four tiers and a gallery; improved by Sanquirico, 1826–30) was built; it opened in 1804 with Mayr's *Zamori, ossia L'eroe dell'Indie*. Opera seasons were given at Carnival and in summer, and from 1831 frequently also in spring. The financing was split between box-owners and the municipality, with the latter paying an increasingly large share. A financial crisis in 1866 had the effect of reducing public support and consequently theatrical standards, but after the boxes were surrendered in 1905, livelier activity resumed; this has continued to the present, though with a traditional repertory.

*

E. Papi: *Il Teatro municipale di Piacenza: cento anni di storia (1804–1912)* (Piacenza, 1912)

U. Benassi: 'Per la storia del teatro e delle fiere di mercanzia', *Bollettino storico piacentino*, x (1916), 214–19

A. Rapetti: *Cronistoria degli spettacoli in Piacenza dal 1230 al 1890* (Piacenza, 1943)

——: 'Il teatro ducale della Cittadella'; 'Il teatro ducale nel Palazzo gotico', *Bollettino storico piacentino*, xlvi (1951), 1–10; 45–51

E. Nasalli Rocca, L. Sidoli and F. Bussi: *Il Teatro municipale di Piacenza* (Piacenza, 1954)

F. Bussi: 'La musica', *Panorami di Piacenza* (Piacenza, 1955), 225–47

L. Bianconi and T. Walker: 'Dalla *Finta pazza* alla *Veremonda*: storie di Febiarmonici', *RIM*, x (1975), 379–454

M. G. Forlani: *Il Teatro municipale di Piacenza (1804–1984)* (Piacenza, 1985)

G. Ferrari, P. Mecarelli and P. Melloni: 'L'organizzazione teatrale parmense all'epoca del Du Tillot: i rapporti fra la corte e gli impresari', *Civiltà teatrale e settecento emiliano*, ed. S. Davoli (Bologna, 1986), 357–80   ALESSANDRO ROCCATAGLIATI

Pia de' Tolomei ('Pia of Tolomei'). *Tragedia lirica* in two acts by GAETANO DONIZETTI to a libretto by SALVADORE CAMMARANO after Bartolomeo Sestini's novella, *Pia de' Tolomei*, in turn after DANTE ALIGHIERI's narrative poem *Commedia*, part 2: *Purgatorio*; Venice, Teatro Apollo, 18 February 1837.

The opera is set in the 13th century. Ghino (tenor) lusts after his sister-in-law Pia (soprano). When she rejects him, he lies to his brother Nello (baritone) that she has been unfaithful. Imprisoned, Pia is secretly visited by her brother Rodrigo (mezzo-soprano); Nello believes her visitor was her lover, and when his suspicions seem to be confirmed he convinces himself that Pia deserves to die. Wounded in battle and dying, Ghino confesses his deceit and reveals the true identity of Pia's nocturnal visitor. Too late to overturn his orders, Nello reaches the prison and discovers that Pia has already drunk the poison. She dies, urging peace between the warring parties of Guelph and Ghibelline.

The score of *Pia de' Tolomei* is uneven, but the tenor role (created by Antonio Poggi) is particularly effective. The arias for Pia are not in the same class as those Donizetti had recently written for Lucia, also a role for Fanny Tacchinardi-Persiani. Nello was originally sung by Giorgio Ronconi.   WILLIAM ASHBROOK

Piano [Piani], **Girolamo** [Geronimo, Giommo, Gelormo] (*b* Naples, *fl* 1726–52). Italian bass. He was heir to a tradition of interpretation that originated with G. B. Cavana and Gioacchino Corrado, and until 1749 he appeared almost exclusively in dialect comedy roles at the Nuovo and Fiorentini theatres in Naples. He sang in important operas such as Pergolesi's *Lo frate 'nnamorato* and *Flaminio* and Latilla's *Gismondo* and *Orazio*, the last two becoming widely successful. In 1738 he appeared at the Teatro S Carlo on the only occasion when a *commedia per musica* was performed there (Auletta's *La locandiera*). In 1745–6 he was in Palermo, but his first true round of performances was in 1751, when he went to Venice to create the roles of Giacinto in Galuppi's *Il mondo alla roversa*, and Roccaforte in *Le donne vendicate* and Beltrame in *La mascherata*, both by Cocchi.

*

P. Weiss: 'La diffusione del repertorio operistico nell'Italia del settecento: il caso dell'opera buffa', *Civiltà teatrale e settecento emiliano*, ed. S. Davoli (Bologna, 1986), 241–56

FRANCO PIPERNO

Piano fantasies and transcriptions. The opera-based fantasy for the piano flourished during much of the 19th century. In an era when operatic music had a strong and immediate popular appeal, as well as an aura of glamour, yet was not generally accessible to a large part of the musical public, it is not surprising that alternative means were derived for its dissemination, mostly through the most popular domestic instrument. The repertory of operatic adaptations, of one kind or another, was very large, and used not only for domestic music-making but also at concerts by virtuoso pianists.

The simplest form of piano music derived from opera is seen in the variations composed during the Classical era, for example those by Mozart on opera themes by Salieri, Paisiello, Gluck and others, or by Beethoven on themes by Dittersdorf, Grétry, Salieri and others. Chopin continued this tradition in his variations on 'Là ci darem la mano' from *Don Giovanni* (1827, with orchestra) and his variations on an air by Hérold (1833). The true opera fantasy, however, came into existence when composers selected two or more melodies from an opera and fashioned them into multi-sectional works, using a variety of titles (fantasy, caprice, potpourri, souvenirs, reminiscences etc.). The selected numbers usually had very little to do with the dramatic character of the opera; typically, they were chosen more for their individual popularity or appeal than for any representative quality. Many works of the kind took the form, favoured by Thalberg, of an introduction, then a presentation of several themes in elaborated form, and a finale in which themes might be combined. Such potpourri-like pieces came to flood the amateur market from the 1830s on, but it was with the rise of the virtuoso concert that the genre came to the fore. The operatic fantasy in fact dominated concert programmes during the middle of the century (in the approximate period 1830–70), and there was scarcely a pianist who did not seek to win audiences by composing

and performing his own. The list of exponents of the genre is a long one, including for example Czerny, Kalkbrenner, Herz, Döhler and Tausig, but two composers in particular were closely associated with the genre, Sigismond Thalberg and Franz Liszt.

Thalberg composed fantasies or similar pieces on more than 30 operas. Those on Bellini's *Norma* (op.12) and Meyerbeer's *Les Huguenots* (op.20) made his reputation, but his fantasy on Rossini's *Moïse* (op.33) was the one that was admired above all: the climactic and totally new effect of the prayer 'Dal tuo stellato soglio', sounding in the tenor register amid powerful cascades of arpeggios, was so overwhelming that members of his audiences sometimes stood on their chairs to see how it was accomplished. But Thalberg, despite his innovations, tended to repeat the same effects, earning for himself the none too flattering nickname 'Old Arpeggio'.

It was Liszt who developed the opera-based piece to its fullest. His works of this sort, some 50 in number, fall into two broad groups, reflecting his activities before and after his retirement from the concert stage in 1847. During his virtuoso years he composed nearly a score of bravura works for his own use. Some concentrate on a single theme, such as the *divertissement* on 'I tuoi frequenti palpiti' from Pacini's *Niobe* (s419), an early warhorse, while others, such as the fantasies on Halévy's *La Juive* (s409a) and Meyerbeer's *Les Huguenots* (s412), feature 'highlights' from the operas. In the best of these works, however – that is, those on Mozart's *Don Giovanni* (s418), Bellini's *Norma* (s394) and Meyerbeer's *Robert le diable* (s413) – Liszt brought a new and deeper musical focus to the genre. Putting aside the usual selection of unrelated themes, he presented a more dramatically cogent choice of thematic material, encapsulating, as it were, the dramaturgical essence of the opera.

After his retirement, Liszt's general approach to opera-based compositions changed. He came to avoid virtuoso display, presenting the music in more literal form as a paraphrase or transcription, and he also shifted his attention from the complete opera to a particular dramatic scene or dance episode (much as he had done earlier with the sextet from Donizetti's *Lucia di Lammermoor* (s397) and the overture to Rossini's *Guillaume Tell* (s552). Thus among the later pieces we have his paraphrase of the waltz from Gounod's *Faust* (s407), the polonaise from Tchaikovsky's *Yevgeny Onegin* (s429), and from Verdi the quartet from *Rigoletto* (s434), the 'Danza sacra e duetto final' from *Aida* (s436) and several others.

Further, as Liszt was well aware that his reputation would help promote the works he presented, his arrangements of excerpts from Wagner's operas deserve special mention. In 1849 he made a brilliant transcription of the overture to *Tannhäuser* (s442), which can only have helped the cause of an opera which within five years of the transcription's appearance was produced for the first time at some two dozen theatres. Liszt also transcribed the closing scene, 'Mild und leise', from *Tristan und Isolde* (s447), dubbing it 'Liebestod'; Wagner had called the scene Isolde's 'Verklärung' ('Transfiguration'), but as the 1867 transcription travelled much faster than the opera itself it was Liszt's designation that has prevailed.

Although a few pianists after Liszt continued to write opera fantasies, the genre fell out of favour towards the close of the century. Not only had it been overexposed but the new operas upon which its vitality depended typically lacked the broad, simple melodies that lent themselves to pianistic elaboration. (One must also allow that, once an opera disappears from the stage, any composition based on it is bound to suffer.) A number of individual works from this later period stand out: Emanuel Chabrier's four-hand quadrille *Souvenirs de Munich*, for instance, a wickedly funny send-up of themes from Wagner's *Tristan*, or two radically different versions of themes from Bizet's indestructible *Carmen*, Ferruccio Busoni's subtly wrought (Sixth) Sonatina *super Carmen* and Vladimir Horowitz's glittering concert-closer. In more recent years, concomitant with an increased interest in the byways of the Romantic era, some of the better fantasies have returned to the concert stage and show signs of again finding a place in the repertory.

*

D. Presser: 'Die Opernbearbeitung des 19. Jahrhunderts', *AMw*, xxxvi (1955), 228–38

C. Suttoni: *Piano and Opera: a Study of the Piano Fantasies Written on Opera Themes in the Romantic Era* (Ann Arbor, 1974)

——: Introductions to Franz Liszt: *Complete Piano Transcriptions from Wagner's Operas* and *Piano Transcriptions from French and Italian Operas* (New York, 1981–2)

S. Döhring: '*Réminiscences*: Liszts Konzeption der Klavierparaphrase', *Festschrift Heinz Becker* (Laaber, 1982), 131–51

H. Loos: 'Liszts Klavierübertragungen von Werken Richard Wagners', *Liszt Studien III: Eisenstadt 1983*, 103–18

CHARLES SUTTONI

Piave, Francesco Maria (*b* Murano, 18 May 1810; *d* Milan, 5 March 1876). Italian librettist. The son of a glass-maker, he studied for the church before obtaining employment as a proofreader. On the failure of his father's business he went to Rome, where he joined a literary circle that included the librettist Jacopo Ferretti, with whom he remained on close terms. He returned to his old position in Venice in 1838, and in 1842 wrote a libretto, *Don Marzio*, for Samuel Levi, but it was not performed. He also provided the third act of Pacini's *Il duca d'Alba*, which Giovanni Peruzzini had been prevented by illness from completing. The autograph survives, heavily corrected by the composer. Piave was recommended to Verdi by Count Mocenigo, and there began a long and successful collaboration from *Ernani* (1844) to *La forza del destino* (1862). Following a period as poet and stage director at La Fenice, Piave moved in 1859 to Milan, where on Verdi's recommendation he obtained the corresponding position at La Scala. On 5 December 1867, on the way to La Scala for a rehearsal, he suffered a stroke which deprived him of speech and movement; he lingered on for nine years in this condition, leaving unfinished a libretto (*Vico Bentivoglio*) for Ponchielli.

Verdi was initially unsure of Piave's abilities and always harried him unmercifully, often having his work revised by others; Piave rewarded him with doglike devotion, and the two remained on terms of sincere friendship. He was frequently summoned to Verdi's side, and they worked together on librettos. Both Verdi and his wife came generously to Piave's aid in his last years.

Throughout his career Piave wrote for many other composers, some well known like Pacini, but most of them insignificant. There is, however, a wide gulf between Piave's Verdian and non-Verdian librettos. Most of the latter are of poor quality and, with the possible exception of *Elisabetta di Valois* (Antonio Buzzolla, 1850; a precursor of *Don Carlos*) and the

extraordinary black comedy *Crispino e la comare* (Luigi and Federico Ricci, 1850), might almost have come from another hand: both dramatic tension and crispness of versification are absent. Verdi, however, used to give Piave explicit instructions on what he wanted, and often wrote out in prose the passages he needed to have versified. Piave had a wide vocabulary and a facile pen, and an uncanny ability for turning Verdi's drafts into verse with an economy of words that satisfied Verdi's insistence on brevity and provided him with the striking, illuminating expressions he sought. It was Piave's willingness to meet Verdi's detailed requirements which provided the basis of their work together, and it is on this partnership that his reputation as a librettist must rest.

mel – *melodramma*   tl – *tragedia lirica*

Il duca d'Alba (tl, Acts 1 and 2 by G. Peruzzini), G. Pacini, 1842; *Ernani* (dramma lirica), Verdi, 1844; *I due Foscari* (tl), Verdi, 1844; *Lorenzino de Medici* (tl), Pacini, 1845; *Estella di Murcia* (mel serio), F. Ricci, 1846 (G. Marcarini, 1856, as Estella); *Attila* (dramma lirico, Acts 1 and 2 by T. Solera), Verdi, 1846; *Tutti amanti* (libretto giocoso), C. Romani, 1847; *Griselda*, F. Ricci, 1847; *Macbeth* (with Maffei), Verdi, 1847; *Allan Cameron*, Pacini, 1848; *Il corsaro*, Verdi, 1848; *Giovanna di Fiandre* (mel), C. Boniforti, 1848; *La schiava saracena* (mel tragico), Mercadante, 1848; *Stiffelio*, Verdi, 1850 (rev. as Aroldo, 1857); *Crispino e la comare* (libretto fantastico-giocoso), L. and F. Ricci, 1850; *Elisabetta di Valois* (tl), Buzzolla, 1850 (Achille Galli, 1852, as Il duca di Foix), *Rigoletto* (mel), Verdi, 1851

La sposa di Murcia (mel), A. Casalini, 1851 (A. Agostini, 1864, as La vendetta); *La baschina*, F. De Liguoro, 1853; *La traviata*, Verdi, 1853; *La prigioniera*, C. Bosoni, 1853; *Pittore e duca*, Balfe, 1854; *Margherita di Borgogna* (mel), F. Petrocini, 1854; *I fidanzati*, A. Peri, 1856; *Simon Boccanegra*, Verdi, 1857; *Vittore Pisani* (mel), Peri, 1857; *Margherita la mendicante* (op semiseria), G. Braga, 1859; *La biscaglina*, S. Levi, 1860; *Guglielmo Shakspeare* (mel), Benvenuti, 1861; *Mormile*, Braga, 1862; *La forza del destino*, Verdi, 1862; *Rienzi*, Peri, 1862; *La duchessa di Guisa*, Serrao, 1865; *Rebecca*, B. Pisani, 1865; *Berta di Varnol*, Pacini, 1867; *Don Diego de Mendoza* (libretto fantastico), Pacini, 1867; *La tombola* (commedia lirica), Cagnoni, 1868; *Olema* (mel), C. Pedrotti, 1872

*

G. Pacini: *Le mie memorie artistiche* (Florence, 1875)

E. Checchi: 'Librettisti e libretti di Giuseppe Verdi', *Nuova antologia di lettere, scienze ed arti*, no.167 (1913), 529–40

L. Miragoli: *Il melodramma italiano nell'ottocento* (Rome, 1924)

D. Rosen and A. Porter, eds.: *Verdi's Macbeth* (Cambridge, 1984)

B. Cagli: '"Questo povero poeta esordiente": Piave a Roma: un carteggio con Ferretti, la genesi di Ernani', *Bollettino dell'Istituto di studi verdiani*, x (1987), 1–18

JOHN BLACK

Piazza, Antonio (*b* Venice, 1742; *d* Milan, 1825). Italian librettist. An imitator of Chiari (some of his *romanze* were, for marketing purposes, attributed by his publishers to Chiari), he was active at the Teatro S Samuele in Venice during the late 1770s. Later he was editor of the *Gazzetta urbana veneta* (1787–98). His shifting political allegiances after the fall of the Republic contributed to his ruin, and he died in poverty. He collaborated with the writer Giovanni Casanova in the polemic between French and Italian writers in his pamphlet *Discorso all' orecchio*. As a dramatist he was influenced by Goldoni; all his known librettos were set by second-rank composers.

L'amor casalingo, Venice, 1776; *L'amor ramingo*, Salari, 1777; *La prepotenza delusa* (dg), G. Cavi, 1777; *L'isola della luna* (dg), Giovanni Valentini, 1780; *L'impresario in rovina* (dg), ?Fabrizi, 1797; *Il secreto*, Vienna, 1817

PATRICIA LEWY GIDWITZ

Piazzola sul Brenta. Italian town near Padua, on the River Brenta. It is dominated by the Villa Contarini, refurbished in the 1660s and 70s by Marco Contarini.

Two theatres were constructed, neither of which exists today. The larger, accommodating 1000 spectators, was intended for occasional festive productions of commissioned operas during the Venetian November *villeggiatura*, and its inaugural production was Carlo Pallavicino's *Le amazzoni nell'isole fortunate* (11 November 1679). This and Domenico Freschi's *Berenice vendicativa* (8 November 1680) follow contemporary Venetian models, providing opportunities for large casts, lavish scenic displays and imaginative instrumentation.

Contarini also established an orphanage ('Luoco delle Vergini') accommodating about 30 girls, whose musical talents were partly fostered in a smaller, 400-seat theatre. Between 1680 and 1686 at least eight operas were staged there, four of which were probably by Freschi. Piccioli was a favoured librettist. The town became a centre for selected members of the local and Venetian nobility, and also attracted visitors from abroad. Opera performances ceased after Contarini's death in 1689, but his collection of scores remained in the library of the villa until 1843 (now in *I-Vnm*).

*

C. Ivanovich: *Minerva al tavolino* (Venice, 1681, 2/1688)

F. M. Piccioli: *L'orologio del piacere* (Piazzola, 1685)

T. Wiel: *I codici musicali contariniani del secolo XVII nella R. Biblioteca di San Marco* (Venice, 1888)

P. Camerini: *Piazzola* (Padua, 1902)   ROBIN WALTON

Piccaluga, Nino (Filippo) (*b* Pavia, 9 June 1890; *d* Milan, 3 Feb 1973). Italian tenor. He made his début in Novara, and in 1919 made a strongly favourable impression on the composer Zandonai, whose Paolo il Bello (*Francesca da Rimini*) he sang in Parma, and who was influential in furthering his career. This was also the year of his marriage to the soprano Augusta Concato (1895–1964). They sang together in the première of Alfano's *La leggenda di Sakùntala* (1921) under Serafin in Bologna and were engaged for La Scala by Toscanini, scoring a notable success there in *Il tabarro*. During the 1920s Piccaluga sang heroic parts throughout Italy. Abroad he was heard widely in South America and toured North America with the Columbia Grand Opera Company in 1930. He sang with the Italian Opera in the Netherlands in 1931 and made some of his last appearances at the S Carlo, Naples, in 1935. His early retirement was due partly to ill-health interacting with vocal problems. His recordings show an ardent style and an ample, though imperfectly focussed, voice.

J. B. STEANE

Piccaver [Peckover], Alfred (*b* Long Sutton, Lincs., 24 Feb 1884; *d* Vienna, 23 Sept 1958). English tenor. He was brought up in New York, where he studied at the Metropolitan School. In 1907 he went to Europe and was engaged for the Prague Opera, where he made his début as Romeo. He continued his studies with Rosario in Milan and Prohaska-Neumann in Prague. In 1910 he joined the Vienna Hofoper, remaining a favourite there until his retirement in 1937. He sang in the first Austrian performances of *La fanciulla del West* and *Il tabarro*. His repertory included Andrea Chénier, Radames, Lohengrin, Walther, Faust, Des Grieux, Don José, Canio, Werther, Florestan and Lensky. He sang with the Chicago Opera from 1923 to 1925 and at Covent Garden in 1924. Piccaver had a large, robust voice and was often compared to Caruso.   HAROLD ROSENTHAL/R

Picchi, Mirto (*b* San Mauro, nr Florence, 15 March 1915; *d* Florence, 25 Sept 1980). Italian tenor. He studied in Florence with Giuseppe Armani and Giulia Tess. He made his début as Radames in the season organized by La Scala at the Milan Palazzo dello Sport in 1946. At first he sang Verdi and Puccini roles in Italy and abroad, with appearances at the Cambridge Theatre, London (1947–8), as the Duke, Rodolfo and Cavaradossi and at the 1949 Edinburgh Festival with the Glyndebourne Company as Riccardo (*Ballo*). In 1952 he sang Pollione at Covent Garden at Callas's London début. From the early 1950s he specialized in contemporary music, creating roles in Castro's *Proserpina y el extranjero* (1952, La Scala), Pizzetti's *Cagliostro* (1953, La Scala) and *La figlia di Iorio* (1954, Naples) and Testi's *La celestina* (1963, Florence), and taking part in the Italian première of *War and Peace* (1953, Florence). He sang Peter Grimes and Captain Vere, and his large repertory included the Drum Major (*Wozzeck*), Tom Rakewell, Tiresias (*The Bassarids*) and Stravinsky's Oedipus. His last appearance was as Don Basilio at La Scala in 1974. Picchi was a highly gifted singer-actor.

HAROLD ROSENTHAL/R

Piccinni. Italian, later French, family of composers.

(1) (Vito) Niccolò [Nicola] (Marcello Antonio Giacomo) Piccinni [Piccini] (*b* Bari, 16 Jan 1728; *d* Passy, nr Paris, 7 May 1800). He was one of the central figures in Italian and French opera in the second half of the 18th century.

1. LIFE. Although his father was a musician and his mother the sister of the composer Latilla, he was destined originally for the church. His precocious musical talent, however, would not be suppressed. Most of the information about his early years comes from La Borde (1780). This, the first substantial notice, was incorporated in Ginguené's memorial biography (1801); Ginguené claimed to have written the notice for La Borde, in which case it originated from a person close to Piccinni at a time when he could have consulted his subject directly, a possibility strengthened by the precision of some of its details. Thus Piccinni is said to have entered the S Onofrio conservatory in Naples in May 1742 and to have studied there until 1754, under Leo (*d* 1744), and then under Durante, who had a special affection for him. Prota-Giurleo has published documents (1954) that throw doubt on this by indicating that Piccinni became a resident of Naples only in 1753. But Piccinni himself called Durante his teacher in a letter published in Alessandro Manfredi's translation of Fux's *Gradus ad Parnassum* (Carpi, 1761). Further, Villarosa (*RosaM*, 1840), using manuscript material left by Giuseppe Sigismondo, wrote that Piccinni was so devoted to his old conservatory that after leaving it he visited it frequently and even acted with some of his old companions in carnival time, as he did in Sigismondo's *I figliastri*.

In 1754 Piccinni embarked on a career of almost exclusively operatic composition. Beginning with comic works, as was the custom, he quickly gained a following in Naples, where the public had formerly been devoted to the *opere buffe* of Logroscino. It was the first of several competitive situations that were later to overshadow the career of this amiable and generous man. The extent of his early success and recognition of his promise are reflected in his soon being invited to compose an *opera seria*, his first, for the Teatro S Carlo.

This work, *Zenobia* (1756), was also a success and was followed by others, so that in the next few years his output was balanced almost evenly between the serious and comic genres. In 1756 he married one of his singing pupils, the 14-year-old Vincenza Sibilla, who sang his music exquisitely in private but never appeared on the stage. The extent of Piccinni's labours in Italy, his resistance to Burney's inducements to visit England, and his subsequent reluctant move to Paris, were dictated by his desire to obtain the best conditions possible to support seven children (two more died in infancy).

The rapid growth of Piccinni's reputation is indicated by the commission from Rome in 1758 for *Alessandro nelle Indie*. His second Rome opera, *La buona figliuola* (1760), created a furore and began a period in which he remained the undisputed favourite of the reputedly fickle Roman public. Goldoni's rather crude adaptation of Richardson's *Pamela* had already been set by Duni in 1756, with scant success. The charm and vitality of Piccinni's music, which according to Ginguené was composed in only 18 days, conquered Europe; it also won the approval of Jommelli: 'Questo è inventore'. Piccinni produced new works in Rome at every Carnival up to 1773 except that of 1767. His fertility became legendary in a period when prolific operatic composition was by no means unusual. Burney reported Sacchini's assertion that Piccinni had written 300 operas. More sober commentators, like La Borde (or Ginguené), gave a figure of 130 that is not much exaggerated. Piccinni remained in Naples, where Burney met him in 1770 and called him 'a lively agreeable little man, rather grave for an Italian so full of fire and genius'. He was second *maestro di cappella* under Manna at Naples Cathedral, taught singing, and on 16 February 1771 was appointed second organist of the royal chapel. Yet from 1758 to 1773 he produced over 30 operas in Naples, over 20 in Rome and others in all the main Italian cities. This period represents the first peak in his achievement.

Piccinni's position in Rome was suddenly undermined by a craze, which began in 1773, for Anfossi, an inferior composer who, although a year Piccinni's senior, had been his pupil in Naples and at first his protégé in Rome. Piccinni's fall was sudden and cruel; a cabal hissed his last Rome opera and he returned to Naples and fell seriously ill. The date of this event is somewhat in doubt. Ginguené placed it in 1775, but Piccinni did not visit Rome in either 1774 or 1775 (1775 was a jubilee year and the theatres were closed). He did go in Carnival 1776, when his *La capricciosa* (also known as *L'incostante*) followed Anfossi's *La vera costanza* at the Teatro delle Dame, and that seems the most likely occasion for his defeat. However, he maintained his reputation in Naples with a second *Alessandro nelle Indie* and the successful comedy *I viaggiatori*, and by 1776 a superficially more alluring prospect had already arisen in Paris. In 1774 the Neapolitan ambassador there, Caraccioli, had commended Piccinni to the court, and negotiations began. A delay was imposed by the death of Louis XV, but in 1776, with the promise of an annual 'gratification', revenue from his operas and employment by the court and nobility, Piccinni left Naples (16 November). He reached Paris on the last day of the year, suffering cruelly from the cold, knowing no French and with little idea of what was in store. In the subsequent squabbles of the 'Gluckistes' and the 'Piccinnistes' he almost alone emerged with dignity and credit; his ability to adapt to the needs of the French stage, a far greater

adjustment than Gluck had had to make, demonstrates both courage and versatility.

The italophile party was large and influential, and Piccinni soon found friends. Marmontel undertook to adapt the librettos of Quinault and reconcile them to a modern, italianate musical idiom. He had also to coach Piccinni daily in French; if his account is to be trusted, he may be considered as much an accessory to Piccinni's music as Calzabigi was to Gluck's. In 1777 Gluck, who claimed to have discarded his *Roland* on hearing that Piccinni was at work on one, produced *Armide*. Battle was joined over La Harpe's review of it, the performance in Paris of Sacchini's *Olympiade* and Marmontel's polemical *Essai*. Isolated at the centre of controversy, Piccinni became depressed, and expected failure; but *Roland*, performed early in 1778, won both respect and affection from the public. Among the cast even the devout Gluckiste Larrivée was won over and performed the title role magnificently.

In 1778–9 Piccinni was engaged to direct a troupe of Italians, giving performances of *opere buffe* at the Académie Royale. The repertory included works by Anfossi, Paisiello, Sacchini and Traetta, as well as Piccinni himself (*Le finte gemelle*, *La sposa collerica*, *La buona figliuola*, *La buona figliuola maritata*, *Il vago disprezzato*). *La buona figliuola* was also known in Paris as *La bonne fille* (Comédie-Italienne, 1771). Later in his Paris sojourn Piccinni was in charge of singing instruction at the Ecole Royale de Musique et de Déclamation, and he undertook private teaching, including well-paid visits to the country home of La Borde, where he seems to have composed *Didon*. He was evidently used unscrupulously by the court, however, and although from 1783 he was granted a pension, the chief promise of Paris – that he would be better off while writing fewer operas – was hardly fulfilled. He also suffered from the chicanery of the Opéra management. He was promised that his *Iphigénie en Tauride* would be staged before Gluck's; in the event it came two years later and was preceded by the composer's nervous disclaimer of any intention to rival Gluck (*Journal de Paris*, 22 January 1781). Nevertheless it survived the problems of a poor libretto (Dubreuil resisted Ginguené's attempts to improve it) and the drunkenness of Mlle Laguerre at the second performance. Only when juxtaposed with a revival of Gluck's work was its undoubted inferiority to that masterpiece demonstrated, albeit crudely, by lower receipts. It was favourably received when revived in 1785. In 1783 Piccinni reached his second peak with a highly successful revival of *Atys* and the introduction of *Didon*, which momentarily eclipsed the rising star of Sacchini. The triumph of *Didon* was partly due to the magnificent performance of St Huberty in the title role; without her at rehearsal it had seemed doomed to failure. Piccinni followed it with two charming and successful comic operas, of which *Le faux lord* would stand revival as well as any of his works.

In 1784 the rival attraction of Sacchini became serious, and Salieri's *Les Danaïdes* diverted attention further from Piccinni. He was no longer a novelty; not only did the dramatically weak *Diane et Endymion* fail to please but he suffered a quite unmerited failure with *Pénélope* in 1785 (it was revived briefly in 1787). A projected revival of *Adèle de Ponthieu*, an inept work which Piccinni had nevertheless revised, came to nothing (1786), and two further tragic operas were never performed, although *Clytemnestre* was rehearsed in 1789. Saddened rather than embittered, Piccinni remained generous; he spoke at Sacchini's funeral and proposed an annual concert in memory of Gluck. With the Revolution and the withdrawal of his pension, his position became precarious, and in 1791 he left for Naples, where he was warmly welcomed. In 1792 his daughter indiscreetly married a Frenchman of Jacobin leanings. Deemed guilty by association in the tense and reactionary atmosphere of Naples in those years, Piccinni, on returning from Venice where he had staged two new works, was quite unjustifiably placed under house arrest in 1794. He remained there in indigence and misery for four years, composing psalms, until political changes enabled him to return to France; his family followed as soon as they could. Financially he fared little better; his pension was only partly restored and he was forced to appeal to Bonaparte. By the time he was granted the post of sixth inspector at the Conservatoire he was too ill to benefit from it.

2. WORKS. It has become customary to describe Piccinni in his Italian operas as a composer whose vein was primarily 'the tender, the intimate, the sad and the higher comic', in the words of Abert, who considered him to have been 'made of far finer and more delicate stuff than most of his predecessors and contemporaries'. The same attitude was sometimes expressed at the time; J. A. Hiller wrote (1768) that Piccinni's forte was 'the naive and the tender'. The sentimental role of Cecchina in his most famous opera, La buona figliuola, encouraged this view. Contemporary manuscript collections of his arias often show a preference for pieces of this sort, and there seems to be a higher proportion of them in his operas than in most others of the time. While his contemporaries had a special affection for this aspect of his work and prized the elegance and grace of his style in general, most of them also stressed its vigour and variety. Burney called him 'among the most fertile, spirited and original' composers then working, while La Borde (or Ginguené) distinguished in his music 'a vigour, a variety, and especially a new grace, a brilliant and animated style'. Piccinni's style in his Italian operas is in fact a rather complex one in the number and variety of its elements and the sources on which it drew. Its originality, also mentioned by most writers of the time, should probably be seen in the way it brought together, balanced and played off against each other elements of simplicity and complexity in vocal lines, accompanying textures and the relationship between the two. The style (if not the form) of many of Piccinni's pieces from the 1750s would not have seemed out of date even in the 1780s. This is most remarkable in the harmonic layout, the way in which accompaniment motifs are used to clarify and articulate it, and the textures that they resulted in; all were to remain typical of the Classical style.

Piccinni's gifts included his dramatic imagination and his ability to adapt his music to the situation at hand. While La buona figliuola is a masterpiece of sentimental comedy, his intermezzo La canterina (1760) is noteworthy for its straightforward comic vigour, particularly in comparison with Haydn's setting of the same text. His French operas, while retaining many italianate characteristics, nevertheless include colourful orchestration, harmonic diversity and an occasional terseness of style that reflect the practices of his adopted country. Although Anfossi's setting of L'incognita perseguitata (1773) contains numbers that are more immediately beautiful than anything in Piccinni's setting

of 1764 (the heroine Giannetta's aria 'Come figlia ubbidiente' is a case in point), Piccinni avoided the saccharine quality of Anfossi's music by using a wide variety of aria forms and types, and by occasionally introducing rather short arias to punctuate the action. Anfossi's characters are more obviously differentiated than Piccinni's; but Anfossi's attempt to distinguish between them results in rigid stereotypes, whereas Piccinni's characters display much greater flexibility.

Piccinni's music grew over the years in fineness of detail and elegance of craftsmanship, if sometimes falling into the perfunctory. That can be seen in his accompanying techniques, which, starting from the standard mid-century texture in which the first violins doubled the vocal line, developed increasing brilliance of orchestral sound and independence and subtlety of interplay between voice and orchestra. The variety of Piccinni's style found freest play in comic opera, which made rapid shifts of dramatic tone (the sentimental, the mock serious or heroic, the farcical) a basic part of its manner. These were reflected in a tendency to sectionalism in the music, marked by changes of metre, tempo and expressive character. The comic arias fall into many formal patterns, of which the most frequent consists of two complete statements of the whole text in a binary tonal scheme. Piccinni is traditionally said to have introduced the musically and dramatically expansive multi-sectional finale – already found in the operas of Galuppi and other northern composers – into Neapolitan comic opera. His earliest use of it is in his first Roman comic opera, La buona figliuola, and he is said to have brought it to Naples in La furba burlata (1760), which is lost. Kretzschmar identified Piccinni with what he called the 'rondo-finale', by which he meant not the return of whole sections within the finale (a technique Piccinni was also to use, but which was certainly known before him), but a departure from and return to significant material within a section, linked to characters or dramatic relationships. The layout of the text in some surviving librettos of earlier Neapolitan operas suggests, however, that something of the sort may have been done earlier. In practice his finales, like his comic arias, took many forms.

Although his comic operas have received more attention, Piccinni was also a central figure in opera seria, and most of his works in that genre have some remarkable numbers. In the first of them, for example, Zenobia (1756), the aria 'Ch'io parta?' begins like an accompanied recitative (and away from the tonic of the key) and retains a fluid, declamatory character, although the form remains that of the da capo aria. The duet 'Va, ti consola' does not, as usually happens, have the second singer enter by repeating the first's solo with different words; rather, he makes a strong expressive contrast, changing to the minor, a favourite device of Piccinni's. In the form of his opera seria arias Piccinni mostly followed the general trends of the time. In the earliest ones the full da capo predominates, giving way in the course of the 1760s to the dal segno form. In the last to be written before his move to Paris the dal segno form was replaced by one close to that of sonata form. A few cavatinas appear (arias of one stanza set like the first part of a da capo), and in the 1770s he was also using a somewhat related, but more expansive form (not called cavatina) in which not just one stanza but the complete poem of two stanzas is set straight through and then repeated in a binary tonal layout (a form perhaps taken over from the comic opera).

In his French operas Piccinni used a wide variety of aria forms, including arias in several movements (Dido, 'Vaines frayeurs') and with contrasting middle sections (Sangaride, 'Malheureuse, hélas', Atys). He also used arioso, and open-ended and incomplete forms. His melodies were much admired, but he was inferior to Sacchini as a lyricist and his line lacks the tautness of Gluck's; too often his cantabile arias seem emotionally uncommitted. Often more effective are arias of that Neapolitan type which, over a motivic continuum, builds a melodic line of short, declamatory phrases (Roland, 'Je me reconnais'; Orestes, 'Cruel et tu dis que tu m'aimes', Iphigénie; Diana, 'Cesse d'agiter mon âme', which Grimm called 'the finest aria M. Piccinni has produced in France'). Piccinni's own ideas on proper aria composition are given by Ginguené and are reflected in the writings of N. E. Framery.

In his Italian works Piccinni was already unusually lavish in his orchestration; in France, where a fuller orchestra was normal, he scored more elaborately still and – the opinions of admirers such as Marmontel notwithstanding – more heavily than Gluck. His sweet, conjunct melodic line is liable to seem insipid in this rich costume, while his recitatives, especially those of Orestes, tend to a self-defeating vehemence in the orchestra, unsupported by harmonic invention. While it is generally true that in Piccinni's French recitatives the orchestral interjections reflect the sense of the words, the effect is often weakened by a rather too regular rhythm of alternation between voice and orchestra and by a certain predictability in the orchestral figures. Piccinni's alternation between short chords and long notes played simultaneously with the voice is often quite dramatic, however, and his occasional use of tremolo accompaniments is effective.

As well as flexible forms and the insertion of ariosos in recitatives, the French heritage in the use of chorus and ballet makes his operas the natural outcome of Encyclopédiste principles, embodied particularly in Marmontel's Essai: Italian music shorn of its unreasonable excesses, and French forms. In Roland the blend is still uncomfortable. The arias and duets are too long for their contexts; but the best recitatives and ariosos, and a few arias, lend the title role, at least, great dramatic force. The monologue 'O nuit, favorisez mes désirs amoureux' and the subsequent mad scene, in which Piccinni boldly juxtaposed a chord of C major, a dominant ending to an 'open-ended' F minor Allegro, with a Grave in Eb minor, were immediately admired and remain impressive even beside Lully's noble setting. In Atys Piccinni achieved a more integrated style, which set the pattern for French opera in the next decade. There are perhaps too many arias (seven for Atys alone), but the interest is better distributed among the roles, as it is in Iphigénie. In Atys Piccinni rose particularly well to the most French features, such as the dream-sequence of song, chorus and dance, and the choral lament at the death of Sangaride. He was able, however, to include without incongruity an italianate quartet, in C minor, some 200 bars long; this forms the dramatic crux. Although his contemporaries favoured Didon, Atys and Pénélope are its equals, and Act 1 of Pénélope is perhaps the finest fruit of Piccinni's collaboration with Marmontel.

Piccinni's French operas are not, as has been suggested, an attempt to oppose Gluck's 'reforms' with the methods of Italian opera seria. The 'rivalry' is over different musical styles; in dramatic organization both composers represent various possibilities of synthesis between a modern musical language and the traditional French forms. Piccinni was doubtless indebted to Gluck, and his French operas are at least as dramatically engaged as Gluck's. There is, however, more emphasis on musical colour and musical expansion for its own sake. Gluck, belonging to an older generation and inimitable through the very qualities for which he is now most admired, had no very substantial following, although aspects of his works, particularly Alceste and the Iphigénie operas, contributed to the genre one may term 'Piccinniste opera'. When Piccinni went to France Italian music was already familiar in concert programmes, and had influenced the establishment of a sophisticated opéra comique to which, with his skill in handling ensembles and his ability, under-used in the serious operas, to write succinct lyrical numbers, Piccinni contributed as to the manner born. At the Opéra he succeeded where the Frenchman Philidor had not in establishing this synthesis of France and Italy by using the lingua franca of the day in the main national theatre. Thereafter French and German composers increasingly adopted an italianate style. Piccinni prepared the way for Sacchini and ultimately for Spontini, who with his omnipresent lyricism, rich orchestration and dramatic vehemence, is more exactly a Piccinnist than a Gluckist.

See also Atys (ii); Buona figliuola, la; Buona figliuola maritata, la; Catone in utica (iii); Didon (ii); Ercole al termedonte; Iphigénie en tauride (ii); and Roland (ii).

NC – *Naples, Teatro di S Carlo*   NFI – *Naples, Teatro dei Fiorentini*
NN – *Naples, Teatro Nuovo*   PO – *Paris, Opéra*
RA – *Rome, Teatro Argentina*   RC – *Rome, Teatro Capranica*
RV – *Rome, Teatro Valle*

Le donne dispettose (ob, A. Palomba), NFI, aut. 1754; also as Le trame per amore; La massara spiritosa [not La marchesa spiritosa]
Il curioso del suo proprio danno (ob, 3, Palomba, after M. de Cervantes: *Don Quixote*), NN, carn. ?1755–6, *I-Nc*; rev., with A. Sacchini, as Il curioso imprudente, NFI, aut. 1761
Le gelosie (ob, G. Lorenzi), NFI, spr. 1755; also as Le gelosie, o Le nozze in confusione; *Nc* [mistitled La sponsale di D. Pomponio]
Zenobia (os, P. Metastasio), NC, 18 Dec 1756, *Nc*, *P-La*
Nitteti (os, Metastasio), NC, 4 Nov 1757, *La*
L'amante ridicolo (int, 2, Pioli), NN, 1757, *D-MÜs, Hs*; also as L'amante ridicolo deluso, *GB-Lbl* (Act 1) [mistitled Il servo padrone], *P-La*; L'amante deluso, *I-Gl*; L'amante ridicolo e deluso, *S-Uu*
La schiava seria (int), Naples, 1757, *D-Bds, Dlb, F-Pn, I-Nc* (? autograph); also as Die Sklavinn, *A-Wn*
Caio Mario (os, G. Roccaforte), NC, ?1757, *I-Nc*, *P-La*
Alessandro nelle Indie [1st version] (os, Metastasio), RA, 21 Jan 1758, *GB-Cfm, Lbl, P-La*; also as Alessandro e Poro, *D-ROu*
Madama Arrighetta (ob, 3, Palomba, after Goldoni: *Monsieur Petiton*), NN, aut. or wint. 1758; also as Petiton (int), *I-Nc*; Monsieur Petiton, *P-La* (Act 1)
La scaltra letterata (ob, 3, Palomba), NN, wint. 1758; *I-Nc*, *P-La*; also as La scaltra spiritosa
Gli uccellatori (ob, ? after C. Goldoni), Naples or Venice, 1758
Ciro riconosciuto (os, Metastasio), NC, Nov or 26 Dec 1759, *I-Nc*, *P-La*
Siroe re di Persia (os, Metastasio), Naples, 1759
La buona figliuola [La Cecchina] (dg, 3, Goldoni), Rome, Dame, 6 Feb 1760, *A-KR, Wn, B-Bc, CH-Zz, D-Dlb, MÜs, Rtt* (in Ger.), *F-Pn, Po, I-Fc* (R1983: IOB, lxxx), *Gl, Mc, MOe, Nc, Rdp, Rsc, P-La, US-Wc*; vs, ed. G. Benvenuti (Milan, 1942); also as La buona figliuola; Cecchina zitella, o La buona figliuola; La buona figliola zitella; La buona figliuola puta; La baronessa riconosciuta; Cecchina nubile, o La buona figliuola; Das gute Mädchen; The Accomplish'd Maid; Der fromme Pige; La bonne fille
L'Origille (ob, 3, Palomba), NFI, spr. 1760, *I-Nc*, *P-La*
La canterina (int), NFI, spr. 1760, *I-Nc, P-La*; perf. with L'Origille
La furba burlata (ob, 3, ?P. di Napoli, after Palomba), NFI, aut. 1760, collab. N. Logroscino; NN, sum. 1762, addns by G. Insanguine; also as I furbi burlati, *F-Pn, I-Nc*

Il re pastore (os, Metastasio), Florence, Pergola, aut. 1760, *Nc**, *P-La*

Le beffe giovevoli (ob, ? after Goldoni), NFI, wint. 1760, aria *I-Nc*

Le vicende della sorte (int, 3, G. Petrosellini, after Goldoni: *I portentosi effetti della madre natura*), RV, 3 Jan 1761, *D-Bds*, *Dlb* (pt.2), *I-Gl*, *Mc*, *Nc**; also as Le vicende del caso ossia della sorte; Der Gluecksweschsel

Olimpiade [1st version] (os, Metastasio), Rome, Dame, carn. 1761, *Nc**

La schiavitù per amore (int), RC, carn. 1761

Tigrane (os, 3, ?after Goldoni's rev. of F. Silvani), Turin, Regio, carn. 1761, *CMc*, *Nc**, *P-La*; also as Farnaspe, *La*

Demofoonte (os, Metastasio), Reggio Emilia, Pubblico, Fiera (May) 1761, *I-Nc**, *P-La*

La buona figliuola maritata (ob, 3, Goldoni), Bologna, Formagliari, May 1761, *A-Wn*, *D-Dlb*, *Mbs*, *F-Pn*, *Po*, *I-Fc*, *MOe*, *Nc*, *P-La*; also as La baronessa riconosciuta e maritata; La Cecchina maritata; La buona moglie

Lo stravagante (ob, 3, A. Villani), NFI, aut. 1761

L'astuto balordo (ob, ?G. B. Fagiuoli), NFI, wint. 1761, *La*; addns by Insanguine

L'astrologa (ob, 3, P. Chiari), Venice, S Moisè, carn. 1761–2, *D-Dlb*, *Rtt*, *F-Pn*, *P-La*

Le avventure di Ridolfo (int), Bologna, Marsigli-Rossi, carn. 1762

Artaserse (os, Metastasio), RA, 3 Feb 1762; *D-Hs*, *Mbs*, *F-Pn*, *I-Fc*, *Nc**, *P-La*, *US-Wc*; rev. Naples, 1772, *I-Nc*

La bella verità (ob, 3, Goldoni), Bologna, Marsigli-Rossi, 12 June 1762, *Nc**

Antigono (os, Metastasio), NC, 4 Nov 1762, *Nc**, *P-La*; rev. RA, carn. 1771

Il cavalier parigino (ob, Palomba), NN, wint. 1762, ? collab. Sacchini

Il cavaliere per amore (ob, 2, Petrosellini), NN, wint. 1762, or RV, carn. 1763, *A-Wn*, *D-Dlb*, *I-Nc**, *Rc*, *Tf*, *P-La* (pt.1); also as Il fumo villano

Amor senza malizia (ob), Nuremberg, Thurn und Taxis, 1762

Le donne vendicate (int, 3, after Goldoni), RV, carn. 1763, *A-Wn*, *D-Dlb*, *F-Pn* (2 copies), *Po*, *I-Gl*, *Nc**, *US-Bp*, *Wc*; also as Il vago disprezzato [Le fat méprisé]

Le contadine bizzarre (ob, 3, Petrosellini), RC, Feb 1763, or Venice, S Samuele, aut. 1763, *A-Wn*, *D-Dlb*, *DS*, *F-Pn*, *I-Fc*, *Nc*, *Rdp*, *P-La** [some MSS ? of 1774 setting]; rev. as La contadina bizzarra, Naples, 1774, *I-Nc**; also as La sciocchezza in amore; Le contadine astute; Le villanelle astute

Gli stravaganti, ossia La schiava riconosciuta (int, 2), RV, 1 Jan 1764, *D-Bds*, *F-Pn*, *GB-Lbl*, *H-Bn* [with addns by Haydn], *I-Nc**, *P-La*; also as La schiava, *A-Wn*, *I-Nc*; Gli stravaganti, ossia I matrimoni alla moda; L'esclave, ou Le marin généreux; Die Ausschweifenden

La villeggiatura (ob, 3, ? after Goldoni), Bologna, Formagliari, carn. 1764, quartet *Gl*; ? rev. of Le donne vendicate, 1763

Il parrucchiere (int), RV, carn. 1764, *Gl*

L'incognita perseguitata (ob, 3, Petrosellini), Venice, S Samuele, carn. 1764, *A-Wn*, *D-Dlb*, *H-Bn* [with addns by Haydn], *I-Gl*, *P-La*

L'equivoco (ob, 3, L. Lantino [A. Villani]), NFI, sum. 1764, *La* (Act 3)

La donna vana (ob, 3, Palomba), NF, Nov 1764, *GB-Lbl*, *I-Mc*, *P-La*

Il nuovo Orlando (ob, after L. Ariosto), Modena, Rangoni, 26 Dec 1764

Il barone di Torreforte (int, 2), RC, 10 Jan 1765, *B-Bc* (Act 2), *Br*, *D-Dlb*, *I-Fc*, *Gl*, *MOe*, *Nc**, *Rdp*, *Tf*, *P-La*

Il finto astrologo (int., ? after Goldoni), RV, 7 Feb or wint. 1765, aria *I-MAc*

L'orfana insidiata (ob), NFI, sum. 1765, addns by G. Astarita

La pescatrice, ovvero L'erede riconosciuta (int, 2, ? after Goldoni), RC, 9 Jan 1766, *A-Wn*, *D-B* (in Ger.), *Dlb*, *DS*, *Rtt*, *F-Pn*, *H-Bn*, *I-Fc*, *Gl*, *Nc**, *P-La*, *US-Bp*, *Wc*; also as L'erede riconosciuta; La pescatrice innocente

La baronessa di Montecupo (int), RC, 27 Jan 1766

L'incostante (int, 2, Palomba), RC, Feb 1766, *I-Gl*, *Nc*, *Rdp*, *P-La* (pt.1); also as Il volubile, *D-Dlb*, *I-Nc**

La fiammetta generosa [Act 1] (ob), NFI, carn. 1766 [Acts 2 and 3 by Anfossi]

La molinarella (ob, 3), NN, aut. 1766, *F-Pn*, *I-Nc**, also as Il cavaliere Ergasto; La molinara

Il gran Cid (os, G. Pizzi), NC, 4 Nov 1766, *D-Wa*, *I-Nc**, *P-La*, *US-Wc*; also as Il Cid

La francese maligna, Naples, 1766–7, or Rome, 1769

La notte critica (ob, 3, Goldoni), Lisbon, Salvaterra, carn. 1767, *I-Nc*, *P-La*; also as Die Nacht, *D-Bds*

La finta baronessa (ob, F. Livigni), NFI, sum. 1767, *I-Nc**

La direttrice prudente (ob, 3), NFI, aut. 1767; also as La prudente ingegnosa, aria *Nc*

Mazzina, Acetone e Dindimento (ob), ?Naples, ?c1767

Olimpiade [2nd version] (os, Metastasio), Rome, 1768, *Nc**, *Rvat*, *P-La*; rev. Naples, 1774, *I-Nc*, *Rdp*, *Rsc*

Li napoletani in America (ob, 3, F. Cerlone), NF, 10 June 1768, *B-Bc*, *F-Pn*

La locandiera di spirito (ob, 3), NN, aut. 1768, *I-Nc*

Lo sposo burlato (int, 2, G. B. Casti), RV, 3 Jan 1769, *A-Wn*, *D-Dlb*, *F-Pc*, *I-Fn*, *Gl*, *Nc**, *Rdp*, *US-Bp*

L'innocenza riconosciuta (ob), Senigallia, 11 Jan 1769

La finta ciarlatana, ossia Il vecchio credulo (ob), NN, carn. 1769

Demetrio (os, Metastasio), NC, 30 May 1769, *I-Nc**, *P-La*

Gli sposi perseguitati (ob, 3, P. Mililotti), NN, 1769, *I-Nc**, *P-La*, *US-Wc*

Didone abbandonata (os, Metastasio), RA, 8 Jan 1770, *I-Nc**, *Rvat*, *P-La*, *US-Wc*; also as La Didone, *I-Mc*

Cesare in Egitto (os, G. F. Bussani), Milan, Ducale, Jan 1770, *F-Pn*, *I-Nc**; also as Cesare e Cleopatra, *P-La*

La donna di spirito (ob), RC, 13 Feb 1770, *F-Pn*

Il regno della luna (ob, not by Goldoni), Milan, Ducale, spr. 1770, *D-Dlb*; also as Il mondo della luna, *I-Nc*

Gelosia per gelosia (ob, G. B. Lorenzi), NFI, sum. 1770, *Nc**

L'olandese in Italia (ob, N. Tassi), Milan, Ducale, aut. 1770

Catone in Utica (dm, 3, Metastasio), Mannheim, Hof, 5 Nov 1770, *D-Mbs**, *Rp*, *GB-Lbl* (R1982: IOB, I), *I-Nc*

Don Chisciotte (ob, Lorenzi, after Cervantes), ? Naples, 1770

Il finto pazzo per amore (ob), ? Naples, 1770

Le finte gemelle (int, 2 or 3, Petrosellini), RV, 2 Jan 1771, *A-Wn*, *D-Dlb*, *F-Pn*, *Po*, *GB-Er*, *I-Bc*, *Bsf* (pt.1), *Fc*, *Nc**, *Tf*, *Vc*; also as Le due finte gemelle; Le germane in equivoco

La donna di bell'umore (ob), NFI, 15 May 1771, *Nc**

La Corsara (ob, 3, Lorenzi), NFI, aut. 1771, *Nc**, *US-Wc*

L'americano (int, 2), RC, 22 Feb 1772, *A-Wn*, *D-Dlb*, *Rtt*, *F-Pn*, *H-Bn*, *I-Fc*; also as L'americano incivilito; L'americano ingentilito

L'astratto, ovvero Il giocator fortunato (ob, 3, Petrosellini), Venice, S Samuele, carn. 1772, *A-Wn*, *D-Dlb*, *F-Pn*; *H-Bn* [with addns by Haydn]; also as Il giocator fanatico per il lotto

Gli amanti dispersi (farsa in prosa and int), NFI, spr. 1772

Le trame zingaresche (ob, Lorenzi), NFI, sum. 1772, *I-Nc**

Ipermestra (os, Metastasio), NC, 4 Nov 1772, *Nc**

Scipione in Cartagena (os, A. Giusti), Modena, Corte, ?26 Dec 1772

La sposa collerica (int), RV, 9 Jan 1773, *D-Dlb*, *F-Po*, *I-Nc**

Il vagabondo fortunato (ob, 3, Mililotti), NF, aut. 1773

Le quattro nazioni, o La vedova scaltra (ob, after Goldoni's spoken comedy), ? Rome, 1773

Alessandro nelle Indie [2nd version] (os, 3, Metastasio), NC, 12 Jan 1774, *Nc**, *P-La*

Gli amanti mascherati (ob), NFI, 1774, *I-Nc**

L'ignorante astuto (ob, 3, Mililotti), NFI, carn. 1775, *US-Wc*

Enea in Cuma (parody, Mililotti), NFI, ?spr. 1775, *A-Wn*, *H-Bn*, *I-Nc**

I viaggiatori (ob, Mililotti, ? after Goldoni), NFI, aut. 1775, *Nc*

Il sordo (int), Naples, 1775, *Nc**

La contessina (ob, 3, Coltellini, after Goldoni), Verona, Filarmonico, aut. 1775

La capricciosa [L' incostanza] (ob, 3), RD, carn. 1776, *D-Dlb*, *I-Nc*

Radamisto (os, A. Marchi), ? Naples, 1776

Vittorina (ob, Goldoni), London, King's, 16 Dec 1777, *Nc* (Acts 1, 3)

Roland (tragédie lyrique, 3, J. F. Marmontel, after P. Quinault), PO, 27 Jan 1778 (Paris, 1778), vs (Paris, 1883)

Phaon (drame lyrique, 2, C. H. Watelet), Choisy, Court, Sept 1778

Il vago disprezzato (ob), PO, 16 May 1779

Atys (tragédie lyrique, 3, Marmontel, after Quinault), PO, 22 Feb 1780, *D-Ds*, *F-Pn*, *Po*, *I-BGc* (Paris, ?1780, 2/*c*1783/*R*1991: FO, lxv)

Iphigénie en Tauride (tragédie lyrique, 4, A. du Congé Dubreuil), PO, 23 Jan 1781, *D-Mbs*, *F-Po*, *I-Fc*, *Nc* (Paris, 1781)

Adèle de Ponthieu (tragédie lyrique, J.-P.-A. des Rasins de Saint-Marc), PO, 27 Oct 1781, *F-Lm*, *Pn*, *Po*; rev. or reset, Paris, 1785, unperf.

Didon (tragédie lyrique, 3, Marmontel), Fontainebleau, 16 Oct 1783, *D-Mbs*, *F-Pn*, *Po*, *I-Nc* (Paris, 1783), vs (Paris, 1881)

Le dormeur éveillé (oc, Marmontel), Paris, Comédie-Italienne, 14 Nov 1783, excerpts pubd separately

Le faux lord (oc, 2, G. M. Piccinni), Versailles, 5 Dec 1783 (Paris,

?1783); also as Der verstellte Lord, *D-Bds*

Diane et Endymion (os, J. F. Espic Chevalier de Lirou), PO, 7 Sept 1784, collab. Espic, *F-Po* (Paris, 1784)

Lucette (oc, G. M. Piccinni), Paris, Comédie-Italienne (Favart), 30 Dec 1784

Pénélope (tragédie lyrique, Marmontel), Fontainebleau, 2 Nov 1785, *Po* (Paris, 1783)

Clytemnestre (tragédie lyrique, ? L. G. Pitra), Paris, comp. 1787; rehearsed but unperf.

La serva onorata (ob, Lorenzi, after L. da Ponte: *Le nozze di Figaro*), NFI, ?carn. 1792

Le trame in maschera (ob), NFI, carn. 1793

Ercole al Termedonte (os, 2), NC, 12 Jan 1793, *I-Nc*; also as La disfatta delle Amazzoni

La Griselda (eroicomico, 2, ? A. Anelli), Venice, S Samuele, 8 Oct 1793, ?*D-Bds, I-Fc, Mc*

Il servo padrone, ossia L'amor perfetto (ob, 2, C. Mazzolà), Venice, S Samuele, 17 Jan 1794

I Decemviri (os), *I-Nc**

Il finto turco (ob), *Nc*

Arias in: Farnace, 1757

Doubtful: Berenice (os, B. Pasqualigo), Naples, *c*1764; Il conte bagiano (int), RV, carn. 1770; La lavandara astuta (ob), Lucca, Pubblico, aut. 1772; L'enlèvement des Sabines, comp. ? Paris, 1787; Der Schlosser (ob), 1793; Sermiculo (int), *F-Pn*; La pie voleuse, ou La servante de Valaiseau [Die Elster] (ob), *D-Bds*; Les mensonges officieux (oc, G. Piccinni), Paris; Les fourberies de marine (oc), Paris; I portenosi effetti (ob), *Dlb*; Le donne di teatro, arias in *I-Mc* and *Nc*; Amante in campagna (int), *Tf*; Le Cigisbé (oc, 2) (Paris, 1804)

(2) Luigi [Lodovico] **Piccinni** (*b* ? Rome or Naples, 1764; *d* Passy, nr Paris, 31 July 1827). He was the third son (the second to survive) of (1) Niccolò Piccinni, who was his teacher. When his father moved to Paris in 1776, Luigi remained in Naples, joining his parents about 1782. In 1784 his first *opéra comique* was performed in Paris, followed by several others until 1790, none of which had much success. In 1791 he returned with his father to Naples and had comic operas performed in several Italian cities in 1793–5. From 1796 to 1801 he was Kapellmeister at the Swedish court in Stockholm. He returned to Paris in 1801 and had several *opéras comiques* performed there, 1804–9; in 1810 he suffered a failure at the Opéra with *Hippomène et Atalante*. He thereafter confined his activities to the teaching of singing, except for one last unsuccessful *opéra comique* in 1819.

Luigi Piccinni seems to have been generally regarded as a mediocre composer. Fétis wrote that he was 'devoid of genius and even of that elegant taste that in the theatre sometimes takes its place'. None of his operas was a great success, although some were published, along with songs and piano pieces.

Les amours de Chérubin (comédie mêlée de musique et de vaudevilles, 3, Desfontaines [F.-G. Fouques]), Paris, Comédie-Italienne (Favart), 4 Nov 1784

Suzette et Colinet, ou Les amants heureux par stratagèmes (cmda, 1, L. C. Person de Bérainville), Paris, Beaujolais, 25 July 1786

Le fat en bonne fortune (opéra bouffe, 2, P.-Y. Barré and J.-B. Radet), Paris, Beaujolais, 30 April 1787

Gli accidenti inaspettati (2, G. Petrosellini), Rome, Capranica, 1792

Il matrimonio per raggiro, Genoa, Falcone, 1793

Le trame in maschera (G. Palomba), Naples, Fiorentini, 1793

L'amante statua (1, A. Valli), Venice, S Cassiano, carn. 1794

Le Cigisbé, ou Le fat corrigé (comédie mêlée de musique, 3, J. F. Marmontel), Paris, Feydeau, 25 Feb 1804; rev. in 2 acts, 1 March 1804

L'aînée et la cadette (1), Paris, Jeunes Artistes, 1806

Avis aux jaloux, ou La rencontre imprévue (1, Chazet), Paris, Feydeau, 25 Oct 1809

Hippomène et Atalante (opéra, 2, later 1, Lehoc), Paris, Opéra, 24 Jan 1810

La rancune trompée (1, Marmontel), Paris, Feydeau, 12 Oct 1819

Doubtful (attrib. by Fétis): La suite des deux chasseurs et la laitière, 1788; Les infidélités imaginaires, 1790; La notte imbrogliata, 1794

(3) Louis Alexandre [Luigi Alessandro; Lodovico Alessandro] **Piccinni** (*b* Paris, 10 Sept 1779; *d* Paris, 24 April 1850). French composer. He was the illegitimate son of Giuseppe Piccinni (*b* 1758), (1) Niccolò Piccinni's eldest child, who wrote the librettos of two *opéras comiques* composed by his father. Louis studied composition with Le Sueur and had advice from his grandfather on his return to France (1799). He became a skilful accompanist and rehearsal pianist, serving in that capacity first at the Théâtre Feydeau and from 1802 at the Opéra. He was also conductor at the theatre of the Porte-St-Martin (1803–7, 1810–16), as well as holding several court posts. In 1816 he became third chorus master at the Opéra, later second and finally chief. He was accompanist at the Théâtre du Gymnase from 1820 to 1824, when he was put in charge of stage design at the Opéra, but was dismissed from there in 1826. In 1827 he managed an unsuccessful theatre season in Boulogne and then was a teacher in Paris (to 1836), Boulogne, Toulouse and Strasbourg. In 1849 he returned to Paris.

A highly prolific composer, Piccinni was best known for his music for a large number of melodramas and ballets at the Porte-St-Martin and other popular Paris theatres.

first performed in Paris unless otherwise stated

Arlequin au village, Jeunes Artistes, 1801

Lui-même (oc, 1, d'Allarde), 4 June 1802

L'entresol (Désaugier), Montansier-Variétés, 1802, collab. G. Lemoyne

L'amant rival de sa maîtresse (1, Henrion), Porte-St-Martin, 14 Nov 1803

L'amoureux par surprise, ou Le droit d'aînesse (oc, 1, Arnoult), OC (Olympique), 4 Oct 1804

Le désastre de Lisbonne (drame héroïque, 3, Bouilly), Porte-St-Martin, 24 Nov 1804

Les billets doux, Jeunes Artistes, 1804

Les deux maîtres, Jeunes Artistes, 1804

Les deux voisins, Montansier-Variétés, 1804

Le pavillon, Jeunes Artistes, 1804

La physionomie, Jeunes Artistes, 1804

Le terme du voyage, Montansier-Variétés, 1804

Rien pour lui (comédie, 3, L.-F. Faur), Jeunes Artistes, 25 Oct 1805

Avis au public, ou Le physionomiste en défaut (comic op, 2, Désaugiers), OC (Feydeau), 22 Nov 1806

Les époux avant le mariage, ou Ils sont chez eux (comic op, 1, Désaugiers), OC (Feydeau), 7 Jan 1808

Alcibiade solitaire (2, Cuvelier de Trie and J. M. Barouillet), Opéra, 8 March 1814

Le sceptre et la charrue (oc, 3, Théaulon and d'Artois), OC (Feydeau), 14 July 1817

La maison en loterie, Gymnase Dramatique, 1820

Le bramine (oc, 1, Delestre-Poirson), 17 June 1822

La petite lampe merveilleuse (opéra-comique-féerie, 3, Scribe and Mélesville [A.-H.-J. Duveyrier]), 29 July 1822

La fête française (oc, 1, Delestre-Poirson), 24 Aug 1823

La prise de Jéricho, Strasbourg, 1847

Others, all given at the Théâtre des Jeunes Artistes: Arlequin bon ami, Les deux issues, La femme justifiée, La pension des jeunes demoiselles

*

BurneyFI; FétisB; RosaM

J. A. Hiller: 'Sechste Fortsetzung des Entwurfs einer musikalischen Bibliothek', *Wöchentliche Nachrichten und Anmerkungen*, iii (1768), 57–64

J. F. Marmontel: *Essai sur les révolutions de la musique en France* (Paris, 1777)

J.-B. de La Borde: *Essai sur la musique ancienne et moderne* (Paris, 1780)

G. M. Leblond: *Mémoires pour servir à l'histoire de la révolution* opérée dans la musique par M. le Chevalier Gluck (Naples and Paris, 1781)

P. L. Ginguené: 'Dessein', 'France', *Encyclopédie méthodique: musique*, ed. N. E. Framery and P. L. Ginguené, i (Paris, 1791)

——: *Notice sur la vie et les ouvrages de Nicolas Piccinni* (Paris, an IX [1800–01])

J. F. Marmontel: *Mémoires* (Paris, 1804)

G. le Brisoys Desnoiresterres: *La musique française au XVIIIe siècle: Gluck et Piccinni 1774–1800* (Paris, 1872)

M. Tourneux, ed.: *Correspondance littéraire, philosophique et critique par Grimm, Diderot, Raynal, Meister, etc.* (Paris, 1877–82)

A. Jullien: *La cour et l'Opéra sous Louis XVI* (Paris, 1878)

E. Thoinan: *Notes bibliographiques sur la guerre musicale des Gluckistes et Piccinnistes* (Paris, 1878)

A. Jullien: *L'Opéra secret au XVIIIe siècle* (Paris, 1880)

H. de Curzon: *Les dernières années de Piccinni à Paris* (Paris, 1890)

A. Cametti: 'Saggio cronologico delle opere teatrali (1754–1794) di Niccolò Piccinni', *RMI*, viii (1901), 75–100

H. Abert: 'Piccinni als Buffokomponist', *JbMP 1913*, 29–42; repr. in *Gesammelte Schriften und Vorträge* (Halle, 1929)

——: *W. A. Mozart*, i (Leipzig, 1919), 250ff

J. D. Popovici: *La buona figliuola von Nicola Piccinni* (Vienna, 1920)

E. Blom: 'A Misjudged Composer', *Stepchildren of Music* (London, 1925), 57–66

A. Della Corte: *L'opera comica italiana nel settecento* (Bari, 1923)

——: *Piccinni: settecento italiano* (Bari, 1928)

P. La Rotella: *N. Piccinni: commemorato nel II centenario della nascita* (Bari, 1928)

A. Parisi: 'Intorno al soggiorno di N. Piccinni in Francia', *RMI*, xxx (1928), 219–25

M. Bellucci la Salandra: 'Opere teatrali serie e buffe di Nicolò Piccinni dal 1754 al 1794', *NA*, xii (1935), 43–54, 114–25, 235–48; see also xiii (1936), 55

A. Gastoué: 'Nicolò Piccinni et ses operas à Paris', *NA*, xiii (1936), 52–4

W. Bollert: 'L'opera *Griselda* de Piccinni', *Musica d'oggi*, xix (1937), 43–50

C. D. Brenner: *A Bibliographical History of Plays in the French Language 1700–1789* (Berkeley, CA, 1947, 2/1979)

N. Pascazio: *L'uomo Piccinni e la 'Querelle célèbre'* (Bari, 1951)

W. C. Holmes: 'Pamela Transformed', *MQ*, xxxviii (1952), 581–94

U. Prota-Giurleo: 'La biografia di Nicola Piccinni alla luce di nuovi documenti', *Il fuidoro*, i (1954), 27

——: 'Sacchini fra Piccinnisti e Gluckisti', *Gazzetta musicale di Napoli*, iii (1957), 57–63, 76–80

——: 'Una sconosciuta cantata di N. Piccinni e il suo ritorno a Parigi nel 1798', *Gazzetta musicale di Napoli*, iv (1958), 8

J. G. Rushton: *Music and Drama at the Académie Royale de Musique, Paris, 1774–1789* (diss., U. of Oxford, 1970)

——: 'The Theory and Practice of Piccinnisme', *PRMA*, xcviii (1971–2), 31–46

M. F. Robinson: *Naples and Neapolitan Opera* (London, 1972)

J. G. Rushton: '"Iphigénie en Tauride": the Operas of Gluck and Piccinni', *ML*, liii (1972), 411–30

G. Allroggen: 'Piccinnis Origille', *AnMc*, no.15 (1975), 258–97

M. Liggett: *A Biography of Piccinni and a Critical Study of his 'La Didone' and 'Didon'* (diss., Washington U., St Louis, 1977)

F. Degrada: 'Due volti d'Ifigenia', *Il palazzo incantato: studi sulla tradizione del melodramma dal Barocco al Romanticismo* (Fiesole, 1979), i, 155–208

R. Strohm: *Die italienische Oper im 18. Jahrhundert* (Wilhelmshaven, 1979)

F. Lippmann: 'Haydn und die Opera buffa: Vergleiche mit italienischen Werken gleichen Textes', *Joseph Haydn: Tradition und Rezeption: Cologne 1982*, 113–40

G. Hardie: 'Neapolitan Comic Opera, 1707–1750: some Addenda and Corrigenda for The New Grove', *JAMS*, xxxvi (1983), 125–7

M. Hunter: '"Pamela": the Offspring of Richardson's Heroine in Eighteenth-Century Opera', *Mosaic: a Journal for the Interdisciplinary Study of Literature*, viii (1985), 61–76

——: 'The Fusion and Juxtaposition of Genres in Opera Buffa 1770–1800: Anelli and Piccinni's "Griselda"', *ML*, lxviii (1986), 363–80

J. Rushton: Introduction to N. Piccinni: *Atys*, FO, lxv (1991)

DENNIS LIBBY
1: with JULIAN RUSHTON, MARY HUNTER
(work-lists with JAMES L. JACKMAN,
MARITA P. McCLYMONDS, DAVID CHARLTON)

Piccola Scala. Theatre in MILAN, built next to La Scala in 1955 for the performance of small-scale works and in use until 1983.

Piccolo Marat, Il ('The Lesser Marat'). *Dramma lirico* in three acts by PIETRO MASCAGNI to a libretto by GIOVACCHINO FORZANO; Rome, Teatro Costanzi, 2 May 1921.

Mascagni turned his attention to the French Revolution, perhaps in the hope of rediscovering the roots of his own poetics, with the example of Giordano's *Andrea Chénier* (written 25 years earlier) before him. But a return to historical drama could only mean the open abandonment of any idea of renewal and an overt adherence to Fascism, which embodied the populist and petit-bourgeois ideals of the immediate postwar period. Forzano was one of the foremost literary figures in Mussolini's circle, and he skilfully devised a functional plot with guaranteed dramatic appeal.

At Nantes in 1790, at the height of the French Revolution, the Prince of Fleury (tenor), to save his mother (mezzo-soprano) from the guillotine, enlists in the revolutionary ranks under the name of Piccolo Marat and wins the confidence of the corrupt and bloodthirsty president of the committee, nicknamed Orco [the Ogre] (bass), and the love of his niece, Mariella (soprano). He frees his mother and manages to escape with Mariella and a carpenter (baritone), who, after a dramatic fight, succeeds in killing the Ogre.

In the previous decade, while continuing to follow the model of *Cavalleria* in general terms, Mascagni had doubted his ability to produce any new work, but after he had rediscovered his lyrical vein in *Lodoletta* he returned without difficulty to *verismo* with *Il piccolo Marat*, as though to set a symbolic seal on the end of the vital part of his career. (*Nerone* was no more than a rhetorical political allegory, though musically subdued and backward-looking.) The chief weakness of *Marat* is the superficiality of the sharp tension between orchestra and voice that characterizes the music. The happy ending – the escape of the hero and heroine contrasted with the death of the wicked Ogre – has a fairy-tale air, whereas the premises of the drama call for a very different conclusion. The condemnation of the French Revolution as a metaphor for the violent and blind rebellion of the masses, as in *Andrea Chénier*, is in line with the ideology of the time and, together with the numerous opportunities the work offers for well-equipped singers to shine, explains the opera's ephemeral success.

MICHELE GIRARDI

Piccolomini, Marietta (*b* Siena, 15 March 1834; *d* Poggio Imperiale, Florence, 23 Dec 1899). Italian soprano. She made her début in 1852 at the Teatro della Pergola, Florence, in *Lucrezia Borgia* and then sang at the Teatro Apollo, Rome, in *Poliuto* and *Don Pasquale*. At Turin in 1855 she sang Violetta, the role for which she became famous; she was the first Violetta in London (Her Majesty's Theatre) and Paris (Théâtre Italien), both in 1856. Her repertory included Luisa Miller, Gilda, Serpina (*La serva padrona*), Zerlina, Lucia, Adina, Marie (*La fille du régiment*), Amina (*La sonnambula*), Elvira (*I puritani*) and Leonora (*Il trovatore*). Her popularity, especially as Violetta, rested more in her youthful, attractive appearance and her acting ability than in her vocal accomplishment.

E. Creathorne Clayton: *Queens of Song* (London, 1865)

ELIZABETH FORBES

Pichl [Pichel], **Václav** [Venceslaus, Wenzel] (*b* Bechyně, nr Tábor, 25 Sept 1741; *d* Vienna, 23 Jan 1805). Czech composer. After early training at Březnice, he was a violinist in Prague and studied at the university there. In 1765 he was engaged by Dittersdorf as a violinist and assistant director for the private orchestra of Bishop Adam Patachich at Nagyvárad, Grosswardein (now Oradea, Romania). After the orchestra's dissolution in 1769 Pichl became music director for Count Ludwig Hartig at Prague, and in about 1770 first violinist of the Vienna court theatre. On the recommendation of the Empress Maria Theresa, who preferred him to Mozart, Pichl became the music director and Kammerdiener (valet) for the Austrian governor of Lombardy, Archduke Ferdinando d'Este, at Milan. Between 1777 and 1796 he lived in Italy, where he visited all the important music centres and was appreciated as one of the foremost European composers; for a time he was music director of the theatre at Monza. From 1796 to his death he again served the archduke in Vienna.

Pichl was a man of broad knowledge and varied interests. At Nagyvárad he wrote Latin librettos which were set to music by both himself and Dittersdorf. Later he compiled a history of Czech musicians in Italy, and translated the libretto of Mozart's *Die Zauberflöte* into Czech (now lost). Pichl's music stands between the early and high Classical styles. One of the founders of the Viennese violin school, he wrote numerous solo violin, chamber and orchestral works, many of which survive together with his sacred works; his operatic output, however, is all lost.

music all lost

3 Lat. operas (Pichl): Olympia Jovi sacra, Grosswardein, 1765; Pythia, seu Ludi Apolloni, Grosswardein, 1766; Certamen deorum, Grosswardein, 1767
Lat. opera 'per Klosterbrack', Vienna, comp. 1770–76
Das Schnupftuch (Spl), Pest, 1774
Der Krieg (Ger. op), Vienna, *c*1775
4 opere buffe, 3 opere serie
It. arrs. of 8 Fr. operas, 1776–96, incl. A.-E.-M. Grétry: La caravana del Cairo (with addl nos.), Monza, 1795, lib. pubd

*

MGG (T. Straková); StiegerO
G. J. Dlabacž: *Allgemeines historisches Künstler-Lexikon*, ii (Prague, 1815), cols.457ff
G. Staud: *Magyar kastélyszinházak* [Hungarian Castle Theatres], ii (Budapest, 1963), 67, 69
J. Hárich: 'Das Opernensemble zu Eszterháza im Jahr 1780', *HayJb*, vii (1970), 5–46   MILAN POŠTOLKA

Pichon, Madame. *See* PUCHON.

Pick-Mangiagalli, Riccardo (*b* Strakonice, 10 July 1882; *d* Milan, 8 July 1949). Italian composer of Czech birth. The family settled in 1884 in Milan, where he studied at the conservatory (1896–1903). Until 1914 he was active as a pianist, spending some time in Vienna; subsequently he concentrated on teaching and composition and from 1936 to 1949 was director of the Milan Conservatory. As a composer he excelled in light ballet music: already in *Il salice d'oro* (composed in 1911–12) there is a pleasing if facile tunefulness, combined with Viennese dance rhythms and spiced with harmonies and orchestration reminiscent of Strauss and Ravel. In the ballet *Il carillon magico* (composed in 1915), Pick-Mangiagalli's most successful stage work, this promise reached fulfilment: though slight, the style is recognizably personal, with frequent unrelated triads, chromatic slithers, unusually placed augmented triads

and diminished 7th chords, etc. Musical means are perfectly matched to dramatic context. The later stage pieces rarely explore fresh territory: in the *commedia dell'arte* opera *Basi e bote* the basic idiom is still that of *Il carillon*, proving less adequate for a full-length work (despite some effective, sometimes vividly parodistic invention, especially in Act 2); and when in *Notturno romantico* Pick-Mangiagalli attempted a more tragic manner, the result sounds merely second-hand from Puccini and others. His best music tends to alternate between the basic moods of gentle nocturnal contemplation and sparkling mercurial exuberance.

Basi e bote op.43, 1919–20 (commedia, 3, A. Boito), Rome, Argentina, 3 March 1927
L'ospite inatteso (1, C. Veneziani), Italian radio, 25 Oct 1931
Notturno romantico op.60 (1, A. Rossato), Rome, Opera, 25 April 1936

*

A. Lualdi: 'Basi e bote di A. Boito e R. Pick-Mangiagalli all'Argentina di Roma', *Serate musicali* (Milan, 1928), 320–24
F. Abbiati: 'Musicisti contemporanei: Riccardo Pick-Mangiagalli', *Emporium* [Bergamo], lxxiii (1931), 34–9
JOHN C. G. WATERHOUSE

Pidhorets'ky [Podgoretsky], **Borys Volodymyrovych** (*b* Lubny, nr Poltava, 25 March/6 April 1873; *d* Moscow, 19 Feb 1919). Ukrainian composer. He studied at Warsaw Conservatory and then in Moscow under Alexander Il'insky. In 1912 he was sent by the Music-Ethnographic Commission of the Russian Geographic Society to collect folksongs in Ukraine. He joined the faculty of the Moscow Conservatory in 1915 and was music critic for *Golos Moskvï* and from 1917 for *Izvestiya*. Besides much choral and piano music, he wrote two operas. *Kupal'na iskra* ('The Spark of Kupalo'; 2, L. Yanovs'ka; 1901, Kiev; rev. version, 1907, Lubny) is based on Ukrainian lore regarding the flame of Kupalo (St John's Eve). The principal dramatic element lies in the contrast of the real and the fantastic; in Act 1 the 'real' rests heavily on the use of folk genres in arias and choruses, while in Act 2 the 'fantastic' is expressed through recitative, arioso and a richer harmonic and instrumental fabric. The true protagonist is the chorus, which Pidhorets'ky handles with great skill. *Bidna Liza* ('Poor Lisa'; 4, M. Vashkevych, after a novel by M. Karamzin; 1916, Moscow; rediscovered only in 1968) deals with everyday life and emotions where an individual is the victim of difficult social circumstances; here Pidhorets'ky uses a sharper harmonic language and relies more on orchestral episodes.

*

K. Cherpukhova, ed.: *Borys Pidhorets'ky: vybrani retsenzii ta statti* [Selected Reviews and Articles] (Kiev, 1970)
K. Cherpukhova: 'Deyaki pytannya muzychnoï dramaturhii oper B. Pidhorets'koho' [Certain Questions regarding the Musical Dramaturgy of the Operas of B. Pidhorets'ky], *Ukraïns'ke muzykoznavstvo*, no.14 (1979), 23–42
——: *Borys Pidhorets'ky* (Kiev, 1990)   VIRKO BALEY

Pièce à machines (Fr.). Term used to describe a French opera, *ballet de cour* or *opéra-ballet* performed during the reigns of Louis XIV and Louis XV whose staging required complicated machinery to produce special effects usually associated with magic and the supernatural. Lully's *Les plaisirs de l'île enchantée* (*comédie-ballet*, 1664) and *Alceste* (*tragédie lyrique*, 1674) and Rameau's *Castor et Pollux* (*tragédie lyrique*, 1737) are examples. While contemporaries emphasized the importance of the 'merveilleux' and its scenic representation as features distinguishing French operatic dramaturgy from that of spoken theatre, the term itself is rarely found in treatises of the period: one notable exception is Perrault (1674) who defined it as a synonym for opera. The term's application is limited to the Baroque. With the changing aesthetic of the late 18th century and the virtual disappearance of magic and gods as prime movers in the action, *spectacle* in French operas was made to serve other ends (such as the representation of natural disasters). Nevertheless, the continuing French interest in machines and the effects they could produce, which can be traced throughout *grand opéra* if not beyond, is in part a distant legacy of the *pièce à machines*.

See also THÉÂTRE À MACHINES.

*

C. Perrault: *Critique de l'opéra, ou Examen de la tragédie intitulée 'Alceste ou le triomphe d'Alcide'* (Paris, 1674)
D. Diderot: 'Opéra', *Encyclopédie, ou Dictionnaire raisonné des sciences, des arts et des métiers*, ed. D. Diderot, J. d'Alembert and others (Paris, 1751–80)
J. Lacombe: 'Opéra', *Dictionnaire portatif des beaux-arts* (Paris, 1752, enlarged 5/1766)
J. J. O. de Meude-Monpas: 'Opéra', *Dictionnaire de musique* (Paris, 1787)
P. Boullet [*machiniste* at the Opéra]: *Essai sur l'art de construire les théâtres, leurs machines et leurs mouvements* (Paris, 1801)
F. Lesure: *L'opéra classique français: XVIIe et XVIIIe siècles* (Geneva, 1972)
J. R. Anthony: *French Baroque Music from Beaujoyeulx to Rameau* (London, 1974, 2/1978; Fr. trans., 1981)
M. ELIZABETH C. BARTLET

Pièce de circonstance (Fr.: 'occasional piece'). Term used in France for an occasional work intended to celebrate state events, laud rulers' actions or arouse patriotism. The term itself rarely appears on the title-pages of scores or librettos (where the more specific type – *drame lyrique*, *opéra* etc. – was preferred), but it (or 'ouvrage de circonstance' or similar phrase) often occurs in contemporary reviews. Rather than portray the extra-theatrical referent directly (as *faits historiques* did), authors selected or invented an episode that permitted their audiences readily to grasp the intended analogy.

The close ties between the Académie Royale de Musique (the Opéra) and the monarchy ensured a long tradition of *pièces de circonstance* there, but they were also popular at the Comédie-Italienne and other theatres. The prologues to Lully's *tragédies lyriques* often function as *pièces de circonstance*: that of *Alceste* (1674), for example, welcomes back the conquering hero, to be identified with Louis XIV. Rameau celebrated metaphorically his successor's victory at Fontenoy in an *opéra-ballet*, *Le temple de la Gloire* (1745). Louis XVI's advent to the throne was greeted by comparisons between him and the most beloved of French kings in J.-P.-E. Martini's *Henri IV* (1774). The tumultuous period of the Revolution favoured *pièces de circonstance* designed to promote love of country; themes of self-sacrifice for the common good, and of collective, as well as individual, heroism were frequent: Grétry's *Callias, ou Nature et patrie* and Méhul's *Horatius Coclès* (both 1794) both sought to present models of bravery in face of seemingly overwhelming odds through subjects from classical history, but the lesson for the beleaguered French Republicans was obvious.

With the Empire, Napoleon, thinly disguised, appeared in many works. As a Roman emperor, his clemency was sung in *Le triomphe de Trajan*, a *tragédie lyrique* by Persuis and Le Sueur (1807, Opéra); as a medieval lord, his marriage to Marie-Louise of Austria formed the backdrop for Méhul's *Les troubadours* (intended for the Opéra-Comique, 1810); as a Greek hero, his son's birth was heralded in an *opéra-ballet*, Rodolphe Kreutzer's *Le triomphe du mois de mars, ou Le berceau d'Achille* (1811, Opéra). Minor theatres extolled his exploits in numerous vaudevilles (such as *L'hôtel de la paix, rue de la Victoire, à Paris* by P.-I. Barré, J.-B. Radet, N. Desfontaines and M. Dieulafoy; 1807, Théâtre du Vaudeville). With the Restoration, *pièces de circonstance* again served the Bourbons, but public taste for the genre was declining. Among the last major examples in Paris is Rossini's *Il viaggio a Reims* (1825, for the coronation of Charles X and performed at the Théâtre Italien). While topical references continued to abound in French opera (for example in the works of Offenbach), *pièces de circonstance*, strictly speaking, virtually disappeared except for the occasional cantata (e.g. Gounod's *A la frontière*, performed at the Opéra during the Franco-Prussian war, 1870).

*

L. H. Lecomte: *Napoléon et l'Empire racontés par le théâtre, 1797–1899* (Paris, 1900)
R. M. Isherwood: *Music in the Service of the King* (Ithaca, NY, 1973)
M. E. C. Bartlet: 'The New Repertory at the Opéra during the Reign of Terror: Revolutionary Rhetoric and Operatic Consequences', *Music and the French Revolution*, ed. M. Boyd (Cambridge, 1992), 107–56
M. ELIZABETH C. BARTLET

Pièce de sauvetage (Fr.). A rarely used translation of the German *Rettungsoper*, or RESCUE OPERA, a 20th-century term applied to French operas of the late *ancien régime* and, more particularly, the Revolution whose plots feature the rescue of the hero or heroine from a villain (e.g. Grétry's *Richard Coeur-de-lion*, 1784; Le Sueur's *La caverne*, 1793), a natural disaster (Cherubini's *Eliza*, 1794), or both (Méhul's *Mélidore et Phrosine*, 1794). Among the latest examples is Cherubini's *Les deux journées* (1800).

Pieri, Maria Maddalena ['La Polpetta'] (*b* Florence, *c*1683; *d* Florence, 2 Jan 1753). Italian contralto. Born into a family living in dire poverty, she had a lifelong love affair with the director of the Florentine Teatro alla Pergola, Marquis Luca Casimiro degli Albizzi, whose protection extended to her sister Maria Teresa Verdiana. The latter, sometimes confused with Maria Maddalena, shared the same nickname and profession, and performed during the same years in Naples, Venice and elsewhere. From the mid-1720s Maria Maddalena also held the title of 'virtuosa' to the Duke of Modena.

Pieri sang in her native town in the 1720, 1726, 1728 and 1733 seasons, at both the Cocomero and the Pergola theatres. Outside Florence, her most significant performances took place in Milan (Gasparini's *Il più fede tra i vassali*, 1720), Turin (Orlandini's *Il carceriere de se stesso*, 1720), Naples at S Bartolomeo and the royal palace (Leo's *Bajazete* and operas by Sarro and Vinci, 1722–3) alongside Faustina Bordoni, and Venice at the S Angelo in 1726 and the S Giovanni Grisostomo in 1729–30 (Hasse's *Artaserse*) alongside Farinelli. In 1731 she sang with her sister in Livorno. Between 1726 and 1735 she sang in Vivaldi operas in Venice, Florence, Verona and Mantua. According to a reference in one of Handel's letters (November 1730) she played male roles successfully, a fact confirmed by analysis of the roles written for her by Vivaldi, sometimes rewritings of tenor parts. Pieri created the title roles for *Farnace* (1726) and *Tamerlano* (1735). Her arias show a lively and forceful singing style, not unlike that of Anna Girò, with whom Pieri shared most of her Vivaldi performances in a kind of cooperative rivalry.

*

S. Sesini: *Il melodramma italiano a Londra nella prima metà del settecento* (Turin, Milan and Rome, 1914)

R. L. Weaver and N. W. Weaver: *A Chronology of Music in the Florentine Theater, 1590–1750* (Detroit, 1978)

A. L. Bellina, B. Brizzi and M. G. Pensa: 'Il pasticcio Bajazet: la "favola" del Gran Tamerlano nella messinscena di Vivaldi', *Nuovi studi vivaldiani*, i (Florence, 1988), 185–271

W. C. Holmes: 'Vivaldi e il teatro La Pergola a Firenze: nuove fonti', *Nuovi studi vivaldiani*, i (Florence, 1988), 117–30

C. Vitali: 'I fratelli Pepoli contro Vivaldi e Anna Girò: le ragione di un'assenza', *Informazioni e studi vivaldiani*, xii (1991), 19–46

CARLO VITALI

Pieri, (Maria) Teresa. Italian soprano, possibly married to PIETRO BARATTA.

Pierné, (Henri Constant) Gabriel (*b* Metz, 16 Aug 1863; *d* Ploujean, Finistère, 17 July 1937). French composer. He settled in Paris with his family at the age of 17. At the Conservatoire he won *premiers prix* for the piano, organ and counterpoint, and in 1882 the Prix de Rome; his teachers included Massenet and Franck, whom he succeeded as organist of Ste Clotilde (1890–98). Later he gained a high reputation as a conductor, becoming principal conductor of the Concerts Colonne in 1910; his name was also associated with the Ballets Russes. He was a member of the Académie des Beaux-Arts and a Chevalier of the Légion d'honneur. Throughout his career he was respected as a musician of the utmost integrity.

Pierné's list of compositions is large and wide-ranging, including operas, ballets, orchestral and chamber music and many songs. It was sometimes said that his willing absorption in the music of other composers adversely affected his style – his compositions give the impression of a cultivated synthesis of many tendencies in the French music of his time. Technically his work is always completely assured; he wrote easily, with virtuosity, always stylishly, and his touch was light even when the subject was serious – a French characteristic. He was perhaps one of the most 'complete' of French composers, and there are two distinct sides to his personality. On the one hand can be seen the serious, solidly based church musician, influenced by Franck; the other side, which gave rise to his operas, relates to his studies with Massenet – the sensual, worldly, popular side, ever present, but kept well in control. One of his most successful works was the comedy *On ne badine pas avec l'amour*, with its refreshing clarity, wit and lightness of touch. Attractive and accomplished also is the one-act comedy *Sophie Arnould*; while a more serious dramatic note is struck in *Fragonard*. It was entirely characteristic of Pierné to pass easily from the light to the thoughtful, from outward sparkle to inner penetration, and readily to find the appropriate style and colour to express many different shades of emotion and feeling. Throughout his work, clarity of texture, colourful orchestration and a fine sense of balance and contrast are characteristic.

Le chemin de l'amour, 1883 (oc, 1), unperf.
Don Louis [Don Luis], 1886 (oc), unperf.

Bouton d'or (fantaisie lyrique, 4, M.-A. Carré), Paris, Nouveau, 3 Jan 1893
Lizarda, 1893–4 (oc, A. Silvestre), unperf.
Salouïe (pantomime lyrique, 1, Silvestre and Melzner), Paris, Comédie Parisienne, 4 March 1895
La coupe enchantée (oc, 2, F. Matrat, after J. de La Fontaine and Champmeslé), Royan, Casino, 24 Aug 1895; rev. version (1), Paris, OC (Favart), 26 Dec 1905
Vendée (drame lyrique, 3 acts and 4 tableaux, C. Foley and A. Brisson), Lyons, Grand, 11 March 1897
La fille de Tabarin (comédie lyrique, V. Sardou and P. Ferrier), Paris, OC (Favart), 8 Feb 1901
On ne badine pas avec l'amour (oc, 3, G. Nigond and L. Leloir, after A. de Musset), Paris, OC (Favart), 20 May 1910
Sophie Arnould (comédie lyrique, 1, Nigond), Paris, OC (Favart), 21 Feb 1927
Fragonard (musical comedy, 3 acts and 4 tableaux, A. Rivoire and R. Coolus), Paris, Porte-St-Martin, 17 Oct 1934

DAVID COX

Pierson [Pearson], Henry Hugo [Hugh] (*b* Oxford, 12 April 1815; *d* Leipzig, 28 Jan 1873). German composer of English origin. Educated at Harrow and Cambridge, he abandoned medical studies in favour of a musical career. His earliest teachers were Corfe, Walmisley and Attwood. From 1839 to 1844 he lived in Germany; Schumann reviewed his op.7 Burns settings in the *Neue Zeitschrift für Musik* in 1842. Two years later he was elected Reid Professor of Music at the University of Edinburgh, but having protested in vain against the mismanagement of the Reid bequest, and swiftly developing a distaste for the bagpipes, he resigned after eight months and settled in Germany.

Pierson's first opera, *Der Elfensieg*, was produced at Brno in 1845; his second, *Leila* (1848, Hamburg), drew favourable notices (*Grove1* commends 'a striking song for bass voice, "Thy heart, O man, is like the sea"'). His father objecting to the family name being associated with operatic music, Pierson for a time adopted the *nom de plume* 'Edgar Mannsfeldt', from his wife's relations; eventually, however, he decided upon 'Henry Hugo Pierson'. In 1852 his oratorio *Jerusalem* was given at the Norwich Festival, where it was well received but condemned by the critics; Pierson resented this and pursued his German career the more vigorously. In 1854 he produced his masterpiece, the incidental music to Part 2 of Goethe's *Faust*, which was widely acclaimed in Germany, where annual performances of the work on Goethe's birthday became a tradition in many leading cities. His opera *Contarini* (1872, Hamburg) further enhanced his reputation in his adopted country. After his death he was lauded in the German press for consistently upholding 'the German spirit, German poetics and German art' (*Augsburger Zeitung*); his standing in Britain remained virtually negligible.

An ultra-Romantic composer, Pierson wrote in a markedly German style, which directly translates his intense emotional reactions to literature into brilliantly conceived musical images. He cannot entirely be acquitted of the charge of amateurishness: his structures often lose their way in a labyrinth of ostensibly unrelated ideas, even if informed by an inherent psychological continuity. *Faust*, however, remains a remarkable achievement: more subjective than Schumann's setting, it deals convincingly with the complex intellectual issues raised by Part 2 of Goethe's poem. Accurately defined by Ernest Newman as 'a musician who is at the same time poet and thinker', Pierson suffered from none of the inhibitions of his English contemporaries, and the finest numbers in *Faust*, such as the chorus 'Heil'ge Poesie', bear the imprint not merely of talent but of genius.

Der Elfensieg, oder Die Macht des Glaubens (C. Pierson), Brno, 7 May 1845

Leila (romantic op, 3, C. Pierson, after her *Schneewittchen*), Hamburg, 22 Feb 1848

Contarini, oder Die Verschwörung zu Padua, 1853 (grand op, 5, M. E. Lindau), Hamburg, 16 April 1872; revived as Fenice, Dessau, 1883

Musik zu Goethe's Faust, zweiter Theil (incidental music), Hamburg, Stadttheater, 25 March 1854 (Mainz, 1858), *US-Wc**

DNB (R. Newmarch); *Grove1* (H. Pearson); *Grove6* (N. Temperley); *MGG* (R. Sietz)

NZM, viii (1842), 32–3; repr. in R. Schumann: *Schriften über Musik und Musiker* (Leipzig, 1888), iii, 113–14

H. Zopff: 'Henry Hugo Pierson und seine Musik zum zweiten Theile von Goethe's Faust', *NZM*, lxix (1873), 529–32; lxx (1874), 2–3, 14–15

E. Newman: *Musical Studies* (London, 1905), 88–91

H. G. Sear: 'Faust and Henry Hugo Pierson', *MR*, x (1949), 183–90

E. Walker: *A History of Music in England* (Oxford, 3/1952, ed. J. A. Westrup), 304–5

P. M. Young: *A History of British Music* (London, 1967), 474–9

N. Temperley: 'Henry Hugo Pierson, 1815–73', *MT*, cxiv (1973), 1217–20; cxv (1974), 30–34   NIGEL BURTON

Pietra del paragone, La ('The Touchstone'). *Melodramma giocoso* in two acts by GIOACHINO ROSSINI to a libretto by LUIGI ROMANELLI; Milan, Teatro alla Scala, 26 September 1812.

A party is in progress in the country house of the wealthy young bachelor Count Asdrubale (bass). The guests include the lovely and demure Marchesina Clarice (contralto), her frustrated admirer the poet Giocondo (tenor) and a notable quartet of society bores and fortune-hunters: the poetaster Pacuvio (baritone), his escort Donna Fulvia (mezzo-soprano), the journalist Macrobio (baritone) and Baroness Aspasia (soprano). While the women vie for Asdrubale's attention, the men carry on various wars of attrition. Pacuvio in particular wishes to win a hearing for his fatuous new poem 'Ombretta sdegnosa del Missipipì' which Rossini turns into one of his most brilliant nonsense arias. Asdrubale is much taken with Clarice and she with him; but she fears that in such company her affection will be thought mercenary. Happily for her, Asdrubale and his servant Fabrizio (bass) decide to test the guests' sincerity by announcing that Asdrubale has lost all his money, Asdrubale himself turning up in the guise of a foreign potentate to slap the seals ('Sigillara') on the Count's possessions. Fulvia and Aspasia are outraged and alarmed as they launch the Act 1 finale, judged by Stendhal to be the funniest Rossini wrote. Clarice, needless to say, remains loyal, but in an epilogue she too is given the chance to test her lover's faith. Dressed as a Captain of the Hussars, she poses as Clarice's brother who has come to take her away from these 'ill-starr'd shores'; Asdrubale's response is desperate enough to convince Clarice of the real depth of his feeling. Rossini's casting Asdrubale as a bass (Filippo Galli in the original production) is an interesting aspect of a work that is overflowing with fresh invention. Act 2 contains a good deal of romantic scene-painting culminating in Giocondo's plaint to Clarice's beauty 'Quell'alme pupille'. There is also a fine trio, later re-used in *La gazzetta*, in which Macrobio is confronted by the Count and Giocondo and proves himself a veritable Aguecheek in the duel that follows.   RICHARD OSBORNE

Pietragrua, Carlo. *See* GRUA, CARLO PIETRO.

Pietragrua, Carlo Luigi. *See* GRUA, CARLO LUIGI PIETRO.

Pietri, Giuseppe (*b* S Ilario, Elba, 6 May 1886; *d* Milan, 11 Aug 1946). Italian composer. At the Milan Conservatory he studied with Amintore Galli (harmony and counterpoint) and Gaetano Coronaro (composition), and from the start concentrated on composition for the theatre. He began with the opera *Calendimaggio* (1910) but achieved his first success with the operetta *Addio giovinezza* (1915). Its favourable reception determined the course of his career (though he returned to opera later in life) and helped establish a native Italian operetta school after World War II. Most successful of his subsequent compositions was *Acqua cheta* (1920) which, with *Addio giovinezza*, well demonstrates Pietri's success in producing works full of local colour, fusing Viennese sensuousness with Italian lyricism.

Calendimaggio (1, P. Gori), Florence, Pergola, 14 March or May 1910

Ruy Blas (A. Colantuoni, after V. Hugo), Bologna, Duse, March 1916

Maristella (M. Salvini, after S. Di Giacomo: *Zi' munacella*), Naples, S Carlo, 22 March 1934

Rondine bionda (A. Rossato, after L. d'Ambra), Livorno, Goldoni, 16 Aug 1937

La canzone di S Giovanni (Rossato), Sanremo, Casinò, 30 Jan 1939

Operettas: In Flemmerland (musical fairy-tale, 3, A. Rubino), Milan, Fossati, 24 Sept 1913; Addio giovinezza (3, Camasio and N. Oxilia), Livorno, Politeama Goldoni, 20 Jan 1915; Modella (A. Lega, after A. Testoni), Rome, Quirino, 29 Jan 1917; Lucciola (3, C. Veneziani), Livorno, Politeama, 26 Sept 1918 or 26 March 1919; Acqua cheta (A. Novelli), Rome, Nazionale, 27 Nov 1920; L'ascensione (Novelli), Florence, Pergola, 17 May 1922; Guarda, guarda la mostarda (G. Colonna di Cesarò), Rome, Piccoli, 4 April 1923; La donna perduta (G. Zorzi and A. Giannini), Rome, Italiani, 26 Sept 1923; Quartetto vagabondo (E. Serretta), Rome, Eliseo, 4 Dec 1924

Namba Zaim (Veneziani), Milan, Lirico, 27 Jan 1926; Primarosa (C. Lombardo and R. Simoni, after Flers and Caillavet: *Primerose*), Milan, Lirico, 29 Oct 1926; Tuffolina (Novelli), Genoa, Politeama Genovese, 26 Oct 1927; Rompicollo (L. Bonelli and F. Paolieri), Milan, Dal Verme, 29 Dec 1928; L'isola verde (3, Lombardo and Bonelli), Milan, Lirico, 16 Oct 1929; Casa mia, casa mia ... (A. Nassi, after Novelli), Rome, Quirino, 5 Oct 1930; Gioconda Zappaterra (G. Bucciolini), Florence, Alfieri, 10 Dec 1930; La dote di Jeannette (Rossato), Rome, Principe, 4 July 1931; Vent'anni (Bonelli), Rome, Quirino, 2 April 1932

R. Carli: *Giuseppe Pietri, cantore dei goliardi* (Livorno, 1956)
                                                                ANDREW LAMB

Pietrobelli, Francesco. *See* PETROBELLI, FRANCESCO.

Pietro von Abano. *Romantische Oper* in two acts by LOUIS SPOHR to a libretto by Carl Pfeiffer after LUDWIG TIECK's novel *Pietro von Abano, oder Petrus Apone: eine Zaubergeschichte*; Kassel, Hoftheater, 13 October 1827.

The plot centres on the lust of a respected scholar, Pietro von Abano (baritone), for Cäcilia (soprano), daughter of the Podesta of Padua (bass). Pietro, however, is in league with the Devil, and when Cäcilia dies unexpectedly he steals her body and uses his magic arts to enthral her soul so that he can satisfy his lust. Antonio (tenor), Cäcilia's betrothed, is instrumental in thwarting Pietro's plans and also in discovering Cäcilia's twin sister, Rosa (soprano), who had been abducted as a child by robbers. The opera concludes with the betrothal of Antonio and Rosa, while Pietro is dragged off to be executed and Cäcilia's soul is released from its bondage by a priest's benediction.

Pietro von Abano was produced four years after the resounding success of Spohr's *Jessonda*, but although it found many admirers, including Meyerbeer, it was seldom produced. Despite the fine and dramatically effective music, the story's gruesomeness and its sexual overtones made it unacceptable on many German stages.

CLIVE BROWN

Pigeon, Madame. *See* PUCHON.

Pigmalion ('Pygmalion'). *Acte de ballet* by JEAN-PHILIPPE RAMEAU to a libretto by Ballot de Sauvot after ANTOINE HOUDAR DE LAMOTTE; Paris, Opéra, 27 August 1748.

The subject and some 30 lines of *Pigmalion* were borrowed from Lamotte's libretto for the entrée 'La sculpture' in *Le triomphe des arts*, an *opéra-ballet* first set by La Barre in 1700. While such resettings were commonplace elsewhere, it was not until *Pigmalion* that the practice was adopted in France, 76 years after the emergence of French opera, and even then the librettist was criticized as the 'corrector' of Lamotte. Nevertheless, the work deservedly became one of Rameau's most popular: by the end of its last 18th-century revival in 1781 it had been given more than 200 performances at the Opéra or at court.

The legend is familiar: the sculptor Pygmalion (*haute-contre*) falls hopelessly in love with his statue and implores the help of Venus. After a sign from L'Amour [Cupid] (soprano), the Statue (soprano and dancer) comes to life and reveals her love to the ecstatic sculptor. This plot, slender but well paced, offers a pleasing variety of moods – the deeply-felt yearning of Pygmalion's opening monologue ('Fatal Amour'), his bewilderment and elation as the Statue comes to life, the uninhibited joy of the final *divertissement*. It also provides an ingenious pretext for the obligatory ballet since the Statue, having come to life, must be taught how to move. Helped by Cupid and the Graces, she learns the characteristics of each dance-type, trying them haltingly at first but with growing confidence. The work is prefaced by a vivacious overture said to depict the sculptor's chisel. Since its first modern revival at the Théâtre des Arts, Paris, in 1913, *Pigmalion* has been one of the most frequently staged of Rameau's operas.

GRAHAM SADLER

Pignatta [Pignati], **Pietro Romulo** (*b* Rome; *d* in or after 1700). Italian composer and librettist. In 1683 he was *maestro di cappella* at S Apollinare, Rome. He may have lived in Venice at least between 1695 and 1700, when five operas by him (whose librettos describe him as an abbot) were given there; three were to his own librettos. None of the music to his operas survives.

all first performed in Venice

Asmiro re di Corinto (Pignatta), SS Giovanni e Paolo, 15 Feb 1695; later as Inganno senza danno and Chi non sa finzere non sa vincere

La costanza vince il destino (Pignatta), SS Giovanni e Paolo, 15 Oct 1695; later as L'Oronta d'Egitto

Sigismondo Primo al diadema (G. Grimani), SS Giovanni e Paolo, 1696

Il Paolo Emilio (F. Rossi), Canal Regio, aut. 1699 [attrib. Pignatta by Bonlini]

Il vanto d'Amore (Pignatta), S Moisè, 1700

*

G. C. Bonlini: *Le glorie della poesia e della musica* (Venice, 1730)

Pijper, Willem (*b* Zeist, 8 Sept 1894; *d* Leidschendam, 18 March 1947). Dutch composer and teacher. He was the most influential composer of his country in the first half of the 20th century. Having studied with Johan Wagenaar in Utrecht (1911–16), he caused quite a stir through his work as a music critic there (1918–23). From 1918 to 1930 he taught at the Amsterdam Conservatory (as professor of composition from 1925), and he directed the Rotterdam Conservatory, 1930–47. His early compositions (up to 1920) show the influence of Mahler, Grieg and Debussy; thereafter his 'germ-cell' principle became an important feature of his style. Pijper compared this principle, which governs the melodic and harmonic growth of a work from a single motif or chord, to the development of an organism from an ovum. He used it in many compositions, including the opera *Halewijn* (2 parts, 9 scenes), to a libretto by his wife at the time, Emmy van Lokhorst, after a ballad by Martinus Nijhoff. Pijper described the work as a 'symphonic drama', and indeed the music, rather than the drama, dominates; purely orchestral passages are as important as the scenes of stage action. The first performance, in Amsterdam on 13 June 1933, drew international attention. Critics compared the work with *Pelléas et Mélisande* and *Wozzeck* but found it insufficiently dramatic; Dutch critics, however, praised its national character (it contains old Dutch folksongs). After *Halewijn* Pijper wrote little apart from some folksong arrangements and concertos for cello and violin. During World War II he was busy with a second opera, *Merlijn* (S. Vestdijk), where the accent was again to be on the symphonic element; in the introduction he mentioned 'three four-part symphonies, of which the 12 episodes are related to the 12 astrological signs of the Zodiac'. Its music is much more dramatic and passionate than that of *Halewijn* and is sometimes Wagnerian in grandeur. The work remained unfinished; the first performance of the existing five and a half scenes was given in Rotterdam on 7 June 1952. Pijper also wrote incidental music for several plays.

*

S. Vestdijk: 'Over de tekst van de opera "Merlijn"', *Mens en Melodie* (1947), 188–93

K. P. Bernet Kempers: *Inleidung tot de opera Halewijn van Willem Pijper* (Rotterdam, 1950)

J. Daniskas: 'Het onvoltooid nagelaten symfonisch drama "Merlijn" van Willem Pijper', *Mens en Melodie* (1952), 131–6

J. Wouters: 'Willem Pijper', *Dutch Composers' Gallery*, i: *Nine Portraits of Dutch Composers* (Amsterdam, 1971), 104–35

O. Ketting: 'From Brigand to Hero of the People', *Key Notes* (1977), no.6, pp.4–11

L. Samama: *Zeventig jaar nederlandse muziek (1915–1985)* (Amsterdam, 1986), 97–108

JOS WOUTERS, LEO SAMAMA

Piket, Frederick (*b* Constantinople [now Istanbul], 6 Jan 1903; *d* Long Island City, NY, 28 Feb 1974). American composer of Austrian descent. He studied at the Vienna Conservatory and later in Berlin with Schreker before emigrating to the USA in 1940. Settling in New York, he taught at the School of Sacred Music at Hebrew Union College and served as music director of the Free Synagogue in Flushing. He composed orchestral, chamber and vocal music, including three one-act operas. *Isaac Levi*, to a libretto by Ray Smolover, was first performed on 11 Dec 1956 in White Plains, New York. In a declamatory style with Romantic elements, it deals with problems facing contemporary Jewry, such as renunciation of faith, intermarriage and the Creator's goodness. *Satan's Trap*, to a libretto by Charles Levy after Gottfried Keller's novel *Romeo und Julia auf dem Dorfe*, had its première in New York on 26 November 1961. The music is in a Romantic style with conservative use of dissonance. Piket's third opera, *Trilby*, was first given in New York on 15 May 1967.

BRADFORD R. DeVOS

Pikovaya dama. Opera by P. I. Tchaikovsky; *see* QUEEN OF SPADES, THE.

Piland, Jeanne (*b* Raleigh, NC, 3 Dec 1945). American mezzo-soprano. She studied at East Carolina University and then sang with the New York City Opera (1974–7). In 1977 she joined Deutsche Oper am Rhein, Düsseldorf, where her roles included Silla (*Palestrina*), Ravel's Child, Fyodor, Cherubino, Hänsel, the Schoolboy (*Lulu*) and Clytemnestra (*Iphigénie en Aulide*, 1991). She has appeared at Vienna, Hamburg, Munich, Zürich, Geneva and Houston. In 1985 she made her Covent Garden début as the Composer, repeating the role at Aix-en-Provence. Her repertory includes Zerlina, Dorabella, Cenerentola, Rosina, Charlotte and Octavia (*L'incoronazione di Poppea*, 1989), also the trouser roles of Idamantes, Annius, Sextus, Smeton (*Anna Bolena*) and Octavian, which she sang at Dresden (1986) and Santa Fe (1988). She has a warm, flexible voice of developing power.

ELIZABETH FORBES

Pilarczyk, Helga (**Käthe**) (*b* Schöningen, nr Brunswick, 12 March 1925). German soprano. She studied in Hamburg, and made her début as Irmentraut (*Der Waffenschmied*), a mezzo-soprano role, at Brunswick in 1951. In 1953–4 she joined the Hamburg Staatsoper, where she specialized in 20th-century opera, becoming particularly identified with the roles of Marie (*Wozzeck*), Lulu, the Woman (*Erwartung*), the Mother (*Il prigioniero*), Renata (*The Fiery Angel*) and Jocasta (*Oedipus rex*). She created Costanza in Henze's *König Hirsch* (1956, Berlin) and took the title role in the first Zürich production of Liebermann's *Penelope* (1961); she sang Salome at Covent Garden (1959), and the Composer (1958) and Colombina (*Arlecchino*, 1960) at Glyndebourne. Having made her American operatic début in *Erwartung* at Washington, DC (1962), she first appeared at the Metropolitan as Marie in 1965, singing in English. Although her voice was not intrinsically beautiful, its intelligent use and her musicianship lent distinction to her performances.

*

H. Pilarczyk: 'On Singing Modern Opera', *Opera*, xiii (1962), 581–5
HAROLD ROSENTHAL/R

Pilgrim's Progress, The. Morality in a prologue, four acts and an epilogue by RALPH VAUGHAN WILLIAMS to his own libretto after John Bunyan's allegory, with interpolations from the Bible and verse by Ursula Vaughan Williams; London, Covent Garden, 26 April 1951.

Although an agnostic, Vaughan Williams had a strong sense of music as a social force, involving himself in church music and regarding it (in the days before radio) as one of the few regular musical focal points for a community. Early in his career, he planned to make an opera from Bunyan's *The Pilgrim's Progress*, not because he shared Bunyan's religious outlook but because he regarded it as a universal dramatic allegory. In the final version of his opera (which he preferred to call a morality), he altered the name of the protagonist from Christian to Pilgrim because 'I want the idea to be universal and appeal to anybody who aims at the spiritual life whether he is Christian, Jew, Buddhist,

Shintoist or 5th Day Adventist' (as he wrote to Rutland Boughton in May 1951).

Vaughan Williams's first stage setting of *The Pilgrim's Progress*, for which he composed music for 12 episodes, was given a semi-amateur performance at Reigate Priory, Surrey, in 1906. The prelude and epilogue were based on the hymn tune 'York', which he connected with Bunyan because of its Roundhead associations; it also opens and closes the opera. In 1921 he made a one-act opera from the episode *The Shepherds of the Delectable Mountains*. This had many performances between the wars and was incorporated into the opera as Act 4 scene ii with its ending changed.

Vaughan Williams worked on Acts 1 and 2 from 1925 to 1936. He then decided that the opera was unlikely to reach the stage and used some of the themes in three of the four movements of his Fifth Symphony (1938–43). His interest was reawakened in 1942 when the BBC commissioned a radio dramatization by Edward Sackville-West of *The Pilgrim's Progress* (first broadcast on 5 September 1943). For this he provided 38 sections of incidental music. He resumed concentrated work on the opera from 1944 to 1949. During rehearsals for the Covent Garden production in 1951 he added Watchful's Nocturne to cover a scene-change, and he revised and expanded the Vanity Fair scene in 1951–2.

The opera begins with a prologue in which Bunyan (bass-baritone) is writing the last words of his book in Bedford Gaol. As he reads from the beginning, Pilgrim (baritone) is seen with a burden on his back crying 'What shall I do?' The Evangelist (bass) directs him to the Wicket Gate. Four Neighbours (two tenors, baritone, bass) try to make Pilgrim turn back, but he sets out in pursuit of 'Life, eternal life'.

At the Wicket Gate, Pilgrim kneels in front of the Cross. Three Shining Ones (soprano, mezzo-soprano, contralto) take his burden and lead him to the gate where the Interpreter (tenor) and the chorus welcome him to the House Beautiful. The Three Shining Ones place a white robe round his shoulders. In the interlude between Acts 1 and 2, Watchful the Porter (high baritone) sings a psalm.

Act 2 opens on the King's Highway. Pilgrim tells a Herald (high baritone) to inscribe his name in the book as one who 'will go on that way'. Pilgrim is given armour and the chorus sings 'Who would true valour see'. In the second scene Pilgrim enters the Valley of Humiliation to the howling of the Doleful Creatures. He is challenged to fight for his soul by Apollyon (bass, often amplified), king of the region. Pilgrim wins, but is wounded. He is revived by Two Heavenly Beings (soprano, contralto). The Evangelist returns with a warning of new trials to come in Vanity Fair and invests Pilgrim with the staff of Salvation, the roll of the Word and the key of Promise.

Act 3 scene i is set in Vanity Fair where 'all that the world can provide is for sale'. Pilgrim is offered samples of the more seductive delights by Lord Lechery (*buffo* tenor), Madam Bubble (mezzo-soprano) and Madam Wanton (soprano), but he rejects them – 'I buy the truth'. He is seized and tried before Lord Hate-Good (bass), who condemns him to death. In prison in scene ii, Pilgrim laments his fate, then remembers the key of Promise. He unlocks the gates and walks away – along the moonlit Pilgrim's Way.

Act 4 begins on the edge of a wood. A Woodcutter's Boy (soprano or treble) directs Pilgrim to the Delectable

'The Pilgrim's Progress' (Vaughan Williams): Arnold Matters as Pilgrim surrounded by the Doleful Creatures in the Valley of Humiliation from Act 2 of the original production at Covent Garden in London, 26 April 1951

Mountains. He encounters Mister and Madam By-Ends (tenor and contralto), who refuse to accompany him. In scene ii, 'The Delectable Mountains', Pilgrim asks three Shepherds (tenor, baritone, bass) if he is on the way to the Celestial City. He stays with them while a Bird (soprano) sings. A Celestial Messenger (tenor) summons him to the Celestial City and pierces his heart with an arrow. Pilgrim enters the River of Death. A trumpet sounds at the start of scene iii, and to the chorus's ecstatic Alleluias, Pilgrim climbs to the gates of the City. The scene fades back to Bunyan in gaol, offering his book to the audience.

Though lacking much of the conventional trappings of opera, *The Pilgrim's Progress*, in the hands of a sensitive director, can be a remarkable theatrical experience; and the music sustains a level of meditative rapture, relieved by the colourful Vanity Fair scene, which sympathetic listeners find spiritually and emotionally powerful.
MICHAEL KENNEDY

Pillet, Léon (François Raymond) (*b* Paris, 6 Dec 1803; *d* Venice, 20 March 1868). French theatre director. He studied law and worked as a journalist and civil servant in Paris before assuming the directorship of the Opéra in 1840. From then until 1847, when he resigned, Donizetti's *La favorite* and *Dom Sébastien* and Halévy's *La reine de Chypre* and *Charles VI* were among the most important premières. His period of tenure was marked by a prolonged liaison with the star mezzo-soprano of the house, Rosina Stoltz, to whose whims he sometimes succumbed with scant regard for sound artis-

tic and financial management. He devoted considerable energy in attempts to persuade Meyerbeer to bring *Le prophète* to the Opéra, but the two never reached a mutually satisfactory agreement. Following Pillet's resignation, he spent the rest of his life as a diplomat, serving as a consul in Nice, Palermo and Venice.
STEVEN HUEBNER

Pillot, Jean-Pierre (*b* Escout, Basses-Pyrénées, 16 Feb 1733; *d* after 1789). French *haute-contre*. He was recruited for the Paris Opéra in about 1755 as a replacement for Jélyotte. His début was as Adonis in Mouret's *Les amours des dieux* in 1757, after which he sang in revivals of Rameau's *Hippolyte et Aricie* (1757), *Dardanus* (1760 and 1768), *Zaïs* (1761) and *Castor et Pollux* (1764), Lully's *Armide* (Renaud, 1761 and 1764) and *Thésée* (1766–7 and 1770), and in a late revival of Desmarets' *Iphigénie en Tauride* (1762). His career was eclipsed by the rise of Legros from the time of the latter's début in 1764.

E. Campardon: *L'Académie royale de musique au xviiie siècle* (Paris, 1884), ii, 242–5
PHILIP WELLER

Pilotti-Schiavonetti, Elisabetta (*d* Hanover, 5 May 1742). Italian soprano. A virtuoso of the Hanover royal house, she was a member of the Queen's (later King's) Theatre company in London from 1710 to 1717, making her début in Mancini's *Idaspe fedele*. She sang in the first performances of Handel's *Rinaldo* (Armida), *Il pastor fido* (Amarillis), *Teseo* (Medea) and *Amadigi* (Melissa), in Francesco Gasparini's *Antioco* and *Ambleto*, Giovanni Bononcini's *Etearco*, the pasticcios *Dorinda*, *Ernelinda*, *Lucio Vero* and *Clearte*, and probably in Handel's *Silla* (Metella). She was the only singer who appeared in all 47 performances of *Rinaldo* between 1711 and 1717. The four parts Handel composed for her, three of them sorceresses, show that she was an exceptional artist with technical agility, dramatic fire and a compass of two octaves (c' to c'''). In 1726 she sang at Stuttgart in a comic opera, *Pyramus und Thisbe*, directed by her husband Giovanni Schiavonetti (*d* 1730), a Venetian cellist and oboist.
WINTON DEAN

Pilou, Jeannette [Pilós, Joanna] (*b* Alexandria, July 1937). Italian soprano of Greek parentage and Egyptian birth. She made her début in 1958 in Milan and then sang throughout Italy, in the Americas (the Metropolitan, San Francisco and Buenos Aires), in Britain (at Covent Garden and with Scottish Opera), and in Paris and Vienna; at Monte Carlo she created Inez de Castro in Renzo Rossellini's *La reine morte* (1973). She took part in the Wexford, Salzburg and Aix-en-Provence festivals. Her repertory ranged from Gluck's Eurydice and Mozart's Susanna and Zerlina to the three female roles in Einem's *Der Prozess*, but her lyrical style and personality were particularly suited to French opera, and Marguerite, Juliet, Micaëla, Manon and Mélisande were among her most successful characterizations. She was also a fine Violetta, while her Puccini roles included Mimì, Butterfly, Manon Lescaut, Liù and Magda (*La rondine*). The timbre of her voice was not without a trace of harshness, which she used skilfully to give dramatic edge to her performances.
ELIZABETH FORBES

Pilsen (Ger.). PLZEŇ.

Pimpinone (i). Comic intermezzos by TOMASO GIOVANNI ALBINONI to a libretto by PIETRO PARIATI; Venice, Teatro S Cassiano, autumn 1708.

This set of three intermezzos is one of very few from the first generation of Venetian comic intermezzos that survive and for which both the composer and the librettist can be identified. The plot employs two of the stock comic characters used in 17th-century *opera seria* – the cunning young servant-girl and the gullible old man. However, the new manner in which these characters are depicted alludes to topical social concerns, such as the aspiration by lower social orders towards the life-style of the nobility; the same themes later appeared in Pergolesi's *La serva padrona*.

In Intermezzo 1 Vespetta (contralto) inveigles Pimpinone (bass), a rich bachelor, into employing her as his housekeeper with pledges of efficiency and probity. In Intermezzo 2 she traps him into promising marriage by threatening to leave his service if her position, which she claims is seen as ambiguous, is not regularized. This achieved, in Intermezzo 3 she shows her true colours by outrageously breaking her earlier promise to avoid pleasure outside the home. Pimpinone protests but finally admits defeat, while ruefully grumbling *sotto voce*.

Pariati provided Albinoni with a sparkling libretto, full of effective repartee and delicious asides. Albinoni's setting, while not as imaginative and rich in musical resources as Telemann's (1725), contains many deft touches. The alert rhythms of its five arias and three duets excellently complement the raciness of the text, while the rumbustious final 'quarrel-duet' looks forward to the mature *buffo* style of the second half of the century. *Pimpinone* quickly became a repertory favourite among comic singers, being revived almost 30 times before 1740 and travelling to operatic outposts as distant as Moscow and Ljubljana.   MICHAEL TALBOT

Pimpinone (ii) [*Pimpinone, oder Die ungleiche Heirat, oder Die herrschsüchtige Cammer-Mädgen* ('Pimpinone, or The Unequal Match, or The Tyrannical Chambermaid')]. Intermezzo in three scenes by GEORG PHILIPP TELEMANN to a libretto by Johann Philipp Praetorius after PIETRO PARIATI; Hamburg, Theater am Gänsemarkt, 27 September 1725.

Seeking a husband, the chambermaid Vespetta (soprano) spies the rich merchant Pimpinone (bass). Vespetta calculatingly flatters Pimpinone, who falls in love with her and offers her a servant's position. In the second scene (some time later), Vespetta threatens to leave Pimpinone because of rumours circulating about the town impugning her virtue. He responds by offering to marry her, but Vespetta laments that she has no dowry. Pimpinone offers a gift of 10 000 thalers as her dowry, on condition that she remain at home and entertain no visitors. She agrees. In the third scene (after their marriage), Vespetta has grown restless under Pimpinone's restrictions. She demands respect and equality, and the freedom to go where she chooses. He threatens her with corporal punishment, and she promises retaliation in kind. They brawl. Finally, Vespetta points to the cleverly written marriage contract, which provides her with the dowry in the event of a divorce. Reminded of this, Pimpinone relents and submits to her will.

Pimpinone shows Telemann in full command of the Italian intermezzo style, eight years before Pergolesi's *La serva padrona*. The arias and duets exhibit the short-breathed parlando style which became the hallmark of *opera buffa*, and they are well integrated into the action. Pimpinone himself is the prototypical *basso buffo*. First performed between the acts of Handel's *Tamerlano*, *Pimpinone* was later repeated as an independent work, and its great popularity encouraged Telemann to compose a sequel, *Die Amours der Vespetta* (Hamburg, 1727), which unfortunately is lost. Telemann published *Pimpinone* in 1728.   BRIAN D. STEWART

Pinacci, Giovanni Battista (*b* Florence, 1694–5; *d* Florence, 1750). Italian tenor. He sang in Rome in 1717 (Francesco Gasparini's *Il Trace in Catena*) and 1723, Milan in 1718, Florence in 1718 and many later seasons (at least 16 operas), Genoa in 1720, Naples in 1721 (A. M. Bononcini's *Rosiclea in Dania* and Porpora's *Gli orti esperidi*), Bologna in 1722 (Orlandini's *Ormisda*), Genoa in 1723, Venice in 1723–4 (operas by Giacomelli and Francesco and Michelangelo Gasparini), Genoa in 1725, Rome in 1728 (Vinci's *Catone in Utica* and Feo's *Ipermestra*), Venice in 1728 and Rome in 1731 (including Vinci's *Artaserse*). Engaged by Handel for London in 1731–2, he probably made his début as Bajazet in *Tamerlano*, sang in the revivals of *Poro*, *Admeto*, *Giulio Cesare* and *Flavio*, in the new operas *Ezio* (Maximus) and *Sosarme* (Haliate), and in Ariosti's *Coriolano* and Handel's pasticcio *Lucio Papirio dittatore*. Handel adapted and recomposed Hercules and Lotario in *Admeto* and *Flavio* for him. His wife, Anna Bagnolesi, was in Handel's company at the same time.

After leaving London Pinacci sang in Florence in 1732–3, 1739, 1743–4 (when he managed the carnival season) and 1748–9, Naples in 1733–4 (three operas, including Hasse's *Cajo Fabricio* and Pergolesi's *Il prigionier superbo*), Rome in 1735 (Pergolesi's *L'olimpiade* and two other operas), Venice in 1740–43 (seven operas, including Galuppi's *Oronte re de' sciti*, Hasse's *Alessandro nell'Indie* and Jommelli's *Semiramide*), 1746 (Jommelli's *Tito Manlio*) and 1747 (Hasse's *Demetrio* and Pescetti's *Ezio*), Livorno in 1746, and Naples in 1747 (Jommelli's *Eumene*). He was one of the leading tenors of his generation, a dramatic singer with powerful low notes, to judge by the parts Handel composed for him; the compass is *c* to *a'*. He was often criticized for bellowing.   WINTON DEAN

Pini, Maria Domenica ['La Tilla'] (*b* Florence, 1670 or 1671; *d* Florence, 15 Oct 1746). Italian soprano. She was a pupil of Martino Bitti and a 'virtuosa' of Prince Ferdinando of Tuscany. She seems to have sung in 16 operas at Pratolino and Florence between 1692 and 1710 and was given permission to sing in Genoa in 1692. In 1696, 1699 and 1700 she appeared in Reggio, in 1702–3 in Turin, and between 1704 and 1710 she sang in 14 operas in Venice.

The Florentine theorist and diarist Nicolò Susier described her as 'una brava cantatrice' and said that she sang in Livorno and 'per tutti i Teatri d'Italia'. Prince Ferdinando evidently had a clear idea of her abilities; he made Alessandro Scarlatti rewrite Act 1 and part of Act 2 of *Il gran Tamerlano* (1705) because he wanted her to sing the role of Rossane, and having cast her as Adalinda in Perti's *Ginevra, principessa di Scozia* he also asked him to recompose one of her arias – to make it 'più staccata' so that she would have more time to take breaths.

M. Fabbri: *Alessandro Scarlatti e il Principe Ferdinando de' Medici* (Florence, 1961)

COLIN TIMMS

Pini-Corsi, Antonio (*b* Zara [now Zadar], Dalmatia, June 1858; *d* Milan, 22 April 1918). Italian baritone. He made his début in 1878 at Cremona as Dandini (*La Cenerentola*) and for 15 years sang throughout Italy, specializing in the comic operas of Rossini and Donizetti. Having made his first appearance at La Scala as Rigoletto, he created Ford in Verdi's *Falstaff* (1893). He also sang Ford at Genoa, Rome, Venice, Brescia and, in 1894, at Covent Garden, where he had made his début as Puccini's Lescaut. He created Schaunard in *La bohème* at Turin (1896), appeared in Franchetti's *Signor di Pourceaugnac* at Genoa and Rome (1898) and made his début at the Metropolitan (1899) as Rossini's Dr Bartolo. At La Scala he sang in the first performances of Giordano's *Siberia* (1903) and Franchetti's *La figlia di Iorio* (1906), and appeared in *La Wally* (1905) and *Der Freischütz* (1906). At the Metropolitan, between 1909 and 1914, he sang many character roles, creating the miner Happy in *La fanciulla del West* and the Innkeeper in Humperdinck's *Königskinder* (1910). His last appearance was in 1917 in Rossini's *Signor Bruschino* at the Teatro dal Verme, Milan, when his voice, if not as powerful, was still as agile as ever and used with the same keen intelligence.

W. H. Seltsam: *Metropolitan Opera Annals* (New York, 1949)
I. Kolodin: *The Story of the Metropolitan Opera* (New York, 1951)
H. Rosenthal: *Two Centuries of Opera at Covent Garden* (London, 1958)
C. Gatti: *Il Teatro alla Scala nella storia e nell'arte 1778–1963* (Milan, 1964)

ELIZABETH FORBES

Pinottini, Maria Teresa Agnesi. *See* AGNESI-PINOTTINI, MARIA TERESA.

Pinsuti, Ciro (*b* Sinalunga, 9 May 1829; *d* Florence, 10 March 1888). Italian composer and singing teacher. He made his début as a pianist at the age of nine, and two years later was made an honorary member of the Accademia Filarmonica, Rome. In 1840 he was taken to London, where he studied the piano, composition and the violin. He returned to Italy in 1845 and took lessons with Rossini in Bologna, while teaching the piano at the Liceo Musicale. In 1848 he settled in London as a singing teacher, and coached many Italian opera singers, among them Grisi, Mario and Ronconi. From 1856 he was on the staff of the RAM. A prolific composer, he had three operas produced in Italy: *Il mercante di Venezia* (4, G. T. Cimino; Bologna, 8 Nov 1873), *Mattia Corvino* (3, C. D'Ormeville; Milan, Scala, 24 March 1877) and *Margherita* (2, A. Zanardini; Venice, Fenice, 8 March 1882). He also composed occasional vocal works, piano pieces and nearly 250 songs, many of which were extremely popular, and was greatly in demand as an accompanist.

ELIZABETH FORBES

Pinto, Mrs. *See* SIBILLA.

Pinza, Ezio (Fortunato) (*b* Rome, 18 May 1892; *d* Stamford, CT, 9 May 1957). Italian bass. Having studied at the Bologna Conservatory, he made his début in 1914 as Oroveso in *Norma* in Soncino, near Cremona. After World War I he began to sing in the principal Italian houses, notably at La Scala under Toscanini (1922–4). His appearance at the Metropolitan Opera in 1926 as the Pontifex Maximus in Spontini's *La vestale* began a

Ezio Pinza in the title role of Mozart's 'Don Giovanni'

period of 22 consecutive seasons as one of the company's leading basses. His repertory there of 52 roles included, besides all the important bass parts in Italian opera, outstanding portrayals of Don Giovanni and Figaro, both of which he also sang frequently at the Salzburg Festival; during the 1930s he appeared in five Covent Garden seasons. After leaving the Metropolitan at the age of 56, he began a second career in musical comedy, operetta and musical films, scoring an enormous success on Broadway in *South Pacific* in 1949. Pinza's beautiful and cultivated *basso cantante*, his handsome presence, engaging personality and spirited acting made him the most richly gifted and accomplished Italian bass of his day, as is shown by his numerous recordings.

GV (J. B. Richards; J. P. Kenyon)
E. Pinza with R. Magidoff: *Ezio Pinza: an Autobiography* (New York, 1958)
J. B. Richards, J. P. Kenyon and J. McPherson: 'Ezio Pinza', *Record Collector*, xxvi (1980–81), 51–95, 101–37 [with discography]

DESMOND SHAWE-TAYLOR

Pinzauti, Leonardo (*b* Florence, 17 Nov 1926). Italian music critic. After studying music in Florence, specializing in music history with Fausto Torrefranca, he began his career as a music critic with the *Giornale del mattino* (1949–57), of which he also became managing editor (1960–63). He joined the editorial boards of *Approdo musicale* (1964) and *Nuova rivista musicale italiana* (1967), to which he contributed a series of interviews with contemporary composers, and became music critic of *La nazione* in 1965. From 1970 he taught music history at the Florence Conservatory. His interests include contemporary Italian music and 19th-century

Italian opera (with particular attention to Florence); he has written articles on Verdi, Busoni, Vittorio Gui and Puccini.

Il Maggio musicale fiorentino dalla prima alla trentesima edizione (Florence, 1967)
Puccini: una vita (Florence, 1974, 2/1975)
La musica e le cose (Florence, 1977)
Musicisti d'oggi: venti colloqui (Turin, 1978)
L'Accademia musicale chigiana: da Boito a Boulez (Milan, 1982)

CAROLYN GIANTURCO

Piovene, Agostin [Agostino] (*b* ?Venice, 17 Oct 1671; *d* after 1721). Italian librettist. Little is known of his life except that he was a count, belonged to the Venetian patriciate and was a member of Venice's most prominent music society, the Accademia Filarmonica, *c*1711. Between 1709 and 1721 he produced eight librettos for the Venetian stage, always for the larger houses favoured by the nobility such as S Cassiano and S Giovanni Grisostomo. From *Publio Cornelio Scipione* (1712) onwards Piovene chose classical subjects, but his most popular librettos were his first two, which were on medieval subjects: *La principessa fedele* (1709) and *Tamerlano* (1711), both set by Francesco Gasparini. A version of *La principessa fedele* with the new title *Cunegonda* was set by Vivaldi (1726, Venice); Vivaldi also used the libretto of *Tamerlano*, much altered, for a pasticcio produced at Verona in 1735. The most famous setting of *Tamerlano* (in a version prepared by Nicola Haym) was that of Handel (1724, London). There is no sign of activity from Piovene after *Nerone* (Orlandini, 1721).

See also TAMERLANO.

La principessa fedele, F. Gasparini, 1709 (Vivaldi, 1726, as Cunegonda); *Tamerlano*, Gasparini, 1711 (Gasparini, 1719, as Il Bajazet; Chelleri, 1720; Leo, 1722, as Bajazete imperador de' turchi; Gasparini, 1723, as Bajazette; Handel, 1724; Giai, 1727; Porpora, 1730; G. Porta, 1730, as Il gran Tamerlano; G. C. de' Bonomi, 1732; Vivaldi, 1735, pasticcio; unknown composer, 1739, as Il Bajazette; Bernasconi, 1742, as Bajazet; E. Duni, 1743, as Bajazette o Tamerlano; Lampugnani, 1748, as Il gran Tamerlano; Jommelli, 1753, as Bajazette; Cocchi and Pescetti, 1754; Sarti, 1764, as Il gran Tamerlano; Scolari, 1764; G. Scarlatti, 1765, as Bajazet; Bertoni, 1765, as Il Bajazetto; P. A. Guglielmi, 1765; Mysliveček, 1772, as Il gran Tamerlano; Sacchini, 1773; Marinelli, 1799, as Bajazette); *Spurio Postumio*, C. F. Pollarolo, 1712; *Publio Cornelio Scipione*, Pollarolo, 1712 (Vinci, 1722); *Porsenna*, Lotti, 1713 (Vignati, 1719); *Marsia deluso*, Pollarolo, 1714; *Polidoro*, Lotti, 1715; *Nerone*, Orlandini, 1721 (Vignati, 1724)

J. M. Knapp: 'Handel's Tamerlano: the Creation of an Opera', *MQ*, lvi (1970), 405–30
A. L. Bellina, B. Brizi and M. G. Pensa: 'Il pasticcio Bajazet: la "favola" del Gran Tamerlano nella messinscena di Vivaldi', *Nuovi studi vivaldiani: edizione e cronologia critica delle opere*, ed. A. Fanna and G. Morelli (Florence, 1988), 185–272
L. Bianconi and G. La Face Bianconi, eds.: *I libretti italiani di Georg Friedrich Händel e le loro fonti* (Bologna, 1992–)

MICHAEL TALBOT (work-list KURT MARKSTROM)

Piper [née Evans], **(Mary) Myfanwy** (*b* London, 28 March 1911). English librettist of Welsh descent. She achieved distinction with three adaptations (two from Henry James and one from Thomas Mann) devised as librettos for Benjamin Britten. Her three librettos for Alun Hoddinott were also adaptations from major authors.

The painter John Piper (1903–92), whom she married in 1935, had long been a friend of Britten's and was the stage designer for *The Rape of Lucretia* (1946). For Britten's *Turn of the Screw* (1954) Myfanwy Piper provided a libretto with strong and telling characterization. Despite the awkwardness of its double prologue and the blunting of James's subtlety (the ghosts become 'real' instead of existing only in the Governess's perception), hers was a significant contribution to the opera's continuing and widespread success.

Owen Wingrave (also after James), televised in 1971, was less well received, but Piper retained the composer's confidence. In the same year she and her husband went with Britten and Peter Pears to Venice, when the composer was planning what was to be his last opera, *Death in Venice*. Thomas Mann's short novel received a necessarily bold reshaping in Piper's text, accommodating dance and mute action. She wrote revealingly about these collaborations in *The Operas of Benjamin Britten* (ed. D. Herbert; London, 1979). Britten's song cycle *Winter Words* (1953) is dedicated to John and Myfanwy Piper.

Later, a sustained association with Alun Hoddinott yielded three opera premières in five years, *The Rajah's Diamond* (like *Owen Wingrave*) having been commissioned for television.

The Turn of the Screw, Britten, 1954; *Owen Wingrave*, Britten, 1971; *Death in Venice*, Britten, 1973; *What the Old Man does is Always Right*, A. Hoddinott, 1977; *The Rajah's Diamond*, Hoddinott, 1979; *The Trumpet Major*, Hoddinott, 1981

ARTHUR JACOBS

Piper of Hamelin, The. Opera by V. E. Nessler; *see RATTENFÄNGER VON HAMELN, DER.*

Pipkov, Lyubomir (*b* Lovech, 19 Sept 1904; *d* Sofia, 9 May 1974). Bulgarian composer. Born into a musical family, he received his first lessons from his father, Panayot Pipkov, entering the Sofia Music School in 1919. From 1926 to 1932 he studied at the Ecole Normale in Paris, where Dukas was his composition teacher. Returning to Bulgaria he became répétiteur, then chorus master and, from 1944 to 1948, director of the Sofia National Opera. Pipkov was a socially aware intellectual with a keen sense of the tragic and dramatic conflict. Having mastered the musical traditions of Western Europe, he reinterpreted the substance of folksong in contemporary language and, influenced by Musorgsky's opera aesthetics, directed his efforts to solving the dichotomy between speech and music and the problems of musical dramaturgy.

In his best-known opera *Yaninite devet bratya* ('Yana's Nine Brothers', 1937), based on a folk ballad, Pipkov attempted exact musical rendering of the rhythmic and metric structure of the prosody of Bulgarian speech, which resulted in a recitative style of declamation. The historical opera *Momchil* (1948), based on a tale of the 14th century, is characterized by 'speech melody', song-like features and epic structure. After the 1950s Pipkov extended his expressive range to include intimate philosophical contemplation and to deal with universal human situations within the framework of contemporary issues. The opera *Antigona '43* (1963) seeks to make philosophical and ethical generalizations in the context of the anti-fascist struggle. It is written in recitative-like style, and uses the chorus in the role of commentator. All three operas were first performed by the Sofia National Opera.

Yaninite devet bratya [Yana's Nine Brothers] (N. Vesselinov and L. Pipkov), Sofia, National, 19 Sept 1937
Momchil (H. Radevski, after S. Zagorchinov: *Den posleden, den*

gospoden [The Last Day, the Day of Our Lord]), Sofia, National, 24 April 1948
Antigona '43 (V. Bashev and P. Panchev, after Sophocles), Ruse, Opera, 23 Dec 1963

*

K. Iliev: *Lyubomir Pipkov* (Sofia, 1958)
L. Koen: *Lyubomir Pipkov* (Sofia, 1968)

MAGDALENA MANOLOVA

Pique Dame. Opera by P. I. Tchaikovsky; *see* QUEEN OF SPADES, THE.

Pirame et Thisbé ('Pyramus and Thisbe'). *Tragédie en musique* in a prologue and five acts by FRANÇOIS FRANCOEUR and François Rebel to a libretto by JEAN-LOUIS-IGNACE DE LA SERRE after OVID's *Metamorphoses*, iv; Paris, Opéra, 17 October 1726.

The first and most successful opera by Francoeur and Rebel, *Pirame et Thisbé* was revived at the Opéra in 1740, 1759, 1761 and 1771; for an outline of the story *see* PIRAMO E TISBE. Servandoni's set design for it was his first commission from the Opéra. A rumour circulated that substantial portions were composed by Rebel's uncle, Michel-Richard de Lalande.

The music displays a fine sense of theatre, as in the interlude for flutes and strings during which dawn gradually lights the stage (5.i), or the dramatic accompanied recitative describing Zoroastre unleashing the wind and the thunder (2.v). The 'air pour les Egiptiens' (2.iv) survived as a 19th-century *contredanse* entitled 'La Camargos'.   LOIS ROSOW

Piramo e Tisbe. *Intermezzo tragico* in two acts by JOHANN ADOLF HASSE to a libretto by MARCO COLTELLINI after OVID's *Metamorphoses*, iv; Vienna, unidentified country estate, autumn 1768 (revised version, Vienna, Laxenburg Palace theatre, September 1770).

Promised to each other since childhood, two young lovers of Babylon learn that their marriage is forbidden by the woman's father (tenor), who, having been insulted by public opinion generated by a dispute between their families, orders his daughter to marry another man. The lovers decide to flee. That night the young woman, Tisbe [Thisbe] (soprano), anxiously awaits her lover Piramo [Pyramus] (soprano) for their tryst in nearby woods. Frightened by a bloodied lion, Thisbe drops her veil and runs. The lion calmly drinks from a spring but leaves blood on the ground and the veil before departing. When Pyramus subsequently arrives, he imagines his beloved brutalized by a beast and stabs himself. Returning and finding Pyramus dying, Thisbe also stabs herself. Finally, as dawn is breaking, Thisbe's father arrives. Blaming himself for his daughter's death, he too stabs himself.

The opera is conspicuously different from any other by Hasse. Using more accompagnato than *semplice* recitative and many through-composed arias and duets (some of which link without a tonic cadence to the following recitative), the work is quite modern for its day. In correspondence with a Venetian friend, G. M. Ortes, Hasse confessed to great satisfaction: 'I place it among the best works I have written; ... while composing I always felt inspiration ... and wish to close my already too-long theatrical career with this opera' (19 November 1768).

The two principals have four arias each and sing three duets; the father has two arias. Four minor keys – G, A, C and F – progressively heighten sadness to fear, while major keys extend Hasse's usual range to include the

quite exceptional B major for the final anguished duet of the dying lovers. The texture is at times very chromatic and orchestrally rich. Though originally sung by amateurs, the vocal parts are demanding and often brilliant.   SVEN HANSELL

Pirata, Il ('The Pirate'). *Melodramma* in two acts by VINCENZO BELLINI to a libretto by FELICE ROMANI after Isidore J. S. Taylor's play *Bertram, ou Le pirate*, a version of Charles Maturin's *Bertram*; Milan, Teatro alla Scala, 27 October 1827.

Bellini had lived in Sicily and Naples until arriving in Milan on 12 April 1827, invited by Barbaia to write for La Scala. *Il pirata* was only his second professional production, and his first collaboration with Romani. Bellini took over six months writing the opera, in order to impress the audience at La Scala. With an excellent cast that included Giovanni Battista Rubini as Gualtiero, Henriette Méric-Lalande as Imogene and Antonio Tamburini as Ernesto, the opera was well received and Bellini was hailed as an exciting new voice. When Rubini and his wife, Adelaide Comelli-Rubini, sang in the opera at the S Carlo, Naples, in 1828, the tenor was probably responsible for major adjustments made to the ending (for illustration *see* RUBINI, GIOVANNI BATTISTA).

Il pirata, with its highly Romantic plot, soon won Bellini international success. The opera was staged in Vienna at the Kärntnertortheater (1828) with Rubini and his wife; in London (the first Bellini opera to be heard there) at the King's Theatre (1830) with Donzelli, Méric-Lalande and V.-F. Santini; and in Paris at the Théâtre Italien (1832), with Rubini and Wilhelmine Schröder-Devrient, who interpolated an aria from Pacini's *Amazilia* and insisted on a happy ending. During the 20th century *Il pirata* was revived at Rome in 1935 to mark the centenary of Bellini's death, while a production at Palermo in January 1958 was transferred to La Scala in May, when the cast included Franco Corelli, Maria Callas and Ettore Bastianini. At Florence during the 1967 Maggio Musicale the cast included Flaviano Labò and Montserrat Caballé.

The scene is Sicily, in and around the castle of Caldora in the 13th century. Ernesto (bass), Duke of Caldora, a follower of the house of Anjou, has forced Imogene (soprano) to marry him against her will and despite her love for Gualtiero (tenor), formerly Count of Montalto and loyal to the rival house of Manfred. Gualtiero, defeated in battle and proscribed, has become the leader of a band of Aragonese pirates, who have just been conquered by a fleet under the command of the Duke of Caldora.

The overture, adapted from one probably played before the first version of *Adelson e Salvini* (1825) and itself deriving from Bellini's E♭ sinfonia of 1823, follows the Rossinian model, with a crescendo after the second subject. Act 1 begins with a storm that wrecks Gualtiero's ship. He and his crew, washed ashore near the castle of Caldora, are given succour by the fishermen. In Gualtiero's cavatina, 'Nel furor delle tempeste', he describes the vision, constantly in his heart, of Imogene as an angel. Imogene is seen approaching and Gualtiero hides, briefly emerging when she narrates her dream of finding him wounded on the beach, 'Lo sognai ferito, esangue' (shortened by Bellini after the première). Imogene thinks she hears Gualtiero's voice. That night the pirates carouse in an echo chorus. Imogene summons the pirate captain and recognizes Gualtiero. In

'Il pirata' (Bellini): lithograph after Alessandro Sanquirico's design for Act 1 of the original production at La Scala, Milan, 27 October 1827

their duet 'Tu sciagurato! ah! fuggi' she tells him that she was forced to marry Ernesto to save her father's life. The chorus announces the triumphant return of Ernesto, whose declaration of victory over the pirates, 'Sì vincemmo e il pregio io sento', derives from 'Obbliarti, abbandonarti' in *Adelson e Salvini*. Over an accompaniment of increasing agitation, Ernesto tries to discover if Gualtiero is among the surviving pirates. He wishes to imprison them but Imogene begs for their release. The impetuous Gualtiero has to be forcibly restrained from giving himself away and attacking Ernesto. The act closes with music from the main crescendo in the overture, also used to end Act 1 of *Adelson e Salvini*.

Act 2 opens with a chorus of Imogene's ladies, leading to a duet, 'Tu m'apristi in cor ferita', in which Ernesto denounces Imogene as a sinful wife and mother; she retorts that he knew of her earlier love for Gualtiero when he forced her to marry him. Imogene warns Gualtiero that her husband is aware of his presence in the castle. He pleads with her to leave with him, but she refuses. Ernesto, at first unnoticed, turns their duet into a trio. Gualtiero challenges him to combat and kills him. To the sound of a Death March, soldiers lament Ernesto's death; Gualtiero appears to surrender his sword, and in 'Tu vedrai la sventurata' expresses his hope that Imogene will forgive him. A cantabile for english horn and harp introduces the entry of the distracted Imogene with her son. In 'Col sorriso d'innocenza' she imagines that the child can win her Ernesto's forgiveness; on hearing the death sentence pronounced on Gualtiero, she loses all sense of reality and sings the dramatic cabaletta 'O sole ti vela' before being led away. In a final scene, neither printed in vocal scores nor usually performed, Gualtiero is surrounded by soldiers, but evades them by leaping from a bridge to his death.

Il pirata played a significant role in establishing the style of the Romantic *melodramma* later developed by Donizetti and Verdi. The tormented, impulsive hero of Italian Romantic opera is presented for the first time in Gualtiero's opening cavatina. Bellini exploited Rubini's talent for flights of passionate expression, avoiding any break in the melodic line by decoration until near the end of the long phrases. However, Bellini maintained the high tessitura of the Rossinian tenor, ascending to *e″* in the opening cavatina (for Rubini he wrote much of Gualtiero's part a tone higher than it appears in printed scores).

Bellini's style was not yet mature and there are some more conservative sections in the score, such as the Larghetto of the duet for Imogene and Ernesto in Act 2, where the voices are in 3rds and dramatically undifferentiated, and which contains the opera's clearest survival of Rossinian *canto fiorito*. Certain features, such as the echo chorus and the complex vocal counterpoint in the Act 1 finale, were experiments that Bellini did not repeat. More significant for his development are the ariosos, such as 'Se un giorno fia che ti tragga' before the duet for Imogene and Gualtiero in Act 1.

SIMON MAGUIRE, ELIZABETH FORBES

Pirates, The. Mainpiece dialogue opera in three acts by STEPHEN STORACE to a libretto by JAMES COBB; London, King's Theatre in the Haymarket, 21 November 1792.

The Pirates is Storace's most italianate English opera, despite its spoken dialogue. It had a successful first season, given by the Drury Lane company, but did not last as long as his two earlier full-length operas. It was revived briefly as *Isidore de Merida* at Drury Lane on 29 November 1827, with a large portion of Storace's music retained but set to new words. The fact that the original libretto was never published probably explains why a new text was provided.

The action takes place in Naples, with mainly Spanish characters. The original backdrop, which featured a view of Naples with Mount Vesuvius in the background and for which Thomas Greenwood received the credit, may have been designed by Storace himself. Don Altador (tenor) sets out to rescue his love Donna Aurora (soprano) from her guardian Don Gaspero de Merida (tenor), a wicked and wealthy pirate who wants her to marry his nephew Don Guillermo (baritone), another pirate. Altador is assisted by his servant Blazio (baritone), Aurora by her maid Fabulina (soprano). Altador attempts to visit Aurora by entering the garden disguised in Gaspero's clothes; foiled in this, he tries to elope with her while the guard at the gate sleeps in a drunken stupor. In Act 2 he tries to abscond with her from a fairground to which her guardian has taken her. This gives Gaspero an excuse to hide her in his castle. Guillermo's pirates land with their booty and are given instructions to capture Altador. After almost taking Gaspero by mistake, they set sail with Altador in a storm. In Act 3 the pirates are themselves taken by the King of Naples's coastguard. In return for Altador's testimony against the pirates, the coastguard captain agrees to help him rescue Aurora. After several more exploits involving disguises, all ends well.

Of all Storace's English operas, *The Pirates* approaches most closely the Italian operatic style and dramatic interaction of text and music that he had studied and used in his early *opere buffe*. His earlier English mainpiece operas, *The Haunted Tower* and *The Siege of Belgrade*, were written in a style carefully modified for an audience familiar with a simpler form of musical theatre. For *The Pirates* Storace and Cobb made significant changes, especially in the two internal finales. They modelled these on the *opera buffa* action finale, scaled down in length. Storace obviously gave directions to Cobb for these sections, as they are unlike anything in the writer's earlier librettos. The finale to Act 1 contains six contrasting sections, each furthering the plot and using a different combination of characters. The finale begins with a stage song by Fabulina, 'Peaceful slumb'ring o'er the ocean', which was published separately and rapidly became known as *Lullaby*. This was by far Storace's most popular song in print, published both in the original solo version and in many different arrangements, for more than half a century. In the vocal score the finale appears, misleadingly, as two separate numbers, with 'Peaceful slumb'ring' given separately. The Act 1 finale runs a typical course, as Altador and Aurora are thwarted in their attempt to escape, Altador fights Aurora's guardian, and then all parties try to tell their side of the story simultaneously to an officer of the guard. The finale to Act 2 has fewer sections but is equally dramatic: Altador is captured by the pirates, Aurora is escorted to her guardian's castle, and a storm springs up.

One of the most colourful airs in *The Pirates* is 'Scarcely had the blushing morn'. Altador's tale of how the pirates captured a prize ship is complete with pictorial effects for the sea, the fight and the dying captain's bravery. Fabulina's 'A saucy knave who pass'd the door' is a skilful blend of a ballad (which she is inventing to get out of an awkward situation), asides in which she calls for help, and hesitations when she stumbles over her story. As usual, Storace borrowed some material for *The Pirates*, most of it from his own earlier works. The opera was Storace's most involved production to date, with its combination of lavish scenes and large-scale musical numbers. Although it was unable to sustain its popularity beyond the 1792–3 season, it holds a significant position in Storace's output because of his use of action finales.   JANE GIRDHAM

Pirates of Penzance, The [*The Pirates of Penzance; or, The Slave of Duty*]. Operetta in two acts by ARTHUR SULLIVAN to a libretto by W. S. GILBERT; Paignton, Royal Bijou Theatre, 30 December 1879; New York, Fifth Avenue Theatre, 31 December 1879.

The nursemaid Ruth (contralto) mistakenly apprentices her charge, Frederic (tenor), to a pirate instead of a pilot. About to come of age, Frederic proposes to leave the outlaws and bring them and their Pirate King (baritone) to justice. Encouraged by his new love, Mabel (soprano), daughter of Major-General Stanley (baritone) – whose 'I am the very model of a modern major-general' is among the best-known Savoy patter songs – Frederic prepares to lead the Sergeant of Police (bass) and his men to arrest the pirates. (That the policemen are not without sympathy for the criminal is, however, clear from the celebrated 'When a felon's not engaged in his employment'.) Frederic learns, however, that since he was born in a leap year on 29 February he has not reached his 21st birthday and is consequently still apprenticed to the pirates. The problem is resolved when it is revealed that the outlaws 'are all noblemen who have gone wrong'.

Having crossed the Atlantic to challenge unauthorized American productions of *HMS Pinafore*, Gilbert and Sullivan crowned their triumphant visit by unveiling their new operetta in New York (securing the British copyright by a token performance in Paignton). Gilbert's libretto drew on his earlier one-act piece *Our Island Home* (1870) as well as on the many melodramatic plays and operas involving robbers or pirates (at the expense of which he contrived much amusing theatrical burlesque). Stylistic burlesque is particularly evident in this work, examples including 'When the foeman bears his steel', evocative of protracted operatic exits, the parody of the Anvil Chorus (*Il trovatore*) found in 'Come friends who plough the sea', and the waltz-song à la Gounod, 'Poor wand'ring one'.
                                              DAVID RUSSELL HULME

Pirchan, Emil (*b* Brno, 27 May 1884; *d* Vienna, 20 Dec 1957). German stage designer and teacher. The son of a well-known painter, he studied art and architecture in Vienna, then taught drawing in a secondary school. He opened an architect's studio in Munich (1908) and a school of stage and graphic design (1913). In 1918 he designed Pfitzner's *Das Christ-Elflein* and Christian Grabbe's play *Hannibal* for the Munich Staatstheater and in 1919 Schiller's *Maria Stuart*, the first of many productions for the Berlin Staatstheater. With the leading expressionist director Leopold Jessner (1878–1945), director of the Staatstheater from 1919 to 1930, he began one of the theatre's most famous artistic collaborations. Influenced by Adolphe Appia's concept of 'rhythmic space', he constructed for each of his productions 'an architecture that adapted to the rhythm of the action'. He conceived the idea of the 'Jessnertreppe' that 'make the stage breathe and render it expressive'.

Pirchan's opera designs include *Salome* (1922), *Falstaff* (1923), *Rigoletto* (1924), *Jenůfa* (1924) and *La traviata* (1925) for the Berlin Staatsoper, *Boris Godunov* (1925) for the Vienna Staatsoper, and *Le nozze di Figaro* (1932), *Samson et Dalila* (1932), *Die Zauberflöte* (1933) and *Lohengrin* and *Tannhäuser* (1933) for the Prague Neues Deutsches Theater. From 1936 to 1948 he was resident designer with the Vienna Burgtheater and he was a professor at the Vienna Academy until his death. He worked in Barcelona (*The Bartered Bride*, 1936), Amsterdam (1939) and for the

1946 Salzburg Festival (Nestroy, *Der Talisman*). He also wrote plays and essays on art and theatre history.

Pirchan designed more than 300 productions, mostly in Germany, Austria and Czechoslovakia. His expressionist style, at its best in the 1920s, became less severe in later productions. Because of the amount and diversity of his work, he significantly influenced European stage design and his basic ideas anticipated the work in the 1950s of the French director Jean Vilar and his Théâtre National Populaire.

ES (F. Hadamowsky)

K. Macgowan and R. E. Jones: *Continental Stagecraft* (New York, 1923)

L. Richard: *The Concise Encyclopedia of Expressionism* (Secaucus, NJ, 1978)   DAVID J. HOUGH

Pirogov, Alexander (Stepanovich) (*b* Novosyolki, Ryazan' province, 22 June/4 July 1899; *d* Moscow, 26 June 1964). Russian bass, brother of Grigory Pirogov. He studied at Moscow University and in Tyutyunik's singing class at the Philharmonic School, Moscow. He became a soloist first with the Zimin Free Opera, Moscow (1922–4), and then from 1924 at the Bol'shoy. His smooth voice – velvety in the low register, full in the middle, free at the top – was finely controlled, and his musicianship and dramatic versatility were combined with a strong temperament. His best roles were Susanin and Ruslan, Boris (which he sang in the film, 1955) and Varlaam, Prince Gremin and the Miller (Dargomïzhsky's *Rusalka*).   I. M. YAMPOL'SKY

Pirogov, Grigory (Stepanovich) (*b* Novosyolki, Ryazan' province, 12/24 Jan 1885; *d* Leningrad, 20 Feb 1931). Russian bass, brother of Alexander Pirogov. He studied with Mikhail Medvedev and Alexander Dodonov at the Philharmonic School, Moscow, until 1908, and made his début at Rostov-na-Donu with the Shumsky company, 1908–9. He sang at the Mariinsky Theatre, St Petersburg (1909–10), and at the Bol'shoy (1910–15, 1917–21). After 1921 he toured in the USSR and abroad (Berlin, Prague and Bucharest in 1923). His voice was a high *basso cantante* of exceptional range (from *F* to *g'*), full and powerful in all registers. He was a contemporary of Shalyapin, who clearly influenced some of his performances. Pirogov's repertory included comic roles (King Dodon and Tsar Saltan, Don Basilio), dramatic (Boris, the Miller in Dargomïzhsky's *Rusalka*) and epic (Ruslan, Wotan). But he was also able to sing with ease the Demon, Tomsky (*The Queen of Spades*) and Escamillo, without transposition.

I. Remezov: *G. S. Pirogov* (Moscow and Leningrad, 1951)
                                                I. M. YAMPOL'SKY

Pironkov, Simeon (Angelov) (*b* Lom, 18 June 1927). Bulgarian composer. He studied composition with Hadjiev and Stoyanov at the State Musical Academy, Sofia, graduating in 1953. From 1947 to 1951 he was a violinist at the National Youth Theatre, and was later the conductor there. Pironkov worked at the Bulgarian film studios for some years from 1961, and in 1980 became vice-president of the Union of Bulgarian Composers. His marked intellectual background and his anti-romantic outlook have brought him close to Ravel, Brecht and Stravinsky, as well as to the irony and tragic disposition of Shostakovich and Prokofiev. The writing of music for films and the theatre has helped shape a laconic and structurally clear musical expression, and

his preference for chamber forces has inclined him towards monologues and soliloquies; moral and philosophical questions are preferred subjects in his stage works. Pironkov's musical language in his operas is based essentially on Bulgarian speech, with its characteristic intervals and rhythms; like Stoyanov and Pipkov, he looks to contemporary European styles and trends to solve creative problems, in preference to adopting popular traditional forms.

librettos by the composer

Istinskata apologiya na Sokrat [Socrates' Real Apology] (1, after K. Varnalis), Sofia, Union of Composers concert hall, 22 March 1967 (concert perf.); staged Sofia, National, 16 June 1982

Dobriyat chovek ot Sechuan [The Good Person of Szechwan], 1969 (after B. Brecht), Stara Zagora, Opera, 24 June 1972

Zhitie i stradanie greshnogo Sofroniya [The Life and Suffering of Sinful Sophronius] (1), Sofia, Zala Bulgaria concert hall, 18 Jan 1977 (concert perf.)

Pustrata ptitsa [The Motley Bird] (comic op, 2 parts), Ruse, Opera, 28 Sept 1980

O, moya mechta [Oh, My Dream] (lyrical comedy, 2 parts), Ruse, Opera, 19 May 1987

M. Manolova: 'Stilistichni belezi v *Pustrata ptitsa*' [Stylistic Features in *The Motley Bird*], *Scientific Conference: Brno, 1985*
                                            MAGDALENA MANOLOVA

Pirro ('Pyrrhus'). *Dramma per musica* in three acts by GIOVANNI PAISIELLO to a libretto by GIOVANNI DE GAMERRA; Naples, Teatro di S Carlo, 12 January 1787.

Pyrrhus (tenor), King of Epirus, has announced his intention to marry Polissena [Polyxena] (soprano), the beautiful daughter of the Trojan King Priam. The news is met with dismay by the Trojan prince Darete (soprano castrato), who expected to marry Polyxena himself, by Polyxena's brother Eleno [Helenus] (tenor) and by the whole Greek court: the Trojans and the Greeks have been enemies since Pyrrhus' father, Achilles, was killed by Paris, Priam's son. Climene [Clymene] (soprano), betrothed to Pyrrhus, is also upset by the news of his impending marriage. She conspires with Ulisse [Ulysses] (alto castrato) to eliminate Polyxena, and this almost succeeds. It is only through Polyxena's calm insistence of her innocence, her constancy to Pyrrhus and her acceptance of her destiny that Pyrrhus realizes Ulysses' treachery.

Polyxena's misfortunes continue, however, when the high priest Calcante [Calchas] (bass) conveys the oracle's pronouncement that Pyrrhus must avenge his father's murder by spilling Trojan blood, otherwise Troy will emerge as the victor. Calchas seizes Polyxena and leads her to the sacrificial altar. Darete, who has shown his love for Polyxena throughout, wants to save her, but she is resigned to her destiny. In a reversal of its previous pronouncement, the oracle frees Polyxena, and Pyrrhus, touched by the constancy of Darete, magnanimously allows him to marry Polyxena.

The story, rooted in Greek mythology, first appeared in Euripides' *Hecuba*; the love scenes, however, were interpolated by 17th-century French poets. As part of his attempt to create a new form of serious opera, Paisiello introduced ensembles into this *dramma per musica*: in his autobiographical letter (see Faustini-Fasini 1940), Paisiello indicated that this opera represents a first attempt to use concerted introductions and finales which was subsequently imitated by others. Act 1 opens with a sextet, and each act ends with an ensemble. The integration of the opening sextet 'La Grecia m'ascolta' with a march using oboes, flutes, horns, bassoons and a wide variety of percussion instruments is indicative of new directions in Italian serious opera. Of specific interest are the Act 2 duet 'Al mio destin deh lasciami' between Polyxena and Darete, full of exclamation and punctuation in the 'larmoyant' tradition, and the Act 3 terzetto 'Incerto, pentito, crudele' between Polyxena, Darete and Pyrrhus. Clarinets assume an important role in the musical texture of the opera. Another innovation for Paisiello occurs during Pyrrhus's Act 2 aria, when a military band marches across the stage, presenting two simultaneous events. The roles of Ulysses and Darete were sung by castratos; the only bass, Calchas, makes only two appearances, in recitatives.

GORDANA LAZAREVICH

Pirro, Nicola de. *See* DE PIRRO, NICOLA.

Pirro, re d'Epiro ('Pyrrhus, King of Epirus'). *Opera seria* in three acts by NICCOLÒ ANTONIO ZINGARELLI to a libretto by GIOVANNI DE GAMERRA; Milan, Teatro alla Scala, 25 December 1791.

The libretto, substantially the same as that used by Paisiello in 1787, tells of the mutual love of Pirro [Pyrrhus] (soprano) and Polissena [Polyxena] (soprano), hindered by their respective rejected lovers Climene [Clymene] (soprano) and Darete (soprano castrato) and by the perfidy of Ulisse [Ulysses] (tenor), who is intent upon exterminating the Trojan line. Through his machinations, Ulysses succeeds in making Polyxena appear to be guilty of plotting against Pyrrhus, but the unexpected prophecy by Calcante [Calchas] (bass) leads to a happy ending. The opera has several scenes combining soloists with chorus (e.g. the Introduction), which Zingarelli treats in expansive musical forms of considerable complexity in an attempt to convey agitation and pathos. The highlights, justly famous in their day, are Polyxena's rondo 'No, non fia mai ch'io perda' (1.vii), the finale to Act 3 (a double duet plus a double trio with chorus), and especially Pyrrhus's rondo 'Cara, negli occhi tuoi', the *cavallo di battaglia* of Marchesi, the role's most famous and successful interpreter.

MARIA CARACI VELA

Pirrotta, Nino [Antonino] (*b* Palermo, 13 June 1908). Italian musicologist. He studied music in Palermo and Florence, and took a liberal arts degree at the University of Florence in 1931. He worked as librarian at the conservatories in Palermo (1936–48) and Rome (1948–56), before visiting the USA, where from 1956 to 1972 he was professor at Harvard University. Returning to Italy in 1972, he took up an appointment as professor of music history at Rome University, from which he retired in 1978. He has edited *Studi musicali* since 1976 and is a member of several academies and the recipient of four honorary doctorates. Pirrotta has made particularly distinguished contributions to the study of Monteverdi, Cesti and the background to the Metastasian tradition, writing with the same breadth of understanding and freshness of approach that characterize his work on 14th-century Italian music. 'Early Opera and Aria' (1968) is an excellent disentanglement of the many interrelated applications of early monodic style, and *Li due Orfei* (1969, 2/1975) ably traces the Orpheus legend in 15th-century dramatic literature and 17th-century opera. His work on the connections between *commedia dell'arte* and opera further demonstrates his ability to recognize relationships between the various traditions he examines.

'Early Opera and Aria', *New Looks at Italian Opera: Essays in Honor of Donald J. Grout* (Ithaca, NY, 1968), 39–107

Li due Orfei: da Poliziano a Monteverdi (Turin, 1969, 2/1975; Eng. trans., 1982) [incl. essay on the scenography by E. Povoledo]

Don Giovanni in musica (Rome, 1974, 2/1991)

Music and Culture in Italy from the Middle Ages to the Baroque (Cambridge, MA, 1984) [collected essays]

Scelte poetiche di musicisti: teatro, poesia e musica da Willaert a Malipiero (Venice, 1987) [collected essays]

CAROLYN GIANTURCO

Pisa. City in Tuscany in central Italy. The first recorded performances of musical drama in Pisa were an 'abatimento di Dario et il finto Alessandro' in 1606 and a 'comedia in musica' in 1607, both with words and music by Ferdinando Gonzaga; they were followed in 1608 with *Orindo* by Cesare Galletti. During the 17th century performances other than those in the grand-ducal residence were given in a hall in the Palazzo dei Consoli del Mare, the 'Stanzone delle Commedie', later called the Teatro Pubblico. In this early period opera production depended on the presence of the Medici court, which usually spent the winter in Pisa, and on the activities of local academies (the Lunatici and the Stravaganti). The inauguration of opera seasons for paying audiences in the early 18th century led to the reconstruction of the Teatro Pubblico in a beehive shape, with three tiers of boxes. In 1770 work began on a new theatre, the Teatro Nuovo or dei Nobili Fratelli Prini, which opened in the following year with Metastasio's *Antigono* (music by various composers). This theatre, whose management passed in 1798 to the Accademia dei Costanti and in 1822 to that of the Ravvivati, was later named after Ernesto Rossi (1878) and remained in use until 1929. Other theatres built during the 19th century were often used for opera: in 1865 the Politeama (destroyed during World War II) opened with *Crispino e la comare* by the Ricci brothers, and from 1872 to 1891 opera was also staged at the Teatro Diurno or Arena Federighi, renamed Arena Garibaldi in 1882. The Regio Teatro Nuovo (Teatro Verdi after 1904), the most important theatre in the city, opened in 1867 with *Guillaume Tell*, and today stages an autumn opera season. It was closed for restoration in 1985, reopening in 1989 with the world première of Roberto De Simone's *Mistero e processo di Giovanna d'Arco*.

A. Segrè: *Il Teatro pubblico di Pisa nel seicento e nel settecento* (Pisa, 1902)

A. Solerti: *Musica, ballo e drammatica alla corte medicea dal 1600 al 1637* (Florence, 1905)

A. Gentili: *Cinquant'anni dopo ... Il Regio teatro Verdi ne' suoi ricordi* (Pisa, 1915)

A. Giusiani: *Notizie storiche sopra il Pubblico teatro o Stanzone delle commedie* (MS, 1935, I-Plu)

I cento anni del Teatro Verdi di Pisa (1867–1967) (Pisa, 1967)

S. Vagelli: *Storia del Teatro Pubblico di Pisa nei secoli XVII e XVIII* (diss., U. of Pisa, 1979)

M. I. Aliverti and M. Alderigi: 'Théâtre et spectacle à Pise au temps de Léopold Ier (1765–1790)', *Fifth International Congress on the Enlightenment: Oxford 1980*, 1432–9

G. Burchielli: 'Il Politeama di Pisa 1865–1943', *La provincia pisana*, ix/Dec (1983), 9–16

G. Dell'Ira: *Il firmamento lirico pisano* (Pisa, 1983)

Il teatro abbandonato (Florence, 1985)

G. Dell'Ira: *I teatri di Pisa (1773–1986)* (Pisa, 1987)

FRANCESCO GIUNTINI

Pisaroni, Benedetta Rosmunda (*b* Piacenza, 16 May 1793; *d* Piacenza, 6 Aug 1872). Italian soprano, later contralto. She studied in Milan and made her début in

Bergamo in 1811 in Mayr's *La rosa bianca e la rosa rossa*. After appearances in Padua, Bologna and Venice, she sang in the première of Meyerbeer's *Romilda e Costanza* (1817, Padua) and was subsequently engaged in Naples, where she created major roles in three of Rossini's operas: Zomira in *Ricciardo e Zoraide* (1818), Andromache in *Ermione* (1819) and Malcolm in *La donna del lago* (1819), repeating Malcolm in Rome (1823) and at La Scala (1824). She also sang in the première of Meyerbeer's *L'esule di Granata* (1821, Milan) and added Arsace in *Semiramide* (1824) and Tancredi (1825) to her repertory. She made her Paris début as Arsace at the Théâtre Italien (1827), and during the next three seasons sang Malcolm, Tancredi and Isabella (*L'italiana in Algeri*) there. In 1829 she appeared in the première of Carafa's *Le nozze di Lammermoor* and sang in London at the King's Theatre. She returned to La Scala in 1831, in Generali's *Romito di Provenza* and Rossini's *Bianca e Falliero*, and then retired.

She had a range of nearly three octaves but a serious illness in 1813 resulted in the loss of her top notes, and she subsequently cultivated her lower register, which increased greatly in volume.   ELIZABETH FORBES

Pishkek. BISHKEK.

Pistocchi, Francesco Antonio Massimiliano [Mamiliano] ['Pistocchino', 'Pistocco'] (*b* Palermo, *c*1659; *d* Bologna, 13 May 1726). Italian composer, singer and teacher. He was probably the most interesting child prodigy before Mozart. The son of Giovanni Pistocchi, a violinist and tenor at S Petronio, Bologna, he was a member of the schola cantorum there and in 1670 was first paid for occasional services as a 'putto musico'. Three years earlier he had published *Capricci puerili*, a set of instrumental pieces; in 1687 he gained admission to the Accademia Filarmonica as a singer and in 1692 as a composer. He was in the service of the Parma court, 1686–95, and in 1696 became Kapellmeister to the Margrave of Brandenburg at Ansbach. He paid visits, with Giuseppe Torelli, to Berlin (1697) and Vienna (1699–1700), returning to Bologna in autumn 1700. He was *principe* of the Accademia Filarmonica in 1708 and 1710 and took holy orders in 1709.

As a contralto Pistocchi was active in the principal theatres. At Ferrara in 1675 a sonnet, *Ai numi dell'Adria*, was published in his honour; in the years that followed he was in Turin (1688), Parma (1688–9, 1690–92, 1699, 1701), Piacenza (1687, 1690), Rome (1693, 1694), Bologna (1694–5), Modena (1686, 1691), Genoa (1693), Pesaro (1692) and Venice (1690–92, 1699, 1704–5). On his last visit to Venice adverse comment was made on the condition of his voice, but he continued to sing for many years in religious services and private entertainments. Great though his fame was as a singer, it was even greater as a teacher of singing; his most celebrated pupils included Luigi Albarelli, Valentino Urbani, Antonio Pasi, Annibale Pio Fabri, Antonio Maria Bernacchi, Gaetano Berenstadt and Giuseppe Cassani. These pupils helped to spread a fame that became almost legendary and contributed to the persistence of various anecdotes, such as Burney's about the loss of his voice. Tosi's panegyric in his *Opinioni* and the fact that Pistocchi was a man of superior literary culture (as is shown by the catalogue of his library, in *I-Bu*) helped to spread an idea of Pistocchi as the defender of a 'pure' style, far removed from the preoccupation with technique of the following gen-

eration. According to Martinelli, however, the corruption of taste originated in his school. In fact he had among his pupils singers who showed a variety of stylistic tendencies, from the emotionalism of Pasi to the many-styled virtuosity of Bernacchi. The trend towards vocal agility around the 1720s and 30s was, moreover, a general phenomenon and not traceable to a single school. The summit of Pistocchi's art must have consisted in the ability to ornament, which according to Tosi involved both melodic and rhythmic variation.

Pistocchi's music has yet to be fully studied. The cantatas are widely disseminated, but he was a proficient composer in every style; unfortunately little of his operatic music survives. His association with the pathetic style is due in part to the fame of an aria, 'E che farei, misera me' from the oratorio *Maria vergine addolorata*, published by Burney, which was apparently quoted by Corelli in the sarabande of his Concerto op.6 no.11 and by Francesco Geminiani in his song 'Gently touch the warbling lyre' (*c*1725).

Il Leandro (dramma per musica, 3, C. Badoaro), Venice, Riva delle Zattere, 15 May 1679 [?Pistocchi]; rev. as Pistocchi Gli amori fatali, Venice, S Moisè, Jan 1682
Il Narciso (pastorale, 5, A. Zeno), Ansbach, Hof, March 1697
Le pazzie d'amore e dell'interesse (idea drammatica per musica), Ansbach, Hof, 16 June 1699
Le risa di Democrito (3, N. Minato), Vienna, Hof, 17 Feb 1700, A-Wn (part of Act 2)
I rivali generosi [Act 2] (dramma per musica, 3, Zeno), Reggio Emilia, Pubblico, April 1710 [Act 1 by C. Monari, Act 3 by G. M. Capelli]

BurneyH; *DEUMM* (A. Chiarelli)
G. B. Martini: *Scrittori de musica* (MS, *I-Bsf*)
P. F. Tosi: *Opinioni de' cantori antichi e moderni* (Bologna, 1723; Eng. trans., 1742, 2/1743, as *Observations on the Florid Song*)
O. Penna: *Catalogo degli aggregati della Accademia Filarmonica di Bologna* (MS, *I-Baf*, 1736/*R* 1971 [sometimes attrib. G. B. Martini])
G. Gaspari: *Miscellanea musicale* (MS, *I-Bc*), iv
V. Martinelli: *Lettere familiari e critiche* (London, 1758), 357ff
A. Ademollo: *La storia del 'Girello'* (Milan, 1890)
A. Einstein: 'Italienische Musiker am Hofe der Neuburger Wittelsbacher 1614–1716', *SIMG*, ix (1907–8), 366–424
H. Mersmann: *Beiträge zur Ansbacher Musikgeschichte* (Leipzig, 1916)
N. Pelicelli: 'Musicisti in Parma nel secolo XVII', *NA*, x (1933), 232–48, esp. 245–7
M. Fabbri: *Alessandro Scarlatti e il Principe Ferdinando de' Medici* (Florence, 1961)
O. Termini: 'Singers at San Marco in Venice: the Competition between Church and Theatre (*c*1675–*c*1725)', *RMARC*, no.17 (1981), 65–96
F. Della Seta: 'I Borghese (1691–1731): la musica di una generazione', *NA*, new ser., i (1983), 139–208, esp. 165ff
                    SERGIO DURANTE

Pistor, Gotthelf (*b* Berlin, 17 Oct 1887; *d* Cologne, 4 April 1947). German tenor. He began his career in 1918 as an actor, then studied singing with Juan Luria and Carl Beines and made his operatic début at Nuremberg in 1923. In the following year he sang at Würzburg, Darmstadt, Magdeburg, Cologne and Berlin, where he became principal Heldentenor in 1930. He first appeared at Bayreuth as Froh in 1925, and later sang most of the leading tenor roles there. His single performance at Covent Garden as Tristan in 1931 brought praise principally for his artistic qualities ('finer, more nervous and distinguished than Melchior', reported Richard Capell in the *Musical Monthly Record*), and he returned to the role in the winter season of 1937, singing with Eva Turner. He appeared as a guest artist in San Francisco and, from 1930 to 1938, as a regular member of the festival company at Zoppot (now Sopot). On recordings he is best remembered for his Parsifal in the 1928 recording of Act 3 conducted by Carl Muck; he had an attractively vibrant timbre, capable of much tenderness and directed with intelligence and imagination. J. B. STEANE

Piticchio, Francesco (*b* ?Palermo; *fl* 1760–1800). Italian composer. He is sometimes said to have been born in Rome, but this seems to result from the confusion of him with the contemporary Roman composer Pietro Paolo Piticchio, some of whose music has also been attributed to Francesco. About 1760 he was a *maestro di cappella* in Palermo. In 1778 he collaborated with Giuseppe Gazzaniga on a comic opera in Rome. His *Didone* was performed in Palermo in 1780, followed by a comic opera in Rome in 1781. He then went to Germany as *maestro al cembalo* of an Italian opera company. For about two years, probably from 1782, he was at Brunswick, in 1784–5 at Dresden and in 1785 at Madrid. He spent the years 1786–91 in Vienna and then apparently returned to Italy. In Naples in 1798 he had an opera performed at the S Carlo, the libretto of which describes him as *maestro di cappella* to the hereditary princess. He probably accompanied the royal family when it fled to Palermo to escape the Revolution of 1799.

Gerber thought highly of Piticchio's operas, calling him a 'passionate and highly expressive' composer, a judgment that has been echoed by later lexicographers. However, to Da Ponte, who collaborated with him on an opera in Vienna, he was a 'maestro bestia' and 'a man of very little intellect and of the most limited musical gifts'.

Il ciarlatano accusato (dg), Florence, Pallacorda, aut. 1777
Il marchese di Verde Antico (int, 2), Rome, Capranica, Jan 1778, collab. G. Gazzaniga
Didone abbandonata (os, P. Metastasio), Palermo, S Cecilia, carn. 1780; rev. Brunswick, wint. 1784, *D-Wa*
Il militare amante (ob), Rome, Dame, carn. 1781
Gli amanti alla prova [Die Liebhaber auf der Probe] (ob, G. Bertati), Dresden, Hof, 4 Jan 1785, *Dlb*
Il Bertoldo (dg, 2, L. da Ponte, after Brunati), Vienna, Hof, 22 June 1787, *F-Pn*
La vendetta di Medea (os, O. Balsamo), Naples, S Carlo, 13 Aug 1798

*

GerberL; GerberNL
L. da Ponte: *Memorie* (New York, 1823–7, enlarged 2/1829–30; Eng. trans., 1929)
O. Tiby: *Il Real Teatro Carolino e l'ottocento musicale palermitano* (Florence, 1957), 271

Pitt, Percy [Percival] **(George)** (*b* London, 4 Jan 1869; *d* London, 23 Nov 1932). English conductor and manager. He studied with Reinecke in Leipzig and with Rheinberger in Munich. He was orchestral keyboard player and accompanist at the Queen's Hall under Henry Wood before moving to opera in 1902, when he was appointed musical adviser to the Grand Opera Syndicate which ran Covent Garden. As musical director there from 1907 to 1924 his post gave him little more than the function of coach, assistant conductor and consultant, but it placed him centrally in the politics of opera. He was a close ally of Hans Richter in the latter's performances of the *Ring* in English at Covent Garden (1908–9) and shared Richter's disappointment that the further establishment of an English repertory was frustrated by the management. On Richter's

nomination, Pitt had already become the first English conductor at Covent Garden during the 'grand season' with Poldini's one-act *Der Vagabund und die Prinzessin* (1907). He also conducted *Don Giovanni* in 1909 (with John McCormack as Don Ottavio) and, in a short season under Beecham's management, Sullivan's *Ivanhoe* (1910). In Beecham's 1919–20 season at Covent Garden, Pitt conducted *Khovanshchina*, *Pelléas et Mélisande* and other works, and on the subsequent financial collapse of Beecham's operatic enterprise Pitt was artistic director of the succeeding British National Opera Company from 1922 until 1924. From 1922 to 1930 he worked for the BBC, first as an adviser and from 1924 as full-time musical director. He conducted the broadcast of parts of *Die Zauberflöte* from Covent Garden on 8 January 1923, one of the earliest opera transmissions. Under Pitt's leadership, the future tone of the BBC's musical enterprise was established. His compositions include a song written for Tetrazzini and a variety of stage music.

*

P. Pitt: 'Broadcasting and the Opera', *Music Masterpieces*, i (London, 1925), 87
J. D. Chamier: *Percy Pitt of Covent Garden and the BBC* (London, 1938) ARTHUR JACOBS

Pittore parigino, Il ('The Parisian Painter'). *Intermezzo comico per musica* in two parts by DOMENICO CIMAROSA to a libretto by GIUSEPPE PETROSELLINI; Rome, Teatro Valle, 2 January 1781.

The story is set in Lyons, where Eurilla (soprano), a learned lady and poet, is writing a play. Baron Cricca (bass), who wants to marry her, has commissioned a portrait of her from Crotignac (tenor), a French painter. Broccardo (baritone), Eurilla's secretary and factotum, reads her father's testament, which promises her a large inheritance if she marries Cricca; but if she marries someone else the money will go to her cousin Cintia (soprano). Eurilla is torn between her growing affection for Crotignac and the prospect of the inheritance, but she commits herself to Cricca for the sake of the money. Cintia, Cricca's jilted mistress who still loves him, arrives from Marseilles disguised as a singer and attempts to discredit Cricca in order to break the engagement. Crotignac's attention to Cintia incites Eurilla's jealousy. She challenges him to a duel to be fought on her behalf by either Cricca or Broccardo. All three men cower at the prospect. In the end, Eurilla decides that love should win over money and elects to marry Crotignac; this enables Cricca to marry Cintia, and all sing a chorus in praise of love, 'Il furbetto amor'.

This rather complex plot parodies the pleasure-seeking, pre-Revolutionary society. Crotignac, through his superficial allegiance to both Eurilla and Cintia, exemplifies the fickleness of love. Eurilla's interest in books and poetry classes her as a 'blue-stocking', a type satirized since Molière's time, and Cricca's aristocratic heritage is also an object of satire. At its première the piece had an all-male cast. It enjoyed performances for 27 years and was reworked several times – for instance, as a three-act *commedia*, *Il barone burlato* with additions by Francesco Cipolla (1784, Naples), and by Cimarosa himself (1792, Vienna). At Eszterháza (1792) Haydn added several vocal numbers, including 'Dolce mi parve un di' from Martín y Soler's *Una cosa rara*, and in Vienna (1792) Haydn's 'Infelice sventurata' was inserted.

Der Onkel aus Amsterdam (1790, Dresden) was a

translation of the text into German with some new arias by an unknown hand added to Cimarosa's music.

GORDANA LAZAREVICH

Pittsburgh. American city in Pennsylvania. The first opera given there was *Il barbiere di Siviglia* (in English) by the visiting Francis Wemyss Troupe on 16 April 1838. In 1873 the Frohsinn Society gave Flotow's *Alessandro Stradella* (in German) to much acclaim, and in 1874 the Gounod Club performed *Martha* in its first operatic series. The city's first permanent company, the Pittsburgh Opera Society, was not established until 1939. Richard Karp was its director from 1939 to 1975, when his daughter Barbara took over; she was succeeded by James de Blasis in 1978 and Tito Capobianco in 1983. The company gives four performances of five works each year. Its first permanent home was the Syria Mosque in 1945; in 1971, with the Pittsburgh SO, it moved to the newly renovated Heinz Hall (formerly the Penn Theatre). In October 1987 the Pittsburgh Opera moved to the Benedum Center for the Performing Arts (formerly the Stanley Theater); the Pittsburgh Opera Orchestra has also been established (principal conductor Theo Alcantara), as well as the Pittsburgh Opera Center training programme for young American artists. Singers who have recently performed at the Pittsburgh Opera include Vladimir Atlantov, John Bröcheler, Mary Jane Johnson, Richard Leech, Ann Panagulias, Bruno Pola and Ludmila Schemtchuk.

The Pittsburgh Opera Theater, formerly the Pittsburgh Chamber Opera, was founded in 1978 by Mildred Miller Posvar, who modelled the company on Boris Goldovsky's New England Opera Theater; its Chamber Opera Series gives three productions each season in the Carnegie Music Hall. The Pittsburgh Savoyards company became a member of the Gilbert and Sullivan Society of London, which provided production assistance for its first operetta, *The Pirates of Penzance*, in 1939; based at the Pittsburgh Center for the Arts (which has no concert hall), the group gives two or three performances each year.

G. M. Rohrer: *Music and Musicians of Pennsylvania* (Philadelphia, 1940)

E. G. Baynham: *A History of Pittsburg Music 1758–1958* (MS, 1970)

Carnegie Magazine, xlix (1975) [whole issue]   IDA REED

Pixérécourt, René Charles Guilbert de (*b* Nancy, 22 Jan 1773; *d* Nancy, 25 July 1844). French librettist and dramatist. Son of a nobleman, he intended to become a lawyer, but his plans were interrupted by the French Revolution and he fled to Germany in 1789. By 1793 he had returned to Nancy, then moved on to Paris, where he began writing plays and librettos. Not until 1797 did one of his works reach the public: *Les petits auvergnats*, at the Théâtre de l'Ambigu-Comique which, along with the Porte-St-Martin and Gaîté theatres, was always eager to produce his melodramas once their appeal was clear.

Throughout the 1820s and into the 30s Pixérécourt continued to write melodramas, *opéras comiques* and other stage works; at the same time, he held government posts and was director of the Opéra-Comique (1822–7). He took over the administration of the Gaîté, but in 1835 fire destroyed this house, along with many of his manuscripts, and he was forced to sell his country estate

and his considerable library in order to survive financially. He retired and returned to Nancy later that year. His total output for the stage, including the works that were not performed, reached 120 pieces.

Dubbed 'the Corneille of the Boulevards', Pixérécourt was practically the inventor, and certainly the codifier, of the popular French stage form *mélodrame*. Noted for its stock characters, complex plots, sensationalism, startling *coups de théâtre*, scenic virtuosity and a strongly moral outlook, the *mélodrame* flourished in the early decades of the 19th century. Pixérécourt built a catalogue of nearly 60 such plays, beginning in 1798 with *Victor, ou L'enfant de la forêt* (originally intended as an *opéra comique*), developing an international reputation. He also wrote comedies, tragedies, vaudevilles, *féeries*, pantomimes and the librettos of some 21 *opéras comiques*. However, he did not emerge in the front rank of librettists for two reasons: his *opéras comiques*, though skilfully written, are quite conventional; and he seldom had the opportunity to collaborate with a really first-rate musician. Yet he certainly was not ignorant of the dramatic potential of music, for he worked a great deal of it into his melodramas. His most frequent collaborators in that genre were Louis Alexandre Piccinni and Adrien Quaisain. In both dramas and librettos he saw himself as a successor of Sedaine.

Though Pixérécourt's melodramas are best known for the influence they exercised on Romantic drama, they were no less influential on the genre that came to be known as French grand opera. Pixérécourt planned innovatory *mises en scène* and more modern approaches to staging than had been used at the Opéra, and called for ballets with authentic period and national dress. Along with these features, the melodramas' frequent historical associations, their use of tableau-like scenes (especially at the ends of acts) and their lavish, highly contrasting sets clearly affected the character of the new style of opera. Also, like French grand opera, Pixérécourt's dramas were ensemble pieces requiring careful preparation and well-rehearsed stage business. Though he was often accused of treating his actors like slaves, his precise, finely honed productions won praise even from those who were not fond of their crowd-pleasing qualities. In addition, many of the Opéra's finest designers, choreographers and dancers in the 19th century first worked with Pixérécourt at the boulevard theatres, where they were encouraged to develop ideas that were to become the hallmarks of French grand opera.

opéras comiques

Jacques et Georgette, 1793, not set; *Marat Mauger*, comp. unknown, 1794; *Le mannequin vivant*, Gaveaux, 1796; *Les petits auvergnats*, Morange, 1797; *Les trois tantes*, Solié, 1797; *Victor, ou L'enfant de la forêt*, Solié, 1797 (planned as oc, but perf. as spoken melodrama); *La forêt de Sicile*, Gresnick, 1798; *Léonidas*, Persuis and Gresnick, 1799; *La musicomanie*, Quaisain, 1800 (It., Carafa, 1806); *Le petit page* (with L. T. Lambert), R. Kreutzer and Isouard, 1800; *Le chansonnier de la paix*, 1801; *Flaminius à Corinthe* (with Lambert), Kreutzer and Isouard, 1801; *Marcel, ou L'héritier supposé*, Persuis, 1801; *Quatre maris pour un*, Solié, 1801; *Raymond de Toulouse*, C. G. Foignet and F. Foignet, 1802; *Avis aux femmes*, Gaveaux, 1804; *Koulouf, ou Les chinois*, Dalayrac, 1806; *La rose blanche et la rose rouge*, Gaveaux, 1809 (It., Mayr, 1813); *Ovide en exil*, Hérold, 1818; *L'amant sans maîtresse*, García, 1821; *Le pavillon des fleurs*, Dalayrac, 1822

PLAYS ON WHICH OPERAS HAVE BEEN BASED

L'homme à trois visages (1801): T. S. Cooke, *c*1813, as Rugantino, or The Bravo of Venice

Tékéli, ou Le siège de Montgatz (1803): Hook, 1806, as Tekeli, or

The Siege of Montgatz
La forteresse du Danube (1805): Hook, 1807, as The Fortress
Les mines de Pologne (1805): Hook, 1808, as The Siege of St
    Quintin, or Spanish Heroism
La cisterne (1809): Donizetti, 1822, as Chiara e Serafina
Marguerite d'Anjou (1810): Meyerbeer, 1820, as Margherita
    d'Anjou
La fille de l'exilé (1819): Donizetti, 1827, as Otto mesi in due ore,
    ossia Gli esiliati in Siberia

*

R. C. G. de Pixérécourt: *Théâtre choisi* (Paris and Nancy, 1841–3)
P. Ginisty: *Le mélodrame* (Paris, 1910)
W. Hartog: *Guilbert de Pixérécourt* (Paris, 1913)
K. Pendle: 'Boulevard Theatres and Continuity in French Opera of
    the Nineteenth Century', *Music in Paris in the 1830s*, ed. P.
    Bloom (Stuyvesant, NY, 1987), 509–35
N. Wild: 'La musique dans le mélodrame des théâtres parisiens',
    ibid, 589–610   KARIN PENDLE

Pixis [Göhringer], Francilla (*b* Lichtenthal in Baden,
1816; *d* 1845 or later). German contralto, adopted
daughter of Johann Peter Pixis. After her stage début at
Karlsruhe in 1834 she appeared in Munich, Leipzig,
Berlin, Paris, London and Milan. She was particularly
successful in Naples, where Pacini wrote for her the
leading role in his opera *Saffo* (1840). She retired from
the stage after her marriage.   GAYNOR G. JONES

Pixis, Johann Peter (*b* Mannheim, 10 Feb 1788; *d*
Baden-Baden, 22 Dec 1874). German composer. As a
pianist he was a child prodigy; he and his brother
Friedrich Wilhelm made a concert tour of Germany in
1796, when Johann Peter was eight. After returning to
Mannheim he also studied composition. The family
moved in 1806 to Vienna, where he studied with
Albrechtsberger and met Beethoven, Meyerbeer and
Schubert. He lived in Vienna, except for a short period,
until 1823 when he moved to Paris, where he won a
reputation as a piano virtuoso and teacher.

Pixis's many compositions include chamber music
and operas, but he was most successful when writing for
the keyboard, in a brilliant if often derivative style. He
wrote several sets of piano variations on operatic
themes.

Almazinde oder Die Höhle Sesam (romantische Oper, 3, H.
    Schmidt), Vienna, An der Wien, 11 April 1820
Der Zauberspruch (romantische Oper, 2, after C. Gozzi), Vienna,
    An der Wien, 25 April 1822
Bibiana oder Die Kapelle im Walde (romantische Oper, 3, L. Lax),
    Aachen, 8 Oct 1829
Die Sprache des Herzens (Operette, 1, P. J. Burmeister-Lyser),
    Berlin, Königstadisches, 15 Jan 1836

*

FétisB; GerberNL
'Memoir of John Peter Pixis', *Harmonicon*, iv (1826), 65–6
R. Batka: 'Aus Joh. Peter Pixis Memoiren', *Kranz: gesammelte
    Blätter über Musik* (Leipzig, 1903)
R. Sietz: *Aus F. Hillers Briefwechsel* (Cologne, 1958)
H. Becker, ed.: *G. Meyerbeer: Briefwechsel und Tagebücher* (Berlin,
    1960)   GAYNOR G. JONES

Pizzetti, Ildebrando [Parma, Ildebrando da] (*b* Parma,
20 Sept 1880; *d* Rome, 14 Feb 1968). Italian composer,
the most respected and influential of the more conservative Italian musicians of his generation.

1. LIFE. The son of a piano teacher, Pizzetti spent most
of his childhood (from 1884) in Reggio Emilia. While at
school there he showed less inclination towards music
than towards the theatre, writing plays for casual
performance among his schoolmates. In 1895, however,
he entered the Parma Conservatory, where he studied
under Telesforo Righi, a modest but outstanding teacher

of harmony and counterpoint, and gained his composition diploma in 1901. Meanwhile he became conversant
with 15th- and 16th-century Italian instrumental and
choral music performed and expounded by Giovanni
Tebaldini, one of the pioneers of Italian musicology,
who directed the conservatory from 1897 and took a
personal interest in his development. Pizzetti's leanings
towards the theatre by no means diminished and he
grew more and more anxious to compose an opera.
Various early attempts, mostly unfinished, already
showed his preference for heroic subjects, exalted
romantic characters and large-scale construction.

In 1905, having read part of the prologue to
D'Annunzio's *La nave* (then a work in progress), he
formed a close friendship with the poet, who invited him
to write incidental music for the play and nicknamed
him 'Ildebrando da Parma' (a pseudonym which
appears on the covers of several of Pizzetti's early published compositions). Their collaboration culminated, in
1909–12, in *Fedra*: D'Annunzio wrote the original
spoken version with the idea of then adapting it as a
libretto for Pizzetti. Meanwhile the composer, who had
lived by giving private lessons and acting as assistant
conductor (1902–4) at the Teatro Regio, Parma, was
appointed to teach harmony and counterpoint at the
Parma Conservatory (1907) and then at the Istituto
Musicale (later Conservatory) of Florence (1908). During this period he published an article in the *Rivista
musicale italiana* on his music for *La nave* (xiv, 1907,
pp.855–62) and another on Dukas' *Ariane et Barbe-
bleue* (xv, 1908, pp.73–111). His years in Florence,
where he lived from 1908 until 1924 (becoming the institute's director in 1917), were decisive: the city's keen
intellectual and cultural life contributed much to his
artistic ripening. This was the time of the famous
Florentine periodical *La voce* (1908–16), round which
gathered many influential Italian philosophers, writers
and other artists: Pizzetti became personally associated
with De Robertis, Prezzolini, Papini, Soffici, Bastianelli
and others, and himself wrote for *La voce*, *Il marzocco*
and the newspapers *Il secolo* (Milan) and *La nazione*
(Florence). That he was more conservative than some
other 'vociani' is, however, shown by his perplexity and
disorientation when he attended the première of *The
Rite of Spring* in 1913, by the speedy break-up of his
collaboration with Bastianelli in editing the anthology-
periodical *Dissonanza* (founded in 1914 and discontinued after only three numbers) and by his largely
nominal links with Casella's Società Italiana di Musica
Moderna (1917–19).

In later life Pizzetti increasingly withdrew from
'advanced' musical circles, until in 1932 he joined with
Respighi, Zandonai and other reactionaries in signing a
notorious manifesto, published in several newspapers,
attacking the more forward-looking trends of the time
and recommending a return to tradition (he later, at
least partly, recanted). Meanwhile he had become
director (1924) of the Milan Conservatory, whence he
moved in 1936 to Rome to teach advanced composition
at the Accademia di S Cecilia (president, 1947–52;
retired 1958). He conducted more often from about
1930 onwards, in the Americas as well as in Europe, and
continued also to write music criticism – notably in *La
rassegna musicale* (1932–47) and the *Corriere della sera*
(from 1953). He remained active well into the 1960s.

2. WORKS. In Italy critical attention has tended to focus
especially on Pizzetti's operas, and it was in that direc-

tion that his greatest ambitions lay (although he also wrote much instrumental music and some fine choral works and songs). After the preliminary gropings of his unpublished juvenilia he formulated, about 1908, a basic set of musico-dramatic principles (first alluded to in his article on *Ariane et Barbe-bleue*) which thereafter, in varying degrees, conditioned his entire operatic output. The exception is *La sacra rappresentazione di Abram e d'Isaac*, whose uncharacteristically self-contained lyrical 'numbers' reflect the work's origin in incidental music to a play. Otherwise (in strong reaction against the melodic indulgences of Mascagni and Puccini) all Pizzetti's operas, from *Fedra* to *Clitennestra*, systematically set out to avoid self-sufficient lyricism, except (as in the beautiful 'Trenodia per Ippolito morto' in *Fedra* or Mara's song near the end of Act 1 in *Dèbora e Jaéle*) when choral groups or individuals are actually depicted as singing songs.

The bulk of Pizzetti's operatic vocal writing consists, rather, of a continuous flexible arioso, sensitive to every nuance of the text and governed by the natural rhythms of the Italian language – the 'Pizzettian declamation' which has been the subject of so much Italian critical discussion, favourable and unfavourable. Although the shade of Wagner can sometimes be perceived in the background, the main models for this arioso are non-Germanic: on the one hand Pizzetti was obviously far from indifferent to the methods of *Pelléas et Mélisande*, and on the other there are recurrent signs of his sympathy with the Florentine monodists and the recitatives of Monteverdi. The result has a distinctive physiognomy and can be intensely expressive, despite a serious risk of monotony in the less inspired scenes (notably those where Pizzetti's characters show a weakness for prolonged ethical discussion).

An outstanding feature of most Pizzetti operas (and the main saving grace of some of the weaker ones) is his richly imaginative, often highly dramatic choral writing. The first act of *Dèbora e Jaéle* in particular brings the chorus right into the foreground as a complex multiple protagonist. This probably remains the most intense and moving act in any Pizzetti opera, even if the elegiac last act of *Fedra* is of comparable stature in its more restrained, contemplative way. None of the later dramatic works can quite equal these two major achievements of his early maturity, although the austere, intermittently intense *Lo straniero* is still well worthy of attention. So is the more colourful and theatrically effective *Fra Gherardo* – though parts of it show clear signs that Pizzetti's operatic methods were degenerating into a routine. By the 1930s he had become so hidebound by his own theories and his lack of stylistic self-renewal that the imaginative tension of his operas was being seriously undermined. Only after the war did the situation improve again, notably in the better – especially (once again) choral – parts of *Ifigenia*, *Assassinio nella cattedrale* and to a lesser extent *La figlia di Iorio*. These works are still notably inferior to *Fedra* and *Dèbora*; but *Assassinio* in particular has been highly successful in Italy, and has had some currency abroad.

See also ASSASSINIO NELLA CATTEDRALE; DÈBORA E JAÉLE; FEDRA (ii); FRA GHERARDO; and SACRA RAPPRESENTAZIONE DI ABRAM E D'ISAAC, LA.

Sabina, 1897 (1, A. Beggi), unperf. [destroyed]
Romeo e Giulietta, 1899–1900 (1, Pizzetti, after W. Shakespeare), unperf. [destroyed apart from 3rd orch int]
Il Cid, 1902–3 (2, Beggi, after P. Corneille and G. de Castro y Bellvís), unperf. [destroyed]
Lena, 1904 (Beggi) [unrealized project]

Aeneas, 1904–7 (prol., 3, Beggi) [sketches only]
Fedra, 1907–8 (1, Pizzetti and M. Silvani, after Euripides), inc., unpubd
Fedra, 1909–12 (3, G. D'Annunzio, after Euripides and Seneca), Milan, Scala, 20 March 1915
Gigliola, 1914–15 (3, after D'Annunzio: *La fiaccola sotto il moggio*), inc., unpubd
Dèbora e Jaéle, 1915–21 (3, Pizzetti, after *Judges* iv–v), Milan, Scala, 16 Dec 1922
La sacra rappresentazione di Abram e d'Isaac, 1917–28 (1, O. Castellino, after F. Belcari), Perugia, Morlacchi, 2 Oct 1937 [expanded from incidental music, 1917 and 1926]
Lo straniero, 1922–5 (2, Pizzetti), Rome, Opera, 29 April 1930
Fra Gherardo, 1924–7 (3, Pizzetti), Milan, Scala, 16 May 1928
Orsèolo, 1928–35 (3, Pizzetti), Florence, Comunale, 4 May 1935
L'oro, 1937–42 (3, Pizzetti), Milan, Scala, 2 Jan 1947
Vanna Lupa, 1943–7 (3, Pizzetti), Florence, Comunale, 4 May 1949, unpubd
Ifigenia (radio op, 1, Pizzetti and A. Perrini), RAI, 3 Oct 1950; stage, Florence, Comunale, 19 May 1951
Cagliostro (radio op, 1, Pizzetti), RAI, 5 Nov 1952; stage, Milan, Scala, 24 Jan 1953; unpubd
La figlia di Iorio (3, D'Annunzio, abridged Pizzetti), Naples, S Carlo, 4 Dec 1954
Povera gente, 1955–6 (1, Pizzetti), inc., unpubd
Assassinio nella cattedrale (int, 2, T. S. Eliot: *Murder in the Cathedral*, trans. A. Castelli, abridged Pizzetti), Milan, Scala, 1 March 1958
Il calzare d'argento (2, R. Bacchelli), Milan, Scala, 23 March 1961
Clitennestra, 1961–4 (2, Pizzetti), Milan, Scala, 1 March 1965

WRITINGS
Musicisti contemporanei (Milan, 1914)
Intermezzi critici (Florence, 1921)
Musica e dramma (Rome, 1945)
La musica italiana dell'800 (Turin, 1947)

*

G. Bastianelli: 'Una conferenza di I. Pizzetti su l'opera', *Il marzocco* [Florence], xviii/3 (1913), 3–4; repr. in G. Bastianelli: *Musicisti d'oggi e di ieri* (Milan, 1914), 85–92
G. Barini: '*Fedra* di Gabriele d'Annunzio e Ildebrando Pizzetti', *Nuova antologia*, no.260 (1915), 652–61, 664
G. Bastianelli: 'La bellezza della *Fedra* di Ildebrando Pizzetti', *Il marzocco*, xx/13 (1915), 2
A. della Corte: 'Ildebrando Pizzetti e la *Fedra*', *Rivista d'Italia* [Rome], xviii/1 (1915), 558–70
D. Sincero: 'La première di *Fedra* alla Scala', *RMI*, xxii (1915), 319–26
R. Fondi: *Ildebrando Pizzetti e il dramma musicale italiano di oggi* (Rome, 1919)
F. B. Pratella: 'Due avvenimenti musicali: *Fedra* di Ildebrando Pizzetti', *L'evoluzione della musica dal 1910 al 1917*, ii (Milan, 1919), 60–69
G. M. Gatti: '*Debora e Jaele* di Ildebrando Pizzetti: guida attraverso il poema e la musica* (Milan, 1922)
G. Barini: '*Debora e Jaele*: dramma di Ildebrando Pizzetti', *Nuova antologia*, no.306 (1923), 80–87
L. Pagano: '*Debora e Jaele* di Ildebrando Pizzetti', *RMI*, xxx (1923), 47–108; repr. in L. Pagano: *La fionda di David* (Turin, 1928), 79–155
G. M. Gatti: 'L'opera drammatica di Pizzetti', *Il pianoforte* [Turin], vii (1926), 227–41
F. Brusa: '*Fra Gherardo* di Ildebrando Pizzetti', *RMI*, xxxv (1928), 386–441
A. Lualdi: '*Dèbora e Jaéle* di I. Pizzetti alla Scala', '*Abramo e Isacco* di Feo Belcari con musiche di I. Pizzetti al Teatro di Torino', *Serate musicali* (Milan, 1928), 3–12, 222–30
S. Musella: '*Fra Gherardo* (riflessioni)', *Bollettino bibliografico musicale*, iii/5 (1928), 21–5
M. Pilati: *Fra Gherardo di Ildebrando Pizzetti* (Milan, 1928)
M. Rinaldi: *L'arte di Ildebrando Pizzetti e 'Lo straniero'* (Rome, 1930)
A. Bonaccorsi: '*Lo straniero* di Ildebrando Pizzetti', *RMI*, xxxviii (1931), 429–36
A. Baronti: 'La *Debora e Jaele* di Ildebrando Pizzetti al Carlo Felice', *Italia musicale* [Genoa], v/3 (1932), 3–5
G. M. Gatti: *Ildebrando Pizzetti* (Turin, 1934, 2/1955; Eng. trans., enlarged, 1951)
M. Pilati: *L'Orsèolo di Ildebrando Pizzetti: guida attraverso il dramma e la musica* (Milan, 1935)

M. Rinaldi: 'Il valore della *Fedra* di d'Annunzio nel dramma di Pizzetti', *Rassegna dorica*, viii (1936–7), 2–17

D. de' Paoli: *La crisi musicale italiana* (Milan, 1939), esp. 185–215

A. Gasco: 'La *Fedra* di Ildebrando Pizzetti alla Scala di Milano (1915)', 'Fra Gherardo al Teatro Reale (1929)', *Da Cimarosa a Strawinsky* (Rome, 1939), 364–84

G. Ponz de Leon: 'Il dramma lirico nell'arte di Ildebrando Pizzetti', *RMI*, xliii (1939), 539–44

L. Tomelleri: 'Fedra: D'Annunzio e Pizzetti', in L. Tomelleri and others: *Gabriele d'Annunzio e la musica* (Milan, 1939), 47–53, repr. in *RMI*, xliii (1939), 207–13

S. Pugliatti: 'Il dramma musicale nella poetica di Ildebrando Pizzetti', *RaM*, xiv (1941), 277–83

V. del Gaizo: 'Considerazioni sull'*Orséolo* di Ildebrando Pizzetti', *Musica d'oggi*, 1st ser., xxiv (1942), 115–17

G. Gavazzeni: 'Brano di un commento all'*Orséolo* di Pizzetti', *RaM*, xvi (1943), 105–12

M. Rinaldi: *Lo straniero' di Ildebrando Pizzetti* (Florence, 1943)

G. Confalonieri: '*Orséolo* di Ildebrando Pizzetti', *Bruciar le ali alla musica* (Milan, 1945), 153–8

G. Gavazzeni: '*L'oro' di Pizzetti: guida musicale* (Milan, 1946)

G. Barblan: '*L'oro*, ultima opera di Pizzetti alla Scala', *RMI*, xlix (1947), 57–68

G. Gavazzeni: 'Commenti alla *Debora e Jaele* di Pizzetti', *La musica e il teatro* (Pisa, 1954), 83–135

M. Mila: 'Ascoltando *La figlia di Iorio* di Pizzetti', *RaM*, xxv (1955), 103–7; repr. in *RaM*, xxxii (1962), 264–9

G. Pannain: '*La figlia di Iorio* di D'Annunzio e Pizzetti', *RMI*, lvii (1955), 51–4

F. D'Amico and others: 'Venti opere da salvare dal diluvio', *Tempo* [Milan], xviii/27 (1956), 26–30

M. La Morgia, ed.: *La città dannunziana a Ildebrando Pizzetti: saggi e note* (Milan and Pescara, 1958)

M. Mila: 'L'assassinio nella cattedrale', *Cronache musicali 1955–1959* (Turin, 1959), 163–6

——: '*L'Ifigenia* di Pizzetti', *Cronache musicali 1955–1959* (Turin, 1959), 167–9

F. Aprahamian: 'Pizzetti in Coventry', *Ricordiana* [London], vii/3 (1962), 1–3 [on *Assassinio nella cattedrale*]

A. Porter: 'Coventry and London: Murder in the Cathedral', *MT*, ciii (1962), 544–5

P. Santi: 'Il mondo della *Debora*', *RaM*, xxxii (1962), 151–68

D. de' Paoli: 'Gabriele d'Annunzio, la musica e i musicisti', in D. de' Paoli and others: *Nel centenario di Gabriele d'Annunzio* (Turin, 1963), 41–118, esp. 102–14 [RAI pubn]

E. Paratore: 'Introduzione a *La figlia di Iorio* di Pizzetti', *Studi dannunziani* (Naples, 1966), 331–7

J. C. G. Waterhouse: *The Emergence of Modern Italian Music (up to 1940)* (diss., U. of Oxford, 1968)

A. Gentilucci: *Guida all'ascolto della musica contemporanea* (Milan, 1969), 314–16

G. P. Minardi: *Ildebrando Pizzetti: la giovinezza* (Parma, 1980)

E. Paratore: 'Pizzetti drammaturgo', *Lettere italiane* [Florence], xxxii (1980), 498–514

B. Pizzetti: *Ildebrando Pizzetti, cronologia e bibliografia* (Parma, 1980) [reviewed and summarized in *ML*, lxiii (1982), 141–6]

F. Nicolodi: *Musica e musicisti nel ventennio fascista* (Fiesole, 1984), esp. 165–99, 431–42

R. Tedeschi: *D'Annunzio e la musica* (Scandicci, 1988), esp. 54–60, 80–90

M. G. Accorsi: 'Fra Bacchelli e Pizzetti: "Devriansi i Giullari molto amare, bramano gioia ed amano il cantare"', *RIM*, xxiv (1989), 131–52 [principally on *Il calzare d'argento*]

A. Zaccaria: 'Il teatro di Pizzetti', *Rassegna musicale Curci*, xlii/3 (1989), 7–12

J. C. G. Waterhouse: 'Pizzetti in Perspective', *Musica senza aggettivi: studi per Fedele d'Amico* (Florence, 1991), 663–73

GUIDO M. GATTI, JOHN C. G. WATERHOUSE

Pizzi, Emilio (*b* Verona, ? 2 Feb 1862 [possibly Feb 1861]; *d* between 19 and 28 Nov 1940). Italian composer. He began his studies in 1869 at the Istituto Musicale in Bergamo; he then studied at the Milan Conservatory (1881–4) under Bazzini and Ponchielli before working in London (1884–97, and from 1900) and in Bergamo (1897–1900); in later life he returned to Italy.

Pizzi's operas were performed throughout Europe, and one, *Gabriella* (1893), commissioned for Adelina Patti, opened in Boston. His musical style was excessively eclectic. *The Bric-a-brac Will* (1895, London) was a comedy-drama in the popular Gilbert and Sullivan manner; *La rosalba* (1899, Turin), to a libretto of Luigi Illica, had Puccini-like melodies; and *La vendetta* (1906, Cologne) was a Corsican tragedy of the *verismo* type, with musical rhetoric to match. His chamber music was very popular.

Lina (2), Milan, Conservatorio di Musica, 1884
Guglielmo Ratcliff (prol., 3, A. Zanardini, after H. Heine: *Wilhelm Ratcliff*), Bologna, Comunale, 31 Oct 1889
Editta (2, S. Arkel), Milan, Verme, 4 June 1890
Gabriella (2, C. Byrne and F. Fulgonio), Boston, Boston, 25 Nov 1893
The Bric-a-brac Will (operetta, 3, J. Fitzgerald and H. Moss), London, Lyric, 28 Oct 1895
La rosalba (novella scenica, 1, L. Illica), Turin, Carignano, 31 May 1899
La vanità e l'amore (5, A. Edel), Milan, Verme, 26 Jan 1900
La vendetta (prol., 3, A. Kaiser), Cologne, Stadt, 1 Dec 1906; as Ivania, Bergamo, 14 Sept 1926   MARVIN TARTAK

Pizzi, (Giuseppe) Gioacchino [Giovacchino] (*b* Rome, 1716; *d* Rome, 8 Sept 1790). Italian librettist. A cleric, he served as secretary to Cardinal M. A. Colonna and was a protégé of Pope Clement XIV. He was admitted to the Arcadian Academy during the custodianship of Francesco Lorenzini (1728–43), with the Arcadian name Nivildo Amarinzio. He was *procustode* under Giuseppe Brogi (1766–72) and was elected *custode generale* in 1772. His aim was to revitalize the Academy, and he advocated a rejection of pastoral simplicity in favour of a more enlightened approach, incorporating philosophy and science, but being careful not to offend the disciples of Metastasio.

Pizzi wrote only a few opera librettos, similar in structure to those of Metastasio. The bulk of his dramatic works were oratorios and *componimenti drammatici* (probably serenatas).

See also CRESO.

Eumene (os), Aurisicchio, 1754; Creso (os), Jommelli, 1757 (Abos and A. Cocchi, 1758; Sacchini, 1765, rev. 1781 as Euriso; Cafaro, 1768; Alessandri, 1774; Borghi, 1777; Anfossi, 1787; P. Terziani, 1788); Il Cidde (os), N. Piccinni, 1766, as Il gran Cid (Sacchini, 1769; Paisiello, 1775, as Il gran Cid); Le donne vendicate (ob, Acts 1 and 2 by Pizzi, rev. G. Bottarelli, Act 3 by Bottarelli), ?1769

*

C. Dionisotti: 'Ricordo di Cimante Micenio', *Arcadia: atti e memorie*, 3rd ser., i/3–4 (1948), 94–121

A. Cipriani: 'Contributo per una storia politica dell'Arcadia settecentesca', *Arcadia: atti e memorie*, 3rd ser., v/2–3 (1971), 101–66

L. Felici: 'L'Arcadia romana tra illuminismo e neoclassicismo', *Arcadia: atti e memorie*, 3rd ser., v/2–3 (1971), 167–82

A. M. Giorgetti Vichi: *Gli Arcadi dal 1690 al 1800: onomasticon* (Rome, 1977)

M. T. Acquaro Graziosi: 'Nuove ricerche per la storia dell'Arcadia', *Arcadia: atti e memorie*, 3rd ser., viii/2–3 (1983–5), 251–98

BRYAN MARTIN

Pizzi, Pier Luigi (*b* Milan, 15 June 1930). Italian stage designer and director. He was trained as an architect at the Milan Polytechnic; his career in the theatre started at the Teatro Comunale, Genoa, where he designed his first opera, *Don Giovanni*, in 1952. Pizzi continued to design for plays, films and television but the light, learned elegance of his *Orlando* (1959, Florence) established him as a leading interpreter of the Baroque tradition and led to an increasing concentration on opera work. His mastery of Baroque theatre was later demonstrated in his series of Rameau productions in France, typically *Hippolyte et Aricie* (1983, Aix-en-Provence). He has worked in all the leading opera houses, from 1977 as a director/designer: his production of *Les Troyens* opened the new Opéra Bastille, Paris, in 1990 (for illustration *see* PARIS, fig.25). Pizzi's design is characterized by an accurate understanding of historical styles interpreted not by pastiche but through informed and intelligent reference (the neo-classical *Alceste*, 1987, La Scala). He favours clear, uncluttered sets and staging (*I Capuleti e i Montecchi*, 1984, Covent Garden), a cool palette (*Don Carlos*, 1989, Vienna) and intellectual rather than emotional solutions to complex design problems.

MARINA HENDERSON

Plaichinger, Thila (*b* Vienna, 13 March 1868; *d* Vienna, 17 March 1939). Austrian soprano. She studied at the Vienna Academy and was engaged at the Hamburg Opera, where she made her début in 1893; she became the leading dramatic soprano at Strasbourg (1894–1901) and then at the Berlin Hofoper (1901–14), where she was the first Berlin Electra and a famous Brünnhilde and Isolde. She appeared at Covent Garden in 1904 as Isolde, Ortrud and Venus, and in Beecham's 1910 season as Electra, Elisabeth and Isolde. Her only Bayreuth appearances, in 1896–7, were in small roles.

HAROLD ROSENTHAL/R

Plaisirs de la campagne, Les ('The Pleasures of the Countryside'). *Opéra-ballet* in a prologue and three acts (entrées) by TOUSSAINT BERTIN DE LA DOUÉ to a libretto by SIMON-JOSEPH PELLEGRIN and MARIE-ANNE BARBIER; Paris, Opéra, 10 August 1719.

Les plaisirs, with its scenes from everyday life – *La pêche*, *La vendange* and *La chasse* – remains one of the most typical stage works of the *Régence* period, although it was, apparently, 'not to the liking of the public'. In each of the opera's three acts, the composer was able to depict the happy-go-lucky, good-natured character of the individual plots. Judging by the autograph manuscript which has been preserved (in *F-Po*), it also seems to have been the first post-Lullian French opera in which the orchestral accompaniment had only four and not five string parts, lacking *quintes de violon*.

JÉRÔME DE LA GORCE

Planché, James Robinson (*b* London, 27 Feb 1796; *d* London, 29 May 1880). English dramatist, librettist, antiquarian and costume authority. He brought his scholarly knowledge of costume to bear on his stage designs, and was the first to perceive that comedy might arise from ancient Greeks in authentic chitons behaving like Victorians. His first play, a 'serio-comic, bombastic, and operatic interlude', was *Amoroso, King of Little Britain* (1818); his first serious play was *The Vampire, or The Bride of the Isles* (1820). After much rapid hack-work Planché went to Covent Garden, where he began to reform the unhistorical costuming of Shakespeare's plays; he also collaborated with Henry Bishop on 'English operas' (dramas with music). In 1826 he wrote a diffuse libretto for Weber's romantic opera *Oberon, or The Elf King's Oath*, the plot based on C. M. Wieland's poem, the words heavily influenced by Shakespeare. This latter quality led Weber to expostulate gently that music needed dramatic situations rather than poetic imagery. In spite of a successful première, the libretto was criticized for lacking human interest, a charge Planché felt keenly. In 1860 he revised

the text for translation into Italian in a production supervised by Benedict (1860). Planché's real talent for fairy plays, however, appeared in his elegant, witty extravaganzas, such as *Riquet with the Tuft* (1836) and *The Island of Jewels* (1849), both of which starred Lucia Elizabeth Vestris, who had created Fatima in *Oberon*. He continued to write prose plays and to adapt operatic plots from Mozart, Auber, Rossini and others. In 1838 he wrote a historical libretto for Mendelssohn, who first liked it, then decisively rejected it.

Planché wrote, adapted or translated nearly 200 works for the stage, including revues and extravaganzas, both of which types of entertainment he introduced into England, and published a *History of British Costume* (1834) and other antiquarian works. His influence on the theatre was pervasive, though, except in costume reform, rarely profound. Nevertheless, his extravaganzas helped to define the subject matter of the Victorian light musical stage, and looked forward to the Savoy operas of Gilbert and Sullivan.

T. F. Dillon Croker and S. Tucker, eds.: *The Extravaganzas of J. R. Planché, Esq., (Somerset Herald, 1825–1871)* (London, 1879)

JANE W. STEDMAN

Pol Plançon as Méphistophélès in Gounod's 'Faust'

Plançon, Pol [Paul-Henri] (*b* Fumay, Ardennes, 12 June 1851; *d* Paris, 11 Aug 1914). French bass. A pupil of Duprez and Sbriglia, he made his début at Lyons in 1877. He first sang at the Paris Opéra on 23 June 1883 as Gounod's Méphistophélès, and remained there for ten seasons, taking part in the premières of Massenet's *Le Cid* (Count of Gormas) and Saint-Saëns' *Ascanio* (François I). He appeared at Covent Garden for 14 consecutive seasons (1891–1904), singing, besides his French and Italian roles, occasionally in German and even in English (as Friar Francis in the première of Stanford's *Much Ado About Nothing*). On 29 November 1893 he appeared for the first time at the Metropolitan Opera, returning as leading bass for 12 of the subsequent seasons there until his farewell to the house on 30 March 1908.

Judging by the recordings that survive, Plançon was the most polished singer of his time. His beautiful *basse chantante* had been admirably schooled, and his style was extremely elegant; his many recordings (1902–8) embody standards otherwise outside the experience of a present-day listener. Not only his flawless trills and rapid scales but his cantabile and pure legato, as in 'Vi ravviso' from *La sonnambula*, are exemplary.

J. Dennis: 'Paul Henri Plançon', *Record Collector*, viii (1953), 149–91 [with discography and commentary by L. Hevingham-Root]
DESMOND SHAWE-TAYLOR

Planelli, Antonio (*b* Bitonto, 17 June 1747; *d* Naples, March 1803). Italian writer. He studied in Altamura and at Montecassino, where he was ordained; he was also a scientist. He held posts in the Mint at Naples and at a museum, and he may have composed some music. He published there in 1772 a book, *Dell'opera in musica*, in which, taking a moral standpoint on the role of music, he wrote in favour of the opera reforms of Gluck and Calzabigi, presenting theories in line with the enlightenment aesthetics of the time and criticizing the artificiality of Metastasian music drama and its devices as contrary to expression and dramatic flow. He stressed the centrality of the verbal text and its meaning, and discussed an ideal synthesis of poetry, music, action and dance. He cited Gluck's *Alceste* as an ideal tragic opera. Planelli's treatise stands within the tradition of such reformist writers of the 18th century as Algarotti, Rousseau and Arteaga.

ES (A. Mondolfi)
F. Degrada: Introduction to A. Planelli: *Dell'opera in musica* (Fiesole, 1981)

Planquette, (Jean) Robert (*b* Paris, 31 July 1848; *d* Paris, 28 Jan 1903). French composer. He studied briefly at the Paris Conservatoire, gaining the *premier prix* for solfège in 1867 and the *second prix* for piano in 1868, and also studied harmony with Duprato. His early works included piano reductions of operas and some songs, among them a set of 12 military songs, *Refrains du régiment*. Planquette sold these outright and thus failed to benefit financially when one of them, *Le régiment de Sambre-et-Meuse*, became widely popular in a march arrangement by François Rauski. For the most part Planquette was forced to make such living as he could from playing the piano and composing songs for *café-concerts*.

His first one-act operettas were performed at music halls, and it was while working as a *café-concert* pianist that he had the opportunity to compose the operetta that was to bring him fame. *Les cloches de Corneville*, originally offered to Hervé, had over 400 consecutive performances after being produced at the Folies-Dramatiques in 1877 and reached a thousand performances within a decade. Its 'Legend of the Bells' was especially popular, and the work's success was repeated around the world, bringing Planquette into considerable demand. He composed the one-act *Le chevalier Gaston* as a commission for the opening of the Monte Carlo Opera House (1879), and for London *Rip van Winkle* (1882), based on Washington Irving's novel. Though lacking the melodic quality of *Les cloches de Corneville*, this latter has remained his second most popular work. For London, too, he composed *Nell*

Gwynne (1884), as well as adapting other works. However, Planquette never quite recaptured the uncomplicated charm, vitality and melodic appeal of *Les cloches de Corneville*, which remains among the most popular of French operettas. Far from finding its success oppressive, Planquette had a villa called 'Les cloches' built on the Normandy coast near Cabourg, where he became a municipal councillor. He was also a Chevalier of the Légion d'honneur. Among his other works are two dramatic monologues performed in 1876, *La confession de Rosette* and *On demande une femme de chambre* (librettos by P. Véron) and some songs; he also contributed, together with Edouard Okolowicz and others, to the revue *Babel* (libretto by P. Burani and E. Philippe), performed at the Athénée, Paris, in 1879.

See also CLOCHES DE CORNEVILLE, LES.

operettas unless otherwise stated; first produced, and vocal scores published, in Paris unless otherwise stated

Méfie-toi de Pharaon (1, Villemer and L. Delormel), Eldorado, 12 Oct 1872 (n.d.)

Paille d'avoine (1, J. Rozale and A. Lemonnier), Délassements-Comiques, 12 March 1874 (?1895)

Le serment de Mme Grégoire (1, L. J. Péricaud and Delormel), Eldorado, 1874 (n.d.)

Le valet de coeur (saynète, 1, Péricaud, Villemer and Delormel), Alcazar d'Eté, 1875 (n.d.)

Le péage (E. André), Eldorado, *c*1876

Les cloches de Corneville (oc, 3, Clairville and C. Gabet), Folies-Dramatiques, 19 April 1877 (1877)

Le chevalier Gaston (1, P. Véron), Monte Carlo, Opéra, 8 Feb 1879 (1880)

Les voltigeurs de la 32ème (3, E. Gondinet and G. Duval), Renaissance, 7 Jan 1880 (1880); rev. as The Old Guard (H. B. Farnie), London, Avenue, 26 Oct 1887 (London, 1887)

La cantinière (3, Burani and F. Rybère), Nouveautés, 1880 (1881)

Rip van Winkle (3, Farnie, after W. Irving), London, Comedy, 14 Oct 1882 (London, 1882); rev. as Rip! (H. Meilhac and P. Gille), Folies-Dramatiques, 11 Nov 1884 (1884)

Les chevaux-légers (1, Péricaud and Delormel (1882)

Nell Gwynne (3, Farnie), London, Avenue, 7 Feb 1884 (London, 1884); rev. as La princesse Colombine (M. Ordonneau and André), Nouveautés, 7 Dec 1886 (1887)

La crémaillère (3, Burani and A. Brasseur), Nouveautés, 28 Nov 1885 (? only 2 songs pubd, 1886)

Surcouf (prol., 3, H. Chivot and A. Duru), Folies-Dramatiques, 6 Oct 1887 (1887); rev. as Paul Jones (Farnie), London, Prince of Wales, 12 Jan 1889 (London, 1889)

Captain Thérèse (3, A. Bisson and F. C. Burnand), London, Prince of Wales, 25 Aug 1890 (London, 1891); Gaîté, 1 April 1901 (1901)

La cocarde tricolore (3, Ordonneau, after Cogniard brothers), Folies-Dramatiques, 12 Feb 1892 (1892)

Le talisman (3, A. P. d'Ennery and Burani), Gaîté, 20 Jan 1893 (1893)

Les vingt-huit jours de Champignolette (Burani), République, 17 Sept 1895

Panurge (3, Meilhac and A. de Saint-Albin), Gaîté, 22 Nov 1895 (Paris, 1895)

Mam'zelle Quat'sous (4, A. Mars and M. Desvallières), Gaîté, 5 Nov 1897 (1897)

Le fiancé de Margot (1, Bisson) (1900)

Le paradis de Mahomet (3, H. Blondeau), Variétés, 15 May 1906 (1906), completed by L. Ganne

GänzlBMT
J. Brindejont-Offenbach: 'Cinquante ans de l'opérette française', *Cinquante ans de musique française*, ed. L. Rohozhinsky (Paris, 1925), 199–232
L'Aubert: 'Audran, Planquette, Varney, etc.', *Le théâtre lyrique en France*, ii (Paris, 1937–9), 316–25 [pubd Poste National/Radio Paris]
R. Traubner: *Operetta: a Theatrical History* (New York, 1983)
ANDREW LAMB

Plantade, Charles-Henri (*b* Pontoise, 14 or 19 Oct 1764; *d* Paris, 18 or 19 Dec 1839). French composer. As a youth he studied the cello; after his arrival in Paris he studied singing, composition, the piano and the harp. His early sonatas for harp and collections of romances won him recognition, and by 1797 he was music master at the Institut de St Denis. From 1799 to 1807 (and later, 1815–16 and 1818–28) he taught singing at the Paris Conservatoire; his most celebrated pupil there was Laure Cinti-Damoreau. After a period of service in the chapel of the Dutch court, he held the posts of singing master and stage director at the Paris Opéra from 1812 to 1815.

Plantade's operas are consistent with French operatic style at the turn of the 19th century. His melodies are pleasant, if undistinguished, and his musical numbers vary in mood, tonality and scoring, with imaginative use of woodwind and brass. (*Palma*, for example, is scored for oboes, horns, bassoons, trombones and strings.) His occasional oboe solo and his orchestral crescendos are both reminiscent of Rossini. He liked extended orchestral unisons. Though he favoured foursquare phrasing, he handled metre changes with skill and occasionally wrote an irregular melodic phrase. His orchestral passage-work tends to be simple and scalar, but he often modulated unexpectedly within an overture or aria. His solo vocal cadenzas reflect his sympathetic writing for the voice and his formal background as a singing teacher.

Until 1815 Plantade composed mostly stage works, but in 1816 he became music master to the French royal chapel, a position he held throughout the reign of Charles X. In this capacity he wrote a number of religious works, including music for Charles's coronation.

PFE – *Paris, Théâtre Feydeau*

Les deux soeurs (oc, 1, [?P. G.] Pariseau), PFE, 22 May 1792
Les souliers mordorés (oc, 2, A. de Ferrières), PFE, 18 May 1793
Au plus brave la plus belle (oc, 1, L. Philippon de La Madeleine), Paris, Amis de la Patrie, 6 Oct 1794
Palma, ou Le voyage en Grèce (opéra, 2, P. E. Lemontey), PFE, 22 Aug 1797 (Paris, ?1798)
Romagnesi (opéra, 1, Lemontey), PFE, 3 Sept 1799
Lisez Plutarque (oc, 1), Paris, Montansier, spr. 1800
Zoé, ou La pauvre petite (oc, 1, J. N. Bouilly), PFE, 3 July 1800 (Paris, ?1800)
Le roman (opéra, 1, E. Gosse), PFE, 12 Nov 1800
Bayard à la ferté, ou Le siège de Mézières (oc, 2, M.-A.-M. Désaugiers and [?M.-J.] Gentil), PFE, 13 Oct 1811
Le mari de circonstance (oc, 2, F. A. E. Planard), PFE, 18 March 1813 (Paris, ?1813)

*

A. Choron and F. Fayolle: *Dictionnaire historique des musiciens* (Paris, 1810–11)
A. Caswell: 'Mme Cinti-Damoreau and the Embellishment of Italian Opera in Paris: 1820–1845', *JAMS*, xxviii (1975), 459–92
LAURIE C. SHULMAN

Plaschke, Friedrich [Plaške, Bedřich] (*b* Jaroměř, 7 Jan 1875; *d* Prague, 4 Feb 1952). Czech bass-baritone. He studied in Prague, and in Dresden with Scheidemantel. He made his début at the Dresden Hofoper in 1900 as the Herald in *Lohengrin* and remained a member of that company until 1937, creating Pöschel (*Feuersnot*), the First Nazarene (*Salome*), Arcesius (*Die toten Augen*), Altair (*Die ägyptische Helena*), Count Waldner (*Arabella*) and Morosus (*Die schweigsame Frau*); he was also the first Dresden Barak, Gérard (*Andrea Chénier*) and Amfortas. He sang Pogner at Bayreuth in 1911 and Kurwenal, Hans Sachs and Amfortas at Covent Garden in 1914. Plaschke toured the USA with the German Opera Company, 1922–4. In Germany he

was considered one of the best singing actors of his day. He was married to the soprano Eva von der Osten.
HAROLD ROSENTHAL/R

Platania, Pietro (*b* Catania, 5 April 1828; *d* Naples, 26 April 1907). Italian composer. He studied in Catania and then at the Palermo Conservatory with Pietro Raimondi. In 1852 his opera *Matilde Bentivoglio* was given in Palermo, so successfully that the city government awarded him 300 ducats. Later that year, when Raimondi resigned as director and counterpoint teacher at the conservatory, he suggested Platania as his successor; however, it was not until 1863 that Platania won the still-vacant post, by competition. He later became *maestro di cappella* at Milan Cathedral (1882) and director of the Naples Conservatory (1885–1902). Recognized as the greatest Italian contrapuntist of his day, admired by Rossini and by Verdi for his doctrines, Platania was the last illustrious practitioner of the old strict tradition of Italian church music, and his gifts appear to have been better suited to elaborate polyphonic construction than to the dramatic demands of stage music. He nevertheless continued to write operas, most notably *Spartaco* (1891), and was one of the first Italian composers of the period to devote himself significantly to instrumental music. In 1889 he was among the most fervent supporters of Mascagni's *Cavalleria rusticana* in the Sonzogno competition for a new opera.

Matilde Bentivoglio (tragedia lirica, 3, G. Bonfiglio), Palermo, Carolino, March 1852, *I-Mr**, vs (Milan, ?1855)
Piccarda Donati (tragedia, 3, L. Spince), Palermo, Carolino, 3 March 1857
La vendetta slava (dramma serio, 2, F. de Beaumont), Palermo, Bellini, 4 Feb 1865, excerpts, pf acc. (Milan, n.d.)
Spartaco (tragedia lirica, 4, A. Ghislanzoni), Naples, S Carlo, 29 March 1891, vs (Milan, 1891)
Unperf.: I misteri di Parigi, *c*1843; Francesca Soranzo; La corte di Enrico III; Lamma; Giulio Sabino

*

M.: 'Pietro Platania', *Musica e musicisti: gazzetta musicale di Milano*, lx (1905), 49–51
F. Guardione: *Pietro Platania* (Milan, 1908)   ANDREA LANZA

Platée ('Plataea'). *Comédie lyrique* ('ballet bouffon') in a prologue and three acts by JEAN-PHILIPPE RAMEAU to a libretto by Adrien-Joseph Le Valois d'Orville after Jacques Autreau's play *Platée, ou Junon jalouse*; Versailles, La Grande Ecurie, 31 March 1745.

Completed for the dauphin's wedding festivities, *Platée* was given a single performance at Versailles in 1745. Its theme, derived from the ancient Greek writer Pausanias, is the mock marriage between Jupiter and an ugly marsh-nymph. As such, it appears grotesquely ill-suited to the occasion, especially as the bride, the Spanish princess Maria Teresa, was evidently unattractive. This aspect of the work, however, seems to have provoked little contemporary comment. The title role, one of the few travesty parts in French opera of the time, was created by the *haute-contre* Pierre de Jélyotte (see illustration), with Marie Fel as Folly. Four years later, the opera was successfully revived at the Paris Opéra, with the libretto revised by Ballot de Sauvot. A further revival, in 1754, remained in the Opéra's repertory until 1759. Although some criticized the 'grossièretés' of the libretto, the work was by now regarded as one of Rameau's finest. Yet only the prologue was subsequently revived: it appeared for the last time in 1773.

Platée [Plataea] *a marsh-nymph*	haute-contre
Jupiter	bass
Cithéron [Cithaeron]	bass
Mercure [Mercury]	haute-contre
La Folie [Folly]	soprano
Junon [Juno]	soprano
L'Amour [Cupid]	soprano
Clarine	soprano
Momus (Acts 2 and 3)	tenor
Thespis	haute-contre
Thalie [Thalia]	soprano
Momus (prologue)	baritone
A Satyr	baritone
A Naiad	soprano

Satyrs, Maenads, grape-pickers, frogs, nymphs, retinue
of Momus and Folly

Setting A Greek vineyard; a marsh at the foot of Mount
Cithaeron

PROLOGUE ('La naissance de la comédie') *A Greek
vineyard* Thespis, represented as the inventor of
comedy, plans with Cupid, Momus (the god of ridicule)
and Thalia (the muse of comedy) to give mortals and
gods a moral lesson: they decide to re-enact the episode
in which Jupiter cures his wife Juno of jealousy. The
prologue culminates in an elaborate chorus, with an independent line for Thespis, 'Formons un spectacle
nouveau'.

ACT 1 *A marsh at the foot of Mount Cithaeron*
After a storm, graphically depicted in the orchestral
prelude, Mercury descends. He explains to King
Cithaeron that the storm is caused by Jupiter's
impatience with Juno's behaviour. The king suggests a

*Pierre de Jélyotte in the title role of Rameau's 'Platée', the
role he created in the original production at La Grande
Ecurie, Versailles, 31 March 1745: portrait by Christian-
Antoine Coypel*

ruse to cure her tiresome jealousy: Jupiter is to pretend
to court the ugly but inordinately vain marsh-nymph
Plataea. Juno will look foolish when she learns that her
jealousy is groundless. The conspirators depart as
Plataea arrives. She is convinced that Cithaeron's aloofness is a sign of his love. To the offstage sounds of frogs
and cuckoos she begins to woo him. Irritated by his
renewed coldness, she accuses him of treachery; her indignant 'Dis donc pourquoi!' is taken up by the frogs in
an onomatopoeic chorus, 'Quoi? quoi?'. Mercury again
descends. Bowing many times, he explains that Jupiter is
infatuated by Plataea's beauty and wishes to marry her.
Sudden lightning presages a storm – a sign, Mercury
explains, of Juno's wrath. But Plataea is undaunted; indeed, in a virtuoso aria ('Quittez, nymphes, quittez vos
demeures profondes', punctuated with rude syncopations associated with the frogs), she summons her fellow
marsh dwellers to enjoy the rain. The ensuing *divertissement* again features frog noises (oboes at the bottom of
their range). It is interrupted by another storm
symphony, during which Aquilons (North Winds) force
the nymphs back into their swamp.

ACT 2 *The same* Mercury explains to Cithaeron that
he has hoodwinked Juno into going to Athens in the
hope of surprising Jupiter and his new love. 'Look, there
she goes', he jokes, pointing to a passing cloud. He and
the king wait for Jupiter to arrive, and hide as his cloud
descends. Plataea cautiously approaches the cloud ('A
l'aspect de ce nuage'). She is amazed when the god
manifests himself first as a donkey (its braying, which
Plataea mistakes for amorous sighs, realistically
portrayed by double stoppings), then as an owl. At the
sight of the owl, other birds are heard taking panic-
stricken flight, a cacophony ingeniously represented by
two flageolets and upper strings. Eventually, amid a
shower of fire, Jupiter appears in his own form. He
declares his love to the frightened nymph and prepares a
divertissement in her honour. After a laughing chorus,
'Quelle est aima-a-a-able', Folly appears with the 'fous
gais' and 'fous tristes', these dressed respectively as
babies and Greek philosophers. In a brilliant parody of
an italianate coloratura aria, she recounts the story of
Apollo and Daphne ('Aux langueurs d'Apollon Daphné
se refusa'), accompanying herself on a lyre stolen from
Apollo. There follow two dances 'dans le goût de vielle',
the hurdy-gurdy represented by sustained double stoppings. Folly then creates 'a masterpiece of harmony', in
which the whole assembly calls on Hymen to unite
Jupiter and his new Juno. Plataea's excited outburst at
being so described, 'Hé, bon, bon, bon!', is taken up in a
final round-like ensemble and chorus.

ACT 3 *The same* Returning in a fury from her fruitless mission, Juno is persuaded by Mercury to hide and
observe the ceremony that is soon to begin. During a
lively chorus 'Chantons, célébrons en ce jour' and
ensuing march, Plataea appears, heavily veiled, in a
frog-drawn chariot flanked by Jupiter and Mercury and
preceded by dryads, satyrs and nymphs. Leading her
bridegroom by the hand, she observes that Cupid and
Hymen are not yet present. (Mercury comments wryly
to Jupiter that these two divinities rarely go together.) In
the course of a long chaconne, Plataea becomes increasingly impatient. At last Momus appears, dressed to look
like Cupid, blindfold and carrying a ludicrously large
bow and quiver. Explaining that Cupid is otherwise engaged, Momus presents Plataea with the god's wedding
gifts: tears, sorrows, cries, languor (string glissandos).

Momus is embarrassed by the nymph's rejection of these gifts and is mocked by Folly (in the virtuoso *ariette* 'Amour, lance tes traits, épuise ton carquois'). Three of Momus's retinue, disguised as Graces, dance in comical fashion. Jupiter then takes Plataea's hand and begins the marriage oath. But when Juno fails to appear, he has to repeat 'I swear ...' several times. At last she strides in, tears off Plataea's veil – and realizes her mistake. The nymph storms out. To the sound of thunder the gods re-ascend, leaving Folly alone. Countryfolk bring Plataea back and begin to mock her ('Chantons Platée, égayons-nous'). The nymph grabs Cithaeron by the throat and threatens revenge. To renewed taunts she runs off to her swamp, while Folly and the assembly celebrate the reconciliation of Juno and Jupiter.

* * *

In the repertory of the Opéra and of French opera presented at court, comedy had traditionally played little part. Lully, after his first three *tragédies*, had eliminated comic episodes; from then until the appearance of *Platée* only a small number of operas had truly comic themes. The libretto was intended to emulate one of these, the burlesque entrée 'Cariselli' included in Campra's compilation of *Les fragments de Monsieur de Lully* (1702) and subsequently much revived. The prologue apart, Le Valois d'Orville's revisions leave little of Autreau's work intact and greatly increase the element of comedy.

An outline of the plot gives the impression that the humour of *Platée* is distasteful. Yet the cruelty of laughing at an ugly but vain nymph is kept at a distance, since the part of Plataea is sung by a man. The work's humour comes not just from the extravagant situations and comic stage business (about which the libretto is unusually explicit) but from the numerous parodies of serious opera, its descents and transformations, its musical and poetic language, its structural conventions. For example, the chaconne that precedes Plataea's marriage is comic not just because of its absurd length or because it is danced in 'le genre le plus noble', but because it is misplaced: chaconnes belong at the culmination of the final *divertissement*. Musical parody takes many forms – exaggerated vocalises, misaccentuations, vocal acrobatics; onomatopoeic imitations of frogs, cuckoos, frightened birds, Folly's lyre and hurdy-gurdy. The burlesque use of language is seen in Plataea's frequent recourse to a frog-like 'quoi!', her comic alliterations and demotic expressions, including such un-operatic expletives as 'Fi!' and 'Ouffe!'. The first modern revivals of *Platée* took place at the Kaim-Saal, Munich (26 January 1901, in German) and Monte Carlo (5 April 1917, in French). The earliest recording, made in 1961, is notable for Michel Sénéchal's superb characterization of the title role.   GRAHAM SADLER

Platonova [Garder], **Yuliya** [Julia] **Fyodorovna** (*b* Mitava, Latvia, 1841; *d* St Petersburg, 4/16 Nov 1892). Russian soprano. After studying in Riga and St Petersburg she made her début in 1862 at the Mariinsky Theatre as Antonida. She possessed a small but cultured voice of pleasing timbre and was noted for the clarity of her diction and her outstanding dramatic talent. She was admired and respected by many of the leading Russian composers of her time, in whose operas she created important roles, among them Mary in Cui's *William Ratcliff* (1869), Donna Anna in Dargomïzhsky's *The Stone Guest* (1872), Olga in Rimsky-Korsakov's *The Maid of Pskov* (1873) and Dasha in Serov's posthumous

Vrazh'ya sila ('The Power of the Fiend', 1871). Her initiative and energy were largely responsible for a revival of *Rusalka* in St Petersburg in 1865, and for the first full production there of *Boris Godunov* in 1874, following a presentation of three scenes the previous year; Platonova sang Marina on both occasions.

BORIS SEMEONOFF

Platt, Norman (*b* Bury, 29 Aug 1920). English baritone and director. After graduating from King's College, Cambridge, he studied singing privately with Elena Gerhardt and Lucy Manen and joined Sadler's Wells Opera in 1946, making his début as Ned Keene (*Peter Grimes*). His other roles included Schaunard, Monterone, Mizgir (*The Snow Maiden*) and Mr Page (*Sir John in Love*). In 1948 he sang Filch in Britten's realization of *The Beggar's Opera* for the English Opera Group, the work of which was a major influence on his subsequent career. He was Vicar Choral at St Paul's Cathedral, 1948–52, and a founder member of the Deller Consort, 1948–64. In 1969 with Roger Norrington he founded KENT OPERA, of which he remained artistic director for 20 years, his productions ranging from *L'incoronazione di Poppea* (1969) to *Peter Grimes* (1989). Platt believed that 'the central priority in opera is to achieve a fusion of ... the purely musical element and the musical-dramatic element' (*Opera*, xli, 1990). He has made several translations of opera librettos, including *Poppea*, *Don Giovanni* and *Fidelio*, and his writings include essays on 'Purcell's Vocal Music' (*Festival of Britain Purcell Handbook*, 1951) and on aspects of opera. He was made an OBE in 1985.

*

N. Platt: 'Justifying the Dunghill', *Opera*, xl (1989), 678–84 [interview]

——: 'Art made Tongue-tied by Authority', *Opera*, xli (1990), 1168–73   NOËL GOODWIN

Platzer, Joseph (*b* Prague, 20 Sept 1751; *d* Vienna, 4 April 1806). Bohemian stage designer, active mainly in Austria. In 1774 he enrolled in the Akademie der Bildenden Künste, Vienna, where he studied architecture. In 1781 he created his first designs, for the first Viennese performances, at the Burgtheater, of Gluck's *Iphigénie en Tauride*; for four designs he received a payment of 51 gulden. He returned to Prague in 1783 with a commission from Count Nostitz to decorate the auditorium of the new National Theatre and to design the sets for the inaugural production, Lessing's *Emilia Galotti*; these were highly praised. Shortly thereafter, at the express wish of the Emperor Joseph II, he returned to Vienna.

Platzer continued to work for the Burgtheater, and in 1787 was named a regular member of the Akademie der Bildenden Künste, a signal honour. In 1791 he became chief stage designer for the court theatres. Gaspare Galliari replaced him in 1793, but Platzer returned the following year to become director of stage design for the Hoftheater (which involved work at both the Burgtheater and the Kärntnertortheater). In 1802 he returned to Prague, and in 1804 designed several National Theatre productions to celebrate the arrival in Prague of the Emperor Francis II.

From 1794 to 1806 Platzer designed over 45 new operas and ballets, several with Lorenzo Sacchetti. He followed a neo-classical style, favouring the *scena per angolo* for architectural sets, in which a scene can be

Set design by Joseph Platzer for an unidentified opera

viewed at different angles, and placing great emphasis on the contrasts of light and shade. Many of his designs survive in the Akademie der Bildenden Künste, Vienna, and in the Oenslager Collection, Pierpont Morgan Library, New York; over 200 were published by Bittner in 1816.

*

ES (F. Hadamowsky)

N. Bittner, ed.: *Theater-Decorationen nach den Original Skitzen des k.k. Hof-Theater-Malers Joseph Platzer* (Vienna, 1816)

O. Teuber: *Geschichte des Prager Theaters* (Prague, 1885), ii, 99–102

M. Dietrich: 'Einige Daten zu Josef Platzer', *Maske und Kothurn*, iv (1958), 134–41

Y. Haase: *Der Theatermaler Joseph Platzer* (diss., U. of Vienna, 1960)

H. C. Wolff: *Oper: Szene und Darstellung von 1600 bis 1900* (Leipzig, 1968, 2/1979), 138, 146

O. Michtner: *Das alte Burgtheater als Opernbühne* (Vienna, 1970)

D. Oenslager: *Stage Design – Four Centuries of Scenic Invention* (New York, 1975), 130–3

E. Berckenhagen: *Bretter die die Welt bedeuten: Entwürfe zum Theaterdekor und zum Bühnenkostüm in fünf Jahrhunderten* (Berlin, 1978), 141–2

W. Greisenegger: 'Bühnenbild und Kostüm', *Die Wiener Oper: 350 Jahre Glanz und Tradition* (Vienna, 1986; Eng. trans., 1987), 175–210

V. Ptáčková: 'Scenography of Don Giovanni in Prague', *Mozart's Don Giovanni in Prague*, ed. J. Kristek (Prague, 1987), 97–113

S. Wiles: *A Study of some Preparatory Drawings by the Theater Painter Joseph Platzer* (thesis, New York U., 1987)

EVAN BAKER

Playbill (Fr. *prospectus, affiche à la main*; Ger. *Theaterzettel, Handzettel*; It. *locandina*). A handbill, normally printed on one side only, announcing the details of a current or forthcoming theatrical or operatic event, distributed both outside and inside the theatre; it is the forerunner of the modern PROGRAMME. Until the second quarter of the 19th century it was generally a single unfolded leaf; subsequently it was sometimes issued with one or (rarely) two vertical folds. This article deals with both playbills and posters.

There is evidence that in Elizabethan times British players advertised their performances on handwritten bills as well as by oral public announcements and word of mouth. The earliest known reference is by a Venetian ambassador to London, who on 6 February 1559 reported to the Doge and Senate that placards were posted at the corners of the streets inviting people to attend plays. Printed bills in London date from about 1587, when a privilege for producing them was granted to John Charlewood. Possibly the earliest printed appearance of the word 'play-bill' itself is in Ben Jonson's *The Devil is an Ass* (1631), where it occurs in a stage direction (Act 1 scene iv).

The word 'poster' derives from the practice of attaching bills to the posts that marked the area for pedestrians in London streets before the Great Fire. From John Dryden we learn that the bills posted by a visiting French troupe in 1672 were notably large in size and that the practice of printing bills wholly or partly in red was introduced to England on the same occasion. The earliest surviving example of a British 'great' bill appears to be that for Lincoln's Inn Fields Theatre on 27 October 1697 (Harvard Theatre Collection, *US-CA*); somewhat trimmed, it measures 39 cm × 29 cm. In 1734, Henry Giffard, manager of Goodman's Fields, is said to have posted bills 'four feet in length', but these were clearly of exceptional size for the day. More normal was the bill advertising *The Beggar's Opera* pasted to a wall in William Hogarth's print *The Enraged Musician* (1741), measuring about 48 cm × 35.5 cm. A London bill for January 1776 measures approximately 80 cm × 37 cm, while at Covent Garden in 1809 the dimensions were about 58.5 cm × 40.5 cm. From the beginning of the 18th century, and possibly earlier, great bills as well as playbills were printed daily; by the end of the century some 200 great bills for each performance were being posted by Drury Lane.

In most countries, the distinction between the great bill and the playbill was one of size and purpose rather than of content: whereas the poster was for public display, the playbill was a smaller and more adaptable object that could both be posted and used as a programme in the theatre (often in conjunction with the libretto, the play-book or the book of songs). Because of their flimsy and ephemeral nature, few early posters and playbills have survived: no more than a score or so of British examples have been traced from before 1718. Of these the earliest dated bill is for the Booth at Charing Cross, 11 November 1672, measuring 23 cm × 18 cm, while the first for a major theatre is for Drury Lane, 22 February 1687, measuring 23.5 cm × 36 cm; other pre-1700 Drury Lane bills were small oblong slips measuring about 7.5 cm × 18 cm. The earliest extant operatic bill is for the first performance of the pasticcio *Clotilda*, given at the Queen's Theatre on 2 March 1709 (fig.1).

From the reopening of the London theatres in 1660 the bills at first seem to have contained little more than the date (without the year), the name of the theatre and beneficiary (if any), and the titles of the works to be performed and whether or not they were revivals; the only extant bill before 1700 to list a cast was printed for an amateur performance in 1681. According to Dryden, none before 1699 gives the author's name; Dryden suggested that the custom of naming the author on bills may have been a foreign one.

Gradually during the 18th century London bills began to carry further information, which it was the prompter's responsibility to convey to the newspapers (the main source for information about contemporary

NEVER PERFORMED.

At the Theatre Royal, Drury Lane,

This present SATURDAY, January 1, 1791,

Will be presented a new Opera, called, The

Siege of Belgrade.

The SCENES ENTIRELY NEW,

Designed and Executed by Mr. GREENWOOD.

With NEW DRESSES and DECORATIONS.

The Musick composed principally by

MR. STORACE,

With a few Pieces selected from *Martini, Saliezi,* and *Paesiello.*

THE CHARACTERS BY

Mr. KELLY,

Mr. PALMER,

Mr. R. PALMER,

Mr. FOX,

Mr. SUETT,

Mr. BANNISTER, Jun.

Mr. DIGNUM,

Mr. COOK,

[Being his FIRST Appearance on any Stage.]

Mr. HOLLINGSWORTH,

Mr. DUBOIS.

Mrs. CROUCH,

Miss HAGLEY,

Signora STORACE,

Mrs. BLAND.

To which will be added

The DEUCE is in HIM.

Col. Tamper by Mr. WROUGHTON,

Major Belford by Mr. WHITFIELD,

Prattle by Mr. BADDELEY,

Emily by Mrs. GOODALL,

Bell by Mrs. WILLIAMES,

Florival by Miss COLLINS.

NO MONEY TO BE RETURNED.

Places for the Boxes to be taken of Mr. FOSBROOK, at the Theatre.

The Doors to be opened at a Quarter past Five, and to begin at a Quarter past Six.

2. Playbill for the first performance of Stephen Storace's 'The Siege of Belgrade' at Drury Lane, London, 1 January 1791

By *Subscription.*

AT THE

QUEEN's THEATRE

In the *Hay-Market :*

On *Wensday* next, being the Second Day of *March,* will be presented,

A New OPERA, call'd,

CLOTILDA.

The Boxes to be open'd to the Pit. And no Person to be Admitted, but by the Subscribers Tickets; which will be delivered on Tuesday and Wensday Morning next, at Mr. *White's's Chocolate-House* in St. *James's-street.*

Boxes upon the Stage 15 s. First Gallery 5 s. Upper Gallery 2 s.

To begin exactly at Six a Clock.

And by Command. No Person to stand upon the Stage.

Vivat Regina.

1. The earliest extant opera playbill, for the pasticcio 'Clotilda' at the Queen's Theatre, London, 2 March 1709

productions) and playbill printers: the names of the composer and choreographer, the name of the author (except, by curious tradition, for new plays), the cast-lists of plays (from about 1714), the names of scene painters, machinists and costume designers, the prices of seats, the times of opening doors and curtain up, and special information relating to the night's performance, such as the suspension of ticket privileges or apologies for the substitution of works or performers. The foot of the bill was used for announcements of the programmes for the following day or days (or, later, for longer periods), below which the printer might add his name and address. The King's Theatre in the Haymarket, the principal theatre for opera, was in one unfortunate respect an exception, for its playbills rarely list the cast for the mainpiece, though details of the dancers and dances and of the vocal and instrumental music between the acts are usually given; to learn the cast it was necessary to purchase a libretto or book of the words of the songs. Pantomimes were well served from the 1780s: playbills normally gave a list of the scenes and, by the end of the century, a brief synopsis of the action.

Information about the distribution of London playbills is sparse. In the second quarter of the 18th century they were sometimes handed out free, at private houses and in coffee houses and taverns, probably on the day of the performance. In the final quarter, however, they were customarily purchased in the foyers from the orange-woman (who also sold the books of words).

3. Orange-woman selling playbills outside Drury Lane Theatre, London: anonymous etching (1804)

There may have been a different system for benefit performances, for around the end of the century there are accounts of beneficiaries distributing their bills at the doors of the well-to-do, presumably gratis.

From Germany comes what may be the oldest surviving of all manuscript theatre bills (for a Passion play in Hamburg, 1466) and also the earliest printed bill, dating from 1520 for a performance in Rostock; this gives the programme, the place and the curtain time. The format and text of a later example, printed for a performance by an English travelling company in Nuremberg about 1630, may well have been modelled on the bills currently printed in England; this gives the date, the title of the comedy, the promise of 'an excellent dance and a laughable farce' to follow, the place of performance and curtain time. A very early French bill was printed in Paris in about 1629; the date and place of performance were left blank, presumably to enable flexibility of use throughout a season, but, contrary to the British custom, the author's name was given. The names of the singers and actors were not stated, however; they were usually omitted from French bills until about 1790.

One of the earliest extant Italian bills is for a 1684 performance of Alessandro Melani's opera *Il carceriere di se medesimo* at Reggio Emilia (as *La calma fra le tempeste*); only the title, the theatre and the dates of performance are stated. A bill for Domenico Gabrielli's *Il Maurizio*, however, given at Modena five years later, names the composer, librettist and singers; another for the same theatre in 1719 also names the set and costume designers. A particularly detailed bill of 1782, published jointly for the Regio and Carignano theatres in Turin, gives detailed information about admission to both theatres, and a 1796 bill for the Teatro S Agostino, Genoa, even names the orchestral principals. In America the earliest surviving bill is for a performance on 2 April 1750 at the Nassau Street Theatre, New York; the author is named, but not the cast. Within two years the Nassau Street bills were being produced in the same informative style as in Britain, that for 12 November 1753 being unusual in providing a brief summary of the action of the mainpiece.

Printers, especially on the mainland of Europe, had from the first made use of heavy and elaborate borders in order to make their bills more striking in appearance; and from early in the 18th century they began to make more imaginative typographical variations, sometimes to give prominence to the names of star performers. In the 19th century, in order to increase the visual impact yet further, they considerably extended this practice, especially in Britain – contrasting sizes and weights of typeface, upper case with lower and italic, by employing a profusion of fonts (as many as 20 may be found in a single bill), by printing on paper of differing sizes, formats and colours and, for additional emphasis, by using coloured inks (*see* BENEFIT, fig.1, and OBERON, fig.1).

Still greater impact was obtained by the use of illustrations, through the medium first of the woodcut (until the late 19th century) and then of lithography. The illustrated bill certainly existed in London in the second half of the 17th century: an undated example from this period, for John Harris's Booth at Bartholomew Fair, is reproduced in *The London Stage*

4. Poster by Jules Chéret for Offenbach's 'Orphée aux enfers', printed at the time of the production of the revised version at the Théâtre de la Gaîté, Paris, in 1874

1660–1800 (i, facing p.400). In France, acrobats had made use of woodcuts to embellish their posters from the beginning of the 18th century, and it was in Paris in 1836 that the lithographic poster first made its appearance, initially for the promotion of new books. Among the earliest monochrome examples for the musical theatre were Victor Coindre's posters for the ballet *La filleule des fées* (1849) and for Auber's opera *Zerline* (1851); and one of the first lithographic posters in colours was that designed by Henri Emy for Auber's *Marco Spada* (1852). Jules Chéret (*see* fig.4), Antonin Chatinière, Alfred Choubrac, Georges Rochegrosse (*see* PARIS, fig. 23), Théophile Steinlen and Alphonse Mucha were among the most successful Parisian exponents of the artistic poster for opera, though much of their output was devoted to subjects in other fields.

Elsewhere, the most distinguished illustrated posters devoted to opera probably appeared in England and Italy. In England they began to appear in the mid-1860s, and among the earliest printed by chromolithography was one for Sullivan's comic opera *The Contrabandista* (1867), designed by R. J. Hammerton. Richard D'Oyly Carte commissioned further posters for the Opera Comique and Savoy theatres and for his tours, including one by Alfred Concanen for *H.M.S. Pinafore* (about 1878–9; *see* OPERETTA, fig.3) and a number by Dudley Hardy in the mid-1890s. Two of the best known British operatic posters were designed for productions at the Lyric Theatre, Hammersmith, in the 1920s – by Claud Lovat Fraser for *The Beggar's Opera* (1920) and George Sheringham for *The Duenna* (1924). In Italy the most eminent poster artists were Adolfo Hohenstein, notably for *La Wally* (1892), *Falstaff* (1893) and *Iris* (1898), and Leopoldo Metlicovitz, for *Tosca* (1900). In Germany and America the illustrated poster began to make headway in the 1890s.

Posters for touring companies were often designed to be overprinted with the name of a specific theatre and the dates of performances there, so that they could be used over a number of years. An even greater economy, regularly adopted by provincial and amateur companies, was to make use of stock posters, choosing from the ready-made designs offered by specialist theatrical printers; many of these were printed by the cheaper silkscreen process.

In France, the illustrated poster was more often the medium of publishers rather than opera companies (except sometimes for galas). Its essential purpose was to promote a new opera in a general way, seeking to fix the work in the minds of the public by graphically expressing its flavour. The traditional playbill had been growing ever larger in size, and the rise of the illustrated poster coincided with the transition of the playbill into the far more convenient programme. Posters and bills of the traditional letterpress type, containing full details of performances, have continued to be printed in varying formats and sizes up to the present day.

From the late 18th century until the early 20th it was customary in many countries to print bills for certain galas, benefits, premières and other royal or special occasions on silk or satin, sometimes fringed with tassels of silver wire or silk. This practice has been occasionally revived in recent years.

*

ES ('Manifesto'; L. H. Eisner)

R. Blum, G. K. R. Herlosssohn and H. Marggraff, eds.: *Allgemeines Theater-Lexikon* (Altenburg, 1842), vii, 239–40

'Posters and Picture Printing', *The Stage* (14 Dec 1883); repr. in

M. R. Booth, ed.: *Victorian Theatrical Trades* (London, 1981), 37–41

A. Pougin: *Dictionnaire historique et pittoresque du théâtre* (Paris, 1885), 17ff, 622

E. Maindron: *Les affiches illustrés* (Paris, 1886)

A. Oppenheim and E. Gettke, eds.: *Deutsches Theater-Lexikon* (Leipzig, 1889)

C. Hiatt: *Pictorial Posters* (London, 1895)

E. Maindron: *Les affiches illustrés, 1886–1895* (Paris, 1896)

W. J. Lawrence: 'The World's Oldest Playbills', *The Stage Year Book* (London, 1920), 23–30

E. Boswell: 'A Playbill of 1687', *The Library*, 4th ser., xi (1930–31), 499–502

J. Laver: *Nineteenth Century French Posters* (London, 1944)

W. Van Lennep: 'The Earliest Known English Playbill', *Harvard Library Bulletin*, i (1947), 382–5

P. Hartnoll, ed.: *The Oxford Companion to the Theatre* (London, 1951, 3/1967) [incl. G. Enthoven: 'Playbill, Programme', 742–4, and 'Posters, Theatrical', 757–9]

G. Speaight: 'The Earliest Known English Playbill', *Theatre Notebook*, vi (1952), 34–5

J. Macleod: 'The Earliest Amateur Playbill', *Theatre Notebook*, ix (1955), 11–14

J. Lewis: *Printed Ephemera* (Ipswich, 1962, 2/1990)

I. K. Fletcher: 'British Playbills before 1718', *Theatre Notebook*, xvii (1963), 48–50

L. Barbara: 'Manifesti e avvisi teatrali', *Il Museo teatrale alla Scala, 1913–1963* (Milan, 1964), 301–10

L. Broido: *French Opera Posters 1868–1930* (New York, 1976)

N. Wild: *Affiches illustrés 1850–1950* (Paris, 1976)

C. Haill: *Theatrical Posters* (London, 1983)

M. Weiss and J.-H. Piettre, eds.: *L'affiche d'opéra: catalogue* (Paris, 1984)

M. Brauneck and G. Schneilin, eds.: *Theater Lexikon* (Reinbek bei Hamburg, 1986), 985

L. Bianconi and G. Pestelli, eds.: *SOI*, iv: *Il sistema produttivo e le sue competenze* (Turin, 1987), pls. between pp.64 and 65

RICHARD MACNUTT

Pleasants, Henry (*b* Wayne, PA, 12 May 1910). American writer on music. Trained as a singer and pianist, he became music critic for the *Philadelphia Evening Bulletin* in 1930 and music editor from 1934. After army service he joined the US Foreign Service (1945–55), when he was also central European music correspondent for the *New York Times*. In 1967, he settled in London and became London music critic for the *International Herald-Tribune*. His writings extend and elaborate a critical principle which accords serious attention to the popular musical vernacular of the 20th century, including theatre music. His study *The Great Singers* (New York, 1966) suggests that the art of singing reached its zenith in the Baroque period, since when it has been in conflict with the demands of emotional expression and compositional techniques; his *Opera in Crisis* (London, 1989) deals in particular with the increasing interpretative role of the director in the last quarter of the century. Pleasants is an authority on German criticism of the Romantic era and has edited and translated volumes of writings by Eduard Hanslick (*Vienna's Golden Years of Music, 1850–1900*, 1950), Spohr (1961), Schumann (1965), Wolf (1970) and Wieck (1988).

NOËL GOODWIN

Pleven. Town in northern Bulgaria. Traces of Thracian, Roman and early Christian culture survive there. Operatic activity began with the Plevenska Samodeina Opera, which opened on 8 October 1970 with Parashkev Hadjiev's *Lud gidiya* ('The Madcap'). The singer and teacher Christo Brumbarov helped the new company with vocal training, and in 1975 the opera became a semi-professional company bearing his name. Among its successful productions have been *Il trovatore*, *Lucia di Lammermoor* and Marin Goleminov's *Nestinarka* ('The

Fire Dancer'). The group cooperated with Hadjiev, and its conductors have included Dimitar Karagyozov, Dimitar Manolov and Georgi Notev, and its directors, Emil Boshnakov and Stefan Trifonov. An important aspect of the company's activity was its participation in the Katya Popova International Music Festival. Until 1980 performances were given in the 19th-century Pleven drama theatre, reconstructed in 1962 with 560 seats.

R. Biks: *Bulgarski operen teatar*, ii (Sofia, 1985)

MAGDALENA MANOLOVA

Pleyel, Ignace Joseph [Ignaz Josef] (*b* Ruppersthal, Austria, 18 June 1757; *d* Paris, 14 Nov 1831). Austrian composer, music publisher and piano maker, active in France. He became Haydn's pupil and lodger in Eisenstadt about 1772 and was probably Kapellmeister to Count Ladislaus Erdődy later in the decade. After travels in Italy, he became assistant and, in 1789, full Kapellmeister of Strasbourg Cathedral. In 1791–2 he conducted the Professional Concerts in London with much success. He settled in Paris in 1795, opened a music shop and founded a publishing house that became one of the foremost in Europe (active until 1834). Meanwhile, in 1807 he opened a piano factory.

Pleyel's music, especially the symphonies and chamber music, enjoyed enormous popularity in his lifetime. Among his several hundred works in all genres are the marionette opera *Die Fee Urgele* (4, von Pauersbach, after C.-S. Favart), performed at Eszterháza in November 1776 and at the Vienna Nationaltheater (autograph score in *A-Wn*), and the three-act opera *Ifigenia in Aulide* (libretto possibly by Zeno), given at the S Carlo, Naples, on 30 May 1785 (Act 3 in *F-Pn* (autograph score), *I-Nc* and *P-La*). The latter was commissioned by Ferdinand IV, King of Naples, for performance on his name-day; it had 18 further performances that summer. Pleyel also wrote the overture to Haydn's puppet opera *Die Feuersbrunst* (1776–8, Eszterháza).

RITA BENTON

Plishka, Paul [Peter] (*b* Old Forge, PA, 28 Aug 1941). American bass. He studied at Montclair, making his début in 1961 with the Paterson Lyric Opera. After singing with the Metropolitan National Company (1965–7), he made his debut at Lincoln Center in 1967 as the Monk (*La Gioconda*). He sang Berlioz's Méphistophélès at La Scala (1974) and has appeared at Hamburg, Munich, Berlin, Chicago and San Francisco, where in 1991 he sang Kutuzov (*War and Peace*), but the greater part of his career has been spent at the Metropolitan. In 25 seasons there he has sung over 50 roles, among them Leporello, Oroveso, Rocco, King Mark, Varlaam, Pimen and Boris; but it is as an interpreter of Verdi that his firm, flexible voice and acting ability are particularly admired: as Zaccaria, the Miller, Banquo, Philip II, Procida, Silva and Fiesco.

ELIZABETH FORBES

Plomer, William (**Charles Franklyn**) (*b* Pietersburg, Transvaal, 10 Dec 1903; *d* Hassocks, Sussex, 21 Dec 1973). South African-born librettist, resident in Britain from 1929. Well known as a poet and novelist, he collaborated as a librettist with Benjamin Britten on *Gloriana* (1953) and the three 'church parables' (1964–8), having abandoned a plan for a children's opera about space travel. Based on the relationship

between Queen Elizabeth I and the Earl of Essex, *Gloriana* hardly 'glorifies' its heroine. Presented at Covent Garden as a coronation tribute to Queen Elizabeth II, and performed in her presence, it was considered by some to be scandalously inappropriate; however, its musical virtues draw strength from Plomer's mastery of a 'distanced' (but not pseudo-archaic) language and the clarity of the plot.

An even greater control of language is evident in the church parables, a language poised between that of the Authorized Version of the Bible and the directly modern. The most startling of the parables is the first, *Curlew River* (1964), because Britten had taken his inspiration from a Japanese noh play. Plomer had lived in Japan and he skilfully accommodated the Buddhist philosophical point to the Christian context. More consistent, and equally powerful in Plomer's shaping, were *The Burning Fiery Furnace* (1966) and *The Prodigal Son* (1968). The trilogy has never become popular in whole or in part but remains a bold and distinctive form of non-traditional theatre. Britten subsequently wrote his Canticle V, *The Death of St Narcissus* (1974), 'in loving memory' of Plomer.

ARTHUR JACOBS

Plovdiv. Town in Bulgaria. It became an important cultural centre soon after the country's liberation from Ottoman domination in 1878. Interest in visiting Italian troupes led to the foundation of a local singers' society in 1896. The earliest attempts to create an opera theatre date from 1910. Ten years later a privately owned Hudozhestvena Opera (Artistic Opera) was organized, and in 1922 the Plovdivska Gradska Opera (Plovdiv City Opera) was formed by Russian immigrants; by 1944 the Plovdivska Oblastna Opera (Plovdiv District Opera) had been established. On 15 November 1953 the Plovdivska Narodna Opera (Plovdiv National Opera) had its official opening in the Naroden Theater (National Theatre) with *The Bartered Bride*. From the very beginning the company's profile was determined by its ensemble, which included the paired soloists Penka Koeva and Aleksei Milkovski, Valentina Alexandrova and Georgi Velchev, and by its varied repertory, from *Die Zauberflöte*, *Les contes d'Hoffmann*, *L'heure espagnole* and *Adriana Lecouvreur* to *Kát'a Kabanová* and Pipkov's *Antigona 43*. The conductors Ruslan Raichev, Krasto Marev and Dimitar Manolov have also contributed to the company's success. Opera performances alternate with drama, and are given chiefly on the stage of the Trade Union Culture House; there are three performances weekly, with three to four premières a year. The season lasts from September until July.

R. Biks: *Bulgarski operen teatar*, ii (Sofia, 1985)

MAGDALENA MANOLOVA

Plowright, Rosalind (**Anne**) (*b* Worksop, 21 May 1949). English soprano. She studied in Manchester and at the London Opera Centre, then made her début in 1975 as the Page in *Salome* with the ENO. Her later roles with the company included Miss Jessel, Elizabeth (*Maria Stuarda*) and Elisabeth de Valois (1992); she also sang with Glyndebourne Touring Opera, Kent Opera and the WNO. In 1980 she made her Covent Garden début as Ortlinde, and has returned as Donna Anna, Maddalena (*Andrea Chénier*), Leonora (*Il trovatore*), Ariadne, Senta and Desdemona. She has sung in Berne, Frankfurt, Munich, Hamburg, Lyons, Bonn, Dallas and San

Francisco. After singing Cherubini's Medea at Buxton (1984), she became a specialist in both the French and Italian versions of the role. Her repertory includes Norma, Fiordiligi, Aida, Leonora (*Forza*), Tatyana and Tosca, which she sang at the Deutsche Oper, Berlin, in 1992. A versatile and dramatic singer, she has a flexible voice that is particularly strong in the middle register.

E. Forbes: 'Rosalind Plowright', *Opera*, xliii (1992), 416–23

ELIZABETH FORBES

Plumlovský, Ignác [Pater Alanus] (*b* Přerov, 18 Jan 1703; *d* Pásztó, Hungary, 2 May 1759). Moravian composer. A member of the Cistercian order from 1724, he was ordained in 1730. In 1747 a performance of a so-called 'Haná Singspiel' was given (with the libretto written in the dialect of Haná, a district of Moravia) at the Premonstratensian monastery of Hradisko at Olomouc; attributed to Plumlovský, it is presumed to be *Opera sanctionis pragmaticae nova atque vera duabus partibus exhibita orbi/Pargamotéka, to je Smlóva hanácká straneva králové cere*. It was composed in the style of Jesuit school plays and deals with the Pragmatic Sanction that guaranteed Maria Theresa the right of accession to the Austrian throne. Plumlovský is also thought to be the composer of the Singspiels *Gront a puvod plesání hanáckýho* ('The Foundations and Origins of the Hanatic Joy', 1751) and *Kterak Landebork od Prahe z královstvi českého … [lotr]* s Bohem hébal ('How the Rascally Brandenburger Escaped from Prague and the Bohemian Kingdom', *c*1757–8), the latter a commentary on the events of the Seven Years War, including the defeat of the English army at Hastenbeck, near Hanover (1758). Of the three, only the music of *Kterak Landebork* has survived (libretto in Burešová and Petrů, pp.63–83); it is written in a late Baroque operatic idiom close to that of the Neapolitan school. In style it is uncomplicated yet attractive and influenced by Moravian folk and dance music.

K. Kyas: 'Autor hanácké opery' [The Author of the Hanatic Opera], *Řád*, viii (1942), 479–80
——: 'Druhá hanácká opera' [The Second Hanatic Opera], *Řád*, ix (1943), 373–4
J. Trojan: *České zpěvohry 18. století* [Czech Operas of the 18th Century] (Brno, 1981)
A. Burešová and E. Petrů: *Copak to ale za mozeka hraje? Hanácké zpěvohry 18. století* [What is the Music I Hear? Hanatic Operas of the 18th Century] (Ostrava, 1985)
J. Tyrrell: *Czech Opera* (Cambridge, 1988)

MICHAELA FREEMANOVÁ

Plumpton, Alfred (William Edward) (*b* London, 1840; *d* London, April 1902). English conductor and composer. He worked first as a music hall pianist in London, then went to India (conducting a theatre company, *c*1875) and soon after settled in Melbourne. There he wrote criticism for *The Age* and composed three stage works. His first, *Alfred the Great*, written in collaboration with Fred Lyster (brother of W. S. Lyster), was an 'extravaganza' including arrangements of popular airs and set pieces, and the third, also incorporating airs, tended towards the genre of pantomime; between them came *I due studenti* (set in 16th-century Spain) which includes large concerted numbers but is chiefly dependant on monologues. In 1891 Plumpton returned to London and the next year was appointed conductor at the Prince of Wales's Theatre; he composed numbers for the burlesque *King Kodak* (Terry's, 30 April 1894) and later served as musical director at the Palace Theatre.

Alfred the Great (M. Clarke and H. Keiley), Melbourne, Academy of Music, 24 Dec 1878, *AUS-Msl*; collab. F. Lyster
I due studenti (3, U. Catani), Melbourne, Alexandra, 27 Dec 1887
Harlequin and the Forty Thieves (3), Sydney, Royal, 24 Dec 1891 (Sydney, 1891); collab. H. T. Harrison

E. Wood: *Australian Opera 1842–1970* (diss., U. of Adelaide, 1979)

Plzeň (Ger. Pilsen). Czech city. After Prague and together with Brno, it has the richest Czech theatre tradition. The first stone theatre, the Města Divadlo (Town Theatre), was constructed (1832) in the empire style according to Lorenzo Sacchetti's design. Mostly plays were performed, in German; operas were staged only sporadically. The first opera given in Czech, Flotow's *Martha*, was staged by amateurs in 1865, but a permanent Czech opera group, the first outside Prague, became active in 1868–9. Mořic Anger conducted performances of *Il trovatore* and, in 1869, *The Bartered Bride*; since that time there has been a tradition of dressing the *Bartered Bride* characters in folk costumes of the Plzeň region. A number of Czech premières of foreign works were given in Plzeň around this time, including *Tannhäuser* in 1888, three years before it was staged in Prague.

The Velké Divadlo (Great Theatre) was built in 1898–1902 by the architect Antonín Balášek, inspired by the neo-Renaissance style of the Prague National Theatre and by *art nouveau*. It opened in 1902 with Smetana's *Libuše*, and was reconstructed in 1980–87 (550 seats). From 1945 to 1965 small-scale operas were performed in the Malé Divadlo (Small Theatre), the former German theatre, built in 1869. In 1966 the new Komorní Divadlo (Chamber Theatre) was opened for the performance of such works.

The Česke Divadlo (Czech Theatre) in Plzeň has always been owned by the municipality. The town council leased it to cooperatives or to private promoters and subsidized them. From 1945 the theatre was administered directly by the town; since 1949 it has been managed by the Regional National Committee as the Krajské Oblastní Divadlo v Plzni (Regional Theatre of Plzeň). The name was changed to Divadlo J. K. Tyla (J. K. Tyl Theatre) in 1955.

Among several notable conductors (including Václav Talich, 1912–15), Bohumír Liška (1955–67) presided over the most remarkable era, with a repertory of both Czech and international operas, especially modern works. Among the most important have been Hanuš's *Plameny* ('Flames', 1956), Prokofiev's *The Gambler* (1957), Britten's *Albert Herring* (1958), Nejedlý's *Tkalci* ('The Weavers', 1961, première), Jeremiáš's *Enšpígl* (1962) and Hurník's *Dáma a lupiči* ('The Lady and the Thieves', 1966, première). Several generations of singers made successful débuts in Plzeň, then continued their careers in the Prague National Theatre, notably Emil Burian.

100 let českého divadla v Plzni 1865–1965 [100 years of Czech theatre in Plzeň] (Plzeň, 1965)
A. Špelda: *Slavní plzeňské opery* [Famous Performers of the Opera in Plzeň] (Plzeň, 1986)
O. Nový: 'Rekonstrukce Divadla J. K. Tyla v Plzni', *Architektura ČSR*, no.1 (1988)

EVA HERRMANNOVÁ

Pocci, Franz, Graf von (*b* Munich, 7 March 1807; *d* Munich, 7 May 1876). German composer. In childhood he showed talent for drawing, painting and music, and although he studied law at the universities of Landshut and Munich, he continued his artistic activities, composed and performed at the piano. From 1847 to 1863 he was a musician at the Bavarian court. As a composer, Pocci excelled at writing miniatures, and was at his most characteristic in children's songs, for which he showed a special gift. His plays with musical settings for the Munich Marionette Theatre, for which he also designed the scenery, added new vitality to puppet opera; they include *Moschopulos*, on which Rudolf Wagner-Régeny later based his opera of the same name (1928), and *Die Zaubergeige*, later set by Werner Egk (1935). He was less successful in his larger works, which include the two-act Singspiel *Der Alchymist*, to a text by L. Koch, given in Munich in 1840.

ADB (H. Holland); *ES* (H. R. Purschke)

H. Holland: *Zur Erinnerung an F. Pocci* (Munich, 1877)

L. Hirschberg: 'Franz Pocci der Musiker', *ZMw*, i (1918–19), 40–70

F. Pocci: *Franz Poccis lustiges Komödienbüchlein* (Munich, 1921)

K. Pastor: *Franz Pocci als Musiker* (diss., U. of Munich, 1932)

GAYNOR G. JONES

Podéšť, Ludvík (*b* Dubňany u Hodonína, 19 Dec 1921; *d* Prague, 27 Feb 1968). Czech composer. He was educated in Brno, first pursuing language studies, and later composition at the conservatory, studying with Kvapil (1945–8), and musicology at the university (1945–9). Podéšť worked for Czech radio and television, and was artistic director of the V. Nejedlý Army Arts Ensemble in Prague. His administrative activities also involved him in artists' organizations. Towards the end of his life he spent much of his time in Casablanca and concerned himself with music theory.

The source of his music's spontaneity may be found in the folk music of Moravian Slovakia, his native region. His music of the 1940s followed the post-Janáček tradition, then, after about 1950, he began to respond to the new policy of socialist realism, writing melodically conventional and readily comprehensible orchestral works. His early operettas (both for radio and for the stage), incidental music and film scores, all display characteristics of Czech and Moravian folk music. These works prepared the way for a series of operas, including *Hrátky s čertem* ('Gossip with the Devil') and *Apokryfy* ('Apocryphas', originally written for TV), whose lighthearted, ironic stories are set in an often musically witty chamber style. *Gossip with the Devil* is a fairy-tale opera inspired by folk music and including jazz rhythms. It is about Martin, an honest man who is not afraid of robbers, devils or ghosts; he justly punishes the evil-doers and, despite saving the royal princess and Káča from hell, he does not manage to save himself from Káča, who wants to marry him.

Hrátky s čertem [Gossip with the Devil], 1957–60 (fairy-tale op, 7, Podéšť, after J. Drda), Liberec, 12 Oct 1963

Apokryfy [Apocryphas] (trilogy of TV ops, Podéšť after K. Čapek), Brno, 17 Dec 1959

Staré zlaté časy [The Good Old Days] (1)

Svatá noc [Holy Night] (1), Brno, 5 June 1959

Romeo a Julie (1)

Emílek a dynamit [Emílek and the Dynamite] (operetta, 2, V. Dubský and J. Barchánek), Prague, Na Fidlovačce, 12 May 1960

Filmova hvězda [The Film Star] (operetta, 3, K. M. Walló), Ostrava, J. Myron, 2 June 1960

Noci na seně [A Night on the Hay] (operetta, 3, Z. Endris and Z. Borovec), unperf.

JIŘÍ FUKAČ, HELENA HAVLÍKOVÁ

Podgoretsky, Boris Vladimirovich. *See* PIDHORETS'KY, BORYS VOLODYMYROVYCH.

Poe, Edgar Allan (*b* Boston, 19 Jan 1809; *d* Baltimore, 7 Oct 1849). American writer. After being orphaned in 1811 he had a disturbed childhood and youth and became prey to alcoholism at an early age. His literary works, memorable in their unifying images and sensitive sound effects, fostered the genres of prose poems, science and detective fiction, and imaginative hoaxes. In his literary theory, he consistently upheld music as the supreme art in its 'indefinite conception' which best embodies man's basic 'poetic sentiment' and enables the 'soul' to create 'supernal beauty'. Poe opposed narrowly imitative programme music and decorative vocal roulades, favouring a suggestive mood and freedom to experiment with form. These critical tenets, along with the obsessive and gripping nature of his popular tales and poems, quickly spread his influence throughout the western world. Baudelaire's sedulous translations of his tales and Mallarmé's of his poems made him an intrinsic part of late 19th-century French cultural heritage.

Both in art and in music, symbolists and impressionists derived from Poe aesthetic principles as well as narrative themes and melancholy or morbid atmospheric effects. Debussy, after contemplating a symphonic piece on *The Fall of the House of Usher* in 1890, devoted much time (1908–17) to an uncompleted opera on it and also to an even more abortive companion piece, the humorous *Devil in the Belfry* (begun 1902), both promised to Gatti-Casazza for the Metropolitan Opera. Rumours of Debussy's efforts led others to consider Poe tales for short operas, and several composers of the avant garde and of experimental tendencies used them for ballets (e.g. G. Scibine's *The Raven*, after *Annabel Lee*, with choreography by B. Schiffman, 1954; Henri Sauget's *Le caméléopard*, after *Four Beasts in One*, with choreography by J. Babilée, 1956; and M. Vittoria's *Ligeia*, 1957) and for fictional musical treatments of Poe's unfortunate life (e.g. Dominick Argento's *The Voyage of Edgar Allan Poe*, 1976; Georges Aperghis's *William Wilson*; and W. Grien's rock opera *The Revelations*, 1986). In the 1970s and 80s public subsidies and patronage, as well as a growing appreciation of Poe's works in America, encouraged versatile and eclectic approaches to musical settings of a wide range of narrative themes including the satires, although the most dialogic works (*Usher* and *Cask of Amontillado*) still predominate.

tales unless otherwise stated

Politian (play, 1835–6): J. M. Zoubaloff, 1927

Ligeia (1838): L. Lackey, 1980; Currie, 1987

The Devil in the Belfry (1839): Lualdi, 1925, as Il diavolo nel campanile; D. P. McKay, 1984

The Fall of the House of Usher (1839): Debussy, comp. 1908–17 [reconstructed 1977]; Claflin, 1921, unperf.; Loomis, 1941; Sitsky, 1965; G. Sandow, 1979; Currie, 1984, as A Dream within a Dream; Glass, 1988

The Masque of the Red Death (1842): M. Ostraglazov, 1896; Saminsky, 1925, as The Gagliarda of a Merry Plague; R. J. Haskins, 1976

The Pit and the Pendulum (1842): Bettinelli, 1967, as Il pozzo e il pendolo

The Tell-Tale Heart (1843): L. Horacek, 1968; R. Nelson, 1978; T. Czerny-Hydzik, 1979; W. Rehrer, 1980; Adolphe, 1982

The Purloined Letter (1844): Blacher, 1975, as Das Geheimnis des entwendeten Briefes

The Facts in the Case of M. Valdemar (1845): M. Rosenstock, 1978

Some Words with a Mummy (1845): Viozzi, 1954, as Allamistakeo

The System of Dr Tarr and Professor Fether (1845): Rogel, 1867, lost; Tosatti, 1951, as Il sistema della dolcezza; J. Bach, 1974

The Cask of Amontillado (1846): C. F. Hamm, 1953; J. Perry, 1954, as The Bottle; Haskins, 1957; A. Provenzano, 1968; D. Para, 1979; Currie, 1982

M. G. Evans: *Music and Edgar Allan Poe* (Baltimore and Oxford, 1939)

R. C. Archibald: 'Music and Edgar Allan Poe', *Notes and Queries*, clxxix (1940), 170–71

I. B. Cauthen: 'Music and Edgar Allan Poe', *Notes and Queries*, cxciv (1949), 103

E. Lockspeiser: *Debussy et Edgar Poe* (Monaco, 1962)

B. R. Pollin: 'More Music to Poe', *ML*, liv (1973), 391–404

——: 'Music and Poe: a Second Annotated Check List', *Poe Studies*, xv (1982), 7–13, 42

J. L. Idol and S. K. Eisiminger: 'Performances of Operas Based on Poe's Fiction: a Supplementary Listing', *Poe Studies*, xv (1982), 42 [suppl. to Evans 1939, Pollin 1973 and Pollin 1982]

BURTON R. POLLIN

Poggi, Antonio (*b* Castel S Pietro, Bologna, 1806; *d* Bologna, 15 April 1875). Italian tenor. He studied with Nozzari and, after an unsuccessful appearance in Paris as James (*La donna del lago*), made his début in 1827 at Bologna as Peter the Great (Pacini's *Il falegname di Livronia*). He sang in the first performance of Persiani's *Saraceni in Catania* (1832, Padua) and created Roberto in *Torquato Tasso* at the Teatro Valle, Rome (1833). He made his début at La Scala as Elvino (*La sonnambula*) in 1834, then sang in the first performance of Donizetti's *Pia de' Tolomei*(1837, Venice). He appeared at Her Majesty's Theatre, London, in 1842. His repertory included Rossini's Almaviva and Idreno; Bellini's Arturo (*La straniera* and *I puritani*), Pollione and Orombello (*Beatrice di Tenda*); Donizetti's Nemorino, Edgardo, Gennaro and Fernando (*Marin Faliero*). He sang Oronte in Verdi's *I Lombardi* at Venice and Florence (1843), Rome and Milan (1844), then created Charles VII in Verdi's *Giovanna d'Arco* at La Scala (1845). He was married to the soprano Erminia Frezzolini, but they separated in 1846 and he retired from the stage.

ELIZABETH FORBES

Poggi, Gianni (*b* Piacenza, 4 Oct 1921 or 1922; *d* Piacenza, 16 Dec 1989). Italian tenor. He studied in Milan and made his début in 1947 at Palermo as Rodolfo. He first sang at La Scala in 1948 and appeared in all the major Italian cities, including Rome and Florence, where he sang the title role of Donizetti's *Dom Sébastien* in 1955. He made his London début at the Prince's Theatre in 1960 as the Duke in *Rigoletto*. His repertory included Edgardo, Fernand (*La favorite*), Riccardo (*Ballo*), Alfredo, Enzo (*La Gioconda*), Boito's Faust, Maurizio (*Adriana Lecouvreur*), Turiddu, Canio and Cavaradossi. He had a powerful, reliable voice but his tone inclined to hardness.

ELIZABETH FORBES

Poglietti, Alessandro [Boglietti, Alexander de] (*b* ?Tuscany, early 17th century; *d* Vienna, July 1683). Austrian composer of Italian birth. He may have received his musical training in Rome or Bologna. At the beginning of 1661 he was a church organist and Kapellmeister in Vienna; by July of that year he was appointed court and chamber organist in the Kapelle of Leopold I. He was highly regarded as a teacher of keyboard playing and as a writer of keyboard pieces imitating natural sounds and various musical instruments. He formed particularly close ties with the Benedictine foundation of Göttweig, Lower Austria, where, on 12 January 1677, his only known opera, *Endimione festeggiante* (J. Dizent; now in *CS-KRa*) was performed, on the occasion of a visit by the emperor.

F. W. Riedel: 'Alessandro Pogliettis Oper *Endimione*', *Festschrift Hans Engel* (Kassel, 1964), 298–313   FRIEDRICH W. RIEDEL

Pohjalaisia ('The Ostrobothnians'). Opera in three acts, op.45, by LEEVI MADETOJA to his own libretto after Artturi Järviluoma's play; Helsinki, Finnish Opera, 25 October 1924.

Set in the west Finnish plains of Ostrobothnia, the opera is on one level a love story with humorous episodes. On a more fundamental plane it depicts the conflict between a proud peasantry and a brutally unfeeling alien authority leading to an inevitable tragedy. The original play, published in 1914 while Finland was under Imperial Russian rule, was indeed intended as a symbol of the nation's struggle for freedom. The play included Ostrobothnian folksongs, and these Madetoja has used extensively and skilfully in his score. His orchestration is highly charged and vividly colourful, making *Pohjalaisia* more than a mere folk opera, although the work belongs firmly in the nationalist romantic tradition and kept its status as the 'national' opera until the arrival of Joonas Kokkonen's *The Last Temptations* in 1975.

ERKKI ARNI

Pohjan neiti ('The Maid of the North'). Opera in three acts by OSKAR MERIKANTO to a libretto by Antti Rytkönen, after the epic Kalevala; Viipuri (now Vyborg) Song Festival, 19 June 1908.

Pohjan neiti was the first opera written to a Finnish-language text, derived from a national epic, though its connection with the Kalevala is somewhat tenuous. The plot concerns the adventures of the sage Vainamoinen (baritone) and other leading figures in Pohjola ('the Northland'). Musically, the opera is unashamedly nationalist-romantic, its tunes as easy to forget as they are on the ear.

ERKKI ARNI

Pohl, Richard (*b* Leipzig, 12 Sept 1826; *d* Baden-Baden, 17 Dec 1896). German critic and translator. He knew Schumann in Leipzig and helped him with several texts. With K. F. Brendel he worked on the *Neue Musikzeitung* and was co-editor of the *Neue Zeitschrift für Musik* under the pseudonym 'Hoplit' – the indomitable, heavily armed infantryman of classical Greece. He lived in Weimar from 1854 to 1864, then in Baden-Baden. Pohl's heroes were his personal friends Berlioz, Wagner and Liszt. He annoyed Wagner by stating publicly that in *Tristan* he had learnt much from Liszt's harmony, but the two remained friends; Wagner called him 'der älteste Wagnerianer', and Pohl wrote a novel based on Wagner's life, *Richard Wiegand* (Brunswick, 1904). His most important German translations of librettos were of *Béatrice et Bénédict* (Weimar, 1863), *Le dernier sorcier* (Weimar, 1869; original text by Turgenev, set by Pauline Viardot), *Samson et Dalila* (Weimar, 1877) and *A Life for the Tsar* (Hanover, 1878). His writings include *Bayreuther Erinnerungen* (Leipzig, 1877), an autobiographical note (*Musikalisches Wochenblatt*, xii, 1881, p3ff) and a volume each on Wagner, Liszt and Berlioz in *Gesammelte Schriften über Musik und Musiker* (Leipzig, 1883–4).

DEREK WATSON

Pohle [Pohl, Pohlen, Pole, Pol, Bohle], **David** (*b* Marienberg, nr Chemnitz, 1624; *d* Merseburg, 20 Dec 1695). German composer. He received his musical training from Heinrich Schütz at Dresden, then worked for short periods at the courts at Dresden, Merseburg (as an instrumentalist), Kassel, Weissenfels and Zeitz before settling at Halle, where he is listed as Konzertmeister in 1660 and as Kapellmeister in 1661. At Halle he composed at least six Singspiels, most of them to texts by the court secretary, David Elias Heidenreich. Between 1674 and 1677 he also worked at the related courts at Weissenfels and Zeitz. He was Kapellmeister at Zeitz, 1678–80 (replaced by J. P. Krieger), but stayed there until 1682, when he moved to a similar position at Merseburg where he remained until his death. Many of his compositions, including the Singspiels, are now lost; those surviving are mostly sacred cantatas and instrumental works.

all Singspiels; most librettos by D. E. Heidenreich

Liebe krönt Eintracht, 1669
Der singende Hof-Mann Daniel, 1671
Aspasia, 1672
Der glückselige Liebes-Fehl Prinz Walrams aus Sachsen, 1673
Der verliebte Mörder Herodes, 1673
Die vermechselte Braut, 1675
Das ungereimte Paar Venus und Vulcanus, 1679

*

W. Serauky: *Musikgeschichte der Stadt Halle*, ii/1 (Halle and Berlin, 1939)
G. Gille: *Der Schützschüler David Pohle (1624–1695): seine Bedeutung für die deutsche Musikgeschichte des 17. Jahrhunderts* (diss., U. of Halle, 1973)   KERALA JOHNSON SNYDER

Poise, (Jean Alexandre) Ferdinand (*b* Nîmes, 3 June 1828; *d* Paris, 13 May 1892). French composer. He studied with Adolphe Adam and Pierre-Joseph Zimmermann at the Paris Conservatoire and gained second main prize for composition in the Prix de Rome of 1852. Devoting himself immediately to *opéra comique*, he found popularity with his first work, *Bonsoir, voisin*, which held the stage at the Théâtre Lyrique for five years (80 performances), then appeared in the repertory of the Opéra-Comique (101 performances from 1872 to 1877). *Les charmeurs* was hardly less successful; it was also given by the Opéra-Comique, in 1862. *L'amour médecin*, in spite of being the production preceding *Les contes d'Hoffmann*, proved durable; by 1893 it had been seen 187 times, being withdrawn only in 1898. Poise made a speciality of setting librettos derived from 18th-century sources, and in 1867 he arranged and reorchestrated Philidor's *Le sorcier*. In 1872 Poise received the music prize founded by Baron Trémont and awarded by the Académie des Beaux-Arts.

all opéras comiques; first performed and published in Paris unless otherwise stated

Bonsoir, voisin (1, A. de Beauplan and Brunswick [L. Lhérie]), Lyrique, 20 Sept 1853 (*c*1855)
Les charmeurs (1, A. de Leuven, after C.-S. Favart), Lyrique, 7 March 1855, vs (*c*1865)
Le thé de Polichinelle (1, E. Plouvier), Bouffes-Parisiens, 4 March 1856
Le roi Don Pèdre (2, E. Cormon [P. E. Piestre] and E. Grangé [E. P. Basté]), OC (Favart), 30 Sept 1857, vs (1857)
Le jardinier galant (2, de Leuven and P. Siraudin), OC (Favart), 4 March 1861 (1861)
Les absents (1, A. Daudet), OC (Favart), 26 Oct 1864, vs (1865)
Jean Noël (1, E. Dubreuil), unperf., vs in *Le magasin des demoiselles* (1865)
Le sorcier (1, J. Adenis, after A. A. H. Poinsinet), Fantaisies-Parisiennes, 9 Feb 1867 [rev. of F. A. D. Philidor: Le sorcier, 1764]
Le corricolo (3, E. Labiche and Delacour [A. C. Lartigue]), OC (Favart), 28 Nov 1868
Les deux billets (1, J. P. Claris de Florian), Athénée, 19 Feb 1870 (1870)
Les trois souhaits (1, Adenis), OC (Favart), 29 Oct 1873, vs (1874)

La surprise de l'amour (2, C. P. Monselet, after Marivaux), OC (Favart), 31 Oct 1877, vs (1878)
La cigale et la fourmi (1, A. Beaumont [A. Beaume], after La Fontaine), unperf., vs in *Le magasin des demoiselles* (1877)
La dame de compagnie (1, Beaumont), unperf., vs in *Le magasin des demoiselles* (1877)
L'amour médecin (3, Monselet, after Molière), OC (Favart), 20 Dec 1880, vs (1881)
La reine d'une heure (1, Beaumont), unperf., vs in *Le magasin des demoiselles* (1881)
Joli Gilles (2, Monselet, after S. d'Allainval), OC (Favart), 9 Oct 1884, vs (1884)
Le médecin malgré lui, 1887 (after Molière), unperf.
Carmosine, Monte Carlo, 1928

1 piece in La poularde de Caux (1861)

*

LoewenbergA; *StiegerO*
A. Soubies and C. Malherbe: *Histoire de l'Opéra-Comique: la seconde Salle Favart* (Paris, 1892–3)
A. Soubies: *Soixante-neuf ans à l'Opéra-Comique en deux pages* (Paris, 1894)
T. J. Walsh: *Second Empire Opera: the Théâtre Lyrique, Paris, 1851–1870* (London and New York, 1981)
                                                            DAVID CHARLTON

Poisoned Kiss, The [*The Poisoned Kiss, or The Empress and the Necromancer*]. Romantic extravaganza in three acts by RALPH VAUGHAN WILLIAMS, to a libretto by Evelyn Sharp, adapted from Richard Garnett's story *The Poison Maid* and Nathaniel Hawthorne's *Rapaccini's Daughter*; Cambridge, Arts Theatre, 12 May 1936.

Vaughan Williams's lighter side found a musical outlet in this uncertain cross between operetta and musical comedy, with its tangos, waltzes and jazz-inflected harmonies for a women's trio of mediums. It was of *The Poisoned Kiss* that he wrote that he had never dared to show the score to his friend Gustav Holst because he believed Holst would not have understood how he regarded it as unimportant yet wanted to write it.

All the characters have botanical names. The plot concerns a magician, Dipsacus (bass), jilted in his youth by the Empress Persicaria (contralto). In revenge he plans to kill her son Amaryllus (tenor) by bringing up his daughter Tormentilla (soprano) on a diet of poison so that when, as he plans, the young couple meet and fall in love, her first kiss will prove fatal. But the Empress has brought up Amaryllus on antidotes. Eventually, Dipsacus and the Empress are reconciled and get married, as do all other couples in the opera.

The music is delightful, but the libretto causes problems. Vaughan Williams composed the opera in 1927–9, revised it in 1934–5 and 1936–7, and again in 1956–7 when his wife Ursula provided new spoken dialogue.
                                                            MICHAEL KENNEDY

Poissl, Johann Nepomuk, Freiherr von (*b* Haukenzell, Lower Bavaria, 15 Feb 1783; *d* Munich, 17 Aug 1865). German composer. He came from a south German aristocratic family and in 1805 settled in Munich where he studied composition with Danzi and Abbé Vogler. With Danzi's encouragement and support (and perhaps assisted by his own aristocratic background), Poissl had his first stage work, the Singspiel *Die Opernprobe*, staged at the Munich Hofoper in 1806, though the work made little impression. Probably influenced by Danzi's through-composed German grand opera *Iphigenie in Aulis* (1807), Poissl turned his attention to grand opera with continuous music, the genre to which all but two of his subsequent operas belong. His next two operas, *Antigonus* (in German) and *Ottaviano in Sicilia* (in

Italian), both to librettos adapted by the composer from Metastasio, enjoyed considerable local success; according to Weber, *Ottaviano* was greeted 'with almost unparalleled enthusiasm'. However, his Singspiel *Aucassin und Nicolette*, produced the following year, was coolly received and Poissl returned to grand opera, determined to retrieve his reputation. With his tragic opera *Athalia* he gained the acclaim he sought. The *Münchner Theaterjournal* hailed its appearance as marking 'the longed-for era of a national art, the creation of a national artistic model which we have so far lacked'. The *Allgemeine musikalische Zeitung* concurred, believing that in this work Poissl had discovered the style of a truly national opera. During the next few years *Athalia* was performed in most of the major German theatres. Poissl quickly produced another opera along similar lines, *Der Wettkampf zu Olympia*, which was highly praised and widely staged. This was the high point of Poissl's operatic career. Of his later operas, *Nittetis*, *La rappresaglia* and *Die Prinzessin von Provence* were moderately successful, but the poor reception of *Der Untersberg*, in 1829, seems to have deterred Poissl from further efforts for more than a decade. His last opera, *Zaide*, roused little interest.

Poissl spent most of his life in financial difficulties; these were temporarily relieved when, in 1823, he was made assistant superintendant of court music in Munich, and he was director of the court theatre, 1825–33. In 1847 he was named first chamberlain and dismissed from his position as superintendant. His last years were again darkened by financial worries. When he died at the age of 82 his music had sunk into almost total oblivion.

Poissl was an important figure in the move to create a German operatic tradition that could challenge the supremacy of foreign operas on the German stage. He was an important link in the chain connecting the Mannheim-Munich German grand opera tradition, which stemmed from Holzbauer, with the Romantic operas of Weber and Spohr. Weber's personal connection with Poissl, which began in 1811, was undoubtedly significant for both composers. Similar aspirations to create a German grand opera tradition were shared by a number of composers at this time, notably Ignaz von Mosel. But in many respects both Mosel and Poissl approached the problem from a rather different angle from Weber, generally relying on classical or mythological texts in the manner of Gluck. Despite the considerable success of several of Poissl's operas, this approach proved a cul-de-sac. It was Weber's and Spohr's more 'Romantic' conception of German opera that paved the way for Wagner's achievements. Poissl's efforts to handle Romantic themes in his last three operas, composed after the appearance of Weber's *Der Freischütz* and *Euryanthe* and Spohr's *Jessonda*, were not successful.

first performed at Munich, Hofoper, unless otherwise stated

Die Opernprobe (komische Oper, 2, after It. lib.), 23 Feb 1806
Antigonus (3, Poissl, after P. Metastasio), 12 Feb 1808
Ottaviano in Sicilia (dramma eroico, 3, Poissl), 30 June 1812, ov. pubd
Aucassin und Nicolette (Singspiel, 3, F. K. Hiemer, after M.-J. Sedaine), 28 March 1813
Athalia (grosse Oper, 3, J. G. Wohlbrück, after J. Racine), 3 June 1814, ov. pubd
Der Wettkampf zu Olympia, oder Die Freunde (grosse Oper, 3, Poissl, after Metastasio: *L'olimpiade*), 21 April 1815, ov. pubd
Dir wie mir, oder Alle betrügen, 1816 (komische Oper, 2, von Zahlhans), unperf.

Nittetis (grosse Oper, 3, Poissl, after Metastasio), Darmstadt, 29 June 1817
Issipile, 1818 (grosse Oper, Poissl, after Metastasio), unperf.
La rappresaglia (opera semiseria, 2, Poissl, after C. Sterbini), 7 April 1820
Die Prinzessin von Provence (Zauberoper, 3, Poissl, after F. Romani), 23 Jan 1825
Der Untersberg (romantische Oper, E. von Schenk), 30 Oct 1829
Zaide (romantisch-tragische Oper, 4, Poissl), 9 Nov 1843

Additions to: Nasolini: Merope, 1812; and operas by Dittersdorf and Rossini

Münchner Theaterjournal, i (1814), 187
E. Reipschläger: *Schubaur, Danzi und Poissl als Opernkomponisten* (Berlin, 1911)
M. Zenger: *Geschichte der Münchener Oper* (Munich, 1923)
E. Bücken: *Der heroische Stil in der Oper* (Leipzig, 1924)
L. Schrott: 'Aus dem Ringen um die deutsche Oper', *Die Musik*, xxxii (1939–40), 299–303
C. M. von Weber: *Writings on Music*, ed. J. Warrack (Cambridge, 1981), 184–7, 289–91
CLIVE BROWN

Poitier, Jane [Mrs Vernon, Mrs Thompson] (*b* 1736; *d* after 1774). English soprano and dancer. As a child she appeared as a dancer but her London singing début was in Arne's *Eliza* (May 1754). She generally played spirited second-woman roles, singing Lucy in *The Beggar's Opera* almost every season and creating the parts of Dorcas in Arne's *Thomas and Sally* (1760) and Fanny the gypsy in *The Maid of the Mill* (1765). In 1762 her immodest costume while dancing shocked the party in the royal box and in *Thespis* she was called 'the liveliest baggage on the modern stage'. Her Savoy Chapel marriage to the tenor Vernon in 1755 was declared invalid; she sang again as Miss Poitier from September 1762 until she became Mrs Thompson in 1767. In the early 1770s she was in burlettas at Marylebone Gardens with her current lover, Charles Bannister. She last appeared on the London stage in 1774 but continued to sing in Ireland and the provinces for several years.

BDA; *LS*
The Theatrical Review, i (1763), 42–3
H. Kelly: *Thespis*, ii (London, 1767)
T. J. Walsh: *Opera in Dublin 1705–1797* (Dublin, 1973)
OLIVE BALDWIN, THELMA WILSON

Polacchine, Le. *See* NANNINI, LIVIA DOROTEA.

Polacco, Giorgio (*b* Venice, 12 April 1873; *d* New York, 30 April 1960). Italian conductor. After studies in Venice, Milan and St Petersburg, he was engaged as an assistant at Covent Garden in 1890 and made his début the next year at the Shaftesbury Theatre, conducting Gluck's *Orfeo ed Euridice*. He quickly became a successful opera conductor in many European cities, in Russia and in South America (including four seasons in Buenos Aires and seven in Rio de Janeiro), and conducted for Tetrazzini's débuts in Mexico in 1905 and at San Francisco in 1906. In 1911 he toured the USA with Henry Savage's company, directing the first English production in the USA of *La fanciulla del West*. He made his Metropolitan début the next year with *Manon Lescaut*, and remained there until 1917, succeeding Toscanini as director of the Italian repertory in 1915. He conducted in Chicago (1918–19, 1921) where he was later principal conductor of the Civic Opera (1922–30). Polacco's performances were noted for their precision and vigour and, in addition to Wagner and Italian operas, he became a leading conductor of French opera under Mary Garden's influence at Chicago. He appeared at Covent Garden in 1912–13, and made his last appearances there, in 1930, conducting *Pelléas et Mélisande* with Maggie Teyte, who, in her autobiography (1958), described him as that opera's 'ideal interpreter'.

RICHARD D. FLETCHER

Poland. Italian opera apparently found its way to at least one aristocratic court in Poland a few years before it was introduced to the royal court by the crown prince Władysław in 1628. When the prince became Władysław IV in 1632 he had an opera theatre built on the first floor of the royal palace, inaugurating it in 1633 with a production of *La fama reale* by Piotr Elert. The music for this, the first opera by a Polish composer, has not survived. It was in any case exceptional, for the subsequent repertory at the royal court was almost exclusively of Italian operas, many of them composed by the court Kapellmeister Marco Scacchi to librettos on classical themes by the royal secretary Virgilio Puccitelli. The singers and players were also in the main Italian.

Opera thrived at the royal court until 1655, when a series of political upheavals, beginning with the Swedish invasions of that year, effectively destroyed the stability of formal culture in Poland. By the early 18th century the royal company had already moved to Saxony (following the coronation of the Saxon prince August the Strong in 1697), so that Warsaw and Kraków were obliged to play host to the opera company from Dresden. It was only in 1724, with the opening of the first public opera house in Warsaw, that regular productions were restored to the city.

By then an active operatic life was beginning to take shape elsewhere in Poland, notably at the courts of that small select group of families making up the wealthy and politically powerful higher nobility. Many of the operas staged at these courts were by aristocratic amateurs, but there were operas to Polish librettos by professional court composers such as the German-born Jan Dawid Holland (1746–1827), Kapellmeister to the Radziwiłłs at Nieśwież, and Wincenty Lessel (*c*1750–*c*1825), who served the Czartoryskis at Puławy. These courts, especially Puławy, were major cultural centres, albeit less well endowed after the partitions than before.

In 1765 the National Theatre was established in Warsaw, giving plays and operas in Polish translation under the direction of Wojciech Bogusławski, so-called 'father of Polish theatre'. The earliest surviving opera by a Polish composer was staged there in 1778, a 'vaudeville', *Nędza uszczęśliwiona* ('Sorrow turned to Joy'), with music by Maciej Kamieński (1734–1821). Such vaudevilles, or Singspiels, were enormously popular in Warsaw and they culminated in a work which remains a landmark of Polish opera, *Cud mniemany* ('The Supposed Miracle') by Jan Stefani, given the first of many productions in 1794.

The following year, for political reasons, the National Theatre moved to Lwów for three years and it was there that Bogusławski encountered the German-born composer Józef Elsner, inaugurating a collaboration which continued when the two men returned to Warsaw in 1799. It is from this point that we may date a growing preoccupation with a Polish national idiom in opera, evidenced in subject matter, attitudes to Polish word-setting (on which Elsner wrote an important treatise) and the incorporation of national dance idioms. The arrival in Warsaw of Karol Kurpiński in 1810 further

consolidated the growing strength of Polish opera in the early 19th century, with native operas as prominent in the repertory as foreign. All this changed with the 1830 uprising. The Polish element declined, as the Russian director at the Grand Theatre ('National' was dropped from the title) increasingly imported French and Italian companies to the Warsaw stage and rigorously censored native productions. Even the renewed vitality that accompanied Moniuszko's appointment as director of Polish productions in 1858 proved short-lived, all but stifled in the aftermath of the 1863 rising.

By then regular opera companies were already established elsewhere in Poland, notably in Kraków and Lwów, though there were extended periods when these companies were closed down, usually due to political unrest. In Lwów, as also in Poznań, political tensions were further reflected in the later 19th century by the separation of German and Polish companies and (in the case of Poznań) German and Polish audiences. Smaller towns often had to make do with concert performances of operas given by local or visiting companies, and it is worth noting that the original version of Moniuszko's *Halka* was given in just this way at Vilnius.

Polish opera was at a low ebb in the late 19th century and the early 20th. Warsaw produced numerous highly acclaimed singers, but few composers capable of assuming with confidence the mantle of Moniuszko. The leading figures were Władysław Żeleński (1837–1921), Zygmunt Noskowski (1846–1909) and Henryk Jarecki (1846–1918), the last one of the few Polish composers to demonstrate an awareness of Wagner's achievement in a climate still dominated by Italian opera and especially by Verdi. In the end it was left to a much later masterpiece – Szymanowski's *Król Roger* ('King Roger') – to shake Polish opera free of its conservatism and provincialism.

Król Roger was completed in 1924 in the early days of a newly independent Poland, a Poland whose return to statehood was marked by a renewed stability and vitality in the cultural (including operatic) life of the major cities – Warsaw, Kraków, Poznań and Lwów (then still a part of Poland). Following World War II, companies also sprang up in Bytom, Gdańsk, Bydgoszcz and Wrocław, and in the cultural thaw of the late 1950s this expansion of the institutional framework for opera was matched by new creative vitality. Composers such as Witold Rudziński, Tadeusz Baird and Krzysztof Penderecki have made outstanding contributions to the genre, and some of these – Baird's *Jutro* ('Tomorrow', 1966) and Penderecki's *Diably z Loudun* ('The Devils of Loudun', 1969), for instance – have now entered the international repertory.

For further information on operatic life in the country's principal centres see BYDGOSZCZ; GDAŃSK; KRAKÓW; ŁÓDŹ; L'VIV; POZNAŃ; SZCZECIN; WARSAW; and WROCŁAW.

JIM SAMSON

Polani, Girolamo (*fl* Venice, 1689–1720). Italian composer. From 2 October 1689, he was employed as a soprano at S Marco in Venice at the low wage of 25 ducats (most other singers received 100). He wrote operas for three Venetian theatres: one for the Teatro SS Apostoli, marking the last time that theatre was used for opera, three for the Teatro S Angelo, the least prestigious of the large Venetian theatres, and seven for the Teatro S Fantino, a tiny theatre that specialized in small-scale works. None of his settings is known to survive. The light-hearted operas at S Fantino contrasted strikingly with the serious opera cultivated at the major Venetian opera houses. Several are set in everyday contexts and involve as few as five characters, some of whom use Venetian dialect. *Chi la fà l'aspetta* is the first libretto for S Fantino labelled comic, but there is no evidence that the explicitly comic repertory of the years 1717 to 1720 bears any connection with contemporary Neapolitan developments in comic opera. Despite its urban setting, it conforms in its pastoral tone to most of the operas staged at the S Fantino from its opening in 1700 until the last opera presented there in 1720.

A letter from Rolli indicates that Polani had arrived in London via Holland by 18 October 1720. He was put forward as a director of one of the Academy operas, but in the event he did not participate.

all in 3 acts; performed in Venice unless otherwise stated

La vendetta disarmata dall'amore (dramma per musica, F. Passarini), S Fantino, carn. 1704 [with attrib. uncertain as La costanza nell'onore, Rovigo, Teatro Campagnella, aut. 1703]
Creso tolto alle fiamme (dramma per musica, A. Aureli), S Angelo, aut. 1705
Prassitele in Gnido (dramma pastorale, Aureli), SS Apostoli, carn. 1707
Vindice la pazzia della vendetta (favola pastorale, B. Pedoni), S Fantino, carn. 1707
Rosilda (dramma favoloso, Pedoni), S Fantino, aut. 1707
La virtù trionfante d'amore vendicativo (favola pastorale, Pedoni), S Fantino, carn. 1708
Il cieco geloso (dramma pastorale, Aureli), S Fantino, Oct 1708
Il tradimento premiato (favola pastorale, G. P. Candi), S Angelo, 3 Nov 1709
Berengario re d'Italia (dramma per musica, M. Noris), S Angelo, week before 22 Feb 1710
Chi la fà l'aspetta (dramma comico, Passarini), S Fantino, carn. 1717

O. E. Deutsch: *Handel: a Documentary Biography* (New York, 1974), 114–15
O. Termini: 'Singers at San Marco in Venice: the Competition between Church and Theatre (*c*1675–*c*1725)', *RMARC*, no.17 (1981), 65–96, esp.85   HARRIS S. SAUNDERS

Polaski, Deborah (*b* Richmond Center, WI, 26 Sept 1949). American soprano. She studied in Cincinnati and Graz, making her début in 1976 at Gelsenkirchen. After appearing at Munich, Hamburg, Karlsruhe and Ulm, she sang Death/Judas in Einem's *Jesu Hochzeit* at Hanover (1980); Marie (*Wozzeck*), Isolde and Kundry at Freiburg (1983–5); Strauss's Electra, and Katerina Izmaylova at Mannheim (1985–6); Amelia (*Ballo in maschera*) at Essen; Chrysothemis at Geneva (1986); Senta at La Scala and in Prague (1988); and Strauss's Electra at Zürich (1991). She has a strong, vibrant voice of true dramatic proportions. Her interpretation of Brünnhilde was not liked when she sang the role at Bayreuth in 1988, although she scored a great success with the same role when she returned there in 1991.

ELIZABETH FORBES

Polcelli, Luigia. *See* POLZELLI, LUIGIA.

Poldini, Ede (*b* Budapest, 13 June 1869; *d* Corseaux, 28 June 1957). Hungarian composer. He studied at the National Conservatory in Budapest and in Vienna. He then spent a year in Geneva and in 1908 settled in Bergeroc, Vevey. He received the Hungarian Cross of Merit, second class (1935), and the Hungarian Medal for Artists (1948).

In Hungary Poldini was renowned chiefly for his stage works, but his success was not limited to his native country. *Vagabund und Prinzessin* (1903) and *Hochzeit*

im Fasching (1924), his two best operas, were both produced in London, the former at Covent Garden in 1906 and the latter, as *Love Adrift*, at the Gaiety Theatre in 1926; *Vagabund* was also seen in about 20 other European cities. His three children's operas were based on stories from Max Kalbeck's *Märchenspielen für die Jugend*. His many piano compositions, too, achieved widespread popularity. Poldini's compositional style differs from that of most of his compatriots at the time, in that his links were rather with contemporary French and German music, the Hungarian element serving merely as decoration.

Cartouche, 1884 (comic op, 1)
Aschenbrödel [Hamupipőke; Cinderella], 1899 (children's op, A. Váradi, after M. Kalbeck), Budapest, 1927, orchd T. Polgár
Dornröschen [Vadrózsa; Sleeping Beauty], 1899 (children's op, Váradi, after Kalbeck), Budapest, 1927, orchd Polgár
Die Knusperhexe [Vasorru bába; The Iron-nosed Witch], 1899 (children's op, Váradi, after Kalbeck), Budapest, 1927, orchd Polgár
Vagabund und Prinzessin [Csavargó és királylány; The Vagabond and the Princess] (1, A. F. Seligmann, after H. C. Andersen), Budapest, 1903
Hochzeit im Fasching [Farsangi lakodalom; Love Adrift], 1913–14 (3, Ger.: B. Diósy, Hung.: E. Vajda), Budapest, 1924
Die gute alte Zeit (operetta, 3, F. Martos), Budapest, 1926
Das Seidennetz [A selyemháló] (comic op), Budapest, 1929
Himfy, 1934 (P. Bodrogh), Budapest, 1938

MELINDA BERLÁSZ KÁROLYI

Poleri, David S(amuel) (*b* Chestnut Hill, PA, 10 Jan 1921; *d* Hanalei, HI, 13 Dec 1967). American tenor. He studied in Philadelphia and New York. In 1949 he made his operatic début in the title role of *Faust* in Chicago with Fortune Gallo's touring San Carlo Opera. He sang with the New York City Opera (Alfredo and Massenet's Des Grieux, both 1951) and with other leading opera companies in the USA. He sang Don Alvaro (*La forza del destino*), with Glyndebourne Opera at Edinburgh in 1951, returning in 1955. At Florence (1953–4) he sang Hermann in *The Queen of Spades* and Andrey in *Mazepa*, and later he appeared at Perugia and Genoa. In 1954 he created the role of Michele in Menotti's *The Saint of Bleecker Street* in New York, and then sang the role in the Italian première at La Scala; he appeared as Prince Troilus in the Italian première of *Troilus and Cressida* in 1956, the year of his Covent Garden début as Riccardo. With the Chicago Lyric Opera (1961–2) he sang Don Alvaro and Vladimir Igorevich (*Prince Igor*). A pioneer in televised opera, in 1955 he sang Cavaradossi for NBC television. Poleri had a strong, ringing voice and a fine stage presence. He died in a helicopter crash.   CHARLES JAHANT, ELIZABETH FORBES

Polgár, László (*b* Budapest, 1 Jan 1947). Hungarian bass. He studied with Eva Kutrucz at the Liszt Academy of Music, Budapest, 1967–72, and later privately with Hans Hotter and Evgeny Nesterenko. He made his début at the Budapest Opera in 1971 as Count Ceprano (*Rigoletto*). His career proper started in the early 1980s: he sang Rodolfo in *La sonnambula* at Covent Garden in 1981, Leporello in Yuri Lyubimov's famous Budapest production of *Don Giovanni* in 1982 and Gurnemanz in Ferencsik's *Parsifal* revival the next year. He has made regular appearances at the Vienna Staatsoper since 1983, and in Munich and Paris from 1985, and has appeared in Zürich and Salzburg as Sarastro (*Zauberflöte*) and Publius (*La clemenza di Tito*). He was a member of the Zürich Opera from 1991. His international fame has been due to his beautifully silky, well-balanced voice and his remarkable declamation and musicality, as well as his outstanding acting.

PÉTER P. VÁRNAI

Polgar, Tibor (*b* Budapest, 11 March 1907). Canadian composer and conductor of Hungarian origin. He studied at the Liszt Academy in Budapest with Kodály. From soon after his graduation in 1925 until 1950 he was conductor of the Hungarian Radio Symphony Orchestra. He was also a conductor at the Budapest State Opera House and conducted the first Hungarian radio performances of a number of operas. In Europe he wrote a wide variety of music, including music for stage and radio dramas, film scores and popular music; he was twice awarded the Ferenc Erkel composition prize. In 1964 he moved to Canada, becoming a Canadian citizen in 1969. The chamber opera *A European Lover*, described as 'a musical satire disguised as an opera' (1965), was his first Canadian opera. He was instructor in the Opera Department at the University of Toronto, 1966–75, and during the same period was a coach for the Canadian Opera Company; his opera *The Glove* was one of the company's touring productions in 1976. In Canada he continued to compose prolifically in many genres. His music has a contemporary sound, but is not atonal, and is characterized by Hungarian rhythms.

Kérők [The Suitors] (comic op, 3, K. Kotzian), Budapest, 11 May 1954
A European Lover (chamber op, 1, G. Jonas), ?1966
The Troublemaker, 1968 (comic op, 1, E. Mohacsi, after *The Thousand and One Nights*)
The Glove (comic op, 1, Jonas, after F. von Schiller), New Liskeard, Ont., 23 Feb 1975
A Strange Night, 1978 (1, Polgar, after C. Szakonyi)

EMC (C. Ford)   RUTH PINCOE

Polič, Mirko (*b* Trieste, 3 June 1890; *d* Ljubljana, Slovenia, 2 Oct 1951). Slovene conductor and composer. He studied composition at the Giuseppe Verdi Conservatory in Trieste, remaining there to conduct at the Slovene Theatre, where he initiated operatic performances. He was then conductor of the Osijek Opera (1914–23), secretary and conductor of the Zagreb Opera (1923–4) and of the Belgrade Opera (1924–5), conductor and director of the Ljubljana Opera (1925–39) and of the Belgrade Opera (1939–41) and director of the Ljubljana Opera (1945–7). The Ljubljana Opera was much indebted to Polič for his efforts in raising standards and modernizing the repertory; he introduced recent operatic works based on indigenous and world literature. As a composer, he was particularly interested in opera and wrote two, which were both produced in Ljubljana. *Mati Jugovićev* ('The Mother of the Jugović Brothers'), in three parts to a libretto by the composer, is based on L. Vojnonić's *Smrt majke Jugovića* ('The Death of Mother Jugović'); composed between 1939 and 1944, it was first performed in 1947. *Deseti brat* ('The Tenth Brother'), a three-act setting of a libretto by M. Mahnič (after J. Jurčič), received its première in 1951. Stylistically, Polič remained more or less in the Romantic tradition, only occasionally enriching his works with neo-Romantic or post-Romantic elements and other more recent modes of expression. *The Tenth Brother*, composed in a style reminiscent of folk music, is particularly significant.

MANICA ŠPENDAL

Poli-Randaccio, Tina [Ernestina] (*b* nr Ferrara, 13 April 1879; *d* Milan, 1 Feb 1956). Italian soprano. She studied in Pesaro and made her début in 1902 at Bergamo in *Un ballo in maschera*. She travelled widely in Italy, Spain, Hungary and South America, mostly in lyric-dramatic and *verismo* roles. Admiring her Santuzza in *Cavalleria rusticana*, Mascagni engaged her in 1908 to sing the heroine of his *Amica* in an Italian tour. In 1910, as Brünnhilde in *Siegfried*, she made her début at La Scala, where she also appeared in the theatre's first presentation of *La fanciulla del West*. Other notable roles were Aida, La Gioconda and the heroine of Mascagni's *Parisina*. In her only season at Covent Garden (1920) she sang Tosca, a performance praised for emotional force but criticized for unevenness. Her career lasted until 1934 with an appearance as Turandot at Bologna. Recordings show a powerful voice, capable of delicacy but inclined to shrillness at the top and having the fast vibrato characteristic of Italian sopranos of the period. She was clearly an imaginative artist, sensitive to nuance and warm in feeling.

J. B. STEANE

Politeama (It.: 'theatre'). Name used for theatres throughout Italy, notably in the late 19th century. One of the best-known remaining examples is the Politeama Garibaldi in PALERMO, inaugurated in 1874.

Poliuto. *Tragedia lirica* in three acts by GAETANO DONIZETTI to a libretto by SALVADORE CAMMARANO after PIERRE CORNEILLE's *Polyeucte*; Naples, Teatro S Carlo, 30 November 1848.

Poliuto was composed in 1838 and originally intended to serve as the vehicle for Adolphe Nourrit's début at the S Carlo. But the work was banned as it depicted the martyrdom of a Christian saint. Soon after, Donizetti went to Paris, where he reworked and expanded the *Poliuto* score as *Les martyrs* (in four acts, with a text by Scribe); more than three-quarters of the music for the French work comes from the Italian original. Donizetti had to make a number of changes: he added an extensive new overture, the requisite ballet *divertissement* and a concertato finale, and he wrote the tenor arias afresh, not only because they needed to suit the voice of Gilbert Duprez rather than Nourrit but also because, for Paris, the character's motivation needed to correspond more closely with that of his counterpart in the Corneille source. Cammarano, in the Italian libretto, had made much of Poliuto's jealousy, in an attempt – in the event a futile one – to play down the religious rivalry central to the conflict.

Never very successful in Paris, *Les Martyrs* enjoyed some circulation in an Italian translation, as *I martiri*, but in Italy the more compact, three-act *Poliuto* was generally preferred. Its performance history began in 1848, when it received its première, in Naples, soon after Donizetti's death; the recent granting of a constitution there made the mounting of the banned work seem a political gesture as well as an artistic one. Throughout the 19th century it was put on periodically as a vehicle for such dramatic tenors as Tamberlik and Tamagno. It has had some notable revivals: at La Scala in 1940 with Gigli and Caniglia and in 1960 with Corelli and Callas; in 1977 at the S Carlo; and in Vienna in 1986, with Carreras. A Rome revival in 1988 followed a text that removed many years' editorial accretions. *Les martyrs* too has been revived, notably in Venice in 1978.

The action takes place in Melitene, the capital of Armenia, in the 3rd century. Filled with unsatisfied longings, Poliuto (tenor; Polyeucte in the French version) comes to the entrance of the cavern where Nearco (tenor; Néarque) and the Christians practise their proscribed faith. While he receives the rite of baptism, his wife Paolina (soprano; Pauline) enters, filled with emotion as she hears the tranquil hymn of the alien rite; she learns that Severo (baritone; Sévère), to whom she was once betrothed, will soon arrive, and her disquiet increases, for she remembers the attraction he exercised on her. Severo receives a hero's welcome but is dismayed to learn that Paolina has married another.

Paolina has made an enemy of Callistene (Callisthènes), the high priest (bass), whose advances she has repulsed. At the start of Act 2, Callistene brings Poliuto to hear an interview between her and Severo, in which she confesses that although she once loved him her heart now belongs to her husband. Poliuto is overcome by jealous doubts. Word is brought that Nearco has been seized as a convert to a false religion and is to be condemned in the Temple of Jupiter. The act concludes with a powerful scene in the temple, consisting of choruses and a massive concertato with contrapuntal effects (a combination that in some ways foreshadows the Triumphal Scene of *Aida*). Callistene and the priests sing to Jove the Thunderer. When Nearco refuses to name the latest convert, Poliuto steps forward and identifies himself as a Christian. To Paolina's grief and Severo's disapproval, Poliuto avows his constancy in his new belief, and as proof he overturns the altar.

Act 3 opens outside the prison where Poliuto is confined; Callistene and his zealots look forward to vengeance on the Christian heretics. Inside, Poliuto has been dreaming of Paolina. She comes to tell him that he will be pardoned if he will forswear his new faith; but so secure is he that she is moved to proclaim herself convinced and converted (their great conversion duet, 'Ah fuggi da morte ... Il suon dell'arpe angeliche', is a further anticipation of Verdi). She joins him in his march into the arena.

Essentially the plot of *Les martyrs* is that of *Poliuto*, without the motivation of the hero's jealousy. The impressive overture, with a slow introduction for four bassoons, and a chorus intoning a Christian hymn were composed for Paris; also new is a women's chorus to precede Paolina's first aria. The role of her father, the Roman governor Felice (Félix), is expanded and changed from tenor to bass. What had been Paolina's cabaletta was detached as pendant to her *sortita* and transferred unchanged to Act 2, following Félix's aria with chorus. Callistene's aria with chorus, preceding the final scene, was suppressed and was replaced by a trio, derived in large part from one of Poliuto's arias (designed for Nourrit) that had been dropped from Act 2.

Among the adjustments made to *Les martyrs* during the lengthy and, for Donizetti, painful rehearsal period at the Opéra was the excision of a beautiful miniature ensemble which replaced the former coda to Severo's cabaletta.

*   *   *

In *Poliuto*, it is possible to see that, before his engagement to compose for the Paris Opéra, Donizetti was anticipating that move by deliberately striving for a grander scale and a greater emphasis on spectacle than he customarily achieved in his works designed principally for Italy. Representative of this tendency are the magnificent second-act finale, which in a typically French manner depicts violent personal conflicts against an impressive scenic tableau; and the final scene, in which Poliuto's and Paolina's fervent cabaletta is boldly superimposed on to the pagan priest's call for their death. *Poliuto* is an important transitional work in Donizetti's deliberate internationalization of his style by the absorption of French influences that he had encountered during his visit to Paris in 1835 and from his familiarity with Rossini's Parisian operas in their Italian translations.

WILLIAM ASHBROOK

Pollak, Anna (*b* Manchester, 1 May 1912). English mezzo-soprano of Austrian parentage. She studied with Joan Cross, then made her début in 1945 at Sadler's Wells as Dorabella and remained with the company until 1961, creating Lady Nelson (Berkeley's *Nelson*) and Mrs Strickland (John Gardner's *The Moon and Sixpence*) and singing several travesty roles, including Cherubino, Siébel, Hänsel, Orlofsky and Lel' (*The Snow Maiden*); she also sang Carmen (1949). With the English Opera Group she created Bianca in *The Rape of Lucretia* (1946), the title role in Berkeley's *Ruth* (1956) and several parts in Williamson's *English Eccentrics* (1964). She sang Fatima in Weber's *Oberon* at the 1950 Holland Festival, Cherubino at Covent Garden (1952) and Dorabella at Glyndebourne (1952–3). Her last public appearance was as Public Opinion in *Orphée aux enfers* at the Coliseum in 1968. Pollak was a musical, versatile and satisfying singer and an actress of accomplishment and style.

HAROLD ROSENTHAL/R

Pollak, Egon (*b* Prague, 3 May 1879; *d* Prague, 14 June 1933). German-Czech conductor. He turned from mathematics to music in 1900 and joined the German Theatre, Prague, as chorus master. He became principal conductor at Bremen in 1905, with similar appointments at Leipzig, 1910–12, and Frankfurt, 1912–17, during which years he was heard at Covent Garden conducting Wagner, including *Parsifal* (1914). In 1917 he was the first to be named Hanseatischer Generalmusikdirektor at Hamburg, where the opera made much progress under his direction; here he conducted one of the two simultaneous premières (with Cologne) of Korngold's *Die tote Stadt* (1920). He left Hamburg in 1931 and conducted at Chicago Opera, 1931–2, then returned to Prague, where he died while conducting *Fidelio*. His performances were said to resemble those of Mahler in intensity and vitality.

NOËL GOODWIN

Pollard. Family of Australian, later New Zealand, impresarios. They directed a series of children's and juvenile opera companies called the Lilliputians or Pollard's Lilliputian Opera Company. The first company was formed in Launceston, Tasmania, in 1881 by James Joseph Pollard (1833–84), who had settled in Australia in 1854. From Tasmania, this company moved to New Zealand and successfully performed Gilbert and Sullivan, an English version of Planquette's *Les cloches de Corneville* and other light opera, before returning for a tour of Australia. After James Pollard's death the Lilliputians worked under the direction of Tom Pollard (1857–1922), who had changed his name from Thomas John O'Sullivan when he became a violinist with the company; he was rapidly promoted to stage director, a position for which he had an outstanding talent. The company was disbanded in 1886 because the children were growing up and losing their appeal.

In 1891 Pollard formed another juvenile company, which became a leading attraction, especially in New Zealand. It numbered 70, with an orchestra of 10, and presented 36 comic opera productions in its touring repertory; it gave the world première of Alfred Hill's romantic Maori comic opera *Tapu* in Wellington in 1903. At the end of that year the company made a tour of South Africa, but after a fire in Durban burnt the costumes and sets, it returned to Australia and was disbanded. As adults, the performers continued to tour extensively in Australia and South Africa, as well as in New Zealand, from 1896 to 1905. A third juvenile group, formed in 1907, toured Australasia until 1910. Under Pollard's direction the three companies staged 58 different productions by 26 composers, their combined repertories included many major 19th-century comic operas, as well as contemporary operettas and musical comedies.

Another company was formed in the 1890s by Charles Pollard (1858–1942), with his sister Nellie. As the Lilliputians, they performed in South Africa during the Boer War, in Mauritius in 1898, in Calcutta in 1897 and 1900 and in Bombay, and made frequent tours of the USA (from where many of their performers were drawn) and of the Far East, including Hong Kong and Shanghai (1897, 1903). They rarely performed in Australia (and never in New Zealand). They too had two companies, a children's company and a post-juvenile one.

M. Hurst: *Music and the Stage in New Zealand: 1840–1943* (Auckland, 1944)

P. Downes: *Shadows on the Stage: Theatre in New Zealand 1840–1910* (Dunedin, 1975)

——: 'The Perennial Pollards', *Opera in New Zealand: Aspects of History and Performance*, ed. A. Simpson (Wellington, 1990), 33–45

J. M. Thomson: *The Oxford History of New Zealand Music* (Auckland, 1991)
PETER DOWNES, CHARLES PITT

Pollarolo, (Giovanni) Antonio (*b* Brescia, bap. 12 Nov 1676; *d* Venice, 30 May 1746). Italian composer, son of Carlo Francesco Pollarolo. He was a pupil of his father. When he was 13 years old, the family moved from Brescia to Venice. He began his career at St Mark's in 1702 as substitute for his father, who was vice-*maestro di cappella*; in 1723 Antonio was elected to that office in his own right. Upon the death of *maestro* Antonio Biffi in 1733 he served as acting *maestro* for three years, and in 1740 he became *primo maestro*. In 1716 Pollarolo was elected *maestro di coro* at one of the Venetian conservatories, the Ospedaletto, and he served in this position, with one interruption (1733–4), until his resignation in 1743. For the Ospedaletto he composed a number of Latin oratorios, including *Sacrum amoris* (1716) and *Sterilis fecunda* (1717); his *Oratorio per il Ss Natale* was performed in Rome (1718).

Pollarolo's operas enjoyed brief periods of popularity in Venice and elsewhere, from 1700 to 1702 and from 1715 to 1729. He composed or contributed to approximately 14 operas, beginning with *L'Aristeo* (1700, Venice) and ending with *La Sulpizia fedele* (1729, Venice). *Cosroë* (1723) was performed in Rome and *I tre voti* (1724) was written for Vienna. Throughout his career Antonio Pollarolo was overshadowed by masters such as his father and Antonio Lotti; the early librettos call him the imitator of his 'gran Padre' (*L'Aristeo*, 1700). However, after about 1715 they recognized him as a '*celebre Maestro*' in his own right (libretto of

Leucippo e Teonoe, Venice, 1719). Pollarolo's operatic style can be only partly judged because his datable music comes from a short period (1719–24) and consists chiefly of arias. These show the influence of the generation of Vivaldi and Orlandini: a melodious vocal line designed to be dramatically effective is embedded in a homophonic orchestral texture, harmonically often slow-moving or static (see Strohm, p.38). *I tre voti*, the only serenata that survives complete, has a five-part sinfonia, terzettos marked *coro* as well as accompanied and ensemble recitatives. Most notable are the arias, which exceed his father's in scope and virtuosity. Basso continuo arias have almost entirely given way to orchestrally accompanied ones. The *A* section is often tripartite, with orchestral introduction. The da capo is sometimes abbreviated, even to the point of recapitulating only the introduction. Interesting rhythmic patterns in the vocal line and wide-ranging coloratura made the arias an ideal vehicle for the virtuoso singers of the period.

For a stage design for *Lucio Papirio dittatore* see BELLAVITE, INNOCENTE.

performed in Venice unless otherwise stated

dm – *dramma per musica*

L'Aristeo (G. C. Corradi), S Cassiano, 1700
Griselda (dm, 3, A. Zeno), S Cassiano, 1701
Demetrio e Tolomeo (dm, 3, A. Marchi), S Angelo, 1702
Leucippo e Teonoe (tragedia per musica, 5, P. M. Suarez), S Giovanni Grisostomo, aut. 1719, arias D-SWl and F-Pc
Lucio Papirio dittatore (dm, 3, Zeno), S Giovanni Grisostomo, carn. 1721, arias D-Mbs and SWl
Plautilla (dm, 3, V. Cassani), S Giovanni Grisostomo, aut. 1721, arias Mbs and SWl
Venceslao [Acts 2 and 3] (dm, 5, Zeno), S Giovanni Grisostomo, 1722 [according to F. Caffi (MS I-Vnm)]
Cosroë (dm, Zeno: Ormisda), Rome, Alibert, carn. 1723, arias D-MÜs and F-Pc
I tre voti (serenata, Cassani), Vienna, 28 Aug 1724, A-Wn
Turia Lucrezia (dm, 3, D. Lalli), S Angelo, carn. 1726
Nerina (favola pastorale, 3, Lalli, after P. D'Averara: Filindro), S Samuele, Ascension 1728
Sulpizia fedele (dm, 3, Lalli and G. Boldini), S Samuele, Ascension 1729, aria I-Rc
Attributed to Pollarolo or 'diversi': La figli che canta (divertimento comica in musica, 3, F. Passarini), S Fantino, 1719; L'abbandono di Armida (trattenimento scenico da cantarsi, 3, Boldini), S Giovanni Grisostomo, carn. 1729

Aria in Nerone fatto Cesare, S Angelo, 1715

O. Termini: *Carlo Francesco Pollarolo: his Life, Time, and Music with Emphasis on the Operas* (diss., U. of Southern California, 1970)

R. Strohm, ed.: 'Italienische Opernarien des frühen Settecento (1720–1730)', *AnMc*, no.16 (1976) [whole issue]

G. Ellero and others: *Arte e musica all'Ospedaletto* (Venice, 1978)
OLGA TERMINI

Pollarolo, Carlo Francesco (*b* *c*1653; *d* Venice, 7 Feb 1723). Italian composer. His operas illustrate the stylistic transition from the late Venetian to the so-called Neapolitan or late Baroque style of Italian opera.

1. LIFE. Probably the pupil of his father Orazio, Carlo Francesco was organist at the Congregazione della Pace, Brescia, before 1676, when he succeeded his father as organist at Brescia Cathedral. Church records in Brescia establish his marriage (1674) and the baptisms of his children there (between 1676 and 1689).

Pollarolo advanced rapidly in his profession, becoming *capo musico* at the cathedral (1680) and in the Accademia degli Erranti (1681), a society devoted to 'letters, arms, and music'. A libretto records the performance of his earliest opera, *Venere travestita*, in 1678. From 1685 Pollarolo's activity as a composer intensified: *I delirii per amore* was given at Brescia in 1686. *Il Licurgo, overo Il cieco d'acuta vista* and *Il demone amante, overo Giugurta* were both given during the opera season of 1686 in Venice. His *Il Roderico* (1687), *La costanza gelosa negl'amori di Cefalo e Procri* (1687) and *Alarico, re de Gotti* (1689) were given at Verona, and a version of *Antonino e Pompeiano*, with most of the music by Pollarolo, at the Teatro Grande in Brescia (1689). Thus he was an established opera composer before his arrival in Venice. He must have left Brescia by the end of 1689, but his younger brother Paolo (*b* 1672) and the latter's son Orazio (*d* 1765) pursued musical careers there; they produced a few operatic compositions. His daughter Giulia married the organ builder Giacinto Pescetti, a fellow Brescian, in 1697; the opera composer Giovanni Battista Pescetti, who spent part of his modest career in England, was their son.

Although Pollarolo's official positions centred on St Mark's, Venice (second organist, 1690; vice-*maestro di cappella*, 1692), his chief activities were in opera. From 1691 at least one of his operas was performed at the Venetian theatres each year. He dominated the most reputable opera house in the city, S Giovanni Grisostomo, from about 1691 to about 1707, and had works staged at S Angelo, S Cassiano, S Fantino and other theatres in and outside Venice.

Pollarolo lived the rest of his life in the parish of S Simone Grande in Venice. In 1702 he was *giubilato*, that is, relieved of his regular duties at St Mark's without loss of status. His family was large, but he supported them with the excellent income derived from his numerous operas; in 1694 the Grimani family owed him 2000 ducats for opera scores (probably four) and stage props (Giazotto 1967). Pollarolo was at the peak of his operatic career from about 1692 to about 1705, although he continued composing opera until the year before his death. He seems to have been musical director of the Ospedale degl'Incurabili (*c*1696–*c*1716), one of the four famous Venetian 'conservatories', and composed several Latin oratorios for it. He wrote music for other institutions and occasions, including the intermezzo *Il giudizio di Paride* (1699) for the Accademia degli Animosi, whose guiding spirit was the opera reformer Apostolo Zeno. In 1716 Pollarolo composed a cantata, *Fede, Valore, Gloria e Fama* (in which Faustina Bordoni sang the part of Fede [Faith], antedating her operatic début in Pollarolo's *Ariodante* of the same year), for the Austrian ambassador to Venice, and the wedding of the ambassador's son was celebrated with Pollarolo's music for *Il pescatore disingannato* in September 1721. On his visit to Venice in 1713–14 Gottfried Heinrich Stölzel sought Pollarolo out, along with Vivaldi; the English translator (possibly John Galliard) of François Raguenet's *Parallèle* (1709; repr. 1946, p.424) mentions him among 'the most famous masters of the harpsichord' in Venice and as 'the Venetian inventor of the unison ariettas which invention has been followed by the most celebrated composers and is at present one of the greatest beauties in the Italian opera'. His son Antonio and grandson G. B. Pescetti became opera composers, and another son, probably Giuseppe, was a librettist or poet (Selfridge-Field 1985, p.251). Pollarolo's last stage work was the opera *L'Arminio*, produced in November 1722; he was already suffering from his final illness, which lasted six months. He was buried in S Maria di Nazaret, known as the Chiesa degli Scalzi, on the bank of the Grand Canal in Venice.

2. WORKS. Pollarolo wrote some 90 operas and 15 oratorios over a period of 44 years (1678–1722). His operas were performed throughout Italy and in Vienna, Brunswick and Ansbach, but his popularity did not outlive him. He belongs to the generation of M. A. Ziani and Perti. His chief librettists were Corradi, Frigimelica Roberti, Noris, Ottoboni, Silvani and Zeno. Of these Noris is known for his deference to Venetian public taste, whereas Frigimelica Roberti and Zeno worked towards a new kind of libretto in the spirit of the Arcadian reforms of the 1690s.

Pollarolo's early operatic style, derived from Legrenzi and Carlo Pallavicino, reflects his concern with dramatic and textual expression. The recitatives range from an epic style with long note values to a quasi-*secco* style with many repeated short notes. A slightly more florid melodic line often appears at cadences just before an aria; fully-fledged coloratura passages sometimes occur. Pollarolo frequently alternated recitatives with ariosos of varying tempo (4/4, 3/4, 3/2). This refreshing flexibility in compositional technique helps to reflect detailed nuances in the text; it contrasts strongly with the more stereotyped scene structure of his later works and those of his contemporaries. His melodic style had not yet crystallized into formulae for questions, exclamations or cadences; short exclamations by a group of people were sometimes set as ensemble recitatives. A repeated phrase in recitative or arioso may function as a refrain, either to unify the section or to define a persistent mood; the result is a kind of miniature rondo form. By 1699, however, in *Il Faramondo*, ariosos had disappeared from Pollarolo's operas. Recitatives approach the *secco* style; expression is concentrated in harmonic shifts, modulations, affective intervals, chromatic bass lines and dissonances between voice and bass. Accompanied recitatives had become a focal point of expression.

The early arias are brief but already in *ABA* form with variations such as an abbreviated or expanded reprise. Arias accompanied only by basso continuo outnumber those with orchestra; the bass may simply give harmonic support or move independently of the vocal line (e.g. 'Non lagrimate, no' from *Il Roderico*, 1.xiii). The expansion and orchestral elaboration of the accompanied aria is one of Pollarolo's chief contributions to Venetian opera. Thematically the arias of his middle period are undistinguished, but they expand to larger da capo forms with a bipartite *A* section. He constantly varied the basic principle of da capo form by some unusual melodic, harmonic or formal trait. In his last works he even approached a tripartite *A* section (e.g. 'O sommo Apollo' from *Astinome*, 1719). The use of recitative to interrupt an aria forms an effective dramatic device (e.g. 'Ha soave e dolce vita' from the undated oratorio *Jesabelle*).

In the 1690s orchestral arias began to increase in number; in *Ariodante* (1716) they outnumber continuo arias by four to one. In Pollarolo's early works the accompaniment usually consists of three-part strings (unmarked in the scores) with the two treble parts widely separated from the bass, in the manner of the early trio sonata. During the 1690s a wide variety of instrumental combinations appears, ranging from one to eight parts, most frequently five. Interesting examples include a solo violin in duet with the voice without bass in

'Usignuoli che cantate' from *Onorio in Roma* (1692, 3.vi); three-part strings without bass in 'Il viver mio si chiude' from *La forza della virtù* (1693, 3.ii); cornett and bass in 'Aure vaghe' from *Ottone* (1694, 2.i); oboe and bass in 'Fede e onor' from *Le pazzie degli amanti* (1701, 2.iv); two tenor violas, violone and theorbo in 'In quel piè legato' from *Onorio in Roma* (2.iv); five-part strings plus two oboes in 'O non ti rivedrò', from *Ottone* (3.ix); and the same with timpani in 'All' armi' in *La forza della virtù* (3.viii). Pollarolo was one of the first Venetian composers to introduce the oboe into the opera orchestra.

In *Onorio in Roma* (3.ii) Pollarolo transferred the concerto grosso principle to the opera stage: a five-part orchestra on the stage alternated with an offstage three-part concertino. Elsewhere the alternation of tutti and concertino serves to reduce the level of accompaniment during the singer's phrases. Devices such as offstage singing, offstage obbligatos and echo effects are frequent. In the late operas this variety of instrumental grouping gives way to a basic four-part texture, and the string writing is more idiomatic, with some virtuosity. The instrumentation of the sinfonias is increased to four-part strings with wind (oboes, trumpets, trombones), as in *Ariodante*. The form of the sinfonia loosely resembles the Scarlattian type, varied by elements from the French overture. Ensemble singing is limited: there are relatively short duets and, only in the finales, brief vocal trios, quartets or quintets. There are no true choruses in the operas.

In Pollarolo's later operas there is an increasing standardization (scenes divided into long passages of *secco* recitative followed by large-scale da capo arias), coupled with a virtuoso vocal style, that links him with the next generation of Venetian and Neapolitan opera composers.

See also INGANNI FELICI, GLI; for a stage design for *La pace fra Tolomeo e Seleuco, see* GALLI-BIBIENA, fig.1.

drammi per musica in three acts, unless otherwise stated

VGG – *Venice, Teatro S Giovanni Grisostomo*

Venere travestita (G. Bottalino), Brescia, Accademia degli Erranti, 1678

I delirii per amore (F. Miliati), Brescia, Jan 1686

Il Licurgo, overo Il cieco d'acuta vista (M. Noris), Venice, S Angelo, Feb 1686

Il demone amante, overo Giugurta (Noris), Venice, S Angelo, 1686

Enea in Italia (G. F. Bussani), Milan, Regio Nuovo, 1686

Il Roderico (Bottalino), Verona, 1687, lib. *I-MOe* [possibly identical with Il Roderico, Brescia, 1684, and with L'Anagilde, ovvero Il Rodrigo, Reggio Emilia, April 1685, *MOe*]

La costanza gelosa negl'amori di Cefalo e Procri, Verona, 1688, *D-Mbs*

Alarico, re de Gotti, Verona, 1689, *Mbs*

Antonino e Pompeiano (Bussani), Brescia, Grande, 1689

Alboino in Italia (G. C. Corradi), Venice, SS Giovanni e Paolo, 1691, collab. G. F. Tosi

Il moto delle stelle osservato da Cupido (serenata, 10 scenes), Padua, 1691

La pace fra Tolomeo e Seleuco (A. Morselli, after P. Corneille: *Rodogune*), VGG, 1691

Venere travestita (A. Scappi), Rovigo and Murano, 1691

Marc'Antonio (Noris), Genoa, Falcone, 19 Sept 1692

Iole, regina di Napoli (Corradi), Venice, SS Giovanni e Paolo, 25 Nov 1692

L'Ibraim sultano (Morselli, after J. Racine: *Bajazet*), VGG, 1692

La forza della virtù (D. David, after Rogatis: *Storia di Spagna*), VGG, week before 3 Jan 1693, *B-Br, CS-K*

Onorio in Roma (G. M. Giannini, after Corneille: *Stilichon*), VGG, 2 Feb 1693, *D-AN*

Gl'avvenimenti d'Erminia e di Clorinda (Corradi, after T. Tasso: *Gerusalemme liberata*), Venice, SS Giovanni e Paolo, 1693

Ottone (tragedia per musica, 5, G. Frigimelica Roberti), VGG, 14 Jan 1694, *CS-K, D-B, US-SFsc*

La schiavitù fortunata (F. M. Gualazzi), Venice, S Angelo, 15 Nov 1694

Irene (tragedia per musica, 5, Frigimelica Roberti), VGG 26 Dec 1694, *CS-K*; rev. Pollarolo and D. Scarlatti, Naples, 1704, arias *I-Nc*

Alfonso primo (Noris, after Rogatis), Venice, S Salvatore, 1694, frag. *D-SHs, US-SFsc*

Amage, regina de' Sarmati (Corradi), Venice, S Angelo, 1694

La Santa Genuinda, overo L'innocenza difesa dall'inganno [Act 3] (dramma sacro per musica, 3, ? P. Ottoboni, after Molano: *Santi di Fiandra*), Rome, Palazzo Doria Pamphili, 1694, *D-Mbs, F-Pc, GB-Lbl* [Act 1 by G. L. Lulier, Act 2 by A. Scarlatti]

Il pastore d'Anfriso (tragedia pastorale, 5, Frigimelica Roberti, after Virgil: *Georgics*), VGG, 22 Jan 1695, *CS-K*

La Falsirena (R. Cialli), Ferrara, 30 Jan 1695

La Rosimonda (tragedia per musica, 5, Frigimelica Roberti), VGG, aut. 1695, *CS-K*

Ercole in cielo (tragedia per musica, 4, Frigimelica Roberti), VGG, carn. 1696

Almansore in Alimena (Giannini), Reggio Emilia, 3 May 1696, 6 arias *I-Bc*

Gli inganni felici (A. Zeno, after Herodotus), Venice, S Angelo, 25 Nov 1696, *GB-Lbl* (*R*1977: IOB, xvi), arias *I-Rvat*

Amor e dovere (David), VGG, 26 Dec 1696

Tito Manlio (Noris), Florence, Villa di Pratolino, 1696, *D-SWl*, 58 arias *Nc*

La clemenza d'Augusto [Act 2] (C. S. Capece), Rome, Feb 1697, *E-Mn*, aria *GB-Lbl* [Act 1 by S. De Luca, Act 3 by G. Bononcini]

L'Oreste in Sparta (P. Luchesi), Reggio Emilia, April 1697

Circe abbandonata da Ulisse (A. Aureli), Venice, SS Giovanni e Paolo, 12 Nov 1697

La forza d'amore (L. Burlini), Venice, SS Giovanni e Paolo, 1697

I reggi equivoci (Noris), Venice, S Angelo, 1697

Marzio Coriolano (Noris), VGG, 18 Jan 1698

L'enigma disciolto (favola pastorale, 3, G. Neri), Reggio Emilia, Communità, 27 April 1698; as Gli amici rivali, Verona, 26 Oct 1710

L'Ulisse sconosciuto (?C. Frigieri), Reggio Emilia, 2 May 1698

Il Faramondo (Zeno, after Calprenede), VGG, 27 Dec 1698, *A-Wn*

Il repudio d'Ottavia (Noris), VGG, week before 14 Feb 1699, 10 arias *I-Bsp*

L'oracolo in sogno [Act 3] (F. Silvani), Mantua, 6 June 1699; rev., Venice, S Angelo, 11 Jan 1700 [Act 1 by A. Caldara, Act 2 by A. Quintavalle]

Il giudizio di Paride (int), Venice, Palazzo Grimani, Accademia degli Animosi, 1699

Il colore fa' la regina (Noris), VGG, 30 Jan 1700, *CS-K*

Il delirio comune per l'incostanza dei genii (Noris), VGG, 12 Dec 1700

Lucio Vero (Zeno, after Capitolino, Ruffo, Vittore and others), VGG, 26 Dec 1700

L'inganno di Chirone (melodramma, 3, P. d'Averara), Milan, Regio Ducal, 1700

Le pazzie degli amanti (dramma in musica, 3, F. Passarini, ? Vienna, Hof, Feb 1701, *A-Wn*; Rovigo, Manfredini, aut. 1711

Catone Uticense (Noris), VGG, 1701

L'odio e l'amore (Noris), VGG, 27 Dec 1702

Ascanio (d'Averara), Milan, Regio Nuovo, 1702

Venceslao (5, Zeno, after Rotrou and Corneille), VGG, 1703

La fortuna per dote (tragicommedia, 5, Frigimelica Roberti), VGG, 30 Nov 1704

L'eroico amore (tragicommedia, 3, M. A. Gasparini), Bergamo, 1704; as L'Alcibiade, ovvero La violenza d'amore, Milan, 1709, ? collab F. Gasparini and F. Ballaroti; as L'amante impazzito, Venice, 1714

Il giorno di notte (Noris), VGG, 1704

Il Dafni (tragedia satirica in musica, 5, Frigimelica Roberti), VGG, 30 Jan 1705

La fede ne' tradimenti (G. Gigli), Venice, S Fantino, aut. 1705

Filippo, re della Grecia (5, P. G. Barziza, after Livius), VGG, week before 16 Jan 1706

Flavio Bertarido, re dei Langobardi (S. Ghisi), VGG, 1706

La vendetta d'amore (pastorale per musica, 3), Rovigo, Manfredini, 1707, *GB-Lam*

L'Ergisto (dramma pastorale, 3, Passarini), Rovigo, Campanella, Oct 1708

Igene, regina di Sparta (A. Aureli), 1708

Il falso Tiberino (P. Pariati ?and Zeno, after P. Quinault), Venice, S

Cassiano, between 12 and 19 Jan 1709

La ninfa riconosciuta (melodramma pastorale, 3, Silvani), Vicenza, Garzeria Fiera, 1709

Il Costantino pio (dramma posto in musica, 3, Ottoboni), Rome, Palazzo della Cancelleria, 20 Jan 1710

Amor per gelosia (favola pastorale, 3), Rome, 1710

La Costanza in trionfo, Brescia, Accademia, carn. 1711

Engelberta, o La forza dell'innocenza, Brescia, Accademia, carn. 1711

Publio Cornelio Scipione (dramma per musica, 5, A. Piovene, after Livy and Plutarch), VGG, week before 16 Jan 1712

Peribea in Salamina (after Plutarch), Vicenza, Grazie, May 1712, *I-Mc*

L'infedeltà punita (Silvani), VGG, 15 Nov 1712, collab. A. Lotti

Spurio postumio (Piovene), VGG, 26 Dec 1712

Eraclio [Act 3] (P. A. Bernardoni), Rome, Palazzo della Cancelleria, 1712 [Act 2 by F. Gasparini]

Giulio Cesare nell'Egitto (A. Ottoboni, after Bussani), Rome, 1713, *US-Wc*

Semiramide (Silvani), Venice, S Giovanni Grisostomo, 6 Jan 1714, 9 arias *D-Dlb*

Marsia deluso (favola pastorale, 5, Piovene), Venice, SS Giovanni e Paolo, carn. 1714, 5 arias *Dlb*

Il trionfo della costanza, Vicenza, Grazie, May 1714

Tetide in Sciro (Capece), Vicenza, Grazie, May 1715

Il germanico (Barziza), VGG, 24 Jan 1716

Ariodante (A. Salvi), VGG, 14 Nov 1716, *B*(R1985: DMV, xiii), *US-Wc* (copy of lost *D-Dlb* score) [? rev. of G. A. Perti: Ginevra, principessa di Scozia, Florence, Villa Pratolino, 1708]

L'innocenza riconosciuta (T. Malipiero), Venice, S Angelo, aut. 1717

Farnace (D. Lalli), Venice, S Cassiano, aut. 1718

Amore in gara col fasto (dramma per musica, Silvani), Rovigo, Manfredini, 1718

Astinome (?G. Lerner), Rome, Capranica, carn. 1719, 10 arias *F-Pn*

Il pescatore disingannato (epitalamio musicale), Venice, Sept 1721

L'Arminio (Salvi), Venice, S Angelo, 14 Nov 1722; aria in Flavio Anicio Olibrio (pasticcio), *D-ROu*, ed. in Strohm, ii, 273

Other operatic: Cinna [Act 2], *E-Mn*; La fede riconosciuta, lib. pubd 1707, *GB-Lam*; Pastorale à tre voci, *Mp*; Il litigio amoroso (serenata à tre voci con istromenti), *US-BE*; unknown opera, *D-Bds*, ed. in Strohm, ii, 200

Doubtful: Alfonso, il sesto re di Castiglia, Naples, 1694 [cast as for Alfonso primo, 1694]; Il re infante (Noris), Bologna, 1694 [possibly by Pollarolo with addns by Perti]; Gl'amori di Paride ed Ennone in Ida, ?1697; De la virtude ha la bellezza onore (?Pariati), Venice, 1704 [possibly by Pollarolo]; La pace fra Pompeiano e Cesarini (Aureli), Venice, 1708; Berenice e Lucilla, o L'amar per virtù, *D-W* [? Pollarolo or D. Freschi; cast as for Lucio Vero, 1700, recits. in Ger.]; La Proserpine, *GB-Lbl*, attrib. Pollarolo on f.136 [pencil note]

*

AllacciD

F. Raguenet: *Paralèle des italiens et des françois en ce qui regarde la musique et les opéra* (Paris, 1702, 3/1710; Eng. trans., 1709); repr. in *MQ*, xxxii (1946), 411–36

G. C. Bonlini: *Le glorie della poesia e della musica* (Venice, 1731)

F. Caffi: *Storia della musica teatrale in Venezia*, (MS, *I-Vnm*)

H. C. Wolff: *Die venezianische Oper in der zweiten Hälfte des 17. Jahrhunderts* (Berlin, 1937)

R. Giazotto: 'La guerra dei Palchi', *NRMI*, i (1967), 497–508

O. Termini: *Carlo Francesco Pollarolo: his Life, Time, and Music with Emphasis on the Operas* (diss., U. of Southern California, 1970)

R. Strohm: *Italienische Opernarien des frühen Settecento (1720–1730)* (Berlin, 1971)

M. Viale Ferrero: 'Antonio e Pietro Ottoboni e alcuni melodrammi da loro ideati o promossi a Roma', *Venezia e il melodramma nel settecento: Venice 1973*, 271–94

F. Valesio: *Diario di Roma*, ed. G. Scano (Milan, 1977–9), iv, 374–5

O. Termini: 'Stylistic and Formal Changes in the Arias of Carlo Francesco Pollarolo', *CMc*, no.26 (1978), 112–24

——: 'Carlo Francesco Pollarolo: Follower or Leader in Venetian Opera?', *Studi musicali*, viii (1979), 223–72

M. T. R. Barezzani: 'L'opera in musica', *La musica a Brescia nel settecento* (Brescia, 1981)

N. J. Clapton: 'RISM Notes', *EMc*, xi (1983), 295 [letter]

L. Bianconi and T. Walker: 'Production, Consumption and Political Function of Seventeenth-Century Opera', *Early Music History*, iv (1984), 209–96

H. Saunders: *The Repertoire of a Venetian Opera House (1678–1714): the Teatro Grimani di San Giovanni Grisostomo* (diss., Harvard U., 1985)

E. Selfridge-Field: *Pallade Veneta: Writings on Music in Venetian Society 1650–1750* (Venice, 1985)

M. Talbot and C. Timms: 'Music and the Poetry of Antonio Ottoboni (1646–1710)', *Händel e gli Scarlatti a Roma: Rome 1985*, 367–438

O. Termini: Introduction to C. F. Pollarolo: *Ariodante*, DMV, xiii (1986), 9–79

——: 'L'Irene in Venice and Naples – Tyrant and Victim, or the Rifacimento Process Examined', *Antonio Caldara: Essays on his Life and Times*, ed. B. Pritchard (Aldershot, 1987), 365–407

E. Rosand: *Opera in Seventeenth-Century Venice* (Berkeley and Los Angeles, 1991)

E. Selfridge-Field: *Chronology of Venetian Operas 1680–1751* (in preparation)   OLGA TERMINI

Pollet, Françoise (*b* Boulogne Billancourt, nr Paris, 10 Sept 1949). French soprano. After initially studying the violin, she studied singing at the Versailles Conservatory (taking the *premier prix* as mezzo-soprano), and at the Staatliche Hochschule für Musik, Munich. Her début was at the Stadttheater, Lübeck, in 1983 as the Marschallin and she remained in the company there until 1986, singing Fiordiligi, Donna Anna, Amelia (*Ballo in maschera*), Arabella, Elisabeth (*Tannhäuser*) and Giulietta (*Les contes d'Hoffmann*). Returning to France, she sang Agathe (*Freischütz*) in Marseilles, Reiza (*Oberon*) in Montpellier and Paris, and Vitellia (*La clemenza di Tito*) at the Opéra-Comique. In 1988 she sang Valentine (*Les Huguenots*) at Montpellier; she sang Catherine of Aragon (*Henry VIII*) under Pritchard at the Montpellier Festival in 1989 and Magnard's Bérénice the following year. Her roles in 1991 included Ariane (*Ariane et Barbe-bleue*) and Countess Almaviva, both in Paris. She has become the most sought-after of French dramatic sopranos.   CHARLES PITT

Pollini, Francesco [Franz] (**Giuseppe**) (*b* Ljubljana, 25 March 1762; *d* Milan, 17 Sept 1846). Italian composer and singer of Slovene birth. A pupil of Mozart in Vienna, he appeared as a pianist and violinist in various Italian cities, while in Verona, Bologna, Milan, Rome, Turin and Naples he became famous as an opera singer. He studied composition with Zingarelli in Milan (1790) and later taught the piano at the new Milan Conservatory. He composed several dramatic works as well as songs, choral music and piano pieces; in recognition of his renown, Bellini dedicated *La sonnambula* to him.

La casetta nei boschi (3), Milan, Cannobiana, 25 Feb 1798, *I-Mc**

L'orfanella svizzera (melodrama, 2, G. Peruzzini), 1856, *Mc**

Date unknown: Le convenienze teatrali, arias *Mc*; Il genio insubre (2), *Mc*; Ines de Castro, selections *Mc*; Ripudio fortunato, selections *Mc*

*

D. Cvetko: *Histoire de la musique slovène* (Maribor, 1967)   DRAGOTIN CVETKO

Pollone [Polon], **Maria Dominichina** (*b* ?Venice, *c*1700; *d* after 1750). Italian soprano. She was engaged in 1716 or 1717 at the court of Arolsen, near Kassel, where she married the musician and chamberlain Leonhard Polon in 1720. In 1724 the couple moved to Hamburg, where 'Mad. Pollone' (not to be confused with 'Signiora Polonia') was engaged at the Opera. After a benefit concert for her in 1730, the couple returned to Arolsen, where they served in the Hofkapelle under J. G. Graun; Pollone left the court service in 1739.

During her years with the Hamburg Opera Pollone took part in over 30 operas or prologues, making her début in 1724 as Octavia in Orlandini's *Nero* and later that year singing Poppaea in Handel's *Agrippina*. In 1725 her roles included Autonoe in Kunzen's *Cadmus*, Gisela in Keiser's *Bretislaus*, Alcmene in Gasparini's *Amfitrione*, Rosalinda in Keiser's *Der Hamburger Jahrmarkt* and Constantine in his *Hamburger Schlachtzeit*, Asteria in Handel's *Tamerlano* and Sextus in his *Giulio Cesare*. The following year she sang only Rixa in Keiser's *Mistevojus*, and in 1727–8 she appeared in six works by Telemann and one by Porpora; in 1729 she sang the title roles in Handel's *Giulio Cesare* and Telemann's *Flavius Bertaridus*.

*

K. Zelm: 'Die Sänger der Hamburger Gänsemarkt-Oper', *HJbMw*, iii (1978), 64–5

F. Brusniak: 'Grundzüge einer Musikgeschichte Waldecks', *Augsburger Jb für Musikwissenschaft 1985*, 69, 71

——: 'Wenig beachtete Quellen zum Musiklexikon Johann Gottfried Walther', *Augsburger Jb für Musikwissenschaft 1986*, 175–6, 183   HANS JOACHIM MARX

Polly. Ballad opera in three acts with musical arrangements attributed to JOHANN CHRISTOPH PEPUSCH to a libretto by JOHN GAY; London, Little Theatre in the Haymarket, 19 June 1777.

Polly, written as a sequel to Gay's highly successful *The Beggar's Opera* (29 January 1728), went into rehearsal in the autumn of 1728 but was not performed. Though the libretto contains little that was politically sensitive, its performance was banned by order of the Lord Chamberlain on 12 December 1728, perhaps through the influence of Sir Robert Walpole. Audiences, however, suspected the actor-manager Colley Cibber of playing a part in the suppression, though Cibber denied this in his autobiography (London, 1740). Because of the controversy, the printed libretto and songs in *Polly* enjoyed brisk sales when they appeared in London in 1729. They include no mention of Pepusch.

In *Polly*, the leading characters of *The Beggar's Opera*, Polly Peachum (soprano) and Macheath (tenor; disguised as a negro, Morano), are transported to the West Indies, where the action takes place. Gay's story of coffee planters, pirates and Indians has 54 interpolated airs; most of the tunes are popular ballads, with a few from Handel and Ariosti. For the first performance in 1777, the libretto was altered by George Colman the elder, and there were additional new songs by SAMUEL ARNOLD.   D. F. COOK

Polovinkin, Leonid Alexeyevich (*b* Kurgan, 1/13 Aug 1894; *d* Moscow, 8 Feb 1949). Russian composer. He entered the Moscow Conservatory in 1914 to study the piano; from 1918 his teachers there included Vasilenko for composition and orchestration and Glier for fugue. After graduating in 1924 he moved to Leningrad and there took part in the establishment of the studio of the Monumental'nïy Teatr Operï i Baleta, known as the Mamont (Mammoth); that same year he joined the Association for Contemporary Music. He was also music director at the Alexandrinsky Theatre, but soon returned to Moscow for postgraduate composition study at the conservatory (1926); he taught orchestration there from 1926 to 1932. In 1926 he began a long career as music director of the Moscow Central Children's Theatre.

In his music Polovinkin had to overcome a dependence on Skryabin before seeking a new language,

influenced by Les Six, by Schoenberg and by an attraction towards urban life. A new phase in Polovinkin's compositional development began with his appointment to the children's theatre; spurred by the sharply negative press reaction to his music, in this later period he turned to a simpler, folksong-like style.

Churilo Plenkovich, 1924 (3, S. Shervinsky), inc., concert perf. of extracts, Moscow, 31 May 1924

Irlandsky: geroy [Playboy of the Western World: the Hero], 1930–32 (3, Polovinkin, after J. M. Synge), unperf., vs (Moscow, 1932)

Sirokko op.32 (musical comedy, 3, W. G. Zak and Yu. Dantsiger, after A. M. Sobol'), Moscow, Chamber Theatre, 1928, extracts, vs (Vienna, 1929)

Dazhe v trikotazhe [Even in Knitting], 1930 (operetta, 3, Dantsiger and V. Tipot), Moscow, Operetta Theatre, ?1931

Skazka o rïbake i rïbke [The Tale of the Fisherman and the Fish] (children's op, 4, after A. S. Pushkin), Kiev, Academic Theatre of Opera and Ballet, 1935

*

N. Sats: *Deti prikhodyat v teatr* [Children are Coming to the Theatre] (Moscow, 1961), 222ff

L. Rimsky: 'Materialï k biografii L. A. Polovinkina' [Materials for the Biography of Polovinkin], *Iz proshlogo sovetskoy muzikal'noy kul'turï* [The Past of the Soviet Musical Culture], ed. T. Livanova (Moscow, 1975), 164–9   INNA BARSOVA

Polpetta, La. *See* PIERI, MARIA MADDALENA.

Polzelli [Polcelli; née Moreschi], **Luigia** (*b* Naples, *c*1760; *d* Kaschau [now Košice], 5 Oct 1830). Italian mezzo-soprano. From 1779 to 1790 she and her husband, the violinist Antonio Polzelli, were in service at Eszterháza, despite their indifferent talents but probably through the intercession of Haydn, who had taken Luigia as a mistress. She was never assigned a leading role at Eszterháza, and her restricted range and musicality made it necessary for Haydn to rewrite even secondary parts for her. She appeared twice in Haydn's operas, as Silvia in *L'isola disabitata* and Lisetta in *La vera costanza*, though most of Haydn's insertion arias were composed for her. After the dissolution of the Kapelle and the death of her husband, she sang in lesser Italian theatres (Bologna, Piacenza). She later married the singer Luigi Franchi; they remained until 1815 in Bologna, and in 1820 went to Hungary.

HORST WALTER

Pomo d'oro, Il ('The Golden Apple'). *Festa teatrale* in a prologue and five acts by ANTONIO CESTI to a libretto by FRANCESCO SBARRA; Vienna, Hoftheater auf der Cortina, 12 July (prologue, Acts 1 and 2) and 14 July (Acts 3–5) 1668.

Based on the myth of the Judgment of Paris, *Il pomo d'oro* was commissioned in 1666 to celebrate the marriage of Leopold I to the Infanta Margherita of Spain. Because her arrival in Vienna was delayed and the Hoftheater auf der Cortina (designed by L. O. Burnacini; *see* VIENNA, fig.2) was not finished, the opera was postponed. Plans to mount it during the winter of 1667–8 to celebrate the birth of the couple's son Ferdinand Wenzel were also thwarted when the child died in January 1668. It eventually received its première on 12 and 14 July 1668 to celebrate Margherita's birthday and was given again on 23 July. Acts 3 and 5 are missing from the full score (in *A-Wn*); only excerpts from these acts remain (in *I-MOe*). Leopold himself wrote music for Act 2 scene ix and Act 5 scene v, including arias; J. H. Schmelzer wrote the ballet music, choreographed by Santo Ventura with combats staged

Spagna [Spain]	soprano
Italia [Italy]	alto
Sardigna [Sardinia]	soprano
Regno d'Hongheria [Kingdom of Hungary]	tenor
Regno di Boemia [Kingdom of Bohemia]	alto
L'Imperio [Crown Lands]	bass
L'America [America]	tenor
Germania [German Empire]	bass
Amore [Cupid] *god of Love*	soprano
Himeneo [Hymen] *god of Marriage*	alto
La Gloria Austriaca [Glory of Austria]	soprano
Proserpina [Persephone] *Pluto's wife*	soprano
Plutone [Pluto] *lord of the Underworld*	bass
Discordia [Discord] *goddess of Strife*	soprano
Apollo *god of Music and Poetry*	alto
Marte [Mars] *god of War*	tenor
Momo [Momus] *court buffoon*	bass
Nettuno [Neptune] *god of the Sea*	bass
Bacco [Bacchus] *god of Wine*	bass
Mercurio [Mercury] *ambassador for Jupiter*	alto
Venere [Venus] *goddess of Love*	soprano castrato
Giove [Jupiter] *king of the gods*	bass
Hebe *goddess of Eternal Youth*	soprano
Giunone [Juno] *goddess of War*	soprano
Ganimede [Ganimedes] *most beautiful of mortal youths*	alto
Pallade [Pallas Athena] *goddess of Wisdom and Power*	soprano
Ennone [Oenone] *youthful nymph in love with Paris*	soprano
Paride [Paris] *son of the King of Troy*	tenor
Aurindo *shepherd in love with Oenone*	alto
Filaura *Oenone's nurse*	tenor
Caronte [Charon] *boatman who transports the dead to Hades*	bass
Megera [Megaera]	alto
Tesifone [Tisiphone] } *three Furies*	soprano
Aletto [Alecto]	soprano
Cecrope [Cecrops] *King of Athens*	bass
Adrasto *Cecrops's general*	alto
Alceste [Alcestis] *Cecrop's wife*	alto
A Soldier	tenor
Adrasto } *seconds-in-command*	contralto
Trittone	silent
Eolo [Aeolus] *god of the Winds*	bass
Austro *god of the South Wind*	[no extant music]
Euro [Eurus] *god of the East Wind*	tenor
Volturno *god of the East-North-East Wind*	[no extant music]
Zeffiro [Zephyrus] *god of the West Wind*	soprano
A Priest *of Pallas Athena*	bass
A Member of the Chorus	tenor
L'Elemento del Foco [Fire]	alto
Eufrosine [Euphrosyne]	soprano
Aglaie [Aglaia] } *three Graces*	soprano
Pasithea [Thalia]	alto

Choruses of gods, Athenian soldiers, Paris's servants, ministers of Athena's temple, winds

Setting Classical antiquity

---

by Agostino Santini. The opera's 23 sets were engraved by Matthäus Küsel and published in various editions of the libretto (see illustration; for further illustration *see* STAGE DESIGN, fig.4) No revivals are known until 1981, when the prologue and Acts 1, 2 and 4 were performed

in Aidenbach, and July 1989, when concert performances of all the extant music were given by Spectaculum in Vienna. Names of performers for the 1668 performances are unknown except for one 'Vincentino', a castrato lent to Vienna by the Archduke of Florence who sang the role of Venus. Sbarra, Cesti's long-standing collaborator, noted in the libretto that 'No small contribution to the success was made by the music, performed by the first virtuosos of this century, which was composed by Signor Cavalier Cesti … who, always marvellous in his compositions, was in this unsurpassed'.

PROLOGUE *Theatre of the Glory of Austria* In a baroque hall, elaborately decorated to glorify Austria and Leopold I, superbly dressed personifications of the Austrian territories sing the double chorus 'Di feste, e di giubili', based on the 3/4 *corrente*-like middle section of the preceding three-part sonata. An antiphonal ritornello for two five-part string ensembles follows. All the gods unite to sing the florid, festive chorus 'Godiamo noi regni', accompanied by two 'trombe'.

ACT 1.i–iii *Pluto's kingdom* Persephone, in the aria 'E dove t'aggiri', accompanied by two cornetts, three trombones, bassoon and organ, laments her life in darkness, in a scene reminiscent of the Underworld scene in Monteverdi's *Orfeo*. Pluto enters with various spirits and infernal monsters, and Discord, lurking above on a fire-breathing dragon, joins them.

1.iv–v *Jupiter's palace; the banquet of the gods* Many gods, each presented in a brief solo passage, assemble for a banquet. Momus, the court buffoon, dispenses advice and social comment here and throughout the opera. Discord arrives unseen and throws the golden apple in their midst. Venus, Athena and Juno squabble about its ownership and Jupiter notices it is inscribed 'to the most beautiful'. He decrees that possession will be decided by Paris, to which they agree in several trios. Left alone, Momus comments on the folly of it all in a strophic-variation aria 'Queste Paride non ha''.

1.vi–x *A forest on Mount Ida* In the first sub-plot, Oenone sings a lengthy aria of four strophes 'Che gioia, che senti felice', in 3/2 time and *ABA'B'* form, with a ritornello after each of the first three strophes. She is joined by Paris for one of Cesti's finest love duets, 'O mia vita! O mio core', but their rapture is interrupted when Mercury discloses the role Paris must play concerning the golden apple. *Recitativo semplice* is used exclusively until Paris again thinks of Oenone, and another duet follows. Aurindo overhears them and he laments his unrequited love for Oenone, his pastoral character depicted by a change of instrumentation to two 'flauti' (recorders), an ensemble of viols and a 'graviorgano'. Viols, used infrequently, are reserved for three characters: Oenone, Filaura (Act 4.i–ii) and Alcestis (Act 4.v). Finally, Oenone's nurse Filaura, another stock comic character, 'consoles' Aurindo with mock sympathy.

1.xi–xiv *A courtyard in Paris's palace* The final scenes belong together, although the set changes for scene xv (*Garden of Beauty*). Momus, in a monologue and a dialogue with Paris, is at his wittiest, commenting on the corruption of power and money. Each of the principal goddesses lobbies Paris for a favourable decision: Juno, Athena and Venus. Venus makes the winning bid by promising Paris Helen in exchange for

'Il pomo d'oro' (Cesti), Act 1 scenes xi–xiv (a courtyard in Paris's palace; Juno lobbies Paris for a favourable decision): set design by Ludovico Burnacini for the original production at the Hoftheater auf der Cortina in Vienna, 12 July 1668; engraving by Matthäus Küsel

the golden apple. When he accepts, she exults in the aria 'Cingetemi il crine' with accompanying ritornello, which displays passage-work requiring as much virtuosity as any Cesti wrote. The act ends with a ballet involving Ideal Beauty and Cupids.

ACT 2.i–v *A seaport* The subplots continue with Paris's departure by ship to claim Helen, much of the action taking place in recitative dialogue. Aurindo discusses his infatuation for Oenone with Filaura, seeking her aid. Momus then tells Filaura about Paris's desire for Helen in an aria in *ABA'* form. Paris rhapsodizes about Helen in the finely crafted accompanied aria 'O del ben', che acquistero' and encounters Oenone and Filaura, who accuse him of breach of trust. Paris reaffirms his love for Oenone in a 3/2 duet, 190 bars in length and equal to the finest mid-century examples. Another Momus monologue in which he complains about everything, especially Jupiter, concludes the group.

2.vi–ix *The mouth of Hell* Accompanied by instruments used in Persephone's aria in Act 1, Charon laments the dearth of people to transport to the Underworld before being joined by three flying Furies, whom he agrees to carry in exchange for the latest gossip. When they tell him of the strife caused by the golden apple, the delighted Charon forecasts an increase in business!

2.x–xii *An armed camp* Adrasto, Cecrops and soldiers gather. In Cecrops's martial aria 'Pugneremo, vinceremo', the accompanying strings imitate and have a duet with the bass voice. Athena, greatly offended by Paris's capitulation to Venus's offer, joins them and implores Cecrops to defend her honour. Cecrops's wife Alcestis laments their frequent separation caused by war. A show of affection ends in his reluctant agreement that she may accompany his next foray.

2.xiii–xiv *Pool of the Tritons* The act ends with Cecrops's army performing mock combat. Athena flies overhead demanding vengeance for Paris's affront, in brilliant coloratura passage-work punctuated by two 'trombe'. In honour of Athena, the concluding ballet depicts an assault by women dressed as Amazons.

ACT 3.i–ii *Aeolus's cavern* New gods including Aeolus and Eurus are introduced. Juno arrives on a cloud and, after raging at Paris, asks Aeolus to destroy Paris's ship.

3.iii–v *Valley of the Xanthus river* The action returns to the subplots. Oenone is heartsick that Paris still eludes her and receives consolation from Aurindo and Momus. Her laments, built on free bass lines as opposed to the ostinatos favoured by Cavalli, are consistently more chromatic than other passages in the opera. Momus's suggestion that Paris is gone forever raises Aurindo's hopes for his future with Oenone.

3.vi *Mars's arsenal* Content with Paris's judgment, Venus invites Mars's support against the Athenian forces. Venus's second aria, 'Troppo Pallade pretende', is a brilliant strophic exit aria in *ABA'* form using extended passage-work and range (*d'* to *a"*).

3.vii–x *The sea* Aeolus unleashes winds at Paris's ship, but Venus intercedes, promising Neptune the nymph Amphitrite if he will calm the sea. Neptune agrees, Venus departs and Paris continues his search for Helen. Meanwhile, Aurindo and Filaura are still unhappy at their inability to locate Paris. The only lengthy passage of extant music is for scene x: Filaura's arietta 'Quand' Ennone ancora', which exhibits Cesti's infrequent uses of 6/8 time and sequential writing, and the unusual concluding strophic aria 'Sei semplice, affè', which includes a sung refrain in 3/4 (*A*) in conjunction with a 4/4 aria in two strophes (*B*), yielding the form *ABABA*.

3.xi–xii *Amphitheatre* Act 3 concludes with a ballet depicting the battle between the armies of Cecrops and Mars. Mars, victorious, takes Cecrops prisoner.

ACT 4.i–ii *A cedar forest* Oenone is still disconsolate at her unsuccessful quest for Paris. As usual, Filaura overhears her complaint and offers advice.

4.iii–v *Temple of Athena* Adrasto and his ministers gather for a solemn sacrificial ceremony. Their invocation leads to an earthquake that causes columns to crumble and the temple to collapse. Athena, cloud-borne, furiously informs the worshippers that King Cecrops is Mars's prisoner along with the golden apple. Adrasto and his army depart for battle; his rallying cry, 'Su, su dunque su al' armi', which contains brilliant coloratura and an unusual chordal accompaniment reminiscent of Monteverdi's *stile concitato* writing, leads to a dramatic outburst, 'Ah' ah' troppo offesa son'. Finally, Alcestis is relieved to hear that her husband is alive.

4.vi–ix *The heavens, with the Milky Way encircled by blazing fire and Venus at the centre* Venus and Juno have their first confrontation since Act 1. Juno asks Fire (whose passage-work is as lively as his name suggests) to destroy Neptune's kingdom as punishment for intervening on behalf of Paris's ship. Noting that this is forbidden by fate, Fire rejects her command and Juno, insulted, departs.

4.x–xiii *An atrium of Venus's palace* Three Graces, including Euphrosyne awkwardly riding a tortoise, are introduced. Venus, with the golden apple over her head, and Mars, with a crown over his, sit in a triumphal machine drawn by lions ridden by little Cupids. King Cecrops lies at their feet and spoils of war plundered from Juno and Athena are evident. In a trio, musically faithful to each principal, Venus and Mars exultantly call Cecrops a slave, while he steadfastly retorts that he is a king. Cupid interrupts with news that Athenians aroused by Athena herself are on their doorstep. Venus and Mars implore the assembled to take arms.

4.xiv–xv *Mars's fortress* Adrasto and his soldiers approach and the assault commences in the concluding ballet, aided by two elephants, ladders and platforms. Observing from above Athena intercedes, giving the Athenians the advantage.

ACT 5.i–viii *Paris's sumptuous palace* The plot remains in disarray with rival goddesses still battling, Oenone unable to locate Paris and Paris without Helen. After Filaura sings an expressive aria, 'O perfido e ingrato', Jupiter returns on his eagle accompanied by Juno on a cloud. Still angry at having been judged by a mortal, Juno is chided by both Jupiter and Momus. Her arias are extant, as well as music for the storm she unleashes to vent her anger on Jupiter, which mostly consists of arpeggiation over a D major pedal point. Unmoved, Momus shows his disdain in a quasi-strophic aria 'Venga pur fiera tempesta', which spans nearly two octaves (*E–d'*) and has an unusual form, $A^1A^2BA^3C$, covering more than 115 bars. Aurindo reappears, suicidal because of Oenone's rejection of him. Music for scene v, composed by Emperor Leopold I, uses shorter phrases than those found in Cesti's music. Finally Oenone, goaded by Filaura and Momus, quits her search for Paris and submits to Aurindo. The extant music ends with a trio for Oenone, Aurindo and Filaura ('Ti cedo, e che vedo').

5.ix–x *A piazza in Mars's castle* The golden apple is visible on a tower before which Jupiter is seated on a golden throne, attended by his eagle. Angered by Juno and Athena's incessant fighting, he makes the tower crumble, dispatching his eagle to pluck the apple from the rubble. Sbarra provides the opera with a sensible yet ingenious conclusion by having the golden apple awarded to Empress Margherita, in whom the wisdom of Athena, the beauty of Venus and the greatness of Juno are embodied.

5.xi *Heaven, earth, the sea* The opera ends with the presentation of three ballets, involving the Spirits of the Air, Knights of the Earth and the Sirens and Tritons of the Sea.

*   *   *

More than eight hours in length, *Il pomo d'oro* has long been recognized as the epitome of Baroque court operas. Its requirements dwarf those of most other 17th-century Italian operas; even the lavish spectacles Lully created for Louis XIV demand nothing more. The variety of the instrumental forces, comic and serious elements, aria types, ensembles, ballets ending each act, and the machines and other scenic effects, make this opera worthy of the Olympian position it has been accorded in the history of theatrical music since Guido Adler edited what was known of its music at the end of the 19th century.
CARL B. SCHMIDT

Pomone ('Pomona'). *Pastorale* in a prologue and five acts by ROBERT CAMBERT to a libretto by PIERRE PERRIN; Paris, Jeu de Paume de la Bouteille, 3 March 1671.

The plot centres on the wooing of Pomona (soprano), goddess of fruits, by Vertumne [Vertumnus] (*haute-contre*), god of autumn. Vertumnus tries to win Pomona's hand by disguising himself as Pluto, Bacchus and finally – in an attempt to persuade her of his worth – Beroë (soprano), Pomona's nanny, who is herself in love with Vertumnus. Pomona eventually returns his affections and joyful wedding celebrations ensue.

Pomone was the inaugural production of the Académies d'Opéra and is generally considered to be the first French opera. Only the overture, prologue, Act 1 and part of Act 2 survive. The simple story provided the opportunity for a host of theatrical devices (thunder, lightning, flights, character metamorphoses etc.), which were designed by the Marquis de Sourdéac, as well as ballets and scenic spectacle. The work was prepared and rehearsed in 1670 but did not open until 1671 because of problems over the leasing of a theatre. Crowds flocked to see it and scuffles broke out when people tried to enter without paying. *Pomone* apparently enjoyed 146 performances and the run lasted seven or eight months. It is believed that Mlle Cartilly sang the title role and François Beaumavielle played Vertumnus.

Critics wrote favourably about the music and machines (the *Mercure galant*, April 1677, claimed that after *Pomone* there was 'no recitative in France that seemed new') but were less enthusiastic about the poetry. It was long thought that *Pomone* was also staged in England, but there is no solid evidence to support this; in 1687 it was performed in Nantes by the Sieur d'Aumont's troupe.
CHRISTINA BASHFORD

Pompadour, Madame de [Poisson, Jeanne Antoinette] (*b* Paris, 29 Dec 1721; *d* Versailles, 16 April 1764). French patron. She married Guillaume Lenormand, Seigneur d'Etioles, in 1741 and established a popular salon frequented by such leading literary figures as

Voltaire, C.-L. de Secondat, Baron de la Brède et de Montesquieu and Fontenelle. In 1745 she became Louis XV's mistress and was granted the title 'Marquise de Pompadour'. In this capacity she was able to encourage many more artists, including the composers François Rebel, Mion and La Garde and the librettists Pierre Laujon, Moncrif and P.-C. Nivelle de La Chaussée. In 1747 she formed her own amateur theatre at Versailles, the Théâtre des Petits Cabinets, which moved to Bellevue in 1752. During the next seven years some 33 operatic works, mainly in the pastoral genre, were performed, with Mme de Pompadour often taking the leading role. The Duke of Luynes judged her voice small but pleasant. She was, moreover, an excellent musician and an attractive, competent actress.

For illustration *see* PARIS, fig.11.

P. Laujon: 'Les spectacles des petits cabinets de Louis XV', *Bibliothèque des mémoires relatifs à l'histoire de France pendant le xviiie siècle*, iii (Paris, 1846)
C. d'Albert, Duc de Luynes: *Mémoires du duc de Luynes sur la cour de Louis XV (1735–1758)* (Paris, 1860–65)
E. Campardon: *Madame de Pompadour et la cour de Louis XV au milieu du dix-huitième siècle* (Paris, 1867)
A. Jullien: *Histoire du théâtre de Madame de Pompadour* (Paris, 1874)
W. H. Kaehler: *The Operatic Repertoire of Madame de Pompadour's Théâtre des Petits Cabinets (1747–1753)* (diss., U. of Michigan, 1971)
ELISABETH COOK

Pompei, Giovanni (*fl* 1865–80). Italian impresario. During the span of only a few years, he was the first impresario to bring Italian opera to the Far East, including Hong Kong (March 1867), Manila (summer 1867), Singapore (May 1869) and Batavia (June 1869). He toured Java extensively in 1869–70, also visiting Semarang, Solo and Surabaya. He joined forces with Augusto Cagli in Melbourne in May 1871, but went to India shortly thereafter. In 1875, after Cagli had left Australia, Pompei returned and gave opera performances in several Australian cities, including Hobart, Brisbane and Sydney. He also gave a number of seasons in Bombay and Calcutta.

H. Love: *The Golden Age of Australian Opera: W. S. Lyster and his Companies 1861–1880* (Sydney, 1981)
TOM KAUFMAN

Pompeo ('Pompey'). *Dramma per musica* in three acts by Alessandro Scarlatti (*see* SCARLATTI family, (1)) to a libretto by NICOLÒ MINATO; Rome, private theatre of Lorenzo Onofrio Colonna, 25 January 1683.

Minato's libretto takes as its starting-point the historical defeat by Pompey of Mithridates' army at Nicopolis. The real Mithridates fled to Colchis and then to the Crimea, and committed suicide in 63 BC, but in the opera he turns up in disguise in Rome, determined to assassinate his conqueror. Pompey (tenor) tries to win over the heart of Giulia [Julia] (contralto), the daughter of Giulio Cesare [Julius Caesar] (bass), who loves Scipione Servilio [Scipio Servilius] (soprano). Mithridates' wife Issicratea [Hypsicrateia] (soprano) is similarly pursued by both Pompey's son, Sesto [Sextus] (alto castrato), and Caesar's son, Claudio [Claudius] (soprano). This leads to a confused situation at the end of Act 2, when Mitridate [Mithridates] (tenor) kills his wife's slave Harpalia (soprano or tenor) with Sextus's sword. Mithridates is forced to confess to the murder in order to save Sextus, but Pompey, when he overhears Mithridates' wife and son, Farnace [Pharnaces]

(soprano castrato), insisting on dying with him, frees them all, accepts Julia as his wife and installs Pharnaces as the new King of Pontus. Minato's libretto had originally been written for Cavalli in 1666 (for a fuller account of the plot, *see* POMPEO MAGNO).

Il Pompeo shows a number of unusual features, not the least being the allotting of the two main male characters, Pompey and Mithridates, to tenors rather than to castratos. That some difficulties were experienced in casting the opera is suggested by the fact that in the only surviving score the part of Harpalia is notated in the soprano clef in Act 1 but in tenor clef in Act 2, probably indicating a change of singer during the composition of the opera. Unusual features in the musical structure – the relatively small number of da capo arias (only 22 out of 52) and the large number of two-strophe arias – may be explained by Scarlatti's having set a libretto written (for Cavalli) almost 20 years earlier.

Handel borrowed from *Il Pompeo* in some of the operas and oratorios he composed in the 1730s, but not the best-known aria, 'O cessate di piagarmi', sung by Sextus in Act 2.   MALCOLM BOYD

Pompeo magno ('Pompeius Magnus'; 'Pompey the Great'). *Drama per musica* in three acts by FRANCESCO CAVALLI to a libretto by NICOLÒ MINATO; Venice, Teatro S Salvatore, 20 February 1666.

The Queen of Pontus, Issicratea [Hypsicrateia] (soprano), and her young son Farnace [Pharnaces] (soprano), whom Sulla had captured in battle, have been living as prisoners of Pompey (alto) in Rome. Hypsicrateia is courted by both Pompey's son, Sesto [Sextus] (soprano), and Caesar's son, Claudio [Claudius] (tenor). Her consort, King Mitridate [Mithridates] (tenor), has escaped Pompey's army in a recent battle and in disguise circulates freely in Rome. He locates his wife and devises a plan for escape. Mithridates reveals to Hypsicrateia that, if his plan to kill Pompey fails, he will commit suicide. He commands that she and their son Pharnaces both kill themselves along with him. Hypsicrateia enters Pompey's bedroom, but Pharnaces, unaware of the plot, awakens Pompey just in time to save his life. The boy proceeds to distract Pompey while Mithridates flees.

Act 2 opens on a scene of triumph as Cesare [Caesar] (bass) and Crasso [Crassus] (tenor) proclaim Pompey's latest victories to the cheering populace. Caesar presents his daughter Giulia [Julia] (soprano) as a bride to the general. Her betrothed Servilio [Servilius] (soprano) realizes that she faces a great destiny as Pompey's wife. Pompey, wishing to reward Pharnaces for saving his life, allows the young man his choice of spoils from the battle won over Mithridates. He selects his father's weapons. Mithridates later reveals his identity to Pharnaces and retrieves his arms. As night falls, Sextus slips into Hypsicrateia's rooms and threatens her with rape. She grabs his sword and swears to kill herself if he comes nearer. Mithridates rushes in to save her; she swoons in his arms and appears to be dead. Her slave Harpalia (soprano), who favours Sextus and has attempted to persuade her mistress to yield to him, aids him in his escape. Mithridates kills Harpalia with Sextus's sword.

During a ceremony in Pompey's theatre Hypsicrateia enters with Sextus's bloody sword. She accuses him of Harpalia's murder. When Pompey confronts his son, the innocent Sextus confesses to the crime. However, when he sees that Hypsicrateia is still alive, he refuses to divulge any more information for fear that she will be incriminated. Pompey vows to disown Sextus and adopt Pharnaces in his place. Mithridates, moved at Sextus's great self-sacrifice, confesses. As he, Hypsicrateia and Pharnaces start to take poison, Pompey stays their hands and grants them their freedom. Adding a note of irony to the happy resolution, Servilius forswears his Julia so that she can marry the great Pompey.

Pompeo magno is one of a trilogy of historical fantasies devised by Cavalli and Minato as a tribute to Roman patronage. This spectacle opera was written after their return from the court of Louis XIV and shows the influence of French taste as well as the gesture of homage in the dedication to Maria Mancini Colonna, mistress of Louis XIV before his marriage and a niece of the recently deceased Cardinal Mazarin.

MARTHA NOVAK CLINKSCALE

Ponce de León, José María (*b* Bogotá, 16 Feb 1846; *d* Bogotá, 21 Sept 1882). Colombian composer. He showed marked precocity in his comic opera *Un alcalde a la antigua y dos primos a la moderna*, performed as part of a Christmas festivity in the drawing-room of the Bogotá doctor Lorenzo Lleras. After other evidences of talent, his father, an army captain, sent him in 1867 to the Paris Conservatoire, where he studied with Gounod and Thomas until the outbreak of the Franco-Prussian War in 1870.

On his return home his biblical opera *Ester* was given by Virginia Florellini de Balma's touring Italian company in 1874. Turning next to Spanish zarzuela, Ponce de León composed music for *El castillo misterioso o La cinta encarnada*, given in 1876 to an enthusiastic public. Another visiting Italian troupe, headed by Emilia Benic, gave in 1880 Ponce de León's operatic masterpiece, *Florinda*, the plot of which deals with the betrayal of Count Julian's daughter by Don Rodrigo, last Visigothic ruler. *Florinda* was revived by Augusto Azzali's company on 20 July 1893.

Ponce de León's musical avatars were Bellini and his Conservatoire teachers. All his productions were successful with the Bogotá élite, to whose circles his own family belonged. Apart from his operas and zarzuelas (three of which were not produced), he composed sacred works and a *Sinfonía sobre temas colombianos* (1887).

all first performances in Bogotá

Un alcalde a la antigua y dos primos a la moderna (comic op, 2, J. M. Samper), 17 Dec 1863
Ester (biblical op, 3, M. Briceño and R. Pombo), 2 July 1874
El castillo misterioso o La cinta encarnada (zar, 3, J. M. Gutiérrez de Alba), 27 April 1876
Florinda (4, Pombo), 22 Nov 1880

*

J. I. Perdomo Escobar: *Historia de la música en Colombia* (Bogotá, 1945), 143–52
——: *La ópera en Colombia* (Bogotá, 1979), 27–38, 102

ROBERT STEVENSON

Ponchard, Louis(-Antoine-Eléonore) (*b* Paris, 31 Aug 1787; *d* Paris, 6 Jan 1866). French tenor. He studied in Paris, making his début there in 1812 in Grétry's *L'ami de la maison* at the Opéra-Comique, where he sang for 25 years. He created roles in Boieldieu's *Le nouveau seigneur du village* (1813), *Le petit chaperon rouge* (1818) and *Les deux nuits* (1829); Isouard's *Joconde* (1814); Auber's *Leicester* and *La neige* (both 1823), *Le concert à la cour* (1824) and *Le maçon* (1825); and

Carafa's *Masaniello* (1827). His best-known role was George Brown, which he sang in the first performance of Boieldieu's *La dame blanche* (1825). His repertory included Grétry's *Zémire et Azor* and *Richard Coeur-de-lion*.

ELIZABETH FORBES

Ponchard [née Carrault], **Marie-Sophie** (*b* Paris, 30 May 1792; *d* Paris, 19 Sept 1873). French soprano. She made her début in 1814 at the Paris Opéra in the title role of Gluck's *Iphigénie en Aulide*. After singing at Rouen, in 1818 she was engaged at the Opéra-Comique, where she remained until 1837. She took part in the premières of Auber's *Emma, ou La promesse imprudente* (1821), *Le timide* (1826) and *Le cheval de bronze* (1835). She created Marguerite de Valois in Hérold's *Le pré aux clercs* (1832) and Jeanie Deans in Carafa's *La prison d'Edimbourg*. She was married to the tenor Louis Ponchard.

ELIZABETH FORBES

Ponchielli, Amilcare (*b* Paderno [now Paderno Ponchielli], 31 Aug 1834; *d* Milan, 16 Jan 1886). Italian composer. He was the leading Italian composer of the generation between Verdi and Puccini.

1. LIFE. Ponchielli was taught the rudiments of music by his father, the local organist. At the age of nine a wealthy benefactor helped him to obtain a free place at the Milan Conservatory, where his teachers included Arturo Angeleri (piano) and from 1851 Alberto Mazzucato (composition). After graduating in 1854 he settled in Cremona as a music teacher and organist of S Ilario. While a student he had contributed with his fellow-pupils Marcora, Cagnoni and Cunio to a composite *opera buffa*, *Il sindaco babbeo*.

Ponchielli then ventured on a full-length opera, *I promessi sposi*, based on Alessandro Manzoni's novel, which had its first performance at the theatre at Cremona in 1856. Its reception was enthusiastic; but the poor libretto, whose authorship remains unknown, discouraged publishers and impresarios alike from acquiring the rights. Ponchielli's next opera, *Bertrando dal Bornio*, was scheduled for the autumn season of 1858 at the Teatro Carignano, Turin, but for undisclosed reasons the performance never took place. *La Savoiarda* (1861, Cremona), an *opera semiseria* in the style of Donizetti's *Linda di Chamounix*, but with a tragic ending, attracted only local attention. *Roderico re dei Goti* (1863, Piacenza) was taken off after a single performance owing to the indisposition of the baritone. An operatic project undertaken with Piave in 1867 (probably *Vico Bentivoglio*) was brought to an end by the stroke that laid the poet low until his death in 1876.

Meanwhile, in order to gain a living, Ponchielli accepted the post of bandmaster at Piacenza (1862), then at Cremona (1864). In 1867 he competed for the professorship of counterpoint at the Milan Conservatory. Although he was adjudged the winner, the nomination went to Franco Faccio, due partly to the influence of Giulio Ricordi. Once more Ponchielli took part in a composite opera, *La vergine di Kermo* (1870, Cremona), his fellow contributors including Pacini, Cagnoni, Lauro Rossi and Mazzucato. Finally, in 1872 a long period of frustration came to an end with the unexpected success of *I promessi sposi* at the Teatro Dal Verme, Milan, with a new text written by the 'scapigliato' poet Emilio Praga and the addition and substitution of several numbers. Part of the enthusiasm was due to the anti-Wagnerian reaction that was gathering strength in Italy, and part to the interest already aroused by Petrella's opera on the same subject. Critics noted, however, a stylistic discrepancy between the old and the new pieces, while Verdi observed that both were behind their respective times. Two minor successes followed: the ballet *Le due gemelle* (1873, La Scala) and a comic monodrama, *Il parlatore eterno*, written for the baritone Antonio Pini-Corsi (1873, Teatro Sociale di Lecco).

Meanwhile Giulio Ricordi had resolved to groom Ponchielli as Verdi's successor and accordingly commissioned a grand opera set in northern Europe to a libretto by Antonio Ghislanzoni. During its composition Ponchielli consulted the editor at every step; and eventually *I Lituani* went on stage at La Scala in March 1874, splendidly cast and mounted. Critics and public were respectful, but found room for improvement, which Ponchielli brought to it the following year, enlivening the subject with a few dances, a drinking-song and a battle scene. Nonetheless, *I Lituani* was not destined for the repertory, though after Ponchielli's death many writers urged it on impresarios as his best work; and indeed a concert performance in Cremona in 1984 showed it to be a powerful, if sombre, score. Later in the year of its première Ponchielli married the soprano Teresa Brambilla, his first Lucia in the revised *I promessi sposi*, and settled in Milan. In 1875 a cantata by him in honour of Donizetti was performed at the Teatro Riccardi, Bergamo.

With his next opera, *La Gioconda* (1876, La Scala), Ponchielli finally hit the mark, though four years were to pass before he succeeded in hammering the score into its definitive shape. Here he allowed free rein to his lyrical impulse, which, fuelled by the deft mechanism of Boito's libretto and his own propensity for vigorous dance rhythms, ensured the opera's lasting vitality. The vocal writing for all six principals is particularly grateful. No such success attended *Lina* (1877, Teatro Dal Verme), a revised version of *La Savoiarda*, rightly judged impossibly old-fashioned. Over the next two years Ponchielli took up a couple of subjects – Ghislanzoni's *I Mori di Valenza* and Carlo D'Ormeville's *Olga* – only to lay them aside in favour of Angelo Zanardini's *Il figliuol prodigo* (1880, La Scala). Although recognized as his most carefully written work to date, the action was considered too slow and the subject too oratorio-like ('not very prodigal towards the management's coffers!!' was the comment of the singer Teresa Stolz).

In the meantime Ponchielli branched out into other fields. In 1878 he deputized for the conductor Luigi Mancinelli at the Teatro Apollo, Rome, where he directed performances of *Lohengrin* and Massenet's *Le roi de Lahore*. In 1881 he at last obtained the teaching post at the Milan Conservatory that had been so unfairly denied him 14 years earlier. His pupils included Puccini and Mascagni, both of whom recalled him with affection (indeed he was instrumental in procuring for Puccini his first libretto). The following year he was appointed organist at S Maria Maggiore, Bergamo, for which he turned out a number of sacred compositions, the most important being the *Lamentazioni di Geremia* (1885). In his last opera, *Marion Delorme* (1885, La Scala), Ponchielli attempted to diversify his style with elements derived from French *opéra comique*; but the growing exhaustion of his melodic invention was becoming apparent. Acting on Verdi's advice he shortened the libretto with the help of Ghislanzoni for a revival at Brescia the same year, without, however,

materially altering the opera's fortunes. His death from pneumonia the following January was mourned throughout Italy, not least by Verdi, whose initial doubts as to his capability had been fully overcome by the success of *La Gioconda*.

2. WORKS. Ponchielli was a highly accomplished musician, whose misfortune it was to have grown up during a difficult period of transition in Italy's musical history. By nature conservative, he was further handicapped by a lack of self-confidence and a retiring temperament which put him at a disadvantage in the competitive world of the theatre. Such success as he obtained there would have been impossible without Ricordi's efforts on his behalf. Though possessed of a genuine dramatic instinct combined with a lyrical flair, he never took charge of an operatic structure as Verdi always did; rather, he remained dependent on the invention of his librettists, among whom Boito alone was able to satisfy his requirements in full. His masterpiece, *La Gioconda*, inevitably suffers by comparison with those of his great contemporary. Bernard Shaw held it up as 'a mere instance of the mischief which great men bring upon the world when small men begin to worship them'.

But if Ponchielli's idiom rarely advances beyond that of mid-1860s Verdi, he is far from a mere imitator. His melodic style is his own, marked by sinuous contours (e.g. the motif of La Gioconda's filial love, or the opening strain of her duet with Laura); and he had the ability to site commonplaces in a context that purges them of vulgarity (e.g. in the Furlana of *La Gioconda*). One does not blame Webster for not being Shakespeare – and in fact the parallel with Verdi and the Ponchielli of *La Gioconda* runs remarkably close. Nor should one overlook Ponchielli's skill in evoking an ambience, whether night on the Venetian lagoon (*La Gioconda*), the contrasting worlds of Judaea and Nineveh (*Il figliuol prodigo*) or the snows of northern Europe (*I Lituani*); while as a writer of dances he heads what is admittedly a slender field south of the Alps. Hackneyed though it be, disfigured by comic arrangements, the 'Danza delle ore' remains the only Italian operatic ballet whose music bears performance on its own, divorced from its theatrical setting.

See also FIGLIUOL PRODIGO, IL; GIOCONDA, LA; LITUANI, I; MARION DELORME; and PROMESSI SPOSI, I (i).

I promessi sposi (melodramma, 4 pts, after A. Manzoni), Cremona, Concordia, 30 Aug 1856, excerpts, vs (Milan, n.d.); rev. (E. Praga), Milan, Dal Verme, 5 Dec 1872, *I-Mr**, vs (Milan, 1872 [defective], 1873)

Bertrando dal Bornio, 1858, *Mr**, unperf.

La Savoiarda (dramma lirico, 3, F. Guidi), Cremona, Concordia, 19 Jan 1861; rev. 1870, *US-CA**; rev. as Lina (C. D'Ormeville), Milan, Dal Verme, 17 Nov 1877, vs (Milan, n.d.)

Roderico re dei Goti (3, Guidi, after R. Southey: *Roderick*), Piacenza, Municipale, 26 Dec 1863

Il parlatore eterno (scherzo comico, 1, A. Ghislanzoni), Lecco, Sociale, 18 Oct 1873, vs (Milan, n.d.)

I Lituani (dramma lirico, prol., 3, Ghislanzoni, after A. Mickiewicz: *Konrad Wallenrod*), Milan, Scala, 7 March 1874; rev., Scala, 6 March 1875, *I-Mr**, vs (Milan, n.d.)

I Mori di Valenza (dramma lirico, 4, Ghislanzoni, after E. Scribe: *Piquillo Alliaga*), begun 1874, Act 4 completed by Annibale Ponchielli and A. Cadore, Monte Carlo, Opéra, 17 March 1914, vs (Turin, 1914)

La Gioconda (dramma lirico, 4, Tobia Gorrio [A. Boito], after V. Hugo: *Angélo, tyran de Padoue*), Milan, Scala, 8 April 1876; rev., Venice, Rossini, 18 Oct 1876, *US-NYpm**; rev., Genoa, Politeama Genovese, 27 Nov 1879, *I-Mr**; (Milan and New York, n.d.)

Il figliuol prodigo (melodramma, 4, A. Zanardini, after Scribe: *L'enfant prodigue*), Milan, Scala, 26 Dec 1880, *Mr** (Milan, n.d.)

Marion Delorme (melodramma, 4, E. Golisciani, after Hugo: *Marion de Lorme*), Milan, Scala, 17 March 1885, *Mr**, vs (Milan, n.d.)

Music in: Il sindaco babbeo, 1851; La vergine di Kermo, 1870

*

H. Wolf: 'Gioconda', *Musikalische Kritiken* (Leipzig, 1911), 54–6 [4 May 1884]; 152–4 [22 Feb 1885]

G. Cesari: *Amilcare Ponchielli nell'arte del suo tempo: ricordi e carteggi* (Cremona, 1934)

M. Mila: 'Caratteri della musica di Ponchielli', *Pan*, ii/2 (1934), 481–9

A. Damerini: 'Una lettera inedita di A. Ponchielli', *Musica d'oggi*, xvii (1935), 141–2

G. De Napoli: *Amilcare Ponchielli (1834–1886): la vita, le opere, l'epistolario, le onoranze* (Cremona, 1936)

A. Damerini: *A. Ponchielli* (Turin, 1940)

G. Gavazzeni: 'Considerazioni di un centenario: A. Ponchielli', *Trent'anni di musica* (Milan, 1958), 57–62

N. Albarosa, ed.: *Amilcare Ponchielli, 1834–1886: saggi e ricerche nel 150º anniversario della nascita* (Casalmorano, 1987)

JULIAN BUDDEN

Poncini Zilioli, Francesco (*b* Parma, 1704; *d* Parma, 20 Feb 1782). Italian composer. A pupil of G. M. Capelli, he was vice-*maestro di cappella* at Parma Cathedral from 1733 and *maestro* from 1736, then became the first *maestro di cappella* at the Bourbon court established in Parma in 1749 (until 1766). He directed the comic opera company at Colorno from 1752 and the Regio Scuola di Canto at Parma, 1769–73. None of his operas survives.

La riprovazione di Saulle, Parma, 1726
Artaserse (os, 3, P. Metastasio), Parma, 1737
Il Temistocle (os, 3, Metastasio), 1739
Zenobia (os, 3, Metastasio), 1741
Il Medo (os, 3, C. I. Frugoni), Milan, 1747
La Didone abbandonata (os, 3, Metastasio), Livorno, 1752
Catone in Utica (os, 3, Metastasio), Parma, 1756

DEUMM; *EitnerQ*; *GerberNL*; *StiegerO*

J. S. Sainsbury: *A Dictionary of Musicians* (London, 1824, repr. 1825)

C. Alcari: *Parma nella musica* (Parma, 1931)

P. E. Ferrari: *Spettacoli drammatico-musicali e coreografici in Parma dall'anno 1628 all'anno 1883* (Parma, 1884)

N. Pelicelli: 'Musicisti in Parma', *NA*, xi (1934), 29–57, esp. 40, 41

DAVID GREENSLADE

Poniatowski, Józef (**Michał Ksawery Franciszek Jan**) (*b* Rome, 20 Feb 1816; *d* London, bur. Chislehurst, 3 July 1873). Polish composer and tenor. He was a great-nephew of the Polish King Stanislas August Poniatowski. He studied in Rome, and then in Florence under C. Zanetti and F. Ceccherini. At the age of 17 he won a prize in mathematics, but devoted himself to composition, also appearing as a singer in the theatres of Florence, Lucca, Bologna and Genoa, mostly in works by Rossini and Donizetti. His first opera, *Giovanni da Procida*, was staged privately in Florence (1838) and publicly in Lucca (1839) with the composer singing the tenor role; it was well received. *Don Desiderio* was performed in Pisa (1840) and then, with great success, in Venice, Florence, Milan, Bologna, Livorno, Rome and Naples; in 1858 it was given at the Théâtre Italien in Paris. Of his other operas *Bonifazio de' Geremei* (1843) was the most popular in Italy. He wrote librettos for some of his own operas.

Poniatowski held diplomatic posts in Brussels (1849), London (1850–53) and finally Paris, where his *Pierre de Médicis* was staged at the Opéra in 1860, and his *Au travers du mur* at the Théâtre Lyrique in 1861. In that year he was appointed director of the Théâtre Italien. He accompanied Napoleon III into exile in England; his *La contessina*, written for Patti, was performed in London as *Gelmina* in 1872. His operas are marked by melodic inventiveness and effective orchestration. Warsaw critics wrote that he sang like Rubini and composed like Donizetti (*Kurier Warszawski*, 3 March 1844). His ballad *The Yeoman's Wedding Song* was long popular in England. He wrote a pamphlet, *Le progrès de la musique dramatique* (Paris, 1859).

MSS lost unless otherwise stated

Giovanni da Procida (os, 3, Poniatowski, after G. N. Niccolini), private perf., Florence, 25 Nov 1838; public, Lucca, Giglio, 1839

Don Desiderio, ossia Il disperato per eccesso di buon cuore (dg, 2, C. Zaccagnini, after G. Giraud), Pisa, Accademia dei Ravvivati, 26 Dec 1840, *F-Pn*, excerpts arr. pf (Milan, *c*1841), vs (Paris, ?1858)

Ruy Blas (os, Zaccagnini, after V. Hugo), Lucca, Giglio, 2 Sept 1843

Bonifazio de' Geremei (os, 3, Poniatowski), Rome, Argentina, 28 Nov 1843, *Po*, excerpts (Milan, *c*1845); rev. as Marzio Coriolano e i Lambertazzi, Florence, Pergola, 1848

La sposa d'Abido (os, 3, G. Peruzzini, after Byron), Venice, Fenice, Feb 1845, lib. (Venice, 1845)

Malek Adel (os, 3, after S. Cottins: *Mathilde*), Genoa, Carlo Felice, 20 June 1846

Esmeralda (os, 3, F. Guidi and Poniatowski, after Hugo), Florence, Palazzo Vecchio, 26 June 1847

Pierre de Médicis (os, 4, J.-H. Vernoy de Saint-Georges and E. Pacini), Paris, Opéra, 9 March 1860, vs (Paris, 1860–61)

Au travers du mur (oc, 1, Saint-Georges), Paris, Lyrique, 9 May 1861, vs (Paris, 1861); rev. version, London, St George's Hall, 6 June 1873

L'aventurier (oc, 4, Saint-Georges), Paris, 26 Jan 1865, vs (Paris, 1870–72)

La contessina [La jeune contesse] (dg, 3, A. de Lauzières, after Saint-Georges and J. Adenis), Paris, Italien, 28 April 1868, *Pn*, vs (Paris, n.d.); rev. as Gelmina (F. Rizzelli), London, CG, 4 June 1872, lib. (London, 1872)

*

A. Busiri Vici: 'La discendenza romana di Stanislao Poniatowski', *I Poniatowski e Roma* (Florence, 1971)

M. de Angelis: *La musica del Granduca: vita musicale e correnti critichi a Firenze 1800–1855* (Florence, 1978)

IRENA PONIATOWSKA

Ponnelle, Jean-Pierre (*b* Paris, 19 Feb 1932; *d* Munich, 11 Aug 1988). French director and stage designer. He studied at the Sorbonne. His first major work was designing the première of Henze's *Boulevard Solitude* at Hanover in 1952, which led to many engagements as a designer throughout the German opera houses. His first production was *Tristan und Isolde* at Düsseldorf in 1962, a work he was later to design and direct to mesmeric effect at Bayreuth. Subsequently he worked regularly at La Scala, as Regisseur at Cologne Opera (a complete Mozart cycle), Zürich (a Monteverdi cycle, much appreciated, with Harnoncourt as conductor) and San Francisco (more than 20 stagings), always as director and designer. His first work at Covent Garden was as designer of *L'heure espagnole* (1962; see illustration); then he worked as director-designer of *Don Pasquale* (1973), *Aida* (1984) and *L'italiana in Algeri* (1988). At Glyndebourne he directed and designed an entertaining *Falstaff* (1977). His productions of Rossini's main comedies travelled to several centres: *La Cenerentola* was seen during the 1970s at La Scala, Covent Garden and the Edinburgh Festival. He worked regularly at the Salzburg Festival, where his stagings of *Le nozze di Figaro*, *Così fan tutte*, *Die Zauberflöte* and *Moses und Aron*, among others, were admired. His work was always innovative, animated and beautiful to view. He had no sympathy with the school of hard realism yet he never succumbed to routine or convention.

Set design by Jean-Pierre Ponnelle for Ravel's 'L'heure espagnole' (Covent Garden, London, 1962)

His knowledge of the texts and music of the operas he directed made him a stimulating colleague for many of the notable conductors of the day, including Kertész, Karajan, Harnoncourt, Pritchard, Abbado and Levine. The flexibility of filming also appealed strongly to him, and he made film versions of many of his productions, which have been seen on television and been made available on video.

See also FILM and FILMING, VIDEOTAPING; for further illustration *see* BOULEVARD SOLITUDE and SALZBURG.

J. Levine: 'Jean-Pierre Ponnelle, an appreciation', *Opera*, xxxix (1988), 1284–6   ALAN BLYTH

Pons, Lily (Alice Joséphine) (*b* Draguignan, nr Cannes, 12 April 1898; *d* Dallas, 13 Feb 1976). American soprano of French birth. A piano student at the Paris Conservatoire, she received her first vocal instruction from Alberti de Gorostiaga, and then studied with Zenatello in New York. She made her operatic début in 1928 at Mulhouse as Lakmé, with Reynaldo Hahn conducting. She then sang in French provincial houses as Gretel, Cherubino, Blonde, the Queen of Night and Mimì. On the recommendation of Zenatello, she went to the Metropolitan, making her début in 1931 as Lucia. She caused a sensation and thereafter remained with the company for 28 seasons. She had success as Gilda, Amina, Marie (*La fille du régiment*), Philine (*Mignon*), Olympia, and, above all, Lakmé. In 1935 she sang Rosina at Covent Garden and Gilda and Lucia at the Paris Opéra. She sang in South America, San Francisco (where her roles included the Queen of Shemakha and Violetta), Monte Carlo and Chicago, and made several films. She was married to André Kostelanetz from 1938 to 1958. She made her stage farewell at the Metropolitan in 1958 as Lucia. Pons possessed an agile, frail and extremely high coloratura voice; she sang the Mad Scene from *Lucia* a whole tone higher than written. Her intonation was not always accurate, but her technique was otherwise exceptionally secure.

B. Park: 'Lily Pons', *Record Collector*, xiii (1960–61), 245–71 [with discography]
L. Rasponi: 'The Money-Makers', *The Last Prima Donnas* (New York, 1982), 405–30
                                         DENNIS K. McINTIRE, MAX DE SCHAUENSEE

Ponselle [Ponzillo], Rosa (Melba) (*b* Meriden, CT, 22 Jan 1897; *d* Green Spring Valley, MD, 25 May 1981). American soprano. She studied singing with her mother and then with Anna Ryan. She began to appear in film theatres and vaudeville, often with her elder sister Carmela (a mezzo-soprano who was to sing at the Metropolitan from 1925 to 1935). In 1918 her coach William Thorner brought her to the attention of Caruso and Gatti-Casazza. In the first Metropolitan *La forza del destino* she made an unprecedented début – the first operatic performance of her life – as Leonora (1918), opposite Caruso and De Luca. She had prepared the role with Romano Romani, who remained her principal operatic and vocal tutor. She sang at the Metropolitan for 19 seasons, undertaking 22 roles. Perhaps most celebrated as Norma, she also enjoyed extraordinary successes in *Oberon*, *Ernani*, *Don Carlos*, *La Gioconda*, *Andrea Chénier*, *Guillaume Tell*, *L'amore dei tre re*, *Don Giovanni* (Donna Anna), *Cavalleria rusticana*, *La traviata*, *La vestale* and *L'Africaine*. She also participated in Breil's *The Legend*, Montemezzi's *La notte di Zoraïma* and Romani's *Fedra*. In 1935 she attempted Carmen, and experienced her only notable failure. Two years later she retired from opera, reportedly after her request for a revival of *Adriana Lecouvreur* was rejected, and vowed never again to set foot in the Metropolitan after her final performance (Carmen, 1937). She made her Covent Garden début as Norma in 1929, returning as Violetta, Leonora (*Forza*) and the heroine of Romani's *Fedra*; at the Florence Maggio Musicale in 1933 she sang Julia (*La vestale*). Although her repertory was broad, she never sang Puccini or Wagner, about which she later confessed regret.

Ponselle's voice is generally regarded as one of the most beautiful of the century. She was universally

Rosa Ponselle as Leonora in Verdi's 'La forza del destino'

lauded for opulence of tone, evenness of scale, breadth of range, perfection of technique and communicative warmth. Many of these attributes are convincingly documented on recordings. In 1954 she made a few private song recordings, later released commercially, revealing a still opulent voice of darkened timbre and more limited range.

GV (L. Riemens and R. Celletti; S. Smolian and R. Vegeto)

O. Thompson: *The American Singer* (New York, 1937), 335–46

I. Cook: 'Rosa Ponselle', *Opera*, iii (1952), 75–81

T. Villella and B. Park: 'Rosa Ponselle Discography', *Grand Baton*, vii/1–2 (1970), 5–14

J. B. Steane: *The Grand Tradition* (London, 1974), 289–94

J. Ardoin: 'A Footnote to Ponselle's Norma', *Opera*, xxvii (1976), 225–8

'Ponselle at 80', *Opera*, xxviii (1977), 13–25

J. Hines: 'Rosa Ponselle', *Great Singers on Great Singing* (Garden City, NY, 1982), 250–57   MARTIN BERNHEIMER

Pont des soupirs, Le ('The Bridge of Sighs'). *Opéra bouffe* in two acts by JACQUES OFFENBACH to a libretto by HECTOR-JONATHAN CRÉMIEUX and LUDOVIC HALÉVY; Paris, Théâtre des Bouffes-Parisiens (Salle Choiseul), 23 March 1861 (revised in four acts, Paris, Théâtre des Variétés, 8 May 1868).

Cornarino Cornarini, Doge of Venice (*buffo*), and his equerry Baptiste (tenor) return to Venice disguised as beggars after defeat in a sea battle. Arriving at the palace, they find the pageboy Amoroso (soprano) singing a serenade to the doge's wife Catarina (soprano), who has become the page's lover. Then an unwelcome admirer of Catarina arrives: Fabiano Fabiani Malatromba (tenor), who uses his position as a member of the dreaded Council of Ten to have Amoroso arrested.

When the town crier announces that Cornarini and Baptiste have been condemned to death, they hastily climb into the palace. There, in Act 2, they become involved in Malatromba's attempts to carry off Catarina, which end with their arrest. Still unrecognized, they offer to give evidence of Cornarini's death to the Council of Ten. However, during the council's session in Act 3, they are recognized and condemned to death anew. Finally, in Act 4, during carnival time in Venice, Cornarini and Malatromba are each given the chance to demonstrate their suitability for the post of doge. Malatromba wins, and Cornarini is despatched to Spain as ambassador, with both Catarina and – to her delight – Amoroso in tow.

The productions of 1861 and 1868 both featured Lise Tautin as Catarina, with José Dupuis as Malatromba in 1868. Principal numbers include a barcarolle for Cornarini and Baptiste, 'Dans Venise la belle', Amoroso's serenade 'Catarina, je chante', Malatromba's Act 2 'Ah! qu'il est doux, mon beau rêve' and a gondoliers' chorus 'Vole, vole, ma gondole' in Act 3. The extension from two acts to four involved the addition of several new numbers (including Malatromba's 'Les affaires sont les affaires' in Act 3) and the suppression of others. Mistaken identities and the hilarious meeting of the Council of Ten are features of the work.

ANDREW LAMB

Ponzo [Ponzio], **Giuseppe** (*fl* 1759–91). Italian composer. He may have been born in Naples, and the Milan *Indice de' spettacoli teatrali* of 1791 listed him as 'still living'. The list of his operatic productions gives some indication of his travels. He also wrote instrumental music.

Demetrio (os, P. Metastasio), Genoa, carn. 1759, *I-Tf*, *P-La*

Arianna e Teseo (os, P. Pariati), Milan, Regio Ducale, Jan 1762, *I-Gl*, *P-La*

Artaserse (os, Metastasio), Venice, S Benedetto, Jan 1766, *La*

Il re alla caccia (dg, C. Goldoni), ?Malta, Reale, ?1775; Vienna, 1777; *I-Gl*, *Nc*

Doubtful: Alceste, Reggio Emilia, 1760, *P-La* (Act 3); L'uomo femmina, Madrid, 1771, ? by Antonio Ponza

JAMES L. JACKMAN

Poole, Elizabeth (*b* London, 5 April 1820; *d* Langley, Bucks., 14 Jan 1906). English mezzo-soprano. She appeared as a child in pantomime and as an actress, making her operatic début in 1834 at Drury Lane. In 1836 at the same theatre she created Ninka in Balfe's *The Maid of Artois*. She also sang in the first performances of *The Bohemian Girl* (1843) and of Wallace's *Maritana* (1845), in which she took the part of Lazarillo. In 1852 she was engaged at the Surrey Theatre. Donna Elvira (sung in English) was one of the finest roles in her extensive repertory.

ELIZABETH FORBES

Poot, Marcel (*b* Vilvoorde, nr Brussels, 7 May 1901; *d* Brussels, 12 Jan 1988). Belgian composer. A son of Jan Poot, director of the Royal Flemish Theatre, Brussels, he studied at the Brussels Conservatory and at the Royal Flemish Conservatory, Antwerp. He also took lessons from Paul Gilson; he was a founder-member in 1925 of the Synthétistes, an association of Gilson's pupils. In 1930 he won the Rubens Prize, and this enabled him to move to Paris, where he worked under Dukas at the Ecole Normale de Musique. Subsequently he taught in Brussels and was director of the conservatory from

1949; he also wrote for many periodicals. He was made a member of the Royal Flemish Academy.

Poot's compositions include the opera *Het ingebeeld eiland* ('The Fabulous Isle'; composed 1925), the operetta *Het vrouwtje van Stavorea* ('The Little Woman of Stavoren'; composed 1928) and the chamber opera *Moretus* (1944, Brussels, Palais des Beaux-Arts). He also composed ballets and music for silent films and radio plays. His brilliant and vigorous style – close to middle-period Stravinsky, or more particularly to Prokofiev – is often used to ironic or humorous effect, and has shown itself better suited to orchestral than to vocal music.

F. de Wever: *Paul Gilson et les Synthétistes* (Brussels, 1949)
CORNEEL MERTENS

Popovici, Doru (*b* Reşiţa, 17 Feb 1932). Romanian composer. He studied in Timişoara (1944–50) with Liviu Rusu and at the Bucharest Conservatory (1950–55) with Mihail Andricu and Mihail Jora (composition), Paul Constantinescu (harmony) and Marţian Negrea (counterpoint), and attended the Darmstadt summer school in 1968. His compositions include vocal and instrumental music for large and small ensembles. His operatic style is lyrical and well suited to voices, the modally derived harmony making frequent references to Byzantine music. His orchestration is light and airy, more akin to chamber music.

Prometheu op.13, 1958 (1, V. Eftimiu), Bucharest, Romanian Opera, 16 Dec 1964 (Bucharest, 1990)
Mariana Pineda op.28 (1, Popovici, after F. García Lorca), TV broadcast, 22 Dec 1966; stage, Iaşi, State Opera, 24 April 1969 (Bucharest, 1970)
Interogatoriul din Zori [Interrogation at Daybreak] op.47, 1975 (1 act, 2 tableaux, V. Bârlădeanu), Galaţi, Muzical, 1979 (Bucharest, 1977)
Noaptea cea mai lungă [The Longest Night] op.52, 1977 (1, D. Mutaşcu), Bucharest, Romanian Opera, 9 June 1983
Statornicie [Firmness] op.102, 1989 (1, Popovici), unperf.
VIOREL COSMA

Popovici-Bayreuth, Dimitrie (*b* Iaşi, 19 July 1860; *d* Cluj [now Cluj-Napoca], 6 April 1927). Romanian baritone. He studied at the Bucharest Conservatory with George Stephănescu, in Venice, and in Vienna with Josef Gänsbacher. He made his début in the musical fairy-tale *Fata aerului* ('The Maid of the Air') by Ion Andrei Wachmann (1881), and continued to appear at the National Theatre in Bucharest. He became established as a Wagner singer in Prague, from 1886, singing Wolfram, the Dutchman, Hans Sachs and Wotan. He first sang at Bayreuth in 1894, as Telramund, and in 1899 sang Alberich and Klingsor there; at Cosima Wagner's suggestion he assumed the toponym Bayreuth. Other cities in which he appeared include Munich, Hamburg, Berlin, Milan and Florence, and he sang Wagner roles in New York. After he retired he assumed the directorship of the conservatory in Bucharest and then of the Romanian Opera House in Cluj. A baritone with a remarkably brilliant and powerful voice, he was a master of Italian bel canto and of Wagnerian lyrical declamation. He also possessed a fine dramatic sense.

G. Sbârcea: *Dimitrie Popovici-Bayreuth: întăreţul pribeag* [Dimitrie Popovici-Bayreuth: the Lonely Singer] (Bucharest, 1965)
VIOREL COSMA

Popp, Lucia (*b* Uhorska Ves, 12 Nov 1939). Austrian soprano of Czechoslovak birth. After studying at Bratislava, she made her début there as the Queen of Night in 1963, then sang Barbarina in Vienna, where she was engaged at the Staatsoper, and First Boy (*Die Zauberflöte*) at Salzburg. She made her Covent Garden début in 1966, as Oscar, returning as Despina, Sophie, Aennchen, Gilda and Eva. She first appeared at the Metropolitan in 1967 as the Queen of Night, and later sang Sophie and Pamina there. Engaged at Cologne, she sang throughout Europe in a repertory including Zerlina, Susanna, Ilia, Blonde, Konstanze, Marzelline, Rosina and Zerbinetta. In the 1980s she took on heavier roles such as Elsa, Arabella and the Marschallin in Munich; subsequently she sang the two Strauss heroines at Covent Garden. Her voice, which was initially light and perfectly suited to the soubrette repertory, has matured to encompass the more intense emotions of the roles undertaken in her later career. She has recorded extensively.
ALAN BLYTH

Porcile, Giuseppe. *See* PORSILE, GIUSEPPE.

Porfirii [Porfiri], **Pietro** (*fl* 1687–1709). Italian composer. He was a member of the clergy and in 1692 a *maestro di cappella* at Fabriano. According to Radiciotti (1893) he lived for many years in the vicinity of Senigallia and was *maestro di cappella* at Ostra, Iesi, Arcevia and Pesaro. It is unclear whether he was born in that region or at Venice, as asserted by the revisers of Allacci. He was a canon at Urbino in 1709 (according to Ricordi); this information probably derives from the libretto to *La Leucippe*.

Zenocrate ambasciatore a' Macedoni (M. A. Gasparini), Venice, S Moisè, 1687 [attrib. by Ivanovich]
Lo schiavo fortunato in Algeri (Gasparini), Treviso, S Margarita, before 1689, pubd lib. *I-Bc*; also perf. Pesaro, 1699 [according to Radiciotti]
Il Vespasiano (G. C. Corradi), Fabriano, 1 June 1692, pubd lib. *Vgc* [rev. of C. Pallavicino]
La forza del sangue, o vero Gl'equivoci gelosi (G. A. Lorenzani), Mondolfo, nr Senigallia, 1696, pubd lib. *Vgc* [rev. of F. Lanciani]
L'Isifile amazzone di Lenno (A. Aureli), Pesaro, Sole, 1697, pubd lib. *Rn*
La Leucippe, Senigallia, 20 June 1709, lib. pubd (Urbino, n.d.)

AllacciD; *RicordiE*
C. Ivanovich: *Minerva al tavolino* (Venice, 2/1688)
G. Radiciotti: *Teatro, musica e musicisti in Sinigaglia: notizie e documenti* (Tivoli, 1893), 43

Porges, Heinrich (*b* Prague, 25 Nov 1837; *d* Munich, 17 Nov 1900). German editor and writer on music. In 1863 he became co-editor with K. F. Brendel of the *Neue Zeitschrift für Musik*, and in 1867 he assumed responsibility, with the editor, Julius Fröbel, of the arts pages of the *Süddeutsche Presse*. He remained in Munich as music critic of the *Neueste Nachrichten* (from 1880). He came to the attention of Wagner in Vienna in 1863, and although he declined to accept Wagner's summons the following year to join him in Munich, he did later act as his assistant, most notably at the rehearsals for the first *Ring* at Bayreuth, which, at Wagner's request, he recorded in detail in *Die Bühnenproben zu den Bayreuther Festspielen des Jahres 1876* (Leipzig, 1881–96; Eng. trans., 1983).
BARRY MILLINGTON

Porgy and Bess. Folk opera in three acts by GEORGE GERSHWIN to a libretto by DuBose Heyward after his novel *Porgy* (1925), with lyrics by Heyward and IRA GERSHWIN; New York, Alvin Theatre, 10 October 1935.

Porgy *a crippled beggar*	bass-baritone
Bess	soprano
Crown *a stevedore, Bess's lover*	baritone
Serena *Robbins's wife*	soprano
Clara *Jake's wife*	soprano
Maria *keeper of the cook-shop*	contralto
Jake *a fisherman*	baritone
Sportin' Life *a dope peddler*	tenor
Mingo	tenor
Robbins	tenor
Peter *the honey man*	tenor
Frazier *a 'lawyer'*	baritone
Annie	mezzo-soprano
Lily *Peter's wife*	mezzo-soprano
Strawberry Woman	mezzo-soprano
Jim *a cotton picker*	baritone
Undertaker	baritone
Nelson	tenor
Crab Man	tenor

Residents of Catfish Row, fishermen, children, stevedores

Setting Catfish Row, a negro neighbourhood in Charleston, South Carolina, in the 1920s

At first glance, it might seem anomalous that a productive sought-after songwriter would devote the better part of two years to a single large work that was his own idea in the first place. But *Porgy and Bess* was Gershwin's magnum opus, nourished by more than a decade of technical study and a longheld interest in African-American experience. Attracted to ragtime as a teenage pianist, borrowing blues vocabulary for songs as early as 1920 and identified publicly as a 'jazz' composer from the time of the *Rhapsody in Blue* (1924), Gershwin held a substantial stake in black American music long before the day in autumn 1926 when he happened upon Heyward's novel. He responded to his reading of *Porgy* as if to the voice of destiny. Though his earlier experience with through-composed music drama had been limited to *Blue Monday* (1922), a 20-minute opera 'à la Afro-American' written for a Broadway revue, *Porgy* fired him with the vision of a full-length opera, and he wrote to Heyward immediately to propose a collaboration. Though the project took nine years to complete, Gershwin's intuition was on the mark. (He never did compose *The Dybbuk*, the 'Jewish opera' for which in 1929 he accepted a Metropolitan Opera commission – ample indication that he was much more at home with *Porgy*'s subject.)

Gershwin called *Porgy and Bess* a 'folk opera'. His belief in the need for a label is understandable, for *Porgy and Bess* is a work whose precise nature was questioned from the beginning. Gershwin's own credentials and prior experience caused some contemporaries to doubt that he was technically equipped to write a fully-fledged opera. The show's original venue (it played nightly on Broadway rather than according to an opera house's schedule, though trained opera singers were required) has raised further questions about its operatic pedigree. The massive cuts that took place before the New York première – to shorten playing time, tighten the drama, ease the singers' burden – have fed the belief that the work's essence lies in the appeal of individual numbers rather than the impact of its overall form. The popularity of some numbers as songs outside the show

has seemed to confirm this point, although Charles Hamm has argued for the dramatic merits of the original version, revised by Gershwin and Rouben Mamoulian, its first director. Moreover, although the first production was by no means a flop (124 performances), it did fail to return its backers' investment. *Porgy and Bess* stripped of its recitative won its first commercial success when played in 1941 as a drama of separate musical numbers linked with spoken dialogue.

If these matters seemed to undermine the 'opera' part of Gershwin's label, the 'folk' part also proved contentious. Gershwin invoked the word at a time when the concept of 'the folk' as a term denoting respect for 'otherness' was gaining popular acceptance. The US government's public works programmes during the Depression years signalled a growing inclination to preserve, study and value the indigenous practices of different American subcultures, including economically disadvantaged ones. From that perspective, a tale about southern blacks by a white novelist, set to music by a New York-based, Jewish songwriter-lyricist team and played on the Broadway stage, was easy to criticize on grounds of authenticity. In addition, the opera was about African-Americans, whose lives, long after slavery and emancipation, were still affected by racial stereotyping – by being seen as a feckless but violent people, given to singing or brawling their troubles away. A work like *Porgy and Bess*, which confirmed that stereotype, was seen in some quarters as yet another hindrance to the quest of black Americans for social respect.

For these reasons and others, commentators traditionally have viewed *Porgy and Bess* as a flawed effort. Rather than taking the work as Gershwin composed it, seeking clues to the meaning of 'folk opera' in his career and the score itself, critics and historians have been more inclined to privilege their own definitions of 'folk' or 'opera' and then to demonstrate how Gershwin fell short. Not until 1976, when the first production of Gershwin's complete score, given by the Houston Grand Opera, was hailed as an artistic triumph, did the critical tide begin to turn. Now it seems obvious that *Porgy and Bess* deserves consideration as a successful work of art, proved by over half a century of performers' commitment and audience acceptance, and worthy of being studied and appreciated on its own terms. With Gershwin's score as its basis, his 'folk opera' label seems straightforward enough: a staged, fully sung drama, using operatic techniques (recitatives, arias, reminiscence themes, leitmotifs), about an American ethnic community whose music Gershwin felt he understood, though an outsider, and many of whose artistic conventions he had already mastered through long experience as a pianist and composer.

Porgy shows kindness to the beautiful but dissolute Bess when her lover, Crown, is forced to flee after killing Robbins in a drunken fight over a crap game. Porgy takes Bess in and falls in love with her, and she becomes his woman, protected by his care against community opprobrium and the advances of Sportin' Life, the local dope peddler. Urged by Porgy to join a picnic excursion to Kittiwah Island, Bess encounters Crown, who is hiding there. Despite her genuine love for Porgy, Crown overcomes her resistance, and after spending the night with him on the island, she returns to Catfish Row in a state of delirium. Porgy helps nurse her back to health and, though intuition tells him she has been with Crown, he reaffirms his love for her. A hurricane hits the coast while fishermen from Catfish Row are at sea. As

'Porgy and Bess'
(Gershwin), Act 2 scene
iv: set design by Sergey
Soudeikin for the original
production at the Alvin
Theatre, New York, 10
October 1935

the community prays for their safety, Crown reappears, mocks Porgy for being less than a man and then rushes out into the storm in the vain hope of saving the fishermen. Surviving this onslaught of nature, he steals back to Catfish Row the next night to reclaim Bess. The waiting Porgy kills him in a brief struggle. When the police find Crown's body, they arrest Porgy as a witness. Freed a week later, he reappears triumphantly on Catfish Row, only to find that Bess, convinced by Sportin' Life that Porgy is gone for good, has sailed for New York in the dope peddler's company. The opera ends as Porgy leaves by goat cart to search for Bess. ('Which way New York?', he asks. 'It's way up North, past the custom house', his neighbours reply.)

* * *

Ira Gershwin once described his brother's imagination as 'the reservoir of musical inventiveness, resourcefulness, and craftsmanship George could dip into'. That 'reservoir' – nourished by a prodigious flow of inspiration and years of regular instruction, and disciplined by the habit of trusting a popular audience's judgments – is the source of *Porgy*'s sweep and power. The work is infused at every level with song of remarkable variety. Most obvious are the free-standing songs, whose melodies Wilfrid Mellers (in *Music in a New Found Land*) has saluted as 'more memorable than those of any twentieth-century opera', including Clara's lullaby ('Summertime', 1.i), Serena's lament ('My man's gone now', 1.ii), Porgy's banjo song ('I got plenty o' nuttin'', 2.i) and the love duet ('Bess, you is my woman', 2.i). In such numbers Gershwin's belief in the emotions of his principal characters leads to the invention of songs that do not need the opera's dramatic setting to make their impact.

But the principals of *Porgy and Bess* are portrayed as members of a larger community whose identity Gershwin creates through communal songs. Virtually omnipresent on stage and given naturally to musical expression, the residents of Catfish Row sing their own richly varied self-portrait. Rather than borrowing 'spirituals', Gershwin composed his own, which range in mood and technique from songful exaltation ('Leavin' for the Promise' Lan'', 1.ii) and consolation ('Clara, Clara', 3.i) to stark desolation ('Gone, gone, gone', 1.ii) and even simultaneously chanted individual prayers ('Oh, doctor Jesus', 2.iv). On the secular side, Catfish Row's uninhibited social mores can be glimpsed in the opening 'Jazzbo Brown' scene, and are more fully revealed in the fisherman Jake's bemused commentary on romance ('A woman is a sometime thing', 1.i) and a barbaric episode, complete with vocables and tom-toms, during the Kittiwah Island picnic ('I ain' got no shame', 2.ii). In that last scene, the amoral Sportin' Life gets the community, softened up by a day of carousing, to join him in a mockery of biblical teaching, sung in call-and-response fashion replete with blue notes ('It ain't necessarily so').

Finally, Gershwin tapped his reservoir of melody not only in arias and choruses but in recitatives, aptly termed by Lawrence Starr 'potential song' – declamatory passages from which songful moments may be coaxed by understanding performers. Among many such places in the score, Bess's plea that Crown allow her to return from the picnic to Porgy's side is one of the most economically effective. Here, Bess's character stands revealed. Lacking a true moral compass, torn between love for the upright Porgy and lust for the formidable Crown, she moves in just eight bars from reasonable explanation to the edge of despair. Gershwin restricts her to a word-bound vocal line that, as it rises over a static chordal background, calls more and more on the singer's expressive powers. Elsewhere in the work, he sometimes shapes the drama through musical complication, as in Crown and Robbins's battle, fought to a savage, portentous fugue (1.i). Here, he trusts the performer to convey the precise moment in which Bess's good intentions collapse, then supports her confession of defeat with the opera's most tortured song of all ('What you want wid Bess?').

RICHARD CRAWFORD

Poro [*Poro, re dell'Indie*] ('Porus, King of the Indians'). Opera in three acts by GEORGE FRIDERIC HANDEL to a libretto anonymously adapted from PIETRO METASTASIO's *Alessandro nell'Indie*; London, King's Theatre, 2 February 1731.

Poro was Handel's only new opera in the season of 1730–31. He began work on it late in December 1730 and completed the score on 16 January 1731, just over a fortnight before the first performance. Metastasio's libretto, written for Vinci's setting given in Rome only a year earlier (the name was presumably changed to avoid confusion with Handel's *Alessandro*), draws on the accounts of Alexander the Great's encounter in 326 BC with the Indian king Porus given by Arrian (*Anabasis*, v) and Curtius Rufus (*History of Alexander*, viii.13–14), in which Porus is portrayed as a brave and worthy opponent of the young conqueror. Curtius (viii.10) also mentioned Cleophis, Queen of the Assaceni, who is said to have offered herself to Alexander to regain her kingdom. These appear in the opera as Alessandro [Alexander] (tenor) and the lovers Poro [Porus] (alto) and Cleofide [Cleophis] (soprano). They are joined by three fictional characters: Erissena [Eryxene] (mezzo-soprano), Porus's sister; her lover, Porus's general Gandarte [Gandartes] (alto); and Alexander's treacherous general Timagene [Timagenes] (bass). The original cast consisted of the castrato Senesino (Porus), Annibale Pio Fabri (Alexander), Anna Maria Strada del Pò (Cleophis), Antonia Margherita Merighi (Eryxene), Francesca Bertolli (Gandartes) and Giovanni Giuseppe Commano (Timagenes). *Poro* had a highly successful run of 16 performances in 1731. Handel revived it twice. For the first revival of 23 December 1731 the ineffective Commano (who had been given no arias) was replaced by the distinguished bass Antonio Montagnana as Timagenes, for whom three arias from earlier Handel operas were added. More extensive revisions were made for the revival at Covent Garden on 8 December 1736, when the mezzo-soprano castrato Domenico Annibali took over the title role and was allowed to include two arias by Ristori and one by Vinci; Alexander was sung by the soprano castrato Conti and Gandartes by the tenor John Beard. Meanwhile, a version prepared by Telemann and translated by C. G. Wendt as *Triumph der Grossmuth und Treue, oder Cleofide, Koenigen von Indien* had been performed in Hamburg on 25 August 1732 and subsequently to 1736, and there was another revival at Brunswick in August 1732 under the title *Poro ed Alessandro*. The first modern revival, in a version by H. Dütschke, was on 21 April 1928, also at Brunswick. Unicorn Opera gave the first modern British production, at the Watermill Theatre, Bagnor (near Newbury), on 11 September 1966, and subsequently at Abingdon and Claydon House.

ACT 1 The action takes place on the banks of the Hydaspes (the Jhelum) during Alexander the Great's Indian campaign. Alexander's troops have defeated the army of the Indian king Porus. Porus decides to kill himself, believing that Alexander will win over his beloved Cleophis; but his general Gandartes tells him to fight on in disguise, and he and Porus exchange helmets. Porus, arrested by Alexander and his general Timagenes, tells them he is a chieftain, Asbites, loyal to Porus. Impressed by his bold spirit, Alexander orders him to return to his master and obtain his acknowledgment of defeat. He gives Porus the sword of Darius as safe conduct. Porus's sister Eryxene (betrothed to Gandartes) is brought as a prisoner to Alexander, who is angry with her captors and orders her release. Timagenes, who secretly seeks revenge on Alexander for the killing of his father, makes ineffectual advances to her.

In the garden of her palace, Cleophis assures Porus that it is for his benefit she feigns affection for Alexander; Porus swears not to be jealous. Eryxene arrives, full of praise for Alexander. Cleophis announces she will seek an audience with Alexander and appear submissive; she reassures Porus by swearing fidelity. Gandartes tries to calm Porus's renewed jealousy and tells him of Timagenes' hatred of Alexander. Eryxene annoys Gandartes by hinting that she is attracted by Alexander.

In a garden, Alexander receives Cleophis and her retinue and is captivated by her charms. Porus appears, disguised, his jealousy once more aroused, and declares that Porus refuses to submit to Alexander; he goes on to accuse Cleophis of treachery. Alexander says he can be an ally only of Cleophis, not of her lover. Porus and Cleophis quarrel, each sarcastically quoting the other's earlier vow.

ACT 2 Alexander's Macedonian troops cross the river Hydaspes and are met by Cleophis; they are attacked by a rebel force of Indians, led by Porus, who however are driven back. Gandartes destroys the bridge and escapes with the rest of the Indians into the river. Porus accuses Cleophis again, but her threat to drown herself persuades him of her fidelity. Rather than allow her to be taken prisoner, he prepares to kill her, but Alexander intervenes. Cleophis prevents Porus from revealing his identity. Timagenes reports that the Macedonians are demanding Cleophis's death, believing her responsible for the Indian revolt. Alexander assures her of his protection and puts Porus into Timagenes' custody. Porus (still as Asbites) accuses Timagenes of breaking his promise to support the Indians. Timagenes replies by releasing his prisoner, with a letter assuring Porus of aid; meanwhile Timagenes will report Asbites' death.

In Cleophis's palace, Alexander tells the queen he has not convinced the Macedonians of her innocence and offers to protect her by marrying her. Gandartes comes forward, claiming to be Porus and taking blame for the revolt: Asbites and Cleophis are innocent, he says. Not to be outdone in virtue by a barbarian, Alexander resigns Cleophis to the supposed Porus. The joy of Cleophis and Gandartes swiftly vanishes as Eryxene brings news that Porus has drowned in the Hydaspes. Cleophis grieves but Gandartes and Eryxene take comfort in their love.

ACT 3 In a garden, Porus explains to Eryxene that the report of his death was put about to delude Alexander; he makes her promise not to tell Cleophis he is alive; she is to instruct Timagenes to bring Alexander to the garden, where Porus will kill him. Cleophis tells Alexander that she will now accept his offer of marriage; delighted, he tells her to await him at the temple. Alexander returns, angry at some treachery; Eryxene produces Timagenes' letter to Porus, proving him the traitor, but Alexander pardons Timagenes when the latter shows remorse. Porus, in hiding, overhears; distraught, he orders Gandartes to kill him. Gandartes turns the sword on himself, but is stopped by Eryxene with news of Cleophis's impending marriage.

In the temple of Bacchus a scented fire is lit. As Alexander approaches Cleophis, Porus, in hiding, prepares to stab him, but is forestalled as Cleophis announces her intention of joining Porus in death. Porus, overjoyed at this proof of her fidelity, is brought forward by Timagenes: Alexander declares him worthy of a crown and grants him freedom to marry Cleophis. Gandartes may marry Eryxene and is given the lands beyond the Ganges conquered by Alexander.

*   *   *

The personal and national confrontations in *Poro* give it considerable dramatic power, which the music sometimes reinforces and sometimes complements. In the latter category are the reflective simile arias 'Senza procelle ancora' for Porus in Act 2, with its echoing horns and recorders, and 'Son confusa pastorella' for Eryxene in Act 3; the languorous pastoral style of the latter brings new calm to an otherwise mercurial character allotted several brisk songs with thin orchestral texture. The excessively magnanimous Alexander is portrayed mainly in soft-grained arias of an amorous nature, but gains heroic status in his final number ('Serbati a grandi imprese'). Porus's jealous and fiery nature perhaps emerges more strongly in recitative than his arias, but Cleophis's noble suffering is finely expressed in all her music, most notably in the prayer 'Spirto amato' as she prepares for immolation. The Act 1 duet, in which the material of two previous songs is quoted and extended with new material, and the linking of the final duet and chorus, add to the variety of a richly inventive score.

For a page from the autograph score, *see* HANDEL, GEORGE FRIDERIC, fig.2.   ANTHONY HICKS

Porpora, Nicola (Antonio) (*b* Naples, 17 Aug 1686; *d* Naples, 3 March 1768). Italian composer and teacher. He was internationally famous during his lifetime both for his vocal music and opera and as a singing teacher.

1. LIFE. Nicola Porpora was the third son of Carlo Porpora, a Neapolitan bookseller, who placed him in the Conservatorio dei Poveri di Gesù Cristo on 29 September 1696. The boy stayed there about ten years. For the first three he paid for his education and upkeep but thereafter was maintained free of charge (the conservatory gave free places to its best music students and by 1699 probably considered him among them). His first important commission after leaving the Gesù Cristo was for an opera, *Agrippina*, performed in the Neapolitan Royal Palace on 4 November 1708. Commissions for further major works came to him slowly at first. *Flavio Anicio Olibrio*, his second opera, was performed in Naples in 1711, and *Basilio re d'oriente*, his third, in 1713. The libretto of *Flavio* calls him *maestro di cappella* to the Prince of Hesse-Darmstadt; that of *Basilio* names him *maestro di cappella* to the Portuguese ambassador. Of these, the Prince of Hesse-Darmstadt played the more important role in Porpora's career. Walker has suggested that the prince may have been responsible for securing the operatic commission Porpora received from the Viennese court in 1714; the work concerned was *Arianna e Teseo*, performed in Vienna on 1 October (the emperor's birthday). For a while Porpora enjoyed considerable favour both at the imperial court in Vienna and at the viceregal court in Naples. His opera *Temistocle* was presented in Vienna on 1 October 1718, his opera *Faramondo* in Naples on 19 November 1719 (the empress's name-day), his serenata *Angelica* in Naples on the emperor's birthday, 1720 (repeated in Vienna the same year on the empress's name-day and in Naples again on 28 August 1722, the empress's birthday), and his serenata *Gli orti esperidi* was given in Naples on the empress's birthday in 1721. The texts of both serenatas were by a young poet who was to become the greatest librettist of the century, Pietro Metastasio; *Angelica* was his first important poem intended for musical setting. One of Porpora's singing pupils, the later much-famed castrato Farinelli, made his début in this same work. By this time Porpora was beginning to make his mark as a teacher. Between April 1715 and the end of December 1721 he served as *maestro di cappella* (i.e. chief teacher of singing and composition) at the Neapolitan Conservatorio di S Onofrio. From his private singing classes there emerged

around this period both Farinelli and the equally renowned castrato Caffarelli (who made his début in 1726). Another student with whom Porpora came into contact was the future composer Johann Adolf Hasse. When Hasse reached Naples from Germany in 1722, he took a few lessons from Porpora before deciding to study under Alessandro Scarlatti.

Porpora had to wait until the 1720s before acquiring popularity as a composer in Rome and northern Italy. The first Roman opera with which he was associated was in fact a joint venture, *Berenice regina d'Egitto*, produced at the Capranica theatre, Rome, in 1718 with music by Porpora and by Domenico Scarlatti. *Eumene*, his first complete opera for a Roman audience, was performed at the Alibert theatre in 1721, and must have been a success for he was invited to produce further operas for the theatre in 1722 and 1723. In 1725 he was for the first time active in northern Italy, providing an opera and an oratorio for Milan and an opera for Reggio Emilia. Fétis claimed to have seen an autograph letter proving that Porpora was also in Vienna that year. In 1726 he settled in Venice, where he was appointed *maestro* to the girl students of the Ospedale degli Incurabili, where he stayed until 1733. In March that year he made an unsuccessful attempt to gain the post of *maestro di cappella* at St Mark's in Venice. Some time during the summer or early autumn he resigned from the Incurabili and travelled to London.

Porpora's invitation to London came from a group of English noblemen who were setting up an opera company, now known as the 'Opera of the Nobility', in competition with the existing Italian opera company in England under Handel. The Opera of the Nobility opened its first season on 29 December 1733 with the première of a new opera by Porpora, *Arianna in Nasso*. Over the next two and a half years he composed four more operas, an oratorio, a serenata and items for three pasticcios, all for this company. In spite of the fact that he had with him one of the finest teams of Italian singers then assembled (it included the castrato Senesino, the soprano Cuzzoni, and from October 1734 Farinelli as well), Porpora and the Opera of the Nobility did not establish a clear superiority over Handel's rival concern. His last work written in London was the serenata *La festa d'Imeneo*, given four times between 4 May and 15 May 1736 in honour of the marriage of the Prince of Wales. Later that summer he left England: perhaps he already foresaw that the two rival companies could not be supported indefinitely by the London public (and in fact both closed for lack of money the following year). Porpora meanwhile returned to Venice where, about February or March of 1737, he took up his old post of *maestro* of the Incurabili on a temporary basis. The permanent holder of the post by this time was Hasse, who was away from Venice for most of 1737 and 1738 (he was Kapellmeister to the Saxon court at Dresden and had duties there). It seems that Porpora stayed at the Incurabili until about September 1738 when Hasse returned to Venice.

Porpora next moved to Naples, where he arrived on 11 October. On 1 July 1739 he was appointed *maestro di cappella* at the Neapolitan Conservatorio di S Maria di Loreto. His opportunities to teach and compose in Naples were many, but he had been there barely three years when he was seized once more with a desire to travel and change jobs. On 6 October 1741 the Loreto governors gave him leave to go to Venice to fulfil an operatic commission. Once in Venice however he ignored his obligations to the Neapolitans and on 26 January 1742 accepted the post of *maestro di coro* at the Venetian Ospedale della Pietà for the particularly handsome annual salary of 500 ducats. For some unknown reason he asked leave to resign from the Pietà on 15 February 1743, and thereafter gave his services to another of the Venetian musical establishments for young ladies, the Ospedaletto. While there he applied unsuccessfully for the post of *maestro di cappella* at the Neapolitan court. He was still working at the Ospedaletto in June 1746 – a manuscript of his *Laudate pueri* (*GB-Lbl*) written for the girls there is so dated. But in 1747 he was on the move again, this time to Dresden.

From 1747 to 1751 Porpora was in Dresden as singing teacher to the Electoral Princess Maria Antonia. For her 23rd birthday (18 July 1747) he composed the opera *Filandro*, produced in the electoral theatre under Hasse's direction. It was the only opera he composed during his stay in Saxony. His time there is said to have been soured by an unfortunate rivalry that developed between his soprano pupil, Regina Mingotti, and the famous though by this time aging soprano Faustina Bordoni, Hasse's wife. Both singers were in the cast of *Filandro*. Porpora was made court Kapellmeister on 13 April 1748 with an annual salary of 1200 thalers. The appointment was 'until further notice', and may temporarily have seemed to undermine Hasse's position as chief musician at court. In 1750, however, Hasse was created Ober-Kapellmeister and so maintained his superior position. At the end of 1751 Porpora's salary ceased and in its place, from 1 January 1752, he was awarded a state pension of 400 thalers a year. Some time during 1752 or at the beginning of 1753 he moved to Vienna: this is clear from two letters of Metastasio, who had been Viennese court poet since 1730, to Farinelli (15 February and 17 March 1753), which show that, on Farinelli's suggestion, Metastasio had considered handing Porpora his new libretto *L'isola disabitata* to set, but had then, in March, changed his mind when Porpora became ill. Porpora afterwards gave singing lessons in Vienna to Wilhelmine, mistress of Pietro Correr, the Venetian ambassador, and also to Marianna Martinez, Metastasio's protégée. Metastasio was probably responsible, directly or indirectly, for the first meeting between Porpora and the young Joseph Haydn. In the mid-1750s Haydn lived in an attic of the Michaelerhaus in Vienna where Metastasio also lived. He became Porpora's valet, pupil and keyboard accompanist during his master's singing lessons. All that is known about the relationship between them comes from Haydn's autobiographical sketch. In it he made clear what he owed to Porpora: 'I wrote fluently, but not wholly correctly, until I had the good fortune to learn the true foundations of composition from the celebrated Porpora who was in Vienna at that time'.

Porpora's financial position in Vienna, which was never very sound, became precarious after the start of the Seven Years War in 1756 and the invasion of Saxony by Prussia. By 1759 his Saxon pension had stopped and he must have made some intimation to his acquaintances in Naples that he wanted to return there. In 1759 the governors of the Conservatorio di S Maria di Loreto, where he had served from 1739 to 1741, elected him 'another *maestro di cappella*' to join the two *maestri* already serving; Porpora took up his responsibilities at the Loreto on 10 April 1760 and shortly after was invited to compose an opera to open at the S Carlo theatre on 30 May. This, his last opera, *Il trionfo di Camilla*, was a revision of an earlier opera of his heard at the same theatre in 1740, and was not a success. When the death of Abos in September 1760 created a vacancy for *maestro* at the Conservatorio di S Onofrio, the post was given to Porpora. The next year, however, he resigned from both his teaching appointments, leaving the Loreto on 30 April and the S Onofrio in September. His final years of retirement were spent in considerable poverty.

2. WORKS. Though Porpora wrote several instrumental works, his output in this field was small by comparison with that of his vocal works. These can be classified under the headings of secular operas, sacred operas and oratorios, secular serenatas and cantatas, other sacred compositions, *solfeggi* and other didactic pieces; the secular operas make up the largest and most important category. Though he wrote his first opera as early as 1708, he only gradually acquired sufficient fame to be constantly in demand as an opera composer. His great period of operatic composition occurred between 1718 and 1742, after which his popularity among theatre audiences declined.

Musical taste in Italy changed considerably during the first years that he was active as a composer. Styles emphasizing melody with a simple homophonic accompaniment (usually for full strings and continuo) came into fashion, and vocal melody acquired both more lyrical, lilting qualities and, at times, more decorative ornament. The development of Porpora's own style ran parallel with this general trend, and it may be argued that he was one of the composers chiefly responsible for the trend towards more embellishment in vocal melody. Being a great singing teacher, he understood as well as anyone the capabilities of the voice, and he exploited its range and flexibility in passages that were unusually florid and sustained. This deep understanding of the art of singing had its drawbacks, for there are signs in his operas of the 1720s and early 1730s that he came to rely too heavily on the ability of singers to sustain the musical interest through virtuoso display. He made little attempt at this stage of his career to strive for variety in his arias (the da capo structure was the norm), and he rarely applied unusual procedures for the sake of dramatic impact. To some extent this attitude changed when he arrived in London in 1733. Faced with competition from Handel, who had an uncommon flair for making opera theatrically effective, Porpora sharpened his powers of characterization: he aimed for more attractive melody, became more willing to vary the da capo formula of the arias, and made much more extensive use of accompanied recitative than hitherto. This stimulant to his ingenuity was no longer present, however, once he returned to Italy in 1736, and his last operas show a slow decline in his compositional powers and a return to conventionality.

See also ARIANNA IN NASSO and SEMIRAMIDE RICONOSCIUTA.

unless otherwise stated, opere serie, music lost

Agrippina (3, N. Giuvo), Naples, Palazzo Reale, 4 Nov 1708, arias *I-Mc, Nc*; with Armilla e Planco (int)

Flavio Anicio Olibrio (3, A. Zeno and P. Pariati), Naples, S Bartolomeo, Jan 1711, Acts 1 and 2 *GB-Lbl**; with Liso e Perletta (int)

Composizione drammatica [title unknown], Naples, palace of the Prince of Hesse-Darmstadt, Nov 1711

Serenata a 3 [Deianira, Iole, Ercole], 1712, *A-Wn*

Basilio re d'oriente (after G. Neri), Naples, Fiorentini, 24 June 1713; with Dorilla e Nesso (int)

Arianna e Teseo [1st version] (Pariati), Vienna, Hof, 1 Oct 1714

Berenice regina d'Egitto, overo le gare di amore, e di politica [Act 3, part of Act 2] (3, A. Salvi), Rome, Capranica, carn. 1718; with Menenio e Sibillina (int) [Act 1 and part of Act 2 by D. Scarlatti]

Temistocle (3, Zeno), Vienna, Hof, 1 Oct 1718

Faramondo, Naples, S Bartolomeo, 19 Nov 1719; with Merillo e Gilbo (int)

Angelica (serenata a 6, P. Metastasio), Naples, Palazzo del Principe di Torella, 28 Aug 1720, Wn, GB-Lbl*

Eumene (Zeno), Rome, Alibert, carn. 1721, arias F-Pc, I-Rc; with Dorilla e Nesso (int)

Gli orti esperidi (serenata a 5, Metastasio), Naples, Palazzo Reale, 28 Aug 1721, GB-Lbl*

Flavio Anicio Olibrio (3, Zeno and Pariati), Rome, Alibert, carn. 1722, arias in B-Bc and F-Pc

Adelaide (Salvi), Rome, Alibert, carn. 1723, D-SWl, arias in D-Hs, MÜs and F-Pc

Amare per regnare (after F. Passarini: Amore e fortunata), Naples, S Bartolomeo, 12 Dec 1723; arias in GB-Lbl and I-Gl; with Besso e Fiordilina (int)

Imeneo (2, componimento drammatico, S. Stampiglia), Naples, 1723, D-Dlb; rev. as Imeneo in Atene, Venice, S Samuele, 1726, Dlb, F-Pn; rev. as Giasone, Naples, 23 April 1732, I-MC

Semiramide regina dell'Assiria (3, after I. Zanelli: Nino), Naples, S Bartolomeo, spr. 1724, 2 arias MC, arias B-Bc, GB-Lcm, I-Nc

Damiro e Pitia, overo Le gare dell'amicitia, e dell'amore (D. Lalli), Munich, 12 Oct 1724

Didone abbandonata (3, Metastasio), Reggio Emilia, Pubblico, Ascension 1725, Acts 2 and 3 GB-Lbl*

Siface (3, Metastasio), Milan, Ducale, 26 Dec 1725; rev. Venice, S Giovanni Grisostomo, carn. 1726, B-Bc, Acts 1 and 3 GB-Lbl*; rev. Rome, Capranica, 7 Feb 1730, B-Bc*, Br, GB-CDp, arias Lcm

La verità nell'inganno (3, F. Silvani), Milan, Regio Ducal, carn. 1726, arias D-SWl, F-Pn, GB-Lbl

Meride e Selinunte (3, Zeno), Venice, S Giovanni Grisostomo, carn. 1726, B-Bc, Br, GB-Lam, Lbl, copy US-Wc, arias GB-Lbl, I-Vnm

Siroe re di Persia (3, Metastasio), Rome, Dame, Feb 1727, arias D-MEIr, F-Pn, GB-Lcm, I-Rsc

Arianna e Teseo [2nd version] (3, Pariati), Venice, S Giovanni Grisostomo, aut. 1727, Act 2 GB-Lbl*, Act 2 copy US-Wc, arias GB-Cfm

Ezio (3, Metastasio ? and Lalli), Venice, S Giovanni Grisostomo, 20 Nov 1728, B-Bc, GB-Lam

Semiramide riconosciuta (3, Metastasio, rev. ?Lalli), Venice, S Giovanni Grisostomo, carn. 1729, Lam, Acts 1 and 2 I-MC, copy US-Wc, arias GB-Lcm; rev. version, Naples, S Carlo, 20 Jan 1739, D-Dlb (R1977: IOB, xxx), I-Nc

Ermenegildo, Naples, 1729 [according to Mondolfi]

Mitridate (3, Zeno and F. Vanstryp), Rome, Capranica, carn. 1730, B-Bc, Br, copy US-Wc

Tamerlano (3, A. Piovene), Turin, Regio, carn. 1730, arias F-Pn, I-Rsc, US-BE

Poro (3, after Metastasio: Alessandro nell'Indie), Turin, Regio, carn. 1731, arias D-B, Dlb, I-PAc

Annibale (3, Vanstryp), Venice, S Angelo, aut. 1731, B-Bc, copy US-Wc

Germanico in Germania (2, N. Coluzzi), Rome, Capranica, Feb 1732, arias B-Bc, 2 copies GB-Lbl, Lcm, Ob, I-Rsc, sinfonia D-Hs

Componimento per musica [title unknown] (G. Lemer), Rome, 28 Aug 1732

Issipile (3, Metastasio), Rome, Rucellai, carn. 1733, Act 1 I-Mc, arias GB-Lcm, Ob

Arianna in Nasso (3, P. A. Rolli), London, Lincoln's Inn Fields, 29 Dec 1733, A-Wgm, Wn, 2 copies GB-Lbl, copy US-Wc, Favourite Songs (London, 1734)

Enea nel Lazio (3, Rolli), London, Lincoln's Inn Fields, 11 May 1734, GB-Lbl

Polifemo (3, Rolli), London, King's, 1 Feb 1735, Lbl, Act 3 Lbl*, Favourite Songs (London, 1735)

Ifigenia in Aulide (3, Rolli, after Zeno), London, King's, 3 May 1735, Lbl, Act 2 Lbl*

Mitridate (3, G. da Gavardo [C. Cibber]), London, King's, 24 Jan 1736, B-Bc, Acts 2 and 3 GB-Lbl*

La festa d'Imeneo (componimento drammatico, Rolli), London, King's, 4 May 1736, 2 copies (1 autograph) Lbl

Lucio Papirio (3, Salvi, rev. G. Boldoni), Venice, S Cassiano, carn. 1737, 21 arias A-Wn

Rosbale (3, after C. N. Stampa: Eumene), Venice, S Giovanni Grisostomo, aut. 1737, Act 3 GB-Lbl*

Carlo il calvo (3), Rome, Dame, spr. 1738, I-Nc, sinfonia, 14 arias,

---

1 duet GB-Lcm

Il barone di Zampano (comic op, P. Trinchera), Naples, Nuovo, spr. 1739

L'amico fedele (comic op, G. di Pietro), Naples, Fiorentini, aut. 1739

Intermezzo for the marriage of the Infante D. Filippo, Madrid, 1739

Il trionfo di Camilla [1st version] (Stampiglia), Naples, S Carlo, 20 Jan 1740, ?D-Dlb

Tiridate (3, after Metastasio: Zenobia), Naples, S Carlo, 19 Dec 1740

Il trionfo del valore (comedia per musica, A. Palomba), Naples, Nuovo, wint. 1741, lib. GB-Lbl, I-Rn, collab. G. di Domenico, A. Palella and G. Signorille

Giasone (?serenata), Naples, 1742, MC

Statira (3, Silvani), Venice, S Giovanni Grisostomo, carn. 1742, D-B, Dlb

Partenope, Naples, 1742 [according to Mondolfi]

La Rosmene (3), Vienna, 1742, GB-Lbl

Temistocle (3, Metastasio), London, Haymarket, 22 Feb 1743, A-Wn, Favourite Songs (London, 1743)

Le nozze d'Ercole e d'Ebe, Venice, S Giovanni Grisostomo, carn. 1744

Filandro-Philander (3, V. Cassani: L'incostanza schernita), Dresden, Hof, 18 July 1747, D-B, Dlb

Il trionfo di Camilla [2nd version] (Stampiglia, rev. G. Lorenzi), Naples, S Carlo, 30 May 1760, Acts 1 and 3 GB-Lbl*

Tolomeo re d'Egitto (3), I-Nc

Il trionfo di Camilla [? 3rd version], US-Wc

Music in: Artaserse (1721)

*

MGG (A. Mondolfi)

G. Carpani: Le Haydine, ossia Lettere sulla vita e sulle opere di G. Haydn (Milan, 1812)

M. Fürstenau: Zur Geschichte der Musik und des Theaters am Hofe zu Dresden (Dresden, 1861–2)

S. Fassini: Il melodramma italiano a Londra nella prima metà del settecento (Turin, 1914)

F. Walker: 'A Chronology of the Life and Works of Nicola Porpora', Italian Studies, vi (1951), 29–62

U. Prota-Giurleo: 'Per una esatta biografia di Nicolò Porpora', La Scala, lxxxvi (1957), 21–9

M. F. Robinson: 'Porpora's Operas for London, 1733–1736', Soundings, ii (1971–2), 57–87

——: 'The Governors' Minutes of the Conservatory S Maria di Loreto, Naples', RMARC, no.10 (1972), 39, 43–5, 47, 94

E. L. Sutton: The Solo Vocal Works of Nicola Porpora: an Annotated Thematic Index (diss., U. of Minnesota, 1974)

R. Strohm: Italienische Opernarien des frühen Settecento, AnMc, no.16 (1976), 200–08

M. F. Robinson: 'How to Demonstrate Virtue: the Case of Porpora's Two Settings of Mitridate', Studies in Music at the University of Western Ontario, vii (1982), 47–64

MICHAEL F. ROBINSON (text, bibliography)
DALE E. MONSON (work-list)

Porrino, Ennio (b Cagliari, 20 Jan 1910; d Rome, 25 Sept 1959). Italian composer. He studied the violin privately and composition with Dobici and Mulè at the S Cecilia conservatory in Rome, graduating in 1932. He then spent three years studying with Respighi, whose influence was decisive and whose last, unfinished opera, Lucrezia, he completed in collaboration with Respighi's widow, Elsa. He taught at the Rome and Naples conservatories and directed the Cagliari conservatory from 1956 until his death. Porrino enthusiastically supported the Fascist regime, some of whose exponents, including Mussolini, granted him awards, subsidies and performances. In his published writings of the 1930s he declared his aversion to 'internationalist and Bolshevist' tendencies, and his most significant opera, Gli Orazi (1941), is based on a cliché-ridden story that exalts the severe virility of ancient Rome, one of Mussolini's chief fixations. After World War II Porrino experimented with more advanced compositional techniques, including the 12-note system. Like Gli Orazi, however, his later operas and other works are rarely performed.

Gli Orazi (1, C. Guastalla), Milan, Scala, 1 Feb 1941
L'organo di bambù (1, G. Artieri), Venice, Fenice, 23 Sept 1955
Hutalabì (3, Porrino), RAI, Turin, 4 April 1956; stage, rev., as I
    Shardana (lyric drama, 3, Porrino), Naples, S Carlo, 21 March
    1959
Esculapio al neon (theatrical and musical fantasy, 1, L. Folgore),
    RAI, 3 Aug 1966; stage, Cagliari, Istituzione Concerti e Teatro
    Lirico G. Pierluigi da Palestrina, 25 Feb 1982   HARVEY SACHS

Porsile [Persile, Porcile, Porsille], **Giuseppe** (*b* Naples, 5
May 1680; *d* Vienna, 29 May 1750). Italian composer.
He was the son of the musician Carlo Porsile, whose
opera *Nerone* was produced, according to Burney, at
Naples in 1686. Giuseppe was a pupil of Ursino,
Giordano and Greco at the Conservatorio dei Poveri di
Gesù Cristo in Naples. At first he held an appointment
as vice-*maestro di cappella* at the Spanish chapel in
Naples, but in 1695 he was called to Spain by Charles II
(who died in 1700) to organize the music chapel at
Barcelona. He remained there under Charles III, the
Habsburg contender to the Spanish throne, and served
as singing-master to Charles's wife Elisabeth Christina.
To what extent he was also active as a teacher and
composer in Naples before 1713 remains unclear, but
his early opera *Il ritorno di Ulisse* was produced there in
1707.

At the end of 1711 Charles III returned to Vienna,
becoming Charles VI, Holy Roman Emperor. Porsile
remained at Barcelona in the service of Elisabeth until
the end of 1713; he then went to Vienna as singing-
master to the empress. While awaiting a more substantial appointment he served as *attuario di camera*.
On 17 December 1720 he succeeded Gregorio Genuesi
as court composer.

Between 1717 and 1737 Porsile produced at least 21
secular dramatic works and 13 oratorios for the Habsburg court. Only a few works received performances
outside Austria, in cities such as Venice and Prague.
During 1725–7 he was active as a member of the
Viennese Caecilien-Brüderschaft, whose deans were Fux
and Caldara. After the death of Charles VI in 1740 he
continued to receive an honorary stipend and was
awarded a final pension on 1 April 1749.

Burney indicated that Porsile's music was greatly
admired by Zeno and by Hasse, whose wife, the
celebrated soprano Faustina Bordoni, sang the role of
Gianisbe in Porsile's *Spartaco* in Vienna in February
1726, shortly before she went to London. In a report to
the emperor in 1715, Fux described Porsile as 'ein guter
Virtuose von gutten Gusto'.

Porsile belongs to the first group of late Baroque
Neapolitan composers. He was probably the only
composer from Naples to receive a prominent post at
Vienna during the Baroque era. His ability to write in a
strict contrapuntal style probably accounts in part for
his acceptance at the Habsburg court, which was largely
dominated by the more conservative north Italian
school. His melodic, harmonic and cadential patterns
contain numerous examples of the formulae typical of
his generation, but his arias also include some expressive
cantabile writing, an avoidance of excessive coloratura
and frequent imitative passages. His assimilation of the
musical techniques preferred in Vienna is reflected by his
frequent use of the French overture, but for *Spartaco* he
adopted the tripartite structure of the Italian *sinfonia*:
an agitated Allegro propelled by motoric rhythms, an
expressive Adagio in pathetic style, and a concluding
binary dance in 3/8. Within the limits of the standard
Viennese orchestra of the period (first and second violins

doubled by oboes, violas and continuo, including
bassoons) there are many subtle colouristic details. In
Spartaco, for example, we find passages marked *senza
oboe* or *senza cembalo*; the intertwining of soprano and
violins without any bass instruments; the interplay of
tenor and obbligato bassoon; and a dazzling trumpet
obbligato in the final score. Although Porsile's music is
overshadowed by that of his Viennese contemporaries,
Fux and Caldara, its fusion of Neapolitan and north
Italian elements was an important ingredient in the
development of pre-Classical style in Vienna.

See also SPARTACO.

first performed in Vienna unless otherwise stated

Il ritorno di Ulisse alla patria (3, G. A. Moniglia), Naples, Fiorentini,
    1707, *I-Rn*, 40 arias and duets *Nc*
Il giorno natalizio dell'imperatrice Amalia Wilhelmina (P. Pariati),
    21 April 1717, *A-Wgm*, *D-Dlb*
La Virtù festeggiata (Pariati), 10 July 1717, *A-Wgm*
Alceste (festa teatrale, Pariati), 19 Nov 1718, *Wgm*, *Wn*
Meride e Selinunte (dramma per musica, 5, A. Zeno), Neue
    Favorita, 28 Aug 1721, *Wgm*, *Wn*, *D-Dlb*
Il tempo fermato (componimento da camera), 15 Oct 1721, *A-Wn*
La Virtù e la Bellezza in lega (serenata), Grosses Hof, 15 Oct 1722,
    Wn
Il giorno felice (componimento da camera, Pariati), 28 Aug 1723,
    Wgm, *Wn*
Spartaco (dramma per musica, 3, G. C. Pasquini), Kleines Hof, 21
    Feb 1726, *Wgm*, *Wn*/R1979: IOB, xxviii, 1 aria *F-Pn*; lib. *US-
    Wc*/R1978: IOB, ix
Il tempio di Giano, chiuso da Cesare Augusto (componimento per
    musica, Pasquini), Neue Favorita, 1 Oct 1726, *A-Wgm*, *Wn*
La clemenza di Cesare (servizio di camera, Pasquini), Neue Favorita,
    1 Oct 1727, *Wgm*, *Wn*
Telesilla (festa teatrale, Pasquini), 19 Nov 1729, *Wgm*, *Wn*
Scipione Africano, il maggiore (festa di camera, Pasquini), Neue
    Favorita, 1 Oct 1730, *Wgm*, *Wn*
La Fama accresciuta dalla Virtù (festa di camera, Pasquini), 15 Oct
    1735, *Wgm*, *Wn*
Sesostri, re d'Egitto, ovvero Le feste d'Iside (dramma per musica, 5),
    carn. 1737, *Wn*
Il giudizio rivocato (festa di camera, Pasquini), 15 Oct 1737, *Wgm*,
    Wn
Psiche (dramma per musica, 3), *D-Dlb*, *US-Wc*

Doubtful: Osmeno e Fileno (dialoghetto), after 1712, *A-Wn*, attrib.
    Porsile or Caldara

Arias: 7 in *A-Wn*, 2 in *B-Bc*, 1 in *D-Dlb*, 1 in *F-Pn*, 3 in *GB-Lbl*,
    ?several in *I-Pca*, 1 in *US-CA*

AllacciD
L. von Köchel: *Die kaiserliche Hof-Musikkapelle in Wien von
    1543–1867* (Vienna, 1869)
La Mara [M. Lipsius]: 'Briefe alter Wiener Hofmusiker', *Musikbuch
    aus Österreich*, vii (1910), 3
P. Nettl: 'Opernaufführung zu Znaim anno 1723', *Beiträge zur
    böhmischen und mährischen Musikgeschichte* (Brno, 1927),
    14–17
U. Manferrari: *Dizionario universale delle opere melodrammatiche*
    (Florence, 1954–5)
F. Hadamowsky: 'Barocktheater am Wiener Kaiserhof', mit einem
    Spielplan (1625–1740), *Jb der Gesellschaft für Wiener
    Theaterforschung 1951–2* (1955), 7–117
U. Prota-Giurleo: 'Giuseppe Porsile e la Real cappella di Barcellona',
    Gazzetta musicale di Napoli, ii (1956), 160–66
R. Brockpähler: *Handbuch zur Geschichte der Barockoper in
    Deutschland* (Emsdetten, 1964)
A. D. McCredie: 'Nicholas Matteis – English Composer at the
    Habsburg Court', *ML*, xlviii (1967), 127–37
O. E. Deutsch: 'Das Repertoire der höfischen Oper, der Hof- und
    der Staatsoper', *ÖMz*, xxiv (1969), 369–421
M. F. Robinson: *Naples and Neapolitan Opera* (Oxford, 1972)
R. Strohm: *Italienische Opernarien des frühen Settecento:
    1720–1730, AnMc*, no.16 (1976)   LAWRENCE E. BENNETT

Porta, Bernardo (*b* Rome, 1758; *d* Paris, 11 June 1829).
Italian composer, active in France. He began his career

as *maestro di cappella* and director of the orchestra at Tivoli, and then moved into the service of the Prince of Salm, the prelate for Rome. In Italy he wrote masses, motets, two oratorios and the opera *La principessa d'Amalfi*, which was produced with little success in Rome (1780). It has commonly been reported that he went to Paris in 1790 when his *opéra comique Le diable à quatre* was badly received at the Opéra-Comique, but he may have been there as early as 1785; he remained in Paris for the rest of his career. Among his many stage works performed there were *Les Horaces* (1800) and *Le connétable de Clisson* (1804); the latter had little success and earned its composer a satirical vengeful song. He taught harmony in various private establishments until 1822. Much of his instrumental music was intended for beginners.

first performed in Paris unless otherwise stated

La principessa d'Amalfi, Rome, Argentina, 1780
Le diable à quatre, ou La double metamorphose (oc, 3, M.-J. Sedaine), OC (Favart), 14 Feb 1790
Pagamin, ou Le calendrier des vieillards (opéra italien), Louvois, 29 March 1792
La blanche Haquenée (oc, Sedaine), OC (Favart), 24 May 1793
Alexis et Rosette, ou Les Huhlans [Houlans] (pièce républicaine, 1, P. Desriaux), Théâtre Français Comique et Lyrique, 3 Aug 1793
La réunion du 10 août, ou L'inauguration de la République française (sans-culottide dramatique, 5, G. Bouquier and P.-L. Moline), Opéra, 5 April 1794, excerpts (Paris, 1794)
Agricole Viala, ou Le héros de 13 ans (oc, 1, Audouin), OC (Favart), 1 July 1794, excerpts (Paris, 1793)
Le pauvre aveugle, ou La chanson savoyarde (oc, 1, J. B. Hapdé and F.-A. D. Philidor), Ambigu-Comique, 24 July 1797
L'oracle (oc, 1, Desriaux), Ambigu-Comique, 1797
Le prisonnier français, ou Le bienfait récompensé (drame historique, 1), Amis des Arts, 2 Oct 1798 (Paris, 1798)
Deux morts qui se volent (oc, 1, Dorvigny), Ambigu-Comique, 26 April 1800
Les deux statues (oc, 1, Milcent), Ambigu-Comique, 29 April 1800
Les Horaces (tragédie lyrique, 3, N.-F. Guillard), Opéra, 18 Oct 1800, F-Po
Le vieux de la montagne, 1802, inc., unperf., Po
Le connétable de Clisson (opéra, 3, E. Aignan), Opéra, 9 or 10 Feb 1804 (Paris, 1804)   PAULETTE LETAILLEUR

Porta, Giovanni (*b* Venice or the Veneto, *c*1675; *d* Munich, 21 June 1755). Italian composer. From 1706 to 1710 he is supposed to have been at Cardinal Ottoboni's household in Rome, where he would have worked under Corelli. He held the post of *maestro di cappella* at Vicenza Cathedral in 1710–11, and at Verona Cathedral in 1714–16. In 1716 he returned to Venice for a busy period of operatic activity beginning with *La costanza combattuta in amore* at the S Moisè theatre. He was also a pupil of Francesco Gasparini at this time and collaborated with him and another pupil on *Il Trace in catena* (1717). Porta was commissioned by the Royal Academy of Music in London to write the opera *Numitore*, which opened the first season on 2 April 1720 and was subsequently published; he is cited on the title-page of the libretto as a 'virtuoso' in the service of the Duke of Wharton (Handel drew on *Numitore* for many important melodic ideas). From 1726 to 1737 Porta was *maestro di coro* at the Ospedale della Pietà in Venice, where, as a contemporary of Vivaldi, he wrote a wealth of sacred vocal music for the female chorus and orchestra of the Pietà. From 1726 he was also included on the roster of the Accademia Filarmonica in Verona. In 1733 he applied for the post of *maestro di composizione* at the Ospedaletto in Venice, but his obligation to the Pietà prevented him from accepting a second position. Three years later he

entered an important competition for the new post of *maestro di cappella* at St Mark's but lost by nine votes to Lotti. He left Venice in 1737 to accept a position as *Hofkapellmeister* at the Bavarian court of the Elector Karl Albrecht in Munich, where he remained until his death.

While Porta was in Italy, operas by him were given almost every year from 1716 to 1733; he continued to write operas for the Bavarian court, although by mid-century the changes in musical style and opera audiences are reflected in a decline in the number of his stage works. His music is representative of the general Venetian trends of the 1720s and 30s, when the close relationship between genres affected the drama and virtuosity of the music. Porta shared the penchant for fast running scales, arpeggios, wide melodic leaps, extended sequences and especially the popular Venetian sonority of the tutti unison texture. Burney deemed him 'one of the most able masters of his time, uniting learning with invention and fire'. Porta was included on the title-page of Benedetto Marcello's popular treatise *Il teatro alla moda* (1720) as a leading representative of early 18th-century opera.

See also NUMITORE.

La costanza combattuta in amore (F. Silvani, after J. Pradon: *Statira*), Venice, S Moisè, 17 Oct 1716, arias *D-Dlb*
Il Trace in catena (A. Salvi), Rome, Capranica, carn. 1717; collab. F. Gasparini and another comp.
L'Argippo (D. Lalli), Venice, S Cassiano, aut. 1717, *Dlb*, 2 arias *F-Pc*
L'amor di figlia (G. A. Moniglia and Lalli), Venice, S Angelo, aut. 1718, arias *I-Vc*, 1 aria *D-SWl*
Numitore [Rhea Silvia; Die heldenmüthige Schäfer Romulus und Remus] (os, 3, P. A. Rolli), London, King's, 2 April 1720, 1 aria *Dlb*, 1 aria *Bds* (*R* in HS, iv, 1986), ov. and arias (London, 1720)
Teodorico (Salvi), Venice, S Giovanni Grisostomo, aut. 1720, arias *Mbs*
Venceslao [Act 1] (A. Zeno), Venice, S Giovanni Grisostomo, carn. 1722 [Acts 2 and 3 by A. Pollarolo, Acts 4 and 5 by Capelli]
L'amor tirannico [Amor della patria] [Act 3] (Lalli), Venice, S Samuele, May 1722 [Acts 1 and 2 by Chelleri]
L'Arianna nell'isola di Nasso (C. N. Stampa), Milan, Regio Ducal, 28 Aug 1723, 6 arias *GB-Lbl*
Antigone, tutore di Filippo, re di Macedonia (tragedia, 5, G. Piazzon), Venice, S Moisè, carn. 1724, collab. Albinoni, 1 aria *D-ROu*
La caduta de' Decemviri (S. Stampiglia), Milan, Regio Ducal, carn. 1724 [pasticcio with music by Albinoni and Sarro]
Li sforzi d'ambizione e d'amore (A. M. Lucchini), Venice, S Moisè, carn. 1724
La Mariane (Lalli), Venice, S Angelo, aut. 1724, 2 arias *D-SHs*, *GB-Cfm*; rev. of Pollarolo's Gli eccessi della gelosia
Agide re di Sparta (L. Bergalli), Venice, S Moisè, carn. 1725
Ulisse (Lalli), Venice, S Angelo, carn. 1725
Amor e fortuna [La sorte nemica; Amore di sangue; Amor odio e pentimento] (F. Passarini), Naples, S Bartolomeo, 1 Oct 1725
La Lucinda fedele (Zeno), Naples, S Bartolomeo, carn. 1726, 1 aria *F-Pn*
Siroe re di Persia (P. Metastasio), Florence, Cocomero, sum. 1726, 3 arias *Cfm*
Il trionfo di Flavio Olibrio (Zeno and P. Pariati), Venice, S Giovanni Grisostomo, aut. 1726, arias *I-Vnm*
Aldiso (after Stampa: *Oronta*), Venice, S Giovanni Grisostomo, carn. 1727, arias *Vnm*, 1 aria *D-Dlb*
Nel perdono la vendetta (C. Paganicesa), Venice, S Moisè, May 1728
Doriclea ripudiata da Creso (G. B. Corte), Venice, S Moisè, carn. 1729
Il gran Tamerlano (A. Piovene), Florence, Pergola, 1730
Farnace (Lucchini), Bologna, Malvezzi, spr. 1731, *Dlb*, arias *F-Pn*
Gianguir (Zeno), Milan, Regio Ducal, carn. 1732, *D-Dlb*
Lucio Papirio dittatore (Zeno), Rome, Alibert, spr. 1732, 1 aria *A-Wn*, *D-ROu*, *GB-Lbl*, *Lcm*, 2 arias *B-Bc*, *GB-Lkc*, *Ob*
L'Issipile (Metastasio), Venice, S Giovanni Grisostomo, aut. 1732
La Semiramide (Metastasio), Milan, Regio Ducal, carn. 1733

1069

Adriano in Siria (Metastasio), Mantua, Ducale, 1737
Ifigenia in Aulide (Teutsch-musicalisches Trauerspiel, Zeno), Munich, Hof, 1738, *D-Dlb*
Der Traum des Scipio (azione teatrale, after Metastasio: *Il sogno di Scipione*), Munich, 1744

Doubtful: Artaserse (Zeno and Pariati), Munich, Hof, 1739

*

Burney H
F. J. Lipowski: *Baierisches Musiklexicon* (Munich, 1811)
J. J. Maier: 'Archivalische Excerpte über die herzoglich bayerische Hofkapelle', *KJb*, vi (1891), 69–81, esp. 77
G. von Westerman: *Giovanni Porta als Opernkomponist* (diss., U. of Munich, 1921)
O. E. Deutsch: *Handel: a Documentary Biography* (London, 1955), 97
J. M. Knapp: 'Handel and the Royal Academy of Music', *MQ*, xlv (1959), 153–8
D. Arnold: 'Orphans and Ladies: the Venetian Conservatories (1680–1790)', *PRMA*, lxxxix (1962–3), 31–47
R. Strohm: *Italienische Opernarien des frühen Settecento (1720–1730)*, *AnMc*, no.16 (1976), 209–14
L. Lindgren: 'Parisian Patronage of Performers from the Royal Academy of Musick (1719–28)', *ML*, lviii (1977), 7–8
G. Rostirolla: 'L'organizzazione musicale nell'ospedale veneziano della Pietà al tempo di Vivaldi', *NRMI*, xiii (1979), 176–9
J. H. Roberts: *Introduction to HS*, iv (1986), pp.vii–xvi
W. Dean and J. M. Knapp: *Handel's Operas 1704–1726* (Oxford, 1987), 299–305
C. Willner: 'Handel's Borrowings from Telemann: an Analytical View', *Trends in Schenkerian Research* (New York, 1990), 145–68, esp. 160–63
F. Tanenbaum: *The Partbook Collection from the Ospedale della Pietà: the Sacred Music of Giovanni Porta* (diss., New York U., in preparation)   FAUN TANENBAUM

Porta, Nunziato (*fl* 1770–after 1790). Italian librettist. He is remembered as Joseph Haydn's collaborator at Eszterháza between 1781 and 1790. His chief job there was to adapt librettos and write texts for insertion arias; he seems also to have served as a music copyist. His talents lay chiefly in the adaptation of already extant texts rather than in the creation of original ones. The *Orlando paladino* set by Haydn, for example, is an adaptation of Porta's 1777 libretto for music possibly by P. A. Guglielmi (no score survives), which was in turn an adaptation of C. F. Badini's libretto on the same subject. Even the apparently new parts of Haydn's *Orlando paladino* were frequently taken from other operas performed at Eszterháza.

Il convitato di pietra (dramma tragicomico), Righini, 1776; *Orlando paladino* (dramma eroicomico), ? P. A. Guglielmi, 1777 (Haydn, 1782); *L'americana in Olanda*, Anfossi, 1778; *I contrattempi*, Sarti, 1778; *Armida*, Haydn, 1784; *L'incontro inaspettato*, Righini, 1785

*

D. Bartha and L. Somfai: *Haydn als Opernkapellmeister* (Budapest, 1960)
H. C. Robbins Landon: *Haydn: Chronicle and Works*, ii: *Haydn at Eszterháza* (London, 1980)   MARY HUNTER

Portamento (It.). In vocal terminology from the Romantic period to the present, the sound that results when the voice, in passing from one note to another, glides audibly through some or all of the intervening pitches without settling on any one of them. The practice itself is one of the fundamental characteristics of Italian vocalism, and is older than the use of the term to describe it.

The literal Italian meaning of 'portamento' is 'carriage' or 'bearing', and it was in this general sense that it was first applied to singing. In Domenico Corri's 'Dialogue between Master and Scholar' (*The Singer's Preceptor*, 1810), the Master says that the 'portamento

di voce' was the chief merit of the singers of the middle 18th century, and that:

'Portamento di voce is the perfection of vocal music; it consists in the swell and dying of the voice, the sliding and blending of one note into another with delicacy and expression – and expression comprehends every charm which music can produce; the Portamento di voce may justly be compared to the highest degree of refinement in elegant pronunciation in speaking.'

The 'sliding and blending' aspect was already at this time becoming the predominant connotation of the term; G. G. Ferrari wrote in 1818 that 'portamento means the carriage of the voice with dignified expression. In carrying the voice from one note to another, the second must receive a slight intonation, previously to its being articulated'. In *c*1824, Richard Mackenzie Bacon (adding a parenthetical objection to the use of the word) described the practice thus:

Another of the most striking distinctions [between Italian and English singing] is the use of *portamento*, as it is now (erroneously) called, or the lessening the abrupt effects of distant intervals, or smoothing the passage between those less remote, by an inarticulate gliding of the voice from one to the other, whether ascending or descending. This is in constant use amongst Italian singers, and sometimes with beautiful effect.

Descriptions of this kind of legato singing are to be found as far back as the middle of the 18th century. (The practice is possibly even older; systematic descriptions of singing style did not become common until the years after Tosi's *Opinioni de' cantori antichi e moderni o sieno osservazioni sopra il canto figurato*, 1723.) Earlier authors sometimes used the term 'cercar la nota' or 'cercar della nota'. J. C. F. Rellstab (*Versuch über die Vereinigung der musikalischen und oratorischen Declamation*, 1786) showed the beginning of a Graun aria and said that 'any good singer' would employ the 'cercar la nota' on the first interval (a rising minor 3rd). Mattheson may well have been referring to what we would understand as portamento when he wrote (*Der vollkommene Capellmeister*, 1739) that appoggiaturas must be 'so lightly touched and slid that the [appoggiatura and its resolution] may hang together completely and emerge almost as a single sound'.

Few composers before the 20th century made systematic efforts to notate portamento, but several notations used by theorists and editors of annotated arias can help us to gauge its use in earlier eras. Rellstab used a dotted rhythm with the short note anticipating the pitch of the next melody note. Several other theorists use this notation, and it appears often in Corri's *A Select Collection* (*c*1779) of aria realizations (ex.1) and in the collection

Ex.1
(a) Gluck: *Orfeo ed Euridice*

l'e-co   ri - spon - de

(b) Corri's realization

l'e- co   ri-spon - de

of Mozart arias annotated about 1799 for Lady Murray (*GB-Lbl*; ex.2). Gluck himself may have had the same thing in mind when he used the notation shown in ex.3

Ex.2 Mozart: *Le nozze di Figaro*

Voi,___ che sa - pe - te

Ex.3 *Orfeo ed Euridice*

om - bre sde - gno - se

in Orpheus's plea to the Furies in 1762. Louis Spohr used the same device to indicate a slide (providing a fingering to leave no doubt as to his intention) in his *Violinschule*, as did Mendelssohn in a letter of 1 December 1830 to Zelter referring to the Sistine Chapel choir's portamento.

Another notation used the short anticipatory note, in small type, without taking a literal part in the rhythm (ex.4: Haydn, 'She never told her love', in Corri's real-

Ex.4

She ne - ver told her love, she ne - ver told

ization from *The Singer's Preceptor*, 1810). Many later composers, from Massenet to Britten, adopted this notation. J. F. Schubert (*Neue Singe-Schule*, 1804), noting that 'we have no sign in music for this melting of tones into one another', which he too called 'cercar della nota', proposed a simple line between notes (ex.5), but

Ex.5

this does not seem to have been used until the 20th century. Later indications include the literal directions 'portando la voce' and (in French scores, Meyerbeer's especially), 'traînez'. General directions such as 'con portamento' and 'con molto portamento' are also found in 19th-century scores (for instance in the lyrical passages of the title character in *Der fliegende Holländer*). Manuel Garcia, in his long and useful series of examples of portamento usage, indicated the device with a simple slur (but felt obliged to explain in prose that in these instances that is what the slur means) or, for more emphatic portamentos (see below), a slur plus the small anticipatory note. Verdi in *Otello* used a wavy line between notes to indicate the pronounced portamentos of a minor 9th in Desdemona's Willow Song.

Several authors caution that if portamento is used too often (or 'on every interval') it produces a disagreeable result (it is 'disgusting and unbearable' when done in the wrong place, according to J. F. Schubert; Garcia warned that 'in overdoing it, one risks making the execution weak and languid'). To these observations must be added the qualification that, on the same authors' evidence, portamento seems to have been used a great deal more in their times than in any period within living memory.

Several accounts also advise that falling portamentos generally be executed with a diminuendo and rising ones with a crescendo. Some writers (including Vaccai, *Metodo pratico di canto italiano per camera*, c1833) describe as a form of portamento the 'old French method' of beginning a new syllable with a quick reiteration of the previous note. Various authors describe the normal Italian portamento as having different degrees of strength, fullness and rapidity in music of different character (Garcia wrote of a

portamento 'strong, full and rapid' for 'vigorous sentiments' and one 'slower and sweeter' for 'tender and gracious movements', giving copious illustrations). Ferrari (*Breve trattato di canto italiano*, 1818; Eng. trans., 1818) described a form of portamento in which the slide to the next note is interrupted, or perhaps replaced, by a kind of emotional accent on the pitch of destination. His colourful term for this device is 'Piagnistei, or Shrieks' (ex.6). On early recordings of Italian singers, for whom

Ex.6

sol____ re a - men

the tradition of portamento was still strong, one often hears a kind of anticipation that answers to Ferrari's description – sometimes with, and sometimes without, a sliding portamento in the usual sense.

Early recordings also give us evidence for the frequency of usage, sound quality and timing of portamento among late 19th- and early 20th-century singers. Over the course of the century, use of portamento in singing has declined radically, even in overtly lyrical Italian arias. An example is the aria 'Eri tu' from *Un ballo in maschera* as recorded in 1907 by Mattia Battistini and in 1989 by Leo Nucci; the former makes audible portamentos between notes 46 times, the latter six times and much less markedly. In many present-day performances of Mozart and Wagner, portamento is entirely absent. Despite the wealth of evidence for its use in earlier times, the early music movement has yet to make a significant effort in this area.

P. F. Tosi: *Opinioni de' cantori antichi e moderni, o sieno Osservazioni sopra il canto figurato* (Bologna, 1723); trans. J. E. Galliard as *Observations on the Florid Song* (1742); trans. and ed. J. F. Agricola as *Anleitung zur Singekunst* (1757)

J. Mattheson: *Der vollkommene Capellmeister* (Hamburg, 1739)

J. C. F. Rellstab: *Versuch über die Vereinigung der musikalischen und oratorischen Declamation* (Leipzig, 1786)

D. Corri, ed.: *A Select Collection of the most Admired Songs, Duets* (Edinburgh, c1779)

J. F. Schubert: *Neue Singe-Schule, oder Gründliche und vollständige Anweisung zur Singkunst* (Leipzig, 1804)

D. Corri: *The Singer's Preceptor, or Corri's Treatise on Vocal Music* (London, 1810)

G. G. Ferrari: *Breve trattato di canto italiano* (London, 1818)

N. Vaccai: *Metodo pratico di canto italiano per camera* (n.p., c1833)

M. P. R. Garcia: *Mémoire sur la voix humaine* (Paris, 1840)

——: *Traité complet de l'art du chant* (Paris, 1840)

WILL CRUTCHFIELD

Port-au-Prince. Capital of Haiti (formerly Saint-Domingue) from 1749. Originally called L'Hôpital, it supported a vigorous operatic life in the second half of the 18th century, when the colony was the richest in the New World because of sugar, coffee and indigo exports. Saint-Domingue could afford to import excellent instrumentalists and singers, who performed works from Rousseau's *Le devin du village* (6 June 1764) to Grétry's *Le huron* (1769), *Silvain* (1770), *Zémire et Azor* (1772) and 20 other operas up to *Richard Coeur-de-lion* (1786), *Le mariage d'Antonio* (1787) and *Panurge dans l'île des lanternes* (1790). Along with these, a host of works by Dalayrac and Philidor were given. Other notable performances in the colony include Monsigny's *Le* *déserteur* (1770) and *La belle Arsène* (1778), Gossec's *Toinon et Toinette* (1777), Piccinni's *La buona figliuola* (1778), and Gluck's *Orphée et Eurydice* (1779) and *Iphigénie en Aulide* (1789). The operas of Piccinni, Pergolesi, Martini, Sacchini and Paisiello, performed from 1765 to 1789, were always given in French.

The first theatre to offer musical spectacles opened at Cap François (now Cap Haïtien) on 23 February 1744, using performers imported from Paris. A modest 'Salle de Spectacles' operated at Port-au-Prince from 1762 to 1768 under the successive directorships of Rouzier (formerly of the Cap François), Beaubrillant and then Claude Clément, a native of the Cap. Jenot inaugurated a new Salle on 15 February 1775, but although most of the actors and singers were from France, a prime draw from 1777 was the native singer Minette. From 1764 to 1790, blacks in Saint-Domingue who were taught the violin, french horn, trumpet, drums and mandolin by French immigrants played in the opera orchestras, and their names crowd contemporary newspapers, including the *Gazette de St.-Domingue*. Minette and Lise were two mulatto sisters who sang in numerous operas in the 1780s. Two local composers saw their operas produced – Dufresne (*Laurette*, 28 October 1775) and Bisséry (*Le sourd dupé*, 21 June 1777; *Bouquet disputé*, 18 June 1783). In January 1782 François Mesplès (who emigrated to Port-au-Prince in 1766) completed a theatre seating 750; its 16 boxes (some shuttered), balcony for 'les gens de couleur', orchestra pit and curtained stage made the Mesplès theatre the best in the island until it burnt down in November 1791. The French Revolution, which led to the expulsion of the French planter class from the island, put an end to the operatic life that had flourished in Port-au-Prince.

*

J. Fouchard: *Artistes et répertoire des scènes de Saint-Domingue* (Port-au-Prince, 1955)
——: *Plaisirs de Saint-Domingue: notes sur la vie sociale, littéraire et artistique* (Port-au-Prince, 1955)
——: *Le théâtre à Saint-Domingue* (Port-au-Prince, 1955)
R. Stevenson: 'Caribbean Music History: a Selective Annotated Bibliography', *Inter-American Music Review*, iv/1 (1981), 28–32
ROBERT STEVENSON

Porter, Andrew (*b* Cape Town, 26 Aug 1928). British writer on music. While at school in Rondebosch he accompanied Albert Coates's rehearsals and played continuo for him; in 1947 he went as an organ scholar to Oxford, where he read English. He embarked on a career in music criticism in London and in 1952 joined the *Financial Times*; there he built up a distinctive tradition of criticism based on his elegant, spacious literary style – which however was informed by a detailed knowledge of music history and textual scholarship as well as an exceptionally wide range of sympathies, with 19th-century opera as their focal point. Porter wrote regularly for *Opera* (of which he was associate editor, 1953–6, and thereafter a member of the editorial board) and *Gramophone*. He was editor of the *Musical Times*, 1960–67, and did much to broaden its scope. He first went to New York to write for the *New Yorker* in 1972; his extended and well informed notices (of which five collections have been published in book form) drew considerable attention, and he later settled there, also undertaking some university teaching and becoming editor of the American Institute for Verdi Studies newsletter in 1976. In 1992 he returned to London as music critic of *The Observer*. Porter has prepared singing translations of more than 30 operas, including works by Handel, Haydn, Mozart, Rossini, Verdi, Wagner (among them the *Ring*, published in 1976) and Strauss; his English texts are distinguished by their clarity of diction and their attentiveness to the line and rhythm of the music. He has directed operas by Handel, Mozart and Verdi. His scholarly work has centred on Verdi; Porter was primarily responsible for the rediscovery of the full original version of *Don Carlos* in the Paris Opéra library, and is author (with David Rosen) of *Verdi's 'Macbeth': a Sourcebook* (New York, 1984).

STANLEY SADIE

Porter, Cole (Albert) (*b* Peru, IN, 9 June 1891; *d* Santa Monica, CA, 15 Oct 1964). American composer and lyricist. He learned the piano as a child and had his first songs published when he was only ten years old. He studied at Yale, then dutifully followed his family's wish that he enter Harvard Law School, but soon abandoned those studies to transfer to the Harvard School of Music. He regularly composed songs to please his friends. These private compositions slowly gained a reputation outside his small coterie; from 1915, when one of his songs was used in Sigmund Romberg's revue *Hands Up*, he began contributing music to Broadway shows. In 1916 his own first work for Broadway, *See America First*, proved a failure. Three years later *Hitchy Koo* (1919) contained his first hit, the atypically sentimental 'An old-fashioned garden'.

Porter spent most of the 1920s in Europe and did not begin to compose steadily for the stage until the end of the decade. Between 1928 and 1955 he composed 20 works for Broadway and two for London, and continued to supply songs for works by other composers. In the mid-1940s Porter had two successive failures and it was bruited that he was written out. He gave the lie to this rumour with what most students consider his masterpiece, *Kiss Me, Kate* (1948), based on *The Taming of the Shrew*. When the play-within-the-play presents scenes from Shakespeare's comedy, Porter often begins his lyric with Shakespeare's lines and employs hints of Elizabethan musical traditions. For songs in more contemporary scenes his musical style is more up to date and his lyrics frequently slangy. Songs from the show that have become standards are the rousing 'Another op'nin', another show', 'So in love' and 'Wunderbar', this last a spoof of waltzes from older operettas. The musical, which was the fourth longest-running show of the decade in New York, enjoyed a worldwide success; it has been revived many times, and since the 1960s has entered the repertory of opera companies in the USA and in Europe. In 1990 it was recorded by a largely operatic cast. Of the dozen or so films and television programmes to which Porter contributed music, *High Society* (1956) and *Aladdin* (1958) were later staged.

Porter wrote all his own lyrics, which were literate, witty and the epitome of contemporary sophistication. Porter's music was, as many scholars have pointed out, the least changing of any major 20th-century theatre composer. His style was essentially the same at the beginning of his career as it was at the end. Among his signatures was his penchant for Latin rhythms and his employment of the minor mode (facetiously he called the latter his 'Jewish music'). His ability to move back and forth between major and minor modes within a single melody, often within a single phrase, was remarkable.

musicals unless otherwise stated; only professional productions listed, with dates of first New York performance, unless otherwise stated; vocal scores or selections published; book author in parenthesis, lyrics by Porter

See America First (T. L. Riggs and Porter), Maxine Elliott, 28 March 1916
Hitchy-Koo (revue), Liberty, 6 Oct 1919
Paris (M. Brown), Music Box, 8 Oct 1928
Wake up and Dream (revue, J. H. Turner), London, 27 March 1929; New York, Selwyn, 30 Dec 1929
Fifty Million Frenchmen (H. Fields), Lyric, 27 Nov 1929
The New Yorkers (Fields, after E. R. Goetz and P. Arno), Broadway, 8 Dec 1930
Gay Divorce (D. Taylor), Barrymore, 29 Nov 1932
Nymph Errant (R. Brent, after J. Laver), Manchester, Opera House, 11 Sept 1933
Anything Goes (G. Bolton, P. G. Wodehouse, H. Lindsay and R. Crouse), Alvin, 21 Nov 1934
Jubilee (M. Hart), Imperial, 12 Oct 1935
Red, Hot and Blue! (Lindsay and Crouse), Alvin, 29 Oct 1936
You Never Know (R. Leigh), Winter Garden, 21 Sept 1938
Leave it to Me! (B. Spewack and S. Spewack), Imperial, 9 Nov 1938
Du Barry was a Lady (Fields and B. DeSylva), 46th Street, 6 Dec 1939
Panama Hattie (Fields and DeSylva), 46th Street, 30 Oct 1940
Let's Face it! (H. Fields and D. Fields), Imperial, 29 Oct 1941
Something for the Boys (H. Fields and D. Fields), Alvin, 7 Jan 1943
Mexican Hayride (H. Fields and D. Fields), Winter Garden, 28 Jan 1944
Seven Lively Arts (revue), Ziegfeld, 7 Dec 1944
Around the World in Eighty Days (O. Welles, after J. Verne), 31 May 1946
Kiss Me, Kate (B. Spewack and S. Spewack, after W. Shakespeare: *The Taming of the Shrew*), New Century, 30 Dec 1948
Out of this World (Taylor and R. Lawrence), New Century, 21 Dec 1950
Can-can (A. Burrows), Shubert, 7 May 1953
Silk Stockings (G. S. Kaufman, L. MacGrath and Burrows, after the film *Ninotchka*), Imperial, 24 Feb 1955

*

G. Eells: *Cole Porter: the Life that Late he Led* (New York, 1967) [incl. list of works]
R. Kimball: *Cole* (New York, 1971) [incl. list of works, biographical essay by B. Gill]
——, ed.: *The Complete Lyrics of Cole Porter* (New York, 1983)
J. P. Swain: *The Broadway Musical: a Critical and Musical Survey* (New York, 1990), 129–52
R. H. Kornick: *Recent American Opera: a Production Guide* (New York, 1991)   GERALD BORDMAN

Portland. American city, in Oregon. The first known opera performances there were given by the itinerant Bianchi (or Bianca) Opera Company at the newly built Oro Fino Hall in July 1867, with visits by other touring companies continuing into the 1950s. Although the elegant New Market Theatre (built 1875), film theatres and (especially in the 1950s and 60s) high-school auditoriums were once used for opera, the city's most important stage has been the Civic Auditorium (built 1917, seating 3000), which, after renovation in 1968, became the base of the Portland Opera Association. A local company existed from 1917 to 1923, but Portland Opera grew out of the Portland Civic Opera, founded in 1950 by Ariel Rubstein, who marked the occasion by conducting *Aida* in the amphitheatre at Washington Park. Run mostly on a shoestring by volunteers, the company suffered financial collapse in 1957, but under the guidance of Dorothea Lensch it was rescued through its incorporation into the city's Bureau of Parks and Recreation. The present company was restructured in 1964 so as to cut its ties with the city and it is now more professionally orientated. Stefan Minde (musical director, 1971–84) brought it to national attention with his 1977 production of *Die Meistersinger* and especially with the American première of Krenek's *Leben des*

Orest (1975) and the world première of Bernard Herrmann's *Wuthering Heights* (1982). Since Minde's controversial departure, guest conductors have been engaged for all productions. Although a new opera, *Lucy's Lapses* by Christopher Drobny, was commissioned for the 1989–90 season, the repertory has remained solidly conservative. In each season (October–June) five operas are given, each receiving three performances.

*

A. H. Ernst: 'Opera comes to Oregon', *Sunday Oregonian Northwest Rotogravure Magazine* (18 and 25 March 1956)
D. Maclaine: 'History of Portland Opera', *Willamette Week* (4, 18 and 25 Nov 1980)   DOUGLAS LEEDY

Porto (Port.). OPORTO.

Porto, Carlo (Ottolini) (*b* *c*1800; *d* 1836 or later). Italian bass. During the 1830s he sang in Milan, Florence, Turin and Naples. He created roles in four Donizetti operas: Ernesto in *Parisina* (1833) and Clifford in *Rosmonda d'Inghilterra* (1834) at the Teatro della Pergola, Florence; Talbot in *Maria Stuarda* (1834), given as *Buondelmonte* owing to censorship, and Raimondo in *Lucia di Lammermoor* (1835) at S Carlo. He was a famous exponent of Henry VIII (*Anna Bolena*) and also sang many Bellini roles: Capellio (*I Capuleti e i Montecchi*), Rodolfo (*La sonnambula*), Oroveso (*Norma*) and Giorgio (*I puritani*), which he sang in Bologna (1836).   ELIZABETH FORBES

Portogallo, Marcos António. *See* PORTUGAL, MARCOS ANTÓNIO.

Portugal. Although zarzuelas and other semi-operatic Spanish works were performed in Lisbon during the first quarter of the 18th century, the beginnings of opera in Portugal stemmed from the italianization of musical life through, for instance, the engaging of Italian singers for the royal chapel and of Domenico Scarlatti as its *mestre* in 1719. Three Italian comic operas were composed by F. A. de Almeida, a former royal scholar in Rome, among them *La Spinalba* (1739), the only one to have survived complete, written in the elegant sentimental vein of Neapolitan composers of Pergolesi's generation. From 1731 onwards several attempts were made to promote public performances of opera, and a number of *opere serie* were staged at two theatres in Lisbon. Another theatre presented puppet operas with spoken dialogues in the style of *opéras comiques*: the Portuguese texts were by the Jewish lawyer António José da Silva, and the italianate music was probably by António Teixeira, another former royal scholar in Rome. But during the last eight years of the reign of King João V (i.e. 1742–50) no operas were given because of the king's illness.

Only after José I's accession and the arrival of the Neapolitan composer David Perez in 1752 did opera again flourish in Portugal, though there was another hiatus following the Lisbon earthquake of 1755. In the court theatres works by Perez and other leading Italian composers of the day were given, including many operas by Jommelli, sent from Naples by the composer in return for a pension paid by the Lisbon court. With the death of José I in 1777 and that of Perez in 1778, there were more opportunities for local composers, but they were mainly called on to write Italian serenatas and oratorios, no doubt for economical reasons, since these required no sets or costumes. Among them were Pedro António Avondano, João Cordeiro da Silva, João de Sousa Carvalho, Jerónimo Francisco de Lima and António Leal Moreira, all of whom were trained at the music school of the royal chapel, the Seminário da Patriarcal, and were conversant with Italian operatic styles. Sousa Carvalho and Lima also studied at the Conservatorio di S Onofrio at Naples: a number of their operas, for example Lima's *Lo spirito di contradizione* and Sousa Carvalho's *Testoride argonauta*, have recently been revived.

It was during the later 18th century that there emerged the first Portuguese singer to achieve international fame, Luisa Todi. Following a further period during which opera was in abeyance, this time as a result of financial problems, there was a brief surge of Italian opera in Lisbon between 1790 and 1792, conducted, apparently for the first time in a public theatre, by a Portuguese composer, Moreira. By now female singers and dancers had been banned from the public stage in Lisbon, a prohibition that remained in force until the end of the century. There seems to have been no such ban, however, in Oporto, where Italian opera was presented irregularly from 1760 on. Italian opera indeed had a decisive influence on the Portuguese theatre in the 18th century. There were many translations and adaptations of librettos, particularly those of Metastasio, often given as spoken dramas. Performances of this type are also documented in the Portuguese provinces, on the island of Madeira and in colonial Brazil. Nevertheless, the early attempts of Silva and Teixeira to establish Portuguese opera were not followed up, and Portuguese composers did not yet play a significant part in the operatic life of the public theatres.

The last decade of the 18th century began a new period for opera in Portugal. Court opera ended, to be replaced by bourgeois opera houses still committed to the Italian repertory. The opera houses of both Lisbon and Oporto generally followed contemporary Italian trends closely. Operas by Portuguese composers that were staged there, such as those of the first two musical directors of the Teatro de S Carlos, Lisbon – Moreira and M. A. Portugal (the latter enjoyed a flourishing international career) – João Evangelista Pereira da Costa, António Luis Miró, Francisco Xavier Migone and, at the end of the 19th century, Frederico Guimarães, Augusto Machado and José Augusto Ferreira Veiga, Viscount of Arneiro, were written in accordance with the prevailing Italian conventions and were almost always performed in Italian (Moreira's Portuguese comic operas *A saloia enamorada*, 1793, and *A vingança da cigana*, 1794, which include spoken dialogue, are exceptional).

Apart from operas on the theme of Inês de Castro (Carlo Valentini, 1827; Persiani, 1835; Manuel Inocêncio Liberato dos Santos, 1839; Coppola, 1841), it was only with the operas of Francisco de Sá Noronha (*Beatrice di Portogallo*, 1863, and *L'arco di Sant'Anna*, 1867) that a consistent attempt was made to use national themes, with librettos based on Portuguese literary works (though still performed in Italian). Such attempts were continued by Miguel Angelo Pereira (*Eurico*, 1870, Lisbon), Alfredo Keil (*Donna Bianca*, 1888), Francisco de Freitas Gazul (*Fra Luigi di Sousa*, 1891) and J. M. Arroio (*Amore e perdizione*, 1907). Only with Keil's *Serrana* (1899) was an opera sung entirely in Portuguese heard at the Teatro de S Carlos, Lisbon. In 1844 the Academia Filarmónica presented

the 'drama lírico português' *Os Infantes em Ceuta*, with a libretto by the Portuguese writer and historian Alexandre Herculano and music by António Luís Miró.

In the second half of the 19th century several theatres specialized in a mixed repertory which included *opéras comiques*, burlettas, burlesque operas, operettas, vaudevilles and Spanish zarzuelas. It is hard to form a clear idea of the works performed, many of which were written in, or translated into, Portuguese. Among the Portuguese composers of this vast and largely forgotten repertory were António José do Rego, Miró, Ciríaco Cardoso, Noronha, João Guilherme Daddi and Joaquim Casimiro. Apparently the standards of training of such composers were generally lower than those of their 18th-century predecessors, a consequence of the political and social situation prevailing during most of the 19th century. Following the decline or disappearance of courtly musical institutions, neither the state nor the middle class was willing or able to promote and support national musical institutions to the extent found during the 18th century. The Teatro de S Carlos and the Teatro de S João in Oporto were the only important operatic venues, but their activities were based on the importing of foreign music and musicians, and the Teatro de S Carlos closed down in 1910. Moreover, the Lisbon Conservatory was never able to overcome fundamental weaknesses as the main centre of training for players, singers and composers.

When the S Carlos theatre reopened in 1940, its repertory became much wider and included regular productions of French and German operas, sung in the original language by foreign companies. After 1974 efforts were made to create a national opera company, the first in Portugal; it was based in Lisbon, first at the Teatro da Trindade and later at the S Carlos. The Acção Nacional de Opera (1934) was an initiative by Rui Coelho that allowed him to present his own operas. More recently the Teatro de S Carlos has staged contemporary Portuguese operas, such as *A igreja do mar* by Frederico de Freitas (1960), *Mérope* (1959) and *Trilogia das barcas* (1970) by Joly Braga Santos, *D. Duardos e Flérida* by Fernando Lopes Graça (1970), *Em nome da paz* by Alvaro Cassuto (1978) and *As três máscaras* by Maria de Lurdes Martins (1986).

For further information on operatic life in the country's principal centres *see* LISBON and OPORTO.

DBP

*

T. Braga: *Historia do theatro portuguez*, iii: *A baixa comedia e a opera no seculo XVIII* (Oporto, 1871)
F. da Fonseca Benevides: *O Real theatro de São Carlos de Lisboa* (Lisbon, 1883)
A. Sousa Bastos: *Diccionário do theatro portuguez* (Lisbon, 1908)
M. Lambertini: 'Portugal', *EMDC*, I/iv (Paris, 1920)
G. de Matos Sequeira: *Teatro de outros tempos* (Lisbon, 1933)
T. Borba and F. Lopes Graça: *Dicionário de música (ilustrado)* (Lisbon, 1956)
J. de Freitas Branco: *História da música portuguesa* (Lisbon, 1959)
J. López-Calo: 'Portogallo', *Storia dell'opera*, ed. G. Barblan and A. Basso, ii (Turin, 1977), 65–77
M. Moreau: *Cantores de ópera portugueses* (Lisbon, 1981–7)
M. C. de Brito: *Opera in Portugal in the Eighteenth Century* (Cambridge, 1989)
M. C. de Brito and D. Cranmer: *Crónicas da vida musical portuguesa na primeira metade do século XIX* (Lisbon, 1990)
M. C. de Brito: 'La penisola iberica', *SOI*, ii (forthcoming) [18th century only]   MANUEL CARLOS DE BRITO

Portugal [Portogallo], **Marcos António** (da Fonseca) (*b* Lisbon, 24 March 1762; *d* Rio de Janeiro, 7 Feb 1830).

Portuguese composer. Baptized simply Marcos, son of Manuel António da Ascenção and Joaquina Teresa Rosa, he was known in childhood and youth as Marcos António; he adopted the surname Fonseca Portugal in the mid-1780s from Captain José Correia da Fonseca Portugal, who had been *padrinho* ('godfather') at his parents' wedding. On 6 August 1771 he was admitted to the Seminário Patriarcal of Lisbon, where he studied composition with João de Sousa Carvalho, as well as singing and the organ. According to Fétis, he had teachers by the names of Borselli and Orao, acted as accompanist at the Madrid Opera at the age of 20 and was sponsored by the Portuguese ambassador there to go to Italy in 1787, but there is no evidence for these assertions. On 23 July 1783 he was admitted to the music guild, the Irmandade de S Cecília, as singer and organist of the Patriarcal.

Portugal's involvement with the theatre began with his appointment as *maestro* at the Teatro do Salitre, Lisbon, in 1785. Between then and 1792 he composed a series of *farsas* and *entremezes* for the Salitre, including Portuguese versions of Goldonian librettos. None of these is extant. During this period he also composed a number of one-act *elogios* (dramatic odes) for performance there on royal birthdays, of which two have survived: *Licença pastoril* (25 July 1787, P-La) and *Pequeno drama* (J. C. de Figueiredo; 17 December 1787, P-La). Under royal patronage he went to Naples in 1792, ostensibly to complete his musical studies, but he quickly became active as an opera composer. He gained instant success with *La confusione della somiglianza* (1793, Florence), one of several *opere buffe* and *farse* he wrote over the next seven years which were subsequently performed throughout Italy and much of Europe. Although Portugal wrote a number of *opere serie* during this period, they were less well received, only *Fernando nel Messico* (1798, Venice) being repeated outside Italy – in London (1803) thanks to Elizabeth Billington, for whom he had written the opera, and in Lisbon (1805), where he revised it for Angelica Catalani.

Portugal returned to Lisbon in 1800, and was appointed *mestre de capela* of the royal chapel and director of the Teatro S Carlos, taking over the post from the violinist and composer Francesco Federici. From summer 1803 the theatre's musical direction was divided between Portugal, conductor of the *seria* company, and Valentino Fioravanti, of the *buffa*, each heading a troupe of the highest calibre. This state of affairs continued until Carnival 1807 and explains why Portugal wrote or revised 12 *opere serie* during the period but only one *opera buffa* (*L'oro non compra amore*, 1804). Only this last subsequently gained widespread popularity in Italy and elsewhere. When Napoleon's troops entered Lisbon in November 1807, Marcos Portugal, in spite of his court position, did not flee to Brazil with the royal family. During the ten-month French occupation he revised *Demofoonte* for Napoleon's birthday in 1808. He was intermittently conductor at the S Carlos until January 1811, after which he sailed with his brother Simão Portugal, a church composer, for Rio de Janeiro. Here he was immediately reappointed *mestre* of the royal chapel and, upon its opening in 1813, director of the new Teatro S João. The only significant stage work he composed in Brazil was *A saloia namorada* (1812), for performance at court; he also revived four of his Lisbon operas.

As well as theatre works, Portugal composed a sub- stantial amount of church music, particularly in his early career and following his return from Italy. He also contributed a number of *modinhas* to the *Jornal de modinhas*, published in Lisbon in the 1790s. But his fame rests above all on his comic works, especially *La confusione della somiglianza*, *Lo spazzacamino principe*, *La donna di genio volubile*, *Le donne cambiate*, *Non irritar le donne* and *L'oro non compra amore*, and on the showpiece arias he wrote or revised for Catalani, most notably 'Son regina' (from *La morte di Semiramide*, revised in *La Sofonisba*). Stylistically Portugal's music is firmly within the Neapolitan tradition of Cimarosa, reliable rather than adventurous, belonging very much to the 18th century rather than the 19th. Interesting experiments such as the form of the overture to *La morte di Semiramide* (which includes a recitative for oboe and has a reference to the introduction theme in the main allegro) were not repeated or developed in later works. Similarly, orchestration is conservative; even in his later works he relied mainly on oboes for solo woodwind obbligatos, where contemporaries such as Giuseppe Nicolini (e.g. the aria 'Parmi sentir nell'anima' from *I baccanali di Roma*, which Portugal directed at Lisbon in 1804) were exploring the expressive possibilities of clarinets.

LIC – *Lisbon, Teatro S Carlos*
LIS – *Lisbon, Teatro do Salitre*
VM – *Venice, Teatro S Moisè*

dg – *dramma giocoso* dm – *dramma per musica*
ds – *dramma serio* e – *entremez*
f – *farsa* tm – *tragedia per musica*

Os bons amigos (f or e), LIS, 1786
A casa de café (f or e), LIS, 1787
A castanheira, ou a Brites Papagaia (e, 1, J. C. de Figueiredo), LIS, 1788
O amor conjugal (ds, 1, J. P. Monteiro), LIS, 25 July 1789
O amor artifice (f or e, ? after C. Goldoni: *L'amore artigiano*), LIS, 1790
A noiva fingida (dg, 2, trans. of G. M. Diodati: *Le trame deluse*), LIS, 1790
Os viajantes ditosos (dg, 2, trans. of F. Livigni: *I viaggiatori felici*), LIS, 1790
O amante militar (e, ? after Goldoni), LIS, 1791
O lunático iludido [O mundo da lua] (drama, 3, trans. of Goldoni: *Il mondo della luna*), LIS, 1791
La confusione della somiglianza, o siano I due gobbi [Le confusioni/ La forza/L'equivoco della somiglianza, La vera somiglianza; Verwirrung durch/Die täuschende Aehnlichkeit, Die beyden Bucklichten, Die Buckeligen] (dg, 2, C. Mazzini), Florence, Pallacorda, spr. 1793, *D-Dlb, F-Pc, I-Fc, Mr*
Il poeta in campagna (2, F. S. Zini), Parma, Ducale, Sept 1793
Il Cinna (ds, 2, A. Anelli), Florence, Pergola, aut. 1793, *Fc*
Rinaldo d'Aste (commedia con musica, 1, G. M. Foppa, after G. Carpani), VM, 4 Jan 1794, *Gl*
Lo spazzacamino principe [Il principe/Il barone spazzacamino; Der Schornsteinfeger Peter, oder Das Spiel des Ohngefährs; O basculho de chaminé] (commedia con musica, 1, Foppa, after Carpani), VM, 4 Jan 1794, *F-Pc, I-Fc, Mr, PAc*
Demofoonte (dm, 3, P. Metastasio), Milan, Scala, 8 Feb 1794; rev. version in 2 acts, LIC, 15 Aug 1808; *B-Bc, I-Mr**, Act 1 *P-Ln, US-Wc*
La vedova raggiratrice, o siano I due sciocchi delusi [L'astuto, L'astuta; Die schlaue Witwe, oder Die beiden angeführten Thoren] (dg, 2), Florence, Pergola, spr. 1794, *I-Fc*
L'avventuriere (f, 1, ? C. Mazzolà), VM, carn. 1795
Lo stratagemma, ossiano I due sordi (int, 1, Foppa), Florence, allacorda, carn. 1795
L'inganno poco dura (commedia, 2, Zini), Naples, Fiorentini, carn. 1796, *Nc*
Zulima (dm, 2, F. Gonella di Ferrari), Florence, Pallacorda, spr. 1796, *F-Pc, I-Fc, Mc*
La donna di genio volubile [La donna bizzarra, I quattro rivali in amore; Die Wankelmüthige] (dg, 2, G. Bertati), VM, 5 Oct 1796, *A-Wgm, F-Pc* (as La sposa stravagante), *I-Fc, Mr*

Il ritorno di Serse (ds, 2, Gonella di Ferrari), Florence, Pallacorda, April 1797, *I-Fc*, *Mr*, *PAc*; rev. as Argenide, LIC, 13 May 1804, *P-VV*

Le donne cambiate [La bacchetta portentosa, Il calzolaio, Il ciabattino, Il diavolo a quattro; Die verwandelten Weiber, oder Der Teufel ist los, Der lustige Schuster; O Mestre Biajo sapateiro, O sapateiro] (f, 1, Foppa, after C. Coffey: *The Devil to Pay*), VM, 22 Oct 1797, *F-Pc*, *I-Fc*

Fernando nel Messico (dm, 3, F. Tarducci), Venice, S Benedetto, 16 Jan 1798, *GB-Lbl* (largely autograph); rev. version in 2 acts, LIC, sum. 1805, Act 1 *P-La*, Act 2 *VV* (partly autograph)

La maschera fortunata [La maschera felice, Il matrimonio in maschera; A mascara] (f, 1, Foppa), VM, 5 Feb 1798, *F-Pc*, *I-Fc*, *Mr*

L'equivoco in equivoco [Quem busca lã fica tosquiado] (f, 1, Foppa), Verona, Filarmonico, spr. 1798

La madre virtuosa (operetta di sentimento, 1, Foppa), VM, 30 Oct 1798

Alceste (tm, 3, S. A. Sografi), Venice, Fenice, 26 Dec 1798, *Mr*

Non irritar le donne, ossia Il chiamantesi filosofo [Il filosofo, Il sedicente filosofo] (f, 1, Foppa), Venice, S Benedetto, 27 Dec 1798, *F-Pc*

La pazza giornata, ovvero Il matrimonio di Figaro (dramma comico per musica, 2, G. Rossi), Venice, S Benedetto, 26 Dec 1799, *Pc*, *I-Fc*

Idante, ovvero I sacrifici d'Ecate (dm, 2, G. Schmidt), Milan, Scala, 13 Feb 1800, *Mr**

Adrasto re d'Egitto (dm, 3, G. De Gamerra), LIC, 21 Dec 1800 [not 17 Dec as in lib.]

La morte di Semiramide (ds, 2, G. Caravita), LIC, 23 Dec 1801, *P-La*, *Ln*

La Zaira (tm, 2, M. Botturini), LIC, 19 Feb 1802; rev. LIC, sum. 1804; *La*, excerpts *VV*

Il trionfo di Clelia (ds, 2, Sografi), LIC, wint. 1802

La Sofonisba (ds, 2, del Mare), LIC, carn. 1803

La Merope (ds, 2, Botturini), LIC, Dec 1804, *La*

L'oro non compra amore (dg, 2, Caravita), LIC, wint. 1804, *F-Pc*, *GB-Lcm*, *I-Mr*, *Nc*, *P-VV*

Il duca di Foix (dm, 2, Caravita), LIC, wint. 1805

Ginevra di Scozia (dramma eroico per musica, 2, Rossi), LIC, wint. 1805

La morte di Mitridate (tm, 2, Sografi), LIC, carn. 1806, *La*

Artaserse (ds, 2, Metastasio), LIC, aut. 1806, *GB-Lcm*

A saloia namorada (f, 1, D. Caldas Barbosa), Rio de Janeiro, Quinta da Boa Vista, 1812

Augurio di felicità, o sia Il trionfo d'amore (serenata, M. A. Portugal, after Metastasio), Rio de Janeiro, court, 7 Nov 1817

Music in: Gli Orazi e i Curiazi, 1798; Didone, 1803; Tito Vespasiano, 1807; Amor non si cela, 1808; Adriano in Siria, 1809; Omar re di Termagene, 1810; Ines de Castro, 1810; Romeo e Giulietta, 1812; Zulema e Selimo, 1815; Il trionfo di Gusmano, 1816; Der Kampf im Vorzimmer, 1816; Lo sprezzatore schernito, 1816; Il feudatario, 1818

Doubtful: A casa de pasto (pequena peça, J. D. Rodrigues da Costa), LIS, 1784; L'eroe cinese (Metastasio), Turin, 1788; O amor da Patria (ds, 1), LIS, 1789; Il molinaro (int), Venice, carn. 1790; Il muto per astuzia (f, 1, Foppa), ?1800, *I-Mr*; Zulema e Selimo, LIC, 1804; Penelope (os, 3), St Petersburg, Mikhailov, 1818

Spurious: Il finto stregone (f, Foppa), VM, aut. 1798 [by F. Gardi]

*

DBP [incl. Portugal's catalogue of his own works]; *FétisB*

C. I. Ruders: *Portugisisk resa* (Stockholm, 1805–9); Port. trans., abridged, as *Viagem em Portugal 1798–1802* (Lisbon, 1981)

F. da Fonseca Benevides: *O Real theatro de São Carlos de Lisboa* (Lisbon, 1883)

M. Pereira Peixoto d'Almeida Carvalhaes: *Marcos Portugal na sua musica dramatica* (Lisbon, 1910, suppl. 1916)

J.-P. Sarraute: *Marcos Portugal: ensaios* (Lisbon, 1979)

D. Cranmer: 'Autógrafo ou cópia? Partituras das óperas de Marcos Portugal e Valentino Fioravanti escritas para o Teatro de São Carlos', *Boletim da Associação portuguesa de educação musical*, lviii (1988), 27–30   DAVID CRANMER

Posen (Ger.). POZNAŃ.

Poser, Hans Wolfgang (*b* Tannenbergsthal, Vogtland, 8 Oct 1917; *d* Hamburg, 1 Oct 1970). German composer.

As a prisoner of war in Canada, he was helped by the Red Cross from 1940 to pursue his musical studies at a distance, and one of his teachers was Hindemith. After World War II he moved to Hamburg and worked as a teacher, becoming professor at the Hamburg Hochschule für Musik in 1962. He composed two television chamber operas, of which *Die Auszeichnung* (Poser, after G. de Maupassant; 1959) was one of his most successful works; the other, *Die Bassgeige* (Poser, after A. P. Chekhov: *Romance with a Double Bass*), was written for Zweites Deutsches Fernsehen in 1964.

KLAUS L. NEUMANN

Posse (Ger.: 'farce', 'broad comedy'). The noun *Bosse* (from the French *bosse*) or *Posse* denoted in 15th-century usage a decorative figure, especially a grotesque one, or ornamental masonry of sculpture such as a well-head or fountain. By the 16th century the term usually denoted a prank or trick, and by the middle of the 17th the term *Possenspil* (or *Possenspiel*) was in use to denote a type of broad comedy, sometimes specifically including music. *Possenspiel* was commonly used until the beginning of the 19th century (e.g. by Goethe and Schiller), but thereafter the shortened form *Posse* was normal, especially in Vienna, for popular comic entertainments. Apart from the non-theatrical *Possenreisser* (a joker, buffoon), various compound nouns specify types of farce, for example *Charakterposse* (a farce which lays emphasis on the characterization), *Lokalposse* (a farce rich in local allusions and dialect), *Situationsposse* (farce of situation) and *Zauberposse* (a farce in which magic and machinery play an important part; *see* ZAUBEROPER).

In Vienna the term *Posse mit Gesang* became the normal appellation for a farce with songs: much the same phenomenon had earlier been known under a variety of names: *Haupt- und Staats-Aktion*, *musica bernesca*, *Maschinen-Comödie*, *opéra comique* etc. The borderline between *Posse* and other kinds of comedy, with and without music, cannot be clearly drawn. In the 19th century, however, the term *Posse mit Gesang* was the most widely used to describe a comic play that, while it contained fewer and shorter musical numbers than would have justified the subtitle Singspiel, nevertheless made extensive use of solo songs, with occasional rather rudimentary ensembles, incidental music and (roughly until the early 1840s) a number of short choruses. The leading authors of *Possen*, whether or not they preferred to use more pretentious subtitles, were Joseph Alois Gleich (1772–1841), Karl Meisl (1775–1853), Adolf Bäuerle (1786–1859), Ferdinand Raimund and Johann Nepomuk Nestroy. The most important musicians who furnished them with scores were Wenzel Müller, Ferdinand Kauer, Adolf Müller and Franz Suppé.   PETER BRANSCOMBE

Post, Joseph (Mozart) (*b* Sydney, 10 April 1906; *d* Broadbeach, Queensland, 27 Dec 1972). Australian conductor. After studying at the New South Wales Conservatorium, he worked for the ABC as a conductor and later as an assistant director of music. He also gained theatrical experience in Sydney as an orchestral player and then as a conductor for visiting companies. He was musical director of the Melbourne-based National Theatre Movement opera company (1947–54) and the Elizabethan Trust (now Australian) Opera (1956–7), thus presiding musically over the coming-of-age of professional opera production in Australia. A conductor with a particularly clear beat, he was at his best in the incident-packed milieu of opera and was shrewdly aware of structural balance, as William Walton acknowledged after Post conducted *Troilus and Cressida* at the Adelaide Festival in 1964. He was the first Australian-born conductor to make a career in opera. ROGER COVELL

Postage stamps. *See* STAMPS.

Postal Coachmen at the Relay Station. Opera by Y. I. Fomin; *see* YAMSHCHIKI NA PODSTAVE.

Postcard from Morocco. Opera in one act by DOMINICK ARGENTO to a libretto by John Donahue; Minneapolis, Cedar Village Theater, 14 October 1971.

From an abstract libretto by the children's theatre director John Donahue (with lines in no set sequence, assigned to no particular character), Argento created a symbolic fantasy based on the guarded interactions of seven people waiting for a train. Their activities are interrupted by abrupt leaps of time and strange entertainments (a cabaret song to nonsense syllables, a puppet show with lifelike puppets, a Viennese operetta duet). Each character performs an aria of minimal self-revelation and carries an item of luggage, the contents of which he or she symbolically protects from the prying of the others. When Mr Owen (tenor), the only named character, is forced to reveal that his suitcase is empty, he is cut off from the group and, in heroic style, sets out on a voyage of self-discovery in a ship built by the puppets.

The score is a collage-like assemblage of musical ideas. In the cabaret song and operetta duet, Argento employed a technique that was to remain important in his operas: the layering of style simulations or borrowings with new musical material in ways that are both musically and dramatically sophisticated. Here such paraphrases and borrowings (an interlude for the eight-piece orchestra, 'Souvenirs de Bayreuth', is a miniature quotation piece) are juxtaposed with aleatory passages, warmly Romantic idioms and the angular, irregularly accented vocal style of most of the arias. A free use of 12-note technique appears, often for colouristic effect, although tonal underpinnings are continually in evidence. The surrealist work lends itself to various stage interpretations, which have ranged from absurdist to poetic. VIRGINIA SAYA

Postdrivers, The. Opera by Y. I. Fomin; *see* YAMSHCHIKI NA PODSTAVE.

Postel, Christian Heinrich (*b* Freiburg, nr Stade, 11 Oct 1658; *d* Hamburg, 22 March 1705). German poet and librettist. He went to Leipzig University to study law but was forced by an outbreak of the plague to move to Rostock University. Following a number of extended educational tours, during which he cultivated his interest in languages and literature, he returned to Hamburg about 1688 and began an illustrious career as a lawyer. In 1700 he became acquainted with the Arcadian movement in Italy, and in Milan he met L. A. Muratori, an exponent of Italian neo-classicism.

Postel was the most important and prolific writer of librettos for the Hamburg Opera towards the end of the 17th century. He wrote texts for the principal composers there, including Conradi, Förtsch, Keiser and Kusser, while the Opera was directed by his friend Gerhard Schott, on whose death in 1702 he apparently severed his association with the Opera. His librettos are fine examples of dramatic poetry, generally patterned on conventional Italian models and full of complex German Baroque imagery. He naturally based his operatic dramas on the standard Baroque concept of alternating affective states. However, many of them, such as *Die schöne und getreue Ariadne* (set by Conradi), do not present simply a pastiche of contrasting emotional statements; rather, within the limitations of a fairly stereotyped plot, the characters are permitted distinctive, dramatic development as personalities. Postel was frequently criticized in the 19th century for being a typical representative of the Second Silesian School, which was overfond of Marinism, but this view is not substantiated by his texts. He was a transitional figure in German libretto writing, standing between such writers as Bostel and Bressand on the one hand and Feind on the other. As such he strove for a simpler poetic language, abandoned the previously favoured alexandrine metre for the simpler, more effective iambic in recitatives, and successfully varied his metres in the arias for affective purposes. His poetry is highly expressive and colourful in the Baroque sense but without an excessive amount of bombast. His intensely dramatic works were the perfect vehicles for the music of composers such as Conradi, Förtsch and Keiser. All of his librettos survive in Weimar (*D-WRtl*).

Die heilige Eugenia, Förtsch, 1688; *Cain und Abel*, Förtsch, 1689; *Das betrübte und erfreute Cimbria*, Förtsch, 1689; *Ancile Romanum, das ist Des Römischen Reichs Glücks-Schild*, Förtsch, 1690; *Bajazeth und Tamerlan* (after C. Marlowe), Förtsch, 1690; *Die grossmächtige Thalestris, oder Letzte Königin der Amazonen*, Förtsch, 1690; *Der fromme und friedfertige König der Römer Numa Pompilius*, J. G. Conradi, 1691; *Die schöne und getreue Ariadne*, Conradi, 1691

Diogenes Cynicus (? after N. Minato), Conradi, 1691; *Der tapffere Kayser Carolus Magnus und dessen erste Gemahlin Hermingardis*, Conradi, 1692; *Der Verstöhrung Jerusalem erster Theil, oder Die Eroberung des Tempels*, Conradi, 1692; *Der Verstöhrung Jerusalem ander Theil, oder Die Eroberung der Burg Zion*, Conradi, 1692; *Der grosse König der africanischen Wenden Gensericus als Rom- und Karthagens Uberwinder*, Conradi, 1693 [according to Mattheson, attrib. Kusser, ?1694]

Der königliche Printz aus Pohlen Sigismundus, oder Das menschliche Leben wie ein Traum (after P. Calderón de la Barca: *La vida es sueño*), Conradi, 1693; *Der durch Gross-Muth und Tapfferkeit besiegete Porus* (Spl, after F. C. Bressand), Kusser, 1694; *Der wunderbar-vergnügte Pygmalion*, Conradi, 1694; *Der geliebte Adonis*, Keiser, 1697; *Die durch Wilhelm den Grossen in Britannien wieder eingeführte Irene*, Keiser, 1698

Der aus Hyperboreen nach Cymbrien übergebrachte güldene Apfel, Keiser, 1698; *Der bey dem allgemeinen Welt-Friede von dem grossen Augustus geschlossene Tempel des Janus*, Keiser, 1698; *Die an dem glücklichen Vermählungs-Tage ... vorgebildete Verbindung des grossen Hercules mit der schönen Hebe* (Spl), Keiser, 1699; *Die wunderbahr-errettete Iphigenia* (after Euripides), Keiser, 1699; *Die wunder-schöne Psyche* (Spl), Keiser, 1701; *Sieg der fruchtbaren Pomona*, Keiser, 1702

*

J. Mattheson: *Der musicalische Patriot* (Hamburg, 1728)
N. Wilckens: *Hamburgischer Ehrentempel* (Hamburg, 1770)
W. Flemming: *Die Oper*, Deutsche Literatur: Sammlung literarischer Kunst- und Kulturdenkmäler in Entwicklungsreihen, ser.13*b*: *Das Barockdrama*, v (Leipzig, 1933)
H. C. Wolff: *Die Barockoper in Hamburg* (Wolfenbüttel, 1957)
D. I. Lindberg: *Literary Aspects of German Baroque Opera: History, Theory and Practice* (diss., UCLA, 1964)
G. Flaherty: *Opera in the Development of German Critical Thought* (Princeton, 1978)
W. Braun: *Vom Remter zum Gänsemarkt: aus der Frühgeschichte der alten Hamburger Oper (1677–1697)* (Saarbrücken, 1987)
GEORGE J. BUELOW

Poster (Fr. *affiche*; Ger. *Plakat*; It. *manifesto*, *cartello*, *cartellone*). A placard or 'great bill', normally printed in eye-catching style, to be displayed in prominent positions for the purpose of announcing details of a forthcoming event and attracting the public. The word originates from the custom of attaching bills to the posts that marked the area for pedestrians in London streets before the Great Fire. *See* PLAYBILL.

Postillon de Lonjumeau, Le ('The Coachman of Longjumeau'). *Opéra comique* in three acts by ADOLPHE ADAM to a libretto by ADOLPHE DE LEUVEN and BRUNSWICK (i) [Leon Lhérie]; Paris, Opéra-Comique (Salle de la Bourse), 13 October 1836.

The coachman Chapelou (tenor) is celebrating his marriage to Madeleine (soprano), owner of the village inn. His spirited rendering of the song, 'Oh qu'il était beau, le postillon de Lonjumeau', with its repeated top D's in imitation of the post horn, is heard by the Marquis de Corcy (tenor), manager of the Paris Opéra, whose coach has broken down nearby. Corcy engages Chapelou for the Opéra on the spot, and insists that they set off at once, abandoning Madeleine on her wedding night.

In Paris ten years later Chapelou, under the name of Saint-Phar, has become a famous singer. Corcy is giving a soirée for Madame de Latour – as Madeleine, now very rich, has become – at which Saint-Phar will sing. Not recognizing her, Chapelou asks 'Madame de Latour' to marry him and arranges for an actor to perform the ceremony. Madeleine substitutes a real priest, then accuses 'Saint-Phar' of bigamy, a crime punishable by death, before revealing her true identity.

Outside France *Le postillon* was the most successful of all Adam's operas, particularly in Germany, where every tenor with the necessary top notes wanted to sing Chapelou. But the work is more than a vocal showpiece; Madeleine is as well characterized as Chapelou, and the various duets between them, first as the young bride and bridegroom, later as Madame Latour and Saint-Phar, are aptly differentiated. The music is in Adam's most tuneful vein and the work kept its popularity well into the 20th century.   ELIZABETH FORBES

Potenza, Pasquale (*b* ?Naples, *c*1730; *d* after 1797). Italian soprano castrato. He began in *opera seria* at Rome during Carnival 1747 in secondary roles and sang as primo uomo from Carnival 1749 at Palermo. In 1757–9 he was in London, where Burney was not impressed, calling him 'an uncertain singer, and an affected actor, with more taste than voice'. In 1765 he was in Jommelli's Stuttgart company. His career was virtually over by 1770, although he sang in 1772 at Treviso and 1777 at Verona; he was later a singer at St Mark's. He seems to have been a good all-round singer (range approximately *d'* to *c'''*) but not extraordinary in any vocal genre.   DENNIS LIBBY

Potestà di Colognole, Il ('The Governor of Colognole') [*La Tancia*]. *Dramma civile rusticale* in three acts by Jacopo Melani (see MELANI family, (1)) to a libretto by GIOVANNI ANDREA MONIGLIA; Florence, Teatro della Pergola, 5 February 1657.

Anselmo (alto), governor of Colognole, wishes to marry his daughter Isabella (soprano) to Flavio (baritone), a wealthy farmer. She is in love with Leandro (tenor), a young nobleman whom Anselmo considers unsuitable because of his poverty. Lisa (mezzo-soprano), Isabella's maid, stirs up various lovers' quarrels by pursuing first Leandro and then Flavio, whom she finally marries when she is discovered to be the lost daughter of Odoardo (tenor), the local judge. Leandro's clever servant Bruscolo (tenor) incites Anselmo's stuttering servant Desso (tenor) to steal a pot of gold from Anselmo and then tricks Desso into giving him the gold. Bruscolo next convinces Anselmo that Leandro has found a pot of gold (actually Anselmo's own) which, according to an oracle, foretells the union of Leandro and Anselmo's families, thus winning Anselmo's approval for Isabella's marriage to Leandro. A lover's triangle among the servants and peasants, who speak Tuscan dialect, simultaneously parodies that of the 'serious' parts.

The plot draws on classical Roman and Sienese comedies of the Renaissance for its themes, motifs and structure. The music favours aria over recitative, except in slapstick comic scenes, where the clarity of the text demands a simple 'dry' parlando recitative. Among operas of its time, *Il potestà* stands out for the formal diversity and expressiveness of its arias and ensembles. Notable also is the skill with which Melani depicted the characters and the dramatic emotional context. It is not accurate to call this work the first Italian comic opera, as has often been asserted, although Melani and Moniglia did attain a well-balanced and regulated conception of the genre. *Il potestà* was revived as late as 1727 at the Teatro del Cocomero in Florence, and melodies by much later Florentine composers, such as the Rutinis and Michele Neri Bondi, show marked similarity to the prototypes that it established.   ROBERT LAMAR WEAVER

Potpourri overture. *See* MEDLEY OVERTURE.

Potter, A(rchibald) J(ames) (*b* Belfast, 22 Sept 1918; *d* Greystones, 5 July 1980). Irish composer. He studied at Clifton College, Bristol, and at the RCM, where he was a pupil of Vaughan Williams (1936–8). He received the DMus from Dublin University in 1953 and was appointed professor of composition at the Royal Irish Academy of Music, Dublin, in 1955. Potter was one of the most prolific of contemporary Irish composers; he also made many Irish folksong arrangements. His through-composed opera for television, *Patrick*, written in 1962 to a libretto by Donagh McDonagh, was broadcast on 17 March 1965 (RTE TV, Dublin), and *The Wedding*, an opera in three acts to his own libretto, had its première at the Abbey Theatre, Dublin, on 8 June 1981. All of his music is characterized by an effective, if conventional, use of instruments, designed to give clear expression to the melodic content. His uncomplicated style recalls Vaughan Williams in its use of block harmonies, and the music is often broadly romantic, as in the idealistic ending of *Patrick*.   SEÓIRSE BODLEY

Pougin [Paroisse-Pougin], (François- Auguste-)Arthur (*b* Châteauroux, 6 Aug 1834; *d* Paris, 8 Aug 1921). French writer on music. Educated at the Paris Conservatoire, he was from the age of 13 a violinist in theatres, including the Opéra-Comique (1860–63), and assistant conductor and répétiteur at the Folies-Nouvelles (1856–9). He began as a writer on music with biographical articles in the *Revue et gazette musicale*, then contributed frequently to *Le ménestrel*, *La France musicale*, *L'art musical*, *Le théâtre* and *Chronique musicale* and was successively musical feuilletonist to *Le soir*, *La tribune*,

L'événement and (from 1878) the *Journal officiel*. In 1885 he became chief editor of *Le ménestrel*.

With his early series of biographies Pougin was, with Ernest Thoinan, one of the pioneers of French musicology. His main interest was always the music theatre and he wrote many books on opera composers and singers. His most important work, on the life of Verdi, was published in Italian (1881) with additions by Folchetto (Jacopo Caponi); he later produced a revision in French of his own and Folchetto's versions (1886). His *Dictionnaire historique et pittoresque du théâtre* (1885) contains valuable information on contemporary French operatic life. He also edited the music articles in the Larousse *Dictionnaire universel*, the supplement to Fétis's *Biographie universelle*(Paris, 1878–80) and a revision of Clément and Larousse's *Dictionnaire lyrique* (as *Dictionnaire des opéras*, suppl. 1904, 3/1905). He wrote a comic opera *Le cabaret de Ramponneau* and an operetta *Perrina*, both unpublished.

Meyerbeer: notes biographiques (Paris, 1864)
Musiciens français du XVIIIe siècle (Paris, 1864) [essays from *Revue et gazette musicale*, xxviii–xxxi, on Campra, Gresnick, Dezèdes, Floquet, Martini, Devienne]
F. Halévy, écrivain (Paris, 1865)
William-Vincent Wallace: étude biographique et critique (Paris, 1866)
Bellini: sa vie, ses oeuvres (Paris, 1868)
Albert Grisar: étude artistique (Paris, 1870)
Rossini: notes, impressions, souvenirs, commentaires (Paris, 1871)
Auber: ses commencements, les origines de sa carrière (Paris, 1873)
Boïeldieu: sa vie, ses oeuvres, son caractère, sa correspondance (Paris, 1875)
Figures d'opéra comique: Madame Dugazon, Elleviou, les Gavaudan (Paris, 1875)
Rameau: essai sur sa vie et ses oeuvres (Paris, 1876)
Adolphe Adam: sa vie, sa carrière, ses mémoires artistiques (Paris, 1877)
Verdi: vita aneddotica (Milan, 1881; Fr. orig., rev., 1886; Eng. trans., 1887)
Les vrais créateurs de l'opéra français: Perrin et Cambert (Paris, 1881)
Molière et l'opéra comique (Paris, 1882)
Dictionnaire historique et pittoresque du théâtre (Paris, 1885)
Méhul: sa vie, son génie, son caractère (Paris, 1889, 2/1893)
L'opéra comique pendant la Révolution (Paris, 1891)
La Comédie-Française et la Révolution (Paris, 1902)
Un ténor de l'Opéra au XVIIIe siècle: Pierre Jélyotte et les chanteurs de son temps (Paris, 1905)
Hérold: biographie critique (Paris, 1906)
Monsigny et son temps: l'Opéra-Comique et la Comédie-Italienne (Paris, 1908)
Marie Malibran: histoire d'une cantatrice (Paris, 1911; Eng. trans., 1911)
Madame Favart: étude théâtrale, 1727–1772 (Paris, 1912)
Marietta Alboni (Paris, 1912)
Un directeur d'opéra au XVIIIe siècle (A. P. J. de Vismes): l'Opéra sous l'ancien régime: l'Opéra sous la Révolution (Paris, 1914)
Massenet (Paris, 1914)
Une cantatrice 'amie' de Napoléon: Giuseppina Grassini 1773–1850 (Paris, 1920)
NORBERT DUFOURCQ

Poulenard, Isabelle (*b* Paris, 5 July 1961). French soprano. She studied at the Ecole Nationale d'Art Lyrique of the Paris Opéra. She made her début in 1981 at Tourcoing as Lisette in Paisiello's *Il re Teodoro in Venezia* which, like many of her early appearances, was conducted by Jean-Claude Malgoire. Since then she has taken a wide variety of roles, including Despina, the Queen of Night, Gluck's Iphigenia and the title role in Rameau's *Zéphyre*. She has sung in Cesti's *Orontea*, Rameau's *Hippolyte et Aricie* (directed by William Christie) and Poulenc's *Dialogues des Carmélites*. Her recordings include *Orontea* (1983), Lully's *Armide*

(1983), Cavalli's *Serse* (1985), Vivaldi's *L'incoronazione di Dario* (1986), Rameau's *Le temple de la Gloire* (1982) and *Platée* (1988), and Charpentier's *Le malade imaginaire* (1990). Poulenard's agile technique and the tonal purity and light texture of her voice are especially well suited to the Baroque and Classical repertory, in which she reveals an informed sense of style.

NICHOLAS ANDERSON

Poulenc, Francis (**Jean Marcel**) (*b* Paris, 7 Jan 1899; *d* Paris, 30 Jan 1963). French composer. His youth and early career were characterized by wealth, happiness and good fortune. His parents were well off and well connected, but it was through a rather worldly 'Oncle Papoum' as well as his piano teacher, the influential Ricardo Viñes, that he secured his entrées into Parisian social and musical life. His good fortune was that his first attempts at composition, though technically insecure, displayed a freshness and insouciant charm which accorded with the contemporary backlash to the sophistication of post-Wagnerian French music. The new fashion, led by Jean Cocteau and endorsed by Erik Satie, was for simplicity: the sounds of the street, *bals musettes* and circuses rather than the once fashionable *belle époque*. Poulenc's early works – the *Rapsodie nègre* (1917), the *Trois mouvements perpetuels* (1918), the miniature song cycles *Le bestiaire* (1918–19) and *Cocardes* (1919) – all displayed the obligatory naivety which went to make up the style of Les Six. Wishing to increase his technical abilities, Poulenc took lessons with Charles Koechlin. Much of his music of the early 1920s displays a desire to be taken seriously, his natural melodic and harmonic gifts becoming engulfed in a welter of atonality, complications and digressions. He was most himself when he began (under the direct influence of Stravinsky, as so often in his career) to explore the *galant* music of the 18th century in a series of works, from *Les biches* (a Dyagilev commission of 1923, first performed in 1924) to the *Concert champêtre* for harpsichord (1927–8) and *Aubade* (1929), a neoclassical ballet for piano and 18 instruments in which he found a free and musically respectable framework for his melodic gifts. The untimely death in 1936 of a friend and colleague, Pierre-Octave Ferroud, triggered a new maturity. The effects were a rediscovery of his Catholic faith, a concern with serious song-writing (mostly to the verse of the humanist surrealist Paul Eluard) and the forging of a lifelong association with the lyric baritone Pierre Bernac. The *Litanies à la vierge noire* (1936) and *Tel jour telle nuit* (to poetry by Eluard, 1937) initiated a long series of religious works and *mélodies* which form the cornerstones of Poulenc's reputation.

The war increased a strain of melancholy in Poulenc's work, evinced by a new willingness to admit the lyrical and harmonic language of Ravel to an already full roster of musical influences (Satie, Stravinsky, Chabrier, Musorgsky, Debussy and Prokofiev are among the others, but as Poulenc said 'I mistrust a child who blushes at his own parentage'). An understandable urge to celebrate all things vital and sensuous and, above all, French, led to wartime works such as the La Fontaine ballet *Les animaux modèles* (1940–41), the Eluard cantata *Figure humaine* (1943) and the opera *Les mamelles de Tirésias* (1944). The postwar years were marked by increasing isolation at the rearguard of French contemporary music (his self-awareness as a harmonic reactionary is revealed in several awkward excursions into serial writing – he could follow

Stravinsky only so far) and by several bouts of depression and nervous exhaustion. His larger works of this period, *Stabat mater* (1950) and *Gloria* (1959), and the opera *Dialogues des Carmélites* (1953–6), consolidate the religious and musical discoveries made in the key years of 1936–40 while displaying a growing technical and formal mastery. The last three wind sonatas show a slight slackening of pure melodic invention, possibly explicable in the light of the tortured introversion of Poulenc's full-scale works, the opera *La voix humaine* (1959) and the *Sept répons des ténèbres* (1962), in which the pulse and panic of manic depression are immediately and terrifyingly audible.

See also DIALOGUES DES CARMÉLITES; MAMELLES DE TIRÉSIAS, LES; and VOIX HUMAINE, LA.

Les mamelles de Tirésias, 1944 (opéra bouffe, prol., 2, Poulenc, after G. Apollinaire), Paris, OC (Favart), 3 June 1947
Dialogues des Carmélites, 1953–6 (3, Poulenc, after G. Bernanos), Milan, Scala, 26 Jan 1957
La voix humaine (tragédie lyrique, 1, J. Cocteau), Paris, OC (Favart), 6 Feb 1959

H. Jourdan-Morhange: 'La voix humaine à l'Opéra-Comique', Lettres françaises (12–18 Feb 1959)
E. Lockspeiser: 'An Introduction to Poulenc's "La voix humaine"', Opera, xi (1960), 527–34
P.-M. Adéma: 'Les mamelles de Tirésias', Revue des lettres modernes, 4th ser., nos.123–6 (1965), 55–63
J. Bellas: 'Les mamelles de Tirésias en habit d'Arlequin', Guillaume Apollinaire, iv (1965), 30–54
Catalogue de l'exposition à Tours: Georges Bernanos, Francis Poulenc et les 'Dialogues des Carmélites' (Paris, 1970)
F. Rauhut: 'Les motifs musicaux de l'opéra "Dialogues des Carmélites"', Revue des lettres modernes, 4th ser., nos.340–45 (1973), 211–49
J. Sams: 'Poulenc's Carmelites: the Background', Opera, xxxiv (1983), 375–9
L'avant-scène opéra, no.52 (1983) [Dialogues des Carmélites issue]
S. Buckland, ed.: Francis Poulenc: Echo and Source: Selected Correspondence 1915–1963 (London, 1991)   JEREMY SAMS

Pound, Ezra (Loomis) (*b* Hailey, ID, 30 Oct 1885; *d* Venice, 1 Nov 1972). American poet and amateur composer. His musical achievements include an idiosyncratic *Treatise on Harmony*, a body of criticism, a role in the revival of early music, and music for two 'operas', *The Testament of François Villon* (1923) and *Cavalcanti* (1932). In his student years Pound's taste was formed by the Provençal troubadours, with their ideal union of composer and poet. Acquaintance with Arnold Dolmetsch deepened his love for early music. In 1913 the pianist Walter Rummel and Pound published arrangements of nine troubadour songs. From this unorthodox base, Pound, under the pseudonym William Atheling, reviewed London concerts from 1917 to 1920 in *The New Age*, attacking current repertory and performing practice. He considered all opera written since Rossini to be aesthetically corrupt. In the 1930s local concerts sponsored by Pound in Rapallo gave impetus to the 1939 Settimana Vivaldiana at Siena, which helped restore Vivaldi's reputation and included the first modern revival of a Vivaldi opera (*L'olimpiade*).

Villon, composed with help from George Antheil, illustrates Pound's theories of song, combining troubadour monody with rhythmic notation intended to reproduce asymmetrical word rhythms with precision. Complex metres like 7/16 or 19/32 are frequent. Harmony is minimal, instrumentation pointillist, dialogue perfunctory, staging stylized, the performer's personality effaced: all operatic resources are subordinated to the rhythmic-melodic verse line. Pound's style is possibly the most original devised by an amateur. The libretto is constructed from passages of Villon's poetry in Old French stitched together with English dialogue. *Villon*, first given in concert performance in Paris (1926), has been produced twice by the BBC (1932, 1962), staged by the Western Opera Theatre of San Francisco (1971) and recorded by Fantasy Records of Berkeley, California (1972). *Cavalcanti* is similarly constructed from Italian lyrics (as well as two in Provençal by Sordello) and English dialogue. The manuscripts of *Villon* (in Antheil's hand) and of the libretto and separate numbers of *Cavalcanti* are in the Pound collection of the Beinecke Library at Yale University.

S. J. Adams: Ezra Pound and Music (diss., U. of Toronto, 1974)
R. M. Schafer, ed.: Ezra Pound and Music (New York, 1977)
A. Henderson: Pound and Music: the Paris and Early Rapallo Years (diss., UCLA, 1983)   STEPHEN J. ADAMS

Pounds, (Charles) Courtice (*b* London, 30 May 1862; *d* London, 21 Dec 1927). English tenor. Short and boyish-looking, he began his career with D'Oyly Carte at the Savoy Theatre, London, in 1881, rising to play Nanki-Poo in New York in 1885, where he remained for several years; he returned to London to create Fairfax in *The Yeomen of the Guard*, Marco in *The Gondoliers* and Indru in Edward Solomon's *The Nautch Girl* (1891). His performance in the comic role of Lancelot in Audran's *La poupée* (1897) marked a turning away from the juvenile roles towards those of character and comedy in both straight and musical theatre. He appeared in Caryll's *The Duchess of Dantzic*, Leslie Stuart's *The Belle of Mayfair*, Fall's *Der fidele Bauer* and *Der liebe Augustin* and, most memorably, as Ali Baba for all the 2000 and more performances of Frederic Norton's *Chu Chin Chow* (1916), proving himself the most complete and versatile singing actor of his age. His youngest sister, Louie, had an equally remarkable and long career in burlesque, musical comedy and comic opera.   KURT GÄNZL

Pountney, David (Willoughby) (*b* Oxford, 10 Sept 1947). English director. After education at Radley College and Cambridge University, where he was director of productions of the Opera Society, he began his career with *Kát'a Kabanová* at Wexford (1972). From 1975 to 1980 he was director of productions at Scottish Opera, where he directed *Die Meistersinger*, *Yevgeny Onegin*, *Die Fledermaus* and *Don Giovanni*, among others, as well as a highly acclaimed Janáček cycle in collaboration with the WNO. He made his American début with *Macbeth* at Houston in 1973 and his Australian début in Sydney in 1978 with *Die Meistersinger*. A series of productions for the Netherlands Opera included the world première of Glass's *Satyagraha* (1980). His work has also been seen in Berlin, Paris, Rome, the Bregenz Festival, Chicago and the Metropolitan, New York, where he directed the world première of Glass's *The Voyage* on Columbus Day, 1992.

In 1977 Pountney made his début at the ENO with the world première of Blake's *Toussaint*. From 1982 to 1993 he was director of productions at the ENO, where, in close collaboration with the designer Stefanos Lazaridis and the music director, Mark Elder, he evolved a definable house style. Characteristic features were the arresting images of dislocated reality, an inexhaustible repertory of stage contrivances, a determination to explore the social and psychological issues latent in the works, and above all an abundant sense of theatricality. Pountney's riotous inventiveness was seen to best advantage in his expressionistic, sometimes anarchic *Doktor Faust* (1986), his savage *Lady Macbeth of the Mtsensk District* (1987) and his *Wozzeck* (1990), in all of which grotesque caricature jostled with forceful emotional engagement.

A range of distancing devices is evident in Pountney's work, from the ironically illuminated hearts and dollar signs in the vibrant, exhilarating ensemble numbers of *Street Scene* (1989) to the desentimentalized treatment of *La traviata* (1988), which drew attention away from the traditional affective preoccupations and towards the hypocritical double standards of 19th-century sexual mores. Especially characteristic are the phantasmagoric evocations seen in *Osud* (1984), with its white-clad figures, surreal lighting and revolving stage, and *Hänsel und Gretel* (1987), with its dream pantomime peopled by fantasy figures from the children's imagination.

The professionalism and conviction of Pountney's productions have earned the sometimes grudging admiration of the more traditionally minded, at the same time winning new audiences for the ENO and maintaining its place at the forefront of international opera for over a decade.

For illustration *see* LAZARIDIS, STEFANOS and LONDON, fig.12.

'Words, Music and Tradition', *Opera*, xxxviii (1987), 1375–9
'The Joy of Rimsky', *Opera*, xxxix (1988), 1405–9

H. Rosenthal: 'David Pountney', *Opera*, xxxiv (1983), 1072–6
R. Fawkes: 'A Different Light', *Classical Music* (11 Feb 1989), 33–5
BARRY MILLINGTON

Pousseur, Henri (Léon Marie Thérèse) (*b* Malmédy, 23 June 1929). Belgian composer. He studied at the Liège Conservatory, notably with the organist Pierre Froidebise, who widened his interest in new music. Pousseur became greatly interested in the aesthetic of the Second Viennese School, Webern in particular. The most important of his works from this period, when he was questioning traditional models, are the *Sept versets des psaumes de la pénitence* (1950), *Trois chants sacrés* (1951), *Symphonies à 15 solistes* (1954–5) and *Quintette à la mémoire d'Anton Webern* (1955). His first electronic experiments at the Studio für Elektronische Musik, Cologne, also date from 1954. In 1957 he created *Scambi* at the Studio di Fonologia in Milan, and in 1958 he participated in the founding of APELAC, the electronic music studio in Brussels.

Most of the major problems which have engaged musical thinking since the early 1950s are deflected, with an exceptionally lucid critical sense, through the personality of Pousseur: serialism, mobile form and the question of the opening of a work, electro-acoustics and the relationship with the interpreter, the wider scope of musical material (and its treatment in real time by means of new technology), and the exploration of previously existing material. A constant factor in his approach is his interest in vocal work and the great possibilities for creative development represented by collaboration with a writer. Many of his concert works, including *Répons* (1960–65), *Votre Faust* (1960–69), *Le procès du jeune chien* (1977–8) and *La rose des voix* (1982) have dramatic elements; his works composed in collaboration with Michel Butor (music drama, opera and oratorio) have been a testimony to his innovatory

treatment of the relationship between text and music, with neither artistic field subordinated to the other.

See also VOTRE FAUST.

L. Berio: 'Notre Faust', *NRMI*, iii (1969), 275–87
D. and J.-Y. Bosseur: 'Collaboration Butor/Pousseur', *Musique en jeu* (1971), no.4, pp.83–111
J.-Y. Bosseur: 'Les scènes de foire dans *Votre Faust*', *Obliques*, iv (1974), 135–47
JEAN-YVES BOSSEUR

Povest' o nastoyashchem cheloveke. Opera by Sergey Prokofiev; *see* STORY OF A REAL MAN, THE.

Power of the Fiend, The. Opera by A. N. Serov; *see* VRAZH'YA SILA.

Powers, Marie (*b* Mount Carmel, PA, 1910; *d* New York, 28 Dec 1973). American contralto. She studied in New York and in the mid-1940s toured the USA with the San Carlo Opera; her roles for the company included Azucena, Amneris and both Laura and La Cieca in *La Gioconda*. She sang Madame Flora in the New York (1947) and London (1948) premières of Menotti's *The Medium*, and in 1948 made her début with the New York City Opera in his *The Old Maid and the Thief*. She also created Azelia in Still's *Troubled Island* in 1949; at the Paris Opéra she sang Fricka (1951) and Mistress Quickly (1952). A very effective actress with a strong, deep-toned voice, she will always be associated with *The Medium*.
ELIZABETH FORBES

Pownall, Mary Ann. *See* WRIGHTEN, MARY ANN.

Poznań (Ger. Posen). City in Poland, capital of the province of Wielkopolska (Great Poland) and the earliest capital of the Polish state (until *c*1038). In the first half of the 18th century the Jesuit school theatre presented operatic interludes. The first operas were given in 1783–4 in the former Jesuit school by Bogusławski's National Theatre company from Warsaw, including works by Audinot, Duni, Grétry, Paisiello and Sacchini, and Polish comic operas by M. Kamieński and Gaetano. Between 1800 and 1814 the company visited regularly, giving *Die Zauberflöte* (1805), Salieri's *Axur, re d'Ormus* and operas by Cherubini, Paisiello, Winter, Elsner and Jan Stefani; from 1804 performances were staged in the newly built municipal theatre. Other Polish companies, mainly from Kraków, gave summer seasons intermittently from 1819 to 1869.

From 1793 until 1918 the city was under Prussian rule, and operas were frequently staged by German companies. During his stay in Poznań, E. T. A. Hoffmann presented his Singspiel *Scherz, List und Rache* (1801). Operas by Mozart, Weber, Rossini, Donizetti and Halévy were often performed, and the first production of *Tannhäuser* outside Germany was given in Poznań as early as 22 May 1853. Not until January 1870 did the Teatr Polski, a permanent professional Polish repertory theatre, establish itself; it moved to a 600-seat hall in 1875, and included standard operas and operettas among its productions. Soon afterwards, in 1879 the German municipal theatre, built in 1804, was replaced by a new one.

After World War I when the country regained its independence, a Polish opera house, the Teatr Wielki (Grand Theatre), was founded. Designed in 1910 by Max Littmann to hold 900 spectators, it opened on 31 August 1919 with Moniuszko's *Halka* and soon became one of the most important opera houses in Poland. During the Nazi occupation in World War II a German company staged, in addition to the standard repertory, performances of Zillig's *Die Windsbraut* (1942) and Orff's *Die Kluge* (1944). After the war the Wielki Theatre was the first Polish opera house to be reopened, in 1945. In 1949 the company came under state control as Państwowa Opera w Poznanin (State Opera of Poznań), and from 1950 the Wielki Theatre was named after Stanisław Moniuszko. More than 500 productions of operas, operettas and ballets have been given there since 1919, with special emphasis on works by Polish composers; among its 22 world premières are operas by Lucjan Kamieński, Feliks Nowowiejski, Henryk Opieński, Ludomir Różycki and Roman Statkowski. Polish premières include operas by Handel, Gluck, Mozart, Janáček, Strauss, Ravel, Britten, Menotti and Liebermann (*School for Wives*, 1966). The Poznań Operetta House, now the Teatr Muzyczny (Music Theatre), has staged operettas and musicals since 1956.

H. Ehrenberg: 'Das Posener Theater in südpreussischer Zeit', *Zeitschrift der Historischen Gesellschaft für die Provinz Posen*, ix (1894), 27–90
M. Laubert: 'Das Posener Theater 1815–1847', *Studien zur Provinz Posen*, i (Posen, 1908), 117–95
Z. Grot: *Dzieje sceny polskiej w Poznaniu 1782–1869* [History of the Polish Stage in Poznań] (Poznań, 1950)
Z. Raszewski: *Z tradycji teatralnych Pomorza, Wielkopolski i Śląska* [The Theatrical Traditions in Pomerania, Great Poland and Silesia] (Wrocław, 1955)
H. Knudsen: *Deutsches Theater in Posen* (Bad Nauheim, 1961)
J. Waldorff, ed.: *Opera Poznańska 1919–1969* (Poznań, 1970)
T. Świtała: *Opera Poznańska 1919–1969* (Poznań, 1973)
——: *Opera Poznańska w latach 1969–1979* (Poznań, 1979)
D. Gwizdałówna, ed.: *Teatr Wielki im. Stanisława Moniuszki 1919–1979* [The Stanisław Moniuszko Grand Theatre] (Poznań, 1979)
T. Świtała: *Teatr Muzyczny w Poznaniu 1956–1981* [The Music Theatre in Poznań] (Poznań, 1982)   KORNEL MICHAŁOWSKI

Pozsony (Hung.). BRATISLAVA.

Pozzi, Anna (*fl* 1776–88). Italian soprano. She was engaged, apparently without prior experience, as prima donna in London in 1776, and proving unequal (though according to Burney 'young, handsome, and possessed of a voice uncommonly clear, sweet and powerful') was demoted to seconda donna, remaining until 1778. Between 1780 and 1788 she was prima donna in leading Italian theatres, and in 1781–3 seems to have been closely associated with Sarti, singing in four of his operas. She had a voice of wide range, rising to *e'''*, described by some as 'brilliant and silvery' but by others as 'birdlike' and mechanical in expression.

DENNIS LIBBY

Pozzoni(-Anastasi), Antonietta (*b* Venice, 1846; *d* Genoa, April 1914). Italian soprano, later mezzo-soprano. She studied in St Petersburg and Milan, making her début at La Scala in 1865 as Marguerite (*Faust*). After singing in Rome, Padua, Turin and Naples, in 1871 she sang *La traviata* in Florence, which led to her engagement to sing Aida at the première of Verdi's opera in Cairo. Her soprano repertory included Lady Macbeth, Hélène (*Les vêpres siciliennes*), Anna Bolena, Lucrezia Borgia, Emilia (Mercadante's *La vestale*) and Norma. In 1874 she took part in the first performance of Gomes's *Salvator Rosa* at Genoa and sang Amneris at Brescia, repeating the role in Rome, Madrid, Milan, Barcelona and Florence. Her mezzo parts included Fidès, Azucena, Ortrud, Léonor (*La favorite*) and Massenet's Herodias. She retired in 1887.

ELIZABETH FORBES

Praetorius, Johann Philipp (*b* Elmshorn, Holstein, ?1696; *d* Trier or Frankfurt, ?1766). German librettist. He was the principal librettist at the Theater am Gänsemarkt, Hamburg, from 1725 to 1727, and produced about nine librettos for Telemann and Keiser. Most are comedies marked by a ready wit and a penchant for social criticism. After taking a law degree at the University of Kiel, he had arrived in Hamburg by August 1724, when he provided Telemann with the text for his 'Kapitänsmusik' *Geliebter Aufenthalt, beglückte Stille*. By October 1724 Praetorius was evidently employed in some capacity at the Gänsemarkt, as he responded to an article that criticized the opera's management by penning a vicious satire, *Il pregio dell'ignoranza, oder Die Bass-Geige*, directed against the supposed authors of the article, including Telemann. The hot-headed Praetorius was soon reconciled with Telemann, and they collaborated on at least five operas over the next three years, the best-known of which is *Pimpinone* (1725). Praetorius's career as a librettist ended with his departure from Hamburg, some time before 1734; his subsequent positions included a magisterial post in Holstein and a professorship in law at Trier. Legal difficulties, financial reversals and unemployment marred his later life, and he died in obscurity.

Bretislaus, oder Die siegende Beständigkeit (Spl), Keiser, 1725; *Der Hamburger Jahrmarkt, oder Der glückliche Betrug* (Spl), Keiser, 1725; *Die Hamburger Schlachtzeit, oder Der misslungene Betrug* (Spl), Keiser, 1725; *Pimpinone, oder Die ungleiche Heyrath* (int), Telemann, 1725; *La caprizziosa e il credulo*, Telemann, 1725; *Adelheid, oder Die ungezwungene Liebe*, Telemann, 1725; *Der stumme Prinz Atis* (int), Keiser, 1726; *Der lächerliche Prinz Jodelet* (Spl), Keiser, 1726; *Calypso, oder Sieg der Weisheit über die Liebe*, Telemann, 1727; *Die verkehrte Welt* (oc), Telemann, 1728; *Circe* (Spl, with J. J. van Mauritius), Keiser and others, 1734   BRIAN D. STEWART

Prague (Cz. Praha; Ger. Prag). City on the River Vltava (Moldau), capital of Czechoslovakia from 1918 and from 1992 the Czech republic, and formerly capital of Bohemia. It has been an important operatic centre since the 18th century, first as an outpost of the Habsburg empire, and later as the focal point of Czech nationalism.

1. 1627–1783. 2. 1783–1862. 3. 1862–1945. 4. From 1945.

1. 1627–1783. The first operatic performance in Prague took place on 27 November 1627 at the castle on the occasion of the coronation of Ferdinand III, when a company from Mantua presented 'eine schöne Pastoral-Comoedia', perhaps composed by G. B. Buonamente. This new art form was unconnected with any native tradition in Bohemia, but its history was naturally influenced by the political situation in the Czech lands in the 17th century. Following the resignation of Rudolf II in 1611 the imperial court had moved from Prague to Vienna; after defeat in the Battle of White Mountain (1620), the greater part of the non-Catholic nobility had to leave Bohemia. Courtly entertainment therefore found little room in Prague; the aristocratic culture that arrived from Vienna developed slowly, at the country seats of the nobility as much as in Prague itself. The imperial court was twice more situated in Prague during the 17th century, when operas

1. Arena of Prague castle during the performance of Fux's 'Costanza e Fortezza', given as part of the festivities celebrating the coronation of Charles VI as Emperor of Bohemia in August 1723: engraving by Birckhart after Giuseppe Galli-Bibiena

were staged: in 1648 G. F. Sances's opera *I trionfi d'Amore*, and in 1680 Antonio Draghi's *La patienza di Socrate con due moglie*, among other works. Of great importance, over 40 years later, were the court festivities marking the coronation of Charles VI as Emperor of Bohemia (August 1723), which included the première of Fux's *Costanza e Fortezza*. The open-air stage was 63 metres in depth, and the sets and machines were designed by Giuseppe Galli-Bibiena (see fig.1; *see also* GALLI-BIBIENA, fig.2). J. D. Zelenka's festival opera *Sub olea pacis* was also given its first performance at that time (November 1723).

The cultivation of Italian opera at the palaces of the aristocracy after 1650 is little documented, since nowhere was a long tradition established. There were theatres in the Eggenberg-Schwarzenberg palace at Hradčany (built in 1660), in the garden of Count Franz Anton Sporck's residence (built in 1701 and open to the public; until 1725 only spoken drama is documented), in the Clam-Gallas palace (after 1700), in the Kolovrat palace in the Old Town (1743), in the Wallenstein palace in the Little Quarter and (after 1770) in the Thun palace, also in the Little Quarter. It was to the Thun palace that the nobility invited the impresario Pasquale Bondini in 1781, and it was there that a castrato appeared for the last time in Prague.

The first opera impresario to work in Prague was apparently G. F. Sartorio, who was there between 1701 and 1705. He staged Italian operas to a paying audience at the Regnard house in the Little Quarter. In 1724

Count Sporck invited Antonio Denzio's Italian company to his summer palace at KUKS, and from 1725 to 1734 the same company also performed at his theatre in Prague. Denzio presented 57 operas by Vivaldi (several of them premières), Albinoni, Porta and others. During the period 1737–40 a company directed by the composer Santo Lapis performed in Prague, first at Count Sporck's theatre and later in the new theatre at Kotce known as the Comoedia-Haus or the Kotzen Opera (sometimes called simply the 'Nuovo Teatro'). This opened in 1738 or 1739 in a former commercial building; the stage measured 13 by 13 metres and the auditorium 46 by 13 metres. It was the main venue for performances (mostly of *opera buffa*) by Italian companies. The most important impresarios at Kotce were Angelo and Pietro Mingotti (1743–6), who put on operas by Pergolesi, Pinazzi, Galuppi, Vinci and Gluck; G. B. Locatelli (1748–57), who mounted the premières of Gluck's *Ezio* (1750) and *Issipile* (1752), as well as operas by Galuppi and others; J. F. von Kurz (1758–64) and his lessee Molinari, with operas by Galuppi, Auletta and Fischietti; and Giuseppe Bustelli (1764–81), who put on works by Galuppi, Piccinni, Guglielmi, Mysliveček and Kozeluch, while his lessees J. J. Brunian (1769–78) and Karl Wahr presented Singspiels, including *Die Entführung aus dem Serail* in 1782. The theatre at Kotce closed in 1783.

2. 1783–1862. On 21 April 1783 the Nostitzsches Nationaltheater, built by Count F. A. Nostitz (1725–94)

with a capacity of over 1000 and a stage measuring 18 by 16 metres, was opened (see fig.2); until 1862 it was Prague's main opera house. Among its early lessees were Bondini (1784–8) and Domenico Guardasoni (1788–1806). They both presented operas by Mozart: *Le nozze di Figaro* in 1786 and subsequent years, the premières of *Don Giovanni* (1787, commissioned by Bondini for royal wedding celebrations) and *La clemenza di Tito* (1791, commissioned by Guardasoni for the festivities surrounding the coronation of Leopold II), and a revival of *Die Zauberflöte* (1792). Guardasoni was the last impresario in Prague to maintain Italian as the language of performance. His productions included works by Cimarosa and Paisiello, as well as German Singspiels. In 1798 the theatre was purchased by the Bohemian Estates; as the Stavovské Divadlo or Ständetheater (Estates Theatre) it became a centre for German opera. C. M. von Weber worked there as con-

Estates Theatre (*Don Giovanni*, 1842; *Figaro*, 1843).

The first serious attempts to stage opera in Czech occurred only in the late 18th century. Czech theatre had for a long time lacked the support of the nobility and the wealthy, and was starved of good professional forces. At Kotce Czech arrangements of Singspiels and, later, translations of Italian operas were presented, and after 1770 Bustelli and Wahr put on original operas in Czech. In 1786 Bondini's Vlastenské Divadlo (Patriotic Theatre) company began to perform in Czech and German at a new wooden theatre, and from 1789 to 1802 the same company presented about 50 works in Czech at the U Hybernů monastery, including Mozart's *Die Zauberflöte* in 1794 and operas by Süssmayr, Dittersdorf, Müller, Kauer and Tuček. Between 1804 and 1806 Guardasoni presented several operas in Czech, but after 1806 there was no Czech opera in Prague again until 1824. During the next ten years

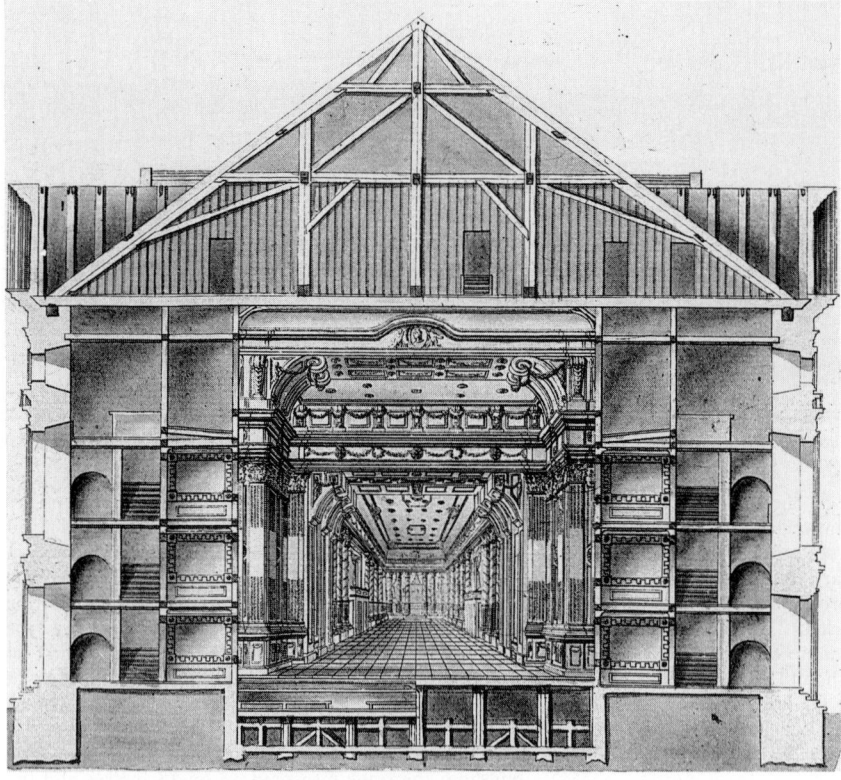

2. Cross-section of the Nostitzsches Nationaltheater, Prague (opened in 1783), showing the stage and proscenium arch: engraving by Filip and Franz Heger

ductor from 1813 to 1816, presenting, among other works, Beethoven's *Fidelio* (1814), the première of Spohr's *Faust* (1816) and a number of French operas. His *Der Freischütz* was performed in Prague 50 times between 1821 and 1823. From 1827 to 1857 the conductor was F. J. Škroup, who chose an exacting repertory: Meyerbeer (from 1835), Verdi (for the first time in 1849), *Tannhäuser* (1854), *Lohengrin* (1856) and *Der fliegende Holländer* (1856). Between 1850 and 1860 Meyerbeer, Donizetti, Flotow, Verdi, Mozart, Rossini and Wagner were the composers most frequently performed. Most of the aristocratic theatres had ceased to exist by 1800, but the nobility continued to support performances by the Prague Conservatory, which presented operas by Mozart between 1828 and 1831 at the theatre of Count Vrtba (*La clemenza di Tito*, 1828; *Die Entführung*, 1829) and later at the Dominican monastery (*Così fan tutte*, 1839) and at the

about 120 performances in Czech were given at the Estates Theatre and its subsidiary theatre in Růžová Street; these were mainly translations of the standard repertory but occasionally included new works such as Škroup's *Dráteník* ('The Tinker', 1826).

3. 1862–1945. In 1862 the Královské Zemské České Divadlo (Royal Provincial Czech Theatre), always known as the Prozatímní Divadlo (Provisional Theatre; cap. 900, stage 9.5 by 9.5 metres), was opened (see fig.3); during the next 20 years its chief conductors were J. N. Maýr (1862–6 and 1874–81) and Smetana (1866–74). In this cramped theatre the premières of several works basic to the Czech repertory were given, in particular Smetana's *The Bartered Bride* in 1866 and works by K. R. Šebor, Karel Bendl and Dvořák (*King and Charcoal Burner*, 1874). French, Italian and German works were also performed. In 1881 the Národní

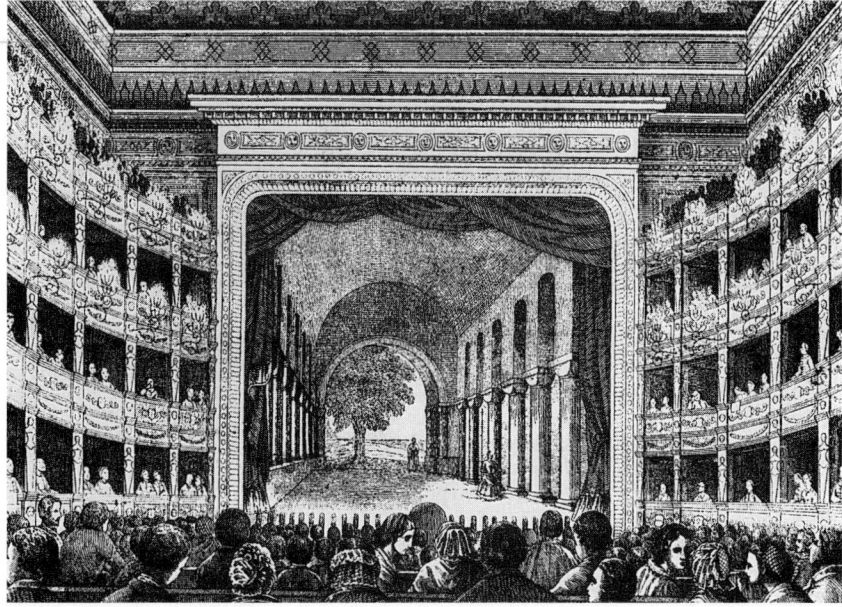

3. *Interior of Prozatímní Divadlo (Provisional Theatre), Prague, opened in 1862 as a home for Czech opera and drama: engraving*

Divadlo (National Theatre; cap. 1500, stage 22 by 20 metres), incorporating the Provisional Theatre, opened with Smetana's *Libuše* (see fig.4). After only two months it was destroyed by fire, but it was rebuilt in 1883. Until 1900 the opera director was F. A. Šubert and the chief conductor Adolf Čech. Under Karel Kovařovic (1900–20) the company reached a high standard; he was succeeded by Otakar Ostrčil (1920–35) and Václav Talich (1935–45). About half of the repertory was by Czech composers; operettas were not included. The most frequently played composers in the years 1888–1918 were Smetana (with 1331 performances), Dvořák (444), Verdi (399), Wagner (355) and Mozart (238). Premières at the National Theatre included those of Dvořák's *Rusalka* (1901) and *Armida* (1904), Janáček's *The Excursions of Mr Brouček* (1920) and Martinů's *Julietta* (1938), as well as operas by Fibich, J. B. Foerster, Ostrčil and Novák.

After 1860 Czech opera was also performed at summer theatres, including the important Novoměstské Divadlo (New Town Theatre; cap. 3000), where from 1859 to 1876 performances (notably the first of Smetana's *Dalibor*, 1868) were given in Czech within the framework of a German-language repertory. From 1876 to 1885 opera was staged in the wooden Nové České Divadlo (New Czech Theatre; cap. 3000), where premières included those of Smetana's *The Secret* (1878) and Dvořák's *Dimitrij* (1882). Between 1907 and 1919 opera was performed in Czech at the Městské Divadlo na Královských Vinohradech (Town Theatre in the Royal Vineyards), under Ludvík Čelanský (until 1913) and Ostrčil (1913–19). 59 operas were given, including Berlioz's *Béatrice et Bénédict* in 1916. Prague Radio also broadcast premières, such as Martinů's *Hlas lesa* ('The Voice of the Forest', 1935) and *Veselohra na mostě* ('Comedy on the Bridge', 1937).

4. *Národní Divadlo (National Theatre), Prague, shortly after its opening in 1881: steel engraving*

For a time from 1862, opera in German was given only at the Estates Theatre, which had to cope with difficult operational problems. From 1885 to 1910 its director was Angelo Neumann, who substantially raised the standard, and in 1885–6 Mahler was conductor. Mozart operas continued to be performed here. But in 1888 the Deutscher Theaterverein opened the Neues Deutsches Theater (cap. 1600, stage size 22 by 16 metres) as the chief German theatre in Prague. It was served by a series of outstanding conductors: Carl Muck (1888–91), Franz Schalk (1895–8), Leo Blech (1899–1906), Otto Klemperer (1907–10), Alexander Zemlinsky (1911–27), William Steinberg (1927–9), Georg Szell (1929–37), Fritz Zweig (1934–8) and Karl Rankl (1937–8).

A speciality of the theatre were 'Maifestspiele' – opera cycles within which Italian seasons were also included during the periods 1899–1914 and 1927–35. The repertory was dominated by Wagner: 719 performances of operas by him were given during the years 1888–1918, as well as 337 of Verdi, 225 of Mozart, 154 of Meyerbeer and 108 of Bizet. German works predominated in the modern repertory as well, which included Strauss (from 1901), d'Albert (whose *Tiefland* received its première in 1903), Schreker, Hindemith and Weill; Schoenberg's *Erwartung* (1924) and Krenek's *Karl V* (1938) received their premières there. Among operas by Prague Germans were Theodor Veidl's *Die Kleinstädter* (1935), Hans Krása's *Verlobung im Traum* (1933) and F. F. Finke's *Die Jakobsfahrt* (1936). The Neues Deutsches Theater also staged operettas.

In 1920 the old Estates Theatre was taken over by Czech actors, and three years later the German Kleine Bühne opened as a substitute, putting on chamber operas by Auletta in 1929, Donizetti in 1933 and Milhaud in 1935. In 1939 the Theaterverein and the company of the Neues Deutsches Theater were dissolved; during World War II companies from Germany gave guest performances in the building.

4. FROM 1945. After 1945 the Estates Theatre became a second stage for the National Theatre under the name Tylovo Divadlo (Tyl Theatre; now the Estates Theatre) and continued to present only operas by Mozart and plays. From 1945 to 1948 the Neues Deutsches Theater was used by the Velká Opera 5. Května (Grand Opera of the Fifth of May), whose director was Alois Hába and conductor Václav Kašlík. This company gave the première of Prokofiev's *Betrothal in a Monastery* in 1946 and performed Hába's *Matka* ('The Mother'), a quarter-tone opera, in the same year. In 1948 all the Prague theatres were merged as the National Theatre complex, the Grand Opera taking the name of Smetanovo Divadlo (Smetana Theatre). Conductors since then have included Zdeněk Chalabala (1936–62), Jaroslav Krombholc (1940–75), Václav Kašlík (1948–89) and Zdeněk Košler (1948–59 and again from 1980). The composers whose works were most frequently performed between 1950 and 1965 were Smetana (with 1846 performances), Dvořák (1186), Verdi (450), Mozart (414), Janáček (397) and Tchaikovsky (376). During the period to 1988 about 20 Czech operas received their premières in Prague, including Martinů's *Mirandolina* (1959) and works by Jaroslav Doubrava, Otakar Jeremiáš, Kašlík, Jaroslav Kvapil, Zbyněk Vostřák, Pavel Bořkovec, Jan Hanuš and Jiří Pauer.

In 1977–83 the National Theatre was reconstructed and the Nová Scéna (New Stage) built to present plays and, occasionally, chamber operas. New operas have been presented by Czechoslovak Radio and Television, the Opera Studio of the Academy of Fine Arts in Prague, the Prague Conservatory and the Chamber Opera, founded in 1984. The Smetana Theatre was renamed the Prague State Opera in 1992.

*

O. Teuber: *Geschichte des Prager Theaters von den Anfängen des Schauspielwesens bis auf die neueste Zeit* (Prague, 1883–8)

F. Šubert: *Dějiny Národního divadla v Praze* [The History of the National Theatre in Prague] (Prague, 1908–11)

R. Haas: 'Beitrag zur Geschichte der Oper in Prag und Dresden', *Neues Archiv für sächsische Geschichte und Altertumskunde*, xxxvii (1916), 68–96

O. Wiener and E. Steinhard: 'Vergessene Prager Bühnen: Topographie alter Prager Theaterstätten', *Prager Theaterbuch*, i (Prague, 1924), 54–62

P. Nettl: 'Giovanni Battista Buonamente', *ZMw*, ix (1926–7), 528–42

——: 'Die erste komische Oper in Prag', *Musikbarock in Böhmen und Mähren* (Brno, 1927), 27–33

H. Teweles: *Theater und Publikum* (Prague, 1927)

J. Borecký: 'Zpěvohra Městského divadla Královských Vinohradů' [The Opera of the Town Theatre in the Royal Vineyards], *Čtvrtstoletí Městského divadla na Královských Vinohradech 1907–1932* (Prague, 1932), 79–87, 138–142 [list of repertory]

J. Port: 'Divadelní výtvarníci staré Prahy' [The Scenographer in Prague in the Past], *Kniha o Praze*, iii (1932), 70–120

'Dějiny operního divadla v Československu' [A History of the Opera House in Czechoslovakia], *Československá vlastivěda*, viii: *Umění* (1935), 667–734

Z. Nejedlý: *Opera Národního divadla do roku 1900* [The Opera of the National Theatre up to 1900] (Prague, 1935)

J. Bartoš: *Prozatímní divadlo a jeho opera* [The Provisional Theatre and its Opera] (Prague, 1938)

R. Rosenheim: *Die Geschichte der deutschen Bühnen in Prag 1883–1918: mit einem Rückblick 1783–1883* (Prague, 1938)

Z. Němec: *Weberova pražská léta* [Weber's Prague Years] (Prague, 1944)

J. Vondráček: *Dějiny českého divadla* [A History of the Czech Theatre] (Prague, 1956–7) [covers 1771–1846]

A. Javorin: *Pražské arény: lidová divadla pražská v minulém století* [Prague Arenas: Prague Folk Theatres in the Last Century] (Prague, 1958)

M. Očadlík: 'Soupis českých tištěných operních textů' [List of Printed Opera Texts in Czech], *MMC*, no.7 (1958), 9–186

T. Volek: 'Repertoár pražské Spenglerovy divadelní společnosti v sezoně 1793–4' [The Repertory of the Prague Spengler Theatre Company, 1793–4], *MMC*, no.14 (1960), 5–26

——: 'Repertoár Nosticovského divadla v Praze z let 1794, 1796–8' [The Repertory of the Nostitz Theatre in Prague, 1794 and 1796–8], *MMC*, no.16 (1961), 3–190

J. Němeček: *Dějiny opery, operety a baletu bývalého Nového německého divadla v Praze* [A History of Opera, Operetta and Ballet at the former New German Theatre in Prague] (typescript, 1962, Library of the Theatre Institute, Prague)

F. Pala: *Opera Národního divadla v období Otakara Ostrčila* [Opera at the National Theatre under Ostrčil], i–iv (Prague, 1962–70); vol. v by V. Pospíšil (Prague, 1983)

J. Hilmera: 'Costanza e Fortezza, Giuseppe Galli-Bibiena und das Barocktheater in Böhmen', *Maske und Kothurn*, x (1964), 396–407

P. Kneidl: 'K pražskému provedení první české zpěvohry před 200 lety' [The Prague Performance of the First Czech Opera 200 Years Ago], *Sborník Národního muzea v Praze*, C9 (1964), 173–186

——: 'Libreta italské opery v Praze v 18. století' [Librettos of the Italian Opera in Prague in the 18th Century], *Strahovská knihovna*, i (1966), 97–131; ii (1967), 115–88

T. Volek and M. Skalická: 'Vivaldis Beziehungen zu den Böhmischen Ländern', *AcM*, xxxix (1967), 64–72

F. Černý, ed.: *Dějiny českého divadla* [A History of the Czech Theatre], i (Prague, 1968), 248–79, 331–46; ii (Prague, 1969) [up to 1848]

J. Němeček: *Opera Národního divadla v období Karla Kovařovice 1900–1920* [Opera at the National Theatre under Kovařovic 1900–1920] (Prague, 1968–9)

Dějiny české hudební kultury [A History of Czech Musical Culture], i: *1890–1918* (Prague, 1972), 95–101; ii: *1918–1945* (Prague, 1981), 63–78

H. Demetz: *Geschichte des deutschen Theaters in Prag, 1737–1945* (typescript, 1974, Library of the Theatre Institute, Prague)

M. Laiske: *Pražská dramaturgie: česká divadelní představení do otevření Prozatímního divadla* [Prague Dramaturgy: Czech Theatrical Performances up to the Opening of the Provisional Theatre] (Prague, 1974)

M. Skalická: 'Die Sänger der italienischen Oper in Prag 1724–1735', *De musica disputationes Pragenses*, ii (Prague, 1974), 147–69

V. Lébl: 'Gustav Mahler als Kapellmeister des Deutschen Landestheaters in Prag', *HV*, xii (1975), 351–71

S. Jareš: 'Prozatímní divadlo v Praze' [The Provisional Theatre in Prague], *HV*, xvi (1979), 252–62

H. Konečná: *Soupis repertoáru Národního divadla v Praze 1881–1983* [List of Repertory of the National Theatre in Prague] (Prague, 1983)

V. Lébl, ed.: *Hudba v českých dějinách* [Music in Czech History] (Prague, 1983, 2/1989)

J. Ludvová: 'Německý hudební život v Praze 1880–1938' [German Musical Life in Prague], *Uměnovědné studie*, iv (1983), 53–173; abbreviated in *Oper heute: Almanach der Musikbühne*, vi (1983), 269–86 [lists repertory of the New German Theatre]

A. Buchner: *Opera v Praze* (Prague, 1985) [text also in Ger., Eng. and Russ.]

T. Volek: 'Šporkovská opera' [Count Sporck's Opera House], *HRo*, xxxix (1986), 135–7

V. Pospíšil, ed.: *Národní divadlo a jeho předchůdci: slovník umělců divadel Vlastenského, Stavovského, Prozatímního a Národního* [The National Theatre and its Predecessors: a Dictionary of the Artists working at the Patriotic, Estates, Provisional and National Theatres] (Prague, 1988)

J. Tyrrell: *Czech Opera* (Cambridge, 1988)

J. Smaczny: *A Study of the First Six Operas of Antonín Dvořák: the Foundations of an Operatic Style* (diss., U. of Oxford, 1989), esp. appx 2

F. Černý, ed.: *Divadlo v Kotcích* [The Theatre in the 'Kotce'] (Prague, 1990)

D. E. Freeman: *The Opera Theater of Count Franz Anton Sporck in Prague* (Stuyvesant, NY, 1992)   JITKA LUDVOVÁ

Praha (Cz.). PRAGUE.

Prandelli, Giacinto (*b* Lumezzane, Brescia, 8 Feb 1914). Italian tenor. He studied in Rome and Brescia, making his début in 1942 at Bergamo as Rodolfo (*La bohème*). Engaged at La Scala, he sang the title role in the first Italian performance of *Peter Grimes* (1947), Loris at the 50th anniversary of *Fedora* (1948) and the Lover in the Italian première of Menotti's *Amelia al ballo* (1954). He sang at the Metropolitan in 1951 and made his London début in 1957 at the Stoll Theatre as Edgardo (*Lucia di Lammermoor*). His repertory included Ruggero (*La rondine*), Hagenbach (*La Wally*), Floreski (Cherubini's *Lodoïska*) and Paolo (*Francesca da Rimini*). A stylish singer, he was also an excellent actor.

ELIZABETH FORBES

Pratella, Francesco Balilla (*b* Lugo di Romagna, 1 Feb 1880; *d* Ravenna, 17 May 1955). Italian composer. He studied at the Pesaro Liceo Musicale, where he had a few lessons from Mascagni; later he directed the Liceo Musicale of Lugo di Romagna (1910–29) and that of Ravenna (1927–45). In 1910 he became associated with Marinetti and the futurists, and he published a number of polemical manifestos; but after World War I he gradually withdrew from the movement. Later, in addition to composing, writing criticism, teaching, and editing early music, he became increasingly absorbed in the study of Italian folk music, which had already influenced such pre-futurist works as *La Sina 'd Vargöun* and the series of symphonic poems *Romagna* (opp. 17–21, 1903–4).

Despite his insecure technique, Pratella's melodic invention has, at its best, an airy, free-ranging lyricism, with modal arabesques that recall both Pizzetti and Romagnan folksong. His most convincing achievements are in small-scale lyrical compositions (especially songs) that have nothing to do with futurism. Of his pre-futurist operas, *Lilia* aroused only ephemeral local interest; but *La Sina 'd Vargöun* won more widespread attention (notably in the *Rivista musicale italiana*) because of the thoroughness with which it is pervaded by Romagnan folklore, in its subject matter and text as well as its music. In *L'aviatore Dro*, Pratella's one ostensibly futurist opera, folkloristic elements nevertheless persist, interacting strangely (yet sometimes creatively) with startlingly naive 'modernisms'. The work had only one stage production, yet has continued to be mentioned and even studied whenever the musical aspects of futurism come under scrutiny. Pratella's later operas have fallen into obscurity: only the unpretentious children's opera *La ninna nanna della bambola* proved modestly successful, whereas *La leggenda di San Fabiano* was a catastrophic failure in the theatre; the composer subsequently recognized that it was really an oratorio. His last opera, *L'uomo*, and two operettas (one of them lost) seem never to have reached the stage.

See also AVIATORE DRO, L'.

Lilia op.15, 1903 (2, Pratella), Lugo di Romagna, Comunale Rossini, 13 Sept 1905; expanded as Il regno lontano, *c*1905 (3, Pratella), ?unperf.

La Sina 'd Vargöun op.22, 1906–8 (scene della Romagna bassa, 3, Pratella), Bologna, Comunale, 4 Dec 1909

L'aviatore Dro op.33, 1911–14 (3, Pratella), Lugo di Romagna, Comunale Rossini, 4 Sept 1920

La vetrina di Venere, *c*1919 (operetta, L. Fiorita), unperf., lost

La ninna nanna della bambola op.44, 1920–22 [incl. music from 1901–2] (children's op, 2, Pratella, after L. de Nardis), Milan, Gran Kursaal del Parco, 21 May 1923

La repubblica delle donne, 1925 (operetta, 3, Pratella and A. Lega), unperf.

Il re dei Cucuberni, *c*1926 (comic op, G. Passini), inc.

La leggenda di San Fabiano op.54, 1928–32 (sacra rappresentazione, prol., 2, epilogue, A. Beltramelli and Pratella), Bologna, Comunale, 9 Dec 1939

L'uomo op.59, 1934–49 (3, Pratella), unperf.

*

A. Toni: 'La Sina 'd Vargöun di F. B. Pratella', *RMI*, xvii (1910), 195–223

G. Guerrini: 'La *Ninna nanna della bambola* di F. Balilla Pratella', *Pensiero musicale*, i (1922), 169–71

A. Lualdi: 'La *Sina di Vargöun* di F. B. Pratella al Dal Verme', *Serate musicali* (Milan, 1928), 140–42

A. Ghigi: *Francesco Balilla Pratella* (Ravenna, 1930)

M. Saint-Cyr: 'Francesco Balilla Pratella', *Rassegna dorica*, iii (1931–2), 165–71; repr. in M. Saint-Cyr: *Musicisti italiani contemporanei* (Rome, n.d.), 103–12

C. Marabini: 'Balilla Pratella: musica e futurismo', *Nuova antologia*, no.489 (Sept–Dec 1963), 67–86

A. Gentilucci: 'Il futurismo e lo sperimentalismo musicale d'oggi', *Convegno musicale*, i (1964), 275–302

Discoteca alta fedeltà [Milan], xii/Jan–Feb (1971), [futurist-music number, incl. G. Tintori: 'Un'opera futurista: L'aviatore Dro', 20–24]

F. B. Pratella: *Autobiografia* (Milan, 1971) [written 1947–55]

G. F. Maffina, ed.: *Francesco Balilla Pratella 1880–1955* (Varese, 1980) [exhibition catalogue]   JOHN C. G. WATERHOUSE

Prati, Alessio (*b* Ferrara, 19 July 1750; *d* Ferrara, 17 Jan 1788). Italian composer. After lessons from Pietro Marzola, *maestro di cappella* of Ferrara Cathedral, he studied composition in Naples and Rome from 1768 to 1775. He then moved to France, where he composed and taught singing and the harpsichord in Marseilles, Paris and possibly Lyons. His first opera, *L'école de la* *jeunesse*, was performed with success at the Théâtre Italien, Paris, in 1779. A short stay in St Petersburg (1782–3) failed to result in a permanent position or operatic commission, and in the summer he returned to Italy, passing through Vienna. From 1784 he was much in demand as a composer of serious opera; he composed at least five operas between 1784 and his death in 1788. Two of these had leading roles for Cecilia Giuliani, a dramatic soprano with whom he was romantically involved. His early death removed from the scene one of the most talented *opera seria* composers of the day.

Prati's skills are apparent in *La vendetta di Nino* (1786), the most widely performed of his operas during the 1780s and 90s and a worthy precursor of Rossini's *Semiramide*. He made the most of the libretto's many large-scale scene complexes, some of which include important choral elements; at its première in Florence a chorus of 22 singers represented priests, soldiers and virgins. The story's macabre qualities are most vividly evoked, perhaps, in the final scene of Act 1, in which the ghost of Nino (Semiramide's husband) makes a sudden, terrifying appearance. The march-like overture, with extensive writing for solo wind, looks forward in some respects to Rossini's overtures.

L'école de la jeunesse, ou Le Barnevelt français (oc, 3, L. Anseaume), Paris, Italien, 11 Oct 1779 (Paris, 1779)
L'Ifigenia in Aulide (dramma per musica, 3, L. Serio), Florence, Pergola, aut. 1784, *US-Wc*
Armida abbandonata (os, 2, G. Sertor, after T. Tasso: *Gerusalemme liberata*), Munich, Hof, 1785, *D-Mbs**
La vendetta di Nino [La morte di Semiramide] (melodramma tragico, 2, P. Giovannini, after Voltaire: *Sémiramis*), Florence, Pergola, carn. 1786, *A-Wn, GB-Ob, I-Bc, Fc, Nc, Rsc, US-Wc*
Olimpia (dramma per musica, 2, after Voltaire), Naples, S Carlo, 6 June 1786, *I-Nc, P-La, US-Wc*
Demofoonte (dramma per musica, 3, P. Metastasio), Venice, S Benedetto, 26 Dec 1786, ? *D-Bds, P-La*
L'Aminta (azione pastorale, G. Muzzarelli Brusantini), Ferrara, ?1787

Doubtful: Semiramide (1780); Didone abbandonata (1783)

*

FlorimoN
C. Laderchi: *Notizie biografiche intorno ad Alessio Prati* (Ferrara, 1825)
R.-A. Mooser: *Annales de la musique et des musiciens en Russie au XVIIIme siècle* (Geneva, 1948–51)   JOHN A. RICE

Pratolino. Villa of Ferdinando de' Medici, near Florence, where operas were staged from 1679 to 1710; *see* FLORENCE, §3.

Pratt, Silas G(amaliel) (*b* Addison, VT, 4 Aug 1846; *d* Pittsburgh, 30 Oct 1916). American composer. He studied the piano in Germany, but a wrist injury caused by too-strenuous practice precluded a career as concert pianist. On returning to the USA, he worked in Chicago as an organist. After another trip to Germany (1875–7), he again lived in Chicago, until 1888. In June 1882 his second opera, *Zenobia, Queen of Palmyra*, was produced in concert form at Central Music Hall and staged the following March at McVicker's Theater. His first opera, entitled *Antonio* when begun in 1870 but renamed *Lucille*, had a three-week run at the Columbia Theater in Chicago during March 1887. His third opera *Ollanta*, on an Inca subject, was never produced. In 1888 Pratt moved to New York; in 1906 he founded the Pratt Institute of Music and Art in Pittsburgh, and was its president until his death.

Antonio, 1870–71, selections perf. Chicago, Farwell Hall, 1874; rev. as Lucille, Chicago, Columbia, 14 March 1887

Zenobia, Queen of Palmyra (4, Pratt), concert perf., Chicago, Central Music Hall, 15 June 1882; stage, Chicago, McVicker's, 26 March 1883; vs (Boston, 1882)
The Musical Metempsychosis (musical entertainment), 1888
Ollanta (Pratt), unperf.

*

DAB (F. L .G. Cole)
W. S. B. Mathews, ed.: *A Hundred Years of Music in America* (Chicago, 1889), 688
E. E. Hipsher: *American Opera* (Philadelphia, 1927), 361
                                        ROBERT STEVENSON

Pré aux Clercs, Le. *Opéra comique* in three acts by FERDINAND HÉROLD to a libretto by François Antoine Eugène de Planard; Paris, Opéra-Comique (Salle de la Bourse), 15 December 1832.

At her inn outside Paris, Nicette (soprano) celebrates her forthcoming marriage to Girot (tenor), hotelier from the Pré aux Clercs, Paris. They sing a charming duet, 'Les rendez-vous de noble compagnie'. Baron de Mergy (tenor) arrives, bringing a request from King Henry of Navarre that his wife, Marguerite de Valois (soprano), sister of the French King Henri III and his virtual prisoner, should be allowed to return to Navarre. Marguerite (who is Nicette's godmother) and her young friend, Isabelle (soprano), abandon the hunt to rest at the inn. In 'Souvenirs du jeune âge' Isabelle sings of her longing for her home in Navarre. She is in love with Mergy and he with her, but the king wishes her to marry Comminge (baritone).

In the palace of the Louvre Marguerite makes plans for Mergy and Isabelle to get married secretly. Mergy is informed that the queen may return to Navarre, but that Isabelle must marry Comminge. The queen revises her plans with the help of Nicette, as Mergy and Comminge arrange to fight a duel. Across the Seine from the Louvre, in the Pré aux Clercs, the crowds dance and stroll around. Marguerite, allowed to leave the palace to attend Nicette's wedding, also witnesses the marriage of Mergy and Isabelle; in a trio, 'C'en est fait! Le ciel même', they express their happiness. Mergy kills his rival in the duel and sets off to Navarre with his bride.

Hérold's opera, acknowledged by composers and musicians as one of the finest of its period, deals with the same subject as *Les Huguenots*, but in a very different way. Instead of the huge, tragic canvas of Meyerbeer's *grand opéra*, Hérold paints a much more intimate picture, though one that is not without serious feelings beneath the surface frivolity, as when the Catholic soldiers accuse the Huguenot Baron de Mergy of eating chicken on a Friday. Mergy could have been killed by Comminge, a noted duellist, but by convention an *opéra comique* should end happily, and in the 1830s most of them did.

The score is a chain of fine numbers, extremely melodious and pretty, but also dramatically well suited to the various characters. The lightweight scenes for Nicette and Girot are balanced by the romantic music of Mergy and Isabelle, while Marguerite, like her namesake in *Les Huguenots*, sparkles and glitters. The second-act finale is particularly effective.

                                        ELIZABETH FORBES

Precauzioni, Le. Opera by Errico Petrella; *see* CARNEVALE DI VENEZIA, IL.

Predieri, Antonio (*b* Bologna, *c*1650; *d* Bologna, 1710). Italian singer, related to Luca Antonio Predieri. He first appeared as a tenor in *L'inganno trionfante* by F. M.

Bassani in 1673. He was in the service of the Duke of Mantua, 1684–7, and then served the Duke of Parma until at least 1699, performing in operas at Milan, Modena, Naples, Rome, Parma and Piacenza. He specialized in comic roles, and many *vecchia* parts were created for him. He later appeared in Genoa (1699), Milan (1704), Florence (1707) and Forlì (1710).

ANNE SCHNOEBELEN

Predieri, Luca Antonio (*b* Bologna, 13 Sept 1688; *d* Bologna, ? 3 Jan 1767). Italian composer, son of Vitale and Maria Menzani. He studied counterpoint with his uncle Giacomo Cesare Predieri, Angelo Predieri and G. A. Perti. He was among the instrumentalists at the church of S Petronio for the patronal feast in 1704, in 1705 as a violist and 1706–11 as a violinist. On 25 June 1716 he was admitted to the Accademia Filarmonica as a composer; he served as *principe* in 1723, *consigliere* in 1724, 1728 and 1733, and *censore* in 1727, 1734 and 1736. He was *maestro di cappella* in several Bolognese churches from 1725, including the cathedral of S Pietro (1728–31). At the end of 1737 Predieri went to Vienna, and after two years was made vice-*maestro* of the court chapel. A series of letters written to G. B. Martini reveals his cordial relationship with Fux, his successes at court and his favour with the emperor, who found in him a worthy successor to Caldara. In 1741, on the death of Fux, he assumed the direction of the court chapel, although he used the title of first *maestro* only in 1746. He retired in 1751, keeping his title and stipend until 1765 when he returned to Bologna.

Predieri wrote many operas, among which his *Partenope* inaugurated the Teatro Marsigli-Rossi, Bologna, in 1710. His operas and oratorios are characterized by careful word-setting in the recitatives and effective use of dynamic contrasts in the arias. He was one of the most famous opera composers of his generation, working in the same years as Vinci, Pergolesi and Porpora but perhaps leaning towards a more traditional musical language. He was mainly active in central Italy and had particularly strong connections with theatres in Tuscany. The librettos he set reflect the taste of the first Arcadian reform of opera, but he also wrote *Il duello d'amore e di vendetta*, described as a 'Spanish opera'. His collaboration with Metastasio and Pasquini on *drammi per musica* and *azioni teatrali* marked the peak of his career, but by the time he retired his operas were almost completely neglected in Vienna.

La Partenope (S. Stampiglia), Bologna, Marsigli-Rossi, 28 Oct 1710; rev., Florence, Cocomero, carn. 1720
La virtù in trionfo, o sia La Griselda (T. Stanzani, after A. Zeno), Bologna, Marsigli-Rossi, 18 Oct 1711, 1 aria *I-Bc*
La Giuditta (F. Silvani), Ancona, Pubblico, 1713
Lucio Papirio (A. Salvi), Pratolino, Villa Medici, 1714, 4 arias *GB-Lbl*
Astarte (Zeno and P. Pariati), Rome, Capranica, 1715
Il pazzo per politica (G. B. Gianoli), Livorno, S Sebastiano, 1717
Il duello d'amore e di vendetta, Livorno, S Sebastiano, 1718
La fede ne' tradimenti (G. Gigli), Florence, Pergola, 1718; rev., Alessandria, Soleri, aut. 1730
Merope (Zeno and Pariati), Livorno, S Sebastiano, 1718
Anagilda (Gigli), Turin, Carignano, 1719
La finta pazzia di Diana, Florence, Pergola, 1719
Il trionfo della virtù (F. Pecori), Florence, Pergola, 1719
Il trionfo di Solimano, ovvero Il trionfo maggiore è vincere se stesso (Pecori), Florence, Pergola, 1719
Astarto, Florence, Pergola, carn. 1720
Tito Manlio (M. Noris), Florence, Pergola, 1721
Sofonisba (Silvani), Rome, Alibert, 1722; rev., Rome, Alibert, carn. 1723
Scipione, Rome, Alibert, 1724

Cesare in Egitto (G. F. Bussani), Rome, Capranica, carn. 1728
Astianatte (Salvi), Alessandria, Soleri, aut. 1729
Eurene (C. Stampa), Milan, Regio Ducal, 1729; rev. as Sirbace, Pistoia, Accademici Risvegliati, 2 July 1730
Ezio (P. Metastasio), ? Milan, Regio Ducal, carn. 1730; Genoa, Falcone, carn. 1731
Scipione il giovane (G. F. Bortolotti), Venice, S Giovanni Grisostomo, aut. 1731, *F-Pc*
Alessandro nell'Indie (Metastasio), Milan, Regio Ducal, 1731
Amor prigionero, Vienna, 1732, *A-Wn*
La serva padrona (F. Vanneschi), Florence, Cocomero, 1732
Il sogno di Scipione (Metastasio), Vienna, 1 Oct 1735
Zoe (Silvani), Venice, S Cassiano, aut. 1736
Gli auguri spiegati (G. C. Pasquini), Laxenburg, 3 May 1738, *Wgm*
La pace tra la virtù e la bellezza (Metastasio), Vienna, 15 Oct 1738, *Wgm*
Perseo, Vienna, 4 Nov 1738, *Wgm*
Astrea placata, ossia La felicità della terra (Metastasio), Vienna, 28 Aug 1739, *Wgm*
Zenobia (Metastasio), Vienna, Favorita, 28 Aug 1740, *Wgm*
Armida placata (Pasquini), 1750; collab. G. C. Wagenseil, Hasse, G. Bonno, G. Abos

*

O. Penna: *Catalogo degli aggregati dell'Accademia filarmonica di Bologna* (MS, *I-Baf*, 1736/R1971) [sometimes attrib. G. B. Martini]
G. B. Martini: *Scrittori di musica: notizie storiche e loro opere*, iii (MS, *Bsf*)
G. Gaspari: *Miscellanea storico-musicale*, i–iv (MS, *Bc* UU/12)
L. von Köchel: *Die kaiserliche Hofmusikkapelle in Wien von 1543 bis 1867* (Vienna, 1869)
C. Ricci: *I teatri di Bologna nei secoli XVII e XVIII* (Bologna, 1888)
A. Bertolotti: *Musici alla corte dei Gonzaga in Mantova nel secolo XV al XVIII* (Milan, 1890)
N. Morini: *La R. Accademia filarmonica di Bologna* (Bologna, 1930)
N. Pelicelli: 'Musicisti in Parma nel secolo XVII', *NA*, x (1933), 233–48
R. Ortner: *Luca Antonio Predieri und sein Wiener Opernschaffen* (Vienna, 1971)
R. Strohm: *Italienische Opernarien des frühen Settecento (1720–1730)*, *AnMc*, no.16 (1976)

ANNE SCHNOEBELEN, SERGIO DURANTE

Preetorius, Emil (*b* Mainz, 21 June 1883; *d* Munich, 27 Jan 1973). German stage designer. He studied law, and later worked as an illustrator. His early graphics set new standards for book illustration in Germany, appearing in children's books, classics and the reviews *Jugend* and *Simplicissimus*. In 1921 the writer Thomas Mann recommended him to Bruno Walter as designer for a new production of Gluck's *Iphigénie en Aulide* at Munich. During the 1920s he designed opera productions for Berlin, Dresden and Munich. His association with Bayreuth began in 1933, when he designed the *Ring* for Heinz Tietjen, with whom he worked both there and in Berlin during the 1930s and 40s. Other important work included *Ring* cycles at La Scala (1938), Rome (1953–4) and Vienna (1958–60), and the 'official' première of Richard Strauss's *Die Liebe der Danae* at Salzburg in 1952.

Preetorius's style dominated mainstream European Wagner design in the two decades preceding Wieland Wagner's revolutionary productions at Bayreuth (his influence on Wieland's early work was great but unacknowledged), forging a link between the weighty, pictorial Wagner settings of the late 19th century and the sparser experimental work of the mid-20th century. His *Ring* included geometrical rock formations that owed much to the sketches of Adolphe Appia, while his imposing Valhalla seemed to come from Fritz Lang's expressionist film *Metropolis*. The ghostly ship in *Der fliegende Holländer* was a frightening apparition of unnatural size. Letters from Bayreuth suggests that

Preetorius sometimes found the Festspielhaus traditions restricting; his later work (e.g. at La Scala in the early 1950s) showed greater abstraction in both sets and costumes. He lectured (mostly in Munich) until 1952, and was elected president of the Bayerische Akademie der Schönen Künste the following year. His published writings include *Richard Wagner: Bild und Vision* (Berlin, 1942) and a collection of essays, *Reden und Aufsätze* (1953).

For illustration *see* LIEBE DER DANAE, DIE and PRODUCTION, fig.21.

ES (H. Vriesen)   MIKE ASHMAN

Prégardien, Christoph (*b* Limburg, 18 Jan 1956). German tenor. He studied at the Frankfurt Hochschule für Musik and later in Milan, Frankfurt and Stuttgart. From 1983 to 1987 he sang with the Frankfurt Opera, making his début there in 1984 as Wenzel (*The Bartered Bride*) and later appearing as Hylas (*Les Troyens*), Fenton and the Steersman. His wide repertory ranges from the Baroque to the 19th century and includes the roles of Don Ottavio, Tamino and Almaviva. His operatic commitments have taken him to many German opera houses, and in 1989–90 he sang in Haydn operas at Cairo and Antwerp. He has acquired an outstanding reputation in cantata and oratorio; his dramatic sense, articulate delivery and lyrical, light-textured voice are well suited to Bach's Evangelist. His recordings include Haydn's *L'infedeltà delusa* and operas by Handel.

NICHOLAS ANDERSON

Preghiera (It.: 'prayer'; Fr. *prière*; Ger. *Gebet*). An aria in one movement consisting of a prayer, usually offered up by the hero or heroine in his or her hour of danger; examples are 'Deh, calma, o ciel, nel sonno' (*Otello*, Rossini, 1816), 'Deh! tu di un'umile preghiera' (*Maria Stuarda*, Donizetti, 1835) and 'Salvami tu, gran Dio' (*Aroldo*, Verdi, 1857). That Verdi in his own *Otello* (1887) should have followed Rossini in assigning a *preghiera* to Desdemona before the final catastrophe bears witness to the strength of the tradition. Curiously, if a prayer forms part of a double aria it is never given the title of *preghiera* (e.g. 'Dio di Giuda'; *Nabucco*, Verdi, 1842). Rare instances of ensemble *preghiere* are the 'Angelus' settings in *Aroldo* and *Le villi* (Puccini, 1884) and, most impressive of all, 'O sacre polve', which concludes Act 2 of Donizetti's *L'assedio di Calais* (1836). 'Del tuo stellato soglio' (*Mosè in Egitto*, Rossini, 1818) constitutes a special case, being built in the manner of a vaudeville-finale.

In French opera the *prière* is rarely confined to a single voice. 'Toi qui du faible es l'espérance' (*Guillaume Tell*, Rossini, 1829) is a terzetto for female voices. 'O Dieu de nos pères' (*La Juive*, Halévy, 1835) and 'Blanche Dourga' (*Lakmé*, Delibes, 1883) both involve choral response. 'O grand Saint Dominique' (*L'Africaine*, Meyerbeer, 1865) is an ensemble piece throughout. Among rare exceptions are 'O ma mère, ombre si tendre' added by Meyerbeer in 1838 to *Robert le diable* (1831) for Mario's début in the title role, and 'O vierge Marie' (*Mignon*, Thomas, 1866).

Prominent examples of the German *Gebet* include 'Allmächt'ger Vater, blick herab' (*Rienzi*, Wagner, 1842) and 'Allmächt'ge Jungfrau, hör mein Flehen' (*Tannhäuser*, 1845), both solo pieces. The choral prayer led by King Henry, 'Herr und Gott nun ruf ich Dich' (*Lohengrin*, 1850), stands out as the one moment of

triple time in the entire score. Particular importance attaches to 'Abends, will ich schlafen gehn' (*Hänsel und Gretel*, Humperdinck, 1893), whose material not only figures in the overture but is developed during the opera into a pantomime of angels.

JULIAN BUDDEN

Preissová [Sekerová], **Gabriela** (*b* Kutná Hora, 23 March 1862; *d* Prague, 27 March 1946). Czech writer and dramatist. Her marriage at the age of 18 took her to Hodonín, in the Moravian ethnographic region of Slovácko. The rich folk culture in the surrounding villages captivated her and provided the setting for her short stories based on her observations and later for her play *Gazdina roba* ('The Farm Mistress'), produced with great success at the Prague National Theatre in 1889. A second play in the same vein, *Její pastorkyňa* ('Her Stepdaughter', 1890), aroused hostility in Prague for its frank subject matter but survived in provincial repertory. Many years later Preissová worked it into a novel, providing interesting background information on the characters involved. Both plays were turned into operas, by Foerster (*The Farm Mistress*, as *Eva*, 1899) and Janáček (*Her Stepdaughter*, 1904; generally known outside Czechoslovakia as *Jenůfa*). Preissová also took a great interest in Janáček's earlier opera, *Počátek románu* ('The Beginning of a Romance', 1894), based on her short story of the same title (1886).

G. Preissová: 'Má setkání s Thalií' [My Encounters with Thalia (i.e. with the theatre)], *Divadlo a hudba*, i/8 (1941–2), 49–51
T. Straková: 'Setkání Leoše Janáčka s Gabrielou Preissovou' [Janáček's Encounter with Gabriela Preissová], *ČMM*, xliii (1958), 145–63
A. Závodský: *Gabriela Preissová* (Prague, 1962) [incl. chaps. on *The Farm Mistress* and *Her Stepdaughter*]
O. Fiala: 'Libreto k Janáčkově opeře Počátek románu' [The Libretto to Janáček's Opera *The Beginning of a Romance*], *ČMM*, xlix (1964), 199–222
B. Štědroň: *Zur Genesis von Leoš Janáčeks Oper Jenůfa* (Brno, 1968, 2/1972)
J. Tyrrell: *Czech Opera* (Cambridge, 1988), 93–4
R. Klos: 'Rozsudek nad Kostelničkou' [The Verdict on the Kostelnička], *OM*, xxi/3 (1989), suppl. pp.xxviii–xxx [on *Her Stepdaughter*]; Eng. trans. in *Glyndebourne Festival Opera 1989*, 126–7 [programme book]
J. Tyrrell: 'The Kostelnička: a Life Before and After', *Glyndebourne Festival Opera 1989*, 121–5 [on Preissová's later novel on the *Jenůfa* topic]
——: *Janáček's Operas: a Documentary Account* (London, 1992)

JOHN TYRRELL

Prelleur, Peter [Pierre] (*b* ?1705; *d* 1741). English composer, probably of French extraction. He was harpsichordist and composer for the Goodman's Fields Theatre from about 1728 until the theatre was closed under the Licensing Act of 1737, whereupon he transferred to the New Wells (or Goodman's Fields Wells) theatre in nearby Leman Street. For the New Wells he wrote much music, including the pantomimes *Harlequin Hermit, or The Arabian Courtezan* (1739) and *Harlequin Student, or The Fall of Pantomime* (1741), and the delightful interlude *Baucis and Philemon* (1740). The last includes an overture (laid out like a trio sonata) for strings, obbligato oboes and continuo, as well as songs and duets (London, *c*1740). Prelleur was also an organist and the author of an *Introduction to Singing* (London, 1735; first published in 1731 as part i of a much larger work entitled *The Modern Musick-Master, or The Universal Musician*).

PETER PLATT

Prelude (Fr. *prélude*; Ger. *Vorspiel*; It. *preludio*, *prologo*). A short or medium-length instrumental number, usually for orchestra, serving to introduce a theatrical work, an act or a scene; also any of various types of instrumental composition for concert use.

The term 'prelude' was frequently used in the 19th century for movements serving as overtures. For some composers the term OVERTURE may have come to mean a work of the size and complexity of Beethoven's *Leonore* no.3 or Mendelssohn's concert overtures; it thus would have been inappropriate for a comparatively slight and unsymphonic number intended to introduce an opera. For some, too, it may have seemed desirable for nationalistic reasons to avoid using a word of French origin. It would appear that 'prelude' was mostly applied to works that were comparatively short, in one tempo and not in sonata form. Verdi maintained a clear distinction between the fully worked-out overtures of works like *Nabucco* and *La forza del destino*, which he termed 'sinfonia', and the more modest sort of number that opens *Rigoletto* and *Aida*, which he called 'preludio', a title he also used for the middle-length, atmosphere-setting prefatory music to *La traviata*. Wagner began using 'Vorspiel' instead of 'Ouvertüre' after *Tannhäuser*; though the opening numbers of most of his later operas are indeed more modest than full-blown overtures (bearing in mind the composer's tendency toward gigantism), he used 'Vorspiel' not only for *Tristan und Isolde* but also for *Die Meistersinger*, which has an overture in the traditional sense.

Paradoxically, this development, which tended to reduce the amount of purely orchestral music at the beginning of the opera, came just as the orchestra's role in providing musical continuity and punctuation within the work was growing considerably. Even in operas without continuous orchestral accompaniment, orchestral numbers to open later acts or scenes became increasingly common. Such numbers could be called 'sinfonia' or, more often, 'interlude' or one of its various synonyms, but were now also frequently called 'prelude'. The terminological distinction between a 'prelude' of this sort and an 'interlude' is essentially arbitrary. It does not necessarily indicate whether the number is musically joined on to the preceding or following numbers; Humperdinck, for instance, gave alternative beginnings for the 'Vorspiel' to the second act of *Hänsel und Gretel* (the 'Hexenritt') depending on whether or not a break is desired after the opening act. At their smallest, internal numbers called 'prelude' may be musically indistinguishable from introductions to vocal numbers. Even at their largest, they are almost always smaller in scale than the overture or prelude at the beginning of the work (an exception is the extensive 'Vorspiel' to Act 2 of Pfitzner's *Palestrina*). This usage reinforces the idea that a 'prelude' is a less substantial piece than an 'overture'.   STEPHEN C. FISHER

Premessa. *See* ARGOMENTO.

Pressburg (Ger.). BRATISLAVA.

Pretoria. City in the Republic of South Africa. It contains the headquarters of the Performing Arts Council of the Transvaal (PACT), which was established in 1963 and is responsible for opera and ballet performances in the Transvaal. Opera was first given at the Johannesburg Civic Theatre and at the Aula in Pretoria. Since its opening in 1981 the Opera, a 1322-seat theatre in the

State Theatre complex in Pretoria, has become the principal venue for opera. Generally, seven productions, including one musical, are given throughout the year. On 24 November 1988 *The Fall of the House of Usher*, a one-act opera by the South African composer Hendrik Hofmeyr, received its première at the Arena, a small experimental part of the State Theatre. The PACT orchestra was founded in 1965, and in 1987 it merged with the National SO to form the National Orchestra. In 1991 this orchestra split again, into the National SO of the South African Broadcasting Corporation and the Transvaal Philharmonic (for PACT). Through its Opera for Youth programme, school tours are also undertaken by PACT. An opera school is attached to the Pretoria Technicon's School of Performing Arts.

Prêtre, Georges (*b* Waziers, 14 Aug 1924). French conductor. He studied the trumpet and composition at the Paris Conservatoire and conducting with Cluytens. His début was in 1946 at the Marseilles Opera in Lalo's *Le roi d'Ys*, and he worked there and at the opera houses of Lille and Toulouse until 1955. After his Paris début the next year at the Opéra-Comique, in the first performance in the city of Strauss's *Capriccio*, he became its music director until 1959; that year he conducted the première of Poulenc's *La voix humaine*. From 1960 he worked frequently at the Opéra, where he was director of music from 1970 to 1971. His American début was at the Chicago Lyric Opera in 1959 with *Thaïs*, followed by débuts at the Metropolitan Opera (*Samson et Dalila*, 1964), La Scala and Covent Garden (1965) and at the Salzburg Festival (1966). Thereafter he was regularly active in those centres and elsewhere, reopening the Théâtre des Champs-Elysées in Paris in 1988 with a concert performance of *Benvenuto Cellini* and conducting the inaugural concert at the Opéra Bastille in 1990.

Prêtre was a favoured conductor of Maria Callas, and recorded *Tosca* and *Carmen* with her in 1964. He also recorded *Samson et Dalila*, *Lucia di Lammermoor*, *La traviata* and *Werther* in the 1960s and *Les pêcheurs de perles* in 1977. His conducting is dynamic, vital and dramatic, but has been criticized for excessive use of rubato and lack of precision. He was made an Officier of the Légion d'honneur in 1984 and is also an Italian Commendatore.

CHRISTIANE SPIETH-WEISSENBACHER / NOËL GOODWIN

Preuss, Arthur (*b* Königsberg, 23 Feb 1878; *d* Vienna, 20 Aug 1944). German tenor. After study in Berlin he made his début at the Vienna Hofoper in 1899. He was successful for many years in such *buffo* roles as Pedrillo, Jaquino, David and Monostatos. He sang at the Vienna Volksoper from 1915, appearing as Schubert in the 1916 première of *Dreimäderlhaus* by Heinrich Berté (1857–1924). He sang at the 1906 Salzburg Festival under Mahler and took part in the Viennese première of Goldmark's *Ein Wintermärchen* (1908).

DAVID CUMMINGS

Prevedi, Bruno (*b* Rovere, Mantua, 21 Dec 1928; *d* Milan, 12 Jan 1988). Italian tenor. He studied with Alberto Soresina in Mantua and Vladimiro Badiali in Milan. His début was in the baritone role of Tonio in *Pagliacci* at the Teatro Nuovo, Milan, in 1958. By 1962 he had been re-trained as a tenor, and sang Cherubini's Jason (*Médée*) and Cavaradossi in Vienna. He appeared at Covent Garden in 1963 as Calaf and in 1965 sang

Pollione at Verona. He was best known in operas by Verdi, appearing variously as Macduff, Ismaele, Ernani and Don Carlos in Berlin, Dallas, Philadelphia, Moscow and Munich. He sang Pollione at Johannesburg in 1982.

DAVID CUMMINGS

Previtali, Fernando (*b* Adria, 16 Feb 1907; *d* Rome, 1 Aug 1985). Italian conductor. He studied at the Turin Conservatory with Alfano (composition) and Pietro Grossi (cello), and joined the orchestra of the Teatro Regio, Turin, as a cellist. In 1928 he moved to Florence to work with Gui at the Comunale, and helped to establish the orchestra of the Maggio Musicale Fiorentino. Gui encouraged Previtali's interest in contemporary music, and he became a leading interpreter of Busoni's music, as well as conducting the premières of many works including Ghedini's *Re Hassan* (1939) and Dallapiccola's *Volo di notte* (1940). As chief conductor of the Rome RSO (1936–43 and 1945–53) he was responsible for many fine opera broadcasts and recordings. In 1953 he was appointed conductor and artistic adviser to the Accademia di S Cecilia. He conducted opera frequently at Buenos Aires from 1959, was appointed principal conductor at the S Carlo, Naples, in 1972, and subsequently became artistic director of the Regio, Turin, and the Comunale, Genoa. He made his American opera début at Dallas in 1975 (with Donizetti's *Anna Bolena*). An accurate interpreter, an authoritative orchestral trainer and a skilled teacher of conducting, he also published a manual, *Guida allo studio della direzione d'orchestra* (Rome, 1951).

LEONARDO PINZAUTI

Prévost [Prévost d'Exiles], Abbé **Antoine-François** (*b* Hesdin, Artois, 1 April 1697; *d* Paris, 25 Nov 1763). French novelist and journalist. The son of a magistrate, he studied at the Jesuit college in Hesdin, but vacillated between holy orders and a military career. After some soldiering experience he was admitted to the Benedictine congregation at St Wandrille, near Rouen, in 1721. Five years later he was ordained priest, but he had already begun writing fiction. Falling foul of the ecclesiastical authorities, he fled to England in 1728 and became a tutor in the household of Sir John Eyles. He lived in the Netherlands and again in London before returning to Paris in 1734, more or less reconciled with the church. His remaining years were devoted mainly to writing. Prévost was founder and editor of *Le pour et contre*, a literary periodical that helped to introduce English literature to the French, as did his somewhat abridged translations of Richardson's *Clarissa* and *Sir Charles Grandison*. Among his own works are the lengthy novels *Histoire de Monsieur Cleveland* (Utrecht, 1732) and *Le doyen de Killerine* (Paris, 1735).

Prévost's most famous work, *L'histoire du Chevalier des Grieux et de Manon Lescaut*, was first published in Amsterdam in 1731 as the seventh volume of *Les mémoires et aventures d'un homme de qualité*, though it has generally been regarded as an independent novel. Considerable realism in the setting, exciting adventure and an apt use of first-person narrative make the naive Des Grieux's account of his total abandonment of principle after falling in love with the wilful Manon entirely persuasive. The death of the heroine in the 'deserts' of Louisiana redeems her character without threatening the society whose values she overturns. A number of 19th-century stage works were based on *Manon*, including a *mélodrame* by Etienne Gosse with music by Propiac (1820), Balfe's *The Maid of Artois* (1836), Auber's *opéra comique Manon Lescaut* (1856), Massenet's *opéras comiques Manon* (1884) and *Le portrait de Manon* (1894) and Puccini's *Manon Lescaut* (1893). Henze's *Boulevard Solitude* (1952) is also based on Prévost's novel.

J. P. Gilroy: *The Romantic Manon and Des Grieux* (Sherbrooke, Quebec, 1980)
R. A. Smernoff: *L'Abbé Prévost* (Boston, 1985)

CHRISTOPHER SMITH

Prévost, Eugène-Prosper (*b* Paris, 23 April 1809; *d* New Orleans, 19 Aug 1872). French composer. He entered the Paris Conservatoire in 1827, studying composition with Le Sueur; Berlioz was a fellow student of his there. He wrote two *opéras comiques* during his student days, *Le grenadier de Wagram* and *L'hôtel des princes*, both of which were produced in Paris in 1831. He won the Prix de Rome in 1831. On his return from Italy in 1835, *Cosimo* was produced at the Opéra-Comique and was very well received. He became the conductor at the theatre in Le Havre, where his wife, Eléonore Colon, was a singer. His conducting career took him to New Orleans, though his operas continued to be staged in Paris as well as in the USA. He returned to Paris to manage the Bouffes-Parisiens for a short time before settling permanently in New Orleans in 1867.

Prévost wrote about ten comic operas, most of which remained unpublished. The critic Gasperini, in his review of Prévost's last work, *L'illustre Gaspard* (1863), made the reasonable judgment: 'It is all clever, light, totally unpretentious; yet it is all written in a masterly fashion'. He also composed a few pieces for orchestra and a mass that shows the influence of Cherubini, Le Sueur and Plantade.

opéras-comiques, first performed in Paris, unless otherwise stated

L'hôtel des princes (1, A. de Ferrière and H. Leblanc de Marconay), Ambigu, April 1831
Le grenadier de Wagram (1, H. Lefebvre and Saint-Amant [A. Lacoste]), Ambigu, 14 May 1831
Cosimo (opéra bouffe, 2, Saint-Hilaire and P. Duport), OC (Bourse), 13 Oct 1835, vs (Paris, ?1835)
Les pontons de Cadix (1, Duport and F. Ancelot), OC (Bourse), Nov 1836
Le bon garçon (1, A. Bourgeois and Lockroy [J. Simon]), OC (Bourse), 22 Sept 1837
Esmeralda (after V. Hugo: *Notre-Dame de Paris*), New Orleans, ? 1840
Alice Clari (op, 3), New York, 1846
Blanche et René (2), New Orleans, 1861
L'illustre Gaspard (1, F.-A. Duvert and A. Lauzanne de Varoussel), OC (Bourse), 11 Feb 1863

JEAN MONGRÉDIEN

Prévôt [Prevot, Prévost], **Ferdinand** (*b c*1800; *d* ?Paris, in or after 1857). French baritone. His father was also a singer, and in the early years of his career he was designated Prévot *fils* or by his full name. He sang in the Opéra chorus as early as 1818 and made his solo début in 1824 in Grétry's *Anacréon chez Polycrate*. His career continued into the 1850s; though he never achieved star status among his peers, his longevity and consistency were remarkable, and he took many minor roles, notably in the premières of Auber's *Gustave III*, Halévy's *La Juive* and *Les Huguenots*. Hervey called him 'a most useful member of the company, who, without being ever positively good, is never positively bad'.

C. Hervey: *The Theatres of Paris* (Paris and London, 1846)
G. Chouquet: *Histoire de la musique dramatique en France* (Paris, 1873)

LAURIE C. SHULMAN

Prey, Claude (*b* Fleury sur Andelle, 30 May 1925). French composer. A graduate of the universities of Paris and Quebec, he engaged in anthropological research before continuing composition studies with Messiaen and Milhaud. One of the most prolific composers for the theatre in postwar France, he has frequently given details for staging requirements as well as writing his own librettos. In addition to adopting a conscious eclecticism, with frequent quotes from the music of the past, he is an innovator who experiments with extended vocal techniques, speech, and juxtapositions and superimpositions of contrasting music. His operas mainly employ chamber groups of 20 or so instruments including percussion and occasionally electronics. He has been one of the most important contributors to the Avignon Festival.

On veut la lumière? Allons-y! concerns the Dreyfus affair and drew from the composer parodies of Satie and Weill as well as a 12-note version of *Die lustige Witwe*. *Jonas* is based on real prison jottings and deals with a prisoner who is both poet and conscientious objector. The partly aleatory *Le jeu de l'oie*, set in a maze, reworks the minotaur myth. *Donna mobile* is more contemporary, and is based on the feminist theme of a mute nymph seduced and transformed, in the kitchen, into a speaking woman. The parodistic *La grand'mère française* mimics Romantic music, the Schola Cantorum and impressionism, while *Les mots croisés*, for one male and one female voice, uses two instrumental groups to represent the crossword-puzzle layout, one for down (the man) and one for across (the woman); each letter of the alphabet has its own note.

librettos by the composer unless otherwise stated

Le phénix, 1958 (ob), unperf.
Lettres perdues, 1960 (opéra épistolaire), RTF, 22 Jan 1961
La dictée, 1961 (monodramme lyrique), unperf.
Le coeur révélateur, 1962 (chamber op, 1, P. Soupault, after E. A. Poe), Paris, Maison de Radio France, 6 Oct 1964; Toulouse, Capitôle, 1974
L'homme occis, 1963 (opéra-clinique), RTF, 10 Oct 1975; Rouen, 24 Feb 1978
Jonas, 1964 (opéra-oratorio), ORTF, 3 Nov 1966; Lyons, Opéra, 2 Dec 1969
Les mots croisés, 1965 (opéra-cruciverbal), OC, 17 Nov 1978
Donna mobile 1 [Donna stabile], 1965 (opéra d'appartement), Tours, Grand, 8 March 1985
Métamorphose d'Echo (opéra de concert), Prague, spr. 1967
La noirceur du lait (opéra-test, 1), Strasbourg, 10 June 1967 (concert perf.)
On veut la lumière? Allons-y! (opéra-parodie, 2), Angers, 12 Dec 1968
Fêtes de la faim (opéra pour comédiens), Avignon Festival, 26 July 1969
Jeu de l'oie, 1970 (opéra), unperf
Donna mobile 2 (opéra pour dames), Avignon Festival, Célestins, 5 Aug 1972
Les liaisons dangereuses (opéra épistolaire, 2, after P. C. de Laclos), Strasbourg, Opéra du Rhin, 5 Feb 1974
Young Libertad (opera-study), Lyons, Opéra studio, 2 March 1976
La grand'mère française (opéra illustré), Avignon, 20 July 1976
Les trois langages, ou Autre jeu de l'oie, 1978 (triple opéra de hasard pour et/ou par enfants), unperf.
Utopopolis (opéra-chanson), Paris, Péniche-Opéra, 11 April 1980
L'escalier de Chambord (drama melodico), Tours, 20 March 1981
Lunedi blu (opéra-brève), Paris, Péniche-Opéra, June 1982 [part of 'collective spectacle' Instantanés]
Paulina (chamber op, 1, after P. J. Jouve), Tourcoing, 6 May 1983
O comme eau (opéra-madrigalesque), Paris, Péniche-Opéra, 30 Nov 1984
Le rouge et le noir (opéra, 2, after Stendhal), Aix-en-Provence, 20 July 1989
Sommaire soleil, 1990 (opéra), unperf.

*

J. Longchampt: *L'opéra aujourd'hui* (Paris, 1970)

J.-R. Julien: 'Prey: repères préliminaires', *Le théâtre lyrique français 1945–1985*, ed. D. Pistone (Paris, 1987)

RICHARD LANGHAM SMITH

Prey, Hermann (*b* Berlin, 11 July 1929). German baritone. He studied in Berlin and made his début in 1952 at Wiesbaden as Moruccio (*Tiefland*). Engaged at Hamburg (1953–60), he created Meton in Krenek's *Pallas Athene weint* (1955). A regular guest in Vienna, Berlin and Munich, he first appeared at Salzburg in 1959 as the Barber in *Die schweigsame Frau*. In 1960 he made his Metropolitan début as Wolfram, returning as Count Almaviva, Papageno and Rossini's Figaro, the role of his San Francisco début in 1963, when he also sang Olivier (*Capriccio*). In 1962 he sang Don Giovanni at Aix-en-Provence; in 1965 he made his Bayreuth début as Wolfram and sang Storch (*Intermezzo*) with the Munich company in Edinburgh. Having made his Covent Garden début in 1973 as Rossini's Figaro, he returned as Guglielmo, Papageno, Eisenstein and Beckmesser, which he first sang at Bayreuth in 1981. His mellifluous tone and keen phrasing, allied with a genial, relaxed manner on stage, were particularly apt in Mozart.

ALAN BLYTH

Preziose ridicole, Le ('The Absurd Précieuses'). *Commedia lirica* in one act by FELICE LATTUADA to a libretto by ARTURO ROSSATO after MOLIÈRE's comedy *Les précieuses ridicules*; Milan, Teatro alla Scala, 9 February 1929.

Faithful to Molière's play, the opera is set in mid-17th-century Paris. Two young men, La Grange (tenor) and Croissy (baritone), are introduced to two young ladies, Madelon (soprano) and Cathos (mezzo-soprano), by Gorgibus (bass), father of one and uncle of the other, but are considered insufficiently refined and educated and are rejected. The young men decide to ridicule the ladies' preciosity and exaggerated formality by sending their servants as Marchese Mascarille (tenor) and Visconte Jodelet (baritone). Their elegant manners win the ladies' hearts, but in the finale La Grange and Croissy reveal the identities of the 'nobles' and humiliate the ladies.

Lattuada set Molière's comedy in a dramatic structure and musical style that recapture the forms prevalent in 19th-century Italian opera. The harmonic idiom is always firmly tonal (e.g. the E Major prelude) and tends to become progressively simpler compared with other theatrical devices whereby the composer seeks to re-create 17th-century atmosphere by using the gavotte and sarabande, thus transforming the music into sonorous comment on the action.   RAFFAELE POZZI

Přibyl, Vilém (*b* Náchod, 10 April 1925; *d* Brno, 21 July 1990). Czech tenor. He made his début in 1952 as Lukáš (Smetana's *The Kiss*) with an amateur group in Hradec Králové and took singing lessons with Jakoubková there (1952–62). In 1960 he joined the opera in Ústí nad Labem and in 1961 the Janáček Opera in Brno (where he had further lessons with Vavrdová). He took heroic tenor parts, to which his ringing yet tender voice and strong temperament were well suited; he inclined towards a psychological interpretation of character by subtle acting and vocal methods. Apart from such roles as Radames, Otello, Don José, Lohengrin and Walther, he achieved his greatest success with Dalibor and Laca. He also took leading roles in *The Greek Passion*, *War and Peace* and *The Fiery Angel*,

Katerina Izmaylova and *The Nose*. He sang at the Holland, Vienna, Salzburg and Edinburgh festivals and at Covent Garden (Florestan).

J. Fukačová: *Vilém Přibyl* (Prague, 1984) [incl. list of operatic repertory and discography]
Postavy brněnského jeviště, i [Personalities of the Brno Stage] (Brno, 1984), 358ff   ALENA NĚMCOVÁ

Price, Curtis (Alexander) (*b* Springfield, MO, 7 Sept 1945). American musicologist. He studied at Southern Illinois University (1963–7) and then at Harvard, where his teachers included John Ward and Nino Pirrotta (AM, 1970; PhD, 1974). He taught at Washington University, St Louis (1974–81), and then at King's College, London (reader 1985, professor 1988). Price's work, chiefly in English dramatic music from Purcell's time to the early 19th century, is concerned with the broader issues of theatrical history, including social and political cross-currents and their influence, as well as the music itself. His vigorous scholarship, some of it conducted in collaboration with Robert D. Hume and Judith Milhous, has thrown much fresh light on the musical theatre of Purcell's time and on London operatic life of the late 18th century.

'The Critical Decade for English Music Drama, 1700–1710', *Harvard Library Bulletin*, xxvi (1978), 38–76
Music in the Restoration Theater: with a Catalogue of Instrumental Music in the Plays, 1665–1713 (Ann Arbor, 1979)
Henry Purcell and the London Stage (Cambridge, 1984)
ed.: H. Purcell: *Dido and Aeneas* (New York, 1986)
'Italian Opera and Arson in Late Eighteenth-Century London', *JAMS*, xlii (1989), 55–107
with J. Milhous and R. D. Hume: *The Impresario's Ten Commandments: Continental Recruitment for Italian Opera in London 1763–4* (London, 1992)
ed.: *Man and Music: The Early Baroque Era* (London, 1993)

Price, (Mary Violet) Leontyne (*b* Laurel, MS, 10 Feb 1927). American soprano. She studied at Wilberforce, Ohio, and at the Juilliard School. After singing St Cecilia (*Four Saints in Three Acts*) on Broadway in 1952, she sang Gershwin's Bess at the Ziegfeld Theatre (1953) and on a two-year world tour (see illustration). She made her San Francisco début in 1957 as Madame Lidoine in the American première of *Dialogues des Carmélites*, then sang Aida, Leonora (*Il trovatore*), Orff's *Die Kluge* and Donna Elvira. In 1958 she made her Verona, Vienna and Covent Garden débuts, as Aida; in 1959 she sang Liù and Thaïs at Chicago, in 1960 Aida at La Scala and Donna Anna at Salzburg. She made her Metropolitan début in 1961 as Leonora (*Il trovatore*), returning as Leonora (*La forza del destino*), Elvira (*Ernani*), Amelia (*Un ballo in maschera*), Tatyana, Butterfly, Manon Lescaut, Minnie, Tosca, Pamina, Fiordiligi, Barber's Cleopatra, which she created in 1966, and Aida, in which role she took her farewell in 1985. Musically a subtle interpreter, she had a true *lirico spinto* voice, full and resonant in tone.

A. Blyth: 'Leontyne Price Talks', *Gramophone*, xlix (1971), 303
J. B. Steane: *The Grand Tradition* (London, 1974), 407ff
                                                    ALAN BLYTH

Price, Margaret (Berenice) (*b* Blackwood, Mon. [now Gwent], 13 April 1941). Welsh soprano. She studied in London, making her début in 1962 with the WNO as Cherubino, then singing Nannetta, Amelia (*Boccanegra*) and Mimì. She first sang at Covent Garden in 1963 as Cherubino; later roles there included Pamina, Marzel-

Leontyne Price and William Warfield in the title roles of Gershwin's 'Porgy and Bess'

line, Donna Anna, Fiordiligi, Countess Almaviva, Desdemona, Norma and Amelia (*Ballo*). At Glyndebourne she sang the Angel (*Jephtha*) in 1966, then Konstanze and Fiordiligi. In 1967 she appeared as Titania at Aldeburgh. She made her American début in 1969 at San Francisco as Pamina, followed by Nannetta, Fiordiligi and Aida. She first appeared at Munich in 1971 as Amelia (*Boccanegra*), then sang her Mozart roles and Ariadne, Adriana Lecouvreur and the Marschallin. She sang in Chicago, at La Scala and at the Paris Opéra, with which she visited New York in 1976, as Countess Almaviva and Desdemona, the role of her Metropolitan début in 1985. Her repertory includes Verdi's Joan of Arc and Elisabeth de Valois. She recorded Isolde with Carlos Kleiber. Her voice, round, brilliant in tone and very flexible, is capable of great dramatic power. She was made a CBE in 1982.

A. Blyth: 'Margaret Price', *Opera*, xxxvi (1985), 607–14
                                                    ALAN BLYTH

Prière (Fr.). PREGHIERA.

Priestman, Brian (*b* Birmingham, 10 Feb 1927). English conductor. After studying at the University of Birmingham and at the Brussels Conservatory, he held various conducting posts with orchestras in Britain, North America and New Zealand. Besides a strong interest in contemporary music he has a scholarly grasp of Baroque performance. He has recorded Handel's *Rodelinda*, *Serse* and *Hercules*, and conducted the first British performance of Alessandro Scarlatti's *Griselda* for BBC radio in 1968.

Prigioniero, Il ('The Prisoner'). Opera in a prologue and one act by LUIGI DALLAPICCOLA to his own libretto after Villiers De l'Isle-Adam's *La torture par l'espérance* and Charles De Coster's *La légende d'Ulenspiegel et de Lamme Goedzak*; Florence, Teatro Comunale, 20 May 1950 (previously broadcast, RAI, 1 December 1949).

The opera is set in Spain in the second half of the 16th century. As the prologue begins the stage is black, but for the deathly white face of the Mother (soprano). She is about to visit her son, who has been imprisoned by the Inquisition, and she sings of her suffering at watching his miserable fate. She is haunted by a nightmare in which a spectral figure forms out of the gloom and advances slowly but relentlessly towards her with heavy steps and eyes shining with the reflections of martyrs' fire: it is Philip II. At the end of the dream, he is metamorphosed into the figure of Death. A choral interlude based on words from the Latin liturgy, 'Fiat misericordia tua, Domine, super nos' ('Have mercy upon us, O Lord') leads into the first scene, set in the dark dungeons of Saragossa prison. The Prisoner (baritone) lies on his pallet, his mother nearby. He tells her of a wonderful moment when, at the height of his sufferings in prison, the Gaoler (tenor) called him 'fratello' ('brother'). This one word has been enough to restore his faith in life, and he has begun to pray again. As he sings of re-discovering his faith and hope, she remembers how he used to pray as a child. At the start of scene ii the Prisoner is again alone, but suddenly the Gaoler appears, once more addressing him as 'brother'. He goes on to instil new hope into the Prisoner's heart, telling him that revolution has broken out in Flanders, and that the town of Flushing has fallen. Roland, the great bell of Ghent which has been silenced by Charles V, will soon ring again, celebrating the end of Philip and of the Inquisition. The Gaoler sings an aria, the Song of the Beggars, resembling a popular revolutionary song. As he evokes the joyous sound of children's voices welcoming the sun as it returns to the liberated cities, the Prisoner tries to take up the song himself, but bursts into sobs. When the Gaoler goes out he leaves the cell door open, seemingly to allow the Prisoner to escape.

In scene iii, the Prisoner finds himself in the dank, labyrinthine passages underneath the prison. Feeling his way furtively along the walls, he repeats his childhood prayer but is forced to cower in a dark corner as a Brother of Redemption (silent role), a torturer, goes by. At the sight of the torturer's instruments the Prisoner feels his courage ebb away but, remembering the story of Lazarus, who also was recalled to life by a word, he finds the strength to continue. He has to hide again as two priests (tenor and baritone) pass by. At last, he feels fresh air on his face and hears the sound of a bell. He interprets this as the great bell of Ghent, indicating the end of Philip II's reign. As he gets nearer the exit, the off-stage chorus once again intones words from the liturgy: 'Domine, labia mea aperies' ('O Lord, open thou my lips').

The final scene is set in a huge garden. It is spring and the sky is full of stars. The Prisoner rushes on, full of joy, and stops in front of a great cedar tree, where he ecstatically spreads his arms wide as a symbolic gesture of love for humanity. Two enormous arms, hitherto hidden by the lower branches of the tree, move out slowly and return his embrace: the Prisoner finds himself locked in the arms of the Grand Inquisitor (tenor; a role usually doubled by the Gaoler). In a flash of intuition, he understands the terrible truth: he has succumbed to the ultimate torture – hope. Now only the flames await him. The Grand Inquisitor, ironically compassionate, leads him away. The opera ends with a barely audible question from the Prisoner: 'La libertà?'

Il prigioniero, Dallapiccola's second opera, was drafted during World War II, and is clearly a response to wartime events. Dallapiccola was never imprisoned, though during World War I he and his family were interned in Austria, and in World War II he was forced into hiding. The opera was conceived in an atmosphere

'Il prigioniero' (Dallapiccola): scene from the original production at the Teatro Comunale, Florence, 20 May 1950

of anonymous denunciation, when petty Fascist officials would 'stare meaningfully when they met you in the street'. Its subject – torture by false hope – is depicted musically by a three-note motif ('fratello'), introduced by the Gaoler, that pervades the music. The friendship suggested by this motif is eventually found to be a delusion, hence the ironic, bittersweet accompaniment (in a 12-note context) of two tonal triads.

The bulk of the opera concerns the Prisoner's solitary attempts to replace despair with hope, and the fluctuations of his moods are traced with remarkable subtlety in music of great passion and lyrical beauty. The music is based on three 12-note rows, each carrying a symbolic status: prayer, hope and freedom. Following the model of Berg, Dallapiccola uses these to construct a series of closed forms, most notably *ricercares*. He also incorporates extended extracts from his *Canti di prigionia* (1938–41), his first piece of overt protest music, though the opera ends without the optimism of the earlier work.

ANTHONY SELLORS

Prigioniero superbo, Il ('The Proud Prisoner'). *Opera seria* in three acts by GIOVANNI BATTISTA PERGOLESI to a libretto after FRANCESCO SILVANI's *La fede tradita e vendicata*; Naples, Teatro S Bartolomeo, 5 September 1733.

In late 1732 Naples was severely damaged by a series of earthquakes. As penance, the Viceroy of Naples banned all theatrical performances in early 1733; the first *opera seria* staged was Pergolesi's *Il prigioniero superbo*, in celebration of the Habsburg Empress Elisabeth Christina's birthday (Naples was in its last year of Austrian rule). The intermezzo *La serva padrona* was written to be performed with this work. Silvani's drama had appeared twice before in Naples: in 1707 set by Gasparini and Vignola, and in 1726 set by Vinci, as *Ernelinda*. Later references to a lost opera, *Ricimero*, must refer to *Il prigioniero*, since the character Metalce was called 'Ricimero' in Silvani's original drama.

Silvani's plot remains largely intact in *Il prigioniero*, although the character names have been changed. Sostrate, who had become King of Norway by slaying Clearco, has been conquered and is being held with his daughter, Rosmene. The King of the Goths, Metalce, plans to restore Clearco's daughter, Ericlea, to the throne by marrying her, and he agrees that his ally Viridate, Prince of Denmark, should marry Rosmene. Ericlea loves Micisda, but wants to preserve the kingdom. Metalce professes his love for Rosmene, but she spurns his pleading and promises. Angered, Metalce commands that Sostrate be executed, but Viridate and Rosmene rise to his defence. If Rosmene will be his bride Metalce offers to spare either Sostrate or Viridate; the other she herself must condemn to death. She chooses to save the life of her father. Metalce insists that Viridate no longer loves her, but Rosmene still abhors Metalce. The people rise in revolt, the temple grows dark and in the ensuing battle Metalce is taken prisoner. He asks forgiveness, but is deposed. A new order is established: Rosmene will marry Viridate, and Ericlea and Sostrate will inherit the throne.

This opera is more advanced than Pergolesi's *Salustia*; the harmonic planning of *Il prigioniero* is more directional, with elaborately constructed dramatic scenes and expressive effects. Sostrate's *aria agitata* at the end of Act 1, 'Salda quercia', uses vivid pictorial imagery, graceful but agile melodies and stable harmonic movement (this is Pergolesi's first use of 'Alberti bass').

Several martial arias in crisp rhythms are orchestrated with trumpets. Rosmene's highly emotional scene to end the second act, where she must choose between her lover and her father, is new to Silvani's drama. The text is set in an *accompagnato* recitative that gradually builds to *allegro*; the ensuing aria is full of expressive effects, such as bare octaves to underscore her terror.

See also RICIMER.

DALE E. MONSON

Prigozhin, Lyutsian Abramovich (*b* Tashkent, 15 Aug 1926). Soviet composer. He studied at the Tashkent Music School from the age of ten and then at the music school of the Leningrad Conservatory, which was evacuated to Tashkent during World War II; he later studied composition at the conservatory and in 1967 returned there as a teacher. In his compositions Prigozhin inclined towards epic and dramatic subjects; his style is characterized by emotional restraint, concentration, severity of colour and sharpness of rhythmic-melodic outline.

Ya sïn trudovogo naroda [I am a Son of the Working People], 1951 (after V. Katayev), unpubd
Doktor Aybolit, 1965 (radio op for children, Prigozhin, after K. Chukovsky), unpubd
Mal'chish-Kibal'chish, 1969 (radio op for children, S. Tikhaya and T. Svirina, after A. Gaydar), unpubd
Robin Gud [Robin Hood], 1972 (Yu. Dimitrin, after Eng. folk ballads), unpubd

E. Ruch'yevskaya: *Lyutsian Prigozhin* (Moscow and Leningrad, 1977)
ABRAHAM I. KLIMOVITSKY

Příhody Lišky Bystroušky. Opera by Leoš Janáček; *see* CUNNING LITTLE VIXEN, THE.

Prima donna (It.: 'first lady'). The leading woman singer in an opera, often though not always a soprano; by extension, a vain, capricious person. The term seems to derive from Italian touring theatre companies, the members of which fitted into set categories (first lover, 'noble father' etc.) and could with minimal dispute be assigned parts in the many plays performed; such a company as a rule had a single leading lady. Operas down to the early 18th century had large casts and, as companies were recruited season by season, did not need to follow so rigid a pattern (though there was some stereotyping and specialization, especially in comic parts). Discussion of status turned on whether a role was a *prima parte*, defined – for instance in a 1699 dispute between the composer Antonio Giannettini and the castrato Adamo Francesco Ghinder (documented in *I-MOs*, Archivio per Materie, Musici b. 2) – by such tests as number of arias, prominence in duets, whether it was the title part, and even whether it was the highest-lying.

The prima donna emerged with the rise of 18th-century *opera seria*, in which a cast of six to eight generally included two women, both with substantial parts but one as a rule more prominent. When the two parts were equally prominent the singers were billed as *prime donne a vicenda* ('co-equal'); to avoid disputes about precedence their names might be printed diagonally across each other. In comic opera the leading lady was known as *prima buffa*. From the 1820s principals in new Italian operas tended to number three or four; by and large the prima donna's part was the emotional centre of the work and might give it its title, while the singer who performed it was at the heart of the opera season as a social occasion. Whether she was typically vainer or more capricious than other singers (or than other people involved in opera) is open to question. With the breakdown from about 1860–70 of the calendar of fixed seasons, soloists came and went, appearing perhaps for a few performances at a time; the term came to be used of any leading woman singer, as it still is.

See also ASSOLUTO, ASSOLUTA; PRIMO MUSICO; PRIMO UOMO; SECONDA DONNA.

G. Valle: *Cenni teorico-pratici sulle aziende teatrali* (Milan, 1823), 35–45
H. S. Edwards: *The Prima Donna* (London, 1888)
C. Clément: *L'Opéra, ou la défaite des femmes* (Paris, 1978; Eng. trans., 1988, as *Opera, or the Undoing of Women*)
K. Honolka: *Die grossen Primadonnen* (Wilhelmshaven, 1982)
R. Christiansen: *Prima Donna: a History* (London, 1984)
S. Durante: 'Il cantante', *SOI*, iv (1987), 349–415

JOHN ROSSELLI

Prima Donna. Comedy opera in one act by ARTHUR BENJAMIN to a libretto by Cedric Cliffe; London, Fortune Theatre, 23 February 1949.

The opera is set in 18th-century Venice, where the impecunious Florindo (baritone) is expecting a visit from his wealthy uncle the Count (bass-baritone), who in turn is hoping to be entertained by the prima donna 'La Filomela'. No longer in a position to invite her, Florindo arranges a substitute, a situation complicated by his friend Alcino (tenor) doing the same; both Olimpia and Fiammetta (coloratura sopranos) try to outdo each other, to the Count's consternation. He is consoled instead by Bellina the maid (soprano) in operatic costume, while the others pair up in the moonlight. Benjamin conducted the première by the London Opera Club 16 years after its composition; at a revival in 1968 (at the RCM) it proved an effective vehicle for student singers. It is a melodious, astutely scored confection in closed forms such as a drinking-trio and quarrelling-quartet, an 'Ariadne' aria in canon for the rival ladies and a period-style gavotte and musette for a small character-ballet. The duration is about 70 minutes, and a small stage band (five players) is employed.

NOËL GOODWIN

Prima la musica e poi le parole ('First the Music and then the Words'). *Divertimento teatrale* in one act by ANTONIO SALIERI to a libretto by GIOVANNI BATTISTA CASTI; Vienna, Schönbrunn Orangerie, 7 February 1786.

Emperor Joseph II commissioned the opera for performance at Schönbrunn Palace; members of the Burgtheater's Italian troupe presented it at one end of the orangery; at the other end members of the German troupe gave Mozart's *Der Schauspieldirektor*, also commissioned for the occasion. Like its companion-piece, *Prima la musica* is a lighthearted look at opera and opera singers. A Music Director (bass) and a Poet (bass) argue about preparations for an opera. The Music Director insists it must be ready for performance in four days, but the Poet says more time is needed. The Music Director explains that the music is already written and the Poet need only write verses to fit the music – it is of little importance that the music express the meaning of the words.

Eleonora (soprano), a role created by Nancy Storace, is a prima donna who specializes in *opera seria*. She demonstrates her abilities by singing excerpts from one of the most popular *opere serie* of the late 18th century,

Sarti's *Giulio Sabino* (1781). Storace's ability to imitate Luigi Marchesi, who had sung the title role of *Giulio Sabino* in Vienna, is exploited to hilarious effect, as the Poet and the Music Director join Eleanora in a ridiculous 'staging' of a scene from Sarti's opera. Some passages are quoted directly from Sarti, along with others composed by Salieri in a parody of *seria* style.

As the Poet and Music Director attempt to put together an aria to suit Eleonora's voice and temperament, they are interrupted by Tonina, a comic-opera soprano who will also sing a role in the performance. She demonstrates her talents in the comic style, and the Poet and Music Director quickly assemble an aria for her. Eleonora returns, and the two quarrel over who is to sing first; they end up singing at the same time, Eleonora in the serious style and Tonina in the comic. The two songs harmonize perfectly. The Poet and Music Director join in the ensemble, bringing the opera to a joyful conclusion.

Salieri responded to Casti's amusing libretto with a light, witty score remarkable for its careful tonal organization. The overture and finale are in the same key (standard procedure for Mozart, but not for most of his contemporaries, including Salieri). Many adjacent numbers are in keys a 3rd apart (e.g. the overture in B♭ is followed by a duet in D; an aria in D precedes the finale in B♭). Like many Viennese operas of the 1780s this one is dominated by ensembles: two duets for the Poet and the Music Director, a trio (actually a serious rondò for Eleonara with comic interpolations by the two basses) and the quartet finale.

JOHN A. RICE

Primo musico (It.: 'first musician'). A term applied *c*1800–1850 to a woman singer performing a leading male part. MUSICO in the 17th century meant any singer or musician of either sex; it then came to mean a castrato. With the decline and then the disappearance of the operatic castrato from about 1800 the habit of assigning a leading male part to a high voice went on, with a woman singing in breeches (as women had from time to time since the early days of opera) now formally described as [*primo*] *musico*. Such a part was generally that of a lover (Tancredi in Rossini's opera, Romeo in *I Capuleti e i Montecchi*) but on occasion that of the hero's or heroine's friend (Pippo in *La gazza ladra*, Maffio Orsini in *Lucrezia Borgia*). A *musico* was often but not invariably a contralto; Giulia Grisi had a contract as both prima donna and *primo musico*, and demanded that it should be rewritten to specify *primo musico soprano* (to Alessandro Lanari, 9 July 1830, *I-Ms* Coll. Casati 659). The last opera still occasionally performed to include a *musico* part was Donizetti's *Linda di Chamounix* (1842). Verdi's rejection of the practice hastened its decline; his later assignment to a high soprano of the page's part in *Un ballo in maschera* (1859) followed a different, mainly French tradition, that of having the parts of children and adolescents sung by women. The principal boy in English pantomime, on the other hand, is a direct descendant of the *musico*.

JOHN ROSSELLI

Primo uomo (It.: 'first man'). The leading male part in an 18th-century *opera seria*, invariably assigned to a high voice – as a rule a castrato, but on occasion a woman. The term emerged alongside PRIMA DONNA. The primo uomo was often a young prince or leading rebel, and almost invariably a lover. Under the conventions of the form, his was not necessarily the title part, which was often that of a ruler – normally assigned to a tenor. In most *opere serie* there was also a secondo uomo, a substantial but less prominent part, likewise sung by a high voice. An example is Mozart's *La clemenza di Tito*, in which Sextus is the primo uomo and Annius the secondo uomo, while the eponymous ruler is sung by a tenor. With the disappearance of the operatic castrato about 1800 the male lead (no longer called primo uomo) went to a tenor or, in a few operas with a subordinate love interest or none (such as Donizetti's *Belisario* and Verdi's *Nabucco* and *Macbeth*), to a baritone. Within the normal range of the male voice the convention that a lover's part should be a high-lying one persists to this day.   JOHN ROSSELLI

Prince Igor [*Knyaz' Igor'*]. Opera in a prologue and four acts by ALEXANDER PORFIR'YEVICH BORODIN to his own libretto after a scenario by VLADIMIR VASIL'YEVICH STASOV largely based on the anonymous (?)12th-century epic *Slovo o polku Igoreve* ('The Lay of the Host of Igor'); St Petersburg, Mariinsky Theatre, 23 October/4 November 1890.

Igor Svyatoslavich *Prince of Seversk*		baritone
Yaroslavna *his second wife*		soprano
Vladimir Igorevich *son by his first marriage*		tenor
Vladimir Yaroslavich [Galitsky] *Prince of Galich, brother of Princess Yaroslavna*		high bass
Konchak ⎫ *Polovtsian khans*		bass
Gzak ⎭		silent
Konchakovna *daughter of Khan Konchak*		contralto
Ovlur *a baptized Polovtsian*		tenor
Skula ⎫ *gudok (rebec) players*		bass
Yeroshka ⎭		tenor
Yaroslavna's Nurse		soprano
Polovtsian Maiden		soprano

Russian princes and princesses, boyars and boyarïnyas, elders, Russian warriors, maidens, crowd; Polovtsian khans, girlfriends of Konchakovna, slave girls of Khan Konchak, Russian prisoners, Polovtsian guards

Setting The city of Putivl' and a Polovtsian encampment, 1185

The opera's protracted gestation – Borodin worked on it between 1869 and 1887, and left it unfinished – has suggested parallels with *Siegfried* and *Les Troyens*, but the most fitting comparison is with that other great unwieldy Russian torso, *Khovanshchina*, like *Prince Igor* a historical opera to the composer's own gradually accumulating and ideologically inconstant libretto. Both were left for others to complete; neither can be said to have achieved definitive form within its author's lifetime. Perhaps most importantly, *Khovanshchina* and *Prince Igor* had Vladimir Stasov in common. The Mighty Kuchka's great tribune (and their christener), a librarian by profession, Stasov had a hand in the conception of many of the group's most characteristic works, but in none did he play so important a role as in Borodin's magnum opus.

The project had its origin in a scenario Stasov prepared, at Borodin's request but at Stasov's own choice, from Russia's earliest literary classic (supplemented by episodes and descriptions from two Kievan chronicles, the *Ipatiyevskaya* and the *Lavrentiyevskaya*). The possibly spurious 'Lay of the Host of Igor', describing a

12th-century princeling's ill-fated campaign against a nomadic Turkic tribe that was interfering with trade routes to the south, seemed to Stasov to answer to all of Borodin's poetic and musical strengths: 'broad epic themes, national character, the most diversified *dramatis personae*, passion, drama, the Orient in all its varied manifestations'.

In short, the opera was to be another *Ruslan and Lyudmila*, the only significant difference being one of tone: earnestly nationalist (as befitted its time and place) rather than innocently 'magical'. From the perspective of the latter 19th century a *Ruslan*-esque opera could not seem anything but anachronistic in concept and design: even Borodin's fellow-kuchkist César Cui called it 'an opera in the narrow and, perhaps, outmoded sense'. Its musical beauties have redeemed it, and the 'epic' genre to which it is said to belong has provided a trusty excuse for its glaring structural gaps (the fates of two major characters being unknown at the final curtain) and its superfluities (much of the love and dance music in the middle pair of acts). At the same time, the work's reputation as an 'operatic picture book' (Dahlhaus) has justified the crudest sort of play-doctoring, such as the 'traditional' omission of Act 3.

Like *Ruslan*, Borodin's opera derived its dramatic rhythm from an opposition of national musical idioms: rigorously Russian versus promiscuously 'oriental'. The former, in *Igor*, is based – though perhaps not as strictly as some have maintained – on 'intonations' from epic ballads and on a small repertory of folksongs such as *Uzh vï gorï moi Vorob'yovskiye* ('About the Sparrow Hills'). The latter ranges in *Igor* from Arabian to Turkic to Finno-Ugric vernaculars.

Stasov sketched out the scenario during a soirée at the home of Glinka's sister, Lyudmila Shestakova, on the

Title-page of the first edition of the full score of Borodin's 'Prince Igor' (Leipzig, 1896)

night of 19–20 April/1–2 May 1869. Three symmetrically disposed acts were planned. The first act portrays the social disintegration of Igor's domain in his absence. The second treats Igor and his son in captivity, corresponding roughly to the two middle acts of the eventual opera. The third act is again set in Putivl', and there is an epilogue, with no counterpart in the opera, set two years later at the wedding of Vladimir and Konchakovna. This epilogue, a transparent derivation from the *Ruslan* finale without precedent in lay or chronicle beyond the tacked-on final chorus, nonetheless epitomizes the scenario's ideology; for while in captivity Igor would not assent to a marriage that would make his son a Polovtsian, he rejoices at home in the same marriage when it 'annexes' the khan's daughter as a Russian and a Christian. Another manifestation of the same double standard is the egregious Ovlur, wholly Stasov's invention (in the scenario he is Yaroslavna's half-Polovtsian retainer), whose treachery against his father's people is heartily approved along with his appeal to Igor to break the bonds of chivalry for the sake of Russian 'honour'. (In the eventual opera Ovlur's connection with Yaroslavna was severed; he appears only in Act 2 as a turncoat-*ex-machina*.) Thus *Prince Igor* made overt the pervasive subtext to 19th-century Russian essays in orientalism: the racially justified endorsement of Russia's militaristic expansion to the east. 'We go with trust in God for our faith, our Russia, our people', the operatic Igor anachronistically proclaims, very much in the spirit of the reigning tsar, Alexander II.

Borodin began composing, in the late summer of 1869, with Stasov's first number 'Yaroslavna's Dream', based in part on sketches for an earlier operatic project on Lev Mey's drama, *Tsarskaya nevesta* ('The Tsar's Bride', later the basis of an opera by Rimsky-Korsakov). According to Stasov, Borodin followed it early in 1870 with its 'oriental' counterpart, Konchakovna's cavatina (it should be noted however that the extant autograph material for that number dates from 1874–5), based in principle on Stasov material but not explicitly provided for. Next (again following Stasov rather than the extant manuscripts) came the chorus of khans, probably adapted from an Oprichniks' chorus in *The Tsar's Bride* – a purely decorative number that could fit here or there or anywhere in the middle act. These were early signs that Borodin's musical fantasy (like Glinka's before him) was going to have its head without concern for dramatic consequences. There is irony in this disregard; as early as March 1870, cold feet about the project's dramatic viability coupled with not unreasonable doubts as to his own competence as a librettist (exacerbated by the humiliating failure of Cui's *William Ratcliff*) caused Borodin to suspend work. Some of his musical sketches went into the Second Symphony, begun the next year, and into *Mlada*, the opera-ballet on which four of the Five worked for a while in 1872. It was only after that project aborted without hope of salvage that Borodin returned to *Igor*. The *Mlada* music, parts of the finale excepted, circled back into the work from which it had mainly been drawn (*see* MLADA (i)).

It would be fruitless to attempt a detailed chronology of the opera's piecemeal accumulation from this point as long as Borodin's manuscripts remain undescribed (Bobéth's checklist is far from complete) and Lamm's annotated 'composite vocal score' – in effect a transcription of all the surviving autographs – remains unpublished. The salient points are:

(*a*) Most of the Polovtsian music (and also Yaroslavna's Lament, which evidently picked up in this way the somewhat oriental flavour that has nonplussed some writers) was written in 1875; for the Act 2 hymn, no.7, the composer relied in part on the same melody from Christianowitsch's *Esquisse historique de la musique arabe* as he did later in the song 'Arabskaya melodiya'; Konchak's Act 2 aria, no.15, seems to have been based on a Chuvash melody from an 1870 collection. The Polovtsian March (no.18) was an obvious emulation of Chernomor's March in *Ruslan*.

(*b*) A 'Carousal chorus' for Galitsky's followers, also written in 1875, became the basis for the eventual Act 1 scene i, which precedes the first number in Stasov's scenario.

(*c*) The 'Chorus of Praise' now in the prologue was originally meant as the culmination of the epilogue, which was never fully composed.

(*d*) Igor's aria, no.13, was originally composed in 1875 as a modest recitative-arioso to an entirely different text (see Dmitriyev 1950); its replacement, based in part on the *Mlada* music, was composed in 1881.

(*e*) In 1878, following another break in his work, Borodin introduced Skula and Yeroshka, the pair of comical *gudochniki* (rebec players) associated with Vladimir Galitsky. Though comparable to minstrel or jester characters in earlier Russian operas such as *Askold's Grave* and *Rogneda*, they were obviously modelled on Varlaam and Missaïl, the tenor-bass pair of vagabond monks in *Boris Godunov*. (This correspondence extends to their musical idiom, largely modelled, in the prologue and finale, on the prose recitatives in Musorgsky's Inn Scene.)

(*f*) 1879 saw the composition of the bulk of Act 1: in addition to nos.2*b*, 4 and 5, Borodin replaced Stasov's narrative of the two merchants with the Chorus of Boyars, no.6, based on the folksong 'About the Sparrow Hills'. A theme from the merchants' narrative went into the unfinished Third Symphony; in 1880 Borodin composed a new conclusion for the act (later dropped, either by the composer or by his posthumous collaborators), in which Galitsky returns to Yaroslavna's quarters after the boyars' report and attempts a mutiny with the aid of the foreign residents of Putivl'.

(*g*) The prologue, which followed in 1883, was an attempt to fill an obvious lacuna caused in Stasov's scenario by the absence of the title character before Act 2; the narration of the fateful eclipse was now replaced by its direct, if slightly anachronistic, portrayal.

(*h*) The last major decision was taken in 1884, when Borodin detached the escape and made it the basis of a separate act, Act 3, in which some of the overflow Polovtsian music (March, Procession of khans, Konchak's song, etc.) might find a home.

By the time of his sudden death Borodin had orchestrated a miscellaneous group of ten numbers from the opera, mostly for concert performances at the Free Music School under Balakirev and Rimsky-Korsakov between 1876 and 1879. Besides the chorus of praise and its reprise in the prologue, the group included nos.2*b*, 4 and 5 from Act 1; 9, 11, 15 and 17 from Act 2; and 25 and 29 from Act 4. Rimsky-Korsakov, who had actually begun a version of the opera in 1885 with the composer's active collaboration (in the process filling some gaps in the prologue), now undertook to complete it. As he had employed his former pupil Lyadov to assist with the orchestration of the Polovtsian dances in 1879, he now enlisted as his assistant the 21-year-old Glazunov – a favourite of Borodin's during the latter's last five years and possessor of a phenomenal musical memory. Rimsky retouched and scored the middle section of the prologue and all the unorchestrated portions of Acts 1, 2 and 4, plus the Polovtsian March in Act 3, adding verbal and musical transitions as needed. Glazunov's role was more creative: he had virtually to compose the bulk of the third act (1252 bars) on the basis of sometimes very fragmentary sketches. His scrupulous account of this work was published in 1896 and translated by Abraham (1939). The extent of his role in the composition of the overture must remain unsettled as he evaluated it differently at different times; Levashov (1985), on the basis of notations on Borodin's manuscripts ('This will do for a first theme', 'Good for a second theme' etc.), has asserted that Glazunov composed it outright.

Doubts about the correspondence between the structurally and dramaturgically lopsided performing version thus produced and the composer's final intentions were inevitable (see Abraham 1939). They were much abetted by Lamm's critical report, the conclusions of which were widely known long before the belated publication of excerpts in 1983. Lamm was able to demonstrate that Rimsky and Glazunov had pruned away some 1787 bars of music, amounting to almost one fifth of the total that Borodin had composed. Several alternative performing versions have been put forth (see Neef 1989), the most substantial being that prepared in the early 1970s by a troika consisting of a young musicologist (Levashov), a veteran composer (Yury Fortunatov) and the chief régisseur of the Moscow Bol'shoy Theatre (Boris Pokrovsky). First produced in Vilnius in 1974, it was given thereafter at the Deutsche Staatsoper in Berlin and published there in 1978. The chief differences naturally pertain to Act 3. In the alternative version a trio of princes, two of them new characters, swear mutual fealty; the familiar trio (no.23) is cut down to a duet (without Igor) to match its counterpart in *Mlada*; the Russian prisoners sing an invocation to the River Don to the music of the *Mlada* finale; most controversially, the 1875 version of Igor's aria is reinstated alongside its 1881 successor, which retains its place in Act 2. In addition, the 1880 ending to Act 1 (Galitsky's rebellion) is restored (culminating in Galitsky's death on the ramparts of Putivl'), and an epilogue corresponding to Stasov's is appended.

PROLOGUE *The market place in Putivl'* Igor sets off on his campaign against the Polovtsï despite an ill-presaging eclipse and the entreaties of Yaroslavna, his wife; Skula and Yeroshka desert (no.1).

ACT 1.i *The court of Prince Vladimir Galitsky* Skula and Yeroshka lead a paean to Igor's profligate brother-in-law and recount how he abducted a maiden for his pleasure (no.2*a*: chorus, 'Slava, slava Volodimiru': 'All hail, Vladimir'). Galitsky announces his philosophy (no.2*b*, recitative and song, 'Greshno tait': ya skuki ne lyublyu': ''Twere a sin to hide it: I hate a dreary life'). He mocks his sister Yaroslavna's disapproval (no.2*c*, recitative). A crowd of maidens rushes in to protest at the abduction; Galitsky sends them on their way (no.2*d*, chorus and *scena*, 'Oy, likhon'ko! Oy, goryushko!': 'Oh, what misfortune, oh, what sorrow'). The men briefly show their fear of Yaroslavna (no.2*e*) but, turning their attention to wine, resume singing Galitsky's praises: he should be their prince, not Igor (no.2*f*: Princely Song, 'Chto u knyazya da Volodomira': 'At Prince Vladimir's').

1.ii *Chamber in Yaroslavna's quarters* Yaroslavna, pining for Igor, suffers from evil dreams (no.3, arioso, 'Nemalo vremeni proshlo': 'No little time has passed'). The Nurse announces the arrival of the maidens, who complain of Galitsky's behaviour in a Glinka-esque 5/4 metre (no.4). Galitsky unexpectedly arrives, frightens off the maidens, attempts to laugh off his sister's reproaches, but in the end agrees to release the abducted girl (no.5); he leaves. A party of boyars comes to Yaroslavna with terrible news: Igor and his son Vladimir have been taken prisoner by the Polovtsï. An alarm sounds: a Polovtsian force under Khan Gzak attacks Putivl' (no.6, finale).

ACT 2 *The Polovtsian encampment; evening* A chorus of Polovtsian maidens entertain Konchakovna with a hymn to the cool refreshment of evening (no.7, 'Na bezvod'ye, dnyom na solntse vyanet tsvetïk': 'In the absence of water the flower withers in the sun by day'), and go into their dance (no.8, 'Dance of the Polovtsian Maidens'). Konchakovna sings of her expected tryst with Vladimir (no.9, cavatina, 'Merknet svet dnevnoy': 'The daylight dies'). Russian prisoners march by on their way back from forced labour. Konchakovna bids the maidens refresh them. The Polovtsian patrol, Ovlur among them, make their round. Ovlur furtively remains onstage when they depart (no.10). Vladimir cautiously makes his way to Konchakovna's tent and sings of their tryst (no.11, recitative and cavatina, 'Gde tï, gde': 'Where art thou, where'). Konchakovna appears, and the lovers sing in ecstasy (no.12, duet, 'Ti li Vladimir moy?': 'Is it you, Vladimir mine?'). They scamper off at the sound of Igor's approach. He sings an elaborate aria in two parts, the first expressing his passionate thirst for freedom, the second his tender thoughts of Yaroslavna (no.13, 'Ni sna, ni otdïkha': 'Nor sleep, nor rest of any kind'). Ovlur seizes the moment: he approaches Igor and proposes a plan of escape. Igor at first refuses to consider such a dishonourable course, but vacillates (no.14); Ovlur disappears. Khan Konchak enters, oozes magnanimity towards his 'honoured guest' (no.15, aria, 'Zdorov li, Knyaz?': 'How goes it, Prince?'). He offers to grant Igor's freedom in return for a pledge of non-aggression, even suggests they become allies; to all of this Igor firmly refuses, much to Konchak's admiration (no.16). The khan orders entertainment from his slaves, offering Igor his pick of the maidens (no.17, Polovtsian dance[s] with chorus).

ACT 3 *An outpost of the encampment* Khan Gzak returns from Putivl', prisoners in tow, to a tumultuous greeting from Khan Konchak and the Polovtsï, while the Russians look on and seethe (no.18, Polovtsian March). Konchak sings a song of triumph (no.19, 'Nash mech nam dal pobedu': 'Our sword has given us victory'). He orders a feast (no.20*a*); the khans go off to divide the spoils (no.20*b*, chorus, 'Idyom za nim sovet derzhat': 'We'll follow him and hold council'); the Russians bewail their defeat and urge Igor to accept Ovlur's offer (no.20*c*). The Polovtsï drink and dance themselves into a stupor (no.21, chorus and dance, 'Podoben solntsu khan Konchak': 'Khan Konchak is like unto the sun'). Ovlur summons Igor (no.22). Konchakovna, having heard of the plan, runs onstage; she contends with Igor over Vladimir, Igor making his appeal to the tune of his 'freedom' aria. Finally she rouses the camp, and Igor must make off without his son (no.23, trio, 'Ya vsyo, ya vsyo uznala': 'I've found out everything'). The Polovtsï threaten Vladimir, but Konchak, ever magnanimous, spares him and even blesses his union with Konchakovna (no.24, finale).

ACT 4 *At the Putivl' town wall* Yaroslavna laments her fate and that of her husband (no.25, Yaroslavna's Lament: 'Akh! plachu ya gor'ko': 'Ah, bitterly I weep'). Some passers-by sing a lament of their own at the fate of Putivl', a masterly and justly famous stylization of folk heterophonic polyphony (no.26, Chorus of villagers, 'Okh, ne buynïy veter zavïval': 'Oh, it was not a stormy wind that howled'). Yaroslavna's dejected mood is broken by the sound of approaching hoofbeats; she recognizes Igor from afar. When he dismounts she rushes to him and they exchange ecstatic greetings (no.27, recitative and duet, 'On – moy sokol yasnïy!': 'It is he, my bright falcon'). Skula and Yeroshka blunder onstage carousing, recognize Igor with panic from afar, save their skins by ringing the tocsin to announce the prince's return and gratuitously declare their loyalty (no.28, song to the rebec, *scena* and chorus). The opera ends with a joyful chorus of greeting (no.29, 'Znat', gospod' mol'bï uslïshal': 'We know the Lord has heard our prayers').

* * *

Act 2 of *Prince Igor*, the only one that Borodin may plausibly be said to have completed (though even this was much retouched by Glazunov and Rimsky-Korsakov: the Prisoners' Chorus was reconstructed from memory by the former to a text by the latter), may serve as paradigm of his operatic manner, and also of the way in which a thoroughly static, formal, conventional (and in some ways inept) conception of the genre is enlivened (and, in corresponding ways, redeemed) by music so fresh and alluring as to keep the opera perpetually alive on the fringes of the repertory.

The act is framed by decorative 'oriental' numbers that set the scene and supply the routine choreographic diversion endemic to grand-operatic second acts. The subplot, the romance of Igor's son Vladimir and his captor's daughter Konchakovna, is given a risibly redundant exposition: lengthy da capo cavatinas for each (Konchakovna's, accompanied by the chorus in Rimsky-Korsakov's version, being a virtual replay of the act's decorative opening), separated by a pair of tiny choral numbers which serve to bring Ovlur furtively on stage, and followed by a duet, longer than the two cavatinas combined, that is cast in equally stereotypical format. The lovers having sung, they depart, almost as if in a Baroque opera, to make way for the title character, who enters to sing his aria of remorse and longing, the opera's centrepiece. This, the largest of all the musical structures in *Prince Igor*, is once again in da capo form but with the reprise modified to produce a climax. After a brief *scena*, Igor's aria is followed by another extended aria for another bass soloist, his captor Khan Konchak, who, like Igor, enters for no other purpose than to sing. The only real dramatic confrontation in the act takes place during the little *scena* between the bass arias when Ovlur steps out of the shadows to propose to Igor an escape plan. Otherwise the act is a classic 'concert in costume', one large vocal number following (but hardly motivated by) another.

The second act of *Prince Igor* would no doubt be just as silly as this description has made it seem were it not for the fact that every number in it is a masterpiece. Borodin's exotic idiom, though it followed and enlarged upon the examples of Glinka (the Ratmir scenes in *Ruslan*) and Balakirev (*Islamey*, *Tamara*), and though it to some extent incorporated source tunes culled from books, was an intensely personal yet flexible style, of all Borodinesque idioms the one most instantly identifiable as the composer's, and adaptable to a great range of emotional expression. At its most *Ruslan*-esque, Borodin's 'orientalism' emphasizes chromatic passes in both directions between the fifth and sixth diatonic degrees over a tonic pedal (and usually with some sort of melismatic ostinato serving as 'melodic pedal': see ex.1). At full sensual strength, the chromatic passes grow to encompass whole scales, accompanied by suitably slithery auxiliaries (ex.2). It is the supreme musical expression of *nega*, the lush languor of the orient as viewed through European eyes. (That it was taken,

Ex.1 No. 7 (Chorus of Polovtsian maidens), bars 32–6

['beneath the chilly dew the flower again revives']

Ex.2 No. 15 (Konchak's aria), bars 168–72

['tenderly and passionately they peep from beneath dark brows.']

along with a concomitant modal instability, as the essential – and influential! – Borodin trait, can be seen from Ravel's pastiche *A la manière de Borodine*.) More *nega* is evoked by the tessitura of Konchakovna's contralto, unexpected in an *ingénue* role. When her voice coils around and eventually beneath Vladimir's as the love duet reaches its climax, the effect is startling, redeeming the insipid verbal text. The concluding Polovtsian dances (which, when performed as a suite, begin with the orchestrally inventive maidens' dance, no.8) marked an epoch for French musicians when introduced by Dyagilev in 1909.

Igor's aria was written twice: first (in 1875) as a dutifully 'kuchkist' arioso over a texture of leitmotifs (all 'petty form, detail, tinycraft', to quote Borodin's operatic credo), then, definitively (in 1881), in full accord with the composer's lyric impulse and in manifest emulation of the title character's battlefield soliloquy in *Ruslan*. The stately themes of its vast da capo structure are concerned, respectively, with Igor's freedom to seek personal glory, and with tender thoughts of his waiting wife, Yaroslavna. The composer's belief in 'artistic truth' over the literal variety (what was then known as realism) is affirmed by Yaroslavna's reprise of Igor's love theme – which, so to speak, we have never seen her hear – when she sings of her corresponding longing in Act 4. It is fascinating to ponder the process by which Igor's aria was amplified alongside the exactly comparable metamorphosis of the title character's central aria in *Boris Godunov* (or, for that matter, that of Kutuzov's big aria in *War and Peace*). In all three cases realistic declamation over a texture of leitmotifs was replaced by lyrical melody adapted from an earlier or abandoned work (in Borodin's case it was *Mlada*; in Musorgsky's,

Salammbô; in Prokofiev's, *Ivan the Terrible*), and for the identical purpose: monumentalization of form and exaltation of tone.

Withal, Borodin could be an excellent musical dramatist when that, rather than totemic portraiture, was his purpose. The terse little scene with Ovlur between the big bass arias is a masterly study in character and contrast. Ovlur retains an 'oriental' tendency towards insinuating melisma as against Igor's syllabic steadfastness, but the fast tempo and the obsessive ostinato repetitions endow his responses with a suitable dramatic tension, and the tellingly sparse accompaniment in two- or three-part counterpoint manages to retain a whiff of the lush Polovtsian harmonic idiom even as it conveys urgency rather than the usual *nega*.

A few more scenes like that (and there is reason to believe they might have been supplied had the composer lived), and *Prince Igor* would have needed no excuses. As it is, the opera is a magnificent farrago, a smörgåsbord from which all listeners and critics seem to find some morsel to their taste. As Borodin put it in a letter, 'Curiously enough, all the members of our circle seem to come together on my *Igor*: from the ultra-innovatory realist Modest Petrovich [Musorgsky], to the lyric-dramatic innovator César Antonovich [Cui], to the martinet with respect to outward form and musical tradition Nikolay Andreyevich [Rimsky-Korsakov], to the ardent champion of novelty and power in all things, Vladimir Vasil'yevich Stasov. Everyone is satisfied with *Igor*, strongly though they may differ about other things'.

RICHARD TARUSKIN

Princesse de Navarre, La ('The Princess of Navarra'). *Comédie-ballet* in three acts by JEAN-PHILIPPE RAMEAU to a libretto by VOLTAIRE; Versailles, La Grande Ecurie, 23 February 1745.

This was Rameau's only *comédie-ballet*, the genre developed by Molière and Lully in the 1660s and consisting of a spoken play with more or less self-contained musical *intermèdes*. It was also the first of Rameau's stage works commissioned by Louis XV's court: like *Platée*, it celebrated the wedding of the dauphin with the infanta Maria Teresa of Spain. The play concerns the ordeals of Constance, Princess of Navarra, who has escaped from the King of Castile and seeks refuge with the ludicrous Don Morillo. Constance does her best to evade the amorous advances of the Duke of Foix, who is disguised as one of Morillo's officers; meanwhile, the naive young Sanchette has become infatuated with the duke and believes she is the true object of his affections.

Rameau's three *intermèdes*, one in each act, are only tenuously linked to this plot. The first creates a necessary diversion to prevent Constance from leaving the castle, while the second celebrates her reunion with the court of Navarra. The final *intermède* relates directly to the dauphin's wedding festivities: at the command of L'Amour [Cupid] (soprano) the Pyrenees collapse and are replaced by a magnificent Temple of Love. Rameau's score, full of interesting and varied music, was to provide an extensive fund of self-borrowings for later operas. The *intermèdes*, but not Voltaire's play, were re-staged at Covent Garden on 24 April 1977 as part of the English Bach Festival.

For illustration *see* ORCHESTRA, fig.6, and PARIS, fig.3.

GRAHAM SADLER

Princesse jaune, La ('The Yellow Princess'). *Opéra comique* in one act by CAMILLE SAINT-SAËNS to a libretto by LOUIS GALLET; Paris, Opéra-Comique (Salle Favart), 12 June 1872.

The third of Saint-Saëns' operas to be composed, *La princesse jaune* was the first to be performed and the first fruit of his friendship and collaboration with Louis Gallet. It was commissioned by Du Locle for the Opéra-Comique as compensation for not being able to mount *Le timbre d'argent* at that time, and was staged in a triple bill with Paladilhe's *Le passant* and Bizet's *Djamileh*; none of the three was well received. Critics were still regularly hostile to Saint-Saëns at that time, and his opera received only five performances. It was occasionally revived in his later years.

The subject was selected to satisfy a craze for Japan, although the opera is actually set in the Netherlands. Léna (soprano) is in love with her cousin, the studious Kornélis (tenor), who is entranced by everything Japanese, particularly his portrait of a Japanese girl he calls Ming. In a fantasy induced by a potion he is transported to Japan, but there realizes that he really loves the Dutch girl Léna after all. The music is brisk and light, with some pentatonic evocation of the orient.

HUGH MACDONALD

Princess Ida [*Princess Ida; or, Castle Adamant*]. Operetta in three acts by ARTHUR SULLIVAN to a libretto by W. S. GILBERT after Tennyson's *The Princess*; London, Savoy Theatre, 5 January 1884.

Behind the mask of a medieval setting, the libretto satirizes contemporary concern with women's education. Prince Hilarion (tenor), son of King Hildebrand (baritone), was betrothed in infancy to the Princess Ida (soprano), the daughter of King Gama (baritone). The marriage is thwarted, however, as Ida has renounced men and founded a women's university. Eventually love overcomes her resolve and she agrees to marry, leaving Lady Blanche (contralto) to run the university.

The blank-verse dialogue and substantial cast requirements of this 'respectful operatic per-version' of Tennyson's poem originate in Gilbert's play *The Princess* (1870), of which the libretto is a reworking. Although the play had been reasonably successful, its operatic reincarnation proved a disappointment at the box office. Gilbert is not at his best in *Princess Ida*, yet the score is among Sullivan's finest. The second act is exceptionally rich: Ida's arias 'Oh, goddess wise' and 'I built upon a rock' contrast with the bubbling gaiety of 'Would you know the kind of maid', the verbal and musical ingenuity of the trio 'Gently, gently' and the poignant quartet 'The world is but a broken toy'. There are good comic songs such as 'Whene'er I spoke sarcastic joke', but the music as a whole has a gentle delicacy that sets it apart from Sullivan's other operettas: even the concluding finale, a reprise of 'Expressive glances', closes quietly. Into such an intimate score the Handelian burlesque of 'This helmet, I suppose' – excellent in itself – seems an intrusion. The operetta was not professionally revived in London until 1919.

DAVID RUSSELL HULME

Principessa fedele, La ('The Faithful Princess'). *Dramma per musica* in three acts by Alessandro Scarlatti (*see* SCARLATTI family, (1)) to a libretto by AGOSTIN PIOVENE, revised probably by Domenico Antonio Parrino; Naples, Teatro S Bartolomeo, 8 February 1710.

The plot of *La principessa fedele* foreshadows both Mozart's *Die Entführung aus dem Serail* and Beethoven's *Fidelio*. The action takes place in Egypt, where the sultan Aladino (tenor) has taken prisoner Ridolfo (soprano castrato), Prince of Germany, who was on a pilgrimage to the Holy Land. Ridolfo's betrothed, Princess Cunegonda of Bohemia (contralto), disguised as a man, arrives with her admiral, Ernesto (soprano), to attempt his rescue, but is shipwrecked and captured by the Egyptian general Arsace (alto castrato) and his men, who take her to the sultan's palace. Aladino is captivated by the 'youth', and his mistress Rosana (soprano) falls in love with 'him', but after various entanglements, in which the two comic characters, Gerina (servant to Rosana, contralto) and Mustafâ (Aladino's jailer, bass), become involved, the sultan magnanimously unites Cunegonda with Ridolfo, promises marriage to Rosana and gives permission for Mustafâ and Gerina to become man and wife.

The backbone of the music, after the Italian-type overture, is formed by the usual succession of recitative-aria units, but the overall shape is somewhat distorted by lacunae in the extant sources. All but four of the 50 surviving arias and duets are in ternary (da capo or dal segno) form. Among the exceptions is 'Tu sei morta – Non son morta', an unusual and dramatically effective extension of the da capo structure in which Ridolfo's conventional reprise is interrupted by Cunegonda's repeat of the whole aria in a different key and to different words, and then taken up again as a duet. Continuo accompaniment, by 1710 rather outmoded in opera, is used for four of the lyrical numbers; in the others the keyboard instrument is joined by strings in two, three or four parts (no other instruments are called for), which also play in some notable stretches of *stromentato* recitative.   MALCOLM BOYD

Pring, Katherine (*b* Brighton, 4 June 1940). English mezzo-soprano. She studied at the RCM, London, and at the Geneva Conservatory, joining Sadler's Wells Opera (later the ENO) in 1968. She made her Covent Garden début in 1972 as Thea (Tippett's *The Knot Garden*), and first sang at Bayreuth the same year. Her wide repertory included Dorabella, Azucena, Preziosilla, Eboli, Carmen, Santuzza, Amneris, and both Waltraute and Fricka in the ENO *Ring* cycle. An intelligent and highly dramatic artist, she appeared in many 20th-century operas, as Jocasta (*Oedipus rex*), Kate (*Owen Wingrave*) and Agave, which she sang in the first British stage performances of Henze's *The Bassarids* (1974). In 1978 she sang Baba the Turk at Glyndebourne. For the ENO she sang the Mother in *Louise* (1981) and Mary in *Der fliegende Holländer* (1982). She then retired for reasons of health. Her voice, of lyrical quality and weight, was well projected and she was a fine actress.

ELIZABETH FORBES

Pringle, John (*b* Melbourne, 17 Oct 1938). Australian baritone. After winning competitions in Melbourne and Adelaide, he made his début in 1967 with the Australian Opera as Frank in *Die Fledermaus* and went on to perform the standard Mozart baritone roles, many of the more lyrical Verdi roles, the Lescauts of Puccini and Massenet, and a considerable number of 20th-century parts: Nick Shadow, the Forester (*The Cunning Little Vixen*), Tarquinius (*The Rape of Lucretia*), Sid (*Albert Herring*) and Andrey (*War and Peace*). His musical and dramatic intelligence and clearly defined stage presence

have made him popular with audiences in Australia and welcome at Glyndebourne – singing Robert Storch (*Intermezzo*) and Olivier (*Capriccio*) – Brussels, Paris and Cologne, between 1980 and 1985. His Beckmesser (1989, Australian Opera) was a complex portrait that avoided caricature and remained theatrically effective.

ROGER COVELL

Printemps [Wigniolle], **Yvonne** (*b* Ermont, Seine-et-Oise, 25 July 1894; *d* Neuilly, nr Paris, 18 Jan 1977). French soprano. She made her début in revue at the Théâtre Cigale in Paris at the age of 12. A career at the Opéra-Comique seemed possible, for she had a voice of delightful quality with prodigious breath control; in 1916, however, she joined the company of actors run by Sacha Guitry, whom she married three years later. Together they enjoyed a great international success in the theatre in plays and *opérettes*, including Messager's *L'amour masqué* and Hahn's *Mozart*, until their divorce in 1932, after which Printemps appeared in films and two musicals – Noël Coward's *Conversation Piece* (1934) and Oscar Straus's *Les trois valses* (1937). In 1949 she appeared as Hortense Schneider, with her second husband (Pierre Fresnay) as Offenbach, in Marcel Achard's film *La valse de Paris*. Several composers wrote specially for her, including Poulenc and Hahn, but she is of interest principally for her recordings, which are good enough to encourage speculation about what opera might have gained had she turned to such roles as Manon and Louise.

P. Henri-Bellier, ed.: *Sacha Guitry et Yvonne Printemps* (Paris, 1926)
J. Tournier, ed.: *Yvonne Printemps ou l'impromptu de Neuilly* (Paris, 1953)
V. Liff and others: *Yvonne Printemps* (Richmond, 1978)
C. Dufresne: *Yvonne Printemps – le doux parfum du péché* (Paris, 1988)
K. Ciupa: *Yvonne Printemps: l'heure bleu* (Paris, 1989)

J. B. STEANE

Prinz von Homburg, Der ('The Prince of Homburg'). Opera in three acts by HANS WERNER HENZE to a libretto by INGEBORG BACHMANN after Heinrich von Kleist's *Prinz Friedrich von Homburg*; Hamburg, Staatsoper, 22 May 1960.

In 1957, when working with Henze on the first production of his ballet *Maratona di Danza*, Luchino Visconti urged the composer to consider Kleist's drama as the basis for an opera. At Henze's suggestion Ingeborg Bachmann saw a stage production of *Prinz Friedrich von Homburg* in Paris and realized that, for all its preoccupations with Prussian militarism, it was a text that commanded respect. She prepared the libretto, drawing arias, ensembles and linking recitatives from Kleist's text, and in the process removing many of the more overtly nationalistic references in the original. Henze completed the music in 1958. The première was conducted by Leopold Ludwig and produced by Helmut Kautners; the cast included Vladimir Ruzdjak as the Prince, Liselotte Fölser as Natalie, Helmut Melchert as the Elector and Heinz Hoppe as Hohenzollern. In 1964 Henze rewrote the title role for a tenor; it was sung by Andor Kaposy with the Frankfurt Opera.

In the following synopsis the numbering of scenes is continuous throughout.

Friedrich Wilhelm *Elector of Brandenburg*	tenor
The Electress *his wife*	contralto
Princess Natalie of Orange *her niece, colonel-in-chief of the dragoons*	soprano
Field Marshal Dörfling	baritone
Friedrich Artur, Prince of Homburg *General of cavalry*	high baritone
Colonel Kottwitz *of the Princess's regiment*	bass
Count Hohenzollern *attached to the Elector*	tenor
First Officer	tenor
Second Officer	baritone
Third Officer	bass
First Lady of the Court	soprano
Second Lady of the Court	mezzo-soprano
Third Lady of the Court	contralto
Sergeant	baritone
First and Second Orderlies	tenor, baritone
Other Officers	tenors, basses

People of the court and military personnel

Setting Fehrbellin, Germany, in 1675

ACT 1.i *The garden of a castle in Fehrbellin* The opening orchestral chords define the strange nocturnal world of the first scene. The Prince of Homburg sits, enraptured, clutching a wreath in his hands. The Elector's courtiers come to find him, and think that he may be ill. The Elector himself takes the wreath from the Prince, places a silver medallion around his neck and gives him the hand of the Princess Natalie before leaving him to his thoughts. Count Hohenzollern wakes the Prince, who is still holding the Princess's glove. It provides a tantalizing link between his fond dream-world and reality.

1.ii *A hall in the castle* The orchestral interlude breaks the unworldly atmosphere of the first scene and prepares for the harsher militaristic world of the second. Field Marshal Dörfling is issuing plans to his commanders for the forthcoming battle. The Prince is ordered not to attack with his cavalry until he receives further instructions, but, still fascinated by the glove and by the thought that the Princess may be searching for it, he remains only dimly aware of his surroundings. When finally he drops the glove, she recognizes what she has lost, and the Prince's worlds of reality and fantasy collide.

1.iii *The battlefield of Fehrbellin, the next day* While they wait for the battle to begin, the Prince tries to clarify with Hohenzollern the details of his orders; he is still fantasizing about the Princess when the first shots are heard. Watched by his fellow officers, the Prince unilaterally orders his cavalry to attack the retreating Swedes; he will not listen to reason and dashes into battle at the sound of a fanfare.

During an interlude dominated by a saxophone solo the scene darkens. The lights go up on the carnage of the following morning; there are rumours that the Elector himself is among the dead. The Prince joins the Electress and Natalie in a trio of mourning. The Prince and Princess declare their love. The Elector appears, unharmed, with his Field Marshal: the premature cavalry attack had jeopardized victory, and whoever was responsible is to be court-martialled and executed. As the Prince offers the Elector the spoils of war, his sword is taken from him; after a large-scale ensemble he is led away to prison.

ACT 2.iv *Prison* The Prince has been found guilty at the court-martial and condemned to death, and he only begins to appreciate the seriousness of his predicament when he is told by Hohenzollern that the Elector is about to sign the death warrant.

2.v *The prison yard* As the Prince goes to appeal against his sentence, he is appalled to see a grave already dug for him.

2.vi *The Electress's room* The Prince appeals to the Electress to intervene with her husband on his behalf, but she feels unable to help him. Natalie assures him of her love and promises to try to get his sentence rescinded.

'Der Prinz von Homburg' (Henze): Vladimir Ruzdjak as the Prince and Liselotte Fölser as Natalie in the original production at the Staatsoper, Hamburg, 22 May 1960

2.vii *The Elector's room* When Natalie pleads with him to pardon the Prince, the Elector is astonished that Homburg should have abandoned so much of his military training as to value his own life above the code of honour of his regiment. Yet he gives Natalie a letter in which he agrees that the Prince can go free if he genuinely believes that the sentence against him was unjust.

2.viii *Prison* Natalie delivers the Elector's letter, telling the Prince that he has his freedom. But the Prince cannot bring himself to write the letter that the Elector demands, as he believes the judgment was a fair one. The couple kiss. Natalie tells him that if he feels he must do what is right, so does she: she will order her own regiment to free the Prince by armed force.

ACT 3.ix *The Elector's room* The Field Marshal tells the Elector that Princess Natalie's dragoons have arrived in Fehrbellin, intending to free the Prince. The Prince's letter is delivered, rejecting the offer of a pardon. Other officers request that he be pardoned, and the Elector agrees to release him, so that his own standards of honour may be upheld. The Prince arrives but still will not change his decision, preferring to purge his guilt in death. The Elector orders him back to prison to await execution; honour has been restored. Despite pleading from Natalie and Hohenzollern he refuses to change his mind, but having re-established the principles of justice tears up the death warrant.

3.x *The castle garden* As a funeral march is played the Prince is brought blindfold to what he still believes will be his execution. He already feels that he has left the real world. Then, as the Elector leads in the remainder of his court, the blindfold is removed and the Prince stands before them, just as in his dream, with the wreath of victory, his silver chain and Natalie as his bride.

* * *

Henze described the pervasive influence of 19th-century Italian opera on the composition of *Der Prinz von Homburg*: 'the angelic melancholy of Bellini, the sparkling brio of Rossini, the passionate intensity of Donizetti, combined and drawn together by Verdi's robust rhythms, his hard orchestral colours and unforgettable melodic lines ... were now to appear as pure melodrama (in the original sense)'. The opera is scored for a large chamber orchestra; each scene uses a different instrumentation and distinct musical structure, some of them based on traditional closed forms: passacaglia, fugue, rondo. In comparison with Henze's earlier operas, and with *König Hirsch* particularly, there is an emphasis on linear counterpoint and a movement away from harmonic concerns.   ANDREW CLEMENTS

Prisoner in the Caucasus, The. Opera by C. A. Cui; *see KAVKAZSKIY PLENNIK*.

Pritchard, Sir **John** (Michael) (*b* London, 5 Feb 1921; *d* Daly City, San Francisco, 5 Dec 1989). English conductor. The son of an orchestral violinist, with whom he studied, he joined the music staff at Glyndebourne in 1947, and in 1949 became chorus master and assistant to Fritz Busch, whose sudden illness during a 1951 performance of *Don Giovanni* led to Pritchard's taking over for an unscheduled début there. He remained associated with Glyndebourne as conductor, music counsellor (from 1963) and music director (1969–78), conducting the British première of Henze's *Elegy for Young Lovers* there in 1961. During this time he made débuts at the Vienna Staatsoper in 1951 and at Covent Garden with *Un ballo in maschera* in 1952, later conducting the premières by the Covent Garden company of Britten's *Gloriana* (1953), Tippett's *The Midsummer Marriage* (1955) and *King Priam* (in Coventry, 1962), as well as various new productions and revivals. His South American début was at the Teatro Colón, Buenos Aires, in 1966, and his American opera début was with the Chicago Lyric Opera in 1969 (*Il barbiere di Siviglia*). In 1971 he made his first appearance at the Metropolitan with *Così fan tutte*. Besides holding various orchestral appointments in Britain, he became widely active in opera as principal conductor at Cologne from 1978, music director at the Théâtre de la Monnaie, Brussels, from 1981, and from 1986 at San Francisco,

where he made his final public appearance in a new production of *Idomeneo* (an opera with which he had been closely associated since his Glyndebourne days). Often praised in Mozart performances, he was also a sympathetic conductor of Bellini, Rossini and Donizetti. His innate musicianship was always admired, but he was sometimes criticized for limp or less than purposeful direction. His recordings include *Idomeneo* (1956); *Lucia di Lammermoor* (1961) and *La traviata* (1962), both with Sutherland; *L'incoronazione di Poppea* (1964); *L'elisir d'amore* (1977); and *Hänsel und Gretel* (1978). He was made CBE in 1962 and knighted in 1983.   NOËL GOODWIN

Procházka, F(rantišek) S(erafinský) (*b* Náměstí na Hané, 15 Jan 1861; *d* Prague, 28 Jan 1939). Czech poet and librettist. He worked as a teacher, then as a librarian and was for many years editor of the magazine *Zvon*. In 1915 Janáček approached him for help with the troublesome libretto of *Výlet pana Broučka do měsíce* ('The Excursion of Mr Brouček to the Moon') and found him so obliging that in 1917 he asked him to write the libretto of its sequel, *Výlet pana Broučka do XV. století* ('The Excursion of Mr Brouček to the Fifteenth Century'), the last commissioned libretto that Janáček set (1917). Procházka also supplied a few lines for Janáček's revision of *Šárka* in 1919. Janáček set several poems by Procházka, mostly for female voices.

*

ČSHS [lists texts used for other musical settings]
A. Rektorys, ed.: *Korespondence Leoše Janáčka s F. S. Procházkou* (Prague, 1949)
R. Šťastný: *Čeští spisovatelé deseti století* [Czech Writers of Ten Centuries] (Prague, 1974) [incl. further bibliography]
J. Tyrrell: *Janáček's Operas: a Documentary Account* (London, 1992)   JOHN TYRRELL

Prodaná nevěsta. Opera by Bedřich Smetana; *see BARTERED BRIDE, THE*.

Prodigal Son, The. Third parable for church performance by BENJAMIN BRITTEN to a libretto by WILLIAM PLOMER; Orford Church, Suffolk, 10 June 1968.

Britten's third church parable takes the familiar New Testament story as its subject. As in *CURLEW RIVER* and *The Burning Fiery Furnace*, singers and players are dressed as monks, acolytes and lay brothers, and perform without a conductor. The main difference is that, after the processional hymn, 'Jam lucis orto sidere', the Abbot (tenor) appears already costumed for his dramatic role as the Tempter, gleefully describing how he will destroy the happiness of a worthy family. After the instrumental interlude in which the other characters are robed and masked, the Father (baritone) expresses the family's pious sense of purpose, rooted in hard work: 'Sin is for idle hands'. In the Father's music a warm major triad (B♭) stands out in music that generally avoids this simple sonority. The Elder Son (bass) willingly goes to work in the fields, but the Younger Son (tenor) holds back, and the Tempter appears, urging him to 'act out your desires'. The Father reluctantly agrees to give the Younger Son his inheritance, despite the recriminations of his elder brother, and to an ensemble of farewell the Younger Son sets out, the Tempter in attendance. As soon as they reach the city they are beset by parasites and beggars. The Younger Son drinks and gambles, and the pieces of his outer robe are progressively removed to symbolize his descent into

'The Prodigal Son'
(Britten): scene from the
original production at
Orford Church, Suffolk,
10 June 1968; Robert
Tear is the Younger Son,
Peter Pears the Tempter

destitution. After the extended ensembles of these scenes there is a return to simpler textures as, in a brief yet eloquent duet with the solo viola, the Younger Son admits his sin and resolves to return home. There he is welcomed with joy, in a dance-like psalm-setting – and, after his words of reproach, the Elder Son is reconciled to his father and younger brother. In the final stages the Abbot discards the guise of Tempter to point the moral, and the work ends with the processional hymn, as the company leaves the acting area.   ARNOLD WHITTALL

Production (Fr. *mise en scène*; Ger. *Regie*; It. *messa in scena*). The presenting of an opera on the stage; the manner of presenting it.

1. Italian opera in the first 100 years. 2. French and English opera before Gluck. 3. *Opera seria*. 4. Enlightenment tendencies. 5. Romantic and Grand Opera. 6. 1876 to World War II. 7. Since World War II. 8. Production planning.

1. ITALIAN OPERA IN THE FIRST 100 YEARS. Operas are theatre works: their texts, verbal and musical, are meant to be staged. Hence there is such an activity as operatic staging, which perhaps has a set of general principles and certainly has a history. What that history is, however, is in some respects difficult to uncover. The aspect of staging concerned with decor has admittedly had quite a high and traceable profile (*see* STAGE DESIGN and COSTUME); but the aspect concerned with actual production – with theatrical interpretation and preparation, with the deployment on stage and the acting techniques of solo singers and chorus, and with the organization and supervision of all this – has rarely drawn much attention to itself, at least not until the coming of 'director's opera' in the later 20th century. A consequence has been the assumption that, before the advent of the modern director (or producer), opera was not 'properly' produced at all; which is untrue. Rather,

production styles have changed along with operatic styles, and a director of the late 20th-century type has not always been considered a *sine qua non* of the process. Indeed, responsibility for the production of opera has been taken by remarkably different people at different times: for instance, by one person per opera or by more than one; by individuals with other jobs to do in the operatic troupe or by individuals without; by dictators or by democrats; by charismatic visionaries or by humble journeyman-enablers.

In the beginnings of the form, the *desideratum* was a knowledgeable enabler. The courtly Italian opera of the 1590s to 1640s saw itself as a multi-media entertainment. Music was not everything; it had to be unified pleasurably with plot, language, musicianship, gesture, dance and decor; and if the show that resulted was to move the audience's passions as it should, each of these things needed to be excellent in its kind. Success could be achieved only by careful preparation, which might well be lengthy (as for instance with Monteverdi's *Arianna*, 1608), though it could on occasion (e.g. Vitali's *Aretusa*, 1620) be very brief. For such a complex enterprise to be properly harmonious and successful called arguably for the universal genius of a Gian Lorenzo Bernini, who is said to have supplied the words, music, scenery, stage machinery and even theatre design for one opera, as well as being a skilled actor who could rehearse his own comedies by demonstrating all the roles to his casts. Failing that, an early opera in rehearsal required either someone on the spot who would organize and integrate the talents of the various artists involved or someone who had provided clear written precepts in advance as to how it was all to be done.

There were venerable precedents for such organizers and preceptors: in the revered theatre of the ancient Greeks; in the sung Latin liturgical dramas of the early

Middle Ages; and in later vernacular religious plays, their performance often rigorously controlled by *maîtres de jeu* or *conducteurs de secrets*. Among more recent forebears were the Mantuan stage manager and lighting expert Leone de' Sommi, who wrote dialogues on his craft in the 1560s; the dancing-master and violinist Balthasar de Beaujoyeulx, who conceived a *Balet comique* at the behest of Queen Louise of Lorraine, contracted out its versification, music and decor, and then supervised the staging at Paris in 1581, also writing the official record of the event; and Angelo Ingegneri, who because of his 'aptitude at arranging and directing tragical matters' was put in charge of the production of *Edipo re* with Andrea Gabrieli's music which opened the Teatro Olimpico at Vicenza in 1585, and who in 1598 published an essay *Del modo di rappresentare le favole sceniche*, taking *Edipo* as its chief example.

Early operatic production developed from all this. For instance, Cavalieri, who was intimately involved with the Florentine *intermedi* of 1589, almost certainly saw to the staging of his own quasi-operatic *Rappresentatione di Anima, et di Corpo* (1600), as well as passing on instructions for 'those who want to stage this work or others like it' through Alessandro Guidotti's preface to the score. Marco da Gagliano's detailed but undictatorial suggestions for subsequent stagings of his *Dafne* (1608), included in its preface, are similarly steeped in this tradition, as are the various sections on operatic production in an anonymous manuscript treatise *Il corago*, dating from about 1630. (The treatise defines a *corago* as someone charged with coordinating, advising, teaching and animating the artists necessary for the successful staging of a dramatic work: something of a blend of the modern impresario, director and stage manager.)

If the organization of early operatic production followed a tradition, so in all likelihood did opera's earliest staging techniques. To exemplify from Monteverdi's *Orfeo* (1607), precedents for the visual and histrionic aspects of the piece are to be found in various later 16th-century Italian entertainments: the courtly ceremonial and choric movement of its Act 4 underworld scene could be traced back to the Vicenza *Edipo re*; its rustic costumes and dances to Renaissance humanist pastoral dramas like the several staged at Florence in the 1590s; its movable scenery, infernal costumes, practicable boat for Charon and descending cloud for Apollo to the 1589 *intermedi*; its lighting effects (if it had any) to the work of Leone de' Sommi at Mantua; and its style of acting in dramatic monody to a tradition of performance to be seen, for instance, in the musical interludes of Gabriele Bombasi's spoken tragedy *Alidoro* (1568), where one performer came to the front of the stage and sang in a persuasive manner closer to speech than to song, 'altering the expression in her face and eyes, and her gestures and movements, to accord with the changes in the meaning of the words she sang'.

Just how detailed and sensitive early operatic acting could be may be gathered from Gagliano's suggestions for the staging of the prologue to *Dafne*: the singer's movements unfussy but pointful, relating clearly but not mechanically to the music. Vitali's tribute to the histrionic skills of the singers in his *Aretusa* – their faces expressive of sincere passion, their vivid, graceful and natural gestures embodying the meaning of the libretto – underlines the fact that true acting (as the late Renaissance understood it) was required from opera singers, not mere standing and chirruping: acting moreover that could range in its mode from the hero's tragic soliloquizing in the last act of *Orfeo* to the antics of such *commedia dell'arte* clowns as Zanni and Coviello in the Roman *Chi soffre speri* (revised version, 1639). Ingegneri and De' Sommi had both stressed the importance of expressive movement and eloquent gesture in spoken drama, and the author of *Il corago* maintains that this applies equally to performers in opera, who should regard any specific operatic skills as additions to such things, not substitutes or alternatives. The specifics of opera in his view include the two rules (both breakable if need be) of making an unhurried entrance to downstage centre before first singing, and of subsequently moving about the stage during instrumental ritornellos and continuo flourishes, not while

1. Precursors of operatic staging I. Sophocles' 'Oedipus tyrannus' (choruses set by Andrea Gabrieli), as staged by Angelo Ingegneri for the inauguration of Palladio's Teatro Olimpico, Vicenza, in 1585; fresco in the ante-odeon of the Teatro Olimpico

2. Precursors of operatic staging II. 'Apollo slays the Python' (words by Rinuccini, music by Marenzio, stage design by Buontalenti), third of the all-sung mythological intermedi staged under Emilio de' Cavalieri's supervision as adjuncts to the performance of Bargagli's comedy 'La pellegrina' at the wedding of Grand Duke Ferdinando I and Christine of Lorraine in Florence, 1589; engraving by Agostino Carracci

one is singing. He adds recommendations to keep gesture as broad and slow as the music requires, to position oneself on the stage naturally rather than forever gravitating towards the centre, and to avoid looking so directly at one's interlocutor that one's face cannot be seen by the audience. He sees more operatic potential in good actors with passable voices than in expert singers with little acting talent; but he allows a role for the latter as supernatural beings, since as such they will have had most of their stage movement done for them by the machinist who devises the descending clouds, airy chariots and mechanical monsters they ride on.

Supporting the principals were the *comparse* (silent supernumeraries), the chorus, and the scenes and machines. *Comparse* are much in evidence in the accounts of the proto-operatic *Edipo re* of 1585 (when there were over 60 of them), while in *Il corago* they are sometimes vividly engaged in battle scenes taught them by a fencing-master and sometimes graciously granted ample stage space by principals playing royalty in ceremonial scenes. Cavalieri, Gagliano and the author of *Il corago* also follow on from *Edipo* in their treatment of the chorus: its size ranging from four to 24, its acting respectful and responsive to the principals, its movements often carefully synchronized and forming geometrical patterns but executed with a graceful

3. Early operatic staging I. Marco da Gagliano's 'La regina Sant'Orsola' (Uffizi, Florence, 1624), Act 2: the battle between the Romans and Huns at Cologne, as directed by the dancing master Agniolo Ricci; engraving by Alfonso Parigi after the design by Giulio Parigi

4. *Early operatic staging II. Stefano Landi's 'Sant'Alessio' (Palazzo Barberini, Rome, c1632), Act 1: Alexis's wife is placed down centre, flanked by his mother and nurse, and backed by a symmetrical arrangement of supernumeraries (the 'comparse'): design variously ascribed to P. da Cortona, F. Buonamici and G. L. Bernini; engraving by F. Collignon*

naturalness avoiding any suggestion of a regimented *corps de ballet*. As for the stage machines and perspective scenes, care was needed to relate these properly to the action. With scenery, opera singers must have tried to follow De' Sommi's advice not to linger near the illusionistic perspectives, as that destroyed their verisimilitude; while with machines Cavalieri insists that they should be moved only in conjunction with music of an appropriate tempo, and *Il corago* stresses that they should move very slowly when the supernatural beings aboard them are singing.

The expansion of Italian operatic activity in the later 1630s to include the public and commercial had its shop window in Venice, where a paying citizen found himself for the first time able to see production methods long established behind private courtly doors. Accounts of the Venetian *Andromeda* (1637) and *Bellerofonte* (1642), for instance, celebrate their spectacular scenic *changements à vue* and machine apotheoses, glittering costumes and stylish acting, their travesty impersonations of goddesses and nymphs by castratos alongside the acting of female roles by women, their crowds of well-dressed, well-drilled *comparse*, their frighteningly realistic monsters and sophisticated dance interludes. For the next 40 years commercial and courtly opera, from Naples to Vienna and beyond, developed a wide spectrum of scale and finesse in performance: from the productions by small companies who toured the Italian cities much in the manner of itinerant *commedia dell'arte* troupes to grandiose and prestigious events like Melani's *Ercole in Tebe* at Florence in 1661 (where 40 pages of the souvenir wordbook are taken up with a breathless account of its many splendours, among them a well-conducted battle between two 30-strong armies of *comparse*, all named; *see* FLORENCE, fig.3) or Cesti's *Il pomo d'oro* at Vienna in 1668 (where the 24 souvenir engravings of L. O. Burnacini's sets during performance illustrate the culmination of the 17th-century tendency to impose a strong axial symmetry on performers as well as scenery; *see* POMO D'ORO, IL and STAGE DESIGN, fig.4). Yet a unified approach to acting in opera – and one the author of *Il corago* would have approved – probably continued in favour until at least the 1670s.

However, 'the bizarre tastes of the city and the extravagant temperaments of the singers' about which the librettist Aurelio Aureli complained in 1673 had begun by then to add to the length, complexity and potential for vocal display of the arias, and consequently to threaten the homogeneity of the acting style and reduce the librettist's firm hold over the composition. By 1699, the Sicilian dramatist Andrea Perrucci was pointing out in his *Dell'arte rappresentativa* that librettists had only a minor share in operatic glory, the greater part going to the machinists, dancers and singers of arias. But he goes on to stress that, apart from voice production and note learning, an opera singer's craft is just the same as that of a speaking actor. Perrucci is as insistent as earlier preceptors on the expressive use of head, eyes, arms and body (deriving much of what he says from the teachings of classical rhetoric), and on a clear frontal presentation of character as the performer advances from the wings. In discussing his particular phobia of collisions in the wings between actors making entrances and those making exits, he suggests that one of his two preferred ways of avoiding these – entrances from behind an upstage flat, exits as close as possible to the proscenium arch – is of special value to the opera singer, who can thus leave from the front of the stage just after the last words of an exit aria. His other idea for avoiding collisions is that someone should number the entrance spaces between flats and provide each performer with an accident-proof personal sequence of numbers. (It is a system which appears earlier in a surviving manuscript of Rospigliosi's libretto for *Dal male il bene*, 1654, along with very detailed notes for scene changes, props and sound-effects.)

Librettists like Rospigliosi were certainly involved with staging, and a function somewhat like the modern director's might well be included *ex officio* in the librettist's. Printed librettos of the late 17th century could be full enough of directorial points to serve as a blueprint for performance: Matteo Noris's text for Legrenzi's *Totila* (1677), for example, averages three to four directions per page on matters of movements, asides, emotional states, props and machines. And that (in the presence of the poet or not) may well have been all the

5. French Baroque opera at the court of Louis XIV. Tapestry (probably from the Gobelins workshop) apparently depicting the 'Divertissement du sommeil' (the scene of good and evil dreams in the Cave of Sleep) during Act 3 of Lully's 'Atys' (1676), first performed before the king under Lully's direction at St Germain-en-Laye, with choreography by Beauchamps and designs by Berain

general direction the cast required. After all, by now they needed little basic instruction in the sort of parts they were called on to perform; machinists could connive directly with the singers who used their machines; and dancing- or fencing-masters could take charge of any complicated ceremonies, battles and the like.

2. FRENCH AND ENGLISH OPERA BEFORE GLUCK. By contrast, the presence of a director at his most absolutist is strongly felt in French opera in the 1670s and 80s, working to the greater glory of the absolutist Louis XIV. Lully directed his operas both musically and dramatically. By the time he acquired control of the Académie in 1672, there had for several years been a golden age of tragic and comic playwriting and acting in Parisian spoken theatre; and he was clearly determined that opera should not suffer in comparison. To this end he seems to have pushed one stage further the techniques of rehearsal by firm instruction and practical demonstration which his former colleague Molière depicts himself using in his *Impromptu de Versailles* (1663). According to Le Cerf de la Viéville, Lully would instruct his casts as to their entrances, moves and proper deportment, sometimes showing a performer every gesture of his role and demonstrating in person the pantomimic parts of his inset ballets. As for the style of acting at the Palais Royal, it is likely that Lully urged his casts to study the grave momentousness of the tragedians in Racine at the Hôtel de Bourgogne, since he is said to have modelled his recitatives on the declamatory accents of one of them, La Champmeslé.

The subtle construction of Lully's operas arguably required a firmer and heavier single hand in the staging than would have been used for operatic production in Italy at the time. That structures almost as complex could be staged without such extreme centralization, however, is demonstrated by the part-spoken 'semi-operas' or 'dramatick operas' of the English Restora-

tion, especially the collaborative *Tempest* of 1674 and the four produced between 1690 and 1695 with music by Purcell. Three of these latter were mounted at the Dorset Garden Theatre in London by a company headed by the actor Thomas Betterton, with Purcell in charge of music, Josias Priest as choreographer and Betterton himself (who had seen Lully's theatrical work in Paris) as animator and presumably general coordinator. The company consisted of actors, of whom most had some singing ability, and their fairly friendly rivals the tribe of Restoration stage singers and dancers, accustomed to taking small supernumerary parts in spoken comedies and tragedies as well as doing inset turns of their own. English theatre companies were kept on a fairly loose rein by their managers in rehearsal, though they were prepared to take advice from authors when this was available and sometimes bowed to an authority figure set over them. For instance, Betterton himself was once paid 50 guineas by the managers of the company to look after rehearsals 'in the nature of a monitor in a school' and a further £50 'for his care and trouble to get up *The Indian Queen*', Purcell's last semi-opera. But an awful warning against too dictatorial a production method was on hand in the Duke of Buckingham's comedy *The Rehearsal* (1671), where all the attempts of the protagonist Mr Bayes to dominate the staging of his own mixed-media extravaganza only serve to make a bad thing worse.

However, Lully's centralization of opera did have a significant result. It established a major, long-lasting Parisian tradition of the mounting of a fixed canon of pieces, something barely known in Italy or England. By securing a copyright, insisting on uncut performances, having his scores printed, staging revivals and training a generation of performers, Lully made his work a national institution and monument. His most distinguished leading lady, Marthe le Rochois (who created several Lully heroines as well as appearing in the premières of works by Charpentier and Campra) can stand as the *fin du grand siècle* opera singer *par excellence*. Though not especially prepossessing in her appearance offstage apart from her large and fiery eyes, she was able to rivet spectators in performance as much by her sheer presence, physical control and *jeu muet* as by her voice. The rich emotional variety she brought to her roles was especially apparent in Lully's *Armide*, where she held audiences breathless in her scene in Act 2 with the sleeping Renaud. (One English theatre-goer thought her 'not inferior to Mrs Barry herself', Elizabeth Barry being one of the greatest actresses of Restoration spoken drama, admired by Betterton for her way of 'living' a part on stage.)

Once retired from the stage, Le Rochois trained effective leading ladies for the future. In the early 18th century there was clearly a need for such training, since even Le Cerf, the loudest champion of France's operatic superiority, was forced to admit that the acting of French singers had reached a low ebb for want of a few sharp rebukes from the late great disciplinarian, Lully. And the major new musical tendency of 18th-century opera did not help: the steadily increasing emphasis being placed by composers, singers and audiences on sheer vocal virtuosity as a prime means of operatic communication. In the French tradition this factor is apparent in the remark attributed to Rameau to the effect that, whereas Lully's operas had needed actors, his own needed singers: even if that permitted the rise to eminence of performers like Jélyotte, the golden-voiced principal tenor of the Opéra in Rameau's time – 'chanteur unique, mais il n'a ni figure ni action' (as the librettist Charles Collé put it).

However, Le Rochois' spirit did live on; and so did much of the Parisian tradition of operatic staging. This set great store by the *merveilleux*, which led to greater emphasis on the vertical axis of the stage – infernal trapdoors, celestial descents and the like – than was called for in the more historical (or pseudo-historical) Italian opera of the age. True to that part of its origins which lay in the *ballet de cour*, the tradition also insisted on the incorporation into the action of frequent dance sequences: hence the presence of a *corps de ballet*, which not only danced the formal and symmetrical *fêtes* for an opera's principal characters but was also the resource for any troupes of warriors, priests, genii and the like that might be required. In these latter roles the dancers were the counterparts of the non-dancing Italian *comparse*; the choreographed battles, ceremonies and visions which resulted at the Opéra seemed to francophiles to be more elegant and eloquent than their mimed equivalents in *opera seria*, while to italophiles they were merely more effete and unnatural.

The other vital distinguishing feature of Parisian opera was its commitment to a major role for a sizable chorus. The entry of the chorus in 18th-century *tragédie en musique* at the Palais Royal continued to be a spectacular moment: its richly dressed members advancing in two ranks, one from each side of the stage, to take up their positions in an elegant U-formation recalling the choric half-moons of the earliest Florentine and Mantuan operas. By framing the activity of principals, dance troupes and theatrical machines in this way, the chorus helped to produce a very strong axial symmetry, which may partly explain the rarity on the French stage (outside the work of Servandoni) of the relatively asymmetric *scena per angolo* so popular in operatic stagings elsewhere in Europe.

The rich counterpoint of various arts characteristic of French operatic performance appealed to sophisticated Parisian tastes; and if a show was to work well, it was doubtless helpful for each artist involved to have some knowledge of the other arts on display. An aspiring opera composer, said Rameau, needed to study also the stage, actors, movement and dance; and there are stories of specialists assisting in spheres outside their own. But in the main, the preparation, rehearsal and performance of *tragédie en musique* and *opéra-ballet* in the first half of the 18th century seem to have involved not so much an organic, chemical compounding of the arts as a benign convergence of them. In the performance itself, for instance, principals sat graciously out of harm's way during the inset *fêtes*; the dancers often wore masks, which set them apart from all other performers; and, once settled into their U-formation, the chorus rarely moved, even when the words they were singing might be thought to demand some physical agitation (if only the unfolding of their much-folded arms).

By the middle of the century, discontented spirits like Noverre and some of the Encyclopedists were arguing that there should be much more creative consultation between librettist, composer, choreographer, designer and machinist at the planning stage of an opera and a greater integration of performing arts during the show itself. That such discontent had not been expressed earlier and that the convergence of the arts had been as benign as it had was largely due to the presence at the Opéra of a potent controlling phantom, that of Lully. Lully in a sense directed the staging of Campra's and Rameau's works from beyond the grave. It was he who ensured that his works were both classics and yardsticks, that there was a strong (though not inflexible) tradition of staging them, and that the company structure necessary for so doing was at the disposal of subsequent makers of operas, always provided that their works – however much more virtuoso musically, cosmopolitan scenically or *galant* in mood than Lully's – fitted the Lullian mould in their stagecraft.

The company structure itself was rationalized by the royal ordinances of 1713 and 1714. Significantly, these edicts (which held in large measure for most of the century) required that the company keep a rehearsed Lully opera in reserve in case of need; and it is significant too that, though they deal with several matters relevant to operatic production (the size of the company, salary gradations, the need for a performer to accept the roles and costumes he is assigned, the teaching of the vocal music and dances, the doubling of small solo parts with chorus work), they say nothing about inter-departmental liaison in the opera house. Making sure that there was at least a bare sufficiency of liaison was presumably the responsibility of 'le syndic chargé de la régie du théâtre', one of the two active syndics the edicts created (the other being concerned with stores and finances).

The syndic *de la régie* in the ordinance of 1714, his every move needing the approval of the inspectorgeneral to the company (a royal appointment), dealt with artistic planning and with the casting (in consultation with the composer, if alive), and oversaw all rehearsals and performances, during which the theatre staff, stage crew and performers were answerable only to him. It is a moot point how far his role in the staging of an opera, and the role of the 'directeurs' who followed him, was a creative and how far a diplomaticadministrative one; but clearly the drawing of the

6. Parisian opera in the 18th century. The confrontation of Armide and Renaud in the enchantress's palace garden in Act 5 of Lully's 'Armide' (1686), as revived six decades later by the Académie Royale de Musique (the 'Opéra') at the Palais Royal in 1747: watercolour by Gabriel de Saint-Aubin

strands together by such figures made for many memorable performances at the Palais Royal, as audiences sometimes acknowledged. ('One cannot praise enough the troubles *MM. les Directeurs* have taken to make the show as brilliant and satisfying as it could be', wrote the *Mercure de France* of the first revival, in 1744, of Rameau's *Dardanus*, enthusing over the contribution of words, music, casting, decor, costumes, choreography and execution.) Other performances, doubtless, were memorable for individual triumphs. Even Rousseau, whose caricature of an Opéra performance in *La nouvelle Héloïse* (1761; ii, 23) is the most vividly cruel thing written about that institution in the 18th century, was impressed enough by Chassé's acting there – he created the roles of Theseus in *Hippolyte et Aricie*, Huascar in *Les Indes galantes* and Pollux in *Castor et Pollux* – to cite him in the *Encyclopédie* as everything a good operatic performer ought to be: never dropping his character to become merely a singer; forever interesting, even in silence; conspiring by steps, looks and gestures to make his audience feel that the music rising from the orchestra pit was rising from his soul.

3. OPERA SERIA. In the Italian tradition, too, increasing emphasis was being placed on sheer vocal expertise as *opera seria* began to establish itself: so much so that Tosi declared in his *Observations on the Florid Song* (1742; Italian original 1723) that, though the ideal for a performer in opera is a double perfection of singing and acting, in the real world of conflicting demands and divided interests it is the perfecting of one's voice that should have the prior claim. Thence sprang a new tribe of vocal virtuosos who were much esteemed in the opera

house although their histrionic skills were rudimentary: singers like the castrato Farinelli, who was for 15 years the toast of operatic Europe for all that his acting (according to J. J. Quantz among others) was perfunctory. Yet the perfect opera singer was generally deemed to be one who (in the words of the Intendant of the royal opera at Lisbon in the 1760s) possessed 'buona voce e grande estensione di corde, buona figura e buona azione'.

With such singers on hand, the staging of *opera seria* was a relatively simple matter. The strong segmentation of the form did not require the firm hand or creative vision of the equivalent of a modern director to make it work in the theatre. Such a figure from the future would have found little to do at an *opera seria* rehearsal. After all, there was likely to be a *maître de danse*, and sometimes an associated fencing-master, seeing to any ceremonies, ballets and battles, a machinist advising performers about such theatrical *coups* as they might be involved in (descents of airy chariots, magical transformations, collapsing of city walls and the like), and a designer independently ringing the changes on a limited range of scenic motifs. What singer needed more? So it is not surprising that, though the most detailed libretto-cum-programme-books of Italian operatic performances at court in the 18th century give the names of cast, composer, librettist, choreographer, fencing-master, costumier, set designer and machinist, they mention no director figure.

It does not follow from this that the stage rehearsal of an *opera seria* by its principals was necessarily anarchic or primitive. For one thing, there were the stage directions in the libretto to be observed: not only for entrances and exits but quite often for characters' moods and stage business as well. For another, performers could apply to their recitatives the age's basic courtly stage deportment. Again, since the staple of *opera seria* was a spectrum of general emotions expressed one after another in a series of arias, an experienced performer coming to a new opera would almost certainly have given formal histrionic expression to all its emotions before – sometimes in exactly the same words (since multiple settings of successful librettos were common), sometimes even, if the new piece were a pasticcio, in the same music.

All these things helped any performer of *opera seria* with a basic theatrical gift to give a strong stage performance after limited rehearsal time. Indeed, a group of competent principals might in a few days achieve a fluent, decorous, pointed and telling staging of an opera (in all but any spectacular or balletic parts) with no external help, or with no more than was necessary in establishing which wings should be used for which entrances and exits, in assigning retinues of *comparse* and pages, and in resolving any disputed points of princely stage etiquette or clashes of artistic temperament. The person responsible for providing such help in practice seems to have been whoever in the company was most serviceable in a given situation: the manager sometimes, or the *maestro di cappella* (who might anyway be the opera's composer). But most often it was the theatre's resident poet, in which case he might take on a rather more consequential role himself at rehearsals.

Maccario in Goldoni's comedy *L'impresario delle Smirne* (1761) typifies this breed of poet. Armed with the works of Metastasio and Zeno, some old plays and a rhyming dictionary, he practises his specialities of writing new librettos, adapting old ones for new settings, fitting new words to old music, instructing the singers in acting, directing the scenes, attending the ladies in their boxes, looking after the *comparse* and blowing the whistle for the scene changes. In his *Mémoires* (1787), Goldoni recalled that his own duties as poet to a Venetian opera house in the 1730s included responsibility 'for directing and coaching the performers'; and Marcello's *Il teatro alla moda* (c1720) implies that a librettist worth his salt should explain his dramatic conception and intentions to the performers in rehearsal, advise them on costumes, gestures and the proper sides of the stage for their entrances and exits, and insist on a clear enunciation of his text.

Marcello's implied ideal, Goldoni's Maccario and Goldoni himself have much in common with the master librettist, Metastasio. Though it was not humanly possible for him to rehearse all the settings of his librettos in person, his letters from Vienna show him to have been a careful director. They include his recollections of 'blocking' an especially touching scene of his *Demetrio* in such a way as to make even bears weep (12 January 1732); references to significant scenic details in the staging of his *Issipile* which he did not choose to incorporate into the printed libretto (19 January 1732); simple but comprehensive diagrams of how he disposed the characters in each scene of his own production of *Demofoonte* (10 February 1748); a recommendation that the detailed analysis of the principal character of *Attilio Regolo* he sent Hasse at Dresden should be passed on to Hasse's leading singer (20 October 1749); and a covering note to go with a sheet of stage business for *Alessandro nell'Indie* suggesting that this might perhaps be of use in Farinelli's Madrid production (4

February 1754). Significantly, these letters are not addressed to theatre poets – they did not have a monopoly of stage supervision – but to composers, singers managing companies and Intendants. They reveal that what Metastasio pictured at his desk while writing a libretto or devised in the theatre while rehearsing a setting of it was just one possible way of doing things. They also reveal that, however formalized the stage action may have been in *opera seria*, the genre's leading librettist was convinced that telling theatricality in the communication of feeling was the essence of staging, not formula or protocol (21 February 1748).

Also evident in his letters (for example 8 January 1734) is Metastasio's nostalgia for the rough and tumble of Italian operatic life, however serious the opera in hand. He caught this aspect of the operatic scene vividly in his libretto for the intermezzo *L'impresario delle Canarie* (1724), a text which helped establish the sub-genre of comic librettos on life backstage, with their

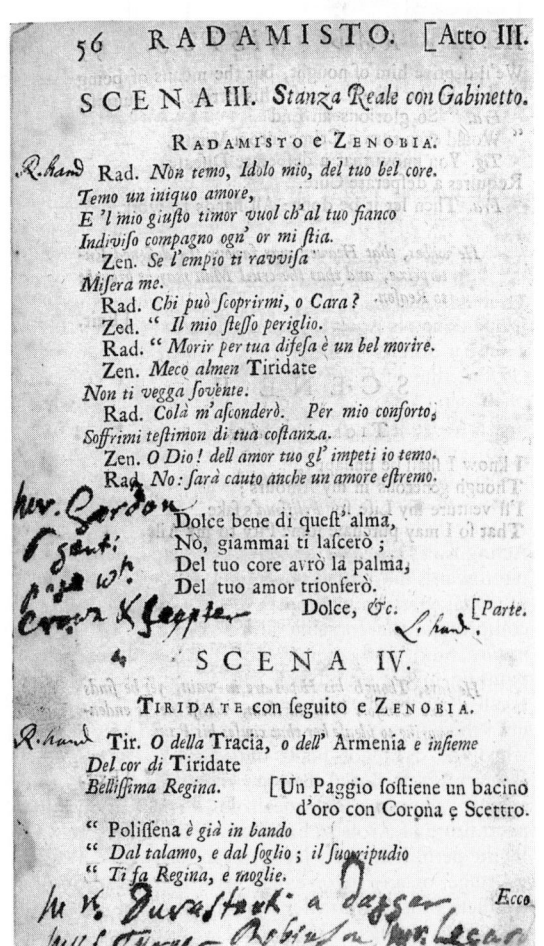

7. The opera seria libretto as prompt-book. Page from a copy of the libretto for Handel's 'Radamisto', partly marked up (probably in draft) as a prompt copy for the original production in London, 27 April 1720. One annotator indicates the sides of the stage for entrances and exits; another gives warnings for the entries of specific singers, noting the props they will need and the number of supernumeraries who will attend them (thus 'Tiridate con seguito' in the printed text has the marginal note 'Mr. Gordon 6 gent:').

8. Instruction in Baroque acting. Two figures from the 'Dissertatio de actione scenica' (1727) by the Bavarian Jesuit drama teacher or 'choragus' Franz Lang. The left-hand figure shows the proper placing of fingers, arms and legs (though Lang rebukes it for presenting its back to the audience). The right-hand figure, falling far short of theatrical actuality (according to Lang), nonetheless gives an idea of a properly managed stage entrance, with body and face immediately turned to the front so that in them the spectator can read the character's state of mind.

audition- and rehearsal-sequences in which leading ladies pointedly ignore the suggestions of librettists, grab inkwells as substitute poison phials in suicide scenes, and arrange composer, poet and various pieces of furniture into a mock-up family tableau to enhance the pathos of a grieving-parent aria.

'Show dignity, and don't move till I've finished', the prima donna instructs her conscripted antagonist before a similar aria in Casti's *Prima la musica, poi le parole* (1786); thus bringing together two grand principles of *opera seria* acting. In many respects such acting was no different from acting in spoken tragedy, and a mid-18th-century singer could find several primers on that subject in print. They preach an acting technique for serious drama of composed stance, deliberate gravity, rhetorically eloquent gesture and expressive face-play. Acting is described as something directed unswervingly out towards the audience, and it is stressed that intensity of characterization must never be allowed to compromise the comeliness and seemliness of *la belle nature*. Study and emulation of classic sculpture and of painting in the grand style are recommended, which recalls Richard Steele's praise of Nicolini's operatic acting ('there is scarce a beautiful posture in an old statue which he does not plant himself in', *The Tatler*, 3 January 1710). But at the same time the actor is warned against allowing this idealized formal and frontal portraiture of a role to breed any lack of concentration by the performers, any lapse in rapport with colleagues on stage, or any involvement with the spectators that conflicts with character portrayal. The tendency for such warnings to be ignored was satirized by Marcello in the 1720s and several decades later by Algarotti, Arteaga and Grétry in their digs at performers taking the opportunity of someone else's aria to bow to the boxes, smile at the orchestra, fiddle distractingly with a watch-chain or leave the stage entirely to suck an orange.

Two aspects of *opera seria* might seem at first to fall outside the sphere of spoken tragic performance: the presence of castratos and the cult of the virtuoso da capo exit aria. But the gap was not a wide one. There is little indication that, apart from a glandular tendency to ponderousness on stage, the castratos as a breed were worse (or better) as actors than other sorts of singer, and Italian audiences cheerfully accepted the convention of castrato as virile warrior or great lover for the various artistic rewards it could bring, much as French audiences for the same reason accepted ancient heroes in spoken tragedy uttering their tirades in rhymed alexandrines. As for performance of the ubiquitous da capo arias, this seems to have been not unlike the classical 18th-century actor's spoken delivery of a tirade or soliloquy. Given the slow pace and composed stances of contemporary serious plays, a fairly static yet sculpted delivery of an aria, visibly embodying one strong emotion (with sometimes another for the central section), would have been wholly acceptable. Two of the elements that distinguish the da capo aria from the soliloquy – the physical demands made by complex melodic writing and the recurrence of lengthy orchestral ritornellos – called for special care. The best performers cultivated a plasticity of the face and a controlled bearing of the neck and chest which disguised the efforts involved in virtuoso singing (some practising before a mirror to monitor this), while for the ritornellos they seem to have hit on a golden mean of deportment between the blockish and the fussy which enabled them, when necessary, to move several momentous steps before striking an apt new attitude for the next vocal paragraph. Their less capable colleagues were criticized throughout the century (by Marcello, Algarotti and Arteaga among others) for breast-heaving, neck-twisting and spitting in the vocal sections of their arias, and in the ritornellos either for standing rooted to the spot in inapposite calm, hand stuck in sword-belt, eyeing the musical director for the cue, or for fussing with fans, gloves and trains, holding mimed conversations with antagonists, wandering aimlessly about the stage, scrutinizing the scenery, even vanishing into the wings for a pinch of snuff.

There is no reason to assume that the spitters or

snuff-takers were in a majority, however. A considerable number of *opera seria* performers were manifestly 'born for singing and acting', as Quantz put it of Faustina. Some, indeed, as Joseph Addison said of Nicolini (*The Spectator*, 14 June 1712), were object lessons in eloquent movement and expressive face-play to the tragedians of spoken drama.

4. ENLIGHTENMENT TENDENCIES. While Nicolini wrestling with the lion in *Idaspe fedele* and Chassé throwing himself into the volcano in *Les Indes galantes* are apt vignettes of Italian and French serious opera in effective performance, their counterpart in the changing operatic world of the later 18th century is Gaetano Guadagni as Gluck's Orpheus mourning Eurydice's second death (Burney said that his 'attitudes' and 'action' earned as much applause as his singing in 'the simple and ballad-like air "Che farò"'). Indeed, Guadagni's whole career can stand as representative of the ethos of operatic staging which was one aspect of the new age of sensibility, sublime simplicity, enlightenment, fresh respect for the arts of comedy and growing concern for theatrical realism. He gained early experience as first *amoroso* in a *buffo* company: a novel way to prepare for a serious career at the time. He was formed as an actor by David Garrick, high priest of the twin cults of Shakespeare and Nature. His acting is said by Burney to have been as distinguished in operatic comedies of genteel life as in the sublimities of Gluck. He had strong views about total impersonation of roles; and Burney's tribute suggests that he reversed in a significantly neo-classic way the old exhortation to a player to imitate idealized painting and sculpture: 'his attitudes and gestures were so full of grace and propriety that they would have been excellent studies for a statuary'. It is apt that he should have created the role of the new Orpheus.

Guadagni's early involvement with *buffo* acting came at a time when the *buffo* manner was growing in its appeal to serious opera lovers. The tiny, often two-person troupes performing the farcical intermezzos set between the acts of *opera seria* and the rather larger companies giving the more extended *opere buffe* had developed a style of acting – part Molièrian, part *commedia dell'arte* – which was brisker, saltier and more immediately alluring, though probably not a great deal less governed by convention, than that seen in loftier opera. The unpretentiousness of this style and the leeway it allowed for sharp observation of contemporary life endeared it to such observers as Charles de Brosses and Arteaga, who saw its vivacity and 'air of truth' as rebukes to the traditional high-operatic stage's tendency to stiffness and frigidity. At a time when the extended operatic ensemble as a form was moving upward from *opera buffa* to the opera of myth and history – a time also when Garrick was influentially shifting the norm of serious acting in spoken theatre away from weighty declamation towards a more energetic, pantomimic mode – it is likely that some of the more seemly aspects of the *buffo* style, along with some Garrickian traits, were sharpening the immediacy of serious operatic acting and increasing its air of truth.

Garrick was a model for several of the new men of theatrical Europe in the mid-18th century: not least Noverre, to whom he was 'the Proteus of our time', his versatility among the dramatic genres and his chameleon-like ability to 'become' a remarkably wide range of characters being inspirations behind Noverre's campaign to unmask the dancers in operatic ballet and so increase their histrionic potential. But if Garrick was a Proteus, it was Gluck who tended to be seen as the modern Prometheus, bringing life to inert operatic clay. To the extent that the new opera of the mid-century associated with him was a blending of *tragédie en musique* and *opera seria*, it risked compounding the stasis of the French chorus – 'ranged motionless like so many organ pipes', one critic said – with the stasis of the fully-blown *seria* aria, of which it was coming to be felt (by Algarotti, Arteaga, Marmontel and Grétry among others) that the ever-lengthening ritornellos and *fioriture* jeopardized any chance of proper dramatic contin-

9. *Baroque acting in practice. Anonymous painting probably representing an opera seria in performance in Italy in the early or mid-18th century (note the page boy on stage holding the diva's train, and the seated gentleman in the pit holding a libretto)*

uity. Both these stases 'chilled the action'; so the slimming of aria form in the work of Gluck and his likeminded contemporaries and their composition of chorus parts which further developed Cahusac's attempts at the Opéra around 1750 'to get the chorus to act in conformity with what they sing' (*La danse ancienne et moderne*, 1754) were hailed as theatrical revitalizations. An article in the *Journal de politique et de littérature* in

10. The influential vivacity and versatility of David Garrick (1717–79): (a) Garrick (as Lord Chalkstone) with members of his Drury Lane company in his own satirical afterpiece, 'Lethe': engraving by Gabriel Smith

10. (b) 'Mr Garrick in Four of his Principal Tragic Characters'; anonymous contemporary engraving

the 1770s describes Gluck as having to deal at first with principal singers whose acting was either lifeless or grotesquely mannered, and with 'a collection of *mannequins* called a chorus'; but 'Prometheus shook his torch and the statues came to life', the principals realizing that the eloquent and expressive idiom of Gluck's music only needed to be felt to bring strong, true stage impersonation along with it, while the chorus members in his operas were 'amazed to discover that they were actors'.

Of course, it should not be supposed that Gluck alone was responsible for theatrical change at this time, or indeed that everything was darkness before him. This encomium nevertheless provides a frame in which to set such things as the poet Verazi's stagings of his own librettos in the 1760s and 1770s, noted as they were for their treating the chorus 'as actors, not statues'; his printing of those librettos with stage directions for elaborate character-revealing business even during da capo arias; the increasing trouble taken by such composers as Jommelli over the construction of *buffo* ensembles which would permit 'natural' acting throughout by everyone involved; the growing tendency for operatic stage space to be characterized by chiaroscuro in lighting, local colour in decor, and asymmetry in the deployment of supernumeraries, dancers and scenery; the praises heaped on the acting of such singers as Sophie Arnould at the Opéra for its tenderness, elevation, energy, soul, sentiment and sensibility; and the determination of Guadagni himself to identify so fully with his roles that he would refuse to acknowledge applause after an aria or to take encores.

Personal vanities, audience enthusiasms and the staying power of the traditions and conventions of *opera seria* all dictated that few singers went as far as Guadagni in this; but his ideal chimes well with a concept of opera as a form involving a conscious and carefully monitored synthesis of theatrical arts, all blending together to present a heightened virtual actuality which will enthrall, elevate and edify. The concept attracted growing support in the later 18th century, though there were differing views as to who should do the careful monitoring. Conscious integration of the arts, as opposed to the traditional *laissez faire*, was urged influentially by Algarotti and Noverre. Both insisted that the librettist (the 'poet') should, as the begetter of an opera, be its monitor, the guardian of its wholeness, and that it was for the other theatre artists to strive to embody the poet's unifying imaginative conception. Noverre further emphasized the need for the executive quintet (composer, designer, machinist, *maître de ballet* and costumier) to work closely together, and for the librettist to be on call throughout: which is much what happened in the case of Calzabigi, Gluck, the choreographer Angiolini, the scenographer G. M. Quaglio and the Intendant Count Durazzo working on *Orfeo*. It was certainly an authority structure assured of some success in court theatres where the librettist (or at least the drafter of operatic scenarios) was the local prince himself: Frederick the Great at Berlin and Potsdam, for instance, or Gustavus III at Stockholm and Drottningholm. Elsewhere, and more humbly, it might be the court's resident theatre poet who would 'stage the performances with good intelligence and good order', as it was put of Gaetano Martinelli at Lisbon in the 1770s, directing the complicated operas he had written with the absentee *maestro di cappella* Jommelli.

It was against the background of these new

11. Enlightenment staging. The obsequies at the tomb of Castor in P. J. Candeille's 'Castor et Pollux' (Paris Opéra, 1791), as conceived by the production's costume designer, Jean-Simon Berthélémy

tendencies, mingling with the persistent traditions of *opera seria* and *opera buffa*, that the operas of Haydn and Mozart were first staged. In the later 1770s and 1780s, Haydn found that a major part of his duties as Kapellmeister at Eszterháza lay in operatic work for the princely theatre. There the day-to-day running of the opera was, for much of the time, in the hands of a triumvirate – Haydn himself as musical director, adapter and resident composer; Pietro Travaglia as principal scenographer and lighting designer; Philipp Bader first, and later Nunziato Porta, as theatre manager – with Prince Nikolaus shaping artistic policy, holding the purse strings and having an important say in the casting. The prince's instructions of 1779 (analogous to Louis XIV's ordinances for the Opéra of 1713–14) require that the musical director be responsible for everything connected with singers and instrumentalists (plus the prompter) once they have been hired, while the scenographer supervises the stage crew and the manager sees to everyone else. Porta's life was a busy one of house management, drawing up costume lists, ordering printing work, approving invoices, copying parts, negotiating over librettos (to say nothing of translating, adapting and writing them) and organizing supernumeraries. One of the principal singers would sometimes arrange the stage battles and other set pieces required for these *comparse* – at Eszterháza they were largely the prince's grenadiers – but generally this was Porta's headache; and a real headache it must have been, as for instance when the first Eszterháza performance of Sarti's *Didone abbandonata* was separated from the second by two day-long additional fencing rehearsals for the 24 grenadiers who impersonated the Moorish and Trojan armies. As for the seasoned Italian principals hired by Prince Nikolaus, one must assume that they were experienced enough histrionically and were cast sufficiently to type to direct themselves in the main, though with the help of Haydn, his prompter and any librettist – Porta or other – who might be on hand.

Assumptions are again called for where the first stagings of Mozart's operas are concerned, since the surviving evidence (as often in the 18th century) is so slight. It is very likely that his librettists were involved in

rehearsals when that was physically possible. Schikaneder clearly was in the case of *Die Zauberflöte*; and Da Ponte states in his memoirs that he 'stayed in Prague for a week in order to direct the actors' before the première there of *Don Giovanni*. But it is also likely that Mozart himself was actively concerned with stage characterization at rehearsals as well as with the notes of the score. He regarded himself as 'a composer who understands the stage'; and plausible anecdotes survive to the effect that he was in favour of friendly theatrical give-and-take between creator and performer.

It is only with the early *Idomeneo* that we have many details of the preparation and rehearsal of a Mozart première. The composer's letters to his father in Salzburg during the three months leading up to the première in 1781 suggest a careful collaboration in Munich between Mozart, Count J. A. von Seeau the court Intendant for music and drama, Cannabich the conductor, Lorenzo Quaglio the scenographer and Le Grand the choreographer. Mozart agreed with Quaglio that the king's disembarkation scene in Act 1 was theatrically far-fetched and needed changing; he settled the action and grouping of the big choric scene of flood, fire and the supernatural at the end of Act 2 with Le Grand, who put their plan into practice; and he rethought the lead into the Act 3 sacrifice scene (presumably in consultation with Quaglio and Le Grand) to make it smoother and scenically more vivid. Much concern was expressed over the proper printing of Varesco's Italian libretto with, if possible, a decent German translation on opposite pages and with scenic descriptions to reflect Quaglio's final arrangement accurately. Yet all this was done without the presence in Munich of Varesco himself. The lack of a librettist on hand to advise the singers about stage action – Varesco in fact had little experience of the theatre – suggests that the principals were expected to be largely self-reliant and to use appropriate modifications of well-tried *seria* and Guadagnian techniques, for all that one of their number had, to Mozart's chagrin, never set foot on any stage before, while another acted 'like a statue' (this led to the composer's insistence that an expository scene between the two be 'shortened as drastically as possible'). However, the principals almost certainly had theatrical advice from Mozart in his role

12. *Two revivals of Mozart's 'Die Zauberflöte' in 1794, three years after the original Vienna production. (a) Goethe's Weimar court theatre, where the work was given in an adaptation by Goethe's brother-in-law, C. A. Vulpius; the director of the scenic workshop was G. M. Kraus, who painted this watercolour of the backstage preparations*

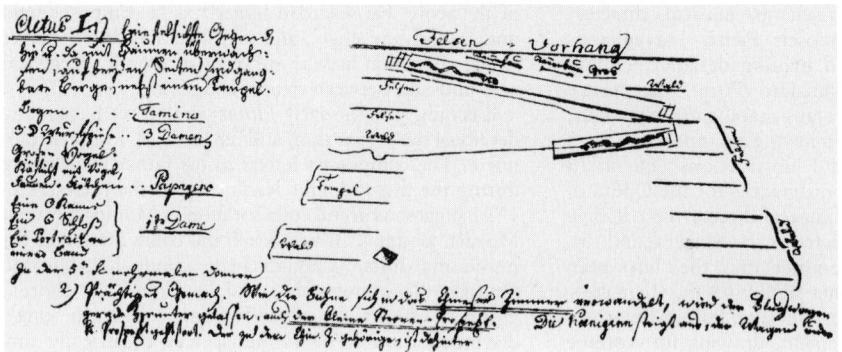

12. *(b) A. W. Iffland's National Theatre, Mannheim, where the prompter Trinkle used his ledger to record details of the staging, as here with the first scenes of Act 1*

of composer-répétiteur, with his earnest concern that recitative should be fast-moving, spirited and fiery in performance and his guiding conviction that the best criterion for librettists, composers and performers alike was theatrical effectiveness. 'Consider it carefully', he said during a discussion of the Subterranean Voice in Act 3; 'picture to yourself the theatre …'.

5. ROMANTIC AND GRAND OPERA. If Mozart had been *maestro di cappella* at Munich in 1781 and not simply a young visitor, he might have chosen to be more auto-cratic about the production of *Idomeneo*. Resident *maestri* certainly were autocratic about staging on occasion: witness Jommelli at Stuttgart in the 1750s and 60s, under the watchful eye of Duke Carl Eugen of Württemberg. According to Christian Schubart, Jommelli confidently revised librettos before setting them and then used his knowledge of singers, instrumentalists, audiences and theatre acoustics, plus the close cooperation of designers, machinists and choreographers, 'to move and uplift the coldest listener's heart and soul with one great totality'. Schubart was writing in the late 18th

century, and his Goethean concept of a Great Totality had a future to it, especially where opera in German was concerned. Indeed, Bayreuth under Richard Wagner does not seem so very far away. The road to Bayreuth was in part via other German-speaking theatres where a particularly strong-minded actor, writer or composer was in control: for instance Gotha under the influence of Konrad Ekhof (1774–78), Weimar under Goethe himself (1791–1817), and most significantly Prague and Dresden under Weber (1813–16, 1817–26).

By the time Weber got to Dresden, he had an intimate knowledge of all the practical elements which needed integrating into a performance totality. At Prague he had been not only musical director, conductor and répétiteur but also chief adviser on costumes and scenery and the overseer of stage movement, as well as an auditioner of performers who was concerned to create an integrated troupe of singer-actors rather than a nest of brilliant songbirds. So he knew what would be involved in bringing German opera in production as close as possible to his ideal of a work where 'every contribution of the related arts is moulded together in a certain way, dissolving to form a new world'. Once at Dresden, he ensured that each of his soloists was versatile enough to be at home in all the relevant operatic styles, and that his chorus members were alert to the need to be genuine actors, not mere standabouts. He employed (for a while at least) a 'literator' to enlighten individual singers about any puzzling aspects of a libretto and to help them with their characterizations. He was minded to appoint a dancing master who would in addition be movement coach to the whole company and devise effective groupings for specific scenes. Above all, he insisted on a careful sequence of music and movement rehearsals under his own supervision, a sequence significantly beginning with a *Leseprobe*: a dramatic reading-aloud of the libretto which was intended to ensure that everyone knew what his or her contribution to the great totality was. (Similar notions about ensemble and rehearsing were held by his younger contemporary, the playwright and director of spoken drama Karl Immermann. In both cases the ideas probably derived from Ekhof's concept of the *Konzertierung des Spiels* and Goethe's development of it in his theatre years at Weimar.)

However, at the centre of Weber's theatre aesthetic was the committed, role-living and hence (in Weber's view) unitalianate singer-actor. One such was his Dresden protégée Wilhelmine Schröder-Devrient, the daughter, perhaps significantly, of a distinguished actress in spoken drama and of a rather less distinguished operatic baritone. Her 'electrifying' impersonations, declared the London *Morning Post* in

13. Early 19th-century instruction in acting. Two figures from Lesson 2, 'On Entering, Exiting and Walking Upon the Stage', of 'Theoretische Lessen over de Gesticulatie en Mimiek' (1827) by the Dutch actor Johannes Jelgerhuis. Above: stage walking ('our walk on stage should be firm and bold'). Below: making entrances and exits (to perform these 'with decorum, that is, with grace and nobility, one must follow one of the continuous lines on the plan; to follow a dotted line is indecorous')

May 1832 on seeing her as Beethoven's Leonore, displayed 'master strokes of that art which seems to have left all art behind and become nature itself'. And Wagner singled out her 'intensely human art' in the same role as the factor which in 1829 pushed him into becoming a composer of music dramas. However, not all nascent 'national operas' could field a Schröder-Devrient, as Weber discovered when he came to London in 1826 to give the première of his English-language *Oberon*, where (in his librettist Planché's words) the leading soprano and tenor were, respectively, 'destitute of histrionic ability' and 'about the worst actor ever seen'. It seems likely, indeed, that for much of the time the staging of British national opera fell uncomfortably between two distinct stools of tried and trusted production: that of London's through-sung Italian opera, with its largely foreign stars and traditional *seria* and *buffa* staging-methods, and that of the native, purely spoken drama which centred on great actor-manager clans like the Kembles and the Keans.

One notable actor-manager who did stage English opera – though not of the most recent vintage and without appearing in it himself – was William Charles Macready. As the painstaking director of a prestigious company, Macready was concerned in spoken plays to embody the dramatist's 'picture' on the stage, 'complete in its parts and harmoniously arranged as to figure, scene and action': something which involved him in meticulous attention to scenic detail (of a romantic-picturesque variety) and also in extracting real performances from minor characters and supers. So it is not surprising that, when he tackled a revival of Handel's *Acis and Galatea* in 1842 (see fig.14 overleaf), the piece became an elegant Sicilian idyll confected out of Poussin and Annibale Carracci, and the members of the chorus found themselves individualized, moulded into groups and integrated into the action. (Such a role for the chorus was still quite a novelty in London. Only ten years before, a visiting German troupe had amazed the critic Henry Chorley, who was used to tolerating choruses made up of 'rueful, shabby people' placed in a 'meagre, motionless semi-circle', by confronting him with 'a company of earnest folk' showing that 'they understood the scene by the assistance their appropriate action afforded to every situation'.) However, the average English Romantic opera in performance seems to have been rather less painstakingly set up than Macready's *Acis*, if we are to trust the reminiscences of Planché and the baritone Charles Santley. In his 1830s anglicizations of French pieces, Planché still faced 'the old obstacle, the want of a singer who would act', while being 'hampered with actors who couldn't sing'; and in his years of appearing in works by Balfe, Benedict, Wallace and Macfarren around 1860, Santley claimed only to have encountered one 'capable stage manager'. (The rest, he said, 'did not deem it necessary to study the drama and prepare the situations'.)

The detailed itemization of stage action that appears in Macready's prompt-books is sometimes quite striking; but across the English Channel it is massively outdone by the quantity of movement, stage business and character revelation (to say nothing of matters of scenery, costumes and props) being recorded behind the scenes at the Parisian *grands spectacles* of the age of Meyerbeer, Auber and Eugène Scribe, for use by stage managers, prompters, répétiteurs and revival-rehearsers. Staging – almost for staging's sake – found itself in the foreground in French grand opera. Of course the

14. Individualizing the
chorus. Groupings of
Sicilian nymphs and
shepherds devised by
William Charles Macready
for his 1842 revival of
Handel's 'Acis and
Galatea' at the Theatre
Royal, Drury Lane:
sketches by John Tenniel,
from his 'Pencillings in the
Pit'

sheer acting skills of such principals as Adolphe Nourrit and (rather later) Pauline Viardot were important to an overall theatrical success; but there was so much else besides to claim the attention. So, given the visual complexity of many of these works, it is not surprising that there were some changes of administration and staffing in the companies mounting them. Thus a Comité de Mises en Scène pour l'Académie Royale de Musique was set up at the Opéra in 1827, and the fairly interchangeable job designations *régisseur de la mise en scène*, *directeur de la scène* and *metteur en scène* began to achieve a considerable currency in the Parisian houses. There was nevertheless an undertow of scepticism about all this from traditionalists who winced at the term 'mise en scène' and even more at its contraction 'mise' as pieces of contemptible backstage argot, and loathed the ostentatiously intricate type of staging they felt the terms stood for. (Such stage directors, it should be said, were not wholly a creation of 19th-century Paris; witness, for instance, the *Instruction für den Regisseur des Schauspiels*, a memorandum drawn up at the Stuttgart court theatre in the 1790s for a figure whose functions focussed on ensuring efficient practical stagecraft and on 'balancing all the individual details to create the overall effect'.)

The newly prominent French operatic *régisseurs*, men like MM. Duponchel, Solomé, Albertin and Palianti, were entrusted with the job of conniving with some or all of the operatic team – librettist, composer, company director, scenic artist, costume designer, choreographer and leading singers – so as to devise a durable staging of the latest score, and then to make sure the staging was kept to. Indeed, it became the custom to set this staging in stone, to make it virtually a part of the work itself, by compiling a sophisticated *livret de mise en scène* which included a movement-by-movement, sometimes almost glance-by-glance, account of the whole complex spectacle (*see* PRODUCTION BOOK). These *livrets*, which evolved from less ambitious attempts in the 1800s to fix the stagings of Parisian melodramas and *opéras comiques* for the benefit of provincial managers, might circulate in manuscript or indeed in print. In the second quarter of the 19th century there were well over 80 of them for grand and comic operas published in Paris (as

small books or in journals), as well as many for spoken dramas. And the age's leading French librettist was enchanted by this practical, responsible and time-saving development. In an open letter to Louis Palianti, who had issued an extensive collection of such *livrets*, Scribe (2 December 1849) wrote that they were a service to theatre art, that they would help hugely in the successful staging of Parisian operas in the provinces and abroad, and that they should also be kept in the archives of the major metropolitan theatres so as to preserve sound traditions.

In Italy at the time, and in italianate opera houses elsewhere in Europe, there would have been little demand for such *livrets*, since, at least in the larger houses, production methods stretching back to the days of Maccario in Goldoni's *Impresario delle Smirne* (1761) seem to have been proving quite adequate: involving the retention by a company of a theatre poet who would organize the *comparse*, do his best to teach acting skills to such singers as lacked them, and block the moves of any sequences the principals could not manage on their own. (Subtleties of characterization expressed through stance and gesture would largely emerge from the rhetoric of the florid song itself and so of course be the singer's responsibility.) Such a poet was put on the *buffo* stage soon after the turn of the century in *La prova di una opera seria* (1805), with words and music by Francesco Gnecco; Gnecco's Grilletto needs no more than nine brisk lines of recitative to enlighten a prima donna about the tragic predicament of the heroine she is playing and then deftly set up a suitably affecting *tableau vivant* around her so that bel canto can commence.

By the second quarter of the 19th century, several notable poet-directors were stationed around Italy: among them Salvadore Cammarano at the S Carlo in Naples and Francesco Maria Piave at the Fenice in Venice. When Piave eventually left Venice for Milan in 1859, he wrote a memorandum listing the duties of a theatre poet beyond the specifically literary. They comprise liaising closely with the scene-, machine- and costume-departments; deciding on the selection of supernumeraries; taking rehearsals – where proper with the *maestro al cembalo* – which might involve the full company or smaller groups or just individuals (the latter being occasions for explaining the dramatic force of particular moments and suggesting means of putting them across the footlights); and, finally, being on hand backstage at premières. Cammarano too left some revealing memoranda (lists, plans, sketches etc.) which, taken with the often quite detailed scene and stage directions in his librettos, show that he was a conscientious planner and rehearser, working out the details of a particular staging in his head before the event, clarifying matters of motivation and psychology for the soloists, arranging effective tableaux of chorus and supers and not skimping on the minutiae of decor. His notes for *Lucia di Lammermoor*, his Donizetti collaboration of 1835, are especially telling: they cover the proper stage sides for entrances and exits, the deployment of huntsmen, villagers and men-at-arms, the placing of baronial props and furniture, matters of consistency in costume, and details of complicated stage business involving hats and swords.

These notes seem to have been compiled for the stage director of a theatre some distance from Cammarano's Naples who was planning to present his own production of *Lucia* after the Neapolitan première. Like

Cammarano himself, he may have been connected with one of the larger theatres and had the title *poeta e concertatore*; or he may have been a rather humbler *direttore del palcoscenico* or *regolatore di scena*: a stage-manager type who saw generally to the stagings at smaller houses which originated no new pieces of their own. However, as Italian operas, largely under the influence of Verdi, became theatrically more complex and less able to rely for proper stagings on traditional production methods, there was an increasing problem of how to ensure that a production put on at some other theatre than the birthplace of the work in question could be faithful to the work as it had been mounted at its première, when librettist and possibly composer and/or company manager and/or publisher had had direct control over what happened on stage.

But if it was Verdi who intensified the problem, it was he who proposed – indeed insisted upon – a particular solution. Louis Palianti's series of Parisian *livrets de mise en scène* had included accounts of two productions Verdi had been particularly closely involved with while in Paris in the 1850s: *Les vêpres siciliennes* (fig.17) and *Le trouvère* (*Il trovatore*). Verdi was passionately

---

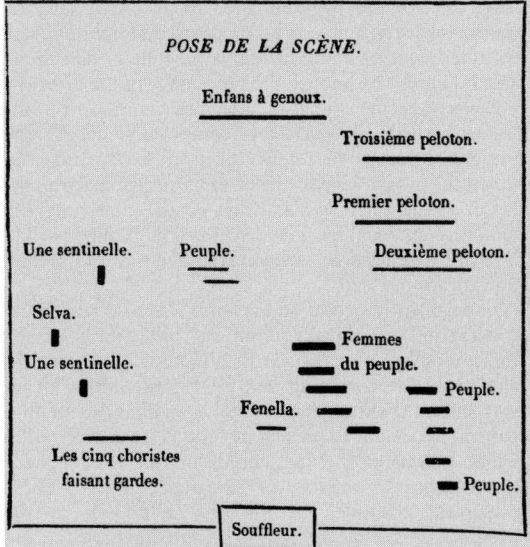

14	LA MUETTE DE PORTICI.

pelle, et se place devant les deux autres, *conservant des distances*. Des enfans venant de la gauche garnissent le dessous de la treille dans toute sa longueur.

Au moment où le chœur commence dans la chapelle, Fenella, le peuple, les enfans se mettent à genoux d'un mouvement spontané, en faisant face à l'autel.

POSE DE LA SCÈNE.

Enfans à genoux.

Troisième peloton.

Premier peloton.

Une sentinelle.   Peuple.   Deuxième peloton.

Selva.

Une sentinelle.   Femmes du peuple.

Peuple.

Fenella.

Les cinq choristes faisant gardes.

Peuple.

Souffleur.

Les soldats tiennent leurs lances à deux mains devant eux, et se courbent seulement; les cinq gardes sur leurs fusils font de même: tout le reste est à genoux.

SELVA.

Dieu! quel spectacle auguste et solennel!
Ce couple heureux s'avance vers l'autel.
Dans leurs regards, quelle tendresse brille!

MISE EN SCÈNE. ACTE Ier.	15

A Paris, le théâtre étant très grand, Selva descend la scène pour chanter ce passage, et retourne ensuite à sa place. En province, l'artiste qui jouera le rôle fera bien de rester sur les marches.

Le chœur reprend: c'est alors que Fenella se lève, regarde en se haussant sur la pointe des pieds. Elle voit Alphonse marcher à l'autel; elle s'élance pour y monter, les cinq soldats croisent leurs armes et lui barrent le chemin.

CHŒUR DES CINQ SOLDATS.

Que voulez-vous?
Retirez-vous,
Ou bien craignez notre courroux.

Selva, pendant ce motif, descend en disant:

Mais que veut cette jeune fille?
Que voulez-vous? (*bis.*)
Retirez-vous.

Il la pousse rudement; il se retourne, a l'air de complimenter les soldats de l'avoir empêché d'entrer: c'est pendant ce temps que les femmes, à genoux, disent à Fenella qui gagne la gauche de la scène, en passant près d'elles:

N'approchez pas, (*bis.*)
Craignez ces farouches soldats.

Selva retourne à sa place, les femmes reprennent l'attitude première de la scène.

Fenella peut à peine se soutenir; deux jeunes personnes de l'extrême gauche s'en aperçoivent, se lèvent, vont à elle, la soutiennent: elle reprend courage. Les deux femmes se remettent à genoux; Fenella reste absorbée dans sa douleur et ses réflexions.

---

15. *The early livret de mise en scène for grand opera. The climactic moment in Act 1 of Auber's 'La muette de Portici' (Fenella recognizing her false former lover at his wedding) as recorded in the 'Indications générales ... pour la mise en scène' (1828) for the opera, compiled by Solomé, 'régisseur général' of the Paris Opéra. There are instructions for the placing, spacing, moves, gestures, emotional states and props of the characters, and at the top of page 15 a distinction is made between what is possible on a big Parisian stage and what may need to be done in a provincial house.*

concerned to get stage business right, and was also much taken with the *livret* idea; indeed, he told Piave enthusiastically that, armed with Palianti's account, a child could stage *Les vêpres*. Hence the *Vêpres livret* was translated into Italian, and from then on each of Verdi's operas had its own *disposizione scenica* prepared and printed by his publishers, Ricordi, with the composer's connivance and blessing: the *disposizioni* increasing in length and elaboration so that the one for *Otello* (the *Falstaff* one has yet to be traced) has all of 270 diagrams of stage positions and moves.

In a sense the Italian wheel was coming full circle. What the prefaces to *La Rappresentatione di Anima, et di Corpo* and *Dafne* were providing in 1600 and 1608, the Ricordi *disposizioni* of Verdi (and others) were finding equivalents for two-and-a-half centuries later. The highly creative, cooperative and labour-intensive preparations for a new piece once over, subsequent stagings could have the benefit of clear instructions as to how to reproduce the event theatrically as well as musically: to reproduce it, according to Cavalieri and Gagliano in the 17th century, with a considerable degree of flexibility and personal input, but according to Giulio Ricordi in the 19th with rigorous and minute (albeit spirited) fidelity. In the Verdi *disposizioni* that he edited, Ricordi asks on the one hand for a mix of intelligence and individuality from soloists and chorus members and on the other for a preparedness to be treated by him like so many puppets or sheep. But it is all in the good cause of a newly minute theatricality in the music. As Ricordi

16. *The librettist as stage director. Salvadore Cammarano's sketches for the staging of two incidents in one of his operas. It has been conjectured that the piece is 'Merope', as set in 1847 by Pacini and staged at the Teatro S Carlo, Naples.*

put it in his epilogue to the *Aida* production book (1872): 'because of recent developments in the music-drama, every moment [prescribed in the book] has its *raison d'être* and the old stage conventions are no longer acceptable'. As to what would happen when these bright new movements themselves came to seem old, conventional or in some other way limiting, Ricordi had too much on his mind to say.

6. 1876 TO WORLD WAR II. It is appropriate to begin the story of modern opera production with the first Bayreuth Festival of 1876, for not only was Wagner the prototype of the 20th-century director, but the festival he inaugurated has for over a century remained one of the chief power-houses of developments in dramaturgy. In contrast to the previous theatrical practice, which could involve a combination of interested parties, Wagner, in collaboration with his choreographer Richard Fricke, imposed himself as the central intelligence. Strong emphasis was placed on the role of improvisation and inspiration in stage blocking. Traditional stock histrionics were replaced by 'natural' expression, and singers were encouraged to ignore the audience and respond only to fellow performers on the stage. This was the apogee of illusionism, the prevailing mode in the spoken theatre, at least, from the mid-18th century.

Wagner naturally took a keen interest in the work of Georg II, the Duke of Saxe-Meiningen, whose coincident innovations with his travelling troupe were a huge influence on the evolution of stagecraft. In Meininger productions, scenery (three dimensional, using the box set) was designed to accommodate the movements of actors; costumes, props and lighting were exploited to create mood and atmosphere. The duke also did much to establish the supremacy of the director.

When Cosima Wagner assumed control of the Bayreuth Festival after the composer's death, she brought a natural dramatic talent to bear, and continued the progressive tendency of naturalistic acting she had observed at the first festivals. At the same time, her pursuit of an 'ideal' performance such as Wagner would have approved led to over-prescriptiveness and stifling of inspiration.

Naturalism in acting and staging was also sought by Konstantin Stanislavsky, who in 1898 founded the Moscow Art Theatre with Vladimir Nemirovich-Danchenko. Recognizing that the representation of inner truth on the stage might involve an abandonment of realism, he sought to project life not as it is perceived in reality but as it is experienced 'in our dreams, our visions, our moments of spiritual uplift'. These principles, grounded in the system known as the 'Method' (based on the actor's personal experience and identification with the role) were embodied in Stanislavsky's work in the Bol'shoy Theatre Opera Studio, which he founded in 1918. Fusion of words, music and movement was the object, but it was the score rather than the libretto that was to provide the cues. More revolutionary was the Moscow Art Theatre Musical Studio, founded in 1919 by Nemirovich-Danchenko, who rejected naturalism and realism in favour of the kind of techniques pioneered by Jaques-Dalcroze, strictly synchronizing movement and gesture in abstract settings.

Nemirovich-Danchenko, like many others, was influenced by the ideas of the Swiss designer Adolphe Appia, who has been described as 'the father of non-

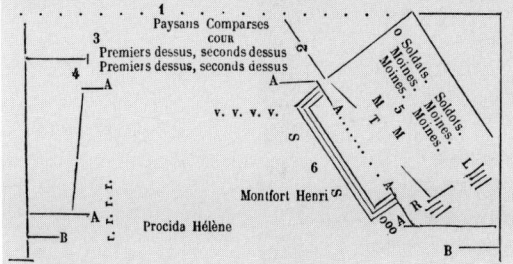

Montfort. — Henri. — Procida. — Hélène.

Après le solo de Procida : *Protégé de Montfort, à lui la honte, etc., etc.*, Hélène, qui a reculé de quelques pas, redescend à la gauche de Henri. *Oui, à nous la gloire ! à nous la mort ! à nous la mort !*—Après le *Ah !* vocalisé, pas général en avant en attaquant le FORTÉ quatre temps : *O noble patrie ! etc., etc.*

Messieurs, mesdames des chœurs, et masses comme ci-dessus.

Vaudemont. — Béthune. — Montfort. — Henri. — Hélène. — Procida. — Mainfroid.

Depuis le changement de mouvement (ALLEGRO 6-8), Procida. Hélène, Mainfroid, Montfort et Henri reculent peu à peu. Dans ce mouvement, Procida se retrouve à la gauche d'Hélène.

Immédiatement après la dernière syllabe chantée, les mouvemens suivans s'exécutent très vite : — Une rue s'ouvre au milieu du théâtre. — Les soldats qui, au fond, sur la terrasse jardin, font face au public, descendent jusqu'au milieu du th âtre former l'aile gauche de la rue. Ils font alors face à leurs camarades qui occupent l'aile droite du théâtre, et qui ne bougent pas de place. — Henri veut s'élancer sur les pas de ses amis, qui le repoussent avec mépris. Vainement il se jette à leurs genoux. — Montfort seul le protège. — Tous les autres personnages qui également ont reculé de quelques pas, prennent part à l'action. — TABLEAU. — Le rideau baisse.

QUATRIÈME ACTE.

Grande pièce en pierres et à voûtes cintrées donnant sur la cour d'une forteresse.

Gauche (jardin.)   Droite (cour).

1. Rideau de fond tombant sur le quatrième plan. Il représente, entourée de hauts murs crénelés, une grande porte donnant accès sur des remparts crénelés, laissant voir la campagne. — 2. Châssis représentant une autre porte conduisant censé à d'autres cours. — 3. Porte conduisant au dehors. — 4. Issue conduisant au logement des prisonniers. — Les plafonds cintrés tombent de A à A. — 5. Pièce sombre, à laquelle on monte par quatre marches de pierre 6. — L'entrée cintrée est entièrement masquée par un rideau en tapisserie devant lequel se trouve une grille haute de deux mètres environ s'ouvrant en deux parties. — Au-dessus de l'ouverture de la pièce 5 sont suspendus quelques vieux drapeaux. — D'autres vieux drapeaux garnissent aussi le haut des murs côté jardin. — B. Manteau d'arlequin. (Les positions indiquées ci-dessus sont celles du commencement du final.)

Le rideau se lève neuf mesures avant le récit d'Henri.

17. The stimulus for the Verdian disposizione scenica. A page from Palianti's French livret de mise en scène based on the original production of Verdi's 'Les vêpres siciliennes' (Paris Opéra, 1855). Palianti details the movements, groupings and pieces of stage business (all closely linked to specific verbal or musical cues in the score) which lead to the big tableau at the end of Act 3: Henri torn between his conspirator friends and his long-lost autocratic father. The diagram, part of the subsequent design specification for Act 4 (the courtyard of a fortress), incorporates the positions the cast are to take up at the beginning of the finale to that act, a finale to which the livret will soon give 750 words of detailed description.

illusionist musical theatre'. Appia aimed to create a theatrical space independent of reality: a 'living background' that projected mood and atmosphere predominantly by imaginative lighting. His set designs were geometrical structures inspired by contemporary Constructivist principles but offset by evocative deployment of light and shadow (fig.18). His theories of opera production, expounded in a series of essays, also proposed simple, stylized costumes and quasi-symbolic, non-realistic stage movements. Similar ideas were espoused by the English theatre designer and director Edward Gordon Craig, but he further attempted to replace painted scenery with screens, variable in shape, size and colour according to the mood of the scene (for illustration *see* CRAIG, EDWARD GORDON). His uncompromisingly anti-realist stance further led him to propose replacing actors altogether with 'Über-Marionetten': puppets manipulated by an omnipotent director. In his notable productions for the Purcell Operatic Society, 1900–03, his rejection of traditional stage conventions and deployment of coloured light bore witness to the symbolist approach that was to

make its effect felt on subsequent generations of directors. As with Appia, Craig's influence was chiefly through his theories rather than his productions. Appia mounted a *Tristan* at La Scala in 1923 and designed an austere, abstract *Rheingold* and *Walküre* in Basle, 1924–5 (the *Ring* thus initiated was abandoned after vigorous protests), but his ideas were contemptuously dismissed by Cosima Wagner and not taken up seriously at Bayreuth until the reforming regime of Wieland and Wolfgang Wagner after World War II.

There were, however, other progressive spirits in the early decades of the century who followed Appia in rejecting pictorialism. Gustav Wunderwald's anti-naturalistic representation of the rocky heights in his *Rheingold* for the Deutsche Oper, Berlin, in 1914 showed an awareness of Appia's ideas, as did the work of Alfred Roller in Vienna, Hans Wildermann in Cologne, Dortmund and Düsseldorf, and Ludwig Sievert, whose *Ring* was first seen in Freiburg im Breisgau in 1912–13, then again, with some variations, in Baden-Baden (1917), Hanover (1925) and Frankfurt (1926–7). Sievert was able to introduce both a cyclorama (such as Appia had wanted but been prevented from executing) and a revolving stage. Appia's influence is also evident in the dark, suggestive, geometric shapes of Sievert's *Ring* designs (the rocky cleft in *Walküre*, Act 2, for example), though the slanting walls and converging perspective here produce a composition that was quite original and in turn widely imitated.

Roller's designs for Mahler's Wagner and Mozart productions in Vienna from 1903 onwards applied elements of neo-romanticism to architectonic structures derived from Appia and Craig (for illustration *see* STAGE DESIGN, fig.17 and VIENNA, fig.8). A more thoroughgoing avant-garde director was Vsevelod Meyerhold, whose determination to draw attention to the artifice and mechanics of the act of stage production foreshadowed Brechtian alienation techniques. Meyerhold's first opera production was an imaginatively reductive *Tristan* at the Mariinsky Theatre in St Petersburg in 1909; on Stanislavsky's death in August 1938 he took over direction of the Studio, by then renamed the Stanislavsky Opera Theatre, but he was arrested soon afterwards as 'an enemy of socialist realism' and deported to a concentration camp in the Arctic.

Another prominent director who gave practical expression to the theories of Appia and Craig was the Austrian Max Reinhardt, who played a key role in establishing the director-impresario in the opera house and is best known for his collaborations with Richard Strauss and Hofmannsthal (*see* ARIADNE AUF NAXOS, fig.1). Reinhardt's approach was an eclectic one, incorporating elements of realism, symbolism and expressionism in an attempt to recapture in modern terms the visionary experience afforded by the traditional theatre. The accusation that his 'obtrusive' production method obscured the author's or composer's intention is an early example of the critical reaction against so-called producer's or director's opera.

A new wave of realism, rooted in the anti-romantic, functional principles of the Bauhaus, informed the most stimulating experiment in opera production in the 1920s: the Berlin Kroll Opera under Klemperer (1927–31). The artist and stage designer Ewald Dülberg, who was responsible for productions of *Fidelio* (fig.19), *Oedipus rex*, *Der fliegende Holländer* and *Rigoletto* there, aimed primarily at creating clearly defined stage spaces, with starkly lit compositions draw-

18. Set design by Adolphe Appia for Gluck's 'Orfeo ed Euridice' (1926)

ing on principles of Cubist abstraction. Dülberg's costumes for the *Holländer* (directed by Jürgen Fehling) were both modern and timeless – Senta sporting a blue pullover, grey skirt and a bright red wig – while the ships were represented as geometric shapes looming in the dark. From 1928 Dülberg's monopoly gave way to the participation of such artists as Caspar Neher, Traugott Müller, Oskar Strnad, Oskar Schlemmer and László Moholy-Nagy. In Moholy's controversial *Les contes d'Hoffmann*, Romantic scenery was replaced by Constructivist designs consisting of geometric and spiral motifs in the style of the Bauhaus; there were sharp contrasts of lighting, and the playing space was occupied by surreal, puppet figures and the first steel furniture to appear on the operatic stage (fig.20).

At Bayreuth, Siegfried Wagner celebrated the reopening of the festival after World War I (1924) with a sustained attempt, in the final six years of his life, to introduce solid three-dimensional sets and other cautious innovations more in tune with the times. The hand of hallowed tradition weighed heavily, but in his last new production, *Tannhäuser* in 1930, there was at last some evidence that the progressive ideas of contemporary music theatre were making headway.

The ascendancy of the Nazis, however, put a stop to virtually all avant-garde experimentation in dramaturgy in Germany. Only at Bayreuth – ironically, in view of the close links forged between the festival and the regime – was there any sign that creative thinking had been allowed to continue. Winifred Wagner's appoint-

19. Design by Ewald Dülberg for Act 2 of 'Fidelio' (Berlin, Kroll Opera, 1927): gouache

ment of Heinz Tietjen as artistic director of the festival brought the scenic designer Emil Preetorius to the centre of attention (fig.21). In his essay *Wagner: Bild und Vision* Preetorius drew attention both to the abundance of natural effects in Wagner's works and to their conception as allegories. On the one hand, he felt that these effects 'must be rendered clearly and with complete illusion'; on the other, he recognized that symbolism must play as important a role in the thinking of the designer as in that of the composer. Like Appia, he laid great emphasis on the use of lighting, allowing its deployment supremacy by reducing stage props to essentials.

At the Metropolitan, New York, at least one cycle of the *Ring* was conducted every year from 1929 to 1939 by Artur Bodanzky, using the faithfully naturalistic sets and bearskins of the Kautsky brothers first seen before World War I. The sets designed for the tetralogy after World War II by Lee Simonson also frequently sprouted foliage, but since Simonson was a Broadway designer, they had more than a touch of modernism as well, with echoes of Sievert and Preetorius.

between the stage directions, which remained bound to 19th-century theatrical modes, and the timeless ideas of the works themselves, which demand constantly new representations. The stage directions, in other words, he regarded as inner visions rather than practical demands.

A diametrically opposed set of dramaturgical principles was evident in the work of another hugely influential director of the same era, Walter Felsenstein. Having founded the Komische Oper in East Berlin in 1947, he remained its director until his death in 1975, establishing 'realistic music theatre' on the basis of long, intensive rehearsal periods and committed ensemble playing, but insisting that 'the central figure is, and remains, the singer-actor'. Felsenstein emphasized the creative contribution to be made by performers, inspiring them to replicate the psychological state of the characters they were playing, drawing on their own emotional reserves and experiences. The dramatic portrayals of characters, and their interaction with one another, had to be persuasive, but Felsenstein also

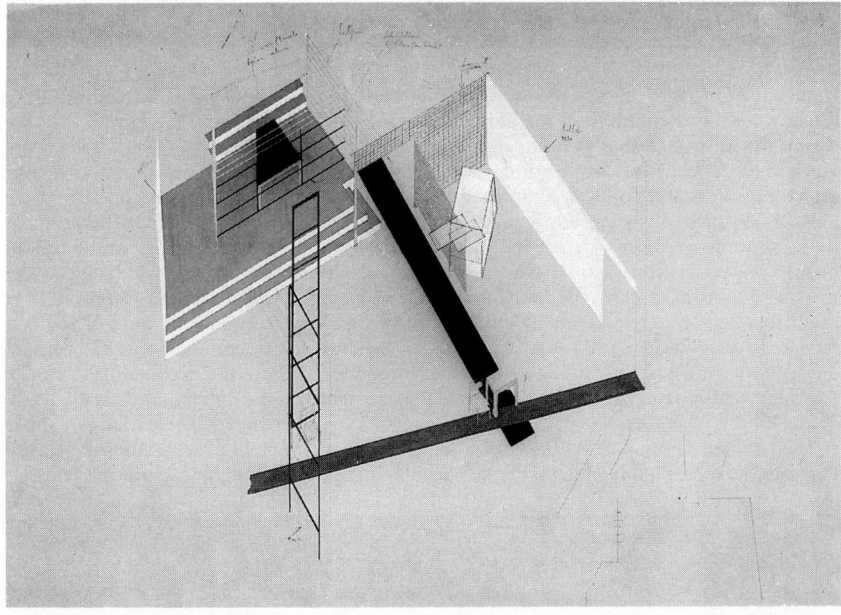

20. Design by László Moholy-Nagy for Act 1 of Offenbach's 'Les contes d'Hoffmann' (Berlin, Kroll Opera, 1929): blueprint with pen, ink and gouache

7. SINCE WORLD WAR II. The most radical shift in the staging of Wagner, and a key moment in the history of 20th-century opera production, occurred with the reopening of the Bayreuth Festspielhaus after World War II in 1951. Bayreuth had become indelibly associated with the Nazi regime, and it was in a conscious attempt to break with the ideology of the past that Wieland and Wolfgang Wagner, the composer's grandsons, discarded all the pictorial sets and their trappings that had become such an outdated fixture. Arguing that there was no incontrovertible reason why Wagner's works had to be given in the naturalistic mode in which they were first performed, Wieland Wagner reduced his sets to the bare essentials, essaying fidelity to the composer not on the surface but in terms of psychological truthfulness. The entire action was set on a circular platform or disc, with a cyclorama effectively suggesting an endless horizon (fig.22). The stated aim was to reveal 'the purely human element, stripped of all convention'. His abandonment of Wagner's specific instructions was justified by the drawing of a distinction

demanded that the act of singing in the theatre had itself to be experienced as a 'convincing, true and utterly indispensable mode of expression'.

Felsenstein's chief legacy was the psychological and social realism he brought to bear, and the emphasis he placed on role identification. His best-known pupils, Götz Friedrich and Joachim Herz, as well as directors such as Harry Kupfer, fused those principles with the quite contrary ones of Brechtian theory to establish the fundamentals of an approach that dominated the stages of Europe, in a variety of contrasting forms, throughout the sixties, seventies and eighties. Brecht's determination to shatter the illusions constructed by traditional, 'culinary' theatre, as he disparagingly named it, led him to formulate the *Verfremdungseffekt*, usually rendered as 'alienation effect', though the intention was to alienate the audience from the action in order to engage it more immediately and intellectually.

Alienation techniques were used conspicuously by Friedrich in his two *Ring* cycles, where, for example, he caused Loge, Alberich and Wotan to step outside the

21. Scene from Act 2 of Heinz Tietjen's production of 'Die Walküre' at the Bayreuth Festspielhaus in 1936, designed by Emil Preetorius

framework of the drama to address the audience directly. Such techniques were used to heighten the contemporary relevance that became the hallmark of the work of Friedrich, Herz, Kupfer and other East German directors. Social and political commitment had been an intrinsic element of Felsenstein's productions too, but the incorporation of Brechtian techniques gave the work of the younger generation a sharper ideological edge. It was no doubt the potency of that ideological element that provoked bourgeois capitalist audiences and critics repeatedly to object to what was dismissed as socialist didacticism on the operatic stage – a stage, moreover, not traditionally associated with ideological engagement of any kind.

The Italian Giorgio Strehler and the Frenchman Patrice Chéreau (notably in his centenary production of the *Ring* at Bayreuth, 1976; fig.24) also attracted criticism for the prominence they accorded the ideological aspects of works. It is no coincidence that the trend they encouraged of directors turning from the spoken theatre to opera was concurrent with the rise of what came to be called (often pejoratively), producer's or director's opera. The age of the producer, or director (as he or she has come, following wider theatrical and American usage, more commonly to be known), may be seen as a response to a set of socio-cultural factors affecting the reception of opera in the modern era. Chief among these are the decline in the cult of the diva and, arguably, in the individuality of expression (though not technique) of singers; the passing of the era of the autocratic, charismatic conductor who fashioned the production in his own image; and the failure of opera in the 20th century

22. Scene from Act 1 of Wieland Wagner's production of 'Tristan und Isolde' at the Bayreuth Festspielhaus, 1962

23. Scene from Act 1 of Götz Friedrich's production of 'Siegfried' at Covent Garden, London, 1975, designed by Josef Svoboda

to regenerate its form or repertory in accordance with the needs of the age. The survival of an antiquated, obsolete genre has necessitated renewal in terms of presentation.

Not all 'interventionist' approaches have a political intention, however: some directors (notably Jonathan Miller) have probed the works from a psychological vantage-point, while others (notably David Freeman) have given priority to emotional directness. Present-day costumes and settings have sometimes, but by no means always, been the chosen means for such explorations. In the 1970s and 80s, some directors attempted to emphasize the universality and timeless relevance of works by incorporating props and costumes from various eras. Friedrich, Chéreau, Kupfer and Lehnhoff all did something of the sort in their productions of the *Ring*, the last-named justifying his deliberate disjunctions of chronology and location as a means of broadening their symbolic and interpretative effect. His Valhalla, for example, which Lehnhoff described as 'a metaphor for immeasurable power', was represented at

different times by a model fairytale castle, by Wall Street skyscrapers, by a petit-bourgeois domestic interior and by a huge military installation. The intention was to stimulate the audience's imagination to make connections of this sort, not to preclude the making of further connections.

'Interventionist' opera productions have also gone hand in hand with the espousal of influential critical theories such as structuralism, post-structuralism (in particular deconstruction), reader-orientated approaches and feminism. The questioning of previous certainties such as the status of the author as the origin of the text, the source of its meaning and the principal authority for its interpretation effected a revolution in the way works, both classic and modern, might be presented. Brechtian theory had already suggested that the bourgeois theatre's illusion of reality could fruitfully be dispelled by disrupting the supposed organic unity of a work, emphasizing instead its discontinuities and contradictions. Now the wider possibilities of exploiting disjunctions between text and music (even of contriving

24. Scene from Act 1 of Patrice Chéreau's production of 'Siegfried' at the Bayreuth Festspielhaus, 1976, designed by Richard Peduzzi

25. Scene from Hans Neuenfels's production of Verdi's 'Aida', Frankfurt, 1981, designed by Erich Wonder

26. Scene from Franco Zeffirelli's production of Puccini's 'Turandot' at the Metropolitan Opera, New York, 1987

them), and of generating creative tension between surface indicators in the score or stage directions and the action as played out on stage began to be realized.

Principles of this sort were initially most evident in the work of continental, primarily German, directors, though by the 1980s the torch had passed to the younger generation active in Britain. Kupfer had already created over 70 productions, mostly in East Germany, before he came to international attention in 1978; Chéreau's Bayreuth *Ring* (1976) was more immediately influential. The Gielen-Zehelein regime at Frankfurt (1977–87) produced a series of radical stagings by a team of guest directors including Ruth Berghaus, Alfred Kirchner, Christof Nel and Hans Neuenfels (fig.25) that pressed such ideas into the service of vibrant music theatre. Berghaus's stagings in particular, drawing also on surrealism and the Theatre of the Absurd, have influenced the work of younger directors such as David Alden and Richard Jones. Others, such as David Pountney in Britain and Peter Sellars in the USA, have ploughed their own furrows, in each case producing a corpus of work that by sheer force of conviction and flair in execution has often been well received even by those of a more traditionalist persuasion.

Alongside such radical developments, a conservative tradition has been maintained in various guises. Visconti's neo-romantic, picturesque opulence has been continued by his protégé Zeffirelli, notably at La Scala and the Metropolitan (fig.26), while 'fidelity to the text' has been the watchword of both those directors cleaving to the humanist, Leavisite tradition (Peter Hall is a prominent example) and, on the continent, those adhering to *Werktreu* principles. It would be misleading, however, to suggest that either the mainstream traditional or the radical interventionist productions had a monopoly on invention and imagination. Peter Stein's *Otello*, *Falstaff* and *Pelléas et Mélisande*, for example, demonstrate that even a conventional concern for harmony of stage action and score can, in resourceful hands, have electrifying theatrical results.

Trends in historical performing practice have affected the playing and singing of operas to various extents, according to the companies concerned (*see* REVIVAL). With a few notable exceptions, energies have not been widely directed, to date, towards the authentic re-creation of sets and stage action stipulated by the works' creators, least of all in the 19th-century repertory. There is a clear contradiction between the demand for rigorous adherence to such prescriptions on the one hand and the increasing acceptance on the other of the legitimacy, if not the necessity, of presenting theatrical works in modes that take account of a modern audience's experiences. Shifts in public taste will no doubt continue to foster experimentation. In a post-modern age uncertain of its cultural identity, iconoclasm and traditionalism seem destined to coexist, giving rise to a multiplicity of stylistic approaches for some time to come.

8. PRODUCTION PLANNING. The mounting of a production in an opera house represents the culminating phase in a long and complex series of decisions and preparations which may occupy a period of as much as five years. No account of operatic production is complete without some indication of what is entailed in this process.

Any opera produced by a standing company presenting a regular season has to be planned within the context of broader repertory management. This will involve the consideration of general factors of local demand and conditions, as well as balance (between different periods, between comic and tragic, between Italian, German and French opera and national representation, between the rare and the familiar); past and future programmes as well as that of the season in question; the workload for chorus and orchestra; coordination with other companies serving the same or a nearby audience; the availability of artists; and budgetary factors. Ultimate decisions about repertory will normally fall to a board of management, on the recommendation of the company's chief executive. Other officers (music director, director of productions, Dramaturg etc.) may also contribute to this recommendation.

The assembly of a production team usually begins with the engagement of one or two key persons to whom the project appears to be ideally suited, and around whose particular abilities and availability it may have been conceived: a conductor, a director, a leading singer or even in rare cases a designer. The remainder of the central creative team will then be engaged with their mutual artistic compatibility in mind. As soon as this group is settled, management autonomy yields to collaboration. Ideally, consultation between the creative team supervenes, with the chief executive as ultimate arbiter. In principle, having chosen the team judiciously, he should be able to rely on it to bring forward a production to which the company will happily devote its energy and resources, but careful monitoring may be needed and, in extreme cases, the replacement of the initial team or part of it may be necessary in the case of projects that are either irreducibly over-budget or seem unlikely to prove successful. If all goes according to plan, the director, after consulting the conductor, will brief his chosen designer and will then produce a 'concept' for his interpretation of the opera, embodied in a model and drawings, to be presented to the senior management team for approval, subject to costing. If the costing is satisfactory, a final model and working drawings are produced, together with costume designs, and the whole physical side of the production is handed over to the workshops – carpentry, metalwork, painting, special processes (such as hydraulics), fabric selection, dyeing, costume-making, wig-making – working to deadlines, which will be a considerable time ahead and geared to the stage rehearsals.

Meanwhile, the process of casting the opera will be continuing; indeed the leading roles will have been settled well before the technical process has begun. While each company must cut its coat according to its cloth, it will want the best possible cast it can afford for its productions and at every level there is competition. This may mean that casting has to be done three or more years ahead in some cases, with the concomitant risk of a singer's deterioration or defection between contract and delivery. The most prudent foresight can still result in cancellation at the last moment, but the vast majority of contracts are honoured and in any case it is pointless to enforce a contract against a singer's will, be the reasons for cancellation respectable or not.

Because of the exacting vocal demands of so many operatic roles, it is hardly surprising that dramatic considerations have often to take second place. For a singer to be dramatically as well as vocally convincing is, if not exactly rare, at least an added bonus. Directors and designers are charged with the task, among others, of rendering the short tall, the bulky slender, the bland exciting and the banal poetic; the voice itself can, in the best examples, help overcome physical unsuitability. Like so much else in opera, casting is a compromise between the ideal and the possible; it is certainly the most important of the contributory functions in the preparation of an opera production.

The question of the language in which the opera is to be sung will have been settled before casting begins. Thereafter, the version must be agreed on. This task ranges in complexity from the agreement of cuts, if any, through the choice between dialogue and recitative for works from the French 19th-century *opéra-comique* repertory to the question of which version should be preferred where more than one has been left by the composer, as in Gluck's *Orfeo* or Verdi's *Don Carlos*. The conductor may need to decide what edition of the work should be followed, particularly if its score has been the subject of new research. Performance material will then be checked, amended and distributed.

The importance of the location and logistics of rehearsals to the success of a production can hardly be overestimated; though factors beyond a director's control – illness in particular – can undermine the best of them. The nimble planner has to show himself able to surmount such obstacles.

See also CASTING; PROMPTER; and REHEARSAL.

*

GENERAL

G. E. Shea: *Acting in Opera* (New York, 1915)

A. Winds: *Geschichte der Regie* (Stuttgart, 1925)

H. C. Wolff: *Oper: Szene und Darstellung von 1600 bis 1900* (Leipzig, 1968)

G. Guccini: 'Direzione scenica e regia', *SOI*, v (1988), 123–74

BAROQUE

Il corago, o vero Alcune osservazioni per metter bene in scena le composizioni drammatiche (MS, *c*1630, *I-MOe*; ed. P. Fabbri and A. Pompilio, Florence, 1983)

B. Marcello: *Il teatro alla moda, o sia Metodo sicuro e facile per il ben comporre ed eseguire l'opere italiane in musica all'uso moderno* (Venice, *c*1720); Eng. trans., in R. G. Pauly: 'Benedetto Marcellos's Satire on early 18th-Century Opera', *MQ*, xxxiv (1948), 222–3, 371–403; xxxv (1949), 85–105, and, abridged, in *Source Readings in Music History*, ed. O. Strunk (New York, 1950)

H. Prunières: 'Lully and the Académie de Musique et de Danse', *MQ*, xi (1925), 528–46

A. Nicoll: *The Development of the Theatre* (London, 1927, 5/1966)

E. Boswell: *The Restoration Court Stage (1660–1702)* (Cambridge, MA, 1932)

H. Tintelnot: *Barocktheater und barocke Kunst* (Berlin, 1939)

J. Eisenschmidt: *Die szenische Darstellung der Opern Händels auf der Londoner Bühne seiner Zeit* (Wolfenbüttel, 1940–41)

T. Cole and H. Krich Chinoy, eds.: *Actors on Acting* (New York, 1949, 2/1970)

G. Guerrieri and E. Povoledo: *Il secolo dell'invenzione teatrale* (Venice, 1951)

A. M. Nagler, ed.: *Sources of Theatrical History* (New York, 1952)

S. T. Worsthorne: *Venetian Opera in the Seventeenth Century* (Oxford, 1954, 2/1968)

T. E. Lawrenson: *The French Stage in the 17th Century: a Study in the Advent of the Italian Order* (Manchester, 1957)

G. Wickham: *Early English Stages 1300 to 1660* (London, 1959–72)

E. Battisti: *Rinascimento e Barocco* (Turin, 1960), 96ff

L. Schrade: *La représentation d'Edipo tiranno au Teatro Olimpico (Vicence, 1585)* (Paris, 1960)

I. Lavin: 'Lettres de Parmes (1618, 1627–28) et débuts du théâtre baroque', *Le lieu théâtral à la Renaissance: CNRS Royaumont 1963*, 105–58

M. McGowan: *L'art du ballet de cour en France, 1581–1643* (Paris, 1963)

A. M. Nagler: *Theatre Festivals of the Medici 1539–1637* (New Haven, CT, 1964)

C. V. Palisca: 'The First Performance of "Euridice"', *Queens College Department of Music Twenty-fifth Anniversary Festschrift (1937–1962)* (New York, 1964), 1–23

A. Boll: 'L'oeuvre théâtrale de Rameau: sa mise en scène', *ReM*, no.260 (1965), 13–20

M. Baur-Heinhold: *Theater des Barock* (Munich, 1966; Eng. trans., 1967)

M. F. Christout: *Le ballet de cour de Louis XIV 1643–1672: mises en scène* (Paris, 1967)

C. Molinari: *Le nozze degli dei: un saggio sul grande spettacolo italiano nel seicento* (Rome, 1968)

N. Pirrotta: *Li due Orfei: da Poliziano a Monteverdi* (Turin, 1969; Eng. trans., 1975)

W. Dean: *Handel and the Opera Seria* (Berkeley and Los Angeles, 1970)

R. A. Griffin: *High Baroque Culture and Theater in Vienna* (New York, 1972)

F. Lesure: *L'opéra classique français: XVIIe et XVIIIe siècles* (Geneva, 1972)

F. Marotti: 'Lo spazio scenico del melodramma, esaminato sulla base della trattatistica teatrale italiana', *Venezia e il melodramma nel seicento: Venice 1972*, 349–57

——, ed.: *Lo spettacolo dall'umanesimo al manierismo* (Milan, 1974)

R. Savage: 'Producing *Dido and Aeneas*: an Investigation into Sixteen Problems', *EMc*, iv (1976), 393–406

C. J. Day: 'The Theater of SS. Giovanni e Paolo and Monteverdi's *L'incoronazione di Poppea*', *CMc*, no.25 (1978), 22–38

C. MacClintock, ed.: *Readings in the History of Music in Performance* (Bloomington, IN, 1979)

J. Milhous: *Thomas Betterton and the Management of Lincoln's Inn Fields, 1695–1708* (Carbondale, IL, 1979)

I. Lavin: *Bernini and the Unity of the Visual Arts* (New York, 1980) [incl. 'Bernini and the Theater', 146–57]

M. Murata: *Operas for the Papal Court, 1631–1668* (Ann Arbor, 1981)

L. Rosow: *Lully's 'Armide' at the Paris Opéra: a Performance History 1686–1766* (diss., Brandeis U., 1981)

J. Milhous: 'The Multimedia Spectacular on the Restoration Stage', *British Theatre and the Other Arts, 1660–1800*, ed. S. S. Kenny (Washington DC, 1984), 41–66

N. Pirrotta: *Music and Culture in Italy from the Middle Ages to the Baroque* (Cambridge, MA, 1984) [incl. 'Monteverdi and the Problems of Opera', 235–53; 'Theater, Sets, and Music in Monteverdi's Operas', 254–70; and *Commedia dell'Arte* and Opera', 343–60]

J. Powell: *Restoration Theatre Production* (London, 1984)

R. W. Vince: *Renaissance Theatre: a Historiographical Handbook* (Westport, CT, 1984)

J. Milhous and R. D. Hume: *Producible Interpretation: Eight English Plays, 1675–1707* (Carbondale, IL, 1985)

——: 'A Prompt Copy of Handel's "Radamisto"', *MT*, cxxvii (1986), 316–21

L. Lindgren: 'The Staging of Handel's Operas in London', *Handel Tercentenary Collection*, ed. S. Sadie and A. Hicks (London, 1987), 93–119

R. Savage and M. Sansone: '*Il Corago* and the Staging of Early Opera: Four Chapters from an Anonymous Treatise *circa* 1630', *EMc*, xvii (1989), 495–511

CLASSICAL AND ROMANTIC

F. Algarotti: *Saggio sopra l'opera in musica* (Bologna, 1755, 2/1763; Eng. trans., 1767)

J. Noverre: *Lettres sur la danse et sur les ballets* (Lyons and Stuttgart, 1760, 2/1783; Eng. trans., 1783, enlarged 1803 and 1930)

C. F. D. Schubart: *Ideen zu einer Ästhetik der Tonkunst* (Vienna, 1806)

E. Campardon: *L'Académie royale de musique au XVIIIe siècle* (Paris, 1884)

A. Beijer: *Slottsteatrarna på Drottningholm och Gripsholm* (Stockholm, 1937)

M. A. Allévy: *La mise en scène en France dans la première moitié du dix-neuvième siècle* (Paris, 1938)

A. S. Downer: 'Nature to Advantage Dressed: Eighteenth Century Acting', *Proceedings of the Modern Language Association of America*, lviii (1943), 1002–37

B. Brunelli, ed.: *P. Metastasio: Tutte le opere* (Milan, 1943–54)

C. Varese: *Saggio sul Metastasio* (Florence, 1950) [esp. appx, 'La regia dal dramma Metastasiano', 103–12]

T. Cole and H. Krich Chinoy, eds.: *Directing the Play: a Sourcebook of Stagecraft* (Indianapolis, IN, 1953, 2/1963, as *Directors on Directing: a Sourcebook of the Modern Theater, with an*

Illustrated History of Directing) [incl. H. Krich Chinoy: 'The Emergence of the Director', 13–67 (1953); 1–77 (1963)]

G. M. Bergman: 'Les agences théâtrales et l'impression des mises en scène aux environs de 1800', *Revue de la Société d'histoire du théâtre*, viii (1956), 228–40

M. Horányi: *Eszterházi vigasságok* (Budapest, 1959; Eng. trans., 1962, as *The Magnificence of Eszterháza*)

M. Kindermann: *Theatergeschichte Europas*, iv–v (Salzburg, 1961–2)

E. Povoledo: 'Les premières représentations des opéras de Rossini et la tradition scénographique italienne de l'époque', *Anatomy of an Illusion: 4th International Congress on Theatre Research: Amsterdam 1965*, 31–4

G. Schöne: 'Trois mises en scène de la "Flûte enchantée" de Mozart: Berlin 1816, Weimar 1817 et Munich 1818', ibid, 45–9

A. Downer: *The Eminent Tragedian: William Charles Macready* (Cambridge, MA, 1966)

D. Steinbeck: 'Die Bildinventare des Münchner Hoftheaters: zur Ausstattungspraxis der Oper im späten 19. Jahrhundert', *Maske und Kothurn*, xiii (1967), 141–7

D. Heartz: 'From Garrick to Gluck: the Reform of Theatre and Opera in the Mid-Eighteenth Century', *PRMA*, xciv (1967–8), 111–27

J. Warrack: *Carl Maria von Weber* (London, 1968, 2/1976)

J. M. da Silva Correira: 'Teatros régios do século xviii', *Bolètim do Museo nacional de arte antiga* [Lisbon], v/3–4 (1969), 24–38

S. Hansell: 'Stage Deportment and Scenographic Design in the Italian *Opera Seria* of the *Settecento*', *IMSCR, xi Copenhagen 1972*, i, 415–424

H. C. Wolff: 'Das Bühnenbild um die Mitte des 19. Jahrhunderts', *Bühnenformen-Bühnenräume-Bühnendekorationen … : Herbert A. Frenzel zum 65. Geburtstag* (Berlin, 1974), 148–59

D. Barnett: 'The Performance Practice of Acting: the 18th Century', *Theatre Research International*, ii (1976–7), 157–86; iii (1977–8), 1–19, 79–93; v (1979–80), 1–36; vi (1980–81), 1–32

H. R. Cohen: 'On the Reconstruction of the Visual Elements of French Grand Opera: Unexplored Sources in Parisian Collections', *IMSCR, xii Berkeley 1977*, 463–81

D. Rosen: 'The Staging of Verdi's Operas: an Introduction to the Ricordi *Disposizioni sceniche*', *IMSCR, xii Berkeley 1977*, 444–53

H. Busch: *Verdi's 'Aida': The History of an Opera in Letters and Documents* (Minneapolis, 1978)

H. R. Cohen and M.-O. Gigou: 'La conservation de la tradition scénique sur la scène lyrique en France au XIXe siècle: les livrets de mise en scène et la Bibliothèque de l'Association de la Régie Théâtrale', *RdM*, lxiv (1978), 253–67

H. C. Robbins Landon: *Haydn: Chronicle and Works*, ii: *Haydn at Eszterháza 1766–1790* (London, 1978)

D. Coe: 'The Original Production Book for *Otello*: an Introduction', *19th Century Music*, ii (1978–9), 148–58

J. Black: 'Cammarano's Notes for the Staging of *Lucia di Lammermoor*', *Donizetti Society Journal*, iv (1980), 29–44

M. McClymonds: *Niccolò Jommelli: the Last Years 1769–1774* (Ann Arbor, 1980)

L. Zeppegno: *Il manuale di Verdi* (Rome, 1980)

J. Black: *The Italian Romantic Libretto: a Study of Salvadore Cammarano* (Edinburgh, 1984)

R. Fajon: *L'Opéra à Paris du Roi-Soleil à Louis le Bien-Aimé* (Geneva, 1984)

H. R. Cohen: 'A Survey of French Sources for the Staging of Verdi's Operas: "Livrets de mise en scène", Annotated Scores and Annotated Libretti in Two Parisian Collections', *Studi verdiani*, iii (1985), 11–44

M. Ottlová and M. Popíšil: 'Oper und Spektakel im 19. Jahrhundert', *Mf*, xxxviii (1985), 1–8

P. Trarieux: *L'Opéra-Comique de Paris et son décor* (diss., U. of Paris-Sorbonne, 1985)

H. R. Cohen and M. O. Gigou: *Cent ans de mise en scène lyrique en France (env. 1830–1930)* (Paris, 1986)

D. Barnett: *The Art of Gesture: the Practices and Principles of Eighteenth-Century Acting* (Heidelberg, 1987)

C. Dahlhaus: 'Operndramaturgie im 19. Jahrhundert', *AcM*, lix (1987), 32–5

H. R. Cohen, ed.: *The Original Staging Manuals for Twelve Parisian Operatic Premières* (New York, 1991)

WAGNER ONWARDS

H. Porges: *Bühnenproben zu den Bayreuther Festspielen des Jahres 1876* (Chemnitz and Leipzig, 1881–96, repr. 1896; Eng. trans.,

1983, as *Wagner Rehearsing the Ring*)

A. Appia: *La mise en scène du drame wagnérien* (Paris, 1895; Eng. trans., 1982)

——: *Die Musik und die Inszenierung* (Munich, 1899; Eng. trans., 1962; Fr. orig., 1963)

C. Hagemann: *Oper und Szene: Aufsätze zur Regie des musikalischen Dramas* (Berlin and Leipzig, 1905)

R. Fricke: *Bayreuth vor dreissig Jahren: Erinnerungen an Wahnfried und aus dem Festspielhause* (Dresden, 1906); Eng. trans., *Wagner*, xi (1990), 93–109, 134–50, and xii (1991), 3–24 [diary kept by production assistant at first Bayreuth Festival]

K. MacGowan and R. E. Jones: *Continental Stagecraft* (New York, 1922)

L. Moussinac: *Tendances nouvelles du théâtre* (Paris, 1931; Eng. trans., 1931)

V. I. Nemirovich-Danchenko: *Iz proshlovo* (Moscow, 1936; Eng. trans., 1936, as *My Life in the Russian Theatre*)

E. Preetorius: *Wagner: Bild und Vision* (Berlin, 1942)

C. Niessen: *Die deutsche Oper der Gegenwart* (Regensburg, 1944)

D. Magarshack, ed.: *Stanislavsky on the Art of the Stage* (London, 1950)

O. F. Schuh: *Salzburger Dramaturgie* (Vienna, 1951)

A. Appia: 'Notes on mise en scène pour l'Anneau de Nibelungen (1891–1892)', *Revue d'histoire du théâtre*, vi/1–2 (1954), 46–59

G. Kernodle: 'Wagner, Appia and the Idea of Musical Design', *Educational Theatre Journal*, vi (1954), 223–30

F. Herzfeld: *Das neue Bayreuth* (Berlin, 1960)

W. Felsenstein and S. Melchinger: *Musiktheater* (Bremen, 1961)

H. Graf: *Producing Opera for America* (New York, 1961)

M. Koerth: *Felsenstein auf der Probe* (Berlin, 1961)

W. E. Schäfer: *Gunther Rennert, Regisseur in dieser Zeit* (Bremen, 1962)

W. Wagner, ed.: *Richard Wagner und das neue Bayreuth* (Munich, 1962)

F. Hadamowsky, ed.: *Max Reinhardt: Ausgewählte Briefe, Reden, Schriften und Szenen aus Regiebüchern* (Vienna, 1963)

O. F. Schuh and F. Willnauer: *Bühne als geistiger Raum* (Bremen, 1963)

Z. Strzelecki: *Polska plastyka teatralna* (Warsaw, 1963)

W. Panofsky: *Wieland Wagner* (Bremen, 1964)

G. Skelton: *Wagner at Bayreuth: Experiment and Tradition* (London, 1965, 2/1976)

W. Felsenstein: 'Towards Music Theatre', *Opera 66*, ed. C. Osborne (London, 1966), 54–75 [Eng. trans. of address in Leipzig, 1965]

V. Gollancz: *The 'Ring' at Bayreuth: and Some Thoughts on Operatic Production* (London, 1966)

G. Friedrich: *Walter Felsenstein: Weg und Werk* (Berlin, 1967)

G. N. Smith: *Luchino Visconti* (London, 1967)

A. Goléa: *Gespräche mit Wieland Wagner* (Salzburg, 1968)

W. R. Volbach: *Adolphe Appia: Prophet of the Modern Theatre* (Middletown, CT, 1968)

N. I. Sokolova, V. F. Rïndin and B. I. Volkov, eds.: *50 let sovetskogo iskusstva: Khudozhniki teatra* [50 Years of Soviet Art: Artists of the Theatre] (Moscow, 1969)

D. Petzet and M. Petzet: *Die Richard Wagner-Bühne König Ludwigs II.* (Munich, 1970)

J. Roose-Evans: *Experimental Theatre: from Stanislavsky to Peter Brook* (London, 1970, 4/1989)

W. E. Schäfer: *Wieland Wagner: Persönlichkeit und Leistung* (Tübingen, 1970)

W. R. Volbach, ed.: *Adolphe Appia: Essays and Scenarios* (Amherst, MA, 1970)

H. Schubert: *Moderner Theaterbau: internationale Situation, Dokumentation, Projekte, Bühnentechnik* (Stuttgart, 1971; Eng. trans., 1971)

G. Skelton: *Wieland Wagner: the Positive Sceptic* (London, 1971)

U. Artioli: *Teorie della scena dal naturalismo al surrealismo* (Florence, 1972)

P. Baldelli: *Luchino Visconti* (Milan, 1973)

G. Zeh: *Das Bayreuther Bühnenkostüm* (Munich, 1973)

H. Fetting, ed.: *Max Reinhardt: Briefe, Reden, Aufsätze, Interviews, Gespräche, Auszüge aus Regiebüchern* (Berlin, 1974)

G. Strehler: *Per un teatro umano* (Milan, 1974)

J. Fiebach: *Von Craig bis Brecht: Studien zu Künstlertheorien in der ersten Hälfte des 20. Jahrhunderts* (Berlin, 1975)

P. P. Fuchs, ed.: *The Music Theatre of Walter Felsenstein* (New York, 1975)

G. Giertz: *Kultus ohne Götter: Emile Jaques-Dalcroze und Adolphe Appia: Versuch einer Theaterreform auf der Grundlage der rhythmischen Gymnastik* (Munich, 1975)

E. R. Hapgood, ed.: *Stanislavsky on Opera* (New York, 1975)

W. Felsenstein: *Schriften zum Musiktheater* (Berlin, 1976)

D. Kranz: *Gespräche mit Felsenstein* (Berlin, 1976)

D. Mack: *Der Bayreuther Inszenierungsstil 1876–1976* (Munich, 1976)

R. Hartmann: *Opera* (New York, 1977) [on production techniques]

H.-J. Irmer and W. Stein: *Joachim Herz: Regisseur im Musiktheater* (Berlin, 1977)

A. Rood: *Gordon Craig on Movement and Dance* (New York, 1977)

P. Barz: *Götz Friedrich* (Bonn, 1978)

C. d'Amico de Carvalho, ed.: *Album Visconti* (Milan, 1978)

C. d'Amico and R. Renzi, eds.: *Luchino Visconti: Il mio teatro* (Bologna, 1979)

H. Barth, ed.: *Bayreuther Dramaturgie: 'Der Ring des Nibelungen'* (Stuttgart, 1980)

C. Baumann: *Bühnentechnik im Festspielhaus Bayreuth* (Munich, 1980)

H. J. Gund: *Die Wagner-Bühnenbilder der Pariser Oper von 1891 bis 1914* (diss., U. of Freiburg, 1980)

R. Hartford, ed.: *Bayreuth: the Early Years* (London and New York, 1980)

A. M. Nagler: *Malaise in der Oper: Opernregie in unseren Jahrhundert* (Rheinfelden, 1980; Eng. trans., 1981, as *Misdirection: Opera Production in the Twentieth Century*)

H. Christian: *Die Wiener Staatsoper 1945–1980: eine Dokumentation* (Vienna, 1981)

R. Hartmann: *Richard Strauss: the Staging of his Operas and Ballets* (New York, 1981)

S. Hughes: *Glyndebourne: a History of the Festival Opera* (Newton Abbot, 1981)

A. Tubeuf: *Bayreuth et Wagner: cent ans d'images, 1876–1976* (Paris, 1981)

O. Bauer: *Richard Wagner: Die Bühnenwerke von der Uraufführung bis heute* (Fribourg, 1982; Eng. trans., 1982)

D. Borchmeyer: *Das Theater Richard Wagners: Idee, Dichtung, Wirkung* (Stuttgart, 1982)

E. Braun: *The Director and the Stage* (London, 1982)

J. Kaut: *Die Salzburger Festspiele, 1920–1981* (Salzburg, 1982)

J. L. Styan: *Max Reinhardt* (Cambridge, 1982)

C. Innes: *Edward Gordon Craig* (Cambridge, 1983)

S. Jaeger, ed.: *Götz Friedrich: Wagner-Regie* (Zürich, 1983)

J.-J. Nattiez: *Tétralogies – Wagner, Boulez, Chéreau: Essai sur l'infidélité* (Paris, 1983)

J. M. Walton, ed.: *Craig on Theatre* (London, 1983)

N. Ely and S. Jaeger, eds.: *Regie heute: Musiktheater in unserer Zeit* (Berlin, 1984)

I. Bontinck: *Angebot, Repertoire und Publikum des Musiktheaters in Wien und Graz* (Vienna, 1985)

M. Ewans: 'Two Centenary Productions of *The Ring* at Bayreuth: the Bayreuth Centenary *Ring* by Patrice Chéreau and Pierre Boulez', *MMA*, xiv (1985), 167–73

R. M. Jacobson: *Magnificence: Onstage at the Met – Twenty Great Opera Productions* (London, 1985)

P. Boulez: 'A Performer's Notebook', *Orientations*, ed. J.-J. Nattiez (London, 1986), 278–91, esp. 286–9 [Eng. trans. of article pubd as 'La tétralogie: commentaire d'expérience' in *Bayreuther Festspiele: Programmheft VI. Siegfried* (Bayreuth, 1977), 9–14]

B. Millington: 'Saucepans of Spaghetti: a Semiology of Opera Criticism', *MT*, cxxvii (1986), 333–5

F. Peixoto: *Opera e encenacão* (Rio de Janeiro, 1986)

D. Harris: 'Full Cycle: how the *Ring* has been Staged since Wagner's Day', *ON*, li/12 (1986–7), 12–14, 45

R. Beacham: *Adolphe Appia* (Cambridge, 1987)

M. Eggert and H. K. Jungheinrich, eds.: *Durchbrüche: Die Oper Frankfurts* (Weinheim, 1987)

B. Millington: 'The *Ring* according to Berghaus', *MT*, cxxviii (1987), 491–2

S. Neef: 'Ein Anfang und kein Ende: Bühnenwerke des 20. Jahrhunderts an der Deutschen Staatsoper Berlin', *Musik und Gesellschaft*, xxxvii (1987), 252–8

J. Tambling: *Opera, Ideology and Film* (Manchester, 1987)

D. Kranz: *Der Regisseur Harry Kupfer: 'Ich muss Oper machen'* (Berlin, 1988)

M. Lewin: *Harry Kupfer* (Vienna and Zürich, 1988)

M. Srocke: *Richard Wagner als Regisseur* (Berlin, 1988)

E. Burzawa: 'Die *Walküre* von Sergej Eisenstein: Versuch der Rekonstruktion', *Richard Wagner und sein Mittelalter*, ed. U. Müller and U. Müller (Salzburg, 1989), 299–313

R. Leach: *Vsevelod Meyerhold* (Cambridge, 1989)

R. Lummer: *Regie im Theater: Harry Kupfer* (Frankfurt, 1989)

S. Neef: *Das Theater der Ruth Berghaus* (Berlin, 1989)

A. Peattie: 'Following Felsenstein', *Opera Now*, no.5 (1989), 52–7

H. Pleasants: *Opera in Crisis: Tradition, Present, Future* (London, 1989)

K. Bertisch: *Ruth Berghaus* (Frankfurt, 1990)

R. Donington: *Opera and its Symbols: the Unity of Words, Music, and Staging* (New Haven, CT, 1990)

I. Kobán, ed.: *Joachim Herz: Interviews* (Berlin, 1990)

M. Ashman: 'Producing Wagner', *Wagner in Performance*, ed. B. Millington and S. Spencer (New Haven, CT, 1992), 29–47

P. Carnegy: 'Designing Wagner: Deeds of Music Made Visible?', ibid, 48–74

ROGER SAVAGE (1–5), BARRY MILLINGTON (6–7), JOHN COX (8)

Production book (Fr., *livret de mise en scène*; Ger. *Regiebuch*; It. *disposizione scenica, messa in scena*). A text in which the setting and action of a production of a stage work is described in detail, usually with diagrams and sometimes incorporating a complete libretto. It is usually prepared by the director in the form of a manuscript or typescript and is sometimes distributed as a booklet printed for restricted use or general sale, often by the publisher of the music.

In France, a tradition developed in the early 19th century of compiling a detailed *livret de mise en scène* for *opéras comiques* and *mélodrames*, to fix their staging for the benefit of provincial directors. It may have been as a result of his experiences in Paris that Verdi initiated the *disposizioni sceniche* that appeared with his operas from *Les vêpres siciliennes* (1855) onwards; eight of these are known, the first, of 38 pages, embodying a clear, rudimentary 'traffic plan' of the opera's action, the last, for *Otello* (1887), containing 100 pages of stage directions and 270 diagrams, in effect a moment-by-moment dramatic analysis. (For further discussion *see* PRODUCTION, §5.)

Such published books were common, especially towards the end of the 19th century, when it was likely that a new opera would be given in several different cities or countries soon after its première. Their usefulness continued only as long as the notion that the composer and librettist's requirements were going to be met by those staging the work elsewhere. The further availability of costume sketches from first performances led to the widespread customs over the clothing of characters which gave certain popular repertory operas such an immediately recognizable look: for example, the high cane, poke bonnet and directoire dress that are immediately identifiable with Tosca, the striped tights worn by Faust, and the boater and battered suitcase carried by Jenny in Weill's *Der Aufstieg und Fall der Stadt Mahagonny* (the score of which contains Brecht's detailed stage directions which themselves amount to a production book) all hark back to the first stagings of the works. Since the rise of the conception of the director as interpreter, wishing to stage operas according to his or her own view of their meaning, the role of the published production book has diminished.

Since very little detailed, descriptive dramatic criticism exists for many early operas, such sets of instructions, where they survive, are invaluable for giving an idea of how the creators of a work envisaged its staging. With a move to follow the period-instrument movement with a corresponding one to re-create authentic stagings, in which not only the original settings and costumes but the use of artificial lighting, make-up and movement might be emulated, these books may be of especial value. Some of the most detailed ones list the furniture and props required on the stage and have diagrams to show exactly where each should be placed.

For illustration of production books *see* GRAND OPÉRA, fig.2 (*Guillaume Tell*); MANON LESCAUT (ii); OTELLO (ii); PRODUCTION, fig.15 (*La muette de Portici*) and 17 (*Les vêpres siciliennes*); SIMON BOCCANEGRA; and for a costume specification ROSENKAVALIER, DER.

PATRICK O'CONNOR

Programme [program] (Fr. *programme*; Ger. *Programm*, *Theaterzettel*; It. *programma*). A leaflet or booklet containing details of the entertainments to be offered, listed in order of performance, which may be either sold or given to the audience; it can range from a single-leaf handbill to an elaborately produced book. The word was also used in the early 19th century to mean the synopsis of the plot of an opera or drama. The origins of the opera programme lie in the libretto and the playbill, and the dividing line between playbill and programme is hazy. Research into the history of the programme is still at a preliminary stage.

From the 17th century, most opera audiences had access during a performance to a copy of the printed libretto, which was usually available for purchase in the theatre (or sometimes given free to subscribers). In many countries, until the late 19th century, a new edition of the libretto was customarily published for each opera production; this would not only give the text of the version being produced but normally, especially after 1700, the name of the theatre, the date or season of the production, the names of the librettist and composer, a list of the cast and other musical and theatre staff, a historical note, a synopsis of any ballet and often further information besides. The playbill, published daily, would usually name all the performers, mention any last-minute changes of cast or programme, provide details of curtain time, admission, benefits and of all the entertainments of music, drama and dancing to be given during the evening; it would also list forthcoming attractions. Armed with libretto and playbill, operagoers had all the information they needed.

Playbills, especially in London, grew enormously in size from the 1820s and by the middle of the century had become too unwieldy to be used conveniently as programmes inside the theatre: Covent Garden's bills of around 1850 measured about 50 cm square, with a central vertical fold. During the 1850s the theatre began to print its standard bill in two sizes, of which much the smaller (25.5×33 cm, folded vertically and still printed on only one side) was more practical for use in a crowded auditorium.

Covent Garden was not, however, the first theatre to issue a small folded leaflet. The true prototype of the modern programme was introduced by Benjamin Lumley at Her Majesty's Theatre (formerly the King's Theatre) in February 1847. This was an eight-page programme (29×19 cm when folded), printed on both sides of a single sheet and folded twice (first horizontally, then vertically). The front page contained the cast-lists and details of admission (see fig.1), the centre pages a synopsis in English and French of the evening's opera and ballet, with engraved vignettes depicting scenes from the action, and the back page the conclusion of the synopses and announcements of future performances; the remaining pages contained advertisements, with occasional notes relating to theatrical matters.

Other London theatres were very slow to follow the pioneering example of Her Majesty's, which itself abandoned the new design after a single season. Drury

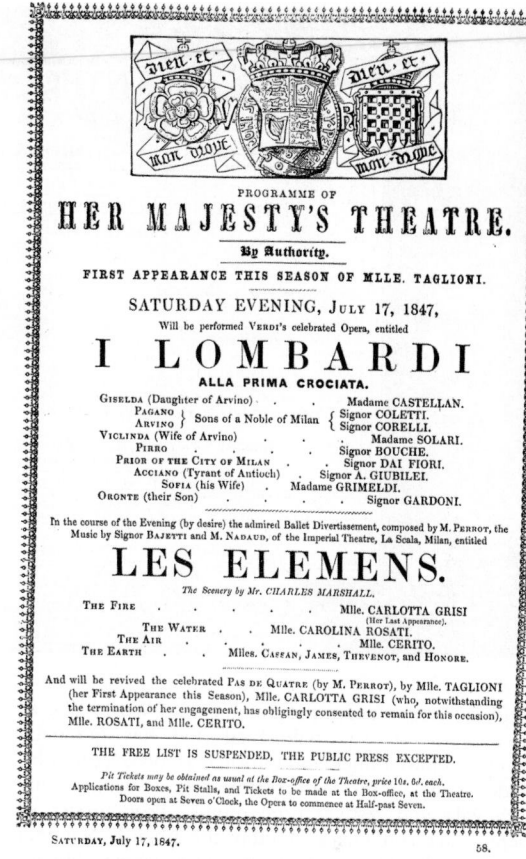

1. First page of a programme for Her Majesty's Theatre, London, for a performance of Verdi's 'I Lombardi' on 17 July 1847

Lane, the Adelphi and the Gaiety, homes of the lighter forms of opera, adopted Covent Garden's two-page format and in the early 1860s started to issue bills that applied to a whole week or even to longer periods; this soon became a widespread practice. By the mid-1860s most programme leaflets were being printed on both sides, and this new four-page programme began to contain features such as puffs and occasional critical or historical articles. From the early 1860s several theatres adopted a style of programme sponsored by the perfumery firm of Eugene Rimmel; embossed with decorative borders, these carried Rimmel's advertisements and were sprayed with their perfume. During the 1870s many theatres personalized their programmes by using decorative title-pages or distinctive designs. Distinctiveness was also achieved from the late 1870s by chromolithographic printing: an early example was the Opera Comique programme for *HMS Pinafore* (1878), and other Gilbert and Sullivan programmes for the Savoy, especially in the 1880s, were printed on card and exquisitely decorated with ornate borders and depictions of the main characters and scenes from the operas (see fig.2). From this period advertising in programmes became more extensive and often carried illustrations.

In the mid-1890s, Covent Garden adopted a four-page programme in which the details of the production and a synopsis of the plot were printed in panels surrounded by advertisements; the inside pages normally contained details of other operas currently in production. This remained the basic format of the

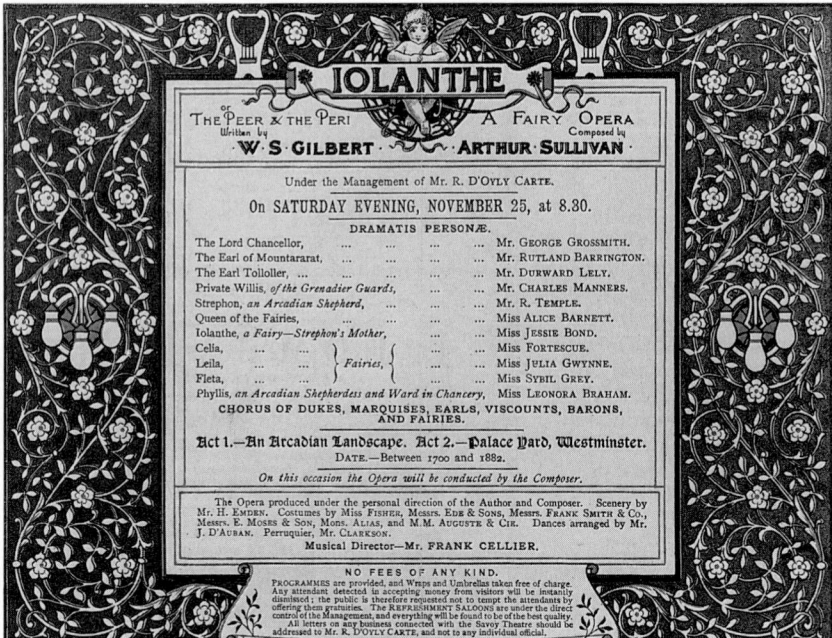

2. Inner pages of the programme for the original production of Gilbert and Sullivan's 'Iolanthe' at the Savoy Theatre, London, 25 November 1882

regular Covent Garden programme until World War II, after which it was redesigned and has gradually developed into a thick and informative booklet that includes many of the features formerly associated only with gala and festival programmes. Programmes of many other companies, notably the English National Opera at the London Coliseum, are comparably informative.

Programmes for galas and special events, as well as those for festivals and seasons given by touring companies, date from early in the 20th century. These are often elaborate publications, sometimes dealing with up to a dozen or so operas; they are likely to include photographs and biographies of the conductor, the principal singers and dancers and others associated with the production, the names of the orchestra, chorus and theatre staff, illustrations of the sets and costumes, articles relating to various aspects of the operas and

their origins, plans of the theatre, the names of patrons and committee members, and numerous advertisements. The Glyndebourne Festival programme book for 1991, which contains no fewer than 190 pages, is by no means exceptional. Programmes of this size and complexity are of course expensive to print and to buy, and sometimes simple cast-lists are available free of charge in the theatre.

Preliminary research suggests that London led the way in the early development of the opera programme and that many of the features present in the modern programme were initiated there; but, during more than half a century when Covent Garden was printing a four-page programme that provided only minimal information, many opera houses worldwide were issuing substantial booklets. In these, however, often only one or two leaves would relate specifically to the day's performance: such leaves would be stapled or loosely in-

3. Front cover of the 'programme illustré' for the original production of Messager's 'Véronique' at the Théâtre des Bouffes-Parisiens, Paris, during the 1898–9 season

4. Front cover of the standard programme of La Scala, Milan, 1911–12

serted into the remainder of the programme, which would contain advertisements and more general matter and would be used unaltered over a period of days, weeks or even for the whole season.

In Paris, importance was given from an early date to the pictorial content of opera programmes. An interesting series of souvenir programmes of dramas and operettas performed at the smaller theatres was published by Le Photo from 1895; 210 numbers appeared within four years (see fig.3). The series was particularly valuable for its photographs of the principal members of the cast and illustrations of the set designs. The regular programmes of the Opéra-Comique from early this century contain excellent photographs of the singers in costume, and the main Paris opera houses have maintained to the present day a high standard in this respect.

See also LIBRETTO (i) and PLAYBILL.

ES ('Programma'; J. Laver)
G. Enthoven: 'Playbill, Programme', *Oxford Companion to the Theatre*, ed. P. Hartnoll (London, 1951, 3/1967), 742–4
J. J. Fuld: 'Music Programs and Posters: the Need for an Inventory', *Notes*, xxxvii (1980–81), 520–32   RICHARD MACNUTT

Prohaska, Felix (*b* Vienna, 16 May 1912; *d* Vienna, 29 March 1987). Austrian conductor, son of Karl Prohaska. He studied the piano with Eduard Steuermann and theory with Hans Gál, Felix Salzer and Oswald Jonas. While teaching at the Graz Conservatory (1936–9) he was also active as co-répétiteur at the opera there. From 1939 to 1941 he conducted at the opera in Duisburg, and from 1941 to 1943 at the German Opera in Strasbourg, at the same time directing the opera class

at the Strasbourg Conservatory. From 1943 to 1945 he conducted the German Opera in Prague and he was a conductor of the Staatsoper in der Volksoper, Vienna, from 1946 to 1955, combining the appointment with a teaching post at the conservatory. Prohaska was Generalmusikdirektor at Frankfurt (1955–61) and after a period back at Vienna he conducted at Hanover (1965–74) and then Kiel. He appeared as a guest conductor at Salzburg (1945–6), Perugia (1951), Copenhagen (1952 and 1956) and South America, and made many recordings.   OTHMAR WESSELY

Prohaska, Jaro(slav) (*b* Vienna, 24 Jan 1891; *d* Munich, 28 Sept 1965). Austrian bass-baritone. He studied at the Vienna Academy (1919–23) and made his début in 1922 at Lübeck. After an engagement at Nuremberg (1925–31) he joined the Berlin Staatsoper, of which he remained a member until 1952, taking part in the première of Graener's *Der Prinz von Homburg* (1935). He sang regularly at Bayreuth (1933–44) as Hans Sachs, Wotan, Gunther, Telramund, Amfortas and the Dutchman. He appeared at the Teatro Colón, Buenos Aires (1935 and 1937) and at the Paris Opéra (1936 and 1940). In addition to Wagner roles his repertory included Ochs, which he sang at the 1949 Salzburg Festival.   HAROLD ROSENTHAL/R

Prohaska, Karl (*b* Mödling, nr Vienna, 25 April 1869; *d* Vienna, 28 March 1927). Austrian composer. His teachers included Eugen d'Albert (for piano), and Brahms showed an interest in his musical development. In 1894–5 he was a stage assistant at the Bayreuth Festival; later he was famous as a teacher of theory and the piano in Vienna. In his compositions, which include the opera *Madeleine Guimard* (L. Braun; Breslau, 28 May 1930; lib. pubd Vienna, 1930), he took the Romantic styles of Schumann and Brahms as a point of departure, but also drew on the harmonic techniques of his own time.

N. Latzko: 'Madeleine Guimard in Aussig', *Rheinische Musik- und Theaterzeitung*, xxx (1929), 15   OTHMAR WESSELY

Prokofiev [Prokof'yev; Prokofieff], **Sergey** [Serge] **(Sergeyevich)** (*b* Sontsovka, Bakhmut district, Yekaterinoslav guberniya [now Krasnoye, Selidovsky district, Donetsk region, Ukraine], 15/27 April 1891; *d* Moscow, 5 March 1953). Russian composer.

1. Pre-Soviet period. 2. The 1930s. 3. The 1940s.

1. PRE-SOVIET PERIOD. Prokofiev's operatic career began at the age of eight (with *Velikan*, 'The Giant', a 12-page opera in three acts), and he always saw himself first and foremost as a composer of music for the lyric stage. If this seems surprising, it is not only because of Prokofiev's great success in the realm of instrumental concert music but also because of the singularly unlucky fate of his operas. Of the seven he completed, he saw only four produced; of the four, only two survived their initial production; and of the two, only one really entered the repertory. As usual in such cases, the victim has been blamed: 'Through all his writings about opera there runs a streak of loose thinking and naivety', wrote one critic, 'and it runs through the works, too'. That – plus a revolution, a world war and a repressive totalitarian regime whose unfathomable vagaries the composer could never second-guess – indeed made for a

frustrating career. Yet time has begun to vindicate some of those long-suffering works, and we may be glad that despite everything (and unlike Shostakovich) Prokofiev persisted as an operatic composer practically to the end.

The charge of 'naivety' derives from Prokofiev's life-long commitment to what might be called the traditions of Russian operatic radicalism. The ideal to which he always remained true, however much circumstances may have eventually mandated departure, was that of the through-composed dialogue opera, following the precedent set in Russia by Dargomïzhsky's *The Stone Guest* and Musorgsky's *Marriage*. Like the later *Pelléas* and *Salome*, these works of the 1860s were already 'sung plays' (to borrow Joseph Kerman's useful term) – that is, verbatim settings of pre-existing stage dramas, in which the whole idea of *dramma per musica* was scrapped in the interests of 'truth', and problems of operatic 'form' and libretto structure finessed. *The Stone Guest* was a setting of one of the four so-called 'little tragedies' in verse that Pushkin had written in 1830. Another of them was *Pir vo vremya chumï* ('A Feast in Time of Plague'), of which Prokofiev made two fragmentary settings as an adolescent, the second of them (1908) a furious declamatory scena on the concluding priestly harangue, which he played the next year at his final examination (in 'form') at the St Petersburg Conservatory and succeeded as planned in exasperating his professors, Anatoly Lyadov and Alexander Glazunov.

By the time of his graduation he had heard *Marriage*, which received its incredibly belated première in 1909 at one of the legendary St Petersburg 'Evenings of Contemporary Music'. An even bolder break with established operatic tradition than the residually lyrical *Stone Guest*, Musorgsky's 'experiment in dramatic music in prose' (to quote its subtitle), on the text of the opening scenes from a terse misogynistic comedy by Gogol, fully deserved the sobriquet 'recitative opera'. Virtually all shaping in it is accomplished by the text and a few rather skimpily deployed leitmotifs, but the musical interest is at all times centred on the voice parts, never the accompaniment.

In 1915 Prokofiev went abroad for the first time and heard Dyagilev and Stravinsky disparage opera as an outmoded form, destined to be superseded by the ballet. The effect of their then-fashionable strictures, curiously, was to imbue the young composer with a mission to revitalize the doomed genre. Returning to St Petersburg, he wangled a commission from Albert Coates, then conducting at the Mariinsky, and went to work on *Igrok* ('The Gambler', on his own prose libretto after Dostoyevsky's novella), in which Musorgsky's principles of one-act anti-opera would be applied at full evening's length. Press interviews Prokofiev gave in 1916, shortly after completing the opera, fairly paraphrase the militant letters Musorgsky had written around the time of *Marriage* and the first version of *Boris Godunov* – letters that had come out in book form that very year. Like Musorgsky, he called for the abolition of set pieces in favour of freely flowing dialogue, dismissing verse texts as 'an utterly absurd convention', and denying that the dramaturgy of opera need differ in any way from that of the spoken drama. But there was an important difference: where Musorgsky's motivation had been a lofty neo-Aristotelian conviction that mimesis of speech was the key to mimesis of emotion, Prokofiev's concerns were more narrowly those of stagecraft (he called it 'scenic flow').

Thus in practice Prokofiev's 'dialogue opera' technique turned out not to be quite so uncompromising as Musorgsky's had been, enabling him, as his friend Nikolay Myaskovsky put it, to solve 'the problem set by *Marriage*' and other works of its kind 'in a way that gives music its due'. More sensitive than either Dargomïzhsky or Musorgsky to considerations of musical form, abstractly conceived (possibly because, unlike them, he was after all a conservatory graduate), Prokofiev was far more disposed than they to give his vocal compositions an easily comprehended general shape. He made considerable use of generalizing accompaniments both to unify long spans and thereafter to return in significant or recapitulatory ways. Often, too, recurrent melodies (whether outright leitmotifs or not) have a way of accompanying his voice parts at formally strategic moments even if they are not actually sung.

Prokofiev's most characteristic and original operatic technique is one that might be termed the 'melodic mould' – a simple melodic idea (i.e. pitch sequence) into which just about any line of prose can be poured by observing Musorgskian rules of good declamation. (These rules, easily inferable from *Marriage*, primarily involve the regular spacing of the tonic accents according to the metrical scheme, and the arrangement of the unaccented syllables around them in freely varying *gruppetti*.) The most compact instance of the technique in Prokofiev's early operas is the small part of the Innkeeper in the first scene of *Ognennïy angel* ('The Fiery Angel', completed 1923, after Bryusov). Her two appearances are framed by lines set to the same melodic mould, which serves not only as an identifying leitmotif but also as a form definer, since it ties her appearances into neat little *ABA* packages (ex.1).

Whatever the concessions to 'purely musical' considerations, however, Prokofiev made sure that not one of his pre-Soviet operas sported so much as a single closed vocal number. The only 'detachable' music in them, so to speak, is orchestral, for example the March and Scherzo from *Lyubov' k tryom apel'sinam* ('The Love for Three Oranges', 1919, after Gozzi by way of Vsevolod Meyerhold). In the case of *The Gambler* and *The Fiery Angel*, detaching the music for concert use required considerable recasting (in the case of *The Gambler* into the suite, *Four Portraits*; in the case of *The Fiery Angel* into the Third Symphony). The composer sought, and in large measure achieved, a truly continuous scenic action, supported by music that asserted perhaps a more conspicuous shaping role than in the works that provided him with his most immediate models, and yet where – in keeping with just about every Russian composer's anti-Wagnerian credo – at least as much melodic interest was concentrated in the voice part as in the orchestra. Though leitmotifs were admitted into Prokofiev's operatic technique, their use is restrained and rather primitive compared with the Wagnerian prototype, lest they subvert the nature of the sung play by turning it into a 'symphonic poem' (to cite the other member of Kerman's dichotomy).

Difficulties with casting and direction prevented *The Gambler* from reaching the stage on schedule; the revolution the next year finished its foreseeable chances. Meyerhold's announced production in 1929 was frustrated by militant opposition from the Russian Association of Proletarian Musicians (RAPM), an omen Prokofiev (naively) chose not to heed. The work was finally produced in Brussels that year in a French

Ex.1 Melodic mould technique in *The Fiery Angel*, Act 1 scene i

['Here, Sir Knight, this is the best room']

['Perhaps Sir Knight would like some wine or some lamb?']

['Ah, Sir Knight, better not ask about her']

['Farewell, Sir Knight, and may Heaven protect thee from her!']

translation; but an operatic style so founded on declamational procedures suffers translation badly. (That Prokofiev continued to write declamational operas on Russian prose texts during his years of emigration indicates that he always had a Russian audience in mind.) *The Love for Three Oranges* could make its way despite the linguistic handicap because of its profusion of visual gags (and its higher proportion of illustrative orchestral music); it was the single Prokofiev opera that could be called a success within his lifetime. *The Fiery Angel*, though, found no favour with Western European or American impresarios (though a Berlin production under Bruno Walter was briefly contemplated). By the time Prokofiev returned to his Soviet homeland (a gradual process complete by 1936), the opera was in a double bind, for Soviet arts policy by then precluded its performance. The utter waste of this score, on which Prokofiev had laboured on and off for eight years and which he regarded as his *chef d'oeuvre*, was the greatest fiasco of his career.

2. THE 1930S. And yet, ironically enough, his inability to get *The Fiery Angel* produced seems in large part to have motivated his return. Frustrated in his bid for leadership in the world of Parisian modernism, where he saw he would always play second fiddle to Stravinsky (and feeling that 'there is no room for me' in America 'while Rakhmaninov is alive'), he beat a tactical retreat to a more provincial pond where he would be beyond dispute the biggest fish. The dissolution of the RAPM in 1932 seemed to remove the last obstacle; it was in that year that Prokofiev accepted Soviet citizenship, though he maintained his Paris apartment until 1936. He finally agreed to give it up when he allowed himself at last to become convinced that he would be exempt from overt political pressure.

That, if anything, was naive. And yet at first Prokofiev managed, even as he appeared to be accommodating himself to a new discipline, to justify writing the kind of opera he believed in. An essay of 1940 describing his first Soviet opera, *Semyon Kotko* (after a novella by Valentin Katayev), is very much to the point. Despite the oft-quoted lip service paid there to 'a new people, new

feelings, a new life [requiring] new means of expression', it is evident that the new means – new, that is, to Soviet audiences – were in fact Prokofiev's accustomed manner. Recognizing that Soviet arts policy was becoming increasingly orientated towards the safest elements in the Russian 'classical heritage', Prokofiev (not usually credited with political adroitness) adopted a sly tactic: he paraphrased a well-known letter to Mme von Meck in which Tchaikovsky, whose centenary was being triumphantly celebrated in 1940, acknowledged his operatic failures and admitted that (in Prokofiev's words now) 'when a person goes to an opera he wants not only to *hear* but to *see*'. Prokofiev cited two kinds of aria, both of which can be found in *Yevgeny Onegin*: the 'Lensky type', which paralyses action, and the type exemplified by Tatyana's Letter Scene, which carries the action along. Prokofiev tacitly expanded the latter category to encompass the whole range of his prosy, through-composed operatic practices, remarking that 'occasionally I have had to substitute vocal parts which, though not arias in the exact sense, offer no less opportunity to the singer'.

Yet there are important differences between *Semyon Kotko* and Prokofiev's earlier operas, suggesting that he did look to the classical Russian tradition for guidance. At this point, however, he did so not directly in response to Soviet pressure (the brunt of which he was yet to feel), but because he was determined not to repeat the staggering failure of *The Fiery Angel*. Most fundamental was a return to basic traditions of contrast-driven dramaturgy he had formerly eschewed as outmoded (e.g. between diatonic good and chromatic evil, between national idioms, between heroic rhetoric and genre detail). Never before in his operatic career had Prokofiev paid the slightest attention to elements of genre or to national character, and his prior dramaturgical convictions had rejected contrast in favour of what he had called in the case of *The Gambler* a 'steady dramatic crescendo'. In *Semyon Kotko* he allowed himself actually to quote one folksong, to imbue tunes of his own devising with characteristically folklike melodic turns and to introduce a limited number of vocal set pieces. Even the prose recitatives were given memorable thematic structure by the use of repeated words and phrases that carry musical repetitions in tow. (Note, for example, all the repetitions of the line 'Nu i s tem dosvidan'ichka', 'Well, with that let's say goodbye', as a transitory leitmotif in Act 2 scene ii, the scene with which Prokofiev began composing the work in March 1939; the leitmotif is then linked motivically with other melodies associated with the positive characters.)

Between the completion of *Semyon Kotko* and its first performance, the Soviet Union signed its non-aggression pact with Germany, making an opera dealing with German interventionism at the time of the post-revolutionary Civil War something of an embarrassment (in the production the Germans became Austrians). Critical opinion was mobilized to retire the opera from the stage on the pretext that its tone did not do justice to the theme of heroism. In fact Prokofiev had given that theme special emphasis of a characteristically Soviet kind. When one of the wedding choruses accompanying the title character's betrothal in Act 2 recurs in the finale, sung to a new text rejoicing in the dawn of Soviet power, the opera palpably crosses the boundary into specifically Soviet aesthetic terrain, as it also does when (using the 'melodic mould' technique) Prokofiev tailors a chorus accompanying the burial of a revolutionary martyr to fit a theme that had previously served as one of Semyon's leitmotifs. To use Semyon's theme as the basis of a general expression of faith in the revolution is to tie the individual to the collective in a way that has obvious connections with the tenets of Socialist Realism (even as the 'realists' of the 19th century had opposed such devices for excessively generalizing the portrayal of character). But it was to no avail: once again a Prokofiev opera fell victim to singularly inopportune timing.

Yet *Semyon Kotko* set the tone for Prokofiev's Soviet operas just as decisively as *The Gambler* had done for the earlier ones. From now on, and definitely under official pressure, Prokofiev would continue in the new direction his work had taken. This meant, first, strengthening the lyric element, both by permitting closed and detachable vocal numbers and by 'musicalizing' his prose declamation (along lines, it should be emphasized, already implicit in his earlier work); secondly, incorporating, at times interpolating, elements of folk and popular music he had formerly shunned; thirdly, fortifying the role of leitmotif, reminiscence and reprise to the point where they could assert their traditional form-governing properties; and, fourthly, seeking ties between his operas and those of the 'classical', rather than the radical, Russian operatic tradition.

3. THE 1940S. Prokofiev's next opera, *Obrucheniye v monastire* ('Betrothal in a Monastery', composed 1940, after Sheridan's *The Duenna*), is usually looked upon as a kind of refuge in comedy, a retreat to a dramatic medium for which Prokofiev's methods were unquestionably suitable, and in which there could be no requirement for heroism. But even in this case there is evidence that Prokofiev consciously 'Sovietized' his style. This can best be seen if *Betrothal in a Monastery* is compared with Prokofiev's other comic opera, *The Love for Three Oranges*. The earlier opera is pure grotesque, and virtually limited in its vocal style to through-composed prose recitative. The later is a lyrical romantic comedy with a heavy reliance on rounded vocal numbers to verse texts (some of them, it is true, inherited directly from Sheridan) and an equally heavy

reliance on the device of reminiscence. Either opera could have been handled in either way; the difference in tone cannot be attributed solely to their literary sources.

Two unfinished projects of the 1940s also involved comic themes. *Khan Buzai*, subtitled 'But the Shah has a Horn!', was planned during summer 1942, during the composer's wartime evacuation to Alma-Ata, capital of the Kazakh SSR. Following a well-known Soviet tradition, it was to have been wholly based on the local folk music (compare Glier's *Shakh-Senem* and *Leyli i Medzhnun*, on Azerbaijani and Uzbek themes respectively), for which the composer could expect to be rewarded with the title 'People's Artist' from the republic in question, a lucrative honorific. At the time Prokofiev was working on three film scores simultaneously – Alma-Ata was the wartime location of the Mosfilm studio – and envisaged the *Khan Buzai* scenario as a series of brief cinematic 'shots'. In summer 1948, under the worst cloud of his career, Prokofiev made a last-ditch effort to compose an ideologically acceptable opera with *Dalyokiye morya* ('Distant Seas'), a sort of operetta with spoken dialogue after *Svadebnoye puteshestviye* ('The Wedding Expedition'), a popular situation comedy by one V. A. Dïkhovichniy about young oceanographers in love. When *The Story of a Real Man* was suppressed for 'formalism' in December of that year a shattered Prokofiev gave up the project with only one scene sketched. It was his farewell to opera.

With *Voyna i mir* ('War and Peace', after Tolstoy), the effort to monumentalize was of course explicit, paramount and – in the opinion of many in the West – fatal. (Ironically, of course, it was just the opposite flaw, pettiness of form and concentration on genre detail, for which the composer was eternally harassed by the Stalinist cultural establishment.) The heroizing process may actually be traced, to the survival of documents from every stage of the opera's arduous gestation. Kutuzov's big aria in Scene 10 – the famous hymn to Moscow, later repeated to form the opera's grand choral finale, and a 'Lensky type' if ever there was one – can serve as object lesson. It was the most rewritten single item in the entire opera. The original conception had been a short arioso linked to the same character's arioso on the battlefield in Scene 8 (in *its* original conception) by shared leitmotivic material. It was conductor Samuil Samosud who goaded Prokofiev into expanding Kutuzov's big moment as befitted the character's manifest role as Stalin-surrogate. After many fruitless attempts, Prokofiev finally adapted a melody he had originally composed in an altogether different context, as part of the score to Sergey Eisenstein's film *Ivan the Terrible*. What was almost uncanny was the way Prokofiev's solution to the problem paralleled Musorgsky's process of revising the title character's central monologue ('I have attained the highest power') in *Boris Godunov*. In both instances declamation over a texture of leitmotifs was rejected in favour of lyrical melody borrowed from a previously composed work (in Musorgsky's case it was the unfinished opera *Salammbô*), and for the identical purpose: exaltation of tone and monumentalization of form.

The final stage of the process was reached in *Povest' o nastoyashchem cheloveke* ('The Story of a Real Man', 1947–8, after a novella by Boris Polevoy), the opera on which Prokofiev was working at the time of his official denunciation in the Zhdanovite 'Resolution on Music' of February 1948. The wish to placate is everywhere apparent. In keeping with the basic requirement of Socialist Realism that art be optimistic, this opera about the agony of an aviator who lost his legs opens with the jolly music of Prokofiev's March for wind band, op.99. The score resounds from first to last with patriotic 'mass songs' and choruses. The dramaturgy and the characterization is at a childish level (as is the harmonic vocabulary, in keeping with Prokofiev's coerced promise in response to the Resolution). And yet even here the composer's basic urge to resolve the question of operatic form in favour of a through-composed 'scenic flow' persists, and finds a novel outlet in the opera's interesting adaptation of cinematic techniques (adumbrated in the *Khan Buzai* libretto) such as flashback and montage.

Through their use Prokofiev managed convincingly to motivate a number of complex ensembles.

Despite all vicissitudes, then, Prokofiev's Soviet operas do not necessarily represent an unmitigated stylistic impoverishment. Setting *War and Peace*, by now a repertory item, alongside *The Gambler*, or especially *The Fiery Angel*, one can see the modifications he made in his methods and resources in response to external demands as introducing a new versatility into his operatic technique, legitimately enriching what had been a rather dogmatic and one-sided approach to musical drama.

See also Betrothal in a Monastery; Fiery angel, the; Gambler, the; Love for three oranges, the; Maddalena; Semyon kotko; Story of a real man, the; and War and peace.

op.	title	genre, acts	libretto	first performance	sources and remarks
			operas unless otherwise stated		
	Velikan [The Giant]	3	Prokofiev and others	Kaluga guberniya, private home, sum. 1901	comp. 1900, MS vs dated 1900, unpubd
	Na pustïnnïkh ostrovakh [On Desert Islands]	ov., 3 scenes of Act 1	Prokofiev		comp. 1900–02, MS vs dated Dec 1900, unpubd
	Pir vo vremya chumï [A Feast in Time of Plague]	1	Prokofiev, after A. S. Pushkin		MS vs dated July–Oct 1903, unpubd
	Undina	4	M. Kilstett, after F. de la Motte Fouqué		comp. 1904–7, partly scored, unpubd
	Pir vo vremya chumï [A Feast in Time of Plague]	1 scene	Prokofiev, after Pushkin		comp. 1908, unpubd
13	Maddalena	1	Prokofiev, after M. G. Liven-Orlova	concert perf., Manchester, 22 Dec 1978 (broadcast BBC, London, 25 March 1979), cond. E. Downes; stage, Graz, Opernhaus, 28 Nov 1981, cond. E. Downes	comp. 1911–13, inc., vs (London, 1990); orchd E. Downes
24	Igrok [The Gambler]	4	Prokofiev, after F. Dostoyevsky	Brussels, Monnaie, 29 April 1929, cond. M. Corneil de Thoran; Russ. concert première, Leningrad radio, 1963, cond. G. Rozhdestvensky; stage, Moscow, Bol'shoy, 1974	comp. 1915–17, vs (St Petersburg, 1917); rev. 1927–8, vs (Berlin, 1930)
33	Lyubov' k tryom apel'sinam [The Love for Three Oranges]	prol., 4	Prokofiev, after C. Gozzi: *L'amore delle tre melarance*	Chicago, Auditorium, 30 Dec 1921, as L'amour des trois oranges; Russ. première, Leningrad, State Academic, 1926	comp. 1919, vs (Berlin, 1922), full score (London, 1981)
37	Ognennïy angel [The Fiery Angel]	5	Prokofiev, after V. Y. Bryusov	Venice, La Fenice, 14 Sept 1955, cond. N. Sanzogno; Act 2, abridged, Paris, Opéra, 14 June 1928, cond. S. Koussevitzky; complete, Paris, Champs-Elysées, 25 Nov 1954, cond. C. Bruck, as L'ange de feu; Russ. première, St Petersburg, Mariinsky, 29 Dec 1991, cond. Downes	comp. 1919–23, rev. 1926–7, vs (Moscow, 1985)
81	Semyon Kotko	5	Prokofiev and V. Katayev, after Katayev: *Ya sïn trudovogo naroda*	Moscow, Stanislavsky, 23 June 1940, cond. M. N. Zhukov	comp. 1939, vs (Moscow, 1960), full score (Moscow, 1967)
86	Obrucheniye v monastïre [Betrothal in a Monastery]/ Duen'ya [The Duenna]	'lyrico-comic' op, 4	Prokofiev and M. Mendel'son, after R. B. Sheridan: *The Duenna*	Prague, National, 5 May 1946; Russ. première, Leningrad, Kirov, 3 Nov 1946, cond. B. Khaikin	comp. 1940, vs (Moscow, 1944, 1960)

op.	title	genre, acts	libretto	first performance	sources and remarks
91	Voyna i mir [War and Peace]	13 'lyrico-dramatic scenes', choral epigraph	Prokofiev and Mendel'son, after L. Tolstoy		comp. 1941–52, vs and full score (Moscow, 1958); ed. in Collected Works, vi–vii (Moscow, 1958)
	orig. version	11 scenes		Moscow, Actors' Club, 16 Oct 1944, concert perf.; stage, Prague, National, 1948	
	expanded (two-evening) version	13 scenes		Leningrad, Malïy, 12 June 1946, cond. S. Samosud (Pt I, 8 scenes); dress rehearsal, July and Dec 1947 (Pt II)	
	abbreviated (one-evening) version	10 scenes		Florence, Maggio Musicale, 26 May 1953, cond. A. Rodziński	
	final version	13 scenes		Leningrad, Malïy, 1 April 1955, cond. E. Grikurov, heavily cut; Moscow, Bol'shoy, 15 Dec 1959, cond. A. Melik-Pashayev, first relatively complete perf., incl. epigraph	
	Khan Buzai				comp. 1942, inc., unpubd
117	Povest' o nastoyashchem cheloveke [The Story of a Real Man]	4	Prokofiev and Mendel'son, after B. Polevoy	private concert perf. Leningrad, Kirov, 3 Dec 1948, cond. Khaikin; stage, with cuts, Moscow, Bol'shoy, cond. M. F. Ermler, 8 Oct 1960	comp. 1947–8, vs (Moscow, 1959, 1962)
	Dalyokiye morya [Distant Seas]		Prokofiev, after V. A. Dïkhovichnïy		comp. 1948, inc., unpubd

MDV – S. Shlifshteyn, ed.: *S. S. Prokof'yev: materialï, dokumentï, vospominaniya* [Material, Documents, Reminiscences] (Moscow, 2/1961)

PSI – V. Blok, ed.: *S. S. Prokof'yev: stat'i i issledovaniya* [Articles and Research Essays] (Moscow, 1972)

PSM – I. Nest'yev and G. Edelman, eds.: *Sergey Prokof'yev: stat'i i materialï* [Essays and Documents] (Moscow, 2/1965)

OPERAS: GENERAL

R. Jahn: 'Von "Spieler" zur "Erzählung von wahren Menschen"', *Musik und Gesellschaft*, xi (1961), 232–8

D. Lloyd-Jones: 'Prokofiev and the Opera', *Opera*, xiii (1962), 513–20

A. Porter: 'Prokofiev's Early Operas', *MT*, ciii (1962), 528–30

M. Sabinina: 'Ob opere, kotoraya ne bïla napisana' [On an Opera that Was Not Written], *SovM* (1962), no.8, pp.41–8 [on *Khan Buzai*]

L. Danko: *Operï S. Prokof'yeva* (Moscow, 1963)

L. Polyakova: '"Dalyokiye morya": o poslednem opernom zamïsle S. Prokof'yeva' [*Distant Seas*: on Prokofiev's Last Operatic Project] *SovM* (1963), no.3, pp.53–6

G. Pugliese: 'The Unknown World of Prokofiev's Operas', *HiFi*, xvi/6 (1966), 44–50

A. Porter: 'Prokofiev's Late Operas', *MT*, cviii (1967), 312–14

L. Danko: 'Prokof'yevskiye traditsii v sovetskoy opere' [Prokofiev Traditions in Soviet Opera], *PSI*, 37–58

E. Kröplin: *Frühe sowjetische Oper: Schostakowitsch, Prokofjew* (Berlin, 1985)

R. Taruskin: 'Tone, Style, and Form in Prokofiev's Soviet Operas: Some Preliminary Observations', *Studies in the History of Music*, ii (1988), 215–39

OPERAS: SPECIFIC

Maddalena

H. Swarsenski: 'Prokofieff: Unknown Works with a New Aspect', *Tempo*, new ser., no.30 (1953–4), 14–16

R. McAllister: 'Prokofiev's Early Opera "Maddalena"', *PRMA*, xcvi (1969–70), 137–47

——: 'Prokofiev's "Maddalena": a Première', *MT*, cxx (1979), 205–6

E. Dawnes [*sic*]: 'Prokofjews Oper "Maddalena"', *ÖMz*, xxxvi (1981), 577–8

E. Downes: Preface to S. Prokofiev: *Maddalena* (London, 1990) [vocal score]

The Gambler

S. Prokofiev: [Two interviews on *The Gambler*], *MDV*, 205–6

V. Karatïgin: 'Dostoyevsky i muzïka', *Izbrannïye stat'i* [Selected Essays], ed. O. L. Dansker (Moscow and Leningrad, 1965), 251–62

E. Mnatsakanova: 'Neskol'ko zametok ob opere Prokof'yeva "Igrok"' [Some Remarks on the Opera 'The Gambler'], *Muzïka i sovremennost'*, iii (1965), 122–44

A. Stratiyevsky: 'Nekotorïye osobennosti rechitativa operï "Igrok" Prokof'yeva' [Some Peculiarities of the Recitative in Prokofiev's Opera *The Gambler*], *Russkaya muzïka na rubezhe XX veka* [Russian Music at the Turn of the 20th Century] (Moscow and Leningrad, 1966), 42–70

S. Prokofiev: 'Pis'ma k V. E. Meyerkhol'du' [Letters to Meyerhold], *Muzïkal'noye nasledstvo* [Musical Heritage], ed. K. Kirilenko and M. Kozlova, ii/2 (Moscow, 1968), 214–31

V. Meyerkhol'd: *Stat'i, pis'ma, rechi, besedï* [Essays, Letters, Speeches, Conversations], ed. A. V. Fevralsky, ii (Moscow, 1968), 70–71

M. Cherkashina: '"Igrok" S. S. Prokof'yeva' [Prokofiev's *The Gambler*], *Iz istorii russkoy i sovetskoy muzïki* [From the History of Russian and Soviet Music], ed. A. Kandinsky, ii (Moscow, 1976), 274–310

B. Yarustovsky: 'Opera', *Muzïka XX veka* [Music of the 20th Century], ed. D. Zhitomirsky (Moscow, 1976), esp.179–81

S. Shlifshteyn: '"Igrok" S. Prokof'yeva v kontsertnom ispolnenii' [Prokofiev's *The Gambler* in Concert Performance], *Izbrannïye stat'i* [Selected Essays] (Moscow, 1977), 124–32

Yu. Fridlyand: *Opera 'Igrok' S. Prokof'yeva* [Prokofiev's Opera *The Gambler*] (Moscow, 1979)

A. Gozenpud: *Dostoyevsky i muzïkal'no-teatral'noye iskusstvo* [Dostoyevsky and the Music-Theatre Arts] (Leningrad, 1981)

D. Zhitomirsky: 'S. Prokof'yev: "Igrok"' [Prokofiev: *The Gambler*], *Izbrannïye stat'i* [Selected Essays] (Moscow, 1981), 365–8

H. Robinson: 'Dostoevsky and Opera: Prokofiev's *The Gambler*', *MQ*, lxx (1984), 96–106

The Love for Three Oranges

D. Mitchell: 'Prokofiev's "Three Oranges": a Note on its Musical-Dramatic Organisation', *Tempo*, new ser., no.41 (1956), 20–24

A. Fevralsky: 'Prokof'yev i Meyerkhol'd', *PSM*, 94–120

E. Szenkar: 'Lyubov' k tryom apel'sinam' [*The Love for Three Oranges*], ibid, 391–5

G. Grigor'yeva: 'Komicheskoye v opere Prokof'yeva "Lyubov' k tryom apel'sinam"' [The Comic Element in Prokofiev's *The Love for Three Oranges*], *Voprosï teorii muzïki* [Questions of Music Theory] (Moscow, 1968)

S. Stompor: '"Die Liebe zu drei Orangen": Dokumente zur Aufführungsgeschichte', *Jb der Komischen Oper Berlin*, ix (1969), 7–15

O. Stepanov: *Teatr masok v opere S. Prokof'yeva 'Lyubov' k tryom apel'sinam'* [The Theatre of Masks in Prokofiev's Opera *The Love for Three Oranges*] (Moscow, 1972)

S. Shlifshteyn: '"Lyubov' k tryom apel'sinam" S. Prokof'yeva na litovskoy stsene' [Prokofiev's *Love for Three Oranges* on the Lithuanian Stage], *Izbrannïye stat'i* [Selected Essays] (Moscow, 1977), 133–41

M. Brown: [review of the first publication of the full score], *Notes*, xxxix (1982–3), 466–8

H. Robinson: 'Love for Three Operas: the Collaboration of Vsevolod Meyerhold and Sergei Prokofiev', *Russian Review*, xlv (1986), 287–304

R. Taruskin: 'From Fairy Tale to Opera in Four Not-So-Simple Moves', *English National Opera 1991* [programme book]

The Fiery Angel

C. Bruck: '"Ognennïy angel" v Parizhe' [*The Fiery Angel* in Paris], *SovM* (1955), no.7, pp.128–30

H. Swarsenski: 'Prokofieff's "The Flaming Angel"', *Tempo*, new ser., no.39 (1956), 16–27

A. Jefferson: '"The Angel of Fire"', *Music and Musicians*, xiii/12 (1965), 32–5

R. McAllister: 'Natural and Supernatural in "The Fiery Angel"', *MT*, cxi (1970), 785–9

N. Rzhavinskaya: 'O roli ostinato i nekotorïkh printsipakh for-moobrazovaniya v opere "Ognennïy angel"' [On the Role of Ostinato and some Formal Principles in *The Fiery Angel*], *PSI*, 96–130

I. Nest'yev: 'Pochemu ne stavyat "Ognennogo angela"? (otkrïtoye pis'mo B. A. Pokrovskomu)' [Why is *The Fiery Angel* not Staged?: an Open Letter to B. A. Pokrovsky], *SovM* (1978), no.4, pp.83–6

B. Pokrovsky: 'Ob "Ognennom angele" (otvet na otkrïtoye pis'mo I. Nest'yeva)' [Concerning *The Fiery Angel*: an Answer to Nest'yev's Open Letter], *SovM* (1980), no.5, pp.37–9

L. Fay: 'The Demonic Prokofiev', *Performing Arts* (Los Angeles Music Center), xxi/9 (1987), 10–15

Semyon Kotko

S. Birman: 'On ves' otdal sebya muzïke' [He Devoted Himself Wholly to Music], *MDV*, 500–05

A. Klimovitsky: *Opera Prokof'yeva 'Semyon Kotko'* [Prokofiev's Opera *Semyon Kotko*] (Moscow, 1961)

S. Prokofiev: 'Semyon Kotko', *MDV*, 235–8

M. Sabinina: *'Semyon Kotko' i problemï opernoy dramaturgii Prokof'yeva* [*Semyon Kotko* and the Problems of Prokofiev's Dramatic Art] (Moscow, 1963)

L. Skorino: *Pisatel' i ego vremya* [The Writer and his Time] (Moscow, 1965), 290–309

M. Aranovsky: 'Rechevaya situatsiya v dramaturgii operï "Semyon Kotko"' [Vocal Style in the Dramaturgy of the Opera *Semyon Kotko*], *PSI*, 59–95

Betrothal in a Monastery

L. Danko: 'Redaktsii "Duen'i"' [The Shaping of *The Duenna*] *SovM* (1961), no.8, pp.94–100

S. Prokofiev: 'Obrucheniye v monastïre (Duenya)' [*Betrothal in a Monastery/The Duenna*], *MDV*, 241–3

L. Danko: 'Sergey Prokof'yev v rabote nad "Duen'yey": sozdaniye libretto' [Prokofiev at work on *The Duenna*: the Making of the Libretto], *Chertï stilya S. Prokof'yeva: sbornik teoreticheskikh*

statey [Aspects of Prokofiev's Style: a Collection of Theoretical Essays], ed. L. Berger (Moscow, 1962), 114–49

H. Stuckenschmidt: 'Serge Prokofieff: "Verlobung im Kloster"', *Oper in dieser Zeit* (Velber, nr Hanover, 1964), 57–9

War and Peace

M. Sabinina: '"Voyna i mir" (opera S. Prokof'yeva)' [Prokofiev's Opera *War and Peace*], *SovM* (1953), no.12, pp.29–38

Yu. Keldïsh: 'Yeshchyo ob opere "Voyna i mir"' [More about the Opera *War and Peace*], *SovM* (1955), no.7, pp.33–40

A. Uteshev: *Opera S. S. Prokof'yeva 'Voyna i mir'* [Prokofiev's Opera *War and Peace*] (Moscow, 1960)

M. Mendel'son-Prokof'yeva: 'O Sergeye Sergeyeviche Prokof'yeve', *MDV*, 370–96

S. Prokofiev: 'Khudozhnik i voyna' [The Artist and *War*], *MDV*, 243–9

A. Shnitke: 'Zametki o dramaturgii pervoy kartinï i o muzïkal'nom tematizme operï S. Prokof'yeva "Voyna i mir"' [Notes on the Form of the First Scene and on the Musical Thematicism of Prokofiev's Opera *War and Peace*], *Chertï stilya S. Prokof'yeva: sbornik teoreticheskikh statey* [Aspects of Prokofiev's Style: a Collection of Theoretical Essays], ed. L. Berger (Moscow, 1962), 32–57

A. Uteshev: 'Istoriya sozdaniya operï S. Prokof'yeva "Voyna i mir"' [The History of the Creation of Prokofiev's *War and Peace*], ibid, 58–81

A. Volkov: 'Pis'ma S. S. Prokof'yeva k V. V. Derzhanovskomu' [Prokofiev's Letters to Derzhanovsky], *Iz arkhivov russkikh muzïkantov* [From the Archives of Russian Musicians], ed. A. Bïkov (Moscow, 1962), 93–118

M. Mendel'son-Prokof'yeva: 'Posledniye dni' [The Last Days], *PSM*, 281–92

L. Prokof'yeva: 'Iz vospominaniy' [From Reminiscences], *PSM*, 224–32

S. Samosud: 'Vstrechi s Prokof'yevïm' [Meetings with Prokofiev], *PSM*, 123–73

E. Mnatsakanova: 'Prokof'yev i Tolstoy: narodnaya ideya operï "Voyna i mir"' [Prokofiev and Tolstoy: the National Idea of the Opera *War and Peace*], *Muzïka i sovremennost'*, iv (1966), 162–85

B. Pokrovsky: 'V rabote nad "Voynoy i mirom"' [At Work on *War and Peace*], *SovM* (1966), no.4, pp.52–6

V. Blok: 'Neopublikovannïye rukopisi Prokof'yeva' [Unpublished Manuscripts of Prokofiev], *SovM* (1967), no.4, pp.93–9

L. Polyakova: *'Voyna i mir' S. S. Prokof'yeva* [Prokofiev's *War and Peace*] (Moscow, 2/1971)

R. McAllister: 'Prokofiev's Tolstoy Epic', *MT*, cxiii (1972), 851–5

C. Osborne: '*War and Peace*: a Repertory Candidate?', *HiFi* (Jan 1975), 67–70

A. Volkov: *'Voyna i mir' Prokof'yeva: opït analiza variantov operï* [Prokofiev's *War and Peace*: an Analysis of the Opera's Variants], (Moscow, 1976)

M. Brown: 'Prokofiev's *War and Peace*: a Chronicle', *MQ*, lxiii (1977), 297–326

S. Shlifshteyn: '"Voyna i mir" v Malom op. teatre' [*War and Peace* in the Malïy Opera Theatre], *Izbrannïye stat'i* [Selected Essays] (Moscow, 1977), 91–100

——: 'Zametki o "Voyne i mire"' [Notes on *War and Peace*], ibid, 60–90

C. Emerson: *Boris Godunov: Transpositions of a Russian Theme* (Bloomington and Indianapolis, 1986), 149–51

The Story of a Real Man

A. Zolotov: 'Ode to Heroism: "The Story of a Real Man" at the Bolshoi Theater', *Current Digest of the Soviet Press*, xlviii (1960), 117–19

L. Aleksandrovsky: 'Muzïkal'naya dramaturgiya operï S. Prokof'yeva "Povest' o nastoyashchem cheloveke"' [Musical Dramaturgy in Prokofiev's Opera *The Story of a Real Man*], *Iz istorii russkoy i sovetskoy muzïki* [From the History of Russian and Soviet Music], ed. A. Kandinsky, i (Moscow, 1971), 189–206

S. Prokofiev: Response to the 'Resolution on Music of the Central Committee of the Communist Party of the Soviet Union (Bolsheviks)', in N. Slonimsky: *Music since 1900* (New York, 4/1971), 1373–4 [orig. in *SovM* (1948), no.1, pp.66–7]

S. Shlifshteyn: 'S. Prokof'yev i ego opera "Povest' o nastoyashchem cheloveke"' [Prokofiev and his Opera *The Story of a Real Man*], *Izbrannïye stat'i* [Selected Essays] (Moscow, 1977), 101–23

RICHARD TARUSKIN

Prologo (It.). PRELUDE.

Prologue. A separate introductory scene to a play or opera serving to clarify and enhance the perceptual and conceptual frame of the drama, often by securing some manner of collusion with the audience. The prologue can variously outline the aesthetic intent of the work, introduce the subsequent action, and/or pay homage to a patron. Thus it will probably consist of one or more of the following elements: invitation or exhortation, explication, justification and dedication. The changing place of the prologue in operatic history holds an intriguing mirror to the fate of opera itself, reflecting the various political, social, cultural and philosophical pressures brought to bear on what is often feared nothing more than an 'exotick and irrational entertainment'.

The first opera librettists and composers exploited the prologue to proclaim the raison d'être of the new genre. In part the precedent was classical, but they also followed the example of the most obvious antecedent to opera, the pastoral play: Poliziano's *La fabula d'Orfeo* (1480) has a prologue recited by Mercury, Tasso's *Aminta* (1573) is introduced by Cupid and Guarini's *Il pastor fido* (1585) by the river Alfeo. In the pastoral, the prologue permitted justification of a genre deprived of classical authority. Similar motives inspired the prologues in early opera. The librettist of the first *dramme per musica*, Ottavio Rinuccini, opted for straightforwardly classical figures – Ovid in *Dafne* (1598), Tragedy in *Euridice* (1600), Apollo in *Arianna* (1608) – although in one case he allowed a modern singer, Giulio Caccini (*Narciso*, ?1608), to explain the rationale behind the entertainment to follow. The choice reflects the insecurity of early opera over its dubious aesthetic foundations, and also the fear that contemporary audiences might find the notion of sung drama unacceptable. Rinuccini responds by producing sententious verse in rigorous quatrains. This is matched by the formalist settings of his composers, who generally employ strophic techniques evoking earlier improvisatory formulae linked to epic verse. The generic associations, plus of course the speakers and their sentiments, claim credibility for an essentially incredible genre.

The manifestos presented in early operatic prologues merit close attention. Tragedy in *Euridice* proclaims her intent to abandon classical garb for more appealing ends, while Music (in Monteverdi's *Orfeo*, 1607) offers an important account of the 'new music'. But with the subsequent acceptance of opera (at least in some quarters), the justificatory prologue gradually lost ground. One can detect its residue in the deities that animate the prologues of Venetian 'public' opera, where disputes between the gods provide a motivation for the opera as exemplar of some moral or emotional issue (as in Monteverdi's *L'incoronazione di Poppea*, 1643): the framing function of the prologue is sometimes enhanced by a balancing epilogue. But here the rationale seems more one of allowing the stage designer leeway to display splendid scenic effects. Similarly, in France the prologue became a more straightforward encomium of the princely patron who motivates the action on stage: Lully's *Alceste* (1674) refers specifically to Louis XIV's recent military campaigns in the Netherlands, equating his return with the Louis/Apollo who provides the *deus ex machina* for the happy ending.

The prologue remained a standard element in French opera until Rameau's *Zoroastre* (1749). Elsewhere, meanwhile, prologues had increasingly lost their place in public opera (Handel's London operas avoid them, with the exception of the ballet for the 1734 revival of *Il pastor fido*). The evident antipathy of Zeno, Metastasio and the Arcadians to superfluous prologues clearly had some influence here, as did the broad familiarity with and acceptance of operatic conventions and themes among an opera-going public. The prologue's function as introduction and explication was instead fulfilled by the printed programme/libretto issued for the performance, and later by the instrumental overture which, according to Gluck, 'ought to apprise the spectators of the nature of the action that is to be represented and to form, so to speak, its argument'.

19th-century aesthetics similarly militated against extraneous prologues. They are generally used only to provide background information (often set some time before the main action) necessary for the understanding of a historical plot: examples include Verdi's *Attila* (1846) and *Simon Boccanegra* (1857), Gounod's *Roméo et Juliette* (1867), Musorgsky's *Boris Godunov* (1874 version) and Borodin's *Prince Igor* (1890). An extreme case is Wagner's *Das Rheingold* (1869), essentially a musical and literary prologue to *Der Ring des Nibelungen*.

The second prologue (1875) to Boito's *Mefistofele* (1868) replaced the first 'Prologo in cielo' with one 'in teatro', involving a debate between the composer, a critic and a member of the audience. Although Boito abandoned the revision, his change was symptomatic. It seems no coincidence that prologues justifying the composer's decision to assay drama through music became more common as opera itself underwent a period of revaluation in the modernist crisis: Leoncavallo's *Pagliacci* (1892) has the protagonist Tonio first appear as the 'Prologo' to emphasize the claims of *verismo*, and Busoni's *Doktor Faustus* (1925) a spoken prologue explaining the composer's choice of subject. Similarly, prologues were used to counter in advance the accusation of irrationality. One technique was to make play of the fictive nature of opera, whether by a direct statement to the audience – as the astrologer in Rimsky-Korsakov's *The Golden Cockerel* (1909), the Animal Tamer in Berg's *Lulu* (1937), the theatre director in Poulenc's *Les mamelles de Tirésias* (1947) and the Choregos in Birtwistle's *Punch and Judy* (1968) – or by some roundabout means, as the theatrical debate in Prokofiev's *The Love for Three Oranges* (1919) and, on a more extended scale, the 'opera within an opera' of Richard Strauss's *Ariadne auf Naxos* (1916).

One can detect similar motives behind prologues that establish an explicit narrative framework for the drama, usually through some 'story-telling' scenario. An early example is Offenbach's *Les contes d'Hoffmann* (1881), and it becomes a standard *topos* through Kodály's *Háry János* (1926), Vaughan Williams's *The Pilgrim's Progress* (1951) and Britten's *The Turn of the Screw* (1954). Indeed, Britten seems to have been particularly interested in using the prologue to mediate between stage and auditorium: in his operas, prologues set a scene (*Peter Grimes*, 1945), establish 'flashback' techniques (*Billy Budd*, 1951), and secure a direct rapport with the audience (the 'Chorus' in *The Rape of Lucretia*, 1946, provides an instructive example).

The various prologue techniques developed in the 20th century encompass both a reversion to early operatic types (in some cases, even to classical antiquity) and experiments influenced by contemporary drama and cinema. They clearly reflect an increasing insecurity over the place and future of opera in the post-modernist period.

O. Jander: 'The Prologues and Intermezzos of Alessandro Stradella', *AnMc*, no.7 (1969), 87–111

B. R. Hanning: 'Apologia pro Ottavio Rinuccini', *JAMS*, xxvi (1973), 240–62   TIM CARTER

Promessi sposi, I (i) ('The Betrothed'). *Melodramma* in four parts by AMILCARE PONCHIELLI to an anonymous libretto after ALESSANDRO MANZONI's novel; Cremona, Teatro della Concordia, 30 August 1856.

The action takes place in Lecco and Milan during the early 17th century. When Part 1 opens, Renzo (tenor) and Lucia (soprano) are engaged to be married, but the wedding is obstructed by the local squire, Don Rodrigo (baritone), who has designs on the bride. In Part 2 he instructs his hired ruffian, Griso (bass), to have her kidnapped just as she and Renzo are about to confront the local priest in the presence of witnesses; but the attempt is thwarted by the monk Fra Cristoforo (bass), who orders the lovers to leave Lecco separately.

Part 3 begins with Lucia lodged in a convent, where the infamous Nun of Monza (mezzo-soprano) arranges for her to be abducted by a robber baron known as L'Innominato (tenor). A prisoner in his castle, Lucia vows solemnly to take the veil if she should escape unharmed. Her wish is granted. In the presence of Cardinal Federico Borromeo (bass), Fra Cristoforo and Lucia's family and friends, L'Innominato solemnly dedicates himself to a virtuous life. Part 4 opens with a carousal, during which Don Rodrigo is stricken with the plague, then raging in Milan. He sends Griso for his personal physician; seeing the 'monatti' (stretcher-bearers appointed for the dying) arriving instead, he shoots himself. In the second scene Fra Cristoforo preaches in the hospital to the convalescent, among them Lucia. When Renzo enters she at first shrinks from him, remembering her vow. But Fra Cristoforo absolves her from it, and so the wedding may at last take place.

Following the première of the revised version of *I promessi sposi*, which took place at the Teatro Dal Verme, Milan on 5 December 1872 and is based on a libretto by Emilio Praga, Ponchielli first sprang into prominence as a theatrical composer. Founded on a literary classic of the time, it owed its appeal to a reaction against modernists such as Boito and against the nascent enthusiasm for Wagner. Indeed its design suggests an opera of the 1840s, employing all the standard post-Rossinian forms together with patterned accompaniments, bursts of coloratura and vocal cadenzas. The musical language, even of the pieces composed subsequently, is essentially that of Donizetti with a wider range of modulation. The most striking number of the score is a *pezzo concertato* in Part 2, which combines an anguished solo for Lucia, a counter-melody of guilt and remorse for the Nun, a religious chorus for female voices and another of lurking bravos in such a way that each emerges totally distinct from the other three.   JULIAN BUDDEN

Promessi sposi, I (ii) ('The Betrothed'). *Melodramma* in four acts by ERRICO PETRELLA to a libretto by ANTONIO GHISLANZONI after ALESSANDRO MANZONI's novel; Lecco, Teatro Sociale, 2 October 1869.

Reducing Manzoni's epoch-making historical novel to practical operatic dimensions posed a problem comparable only to the similar transformation of *War and Peace*, and it must be admitted that Prokofiev did a better job for himself than Ghislanzoni did for Petrella. The original novel, subtitled 'A Tale of 17th-century Milan', is a story of war, famine and plague, tracing the attempts of two poor silk weavers to marry amid the corruption and oppression of Spanish rule in Lombardy. (For details of the plot, *see* PROMESSI SPOSI, I (i).) The conventions of Ghislanzoni's operatic diction allow no hint of the linguistic originality that was Manzoni's greatest achievement; the wide-ranging plot is trivialized, and the characters are pitilessly reduced to their 19th-century operatic equivalents.

The deep humanity with which Manzoni treats his subject is clearly beyond Petrella's grasp: Don Abbondio (bass) becomes a typical *buffo* role, Don Rodrigo (baritone) an operatic grandee, Perpetua (mezzo-soprano) the character role and so on. Nevertheless the opera as a whole is less blatant, more inventively accompanied and delicately scored than Petrella's earlier operas, and the predicament of the two lovers (though much simplified) drew a spark of fragile lyricism from this wholly intuitive composer: the departure of Lucia (soprano) and Renzo (tenor) across the waters of the Adda at the end of Act 2 has a certain lingering charm even today. The popularity of the subject, and the publicity that surrounded the first performance of the work, ensured its success on the Italian opera market for a few years, but it has not been recently revived.   MICHAEL ROSE

Prometheus. *Szenisches Oratorium* in five scenes by RUDOLF WAGNER-RÉGENY to a libretto by the composer after AESCHYLUS; Kassel, Staatstheater, 12 September 1959.

Zeus's executioners, Macht [Power] (baritone) and Gewalt [Force] (bass), bring on Prometheus (baritone), who is chained to a rock by Hephaistos [Hephaestus] (tenor). The song of the Okeanides [Oceanides] is heard. In Scenes ii and iii the Oceanides pity Prometheus and wait near him, and then Okeanos [Oceanus] (bass) tries to induce him to submit to Zeus. Scene iv introduces Io (mezzo-soprano), who hears Prometheus prophesy that after ten generations the saviour of mankind will be born, descended from the son she has conceived by Zeus. Along with this visionary promise Goethe's poem *Prometheus* is recited. In the final scene Hermes (tenor), on Zeus's behalf, tries to discover what it is that Prometheus prophesied, but Prometheus will not tell him and falls into the Tartarus, together with the Oceanides.

Prometheus was commissioned for the opening of the Staatstheater, Kassel, in 1959. Musically it is Wagner-Régeny's most powerful and 'modern' opera, combining a tonally controlled dodecaphony with a rhythmically terse manner in a style between that of Weill and Stravinsky. Wagner-Régeny's own sensitivity is felt in the cantabile expression of the soloists and, even more, of the women's chorus. In writing his own libretto the composer was advised and assisted by Karl Holl. *Prometheus* received three concert performances in East Berlin between 1960 and 1984, but has not been revived on stage.   TILO MEDEK

Prompter (Fr., Ger. *souffleur*; It. *rammentatore*, *suggeritore*). One who assists performers with their lines and cues. In *My Life in Art* the Russian actor-director Constantin Stanisklavsky wrote:

If you look into the kennel of the prompter you are reminded of mediaeval inquisition. The prompter in the theatre is sentenced to eternal torture that makes one fear for his life. He has a dirty box lined with dusty felt. Half of his body is beneath the floor of the stage in the dampness of a cellar, the other half, at the level of the stage, is heated by the hundreds of lamps in the footlights on both sides of him. All the dust created at the rising of the curtain or the sweeping of robes across the stage strikes him square in the mouth. And he is forced to speak without stop during performance and rehearsal in an unnaturally squeezed and often strained voice so that he may be heard by the actors alone, and not by the spectators.

Stanislavsky was writing in the 1920s, and of the straight theatre, but his comments are just as applicable to opera prompters now and in the past.

Since prompters are not supposed to be seen or heard by audiences, they and their contribution to theatrical productions are often forgotten. Someone must have helped ancient actors with their lines in Greece and Rome, but who did it, what the person was called, and what other responsibilities came with the post are not known. In medieval stage performances the prompter, sometimes called a regent or ordinary, was usually the director; according to some historians he stood on stage, script in one hand and baton in another, conducting the show and feeding the often illiterate performers all of their lines. There are at least three pictures of what appear to be medieval prompters, and the practice of feeding lines still exists today in Moro-Moro folk productions in the Philippines.

With the advent of the proscenium arch in the early 16th century the presence of the prompter on stage became inappropriate, because he destroyed the scenic 'illusion'. He found a new position off stage on one side or the other (hence 'PS' for prompt side and 'OP' for opposite prompt in his book); in that position he could also cue such things as entrances, special effects and the curtain. He usually had an assistant on the opposite side of the stage and a callboy who fetched performers for entrances.

As opera grew in popularity and complexity in the 17th century, most of the prompter's duties shifted to the stage manager, and the prompter devoted his full time to aiding performers. Probably about the same time his position was moved to downstage centre (*see* LIGHTING, fig.5c). Drawings of stages do not always show a prompter's hole or box, whether a theatre had one or not, and in some houses there was simply a small trap which could be opened and hooded, or not, as needed.

Prompters today can sometimes be found off stage, in the wings, especially in theatres with unusually wide stages, where two prompters are needed, one on each side. But the usual position is in the box downstage centre, assisted by television monitors in the wings. At La Scala the box can accommodate two prompters. The standard prompting practice (described in Pauly and in a letter written by David Syrus of the Royal Opera House, Covent Garden, to E. A. Langhans, 26 October 1989) is for the prompter, working from a vocal score, to give all cues to all singers (unless they do not want to be prompted). From his box he can see the singers, and through one or more mirrors or, better still, a television monitor, he has a view of the conductor. Depending on the volume of the music, the prompter can speak loudly or softly. Ideally, the audience will be unaware of him, though his voice may be picked up by microphones if the opera is being broadcast or televised. At Covent Garden the sound is piped into the box to boost what the prompter hears naturally.

The prompter motions to singers if they are out of place on stage or have got ahead of the beat, and he sometimes gives the pitch for a difficult vocal entrance. In Italy he gives cues with hand signals, like a conductor, while in Germany he usually gives verbal cues. Prompters are especially necessary in companies operating in repertory, as is the case with most opera troupes. Covent Garden follows the Italian system of having all members of the music staff share duties, including that of prompting in performances.

A film of the 18th-century Drottningholm Court Theatre in Sweden shows the prompter getting into her prompter's box; her location makes it all the more understandable why stage directors so frequently place singers down centre – or why singers so often gravitate to a position where they can easily see and hear one of the most important members of the company.

*

A. Hill and W. Popple: *The Prompter*, no.1 (12 Nov 1734)

C. Stanislavsky: *My Life in Art* (Boston, 1924), 297

W. J. Lawrence: 'Early Prompt-Books and What They Reveal', *Pre-Restoration Stage Studies* (Cambridge, MA, 1927), 373–413

A. Nicoll: *The Development of the Theatre* (New York, 1927, 5/1966)

W. J. Lawrence: 'The Prompter', *Old Theatre Days and Ways* (London, 1935), 22–41

A. M. Nagler, ed: *Sources of Theatrical History* (New York, 1952)

R. G. Pauly: *Music and the Theater* (Englewood Cliffs, NJ, 1970), 9

J. Chatfield-Taylor: *Backstage at the Opera* (San Francisco, 1982)

E. A. Langhans: *Eighteenth Century British and Irish Promptbooks* (New York, 1987)　　　　　EDWARD A. LANGHANS

Properties [props] (Fr. *accessoires*; Ger. *Requisiten*; It. *accessori*; Sp. *utilería*). Any objects used on stage that cannot be designated as costumes, scenery or lights: furniture, table lamps, food, flowers, carried spears, statuary and the like. A property may be as small as a snuff box or as large as a fabricated horse; it may be part of a costume (like a cap, which is a costume if worn but a prop if handled); it may be a personal or a hand prop, used by performers (carried, thrown, eaten from, read etc.); or it may serve only as trim or 'dressing' (such as pictures on a wall or chairs that are not used but decorate the stage and complete the design).

The dividing lines between properties, scenery and costumes are sometimes hazy. But the Scene Shop will usually see to the horse in *Les Troyens*, Siegfried's anvil or a cannon, which are as much machines as props or scenic units, while the Costume Shop will probably take care of canes, sceptres, magic wands and Desdemona's handkerchief. Many theatres have in-house departments for wigs, costumes, properties and scenery, but some have such shops scattered around town and/or use outside suppliers. Though some props can be purchased, many are specially designed and built, just as are costumes and wigs. Since most operas are set in past periods or realms of the imagination, they rarely call for modern costumes and properties. In his own day Mozart might have seen *Le nozze di Figaro* produced with almost everything borrowed or bought in the marketplace; today the same things would have to be designed and constructed from scratch.

The French and the Italian terms carry interesting designations and derogations; the German makes props more important, and the Spanish compromise. The English 'prop' is not just a shortening of 'property' but a description, for many are supports and some, such as Desdemona's handkerchief or Siegfried's sword or Marguerite's jewels, are absolutely essential to the action.　　　　　EDWARD A. LANGHANS

Prophète, Le ('The Prophet'). Grand opera in five acts by GIACOMO MEYERBEER to a libretto by EUGÈNE SCRIBE; Paris, Opéra, 16 April 1849.

Jean de Leyde [John of Leyden]	tenor
Fidès *John's mother*	mezzo-soprano
Berthe *betrothed to John*	soprano
Jonas	tenor
Mathisen } *Anabaptists*	bass or baritone
Zacharie }	bass
Count Oberthal	bass

Peasants, Anabaptists, soldiers, burghers and children

Setting The Low Countries and Westphalia, 1530

Among the opera projects that Meyerbeer contemplated following the première of *Les Huguenots* in 1836 were a *Cinq-Mars* with the librettist J.-H. Vernoy de Saint-Georges as well as *L'Africaine* and *Le prophète* with his seasoned collaborator Eugène Scribe. The first did not get beyond the rough sketching stage and the second was abandoned after one act had been drafted, when it became clear that the soprano Cornélie Falcon, for whom Meyerbeer had intended the title role, was losing her voice. On 2 August 1838 Meyerbeer and Scribe signed a formal contract for *Le prophète*, by the terms of which the composer agreed to complete the opera within two years.

The first edition of the libretto includes an excerpt from Voltaire's *Essai sur les moeurs* outlining the historical context of the Anabaptist revolt in 16th-century Germany and the role in that uprising of a certain Jean from Leyden. Other possible literary sources for the libretto include a novel, *Die Anabaptisten* (1826), by Van Der Welde and the *Mémoires de Luther*, a collection of letters, anecdotes and articles assembled by the French historian Jules Michelet. In an essay entitled 'Anabaptistes de Münster' Michelet actually refers to Jean as a 'prophète' and suggests that well before the event he had premonitions about being crowned, like the protagonist in Meyerbeer's work. The dramatic highlight of the opera is the encounter between John and his mother during his coronation; the parallel between this episode and the scene in Schiller's *Jungfrau von Orleans* where Joan is confronted by her father was certainly not lost on Meyerbeer, though whether *Jungfrau* actually provided the creative spark for the operatic scene is unclear.

On assuming directorship of the Opéra in 1840, Léon Pillet informed the composer that a production of *Le prophète* was a priority. Meyerbeer, however, harboured doubts about the suitability of the Opéra roster for his new work. At first he thought that Rosine Stoltz, the Opéra's leading contralto and mistress of the director, would not project well the role of Fidès. His increased confidence in her abilities was soon counterbalanced by growing suspicions about Pillet's commitment to his work. In 1843 it became clear that the powers of Gilbert Duprez, the house's leading tenor, were in decline. Subsequently, the selection of a tenor for the title role became the main issue of contention between Meyerbeer and Pillet: Meyerbeer's two preferred candidates, Gaetano Fraschini and Mario de Candia, were never engaged by the Opéra in this period.

Renewed impetus for a production came when Duponchel and Roqueplan were made directors in 1847. By that time Rosine Stoltz was no longer a viable

Fidès, and Meyerbeer settled upon Pauline Viardot, whom he had actually wanted from the start. He agreed to Gustave-Hippolyte Roger, a veteran singer from the Opéra-Comique, for the role of John, though with some reservations about stamina which were in part borne out, since Meyerbeer found himself having to reduce the role for him. Jeanne Castellan was chosen as Berthe and Meyerbeer indulged her request for an exit aria by supplying the *cavatine* 'Mon coeur s'élance et palpite' in Act 1, which he explicitly excluded from complete vocal scores. *Le prophète* was a great success at its première, due not only to effective musico-dramatic situations but also to the skaters' ballet and the sensational effect of the rising sun in Act 3, the first use of electricity on the stage of the Opéra (*see* LIGHTING, fig.11).

ACT 1 *Outside Count Oberthal's castle near Dordrecht* Following a brief instrumental prelude, the scene is prepared by a pastoral chorus with such conventional rustic *topoi* as open 5ths in the low strings and imitation of shepherds' pipes, as well as a more unusual orchestral effect of small sheep bells rendered by triangle, piccolo and pizzicato strings. Berthe meets her prospective mother-in-law, Fidès, and explains that she must obtain authorization from Count Oberthal to marry her son John. Three Anabaptists enter, intoning Latin words in unison to a dark accompaniment of bassoons and horns. The architecture of the subsequent number mirrors the spread of discontent among the peasants: an exposition of social evils by each of the three Anabaptists is punctuated by statements of 'Ad nos ad salutarem'; individual peasants begin to show interest, the tempo increases and a long dominant preparation gives way to a unison choral rendition of 'Ad nos'; the number closes with an even more rousing march chorus as the peasants arm themselves with pitchforks and axes and assume ranks. This brings the feudal lord Count Oberthal out of his castle. He does not establish a strong musical presence as he dismisses the seditious activities of the Anabaptists in nondescript recitative; from the musical point of view, the stage instructions for peasants to cower before him are scarcely credible. Berthe asks Oberthal for permission to marry John in a strophic *romance*, 'Un jour dans les flots de la Meuse', in which Fidès echoes the end of Berthe's phrases and the two combine in the refrain. Oberthal refuses and orders his soldiers to seize Berthe and Fidès and disperse the peasants; 'Ad nos' is heard in the distance as the two women are led away.

ACT 2 *The interior of John's inn at Leyden* A rustic waltz chorus is the musical backdrop for John's expressions of longing for Berthe, and for the discovery by the three Anabaptists that he bears a striking resemblance to an altar painting of King David in Münster. When alone with the Anabaptists, John reveals a recent dream: to music that will be heard in the coronation scene in Act 4 he tells of being heralded as the Messiah and then dragged to hell by Satan. In a strophic pastorale, 'Pour Berthe moi je soupire', he sings of his love for Berthe; between the stanzas the Anabaptists, who see John as politically useful, try to enlist him by suggesting softly, with staccato singing, that, just as in his dream, he is destined to rule. These words do not strike a responsive chord, but just then Berthe rushes in, begging John to hide her. Oberthal follows and threatens to execute Fidès if Berthe is not given up; disgusted, John throws her into the hands of the soldiers and Fidès is freed. In a tender number with reduced scoring featuring muted cellos, Fidès blesses John. The Anabaptists reappear, and this time John, eager to wreak revenge upon Oberthal, places his faith in them. He is told, however, that in order to assume leadership of their forces he must leave his homeland and mother for ever. Recalling Fidès's arioso, John balks at first, but cannot resist the call of the Anabaptists after a twofold rendition of a martial ensemble promising the end of feudal tyranny.

ACT 3.i *The camp of the Anabaptists in the Westphalian forest* While sounds of battle are heard in the distance and aristocratic prisoners are led in, the Anabaptist forces express their fanaticism with repeated snap rhythms on strong beats and a unison passage in which they voice their hatred. In strophic *couplets* of swaggering bravado Zacharie revels in the apparent might of the Anabaptist forces ('Aussi nombreux que les étoiles'). Men and women bearing provisions skate towards the camp: a sforzando followed by a rapid diminuendo on a sustained chord in each bar suggests the motion of skating. The soldiers enjoy a moment of repose as they are served food and drink and are entertained with a ballet.

3.ii *Inside Zacharie's tent* Mathisen agrees with Zacharie that Münster must be taken soon and leaves to rouse the soldiers. Oberthal has stumbled into the Anabaptist camp and is brought before Jonas and Zacharie, who do not recognize him in the dark. Seeing a chance to enter Münster, Oberthal declares that he will join the Anabaptist cause. In a trio with ensemble refrains he swears, tongue in cheek, that he would gladly hang assorted aristocrats at the first opportunity; in a lilting 6/8 passage with interspersed 'tra-la-las' Jonas casually tells him that Oberthal *père* has been executed. When Jonas lights a lamp the real identity of the guest is discovered and the final refrain follows, with grim ironic effect: whereas the first two refrains were those of a drinking-song, the third retains the same music but Jonas and Zacharie sing about Oberthal's impending execution and Oberthal expresses unbridled hatred of the Anabaptists. Just as Oberthal is about to be led off, John appears, in deep reflection about the Anabaptists as well as the intertwined fates of the two women in his life: the orchestra sounds the music of his earlier pastorale about Berthe as he actually sings of his mother. Oberthal informs him that Berthe has been seen alive in Münster. John immediately orders that he be spared, and an attack on the city mounted. Mathisen runs in with the news that there is a revolt among Anabaptist soldiers.

3.iii *The Anabaptist camp* A chorus of rebellious soldiers is the first section of a multi-sectional finale; a long dominant preparation in C major veers suddenly to B major to underscore a fortissimo 'mort à l'imposteur'. In a remarkable passage of declamation following the chorus, John forces his disenchanted troops to kneel. A prayer led by the prophet forms the slow section of the number. Following a transition in which, to the accompaniment of harps, John tells of a celestial vision, a 'Hymne triomphal' functions as the *strette*. This culminates in a scenic *coup* before the curtain: the sun rising as the troops prepare for battle.

ACT 4.i *A public square in Münster* The city has been taken and a chorus of inhabitants alternates *piano* complaints about the oppressive rule of the Anabaptists with *forte* affirmations of loyalty to the prophet as his patrols pass by. Fidès appears, begging for alms ('Donnez pour une pauvre âme'). The number is strophic, but in the second strophe Meyerbeer brings in the voice part on an E♭, taking the music to G minor after the prevailing E tonic, thereby intensifying Fidès's expression of distress. Berthe appears and recognizes Fidès. In the agitated first section of a duet she tells of her futile search for John and then, to a broadening of the tempo, exudes joy that she is in Fidès's arms. The latter has been tricked by the Anabaptists into believing that John is dead; following a static ensemble in which both commiserate in extensive parallel singing, Fidès attributes John's demise to the work of the prophet. In the *cabalette* of the duet Berthe vows that she will kill the odious tyrant, while Fidès assumes a more passive position in prayer.

4.ii *The cathedral at Münster* A large crowd has gathered to witness the coronation of John the prophet as a new emperor. To a grand processional march, featuring a family of saxhorns and a trumpet melody (foreshadowing that in Act 2 of Verdi's *Aida*), the electors enter with various imperial accoutrements, followed by John himself. The entire populace kneels in prayer. Fidès, appears and, in a fine passage marked 'avec exaltation' in which the voice sweeps rapidly between extremes of tessitura, she vows to strike the prophet. A chorus of children hails John as the prophet-king, and with halting pianissimo declamation John concludes that he must be the son of God. His personal reverie and the entire public ceremony are abruptly cut off by Fidès's exclamation of 'Mon fils!' in recognition of her own son, the *coup de théâtre* that spawns the slow section of this finale. John refuses to admit that he knows the woman. In response to a faction that questions his legitimacy, John forces Fidès, by means of a ruse, to repudiate her relationship to him: when he offers to give up his life on the spot if her claim can be substantiated, maternal instinct leads Fidès to declare that he is not her son after all.

ACT 5.i *A vaulted cellar beneath the Münster palace* In a brief exchange Jonas, Mathisen and Zacharie agree that, to ensure their own safety, they will deliver the prophet to the imperial armies advancing on the city. Fidès is led in as a prisoner. In the slow section of a *grand air* ('O toi qui m'abandonnes') she pardons her son; learning that he intends to appear, she expresses hope that he will see reason, the music of her *cabalette* returning to the heroic sweep of the music marked 'avec exaltation' in the coronation scene. Fidès assumes the dominant position dramatically, as well as in sheer quantity of music, in the subsequent duet. First she unleashes her anger in a driving allegro replete with dotted rhythms. She orders John to give up power and assures him that, if he does this, celestial pardon will be his. John's direct acknowledgement of Fidès as his mother ignites the final *cabalette*. Berthe happens upon the two and explains that she intends to set fire to the palace in order to destroy the prophet. She is overjoyed to see John alive and, in music that recalls the pastoral vein and tonality of the Act 2 waltz, the three sing of the joy of a humble existence. When an officer enters and addresses John as the prophet, Berthe is horrified; following an *alla breve strette* capped by a torrent of coloratura, she stabs herself. John resolves to seek revenge on the Anabaptists and the advancing forces of order.

5.ii *A large hall in the palace* Those assembled celebrate the glory of the prophet in song and dance. John tells two officers to allow the enemy to enter and

'Le prophète' (Meyerbeer), Act 4 scene ii (the cathedral at Münster), John of Leyden forces his mother Fidès to repudiate him: engraving from 'L'illustration' (24 April 1849) showing the original production, with sets by Charles-Antoine Cambon and Joseph Thierry, at the Paris Opéra (Salle Le Peletier), 16 April 1849

warns them that he has ignited the saltpetre in the cellar. Assuming a convivial air, he launches a strophic drinking song; the second strophe is interrupted by the entry of the three Anabaptists, Oberthal and imperial troops. As Fidès joins her son in the final strophe of the song, an explosion is heard, and the walls of the palace collapse.

*   *   *

The première of *Le prophète* took place at a time that was particularly propitious for its box office fortunes and offers one example among several of how Meyerbeer's operas benefited from political events. Since the performance occurred less than a year after the popular uprising of June 1848, *Le prophète* could readily be appropriated by authorities as a piece about the dangers of popular sedition ignited by demagoguery. This was possible especially because the evils of aristocratic authority, the ostensible cause of the Anabaptist revolt, receive very little musico-dramatic projection in the work. The sympathies that are engendered lie mainly with Fidès, the most striking character in *Le prophète* and one with little competition from a romantic female lead whose musical personality is sketchily articulated. Fidès can be seen as a forerunner to La Cieca in Ponchielli's *La Gioconda* and also could not have been far from Verdi's mind as he forged Azucena in *Il trovatore* within three years of Meyerbeer's première (which he witnessed): like *Le prophète*, *Il trovatore* features an intimate scene between mother and son before the final catastrophe is unleashed.

STEVEN HUEBNER

Prophetess, The. Semi-opera by Henry Purcell; *see* DIOCLESIAN.

Propiac, (Catherine Joseph Ferdinand) Girard de (*b* Dijon, 1759; *d* Paris, 31 Oct 1823). French composer. He began composing at an early age and made his début in 1787 at the Comédie-Italienne with *Isabelle et Rosalvo* and *Les deux morts*, both *opéras comiques*.

Betwen 1787 and 1790 he composed three more, which had some success. He emigrated in 1791, served in Condé's anti-Revolutionary army and stayed for a time in Hamburg. He returned to Paris after Napoleon came to power in November 1799 and obtained a post as archivist to the Prefecture of the Seine. Thereafter he devoted himself almost exclusively to literature, although he composed two minor *opéras comiques*, *La double apothéose* (1800) and *La pension des jeunes garçons* (1801), which were probably occasional works, performed in small theatres.

first performed at the Comédie-Italienne (Salle Favart), Paris, unless otherwise stated

Isabelle et Rosalvo (comédie mêlée d'ariettes, 1, M.-V. Patrat), 18 June 1787 (Brussels and Paris, 1788)

Les deux morts (oc), 20 June 1787 (Brussels, 1788)

Les trois déesses rivales, ou Le double jugement de Paris (comédie lyrique, 1, J. de Piis), 28 July 1788 (Paris, 1788)

La fausse paysanne, ou L'heureuse inconséquence (comédie, 3, de Piis), 26 March 1789 (Paris, ?1789)

Les savoyards, ou La continence de Bayard (comédie, 1), 30 May 1789

La double apothéose (oc, 2), Paris, Troubadours, 1800

La pension des jeunes garçons (oc, 1), Paris, Jeunes Artistes, 1801   PAULETTE LETAILLEUR

Proserpin ('Proserpina'). Opera in one act by JOSEPH MARTIN KRAUS to a libretto by JOHAN HENRIK KELLGREN after an outline by GUSTAVUS III of Sweden; Stockholm, Ulriksdal Castle Theatre, 1 June 1781.

Based loosely on Philippe Quinault's *Proserpine*, the plot revolves around a young shepherd, Atis [Attis] (tenor), who is in love with Proserpina (soprano), the daughter of Ceres (soprano). Attis's lover, the nymph Cyane (soprano), is jealous and plots with Pluto (bass) to abduct Proserpina while she is out picking flowers. When the despondent Attis rejects her and commits suicide, she confesses her guilt to Ceres. Mercurius [Mercury] (tenor) arrives, bringing both Attis and

Proserpina; the former is restored to Cyane while the latter is returned to her mother. Jupiter (bass) banishes Pluto from the final festivities.

Composed as a trial piece to test Kraus's talent as a composer, *Proserpin* was never intended to be performed on the main Stockholm stage without extensive revisions to tighten the musico-dramatic language. Though plans were made to revise the work for the regular season of the Royal Opera, it was not performed again until 1980. It contains numerous choruses, and the recitative, apart from two four-bar passages, is entirely accompagnato, creating a through-composed feeling. Kraus's setting owes much to Gluck in its careful treatment of the thin drama; his often dark orchestration and rich harmonic palette show distinct traces of the *Sturm und Drang* musical style.

BERTIL H. VAN BOER

***Proserpina*.** Monodrama [melodrama] in one act by KARL SIEGMUND VON SECKENDORFF to a text by JOHANN WOLFGANG VON GOETHE; Weimar, Neues Theater, 30 January 1778.

In the depths of Hades, Proserpina (spoken) laments her situation. She relives her carefree days on earth and also her abduction by Pluto. Unseen, the Fates welcome their new queen, who pours out her hatred and despair. Goethe wrote this stern, gloomy scene in response to Gluck's request for a poem in memory of his niece Marianne. Seckendorff's setting, beholden to Georg Benda's melodrama style, was first performed by Corona Schröter as part of Goethe's comedy *Der Triumph der Empfindsamkeit* – a gross incongruity, as the poet later admitted. THOMAS BAUMAN

Proserpina y el extranjero ('Proserpina and the Visitor'). Opera in three acts by JUAN JOSÉ CASTRO to a libretto by Omar del Carlo after his own play; Milan, Teatro alla Scala, 17 March 1952 (as *Proserpina e lo straniero*).

Castro's second opera, an adaptation of the Persephone myth, is based on a play by the Argentine dramatist Omar del Carlo (1918–75). Proserpina (soprano) is abducted by Porfirio Sosa (tenor) and carried to a brothel in suburban Buenos Aires owned by Marfa (contralto). The grief of Proserpina's mother Demetria (mezzo-soprano) causes her to neglect the harvests, and famine spreads. A Visitor (baritone) returns to the brothel, a house that was once his own, to seek reconciliation with his dead wife Flavia (soprano). Bonded to Flavia, the Visitor cannot reciprocate Proserpina's love for him; he is attacked and murdered by Sosa and Marcial Quiroga (tenor), Proserpina's seducers. His death releases Proserpina from her fate, redeems her from the moral corruption of the city and allows her to return to the country. The idea of seasonal rebirth in the Greek myth is thus transferred to the idea of redemption through the death of an innocent man.

Castro differentiated between the story's banal realism and the myth's poetic strength through distinct compositional approaches: motivic material characterizing conceptual abstractions (e.g. fate, the past, death, redemption) is subjected to complex treatment, while elements from the urban popular tradition portray characters who never transcend reality, as mirrors of their social milieu. The main characters (Proserpina, Demetria, the Visitor) bridge the gap between the two styles through the parts they play in both the symbolic and the realistic aspects of the drama.

Although this scheme affects the work's dramatic continuity Castro maintains a climate of suggestive symbolism by combining motivic characterization with technical virtuosity. The parallel actions are also differentiated by basic pitch intervals: 4ths outline motifs associated with symbolism, while 3rds are emphasized in realistic characterizations. Myth (tenor) and the Chorus function as allegorical characters that narrate or comment on the action.

The opera was awarded the Verdi Prize in 1951; it had its Argentine première at the Teatro Colón, Buenos Aires, on 13 September 1960. MALENA KUSS

Proserpine ('Proserpina'). *Tragédie en musique* in a prologue and five acts by Jean-Baptiste Lully (*see* LULLY family, (1)) to a libretto by PHILIPPE QUINAULT after OVID's *Metamorphoses*; St Germain-en-Laye, court, 3 February 1680.

The plot tells the story of the abduction by Pluton [Pluto] (baritone) of Proserpina (soprano) but is overladen with extraneous actions, including the love of Cérès [Ceres] (soprano) for Jupiter (baritone) – understood to represent Mme de Montespan's love for Louis XIV – and an extended love intrigue for the minor deities Alphée [Alpheius] (*haute-contre*) and Aréthuse [Arethusa] (soprano). The interplay between Jupiter – represented by his messenger Mercure [Mercury] (*haute-contre*) – Ceres and Pluto permits spectacular movement from heaven to earth to Hades, and the entire story lends itself to charming pastoral imagery, for instance an echoing chorus of forest deities, alternately loud and soft, as Mount Aetna is seen spewing fire in the background (3.i).

For illustration *see* COSTUME, fig.4b. LOIS ROSOW

Prot, Félix-Jean (*b* Senlis, Oise, 1747; *d* Paris, early 1823). French composer. He studied the violin, and composition with Pietro Gianotti. When he was 14 his one-act *opéra comique*, *Le bal bourgeois*, for which Favart wrote some music, was performed with great success at the Foire de St Laurent. He joined the orchestra of the Comédie-Française as a violist in 1775 and remained there for 47 years. In 1779 his *Les rêveries renouvelées des Grecs*, a parody of Gluck's *Iphigénie* operas, was performed at the Théâtre Italien. Two more operas followed in the 1780s, but although he had Favart behind him, Prot could not compete with Grétry, Duni, Philidor and Monsigny during a period in which French musical theatre received poor support; therefore he turned to teaching and the composition of chamber music, particularly duos and trios.

all published in Paris

Le bal bourgeois (oc, 1, C.-S. Favart), Paris, OC (Foire St Laurent), Aug 1761 (1762), collab. Favart
Les rêveries renouvelées des Grecs (parodie en vers mêlée de vaudevilles, 3, Favart, C. H. F. de Voisenon and J. N. Guérin de Frémicourt), Paris, Italien, 26 June 1779 (1779)
Le printemps (divertissement pastoral, 1, A. P. A. di Piis and P. Y. Barré), Marly, 19 May 1781 (1781)
L'amour à l'épreuve (oc, 1, L.-F. Faur), Paris, Italien, 13 Aug 1784 (1784) ARISTIDE WIRSTA

Prota. Italian family of composers, active in Naples in the 18th and early 19th centuries.

(1) **Ignazio Prota** (*b* Naples, 15 Sept 1690; *d* Naples, Jan 1748). Composer. Trained in Naples, he con-

tributed a prologue, several arias and three *buffo* scenes to a performance of C. F. Pollarolo's *Tito Manlio* at the Teatro S Bartolomeo in Naples in 1720. The following year he composed his first *opera buffa*, in Neapolitan dialect, *La finta fattucchiera*, for the Teatro dei Fiorentini. After his appointment to the Neapolitan conservatory S Onofrio a Capuana in 1722, he curtailed his promising career as an operatic composer in favour of teaching. His pupils included Gennaro Manna, Jommelli, Latilla and Domenico Fischietti. Several of his descendants became musicians. In 19th-century literature (Fétis, Florimo, Eitner) various members of the family are confused, and Ignazio's biography is discussed under the name of his son Giuseppe (1737–1807), an oboist.

La finta fattucchiera (ob, A. Birini), Naples, Fiorentini, spr. 1721
La vedova ingegnosa [Strabone e Drusilla] (int, T. Mariani), Naples, S Bartolomeo, 12 July 1735 [perf. with L. Leo: Emira]
La Camilla (ob, A. Palomba), Naples, Nuovo, wint. 1737

Contribs. to: C. F. Pollarolo: Tito Manlio, 1720, 1 aria I-Nc

(2) Tommaso Prota (*b* Naples, ?1727; *d* after 1768). Composer, son of (1) Ignazio Prota. Probably an approximate contemporary of Tommaso Traetta (*b* 1727), he presented himself to the Neapolitan public with *La moglie padrone*, an *opera buffa* on a libretto by Lantino Liviano (pseudonym of Antonio Villano), at the Teatro Nuovo in 1748. From existing manuscripts, performance records and publications of his instrumental works it seems that he left Naples for Malta, worked in various Italian cities and perhaps also in Paris and London. His *opera buffa L'abate, ossia Il poeta moderno* was staged in Malta (Teatru Manoel, 1752), and his intermezzo *Il cicisbeo burlato* in Bologna (Teatro Marsigli-Rossi, January 1764). All three stage works are lost.

(3) Gabriele Prota (*b* Naples, 19 May 1755; *d* Naples, 22 June 1843). Composer, grandson of (1) Ignazio Prota. He was a *maestro di cappella* in Naples. In 1785, according to Prota-Giurleo, he married a young Parisian, Rosalie Laurent, who had been raised and educated in Naples. During the 1790s he composed several successful *opere buffe*, among them *I studenti*, for Neapolitan theatres. Gabriele and his wife became politically associated with the Jacobin cause and the 1799 republican uprising, and were incarcerated after the Bourbons had crushed the revolution. In 1806, when the French began to rule Naples, King Joseph Bonaparte appointed Mme Prota director of the newly formed music school for women, the Collegio delle Donzelle, and Gabriele became *maestro di cappella* and singing teacher there.

Ezio (os, P. Metastasio), Perugia, Civico de' Verzaro, carn. 1784 [acc. to Stieger]
Le donne dispettose (ob, G. Palomba), Naples, Fondo, carn. 1793
Le furberie deluse (ob, Palomba), Naples, Nuovo, carn. 1793
I studenti (ob, Palomba), Naples, Fondo, May 1796, I-Nc

(4) Giovanni Prota (*b* Naples, *c*1786; *d* Naples, ? 13 June 1843). Composer and teacher, son of (3) Gabriele Prota and Rosalie Laurent. His approximate date of birth is based on Prota-Giurleo's claim that the parents were married in 1785; a Requiem mass attributed to Giovanni and dated 20 December 1798 would therefore represent the efforts of a 12-year-old. His first opera, *Il servo furbo*, was staged at the Teatro dei Fiorentini in Naples in 1803. After the performance of his *opera buffa, Amor dal naufragio*, at the Teatro Nuovo in

1810, the *Corriere di Napoli* praised the 'giovanine maestro di cappella' for his accomplishments in the genre. About 1820, Giovanni became a teacher at the Educandato dei Miracoli.

Il servo furbo (ob, G. Palomba), Naples, Fiorentini, carn. 1803, I-Nc
Amor dal naufragio (ob, A. L. Tottola), Naples, Nuovo, Jan 1810, sinfonia Nc
Il cimento felice (dg, M. Cimorelli), Naples, Fiorentini, aut. 1815, Nc, aria and duet Mc

EitnerQ; ES; FétisB; FlorimoN; SteigerO
U. Rolandi: *Musica e musicisti in Malta* (Livorno, 1932)
U. Prota-Giurleo: *La famiglia napoletana dei Prota nella storia della musica* (Milan, 1957)   HANNS-BERTOLD DIETZ

Prota-Giurleo, Ulisse (*b* Naples, 13 March 1886; *d* Perugia, 9 Feb 1966). Italian musicologist. He devoted himself to the history of Neapolitan music and theatre, assisting his teacher, Salvatore di Giacomo, with his two volumes on the conservatories (1924–8). From 1920 to 1930 he gathered information on the history of music and theatrical and artistic life in the city, and made important contributions to knowledge of the Scarlatti family, Logroscino and the early history of *opera buffa*, Sacchini, Cimarosa, Porpora, Piccinni, Provenzale, Insanguine and others, including his own family, the Prota. He was unable to find a publisher for a planned comprehensive history of Neapolitan music, but part of his research appeared in the article 'Breve storia del teatro di corte', one of the most important 20th-century essays in that field.

Musicisti napoletani in Russia (Naples, 1923)
Musicisti napoletani alla corte di Portogallo (Naples, 1924)
Alessandro Scarlatti 'il Palermitano' (Naples, 1926)
La grande orchestra del Teatro San Carlo nel '700 (Naples, 1927)
Nicola Logroscino 'il dio dell'opera buffa' (Naples, 1927)
'Breve storia del teatro di corte e della musica a Napoli nei secoli XVII e XVIII', Il teatro di corte del Palazzo Reale di Napoli (Naples, 1952), 19–146
Francesco Cirillo e l'introduzione del melodramma a Napoli (Grumo Nevano, 1952)
La famiglia napoletana dei Prota nella storia della musica (Milan, 1957)
I teatri di Napoli nel '600: la commedia e le maschere (Naples, 1962)
'Notizie biografiche intorno ad alcuni musicisti, d'oltralpe a Napoli nel settecento', AnMc, no.2 (1965), 112–43
with A. Giovine: Giacomo Insanguine detto Monopoli, musicista monopolitano: cenni biografici, elenco di rappresentazioni, bibliografia, indice vari e iconografia (Bari, 1969)
                                                    CAROLYN GIANTURCO

Protagonist, Der ('The Protagonist'). Opera in one act, op.14, by KURT WEILL to a libretto by Georg Kaiser after his own play; Dresden, Staatsoper, 27 March 1926.

The setting is Shakespeare's England. A troupe of players, led by the Protagonist (tenor), are to entertain the Duke. They are accompanied by the Protagonist's sister, Catherine (soprano), who alone is capable of easing him back to reality after intense theatrical performances. Almost incestuously close to her, he is ignorant of her love affair with a young gentleman (baritone). After tortured deliberation, however, she has resolved to tell him about it. Meanwhile, to entertain the Duke's guests, who include foreign dignitaries, the players rehearse a wordless pantomime. It is a bawdy farce: a man enlists a monk to distract his wife while he himself commits adultery with his mistress. When Catherine tries to make her confession, the Protagonist is genial and incredulous. The Major-Domo (tenor) announces the unexpected arrival of a Bishop: a serious drama is now required, and comedy must yield to tragedy. A second pantomime is rehearsed, the monk replaced by a rich and dissipated elderly gentleman. Catching sight of his wife from the street, the Protagonist dashes into the house in a jealous rage. Wielding a dagger, he hurls himself against the door of the room in which she is extravagantly caressing her elderly paramour. The players are confused. How will the pantomime end? As his sister enters to tell him of her happiness, the Protagonist plunges the dagger into her neck. Still in the grip of passion, he begs that his arrest be postponed. Otherwise he will forfeit his best role, which 'can no longer distinguish between real and feigned insanity'. The stage musicians, who have accompanied the pantomimes, gradually descend into the orchestra pit.

Der Protagonist was Weill's first mature opera (two earlier operas have not survived). Like Berg's *Wozzeck* and Zimmermann's *Die Soldaten*, it is a *Literaturoper*: its libretto was derived, with little alteration, from Georg Kaiser's play *Der Protagonist* (1920). The two pantomime scenes, already part of Kaiser's scenario, prompted Weill to alternate musical idioms in order to distinguish the layers of the action. In sharp contrast to the late-romantic lyricism of the opera proper, which teeters on the brink of atonality, the stage band performs music whose rhythmic discipline and ambiguous diatonicism suggest a debt to the neo-classical Stravinsky. The first pantomime lends itself also to performance as a separate concert item.

STEPHEN HINTON

Protschka, Josef (*b* Prague, 5 Feb 1944). German tenor of Czech birth. He studied in Cologne and made his début in 1977 at Giessen; after singing in Saarbrücken, in 1980 he was engaged at Cologne. He has also appeared in Düsseldorf, Mannheim, Munich and Hanover and has sung Peisander (*Il ritorno d'Ulisse*) in Salzburg (1985), Idomeneus at Drottningholm (1986), Flamand (*Capriccio*) in Florence and Hoffmann at Bregenz (1987) and the title role of *Fierrabras* in Vienna (1988). His repertory includes Tamino, Don Ottavio, Max, Lionel, Faust, Werther, Jeník, Loge and Tom Rakewell. He has a strong, warm-toned and lyrical voice which has become larger and more dramatic through tackling heavier roles such as Florestan, which he sang at Hamburg (1988), Brussels (1989) and Covent Garden (1990), and Lohengrin, which he sang in Zürich (1991).

ELIZABETH FORBES

Protti, Aldo (*b* Cremona, 19 July 1920). Italian baritone. He studied in Parma and made his début as Figaro in *Il barbiere di Siviglia* in 1948. At La Scala he first appeared in *Aida* in 1950, then in *Rigoletto* in 1954; he continued to sing at the house for many years. Described by Giorgio Gualerzi in 1972 as 'one of the most reliable baritones in the business' (*Opera*, xxiii, 1972, p.744), he sang the standard Italian repertory in most of the major European houses (though not at Covent Garden) and in the USA, making his Metropolitan début at the age of 65 as Rigoletto. His performances, never subtle, have been increasingly criticized for lack of character in the voice and the acting; this view of his work is largely borne out by the many recordings of complete operas he made in the 1950s and 60s, which, however, show a sturdy, serviceable voice and an authoritative manner.

J. B. STEANE

Provenzale, Francesco (*b* Naples, *c*1626; *d* Naples, 6 Sept 1704). Italian composer. He was the first prominent Neapolitan musician to compose opera, and he is now recognized as the forerunner of the long line of Neapolitan composers of opera and other forms of vocal music, sometimes called the Neapolitan school, active in the 18th century. Some indication of Provenzale's date of birth comes from the records of his marriage banns, which are dated 5 January 1660 and state that he was at the time 'about 33 years old'. It is known that he became associated with the opera company in Naples around 1652–3 and that this company presented his first opera, *Il Ciro*, probably in 1653. The total extent of his composition for the Neapolitan operatic stage in the 1650s remains a matter for conjecture. But the preface to the libretto of his *Il Theseo, o vero L'incostanza trionfante* (1658, Naples) testifies that he had a hand in at least four operas during that decade:

This time you have a drama that cannot fail to please you. The poet is able, and much more so is the composer of the music, your Neapolitan Sig. Francesco Provenzale, who, if he knew how to satisfy you in Ciro, Xerse and Artemisia, certainly knows how to please you even more in this one, in which he has managed to demonstrate the vivacity of his spirit to better advantage.

An opera with the title *Il Ciro* and with music by an unstated Neapolitan composer was presented at the Teatro SS Giovanni e Paolo, Venice, in 1654, with additional music by Cavalli. There seems no doubt that this opera was Provenzale's. Provenzale may afterwards have returned the compliment that Cavalli paid him by adapting his *Il Ciro*. Cavalli wrote two original operas called *Xerse* and *Artemisia* for Venice, in 1654 and 1656 respectively. Since the operatic company then in Naples was in the habit of borrowing extensively from the Venetian repertory, it is possible that Provenzale's *Xerse* and *Artemisia* were arrangements of Cavalli's operas rather than compositions totally his own. Equal uncertainty surrounds Provenzale's work for the professional theatre in the 1660s. Prota-Giurleo has used circumstantial evidence to ascribe to him two operas to which no contemporary document of the 1660s puts a composer's name. These are *La Cloridea* (1660, Naples) and *La Bisalba, o vero Offendere chi più s'ama* (1667–8, Naples), credited to Provenzale on the grounds that the librettist, Pedro Sanz Palomera y Velasco, was witness at his wedding and was evidently a friend of his. As regards the operas *Lo schiavo di sua moglie* and *Difendere l'offensore* (usually known as *La Stellidaura vendicata*), there is no doubt either about dates or about attribution. The music of both these works has survived. The score of the first gives the year of composition as 1671; the second was, according to documentary evidence, first performed in the Naples suburb of Mergellina in September 1674. Some authorities have expressed the view that Provenzale was involved in another opera presented in Naples in 1678, *Chi tal nasce tal vive, o vero L'Alessandro Bala*, but this has not been proved. There is no evidence that he was engaged in opera for the professional stage after 1678.

Provenzale's dissociation from opera at Naples in his later years is a fact of some interest. It may partly be explained by the increasing competition created by other, non-Neapolitan opera composers, notably P. A. Ziani and Alessandro Scarlatti, who came to work in Naples at one time or another during the last quarter of the century. It may also be accounted for by the growing scope of his other activities. These included composing

Ex.1 *Lo schiavo di sua moglie*, Act 1

['How many of these ladies are in the situation of desiring a husband and of looking for one all the time.']

and directing music in his capacity as *maestro di cappella* to the city of Naples, a post he gained on 17 September 1665. Since 1663 he had also been busy as a teacher, having been appointed chief *maestro* at the Neapolitan Conservatorio S Maria di Loreto that year (he was paid from 1 March). Provenzale's teaching methods included making his pupils perform operas on sacred subjects in the conservatory, a good way of training them for the professional theatre. He himself composed one such work, *La fenice d'Avila Teresa di Giesù* (1672), and he probably composed others too. The libretto of another sacred opera with music by Provenzale, *La colomba ferita*, was published in Naples in 1670. He left the Loreto at the end of October 1675, having undertaken to head the music staff at another conservatory, the S Maria della Pietà dei Turchini. Here he taught until old age forced his retirement in April 1701.

Provenzale's other posts included that of *maestro di cappella* to the treasury of S Gennaro (1686–99). Another position in Naples in which he was interested was that of *maestro di cappella* to the viceregal court. He was made *maestro onorario* in 1680, but when the *maestro*, P. A. Ziani, died on 12 February 1684 his job was given not to Provenzale, as had been expected, but to the 23-year-old Alessandro Scarlatti. Provenzale resigned in protest, but returned to court service between 24 January and 11 March 1688 as *maestro di cappella di camera*, and was reinstated *maestro onorario* in 1690.

The music of the two surviving operas whose music is entirely by Provenzale, *Lo schiavo di sua moglie* and *La Stellidaura vendicata*, consists of a free alternation of recitatives, ariosos, arias and ensembles such as is found in other Italian operas of the period. His lyrical items are variously structured, only a minority being in the da capo form that later, 18th-century Neapolitan composers used so often. The chromatic, highly expressive style he adopted in certain laments has been praised by historians ever since Rolland first drew attention to them. However, his style is generally more lively and genial than this. Although he often modelled it on that of Cesti and other Venetian contemporaries, he was

capable of producing melodies with a warm individuality, and some of his songs too have a dance-like, popular flavour that recent commentators have claimed is akin to southern Italian folk music (see ex.1).

See also SCHIAVO DI SUA MOGLIE, LO.

Il Ciro (drama per musica, 3, G. C. Sorrentino), Naples, S Bartolomeo, ? 1653; with musical addns by F. Cavalli, Venice, SS Giovanni e Paolo, 4 Feb 1654; further musical addns by A. Mattioli, Venice, 1665, *I-Vnm*
Xerse (drama per musica, N. Minato), Naples, S Bartolomeo, 1657, [? adaptation of Cavalli's Xerse]
Artemisia (Minato), Naples, S Bartolomeo, ?1658 [? adaptation of Cavalli's Artemisia]
Il Theseo, o vero L'incostanza trionfante (drama per musica, 3, G. delle Chiavi), Naples, S Bartolomeo, 20 Nov 1658
La colomba ferita (op sacra, prol., 3, G. Castaldo), Naples, 1670
Lo schiavo di sua moglie (melodrama, prol., 3, F. A. Paolella), Naples, Palazzo Reale, 21 April 1672, *Rsc*
La fenice d'Avila Teresa di Giesù (melodrama sacro, 3, Castaldo), Naples, Conservatory S Maria di Loreto, 6 Nov 1672
Difendere l'offensore, o vero La Stellidaura vendicata (melodrama, 3, A. Perrucci), Naples, Villa Cursi Cicinelli, Mergellina, 2 Sept 1674, *Rsc*, arias *Nc*

ES (W. Stalnaker)
R. Rolland: *Les origines du théâtre lyrique moderne: l'histoire de l'opéra en Europe avant Lully et Scarlatti* (Paris, 1895, 4/1936)
H. Goldschmidt: 'Francesco Provenzale als Dramatiker', *SIMG*, vii (1905–6), 608–34
G. Pannain: 'Francesco Provenzale e la lirica del suo tempo', *RMI*, xxxii (1925), 497–518
U. Prota-Giurleo: 'Francesco Provenzale', *Archivi*, xxv (1958), 53
A. Mondolfi Bossarelli: 'Vita e stile di Francesco Provenzale: la questione di "Alessandro Bala" ', *Annuario del Conservatorio S. Pietro a Maiella, Naples*, x (1962–3), 15
L. Bianconi: 'Funktionen des Operntheaters in Neapel bis 1700 und die Rolle Alessandro Scarlattis', *Colloquium Alessandro Scarlattis: Würzburg 1975*, 13–111
MICHAEL F. ROBINSON (with DALE E. MONSON)

Provisional Theatre (Prozatímní Divadlo). Opera house in Prague, opened in 1862; *see* PRAGUE, §III, 1.

Prowse, Philip (*b* Worcestershire, 29 Dec 1937). English designer and director. He studied at the Slade School of Fine Art in London, and later taught at the Birmingham College of Art and then the Slade. He designed many drama productions in the 1960s in England, Belgium, Sweden and Germany. His first designs for Covent Garden (1961) were for ballets, followed by Gluck's *Orfeo* in 1969 and Strauss's *Ariadne auf Naxos* in 1976. In 1970 he became Associate Director of Glasgow Citizens' Theatre, where he directed and designed many productions, later doubling the two tasks in opera (Handel's *Tamerlano*, 1982, WNO; Bizet's *Les pêcheurs de perles*, 1987, ENO). He had notable successes during the first ten years of Opera North, with productions of Weill's *Die Dreigroschenoper*, Verdi's *Aida* and Strauss's *Daphne*. In 1986 he designed Jonathan Miller's production of *Don Giovanni* for ENO. While his work has often aroused controversy, Prowse's productions fuse traditional stagings with updated designs more successfully than most.
PATRICK O'CONNOR

Prozess, Der ('The Trial'). Opera in nine scenes (two parts) by GOTTFRIED VON EINEM to a libretto by BORIS

BLACHER and Heinz von Cramer after Franz Kafka's novel; Salzburg, Festspielhaus, 17 August 1953.

Von Einem selected nine episodes from Kafka's chilling novel about the bank signatory Josef K., who is placed on trial for an unspecified crime. Part 1 opens in Josef K.'s lodgings. Two men enter his room and tell Josef K. (tenor) that he is to be arrested. He is instructed to dress and report immediately to the warder who is waiting for him in the next room. Nevertheless, his arrest should not necessarily prevent him from going to work. In the evening, Josef returns from the bank and tries to explain the situation to his neighbour Fräulein Bürstner (soprano), for it was in her room that he was arrested. He loses his nerve and starts to scream. When Fräulein Bürstner pushes him out of the room he kisses her passionately. Later that evening, Josef becomes more uncertain and feels that he is under constant observation. The court committal is held later, in the loft. Josef tries to ridicule the senselessness of the trial, but a scream from the bailiff's wife interrupts his speech. The investigating Magistrate (baritone) resumes the trial as a crowd gathers, but Josef abuses the court and runs away. In Part 2 the two men who were present when Josef was initially arrested beat him up. His uncle brings him to a Solicitor (baritone) who is already well-informed about the trial, more so than the accused. Even at the bank, the trial has become common knowledge. A Business Acquaintance (baritone) suggests that he should enlist the help of the painter Titorelli (tenor). However, the painter convinces Josef that it is impossible for him to be free and suggests that he might try to delay the trial. The final scene takes place in the cathedral. Josef appeals to the Prison Chaplain (baritone) for help, but two thugs carry him off to his execution.

Der Prozess, von Einem's second opera, is a parable about the individual pitted against a bureaucratic society. It is probably the first attempt by a postwar composer to meet the challenges of Kafka's almost surrealist mixture of fantasy and realism. The musical language is harsh, with obsessive rhythmic ostinatos and neutral vocal lines that follow the rise and fall of natural speech.   ERIK LEVI

Prudent [first name unknown] (*d* 1780 or 1781). French composer. Very little is known of his life except that he taught the violin and composition. He published some *cantatilles* in 1745 and wrote a successful motet for the Concert Spirituel in 1766. He may also be the Prudent mentioned by *Les spectacles de Paris* of 1758 as a violinist in the orchestra of the Concert Spirituel. Prudent's principal opera, *Les jardiniers*, is a *comédie mêlée d'ariettes* in two acts to a libretto by Davesne, first given in Paris at the Comédie-Italienne (Hôtel de Bourgogne), on 15 July 1771; arias from it were published in 1771 and the score in 1772. The work is interesting in that it represents the *opéra comique* of the 1760s and 70s at its least complex. Comic elements play a large part in descriptive arias and in ensembles expressing contradictory feelings; the music for the two lovers, however, ranges from the sentimental to the pathetic, with various instrumental effects and frequent recourse to the key of G minor. The public was clearly avid for this kind of opera, for *Les jardiniers* was revived in 1781. Prudent also wrote *L'heureux engagement*, an *opéra comique* to a libretto by Roger-Timothée Pleinchesne (Paris, Ambigu-Comique, 8 October 1772).   MICHEL NOIRAY

Pruett, Jerome (*b* Poplar Bluff, MO, 22 Nov 1941). American tenor. He studied in St Louis and Colorado, making his début in 1974 at Carnegie Hall as Ugo in *Parisina*, then singing with the New York City Opera. In 1975 he was engaged at the Vienna Volksoper singing in the première of Wolpert's *Der eingebildete Kranke*. In 1977 he sang Henry Morosus at Glyndebourne, returning in 1985 as Matteo (*Arabella*). In 1983 he sang Julien (*Louise*) and Boris (*Kát'a Kabanová*) at Brussels and Pelléas at Geneva. For Opera North (1986–7) he sang Faust and Alfredo. He has appeared in Paris, Amsterdam, Bologna and Lausanne. His repertory includes Belmonte, Tamino, Ferrando, Don Ottavio, the Podestà (*La finta giardiniera*), Tonio (*La fille du régiment*), Ernesto, Fenton (Nicolai and Verdi), Fritz (*La Grande-Duchesse de Gérolstein*) and Armand (*Boulevard Solitude*). An excellent actor, he uses his light, lyric voice with intelligence.   ELIZABETH FORBES

Prunières, Henry (*b* Paris, 24 May 1886; *d* Nanterre, 11 April 1942). French musicologist. A pupil of Rolland at the Sorbonne from 1906, he took the doctorat ès lettres in 1913 with dissertations on Italian opera and the *ballet de cour* in France before Lully. He taught at the Ecole des Hautes Etudes Sociales, 1909–14. In 1920 he founded and directed (until 1939) the *Revue musicale* and from 1921 its series of concerts, largely of contemporary music; concurrently he was Paris music correspondent of the *New York Times* (1924–35).

Prunières' writings are largely centred on French 17th-century music, above all Lully, whom he identified as the founder of French music. He returned repeatedly to the period. One of his last enterprises was a collected edition of Lully's music (*Oeuvres complètes*, Paris, 1930–39), sadly left incomplete. The most useful volume is *Alceste* since there is no complete full score of this work dating from Lully's lifetime; Prunières' collation of librettos, part-books and incomplete versions is masterly. His book on Cavalli is probably his most successful for the general reader, combining something of the breadth of scope of his scholarly writing with a lively anecdotal style.

Lully (Paris, 1910, 2/1927)

L'opéra italien en France avant Lulli (diss., U. of Paris, 1913; Paris, 1913)

Le ballet de cour en France avant Benserade et Lully (supplementary diss., U. of Paris, 1913; Paris, 1914)

ed.: Stendhal: *Vie de Rossini* (Paris, 1922)

Claudio Monteverdi (Paris, 1924)

La vie et l'oeuvre de Claudio Monteverdi (Paris, 1926; Eng. trans., 1926)

La vie illustre et libertine de Jean-Baptiste Lully (Paris, 1929)

Cavalli et l'opéra vénitien au XVIIe siècle (Paris, 1931)

Nouvelle histoire de la musique (Paris, 1934–6; Eng. trans., 1943)
                                          PATRICIA HOWARD

Pruslin, Stephen (**Lawrence**) (*b* New York, 16 April 1940). American librettist and writer. He studied music at Brandeis University and at Princeton and in 1964 settled permanently in London to pursue a career as a concert pianist. In 1967 he was a founder-member of the Pierrot Players and in 1970 of the Fires of London, appearing with the groups in the first performances of many of Maxwell Davies's music-theatre works and chamber operas. He provided the librettos for Birtwistle's *Monodrama* (1967, withdrawn) and *Punch and Judy* (1968). In the latter he constructed a thoroughly adult, highly ritualized scenario from the historical tangle of tales that have been woven around the children's entertainment; the text is sustained upon a fabric of dense allusion and skilful word play. Pruslin has written extensively on the music of Maxwell Davies, and was the editor of *Peter Maxwell Davies: Studies from Two Decades* (London, 1979).

ANDREW CLEMENTS

Pryanishnikov, Ippolit Petrovich (*b* Kerch', 14/26 Aug 1847; *d* Moscow, 11 Nov 1921). Russian baritone and director. He studied in St Petersburg and Milan and sang in Italy until 1877. He made his début at the Mariinsky Theatre, St Petersburg, as Rubinstein's Demon (1878) and sang there until 1886, notably as Lionel in the première of Tchaikovsky's *Maid of Orleans* and Mizgir' in the première of Rimsky-Korsakov's *Snow Maiden*. Highly valued by Tchaikovsky, he was the first St Petersburg Yevgeny Onegin and Mazeppa. He directed operas by Borodin, Rimsky-Korsakov and Leoncavallo in both Tbilisi and Moscow.

DAVID CUMMINGS

Pskovityanka. Opera by N. A. Rimsky-Korsakov; *see* MAID OF PSKOV, THE.

Psyche. Tragic semi-opera in five acts by MATTHEW LOCKE to a libretto by Thomas Shadwell, after the *tragédie-ballet* of the same name by Lully to words by Molière, Corneille and Quinault (*see* PSYCHÉ below); London, Dorset Garden Theatre, 27 February 1675.

Probably commissioned by Thomas Betterton in October 1673 for the celebration of the marriage of the Duke of York (later James II) and Mary of Modena, the opera had its production delayed 16 months for political reasons. *Psyche* was then brought out to capitalize on the huge popularity of the semi-operatic *Tempest*; though far less successful, it was strikingly original and influenced Purcell's *Dido and Aeneas* and *King Arthur* as well as serving as a model for Congreve and Eccles's opera *Semele* some 30 years later. *Psyche* was Locke's last stage work; he claimed for it the title 'English Opera' even though, as he explained in a preface to the published score (1675), 'all the Tragedy be not in Musick', but mixed 'with interlocutions, as more proper to our [English] Genius'. In fact, *Psyche* came very close to being a true opera.

Princess Psyche, the most beautiful woman in the world, is in retreat, enjoying rustic entertainments offered by Pan (bass) and his followers. Her peace is disrupted first by Envy (bass) and Ambition and then by the rival princes Nicander and Polynices, who come courting. Her older sisters Cidippe and Aglaura, envious of Psyche's beauty, arouse Venus's (soprano) jealousy of her. The goddess descends and in a recitative ('With kindness I your pray'rs receive') offers to suborn Apollo (countertenor) into condemning Psyche to marry a poisonous serpent. The procession to the temple is accompanied by grand choruses of priests interspersed with recitatives and ariettas. Psyche's abandonment at the mouth of the serpent's cave is preceded by a portentous scene for despairing lovers, who exchange spoken and sung farewells, then commit mass suicide.

Psyche is whisked away by zephyrs to Cupid's palace, where she is entertained by Vulcan (tenor) and the Cyclops hammering on anvils in 'Ye bold sons of earth', an air and chorus of comic relief which anticipates the Sailors' Song in *Dido and Aeneas*. Cupid, disguised in human form, seduces Psyche with a musical *carpe diem*. Meanwhile back on earth, Nicander and Polynices are fêted for having killed the serpent in another grand and somewhat ponderous musical scene. This is followed without pause by a dialogue between Venus and Mars (tenor), who plot Psyche's downfall. Much of the third act is thus conducted in almost continuous music.

In Act 4 the evil sisters arrive at the heavenly palace, only to be insulted by the song and chorus 'Let old age in its envy'. They persuade Psyche to ask Cupid to reveal his true identity, a violation of Olympian law. As a mortal, Psyche is cast back to earth, where she is prevented from killing herself by river nymphs, who sing a highly contrapuntal trio. Venus then takes her revenge: Psyche is pulled down to Hell, and the rival princes commit suicide. The final act opens in the Underworld with a jolly entertainment of furies and devils, another long musical scene which includes a recitative-arioso for Pluto (baritone), who pardons Psyche and arranges her return to Cupid's palace. Proserpina (soprano) gives her a box to be delivered to Venus. Overcome by curiosity during her journey (notice the parallels with the Orpheus myth), Psyche opens the box and is killed by the 'dark fumes' intended for Venus. Apollo appears and the drama concludes with a grand musical entertainment to celebrate Psyche's apotheosis.

Psyche was a lavish production, and the printed score (though lacking much of the dance music) indicates rich orchestration with a great variety of instruments. But the choral music sacrifices melodic interest to contrapuntal artifice, and the recitatives and ariosos are forced and less natural than Locke's previous efforts. This work is still noteworthy for ingeniously blurring the boundary between speech and song. It pointed the way towards a distinctive kind of English music drama and served as a worthy model when Purcell began to compose semi-operas in 1690.

CURTIS PRICE

Psyché ('Psyche'). *Tragédie en musique* in a prologue and five acts by Jean-Baptiste Lully (*see* LULLY family, (1)) to a libretto by THOMAS CORNEILLE after Apuleius's *The Golden Ass*; Paris, Opéra, 19 April 1678.

The plot, based on the story of Psyche (soprano) and L'Amour [Cupid] (soprano), was first used by Lully in 1671 for his *tragédie-ballet Psyché* to a libretto by Molière, Pierre Corneille and Phillippe Quinault. The authors retained the *intermèdes* from the *tragédie-ballet* version (including an old-fashioned *plainte italienne*), replaced spoken dialogue with recitatives and strengthened the roles of the gods at the expense of the mortal characters. *Psyché* was the first of two collaborations between Lully and Thomas Corneille, necessitated by Quinault's disgrace at court. The première met with little enthusiasm but a Paris revival in 1703 was more successful.

LOIS ROSOW

P'tites Michu, Les ('The Little Michus'). *Opérette* in three acts by ANDRÉ MESSAGER to a libretto by ALBERT VANLOO and Georges Duval; Paris, Théâtre des Bouffes-Parisiens, 16 November 1897.

The plot revolves around the similarity between Marie-Blanche and Blanche-Marie (soprano, mezzo-soprano), the daughters of Parisian shopkeepers M. and Mme Michu (tenor, mezzo-soprano). Only one of the girls is really their daughter, the other having been entrusted to the Michus by the Général des Ifs (baritone), who subsequently returns and wishes to marry her to one of his officers, Captain Gaston (baritone). Unfortunately, nobody knows which of the two girls is the general's daughter. Gaston loves both girls, but finally chooses Marie-Blanche who, guessing that he has in fact chosen wrongly, and that she is a Michu, manages to convince everyone that Blanche-Marie is the general's daughter. A double wedding follows, with Marie-Blanche marrying Aristide (tenor), the Michus' shop assistant.

Les p'tites Michu was an important turning-point in Messager's career, following the failure of his more serious *Le chevalier d'Harmental* in May 1896. Its success led to a further collaboration (*Véronique*) with Duval and Vanloo a year later. The first British performance on 29 April 1905 (as *The Little Michus*, Daly's Theatre, London, with words by Henry Hamilton and Percy Greenbank) included some extra numbers, such as 'Miss Nobody from nowhere' (Act 2, no.13a). The most popular number from the operetta was the waltz-tempo 'Blanche-Marie et Marie-Blanche' (Act 1, no.2).   JOHN WAGSTAFF

Publishing.

1. Forms of publication: definitions. 2. General survey. 3. The 17th and 18th centuries: (i) Italy (ii) Germany (iii) France (iv) England (v) Other countries. 4. The 19th and 20th centuries: (i) General (ii) Germany and Austria (iii) France (iv) Italy (v) England (vi) Other countries.

1. FORMS OF PUBLICATION: DEFINITIONS. The music of operas has traditionally been written out or published in a number of forms designed to meet the needs of performers, amateurs and students. Whether in manuscript or in print, in whole or in part, the music may be presented in various forms, of which the following are the most common:

(a) 'Full score, Orchestral score, Conductor's score' (Fr. *partition d'orchestre, grande partition*; Ger. *Orchesterpartitur, Dirigierpartitur, Direktionspartitur*; It. *partitura d'orchestra*): the complete vocal and instrumental parts, or groups of parts, that comprise the work, aligned vertically – typically in a large format suitable for use by a conductor. A 'conductor's' score may also signify a vocal score marked up with details of instrumentation, for use when no full score exists. A full score in smaller format (but larger than miniature), designed primarily for consultation rather than performance, is known as a 'study' score (Fr. *partition d'étude*; Ger. *Studienpartitur*; It. *partitura da studio*). Smaller still, typically about 19 by 14 cm, is a 'miniature' or 'pocket' score (Fr. *partition de poche, partition in 8°, petite partition*; Ger. *Taschenpartitur, kleine Partitur*; It. *partitura tascabile, partitura in 8°*).

(b) 'Orchestral parts, Orchestral material' (Fr. *parties d'orchestre, matériel d'orchestre*; Ger. *Orchesterstimmen*; It. *parti d'orchestra, materiali d'orchestra*): the individual parts for each instrument or a complete set of such parts, printed separately for the use of the players, normally in large format. 'Stage band' parts (Fr. *parties d'orchestre sur le théâtre*; Ger. *Bühnenorchesterstimmen, Bühnenmusikstimmen, Bühnen[stimmen]*; It. *parti [per] banda*) are for the use of on- and offstage instrumentalists; there is sometimes a separate 'stage band' score (Fr. *partition d'orchestre sur le théâtre*; Ger. *Bühnenmusikpartitur*; It. *guida-banda, partitura banda*).

(c) 'Short score, Reduced score' (Fr. *partition réduite*; Ger. *Particell*; It. *particella*): a score containing the vocal lines and the complete instrumentation, or a selection from it, condensed on to a smaller number of staves.

(d) 'Vocal score, Piano-vocal score' (Fr. *partition [pour] piano et chant, partition [pour] chant et piano, partition piano-chant*; Ger. *Klavierauszug*; It. *spartito [per canto e pianoforte], riduzione per canto e pianoforte*): a score having the vocal lines on separate staves and the orchestral music arranged for keyboard. A 'rehearsal' or 'provisional' score is a vocal score for use in rehearsals for early productions, normally reproduced from the composer's or a copyist's manuscript before publication. A 'production' score is usually a vocal score interleaved with blank folios on which production details are entered.

(e) 'Piano score, Piano reduction' (Fr. *partition réduite pour piano seul*; Ger. *Klavierauszug ohne [or mit] Text*; It. *riduzione per pianoforte [solo]*): the score, including all vocal lines, arranged for piano, sometimes with the words printed above or between the staves; for use domestically, not in the opera house. Piano solo is assumed unless otherwise stated; a common alternative is the 'piano duet' score (Fr. *partition [réduite] pour piano à quatre mains*; Ger. *Klavierauszug zu vier Händen*; It. *riduzione per pianoforte a 4 mani*).

(f) 'Chorus score' (Fr. *partition de choeurs*; Ger. *Chorpartitur*; It. *spartito del coro*): a score giving the chorus music only, usually with each part on a separate stave and without accompaniment, often with cues.

(g) 'Vocal/Chorus part' (Fr. *soliste, partie de chant, rôle/partie de choeurs*; Ger. *Sing-/Chorstimme*; It. *parte per canto, parte scannata/parte per* (or *del*) *coro*): the music for each solo or chorus singer, presented separately or in pairs, often with cues.

(h) 'Violin-conductor' (Fr. *[partition de] violon-conducteur, violon principal*; Ger. *Direktionsstimme*; It. *[parte per] violino principale*): a first violin part in which important entries for other instruments are cued in, for use by the principal violinist, primarily during the period before the mid-19th century when he was responsible for directing the orchestra in rehearsals or performances.

(i) 'Excerpt, Separate number' (Fr. *extrait, morceau détaché*; Ger. *Einzelstück, Einzelnummer*; It. *pezzo staccato, pezzo sciolto*): a vocal or orchestral number or segment of an opera, copied or published separately. Sometimes excerpts were issued first, later to be assembled to form a more or less complete score.

(j) 'Arrangement' (Fr. *arrangement*; Ger. *Übertragung, Bearbeitung*; It. *arrangiamento*): any version of the music in which the designated voices or instruments are changed, for the use of performers other than those originally intended. Often the music is freely arranged so as to become more in the nature of a transcription.

(k) 'Critical edition, Scholarly edition' (Fr. *édition critique*; Ger. *kritische Ausgabe*; It. *edizione critica*): an edition in which the musical and literary texts incorporate the findings of a thorough appraisal of the original sources. Such editions are published in full score (and sometimes also in vocal score), normally with critical notes and lists of variant readings, and often with supplements containing items (such as alternative arias) composed for particular performances in the past.

(l) 'Performing edition' (Fr. *réalisation*; Ger. *praktische Ausgabe*; It. *realizzazione, revisione*): a full or vocal score in which certain performing details (e.g. tempos, dynamics, ornamentation, phrasing and the realization of the continuo harmonies) not indicated in the sources are supplied by the editor. It may incorporate some of the advantages of a critical edition when the editorial interventions are clearly identified.

(m) 'Adaptation, Revision' (Fr. *reconstitution, adaptation*; Ger. *Rekonstruktion, Neubearbeitung, Neufassung*; It. *adattamento*): a vocal or full score of a work whose extant sources are incomplete and have been supplied by the editor; or a performing version intended to make a work more acceptable to modern ideas of what is stageworthy. Such editions may be designed to circumvent the unavailability of original instruments and voice-types (especially castratos), to rectify the deficiencies of a weak or outmoded libretto, or in some way to render a work more acceptable to prevailing tastes (as Rimsky-Korsakov sought to do in his versions of Musorgsky's operas).

Performance materials are frequently marked up by the conductor, the librarian or the performers themselves. Such markings, which are often not erased, may relate to dynamics, phrasing, bowing, or important entries; they may give the players' names, details of conductors, casts and running times; or (especially in orchestral parts) they may include cartoons, scurrilous verses and humorous annotations. A cut in performance may be indicated in various ways. One traditional notation is 'vi==de', the beginning of the cut being indicated by 'vi=' and the end by '=de'; the excised section is sometimes crossed through. In addition, paper may be stuck over the excision or, for longer cuts, pages may be stitched, stapled or even glued together.

2. GENERAL SURVEY. The publication of operas originated almost at the beginning of opera itself when, in 1601, Marescotti published scores of Peri's and Caccini's settings of *Euridice*. Throughout the history of the genre, the music of operas has regularly been printed in some form wherever music publishing has flourished; where it has not, the music has had to circulate exclusively in manuscript copies. A successful opera may well have been copied many times, for productions in several theatres and for private or institutional libraries: in such cases several copies may still be extant. Frequently, however, the music for unpublished and less well-travelled operas survives in only one or two manuscript sources, possibly fragmentary, or has been lost altogether.

It is likely that the early Italian operas were published by Marescotti and his immediate successors as much to bring honour to the patrons as to fill a specific public demand for copies of the music; and when contemporary editions of Lully's operas were issued in handsome folios the purpose was no doubt partly to present a suitably monumental record of what was regarded as the musical equivalent of the French classical theatre of Corneille, Molière and Racine. Such publications were expensive to produce and to buy, however, and did not satisfy the growing domestic market for operatic music. By the end of the 17th century, especially in Paris, Amsterdam and London, publishers had begun to cater for this new market with instrumental arrangements and keyboard reductions of songs from the current repertory, both in the form of anthologies and as separate numbers. It was not until the 19th century that the vocal score gradually became the standard form in which complete operas were published. Full scores, in large, study or miniature format, have normally been published only for the most regularly performed works: for other operas full scores have sometimes been printed in small quantities but have usually been available only direct from the publishers, together with the performance materials. Pub-

lishers have traditionally preferred to hire out rather than to sell performance materials, both for copyright and non-copyright operas; hire fees are normally levied per performance and are likely to be higher for a copyright work.

It has always been rare for orchestral, chorus and vocal parts of operas to be published (which by definition means put on sale). Ballard published parts for Lully's *Isis* in 1677, Walsh for several operas about 1710, Dalayrac and Pierre Gaveaux for several of their own operas about 1800, Schonenberger for a few operas about 1840 (including four by Donizetti) and Breitkopf & Härtel for operas by Mozart, Beethoven and Wagner in the second half of the 19th century. But these are among the rare exceptions. From the beginning until well into the 19th century performance materials normally circulated in manuscript copies, prepared under the supervision of the composer, an impresario or the publisher of the score, or by the theatre itself. The larger theatres have traditionally employed a copyist or librarian, whose responsibilities include obtaining the score and parts and ensuring that they agree with each other textually (for the version being produced) and are uniformly marked with bowings and rehearsal numbers or letters. Smaller theatres, offering only occasional and brief seasons, have relied on the impresario or visiting company to provide performance materials.

Most theatre libraries either perished in theatre fires or were discarded or dispersed as the repertory changed: there is consequently a dearth of extant manuscript as well as printed performance material available for study. Fortunately, however, some opera house collections have survived, including that of the Paris Opéra, whose library dates back to 1671. Théodore de Lajarte's catalogue of the surviving material for each opera is arranged chronologically and shows that from the beginning there was either a manuscript or printed full score available (sometimes both, and often with manuscript annotations); further, there were multiple vocal, chorus and orchestral parts and sometimes also chorus scores, all in manuscript. By the end of the 18th century there were prompter's and répétiteur's scores; and in 1808 mention is made of a 'conducteur d'orchestre' part, which would have been used by the keyboard player (responsible for the singers), and a 'violon principal' part, for the first violin (responsible for the orchestra). Soon afterwards printed vocal scores were regularly available to the company and are preserved in the library.

Until the beginning of the 20th century the manner and extent of printing operas varied considerably between the main centres of operatic performance and music publishing. It is only since 1900 that printing techniques and published editions have acquired a fairly close degree of international conformity.

3. THE 17TH AND 18TH CENTURIES.

(i) Italy. The birth of opera coincided with a period of lively activity among northern Italian music publishers. The music of the first opera, *Dafne*, was not published at the time, but the next two – Peri's and Caccini's settings of *Euridice* – were published in Florence by Giorgio Marescotti early in 1601, Caccini's setting being narrowly the first to appear (fig.1). Marescotti's heirs published excerpts from the fourth opera, Caccini's *Il rapimento di Cefalo*, in 1602. Further editions of these three works as well as six new operas were published between 1606 and 1626 in Venice, the new

1. The opening page of Caccini's 'Euridice', the first complete opera score to be published, printed from movable type (Florence: Marescotti, 1601)

operas including Monteverdi's *Orfeo* (two editions, 1609 and 1615). The first opera to be published in Rome was Vitali's *Aretusa* (1620); four further operas of Roman origin were published there between 1629 and 1639. Meanwhile, the first opera by a woman composer, Francesca Caccini's *La liberazione di Ruggiero dall'isola d'Alcina* (1625), and Gagliano and Peri's *La Flora* (1628) had been performed and published in Florence.

By 1639 as many as 17 operas had been published in Florence, Venice or Rome. The editions were printed from type in upright folio format in an open score; the degree to which the instrumentation is specified varies. From 1640 onwards, however, the picture is very different, for the general decline in music publishing in Italy drastically affected the survival of the music of many operas known to have been performed there. In the next 150 years the only complete operas published in Italy were Marazzoli's *La Vita humana* (Rome, 1658), Bertoni's *Orfeo* (two editions: Venice, c1776, and, without imprint, c1783) and Millico's *La pietà d'amore* (two Naples editions: 1782 and slightly later). For the music of later 17th- and 18th-century operas by Italian composers we have to rely on their survival as manuscripts (see fig.2) and to a limited extent on publication elsewhere (principally in London and Paris). In any case, the nature of Italian opera performance during this period made the genre inapt for publication; since each opera was conceived in terms of a single run of performances, by a particular cast in a particular city (and were it to be revived it would be altered to suit changed circumstances), the fixity of a published text

was inappropriate and there would have been little market for it. A revival of Italian music publishing from about 1770 was initiated by Luigi Marescalchi, first in Venice and then in Naples. Most of his output consisted of excerpts in full score (sometimes also with parts); he also ran a *copisteria* and hire library.

(ii) Germany. The earliest German opera whose music is extant is the Singspiel *Seelewig* by Sigmund Staden, published in 1644 in full score in a small oblong octavo format. Bontempi's *Paride*, the first Italian opera to be staged in north Germany, was published in Dresden by Melchior Bergen (1662). Excerpts from a few operas by Franck, Steffani, Kusser, Keiser and Mattheson were published from the 1680s, usually in vocal score or parts, but it was not until J. G. I. Breitkopf established his business in the middle of the 18th century that opera in Germany started to be published on a regular basis.

Breitkopf's first landmark was the full score of *Il trionfo della fedeltà* (1756), by Maria Antonia Walpurgis of Bavaria, an oblong folio of great elegance printed from a new movable type that enabled the printing of far larger editions than previously (fig.3). But although he published a full score of the same composer's *Talestri* (1765), it was and has remained unusual for German publishers to put full scores of operas on sale contemporaneously with their early productions (Wagner's works were a notable exception). Instead, from about 1770, the custom of publishing vocal scores of the most successful operas was initiated, including works by J. A. Hiller, E. W. Wolf, Georg Benda, Dittersdorf and their contemporaries. During this period the great firms of Schott (1770) and Simrock (1793) were founded, and it was Schott who published the first vocal scores of *Die Entführung* (1785) and *Don Giovanni* (1791; fig.4), the only two Mozart operas to be published complete in the composer's lifetime.

(iii) France. The first operas to be printed in France were Cambert's *Pomone* (1671) and *Les peines et les plaisirs de l'amour* (1672), both published by Christophe Ballard; only fragments of the two scores are extant. In 1672 Lully, appointed director of the Académie Royale de Musique, acquired a monopoly for producing works at the Opéra, while the house of Ballard had the sole right to publish the music performed there. Lully's first published opera was *Isis*, which was issued as separate vocal and orchestral parts in 1677. From *Bellérophon* (1679) until his death in 1687 each new Lully opera and ballet was published by Ballard in tall folio full scores printed from movable type, with each vocal part on a separate staff and the orchestral parts laid out on five or six staves (fig.5).

For some 40 years after Lully's death the firm of Ballard published most of the operas successfully performed at the Paris Opéra. At first they continued to issue folio full scores; but from 1695 onwards, beginning with Desmarets' *Théagène et Cariclée*, almost all their publications of complete operas were issued in short score, in oblong quarto format. All but a handful of these were printed from type, and it was the firm's unwillingness to adopt the techniques of engraving that contributed to its gradual decline from the 1720s. Nonetheless it established almost from the outset the twin French traditions of publishing complete scores of most of the operas in the current Paris repertory and of issuing revised editions conforming to the versions in production. Consequently, the surviving printed sources for operas performed in France, certainly until the late

2. Manuscript full score of Paolo Magni's 'Agrippina' (here called 'Nerone infante'), prepared by a professional copyist, c1703 (Milan), the only surviving source

3. Full score of Maria Antonia Walpurgis's 'Il trionfo della fedeltà', printed from movable type (Leipzig: Breitkopf, 1756)

4. First edition of the vocal score of Mozart's 'Don Giovanni' (opening of the duettino 'Là ci darem la mano', Act 1), printed from engraved plates (Mainz: Schott, 1791)

5. Full score of Lully's 'Atys' (opening of Act 2 scene iv), printed from movable type (Paris: Ballard, 1689)

19th century, are far more extensive than for those performed in other countries.

The Ballard monopoly was first challenged by Henri Foucault, who in 1702 published Theobaldo di Gatti's *Scylla*, and by Pierre Ribou, who published Campra's *Alcine* in 1705. Both were short scores engraved by Henri de Baussen, who went on to engrave a series of eight Lully scores between 1708 and 1711. Other publishers, principally Boivin, Le Clerc and Leclair, continued the tradition of regular publication of the current repertory. Almost all their output was engraved and in short score.

From the 1720s comic operas appeared in a new type of publication that was to become popular in England with the advent of ballad opera: the music of some or all of the airs, though usually only the melodic lines, was printed within, or as a supplement to, an octavo libretto. This format was continued, principally by the publisher Duchesne, in librettos of many comic operas and parodies from the 1730s to the 1770s, especially those of C.-S. Favart. Musically thin though this material may be, it provides the main surviving source for this period of French *opéra comique*.

In 1742 the score of Mondonville's *Isbé*, published by Boivin and Le Clerc, marked the beginning of a new and important phase in operatic publishing, for it initiated the custom of publishing full rather than short scores of most new operas given at the main Paris opera houses. These scores appeared in a new format, a rather squat folio (approximately 34 by 26 cm), which remained the regular size for French full scores for more than a hundred years. A host of new publishers set up in business before 1800, the most active being La Chevardière, Sieber, the Bureau d'Abonnement Musical, Leduc, Des Lauriers, Cousineau, Imbault and Nadermann.

The first contemporary foreign opera composer after Lully to make an impact in Paris was Duni, and it is to the Parisian taste for Italian music that is due the survival in printed form of so many complete operas by Piccinni, Sacchini, Paisiello, Salieri, Cimarosa and Cherubini. The most influential foreign visitor in the

6. First edition of the French version of Gluck's 'Alceste' (opening of Alcestis's aria 'Divinités du Stix'), printed from engraved plates in full score (Paris: Bureau d'Abonnement Musical, c1776)

18th century was of course Gluck. Already in 1764, nine years before the composer's arrival in Paris, Duchesne had published the original Italian version of *Orfeo ed Euridice*, and between 1774 and 1787 all his French operas were published there in full score (see fig.6).

In addition to complete scores, various periodical collections of individual numbers from current operas, set for the voice with, typically, harp, keyboard or guitar accompaniment, began to appear (weekly, fortnightly or monthly) from the 1760s. Successful examples were the *Journal hebdomadaire* (La Chevardière, 1764–83; Leduc, 1784–1808) and *Feuilles de Terpsichore*, which appeared with either harp or keyboard accompaniment (Cousineau, 1784–99).

(iv) England. The first English operatic work of which the music survives is Matthew Locke's *Psyche*, performed in 1675 and published the same year in short score (though Draghi's act tunes are lost). Extracts from this and other operas appeared in a succession of anthologies published by Playford and others from 1676 onwards. The earliest English full scores were typeset folios of Grabu's *Albion and Albanius* (1687) and Henry Purcell's *Dioclesian* (1691); these were the only complete operatic scores published in London in the 17th century.

In 1706 John Walsh initiated a new era in British music publishing by engraving in vocal score the songs from Clayton's *Arsinoe*. Thereafter most of the successful operas (many of them pasticcios) performed in London were published in engraved vocal, short or full scores, initially in folio format and substantially complete (though often without recitatives and choruses). The majority of Handel's London operas

were published, starting with *Rinaldo* (1711; see fig.7); in 1724 his *Giulio Cesare* was the first octavo score of any complete opera to appear, beautifully printed by Cluer. A few of the London operas of Bononcini and Ariosti were published complete, but from as early as 1721 Walsh more commonly printed only collected excerpts, entitled 'Favourite Songs', a practice the firm continued until its demise in the 1760s. These were folio editions, normally about 20 or 30 pages in short score, containing about five or six of the most popular arias and duets from operas currently in production. Most Italian operas performed in London until the 1780s were published in this way and some, particularly under Welcker's and Bremner's imprints from the 1760s onwards, were issued in more complete form (including operas of J. C. Bach, Piccinni and Sacchini).

In 1728 the libretto of *The Beggar's Opera* was published in two octavo editions, the first having the melodic lines of the airs printed as a supplement, the second having them interspersed with the text (see fig.8), preceded by the overture in score. This remained the standard format in which the early ballad operas appeared (the tunes usually being printed from woodcuts). Around the middle of the century a few English operas, by Thomas Arne, Lampe, Boyce, J. C. Smith and others, were published in full or short score, but publishers in the second half of the century (notably

7. Handel's first published opera 'Rinaldo', printed from engraved plates in short score, apart from the overture and final chorus which are in full score (Walsh & Hare, 1711)

The BEGGAR's *Opera.*

ACT I. SCENE I.

SCENE Peachum's *House.*

Peachum *sitting at a Table with a large Book of Accounts before him.*

AIR I. *An old Woman cloathed in Gray, &c.*

THROUGH *all the Employments of Life*
Each Neighbour abuses his Brother;
Whore and Rogue they call Husband and Wife:
All Professions be-rogue one another.
The Priest calls the Lawyer a Cheat,
The Lawyer be-knaves the Divine;
And the Statesman, because he's so great,
Thinks his Trade as honest as mine. •

A Lawyer is an honest Employment, so is mine. Like me too
he acts in a double Capacity, both against Rogues and for 'em;
C   for

8. 'The Beggar's Opera', second edition (John Watts, 1728), in which the airs, printed from engraved woodblocks, are interspersed in the text

Thompson, Welcker, Bremner, Longman & Broderip, Preston and Dale) issued almost exclusively vocal scores for the popular repertory – pasticcios such as *Love in a Village* (1762) and *The Maid of the Mill* (1765) and the operas of Michael Arne, Linley, Arnold, Shield and Storace; these were normally in the oblong folio format first introduced for operas in the 1750s by Walsh.

From the end of the 17th century right through the 18th it was common to publish individual songs from operas, usually with keyboard accompaniment and often, added at the foot, a transposition for the flute or guitar. These began as single (occasionally double) sheets and were often, especially up to about 1750, printed on one side of the leaf only. From the 1770s the excerpts tended to become longer, often consisting of several pages and sometimes (especially for excerpts from Italian operas) printed in full score. At the head of each songsheet it was customary to name the singer or singers – a practice that enables study of individual repertories and vocal styles.

(v) Other countries. The principal centres, described above, strongly influenced the development of opera publishing in other countries. In the Low Countries,

however, the earliest operatic publication was in the innovatory form of a libretto interspersed with the music in full score: this was Carolus Hacquart's *De triomfeerende min*, traditionally considered to be the first Dutch example of opera, published in 1680 by Jacob Lescailje at Amsterdam. For many years thereafter Dutch publishers concentrated primarily on producing scores and arrangements of operas originally performed in Paris. Between 1682 and 1685 J. P. Heus published selections in parts from Lully's *Cadmus* (the first music from the opera published anywhere) and from four other operas of Lully, and from 1687 to 1700 Antoine Pointel issued several further selections from Lully's works as well as, in 1688, the first folio full score to appear in the Netherlands, Collasse's completion of Lully's *Achille et Polyxène*.

In 1697 Estienne Roger began his distinguished career, publishing from engraved plates vocal and instrumental arrangements of Lully's operas and full scores of *Phaëton* and *Roland* and a short score of Campra's *L'Europe galante*. Between 1708 and 1711 Pierre Mortier brought out rival and cheaper editions of these and other scores. About 1720 Roger's daughter Jeanne published the full score of Fux's *Elisa*, a rare example of an Italian *opera seria* printed on the Continent at this period. Subsequent Amsterdam 18th-century publishers were better known for their instrumental than for their operatic output.

In Spain the only notable operatic publication from the 18th century was the full score of Martínez de la Roca's *Los desagravios de Troya*, published in Madrid in 1712. In Scandinavia, Sarti's *Ciro riconosciuto* was published in full score by Thiele of Copenhagen as early as 1756. The Danish publisher most active in the field of opera was Søren Sønnichsen, who published typeset vocal scores of Danish operas by Kunzen and Schulz in the 1790s.

In Vienna the earliest notable publications were Trattner's first editions in full score of Gluck's *Alceste* (1769) and *Paride ed Elena* (1770). Artaria's first operatic publication was an aria in full score from Haydn's *L'incontro improvviso* (1783) and their second the complete full score of Salieri's *La grotta di Trofonio* (1786). Their series *Raccolta d'arie*, consisting of excerpts in vocal score from operas in the current repertory, began in 1787 and ran until about 1810; it included a substantial set of 24 individual numbers from *Die Zauberflöte* (1791–2) and isolated posthumous excerpts from other Mozart operas. Artaria published no further full scores and no complete vocal scores in the 18th century, though a handful of vocal scores were put out by other publishers (including a complete *Die Zauberflöte*, published by the Musikalisches Magazin in 1791–3 in the form of 38 individual numbers).

In Russia the first opera to be published was Pashkevich's *Fevey*, of which a vocal score was printed in 1789. The first operatic full score to appear in print (1791) was *Nachal'noye upravleniye Olega*, composed jointly by Pashkevich, Sarti and Cannobio. Both these scores were printed in St Petersburg by Tipografiya Gornago Uchilishcha.

4. THE 19TH AND 20TH CENTURIES.

(i) General. By 1800 the number of active music publishers had multiplied greatly. Their output had increased at least tenfold during the previous century and was to increase perhaps five times further by 1900. Operatic publications increased at least in proportion to

those of other genres and account for a sizeable proportion of the total. During the second half of the 20th century there has been a decrease in separate musical publications of all genres, including operas. There has also been a sharp decline in the publishing of excerpts and arrangements. When a new Verdi opera came out in the 1840s Ricordi devoted some 150–200 publications to it – each separate number in vocal score, a complete vocal score, and numerous arrangements of the popular numbers for solo instruments and various instrumental combinations. Furthermore, the publisher of a successful opera would have agents in several countries, each of whom might publish a new edition of the vocal score and numerous arrangements. Nowadays a major publisher is unlikely to publish anything other than the vocal score of a new opera, and foreign sales will be of copies of that same edition rather than a newly printed one. On the other hand, for well-known operas of earlier periods not only a vocal score but also a full score or facsimile is likely to be in print.

An important development that significantly affected opera publishing from the beginning of the 19th century was the invention of lithography. Although the basic form of lithography, which involves writing directly on to stone or at one remove via transfer paper, was used as an alternative to typesetting and engraving as early as 1796 and was employed sporadically by a number of publishers from the early 1800s, a more valuable application to music printing was the transfer to stone of an image taken from engraved plates on to transfer paper. This saved wear on the plates and so enabled far larger editions to be printed from one set; the invention of the lithographic steam press in the 1860s introduced the additional advantage of speed. Meanwhile the invention and development of photography meant that by 1860 it was possible to transfer to lithographic stone an image written or printed on, or otherwise applied to, ordinary paper.

There were other 19th-century developments. One was the general acceptance of the vocal score as the normal medium in which complete operas were published; by the 1830s the most successful new operas performed in the main centres were automatically published in this way. Another, which arose from the establishment of a historically based repertory, was the gradual growth of collected editions and historical sets, increasing in the 20th century, in which many operas were first printed or were reprinted in newly edited texts. Miniature scores and various formats of study score also became popular from the turn of the century. Since World War II a further development has been the enormous expansion of reprint publishing, which has made many operas readily available through facsimile reproduction of original printed sources and manuscripts.

(ii) Germany and Austria. In Germany the publication of vocal scores had already been initiated in the 1770s, and it was now continued by several great firms, of which some, already active by the 1820s, are still (themselves or their successors) in business today – Breitkopf & Härtel (the first to publish Beethoven's *Leonore*, in 1810), Schott, Simrock, Peters and A. M. Schlesinger. Other publishers associated with opera include J. Schuberth, Bote & Bock, Meyer, Litolff, Senff, Rahter, Brockhaus and the Drei Masken Verlag (who produced some splendid facsimiles of Wagner's autograph scores in the 1920s). Another was C. F. Meser,

who published Wagner's first three operas in vocal score and was eventually succeeded by Fürstner, publisher of most of the operas of Richard Strauss.

The publication of full scores was uncommon in Germany and was generally confined to posthumous editions of the works that stayed longest in the repertory. In 1801 Breitkopf & Härtel published *Don Giovanni*, the earliest full score of a Mozart opera; his other operas were first published by Breitkopf or Simrock between 1805 and 1814, though *Le nozze di Figaro* was published first in Paris. *Fidelio* too first appeared in Paris, in 1826, and not in Germany until 1847. The full scores of Weber's operas were all posthumous – for instance *Der Freischütz* (c1849), *Euryanthe* (1866) and *Oberon* (1874). A few operas of Spohr, Nicolai and Lortzing appeared in the 1880s and 90s and three more of Lortzing in the 1920s; but until the end of the 19th century few current works were issued in full score. Wagner was the great exception: he printed privately by lithography a small number of copies of *Rienzi* (1844), *Der fliegende Holländer* (1845) and *Tannhäuser* (1846; fig.9), the latter prepared for lithography entirely in his own hand; his subsequent operas were published contemporaneously by Breitkopf & Härtel or Schott.

Wagner had marked his lithographed scores 'als Manuskript autographirt' or 'als Manuskript gedruckt', which acted as a copyright warning. Many scores and librettos printed in Germany and Austria until well into the 20th century carried such a warning. In the later 19th century most full scores were lithographed from copyists' manuscripts, and these were invariably only for hire; later, for the more important composers such as Humperdinck, Richard Strauss, Pfitzner and Schoenberg, engraving was usually preferred and purchase was in some cases allowed.

In Vienna Artaria published the earliest vocal scores of *Fidelio* (1814) and of a number of Rossini operas, but rival publishers, such as Mechetti, Diabelli and Pennauer, active in other genres only dabbled in opera, and it was not until later in the century that the popularity of the lighter operatic forms encouraged Austrian publishers to turn their attention to works for the stage. Spina, Cranz, Doblinger, Lewy, Weinberger and Karczag became pre-eminent in operetta, publishing vocal scores and numerous excerpts and arrangements. For opera itself the outstanding event was the founding in 1901 of Universal Edition, which is still in business. From about 1910 they began to publish operas in the current repertory, printing vocal scores and frequently also full scores, though the latter were seldom for sale. Among the operas first published by the firm were Schoenberg's *Erwartung* and *Die glückliche Hand*, Zemlinsky's *Der Zwerg*, Bartók's *Bluebeard's Castle*, Berg's *Wozzeck* and *Lulu*, Krenek's *Jonny spielt auf*, Weinberger's *Švanda dudák* (fig.10), Weill's *Die Dreigroschenoper* and *Aufstieg und Fall der Stadt Mahagonny*, Kodály's *Háry János* and several by Janáček and Schreker.

(iii) France. The publishing of full scores of successful operas continued into the 1850s before dwindling to a trickle. Thus most of the operas of Méhul, Boieldieu, Hérold, Auber, Halévy, Adam and a host of other composers, as well as the French operas of Cherubini, Spontini, Rossini, Meyerbeer, Donizetti and Balfe, were all put on public sale; the format remained folio and all were printed direct from engraved plates. Furthermore,

French publishers were the first to publish full scores of *Le nozze di Figaro* (Magasin de Musique, *c*1807–8) and *Fidelio* (Farrenc, 1826). The most active publishers of full scores were Gaveaux, Pleyel, Erard, the Magasin de Musique, Richault, Frey, Maurice Schlesinger, Troupenas and Schonenberger. After the 1860s full scores were still printed, but normally only for hire.

Vocal scores of complete operas first appeared in France in the first decade of the 19th century, and very soon it became routine for almost every new opera or operetta performed in Paris to be published in this way, sometimes in several rival editions. Among the most active publishers in the early part of the century, in addition to those already mentioned who regularly published full scores, were Janet & Cotelle, Pacini, Carli, Boieldieu, Launer and Latte. From the 1820s to the 60s the normal pattern of publication was that the excerpted numbers from an opera were published first (often with a thematic index on the first *recto*), the complete vocal score soon afterwards and the full score last of all. Somewhat curiously, publishers often chose to print the complete vocal score not from the plates of the *morceaux détachés* but from a freshly engraved set of plates; there are sometimes musical differences between these two sources.

The early vocal scores were published in the same folio format as the full scores, but at the beginning of the 1840s Schonenberger, Launer and Schlesinger introduced octavo editions (sometimes in addition to folios) which gradually became the commonest format for vocal scores worldwide. Printing was generally direct from engraved plates until the 1860s, when it became more usual to use lithographic transfer (see fig.11). Plates were easily altered, and new versions conforming with the latest changes in a production were often issued. From about 1840 to the end of the century several new publishers emerged, including Heugel, Alphonse Leduc, Escudier, Brandus, Choudens, Lemoine (founded in 1772), Hartmann, Durand, Enoch, Michaelis and Costallat; since 1900 Eschig and La Sirène have also published opera. Among these firms are several that remain in business today.

(iv) Italy. Music publishing in Italy after 1808 was dominated by the Milan firm of Ricordi. Many of their early publications were excerpts from operas, usually in vocal score, but in 1816 they published their first complete opera in vocal score, Mayr's *Adelasia e Aleramo*. From the mid-1820s they regularly published vocal scores, separate numbers and arrangements of the current repertory, and in 1839 they took the important step of publishing Verdi's first opera, *Oberto*, thenceforward remaining his main publisher. Their normal procedure until the 1860s was first to issue the

9. First edition of the full score of Wagner's 'Tannhäuser', showing the opening of Act 1. Wagner himself wrote out the score on lithographic transfer paper which was then laid down on to the stone; 100 copies were privately printed (Dresden, 1845).

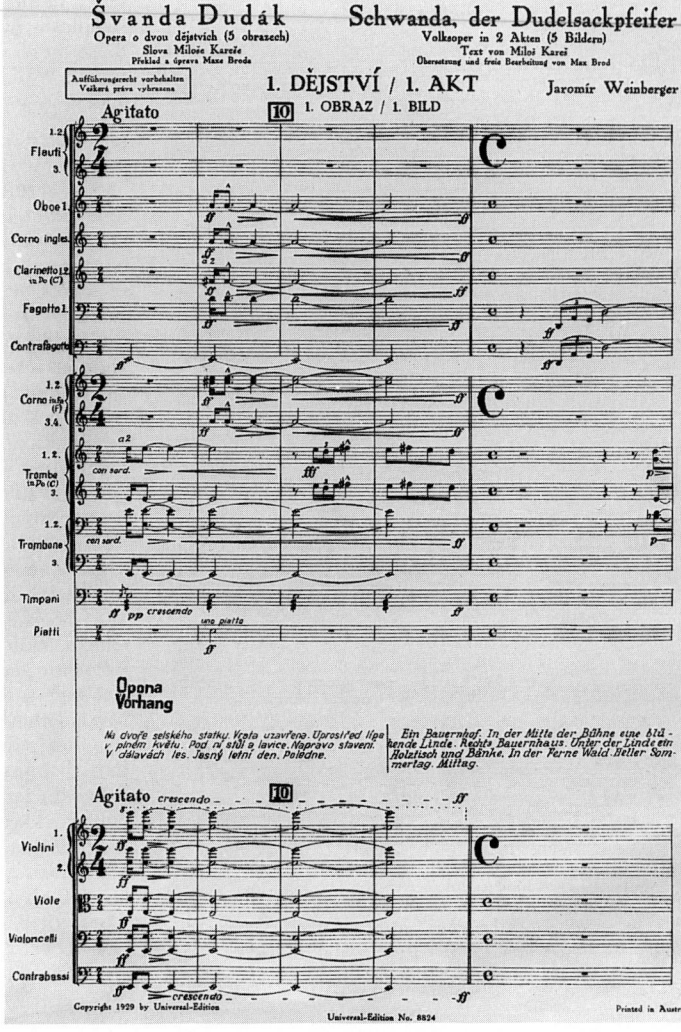

10. First edition of the full score of
Weinberger's 'Švanda Dudák' ['Švanda the
Bagpiper'], printed by lithography from
manuscript (Vienna: Universal, 1929)

separate numbers and then to combine them from the
same plates for the complete vocal score, substituting individual plates where necessary (see fig.12). Italian vocal
scores were invariably oblong folios until about 1860,
after which Ricordi and others occasionally
experimented with folios before instituting in the 1870s
a quarto format (broader than the French octavo),
which has survived to the present day.

In the first half of the century Ricordi competed
principally with Artaria of Milan, Girard (later Cottrau)
of Naples and with Lucca of Milan (absorbed by
Ricordi in 1888); from 1857 Giudici & Strada became a
force in Turin, and after 1874 Sonzogno of Milan published some major composers. The important publishers, especially in Italy, exerted considerable sway
over opera houses, commissioning scores, influencing
casting, controlling stage production (by supplying
production books and designs) and generally representing their composers' business interests – and, of course,
their own, particularly in establishing copyright and
suppressing piracy.

The only full scores of complete operas to be published in Italy during the first half of the century were
eight Rossini scores printed in lithography by Ratti,
Cencetti & Comp. in Rome in the 1820s (see fig.13) and
a single Bellini opera, Beatrice di Tenda, published by

Pittarelli about 1833, also in Rome. A notable event in
the 1860s was the publication by Guidi of Florence of
the first miniature scores of operas ever printed. Starting
with Rossini's Guillaume Tell, these included Peri's Euridice, Paisiello's and Rossini's settings of Il barbiere di
Siviglia and operas by Meyerbeer. From the 1850s
Ricordi began printing full scores of important operas
but never for general sale: it was not until 1912 (Falstaff) that they started to sell full scores, in small quarto
format, of about 20 of their main operas, most of them
by Verdi and Puccini. Among active publishers of opera
since World War II, Suvini Zerboni (Dallapiccola's publisher) should be mentioned.

(v) England. The tradition of publishing complete full
scores of new operas, or selections from them, died out
in the 1780s and has seldom been revived; among the
rare exceptions are Sullivan's Ivanhoe (Chappell, 1891),
Tippett's The Midsummer Marriage (Schott, 1954), and
most of Britten's operas (Boosey & Hawkes and Faber
Music). Vocal scores of operas performed in Britain,
both native and foreign – of which the most famous to
have its première in England was Oberon (Welsh &
Hawes, 1826) – were regularly published, originally as
folios and then from the 1850s more normally as
quartos; in the 1870s both Novello and Boosey started

1163

11. *First edition of the vocal score of Bizet's 'Carmen', printed by lithographic transfer from engraved plates (Paris: Choudens, 1875)*

series in the octavo format initiated in Paris. Other significant publishers of opera and light opera include those mentioned above and Birchall, Lavenu, Cramer, Joseph Williams, Augener, Chester, Curwen, Bosworth and, more recently, Oxford University Press.

(vi) Other countries. In Denmark, 19th-century opera publishing was mainly in the hands of the firms of Lose and its eventual purchaser (in 1879), Wilhelm Hansen, founded in 1853 and still in business. From the beginning of the 20th century Hansen has also dominated music publishing in Norway and Sweden and specializes in works by Scandinavian composers. In Spain many zarzuelas were published in vocal score in Madrid from the middle of the 19th century. Eslava, Casa Romero and Casa Dotesio were leading publishers, the latter changing its name in 1914 to Unión Musical Española, which has absorbed most of the other Spanish publishers. Ricordi capitalized on the popularity of opera in South America by setting up branches in Buenos Aires and São Paulo in the 1920s.

Other than excerpts and a few vocal scores put out by Dalmas, little opera was published in Russia until the firms of Stellovsky, Gutheil, Jürgenson and Bessel were founded in the 1850s and 60s and that of Belyayev in 1885; between them they brought out the operas of Glinka, Borodin, Musorgsky, Tchaikovsky, Rimsky-Korsakov and many others, mainly in folio vocal scores – though some full scores were also printed. The State Music Publishing House that emerged after the Revolution has published the operas of Russian composers since that time.

In Hungary the three most important 19th-century publishers were József Wagner, József Treichlinger and the firm that took them over (respectively in 1858 and 1874), Rózsavölgyi és Társa. In Poland the two leading firms, both of whom published contemporaneous vocal scores of Moniuszko's operas, were Sennewald and Gebethner & Wolff. In Czechoslovakia the publishers specializing in opera were Starý, Hudební Matice and

12. *First complete edition of the vocal score of Verdi's 'Un ballo in maschera', printed from engraved plates (Milan: Ricordi, 1860)*

13. *Full score of Rossini's 'Mosè in Egitto', printed by lithography (Rome: Ratti, Cencetti & Comp., c1825)*

Urbánek, founded between 1867 and 1872; they published many works by Smetana, Fibich, Dvořák and Janáček. Other than Sennewald, all these eastern European firms were still in business until they were replaced by state publishers after World War II.

In the USA, although a few operatic publications had appeared at the end of the 18th century, it was not until the first quarter of the 19th that publishers such as Hewitt, the Carrs, Willig, Dubois & Stodart, Graupner and Blake fully exploited the market for opera songs, overtures and arrangements of familiar airs, both in anthologies and single publications; many were pirated from European editions, but a small percentage of the stage works published were of American origin. Vocal scores of the earliest significant native operas, W. H. Fry's *Leonora* and G. F. Bristow's *Rip Van Winkle*, were published in New York, by E. Ferrett (1846) and W. Corbyn (1855) respectively; Fry's *Notre Dame of Paris* was printed about 1864 without imprint. Among the publishers of other 19th-century operas by American composers were Oliver Ditson and G. Schirmer. Around the turn of the century there was an increase both in operatic output (Victor Herbert, Reginald De Koven and Walter Damrosch, for example) and in publishing activity; among the new firms were J. W. Stern, Witmark and E. Schuberth, and, specializing in musicals, Chappell and T. B. Harms.

See also EDITING; EDITIONS; and LIBRARIES AND ARCHIVES.

EitnerQ; Grove6
T. de Lajarte: *Bibliothèque musicale du Théatre de l'Opéra: Catalogue historique, chronologique, anecdotique* (Paris, 1878)
B. and F. Pazdírek, eds.: *Universal-Handbuch der Musikliteratur aller Zeiten und Völke: als Nachschlagewerk und Studienquelle der Welt-Musikliteratur* (Vienna, 1904–10) [34 vols.]

O. G. T. Sonneck: *Dramatic Music: Catalogue of Full Scores in the Collection of the Library of Congress* (Washington, 1908)
W. A. Fisher: *One Hundred and Fifty Years of Music Publishing in the United States: an Historical Sketch with Special Reference to the Pioneer Publisher Oliver Ditson Company, Inc., 1783–1933* (Boston, 1933)
C. L. Day and E. B. Murrie: *English Song-Books, 1651–1702: a Bibliography* (London, 1940)
A. Loewenberg: *Annals of Opera 1597–1940* (Geneva, 1943, 3/1978)
O. G. T. Sonneck and W. T. Upton: *A Bibliography of Early Secular American Music (18th Century) … Revised and Enlarged by William Treat Upton* (Washington, 1945)
O. E. Deutsch: *Music Publishers' Numbers: a Selection of 40 Dated Lists, 1710–1900* (London, 1946; Ger. trans., rev., 1961 as *Musikverlagsnummern*)
W. C. Smith: *A Bibliography of the Musical Works published by John Walsh during the Years 1695–1720* (London, 1948, 2/1968)
R.-A. Mooser: *Annales de la musique et des musiciens en Russie au XVIIIme siècle* (Geneva, 1948–51)
A. Weinmann: *Beiträge zur Geschichte des alt-Wiener Musikverlages* (Vienna, 1948–)
C. Hopkinson: *A Dictionary of Parisian Music Publishers, 1700–1950* (London, 1954, 2/1979)
C. Humphries and W. C. Smith: *Music Publishing in the British Isles from the Beginning until the Middle of the Nineteenth Century* (London, 1954, 2/1970)
C. Johansson: *French Music Publishers' Catalogues of the Second Half of the Eighteenth Century* (Stockholm, 1955)
A. Weinmann: *Wiener Musikverleger und Musikalienhändler von Mozarts Zeit bis gegen 1860* (Vienna, 1956)
A. H. Heyer: *Historical Sets, Collected Editions, and Monuments of Music: a Guide to their Contents* (Chicago, 1957, 2/1969)
E. B. Schnapper, ed.: *The British Union-Catalogue of Early Music* (London, 1957)
B. L. Vol'man: *Russkiye pechatnïye notï XVIII veka* (Leningrad, 1957)
C. Sartori: *Dizionario degli editori musicali italiani* (Florence, 1958)
C. Hopkinson: *Notes on Russian Music Publishers* (London, 1959)

G. A. Glaister: *Glossary of the Book* (London, 1960, 2/1979 as *Glaister's Glossary of the Book*)

Répertoire international des sources musicales [*RISM*], ser. B/I, II (Munich and Duisburg, 1960–64); ser. A/I (Kassel, 1971–)

A. Hyatt King: *Four Hundred Years of Music Printing* (London, 1964)

R. J. Wolfe: *Secular Music in America 1801–1825: a Bibliography* (New York, 1964)

B. S. Brook, ed.: *The Breitkopf Thematic Catalogue: the Six Parts and Sixteen Supplements 1762–1787* (New York, 1966)

K. G. Fellerer: 'Opernbearbeitungen im Musikverlag um die Wende des 18./19. Jahrhunderts', *Musik und Verlag: Karl Vötterle zum 65. Geburtstag* (Kassel, 1968), 279ff

W. C. Smith and C. Humphries: *A Bibliography of the Musical Works published by the Firm of John Walsh during the Years 1721–1766* (London, 1968)

F. Lesure: *Bibliographie des éditions musicales publiées par Estienne Roger et Michel-Charles Le Cène (Amsterdam, 1696–1743)* (Paris, 1969)

R. Fiske: *English Theatre Music in the Eighteenth Century* (London, 1973, 2/1986), esp. 586ff

D. W. Krummel, ed.: *Guide for Dating Early Published Music* (Hackensack and Kassel, 1974)

A. Devriès: *Edition et commerce de la musique gravée à Paris dans la première moitié du XVIIIe siècle: les Boivin, les Leclerc* (Geneva, 1976)

D. Fog: *Dansk Musikfortegnelse 1. del 1750–1854: ein dateret katalok over trykte danske musikalier* (Copenhagen, 1979)

A. Devriès and F. Lesure: *Dictionnaire des éditeurs de musique français*, i: *Des origines à environ 1820* (Geneva, 1979) [in 2 pts]; ii: *De 1820 à 1914* (Geneva, 1988)

F. Lesure, ed.: *Catalogue de la musique imprimée avant 1800 conservée dans les bibliothèques publiques de Paris* (Paris, 1981)

The Catalogue of Printed Music in the British Library to 1980 (London, 1981–7) [62 vols.]

Catalogue of the Opera Collections in the Music Libraries: University of California, Berkeley; University of California, Los Angeles (Boston, 1983)

A. Z. Laterza: *Il catalogo numerico Ricordi 1857 con date e indici* (Rome, 1984)

O. Mischiati: *Indici, cataloghi e avvisi degli editori e librai musicali italiani dal 1591 al 1798* (Florence, 1984)

J. Rosselli: *The Opera Industry in Italy from Cimarosa to Verdi: the Role of the Impresario* (Cambridge, 1984), 56ff, 175ff

D. Fog: *Notendruck und Musikhandel im 19. Jahrhundert in Dänemark: ein Beitrag zur Musikaliendatierung und zur Geschichte der Musikvermittlung* (Copenhagen, 1986)

T. Carter: 'Music Publishing in Italy, c1580–c1625: some Preliminary Observations', *RMARC*, xx (1986–7), 19–37

D. W. Krummel: *Bibliographical Handbook of American Music* (Urbana, IL, 1987)

D. C. Hunter: *English Opera and Song Books, 1703–1726: their Contents, Publishing, Printing, and Bibliographical Description* (Ann Arbor, 1988)

T. Carter: 'Music Publishing in Florence', *EMH*, ix (1990), 27–72

D. W. Krummel and S. Sadie, eds.: *Music Printing and Publishing* (London, 1990)

J. A. Parkinson: *Victorian Music Publishers: an Annotated List* (Warren, MI, 1990)

D. C. Hunter: 'The Publishing of Opera and Song Books in England, 1703–1726', *Notes*, xlvii (1990–91), 647ff

RICHARD MACNUTT

Puccini, Domenico (Vincenzo Maria) (*b* Lucca, 5 April 1772; *d* Lucca, 25 May 1815). Italian composer, grandfather of Giacomo Puccini. He was first taught by his parents and continued his studies in Bologna under Mattei and in Naples under Paisiello, with whom he remained on excellent terms. From 1806 to 1809 he was director of the small Cappella di Camera in Lucca (founded by Napoleon's sister, Elisa Baciochi, and later transformed into an even smaller Cappella di Palazzo), where Niccolò Paganini was also employed. In January 1807 he conducted *Il matrimonio segreto* in the court theatre, performed by amateur singers who were members of the nobility. He went on to direct the Cappella Municipale from 1811 until his sudden death.

Puccini had early successes with two *tasche*, political serenatas of a kind then popular in Lucca: *Spartaco* in 1793 and *Castruccio* in 1797. His career as a composer of opera, however, had a slow start, perhaps due to the crisis in the theatres of Lucca; his first operas were given by amateurs in private performances. Even the success of *Il trionfo di Quinto Fabio*, with Marietta Marcolini taking part, failed to secure his fame. A portrait of the composer was nonetheless included among those of other well-known musicians in an engraving by Luigi Scotti from the early years of the 19th century. The scores of Puccini's operas reveal a real theatrical talent. The structure and orchestration of *Quinto Fabio* are apt and stylish; the comic operas show an outstanding dramatic sense and a fresh and spontaneous inspiration, along with the assimilation of styles present in the comic operas of the time, particularly those of the *farsa*.

Le frecce d'amore (opera pastorale, 2, Francesconi), Lucca, private perf., ?1800, *I-Li* (inc.)

L'ortolanella (farsa, 1), Lucca, ?1800, *Li*; rev. version, Lucca, Camaiore, ?1811

Il trionfo di Quinto Fabio (dramma serio, 2, M. Prunetti), Livorno, Floridi, 19 May 1810, *Li*

La scuola dei tutori (farsa, 1, G. A. Andreini), Lucca, Castglioncelli, 16 Feb 1813, *Bc*

Il ciarlatano, o sia I finti savoiardi (commedia in musica, 1, L. G. Buonavoglia), Lucca, Castiglioncelli, 21 Jan 1815, *Li*

La villana [?rev. of L'ortolanella]

L. Nerici: *Storia della musica in Lucca* (Lucca, 1880)

A. Bonaccorsi: *Giacomo Puccini e i suoi antenati musicali* (Milan, 1950)

H. Handt: *Il ciarlatano* (Lucca, 1971–2) [programme notes]

G. Biagi Ravenni: *Il ciarlatano* (Lucca, 1973–4) [programme notes]

B. Cagli: *Il trionfo di Quinto Fabio* (Lucca, 1975–6) [programme notes]

M. Bianchi: 'Il trionfo di Quinto Fabio' di Domenico Puccini (diss., U. of Pisa, 1984)

H. Handt and G. Biagi Ravenni: *Il ciarlatano* (Monte Carlo, 1984–5) [programme notes]   GABRIELLA BIAGI RAVENNI

Puccini, Giacomo (Antonio Domenico Michele Secondo Maria) (*b* Lucca, 22 Dec 1858; *d* Brussels, 29 Nov 1924). Italian composer. He was the most successful composer of Italian opera after Verdi.

1. Education and early compositions. 2. The first operas: *Le villi*, *Edgar* and *Manon Lescaut*. 3. 1894–1904: *La bohème*, *Tosca* and *Madama Butterfly*. 4. Middle and late years. 5. Dramaturgy and musical style. 6. Assessment.

1. EDUCATION AND EARLY COMPOSITIONS. Born into a family that had supplied his native city with cathedral organists and composers for four generations, Puccini was taught the rudiments of music by his maternal uncle, Fortunato Magi, his father having died when he was five years old. He sang as a treble in the choir of the Cathedral of S Martino and the church of S Michele; at 14 he was able to deputize for organists in the neighbourhood. At the Istituto Musicale Pacini, which he entered in 1874, he studied under Carlo Angeloni, Magi's successor as director, a respectable composer mainly of motets and masses. Lucca's cultural life was remarkably rich for a provincial town. Operatic fare was supplied at its three theatres at different times of the year. No less important for Puccini's future was a strong tradition of spoken drama, with regular visits by Italy's most distinguished touring companies, offering a repertory that reached from Vittorio Alfieri and Carlo Goldoni to the latest Parisian products of the Dumas *père et fils*, Sardou and Alfred de Musset. At a time when the canons of play and opera were drawing ever closer together, their influence on the future composer

of *La bohème* and *Tosca* can hardly be overestimated; indeed it was to his early familiarity with a wide range of dramatic literature that Puccini later owed his flair for discovering the operatic possibilities of plays that he saw performed in a language of which he understood not a word. Luccan opera, by contrast, was for the most part poorly mounted and inadequately sung by second-rate artists, often recruited locally. It was not until he saw a performance of Verdi's *Aida* in Pisa in 1876 that Puccini awoke to the full possibilities of the genre and decided once and for all where his future lay. That same year saw his first composition of any significance: a prelude in E minor for orchestra, the autograph of which is in the private collection of Natale Gallini, Milan. In 1877 he wrote the motet for baritone, mixed chorus and orchestra *Plaudite populi*, which was performed at a students' concert in April that year. The motet was repeated the following year, with a newly-composed Credo that was subsequently incorporated in the *Messa a quattro voci* of 1880, Puccini's passing-out piece for the Istituto Musicale Pacini. Known for a long time only to Puccini scholars, this work was first published in 1951 under the title *Messa di gloria*. Though not especially devotional in character, it shows a sureness of musical touch and a complete control of material. The Kyrie and Agnus Dei were recycled in *Edgar* and *Manon Lescaut* respectively.

With the aid of a grant from the Queen of Italy, augmented by a subsidy from a bachelor relation, Puccini proceeded to the Milan Conservatory, although he was well over the age limit for entrance (he was in his 22nd year). He did well enough at the examination to be accepted into the senior composition class. His first teacher was the well-known violinist and composer Antonio Bazzini, one of the few Italian professors with a European background. For him Puccini composed a string quartet in Mendelssohnian style, only one movement of which survives. When in 1882 Bazzini succeeded to the directorship Puccini passed under the tuition of Ponchielli, who, in the short time remaining to him (he died in 1886), did all he could to further Puccini's career in opera. However, the two principal fruits of his studies were a *Preludio sinfonico* in A major (1882) and the *Capriccio sinfonico* with which he graduated in 1883. Both show a new richness of orchestral imagination and a number of harmonic and melodic features that are characteristic of the mature composer. Of the *Capriccio*, which later provided the opening theme for *La bohème*, Milan's leading critic, Filippo Filippi, wrote in *La perseveranza* that it denoted a 'specifically symphonic talent'. Nonetheless, opera remained Puccini's goal.

2. THE FIRST OPERAS: 'LE VILLI', 'EDGAR' AND 'MANON LESCAUT'. That same year – 1883 – Puccini entered a competition for a one-act stage piece promoted by the publisher Edoardo Sonzogno. Ponchielli found him a librettist in the young 'scapigliato' poet Ferdinando Fontana, who took the subject from a short story, *Les willis*, by the French writer Alphonse Karr. Puccini declared himself delighted with it 'since it will mean working a good deal in the symphonic-descriptive vein, and that will suit me very well'. But despite Ponchielli's presence among the adjudicators the prize was awarded elsewhere and *Le villi* did not even receive an honourable mention. Fortunately friends and acquaintances subscribed to a performance in May 1884 at the Teatro Dal Verme, Milan, which prompted one critic to declare

that 'Puccini could be the composer for whom Italy has been waiting a long time'. Filippi was again complimentary, adding, however, that 'Puccini's nature is essentially that of a symphonist and ... he exaggerates the *symphonic element*, and frequently overloads the pedestal to the detriment of the statue'. Verdi wrote to a friend, Count Arrivabene, that he had

heard many good things said about the composer Puccini. It seems however that the symphonic element predominates in him. No harm in that! But here we should tread carefully. Opera is opera and symphony is symphony; and I don't think that in an opera it's a good idea to write a symphonic piece merely for the pleasure of making the orchestra dance.

The publisher Giulio Ricordi, however, was in no doubt that in the composer of *Le villi* he had found Verdi's successor. He persuaded Fontana and Puccini to expand it into two acts, in which form it achieved a modest circulation over the next few years. He also commissioned a new, full-length opera from poet and composer and arranged for the firm to provide Puccini with a monthly stipend so that he could compose the music at leisure. Until his death in 1912 Giulio Ricordi acted as the composer's 'guide, philosopher and friend', advising him on subjects, finding him librettists and smoothing out his perennial difficulties with them.

Puccini's letters home shed a revealing light on his enthusiasms at the time, *Carmen* ('a most beautiful opera') and *Dejanice*, by his fellow Luccan Alfredo Catalani ('the public don't go into ecstasies over it, but I say that artistically speaking it's a fine opera, and if they do it again I shall go back to see it'). Other formative influences noted by Ponchielli (without approval) were Massenet, evident in the soft suppleness of his vocal lines, and Wagner, for whom Puccini nurtured a lifelong admiration. In 1889 he accompanied the conductor Faccio to Bayreuth to advise on cuts for the forthcoming production at La Scala of *Die Meistersinger* (as *I maestri cantori di Norimberga*).

For their next collaboration Fontana and Puccini turned to a dramatic poem by Alfred de Musset, which became the four-act opera *Edgar*. Progress on the composition was painfully slow, largely due to domestic circumstances. Shortly after his mother's death in 1884 Puccini set up house with Elvira Geminiani, wife of a Luccan grocer, who brought with her two children. A year later their own son Tonio was born; but it was not until Geminiani's death in 1903 that the union was regularized. Eventually produced at La Scala in 1889, *Edgar* achieved a mere *succès d'estime*. The critics noted an advance on *Le villi*, especially in orchestral and harmonic resource, but admitted that in general the work was a disappointment. Puccini later condensed the four acts into three without, however, improving its fortunes. Ricordi was now under pressure from shareholders to withdraw Puccini's allowance; but he held firm, to find his faith in his protégé triumphantly vindicated by the immediate success of *Manon Lescaut* (1893, Turin). The opera's genesis had been more than usually tormented. Four librettists, including Leoncavallo, had been successively involved in the text; and though the final product was effectively the work of Domenico Oliva and Luigi Illica it was decided to publish the libretto without an attribution. But the critics and public were unanimous in their praise. When the opera reached London in 1894 Bernard Shaw noted in *The World* that in it 'the domain of Italian opera is enlarged by an annexation of German territory', adding that 'Puccini looks to me more like the heir of Verdi than any of his rivals'. From that time Puccini's financial problems were at an end. He was able not only to repay Ricordi's advances in full but also to acquire a spacious villa at Torre del Lago, which was to remain his home for most of his life and has since become the composer's museum.

3. 1894–1904: 'LA BOHÈME', 'TOSCA' AND 'MADAMA BUTTERFLY'. Unlike most of his contemporaries Puccini produced his operas at long intervals, partly because of his fastidiousness in choosing subjects, several of which he took up only to abandon after several months, and partly because of his constant demands for modification of the texts. Much of his time, too, was spent in hunting in the marshes round his new home and in trips abroad to supervise revivals of his works. For his librettos over the next decade Ricordi secured him the team of Luigi Illica, who worked out the scheme and drafted the dialogue, and the poet and playwright Giuseppe Giacosa, who put the lines into verse. The first fruit of their partnership was La bohème (1896, Turin), drawn from Henry Murger's picaresque novel of life among the artists of the Latin Quarter in Paris. The critics were cool, several of them finding in the opera's comparative restraint a certain falling-off of invention after the emotional ardour of Manon Lescaut. But the public soon took it to their hearts; and it quickly outstripped its predecessor in popularity abroad. Only in Vienna was it excluded for some years from the repertory, because of the hostility of Mahler, who much preferred Leoncavallo's treatment of the same subject.

Even before he had completed La bohème Puccini had already decided on an operatic setting of Victorien Sardou's play, La Tosca, for which Illica had in the meantime prepared a libretto for Alberto Franchetti. But although it had won the approval of Verdi, Franchetti was dissatisfied with it and was persuaded without difficulty to hand it over to his rival. Over the next three years Illica and Giacosa shaped it to Puccini's requirements, and the opera was launched at the Teatro Costanzi, Rome, in 1900. Again the critics were guarded in their appraisal, but Tosca was soon going the rounds as successfully as La bohème. Here Puccini harnessed to his lyrical gift a leitmotif technique, loosely indebted to Wagner, in the service of a powerful, swiftly moving action, while transforming Sardou's mildly ridiculous heroine, conceived as a vehicle for the virtuosity of Sarah Bernhardt, into a credible and moving personality. Nor would it be the last time that Puccini succeeded in vastly improving on his literary source. For his next opera he turned to David Belasco's one-act play Madame Butterfly after seeing it performed in London. With the help of Illica and Giacosa he expanded the slender plot to the dimensions of a full evening's entertainment. Completion was delayed, however, by a severe motor accident, from which Puccini's slow recovery was found to be due to a diabetic condition that remained with him to the end of his life. When the première of Madama Butterfly eventually took place (1904, Milan), the opera was subjected to what Puccini described as 'a veritable lynching'. That the audience's hostility was deliberately engineered none of his biographers has ever doubted, though they are not prepared to say by whom. All the evidence points, however, to Ricordi's chief rival, Sonzogno, as the prime mover. Such members of the 'giovane scuola' as had flocked to his banner – Mascagni, Leoncavallo, Giordano, Cilea – had by now clearly given their best work. None had

equalled Ricordi's protégé in achieving three major successes in a row; a fourth was bound to be unwelcome. The few modifications that Puccini brought to the score for its second performance at Brescia that year would not have been sufficient to turn the tide in its favour, had the public's initial reaction to it been spontaneous. As it was, Madama Butterfly quickly joined its two predecessors as one of the cornerstones of the contemporary operatic repertory. As well as enriching his idiom with oriental elements, Puccini had here won through to a new scale of musical thought, to which the love duet of Act 1 bears special witness.

4. MIDDLE AND LATE YEARS. A lean period followed. Among the subjects taken up and laid aside were Victor Hugo's Notre Dame de Paris, Oscar Wilde's unfinished play A Florentine Tragedy and Pierre Louÿs's La femme et le pantin (later set by Riccardo Zandonai as Conchita). At one point Puccini considered a collaboration with Italy's foremost poet, Gabriele D'Annunzio, but that too came to nothing. Of his two librettists, Giacosa died in 1906, while Illica remained for years engaged in drawing up a Maria Antonietta which he never finished to the composer's satisfaction. Almost faute de mieux Puccini turned to another Belasco play, The Girl of the Golden West, with a tougher, more resilient heroine. Work on La fanciulla del West was interrupted by a particularly unpleasant domestic crisis. An unfaithful husband, Puccini was suspected by his wife of having an affair with their maidservant, Doria Manfredi. She persecuted Manfredi to such an extent that the girl committed suicide. A subsequent autopsy proved her to be a virgin, whereupon her family sued Elvira Puccini for gross defamation of character. Ultimately a settlement was reached whereby she escaped a prison sentence, and peace was gradually restored to the Puccini household. But the scandal had resulted in a hiatus of nine months in the composition of La fanciulla del West, which finally had its première at the Metropolitan Opera House, New York, in December 1910. To outward appearance it was a triumphant success, but its new harmonic elaboration, combined with a curbing of the lyrical impulse that had marked Puccini's earlier scores, alienated many of the composer's admirers; the opera has never entered the circle of steady favourites. At the same time Puccini found himself under attack from another quarter. A new generation of Italian composers had arisen, represented by Casella, Pizzetti and Gian Francesco Malipiero, who, in their concern to revive the glories of their country's polyphonic past and with it a long defunct instrumental tradition, set their faces firmly against Italian opera, especially its latest manifestations. Their standard-bearer, the critic Fausto Torrefranca, launched a savage diatribe against the author of La bohème and Madama Butterfly under the title Giacomo Puccini e l'opera internazionale, which called into question not only his taste but also his musicianship. Puccini, however, refused to be deflected from his chosen path. His next venture was into the world of Lehár with his operetta-like (though through-composed) La rondine (1917, Monte Carlo). A Viennese commission, originally intended for the Carltheater, its composition covered the years of Italy's entry into World War I – another difficult period for Puccini, who was suspected, not without reason, of lacking enthusiasm for the Allied cause. He had refused to join Debussy, Elgar, Mascagni and others in contributing to Hall Caine's King Albert's Book in honour

1. Giacomo Puccini (right), with (left to right) Giulio Gatti-Casazza, David Belasco and Arturo Toscanini in New York at the time of the première of 'La fanciulla del West' in December 1910

of 'brave little Belgium', and for this was ferociously attacked in an open letter by Alphonse Daudet's son Léon. (He later placated French hostility by devoting a year's profits from performances of *Tosca* by the Opéra-Comique to the benefit of the country's wounded.) His own son, Tonio, then in uniform, was likewise a source of anxiety. Nonetheless, he managed to finish *La rondine*, which had its première on neutral soil before reaching Italy. Neither at home nor abroad did it ever enjoy an enduring success. In the meantime Puccini had been working on the long-cherished project of a triple-bill of contrasted one-act operas. Here he enjoyed the benefit of two young librettists of outstanding ability: Giuseppe Adami, his collaborator on *La rondine*, who drew up the text for *Il tabarro* from a Grand Guignol melodrama by Didier Gold, and Giovacchino Forzano, whose *Suor Angelica* and *Gianni Schicchi* were his own invention. The so-called *Trittico* was first given (in Puccini's absence) at the Metropolitan Opera House, New York, in December 1918. Though in subsequent revivals *Suor Angelica* failed to stay the course, all three operas were recognized as showing a new strength and confidence. Puccini's position as Italy's leading opera composer was now unchallenged even by Mascagni (though in 1921 the latter scored a momentary, unexpected triumph with *Il piccolo Marat*). His last efforts were directed towards a large-scale opera which should explore entirely new territory. This was to be *Turandot*, derived from a *fiaba* (fairy-tale) by the 18th-century Venetian playwright Carlo Gozzi. Its gestation was long and difficult; nor did the librettist Adami and his partner Renato Simoni ever succeed in working out to the composer's satisfaction the text of a final duet which would bring about a convincing denouement, with the result that by the time of Puccini's death in 1924 (from heart failure while under surgical treatment for cancer of the throat) the opera was un-

finished. In the meantime his status had been confirmed by his nomination as Senator of the Realm.

5. DRAMATURGY AND MUSICAL STYLE. Puccini stands as the supreme exponent of a style of opera which first became popular following the success of Mascagni's *Cavalleria rusticana* (1890). Often loosely, and indeed misleadingly, labelled 'verismo', it is characterized by a swift, naturalistic action similar to that of a spoken play and a full-blooded romantic rhetoric that owes much to Massenet and something to Wagner. In a letter of 1895 written to Carlo Clausetti of Ricordi, Puccini complained that as early as *Le villi* (1884) he had already established the 'stile mascagnano' but that nobody gave him the credit for it. Musically speaking, his claim was justified. In *Le villi* all the basic traits of the 'giovane scuola' (as Puccini's generation came to be called) are already present, while *Edgar* shows the establishment of a strongly personal idiom with fingerprints that were to remain constant throughout the composer's career: diatonic melodies without chromatic inflection that move mostly by step while incorporating many a falling 5th, sequences with a heavy subdominant bias, successions of parallel, often unrelated chords, frequent use of added notes and unresolved dissonances, climaxes built on alternating progressions, and a habit of doubling the outer parts with harmonies sandwiched in between. If the style appears relatively narrow, it is sufficiently flexible to absorb in the course of its evolution elements from more advanced contemporaries such as Debussy, Richard Strauss and Stravinsky, as well as those of exotic folk music. In matters of construction Puccini was far ahead of his Italian rivals, avoiding their tendency to formless rhapsodizing by organizing his acts motivically and even weaving motifs into the fabric of a detachable number (e.g., 'Che gelida manina' in *La bohème* and 'Vissi d'arte' in *Tosca*). At the same time a

remarkable capacity for self-renewal, comparable to Verdi's, ensured a steady progress from one opera to the next, sometimes accompanied by a modification of technique. The symphonic tendencies evident in much of *Manon Lescaut* (much of the first act is like an elaborate scherzo) give way in *La bohème* to a more relaxed procedure in which thematic reminiscence and leitmotif play a prominent role – a method which reached its apogee in *Tosca*. It should be noted, however, that Puccini's use of leitmotif was rarely as systematically referential as Wagner's. Ernest Newman's gibe that Puccini often seemed to have forgotten where his motifs had first occurred is beside the point. Over and above their power of recall, Puccini exploited them for their cohesive force and their emotional charge, which may vary according to their dynamic and scoring. In his orchestral perorations (a device derived from Ponchielli) he has been accused of quoting inappropriate themes – Colline's farewell to his overcoat at the end of *La bohème*, 'E lucevan le stelle' for the final curtain of

Tosca; yet each strikes the right note of personal grief. In *Suor Angelica* not one of the many motifs can be related to a particular person or idea. By that time Puccini had arrived at yet another structural method, involving large musical blocks, each hewn from the same material (this too could be said to have a Wagnerian precedent in Isolde's narration, King Mark's lament for Tristan's betrayal and Pogner's address in Act 1 of *Die Meistersinger*). Such is the organizing principle behind *Il tabarro* and, above all, *Turandot*.

In the domain of stagecraft Puccini remains unsurpassed. Not even Wagner was more concerned than he to integrate music, words and gesture into a single scenic concept, with the result that his operas are virtually director-proof. None of his detailed stage directions can be ignored without detriment to the general effect. As early as *Manon Lescaut* he breached the time-honoured convention of the static *pezzo concertato* with an ensemble of action, namely the roll-call of the prostitutes in Act 3. From then on his massed choral

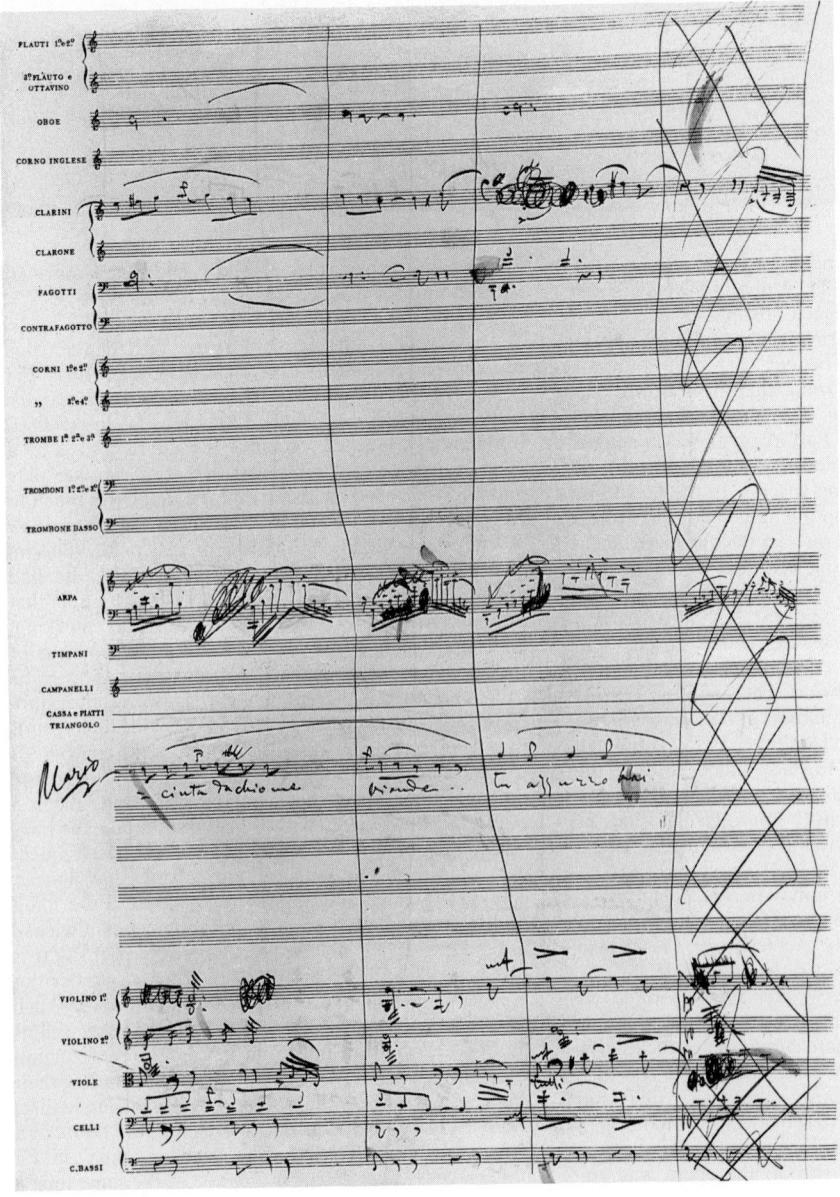

2. Autograph score of a page from Cavaradossi's aria, 'Recondita armonia', from Act 1 of Puccini's 'Tosca' (1900)

scenes conform to this type, with the sole exception of the consciously operetta-style brindisi ('Beviam al tuo fresco sorriso') of *La rondine*. Following the example set by Bellini in *I puritani* the majority of his heroines are heard before they are seen, so that they are established first and foremost as voices. In *Turandot*, on the other hand, the procedure is no less happily reversed. Several of the later operas show a characteristic scheme whereby the action proceeds through a number of apparently unrelated incidents until at a certain moment the listener is made aware that the central drama has been launched: the entrance of Dick Johnson alias Ramerrez (*La fanciulla del West*), the sighting of the Princess's carriage (*Suor Angelica*) and the point at which Luigi and Giorgetta are alone for the first time (*Il tabarro*). To all this must be added Puccini's rare gift of evoking an ambience, often mixing music with extraneous noise (the bells in *Tosca*, the ship's sirens in *Il tabarro*). Even Debussy, no friend to the contemporary school of Italian opera, once confessed to Paul Dukas that he knew of no one who had described the Paris of the age of Louis-Philippe 'as well as Puccini in *La bohème*'.

6. ASSESSMENT. Puccini's limitations as an artist were, in a sense, spiritual. His values were those of 'L'italietta', the bourgeois, unadventurous Italy before World War I. 'Great sorrows in little souls' was his watchword, he told Gabriele D'Annunzio; and that alone would have rendered him incapable of matching in music the poet's daring aesthetic flights. His love of tugging the heartstrings led him to favour – though by no means exclusively, as is sometimes implied – the soft, wilting heroines and to wind up almost sadistically the agony of their destruction. That this did not preclude a genuine talent for comedy is demonstrated by parts of *La bohème* and all of *Gianni Schicchi*, but it debarred him from the highest level of tragedy. The wider issues, whether of politics or religion, lay outside his grasp. For him there was no glory beyond the grave. Each of his victims could have echoed Shakespeare's Iras in *Antony and Cleopatra*: 'Finish, good lady; the bright day is done, And we are for the dark.' Hence his refusal to end *Tosca* on the note of facile uplift that marks the conclusion of Giordano's *Andrea Chénier*. Inevitably, when an element of transfiguration was required he was found wanting: a defect that prevented him from finishing *Suor Angelica* satisfactorily and *Turandot* at all.

Puccini still has his detractors, who have expressed themselves as savagely as Torrefranca in 1912. Nevertheless, his hold on the public remains as strong as ever; and it can be safely maintained that, however prejudiced to start with, anyone who has worked practically on his operas has ended with a profound respect for Puccini as musician and man of the theatre.

See also BOHÈME, LA (i); EDGAR; FANCIULLA DEL WEST, LA; GIANNI SCHICCHI; MADAMA BUTTERFLY; MANON LESCAUT (ii); RONDINE, LA; SUOR ANGELICA; TABARRO, IL; TOSCA; TRITTICO, IL; TURANDOT (ii); and VILLI, LE.

published in Milan unless otherwise stated; detailed bibliographical information in Hopkinson

title	genre, acts	libretto	first performance	sources; publication; remarks
Le villi	leggenda drammatica in due quadri, 1	F. Fontana, after A. Karr: *Les willis*	Milan, Dal Verme, 31 May 1884	*I-Mr**; unpubd
2nd version	opera ballo, 2		Turin, Regio, 26 Dec 1884	vs (1885); rev. edns (1888 and 1892)
Edgar	dramma lirico, 4	Fontana, after A. de Musset: *La coupe et les lèvres*	Milan, Scala, 21 April 1889	*Mr** (Acts 1 and 3); vs (1890)
2nd version	3		Ferrara, Comunale, 28 Feb 1892	copy of 1st version with autograph changes, *Mr*; vs (1892)
3rd (definitive) version	3		Buenos Aires, Opera, 8 July 1905	vs (1905)
Manon Lescaut	dramma lirico, 4	D. Oliva and L. Illica, after Abbé Prévost: *L'histoire du chevalier des Grieux et de Manon Lescaut*	Turin, Regio, 1 Feb 1893	*Mr**; full score and vs (1893)
La bohème	opera, 4	Illica and G. Giacosa, after H. Murger: *Scènes de la vie de bohème*	Turin, Regio, 1 Feb 1896	*Mr**; full score (1898), vs (1896)
Tosca	melodramma, 3	Illica and Giacosa, after V. Sardou: *La Tosca*	Rome, Costanzi, 14 Jan 1900	*Mr**; full score and vs (1899)
Madama Butterfly	tragedia giapponese, 2	Illica and Giacosa, after D. Belasco's stage version of a magazine story by J. L. Long	Milan, Scala, 17 Feb 1904	*Mr**; vs (1904)
2nd version	2		Brescia, Grande, 28 May 1904	changes in autograph, *Mr*; vs (1904)
3rd version	2		London, CG, 10 July 1905	vs (1905)
4th version	3		Paris, OC (Feydeau), 28 Dec 1906	full score (1906; 1907, with changes to text)
La fanciulla del West	opera, 3	G. Civinini and C. Zangarini, after Belasco: *The Girl of the Golden West*	New York, Met, 10 Dec 1910	*Mr**; full score (1911), vs (1910)
La rondine	commedia lirica, 3	G. Adami, after A. M. Willner and H. Reichert	Monte Carlo, Opéra, 27 March 1917	autograph lost; full score and vs (1917)

title	genre, acts	libretto	first performance	sources; publication; remarks
Il trittico			New York, Met, 14 Dec 1918	*Mr**; full score and vs (1918)
Il tabarro	opera, 1	Adami, after D. Gold: *La houppelande*		
Suor Angelica	opera, 1	G. Forzano		
Gianni Schicchi	opera, 1	Forzano, developed from a few lines in Dante: *Inferno*, xxx: 32–3, 42–5		
Turandot	dramma lirico, 3	Adami and R. Simoni, after C. Gozzi and F. von Schiller	Milan, Scala, 25 April 1926	*Mr**; vs (1926); inc., completed by F. Alfano

SOURCE MATERIAL

G. Adami: *Giacomo Puccini: epistolario* (Milan, 1928; Eng. trans., 1931, 2/1974)
V. Seligman: *Puccini among Friends* (London, 1938)
L. Marchetti: *Puccini nelle immagini* (Milan, 1949)
L. Ricci: *Puccini interprete di se stesso* (Milan, 1954)
E. Gara: *Carteggi pucciniani* (Milan, 1958)
C. Paladini: *Giacomo Puccini* (Florence, 1961)
C. A. Hopkinson: *Bibliography of the Works of Giacomo Puccini 1858–1924* (New York, 1968)
A. Marchetti: *Puccini com'era* (Milan, 1973)
G. Magri: *Puccini e le sue rime* (Milan, 1974)
G. Pintorno: *Puccini: 276 lettere inedite* (Montecatini, 1974)
S. Puccini, ed.: *Giacomo Puccini: lettere a Riccardo Schnabl* (Milan, 1981)
M. Kaye: *The Unknown Puccini* (Oxford, 1985)

BIOGRAPHY AND CRITICISM

F. Fontana: 'Giacomo Puccini', *Gazzetta musicale di Milano*, xxxix (1884), 381–2; repr. as 'Giacomo Puccini visto dal suo primo librettista', *Musica d'oggi*, xv (1933), 148–50
F. Torrefranca: *Giacomo Puccini e l'opera internazionale* (Turin, 1912)
I. Pizzetti: 'Giacomo Puccini', *Musicisti contemporanei: saggi critici* (Milan, 1914), 49–106
A. Fraccaroli: *La vita di Giacomo Puccini* (Milan, 1925)
G. Adami: *Puccini* (Milan, 1935)
P. Panichelli: *Il 'Pretino' di Giacomo Puccini racconta* (Pisa, 1940, 3/1949)
G. Marotti: *Giacomo Puccini* (Florence, 1949)
A. Bonaccorsi: *Giacomo Puccini e i suoi antenati musicali* (Milan, 1950)
G. R. Marek: *Puccini: a Biography* (New York, 1951)
D. Del Fiorentino: *Immortal Bohemian: an Intimate Memoir of Giacomo Puccini* (London, 1952)
M. Carner: *Puccini: a Critical Biography* (London, 1958, 2/1974)
E. Greenfield: *Puccini: Keeper of the Seal* (London, 1958)
C. Sartori: *Puccini* (Milan, 1958, 4/1978)
P. C. Hughes: *Famous Puccini Operas* (London, 1959)
W. Ashbrook: *The Operas of Puccini* (New York, 1968; London, 1969, 2/1985)
L. Pinzauti: *Puccini: una vita* (Florence, 1974)
L'avant-scène opéra, no.11 (1977) [*Tosca* issue]
S. Martinotti: 'I travagliati Avant-Propos di Puccini', *Il melodramma italiano dell'ottocento: studi e ricerche per Massimo Mila* (Turin, 1977), 451–510
C. Casini: *Giacomo Puccini* (Turin, 1978)
J. Smith: 'A Metamorphic Tragedy', *PRMA*, cvi (1978–80), 105–14
L'avant-scène opéra, no.20 (1979) [*La bohème* issue]
H. Greenfeld: *Puccini* (London, 1980)
J. Nicolaisen: *Italian Opera in Transition, 1871–1893* (Ann Arbor, 1980)
L'avant-scène opéra, no.33 (1981) [*Turandot* issue]
M. Girardi: '*Turandot*: il futuro interrotto del melodramma italiano', *RIM*, xvii (1982), 155–81
L'avant-scène opéra, no.56 (1983) [*Madama Butterfly* issue]
L'avant-scène opéra, no.82 (1985) [*Gianni Schicchi* issue]
M. Carner: *Giacomo Puccini: Tosca* (Cambridge, 1985)
J. Maehder, ed.: *Esotismo e colore locale nell'opera di Puccini* (Pisa, 1985)
C. Foucart: 'De la conversation romanesque à l'air d'opéra: d'Henry Murger à Giacomo Puccini', *Oper als Text: romantische Beiträge zur Libretto-Forschung*, ed. A. Gier (Heidelberg, 1986), 277–87
A. Groos and R. Parker: *Giacomo Puccini: La bohème* (Cambridge, 1986)

J. Maehder: 'Paris-Bilder: zur Transformation von Henry Mürgers Roman in den 'Bohème'-Opern Puccinis und Leoncavallos', *JbO*, ii (1986), 109–76
J. L. DiGaetani: *Puccini the Thinker: the Composer's Intellectual and Dramatic Development* (New York, 1987)
A. Groos: 'Lieutenant F. B. Pinkerton: Problems in the Genesis of an Operatic Hero', *Italica*, lxiv (1987), 654–75
J. Budden: 'The Genesis and Literary Source of Giacomo Puccini's First Opera', *COJ*, i/1 (1989), 79–85
M. Girardi: *Puccini: la vita e l'opera* (Rome, 1989)
A. Groos: 'Return of the Native: Japan in *Madama Butterfly/ Madama Butterfly* in Japan', *COJ*, i/2 (1989), 167–94
M. Sansone: 'Verga, Puccini and *La lupa*', *Italian Studies*, xliv (1989), 63–76
G. Musco: *Musica e teatro in Giacomo Puccini*, i (Cortona, 1989)
D. Schickling: *Giacomo Puccini: Biographie* (Stuttgart, 1989)
W. Ashbrook and H. Powers: *Puccini's Turandot: the End of the Great Tradition* (Princeton, NJ, 1991)
A. W. Atlas: 'Newly Discovered Sketches for Puccini's *Turandot* at the Pierpont Morgan Library', *COJ*, iii/2 (1991), 173–93
A. Groos: 'Madame Butterfly: the Story', *COJ*, iii/2 (1991), 125–58

JULIAN BUDDEN

Puccitelli, Virgilio (*b* San Severino Marche, 1599; *d* San Severino Marche, 26 Dec 1654). Italian librettist. He was educated and ordained in Rome. About 1630 (or perhaps earlier) he entered the service of Prince Władysław Sigismund of Poland, later King Władysław IV (1633–48). From 1634 he acted as secretary to the king, undertaking private missions (to Italy in 1638–9 and France in 1640) connected with, among other things, the organization of musical life at court. In 1649 he returned to Italy, where he lived first in Naples and then in San Severino.

Puccitelli wrote the texts for nine operas performed at the Polish court and probably for a number of ballet introductions. The themes of his *drammi* range from the pastoral and the hagiographic to the epic, and the ideology is a restrained fusion of neo-Platonic theory of love and Baroque moralism. The texts are written in *versi sciolti* for recitative, and in stanzas (with short lines) for choruses and solo arias. In the choruses a solo voice usually alternates with tutti. The structure of the works combines features from different dramatic genres, with strong emphasis on tragic hieratic elements; heroic characters are identified panegyrically with the king. Much use was made of the theatrical machinery of the time, especially in the mythological *intermedi*, examples of which were introduced between the acts of *La Santa Cecilia*, staged for the king's wedding. The music of these operas is lost, but it is known that it was composed exclusively by members of the royal chapel, probably mostly by Marco Scacchi, but possibly also by Kaspar Förster, Marcin Mielczewski and Bartłomiej Pękiel.

Dafne, 1635; *Il ratto di Helena* (dramma musicale), M. Scacchi, 1636; *La Santa Cecilia* (dramma musicale con gl'intermedii favolosi), ?Scacchi, 1637; *Narciso trasformato* (favola pastorale recitata in musica), Scacchi, 1638; *Armida abbandonata* (azzione rappresentata in musica), ?Scacchi, 1641; *L'Enea* (favola drammatica rappresentata in musica), ?Scacchi, 1641; *L'Andromeda* (favola drammatica rappresentata in musica), ?Scacchi, 1644; *Le nozze d'Amore e di Psiche* (dramma musicale), ?Scacchi, 1646; *Circe delusa* (dramma musicale), ?Scacchi, 1648

*

S. Windakiewicz: 'Teatr Władysława IV (1633–48)', *Przegląd Polski*, xxviii (1893), 231–97; pubd separately (Kraków, 1893); suppl., *Czas*, xlviii (1895), no.285
K. Targosz-Kretowa: *Teatr dworski Władysława IV* (Kraków, 1965)
A. Panicali: 'Un librettista italiano in Polonia: Virgilio Puccitelli (1599–1654)', *Studi secenteschi*, ix (1968), 287–98
A. Panicali and A. Szweykowska: 'La maga sdegnata Virgilio Puccitellego', *Pamiętnik teatralny*, xviii (1969), 511–31
A. Szweykowska: 'Qualche osservazione sulla struttura letteraria del dramma musicale del primo seicento (sull'esempio delle opere di Virgilio Puccitelli: 1599–1654)', *Quadrivium*, xii/2 (1971), 77–88
——: 'Virgilio Puccitelli e l'opera italiana alla corte di Ladislao IV di Polonia', *RIM*, vii (1972), 182–95
J. Lewański: 'Świadkowie i świadectwa opery władysławowskiej' [Witnesses and Evidence of Władisławian Operas], *Studia staropolskie*, xxv (1973), 50–60
G. L. Masetti-Zannini: 'Due re di Polonia ed un poeta e musicista settempedano', *Miscellanea settempedana*, i (1976), 61–80
A. Szweykowska: *Dramma per musica w teatrze Wazów 1635–1648* (Kraków, 1976)
Miscellanea settempedana, ii (1979) [whole vol.]
A. Szweykowska: 'Sulle analogie fra i melodrammi polacchi e veneziani negli anni quaranta del seicento', *Vita teatrale in Italia e Polonia fra seicento e settecento*, ed. N. Bristiger and J. Kowalozyk (Warsaw, 1984), 177–83
——: 'Melodramma Andromeda 1644', *Muzyka*, xxxii/4 (1987), 17–28
ANNA SZWEYKOWSKA

Pucitta, Vincenzo. *See* PUCITTA, VINCENZO.

Puchon [Pichon, Pigeon], **Madame** (*b* c1700; *d* after 1722). Soprano. She went to the Hamburg Opera in 1722 with the soprano Christina Louisa Koulhaas and the alto castrato Antonio Campioli; they had previously been engaged in Brunswick, where Puchon was also a dancer. Mattheson mentions her with Campioli in his autobiography but says nothing about her qualities as a singer. In 1722 she sang Rosmiris in *Arsaces* by Orlandini and Amadei, conducted by Telemann, Pulcheria in Telemann's *Sieg der Schönheit*, Dorothea in Conti's *Don Chisciotte in Sierra Morena* and the title role in Keiser's *Ariadne*. The last known appearance of Puchon was as Clelia in *Muzio Scevola*, by Amadei, Giovanni Bononcini and Handel (1723).

*

K. Zelm: 'Die Sänger der Hamburger Gänsemarkt-Oper', *HJbMw*, iii (1978), 65–6
HANS JOACHIM MARX

Pucitta [Puccitta], **Vincenzo** (*b* Civitavecchia, nr Rome, 1778; *d* Milan, 20 Dec 1861). Italian composer. After studying at the Conservatorio della Pietà dei Turchini in Naples with Fenaroli and Sala, he began his career as an opera composer in Senigallia in 1799 (according to Fétis) with a work of unknown title, followed by two farces for Parma and Lucca. During the next five years he produced mostly farces or one-act comedies for theatres in Venice and Milan, including a one-act opera inspired by Goethe's *Werther* in 1802. In the same year his *opera buffa Il puntiglio* was given at La Scala, establishing his reputation, and in 1804 he had his first great success with the farce *La burla fortunata*, which was widely revived until 1833 under various titles. Fétis reports that he went to Lisbon in 1806, where an *Andromaca* was performed. He was then music director of the Italian opera in Amsterdam and from 1809 to 1814 composer and music director at the King's

Theatre, London, which was at that time a showcase for the soprano Angelica Catalani. For her Pucitta composed a series of operas, both *buffa* and *seria*, tailoring his music to her elaborate vocalism, as in the brilliant part of Marietta in *La caccia di Enrico IV* (1809) and the principal role in *La vestale* (1810), his most widely acclaimed serious opera. The peak of his success in London was the gala performance of his opera based on Monti's tragedy *Aristodemo* in June 1814 in the presence of the king and queen, the tsar and the king of Prussia. During this time Pucitta was Catalani's accompanist and provided much of the repertory for her solo concerts, at which he often conducted the orchestra; he went with her on tours in Scotland and Ireland and throughout Europe. In 1815, when she was director of the Théâtre Italien in Paris, he became her house composer. However, the Paris public took such a dislike to him and his music that when Catalani appeared in his new opera *La principessa in campagna* in 1817, she had it advertised without his name. Because of this situation and after disputes with her husband, he returned to Italy that year.

In 1819 Pucitta made a successful tour of Austria and Germany with his pupil, the English soprano Elizabeth Ferron (or Feron). In April 1820 her début at La Scala in *La principessa in campagna* was well received, but the opera was not. The two works that Pucitta composed for the next carnival season in Rome and Milan were fiascos and he ceased to write for the stage. His output included about 34 operas and some sacred works; in his later years he edited collections of popular Marian melodies.

Le nozze senza sposa (farce, 1), Parma, Ducale, carn. 1800; Venice, S Benedetto, May 1802, *I-Mr**
L'amor platonico (farce, 1, G. D. Camagna), Lucca, Pubblico, spr. 1800; Venice, S Benedetto, 31 May 1803, *Mr**
Bianca de' Rossi (azione tragica), Florence, Pallacorda, spr. 1800
Il fuoruscito (op semiseria, 2, A. Anelli), Milan, Scala, 16 June 1801, excerpts *Rsc*
Teresa e Wilk (farce, 1, Camagna), Venice, S Benedetto, Feb 1802, *Fc, Mr*
Werter e Carlotta (1, Camagna, after J. W. von Goethe), Venice, S Moisè, spr. 1802, *Mr*
Il puntiglio [Furberia e puntiglio] (ob, 2, L. Romanelli), Milan, Scala, 7 July 1802, *Mr**
La perfidia scoperta (farce, Camagna), Venice, S Giovanni Grisostomo, spr. 1803
Zelinda e Lindoro (farce, 1, Camagna, after C. Goldoni), Venice, S Giovanni Grisostomo, 3 May 1803, *Mr*
Oh, che bel-caso! (farce, Camagna), Venice, S Giovanni Grisostomo, June 1803
Lauretta (farce, Camagna), Padua, Nuovo, 9 July 1803, *Mr*, Pl*
L'imbroglio della lettera, ossia Il pittore (farce, after G. Foppa), Milan, Carcano, carn. 1804
La burla fortunata, ossia I due prigionieri (farce, 1, Camagna, after B. J. Marsollier: *Adolphe et Clara*), Venice, S Moisè, 9 April 1804, *Fc, Nc* (2 copies with variants); as Adolfo e Chiara, Turin, Carignano, aut. 1812, excerpts *Tf* and *Tn*; as Li due prigionieri, ossia Adolfo e Clara, London, King's, 1814, *GB-Lbl, D-Mbs*, excerpts (London, 1813)
Il duello per complimento (farce), Milan, Carcano, carn. 1805
Lo sposo di Lucca (farce, Camagna), Venice, S Moisè, spr. 1805, *I-Mr**
La finta pazza, ossia Il vero recipe (farce), Zara, 1805
Andromaca (os, 3, Romanelli), ? Lisbon, S Carlos, 1806; ?rev. version, Milan, Scala, 26 Dec 1821, *Mr**
Il marchese d'un giorno, ovvero Gli sposi felici (ob, 2), Livorno, Avvalorati, carn. 1808
La caccia di Enrico IV (S Buonaiuti, after C. Collé), London, King's, 7 March 1809, excerpts *Rsc*, excerpts (London, c1812); rev. version, Paris, Italien, 28 Oct 1815
La vedova di spirito (2, Buonaiuti), ?London, spr. 1809
Le quattro nazioni, London, King's, 11 July 1809
I viaggiatori bizzarri, London, King's, 1809

La vestale (os, 3, Romanelli, after E. Jouy), London, King's, 3 May 1810; rev. version, Lisbon, S Carlos, May 1816, and Milan, Re, sum. 1816, *BGc*, *Mr*, vs (London, *c*1810)

Il trionfo di Rosselane, ossia Le tre sultane (op comica, 3, G. Caravita), London, King's, 22 Jan 1811, *GB-Lbl*, vs (London, 1811)

Ginevra di Scozia (os, 2, G. Rossi), London, King's, 16 April 1812, vs (London, 1812)

Boadicea (os, 2), London, King's, 23 March 1813, excerpts (London, 1813–15)

Il feudatario (2), Trieste, Nuovo, Oct 1813

Aristodemo (os, 3, L. Buonavoglia, after V. Monti), London, King's, 9 June 1814, full score, Bucharest, Ciprian Porumbescu Conservatory; excerpts *I-Rsc*, *Vnm*, vs (London, 1814)

L'orgoglio avvilito (2), Paris, Italien, 30 Nov 1815

La principessa in campagna, o Il marchese nell'imbarazzo [La principessa bizzarra] (ob, 2) Paris, Italien, 20 Nov 1817, *GB-Lbl* (with autograph addns), *I-Mr**, excerpts (Milan, 1820)

Il maestro di cappella (ob, A. Palomba), Trieste, Nuovo, March 1818

La festa del villaggio (dg, 2, J. Ferretti), Rome, Apollo, Jan 1822

La fausse Agnès (ob, 3, Castil-Blaze [F.-H.-J. Blaze], after P. N. Destouches), Paris, Gymnase, 6 July 1824, vs (Paris, n.d.) [pasticcio with music of Cimarosa, Mozart, Meyerbeer, Rossini and Puccitta]

Muta per amore, excerpt *Nc*

*

FétisB
AMZ, xx (1818), 176; xxii (1820), 499–500   ANDREA LANZA

Puerto Rico. For a discussion of opera in Puerto Rico *see* SAN JUAN.

Pugnani, Gaetano (*b* Turin, 27 Nov 1731; *d* Turin, 15 July 1798). Italian composer. At the age of ten he began his career as a second violinist in the orchestra at the Teatro Regio, Turin. A royal stipend enabled him to study composition with Ciampi in Rome (1749–50). On 2 February 1754 he performed one of his own compositions at the Concert Spirituel in Paris, where his first published works appeared the same year. From 1767 to 1769 he served as conductor at the King's Theatre in London, where his first opera, *Nanetta e Lubino* (1769), met with success. In 1770 he became first violinist of the king's music in Turin, a post his teacher G. B. Somis had held and which included the leadership of the Teatro Regio orchestra. In 1776 he also became general director of instrumental music, and in 1786 was appointed supervisor of military bands. From 1780 to 1782 he toured northern Europe with his illustrious pupil Viotti. A commission for Naples in 1784 initiated a period of activity in which he wrote four operas in five years, as well as some ballet music. His last foreign journey took him to Vienna, where on 22 March 1796 he conducted his orchestral suite based on Goethe's *Werther*. During his last years he saw the decline and ultimate dissolution of Turin's musical establishment as a result of the war with France.

Burney observed that Pugnani, 'though an able and celebrated professor on the violin, seems to have begun writing for the voice too late in life to arrive at great excellence in lyric compositions'. Nevertheless, his modest accomplishments in opera are not without interest or merit. After his initial comic opera for London, the rest of his works were either serious operas or *feste teatrali*, which traditionally incorporate machinery, spectacle, choruses and dance. Typically, the librettos of the Turin court poets Cigna-Santi and Boggio emphasize the exotic and spectacular but remain traditional in formal structure, which made them attractive to Italian theatres. Pugnani's *Tamas Kouli-Kan nell'India* (1772), with its military display, staged battles and burning

cities all within an exotic Persian setting, earned another performance in Florence in 1774.

His two serious operas of the mid-1780s are quite unusual, and their formal innovations reflect the influence of the librettist Verazi. In *Achille in Sciro* (1785), which includes all Metastasio's choruses, the second and third movements of the sinfonia are used as dance music for an opening spectacle. In a new action ensemble Deidamia interrupts a duet between Achilles and Ulysses, thwarting the latter's efforts to lure Achilles away to his military duties. Even more unusual is Achilles' cavatina of three stanzas in Act 3, where he is twice interrupted by Deidamia and finally by Ulysses who leaves before the last stanza. Almost more surprising is his serious opera for Naples, *Adone e Venere* (1784), based on a mythological subject with lavish use of chorus and ballet, normally excluded from *opera seria*.

Pugnani's orchestration contains excellent string writing, often in four parts. He treated wind instruments both as soloists and as ensemble players, as well as writing wind dialogue with strings and with the voice. His operas of the 1780s have clarinet parts. He wrote imaginative programme music for battles and storms, and indulged a penchant for melismatic display in word-painting and programmatic effects in his obbligato recitatives and arias.

Nanetta e Lubino (ob, C. F. Badini), London, King's, 8 April 1769, *D-Bds**, *I-Vlevi*, Favourite Songs (London, 1769)

Issea (favola pastorale, 2, V. A. Cigna-Santi), Turin, Regio, 1771, *D-Bds**, *P-La*; rev. as Apollo e Issea, London, 30 March 1773

Tamas Kouli-Kan nell'India (os, 3, Cigna-Santi), Turin, Regio, 1 Feb 1772, *La*

Aurora (festa, 2, G. D. Boggio), Turin, 1775 [for wedding of Carlo Emanuele IV and Adelaide Clotilde of France], *I-Rsc*, *P-La*

Adone e Venere (os, 3, G. Boltri), Naples, S Carlo, 12 Jan 1784, *D-Bds**, *I-Tf*, *P-La*

Achille in Sciro (os, 3, P. Metastasio), Turin, Regio, 15 Jan 1785, *F-Pn* (inc.), *I-Tf*, *P-La*

Demofoonte (os, 3, Metastasio), Turin, Regio, 26 Dec 1787, *D-Bds** (arias), *F-Pn* (Act 1), *P-La*

Demetrio a Rodi (festa, 2, Boggio), Turin, 1789 [for wedding of Vittorio Emanuele, Duke of Aosta, and Maria Teresa of Austria], *I-Mr*

*

BurneyH

F. Fayolle: *Notices sur Corelli, Tartini, Gaviniès, Pugnani et Viotti* (Paris, 1810)

A. Bertolotti: *Gaetano Pugnani e altri musici alla corte di Torino nel secolo XVIII* (Milan, 1892)

D. Carutti: 'Della famiglia di Gaetano Pugnani', *Miscellanea di storia italiana*, iii/2 (Turin, 1896)

A. Della Corte: 'Due inedite opere teatrali di Gaetano Pugnani', *Musica d'oggi*, xiii (1931), 490–97

——: *Notizie di Gaetano Pugnani* (Turin, 1931)

E. M. von Zschinsky-Troxler: *Gaetano Pugnani* (Berlin, 1939)

G. Barblan: 'Ansia preromantica in Gaetano Pugnani', *Chigiana*, xvi (1959), 17–25

U. Zelaschi: *L'opéra italien jusqu'en 1900* (Brussels, 1982)

C. Sartori: *I libretti italiani a stampa dalle origini al 1800: catalogo analitico con 16 indici* (Cuneo, 1990–)

BORIS SCHWARZ/MARITA P. McCLYMONDS

Pugni, Cesare (*b* Genoa, 31 May 1802; *d* St Petersburg, 14/26 Jan 1870). Italian composer. From 1815 to 1822 he studied in Milan, with Asioli among his teachers of composition. In 1823 he contributed to the ballet *Il castello di Kenilworth* (La Scala), and his own ballet *Elerz e Zulmida* was given in 1826. In the following years he specialized in this genre, but from 1831 to 1834 attempted opera with a series of five works which began successfully with *Il disertore svizzero* and ended with the fiasco of *Un episodio di San Michele*. He was *maestro al cembalo* and music director at La Scala, 1832–4, then spent some years in Paris, where he was briefly associated with Bellini. He worked in London from 1843 and St Petersburg from 1851. Pugni is said to have written all or part of the music for more than 300 ballets; he also wrote sacred and orchestral works. The *brio* and the easy expressiveness of his music, together with the conventionality of its style, contributed largely to the success of his stage works.

Il disertore svizzero, o La nostalgia (melodramma, 2, F. Romani), Milan, Cannobiana, 28 May 1831, vs (Milan, 1831)
La vendetta (melodramma tragico, 2, C. Bassi), Milan, Scala, 11 Feb 1832, *I-Mr**
Ricciarda di Edimburgo (dramma serio, 2, Bassi), Trieste, Grande, 29 Sept 1832
Il contrabbandiere (melodramma, 2, Romani), Milan, Cannobiana, 13 June 1833, *Mr**, excerpts, pf acc. (Milan, ?1833)
Un episodio di San Michele (melodramma giocoso, 2, Romani), Milan, Cannobiana, 14 June 1834   ANDREA LANZA

Pugno, (Stéphane) Raoul (*b* Montrouge, nr Paris, 23 June 1852; *d* Moscow, 21 Dec 1913/3 Jan 1914). French composer. He made his début as a pianist in 1858, then studied at the Ecole Niedermeyer in Paris. From 1866 to 1869 he was a student at the Conservatoire. He took an active part in the Commune of 1871 and in May was made music director of the Opéra. On the fall of the Commune he escaped any retribution and in 1872 became organist at the church of St Eugène. In 1874 he also became choirmaster at the Théâtre Ventadour. From 1892 he taught at the Conservatoire. In 1893 Pugno resumed his concert career and was soon recognized as perhaps the leading French pianist of the time (he made several recordings in 1903). An early exponent of Wagner in France, he and Debussy provided the two-piano accompaniment for a famous concert performance of parts of *Das Rheingold* on 6 May 1893. He composed, mostly before resuming his concert career, a considerable number of stage works in the lighter genres, and salon music, now forgotten.

unless otherwise indicated, first performed in Paris and published there shortly afterwards in complete vocal score or excerpts

A qui la trompe (opérette, 1, M. Richard [H. de Sartem]), Asnières, 13 Dec 1877, unpubd
La fée Cocotte (féerie-ballet, 3, G. Marot and E. Phillipe), Palace, 26 Jan 1881, vs (Paris, 1882), collab. Bourgeois
Ninetta (opéra-comique, 3, M. Hennequin and A. Bisson), Renaissance, 26 Dec 1882
La brigue Dondaine, 1890
Le sosie (opéra-bouffe, 3, A. Valabrègne and H. Kéroul), Bouffes-Parisiens, 8 Oct 1887
Le valet de coeur (opérette, 3, P. Ferrier and C. Clairville), Bouffes-Parisiens, 19 April 1888
Le retour d'Ulysse (opérette-bouffe, 3, F. Carré), Bouffes-Parisiens, 1 Feb 1889
La vocation de Marius (opéra-bouffe, 3, Carré and A. Debelly), Nouveautés, 29 March 1890
La petite Poucette (vaudeville-opérette, 3, Hennequin and M. Ordonneau), Renaissance, 7 March 1891
Tai-Tsoung (grand opéra, 5, E. d'Hervilly), Marseilles, 11 April 1894, collab. E. Guinet
La ville morte (G. D'Annunzio), unperf., unpubd, completed N. Boulanger

*

H. Imbert: *Médaillons contemporains* (Paris, 1902) [with list of works]
E. Berteaux: *En ce temps-là (souvenirs)* (Paris, 1946)
G. Samazeuilh: *Musiciens de mon temps* (Paris, 1947)
          GUY BOURLIGUEUX

Pujman, Ferdinand (*b* Nížkov, Bohemia, 23 May 1889; *d* Prague, 17 Dec 1961). Czech director and writer. While studying engineering in Prague (1906–12) he attended Nejedlý's music lectures and later joined Nejedlý's circle, contributing to *Smetana* and writing reviews for the daily *Samostatnost*. He was able to put into practice the insights he gained as a theatre critic and admirer of Appia and Meyerhold when he left engineering to become opera director at the Brno Theatre (1920) and the Prague National Theatre (1921–50; 1956–9). There he began a fruitful collaboration with the musical director Otakar Ostrčil. His 92 productions included the Czech premières of *Pelléas et Mélisande* (1921), *Wozzeck* (1926) and *The Cunning Little Vixen* (1925, a production much disliked by Janáček). His spare style, omitting inessentials and making more use of space, motion and lighting resources (Dalcroze was an influence), had a profound effect on Czech opera production. Pujman also lectured at the Prague Conservatory and, after World War II, at the new Academy of Musical Arts, where in his student productions he was able to explore a more adventurous repertory than at the National Theatre. He wrote the libretto for Alois Hába's opera *New Land*, adapted Hába's own text for *Thy Kingdom Come*, and translated many Russian vocal texts.

K zpěvoherní dramaturgii [Operatic Dramaturgy] (Prague, 1917)
Poznámky o dramaturgii smetanovských oper [Remarks on the Production of Smetana's Operas] (Prague, 1919)
Operní sloh Národního divadla [The Operatic Style of the National Theatre] (Prague, 1933)
Zhudebněná mateřština [The Musical Setting of one's Mother Tongue] (Prague, 1939)
Operní režie [Opera Production] (Prague, 1940)
Stati o režii a dramaturgii zpívané hry [Essays on the Production and Dramaturgy of the Sung Play] (Prague, 1958)
Smetanovský breviř [A Smetana Breviary] (Prague, n.d.)

*

O. Bartoňková: 'Ferdinand Pujman', *Prolegomena Scénografické encyklopedie*, x (Prague, 1972), 72–80
M. Dosoudilová: 'Pujmanova režijní koncepce Smetanova Dalibora' [Pujman's Conceptualization as a Director of Smetana's *Dalibor*], *HRo*, xxxviii (1985), 178–84, 221–4, 284–7
M. Bergerová: 'Ferdinand Pujman a česká scénografická avantgarda' [Ferdinand Pujman and Czech Avant-garde Scenography], *Divadelní revue*, i/3 (1990), 52–62
A. Scherl: 'Ferdinand Pujman a evropská operní režie' [Ferdinand Pujman and European Opera Production], *Divadelní revue*, i/3 (1990), 45–51
M. Dosoudilová: 'Geneze Pujmanova pojetí Prodané nevěsty' [The Genesis of Pujman's Conception of *The Bartered Bride*], *HV*, xxviii (1991), 125–33   JOHN TYRRELL

Pulli, Pietro (*b* Naples, *c*1710; *d* 1759 or later). Italian composer. His earliest known activity as a composer dates from autumn 1731, when he provided six arias for the revival, with musical alterations by Giuseppe Sellitto, of Vinci's *La mogliere fedele* at the Teatro Nuovo, Naples; the libretto, by B. Saddumene, calls him 'famosissimo sonatore de arceliuti e contrapuntisto'. In other works he is named simply as Neapolitan *maestro di cappella*. He worked at least until 1734 in Naples, where he set the two dialect operas by Saddumene, *Li zitelle de lo vòmmero* (1731) and *La marina de Chiaja* (1734), both for the Teatro dei Fiorentini. These works are of some historical interest, since they involve quasi-Arcadian settings, a new, scenographically decorative element.

The remainder of Pulli's operas were produced in north Italy, suggesting that he had moved there at least as early as 1739. He probably went first to Modena, where De Brosses found his music for the translation of Lamotte's comedy *Le Carnaval et la Folie* (*Il Carnevale e la Pazzia*) not at all to his Gallic taste; he grumbled that only a Pergolesi or a Hasse could have done justice to the play. Pulli's other operas were all serious. *Caio Marzio Coriolano*, for Reggio Emilia in 1741, was his most successful work, revived in Naples (1745), Venice (1747) and Modena (1750).

Li zitelle de lo vòmmero (chelleta, B. Saddumene), Naples, Fiorentini, 1731

La marina de Chiaja (chelleta, Saddumene), Naples, Fiorentini, 1734 [? rev. of 1731 setting, with lib. rev. by G. A. Federico]

Il Carnevale e la Pazzia (ob, after A. H. de Lamotte: *Le Carnaval et la Folie*), Modena, Ducale, carn. 1739–40

Le nozze del Piacere e dell'Allegria (festa teatrale), Modena, Molza, carn. 1739–40

Vologeso re dei Parti (os, after A. Zeno: *Lucio Vero*), Reggio Emilia, Pubblico, spr. 1741, arias *I-Fc*

Caio Marzio Coriolano (os, 3, Z. Seriman), Reggio Emilia, Pubblico, 1741, *Vnm*

Zenobia (os, P. Metastasio), Milan, Regio Ducal, 26 Dec 1748

Il Demetrio (os, Metastasio), Milan, Regio Ducal, carn. 1749, arias *MOe*

Olimpiade (os, Metastasio), Modena, Corte, Jan 1751

Andimione, *F-Pn*

Arias in: La mogliere fedele, 1731

*

C. de Brosses: *Lettres familières écrites d'Italie en 1739 et 1740* (Paris, 1799), letter to M de Neuilly, Ash Wednesday 1740

A. Gandini: *Cronistoria dei teatri di Modena dal 1539 al 1871* (Modena, 1873), i, 22–3, 61; ii, 25–6

M. Scherillo: *L'opera buffa napoletana durante il settecento: storia letteraria* (Naples, 1883, 2/1916), 171–2

O. G. T. Sonneck: *Library of Congress: Catalogue of Opera Librettos Printed before 1800* (Washington DC, 1914), i, 769

V. Viviani: *Storia del teatro napoletano* (Naples, 1969), 294–5

JAMES L. JACKMAN (with MARITA P. McCLYMONDS)

Punainen viiva. Opera by Aulis Sallinen; *see* RED LINE, THE.

Punch and Judy. 'Tragicomedy or comitragedy' in one act by HARRISON BIRTWISTLE to a libretto by STEPHEN PRUSLIN; Aldeburgh, Jubilee Hall, 8 June 1968.

Punch	high baritone
Judy/Fortune Teller	mezzo-soprano
Pretty Polly/Witch	high soprano
Choregos/Jack Ketch	baritone
Lawyer	high tenor
Doctor	deep bass

Birtwistle's first opera was commissioned by the English Opera Group for the Aldeburgh Festival; the original production by Anthony Besch, conducted by David Atherton, was subsequently seen in Edinburgh and London. Despite its critical success and an American première in Minneapolis in 1970, the work was not heard again in Britain until 1979, when Atherton conducted a concert performance in London and a subsequent recording. In 1982 David Freeman staged it for Opera Factory London, a version that was widely seen and subsequently televised. In June 1991 the composer directed a new production at the Aldeburgh Festival.

Cast in a prologue, four scenes and an epilogue, the musical and dramatic structure of *Punch and Judy* is a mosaic of small-scale closed forms; it combines the ritualized rigour of classical Greek drama with a continuous structure of self-contained numbers borrowed from Baroque opera and oratorio (Bach's *St Matthew Passion* was a declared model). There are more than 100 separate musical items labelled in the score, grouped in recurring sequences and cycles.

PROLOGUE After a parody fanfare the Choregos appears in front of the curtain to welcome the audience. He underlines the work's mixture of comedy and menace: 'Please to enjoy our little play. If we make you laugh then you need not pay.'

MELODRAMA 1 The curtain rises on Punch, rocking the baby and singing a threatening lullaby, which ends with his war-cry ('Roo-it-too-it-too-it-too-it-too-it!') as he throws the baby on the fire. Judy enters with her own lullaby and discovers her dead baby; after a word game with Punch she is led to the Altar of Murder while the Choregos offers a commentary. The Murder Ensemble is briefly interrupted by the first Passion Aria, sung by the Doctor and Lawyer as chorus, but Punch stabs Judy and the Choregos leads her to the gibbet. Punch sets off on his search for Pretty Polly.

PASSION CHORALE 1 Framed by short instrumental toccatas, the Choregos with Judy, the Doctor and the Lawyer comment on the crime just committed.

'Punch and Judy' (Birtwistle): The Quest for Pretty Polly 1 from the original production at Jubilee Hall, Aldeburgh, 8 June 1968

THE QUEST FOR PRETTY POLLY 1 In a sequence of six short numbers (Travel Music, Weather Report, Prayer, Serenade, Pretty Polly's Rhapsody and Moral) that will be repeated three times in the course of the opera, Punch travels on Horsey to seek out Pretty Polly. An astronomical clock shows that Punch is suspended between heaven and earth, under the sign of the Crab on a summer's afternoon; the Weather Report foretells a tempest from the east at three o'clock. Polly is discovered sitting on a pedestal in a green spotlight. Punch serenades Polly but he fails to impress her with his offer of a huge sunflower (it is tainted by the fire in which the baby died), and the Choregos is left to offer commiserations: 'Weep, my Punch, Weep out your unfathomable, inexpressible sorrow.'

MELODRAMA 2 After a short instrumental sinfonia the Doctor and Lawyer confront Punch with his crime: 'The law of the land is the medicine of mankind'. Punch lures them into a game of riddles and eventually leads them both to the Altar; the Choregos announces their deaths, and Punch stabs them both, the Doctor with a giant syringe, the Lawyer with a huge quill pen.

PASSION CHORALE 2 After they have been taken to the gibbet, Punch resumes his quest for Pretty Polly.

THE QUEST FOR PRETTY POLLY 2 The sequence of events and musical numbers is repeated: Punch is now suspended between heaven and earth under the sign of the Scorpion at twilight in autumn. Pretty Polly is found this time in a red spotlight, and she dismisses Punch's offering of a huge jewel because it is flawed by the suffering of his victims. The Choregos is again ironically sympathetic.

MELODRAMA 3 After 'A Little Canonic Prelude to Disaster', the second half of the work begins with the Choregos entering the action of the opera. He confronts Punch as they celebrate Pretty Polly: 'Let her be praised in singsong and psalm'. But despite Judy's intervention from the Chorus Gibbet in a Recitative and Passion Aria 2, the Doctor and Lawyer proclaim the Choregos's demise and at the height of the jollity Punch saws him to death inside a bass-viol case. But the Choregos's murder has destroyed the ritual symmetries of the action, as the chorus sings his lament.

NIGHTMARE There is no search this time; after a Transition and the third Travel Music and Weather Report, now showing Punch between heaven and hell at midnight, the Choregos and the Chorus describe a nightmare: 'United in fear, man and landscape dissolve into the whiteness of a shriek'. Punch appears at a fortune teller's booth to consult the Tarot cards; after three Tarot games Judy is revealed as the Fortune Teller. There is a Black Wedding: Punch and Judy are led to Pretty Polly's pedestal, now transformed into a wedding altar; Pretty Polly herself is disguised as a witch. Punch is taunted and scourged, and confronted with the details of his crimes in an Adding-song: 'A fractured skull, a bleeding face, a severed limb, an oozing eye, a twisted neck'. At its climax Punch calls out for Horsey and faints.

THE QUEST FOR PRETTY POLLY 3 The quest is shortened to four numbers; Punch is between heaven and earth under the sign of the Goat, at dawn in winter. But Pretty Polly's pedestal is empty under a blue spotlight; again Punch is comforted by the Choregos.

PASSION CHORALE 3 Framed by toccatas, Punch's four victims envisage the possibility of a redemptive love.

MELODRAMA 4 Punch is in prison and condemned to death. The Choregos appears disguised as Jack Ketch the hangman, though Punch soon establishes who he really is and persuades him to put his own head in the noose. After a final war cry, he hangs Jack Ketch. This time he has unwittingly done a good deed; Pretty Polly is bathed in brilliant white light.

PUNCH TRIUMPHANS Pretty Polly sings a rhapsody to spring and joins Punch in a love duet. The gallows is transformed into a maypole, as everyone except the Choregos hymns the happy couple.

EPILOGUE The Choregos brings down the curtain on what he originally announced as a tragedy but has turned out to be a comedy.

* * *

In the detailed stage directions in the score, as well as in the musical treatment, Birtwistle is at pains to emphasize the ritual aspects of *Punch*: the Choregos is directed to sing from a booth downstage left, Pretty Polly's pedestal is upstage right, and so on. A group of five wind instruments from the 15-piece ensemble is to be seated on stage. Much of the instrumental writing in the score employs extreme tessituras, and that characteristic gives the opera its distinctive pungency. Yet the vocal writing is widely varied, from rapt ensembles (the Passion Chorales, the Prayers) through fine-spun arias (Punch's Prayer, Judy's Passion Aria 2) to ditties and declamation (Punch's Rules and War Cries); and the music juxtaposes similar contrasts of style. Pruslin's libretto, intricately worked and saturated with alliteration and puns, is extremely effective in conjuring up the stylized world of the opera, in which human weaknesses and emotions are exaggerated to the point of surreal caricature.   ANDREW CLEMENTS

Puntatura (It.: 'pointing'). Term used for the recomposition of a vocal line to adjust its tessitura, while the accompaniment remained unaltered. There are numerous examples in Italian 19th-century opera, for example Rossini's rewriting of the final aria of *La Cenerentola* for soprano instead of mezzo-soprano (autograph, *US-NYpm*).

Puntila. Opera in 13 scenes and an epilogue by PAUL DESSAU to a libretto by Peter Palitzsch and Manfred Wekwerth after BERTOLT BRECHT's play *Herr Puntila und sein Knecht Matti*; Berlin, Deutsche Staatsoper, 15 November 1966.

Dessau discussed his plans for an opera based on Brecht's 1948 play with the author, but the libretto was created after Brecht's death in 1956 by two of his pupils. The plot concerns Johannes Puntila (bass), a Finnish landowner, who behaves like a tyrant when sober yet becomes quite human when drunk. In providing a husband for his daughter Eva (soprano) he has to choose between two suitors: his attaché Eino (tenor), whom Eva loves but who will demand a lavish dowry, and Matti (baritone), Puntila's chauffeur and unswerving antagonist. Puntila's inconstant behaviour provokes Eva into running away (he later disowns her) and, following a near-riot by the servants, Matti leaves too: anyone who trusts the drunk and therefore affable Puntila is all the more harshly disillusioned by the same man when sober.

Brecht's play attempts to show the intransigence of class difference; Dessau's music combines dodecaphony with 'colloquialism' and folklike melodies, linking seemingly opposing principles. The intention is to provide a critical commentary, the 12-note structures producing an effect of distortion as they enter tonal spheres.

FRITZ HENNENBERG

Puppet opera. Usually a mixed genre containing both music and spoken dialogue, performed on a specially designed stage by puppets (string, hand or rod). The works may take the form of serious or comic operas, plays with incidental music or interpolated songs, or ballets. Because of the caricature nature of puppets, most works written for them have been comic adaptations, mock-heroic dramas or satires of popular dramas. Before the 5th century BC, puppets had a widespread existence in all civilized lands, and they continued to have a place in the performances of mystery plays and liturgical dramas as well as the *commedia dell'arte* throughout the Middle Ages and the Renaissance.

The earliest known Italian operas for puppets (*fantoccini*) were 17th-century burlesques staged in Venice at the Teatro S Moisè by the Florentine nobleman, Filippo Acciaiuoli (1637–1700). *Leandro* (1679), *Damira placata* (1680), *Ulisse in Feaccia* (1681) and *Girello* (1682) were staged during the carnival season using wooden or wax figures while the music was performed by singers behind the stage.

A serious attempt to mount a permanent marionette theatre in Paris was made by Dominique de Normandin, Sieur de La Grille, one of Lully's singers in the Académie Royale de Musique, in 1676. La Grille obtained royal permission to establish a troupe and a Théâtre des Pygmées in the Marais. The marionettes, or 'Pygmées', were finely crafted, 1.20 m tall, and capable of dancing and of miming singing; they were dressed in costumes specially designed by Jean Berain. Elaborate scenery with machines was constructed for *Les pygmées*, the five-act tragedy that inaugurated the theatre, and *Les amours de Microton ou Les charmes d'Orcan* (1676); the services of an expert marionettist was also secured. It had been La Grille's intention eventually to present operas and the *livrets* of *Les pygmées* and *Les amours de Microton* reveal the use of singers and instrumentalists in Lullian parodies. The popularity of these works, together with La Grille's evident ambition, no doubt aroused in Lully the memory of Molière. In consequence, he initiated a campaign of harassment against La Grille, who was forced to change the name of the troupe to the Théâtre des Bamboches, then discontinue the employment of musicians. As a result, the theatre closed in 1677.

In 18th-century France, the development of the Parisian Théâtres de la Foire and their continual struggle for survival helped towards the establishment of the puppet (marionette) theatre. The Théâtres de la Foire were constantly harassed by the licensed Comédie-Française and the Académie Royale de Musique, and the puppet theatres, considered beneath official contempt, became a haven for persecuted or aspiring directors, actors, authors and musicians. This incessant rivalry stimulated a renewed interest in dramatic parody. The enlivening of these burlesques and operatic travesties by vaudeville played a part in the birth of the *opéra comique*. Without the marionette theatres at the annual fairs of St Germain and St Laurent, the production of parodies and *opéras comiques* would have been limited to the short periods of tenure of the human theatres. About 40 puppet *opéras comiques* have survived. Several of them, by such authors as Carolet, Favart, Fuzelier, d'Orneval, Le Sage, Piron and d'Orville, found their way into the publication series *Le Théâtre de la Foire ou l'Opéra-Comique* (Paris, 1721–37). The importance of the marionette theatres, however, stood in direct proportion to their necessity; with the establishment of the Opéra-Comique and the Théâtre-Italien and the replacement of the vaudeville by the *ariette*, they were quickly abandoned.

Puppet theatres have played a small but significant role in the history of the English stage. For a short time, when the Puritans closed the orthodox theatres during the interregnum, this form of popular entertainment provided the only home for dramatic activities. Descriptions of the puppet theatres at Bartholomew and Southwark fairs are noted in the diaries of Samuel Pepys and John Evelyn. It was in these humble surroundings that the notable Punch made his début and became synonymous with English puppetry. By the end of the 17th century, puppets had been immortalized in numerous literary works including D'Urfey's *Don Quixote*, Jonson's *Bartholomew Fayre* and Addison's Latin poem *Machinae gesticulantes*.

In the 18th century, operas, satires and artificial heroics filled the puppet theatres, now referred to as 'Punch's theatre'. Martin Powell opened a well-fitted one in London in 1710; *The Tatler* and *The Spectator* regarded Powell's theatre in Covent Garden and the opera at the Haymarket as the two leading diversions of London. For three seasons, Powell responded to the craze for Italian opera by staging satires of contemporary society, opera burlesques and mock-heroic tragedies. Following Powell's success, Punch theatres opened yearly in unused concert halls or even in converted tennis courts. The Licensing Act of 1737 restricted regular theatrical activities and many actors, musicians and playwrights sought refuge in the less conspicuous puppet theatres. Ballad operas now made up the bulk of the puppet theatres' repertory, and contributions were made by such notable 'proprietors' as Charlotte Charke, Henry Fielding, Samuel Foote and Charles Dibdin.

Between 1770 and 1790 London was invaded by Italian *fantoccino* troupes, who staged mostly popular French comedies and light operas. Joseph Haydn visited

Götz Friedrich rehearsing puppets of the Salzburger Marionettentheater for their 1991 production of Mozart's 'Così fan tutte'

one of these theatres, the Théâtre de Variétés Amusantes in Savile Row, in November 1791, and wrote in his diary: 'The puppets were manipulated well; the singers were bad, but the orchestra was quite acceptable'. By this time, puppet theatres were as brilliantly fitted as Europe's finest opera houses. It was at this level of existence that puppets found favour with the royal courts throughout Europe.

Puppets were displayed in their own elaborate theatre in plays and operettas at the summer palace of Prince Nikolaus Esterházy. The theatre flourished between 1773 and 1783 under Haydn's musical guidance. At least two of Haydn's own creations were among the productions: *Philemon und Baucis* and *Die Feuerbrunst*. Other puppet works attributed to Haydn are: *Hexenschabbas*, *Genovefens vierter Theil*, *Die bestrafte Rachbegierde* and *Demofoonte*. Two more works were included in the puppet repertory: *Alceste* by Carlos d'Ordonez and *Die Fee Urgele* by Ignace Pleyel. In the closing years of the 18th century, the craze for puppets faded. The success enjoyed by the puppet theatre, usually at the expense of the human theatre, had now shifted to its living counterpart.

During the late 19th century and the first half of the 20th, there was an enthusiastic regeneration of interest in the puppet theatre, and in several countries puppetry reached an artistic level of significant potential. Illustrious names from the fields of theatre, opera and stage design rediscovered in the puppet theatre an ideal medium for experimental work; many men of letters turned to it as a means of legitimate dramatic expression, including Craig, Shaw, García Lorca, France and Jarry. Among operas composed specifically for marionette performance during this period are Hindemith's *Das Nusch-Nuschi* (1921, Stuttgart), Falla's *El retablo de maese Pedro* (1923, Paris), Satie's *Geneviève de Brabant* (1926, Paris) and Ernst Toch's *Die Prinzessin auf der Erbse* (1927, Baden-Baden); other composers who added to the puppet-opera repertory include Britten, Casella, Caturla, Chausson, Copland, Honegger, Krenek, Liuzzi, Lualdi, Malipiero and Smetana.

The early 20th century saw the establishment of a number of permanent puppet theatres, the majority of which included productions of operas and operettas that were not originally conceived for the puppet medium; among these were the marionette theatres of Munich (one founded in 1905, a second in 1934), Baden-Baden (1911) and Salzburg (1913), the Teatro dei Piccoli of Milan (1913), the Arc-en-Ciel Théâtre in Paris (1925), the Central State Puppet Theatre in Moscow (1931) and the Kungsholm Puppet Theatre of Chicago. The techniques employed in staging an opera with marionettes or puppets depend on the elaborateness of the theatre facility. Directors have usually tried to create a visual effect as close to the 'live' theatre as possible, with the singers hidden behind a screen, to encourage the illusion that the puppets are singing, and the instrumentalists placed before the stage in full view of the audience. In more recent times some puppet theatres, such as the one in Salzburg, have resorted to playing recordings to reduce the cost and to expand the repertory.

W. J. Lawrence: 'Marionette Operas', *MQ*, x (1924), 236–43

F. Lindsay: *Dramatic Parody by Marionettes in Eighteenth-Century Paris* (New York, 1946)

G. Speaight: *The History of the English Puppet Theatre* (London, 1955)

H. C. R. Landon: 'Haydn's Marionette Operas', *Haydn Yearbook*, i (1962), 111–99

J. M. Minniear: *Marionette Opera: its History and Literature* (diss., U. of North Texas, 1971)

J. de La Gorce: 'Un théâtre parisien en concurrence avec l'Académie Royale de Musique dirigé par Lully: l'Opéra des Bamboches', *Lully: Heidelberg and St Germain-en-Laye 1987*, 223–33

M. Ohana: 'La marionette à l'opéra', *ReM*, no.351–2 (1982), 75

JOHN MOHR MINNIEAR

Purcell, Daniel (*b* London, *c*1660; *d* London, 12 Dec 1717). English composer. Although inevitably a victim of invidious comparison with his older brother Henry, he was a talented composer of vocal music and author or co-author of four major semi-operas. Daniel Purcell was organist of Magdalen College, Oxford, until 1695, when he began to supply music for the Theatre Royal, Drury Lane, London. The change of career may have been prompted by his brother's illness and death in November 1695; the two men shared the composition of the music for Richard Norton's tragedy *Pausanias* (late 1695) and Daniel supplied the fifth-act masque in *The Indian Queen*, 'Mr Henery Purcell being dead'.

Daniel Purcell succeeded his brother as house composer at the Theatre Royal, Drury Lane. He supplied songs for plays and advised the manager Christopher Rich on the purchase and rental of harpsichords. His major stage works include the vocal music of several semi-operas: *Brutus of Alba, or Augusta's Triumph* (1696), a pastiche based partly on Dryden's libretto for *Albion and Albanius*; *The Island Princess* (1699), with Jeremiah Clarke and Richard Leveridge; *The Grove* (1700), an original work; and *The Rival Queens* (1701), a collaboration with Gottfried Finger, to a libretto based on Nathaniel Lee's play of the same name. Daniel Purcell's setting of Congreve's masque *The Judgment of Paris* for the Musick Prize in 1701 came third, though Finger claimed it was the best music (after his own).

His style, especially in declamatory songs, owes much to his brother. Motteux's opinion of Daniel's music for *The Island Princess* as 'so fine, that as he seems inspir'd with his Brother's wonderful Genius, it cannot but be equally admir'd' is an exaggeration. The music is often too ornate, but never dull or incompetent. His simpler folklike tunes, such as 'All the pleasures Hymen brings' in *The Island Princess*, do not suffer comparison with similar pieces by Henry. Daniel's stage career was cut short by the growing taste for Italian music in the first decade of the 18th century. Though he continued in employment at the Theatre Royal, his rumoured setting of *Orlando furioso* (after Quinault) in 1707 never materialized, being pushed aside by the Italian pasticcios that were then in fashion.

See also ISLAND PRINCESS, THE; and JUDGMENT OF PARIS, THE.

CURTIS PRICE

Purcell, Henry (*b* London, 1658 or 1659; *d* London, 21 Nov 1695). English composer and organist. Generally acknowledged as the greatest English opera composer, Purcell wrote only one true opera, *Dido and Aeneas*. His main contribution to the professional stage includes substantial scores for four semi-operas and miscellaneous incidental music for some 50 plays, including Dryden's *Amphitryon* and Congreve's *The Double-Dealer*. Possessed of an unparalleled genius for setting the English language, Purcell was also unerring in his depiction of human passions; in *Dido and Aeneas* he created a musical tragedy of unsurpassed pathos and concision.

Purcell's stage career, which occupied only the last five years of his life, and accounts for less than a third of his total output, must be assessed in terms of the 17th-century English attitude towards all-sung opera, which ranged from indifference to hostility. During the 1670s, Purcell's formative years, attempts to introduce both French and Italian opera into England had failed miserably. Among other writers, John Dryden, the poet laureate, dramatist and formidable critic of the arts, declared the English language and temperament incompatible with the aesthetic of Italian opera. Though he later changed his mind and became Purcell's eloquent advocate and enthusiastic collaborator, all-sung opera in English did not take root in England until the 20th century.

1. Early theatrical career, 'Dido and Aeneas'. 2. The first semi-operas. 3. The late stage works.

1. EARLY THEATRICAL CAREER, 'DIDO AND AENEAS'. Trained as a chorister at the Chapel Royal (*c*1669–73), Purcell was appointed composer-in-ordinary to the king in 1677 and organist of Westminster Abbey in 1679 and of the Chapel Royal in 1682, posts he retained for the rest of his life. Accordingly, his main duty was to provide anthems, welcome songs, birthday odes and coronation music for the four monarchs whom he served – Charles II (to 1685), James II (1685–8) and William and Mary (1689–95). He also contributed to virtually all vocal and instrumental genres known in England, from the obsolete viol fantasia to the modern italianate sonata, from devotional cantatas to racy catches. The bulk of his music is, however, connected with the court. His decision in 1690 to become a full-time theatre composer may have resulted from the accession of William and Mary the year before. Under the new monarchy, the Royal Musick was severely cut back, forcing Purcell and his colleagues to seek supplementary income by teaching, publishing, organizing public concerts and composing for the commercial stage.

Purcell's first known contact with the theatre was in 1680, when he composed vocal music for Nathaniel Lee's tragedy *Theodosius*. The death in 1677 of his teacher Matthew Locke, who was noted for his dramatic music, had left a vacuum in the London theatrical world, and no new semi-opera had been produced for several years. But Purcell seems to have made little impact with *Theodosius* and wrote only sporadically for the stage during the next decade. In 1684 King Charles II commanded the creation of a grand opera to celebrate his restoration and reign; this was *Albion and Albanius*, with a libretto by Dryden. Surprisingly, both Purcell and his colleague John Blow were passed over in favour of the French-trained Catalan Luis Grabu, who produced a huge score after the manner of a *tragédie lyrique*. Presumably among those native composers said to have been chagrined at the slight, Purcell was nevertheless influenced by this, the first full-length, all-sung opera in English, despite its abject failure and the contempt generally held for its foreign composer.

The origins and première of *Dido and Aeneas* are shrouded in obscurity and scholarly controversy. The only known performance during Purcell's lifetime was at a girls' boarding school in Chelsea run by the dancer and choreographer Josias Priest; it is usually dated to 1689. It was composed some time after Blow's *Venus and Adonis*, on which it is closely modelled. Blow's opera was originally performed for the private en-

tertainment of Charles II in 1682 or 1683 and then revived at Priest's school in April 1684. *Dido and Aeneas* may have been composed at any time from the mid-1680s and have followed a similar gestation. Given the eminence of those involved in the production – Purcell was already acknowledged as the greatest living English composer, and the librettist Nahum Tate later became poet laureate – the opera would hardly seem like a mere school production.

The stylistic connections between *Venus and Adonis* and *Dido and Aeneas* are also manifest. Both are three-act tragedies with florid recitatives and no spoken dialogue. But whereas Blow's opera is virtually *sui generis*, dominated by more or less continuous arioso and choruses, *Dido* more closely resembles contemporary French and Italian opera: the first in its preference for repeating units of *ariette*-chorus-dance, the second in its reliance on self-contained, modern-style arias. Of the heroine's two set pieces, one ('Ah Belinda') is a written-out da capo and the other ('When I am laid in earth') is a lament on a ground bass, a cliché of Venetian opera.

2. THE FIRST SEMI-OPERAS. *Dido* elicited no contemporary comment and does not appear to have been performed again during the composer's lifetime, but contact with Priest, who was also a choreographer at the Theatre Royal, may have proved a turning-point in Purcell's career. In 1689–90 he was commissioned to compose the music for the first new semi-opera since 1677. This was *The Prophetess, or the History of Dioclesian*, first given in late May 1690. All previous semi-operas had been composed by committee; the managers of the Theatre Royal were thus expressing unusual confidence in Purcell by giving him sole control of the music. The production and adaptation of Massinger and Fletcher's original play was undertaken by the eminent actor Thomas Betterton, who had been involved in nearly all the previous semi-operas and was especially keen to adopt French stage techniques and design. The music of *Dioclesian*, as the work came to be known, is sumptuous and varied, though sometimes awkwardly coordinated with the play itself. Purcell modelled the climactic ground in the fifth-act masque ('Triumph, victorious Love') on the chaconne in *Albion and Albanius* and, like Grabu, published a handsome full score of the opera.

Despite some contemporary criticism of the dramatic absurdity of the choral scene in the second act, *Dioclesian* was a notable financial success. The production involved all members of the company – actors, singers, orchestra, dancers, scene painters and machinists – and was thus very expensive, but it could also be profitably revived season after season. For the performance of semi-operas the Theatre Royal company, which normally operated at the Drury Lane playhouse, transferred to the larger theatre at Dorset Garden on the Thames at Blackfriars, erected in 1674 and specially equipped for opera. *Dioclesian* was also an artistic triumph for Purcell. Dryden publicly apologized for having passed him over in 1684 ('we have at length found an *English-man*, equal with the best abroad') and immediately offered him the libretto of *King Arthur* (première May–early June 1691). This is the only semi-opera by Purcell or any of his contemporaries which is not an adaptation of an earlier play; focussed on King Arthur and the blind heroine Emmeline (though they, like all semi-opera leading characters, do not sing), the music is integral to the action and hence far more dramatic than anything in *Dioclesian*. *King Arthur* is also notable for its coopting of existing musical styles and forms, especially the verse anthem and welcome ode with their interplay of soloists, chorus and instrumental symphonies. The finest numbers of the score, the fourth-act chaconne 'How happy the lover' and the Frost Scene, are both heavily indebted to Lully's operas.

King Arthur was outstandingly popular and remained firmly in the repertory well into the 18th century (Garrick revived it in an arrangement by Arne in 1770); music was the key to its success, for the first production was modest in comparison to other semi-operas, and Dryden's libretto, while perhaps underrated, is an obscure political allegory tainted by sexual innuendo.

Following the production schedule established in the previous two seasons, the Theatre Royal commissioned the third and most lavish of Purcell's semi-operas, *The Fairy-Queen* (première 2 May 1692). Based on *A Midsummer Night's Dream*, it departed from Purcell's usual practice in that its four masques (a fifth was added for the 1693 revival) are self-contained and effectively insulated from the play itself; nor did Purcell set a single line of Shakespeare. Instead the masques, all of which are associated with the fairy kingdom, capture the atmosphere of the original play in a way that admits of no other reading. For the first time Purcell was able to write for professional stage singers (Messrs Pate and Reading, Mrs Ayliff and others) rather than actors who also happened to sing (for example John Bowman and Charlotte Butler, the leads in *King Arthur*); the vocal music of *The Fairy-Queen* is thus much more technically demanding. Also apparent is a growing concern for motivic and harmonic coherence across the whole diverse score; even the instrumental act tunes are imbued with the dissonant, somewhat mysterious style of counterpoint heard most prominently in the Masque of Sleep (Act 2).

The Fairy-Queen, though another triumph for Purcell, emptied the Theatre Royal's treasury. No new semi-opera could be commissioned for 1693; rather *Dioclesian* and *The Fairy-Queen* were revived with extra songs and to the latter was added a satirical scene of a drunken poet in Act 1. During this and the 1694–5 seasons, Purcell's stage career suffered a setback. While he continued to supply most of the orchestral incidental music for plays (published posthumously in the collection *Ayres for the Theatre*, 1697), he found his position as head composer challenged by John Eccles. With no new semi-opera in prospect, playwrights relied increasingly on added songs and masques in ordinary plays, music performed mostly by the actor-singers rather than by the professionals for whom Purcell wrote *The Fairy-Queen*. Eccles was much more adept than Purcell at providing simple but highly dramatic music for actors such as William Mountfort, Thomas Doggett and especially the 'celebrated virgin' Anne Bracegirdle, who sang exclusively his music. So, for example, in Thomas D'Urfey's ambitious trilogy *Don Quixote* (parts 1 and 2, May 1694; part 3, November 1695), the two composers were equal collaborators; though Purcell produced splendid music in parts 1 and 3 (including 'Let the dreadful engines' and 'From rosy bowers'), the great success of the show was Mrs Bracegirdle's rendering of Eccles's 'I burn, I burn' in part 2. Purcell's reaction to shifting theatrical taste during these lean years can be seen in the rechannelling of his best inspiration into pieces such as *Come ye Sons of Art Away*, the 1694 Queen Mary Birthday Ode.

3. THE LATE STAGE WORKS. At the end of 1694 Purcell's stage career was further affected by the Actors' Rebellion. Furious at the stingy and dictatorial management of the notorious Christopher Rich, Betterton led the secession of most of his fellow players in setting up a rival theatre in Lincoln's Inn Fields. He also took with him Eccles and virtually all of Purcell's professional singers. Rich, who was left with young and inexperienced actors, decided the only way to compete with the new company was to exploit Purcell's talent: several major new works or revivals requiring musical entertainments were put into production (*Bonduca*, *The Libertine*, *Timon of Athens*) and a new semi-opera, *The Indian Queen*, was planned. Between early spring 1695 and his untimely death in November, Purcell composed more theatre music than in any similar period of his life. Bereft of his favourite singers, including the mainstays Bowman and Mrs Ayliff, he had to rely on three inexperienced performers during this hectic season: the boy treble Jemmey Bowen, who was capable of executing the most difficult passagework and of improvising his own ornaments ('"Oh let him alone", said Mr. Purcell; "he will grace it more naturally than you, or I, can teach him"'); the soprano Letitia Cross, a 16-year-old actress of dubious personal reputation; and the young bass Richard Leveridge, at the beginning of a long and distinguished career as both performer and composer.

Under these difficult circumstances, Dryden and Sir Robert Howard's heroic play of 1664, *The Indian Queen*, was rather crudely adapted into a semi-opera (première probably late autumn 1695). The scaled-down production included little dancing or scenic spectacle. Because of Purcell's illness, lack of time or death, his younger brother Daniel had to be brought from Oxford to compose the final masque. Despite these problems and the diminished resources available to the Theatre Royal, the music of *The Indian Queen* is probably Purcell's finest for the stage, the most impressive pieces being the masque of ariel spirits in Act 3 and Ismeron's 'You twice ten hundred deities', which Burney called 'the best piece of recitative in our language'.

During the last months of his life, Purcell wrote a song ('Dear pretty youth') for an unrecorded revival of the 1674 operatic version of *The Tempest*, but he is almost certainly not the composer of the version of the semi-opera published in vol. xix of his complete works: this is clearly a later composite score which includes some highly italianate music, much of it in da capo form. John Weldon (1676–1736) has been suggested as the main composer. The apparent misattribution of *The Tempest* to Purcell has given rise to the idea that his style changed radically during the final year of his life. But *The Indian Queen*, his last major work, is remarkably conservative, being purged of much of the irregular dissonance of his youth, yet still displaying sophisticated counterpoint and the highly flexible rhythms and phrase lengths that characterize his earlier music.

In sheer dramatic intensity, Purcell did not surpass *Dido and Aeneas*, but of course never again was he able to write for tragic protagonists who sing; most of the singers in the semi-operas are minor characters – spirits, priests, soldiers, fairies and the like. Yet in each of the mature stage works there are brilliantly dramatic moments (the entrance of the Baccanalians in the masque in *Dioclesian*, the rising of the Cold Genius in *King Arthur*, the singing to sleep of Titania in *The*

Fairy-Queen, the appearance of the God of Dreams in *The Indian Queen*). What the semi-operas inevitably lack is *Dido*'s sustained characterization and interaction at the human level. Thus there are no real successors to the recitatives in *Dido*. In the semi-operas characters rarely converse, except in so-called dialogues (such as 'Now the maids and the men' in *The Fairy-Queen*), in which lines are sung alternately before the piece culminates in a homophonic 'chorus'; duets, of which there are many fine examples among Purcell's late works, make little dramatic distinction between the parts, treating them rather as a harmonious manifestation of a single voice. In *Dido*, especially in the final confrontation of the lovers, recitative (*secco* and florid) and dialogue are combined to express genuine human conflict. While the later semi-operas probably contain consistently finer music, *Dido* uncannily anticipates many aspects of 19th-century opera.

See also DIDO AND AENEAS; DIOCLESIAN; FAIRY-QUEEN, THE; INDIAN QUEEN, THE; KING ARTHUR; and TEMPEST, THE (i).

Catalogue: F. B. Zimmerman: *Henry Purcell, 1659–1695: an Analytic Catalogue of his Music* (London, 1963) [Z]

Edition: *The Works of Henry Purcell*, The Purcell Society (London, 1878–1965; newly ed. or rev. 2/1961–) [PS]

all first performed in London

Z	title	genre, acts	libretto	first performance	PS
626	Dido and Aeneas	tragic op, 3	N. Tate	Josias Priest's School for Young Ladies, Chelsea, before Dec 1689 [first known perf.]	iii
627	Dioclesian [The Prophetess, or The History of Dioclesian]	semi-op, 5	T. Betterton, after J. Fletcher and P. Massinger	Dorset Garden, late May 1690	ix
628	King Arthur, or The British Worthy	semi-op, 5	J. Dryden	Dorset Garden, late May–early June 1691	xxvi
629	The Fairy-Queen	semi-op, 5	after W. Shakespeare: *A Midsummer Night's Dream*	Dorset Garden, 2 May 1692	xii
630	The Indian Queen [final masque by D. Purcell]	semi-op, prol., 5	Dryden and R. Howard	Drury Lane, ? late aut. 1695	xix

W. B. Squire: 'Purcell's Dramatic Music', *SIMG*, v (1903–4), 489–564

A. C. Sprague: *Beaumont and Fletcher on the Restoration Stage* (Cambridge, MA, 1926)

E. J. Dent: *Foundations of English Opera* (London, 1928)

E. W. White: 'New Light on "Dido and Aeneas"', *Henry Purcell 1659–1695*, ed. I. Holst (London, 1959), 14–34

R. E. Moore: *Henry Purcell & the Restoration Theatre* (London, 1961)

A. M. Laurie: *Purcell's Stage Works* (diss., U. of Cambridge, 1961)

J. Buttrey: *The Evolution of English Opera between 1656 and 1695* (diss., U. of Cambridge, 1967)

R. Savage: 'The Shakespeare-Purcell *Fairy Queen*: a Defence and Recommendation', *EMc*, i (1973), 201–21

——: 'Producing *Dido and Aeneas*: an Investigation into Sixteen Problems', *EMc*, iv (1976), 393–406

R. Luckett: 'Exotick but Rational Entertainments: the English Dramatick Operas', *English Drama: Forms and Development*, ed. M. Axton and R. Williams (Cambridge, 1977), 123–41; 232–4

L'avant-scène opéra, no. 18 (1978) [*Dido and Aeneas* issue]

C. A. Price: *Music in the Restoration Theatre* (Ann Arbor, 1979)

J. A. Westrup: *Purcell* (London, 4/1980)

D. Charlton: ' "King Arthur": Dramatick Opera', *ML*, lxiv (1983), 183–92

C. Price: *Henry Purcell and the London Stage* (Cambridge, 1984)

Henry Purcell: Dido and Aeneas, ed. C. Price (New York, 1986)

E. T. Harris: *Henry Purcell's Dido and Aeneas* (Oxford, 1987)

J. J. G. Muller-van Santen: *Producing The Prophetess or the History of Dioclesian* (diss., U. of Amsterdam, 1989)

A. Pinnock: 'Play into Opera: Purcell's *The Indian Queen*', *EMc*, xviii (1990), 3–21

M. Goldie: 'The Earliest Notice of Purcell's *Dido and Aeneas*', ibid., 392–400

B. Wood and A. Pinnock: ' "Unscarr'd by turning times"?: the Dating of Purcell's *Dido and Aeneas*', *EMc*, xx (1992), 372–90

CURTIS PRICE

Purchase. American village, in the township of Harrison, New York. It was founded in 1696 as part of the town of Harrison's Purchase, and began to assume its own identity after 1972, when a branch of the State University of New York opened. From 1980 to 1989 it was the home of the Pepsico Summerfare, a festival that became known for its opera. Beginning with productions of Britten's *Noye's Fludde* (1981–4), the festival embraced more experimental productions with Eaton's *The Cry of Clytaemnestra* (1982) and Peter Sellars's combination of Bach and Weill in his *Little Mahagonny/Cantata 60: Conversations with Fear and Hope After Death* (1985). Most famous of the Pepsico productions were those by Peter Sellars of Mozart's *Così fan tutte* (1986), *Don Giovanni* (1987) and *Le nozze di Figaro* (1988). The State University mounts one opera each year.

R. Dyer: 'Purchase, New York: Disturbing and Rewarding', *Opera* (1986), festival issue, 116–18

M. Mayer: 'Purchase, New York: Sellars Market', *Opera* (1987), festival issue, 51–3

——: 'Purchase, NY: Social Distances', *Opera* (1988), festival issue, 118–21

R. Milnes: 'Purchase: the Sellars Watershed', *Opera* (1989), festival issue, 11–15

Purgatory. Opera in one act, op.18, by GORDON CROSSE after the play by William Butler Yeats; Cheltenham, Everyman Theatre, 7 July 1966.

Adapted by the composer from a short verse play by Yeats, Crosse's first opera is narrowly focussed on the drastic efforts of an Old Man (high baritone) to release his mother's soul from the purgatory of eternally reliving the first night of a disastrous marriage. By killing his own son (named as Boy, tenor) at the ruins of the house where he was born and where he, as a boy, had killed his drunken father, the Old Man succeeds in breaking the line of degeneracy which he had inherited. But, as he recognizes in a final prayer, he cannot alone save his mother's soul.

The terrible irony of the text is reflected in a serially organized score which, owing much to Britten's example in *The Turn of the Screw*, persistently contradicts the triadic harmonies postulated by an offstage female chorus. Lyricism is eschewed until the deed is done but even then the harmonic resolution is withheld until the very last bar – a C major chord suggesting perhaps that the Old Man's prayer is answered.

Purgatory was first performed by the New Opera Company at the Cheltenham Festival in 1966, directed by Cyrile Fradan and conducted by Leon Lovett.

GERALD LARNER

Puritani, I ('The Puritans'). *Melodramma serio* in three parts by VINCENZO BELLINI to a libretto by CARLO PEPOLI after the play by J.-A. F.-P. Ancelot and Xavier (J. X. Boniface *dit* Saintine), *Têtes Rondes et Cavaliers*; Paris, Théâtre Italien, 24 January 1835.

Lord Gualtiero Walton *Governor General of the fortress*	bass
Sir Giorgio *brother of Lord Walton, retired Puritan colonel*	bass
Lord Arturo Talbo *Cavalier, Stuart sympathizer*	tenor
Sir Riccardo Forth *Puritan colonel*	baritone
Sir Bruno Robertson *Puritan officer*	tenor
Enrichetta di Francia [Queen Henrietta Maria] *widow of Charles I*	mezzo-soprano
Elvira *daughter of Lord Walton*	soprano

Puritan soldiers, Arturo's followers, ladies, pages and servants

Setting A fortress near Plymouth (during the English Civil War)

I puritani was Bellini's final opera. He had left Italy for Paris in 1833 and was in negotiations with both the Opéra and the Théâtre Italien during October, signing a contract with the latter by early February 1834. He had broken with his regular librettist, Felice Romani, over *Beatrice di Tenda* the year before; by 11 March Carlo Pepoli was suggesting plots to him. The story and casting were decided by 11 April, and Bellini began composition on about 15 April. The division into three acts was made at the last moment. The title in the Paris libretto is 'I Puritani e i Cavalieri/opera-seria in due Parti', but Bellini referred to it as 'I Puritani' in a letter of 4 September 1834. This form of the title was finally chosen because of the fame of Scott's *Old Mortality* (1816), translated as *Les puritains d'Ecosse* (1817) and *I puritani di Scozia* (1825), with which the opera has little connection.

The original cast included Giulia Grisi (Elvira), Giovanni Battista Rubini (Arturo), Antonio Tamburini (Riccardo) and Luigi Lablache (Giorgio), who collectively became known as the *Puritani* quartet. On 21 May the opera was performed in London at the King's Theatre with the same cast. Three days before, the Princess Victoria had heard a preview of the main pieces, sung by the quartet at a private concert at Kensington Palace in celebration of her sixteenth birthday; throughout her life she was to refer to it as 'the dear *Puritani*'. The English critic Chorley recounted how London was smitten with 'Puritani-fever' ('Errand-boys whistled it, barrel-organs ground it …'). Meanwhile the opera spread rapidly round Europe. It was performed at La Scala in December 1835, possibly in a pirated version. To avoid religious censorship the title was changed

to *Elvira e Arturo* (1835, Palermo) and *Elvira Walton* (1836, Rome). At La Fenice in 1836 Elvira was sung by Giuseppina Strepponi, who became a frequent exponent of the role. At the S Carlo, Naples, in 1837 the Elvira was Caterina Barilli-Patti, mother of Adelina Patti, who sang the role at Covent Garden in 1870. *I puritani* was given during 1883, the inaugural season at the Metropolitan, with Marcella Sembrich as Elvira. Maria Callas sang Elvira for the first time in 1949 at La Fenice; she repeated the role at Catania in 1951, the 150th anniversary of Bellini's birth. Joan Sutherland sang Elvira at Glyndebourne in 1960 and at Covent Garden in 1964, where *I puritani* had not been heard for 77 years.

Bellini prepared a separate version for Maria Malibran to sing (as Elvira) at Naples. He had been negotiating to write a new opera for the S Carlo since February 1834, but work on *I puritani* had progressed slowly because of Pepoli's inexperience, and in early October Bellini decided to adapt it for Naples. The 'Malibran' version contains little new music but, because he had to send off the manuscript before the final cuts were made for Paris, it preserves the original division into two parts and contains three sections not in the standard version: a trio in Part 1, a central cantabile to the duet now in Part 3 and a final stretta (reinstated by Sutherland in a 1975 recording). Neapolitan censorship precluded the duet 'Suoni la tromba'. Transpositions made Riccardo a tenor and much of Elvira's music was taken down to the mezzo range, while Elvira, not Arturo, now led the Part 2 finale. The manuscript arrived at Naples too late and the version was not heard until a concert performance at the Barbican Centre, London, on 14 December 1985; it was staged at Bari the following year with Katia Ricciarelli and Chris Merritt.

PART 1.i *A large open courtyard in the fortress* There is no overture. The introduction announces several themes used at the end of the opera. Horn-calls sound from the surrounding countryside as the Roundheads hail the dawn and threaten death for the Cavaliers. A bell announces matins, and Bruno leads the soldiers in prayer. The ladies and gentlemen inhabiting the fortress announce the start of the festivities in celebration of Elvira's wedding. Riccardo tells Bruno that he had hoped to marry Elvira himself, though he knows that his love for her is not returned, and that Lord Walton has consented to her wish to marry Arturo instead. His cavatina, 'Ah! per sempre io ti perdei', expresses his grief.

1.ii *Elvira's chambers* Giorgio finds his niece in great distress, afraid that she will have to marry Riccardo. She pours out her feelings in the first part of their duet, 'Sai com'arde in petto mio'. Giorgio tells her that he has persuaded her father to agree to her marriage to Arturo. She does not believe him at first; then horns sound again in the distance, heralding Arturo's arrival. As the soldiers call out his name, Elvira at last gives way to her joy in 'A quel nome'.

1.iii *The Hall of Arms* A chorus welcomes Arturo as Elvira's bridegroom. He makes a grand formal entrance, bearing gifts that include a magnificent white bridal veil. Arturo's cavatina 'A te, o cara, amor talora', becomes a quartet as each of the two verses is taken up by Elvira, Giorgio, Walton and the chorus. Walton gives Arturo a safe conduct for Elvira and himself; he cannot attend his daughter's wedding as he has to escort a female prisoner, believed to be a Royalist

'I puritani' (Bellini), Part 1 scene iii (the Hall of Arms) designed by Domenico Ferri for the original production at the Théâtre Italien, Paris, 24 January 1835: engraving

spy, to London. The prisoner is brought in and, when left alone with Arturo, she reveals that she is Queen Henrietta Maria, widow of Charles I. Realizing that she will be put to death once she is recognized, Arturo resolves to save her, but is interrupted by the voice of Elvira; she runs in wearing her bridal veil and singing 'Son vergin vezzosa' ('Donzella vezzosa' at Rome), a *polacca* expressing her joyful exuberance. She places the white veil on Henrietta's head to admire it and then runs out again. Arturo decides to use the veil to smuggle Henrietta out of the castle. Riccardo enters, confronts Arturo and challenges him to a duel (the melody is from the 1828 version of *Bianca e Fernando*); this was originally a trio which included a slow central section, preserved in the Naples score. When Riccardo sees that the woman is the Royalist prisoner, he allows them to leave, promising not to give the alarm until they are outside the fortress walls. Elvira comes in, calling for Arturo; there is general consternation when his flight is discovered. Orders are given for the capture of the traitors. Elvira, her reason slipping away, leads the main ensemble with 'Oh vieni al tempio, fedele Arturo', imagining his return to her. Giorgio, Riccardo and the other Puritans express their pity for Elvira and hatred for Arturo.

PART 2 *A hall with side entrances* The ladies and gentlemen lament the fate of the distracted Elvira. In 'Cinta di fiori e col bel crin disciolto', Giorgio describes how she wanders about garlanded with flowers, her hair dishevelled. Riccardo enters, declaring that Arturo has been condemned to death and is to be hunted down. Elvira's voice is heard outside and she comes in, her reason obviously gone. In the mad scene, 'Qui la voce sua soave', she imagines Arturo's voice, laments his departure and comforts Giorgio and Riccardo, both of whom weep as they comment on her words; finally she conjures up an ecstatic vision of Arturo. After she has left, Giorgio works on Riccardo's love for Elvira in the duet 'Il rival salvar tu dêi', pointing out that Arturo's death would kill her, in order to persuade Riccardo to

help save the cavalier. Riccardo resists at first, but realizes that he could not bear the prospect of her phantom pursuing him. Both agree, however, that Arturo must die if he is with the Cavalier troops when they attack the fortress. A trumpet sounds and in the celebrated 'Suoni la tromba, e intrepido' they proclaim 'libertà' (replaced by 'lealtà' in Milan and 'fedeltà' in Rome).

PART 3 *A loggia in a wooded garden near Elvira's apartments* An orchestral storm rages as Arturo enters, having for the moment eluded his pursuers. He hears a harp, then the voice of the still distracted Elvira, singing 'A una fonte, afflitto e solo', a song that he once taught her. Her voice fades and he takes up the melody himself. He is interrupted by a posse of Puritan soldiers searching for him and hides until they have gone, then continues with his song. Elvira appears, drawn by the sound of his voice, and, to a reminiscence of Arturo's first cavatina, sadly conjures up happy memories. When she sees and recognizes him the shock momentarily restores her senses. In the duet 'Nel mirarti un solo istante' they sing of their love for each other and of the sorrow brought by three months' separation – more like three centuries, says Elvira. Arturo explains why he left with another woman, a prisoner who would have been executed but for his intervention. The sound of a drum upsets Elvira's fragile sanity and she suffers a relapse. Arturo tries to lead her away, but she will not go and calls for help. Riccardo, Giorgio, the soldiers and inhabitants of the fortress run in and recognize Arturo. Accompanied by a funeral march, Riccardo condemns the traitor. At the pronouncement of the death sentence, Elvira is finally shocked back to sanity. In the ensemble 'Credeasi misera', launched by Arturo, he assures her of his love, while Elvira vows to die with him. The soldiers impatiently call for Arturo's death, and are accused of cruelty by Riccardo and Giorgio. A hunting horn announces a herald, who brings a message from Cromwell: the Stuarts have been defeated and a general amnesty is declared. All rejoice at Cromwell's victory and wish Elvira and Arturo happiness.

* * *

Bellini anticipated Verdi in attributing to *I puritani* an individual 'colorito', which he described as 'basically the genre of *La sonnambula* and Paisiello's *Nina* with a touch of military robustness and something of Puritan severity'. In its harmony and scoring *I puritani* is Bellini's most sophisticated opera – a direct consequence, no doubt, of its having been written for a Parisian audience. To the same cause we may ascribe its unusual wealth of thematic recall, which was a regular feature of contemporary French opera. Bellini's concern to establish a spacious time-scale (his chief point of contact with Wagner) is evident in the introduction, with its parade of slow triplets against the beat. The role of Elvira offers a *ne plus ultra* of romantic madness, conceived less as a morbid condition than one of the transfiguration – part lyrical, part virtuoso – of fragile womanhood, such as would find an echo in Donizetti's *Lucia di Lammermoor*. Be it noted, too, that in every act Elvira is heard before she is seen, as happens so often in the operas of Puccini. The storm that opens Act 3, intended to 'describe the sadness whereby nature is afflicted beneath the lightnings of the heavens', is Bellini's nearest approach to the Beethovenian ideal of 'Mehr Ausdruck der Empfindung als Malerei'. The opera contains two classic instances of Italian romantic lyricism in the quartet 'A te, o cara' and Elvira's cantabile 'Qui la voce sua soave'; on the other hand there is a striking departure from the norm both in Giorgio's 'Cinta di fiori e col bel crin disciolto', a setting of eleven-syllable lines such as were usually reserved for recitative and Venetian serenades, and in the duet-cabaletta 'Vieni fra queste braccia' in which two five-bar phrases are balanced by a concluding period of nine. Each is a tantalizing hint as to how Bellini's melodic style might have developed had he lived longer.

For further illustration *see* COSTUME, fig.10.

SIMON MAGUIRE, ELIZABETH FORBES, JULIAN BUDDEN

Púrpura de la rosa, La ('The Blood of the Rose'). Opera in one act attributed to JUAN HIDALGO to a libretto by PEDRO CALDERÓN DE LA BARCA; Madrid, Coliseo of the Buen Retiro, probably 17 January 1660.

Calderón's libretto, based on the myth of Venus and Adonis, was written in 1659 to commemorate the Peace of the Pyrenees between Spain and France. The Peace was crowned by the marriage of Louis XIV and the Infanta María Teresa of Spain. Hidalgo's setting was the first Spanish opera since the unsuccessful experiment of *La selva sin amor* in 1627 (text by Lope de Vega, music by Filippo Piccinini). In 1659 and 1660, the extreme importance of the occasion and rivalry with France motivated the unusual production of fully-sung operas (the second was Hidalgo's *Celos aun del aire matan*), rather than a zarzuela or semi-opera, as part of an elaborate artistic campaign at the court in Madrid. Hidalgo's music, now lost, was later performed in 1680 to honour another Spanish-French alliance, the marriage of Charles II of Spain to Marie-Louise of Orleans.

Another setting of the Calderón text by TOMÁS DE TORREJÓN Y VELASCO (1701) was commissioned in Lima to celebrate the birthday of Philip V, Louis XIV's grandson and first Bourbon king of Spain; scored for voices and continuo, it is clearly within Hidalgo's stylistic orbit, with its strophic airs for long sections of narrative and dialogue, and restricted use of recitative. Alongside Hidalgo's score for *Celos aun del aire matan*, La

púrpura de la rosa provides important evidence for the independent musical and dramatic conventions of Spanish opera and semi-opera in the later 17th century, and the close relationship between musical conventions in Spain and the New World.   LOUISE K. STEIN

Pushkin, Alexander Sergeyevich (*b* Moscow, 26 May/6 June 1799; *d* St Petersburg, 29 Jan/10 Feb 1837). Russian poet. Two factors determine the enormous appeal that his writings have had for Russian composers – the extraordinary breadth and variety of their character and the purely musical appeal of their language. Pushkin combined a knowledge of French and English literature (Shakespeare and Byron in particular) and the sophistication characteristic of the upper class in Moscow and St Petersburg with a deep attachment to the Russian countryside and Russian legends and fairy stories. A liberal by nature, he was always suspect to the authorities and spent six years of his short life relegated to the provinces. His writings, prose stories, verse and verse dramas show a protean ability to identify himself with the most widely different characters and temperaments; and the lively, irreverent, sardonic tone of his correspondence, though echoed closely in such works as *Graf Nulin*, *The Golden Cockerel* and *The Queen of Spades*, disappears entirely not only in many of the lyrics but in such deeply compassionate and profound dramas as *Boris Godunov*, *The Miserly Knight* and *Mozart and Salieri*, where Shakespeare's influence is unmistakable. In his handling of the Don Juan legend (*The Stone Guest*) Pushkin combined a Byronic disillusion and worldliness of tone with astonishingly original touches of erotic psychology and an ability to evoke atmosphere by the most economical means.

In his use of words Pushkin emancipated the Russian language from its adolescent conventions and achieved a simplicity and directness of speech and imagery that have few parallels outside the language of ancient Greece. His ear, untrained and uninterested in music proper, had a unique instinct for combining, contrasting and exploiting the various vowel sounds and the extraordinary wealth of liquid, sibilant and guttural consonants that give the Russian language its beauty and variety, while he retained a simplicity and a naturalness of expression that often give his poetry and prose an almost conversational character.

Each composer has taken what he needed from Pushkin, beginning with his contemporary Glinka, who set an early fairy story in the form of a narrative poem (*Ruslan and Lyudmila*). Dargomïzhsky also set a fairy story and then took *The Stone Guest* for his attempt to write an opera in a style characterized by César Cui as 'melodic recitative'. Musorgsky chose a historical drama (*Boris Godunov*), Rimsky-Korsakov two fairy stories (*Tsar Saltan* and *The Golden Cockerel*) and one of the dramatic scenes (*Mozart and Salieri*). Tchaikovsky took Pushkin's somewhat Byronic verse novel (*Yevgeny Onegin*), a verse historical romance (*Mazepa*) and an enigmatic psychological *conte* (*The Queen of Spades*), Rakhmaninov another of the dramatic scenes and the romantic narrative poem *The Gypsies* (as *Aleko*). Stravinsky made his opera *Mavra* from the ironic and mysterious *Little House at Kolomna*. Pushkin's life has furnished the subject for Boris Shekhter's opera *Pushkin v Mikhaylovskom* ('Pushkin in Mikhaylovskoye, 1954–5, performed as *Pushkin v izgnanii*, 'Pushkin in Exile', 1958), and for—Vladimir Kobekin's *Prorok: Pushkinskiy triptikh* ('The Prophet: a Pushkin

1185

Triptych', 1984), which incorporates settings of two of the 'little tragedies' and of reminiscences by Pushkin's contemporaries.

Andzhelo [Angelo] (narrative poem, 1833); A. V. Kuznetsov, 1894, as Iskusheniye [Temptation]

Arap Petra Velikogo [The Negro of Peter the Great] (unfinished novella, 1834–7): G. N. Dudkevich, inc., lib. 1937; Arapov, 1959, as Fregat 'Pobeda' [The Frigate 'Victory']; Lourié, 1961

Bakhchisarayskiy fontan [The Fountain of Bakchisarai] (narrative poem, 1822): Měchura, 1871, as Marie Potocká; A. F. Fyodorov, 1895; M. M. Zubov, 1898; A. A. Il'insky, 1899; G. A. Smetanin, 1935, as Girey-khan; I. K. Shaposhnikov, 1937

Barïshnya-krest'yanka [Mistress into Maid] (tale, 1830): I. P. Larionov, 1875; Zajc, 1878, as Lizinka; Shutke, 1888; F. Ekkert, 1911, as Liza Muromskaya; Y. S. Biryukov, 1947; I. N. Kovner, 1948, as Akulina; V. Duke, 1958 (orig. in Fr. 1926, as Demoiselle paysanne)

Boris Godunov (tragedy, 1825): Musorgsky, 1874

Domik v Kolomne [The Little House in Kolomna] (narrative poem, 1830): Solov'yov, inc., excerpts pubd 1899; Stravinsky, 1922, as Mavra

Dubrovsky (unfinished novella, 1833): Nápravník, 1895; Napoli, 1973, as Dubrowski II

Graf Nulin [Count Nulin] (narrative poem, 1825): G. A. Lishin, 1882; A. A. Arkhangel'sky, 1915; Koval', comp. 1929 (rev. 1949, as Usad'ba [The Farmstead]); N. M. Strel'nikov, 1949; A. A. Nikolayev, 1983

Grobovshchik [The Undertaker] (tale, 1830): I. G. Admoni, 1935

Kammenïy gost' [The Stone Guest] ('little tragedy', 1830): Dargomïzhsky, 1872; Y. S. Biryukov, 1937, as Don-Zhuan i Leporello; N. A. Timofeyev, inc., 1933; Malipiero, 1963, as Don Giovanni; Kobekin, 1984, as Prorok [The Prophet] (with excerpts from *Pir vo vremya chumï*)

Kapitanskaya dochka [The Captain's Daughter] (novella, 1836): Cui, 1911; S. A. Katz, 1941

Kavkazskiy plennik [The Captive in the Caucasus] (narrative poem, 1821): Cui, 1883 (orig. version 1857–8); D. Lari, 1909, as Jela

Mednïy vsadnik [The Bronze Horseman] (narrative poem, 1833): Asaf'yev, 1939–40

Metel' [Blizzard] (tale, 1830): Kryukov, inc., 1941; Dzerzhinsky, 1946, as V zimnyuyu noch' [On a Winter's Night]

Motsart i Sal'yeri [Mozart and Salieri] ('little tragedy', 1830): Rimsky-Korsakov, 1898

Pikovaya dama [The Queen of Spades] (novella, 1833): Halévy, 1850, as La dame de pique; Suppé, 1862, as Die Kartenschlägerin; Tchaikovsky, 1890

Pir vo vremya chumï [Feast in Time of Plague] ('little tragedy' [purported trans. from J. Wilson: *The City of the Plague*], 1830): Cui, 1901; N. S. Rechmensky, 1927; Lourié, 1935; V. M. Tarnopol'sky, 1937; Goldenweiser, 1945; Firsova, 1972; A. A. Nikolayev, 1982; Kobekin, 1984, as Prorok [The Prophet] (with excerpts from *Kamennïy gost'*)

Poltava (narrative poem, 1828): B. A. Vietinghoff-Schell, 1858, as Mazepa; P. P. Sokal'sky, 1859, as Mariya; Tchaikovsky, 1884, as Mazepa

Roslavlev (novella frag., 1831): M. M. Bagrinovsky, 1944, as 1812 god [The Year 1812] (with excerpts from G. Danilevsky's novel *Sozhzhyonnaya Moskva* [Moscow Aflame])

Rusalka [The Mermaid] (unfinished dramatic poem, 1826–32): A. A. Alyab'yev, comp. 1841–3, as Rïbak i rusalka, ili Zloye zel'ye [The Fisherman and the Mermaid], inc.; Dargomïzhsky, 1856; Baroness de Maistre, 1870, as Les roussalkas

Ruslan i Lyudmila [Ruslan and Lyudmila] (narrative poem, 1820): Glinka, 1842

Skazka o myortvoy tsarevne i o semi bogatïryakh [Tale of the Dead Princess and the Seven Heroes] (imitation folktale, 1833): A. Y. Mittel'shtedt, vs pubd 1913; M. I. Krasev, 1924; A. A. Yemel'yanov, 1937; Veysberg, 1938, as Myortvaya tsarevna [The Dead Princess]; A. A. Kotilko, 1947; M. Y. Chernyak, 1949; V. N. Tsïbin, 1949

Skazka o pope i rabotnike ego Balde [Tale of the Priest and his Workman Balda] (folktale, 1830): L. I. Voinov, 1929; V. B. Karagichev, 1931; L. O. Bakalov [Popov], 1938

Skazka o ribake i ribke [Tale of the Fisherman and the Fish] (imitation folktale, 1833): L. A. Polovinkin, 1935; B. D. Gibalin, 1936; N. M. Parkhomenko, 1936; A. M. Manukian, 1937 (in Armenian); G. Croses, 1942, as Le poisson fée

Skazka o Tsare Saltane [Tale of Tsar Saltan] (imitation folktale, 1831): Rimsky-Korsakov, 1900; A. V. Nikol'sky, 1912

Skazka o zolotom petushke [Tale of the Golden Cockerel] (imitation folktale, 1834): Rimsky-Korsakov, 1909, as Zolotoy petushok [The Golden Cockerel]

Skupoy rïtsar' [The Miserly Knight] ('little tragedy', 1830): Rakhmaninov, 1906; Napoli, 1970, as Il barone avaro

Stantsionnïy smotritel' [The Stationmaster] (tale, 1830): L. Karlovsky, 1893, as Dunyasha – doch' stantsionnogo smotritelya [Dunyasha, the Stationmaster's Daughter]; Grechaninov, 1906; Kryukov, 1940; F. Reuter, 1947, as Postmaster Wyrin; Z. Y. Stel'nik, inc., 1948

Torzhestvo Vakkha [The Triumph of Bacchus] (anacreontic verses, 1817): Dargomïzhsky, 1867

Tsiganï [The Gypsies] (narrative poem, 1824): Kashperov, inc., c1850; G. A. Lishin, inc., frags. pubd 1876; Rakhmaninov, 1893, as Aleko; P. F. Yuon, 1896, as Aleko; N. N. Mironov, 1899; V. Sacchi, 1899, as Gli zingari; A. Ferretto, 1900, as Gli zingari; A. N. Shefer, 1901; K. M. Galkaukas, 1908; Leoncavallo, 1912, as Zingari; L. I. Levankovsky, 1913, as Zemfira; N. M. Shakhmatov, 1949; I. Csenki, 1973, as Tsiganyok

Vïstrel [The Shot] (tale, 1830): S. K. Shtrassenburg, 1936

Yevgeny Onegin [Eugene Onegin] (verse novel, 1830): Tchaikovsky, 1879

Zhenikh [The Bridegroom] (ballad, 1825): I. Blyum, c1900

*

C. Cui: 'Vliyaniye Pushkina na nashikh kompozitorov i na ikh vokal'nïy stil'' [The Influence of Pushkin on our Composers and on their Vocal Style], *Novosti i birzhevaya gazeta* (26 May 1899); repr. in C. Cui: *Izbrannïye stat'i*, ed. Yu. A. Kremlyov (Leningrad, 1952), 501–5

N. Kashkin: 'Znacheniye poèzii A. S. Pushkina v russkoy muzïke' [The Importance of Pushkin's Poetry in Russian Music], *Zhizn'* (1899), no.5, pp.126–30

L. Sacchetti: 'Otnosheniye Pushkina k muzïke' [Pushkin's Attitude to Music], *Sbornik statey v chest' D. F. Kobenko* (St Petersburg, 1913), 26–33

B. Tomashevsky: 'Pushkin i ital'yanskaya opera', *Pushkin i ego sovremenniki* [Pushkin and his Contemporaries], xxxi–xxxii (Leningrad, 1927), 49–60

I. Eyges: *Muzïka v zhizni i tvorchestve Pushkina* [Music in the Life and Work of Pushkin] (Moscow, 1937)

M. Pekelis: 'Dramaturgiya Pushkina i russkaya opera', *SovM* (1937), no.5, 45–9

V. Yakovlev: 'Pushkin i russkiy opernïy teatr', *SovM* (1937), no.3, pp.19–25; no.6, pp.42–7

G. Abraham: 'Moussorgsky's *Boris* and Pushkin's', *ML*, xxvi (1945), 31–8

V. Yakovlev: *Pushkin i muzïka* (Moscow, 1949)

E. Berlyand-Chyornaya: *Pushkin i Chaykovsky* (Moscow, 1950)

A. Glumov: *Muzïkal'nïy mir Pushkina* [The Musical World of Pushkin] (Moscow and Leningrad, 1950)

S. Shlif'shteyn: *Glinka i Pushkin* (Moscow and Leningrad, 1950)

M. Cooper: 'Pushkin and the Opera in Russia', *Opera*, xxii (1971), 96–111

A. Gozenpud: 'Pushkin i russkaya opernaya klassika', *Izbrannïye stat'i* (Leningrad and Moscow, 1971), 5–27

E. Stöckl: *Puškin und die Musik* (Leipzig, 1974)

N. Vinokur and R. Kagan: *Pushkin v muzïke: spravochnik* [Pushkin in Music: a Guide] (Moscow, 1974)

J. Baker: 'Dargomïzhsky, Realism, and *The Stone Guest*', *MR*, xxxvii (1976), 193–208

S. Campbell: 'The "Mavras" of Pushkin, Kochno and Stravinsky', *ML*, lviii (1977), 304–17

A. Orlova and M. Schneerson: 'After Pushkin and Karamzin: Researching the Sources for the Libretto of Boris Godunov', *Musorgsky: in memoriam*, ed. M. H. Brown (Ann Arbor, 1982), 249–70

M. Pritsker: 'Novïye proizvedeniya na Pushkinskiye Syuzhetï' [New Compositions based on Pushkin], *Muzïkal'naya zhizn'* (1983), no.14, p.5

B. Shteynpress: 'Russkaya literatura v zarubezhnoy opere' [Russian Literature in Foreign Operas], *SovM* (1985), no.6, pp.83–8

MARTIN COOPER (text),
RICHARD TARUSKIN (work-list, bibliography)

Putnam, Ashley (Elizabeth) (*b* New York, 10 Aug 1952). American soprano. She studied at Michigan University, then became an apprentice at Santa Fe. She made her début in 1976 as Lucia at Norfolk, Virginia, where she later sang the title role in the American première of Musgrave's *Mary, Queen of Scots* (1978). She sang Angel More (*The Mother of Us All*) and Gilda at Santa Fe, Donna Elvira and Ophelia (*Hamlet*) at San Diego, Zdenka at Houston and Konstanze at Miami. At the New York City Opera (1978–83) her roles included Violetta, Elvira (*I puritani*), Giselda (*I Lombardi*) Adèle (*Le comte Ory*), Marie (*La fille du régiment*) and Donizetti's Mary Stuart. She made her European début in 1978 as Musetta at Glyndebourne, where she later sang Arabella (1984) and Vitellia (1991). Returning to Santa Fe she sang Strauss's Danae (1982), Fiordiligi (1988) and the Marschallin (1989). In 1983 she sang Xiphares (*Mitridate*) at Schwetzingen and Aix-en-Provence. She made her Covent Garden début in 1986 as Jenůfa and her Metropolitan début in 1991 as Marguerite (*Faust*). She has appeared at San Francisco, Chicago, Brussels, Amsterdam, Florence and Zürich. Her flexible, silver-toned voice is ideal for the bel canto repertory, but she has also taken more dramatic roles such as Donna Anna, Kat'a Kabanova and Ellen Orford, which she sang at Geneva in 1991.   ELIZABETH FORBES

Py, Gilbert (*b* Sète, 9 Dec 1933). French tenor. A gypsy by birth, he trained as an acrobat and a dancer before becoming a singer. He made his début in 1964 at Verviers as Pinkerton. He sang Sutermeister's Raskolnikoff at Nice, Hoffmann at the Opéra-Comique (1969), Adoniram (*La reine de Saba*) at Toulouse (1970), and has also appeared at the Paris Opéra and La Scala, and in Vienna, Berlin, Verona and throughout France. His repertory included Don José, Faust (Berlioz and Gounod), John the Baptist (*Hérodiade*), Werther, Licinius (*La vestale*), Radames, Manrico, Otello, Cavaradossi, Florestan, Lohengrin, Tannhäuser and Siegmund. His favourite role was Saint-Saëns' Samson, which he sang at New Orleans (1972), for Opera North and in Dublin (1978), in Santiago (1984) and elsewhere. His voice, robust but mellow at the height of his career, later became somewhat hard in tone.

                ELIZABETH FORBES

Pygmalion. *Acte de ballet* by J.-P. Rameau; *see* PIGMALION.

Pylkkänen, Tauno (*b* Helsinki, 22 March 1918; *d* Helsinki, 13 March 1980). Finnish composer. He studied music in Helsinki at the academy (1937–40) and at the university (MA 1941). Appointments followed with Finnish radio (1942–61), as music critic for the newspaper *Uusi Suomi* (1941–69), as artistic director of the Finnish National Opera (1960–70) and as lecturer in the history of opera at the Helsinki academy (1967). He published *Oopperavaeltaja* ('The Opera Wanderer', Helsinki, 1953) and opera has been his chief interest as a composer. His style has been categorized as a kind of Finnish *verismo*, a description that applies both to his handling of dramatic situation and to his musical idiom, which is deeply influenced by Puccini. The success of his operas is largely due to his natural theatrical ability; *Varjo* ('The Shadow', 1952), his most wholly satisfactory piece, has, for its thrilling dramatic effect, been compared with *The Consul*. On the other hand, at a time when new trends were beginning to revolutionize musical thought, Pylkkänen's idiom tended to drift from one style to another. Sometimes the dramatic force of the libretto somewhat overshadowed the impact of the music. His strength lay in his skilfully crafted and

dramatically convincing one-act operas, several of which were specifically written for radio. In 1950 he won the third Italia Prize for his radio opera *Sudenmorsian* ('The Wolf's Bride'). His instrumental music clearly reveals the limitations of his style.

first performed in Helsinki, Aleksanterinteatteri, unless otherwise stated
Batsheba Saarenmaalla [Bathsheba at Saarenmaa] op.10, 1940 (1, A. Kallas), Finnish Radio, 1948; rev. 1958
Mare ja hänen poikansa [Mare and her Son] op.22, 1942–3 (3, Kallas), 27 Sept 1945
Simo Hurtta op.43 (4, E. Leino), 21 Nov 1948
Sudenmorsian [The Wolf's Bride] op.47 (radio op, 1, Kallas), Turin, 1950
Varjo [The Shadow] op.52, 1952 (1, H. Bergman), Tampere, 18 Nov 1954
Ikaros, 1956–60, (3, P. Knudsen), 8 Dec 1960
Opri ja Oleksi op.61, 1957 (3, K. Mäntylä), 23 Jan 1958
Vangit [The Prisoners] op.69 (1, A. Kivimaa), Finnish Television, 1965
Tuntematon soilas [The Unknown Soldier] op.73 (3, E. Laine and Pylkkänen, after V. Linna), 15 Nov 1967   ILKKA ORAMO

Louisa Pyne in the title role and William Harrison as Count Rupert in the original production of Balfe's 'Satanella' by the Pyne-Harrison Opera Company (Covent Garden, 1858–9): lithograph from a contemporary sheet music cover

Pyne, Louisa (Fanny) (*b* ?27 Aug 1832; *d* London, 20 March 1904). English soprano. She studied with Sir George Smart and made her début in 1849 as Amina in *La sonnambula* at Boulogne. She then sang Zerlina and Amina at the Princess's Theatre, London, and created Fanny in Macfarren's *Charles II*. In 1851 she appeared in an English season at the Haymarket and then replaced Anna Zerr as the Queen of Night with the Royal Italian Opera at Covent Garden, where her voice was said to be beautiful and flexible.

In 1854 she appeared in New York as Amina and as Arline in *The Bohemian Girl*. In the same year, with the tenor WILLIAM HARRISON, she formed the Pyne-Harrison Opera Company, which then undertook a successful tour of eastern America. After appearances at the

Lyceum and Drury Lane in 1857, the company appeared at Covent Garden each winter from 1859 to 1864. During this period Pyne sang the leading soprano roles in the first performances of Balfe's *Rose of Castille*, *Satanella, or The Bravo's Bride*, *Bianca*, *The Puritan's Daughter* and *The Armourer of Nantes*, Wallace's *Lurline*, Benedict's *Lily of Killarney* and Glover's *Ruy Blas*.

For further illustration *see* BALFE, MICHAEL WILLIAM.

HAROLD ROSENTHAL/R

Pyne-Harrison Opera Company. English touring company, assembled in New York by Louisa Pyne and William Harrison, who arrived in the USA in 1854. The company travelled throughout the eastern half of the country, performing English and Irish opera (Wallace and Balfe) as well as English translations of French (Auber), German (Weber and Mozart) and Italian works (Bellini, Rossini and Donizetti). On their return to England in 1857, Pyne and Harrison organized several successful seasons of English opera at Drury Lane and Covent Garden. *See* LONDON, §II, 1 and TRAVELLING TROUPES, §5(i).

Pyotr I ('Peter I'). 'Musical-dramatic frescoes' in three acts by ANDREY PAVLOVICH PETROV to a libretto by Natal'ya Kasatkina and Vladimir Vasilyov; Leningrad, Kirov Theatre, 14 June 1975.

Peter	bass
Marta, subsequently Yekaterina *Peter's wife*	mezzo-soprano
Tikhon *a soldier*	baritone
Anastasiya *Tikhon's fiancée*	soprano
Men'shikov } *Peter's comrades-in-arms*	tenor
Lefort }	baritone
Prince Romodanovsky	bass
Sof'ya *Peter's sister*	soprano
Makary *Sof'ya's attendant*	bass
Vladimir *a painter*	tenor
Rzhevskaya *Prince/Mother Superior of the 'All-Fools Council'*	mezzo-soprano
Gerrit *Dutch ship's captain*	tenor
A Boyar	tenor
First Soldier	tenor
Second Soldier	bass

The people, Peter's troops, strel'tsï, monks, Dutch citizens, sailors

Setting Russia and the Netherlands, 1689–1703

As a preliminary to embarking on his first opera, *Peter I*, Petrov composed four vocal-symphonic frescoes for soloist, chorus and orchestra on the same subject. After the successful concert première of this score in April 1973, the composer used the four original frescoes as the basis for the expanded operatic concept, which consists of ten frescoes and was completed in 1975. Petrov and his librettists drew on historical documents and letters as well as specific musical styles ranging from military fanfares and marches, *kantï* and Orthodox chant to lend authenticity to the work, though the musical language as a whole is not stylized; in a fundamentally tonal framework, it makes eclectic use of modern devices and popular idioms. The work is appropriately labelled 'musical-dramatic frescoes': the major conflicts and accomplishments of Peter the Great's reign are etched by means of a series of illustra-

tive episodes rather than traced through a progressive narrative. Petrov was awarded the USSR State Prize for this work in 1976.

ACT 1 The four frescoes of Act 1 depict the young Peter as he attains maturity. Anastasiya's opening prayer-lament, 'Chudnaya Mati-zemlya' ('O glorious mother-earth'), and the answering choral chant, 'Kak na nas gospod' porazgnevalsya' ('How God became angry with us'), which symbolizes the fear and resistance of the old Russia, reappear periodically as refrains during the opera. In the first fresco, 'Sof'ya', Peter's sister and her supporter Makary, threatened by the destruction of the old order if Peter becomes tsar and greedy for power, plot to have the strel'tsï – an élite military unit founded by Ivan the Terrible – assassinate Peter and then accuse him of planning to overthrow his elder brother Ivan. The streletz Tikhon is horrified by what he has heard and resolves to save the young tsar. The sombre, ominous tone of the first fresco contrasts sharply with the bright, festive fanfares and drumrolls of the second, 'Peter at Preobrazhenskoye', in which Peter's troops drill happily under the guidance of Men'shikov while Peter works on his boat. As the ominous strains of the choral chant 'How God became angry' begin to clash with the march music, Tikhon rushes in with the news that the strel'tsï, incited by Sof'ya, are marching on Preobrazhenskoye to kill Peter. Peter and his men hastily take shelter in Troitskoye monastery.

The third fresco, 'Accession to the Throne', consists of two parts. In the first, which takes place in the monastery, Lefort and Peter's followers urge Peter to take decisive action against Sof'ya and take power in his own hands. Military fanfares are heard in the distance as regiments rally to Peter's support. As he prepares for battle, Peter's arioso 'Pridyot vremya' ('The time is coming') rises to the orchestral presentation of a theme which symbolizes the greatness of Russia. Peter composes a letter to Ivan while in the background the painter Vladimir, accompanied by the sound of church bells, predicts a difficult path for the young leader. Peter reads his letter before Ivan, Sof'ya and the boyars at the Kremlin. Despite the hysterical protestations of Sof'ya, he assumes the throne, banishing his sister to a nunnery. Against a reprise of Anastasiya's prayer-lament, Makary's curses of 'Antichrist' can be heard.

In the fourth fresco, 'All-Fools Council', Peter carouses with his hard-drinking companions. Mocking the rituals of the Church, they robe Men'shikov as Bacchus and crown him Patriarch of the drunken assembly. The songs of 'Mother Superior' Rzhevskaya and Lefort (the latter's being a French chanson) lead to an orgy of dancing from which the participants gradually drop into a drunken stupor. The debauchery gives way to more serious reflection as Peter looks around and wonders if such ignorance and decay are found everywhere. In a song of inspiration, he resolves 'Pora! Pora na mir vzglyanut'' ('It's time to see the world!').

ACT 2 In 'Holland', the first of three frescoes in Act 2, the music takes on more stylized characteristics to evoke the cultivated European setting. Peter has been successfully apprenticed as a shipbuilder, and the residents of Amsterdam have gathered at the port to celebrate the launching of a frigate. Men'shikov and Tikhon are homesick, a feeling reinforced by the offstage reprise of Anastasiya's prayer-lament, and beg Peter to return home. The theme of Russia's greatness is heard as Peter

'*Pyotr I' (Petrov): final fresco of Act 1 from the original production at the Kirov Theatre, Leningrad, 14 June 1975, with Vladimir Morozov (centre) as Peter*

dreams of opening Russia to the sea. His hopes of further discovery are cut short, however, by the news that the strel'tsï are in rebellion in Russia.

The famine and suffering of 'Old Moscow' are underlined by the choral chant 'How God became angry'. The voices fragment into chaos. Peter learns that Sof'ya is fomenting sedition from within her monastery, and in a monologue, 'Nikto ne mozhet pomïslov moikh urazumet'' ('No one can comprehend my aspirations'), reminiscent of Boris Godunov's, he reflects sadly on the blood which will have to be shed to prevent Russia from dragging backwards. Confronting Sof'ya in her cell as she prays fervently, Peter tries to persuade her to stop her plotting, but tempers flare and Peter informs her of the execution of the strel'tsï.

In 'The Encampment at Narva', the final fresco of Act 2, Peter's soldiers sing a satirical song about the King of Sweden. They flirt with Marta, a captive washerwoman, who takes a liking to Tikhon. Men'shikov tries to compete for her attentions, but he is outranked by Peter, who takes charge of the maiden and changes her name to the Orthodox Yekaterina. She introduces herself to the infatuated tsar with the lyrical ballad 'Kak ptichka vol'naya zhila' ('I lived as free as a bird'). A wounded soldier arrives with the tragic news that Swedish troops have routed the Russians at Narva.

ACT 3 The three frescoes of Act 3 depict Peter's victory over internal and external enemies. In 'The Removal of the Bells', Peter has ordered all church bells to be melted down for munitions in his war against the Swedes, a move passionately resented by the Old Believers. Makary persuades them to resist the Anti-

christ, but the soldiers continue their work and the people scatter in terror from the falling bells. Anastasiya is crushed, and Makary persuades the grieving Tikhon to murder Peter. In Peter's tent on the eve of battle, after Yekaterina proudly anticipates her future as tsarina in 'Den' prishyol' ('The day has come'), Tikhon's pistol misfires in 'The Assassination Attempt'. Peter orders the execution of Makary, but he forgives Tikhon and sends him to spread the news that God has saved the tsar.

The final fresco, 'The Battle with the Swedes', provides a suitably monumental and heroic conclusion. With appeals to their national pride, Peter inspires his troops to battle, which is played out in a vivid orchestral interlude. The victory of Peter's troops is signalled by the great Russia theme and Peter appears at the gate of the fortress to announce that the first stone for the city of Petersburg will be laid here. He expresses his faith in the future of Russia in his final monologue, 'Moya doroga tol'ko nachalas'' ('My path has just begun'), before the victory celebrations lead to a massed choral and orchestral apotheosis.   LAUREL E. FAY

Pyramus and Thisbe. Libretto subject popular in the 18th century, taken from OVID's *Metamorphoses*, iv.

A young Babylonian couple, Pyramus and Thisbe, were betrothed; but the families quarrelled, broke off relations and forbade the young people to see each other. They decided to meet at night and elope. Then the tragic chain of events began that has given their story immortality: while waiting for Pyramus, Thisbe is frightened away by a lion and leaves her scarf behind; Pyramus arrives, finds the scarf bloody and mauled by the lion, and stabs himself, believing that Thisbe is dead;

returning, Thisbe finds him dying, and she stabs herself; and finally her father arrives to find both young people dead, and he stabs himself too. The plot of course appears as the rustics' play in Shakespeare's *A Midsummer Night's Dream*, and in operas based on it, notably Britten's.

Pirame et Thisbé, a *tragédie en musique* by Rebel and Francoeur, was performed at the Paris Opéra in 1726, but the Italian settings by Giuseppe Merola and Lorenzo de' Rossi (1740, Urbino) were of the modest *azione dramatica* type rather than full-length *opere serie*, which would have been subject to the usual conventions that prohibited staged deaths. The same is true of the *intermezzo tragico* on the subject by Hasse to a libretto by Coltellini, produced for Vienna in 1768; this is in two parts, with three characters, and has many short ensembles and cavatinas without exit. Revivals are recorded in Vienna (1770) and Potsdam (1771). Botturini translated Coltellini's version into English; it was set by Venanzio Rauzzini for Munich in 1769 and revised for London in 1775. This version names Thisbe's father, Eupalte, and adds a fourth character, Corbeo.

In Venice in 1783 the plot was presented as a full-length *opera seria* in three acts with six characters, with music by Francesco Bianchi and libretto by Gaetano Sertor. Here Thisbe's father is Zoroa, King of Babylon, and each of the three principals has acquired a noble confidant (Belesi, Zulima and Zopiro). The libretto carries both the tragic ending and an alternative one which was actually performed. In the latter, Zoroa finds Pyramus wild with grief, but both are so relieved when Thisbe returns alive that all is forgiven. Sartori lists revivals of Bianchi's setting for Cremona in 1784 and Perugia. In autumn 1783 the Pergola Theatre in Florence took the unprecedented step of presenting Sertor's libretto with the tragic ending intact. Set again that year by G. B. Borghi, it marked an important move towards the abrogation of the old rules and the more frequent depiction of death on the stage in Italian *opera seria* during the late 1780s.

See also FAIRY-QUEEN, THE [Purcell]; *MIDSUMMER NIGHT'S DREAM, A* [Britten]; *PIRAME ET THISBÉ* [Francoeur and Rebel]; *PIRAMO E TISBE* [Hasse]; and *PYRAMUS AND THISBE* [Lampe].

MARITA P. McCLYMONDS

Pyramus and Thisbe. Mock opera in one act by JOHN FREDERICK LAMPE to an anonymous libretto based on RICHARD LEVERIDGE's libretto of the same name after the play-within-a-play in WILLIAM SHAKESPEARE's *A Midsummer Night's Dream*; London, Covent Garden, 25 January 1745.

This was the last of Lampe's operas, and was a much-needed success after a difficult period for musicians in the London theatre. In 1741 the revolution in Shakespearean acting initiated by Macklin and Garrick diverted attention away from music, and Lampe produced no new work in the major theatres for four years. *Pyramus* returns to the vein of burlesque that he mined in *The Dragon of Wantley* (1737), his first popular success; it ridicules Italian-style opera and opera singers rather than Shakespeare's plays and players. The onstage audience, originally Duke Theseus and his entourage, consists of Mr Semibrief (the impresario) and two gentlemen, one of whom has experienced Italian opera at first hand on the grand tour; they interject facetious spoken comments as the all-sung opera proceeds. The story follows Shakespeare closely: the Wall (tenor) sports a chink through which Pyramus (tenor) and Thisbe (soprano) arrange to meet 'at Ninny's tomb'. Thisbe arrives first and is frightened away by the Lion (bass), who sings a splendid roaring aria. After the Moon (tenor) has sung a lyrical Arne-like number, Pyramus appears, fears the worst and stabs himself 'like a hero in Italian opera, to very good time and tune'; Thisbe follows suit. But they are revived by Mr Semibrief in time to sing the epilogue. Lampe's music is charming and largely deadpan, though there are the standard Handelian rage and revenge arias. The full score (London, 1745/*R*1988) omits the *secco* recitatives, a dance and the last chorus.

PETER HOLMAN

Q

Quadri, Argeo (*b* Como, 23 March 1911). Italian conductor. He studied composition, piano and choral singing at the Milan Conservatory, graduating in 1933. He was successful in Italy for more than 20 years, giving a wide range of operas at all the major houses. He conducted *Rigoletto* at the end of the 1955–6 season at Covent Garden, returning early the following season for a *Ballo in maschera* that was described as 'noisy and violent' (H. D. Rosenthal, *Two Centuries of Opera at Covent Garden*, 1958). Quadri conducted Italian repertory in Vienna (Volksoper and Staatsoper) from 1957. *Don Pasquale*, *Tosca* and *Fedora* are among his recordings.   DAVID CUMMINGS

Quadrio, Francesco Saverio (*b* Ponte in Valtellina, 1695; *d* 1756). Italian scholar. At first a Jesuit, he left the order to devote himself to secular studies. His most important work, in seven volumes, was a history of poetry from classical antiquity to his own era, *Della storia e della ragione di ogni poesia* (Bologna, 1739–52). It alternates discursive articles with brief subject and biographical entries, and explores the relationship between poetry and music. Much of the work concerns the history of music and early instruments, of which there are illustrations. Volumes ii and iii contain articles on *melodramma*, oratorio and cantata. Part 2 of volume iii (pp.425–563), which contains lists of singers, actors, writers, stage designers, costume designers and inventors of stage machines, as well as comments on production, is invaluable for historians of opera.

S. Quadrio: *Di F. S. Quadrio e delle sue opere* (Brescia, 1911)
B. Pinchetti: *La vita di F. S. Quadrio* (Milan, 1913)
——: *Ricerche sulle opere letterarie di F. S. Quadrio* (Catania, 1915)
M. Costanzo: *Dallo Scaligero al Quadrio* (Milan, 1961)
                                      BARBARA REYNOLDS

Quaglio. Italian-German family of stage designers. Giovanni Maria (i) (*b* Laino, Como, *c*1700; *d* Vienna, *c*1765) and Domenico (i) (1708–73), a portrait and historical painter, were sons of the painter Giulio Quaglio (1668–1751); their descendants constitute two distinct branches of the family.

G. M. Quaglio studied in Rome and Milan and moved to Vienna, probably in the early 1730s, as an architect and stage designer. He was involved in the reconstruction of the Redoutensaal (1748–52) and designed sets for the Burgtheater and Kärntnertortheater in Vienna (1748–51), becoming the leading designer for both (1752–65). His sets encompassed the Viennese repertory during the transition from courtly to middle-class theatre – *opera seria*, *opera buffa*, *opéra comique* and ballet. He designed nearly all the sets for the reformers Durazzo, Calzabigi, Angiolini and Gluck (*Orfeo ed Euridice*, 1762; *Telemaco*, 1765). His art was rooted in the *opera seria* tradition of formalized illusionistic architecture painting, but he also developed staging as a means of expression, particularly in association with Gluck, through picturesque natural structures aiming at truth and universal appeal.

His son Lorenzo (i) (*b* Laino, 23 July 1730; *d* Munich, 2 May 1805) was appointed theatre artist at the palatine court of Carl Theodor in 1752. As court theatre architect from 1758 he was responsible for scenery at the Mannheim and Schwetzingen court theatres, and for enlarging the Mannheim Hofoper (1758) and reconstructing the Nationaltheater (1777). During that period he also worked at Reggio Emilia, Frankfurt, Dresden and Zweibrücken (1775). He moved to Munich in 1778 with the court and retired in 1799. As designer for works of the Mannheim school, especially Holzbauer's operas and Cannabich's ballets, Quaglio gave a considerable impulse to German musical theatre. He followed his father in continuing to reconcile the courtly formalism of the Galli-Bibiena school with bourgeois intimacy and objectivity, with its genre pieces (Hiller's *Der Dorfbalbier*, 1771) and classical (Schweitzer's *Alceste*, 1773) or national themes (Holzbauer's *Günther von Schwarzburg*, 1777). For late 18th-century *opera seria* (Mozart's *Idomeneo*, 1781; Vogler's *Castore e Polluce*, 1787) extravagances of perspective were replaced by clearly structured neo-classical architectural and landscape views. Carlo (*fl c*1761–78), son of G. M. Quaglio (i), was assistant and second theatre engineer (1762–5) to his father in Vienna; in 1761 he designed the stage of the palace theatre in Eisenstadt, where Haydn worked, and from 1765 to about 1778 he was stage designer in Warsaw. A third brother, Martin (*fl c*1764–73), was assistant to Lorenzo (i) in Mannheim in 1764–8 and then became stage designer in Kassel, where he was still active in 1773. Lorenzo's son Giovanni Maria (ii) (1772–1813) was court theatre painter in Munich (1795–9 and 1802–3) and in Mannheim (1800–02).

The family's other line of influential stage designers was founded by Giuseppe (or Joseph) Quaglio (*b* Laino,

The Queen of Night, design by Simon Quaglio for Act 1 scene vi of Mozart's 'Die Zauberflöte', performed at the Hof- und Nationaltheater, Munich, 1818: pen, ink and watercolour

2 Dec 1747; *d* Munich, 2 March 1828), son of Domenico (i) and nephew of G. M. Quaglio (i), with his brother Giulio. Their work was closely connected with Romantic musical theatre and the rise of historical stage design in Germany. Giuseppe went to Mannheim about 1770 as a theatre painter and followed his cousin Lorenzo (i) to Munich in 1779; until 1823 he was stage designer there, from 1801 court theatre architect. He completed the transition to a pictorially composed scene begun by the older members of the family, especially as regards historical milieu: his sets, using the devices of Romantic landscape painting, exploited mood and local colour and achieved striking expressive variety. This historical eclecticism catered for the contemporary repertory, serving historical opera (Vogler's *Albert der Dritte von Bayern*, 1781) as well as comic (Winter's *Der Frauenbund*, 1805) and mixed genres (*Don Giovanni*, 1791); it was strongest in the large-scale sets for post-revolutionary grand opera (Paer's *Achille*, 1802; Méhul's *Joseph*, 1809).

His brother Giulio (or Julius) Quaglio (*b* Laino, 1764; *d* Munich, 21 Jan 1801) was a theatre artist in Munich (*c*1781–5), Mannheim (1785–98) and Dessau (1798) before succeeding his cousin Lorenzo (i) as Munich court theatre architect in 1799. His designs, particularly those created after 1785 for the Mannheim Nationaltheater, followed essentially the principles of his brother, but he made less use of historical scenery and his setting of *Die Zauberflöte* (1794, Mannheim), partly composed of older sets from the theatre's stock, showed a multiplicity of different stylistic elements, notably exotic motifs including a 'Chinese' hall, a 'Gothic' temple and an 'Egyptian' vault.

Giuseppe's son Angelo (i) (*b* Munich, 13 Aug 1784; *d* Munich, 2 April 1815) was an artist at the Munich Hoftheater from 1801 and also at the Isartortheater after 1812. Like his brothers Domenico (ii) (1787–1837), only very briefly a stage designer, and Lorenzo (ii) (1793–1869), Angelo made a considerable contribution to the popularization of the Gothic style. His work for the stage, which has survived mainly through his illustrated inventory of the court theatre (1803–10), inclined not only to the Gothic period but

also to other historical epochs – classical antiquity in particular was glorified in the idealized landscapes and architecture of heroic opera (Salieri's *Palmira*, 1814).

A fourth son of Giuseppe, Simon (Joseph) (*b* Munich, 23 Oct 1795; *d* Munich, 8 March 1878), was an assistant from 1812 and from 1814 a permanent stage designer at the Munich court theatre, where he supervised the scenery from 1824 up to his retirement in 1877. After his classical early works he devoted himself to Romantic stage painting with mystical characteristics (*Die Zauberflöte*, 1818, Hof- und Nationaltheater; *Der Freischütz*, 1822). Influenced by grand opera, which dominated the Munich repertory, he later developed a more solemn historical style (*La Juive*, 1844). His son Angelo (ii) (*b* Munich, 13 Dec 1829; *d* Munich, 5 Jan 1890) worked from 1850 at the court theatre and managed a commercial scenic studio which supplied theatres in Dresden, Berlin, Stuttgart, St Petersburg and elsewhere. His designs remained within his father's illusionistic historical style. Closely connected with the aesthetic ideas of Ludwig II of Bavaria, Quaglio was the principal designer for the Munich Wagner premières (*Tannhäuser*, 1855; *Lohengrin*, 1858, 1867; *Der fliegende Holländer*, 1864; *Tristan und Isolde*, 1865; *Die Meistersinger*, 1868; *Das Rheingold*, 1869; *Die Walküre*, 1870) and for Ludwig's private performances (including *Aida*, 1877, and *Oberon*, 1881). He worked with his father and others. His son Eugen (*b* Munich, 3 April 1857; *d* Berlin, 25 Sept 1942) worked in his father's studio from about 1877, later (1891) becoming court theatre painter in Berlin, a post he held until 1923. He carried on the family tradition of historical stage designs, above all in Wagner productions (*Tannhäuser*, 1890; *Lohengrin*, 1891; *Rienzi*, 1895; *Tristan und Isolde*, 1903). Although he was influenced by naturalism and *verismo*, his romanticizing productions were basically historical idylls (D'Albert's *Der Improvisator*, 1902; Strauss's *Feuersnot*, 1902).

See also STAGE DESIGN, §§4 and 5. For further illustration *see* FEUERSNOT; STAGE DESIGN, fig.15; and *TRISTAN UND ISOLDE*.

F. Walter: *Geschichte des Theaters und der Musik am kurpfälzischen Hofe*, i (Leipzig, 1898), 173ff

L. Malyot: 'Die Künstlerfamilie Quaglio', *Theaterzeitung der Staatlichen Bühnen Münchens*, ii (1921), no.56, p.7

J. Kaap: *200 Jahre Staatsoper im Bild* (Berlin, 1942), 68–9, 80ff

W. Niehaus: *Die Theatermaler Quaglio* (diss., U. of Munich, 1956)

G. Schöne and H. Vriesen: *Das Bühnenbild im 19. Jahrhundert* (Munich, 1959) [exhibition catalogue]

K. Hommel: *Die Separatvorstellungen vor König Ludwig II. von Bayern* (Munich, 1963)

F. Cavarocchi: 'Artisti della Valle Intelvi e della Diocese Comense attivi in Baviera alla luce di carte d'archivio del Ducato di Milano', *Arte lombarda*, x/2 (1965), 135–48

G. Schöne: 'Trois mises en scène de la "Flûte enchantée" de Mozart: Berlin 1816, Weimar 1817 et Munich 1818', *Anatomy of an Illusion: 4th International Congress on Theatre Research: Amsterdam 1965*, 45–9

D. Petzet and M. Petzet: *Die Richard-Wagner-Bühne Ludwigs II.* (Munich, 1970)

B. Król-Kaczarowska: *Teatr dawney polski: budynki, dekoracje, kostiumy* (Warsaw, 1971), 123–4

G. Zechmeister: *Die Wiener Theater nächst der Burg und nächst dem Kärtnerthor von 1747 bis 1776* (Vienna, 1971)

M. Boetzkes: 'Quaglio', *The Age of Neo-classicism* (London, 1972), 938–44 [exhibition catalogue]

B. Trost: *Domenico Quaglio 1787–1837: Monographie und Werkverzeichnis* (Munich, 1973)   MANFRED BOETZKES

Quartararo, Florence [Fiorenza] (*b* San Francisco, 31 May 1922). American soprano. Her teachers were Pietro Cimini in Los Angeles and Elizabeth Wells in San Francisco. She made her début as Leonora in a concert performance of *Il trovatore* at the Hollywood Bowl in 1945. Her stage début took place the next year at the Metropolitan Opera as Micaela. For the four seasons following she appeared regularly at the Metropolitan, performing roles including Desdemona, Nedda, Pamina and Violetta. She made her début in San Francisco in 1947 as Donna Elvira, and in Europe in 1953 at the Arena Flegrea in Naples as Margherita in *Mefistofele*. Soon afterwards she curtailed her career. Her voice combined lyricism and power, lending her the versatility to range from Mozart heroines to Verdi and spinto *verismo* roles.   CORI ELLISON

Quartet (Fr. *quatuor*; Ger. *Quartett*; It. *quartetto*). An ensemble for four voices. Quartets appeared in opera as early as the mid-17th century; Cavalli's *Calisto* (1651) ends with one and Alessandro Scarlatti wrote some in his late Roman operas. They were uncommon in Italian opera during the first half of the 18th century, although notable examples may be found in Handel's *Radamisto* (1720) and *Partenope* (1730); there is a striking quartet in Feo's *Andromaca* (1730) and three appear in Latilla's comic opera *Angelica ed Orlando* (1735). Throughout this period quartets generally tend to appear within scenes as short collective expressions of emotion, as part of a *divertissement*, or at the close of an opera. In Italian opera, where present they normally appear in Act 3. Early in his career, Metastasio wrote such a quartet for *Catone in Utica* (1728), which he retained in his approved Paris edition of 1780–82; it was however seldom set and he himself omitted it in a new ending written for the opera soon after the first performance. In his setting of Metastasio's *Artaserse* for Vienna (1749), Galuppi added a quartet at the end of Act 1, replacing a series of arias; it produces (according to Heartz 1978) a moment of considerable dramatic power: 'One of the most expressive effects of this quartet is the way the music enhances the tragic isolation and moral strength of the hero. Arbace controls most of the modulation, confirms the tonal arrivals, and stands out alone, vocally, against the others.' Galuppi's quartet was not included in a revival in Padua in 1751, possibly because

singers were averse to the loss of their arias in favour of ensembles. Metastasio himself disapproved of elaborate concerted numbers, as he wrote to Saverio Mattei 20 years later, referring to Mattei's addition of a quartet to *Ezio* for a setting by Sacchini (Jommelli and Anfossi also set *Ezio* in the 1770s with a quartet at this point):

The *Quartetto* you have written is decent, convenient, and happy; and if it is well treated by the composer and performers, I believe it will have a good effect. Indeed it will render Act 2 somewhat barren of airs, in which the two principal personages will have but one song apiece: which would have been thought a sacrilege when I wrote the opera. ... On the other hand, it is a false supposition, that I ever wrote a *quartet* for *Ezio*, or that I ever requested one.

Quartets became more frequent in *opera seria* after 1750; Metastasio himself wrote one for his *Il rè pastore* in 1751. They appear fairly regularly (though less so than duets or trios) from about 1765. Verazi provided quartets of diminishing personnel for Jommelli (down to a duet) and J. C. Bach (to a duet and then a solo). They began to acquire action in Italian opera during the 1780s, and in the 1790s both reflective and action quartets appear, both within the acts and as finales. In comic opera, quartets mainly appeared as act endings in the first half of the century; in the 1750s they began to acquire action, though more as finales than within acts. They also served as introductory ensembles. Mozart wrote a contemplative quartet in Act 3 of *Idomeneo* (1781; the original libretto had included a second quartet) and one that is a blend of action and contemplation as the Act 2 finale of *Die Entführung aus dem Serail* (1782); his Act 1 quartet in *Don Giovanni* (1787) serves to draw together different threads of the evolving drama. In France quartets were common in *opéra comique* from the early 1760s, as finales and elsewhere; a notable example is the Act 2 finale of Monsigny's *Le roi et le fermier* (1762).

In the 17th century, quartets were usually made up of a succession of points of imitation, as in 'Così va chi d'amor' from Provenzale's *Lo schiavo di sua moglie*. By the early 18th century this had given way to the favoured succession of textural thickenings beginning with long solos for each participant, moving to short comments and then imitatively into a predominantly homophonic tutti with antiphonal alternation and short solos, again moving from imitative to tutti textures. Examples include 'Saprò morire' in Porsile's *Spartaco*, 'Deh in vita ti serba' in J. C. Bach's *Catone in Utica*, and of course 'Andrò ramingo e solo' in *Idomeneo*. Sometimes quartets take the form, texturally speaking, of 'double duets'. Philidor wrote a canonic quartet to open *Tom Jones* (1765); other canonic quartets include Mozart's in the Act 2 finale of *Così fan tutte* (1790; a three-voice canon with one free part), in a tradition established by Martín y Soler (*see* CANON), and Beethoven's 'Mir ist so wunderbar' from *Fidelio* (1805).

In the early part of the 19th century quartets remained rare outside *opera buffa* and *semiseria*. An example is Bellini's 'A te, o cara' from *I puritani* (1835), which was performed at the composer's funeral by the four star singers for whom the opera was written, Grisi, Rubini, Tamburini and Lablache (although Tamburini was not originally involved in the quartet itself). With its long initial tenor solo Bellini's quartet probably formed the starting-point for the most famous of all operatic quartets, 'Bella figlia dell'amore' from *Rigoletto* (1851), an inspired simultaneous expression of different feelings (ardent wooing, coquettish banter, anguish and vengefulness). Other fine Verdi quartets include 'Ah, mon pays' from *Les vêpres siciliennes* (1855) and 'D'un uom che geme' from *Otello* (1887), as well as the all-female 'Quell'otre! quel tino!' from *Falstaff* (1893), which was encored at the première. Quartets that feature two couples mostly in alternation include 'Prenez mon bras un moment' from Gounod's *Faust* (1859) and the corresponding ensemble in Boito's *Mefistofele* (revised 1875); another is the ensemble concluding the garden scene in Tchaikovsky's *Yevgeny Onegin* (1879); to these may be added the whole of Act 2 scene ii of Janáček's *Kát'a Kabanová* (1921). In Puccini's 'Addio dolce svegliare alla matina', from *La bohème* (1896), the quarrelling of one pair of lovers forms a counterpoint to the tender exchanges of the other.

See also FINALE.

D. Heartz: 'Hasse, Galuppi and Metastasio', *Venezia e il melodramma nel settecento: Venice 1973*, i (Florence, 1978), 326–31

MARITA P. McCLYMONDS, ELISABETH COOK, JULIAN BUDDEN

Quatro rusteghi, I [*Die vier Grobiane*] ('The Four Curmudgeons' [*School for Fathers*]). Comic opera in three acts by ERMANNO WOLF-FERRARI to a libretto by Luigi Sugana and Giuseppe Pizzolato after CARLO GOLDONI's play *I rusteghi* (1760); Munich, Hoftheater, 19 March 1906.

After the promise revealed in Wolf-Ferrari's first Goldoni opera *Le donne curiose*, this second of his five operatic versions of comedies by the great Venetian playwright is regarded by many as his masterpiece. Certainly it is far superior to the relatively trivial *Il segreto di Susanna* and *I gioielli della Madonna*, which have become disproportionately familiar to the English-speaking world.

In adapting and shortening the play for operatic purposes, the librettists transformed much of Goldoni's dialogue into verse. Yet important aspects of the original text were retained: for example, almost all the characters – apart from the aristocratic outsider Count Riccardo (tenor) – express themselves in Venetian dialect, which in *Le donne curiose* had been confined to the parts of Pantalone and Arlecchino. The distinctive atmosphere and spirit of *I quatro rusteghi* is closely bound up with the colourful eccentricities of that remarkable dialect, a fact which performance in other languages inevitably disguises. However, when first staged in English (at Sadler's Wells, London, on 7 October 1946, under the title *School for Fathers*) the work won a resounding success, helped by Edward Dent's splendidly witty translation. The rarity with which the opera has been professionally revived in Britain since then is a gross injustice to one of the liveliest Italian comic operas since *Falstaff*.

The Venetian word *rusteghi* has special implications, which its counterpart in standard Italian does not share. It may be translated here as 'curmudgeons' or 'pedantic boors', since the characters in question are stubbornly hidebound by the absurd social conventions of their time. Two of them, Lunardo and Maurizio (both basses), have arranged that the former's daughter Lucieta (soprano) should marry the latter's son Filipeto (tenor) – on the rigid condition that they should wait until the wedding before they may even see each other. Fiercely resenting this, the young people enlist the aid of the older female characters and of Count Riccardo: Filipeto thus manages to enter Lunardo's house dressed as a woman, the couple are brought face to face at last,

and they instantly fall in love. But the perversity of their fathers, and of the conventions that the *rusteghi* unthinkingly uphold, now takes a new turn: such flagrant anticipation of marriage can be adequately punished (according to Lunardo) only by cancelling the wedding. The more enlightened characters – notably the volatile Felice (soprano), wife of a third *rustego* called Cancian (bass) – have to exert enormous psychological pressure before Lunardo and his cronies will change their minds. Eventually, however, all is resolved in a happy ending.

As in *Le donne curiose*, the slender plot is little more than a pretext for wittily inventive satirical dialogue and characterization, which are abundantly reinforced by the no less inventive music. Again deriving important aspects of his inspiration from 18th-century *opera buffa*, Wolf-Ferrari drew on that tradition flexibly enough to accommodate sly references to both Verdi and Wagner and numerous touches of subtly ingenious orchestration. A familiar Venetian popular melody plays a prominent part at several points; and there are occasional touches of obstinately unresolved dissonance – notably at the beginning of the third act, where three of the *rusteghi* are in a state of high dudgeon about the youngsters' flagrant breach of the rules. These various elements are held together with remarkable spontaneity and sure-footedness, by the unassuming yet unmistakable controlling force of Wolf-Ferrari's personality. The quintessence of this personality is winsomely distilled in the sweet, refined innocence of the well-known orchestral prelude and intermezzo. But the vitality and expressive range of the opera as a whole are far greater than those modest little pieces can indicate.

JOHN C. G. WATERHOUSE

Quatuor (Fr.). QUARTET.

Quebec (Fr. Québec). Canadian city, capital of Quebec province. The first opera to be heard there was Dibdin's *The Padlock*, performed at the Thespian Theatre in 1783. It was followed by Shield's *The Choleric Fathers* and *The Poor Soldier* (1794–5). A touring company gave Rossini's *Il barbiere di Siviglia* in 1864 (possibly the Canadian première), and *La dame blanche* was performed in 1879. Later there were visits from the Montreal Opera Company (1910–13) with programmes of French operas; *Manon* and *Thaïs* were banned in 1911. In 1948 the Opéra National de Québec was formed for students to perform in Quebec, Montreal and other cities. Operas produced between 1949 and 1952 included *Faust*, *Lakmé*, *Carmen*, *Roméo et Juliette*, *Rigoletto* and *La bohème*. The Théâtre Lyrique de Nouvelle-France (later de Québec) produced one opera a year from 1961 to 1970, including *Werther*, *Les pêcheurs de perles*, *Mignon*, *Mireille* and *Manon*; the Société Lyrique d'Aubigny (1969–80) performed much the same repertory. The Opéra de Québec (1971–5), giving annual four-opera seasons, produced *Samson et Dalila*, *Il trittico*, *La fille du régiment*, *Salome*, *Otello*, *Don Giovanni*, *Falstaff* and *Tristan und Isolde*. In 1981 the Grand Théâtre de Québec, which shortly became the second Opéra de Québec, opened with *Les contes d'Hoffmann*. Its repertory of two operas a season has included *Nabucco*, *Madama Butterfly*, *Carmen*, *Faust*, *Le nozze di Figaro*, *Rigoletto*, *Manon*, *Lucia di Lammermoor* and the world première of André Gagnon's *Nelligan* (1990), later performed in Montreal and Ottawa.

ELIZABETH FORBES

Queen of Spades, The [*Pikovaya dama (Pique Dame)*]. Opera in three acts, op.68, by PYOTR IL'YICH TCHAIKOVSKY to a libretto by MODEST IL'YICH TCHAIKOVSKY and the composer after ALEXANDER SERGEYEVICH PUSHKIN's novella (1833); St Petersburg, Mariinsky Theatre, 7/19 December 1890.

Gherman [Hermann]	tenor
Count Tomsky	baritone
Prince Yeletsky	baritone
Countess ***	mezzo-soprano
Liza [Lisa] *her granddaughter*	soprano
Pauline *Lisa's confidante*	contralto
Chekalinsky	tenor
Surin	bass
Chaplitsky	tenor
Narumov	bass
Master of Ceremonies	tenor
Catherine the Great	silent
Governess	mezzo-soprano
Masha *Lisa's maid*	soprano
Make-believe Commander	spoken (boy)
In the intermède (Act 2)	
Prilepa/Chloë	soprano
Milovzor/Daphnis (Pauline)	contralto
Zlatogor/Plutus (Tomsky)	baritone

Nursemaids, governesses, wet-nurses, strollers, children, gamblers etc.

Setting St Petersburg at the close of the 18th century

Modest Tchaikovsky's libretto was originally prepared not for his brother but for the minor composer Nikolay Semyonovich Klenovsky (1853–1915), then a conductor at the Bol'shoy Theatre, Moscow, who had received a commission from Ivan Vsevolozhsky, the Intendant, to write an opera on Pushkin's famous story. Pyotr Tchaikovsky had expressed an interest in the tale as early as 1885, but once a lesser composer had been offered Modest's libretto by the theatre directorate he had to wait until not only Klenovsky but also Nikolay Solov'yov had exercised their right of refusal before he could tackle it himself.

The entire opera was composed in Florence in 44 days of frenzied inspiration (30 January–14 March 1890), the composer freely supplementing his brother's text at the dictate of his hectic muse. By mid-June the orchestration was complete and the opera had been submitted to the theatre and to Tchaikovsky's publisher Jurgenson. The inordinate speed of composition was matched by an unusually tight construction and a quality of imagination unmatched in its way in the whole of Russian opera. The composer's many letters to his brother librettist abound with expressions of happy amazement at his own powers of disciplined invention: 'Either I am horribly mistaken, Modya, or the opera is a masterpiece' was the final verdict – one which the international operatic audience has ratified. Earlier he had written 'I am so far firmly convinced that *The Queen of Spades* is a good, and mainly, a very original piece, speaking not from the musical point of view but in general'.

Pushkin's novella, at barely 10 000 words a masterpiece of 'cold fury' (Dostoyevsky) and ironic narrative dispatch, might have seemed a natural for brisk one-act treatment, insofar as a study in ugly monomania suggested musical adaptation at all: having overheard that a certain old countess possesses the secret of winning infallibly at cards, an impoverished young officer resolves to wrest it from her. Under the pretext of a rendezvous with his quarry's young ward and poor relation in whom he has been feigning a romantic interest, he gains entry to the countess's house and hides in her bedroom, where, in Pushkin's unforgettable phrase, he is 'witness to the repulsive mysteries of her toilette'. He frightens the old woman to death with his entreaties but is later visited by her ghost, who discloses the secret ('Three, Seven, Ace'). When he tries to play, however, he finds he is holding the Queen of Spades in place of the ace, and loses not only his fortune but his mind.

The libretto Tchaikovsky set, composed on order from the Imperial Theatres and reflecting many of Vsevolozhsky's suggestions and demands, opened up the terse, tense narrative with all kinds of leisurely interpolations that at times appear to dwarf the original plot altogether; transposed the action into the 19th-century fairyland known as 'the 18th century' so as to provide a pretext for the most sumptuous interpolation of all; and supplemented Pushkin's proto-Poeish 'horror' with an admixture of more typically operatic 'tragedy' – a genuine romantic intrigue between officer (Hermann) and ward (Lisa), now the countess's granddaughter and his social superior, which ends in their double suicide.

For these deeds the Tchaikovsky brothers have been castigated many times over by guardians of literature, second-guessed by a Soviet production team under Meyerhold (their attempted 'repushkinization' of the opera was shown at the Leningrad Malïy Theatre in 1935), and rebuked by puritanical but unimaginative critics who cannot hear the music to which the cannily adulterated libretto gave rise. What critics have been slow to recognize is precisely what the composer meant when he wrote with such uncharacteristic confidence about his originality: Tchaikovsky's penultimate opera is the first and possibly the greatest masterpiece of musical surrealism.

The première was conducted by Eduard Nápravník, with Nikolay Figner as Hermann, Ivan Mel'nikov as Tomsky, Mariya Slavina as the Countess and Medea Mei-Figner as Lisa.

ACT 1.i *Spring: Square in the Summer Garden* Nursemaids, governesses and wet-nurses are enjoying the weather along with their charges, who are playing catch, jumping with skipping ropes, playing at soldiers (this last possibly borrowed from *Carmen*, Tchaikovsky's favourite opera) and so on. Two officers, Chekalinsky and Surin, enter discussing the strange behaviour of their friend Hermann, who watches them gamble the whole night through but never plays himself. Hermann enters with Count Tomsky, who asks him why he is so glum. Out of their conversation, prefigured by the solo cello, Hermann's 'arioso' – actually a rather formal aria in two parts – emerges, in which he confesses he has fallen in love with a beauty above his station ('Ya imeni yeyo ne znayu': 'I don't even know her name'). They wander off. The crowd which has been gathering breaks into a paean to the glorious weather. Hermann and Tomsky wander back in time to congratulate the radiant Prince Yeletsky on his engagement, but to himself Hermann broods enviously in a curious little near-canonic duet with his happy friend.

The Countess enters with Lisa; Yeletsky rushes to greet his betrothed and, to his horror, Hermann recognizes her as the object of his hopeless obsession. All the principals now briefly join in individual though simultaneous expressions of dread ('Mne strashno!': 'I'm frightened!'): Lisa and the Countess of Hermann, whose strange behaviour they have noticed; Hermann of the awful old Countess; Tomsky, knowing Hermann, on Lisa's account; Yeletsky on seeing Lisa's unaccountable change of mood. This tiny quintet has aptly been called the opera's dramatic 'knot'. Surin and Chekalinsky ask Tomsky why the old woman, rich as she is, never gambles. Tomsky regales them with the tale, foreshadowed in the orchestral introduction, of 'The Three Cards' – the secret winning combination imparted to the Countess by the Count of Saint-Germain, long ago when she was known to all of Paris as 'la Vénus moscovite', through which she recouped some ruinous losses on condition that she never play again. It is just an old canard (as its setting in three formal strophes with refrain assures us), but Hermann overhears it with great agitation. His friends tease him with the end of the story, a prophecy that the Countess, who has revealed the secret only twice in her life, will die at the hands of the third, 'who, full of love's fiery passion, will come to learn the three cards by force'. A thunderstorm breaks out; all run for cover, leaving Hermann alone on stage, oblivious. He vows that he will win Lisa from Prince Yeletsky by means of the cards.

1.ii *Lisa's room; a door to the balcony overhanging the garden* At the harpsichord (piano in the pit), Lisa accompanies herself and Pauline in a setting of Vasily Zhukovsky's lyric 'Uzh vecher, oblakov pomerknuli kraya' ("Tis evening, the edges of the clouds have darkened', 1806). Their girl friends having received their song with enthusiasm, Lisa asks Pauline to sing a solo; she complies, after hesitating, with a gloomy *memento mori* by Konstantin Batyushkov ('Podrugi milïye': 'Dear girls', 1810); bemused at her own choice, Pauline proposes to offset the lowering mood with a merry *russkaya* (to an imitation folk text by the composer) in which all join, clapping and dancing gaily: 'Nu-ka, svetik-Mashen'ka, tï potesh', poplyashi' ('Well now, Masha, sweetie-pie, amuse us, go into your dance'). The noisy dancing *à la russe* brings the Governess on stage with a stern reproof from the Countess at the girls' lack of breeding ('Fi, quel genre, mesdames!'). She gives them a little lesson in *noblesse oblige*, then breaks up the party. After the guests leave, Lisa goes out to the balcony and expresses to the night her ambivalent feelings about her bridegroom (arioso: 'Zachem zhe eti slyozï': 'But why these tears'). At its height she is surprised by Hermann, who suddenly appears out of the shadows. A new wave of dramatic tension begins to build. The couple's first exchange is accompanied by music previously heard at the climax of the orchestral introduction, and for that reason obviously the authentic love music of the opera. Still, Hermann must win Lisa over in good conscience; he delivers an arioso on one knee ('Prosti, prelestnoye sozdan'ye': 'Forgive me, adorable creature'). It, too, is broken off at the climax when the Countess knocks on the balcony door from inside the house and orders Lisa to go to bed; at the sound of her voice Hermann thinks obsessively about Tomsky's prophecy regarding the 'third man'. The final portion of the scene, an amplified reprise of the first exchange, ends with Lisa's declaration, 'I am thine!'

ACT 2.i *Masquerade ball in a rich house* The scene begins with a chorus, the first of the scene's many 'neoclassical' stylizations. The Master of Ceremonies invites the guests outdoors to see a fireworks display. Left alone, Yeletsky sings to Lisa an aria, to words by the composer ('Ya vas lyublyu bezmerno': 'I love you beyond measure'), interpolated in order to place Yeletsky among the major characters; from the first a popular recital item, it is strongly reminiscent of Prince Gremin's aria in *Yevgeny Onegin*. Hermann wanders on stage, reading a note from Lisa requesting a rendezvous; his agitation is reflected in the syncopations and the sudden halts that characterize the orchestral accompaniment to this scene throughout. Surin and Chekalinsky steal up behind him and tease him with whispers naming him as the 'third' who will wrest the secret of the three cards; Hermann is dumbfounded.

The Master of Ceremonies announces a pastoral play, 'The Faithful Shepherdess', an extended *divertissement* 'à la Mozart' based on the story of Daphnis (Milovzor, sung by Pauline) and Chloë (Prilepa): (*a*) 'Chorus of Shepherds and Shepherdesses', a parody of the peasant chorus from *Don Giovanni*; (*b*) Dance of the Shepherds and Shepherdesses, a 'sarabande' (in 4/4 time!); (*c*) 'Duet of Prilepa and Milovzor', a take-off of 'Plaisir d'amour' (by J.-P.-E. Martini), in which the lovers declare themselves; and (*d*) 'Tempo di minuetto', in which Plutus (Zlatogor, played by Tomsky) arrives, bearing fantastic gifts, in a golden chariot, but cannot entice Chloë from her shepherd love; the intermède concludes with general rejoicing, including reprises of (*c*) and (*a*). There is a brief confrontation between Hermann and his teasing friends, and an encounter with Lisa in which she tells him how to reach the Countess's bedroom on his way to hers, giving him the final proof of his main chance; then the guests burst into frenzied acclamation at the sudden appearance of the tsaritsa herself, Catherine the Great, in their midst.

2.ii *The Countess's bedroom, lit by icon-lamps* Hermann has stolen into the room; his breathless monologue on the fate that has brought him there is accompanied throughout by a magnificently sustained orchestral ostinato comprising three elements in everchanging juxtapositions, a strikingly modern concept. Footsteps announce the arrival of the Countess and a bevy of attendants who sing her to her armchair. She waves them off, expressing her irritation at the *mauvais ton* she encountered at the ball; her mind goes back to her youth and she sings herself to sleep to the anachronistic strains of a tune ('Je crains de lui parler la nuit'), which Tchaikovsky copied out of *Richard Coeur-de-lion*, an *opéra comique* by Grétry (1784). For the second time Hermann reveals himself as intruder, this time rousing the Countess, pleading with her, encountering silence, threatening her with his revolver, at last finding her dead. Lisa enters, drawn by the noise. Horrified both at the scene she has discovered and at the thought that Hermann was interested in her only as a conduit, she orders him out. Having lost everything, he rushes out in despair, the air heavy with leitmotifs.

ACT 3.i *Hermann's barracks room, late at night* After an orchestral fantasy evocative of Hermann's ravings, he is seen tormented by conscience, obsessively recalling the Countess's obsequies and rereading a forgiving letter from Lisa in which she insists on a midnight meeting. He hears footsteps, the audience hears a whole-tone scale, and the Countess's ghost heavily enters the room, telling him she is there against her will, enjoining him to marry Lisa, and finally imparting the secret of the cards: Three, Seven, Ace.

3.ii *An embankment* Lisa is waiting, distraught, fearing Hermann's failure to appear, which will finally establish his depravity and consequently her own; at last, exhausted, she reflects on her lost happiness in a short, perfectly shaped aria that has become a favourite of the Russian recital stage ('Akh, istomilas' ya gorem': 'Ah, I am worn out by grief'). The clock in a nearby fortress tower strikes midnight and Lisa laments the confirmation of her fears in what sounds at first like the cabaletta to the preceding arioso ('Tak eto pravda!': 'So it's true!'). But Hermann arrives and quells her misgivings (she responds to his appearance with a phrase that seems to quote Tatyana's Letter Scene in *Yevgeny Onegin*, when she sings, 'Resolve my doubts'). Their momentary idyll ('O da, minovali stradan'ya': 'Oh yes, the pain is gone', based on a leisurely 9/8 variation of the main love theme) is shattered when Hermann announces he is on his way to the gaming house, having learnt the secret from Lisa's grandmother's ghost. He rushes off and Lisa, knowing him now to be hopelessly insane, jumps from the embankment and drowns herself in the Neva.

3.iii *The gaming house; supper in progress* The assembled players give free rein to their high spirits. They welcome Yeletsky with surprise; he admits he is there to compensate his loss of Lisa. All call for Tomsky to sing; his song 'Yesli b milïye devitsï tak mogli letat' kak ptitsï' ('If pretty girls could fly like birds') is followed by a gamblers' chorus. Hermann arrives, makes straight for the gaming table, to everyone's delighted surprise, and places an unheard-of 40 000-ruble bet. It is reluctantly accepted; his three wins as per the formula. He doubles; his seven wins. Before staking his last card (against Yeletsky, who eagerly volunteers

himself as nemesis) Hermann sings a maniacal song whose incipit could serve as the opera's epigraph ('Chto nasha zhizn'? Igra!': 'What is our life? A game!'); finally his 'ace' turns out to be the Queen of Spades, which – he is certain – looks back at him sarcastically with the Countess's face. Mad, he stabs himself; the opera ends with a brief chorus of ritual farewell.

*   *   *

Reasons for associating Tchaikovsky's phantasmal romanticism with the incipient symbolist movement include a network of sinister doubles that haunt the opera on every level and the many subtly drawn correspondences (to use Baudelaire's word) between the surface action and its occult underpinnings. To analyse Tomsky's ballad from Act 1 scene i as a source of leitmotifs, for example, is to penetrate in unexpectedly ironic fashion from the one level straight to the other. A jovial set piece characterized by an especially 'enlightened' formal symmetry yields up, on the one hand, a phrase ('x') that, tortured and skewed beyond belief (but not beyond recognition), governs all those moments in which Hermann makes contact, through the Countess, with the world beyond (or it, through her, with him), until, in the last scene, it crushes him with the full weight of the orchestra. On the other hand, the ballad's refrain ('y') resonates as a sinister double with Hermann's just-completed cavatina, linking his love for Lisa with the fatal imperative that will doom them both (ex.1).

Another way of invoking malign destiny is by the use of intertextual resonance: for example, the adaptation of Tomsky's ballad to the rhythm of the main theme in the first movement of Tchaikovsky's recently completed Fifth Symphony, whose motto clearly echoes as well through the E minor orchestral music at the beginning

Ex.1

Act 1 scene i, Tomsky's ballad

Od – nazh – dï v Ver–sa – le 'au jeu de la Reine'...
['Once at Versailles 'au jeu de la Reine . . .

[refrain]
...tri kar – tï, tri kar–tï, tri kar – tï!
. . . three cards, three cards, three cards!']

Introduction
cl, bn

Symphony no. 5, 1st movt
cl, bn

Act 1 scene i, Hermann's arioso
Ya i – me – ni e – yo ne zna–yu
['I do not know her name']

Queen of Spades, Act 1 scene ii, Countess and Lisa, accompaniment

Act 2 scene ii, Hermann steals up to the countess

Ex.2

Act 1 scene ii, Pauline's romance

Po - dru - gi___ mi - lï-ye, po - dru - gi___

mi - lï-ye v bes-pech... etc.

['Sweet companions . . .']

Act 1 scene ii, Hermann's confession [transposed]

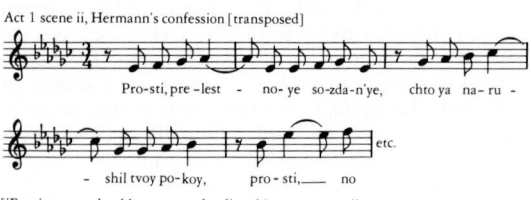

Pro-sti, pre -lest - no-ye so-zda-n'ye, chto ya na - ru -

- shil tvoy po- koy, pro - sti,___ no etc.

['Forgive me, adorable creature, for disturbing your peace']

and the end of the opera's penultimate scene, which ends in Lisa's suicide. An intertextual linkage within the opera itself – and one that goes far towards explaining both the sheer abundance of genre and digression in the work and its uncanny equiponderance with the terse main line of action – comes when Hermann confesses his love for Lisa in Act 1 scene ii to an unwitting echo of Pauline's melancholy romance. All at once the opera's heroine is identified with the dead maiden in the song; fate has left another calling card (ex.2).

RICHARD TARUSKIN

Queensbury. American town, in the state of New York; it is the home of the Lake George Opera Festival. Founded in 1962, the festival moved from a small barn at Diamond Point on Lake George, in the scenic Adirondack region, to its present home in the one-level, 875-seat Queensbury High School Auditorium three years after its inception. Although the Lake George company performs primarily in Queensbury, it occasionally offers fully staged productions nearby in the state capital of Albany, in Schenectady and in Saratoga Springs. Three to seven operas are produced annually in repertory, for four to six weeks each summer. The company's threefold purpose is to present opera in English, to search out and employ fine young singers, and to perform new American works.

During its three decades, Lake George has produced more than 70 operas, operettas, music-theatre and children's works. Two dozen have been by American composers; seven, including Richard Waigo's *The Seduction of a Lady* (1985) and Kirke Mechem's *Tartuffe* (1982), received their premières (a workshop production in the case of the latter) at Lake George. Six seasons in the 1980s and early 90s included at least one new American work. The company maintains an apprentice artist programme, the American Lyric Theatre Young Artists Program, which provides training, coaching and performing opportunities for young singers. The festival has given impetus to the careers of singers including Jerry Hadley, Johanna Meier and Florence Quivar.

ROBERT V. PALMER

Queen's Theatre. The name of the King's Theatre, London, during Queen Anne's reign; *see* LONDON, §II, 2.

Nikolay and Medea Figner as Hermann and Lisa in the original production of Tchaikovsky's 'The Queen of Spades' at the Mariinsky Theatre, St Petersburg, 7/19 December 1890

Queler, Eve (*b* New York, 1 Jan 1936). American conductor. She studied at Mannes College, New York, and with Susskind and Slatkin at St Louis and Markevitch and Blomstedt in Europe. After working as musical assistant with New York City Opera and the Metropolitan Opera National Company, she founded in 1968 and has since directed the Opera Orchestra of New York, the main focus of her work. Based from 1971 at Carnegie Hall, it has given regular concert performances of rarely heard operas (many of them New York premières), including Donizetti's *Parisina* and *Gemma di Vergy*, Verdi's *Aroldo*, Massenet's *Le Cid*, Boito's *Nerone*, Puccini's *Edgar*, Strauss's *Guntram* and Respighi's *Belfagor*; some were also recorded. Her conducting début with New York City Opera was in 1978 in *Le nozze di Figaro*, and that year the University of Maryland created for her a National Opera Orchestra Workshop project. She has also conducted at Barcelona, Las Palmas, Lyons, Nice, Prague, Budapest, Sydney and Caracas, and in several other American cities. An authoritative and dynamic conductor, she communicates her enthusiasm for out-of-the-way repertory to her audiences.

ELIZABETH WOOD, NOËL GOODWIN

Querelle des Bouffons. A musical and literary dispute waged in Paris between 1752 and 1754 over the respective merits of French and Italian opera. The performance at the Opéra, on 1 August 1752, of Pergolesi's intermezzo *La serva padrona* by an Italian troupe under the direction of Eustachio Bambini is commonly believed to have instigated this controversy, but the seeds of the crisis had in fact been sown months before the Italians' arrival in Paris. The subsequent quarrel, which engaged many leading philosophical figures of the time and resulted in the publication of over 60 letters and pamphlets, merely used Bambini's troupe, popularly known as the 'Bouffons', as a cover for voicing ideas of a profound political significance.

By the middle of the 18th century the Opéra had lost much of its former glory. Far more old works than new had held the repertory together, and an impasse had been reached in that the public regarded Lully's operas as outmoded yet those by Rameau too bold and daring. This artistic crisis ran hand in hand with financial difficulties, substantial debts having accrued over several years as a result of administrative problems. In 1749, therefore, Louis XV handed the privilege of the Opéra to the city of Paris, a political move intended to ease the pressure on the royal purse-strings. Alterations to the repertory, designed to restore public support and fight off insolvency, were introduced, and it is against this background of change that the arrival of the Bouffons may in part be explained.

In May 1752 Bambini's comedians had been engaged to perform for several months in Rouen. The Opéra administrators probably revoked this agreement and summoned the troupe to Paris in order to dampen the pretensions of provincial theatres and ensure that their own privilege was not infringed. Even more complicated motives may have underlain this decision: either the *inspecteurs-généraux* of the Opéra felt the need to introduce an element of much-needed novelty into their repertory, particularly in the wake of the public exchange of letters between Grimm (*Lettre de M. Grimm sur Omphale*) and Rousseau (*Lettre à M. Grimm au sujet des remarques ajoutées à sa Lettre sur Omphale*) in the early months of 1752, questioning the substance of French opera; or, by deliberately inviting an unknown and obscure band of Italian comedians to present a limited repertory of short, farcical pieces in the dignified setting of the Opéra, they may have hoped to quell the popular support for Italian music that had been gathering throughout the first half of the 18th century. Whatever their motives, the Bouffons were certainly not an overnight success. The *Mercure de France* (September 1752) noted that for the first performance the troupe was clearly unaccustomed to its spacious surroundings and lacked vivacity. The review also criticized the recitative and some of the *ariettes*, which were apparently to the taste only of 'un petit nombre de connoisseurs'. Cuts were implemented before the second performance, which met with greater public approval. Thereafter the troupe gradually won over Parisian audiences, although the *Mercure* still voiced some reservations: 'il est à souhaiter cependant qu'ils n'excédent pas dans la charge'.

Masson (1945) has already identified Grimm's *Lettre ... sur Omphale* as a continuation of the earlier controversy between the Lullistes and the Ramistes rather than as the opening salvo in the Querelle des Bouffons. The first exchange of pamphlets in this new debate did not take place until January 1753, with the publication of Grimm's *Le petit prophète de Boehmischbroda*. (D'Holbach's *Lettre à une dame d'un certain age*, published in November 1752, had elicited no rejoinders.) The Bouffons had, by this time, spent nearly six months in Paris without inspiring the *littérateurs* to take up their pens. Why, therefore, the literary dispute should have erupted at this point is a complex matter. Certainly, one impetus for the pamphlet war was the success, at the Opéra in January 1753, of Mondonville's *pastorale héroïque Titon et Aurore*, a success deliberately engineered by the supporters of French opera (see Pougin 1860). But of more significance was the severe

constitutional crisis that shook France at exactly the same time.

Since the early years of the 18th century, Jansenists and Jesuits had been arguing over the controversial papal bull, *Unigenitus* (1713). Matters came to a head around 1750 when a radical group within the episcopacy began to refuse sacraments to those opposed to the bull. (Appellants were often, although not always, Jansenists.) The Parlement de Paris, whose Jansenist sympathies dated back to the Fronde, began to intervene, only to have their judgments continually annulled by the king's council, which comprised many Jesuit supporters. By August 1752 the two sides had begun a fierce exchange of pamphlets; in December the Parlement attempted to bring the Archbishop of Paris to trial. In February 1753 the king expressly forbade the *parlementaires* to continue with their legal proceedings; they ignored his edict and, in May 1753, were sent into exile.

The stance of the *parlementaires* embodied a real challenge to royal absolutism. The leaders of the Enlightenment realized that the same line of attack was available to them if disguised as a musical dispute. Opera, since its inception in France, had been an overt celebration of absolutism. The transfer of allegiance in taste from French to Italian music was therefore understood to symbolize freedom of thought by the individual and weakening of the monarch's influence. Support for the Bouffons implied criticism of the way in which the king controlled not only the arts but all aspects of French life: 'dans le Dictionnaire de certaines gens, Bouffoniste, Républicain, Frondeur, Athée ... sont autant de termes synonimes' (D'Alembert, *De la liberté de la musique*, 1759). The mock-biblical style of *Le petit prophète*, together with Grimm's deliberate identification of his 'prophet' as a Jesuit, underlines the musical and political analogies. The 25 known responses to this pamphlet were, in all probability, a direct imitation of events in the political arena. These comprised the first real stage of the quarrel; the second, inspired by Rousseau's vitriolic *Lettre sur la musique française* (November 1753), elicited over 30 further replies and led the dispute to new ground. Arguments centred around vindications or condemnations of Rousseau's strong personal views; opinions of the Bouffons and comparisons of French and Italian operatic styles took second place to the defence or attack of French language and prosody.

Supporters of the national style, aptly named the *coin du roi*, were quick to assert the dramatic power of the *tragédie lyrique*, the nobility of its declamatory recitative and its close matching of music and poetry. They were critical of the overemphasis Italian composers had placed on the aria and the resulting weakness of simple recitative. The *coin de la reine*, strongly influenced by the Encyclopedist camp, preferred the graceful charm and clear harmonic structure of Italian cantilena. They ridiculed the manner in which French composers crammed their works with complicated, elaborate harmonies and overdeveloped, declamatory recitative, all at the expense of melody. Laying aside the political implications of the quarrel, its participants argued largely along the lines of whether opera should be regarded as a primarily musical, or primarily literary, phenomenon. Few, however, seem to have realized the futility of comparing two vastly different genres: the one light, farcical and comic, the other noble, elevated and tragic.

The exchange of pamphlets ceased one month before the Bouffons left Paris in March 1754, which would suggest that literary polemics were not directly accountable for the troupe's departure. The Italians did not leave in a blaze of glory, because their last production, Leo's *I viaggiatori*, proved unsuccessful with Parisian audiences; but they had spent some 20 months in France and given over 150 performances of 13 different works (many of which were not intermezzos but cleverly adapted *opere buffe* accommodating up to seven characters). Essentially a wandering band of comedians, the Bouffons probably wanted either to move on to another city or to return to Italy. What they thought of their eventful stay in Paris remains unknown because they took no active part in the literary dispute; but they certainly owed the highpoint of their careers to a chance combination of factors. Crises at the Opéra, major political upheavals and philosophical agitation by the Encyclopedists brought them success where previous Italian troupes in 1729 and 1746 had failed.

The position of the Opéra vis-à-vis the Bouffons was extremely awkward. On the one hand, the Italian troupe usurped the prowess of the native *tragédie lyrique*, while on the other, it brought valuable revenue to an establishment in considerable financial straits. The Opéra may have emerged as the temporary victor in the Querelle des Bouffons since the *tragédie lyrique* continued to dominate its repertory for a further two decades; but the Bouffons proved highly influential in shaping a native style of comic opera in France, and by the late 1750s the first generation of *opéra comique* composers – Egidio Duni, Pierre-Alexandre Monsigny and François-André Danican Philidor – were making their mark. This new genre was eventually to rival the established *tragédie lyrique* in popularity and success, for which, as Rousseau observed in *Les confessions* (1782), the Querelle des Bouffons was entirely responsible: 'Quelque temps avant qu'on donnât *Le devin du village*, il était arrivé à Paris des Bouffons italiens, qu'on fit jouer sur le théâtre de l'Opéra sans prévoir l'effet qu'ils y allaient faire … elles ne laissèrent pas de faire à l'opéra français un tort qu'il n'a jamais réparé'.

A. Pougin: 'Mondonville et la guerre des coins', *Revue et gazette musicale de Paris*, xxvii (1860), 193–4, 201–3, 217–8, 225–6, 241–2

E. Hirschberg: *Die Encyclopädisten und die französische Oper im 18. Jahrhundert* (Leipzig, 1903)

L. de La Laurencie: 'La grande saison italienne de 1752: les Bouffons', *BSIM*, viii/6 (1912), 18–33; viii/7 (1912), 13–22

L. Richebourg: *Contribution à l'histoire de la 'Querelle des Bouffons'* (Paris, 1937)

N. Boyer: *La Guerre des Bouffons et la musique française* (Paris, 1945)

P.-M. Masson: 'La lettre sur Omphale', *RdM*, xxvii (1945), 1–19

A. R. Oliver: *The Encyclopedists as Critics of Music* (New York, 1947)

A. M. Whittall: *La Querelle des Bouffons* (diss., U. of Cambridge, 1963)

S. Sacaluga: 'Diderot, Rousseau, et la querelle musicale de 1752: nouvelle mise au point', *Diderot Studies*, x (1968), 133–73

D. Launay, ed.: *La Querelle des Bouffons* (Geneva, 1973) [facs. of 61 pamphlets pubd 1752–4]

——: 'La Querelle des Bouffons et ses incidences sur la musique', *IMSCR, xii: Berkeley 1977*, 225–33

D. Heartz: 'Diderot et le théâtre lyrique: "le nouveau stile", proposé par *Le neveu de Rameau*', *RdM*, lxiv (1978), 229–52

W. Weber: '*La musique ancienne* in the Waning of the Ancien Régime', *Journal of Modern History*, lvi (1984), 58–88

E. Cook: *The Operatic Ensemble in France, 1673–1775* (diss., U. of East Anglia, 1989), 76–127

M. Noiray: 'L'opera italiana in Francia nel secolo xviii', *SOI*, ii (forthcoming)
ELISABETH COOK

Querzoli [Quercioli] Laschi, Anna Maria (*b* Bologna, *fl* 1737–68). Italian soprano. One of the most acclaimed singers of *opera buffa* in the mid-18th century, she sang in central and northern Italy and elsewhere in Europe with her husband, Filippo Laschi. Initially she sang serious roles (Mitrane in Hasse's *Demetrio*, 1737, Rimini), but she soon began to specialize in comedy, particularly after appearing in Latilla's *La finta cameriera* (1741, Modena) with the Roman bass Francesco Baglioni, who introduced her to the most flourishing *opera buffa* circuits. In 1743 she sang in Venice in a company led by Pellegrino Gaggiotti and a group of Florentine singers that included her future husband, and with these she visited Brussels (1750 and 1755) and London (1748–9 and 1766–8), where she was admired by Burney. She used the title of *virtuosa di camera* of Duke Charles of Lorraine and Bar.

P. Weiss: 'La diffusione del repertorio operistico nell'Italia del Settecento: il caso dell'opera buffa', *Civiltà teatrale e settecento emiliano*, ed. S. Davoli (Bologna, 1986), 241–56
FRANCO PIPERNO

Quesnel, (Louis) Joseph (Marie) (*b* St Malo, 15 Nov 1746; *d* Montreal, 3 July 1809). Canadian composer and playwright of French birth. After visiting several exotic countries as a young sailor, he arrived in Canada unintentionally in 1779 when his ship, carrying supplies to the USA, was captured by the British off Nova Scotia. He was allowed to settle in Montreal and later moved to nearby Boucherville. A well-educated amateur anxious to promote music and theatre in a pioneer society, he was a co-founder of Montreal's Théâtre de Société in 1789. On 14 January 1790 this company gave the première of the 'comédie en prose, mêlée d'ariettes' *Colas et Colinette, ou Le bailli dupé* with music and words by Quesnel, the first Canadian opera. After revivals in Quebec in 1805 and 1807 the text was published there in 1808, but the music printing did not continue beyond the first few pages of proof. Only the vocal and second violin parts survive in manuscript (in *C-Qsl*); the accompaniment was reconstructed by Godfrey Ridout for a modern revival in 1963, and published at Toronto in 1974. Quesnel also wrote the words and music for the comic opera *Lucas et Cécile*, of which only the vocal parts survive (*Qsl*); the work's 16 musical numbers were reconstructed in 1989–90 by John Beckwith and a piano-vocal score published at Quebec City. Quesnel's church and instrumental music is lost.

See also COLAS ET COLINETTE, OU LE BAILLI DUPÉ.

*

EMC (H. Kallmann, D. Ménard and A. Poussart)
HELMUT KALLMANN

Quiet Flows the Don [*Tikhiy Don* ('The Quiet Don')]. Opera in four acts by IVAN IVANOVICH DZERZHINSKY to a libretto by Leonid Ivanovich Dzerzhinsky on motifs from Mikhail Alexandrovich Sholokhov's novel;

Dzerzhinsky based his first opera on books 1 and 2 of Mikhail Sholokhov's as yet incomplete novel *Tikhiy Don*. As it turned out, composer and novelist resolved the plot in different ways. Dzerzhinsky entered his opera in a contest sponsored by the Bol'shoy Theatre and the newspaper *Komsomol'skaya pravda*. When the results were made known in 1934, there was no inkling that *Quiet Flows the Don* would soon become a pivotal

Panteley Melekhov	tenor
Il'inichna *his wife*	mezzo-soprano
Grigory ⎫ *their sons*	tenor
Pyotr ⎭	bass
Dasha *Pyotr's wife*	soprano
Lukinichna Korshunova	soprano
Natal'ya *her daughter*	soprano
Mit'ka *her son*	low bass
Aksin'ya	mezzo-soprano
General Listnitsky	bass
Yevgeny *his son*	baritone
Mishuk *Grigory's friend*	tenor
Sashka *the Listnitsky family's coachman*	bass
An Insane Soldier	tenor
Esaul	baritone

Guests, muzhiks, cossacks, soldiers, deserters, prisoners

Setting By the River Don and the Austrian front, 1914–17

opera of the early Soviet period, the prototype Socialist Realist 'song opera': it received no award, and was censured by the jury for its fragmentary libretto, dramaturgical weakness, primitive orchestration and musical monotony. Dmitry Shostakovich, however, recognized in it a glimmer of talent and helped the inexperienced Dzerzhinsky to rework and reorchestrate his opera. In gratitude, Dzerzhinsky dedicated the work to him. Shostakovich also brought the opera to the attention of Samuil Samosud, artistic director and chief conductor of the Malïy Theatre in Leningrad, who accepted it for production and helped develop its stage potential. Samosud conducted the première in October 1935.

Two months after the première the Malïy company went on tour to Moscow, and on 17 January 1936 Stalin and a delegation of high government officials attended a performance of Dzerzhinsky's opera. In the final interval Stalin summoned the composer and principals to his box for a creative discussion, which was widely reported in the press. Despite some criticism, Stalin gave positive marks to the ideological work of the theatre and its efforts on behalf of Soviet opera. Nine days later Stalin and his entourage went to the opera again, this time to see a performance of Shostakovich's *Lady Macbeth of the Mtsensk District*, a work which had been playing with enormous success for two years. On this occasion Stalin did not stay to talk with the creators; indeed he left before the end of the performance. Two days later the notorious unsigned editorial 'Muddle instead of Music' – which savagely condemned Shostakovich's opera – was published in *Pravda*. The sequence of events left little doubt that this was a carefully calculated campaign to exert aesthetic control over the creativity not just of Soviet musicians, but of the entire artistic élite; the operas of Dzerzhinsky and Shostakovich became synonymous, respectively, with the aesthetic antipodes of Socialist Realism and formalism.

Among the characteristics of *Quiet Flows the Don* which contributed to its official recognition is its unpretentious and immediately accessible tunefulness; much of its melodic inspiration derives from simple folk or genre types with well-defined tonal, rhythmic and structural features. Complex ensemble numbers and dissonance are conspicuously absent. The revolutionary

dramatic theme and its heroic treatment are clearly also of importance: the hero, Grigory, from a rich cossack family, rejects the heritage of his class for the love of a poor girl and, concurrently, develops into a committed Bolshevik. In the context of emotional conflict, personal suffering and sacrifice, the uplifting spirit of revolutionary virtue triumphs.

While Shostakovich's opera disappeared immediately from the boards, *Quiet Flows the Don* enjoyed a burst of new productions. In the next few years it was staged twice in Moscow as well as in another 22 cities throughout the USSR. The opera was first performed in a revised version at the Malïy Opera Theatre, Leningrad, on 7 November 1947.

ACT 1.i Panteley Melekhov has arranged the marriage of his son Grigory to Natal'ya Korshunova, the daughter of a rich cossack. The characteristic colour of wedding songs, exemplified in the chorus 'Okh matushka, toshno mne' ('Oh matushka, I feel terrible') forms the backdrop to the scene. For Grigory, however, the festivities are spoilt by thoughts of his love for Aksin'ya. Consumed by jealousy, Aksin'ya appears at the wedding and registers a claim to Grigory.

1.ii Aksin'ya and Grigory cannot live without each other. Despite the curses of his father, the tears of his mother and wife and the loss of his cossack rights, Grigory leaves his village to begin a new life with Aksin'ya.

ACT 2.i This scene, in contrast with the previous one, is dominated by the activity of the crowd and choral songs. Grigory and Aksin'ya have become labourers at the Listnitsky farm. A crowd gathers at the mill waiting for the flour to be ground. A fight between rich cossacks and poor peasants is interrupted by the arrival of cossack General Listnitsky, who announces that war has broken out. His appeal for all to stand up for the tsar is greeted with silence.

2.ii In the servants' quarters the old coachman, Sashka, entertains the assembly with a lively story fleshed out by clever colouristic details in its accompaniment. Aksin'ya is saddened by the illness of her daughter. The young master of the farm, Yevgeny, tries to seduce her in the strains of a deliberately banal romance, but she rebuffs him coldly; she pines for word from Grigory, now at the front. Natal'ya brings tragic news: Grigory has been killed. Aksin'ya continues to rock the cradle and her lullaby turns to sobbing. She looks at their beloved daughter with grief and suddenly howls: the child has died. Like a hunter tracking his prey, Yevgeny returns. Aksin'ya does not have the strength to resist his caresses.

ACT 3 Near the Austrian front, Grigory unexpectedly returns from the hospital to join his cossack comrades, who have given him up for dead. All miss their families and homes. When Grigory tells them that the tsar has been overthrown, they resolve to quit the senseless war. To the strains of a revolutionary song, the cossacks join the stream of soldiers deserting the front.

ACT 4 On returning home, Grigory learns of the death of his daughter and the faithlessness of Aksin'ya. Overcome with anger, he kills Yevgeny. Grigory forgives Aksin'ya but goes off to join a revolutionary detachment to fight for a new and better life. The concluding chorus of patriotic resolve and inspiration, the marching song 'Ot kraya do kraya' ('From border to border'), became widely popular outside the context of the opera.

'A Quiet Place'
(Bernstein): scene from
the original production at
Jones Hall, Houston, 17
June 1983, with (left to
right) Chester Ludgin as
Sam, Timothy Nolen as
Junior, Peter Kazaras as
François and Sheri
Greenawald as Dede

    *   *   *

The early success of *Quiet Flows the Don* led many composers to emulate its 'song opera' formula, though with little success. Dzerzhinsky, catapulted so unexpectedly into the annals of operatic fame, tried repeatedly throughout the rest of his career to duplicate his initial success, but, even though he wrote three more operas on works by Sholokhov, including a revised continuation of *Quiet Flows the Don* (*Grigory Melekhov*, 1967), he was never able to satisfy the heightened expectations.   LAUREL E. FAY

Quiet Place, A. Opera in one act by LEONARD BERNSTEIN to a libretto by STEPHEN WADSWORTH; Houston, Jones Hall, 17 June 1983 (revised in three acts, incorporating *Trouble in Tahiti*; Milan, Teatro alla Scala, 19 June 1984).

An estranged family reunites for the first time in 20 years at the funeral of the mother, Dinah, killed in a car accident and survived by her husband Sam (baritone). Their son Junior (baritone) and daughter Dede (soprano) arrive from Canada, with Dede's husband François (tenor), who used to be Junior's lover. Confrontations give way to an outburst from Junior, a sign of his longstanding mental disturbance. At home that night, the four of them recall their history with each other and with Dinah. The next morning, after breakfast and games in the garden – Dinah's 'quiet place' – their anger with each other finally gives way to reconciliation. *A Quiet Place* was jointly commissioned by the Houston Grand Opera, the Kennedy Center and La Scala, Milan. Its reception at the Houston première was largely hostile, and this, together with the authors' dissatisfaction, led to a revision for the Milan performances.

The opera was written as a sequel to Bernstein's 1952 opera *Trouble in Tahiti*, which depicts a younger Sam and Dinah (mezzo-soprano) in more satirical vein. In the earlier work, commentary by an amplified jazz trio (soprano, tenor, baritone) encloses a series of short scenes in the couple's day, Sam at work and in the gym, Dinah telling her dreams to a psychiatrist and sentimentally reliving a musical film she's just seen. At home that night they try to talk out their problems, but give up and instead go out to a film of glamorous exotic love, *Trouble in Tahiti*, the same one Dinah has seen. In the original version of *A Quiet Place*, the earlier opera served as a curtain-raiser. In the revision, *Trouble in Tahiti* is incorporated in its entirety into the second act, as the older Sam's reverie. *Trouble in Tahiti* also remains available for separate performance.

The two operas differ markedly in musical style and structure. *Trouble in Tahiti* defines its short scenes through straightforward closed forms, sometimes linked motivically. The trio's prologue in praise of suburban life successfully applies harmonic and rhythmic sophistication to a popular idiom; in a typically Bernstein manner, it is an irresistible example of the genre being mocked. The solo scenes are strophically organized, with special emphasis on Dinah's refrains – the wistful 'There is a garden' and the ultra-typical beguine, 'Island Magic', both of which recur later. The two scenes of Sam and Dinah at home also share musical material, with the morning argument later serving as accompaniment to an evening hymn by the trio, and the soliloquies following that argument transformed into a soaring duet that ends the last scene. The final chord is a verticalization of the duet's theme.

The same chord begins *A Quiet Place*, and the jazz trio of the earlier work finds a counterpart in the off-stage chorus which offers echoes and comments throughout the later opera. Dinah's 'garden' theme returns intermittently as a memory of the missing mother. A considerable part of *A Quiet Place*, however, is independent of the earlier opera. A new chorale theme undergoes a series of variations and transformations before aiding in the final healing, and the overall organization avoids the self-contained, detachable numbers of *Trouble in Tahiti*.

Most noticeable about *A Quiet Place* is the kind of word-music interaction decided on by its authors, a combination of mundane, colloquial, sometimes coarse language with emotionally searching music. At times the conversations suggest speech which has been only heightened, not transformed, by music, with the orchestra providing the depth for which the characters cannot find words. At other times there is a higher degree of stylization; orchestral and word-setting strategies are chosen to meet the needs of the drama. If some of the story skirts banality, that is the risk the authors took in order to find the true feelings masked by inarticulate attempts at communication. Like *Porgy and Bess* and *The Knot Garden*, *A Quiet Place* explores the central 20th-century subject of alienation – from oneself and from those one wants to love.　　　JON ALAN CONRAD

Quilico, Gino (*b* New York, 29 April 1955). Canadian baritone, son of Louis Quilico. He studied music at the University of Toronto and continued vocal studies with his parents, making his début in 1978 as Mr Gobineau in a nationwide television performance of *The Medium*. After engagements in Canada and the USA, in 1980 he made his European début in Paris as Gounod's Mercutio, which brought him a three-year contract at the Opéra. He made his British début as Puccini's Lescaut with Scottish Opera at the 1982 Edinburgh Festival, followed by Valentin at Covent Garden the next year and Escamillo in 1991. Besides many roles in the French and Italian repertory and in Mozart, he has sung in the premières of *L'héritière* (Damase) and *Montségur* (Landowski). He made his Metropolitan début in 1987 as Massenet's Lescaut, returning as Valentin (1990) and Figaro in the première of Corigliano's *The Ghosts of Versailles* (1991). His roles include Yeletsky, and Onegin, which he sang at Montreal in 1992. His high baritone voice, full-toned and pungent in character, is combined with an elegant presence. He has made several video recordings, and his audio recordings include Lescaut, Marcello, Mercutio, Orpheus (Monteverdi), Raimbaud and the title role in *Le roi Arthus*.　　　NOËL GOODWIN

Quilico, Louis (*b* Montreal, 14 Jan 1929). Canadian baritone. He studied at the Montreal Conservatoire, the S Cecilia Academy, Rome, and the Mannes School, New York; his teachers were Lina Pizzolongo (who became his wife) and Martial Singher. He made his débuts with the New York City Opera in 1953, at San Francisco in 1955, Covent Garden in 1961, Paris in 1962, and – as Golaud – at the Metropolitan Opera in 1972, where he soon became a leading member of the company. He was also principal baritone of the Canadian Opera Company. Quilico has a clear and ringing dramatic voice, well suited to Verdi; his roles include Germont, Rigoletto, Posa, Iago, Falstaff and principal roles in Puccini and Donizetti operas. He sang in the premières of Jolivet's *Les coeurs de la matière* (1965) and Milhaud's *La mère coupable* (1966). He has recorded with Nilsson, Sills and Caballé.　　　EZRA SCHABAS

Quilter, Roger (*b* Brighton, 1 Nov 1877; *d* London, 21 Sept 1953). English composer. He was educated at Eton, then studied under Knorr at the Hoch Conservatory, Frankfurt. He became known as a song composer late in 1900 when his *Songs of the Sea* were given at the Crystal Palace, London. The light opera *Julia* (3, J. Lambourne, lyrics by R. Bennett), based on the courtship of the artist George Morland and Anne, the sister of James Ward the engraver, was performed at Covent Garden on 3 December 1936, conducted by Albert Coates. It was not a success, no doubt partly because it fell between genres, being too sentimental for an opera audience and too integral a score for devotees of Ivor Novello. Its best moments, such as the Act 2 gavotte, are excellent light music, but as an art song composer, which is how Quilter is best remembered, he was not at home with

refrain structures. Nevertheless, the work was later published as *Love at the Inn*. More popular were the music for the fairy play *Where the Rainbow Ends* and the light orchestral pieces performed at the Promenade Concerts.
　　　STEPHEN BANFIELD

Quinault, Jean-Baptiste-Maurice [l'aîné] (*b* Verdun, 9 Sept 1687; *d* Gien, 30 Aug 1745). French composer and singer. A son of the actor Jean Quinault (1656–1728), he was the eldest of five children, all active in the theatre. He made his début as an actor at the Comédie Française as Hippolytus in Racine's *Phèdre* on 6 May 1712. He retired with a pension on 22 March 1733, but returned for three performances the following year. Although Voltaire chose him for leading roles in his tragedies, he was most applauded for comic roles. His gift for comic characterization is seen in his music for M. A. Legrand's *Impromptu de la folie* (1725).

He composed more than 24 *divertissements* and *intermèdes* for the French stage from 1714 to 1732 (listed in *La MusicaD*). They include music for plays by Legrand, P.-C. Roy, Louis Fuzelier, S.-J. Pellegrin and Molière (*Le bourgeois gentilhomme*, 1716, and *La princesse d'Elide*, 1722). It was not uncommon for Quinault to have composed the music as well as appearing as an actor and singer in a work. His *divertissements* for Roy's comedy *Les captifs* (1714) were described as 'extraordinary, beautiful and well characterized' (*Mercure galant*, October 1714).

Quinault's only work for the Paris Opéra is the *ballet-héroïque Les amours des déesses* (libretto by Fuzelier). At its first performance, 9 August 1729, it consisted of a prologue and three entrées ('Vénus et Adonis', 'Diane et Endimion' and 'Melpomène et Linus'); a fourth entrée, 'L'Aurore et Céphale', was added for the performance on 25 August 1729.　　　JAMES R. ANTHONY

Quinault, Philippe (*b* Paris, bap. 5 June 1635; *d* Paris, 26 Nov 1688). French librettist. He was the principal librettist of Jean-Baptiste Lully. The son of a Parisian baker, he studied law and was certified as a jurist while still in his teens. At the same time he began writing plays; public performances of his works began around 1653. He described the poet Tristan l'Hermite as his teacher and mentor. The traditional belief that he had been Tristan's valet is called into question by evidence that he began a formal Latin education at the age of 11. Through Tristan Quinault met the Duc de Guise, his first patron, and was introduced to the salons of the Précieuses, who influenced his literary style and helped establish his career. In 1660 he married a young widow, whose great wealth permitted him to insinuate himself into the circles of the royal court, and in 1664 he became a royal pensioner. His earliest collaborations with Lully were on court entertainments: the brief eclogue *La grotte de Versailles* (1668) and the *tragédie-ballet Psyché* (1671, with Molière and Pierre Corneille). In 1670 Quinault was elected to the Académie Française, and in 1674 to the Académie des Inscriptions et Belles-Lettres.

In 1672, the year in which Lully acquired the fledgling Paris Opéra, Quinault's career turned definitively away from spoken plays. (His output up until then, besides *La grotte* and *Psyché*, included 17 tragedies, comedies and tragicomedies, along with numerous song texts and poems.) The success of *Cadmus et Hermione* (1673) led Lully to offer him a formal contract: he was paid to write one libretto per year at 4000 livres each. The partnership resulted in 11 *tragédies en musique* and two large-scale ballets (*Le triomphe de l'Amour*, 1681; *Le temple de la paix*, 1685); most of these works were performed both at Louis XIV's court and at the Opéra. It was a close collaboration: Quinault rewrote extensively at Lully's request. The partnership was interrupted between 1677 and 1680, when Quinault was temporarily banished from court because his unflattering portrayal of Juno in *Isis* was taken to represent the king's mistress. In 1686 he retired from the stage, possibly because he developed religious scruples about opera, but more likely because he was suffering from tuberculosis.

Quinault and Lully invented a new genre, the *tragédie en musique*, which influenced the development of French opera for more than a century. The five-act structure and scene elisions follow the conventions of spoken tragedy. Rather than alexandrines, however, the poetry consists of *vers libres*, as in the *pastorale* libretto; Perrin had called these irregular, short-breathed lines *vers lyriques*. Scenes are flexible in poetic organization; they are given structure by repetitions and refrains, frequent aphoristic couplets (set by Lully as sections of binary *maxim airs*) and choral interjections like those in the *tragédie à machines*. The heroic plots, the first eight based on ancient mythology and the last three on tales of medieval chivalry, were heavily veiled allegories of life at court; sycophantic prologues praised the king more directly and referred openly (though not explicitly) to topical political events. The central plot element in each case is a tender and delicate love intrigue involving high-born heroes and heroines; it is sometimes a simple love triangle but often a complex love chain including multiple relationships. The attitudes towards elegant, decorous love, combining male sacrifice with female pride, are based on those of the Précieuses; the metaphorical language (e.g. 'my flame burns for him') is traditional, antedating the *précieux* movement. The love intrigue gives rise to considerable non-erotic action and adventure, such as fights, celebrations, heroic quests, *sommeils* (sleep scenes), prayers and journeys to the underworld. Comic scenes and subplots for lower-class characters, as in Roman or Venetian opera, were criticized as unseemly and destructive of unity of action; they disappeared after 1675.

Heroic *gloire*, which might roughly be defined as a sense of personal integrity achieved by behaving in a way appropriate to one's standing in society, is often attained; in *Alceste*, for instance, Admetus finds it 'sweet' to die for Alcestis (and she returns the favour), while Alcides triumphs over an army, the forces of hell and his own desires. Yet the political dilemma found at the heart of Corneillian tragedy is either altogether absent from these plots or virtually eclipsed by the love story. In *Atys* (the only plot whose outcome is unrelievedly tragic) Attis and Sangaride are apparently punished because they choose their love for each other over their duty to Celaenus and Sangarius – fealty in his case, filial duty in hers – but the main tragic figure is Cybele, whose indecorous demand of Attis's love is without social merit. *Armide* is a rare case in which a character's vacillating indecision controls the story; still, Armide is preoccupied by questions of hurt pride (central to a woman's *gloire*, to be sure), not by the fate of Damascus. Armide and Glory's rivalry for Renaud's affections – the knight's need to choose between an inglorious love and glorious duty – is a false dilemma: it disappears as soon as Renaud's enchantment is broken.

The hero of *Roland* is so blinded by love that he perceives no political dilemma; a *dea ex machina* has to point it out.

Contemporaries made much of Quinault's extreme *tendresse*. One remarked that no author had ever conjugated the verb *aimer* so many times, and Quinault's enemy Boileau wrote sarcastically, 'Everything is said tenderly, right up to "I hate you"' (*Satire III*, 1666). Yet when Quinault slips from tender Corneillian love into the obsessive Racinian love that devours characters, he often sets *tendresse* aside (e.g. Medea's 'Dépit mortel', *Thésée*, 2.ix). Furthermore, the explicit depiction of horror – for instance, torture of prisoners or attack by monsters – was permitted in this genre. *Tendresse* coexists with violence and cruelty.

As in various 17th-century pastoral genres, the human drama unfolds in an atmosphere controlled by magical and supernatural forces. Here they are visible: pagan deities make frequent appearances, sometimes in response to invocations by humans and sometimes on their own initiative, and they often use humans as pawns in their private battles. In some cases magicians and gods are protagonists in the central love intrigue; despite their superhuman powers, they display human frailties as lovers and rivals. A profusion of mythological supernumeraries, from zephyrs and fairies to monsters and furies, take part in the action when it enters the supernatural realm.

Spectacle is abundant. The supernatural element permits characters to metamorphose into objects. It also justifies violation of unity of place: at least once per act the setting is magically transformed. In addition, each act contains a ballet *divertissement*: a stylized presentation of some collective action central to the plot (celebration, ceremony, battle, enchantment etc.), structured as a more or less symmetrical arrangement of dances, *airs* and choruses. The dances are indicated in the librettos simply by 'On danse' or by instructions for pantomime.

In France Quinault's librettos were judged as literature. They were controversial at first but were highly regarded by most 18th-century critics. In the latter half of the century, when it became fashionable for Italian poets to rework old French librettos, Villati provided *Angelica e Medoro* (1749, based on *Roland*), *Fetonte* (1750, based on *Phaëton*) and *Armida* (1751, based on *Armide*) for C. H. Graun; Migliavacca and Giacomo Durazzo wrote an *Armida* (1761) for Traetta, a version that was also set by Mysliveček (1779); and Verazi wrote a *Fetonte* for Jommelli (1768). French reworkings were made as well: Marmontel provided *Roland* (1778) and *Atys* (1780) for Piccinni, as well as *Persée* (1780) for Philidor; and Morel reworked *Thésée* (1782) for Gossec.

tragédies en musique unless otherwise stated; all first settings by Lully

La grotte de Versailles (eclogue), 1668; *Psyché* (tragédie-ballet, with Moliere and P. Corneille), 1671; *Les fêtes de l'Amour et de Bacchus* (pastorale, with I. de Benserade and the Président de Périgny), 1672; *Cadmus et Hermione*, 1673; *Alceste*, 1674; *Thésée*, 1675 (Strungk, 1683; Mondonville, 1765); *Atys*, 1676; *Isis*, 1677; *Proserpine*, 1680 (Paisiello, 1803); *Persée*, 1682; *Phaëton*, 1683; *Amadis*, 1684 (La Borde, 1771; J. C. Bach, 1779); *Roland*, 1685; *Armide*, 1686 (Gluck, 1777)

ES (P. F. Butler)

F. Lindemann: *Die Operntexte Ph. Quinaults vom literarischen Standpunkte aus betrachtet* (diss., U. of Leipzig, 1904)
H. Prunières: 'La Fontaine et Lully', *ReM*, ii/10 (1921), 98–112
X. de Courville: 'Quinault, poète d'opéra', *ReM*, vi (1925), 74–88

E. Gros: *Philippe Quinault: sa vie et son oeuvre* (Paris, 1926) [incl. comprehensive lists of 17th- and 18th-century literature, and of literary edns]

——: 'Les origines de la tragédie lyrique et la place des tragédies en machines dans l'évolution du théatre vers l'opéra', *Revue d'histoire littéraire de la France*, xxxv (1928), 161–93

J. van Eerde: 'Quinault, the Court and Kingship', *Romantic Review*, liii (1962), 174–86

L. Maurice-Amour: 'Comment Lully et ses poètes humanisent dieux et héros', *Cahiers de l'Association internationale des études françaises*, xvii (1965), 59–95

C. Trichet: *Quelques aspects des formes lyriques dans les opéras de Quinault* (diss., U. of Grenoble, 1969)

P. Smith: *The Tenth Muse: a Historical Study of the Opera Libretto* (New York, 1970)

C. Girdlestone: *La tragédie en musique (1673–1750) considérée comme genre littéraire* (Geneva, 1972) [incl. details of 17th- and 18th-century literature]

J. R. Anthony: *French Baroque Music from Beaujoyeulx to Rameau* (London, 1973, 2/1978)

Y. Giraud: 'Quinault et Lully ou l'accord de deux styles', *Marseille*, no.95 (1973), 195–212

R. Fajon: *L'Opéra à Paris du Roi Soleil à Louis le Bien-Aimé* (Geneva, 1984)

P. Gethner: 'La "morale lubrique" dans les opéras de Quinault', *Les visages de l'amour au XVIIe siècle* (Toulouse, 1984), 145–54

T. Wright: *Lully and Quinault: Musico-Dramatic Synthesis in the tragédie en musique* (diss., U. of Kansas, 1984)

L. Auld: '*Intrigue* and *raisonnement* in the Opera *livret*', *Actes de Baton Rouge: Biblio 17: Papers on 17th-Century French Literature*, xxv (1986), 5–18

G. Cowart: 'Lully *enjoué*: *galanterie* in Seventeenth-Century France', ibid, 35–51

F. Karro: 'Le prologue d'Armide (Quinault-Lully)', *Les écrivains français et l'opéra*, ed. J.-P. Capdevielle and P.-E. Knabe (Cologne, 1986), 39–47

C. Kintzler: 'De la pastorale à la tragédie lyrique: quelques éléments d'un système poétique', *RdM*, lxxii (1986), 67–96

A. Mansau: '*Amadis de Gaule* de Maynard à Quinault', *Cahiers Maynard*, no.15 (1986), 33–40

L. Quetin: 'Quinault, librettiste entre le tragique et le romanesque: *Amadis de Gaule*', *Les écrivains français et l'opéra*, ed. J.-P. Capdevielle and P.-E. Knabe (Cologne, 1986), 19–37

L'avant-scène opéra, no.94 (1987) [*Atys* issue]

P. Gethner: 'Alceste, or How to Rewrite Greek Tragedy in the Age of Louis XIV', *Cahiers du dix-septième: Journal of the Southeast American Society for French Seventeenth-Century Studies*, i (1987), 103–15

P. Howard: 'The Positioning of Woman in Quinault's World Picture', *Lully: Heidelberg and St Germain-en-Laye 1987*, 193–9

W. Brooks: *Bibliographie critique du théâtre de Quinault* (Paris, 1988)

——: 'Lully and Quinault at Court and on the Public Stage, 1673–86', *Seventeenth-Century French Studies*, no.10 (1988), 101–21; suppl. note, no.11 (1989), 147–50

J. de La Gorce: 'Un proche collaborateur de Lully: Philippe Quinault', *XVIIe siècle*, xl (1988), 365–70

B. Norman: 'The Vocabulary of Quinault's Opera Libretti: Drama without Drama', *L'âge du théâtre en France/The Age of Theatre in France*, ed. D. Trott and N. Boursier (Edmonton, Alta., 1988), 287–98

M. Couvreur: *Le livret d'opéra en France de "Cadmus et Hermione" de Quinault et Lully (1673) aux "Boréades" de Cahusac et Rameau (1763): Essai de définition pluridisciplinaire d'un "genre d'écriture"* (diss., U. Libre de Bruxelles, 1989)

P. Gethner: 'La fonction des sentences dans les livrets de Quinault', *Cahiers de l'Association internationale des études françaises*, xli (1989), 129–44

B. Norman: 'Ancients and Moderns, Tragedy and Opera: the Quarrel over *Alceste*', *French Musical Thought, 1600–1800*, ed. G. Cowart (Ann Arbor, 1989), 177–96

C. Kintzler: *Poétique de l'opéra français de Corneille à Rousseau* (Paris, 1991)

P. Howard: 'The Influence of the Précieuses on Content and Structure in Quinault's and Lully's Tragédies Lyriques', *AcM*, lxiii (1991), 57–72

P. Howard: 'Quinault, Lully and the Précieuses: Images of Women in Seventeenth-Century France', *Cecilia: Feminist Perspectives on Women and Music*, ed. S. Cook and J. Tsou (Urbana, IL, 1993)

M. Browne: *The Aesthetics of the Précieux: its Influence on Early French Opera* (diss., U. of North Texas, in preparation)

LOIS ROSOW

Quintavalle, Antonio (*fl* 1688–?1724). Italian composer. In 1703 and perhaps earlier he was chamber organist at the Mantuan court. He wrote music for three operas produced there, one in collaboration with the *maestro di cappella* Caldara. According to Lunelli Quintavelle was *maestro di cappella* of Trent Cathedral from 1712 to 1724. An Antonio Quintavalle, chaplain at Torcello, near Venice, died on 28 January 1721 at the age of 45.

music lost

L'oracolo in sogno [Act 2] (F. Silvani), Mantua, Mantova, 6 June 1699, pubd lib. *I-Bc* [Act 1 by A. Caldara, Act 3 by C. F. Pollarolo]

Il trionfo d'amore, Mantua, 19 Dec 1703, pubd lib. *US-Wc*

Paride sull'Ida, ovvero Gli amori di Paride con Enone (F. Mazzari), Mantua, 1704, pubd lib. *I-Bc*

Partenope (S. Stampiglia), Trent, Gaudenti, 1713

RicordiE; *SchmidlD*

O. G. T. Sonneck: *Library of Congress: Catalogue of Opera Librettos Printed Before 1800* (Washington DC, 1914)

U. Kirkendale: *Antonio Caldara: sein Leben und seine venezianisch-römischen Oratorien* (Graz and Cologne, 1966)

R. Lunelli: *La musica nel Trentino dal XV al XVIII secolo* (Trent, 1967)

Quintet (Fr. *quintette, quintuor*; Ger. *Quintett*; It. *quintetto*). An ensemble for five voices. Quintets are rare in 17th-century opera except occasionally as finales or as collective, sometimes quite brief, expressions of emotion within acts. They appear on occasion in comic operas, chiefly as act finales, during the first half of the 18th century. After 1750 they function more variously. As finales, they gradually expand in personnel (that is, they might begin as a duet, to which further characters accrue) and might contain action as well as reflection; appearing within acts and as *introduzioni* they come to take on the freer construction of a finale later in the century, encompassing action. There are several quintets in Mozart's comic operas, notably *Così fan tutte* (1790).

In serious opera, quintets are rare. One was provided by Verazi for Jommelli in *Enea nel Lazio* as early as 1755 (Stuttgart), and for Sacchini's *Calliroe* (1770, Stuttgart) in which he constructed a quintet of diminishing personnel involving a battle (five characters are reduced to three and then to one). There are several quintets in Sarti's operas (*Semiramide*, 1768, Venice; *Ifigenia*, 1777, Rome; *Olimpiade*, 1778, Florence), and one in Paisiello's *Sismano nel Mogol* (1773, Milan). From the late 1770s quintets are increasingly frequent, often having finale-like construction even when they are not finales (which they usually were until the 1790s).

The earliest known example in a French opera is in the manuscript score of Boismortier's *Don Quichote chez la duchesse* (1743): in 2.viii a solo voice ('Arrestez, redoutez mon courroux') is superimposed above a double duet ('Dieux quelle violence'). This may have been regarded as an over-ambitious experiment in French serious opera, since neither the printed score nor the libretto (both 1743) reproduce the ensemble. An early example from *opéra comique* is in Laruette's *L'heureux déguisement* (1758), which although not a finale involves action; the music does not survive. Quintets appear more often in *opéras comiques* of a slightly later period, probably because of the interest of such librettists as Anseaume and particularly Sedaine, who includes quintets in, among other works, Philidor's *Blaise le savetier* (1759) and Monsigny's *Le déserteur* (1769). The texts become increasingly complex with each character's lines divergent in expression. Quintets developing from quartets appear in some operas, for example Egidio Duni's *L'isle des foux* (1760). Various textures are found, from simple dialogue to homophonic writing and counterpoint. Philidor wrote a quintet in his italianate *tragédie lyrique Ernelinde, princesse de Norvège* (1767, Paris).

Like the quartet, the quintet is chiefly found in the comic forms of opera in the first three decades of the 19th century, where it may be laid out on quite a large scale. That in Rossini's *L'italiana in Algeri* (1813), 'Ti presento di mia mano', is in three movements, while 'Signor, una parola' from *La Cenerentola* (1817) and 'Don Basilio! che veggo?' from *Il barbiere di Siviglia* (1816) are each in four, though in the latter, one of the characters has left the stage before the beginning of the third movement. The more elevated 'Celeste man placata' (*Mosè in Egitto*, 1818) is again in three movements, starting with a *falso canone* and ending with a stretta. Among single-movement quintets later in the century are the mercurial 'Nous avons en tête une affaire' (*Carmen*, 1875), 'Quand une femme est si jolie' (Delibes' *Lakmé*, 1883) and, in serious vein, 'Selig wie die Sonne', from Act 3 of *Die Meistersinger* (1868), which violates the precepts of Wagner's *Oper und Drama* in the interests of pure music, the dramatic action being suspended while the characters take stock of the situation. 'È scherzo od è follia' from Verdi's *Un ballo in maschera* (1859) is sometimes referred to as a quintet, though it is strictly the *pezzo concertato* of the Act 1 finale and accordingly involves the chorus (comparable with the sextet from Donizetti's *Lucia di Lammermoor*).

See also FINALE.

MARITA P. McCLYMONDS, ELISABETH COOK, JULIAN BUDDEN

Quinto Fabio ('Quintus Fabius'). *Opera seria* in three acts by FERDINANDO BERTONI to a libretto by APOSTOLO ZENO after his *I due dittatori*; Milan, Teatro Interinale, 31 January 1778.

Written to display the remarkable qualities of the castrato Gasparo Pacchierotti, *Quinto Fabio* proved a great success. Pacchierotti was invited back to Milan as primo uomo in the first opera at the new Teatro alla Scala seven months later; the opera also launched the international careers of Bertoni and Pacchierotti as a team. After Milan, *Quinto Fabio* was given 'twenty times at Padua with the greatest applause' (Burney, ii, 890) from 12 June 1778 with Pacchierotti again as Quintus Fabius (soprano castrato), the Roman military

leader who disobeyed his father-in-law, the dictator Lucio Paperio [Lucius Papirius] (tenor), by engaging the enemy in battle, and who was condemned to die by the axe but was saved by the tears of his father and the entreaties of the people. Also in the Padua cast were Giacomo Davide as Lucius Papirius, Luigi Mazzoni as Marco Fabio [Marcus Fabius] (tenor), Giovanina Gardi as Emilia (soprano), Quintus's wife, Marianna Moltez as Faustina (soprano) and Francisco Bellaspica as Volunnio [Volumnius] (soprano castrato).

Bertoni and Pacchierotti were engaged by the King's Theatre, London, for the 1778–9 season. After this their contracts were renewed, and *Quinto Fabio* was performed there 12 times from 22 January 1780; it was revived on 7 March 1782 during Bertoni's second London sojourn. *The Favorite Songs* (London, 1780) contains a duet and four arias, one of which, the cantabile 'Teco resti anima mia', ends with an Allegro duettino. Emilia's florid aria 'Va crescendo il mio tormento' was published in Bailleux's *Journal d'ariettes italiennes* (Paris, 1781) with a note that it was 'added to *Le devin du village*' with a French text 'Je respire après la crainte'. The arias in *Quinto Fabio* exhibit great structural variety, using da capo, *ABA'*, composite, rondo and cavatina forms. The orchestration for the London performances adds flutes, clarinets and a solo bassoon. Other productions of *Quinto Fabio* were mounted in Lucca (1781), Venice (1784), Rome (1786) and again in London (1791), all with Pacchierotti in the title role. The large number of extant manuscript copies of individual arias attests to the popularity of the music.

Further operas of the same title, by Anfossi and others, were composed in the 18th century. The plot is essentially the same as that of operas on the subject of LUCIUS PAPIRIUS, settings of texts by Salvi and Zeno, in which Quintus Fabius Maximus Rullianus is a leading character.

GEORGE TRUETT HOLLIS

Quivar, Florence (*b* Philadelphia, 3 March 1944). American mezzo-soprano. She studied in Philadelphia and in New York, where in 1975 she sang Ježibaba and the Foreign Princess (*Rusalka*) at the Juilliard Opera Center. She made her Metropolitan début in 1977 as Marina (*Boris Godunov*) and later Jocasta, Suzuki, Isabella (*L'italiana in Algeri*), Fidès (*Le prophète*), Mother Marie (*Dialogues des Carmélites*) and Serena (*Porgy and Bess*). She has also sung in Berlin, Venice, Rome, Rio de Janeiro, Buenos Aires and Los Angeles. Her repertory includes Adalgisa, Carmen, Erda, Brangäne and Gluck's Orpheus, the role that best displays the rich beauty of her voice and the dignity of her presence.

ELIZABETH FORBES

R

Raab [*née* Bilik], **Vil'gel'mina Ivanovna** (*b* 1848; *d* St Petersburg, 10/23 Nov 1917). Russian soprano. She studied in Vienna with Buchholz-Calconi and in St Petersburg with Nissen-Saloman. She made her début as Mathilde (*Guillaume Tell*) at the Mariinsky Theatre in 1871 and continued to sing there until her retirement in 1885. Her extensive repertory covered both dramatic and lyric coloratura roles. She was particularly noted for taking contrasting roles in the same opera: Gorislava and Lyudmila; Kupava and the title role in *The Snow Maiden*; Marguerite and the Page (*Les Huguenots*); and Donna Anna and Donna Elvira. Roles she created (all in St Petersburg) were Natal'ya (Tchaikovsky's *Oprichnik*, 1874), Tamara (Rubinstein's *The Demon*, 1875) and Oxana (*Vakula the Smith*, 1876). Other admired roles included Gilda, Aida, the name part in Serov's *Judith*, Elsa and, particularly, Marguerite (*Faust*). From 1884 she taught at the St Petersburg Conservatory.

BORIS SEMEONOFF

Raaff [Raff], **Anton** (*b* Gelsdorf, nr Bonn, bap. 6 May 1714; *d* Munich, 28 May 1797). German tenor. After being appointed to the service of Clement Augustus, Elector of Cologne, Raaff was sent in 1736 to Munich, where he studied with Ferrandini and sang in one of his operas. The following year he studied with Bernacchi in Bologna, remaining in Italy until 1741–2, when he returned to electoral service in Bonn. In 1749 he left for Vienna where he sang in several operas composed and directed by Jommelli. He was in Italy in 1751–2, when he was called to the court of Lisbon; from there he went in 1755 to Madrid and, in 1759, he travelled with Farinelli to Naples.

For the next decade Raaff was the principal tenor on the Neapolitan and Florentine stages, appearing in operas by Hasse, Majo and J. C. Bach, as well as Sacchini, Piccinni, and Mysliveček. In August 1770 he arrived at Mannheim, Carl Theodor's seat, where he sang the title roles in Piccinni's *Catone in Utica* (1770) and Bach's *Temistocle* (1772) and *Lucio Silla* (1775). Mozart was severely critical of his singing and acting in the title role of Holzbauer's *Günther von Schwarzburg* (1777), but was more sympathetic after hearing him sing Bach's 'Non so d'onde viene' from *Alessandro nell'Indie* at the Concert Spirituel in Paris during June 1778; Mozart tried to win his favour by composing a setting of one of the tenor's favourite texts, 'Se al labbro mio' (κ295). Raaff's last role was the title part in

Anton Raaff in a costume for a role in an unknown opera seria: watercolour

Idomeneo (1781), composed for Munich where Carl Theodor had transferred his court. Though Raaff's voice was praised by Schubart as having an unusually large range from bass to alto, with flexible coloratura throughout, Mozart found it small in range and limited in technique. Yet Raaff sang well enough in 1787 to impress Michael Kelly, who wrote that 'he still retained his fine *voce di petto* and sostenuto notes, and pure style of singing'. He was one of the last and greatest representatives of the legato technique and portamento, brought to perfection by Bernacchi and his school.

1207

C. F. D. Schubart: *Ideen zu einer Ästhetik der Tonkunst* (Vienna, 1806)

AMZ, xii (1810), 857–77

F. J. Lipowsky: *Baierisches Musiklexikon* (Munich, 1811)

M. Kelly: *Reminiscences* (London, 1826, 2/1826), i, 282; ed. R. Fiske (London, 1975)

H. Freiberger: *Anton Raaff (1714–1797): sein Leben und Wirken* (Cologne, 1929)

E. Anderson, ed.: *The Letters of Mozart and his Family* (London, 1938, 3/1985)

S. Kunze: 'Die Vertonungen der Aria "Non so d'onde viene" von J. C. Bach und Mozart', *AnMc*, no.2 (1965), 85–110

U. Prota-Giurleo: 'Notizie biographiche intorno ad alcuni musicisti d'oltralpe a Napoli nel settecento', *AnMc*, no.2 (1965), 112–43, esp. 136–9

P. Petrobelli: 'The Italian Years of Anton Raaff', *MJb 1973–4*, 233–73

D. Heartz: 'Raaff's Last Aria: a Mozartian Idyll in the Spirit of Hasse', *MQ*, lx (1974), 517–43

P. Corneilson: *Opera at Mannheim, 1770–1778* (diss., U. of North Carolina, 1992)   DANIEL HEARTZ (with PAUL CORNEILSON)

Rabaud, Henri (*b* Paris, 10 Nov 1873; *d* Paris, 11 Sept 1949). French composer and conductor. His great-aunt was the soprano Dorus-Gras. Rabaud showed prodigious talent and a somewhat academic spirit: 'modernism is the enemy' was his watchword. At the Paris Conservatoire he studied composition with Massenet, but gained more from his studies of the Viennese Classics – the music of Wagner, Franck and Debussy left him indifferent. In 1894 he won the Prix de Rome, and his sojourn at the Villa Medici opened his mind to newer music; he came to admire Verdi, Mascagni and Puccini. A trip to Bayreuth was enough to complete the demolition of the barriers he had imposed; turning in the direction of Wagner and Franck, he composed a mystical oratorio, *Job* (1900), which enjoyed an immense success. However, he was still capable of writing such drily academic music as the opera *La fille de Roland*. For his second opera, *Mârouf, savetier du Caire*, Rabaud welded together Wagnerian form and oriental picturesqueness; the work was greeted with enthusiasm both in France and abroad. During this period Rabaud was a frequent conductor of the Opéra-Comique and at the Opéra, directing the latter house from 1914 to 1918, in which year he was admitted to the Institut de France. He succeeded Fauré as director of the Conservatoire in 1922, retiring in 1941. As well as operas he composed film scores, other incidental music and orchestral and choral works.

La fille de Roland (4, P. Ferrari, after H. de Bornier), Paris, OC (Favart), 16 March 1904

Mârouf, savetier du Caire (5, L. Népoty, after *The Thousand and One Nights*), Paris, OC (Favart), 15 May 1914

L'appel de la mer (1, Rabaud, after J. M. Synge), Paris, OC (Favart), 10 April 1924

Rolande et le mauvais garçon (5, Népoty), Paris, Opéra, 28 May 1934

Martine (5 scenes, after J.-J. Bernard), Strasbourg, 26 April 1947

Le jeu de l'amour et du hasard, 1948 (3, after P. C. de Chamblain de Marivaux), Monte Carlo, 19 Nov 1954

*

P. Landormy: 'Henri Rabaud, Max d'Ollone, Roger Ducasse', *Le théâtre lyrique en France* (Paris, 1937–9) [pubn of Poste National/Radio-Paris], iii, 149–54

G. Samazeuilh: *Musiciens de mon temps* (Paris, 1947)

M. d'Ollone: *Henri Rabaud: sa vie et son oeuvre* (Paris, 1958)
ANNE GIRARDOT

Racconto (It.: 'tale'). A term used in Italian 19th-century opera to denote a narrative aria, the form of which is determined by the events it describes, e.g.

Massimiliano's 'Un ignoto tre lune or saranno' (*I masnadieri*, Verdi, 1847), Azucena's 'Condotta ell'era in ceppi' (*Il trovatore*, Verdi, 1853) and Amenofi's 'Di Gerzabel nell'oasi poco lontana' (*Il figliuol prodigo*, Ponchielli, 1880). Arias which tell a story within a traditional 'cantabile' pattern, however modified, such as Maffio Orsini's 'Nella fatal di Rimini' (*Lucrezia Borgia*, Donizetti, 1833), are never thus designated.

JULIAN BUDDEN

Racine, Jean (*b* nr Soissons, bap. 22 Dec. 1639; *d* Paris, 21 April 1699). French dramatist, in whose tragedies the epitome of French classical style was reached. He was educated at Port-Royal, where he received a thorough grounding in Latin and Greek, and was introduced to Jansenist philosophy, two factors which were to influence his playwriting. A natural ability to write poetry provided an entrée into the theatrical circles of Paris, where he became friendly with Molière, La Fontaine and Boileau. The internal conflict between the austere philosophy of Jansenism and the more libertine world of the stage was to influence him for the rest of his life. His first play, *La Thébaïde*, was performed in Paris in 1664. Given the extent of his influence on French theatre, it is remarkable that Racine wrote only 12 plays, all tragedies except one, the comedy *Les plaideurs* (1668). Eight of the tragedies derive their subject matter from classical history or mythology, the other three from contemporary history. His two greatest successes were *Iphigénie en Aulide* (1674) and *Phèdre* (1677).

After *Phèdre* Racine turned his attention to *tragédie lyrique*. In 1679 he and Boileau were invited by Mme de Montespan to write the libretto for Lully's *La chute de Phaëton*, but Louis XIV insisted that Lully work with Quinault, with the result that the Racine-Boileau libretto was never completed. Two contemporary sources allude to an unnamed 'petit opéra' (more likely a ballet) by Racine and De Préaux, apparently written in three days and performed at court during the carnival celebrations of 1683. Racine's best-known venture into musical drama can be found in *L'idylle sur la paix* (1685), a *divertissement* with music by Lully written to celebrate the signing of the Treaty of Regensburg.

Racine's tragedies respect the dramatic unities and have simple plots in which internal conflicts lead to psychological disintegration. In Corneille's plays the indomitable will of the protagonist wrestles with external forces greater than itself; but with Racine, tragic heroes and heroines, like Nero (*Britannicus*) or Phaedra, are driven by inner passions beyond their control and battle in vain with their inevitable destinies. His portrayal of such strong-willed women as Iphigenia is particularly commendable.

All Racine's plays except *Les plaideurs* have provided material for operas. The two religious plays, *Esther* (1689) and *Athalie* (1691), had recitatives and choruses set to music by J.-B. Moreau, Racine's favourite composer, and were later chosen as the basis of oratorios composed by Handel. Zeno acknowledged his debt to Racine in the *argomento* to three librettos based on his plays: *Andromaca*, *Ifigenia in Aulide* and *Mitridate*; the last borrows characters and situations from Racine's *Mithridate* (1673) but does not follow the plot closely. *Andromaque* (1667) also provided the foundation for Tottola's *Ermione*, set by Rossini in 1819. Metastasio's libretto *Alessandro nell'Indie* shows similarities with *Alexandre le grand* (1665), as does his *Ipermestra* with *Britannicus* (1668) and *Antigono* with

Mithridate. Of all Racine's plays, however, it is *Bérénice* (1670) that had the greatest influence on Metastasio. Its psychological conflicts resurface in *Adriano in Siria* and *Artaserse*, its love relationships in *Didone abbandonata* and *Demofoonte*, and its similarities of plot in *Demetrio*. In addition, situations, characterizations and relationships from this tragedy are echoed in *La clemenza di Tito*. *Bérénice* found further operatic expression in C. S. Capece's libretto for Caldara's *Tito e Berenice* (1714), as well as in Antonio Salvi's text for Handel's *Berenice* (1737).

Other librettos based on Racine's tragedies include adaptations of *Phèdre* – one by Pellegrin entitled *Hippolyte et Aricie* and set by Rameau (1733), another by Gioseffe Corio for Gluck's *Ippolito* (1745) and, in the 20th century, Bussotti's *Le Racine* (1980). Librettos based on *Iphigénie en Aulide* were set by Domenico Scarlatti (1713), Gluck (1774) and Cherubini (1788), and one, set by Graun (1748), was supposedly co-written by Frederick the Great. Mozart's youthful opera *Mitridate, re di Ponto* (1770) follows the plot of *Mithridate*.

La Thébaïde, ou Les frères ennemis (play, 1664): Graun, 1756, as I fratelli nemici
Alexandre le grand (play, 1665): J. S. Kusser, 1693, as Porus; set as Alessandro nell'Indie: *see* METASTASIO, PIETRO
Andromaque (play, 1667): Caldara, 1724; G. Bononcini, 1727, as Astianatte; Bioni, 1730; Feo, 1730; Sacchini, 1761; Grétry, 1780; Martín y Soler, 1780; Paisiello, 1797; Rossini, 1819, as Ermione
Britannicus (play, 1668): Porpora, 1708, as Agrippina; Graun, 1751
Bérénice (play, 1670): Freschi, 1680, as Berenice vendicativa; ?Bronner, 1702; Ruggieri, 1711, as Le gare di politica e d'amore; Caldara, 1714, as Tito e Berenice; Orlandini, 1725; Araia, 1730; Ferrandini, 1730; Handel, 1737; Galuppi, 1741; I. Platania, 1771; Rust, 1785; Nasolini, 1793, as Tito e Berenice; P. Raimondi, 1824, as Berenice in Roma; Magnard, 1911
Bajazet (play, 1672): Leo, 1722, as Bajazete, imperator dei turchi; Giai, 1727, as Tamerlano; Vivaldi, 1735, as Tamerlano; Bernasconi, 1742; Cocchi, 1746; Lampugnani, 1746, as Il gran Tamerlano; Cocchi and Pescetti, 1754, as Tamerlano; Scolari, 1763, as Il Tamerlano; Bertoni, 1765; Andreozzi, 1783; Generali, 1814; Burghersh, 1821; Hervé, 1869, as Les Turcs
Mithridate (play, 1673): A. Scarlatti, 1707, as Il Mitridate Eupatore; Bioni, 1722; Capelli, 1723, as Mitridate re di Ponto, vincitor de sè stesso; Caldara, 1728; Giai, 1730; Porpora, 1730; Aliprandi, 1738; Terradellas, 1746; Graun, 1750; ? Sarti, 1765; Q. Gasparini, 1767; Mozart, 1770; Sarti, 1779; Sacchini, 1781; Tarchi, 1785; Nasolini, 1796, as La morte di Mitridate; Zingarelli, 1797, as La morte di Mitridate; Tadolini, 1827
Iphigénie en Aulide (play, 1674): A. B. Coletti, 1707; D. Scarlatti, 1713; Caldara, 1718; Orlandini, 1732; Porpora, 1735; Porta, 1738; Graun, 1748; Jommelli, 1751; Bertoni, 1762; ? Majo, 1762; Guglielmi, 1768; Gluck, 1774; Sarti, 1777; Martín y Soler, 1779; Prati, 1784; Lorenzo Rossi, 1784; Tarchi, 1785; Zingarelli, 1787; Cherubini, 1788; G. Mosca, 1799; Trento, 1804; Federici, 1809; Mayr, 1811, as Il sacrifizio d'Ifigenia
Phèdre (play, 1677): Rameau, 1733, as Hippolyte et Aricie; Gluck, 1745, as Ippolito; ? Holzbauer, 1759, as Ippolito ed Aricia; Traetta, 1759, as Ippolito ed Aricia; Lemoyne, 1786; Paisiello, 1788; G. Nicolini, 1803, as Pedra, ossia Il ritorno di Teseo; Mayr, 1820; Burghersh, 1824; Mihalovici, 1951; Rochberg, 1973–4; Bussotti, 1980, as Le Racine, rev. 1988 as Fedra
Esther (play, 1689): Meyerowitz, 1957
Athalie (play, 1691): J. A. P. Schulz, 1785; Poissl, 1814; Weisgall, 1964

Libretto: *La chute de Phaëton*, Lully, 1679, inc.

*

W. Pietzsch: *Apostolo Zeno in seiner Abhängigkeit von der französischen Tragödie* (Leipzig, 1907)
G. Orcibel: 'Racine et Boileau librettistes', *Revue d'histoire littéraire de la France*, xlix (1949), 246–55
A. Trigiani: *Il teatro raciniano e i melodrammi di Pietro Metastasio* (Turin, 1951)
J. Vanuxem: 'Sur Racine et Boileau librettistes', *Revue d'histoire littéraire de la France*, li (1951), 78–81
R. Picard: *La carrière de Jean Racine* (Paris, 1956)
R. B. Moberly: 'The Influence of French Classical Drama on Mozart's *La clemenza di Tito*', *ML*, lv (1974), 286–98
M. Aranda: *Iphigénie de Racine à Du Roullet: illustration concrète d'une confrontation tragédie/opéra* (diss., U. of Paris-Sorbonne, 1986)
C. Dahlhaus: 'Tragödie, Tragédie, Reformoper: zur *Iphigenie in Aulis* von Euripides, Racine und Gluck', *Oper als Text: romantische Beiträge zur Libretto-Forschung*, ed. A. Grier (Heidelberg, 1986), 95–100
R. Strohm: '"Tragédie" into "Dramma per musica"', *Informazione e studi vivaldiani*, ix (1988), 14–24; x (1989), 57–101; xi (1990), 11–25; xii (1991), 47–74
ALISON STONEHOUSE

Racine, Le. Opera balletto in three acts by SYLVANO BUSSOTTI to his own libretto after JEAN RACINE's *Phèdre*; Milan, Piccola Scala, 9 December 1980.

The action takes place in a Parisian 'pianobar' called *Le Racine*, run by a former actress at the Comédie Française, Madame Phèdre (soprano), who recites Racine's verses in everyday life. As in other operas by Bussotti, the author (Racine, bass) takes part in the action. The main conflict of Racine's tragedy, the incestuous relationship between Hippolytus and Phaedra, is gradually transferred from Hippolyte (dancer) and Madame Phèdre to Hippolyte and Racine, who as a father figure to all the characters on stage commits incest with Hippolyte.

The opera was intended to be a preparation for a more ambitious work, *Fedra*, which Bussotti was planning; *Le Racine* is accompanied only by the piano, in imitation of a stage rehearsal of an imaginary score for full orchestra. The libretto retains the original French verse of Racine's drama, though Racine's text is shortened and redistributed among the characters. The vocal lines are dodecaphonic, in homage to Racine's alexandrines. Large sections of the text are spoken rhythmically. The famous 'récit de Théramène', which in Racine's tragedy announces Hippolyte's death, is sung in the opera by Xio Leblanc (baritone). Bussotti's score may be interpreted as a reverse form of *Literaturoper*, for instead of shortening the poetic text and keeping the action intact, he builds a monument to Racine's verses, but destroys their dramatic coherence. As in Bussotti's other operas, all sets and costumes are specified by the composer.

Bussotti's reworking of *Le Racine*, as the three-act *tragedia lirica Fedra*, was first performed at the Teatro dell'Opera in Rome on 19 April 1988. *Fedra* is on a larger scale, with orchestra, and adds the complication of a shifting time of action from antiquity to 1931, the year of the composer's birth. The text and vocal lines are virtually the same as for *Le Racine* but are distributed differently among the characters. Chorus and orchestra have an important commenting function. Notwithstanding their musical similarities the two operas give a profoundly different impression on stage, the wide spaces called for in Bussotti's designs for *Fedra* contrasting markedly with the closed 'pianobar' atmosphere of *Le Racine*.
JÜRGEN MAEHDER

Račiūnas, Antanas (*b* Užliaušiai, 4 Sept 1905; *d* Vilnius, 3 April 1984). Lithuanian composer. He graduated in composition from the Kaunas conservatory (1933) and continued his studies in Paris with Boulanger, Koechlin and Stravinsky (1936–9). He taught at the Kaunas conservatory from 1939 and at the Lithuanian conservatory in Vilnius from 1949 (professor in 1958). Račiūnas's music is rather conservative in harmony and form; in many of his compositions, including the large-scale works, he makes use of traditional folk elements such as the *sutartinés* (a song and dance form). In *Trys talismanai* ('The Three Talismans') Račiūnas used simple means of expression in a modern idiom; the opera, using fairytale subjects, depicts the struggle between good and evil. *Saulès miestas* ('The City of the Sun'), after Tommaso Campanella's book *La città del sole*, tells of the 17th-century Lithuanian free-thinker Kazimieras Liščinskis.

Trys talismanai [The Three Talismans] (6 scenes, K. Inčiūra, after Lithuanian folktales), 1936, Kaunas, Valstibės, 19 March 1936
Marytė (4, A. Venclova, P. Keidošius and J. Gustaitis), Vilnius, Theatre of Opera and Ballet, 19 Sept 1953
Saulės miestas [The City of the Sun] (3, J. Mackonis, after T. Campanella), Vilnius, Theatre of Opera and Ballet, 13 March 1965

*

D. Palionytė: *Valanda su kompozitorium A. Račiūnu* [An Hour with the Composer A. Račiūnas] (Vilnius, 1970)

Radamisto ['Radamistus', 'Rhadamistus']. Opera in three acts by GEORGE FRIDERIC HANDEL to an anonymous libretto adapted from DOMENICO LALLI's *L'amor tirannico, o Zenobia* (1710, Venice) as revised for Florence (1712); London, King's Theatre, 27 April 1720.

Radamisto *son of Farasmane*	soprano
Zenobia *his wife*	contralto
Farasmane *King of Thrace*	bass
Tiridate *King of Armenia*	tenor
Polissena *his wife, daughter of Farasmane*	soprano
Tigrane *Prince of Pontus*	soprano
Fraarte *brother of Tiridate*	soprano

Setting Asia Minor, 1st century AD

Radamisto was Handel's first opera for the newly formed Royal Academy of Music and the Academy's second production. The wordbook, unusually, bears the composer's own dedication to King George I. Both the King and the Prince of Wales, recently reconciled after an estrangement of nearly three years, attended the first night and the initial run of ten performances was enthusiastically received. A substantially revised version of the opera was produced at the King's Theatre on 28 December 1720 with revisions to suit a much changed cast; there were further revivals with revisions the following year and in January 1728. A version of *Radamisto*, under the title *Zenobia*, was produced at Hamburg on 28 November 1722 and was frequently repeated. The first 20th-century revival, in a version by Joseph Wenz, was at Göttingen on 27 June 1927; the first in Britain was by the Handel Opera Society under Charles Farncombe at Sadler's Wells Theatre, London, on 6 July 1960. Chrysander's Händel-Gesellschaft edition presents the April 1720 version with deficiencies in detail and sadly misrepresents later versions by muddling their variants. Though a few recitatives are lost, the version of December 1720 merits a complete score of its own.

Burney's attribution of the libretto to Nicola Haym is plausible but cannot be confirmed. The basis of the story is a passage in Tacitus's *Annals of Imperial Rome* (xii.51), describing an incident in Asia Minor around 51 AD. The action takes place in and near an unnamed city on the banks of the river Araxes. Tiridate, King of Armenia, unmoved by the loyalty of his wife Polissena, has become infatuated with Zenobia, the wife of Radamisto. Radamisto is the son of King Farasmane of Thrace and Polissena's brother. In an attempt to capture Zenobia, Tiridate is laying siege to the city, which Radamisto is holding; he has already taken Farasmane prisoner. The opera begins with Polissena in despair, praying for divine help. Tiridate's ally Tigrane, Prince of Pontus, who loves her, fails to persuade her to leave Tiridate. Tiridate orders the destruction of the city, but allows his brother Fraarte to take Farasmane to the city walls to speak with Radamisto. When Radamisto appears Fraarte tells him that he must yield the city or his father will be executed on the spot. Farasmane urges his son to be defiant, and Fraarte gives the signal for his execution; but Tigrane intervenes. Tigrane and Fraarte then lead a successful attack on the city. Tiridate, annoyed at the sparing of Farasmane, agrees that he may live if Radamisto and Zenobia are brought to him. Fraarte remembers his own former love for Zenobia. Radamisto and Zenobia escape from the city via a subterranean passage and emerge in open country near the Araxes. Soldiers approach, and in despair Zenobia begs her husband to kill her. He makes a reluctant attempt to do so, but merely wounds her. Zenobia tries to fulfil her intentions by throwing herself into the river. The soldiers, under Tigrane's command, capture Radamisto. Fraarte saves Zenobia from drowning and brings her to Tiridate. He learns that he is his brother's rival in love. Zenobia resists the advances of both brothers. Tigrane brings Radamisto, disguised as a soldier, to Polissena. As Tiridate pays court to Zenobia, Tigrane enters with Radamisto's clothes and announces that he is dead; a 'messenger' will report what happened. The messenger, named Ismene, is the disguised Radamisto, immediately recognized by Zenobia. Tiridate is annoyed by Radamisto's account of his supposed dying speech, but feels that Ismene will be useful and asks him for help in gaining Zenobia. Tigrane and Fraarte, wearying of Tiridate's tyranny, plan to make the king see the error of his ways. Tiridate greets Zenobia as Queen of Armenia and offers her a crown and sceptre. She rejects the offer and Tiridate tries to catch hold of her. Radamisto enters, together with Polissena and Farasmane, and threatens Tiridate with his sword, but Polissena intervenes. Farasmane reveals Radamisto's identity. Tiridate orders his execution and refuses to spare him despite Polissena's pleas; she warns him that her sorely tried fidelity may yet change to anger. Tiridate agrees to pardon Radamisto if Zenobia will be his. In the temple Zenobia makes the choice: she rejects Tiridate and will die with her husband. But Polissena announces that Tiridate's army has revolted and, led by Tigrane and Fraarte, surrounds the temple. Tiridate is abandoned by his attendants and is held. Tigrane offers the throne of Armenia to Farasmane. Radamisto asks Polissena to pardon the repentant Tiridate and tells them to rule in Armenia as before; his reunion with Zenobia has banished his sorrows.

* * *

The serious tone and powerfully motivated action of *Radamisto* mark a decisive break from the more carelessly assembled operas that Handel had composed for London in the previous decade. Both the female roles are memorably portrayed in their music, the submissive Polissena (first sung by Ann Turner Robinson) showing strength in her unswerving if apparently unmerited love for her tyrannous husband, and Zenobia (Anastasia Robinson) brave and passionate in her faithfulness to Radamisto. Only in Polissena's 'Sposo ingrato', the lengthy and over-elaborate Act 3 aria in which she turns on Tiridate, does Handel falter; and the fault was to be splendidly corrected in the first revision of the opera. The part of Radamisto was written for the soprano Margherita Durastanti: his F minor lament 'Ombra cara', sung in Act 2 when he believes Zenobia to be dead, is perhaps the greatest of all the arias, but the standard is consistently high throughout.

For the December 1720 revival, the alto castrato Senesino took over Radamisto, Durastanti transferring to Zenobia and the bass Giuseppe Boschi playing Tiridate; Handel took the opportunity to make several changes for what seem to be purely artistic reasons. Certain features of the earlier score – such as Tiridate's aria with trumpet 'Stragi, morti' – are regrettably lost, but in general the new version improves on the old, especially in Act 3: Polissena turns on Tiridate with the wonderfully dramatic aria 'Barbaro, partirò' (begun without ritornello), and a remarkable quartet marks the climax. Ten arias, a duet and the quartet were newly composed. In 1721 Handel removed the part of Fraarte; the revisions for the 1728 revival, to allow the roles of Zenobia and Polissena to be taken over by the rival sopranos Faustina and Cuzzoni, and Tigrane by the alto castrato Baldi, severely weaken the characterization.

For a page from a prompt copy of the libretto for *Radamisto*, see PRODUCTION, fig.7.   ANTHONY HICKS

Radford. English sisters, founders and directors of the Falmouth Opera Singers, a company dedicated to giving opera in English. Maisie (*b* Plymouth, 26 April 1885; *d* St Anthony in Roseland, nr Truro, 16 July 1973) and Evelyn (*b* Plympton, 21 Jan 1887; *d* Hayle, 30 March 1969) formed the enterprising amateur company in 1923. Beginning with Gluck's *Orfeo ed Euridice*, and using local soloists, chorus and orchestra, they put on operas yearly until 1968; Maisie conducted, Evelyn was répétiteur, and together they coached and directed. In Falmouth and London they translated and staged revivals of *La clemenza di Tito* (1931), the first in England since 1840, and of *Idomeneo* (1937), the first ever in England. Evelyn, the linguist, and Maisie, the singer and poet, wrote accurate, elegant and singable translations. They also translated and staged Pergolesi's *La serva padrona* (1927, 1950), Gluck's *Armide* (1936) and *La Cythère assiégée* (1950), Spontini's *La vestale* (1954) and Monteverdi's *Combattimento di Tancredi e Clorinda* (1965); Cherubini's *Eliza* was only translated. Gluck's *Orfeo* was given several times (1925, 1940, 1955), as was *Die Entführung aus dem Serail* (1926, 1932, 1952); further productions included Purcell's *King Arthur* (1924, 1959) and *Dido and Aeneas* (1942), Gluck's *Iphigénie en Tauride* (1934) and *Alceste* (1949), Mozart's *Der Schauspieldirektor* (1943) and Rossini's *Mosè in Egitto* (1954). They gave the first stage performances of several Handel oratorios and Mendelssohn's *Elijah* (1927). Philip Cannon was commissioned to compose *Morvoren* (1964), to a libretto by Maisie based on a Cornish legend. The company also revived English operas by Stanford, Holst, Vaughan Williams and Rutland Boughton.

M. Radford and E. Radford: *Musical Adventures in Cornwall* (London, 1965)   JENNET CAMPBELL

Radford, Robert (*b* Nottingham, 13 May 1874; *d* London, 1 March 1933). English bass. He studied in London, making his début in 1904 at Covent Garden as the Commendatore. He sang Hunding and Hagen in 1908 in the first *Ring* cycle in English, conducted by Richter; Pogner (*Die Meistersinger*) and Abbot Tunstall in the première of Naylor's *The Angelus*, 1909; and, in 1910, Claudius (*Hamlet*) and Tomasso in the British première of *Tiefland*. During the war years he sang with the Beecham Opera Company on tour and in London, when his roles included Boris. Returning to Covent Garden as a founder-member of the British National Opera Company in 1922–3, he appeared as Méphistophélès, the Father (*Louise*), King Mark and Osmin. His firm, resonant voice was particularly admired in Wagner.

W. G. Kloet: 'Robert Radford', *Record Collector*, xiv (1961–2), 200–30 [with discography by J. P. Kenyon]
W. Radford: 'Robert Radford', *Recorded Sound*, no.39 (1970), 632–8   ELIZABETH FORBES

Radić, Dušan (*b* Sombor, 10 April 1929). Serbian composer. After studying at the Academy of Music in Belgrade and with Milhaud and Messiaen in Paris, he worked as a freelance artist, composing theatre music in a neo-classical style close to that of Stravinsky, Prokofiev and Bartók. After writing incidental music for Molière's farce *Monsieur de Pourceaugnac* he composed the *comédie-ballet Ljubav, to je glavna stvar* ('Love, that is the Principal Thing'; Belgrade, 15 Dec 1963), on a shortened translation of the same work by Stanislav Vinaver. The impressions conveyed by this comic opera are direct and grotesque. The musical language is simple and tonal, and the vocal parts range from speech to arioso, as in *opéra comique*; there are many ballet numbers. In addition to an earlier ballet Radić also composed film music. In 1979 he became professor at the Academy of Art in Novi Sad.

V. Peričić: *Muzički stvaraoci u Srbiji* [Musical Creators in Serbia] (Belgrade, 1969)   ROKSANDA PEJOVIĆ

Radicati, Felice Alessandro (*b* Turin, 1775; *d* Bologna, 19 March 1820). Italian composer. He studied the violin with Pugnani and played in the Turin *cappella* until it disbanded in 1798. He married the soprano Teresa Bertinotti in 1801. They spent the years 1805–8 in Germany and Austria, where Felice played and composed chamber music. He was welcomed in Viennese social and artistic circles that included such figures as Haydn and Ferdinand Fränzl. In 1809 Felice's opera *Coriolano* was produced in Amsterdam, and while the Radicatis were in England, 1810–12, *Fedra* had its première at the King's Theatre, London (5 March 1811). *Fedra* did not, according to the *Morning Herald*'s critic, show 'any material sign of either genius or perfect knowledge'. However, the oboist William Parke thought the music good and 'the finale of Act 1 and the duet "con sola quest'anima" masterly compositions'. For two years they lived and performed in Lisbon, then returned to Italy. Felice held posts in Turin and Bologna, and two more of his operas were given: *Castore e Polluce* (1815, Bologna) and *Blondello* (1816, Turin).

Il sultano generoso, c1805, unperf.
Coriolano, Amsterdam, 1809
Fedra, London, King's, 5 March 1811
L'intrigo fortunato, 1815

Castore e Polluce (2, L. Romanelli), Bologna, Corso, 27 May 1815
Blondello, ossia Riccardo Cuor di Leone (A. L. Tottola), Turin, Carignano, aut. 1816
La lezione singolare, ossia Un giorno a Parigi, c1819, unperf.
I due prigioneri, c1820, unperf.
Il medico per forza, c1820, unperf.

*

DEUMM (R. Cognazzo)
W. T. Parke: *Musical Memoirs* (London, 1830)   ALBERT MELL

Radio. It is the peculiar achievement of 20th-century technico-musical developments to have isolated the sound from the sight of music-making, creating disembodied sound; and it is a curious but undeniable fact that the most extensive coverage of the operatic repertory and its widest dissemination among the public have been due to two media, sound recordings and the radio, which lack all the visual elements of the art (acting, costume, scenery, lighting) that are essential to its full representation. Nevertheless, radio from its earliest days has involved itself with opera – as early as 1910 an attempt was made to relay Caruso in *Pagliacci* from the Metropolitan Opera House, New York – and during the course of the century a huge range of works, familiar, neglected or quite unknown, from 17th-century beginnings to contemporary compositions, has been broadcast by radio organizations, especially in Europe and North America. (BBC Radio, for example, broadcasts about 120 operas each year.) Stations have had three sources of supply: commercial records; relays, either live or recorded, from opera houses and festivals; and studio productions.

1. Early history. 2. Special problems. 3. Opera-house relays. 4. Studio performance.

1. EARLY HISTORY. The scarcity of commercial recordings of complete operas until the second half of the century, with the advent first of long-playing and then of compact discs, and the limited production facilities and technical expertise of pioneering radio stations, meant that at the beginning, opera-house relays (perforce live, since recording was not yet a possibility) provided the first manifestations of opera on radio. Programme heads, understandably anxious to appeal to known public tastes when launching a new medium, chose well-known popular works for these relays: for example, *Madama Butterfly* from the Unter den Linden house in Berlin in 1921; *La bohème* from Salt Lake City in 1922; Act 1 of *Die Zauberflöte* from Covent Garden in 1923; Smetana's *The Two Widows* (at least locally familiar) from the Prague National Theatre in 1925; Gounod's *Faust* from the Chicago Civic Opera in 1926. Annual broadcasts from the Bayreuth Festival began in 1930 with *Tristan und Isolde*. The Metropolitan Opera began a long and influential series of Saturday afternoon live relays in 1931. However, more adventurous programme executives soon realized that the standard repertory offered by opera houses, although much appreciated by the general public, could become unduly restrictive, and sought to extend the range of works by producing less familiar operas in the studio. The BBC was among the first to do so, broadcasting Gounod's *Roméo et Juliette* in 1923, and in 1926 breaking fresh ground by giving the first UK performance of Rimsky-Korsakov's *Legend of the Invisible City of Kitezh*.

As radio developed, composers, initially slightly suspicious of the new medium, began to take it seriously and – with or without commissions from radio organizations – started to write works specifically

designed for it, capitalizing on radio's potential for stimulating the listener's imagination. Most such works were shorter than stage operas, some included elements of fantasy, and the best of them avoided elaborate plots that might confuse the unaided ear. Among such radio operas may be mentioned Egk's *Columbus* (Bavarian Radio, 1933), Cadman's *The Willow Tree* (NBC, 1932), Sutermeister's *Die schwarze Spinne* (Radio Beromünster, 1936), Martinů's *The Voice of the Forest* and *The Comedy on the Bridge* (Czech Radio, 1935 and 1937 respectively), Louis Gruenberg's *Green Mansions* (CBS, 1937, described as a 'non-visual opera'), Menotti's *The Old Maid and the Thief* (NBC, 1939), Randall Thompson's *Solomon and Balkis* (CBS, 1942), Ibert's *Barbe-bleue* (Radio Lausanne, 1943), Dallapiccola's *Il prigioniero* (RAI, 1949), Harsányi's *Illusion* (RTF, 1948), Chevreuille's *D'un diable de briquet* (Radiodiffusion-Télévision Belge, 1950), Reizenstein's *Anna Kraus* (BBC, 1952), Pizzetti's *Cagliostro* (RAI, 1952), Henze's *Ein Landarzt* and *Das Ende einer Welt* (Norddeutscher Rundfunk, 1951 and 1953 respectively), Mihalovici's *Die Heimkehr* (Hessischer Rundfunk, 1954), Sven-Erik Bäck's *Tranfjädrarna* ('The Crane Feathers'; Swedish Radio, 1957), Badings's *Asterion* (South African Radio, 1957), Petrovics's *C'est la guerre* (Hungarian Radio, 1961) and Searle's *The Photo of the Colonel* (BBC, 1964).

An extra fillip was given to musical works commissioned for radio and produced by members of the European Broadcasting Union (EBU) by the institution in 1948 of the Prix Italia: among its award-winning operas were Pizzetti's *Ifigenia* (RAI, 1950) and Badings's *Orestes* (Netherlands Radio, 1954); but most Prix Italia entries lay outside the purely operatic category, focussing more on 'mixed forms' and technological experimentation. Not many of these new operas were taken up by other than their originating stations, however; and as their brevity (and, in some cases, their particularly radiogenic qualities) militated against their adoption by opera houses, financial returns from performing rights were scanty. Accordingly, composers have become increasingly less tempted by the form, especially since the advent of television opera, which commands larger audiences and is not subject to radio's visual limitations.

2. SPECIAL PROBLEMS. A consequence of 'blind opera' (as operatic radio transmissions have been called), like that of concert performances, is to limit attention to the music and its performers: even the words take second place, since not all of them, no matter how clear the singers' enunciation, are likely to be picked up by the listener, however keen-eared, on a first hearing. This weakening of the dramatic aspect, in an art which by definition is basically 'dramma per musica', is severe, and has contributed to the heresy (taking as dogma Rossini's desideratum of 'voce, voce e poi voce') of regarding operas as showpieces for singers, a kind of vocal point-to-point linked somehow or other with connecting material, and to exaggerated personality cults of operatic stars; on the other hand, it must be admitted that many works of musical interest that are unstageworthy or handicapped by a poor libretto have been rescued from oblivion in this way.

A major and seemingly insoluble problem in radio opera, whatever its source, is how to keep the listener abreast of the action. Here the medium is under a disadvantage even as compared with commercial records, which now commonly include a libretto, or at least a synopsis of the plot, which can be referred to at any moment. Attempts have been made to supply summaries of the action (sometimes with a timetable of its events, related to the programme transmission time), either by publication in radio journals or by post to those interested enough to write in beforehand; but patently these cannot reach the whole audience, some of whom will probably have tuned in by chance. The usual practice of introducing an opera by a presenter or announcer outlining the plot is very much a makeshift, since even when each scene is prefaced with a résumé it is often very difficult, in an unfamiliar work, for a listener to bear in mind all the details of the action, particularly if it is at all complex, and to relate them to what is heard: instead, the listener is faced (especially if the work is being given in a foreign tongue) with uncomprehended expanses of singing. It cannot be lightly assumed, either, that the details of the plots of frequently performed works are known: could even seasoned operagoers be certain of the details of the action in, say, Act 4 of *Figaro*? Some radio producers, in their endeavours to clarify matters, have gone so far as to intervene with explanatory commentaries at natural breaks or pauses within a work; but many listeners resent such intrusions in its artistic continuity, especially when a sudden intervention in the vernacular disrupts the atmosphere of a foreign-language performance.

3. OPERA-HOUSE RELAYS. This particular problem is highlighted in the many live relays or recordings from opera houses which, since soon after World War II, have been made available outside the initiating country in international exchanges, either direct between stations or through the EBU as an intermediary, and which conspicuously enrich locally available fare. Though paid for by the originating station, such exchanges are usually cost-free to recipients abroad. Programme heads tend to welcome broadcasts from opera stages as lending a 'sense of occasion', but direct relays, as well as being technically full of pitfalls, can cause anxieties over timing to the radio producer: not only has he or she to ensure that the duration – easily affected by small mishaps in the theatre, stage-waits or vagaries of tempo by singer or conductor – does not exceed its allocation in the programme schedule, but every interval and scene change, and even the conductor's entries into the pit, ideally should be timed at a previous performance so that such pauses can be filled on the night with a commentary that fits exactly. Breakdowns in transmission lines from abroad have been known to disrupt a foreign relay or even cause it to be abandoned.

It is highly desirable too for the sound engineers to have heard a performance before that being broadcast so that they can secure a satisfactory overall sonority, balance between singers and orchestra and spatial perspectives: failure to do so has often resulted in its becoming plain that they were groping their way, grappling with troublesome acoustics, poor orchestral sound quality and unwanted stage noises, including the contribution of the prompter. Sound engineers in different countries and different organizations have their own ideas on microphone placing. Some idea of the complexity of their task may be gained from an outline of the 1990 set-up adopted by BBC technicians for relays from Covent Garden: this consists of a stereo mix from two stereo microphones, one above the conductor's head and one slung from the roof halfway down the auditorium (for perspective and atmosphere), a number of mono microphones in the orchestra pit to highlight various instrumental sections, four to six 'pressure-zone' mono microphones across the front of the stage (each covering a limited area), plus possible extra microphones (e.g. hanging from a stage lighting gantry) for any important upstage or offstage action.

4. STUDIO PERFORMANCE. Studio productions of operas present rather fewer purely technical problems, since the producer can position his singers as he pleases instead of having to conform to a plan designed for visual presentation. Works chosen are those unlikely to be available from stage sources, such as rarely heard Baroque or early Classical operas or new contemporary operas; but radio has also rendered valuable service in producing works that, in the theatre, would make intolerably heavy demands on casting, rehearsal time and costs. For some years the EBU organized jointly-funded productions of such works – beginning in 1973 with Milhaud's highly elaborate *Christophe Colomb*, which calls for a large cast of singers and speaking actors and a big double chorus (and, in the theatre, cinematography), and in 1977 including Schreker's *Der ferne Klang*, with a cast of two dozen and multiple orchestral and choral groups – which were transmitted in about a dozen countries. The EBU was also active in initiating and making possible the recording of the pioneer series of Haydn operas conducted by Antal Dorati that were later released on commercial discs.

Considerable differences of approach are found among opera producers for radio. Some are content with what is no more than a concert performance, each singer making his or her contribution from a set position. Others try to suggest a stage production, using distant placing for offstage effects, changing perspectives to follow characters' entrances or exits, and creating, by the use of a 'stereo image', the illusion that characters are moving about the scene in accordance with the course of the action. The most radical approach is that of imaginative producers who argue that, as it is common practice to adapt stage dramas for the radio medium, similar treatment logically should be applied to opera. This is not a question merely of employing differentiated acoustics (e.g. a rather hollow, reverberant atmosphere for supernatural voices, such as that of the graveyard statue in *Don Giovanni* or the initial appearance, from the background, of Death in Holst's *Sāvitri*), manipulating sound levels (for violent orchestral outbursts accompanying some dramatic climax like the oven explosion in *Hänsel und Gretel*), electronically 'panning' a procession across the sound spectrum (as in Berlioz's *Les Troyens*) or discreetly adding realistic sound effects (the clinking of coins, the clashing of swords in a duel, the smashing of china in Donizetti's *Campanello di notte*, or the flutter of the magpie's wings in Rossini's *La gazza ladra* as it flies off with the silver). All these treatments, however, call for the nicest judgment, since excessive recourse to noises (as of footsteps or shutting of doors) sounds merely ridiculous.

The producer needs to remember that the listener has no way of knowing to whom a new voice that appears unannounced belongs, or of telling when a character addresses his words first to one person and then turns to another: in an endeavour to compensate for the lack of sight which would make such things instantly understandable, words may be changed slightly so as to identify the newcomer or the person being addressed. On the stage the presence of a chorus is obvious even when it has nothing to sing for long periods; but on the radio the listener may well forget its existence, and in order to integrate it into the action it could with advantage be given appropriate noises of reaction to what is taking place – laughter, applause, murmurs of indignation or encouragement, and so on; indeed, the absence of any such sounds can lend an air of unreality to its sudden outbursts of singing. It may even be necessary to write in an occasional spoken line for one or other of the characters in order to make the situation clear. This is particularly so in what are the extreme cases of difficulty, mime scenes: from the music alone, no one could tell what is happening at the end of Act 2 of *Tosca* or Act 1 of Hindemith's *Cardillac*, in the pantomime in Weill's *Der Protagonist*, or in the scene of the convicts' crude entertainment in Act 2 of Janáček's *From the House of the Dead*. For these it is necessary to invent evocative sound montages. Much can be done by an ingenious producer to adapt opera to the radio medium while leaving the music itself inviolate, as it must be.

K. Blum: *Die Funkoper* (diss., U. of Cologne, 1951)
Opera in Radio, TV and Film (Salzburg, 1956) [pubn of Internationales Musikzentrum]
N. Goodwin: 'BBC Plans and Policy', *Opera*, xv (1964), 233–7
L. Salter: 'Opera at Home', *EBU Review*, no.96*b* (1966), 12–18
B. Paulu: *Radio and Television Broadcasting on the European Continent* (Minneapolis, 1967)
J. Bornoff, ed.: *Music Theatre in a Changing Society* (Paris, 1968)
S. Goslich: 'Brief History of Opera on Radio', *IMZ Congress: Salzburg 1971*
——: *Musik im Rundfunk* (Tutzing, 1971) [incl. extensive bibliography]
J. Bornoff and L. Salter: *Music and the 20th-century Media* (Florence, 1972) [pubn of International Music Council]
IMZ Symposium: Opera in Television (Vienna, 1978) [pubn of Internationales Musikzentrum]
A. Dean: 'The Operas of Haydn: an Example of EBU Radio Co-operation', *EBU Review*, xxx/5 (1979), 23–7   LIONEL SALTER

Radnai, Miklós (*b* Budapest, 1 Jan 1892; *d* Budapest, 4 Nov 1935). Hungarian director, composer and critic. He studied composition with Koessler and Viktor Herzfeld at the Budapest Academy of Music (1906–11) and later taught at the Fodor Conservatory (1912–19) and at the Budapest College of Music (1919–25). He also wrote music criticism for various daily newspapers in the Hungarian capital from 1919 to 1925. From August 1925 until his early death he was artistic director of the Royal Hungarian Opera House in Budapest. His tenure brought consolidation and higher artistic standards to the institution between the two world wars. By engaging young artists (János Ferencsik as co-répétiteur, later conductor, and Kálmán Nádasdy and Gusztáv Oláh as directors), he ushered in a new phase in the history of the opera house. Radnai engaged the leading Italian conductor Sergio Failoni as chief conductor for the Wagner, Verdi, Bartók and Kodály repertory. He was as eager to produce the works of contemporary Hungarian composers (Jenő Ádám, Bartók, Ernő Dohnányi, Hubay, Kodály, Kósa, Albert Siklós, Tivadar Szántó, Leó Weiner) as those of earlier masters of Hungarian music (Erkel, Liszt, Mosonyi) and of his foreign contemporaries (Debussy, Falla, Hindemith, Malipiero, Milhaud, Ravel, Respighi, Richard Strauss, Stravinsky, Zandonai). In revitalizing the design and production side, establishing discipline during rehearsals and performances, and educating a young

and gifted generation of singers, Radnai created one of the most successful chapters in the history of Hungarian opera. He also contributed knowledgeable studies of works by Gounod, Erkel, Poldini and Goldmark to the literature of operatic analysis.   FERENC BÓNIS

Radoux, Jean-Théodore (*b* Liège, 9 Nov 1835; *d* Liège, 20 March 1911). Belgian composer. After studying at the Liège Conservatory, he was appointed bassoon professor there as early as 1856. He won the Belgian Prix de Rome in 1859 and continued his training in Paris with Halévy. He was director of the Liège Conservatory, 1872–1911, and was elected to the Académie Royale de Belgique in 1874. Radoux left many vocal works (songs, choruses and cantatas), piano music and several orchestral overtures. His opera *Le Béarnais*, which observes all the conventions of *opéra comique*, had some success thanks to its many numbers containing local colour, to its use of familiar themes (including 'Vive Henri IV') and to the orchestral accompaniment, which is often more original than the vocal parts. After the failure of *La coupe enchantée*, Radoux wrote little operatic music. His brother Jean-Toussaint Radoux (1825–89) wrote two *épisodes lyriques*, *Marie de Brabant* (F. Chaumont; Liège, 2 March 1854) and *Le Juif errant* (P. Bracaval; Liège, 26 March 1871).

Le Béarnais (oc, 3, A. Pellier-Quensy), Liège, Royal, 14 March 1866; lib. rev. H. Kirsch, 1868
La coupe enchantée (oc, 2, Pellier-Quensy and Kirsch), Brussels, Monnaie, 15 Jan 1872
Une aventure sous la Ligue (oc, 1)
Le miracle (oc, 1, J. Demoulin), ?unperf.
André Doria (oc, 3, Pellier-Quensy), inc.

S. Dupuis: 'Notice sur Jean-Théodore Radoux', *Annuaire de l'Académie royale de Belgique*, xci (1925), 71–111
C. van den Borren: *Geschiedenis van de muziek in de Nederlanden*, ii (Antwerp, 1951), 215–17   HENRI VANHULST

Radoux-Rogier, Charles (*b* Liège, 30 July 1877; *d* Liège, 30 April 1952). Belgian composer, son of Jean-Théodore Radoux. He studied at the Liège conservatory and in 1907 won the Belgian Prix de Rome. Appointed professor of harmony at the Liège conservatory in 1905, he was later inspector of music education and was also active as a pianist and music critic. His operatic works, though hardly original in musical style, are among his best works, displaying his pleasing lyrical facility. *Le sanglier des Ardennes*, incidental music for a drama by Jules Sauvenière, was first performed in Liège (12 June 1905); the four-act *drame lyrique Oudelette*, to a libretto by Richard Ledent, had its première in Brussels (Théâtre de la Monnaie, 11 April 1912). Radoux-Rogier employed leitmotifs, and the vocal style of the music is clearly influenced by Wagner, as is the composer's use of the orchestra to comment on the actions and emotions of the characters.   HENRI VANHULST

Raff, (Joseph) Joachim (*b* Lachen, nr Zürich, 27 May 1822; *d* Frankfurt, ?24/25 June 1882). German composer and teacher. Despite early success as a composer of piano pieces, he was unsuccessful in trying to secure a performance of a grand heroic opera, *König Alfred*, in Stuttgart in 1845. However, on moving to Weimar as Liszt's assistant in 1850, he conducted his opera at the Weimar Hoftheater in 1851. Liszt thought *König Alfred* dramatically effective and wrote a fantasy on its themes, but Raff was disappointed that its success failed to spread beyond Weimar. His next opera,

Samson, was more ambitious still, drawing upon his symphonic writing and also his new enthusiasm for Wagner, as revealed in his Wagner piano fantasies of 1853, but the difficulty of the singers' roles prohibited its performance. Raff left for Wiesbaden in 1856, discouraged by the lack of support now offered by the Lisztian circle. With the comic opera *Die Parole* (1868), he embraced a lighter Italian or French idiom, reminiscent of his salon writing. Raff lacked sympathy with Wagner's style from the *Ring* onwards and in later years became seen as a conservative figure, turning towards a lyrical rather than dramatic view of opera.

König Alfred (4, G. Logau), Weimar, Hof, 9 March 1851; rev. 1852, Weimar, 13 March 1853
Samson, 1853–7 (5, Raff), unperf.
Die Parole, 1868 (3, Raff, after von Saldern), unperf.
Dame Kobold (komische Oper, 3, P. Reber, after P. Calderón de la Barca), Weimar, 9 April 1870, vs (Berlin, 1871)
Benedetto Marcello, 1877–8 (3, Raff), unperf.
Die Eifersüchtigen, 1881–2 (komische Oper, 3, Raff), unperf.

J. Raff: *Die Wagnerfrage*, i: *Wagners letzte künstlerische Kundgebung im Lohengrin* (Brunswick, 1854)
F. Liszt: 'Dornröschen, Genast's Gedicht und Raff's Musik gleichen Namens', *Gesammelte Schriften*, v, ed. L. Ramann (Leipzig, 1882), 133–81
A. Schäfer: *Chronologisch-systematisches Verzeichnis der Werke Joachim Raffs* (Wiesbaden, 1888)
P. Marsop: 'Joachim Raff und "Die Wagnerfrage"', *Neue Musik-Zeitung*, xliii (1922), 252–4
H. Raff: *Joachim Raff: ein Lebensbild* (Regensburg, 1925)
M. Römer: *Josef Joachim Raff (1822–1882)* (Wiesbaden, 1982)
AMANDA GLAUERT

Raffaelli, Francesca. *See* CACCINI family, (2).

Raffanelli [Rafanelli], **Luigi** (*b* Pistoia, 21 March 1752; *d* Milan, 1821). Italian bass. He studied at Pistoia with a certain Renai and first appeared, so far as is known, in Venice in 1781. Shortly thereafter he married the singer Giulia Moroni, with whom he performed in Venice and Genoa (1783–6). He sang in Genoa and Rome in 1787–8 and then took part in a production at the Théâtre Italien, Paris, where he was engaged until 1792. After further appearances in Genoa (1795) and Rome (1796), he returned to both Venice (1796–1800) and Paris (1801–7). His last appearance was at La Scala in 1815. He was one of the leading performers of his day in comic opera, and his repertory included works by Paisiello, Cimarosa and Rossini. COLIN TIMMS

Raffanti, Dano (*b* Lucca, 5 April 1948). Italian tenor. While studying in Milan, he made his début at La Scala in 1976 in Bussotti's *Nottetempo*. In 1978 he sang Medoro in Vivaldi's *Orlando furioso* in Verona, repeating the role for his American début in 1980 in Dallas. He made his Metropolitan début in 1981 as Alfredo, later singing the Duke, Edgar, and Goffredo in Handel's *Rinaldo*. He has sung throughout Italy, in Paris, San Francisco, Hamburg, Berlin and at Covent Garden, where he sang Tebaldo in *I Capuleti e i Montecchi* (1984). His roles include Titus, Lyonel (*Martha*), Almaviva, Nemorino, Roderick Dhu (*La donna del lago*), Fra Diavolo, Rinuccio, Rodolfo, Idomeneus and Don Carlos, which he sang at Turin in 1990. He has a lyrical, silver-toned voice and is a stylish interpreter of bel canto opera. ELIZABETH FORBES

Raffeiner, Walter (*b* Wolfsberg, 8 April 1947). Austrian tenor. He studied in Vienna, making his début in 1973 at Hagen as a baritone. Engaged at Darmstadt, he sang Pedro (*Tiefland*), his first tenor role. In 1979 he moved to Frankfurt, where he sang Painter/Negro (*Lulu*), Stolzius (*Die Soldaten*), Max, Florestan and Parsifal. He has sung at Kassel, Munich, Hamburg, Vienna, Düsseldorf and Salzburg, where he created Silvanus Schuller in Penderecki's *Schwarze Maske* in 1986. His repertory includes Siegmund, Tristan, Shuisky, Tichon (*Kát'a Kabanová*), Yannakos (*Greek Passion*), Sergey (*Lady Macbeth of the Mtsensk District*), Herod, Drum Major (*Wozzeck*) and Alexey (*The Gambler*). An excellent actor, he has a strong voice which is particularly effective in modern music.
ELIZABETH FORBES

Raftery, J(ohn) Patrick (*b* Washington DC, 4 April 1957). American baritone. He studied with Armen Boyajian, making his début in 1980 at Chicago as Shchelkalov (*Boris Godunov*). In 1982 he sang Zurga at Paris Châtelet and Harald in the American première of *Gwendoline* at San Diego; and in 1984 Guglielmo at Glyndebourne and Pasha Seid (*Il corsaro*) at San Diego. He has sung with NY City Opera and at Santa Fe, Hamburg, Bonn, Cologne, Brussels and Covent Garden, where he made his début in 1985 as Almaviva. His repertory includes Enrico Ashton, Belcore (*L'elisir d'amore*), Malatesta, Riccardo (*I puritani*), Yevgeny Onegin, Yeletsky (*The Queen of Spades*), Escamillo, Mercutio, Valentin, Luna, Marcello, Lescaut (*Manon*), Germont and Sharpless. His light, flexible voice and acting ability are ideally displayed as Rossini's Figaro, a role he sang in Vancouver in 1991. ELIZABETH FORBES

Ragin, Derek Lee (*b* West Point, NY, 17 June 1958). American countertenor. He studied at the Oberlin College Conservatory of Music, Ohio, and at the age of 26 won the ITT International Fellowship, which enabled him to study in Amsterdam. He has won several major prizes, including first prize in the 1986 Munich International Competition. In 1983 he made his operatic début in Cesti's *Tito* at the Festwoche der Alten Musik, Innsbruck. His American début was as Nirenus in Handel's *Giulio Cesare* at the Metropolitan in 1988. He has appeared at the Aldeburgh, Maryland and Aix-en-Provence festivals, and in 1990 made his Salzburg Festival début as Orpheus in Gluck's *Orfeo ed Euridice*. His recordings include Handel's *Tamerlano* and *Flavio*, and Hasse's *Cleofide*.

He sings in concerts in Germany and elsewhere, but is particularly renowned for his interpretations of operatic roles. NICHOLAS ANDERSON

Ragué, Louis-Charles (*b* before 1760; *d* Moulins, after 1793). French composer and harp teacher. He appeared on the musical scene in Paris in 1783, when the press described him as an 'amateur distinguished in more than one genre' (*Mercure de France*, October 1784, p.239). He had an active and highly successful career for a decade, after which he disappeared. His two *opéras comiques* were first performed at the Opéra-Comique (Salle Favart): *Memnon* on 26 August 1784 and *L'amour filial* on 2 March 1786. *Memnon* was unsuccessful because of its weak libretto, although some musical numbers were praised for their melodic charm; *L'amour filial* was more favourably received. Ragué's name appeared frequently in the Parisian press until December 1793, when his ballet *Les muses* was presented at the Opéra. According to Fétis, he retired to the environs of Moulins in 1792 (1794, after the première of his ballet, seems a more likely date).

Although Ragué was not known as a harpist, almost all his compositions (including two methods) were for the harp, which was much in vogue in Paris at the time.

Memnon (oc, 3, J.-F. Guichard, after Voltaire), Paris, OC (Favart), 26 Aug 1784; 3 airs pubd in P. Le Roy: *Airs de Richard Coeur de Lion, Memnon etc.* (Paris, 1784)

L'amour filial (oc, 2, B. F. de Rosoi, after J. J. Engel: *Der dankbare Sohn*), Paris, OC (Favart), 2 March 1786; excerpts pubd in contemporary anthologies

*

Notices in contemporary Parisian periodicals, incl. *Almanach musical* (1783); *Mercure de France* (1783–7); *Annonces, affiches et avis divers* (1783–93); *Journal général de France* (1785–6)

A. d'Origny: *Annales du Théâtre Italien depuis son origine jusqu'à ce jour*, iii (Paris, 1788), 166–7

A. Choron and F. Fayolle: *Dictionnaire historique des musiciens* (Paris, 1810–11)   BARRY S. BROOK, SUSAN KAGAN

Raguenet, François (*b* Rouen, *c*1660; *d* 1722). French writer on music. A doctor of medicine and a priest, he was tutor to the nephews of Cardinal de Bouillon, whom he accompanied to Rome in 1697. In Italy he developed a passionate interest in both Roman architecture and contemporary Italian music, which after his return to Paris he expressed in *Les monumens de Rome* (1700) and *Paralèle des italiens et des françois, en ce qui regarde la musique et les opéra* (1702). He may have worked in Rome on his edition of *Nouvelles oeuvres meslées de Saint-Evremond* (1700). He was already well known as the author of an epic two-volume novel, a history of the Old Testament and a biography of Oliver Cromwell; in 1689 he won the Académie Française's *prix d'éloquence* for his *Discours sur … le martyre*. His biography (1738) of Vicomte de Turenne (the uncle of Cardinal de Bouillon), for which he had access to secret state papers, earned him posthumous acclaim.

The title of his *Paralèle*, inspired by Charles Perrault's *Parallèle des anciens et des modernes en ce qui regard les arts et les sciences* (1692), compares Italian with French music, strongly favouring the former. Taking opera as his focus, he is unstinting in his praise for the Italian-born Lully. But he damns the French with faint praise by considering Lully the only French opera composer worth mentioning and suggests that parity between the two musics can be achieved only when a French-born composer succeeds in winning Italian approbation, as Lully did. For him, the Italians are born musicians and their castratos, with their 'voix de rossignol' and 'haleines infinies', are indispensable to opera. Raguenet praises the instrumentalists' technical training, their ability to sight-read and to play without a conductor and, noting the lowly status of French musicians, remarks on the prestige the Italians enjoy at home and abroad.

The warm reception accorded to the *Paralèle* by the press was starkly contrasted by the criticism voiced in the Première Partie of the *Comparaison de la musique italienne et de la musique françoise* (published anonymously in 1704). The author of the *Comparaison* was JEAN LAURENT LE CERF DE LA VIÉVILLE, vigorous champion of French music and a fellow *rouenais*. The controversy reached a climax in 1705 with the publication of Raguenet's bitter and often carping *Défense du Paralèle des italiens et des françois* (to which he appended André Maugars' 1639 *Réponse faite à un*

curieux sur le sentiment de la musique d'Italie, expurgated of any praise of French music), the Seconde Partie of Le Cerf's *Comparaison*, and, more particularly, Le Cerf's *Réponse à la Défense du Parallèle*. They were joined by Nicolas de Boisregard Andry, a physician and medical journalist who supported Raguenet in the *Journal des Sçavans* of 7 December 1705. Though Raguenet bowed out of the polemic, Le Cerf and Andry issued further publications in 1706.

Raguenet's *Paralèle* was translated, with copious annotations, into English in 1709 and twice into German, by Mattheson (1722) and Marpurg (1759). An anonymous, updated and annotated version was published in Amsterdam in 1753.

Paralèle des italiens et des françois, en ce qui regarde la musique et les opéra (Paris, 1702, 3/*c*1710); repr. with changes as *La paix de l'opéra, ou Parallèle impartial de la musique françoise et de la musique italienne* (Amsterdam, 1753); Eng. edn (London, 1709); repr. in *MQ*, xxxii (1946), 411–36, and in Strunk); Ger. edns in J. Mattheson: *Critica musica*, i (Hamburg, 1722) and F. W. Marpurg: *Kritische Briefe über die Tonkunst*, i (Berlin, 1759)

Défense du Paralèle des italiens et des françois, en ce qui regarde la musique et les opéra (Paris, 1705)

*

J. Ecorcheville: *De Lulli à Rameau 1690–1730: l'esthétique musicale* (Paris, 1906)

P.-M. Masson: 'Musique italienne et musique française: la première querelle', *RMI*, xix (1912), 519–45

M. E. Storer: 'Abbé François Raguenet: Deist, Historian, Music and Art Critic', *Romanic Review*, xxxvi (1945), 283–96

O. Strunk, ed.: *Source Readings in Music History* (New York, 1950), 473–88

G. Cowart: *The Origins of Modern Musical Criticism: French and Italian Music 1600–1750* (Ann Arbor, 1981)
                                    ALBERT COHEN, JULIE ANNE SADIE

Raichev, Alexander (*b* Lom, 11 April 1922). Bulgarian composer. He studied with Vladigerov at the State Musical Academy in Sofia, graduating in 1947, then with Kodály at the Budapest Conservatory (1949–50). Later he taught at the Bulgarian State Conservatory, where he was Rector from 1970 to 1978. Raichev's music shows the influence of Bach, Mozart and Beethoven, as well as Shostakovich, Stravinsky and Britten, and he has written in all genres. His operas show new developments in his style: *Most* ('The Bridge', 1965) is the first of two dealing with the struggle against fascism in Bulgaria; urban popular songs contribute a contemporary feel, while dramatic tension is built up in the music. The realistic treatment in *Trevoga* ('Anxiety', 1974), dealing with nationalist troubles before 1944, is an important development in Bulgarian opera. For the large-scale *Khan Asparouh* (1981), written to commemorate the 13th centenary of the founding of the Bulgarian state, Raichev took a historical subject, the settlement in the 7th century of the Balkan region by nomads from the Byzantine empire, led by Khan Asparouh. Both this and *Anxiety* are traditional number operas in *verismo* style; the musical language is modern, polytonal and dissonant. *Vasheto prisastvie* ('Your Presence', 1969) was the earliest Bulgarian radio opera to be broadcast.

Slaveyat na Orkhideyata [The Nightingale of the Orchid] (operetta, 7 scenes, V. Bashev, after P. Panchev), Sofia, State Music, 6 March 1962

Most [The Bridge] (3, Bashev), Ruse, Opera, 2 Oct 1965

Vasheto prisastvie [Your Presence] (radio op, 1), Radio Sofia, 5 Sept 1969; stage, Blagoevgrad, Chamber Opera, 1980

Trevoga [Anxiety] (3, O. Orlinov, after O. Vassilev: *Trevoga*), Sofia, National Opera, 1974

Khan Asparouh (N. Gounov), Ruse, Opera, 9 March 1981

D. Zenginov: 'Trevoga na Burgaska scena' [Anxiety Staged in Burgas], Bulgarska muzika, iii (1981), 55–6
B. Arnaudova: 'Khan Asparouh', Bulgarska muzika, v (1985), 60
A. Raichev: Kompozitor i suvremennost [Composer and Contemporaneity] (Sofia, 1985)   MAGDALENA MANOLOVA

Raichev, Peter (b Bulgaria, 9 March 1887; d Sofia, 3 Aug 1960). Bulgarian tenor. After studying in St Petersburg and at Naples with De Lucia, he made his début in 1913 at St Petersburg, where his roles included Lensky, Hermann (*The Queen of Spades*), Rodolfo and Canio. In 1920 he left Russia and sang in Italy, Vienna, Berlin, Leipzig, Dresden, Hamburg and Paris, touring in Europe and South America with Opéra Russe. Later he was engaged at Zagreb and Sofia. He retired in 1950 and concentrated on teaching. He had a strong, lyrical voice, most effective in Russian and Italian opera.

ELIZABETH FORBES

Raimondi, Gianni (b Bologna, 13 April 1923). Italian tenor. A pupil of Gennaro Barra-Caracciolo, he made his début in 1947 at the Teatro Comunale, Bologna, in *Rigoletto*. After appearing at the Comunale, Florence (1952), the Opéra (1953) and at the Stoll Theatre, London (*Rigoletto*, 1953), he sang for many years at La Scala, from 1955–6, also appearing at the Vienna Staatsoper (1958 and 1962) and at the Metropolitan (1965–6). Endowed with an ample voice of pure, warm timbre, he has clear enunciation and an exact sense of phrasing. The facility, range and brilliance of his top register have enabled him to take part in many important revivals such as Rossini's *Armida*, *Semiramide* and *Guillaume Tell*, and *Anna Bolena* and *Les vêpres siciliennes*. His other notable roles from the standard repertory include Rodolfo and Pinkerton.

GV (G. Gualerzi; R. Celletti)   RODOLFO CELLETTI

Raimondi, Pietro (b Rome, 20 Dec 1786; d Rome, 30 Oct 1853). Italian composer. After completing studies with Tritto at the Conservatorio di S Maria della Pietà in Naples, he embarked on a series of operas, mostly comic, for Genoa, Florence, Naples and Rome. In 1815 he took his first post as *maestro di cappella* in Acireale, Sicily, and apart from reviving two earlier operas for Messina and Catania, he was occupied mainly with cantatas and sacred music during this period. He resumed operatic composition after settling in Naples in 1820, reaffirming the gift for light farcical works, partly in Neapolitan dialect and with spoken dialogue, that was largely to sustain his theatrical career. His skill in treating comic dialect parts is shown in the first-act duet of *Il finto feudatario* (1826), in which the disguised Baron Folpo affects a lofty Italian while attempting to trick Albina into marrying him, reverting to dialect in an explosion of patter-singing as he sees his plan fail. The performance of such works was naturally restricted to Naples, though *La donna colonello* (1822), profiting by its association with Rubini, who had created the lead tenor role, was revived in Dresden in an all-Italian version. Rubini also included arias written for him in *La caccia di Enrico IV* (1822) and *Argia* (1823) on concert tours, and inserted them into other operas, helping to spread Raimondi's fame.

The serious operas of Raimondi's Neapolitan period were generally unsuccessful; even the most touching scenes found him incapable of rising to the requisite pathos. In 1824 he was appointed music director of the royal theatres in Naples, and became an instructor in counterpoint at the Naples conservatory the following year. In addition to his own steady operatic production, he supplied numbers for insertion into other composers' operas; his tampering with the score of Bellini's *Il pirata* at the time of its first Neapolitan performance in 1828 brought the wrath of the young composer upon him. Better appreciated were the sacred works he provided for the royal chapel, which led to Pacini's calling him the most celebrated contrapuntist of his day.

Il ventaglio (1831), after Goldoni, was both the greatest success and the undoing of Raimondi's operatic career, a model against which his later operas were compared and found wanting. Exceptions were *La vita di un giuocatore* (1831), *La verdummara de puorto* (1832), which survived to the 1860s, and *Isabella degli Abenanti* (1836). In June 1833 Raimondi left Naples for Palermo to become director of both the conservatory and the Teatro Carolino. His frequent return visits to Naples, where he continued to receive operatic commissions, soon aroused complaints at both institutions. Rejected in his applications for posts in Paris and Milan, and aware that he was being eclipsed by Donizetti and Bellini as he had earlier been by Rossini, he turned with renewed interest to sacred music and contrapuntal theory. In 1835 his first didactic text *Bassi imitati e fugati* was published, and the following year a *messa di gloria* for double chorus and double orchestra was performed in Palermo. This was the first in a series of experiments in musical simultaneity which culminated in his 'triple oratorio' *Putifar-Giuseppe-Giacobbe* (1847–8), a set of three oratorios to be performed first separately and then simultaneously. The great success of this work led to Raimondi's appointment in 1852 as *maestro di cappella* at St Peter's, Rome.

After the relative failure of the tragic melodrama *Francesca Donato* (1842), a sincere if belated attempt to employ the flexible structures introduced by his more advanced contemporaries, Raimondi's renunciation of opera had been nearly total. But the reception given to his triple oratorio now encouraged him to plan a definitive demonstration of his operatic prowess with the serious opera *Adelasia* and the comic *I quattro rustici*, works that could be performed both separately and as a combined 'double opera'. He planned to have the piece ready for Carnival 1854, but his duties at St Peter's and his final illness prevented him from completing the instrumentation of many passages. As in the triple oratorio, Raimondi exercised great ingenuity in differentiating component parts of the work, juxtaposing different tempos, textures (such as aria and recitative) and, so far as can be seen from the completed orchestral parts, accompaniment patterns and instrumentation. Scene changes in the two operas overlap, as do the beginnings and endings of individual numbers. Dramatically each opera forms an oblique commentary upon the other, in the larger theme of parental authority – treated comically in *I quattro rustici* and seriously in *Adelasia* – as well as in individual scenes.

The complicated appearance of some of Raimondi's experiments has led to an erroneous impression of him as a musical radical. But the extreme simplicity of his harmonic language (surprising in one admired for his doctrine and learning), the prevalence of neat, symmetrical formal patterns and the abundance of spoken dialogue in his operas, which naturally worked against the progressive trend towards larger musical unities, all mark Raimondi as a most conservative musician. Certainly he was seen as such by his contemporaries; *Il ventaglio*, his only national success, was universally considered a throwback to an essentially pre-Rossinian idiom. Even so spectacular a novelty as the 'double opera' may be viewed as an attempt to breathe life into forms and procedures which by the mid-19th century were artistically dead.

See also VENTAGLIO, IL.

first performed in Naples unless otherwise stated

NC – Teatro S Carlo   NFO – Teatro del Fondo
NN – Teatro Nuovo

Le bizzarie dell'amore, ossiano I due viaggiatori (dg, 2), Genoa, S Agostino, carn. 1808
La forza dell'imaginazione, ovvero Il battuto contento (farsa, 1, P. Calvi, after Boccaccio), Genoa, S Agostino, 18 June 1810
Eloisa Werner (dramma di sentimento per musica, 1), Florence, Pergola, aut. 1810
L'oracolo di Delfo (staged cantata, 1, S. Scrofani), NC, 15 Aug 1811
Il fanatico deluso (commedia in musica, 2, G. Palomba), Fiorentini, 21 Oct 1811, *I-Nc*
Lo sposo agitato (commedia per musica, 2, Palomba), Fiorentini, 23 May 1812
Amuratte II (dramma serio, 2, F. Tarducci), Rome, Argentina, 3 Feb 1813
La lavandaia, ovvero Il ritorno di maggio (2, G. Schmidt), NFO, 3 Dec 1813 [parody of Spontini: La vestale]
Ciro in Babilonia (dramma per musica, 2, G. B. Bordese), NC, 19 March 1820
I minatori scozzesi (dramma per musica, 2), NN, 31 Jan 1821
La caccia di Enrico IV (commedia per musica, 2, Palomba), NFO, 4 March 1822, *Nc*
La donna colonello (farsa per musica, 1), NFO, 22 May 1822, *Nc*
Le finte Amazzoni (melodramma giocoso, 2, L. Romanelli), Milan, Scala, 15 May 1823
Argia (componimento drammatico, 1, Schmidt), NC, 6 July 1823, *Nc*
Le nozze de' Sanniti (dramma per musica, 2, Schmidt), NC, 24 Feb 1824
Berenice in Roma (dramma per musica, 2, Bordese), NC, 4 Nov 1824
Il disertore (melodramma, 1, A. L. Tottola), NFO, 23 Jan 1825
Il morto in apparenza (melodramma, 2, G. Checcherini), NN, 29 Aug 1825, *Nc*
Sapienti pauca (melodramma, 2, L. Ricciuti), NFO, 31 Dec 1825
Il finto feudatario (melodramma, 2, Checcherini), NN, 18 May 1826, *Nc*
Don Anchise Campanone (ob, 2, G. B. Lorenzi), NN, 13 Aug 1826
Giuditta (azione tragico-sacra, 2, Tottola), NC, 6 March 1827
Un cestellino di fiori (melodramma, 1, Tottola), NFO, 6 July 1827
L'infanzia accusatrice, ovvero Innocenza e perfidia (melodramma comico-sentimentale, 3, Tottola), NN, 29 Dec 1828
Costanza ed Oringaldo (melodramma, 1, Tottola), NC, 30 May 1830, collab. Lauro Rossi
Il ventaglio (commedia per musica, 2, D. Gilardoni, after Goldoni), NN, 22 Jan 1831, *Mr*, *Nc*
A mezzanotte (melodramma comico, 2, Tottola), NFO, 6 Aug 1831
La vita di un giuocatore (azione melodrammatica, 3, Checcherini), NN, 28 Dec 1831
La verdummara de puorto (commedia, 1), NN, 4 April 1832, *Mc*
Il nemico degli ammogliati (ob), NFO, 2 June 1832
La fidanzata del parrucchiere (dg, 2, A. Passaro), NN, 11 June 1832
Clato (tragedia lirica, 2, F. Livini), NC, 26 Dec 1832
Peggio il rimedio del male (commedia per musica, 2, V. Torelli), NN, 20 April 1833
Il biglietto del lotto stornato (commedia buffa, 2, Passaro), NN, 3 June 1833
I parenti ridicoli (melodramma, 2, Checcherini), NN, 21 June 1835
L'orfana russa (azione romantica, 2, Passaro), NFO, 26 Aug 1835, *Nc*
Isabella degli Abenanti (melodramma tragico, 3, G. Sapio), NC, 26 Sept 1836
Il tramonto del sole (2, A. Macedonio), NN, 8 April 1837
Gli artifizi per amore (melodramma giocoso, 1, R. D'Ambra), NFO, 21 April 1837
Vinclinda (melodramma, 1, Sapio), NC, 30 May 1837; rev. as Sveno, Palermo, Carolino, carn. 1839

Palmetella maritata (commedia buffa, 2, Passaro), NFO, 3 Aug 1837 [sequel to Il ventaglio]
Raffaello Sanzio da Urbino e la Fornarina (ob, 3, Checcherini), NN, 17 March 1838
Il caffettiere (melodramma comico, 2, Sapio), Palermo, Carolino, 6 July 1838
Il presidente disgraziato (commedia per musica, 2, Passaro), NFO, 30 Oct 1838
Il trionfo delle donne (farsa, 1, Sapio), Genoa, Carlo Felice, 4 Dec 1841
Francesca Donato (melodramma tragico, 3, F. Romani), Palermo, Carolino, 12 Dec 1842, vs (Milan, 1845)
Il No (commedia, 2), Palermo, Carolino, March 1851

Unperf.: La stanza di letto, 1840
Inc.: Adelasia (os, L. Scalchi), *Rsc**; I quattro rustici (ob, Scalchi, after Goldoni: *I rusteghi*), *Rsc**

*

FlorimoN
G. Pacini: *Cenni storici sulla musica e trattato di contrappunto* (Lucca, 1834), 23
F. Cicconetti: *Memorie intorno a Pietro Raimondi* (Rome, 1867)
O. Chilesotti: *I nostri maestri del passato* (Milan, 1882), 373–83
H. Wichmann: 'Il più artificioso pezzo di musica', *Gesammelte Aufsätze von Hermann Wichmann* (Leipzig, 1887), 78–92
U. Rolandi: 'Tre parodie de La vestale', *I° congresso internazionale di studi spontiniani: Iesi, Maiolati, Fabriano, Ancona 1951*, 41–7
O. Tiby: *Il Real Teatro Carolino e l'ottocento musicale palermitano* (Florence, 1957)
L. Kantner: *Aurea Luce: Musik an St Peter in Rom 1790–1850* (Vienna, 1979)
P. Gossett: Introduction to P. Raimondi: *Il ventaglio*, IOG, xl (New York, 1990)   JESSE ROSENBERG

Raimondi, Ruggero (*b* Bologna, 3 Oct 1941). Italian bass. A pupil of Teresa Pediconi and of Piervenanzi, he made his début at Spoleto in 1964 as Colline, followed immediately by Procida (*Les vêpres siciliennes*) at the Rome Opera; he continued to appear in Italy, notably at La Fenice and La Scala (1967–8). In 1969 he sang an acclaimed Don Giovanni at Glyndebourne and in 1970 he made his Metropolitan début as Silva (*Ernani*). At Covent Garden he sang Verdi's Fiesco in 1972, and he appeared as Boris at La Fenice later that year. His repertory includes Massenet's Don Quichotte (1982, Vienna), Gounod's Méphistophélès (1985, Hamburg) and Selim in *Il turco in Italia* (1986, Pesaro). He has the full, smooth and resonant voice of a *basso cantante* (with a certain baritonal quality and colour in the upper register), a very accurate and stylish technique and an imposing stage presence. He is considered one of the finest contemporary basses for early 19th-century repertory.   RODOLFO CELLETTI

Raimund [Raimann], Ferdinand (*b* Vienna, 1 June 1790; *d* Pottenstein, Lower Austria, 5 Sept 1836). Austrian dramatist, actor and theatre director. He became fascinated by the theatre as a boy and determined to become an actor. He spent some years as a member of small touring troupes, and in 1814 was engaged at the theater in der Josefstadt in Vienna, three years later joining the famous ensemble of the Theater in der Leopoldstadt. His rise to pre-eminence was steady rather than meteoric, and was based above all on his remarkable powers of mime and timing. He became director of the Leopoldstadt company in 1828, but in 1830 he left and spent the rest of his life making guest appearances and touring. During his years at the Josefstadt theatre he contracted an ill-advised marriage to Luise Gleich (daughter of the playwright and director Joseph Gleich) which broke up after a year and left him unable to legalize a later union. He died by his own hand, believing that a dog that had bitten him was mad.

Raimund was the most poetic of the dramatists of the Viennese popular theatre, though he became a playwright only out of necessity – when Karl Meisl failed to provide him with a satisfactory play for a benefit performance, he wrote *Der Barometermacher auf der Zauberinsel* (1823, music by Wenzel Müller, 96 performances in the Leopoldstadt until 1855). Raimund followed this success with a further seven dramas: *Der Diamant des Geisterkönigs* (1824, music by Drechsler, 160 performances until 1854), *Das Mädchen aus der Feenwelt, oder Der Bauer als Millionär* (1826, music by Drechsler, 207 performances until 1859), *Moisasurs Zauberfluch* (1827, music by Riotte), *Die gefesselte Phantasie* (1828, music by Müller), *Der Alpenkönig und der Menschenfeind* (1828, music by Müller, 163 performances until 1859), *Die unheilbringende Zauberkrone* (1829, music by Drechsler), and *Der Verschwender* (1834, music by Conradin Kreutzer, 142 performances in the Leopoldstadt until 1859). Raimund himself wrote the melodies for some of his best-known songs (sketches survive in his hand for the 'Aschenlied' and 'Brüderlein fein' from *Das Mädchen aus der Feenwelt*, to mention but two of the songs that became *Volkslieder*). Though his voice was neither beautiful nor particularly strong, he was acclaimed for his skill at putting across the songs in his own and other authors' plays. Along with his younger contemporary and antipode, Nestroy, Raimund marks the peak and the end of a long and distinguished tradition; though the most ambitious and tragic of his plays (*Moisasur, Phantasie* and *Zauberkrone*) enjoyed little success in Raimund's lifetime and even now are less popular than the great comedies, his achievement as a dramatist is broad, unified and powerful. The role of music in his plays is considerable, averaging 20 numbers.

*

W. A. Bauer and H. Kraus, eds.: *Raimund-Liederbuch* (Vienna, 1924)

A. Orel, ed.: *Die Gesänge der Märchendramen in den ursprünglichen Vertonungen*, [F. Raimund:] *Sämtliche Werke* (Historisch-kritische Säkularausgabe), vi (Vienna, 1924)

A. Orel: 'Raimund und die Musik', *Raimund-Almanach 1936* (Innsbruck, 1936)

D. Prohaska: *Raimund and Vienna* (Cambridge, 1970)

J. Hein: *Ferdinand Raimund* (Stuttgart, 1970)

L. V. Harding: *The Dramatic Art of Ferdinand Raimund and Johann Nestroy: a Critical Study* (The Hague, 1974)

PETER BRANSCOMBE

Rainforth, Elizabeth (*b* ?23 Nov 1814; *d* Bristol, 22 Sept 1877). English soprano. She studied with George Perry and Tom Cooke in London, making her début there in 1836 as Mandane in Arne's *Artaxerxes* at St James's Theatre. After further study with Crivelli she sang at Covent Garden, where her repertory included Zerlina in *Fra Diavolo*, Susanna and Countess Almaviva, and the title role in Cherubini's *Lodoïska* (a pastiche version). In 1843 she joined the company at Drury Lane, where she created Arline in *The Bohemian Girl*. She retired in 1856. Her voice was a high soprano, even and sweet in quality.
HAROLD ROSENTHAL/R

Rains, Leon (*b* New York, 1 Oct 1870; *d* Los Angeles, 11 July 1954). American bass. He began his training in 1890 at the National Conservatory, New York, and later studied with Oscar Saenger, going in 1896 to Paris to study with Jacques Bouhy. His début was in 1897 with the Damrosch-Ellis Opera Company, with which he toured the USA in 1899. The same year he sang for the first time with the Royal Opera in Dresden, and remained a member of the company for 18 seasons. Guest engagements took him to Bayreuth and Covent Garden in 1904. He spent one season (1909–10) with the Metropolitan Opera, singing Méphistophélès and Hagen. The outbreak of World War I obliged him to leave Dresden and return to the USA, where he occasionally appeared in concert. After 1924 he lived and taught in Los Angeles. Rains's powerful bass and his musicality made him an estimable interpreter equally of Wagner and lieder, as his recordings attest.
CORI ELLISON

Raisa, Rosa [Burchstein, Rose] (*b* Białystok, 23 May 1893; *d* Los Angeles, 28 Sept 1963). American soprano of Polish birth. When she was 14 she fled to escape a pogrom and settled in Naples, where she studied with Barbara Marchisio. She made her début as Leonora in *Oberto* during the 1913 Verdi celebrations at Parma. Later that year she sang Queen Isabella (*Cristoforo Colombo*) at Philadelphia; she then sang in Chicago (1913–14) and at Covent Garden in 1914. She sang regularly in Chicago, 1916–32 and 1933–6, appearing in the first American performances of Mascagni's *Isabeau*, Montemezzi's *La nave* and Respighi's *La fiamma*. In 1936 she sang Leah in the American première of Rocca's *Il dibuk* at Detroit.

Engaged at La Scala, she created Asteria in Boito's *Nerone* in 1924 and Turandot in 1926. She returned to Covent Garden in 1933 as Tosca. She was a thrilling singer and actress, and a great dramatic soprano.

GV (R. Celletti; J. Stratton)   HAROLD ROSENTHAL/R

Raitio, Väinö (Eerikki) (*b* Sortavala, 15 April 1891; *d* Helsinki, 10 Sept 1945). Finnish composer. He studied at the Helsinki Conservatory (1911–16) and in Moscow (1916–17), Berlin (1921) and Paris (1925–6). After a period of teaching at the Viipuri Music Institute (1926–32) he lived as a freelance composer, in difficult circumstances.

With Ernest Pingoud and Aarre Merikanto, Raitio was responsible in the 1920s for introducing the first period of modernism in Finnish music. His early output was bound by Romanticism, but in Moscow and Berlin he received new influences that made his style more radical: his harmony was affected by Skryabin and German expressionism, his orchestration by Debussy and other French impressionists. His most important works from the end of that decade and the 1930s are operas. Some of them suffer from weak texts, but they do not lack a certain musical interest, even if they (as well as the orchestral works of this period) fall short of the level of his earlier tone poems. Raitio's vocal writing makes extensive use of recitative in order to have every detail of the text faithfully reflected in the music. His ideas on the relationship between drama and music, as well as his use of leitmotifs, were evidently based on Wagner, but in general atmosphere his operas are closer to *Pelléas*. The best of them are the first, *Jephtan tytär* ('The Daughter of Jephtha', 1929), and *Lyydian kuningas* ('The King of Lydia', 1937).

Jephtan tytär [The Daughter of Jephtha] op.30, 1929 (2, J. Linnankoski and S. Ranta), Helsinki, Finnish Opera, 2 Dec 1931

Prinsessa Cecilia, 1933 (6 scenes, H. Jalkanen and C. Lilius), Helsinki, Finnish Opera, 1 April 1936

Wäinämöisen kosinta, 1934–6 (1, E. Leino), Helsinki, Workers' Institute, 28 Feb 1971

Lyydian kuningas [The King of Lydia], 1937 (Leino, after Herodotus), Finnish Radio, 4 Dec 1955

Kaksi kuningatarta [Two Queens] (3, L. Haarla), Helsinki, Finnish Opera, 11 Oct 1944

*

S. Ranta: 'Väinö Raitio', *Suomen säveltäjiä*, ed. E. Marvia, ii (Borgå, 2/1966), 103

ILKKA ORAMO

Rajičić, Stanojlo (*b* Belgrade, 16 Dec 1910). Serbian composer. He studied at the Prague Conservatory with Rudolf Karel and took part in Josef Suk's masterclasses; later he taught in Belgrade. A prolific composer, he wrote four operas in which he retained Classical form and tonality, but enriched them with freer harmonic treatment, sometimes using polytonality. Having already produced orchestral song cycles, concertos and symphonies, Rajičić wrote his major opera, *Simonida*, as a mature composer. The work, concerning the events at court during the reign of the Serbian king Milutin and his consort, the Byzantine princess Simonida, features vocal arioso, scenes with both soloists and choruses, symphonic orchestration and bitonal harmonies. His later television operas show the same organization of musico-dramatic form and also use arioso declamation and bitonal writing; leitmotifs are used to create dramatic intensity and psychological characterization. *Dnevnik jednog ludaka* ('The Diary of a Fool') is scored for one solo singer.

Simonida (2, after M. Bojić: *Kraljeva jesen* [The King's Autumn]), Sarajevo, 24 May 1957; rev. (3), 17 June 1958; rev. (1), 26 Sept 1968, vs of one act (Belgrade, 1968)
Karadjordje, 1972 (television op, 1, after I. Studen: *Vožd* [The Leader]), Belgrade, 26 June 1977
Dnevnik jednog ludaka [The Diary of a Fool] (television op, 22 scenes, after N. V. Gogol), Belgrade, 4 April 1981
Bele noći [White Nights] (television op, 1, after F. M. Dostoyevsky), Belgrade, 14 April 1985

*

V. Peričić: *Stvaralački put Stanoja Rajičića* (Belgrade, 1971)
K. Tomašević: *Tri pozna operska opusa Stanojla Rajičića* [Three Late Operatic Works by Stanojlo Rajičić] (diss., U. of Art, Belgrade, 1986)

ROKSANDA PEJOVIĆ

Rake's Progress, The. Opera in three acts (nine scenes and an epilogue) by IGOR STRAVINSKY to a libretto by W. H. AUDEN and CHESTER KALLMAN after William Hogarth's series of paintings (1732–3); Venice, Teatro La Fenice, 11 September 1951.

Tom Rakewell	tenor
Nick Shadow	baritone
Trulove	bass
Anne *Trulove's daughter*	soprano
Mother Goose	mezzo-soprano
Baba the Turk	mezzo-soprano
Sellem *an auctioneer*	tenor
Keeper of the Madhouse	bass

Whores and roaring-boys, servants, citizens, madmen

Setting 18th-century England

Stravinsky happened on Hogarth's paintings at the Chicago Art Institute on 2 May 1947; they struck him as a series of scenes from a drama and suggested the subject for the English-language opera he had wanted to write since arriving in the USA eight years before. His California neighbour Aldous Huxley suggested Auden as librettist, and the latter, after working out a draft scenario with the composer in November, called in his friend Kallman as collaborator. The draft scenario is printed as an appendix to I. Stravinsky and Craft 1960;

a detailed chronology of the opera's genesis may be found in V. Stravinsky and Craft 1978, pp.396–415; the librettists' textual contributions are as follows:

1.i – Auden, to end of Tom's aria, then Kallman; 1.ii – Kallman; 1.iii – Auden
2.i – Kallman, opening *scena* (aria, recitative, aria, reprise), then Auden; 2.ii – Kallman, revised at Stravinsky's request by Auden; 2.iii – Auden
3.i – Kallman, except for offstage song of Tom and Shadow; 3.ii – Kallman; 3.iii – Auden
Epilogue – Auden

Stravinsky received the text of the first act on 16 January 1948 and went to work in May (the previous December, anxious to get started, he had composed the icy string-quartet introduction to the graveyard scene, 3.ii). The libretto was finished and handed over to the composer in Washington, DC, on 31 March. The place and date are doubly important for the opera, and for Stravinsky's late career generally, because it was also the place and date of his earliest meeting with the conductor Robert Craft, one of whose first duties as musical assistant was to read the text of *The Rake's Progress* aloud so that the composer might learn its proper intonation and accentuation. (True to his established habit, Stravinsky frequently honoured these niceties in the breach; but his music-motivated departures from standard spoken English were informed ones.)

The opera was composed on a rough one-act-per-year schedule. The epilogue was completed on 7 April 1951, but the last music to be composed was the first to be heard: the undated fanfarish prelude to Act 1. Among the few Stravinsky compositions not written on commission (a circumstance made possible by an advance from the publishers Boosey & Hawkes), *The Rake* was 'bought' by the managers of the 14th Festival of Contemporary Music at Venice (the 'Biennale'), the composer's old friend Nicolas Nabokov acting as his agent. The orchestra and chorus of La Scala were engaged for the première, as was the conductor Ferdinand Leitner (after Stravinsky's first choice, Igor Markevich, was rejected by the Italians), who conducted all performances but the 'prima assoluta', which was conducted by the composer. Elisabeth Schwarzkopf sang Anne, Robert Rounseville sang Tom, and Nick Shadow was played by Otakar Kraus. The first commercial recording, under the composer's baton (and with the harpsichord, mainly played by an uncredited Ralph Kirkpatrick, finally in place instead of the piano cautiously employed in earlier performances), followed a production at the Metropolitan (1953), conducted in the house by Fritz Reiner. Despite some early disappointment with its retrospective manner (not entirely a philistine reaction, for the composer, embarrassed, quickly sought stylistic renewal in serialism), *The Rake* has become a stout repertory item, with more productions, as Griffiths has noted, than any other opera written after the death of Puccini. Its success may have been abetted in the first instance by Kerman's influential praise, but the crucial factor has surely been its adaptability to the resources of workshop and student theatres. Among its later productions, that of the Royal Swedish Opera (1961) under Ingmar Bergman's direction deserves mention because of the composer's enthusiastic endorsement, reported by Craft, extending to the director's decision to break for an interval only once, after 2.ii.

'The Rake's Progress' (Stravinsky): the quartet from Act 1 scene i (Trulove's garden) of the original production at La Fenice, Venice, 11 September 1951, including (left to right) Elisabeth Schwarzkopf as Anne, Robert Rounseville as Tom and Otakar Kraus as Nick Shadow

ACT 1.i *The Garden of Trulove's house in the country on an afternoon in spring* Tom and Anne celebrate the season and their love ('The woods are green'), while Trulove hopes his doubts about Tom will prove unfounded. In a recitative, Trulove dispatches his daughter to the kitchen and proposes that Tom take a position in a friend's counting-house. When Tom refuses, Trulove warns him that he will not allow his daughter to marry a lazy man. Left alone, Tom angrily reflects that he is not made for a life of drudgery but will trust to fortune (recitative and aria, 'Here I stand', 'Since it is not by merit'). He makes the first of the spoken wishes that provide the plot with its mainspring: for money. Nick Shadow materializes instantly, bids him call Anne and Trulove to hear the news, and informs them all that an obscure uncle of Tom's has died and left him a fortune (recitative [so called, evidently, after the draft scenario, despite its well-articulated aria structure], 'Fair lady, gracious gentlemen'). All react gratefully in their various ways, the ensemble taking shape out of an ironic fugato on the words 'Be thanked', set to a dissonant drooping minor 9th; Tom agrees to employ Shadow and at the latter's suggestion decides to establish himself in London before marrying Anne (quartet, 'I wished but once'). Tom and Anne take their tender leave (duettino, 'Farewell for now'). Tom promises Trulove that he will soon send for him and for Anne; he gaily makes off with Nick, having agreed to pay the latter after a year and a day have passed; Anne suppresses a tear; Trulove expresses misgivings (arioso and terzettino, 'Dear Father Trulove', 'Laughter and light'). Just before the curtain, Nick Shadow turns to the audience – showing that he is not merely Tom's alter ego (shadow) but truly the devil (Nick) – and announces, 'The progress of a rake begins'.

1.ii *Mother Goose's Brothel, London* The Roaring-Boys and Whores cavort in the chorus 'With air commanding'. Shadow and Mother Goose catechize Tom in the ways of cynicism, the harpsichord punctuating the lesson with arch cadences. Tom falters meaningly at the mention of love. He makes as if to flee, but is reassured by Nick, who sets the cuckoo clock back an hour to midnight to show that Tom has time on his side ('Fear not. Enjoy. You may repent at leisure.'). Tom drinks, the company egging him on (chorus, 'Soon dawn will glitter'). Nick formally presents him and he sings an initiation song (cavatina, 'Love, too frequently

betrayed'). Its excessive sincerity discomfits the whores briefly and strangely attracts them ('How sad a song'). But Mother Goose banishes care and claims Tom for herself while the company serenades their withdrawal to a room off stage ('The sun is bright, the grass is green. Lanterloo'). The scene ends in a dreamlike diminuendo, Shadow warning that when his dreams end the Rake will die.

1.iii *Trulove's garden* The scene is given over to a two-part solo *scena* for Anne, in which she refuses to acknowledge Tom's silence as rejection, invoking night and moon as her allies in caring quest of him (aria, 'Quietly, night') and then, reflecting on Tom's greater need, resolves forthwith to leave her father and follow Tom to London (cabaletta, 'I go, I go to him').

ACT 2.i *The morning room of Tom's house in a London square* The Rake, disillusioned with his decadent urbanity, longs for the simple country joys he left behind ('Vary the song'). He pronounces the second wish: to be happy. Shadow enters, a broadsheet in hand. It is an advertisement for Baba the Turk, the lady freak on display at the St Giles Fair. Shadow proposes that Tom marry her to assert his freedom from ordinary appetites and constraints and thereby know true happiness (aria, 'In youth the panting slave'). With a loud laugh Tom sees the point and agrees (duet finale, 'My tale shall be told both by young and by old').

2.ii *The street in front of Tom's house* Anne is waiting apprehensively for Tom's return (recitative and arioso, 'How strange!', 'O heart be stronger'). She is surprised by a procession of lackeys carrying all sorts of odd packages into the servant's entrance as night falls; last, a sedan chair is carried in and deposited at the main entrance; Tom alights and, all confusion, recognizes Anne; confessing himself unworthy, he bids her go (duet, 'Anne! Here!'). Baba, heavily veiled, pokes her head out from the carriage and expresses her impatience; Tom admits to the astonished Anne that he is married (Anne: 'I see, then, it was I who was unworthy'). They separately reflect on what might have been, while Baba, periodically appearing at the carriage window, waxes ever more indignant at the delay (trio, 'Could it then have been known', 'It is done, it is done', 'Why this delay?'). Anne exits hurriedly; Tom escorts Baba from the sedan chair, identifying Anne to her as 'a milkmaid to whom I was in debt'. A crowd of passers-by recognize Baba and hail her; she turns to receive their plaudits and, 'with the practiced manner of a great artiste', removes her veil, revealing a full and flowing black beard (finale, 'Baba the Turk is here!').

2.iii *The same room as 2.i, except that now it is cluttered up with every conceivable kind of object* Baba is chattering away over breakfast while Tom sulks (aria, 'As I was saying'). Noticing that he is out of sorts she attempts to cajole him (Baba's song, 'Come, sweet, come'), but he shoves her away. Enraged, she strides about breaking anything to hand until Tom covers her head with his wig, which cuts her off mid-roulade (aria, 'Scorned! Abused! Neglected! Baited!'). He falls into an exhausted sleep upon the sofa; Shadow enters, singing to himself and wheeling a 'fantastic baroque machine' with which he seems to turn a shard from one of Baba's broken vases into a loaf of bread; but as he shows the audience, it is just a device with a false bottom (pantomime; the octatonic machine-music recalls that of the mechanical Japanese bird in *The Nightingale*). Tom awakens with his third wish on his lips: that by means of a miraculous machine he has just seen in a dream he might perform a great good deed and (to the melody of the recitative line immediately preceding the cabaletta in 1.iii) 'deserve dear Anne at last' (recitative-arioso-recitative, 'O Nick I've had the strangest dream'); he is elated to find Shadow standing before him with the very machine he had imagined. Tom exults in his impending salvation while Shadow, addressing the audience, mocks his credulity (duet, 'Thanks to this excellent device', 'A word to all my friends'). Shadow reminds Tom that the machine must be mass-produced and marketed, and proposes a stock issue. They go off in pursuit of backers, Tom meanwhile informing Shadow that he has disposed of his wife.

ACT 3.i *The same as 2.iii, except that everything is covered with cobwebs and dust* The marketing enterprise having failed and ruined the Rake, his possessions are up for auction. A crowd gathers gossiping for the sale ('Ruin, disaster, shame'). Anne wanders in looking for Tom, but no-one can tell her where he is. Sellem, the auctioneer, enters and gets down to business, selling off a stuffed auk, a mounted fish and so on, to the tune of a waltz with an inanely stylized refrain, each sale greeted with idiotic huzzas from the crowd (aria, interrupted by periodic 'bidding scenes', 'Who hears me, knows me ... La! come bid, Hmm! come buy'). The final object auctioned turns out to be Baba ('An unknown object draws us near'). As soon as the wig is removed from her head she resumes her interrupted roulade from where she left off in 2.iii (aria, with chorus, 'Sold! Annoyed!'). The voices of Tom and Shadow are heard offstage ('Old wives for sale!'), showing them to be at large. Baba advises Anne to pursue Tom, who still loves her (recitative and duet with chorus and Sellem, 'You love him, seek to set him right'). Tom and Shadow are heard again from the street (ballad tune, 'If boys had wings and girls had stings'). Anne rushes off full of hope (stretto-finale, 'I go to him'), while Baba, with Sellem's reluctant assistance, makes a dignified exit ('The next time you see Baba, you shall pay!').

3.ii *A churchyard with tombs on a starless night* It is a year and a day since Tom and Shadow struck their bargain. 'Servant' now reveals his true identity to 'master' and demands the latter's soul in payment. Tom pleads, but his grave is dug, the clock begins to strike

midnight, and Shadow offers him no choice but that of his means of suicide (duet, 'How dark and dreadful is this place'). On the ninth stroke, sporting as ever, Shadow relents and proposes a game of cards, accompanied by the suddenly (and wildly) soloistic harpsichord: he will cut the deck three times and Tom must guess which card he holds. First, thinking of Anne, Tom correctly guesses the Queen of Hearts; second, startled by a falling gravedigger's spade, he involuntarily shouts 'The deuce!' – again correct. Now Shadow is upset, and cheats: he replaces the Queen of Hearts in the deck and chooses it again; but Tom, hearing Anne's voice singing a reprise of her Act 2 aria, divines the ruse and wins. He wishes a fourth, uncontracted time, for the return of her love. Defeated, Shadow sinks at the twelfth stroke of the clock into the grave meant for Tom ('I burn! I freeze!'), but as he goes he takes away Tom's reason, leaving him to greet the spring dawn believing himself to be Adonis ('With roses crowned I sit on ground'). This dramatic turning-point is underscored by an anthology of thematic reminiscences – Tom's of Anne's cabaletta in 1.iii, Shadow's of his own aria in 2.i, and, finally, the ballad tune in 3.i.

3.iii *Bedlam* Tom/Adonis calls upon the other inmates to celebrate his wedding to Venus (arioso, 'Prepare yourselves, heroic shades'). The others mock him (dialogue with chorus, 'Madmen's words are all untrue'). Anne appears with the Keeper, who points Tom out to her. He takes her for Venus (arioso, 'I have waited for thee so long'). He asks forgiveness (duet, 'In a foolish dream', 'What should I forgive?'). She comforts him and, accompanied by a pair of flutes, lulls him to sleep while the others marvel at her song (lullaby with chorus, 'Gently, little boat', 'O sacred music of the spheres!'). Her father bids her leave with him (duet, 'Every wearied body', 'God is merciful and just'). Tom awakens, looks in vain for Venus, sinks back heartbroken and dies (finale and mourning-chorus, 'Where art thou, Venus?', 'Mourn for Adonis').

EPILOGUE *Before the curtain, house lights up* Enter Baba, Tom, Nick, Anne, Trulove, the men without wigs, Baba without her beard. They sing a vaudeville culminating in the fable's moral: 'For idle hands/And hearts and minds/The Devil finds/A work to do'.

*   *   *

There is no work by Stravinsky, or by anyone else, that embodies more conspicuously than *The Rake's Progress* the artistic self-consciousness – the consciousness of art in crisis – that is the nub and essence of 'neo-classicism'. On its every level – plot, scenario, text, music – the opera can seem to throw up such a din of super-erogatory allusion as to imperil its own dramatic integrity. The plot, ostensibly a device to link Hogarth's painted scenes, makes explicit or implicit reference (and sometimes both at once) to the myths of Venus and Adonis as well as Orpheus (on which Stravinsky had just completed a ballet), to the Faust legend and to the Don Juan tradition, while at the same time embodying the distinctive structure of a fairy-tale, moreover inserting (in place of Hogarth's rich bride and the 'Ugly Duchess' of the draft scenario) a 'homosexual joke' in the person of Baba the Turk that so outraged Stravinsky's lawyer that he counselled the composer to withdraw from the project. Over and above its newsworthy general aspect of revival, resurrecting stilted 18th-century convention right down to harpsichord-accompanied *secco*, the scenario parodies such famous predecessors as *Don Giovanni* (the Epilogue, but also the Graveyard Scene) and even *Carmen* (the Micaëla-like Anne, ever in gentle-hearted pursuit). The libretto language, much criticized for its difficulty of immediate apprehension ('how', wondered Kirkpatrick, 'does one understand across the orchestra pit of an opera house the words, "London, green unnatural mother" ?'), was consciously educed from Pope and Congreve.

As for the music, Stravinsky confessed the late Mozart operas to have been his sources not only of inspiration but of style, even specific figurations. Later, more boldly, he was to declare himself 'Mozart's continuer', even though the opera's musical structure is actually far less ambitious than Mozart's, relying to a great extent on the simple verse and refrain of the ballad opera. The list of additional creditors cited by critics would include – at a minimum, and in chronological order – Handel, Gluck, Beethoven, Schubert, Weber, Rossini, Donizetti (*Don Pasquale*) and Verdi. Nor will anyone approaching *The Rake* from a Russian perspective miss the resonances from Tchaikovsky's Pushkin operas (*Yevgeny Onegin* and *The Queen of Spades*) – doubly ironic in that the originals were themselves concerned with period stylization, the latter with its own variety of 18th-century pastiche.

The overt display of precedents has been deplored as reactionary, but it issues from what Auden identified, in an essay on Yeats, as the central 'modern problem': that of being 'no longer supported by tradition without being aware of it'. It is the forced awareness, not the traditionalism as such, that has grated. Yet while inevitably jutting out at first, the impression of pastiche has waned as the opera has joined its models in history, has matured in repertory, and as a fluent performing practice for it has evolved. (Now we are more apt to notice affinities with Stravinsky's own earlier output for the stage, despite the composer's arch suggestion in the Metropolitan Opera programme that *The Nightingale*, his first opera, 'seems more remote to me now than the English operas of three centuries ago'; compare, for example, the harpsichord flourishes that accompany Shadow's appearances in 1.i and 2.i with the cimbalom arpeggios that herald the title character in *Renard*.)

The best performances of *The Rake* are those that, taking its style(s) for granted, seriously address its moralizing purpose; and that locate the morality not in the epilogue's persiflage (another concession to the 'modern problem') but in the traditional if not 'classical' operatic theme of redemption through love. Tom's final madness, though it complicates this interpretation as modernity complicates everything traditional, does not preclude it. The asylum scene, it is worth noting, was the one Hogarthian vestige on which Stravinsky had set his heart from the very beginning, as we learn from his first feeler to Auden; and Auden's answer explains its survival into the finished opera: 'it is the librettist's job to satisfy the composer, not the other way around'.

RICHARD TARUSKIN

Rakhmaninov [Rachmaninoff], **Sergey Vasil'yevich** (*b* Semyonovo, nr Staraya Russa, Novgorod district, 20 March/1 April 1873; *d* Beverly Hills, CA, 28 March 1943). Russian composer, pianist and conductor. Opera occupies a minor place in his many-sided career and in his creative output, but for a short time around the turn of the century the musical stage was his primary focus.

While a pupil of Taneyev and Arensky at the Moscow Conservatory, in autumn 1888, Rakhmaninov began

sketching an opera on the libretto of Dargomïzhsky's *Esmeralda* (based on Victor Hugo's *Notre-Dame de Paris*), getting only as far as the instrumental introduction to Act 1 and Claude Frollo's Act 3 *scena*, all in piano score. During the 1890–91 school year he composed, presumably on assignment, a pair of settings from Pushkin's drama *Boris Godunov*, one of which, Pimen's monologue, had a famous counterpart in Musorgsky's opera (Rakhmaninov's version was published posthumously in the USSR, in *Vokal'nïye proizvedeniya, neopublikovannïye avtorom*, 'Vocal Works, Unpublished by the Composer', ed. P. Lamm, Moscow, 1947). A vocal quartet based on a libretto for an opera *Mazepa* (after Pushkin's *Poltava*), and a setting of Arbenin's monologue from Lermontov's play *Masquerade*, also date from this period.

Rakhmaninov's graduation piece from Arensky's class was a one-act opera, *Aleko*, to a patchy libretto prepared for the occasion by Vladimir Nemirovich-Danchenko after Pushkin's *The Gypsies*. Rakhmaninov received his usual '5+' (A+) for his effort, as well as the rarely awarded large gold medal on graduation in spring 1892; more important, the opera was accepted for publication and performance, and launched the young composer's professional career. (In 1897 Shalyapin appeared in St Petersburg in the title role, with his usual wild success; thanks to him Aleko's cavatina became a recital favourite.) Alone among Rakhmaninov's operas, this modest but appealing student piece has maintained a toehold in the Russian repertory, largely in workshop and amateur productions for which it is well suited.

In spring 1897 Savva Mamontov, the fabled railway tycoon and arts patron, engaged the young Rakhmaninov as deputy to the principal conductor (an Italian named Eugenio Esposito) of his Moscow Private Opera Company. Here he made friends with Shalyapin, then starting his career as a Mamontov protégé. During the 1897–8 season Rakhmaninov conducted operas by Verstovsky, Glinka, Dargomïzhsky, Serov and Rimsky-Korsakov. After spending the summer with Shalyapin working intensively on *Boris Godunov*, then recently resurrected in Rimsky-Korsakov's version, Rakhmaninov was moved to try his hand at opera composition again. He turned to Modest Tchaikovsky (who since his brother's death had gone on supplying librettos to other Russian composers, including Rakhmaninov's teacher Arensky and his sometime fellow student Arseny Koreshchenko) with a request for a libretto after Shakespeare. Instead he received an execrable libretto on *Francesca da Rimini*, which he began setting, in a suitably veristic style, while staying with Shalyapin in Italy in July 1900. After composing one scene Rakhmaninov embarked on his Second Piano Concerto, following which a whole series of instrumental pieces intervened before he returned to opera composition.

When he did so, in summer 1903, he did not immediately resume work on *Francesca da Rimini*, but turned instead to Pushkin's 'little tragedy' *Skupoy rïtsar*', 'The Miserly Knight', which he set to music virtually as it stood (à la *Pelléas*, it would have appeared to Western operagoers), completing it in vocal score in February 1904. There was in fact a tradition for this sort of libretto-less opera in Russia, going back to Dargomïzhsky's *The Stone Guest* (1872), also based on one of Pushkin's four 'little tragedies' of 1830, ideal sources for 'sung plays' because of their concentration and brevity. In the meantime the remaining pair had been set by Rimsky-Korsakov (*Mozart and Salieri*, 1897) and Cui (*Pir vo vremya chumi*, 'A Feast in Time of Plague', 1901), so that Rakhmaninov's opera exhausted the series. His essay differs considerably from its Russian predecessors, however, in its quasi-Wagnerian symphonic facture; perhaps it is significant that the composer and his bride had visited Bayreuth on their honeymoon in 1902. On its face *The Miserly Knight* seems an unpromising subject for opera, since there are only male roles. But the title character has a huge and lurid soliloquy in his subterranean money vault that must have seemed a surpassing vehicle for Shalyapin. More's the irony, then, that Shalyapin never sang the opera (though he did sing the soliloquy in concert); at both the Moscow (1906) and the St Petersburg (1912) premières, the title role was sung by Georgy Baklanov.

In spring 1904 Rakhmaninov accepted an invitation from the Moscow Bol'shoy Theatre to become chief conductor of Russian opera, a post he held from September of that year until February 1906. He now threw himself with a will into opera composition, completing *Francesca da Rimini* in vocal score in summer 1904 and orchestrating both his new operas during summer 1905. Both are longish one-act operas that between them make up a very substantial double bill.

During his first season at the Bol'shoy, besides his own *Aleko*, Rakhmaninov conducted operas by Glinka (*A Life for the Tsar*), Dargomïzhsky (*Rusalka*), Rubinstein (*The Demon*), Tchaikovsky (*Oprichnik, Yevgeny Onegin, The Queen of Spades*), Borodin (*Prince Igor*) and Musorgsky (*Boris Godunov*), many of them with Shalyapin. The high points of his career there came the next season: on 27 September/10 October 1905, with the Moscow première of Rimsky-Korsakov's *Pan Voyevoda*; and on 11/24 January 1906, with his own double bill. A month later Rakhmaninov abruptly resigned his Bol'shoy position and left for an extended stay abroad. (It has been suggested that his behaviour was a reaction to political unrest that made creative work difficult; but the height of the so-called Revolution of 1905 had coincided with Rakhmaninov's most fruitful burst of artistic activity.) A blossoming operatic career was cut short; he was never to complete another work for the stage.

Almost immediately on arriving in Italy in March 1906 Rakhmaninov busied himself with a new operatic project involving Flaubert's *Salammbô*, which had previously served Musorgsky and Reyer. He drafted a detailed scenario, but though he appealed to three different potential collaborators, he could not obtain a satisfactory libretto to his specifications. In the early months of 1907 he began an opera based on Maeterlinck's play *Monna Vanna*, to a libretto by his close friend the singer and composer Mikhail Slonov (1869–1930). The first act was completed in vocal score on 2/15 April and Rakhmaninov began sketching the second act as well; but when he learnt that Maeterlinck had assigned exclusive operatic rights to Henry Février he abandoned work, never to return to opera although he lived another 36 years. The existing act, orchestrated by Igor Buketoff, was given at Saratoga Springs, New York, in August 1984, after the manuscript, thought lost, was discovered at the Library of Congress.

Because his completed operas were all one-act pieces, and because they were all more or less seriously handicapped by their librettos, Rakhmaninov was never a serious contender on the world operatic stage. Nevertheless, *Aleko*'s cavatina from his first opera, the cupidity monologue from his second and the love scene from his third testify to enormous flair for the medium. While one cannot exactly deplore the ultimate shape of Rakhmaninov's career as legendary composing virtuoso, one cannot contemplate his stunted operatic legacy without some sense of loss.

See also ALEKO; *FRANCESCA DA RIMINI* (i); and *MISERLY KNIGHT, THE*.

op.	title	acts	libretto	first performance	sources and remarks
	Esmeralda		after V. Hugo: *Notre-Dame de Paris*		comp. 1888, introduction to Act 1 and frag. of Act 3 only, pf score
	Aleko	1	V. Nemirovich-Danchenko, after A. S. Pushkin: *Tsïganï* [The Gypsies]	Moscow, Bol'shoy, 27 April/9 May 1893, cond. I. Al'tani	comp. 1892, vs (Moscow, 1892), full score (Moscow, 1953)
24	Skupoy rïtsar' [The Miserly Knight]	1	Pushkin	Moscow, Bol'shoy, 11/24 Jan 1906, cond. S. Rakhmaninov	comp. 1903–5, vs (Moscow, 1904), full score (Moscow and Leipzig, 1972)
25	Francesca da Rimini	1	M. I. Tchaikovsky, after Dante: *Inferno*, v:97–142	Moscow, Bol'shoy, 11/24 Jan 1906, cond. Rakhmaninov	comp. 1900, 1904–5, vs (Moscow, 1905), full score (Moscow, 1974)
	Salammbô		M. Slonov, after G. Flaubert		comp. 1906, scenario only
	Monna Vanna	7 scenes	Slonov, after M. Maeterlinck	concert perf. of Act 1, Saratoga, NY, Saratoga Performing Arts Center, 11 Aug 1984	comp. 1907, pf score of Act 1 and sketches for Act 2 only; orchd I. Buketoff

I. F. Bel'za, ed.: *S. V. Rakhmaninov i russkaya opera: sbornik statey* [Rakhmaninov and Russian Opera: a Collection of Essays] (Moscow, 1947)

L. Polyakova: '*Aleko*' *S. Rakhmaninova* (Moscow and Leningrad, 1949)

A. Kandinsky: *Operï S. V. Rakhmaninova* (Moscow, 1956, 2/1979)

G. Norris: 'Rakhmaninov's Student Opera', *MQ*, lix (1973), 441–8

——: *Rakhmaninov* (London, 1976)

Z. Apetyan, ed.: *S. Rakhmaninov: literaturnoye naslediye* [Literary Legacy] (Moscow, 1978–81)

H. Macdonald: 'Opera in America', *MT*, cxxxi (1990), 321 [on *Francesca da Rimini*]

RICHARD TARUSKIN

Raleigh. American city, capital of North Carolina. It is the home of a small but respected touring company, the National Opera Company, valued as both an educational resource and a stepping-stone for aspiring singers. It was founded in 1948 by the philanthropist A. J. Fletcher, since whose death it has been funded by the

Fletcher Foundation as part of the Fletcher School for Performing Arts in Raleigh. The company has given more than 3000 performances in 35 states and has appeared before more than 2 million schoolchildren in North Carolina alone. In Raleigh it performs twice a year with the North Carolina Symphony in its home, the 2300-seat Memorial Auditorium.

The company gives about a hundred performances of four operas a year, in English, in a repertory ranging from *La fille du régiment* to Oscar Straus's *Der tapfere Soldat* and Boieldieu's *La dame blanche*, which was given its American première by the company in 1990. Former members include the baritone Samuel Ramey.

DEAN SMITH

Ralf, Oscar (Georg) (*b* Malmö, 3 Oct 1881; *d* Stockholm, 3 April 1964). Swedish tenor. He studied in Stockholm with John Forsell and Gillis Bratt, and in Berlin and Munich. After making his stage début in 1905 at Oscarsteatern, Stockholm's operetta theatre, he sang there until 1915, when he began to study the Heldentenor repertory with Bratt. He made his operatic début in 1918 as Siegmund with the Swedish Royal Opera, of which he remained a member until 1940, specializing in the Wagner and Verdi repertories and giving notable performances as Florestan and Samson. He was the first Swedish tenor to appear at Bayreuth, as Siegmund in 1927. He wrote an autobiography, *Tenoren han går i Ringen* ('The Tenor goes into the Ring'; Stockholm, 1953).

HAROLD ROSENTHAL/R

Ralf, Torsten (Ivar) (*b* Malmö, 2 Jan 1901; *d* Stockholm, 27 April 1954). Swedish tenor, brother of Oscar Ralf. He studied in Stockholm and in Berlin with Hertha Dehmlow and made his début at Stettin (now Szczecin) in 1930 as Cavaradossi. After engagements at Chemnitz (1932–3) and Frankfurt (1933–5) he joined the Dresden Staatsoper, of which he remained a member until 1944. At Dresden he created Apollo in Strauss's *Daphne* (1938) and appeared in the première of Sutermeister's *Die Zauberinsel* (1942). He sang regularly at Covent Garden (1935–9) as Lohengrin, Walther, Parsifal, Erik and Tannhäuser, and in 1936 was heard as Bacchus in a single performance of *Ariadne auf Naxos* given in London by the Dresden company with Strauss conducting. He returned to Covent Garden in 1948 as Radames. He sang at the Metropolitan (1945–8) in the Wagnerian repertory and as Radames and Otello, and appeared at the Teatro Colón, Buenos Aires, in 1946.

HAROLD ROSENTHAL/R

Rameau, Jean-Philippe (*b* Dijon, bap. 25 Sept 1683; *d* Paris, 12 Sept 1764). French composer and theorist. He has long been recognized as one of the greatest figures in French musical history. A theorist of European stature, he was also France's leading composer in the 18th century. While he made important contributions to the cantata, the motet and, more especially, keyboard music, many of his finest and most ambitious works are in the field of dramatic music, where they stand alongside those of Lully and Gluck as the pinnacles of pre-Revolutionary French opera.

1. Early life. 2. Operatic career, 1733–44. 3. Operatic career, 1745–64. 4. Dramatic music.

1. EARLY LIFE. Rameau spent most of his first 40 years in the relative obscurity of the French provinces. His early musical education came mainly from his father, a Dijon organist, and he also attended the local Collège des Godrans, where he doubtless experienced the didactic music theatre that was an important feature of the Jesuit curriculum. Such productions may indeed have fired Rameau's enthusiasm for opera which, he later admitted, began when he was 12. No details of any Dijon productions have however come to light.

Rameau spent the next two decades mainly as a church and cathedral organist, teacher or freelance musician, in Avignon (1702), Clermont (1702–6), Paris (1706–*c*1709), Dijon (1709–13), Lyons (1713–15) and Clermont again (1715–22). His surviving output from these years is small: a published harpsichord collection (1706), a handful of cantatas and several motets, drinking songs and canons.

Travelling to Paris in 1722 to supervise publication of his first theoretical work, *Traité de l'harmonie*, Rameau decided to settle there. Though nearly 40, he was still virtually unknown in the capital. However, the appearance of this monumental treatise earned him a formidable reputation, consolidated during the next 40 years by some three dozen books and pamphlets on music theory. Incongruous as it seems in view of his new-found eminence, Rameau's first compositions in Paris included a substantial amount of music for Alexis Piron's knockabout *opéra comique*, *L'Endriague* (1723), at the Foire St Germain. In three further collaborations with Piron at the Fair Theatres, he contributed less. Despite their lack of prestige, however, the Fairs gave him valuable experience. It was probably there, too, that he met Louis Fuzelier, future librettist of *Les Indes galantes*.

During the 1720s Rameau acquired a growing reputation as composer and teacher. Most of his best-known harpsichord music appeared at that time. By now, however, he was planning his operatic début: a letter to Antoine Houdar de Lamotte (25 October 1727) reveals that Lamotte had refused him a libretto and had cast doubts on his chances of success. Stung by this, Rameau set down with unusual clarity his credentials as a potential opera composer, but to no avail.

2. OPERATIC CAREER, 1733–44. It was not until he was 50 that Rameau made his operatic début. The impact of *Hippolyte et Aricie* (1733) was immense. Never had French audiences encountered music so intensely dramatic. While there were some who hailed him as 'the Orpheus of our century', others found the music overcomplex, unnatural, misshapen – in a word, *baroque*. (*Hippolyte* has the dubious distinction of being the first musical work to which that epithet, still then pejorative, seems to have been applied.) The opera sparked off a dispute between Rameau's supporters – Ramistes (or *ramoneurs*, chimney-sweeps) – and the Lullistes, a small but vociferous cabal motivated by a distaste for his style and a fear that it would annihilate the traditional repertory, above all the operas of their revered Lully. There was some professional jealousy on the part of composers and librettists, and Rameau had to contend with the ill-will of performers at the Paris Opéra. The dispute reached a climax with the production of *Dardanus* (1739); while it abated during the next decade as the public came to terms with Rameau's powerful idiom, echoes could still be heard in the 1750s and beyond. Even so, his first five operas were by no means failures: *Les Indes galantes* was given 64 times between 1735 and 1737, *Les fêtes d'Hébé* 71 times in

1739 and 1740. *Castor et Pollux* was less successful, yet its first run nevertheless included 21 performances.

By the standards of Rameau's mature years the period 1740–44 was uncharacteristically slack: he produced no new theoretical writings, and composition was limited to the *Pièces de clavecin en concerts* (1741) and the revision for their first revivals of three of his existing operas. There are hints of dissatisfaction with the Opéra management; certainly his productivity revived sharply after the directorship passed from Eugène de Thuret to Jean-François Berger in May 1744.

3. OPERATIC CAREER, 1745–64. A series of commissions, three from the court, stimulated Rameau to complete no fewer than four dramatic works in 1745. For the dauphin's wedding festivities he wrote *La princesse de Navarre* and *Platée*; for the court celebration of the Battle of Fontenoy he composed *Le temple de la Gloire*; and for the Paris Opéra's commemoration of Fontenoy he completed *Les fêtes de Polymnie* – the first of at least seven collaborations with Louis de Cahusac. On 4 May, after the dauphin's wedding, Rameau received the first of two royal pensions and the title *compositeur de la musique de la chambre du roy*. From 1745 he was increasingly involved at court: more than half his remaining works were intended for performance there. *Les surprises de l'Amour* (1748) was even written as a vehicle for Mme de Pompadour's theatrical talents in her Théâtre des Petits Cabinets.

The years 1745–9 were Rameau's most prolific: altogether he completed nine operas, including the *tragédie Zoroastre*, the *comédie lyrique Platée*, two *pastorales* and three *opéras-ballets*. By 1749 his works dominated the stage to the extent that the marquis d'Argenson, among the last of the Lullistes, forbade the Opéra to stage more than two of his works in any one year. By now, however, Rameau enjoyed the esteem of an increasingly wide cross-section of the French public. His standing at court was high, he had the support of most of the intellectuals (including many who were later to side against him), and his works were widely performed in Paris and throughout the provinces.

During his final 13 years (1752–64), Rameau's operatic activity declined sharply. Apart from two major works – *Les Paladins* and *Les Boréades* – his composition was limited to small-scale *pastorales*, *actes de ballet* and the revision of earlier operas (notably *Castor et Pollux* and *Zoroastre*). Of the new works, only *Les Paladins* appeared at the Opéra; the rest were performed solely at court. Even *Les Boréades*, formerly thought to have been in rehearsal at the Opéra when Rameau died, is now known to have been prepared instead for court performance at Choisy in 1763 (Bouissou 1983). This reduction in the quantity (if not necessarily the quality) of new works was partly the result of ill-health and advancing age (he was almost 81 when he died). Nevertheless, these years saw a remarkable resurgence in his theoretical work: from 1752 he produced some 23 books or pamphlets. A significant number of these were stimulated by his rift with the Encyclopedists, notably J.-J. Rousseau and, later, Diderot and D'Alembert. This rift became rapidly wider in the wake of the QUERELLE DES BOUFFONS (1752–4), that notorious pamphlet war ostensibly between the supporters of *opera buffa* and those of serious French opera.

It was during the Querelle that Rameau found himself once more under attack, this time not as a threat to the musical establishment but as an establishment figure; his opponents were those who for a variety of reasons wanted French opera to conform more with the italianate pan-European tradition. And although he was generally viewed by the wider musical public as the Grand Old Man of French opera, criticism that his style was outmoded could now more often be heard. While a number of Rameau's works remained in the repertory after his death, few survived the radical change in taste brought about by the arrival of Gluck's operas in the mid-1770s.

4. DRAMATIC MUSIC. Although Rameau's composing career covers the best part of six decades (1706–c1764), his operas belong entirely to the last three. By contemporary French standards his output was large. Taking into account prologues, extensive revisions and works now lost, it amounts to the equivalent of more than a hundred separate acts – a remarkable quantity in view of the composer's late start and his prolific theoretical output.

Rameau's *oeuvre* includes virtually all the sub-species of French opera then current – *tragédie en musique, opéra-ballet, pastorale-héroïque, comédie lyrique, comédie-ballet* – but is perhaps most remarkable for its emphasis on the *tragédie*: at a time when fellow composers generally shunned this most risky and demanding of French genres, Rameau devoted to it almost a quarter of his output. True, only four of his seven *tragédies* were staged during his lifetime (performances of *Samson, Linus* and *Les Boréades* were for various reasons abandoned), but *Dardanus* and *Zoroastre* were so comprehensively revised for their first revivals that the later versions may almost be considered autonomous works. He was perhaps never as fortunate as Lully in his choice of librettist (he shied away from the idea of resetting Quinault), but the librettos of several of his *tragédies*, notably those by Pellegrin, Bernard and Voltaire, are among the finest of their kind.

Rameau was indebted to the French operatic tradition for his musical forms and for many elements of his style. Few of these elements survive unmodified, however. In his recitative, for instance, he accepted the fundamental character of the Lullian model, with its meticulously notated declamatory rhythms, its active bass line and frequent changes of metre; he even retained many of its turns of phrase. Yet his recitative is musically more sophisticated than that of his predecessors. It makes greater use of syncopation and cross-accents and contains a wider variety of note values (ex.1). Bold leaps are

Ex.1 *Les Boréades*, Act 2 scene v

Con-ten-te toi___ d'u-ne vic - ti - me, frap - pe,

frap - pe, Je me livre à tes coups.

['Be content with one victim. Strike! I surrender to your blows.']

frequent, especially those involving augmented or diminished intervals (ex.2), while the traditional, severely syllabic style of word-setting is increasingly relieved by discreet use of decorative or expressive detail (ex.3). Above all, Rameau brings to the recitative – as to all his music – one of the richest harmonic idioms of his age, full of 7ths, 9ths and other dissonant chords, and numerous appoggiaturas. Modulations are frequent and

Ex.2 *Hippolyte et Aricie*, Act 2 scene i

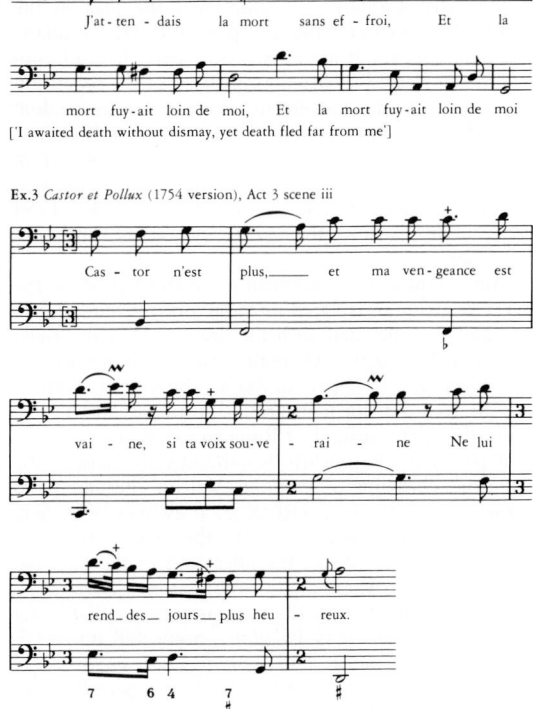

[`I awaited death without dismay, yet death fled far from me']

Ex.3 *Castor et Pollux* (1754 version), Act 3 scene iii

[`Castor is dead, and my vengeance is useless unless your sovereign voice restore happier days to him.']

often to remote keys. Many of these developments arise from a desire to enhance and intensify the declamation. At the same time, Rameau could not help allowing purely musical considerations to invade his recitative: 'Lully needs actors', Voltaire reports him as saying, 'but I need singers'. It was this greater elaboration and complexity that caused some contemporaries to compare his recitative style unfavourably with 'le beau naturel' of Lully's.

Accompanied recitative, though by no means absent from the operas of his predecessors, is used by Rameau with increasing frequency, especially from the mid-1740s onwards. In style it is uniquely French. The vocal line remains much as in simple recitative, while the accompaniment takes one of two principal forms: the first, reserved for solemn pronouncements, consists of organ-like sustained chords involving double-stopped strings, occasionally with independent wind; the second, found in agitated contexts, consists of a variety of energetic figures demanding considerable orchestral agility and coordination. Rameau broke new ground in using this sort of accompaniment in passages of dialogue (e.g. *Hippolyte et Aricie*, 4.iii).

The vocal *airs* in his operas, like those of his contemporaries, are of four main varieties: the dance-songs and *ariettes* found exclusively in the *divertissements*, and the *airs de mouvement* and *monologues* of the main scenes. In many of his dance-songs, Rameau adopts the traditional practice of 'parodying' (in this context, adapting words to) an existing dance. Increasingly, though, he reworks his material, sometimes so extensively that *air* and dance have wholly different musical forms (e.g. 'Pénétrez les humains' and the 'Air vif pour les héros' in the prologue of *Le temple de la Gloire*).

Rameau's treatment of the *ariette* underwent considerable development. In his first operas, these large-scale but essentially decorative da capo arias are relatively few. Moreover, vocal display is limited to long-held notes and to occasional, fairly brief *vocalises* on certain standard words ('ramage', 'brillez' etc.). It was doubtless the growing virtuosity of such singers as Marie Fel and Pierre de Jélyotte that encouraged him not only to include more *ariettes* in his later operas and revivals but also to increase the element of display. The demands of an *ariette* like 'Un horizon serein' (*Les Boréades*, 1.iv), with its high tessitura and extended melismas (ex.4), would have been unthinkable 30 years

Ex. 4 *Les Boréades*, Act 1 scene iv

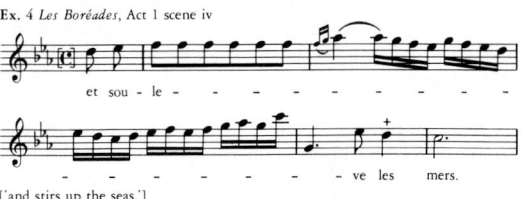

['and stirs up the seas.']

earlier. Even so, the technique required in Rameau's vocal music remained modest by contemporary Italian standards.

Quite different in character are the vocal set pieces outside the *divertissements*. Much the simplest are the *airs de mouvement* (also known as *petits airs* or *airs tendres*) scattered throughout the recitative. Rameau's treatment of these short pieces – some only two or three bars long, few more than two dozen – differs little from that of his predecessors. He is, however, inclined to make occasional use of orchestral accompaniment and to decorate the melodic line with more ornament (e.g. 'Que d'un objet aimé', *Les Boréades*, 3.ii).

By far the weightiest 'arias' are the large-scale *airs de monologue*, often situated at the beginnings of acts and employed for expressions of high emotion. Rameau was drawn to this type of air which, in the hands of composers such as Campra, Destouches and Montéclair, had already developed into a potent, highly-charged mode of expression. Yet of his precursors only Charpentier, in *Médée* (1694), approached the emotional impact of 'Cesse, cruel Amour' (*Dardanus*, 1.i) or Theseus's two prayers to Neptune (*Hippolyte*, 2.iii and 3.ix). Indeed, the first of these prayers, with its arpeggio accompaniment, bold leaps and rich harmony, comes closer to the ariosos in Bach's Passions than to anything in the French tradition. While many of these *monologues* involve a da capo, they have little else in common with the contemporary Italian aria. The vocal lines, slow-moving, intense and almost entirely syllabic, have the character of heightened recitative. The opening ritornello introduces thematic ideas that are employed, often only loosely, in the subsequent accompaniments but not necessarily in the vocal line (*Dardanus*, 3.i). Accompaniments tend to be rich and sombre, as in 'Tristes apprêts' (*Castor et Pollux*, 1.iv) and 'Lieux funestes' (*Dardanus*, 1744 version, 4.i), both with important lines for bassoons.

Unlike contemporary *opera seria*, French opera in Rameau's day was as rich as ever in ensembles and choruses. Yet even by French standards, Rameau's first opera contains a high proportion of ensembles, several very extensive (e.g. the enharmonic Trio des Parques, *Hippolyte*, 3.iv). It includes several duets in which the characters express conflicting ideas in terse, vigorous counterpoint. In response to the criticism that such ensembles were irrational, Rameau shortened several of them during the opera's first run and thereafter composed fewer ensembles of this sort. Duets in which singers express the same sentiment remain an important ingredient, however.

In their richness, variety and dramatic power, Rameau's choruses are comparable with those of the Handel oratorios and Bach Passions. Choruses are deployed in the traditional French manner, either as important decorative elements in the *divertissements* or as agents in the drama itself. It is in the latter role that the chorus is at its most expressive, whether in reacting to dramatic events such as battles (*Castor*, 1754 version, 1.v), spectacular natural or supernatural phenomena (*Les fêtes de l'Hymen*, 1.vii) or, above all, to the deaths of protagonists (*Hippolyte*, 4.iii and iv; *Castor*, 1.i). Often the distinction between *divertissement* and action choruses is blurred, as in those which occur during Theseus's trial by Pluto's court (*Hippolyte*, 2.iii and iv) or during Abramane's occult sacrifice (*Zoroastre*, 4.vi and vii).

In his treatment of the orchestra Rameau is generally more original than in his writing for voices, eloquent though that often is. His eclectic approach and imaginative orchestration (the latter often misrepresented in the *Oeuvres complètes*) help create music of almost symphonic richness and variety. His introduction of instruments new to France (orchestral horns from about 1745, clarinets from 1749) is paralleled by his experimentation with instrumental techniques seldom before used at the Opéra: pizzicato from 1744, glissando in 1745. With younger contemporaries like Royer and Mondonville, he developed a more imaginative approach to the combining of wind and strings. In such late works as *Acante et Céphise* and *Les Paladins* he pioneered a style of orchestration less concerned with blend than with a 'counterpoint of timbres' – scoring, well illustrated by the overture to *Acante et Céphise* and the ballet music of the 1757 *Les surprises de l'Amour* and of *Les Paladins*, in which superimposed layers are distinguished not only by timbre but also by thematic material.

It is in the purely instrumental movements – dances and the various sorts of dramatic *symphonie* – that Rameau's orchestral virtuosity is at its greatest. In its freshness and variety his ballet music is second to none. Diderot exaggerated, of course, when he claimed that before Rameau 'no one had distinguished the delicate shades of expression that separate the tender from the voluptuous, the voluptuous from the impassioned, the impassioned from the lascivious'. But the composer's ability to capture a huge range of moods – from the aching nostalgia of his pastoral music to the Dionysiac frenzy of his tambourins – is indeed one of his most remarkable gifts, the more so given the limitations of form, phrase-structure and rhythm imposed by contemporary choreography. His dances cry out for physical gesture, a quality much appreciated by the ballet-masters of his day.

Symptoms of Rameau's desire to integrate the instrumental movements can be seen in his development of the *ballet figuré* and dramatic entr'acte and in his rethinking of the role of the overture. The *ballet figuré*, in which dancers presented a stylized action linked to that of the drama, may be found sporadically in the earlier history of French opera, but it was not until Rameau – or rather his librettist Cahusac – championed the idea in the 1740s that examples become plentiful. The dramatic entr'acte appears at about the same period. Traditionally the entr'acte had usually consisted of the repetition of an instrumental movement taken almost at random from the preceding act. The 1744 *Dardanus*, however, includes a *bruit de guerre* accompanying offstage action between Acts 4 and 5; further specially composed entr'actes appear in *Naïs*, *Acante et Céphise*, the 1754 version of *Castor*, the 1756 *Zoroastre* and *Les Boréades*.

More significant is Rameau's transformation of the overture from an isolated introductory movement into one closely connected with the drama. Though briefly anticipated in *Castor* (where the first section of the overture reappears, reshaped, in Act 5), the idea of connecting the two did not gain ground until the mid-1740s. From that date, several of Rameau's overtures contain tone-paintings that clearly foreshadow the action: the sculptor's chiselling (*Pigmalion*), Vulcan's hammer (*Les surprises de l'Amour*), celebratory fireworks (*Acante et Céphise*), the distillation of the elements from primordial chaos (*Zaïs*), the liberation of the Bactrian citizens after Abramane's oppression (*Zoroastre*). Others are linked musically to a later scene (*Platée*, *La naissance d'Osiris*, *Les Paladins*). Some fall into both categories (*Les fêtes de Polymnie*, *Les surprises de l'Amour*, *Naïs*, *Les Boréades*). In this respect Rameau anticipated the Gluck of *Iphigénie en Tauride* by several decades. He was also the first in France to diversify the form and style of the overture. Only those of his first few operas can truly be said to preserve something of the spirit of the Lullian French overture. Several of Rameau's later works adopt the general form – or even, in the case of *La princesse de Navarre*, the style – of the contemporary Italian overture, with its two fast movements flanking a slower one.

In spite of such developments, it is remarkable how little Rameau's concept of opera seems to have changed when one views his output as a whole. *Hippolyte et Aricie* and *Les Boréades*, for instance, have much in common though separated by some 30 years – the same division into five acts, each with an obligatory *divertissement* more or less integrated into the action, the same alternation of tension and relaxation, the same flexibility of movement between recitative and set piece. The main structural difference is the absence in the later work of the traditional prologue, considered redundant from the time of *Zoroastre* (1749) onwards. Yet even in his 60s and 70s Rameau remained receptive to new musical fashions. His lofty and dignified idiom of the 1730s became noticeably influenced during the next two decades by the lighter German and Italian styles of the mid-18th century and softened by a proliferation of ornamental detail. The differences of style appear most acute from the 1750s onwards, whenever Rameau composed new music for the revival of an older opera.

See also ACANTE ET CÉPHISE; ANACRÉON; BORÉADES, LES; CASTOR ET POLLUX; DARDANUS (i); FÊTES DE L'HYMEN ET DE L'AMOUR, LES; FÊTES DE POLYMNIE, LES; FÊTES D'HÉBÉ, LES; GUIRLANDE, LA; HIPPOLYTE ET ARICIE; INDES GALANTES, LES; NAÏS; NAISSANCE D'OSIRIS, LA; NÉLÉE ET MYRTHIS; PALADINS, LES; PIGMALION; PLATÉE; PRINCESSE DE NAVARRE, LA; SURPRISES DE L'AMOUR, LES; TEMPLE DE LA GLOIRE, LE; ZAÏS; ZÉPHYRE; and ZOROASTRE.

Edition: *J.-P. Rameau: Oeuvres complètes*, ed. C. Saint-Saëns, C. Malherbe and others (Paris, 1895–1924) [OC]

first performed at the Paris Opéra unless otherwise stated; information given only for premières and principal revivals in Rameau's lifetime

* – wholly or largely autograph

† – contains autograph sections, passages, revisions, annotations

title	genre, acts	libretto	performances	remarks	sources	edition
Hippolyte et Aricie	tragédie en musique, prol., 5	S.-J. Pellegrin	1 Oct 1733 11 Sept 1742 25 Feb 1757	major cuts and substitutions during first run without prol.	*F-Dc, Pa, Pc, Pn* (incl. 1 pr. title, Paris, 1742), *Po, V, GB-Cfm*; reduced score (Paris, *c*1733) [some copies with 'Changements conformes à la représentation'; some with revs. made for 1742 revival; *F-Pc, Pn, US-MED*, with MS rev.; copy *F-Po* †	OC vi
Samson	tragédie en musique, prol., 5	Voltaire	unperf.	lib. begun by Dec 1733; ov., chaconne, dances, Acts 3 and 5 rehearsed ?Oct 1734, subsequently abandoned; music said to have been reused in Les Indes galantes (entrée Les Incas), Castor et Pollux, Les fêtes d'Hébé and Zoroastre; text (and probably music) of air 'Echo, voix errante' used in La princesse de Navarre and rev. of Les fêtes de Polymnie (1753) [see Sadler 1989]	lib. (Paris, 1745); MS libs. in *Pa, S-Sk* and St Petersburg, Hermitage	lib. in L. Morland, ed.: *Voltaire: Oeuvres complètes*, iii (Paris, 1877–85)
Les Indes galantes [formerly Les victoires galantes]	opéra-ballet, prol., 2–4 entrées: Le Turc généreux Les Incas du Pérou Les fleurs Les sauvages	L. Fuzelier	23 Aug 1735 28 Aug 1735 10 March 1736 28 May 1743 8 June 1751 14 July 1761	prol., 2 entrées 3rd entrée added; some rev. of prol. and first 2 entrées 4th entrée added prol., various combinations of 3 or 4 entrées; from Feb 1744, prol. and 2nd entrée perf. with other works prol., entrées 1–3; from 3 Aug, Les sauvages replaced Le Turc généreux; from 21 Sept, Les sauvages perf. with other works; from 24 Oct, prol., Les sauvages, Les Incas, Les fleurs prol., entrées 1–3; from 18 Aug, Les sauvages replaced Le Turc généreux; from 20 July 1762, prol. and Les sauvages perf. with La guirlande	*F-AG, Pa, Pc, Pn, Po* (incl. 1 pr. title, Paris, 1735), *TLm, GB-Cfm*; reduced score (Paris, *c*1736) [prol. and 1st 3 entrées arr. as Quatre grands concerts; also contains new entrée Les sauvages]	OC vii

title	genre, acts	libretto	performances	remarks	sources	edition
Castor et Pollux	tragédie en musique, prol., 5	P.-J. Bernard	24 Oct 1737 8/11 Jan 1754 24 Jan 1764	no prol., new Act 1, former Acts 1–5 reworked as Acts 2–5; some new music minor rev.	*F-A, AG, AIXc, CLO, Dc, Mc, NAc, Pa, Pn, Po, TLm, GB-Cfm, I-Baf, US-I*; reduced scores (Paris, *c*1737), (Paris, *c*1754) [copy in *F-Pc* with MS rev.]	OC viii
Les fêtes d'Hébé, ou Les talents lyriques	opéra-ballet, prol., 3 entrées: La poésie La musique La danse	A. G. de Montdorge [addns by Bernard, Pellegrin and A.-J.-J. Le Riche de La Pouplinière and possibly others]	21 May 1739 27 July 1747 18 May 1756 5 June 1764	from 23 June with rev. 2nd entrée minor rev.; incl. 1 air by Le Vasseur 1st entrée rev. without prol.; from 10 Jan 1765 prol. reinstated	*AG, Pa, Pc, Pn* (incl. 1 pr. title, Paris, 1739), *GB-Cfm*; reduced scores (Paris, *c*1739) [some copies with rev. 2nd entrée], (Paris, *c*1756 or later) [copies with rev. 2nd entrée, either scenes i–iv or i–vi]	OC ix; ed. in Cyr 1975
Dardanus	tragédie en musique, prol., 5	C.-A. Le Clerc de la Bruère	19 Nov 1739 23 April 1744 15 April 1760	cuts, addns and other changes (?collab. S.-J. Pellegrin) during 1st run rev. as Nouvelle tragédie; major changes to plot, Acts 3–5 largely new music without prol., further rev.	*F-AG, Pa, Pc, Pn* (incl. 1 pr. title, Paris, 1739), *Po, TLm, GB-Cfm*; reduced scores (Paris, *c*1739), (Paris, *c*1744) [proof copy *F-Po* †, copies in *Po* with MS rev.]	OC x
La princesse de Navarre	comédie-ballet, 3	Voltaire	Versailles, 23 Feb 1745 Bordeaux, 26 Nov 1763	for wedding of dauphin with Maria Teresa of Spain; incl. spoken dialogue with new prol. by Voltaire	*BO, Pc, Pn*; lib. (Paris, 1745)	OC xi
Platée	comédie lyrique, prol.: La naissance de la Comédie, 3	A.-J. Le Valois d'Orville, after J. Autreau	Versailles, 31 March 1745 9 Feb 1749 21 Feb 1754	for wedding of dauphin with Maria Teresa of Spain lib. altered by Ballot de Sauvot	*Pa, Pn, Po*; reduced score (Paris, *c*1749) [proof copy *Po* †]	OC xii
Les fêtes de Polymnie	opéra-ballet, prol.: Le temple de Mémoire, 3 entrées: La fable L'histoire La féerie	L. de Cahusac	12 Oct 1745 21 Aug 1753	prol. for victory of Fontenoy; cuts during 1st run most cuts reinstated; some new music	*Pa, Pn* (incl. 1 pr. title, Paris, 1745), *Po* †; reduced score (Paris, *c*1753) [proof copy *Po* †]	OC xiii
Le temple de la Gloire	opéra-ballet, 5	Voltaire	Versailles, 27 Nov 1745 7 Dec 1745 19 April 1746	for victory of Fontenoy rev. as prol. (La caverne de l'Envie) and 3 entrées (Bélus, Bacchus, Trajan)	*Pa, Pmeyer, Pn* †, *Po* †, *V, US-BE*	OC xiv
Les fêtes de Ramire	acte de ballet, 1	Voltaire (rev. J.-J. Rousseau)	Versailles, 22 Dec 1745	re-use of divertissements from La princesse de Navarre, linked by new lib. and without spoken dialogue; copy in *F-V* has at least one air (? and recit.) by Rousseau, but not ov. or other nos. he claims to have written	*F-V*; lib. (Paris, 1745)	OC xi

title	genre, acts	libretto	performances	remarks	sources	edition
Les fêtes de l'Hymen et de l'Amour, ou Les dieux d'Egypte	opéra-ballet, prol., 3 entrées: Osiris Canope Aruéris ou Les Isies	Cahusac	Versailles, 15 March 1747 5 Nov 1748 9 July 1754	for wedding of dauphin with Maria-Josepha of Saxony without prol.	AG, Pa, Pn; reduced score (Paris, c1748) [proof copy Po †]	OC xv
Zaïs	pastorale-héroïque, prol., 4	Cahusac	29 Feb 1748 19 May 1761	without prol.	COM, Pa, Pn; reduced score (Paris, c1748) [some copies with suppl. of addns; 2 copies, Pc, with MS addns; proof copy Po †]	OC xvi
Pigmalion	acte de ballet, 1	Ballot de Sauvot, after A. H. de Lamotte: Le triomphe des Arts (entrée: La sculpture)	27 Aug 1748 9 March 1751 10 Aug 1760 31 March 1764	perf. with other works perf. with other works perf. with other works perf. with other works	AG, BO, LYm, Pa, Pc, Pn, Po †; reduced score (Paris, c1748) [copy in V, annotated and corrected]	OC xvii/1
Les surprises de l'Amour	opéra-ballet, prol.: Le retour d'Astrée, 2 entrées: La lyre enchantée Adonis [from 1757, L'enlèvement d'Adonis]	Bernard	Versailles, 27 Nov 1748 31 May 1757 10 Oct 1758	prol. for Peace of Aix-la-Chapelle without prol., major rev. of entrées, with Anacréon (ii) as 3rd entrée; from 12 July, Les sibarites (1753) replaced La lyre enchantée as 31 May 1757 but with rev. of La lyre enchantée and Anacréon (ii); from 7 Dec, Les sibarites replaced Anacréon	1st version: Pn, Po* (prol. only) later versions: Pn, Po †; reduced scores (Paris, c1757) [incl. L'enlèvement d'Adonis, La lyre enchantée and Anacréon; some copies incl. Les sibarites]; all entrées also issued separately (Paris, c1757); La lyre enchantée repr. (Paris, c1758) with changes	OC xvii/1
Naïs	pastorale-héroïque, prol.: L'accord des dieux, 3	Cahusac	22 April 1749 7 Aug 1764	prol. for Peace of Aix-la-Chapelle P.-M. Berton claims to have made addns and revs.	Lm, Pa, Pc, Pn, Po, US-Bp, Wc	OC xviii
Zoroastre	tragédie en musique, 5	Cahusac	5 Dec 1749 19 Jan 1756	major rev. of plot; music of Acts 2, 3 and 5 largely new	reduced score (Paris, c1749) [annotated copies in F-Pa, Pc, Po, V] Pa, Pc, Pn, Po, TLm, GB-Cfm	1749 version ed. T. Lajarte (Paris, n.d.); 1756 version ed. F. Gervais (Paris, 1964)
Linus	tragédie en musique, 5	La Bruère	unperf.	rehearsed in or before 1752	F-Pn (2 copies of vn 1 only, 1 with autograph addns); MS lib. in Pn	——
La guirlande, ou Les fleurs enchantées	acte de ballet, 1	J. F. Marmontel	21 Sept 1751 11 April 1752 20 July 1762	with Les sauvages (from Les Indes galantes) and Les génies tutélaires (by F. Rebel and F. Francoeur) with Zélindor, roi des sylphes (by Rebel and Francoeur) and Pigmalion with prol. and Les sauvages (from Les Indes galantes)	AG, Pa, Pn; reduced score (Paris, c1751) [proof copy, and copy with addns and rev. in Po †]	ed. G. Beck (Paris, 1981)
Acante et Céphise, ou La sympathie	pastorale-héroïque, 3	Marmontel	19 Nov 1751	for birth of Duke of Burgundy	Pa, Pc, Pn, Po †; reduced score (Paris, c1751) [copy in Pn with MS rev.; proof copies Po †]	——
Daphnis et Eglé	pastorale-héroïque, 1	C. Collé	Fontainebleau, 30 Oct 1753	——	Pn, Po*	——

title	genre, acts	libretto	performances	remarks	sources	edition
Lysis et Délie	pastorale, 1	Marmontel	unperf.	intended for perf. at Fontainebleau, 6 Nov 1753, but considered too similar to Daphnis et Eglé, abandoned	lib. (Paris, 1753)	——
Les sibarites	acte de ballet, 1	Marmontel	Fontainebleau, 13 Nov 1753	perf. with La coquette trompée (A. Dauvergne); entitled Sibaris in some sources	*Pn*, *Po*; reduced score (Paris, *c*1757)	OC xvii/2
			12 July 1757	rev., added to revival of Les surprises de l'Amour		
			7 Dec 1758			
La naissance d'Osiris, ou La fête Pamilie	acte de ballet, 1	Cahusac	Fontainebleau, 12 Oct 1754	for birth of Duke of Berry; with Les Incas du Pérou (from Les Indes galantes) and Pigmalion; at one stage entitled Les fêtes Pammilies; orig. intended as prol. to (?projected) opéra-ballet Les beaux jours de l'Amour	*Pc*, *Pn*, *Po**	——
Anacréon (i)	acte de ballet, 1	Cahusac	Fontainebleau, 23 Oct 1754		*Pc* †, *Pn*, *Po*	——
Anacréon (ii)	acte de ballet, 1	Bernard	31 May 1757	added to revival of Les surprises de l'Amour as 3rd entrée	*Pn*, *Po*; reduced score (Paris, *c*1757)	OC xvii/2
Les Paladins	comédie lyrique, 3	anon.	12 Feb 1760	lib. attrib. D. de Monticourt by Beffara (1783–4) and in the Soleinne lib. collection (*F-Pn*); attrib. P.-J. Bernard by Collé, who mentions C.-H. de Voisenon and de Tressan as possibilities	*Pc*, *Pn**, *Po* †, *GB-Cfm*	ed. in Wolf 1977; FO, xliv (1986)
Les Boréades	tragédie en musique, 5	anon.; attrib. Cahusac	?unperf.	entitled Abaris in some sources; rehearsed Paris (25 April 1763), Versailles (27 April 1763); court perf. planned; lib. attrib. Cahusac in Decroix (1776) and A. B. Teulières, continuator of Cathala-Coture: *Histoire politique, ecclésiastique et littéraire du Querci* (Montauban, 1785)	*F-Pc*, *Pn* †, *US-Bp*	ed. in Térey-Smith 1971; facs. (Paris, 1982); autograph frags. in Green 1983
Nélée et Myrthis	acte de ballet, 1	anon.	?unperf.	entitled Mirthis in autograph; intended as 1 entrée in (?projected) opéra-ballet Les beaux jours de l'Amour (as with La naissance d'Osiris, 1754)	*F-Pc**, *Pn*	OC xi
Zéphyre	acte de ballet, 1	anon.	?unperf.	orig. entitled Les nymphes de Diane	*Pc**, *Pn*	OC xi
Io	acte de ballet, 1	anon.	?unperf.	all sources lack final divertissement; possibly dates from before 1745 [see Sadler 1989]	*Pc*, *Pn*	——

Doubtful: Le procureur dupe sans le savoir (opéra comique mêlé de vaudevilles, 1), *c*1758, music lost; anon. lib. in *F-Pn* apparently copied from a score with autograph annotations found among Rameau's papers

GENERAL

M.-P.-G. de Chabanon: *Eloge de M. Rameau* (Paris, 1764)

H. Maret: *Eloge historique de M. Rameau* (Dijon, 1766)

C. Palissot de Montenoy: 'Rameau', *Necrologe des hommes célebres de France 1765* (Paris, 1765), 85–116

J.-J.-M. Decroix: *L'ami des arts, ou Justification de plusieurs grands hommes* (Amsterdam, 1776)

J.-B. de La Borde: 'Rameau (Jean-Philippe)', *Essai sur la musique ancienne et moderne* (Paris, 1780), iii, 464–9

L.-F. Beffara: *Dictionnaire de l'Académie royale de musique* (MS, 1783–4, F-Po Rès.602)

C. Malherbe: 'Commentaire bibliographique', *Jean-Philippe Rameau: Oeuvres complètes*, vi–xvi (Paris, 1895–1924)

M. Emmanuel and M. Ténéo: 'Commentaire bibliographique', *Jean-Philippe Rameau: Oeuvres complètes*, xvii–xviii (Paris, 1895–1924)

P.-M. Masson: 'Lullistes et Ramistes, 1733–1752', *L'année musicale*, i (1911), 187–211

——: *L'opéra de Rameau* (Paris, 1930)

E. Lebeau: 'J. J. M. Decroix et sa collection Rameau', *Mélanges d'histoire et d'esthétique musicales offerts à Paul-Marie Masson* (Paris, 1955), ii, 81–91

E. G. Ahnell: *The Concept of Tonality in the Operas of Jean-Philippe Rameau* (diss., U. of Illinois, 1957)

A. M. Nagler: 'Maschinen und Maschinisten der Rameau-Ära', *Maske und Kothurn*, ii (1957), 128–40

C. Girdlestone: *Jean-Philippe Rameau: his Life and Work* (London, 1957, 2/1969)

G. Seefrid: *Die 'Airs de danse' in den Bühnenwerken von Jean-Philippe Rameau* (Wiesbaden, 2/1971)

C. Girdlestone: *La tragédie en musique (1673–1750) considérée comme genre littéraire* (Geneva, 1972)

J. R. Anthony: *French Baroque Music from Beaujoyeulx to Rameau* (London, 1973, 2/1978; Fr. trans., 1981)

G. Sadler: 'Rameau, Piron and the Parisian Fair Theatres', *Soundings*, iv (1974), 13–29

R. Cotte: *La musique maçonnique et ses musiciens* (Braine-le-Comte, 1975, 2/1987)

M. Cyr: 'Rameau et Traetta', *NRMI*, xii (1978), 166–82

E. Lang-Becker: *Szenentypus und Musik in Rameau's Tragédie lyrique* (Munich, 1978)

M. Cyr: 'Eighteenth-Century French and Italian Singing: Rameau's Writing for the Voice', *ML*, lxi (1980), 318–37

C. Kintzler: 'Rameau et Voltaire: les enjeux théoriques d'une collaboration orageuse', *RdM*, lxvii (1981), 139–68

G. Sadler: 'Rameau and the Orchestra', *PRMA*, cviii (1981–2), 47–68

T. Green: '"Chants d'allégresse": le travail contrapuntique de Rameau', *IMSCR, xiii Strasbourg 1982*, 555–78

T.-G. Boucher: 'Rameau et les théâtres de la cour (1745–64)', *Jean-Philippe Rameau: Dijon 1983*, 565–77

M. F. Christout: 'Quelques interprètes de la danse dans l'opéra de Rameau', *Jean-Philippe Rameau: Dijon 1983*, 533–49

R. Fajon: 'Le préramisme dans le répertoire de l'Opéra', *Jean-Philippe Rameau: Dijon 1983*, 307–29

C. Kintzler: *Jean-Philippe Rameau: splendeur et naufrage de l'esthétique du plaisir à l'âge classique* (Paris, 1983, 2/1988)

J. de La Gorce, ed.: *Jean-Philippe Rameau: Dijon 1983*

——: 'Twenty Set Models for the Paris Opéra in the Time of Rameau', *EMc*, xi (1983), 429–40

N. Lecomte: 'Les divertissements exotiques dans les opéras de Rameau', *Jean-Philippe Rameau: Dijon 1983*, 551–63

B. Lespinard: 'De l'adaptation des airs de danse aux situations dramatiques dans les opéras de Rameau', *Jean-Philippe Rameau: Dijon 1983*, 477–99

N. McGegan and G. Spagnoli: 'Singing Style at the Opéra in the Rameau Period', *Jean-Philippe Rameau: Dijon 1983*, 209–26

C. Massip: 'Rameau et l'édition de ses oeuvres: bref aperçu historique et méthodologique', *Jean-Philippe Rameau: Dijon 1983*, 145–57

S. Milliot: 'Rameau et l'orchestre de l'Académie royale de musique d'après les exemplaires des répétitions de ses opéras', *Jean-Philippe Rameau: Dijon 1983*, 201–8

F. Moureau: 'Les poètes de Rameau', *Jean-Philippe Rameau: Dijon 1983*, 61–73

J.-B. Rivaud: 'Approche thématique et structurelle des livrets d'opéra de Jean-Philippe Rameau', *Jean-Philippe Rameau: Dijon 1983*, 75–87

M. Roland-Michel: 'Costumes de ballet au temps de Rameau', *Jean-Philippe Rameau: Dijon 1983*, 595–600

G. Sadler: 'Rameau's Singers and Players at the Paris Opéra: a Little-known Inventory of 1738', *EMc*, xi (1983), 453–67

——: 'The Paris Opéra Dancers in Rameau's Day: a Little-known Inventory of 1738', *Jean-Philippe Rameau: Dijon 1983*, 519–31

L. Sawkins: 'Nouvelles sources inédites de trois oeuvres de Rameau: leur signification pour l'instrumentation et l'interprétation du chant', *Jean-Philippe Rameau: Dijon 1983*, 171–200

H. Schneider: 'Rameau et la tradition lulliste', *Jean-Philippe Rameau: Dijon 1983*, 287–306

R. P. Wolf: 'An Eighteenth-Century *oeuvres complètes* of Rameau', *Jean-Philippe Rameau: Dijon 1983*, 159–69

G. Sadler: 'Patrons and Pasquinades: Rameau in the 1730s', *JRMA*, cxiii (1988), 314–37

D. Foster: *Jean-Philippe Rameau: a Guide to Research* (New York, 1989)

P. F. Rice: *The Performing Arts at Fontainebleau from Louis XIV to Louis XVI* (Ann Arbor, 1989)

G. Sadler: 'A Re-examination of Rameau's Self-Borrowings', *Jean-Baptiste Lully and the Music of the French Baroque: Essays in Honor of James R. Anthony* (Cambridge, 1989), 259–89

T. Green: *Early Rameau Sources: Studies in the Origins and Dating of the Operas and other Musical Works* (diss., Brandeis U., 1992)

INDIVIDUAL WORKS

E. Dacier: 'L'opéra au XVIIIe siècle: les premières représentations du 'Dardanus' de Rameau (novembre-décembre 1739)', *RHCM*, iii (1903), 163–73

C. Wahlund: 'Un acte inédit d'un opéra de Voltaire, publié d'après deux anciennes copies manuscrites de la Bibliothèque royale de Stockholm', *Studier i modern sprakvetenskap, utgifna af Ny-filologiska sällskapet i Stockholm*, iii (1905), 1–60 [on *Samson*]

C. Girdlestone: 'Voltaire, Rameau et "Samson"', *RMFC*, vi (1966), 133–43

J. Malignon: 'Zoroastre et Sarastro', *RMFC*, vi (1966), 145–58

M. Térey-Smith: *Jean-Philippe Rameau: 'Abaris ou Les Boréades': a Critical Edition* (diss., U. of Rochester, 1971)

S. Pitou: 'Rameau's *Dardanus* at Fontainebleau in 1763', *Studies on Voltaire and the Eighteenth Century*, cxvi (1973), 281–305

M. Cyr: *Rameau's 'Les fêtes d'Hébé'* (diss., U. of California, Berkeley, 1975)

R. P. Wolf: *Jean-Philippe Rameau's comédie lyrique 'Les Paladins' (1760): a Critical Edition and Study* (diss., Yale U., 1977)

C. Ayrey: *Rameau and the 'pastorale héroïque': a Dramatic and Structural Analysis of 'Zaïs'* (diss., U. of Auckland, 1978)

T. Green: 'La genèse d'une ariette de Rameau', *Les sources en musicologie: Orléans La Source 1979*, 151–7 [on *Zoroastre* and *La naissance d'Osiris*]

J. Sgard: 'Le premier *Samson* de Voltaire', *L'opéra au XVIIIe siècle: Aix-en-Provence 1977*, 513–25

G. Sadler: '*Naïs*, Rameau's "Opéra pour la paix"', *MT*, cxxi (1980), 431–3

C. Berger: 'Ein "Tableau" des "principe de l'harmonie": *Pygmalion* de Jean-Philippe Rameau', *Jean-Philippe Rameau: Dijon 1983*, 371–84

S. Bouissou: '"Les Boréades" de J.-Ph. Rameau: un passé retrouvé', *RdM*, lxix (1983), 157–85

T. Green: 'Les fragments d'opéras dans la partition autographe de *Zéphyre*', *Jean-Philippe Rameau: Dijon 1983*, 265–76

R. Langellier-Bellevue: 'Le concept d'exotisme chez Rameau: un exemple, 'Les sauvages' des *Indes galantes*', *RMFC*, xxi (1983), 158–60

J. Morel: '*Hippolyte et Aricie* de Rameau et Pellegrin dans l'histoire du mythe de Phèdre', *Jean-Philippe Rameau: Dijon 1983*, 89–99

M. Noiray: '*Hippolyte et Aricie* travestis: Rameau à l'Opéra-comique', *Jean-Philippe Rameau: Dijon 1983*, 109–25

O. Opdebeeck: '*Pigmalion* de Rameau: étude des sources et propositions pour une édition', *Jean-Philippe Rameau: Dijon 1983*, 245–64

G. Sadler: 'Rameau, Pellegrin and the Opéra: the Revisions of "Hippolyte et Aricie" during its First Season', *MT*, cxxiv (1983), 533–7

R. Savage: 'Rameau's American Dancers', *EMc*, xi (1983), 441–52 [on *Les Indes galantes*]

L. Sawkins: 'New Sources for Rameau's *Pigmalion* and other Works', *EMc*, xi (1983), 490–96

J. Van den Heuvel: '*Platée*, opéra-bouffe de Rameau au milieu du XVIIIe siècle', *Jean-Philippe Rameau: Dijon 1983*, 101–7

R. P. Wolf: 'Rameau's *Les Paladins*: from Autograph to Production', *EMc*, xi (1983), 497–504

L. Sawkins: 'Rameau's Last Years: some Implications of Rediscovered Material at Bordeaux', *PRMA*, cxi (1984–5), 66–91 [on *La princesse de Navarre*]

H. Brofsky: 'Rameau and the Indians: the Popularity of *Les sauvages*', *Music in the Classic Period: Essays in Honor of Barry S. Brook* (New York, 1985), 43–60

R. P. Wolf and G. Sadler: Introduction to J.-P. Rameau: *Les Paladins*, FO, xliv (1986), vii–lix

P. Russo: 'Les incertitudes de la tragédie lyrique: *Zoroastre* de Louis de Cahusac', *RdM*, lxxv (1989), 47–64

S. Bouissou: *Jean-Philippe Rameau: Les Boréades ou La tragédie oubliée* (Paris, 1992)
GRAHAM SADLER

Ramey, Samuel (Edward) (*b* Colby, KS, 28 March 1942). American bass. He studied in Wichita and New York, making his début in 1973 as Zuniga at New York City Opera; later roles with the company have included Mephistopheles (Gounod and Boito), Don Giovanni, Leporello, the *Hoffmann* villains, Henry VIII (*Anna Bolena*), Archibaldo, Olin Blitch (Floyd's *Susannah*), Attila and Don Quichotte (1986). At Glyndebourne (1976–7) he sang Mozart's Figaro and Nick Shadow. He made his Chicago and San Francisco débuts (1979) as Colline. At Aix-en-Provence (1980) he sang Assur (*Semiramide*), returning as Nick Shadow (1992). He first appeared at La Scala and the Vienna Staatsoper (1981) as Figaro, the role of his début at Covent Garden (1982), where he later sang Don Basilio, Méphistophélès, the *Hoffmann* villains and Philip II (1989). At Pesaro (1981–9) he sang Rossini's Mustafà, Douglas, Selim, Lord Sidney (*Il viaggio a Reims*), Maometto II and the Mayor in *La gazza ladra*. He made his Opéra début as Rossini's Moses (1983), and then sang Bertram in *Robert le diable* (1985). He made his Metropolitan début in 1984 as Argante (*Rinaldo*), returning as Giorgio, Escamillo, Bartók's Bluebeard, Don Giovanni and Philip II (1991–2). He has sung Don Giovanni at Salzburg in 1987 and has also appeared at Hamburg, Brussels, Berlin, Amsterdam, Florence, Geneva and Venice. His other roles include Arkel and Rodolfo (*La sonnambula*). A compelling actor with a magnificent stage presence, he has a resonant, flexible voice equally at home in Rossini and the Verdi bass roles such as Philip or Attila, which he has sung at La Scala (1991) and in Geneva (1992) and other cities.

*

M. Mayer: 'Samuel Ramey', *Opera*, xxxvii (1986), 399–405
CHARLES JAHANT/ELIZABETH FORBES

Rammentatore (It.). PROMPTER.

Ramondon, Littleton [Lewis] (*b* London, 28 Jan 1684; *d* after 1715). English baritone. Although he was christened Lewis and so called by Burney and Hawkins, he signed himself Littleton on theatre documents. Ramondon made his stage début in April 1705, performing songs in Italian and English. He created minor roles in English in *Camilla* (1706), *Pyrrhus and Demetrius* (1708) and *Clotilda* (1709) but lost his place in the Queen's Theatre Opera Company when performances were given completely in Italian. He made instrumental arrangements of opera tunes, mainly from *Camilla*, and composed songs, often to his own words. The tune of his 'All you that must take a leap in the dark' was used in *The Beggar's Opera*.

*

BurneyH; HawkinsH; LS
J. Milhous and R. D. Hume: *Vice Chamberlain Coke's Theatrical Papers 1706–1715* (Carbondale, IL, 1982)
OLIVE BALDWIN, THELMA WILSON

Ramos Carrión, Miguel (*b* Zamora, 17 May 1845; *d* Madrid, 8 Aug 1915). Spanish zarzuela librettist. He began his studies in Zamora before moving to Madrid, where he studied at the conservatory. At the age of 18 he collaborated on a libretto for the Bufos Madrileños, and he went on to a successful career as a writer of poetry and satirical pieces for periodicals as well as writing prolifically for the theatre, most often in collaboration with Vital Aza (1851–1911). His early zarzuela collaborations were with Arrieta, for whom he adapted Campodrón's original libretto for *Marina* into a three-act opera. The most successful of his later works include *Los sobrinos del Capitán Grant* (Caballero, 1877), *La bruja* (Chapí, 1887), *El rey que rabió* (Chapí, 1891) and *Agua, azucarillos y aguardiente* (Chueca, 1897). His librettos were noted for their strength of outline and the cleverness of their development. His sons, Antonio Ramos Martín (1885–1970) and José Ramos Martín (1892–1974), were also zarzuela librettists.

selective list; zarzuelas unless otherwise stated

Un sarao y una soirée (with E. de Lustanó), Arrieta, 1866; *El figle enamorada*, Arrieta, 1867; *De Madrid a Biarritz* (with C. Coello), Arrieta, 1870; *Marina* (ópera), Arrieta, 1871; *Esperanza*, G. Cereceda, 1872; *La gallina ciega*, Caballero, 1873; *El domador de fieras* (with C. Arana), F. A. Barbieri, 1874; *La clave* (with Arana), Caballero, 1875; *La marsellesa*, Caballero, 1876; *El siglo que viene* (with Coello), Caballero, 1876; *Los sobrinos del Capitán Grant*, Caballero, 1877; *El carbonera de Subiza* (with S. M. Granés), A. Rubio and Aceves, 1878; *El diablo cojuelo* (with M. Pina), Barbieri, 1878

Las dos princesas, Caballero, 1879; *Periquito*, Rubio, 1879; *La calandria* (with V. Aza), Chapí, 1880; *La tempestad*, Chapí, 1882; *El coro de señoras* (with Aza and Pina), M. Nieto, 1886; *Los lobos marinos* (with Aza), Chapí, 1887; *La bruja* (with Aza), Chapí, 1887; *El chaleco blanco*, Chueca, 1890; *El rey que rabió* (with Aza), Chapí, 1891; *Per salvar a mi tenitente*, Costa, 1896; *Agua, azucarillos y aguardiente*, Chueca, 1897; *Los hijos de la calle de Toledo* (with Samper), Piquer, 1900; *Circe* (ópera), Chapí, 1902; *Pasacalle* (with A. Ramos Martín), Valverde hijo, 1905; *La joroba* (with Ramos Martín), Chapí, 1906; *Pepe Botella*, Vives and Lleó, 1908
ANDREW LAMB

Ramos Martín, José (*b* Madrid, 10 March 1892; *d* Madrid, 16 Oct 1974). Spanish librettist. Son of Miguel Ramos Carrión, he assumed the latter's position as one of the premier zarzuela librettists, alternating such work with writing for journals such as *ABC*, *Blanco y negro* and *El liberal*. His first work, *El nido de la paloma*, was staged when he was only 20, and he went on to write numerous short stage works. These included several spectacular revues, but his most durable successes were the librettos for Jacinto Guerrero's zarzuelas *La alsaciana* (1921), *La montería* (1922) and *Los gavilanes* (1923). He was for many years director of the theatrical section of the Sociedad General de Autores de España.

selective list; all zarzuelas

Esta noche es Nochebuena, J. Jiménez, 1917; *Abejas y zánganos*, Jiménez, 1918; *Tras Tristán*, Jiménez, 1918; *Soleares*, Jiménez, 1919; *La alsaciana*, Guerrero, 1921; *La montería*, Guerrero, 1922; *El niño de la suerte*, T. Barrera, 1922; *Los gavilanes*, Guerrero, 1923; *La virgen capitana*, Barrera, 1923; *Campanela*, Guerrero, 1930; *Xuanón*, Moreno Torroba, 1933; *¡Qué sabes tú!*, E. Rosillo, 1943
ANDREW LAMB

Rampini [Rampin], (Giovanni) Giacomo (*b* Padua, 1680; *d* Padua, 27 May 1760). Italian composer. Of modest family background, he became a priest when little more than 20 and was elected to succeed Pignatta as *maestro di cappella* of Padua Cathedral in 1704. He held this position until his death, when Adolfati was named his successor. La Borde described Rampini as an excellent composer of sacred music and a successful one of operas. His reputation as a teacher attracted numerous students, including his nephew, Giacomo Rampini.

all opere serie

Armida in Damasco (3, G. Braccioli, after T. Tasso: *Gerusalemme liberata*), Venice, S Angelo, 17 Oct 1711

La gloria trionfante d'amore (3, Braccioli), Venice, S Angelo, 16 Nov 1712

Marco Attilio Regolo (3, M. Noris), Verona, Accademia Vecchia, aut. 1713

Ercole sul Termodonte (3, G. F. Bussani), Padua, Obizzi, June 1715

*

J.-B. de La Borde: *Essai sur la musique ancienne et moderne*, iii (Paris, 1780), 226

N. Pietrucci: *Biografia degli artisti padovani* (Padua, 1859), 224–5

A. Garbelotto: 'Piccola enciclopedia musicale padovanna', *Padova e la sua provincia*, xx/April (1974), 24   SVEN HANSELL

Ramponi, Virginia. *See* ANDREINI, VIRGINIA.

Ranalow, Frederick (Baring) (*b* Dublin, 7 Nov 1873; *d* London, 8 Dec 1953). Irish baritone. He trained at the RAM under Randegger. As a leading baritone in the Beecham Opera Company his roles ranged from Hans Sachs to Papageno, and he was one of the best Figaros of his generation. In 1920 he gave up serious opera to take part in Frederic Austin's revival of *The Beggar's Opera* at the Lyric Theatre, Hammersmith. Ranalow's Macheath was an essential feature of its success; he played the part almost 1500 times and was thereafter associated with the role whatever part he was playing.

Ranczak, Hildegard (*b* Witkowitz in Mähren [now Vitkoviče], 20 Dec 1895; *d* Vienna, Feb 1987). Bohemian soprano. She studied in Vienna with Irene Schlemmer-Ambros and made her début in Düsseldorf in 1919 as Pamina. After engagements in Cologne (1923–5) and Stuttgart (1926–8) she became a member of the Munich Staatsoper. Under the direction of Clemens Krauss she often appeared in operas by Strauss, creating Clairon in *Capriccio* (1942) and singing Octavian, Zdenka, Aithra (*Die ägyptische Helena*) and the Dyer's Wife. Guest appearances took her to Vienna (1931, 1943), London (as Salome, 1937), Paris (as Octavian, 1937), Rome and Dresden. Her last appearance was in 1950 as Carmen in Munich.

DAVID CUMMINGS

Randegger, Alberto (*b* Trieste, 13 April 1832; *d* London, 18 Dec 1911). English conductor and composer of German and Italian descent. He studied composition with Luigi Ricci. His first works included two operas, one a pasticcio, *Il lazzarone* (1852, Trieste, in collaboration with three more of Ricci's pupils), the other a tragedy, *Bianca Capello* (3, C. Wilten; Brescia, Grande, 23 Feb 1854). He was also musical director of theatres in Fiume, Senigallia, Brescia and Venice (1852–4). In 1854 he moved to London, where he became widely known as a singing teacher, conductor and composer. His comic opera *The Rival Beauties* (2, J. P. Wooler) was produced in Leeds in 1864. He became professor of singing at the RAM (1868) and at the RCM. As an opera conductor he directed an Italian season at St James's Theatre (1857) and also worked with the Carl Rosa company (1879–85) and at Covent Garden and Drury Lane (1887–98).

Randegger did much to encourage a following for Wagner's early operas, and was admired for his Verdi interpretations: he had known the composer in Italy, particularly in Trieste at the time of *Stiffelio* (1850). At Covent Garden in 1888 he conducted *Die Zauberflöte* with an inserted ballet to Mozart's chamber music; in later Mozart performances he was more scrupulous, discarding for instance the extra orchestration that had been introduced into *Don Giovanni* by Costa and others. He collaborated with T. J. H. Marzials on the libretto for Arthur Goring Thomas's *Esmeralda* (1883).

Randle, Thomas (*b* Hollywood, CA, 21 Dec 1958). American tenor. He studied at Los Angeles and in Germany, then began his career as a concert singer. A performance in Los Angeles of Tippett's *Songs for Dov*, conducted by the composer, led to his engagement at the ENO, where he made his operatic début in 1988 as Tamino. In 1989 he sang in *The Fairy-Queen* at Aix-en-Provence and appeared as Monteverdi's Orpheus at Valencia. He has sung Ferrando in Brussels and for Scottish Opera, Pelléas (1990) at the ENO, Olympion in *The Ice Break* at the Royal Albert Hall (1990) and Tamino at Glyndebourne (1991); at the ENO he also created Dionysus in Buller's *Bakxai* ('The Bacchae', 1992). An excellent actor and a musical singer, he has a strong, lyrical voice of great beauty of timbre.

ELIZABETH FORBES

Randová, Eva (*b* Kolín, 31 Dec 1936). Czech mezzo-soprano. After teaching mathematics and sport she took singing lessons, making her début as Eboli at Ostrava in 1962; she learnt the main mezzo roles before joining the Prague National Theatre in 1968. She became a member of the Stuttgart Opera in 1971, made her Bayreuth début as Waltraute in 1973, and later had conspicuous success there as Ortrud, Kundry, and Fricka in the 1976 *Ring* directed by Chéreau. At Salzburg in 1975 she sang Eboli under Karajan, and in 1977 made her Covent Garden début as Ortrud. Her American début was at San Francisco, followed by the Metropolitan in 1981 as Fricka. She is renowned as the Kostelnička in *Jenůfa*, which she sang in Lyubimov's production at Covent Garden (1986) and in a recording under Mackerras (1983). Other recordings include Ortrud under Solti (1987) and Vlasta in Fibich's *Šárka* (1988). Her dark-toned, firmly sustained voice and incisive diction and character make for exciting stage performances.

*

J. Higgins: 'The Competitive Spirit', *The Times* (17 Nov 1986) [interview]   NOËL GOODWIN

Rangström, (Anders Johan) Ture (*b* Stockholm, 30 Nov 1884; *d* Stockholm, 11 May 1947). Swedish composer. He was largely self-taught as a composer, but studied for a short time with Johan Lindegren (1903–4) and Pfitzner (1905–6); as his main interest was in vocal music, he studied singing, latterly in Munich (1906–7). Back in Sweden he worked for a number of years as a singing teacher. He was also a conductor and critic, and in 1930–36 was press adviser at the Swedish Royal Opera. His main compositions are his songs; his instrumental works are dominated by the four symphonies, which stand out among Swedish music for their original language and free declamatory style. Rangström followed a similar approach in his operas, above all in the first, *Kronbruden* ('The Crown Bride'), composed in a short time in 1915. It is based on the play by Strindberg, omitting the last two acts, and uses the original text itself, with only one word changed. Strindberg sanctioned the four-act version when the two men met in 1909. Reflecting the abrupt character of Strindberg's dialogue, Rangström uses a melodramatic style in which melodic expression predominates. The strength of the work lies in its transformation of musically fixed declamation, which floats over expressive motivic orchestral writing, into powerful dramatic singing. The opera keeps close to the original character of the drama, as a lyrical-dramatic ballad, and may be regarded as a scenic folksong. It deals with universal issues such as debt and reconciliation, and in the parts where this is woven with the mysterious powers of nature and with Swedish saga and myth, it touches the 'Swedish soul' as no other opera has done. The Swedish première of Kronbruden was delayed for three years (until 1922); the first night took place in Stuttgart in 1919, and from then on the opera had considerable success. In Rangström's last opera, Gilgamesj, the expansive features of his style are developed into an ecstatic, suspended, free structure which contrasts with the thin melodic lyricism. The extensive use of ostinato and rhythmic sequences indicates a neo-classical influence, and the taut integration of the chorus with both music and drama compensates for the somewhat static dramaturgy. The opera was planned in two parts, each in two acts, but because of an illness which proved fatal Rangström was able to complete only the vocal score of the first part and two-thirds of the orchestration; the orchestration was completed by John Fernström and the work was posthumously performed in 1952. In addition to another opera, Middelalderlig ('In the Middle Ages'), Rangström also composed incidental music.

autographs in S-Skma

Kronbruden [The Crown Bride], 1915 (4, A. Strindberg), Stuttgart, Hof, 21 Oct 1919

Middelalderlig [In the Middle Ages] (prelude and melodrama, H. Drachman), Stockholm, Royal Opera, 11 May 1921

Gilgamesj, 1943–4 (2, E. Linde), Stockholm, Royal Opera, 20 Nov 1952, orchestration completed J. Fernström

*

F. H. Törnblom: 'Ture Rangström', *Ord och bild*, lxiii (1934), 551–4

G. Österberg: 'Gilgamèsj – en ny svensk opera', *Musikvännen* (1945), 2–9

P. Lindfors: 'Ture Rangström och August Strindberg', *Musikrevy*, x (1955), 75–85 [Eng. trans. in *Musikrevy international* (1954)]

A. Helmer: 'Ture Rangströms "Kronbruden", ett sjunget drama', *Operan 200 år*, ed. K. Ralf (Stockholm, 1973), 136–9

ANDERS WIKLUND

Ranieri, Francesco. *See* HORBOWSKI, MIECZYSŁAW APOLINARY.

Ránki, György (*b* Budapest, 30 Oct 1907). Hungarian composer. He studied with Kodály at the Budapest Academy of Music (1926–30), and he also visited Paris to study ethnomusicology with André Schaeffner. Thereafter he lived mainly as a freelance composer. Awards made to him include the Erkel Award (1951), the Kossuth Prize (1954) and the Bartók-Pásztory Award (1987).

Ránki draws upon Hungarian and other folk music, contemporary popular music and jazz as sources of inspiration. He has a special talent for the musical illustration of characters and situations with a few sharply contoured, grotesque lines. His witty, swift and satirical comic opera, Pomádé király új ruhája ('King Pomádé's New Clothes'), was originally composed for Hungarian Radio in 1951; it proved to be the happiest achievement of Hungarian opera in the first two decades after World War II. Ránki introduced to Hungary the genre of musical tragedy with Egy szerelem három éjszakája ('Three Nights of Love', 1961), actually a song-opera of the Brecht-Weill type, but his most ambitious operatic endeavour was Az ember tragédiája ('The Tragedy of Man').

all first performed at the Hungarian State Opera House, Budapest

Pomádé király új ruhája [King Pomádé's New Clothes] (comic op, 3, A. Károlyi, after H. C. Andersen), 6 June 1953; rev. in 1 act, 17 Dec 1972

Egy szerelem három ejszakája [Three Nights of Love], 1961

Muzsikus Péter [Peter the Musician] (children's op), 1962

Az ember tragédiája [The Tragedy of Man] (2 pts, after I. Madách), 4 Dec 1970

A holdbéli csónakos [The Boatman of the Moon] (opera-fantasy), 1979

Végelszámolás [Terminal] (music drama), 1982

*

A. Boros: *Harminc év magyar operái 1948–1978* [30 Years of Hungarian Opera 1948–1978] (Budapest, 1979)

G. Staud, ed.: *A budapesti operaház száz éve* [A Hundred Years of the Budapest Opera House] (Budapest, 1984)   TIBOR TALLIÁN

Rankin, Nell (*b* Montgomery, AL, 3 Jan 1926). American mezzo-soprano. She studied at the Birmingham (Alabama) Conservatory and in New York. Her opera début was in 1949 as Ortrud at Zürich, and in her first season she sang 126 performances in a variety of roles. Engagements followed at La Scala, and at the Vienna Staatsoper in 1951 as Amneris, which she also sang for her Metropolitan début in the same year. She appeared regularly in New York for some 20 seasons and in almost as many roles, notably Ortrud, Gutrune, Ulrica and Azucena. For her débuts at Covent Garden (1953) and San Francisco (1955) she sang Carmen. Her recordings include Suzuki with Tebaldi, conducted by Erede (1951). She impressed with fullness of tone and generous phrasing more than with vitality of character.

NOËL GOODWIN

Rankl, Karl (*b* Gaaden, nr Vienna, 1 Oct 1898; *d* Salzburg, 6 Sept 1968). British conductor and composer of Austrian birth. He studied privately in Vienna with Schoenberg and later Webern, yet for all this modern influence he was a musician in the Kapellmeister tradition, who combined composition with the direction of opera. He was conductor at Liberec (1925), Königsberg (1927) and the Kroll Oper in Berlin (1928–31), where he assisted Klemperer. After a spell at Graz, he was appointed in 1937 director of the Neues Deutsches Theater in Prague, where in 1938 he conducted the first performance of Krenek's Karl V. At the outbreak of World War II he took refuge in England and became a British citizen.

His experience made him an ideal musical director for the new establishment of opera at Covent Garden set up in 1946. He recruited a company of British singers and persuaded international singers including Schwarzkopf, Welitsch and Silveri to join it and perform a wide repertory of German, Italian, Russian and English opera, most of it in the vernacular in accordance with the policy first adopted for the reopened London opera house. By 1951 he had made it a going concern in what promised to be a stronger operatic tradition than London had had for decades, but had reached, notably in his 1950 performances of the Ring, the limits of his ability as a conductor. His reluctance to create a broader conducting base led eventually to his resignation in 1951, and he took up an orchestral post in Glasgow. He was music director of the Elizabethan Trust Opera

Company (later Australian Opera), 1958–60. His opera *Deirdre of the Sorrows* (based on J. M. Synge's play) won an Arts Council prize for the Festival of Britain in 1951, but was never produced.　　　FRANK HOWES

Rannstädter Tor [Theater am Rannstädter Tor]. Theatre built in LEIPZIG in 1766.

Ranzato, Virgilio (*b* Venice, 7 May 1882; *d* Como, 19/ 20 April 1937). Italian composer. He studied with Pier Adolfo Tirindelli in Venice, then with Rampazzini and Vincenzo Ferroni at the Milan Conservatory. He began a career as a violinist and conductor, was a member of the Trio Italiana (1906–9) and was leader of the orchestra of La Scala, Milan, which toured under Toscanini in 1920–21. In 1927 he reconstituted the Trio Italiana, but the latter part of his life was devoted largely to composition; he wrote violin, chamber and orchestral music, but his chief success was in operetta. In particular *Il paese dei campanelli* (1923), a work distinguished by warm melody and lyricism, has remained a classic of the Italian school and, together with works such as *Cin-ci-là* (1925, set in Macao), evokes the lighter, sensuous style of Lehár.

Campane di guerra (C. Ravasio), Milan, Puccini, 19 April 1933

Operettas: Velivolo (3, G. Guidi), Turin, Balbo, 28 Jan or Feb 1911; Yvonne (3, G. Antona-Traversi and C. Vizzotto), Rome, Apollo, 16 Nov 1912; La leggenda delle arance (3, C. Caretta and P. Lampugnani), Milan, Diana, March 1916; Quel che manca a Sua Altezza (G. Forzano, after V. Soldini), Rome, Quirino, 8 May 1919; I gigli del Redentore (G. M. Sala), 1920; Il paese dei campanelli (C. Lombardo), Milan, Lirico, 23 Nov 1923; Luna Park (Lombardo), Milan, Lirico, 26 Nov 1924; Cin-ci-là (Lombardo), Milan, Dal Verme, 18 Dec 1925; Zizì (Ravasio), Milan, Lirico, 13 April 1927; La città rosa (Ravasio), Milan, Lirico, 13 April 1927, collab. Lombardo; Cri-Cri, Milan, Dal Verme, 28 March 1928, collab. Lombardo
La danza del globo, Genoa, Politeama Genovese, 30 Oct 1928; I merletti di Burano, Milan, Lirico, 22 Dec 1928; Lady Lido (D. Marchi), Milan, Nazionale, 31 July 1929; Fuoco fatuo, Messina, Savoia, 16 March 1930; I monelli fiorentini (L. Bonelli), Palermo, Nazionale, 13 June 1930; La duchessa di Hollywood (Lombardo), Milan, Dal Verme, 31 Oct 1930; Re Salsiccia (G. Bucciolini), Florence, Politeama Nazionale, 29 Jan 1932; Prigioni di lusso (Ravasio and Lombardo), Milan, Odeon, 26 March 1932; Parigi che dorme, 5 Aug 1935 [radio broadcast]; A te voglio tornar (Sala), Alessandria, Municipale, 24 Feb 1936; Briciolina (musical fable, M. Tibaldi-Chiesa), Milan, Arcimboldi, 7 Dec 1936; Valentina (Sala, after G. Cenzato: Ho perduto mio marito), 1936　　　ANDREW LAMB

Rape of Lucretia, The. Opera in two acts, op.37, by BENJAMIN BRITTEN to a libretto by RONALD DUNCAN after ANDRÉ OBEY's play *Le viol de Lucrèce*; Glyndebourne, 12 July 1946.

Britten's first chamber opera, for eight solo singers and an instrumental ensemble of 13 players, was written to a Glyndebourne commission soon after *Peter Grimes*, at a time when the composer was particularly conscious of the problems that could arise when working with an established opera company. (The potential and practicality of the chamber medium encouraged Britten to become involved in the foundation of the English Opera Group in 1946.) *The Rape of Lucretia* is rare among Britten's operas in giving the central role to a female singer; the cast for the première, conducted by Ernest Ansermet, included Kathleen Ferrier as Lucretia (recordings of excerpts with this cast were issued). Perhaps because of the stylized form and at times rather strained poeticisms of the text, the work has not enjoyed

the relatively widespread success and frequent production of most of Britten's operas, but it was successfully revived at Aldeburgh in 1966 with Janet Baker – a recording followed in 1971 – and there was a well-regarded production by the ENO (1983).

The opera is in two acts, each divided into two scenes linked by interludes. Act 1 scene i begins with the Male Chorus (tenor) and Female Chorus (mezzo-soprano), who function as narrators and commentators from outside the main action. They describe the unhappy state of Rome under the Etruscan prince Tarquinius, first in brisk recitative (the orchestra includes piano), finally with a strongly-shaped melody that returns twice in Act 2 to words underlining the fact that a pagan tale is being given a Christian perspective. As the action begins, Collatinus (bass), Junius (baritone) and Tarquinius (baritone) are drinking in their tent at an army camp outside Rome. The night is sultry – magically and economically invoked by flutterings and oscillations in the orchestra – and the men are bemoaning the general unreliability of women. Only Lucretia, the wife of Collatinus, is held to be of unshakable virtue, and Tarquinius is provoked, as he deviously tells Junius, to 'prove Lucretia chaste'. An exciting, uninhibited interlude, narrated by the Male Chorus, depicts Tarquinius's furious ride to Rome, and ends with the reiteration of Lucretia's name to the sinuous chromatic motif consistently associated with it. In scene ii Lucretia (contralto) is at home with her attendants Bianca (mezzo-soprano) and Lucia (soprano), spinning. In a haunting, lyrical ensemble they sing of the routine of their lives, and in a brief but intense arioso Lucretia declares 'How cruel men are to teach us love!'. The Female Chorus recounts how the women prepare for the night; meanwhile, as the Male Chorus's music makes clear, Tarquinius is approaching. When he is admitted to the house and requests a bed for the night, the Choruses describe the atmosphere of strained formality. Only as 'Lucretia leads Prince Tarquinius to his chamber' do the characters in the main action sing again, in a short, ironically decorous ensemble, bidding each other, repeatedly, 'good-night'. The act ends with the orchestra revealing the passionate feelings underlying this deceptive calm.

Act 2 scene i begins with another episode of narration in which the Choruses outline the depredations wrought by the Etruscans in Rome. As in Act 1 scene i this ends with the serene melody pointing the Christian perspective. Then Lucretia is shown asleep, the Male Chorus describing Tarquinius's approach. Tarquinius kisses Lucretia while she is still asleep, and she responds, imagining the presence of her husband. Then she wakes and a terse dialogue begins as she struggles vainly to resist Tarquinius's demands. The text here may be tortuously allusive, but there is genuine anger and passion in the music, leading into an interlude in which the Choruses sing a chorale describing the sorrow of Christ when virtue is 'assailed by sin', and the consolation offered to Christians by the purity of the Mother of God. During this interlude the music gradually quietens, and Act 2 scene ii begins with Lucia and Bianca ecstatically welcoming the bright sunshine of a summer morning. Their duet illustrates Britten's skill at using a relatively strict compositional technique – close contrapuntal imitation – to create a strongly built yet naturally expressive form. When Lucretia enters the mood changes instantly. Coolly calm, then hysterical, she sends Lucia to summon her husband to witness the full

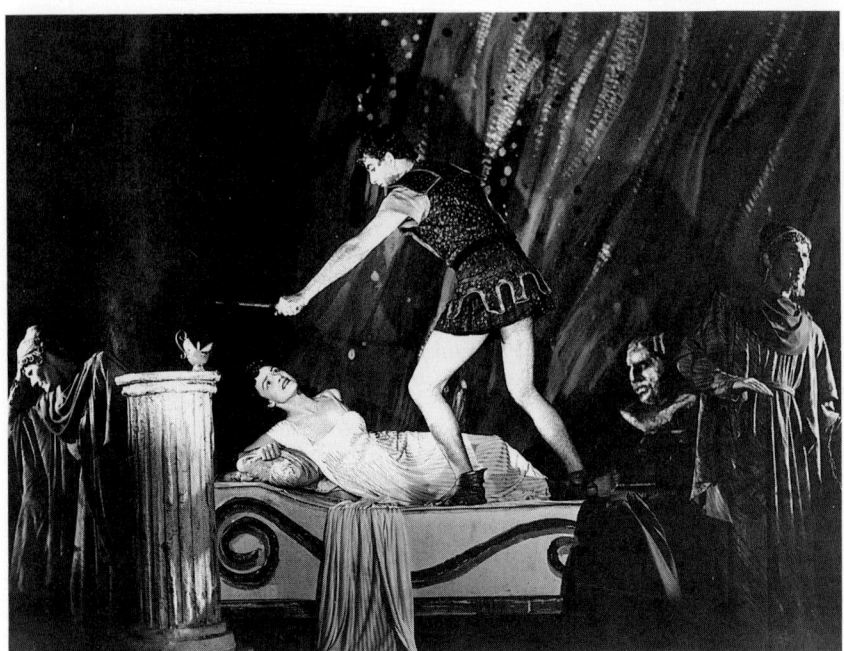

*'The Rape of Lucretia'
(Britten): Act 2 scene i
from the original
production at
Glyndebourne, 12 July
1946, with Kathleen
Ferrier as Lucretia and
Otakar Kraus as
Tarquinius*

extent of her shame. She then sings a sad, simple aria as she makes a wreath from the flowers the servants had been arranging. Fearing the worst, Bianca seeks to prevent Collatinus's arrival, but it is too late. He enters with Junius and quickly realizes, from what Bianca tells him, what has happened. Lucretia now returns to processional music of funereal gravity, and despite Collatinus's expression of love, she declares – in an impassioned arioso (a fully-developed aria would be out of proportion here) – that her shame is too great for her to survive. She stabs herself and dies. A final ensemble of mourning, a passacaglia, follows, and gradually intensifies to the point where all eight singers cry out the question 'Is this it all?', seeking consolation for the needless death of a pure woman and the unbearable grief of the survivors.

In an epilogue the question is answered by the Choruses with the Christian promises of eternal life and redemption. This ending was not part of Duncan's original scheme. Britten wanted it primarily for musical reasons, since he felt that to end the work with the mourning ensemble, when the whole opera depended on the double perspective of characters in time and narrators outside time, would have been too abrupt. The imagery of the epilogue may seem contrived, but the gradual transformation of the mourning passacaglia into the serene melody to words that refer not directly to Christian values but to 'great love', 'human tragedy' and 'song', proves the rightness of Britten's dramatic instinct. *The Rape of Lucretia* confirms the mastery, already displayed in *Peter Grimes*, of the difficult art of giving a personal slant to traditional operatic forms – recitative, arioso, aria, ensemble – and a fresh feeling to the basic linguistic conventions of tonality, without excessive resort to neo-classical features. *Lucretia* may lack the psychological penetration, and the satisfying ambivalence, of Britten's best stage works – the ironies of Act 1 seem awkward alongside the earnestness of Act 2 – but the resourcefulness of its music and the tautness of its structure create a powerful theatrical experience.

ARNOLD WHITTALL

Rapimento di Cefalo, Il ('The Abduction of Cephalus'). Opera in a prologue, five scenes and an epilogue by GIULIO CACCINI (*see* CACCINI family, (1)) to a libretto by GABRIELLO CHIABRERA; Florence, Palazzo Uffizi, 9 October 1600.

Chiabrera's libretto embroiders the story of Cefalo [Cephalus] who, although he loves a mortal woman, is seduced by Aurora [Dawn] who descends from heaven to woo him (Scene 1). Jealous old Titone [Tithonus] (bass) laments Dawn's disappearance and searches for her in vain, and an outraged Oceano [Oceanus] asks Febo [Helius], the sun god, to explain the delay of daybreak. Amore [Cupid] triumphantly celebrates Dawn's new love (Scene 2). Cephalus succumbs to her advances and they go off together, leaving Notte [Night] to preside (Scene 3). Berecyntia complains that, as a result of Dawn's dalliance, the earth is deprived of warmth and light. Cupid assures her of a happy outcome, but Mercurio [Mercury] rebukes Cupid and pursues him as he tries to escape (Scene 4). Giove [Jupiter] ordains that Cupid bring Dawn back to heaven with Cephalus. The transformation of mortal into divine love having assuaged her yearnings, Dawn resumes her function, thus ensuring the continued existence of the world (Scene 5).

The production, for which there was an open rehearsal on 7 October, was the most lavish in the series of entertainments mounted to celebrate the wedding of Maria de' Medici and Henri IV of France. Charged with supervising the music, Caccini composed everything but the choruses at the ends of Scenes 1 and 2 (by Stefano Venturi del Nibbio and Piero Strozzi) and Scenes 3 and 4 (by Luca Bati). A detailed *Descrizione* of the spectacular staging, designed by Bernardo Buontalenti, was published by Michelangelo Buonarroti the younger (Florence, 1600). Caccini's setting was never published in full and the music is presumed lost, except for two excerpts that were included in his *Nuove musiche* (Florence, 1601/2): the final chorus, 'Ineffabil ardore', in which are embedded three solo airs, originally sung by the virtuosos Melchior Palantrotti, Jacopo Peri and

Francesco Rasi, and Tithonus's air at the beginning of Scene 2, 'Chi mi confort' ahimè, chi più consolami'.

BARBARA R. HANNING

Rappold [née Winterroth], **Marie** (*b* London, 1873; *d* Los Angeles, 12 May 1957). American soprano. She appeared on the London stage at the age of five before emigrating with her parents to the USA. She studied singing in New York with Oscar Saenger and was coached in stage deportment by Heinrich Conried, manager of the Metropolitan Opera. Her début there in 1905 as Sulamith in *Die Königin von Saba* was well received, and she followed it with a 'singularly sweet and fresh' Elsa in *Lohengrin*. Other roles included Inès (*L'Africaine*), Helen of Troy (*Mefistofele*) and Bianca (in Hermann Goetz's *Der Widerspenstigen Zähmung*). In 1910 and 1912 she appeared with the Boston Opera Company as Aida and Leonora (*Il trovatore*). She also toured Europe and in the 1920s sang in Naples, Havana and Chicago. Her first husband was Dr Julius Rappold, her second the tenor Rudolf Berger. Though failing to fulfil the promise of her début, she had a fine voice which took well to recording.

J. B. STEANE

Rappresentatione di Anima, et di Corpo ('Drama of the Soul and the Body'). Sacred opera in a prologue and three acts by EMILIO DE' CAVALIERI to a text probably by Agostino Manni; Rome, Oratorio di S Maria in Vallicella, February 1600.

It is the earliest opera of which all the music survives, and the first to be published (Rome, autumn 1600; both a score with libretto appended and a separate libretto); the music was the first to appear in print with a figured *basso continuo*. The score is preceded by informative, if brief, essays: a dedication to the powerful Roman prelate Cardinal Pietro Aldobrandini signed by the editor of the score, the Bolognese Alessandro Guidotti, and notes for directors and performers (unsigned). These essays, which include the earliest considered statements of operatic dramaturgy, may in fact have been by Cavalieri himself, who, though named as composer of the score, as a nobleman remained officially in its background. Manni, the probable librettist, was a poet associated with the Congregazione dell'Oratorio of Filippo Neri.

The crux of the opera, reminiscent of both the old tradition of the *sacra rappresentazione* and the more recent Counter-Reformation *lauda*, is the conflict between Anima [Soul] (soprano) and Corpo [Body] (tenor); their first contentious dialogue (Act 1 scenes iv–xiv) is a monodic setting of a text borrowed from a strophic partsong in a Roman collection of *laude* of 1577. 12 other, mostly allegorical characters – Intelletto [Intellect] (alto), Consiglio [Good Counsel] (tenor), Piacere [Pleasure] (alto) and the like – figure in the work, plus various choruses: Angeli in coelo [Angels in heaven], Anime dannate [Damned Souls], Anime beate [Blessed Souls]. The axis of the action is the struggle between the temptations held out by Il mondo [the World] (tenor) and Vita mondana [Worldly Life] (soprano) and the eternal delights of heaven promised to those who reject such temptations. In the original production, three stage areas, possibly on different levels, represented heaven, earth and hell. By the end of Act 2, Body and Soul, finally united with the help of an Angelo custode [Guardian Angel] (soprano), have driven away the World and Worldly Life; in Act 3 the mouth of hell opens to reveal the suffering of the Damned Souls, and closes again as heaven opens to

reveal the bliss of the Blessed Souls. Cavalieri's score offers two possible endings: a climactic eight-part chorus, or a festive ballo in six stanzas for five-part chorus alternating with instrumental ritornellos.

The *Rappresentatione* is to begin with 'some full music, with doubled voices and a good quantity of instruments', according to the prefatory notes, which suggest for this the madrigal 'O Signor santo e vero', 86th of the 91 numbers (many extremely brief) that make up the work. Then follows a prologue – a discussion, summarizing the themes of the opera, between two youths named Avveduto [Wary or Careful] and Prudentio [Prudent]; Cavalieri left this to be spoken, not sung. The three-act text that follows must have been a challenge to the composer: its verses are cast almost exclusively in rhymed couplets, making it difficult for him to avoid frequent and repetitive cadential punctuation. The varied means by which he sought to overcome this constraint is admirable. The solo passages are set either in declamatory recitative over a static basso continuo or, less frequently, in a more lyrical arioso manner. To lighten the predominantly sombre tone, occasional small ensembles are given music in dance metres – notably some trios in Act 2 for Pleasure and Two Companions who are to play (the preface suggests a chitarrone and a Spanish tambourine) as they sing. Many choruses appear – some two dozen in all – mostly in homophonic textures or even choral recitative, but sometimes in more interesting contrapuntal style. Each of the three acts concludes brilliantly, the first and second with big orchestral *sinfonie*, the third with the full chorus or the ballo and its ritornellos. (The preface counsels performance of the *sinfonie* and the ritornellos by 'a great number of instruments', saying that 'a solo violin, specifically assigned to the treble part, will make a fine effect'.)

The two performances of the *Rappresentatione* in February 1600 had a good reception (many cardinals attended), and Cavalieri was pleased: later that year, comparing it with Peri and Caccini's *Euridice*, the writer of the preface to the printed score said the *Rappresentatione* was adjudged the better work because it 'moved [the listeners] to tears and laughter and pleased them greatly'. Such a demonstratively emotional response depended partly on a production extraordinarily colourful in costumes, stage action, vocal virtuosity and instrumental participation, all matters that are touched on in the score's preface.

Cavalieri's *Rappresentatione* can be viewed as a Counter-Reformation counterpart to the humanist pastorales and 'fables', exploiting the new musical style of text-dominated *musica recitativa* for solo voices accompanied by a subordinate basso continuo, which had recently made such an impression, especially in Florence. Indeed, in his dedication Guidotti cites several such Florentine works of the 1590s (by Cavalieri) and specifically points to the great success of the *Rappresentatione* as having proved that 'this style can also move [listeners] to devotion'. He also implies that it had been Cavalieri who invented the style, in imitation of ancient Greek and Roman theatrical productions – an opinion shared by Cavalieri (and by Peri, if not by the self-serving Caccini, who always claimed himself as the inventor of recitative).

H. WILEY HITCHCOCK

Rappresentazione sacra [*sacra rappresentazione*] (It.: 'sacred performance'). A religious play with music, cultivated in Italy, mainly in the 15th and 16th centuries, and one of the precursors of opera, oratorio and school drama. The chief centre for the genre would seem to have been Florence, but *rappresentazioni sacre* were also performed elsewhere. Recent research (Distaso 1987) has revealed sources in southern Italy, particularly in Apuglia, where an interest in such works continued well into the 17th century.

The origin of the *rappresentazione sacra* is not clear, but it probably developed from the Umbrian *devozioni* (musical-dramatic dialogue *laudi*) and mystery plays of the late Middle Ages. The *rappresentazione sacra* is a complex genre with a large number of characters, often elaborate staging with machines, and music. The subject matter is usually derived from the Bible or the lives of saints. From the approximately 100 surviving Florentine texts, a few examples are the *Rappresentazione di Abramo e Isacco*, *Rappresentazione dell'Annunciazione* and *Rappresentazione di S. Pannunzio* by Feo Belcari (1410–84); the *Rappresentazione di Baarlam e Josafat* by Bernardo Pulci (c1438–c1488); the *Rappresentazione della Cena e Passione di N. S. Gesù Cristo*, *Rappresentazione del Filiuol Prodigo*, *Rappresentazione di S. Tommaso* and *Rappresentazione di S. Eufrasia*, by Castellano Castellani (c1461–c1519); and the most famous of the *rappresentazione sacre*, *S. Giovanni e Paolo* by Lorenzo de' Medici. Despite the religious subject matter, however, the plays include secular and comic elements. The actors, usually boys who belonged to confraternities, seem to have declaimed most of the poetry (in *ottava rima*) to melodic formulae (Becherini 1951). The purely musical numbers included *laudi*, frottolas, canzoni and (in the 16th century) madrigals, as well as instrumental music. In the later *rappresentazioni sacre*, in both Florence and Apuglia, the musical numbers formed part of the *intermedi*, scenic-dramatic interludes between the scenes of the play. The 16th-century Florentine *Rappresentazione di Santa Uliva* included 13 *intermedi*, among which were an echo scene, a banquet and a scene with fireworks.

Emilio de' Cavalieri apparently intended his *Rappresentatione di Anima, et di Corpo* (1600) as a renewal of the *rappresentazione sacra*. This pivotal work is of considerable significance to the history of both oratorio and opera. Unlike the old *rappresentazione sacra*, with its melodic formulae, Cavalieri's work requires the actors to sing in the new Florentine style of recitative, called on the title page of the printed score (Rome, 1600) 'recitar Cantando'. As a work acted and sung throughout, it clearly falls within the genre of opera of which it is among the outstanding early examples. Yet the religious subject matter, the origin of the text and the place of first performance clearly suggest an influence on the oratorio, a genre that was to emerge during the first half of the 17th century. The text, probably by Agostino Manni, the chief poet of the Congregazione dell'Oratorio at the Chiesa Nuova (S Maria in Vallicella) in Rome, takes its point of departure from a *lauda*, 'Anima mia che pensi', a dialogue between the body and the soul. That *lauda* had long been sung in the Oratorio and had been published in *Il terzo libro delle laudi spirituali stampate ad instantia delli Reverendi Padri della Congregatione dell'Oratorio* (Rome, 1577). The text for Cavalieri's *Rappresentatione* is an expansion and elaboration of the *lauda*. The work was first performed in the Oratorio of the Chiesa Nuova in February 1600, and thus its function is similar to that of the oratorio. Yet it was a highly exceptional work for the Congregazione dell'Oratorio, an elaborate production for carnival season in a Holy Year.

During the second half of the 17th century in Vienna, the term *rappresentazione sacra* was often applied to the SEPOLCRO.

MGG (B. Becherini; 'Intermedium', N. Pirrotta)

A. d'Ancona, ed.: *Sacre rappresentazioni dei secoli XIV, XV e XVI* (Florence, 1872)

A. d'Ancona: *Le origini del teatro italiano* (Turin, 1891)

D. Alaleona: 'Su Emilio de' Cavalieri, la *Rappresentatione di Anima e di Corpo* e alcune sue composizioni inedite', *La nuova musica*, anno 10 (1905), nos.113 and 114

V. de Bartholomaeis: *Le origini della poesia drammatica italiana* (Bologna, 1924)

A. Bonfantini: *Le sacre rappresentazioni italiane* (Milan, 1939)

V. de Bartholomaeis, ed.: *Laude drammatiche e rappresentazioni sacre* (Florence, 1943)

B. Becherini: 'La Rappresentazione di Anima e Corpo di Emilio de' Cavalieri', *RaM*, xvi (1943), 1–9

——: 'Un canta in panca fiorentino: Antonio di Guido', *RMI*, l (1948), 241–8

——: 'La musica nelle "sacre rappresentazioni" fiorentine', *RMI*, liii (1951), 3–48

H. E. Smither: *A History of the Oratorio*, i (Chapel Hill, NC, 1977)

G. Distaso: *De l'altre meraviglie: Teatro religioso in Puglia (secoli XVI–XVIII)* (Milan, 1987)　　　　HOWARD E. SMITHER

Rasa, Lina Bruna (*b* Padua, 24 Sept 1907; *d* Milan, Oct 1984). Italian soprano. She studied in Padua and Milan. Her début at Genoa in 1926 as Helen of Troy (*Mefistofele*) was so great a success that Toscanini engaged her for the same role at La Scala later that year. She appeared regularly in Milan from 1927 to 1936, being especially successful in the *verismo* repertory and as Dolly in Wolf-Ferrari's *Sly*, a role she created in 1927. Mascagni chose her to create Atte in *Nerone* (1935), and she sang Santuzza throughout Italy for the *Cavalleria rusticana* 50th-anniversary celebrations in 1940, the year in which she also recorded the role under the composer's direction. She sang with success in the Netherlands, Germany and South America.

HAROLD ROSENTHAL/R

Rascarini [Lascarini], **Francesco Maria** (*b* Reggio Emilia; *d* Turin, July 1706). Italian alto castrato. He was in the service of the Duke of Savoy at Turin from 1662 to 1706 (except 1691–7). His popularity as an opera singer took him to Bologna in 1658 (P. A. Ziani's *Le fortune di Rodope e Damira*), Bergamo in 1660 (again *Le fortune*), Venice in 1666 (Cesti's *Tito* and *Orontea*), Milan in 1670 (Busca, P. S. Agostini and P. A. Ziani's *Ippolita reina delle amazzoni*) and Piacenza (Uccellini's *Gli eventi di Filandro ad Edessa*) and Parma (Uccellini's *Giove d'Elide fulminato*) in 1677. He was to have taken part in Cesti's *La Dori* in Venice in 1667 but was recalled for a ballet in Turin. He also composed; his only surviving works are two cantatas.

LORENZO BIANCONI

Rasheed, Hassan (**Ahmed**) (*b* Cairo, 1896; *d* Cairo, 1969). Egyptian composer. As a boy he played the violin in Egypt and in England. He read agriculture at Durham University (also singing baritone and composing), and returned to Cairo in 1918. He began to compose vocal music to Arabic texts, an activity which culminated in the first opera composed by an Egyptian, *Anthony's Death*, to the first part of Ahmed Shawky's *Cleopatra's Death*. Parts of it were produced in 1942 and again in 1973 (by the Egyptian Opera Troupe); the overture and the aria 'Isis, O fount of tenderness' are often performed separately. Rasheed was influenced by Italian opera performed in Cairo, yet his melodic invention is not without originality. However, the Egyptian public found it difficult to accept the conventions of Western operatic style, particularly when associated with familiar poetry in Arabic, and Rasheed's opera had few immediate successors.

SAMHA EL-KHOLY

Rasi, Francesco (*b* Arezzo, 14 May 1574; *d* Mantua, by 9 Dec 1621). Italian tenor and composer. Born into a noble Tuscan family, he studied with Caccini and as an adolescent was a singer and chitarrone player at the Florentine court. In 1593 he accompanied Emilio de' Cavalieri to Rome, where his performances were enthusiastically received, and thereafter he travelled with Gesualdo in Italy, with the Bishop of Caserta to Poland and with the Gonzaga family, whom he served from 1598 until his death, both in Mantua and on their European travels. He took part in Peri's *Euridice* (as Amyntas) and in Caccini's *Il rapimento di Cefalo*, both staged in Florence in 1600 for the wedding of Maria de' Medici and Henri IV of France. He sang the title role in Monteverdi's *Orfeo* in Mantua in 1607. The following year he performed the part of Apollo in Marco da Gagliano's *Dafne* and probably took major roles in entertainments in Mantua and Turin – including Monteverdi's *L'Arianna* – celebrating the marriage of Francesco II Gonzaga and Margherita of Savoy.

In 1610, after his implication in a murder, Rasi was banned from Tuscany (until 1620) and sent to Turin, where he took part in a restaging of *Orfeo*. In 1611 he sang in G. C. Monteverdi's *Il rapimento di Proserpina* at Casale Monferrato, and in the years following performed in many north Italian courts. A year before his death he sang again in Florence and Rome. Giustiniani and Bonini cited his ability to execute ornaments and diminutions brilliantly in both tenor and bass ranges, and also to sing with grace and feeling; in Bonini's words, 'he was a handsome and jovial man, and his sweet and robust voice together with his majestic and cheerful countenance made his singing seem angelic and divine'. Rasi's compositions include an opera, *Cibele ed Ati*, intended for the wedding of Ferdinando Gonzaga and Caterina de' Medici in 1617 but not performed then, and another dramatic work, *Elvidia rapita* (music for both lost; librettos in his *La cetra di sette corde*, Venice, 1619).

P. Canal: 'Della musica in Mantova', *Memorie del reale istituto veneto di scienze, lettere ed arti*, xxi (1879), 655–774, esp. 737–9; pubd separately (Venice, 1881)
A. Ademollo: *La bell'Adriana ed altre virtuose del suo tempo alla corte di Mantova* (Città di Castello, 1888)
A. Bertolotti: *Musici alla corte dei Gonzaga in Mantova dal secolo XV al XVIII* (Milan, 1890)
C. MacClintock, ed. and trans.: *Vincenzo Giustiniani: Discorso sopra la musica*, MSD, ix (1962), 71
C. V. Palisca: 'Musical Asides in the Diplomatic Correspondence of Emilio de' Cavalieri', *MQ*, xlix (1963), 339–55
A. Newcomb: 'Carlo Gesualdo and a Musical Correspondence of 1594', *MQ*, liv (1968), 409–36
M. A. Bonino, ed. and trans.: *Severo Bonini: Discorsi e regoli* (Salt Lake City, 1979), 149
I. Fenlon: 'Monteverdi's Mantuan *Orfeo*', *EMc*, xii (1984), 163–71
W. Kirkendale: 'Zur Biographie des ersten Orfeo, Francesco Rasi', *Claudio Monteverdi: Festschrift Reinhold Hammerstein* (Laaber, 1986), 297–335
S. Parisi: *Ducal Patronage of Music in the Court of Mantua, 1587–1627: an Archival Study* (diss., U. of Illinois, 1989)

SUSAN PARISI

Raskin, Judith (*b* New York, 21 June 1928; *d* New York, 21 Dec 1984). American soprano. She studied at Smith College, Northampton, Massachusetts, and with Anna Hamlin. She made her début at Colorado in 1956 in the title role of *The Ballad of Baby Doe*. The following year she joined NBC Opera and sang Susanna at Ann Arbor. She made her New York City Opera début in 1959 as Despina and her Metropolitan début in 1962 as Susanna, later singing Nannetta, Pamina and Sophie. In 1963 she created the Wife in Menotti's *The Labyrinth* for television and sang Pamina at Glyndebourne. A noted exponent of Baroque music, she appeared in *L'Orfeo, L'incoronazione di Poppea, The Fairy-Queen* and *Les Indes galantes*. She also sang Sister Constance (*Dialogues des Carmélites*) and Anne Trulove, which she recorded under Stravinsky. A performer of charm and refinement, she was compared to Elisabeth Schumann for vocal flexibility and purity.

HAROLD ROSENTHAL/R

Rasse, François (Adolphe Jean Jules) (*b* Helchin, Hainaut, 27 Jan 1873; *d* Ixelles, Brussels, 4 Jan 1955). Belgian composer. At the Brussels conservatory he studied the violin (with Ysaÿe) and composition, winning the Belgian Prix de Rome in 1899. Later he took up a career as a chamber music player and conductor, notably at the Théâtre de la Monnaie in Brussels. He taught at the conservatories in Brussels and Liège. He composed a large quantity of music in a late-Romantic style, including the *drame lyrique Déïdamia* (3, L. Solvay, after A. de Musset; Brussels, Monnaie, 3 April 1906) and *Soeur Béatrice* (3, M. Maeterlinck; Brussels, Monnaie, 22 Dec 1944), which was defined as a *miracle*. He also composed a ballet and many song cycles. *Soeur Béatrice* in particular displays a considerable dramatic sense. Rasse was influenced by Wagner, using leitmotifs in the orchestra and beginning each opera with a long Vorspiel.

D. von Volborth-Danys: *CeBeDeM and its Affiliated Composers* (Brussels, 1977–80)

HENRI VANHULST

Rastrelli, Joseph [Gioseffo, Giuseppe] (*b* Dresden, 13 April 1799; *d* Dresden, 15 Nov 1842). Italian composer and conductor. His first teacher was his father, Vincenzo, a composer at the Dresden Hofkapelle, who in 1805 introduced his child-prodigy son to the public at a violin recital in Moscow. He continued his studies in Dresden with the organist Fiedler and in 1814 went with his father to Italy, where he was a counterpoint pupil of Padre Mattei in Bologna. In 1816 he made his début as a composer at Ancona with the sacred drama *La distruzione di Gerusalemme*. In 1817 he returned to Dresden, where his opera *La schiava circassa* was successfully performed in 1820, and in the same year he became a violinist in the royal chapel. He had two more operatic successes, in 1821–3. Given a royal grant, he went to Italy, where his opera *Amina* had one performance at La Scala in 1824.

In 1829 Rastrelli was appointed deputy music director under Morlacchi at the Dresden Hoftheater, and in 1830 royal *maestro di cappella*, together with Morlacchi and Reissiger. In 1832 he produced *Salvator Rosa, oder Zwey Nächte in Rom*, a Singspiel reflecting both German and Italian influences. This was the first new opera performed in Dresden after the liquidation in that year of the Italian Opera and it was followed by two others, also in German, in 1835 and 1839. Highly esteemed in Dresden, particularly as a conductor, Rastrelli declined in 1836 an advantageous offer from Moscow. With his death and that of Morlacchi, the Dresden dynasty of Italian musicians came to an end. In 1843 they were replaced at the Hoftheater and at the royal chapel by Wagner.

performed in Dresden, Hoftheater, unless otherwise stated

La distruzione di Gerusalemme (dramma sacro), Ancona, 1816

La schiava circassa, ossia Imene e Virtù (2, Celani), 26 Feb 1820, *D-Dlb*

Le donne curiose (dg, 3, Montucci, after C. Goldoni), 14 April 1821, *Dlb**

Velleda, ossia Il paladino mutolo (op magica, 4, Montucci, after A. von Kotzebue: *Die kluge Frau im Walde*), 15 Jan 1823, *Dlb*

Amina, ovvero L'innocenza perseguitata (op semiseria, 2, F. Romani), Milan, Scala, 16 March 1824

Salvator Rosa, oder Zwey Nächte in Rom (2, P. J. Burmeister-Lyser, after E. T. A. Hoffmann: *Signor Formica*), 22 July 1832, *Dlb**, vs (Dresden and Leipzig, ?1832)

Bertha von Bretagne (romantische Oper, 3, C. Leonhardt-Lyser), 12 Sept 1835, *Dlb*

Die Neuvermählten (komische Oper, 2, Prinzessin Amalie von Sachsen), 10 March 1839, *Dlb*

Il trionfo di Nabucco il Grande, ossia Punizione di Sedacia (dramma serio per musica, 2), ?unperf., *Dlb*

*

FétisB; StiegerO

M. Fürstenau: *Beiträge zur Geschichte der königlich-sächsischen musikalischen Kapelle* (Dresden, 1849)

M. Börner-Sandrini: *Erinnerungen einer alten Dresdnerin* (Dresden, 1876), 123, 233ff

H. von Brescius: *Die königliche sächsische musikalische Kapelle von Reissiger bis Schuch (1826–1898)* (Dresden, 1898)

ANDREA LANZA

Rathaus, Karol (*b* Tarnopol, 16 Sept 1895; *d* New York, 21 Nov 1954). American composer of Polish birth. He studied under Schreker in Vienna and Berlin; in the 1930s he lived first in Paris and then in London, settling in the USA in 1938, where he was highly influential as professor of composition at Queens College, New York. The Polish tradition and German expressionism are among the influences on his own music, which is imaginative, colourful and often rhapsodic in style, bold in its use of dissonance but not atonal. His only opera is *Fremde Erde* (5, K. Palffy-Wanieck; Berlin, Staatsoper, 10 Dec 1930); he also wrote ballets and music for films, among them a classic score to *The Brothers Karamazov* (1931). In 1952 he was commissioned by the Metropolitan Opera to rework the orchestration of *Boris Godunov*, a task he performed with exemplary discretion.

K. Rathaus: 'Meine Oper "Fremde Erde"', *Musikblätter des Anbruch*, xii (1930), 13–14

B. Schwarz: 'Karol Rathaus', *MQ*, xli (1955), 481–95 [with list of works]
BORIS SCHWARZ/R

Ratisbon. REGENSBURG.

Rattenfänger von Hameln, Der ('The Rat-Catcher of Hamelin', 'The Piper of Hamelin'). *Grosse Oper* in five acts by VIKTOR E. NESSLER to a libretto by Friedrich Hofmann after the verse romance by Julius Wolff; Leipzig, 19 March 1879.

Hunold Singuf (baritone) is presented as both romantic vagabond and demonic foreigner. The councillors of Hamelin engage him to rid the town of rats. He fascinates the fisher-girl Gertrud (soprano), who abandons her betrothed for him. Hunold's piping lures the rats to drown in the river, but the councillors cheat him of his reward and accuse him of bewitching the mayor's daughter Regina (soprano). Thinking Hunold has deserted her, Gertrud throws herself into the river; the townsfolk repair to the church to pray. Hunold, grieving, vengefully pipes the children out into the square and across the river. Their parents reappear, but Hunold magically destroys the bridge and leads the children into the mountainside, where they all disappear. The opera was considered thoroughly out of date by Hanslick at the time of its first performance in Vienna in 1897. Observing that the uncut version lasted longer than *Les Huguenots*, he found the material to be ineptly derived from Lortzing while accepting that its mixture of strophic songs and strategic ensembles satisfied conservative north German popular taste.
PETER FRANKLIN

Ratti, Eugenia (*b* Genoa, 5 April 1933). Italian soprano. She made her début in 1954 at Sestri Levante. In 1955 she sang in the stage première of Milhaud's *David* at La Scala and made her Glyndebourne début as Nannetta. In 1957 she created Sister Constance (*Dialogues des Carmélites*) at La Scala and sang Fiorilla (*Il turco in Italia*) and Elisetta (*Il matrimonio segreto*) with the Piccola Scala in Edinburgh. She made her American début in 1958 at San Francisco, singing Rosina, Musetta and Susanna. Returning to Glyndebourne, she sang Adina (1961) and the Italian Soprano in *Capriccio* (1973). She also appeared in Vienna, Munich and Paris. A spirited comic actress with a keen, expressive voice, she excelled in such roles as Vespina (*L'infedeltà delusa*), which she sang at Wexford (1969) and the Holland Festival (1970).
ELIZABETH FORBES

Rattle, Simon (Denis) (*b* Liverpool, 19 Jan 1955). English conductor. He studied the piano and percussion in Liverpool, where he formed and conducted the Liverpool Sinfonia (1970) and played with the Royal Liverpool PO and National Youth Orchestra before entering the RAM in 1971 for studies in conducting and the piano. In 1974 he won the first John Player International Conductors' Competition as the youngest entrant, which brought him a two-year contract with the Bournemouth orchestras. He made his opera début with *The Rake's Progress* for Glyndebourne Touring Opera (1975). After *The Threepenny Opera* for English Music Theatre (1976), he conducted *The Cunning Little Vixen* at Glyndebourne (1977) and for his Covent Garden début in 1990. While principal conductor and music director at Birmingham (CBSO) since 1980, and an artistic director of the Aldeburgh Festival from 1982, he first appeared with the ENO in *Kát'a Kabanová* (1985) and made his American opera début in *Wozzeck* at Los Angeles (1988). His performance and recording of the first Glyndebourne production of *Porgy and Bess* in 1986 was widely acclaimed. At Glyndebourne he also conducted *Idomeneo*, *Figaro*, Haydn's *La fedeltà premiata*, Strauss's *Ariadne* and *Der Rosenkavalier*, Prokofiev's *Love for Three Oranges* and the two Ravel operas as a double bill. His performances combine self-discipline, strength of musical purpose and rhythmic vitality over a wide repertory. He was appointed CBE in 1987, and is married to the soprano Elise Ross.

*

N. Kenyon: *Simon Rattle: the Making of a Conductor* (London, 1987)
NOËL GOODWIN

Ratto della sposa, Il ('The Kidnapped Fiancée'). *Opera buffa* in three acts by Pietro Alessandro Guglielmi (*see*

GUGLIELMI family, (1)) to a libretto by GAETANO MARTINELLI; Venice, Teatro S Moisè, autumn 1765 (revised version, London, 1768).

This opera is a typical Goldonian farce, involving trickery, disguise and the inevitable trials and tribulations of love. Gaudenzio (tenor) and his sister Aurora (mezzo-soprano) are forced into servitude through Gaudenzio's spendthrift habits. Gaudenzio's employer, Donna Ortensia (soprano), hopes to marry him, as does the maid Dorina (soprano). Aurora is in love with Gentilino (tenor). Gaudenzio persuades Gentilino to help him rob old Polidoro (tenor) of his treasure by pretending to be his long-lost nephew. This plan is complicated by the appearance of Polidoro's real nephew Biondino (tenor). Polidoro takes Aurora under his protection and plans to marry her, but she is kidnapped by Gentilino and Gaudenzio. All confusions are eventually resolved and the couples are paired off appropriately. Guglielmi's setting includes many short, attractive arias in simple binary and sonata-like forms, and the concise chain finales are in three and four sections respectively. The work was moderately successful for a decade, and produced until the 1780s; it was given also as *La sposa rapita* and *Il vecchio deluso*.

MARY HUNTER

Rauchfangkehrer, Der [*Der Rauchfangkehrer, oder Die unentbehrlichen Verräther ihrer Herrschaften aus Eigennutz* ('The Chimney-Sweep, or The Indispensable Betrayers of Their Lordships' Self-interest')]. *Musikalisches Lustspiel* in three acts by ANTONIO SALIERI to a libretto by JOSEPH LEOPOLD AUENBRUGGER; Vienna, Burgtheater, 30 April 1781.

As the playful subtitle suggests, the opera is in the spirit of those late 18th-century Italian comic operas that deal with conflict between social classes. Volpino (tenor), an Italian chimney-sweep, is engaged to Lisel (soprano), a cook in the house of the young widow Frau von Habicht (soprano). Frau von Habicht and her daughter Nannette (soprano) are the objects of amorous advances by the impoverished noblemen Herr von Bär (bass) and Herr von Wölf (tenor). Volpino puts into action an elaborate trick that promises to result in a dowry for him and Lisel. With his musical skills he charms both mother and daughter into falling in love with him; then to Bär and Wölf he proposes to reject the two women in exchange for a handsome dowry. After a suitable amount of confusion and misunderstanding, his plan is successful and all the principal characters are happily engaged.

Salieri composed this opera at the command of Joseph II for performance by his German troupe, which included Caterina Cavalieri (who sang the role of Nannette) and Ludwig Fischer (Herr von Bär), but it is in many ways more Italian than German: both libretto and music resemble an *opera buffa* more than a north German Singspiel. It was moderately successful in Vienna, performed 13 times in 1781–2. The last performance was on 5 July 1782, less than two weeks before the première of Mozart's *Entführung*, the success of which must have contributed to the abandonment of *Der Rauchfangkehrer* by the Viennese court theatres.

JOHN A. RICE

Raum, Elizabeth (*b* Berlin, NH, 13 Jan 1945). Canadian composer of American birth. She was brought up in Boston and graduated from the Eastman School of Music in 1966. She had a career as a freelance oboist in Boston before moving in 1968 to Halifax, Nova Scotia, where she became principal oboist in the Atlantic SO. In 1975 she moved to Regina, Saskatchewan, where she joined the Regina SO and became principal oboist. She was a founder member of the contemporary-music chamber group of Regina, Contemporary Directions Ensemble. She took Canadian citizenship in 1984.

Before composing operas, Raum wrote short stories and the poetry for *Winterpiece*, a musical composition by Tom Schudel. Her first opera, *The Garden of Alice* (1979) was completed before she received the MMus in composition from the University of Regina (1985). A Kafkaesque *Alice in Wonderland* (to her own libretto, after Lewis Carroll), it established her as an opera composer. Raum has written the librettos for all her operas. Her musical style is conservative, which makes her music accessible and frequently more popular with audiences than with critics. Each opera is scored idiomatically for chamber ensemble. *Eos: the Dream of Nicholas Flood Davin* explores the struggles facing Davin, the Canadian politician who brought culture to western Canada; he committed suicide in 1901.

all librettos by Raum

The Garden of Alice, 1979 (2, after Lewis Carroll: *Alice in Wonderland*), Regina, Norman Mackenzie Art Gallery, 4 March 1984 [condensed version]; Regina, Globe, 19 Jan 1985

The Final Bid (1), Regina, Open Stage, 27 Feb 1981

Thunder in a Concave Vacuum (multi-media theatre work), Regina, Globe, 10 May 1986

Mulligan's Toy Shop (children's musical)

Eos: the Dream of Nicholas Flood Davin (3, after Davin's epic poem), Regina, Norman Mackenzie Art Gallery, 26 Jan 1991

GAYNOR G. JONES

Raupach, Hermann Friedrich (*b* Stralsund, 21 Dec 1728; *d* St Petersburg, Dec 1778). German composer. He was engaged as a harpsichordist and conductor at the Russian court in St Petersburg, 1755–62 and 1768–78. While serving as continuo player in the court orchestra, he wrote an *opera seria*, *Al'tsesta* ('Alceste'), to a Russian text by the classical dramatist Alexander Sumarkov. Performed at Peterhof in summer 1758, it was a great success and assured his appointment the following year as court Kapellmeister in succession to Araia. In his first year as Kapellmeister Raupach produced an *opéra-ballet* to a text by Sumarkov entitled *Pribezhishche dobrodeteli* ('The Refuge of Virtue') with dance numbers by Joseph Starzer. He next produced a setting of an untranslated libretto by Metastasio, *Siroe*, performed (with interpolated ballets by Starzer) at the Winter Palace in 1760. In 1762 he was replaced as Kapellmeister by Vincenzo Manfredini.

After a sojourn in Paris (where he observed and helped test the powers of the child Mozart, who incorporated movements from Raupach's violin sonatas in his early keyboard concertos), Raupach was re-engaged at St Petersburg as harpsichordist under the new Kapellmeister, Tommaso Traetta. From 1777 he also taught at the Academy of Fine Arts in St Petersburg, where his pupils included Yevstigney Fomin. For the court he thenceforth produced only ballets. For the public theatre, however, Raupach composed a Singspiel that made him posthumously famous: *Dobrïye soldatï* ('The Good Soldiers'), his setting of a *comédie larmoyante* by Mikhail Kheraskov, opened at the Orphanage theatre in Moscow early in 1779, shortly after the composer's death. A story of mistaken identity and constancy rewarded, it played steadily in Moscow and St Petersburg until after the Napoleonic wars. The soldiers' chorus in praise of their captain, 'Mï tebya lyubim serdechno' ('We love you heartily'), became a household favourite and lived on in oral tradition.

Al'tsesta [Alceste] (os, 3, A. Sumarkov), St Petersburg, Peterhof, 28 June/9 July 1758, *RU-SPtob*
Pribezhishche dobrodeteli [The Refuge of Virtue] (opéra-ballet, 5, A. Sumarkov), St Petersburg, court, ?5/16 Sept 1759; collab. Starzer
Siroe, re di Persia (os, 3, P. Metastasio), St Petersburg, Winter Palace, 1760, *B-Bc*
Dobrïye soldatï [The Good Soldiers] (Spl, 3, M. Kheraskov), Moscow, Orphanage, 26 Feb/9 March 1779, *RU-SPtob*, ov. excerpt in Findeyzen, 1 scene in Ginzburg

*

N. F. Findeyzen: *Ocherki po istorii muzïki v Rossii s drevneyshikh vremyon do kontsa XVIII veka* [Studies in the History of Music in Russia from Ancient Times to the End of the 18th Century], ii (Moscow and Leningrad, 1929)
R.-A. Mooser: *Annales de la musique et des musiciens en Russie au XVIIIme siècle*, i (Geneva, 1948)
A. A. Gozenpud: *Muzikal'nïy teatr v Rossii ot istokov do Glinki: ocherk* [Musical Theatre in Russia from its Origins up to Glinka: a Study] (Leningrad, 1959)
S. Ginzburg: IRMO, i   RICHARD TARUSKIN

Rautavaara, Einojuhani (*b* Helsinki, 9 Oct 1938). Finnish composer. After attending the Sibelius Academy, he was awarded a scholarship (on Sibelius's recommendation) to the Juilliard School in New York (1955–6) and subsequently to Tanglewood, where he studied with Sessions and Copland. Later studies with Wladimir Vogel in Ascona were to be significant in the development of a style that combines elements from, and explores the creative tensions between, a fairly straightforward and tonal nationalism and an intellectually based modernism. His musical language has continued to evolve largely through his willingness to experiment.

Rautavaara's output includes several operas in a wide range of styles. *Kaivos* ('The Mine', 1957–63), composed in a strictly 12-note idiom, is a study of the conflicts between individual liberty and state power in a closed society; it was inspired by the 1956 Hungarian uprising. A miners' strike brings hope of a new order, but is weakened by internal dissension and finally crushed brutally by 'the Party'. Because of its political overtones, *The Mine* was rejected by the Finnish National Opera but was presented by Finnish Television in 1963.

Apollo ja Marsyas ('Apollo and Marsyas', 1973) is a version of the Greek legend of the musical contest between the god Apollo and the satyr Marsyas. Set alternately in ancient Greece and the modern world, the work ironically contemplates the contrasts between 'high' and 'popular' culture, invoking serialism, jazz and pastiches of the Viennese classics. Two years later came *Marjatta matala neiti* ('Marjatta the Lowly Maiden') and in 1981 *Runo 42, Sammon ryöstö* ('Canto 42, The Abduction of the Sampo'), both short 'choral operas' based on themes from the Kalevala, the Finnish national epic. In *Thomas* (1985) and *Vincent* (1990) Rautavaara adopted the convention of allowing a central character to recall the turbulent events of his past life. *Thomas* tells the story of the first Bishop of Finland, a fallible man motivated by ambition, while *Vincent* explores the troubled genius of Van Gogh.

See also THOMAS and VINCENT (ii).

Kaivos [The Mine] (3, Rautavaara), Helsinki, Finnish Television, 10 April 1963
Apollo ja Marsyas [Apollo and Marsyas] (3, Rautavaara, after B. V. Wall), Helsinki, Finnish National Opera, 30 Aug 1973

Marjatta matala neiti [Marjatta the Lowly Maiden] (1, Rautavaara, after the Kalevala), Espoo, 3 Sept 1977
Runo 42, Sammon ryöstö [Canto 42, The Abduction of the Sampo] (1, Rautavaara, after the Kalevala), Helsinki, 1981
Thomas (3, Rautavaara), Joensuu, 21 June 1985
Vincent (3, Rautavaara), Helsinki, Finnish National Opera, 17 May 1990

*

M. Heiniö: 'A Portrait of the Artist at a Certain Moment', *Finnish Music Quarterly* (1988), no.2, pp.3–14
H. Bacon: 'The Sorrows and Grandeurs of *Vincent*', *Nordic Sounds* (1990), no.2, pp.22–4
R. Fairman: 'Vintage Van Gogh', *Opera*, xli (1990), 1228–9
S. Rautavaara: record notes, *Thomas* (Ondine ODE 704–2, 1990)
A. Sivuoja: 'Rautavaara's *Vincent* – not a Portrait', *Finnish Music Quarterly* (1990), no.2, pp.4–11   ERKKI ARNI

Rautawaara, Aulikki (*b* Vaasa, 2 May 1906; *d* Helsinki, 29 Dec 1990). Finnish soprano. She studied in Helsinki and Berlin, making her début in 1932 in Helsinki. In 1934 she sang Countess Almaviva (*Le nozze di Figaro*) in the inaugural season at Glyndebourne, returning each year until 1938 as Countess Almaviva and Pamina (*Die Zauberflöte*). In 1937 she appeared at the Salzburg Festival. She also sang in Berlin, Vienna, Munich and Stockholm. A stylish Mozart singer, she can be heard on the Glyndebourne recording of *Le nozze di Figaro*, conducted by Fritz Busch.   ELIZABETH FORBES

Rauzzini, Matteo (*b* Camerino, nr Rome, 1754; *d* Dublin, 1791). Italian composer. He followed his more successful brother Venanzio to Munich, where his two comic operas *Il kam cinese* and *Le finte gemelle* were produced in 1772. Hearing the latter, Burney described the music as 'common, but pretty and in good taste'. He was later active in Venice, where he wrote two comic operas and two oratorios and taught at the Incurabili. He passed his last years as a singing teacher in Dublin where *Il re pastore*, his only *opera seria*, had been performed in the 1783–4 season.

Il kam cinese (dg, G. Fioroni), Munich, Residenz, 1772
Le finte gemelle (ob, 2, ? G. Petrosellini), Munich, Residenz, 1772; also as I finti gemelli
Li due amanti in inganno [Act 2] (ob, 3), Venice, S Cassiano, carn. 1775 [Acts 1 and 3 by G. Rust]
L'opera nuova (ob, 2, G. Bertati), Venice, S Moisè, carn. 1781
Il re pastore (os, 3, P. Metastasio), Dublin, Smock Alley, carn. 1784

*

BurneyGN   KATHLEEN KUZMICK HANSELL

Rauzzini, Venanzio (*b* Camerino, nr Rome, bap. 19 Dec 1746; *d* Bath, 8 April 1810). Italian soprano castrato and composer. After early studies in Rome and possibly also in Naples with Porpora, he made his début at the Teatro della Valle in Rome in Piccinni's *Il finto astrologo* (7 February 1765). His first major role was in Guglielmi's *Sesostri* at Venice during Ascension Fair 1766. In the same year he entered the service of the Elector Maximilian III Joseph at Munich, where he remained until 1772. He first appeared there in Traetta's *Siroe* (Carnival 1767) and later that year was given leave to perform at Venice and at Vienna, where Mozart and his father heard him in Hasse's *Partenope*. Burney, visiting Rauzzini in August 1772, praised his virtuosity and the quality of his voice, but was most impressed by his abilities as a composer and harpsichordist. His last known operatic performance in Munich was in Bernasconi's *Demetrio* (Carnival 1772). According to Michael Kelly he was forced to leave because of difficulties with noblewomen engendered by his good looks.

Venanzio Rauzzini and Signora Schinderlin in the original production of Sacchini's 'Montezuma' at the King's Theatre, London, 7 February 1775: etching

MONTESUMA. MUSICHA. DEL. CELEBRE. MAESTRO. SACHINI
CARA. ASCHONDI. A. ME. QUEL. PIANTO.
My dearest hide these precious tears; Your griefs impress my soul with woe
My fate more cruel far appears. To see your eyes like fountains flow.

Rauzzini performed for two more years in Italy before moving permanently to England. Engaged for Carnival 1773 at Milan, he was primo uomo in Mozart's *Lucio Silla* (26 December 1772) and in Paisiello's *Sismano nel Mogol* (30 January 1773). In January Mozart wrote for him the brilliant motet *Exsultate, jubilate* K165/158a. Later that year he sang at Venice and Padua, and in 1774 at Turin (Carnival) and Venice (Ascension Fair).

From November 1774 to July 1777 Rauzzini sang regularly at the King's Theatre in London, making his simultaneous début as singer and composer in the pasticcio *Armida*. Bingley reported that his acting in Sacchini's *Montezuma* (7 February 1775; see illustration) greatly impressed Garrick. Both Burney and Lord Mount Edgcumbe, however, deemed his voice sweet but too feeble, a defect Burney ascribed to Rauzzini's devoting too much time to composition. Indeed, Rauzzini contributed arias to four other pasticcios in the season 1775–6 and wrote a comic opera, *L'ali d'amore*. *Piramo e Tisbe*, his best-loved opera, was first staged in London on 16 March 1775 (and probably not in Munich, 1769, as claimed in many biographical sketches); it was revived there in three other seasons and performed at many continental theatres. In the following years many of his works, both vocal and instrumental, were published in London.

In autumn 1777 Rauzzini took up residence in Bath, where he managed concerts by many renowned performers, among them his pupils John Braham, Nancy Storace, Charles Incledon, Mrs Billington and Mme Mara. At Dublin in 1778 he met and taught Michael Kelly and promoted his career with advice to study in Naples. In spring 1781, again in London, Rauzzini sang in concerts with Tenducci and others and wrote the second act of the opera *L'omaggio di paesani al signore del contado*. He was intermittently in London during the next three seasons to stage his operas *L'eroe cinese*, *Creusa in Delfo* and *Alina, o sia La regina di Golconda*, which was heavily criticized by the *Public Advertiser* (10 May 1784). Ballets with music by him were performed at the King's Theatre in the season 1783–4, and he also directed the production of Sarti's *Le gelosie villane* (15 April 1784). During this period a scandal arose over his claim that certain arias in Sacchini's operas were his own. The London première of his opera *La vestale* (1 May 1787) was unsuccessful, and thereafter he remained permanently at Bath. Near the end of his life Rauzzini published a set of 12 vocal exercises with an introduction summing up his ideas on the art of singing and reflecting his own tasteful execution.

first produced in London, King's Theatre, unless otherwise stated

Armida (os, pasticcio, 3), 19 Nov 1774, Favourite Songs (London, *c*1774)

Piramo e Tisbe (azione tragico, 2, R. Calzabigi, after M. Coltellini), 16 March 1775, *A-Wn*, *F-Pn*, *I-Bc*, arias (London, 1775) and in A Select Collection of the Most Admired Songs, Duetts &c (Edinburgh, 1779)

La sposa fedele (opera comica, pasticcio, 3, P. Chiari), 31 Oct 1775, Favourite Songs (London, *c*1775)

Didone abbandonata (os, pasticcio, 3, P. Metastasio), 11 Nov 1775, Favourite Songs (London, *c*1775)

The Duenna, or Double Elopement (comic op, pasticcio, 3, R. Sheridan), London, CG, 21 Nov 1775; aria, By him we love offended [= Fuggiam dove sicura], in The Duenna (London, *c*1775) and A Select Collection of the Most Admired Songs, Duetts &c (Edinburgh, 1779)

L'ali d'amore (opera comica, 3, C. F. Badini), 29 Feb 1776; rev., 13 March 1777, Favourite Songs, op.3 (London, *c*1777) and in A

Select Collection of the Most Admired Songs, Duetts &c (Edinburgh, 1779)

Astarto re di Tiro (os, pasticcio, 3, G. Bottarelli), 2 Nov 1776, Favourite Songs (London, c1776)

L'omaggio di paesani al signore del contado (os, 3), 5 June 1781; only Act 2 by Rauzzini

Ezio (os, pasticcio, 3, Metastasio), 17 Nov 1781, Favourite Songs (c1781)

L'eroe cinese (os, 3, Metastasio), 16 March 1782, arias (London, 1782)

Creusa in Delfo (os, 2, G. Martinelli), 29 April 1783; aria, Spiegar non posso (London, ?c1783)

Alina, o sia La regina di Golconda (os, 3, A. Andrei, after M.-J. Sedaine), 18 March 1784, ov. and arias (London, c1784)

La vestale, o sia L'amore protetto dal cielo (os, 2, Badini), 1 May 1787, 3 arias GB-Lbl

The Village Maid (comic op, pasticcio, 3), lib. (London, 1792); aria, Silent I tread, Cpl

Doubtful: Astarto (os, 3, A. Zeno and P. Pariati), Munich, Residenz, sum. 1769/72; Pompejo (os, 3), Munich, Residenz, 1773

Spurious: L'eroe cinese, Munich, 27 April 1770 [by Sacchini]

*

BurneyGN; BurneyH; LS
Indice de' spettacoli teatrali per il carnovale (Milan, 1772), 35; ibid (1773), 29; ibid (1774), 60
W. Bingley: Musical Biography (London, 1814), ii, 315ff
M. Kelly: Reminiscences (London, 1826, 2/1826), 10ff, 118ff
R. Mount Edgcumbe: Musical Reminiscences … Respecting Italian Opera in England … from 1773 to 1823 (London, 2/1827), 14–15, 18
F. Rudhart: Geschichte der Oper am Hofe zu München (Freising, 1865), 149–50, 156–7
M. Sands: 'Venanzio Rauzzini – Singer, Composer, Traveller', MT, xciv (1953), 15–19, 108–11
H. Bolongaro-Crevenna: L'arpa festante: die Münchner Oper 1651–1825 (Munich, 1963), 88, 238–9
KATHLEEN KUZMICK HANSELL

Raveau, Alice (b 1884; d Paris, 1951). French contralto. She studied at the Paris Conservatoire and made her début at the Opéra-Comique in 1908, singing the role which was to remain most closely associated with her: Gluck's Orpheus. She was still singing it at the company's revival in 1924, and in 1936 she took part in the first complete recording, a performance that continues to impress, as much by its intensity of feeling and care for words as by the beauty and noble power of the voice. She sang the title role in the world première of Gaston Salvayre's Solange (1909) and the leading female role of Diana in Samuel-Alexandre Rousseau's Léone (1910). At Monte Carlo in 1913 she sang Eurycleia in the world première of Fauré's Pénélope and created the title role in Yato by Marguerite Labori. She was also a noted Charlotte in Werther and in 1929 sang Delilah at the Opéra. Though her fine art and rich voice can be heard in many recordings, the Orphée remains her most memorable achievement for the gramophone.

J. B. STEANE

Ravel, (Joseph) Maurice (b Ciboure, Basses Pyrénées, 7 March 1875; d Paris, 28 Dec 1937). French composer. His family went to Paris when he was three months old and the city remained his home until 1921, when he moved to a village some 30 miles to the south-west. He entered the Paris Conservatoire in 1889, left in 1895 after an undistinguished career, but returned to join Fauré's composition class in 1898, the year of his first known operatic project, Shéhérazade, of which only the overture survives.

During the next ten years he made a name for himself with works for piano like Jeux d'eau and Miroirs, and the String Quartet, but he continued to work at operatic projects, including La cloche engloutie, based on Gerhart Hauptmann's play Die versunkene Glocke, and Olympia, based on E. T. A. Hoffmann's Der Sandmann. One of Ravel's pupils has claimed that parts of Olympia were used in the first of Ravel's two completed operas, L'heure espagnole (1907–9).

In 1909 Dyagilev commissioned him to write Daphnis et Chloé, which was performed by the Ballets Russes three years later. In 1915 Ravel enlisted in the French army as a truck driver, but was invalided out after 18 months. In 1917 his mother died, and many of his friends felt that this was a blow from which he never recovered. For the last 20 years of his life he lived a solitary existence, broken by visits from friends, concerts in Paris and foreign tours. He now composed more slowly than ever and for his second opera, L'enfant et les sortilèges, took five years (1920–25) to compose an hour's music. (He took less time and trouble over Boléro and was amazed at its success.) Shortly after completing the two piano concertos in 1931, he began to show signs of a brain illness, and for the last four years of his life he was unable to compose. Not even sketches remain of his last operatic project, a setting of Delteil's Jeanne d'Arc, in which he intended to 'bring out Jeanne's peasant simplicity and her brutal, warlike side'.

Ravel found his style early – the Habanera (for two pianos), which he later included in the orchestral Rapsodie espagnole, dates from 1895. He suffered for years from being labelled a follower of Debussy, but although there are some superficial resemblances of harmonic and textural practice (Ravel was a passionate admirer of Pelléas et Mélisande), these are far outweighed by the differences: Ravel was always more contrapuntal in his thinking and liked to base his works on pre-existing models, even if he was an indefatigable searcher after novelty in the matter of detail. After Daphnis et Chloé (1909–12), in which he proved once and for all that he was far more than a miniaturist, he followed (or in some cases set) the Paris postwar fashion for using smaller forces to produce clearer, harder textures – the so-called 'style dépouillé'. Bitonality and jazz elements, heard to good advantage in L'enfant et les sortilèges, gave a new edge to his music, while the two piano concertos demonstrated to what differing uses these techniques could be put. Even if Ravel marks an end rather than a new beginning, and if he was notably cautious in the musical boundaries he set himself, few composers have cultivated their chosen terrain with such fastidious single-mindedness or found such favour with critics and general public alike.

See also ENFANT ET LES SORTILÈGES, L' and HEURE ESPAGNOLE, L'.

L'heure espagnole, 1907–9 (comédie musicale, 1, Franc-Nohain), Paris, OC (Favart), 19 May 1911

L'enfant et les sortilèges, 1920–25 (fantaisie lyrique, 1, Colette), Monte Carlo, 21 March 1925

*

Roland-Manuel: Maurice Ravel et son oeuvre dramatique (Paris, 1914)
——: A la gloire de Ravel (Paris, 1938, 2/1948; Eng. trans., 1947)
J. Bruyr: Maurice Ravel, ou Le lyrisme et les sortilèges (Paris, 1950)
A. Orenstein: 'L'enfant et les sortilèges: correspondance inédite de Ravel et Colette', RdM, lii (1966), 215–20
H. H. Stuckenschmidt: Maurice Ravel: Variationen über Person und Werk (Frankfurt, 1966; Eng. trans., 1968)
F. Lesure and J.-M. Nectoux: Maurice Ravel (Paris, 1975) [catalogue of exhibition at Bibliothèque Nationale]
A. Orenstein: Ravel: Man and Musician (New York, 1975)
J.-M. Nectoux: 'Maurice Ravel et sa bibliothèque musicale', FAM, xxiv (1977), 199–206
M. Marnat: Maurice Ravel (Paris, 1986)

L. Dallapiccola: 'L'enfant et les sortilèges', *Selected Writings*, i (London, 1987), 117–25

P. Saint-André: 'L'enfant et les sortilèges: l'esthétique d'un conte', *Musical*, iv (1987), 108–15

A. Orenstein, ed.: *Lettres, écrits, entretiens* (Paris, 1989; Eng. trans., 1990)

L'avant-scène opéra, no.127 (1990) [*L'enfant et les sortilèges* and *L'heure espagnole* issue]
ROGER NICHOLS

Ravenna. City in Romagna, Italy. The earliest certain references to operatic activity date back only to 1683: on 23 March a 'musical drama' was performed privately in the home of the Cavalli family for a wedding; and between 18 May and 25 June there were 13 performances to a paying audience of *Idalma* (probably by Pasquini). Organized by a group of local nobles with Pompeo Capranica of Rome, the performances took place in the hall of the Palazzo Pubblico, which had long been used as a theatre and was equipped with a permanent stage, boxes and a balcony. It was subsequently used in 1685, 1686 and 1696, during Carnival and at the time of the fair (May–June), for performances probably organized by the same aristocratic impresarios under Academy pseudonyms (Riuniti, Arditi). The works performed were predominantly by Alessandro Scarlatti (one or two a season, with 10–15 performances each). This theatre was dismantled in 1702.

In 1721 the municipality decided to build a public theatre (Teatro Pubblico or Comunitativo); the exterior was completed in 1723, the work of Giacomo Anziani, and the interior was designed by Antonio Mauro the following year. It had a flattened U-shaped plan, with 97 boxes in four tiers, and was used for opera at Carnival and the May fair until 1852 (25–30 performances a year); it closed in 1857. For a short time (1726–9), there were performances at the private Teatro dell'Industria of Pier Giovanni Bruni, and in 1777 opera was staged in the small theatre of the Collegio dei Nobili, where *La vaga frascatana* (possibly by Anfossi) received its first performance. Between 1840 and 1852 the municipality built a new theatre, the Alighieri, inaugurated on 15 May 1852 with 26 performances of *Robert le diable*. Designed by Tomaso and G. B. Meduna on a horseshoe plan, it has 124 boxes in five tiers and is still in use. During the 19th century, opera was presented in four other theatres: Teatro Bertoldi (Filodrammatico after 1867), built in 1846–7, staging opera sporadically from 1849 to 1858 and in 1876, in the minor seasons (summer and autumn); the Arena Zinanni, built in 1851, where opera was performed especially in 1867–76, and operetta from 1878 until it closed in 1896; Teatro Patuelli (Mariani after 1877), built in 1863–4, used from 1865 to 1928 and after World War II converted into a cinema; and Teatro Filodrammatico (1892, later Rasi), in the former church of S Chiara, rebuilt and opened in 1979.

*

P. Gironi: *Il teatro Comunale di Ravenna nel secolo XIX* (Ravenna, 1902)

L. Miserocchi: *Musica e teatro in Ravenna dal 1800 al 1920* (Ravenna, 1921)

F. Farneti and S. Van Riel: *L'architettura teatrale in Romagna 1757–1857* (Florence, 1975)

P. Fabbri: 'Scena e musica nella Ravenna del seicento', *Quadrivium*, xviii (1978), 67–84

G. Ravaldini: *Spettacoli nei teatri e in altri luoghi di Ravenna* (Imola, 1978)

P. Fabbri and N. Pirazzoli: *Il teatro Alighieri: un'opera veneziana a Ravenna* (Ravenna, 1988)

P. Fabbri and S. Monaldini: *Periferie operistiche del seicento: il teatro per musica nella legazione di Romagna* (Ravenna, 1989)
PAOLO FABBRI

Rawnsley, John (*b* Colne, Lancs., 14 Dec 1950). English baritone. He studied in Manchester and made his début in 1975 with Glyndebourne Touring Opera as Kilian (*Freischütz*); he also sang Ford and Nick Shadow on tour, and Masetto, Marcello, Rossini's Figaro and Paolo (*Simon Boccanegra*) at Glyndebourne. He sang Mozart's Figaro with the WNO in 1977 and made his Covent Garden début in 1979 as Schaunard, returning for Sonora (*La fanciulla del West*) and Enrico Ashton. He made his début at La Scala in 1987 as Tonio. His repertory includes Papageno, Don Alfonso, Taddeo (*L'italiana in Algeri*) and Verdi's Renato, Macbeth, Ezio (*Attila*) and Amonasro. A powerful actor, with a firm voice which is particularly strong in the upper register, he is a very fine Rigoletto, a part he first sang with Opera North in 1979 and has repeated for the ENO and Scottish Opera. He has also sung at Paris, Brussels, Geneva and Toronto.
ELIZABETH FORBES

Rayam, Curtis (*b* Belleville, FL, 4 Feb 1951). American tenor. He studied in Miami, making his début there in 1971 in *Manon Lescaut*, then sang in Houston, Dallas and Jackson. His European début was in 1976 at Wexford as Charles VII (*Giovanna d'Arco*), returning as Lenny (Floyd's *Of Mice and Men*), Sultan Soliman (*Zaide*) and Wilhelm Meister (*Mignon*). In 1979 he sang Olympion in the American première of Tippett's *The Ice Break* at Boston. He has sung at Frankfurt, Amsterdam, Venice, Salzburg, Paris, Naples and La Scala, where he made his début in 1985 in *Alcina*. His wide repertory includes Belmonte, Idomeneus, Mithridates, Titus, Irus (*Il ritorno d'Ulisse*), Gluck's Achilles, Rossini's Otello and Cléomène (*Le siège de Corinthe*), as well as Berlioz's Faust, Grigory (*Boris Godunov*) and Werther. In 1988 he sang Creon (Traetta's *Antigone*) at Spoleto and Orcane (Jommelli's *Fetonte*) at La Scala. He has a firm, flexible voice, but some of the florid roles that he attempts are beyond his range.
ELIZABETH FORBES

Raybould, (Robert) Clarence (*b* Birmingham, 28 June 1886; *d* Bideford, 27 March 1972). English conductor. He took the the BMus degree at Birmingham University in 1912, and that year he joined the staff of the Midland Institute of Music. He assisted Rutland Boughton as pianist, coach and conductor at the early Glastonbury Festivals, and after World War I he performed the same service for the Beecham Opera Company and then for the British National Opera Company. His opera *The Sumida River* was produced in Birmingham in 1916. Raybould, best known as an orchestral conductor, directed the British concert premières of Hindemith's *Cardillac* (1936) and *Mathis der Maler* (1939).

Raymond [Raimond, Raymont], **B. Louis** (*fl* 1785–1806). French composer and librettist. He was among the composers whose works were most frequently performed at the Théâtre des Beaujolais in Paris during the last years of the *ancien régime*; he became conductor of its orchestra in 1787. In 1789 Raymond was conducting the orchestra of the Théâtre de Lille, and subsequently returned to Paris as prompter at the Théâtre du Délassement Comique, for which he wrote several librettos. According to Wild (1989), his works were performed at two small theatres founded under the Revolution, the Théâtre des Jeunes Artistes and the Théâtre des Jeunes Elèves; he was conductor at the Jeunes Elèves when it opened in 1799. The only work by Raymond which has survived is the libretto for *L'amateur de musique*.

in one act and first performed in Paris, Théâtre des Beaujolais, unless otherwise stated; texts by Raymond unless otherwise stated

Anacréon (after Colomb de Seillans), 12 May 1785
L'amant écho, 27 May 1785
L'amateur de musique (comédie), 3 July 1785
L'armoire, ou La cachette (C. J. Guillemain), 6 Sept 1785
La vraie ruse d'amour, 1785
Le braconnier (cmda, Rauquil-Lieutaud), 11 July 1786
Le Français à Constantinople, ou Le chevalier de Sérigny (comédie lyrique, 3), 26 May 1787
Jean-Jeannot (opéra bouffon, J. B. Radet), ?1787, collab. others
La faillite réparée, ou L'école des fils (cmda), Lille, 6 Sept 1789
La muette (opéra bouffon), Paris, Montansier, 16 Oct 1790

*

Calendrier musical universel pour l'année 1788, 103–6
Almanach général de tous les spectacles (1791), 216, 220
L. Lefebvre: *Histoire du Théâtre de Lille de ses origines à nos jours* (Lille, 1901), ii, 59, 62, 65
L. Péricaud: *Théâtre des Petits Comédiens de S.A.S. Monseigneur le comte de Beaujolais* (Paris, 1909)
C. D. Brenner: *A Bibliographical List of Plays in the French Language, 1700–1789* (Berkeley, 1947, 2/1979)
N. Wild: *Dictionnaire des théâtres parisiens au XIXe siècle* (Paris, 1989)   MICHEL NOIRAY

Raymond and Agnes. Romantic opera in four acts by EDWARD LODER to a libretto by EDWARD FITZBALL after an episode in Matthew Gregory Lewis's novel *Ambrosio, or The Monk*; Manchester, Theatre Royal, 14 August 1855.

A version in three acts was given in London at the St James's Theatre on 11 June 1859. The original libretto is lost. Details of the plot given below are from the reconstruction, in three acts, by Max Miradin, with music edited by Nicholas Temperley, for the revival at Cambridge Arts Theatre on 2 May 1966.

Inigo, Baron of Lindenberg (bass-baritone), lives under a curse put upon his family by St Agnes, a nun who stabbed herself when threatened with rape by one of his ancestors. Only when he marries one of her related descendants will the curse be lifted. He has therefore determined to marry Lady Agnes (soprano), his ward and the last of St Agnes's line. Brought up in strict confinement at a convent in Madrid, she has nevertheless fallen in love with the Spanish nobleman Don Raymond (tenor). Agnes reluctantly consents to return to Bavaria with Inigo, but Raymond secretly follows them. Arriving at Castle Lindenberg, he confronts the Baron, who inadvertently reveals himself as the murderer of Raymond's father. The two men fight and Raymond is overpowered. Inigo promises to free Raymond, but arranges that his retainer, Antoni (baritone), shall shoot him. At the crucial moment, however, the nun's blood-stained ghost appears, and Antoni, panicking, fires wildly and kills the Baron by mistake.

Though Fitzball's libretto was the kind of 'blood and thunder' melodrama that Gilbert was later to satirize in *Ruddigore*, its dramatic force was sufficient to inspire Loder to write music of a surprising emotional intensity. The opera was not successful in the 19th century, but the 1966 revival effected a re-evaluation, and it is now generally recognized as Loder's masterpiece.
                                                                      NIGEL BURTON

Re, Il ('The King'). Novella in three scenes by UMBERTO GIORDANO to a libretto by GIOVACCHINO FORZANO; Milan, Teatro alla Scala, 12 January 1929.

The action takes place in the 18th century. Rosalina (soprano), a miller's daughter, is causing grave concern to her family and her betrothed, Colombello (tenor), by her giddy behaviour and refusal to speak when spoken to. A priest (tenor), a lawyer (bass) and a female astrologer (mezzo-soprano) are asked for their opinion; but none can help. At length the girl herself explains: while listening to the song of a blackcap beneath a tree she saw a royal procession pass by. According to an ancient legend this means that she is destined to be a royal bride. Perplexed, the family decide to seek advice from the King (baritone). His answer is that Rosalina must spend the night in his palace. Her parents are suitably shocked, but dare not offer resistance. That evening Rosalina is decking herself for the wedding and musing on her altered fortunes ('In un mattin sereno'), when the King enters and divests himself of his royal robes, to be revealed as old, bald and wizened. Rosalina is only too thankful to return to the arms of Colombello, having learnt the valuable lesson that '' 'tis distance lends enchantment to the view'.

Il re is unusual in 20th-century opera as having been written as a vehicle for an old-style coloratura soprano, Toti Dal Monte, with whose retirement from the stage it quickly passed out of circulation. In it, Giordano assimilated into a late Romantic style the lighter, transparent textures of Wolf-Ferrari in his Venetian vein. The three scenes are linked by continuous music.
                                                                      JULIAN BUDDEN

Re [Dal Re, Del Re], **Vincenzo** (*b* Parma, *c*1700; *d* Naples, 8 July 1762). Italian designer. He was a pupil of Pietro Righini, under whom he worked in Parma and possibly in Turin and Milan; in 1737 he followed him to Naples, where Righini was commissioned to provide the scenery for the inaugural performance at the S Carlo theatre. When Righini returned to Parma in 1740, Re succeeded him as scenographer in Naples and remained there until his death. His name was associated with many opera productions, including Leo's *Demofoonte* (1741), Hasse's *Ipermestra* (1746), Gluck's *La clemenza di Tito* (1752), a pasticcio of Jommelli's *Attilio Regolo* (1761), and with elaborate staging for court festivities, in particular, Giuseppe de Majo's *Il sogno d'Olimpia* (1747).

A large number of Re's scenographic drawings survive in libraries (Metropolitan Museum of Art, New York; Royal Institute of British Architects, London; Rava collection, Milan); others have been found in private collections or on appearance at auction (an important group was sold at Sotheby's in 1969). Re's style is influenced by Righini and by the Bibiena family, but he is less concerned with sumptuousness and caprice, preferring a perhaps equally artificial naturalness. The close adherence of the visual images to the dramatic text is remarkable, especially for the Metastasian operas. The faithfulness with which Re followed directions in the librettos often makes it possible to recognize the works to which the drawings refer even when they are not identified. This rational relationship between the literary and the scenic elements of the operas did not, however, exclude some surprising effects, as for instance the presence of an elephant on stage in Sarro's *Alessandro nell'Indie* in 1743.

For further illustration *see* NAPLES, fig.2 and SEATING, fig.1.

*

Narrazione delle solenni reali feste fatte celebrare in Napoli da S. M. il re delle due Sicilie (Naples, 1747)

Design by Vincenzo Re for Sarro's 'Alessandro nell'Indie' (Alexander's camp on the banks of the Hydaspes), performed at the Teatro S Carlo, Naples, in 1743

H. Tintelnot: *Barocktheater und barocke Kunst* (Berlin, 1939)
J. Scholz and A. Mayor: *Baroque and Romantic Stage Design* (New York, 1950)
F. Mancini: *Scenografia napoletana dell'età barocca* (Naples, 1964)
J. Harris: *Italian Architectural Drawings Lent by the R. I. B. A.* (London and Washington DC, 1966) [exhibition catalogue]
W. Jeudwine: *Stage Designs ... the RIBA Drawings* (London, 1968)
Catalogue of Important Old Master Drawings (London, 1969) [exhibition catalogue]
D. Oenslager: *Four Centuries of Scenic Invention: Drawings from the Collection of Donald Oenslager* (Washington DC, 1974)
C. Sorgato and D. Lenzi: 'Vincenzo Re', *L'arte del settecento miliano: architettura, scenografia, pittura di paesaggio* (Bologna, 1980), p.279, nos.191, 352–5 [exhibition catalogue]
F. Mancini: *Il Teatro di S Carlo, 1737–1987*, iii: *Le scene, i costumi* (Naples, 1987)   MERCEDES VIALE FERRERO

Rea, John (*b* Toronto, 14 Jan 1944). Canadian composer. He studied with John Weinzweig and Gustav Ciamaga at the University of Toronto and with Milton Babbitt at Princeton. In 1973 he was appointed to teach at McGill University, Montreal, where he was later Dean of the Faculty of Music (1986–91). He lived in Berlin (1979–80), and was composer-in-residence in Mannheim in 1984. He was a founder-member of the Montreal new-music society Les Evénements du Neuf, and joined the board of directors of the Société de Musique Contemporaine du Québec in 1982.

Rea's first opera, *The Prisoners Play*, to a libretto by Paul Woodruff, was commissioned in 1972 by the University of Toronto opera department and had its première on 12 May 1973 at the MacMillan Theatre. A serial work written for children, it combines the magical and enchanted world of Circe with that of discovery in the music. His second opera, *Le petit livre des 'Ravalet'* (1983), to a text by the Belgian poet and sculptor Joseph Mignolet, was commissioned by Radio Canada and conceived for the Ensemble Claude-Gervaise, Montreal. It is based on Jules Barbey d'Aurevilly's true story of a 16th-century Norman family and was written as a one-act 'opéra parlé' in which spoken and sung texts are deliberately separated. This procedure polarizes the domains of speech and song and makes the sung sections particularly telling. Subsequently Rea has worked on short operatic scenes. His *Offenes Lied* (1986, performed at the International Festival in Montepulciano in 1987) was inspired by Heine's poem. In the early 1990s he began composing further operatic scenes based on Beatrice's monologue at the end of Dante's *Inferno* and Edgar Allan Poe's *Morella* in Baudelaire's translation.   GAYNOR G. JONES

Reading, John (*fl* 1684–1724). English bass. He was singing on the London stage by 1684 and was the first Coridon in Purcell's *The Fairy-Queen* (1692). He sang Vulcan in the masque *The Loves of Mars & Venus* by Eccles and Finger (1696) and the title role in Eccles's *Hercules* in *The Novelty* (1697). From 1715 he performed at Lincoln's Inn Fields in musical afterpieces and revivals of dramatic operas. A Mrs or Miss Reading sang Peace in Clayton's *Rosamond*.

BDA; LS   OLIVE BALDWIN, THELMA WILSON

Reardon, John (*b* New York, 8 April 1930; *d* Santa Fe, 16 April 1988). American baritone. After studying with Martial Singher and Margaret Harshaw, he made his début in 1954 at the New York City Opera and subsequently sang with numerous companies in the USA – his Metropolitan début was in 1965 as Tomsky in *The Queen of Spades* – and Europe. His recordings include Nick Shadow. The possessor of a well-controlled lyric voice and notable acting ability, Reardon was best known for his large repertory of over a hundred roles (Scarpia, Pelléas, Britten's Tarquinius and roles in works by Mozart and Strauss) and for the number of premières he gave, mostly with the Santa Fe Opera. These included works by Douglas Moore, Lee Hoiby, Marvin David Levy and Thomas Pasatieri, as well as American premières of *The Nose, Cardillac, Dantons Tod, The Devils of Loudun, The Bassarids* and *Help, Help, the Globolinks!*. He directed the opera workshop at the Wolf Trap Summer Theatre in Virginia.

J. Reardon: 'The Challenges of Modern Opera', *Music Journal*, xxix/4 (1971), 28ff   PATRICK J. SMITH

Rebecca. Opera in two acts by WILFRED JOSEPHS to a libretto by Edward Marsh after Daphne du Maurier's novel; Leeds, Grand Theatre, 15 October 1983.

The (unnamed) Girl (soprano) meets Maxim de Winter (baritone) at Biarritz and accepts his offer of marriage. At Manderley, Maxim's family home in Cornwall, the family welcomes her, but the housekeeper Mrs Danvers (mezzo-soprano) undermines her confidence with reminiscences of Maxim's first wife, now dead, the brilliant and much admired Rebecca. After Mrs Danvers has attempted to drive her to suicide, the Girl discovers that Rebecca had been an unfaithful wife, aided and abetted in her many affairs by Mrs Danvers and hated by Maxim. During a great storm Mrs Danvers dies as Manderley is burnt to the ground and Rebecca's ghost is laid.

Rebecca met with a mixed response from the critics, but scored an immediate success with the general public. Colin Graham's production was closely integrated with both libretto and music, and Ann Howard's portrayal of Mrs Danvers (at the première and at the 1988 revival) showed that the role offers great opportunities for a dramatic mezzo-soprano. The music is apt and atmospheric, action is rapid and fruitful use is made of familiar musico-dramatic formulae, ranging from a Poulenc-like waltz to music of ferocious dissonance in the climactic scenes of storm and stress. Josephs's own character emerges most distinctly in the quieter, more lyrical scenes; at other times he is content to act as musical illustrator.

HUGO COLE

Rebel, François [*le fils*] (*b* Paris, 19 June 1701; *d* Paris, 7 Nov 1775). French composer, director and administrator, son of Jean-Féry Rebel. He entered the Opéra orchestra in 1714 and three years later was granted the right of succession to his father's place in the 24 violons du roi. From early in his career until his death he was a colleague, and later a close collaborator, of François Francoeur; *Pirame et Thisbé*, their first operatic venture, appeared in 1726. Although Rebel's activities as a court musician ranged from playing the violin and conducting the orchestra to directing and staging operas, and included the duties of composer and *surintendant* of the Musique de la Chambre du Roi, his greatest achievement probably lay in his efforts to keep French opera alive in the troubled times of the 1750s and 60s when he (and Francoeur) held administrative posts at the Opéra. For a more detailed account of his career and a list of his operatic collaborations, *see* FRANCOEUR, FRANÇOIS.

Rebel, Jean-Féry [*le père*] (*b* Paris, bap. 18 April 1666; *d* Paris, 2 Jan 1747). French composer, father of François Rebel *le fils*. His musical versatility is demonstrated by the many positions he held at the court of Louis XIV and at the Opéra. He began his professional career in 1699 as a violinist at the Opéra, later serving as harpsichordist (1702–15), *batteur de mesure* (1715–*c*1727) and *maître de musique* (*c*1727–33). Concurrently he held positions at court as a member of the 24 violons du roi (1705–17) before becoming their leader, and as *compositeur de la musique de la chambre* (1718–27). To the vocal repertory he contributed many songs and one *tragédie lyrique*, *Ulysse*, in a prologue and five acts to a libretto by Henry Guichard, given at the Opéra on 23 January 1703 and published in Paris in that year. His long tenure at the Opéra as *batteur* and *maître de musique* left an imprint on the *tragédie lyrique* repertory. His awareness of new trends resulted in

pioneering suites and sonatas for violin, as well as introducing a number of works in a new genre, the 'choreographic symphony'; some of his own works were given in this form, notably *Les caractères de la danse* (1715) and *Les élémens* (1737).
See also ULYSSE.

*
L. de La Laurencie: 'Une dynastie de musiciens aux XVIIe et XVIIIe siècles: les Rebel', *SIMG*, vi (1905–6), 253–307
A. Ducrot: 'Les représentations de l'Académie Royale de Musique à Paris au temps de Louis XIV (1671–1715)', *RMFC*, x (1970), 19–55
M. Benoit: *Versailles et les musiciens du roi: étude institutionnelle et sociale, 1661–1733* (Paris, 1971)
J. R. Anthony: *French Baroque Music from Beaujoyeulx to Rameau* (London, 1973, 2/1978; Fr. trans., 1981)
L. E. Brown: *The 'Tragédie Lyrique' of André Campra and his Contemporaries* (diss., U. of North Carolina, 1978)
J. de La Gorce: 'L'Académie Royale de Musique en 1704', *RdM*, lxv (1979), 160–91
C. Wood: *Jean-Baptiste Lully and his Successors: Music and Drama in the 'tragédie en musique', 1673–1715* (diss., U. of Hull, 1981)
G. Sadler: 'Rameau and the Orchestra', *PRMA*, cviii (1981–2), 47–68
VLADIA KUNZMANN

Rebellón, Eduardo Rodríguez-Losada. *See* RODRÍGUEZ-LOSADA REBELLÓN, EDUARDO.

Reber, (Napoléon-)Henri (*b* Mulhouse, 21 Oct 1807; *d* Paris, 24 Nov 1880). French composer. Intended for a career in industry, he began studying music on his own and was briefly a pupil of Reicha and Le Sueur at the Paris Conservatoire. A successful series of *opéras comiques* followed between 1848 and 1857. In these, 'he strove to counteract the tendency towards noise and bombast then prevalent both in French and Italian opera and to show how much may be made out of the simple materials of the old French *opéra comique* by the judicious use of modern orchestration' (Chouquet). In 1851 he began teaching at the Conservatoire, succeeding Halévy as professor of composition in 1862. The success of *Le père Gaillard* resulted in his election to the Institut as Onslow's successor in 1853. Reber is also noted for his *Traité d'harmonie* (Paris, 1862, 2/1889).

opéras comiques, published in vocal score in Paris shortly after first performance unless otherwise stated; MSS in F-Pc

POC – Paris, Opéra-Comique

La nuit de Noël (3, E. Scribe), POC (Favart), 9 Feb 1848
Le père Gaillard (3, T. Sauvage), POC (Favart), 7 Sept 1852 (Paris, 1852)
Les papillottes de Monsieur Benoist (1, J. Barbier and M. Carré), POC (Favart), 28 Dec 1853
Les dames-capitaines (3, Mélesville [A.-H.-J. Duveyrier]), POC (Favart), 3 June 1857
Naïm, ou Les maures en Espagne (grand opéra, 5), unperf., unpubd; ov. (Paris, n.d.)
Le ménétrier à la cour, unperf., unpubd; ov. (Paris, n.d.)

*
Grove5 (G. Chouquet)
E. Legouvé: 'Reber', *La France musicale*, vi (1843), 98–9
C. Saint-Saëns: *Notice sur M. Henri Reber* (Paris, 1881)
F. Raugel: 'Autour de Sauzay, de Boely et de Reber', *RMFC*, xv (1975), 146–52
FRÉDÉRIC ROBERT

Rebikov, Vladimir Ivanovich (*b* Krasnoyarsk, Siberia, 19/31 May 1866; *d* Yalta, 4 Aug 1920). Russian composer. He studied at the Moscow Conservatory and in Berlin. From 1894 to 1898 he lived in Odessa and thereafter in Kishinyeu, founding branches of the Society of Russian Composers in both cities. After a period in Berlin and Vienna, he took up residence in Moscow (1901–19), appearing as a pianist at home and abroad. His early compositions are in a Tchaikovskian style, but around 1900 he began to be much more experimental. His use of whole-tone harmony earned him a reputation as the finest Russian impressionist, and he also became known as the father of Russian modernism. His 'musico-psychological dramas' are among his most adventurous and celebrated (though seldom heard) pieces, in which an expressionist style is combined with the continuing influence of Tchaikovsky; the conception of these works was largely influenced by the realistic productions at the Moscow Arts Theatre. *Bezdna* ('The Abyss', 1907), *Zhenshchina s kinzhalom* ('The Woman with the Dagger', 1910) and *Dvoryanskoye gnezdo* ('A Nest of Gentlefolk', 1916) are the most advanced examples of his 'psychographic' music; the last also contains detailed instructions on the use of scenic effects such as damp earth, grass, flowers and trees. The fairy play *Yolka* ('The Christmas Tree', 1903) was particularly popular on the Russian stage and was also performed in Prague and Berlin.

V grozu [In the Thunderstorm] op.5 (2, S. Plaksin, after V. Korolenko), Odessa, City Theatre, 15/27 Feb 1894
Yolka [The Christmas Tree] op.21, 1894–1900 (musico-psychological drama, 1, Plaksin, after F. M. Dostoyevsky, H. C. Andersen and G. Hauptmann), Moscow, Aquarium Theatre, 17/30 Oct 1903
Tea: boginya [Thea: the Goddess] op.34, 1904 (spiritual drama, 4 scenes, after A. P. Vorotnikov)
Bezdna [The Abyss] op.40, 1907 (musico-psychological tale, Rebikov, after L. N. Andreyev)
Zhenshchina s kinzhalom [The Woman with the Dagger] op.41, 1910 (musico-psychological drama, 3 scenes, Rebikov, after A. Schnitzler)
Al'fa i omega [Alpha and Omega] op.42, 1911 (musico-psychological drama, 2 scenes, Rebikov)
Nartsiss [Narcissus] op.45, 1913 (1, T. L. Shchepkina-Kupernik, after Ovid)
Arakhne [Arachne] op.49, 1915 (2, Shchepkina-Kupernik, after Ovid)
Dvoryanskoye gnezdo [A Nest of Gentlefolk] op.55, 1916 (musico-psychological drama, 4, Rebikov, after I. Turgenev)
Prints krasavchik i printsessa chudnaya prelest' [Prince Charming and Princess Beautiful] (children's fairy-tale op)

*

ES (W. H. Dale)
M. Montagu-Nathan: 'Rebikof', *Contemporary Russian Composers* (London, 1917)
A. Rowley: 'Rebikoff', *MR*, iv (1943), 112–15
W. H. Dale: *A Study of the Musicopsychological Dramas of Vladimir Ivanovich Rebikov* (Rochester, NY, 1958)
O. Tompakova: *Vladimir Ivanovich Rebikov: ocherk zhizni i tvorchestva* [Rebikov: Life and Work] (Moscow, 1989)

Re cervo, Il. Opera by Hans Werner Henze; see KÖNIG HIRSCH.

Rech, Géza (*b* Vienna, 25 June 1910). Austrian director and musicologist. He studied at Vienna University with Lach, Orel and Wellesz (1929–35) and took the doctorate in 1935 with a dissertation on the Viennese stage director Friedrich Strampfer. After serving as stage manager and director at various German and Austrian theatres (1935–44) he worked for Salzburg radio, and in 1950 he was appointed to the Salzburg Mozarteum to teach opera production and direction, also lecturing in drama at Salzburg University. In 1950 he became editor of the *Mozart-Jahrbuch* and director of the musicology section of the Internationale Stiftung Mozarteum. Most of his writings are on Mozart and his operas; with R. Thomasberger he wrote a study, *Salzburger Szenenbilder* (Salzburg, 1977).   RUDOLF KLEIN

Récit (Fr.). In French 17th-century opera and related forms, as well as sacred music, a term used to designate solo vocal music, particularly, according to Furetière, for the soprano. It should not be confused with *récitatif* (see RECITATIVE).

The term was borrowed from spoken *tragédie* where *récits*, generally monologues or long speeches, were used as a narrative device. This primarily dramatic definition remained significant for its musical use. In the *ballet de cour*, *récits* were at first declaimed, and after 1605 sung, generally at the beginning of an act or entrée: here a minor character set the scene and tone of what was to follow.

In Lully operas *récits* (most often in monologues, but occasionally in dialogues) were similarly placed and often included *airs*, *récitatifs* and instrumental interludes in quite a fluid structure. The prologue of *Alceste* provides a typical example: the Nymph of the Seine, alone on stage, sings of her anxiety while waiting for the return of the hero victorious in battle ('Le héros que j'attens ne reviendra-t-il pas?'). Not a principal figure, she nonetheless makes the initial situation clear to the audience and represents metaphorically the prevailing emotional state.

In the 18th century there are numerous *récits* for other voice types, including the bass, but flexibility in style and variety of forms remained important features in the operas of Campra and his contemporaries. Their dramatic function, as well as narration, instruction and expression of feelings, could include persuasion, and now more often *récits* were sung by main characters, such as Ismenor's 'Mânes des rois les plus terribles' from Campra's *Tancrède* (see Brown 1984). Probably the prominence of instrumental solos led to the extension of the term to violins and other melody instruments outside the vocal context (as in *récit de violon*, *récit de flûte* and so on). By the mid-century vocal *récit* was no longer in general use as an operatic term, although monologue scenes to open acts fulfilling similar dramatic aims remained an important feature of French opera. Later, and into the 19th century, 'récit' was employed as an abbreviation for *récitatif*.

*

A. Furetière: *Dictionnaire universel* (The Hague, 1691)
L. de Jaucourt: 'Récit dramatique', *Encyclopédie, ou Dictionnaire raisonné des sciences, des arts et des métiers*, ed. D. Diderot and others (Paris, 1751–80)
J.-J. Rousseau: 'Récit en musique', ibid
——: *Dictionnaire de musique* (Paris, 1768)
H. Prunières: *Le ballet de cour en France avant Benserade et Lully* (Paris, 1914)
L. E. Brown: 'The *Récit* in the Eighteenth-Century *tragédie en musique*', *MR*, xlv (1984), 96–111   M. ELIZABETH C. BARTLET

Recitative (Fr. *récitatif*; Ger. *Rezitativ*; It. *recitativo*). A type of vocal writing, normally for a single voice, with the intent of mimicking dramatic speech in song. In practice its nature has varied widely by era, nationality, origin and context.

1. Up to 1800: (i) History (ii) Performance. 2. After 1800.

1. UP TO 1800.

(*i*) *History*. *Recitativo* is properly an adjective. As a noun, short for *stile recitativo*, it occurs as early as 1626 (Domenico Mazzocchi, *La catena d'Adone*). It derives from the verb *recitare*, 'to recite', which was also used in the 16th century for vocal performance, for example in Baldassare Castiglione's *Il libro del cortegiano* (1528), where the phrase 'cantare alla viola per recitare' occurs. The liberalization of poetic forms and blank verse in late

16th-century Italy fostered approximations of the affects of dramatic speech through pitch and rhythm in many different places and circumstances. These attempts, by such groups as the Florentine Camerata, had a number of typical traits: the text was generally not repeated, the rate of harmonic change varied with the affect of the text, an overall slow harmonic rhythm unfolded over a generally static bass line (which gave the impression of declamatory freedom, though chord progressions were still clearly derived from the madrigal), the poetic accents were reinforced by harmonic change, and particularly affective passages or individual words were often supported with strong dissonance (another madrigal borrowing). These sections were not initially known as recitative, although this is implied by Agazzari (*Del sonare sopra 'l basso*, 1607) in his reference to 'lo stile moderno di cantar recitative', and by Gagliano in the preface to *Dafne* (1608), where he speaks of the 'artifiziosa maniera di recitare cantando'. More generally it was called the *stile rappresentativo*, as Monteverdi suggested in his seventh book of madrigals (1619). Peri's preface to his opera *Euridice* (1600/01) is perhaps the earliest attempt to describe this middle ground between speech and song, but both the extant portions of this work and his *Dafne* (1597–8) are still closely linked with general 16th-century practice. Peri's reciting style was imitated by Monteverdi in *Orfeo* (1607, 'In un fiorito prato,' from Act 2, has clear parallels to Peri's 'Per quel vago berchetto' in *Euridice*), although the model is surpassed in Monteverdi's variety of rhythm and imaginative continuo progressions. Caccini later claimed precedence over Peri in establishing the style; in the preface to his *Le nuove musiche* (1601/2) he advertised a music in which one might be said to speak in music ('in armonia favellare'), employing a certain 'sprezzatura di canto'. It has also been suggested (Bettley 1976–7) that the Italian *falsobordone* tradition, sharing many traits with the early recitative of Peri and Monteverdi, may have played a greater role in the development of Italian recitative than is generally thought. The virtues of recitative were not everywhere admired; at times it was found tedious when unenlivened by the frequent interpolation of arias, as Saint-Evremond (*Sur les opéra*, 1705) reported concerning the Parisian reception of Luigi Rossi's *Orfeo* in 1647.

A clear separation of recitative monody from more lyrical writing appeared only gradually during the 17th century, with many passages sharing qualities of both recitative and aria, perpetuating the use of strophic variation or other aria-like forms (as in the prologue to Monteverdi's *Orfeo* and in Mazzocchi's *La catena d'Adone*), or providing other textual or musical repetition to lend coherence. In the course of the 17th century the aria became the more dominant element in opera, partly through the influence of the solo cantata and partly as the result of the opening of public theatres in Venice from 1637 onwards. Still, before 1650 the moments of most intense passion were generally rendered in recitative, often in long soliloquies.

There were fundamental differences among the recitative writing of Italian, French, German and English composers in the 17th century. The French modelled recitative on the highly stylized declamation of the spoken theatre (particularly in Lully's imitation of Mlle Champmeslé) and on French traditions of metric freedom (as in the 16th-century *musique mesurée*), stressing the lyric accents of the text by marking both the rhyme and the caesura; this had only loose analogy in Italian recitative, which regularly accentuated only punctuation (through harmonic change and rests in the vocal line). French recitative also favoured a more flowing melodic style, emphasized by the frequent change of time signature. By the mid-18th century Rousseau noted a confusion of French terminology, in which RÉCIT (which properly referred to everything 'sung by the solo voice', including *airs*) was often confused with *récitatif*. Schütz may well have introduced the Italian, Monteverdian style of recitative to Germany in his opera *Dafne* (1627), but this can only be a conjecture since the music is lost. Recitative in 17th-century Germany largely developed in the *historia*, which followed conventions of chanting biblical prose texts, an adaptation first introduced to Germany in Schütz's *Psalmen Davids* (1619). In the preface to this work Schütz noted that the 'stylo recitativo' was 'almost unknown in Germany at present'. By the end of the century the *historia* type of recitative was the most effusive and unpredictable in Europe, striking bold and unexpected harmonic progressions, affective melodic intervals and other musical means to elevate textual expression. Unique approaches developed for the treatment of specific texts and situations, such as setting the Evangelist as a tenor and Christ as a bass, surrounding the Lord's texts with a 'halo' of string sound. A new wave of italianate influence entered North German sacred music in Hamburg through Keiser, Mattheson and others, where German opera struggled for ascendancy. The unusually diverse, expressive recitative of such 18th-century German composers of Italian opera as Handel and Hasse was also coloured by German traditions. In England, monody had its adherents early in the 17th century, particularly in the masque; but although Ben Jonson stated that the music of his *Lovers Made Men* (1617) was 'sung after the Italian manner, stylo recitativo' by Nicholas Lanier, who wrote it, it is not until Lanier's *Hero and Leander* (*c*1630) that the first unequivocal use of recitative is found in English music. The style of the English compositions is, in any case, nearer to arioso than to recitative in the Italian sense, and this is true even of Purcell's music. Italian recitative was a complete novelty to most people when it arrived in England at the beginning of the 18th century, as Addison observed in the *Spectator* (no. 29): 'there is nothing that has more startled our *English* Audience, than the *Italian Recitativo* at its first Entrance upon the Stage. People were wonderfully surprized to hear Generals singing the Word of Command, and Ladies delivering Messages in Musick.'

By the 18th century recitative came to be the principal vehicle for dialogue and dramatic action in opera, with the arias carrying the more lyric portions, although this traditional understanding of the separation of dramatic function is less rigorous than is sometimes supposed – in Metastasio's librettos there are clear examples of dramatically active arias (such as 'Se cerca, se dice' from *L'olimpiade*) and contemplative recitatives. Italian recitative of the 18th century was routinely separated into two distinct types (as John Brown proposed): texts 'of passion and sentiment, or such as are not so'. The more common type, for voice and continuo alone, was most widely known as *recitativo semplice*, although the term *secco* apparently gained parlance by the late 18th century (C. F. Cramer used it in an article in his *Magazin der Musik* in 1784). Moments of intense dramatic crisis (disasters, irreconcilable decisions, general stress), mental confusion (particularly madness), magic scenes

and other suitable moments were clothed with an enriched, colourful background, and were variously
known as *accompagnato* (in France *récitatif
accompagné*), *stromentato*, *obbligato* and the like. This
perpetuated an infrequent usage of the 17th century,
found in scores of Cavalli, Antonio Cesti, Lully,
Steffani, Purcell and others, which gradually rose in
prominence after 1700, with theatre poets in the latter
half of the 18th century often adding new verses to
established texts to facilitate these musical diversions.
Distinct from *recitativo semplice* by virtue of its
rhythmic and melodic figuration in the accompanimental parts, rapidly shifting character and imitation of
the passions of the text, over time it became customary
to enlist the orchestra's aid. In practice, the accompanimental orchestral voices generally sustained chords or
played scales and short melodic figures (particularly
after about 1740). Such passages were also more likely
to be treated formally, in sections. Metastasio was well
aware of the dramatic function of *recitativo obbligato*.
In a letter to Hasse, dated 1749 and published in his
posthumous works, he set out in detail how a scene in
Attilio Regolo was to be set – where the instruments
should accompany, where they should be silent, where
they should have ritornellos. In *Orfeo ed Euridice*
(1762) Gluck, in accordance with his and Calzabigi's
reform principles, accompanied all the recitatives with
orchestra, mostly in a simple and straightforward style.

The harmonically diverse, melodically expressive
recitative of Monteverdi's day gave way over time to an
array of conventions, more or less routinely applied by
the 1700s. This was widely lamented by Italian literati,
such as Gravina, Muratori, and Crescembeni, who, in
seeking to defend and reform Italian poetry and drama
(that is, opera) against French claims of newly won
superiority and allegiance to classical models, constantly
held up the ideals of the Camerata as the best model.
Within these conventions, it should be stressed,
composers were able to tailor their recitative closely to
the expressive needs of the drama; one of the best such
examples is Hasse's early *Artaserse* (1730, Venice).

The carefully notated rhythmic declamation of early
recitative was replaced by a more rapid and even
delivery, notated almost entirely in quavers with occasional crotchets and semiquavers. Easily identifiable
melodic formulae, often of several bars in length, occur
repeatedly to widely varied texts and across dozens of
composers. Typical Italian recitative was organized
around a simple harmonic scheme: (*a*) secondary
dominant chains, (*b*) chains of interlocking I–IV–V–I
progressions, in which the concluding V–I became the
I–IV of the next sequence, and (*c*) the juxtaposition of
relative major/minor harmonies. By the time of the
operas of such composers as Vinci, Porpora and Caldara
this had become the norm, and up to the end of the 18th
century it is the expected background against which
variation is best understood; deviation from these
patterns was almost always textually motivated, and
modern audiences miss expressive nuances when unfamiliar with the patterns. By this means recitatives
could modulate rapidly in either direction (towards flats
with secondary dominants, towards sharps with
I–IV–V–I chains) to connect to the keys of both the preceding and subsequent arias. It was often German
composers, or those who worked extensively outside
Italy (such as Handel, Hasse and Jommelli), who
experimented most widely with expressive harmonic
interpolations within this basic outline. Similarly,

towards the end of the 17th century the practice arose of
beginning a recitative with a 6-3 chord, no doubt also to
preserve continuity with the preceding aria or, in the
case of an initial recitative, to convey the impression of a
continuing narrative or dialogue. By its very nature,
recitative is designed primarily for solo singing.
Examples of recitative in two (rarely more) parts are not
uncommon in late 17th- and 18th-century opera, but
they are confined to very brief passages in which both
characters sing the same words. In a similar way choral
recitative is employed for turba interjections in Passion
settings.

(*ii*) *Performance.* In *Orfeo* Monteverdi prescribed three
keyboard instruments for the continuo – harpsichord,
organ and regal – in addition to plucked string instruments. With the development of opera as a public spectacle, variety of this kind was impractical and the
harpsichord became the standard instrument in secular
music, the organ in sacred music. The complete
accompanimental ensemble for simple recitative varied,
but most houses had, in addition to one or two
harpsichords, lutes, archlutes and other chord-playing
instruments, as well as sustaining instruments, such as
cellos, basses and bassoons. Their manner of
accompaniment is debated, as a result of differences
among the clear testimonies of North German practice
and scattered accounts of Italian traditions. The most
widespread accompanimental style for sacred recitative
in early 18th-century Germany apparently was 'short
declamation', or a performance in which tied semibreves
and minims in the continuo line were played as brief
strokes, often transcribed in contemporary theory
treatises (Heinichen, Niedt, Kellner, Telemann and
others) as crotchets; according to G. J. J. Hahn (*Der ...
General-Bass-Schüler*, 1751) and C. P. E. Bach (*Versuch
über die wahre Art*, 1753–62), in organ accompaniment
the player should, after a chord is struck, raise his right
hand and rest until the next chord is reached. Evidence
for similar practices in harpsichord performance of
Italian opera is ambiguous – in any case the fleeting,
ephemeral sound of a harpsichord in an opera house
could be sustained only through arpeggiation, recommended by J. J. Quantz (*Versuch einer Anweisung*,
1752), N. Pasquali (*Thorough-bass Made Easy*, 1757)
and others. Some evidence suggests that the German
practice of 'short declamation' arose directly from the
influence of Italian opera on German centres at the
beginning of the century, as it is clear that a short style
was used in at least some Italian opera performances in
foreign locations, such as in London and France;
Rousseau is unambiguous in this regard. Within Italy
the picture is less clear, but occasional oblique
references to short declamation (such as the Verri
brothers' reference to the disagreeable 'strokes of the
bass' in Roman recitative) suggest it may have been
widely practised. The term *secco*, in fact, may have
originally referred to an accompanimental style rather
than a dramaturgical deficiency (a meaning inferred by
the 19th century); in French scores *sec* routinely
describes short, punctuated quaver passages in
accompagnato, and *secco* was first used in a published
score in Jommelli's *L'olimpiade* (1783) for the
francophile Stuttgart court.

It became customary for the singer to add expressive
appoggiaturas at the final cadence and at appropriate
intermediate points. In his *Anleitung zur Singekunst*
(1757, an enlarged German version of P. F. Tosi's

Opinioni de' cantori antichi e moderni), J. F. Agricola gave examples to show how this was done (ex.1). In the

Ex.1

earliest operas and cantatas the voice and accompaniment always end together, as in the late madrigal. The practice of cutting off the voice before the cadence and leaving the accompaniment to complete the progression seems to have arisen in recitatives of a pathetic character, where the singer was so overcome with emotion as to be unable to continue; there are examples in Michelangelo Rossi's *Erminia sul Giordano* (1633), Cavalli's *Didone* (1641) and Monteverdi's *L'incoronazione di Poppea* (1642). Confusion in later repertories has partly resulted from Tosi's complaint against the *cadenza tronca*, which has variously been interpreted as a 'foreshortened' cadence (i.e. one in which the dominant harmony in the accompaniment – with a 4–3 suspension – coincides with a tonic appoggiatura in the voice) or (more likely) merely as the repetitious and premature cadencing of the vocal part itself. By the early 18th century both the delayed and the 'foreshortened' cadence were amply borne out in Italian manuscripts and by contemporary German theorists, such as C. P. E. Bach, Telemann and Heinichen.

The speed at which recitative was sung depended entirely on expression. Tosi, writing about *opera seria*, said that singers should learn 'a certain natural Imitation, which cannot be beautiful, if not expressed with that Decorum with which Princes speak, or those who know how to speak to Princes' (*Opinioni*, Eng. trans., 2/1743). On the other hand, Grimm (*Encyclopédie*, xii, 1763, 'Poème lyrique') regarded recitative as the medium for ordinary conversation. These views are not easily reconciled, because neither takes into account the context of a recitative or the type of work in which it occurs.

2. AFTER 1800. During the first decade of the 19th century the distinction remained intact between the conversational *recitativo secco* and the more declamatory *recitativo accompagnato*, both varieties being marked off from the set numbers by the use of 'versi sciolti' (freely alternating lines of seven-syllable and eleven-syllable verse). Subsequently, however, under the reign of Murat in Naples, which saw the importation of early French grand opera, the fashion started of scoring the *secco* recitative for strings, exemplified by Mayr's

Medea in Corinto (1813) and Rossini's *Elisabetta, regina d'Inghilterra* (1815). By 1820 this had become the rule for serious works, keyboard accompaniment being restricted to *opera buffa* and *semiseria*. In due course both types of recitative became subsumed into the SCENA. All passages, however, intended to be delivered in the rhythm of ordinary speech continued to be marked 'recitativo', even for only a few bars, a practice that continued until the 1890s, as in Verdi's *Otello* (1887) and Catalani's *La Wally* (1892). In the operas of Puccini and his successors, on the other hand, the term vanishes, being replaced by the marking 'a piacere' in the voice-part and 'col canto' in that of the orchestra.

In France recitative was confined to works produced at the Opéra and, during the 1860s, at the Théâtre Lyrique, as for example in Gounod's *Faust* (1862, revised version), Berlioz's *Les Troyens* (1863) and Bizet's *Les pêcheurs de perles* (1863) and *La jolie fille de Perth* (1867). Traditionally its text was set out in 'vers libre', consisting of lines of varying length with an alexandrine basis, to the setting of which the weak tonic accents of the French language permitted considerable flexibility. For most of the century *opéra comique* employed spoken dialogue and 'mélodrame' as a link between its set numbers, with the exception of Delibes' *Lakmé* (1883) and Chabrier's *Le roi malgré lui* (1887); but during the 1880s, it too became through-composed, as for example in Massenet's *Manon* (1884). The recitatives added by Guiraud to Bizet's *Carmen* (1875), though they ensured the opera's international circulation, were never performed at the Opéra-Comique; nor were they heard in Paris before the opera's first performance at the Palais Garnier during the 1950s.

German Singspiel, in which the dialogue was spoken, admitted only accompanied recitative, as exemplified by 'Abscheulicher!' in Beethoven's *Fidelio*. The move towards continuous music began, as Meyerbeer's diaries show, about 1816, though it yielded no work of substance until 1823 with Spohr's *Jessonda* and Weber's *Euryanthe* (Schubert's *Alfonso und Estrella*, though completed in 1822, was not performed until 1854 under Liszt's direction at Weimar). Here there is no fixed pattern of verse for the recitatives, some of which approximate to prose. Recitative is found in Wagner's early works up to *Der fliegende Holländer* (1843), but not in the more continuous texture of *Tannhäuser* (1845). In *Lohengrin* (1850), even passages such as the exchanges between Ortrud and Telramund at the start of Act 2, which are delivered in the rhythm of ordinary speech, are no longer qualified by the term; while in the music dramas from *Das Rheingold* onwards, where the bounds between lyrical and declamatory elements are quite differently defined, it does not apply at all.

The only English operas of the 19th century to have endured are constructed on the model of French *opéra comique*, using spoken dialogue with occasional melodrama. Balfe, however, made two through-composed settings, *Catherine Grey* (1837) and *The Daughter of St Mark* (1844), both of which revert to the 18th-century English tradition of recitative in heroic couplets (as used in Arne's *Artaxerxes*, 1762). A less clumsy, more flowing expedient based on blank verse can be found as late as 1891 in Sullivan's *Ivanhoe*.

Recitative in Russian opera is more measured and even-paced because of the nature of the language; nor is it marked off metrically from the closed numbers. Hence the development of Dargomïzhsky's 'melodic recitative' as the basis of an entire opera, examples of which are furnished by Musorgsky's uncompleted *Marriage* (composed 1868), Dargomïzhsky's *The Stone Guest* (1872) and Rimsky-Korsakov's *Mozart and Salieri* (1898).

As operas became more continuous during the course of the 19th century, recitative as such inevitably disappeared. Its legacy, however, can be found in the comparatively unvocalized delivery required in such operas as Debussy's *Pelléas et Mélisande* (1902), Vaughan Williams's *Riders to the Sea* (1937) and the SPRECHGESANG employed in the operas of Berg and Schoenberg. A modern variant of *recitativo secco* occurs accompanied by piano in Britten's *The Rape of Lucretia* (1946) and by harpsichord in Stravinsky's *The Rake's Progress* (1951).

*

J.-L. le Gallois: *Traité du récitatif* (Paris, 1707, 2/1740)

G. H. Stölzel: *Abhandlung vom Recitativ* (MS, *A-Wgm*); ed. in W. Steger: *Gottfried Heinrich Stölzels 'Abhandlung vom Recitativ'* (diss., U. of Heidelberg, 1962)

C. G. Krause: *Von der musikalischen Poesie* (Berlin, 1753)

J. Adlung: *Anleitung zu der musikalischen Gelahrtheit* (Erfurt, 1758)

F. W. Marpurg: 'Unterricht vom Recitativ', *Kritische Briefe über die Tonkunst*, ii (1762), 253–416 passim

J. A. Scheibe: 'Abhandlung über das Recitativ', *Bibliothek der schönen Wissenschaften und freien Künste*, xi (1764), 209–68; xii (1765), 1–41, 217–66

J.-J. Rousseau: 'Récitatif', *Encyclopédie, ou Dictionnaire raisonné des sciences, des arts, et des métiers*, xiii (Paris, 1765)

——: 'Récitatif accompagné', 'Récitatif mesuré', *Supplément à l'Encyclopédie*, iv (Amsterdam, 1777)

G. J. Vogler: 'Praktische Abhandlung vom Accent im Recitative', *Betrachtungen der Mannheimer Tonschule*, i (Mannheim, 1778), 398–402

C. F. Cramer: Editor's note to 'Schlechte Einrichtung des Italiänischen Singgedichts: Warum ahnen die Deutsche sie nach?', *Magazin der Musik*, ii (1786), 629–50, esp. 629–31

J. C. F. Rellstab: *Versuch über die Vereinigung der musikalischen und oratorischen Declamation* (Berlin, 1786)

J. Brown: *Letters upon the Poetry and Music of the Italian Opera: Addressed to a Friend* (Edinburgh, 1789, 2/1791)

G. Weber: 'Begleitung des Recitativs', *AMZ*, xiii (1811), 93–7

E. Schmitz: 'Zur Frühgeschichte der lyrischen Monodie Italiens im 17. Jahrhundert', *JbMP 1911*, 35–48

B. Zeller: *Das Recitativo accompagnato in den Opern J. A. Hasses* (Halle, 1911)

M. Schneider: 'Die Begleitung des Secco-Rezitativs um 1750', *Gluck-Jb*, iii (1917), 88–107

R. Meyer: 'Die Behandlung des Rezitativs in Glucks italienischen Reformopern', *Gluck-Jb*, iv (1918), 1–90

C. Spitz: 'Die Entwicklung des Stile recitativo', *AMw*, iii (1921), 237–44

P. Mies: 'Über die Behandlung der Frage im 17. und 18. Jahrhundert', *ZMw*, iv (1921–2), 286–304

F. Corder: *Vocal Recitative Historically and Practically Described* (London, 1922)

H. Abert: 'Wort und Ton der Musik des 18. Jahrhunderts', *AMw*, v (1923), 31–70; repr. in *Gesammelte Schriften und Vorträge von Hermann Abert* (Halle, 1929), 173–231

H. Ritscher: *Die musikalische Deklamation in Lullys Opernrezitativen* (diss., U. of Berlin, 1925)

E. Borrel: 'L'interprétation de l'ancien récitatif français', *RdM*, xii (1931), 13–21

H. Nathan: *Das Rezitativ der Frühopern Richard Wagners: ein Beitrag zur Stilistik des Opernrezitativs in der ersten Hälfte des 19. Jahrhunderts* (diss., U. of Berlin, 1934)

A. Boll: 'L'art lyrique: évolution du récitatif', *ReM*, no.217 (1952), 19–32

A. A. Abert: 'Wort und Ton', *GfMKB, Hamburg 1956*, 43–5

J. A. Westrup: 'The Nature of Recitative', *Proceedings of the British Academy*, xlii (1956), 27–43

W. Heinitz: 'Rezitativ-Gestaltung in Händelschen Werken', *Händel-Ehrung: Halle 1959*, 135–40

E. O. Downes: 'Secco recitative in Early Classical Opera Seria (1720–80)', *JAMS*, xiv (1961), 50–69

B. Challis: 'La déclamation théâtrale aux XVIIe et XVIIIe siècles d'après les récitatifs', *Saggi e ricerche in memoria di Ettore Li Gotti* (Palermo, 1962), 355–7

F.-H. Neumann: *Die Theorie des Rezitativs im 17. und 18. Jahrhundert unter besonderer Berücksichtigung des deutschen Musikschrifttums des 18. Jahrhunderts* (diss., U. of Göttingen, 1955; chap. 1 pubd as *Die Ästhetik des Rezitativs*, Strasbourg, 1962)

J. A. Westrup: 'The Cadence in Baroque Recitative', *Natalicia Musicologica Knud Jeppesen* (Copenhagen, 1962), 243–52

H. C. Wolff: 'Die Sprechmelodie im alten Opernrezitativ', *HJb 1963*, 93–134

T. Dart: 'Handel and the Continuo', *MT*, cvi (1965), 348–50

W. M. Vos: *English Dramatic Recitative before ca. 1685* (diss., Washington U., St Louis, 1967)

R. Allorto: 'Il prologo dell'Orfeo: note sulla formazione del recitativo monteverdiano', *Monteverdi e il suo tempo: Venice, Mantua and Cremona 1968*, 157–70

J. H. Baron: 'Monody: a Study in Terminology', *MQ*, liv (1968), 462–74

C. Gallico: 'Discorso di G. B. Doni sul recitare in scena', *RIM*, iii (1968), 286–302

S. H. Hansell: 'The Cadence in 18th-Century Recitative', *MQ*, liv (1968), 228–48

P. Mies: *Das instrumentale Rezitativ von seiner Geschichte und seinen Formen* (Bonn, 1968)

S. Kunze: 'Aufführungsprobleme im Rezitativ des späteren 18. Jahrhunderts', *MJb 1968–70*, 132–44

Z. Pilkova: 'The Differences in the Relationship between the Music and the Word in Melodrama: Recitative and Aria in the Second Half of the Eighteenth Century', *Music and Word: Brno 1969*, 59–66

V. Köhler: 'Rezitativ, Szene und Melodram in Heinrich Marschners Opern', *GfMKB, Bonn 1970*, 461–4

K.-H. Viertel: ' "Singend sprechen" – zur Aufführungspraxis von Opern des 18. Jahrhunderts', *Musik und Gesellschaft*, xx (1970), 672–3

S. Hermelink: 'Die innere Logik der Rezitativ-Kadenz', *GfMKB: Berlin 1974*, 286–91

M. Seares: 'Aspects of Performance Practice in the Recitatives of Jean-Baptiste Lully', *SMA*, viii (1974), 8–16

H. Seifert: 'Das Instrumentalrezitativ vom Barock bis zur Wiener Klassik', *De ratione in musica: Festschrift Erich Schenk* (Kassel, 1975), 103–16

A. Verchaly: 'A propos du récit français au début du XVIIe siècle', *RMFC*, xv (1975), 39–46

M. Ruhnke: 'Das italienische Rezitativ bei den deutschen Komponisten des Spätbarock', *AnMc*, no.17 (1976), 79–120

G. Stefani: 'Dal parlato al canto: l'intonazione recitativa', *Studi musicali*, v (1976), 3–28

J. Bettley: 'North Italian "falsobordone" and its Relevance to the Early "Stile Recitativo" ', *PRMA*, ciii (1976–7), 1–18

W. Dean: 'The Performance of Recitative in Late Baroque Opera', *ML*, lviii (1977), 389–402

P. Beaussant: 'Le récitatif lulliste', *Gouts réunis*, iii (1978), 1

R. Fajon: 'Propositions pour une analyse rationalisée du récitatif de l'opéra lullyste', *RdM*, lxiv (1978), 55–75

R. Monelle: 'Recitative and Dramaturgy in the Dramma per musica', *ML*, lix (1978), 245–67

R. P. Wolf: 'Metrical Relationships in French Recitative of the Seventeenth and Eighteenth Centuries', *RMFC*, xviii (1978), 29–49

W. Hübner: 'Improvisation und Verzierung bei Ausführung des Generalbasses, insbesondere bei der Begleitung von Rezitativen', *Improvisation in der Instrumentalmusik der ersten Hälfte des 18. Jahrhunderts: Blankenburg/Harz 1979*, 87

M. Murata: 'The Recitative Soliloquy', *JAMS*, xxxii (1979), 45–73

J. E. W. Newman: *Formal Structure and Recitative in the 'Tragédies lyriques' of Jean-Baptiste de Lully* (Ann Arbor, 1979)

K. Zauft: 'Zu einigen Aspekten der Gestaltung des Secco-Rezitativs auf der theatralischen Szene', *Aufführungspraxis und Interpretation Händelscher Werke: Halle 1978*, 59–67

D. Muller: 'Aspects de la déclamation dans le récitatif de Jean-Baptiste Lully', *Basler Studien zur Interpretation der alten Musik*, ed. H. Oesch, ii (Winterthur, 1980), 234–51

T. Bauman: 'Benda, the Germans, and Simple Recitative', *JAMS*, xxxiv (1981), 119–31

C. V. Palisca: 'Peri and the Theory of Recitative', *SMA*, xv (1981), 51–61

G. Tomlinson: 'Madrigal, Monody, and Monteverdi's *via naturale alla immitatione*', *JAMS*, xxxiv (1981), 60–108

K.-H. Viertel: 'Zur Tradition der vokalen Ausführung des *Rezitativo semplice* im 18. und 19. Jahrhundert', *Die Bedeutung Georg Philipp Telemanns für die Entwicklung der europäischen Musikkultur im 18. Jahrhundert: Magdeburg 1981*, 94–103

T. Carter: 'Jacopo Peri's *Euridice* (1600): a Contextual Study', *MR*, xliii (1982), 83–103

D. Charlton: 'Instrumental Recitative: a Study in Morphology and Context, 1700–1808', *Comparative Criticism*, iv (1982), 149–68

C. Gianturco: 'Nuove considerazioni su *il tedio del recitativo* delle prime opere romane', *RIM*, xvii (1982), 212–39

D. E. Monson: *Recitativo semplice in the opere serie of G. B. Pergolesi and his Contemporaries* (diss., Columbia U., 1982)

F. Neumann: 'The Appoggiatura in Mozart's Recitative', *JAMS*, xxxv (1982), 115–37

L. Rosow: 'French Baroque Recitative as an Expression of Tragic Declamation', *EMc*, xi (1983), 468–79

F. W. Sternfeld: 'A Note on *Stile Recitativo*', *PRMA*, cx (1983–4), 41–4

P. Walls: 'The Origins of English Recitative', *PRMA*, cx (1983–4), 25–40

L. E. Brown: 'The *récit* in the Eighteenth-Century *Tragédie en musique*', *MR*, xlv (1984), 96–111

M. Collins: 'Cadential Structures and Accompanimental Practices in 18th-Century Italian Recitative', *Opera & Vivaldi*, ed. M. Collins and E. K. Kirk (Austin, 1984), 211–32

J. P. Pinson: 'L'*action* dans le récitatif pathétique de Lully: la déclamation', *Canadian University Music Review*, v (1984), 152–78

M. A. Radice: 'Heinrich Schuetz and the Foundations of the Stile Recitativo in Germany', *Bach*, xvi (1985), 9

B. L. Glixon: *Recitative in Seventeenth-Century Venetian Opera: its Dramatic Function and Musical Language* (diss., Rutgers U., 1986)

C. Kintzler: 'Essai de définition du récitatif, le chaînon manquant', *RMFC*, xxiv (1986), 128–41

D. Tunley: 'Grimarest's *Traité du récitatif*: Glimpses of Performance Practice in Lully's Operas', *EMc*, xv (1987), 361–4

L. Rosow: 'The Metrical Notation of Lully's Recitative', *Lully: Heidelberg and St Germain-en-Laye 1987*, 405–22

J. Tyrrell: 'Janáček's Concept of Recitative', *Leos Janáček and Czech Music: St Louis, Missouri 1988* (forthcoming)

DALE E. MONSON (1, with JACK WESTRUP), JULIAN BUDDEN (2)

Řecké pašije. Opera by Bohuslav Martinů; *see* GREEK PASSION, THE.

Reconstructie ('Reconstruction'). Morality in two parts (26 sections) by LOUIS ANDRIESSEN, Reinbert de Leeuw, Misha Mengelberg, PETER SCHAT and JAN VAN VLIJMEN to a libretto by Hugo Claus and Harry Mulisch; Amsterdam, Carré Theatre, 29 June 1969.

The composition is enacted roughly on three levels: on the lowest platform the vicissitudes of the management members of the Total American Company are shown. On the second platform imperialism appears in the figure of Don Juan, and on the third level a statue of Che Guevara is being built by seven labourers. The action concerns reconstructions of the murder of Che Guevara, the statue of Che Guevara and the Don Juan theme. The imperialist Don Juan (baritone) kills the Commendatore, alias Che Guevara, who is reconstructed as a stone guest. Don Juan's victims are Bolivia (soprano) and Cuba (spoken). Another central theme is the relation between masters and servants: Bormann is the servant of Tarzan (both spoken roles), Erasmus (spoken) of Don Juan.

Reconstructie is divided into two parts with 15 and 11 sections respectively, symbolized by the 26 letters of the alphabet. Each letter leads to a word with a concrete or symbolic meaning: A = America, B = Bolivia, C = Culture, D = Devotion etc.

The work contains an extraordinary combination of singing and acting, art and pop music, electronic and instrumental groups, avant-garde techniques and pastiche Mozart, and it is hardly possible to trace specific moments of the score to any particular of the five composers. *Reconstructie* aroused much controversy because of its political theme, and had considerable influence on contemporary music in the Netherlands.

R. Koopmans: 'On Music and Politics – Activism of Five Dutch Composers', *Key Notes*, iv (1976), 19–35

E. Schönberger: 'From a Personal Point of View', *Key Notes*, iv (1976), 36–8

L. Samama: *Zeventig jaar Nederlandse muziek (1915–1985)* (Amsterdam, 1986), 228, 261   LEO SAMAMA

Recording.

1. Introduction. 2. Acoustic recording. 3. The electric era. 4. After World War II. 5. Records as historical documents.

1. INTRODUCTION. For a long while successive periods in the history of the gramophone (or phonograph) tended to follow one another at approximately 25-year intervals. The invention itself dates from 1877, the year in which the Frenchman Charles Cros (1842–88) deposited with the Académie des Sciences a paper containing proposals for the reproduction of sound, without putting his theories to a practical test, and in which an American, Thomas Edison (1847–1931), independently began to study sound recording and reproduction as part of his wider researches into telegraphy, and was soon able to recite *Mary had a Little Lamb* into a crude recording horn and to hear his words immediately and recognizably played back.

Thereafter, nothing very momentous happened until the last decade of the century. The early death of Cros and Edison's lack of interest in the musical possibilities of his invention left the field open for a while to the apparently extensive and important but somewhat shadowy achievements of an Italian cavalry officer, Lt Gianni Bettini, who indulged in activities of considerable scope and value, and actually recorded the voice of Pope Leo XIII in his 93rd year. With the exception of an undoubtedly genuine recording of the great Polish soprano, Marcella Sembrich, which was romantically discovered in the attic of a New Zealand hotel, scrupulously dubbed and made generally available in 1965, remarkably little has physically survived from the numerous and lengthy catalogues of both popular and classical titles, including the work of many fine artists, issued by Bettini around the turn of the century.

At roughly the same time serious recording began in more conventional commercial form. About 1890 Emile Berliner, a German émigré in the USA, had begun to use flat discs, capable of being reproduced in quantity from a stamper, with an instrument which he called a 'gramophone' (the etymologically correct 'phonograph' has continued to be preferred in the USA). Towards the end of the century this invention was commercially developed in the USA, England, Germany and Russia; about 1900, famous singers and a few instrumental soloists began to make records, while the original cylinder system continued to survive beside the increasingly popular disc for another 25 years. Early in the century many of the best-known opera and concert singers of the day had begun to sing favourite items from their repertory into the recording horn; and such excerpts, supplemented by instrumental solos, formed

Lionel Mapleson with his recording horn and wax cylinders at the Metropolitan Opera House, New York, where he was librarian at the turn of the century. Between 1900 and 1904 he made numerous recordings during actual performances. Many of these survive and have been successfully transferred to modern discs; they show high standards not only of individual singing but of ensemble.

the musical backbone of the catalogues until the arrival of the electric recording system in 1925.

After electric recording, the next step was the arrival of the long-playing record or LP (USA 1948, Europe 1950), which increased the average playing length of a side from under five minutes to 20 or 30 minutes or even longer. More than anything else, this development put the recording of large-scale symphonic and other concert music – together with that of complete operas, even the *Ring* – effectively in the centre of the picture. Thereafter, our pattern of quarter-century dates begins to falter, with the introduction of stereophonic recording in 1958 and the revolutionary arrival of the compact disc (CD) in 1983.

2. ACOUSTIC RECORDING. Throughout all these periods opera occupied a leading role in the output of classical music on record. The main reason for this preference, in the early days, was that during the pre-electric (or acoustic) period of recording the sound of the human voice could be captured with greater fidelity and realism than that of any other musical source – an advantage artificially exaggerated by the practice of recording the singer as close as possible to the old-style recording horn, and of urging him or her to step back at the approach of loud high notes such as could distort on the wax and cause the resulting shellac disc to become subject to rapid wear in the course of playing.

Among other attractions in the choice of operatic excerpts for early recording we must include the marked popularity and suitability of such pieces in themselves, and their convenient brevity; for the same reason arias from Italian and French operas already provided a great part of the typical 'celebrity' concert programmes of that period. At one time it used even to be said that Puccini deliberately wrote his most famous arias in this brief form so as to fit neatly on a 10-inch or 12-inch record side; this was, in fact, an absurd notion, since his most popular works up to and including *Tosca* (1900) had been composed before the arrival of the 'red-label celebrity record', and from *Madama Butterfly* (1904) onwards his later works proved, in layout and structure, to be noticeably less amenable to such sectional treatment. Nevertheless, there is no doubt that 'highlights'

from Puccini, and still more from Verdi, provided for many years a solid basis for the celebrity catalogues of The Gramophone Company (later known as His Master's Voice), of its American partner, Victor, of the Columbia Graphophone Company and of many smaller companies on both sides of the Atlantic – among which should be mentioned Fonotipia in Italy, Pathé in France, Edison in the USA, and Odeon and Deutsche Grammophon (soon to be allied with the English-based Gramophone Company) in Germany.

Among the earliest opera singers to make records were Jean-Baptiste Faure (1830–1914) – although there is a slight doubt as to the authenticity of the two records ascribed to him – and Sir Charles Santley (1834–1922); among the earliest operatic excerpts is a version of the 'Miserere' scene from *Il trovatore* recorded about 1896 by the tenor Ferrucio Giannini (1868–1948; father of the famous soprano, Dusolina), without either chorus or a soprano to sing the music for Leonora.

While we must lament the fact that recording came too late to capture the art of the great 19th-century performers in their prime, it is fortunate that several of them – more especially singers such as Adelina Patti, Santley, Lilli Lehmann, Nikolay Figner and Medea Mei-Figner (Tchaikovsky's first Hermann and Lisa), Tamagno (Verdi's first Otello) and Victor Maurel (his first Iago and Falstaff) – contrived to leave us brief and tantalizing glimpses of their art and style, which have been preserved and transferred to modern formats, often with remarkable results. Not only is our natural curiosity to some extent answered by such survivals, but we are enabled to note features of performing practice which would otherwise have to be deduced or taken on trust – or perhaps simply disbelieved. If a modern singer introduces appoggiaturas and other ornaments into an aria, it is because he has been persuaded (often with difficulty) that it is 'correct' to do so, whereas a singer like Santley used appoggiaturas freely because it had never occurred to him to do otherwise, and even introduced an octave-and-a-half downward scale before a reprise of the tune in Figaro's 'Non più andrai', no doubt because he had heard many older singers make play with just such elegant variations in a style that may go back to the time of Mozart himself. In short, already at this early stage of recording it is possible to discern the historical value of what is being preserved – a value all the more evident since so many of these early recording artists were performing the music of their own day, and had frequently worked with the composers concerned or with conductors who had direct knowledge of the composers' intentions. Besides some of the original Tchaikovsky, Verdi and Puccini interpreters, records exist of the first performers of many pre-1914 operas, notably those of Strauss.

The younger and even the middle-aged generation of singers soon adopted the habit of regular record-making, finding that it greatly increased their renown and their earnings. Though Melba was already 45 at the time of her first records, her beautifully placed and well-preserved voice with its strongly individual timbre proved to be admirably suited to reproduction, and she continued to visit the studios regularly until the early days of electric recording. Caruso flung himself with typical Neapolitan gusto into the somewhat hectic and careless task of early record-making in a Milan hotel room, and soon found that by his records alone he had vastly spread his fame and increased his income. His predecessor, Fernando De Lucia, was already past his brief youthful flowering at the time of his first recordings in 1902; but something uniquely personal in his style and utterance proved nonetheless irresistible, and he was to become perhaps the most prolific of all the early recording artists, producing within a period of 20 years as many as 400 record sides, including two more or less complete operas (*Il barbiere di Siviglia* and *Rigoletto*).

The practice of recording complete operas – or at any rate of assembling an adequate tally of sides to count as such – had already begun, mostly in Berlin, in about 1906; and two of these early sets (a 36-side *Carmen* and a 34-side *Faust*) had the distinction of listing Emmy Destinn in the leading roles. French Pathé followed suit in 1918 with several popular French operas, and Verdi favourites in French translation, using leading native singers of the day. But the notion then enjoyed only a limited success, and the practice was soon dropped by the few companies which had attempted it. Commercial considerations seem to have been the main drawback: customers were no doubt reluctant to pay a high price for a complete opera of which the most famous numbers, sung by their leading exponents, were perhaps already in their collections; moreover, previously unrecorded ensembles and complex finales did not take kindly to the restrictions of the early recording horn.

3. ELECTRIC RECORDING. The introduction of electric recording, in 1925, which was of decisive importance to the complete recording of the concert repertory, had nearly as great an influence on that of opera. At last the preponderance in the catalogues of favourite arias and duets began to yield to the increasingly frequent appearance of complete recorded operas. At first there was an element of cheeseparing in this development. Purely for economic reasons, it was then rare for such complete recordings to make use of the leading singers of the day – evidently, in order that these multi-record sets could be issued in the lower price categories. Collectors whose memories go back to that period will recall the excitement that was aroused when, at long last, extensive excerpts (though still not complete versions) of famous operas began to appear with leading exponents in the principal roles – as happened first with

Wagner during the period 1925–39 (which happened to be a great epoch in Wagner singing and conducting), and especially with the still celebrated abridged *Rosenkavalier* set of 1933 sung by the 'classic' cast of Lotte Lehmann, Maria Olszewska, Elisabeth Schumann and Richard Mayr. Unfortunately, the economic collapse of 1931 discouraged the all-star complete recordings of Italian opera which might otherwise have been expected from the Victor company because of the unparalleled availability of the world's leading singers during the long annual seasons at the Metropolitan Opera and at Chicago. The most that was then achieved in that line was the occasional appearance of isolated scenes, such as the Nile Scene from *Aida* with Rethberg, Lauri-Volpi and De Luca, and the final Tomb Scene from the same opera with Rosa Ponselle and Giovanni Martinelli.

It was indeed tantalizing, in those days, to scan, week after week, the star-studded casts at the Metropolitan and at the Chicago Opera, and to realize that only isolated arias and duets by such artists would ever become available on the gramophone. Long afterwards, semi-private and mainly unauthorized sources gathered together surviving tape-recordings made during the weekly Metropolitan broadcasts, and issued them to the public on LP in a more or less clandestine way. The big companies and many of the artists involved were at first understandably incensed at this invasion of their legal rights, but soon shrugged their shoulders at what they found themselves unable to suppress; and in more recent years the 'pirate' firms have come to be regarded as benefactors rather than as villains. Later still, changes in copyright law enabled such recordings to be made more widely available; some of the most notable Metropolitan broadcasts of the period – among them a complete *Rosenkavalier* with Lehmann, an *Otello* with Giovanni Martinelli, Rethberg and Tibbett, and a *Tristan* with Flagstad and Melchior – have even been officially issued by the Metropolitan, though sometimes at very high, fund-raising prices.

Meanwhile in Europe recordings of complete operas had become increasingly frequent. Even in Russia, with its long history of operatic recording dating back to the first years of the century, activity resumed in this field soon after the local adoption of electric recording in 1929. At that time, as during the previous post-revolutionary years, confusion prevailed in the matter of labels; of these there existed a great variety, such as Muzpred and Mustrest or Mustrust, which often took their names from various factories in or near Moscow still in operation after the Bolshevik coup of November 1917. The numerical confusion was largely resolved in 1933, when all factories came under the single control of Gramplasttrest; this organization used a single numbering system, notable for the fact that all 12-inch (30 cm) discs bore the prefix '0' – a system borrowed from that of the western Gramophone Company, and perpetuated from 1965 to this day, both for 78 r.p.m. and LP issues, by the sole eventual successor, Melodiya.

Even before World War II complete operas with casts drawn from those heard in the leading Russian theatres, more especially in the Bol'shoy of Moscow, had begun to appear; and these quickly became more numerous until even relatively obscure Russian operas were added to the list (together with the more popular Western operas, invariably in Russian translation). Sometimes these versions were inadequately cast and poorly recorded; but the standard soon improved in both respects, and even the Western collector began to realize that a remarkable generation of singers – among them, the contralto Nadezhda Obukhova, the tenors Ivan Kozlovsky and Sergey Lemeshev, the baritone Pavel Lisitsyan and the bass Mark Reyzen – had arrived on the Russian operatic scene (the sopranos, with the marked exception of the expatriate Oda Slobodskaya, were of a generally lower standard).

Among other Slavonic and East European countries, Czechoslovakia had during this time naturally been foremost, its national treasure of operas by Smetana, Dvořák and Janáček eventually finding their way into circulation as LPs, and doing much in that form to spread the knowledge of such fine works in the West; Poland and Hungary were not slow to follow suit. In Western Europe itself, quite large-scale, and eventually complete, recordings of famous operas with important and even 'historic' casts forged ahead. In 1928 French Columbia made an abridged recording of *Pelléas et Mélisande* including in the cast the original Golaud (Hector Dufranne), together with a Geneviève (Claire Croiza) and a Pelléas (Alfred Maguenat), both of whom Debussy had valued highly. In 1904 the original Mélisande, Mary Garden, had made a primitive disc of the song from the tower, accompanied by the composer; and it is tantalizing, now, to reflect that her active career lasted well into the period of electric recording without including another recorded note of *Pelléas*.

In those later years, unfortunately, and well into the postwar LP era, the French were not very active in the recording of such operas as might have been expected to form the pride of their repertory. For example, it was left to Colin Davis and Covent Garden to record for the first time (as late as 1969) the whole of Berlioz's *Les Troyens*; and while French singers and companies were enthusiastically involved in the first recordings of works by Lully, Rameau and Leclair (his *Scylla et Glaucus*), in the first worthy version of Gluck's *Iphigénie en Tauride*, and even in Chabrier's delightful trifle *L'étoile*, these sets would not have appeared without the stimulus of such American and English scholar-conductors as William Christie of Les Arts Florissants and John Eliot Gardiner of the Monteverdi Choir and the Lyons Opéra. It is only fair to add that, especially since the arrival of CD, the net of complete opera recording, in France and elsewhere, has been more and more widely flung.

French operas of more widely popular appeal had begun to appear in complete form during the inter-war period: among them a *Faust* with the veteran but still impressive bass, Marcel Journet, as Méphistophélès, and a *Carmen* with the admired tenor, Georges Thill, as Don José. Less characteristic of the period, but so artistically successful as still to be cherished in CD transfer more than half a century later, was the 1933 *Werther* of Massenet with Thill as the hero and Ninon Vallin as the heroine, Charlotte. Casting on that level was uncommon in France, as elsewhere; and it was not until 1942, in the dark years of the German occupation, that the French at last recorded, under Roger Désormière, a complete and exquisite version of their national treasure, *Pelléas et Mélisande*. In this labour of love the young and then unfamiliar principals were Jacques Jansen and Irène Joachim, who had lately appeared with the rest of the cast (notably Henri Etcheverry as Golaud) and the same conductor in an Opéra-Comique revival. Such were the sense of dedication and level of achievement among all those concerned in this enterprise that recent transfers of the set, both to LP and to CD, have found a ready welcome among numerous technically superior successors. It is ironical, now, to reflect that about the same time German radio developed and improved the taping of live operatic performances and broadcasts, as can be heard in such preserved radio broadcasts as those of Strauss's *Capriccio*, of a *Salome* planned to celebrate his 80th birthday (1944) with the young Ljuba Welitsch in the title role, and of a notable Karl Böhm *Ariadne auf Naxos* with the young Irmgard Seefried as the Composer.

During the inter-war period, when such facilities as we have just been describing were not yet available, one of the most ambitious attempts at operatic recording *in situ* was the despatch of a recording team to the 1927 Bayreuth Festival by the English Columbia Company (at that time not yet affiliated with HMV and the Parlophone-Odeon group to form the composite EMI), in order to capture excerpts from the *Ring* and *Parsifal* in the Festspielhaus, although not as yet during actual performances. That this was a pioneer effort beset by difficulties in practice is clear from the published results; yet there were successful passages, notably the Transformation Music from the first act of *Parsifal*, where the sound of the specially cast temple bells of Bayreuth could be impressively heard – which encouraged the company to embark on a considerably more extensive recording programme in the following year. This was apparently intended to provide a virtually complete recording of the *Tristan* performances of that year under Karl Elmendorff, and achieved that result with fair success throughout the first two acts; in Act 3 either the company's courage or their resources failed them, and only a very small part of this act found its way on to the published records.

4. AFTER WORLD WAR II. During the LP epoch, and still more in the present CD period, a great many operatic recordings have been made, both from live performances and from specially assembled forces in the studio. Argument has raged between the advocates of the two methods, the advantage in stage excitement and authenticity captured during a live performance being held by some to compensate for and even outweigh such attendant defects as uncorrectable inaccuracies and faulty balance caused by the stage movements of the performers; at the present time, moreover, a great deal of live recording is published simply because of the availability of high-quality broadcast tapes in circumstances where studio repeats might well have proved impossible to arrange.

In the inter-war period, before such problems arose, some historically valuable performances had been already captured in part or in whole. In Germany, selections from Kurt Weill's early successes, with original casts including Lotte Lenya in her prime, had appeared on Telefunken and German HMV (Electrola) discs; and these would doubtless soon have been followed by complete versions but for the arrival of Hitler and the Third Reich and the flight of the composer from his now hostile and dangerous homeland. In general, not much modern opera had been recorded, partly because of the timidity of the companies and the relative unpopularity of the music, and partly because of the difficulty of recording such music on 78 r.p.m. From the operas of Berg, Prokofiev and Stravinsky only a few standard 'concert suites' and transcriptions found their way on to 78 r.p.m. discs.

The situation was rather different in Italy, owing to the greater public esteem enjoyed by contemporary operas. Towards the end of Beniamino Gigli's career – in the years shortly before, during and after World War II – complete recordings of eight of his most famous operatic roles were made with the forces either of La Scala, Milan, or of the Rome Opera; although the casts were not especially distinguished, they were about the best that were then and there available. But none of these issues could truly be described as 'modern', even though one of them, *Cavalleria rusticana*, was actually conducted by its composer. After the war, the long-lived and still masterful Toscanini began to add complete opera recordings to the extensive scheme of his regular New York NBC broadcasts. Although some members of their casts seemed to have been chosen rather for their pliability than for their intrinsic merits, these sessions – all eventually issued and reissued by RCA Victor – yielded material of the utmost value, most of all in the sets of Verdi's *Otello* and *Falstaff*, in the early or even first performances of which the conductor had as a young man been personally involved.

Already in the inter-war years the gramophone had spread the renown of singers and of instrumentalists to an extent previously unimaginable. In Nancy Mitford's popular novel *The Pursuit of Love* (1945), Uncle Matthew (a figure based on the eccentric character of the author's father) is an avid enthusiast for the spectacular records of coloratura arias made by the American-based soprano Amelita Galli-Curci. When at last she crosses the Atlantic and begins (in 1924) her first English concert tour, Uncle Matthew makes a special journey to Liverpool in order to hear her in person, with disappointing results; thereafter, Galli-Curci's records remain silent. A few years later, in 1929, a series of Covent Garden performances starring the celebrated American soprano, Rosa Ponselle, had drawn very large audiences simply on the strength of her well-known recordings – in this case, fortunately, without any element of disappointment. Both these were no more than early instances of a process now too regular and too universal to arouse comment.

A landmark in the history of recorded opera was the first appearance – spread over a seven-year period and completed in 1966 – of the complete *Ring*, uncut, in a series of strongly cast and technically brilliant studio recordings under Solti. This derived from the enterprise of John Culshaw of the Decca company; his opposite number at EMI, the distinguished impresario and first-rate musician Walter Legge, was responsible for a long and still more enterprising series of recordings, largely orchestral but including much opera, in which he could draw on that company's brilliant roster of international artists, such as Karajan, Klemperer and Callas, guided by his own outstanding flair and taste.

About this time, however, and still more during the CD era of today, a change gradually took place in the contractual habits and attitudes of recording artists. They became less and less firmly tied to a single recording company or group of companies. This development – on the whole musically beneficial, since it allowed the most appropriate performers to appear freely together on records just as they already did in live performances – has been ascribed to the enterprise of an operatic tenor, who took legal action against a powerful record company for placing him under contract and then failing to record him, and established the principle that such a procedure was illegal, thereby heralding the end of the exclusive contract system. Whether this explanation is true or not, leading artists seem gradually to have discovered that it was worth their while, financially as well as artistically, to retain a large measure of personal freedom; and this new freedom simplified the task of the recording manager, who no longer found himself in an impasse because the indispensable star required for some cherished and ambitious project could not be weaned away from his own professional stable in order to take part in recording activity elsewhere.

Such developments certainly eased the introduction and circulation of new, unfamiliar and once reputedly difficult operas, which began to appear on disc in the 1950s – with Berg's *Wozzeck* (first performed 1925, first recorded 1951) and Britten's *Peter Grimes* (first performed 1945, first recorded 1959) in the vanguard. The CD format, at first expected to narrow an adventurous choice of repertory just as the first days of the LP process had once had a restrictive effect, turned out before long to produce diametrically opposite consequences – so that every month has for some time brought recordings of operas such as could hardly have been expected to turn up in a lifetime of the most assiduous and cosmopolitan opera-going. Not only do more and more of the voluminous works of Rossini, Donizetti and Verdi reach the catalogues, but also the operas of Franz Schreker, George Enescu, Albéric Magnard and many more. A cautious writer now hesitates to describe any opera as inaccessible on disc for fear of being proved wrong by the time his words are printed. As for the standard classics, it is scarcely possible to exaggerate the 'mushrooming', during the 1980s, of the record industry and its activities. All this, it may well be thought, is by and large to the good, in constantly increasing the choice available to the musical public; but it also makes that public increasingly dependent on the guidance of experts who themselves can scarcely contrive to keep abreast of the flood and to provide an adequate critical coverage of the available choice. There is now the corresponding danger of some long-desired recording turning out to have been already consigned to the ever-expanding scrapheap of gramophone history before it has reached an eager applicant.

5. RECORDS AS HISTORICAL DOCUMENTS. Fortunately, the increasing availability of publicly funded and administered record libraries has gone some way towards correcting the tendency towards impermanence encouraged by the sheer profusion of issued material. Public broadcasting companies, such as the BBC, soon discovered the need to preserve and make speedily available, for their own requirements, whatever uncommon material had been previously broadcast or commercially recorded; and many firms or private individuals have shown themselves willing to help in the task of preservation and dissemination. In Great Britain the principal public collection is that of the National Sound Archive (formerly British Institute of Recorded Sound, and now administered by the British Library). In the USA there are many such collections which enjoy a generally greater degree of financial support. The Library of Congress, which occupies the foremost position in this field, is rivalled and supplemented by public collections, such as the Rodgers and Hammerstein Archive of Recorded Sound (a part of the New York Public Library at Lincoln Center), and by several university collections, most notably those of Yale University at New Haven, Connecticut, and of Stanford University at Palo Alto,

California. These and other such institutions have shown the way to many others by supplementing their collections of printed and manuscript sources with similarly catalogued and organized collections of recorded material; and scholars have shown themselves to be not slow in profiting from this new availability of material for their studies.

To take a single instance: for some years past Will Crutchfield, a critic who previously wrote for the *New York Times*, has devoted much time and attention to the extensive recorded evidence of 19th-century performing practice as shown, for example, in the very numerous surviving records of the tenor Fernando De Lucia (1860–1925) and the baritone Mattia Battistini (1856–1928). His careful and detailed studies and musical transcriptions have shown that such a composer as Verdi must have expected to hear cadenzas and other ornaments spontaneously improvised and widely different from those to be found (themselves often very elaborate) in the printed scores; they have suggested, by extension, that a similar or still greater freedom from the printed scores of Rossini, Bellini and Donizetti would formerly have been expected, as also in the case of Mozart and of 18th-century composers in general. Similar studies (although in these categories the source material is less abundant) have been devoted to the work of the older keyboard or string performers, and also to orchestral practice as shown in recordings conducted by Sir Edward Elgar or Richard Strauss (notably in the work of Robert Philip). The general impression conveyed both in the instrumental and the operatic repertories is that performance styles were formerly much less rigid and less circumscribed by the printed notes than had been previously supposed.

In the present and the recent past, however, the record catalogues have supplied an increasingly full documentation of the styles in which earlier and contemporary operas were customarily performed. For example, during the inter-war years, recordings of extensive excerpts from the Wagner and Strauss operas were made by such authoritative conductors as Carl Muck, Bruno Walter, Beecham, Furtwängler and Toscanini, as well as by a splendid group of singers, several of whom have been already named. Personal observation and report suggest, however, that not many young students have in fact availed themselves of these easily accessible models, which their predecessors in earlier days crossed Europe and the Atlantic to consult in their student years. It has rather seemed as though an excessive passion for originality at all costs, for studying the score and then choosing their own way without further guidance, has inclined present-day beginners to neglect recorded models whose example could have been at least useful.

Perversely, perhaps, the best-known exception to this has been the numerous output of complete recorded operas and of extended operatic scenes by the Greek-American soprano and world-famous exponent of popular and also of long-neglected roles, Maria Callas. Callas did indeed furnish an incomparable model as regards the seriousness, fine taste and intensity of her phrasing and declamation; on the other hand, increasing and evidently ineradicable faults of tonal emission made her an unreliable exemplar of vocal purity and technical control. It has been said that disciples often copy not the virtues but the faults of a model. No doubt a generation of budding sopranos nourished on the bel canto mannerisms and insecurities of Callas would prove

hardly more satisfactory than a school of operatic basses who had taken as their exemplar, in Western as well as in Russian music, the highly individual style, often amounting to downright eccentricity, of that extraordinary genius, Fyodor Shalyapin.

Composers' recorded interpretations of their own music, whether operatic or symphonic, are often and naturally expected to provide better models of style than those of even the most notable contemporary or subsequent conductors. But such a preference cannot be taken for granted. While some composers are admirable conductors, others are not. Benjamin Britten belonged to the former category; and there can be no doubt that the long series of complete recordings of his operas made under his direction or supervision, from *Peter Grimes* (1959) to *Death in Venice* (1974), will retain their value as models of style so long as the operas themselves remain in the repertory – as can be said likewise, to some extent, of the performances by members of the original casts, notably Peter Pears.

At all events, the ever-increasing profusion and availability of even the rarest operas in complete recorded form should ensure that future students will suffer from no lack of models. The problem will be rather to discriminate between innumerable potential exemplars than to ensure their survival and accessibility. Nor can we always be sure of the status and suitability of many of these likely models. At the moment of writing, for example, the spread and popularity of CD-Video is in its infancy. It may seem possible – some might think even desirable – that a tendency may arise whereby the vocal and orchestral elements of such issues are subordinated to the visual; or even whereby the vocal and orchestral elements would be entrusted, as at present, to the leading available exemplars of the roles in the major opera houses of the world, while the visual aspect might be handed over to the latest and most fashionable director and designer, however eccentric, on the one hand, and to the most personable and glamorous of actresses, on the other hand, whose conception of operatic art as understood at the time of composition of the work in question is likely to be no more than rudimentary. Optimists might suppose that such a combination of talents might herald a new golden age of recorded opera, while more cautious observers are likely to fear that the introduction of elements so far removed from the conception of composer and librettist might well result in artistic chaos.

Grove5 (D. Shawe-Taylor); *Grove6* ('Gramophone'; D. Bicknell and R. Philip)

R. D. Darrell, ed.: *The Gramophone Shop Encyclopedia of Recorded Music* (New York, 1936–48)

F. W. Gaisberg: *Music on Record* (London, 1946)

R. Bauer: *The New Catalogue of Historical Recordings, 1898–1908/9* (London, 1947)

P. G. Hurst: *The Golden Age Recorded: a Collector's Survey* (London, 1947)

J. M. Moses: *Collectors' Guide to American Recordings 1895–1925* (New York, 1949)

B. Semeonoff: *Record Collecting* (Chislehurst, 1950)

F. F. Clough and G. J. Cuming: *The World's Encyclopedia of Recorded Music* (London, 1952, suppls. 1953, 1957)

Bielefelder Katalog (1953–) [biannual]

Gramophone Classical Catalogue (1953–) [quarterly to Dec 1990; biannual]

R. Gelatt: *The Fabulous Phonograph* (Philadelphia, 1954, 3/1977)

Voices of the Past (Lingfield, 1955–74) [catalogues of recordings issued by HMV and associated companies]

R. Philip: *Some Changes in the Style of Orchestral Playing 1920–1950 as shown by Gramophone Recordings* (diss., U. of Cambridge, 1974)

J. B. Steane: *The Grand Tradition: Seventy Years of Singing on Record, 1900–1970* (London, 1974)
Gramophone Records of the First World War: an HMV Catalogue 1914–18 (Newton Abbot, 1975)
B. Jewell: *Veteran Talking Machines: History and Collectors' Guide* (Tunbridge Wells, 1977)
M. Scott: *The Record of Singing* (London, 1977–) [with discs]
A. Blyth, ed.: *Opera on Record* (London, 1979–85)
P. Gammond: *Illustrated Encyclopedia of Recorded Opera* (New York, 1979)
A. Payne: *Grands opéras du repertoire: résumés des livrets, analyses musicales, discographie* (Paris, 1979)
W. Crutchfield: 'Vocal Ornamentation in Verdi: the Phonographic Evidence', *19th Century Music*, vii (1983–4), 3–54
E. Mordden: *A Guide to Opera Recordings* (New York, 1987)
W. Crutchfield: 'Voices', *Performance Practice: Music after 1600*, ed. H. M. Brown and S. Sadie (London and New York, 1989), 292–319, 424–58
C. H. Parsons, ed.: *The Mellen Opera Reference Index*, x–xii: *Opera Discography* (Lewiston, NY, 1990)

DESMOND SHAWE-TAYLOR

Redding, Joseph Deighn (*b* Sacramento, CA, 13 Sept 1859; *d* San Francisco, 21 Nov 1932). American composer and librettist. After graduating from the California Military Academy in 1874, he attended Harvard Law School (1877–9) and practised law in San Francisco. He served as president of the San Francisco Art Association (1885–7) and was active in the Bohemian Club. In 1902 he composed the score for the first of the 'Grove' plays presented at the open-air Bohemian Grove near San Francisco; subsequently he wrote librettos and incidental music for several productions, including the libretto for Henry Hadley's *The Atonement of Pan*. His earliest published compositions, chiefly for piano, voice and string quartet, date from the 1880s. The libretto he wrote for Victor Herbert's *Natoma* (1911), a romanticized treatment of an American Indian theme, demonstrates his preference for exotic subject matter. Redding's three-act opera *Fay-Yen-Fah* had its première at the Monte Carlo Opera House on 26 February 1925. The libretto by Charles Templeton Crocker, based on his Grove play *The Land of Happiness*, concerns a young Chinese nobleman who defies the evil fox-god to win the hand of the viceroy's daughter. Redding's arioso-like vocal lines and atmospheric use of oriental motifs recall both Debussy and Puccini. The San Francisco Opera Company presented *Fay-Yen-Fah* at the Columbia Theater on 11 January 1926. Both productions were sung in French. The vocal score was published in Paris in 1925.   HARRY HASKELL

Red Line, The [*Punainen viiva*]. Opera in two acts by AULIS SALLINEN to his own libretto after Ilmari Kianto's novel; Helsinki, Finnish National Opera, 30 November 1978.

Sallinen's second opera is set in 1907, the year of the first election under universal suffrage in Finland. Topi, a poor crofter (baritone), with his wife Riika (soprano) and children, is struggling to eke out a miserable livelihood in the bleak north Finnish backwoods. A marauding bear has killed their last remaining sheep; the Church coldly rejects appeals for help. Topi goes off to sell some game he has caught, and in the meantime a wandering pedlar turns up. He entertains the children with a ballad.

Soon afterwards a professional socialist agitator appears in the village. If only the poor peasants and their wives will draw a red line on the ballot paper, their oppression will be at an end, and a new era of justice and prosperity will dawn. However, for Topi and Riika the agitator's promises turn out to be hollow. When Topi returns from a logging camp, he finds his children dead from sickness and malnutrition, and Riika desperate with grief. In the end the bear attacks again. Topi rushes out to fight it; and finally Riika finds him dead, his throat cut in a red line.

The music of *The Red Line* is much more vivid than the starkness of the subject would suggest, and variations of mood are carefully structured. There is lyricism in the opening scenes, where Topi and Riika are bickering in their desperate plight; the pedlar's ballad is an attractive pastiche of folksong. A confrontation between two choruses, representing the old order and the new, contrasts traditional folk melody with revolutionary fervour. At the end, an anguished funeral march culminates in a searing cry of bitterness and pain.

ERKKI ARNI

Redondo (Valencia), Marcos (*b* Pozoblanco, Córdoba, 24 Nov 1893; *d* Barcelona, 17 July 1976). Spanish baritone. He was a choirboy in the cathedral of Ciudad Real, won a scholarship to the Madrid Conservatory, and in 1919 appeared with great success in *La traviata* at the Gran Teatro, Madrid. He studied further in Milan and sang in opera in Italy and the USA, but it was his zarzuela stage performances and recordings during the 1920s and 30s that made him one of the best-loved of Spanish singers. He had particular success in Alonso's *La calesera* (1925) and *La parranda* (1928), other composers with whose zarzuelas he was particularly associated including Millán, Guerrero, Luna, Díaz Giles and Moreno Torroba. He was the finest Spanish baritone of his time, and his recordings (which include duets with Conchita Supervia) reveal a voice of wide range and exceptional flexibility, clarity and expressiveness, with a particularly thrilling *pianissimo*.   ANDREW LAMB

Reece, Arley (*b* Yoakum, TX, 27 Aug 1945). American tenor. After studying in Texas and New York, he made his début in 1970 with the American Opera Society as Assad (*Die Königin von Saba*) and then joined the New York City Opera. He sang Alexey (*The Gambler*) and Jason (*Medea in Corinto*) at Wexford (1973–4); Hermann with the WNO (1977); Monteverdi's Irus (*Il ritorno d'Ulisse*) at Zürich and Edinburgh (1978); and the Drum Major (*Wozzeck*) for Scottish Opera (1979). He has sung at Amsterdam, Vancouver, Kassel, Gelsenkirchen, Berne, Madrid, Barcelona and Wiesbaden (Hugo von Ringstetten in Lortzing's *Undine*, 1991).

His roles include Florestan, Manrico, Otello, Canio, Calaf, Bluebeard, Don José, Filka Morozov (*From the House of the Dead*), Laca, Bacchus, Lohengrin, Tannhäuser and Tristan. His huge stature and a solid, well-focussed voice are appropriate to Siegmund and Siegfried (*Götterdämmerung*), which he sang at Warsaw (1988–9).   ELIZABETH FORBES

Reed, H(erbert) Owen (*b* Odessa, MO, 17 June 1910). American composer. He studied with Howard Hanson and Bernard Rogers at the Eastman School; he also studied privately with Roy Harris and at the Berkshire Music Center with Copland and Bernstein. From 1939 until his retirement he taught at Michigan State University. His awards include a Guggenheim Fellowship (1938–9) and many commissions, including one from Michigan State University for *Peter Homan's Dream*, a folk opera in two acts written for the university's centenary (1955). Reed's three chamber dance-operas, *Earth Trapped* (1962), *Living Solid Face* (1974) and *Butterfly Girl and Mirage Boy* (1980), all based on American Indian legends, blend ethnic and contemporary idioms.

Peter Homan's Dream (folk op, 2, J. Jennings), East Lansing, MI, 13 May 1955; arr. as musical, 1971
Earth Trapped (chamber dance-op, H. Alexander), concert perf., East Lansing, 24 Feb 1962; stage, San Francisco, Western Opera, 23 May 1970
Living Solid Face (chamber dance-op, Alexander and F. W. Coggan), Brookings, SD, 10 Feb 1976
Butterfly Girl and Mirage Boy, 1980 (chamber dance-op, Alexander and Coggan), Brooklyn, NY, 8 Feb 1985   RICHARD S. JAMES

Reed, Thomas German [German Reed, Thomas] (*b* Bristol, 27 June 1817; *d* Upper East Sheen, Surrey [now London], 21 March 1888). English impresario and composer. He first studied music with his father, Thomas Reed, who was conductor at the Haymarket Theatre and later the Garrick Theatre in London. Reed's first appointment was as organist at the Catholic Chapel in Sloane Street. In 1838 he became musical director at the Haymarket Theatre, where he remained until 1851 (during the temporary closure of the theatre, he produced Pacini's *Sappho* at Drury Lane in 1843). In 1852 he conducted a season of opera presented at Sadler's Wells by his wife Priscilla Horton (1818–95), a popular contralto and actress who had first appeared, aged ten, at the Surrey Theatre, London. Following their marriage in 1844 Reed directed the production of English opera at the Surrey, and together they made prolonged provincial tours. On 2 April 1855 the first of 'Miss P. Horton's Illustrative Gatherings' was held at St Martin's Hall. These performances evolved into 'Mr and Mrs German Reed's Entertainments' at the Royal Gallery of Illustration, Regent Street, and typically consisted of one or two short comic operas composed or adapted for the resident company of from four to six characters with accompaniment of pianoforte and harmonium (much later, an instrumental ensemble). Reed directed the entertainments, and he and his wife invariably appeared in the programme. Over the next three decades he commissioned nearly a hundred musical pieces, providing early training for many of the important composers and dramatists of the late 19th century. Among the composers who were enlisted by Reed were Arthur Sullivan, Frederic Clay, George Macfarren, Alfred Cellier, J. L. Molloy and Hamilton Clarke; among the librettists were W. S. Gilbert, F. C. Burnand, William Brough, Gilbert à Beckett, Robert Reece and Arthur Law.

In 1867 Reed leased the new St George's Hall, Langham Place, for the production of comic opera. Here he produced full-length musical pieces, with full cast and orchestra, including Sullivan's *The Contrabandista* (18 December 1867), Auber's *L'ambassadrice*, and *The Beggar's Opera*. This endeavour, however, was not a commercial success. Reed also played an important role in the development of the 'Savoy opera'. He produced six early pieces by W. S. Gilbert, whose *Ages Ago* (1869, music by Frederic Clay) was one of Reed's longest-running attractions. It was at the Gallery of Illustration that Gilbert and Sullivan were first introduced in 1869 by Clay; and the German Reed entertainments were later recognized as the breeding-ground for the Savoy

operas: many situations in the Gilbert and Sullivan operas have antecedents among Gilbert's early pieces.

As the composer of more than a dozen of the entertainments, Reed proved to be an imaginative and effective writer of music for the stage. Most of his librettos were provided by Burnand and Gilbert à Beckett, but of particular importance were his three collaborations with W. S. Gilbert: *Our Island Home* (1870), *A Sensation Novel* (1871) and *Eyes and No Eyes; or, The Art of Seeing* (1875). Apart from a few individual songs, his scores were unpublished, and with the exception of *Our Island Home* (autograph, US-NYpm) they appear to have been lost. When Reed's lease of the Gallery of Illustration expired in 1873 the entertainments continued at St George's Hall. After his death the enterprise continued under the direction of his son Alfred and the comedian Richard Corney Grain until they died, both in 1895.

selective list; all in one act unless otherwise stated; all first performed in London

The Drama at Home; or, An Evening with Puff (review, J. R. Planché), Haymarket, 8 April 1844
A Match for the King (comedy, C. J. Mathews, after A. P. d'Ennery and P. F. P. Dumanoir: *Don César de Bazan*), Haymarket, 7 Oct 1844
The Golden Fleece; or, Jason in Colchis and Medea in Corinth (extravaganza, Planché), Haymarket, 24 March 1845
Who's the Composer? (farce, J. M. Morton), Haymarket, 28 Oct 1845
The Wonderful Water Cure (operetta, B. N. Webster, after T. M. F. Sauvage: *L'eau merveilleuse*), Haymarket, 15 July 1846 [rev. of Grisar's opéra comique, 1839]
Our Island Home (W. S. Gilbert), Gallery of Illustration, 20 June 1870
A Sensation Novel (Gilbert), Gallery of Illustration, 30 Jan 1871
Mildred's Well, a Romance of the Middle Ages (F. C. Burnand), Gallery of Illustration, 5 May 1873
He's Coming (Via Slumborough, Snoozleton & Snoreham) (Burnand), St George's Hall, 17 May 1874
The Three Tenants (G. à Beckett), St George's Hall, 16 Dec 1874
The Ancient Britons (Beckett), St George's Hall, 25 Jan 1875
Eyes and No Eyes; or, The Art of Seeing (Gilbert), St George's Hall, 5 July 1875
A Spanish Bond (Beckett), St George's Hall, 1 Nov 1875
An Indian Puzzle (Beckett), St George's Hall, 28 Feb 1876
The Wicked Duke (Beckett), St George's Hall, 9 June 1876
Matched and Mated (Burnand), St George's Hall, 6 Nov 1876
A Night's Surprise (West Cromer [A. Law]), St George's Hall, 12 Feb 1877
No. 204 (Burnand), St George's Hall, 7 May 1877

DNB (G. C. Boarse)
C. E. Pascoe: *The Dramatic List* (London, 1880), 282–4
D. Williamson: *The German Reeds and Corney Grain* (London, 1895)
J. W. Stedman: *Gilbert Before Sullivan* (Chicago, 1967), 1–51
        FREDRIC WOODBRIDGE WILSON

Reeve, William (*b* London, 1757; *d* London, 22 June 1815). English composer. After working as an organist in Devon in the early 1780s, he went to London to help with the music at Astley's Amphitheatre, where the more popular performers were all horses; two songs survive from a burletta called *The Double Jealousy*. In June 1787 John Palmer opened his ill-fated Royalty Theatre. When he found that spoken dialogue would be illegal there, he was forced to present all-sung burlettas in which, being a poor singer, he could take little part. Of Reeve's contributions only *Thomas and Susan* was published in vocal score; most of the song tunes were traditional ballads. Palmer also staged a ballet called *Don Juan* so that he could mime the title role, and Reeve wrote much of the music. Dramatic miming was almost unknown at the playhouses. Covent Garden's first successful attempt at what we would call *ballet d'action* was *Oscar and Malvina* (1791); the plot, developed from hints in Ossian, was carried on entirely in mime and dance, but a few songs and choruses were added for variety. Shield was to have written the music, but he quarrelled with the management and went abroad, with the result that Reeve, who had been a minor Covent Garden singer for two seasons, was asked to complete the score. The success of *Oscar and Malvina* and the absence of any rival of the least ability made it possible for him to compose Covent Garden operas and pantomimes for the next 15 years; in their more ambitious productions he was told to collaborate with Mazzinghi. By chance rather than inclination he continued to be involved in ballet experiments. *Hercules and Omphale, Raymond and Agnes, The Round Tower* and *Joan of Arc* had no spoken dialogue or recitative to carry forward their elaborate plots, though all contained a few songs. As only his songs were published, one cannot tell how Reeve dealt with the more dramatic moments. He was much less interested in ballet than was John C. Cross, the librettist for many of his early operas. Cross devised the action of *The Round Tower* and *Joan of Arc*, and then went off to the Royal Circus Theatre where, with James Sanderson, he created much more adventurous story ballets of which all the music survives.

Reeve was a composer of negligible talent, and when an opera of his succeeded it was not because of the music. *The Caravan* drew crowded houses because, at the climax, a dog jumped into a tank of water and rescued a child. The success of this piece led Charles Dibdin (the older son of the composer Charles Dibdin, who was running Sadler's Wells from 1803, to install there a large tank of usually fetid water round which he devised his 'aqua dramas'. From 1808 until his death, Reeve, seldom now wanted at Covent Garden, wrote nearly all the Sadler's Wells music; he had earlier become one of the proprietors by buying five of the 40 shares. Dibdin admired his honesty and benevolence. The George Reeve who also composed for Sadler's Wells was presumably his son.

only works from which music survives are listed; all first performed in London and published in London shortly after first performance

LCG – *Covent Garden*   LSW – *Sadler's Wells*

Hobson's Choice (burletta, W. C. Oulton), Royalty, 3 July 1787, 1 song (?1790)
Hero and Leander (burlesque, I. Jackman), Royalty, ov., 2 songs (1787)
Thomas and Susan (musical entertainment), Royalty, vs (1787)
Don Juan (ballet, Delpini), Royalty, 23 June 1788, 3 dances, 4 songs
Tippoo Saib (pantomime ballet, M. Lonsdale), LCG, 6 June 1791, vs (songs)
Oscar and Malvina (pantomime ballet, Byrne), LCG, 20 Oct 1791, vs [Reeve's contribution], collab. W. Shield
The Purse (musical entertainment, J. C. Cross), Little, Haymarket, 8 Feb 1794, vs
British Fortitude (musical entertainment, Cross), LCG, 29 April 1794, vs
The Apparition (musical entertainment, Cross), Little, Haymarket, 3 Sept 1794, vs
Hercules and Omphale (pantomime ballet, Byrne), LCG, 17 Nov 1794, collab. Shield
Merry Sherwood (pantomime, Pearce and J. O'Keeffe), LCG, 21 Dec 1795, vs
The Charity Boy (musical entertainment, Cross), Drury Lane, 5 Nov 1796, ov., 2 songs
Harlequin and Oberon (pantomime, Wild and Follet), LCG, 19 Dec 1796, ov., 1 song

Olympus in an Uproar, or The Descent of the Deities (afterpiece, O'Keeffe, after K. O'Hara: *The Golden Pippin*), 1796
Bantry Bay (musical entertainment, G. N. Reynolds), LCG, 18 Feb 1797, vs
Raymond and Agnes (pantomime ballet, Farley, after M. G. Lewis: *Ambrosio, or The Monk*), LCG, 16 March 1797, ov., 4 songs
The Round Tower (pantomime ballet, Cross), LCG, 24 Nov 1797, songs, lib. in Cross: *Circussiana*
Harlequin and Quixote (pantomime, Cross), LCG, 26 Dec 1797, ov., 1 song
Joan of Arc (historical ballet of action, Cross), LCG, 12 Feb 1798, ov., 6 songs in short score
The Raft (Cross), LCG, 31 March 1798, ov., 2 songs
Harlequin's Return (pantomime, Cross), LCG, 9 April 1798, ov., 4 songs, MS lib. *US-SM*
Ramah Droog (comic op, J. Cobb), LCG, 12 Nov 1798, vs, collab. J. Mazzinghi
The Embarkation (musical entertainment, 2, A. Franklin), Drury Lane, 3 Oct 1799, vs
The Turnpike Gate (comic op, Knight), LCG, 14 Nov 1799, vs, collab. Mazzinghi
Paul and Virginia (musical drama, Cobb), LCG, 1 May 1800, vs, collab. Mazzinghi
The Blind Girl (comic op, T. Morton), LCG, 22 April 1801, vs, collab. Mazzinghi
The Chains of the Heart (comic op, P. Hoare), LCG, 9 Dec 1801, vs, collab. Mazzinghi
Harlequin's Almanack (pantomime, T. J. Dibdin), LCG, 28 Dec 1801, ov., songs
Jamie and Anna (Scots pastoral, 1), *c*1801, vs
The Cabinet (comic op, T. J. Dibdin), LCG, 9 Feb 1802, vs, collab. J. Braham, D. Corri, J. Davy, J. Moorehead
Family Quarrels (comic op, T. J. Dibdin), LCG, 18 Dec 1802, vs, collab. Braham, Moorehead
The Caravan (Reynolds), Drury Lane, 5 Dec 1803, vs
Thirty Thousand, or Who's the Richest? (comic op, T. J. Dibdin, after M. Edgeworth), LCG, 10 Dec 1804, vs, collab. Braham, Davy [Reeve also set a pantomime with same title, LSW, 18 April 1808]
Out of Place, or The Lake of Lausanne (operatic romance, Reynolds), LCG, 1805, vs, MS lib. *SM*, collab. Braham
Kais, or The Love in a Desert (4, Brandon), Drury Lane, 11 Feb 1808, songs, collab. Braham
The White Witch (C. I. M. Dibdin), LSW, 18 April 1808, ov., songs
The Magic Minstrel (aqua drama, C. I. M. Dibdin), LSW, Whitsun 1808, ov., songs
Harlequin High Flyer (pantomime, C. I. M. Dibdin), LSW, 4 July 1808, ov., 1 song
Castles in the Air (pantomime, C. I. M. Dibdin), LSW, 31 July 1809, 2 songs
The Red Beaver (melodrama, C. I. M. Dibdin), LSW, 15 April 1811, ov., 1 song
Dulce Domum (pantomime, C. I. M. Dibdin), LSW, 15 April 1811, 2 songs
The Council of Ten (Venetian water romance, C. I. M. Dibdin), LSW, 3 June 1811, vs
Rokeby Castle (aqua drama, C. I. M. Dibdin, after W. Scott), LSW, 19 April 1813, 2 songs
Who's to have her? (musical farce, T. J. Dibdin), Drury Lane, 22 Nov 1813, vs, collab. J. Whitaker
The Farmer's Wife (comic op, C. I. M. Dibdin), LCG, 1 Feb 1814, 1 song, collab. H. Bishop, Davy and others
The Corsair (aqua drama, C. I. M. Dibdin, after Byron), LSW, 1 Aug 1814, 3 songs
Brother and Sister (musical entertainment, 2, W. Dimond, after J. Patrat: *L'heureuse erreur*), LCG, 1 Feb 1815, *GB-Lbl, Lcm*, songs, collab. Bishop

30 other items listed in *NichollH*, music lost; many songs pubd singly and in contemporary anthologies, probably from theatrical works: see *RISM* and *BUCEM*

*

BUCEM; NichollH
J. S. Sainsbury, ed.: *A Dictionary of Musicians* (London, 2/1825)
C. I. M. Dibdin: *Professional and Literary Memoirs of Charles Dibdin the Younger*, ed. G. Speaight (London, 1956)
                                    ROGER FISKE/IRENA CHOLIJ

Reeves, Sims [John] (*b* Shooters Hill, now in London, ?26 Sept 1818, bap. 25 Oct 1818; *d* Worthing, 25 Oct 1900). English tenor. He made his début as a baritone in 1838 at Newcastle upon Tyne in Bishop's *Guy Mannering*. After three seasons he found that his voice was changing and studied with Tom Cooke. He sang second tenor roles with Macready's company at Drury Lane (1841–3) and then went to Paris and Milan for further study with Bordogni and Mazzucato. He made his début at La Scala in 1846 as Edgardo (*Lucia di Lammermoor*), returning to London to sing the same role at Drury Lane, where the next year he created Lyonnel in Balfe's *The Maid of Honour*. He appeared at Her Majesty's Theatre, singing the title role in *Faust* in the opera's first performance in English (1864) and Huon in *Oberon* (1866). He also sang Florestan, Carlo (*Linda di Chamounix*) and Macheath. His writings include an autobiography, *My Jubilee, or Fifty Years of Singing* (London, 1889).

H. Sutherland Edwards: *The Life and Artistic Career of Sims Reeves* (London, 1881)

C. E. Pearce: *Sims Reeves: Fifty Years of Music in England* (London, 1924)   HAROLD ROSENTHAL/R

Refice, Licinio (*b* Patrica, Frosinone, 12 Feb 1883; *d* Rio de Janeiro, 11 Sept 1954). Italian composer. After studying at the Rome Conservatory and taking priest's orders (1910), he taught at the Scuola Pontificia di Musica Sacra (1912–50) and was *maestro di cappella* at the Basilica of S Maria Maggiore (1911–47). Besides composing church music, 'mysteries', 'biblical scenes' and oratorios in the tradition of Lorenzo Perosi, he developed a tendency towards dramatic and theatrical music on religious themes, which led him to compose two operas with hagiographical subjects. *Cecilia*, written in 1923 to a libretto by Emidio Mucci, was performed in Rome at the Teatro Reale dell'Opera on 15 February 1934, with Claudia Muzio in the title role. The success of the opera led Refice to undertake another, *Margherita da Cortona*, a 'legend in a prologue and three acts', also to a libretto by Mucci; it was performed with success at La Scala, Milan, on 1 January 1938 (the stage design of Nicola Benois and Michele Cascella was particularly remarked upon). The careful and accurate reconstruction of historical setting, the juxtaposition of mysticism and passion, the visual interest and a musical style combining echoes of Gregorian chant with 20th-century harmony, together with a developing sensitivity in the orchestral writing, give these works a place in the Italian post-*verismo* tradition. *Cecilia* in particular won a degree of international fame, not least because Refice died while conducting a performance of it in Brazil. He left unfinished *Il mago*, an opera to a libretto by Mucci after a play by Calderón.

See also CECILIA.

DEUMM (R. Cognazzo)

M. Rinaldi: 'Le opere nuovissime: "Cecilia" di Licinio Refice', *Rassegna dorica*, v (1933–4), 143–6

G. Sallustio: ' "Cecilia" ', *Musica d'oggi*, xvi (1934), 98–101, 113

G. Gavazzeni: 'Lettera da Milano', *RaM*, xi (1938), 28–31 [on *Margherita da Cortona*]

E. Mucci: *Licinio Refice* (Assisi, 1955)

T. Onofri and E. Mucci: *Le composizioni di Licinio Refice* (Assisi, 1966)

A. Bartocci: 'Licinio Refice (1883–1954) a vent'anni dalla morte', *Bollettino ceciliano*, lxix (1974), 106–11

——: 'Ricordo di Licinio Refice e Raffaele Casimiri, maestri di

Mons. Haberl', *Festschrift Ferdinand Haberl zum 70. Geburtstag: sacerdos et cantus gregoriani magister* (Regensburg, 1977), 39–48
                                                        LUCA ZOPPELLI

Reform. A term much used in the literature of opera in respect of changes in methods of writing operas which are supposed to represent improvement. It has been used at many stages in the history of opera, including in particular the Arcadian reforms of the libretto and its treatment at the end of the 17th century (with the elimination of comic episodes and the depiction of heroic or pastoral themes; *see* ROME, §2), and above all the changes, identified especially with the rejection of Metastasian tradition or its abuse, as seen in the operas of Calzabigi and Gluck of the 1760s (*see* GLUCK, CHRISTOPH WILLIBALD, esp. §6, and *ALCESTE* (ii)) but also present in the work of many other composers, notably Jommelli and Traetta. Another conscious reformer, who tried to banish 'trivial' elements that were detrimental to the drama, was Mercadante. Wagner's changes were also regarded as in some respect 'reforms'. Most 'reforms' of opera have been viewed by their proponents as favouring dramatic elements, and especially dramatic realism, against abuses that had arisen from giving priority to purely musical factors.

Regamey, Constantin (*b* Kiev, 15/28 Jan 1907; *d* Lausanne, 27 Dec 1982). Swiss composer. Born of a Swiss (Vaudois) father and a Russian mother, he was self-taught as a composer. During World War II he was deported by the Germans, but escaped to Switzerland in 1944 and was appointed to the chair of Slavonic and oriental languages at the universities of Lausanne and Fribourg; he also toured as a pianist. Among his works are the operas *Don Robott* (1962; 5 scenes and 2 acts, E. Tauber), which was performed in 1970, and the children's opera *Mio, mein Mio* (G. Bächli, after A. Lindgren), performed in Hamburg in 1973. His music is a refined synthesis of oriental and Western thinking, and has an extremely complex style which makes use of some of the developments of serialism, atonality and modality. In his highly self-critical quest for original expression, Regamey did not stifle the emotive message, but nonetheless refrained from excessive expansiveness and violent contrasts. He treated the voice as if it were another instrument; the writing is always assured.

                                                        PIERRE MEYLAN/R

Regensburg. City on the Danube in Bavaria, southern Germany, formerly Ratisbon. In 1748 the princes of Thurn und Taxis moved from Frankfurt to Regensburg. Prince Alexander Ferdinand built a court theatre, where Italian opera was performed (1774–8 and 1784–6, directed by Theodor von Schacht). The Kapelle numbered 35 in 1777. The theatre was subsequently used by visiting directors, including Schikaneder (1786–9) and Ignaz Walter (1804–22). At the beginning of the 19th century a theatre with a drama school, on the model of Weimar, was built by the architect Emanuel d'Hérigoyen. It was destroyed by fire on 18 July 1849, and a new theatre, the Neues Haus, was built by Karl Kein to plans by d'Hérigoyen. In a neo-Baroque style with four tiers of seats, it opened on 12 October 1852 with *Les Huguenots*. The façade was renovated in 1859, and an iron curtain fitted in 1882. The theatre saw its heyday when Martin Wihrler was director (1857–73) and there was a permanent opera company with an extensive repertory. Prince Albert of Thurn und

Taxis was a distinguished patron from 1888 to 1935. Berti Eilers, director from 1900 to 1905, brought the *Ring* to Regensburg for the first time. The theatre was partly closed during World War I and did not resume regular performances until after 1918. In the mid-1920s the Munich Staatsoper gave guest performances under Knappertsbusch. The house became the Städtische Bühnen in 1933. It survived World War II undamaged, and underwent alterations in the 1950s and 60s; it now has 538 seats. The season runs from October to mid-July, and the repertory consists chiefly of drama and operetta.

D. Mettenleiter: *Musikgeschichte der Stadt Regensburg* (Regensburg, 1866)

S. Färber: 'Der fürstlich Thurn und Taxische Hofkomponist Theodor von Schacht und seine Opernwerke', *Studien zur Musikgeschichte der Stadt Regensburg*, ed. H. Beck, i (1979), 11–122
KLAUS J. SEIDEL

Reggente, Il ['The Regent']. *Dramma lirico* in three acts by SAVERIO MERCADANTE to a libretto by SALVADORE CAMMARANO after EUGÈNE SCRIBE's play *Gustave III*; Turin, Teatro Regio, 2 February 1843.

The libretto is drawn from the same source as Auber's *Gustave III* and Verdi's *Un ballo in maschera*, but the action is transferred to Scotland and the date changed to 1570. Gustave III becomes Count Murray (the *reggente* of the title; tenor); Ankastrom becomes the Duke of Hamilton (bass); and Madame Arvedson Meg (soprano). The leaders of the conspirators are Lords Howe (tenor) and Kilkardy (bass; more convincingly, it must be admitted, than the Sam and Tom of Verdi's Boston version); only Oscar (contralto) and Amelia (soprano) keep the names that Scribe originally gave them. The sequence of scenes is practically identical to that in Verdi's opera and many of the situations are strikingly familiar. There is little in Mercadante's music of the human intensity or lyrical strength that makes a masterpiece of Verdi's opera; nevertheless it has a refinement and richness of invention and a greater sense of personal involvement than is usual with Mercadante, giving this opera a special place in its composer's output.
MICHAEL ROSE

Reggio Emilia [Reggio nell'Emilia]. City in Emilia Romagna, northern Italy. Opera began in the second city of the duchy of Modena through the activity of local impresarios (Landi's *Sant'Alessio*, 1645) and travelling companies (Sacrati's *La finta pazza*, 1648). Performances, usually of directly imported Venetian works, were organized until the early 1670s by and for the aristocracy and given in the Teatro (or Sala) delle Commedie in the Palazzo del Monte di Pietà (in the present Piazza Battisti). Contemporary theatre plans show that seats were not for sale for single performances. The Commedie, which had been built in 1637 in stepped rows, subdivided in sectors, and enlarged with superimposed boxes and benches in the stalls, 1645–74, was rearranged in 1675 and a ducal box installed. The linking of the opera season and the spring Fair (only occasional before 1674, but a novelty in Italy) was mutually beneficial and became an institution.

In the decades spanning the 17th and 18th centuries works performed were mainly original, sometimes to specially written texts (e.g. Ballarotti's *Ottaviano in Sicilia*, 1692). Some were commissioned from local composers (Giannettini, *Tito Manlio*, 1701; A. M. Bononcini, *La conquista del vello d'oro*, 1717), others

from more celebrated musicians (Gasparini, *L'Eumene*, 1714, *Il tartaro nella Cina*, 1715, and *Bajazet*, 1719, a new setting of his *Tamerlano*; Porpora, *Didone abbandonata*, 1725; Vivaldi, *Siroe, re di Persia*, 1727); few were revived. The quality and frequency of productions declined in the 1730s and 40s, during the wars of succession and the Austrian occupation. An exception was a sumptuous production of Pulli's *Vologesco* (1741), which inaugurated the new Teatro 'dell'Illustrissimo Pubblico' in the Cittadella, built after the Commedie burnt down in 1740, in what is now Piazza della Libertà. This new theatre was designed by Antonio Cugini, with 130 boxes in four stepped rows and a gallery. After Francesco III's reinstatement in 1749 Metastasian *opera seria* dominated the fair seasons. Comic opera caught on after 1766 when a second season, at carnival, was established; even the principal season reverted to well-known *opere giocose*. Only with a grand first performance of Anfossi's *Motezuma* (1776) did both types of opera begin to co-exist in playbills.

After such significant events during the republican period as the first performance of Nasolini's *Timoleone* (1798), opera in the early 19th century continued along well-tried lines, maintaining a high standard. Fashionable composers had their works opportunely staged at the Pubblico. After a fire there in 1851 a small theatre, the Teatro Filodrammatico (43 boxes in three tiers), was built in the surviving foyers; operas were staged here, 1852–7, while a new, imposing theatre was being built at the eastern end of the Cittadella. This, the Teatro Comunitativo, now Teatro Municipale Valli, designed by Cesare Costa with 106 boxes in four tiers and a gallery, was inaugurated in 1857 with Achille Peri's *Vittore Pisani*; it suffered as a result of the financial uncertainties that followed the unification of Italy, yet the première of Franchetti's *Asrael* was nevertheless given there in 1888. By then other more popular theatres were presenting opera and operetta: the Teatro Croppi (1870, in via Emilia) and the Politeama (from 1927 Teatro) Ariosto (1878, on the site of the old Cittadella). The latter substituted for the Municipale in several fair seasons between 1890 and 1915, replacing it in 1925–38.

After some postwar seasons organized by impresarios, in 1957 the city decided to take over direct management of the Teatro Municipale. It became a 'teatro di tradizione' (one that is only partly funded by the state) in 1967, and was among the promoters of the Associazione Teatri Emiglia Romagna, a regional circuit for local and imported opera productions (chiefly from the main eastern European theatres). Renamed Municipale Valli in 1980, the theatre staged notable productions in the 1980s, especially with the director and designer Pier Luigi Pizzi. It also houses the Discoteca Storica Agosti, an important collection of historic opera recordings.

C. Ritorni: *Annali del teatro della città di Reggio* (Bologna, 1826–39)

G. Crocioni: *I teatri di Reggio nell'Emilia* (Reggio Emilia, 1907)

O. Rombaldi: 'Profilo della storia del teatro in Reggio Emilia dal 1568 al 1857', *Il teatro a Reggio Emilia* (Reggio Emilia, 1958), 57–97

G. Degani and M. Grotti, eds.: *Teatro municipale di Reggio Emilia*, iv: *Opere in musica (1857–1976)* (Reggio Emilia, 1976)

A. Cavicchi: 'Musica e melodramma nei secoli XVI–XVIII', *Teatro a Reggio Emilia*, ed. S. Romagnoli and E. Garbero (Florence, 1980), i, 97–133

M. Conati: 'La musica e Reggio nel secondo ottocento'; 'Primo novecento musicale reggiano', ibid, ii, 127–60; 265–86

P. Fabbri: 'Il melodramma tra metastasiani e romantici', ibid, ii, 111–25

L. Bianconi and T. Walker: 'Production, Consumption and Political Function of Seventeenth-Century Opera', *Early Music History*, iv (1984), 209–96

M. Conati: *Il 'Simon Boccanegra' di Verdi a Reggio Emilia (1857): storia documentata: alcune varianti alla prima edizione dell'opera* (Reggio Emilia, 1984)

S. Durante: 'Cantanti per Reggio (1696–1717): note sul rapporto di dipendenza', *Civiltà teatrale e settecento emiliano: Reggio Emilia 1985*, 301–7

P. Fabbri: 'Il municipio e la corte: il teatro per musica tra Reggio e Modena nel secondo seicento', *Alessandro Stradella e Modena* (Modena, 1985), 160–84

P. Fabbri and R. Verti: 'Struttura del repertorio operistico reggiano nel settecento', *Civiltà teatrale e settecento emiliano: Reggio Emilia 1985*, 257–99

L. Lindgren: 'Antonio Maria Bononcini e *La conquista del vello d'oro* (Reggio Emilia 1717)', ibid, 309–33

M. Pigozzi, ed.: *In forma di festa: apparatori, decoratori, scenografi, impresari in Reggio Emilia dal 1600 al 1857* (Bologna, 1985)

P. Fabbri and R. Verti: *Due secoli di teatro per musica a Reggio Emilia: repertorio cronologico delle opere e dei balli 1645–1857* (Reggio Emilia, 1987)

D. Seragnoli: *L'industria del teatro: Carlo Ritorni e lo spettacolo a Reggio Emilia nell'ottocento* (Bologna, 1987)

ALESSANDRO ROCCATAGLIATI

Regina. Opera in three acts by MARC BLITZSTEIN to his own libretto after Lillian Hellman's play *The Little Foxes*; New York, 46th Street Theatre, 31 October 1949.

William Marshall (tenor) from Chicago visits Alabama in the spring of 1900 to plan a new financial venture with three rapacious siblings, Regina Giddens (soprano) and Ben and Oscar Hubbard (baritones). Only the investment of her kindly banker husband Horace Giddens (bass) will ensure Regina's participation, but Horace is ill in Baltimore. Regina sends her daughter Alexandra (soprano) to fetch him. Oscar's aristocratic wife Birdie (soprano) fears that the family plan to marry her wastrel son Leo (tenor) to Alexandra. On Horace's return, Regina arranges a ball to celebrate the financial deal, but Horace refuses to cooperate. Leo steals Horace's bonds from a safe-deposit box at the bank; with these, Ben completes the deal with Marshall. Regina, baffled, turns against Horace. Next day, Horace changes his will, leaving only the bonds to Regina, knowing they are stolen. Regina taunts Horace, who has a heart attack and dies. Under Regina's threat of legal action, her brothers agree to her 75% share. She has won, but loses Alexandra, who breaks with her mother.

Commissioned by the Koussevitzky Music Foundation, *Regina* uses American forms such as field songs, spirituals, blues, minstrel, early Dixieland jazz and salon music, as well as formal arias, extended scenas and choruses, and unaccompanied speech to create a musical portrait of the country by turns dramatic and comic.

ERIC A. GORDON

Regio (It. 'royal'). Title used for many 'royal theatres' in Italy. The Teatro Regio of TURIN was built in the 1730s, burnt down in 1936 and was rebuilt in 1973; the Teatro Regio of PARMA was so named in 1849, having previously been the Teatro Ducale and Nuovo Teatro Ducale. The Regio Ducal Teatro (or Teatro Regio Ducale) of MILAN was opened in 1717 and burnt down in 1776, to be replaced by the Teatro alla Scala.

Re Hassan ('King Hassan'). Opera in three acts by GIORGIO FEDERICO GHEDINI to a libretto by Tullio Pinelli; Venice, Teatro La Fenice, 26 January 1939 (new version, reorchestrated and with drastically revised last act, Naples, Teatro S Carlo, 20 May 1961).

Though less convincing than his operatic masterpiece *Le baccanti* (composed during 1941–4), *Re Hassan*, written in 1937–8, represents a big step forward in Ghedini's belated development towards stylistic maturity. The rugged, starkly dissonant if at times rather static world of sound underlines a no less stark dramatic confrontation between opposing political forces, and between members of the same family, at the very end of Moorish rule in 15th-century Granada. The aging King Hassan (bass) refuses to pay tribute to Spain, thus causing a war between the two peoples for the first time in 200 years. Meanwhile his estranged queen Jàrifa (mezzo-soprano) has been encouraging their son Hussein (tenor) to try to usurp his father's throne. Family tensions reach breaking-point after Hussein has been taken prisoner by the Spaniards: he is offered his freedom on the condition that he should fight against his father and take over the Moorish kingdom, but hand over Granada to Spain. The Spanish king (who never appears in person) asks for Hussein's child as a hostage, thus causing Moraima (mezzo-soprano) – Hussein's wife and the child's mother – to die of grief. The opera ends (in the definitive 1961 version) with Hassan abdicating and committing suicide, having accepted the loss of Granada as inevitable.

The musical language of *Re Hassan* retains few of those direct signs of Pizzetti's influence that were evident in parts of Ghedini's earlier opera *Maria d'Alessandria* (composed in 1936). Yet the general reliance in the solo vocal writing on rapid, often highly charged (though sometimes rather monotonous) declamation can still be related, in a general way, to the older composer's example – as can the dramatic use of the chorus at several points. The orchestral imagery, however, already directly foreshadows that of *Architetture* (1940), often regarded as Ghedini's first fully mature instrumental work.

JOHN C. G. WATERHOUSE

Rehearsal (Fr. *répétition*; Ger. *Probe*; It. *prova*). By its nature, rehearsal is an elusive subject, no less so in opera than in other types of musical or dramatic performance, and one that has been little studied. Historical documentation is scanty, not only because it has been destroyed in the regular opera-house fires of the past but also because it has rarely been considered worth retaining. Reports on rehearsals do not often survive even in theatre accounts because rehearsal has not normally been specifically paid for but rather treated as an understood adjunct to performance. Diaries, reports, memoirs and other such sources supply most of such material as has come down to us.

The present article, then, makes no attempt at a comprehensive survey of the history of rehearsal. In its historical section, some of the surviving information regarding rehearsal patterns, procedures and timetables is presented. These have changed in the course of time as opera-house circumstances and priorities have changed: as the relative roles of singer, conductor, sometimes composer, stage architect or designer, and director – not to mention impresario or patron – have assumed more or less importance, rehearsal procedures have reflected it. In particular, the role of the director has altered: dominant by the late 20th century, he did not exist until the late 19th, and until that time the direction of rehearsals normally fell to the librettist or the theatre poet, although there are instances where the intendant and the ballet master, and even the composer, played a role in determining aspects of the staging (and certainly numerous instances too where established singers did precisely what they wished on the stage irrespective of any other supposed authority).

1. History: (i) Italy (ii) Germany and Austria (iii) France (iv) England. 2. Present-day practices: (i) Introduction (ii) Music (iii) Costumes, sets, lighting (iv) Staging rehearsals (v) New productions, revivals.

1. HISTORY.

(i) Italy. After early court performances, where the timing of rehearsals was set at the wish of the ruler – those for Monteverdi's *Arianna* at Mantua were reportedly prolonged over several months – the Italian norm down to the late 19th century was a short, intensive rehearsal period for new operas; this often had to run alongside performances of another work. About 1660 some singers were learning their parts, including long recitatives, in the summer preceding the Venice carnival season; but then as later the company rehearsed together for about 20 days, sometimes less. As little as a week was sometimes allowed for an 18th-century *opera seria*, with its small amount of ensemble work. The Mozart family letters from Milan, preceding the production of his carnival operas *Mitridate* and *Lucio Silla* respectively on 26 December 1770 and on the same date in 1772, both new productions, give a picture of how rehearsals were organized. For the former there were three recitative rehearsals, on 6, 8 and 21 December; there was a rehearsal with reduced orchestra on the 12th, the first with full orchestra (held in the *sala di ridotto*) on the 17th, two in the theatre itself on the 19th and the 22nd and the dress rehearsal on the 24th. For *Lucio Silla* (which unlike *Mitridate* calls for a chorus), there were only two recitative rehearsals, on 12 and (probably) 18 December, and three with orchestra, on the 19th, 20th and 22nd, before the dress rehearsal on the 24th.

By 1823 a guide to opera management stated, as the time allowed by custom for a singer to learn a part, 15 days for *opera seria*, ten for *opera semiseria* or *buffa*, but, for a 'fall-back opera' (rushed on because a new work had failed), only a few days. In 1853 *Il trovatore*, then new, was rehearsed from scratch at Reggio Emilia in 17 days, *Le prophète* at Bologna in 1860 in 16 (but the ballets had gone into rehearsal earlier). Experienced British and French observers testified to the disciplined routine that enabled Italian companies swiftly to put together an acceptable performance. Sometimes, however, operas were being written right up to the first night or beyond, like some musical comedies today; the rush might tire out the singers and make for a semi-failure on the first night, as with Rossini's *Il barbiere di Siviglia*. When repertory opera became the norm, performances were sometimes thrown on to the stage with one piano and one orchestral rehearsal; at the Teatro Colón, Buenos Aires, about 1910, the contracts of leading Italian singers provided that they would be fined if they needed more.

(ii) Germany and Austria.

(a) Before Wagner. The dispersed state of operatic activity in Germany in the 17th and 18th centuries, along with the variety of genres and institutional arrangements, made for marked differences in the care with which musical works were prepared for stage presentation.

At the courts that sponsored Italian opera, the music director or Kapellmeister was expected to devote considerable attention to rehearsals. Responsibility for preparing the solo numbers of individual singers was often delegated to a Korrepetitor, normally the leading violinist of the opera orchestra. For a new opera the composer, when present, ran the final rehearsals of the entire ensemble. As in Italy, the court's Theaterdichter or Hof-Poete was usually expected to serve as stage director. In addition, a music-loving ruler often participated directly in the supervision of rehearsals. Examples include Frederick the Great of Prussia and his successor Friedrich Wilhelm II, who sometimes played the cello in the orchestra during rehearsals.

Travelling German companies could at first devote little attention to musical rehearsals of Singspiels. The company of Abel Seyler was the first to hire both a music director (Anton Schweitzer) and a Theaterdichter (J. B. Michaelis), in 1769; F. L. Benda served from 1775 to 1779 as the troupe's rehearsal violinist (répétiteur). At the Bonn court theatre under Maximilian Friedrich rehearsals involved a keyboard player, a role frequently assigned to the young Beethoven by his teacher and the company's music director, C. G. Neefe.

Although singing skills were often indifferent in German companies, standards of gesture and ensemble were usually high, partly because most singers were also trained actors, partly because companies stayed together for many years (unlike the Italian opera establishments, which typically gave only yearly contracts to leading singers). Following French practice, at a first rehearsal a new text was read and its dramatic potential discussed by the entire company.

After 1750, the French theatre at Vienna under Maria Theresa required a general coordinator of rehearsals (this was Philipp Gumpenhuber, *sous-directeur des ballets*). Later, under the National-Singspiel (1778–83), Salieri's deputy Ignaz Umlauf supervised musical rehearsals while the actors J. H. F. Müller and later Stephanie the younger instructed the singers in gesture and declamation. For the enterprise's inaugural performance of Umlauf's *Die Bergknappen*, the ensemble held two daily rehearsals lasting several hours over a four-week period. At the rehearsals of the Italian *opera buffa* company that succeeded the National-Singspiel, the newly appointed theatrical poet Lorenzo da Ponte supervised the stage action while the Kapellmeister, Salieri, devoted meticulous care to musical preparations.

By the 19th century, the number of rehearsals given to a new work could range from just a few to several dozen. While head of the German company at Dresden from 1817 to 1821, C. M. von Weber, himself born into a German theatrical family, participated in all phases of rehearsal; first came the Leseprobe (at which he read and even acted the work), next rehearsals with individual singers, then two ensemble rehearsals without action, and finally two to four *Generalproben*.

In religious institutions, such as those run by Jesuits in Bavaria and Austria, responsibility for rehearsing and staging school dramas with music rested with the author, usually a senior professor of rhetoric. In many places schools routinely provided the chorus for civic or court operatic productions; they were rehearsed separately by the chorus master prior to the dress rehearsals.

(b) The Wagner era. From the early 1840s Wagner was concerned with the detailed preparation of his works as dramatic representations. He expected singers to familiarize themselves with the text, even before learning the music – a request that met with considerable resistance – and he insisted that the stage manager should not simply coordinate the activities of the singers, but should intervene, explain and direct. The notion of this kind of production rehearsal became an intrinsic part of Wagner's programme for a revolution in theatrical practice. Following his experiences in Paris, where incompetence and lack of cooperation necessitated no fewer than 164 rehearsals over a six-month period for the production of *Tannhäuser* (1861), and in Vienna, where the projected première of *Tristan* was aborted in 1862–3, Wagner called for a system of thoroughgoing collaboration between the chief musical coach, conductor and stage director, the last, in an historical innovation, to be 'an official of equal standing with the other two directors'.

This principle was put into practice at the first Bayreuth Festival, when Richard Fricke was invited to assist as choreographer and 'Regisseur' under Wagner's general supervision. In an intensive six-week period of preliminary rehearsals in 1875 Wagner himself sang through and acted the part with each individual singer. Fricke played a greater role in 1876, when three cycles of intensive rehearsals were held from the beginning of June to the opening of the festival in mid-August. The detailed preparation of the work, both musical and dramatic, was unprecedented in operatic history. Yet Wagner's apparently idealistic demands have become the norm, at least for productions of the *Ring*, in many houses in the 20th century. The unique conditions obtaining at Bayreuth, where the entire resources of the theatre can be given over to the preparation of productions for several weeks each year, are, however, regarded with some envy by directors elsewhere.

(iii) France. Unauthenticated details about Lully's rehearsal techniques in the later 17th century are reported by Durey de Noinville (*Histoire*, i, 64–5).

In the rehearsals that he took himself he allowed in only those people who were needed: the librettist, the particular musician, etc. He was at liberty to reprove his singers; he would advance defiantly on them … He had such a quick ear for his orchestra that he could discern an out-of-tune violin from the back of the theatre; he would run up and say to them, 'it's you! that isn't in the part!'

When the Paris Opéra rules were drawn up in 1714, Articles 26, 27 and 28 affected conducting and rehearsing (ibid, 135–7). Article 26, reporting that hitherto the tasks of *batteur de mesure* ('time-beater') and *maître de musique* had been confused, now proposed to separate them. Article 27 defined duties of the *batteur de mesure* 'not only to beat time both in performances and in rehearsals, but also to watch over the orchestral personnel, to ensure they go punctually to their work'. Article 28 concerned the *maître de musique*, who

will attend at least three times a week at 9am exactly at the *Magasin* [ancillary building], where a hall or room will be set aside, in which he will teach and rehearse the roles to the female singers who will go there for this purpose. He will also be obliged to teach [theory of] music to those ignorant of it. In all [stage] rehearsals and performances, he will be among the first present, to see that the female choristers are costumed and ready to sing; he will show equal care during the piece, and remain in one of the wings, a [scroll of] paper in hand, to start the choruses off and make them keep the beat.

No one was officially assigned to superintend the preparation of male singers. In the case of new works, Article 12 made different provision:

As it has often been observed that the poor direction on the part of those taking rehearsals very often prejudices a work's success, the composer of an opera may on his own, if it seem good to him, direct the rehearsals and may beat time even in the performances, without anyone else being able to join in except with his consent.

A document written by Mme de Graffigny describes Rameau taking a rehearsal of *Dardanus* in 1739 (see Sadler). It seemed chaotic to her, with 'interruptions', 'scoldings' and quite separate distractions from some 150 members of the public seated in the stalls. The orchestra, singers and dancers were taking part. Problems with the public at such rehearsals went on for some time; Meude-Monpas (*Dictionnaire*) protested that artists were thereby inhibited from working properly.

Just as today, the personality of those taking rehearsals was all-important. Grétry (*Réflexions*, ii, 102) shows how the librettist J.-F. Marmontel (who had also worked with Rameau) fared at the Opéra:

He was ambiguous: friendly when speaking privately to actors, supercilious when making observations to them in front of witnesses. If he delivered an opinion on stage, or if he shouted from the boxes, he caused laughter. At a general rehearsal of [Grétry's] *Céphale et Procris* at the Opéra [1775 or 1777], he had a well-lit table placed in the middle of the *amphithéâtre* in order to make notes, and each time someone made a mistake or sang out of tune, a person would call out from the auditorium: 'Write it down, clerk of the court!' His expedient was good, but ought to have been put to use in a grilled box, as Monnet did in his Opéra-Comique at the Foire.

This refers to the period before 1762; the evidence is seemingly corroborated by Sedaine, who noted (1769) that such a device enabled rapid improvements to be made to ensemble performance at the Foire St Laurent.

Papillon de La Ferté's 1774 *règlement* for the Comédie-Italienne (see Campardon) is not specific about regular rehearsals. However, newly engaged soloists had the right to appear in three works of their choice, and each was supposed to be given 'a full stage rehearsal' (Article 6). For totally new *opéras comiques* the finished score was supposed to be subject to approval by the governing committee during a prepared run-through in the theatre itself, where 'all indispensable members of the orchestra will have been summoned, and the actors, each in their style [*genre*], will sing the roles that will duly have been sent them in advance in order to give them time to prepare' (Article 7). Grétry mentions in his *Mémoires* (i, 416) that he coached Mme Dugazon in the 1780s at her own request, in roles he wrote for her; he goes on to remark that Pierre Garat, who was untrained, did just as well or better by native instinct in preparing roles. This is a salutary reminder that opera singers were appreciated as individual artists first and interpreters second.

Some rehearsals at the Comédie-Italienne from 1774 were accompanied by two violins and a cello. Framery (*De l'organisation*, 132) pointed out the disadvantages in not using a piano for rehearsals, a method the native Italians were practising at the new Théâtre de Monsieur, but the French *opéra comique* musicians were not: 'A difficult passage can easily be repeated ten times; one is reluctant to have seven or eight instruments repeat in the same way. With the Italians' method three or four general rehearsals are sufficient'.

In the 19th century, the complexity of works by Spontini and Meyerbeer, for example, could provoke enormous numbers of rehearsals at the Opéra. In December 1819 the *Allgemeine musikalische Zeitung* reported of Spontini's *Olimpie*: 'the first two acts have been in rehearsal for a year and a half and ... the singers received the parts for the third and last act only four weeks ago' (see Libby, 191). Further details are strikingly recalled by Véron in his *Mémoires*. The librettist Scribe took an active part in rehearsals, at least when Véron was director (1831–5). One dress rehearsal for Meyerbeer's *Robert le diable* lasted until 3.00 a.m.; it was without spectators; the music was accompanied by a quartet of strings. Meyerbeer's attention to detail is seen in a letter to Halévy (*chef de chant* of the Opéra) concerning rehearsal plans for *Les Huguenots* (1836): he requested two soloists and female choristers at 11.30 a.m. for specific work on Acts 2 and 3, then male choristers and soloists at 12.30 p.m. for work on Act 1. This will take place in the foyer, whose piano, he demands, be thoroughly improved from its dismal state in the last rehearsal (see Tiersot, 129).

By now, theatre composers in France were paradoxically 'not entitled to direct their own works', as Berlioz ruefully noted in his *Mémoires* (chapter 48). His account of *Benvenuto Cellini* in rehearsal vividly illustrates the problem of a conductor (Habeneck) failing to grasp the composer's personally expressed intentions in Tableau 2, going at half speed and thus incommoding the dancers. Habeneck 'stopped and, turning round to the orchestra, said, "Since I am unfortunately unable to satisfy M. Berlioz, we will leave it at that for today. You may go, gentlemen." And there the rehearsal ended' (Cairns, 244). Gounod exerted more control by having a minister agree to exclude the public from final Opéra rehearsals; for 20 years he struggled in print to end the very abuse from which Rameau had suffered over a century earlier.

(iv) England. In London, rehearsals were in some degree open to the public. Until the Licensing Act of 1737, which required librettos to be submitted for censoring a fortnight before the first public performance, firm dates were only exceptionally assigned in advance to a première. Instead, opera was rehearsed until sufficiently polished for money to be taken at the door. For Purcell's semi-operas, two or three months' rehearsal time was normal (as opposed to a week or less for a straight play). Sometimes rehearsals were held at court, apparently without scenery or costumes, as in the case of *Albion and Albanius* (1685); for *The Fairy-Queen*, rehearsals began in November 1691 for a première probably planned for January 1692 but which in fact was postponed until 2 May 1692. For Italian opera (later in the 18th century) the initial rehearsals concentrated on scenery, machines and dancers; arias and *secco* recitative were rehearsed separately. A number of full orchestral rehearsals for the subscribers and their friends followed.

In the second half of the 18th century, dress (or 'general') rehearsals were not necessarily in costume; they were often sung through without breaks, with the singers using only half voice (the subscribers protesting that they were inaudible), and the lighting too was greatly reduced in the auditorium to save cost. Later in the century, especially for operas with ballet, special lighting rehearsals were held. The French-Swiss choreographer J.-G. Noverre, who worked in London in the 1780s, demanded numerous production rehearsals of lighting and scene changes to ensure their smooth running. Singers were expected to know their parts by the time of the dress rehearsals; and at least in the early years of the century the principals each had a harpsichord or spinet in their dressing-rooms.

For an Italian opera a month of rehearsal was normally regarded as a minimum. When, under Giardini in the early 1760s, the London opera season was planned to begin at the end of October, he required the singers to be available by the end of September (in fact, they did not arrive until much later, and the opening night was accordingly delayed). In the 1780s and 90s rehearsals were all held in the opera house itself, those for the recitatives in small ante-rooms, while arias and en-

1. Rehearsal for a revival of Thomas' 'Hamlet' at the Paris Opéra (Salle Garnier) on 31 March 1875: engraving from 'Le monde illustré' (10 April 1875)

2. 'Rehearsal of an Opera' (c1709), by Marco Ricci, one of a complex series of paintings dating from the artist's period in London as a scene painter at the Queen's (later King's) Theatre, Haymarket; it has been suggested that the central figure may be the castrato Nicolini, and that the rehearsal may be for Nicola Haym's 'Pyrrhus and Demetrius' (Ricci was designer for the 1709 revival)

sembles were practised with piano or harpsichord in the large coffee-room above the foyer. There was no fixed time for rehearsals, though they were usually held on Monday, Wednesday and Friday mornings (Tuesday and Saturday being the nights of public performances). When word got round that a new work was being rehearsed, large crowds assembled, even to hear the *secco* recitatives.

No single person was in charge; the composer or arranger presided at the keyboard and attended to the singers, but the leading violinist had sole authority over the orchestra (in matters of tempo and tuning), and singers' suggestions and complaints normally had to go through him. In a pasticcio each singer in effect directed his or her own arias. In the course of rehearsal extensive changes and cuts might well be made; in some degree this was the final stage of composition. In spite of elaborate preparations, things could go badly wrong. In April 1780 during a performance of Sacchini's *Rinaldo*, Pacchiarotti was hurt when attacked by 12 under-rehearsed Furies and complained of bruising and burning from their torches.

2. PRESENT-DAY PRACTICES.
(i) *Introduction.* Rehearsal is the final and most crucial stage in the production process of an opera. Ideally, contractual arrangements with artists and suppliers will be complete by the time it begins so that the energy of all concerned can be directed towards the artistic realization of the project. Up to this point, artistic decisions will have been entirely in the hands of the production team – conductor, director, designer – chosen by the management. Their decisions will have foreclosed on most of the available options to arrive at an agreed conceptual framework for the production. The amount of leeway will depend largely on the personalities involved and their degree of methodological rigidity. In any case, the purpose of rehearsal is to close all the remaining options in order to determine the unique nature of the production.

Those elements requiring rehearsal will be the principal singers, the chorus and the orchestra, as well as the scenery, costumes, lighting and any dancers and extras. Each of these will be capable of separate rehearsal and in the early stages this is normally done. As the rehearsals progress, they are gradually brought together – the principals will be joined by the chorus, then any ballet and extras. Early rehearsals are usually held on a rehearsal stage or in a room of suitable size where some but probably not all of the scenery can be erected and the correct furniture and properties or suitable substitutes provided. When rehearsals move to the stage itself, the full scenery will be available. Meanwhile, technical rehearsals will have been conducted to establish the smooth running of any mechanized procedures and to perfect scene changes.

Lighting rehearsals will then complete the creation of the imaginary world in which the events of the drama will take place. Usually the next additions will be costumes, wigs and make-up. Most designers prefer this stage to occur after the lighting is completed, for obvious reasons, although elements of costume which may present handling difficulties for the artists or which are deemed helpful in the development of character may be added at an earlier stage (such as Falstaff's padding, Turandot's train or *commedia dell'arte* masks).

Some time after the production reaches the stage, the orchestra will join rehearsals in the pit, having already been at work with the conductor. A particularly important occasion is the *Sitzprobe* (the German word is current in all English-speaking countries), a rehearsal where the singers sit and work with the orchestra and conductor to sort out purely musical problems, undistracted by the demands of the staging.

The final rehearsals unite every element of the production as developed over the rehearsal period. Interruptions for corrections become fewer as the collective will grows to achieve something close to a complete run-through, so that the performance gathers its own momentum and the performers can pace themselves.

After this, the next significant stage is performance before the public. It has become a common if not universal practice to invite a public audience to the final dress or general rehearsal (*Generalprobe*); this is more likely to be a select group than the public at large. Much can be learned from its reaction, and valuable last minute fine-tuning done.

(ii) Music. For the chorus, musical rehearsals will consist of teaching the notes before matters of balance and interpretation are taken in hand. In most cases language coaching will be a necessary adjunct. For the orchestra, a complex or new work will involve sectional rehearsals where individual groups will tackle the score in detail to save time and tedium later; then there will be a number of sessions for orchestra alone, presided over by the conductor, before forces are joined with the stage.

Whereas in a play the actor will probably arrive not knowing the part, it is traditional, not to say obligatory, for a solo singer to know his or her music before rehearsals begin. This obviously saves time and facilitates dialogue with the director and conductor from a position of strength. Thus, for the soloists, pre-production rehearsals consist of coaching sessions with a pianist (the répétiteur) where musical and linguistic correction will certainly be made but where interpretation will be the main thrust of the work. A répétiteur can make a major contribution to the success or otherwise of a singer's portrayal. Ensemble rehearsals, involving anything from two to four artists, will also be held, where in addition to the foregoing points vocal and dramatic balance are established.

(iii) Costumes, sets, lighting. Costume and wig rehearsals, or fittings, must be carried out in the workshops on every individual involved in the performance. In a new production, the designer will be present and much is liable to be changed as the realities of a face or figure prevail over the ideal usually projected by the design sketch. These adjustments are liable to continue until the final dress rehearsal or even beyond. In a revival, compromises are often necessary owing to the infinite variety of shapes and sizes of body surrounding the great voices of the world. The star singer who brings 'the costume', along with 'the interpretation', in a much-travelled suitcase has not yet disappeared from the operatic scene, though he or she is increasingly discouraged.

Technical rehearsals begin with the installation of the scenery on stage for the first time. This involves such varied tasks as flying all the painted cloths, borders and other pieces on predetermined lines in such a way that they function smoothly in relation to one another, to the lighting equipment and to the scenery standing below. Revolves, mobile stages and trucks, traps, towers and winches and all the usual installations of a stage are mobilized and any errors or awkwardness of construction or function identified and eliminated, if possible before the artists use the scenery. Scene changes are then roughly rehearsed to ensure ease of handling. In many cases these changes have to be completed within a prescribed musical time, or with sensitivity to musical mood; such aspects have gradually to be perfected in the course of later rehearsals.

Once the setting has been finalized, lighting rehearsals may be conducted with confidence, for now it is possible to determine the setting of many hundreds of lamps, from above, below and the side of the stage as well as from the auditorium itself, so that they are correctly angled, focussed and coloured for each scene, and positioned in such a way that they do not impede the movement of the performers, cause unwanted shadows or cast light on to surfaces where not required. Then the intensity of each lamp must be adjusted for each individual lighting state (or 'cue'), according to the exigencies of the atmosphere required and the performers within it. This is a long and painstaking process, and the one perhaps least susceptible to advance determination, but which happily can, thanks to modern, computerized technology, be continuing unobtrusively throughout the later staging rehearsals.

(iv) Staging rehearsals. Throughout the rehearsal period the main field of activity is the staging rehearsal, led by the director and focussed on the principal singers. His supporting personnel would be an assistant director or two, a stage manager and a property manager who

3. Boris Goldovsky directing the New England Opera Theater in a rehearsal (1948) of the quintet from Act 2 of Bizet's 'Carmen'; to promote the singers' self-reliance and dramatic integrity in the performance the company frequently rehearsed with the singers facing away from the conductor

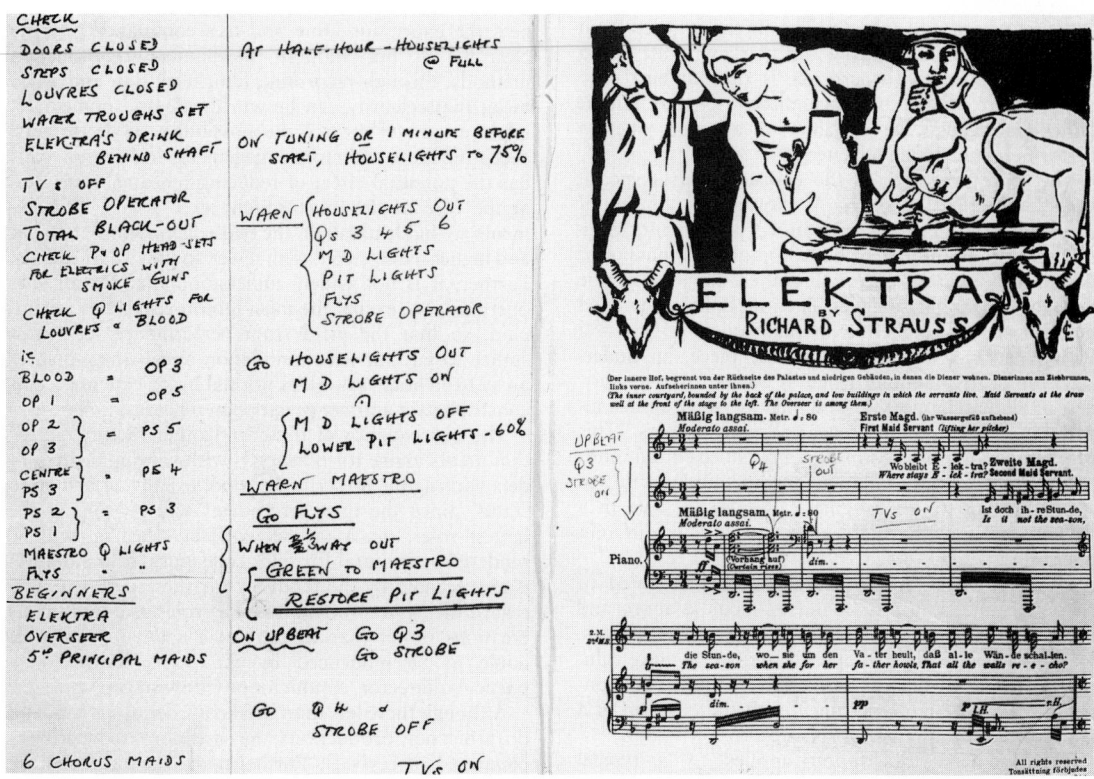

4. Opening pages of the stage manager's prompt score for the Götz Friedrich production of Richard Strauss's 'Elektra' at Covent Garden, London, 1990: the numbers refer to wings (numbered from downstage); PS – prompt side (normally stage left); OP – off prompt side; Q – cue; FLYS – fly tower

between them are responsible for the smooth operation of the rehearsal, the provision of necessary props, furniture and rehearsal clothes, the marking of the floor to indicate the available performing space and constraints and the keeping of a daily record (constantly updated) of the staging. The assistant director's records are designed to assist the director in developing his ideas and to provide information for the singers. The stage manager's records are designed to facilitate the transfer from rehearsal room to stage and to provide a framework of organization for what can be hundreds of people responding at innumerable points on and off stage to a variety of musical or visual cues. The master score that finally emerges from the rehearsal process will be called the 'prompt score' (see fig.4), and will contain, in addition to a simplified outline of the production, all the cues and information necessary for running a performance. The stage manager charged with this task is said to be 'on the book'; his importance cannot be overstated. The master score prepared by the assistant director will contain much more detail of stage movement, together with notes on motivation and character, and will provide the rubric for future revivals.

On the musical side, the personnel at the director's rehearsals will consist of a pianist, a prompter, a language coach and a conductor. The last named will often be the conductor of the performances, and when this is so the production as a whole is likely to be best served, because ideally it should be a close collaboration between conductor and director as artistic equals. When the conductor is too busy, or indifferent to the production, or unwilling to be bored by the sometimes lengthy and tedious business of staging, there is a risk of

divergences of opinion surfacing too late to be anything other than damaging. When the conductor himself is not present, a substitute will be provided from the theatre's music staff. If the chorus is present, the chorus master is on hand to provide assistance with questions of balance and vocal grouping within the framework of the director's requirements. Likewise, a choreographer and a fight director might also be present, and, where children are involved, a chaperone.

On the first day of rehearsal, most directors like to discuss with the company their general concept of the production, reveal the set and costume designs, and explain how they embody the concept. Any historical and geographical relocation would be discussed in terms of its gestural or expressive consequences, and major questions of style would be examined.

Thereafter the staging would be developed as a symbiosis of human interaction and stage movement (or 'blocking'). The latter should arise naturally and expressively from the former. Occasionally the exigencies of vocal balance with heavy orchestration lead to hard-fought compromises but excellent results can be achieved with a sympathetic conductor, while the general use of TV monitors has all but disposed of the old tell-tale sight of the singer addressing passionate emotions to the conductor instead of the appropriate recipient on stage.

Singing at full voice is not a practical proposition throughout rehearsals as the constant strain on the vocal cords could be damaging. A special vocal technique has been developed specifically for rehearsal purposes, called 'marking'; it entails singing the notes at pitch or an octave either way in a vocal position somewhere between speech and falsetto. The method varies from singer to singer, and not all can mark without losing dramatic intensity. The practice is thus at best only grudgingly tolerated by stage directors, who find it difficult to gauge the dynamic of a scene when a performer is not giving full energy.

The stage rehearsal of the chorus requires special skills and great patience. A chorus can be moral commentator, detached spectator, participant, even protagonist: an indifferent backdrop or an impassioned populace. Sometimes any or all of these elements can be brought to bear in a single production. Imbuing a mixed body of people numbering anything up to 150 with a strong personal commitment to the piece, an understanding of its manifold demands and a reactive alertness to all that happens around them on stage almost invariably requires more rehearsal than it gets. This problem is compounded in that any chorus in an international opera house will be singing in – and reacting to – anything up to six languages besides its own in a season, and may be performing up to four different operas in a week.

However well a role has been prepared ahead of rehearsal, uncertainty is bound to recur as more and more details of staging are loaded on to the singers. Hence the role of the prompter is frequently more valuable in rehearsal than in performance, just as his contribution can be more detrimental to the creation of a concentrated dramatic atmosphere.

The foregoing description applies to a typical rehearsal process in a well-run and properly funded opera house. There are likely to be differences of emphasis and timing between new productions and revivals.

(v) New productions, revivals. A new production of a standard-length work will not normally be rehearsed for less than four weeks by a self-respecting company. This period might be extended for a larger or specially complex work or for a director who claims he cannot manage in the time. The character and quality of the rehearsals will be determined largely by the director. Some are tough disciplinarians, others prefer a loose rein; some are well prepared, others prefer to let their knowledge of the piece grow with rehearsals; some come with a strict blueprint of requirements, others prefer to work with the singers towards a pre-determined goal; some welcome suggestions, others resent them; some work closely with the verbal text, others let the music determine the basic course of the production. Most are a mixture of all elements.

The rehearsal of a new work would involve an additional and potentially very far-reaching process, namely the shaping of the work itself. It is rare for a new composition to transfer unmodified from page to stage, and few major works are without their history of cutting, transplanting and re-composing right up to the last minute as rehearsals reveal damaging flaws or exciting new possibilities. These changes could vary from the adjustment of a vocal line to suit a singer to the excision of a whole scene for reasons of brevity; historically, there are numerous instances of the shortening of arias and of the trimming – or the extending – of orchestral passages to accommodate the stage action or scene changes.

The realities of the late 20th-century opera industry do not always conform to the standard procedures already outlined. The celebrity factor is not new – witness the enormous fame and fees commanded by the castratos – but modern mechanical reproduction methods, through recording, film, television and video mean that celebrity can be worldwide and immediate, while air travel creates the possibility of performers' accepting more and more engagements in a season. This has the potential effect of reducing rehearsal time, and in the case of the most sought-after artists, managements are liable to fall on the two-edged sword of higher and higher fees coupled with fewer and fewer rehearsals. Further, it is not widely understood that for all solo opera singers, except the most junior, rehearsals are unpaid, so that the yield from performance fees must suffice to pay for accommodation and living expenses away from home as well as normal living expenses. This constitutes yet another pressure on rehearsal time.

The consequence of these and other factors can be that artists arrive for rehearsals with varying degrees of delay during the prescribed period, usually according to status. Since the most prominent will be singing the largest roles, much of the work at rehearsal will be rendered conjectural for their colleagues. This situation is exacerbated by the tendency for these performers to regard their interpretations of key roles as autonomous creations rather than as part of a dramatic ensemble liable to be influenced by the interpretation of a particular director, conductor or fellow singer.

Although these less than ideal considerations can, and do, afflict new productions, they are more frequently encountered in revivals. Furthermore, such revivals are understandably subjected to time-constraints on rehearsal, which must often be carried on without the presence of the original director. Maintaining high standards here is a major task, but it must be allowed that some of these performances succeed as if by magic at a very high level. That is often because, thanks to the foregoing circumstances, there evolves a standard interpretation of each major repertory piece which is highly developed and convincing. In such an opera as *Tosca* the experience is somewhat akin to three ocean liners docking at the production while all the supporting roles move in like tugs and tie up to them; rehearsals are largely a matter of avoiding collision.

In the conveyor-belt conditions prevailing in many international houses and indeed in many German provincial houses, singers often perform demanding roles with no more rehearsal than a quick word on tempos with the conductor and a same-day indication from a staff assistant of the positions of relevant doors, windows and furniture. Many is the time that the Marschallin has met her Octavian for the first time in bed.

*

ITALY

Marco Faustini papers (*I-Vas*, Scuola Grande di S Marco, b. 188 c. 170–1, 174, 208)

Notarial documents for Giuseppe Scolari's *Il ciarlatano* [Venice, S Moisè, aut. 1759] (*I-Vas*, notarile atti, *buste* 4290 ff. 549v–551r, 555r–v)

G. Valle: *Cenni teorico-pratici sulle aziende teatrali* (Milan, 1823), 90–91

J. Ebers: *Seven Years of the King's Theatre* (London, 1828), pp.xxvii, 85

Alessandro Lanari papers, 1838, 1849 (*I-Fn*, Carteggi Vari 365/23, 34, 59, 393/47–59)

'Promemoria serale per lo spettacolo autunnale 1852', 'Giornale delle prove e delle recite', 1860 (*I-Bas*, Deputazione dei Pubblici Spettacoli, tit. I, rub. 1, 1853, 1860)

Correspondence: Settimio Malvezzi to Giovanni Ricordi, 1853 (*I-Mr*)

L. Quicherat: *Adolphe Nourrit* (Paris, 1867), i, 436–7; iii, 310, 330, 338

Correspondence: Teresa Brambilla Ponchielli to Amilcare Ponchielli, 1876 (*I-Ms*, CA 2439–42)

Cesare Ciacchi: contracts with G. De Luca, F. Constantino, G. Pareto, A. Pintucci, F. Anitua, 1909–10 (*ARG-BAc*)

W. Armstrong, ed.: *Lillian Nordica's Hints to Singers, together with an Account of Lillian Nordica's Training for the Opera* (New York, 1923), 30–34

B. Brunelli: 'L'impresario in angustie', *Rivista italiana del dramma*, v (1941), 311–41, esp. 336–8

A. Basso, ed.: *Storia del Teatro Regio di Torino* (Turin, 1976–82), i, 217–9; ii, 705–11

M. Rinaldi: *Due secoli di musica al Teatro Argentina* (Florence, 1978), i, 492–501

J. Rosselli: *The Opera Industry in Italy from Cimarosa to Verdi* (Cambridge, 1984), 6–9

GERMANY

H. Porges: *Die Bühnenproben zu den Bayreuther Festspielen des Jahres 1876* (Leipzig, 1877, repr. 1896; Eng. trans., 1983)

R. Fricke: *Bayreuth vor dreissig Jahren: Erinnerungen an Wahnfried und aus dem Festspielhaus* (Dresden, 1906; Eng. trans. in *Wagner*, xi (1990), 93–109, 134–50; xii (1991), 3–24)

J. Hey: *Richard Wagner als Vortragsmeister: Erinnerungen*, ed. H. Hey (Leipzig, 1911)

G. Skelton: *Wagner at Bayreuth: Experiment and Tradition* (London, 1965, 2/1976)

M. Srocke: *Richard Wagner als Regisseur* (Berlin, 1988)

M. Ashman: 'Producing Wagner', *Wagner in Performance*, ed. B. Millington and S. Spencer (New Haven, 1992)

FRANCE

J.-B. Durey de Noinville: *Histoire du théâtre de l'Académie royale de musique en France* (Paris, 2/1757)

M.-J. Sedaine: 'Avertissement', *Le déserteur* (Paris, 1769)

J. J. O. de Meude-Monpas: 'Répétition', *Dictionnaire de musique* (Paris, 1787), 173–4

[E.-N. Framery]: *De l'organisation des spectacles de Paris* (Paris, 1790)

A.-E.-M. Grétry: *Mémoires, ou Essais sur la musique* (Paris, 1796–7)

E. Campardon: *Les comédiens du roi de la troupe italienne pendant les deux derniers siècles* (Paris, 1880)

A.-E.-M. Grétry: *Réflexions d'un solitaire*, ed. L. Solvay and E. Closson (Brussels and Paris, 1919–24)

J. Tiersot: *Lettres de musiciens écrites en français*, ii (Paris and Milan, 1936)

E. Véron: *Mémoires d'un bourgeois de Paris*, ed. P. Josserand (Paris, 1945), ii, 79–80

D. Libby: *Gaspare Spontini and his French and German Operas* (diss., Princeton U., 1969)

D. Cairns, ed.: *The Memoirs of Hector Berlioz* (London, 1969, 2/1977)

G. Sadler: 'Patrons and Pasquinades: Rameau in the 1730s', *JRMA*, cxiii (1988), 314–37

S. Huebner: *The Operas of Charles Gounod* (Oxford, 1990)

ENGLAND

BurneyH

Susanna Elizabeth Burney, letter-journal, 1779–80 (*GB-Lbl* Egerton 3691)

An Apology for the Life of Colley Cibber, ed. B. R. S. Fone (Ann Arbor, 1968)

J. Milhous and R. D. Hume: 'A Prompt Copy of Handel's *Radamisto*', *MT*, cxxvii (1986), 316–21

J. Milhous: 'Lighting at the King's Theatre, Haymarket, 1780–82', *Theatre Research International*, xvi (1991), 215–36

JOHN ROSSELLI (1, i), THOMAS BAUMAN (1, ii, a), BARRY MILLINGTON (1, ii, b), DAVID CHARLTON (1, iii), CURTIS PRICE (1, iv), JOHN COX (2)

Rehfuss, Heinz (Julius) (*b* Frankfurt, 25 May 1917; *d* Rochester, NY, 27 June 1988). Swiss bass-baritone, later naturalized American. He studied singing with his father, Carl Rehfuss, and operatic production with Otto Erhardt. In 1938 he made his début as a singer and producer at the Städtebundtheater in Biel-Solothurn; he sang in 1938–9 in Lucerne and from 1940 to 1952 at the Zürich Opera, where he undertook more than 80 roles. From 1952 he sang at many European opera houses, including La Scala, the Paris Opéra and the Vienna Staatsoper, notably as Don Giovanni, Boris and Golaud. He made a speciality of roles in 20th-century music, appearing as Dr Schön in *Lulu* and taking part in the première of Nono's *Intolleranza 1960* (1961, Venice Biennale).

JÜRG STENZL

Rehkemper, Heinrich (*b* Schwerte, 23 May 1894; *d* Munich, 30 Dec 1949). German baritone. He studied in Hagen, Düsseldorf and Munich, making his début in Kálmán's *Die Faschingsfee* at Coburg in 1919. At Stuttgart (1921–4) he sang over 40 roles and in 1925 he joined the Munich Opera where he remained until 1943. He was a popular Papageno but also sang dramatic roles such as Macbeth, Rigoletto, Amfortas and Telramund. In 1931 he appeared in the première of Pfitzner's *Das Herz*. He was also much in demand throughout Germany as a recitalist. His recordings reveal a somewhat dry voice with limited appeal, though his singing can be tender and intense in feeling.

J. B. STEANE

Reich, Günter (*b* Liegnitz, 22 Nov 1921; *d* Heidelberg, 15 Jan 1989). Israeli bass of German birth. He studied in Berlin and Mannheim, making his début in 1961 at Gelsenkirchen as Iago. Engaged at Stuttgart, he sang regularly at Munich, Hamburg, Frankfurt, Düsseldorf and Berlin, where he created Soroker in Blacher's *200000 Taler* (1969). Though his vast repertory included Don Alfonso and Hans Sachs, he specialized in 20th-century opera; he sang Dallapiccola's Ulysses, Morone (*Palestrina*), Duke Adorno (Schreker's *Die Gezeichneten*), Busoni's Faust, Satan (Penderecki's *Paradise Lost*), Reimann's Lear and Schoenberg's Moses (he has twice recorded the role of Moses). He created Löwel Perl in Penderecki's *Schwarze Maske* at Salzburg (1986). The role that best displayed his outstanding musical and dramatic gifts was Dr Schön in *Lulu*, which he sang at Covent Garden (1981), at the Teatro Real in Madrid (1988) and at many other theatres.

ELIZABETH FORBES

Reich, Willi (*b* Vienna, 27 May 1898; *d* Zürich, 1 May 1980). Swiss music critic and musicologist of Austrian birth. He studied with Lach, Orel and Haas at Vienna University, where he took the doctorate in 1934; he was also a pupil of Berg and Webern. From 1920 he worked as a music critic for several Viennese and foreign newspapers. Encouraged by Berg, he edited the journal *23 – eine Wiener Musikzeitschrift*, 1932–7, which took vehement issue with the defects of Viennese musical life and supported the new music, particularly that of the Second Viennese School. In 1938 he moved to Basle where he worked as a freelance writer, and from 1948 on the *Neue Zürcher Zeitung*; he also lectured at the Technische Hochschule in Zürich (1959–70). Reich's two monographs on Berg (1937; 1963, Eng. trans. 1965) and his book on Schoenberg (1968, Eng. trans., 1971) are fundamental accounts of the life and works of the two composers. His numerous other books, many of which aim to characterize musicians in their own words, include studies of Wagner (1948) and Verdi (1951).

JÜRG STENZL

Reicha [Rejcha], Antoine(-Joseph) [Antonín, Anton] (*b* Prague, 26 Feb 1770; *d* Paris, 28 May 1836). Bohemian, later French, composer and teacher. He studied at Bonn University, where he knew Beethoven and was profoundly influenced by the philosophy of Kant; he

1275

conducted several of his *scènes italiennes* there in 1787. In 1794 he moved to Hamburg where his earliest known opera *Godefroid de Montfort* was given in about 1796, probably its second private performance. Hoping to achieve greater success, he went to Paris in 1799. On Grétry's recommendation he set *L'ouragan* but was unable to have it performed; frustrated, he left for Vienna in late 1801 or early 1802. There Prince Lobkowitz had *L'ouragan* staged in about 1801 and Empress Marie Thérèse (wife of Francis II) commissioned Reicha to write *Argine, regina di Granata*, in which she sang at a private performance in the Hofburg.

Reicha returned to Paris in 1808. His opera *Cagliostro* (1810) ran for eight performances, its initial concept serious but transformed into an *opera buffa* in the production process. The *Journal de Paris* (28 Nov 1810) mentioned some 'truly excellent pieces, especially the overture'. Reicha's only other produced operas, *Natalie* (1816) and *Sapho* (1822), fared only slightly better commercially, though Berlioz recalled hearing in *Sapho* a 'magnificent duet, filled with verve and passion'. Reicha considered *Sapho* and the unperformed *Philoctète* to be his masterpieces.

His operas failed but his teaching (his pupils included Berlioz, Gounod and Pauline Viardot), wind quintets and treatises made him famous. His *Traité de mélodie* (1814) treats melody apart from its relation to harmony and also discusses singers' embellishments and the use of national airs to impart local colour. In his *Art du compositeur dramatique* (1833) Reicha methodically leads the student, by use of examples from his three most important operas, from basic matters of prosody and libretto, types of vocal and instrumental numbers appropriate to opera, the role of the orchestra and staging, through to the composition of an entire act. It offers one of the most comprehensive views of opera aesthetics and contemporary performing practice of the late 18th and early 19th centuries. The ideas expressed in his treatises and in his autobiography (*Notes sur Antoine Reicha*, c1824) are in the tradition of Haydn, Mozart, Rameau and Gluck and are strongly coloured by his admiration for Racine. Continuing the trend of merging the Italian and French serious and comic opera traditions into what was becoming the supranational grand opera, Reicha includes in his discussions approbatory references to Grétry, Dalayrac, Berton, Della Maria, Catel, Le Sueur, Méhul, Boieldieu and Auber, and to Carissimi, Piccinni, Sarti, Paisiello, Sacchini, 'Giordanello', Cimarosa, Zingarelli, Cherubini, Spontini and Rossini. His Kantian ideals dictated that operas should not be mere shallow diversions and for this reason he criticized the librettos of *Don Giovanni*, *Figaro* and *Der Freischütz*.

For him music must act together with and serve dramatic truth, yet not be subordinate to the libretto. Simple recitative should be kept to a minimum, accompanied recitative and arioso increased. These, along with arias, ensembles, choruses and dance and instrumental numbers, should be well integrated with the plot. Through his writings Reicha exerted an influence on opera, with composers such as Meyerbeer, Thomas and Smetana, which extended beyond Paris and his own time.

Armide (?scène italienne, R. de Calzabigi), c1787, lost [mentioned in Vysloužil 1970]
Godefroid de Montfort [Godfried von Montfort], ?c1794, Hamburg, ?1796 [mentioned in *FétisB*]

L'ermite dans l'île Formose, ?1794–8 (?Spl, A. von Kotzebue), lost [mentioned in Vysloužil 1970]
Obaldi, ou Les Français en Egypte, before 1798 (opéra, 2), *F-Pc**
Amor, der Joujou-Spieler, before c1800 (Spl), 1 aria *D-Lr*
Rosalia, ?before 1800 (Spl), *Rtt*
Télémaque, ?1800–01 (grand opéra, ?Devismes), inc., lost [mentioned in Vysloužil 1970]
L'ouragan (opéra, 3, J. H. Guy); in Ger., Vienna, Prince Lobkowitz's palace, c1801 or 1804; entr'acte between Acts 2 and 3 *F- Pc**
Argine, regina di Granata (os, 2, ? Calzabigi or L. da Ponte), Vienna, Hofburg, c1802 or 1805, *Pc**, *A-Wn*
Bégri, ou Le chanteur à Constantinople, after c1809 (oc, 1), *F-Pc**
Gusman d'Alfarache, after c1809 (oc, 1, E. Scribe and J. H. Dupin), frags. *Pc**
Cagliostro, ou La séduction [Les illuminés] [Acts 2 and 3] (oc, 3, J. A. Révéroni de Saint-Cyr and E. Mercier-Dupaty), Paris, OC (Feydeau), 27 Nov 1810, frags., sketches *Pc** [Act 1 by V.-C.-P. Dourlen]
Natalie, ou La famille russe, c1810–12 (grand opéra, 3, Guy), Paris, Opéra, 30 July 1816, frag. *Pc**, *Po* (2 versions), vs, ov. and selected scenes (Paris, n.d.), excerpts in Reicha (1833)
Olinde et Sophronie, c1819 (opéra), inc. [mentioned in Emmanuel 1937]
Philoctète, before 1822 (grand opéra, 2, ?after Sophocles), lost except for 3 choruses in Reicha (1833)
Sapho (tragédie lyrique, 3, H. Cournol and A. J. S. Empis), Paris, Opéra, 16 Dec 1822, *Pc** (almost complete), *Po*, ov. and selected scenes (Paris, c1822), excerpts in Reicha (1833)
Gioas, re di Giuda, before 1826 (P. Metastasio), ?inc., aria and chorus in Reicha (1833)
Venne ed il nostro addio (?scène italienne), frags. (finale, cavatina, recit. and duet) *A-Wn* [?from Argine]

Ovs., arias, ensembles ?written for operas: *D-Rtt*, *Hs*, *F-Pc*, *Pn*; Scènes italiennes, 1787 [mentioned in Vysloužil 1970]

*

ČSHS; *FétisB*
Journal de Paris (28 Nov 1810)
A. Reicha: *Traité de mélodie* (Paris, 1814); ed. C. Czerny as *Vollständiges Lehrbuch der musikalischen Composition*, ii (Vienna, 1832) [Fr. and Ger. text]
——: *Notes sur Antoine Reicha* (MS, c1824, *F-Po* Carton 2073)
——: *Traité de haute composition musicale* (Paris, 1824–6)
——: *Art du compositeur dramatique, ou Cours complet de composition vocale* (Paris, 1833); ed. C. Czerny as *Die Kunst der dramatischen Composition* (Vienna, 1835)
H**** [H. Berlioz]: 'Antoine Reicha', *Journal des débats* (3 July 1836)
H. Blanchard: 'Des successeurs de Reicha', *Revue et gazette musicale de Paris*, iii (1836), 200–01
H. Berlioz: 'Biographies: Reicha (Antoine)', ibid, v (1838), 287–9
——: *Mémoires* (Paris, 1870; Eng. trans. 1969, 2/1977)
E. Bücken: *Anton Reicha: sein Leben und seine Kompositionen* (Munich, 1912)
——: 'Anton Reicha als Theoretiker', *ZMw*, ii (1919–20), 156–69
M. Emmanuel: *Antonin Reicha* (Paris, 1937)
K. Blum: 'Bemerkungen Anton Reichas zur Aufführungspraxis der Oper', *Mf*, vii (1954), 429–40
H. Fredericks: 'Das Rezitativ in den "Hugenotten" Giacomo Meyerbeers', *Beiträge zur Geschichte der Oper*, ed. H. Becker (Regensburg, 1969), 55–76
H. Becker, ed.: *Giacomo Meyerbeer: Briefwechsel und Tagebücher* (Berlin, 1970)
HV, vii (1970) [Reicha issue]
J. Vysloužil, ed.: *Zápisky o Antonínu Rejchovi/Notes sur Antoine Reicha* (Brno, 1970) [with annotated edn of A. Reicha: *Notes sur Antoine Reicha*]
A. Krutová: *Opera v projetí Antonína Rejchy* (MS, Brno, 1971)
J. Vysloužil: 'Antonín Josef Rejcha', *OM*, iii (1971), 1–7
H. Becker, ed.: *Die 'Couleur locale' in der Oper des 19. Jahrhunderts* (Regensburg, 1976)
O. Šotolová: *Antonín Rejcha* (Prague, 1977) [incl. thematic catalogue]
M. D. Smith: *Antoine Joseph Reicha's Theories on the Composition of Dramatic Music* (diss., Rutgers U., 1979)

PETER ELIOT STONE

Reichardt, Johann Friedrich (*b* Königsberg [now Kaliningrad], 25 Nov 1752; *d* Giebichenstein, nr Halle,

27 June 1814). German composer. The son of a lutenist, he enjoyed extensive practical training in music as a young man in East Prussia. At Königsberg University, where he studied for three years, he fell under the spell of Kant's lectures in philosophy. At 19 he embarked on three years of travel, setting a pattern of restlessness that he was to maintain to the end of his life. On this journey he performed as a violinist in various cities of northern Germany and Bohemia and met many prominent composers, writers and musicians. He studied briefly with several composers, including J. A. Hiller at Leipzig, under whose guidance he completed a one-act German comic opera begun at Königsberg, and set another, *Amors Guckkasten* (also set by Hiller's pupil C. G. Neefe). Reichardt later published an extended, laudatory analysis of Hiller's *Die Jagd* (*Über die deutsche comische Oper*, Hamburg, 1774) and two volumes of travel notes in his *Briefe eines aufmerksamen Reisenden, die Musik betreffend* (Frankfurt, 1774–6).

The most singular event in Reichardt's career was his appointment in 1775 to succeed J. F. Agricola as Frederick the Great's Kapellmeister of the Italian opera establishment at Berlin, apparently on the strength of the score of his first Italian opera, *Le feste galanti*, a direct imitation of the Hasse-Graun style dear to the king's heart (it uses a libretto set earlier by Graun). The position itself was poorly paid and amounted to a curatorship of the very style Reichardt had aped. Frederick refused to let his young Kapellmeister compose another Italian opera, restricting him to occasional celebratory prologues and cantatas. Reichardt travelled frequently, especially after 1781, when the king ceased attending the opera. He visited Italy, England and France, among other places, and went often to Hamburg and Dessau.

The death of Frederick in 1786 brought Friedrich Wilhelm II to the throne and new opportunities for Reichardt. His *Andromeda*, mounted at lavish expense in 1788, was a triumph and kindled visions of international fame, but attempts to gain a foothold in Paris with two Gluckian operas were thwarted. At this time Reichardt cemented an artistic friendship with Goethe at Weimar. He set the revised version of the poet's *Claudine von Villa Bella* for the royal stage at Berlin in 1789, then his other librettos (as well as writing incidental music to *Lila*, 1791) and virtually every poem by Goethe he could get his hands on. But the high water mark of Reichardt's operatic career at Berlin came with his heroic Italian opera *Brenno* (its title role for the bass Ludwig Fischer), a work of frankly Gluckian inspiration that remained popular in a German concert version well into the next century.

A combination of intrigues against Reichardt during his frequent absences and his increasingly outspoken support of French revolutionary ideals led to his summary dismissal, without pension, in 1794. Inflammatory writings in two journals he founded, *Deutschland* and *Frankreich*, also alienated both Goethe and Schiller. But Reichardt was equally the valued host to a coterie of young Romantics, including Wackenroder and Tieck, who formed a stimulating intellectual circle at his country home in picturesque Giebichenstein.

By 1796 Reichardt was back in favour with Friedrich Wilhelm II, and after the latter's death in 1797 his successor, Friedrich Wilhelm III, reinstated the composer as Kapellmeister. His late operas for Berlin include alike German ones for the Nationaltheater

(notably *Die Geisterinsel*, 1798) and Italian ones for the declining Italian company (the most successful was *Rosmonda*, 1801). He also sought, with short-lived success, to initiate a German parallel to French vaudeville comedy with a new genre, the LIEDERSPIEL – an entertainment mixing comfortable, familiar scenes of everyday life with a musical content consisting of 'the lied and nothing but the lied'. Reichardt himself wrote the libretto to *Lieb' und Treue*, his first Liederspiel (1800, Berlin), and based it partly on his own family life.

Reichardt's last years were ones of increasing obscurity and poverty. His country estate was destroyed during the Napoleonic invasion in 1806. A year later Jérôme Napoleon appointed him theatrical and orchestral director at Kassel, where he found little favour and left after a year of service. A journey to Vienna and Prague in 1808–9 resulted in his last significant work of musical journalism, *Vertraute Briefe geschrieben auf einer Reise nach Wien* (Amsterdam, 1810).

Reichardt's early German operas emphasize the farcical rather than the sentimental strain in Hilleresque comic opera. He continued to write German opera as well as melodramas for the German stages at Berlin and Dessau in the 1780s, and even sought a marriage of the two genres in *Liebe nur beglückt* (1781, Dessau), but his major efforts went into serious opera, at first for Paris (*Panthée*, 1786; and *Tamerlan*, unperformed there) and, after Frederick's death, for Berlin. In these works he sought consciously to emulate the style of Gluck (whom he had met in Vienna in 1783), as yet little known in Berlin. His *Andromeda* (1788) incorporated ballet into the opera itself (dance figures in nearly all the choruses). Of all his operas, Reichardt himself considered *Brenno* (1789) to be 'written more than any other after my own mind and with reliance on my own powers'. Its large orchestra (including a full Janissary band) and mass crowd scenes anticipated traits of heroic opera during the age of Napoleon.

Reichardt's friendship with Goethe in the late 1780s renewed his interest in German opera. In all his settings of the poet's librettos, even in large-scale works such as *Claudine von Villa Bella* (1789), he followed Goethe's own strong predilection for simplicity of musical means. His one abiding success in German opera during this period was a different sort of work – *Die Geisterinsel* (1798, based on Shakespeare's *Tempest*), a variegated, colourful spectacle that held the stage in Berlin until 1825.

See also BRENNO; CLAUDINE VON VILLA BELLA (ii); and ERWIN UND ELMIRE (ii).

Hänschen und Gretchen, 1771–2 (Operette, 1, J. C. Bock, after M.-J. Sedaine: *Rose et Colas*), unperf., ov. *A-Wgm*, vs (Riga, 1773 [pubd with Amors Guckkasten])

Amors Guckkasten, 1772 (Operette, 1, J. B. Michaelis), unperf., vs (Riga, 1773 [pubd with Hänschen und Gretchen])

Le feste galanti [La gioja dopo il duolo, ò Le feste superbe] (os, 3, L. de Villati, after Duché de Vancy), Potsdam, Hof, 1775, *D-B*, *F-Pc*

Der Holzhauer, oder Die drei Wünsche, c1775 (komische Oper, 1, after Castet and J. F. Guichard: *Le bûcheron*), unperf.

Cephalus und Prokris (Melodram, 1, K. W. Ramler), Hamburg, Gänsemarkt, 7 July 1777, *D-B*, vs (Berlin, 1777)

Ino (musikalisches Drama, 1, J. C. Brandes), Leipzig, 4 Aug 1779, *B*, *DK-Kk*, vs (Leipzig, 1779)

Liebe nur beglückt (Schauspiel mit Zwischenmusik und Gesang, 3, Reichardt), Dessau, Hof, aut. 1781, *D-B*, *Bds**

Tamerlan, 1786 (tragédie lyrique, 4, E. Morel de Chédeville, after Voltaire: *L'orphelin de la Chine*), unperf.; in Ger., Berlin, Kgl, 16 Oct 1800, *B*, *US-Wc*

Panthée (tragédie lyrique, 4, Berquin), Paris, Opéra, 1786, *F-Pc*

Andromeda (os, 3, A. de' Filistri da Caramondani), Berlin, Kgl, 11 Jan 1788, *D-B*, *Bds*, *Mbs*, *US-Wc*

Protesilao [Act 1] (os, 2, G. Sertor), Berlin, Kgl, 26 Jan 1789, *D-B* (Act 1), *Bds* (Act 2) [Act 2 by J. G. Naumann]

Claudine von Villa Bella (Spl, 3, J. W. von Goethe), Charlottenburg, Schloss, 29 July 1789, *B*, *Bds* (pts), *WRdn*

Brenno (os, 3, Filistri), Berlin, Kgl, 16 Oct 1789, vs (Berlin, 1789), full score (Berlin, *c*1797)

Jery und Bätely, 1789 (Spl, 1, Goethe), Berlin, National, 30 March 1801, *A-Wn*, *D-B*, *WRdn*, *US-Wc*, vs (Berlin, *c*1789)

L'olimpiade (drama per musica, 3, P. Metastasio), Berlin, Kgl, 2 Oct 1791, *D-B*, *Bds*

Erwin und Elmire (Spl, 2, Goethe), Berlin, concert perf., early 1793, *B*, *WRdn*, *US-Wc*, vs (Berlin, 1791)

Die Geisterinsel (Spl, 3, J. F. W. Gotter, after W. Shakespeare: *The Tempest*), Berlin, National, 6 July 1798, *D-B*, *Bds* (pts), *WRdn*, vs (Berlin, 1799)

Lieb' und Treue [Lieb' und Frieden] (Liederspiel, 1, Reichardt), Berlin, National, 31 March 1800, *B*, *Dlb*, vs (Berlin, 1800)

Der Jubel, oder Juchhei (Liederspiel, 1, Reichardt), Berlin, National, 21 June 1800, *B*, *DT*, vs (Strasbourg, 1805)

Rosmonda (tragedia per musica, 3, Filistri), Berlin, National, 6 Feb 1801, *B*, *Bds*

Das Zauberschloss (Spl, 3, A. von Kotzebue), Berlin, National, 2 Jan 1802, *F-Pc*

Hercules Tod (Melodram, 1, after Sophocles), Berlin, National, 10 April 1802, *D-B*, *Bds*, *US-Wc*

Kunst und Liebe, *c*1803 (Liederspiel, 1, Reichardt), Berlin, National, 30 Nov 1807, vs (Strasbourg, 1805)

L'heureux naufrage (comedy, 1), Kassel, Hof, aut. 1808, *D-Bds*

Bradamante (4, H. J. von Collin), Vienna, 3 Feb 1809, *Tu*

Der Taucher (Spl, 2, S. G. Bürde, after F. von Schiller), Berlin, National, 18 March 1811, *B*, *Bds*

Music in: Hasse: *Artemisia*, 1778; Bertoni: *Orfeo ed Euridice*, 1788

*

J. F. Reichardt: *An das musikalische Publikum seine französischen Opern Tamerlan und Panthée betreffend* (Hamburg, 1787)

——: 'Autobiographie', *AMZ*, xv-xvi (1813–14)

H. M. Schletterer: *Johann Friedrich Reichardt* (Augsburg, 1865)

C. Lange: *Johann Friedrich Reichardt* (Halle, 1902)

F. Flössner: *Reichardt, der Hallische Komponist der Goethezeit* (Halle, 1929)

P. Sieber: *Johann Friedrich Reichardt als Musikästhetiker: seine Anschauungen über Wesen und Wirkung der Musik* (Strasbourg, 1930)

W. Salmen: *Johann Friedrich Reichardt: Komponist, Schriftsteller, Kapellmeister und Verwaltungsbeamter der Goethezeit* (Freiburg and Zürich, 1963)

R. Pröpper: *Die Bühnenwerke Johann Friedrich Reichardts* (Bonn, 1965)

T. Bauman: *North German Opera in the Age of Goethe* (Cambridge, 1985)   THOMAS BAUMAN

Reichenberg (Ger.). LIBEREC.

Reicher-Kindermann, Hedwig (*b* Munich, 15 July 1853; *d* Trieste, 2 June 1883). German dramatic soprano. She studied with her father, August Kindermann, and after singing in the chorus of the Munich Hofoper, in 1871 she was engaged at Karlsruhe and then sang in Berlin as Pamina and Agathe. She sang Orlofsky in the first Munich performance of *Die Fledermaus* (1875), Grimgerde in the first complete *Ring* cycle at Bayreuth in 1876 and also Erda in the second cycle. In 1877 she sang at Hamburg, making her début there as Gluck's Orpheus. Engaged at Leipzig from 1880, she sang Fricka in Angelo Neumann's production of the *Ring* at the Victoria Theatre, Berlin (1881), Isolde in the first Leipzig performance of *Tristan und Isolde* (1882), Ortrud and Eglantine (*Euryanthe*). In the first London performances of the *Ring*, at Her Majesty's Theatre (1882), she sang Fricka and Waltraute in the first cycle, and Brünnhilde in the second and third. She accompanied Neumann's Wagner tour through Europe, singing Brünnhilde at the opening performances in

Breslau. Forced to leave the company because of illness, she rejoined it for the Italian part of the tour. After performances in Venice, Bologna, Rome, Turin and Milan, she sang Brünnhilde in *Götterdämmerung* at Trieste. 12 days later she died, aged only 29. Her passionate intensity, dramatic abandon and glorious voice combined to make her an outstanding interpreter of Wagner's heroines.

*

H. Klein: *Thirty Years of Musical Life in London* (London, 1903)

A. Neumann: *Erinnerungen an Richard Wagner* (Leipzig, 1907; Eng. trans., 1908)

H. von Wolzogen: *Lebensbilder* (Regensburg, 1923)

E. Newman: *The Life of Richard Wagner* (London, 1933–47)

H. Wagner: *200 Jahre Münchner Theaterchronik 1750–1950* (Munich, 1958)

G. Skelton: *Wagner at Bayreuth* (London, 1965)

ELIZABETH FORBES

Reichert, Heinz [Blumenreich, Heinrich] (*b* Vienna, 27 Dec 1877; *d* Hollywood, 16 Nov 1940). Austrian librettist. In the years immediately preceding World War I he collaborated on various Viennese operetta librettos with Fritz Grünbaum (1880–1941). Then, with A. M. Willner, he was contracted to provide the operetta libretto sought by Puccini and eventually adapted by Giuseppe Adami for *La rondine* (1917). Meanwhile Willner and Reichert had enjoyed success with their adaptation of music by Schubert for *Das Dreimäderlhaus* (1916; known in English as *Lilac Time* or *Blossom Time*), and the partnership went on to provide various further librettos, notably for works for Lehár and for *Walzer aus Wien* (1930; *Waltzes from Vienna* or *The Great Waltz*), which uses music by Johann Strauss father and son.

operettas unless otherwise stated

Madame Flirt (with F. Grünbaum), A. Götzl, 1908; *Das Himmelbett* (Vaudeville-Operette, with F. Wagner), F. Lehner, 1909; *Miss Dudelsack* (with Grünbaum), R. Nelson, 1909; *Don Quichotte* (with Grünbaum), Heuberger, 1910; *Der ledige Gatte* (with Grünbaum), G. Wanda, 1910; *Die teuerste Frau von Paris* (with Grünbaum), L. Schottländer, 1910; *Der Frechling* (with Grünbaum), C. Weinberger, 1912; *Die Prinzenjagd* (with Grünbaum), L. Friedmann, 1913; *Man steigt nach* (Posse, with V. Léon), Straus, 1915

Papa wider Willen (Posse, with Wagner), E. Pfau, 1915; *Das Dreimäderlhaus* (Spl, with A. M. Willner, after R. H. Bartsch: *Schwammerl*), H. Berté, after Schubert, 1916; *Wiener Kinder* (Spl, with Léon), O. Stalla, after J. Schrammel, 1917; *Die schöne Saskia* (with Willner), O. Nedbal, 1917; *Hannerl* [Dreimäderlhaus, 2. Teil] (Spl, with Willner), K. Lafite, after Schubert, 1918; *Seine einzige Rettung* (Schwank, with Grünbaum), G. Benedict, 1918; *Wo die Lerche singt* (with Willner), Lehár, 1918; *Hol' mich der Teufel* (with Léon), L. Reichwein, 1920

Der Herzog von Reichstadt (with Léon), Stojanović, 1921; *Frasquita* (with Willner), Lehár, 1922; *Drei arme Teufel* (with R. Oesterreicher), C. Weinberger, 1923; *Glück bei Frauen* (with Léon), B. Granichstaedten, 1923; *Donna Gloria* (with Léon), Nedbal, 1925; *Der Zarewitsch* (with B. Jenbach), Lehár, 1927; *Ade, du liebes Elternhaus* [Die Lori] (Spl, with Willner), O. Jascha, 1928; *Rosen aus Florida* (with Willner), Korngold, after Fall, 1929; *Walzer aus Wien* (Spl, with Willner and E. Marischka), Bittner and Korngold, after J. Strauss father and son, 1930; *Ein Liebestraum* (Spl), K. Komjathi, 1933

ANDREW LAMB

Reichmann, Theodor (*b* Rostock, 15 March 1849; *d* Marbach, 22 May 1903). German baritone. He studied in Berlin, Prague and with Lamperti in Milan, making his début in 1869 at Magdeburg. After singing at Rotterdam, Strasbourg and Hamburg, he appeared for the first time in Munich in 1874 in *Guillaume Tell*, and

Theodor Reichmann as Amfortas in Wagner's 'Parsifal', the role he created in the original production at Bayreuth in 1882

the following year began a permanent engagement there in Marschner's *Hans Heiling*. He sang Amonasro in *Aida* (1877), the Wanderer in *Siegfried* (1878) and the title role of Nessler's *Der Rattenfänger von Hameln* (1881), all first Munich performances. He sang Amfortas at all 16 performances of *Parsifal* at Bayreuth in 1882, returning to the festival in that role regularly until 1902, as Hans Sachs in 1888–9 and as Wolfram in 1891. He made his London début in 1882 as Wotan in the second and third *Ring* cycles presented by Angelo Neumann at Her Majesty's Theatre. He first sang at Covent Garden in 1884 as Telramund, the Dutchman and Hans Sachs and returned in 1892 to sing Wotan (*Siegfried*, then *Die Walküre*) in the *Ring* cycles conducted by Mahler. From 1883 to 1889 he was engaged at the Vienna Hofoper, where he sang Iago in the first Vienna performance of Verdi's *Otello* (1888). He made his Metropolitan début in 1889 in *Der fliegende Holländer*, and during his two seasons there he sang 16 parts, which included Don Giovanni, Count di Luna, Renato, Solomon (*Die Königin von Saba*), Amonasro, Werner (*Der Trompeter von Säkkingen*), Nélusko (*L'Africaine*) and Escamillo, as well as his Wagner roles. Then he returned to Vienna. He made his final appearance in Munich at the Prinzregententheater as Hans Sachs in 1902, when the resonance of his magnificently warm and even voice was said to have been as powerful as at the beginning of his career.

*

H. Klein: *Thirty Years of Musical Life in London* (London, 1903)

T. W. Elbertshagen: *Der Roman eines Sangesfürsten* (Brunswick, 1932)

E. Newman: *The Life of Richard Wagner* (London, 1933–47)

W. Beetz: *Das Wiener Opernhaus 1869 bis 1945* (Vienna, 1949)

W. H. Seltsam: *Metropolitan Opera Annals* (New York, 1949)

E. Pirchan, A. Witeschnik and O. Fritz: *300 Jahre Wiener Operntheater* (Vienna, 1953)

H. Rosenthal: *Two Centuries of Opera at Covent Garden* (London, 1958)

H. Wagner: *200 Jahre Münchner Theaterchronik 1750–1950* (Munich, 1958)

G. Skelton: *Wagner at Bayreuth* (London, 1965)

ELIZABETH FORBES

Reimann, Aribert (*b* Berlin, 4 March 1936). German composer and pianist. Born into a family of musicians (his father was a professor at the Berlin Academy of Music, his mother a singer), Reimann studied composition with Blacher and Ernst Pepping between 1955 and 1960, at the same time developing his career as a pianist. He has continued to work as an accompanist with such singers as Grümmer, Haefliger and Fischer-Dieskau, and most of his own works are vocal. His musical language has been consistently rooted in the Second Viennese School and in the works of Webern and Berg in particular.

Reimann's earliest theatre work was the ballet *Stoffreste*, a collaboration with Günter Grass in 1957. With *Ein Traumspiel* after Strindberg (1965) and especially *Melusine* (1971), which was widely performed in German opera houses, he began to establish a distinctive musical style, in which the terms of musical reference and the expressive range were dictated by the dramatic context rather than by predetermined aesthetic principles. The most spectacular product of this reorientation was *Lear*. The title role was created specifically for Fischer-Dieskau, and after its first production in Munich in 1978 the work rapidly became one of the most widely performed of all European postwar operas.

If in *Lear* much of the dramatic effect is achieved by employing musical extremes – dense orchestral tone clusters, expressionist vocal lines – and bold dynamic curves, Reimann's next opera, *Die Gespenstersonate*, moved back to a world of suggestion and restraint, in which the ambiguities and illogicalities of Strindberg's drama are rendered in deliberately elusive and mysterious terms. Whatever the apparent thinness of its musical invention (certainly in the wake of *Lear*) it was widely performed (and reached London in a production by Opera Factory in 1989 that twinned it with Strindberg's original). With *Troades* (see illustration overleaf), first staged in Munich in 1986, Reimann returned to epic tragedy of the kind that he had exploited so successfully with *Lear* and to which his operatic style seems to

Scene from the original production of Reimann's 'Troades' at the Bayerische Staatsoper, Munich, 7 July 1986; designed by Pet Halmen

be most naturally suited. *Das Schloss* (1992) followed in the same large-scale lineage. Based upon Brod's dramatization of the Kafka novel, it pivots around the central baritone role of K., as exacting in its demands as that of Lear. Despite a similar structural use of black sonorities and intense orchestral interludes, the atmosphere is far more inward-looking than that of the earlier opera, fusing the physical intensity of *Lear* with the psychological probings of *Die Gespenstersonate*.

See also LEAR.

Ein Traumspiel (1, C. Henius, after A. Strindberg), Kiel, Städtische Bühnen, 20 June 1965
Melusine (4, C. H. Henneberg, after Y. Goll), Schwetzingen, Schwetzinger Festspiele, 29 April 1971
Lear (2 pts, Henneberg, after W. Shakespeare), Munich, National, 9 July 1978
Die Gespenstersonate (1, Riemann and U. Schendel, after Strindberg), Berlin, Hebbel, 25 Sept 1984
Troades (1, G. Albrecht and Reimann, after Euripides), Munich, Bayerische Staatsoper, 7 July 1986
Das Schloss (2, Reimann, after M. Brod and F. Kafka), Berlin, Deutsche, 2 Sept 1992

*

W.-E. von Lewinski: 'Aribert Reimann: "Ein Weg in der Freiheit" ', *Melos*, xxxviii (1971), 129–33 [on *Melusine*]
R. Samuel: 'Music in Command', *Lear*, English National Opera 1989 [programme book]   ANDREW CLEMENTS

Reims (Ger. Rheims). City in Champagne, north-east France. The first Grand Théâtre, seating 600, dated from 1777 and was built in what is now the rue Talleyrand. It served until 1873 when the second Grand Théâtre (1200 seats) was built on the present site, rue de Chanzy, by the local architect Alphonse Gosset. This theatre gave six or seven performances each week, with opera and operetta taking their place beside comedy and drama. The stars of the Paris Opéra appeared as guest artists, Massenet conducting his *Manon* there in 1884, Gounod his *Mireille* in 1885. Partially destroyed by German shelling in 1914, the theatre was rebuilt in 1931, seating 1300 in stalls and three galleries; it was constructed behind Gosset's surviving façade by Maille and

Sollier, respecting Gosset's plans but with an interior decorated in the style of the 1930s. Once again the stars of the Paris Opéra – Thill, Verdière, Pernet, Luccioni – appeared as guest artists. The company is now run on a tiny municipal subsidy. The season runs from October to March, during which four or five operas and as many operettas are performed, the operas usually for one performance only (Sunday matinée), the operettas slightly more frequently. The orchestra consists only of a permanent nucleus of the teachers at the local conservatory, supplemented for performances by their best pupils and supernumeraries.   CHARLES PITT

Reina, Domenico (*b* Lugano, 1797; *d* Lugano, 29 July 1843). Italian tenor. He studied in Milan, making his début in 1820. At the King's Theatre in 1823 he sang in the first London performances of Rossini's *Ricciardo e Zoraide*, *La donna del lago* and *Matilde di Shabran*. Engaged at La Scala, he created Arturo in Bellini's *La straniera* (1829) and Tamas in Donizetti's *Gemma di Vergy* (1834). He also sang in Rome, Venice, Bergamo and Naples. His repertory included Rossini's Ilo (*Zelmira*); Donizetti's Leicester (*Maria Stuarda*), Fernando (*Marino Faliero*) and Alamiro (*Belisario*); and Bellini's Tebaldo (*I Capuleti e i Montecchi*), Orombello (*Beatrice di Tenda*), Elvino (*La sonnambula*) and Pollione.   ELIZABETH FORBES

Reinagle, Alexander (*b* Portsmouth, bap. 23 April 1756; *d* Baltimore, 21 Sept 1809). English composer of Austrian descent. He was a pupil of his father Joseph, a trumpeter, and of Raynor Taylor, musical director of the Theatre Royal in Edinburgh. By 1778 he was teaching the harpsichord in Glasgow; later he spent time in London, Hamburg (*c*1784, visiting C. P. E. Bach) and Lisbon. In 1786 he settled in Philadelphia, where he was active as a composer, pianist and teacher. From 1790 or 1791 until his death he was a partner with the English actor Thomas Wignell (*d* 1803) and Wignell's successors in a theatrical company operating in Philadelphia and Baltimore. The New Company, as it was called, erected spacious and elegant theatres in Philadelphia (the New Theatre in Chestnut Street, February 1793) and Baltimore (Holliday Street, September 1794). The company's repertory was divided equally between spoken and musical works, the latter usually English light opera or ballet. In his 15 years with the company Reinagle directed the theatre orchestra from the piano, and composed or arranged music for hundreds of productions, including operas, melodramas, pantomimes and plays; the extent of his responsibility ranged from a single incidental song to a completely new score, or the orchestration of an existing score. All this music, except for a few published excerpts, perished in the fire that destroyed the Philadelphia New Theatre on 2 April 1820, though many of his non-theatrical works survive. The largest extant fragment of any of Reinagle's stage works is a collection of 14 songs from *The Volunteers*, printed in a piano reduction in 1795. Typical of ballad opera numbers, they are mostly strophic and written to a binary pattern framed by an instrumental introduction and coda. The music may not exemplify Reinagle's best stage style: *The Volunteers* was not a success, playing only once during the 1794–5 season and never revived. Reinagle was the first in America to replace the harpsichord with the piano in the orchestra pit. His high standard of performance and refined taste, greatly admired by his contemporaries, widely influenced the musical life of the young republic.

all first performed at Philadelphia, New Theatre; music lost unless otherwise stated

La forêt noire (pantomime), 26 April 1794
The Volunteers (comic op, 2, S. H. Rowson), 21 Jan 1795, vs (Philadelphia, 1795), facs. in Early American Imprints (Worcester, MA, 1967–74), no.29440
The Sicilian Romance, or The Apparition of the Cliffs (musical play, 2, H. Siddons), 6 May 1795
The Warrior's Welcome Home (pantomime), 10 Feb 1796
The Witches of the Rocks, or Harlequin Everywhere (pantomime), 26 Feb 1796
Columbus, or The Discovery of America (melodrama, 5, T. Morton), 30 Jan 1797, selection (Philadelphia, 1797)
The Savoyard, or The Repentent Seducer (musical farce, 2), 12 July 1797
The Italian Monk (melodrama, 3, J. Boaden), 11 April 1798 [?rev. of S. Arnold]
The Arabs of the Desert, or Harlequin's Flight from Egypt (pantomime), 13 April 1799
The Constellation, or A Wreath for American Tars (dramatic sketch), 30 Dec 1799, selection arr. pf in Mr Francis's Ballroom Assistant (Philadelphia, c1802)
A Wreath for American Tars, or Huzza Again for the Constitution (dramatic sketch), 8 April 1800, selection arr. pf in Mr Francis's Ballroom Assistant (Philadelphia, c1802)
The Double Disguise (musical farce, 2, H. H. Hook), 18 April 1800
The Sailor's Daughter (comedy, 5, R. Cumberland), 10 Dec 1804, selection (Philadelphia, 1807)
Mary, Queen of Scots (tragedy, 5, J. St John), 15 Jan 1806

Contribs to: Robin Hood, or Sherwood Forest, 1794; St Patrick's Day, or The Scheming Lieutenant, 1794; The Spanish Barber, or The Fruitless Precaution, 1794; Harlequin Shipwrecked, 1795; The Purse, or Benevolent Tar, 1795; Auld Robin Gray, or Jamie's Return from America, 1795; Harlequin's Invasion, 1795; The Lucky Escape, or The Ploughman Turned Sailor, 1796; Harlequin Freemason, 1800; The Wife of Two Husbands, 1805; The Travellers, or Music's Fascination, 1807

DAB (E. C. Krohn); *DNB* (J. C. Hadden)
O. G. T. Sonneck: 'Early American Operas', *SIMG*, vi (1904–5), 428–95; repr. in *Miscellaneous Studies in the History of Music* (New York, 1921), 16–92
——: *A Bibliography of Early Secular American Music* (Washington DC, 1905, enlarged 2/1945)
R. R. Drummond: *Early German Music in Philadelphia* (New York, 1910), 57ff
O. G. T. Sonneck: *Early Opera in America* (New York, 1915)
R. J. Wolfe: *Secular Music in America, 1801–1825: a Bibliography* (New York, 1964)
R. Hopkins: Preface to A. Reinagle: *The Philadelphia Sonatas* (Madison, WI, 1978), pp.xvi–xxiii   ROBERT HOPKINS

Re in ascolto, Un ('A Listening King'). *Azione musicale* in two parts by LUCIANO BERIO to a libretto assembled by the composer from texts by Italo Calvino, W. H. AUDEN, Friedrich Einsiedel and FRIEDRICH WILHELM GOTTER; Salzburg, Kleines Festspielhaus, 7 August 1984.

As Berio's description indicates, this is a work whose inner consistency depends intimately on its musical development. Its final simplicity – the story of an old theatrical impresario losing his hold upon his one-time realm, the theatre, as he moves towards death – conceals a complex genesis. Calvino had originally proposed a scenario based on the way in which we apprehend the world through listening: an old king deduces the waning of his authority and the infidelity of his wife from snatches of sound heard through listening-tubes in his palace. But Berio placed the poetic monologues that Calvino had written for the listening king in the mouth of his preferred protagonist, the impresario, on whom, in homage to Shakespeare's *The Tempest*, he conferred the name Prospero (bass-baritone).

Within the 'island' that is his theatre, Prospero is intent on developing a fantastic spectacle that both echoes and transforms *The Tempest*. Berio accordingly constructs much of his text from two of *The Tempest*'s literary offshoots: the libretto prepared in 1791 by Friedrich Einsiedel and Friedrich Wilhelm Gotter for a Singspiel based on the play, and W. H. Auden's *The Sea and the Mirror*, a poetic elaboration on matters left unresolved by Shakespeare's happy ending. Intent on finding a singer who can realize his vision of the female protagonist, Prospero starts auditions, but is left unsatisfied. His unhappiness is increased by the ambitious Producer (tenor) whom he has engaged to realize his project, but who has grandiose plans of his own. Increasingly enraged by his pretentions, Prospero attempts at the end of Part 1 to tear down part of the elaborate scenery, but collapses.

When Prospero is found at the start of Part 2, those nearest to him react to the prospect of his death with unblushing self-interest. But his players instead instigate an ill-disciplined but affectionate ritual of farewell. Prospero retreats further into his own world: in the third and final audition he assumes the role of Calvino's listening king. Indeed, left to his own meditations he finally realizes that the 'other' theatre towards which he has aspired is not that created by lighting and scenery, but that of music. As if summoned by this moment of truth, the female Protagonist (soprano) for whom he has been searching materializes before him. She sings an aria that sums up both music and words of the auditions, giving final form to the strangely intimate message that Prospero has heard in the singing of all the other women who aspired to her role: there is an irremediable gap between the world of the desirer and that of the desired. Her person, her will and her voice are her own. With these hard truths confronted, Prospero is free. His players bid him farewell, and left alone on the stage of his theatre, he dies.

The musical processes that carry this action through to its final point are articulated as a network of closed

'Un re in ascolto' (Berio):
scene from the original
production at the Kleines
Festspielhaus, Salzburg, 7
August 1984, with Theo
Adam (front) as Prospero
and Patricia Wise (centre)
as the Protagonist

but strongly interrelated numbers. A pivotal point is
provided by Prospero's five arias on listening, all of
which use the same fixed field of pitches and thus share
strong common melodic characteristics, but are fleshed
out with a rich range of textures and orchestration.
Three of the four *Concertati* frame the bustling variety
of Prospero's theatre (itself an invitation to inventive
producers) with shared materials that have strong tonal
echoes. As already noted, the three Auditions resolve
into the Protagonist's Aria. In a more unexpected
reworking, the argument between Prospero and his
Producer (Duet 2) is re-enacted as a Duet 3 between
Prospero's two familiars, the Caliban-like (but faithful)
Venerdì (speaker) and a mute Ariel (mime). The teeming
abundance of the stage, so dear to Berio's all-inclusive
aspirations, is thus unified by the discipline of musical
structure.   DAVID OSMOND-SMITH

Reindl, Constantin (*b* Jettenhofen, Upper Palatinate, 29
June 1738; *d* Lucerne, 25 March 1799). German
composer active in Switzerland. A Jesuit priest, he
studied in Ingolstadt, Dillingen and Freiburg, after
which he taught in Freiburg and, from 1772, at the
Gymnasium in Lucerne, also succeeding Abbé Joseph
Bullinger (known for his association with the Mozart
family) as the city's director of music (*Musikpräfekt*).
He continued in these posts even after the dissolution of
the Jesuit order in 1773, and from 1775 to 1777 he also
worked at the seminary in St Urban. Reindl's stage
works – the peak of his creative output – consist of
Singspiels and comic operettas in a light *buffo* style (generally without overtures); they became the characteristic
repertory of the Lucerne school theatre in its heyday.

mostly Singspiels, first performed in Lucerne

Die Sempacherschlacht, 1779, *CH-Lz*
Der Dorfschulmeister, 1784, *Lz*
Das Donnerwetter oder Der Bettelstudent, 1787, *Lmg, Lz*
Der Dorfhirt, 1789, *Lmg, Lz*
Der betrogene Dieb, 1791, *Lz*
Der eingebildete Kranke, 1792, *Lz*
Lebet wohl, 1795, *Lz*
Das neugierige Frauenzimmer, 1796, *Lmg*
Abraham und Isaack, frag. *Lmg*

2 pantomimes, *Lz*; 9 other stage works, lost

*

A. Geering: 'Von der Reformation bis zur Romantik', *Schweizer
    Musikbuch*, ed. W. Schuh, i (Zürich, 1939), 54–114, esp. 96
W. Jerger: 'Constantin Reindl, ein unbekannter Zeitgenosse W. A.
    Mozarts', *MJb 1954*, 143–9
——: *Constantin Reindl* (Fribourg, 1955)
——: 'Zur Musikgeschichte der deutschsprachigen Schweiz im 18.
    Jahrhundert', *Mf*, xiv (1961), 303–12   WILHELM JERGER

Reinecke, Carl (Heinrich Carsten) (*b* Altona, 23 June
1824; *d* Leipzig, 10 March 1910). German composer
and conductor. He studied with his father, a music
teacher, and after travels through Europe (1845) he was
appointed court pianist in Copenhagen in 1846. In 1851
he moved to Cologne, where he taught at Hiller's conservatory. After a period as musical director and conductor in Barmen, 1854–9, he spent ten months in
Breslau as director of music at the university and conductor of the Singakademie. From 1860 he taught at the
Leipzig Conservatory, becoming director in 1897, and
was also conductor of the Gewandhaus Orchestra until
1895 (when he was succeeded by Nikisch); a stern disciplinarian, he achieved a high standard of virtuosity
from his players. He became a member of the Berlin
Academy in 1875, and a professor in 1885. He retired in
1902, though his creative work continued.

As a composer Reinecke was a master of the so-called
'Hausmusik' and of the simpler forms popular at the
time. Among his vocal works are several musical fairy-
tales, based in part on his own texts (written under the
name Heinrich Carsten) and set in a folklike style. As an
opera composer he was best known for his lighter
works, among which *Der Gouverneur von Tours* excels.
The large-scale *König Manfred*, markedly influenced by
Wagner, is notable for its preludes.

all published in Leipzig

Der vierjährige Posten op.45 (operetta, 1, after T. Körner), Barmen,
    1855, vs (1856)
König Manfred op.93 (grosse Oper, 5, F. Röber), Wiesbaden, 26
    July 1867 (?1870)
Kathleen und Charlie (Liederspiel, H. Grans), Leipzig, 12 Nov
    1870; rev. as Ein Abenteuer Händels, oder Die Macht des Liedes
    op.104 (Spl, 1, W. te Grove), Schwerin, 18 March 1874 (1874)

Glückskind und Pechvogel op.117 (Märchenoper für Kinder, 2, H. Carsten and R. Leander), unperf. (1883)
Auf hohen Befehl op.184 (komische Oper), Hamburg, Stadt, 1 Oct 1886, vs (c1886)
Der Gouverneur von Tours (komische Oper, 3, E. Bormann), Schwerin, 22 Nov 1891 (1891)

*

StiegerO
F. Reinecke: *Verzeichniss der Compositionen von Carl Reinecke* (Leipzig, 1889)
W. J. von Wasielewski: *Carl Reinecke* (Leipzig, 1892)
E. Segnitz: *Carl Reinecke* (Leipzig, 1900)
H. J. Moser: *Geschichte der deutschen Musik*, ii/2 (Stuttgart and Berlin, 1924)
R. Sietz: 'Reinecke, Carl Heinrich Carsten', *Rheinischer Musiker*, iii, ed. K. G. Fellerer (Cologne, 1964), 68–73   REINHOLD SIETZ/R

Reine de Chypre, La ('The Queen of Cyprus'). *Opéra* in five acts by FROMENTAL HALÉVY to a libretto by JULES-HENRI VERNOY DE SAINT-GEORGES; Paris, Opéra, 22 December 1841.

This opera is famous for its association with Wagner, who was employed during his first stay in Paris arranging the vocal score, and who wrote admiringly of it in his reports to the *Dresdener Abend-Zeitung*. Set in 1469 at the time of the Venetian annexation of Cyprus, the opera was regarded by some as superior even to *La Juive*, and the last act duet between Catarina Cornaro (contralto) and her lover Gérard (tenor) is one of Halévy's greatest scenes. Catarina, a Venetian, is betrothed against her will to Lusignan, king of Cyprus (baritone). When Gérard is set upon by assassins acting on the orders of Mocenigo (baritone), member of the Council of Ten, he is saved by an unknown man who turns out later to be Lusignan, his rival for the hand of Catarina. Lusignan dies defending his kingdom against the Venetians.

Halévy's word-setting is fallible but his craft in building big scenes and in engineering harmonic surprises is highly developed. The choruses are usually long and homophonic in style, supporting the spectacular scenes.
HUGH MACDONALD

Reine de Saba, La ('The Queen of Sheba'). *Opéra* in five acts by CHARLES-FRANÇOIS GOUNOD to a libretto by JULES BARBIER and MICHEL CARRÉ after GÉRARD DE NERVAL's collection of stories *Le voyage en Orient*; Paris, Opéra, 28 February 1862.

The biblical king Soliman [Solomon] (bass – 'première basse de grand opéra') wishes to marry Balkis, Queen of Sheba ('falcon' soprano), but unknown to him she and his principal sculptor and architect Adoniram ('fort' tenor) are drawn together because of their common divine forefather, Tubalkaïn. Three dissatisfied workers sabotage Adoniram's magnum opus, the casting of a mammoth bronze vessel, but he recovers from this setback with the help of spirits from the underworld realm of Tubalkaïn. In an attempt to elope, Adoniram abruptly announces his departure from Solomon's service and Balkis drugs the king. The plan is foiled, however, when the three workers murder Adoniram at the isolated location of his rendezvous with Balkis.

The work was severely condemned by almost the entire Parisian press. In spite of Gounod's efforts to clarify motivations of the characters through thematic recollections, critics were mystified by the racial origin of and ideological imperatives for the Balkis-Adoniram union; the opera was withdrawn after only 15 performances. With some revisions, it fared better at the Théâtre de la Monnaie and became part of the repertory there in the 1860s and 70s. Performances in England in 1865, at the Crystal Palace (where the title role became Irene and the setting was shifted to Turkey), as well as a Parisian revival in 1900 were unsuccessful.   STEVEN HUEBNER

Reiner, Fritz (*b* Budapest, 19 Dec 1888; *d* New York, 15 Nov 1963). American conductor of Hungarian birth. He studied composition with Koessler and piano with Bartók at the Liszt Academy of Music, Budapest. In 1909 he made his conducting début with *Carmen* for the Vigopera company in Budapest, and in 1910 he became conductor at the Landestheater in Laibach (now Ljubljana). He conducted the Népopera company in Budapest from 1911 until 1914, when he was appointed conductor and musical director at the Dresden Staatsoper. There he came into contact with Arthur Nikisch (a major influence on his conducting style) and Richard Strauss, with whose works he became closely associated (he conducted the first German production of *Die Frau ohne Schatten* in 1919).

After brief periods in Barcelona, Rome and elsewhere, Reiner settled in the USA, becoming an American citizen in 1928. He conducted opera in Philadelphia (1932–3) and San Francisco (1936–8) and gave the premières of Menotti's *Amelia al ballo* (1937, Philadelphia) and Douglas Moore's *The Devil and Daniel Webster* (1939, New York). After spending some years teaching at the Curtis Institute, Philadelphia, where his pupils included Bernstein and Foss, he conducted at the Metropolitan Opera (1948–53), giving the American première of *The Rake's Progress* in 1953. Reiner's visits to Europe included his Covent Garden début in 1936–7 at Beecham's invitation, when he conducted *Tristan und Isolde* for Flagstad's London début, and *Die Meistersinger* at the rebuilt Vienna Staatsoper in 1955.

Reiner was irascible and impatient with his musicians, but he placed great emphasis on rhythmic precision and clarity of texture. His performances were elegant and unsentimental, but capable of great dramatic impact, and his gestures were sparing: his beat ('a short man who used a big baton') was the smallest since Richard Strauss's, and his performances sounded correspondingly alert.

*

H. C. Schonberg: *The Great Conductors* (New York, 1967), 335ff
PHILIP HART, ROBERT PHILIP

Reinhardt, Delia (*b* Elberfeld, 27 April 1892; *d* Arlesheim, 3 Oct 1974). German soprano. She studied in Frankfurt with Strakosch and Hedwig Schako and made her début at Breslau in 1913. Three years later she was engaged by the Munich Hofoper, where she remained until 1923, being especially admired in the Mozart repertory. From Munich she went to the Berlin Staatsoper, where she appeared regularly until 1938, singing more than 60 roles including Octavian, the Empress (*Die Frau ohne Schatten*), the Composer, Christine (*Intermezzo*), Elsa, Elisabeth (*Tannhäuser*) and Eva, as well as roles in works by Milhaud, Schreker and Weill. She appeared at Covent Garden between 1924 and 1929 and sang Octavian in the famous performances of *Der Rosenkavalier* under Bruno Walter, with Lotte Lehmann, Elisabeth Schumann and Richard Mayr. In London she also sang Cherubino, Freia, Gutrune, Micaëla, Mimì and Butterfly. She appeared at the Metropolitan Opera for two seasons, 1922–4. Her first husband was the baritone Gustav

Schützendorf, her second the conductor Georges Sébastian.   HAROLD ROSENTHAL/R

Reinhardt, Heinrich (*b* Pressburg [now Bratislava], 13 April 1865; *d* Vienna, 31 Jan 1922). Austrian composer. He studied in Vienna at the conservatory of the Gesellschaft der Musikfreunde, where he was one of Bruckner's pupils. He became an accomplished pianist and organist, and his familiarity with several other instruments later served him well as orchestrator of his own works and those of others. Between 1890 and 1900 he published numerous songs, piano and salon pieces, as well as an opera, *Die Minnekönigin* (1895). He also wrote music criticism but abandoned this after the tremendous success of his first operetta *Das süsse Mädel* in 1901. Somewhat in the style of a musical comedy, it opened a new phase for Viennese operetta, though Reinhardt's later works in the genre were eclipsed by those of Eysler, Lehár, Straus and Fall.

operettas unless otherwise stated

Die Minnekönigin (komische Oper, 1, H. Koppel), 1895, vs (Vienna, 1895)
Das süsse Mädel (3, A. Landesberg and L. Stein), Vienna, Carl, 25 Oct 1901, vs (Vienna, 1902)
Der liebe Schatz (3, Landesberg and Stein), Vienna, Carl, 30 Oct 1902, vs (Vienna, ?1902)
Der Generalkonsul (3, Landesberg and Stein), Vienna, Wien, 29 Jan 1904, vs (Vienna, ?1904)
Krieg im Frieden (3, J. Wilhelm, after G. Moser and F. von Schönthan), Vienna, Carl, 24 Jan 1906, vs (Vienna, ?1906)
Die süssen Grisetten (1, Wilhelm), Vienna, Cabaret Hölle, 1 Dec 1907, vs (London, 1912)
Ein Mädchen für Alles (3, H. von Waldberg and A. M. Willner), Munich, Gärtnerplatz, 8 Feb 1908, vs (Vienna, ?1908)
Die Sprudelfee (2, Wilhelm and Willner), Vienna, Raimund, 23 Jan 1909, vs (?Zürich, ?1909)
Die siamesischen Zwillinge (1, A. Ress and L. Windhopp), Vienna, Cabaret Hölle, 16 March 1909
Studentenhochzeit (1, Reinhardt), Vienna, Cabaret Hölle, 1 Oct 1910
Miss Exzentrik (1, A. Engel and A. Friedmann), Vienna, Apollo, 1 Nov 1910
Napoleon und die Frauen (3 parts: Die Frau Oberst, Die Putzmacherin, Die Wienerin) (Spl, Reinhardt), Vienna, Volksoper, 1 May 1912, vs (Vienna, 1912)
Prinzess Gretl (3, Willner and R. Bodanzky), Vienna, Wien, 31 Jan 1913, vs (Zürich, ?1913)
Die erste Frau (3, Willner and R. Oesterreicher), Vienna, Carl, 22 Oct 1915, vs (Vienna, ?1915)
Der Gast des Königs (komische Oper, 3, Friedmann, after Dickens), Vienna, Volksoper, 9 Jan 1916, vs (Vienna and Leipzig, 1916)
Der Glückstrompeter (3, G. Beer and Friedmann), Vienna, Komödienhaus, 7 Dec 1922
Der Söldner (dramatische Oper), 1922
Grisettenliebe (3, Wilhelm), Vienna, Rolandbühne, 23 March 1928

*

StiegerO   ANDREW LAMB

Reinhardt [Goldmann], **Max** (*b* Baden, Austria, 9 Sept 1873; *d* New York, 31 Oct 1943). Austrian director. He began as an actor in Salzburg, but by 1903 he was devoting himself exclusively to production, responding with enthusiasm and taste to the new theatrical ideas and methods then evolving. He is generally associated with stage spectacle, having effectively mounted many scenic extravaganzas with huge casts, such as *Oedipus rex* (1910) in a Vienna circus, *The Miracle* at Olympia, London (1911), and the annual Salzburg Festival presentations of the morality *Jedermann* in the Domplatz. Like Dyagilev he was a remarkable entrepreneur with a talent for choosing the ideal actors, designers, choreographers and musicians for each production. Music played a substantial part in all his productions, and he

supervised the choice of music. He carefully stage-managed musicians, concealing them, costuming them to mix with actors, or leaving them in the orchestra pit, as required. He worked closely with the composers he commissioned, who included Humperdinck for *The Miracle* and *Twelfth Night*; Weill for Werfel's *The Eternal Road*; Leo Blech for *The Taming of the Shrew*; Pfitzner for Kleist's *Kätchen von Heilbronn*; and Einar Nilson, his musical director and staff composer for over 15 years.

One of Reinhardt's most popular productions was *Orphée aux enfers*, which he first staged with singing actors at the Neues Theater, Berlin, in 1906; Klemperer, then a student, was first choirmaster and then conductor. In 1911 he produced Offenbach's *La belle Hélène* in Venice, and in 1930 the first of several revivals of *Die Fledermaus*. He is best remembered on the opera stage, however, for directing the première of *Der Rosenkavalier*, with sets and costumes by Alfred Roller (1911, Dresden); he also staged the première of the original version of *Ariadne auf Naxos* in Stuttgart (1912), with designs by Ernst Stern. His influence on Strauss and Hofmannsthal was considerable; both *Salome* and *Elektra* were directly inspired by his productions of dramatic versions. In 1920 Strauss, Hofmannsthal and Reinhardt united to create the Salzburg Festival. The idea for the festival, its location and its emphases (Mozart and the Austrian dramatic tradition), were his, and he remained active in it until forced into exile in America in 1937. Among his accomplishments there were the annual productions of *Jedermann* and *Faust*, and his last new opera production, Offenbach's *Les contes d'Hoffmann* (1931). His letters and other writings were published as *Ausgewählte Briefe, Reden, Schriften und Szenen aus Regiebüchern* (ed. F. Hadamowsky; Vienna, 1963) and *Briefe, Reden, Aufsätze, Interviews, Gespräche, Auszüge aus Regiebüchern* (ed. H. Fetting; Berlin, 1974).

For illustration *see* DRESDEN, fig.7.

*

ES (H. Jhering and G. C. Castello)
H. Herald and E. Stern: *Reinhardt und seine Bühne* (Berlin, 1918)
O. M. Sayler, ed.: *Max Reinhardt and his Theatre* (New York, 1924)
F. Horch, ed.: *Die Spielpläne Max Reinhardts 1905–1930* (Munich, 1930)
E. Stern: *My Life, My Stage* (London, 1951)
F. Hadamowsky: *Reinhardt und Salzburg* (Salzburg, 1964)
H. Braulich: *Max Reinhardt* (Berlin, 1969)
G. Reinhardt: *Der Liebhaber* (Munich, 1973)
J. Styan: *Max Reinhardt* (Cambridge, 1982)   PAUL SHEREN

Reinhold, Frederick Charles (*b* London, 1737; *d* Somers Town, London, 28 Sept 1815). English bass, son of Henry Reinhold. As 'Master Reinhold' he sang from 1752 and created Oberon in J. C. Smith's opera *The Fairies* (February 1755). His first recorded appearance as a bass was in the chorus for the Foundling Hospital *Messiah* in 1758. His adult stage career developed slowly, with burlettas in Marylebone Gardens, chorus parts at Drury Lane, a Haymarket summer season and a role in Bates's *Pharnaces* (1765, Drury Lane). He was engaged at Covent Garden from 1769, singing traditional bass parts such as Hecate in *Macbeth* but also Hawthorne in *Love in a Village* and Giles in *The Maid of the Mill*, roles created by John Beard. His performance of the traitor Artabanes in Arne's *Artaxerxes* was much admired. Dibdin wrote that he was 'really possessed of a voice' but spoiled it by too much falsetto. He became organist of St George the Martyr, Bloomsbury, in 1783 and left Covent Garden the next year. He continued to sing in oratorios (Polyphemus in *Acis and Galatea* was a favourite part) until March 1798.

BDA; LS
C. Dibdin: *A Complete History of the English Stage*, v (London, 1800)
J. Boaden: *Memoirs of Mrs Siddons*, i (London, 1827)
J. Brown: *Biographical Dictionary of Musicians* (Paisley, 1886)
OLIVE BALDWIN, THELMA WILSON

Reinhold, Henry [Theodore] (*d* London, 14 May 1751). English bass of German descent. He was second bass in Handel's *Atalanta* in May 1736 and the sole bass the following season, when he sang in the premières of *Arminio*, *Giustino* and *Berenice*. Later in 1737 he created the comic role of the Dragon in Lampe's *The Dragon of Wantley*, which received 68 performances in its first season. His other English stage roles included Sir Trusty in Arne's *Rosamond* and the Lion in Lampe's *Pyramus and Thisbe*. He sang in Handel's last two operas, *Imeneo* (1740) and *Deidamia* (1741), by which time he was the composer's principal oratorio bass. The roles of Harapha in *Samson*, Cadmus, High Priest and Somnus in *Semele*, the title role in *Hercules* and many others were written for him. On his death the *General Advertiser* described him as 'not less admired for his private Character than his publick Performance'. In the records of the Royal Society of Musicians, of which he was a founder member, his name is given as Theodore, but the burial register at St Anne's Soho calls him Henry.

BDA; LS
W. Dean: *Handel's Dramatic Oratorios and Masques* (London, 1959)
OLIVE BALDWIN, THELMA WILSON

Reining, Maria (*b* Vienna, 7 Aug 1903; *d* Vienna, 11 March 1991). Austrian soprano. She studied in Vienna, making her début in 1931 at the Staatsoper as a soubrette and remaining for two seasons. After appearances in Darmstadt (1933–5) she joined the Staatsoper in Munich. She returned to Vienna in 1937, singing there regularly until 1958. She appeared at Salzburg from 1937 to 1941, as Eva, Euryanthe, Elisabeth (*Tannhäuser*), Countess Almaviva and Pamina, and returned as Arabella (1947) and the Marschallin (1949 and 1953). In 1938 she sang Elsa at Covent Garden and Eva and Butterfly at Chicago; in 1949, the Marschallin at the Paris Opéra and the Marschallin and Ariadne at the New York City Opera. She had a beautiful, well-schooled voice and an elegant and aristocratic stage presence.

A. Blyth: 'Maria Reining', *Opera*, xxxix (1988), 545–50
HAROLD ROSENTHAL/R

Reinmar [Wochinz], **Hans** (*b* Vienna, 11 April 1895; *d* Berlin, 7 Feb 1961). Austrian baritone. He studied in Vienna and Milan, making his début at Olomouc in 1919. Nuremberg, Zürich, Dresden and Hamburg claimed him in turn, until in 1928 he sang at the Staatsoper in Berlin where, apart from a break in the 1940s, he remained until his death. At Bayreuth his roles included Gunther and Amfortas, and at Salzburg in 1942 he sang an admired Mandryka. He was also a guest artist at La Scala and in Vienna, Paris and Rome.

His Italian training helped him to play a leading part in the Verdi revivals, such as those of *Simon Boccanegra* and *Don Carlos* in Berlin. His many recordings cover both the Italian and the German parts of his repertory, showing a voice of considerable power and beauty, used with scrupulous care for evenness of production.

J. B. STEANE

Reinthaler, Karl (Martin) (*b* Erfurt, 13 Oct 1822; *d* Bremen, 13 Feb 1896). German composer. He studied with A. B. Marx in Berlin and took singing lessons from Giulio Bordogni in Paris. In 1853 he obtained a post at the Cologne Conservatory and in 1858 became organist of Bremen Cathedral and conductor of the Singakademie. He was a friend of Brahms. In 1875 his opera *Edda* (4, E. Hopffer) was successfully produced at Bremen, Hanover and elsewhere. His only other opera, *Käthchen von Heilbronn* (4, F. Bulthaupt), based on Kleist's drama, was chosen by competition for the opening in 1881 of the new opera house at Frankfurt.

FRANZ GEHRING

Reise, Jay (*b* New York, 9 Feb 1950). American composer. He was a student at Hamilton College and McGill University before doing graduate work at the University of Pennsylvania, where he studied with George Crumb and Richard Wernick. He taught at Hamilton and at Kirkland College, then at the University of Pennsylvania, where he became Professor of Music. He has received fellowships from the Fromm, Guggenheim and Rockefeller foundations.

Reise's two-act opera *Rasputin* was commissioned by Beverly Sills and the New York City Opera and first performed by that company at the New York State Theater, Lincoln Center, on 17 September 1988, with Christopher Keene conducting and Frank Corsaro directing. Reise himself wrote the libretto, basing it on historical accounts of the life of Rasputin (bass-baritone), depicting his ritual orgies (there are scenes involving total nudity), his gradually increasing influence over Tsar Nicholas II (tenor) and Tsarina Alexandra (soprano), his murder by the effeminate Prince Yusupov (tenor), who earlier sings a cabaret-style aria in drag, and the eventual murder of the Romanov family at the hands of Bolshevik revolutionaries. The amplified voice of Lenin (a speaking role) goads the proletariat on to still bloodier deeds.

Imaginatively scored for large orchestra, *Rasputin* is predominantly atonal and strongly dissonant. The music for the Romanovs, however, is often tonal in a lush, early 20th-century style, reminiscent of Richard Strauss and Berg, symbolically depicting the decay of 19th-century aesthetics and politics in juxtaposition with the harsh (atonal) reality of anarchy and the Revolution. The clash of contrasting styles and centuries is further reflected in a ballroom scene churning with distorted references to one of the waltzes from Tchaikovsky's *Swan Lake*. Touches of minimalism depict Rasputin's hypnotic powers.

Reise's other works include three symphonies and pieces for large and small instrumental ensembles.

D. Burgwyn: 'Rasputin's Song', *Philadelphia Magazine*, lxxix/12 (1988), 117–21
R. H. Kornick: *Recent American Opera: a Production Guide* (New York, 1991), 239–41
JAMES FREEMAN

Reisen, Mark. *See* REYZEN, MARK.

Reisinger, Barbara. *See* GERL, BARBARA.

Reiss, Albert (*b* Berlin, 22 Feb 1870; *d* Nice, 19 June 1940). German tenor. He studied in Berlin with Vilmar and later with Stolzenburg and Lieban, making his début at Königsberg in 1897 as Ivanov (*Zar und Zimmermann*). After engagements at Posen and Wiesbaden, in 1901 he was engaged by the Metropolitan, where he sang every season until 1919–20, being especially acclaimed for his David in *Die Meistersinger* and Mime in the *Ring*; he also appeared with success as the Witch in *Hänsel und Gretel*. In New York he created Nick in *La fanciulla del West* (1910), the Broom-maker in Humperdinck's *Königskinder* (1910), Nial in Parker's *Mona* (1912) and Richard in De Koven's *Canterbury Pilgrims* (1917). He sang Alfred in the Metropolitan première of *Die Fledermaus* (1905), Vašek in the Metropolitan première of *The Bartered Bride* (1909) and Valzacchi in the American première of *Der Rosenkavalier* (1913). At Covent Garden (1902–5, 1924–9) he sang David, Mime and Valzacchi. Returning to Germany, he sang at the Berlin Volksoper (1923–5) and later at the Städtische Oper. He was one of the most successful comprimario tenors of his day. HAROLD ROSENTHAL/R

Reissiger, Karl Gottlieb (*b* Belzig, 31 Jan 1798; *d* Dresden, 7 Nov 1859). German composer. He studied the piano and composition at the Thomasschule in Leipzig, and on the advice of his teacher, Schicht, abandoned his theological studies at the University of Leipzig in order to pursue a musical career. He took theory lessons from Salieri in Vienna in 1821 and the following year moved to Munich to study composition and singing with Winter. His opera *Didone abbandonata* was given in Dresden in 1824 under the direction of Weber with moderate success, and Reissiger was given 500 thalers by the King of Prussia to study methods of music education in France and Italy and to advise on its reorganization in Berlin.

On his return to Berlin in 1825 he taught composition until invited in the following year to succeed Weber as director of the Hofoper in Dresden. As a champion of German opera, he was at first harassed by pro-Italian factions, but his excellent performances of *Oberon* and *Euryanthe* won him approval, and in 1828 he was appointed Hofkapellmeister, with responsibility for sacred music, chamber music and the music for the court theatre, a post he held until his death. Under Reissiger's direction the Dresden Opera became acknowledged as the best in Germany; in 1842 he gave the first performance of Wagner's *Rienzi* and in 1843 welcomed its composer as second Kapellmeister. Relations between the two men deteriorated when Reissiger declined to set Wagner's libretto *Die hohe Braut*, after which Wagner portrayed him, apparently quite falsely, as a philistine opponent of his progressive artistic views. Reissiger was a gifted conductor and was also regularly called upon to direct music festivals, adjudicate at competitions and advise on music education. Clara Schumann was one of his theory pupils.

Reissiger embodied the dying tradition of the Kapellmeister-composer, and despite sound craftsmanship his music has been forgotten, perhaps because of lack of individuality. Weak librettos and lack of dramatic sense hampered him in opera, his favourite but least successful form; only *Die Felsenmühle* (1831) was successful outside Dresden, though the melodrama *Yelva* (1828) enjoyed a certain popularity.

Reissiger's younger brother Friedrich August (1809–83) gained a modest reputation in Christiania (now Oslo) as a conductor, military bandmaster and composer; his works include four operas.

first performed at the Hofoper, Dresden, unless otherwise stated

Das Rockenweibchen, 1821, unperf., ov. pubd
Didone abbandonata (os, 2, P. Metastasio), 31 Jan 1824
Der Ahnenschatz (G. Döring), 1825, inc., unperf.
Yelva (melodrama, 2, T. Hell, after E. Scribe), 21 Oct 1828
Libella (grosse Oper, 2, Theophania), 4 Jan 1829
Die Felsenmühle zu Etalières (romantische Oper, 2, B. von Miltitz), 10 April 1831
Turandot (grosse Oper, 2, C. Gozzi), 22 Jan 1835
Adèle de Foix (grosse Oper, 4, R. Blum), 26 Nov 1841
Der Schiffbruch der Medusa (4, after Brothers Cogniard), 16 Aug 1846

*

W. Neumann: *K. G. Reissiger* (Kassel, 1854)
R. Prölss: *Geschichte des Hoftheaters zu Dresden* (Dresden, 1878)
H. von Brescius: *Die königliche sächsische musikalische Kapelle von Reissiger bis Schuch (1826–1898): Festschrift des 350jährigen Kapelljubiläums* (Dresden, 1898)
A. Kohut: 'R. Wagner und K. G. Reissiger', *AMz*, xxxvii (1910), 33–5
J. Reichelt: 'R. Wagner und sein Kollege Reissiger', *AMz*, xl (1913), 505–7
B. Kortsen, ed.: *Bref fra F. A. Reissiger* (Bergen, 1976)
JOHN RUTTER

Reissmann, August (Friedrich Wilhelm) (*b* Frankenstein, Silesia, 14 Nov 1825; *d* Berlin, 13 July 1903). German writer on music and composer. In 1850 he settled in Weimar and from 1863 to 1880 lived in Berlin, where he remained for the rest of his life, teaching at the Stern Conservatory from 1866 to 1874. Most of his writing, which includes books on the life and works of Haydn, Gluck, Handel and Weber, shows a conservative bias; but the *Musikalisches Conversations-Lexikon*, which he edited after the death of its previous editor Hermann Mendel, is still useful as a wide-ranging reference book for 19th-century music (vii–xi and suppl.; Berlin, 1877–80, 3/1890–91). Though he never won a reputation as a composer, Reissmann wrote three operas. *Gudrun* was based on a German poem, and the remaining two on historical events.

Gudrun (3, Reissmann), Leipzig, 7 Oct 1871
Die Bürgermeisterin von Schorndorf (komische Oper, 3, Reissmann), Leipzig, 1 Nov 1880
Das Gralspiel (3, Reissmann), Düsseldorf, 19 Jan 1895

*

*Stieger*O
J. Göllrich: *August Reissmann als Schriftsteller und Komponist* (Leipzig, 1884) MARTIN ELSTE

Reiter, Josef (*b* Braunau, 19 Jan 1862; *d* Bad Reichenhall, 2 June 1939). Austrian composer. After studying music with his father in Braunau, in 1886 he went to Vienna, where he worked as a music teacher and conductor. From 1908 to 1911 he was director of the Mozarteum in Salzburg, and in 1917–18 Kapellmeister at the Hofburgtheater in Vienna. Primarily a composer of lieder and choral music, Reiter wrote a number of operas in a neo-Wagnerian style, none of which achieved any lasting success. *Der Bundschuh* (1897) is a setting of a love story between the peasant Hans Fuchs and the chatelaine Ehrengard, which takes place against the background of the Thirty Years War. It was given by Mahler at the Hofoper in Vienna in 1901, but withdrawn after five performances. When in 1904 Reiter submitted his next opera, *Der Totentanz*, for performance in Vienna, it was rejected by Mahler. Both works were revived some 30 years later at the Deutsches Opernhaus in Berlin in 1938 as a result of the composer's fervent support for Hitler and the *Anschluss*. An early opera, *Fritjof*, was never performed.

Fritjof, 1884–5, unperf.
Klopstock in Zürich (1, M. Morold), Linz, 12 April 1893
Der Bundschuh (1, Morold), Troppau, 18 March 1897, vs (Leipzig, 1901)
Der Totentanz (3, Morold), Dessau, 5 Nov 1905, vs (Vienna, 1905)
Der Tell (3, Morold), Vienna, Volksoper, 3 Nov 1917, vs (Leipzig and Zürich, 1917)

M. Morold: *Josef Reiter* (Vienna, 1904)
L. Etzmansdorfer: *Josef Reiter* (Braunau, 1923)
M. Morold: 'Josef Reiter zu seinem 75. Geburtstag', *ZfM*, Jg.104 (1937), 21–4
M. Langer: 'Dem Tondichter Joseph Reiter zum Gedenken', *Unsere Heimat*, xxxiii (Vienna, 1962), 72–4　　ERIK LEVI

Reizenstein, Franz (Theodor) (*b* Nuremberg, 7 June 1911; *d* London, 15 Oct 1968). English composer of German birth. From 1930 he studied composition with Hindemith at the Berlin State Academy. When the Nazis came to power he left for London, where he studied composition with Vaughan Williams at the RCM and the piano privately with Solomon. He taught the piano at the RAM (1958–68) and the RMCM (1962–8), and went to Boston University as visiting professor of composition in 1966. His early output consisted largely of piano and chamber music. In 1951 the success of his major choral work, *Voices of Night*, led to a commission for the one-act radio opera *Anna Kraus* op.30; this was first broadcast on 5 March 1952. The texts for both were written by his friend Christopher Hassall. *Anna Kraus* was the first British opera written specifically for radio; the style is simple and direct, with no concerted numbers, underlying unity depending on the close working of a few leading motifs. The opera (which dispenses with any narrator) tells the tragic story of Anna, who has lost her family in a Polish pogrom, and is finally driven to murder and suicide.

C. Mason: 'An Opera for Broadcasting', *The Listener* (26 Feb 1953)　　HUGO COLE

Rellstab, (Heinrich Friedrich) Ludwig (*b* Berlin, 13 April 1799; *d* Berlin, 27 Nov 1860). German music critic and poet, son of the music publisher and composer J. C. F. Rellstab. Before abandoning a military career in 1821, he had begun keyboard lessons with Ludwig Berger and the study of theory with Bernhard Klein, with both of whom as well as Gustav Reichardt he helped found the Jüngere Liedertafel in 1819. His first set of poems appeared in 1823, and he completed the libretto for Klein's *Dido* the same year. In 1826 he became the music critic for the *Vossische Zeitung*; he also edited the periodical *Berlin und Athen* (1836) and in 1830 founded *Iris im Gebiete der Tonkunst*. By the late 1830s he had become Berlin's most influential critic.

As an outspoken supporter of Weber and proponent of German opera, Rellstab in 1826 produced a booklet which satirized not only the singer Henriette Sontag, who had created a vogue for Rossini, but also many of her Berlin admirers. The situation became highly politicized, and Rellstab was forced to serve a three-month 'Festungsarrest' at Spandau in 1827. He was severely critical of Spontini, who was Generalmusikdirektor in Berlin and the personal favourite of King Friedrich Wilhelm III, and was again imprisoned in

1836. His attitude towards Meyerbeer was initially unfavourable, and he had reported negatively on the Berlin presentation of *Les Huguenots* in 1842; but a reconciliation was brought about with the help of Liszt, and Rellstab was entrusted with the German versification of Scribe's adjusted scenario for Meyerbeer's *Ein Feldlager in Schlesien* celebrating the reopening of the royal opera house on 7 December 1844. He also made German translations of numerous works including the librettos to Lord John Fane Burghersh's *L'eroe di Lancastro*, Halévy's *Le val d'Andorre* and *Le Juif errant*, and Meyerbeer's *Le prophète* and *L'étoile du nord*.

LIBRETTOS
Dido (Oper, 3), B. Klein, 1823; Irene (grosse Oper, 3), C. Arnold and Klein, 1832; Ein Feldlager in Schlesien (Spl, 3, after E. Scribe), Meyerbeer, 1844 [with C. Birch-Pfeiffer]

WRITINGS
Henriette oder Die schöne Sängerin (Leipzig, 1826) [under pseud. F. Zuschauer]
Über mein Verhältnis als Kritiker zu Herrn Spontini (Leipzig, 1827)
Beurtheilung der Kompositionen des Fürsten Anton Radziwill zu Goethes Faust (Berlin, 1836)
Die Gestaltung der Oper seit Mozart (Sondershausen, 1859)

C. F. Müller: *Spontini und Rellstab: einige Worte zur Beherzigung der Partheien* (Berlin, 1833)
L. E. Kossatz: *Aphorismen über Rellstabs Kunstkritik* (Berlin, 1846)
E. König: *Ludwig Rellstab: ein Beitrag zur Geschichte der Unterhaltungsliteratur in Deutschland* (Würzburg, 1938)
K. Goedeke: *Grundriss zur Geschichte der deutschen Dichtung aus den Quellen*, xi/1 (Düsseldorf, 2/1951); xiv (Berlin, 2/1959)
W. Franke: *Der Theaterkritiker Ludwig Rellstab* (Berlin, 1964)　　SHELLEY DAVIS

Remedios, Alberto (Telisforo) (*b* Liverpool, 27 Feb 1935). English tenor. He studied at the RCM and made his début at Sadler's Wells in 1957 as Tinca (*Tabarro*). Other roles for Sadler's Wells were Don Ottavio, Tamino, Alfredo, Jake (*Aufsteig und Fall der Stadt Mahagonny*), Bacchus, Erik, Max, Florestan and Samson. In 1965 he toured Australia with the Sutherland-Williamson company, as Faust and Lensky, then made his Covent Garden début as Dmitry, followed by Erik and Mark (*The Midsummer Marriage*). In 1968 he sang Walther at Sadler's Wells and was then engaged for two seasons at Frankfurt. His roles for Sadler's Wells/ENO included Berlioz's Faust, Don Alvaro, Siegmund, Siegfried, Lohengrin, Massenet's Des Grieux and Tristan (1981). In 1973 he made his American début at San Francisco as Dmitry, then sang Don Carlos. In 1975 he sang Otello for the WNO and in 1976 made his Metropolitan début as Bacchus. For Scottish Opera he has sung Aeneas (*Les Troyens*), Stravinsky's Oedipus and Laca. His repertory included Peter Grimes and Radames. With a strong yet lyrical voice, capable of singing Mozart and Wagner, he excelled as Bacchus, Walther and the young Siegfried. He was made a CBE in 1981.

E. Forbes: 'Alberto Remedios', *Opera*, xxiv (1973), 15–21　　ALAN BLYTH

Remedios, Ramon (*b* Liverpool, 9 May 1940). English tenor, brother of Alberto Remedios. After studying at the GSM, he sang with Opera for All (1965–7). He joined the WNO in 1968, and has sung Ismaele (*Nabucco*), Grigory, Alfredo, Macduff, Almaviva, Tamino, the Painter (*Lulu*), the Novice (*Billy Budd*), Don Ottavio, the Duke, Rodolfo and Skuratov (*From the House of the Dead*). His roles for the ENO include

Don José and David. At Cologne he sang Ernesto, Lensky, Froh and Pinkerton. He made his Covent Garden début in 1982 as Narraboth, returning as Uldino (*Attila*) in 1990, and has also sung at Frankfurt and in France. His sweet-toned, lyrical voice is well suited to such roles as Nadir.   ELIZABETH FORBES

Reminiscence motif (Ger. *Reminiszenzmotiv, Erinnerungsmotiv*). A theme, or other coherent musical idea, which returns more or less unaltered, as identification for the audience or to signify recollection of the past by a dramatic character. It is an important ancestor of the LEITMOTIF.

The systematic use of motifs for dramatic purposes first developed in France and Germany in late 18th-century opera, though earlier examples may be found (for example where one character quotes another's music allusively). With the weakening of the closed aria form, greater importance began to pass to arioso, recitative and scena; and the association of motifs with characters and events began now to provide not only a useful system of illustration but, gradually, the means of applying formal control through quasi-symphonic techniques. An early formulation of the principle of associating a musical idea with a character occurs in Lacépède's *La poétique de la musique*, ii (1785): a chapter on 'Des caractères des personnages considérés relativement à la tragédie lyrique' proposes for the musician that, in 'chaque morceau qu'il composera, il comparera ce sentiment qu'il aura, pour ainsi dire, créé, avec celui que le morceau devra montrer et faire naître' ('in each piece that he composes, he shall match this feeling that he will have, so to speak, created, with the person whom the piece is to show and bring to life').

Mozart's use of motif was generally confined to such straightforward devices as the recurrence, in *Le nozze di Figaro* (1786), of Figaro's 'Se vuol ballare' to re-emphasize his intentions towards Count Almaviva, but there are prefigurations of later techniques in *Idomeneo* (1781), particularly in figures associated with the emotions of Ilia and the sacrifice of Idamantes. Other operas of the closing decades of the 18th century make effective use of reminiscence motifs. A celebrated instance is Blondel's song in Grétry's *Richard Coeur-de-lion* (1784); the device was also used by Méhul (*Ariodant*, 1799) and Catel (*Sémiramis*, 1802), among many others, to provide a reminder of a previous dramatic event. The quotation of a substantial part of a whole number for dramatic effect remained a familiar device, as with 'The Last Rose of Summer' in Flotow's *Martha* (1847) or 'La donna è mobile' in Verdi's *Rigoletto* (1851). Verdi also used reminiscence more subtly, for example in the moving recall, in *Otello* (1887), just before Otello kills Desdemona, of the theme associated with their loving embrace.

Although composers have continued to use simple thematic recall, or thematic 'labels', to identify or characterize individuals, ideas and events on their recurrence, most have chosen to avail themselves of the additional dramatic and expressive resources offered, in the light of the Wagnerian leitmotif, by thematic transformation and development.

For bibliography *see* LEITMOTIF.

Renard ('Reynard') [*Bayka pro lisu, petukha, kota da barana* ('Fable of the Vixen, the Cock, the Cat and the Ram')]. A 'merry performance with singing and [instru-

mental] music' by IGOR STRAVINSKY to his own libretto after Alexander Afanas'yev's *Russkiye narodnïye skazki* ('Russian Folktales', 1855–64); Paris, Opéra, 18 May 1922.

Scored for two tenors, two basses and an 'orchestra' of 15 performers (with a featured cimbalom standing in for the *gusli*, a Russian folk psaltery), this little minstrel show is an opera to the extent that its story unfolds through continuous singing. The singers are placed within the orchestra, however, while the four roles of the title are played by clowns, ballet dancers or acrobats on a trestle stage. The action is slight: a vixen twice succeeds in coaxing a cock down from a tree and into her clutches; the first time the cock is rescued by the cat and the ram, and the vixen runs away; the second time the cat and the ram slay the vixen. The little tale is tricked out with a variety of folk verses, virtuosically set to original music and performed without any fixed correspondence between the voice part and onstage character. Ernest Ansermet conducted the first performance, which was given by the Ballets Russes. The standard Western title, *Renard*, comes from Charles Ferdinand Ramuz's French translation of the libretto.

For illustration *see* STAGE DESIGN, fig. 18.   RICHARD TARUSKIN

Renaud [Croneau], **Maurice** (**Arnold**) (*b* Bordeaux, 24 July 1860; *d* Paris, 16 Oct 1933). French baritone. He made his début in autumn 1883 at La Monnaie, where he later sang in the premières of Reyer's *Sigurd* (1884) and *Salammbô* (1890) in addition to singing a wide variety of French, Italian and Wagnerian roles. From 1890 (début 19 September as Karnac in *Le roi d'Ys*) to 1891 he appeared with the Opéra-Comique and from 1891 (début 17 July as Nélusko in *L'Africaine*) to 1902 he was a member of the Opéra, returning frequently until 1914. He sang at Monte Carlo, 1891–1907, and at New Orleans in 1893. His Covent Garden début was in 1897; he returned for the next two seasons and again (1902–4) as, among others, Don Giovanni, Wolfram, Nevers (*Les Huguenots*), Escamillo, Rigoletto and Lescaut (*Manon*). He appeared with the Manhattan Opera (1906–7, 1909–10), at the Metropolitan (1910–12), in Boston and in Chicago, where he sang Rigoletto, Athanaël, Rance (*La fanciulla del West*) and Coppélius, Dapertutto and Dr Miracle (*Les contes d'Hoffmann*). Renaud had a warm, expressive voice and was considered one of the most versatile singing actors of his day.

*

GV (R. Celletti; R. Vegeto)
A. de Cock and P. G. Hurst: 'Maurice Renaud', *Record Collector*, xi (1957), 75–119, 166–7; xii (1958), 37 [with discography by L. Hevingham-Root]   HAROLD BARNES

Rencontre imprévue, La ('The Unexpected Meeting'). *Opéra comique* in three acts by CHRISTOPH WILLIBALD GLUCK to a libretto after the *opéra comique Les pèlerins de la Mecque* (1726) by Alain-René Lesage and D'Orneval, as revised by Louis Hurtaut Dancourt; Vienna, Burgtheater, 7 January 1764.

Gluck's resetting of this vaudeville classic was his last *opéra comique* for Vienna. Its libretto underwent two revisions: one as Dancourt recast the work as a *comédie mêlée d'ariettes*, and another when, during rehearsals, the death of Isabella of Parma (wife of Joseph II) was seen as resembling too closely the feigned demise of Princess Rezia in the opera. In the work's final form (that generally known), much word-painting is left unexplained; Dancourt and Gluck's original version (which retained the 1726 title) was unperformed until 1990. *La rencontre imprévue* is a 'Turkish' opera, related in plot to Mozart's *Die Entführung aus dem Serail*. Prince Ali's love for Princess Rezia is thwarted by her father's opposition, and the lovers are separated by stratagem and misunderstanding. As the opera opens, Ali (*haute-contre*) and his servant Osmin (baritone) have arrived in Cairo, where Rezia (soprano) is a captive in the Sultan's harem. The couple plan to escape disguised as pilgrims to Mecca, but are betrayed by a mendicant dervish, or Calender (baritone), and threatened with death. The Sultan (bass) is moved to mercy on hearing of their long devotion. Peripheral characters include a 'peintre fou', Vertigo (baritone), who exhibits his canvases with much musical display, and three attendants (all sopranos) to Rezia, who successively test Ali's constancy to the princess he thinks is dead.

Despite a loosely constructed plot, *La rencontre imprévue* was enormously successful in Vienna and elsewhere, on account of its exotic subject and Gluck's highly varied score. To the noble lovers Gluck gave music of a seriousness and difficulty unprecedented in *opéra comique* (Ali was played by an *haute-contre* from the Paris Opéra); elsewhere he employed 'Turkish' music, French-inspired musical coquetry and italianate finales. Mozart paid tribute to Osmin's folklike air 'Les hommes pieusement' ('Unser dummer Pöbel meint') with his piano variations K455.   BRUCE ALAN BROWN

Rendall, David (*b* London, 11 Oct 1948). English tenor. He studied at the RAM and the Salzburg Mozarteum and in 1973 won a Young Musician of the Year Award from the Greater London Arts Association, followed by a Gulbenkian Fellowship in 1975. He made his début with Glyndebourne Touring Opera in 1975 as Ferrando, and then sang the Italian Singer in *Der Rosenkavalier* at Covent Garden, where his roles have included Almaviva, Massenet's Des Grieux, Matteo (*Arabella*), Rodrigo (*La donna del lago*), Flamand (*Capriccio*) and the Duke. In 1976 he first sang at Glyndebourne as Ferrando, returning as Tom Rakewell and Belmonte. At the ENO (1976–92) he has sung Leicester (*Maria Stuarda*), the Duke, Rodolfo and Pinkerton. His North American début was at Ottawa as Tamino in 1977, followed the next year by Rodolfo and Alfredo with New York City Opera and Don Ottavio at San Francisco. His Metropolitan début (1980) was as Don Ottavio, and he returned for Lensky, Matteo, David and Idomeneus. He has sung in Paris, Vienna, Berlin, Hamburg, Buenos Aires, San Francisco, Chicago, Santa Fe and Aix-en-Provence, where he sang Mozart's Titus in 1988. A lyric tenor of accomplished style and versatility, he is an ardent and convicing actor. His recordings include *Maria Stuarda* under Mackerras (1982) and *La rondine* under Maazel (1985).

ELIZABETH FORBES, NOËL GOODWIN

Rendano, Alfonso (*b* Carolei, nr Cosenza, 5 April 1853; *d* Rome, 10 Sept 1931). Italian composer. He studied in Naples, Leipzig and Paris, and his teachers included Thalberg and Reinecke; he became a virtuoso pianist. His few compositions include the lyric drama *Consuelo* (prol., 3, F. Cimmino; Turin, Vittorio Emanuele, 25 May 1902; published Milan, n.d.), based on a novel by George Sand in praise of artistic life and on the consoling power of music. Its première was followed by another successful production, in German (1903, Stuttgart). The libretto was considered untheatrical by critics, including Torchi, because its succession of scenes lacks coherence and hence dramatic power; also, the characterization is colourless and muted – especially the visionary delirium of Alberto (baritone) and the naive and loving courage of Consuelo (soprano). The love duet in Act 2, however, is one of the highlights of the opera. The lengthy score includes arias, songs, dances and ensembles, and makes some use of Wagnerian leitmotifs. The style tends towards the terse elegance of French composers such as Gounod and Saint-Saëns, but the music is unoriginal and pianistic, and the essentially syllabic declamation is overshadowed by the orchestral writing.

*

L. Torchi: '"Consuelo" di Alfonso Rendano', *RMI*, x (1903), 564–80

G. Puccio: *Alfonso Rendano* (Rome, 1937), 105–15

F. Perrino: 'Alfonso Rendano', *Rassegna musicale Curci* [Milan], xv (1961), 10–11   FRANCESCO BUSSI

Rendez-vous bourgeois, Les ('The Bourgeois Rendezvous'). *Opéra-bouffon mêlé d'ariettes* in one act by NICOLAS ISOUARD to a libretto by FRANÇOIS-BENOÎT HOFFMAN; Paris, Opéra-Comique (Salle Feydeau), 9 May 1807.

The retired timber merchant, Dugravier (bass), leaves for Paris with his servant, Bertrand (tenor), to arrange the marriages of his daughter, Reine (soprano), and his niece, Louise (soprano), with the sons of the goldsmith Josse and the restaurant proprietor Rose. Reine and Louise independently confess to their servant Julie (mezzo-soprano) that their secret lovers – César (tenor) and Charles (tenor) – are waiting outside. Julie hides the men in different compartments of a cupboard, her own lover Jasmin (baritone) having already hidden under a table. The unexpected return of Dugravier and Bertrand interrupts Louise's attempt to find her lover in the cupboard. Left alone in the room, Dugravier and his servant are terrified at the sight of the three men escaping through a window. Shortly afterwards the three return, claiming to have chased away some thieves who were in the house. They present themselves as César Josse and Charles Rose. Dugravier gratefully agrees to their marriage with Reine and Louise, while Jasmin can marry Julie.

Isouard adopted a simple and superficially brilliant style for this plot. Most of the musical numbers (*airs*, *couplets*, *romance*, rondò and four ensemble pieces) are found in the first part of the opera, in which a carefree or lyrical mood prevails (nine of the ten musical numbers occur in the first 17 of 28 dramatic scenes), whereas the second, more exciting part is conveyed as a spoken drama. The opera was successfully performed in various European countries and was revived in Paris in 1933.   MICHAEL FEND

Rennert, Günther (*b* Essen, 1 April 1911; *d* Salzburg, 31 July 1978). German director and administrator. He studied law, music, drama and film in Munich, Berlin and Halle. He began his career in 1933 as a film director, but soon moved towards the theatre, encouraged by Walter Felsenstein, whose assistant he became at the Frankfurt opera house. In 1939 he was appointed resident director at the theatre in Königsberg (now Kaliningrad) where he remained until 1942, when he took up a similar post at the Berlin Städtische (now Deutsche) Oper. At the end of the war he was back in

Munich to open the 1945 opera season there with *Fidelio*. In 1946 he was appointed Intendant of the Hamburg Staatsoper, where in addition to strengthening the contemporary repertory with *Peter Grimes* and *The Rake's Progress* he also spearheaded a revival of interest in Rossini's comedies. His productions of *Il barbiere di Siviglia* in Hamburg and *Il turco in Italia* in Stuttgart were regarded as landmarks. In 1959 he staged *Fidelio* at Glyndebourne and the following year was appointed joint artistic director with Vittorio Gui. His productions there included *La pietra del paragone*, *Jephtha*, *Capriccio*, *Elegy for Young Lovers* and *Don Giovanni*. With Raymond Leppard he inaugurated Glyndebourne's series of pre-Classical operas with *L'incoronazione di Poppea* (1962) and Cavalli's *Ormindo* (1967). In 1967 he was appointed Staatsintendant of the Bayerische Staatsoper in Munich, where he remained until 1977, concentrating on the standard German repertory with particular emphasis on the works of Mozart, Wagner and Strauss. His Munich productions of *Die schweigsame Frau* and *Ariadne auf Naxos* were seen at Covent Garden in 1972.

His brother, Wolfgang Rennert (*b* Cologne, 1 April 1922), was appointed Generalmusikdirektor of the Mannheim Opera in 1980. He studied at the Salzburg Mozarteum under Clemens Krauss and made his conducting début (1947) with *Un ballo in maschera* at Düsseldorf in 1947. From 1971 to 1980 he was a Kapellmeister at the Berlin Staatsoper; he specializes in the German repertory and frequently conducts Strauss operas as a guest in the principal German houses. His book *Opernarbeit: Inszenierungen 1963–1973* was published in Munich in 1974.

*

G. Christie: 'Günther Rennert', *Opera*, xxix (1978), 956–8

HUGH CANNING

Rennes. French town, one of the two capitals of Brittany. In 1689 Lully's *Atys* was performed there for the opening of the Parlement, with a new prologue by Pascal Collasse including local colour in its 'Passe-pieds à la manière de Bretagne'. The Théâtre de la Ville in the Place de l'Hôtel de Ville was built by the local architect Charles Millardet and inaugurated in 1836. Its convex façade surmounted by statues of the Muses and Apollo is finely representative of its period. It seats 800 in stalls and three galleries. The interior was destroyed by fire in 1856 and the current interior decoration, with its fine circular ceiling depicting Breton costumes and flora by J. J. Lemordant, dates from 1913. The opera season runs from October to May with, typically, productions of five operas and five operettas, each opera being given three or four performances, the operettas slightly more frequently.

CHARLES PITT

Reno. American city in the state of Nevada. It is the home of Nevada Opera, founded in 1968, which performs in the Pioneer Center for the Performing Arts. Since its inception the company has presented over 80 operas, including the American stage premières of Honegger's *Jeanne d'Arc au bûcher* and Busoni's *Doktor Faust*. Performances of three operas, the *Nutcracker* ballet and a summer musical attract an annual audience totalling 20 000. An apprentice programme aims to help launch singers' careers. For its 25th season (1992–3) an opera on Mark Twain's years on the Comstock Lode in Nevada was commissioned from Bern Herbolsheimer.

WES BLOMSTER

Renosto, Paolo (*b* Florence, 10 Oct 1935; *d* Reggio Calabria, 10 Feb 1988). Italian composer. A pupil of Dallapiccola and Lupi in Florence and Maderna at Darmstadt, he taught composition at Pescara, Pesaro and L'Aquila. The first of his operas shows the closest affinity with the radical innovations of the 'Neue Musik': *La camera degli sposi* (19 May 1972, Milan, Piccola Scala), a one-act opera to a libretto by Aldo Rostagno, centres on the alienation of the individual shown through the crisis of a couple who find themselves involved in dramatic events in the external world. In *L'ombra di Banquo* (11 Oct 1976, Spoleto, Teatro Belli), Bruno Cagli's libretto goes beyond Shakespeare's text to show the continuing violence of power personified in Lady Macbeth, who has the anguished and remorseful Macbeth killed and marries Fleance. In this work Renosto borrows ideas from Berg and expressionism. *Le campanule*, a 'commedia mistica in tre momenti' to a libretto by Cagli, is for soprano, mezzo-soprano, tenor and nine instruments. It was first performed on 5 August 1981 at Casale Monferrato and a revised version appeared two years later. The opera is more traditional in character than the other two, returning to closed forms and making many stylistic allusions. Set in a mountain resort, it shows how a reversal of time is brought about in the meeting of an elderly official who regresses to a childlike state and an adolescent who rapidly grows old and dies.

PAOLO PETAZZI

Renzi [Rentia, Renzini], **Anna** (*b* Rome, *c*1620; *d* in or after 1660). Italian soprano. She began her operatic career at the house of the French ambassador to Rome, probably in Castelli's dramas *La sincerità trionfante* (music by Angelo Cecchini, 1639) and *Il favorito del principe* (music by her teacher Filiberto Laurenzi) in which she sang Lucinda at the French embassy. In 1640 she went with Laurenzi to Venice, where her leading roles included Deidamia in Sacrati's *La finta pazza* (Teatro Novissimo, 1641), Archimene in Sacrati's *Bellerofonte* (Novissimo, 1642), Aretusa in *La finta savia* (Teatro SS Giovanni e Paolo, 1643, music largely by Laurenzi), Octavia in *L'incoronazione di Poppea* (SS Giovanni e Paolo, 1643) and the title role in *Deidamia* (Novissimo, 1644). She also sang in Rovetta's *Ercole in Lidia* (Novissimo, 1645) and in *Torilda* (1648) and *Argiope* (1649, dedicated to her in 1645), both at the Teatro SS Giovanni e Paolo. In 1653 she probably sang at Genoa (in *Torilda* and *Cesare amante*) and was then at the Innsbruck court (1653–4, 1655), when she would have sung the title role in Cesti's *Cleopatra* and Dorisbe in his *Argia*, returning to Venice for P. A. Ziani's *Le fortune di Rodope e di Damira* (Teatro S Apollinare, 1657). According to Strozzi her performances were distinguished by understanding of the text, a sweet but unaffected pronunciation and easy ornamentation.

*

G. Strozzi: *Le glorie della signora Anna Renzi romana* (Venice, 1644)
G. F. Loredan: *Bizzarrie academiche*, ii (Bologna, 14/1676), 180
C. Sartori: 'La prima diva della lirica italiana: Anna Renzi', *NRMI*, ii (1968), 430–52
L. Bianconi and T. Walker: 'Dalla *Finta pazza* alla *Veremonda*: storie di Febiarmonici', *RIM*, x (1975), 379–454

THOMAS WALKER

Re pastore, Il ('The Shepherd King'). Libretto by PIETRO METASTASIO, first set by Giuseppe Bonno (1751, Schönbrunn).

'Il re pastore', Act 1 scene i (the countryside beyond the walls of Sidon, as described in the libretto); engraving from the 'Opere' of Pietro Metastasio (Venice: Bettinelli, 1758)

ACT 1   Alessandro [Alexander], King of Macedonia, has freed Sidon from the tyrant, Straton, and wants to restore the rightful heir to the throne. He and the Sidonian nobleman Agenore [Agenor] approach the shepherd, Aminta [Amyntas], and are impressed by the noble manner in which he declines their offers to improve his lot. Amyntas plans to marry the nymph Elisa and is content. Tamiri [Tamyris], daughter of the deposed Straton, has disguised herself as a shepherdess and is in hiding with Elisa. She is in love with Agenor but too proud to seek clemency from Alexander. Just as Amyntas is about to approach Elisa's father for a marriage blessing, Agenor arrives and informs him that he is not a lowly shepherd, but Abdalonimo [Abdalonimus], the closest relative to the royal line of Sidon. He summons Amyntas/Abdalonimus to the presence of Alexander.

ACT 2   Hoping to ensure peace in the country, Alexander decides that Tamyris should marry Amyntas. Agenor dutifully complies but carefully avoids revealing Alexander's decision to Amyntas.

ACT 3   Elisa, angered by Alexander's plan, demands that Amyntas publicly confess his breach of faith. Tamyris likewise is displeased with Agenor who, for his part, struggles between love and patriotic duty. Amyntas decides to renounce the throne for Elisa, but Alexander reconsiders. He unites the lovers, restores Amyntas, and promises a kingdom to Agenor and Tamyris.

*   *   *

The Curtius Rufus *Historiarum* (book 4) and the Diodorus Siculus *Bibliotheca* (book 17) contain full accounts of this story, and further reference may be found in Justin's epitome of the Trogus *Historiae* (book 11). Mindful also of the *Aminta* of Torquato Tasso, Metastasio reluctantly completed his drama in April 1751, at the request of Maria Theresa, for performances in December by a gentleman and four ladies of the imperial court. The October première, in which Count Bergen sang the role of Alexander and Mmes Frankenberg, Kollonitz, Lamberg and Rosemberg portrayed the two sets of lovers, came upon Metastasio unexpectedly. Furthermore, he was made responsible not only for all the staging involved but also for the dramatic and vocal coaching of the amateur performers. Although initially negative towards the enterprise, Metastasio sub-

sequently expressed his satisfaction with the performers, the costumes, the settings and the music. To his chagrin, however, success led to his writing L'EROE CINESE for the same group of performers with the same requirements applied.

One month after its première, Metastasio recommended *Il re pastore* to Carlo Broschi (Farinelli), then theatre director in Madrid. At that time Metastasio was revising four of his other dramas for Farinelli's use. *Il re pastore* achieved moderate success, with approximately 25 settings between 1751 and the end of the 18th century. For Sarti, it provided the text for a triumphant first commission for Venice (1752), for Uttini (1755, Drottningholm) it inspired his only Italian opera score to be printed, and for Maria Agnesi, it prompted her only Metastasian opera. The sisters Caterina and Francesca Gabrielli sang the roles of Elisa and Tamyris in the Vienna première of Gluck's setting, which coincided with the birth of the Archduke Maximilian Franz on 8 December 1756. The archduke's visit to Salzburg in 1775 was, in turn, honoured by Mozart's setting of a curtailed version of the text. Mozart had probably seen the opera in Giardini's setting in London in 1765, the year after George Rush had set the text as *The Royal Shepherd*, to be performed in competition with Arne's *Artaxerxes*.

For a list of settings *see* METASTASIO, PIETRO.   DON NEVILLE

Re pastore, Il ('The Shepherd King'). Serenata in two acts, K208, by WOLFGANG AMADEUS MOZART to a libretto by PIETRO METASTASIO (*see* RE PASTORE, IL above); Salzburg, Archbishop's Palace, 23 April 1775.

Il re pastore was written immediately after Mozart's return from Munich to oversee the performance of *La finta giardiniera*. It was one of two short works performed in honour of Archduke Maximilian, who broke a journey from Vienna to Italy at Salzburg (the other was *Gli orti esperidi* by Fischietti). The reduced form of Metastasio's libretto compresses Acts 2 and 3 into one, cutting five arias and reducing the recitatives so that what was originally a pastoral *opera seria* is scaled down to the proportions of a serenata. This version of the libretto had been devised for a performance in Munich in 1774, with music from Guglielmi's 1767 setting for Venice, and was Mozart's principal source;

further alterations may have been made by Giambattista Varesco.

The performance took the semi-staged form, without scenery, appropriate to a serenata. The castrato Tommaso Consoli came from Munich to sing Aminta [Amyntas]; with him came the flautist Johann Baptist Becke. The exact disposition of the other roles, taken by members of the Salzburg Hofkapelle, is unknown.

Il re pastore, based on an episode in the career of Alexander the Great, is designed to show the magnanimity and understanding of this imperial archetype. The title role is the shepherd Amyntas (soprano castrato) who, unknown to himself, is Abdalonimo [Abdalonimus], legitimate heir to the kingdom of Sidon. He is betrothed to Elisa (soprano), despite her noble birth.

The first act is almost unchanged from Metastasio's. As in Gluck's setting (1756), the single-movement overture runs into Amyntas's first aria ('Intendo amico rio'), really a short song in a pastoral 6/8; it is interrupted in turn by the arrival of Elisa. Amyntas is worried by the proximity of Alexander's army; Elisa is sanguine ('Alla selva, al prato'); the country and her beloved will provide a sanctuary. Alessandro [Alexander] (tenor) comes disguised with the Sidonian nobleman Agenore [Agenor] (tenor) to question Amyntas, who praises the simplicity and honesty of his pastoral existence (obbligato recitative and aria, 'Aer tranquillo', a replacement text present in the 1774 Munich libretto).

Alexander looks forward to restoring the instinctively noble young man to his rightful station (the martial aria 'Si spande al sole in faccia'). Tamiri [Tamyris] (soprano), friend of Elisa and daughter of the tyrant Straton whom Alexander has deposed, is in hiding, but she comes to Agenor, her betrothed. He assures her of his love ('Per me rispondete'); she, however, fears the wrath of Alexander ('Di tante sue procelle'). Agenor tells Amyntas of his change in fortune; he fears parting from Elisa but she remains confident (obbligato recitative). The lovers' duet ends the first act.

In this compressed form of the libretto the lovers' problems are quickly resolved. First Agenor is obliged to prevent Elisa from seeing Amyntas; her anguish is expressed in her second aria ('Barbaro, oh Dio!'), a lamenting Andante in which the coloratura is deeply expressive, and a protesting Allegro. Amyntas is likewise prevented from following Elisa. Alexander sends him to deck himself like a king.

On learning from Agenor that Tamyris is near, Alexander announces his intention to marry her to Amyntas; through his conquests he wishes people to be made happy (a virtuoso aria in F major, 'Se vincendo vi rendo felici'). In Amyntas's next aria ('L'amerò, sarò costante'), a ravishing rondò with violin obbligato, muted strings, two flutes and two english horns, the noble arches of his melody support a declaration of the constancy of his love. Elisa and Agenor believe that he is talking of Tamyris, who, however, accuses Agenor of faithlessness ('Se tu di me fai dono': surprisingly, a Grazioso in A). His misery induces the only minor-mode aria, a vehement Allegro protesting his constancy ('Sol può dir'). Alexander enters, his final aria ('Voi che fausti ognor donate') a kingly showpiece. Tamyris and Elisa throw themselves on his mercy, and as soon as he understands he unites the four lovers and declares that the Shepherd King and Elisa will rule in Sidon, while Agenor and Tamyris will be granted another kingdom. All join in a 'coro' in praise of the unconquered Alexander ('Viva l'invitto Duce').

*   *   *

The second and third arias of Act 2 add two flutes to the standard Salzburg group of two oboes and two horns; the virtuoso flourishes in the first of these were doubtless intended for Becke. Trumpets appear in Alexander's other arias, so that all three are distinguished instrumentally. So, however, are the crucial arias in the roles of the characters who are facing real dilemmas: Amyntas (see above) and Agenor ('Sol può dir', where the minor mode is supported by two horns in different keys). The arias with strings only (Agenor's first and Tamyris's second) act as a foil to these more elaborate movements. Mozart shows equal resource in the handling of the now standard aria design, the 'modified da capo' or small-scale sonata-form aria. If *Il re pastore* is not as original as *La finta giardiniera*, it nevertheless makes the most of its slender dramatic basis, and helped Mozart to develop characterization in the serious style, a useful preparation for *Idomeneo*.   JULIAN RUSHTON

Repertory. (1) A stock of operas; the operatic repertory is generally understood to consist of a central body of operas (by Mozart, Rossini, Verdi, Wagner, Bizet, Puccini, Strauss and others) that, with a further selection determined by local taste, form the basis of performances in most opera houses. The concept of a central repertory of opera, like that of concert music, dates from the early 19th century, although it was anticipated in France when Lully's operas were kept in repertory for much of the 18th century. In German-speaking countries, then in France and elsewhere, Mozart's operas came to enter the repertory in the early 19th century; in Italy it was chiefly Rossini's operas that did so. The term 'opera di repertorio' is first met with shortly before the middle of the 19th century.

(2) The term is used to describe a particular manner of organizing the programme planning of an opera house, to refer to a system based on the holding of a large number of productions in preparation at the same time (as opposed to the STAGIONE system, where only one or two operas are prepared for performance, in short seasons, at any particular moment). The repertory system, generally favoured in German opera houses, is particularly appropriate for a resident company with a regular opera-going public but is not suitable for most international opera houses.

Répétiteur. A musician on the staff of an opera house or of a management, entrusted with guiding singers through the learning and interpretation of their roles, and sometimes with rehearsing sections of the orchestra or even the entire orchestra.

The role of the répétiteur has its origins in that of the *maestro concertatore* in the Italian opera orchestra until about 1860. The orchestra in performance had a leader (*maestro direttore*), then as now the leader of the first violins, who might also be in charge of the orchestra's administrative arrangements and of hiring and paying the players. (There was no conductor in the modern sense.) The *maestro concertatore*, almost invariably paid somewhat less than the leader, was a keyboard player who played continuo in performances and was in charge of individual preparation of singers and of orchestral rehearsals. If the opera was new, as in this period it often was, the composer was expected to do part of this job and to accompany the first three performances at the keyboard. As orchestration became more complex, this division of labour came to seem unsatisfactory; even in the early 19th century the excellence of the S Carlo orchestra at Naples was due in part to Giuseppe Festa's being, unusually, both leader and *concertatore*. Some *concertatori* were nevertheless highly gifted and influential, in particular Pietro Romani, who on behalf of the impresario Alessandro Lanari coached such singers as Gilbert Duprez and Giorgio Ronconi. With the coming of the modern conductor and the disappearance of continuo playing the répétiteur withdrew to the rehearsal room or stage.

In modern opera houses a répétiteur may go on to become a conductor, and anyhow needs to work closely with the conductor and, nowadays, the director. Some répétiteurs, on the other hand, also work as singing teachers. In ballet, where the choreographer is usually present at rehearsals, the répétiteur is generally limited to playing the piano.   JOHN ROSSELLI

Reprise overture. A type of OVERTURE in three sections, the first and third in a quick tempo and employing the same thematic material, with a contrasting middle section usually in a different key or mode and in a slower tempo. 'Reprise overture' seems the best term because others – 'ABA overture' (LaRue) and 'da capo overture' (Churgin) – imply a literal return of the opening section, which is rare.

Though works of this type were written in the 17th century (Draghi, *L'albero del ramo d'oro*, 1681) and the 19th (Weber, *Euryanthe*, 1823), the reprise overture is primarily an 18th-century form. Its heyday came in the 1770s and 80s, when many composers found it an attractive multi-sectional alternative to the three-movement Italian overture. The overture to Piccinni's *Iphigénie en Tauride* (1781) is a good example. The opening Allegro in D major represents the exposition of a sonata design; the following Andantino sans lenteur in D minor, in which the trumpets and timpani are silent, resembles the slow movement of a three-movement overture; and the reprise of the Allegro, once more fully scored, constitutes a free recapitulation of the opening section.

The best-known reprise overture is that to Mozart's *Die Entführung aus dem Serail* (1782); it is atypical only in its close connection to the opening scene of the opera. Its anticipation of a later number in the slow middle section is not unique (one occurs in the overture to Piccinni's *La finta baronessa*, 1767), but the transitional passage leading to the opening number and the thematically and tonally unified opening complex that results do not occur in other reprise overtures. Mozart's Symphony in G K318 (1779), which has been used as an overture to his *Zaide*, is another well-known example of a reprise overture.

*

Grove6 ('Sinfonia', J. LaRue)

H. Abert: *W. A. Mozart* (Leipzig, 8/1973), 367

B. Churgin: 'The Italian Symphonic Background to Haydn's Early Symphonies and Opera Overtures', *Haydn Studies: Washington 1975*, 331

S. C. Fisher: *Haydn's Overtures and their Adaptations as Concert Orchestral Works* (diss., U. of Pennsylvania, 1985), 57–66, 351–3   STEPHEN C. FISHER

Rescigno, Nicola (*b* New York, 28 May 1916). American conductor. Born into a musical family (his father played the trumpet in the Metropolitan Opera orchestra), he studied with Pizzetti, Giannini and Polacco. His début was in 1943, conducting *La traviata* at the Brooklyn Academy of Music. He then toured the USA with the San Carlo Opera and served as music director for Connecticut Opera and Havana Opera. In 1953 he co-founded the Chicago Lyric Opera and that year presented the American début of Maria Callas, with whom he was closely associated. In 1957 he co-founded the Dallas Opera, remaining as artistic director until 1990; there he introduced to American audiences many artists including Berganza, Caballé, Domingo, Olivero, Sutherland, Vickers and Zeffirelli, and presented the American premières of *Alcina*, *Giulio Cesare*, *L'incoronazione di Poppea* and *Orlando furioso* (Vivaldi), as well as the première of Argento's *The Aspern Papers* (1988). He made his Metropolitan début in 1978, directing *Don Pasquale*. He has conducted at Glyndebourne, in Buenos Aires, London, Paris, San Francisco, Vienna, Zürich and most Italian major musical centres.   CORI ELLISON

Rescue opera.

1. The term. 2. Background. 3. Redefinition.

1. THE TERM. 'Rescue opera' is an unhistorical term of limited usefulness. It is not an authentic genre like 'opera buffa', and was coined only in the late 19th or early 20th century. In origin it has been traced to German criticism, as part of its tendency to label musical phenomena in a single word (e.g. 'Humanitätsmelodie' for the slow F major music, 3/4, in the Act 2 finale of *Fidelio*, 'O Gott! welch ein Augenblick').

R. M. Longyear (1959) revealed that Dyneley Hussey had noted the phrase 'rescue opera' in an article on *Fidelio* in 1927, mentioning German provenance, and that Karl M. Klob wrote of 'das sogenannte Rettungs-oder Befreiungsstück' in *Die Oper von Gluck bis Wagner* (Ulm, 1913; p.281). Resulting from the attempt in opera criticism to set Beethoven's opera in its intellectual context, the idea of 'rescue opera' has provided a superficial means of relating *Fidelio* to French tradition. The attempt was founded on little knowledge, and the dangerous consequence of using the term is to distort historical values.

The very vagueness of the term's pedigree has, in part, the obvious result that no two published definitions of 'rescue opera' in English will be found to agree, and no one definition will satisfactorily cover the range of operas that are called as evidence of a 'rescue' tendency in the later 18th century. This is because to take the concept 'rescue' as a cardinal criterion is false to dramatic history. In the broadest sense, a 'rescue' is a form of happy dramatic resolution, or turn of events, that can be related to the *deus ex machina* of classical *opera seria*. (Significantly, no one has proposed a category of *deus ex machina* operas.)

2. BACKGROUND. One particular librettist was responsible for developing *opéras comiques* in France stressing the dimension of 'freedom': MICHEL-JEAN SEDAINE (1719–97). In *Le roi et le fermier* (1762) Jenny has escaped from her place of abduction; in *Le déserteur* (1769) Alexis is freed from the death cell through the exertions of his betrothed, Louise; in *Le magnifique* (1773) Horace, the heroine's father, is freed from slavery; in *Richard Coeur-de-lion* (1784) the king is freed from detention in an Austrian castle; in *Le comte d'Albert* (1786) the count's wife enters his prison (effectively, the Bastille) and assists in his escape. In each case Sedaine was concerned to set up a moral dilemma, in

which the theme of 'unjust detention' should provide one of the dramatic mainsprings. The reasons for the detention are different in each opera, and there is no uniformity of treatment concerning the character or characters responsible for the detention, or the degree of their culpability. Popular theatre (e.g. melodramas) was exploiting similar themes at the same period but emphasized scenic effects, danger and the act of physical rescue. Sedaine exploited the excitements of danger and tension, but he approached the simplistic moral structure of a melodrama only in *Richard Coeur-de-lion*. That is precisely why he agreed only reluctantly to have it staged in the form we now recognize, at the behest of colleagues and public alike (see Charlton 1986).

3. REDEFINITION. The 1789 revolution ensured the true popularization of theatre and opera in certain French cities, and many operas thereafter had a simple, melodramatic moral structure. The end (the actual celebration of social freedom) justified the means (the simplistic dramatic portrayal of right and wrong). The operas that influenced *Fidelio*, via Bouilly's and Gaveaux's *Léonore* of 1798, nevertheless fall into two classes: 'tyrant' operas and 'humanitarian' operas. 'Tyrant' operas personified injustice by means of an evil character, who deprives some person of their liberty. Examples are Méhul's *Euphrosine* and H.-M. Berton's *Les rigueurs du cloître* (both 1790); the *Lodoïska* operas by Cherubini and Rodolphe Kreutzer (both 1791); Dalayrac's *Camille* (also 1791) and Le Sueur's *La caverne* (1793). 'Humanitarian' operas did not portray the tyrant, if there was one at all, but stressed the individual sacrifices necessary in righting a wrong, and in obtaining a person's freedom. Examples are Dalayrac's *Raoul sire de Créqui* (1789) and Bouilly's and Cherubini's *Les deux journées* (1800), together with Sedaine's pre-1789 works discussed above.

Opera outside France occasionally emulated Sedaine's librettos, and sometimes French librettos of this type were translated and set to music anew, as in the case of Paer's *Camilla* and his *Leonora*. By and large, however, 'tyrant' and 'humanitarian' themes were associated with the French tradition.

A separate, third class of opera had no connection with detention, but used the culmination of a natural catastrophe (at some level equating with divine justice) and a rescue from it: the *Paul et Virginie* operas by Rodolphe Kreutzer (1791) and Le Sueur (1794), and Cherubini's *Elisa* (also 1794).

Bouilly's libretto *Léonore* effectively combined 'tyrant' and 'humanitarian' traditions; and François-Benoît Hoffman also combined these types, to new purpose, in his *Léon, ou Le château de Monténéro*, set by Dalayrac (1798). Historically, all these works had the purpose of demonstrating an act of humanity. In painting, the same trend is called the *exemplum virtutis* by Rosenblum (1967).

For illustration see *DÉSERTEUR, LE* and *RICHARD COEUR-DE-LION*.

R. M. Longyear: 'Notes on the Rescue Opera', *MQ*, xlv (1959), 49–66

R. Rosenblum: *Transformations in Late Eighteenth-Century Art* (Princeton, 1967)

W. Dean: 'French Opera', NOHM, viii (1982)

D. Charlton: *Grétry and the Growth of Opéra-Comique* (Cambridge, 1986)

——: 'On Redefinitions of Rescue Opera', *Music and the French Revolution*, ed. M. Boyd (Cambridge, 1992), 169–88

DAVID CHARLTON

Residenztheater. Theatre in Munich, commissioned by Maximilian III Joseph and opened in 1753; it is also known as the Cuvilliéstheater. *See* MUNICH, §§2 and 3(i).

Resnik, Regina (*b* New York, 30 Aug 1922). American mezzo-soprano (formerly soprano) and director. She studied at Hunter College, New York, and sang Lady Macbeth with the New Opera Company, New York, in 1942. She sang with the Metropolitan (1944–74), making her début as Leonora (*Il trovatore*); her roles there included Ellen Orford in the New York première of *Peter Grimes*, Alice Ford, Leonore, Donna Anna and Donna Elvira, and Sieglinde. At Bayreuth she sang Sieglinde in 1953 and Fricka in 1961. In 1955 she began to concentrate on the mezzo-soprano repertory, singing Azucena, Eboli and Herodias (*Salome*). She created the Baroness in Barber's *Vanessa* (1958) and also sang Lucretia in *The Rape of Lucretia* at Stratford, Ontario (she had sung the Female Chorus in the American première at Chicago in 1947). In 1972 she sang Claire in the American première of *Der Besuch der alten Dame* at San Francisco.

Resnik made her Covent Garden début in 1957 as Carmen; her roles there included Marina (*Boris Godunov*), a brilliant Mistress Quickly and a decadent Clytemnestra. She also appeared in Vienna, Salzburg and in the leading American and German opera houses. In 1971 she directed *Carmen* at Hamburg and *Elektra* in Venice. She had a vibrant voice with a strong upper register. Her acting was full of subtle detail, and her fine musicianship and keen intelligence were apparent in all her work.

I. Cook: 'Regina Resnik', *Opera*, xiv (1963), 13–18

H. Rosenthal: *Great Singers of Today* (London, 1966)

HAROLD ROSENTHAL/R

Respighi, Ottorino (*b* Bologna, 9 July 1879; *d* Rome, 18 April 1936). Italian composer. He studied at the Liceo Musicale, Bologna (1891–1901), where his teachers included Luigi Torchi and Giuseppe Martucci. In 1900–01 and again in 1902–3 he visited Russia, where he had lessons from Rimsky-Korsakov that crucially influenced his orchestration. He was active as a string player and pianist in the first decade of the century and began to take an interest in neglected Italian music of the remoter past. In 1908–9 he was in Berlin, where he absorbed much from the rich musical environment but little from the few of Bruch's lectures that he attended. After a further period in Bologna, he settled in Rome in 1913, having been appointed professor of composition at the Liceo (later Conservatorio) di S Cecilia; in 1924 he became director but resigned two years later to devote himself mainly to composing. During his last decade he nevertheless continued to teach, to conduct in many countries and to accompany singers, notably his wife Elsa Olivieri-Sangiacomo (*b* 1894), herself a composer and later her husband's biographer.

Though not the most important or original Italian composer of his generation, Respighi was much the most successful internationally, thanks especially to the advocacy of certain conductors (notably Toscanini). The limitations of his art were closely bound up with the limitations of his personality. Though a man of culture, he remained at heart very simple, even childish. He was an avid observer rather than a thinker, and the best aspects of his work tend to be 'sensory' in character: his preoccupation with vivid orchestral colours, and his eager, magpie-like appropriation of decorative elements in the styles of predecessors and contemporaries, were symptomatic. A prime example is the justly celebrated, richly colourful tone poem *Fontane di Roma* (1914–16), in which influences from, among others, Ravel and Strauss are completely assimilated; here Respighi showed both a perfect knowledge of his limitations and a superb command of his gifts. His later symphonic poems resemble their prototype in their hedonistic pictorialism, but he continued to explore new possibilities within the same general aesthetic. The years immediately following *Fontane* were a turning-point in one respect, for it was then that he increasingly admitted archaic elements into his works, a trend probably best known through his arrangements of early music and his use of Gregorian motifs in the later symphonic poems (notably *Vetrate di chiesa*, 1925). The most perfect example of his 'archaizing' side is, however, the radiantly charming *Lauda per la Natività del Signore* (1928–30), pervaded by suggestions of 16th-century madrigals, Monteverdian arioso and other pre-Classical music.

Respighi's operas are a secondary and uneven yet by no means negligible branch of his output, in which, however, he matured relatively slowly. *Re Enzo*, his first theatrical venture, seems to have been little more than an operetta and has remained unpublished, although it was well received when performed by students when new. *Marie Victoire* was neither published nor performed: the composer was evidently dissatisfied with it; and even *Semirâma* – his only pre-war opera which did reach both print and the professional stage – was not revived, after its initial 1910 production, until 1987 (Palermo, Teatro Massimo, 7 January). When new, the work (which is set in ancient Babylon) attracted interest as supposedly the first Straussian opera by an Italian composer. In fact it is only superficially and intermittently indebted to *Salome*: turbulent quasi-Straussian textures interact with a pseudo-oriental (often pentatonically tinged) colourfulness in which one can already sense the extent of Respighi's debt to Rimsky-Korsakov. Two decades later the composer reused the exotic 'Danza dell'aurora' from *Semirâma* in his unrestrainedly opulent ballet score *Belkis, regina di Saba* (1930–31).

Only after World War I did Respighi start to win more widespread acclaim with his operas. *La bella dormente nel bosco* – still (in its small way) arguably his most perfect dramatic work – was first launched as an opera for puppets, and was taken all over the world by Vittorio Podrecca's famous Teatro dei Piccoli. *Belfagor*, Respighi's first full-size opera of the inter-war years (and the first of his several collaborations with Claudio Guastalla), was a relative failure, handicapped as it was by an unsatisfactory libretto that has surprisingly little connection with Machiavelli's famous story of the same name. Yet the music, though uneven, has qualities that merit attention. The two remaining full-length operas, *La campana sommersa* and *La fiamma*, have enjoyed successes on both sides of the Atlantic which they to a fair extent deserve, although they too have weaknesses which have prevented them from winning firm places in the repertory. In Italy the most often performed Respighi opera has been the small and stylized *Maria egiziaca*, in which Guastalla's selfconsciously 'archaic'

text is matched by overt (though by no means all-pervading) archaisms in the music. Quasi-Monteverdian archaisms reappear in Respighi's last opera *Lucrezia*, which shows all too clearly, however, that his creative powers were being undermined by illness: his lifelong eclecticism here became a liability rather than an asset. After his death the orchestration was completed by his widow, with the help of Ennio Porrino. Elsa Respighi in due course wrote two operas of her own, *Alcesti* (1941) and *Samurai* (1945), to libretto by Guastalla.

In 1920 Respighi prepared versions of Paisiello's *La serva padrona* and Cimarosa's *Le astuzie femminili*, and in 1935 a free transcription of Monteverdi's *Orfeo*.

See also BELFAGOR; BELLA DORMENTE NEL BOSCO, LA; CAMPANA SOMMERSA, LA; FIAMMA, LA; and MARIA EGIZIACA.

Re Enzo (comic op, 3, A. Donini), Bologna, Corso, 12 March 1905, unpubd
Al mulino, 1908, inc. (2, Donini), unpubd
Semirâma, 1908–10 (3, A. Ceré), Bologna, Comunale, 20 Nov 1910
Marie Victoire, 1913–14 (4, E. Guiraud), unperf., unpubd
La bella dormente nel bosco [La bella addormentata nel bosco], 1916–21 (fiaba musicale, 3, G. Bistolfi, after C. Perrault), Rome, Piccoli di Podrecca, Palazzo Odescalchi (Sala Verdi), 13 April 1922 (marionette version); rev. for child mimes, Turin, Torino, 9 April 1934; 3rd version, rev. G. L. Tocchi, RAI, 13 June 1967
Belfagor, 1921–2 (comic op, prol., 2, epilogue, C. Guastalla, after E. L. Morselli), Milan, Scala, 26 April 1923
La campana sommersa, c1924–7 (4, Guastalla, after G. Hauptmann: *Die versunkene Glocke*), Hamburg, Stadt, 18 Nov 1927
Maria egiziaca, c1929–31 (trittico per concerto/mistero, 1, Guastalla, after D. Cavalca: *Le vite dei santi padri*), New York, Carnegie Hall, 16 March 1932 (semi-staged); staged Venice, Goldoni, 10 Aug 1932
La fiamma, 1931–3 (3, Guastalla, after H. Wiers-Jenssen: *Anne Pedersdotter*), Rome, Opera, 23 Jan 1934
Lucrezia, 1935 (1, Guastalla, after W. Shakespeare: *The Rape of Lucrece* and Livy: *Ab urbe condita libri*), Milan, Scala, 24 Feb 1937 [completed by E. Respighi and E. Porrino]

*

I. Pizzetti: 'Semirama di Ottorino Respighi al Comunale di Bologna', *Il secolo* [Milan] (21 Nov 1910), 2
G. Bastianelli: 'Le nuove tendenze dell'opera italiana: Semirama di Ottorino Respighi', *Musicisti d'oggi e di ieri* (Milan, 1914), 48–58
S. A. Luciani: 'Belfagor' di Ottorino Respighi (Milan, 1923)
A. Lualdi: ' "Belfagor" di Ottorino Respighi alla Scala', *Serate musicali* (Milan, 1928), 34–43
M. Barbieri: ' "La campana sommersa" di Ottorino Respighi', *Italia musicale* [Genoa], iii/7 (1930), 2
R. de Rensis: *Ottorino Respighi* (Turin, 1933; Fr. trans., 1957), esp. 14–19, 34–6, 40–45, 47–50, 55–95
M. Rinaldi: ' "La fiamma" di Ottorino Respighi', *Rassegna dorica* [Rome], v (1933–4), 100–05
D. de' Paoli: *La crisi musicale italiana* (Milan, 1939), esp. 269–78
A. Gasco: 'La ripresa della *Campana sommersa* di Respighi al Teatro Reale'; '*La fiamma* al Teatro Reale', *Da Cimarosa a Strawinsky* (Rome, 1939), 243–6; 247–53
E. Respighi: *Ottorino Respighi: dati biografici ordinati* (Milan, 1954; Eng. trans., abridged, 1962)
C. Guastalla: 'L'opera di Ottorino Respighi nei ricordi di Claudio Guastalla', *Ricordiana* [Milan], new ser., i (1955), 44–7
F. Abbiati: 'Il teatro di Ottorino Respighi', *Ricordiana* [Milan], new ser., ii (1956), 279–83
R. Rossellini: 'Il teatro di Respighi', *Musica d'oggi*, new ser., iv (1961), 158–61
L. Bragaglia and E. Respighi: *Il teatro di Respighi* (Rome, 1978)
'Il teatro per musica di Ottorino Respighi', *Vita italiana* [Rome], xxix/4 (1979), 117–29
F. D'Amico: 'Situazione di Ottorino Respighi (1879–1979)', *Vita italiana*, xxix/8 (1979), 3–15; repr. in Rostirolla (1985); Eng. trans. in *Italy: Documents and Notes* [Rome], xxix/9 (1980), 43–54
L. Bragaglia: 'Respighi's Theatre and its Interpreters', *Italy: Documents and Notes*, xxix/10 (1980), 37–53
M. Modugno: 'Fortuna e sfortuna di Ottorino Respighi', *Musica italiana del primo novecento: 'la generazione dell'80': Florence 1980*, 125–34

F. Nicolodi: *Musica e musicisti nel ventennio fascista* (Fiesole, nr Florence, 1984), esp. 151–7

P. Mioli: 'Il teatro di Respighi', in A. Cantù and others: *Respighi compositore* (Turin, 1985), 194–216

G. Rostirolla, ed.: *Ottorino Respighi* (Turin, 1985) [incl. D. Spini: 'Ottorino Respighi: profilo biografico', 7–84; G. Gavazzeni: 'Ricordi ed esperienze su Respighi', 87–93; F. D'Amico: 'Situazione di Ottorino Respighi (1879–1979)', 107–16; L. Bellingardi: 'Il teatro di Respighi nei giudizi della critica', 263–311; G. Gualerzi and C. Marinelli Roscioni: 'Le rappresentazioni in Italia delle opere di Ottorino Respighi: cronologia', 315–23; P. Pedarra: 'Catalogo delle composizioni di Ottorino Respighi', 327–404]

Il novecento musicale italiano tra neoclassicismo e neogoticismo: Venice 1986 [Studi di musica veneta, xiii, ed. D. Bryant (Florence, 1988)]

JOHN C. G. WATERHOUSE

Resse, Celeste. *See* GISMONDI, CELESTE.

Resta, Natale (*fl* ?Milan, 1748). Italian composer. The only known evidence of his existence is one comic opera, *Li tre cicisbei ridicoli* (3, C. A. Vasini; Bologna, Formagliari, Carnival 1748), the libretto of which names him as 'maestro di cappella Milanese'. The work, which enjoyed some popularity (with performances in Venice and London) and earned contemporary praise (Burney said it 'had great comic merit' among the works introduced in London's first season of Italian comic opera in 1748–9; La Borde called it 'charming'), is one of the few north Italian comic operas to survive before Galuppi pre-empted the field.

Although the surviving score (I-MOe; catalogued under Galuppi's name) represents a later version, it retains approximately half the original musical numbers, including all the finales. These show Resta to have been an able composer. The arias are written in short-breathed, often irregular phrases, with a sharp ear for expressive rhythms; some are in da capo form and some, which repeat the entire text, are in a shape resembling binary sonata form. In the finales Resta departs from the 'chain' arrangement of musically independent segments which was usual for this time and makes some attempt at internal formal organization.

JAMES L. JACKMAN

Restorini, Antonio Maria. *See* RISTORINI, ANTONIO MARIA.

Reszke, de. *See* DE RESZKE.

Retablo de maese Pedro, El ('Master Peter's Puppet Show'). Puppet opera in six scenes by MANUEL DE FALLA to his own libretto after an episode from MIGUEL DE CERVANTES's *Don Quixote*; concert performance, Seville, San Fernando, 23 March 1923; stage, Paris, home of Princess Edmond de Polignac, 25 June 1923.

The setting is the courtyard of an inn with a trestle stage on which Maese Pedro's puppets perform the following scenes, the action of which is explained by a youthful narrator or *trujamán* (boy soprano). Scene 1 takes place at the court of Charlemagne. The emperor's daughter Melisendra is in captivity at Saragossa. He appeals to the knight Gayferos, Melisendra's husband, to rescue her. In Scene 2, at a tower at Saragossa, a Moorish soldier steals a kiss from the doleful Melisendra. The king, Marsilius, orders due punishment; the boy, enlarging upon the theme of punishment under the Moors, is chided by Quixote (bass-baritone) and Maese Pedro (tenor) for digressing. The punishment takes place in Scene 3 to the strains of a march. In the next scene, Gayferos rides through the Pyrenees towards Saragossa, his horn resounding. Scene 5, entitled 'The Flight', begins with Melisendra espying the knight from afar. When she recognizes Gayferos she leaps from the tower into his arms. Joyfully the couple ride off towards Paris. At the start of the final scene ('The Pursuit'), both Maese Pedro and Quixote interrupt the action with complaints about the boy's narration. When Quixote sees Moors in pursuit of the Christian couple he is outraged. Advancing on the stage, convinced that the puppets are real, he attacks them with his sword, wrecking Maese Pedro's puppets and his livelihood. Quixote then declares himself knight errant in thrall to the fair Dulcinea, to whom he sings a short prayer before addressing the audience on the virtues of knighterrantry.

El retablo was the result of an invitation from Princess Edmond de Polignac for a chamber opera. With her permission, a concert performance was given in Seville with Falla conducting. The first stage performance was given (privately) on a stage fitted up in the princess's Paris music room. Wanda Landowska played the harpsichord and Hector Dufranne sang Quixote. The first public stage performance took place on 14 October 1924 at Clifton, Bristol.

Falla adapted his own text from that of Cervantes. The original intention, not always followed in performance, was to have two sets of puppets, large ones for the singing characters (with the singers in the orchestra) and small ones for the performers of the play within a play. The score represents a great advance on the strong, but still naive, theatrical instinct shown in *La vida breve*. *El retablo* is an original, delightful work of art, in which Falla used a small orchestra with consummate skill, nowhere more evident than in the scoring of the ride in Scene 4. Equally remarkable is the range of expression, through pungent rusticity and feminine delicacy (Melisendra) to knightly dignity. The scenes, which are continuous, are tightly compressed, but so adroitly contrasted and finely proportioned that the work seems bigger than it is in reality.

RONALD CRICHTON

Re Teodoro in Venezia, Il ('King Theodore in Venice'). *Dramma eroi-comico* in two acts by GIOVANNI PAISIELLO to a libretto by GIOVANNI BATTISTA CASTI; Vienna, Burgtheater, 23 August 1784.

The plot is based on an incident in Voltaire's *Candide*. Teodoro (baritone), the deposed King of Corsica, hoping to avoid his creditors and would-be assassins, is staying incognito with his chamberlain Gafforio (tenor) in Venice at the inn of the rich Taddeo (baritone) and his daughter Lisetta (soprano). Teodoro loves Lisetta, but his attempts to marry her, and thereby enlist Taddeo's financial assistance, ultimately fail; she is reconciled instead with her lover Sandrino (tenor), while Teodoro finds himself in debtors' prison. A subplot involves the comic efforts of the brusque Acmet (baritone), a deposed sultan also in exile and in disguise, to woo Belisa (soprano), Teodoro's long-lost sister.

Commissioned after the Viennese success of Paisiello's *Il barbiere di Siviglia*, *Il re Teodoro* won great favour both in Vienna (where it was performed nearly 60 times by 1791) and elsewhere (over a dozen productions by 1791). While Casti's libretto has the normal comic play of misunderstandings and deceptions, it is unusual for its serious elements (including the king's unhappy fate) and the degree to which some characters, particularly Teodoro and Belisa, transcend mere stereotypes. Paisiello's music does not achieve any great emotional depth; instead, its light, accessible and theatrically effective style succeeds best in comic or in tender scenes. The first-act finale is a tour de force in both the libretto and the music. The intrigue works up to an unusually convincing scene of comic confusion, and Paisiello's final stretta builds in volume and intensity in a masterly way to a rousing high point, after which the characters leave one by one. The act closes, without precedent, in a purposely anticlimactic recitative for Taddeo, who is left alone on stage.

Il re Teodoro influenced both Da Ponte and Mozart in the creation of *Le nozze di Figaro* (1786). Da Ponte's libretto for *Figaro* relies on the same characters as the earlier libretto for *Il barbiere*, but the stereotyped figures of Paisiello's opera (1782) lack the depth of characterization found in Mozart's *Figaro*, whose more convincing characters were inspired in part by those in Casti's libretto for *Il re Teodoro*. The music of *Il re Teodoro* (as well as that of *Il barbiere*) made a great impression on Mozart, who probably regarded Paisiello as the leading operatic composer with whom he had to compete. Not surprisingly, there are a number of musical connections between *Figaro* and these two operas. Some are similarities of tone and affect, as between the Countess's 'Porgi amor' and another E♭ cavatina, 'Giusto ciel', sung by the same character (Rosina) in *Il barbiere*. Others are melodic relationships too striking to be coincidental: for example, a passage of angry patter in Figaro's 'Aprite un po' quegl'occhi', in which he complains of the faithlessness of women, is virtually identical with part of Sandrino's aria 'Voi semplici amanti' (in *Il re Teodoro*) on the same subject.

JOHN PLATOFF

Rethberg, Elisabeth [Sattler, Lisbeth] (*b* Schwarzenberg, nr Zwickau, 22 Sept 1894; *d* Yorktown Heights, NY, 6 June 1976). German soprano. She studied at Dresden, made her début in 1915 with the Dresden Opera, and remained with the company for seven years. She made her Metropolitan début in 1922 as Aida, remaining as leading soprano for 21 consecutive seasons. During those years she returned regularly to Dresden, sang at Covent Garden in five seasons, and frequently appeared at the Salzburg Festivals. On one return trip to Europe she sang the title role at the Dresden première of Strauss's *Die ägyptische Helena* in 1928. Her other Verdi roles were Desdemona, Amelia (*Un ballo in maschera*), Maria Boccanegra and the Leonoras of both *Il trovatore* and *La forza del destino*. In Wagner she excelled in the 'youthful-dramatic' parts of Elisabeth, Elsa, Eva and Sieglinde; she was also an accomplished Mozart singer. Her beautiful *lirico spinto* soprano was perfectly equalized between the registers, and a combination of natural musicianship and sound training enabled her to maintain an unusually even legato in the most difficult passages.

For illustration see ÄGYPTISCHE HELENA, DIE.

GV (J. B. Richards; S. Smolian)
J. B. Richards: 'Elisabeth Rethberg: the Discography', *Record Collector*, iii (1948), 51–6
——: 'Elisabeth Rethberg's Recordings', *Record Collector*, viii (1953), 5–19   DESMOND SHAWE-TAYLOR

Réthy, Esther (*b* Budapest, 22 Oct 1912). Hungarian soprano. She studied in Budapest and Vienna, making her début in Budapest in 1934 as Micaëla (*Carmen*). In 1937 she was engaged at the Vienna Staatsoper, where she remained until 1949. She sang Susanna (*Le nozze di Figaro*) and Sophie (*Der Rosenkavalier*) at Salzburg (1937–9), returning as Donna Elvira (1950) and Europa in the first public performance of Richard Strauss's *Die Liebe der Danae* (1952). Her repertory included Handel's Rodelinda and Eva (*Die Meistersinger*). From 1948 she sang frequently at the Vienna Volksoper in the operettas of Johann Strauss, Kálmán and Lehár. A very beautiful woman, she scored a particular success in Heuberger's *Der Opernball*.   ELIZABETH FORBES

Reuss-Belce [Baumann], **Luise** (*b* Vienna, 24 Oct 1860; *d* Aibach, Augsburg, 5 March 1945). Austrian soprano. She studied in Vienna, making her début in 1881 as Elsa at Karlsruhe, where she sang Cassandra in the first complete performance of *Les Troyens* (1890). In 1897 she moved to Wiesbaden and in 1901 to Dresden, where she remained until 1911. Having made her Bayreuth début in 1882 as a flowermaiden in the première of *Parsifal*, she returned (1889–1901) as Eva, Gutrune, Fricka and Second Norn. She made her Covent Garden début in 1893 as Sieglinde and then sang Fricka (1900). Engaged at the Metropolitan (1901–3), she sang Elisabeth, Fricka and Gutrune; she also sang Iolanthe in the American première of Ethel Smyth's *Der Wald* (1903). One of the longest-living singers to have participated in a performance under Wagner's aegis, she had a fine, substantial voice, particularly strong in the middle register.   ELIZABETH FORBES

Reutter, (Johann Adam Joseph Karl) Georg (von) (*b* Vienna, bap. 6 April 1708; *d* Vienna, 11 March 1772). Austrian composer. He was a composition pupil of Caldara and by the age of 14 was deputizing for his father, the composer Georg Reutter, as Viennese court organist. After studying in Venice and Rome (from 1729 or 1730), he obtained the post he wanted as court composer in 1731. He was a prolific composer of operas and oratorios, with 38 dramatic works performed between 1727 and the death of Charles VI in 1740. His requests for a salary increase found little or no support from Fux, the first court Kapellmeister, and were mostly rejected.

About 1736 Reutter took over the duties of first Kapellmeister at St Stephen's Cathedral, and the post was made over to him officially on his father's death in 1738. In 1739–40 he engaged the young Haydn as a chorister; in 1740 he was ennobled. On Fux's death in 1741, L. A. Predieri was promoted to first court Kapellmeister; Reutter occasionally undertook the Kapellmeister's duties and became second Kapellmeister in 1747. He assumed full control of the court Kapelle in 1751, although he bore the title of first Kapellmeister only after Predieri's death in 1769. When Reutter took over, Maria Theresa severely reduced the budget for court music: the number of court musicians steadily declined, as did the level of performance.

In 1751 the administration of the court theatre was handed over to the city authorities. The number of Italian opera performances had dwindled to a minimum since the beginning of Maria Theresa's reign. When Durazzo was appointed director of court and chamber music in 1760 and took over the supervision of both theatres, the city council retained control of the Kärntnertortheater. Durazzo's efforts to appoint Gluck in Reutter's place, or to transfer to him as second

Kapellmeister the direction of court secular music, failed, and the consequent dispute was resolved in Reutter's favour (see Haas, 39ff).

Reutter seems to have been little concerned with his obligations at the cathedral; but he was nevertheless able to secure in 1756 both Kapellmeister positions at court and also both at the cathedral.

Reutter was one of the most prolific composers of his time and enjoyed a high reputation at court, but his work is uneven. His operas, modelled on those of Caldara, lack the cantabile mellifluousness that distinguishes Caldara's arias. His harmonic progressions are simple and he overused sequence. Though talented, he apparently lacked self-criticism. His output includes occasional dramatic pieces, numerous sacred works and instrumental music.

first performed in Vienna unless otherwise stated

Archidamia (festa teatrale, 1, G. C. Pasquini), 22 Nov 1727, A-Wgm, Wn

La forza dell'amicizia (dramma per musica, 3, Pasquini), Graz, 17 Aug 1728, collab. Caldara, Wgm, Wn

La magnanimità di Alessandro (Pasquini), 1 Oct 1729, Wn

Alcide trasformato in dio (dramma per musica), 1729, Wn

Plotina (festa teatrale, 1, Pasquini), 19 Nov 1730, Wn

La pazienza di Socrate con due mogli (scherzo drammatico, 3, N. Minato), Hof (Teatrino), 17 Jan 1731, collab. Caldara, Wn

La generosità di Artaserse con Temistocle [Act 1] (dramma per musica, 3, Pasquini), 1 Oct 1731, Wn

Il tempo e la verità (Pasquini), 15 Oct 1731, Wn

Alessandro il Grande (festa di musica, Pasquini), 1 Oct 1732, Wgm, Wn

Zenobia (festa teatrale, 1, Pasquini), Neu-Wartenburg, 28 Oct 1732, Wgm, Wn

Ciro in Armenia (festa teatrale, 1, Pasquini), 1 Oct 1733, Wgm, Wn

La gratitudine di Mitridate (1, Pasquini), 1 Oct 1734, Wn

Dafne (festa teatrale, 1, Pasquini), 19 Nov 1734, Wgm, Wn

Il Palladio conservato (azione teatrale, 1, P. Metastasio), 1 Oct 1735, Wn

Il sacrifizio in Aulide (festa teatrale, 1, P. Pariati), 19 Nov 1735, Wn

La speranza assicurata (serenata, Pasquini), Laxenburg, 13 May 1736, Wgm, Wn

Diana vendicata (festa teatrale, 1, Pasquini), 19 or 21 Nov 1736, Wgm, Wn

Statira (3, A. Zeno and Pariati), 1736

Il Parnasso accusato e difeso (festa teatrale, 1, Metastasio), 28 Aug 1738, Wn

L'alloro illustrato (festa teatrale, 1, Pasquini), 19 Nov 1738, Wgm, Wn

L'eroina d'Argo (Pasquini), 15 Oct 1739, Wgm, Wn

La gara (componimento drammatico, 1, Metastasio), 13 May 1755, Wn

Other stage works, libs. by Metastasio: L'amor prigioniero, 1741; La rispettosa tenerezza, 1750; Il tributo di rispetto, 1754; Il sogno, 1756; Le grazie vendicate, 1758

*

L. von Köchel: *Die kaiserliche Hof-Musikkapelle in Wien von 1543 bis 1867* (Vienna, 1869)

L. Stollbrock: 'Leben und Wirken des k.k. Hofkapellmeisters und Hofkompositors Johann Georg Reutter jun.', *VMw*, viii (1892), 161–203

R. Haas: *Gluck und Durazzo im Burgtheater* (Vienna, 1925)

G. Zechmeister: *Die Wiener Theater nächst der Burg und nächst dem Kärntnerthor von 1747 bis 1776* (Vienna, 1971)

EVA BADURA-SKODA

Reutter, Hermann (*b* Stuttgart, 17 June 1900; *d* Heidenheim an der Brenz, 1 Jan 1985). German composer. He studied the piano and cello before moving to Munich, where he became a pupil of Courvoisier and Dorfmüller at the Akademie der Tonkunst, 1920–25. During the 1920s and 30s he established a reputation as a fine lieder accompanist, working with such singers as Sigrid Onegin. In 1932 he was appointed a teacher in composition at the Stuttgart Musikhochschule and from 1936 to 1945 was director of the Hoch Conservatory in

Frankfurt. After the war he retired from teaching until 1952, when he took over classes in lieder and composition at the Staatliche Hochschule für Musik, Stuttgart, becoming director in 1956. From 1966 to 1974 he was in charge of a masterclass for lieder interpretation at the Munich Musikhochschule.

Reutter's initial development as an operatic composer was to some extent shaped by external factors connected with the political situation in Germany. In the 1920s he was closely associated with the Donaueschingen Festival and came under the influence of Hindemith and Stravinsky. The stylized nature of his two early one-act operas *Saul* and *Der verlorene Sohn* represent a compromise between expressionism and the static, oratorio-like nature of Stravinsky's *Oedipus rex*. Indeed, the later of these works was recast as a scenic oratorio *Die Rückkehr des verlorenen Sohnes* in 1952. However, after following Hindemith's example in writing a *Lehrstück*, *Der neue Hiob* (1930), Reutter reacted against his earlier style and embraced a more consciously popular language in the cantata *Der grosse Kalender* (1930–32). This particular work marked the beginning of a long collaboration with the librettist and publisher Ludwig Andersen, who subsequently produced the material for three of the composer's later operas. The first of these works, *Doktor Johannes Faust* (composed 1934–6), based on the old puppet play in the Karl Simrock version, represents a genuine attempt to write a 20th-century Volksoper with song and dance episodes and closed forms. Despite the fact that the opera received over 100 performances between 1936 and 1944, it was censured by certain sectors of the Nazi establishment for being 'constructivist'. Opposition to Reutter and his works reached its apogee in 1938 when the composer's portrait was featured at the 'Entartete Musik' exhibition in Düsseldorf. Nevertheless, these criticisms subsided in the wake of wartime activity, and in his next opera, *Odysseus* (1942), he achieved a genuinely patriotic feeling while following the contemporary German fashion of drawing material from an episode in classical mythology.

After 1945 Reutter further exploited the stark linearity of style which had appeared in embryo in *Odysseus*. For the first time, he tackled a contemporary theme: in *Der Weg nach Freudenstadt* a young woman searches in vain for her soldier husband after the end of a war. Characteristically, this moving scenario is set in an epic and detached manner, but such restraint ultimately enhances the emotional impact. Similarly, in *Die Brücke von San Luis Rey* (1954), based on Wilder's novel about the lives of several people united in catastrophe when a bridge collapses in Peru carrying them to their deaths, the composer avoids exaggerated emotionalism and his harmonic language achieves a greater toughness through the influence of serialism. *Der Tod des Empedokles* (composed 1965) demonstrates further preoccupation with 12-note procedures, especially in its fugal intermezzo, but ends with an unequivocal C major chord. Unusually, the work is designated not as an opera but as a 'concerto scenico', and it often employs forms associated with absolute music. For example, the three monologues sung by Empedokles are cast as variations on a theme first stated by the orchestra, and the final song of the three loyal followers is a trio in canon form. The composer considered his final opera, *Hamlet* (1980), which he had planned over a period of 40 years, as representing the summation of his achievements in the operatic medium. Described as a drama for singers, actors and dancers, the work is remarkable for the absence of lengthy arias or dramatic choral finales. Even the fatal duel scene at the end of the opera takes place within an intimate family atmosphere. Such understatement runs the risk of undermining the dramatic tension of Shakespeare's play, although the dance scene which depicts Ophelia's madness, accompanied by *a cappella* chorus, is peculiarly affecting.

Saul (1, A. Lernet-Holenia), Baden-Baden, 20 July 1928 (Mainz, 1928); rev. version, Hamburg, 21 Dec 1947, vs (Mainz, 1947)

Der verlorene Sohn (1, A. Gide, trans. R. M. Rilke), Stuttgart, 20 March 1929 (Mainz, 1929); rev. as Die Rückkehr des verlorenen Sohnes, Dortmund, 2 Oct 1952 (Mainz, 1952)

Doktor Johannes Faust, 1934–6 (3, L. Andersen), Frankfurt, 26 May 1936, vs (Mainz, 1936); rev. version, Stuttgart, 8 June 1955 (Mainz, 1956)

Odysseus (3, R. Bach), Frankfurt, 7 Oct 1942 (Mainz, 1942)

Der Lübecker Totentanz (1, after poems in the Marienkirche), Göttingen, 25 Jan 1948 (Mainz, 1950)

Der Weg nach Freudenstadt (szenisches Spiel, 5 scenes, S. Korty), Göttingen, 25 Jan 1948 (Mainz, 1950)

Don Juan und Faust (7 scenes, Andersen, after C. D. Grabbe), Stuttgart, 11 June 1950 (Mainz, 1950)

Die Witwe von Ephesus (1, Andersen, after Petronius), Cologne, 23 June 1954, vs (Mainz, 1954); rev., Schwetzingen, 1966 (Mainz, c1970)

Die Brücke von San Luis Rey (1, Reutter, after T. Wilder), Frankfurt Radio, 20 June 1954; staged Essen, 18 Dec 1954 (Mainz, 1954)

Der Tod des Empedokles, 1965 (conc. scenico, 2, Reutter, after F. Hölderlin), Schwetzingen, 29 May 1966, vs (Mainz, 1966)

Bauernhochzeit (1, H. Roth, after J. G. von Herder), Mainz, 15 Feb 1967

Nausikaa (1, after J. W. von Goethe), Mainz, 15 Feb 1967

Hamlet (2, Reutter, after W. Shakespeare), Stuttgart, 6 Dec 1980 (Mainz, 1980)

*

W. Fröhlich: 'Hermann Reutter', *ZfM*, Jg.103 (1936), 657–61

C. Niessen: *Die deutsche Oper der Gegenwart* (Regensburg, 1944)

K. Laux: 'Hermann Reutter', *Musik und Musiker der Gegenwart* (Essen, 1949), 203–15

W. Fröhlich: ' "Don Juan und Faust" von Hermann Reutter', *Neue Musikzeitschrift*, iv (1950), 181–4

H. Reutter: 'Wort und Ton in der zeitgenössischen Musik', *Musica*, iv (1950), 121–4

——: 'Dramma per musica. Betrachtungen eines Befangenen', *Musica*, vii (1953), 550–53

G. Gilhoff: 'Hermann Reutter's Faust Opera', *Monatshefte*, lii (1960), 242–8

H. Lindlar, ed.: *Hermann Reutter, Werk und Wirken* (Mainz, 1965)

H. Reutter: *Zur Dramaturgie meines 'Hamlet'* (Mainz, 1980)

ERIK LEVI

Reval (Ger.). TALLINN.

Revelation in the Courthouse Park. Music-dance drama in one act by HARRY PARTCH to his own libretto after *The Bacchae* of EURIPIDES; Urbana, University of Illinois, 11 April 1961.

Partch actually used the term 'music-dance drama' only with reference to *Oedipus*, but it serves for all five of his major theatre works, some of which are more overtly operatic than others. *Revelation*, like the others, features Partch's unique musical instruments prominently on stage, and their players contribute both movement and voices to the choral and dance climaxes. In addition the work features an eight-piece marching band and two guitarists, all of whom participate directly in the action.

The events of the drama take place from the late afternoon of one day to the dawn of the next, but shuttle between ancient Thebes and contemporary small-town America. The American scenes, labelled 'choruses', replace Euripides' choruses; choral passages are also found in the Theban scenes. A single set serves to represent the exterior of the palace of Thebes and an American neo-classical county courthouse.

Chorus 1 begins with a 'Park Prologue' in which Mom (= Agave, soprano) declares her emotional independence from conservative Sonny (= Pentheus, tenor-baritone). The townspeople, complete with brass band, majorettes and clog dancers, gather to celebrate the arrival of Dion, 'Hollywood king of Ishbu Kubu' (= Dionysus, baritone), a character modelled in part on Elvis Presley, whom Partch greatly admired. They greet him with cult catch-phrases, which Mom enthusiastically leads while Sonny watches from the sidelines in distress. In Thebes (Scene 1), Dionysus announces that he had come to punish the city, and particularly King Pentheus, for its unbelief. He has 'laid a craze upon the women', and only Pentheus remains untouched. Even the aged seer Tiresias (bass-baritone) and the king's grandfather, Cadmus (baritone) have been caught up in the cult, but Pentheus angrily denounces the god and his followers. In the courthouse park (Chorus 2) Sonny has a nightmare vision that he will be offered up as a sacrifical victim. As Pentheus in Thebes (Scene 2), he has Dionysus imprisoned, but the god miraculously escapes as the Bacchantes sing his praises. Later that night in the courthouse park (Chorus 3) the revels are in full swing: the already lavish forces of Chorus 1 are augmented by gymnasts and a filmed fireworks display as Dion leads the assembled multitude in an orgy of 'Ishbu Kubu' nonsense syllables. In Thebes (Scene 3) a Herdsman (tenor-baritone) who has witnessed the Baccanale tells Pentheus of it in vivid language. Dionysus, playing on the king's unacknowledged salacious curiosity, convinces him to spy on the Bacchantes. At midnight in the courthouse park (Chorus 4) Mom, in a nightmare paralleling her son's in Chorus 2, dreams that Sonny is attacked by a mob while she stands helpless. At dawn in Thebes (Scene 4) the Herdsman tells of the King's fate: Pentheus has been torn apart by the maddened Bacchantes, under the leadership of his own mother, Agave. She enters bearing her son's mask, his head, which she thinks is a lion's. Cadmus gently calls her attention to what she is holding, and she drops the mask with a great crash of percussion, drops her own on top of it (another crash) and slowly backs away as the Coda draws to a close.

Partch's updating of Euripides makes the tragedy a modern one of sexuality and sex roles, of ecstatic ritual and the majoritarian tyranny it may conceal. The composer clearly identified both with Dion/Dionysus, master of the sacred revels, and Sonny/Pentheus, the nonconformist outsider; the irreconcilability of these roles constitutes the heart of the tragedy. ANDREW STILLER

Revival. A term generally applied to the production of an opera that has disappeared from the active repertory. It is however used in a variety of senses, particularly for the restoration to an opera house's repertory of an existing production; it is also occasionally applied to a new production of a work formerly in repertory. Further, it is sometimes applied to entire repertories ('the Handel revival'; 'the bel canto opera revival'). In the 17th and 18th centuries popular works were repeatedly revived, often with extensive changes by the original composer or others, to the extent that any revival might in effect become a PASTICCIO.

The present article is concerned principally with the revival, since the late 19th century, of operas from the Baroque or Classical periods, and in particular with the way in which such revivals have increasingly been animated by a desire to recover a lost or interrupted mode of performance.

Opera was often represented in 19th-century historical concerts illustrating various schools or genres of composition. In 1832 Fétis conducted a concert at the Paris Conservatoire surveying the history of opera; it included excerpts from Peri's *Euridice*, Monteverdi's *Orfeo*, Lully's *Armide*, Rameau's *Zoroastre* and Handel's *Berenice*, and some historical instruments were used. In the late 19th century interest in early French, German, Italian and English opera grew steadily, fuelled partly by the rising nationalism of the period and partly by the expanding horizons of musical scholarship. The first full-scale stage revival seems to have been Handel's *Almira*, produced in 1878 as part of a festival of German opera in Hamburg. The procrustean cuts and alterations in the score drew sharp criticism from Chrysander, whose scholarly edition of the work had recently been published. But most commentators accepted that early music had to be adapted or 'improved' for modern listeners. Charles Wood supplied lushly Romantic orchestration for a London staging of *Dido and Aeneas* in 1895 marking the bicentenary of Purcell's death. D'Indy similarly modernized the music of Rameau, Lully, Monteverdi and Destouches for the pioneer performances, both staged and concert, presented by the Schola Cantorum in France in the first quarter of the 20th century.

D'Indy's performing editions represented a compromise between practicality and historical fidelity as then conceived. For the 1904 revival of *Orfeo*, involving some 150 singers and instrumentalists, he omitted the first and last acts as undramatic and made substantial cuts in the remaining three; he justified his procedure by arguing that the opera was 'a work of art, not of archaeology'. His orchestra, modelled closely on Monteverdi's own, included pairs of flutes, oboes and trumpets, five trombones, strings, harp-lute, chromatic harp, harpsichord and organ. Harpsichords were often employed in early revivals, though even the resonant modern instruments proved inadequate for larger opera houses. When the Paris Opéra presented d'Indy's version of *Hippolyte et Aricie* in 1908, it was deemed necessary to reinforce the Pleyel harpsichord with a double string quartet in the recitatives, producing what one listener called 'a sensation of devastating monotony'. The following year, when *Orfeo* was given in Milan in a version by Giacomo Orefice, the critic Carlo Censi defended the use of modern instruments on the grounds that it was impossible to reproduce the effect of the original orchestra on 17th-century listeners. This argument has been echoed by other critics and editor-arrangers unsympathetic to any trend in favour of historical productions.

It is clear from contemporary recordings and reports that little effort was made in early revivals to re-create the vocal practices of the Baroque period. The singing tended to be heavily Romantic in style, with unvaried, legato phrasing, little ornamentation, frequent ritardandos and sluggish recitatives. The lack of concern for musical authenticity in the modern sense was reflected in the work of stage directors and choreographers, few of whom valued historical accuracy for its own sake. Gordon Craig announced that he had 'taken care to be entirely incorrect in all matters of detail' in his production of *Dido and Aeneas* for the Purcell Operatic Society in 1900. The first modern staging of Monteverdi's *Orfeo*, at the Théâtre Réjane in Paris in 1911, took place against the incongruous backdrop of sets for Maeterlinck's *L'oiseau bleu*. Static tableaux and statuesque poses seem to have been the norm; costuming and decor tended towards the generically 'antique'. Occasionally designers evoked a specific period, as in a 1901 production of Rameau's *Platée* in Munich, in which the singers wore costumes described as 'half Greek, half Louis XIV'. As early as 1925 the Paris Opéra attempted to re-create 17th-century dances in a production of Lully's *Le triomphe de l'Amour*. But little serious consideration was given to Baroque choreography, stagecraft and dramaturgy until after 1945.

The German 'Handel Renaissance' of the 1920s and 30s initiated a more intensive phase in the Baroque opera revival. Oskar Hagen, an art historian at the University of Göttingen, led the movement in 1920 with the first modern staging of *Rodelinda*; it elicited an unprecedented response in the nationalistically charged atmosphere of postwar Germany. A rash of Handel productions ensued, ranging in style from expressionist to quasi-Baroque, and in scale from modest academic stagings to lavish outdoor spectacles with massed dancers and amplified music. Hagen's heavily abridged and rearranged editions were adopted by Werner Josten at Smith College in Massachusetts, where a series of Handel and Monteverdi productions took place in the late 1920s and early 30s. Other notable revivals with academic support in the interwar years were given by the Juilliard School in New York and in England by the Cambridge University Musical Society and the Oxford University Opera Club. Westrup's editions of *Orfeo* and *L'incoronazione di Poppea*, first heard in Oxford, set new standards of scholarly fidelity, as did Dent's widely used version of *Dido and Aeneas*. Yet the period also produced a spate of freely modernized editions of Baroque operas by composers such as Krenek, Respighi and Orff. The latter's adaptation of *Orfeo* was perhaps freest of all: the allegorical figures were eliminated, a narrator was introduced to relate the Orpheus story, and the scenes were reordered to fit the revised libretto.

The trend towards greater historical awareness, sporadically evident in earlier revivals, became firmly established after World War II. Two notable productions of Monteverdi's *Orfeo* – Hindemith's in Vienna in 1954 and August Wenzinger's in Hitzacher in 1955 – used historical instruments as well as sets and costumes based on Baroque designs. A new generation of conductors concerned with the findings of recent scholarship, among them Charles Farncombe, Anthony Lewis, Newell Jenkins and Nikolaus Harnoncourt, exercised a strong influence on the performance of early opera. As in the Early Music revival generally, there was a growing body of opinion in favour of presenting operas in a form as close as possible to the original. Raymond Leppard's popular but controversial arrangements of Cavalli and Monteverdi operas, however, with many cuts and rich orchestral textures, commissioned by the Glyndebourne Festival in the 1960s and 70s, attest to the durability of the dissenting view, and they undoubtedly won the composers many admirers.

Much recent scholarship has been devoted to the re-creation of every aspect of original opera production: singing, playing, staging, gesture, the disposition of the orchestra, costumes, sets, choreography and lighting. A rigorously historical approach, however, is unsuited to the resources or the size of most modern opera houses and many memorable productions have been the work of smaller and more adventurous companies, festivals and workshop groups. Many such revivals have been associated with early theatres that survive in their original form or in reconstruction. Of these, the leading example is the Drottningholm theatre, near Stockholm, which has been a centre of period-performance revival (of Mozart, Gluck and others) under Farncombe and Arnold Östman, though generally with modern settings; other surviving houses include those at Schwetzingen, near Mannheim, and Versailles, which has been used for Rameau revivals. In the Low Countries there have been revivals, at Amsterdam and elsewhere, of Monteverdi and the Classical repertory, under Gustav Leonhardt and Sigiswald Kuijken; Harnoncourt has directed similar repertories in Vienna and Zürich. Period-style performances have been given at Innsbruck under Alan Curtis and René Jacobs. In London they have been given by the English Bach Festival (particularly attentive to costume and staging in their favoured French repertory) and by Kent Opera under Roger Norrington and others. In the USA the chief centres have been Boston and Berkeley (where Nicholas McGegan, who also conducts period opera in Hungary, and Curtis are active) and Bloomington, Indiana. Among the particularly successful directors of recordings have been Östman (of the Da Ponte-Mozart operas), John Eliot Gardiner (Rameau, Gluck and Mozart), Jacobs (Cavalli, Cesti and Handel), William Christie (Lully and other French repertory), Kuijken (Handel) and Nigel Rogers (Monteverdi). A school of singers has developed techniques apt to singing in an appropriate historical style with period instruments, including Julianne Baird, Emma Kirkby, Judith Nelson, Agnès Mellon and Jennifer Smith (sopranos), James Bowman, Jacobs, Drew Minter and Dominique Visse (countertenors) and Rogers (tenor).

Although the postwar bel canto opera revival owed little directly to the Early Music movement, both can be seen as manifestations of a widespread growth of interest in historical repertories and modes of performance. The cultivation of bel canto vocal technique and especially ornamentation by such singers as Joan Sutherland and Maria Callas has had a far-reaching impact on the performance of early opera. As the Early Music revival has moved forward into the Classical and Romantic eras, directors have begun to apply historical principles to the mainstream 19th-century repertory.

*

R. Steglich: 'Die neue Händel-Opern-Bewegung', *HJb*, i (1928), 71–158

H. C. Wolff: *Die Händel-Oper auf der modernen Bühne* (Leipzig, 1957)

W. Meyerhoff, ed.: *50 Jahre Göttinger Händel-Festspiele* (Kassel, 1970)

W. Dean: 'Twenty Years of Handel Opera', *Opera*, xxvi (1975), 924–30

N. Fortune: 'The Rediscovery of "Orfeo"', *Claudio Monteverdi: 'Orfeo'*, ed. J. Whenham (Cambridge, 1986), 78–118

E. T. Harris: *Henry Purcell's 'Dido and Aeneas'* (Oxford, 1987)

H. Haskell: *The Early Music Revival: a History* (London, 1988)

HARRY HASKELL

Revoltosa, La ('The Siren'). Zarzuela in one act by RUPERTO CHAPÍ to a libretto by J. López Silva and CARLOS FERNÁNDEZ SHAW; Madrid, Teatro Apolo, 25 November 1897.

In a Madrid apartment-block Mari-Pepa (soprano) flirts coquettishly with all the men around and dazzles them with her beauty. Their outraged wives plan revenge by sending their husbands a note purporting to come from her, inviting them to an assignment late that night. After an evening of festivities (during which a lively *guajiras* is sung), the men slip out for their rendezvous, only to retreat in embarrassment at finding the others with the same idea, and then are confronted by their angry womenfolk. Felipe (baritone) is the only man whom Mari-Pepa, to her annoyance, has failed to arouse, although he is secretly attracted to her. He is finally fired to jealousy by the commotion, and in the end she realizes the worth of true love and gives him her heart. The principal number of this very popular work (which was highly praised by Saint-Saëns) is the duet between Mari-Pepa and Felipe.   LIONEL SALTER

Rexroth-Berg, Natanael. *See* BERG, NATANAEL.

Rey, Cemal Reşit (*b* Jerusalem, 25 Oct 1904; *d* Istanbul, 14 Oct 1985). Turkish composer, pianist and conductor. He completed his musical education at the Paris Conservatoire with Marguerite Long and Raoul Laparra. Returning to Turkey in 1923 he took up a teaching appointment at the Istanbul Municipal Conservatoire, and in the 1940s was a founder of the Istanbul Municipal Orchestra and the Philharmonic Society. From 1940 to 1942 he was musical director of Ankara Radio and between 1949 and 1960 conducted his own works in various European countries. He composed in every genre and all his works show the influence of French impressionism combined with the rich Turkish folklore tradition. His theatre music falls into two categories: operas, which he began writing at an early age, and operettas and musicals aimed at arousing a wider appreciation of music. His brother Ekrem Reşit Rey was librettist for all his stage compositions.

all librettos by E. R. Rey

Sultan Cem (5), 1923

Lükus Hayat [High Society] (operetta, 3), Istanbul, 1923

Zeybek (3), 1926

Koyde bir Facia [A Village Tragedy] (1), 1929

Deli Dolu [Daredevil] (operetta, 3), Istanbul, 1934

Maskara [The Buffoon; The Masquerader; Masquerade] (musical comedy, 3), Istanbul, 1936

Çelebi, 1943, Ankara, State Opera, spr. 1991   FARUK YENER

Rey, (Louis-Etienne-)Ernest. *See* REYER, ERNEST.

Rey, Jean-Baptiste (*b* Lauzerte, 18 Dec 1734; *d* ?Paris, 15 July 1810). French conductor and composer. He was taught at the choir school at St Servin and had become *maître de chapelle* at Auch Cathedral by the age of 17. After three years he went as a conductor to the opera houses of Toulouse, Montpellier, Marseilles, Bordeaux and Nantes. In 1776 he was engaged as a conductor at the Paris Opéra, where he conducted works by Gluck and Piccinni, among others, and in 1781 he became director of the Opéra orchestra. From 1779 he was master of the *musique de chambre* at the court of Louis XVI, and from 1781 occasionally conducted at the Concert Spirituel. In 1792, during the Revolution, he joined the committee in charge of the Opéra. During 1793 he conducted at the Théâtre de la République (the Comédie-Française), notably some incidental music by Méhul for André Chénier's *Timoléon*, in which Talma took the leading part. He went to the Paris Conservatoire in 1799 as professor of harmony. Five years later he became *maître de chapelle* to Napoleon, but just before his death resigned from all his positions.

Rey is best remembered as a conductor. After the revival of Gluck's operas in 1786, the *Mercure de*

France (4 March 1786) called him 'the foremost conductor in all Europe'. As a composer he mostly limited himself to arrangements of works he was about to conduct. His most important work was his completion of Sacchini's *Arvire et Eveline* (1788); he also made additions to works by J. J. Mouret and his brother Louis-Charles-Joseph Rey, and he wrote one opera, *Diane et Endymion* (Opéra, 1791), in which Rameau's influence is apparent.

R. Cotte: *Musiciens F … M … à la cour de Versailles* (Paris, 1983)

ROGER J. V. COTTE

Reyer [Rey], (Louis-Etienne-)Ernest (*b* Marseilles, 1 Dec 1823; *d* Le Lavandou, Var, 15 Jan 1909). French composer and critic. He received his musical education from his cousin, the pianist Louise Farrenc, in Paris. His 'oriental symphony', *Le sélam*, was successfully performed in 1850, and his ballet *Sacountalâ* was played at the Opéra in 1858. Both these works had texts by Gautier, the most prominent of Reyer's many literary friends. He also won the admiration of Berlioz and became one of the older composer's few close friends in his last years.

Reyer's first opera was *Maître Wolfram*, again with a text by Gautier, staged at the Théâtre Lyrique in 1854. Wolfram, an organist, decides to devote himself to music when he discovers his beloved does not love him. *La statue*, given at the same theatre in 1861, has a story derived from *The Thousand and One Nights*. The setting – the ruins of Baalbek – was much admired, and the opera was successful for many years. Its kinship with Weber, whom Reyer greatly admired, was widely observed. *Erostrate* (1862) tells the legend of how the Venus de Milo lost her arms.

Despite his early success as an opera composer Reyer's career was diverted in the mid-1860s towards journalism. His two remaining operas, *Sigurd* and *Salammbô*, were long in gestation, though both made a profound and lasting impression on the French public; in the 1890s Reyer was regarded as a major opera composer of the time. He was accused of Wagnerism but made his own position very clear: 'I admire both of them [Berlioz and Wagner] in their very different types of genius too much ever to have the audacity to imitate them'. He displayed a characteristically French taste for orientalism, but his music is never frail or lacklustre; it has considerable weight, if not much real melodic distinction, and he took great pains with his orchestration. His work was serious and disciplined, despite being accused of amateurishness by his critics, and he exercised the sternest self-discipline.

See also SALAMMBÔ (ii) and SIGURD.

all published in Paris

Maître Wolfram (oc, 1, J. Méry and T. Gautier), Paris, Lyrique, 20 May 1854, (*c*1855)

La statue (oc, 3, M. Carré and J. Barbier), Paris, Lyrique, 11 April 1861, vs (*c*1861)

Erostrate (2, Méry and E. Pacini); in Ger., Baden-Baden, 21 Aug 1862; in Fr., Paris, Opéra, 16 Oct 1871; vs (1862)

Sigurd (4, C. Du Locle and A. Blau), Brussels, Monnaie, 7 Jan 1884, (*c*1884)

Salammbô (5, Du Locle, after G. Flaubert), Brussels, Monnaie, 10 Feb 1890, vs (*c*1890)

H. de Curzon: *La légende de Sigurd dans l'Edda: l'opéra de Reyer* (Paris, 1890)

——: *Salammbô: le poème et l'opéra* (Paris, 1890)

H. Imbert: *Nouveaux profils de musiciens* (Paris, 1892)

A. Jullien: *Musiciens d'aujourd'hui* (Paris, 1892–4), 209–30

G. Servières: *La musique française moderne* (Paris, 1897)

A. Bruneau: *Musiques de Russie et musiciens de France* (Paris, 1903)

J. Combarieu: 'Ernest Reyer', *RHCM*, ix (1909), 88–9

A. Jullien: *Ernest Reyer: sa vie et ses oeuvres* (Paris, 1909)

A. Pougin: *Musiciens du XIXe siècle* (Paris, 1911)

H. de Curzon: *Ernest Reyer: sa vie et ses oeuvres* (Paris, 1924)

A. Jullien: 'Reyer intime d'après des lettres inédites', *ReM*, v/3 (1924), 12–21

A. Boschot: *Portraits de musiciens*, i (Paris, 1946)

T. J. Walsh: *Second Empire Opera: the Théâtre Lyrique, Paris, 1851–1870* (London, 1981)

HUGH MACDONALD

Reykjavík. Capital of Iceland. Regular professional opera in Iceland dates only from the foundation in 1950 of the National Theatre in Reykjavík, which seats 661 and can accommodate 40 in the pit; it is legally required to produce at least one opera a year. Its first production was *Rigoletto*, sung in Icelandic; *Tosca* (1957–8) was the first opera given by an all-Icelandic cast, though most of the singers had received training in Scandinavia or Italy. The first performance by local musicians was *Carmen* in 1975. Iceland Opera was formed in 1979, with the tenor Gardar Cortes as director; it opened with *Pagliacci*. A sizable bequest from Sigurlidi Kristjánsson in 1980 enabled the company to purchase the Gamla Bíó, a cinema built in the 1920s. Modifications were carried out and new lighting installed, leaving a capacity of 505 and excellent acoustics. The house opened on 9 January 1982 with *Der Zigeunerbaron*, which ran for 49 sold-out performances. In June of that year the National Theatre replied with perhaps the greatest operatic success by an Icelandic composer, Atli Heimir Sveinsson's *Silkitromman* ('The Silken Drum'), first performed at the start of the seventh Biennial Reykjavík Arts Festival (begun 1970). A similar triumph was Karólína Eiríksdóttir's *Någon har jag sett* ('Someone I have Seen'), given by Iceland Opera in 1989, a year after its première in Sweden.

Iceland Opera maintains a schedule of three or four productions a year, with both local and foreign singers and conductors, and regularly plays to full houses. The state underwrites only about one-third of its budget, leaving the balance to be found at the box office. A large proportion of Icelanders sing in choirs, and the opera chorus is known for its high standards. Accompaniment is provided mainly by members of the Iceland SO. Most operas are now sung in the original language with Icelandic surtitles.

MARTIN DREYER (with CHARLES PITT)

Reynard. 'Merry performance' by Igor Stravinsky; *see* RENARD.

Reynolds, Anna [Ann] (*b* Canterbury, 4 Oct 1931). English mezzo-soprano. She studied in Rome, making her début in 1960 at Parma as Suzuki. She first sang at Glyndebourne in 1962 as Debussy's Geneviève (a part she also sang at Aix-en-Provence and La Scala), returning for Ortensia (Rossini's *La pietra del paragone*) and Annina (*Der Rosenkavalier*). She made her Covent Garden début in 1967 as Adelaide (*Arabella*), then in 1975 sang Andromache (*King Priam*). Having made her Metropolitan début in 1968 as Flosshilde (*Das Rheingold*), she sang Fricka in 1969. She appeared at the Salzburg Easter Festival (1970), in Rome (1970) as Elizabeth (*Maria Stuarda*) and at Bayreuth (1970–75) as Fricka, Waltraute and Magdalene. Her roles included Purcell's Dido, Rossini's Tancredi and Charlotte (*Werther*). She had an evenly produced, flexible voice and excellent diction.

ALAN BLYTH

Rey que rabió, El ('The King who was Rabid'). Zarzuela in three acts by RUPERTO CHAPÍ to a libretto by MIGUEL RAMOS CARRIÓN and Vital Aza: Madrid, Teatro de la Zarzuela, 20 April 1891.

This comic satire centres on a young King (soprano) who determines to go among his people dressed as a shepherd in order to see whether the country is as well run as his ministers would have him believe. His General (baritone), similarly disguised, accompanies him; but as a precaution, unknown to them the governor precedes them to organize favourable reactions wherever they go. Rosa (soprano), the niece of an innkeeper, has scorned the wooing of the perpetually complaining Jeremías (tenor), and when the King falls in love with her she responds wholeheartedly. An army patrol taking men due for military service seizes Jeremías and the supposed shepherds; but a few days later the King runs away, taking Rosa with him. The King's identity is revealed by the governor, and a search party is sent out for him. Meanwhile Jeremías, who has also gone on the run to search for Rosa, has been bitten by a dog. This accident is related to the search party, who assume that the fleeing Jeremías is the King. General consternation: was the dog rabid? A huddle of doctors shilly-shally. Finally all is happily resolved, and the King, rejecting various brides proposed by ambassadors, marries Rosa.

LIONEL SALTER

Reyzen [Reisen], **Mark** (Osipovich) (*b* Zaytsevo, Dnepropetrovsk province, 21 June/3 July 1895). Ukrainian bass. He studied at the Kharkiv Conservatory and made his début with the Kharkiv Opera as Pimen in *Boris Godunov* in 1921. In the following seasons he appeared in a wide variety of roles, including Méphistophélès in *Faust*, Saint-Bris in *Les Huguenots*, Ruslan and Farlaf in *Ruslan and Lyudmila* and Dosifey in *Khovanshchina*. From 1925 to 1930 he was a member of the Leningrad Opera, where in 1928 he sang his first Boris. He then became principal bass at the Bol'shoy, Moscow, remaining there for the rest of his long career. He also sang in Germany, Hungary and France, with appearances at the Paris Opéra and at Monte Carlo in *Mefistofele* and *Il barbiere di Siviglia*. One of the greatest of Russian singers, he had a voice of exceptional beauty, scrupulously used and so well preserved that he could sing at the Bol'shoy to celebrate his 90th birthday. He was also an imposing figure and an accomplished actor. His recordings, dating from 1929 to 1980, include complete performances of *Boris Godunov*, *Khovanshchina* and *Mozart and Salieri*.

M. Reyzen: *Avtobiograficheskiye zapiski* [Autobiographical Notes] (Moscow, 1980)
N. Linnell: 'Mark Reizen', *Record Collector*, xxviii (1983), 5–31
J. B. STEANE

Rezniček, E(mil) N(ikolaus) von (*b* Vienna, 4 May 1860; *d* Berlin, 2 Aug 1945). Austrian composer and conductor. He came from a line of military musicians and read law at the University of Graz from 1878, at the same time studying music with Wilhelm Mayer (W. A. Rémy). He completed his studies at the Leipzig Conservatory from 1881 to 1884 under Reinecke and Jadassohn. After a time as a répétiteur in Graz, he served as theatre conductor in Zürich, Mainz, Stettin, Berlin, Jena and Bochum. At the German Opera House in Prague he was engaged by Angelo Neumann as house composer, and it was there that his first operas were

performed in 1887. From 1888 he was for seven years military bandmaster in Prague; it was towards the end of that time that his comic opera *Donna Diana* was produced, in 1894. The work was subsequently performed in several German theatres, and it has remained Rezniček's best-known work thanks to its sparkling overture. In 1896 he was for a short time court conductor at Weimar and from 1896 to 1899 at Mannheim, where he also conducted the academy concerts. He went to Berlin in 1902 as a conductor, gave chamber concerts there, and for a brief time from 1906 taught theory at the conservatory. From December 1906 until 1909 he was conductor of the Warsaw Opera and PO, making frequent journeys into Russia. In November 1907 he conducted two concerts in London, introducing his Symphony in B♭. He was conductor of the Komische Oper, Berlin (1909–11), and of the Italian seasons under Hermann Gura until 1912, after which he largely concentrated on composition. In 1919 he was elected to the Berlin Akademie für Künste and from 1920 to 1926 taught at the Hochschule für Musik. He composed very much in the German Romantic tradition, his lighter compositions evoking the shades of Weber and Mendelssohn, his more serious operas inviting comparisons with the style of Richard Strauss.

Die Jungfrau von Orleans (3, Rezniček, after F. von Schiller), Prague, Stände, 19 June 1887, lost
Satanella (2, Rezniček), Prague, Stände, 3 May 1887, lost
Emmerich Fortunat (Rezniček), Prague, Neues Deutsches, 8 Nov 1889
Donna Diana (komische oper, 3, Rezniček, after A. Moreto y Cavana: *El desdén con el desdén*), Prague, Neues Deutsches, 16 Dec 1894, vs (Leipzig, 1895); rev. 1908; rev. (J. Kapp), Wuppertal, 15 Nov 1933, vs (Vienna and Leipzig, 1933)
Till Eulenspiegel (2, Rezniček, after J. Fischart: *Eulenspiegel Reimensweiss*), Karlsruhe, 12 Jan 1902, vs (Wiesbaden, 1901); rev., Cologne, 17 June 1937
Eros und Psyche (2, Rezniček), Breslau, Hof, 1917
Ritter Blaubart (3, H. Eulenberg), Darmstadt, 29 Jan 1920 (Vienna and Leipzig, 1920)
Holofernes (2, Rezniček, after F. Hebbel: *Judith und Holofernes*), Berlin, Deutsches Opernhaus, 27 Oct 1923, vs (Vienna and New York, 1923)
Satuala (4, R. Lauckner), Leipzig, Stadt, 4 Dec 1927, vs (Vienna and Leipzig, 1928)
Benzin, 1929 (2, after P. Calderón de la Barca), unperf.
Spiel oder Ernst? (1, P. Knudsen), Dresden, 11 Nov 1930; as Fact and Fiction, Philadelphia, 1941
Der Gondoliere des Dogen (1, Knudsen), Stuttgart, Stadt, 29 Oct 1931 (Berlin, 1931)
Das Opfer, 1932
Tenor und Bass (1), Stockholm, State Opera, 1934

Operettas: Die verlorene Braut, 1910; Die Angst vor der Ehe, Frankfurt an der Oder, 1914, vs (Berlin, 1914)

O. Taubmann: *Emil Nikolaus von Rezniček* (Leipzig, 1907)
M. Chop: *Emil Nikolaus von Rezniček: sein Leben und sein Werk* (Vienna, 1920)
R. Specht: *Emil Nikolaus von Rezniček: eine vorläufigfe Studie* (Vienna, 1923)
H. Killer: 'Gedanken über einen Meister: zur Vollendung des 80. Lebensjahres von E. N. von Rezniček', *Die Musik*, xxxii (1939–40), 224–6
W. Altmann: 'Emil Nikolaus von Rezniček zum Gedächtnis', *Neue Musikzeitschrift*, iv (1950)
F. von Rezniček: *Gegen den Strom* (Vienna, 1960) [with survey of works by L. Nowak]
ANDREW LAMB

Rheims (Ger). REIMS.

Rheinberger, Joseph (Gabriel) (*b* Vaduz, 17 March 1839; *d* Munich, 25 Nov 1901). Liechtenstein composer and organist. He studied the organ, piano and theory at the Munich Conservatory, later taking instruction from Franz Lachner. By 1853 he was organist at a number of churches and also earned his living as a private music teacher. In the next few years he wrote well over 100 widely varied works. From 1859 Rheinberger taught the piano and then theory at the conservatory; he also became organist at St Michael's Church and soon achieved some notable early success with compositions, including incidental music to Calderón's *El mágico prodigioso*. In 1864 he succeeded Perfall as conductor of the Munich Choral Society, a post he held until 1877, proving himself an able choral conductor. He also worked for a time as a coach at the court opera. In 1867 he became a professor at the conservatory, remaining highly revered until his death. In his latter years he won many honours.

Rheinberger's stage works include the operas *Die sieben Raben* (1869) and *Türmers Töchterlein* (1873), and the children's Singspiels *Der arme Heinrich* and *Das Zauberwort*. In his compositions as in his teaching Rheinberger remained aloof from the new currents that developed in the mid-19th century. The strength of his works lies in the indisputable mastery and planned coherence of his compositional style, imbued with the spirit of polyphonic thinking rather than compelling inventiveness or vivid conception. The survival of his work is thus prejudiced by a certain academic approach and want of lively intensity of expression.

autographs in D-Mbs unless otherwise stated

Scherz, List und Rache, 1854 (komische Oper, 4, J. W. von Goethe), ?unperf.

Die Wette, 1856 (ob, 1), ?unperf.

Die sieben Raben op.20, 1860–63, rev. 1868 (dramatisiertes Märchen, 3, F. Bonn), Munich, Hof, 23 May 1869, vs (Leipzig, 1869)

Der arme Heinrich op.37, 1863 (komisches Spl for children, Bonn), unperf., vs (Nuremberg and Munich, 1870)

Türmers Töchterlein op.70 (komische Oper, 4, M. Stahl), Munich, Hof, 23 April 1873, vs (Bremen, 1874)

Das Zauberwort op. 153 (Spl for children, 2, F. von Hoffnaass), 1889, vs (Leipzig, 1888)

Lucius Aula (grosse Oper, G. A. Hemmerich), inc., autograph lost, lib. of Act 1 in Mbs

*

A. Maczewski: 'Die sieben Raben', *Musikalisches Wochenblatt*, i (1870), 164–6, 181–3, 195–7

Review of vs of Der arme Heinrich, *Musikalisches Wochenblatt*, i (1870), 628–9

H. Hoffmann: 'Die sieben Raben', *Neue Berliner Musikzeitung* (1871), 282–3

Review of vs of Das Zauberwort, *Musikalisches Wochenblatt*, xxi (1890), 76

L. Schmidt: *Zur Geschichte der Märchenoper* (Halle, 1895), 62–3

ANTON WÜRZ/R

Rheingold, Das ('The Rhinegold'). *Vorabend* (preliminary evening) of DER RING DES NIBELUNGEN, in four scenes, by Richard Wagner (*see* WAGNER family, (1)) to his own libretto; Munich, Königliches Hof- und Nationaltheater, 22 September 1869 (first performance as part of cycle: Bayreuth, Festspielhaus, 13 August 1876).

The first prose sketch for *Das Rheingold*, at that time conceived in three acts, dates from autumn (probably October) 1851. The sketch was then developed into a prose draft (23–31 March 1852) entitled *Der Raub des Rheingoldes/Vorspiel (oder: das Rheingold)?*. The verse draft was made between 15 September and 3 November 1852 and the final poem was incorporated into the private printing of the entire *Ring* text in February 1853.

Gods	
Wotan	bass-baritone
Donner	bass-baritone
Froh	tenor
Loge	tenor
Fricka	mezzo-soprano
Freia	soprano
Erda	contralto
Nibelungs	
Alberich	bass-baritone
Mime	tenor
Giants	
Fasolt	bass-baritone
Fafner	bass
Rhinemaidens	
Woglinde	soprano
Wellgunde	soprano
Flosshilde	mezzo-soprano
Nibelungs	

According to Wagner's account in *Mein Leben*, the initial musical inspiration for *Rheingold* – rushing arpeggio figures in E♭ major – came to him as he lay in a trance-like state in an inn at La Spezia. Doubt has been cast on the likelihood of such a 'vision' but it has also been argued that the documentary evidence neither supports nor contradicts Wagner's account (see Deathridge 1984 and Darcy 1989–90). Discounting a handful of musical jottings, the composition of *Rheingold* was begun on 1 November 1853, with the first complete draft, a continuous setting of the poem that occupied him until 14 January 1854. In view of the unprecedented problems of writing for the *Ring*'s expanded forces (including quadruple woodwind), Wagner elaborated the orchestration in a draft of a full score (a procedure he was not to repeat), between 1 February and 28 May 1854. The fair copy of the full score was written out between 15 February and 26 September 1854.

SCENE i *At the bottom of the Rhine* The simple, protracted E♭ chords that open the tetralogy do more than depict the depths of the Rhine: they also suggest the birth of the world, the act of creation itself. Eight double basses sound a low octave E♭, to which is added the B♭ a 5th higher on bassoons. Eight horns introduce the Nature motif (ex.1), one by one, building up a

Ex.1

complex polyphonic texture. The motion is increased by first flowing quavers and then rushing semiquavers, both rising through the strings from the cellos. The curtain rises towards the end of this orchestral introduction – 136 bars of unadulterated E♭ – to reveal the three Rhinemaidens swimming in the water. Maintaining the E♭ harmony, but now with pentatonic colouring, the sisters enunciate the first lines of text: an alliterating assemblage of primitive-sounding syllables chosen for aural effect rather than linguistic sense, 'Weia! Waga!'. The falling-tone motif, heard again a little later in the ensemble cry of the Rhinemaidens (ex.2), is one of the

Ex.2

Rhein - gold!

most frequently recurring motifs, in its many different forms, in the cycle. Flosshilde chides her sisters for failing to watch over the 'sleeping gold'.

From a dark chasm lower down emerges the hunchbacked dwarf Alberich, his crabbed nature and ungainly movements suggested by stabbing semiquavers accented off the beat and by acciaccaturas. The Rhinemaidens decide to reward his lubricious advances by teaching him a lesson. Woglinde leads him on, and his slithering on the rocks and sneezing are graphically portrayed in the music (accented demisemiquaver slides and more acciaccaturas). Both Woglinde and Wellgunde in turn elude him. Flosshilde too seems to offer him love and consolation (against a harmonic background redolent of a traditional love scene), but she also turns out to be mocking him. Alberich's cry of rage and misery (ex.3) turns the Rhinemaidens' motif (ex.2) from major

Ex.3

We - he!   ach   we - he!
['Woe! oh woe!']

to minor, the form in which it is to make by far the greater number of appearances.

Failing in a last desperate bid to seize hold of the Rhinemaidens, Alberich sees a bright light illuminating the large rock in the centre. Against a background of shimmering strings, the announcement of the Gold motif (perhaps symbolically a brass fanfare) anticipates the Rhinemaidens' joyous hymn to the treasure they guard. To a motif in 3rds tracing the outline of an ellipsis, known as the Ring or World Inheritance motif, Wellgunde tells that a ring conferring limitless power can be fashioned from the Rhinegold. Only he who forswears the power of love can fashion the ring, adds Woglinde, to the solemn Renunciation of Love motif – in which case they have nothing to fear from the lascivious dwarf. But as they watch, Alberich climbs to the top of the central rock, declares his curse on love, and wrests the gold away with terrible force. He scrambles away with it, deaf to the lamenting cries of the Rhinemaidens.

This primeval first scene lies outside the time zone of the main action, just as it lies outside its tonal structure: the chief tonality of *Rheingold* can be seen as D♭ (the beginning of scene ii and end of scene iv, as of the *Ring* as a whole). Thus the formal structure of *Rheingold* (three scenes and a prologue) replicates that of *Götterdämmerung* and of the entire *Ring*.

SCENE ii *An open space on a mountain height, near the Rhine* A pair of horns take over the Ring motif, elongating it into something more noble and visionary; this is the transition into the second scene, where Wotan and Fricka are lying asleep on a mountain height. The vision is that of Valhalla, Wotan's newly built fortress, and its grand motif is given out by a chorus of brass instruments, including the Wagner tubas. Fricka, waking first, rouses her husband, who sings a paean to the completed work: 'Vollendet das ewige Werk!' Fricka reminds him that it was her sister, Freia, the goddess of love, that was rashly offered to the giants in payment for

the work. Wotan brushes aside her fears. She chides him for trading love and the virtues of woman (echoes of the Renunciation of Love motif) in exchange for power and dominion. Reminding her that he once pledged his only remaining eye to court her (a pledge he was not called upon to fulfil), Wotan says that he never intended to give up Freia.

Even as he speaks, Freia enters in terrified haste, followed closely by the giants Fasolt and Fafner. The second part of the accompanying motif (*x* of ex.4), for

Ex.4

x

long mislabelled that of Flight, has been described as Wagner's 'basic love-motive' (see Cooke 1979), a theme central not only to the *Ring* but to all his works. When Wotan refuses to hand over Freia as payment, Fasolt indignantly reminds Wotan that the runes on his spear symbolize his contractual agreements and it is they that legitimize his power. This exchange is punctuated by the measured, stepwise-descending motif (ex.5) that

Ex.5

represents Wotan's spear, his authority and the bargains he has struck. Fasolt's eloquent music alternates between anger at Wotan's behaviour and the tenderness he feels towards Freia. Fafner is interested in Freia only as a possible ransom: he knows that without her youth-perpetuating apples the gods will wither and die.

As the giants prepare to take Freia away, her brothers Froh and Donner (the god of thunder) rush in to protect her. Wotan prevents Donner from exercising force and is relieved to see Loge arrive at last. The flickering chromatic semiquavers that accompany him remind us that he is the god of fire; his motif, artfully combining both the falling tone and semitone, hints at his moral ambivalence (ex.6). Pressed by Wotan, Loge relates how

Ex.6

he has circled the world to find out what men hold dearer than the virtues of womankind ('So weit Leben und Weben'). His account begins like a conventional aria in D major, but as he tells of Alberich's capture of the gold, the motifs of the Rhinemaidens and their treasure become coloured by minor tonalities. As Loge repeats the Rhinemaidens' plea for the gold to be returned to the water, the same motifs are heard in their original bright C major.

Loge's explanation of the power of the ring forged from the gold sets everybody thinking. Wotan determines to acquire it and Fafner demands that it then be handed over in payment. The giants trudge away, dragging behind Freia as hostage. A mist descends on the gods who, denied Freia's golden apples, begin to wilt; a sense of suspended animation is created by muted tremolando strings and a slow tempo. Wotan, accompanied by Loge, descends through a sulphur cleft in pursuit of the gold. A masterly transition passage for

'Das Rheingold' (Richard Wagner)
(a) Joseph Hoffmann's design for Scene i (at the bottom of the Rhine; the theft of the Rhinegold) in the first Bayreuth production, 1876

(b) stage wagons used in the same production to create the illusion of the Rhinemaidens swimming underwater; note the use of gas lighting in the wings and borders

orchestra depicts the descent to Nibelheim. Ex.5 alternates with the motif of the Renunciation of Love. As the tempo quickens, the falling semitone (ex.4) suggests the proximity of greed, evil and servitude, while an obsessively repeated perversion of the Love motif (ex.3) warns of the dangerous forces unleashed in Alberich by sexual frustration. B♭ minor gradually emerges through the sulphurous mists as the primary key, which is then reinforced by a symphonic working of the motifs associated with the Nibelungs and servitude. Eighteen anvils behind the scenes thunder out the dotted rhythm of the Nibelungs' motif. The F they sound is not an arbitrary note, but part of a gigantic dominant preparation for the Nibelheim scene.

SCENE iii *The subterranean caverns of Nibelheim* B♭ minor is to dominate this scene, as it does others featuring the Nibelungs later in the *Ring*. In the depths of Nibelheim, Alberich is tormenting his weaker brother Mime, and demands the magic Tarnhelm that he has forced him to make. The Tarnhelm (represented by a mysterious-sounding motif on muted horns) renders its wearer invisible, and Alberich proves its efficacy by disappearing and raining blows on the defenceless Mime.

Alberich eventually leaves, and Wotan and Loge arrive. Loge, offering to help Mime, hears from him (against a background of first the Ring and then the motif of the Nibelungs, with the falling semitone now identified with servitude) how the carefree race of Nibelung blacksmiths has been held in thrall by Alberich since he forged a ring from the Rhinegold.

Alberich returns, driving his slaves with whiplashes to pile up the gold. He brandishes the ring, in a climactic eight-bar passage of immensely compressed power, and they scatter in all directions. Alberich now turns his attention to the strangers. Scornfully dismissing Loge's reminders of their earlier friendship, Alberich boasts about his newfound power and threatens one day to vanquish the gods and force his favours on their women. The threat is made in a stark recitative-like passage following a striking appropriation by Alberich of the sumptuous Valhalla music. Loge pretends to flatter him, but asks how, mighty as he is, he would protect himself against a thief in the night. Alberich shows him the Tarnhelm and Loge asks for a demonstration. To a coiling serpentine theme Loge turns himself into a dragon. Loge feigns terror and goads Alberich into turning himself into something small like a toad. Alberich duly obliges and is trapped by the gods. Each of Alberich's transformations switches the tonality briefly to G♯ minor (the key associated with the Tarnhelm) within a broader context of A major. The latter is the closest the tonally unstable Loge comes to having a key; the chief tonality of the scene remains B♭, that of the Nibelungs. Wotan and Loge tie Alberich and drag him to the surface to the accompaniment of another transition passage in which many prominent motifs are subjected to symphonic development.

SCENE iv *An open space on a mountain height, near the Rhine* Wotan and Loge deride Alberich's pretensions to world domination: if he wants to be free, they tell him, he will have to give up the gold. Intending to keep the ring to generate more gold, Alberich agrees to hand over the treasure. His right hand is untied – a series of demisemiquaver slides illustrate the rope slipping away – and he summons the Nibelungs with the ring. To the obsessive accompaniment of their dotted figure, the Nibelungs drag in the gold; the continually repeated falling semitone alludes both to the servitude of the Nibelungs and to Alberich's fuming disgrace at being seen in captivity by his slaves. Loge adds the Tarnhelm to the pile of gold, and to Alberich's horror, Wotan demands the ring on his finger too. It is eventually wrested from him by force, at which Alberich delivers, against a single, sinister drum roll, his fateful curse, 'Wie durch Fluch er mir geriet': the ring will bring anxiety and death to whoever owns it; those who possess it will be racked with torment, those who do not will be consumed with envy.

Alberich vanishes, the atmosphere clears and, to the sound of divided violins soaring and descending together, it gets lighter. Donner, Froh and Fricka welcome back Wotan and Loge, who show them Freia's ransom: the pile of gold. Freia returns with the giants, but Fasolt, reluctant to relinquish her, insists that the gold be stacked so as to hide her from sight. Loge and Froh pile up the treasure, filling all the gaps. But Fafner can still see Freia's hair: the Tarnhelm has to be thrown on the heap. Fasolt too can see her shining eyes through a chink, and Fafner demands that the ring on Wotan's finger be used to stop the gap. The Rhinemaidens' fall-

ing tone (ex.2) is heard as Loge suggests that Wotan will be returning the ring to them. But Wotan refuses to yield the ring, remaining impervious both to the giants, who threaten to take away Freia again, and to the other gods, who beg him to relent. Finally Erda, the earth goddess, appears in a blue light from a rocky cleft. Her motif (ex.7), intoned initially on bassoons and Wagner tubas,

is a minor variant of the Nature motif (ex.1). The new tonal area (C♯ minor), slow tempo and sombre colouring of the Erda scene mark it out as one of considerable individuality and importance: 'Weiche, Wotan! weiche!'. Erda warns Wotan that possession of the ring condemns him to irredeemable dark perdition. A dark day is dawning for the gods: he should yield up the ring. The prophecy evokes an inversion of Erda's theme, the descending form being known as the Twilight of the Gods (ex.8).

Erda disappears from sight and Wotan decides to heed her advice. He tosses the ring on the pile, but the joyfully expansive phrases greeting Freia's release give way to nagging figures of worry and greed as Fasolt and Fafner bicker over the treasure and Fafner kills his brother. This passage also effects a large-scale modulation to B minor, for the sole purpose of allowing the Curse motif to ring out in its original tonality, on a trio of trombones, at the killing. Thus the tonality of a single motif sometimes determines the key of an entire structural unit. A proliferation of motifs – associated with the curse, the Nibelungs, the ring and Erda – conveys Wotan's agitation.

The gods prepare to enter the fortress. Donner swings his hammer to gather the mists ('Heda! Hedo!'), with brass fanfares over an exhilarating background of swirling string arpeggios (multiple divisions in all departments). There is thunder and lightning; the clouds lift and a rainbow bridge is visible, stretching across the valley to the fortress. Yet more shimmering effects on strings and winds accompany the theme of the Rainbow Bridge (a radiant transformation of the Nature motif). Wotan greets Valhalla, as a motif later to be associated with the sword rings out on a trumpet. The gods walk in procession to the bridge, though Loge looks on nonchalantly. The wail of the Rhinemaidens, lamenting their lost gold, rises poignantly out of the valley. Wotan ignores it and as the curtain falls he leads the gods over the bridge to the triumphant strains of the Valhalla motif. The dramatic situation suggests that the triumph will be a hollow one, but there are few intimations of that in the blaze of D♭ major with which the work ends.

* * *

Das Rheingold, the first dramatic work to be written according to the theoretical principles laid down in *Oper und Drama*, also represents the most rigorous application of those principles – an extreme position which Wagner subsequently modified. If melodic distinction is occasionally sacrificed in the process, there are nevertheless many memorable and accomplished passages in the work, both involving word-setting

(Loge's narration in scene ii, for example) and in purely orchestral writing (notably the transitions between scenes ii and iii, and iii and iv). Though described as a 'preliminary evening' to the *Ring* tetralogy, *Das Rheingold* is a substantial work in its own right, with characteristics not shared by other works in the cycle.

BARRY MILLINGTON

Rhodes, Jane (Marie Andrée) (*b* Paris, 13 March 1929). French mezzo-soprano. She made her début in *La damnation de Faust* at Nancy in 1953, and took part in the première of Landowski's *Le fou* (1956). Her Opéra début was in 1958 as Berlioz's Marguerite; incursions into the dramatic soprano repertory, notably as Strauss's Salome (Opéra, 1958), were less successful, though she sang an internationally admired Carmen at the Metropolitan (where she made her début as Salome in 1960), on American television, and in Tokyo, Buenos Aires and France. She developed an impressively 'French' portrayal, aided by a voice not large or intrinsically beautiful, but capable of exquisitely seductive inflections. In addition to a repertory that includes *Bluebeard's Castle*, *L'incoronazione di Poppea*, *L'heure espagnole* and Poulenc's *La voix humaine* (the last two played in a 1968 Opéra-Comique double bill), she has appeared in much Offenbach. In 1974 she sang Kundry in Paris. She married the conductor Roberto Benzi in 1966.

MAX LOPPERT

Ribeiro, [Julio] León [Alfredo] (*b* Montevideo, 11 April 1854; *d* Montevideo, 12 March 1931). Uruguayan composer. He studied with Luigi Sambucetti and Carmelo Calvo (whose opera *Ofelia*, to a libretto by Juan Zorrilla de San Martín, was given at the Teatro Solís on 28 October 1880). He later taught at the conservatory La Lira, becoming director in 1891. Among his substantial output, which includes symphonies, chamber music and piano music, are seven operas, of which only one was performed in full; *Liropeya*, composed in 1881, which treats the wars between the Spanish invaders and the indigenous tribes, was given by an Italian troupe more than 30 years later, when it was criticized for its italianate style. Material for this and others of his operas survives in the Instituto Estudios Superiores de Montevideo.

Colón (alegoría melodramática, 1, N. Granada), excerpts, Montevideo, Solís, 21 Oct 1892
Liropeya, 1881 (3, Ribeiro, after P. Bermúdez: *El Charrua*), Montevideo, Solís, 28 Aug 1912
Unperf.: Don Ramiro (3, after H. Heine); Nidia (3, L. Ambruzzi); Nora (L. Eridano); Yole (Ambruzzi); Harpago y Helena (E. U. Genta)

F. C. Lange: 'León Ribeiro – documentos de su vida', *Boletín latino-americano de música*, iii (1937), 519–36
S. Salgado: *Breve historia de la música culta en el Uruguay* (Montevideo, 1971), 93–9, 209–11

ROBERT STEVENSON

Riccardi [Ricardi, Riccardo], Carl'Antonio (*b* ?Parma; *fl* 1663–90). Italian soprano castrato. He served at the court of Parma from 18 April 1663 to 15 February 1695 as 'court and theatre singer', and from 4 February 1668 to April 1696 was in the choir of the Steccata chapel in Parma. His theatrical career was based on the duchy of Parma-Piacenza. In Piacenza he sang in Cavalli's *Coriolano* (1669) and in Parma he appeared in Marco Uccellini's *Gli eventi di Filandro et Edessa* (1677) and *Il Giove d'Elide fulminato* (1677), F. M. Bazzani's *Ottone in Italia* (1679), G. B. Policci's *Amalasonta in Italia*

(1681) and *Amore riconciliata con Venere* (1681), and Sabadini's *Il favore degli dei* (1690). He also sang in Reggio Emilia in Cesti's *La Dori* (1668) and in P. A. Ziani's *Il talamo preservato dalla fedeltà d'Eudossa* (1683), together with such star performers as the Salicola sisters, Antonio Cottini and Giovanni Buzzoleni. In Mantua he sang in Antonio del Gaudio's *Eudosia* (1669) and G. B. Tomasi's *Il gran Costanzo* (1670), and in Bologna in G. L. Carpani's *Antioco* (1673).

P. Besutti: *La corte musicale di Ferdinando Carlo Gonzaga ultimo duca di Mantova: musici, cantanti e teatro d'opera tra il 1665 e il 1707* (Mantua, 1989)

PAOLA BESUTTI

Riccardo Primo [*Riccardo Primo, re d'Inghilterra* ('Richard I, King of England')]. Opera in three acts by GEORGE FRIDERIC HANDEL to a libretto by PAOLO ANTONIO ROLLI adapted from FRANCESCO BRIANI's *Isacio tiranno* (1710, Venice); London, King's Theatre, 11 November 1727.

Handel composed a draft score of *Riccardo Primo* in the spring of 1727, completing it (according to the date entered in the autograph) on 16 May. It was written for the seven singers engaged for the Royal Academy's opera season of 1726–7 – Senesino (Richard), Francesca Cuzzoni (Costanza), Faustina Bordoni (Pulcheria), Antonio Baldi (Oronte), Giuseppe Boschi (Isacio [Isaac]), Giovanni Palmerini (Berardo) and the contralto Anna Vincenza Dotti (the Bohemian prince Corrado, an ally of Richard) – and was presumably intended as the final production of the season. The financial difficulties of the Academy, exacerbated by the disputes between Cuzzoni and Faustina and their factions, seem to have delayed its performance, and the production was postponed until early in the next season, the Royal Academy's last. By that time both librettist and composer had reasons to make changes to their work; the role of Corrado had to be removed as Dotti was no longer in the company, and the accession of George II to the throne on 6 June prompted Rolli to dedicate the opera to the newly crowned king and to emphasize the patriotic elements in the story. Handel's pre-performance revisions to the score were extensive, however, and go beyond what was necessary to meet the new circumstances. *Riccardo* received at least 11 performances in 1727 and was not revived, but Handel re-used some of its arias in later operatic performances, notably the 1730 revival of *Scipione* and the 1733 revival of *Tolomeo*.

German versions of *Riccardo* were given in Hamburg and Brunswick in 1729. The first modern revival was given by the Handel Opera Society at Sadler's Wells Theatre, London, on 8 July 1964. The main text of Chrysander's edition corresponds to Handel's performing version, but his appendix includes only the aria 'Quando non vedo' from the pre-performance version, much of which is reconstructable.

The libretto is based on early accounts of the conquest of Cyprus by Richard I of England ('Richard Coeur-de-lion') and his marriage while on the island to Princess Berengaria of Navarre (named Costanza in the opera). (Richard landed on Cyprus on 6 May 1191, after being delayed by a storm, and married the princess six days later.) The characters of Isaac Comnenus, governor of Cyprus, and his daughter (named Pulcheria in the opera) are also historical, though the latter was actually a child whom Berengaria took into care. The action of the opera begins with Costanza (soprano) on the coast at Limassol watching a violent storm at sea; she threatens suicide, fearing that Richard is drowned, but is restrained by Berardo (bass), her cousin and tutor. Though she and Richard have never met, she is deeply in love with him. Costanza and Berardo are found by Isaac (bass), Pulcheria (soprano) and Pulcheria's lover Oronte, Prince of Syria (alto); they give their names as Doris and Narsete and are invited to the marriage of Pulcheria and Oronte. Richard (alto) has arrived safely further round the coast and learns that Costanza is in the governor's palace. Oronte pays court to Costanza, arousing Pulcheria's jealousy. Isaac also makes advances to her, but she remains unmoved. Richard appears before Isaac disguised as his own ambassador, demanding Costanza and warning of the presence of British troops on the island. Isaac realizes that 'Doris' is Costanza and deceitfully pledges to release her. Aware, however, that Richard and Costanza have never met, he orders Pulcheria to offer herself as Richard's bride so that he can have Costanza for himself. She reluctantly obeys, but Oronte, knowing of the plan from Berardo, reveals the truth to Richard, whom he decides to support against Isaac. Richard, still disguised, again demands Costanza. Isaac refuses, declaring war, but Pulcheria pacifies him and brings Costanza and Richard together. Isaac again proves treacherous and abducts Costanza. The troops of Richard and Oronte breach the walls of Limassol. Isaac tries to evade capture by threatening to kill Costanza and is unmoved by Pulcheria's resolve to die with her; but Oronte disarms him. Richard spares his life, Pulcheria nominates Oronte as future governor of Cyprus and the two couples look forward to future happiness.

* * *

Though Rolli's condensation of Briani's libretto shows more concern with polishing the Italian verse than with clarifying the action, *Riccardo* is an effective and colourful work, opening (after the overture) with a striking orchestral description of a storm. Several of the arias have unusual instruments in their accompaniments. (The aria 'Quando non vedo', with two chalumeaux, was removed in the pre-performance revisions, however; the two touring clarinettists for whom the parts were written had left London in the spring of 1727.) A contrast is drawn between the characters of Pulcheria and Costanza: the former is a trifle coquettish, her arias predominantly in major keys, while the latter, always noble, has several expressive minor-key arias – one of which ('Bacia per me la mano') is among Handel's most profound. Two of the heroic arias for Richard demand spectacular virtuosity, and both the arias for the villanous Isaac (the first, 'Ti vedrò', full of ingenious counterpoint) are excellent examples of Handel's vigorous style.   ANTHONY HICKS

Ricci [Rizzi, Riccio], **Domenico** ['Menicuccio'] (*b* Fano, *c*1700; *d* 6 March 1751). Italian soprano castrato. He was a pupil of Francesco Gasparini and lived with him in Rome from 1723 to 1726, when he entered the service of Cardinal Pietro Ottoboni. In March 1728 he became a papal singer, and he was often granted permission to sing in theatres at the request of Cardinal Corsini. His theatrical career developed at a time when Gasparini's musical style was being superseded by that of a new generation of composers including Sarro, Porpora, Leo and Broschi. Ricci was active initially as a *buffo* singer in both male and female parts. The height

of his career was around the years 1734–7, during which he took leading or second-lead serious male roles at the Tordinona theatre in Rome (*L'olimpiade*, 1735; *Adriano in Siria*, 1736). At the end of his career he reverted to *buffo* parts in intermezzos with music by Costanzi, performed in Rome in 1746.

E. Celani: 'I cantori della cappella pontificia nei secoli XVI–XVIII', *RMI*, xv (1908), 55–112, esp. 92
——: 'Musica e musicisti in Roma', *RMI*, xviii (1911), 1–63, esp. 16
F. Piperno: 'Francesco Gasparini: le sue abitazioni romane, i suoi allievi coabitanti (1717–1727)', *Esercizi: arte, musica, spettacolo*, iv (1981), 104–15   SERGIO DURANTE

Ricci, Federico (*b* Naples, 22 Oct 1809; *d* Conegliano, nr Treviso, 10 Dec 1877). Italian composer, brother of Luigi Ricci. He was educated at the Naples Conservatory from 1818. His teachers included Zingarelli, Pietro Raimondi and, in their capacity as *maestrini*, his own brother and Bellini. In 1829 he cut short his studies to follow Luigi to Rome, where he became intimate with the painter Horace Vernet and his circle. About this time he was recommended to Bellini, who, it was hoped, might secure him an opera contract at La Scala. But Bellini was either unable or unwilling to do this, and the start of Federico's theatrical career was delayed until the production in 1835 at the Teatro Fondo, Naples, of *Il colonello*, the first of four comedies composed jointly with Luigi. This was followed by Federico's first venture on his own, *Monsieur de Chalumeaux* (1835, Venice), and a second collaboration, *Il disertore per amore*, written for Naples in 1836. Then came one of his most sensational successes, *La prigione di Edimburgo* (1838, Trieste), an *opera semiseria* drawn from Scott's *The Heart of Midlothian*. Besides the popular barcarolle 'Nella poppa del mio brick', it contains a remarkable mad role for the seconda donna (Madge Wildfire in the novel), in which the singer Rita Gabussi created a furore.

Federico's La Scala début with *Un duello sotto Richelieu* (1839) was not specially glorious, but in 1841 he achieved a double success with *Luigi Rolla* (Florence), written for and dedicated to the tenor Napoleone Moriani, and *Corrado d'Altamura* (Milan), based on the same plot as Verdi's *Oberto, conte di San Bonifacio* and widely considered to be his masterpiece in the tragic genre (it was the only one of his serious operas to be printed outside Italy). Ricci was now famous; he travelled widely and was known in the salons of Paris. But his serious operas written subsequently aroused less and less interest. Like his brother he succeeded mainly in comedy, to which he devoted himself exclusively after 1847. Two years after *Crispino e la comare* (1850, Venice), his final collaboration with Luigi, Federico triumphed in Vienna with *Il marito e l'amante*, not surprisingly, perhaps, for what is an obvious forerunner of Strauss's *Die Fledermaus*. But the failure of *Il paniere d'amore* (1853) persuaded him to accept the offer of an appointment as *maître de chapelle* of the imperial theatres at St Petersburg, a sinecure involving no more than the supervision of vocal studies at the conservatory. His compositions over the next 16 years did not include works for the stage. In 1869 he left Russia for Paris, where he enjoyed an Indian summer of popularity as a composer of *opéras bouffes*. The most famous of these, *Une folie à Rome* (1869, Paris), was originally composed in Italian as *Carina* (though first performed in Italian as *Una follia a Roma*) and was also performed with great success at Genoa under Angelo

Mariani. In 1876 Ricci retired to Conegliano in the Veneto, where he died the following year leaving his last opera, *Don Quichotte*, uncompleted.

Less obviously original than his brother, Federico was the more accomplished and versatile composer. In comedy he had a lighter, more graceful touch, which would make his contributions to *Crispino e la comare* relatively easy to pick out, even if they were not indicated in the first printed score. His serious works are worthy to stand beside Mercadante's, though they do not aspire to the same grandeur. Late offshoots of the Bellini tradition, they were inevitably among the casualties of the post-*Nabucco* era. But *La prigione di Edimburgo*, which holds a delicate balance between pathos and comedy, might well bear revival. The late *opéras comiques* show an unexpected ability to keep up to date in matters of harmony and scoring, but they remain tied to the expansive traditions of Italian *opera buffa*.

See also CRISPINO E LA COMARE.

mel – *melodramma*

Il colonello [La donna colonello] (opera giocosa, 2, J. Ferretti), Naples, Fondo, 14 March 1835, *I-Mr*, *Nc*, excerpts (Milan, 1835), vs (Paris, *c*1840), collab. L. Ricci
Monsieur de Chalumeaux (mel comico, 2, Ferretti), Venice, S Benedetto, 14 June 1835, *Mr**, excerpts (Milan, 1835)
Il disertore per amore (op giocosa, 2, Ferretti), Naples, Fondo, 13 Feb 1836, *Mr*, *Nc*, excerpts (Milan, 1836), collab. L. Ricci
La prigione di Edimburgo (mel semiserio, 3, G. Rossi, after W. Scott: *The Heart of Midlothian*), Trieste, Grande, 13 March 1838, *Mr**, vs (Milan, 1840); rev., Milan, *Mr*
Un duello sotto Richelieu (mel serio, 2, F. dall'Ongaro), Milan, Scala, 17 Aug 1839, *Mr**, excerpts (Milan, 1839)
Luigi Rolla [Michelangelo e Rolla] (mel tragico, 3, S. Cammarano), Florence, Pergola, 30 March 1841, vs (Milan, 1841)
Corrado d'Altamura (dramma lirico, prol., 2, G. Sacchéro), Milan, Scala, 16 Nov 1841, *Mr**, vs (Milan, 1842); rev., Paris, 1844, *Mr*, added nos. (Milan, 1844), vs (Paris, n.d.)
Vallombra (dramma lirico, 2, Sacchéro), Milan, Scala, 26 Dec 1842, *Mr**, excerpts (Milan, 1843)
Isabella de' Medici (os, 3, A. Gazzoletti), Trieste, Grande, 9 March 1845
Estella di Murcia (mel serio, 3, F. M. Piave), Milan, Scala, 21 Feb 1846, *Mr**, vs (Milan, 1846); rev., Venice, *Mr*
L'amante di richiamo (op giocosa, 2, dall'Ongaro), Turin, Angennes, 13 June 1846, collab. L. Ricci
Griselda (mel serio, 4, Piave), Venice, Fenice, 13 March 1847, *Mr**, vs (Milan, n.d.)
Crispino e la comare (mel fantastico-giocoso, 4, Piave), Venice, S Benedetto, 28 Feb 1850, *Mr**, vs (Milan, 1850), collab. L. Ricci; trans. C.-L.-E. Nuitter and Beaumont as Le docteur Crispin, Liège, 17 Dec 1866, with added nos. by F. Ricci, vs (Paris, n.d.)
I due ritratti (ob, 2, ?Ricci), Venice, S Benedetto, 21 Nov 1850
Il marito e l'amante (mel comico, 3, Rossi), Vienna, Kärntnertor, 9 June 1852, *Mr**, vs (Milan, 1852); in Fr. as Une fête à Venise, Paris, 1872, with added nos. by Ricci, vs (Paris, n.d.)
Il paniere d'amore (ob, 2, ?Ricci), Vienna, Kärntnertor, 25 May 1853
Une folie à Rome (opéra bouffe, 3, V. Wilder), Paris, Fantaisies-Parisiennes, 30 Jan 1869; in orig. It. as Una follia a Roma, Paris, 1870; *Nc**, vs (Paris, n.d.; Milan, 1870)
Le docteur Rose, ou La dogaresse (oc, 3, E. de Najac), Paris, Bouffes-Parisiens, 10 Feb 1872, vs (Paris, n.d.)
Don Quichotte, 1876 (after M. de Cervantes), inc.

L. Escudier: *Mes souvenirs* (Paris, 2/1863), 20–21
F. de Villars: *Notices sur Luigi et Federico Ricci, suivies d'une analyse critique de 'Crispino e la comare'* (Paris, 1866)
A. Heulard: *Etude sur 'Une folie à Rome'* (Paris, 1870) [with work-list]
P. Cambiasi: 'Prospetto delle composizioni musicali del maestro cav. Federico Ricci', *Gazzetta musicale di Milano*, xxxii (1877), suppl. to no.51
L. de Rada: *I fratelli Ricci* (Florence, 1878)
G. Cottrau: *Lettres d'un mélomane pour servir de document à l'histoire musicale de Naples de 1829 à 1847* (Naples, 1885)

A. Cametti: *Un poeta melodrammatico romano: appunti e notizie in gran parte inedite sopra Jacopo Ferretti e i musicisti del suo tempo* (Milan, 1898)
JULIAN BUDDEN

Ricci, Francesco Benedetto (*fl* 1790–1814). Italian impresario. He had already had experience as impresario at Genoa when in 1798 he took on the management of La Scala, Milan, under the republican regime installed by Napoleon. He remained in charge until 1814 (with a brief hiatus caused by the French retreat in 1799), with a series of partners including Barbaia. Thanks to wartime prosperity in Milan from 1802, and to the decision of the Napoleonic government to reintroduce a gambling monopoly centred on the opera house, he enjoyed large profits, some of which he invested in lavish productions of opera and ballet, employing Rossini, the librettist Felice Romani, the scene designers Paolo Landriani and Alessandro Sanquirico, and the choreographer Salvatore Viganò; these established La Scala as the leading Italian opera house. When the new Austrian government forbade gambling, in 1814, Ricci, who had invested large sums in property, retired.

J. Rosselli: 'Governi, appaltatori e giuochi d'azzardo nell'Italia napoleonica', *Rivista storica italiana*, xciii (1981), 346–83
JOHN ROSSELLI

Ricci, Luigi (*b* ?Naples, 8 June or 8 July 1805; *d* Prague, 31 Dec 1859). Italian composer, brother of Federico Ricci. At the age of nine he entered the Naples Conservatory, where he studied the violin before turning to the keyboard and to composition. His teachers included Zingarelli and, privately, Generali, at whose instigation he composed his first comic opera, *L'impresario in angustie*, to the libretto set by Cimarosa in 1786; it was performed in 1823 by the students of the conservatory. In 1824 Ricci made his début at the Teatro Nuovo, Naples, with *La cena frastornata*, in which Generali had a hand; it was followed by four more works there in the years 1825 to 1827. His attempt to capture the S Carlo with *Ulisse in Itaca* in 1828 failed, as did most of his essays in the serious genre. The moderately successful *Colombo* (Parma) and *L'orfanella di Ginevra* (Rome) in 1829 were followed by four disasters: *Il sonnambulo* and *L'eroina del Messico* (Rome), *Annibale in Torino* (Turin) and *La neve* (Milan). But with *Chiara di Rosembergh* (1831, Milan), an *opera semiseria* composed for the mezzo-soprano Giuditta Grisi, Ricci not only redeemed his reputation but also created one of the favourite pieces of the decade. From then on he continued mainly in comedy, achieving a notable success with *Un'avventura di Scaramuccia* (1834, Milan), written to a witty libretto, part romance, part theatrical satire, by Felice Romani. A performance at Pavia the following year earned him a benefit night, for which he added the one-act *farsa La serva e l'ussero*, an amusing piece that has enjoyed modern revival. In the same year *Il colonello*, the first of four works written jointly with his brother Federico, was produced in Naples. The series culminated in the fantastic comedy *Crispino e la comare* (1850, Venice), which held the stage until the end of the century.

In 1836 Ricci became *maestro di cappella* at Trieste. After the predictable disaster of his *Le nozze di Figaro* (1838, Milan), written to a new and undistinguished libretto by Gaetano Rossi, he gave up composing operas for seven years and devoted himself to religious music, also serving as *maestro concertatore* at the Teatro

Grande (in this capacity he directed the première in 1848 of Verdi's *Il corsaro*).

The twins Franziska (Fanny) and Ludmilla (Lidia) Stolz (both sopranos; *b* 1827) accompanied Ricci to Odessa, where he directed the 1844–5 opera season. There he lived more or less openly with both, causing confusion as well as scandal. After returning to Trieste, the three were at Copenhagen (1847–8), where the sisters' engagement at the Opera was cut short by the king's death. Back in Trieste, Ricci married Lidia in 1849 without discontinuing the *ménage à trois*. (Lidia's daughter Adelaide, 1850–71, had a brief career as a singer, appearing at the Théâtre Italien, Paris. Fanny's illegitimate son Luigi, 1852–1906, was a theatre conductor and composer of operas and operettas. He called himself Ricci-Stolz after becoming the heir of his aunt, the soprano Teresa Stolz, sister of the twins and a pupil of Luigi Ricci.)

By the middle of the century Ricci was once more doing well with *opere buffe* such as *Il birraio di Preston* (1847, Florence) and, more notably, *La festa di Piedigrotta* (1852, Naples), whose tarantella remains a popular classic of light music. After the appearance of his last opera, *Il diavolo a quattro* (1859, Trieste), which had been commissioned at Copenhagen but not performed there, symptoms of mental illness became evident. He was transferred to an asylum at Prague, his wife's birthplace, where he died.

Luigi Ricci's is one of the more individual voices in Italian opera of the period. His chief gift was for comedy, to which he brought not only a complete mastery of the traditional devices but also a new, robust *buffo* manner characterized by a wealth of bouncing *allegretto* melodies, mostly in duple time, and a not infrequent use of folktune. Not even at his most sophisticated, as in *Scaramuccia*, did he match Donizetti's elegance and sentimental charm. He was clearly the leading spirit in the collaborations with his brother Federico, and most of *Crispino* is by him. The comic numbers of *Chiara di Rosembergh* were the most celebrated, but elsewhere there are bold strokes of harmony and rhythm that show an ability to rise to the serious dramatic occasion.

See also CRISPINO E LA COMARE.

mel – *melodramma*
mels – *melodramma serio*
melss – *melodramma semiserio*

L'impresario in angustie (farsa, 1, G. M. Diodati), Naples, Conservatory, 1823, *I-Nc*
La cena frastornata (op semiseria, 2, A. L. Tottola), Naples, Nuovo, aut. 1824, *Nc*
L'abbate Taccarella [La gabbia de' matti; Aladino] (ob, 2, Tottola), Naples, Nuovo, carn. 1825, *Mr*, *Nc*, excerpts (Milan, 1832)
Il sogno avverato (azione teatrale, Tottola), Naples, Nuovo, for king's return, sum. 1825, collab. D. Pogliani-Gagliardi
Il diavolo condannato a prender moglie [Il diavolo mal sposato] (azione comico-favolosa, 2, Tottola), Naples, Nuovo, 27 Jan 1827, *Mc*, *Nc*
La lucerna di Epitteto (op semiseria, 2, G. Checcherini), Naples, Nuovo, carn. 1827, *Nc*
Ulisse in Itaca (os, 2, D. Gilardoni), Naples, S Carlo, 12 Jan 1828, *Nc*
Colombo (mels, 2, F. Romani), Parma, Ducale, 27 June 1829, *Mr*, excerpts (Milan, 1830)
L'orfanella di Ginevra [Amina] (melss, 2, J. Ferretti), Rome, Valle, 9 Sept 1829, *Mc*, *Mr*, *Nc*, excerpts (Milan, 1830), rev. version, *Mr*
Il sonnambulo (op semiseria, 2, Ferretti), Rome, Valle, 26 Dec 1829, excerpts (Milan, 1830)
L'eroina del Messico, ovvero Fernando Cortez (mels, 2, Ferretti), Rome, Tordinona, 9 Feb 1830, *Mr**, excerpts (Milan, 1830)

Annibale in Torino (mels, 2, Romani), Turin, Regio, 26 Dec 1830
La neve (commedia lirica, 2, Romani), Milan, Cannobiana, 21 June 1831, *Mr* (?autograph)
Chiara di Rosembergh (op semiseria, 2, G. Rossi), Milan, Scala, 11 Oct 1831, *Mr**, vs (Milan, 1832)
Il nuovo Figaro (mel giocoso, 2, Ferretti), Parma, Ducale, 15 Feb 1832, *Mr**, excerpts (Milan, 1832)
I due sergenti (op semiseria, 2, Romani), Milan, Scala, 1 Sept 1833, *Mr**, excerpts (Milan, 1833)
Un'avventura di Scaramuccia (mel comico, 2, Romani), Milan, Scala, 8 March 1834, *Mr**, *Mc*, vs (Milan, 1834)
Eran due, or son tre, ovvero Gli esposti (mel buffo, 2, Ferretti), Turin, Angennes, 3 June 1834, *Mr**, excerpts (Milan, 1839)
Chi dura vince, ovvero La luna di miel (mel eroicomico, 2, Ferretti), Rome, Valle, 26 Dec 1834, *Mr**, vs (Milan, 1841); as La petite comtesse, Paris, 1876, vs (Paris, n.d.)
Il colonello [La donna colonello] (op giocosa, 2, Ferretti), Naples, Fondo, 14 March 1835, *Mr*, *Nc*, excerpts (Milan, 1835), vs (Paris, *c*1840), collab. F. Ricci
La serva e l'ussero (farsa, 1), Pavia, Compadroni, spr. 1835, *Mr**, vs (Milan, 1841)
Chiara di Montalbano [in Francia] (melss, 2, Rossi), Milan, Scala, 15 Aug 1835, *Mr**
Il disertore per amore (mel, 2, Ferretti), Naples, Fondo, 13 Feb 1836, *Mr*, *Nc*, excerpts (Milan, 1836), collab. F. Ricci
Le nozze di Figaro (mel comico, 2, Rossi), Milan, Scala, 13 Feb 1838, *Mr**, excerpts (Milan, 1838); rev., Milan, Scala, 1841, *Mr**, excerpts (Milan, 1841)
La solitaria delle Asturie (os, 2, Romani), Odessa, Italiano, 20 Feb 1845
L'amante di richiamo (op giocosa, 2, F. Dall'Ongaro), Turin, Angennes, 13 June 1846, collab. F. Ricci
Il birraio di Preston (mel giocoso, 3, F. Guidi), Florence, Pergola, 4 Feb 1847, *Mo*, vs (Milan, ?1847)
Crispino e la comare (mel fantastico-giocoso, 4, F. M. Piave), Venice, S Benedetto, 28 Feb 1850, *Mr**, vs (Milan, 1850), collab. F. Ricci; trans. C.-L.-E. Nuitter and Beaumont as Le docteur Crispin, Liège, 17 Dec 1866, with added nos. by F. Ricci, vs (Paris, n.d.)
La festa di Piedigrotta (ob napolitana, 4, M. D'Arienzo), Naples, Nuovo, 23 June 1852, *Nc*, vs (Naples, n.d.)
Il diavolo a quattro (mel comico, 3, Rossi), Trieste, Armonia, 15 May 1859, *Mr**, vs (Milan, 1859)

V. dal Torso: *Luigi Ricci* (Trieste, 1860)
L. Escudier: *Mes souvenirs* (Paris, 2/1863), 20–21
F. de Villars: *Notices sur Luigi et Federico Ricci, suivies d'une analyse critique de 'Crispino e la comare'* (Paris, 1866)
L. de Rada: *I fratelli Ricci* (Florence, 1878)
G. Cottrau: *Lettres d'un mélomane pour servir de document à l'histoire musicale de Naples de 1829 à 1847* (Naples, 1885)
F. Walker: *The Man Verdi* (London, 1962)   JULIAN BUDDEN

Ricci, Marco (*b* Belluno, June 1676; *d* Venice, 21 Jan 1730). Italian scene painter. He went to England in 1708 in the train of the Duke of Manchester with Giovanni Pellegrini, the first of a long line of Italian designers to be thus employed. They provided a set of new scenes for a revival of Haym's *Pyrrhus and Demetrius* on 2 April 1709, and three days later their scenes were used for a revival of Haym's *Camilla*. In 1710 Ricci alone painted scenery for Francesco Mancini's *Hydaspes* at the Queen's Theatre in the Haymarket. He seems to have quarrelled with Pellegrini and returned to Italy. He was back in England in 1711–12 with Sebastiano, but in 1718 returned to Venice, where he provided scenery for two opera houses.

The Royal Collection at Windsor includes several of Ricci's drawings for scenery but none can be specifically attributed to his work in England. They are in the Baroque style and seem to have been influenced by Juvarra.

For illustration *see* REHEARSAL, fig.2.

BDA
A. Blunt and E. Croft-Murray: *Venetian Drawings of the XVII and XVIII Centuries in the Collection of Her Majesty the Queen at Windsor Castle* (London, 1957)
E. W. White: 'The Rehearsal of an Opera', *Theatre Notebook*, xiv (1959–60), 79–90
M. Sands: 'The Rehearsal of an Opera', *Theatre Notebook*, xix (1964–5), 30–31
                                                           SYBIL ROSENFELD

Ricciardo e Zoraide ('Ricciardo and Zoraide'). *Dramma* in two acts by GIOACHINO ROSSINI to a libretto by Francesco Berio di Salsa after cantos xiv and xv of Niccolò Forteguerri's epic poem *Il Ricciardetto*; Naples, Teatro S Carlo, 3 December 1818.

The Asiatic prince Ircano (bass), father of Zoraide (soprano), has angered the tyrannical Agorante (tenor) by withholding from him Zoraide's hand in marriage. As a result, Agorante has driven Ircano from the Nubian lands over which Ircano briefly ruled. During the flight from Nubia, Zoraide has met and fallen in love with the paladin knight Ricciardo (tenor); but she is later captured by the marauding Agorante, much to the fury of Agorante's wife Zomira (contralto). In Act 1 the Christian knights, led by Ernesto (tenor) and accompanied by an 'African Guard' (the disguised Ricciardo), attempt to negotiate with Agorante but to no avail. In Act 2 Ricciardo, under cover of his disguise, takes Agorante into his confidence, claiming that he too has been wronged by 'Ricciardo'. A meeting is arranged between Ricciardo and Zoraide but the lovers' ploy is foiled by Zomira's confidante, Elmira (mezzo-soprano), who overhears their meeting. In the meantime, while Zomira plots the death of the lovers, Agorante has lost patience with Zoraide and threatens jail and death, weakening only to permit a final trial in which two knights will joust on her behalf. Agorante chooses Ricciardo as his champion; an anonymous 'Knight of the Tears', in reality Ircano, comes forward to defend Zoraide's name. Ircano is defeated and Ricciardo and Zoraide are arrested as they prepare to flee, leaving all three in Agorante's power. The situation is saved by Ernesto: Agorante is overthrown, leaving Ricciardo, the true Christian knight, to spare Agorante's life and to seek from Ircano Zoraide's hand in marriage.

The weakness of the opera lies not so much in the plot as in the libretto's failure to cope with the fantastical nature of Forteguerri's original poem. Musically, the work shows Rossini's evolving powers in handling such things as choral writing, orchestration and accompanied recitatives being put at the service of stereotyped forms and picture-book characterization.   RICHARD OSBORNE

Ricciarelli, Katia (*b* Rovigo, 18 Jan 1946). Italian soprano. She studied in Venice, making her début in 1969 at Mantua as Mimì. After winning the 1970 Verdi Award at Parma, she sang Leonora (*Il trovatore*) there and Verdi's Joan of Arc in Rome, both in 1971. She made her American début at Chicago in 1972 as Lucrezia (*I due Foscari*) and first sang at La Scala in 1973 as Angelica. Having made her Covent Garden début in 1974 as Mimì, she sang Amelia (*Ballo*), Elisabeth de Valois, Luisa Miller, Lucia, Aida, Alice Ford (*Falstaff*), Desdemona and Bellini's Giulietta. She made her Metropolitan début in 1975 as Mimì, then sang Micaëla and her Verdi roles. At Pesaro (1981–9) she sang Ellen (*La donna del lago*), Amenaide (*Tancredi*), Madama Cortese (*Il viaggio a Reims*), Bianca (*Bianca e Falliero*) and Ninetta (*La gazza ladra*). Her repertory includes Cherubini's Medea, Mathilde

(*Guillaume Tell*), Norma, Imogene (*Il pirata*), Paolina (*Poliuto*) and the title roles of *Maria Stuarda, Caterina Cornaro, Lucrezia Borgia* and *Maria di Rohan*. In 1989 she sang Maddalena (*Andrea Chénier*) at Versailles. She has recorded many of her bel canto roles and also Aida, Tosca and Turandot. Her phrasing is spacious and her voice is vibrant and warm-toned if apparently sometimes hard to control. She is a truthful, appealing actress.

A. Blyth: 'Katia Ricciarelli', *Opera*, xli (1990), 28–33
                                                                ALAN BLYTH

Riccio [Ricci], **Benedetto** (*b* ?Naples, ?1678; *d* after 1710). Italian composer. He was listed by Prota-Giurleo among the 'dilettanti' (together with Faggioli, Antonio Orefice and Mauro) who originated the Neapolitan dialect *opera buffa*. His *L'alloggiamentare* (N. Gianni; Fiorentini, ?autumn 1710; music lost) belongs, formally speaking, among the earliest examples of the genre, with its many (57) short musical numbers, frequent ensemble pieces, use of short and probably sometimes strophic arias, lack of exit arias, and in general rapid, fluid movement between recitative and song. As far as can be judged from the libretto, however, it is progressive in intent: the verse forms in the arias are often longer and more complex than those in the opera's predecessors; the possibilities of onstage music begin to be exploited, for example in Act 3 a serenata (which Viviani considered possibly a popular song of the day) and a dance; and there is some evidence that the dramatic material was shaped in terms of the musical, as in Act 2 scene iii, with its increasingly complex series of numbers. Riccio had earlier composed a serious opera, *Ateone* (I. Romani, Naples, Fiorentini, 1708), and two *melodrammi sacri*.

CroceN
M. Scherillo: *L'opera buffa napoletana durante il settecento: storia letteraria* (Naples, 1883, 2/1916), 90ff
U. Prota-Giurleo: *Nicola Logroscino: 'il dio dell'opera buffa'* (Naples, 1927), 16
A. Sacchetti-Sassetti: 'La cappella musicale del duomo di Rieti', *NA*, xvii (1940), 170
V. Viviani: *Storia del teatro napoletano* (Naples, 1969), 266
                                                           JAMES L. JACKMAN

Riccio, Domenico. *See* RICCI, DOMENICO.

Riccioni, Barbara ['La Romanina'] (*b* ?Bologna or Rome; *fl* 1684–1707). Italian singer. She is first mentioned at Reggio Emilia in 1684, when she sang Isabella in Alessandro Melani's *La calma fra le tempeste, overo Il prencipe Roberto fra le sciagure felice*. In 1685 she sang again in Reggio, in C. F. Pollarolo's *L'Anagilde, ovvero Il Rodrigo*, and in Milan in Carlo Pallavicino's *Massimo Puppieno*; the following year she sang in Modena. At least from 1687 probably until 1701 she was in the service of Duke Ferdinando Carlo Gonzaga of Mantua, who granted her a salary from 31 January 1695. She sang in many Italian cities, including Rome (in 1687 and 1693 at the court of Queen Christina of Sweden), Genoa, Turin, Parma, Piacenza, Milan, Ferrara, Bologna and Padua. In Mantua she appeared in *L'oracolo in sogno* (music by A. Caldara, A. Quintavalle and C. F. Pollarolo; 1699), A. F. Martinengo's *L'Arsiade* (1700) and M. A. Ziani's *Il duello d'amore e di vendetta* (1701). She is last known to have sung at performances in Genoa in 1702 and 1704 and in 1707 in Albinoni's *La prosperità di Elio Sejano*.

C. Sartori: 'Profilo di una cantante della fine del secolo XVII: Barbara Riccioni', *Festschrift Karl Gustav Fellerer* (Regensburg, 1962), 454–60

P. Besutti: *La corte musicale di Ferdinando Carlo Gonzaga ultimo duca di Mantova: musici, cantanti e teatro d'opera tra il 1665 e il 1707* (Mantua, 1989)   PAOLA BESUTTI

Rice, Edward Everett (*b* Brighton, MA, 21 Dec 1848; *d* New York, 16 Nov 1924). American composer and director. His best-known work is *Evangeline* (1874), the most popular American musical stage work of its decade, one of the first works to be called a 'musical comedy', and perhaps the first of its genre in the USA to have a fully original score without adapted or interpolated songs. Advertisements for *Evangeline* referred to it as a 'refined extravaganza embracing all the beauties of opera bouffe and burlesque, without titillating costumes'; Rice reportedly suggested writing the show as 'a burlesque diversion to which an entire family might be taken, in lieu of the imported entertainment at which only the black sheep from every fold were expected'. During the 1870s Rice also wrote songs for revivals of John Brougham's burlesques *Po-ca-hon-tas* and *Lotos*. His own later works were 'leg-drama' burlesque comedies with mostly perfunctory music.

Rice formed his own troupe, Rice's Extravaganza Combination, later Rice's Surprise Party, to introduce new burlesque extravaganzas in Boston; it revived his works for many years, continually adding new dialogue and topical songs. Rice could neither read nor write musical notation, but in the manner of several prominent Tin Pan Alley songwriters of the next generation he picked out melodies at the piano for an amanuensis to transcribe, and gave instructions for orchestration, tempo and dynamics. He led in the reform of burlesque; while his productions succeeded largely on account of their comic routines, his best music adeptly portrays the humorous and sentimental characters, and his graceful and varied melodies skilfully match the nature of the texts. Rice was a leading director for two decades in New York. His production of *Little Christopher* (1895) was the first show Jerome Kern saw, and Rice in 1904 gave Kern his first opportunity to write for the theatre. Rice also directed the first 'Negro operetta', Will Marion Cook's *Clorindy, or The Origin of the Cakewalk* (1898), and owned the American rights for Gilbert and Sullivan's *Patience*, in which he introduced the young actress Lilian Russell (1881). Irving Berlin first appeared on stage in Rice's production of *Show Girl* (1902).

selective list; dates are those of first New York performance

Evangeline (musical comedy, J. C. Goodwin), Niblo's Garden, 27 July 1874

Hiawatha (burlesque, N. L. Childs), Standard, 21 Feb 1880

Revels (burlesque, J. J. McNally), Haverly's 14th Street, 25 Oct 1880

Adonis (burlesque, W. Gill), Bijou Opera House, 4 Sept 1884

The Corsair (burlesque, J. Braham, after Byron), Bijou Opera House, 18 Oct 1887

Several songs in shows by other composers

C. Smith: *Musical Comedy in America* (New York, 1950)

G. Bordman: *Jerome Kern: his Life and Music* (New York and Oxford, 1980)

D. L. Root: *American Popular Stage Music, 1860–1880* (Ann Arbor, 1981)

R. Sanjek: *American Popular Music and its Business* (New York and Oxford, 1988)   DEANE L. ROOT

Rich, John (*b* ?London, 1692; *d* London, 26 Nov 1761). English theatre manager. He was the elder son of Christopher Rich (*d* 1714), who became patentee at Drury Lane in 1693 and was 'silenced' by the Lord Chamberlain in 1709. Rich senior then built the third Lincoln's Inn Fields theatre and obtained permission from George I to operate it, but died before it opened. John Rich carried on (1714–32), surviving some financially difficult early seasons. Under the name of Lun he eventually found his métier as Harlequin in the series of pantomimes he staged at Lincoln's Inn Fields (with music by Galliard), and later at Covent Garden (composers unknown), which he managed from 1732 to his death. His importance to the history of opera is twofold: he launched ballad opera as a genre when he staged John Gay's *The Beggar's Opera* (1728), and he gave Handel's beleaguered opera company a home at Covent Garden from 1734 to 1737. At Lincoln's Inn Fields Rich occasionally mounted new productions in English of proven musical works, both semi-operas such as *The Island Princess* (revived in 1715) and all-sung italianate works such as Bononcini's *Camilla* as arranged by Haym (revived triumphantly in 1726–7). Rich apparently employed J. C. Pepusch as musical director at Lincoln's Inn Fields; by 1724 Pepusch was making the unusually high salary of £4 per week. Pepusch is generally credited with arranging the music for *The Beggar's Opera* in 1728, and may have provided the overture. Despite the fantastic success of that work (said to have made 'Gay Rich and Rich Gay'), John Rich did not aggressively pursue the possibilities of ballad opera form, perhaps because he preferred to invest the company's resources in pantomime.

Rich was known in his own day as a brilliant dancer and mime, as the *bon vivant* founder of the Sublime Society of Beefsteaks and also as a parsimonious anti-intellectual. His standard dismissal to the author of a new play was merely 'It will not do'. The first Covent Garden theatre was built in 1732 to his specification; characteristically, he sold £15 000 worth of 'renter's shares' and spent only £5600 on the building. Why he welcomed Handel in 1734 remains a puzzle. Rich's view of Italian opera in his dedication to *The Rape of Proserpine* (1727) is decidedly hostile:

Though my Inclination to Musick frequently leads me to visit the *Italian* Opera; yet, I confess, it is not in the Power of the present Excellent Performers to prevent my falling into the very common Opinion, that there are many essential Requisites still wanting, to establish that Entertainment on a lasting Foundation, and adapt it to the Taste of an *English* Audience.

For not to mention the trite Objection of the Performances being in *Italian*, and the general ill Choice of the Subjects for those Compositions; it is evident, that the vast Expence of procuring Foreign Voices, does necessarily exclude those various Embellishments of Machinery, Painting, Dances, as well as Poetry it self, which have been always esteemed (except till very lately in *England*) Auxiliaries absolutely necessary to the Success of Musick; and, without which, it cannot be long supported, unless by very great Subscriptions, of which we naturally grow tired in a few Years.

Notwithstanding these views, when the 'Opera of the Nobility' dispossessed Handel of the King's Theatre, Haymarket, in 1734, Rich allowed him to mount operas and oratorios at Covent Garden for three seasons; the works first performed there included *Ariodante*, *Alcina*, *Atalanta*, *Arminio*, *Giustino* and *Berenice*. The financial arrangements between them are unknown, but in March 1737 Rich wrote to the Duke of Bedford claiming to be unable to pay ground rent because of substantial losses due to the opera. Yet relations between Rich and Handel evidently remained cordial. Handel continued to give his oratorios at Covent Garden in the 1740s and 50s, and he willed to Rich his 'Great Organ', which was duly installed at Covent Garden after his death in 1759. In the same year Rich's daughter Charlotte married Handel's favourite tenor, John Beard, who succeeded Rich as principal manager at Covent Garden in 1761.

BDA; LS
C. A. C. Davis: 'John Rich as "Lun"', *Notes & Queries*, cxcii (1947), 222–4
R. Fiske: *English Theatre Music in the Eighteenth Century* (London, 1973, 2/1986)
P. Sawyer: *The New Theatre in Lincoln's Inn Fields* (London, 1979)
R. D. Hume: 'Handel and Opera Management in London in the 1730s', *ML*, lxvii (1986), 347–62　　　JUDITH MILHOUS

Richard Coeur-de-lion ('Richard the Lionheart'). *Comédie mise en musique* in three acts by ANDRÉ-ERNEST-MODESTE GRÉTRY to a libretto by MICHEL-JEAN SEDAINE after an anonymous account in the *Bibliothèque universelle des romans*, ii (July 1776), pp.163–94; Paris, Comédie-Italienne (Salle Favart), 21 October 1784 (revised in four acts, Fontainebleau, 25 October 1785).

The opera is set in the environs of Linz Castle, around the year 1193. Peasants are returning home for the night. Blondel (baritone), a troubadour and squire to King Richard (tenor), enters in disguise and feigning blindness. A local boy, Antonio (soprano), guides him and goes to find him lodgings. Blondel, alone, thinks the castle may hold Richard: he sings of the master he seeks ('O Richard! ô mon Roi!'), who has been imprisoned during his return from the Third Crusade. The expatriate Welsh knight Williams (bass) and his daughter Laurette (soprano) live close by. Blondel has intercepted a letter to Laurette: its contents reveal to him that its author is Florestan (baritone), the castle governor who is courting Laurette, and that there is a secret, important prisoner. After Laurette's account of her love, and Blondel's reply ('Un bandeau couvre les yeux'), a retinue of knights and ladies enters together with Marguerite of Flanders (soprano). Blondel recognizes her as Richard's declared love, and plays on his violin the *romance* his master composed for her, 'Une fièvre brûlante': she recognizes it. Blondel says he has picked it up from a passing crusader, and then, as night falls, performs the crusader song 'Que le Sultan Saladin'.

Act 2 shows dawn over the castle, and Richard on a terrace. He sings of past glory and Marguerite ('Si l'univers entier'). Blondel, out of Richard's sight, sings the opening strains of 'Une fièvre brûlante'. Richard, recognizing the voice, joyfully continues the song. Blondel, playing his violin, attracts soldiers' attention and manages to pass a false invitation to Florestan to attend a party for Marguerite later in the day.

Act 3 scene i shows the interior of Williams's house; Marguerite talks of entering a convent. Blondel, now in his own person, reveals Richard's location. A plan is hatched to capture Florestan and breach the castle wall. Florestan duly appears after some dancing, and is held. The scene changes to the siege. Battle music resounds as Blondel leads the successful attack. Richard and Marguerite are united, and the *romance* melody is finally recalled, before closing acclamation.

This *opéra comique* stands at the high point of Grétry's career and of his partnership with Sedaine. Although its royalist sentiments caused it to be banished from the French stage in 1791 (and also during the 1830 and 1848 revolutions), the opera was seen throughout the 19th century and became perhaps the most universally familiar 18th-century *opéra comique*.

In design, the work presents a highly original approach. Many surrounding characters, and the chorus, depict an idealized medieval community. The use of historical subject matter, combined with the decisive role of an individual (Blondel), locate *Richard Coeur-de-lion* as an ancestor of Romantic grand opera. Grétry's music frequently evokes archaic qualities, and the whole score is a point of reference for 'gothic' local colour. Structurally important are the nine dramatically vital appearances of the *romance*, which thereby becomes a significant feature in the opera's dramaturgy.

DAVID CHARLTON

'Richard Coeur-de-lion' (Grétry), Act 3 (the assault on Linz Castle): engraving (1786) by Claude Bornet after his own original

Painting (1765) by John Inigo Richards for a scene from Arnold's pasticcio 'The Maid of the Mill'

Richards, John Inigo (*b* 1728–9; *d* London, 18 Dec 1810). English scene painter. He worked at Covent Garden (1759–1803) in collaboration with Nicholas Dall, on whose death in 1776 he succeeded as chief scenic artist. His first known design was for Arnold's pasticcio *The Maid of the Mill*, an original painting for which is in the Paul Mellon Collection at the Yale Center for British Art, New Haven, Connecticut (it was engraved by William Woollett, 1768). It depicts a farmyard scene in which the water-mill worked and a girl was seated at a practicable window (see illustration). In contrast is a violent Baroque scene of Tartarus for Dibdin's pantomime *The Mirrour, or Harlequin Everywhere* (1779) on which he collaborated with G. B. Cipriani (see Rosenfeld, pl. 22). It consists of a rocky cave with a great falling rock, a St Catherine's wheel and a background of flames. A critic of scenery for Richard Cumberland's *Joanna of Montfaucon* (1800; music by Busby) commented on 'The appropriate beauty of the scenery, in which the rules of perspective are critically observed, the splendour of the decorations and the richness of the dresses have rarely been equalled'.

Little is known of his scenery for comic operas, many of which were by Shield, including *The Woodman* (1791), *The Travellers in Switzerland* (1794) and *Abroad and at Home* (1796). For Arne's pasticcio *Tom Jones* (1769) he designed a garden flat, for Shield's *Siege of Gibraltar* (1780) he and Robert Carver depicted English and French fleets entering the bay, and for Cobb's *Ramah Droog* (1798; music by Mazzinghi and Reeve) he used Thomas Daniell's drawings of Indian landscape and architecture. He was also employed on widening Covent Garden and decorating the auditorium in 1784 and in supplying a model, scenes and a drop curtain for the Chesnut Street Theatre, Philadelphia, in 1794.

BDA
S. Rosenfeld and E. Croft-Murray: 'A Checklist of Scene Painters Working in Great Britain and Ireland in the 18th Century', *Theatre Notebook*, xix (1964–5), 142
S. Rosenfeld: *A Short History of Scene Design in Great Britain* (Oxford, 1973)
                                                           SYBIL ROSENFELD

Richardson, Marilyn (*b* Sydney, 10 June 1936). Australian soprano. After study at the New South Wales Conservatorium she sang roles in many contemporary works in the 1960s (including the Governess in *The Turn of the Screw*), before going to Europe for further study with Pierre Bernac in Paris and Conchita Badía in Barcelona. She sang the title roles of *Lulu* (1972) and *Salome* (1974) at Basle, and in Australia established herself immediately with her Aida of 1975 for the Australian Opera. She has since been a leading principal with that and other Australian companies, especially effective as Salome and the Marschallin. She is noted for her musicianship and stage presence. Many felt that the girlish mobility and luminous ardour of her Isolde (1990) helped balance some lack of ideal vocal power and stamina. Her striking portrayal of Laura in Meale's *Voss* can be heard on the complete recording of 1987.

                                                           ROGER COVELL

Richings [Reynoldson], (Mary) Caroline (*b* England, 1827; *d* Richmond, VA, 14 Jan 1882). American impresario and singer. Taken to the USA at an early age and adopted by the actor Peter Richings, she began her musical career as a concert pianist. She later studied singing and made her operatic début at the Walnut Street Theatre, Philadelphia, as Marie in Donizetti's *La fille du régiment* (9 February 1852). She performed as pianist and singer in the Richings Opera Company, which her father had formed in 1859, and became its director on his retirement in 1867. In the same year she married Peter Bernard, a tenor in the troupe, which, under the name Richings-Bernard Company, toured the USA extensively. In 1870 they joined forces briefly with Euphrosyne Parepa-Rosa, their chief rival, as the Caroline Richings-Bernard Grand Opera Combination; but Clara Kellogg lured most of the good singers away and the venture failed financially.

Richings was dedicated to presenting French, German and Italian opera in English and often translated and edited the librettos herself. After her last venture, a concert group called the Old Folks Opera Company (1874–5), she appeared in light opera and in concerts in Baltimore, where she was also a sought-after singing teacher. Her last stage appearance was in her own operetta, *The Duchess* (August 1881, Baltimore).

See TRAVELLING TROUPES, §5(i, ii).

DAB ('Richings, Peter'; E.F. Edgett)
G. P. Upton: *Musical Memories* (Chicago, 1908), 137   DEE BAILY

Richter, Ferdinand Tobias (*b* Würzburg, 22 July 1651; *d* Vienna, 3 Nov 1711). Austrian composer of German birth. He probably received his musical training from his father Tobias (*d* 1682) and his godfather P. F. Buchner (1614–69). He went on to become organist at the Cistercian monastery of Heiligenkreuz (1675–9) and then imperial court and chamber organist (1683–1711). Though best known as an organist and teacher and for his instrumental compositions, he also wrote dramatic music for 15 Jesuit Latin plays. These were produced between 1677 and 1710 for the imperial family in Vienna, who encouraged high artistic standards. The plays depart from the Jesuit tradition in that the use of music is no longer confined to the prologue, epilogue and conclusions of individual acts, but frequently permeates the texts of the remainder of the drama. Moreover, Richter's music in these works follows the operatic style of the day, including recitatives, arias and ballets.

Richter also wrote two one-act serenatas for the birthday celebrations of Duchess Eleanora Maria of Lorraine (*L'istro ossequioso*, 31 May 1694) and Leopold I (*Le promesse degli dei*, 9 June 1697, to a libretto by Nicolò Minato). Manuscript scores of both serenatas survive (*A-Wn*); *Le promesse degli dei* is notable for its rich instrumentation.

A. von Weilen: *Zur Wiener Theatergeschichte: die vom Jahre 1629 bis zum Jahre 1740 am Wiener Hofe zur Aufführung gelangten Werke theatralischen Charakters und Oratorien* (Vienna, 1901)
E. Wellesz: 'Die Opern und Oratorien in Wien, 1660–1708', *SMw*, vi (1919), 5–138
F. Hadamowsky: 'Barocktheater am Wiener Kaiserhof; mit einem Spielplan (1625–1740)', *Jb der Gesellschaft für Wiener Theaterforschung* (1951–2), 7–117; repr. separately (Vienna, 1955)
H. Wlczek: *Das Schuldrama der Jesuiten zu Krems (1616–1763)* (diss., U. of Vienna, 1952)
A. Bauer: *Opern und Operetten in Wien: Verzeichnis ihrer Erstaufführungen in der Zeit von 1629 bis zur Gegenwart* (Graz, 1955)
J. Fröhler: 'Zur Schauspieltätigkeit der Studenten am Linzer Jesuitengymnasium', *Historisches Jb der Stadt Linz 1955*, 197–270
——: 'Überlieferte Linzer Jesuitendramen', *Historisches Jb der Stadt Linz 1957*, 69–130
K. Adel: 'Handschriften von Jesuitendramen in der Österreichischen Nationalbibliothek in Wien', *Jb der Gesellschaft für Wiener Theaterforschung*, xii (1960), 83–112
——: *Das Wiener Jesuitentheater und die europäische Barockdramatik* (Vienna, 1960)

A. Sturm: *Theatergeschichte Oberösterreichs im 16. und 17. Jahrhundert* (Vienna, 1964)
W. Kramer: *Die Musik im Wiener Jesuitendrama von 1677–1711* (diss., U. of Vienna, 1965)
I. Bartels: *Die Instrumentalstücke in Oper und Oratorium der frühvenezianischen Zeit* (diss., U. of Vienna, 1970)
A. Niemetz: *800 Jahre Musikpflege in Heiligenkreuz* (Heiligenkreuz, 1977)
H. Seifert: 'Die Entfaltung des Barock', *Österreichische Musikgeschichte*, ed. R. Flotzinger and G. Gruber, i (Vienna, 1977), 323–79
——: *Die Oper am Wiener Kaiserhof im 17. Jahrhundert* (Tutzing, 1985)   RUDOLF SCHNITZLER

Richter, Hans (*b* Raab [now Győr], 4 April 1843; *d* Bayreuth, 5 Dec 1916). Austro-Hungarian conductor. He received his first musical training from his parents – his mother was an opera singer, his father Domkapellmeister. On his father's death, in 1853, Richter became a chorister at the Hofkapelle and from 1860 to 1865 studied the piano, violin and horn, together with theory (under Sechter), at the Vienna Conservatory. He mastered all instruments save the harp, and while a student earned his living as a horn player (after just 19 months' study) in the Kärntnertortheater (1862–6). In October 1866 he was sent to Wagner at Tribschen as copyist of *Die Meistersinger*; he assisted as répétiteur and chorus master for the opera's première in Munich (1868) under von Bülow, whom he succeeded at the Hoftheater in 1869. He resigned in protest when the staging of the first performance of *Das Rheingold* did not meet with Wagner's approval and, after a short stay in Paris, went to Brussels in 1870 to conduct the première there of *Lohengrin*. He then returned to Tribschen to copy *Siegfried* for Wagner, who, together with Liszt, secured him a post as Kapellmeister (and later music director) at the Budapest Opera (1871–5). After a guest appearance in Vienna in 1875 he virtually took over conducting all the major musical organizations of that city, including the Hofoper, where he remained until 1899.

In 1876 he conducted the première of Wagner's *Ring* at the first Bayreuth Festival, and the following year joined the composer in London to share the conducting of the Wagner Festival. His reception in England was enthusiastic, and he conducted an annual series in London, 1879–97, the Birmingham Triennial Festival, 1885–1909, the Hallé Orchestra, 1899–1911, and the newly formed LSO, 1904–11. His operatic work was largely confined to Vienna, with regular appearances at Bayreuth and in London, where he conducted the German Opera seasons of 1882 and 1884 (at Drury Lane) and the first *Ring* in English in 1908. His final performance was in 1912 at Bayreuth where he conducted the work he had made his own, Wagner's *Die Meistersinger*.

Richter's operatic repertory was dominated by Wagner (he conducted all the operas after *Rienzi* except *Parsifal*), Mozart, Beethoven, Bizet, Auber, Meyerbeer and Gounod. His interest in Italian opera was limited to a handful of operas by Cherubini, Bellini, Donizetti, Ponchielli and Verdi (*La traviata*, *Il trovatore* and *Aida*). Hans Richter was one of the most prominent musical personalities of his day, and for nearly 40 years his influence upon the opera houses and concert halls of Vienna and London was second to none.

CHRISTOPHER FIFIELD

Ricimer. Libretto subject used in the 17th and 18th centuries. Its source is Roman history. Flavius Ricimer,

Roman patrician and *magister militum* (Master of the Roman Soldiers), 456–72, directed Roman policy in the western empire through a succession of weak emperors under his control. His most amenable puppet, Livius Severus, ruled from 461 until his death in 465. With the installation of Anthemius in 467, Ricimer received the hand of the new emperor's daughter in marriage. Dissatisfied with Anthemius's failure to defend the empire against the Vandals, Ricimer laid siege to Rome in 472 and installed the Roman senator Flavius Anicius Olybrius as emperor. Both Ricimer and Olybrius died later that same year. While the most common Italian title for the story was simply *Ricimero* (and thus *Ricimero, re de' Goti*; *Ricimero, re de' Vandali*), operas on the subject were also called *Flavio Anicio Olibrio*.

The first libretto based on the character Ricimer was written by Matteo Noris for Carlo Pallavicino (1684). Noris added traditional amorous and political subplots and ignored the death of Severus two years before Anthemius's arrival. In Noris's libretto the Vandal Ricimero [Ricimer] is given entrance into Rome by Antemio [Anthemius] and a promise of marriage to his daughter, Domizia. The deposed emperor Severo [Severus], his wife Pulcheria, his father-in-law Cina and his son Lidio are taken prisoner by Ricimer and face execution despite their pleas for mercy. Domizia falls in love with Ricimer and rejects the entreaties of her former beloved, Celso. Ricimer, however, desires the hand of his prisoner, Pulcheria, who rejects him, even after being informed of Severus's apparent suicide. Anthemius and Celso vow revenge on Ricimer for his violation of Domizia's honour and join with Severus and his family to depose the barbarian.

Zeno's libretto *Flavio Anicio Olibrio*, written in collaboration with Pariati and first set by Francesco Gasparini (1708), is based on a later episode in Ricimer's life. Zeno also embellished history by adding amorous subplots and rearranging political allegiances. Olibrio [Olybrius] arrives in Rome to find that Ricimer has captured the city and imprisoned his beloved, Placidia. Olybrius enters the city in disguise to liberate her, but is taken prisoner when his identity is revealed. Ricimer, who (as before) has fallen for his prisoner, forces Placidia to choose between marriage and the death of her beloved. Ricimer's sister Teodolinda, who secretly loves Olybrius, continually rejects the entreaties of her former beloved, Olderico, and arranges for the release of Olybrius in exchange for his promise to love her. After his release Olybrius rejects Teodolinda and challenges Ricimer to combat for the hand of Placidia. Ricimer agrees and is defeated in battle. Zeno's text was later set by Porpora (1711), Vinci (1728) and Jommelli (1740).

Ricimero is also the name given by Francesco Silvani to the Visigothic king Athaulf (also called Ataulfo) in his largely fictional *La fede tradita e vendicata*, first set to music by Francesco Gasparini (1704) and later set as *Ricimero* and as *Ernelinda*; it is related to Pergolesi's IL PRIGIONIERO SUPERBO (1733) and Philidor's *ERNELINDE, PRINCESSE DE NORVÈGE* (1767).

PAUL CAUTHEN

Ricordi. Firm of publishers, the most important Italian publishers of opera. The firm was founded in Milan in 1808 by Giovanni Ricordi (*b* Milan, 1785; *d* Milan, 15 March 1853); it was directed from 1853 to 1888 by his son Tito (i) (*b* Milan, 29 Oct 1811; *d* Milan 7 Sept 1888), from 1888 to 1912 by Tito's son Giulio (*b* Milan, 19 Dec 1840; *d* Milan, 6 June, 1912) and from 1912 to 1919 by Giulio's son Tito (ii) (*b* Milan, 17 May 1865; *d* Milan, 13 March 1933). It was managed from 1919 to 1940 jointly by Renzo Valcarenghi and Carlo Clausetti, from 1940 to 1944 by Valcarenghi and Alfredo Colombo, and from 1944 to 1952 by Colombo, Eugenio Clausetti and Camillo Ricordi. In 1952 it became a limited company, under the presidency first of Colombo, then of Guido Valcarenghi (1961–76), Carlo Origoni (for a few months during 1976), Gianni Babini (1976–88), and of Guido Rignano (from 1988).

Giovanni Ricordi, a violinist, was leader of the orchestra of a small Milanese theatre, the Fiando. Probably in 1803 he had started a *copisteria* (copying establishment) beneath the portico of the Palazzo della Ragione. From 1804 to 1807 he was under contract as official copyist and prompter to the Teatro Carcano and in 1807 to the Teatro del Lentasio. In 1807 he went to Leipzig to study the techniques of Breitkopf & Härtel; after returning to Milan, he formed a publishing partnership with Felice Festa, an engraver and music seller, on 16 January 1808. Their first and probably only joint publication was a duet from Farinelli's *Calliroe*, issued as the first in a series entitled *Giornale di musica vocale italiana*; the partnership was terminated on 26 June 1808.

The firm occupied several different premises (including one, from 1844, at the side of La Scala). The present premises, in via Berchet, were rebuilt after World War II and opened in 1950. The most valuable of Ricordi's rich archives survived the war and are still in the possession of the firm; housed at the production plant in via Salomone, they include some 4000 music manuscripts (chiefly autograph), a large quantity of correspondence, and approximately 25 000 printed editions; details of much of the collection are listed at the Ufficio Ricerca Fondi Musicali (the Italian RISM centre) in Milan.

During his first decade in business Giovanni Ricordi issued an average of 30 publications a year; in his second the yearly average was about 300. This expansion was largely the result of a succession of contracts, starting from December 1814, which he won as prompter and exclusive copyist to La Scala, giving him the right to publish the music performed there; in 1825 he purchased their entire musical archives. In 1816 he had a similar contract as copyist to the Teatro Re, and in the 1830s and 40s concluded highly favourable agreements with the opera houses of Venice and Naples. By the end of 1837 he had not only purchased the stock and plates of Ferdinando Artaria but was able to boast more then 10 000 publications, the exclusive rights to operas written for Milan and Naples, an archive of 1800 autograph manuscripts and a branch in Florence. By his death in 1853 Giovanni had issued 25 000 publications.

Tito (i), a good pianist, had worked in the firm since 1825. Under his management, new printing methods were introduced, branches in Naples (1860), Rome (1871), London (1875), Palermo and Paris (both 1888) were opened, and the substantial businesses of Clausetti (1864), Del Monaco and Guidi (both 1887) and finally Lucca (30 May 1888) were taken over. The acquisition of Lucca, which had been Ricordi's chief rival from the 1840s and had itself between 1847 and 1886 absorbed five firms (including Canti), brought to the Ricordi catalogue some 40 000 editions as well as the Italian rights to Wagner's operas.

Shortly before his death, Tito (i) gave over the management of the firm to his son Giulio, a highly cultured man and the best musician in the family. He composed piano pieces and songs as well as orchestral music and stage works, culminating in a comic opera *La secchia rapita* (1910, Turin). He worked for his father for a short time from 1856 and permanently from 1863. It was he who regularly dealt with Verdi on the firm's behalf from about 1875 and who played a central role in Puccini's artistic development. Under his management, branches at Leipzig (1901) and New York (1911) were opened, part of the stock of Escudier, Ricordi's former Paris agent, was acquired (1889), and the firms of Pigna and Schmidl (both 1902) and Carelli (1905) were taken over. His son Tito (ii), who succeeded him, appears to have lacked both charm and judgment. He and Puccini disliked each other, and Puccini had *La rondine* published by Ricordi's rival Sonzogno. When Tito (ii) retired in 1919, the management of the firm passed out of the hands of the family. Business expansion continued, however, and in South America several publishers were taken over; the Walter Mocchi musical archives were acquired in 1929, and the Naples firm of Pasquariello absorbed in 1946. Branches were set up in São Paulo (1927), Basle (1949), Genoa (1953), Toronto (1954), Sydney (1956) and Mexico City (1958). Since then, branches or agencies have been opened in Bari, Florence, Turin and Munich, and the branch in Leipzig has closed. The New York branch was purchased by Alfredo Colombo's son, Franco (*b* Milan, 4 Aug 1911), who had been its managing director since 1949, and became known as Franco Colombo Inc. in 1962. By 1991 Ricordi had published more than 135 500 editions.

Ricordi's first catalogue (1814) lists his first 176 publications, mainly piano arrangements of and variations on operatic tunes, pieces for guitars and the operatic numbers that formed part of his *Giornale di musica vocale italiana* (which did not run beyond its fourth volume). The most notable single items include Ricordi's first complete vocal score, Mayr's *Adelasia ed Aleramo*, issued in association with the firm of G. C. Martorelli. By 1824 the firm was offering a range of instrumental music, a large selection of Italian operatic numbers for piano solo and piano and voice (including many pieces by Rossini) and vocal scores of five complete operas. The 1825 catalogue lists about 60 operatic excerpts in full score.

By 1840 Giovanni Ricordi had, through his connections with opera houses, established both an extremely powerful position for himself in the operatic world and a highly profitable business. Rossini had effectively retired and Bellini was dead; but Ricordi had published vocal scores and was in a position to hire out performing material of 19 operas by Rossini and eight by Bellini. Donizetti was still flourishing, and Ricordi either already had published, or was about to publish, all but a handful of his works composed after 1830. Also on Ricordi's books were the best of the other Italian opera composers – Mercadante, Vaccai, Pacini and Luigi and Federico Ricci – as well as Meyerbeer, whose *Il crociato in Egitto* had been published by the firm in 1824 and whose French operas were now achieving widespread success. In 1839, by publishing Verdi's first opera, *Oberto, conte di S Bonifacio*, Ricordi took the most significant single step in the history of the firm. Except for *Attila*, *I masnadieri* and *Il corsaro*, published by Lucca between 1846 and 1848, Ricordi published all Verdi's remaining operas. In 1842 he founded an important and long-running house journal, the *Gazzetta*

musicale di Milano, which served to focus attention on the successes of his stable of authors.

The Italian passion for operatic and vocal music coupled with the paucity of original instrumental works composed in Italy during the 19th century was reflected in Ricordi's catalogues, and during the second and third quarters of the century a large proportion of the immense quantity of instrumental music, especially for piano, put out by the firm consisted of operatic arrangements. The catalogue of 1875 advertised the *Biblioteca di musica populare*, which came to be known as the *Edizioni economiche*. Designed to be produced inexpensively, this at first consisted only of vocal and piano scores of operas, in a new smaller format (subsequently used for all Ricordi's vocal scores). This catalogue shows that in the second half of the century the firm was maintaining its operatic tradition. Pedrotti and Boito had already been taken on, and from the 1870s operas by Ponchielli and Catalani were published. In 1884 Ricordi published Puccini's first opera, *Le villi*, after it had been turned down by Sonzogno; apart from *Le rondine*, the firm went on to publish all Puccini's operas. After Verdi, Puccini has been Ricordi's most valuable asset by far. Sonzogno, however, proved to be their strongest rival since Lucca; he was the main publisher of Puccini's most successful contemporaries, Mascagni and Leoncavallo, leaving Ricordi the less profitable Alfano, Franchetti, Montemezzi and Zandonai. Ricordi have continued to publish, though with far more competition and rather less energy and inspiration than in the 19th century, the works of contemporary Italian composers, including operas and other music by Pizzetti, Malipiero, Respighi, Wolf-Ferrari, Rocca, Tosatti, Rossellini, Bettinelli, Rota and Testi.

In the entire history of music publishing there has been no other firm that through its own efforts, astuteness, initiative and flair has achieved a position of dominance such as Ricordi enjoyed in Italy in the 19th century, nor of power such as it has been able to maintain (on account of its rights on Verdi's and Puccini's operas) in the 20th. Yet with power should go responsibility, and Ricordi have been criticized in the past for allowing considerations of art to take second place to those of commerce. Verdi himself complained bitterly about the elder Tito's sanctioning, for financial gain, of mutilated performances of his works. There is a clear moral obligation for the publisher owning the rights and autograph manuscripts of almost every one of Verdi's and Puccini's operas to make those works available, and in correct texts. Although all the major works of Puccini are now available in full score, only about a third of Verdi's operas are offered for sale in this format (though most others are available for hire), and the fraction of Rossini's, Bellini's and Donizetti's works is far smaller still. Furthermore, there is a widely held view that the existing scores (particularly of operas from the first half of the 19th century), whether for sale or hire, often offer inaccurate or incomplete texts.

During the last 20 years, Ricordi have been making considerable efforts to remedy this situation. Scholarly access to the autograph scores is now much freer than it once was, and – more important still – the firm has become collaboratively involved in a number of critical editions, most notably those of Rossini and Verdi (both under the general editorship of Philip Gossett) and of Donizetti (under the general editorship of Gabriele Dotto and Roger Parker). Though the pace of such editions is necessarily slow, they have served gradually to enhance Ricordi's reputation among scholars and performers.

See also PUBLISHING.

N. Tabanelli: 'Giurisprudenza: la causa Ricordi-Leoncavallo', *RMI*, vi (1899), 833–45
——: 'Giurisprudenza teatrale: la ditta Ricordi contro il tenore Bonci', *RMI*, viii (1901), 703–14
G. Adami: *Giulio Ricordi e i suoi musicisti* (Milan, 1933)
——: *Giulio Ricordi: l'amico dei musicisti italiani* (Milan, 1945)
O. Vergiani: *Piccolo viaggio in un archivio* (Milan, 1953)
C. Sartori: *Casa Ricordi 1808–1958, profilo storico* (Milan, 1958)
D. Vaughan: 'Discordanze tra gli autografi verdiani e la loro stampa', *La scala* (1958), no. 104, pp.11–15
G. Gavazzeni: *Problemi di tradizione dinamico-fraseologica e critica testuale, in Verdi e Puccini* (Milan, 1961) [in It., Eng. and Ger.]
C. Hopkinson: *A Bibliography of the Works of Giuseppe Verdi* (New York, 1973–8)
F. Degrada and others: *Musica, musicisti, editoria: 175 anni di Casa Ricordi, 1808–1983* (Milan, 1983)
A. Zecca Laterza, ed.: *Il catalogo numerico Ricordi 1857, con date e indice*, i (Milan, 1984)
P. Gossett: 'The Ricordi Numerical Catalogues: a Background', *Notes*, xlii (1985–6), 22–8
P. Petrobelli, M. Di Gregorio Casati and C. M. Mossa, eds.: *Carteggio Verdi-Ricordi (1880–1881)* (Parma, 1988)
L. Jensen: *Giuseppe Verdi and Giovanni Ricordi with Notes on Francesco Lucca: from 'Oberto' to 'La traviata'* (New York, 1989)　　　RICHARD MACNUTT (with ROGER PARKER)

Ridderbusch, Karl (*b* Recklinghausen, 29 May 1932). German bass. He made his début at the Städtisches Theater, Münster, in 1961. He was a member of the Essen Opera before moving to Düsseldorf in 1965, where he made the Deutsche Oper am Rhein his artistic base. In 1967 he made his débuts at Bayreuth and the Metropolitan in Wagner, and at Covent Garden in 1971 where he sang Fasolt, Hunding and Hagen. He has sung regularly at the Vienna Staatsoper since his first appearance there in 1968, and was a notable Hans Sachs in Karajan's production of *Die Meistersinger* at the 1974 and 1975 Salzburg Easter festivals. Ridderbusch's voice is firm, clear, sonorous and rich in timbre; his style is direct, his stage presence imposing. He has appeared successfully in Verdi, and in *buffo* roles including Ochs, Rocco and Mozart's Bartolo, but he is at his best in the serious, dramatically demanding repertory, for example the Commendatore, Pizarro, Hunding, Hagen, Hans Sachs and Caspar (*Der Freischütz*).　　　GERHARD BRUNNER

Riders to the Sea. Opera in one act by RALPH VAUGHAN WILLIAMS to his own libretto after JOHN MILLINGTON SYNGE's play; London, Royal College of Music, 1 December 1937.

This is Vaughan Williams's most successful opera, perhaps because the subject – man against nature – was one which always drew strong and characteristic music from him, as in *A Pastoral Symphony* and *Sinfonia antartica*. The desolation of the Arran landscape as a background for the tragic lives of the fisherfolk inspired music of a kind which later found abstract expression in the finale of the Sixth Symphony (1944–7).

After a short prelude depicting a stormy sea, Nora (soprano) asks her sister Cathleen (soprano) to help her identify some clothes taken off a drowned man as belonging to their brother, Michael. Like his father and four other brothers, he has lost his life at sea. They talk quietly because their mother Maurya (contralto) is rest-

ing in the next room, and they hide the clothes in the loft.

But Maurya cannot sleep. She is worried that her last surviving son Bartley (baritone) is taking horses in a boat to Galway Fair. Bartley arrives to fetch a rope. The women beg him to stay, but he tells them how to manage while he is away. He will ride the red mare with the grey pony behind. The sisters reproach Maurya for not giving Bartley her blessing and send her after him with some bread. While Maurya is away, the sisters confirm that the clothing was Michael's but hide it from their mother. Maurya returns in some distress. She has seen Bartley riding to the sea on the red mare, with Michael, in new clothes and shoes, on the grey pony. Cathleen tells her Michael is dead. Maurya says her vision means Bartley will die too. As she sings of the deaths of her men, Bartley's body is carried in. He has been knocked into the sea by the grey pony. Maurya, in a noble elegy, sings that the sea can hurt her no more. She blesses the dead and the living.　　　MICHAEL KENNEDY

Ridler [née Bradby], **Anne** (**Barbara**) (*b* Rugby, 30 July 1912). English librettist and translator. Best known as a poet, she was the librettist of two operas by Elizabeth Maconchy, *The Jesse Tree* (1970) and *The King of the Golden River* (after Ruskin; 1975), and one by Robert Sherlaw Johnson, *The Lambton Worm* (1978). She won wider acclaim with her English versions of operas by Cavalli (*Rosinda*) and Monteverdi (*Il ritorno d'Ulisse in patria*), both admirably and unusually matching poetic image with musical flow. She has also translated operas by Handel, Gluck and Mozart.　　　ARTHUR JACOBS

Ridout, Alan (**John**) (*b* West Wickham, Kent, 9 Dec 1934). English composer. He studied composition with Gordon Jacob and Herbert Howells at the RCM, privately with Fricker and Tippett, and with Henk Badings in the Netherlands. He was a professor at the RCM (1961–84), and has taught composition at Birmingham, London, Cambridge and Oxford universities. His works include eight symphonies and much church music; his operas show him to be equally resourceful whether writing for professionals, for amateurs or for choirboys. Writing of *The Rescue*, Peter Dickinson has remarked that Ridout 'achieves simple effectiveness without concessions', comparing his sense of timing and emotional calculation to that of Kurt Weill. Ridout's idiom, however, is generally nearer to Britten's than to Weill's, while his lean and trenchant style reflects his interest in music of many periods, from medieval polyphony to 12-note serialism.

The Greek Kalends (children's op, 2, J. H. Oldham), Tunbridge Wells, 1956
The Rescue (chamber op, 1, D. Holbrook), Hastings, 1963
The Boy from the Catacombs (church op, 2, F. H. Wilkinson), Canterbury Cathedral, 1965
Children's Crusade (church op, 1, Holbrook, after B. Brecht), Canterbury Cathedral, 1968
The Pardoner's Tale (N. Platt, after G. Chaucer), Canterbury, 1970
Angelo (chamber op, 2, J. Platt, after Q. Blake), Canterbury, 1971
The Cat (1, J. Platt and N. Platt, after Aesop), Berkshire, NY, 1971
The Gift (children's op, 1, A. Wicks, after C. Rossetti: *Goblin Market*), Canterbury Cathedral, 1971
Creation (church op, 7 scenes, P. Dickinson, after *Genesis*), Ely Cathedral, 1973
Phaeton (radio op, Dickinson), BBC, 1974
A Vision (monodrama, 9 scenes, Ridout, after R. Jefferies: *Story of my Heart*), Manchester, 1974
The Selfish Giant (chamber op, 1, J. Platt, after O. Wilde), Wye Church, Kent, 1977

Wenceslas (church op, 2, Dickinson), Bournemouth, 1978
The White Doe (church op, 2, Wicks, after W. Wordsworth), Ripon
    Cathedral, 1987

*

P. Dickinson: 'Composer of Today', *Music and Musicians*, xv/4
    (1966), 28–30
J. Harding: 'Alan Ridout', *Performance* (wint. 1980–81), 45–7
HUGO COLE

Ridout, Godfrey (*b* Toronto, 6 May 1918; *d* Toronto,
24 Nov 1984). Canadian composer. He studied with
Ettore Mazzoleni, Charles Peaker and Healey Willan at
the Toronto Conservatory, where in 1940 he began
teaching. In 1948 he was appointed to the Faculty of
Music of Toronto University, where he became senior
professor. Proud of his status as the eccentric
traditionalist among Canadian composers, he has
acknowledged the particular influence of such Victorian
and Edwardian composers as Sullivan, Elgar and Holst,
but his music is much more widely informed, even to the
extent of occasional forays into serial techniques – without, however, following their stylistic implications. He
is best known for his tuneful orchestral works.

Ridout's two operatic ventures are typically eclectic.
In 1963 he reconstructed from the surviving vocal and
second violin parts the orchestral score of the first
Canadian opera, Jacques Quesnel's *Colas et Colinette*
(1790); the opera was published at Toronto in 1964 and
is frequently performed. Less successful was his three-
act opera for CBC television, *The Lost Child* (J. Reid;
1975), which though based on a charming Christmas
tale suffered from an overambitious libretto.
HARVEY OLNICK

Ried, Aquinas (*b* Bavaria, *c*1810; *d* Valparaíso, Chile,
17 May 1869). German composer. After receiving a
doctorate in philosophy at the Royal University
Ludovica Maximiliana in Munich in 1830, he emigrated, first to London and later to Australia, where he
worked as a surgeon in a penal colony for seven years.
On his return journey to Europe in 1844, he dis-
embarked permanently at Valparaíso. In 1846 he
composed a three-act opera in Spanish, *Telésfora* the
first lyric drama to be attempted in Chile; it was
dedicated to the country's grandeur, but only one
chorus was ever performed. All his works are lost, but in
addition to *Telésfora* he is known to have completed
three other operas (*Il granatiere*, 1860, to an Italian
libretto, *Ismenilda* and *Ondega*) and to have left four incomplete (*Walhala*, 1863, to a German libretto, *Diana*,
Atacama and *Idoona*).

*

A. Ried: 'Diario', *Revista chilena de historia y geografía*, xxxvi/40
    (1920), 212–66
E. Pereira: *Los orígenes del arte musical en Chile* (Santiago, 1941)
R. Stevenson: 'Chilean Music in the Santa Cruz Epoch', *Inter-
American Music Bulletin*, lxvii (1968), 1–17
M. Cánepa: *La opera en Chile (1839–1930)* (Santiago, 1976)
SAMUEL CLARO-VALDÉS

Riedel, Deborah (*b* Sydney, 31 July 1958). Australian
soprano. She studied in Sydney, and made her début in
1986 with Australian Opera as a mezzo-soprano, singing Countess Ceprano, then Hänsel, Mrs Meg Page,
Mignon and Queen Henrietta (*I puritani*). After becoming a soprano she sang Arminda (*La finta giardiniera*)
and the Drummer (*Der Kaiser von Atlantis*) at Adelaide
(1987–8); Zerlina, Susanna, Mimì, Pamina, Micaëla
and Juliet for Australian Opera (1988–92); and
Gounod's Marguerite and Leïla at Melbourne (1990).

She made her Covent Garden début as Freia (1991), and
sang Teresa (*Benvenuto Cellini*) at Geneva and Donna
Elvira at Bordeaux (1992). A fine actress, she has a flexible, bright and well-focussed voice.   ELIZABETH FORBES

Riegel, Kenneth (*b* Womelsdorf, PA, 19 April 1938).
American tenor. He studied in New York, making his
début in 1965 at Santa Fe as an Alchemist in *König
Hirsch*. Engaged at the New York City Opera
(1969–74), he made his Metropolitan début in 1973 as
Iopas (*Les Troyens*), later singing Tamino, Titus, David
and Hoffmann. He has also sung at Houston, San
Francisco, Seattle, Munich, Geneva, Brussels, Berlin and
the Paris Opéra, where he sang Alwa in the first three-
act performance of *Lulu* (1979) and created the Leper in
Messiaen's *Saint François d'Assise* (1983). His repertory
included Don Ottavio, Ferrando, Belmonte and
Idomeneus, but in the 1980s his voice grew heavier and
he sang Berlioz's Faust, Erik, Loge, Shuysky, Albert
Gregor (*The Makropulos Affair*), Oedipus, Busoni's
Mephistopheles, and Gustav von Aschenbach. A power-
ful and subtle actor, he scored a huge success at Hamburg in 1981 as the Dwarf in Zemlinsky's *Der Zwerg*,
which he later repeated at Edinburgh, Amsterdam and
Covent Garden (1985). He later returned to Covent
Garden as Loge (1991) and Herod (1992).
ELIZABETH FORBES

Riemschneider [Riemenschneider], **Johann Gottfried** (*b*
?Halle; *fl* 1720–40). German bass and composer. He
was the son of Gebhard Reimschneider (1657–1701),
Kantor of the Marienkirche at Halle, and is said to have
been a schoolfellow of Handel's. He sang at Hamburg
from about 1720, appearing in at least five operas by
Keiser (1723–7) and arrangements of Handel's
Tamerlano and *Giulio Cesare*. In 1729 Handel engaged
him for London where he made his début as Clodomiro
in *Lotario* and sang in *Giulio Cesare* (Achillas),
Partenope (Ormonte) and the pasticcio *Ormisda*
(1730). Rolli wrote that his voice was 'more of a natural
contralto than a bass. He sings sweetly in his throat and
nose, pronounces Italian in the Teutonic manner, acts
like a sucking-pig, and looks more like a valet than anything'. The small parts given him by Handel suggest no
great confidence in his powers; his voice was a high baritone (compass of *A* to *g'*). In 1730 Riemschneider
returned to Hamburg, where he sang in *Cleofide* (Handel's *Poro*) in 1732 and was later appointed Kantor and
musical director at the cathedral. His brother Gebhard
Julius also sang at the Hamburg Opera.   WINTON DEAN

Rienzi, der Letzte der Tribunen ('Rienzi, the Last of
the Tribunes'). *Grosse tragische Oper* in five acts by
Richard Wagner (*see* WAGNER family, (1)) to his own
libretto after EDWARD BULWER-LYTTON's novel of the
same name; Dresden, Königlich Sächsisches Hoftheater,
20 October 1842.

Wagner's reading of Bulwer-Lytton's novel *Rienzi,
the Last of the Roman Tribunes* in Blasewitz, near
Dresden, in the summer of 1837 confirmed his intention
of writing an opera on the subject (the idea had
apparently been implanted earlier by his friend Apel).
He immediately sketched an outline, followed by a
prose draft and then, the following summer, a verse
draft. A series of fragmentary composition sketches preceded a continuous composition draft, the first two acts
of which were completed by 9 April 1839. After a short
gap, Act 3 was begun in February 1840 and the work

Cola Rienzi *papal notary* — tenor
Irene *his sister* — soprano
Steffano Colonna *head of the Colonna family* — bass
Adriano *his son* — mezzo-soprano
Paolo Orsini *head of the Orsini family* — bass
Raimondo *papal legate* — bass
Baroncelli ⎱ *Roman citizens* — tenor
Cecco del Vecchio ⎰ — bass
The Messenger of Peace — soprano

Herald, Ambassadors from Milan, the Lombard States, Naples, Bohemia and Bavaria, Roman nobles and attendants, followers of Colonna and Orsini, priests and monks of all orders, senators, Roman citizens (male and female), messengers of peace

Setting Rome, about the middle of the 14th century

completed in draft, with the overture being written last, in October 1840.

The première lasted, according to *Mein Leben*, more than six hours (including intervals), but the work was received with immense enthusiasm, and Joseph Tichatschek and Wilhelmine Schröder-Devrient scored personal successes in the roles of Rienzi and Adriano. The work was subsequently given both over two evenings and in a truncated version prepared by Wagner himself. The absence of the autograph score (which was in the possession of Hitler) and of any original printed score without cuts has bedevilled the preparation of an authoritative complete edition (see Deathridge 1977).

In spite of the practical problems it posed, and somewhat to the composer's embarrassment on account of its stylistic nature, *Rienzi* was one of Wagner's most successful works in the latter years of his life and up to the end of the century. In Dresden alone, 100 performances had been given by 1873 and 200 by 1908. The first production in the USA was at the Academy of Music, New York, in 1878, and in England at Her Majesty's Theatre, London, in 1879.

ACT 1 *A street in Rome* Rienzi's sister Irene is about to be abducted by Paolo Orsini and his followers when they are confronted by their rivals, the Colonnas. Adriano Colonna, in love with Irene, attempts to protect her in the ensuing brawl. The commanding presence of Rienzi, when he arrives on the scene (with a sudden shift of tonality from D to E♭), quells the fighting; his friends and the crowd all urge him to take power and bring order to the city.

Alone with Irene and Adriano (terzet, 'O Schwester, sprich'), Rienzi tells how he has sworn to avenge his brother, murdered by a Colonna; the motif (sometimes called the Vengeance motif) first heard here is a forerunner of the motif of reminiscence as used in the *Ring*. Adriano atones for his family's guilt by pledging himself to Rienzi; in return, he is entrusted with Irene and they sing of their love in an impassioned duet ('Ja, eine Welt voll Leiden').

A single sustained note is sounded on a trumpet (first heard at the start of the overture, it returns periodically to symbolize Rienzi's revolutionary authority). An excited crowd gathers and acclaims Rienzi as their liberator and saviour ('Gegrüsst'). Refusing the title of king, he tells them that the state should be governed by a senate; he himself will be their tribune.

ACT 2 *A great hall in the Capitol* An effulgent orchestral introduction heralds the Chorus of the Messengers of Peace: a triumphal song by the patrician youths, clad in white silk, celebrating the success of their peace mission throughout Italy. The Colonnas and Orsini, compelled to obey the law just as the plebeians do, conspire together against Rienzi. Rienzi receives the foreign ambassadors and claims for the Roman people the historic right to elect the German emperor.

A ballet, allegorizing the union of ancient and modern Rome, is performed. Orsini stabs Rienzi with a dagger, but his assassination attempt is thwarted by Rienzi's steel breastplate. Colonna's men have meanwhile attempted to seize the Capitol. Senators and people demand death for the traitors. Adriano and Irene plead for Colonna's life and Rienzi pardons the nobles. In a final ensemble Rienzi's clemency is praised by Adriano and Irene but condemned as weakness by his friends Baroncelli and Cecco; the nobles plot vengeance while the people hail their leader.

ACT 3 *The large square in the ancient forum* The nobles are preparing to attack Rienzi, who, with the battle-cry 'Santo Spirito, Cavaliere!' rouses the people to take up arms. Adriano agonizes over his divided loyalty to his father and to the brother of Irene: 'Gerechter Gott!' A grand procession of senators and armed citizens is led by Rienzi, fully armed and on horseback: the battle-cry 'Santo Spirito, Cavaliere!' is re-echoed, and there is some heavily scored military music.

Adriano begs in vain to be sent as an ambassador to his father. He tells Irene that death is calling him, but finally yields to her entreaties to stay and protect her. Irene and the women pray for victory and in due course Rienzi returns in triumph; the bodies of Orsini and Colonna are borne in on litters. Adriano curses Rienzi and vows revenge. Rienzi is borne aloft on a triumphal chariot, crowned with a laurel wreath.

ACT 4 *A square in front of the Lateran church* A series of taps on the timpani open the act in an atmosphere of mystery and conspiracy as Baroncelli, Cecco and some citizens discuss the situation. They deplore Rienzi's arrogance in interfering with the election of the German emperor: the Germans have, as a result, withdrawn their ambassador from Rome. The new emperor, moreover, is an ally of the pope, who was Colonna's protector. Cardinal Raimondo has also turned to the pope for protection. Baroncelli alleges that Rienzi sought an alliance with the nobles, offering his sister Irene in return. The crowd demands evidence of this treachery and Adriano, throwing off his disguise, endorses the charge. The conspirators vow to strike at Rienzi during the victory celebrations later that day. As they turn to go, they see a procession of priests and monks, led, to their surprise, by Raimondo; they assume they are entering the church in preparation for the celebratory *Te Deum*.

Rienzi enters in festal garb. Adriano baulks at assassinating Rienzi in view of Irene, while the other conspirators are won over by his rhetoric. Suddenly Raimondo appears on the steps of the Lateran to proclaim the excommunication of Rienzi. As his followers desert him, Adriano tries to persuade Irene to abandon him too, but she remains, in her brother's embrace.

ACT 5.i–iii *A hall in the Capitol* Rienzi prays to God for strength: 'Allmächt'ger Vater'; the music of his

1321

'Rienzi' (Wagner): painting by Baron von Leyser showing the finale of Act 2 in an 1843 Dresden production with Henriette Kriete as Adriano and Joseph Tichatschek (who had created the role at the original Dresden production in 1842) as Rienzi

Prayer draws on the dignified, eloquent main theme of the overture. Joined by Irene, he tells her that he has been deserted by everybody; she refuses to leave him for Adriano and they fondly embrace. Rienzi leaves to arm himself and Adriano enters in agitation. As the commotion outside increases, he tries to carry away Irene by force, but she pushes him away and runs out.

5.iv *A square in front of the Capitol* Deaf to Rienzi's pleas, the people, led by Baroncelli and Cecci, try to stone him. They set fire to the Capitol and Rienzi and Irene are seen on the balcony, clasped in each other's arms. Adriano and the nobles attack the people and try to reach Irene. But as he approaches, the building collapses, burying Adriano as well as Rienzi and Irene.

*   *   *

Wagner's conception of *Rienzi* was that of a grand opera, one, moreover, that 'should outdo all previous examples with sumptuous extravagance'. Deliberately planned so that it could not be given in a small theatre, *Rienzi* is generously endowed with marches, processions and ballets. The models of Italian and French grand opera are, however, more evident in Acts 1 and 2 than in the remainder of the work, written after a gap during which Wagner had begun to rethink his stylistic principles.

For further illustration *see* DRESDEN, fig.5.   BARRY MILLINGTON

Ries, Ferdinand (*b* Bonn, bap. 28 Nov 1784; *d* Frankfurt, 13 Jan 1838). German pianist and composer. After early studies with his father and with B. H. Romberg (cello) and Peter von Winter, he moved to Vienna in 1801 to study with Beethoven, a former pupil of Ries's father. Beethoven taught him the piano (Ries often acted as the composer's secretary and copyist), but sent him to Albrechtsberger for composition. Beethoven also secured him appointments as pianist to Count Browne in Baden (1802) and with Prince Lichnowsky (1805). For four years from summer 1809, Ries seems to have been constantly on tour (Kassel, Hamburg, Copenhagen, Stockholm and St Petersburg), and from 1813 to 1824 he was in London, where he was regarded as one of the finest pianists of the day (his works frequently appeared in the programmes of the Philharmonic Concerts). On his return to the Rhineland he did much for the Lower Rhine Music Festivals, writing several works and conducting for a number of years. He was appointed head of the town orchestra and the Singakademie of Aachen in 1834. He collaborated with F. G. Wegeler on one of the most important early biographies of Beethoven.

Ries was a prolific composer, especially of piano and chamber music. His most successful opera was *Die Räuberbraut* (1828, Frankfurt), given in England in 1829 by rival companies, at the Lyceum in July and Covent Garden in October, as well as in Paris, Amsterdam and various German cities. Such was the success of *Die Räuberbraut* that Ries was invited to write specially for the London stage. *The Sorceress* was judged a failure, however. According to the librettist, Edward Fitzball, the opera was 'too heavy, and too Germanic, and required, above all things, melody, without which, no opera can ever succeed, whatever merit else it may possess'.

Die Räuberbraut op.156 (3, G. Döring, after C. W. Häser), Frankfurt, 15 Oct 1828, *D-Bds**, vs (Leipzig, 1828)

The Sorceress op.164 (grand romantic op, 2, E. Fitzball), London, Adelphi, 4 Aug 1831, vs (London, 1831); in Ger. as Liska, oder Die Hexe von Gyllensteen, Cologne, 5 Feb 1832, vs (Bonn, 1831)
Die Nacht auf dem Libanon woo51, 1834 (romantische Oper, 3, C. M. Heigel), excerpts, Paris, 1837, F-Pn*
Die Zigeunerin woo53, 1835 (melodrama, 2), D-MBs*

*

LoewenbergA; StiegerO
'Memoir of Ferdinand Ries', The Harmonicon, ii (1824), 33–5
G. A. von Maltitz: Denkmal, den berühmten musikalischen Künstlern (Leipzig, 1835)
C. Hill: Ferdinand Ries: a Thematic Catalogue (Armidale, NSW, 1977)
——: Ferdinand Ries, Briefe und Dokumente (Bonn, 1982)
CECIL HILL/R

Riese, Friedrich Wilhelm. See FRIEDRICH, W.

Rieti, Vittorio (b Alexandria, Egypt, 28 Jan 1898). American composer of Italian descent. He studied with Giuseppe Frugatta in Milan and later in Rome with Ottorino Respighi. During the 1920s and 30s he was allied with the French composers known as Les Six and spent most of his time in Paris, where he composed ballet and theatre music in a neo-classical vein. After abandoning work on a dramatization of the Orfeo myth, he was invited to compose an opera for the 1934 Venice Biennale. Teresa nel bosco, to Rieti's own libretto about an unhappy woman who deserts her family to live in the wild, was badly received and disappeared after a single performance.

After moving to the USA in 1940, Rieti concentrated on symphonic and chamber music. His next opera, Don Perlimplin, was staged in Paris in May 1952. Adapted from a tragedy by García Lorca, it is distinguished by finely drawn musical characterizations and mercurial changes of atmosphere. The score is organized in traditional set pieces; the music is chromatic and rhythmically sophisticated. Stravinsky's influence is also pronounced in Viaggio di Europa, based on the myth of Europa and the bull. It was commissioned by Italian radio and broadcast in December 1954.

Rieti's subsequent three operas, all collaborations with the writer Claire Nicolas, are similarly intimate in scale but generally lighter in musical texture. The Pet Shop, first performed in 1958 by students of the Mannes College of Music, satirizes New York high society. The Clock and Maryam the Harlot are darker and more ambitious works. The former suffers from a turgid and convoluted libretto; the latter, a religious morality tale, is musically eventful but lacking in dramatic tension. Neither has been staged and, like Rieti's other operas, both remain unpublished.

Orfeo tragedia, 1928–9 (A. Poliziano), withdrawn
Teresa nel bosco (1, Rieti), Venice, Goldoni, 15 Sept 1934
Don Perlimplin (1, Rieti, after F. García Lorca), Paris, Champs-Elysées, 7 May 1952
Viaggio di Europa (radio op, 1, P. Masino), RAI, 12 Dec 1954
The Pet Shop (1, C. Nicolas), New York, Mannes College of Music, 14 April 1958
The Clock, 1959–60 (2, Nicolas), unperf.
Maryam the Harlot, 1966 (1, Nicolas), unperf.

*

A. Jacobs: Review of Don Perlimplin, Opera, iii (1952), 396–8
F. C. Ricci: Vittorio Rieti (Naples, 1987)
HARRY HASKELL

Riga (Latvian Rīga). Capital city of Latvia. After centuries of German rule, Latvia was conquered by Russia during the 18th century; however, the capital city's cultural life retained a strong German influence for the next hundred years. There were performances by touring companies during the mid-18th century, but a regular opera season did not begin until 1772, when O. H. von Vietinghoff established the Place de Parade Theatre, which for three years staged Singspiels and opéras comiques. A few operas were also given in 1778–9. Vietinghoff then constructed a new building which was inaugurated with a new opera troupe as the Riga City Theatre in 1782. Its repertory at first consisted mostly of opere buffe and Singspiels, but expanded over the next 50 years to include operas by (among others) Grétry, Monsigny, Cherubini, Mozart, Dittersdorf, Beethoven (Fidelio, 1818) and Georg Benda, who himself visited Riga in 1788 to conduct his works; visiting Russian and Polish troupes also performed there. As a result of Wagner's association with the city (he was conductor of the opera from 1837 to 1839), Riga's opera house became one of the first to set up and maintain a tradition of performing his operas. Upon Wagner's departure for Paris, Heinrich Dorn became conductor, and two of his operas had their premières there.

The Riga opera house, built in 1863 with 1240 seats, burnt down in 1882 but was rebuilt by 1887. A major production of the Ring was mounted there for Wagner's centenary, and there were frequent visits by Russian troupes. P. Jurjāns set up the first Latvian opera company in 1913. They suspended operations during World War I, but in 1919 the company became the Latvian National Opera; in 1920, two years after Latvia proclaimed its independence from Russia, the company staged the première of the first truly Latvian opera, Baņuta by Alfrēds Kalniņš (the earlier one-act Spoku stunda by Jēkabs Ozols, 1893, had been an amateurish affair). The brothers Jāzeps and Jānis Mediņš conducted there (1922–5 and 1920–28 respectively), and each wrote operas which had their premières in Riga. When the Soviet Union annexed Latvia in 1940, the theatre was renamed the State Ballet and Opera Theatre of the Latvian SSR. During the Nazi occupation (1941–4) the company continued to perform, but was gradually dispersed by emigrations to the West. After the war the Soviet state encouraged a concentration on ballet, but during the 1960s the opera company began to flourish, its repertory including Wagner and 20th-century works; the name Latvian National Opera was restored in 1990. Premières of Latvian operas since the war have included Zaļās dzirnavas ('The Green Mill') by Marģers Zariņš (1958) and Ādolfs Skulte's Princese Gundega (1971).

*

ME ('Latviyskiy Teatr Operï i Baleta'; Ya. Vitolin)
M. Rudolph: Rigaer Theater- und Tonkünstler-Lexikon (Riga, 1890)
K. Kundzin': Latishskiy teatr (Moscow, 1963)
E. Arro: 'Richard Wagners Rigaer Wanderjahre', Musik des Ostens, iii (1965), 123–68
S. Verina: 'Russkaya opera v Latvii', Ocherki muzikal'noy kul'turi Sovetskoy Latvii [Essays on the Musical Culture of Soviet Latvia], ed. L. Karklin'sh (Leningrad, 1971)
——: Muzikal'niy teatr Latvii i zarozhdeniye latishskoy natsional'noy operi [The Musical Theatre of Latvia and the Origins of Latvian National Opera] (Leningrad, 1973)
V. Briede-Bulavinova: Latviešu opera (lidz 1940 q.) (Riga, 1975)
A. Darkevics, ed.: Mūzikas dzīve padomju Latvijā [Musical Life in Soviet Latvia] (Riga, 1980)
V. Briede: Latviešu opereteātris (Riga, 1987)
ARNOLDS KLOTIŅŠ, MITCHELL MORRIS

Rigby, Jean (b Fleetwood, 22 Dec 1954). English mezzo-soprano. She studied at the Birmingham School of Music, the RAM and the National Opera Studio. After winning the ENO Young Artists competition in 1981 she joined the company the next year and made her début as Mercédès (*Carmen*). A wide range of roles followed including Britten's Lucretia in 1984; she created Eurydice in Birtwistle's *The Mask of Orpheus* (1986) and won special distinction as Penelope in *Il ritorno d'Ulisse* (1989). Her Covent Garden début was as Thibault (*Don Carlos*) in 1983, and she appeared at Glyndebourne in 1985 as Mercédès; at Zürich in 1986 she sang Cornelia in *Giulio Cesare* under Harnoncourt. Her video recordings include Dorabella, directed by Jonathan Miller, for whose *Rigoletto* production in English she sang and recorded Maddalena, and Britten's Lucretia. Her rich, velvety tone, ease of production and musical sensitivity are also heard frequently in concerts.

NOËL GOODWIN

Rigel [Riegel], **Henri-Joseph** (*b* Wertheim, 9 Feb 1741; *d* Paris, 2 May 1799). German composer active in France. His early musical education may have been furthered by Prince Löwenstein, and according to La Borde he studied with Jommelli in Stuttgart. He probably arrived in Paris early in 1767, and there, for more than a decade, he composed numerous instrumental works and earned a distinguished reputation before turning to the stage. He worked with a variety of librettists and for a number of Parisian theatres, including initially the established Comédie-Italienne and then the newer Théâtre Beaujolais, which had opened in 1784. *Le savetier et le financier* (1778) and *Blanche et Vermeille* (1781) must have been two of Rigel's most popular early stage works, since they were revived fairly regularly at the Comédie-Italienne. *Le savetier* includes a substantial overture, several extensive *airs* and a high proportion of ensembles, all evidence of Rigel's experience as an instrumental composer, although some contemporaries were of the opinion that 'even the style of the best symphonies and keyboard pieces is not always suited to vocal music' (d'Origny). There is also an interesting scene towards the end of Act 1 in which oboes, bassoons and horns (the *musiciens du château*) alternate repeatedly with the soloists accompanied by strings. *Rosanie* (1780) is based on the story of Richard the Lionheart, thus predating Grétry's version of 1784 but following the fashion for medieval subject matter; one particular *air*, 'Si jeune et tendre femelle', was claimed to have been written by Richard himself, Rigel having merely provided the accompaniment (see Charlton). In reviewing this opera, the *Mercure* wrote of Rigel: 'his style is pure; his workmanship is learned; his composition is full of ideas; his expression is true; his accompaniments well conceived, and his melodies of a fluent and graceful nature'.

first performed in Paris unless otherwise stated: printed works published in Paris

Le savetier et le financier (oc, 2, J.-B. Lourdet de Santerre, after J. de La Fontaine), Marly, 23 Oct 1778 (1782), airs (1778), ov. (1779)

Le départ des matelots (cmda, 1, ?J. Rutlidge), Comédie-Italienne (Bourgogne), 23 Nov 1778

Cora et Alonzo (grand opéra, 4, P.-U. Dubuisson), commissioned by Opéra, 1779, unperf.

Rosanie (comédie lyrique, 3, A.-M.-D. Devismes), Comédie-Italienne (Bourgogne), 24 July 1780, excerpts (1780); rev. as Azélie, Monsieur, 4 July 1790, *F-Mc*, excerpts (n.d.)

Blanche et Vermeille (comédie pastorale, 2, J.-P. Florian), Comédie-Italienne (Bourgogne), 5 March 1781; rev. (2), 26 May 1781 (1781); rev. (1), 26 March 1782, excerpts (n.d.)

L'automate (cmda, 1, Cuinet-Dorbeil), Comédie-Italienne (Bourgogne), 20 Aug 1781

Ariane fille de Minos (comédie mêlée de couplets, 1, L. H. Dancourt), Beaujolais, 1784

Les amours du Gros-Caillou (oc, 1, C.-J. Guillemain), Beaujolais, 10 April 1786

Aline et Zamorin, ou L'amour turc [also listed as Atine et Zamorin] (opéra bouffon, 3, Dancourt), Beaujolais, 26 Sept 1786, excerpts (n.d.)

L'entrée du seigneur (oc, 1, Lebas), Beaujolais, 21 Oct 1786

Lucas et Babet, ou La veillée (oc, 1, ? J.-L. Gabiot de Salins), Beaujolais, 15 June 1787, *Pc**

Alix de Beaucaire (drame lyrique, 3, M.-J. Boutillier), commissioned by Comédie-Italienne, 1787, perf. Montansier, 10 Nov 1791, *Mc*, *Pc**

Estelle et Némorin (mélodrame pastoral, 2, Gabiot de Salins, after Florian), Ambigu-Comique, 25 June 1788 (1788)

Le bon fermier (cmda, 1, ?E. J. B. Delrieu or Gabiot de Salins), Beaujolais, 18 May 1789, *Pc**

Pauline et Henri (cmda, 1, Boutillier), Feydeau, 9 Nov 1793, *Pc*; as Edmond et Caroline, *Pc**

Le magot de la Chine (opéra bouffon, 1, Dancourt), Ambigu-Comique, 6 Aug 1800 [posth.]

*

Mercure de France (Aug 1780), 43–7

J. B. de La Borde: *Essai sur la musique ancienne et moderne* (Paris, 1780)

A. d'Origny: *Annales du théâtre italien depuis son origine jusqu'à ce jour* (Paris, 1788)

Correspondance littéraire, philosophique et critique par Grimm, Diderot, Raynal, Meister, etc., ed. M. Tourneux (Paris, 1877–82)

L. Péricaud: *Théâtre des Petits Comédies de S.A.S. Monseigneur le Comte de Beaujolais* (Paris, 1909)

D. Charlton: *Grétry and the Growth of Opéra-Comique* (Cambridge, 1986), 230–31

ELISABETH COOK (text), MICHEL NOIRAY (work-list)

Righenzi [Righensi], **Carlo** (*b* ?Verona, *fl* 1648–67). Italian tenor and librettist. The earliest reference to him dates from 1648, when he signed the dedication of Cavalli's *La virtù de' strali d'Amore* at Bologna and perhaps sang in Cavalli's *Egisto* at Ferrara. Between 1657 and 1663 he sang in Florence in several operas by Jacopo Melani: Desso in *Il podestà di Colognole* (1657), Flavio in *Il pazzo per forza* (1658), Sifone in *Ercole in Tebe* (1661), and *Amor vuol inganno* (in preparation in 1663 and then suspended). Also at Florence he sang in *La serva nobile* (1660), probably by Domenico Anglesi, and *Erismena* (1661), possibly by Cavalli. During the same years he signed the dedications to some operas in Florence and Milan. The librettos of *Crispo* (1663) and *La farsa musicale* (1664), both of which were performed in Milan with music by the Abate F. Rossi of Bari, are also attributed to him. With *La farsa musicale* Righenzi transferred to northern Italy the fashion for comedy with the comic use of dialect that had been tried in Tuscany. In 1665 he was responsible for performances of Cavalli's *Xerse* in Milan and then Verona after making alterations to Minato's text, enlarging the part of Elviro, which he himself took in the Verona production. The same version of *Xerse* was performed in Turin in 1667. Righenzi was remembered for his acting ability and as a specialist in comic roles.

*

F. S. Quadrio: *Della storia e della ragione d'ogni poesia* (Bologna, 1739–52)

H. S. Powers: 'Il Serse trasformato', *MQ*, xlvii (1961), 481–92

M. Viale Ferrero: 'Repliche a Torino di alcuni melodrammi veneziani e loro caratteristiche', *Venezia e il melodramma nel seicento: Venice 1972*, 145–72

C. B. Schmidt: 'An Episode in the History of Venetian Opera: the Tito Commission', *JAMS*, xxxi (1978), 442–66

F. Piperno: 'Il sistema produttivo, fino al 1780', *SOI*, iv (1987), 1–75

P. Fabbri: *Il secolo cantante: per una storia del libretto d'opera nel seicento* (Bologna, 1990)

PAOLA BESUTTI

Design by Pietro Righini for the entrance to Neptune's temple in Vinci's tournament 'Le nozze di Nettuno l'equestre con Anfitrite' at the Teatro Farnese, Parma, 1728: engraving by Jacopo Vezzani

Righetti [Giorgi-Righetti, Righetti-Giorgi], **Geltrude** (*b* Bologna, 1793; *d* Bologna, 1862). Italian contralto. She studied in Bologna and gave her first public performance there in 1814. In September 1815 she was invited by the Duke of Sforza Cesarini to sing, at the express wish of Rossini, in the première of *Il barbiere di Siviglia* (1816, Teatro Argentina, Rome). In 1817 she created the title role in *La Cenerentola* at the Teatro Valle in Rome. During her brief career, she was appreciated for her coloratura singing, her range extending from *f* to *bb"*. She retired from the stage, probably for health reasons, in 1822. Her *Cenni d'una donna già cantante sopra il Maestro Rossini ...* (Bologna, 1823), a reply to an article by Stendhal published under a pseudonym in the *Revue mensuelle de Paris* (1822), gives an interesting account of the première of *Il barbiere di Siviglia*.

*

A. Cametti: *La musica teatrale a Roma cento anni fa* (Rome, 1916)
BRUNO CAGLI

Righini, Pietro (*b* Parma, 2 Aug 1683; *d* Parma, 20 Dec 1742). Italian stage designer. He began his career in Parma, perhaps under the direction of Ferdinando Galli-Bibiena whom he succeeded in 1727 as theatre architect to the Duke of Parma. By 1717 his fame was such that he was called to Milan to design the scenery for Francesco Gasparini's *Costantino*, the inaugural work at the Regio Ducal Teatro. He also worked in Milan in the following season, and returned there in 1734 and 1735. There is evidence of intense activity between 1719 and 1737, mostly in northern Italy. In Turin he designed the scenery for *Artenice* (the alternative title of G. M. Orlandini's *Ormisda*, with additions by G. A. Giai, 26 December 1722), for the inauguration of the Teatro Regio, which had been rebuilt by Filippo Juvarra. He returned there for the carnival seasons of 1730, 1732 and 1737. At the Teatro S Agostino in Genoa he worked with Giuseppe Palmieri on P. G.

Sandoni's *Adriano in Siria* (Carnival 1734). Among his many productions in Parma, of particular interest were those for the marriage of Antonio Farnese in spring 1728 (Vinci's *Medo* at the Teatro Ducale and the tournament *Le nozze di Nettuno l'equestre con Anfitrite* at the Teatro Farnese) and other festive occasions (*La venuta d'Ascanio in Italia*, Teatro Farnese, October 1732). He also worked in Reggio Emilia and Piacenza; and sometime between 1729 and 1735 he visited Vienna. In 1737 he was summoned to Naples as designer for the inaugural production at the Teatro S Carlo, D. N. Sarro's *Achille in Sciro*, and he provided scenery for Naples until 1740, when he was succeeded by his pupil and collaborator Vincenzo Re.

Only a few scene drawings attributed to Righini survive, but engravings by Jacopo Vezzani reproduce the settings for *Le nozze di Nettuno* (see illustration) and *Medo* in Parma (the *Medo* scenes were also engraved later by Martin Engelbrecht); and there is an engraving of Sarro's *Nozze di Peleo e Teti* (Naples, Real Palazzo, December 1739).

Righini's early training with Bibiena was enriched by other contacts, in particular with Juvarra: the scenery for *Artenice* and A. S. Fiorè's *Trionfo della Fedeltà* at the Teatro Regio, Turin, was executed by Righini to designs by Juvarra (Turin, Musei Civici). These experiences led him to develop his own ideas on scenic space, based on the variety of possible viewing points and on virtuoso illusionist effects. His work was admired by intellectuals such as C. I. Frugoni and F. S. Quadrio, and had an important influence on other designers: some of his compositional plans were used again by Re, Fabrizio Galliari, G. P. Gaspari and G. M. Quaglio.

*

F. S. Quadrio: *Della storia e della ragione d'ogni poesia*, iii (Milan, 1744), 425–563
H. Tintelnot: *Barocktheater und Barocke Kunst* (Berlin, 1939)

M. Viale Ferrero: 'Scene e scenografi del '700', *Tempi e aspetti della scenografia* (Turin, 1954), 65–121, 243

F. Mancini: *Scenografia napoletana dell'età barocca* (Naples, 1964)

F. Mancini and M. T. Muraro: 'Pietro Righini: il modello replicato', *Illusione e pratica teatrale*, (Venice, 1975), 102–8 [exhibition catalogue]

D. Lenzi and M. Pigozzi: 'Pietro Righini', *L'arte del settecento emiliano: architettura, scenografia, pittura di paesaggio* (Bologna, 1980), 189–91 [exhibition catalogue]

M. Viale Ferrero: *Storia del Teatro Regio di Torino*, iii: *La scenografia dalle origini al 1936* (Turin, 1980)

G. Botti: 'Il "Medo" di Pietro Righini: lo spettacolo fra tradizione bibienesca e scena-quadro', *Civiltà teatrale e settecento emiliano: Reggio Emilia 1985*, 223–38

F. Mancini: *Il Teatro di S Carlo 1737–1987*, iii: *Le scene, i costumi* (Naples, 1987)
MERCEDES VIALE FERRERO

Righini, Vincenzo (*b* Bologna, 22 Jan 1756; *d* Bologna, 19 Aug 1812). Italian composer, singing teacher and conductor. Because of his excellent voice he was soon made a choirboy at S Petronio in Bologna. According to his obituary in the *Allgemeine musikalische Zeitung*, he sang too much, so that his voice became somewhat husky and dull, and it is true that in later years he had little success as a singer. He is sometimes said to have been a composition pupil of Martini, but this was doubted even in his obituary. He certainly did not have singing lessons from Bernacchi (*d* 1756), but he was trained in the Bologna school of singing, which Bernacchi had raised to its greatest heights. In 1775 Righini made his début as a tenor in Parma and in 1776 joined the Bustelli opera troupe in Prague, for which he wrote his first stage music – arias, scenes and whole operas. *Il convitato di pietra* (1776), his first opera, was successful and in the next few years was performed in Vienna (in both Italian and German), Eszterháza (through Haydn), Brunswick and Hanover. In 1780 Emperor Joseph II called him to Vienna to be singing master to Princess Elisabeth of Württemberg and director of the Italian Opera. In Vienna – and later in Berlin – Righini was a singing teacher much sought after by society, but he also trained a large number of professional singers. His *Exercices pour se perfectionner dans l'art du chant* (Paris, n.d.) were called by Gerber 'undoubtedly the most beautiful solfeggios we have' and were also highly praised by Reichardt. His Viennese operas show his thorough knowledge not only of the voice but also (as in the echo aria for coloratura soprano and clarinet in *Armida*) of instrumentation. In 1787 Righini became the first Italian to be appointed Kapellmeister at the electoral court in Mainz. His first important undertaking in this post was a performance of *Armida*, probably revised for the occasion, in Aschaffenburg (1788). Also in 1788 he married the contralto Anna Maria Lehritter (1762–93). Among the significant works of this period were the *azione teatrale Alcide al bivio* (1790), written for the Elector of Trier (Righini's correspondence with the Elector reveals his attempts to increase the proportion of duets, trios, quartets and other ensemble pieces in the work), an oratorio and the *Missa solemnis* op.59. In 1793 Righini was appointed successor to Alessandri as court Kapellmeister and director of the Italian Opera in Berlin, alongside Reichardt, who was succeeded in 1794 by Himmel. Also in 1793 he composed *Arianna* for the wedding of the future King Friedrich Wilhelm III. He worked hard for the advancement of Italian opera in Berlin; a number of excellent singers were at his disposal, among them the bass Ludwig Fischer, who as a pupil of Raaff had been trained in the Bologna school of singing. Righini's decisive effect on the development and cultivation of the bass aria resulted from his collaboration with Fischer.

In contemporary accounts Righini is described as a straightforward, unpretentious and likeable person who enjoyed general respect, so that on the death of Friedrich Wilhelm II in 1797 he was able to keep his post. In 1798 he visited Hamburg, where his second wife, the singer Henriette Kneisel (1767–1801) was engaged; he had married her in 1793 and was to divorce her in 1800. His activities in the years 1802–5 are not entirely clear. Reichardt (in the *Berliner musikalische Zeitung*, ii, 1806, p.100) stated that Righini composed his *La selva incantata* shortly before a journey to Italy and that because of an illness he was unable to conduct or hear it when it was first performed in January 1803. The following month the *Allgemeine musikalische Zeitung* reported that he was dangerously ill but did not say where he was at the time. In 1804 he visited Leipzig, Hamburg and Vienna, the last probably on a second journey to Italy, during which he was at Bologna, Venice and Naples. He returned to Berlin with the singer Brizzi in November 1805. In 1806, following the outbreak of war, the Italian Opera was disbanded, but Righini remained in Berlin, and when the royal theatre was reorganized in 1811, he was by general consent appointed Kapellmeister, along with B. A. Weber. His last major work was a *Te Deum* for the return of the king and queen to Berlin in 1810. The unexpected death of his only son in 1810 is supposed to have brought on his fatal illness; in 1812 he went to Italy and died after an operation in Bologna.

The Berlin operas represent the peak of Righini's work; their direction is already apparent in *Enea nel Lazio* (1793), which is defined as being 'con cori e balli analoghi'. The criticism that he sacrificed the dramatic concept by expanding the ballets misses the point: it is precisely in these ballets that he broke free from the traditional musical language and turned to a more dramatic expression. Criticism has also been levelled – and rightly – at Filistri's librettos, but as Filistri was court poet and (from 1797) also Intendant of the royal theatres and had, through the Countess Lichtenau, considerable influence on the king, Righini was in no sense free in his choice of librettist. In spite of his limitations and of unfavourable comparisons – with Mozart, for example – Righini's operas were famous in their time and were praised for the way in which they combined expressive, authentically Italian vocal writing with German craftsmanship, but above all for their instrumentation, as in the 'sublime' horn, bassoon and cello trio in *Tigrane* (*AMZ*, iii, 1800, col.620). Gerber warmly remembered *Atalante*, with its 'sublime music', and the author of Righini's obituary (in *AMZ*) rightly stated that although his operas were really concert music, the best parts of them were among the most splendid music ever written for the voice. A thorough evaluation of Righini's work is still lacking, especially of his numerous songs and instrumental pieces, also popular in their day. In these the composer by no means followed the usual paths, as his songs with variations prove.

Il convitato di pietra, ossia Il dissoluto punito [Don Giovanni] (dramma tragicomico, 3, N. Porta), Prague, 1776, *H-Bn* (with addns by J. Haydn); as Das steinerne Gastmahl, oder Der Ruchlose, Vienna, 1777

La bottega del cafè (commedia giocosa, 2, C. Goldoni), Prague, 1778, *Bn* (with addns by Haydn)

La vedova scaltra (dg, 2, Goldoni), Prague, 1778, *Bn* (with addns by Haydn)

Armida (dramma, 2, M. Coltellini, after T. Tasso: *Gerusalemme liberata*), Vienna, 1782; rev. as La Gerusalemme liberata, ossia Armida al campo de' franchi (A. Filistri de Caramandani), Berlin, 1799; *D-Bds, DS, GB-Lbl, I-Fc*, vs (Bonn and Leipzig, *c*1799)

L'incontro inaspettato (dg, 3, Porta), Vienna, 1785, *D-Bds, H-Bn* (with addns by Haydn); as Die unvermutete Zusammenkunft, Berlin, 1793

Il Demogorgone, ovvero Il filosofo confuso (ob, 2, L. da Ponte, after Brunati), Vienna, 12 July 1786, *D-Bds*, Act 2 *F-Pn*

Antigono (dramma serio, Coltellini), Mainz, 1788, aria *I-Mc*

Alcide al bivio (azione teatrale, 1, P. Metastasio), Koblenz, 1790; rev. as cantata, Vienna, 1804; *Bc**, copy *A-Wgm*

Enea nel Lazio (dramma eroi-tragico, 3, Filistri), Berlin, 1793, *Wgm, D-Bds, DS, GB-Lbl*, vs (Leipzig, n.d.)

Il trionfo d'Arianna (dramma, 3, Filistri), Berlin, 1793, *D-Bds*, Act 2 *Hs*

Atalante e Meleagro (festa teatrale, 1, Filistri), Berlin, 1797, *Bds, Hs*

Tigrane (dramma eroico, 3), Berlin, 1800, ballets *Bds, DS*, excerpts (Leipzig, n.d.)

La selva incantata (Filistri, after Tasso: *Gerusalemme liberata*), Berlin, 1803, *Bds, DS, Hs, I-Fc*, vs (Leipzig, ?1803); as Der Zauberwald, Berlin, 1811

Music in: Vasco di Gama, 1792

ES (G. Tintori and W. Bollert); *MGG* (H. Engel)

Obituary, *AMZ*, xiv (1812), col.687

C. von Ledebur: *Tonkünstler-Lexikon Berlins* (Berlin, 1861)

H. Mendel and A. Reissmann: *Musikalisches Conversations-Lexikon* (Berlin, 1877)

A. Weissmann: *Berlin als Musikstadt* (Berlin and Leipzig, 1911)

A. Gottron: *Tausend Jahre Musik in Mainz* (Berlin, 1941)

H. Fetting: *Die Geschichte der deutschen Staatsoper* (Berlin, 1955)

A. Gottron: *Mainzer Musikgeschichte von 1500–1800* (Mainz, 1959)

D. Bartha and L. Somfai: *Haydn als Opernkapellmeister* (Budapest and Mainz, 1960)

J. Harich: 'Das Repertoire des Opernkapellmeisters Joseph Haydn in Esterháza (1780–1790)', *HayJb 1962*, 9–110

G. Bereths: *Die Musikpflege am Kurtrierischen Hofe zu Koblenz-Ehrenbreitstein* (Mainz, 1964)

H. Federhofer: 'Vincenzo Righinis Opera Alcide al bivio', *Essays Presented to Egon Wellesz* (Oxford, 1966), 130–44

O. Michtner: *Das alte Burgtheater als Opernbühne* (Vienna, 1970)

S. Kunze: *Don Giovanni vor Mozart: die Tradition der Don Giovanni-Opern im italienischen Buffo-Theater des 18. Jahrhunderts* (Munich, 1972)   GUDRUN BECKER-WEIDMANN

Rigoletto. *Melodramma* in three acts by GIUSEPPE VERDI to a libretto by FRANCESCO MARIA PIAVE after VICTOR HUGO's play *Le roi s'amuse*; Venice, Teatro La Fenice, 11 March 1851.

The Duke of Mantua	tenor
Rigoletto *his court jester*	baritone
Gilda *Rigoletto's daughter*	soprano
Sparafucile *a hired assassin*	bass
Maddalena *his sister*	contralto
Giovanna *Gilda's duenna*	soprano
Count Monterone	bass
Marullo *a nobleman*	baritone
Borsa *a courtier*	tenor
Count Ceprano	bass
Countess Ceprano	mezzo-soprano
Court Usher	bass
Page	mezzo-soprano

Noblemen

Walk-on parts Ladies, pages, halberdiers

Setting In and around Mantua during the 16th century

Verdi first mentioned the idea of setting a version of Victor Hugo's drama as early as September 1849, with Salvadore Cammarano to be the librettist; but it was a contract with La Fenice, Venice, signed in April 1850, that eventually brought the opera into being. Perhaps encouraged by the presence in Venice of the accomplished baritone Felice Varesi (who had created the title role of *Macbeth* in 1847), Verdi suggested to Piave, the resident poet at La Fenice, that they adapt Hugo's *Le roi s'amuse*, 'one of the greatest creations of the modern theatre'. He had fears that there might be problems with the censor, but Piave – after seeking advice in Venice – managed to reassure him and the plan went ahead under the working title of *La maledizione*. By summer 1850, however, signs from Venice over the suitability of the subject were not encouraging. Verdi insisted on continuing, saying that he had now found the 'tinta musicale' of the subject and so could not turn back.

By early October 1850 the cast for the première had been fixed and Piave had submitted a draft libretto. Verdi, still involved with *Stiffelio* at Trieste, had little time to begin composition in earnest and probably did not start drafting the score until late November. However, soon after that, the Venetian police censors intervened: calling attention to the 'disgusting immorality and obscene triviality' of the libretto, they imposed an absolute ban on its performance in Venice. Verdi was enraged, blamed Piave and, refusing to consider writing a fresh opera, offered La Fenice *Stiffelio* instead. Piave hastened to make an acceptable adaptation, entitled *Il duca di Vendome*, which accommodated the censor's objections and was officially approved on 9 December. But Verdi remained steadfast. In a long letter of 14 December, he went into great detail about the dramatic essentials of the subject, insisting (among many aspects that *Il duca di Vendome* had obscured or excised) that the principal tenor retain absolute power over his subjects, and that Triboletto (as the protagonist was then called) remain a hunchback. By the end of the month, a compromise had been reached with the authorities at La Fenice – one which in effect allowed Verdi to retain what he considered dramatically essential – and, soon after, the opera acquired a new title, *Rigoletto*.

Verdi spent the first six weeks of 1851 busy with his score, and arrived in Venice in mid-February to begin piano rehearsals with the principals and to complete the orchestration. The première, with a cast that included Raffaele Mirate (Duke), Felice Varesi (Rigoletto; for illustration *see* VARESI, FELICE) and Teresa Brambilla (Gilda), was an enormous success, and the opera, in spite of continuing problems with local censors, almost immediately became part of the basic repertory, being performed more than 250 times in its first ten years. *Rigoletto* has never lost this position and remains one of the most frequently performed operas in the international repertory.

The prelude, as was to become common in mature Verdi, is a kind of synopsis of the opera's dramatic essentials. The brass, led by solo trumpet and trombone, intone a restrained motif later to be associated with the curse placed on Rigoletto; this builds in intensity and eventually explodes into a passionate sobbing figure for full orchestra; the figure peters out, the brass motif returns, and simple cadences effect a solemn close.

1. 'Rigoletto' (Verdi): design by Giuseppe and Pietro Bertoja for Act 1 scene ii (the most deserted corner of a blind alley) of the original production at La Fenice, Venice, 11 March 1851

ACT 1.i *A magnificent hall in the ducal palace* The opening scene begins with a lengthy sequence of dance tunes played by an offstage band, over which the Duke and his courtiers converse casually. The Duke has seen a mysterious young woman in church and is determined to pursue her. To drive home his libertine character, he sings a lively two-verse ballad in praise of women, 'Questa o quella'. The Duke then turns his attention to Countess Ceprano, courting her to the accompaniment of a graceful minuet, before Rigoletto enters to mock the unfortunate Count Ceprano. To a reprise of the opening dance sequence, two conversations take place: Marullo tells the courtiers that Rigoletto has been seen with a mistress; and Rigoletto advises the Duke to banish or even execute Ceprano. The ensuing ensemble (Ceprano and others muttering vengeance against Rigoletto) is interrupted by Monterone, come to upbraid the Duke for dishonouring his daughter. Rigoletto's sarcastic reply brings down on him Monterone's terrifying anathema; the scene ends in a further ensemble, with Rigoletto visibly shaken by the old man's curse. This opening sequence is clearly based on the traditional *introduzione* format, but with the difference that it boasts an unprecedented level of musical variety: from the brash *banda* dances, to the Duke's light, comic-opera ballad, to the elegant minuet, to Rigoletto's grotesque musical parodies, to Monterone's high drama and the stunned reaction it provokes. But there are also connecting devices (for example the descending melodic motif that opens the dance sequence) and a superb sense of dramatic economy; these serve to bind the episode together, making it one of the richest and most complex opening scenes hitherto attempted in 19th-century Italian opera.

1.ii *The most deserted corner of a blind alley* Rigoletto, returning home, meets the hired assassin Sparafucile, who offers his services. Rigoletto questions him but eventually sends him away. This brief duet, which is preceded by Rigoletto's intoned reminiscence of Monterone's curse, 'Quel vecchio maledivami!', bears no relation to the formal norms of Italian opera. It is in a single movement, and the primary continuity is supplied by an orchestral melody played on

solo cello and bass. Over this, the voices converse with the greatest naturalness, indeed with a restraint that belies the violence of the subject matter. The effect is calm, sinister and seductive: a necessary pause after the preceding hectic activity, but one that adds an important new colour to the dramatic ambience.

Rigoletto reaches his house and offers the first of his long, freely structured soliloquies, 'Pari siamo', in which the contrasting aspects of his personality are tellingly explored within the flexibility of recitative but with the potential emotional charge of aria. The ensuing duet with Gilda returns us to the formal world of early 19th-century opera, with a conventional four-movement sequence. An opening movement dominated by a syncopated violin melody gives way to 'Deh non parlare al misero', in which Rigoletto's increasingly agonized reminiscences of Gilda's mother are answered by his daughter's broken semiquavers and sobbing appoggiaturas. The *tempo di mezzo* transition section, as will happen increasingly in later Verdi, also develops lyrical ideas, notably 'Culto, famiglia, patria', in which Rigoletto tells Gilda that she is everything to him. But Gilda wishes for freedom to leave the house. Rigoletto, horrified, calls Giovanna and, in the cabaletta 'Ah! veglia, o donna', enjoins her to watch carefully over her charge. This final movement has none of the driving energy of the early Verdian cabaletta, being far more reminiscent of the relaxed, Donizettian type. But there is room for a remarkable intrusion of stage action: having reached the reprise of the main melody, Rigoletto breaks off, hearing a noise outside; as he goes to investigate, the Duke slips in unnoticed. The cabaletta then continues, but with a hidden presence that will lead the action forward.

Left alone with Giovanna, Gilda muses on the young man she has seen at church, hoping that he is poor and of common blood. The Duke emerges from his hiding place to declare his love and so initiate a further four-movement duet, though one much reduced in scope and duration in comparison with the preceding number. After a hectic dialogue movement in which Gilda begs him to leave, the Duke declares his love in a simple 3/8 Andante, 'È il sol dell'anima', at the end of which he is joined by Gilda in an elaborate double cadenza. In a brief connecting movement he declares himself to be 'Gualtier Maldè', a poor student; Ceprano and Borsa appear in the street outside and Giovanna warns the lovers to part. The cabaletta of farewell, 'Addio ... speranza ed anima', is extremely condensed, with the principals sharing the exposition of melodic material.

Gilda, again left alone, muses on her lover's name in the famous aria 'Caro nome'. The opening melodic phrases, as befits the character, are of extreme simplicity, but the aria develops in a highly unusual manner, as a contrasting series of strictly controlled ornamental variants, quite unlike the 'open'-structured ornamental arias of the previous generation. The aria is further held together by its delicately distinctive orchestration, in which solo woodwind play an important part. As the opening melody returns in a coda-like ending, Marullo, Ceprano, Borsa and other courtiers again appear outside and can be heard preparing Gilda's abduction.

Rigoletto returns to the scene, and briefly recalls Monterone's curse before Marullo tells him that they are planning to abduct Countess Ceprano, who lives nearby. While fitting Rigoletto with a mask, Marullo succeeds in blindfolding him. The courtiers sing a conspiratorial chorus, 'Zitti, zitti', mostly *pianissimo* but full of explosive accents. Rigoletto holds a ladder as the courtiers emerge with Gilda, her mouth stopped by a handkerchief. He does not hear her cries for help, but soon tires of holding the ladder and takes off the mask to find his house open and Gilda's scarf lying in the street. To an inexorable orchestral crescendo he drags Giovanna from the house but is unable to speak except once more to recall Monterone's curse, 'Ah! ah! ah! ... la maledizione!'

ACT 2 *A hall in the Duke's Palace* First comes a Scena ed Aria for the Duke, in the conventional mode and a necessary close focus on a character who will see no more of the action during Act 2. 'Ella mi fu rapita!' ('She was stolen from me!'), he cries, and in a lyrical Adagio pours out his feelings at the presumed loss of Gilda. 'Parmi veder le lagrime' is formally structured along familiar lines, but is intricately worked, proving not for the first or the last time that formal conventionality in no sense blunted Verdi's musical or dramatic skills. The courtiers enter to announce in a jaunty narrative that they have duped Rigoletto and have his 'mistress' (actually of course Gilda) nearby, a change of perspective that immediately allows the Duke to launch into a cabaletta of joy and expectation, 'Possente amor mi chiama'. This aria's rather backward-looking melodic and orchestral brashness causes it often to be cut in performance, although doing so unbalances both the scene and the characterization of the Duke, who needs the somewhat vulgar catharsis of this moment to be fully convincing in his Act 3 persona.

The Duke leaves to take advantage of Gilda and Rigoletto enters for a very different kind of Scena ed Aria. Affecting indifference before the courtiers, he mixes a nonchalant, public 'la ra, la ra' – though one in which the 'sobbing' appoggiaturas are all too apparent – with stifled asides as he searches for his daughter. The innocent questions of a page eventually reveal to him that Gilda is with the Duke, and against the background of a string figure of gathering intensity he reveals that Gilda is his daughter and demands access to her. The courtiers block his way, and in frustration he unleashes

a remarkable aria. 'Cortigiani, vil razza dannata', unclassifiable in conventional formal terms, is in three distinct parts, each marking a stage in Rigoletto's psychological progress. First, against an obsessively repeated string figure, he rails against the courtiers with fierce declamatory force, concentrating almost exclusively on the range from a 3rd above to a 3rd below middle C. Then comes fragmentation, a breaking of the accompaniment rhythm, and of the voice: a frightening disintegration. And finally, the third stage, Rigoletto gains a new dignity and continuity: aided by a solo cello and english horn he asks pity for a father's sorrow.

Gilda enters and throws herself into her father's arms, and so begins yet another four-movement duet. Rigoletto solemnly dismisses the courtiers and bids her tell her story. 'Tutte le feste al tempio', unlike the parallel lyrical duet movements of Act 1, is begun by Gilda: it is she who now achieves a new status from the circumstances that have befallen her. And as with Rigoletto's previous monologue, the duet moves through strongly contrasting sections, from her opening narration, a kind of duet with solo oboe, to Rigoletto's obsessively fixed response, and finally to another clarifying third stage, in which Rigoletto bids his daughter weep and in which she joins him with a completely new kind of vocal ornamentation, only superficially resembling that found in Act 1. Monterone passes by on his way to prison, and this time Rigoletto assures him that he will have vengeance. Staring at a portrait of the Duke, the jester joins with his daughter in a cabaletta, 'Sì, vendetta, tremenda vendetta', that brings the act to a close.

ACT 3 *A deserted bank of the River Mincio* An orchestral prelude, in Verdi's severe, 'academic' vein, leads to a brief exchange between Rigoletto and Gilda. Time has passed, but Gilda still loves the Duke. Rigoletto, promising to show her the true man, has her gaze into Sparafucile's house through a chink in the wall. The Duke appears, asks loudly for wine and the woman of the house, and breaks into a song in praise of women's fickleness. 'La donna è mobile' is certainly the best-known music in the score, perhaps unfortunately, as its brashness and simplicity make their full effect only in the surrounding gloomy context. The Duke's song dies away, to be followed by the famous quartet. Its first half, 'Un dì, se ben rammentomi', is dominated by a violin melody that carries reminiscences of earlier material (in particular Gilda's 'Caro nome'), over which the Duke and Maddalena converse lightheartedly. Then comes the main lyrical portion, 'Bella figlia dell'amore', in which Rigoletto and Gilda join them in a static portrayal of contrasting emotional states. The dramatic aptness of this section is made especially powerful by the manner in which the three principals involved all offer a kind of digest of their vocal characters elsewhere in the opera: the Duke (who carries the main melodic thread) ardent and lyrical, Gilda overcome with appoggiatura 'sobbing', Rigoletto declamatory and unmoving.

A storm is gathering, and over fragmentary bursts of orchestral colour Sparafucile and Rigoletto agree on a price for the murder of the Duke. Rigoletto will return at midnight to throw the body in the river. The hunchback retires and the Duke is conducted to a room, there dreamily recalling 'La donna è mobile' before falling asleep. As the storm gathers force, Maddalena tries to persuade Sparafucile to spare the Duke. Professional honour forbids that he kill Rigoletto instead, but he

2. *Title-page of the first edition of the vocal score of Verdi's 'Rigoletto' (Milan: Ricordi, 1851), with a vignette showing the opening scene of Act 3; the costumes are identical with those in Ricordi's published 'figurini' for the opera*

agrees that, if another should come along before the time allotted, a substitution can be made. Gilda over-hears this and, in a trio characterized by its relentless rhythmic drive ('Se pria ch'abbia il mezzo'), decides to sacrifice herself. She enters the house, and a terrifying orchestral storm depicts the gruesome events that occur within.

The final scene shows great economy of means. The storm recedes as Rigoletto reappears to claim the body, which has been placed in a sack for easy disposal. He is about to dispatch it when he hears the voice of the Duke, again singing 'La donna è mobile'. Horrified, he opens the sack to find Gilda, on the point of death. Their final duet, 'V'ho ingannato!', is necessarily brief, leaving time only for Gilda to look towards her arrival in heaven – with the obligatory flute arpeggios – and for Rigoletto to declaim in ever more broken lines. He recalls the curse one last time, and the curtain falls.

* * *

Rigoletto is almost always placed as the true beginning of Verdi's maturity, the essential dividing line between 'early' works and the succession of repertory pieces that will follow; and this special placing is commonly seen as exemplified in the striking formal freedom of various scenes. But thus to concentrate on such matters risks a certain distortion: most of the opera's formal innovations have been prefigured in earlier works, and many of

its most powerful sections exist unambiguously and comfortably within the formal conventions of the time. However, no earlier work is as impeccably paced as *Rigoletto*, nor does any show its overall consistency of style; and perhaps these matters are best seen as linked not so much to formal matters as to a new sense of musical characterization. With Rigoletto and Gilda in particular, Verdi managed to create musical portraits that function for the most part within the formal norms of Italian opera but that nevertheless manage to develop individually as the drama unfolds. This was as much a technical as an emotional advance; it entailed, that is, a kind of mature acceptance of conventional discourse, as well as an acutely developed perspective on precisely when it could be ignored and when exploited. Though this acceptance was to appear in various guises in the works of Verdi's maturity, it was something that rarely left the composer during the remainder of his long career.
ROGER PARKER

Rihm, Wolfgang (*b* Karlsruhe, 13 March 1953). German composer. He studied at the Musikhochschule, Karlsruhe, with Eugen Werner Velte from 1968, the year in which he completed his First Symphony, and then with Stockhausen in Cologne (1972) and Klaus Huber in Fribourg (1973). During that period he also worked with Fortner and Searle and from 1970 attended the Darmstadt summer courses, where he has taught since 1978. Though Rihm came into contact with many of the prevailing trends and styles in European music of the 1970s and 80s, he has always preserved his independence from technical dogma and avoided overt subscription to any compositional school. He has consistently advocated the pre-eminence of musical freedom; his works of the late 1980s began to reveal the influence of Nono's late phase.

Rihm's first stage works were the chamber operas *Faust und Yorick* (1977) and *Jakob Lenz* (1979), in which he adhered closely to conventional narrative theatrical devices. *Jakob Lenz* in particular has achieved notable success; it is a taut realization of Büchner's portrayal of the final decline of the poet and dramatist, conceived in an economical sequence of sharply characterized scenes and coloured by a fastidiously deployed chamber ensemble. In his two major music-theatre works of the 1980s, however, Rihm moved towards a much less linear conception of dramatic form. In *Die Hamletmaschine* (1987), Heiner Müller's text is used as the basis for a conception that blurs distinctions between opera, oratorio and symphonic form; it is a fantasy around the central Shakespearean characters Hamlet and Ophelia that also introduces Marx, Mao and Lenin. *Oedipus* (1987) contrives to offer a central narrative thread derived from Sophocles but surrounds it with material from Hölderlin, Nietzsche and Müller that glosses and comments on the myth. The dramatic apparatus is framed within a rigorous sequence of images, scenes and commentaries; in both works Rihm's wide musical range and dramatic extremes are contained within lucid formal structures.

With *Die Eroberung von Mexiko* (1992), Rihm's work for the stage reached its most satisfying synthesis of music and gesture so far. Based upon Antonin Artaud's outline scenario of the same title, it chronicles the encounters between the Spanish *conquistadores* and the Mexican people, centred upon the confrontation between Cortez and the Aztec emperor Montezuma. Cortez's lines are given to a baritone and doubled by two speakers in the orchestral pit; those for Montezuma are delivered by an onstage soprano, shadowed off stage by soprano and contralto. In its range of musical expression, use of massed choral and orchestral effects, and its sustained dramatic scheme, *Die Eroberung* appeared one of the most distinguished European operas of the 1980s and 90s.

Faust und Yorick (chamber op, 1, M. Fusten, after J. Tardieu), Mannheim, National, 29 April 1977
Jakob Lenz (chamber op, 1, M. Fröhling, after G. Büchner: *Lenz*), Hamburg, Staats, 8 March 1979
Die Hamletmaschine (music theatre, 5 pts, Rihm, after H. Müller), Mannheim, National, 25 March 1987
Oedipus (music theatre, text compiled by Rihm, after Sophocles, F. Nietzsche and Müller), Berlin, Deutsche, 4 Oct 1987
Die Eroberung von Mexico (music theatre, 4 pts, Rihm, after A. Artaud), Hamburg, Staats, 9 Feb 1992

*

D. Rexroth, ed.: *Der Komponist Wolfgang Rihm* (Frankfurt, 1985)
ANDREW CLEMENTS

Rijeka (It. Fiume). City in Croatia. The old Adamić civic theatre in Rijeka was replaced in 1885 by the Teatro Comunale (designed by Ferdinand Fellner and Hermann Helmer). It was directed by impresarios who for the most part engaged Italian companies; the operas performed were usually from the Italian bel canto repertory, but French and German works were also

staged. Prominent singers and composers were invited: Caruso appeared in *La bohème* in May 1898, and Puccini had an enthusiastic reception at a performance of *Manon Lescaut* in May 1895.

The opera was run on a basis of guest performances until 20 October 1946, when the theatre became a permanent institution with its own opera company. Since 1953 it has borne the name of the composer Ivan Zajc, who was born in Rijeka. During extensive renovations (1970–81) operas and operettas were performed on temporary stages with many guest performances. After World War II the repertory was extended to include operas by Mozart, Gluck, Richard Strauss and Croatian composers (Dobronić, Papandopulo and Vidošić). Since 1957 the opera company has participated in the summer festival in Opatija, and also performed on other open-air stages along the coastland of Croatia. Prominent conductors to have appeared in Rijeka include Boris Papandopulo, Lovro von Matačić and Berislav Klobučar.

*

Narodno kazalište 'Ivan Zajc' Rijeka 1945–1955 [The Ivan Zajc National Theatre in Rijeka, 1945–55] (Rijeka, 1955)
V. Cihlar: 'Kroz historiju riječkog kazališta' [Through the History of the Theatre in Rijeka], *Kazališni list* (Rijeka, 1961), 1–4
J. Andreis: *Music in Croatia* (Zagreb, 1974)
Narodno kazalište 'Ivan Zajc' Rijeka [The Ivan Zajc National Theatre in Rijeka] (Rijeka, 1981)
KORALJKA KOS

Riley, Dennis (*b* Los Angeles, 28 May 1943). American composer. He studied at the universities of Colorado (BM 1965), Illinois (MM 1968) and Iowa (PhD 1973), his principal composition teachers being George Crumb, Thomas Frederickson, Ben Johnston, Richard Hervig and Donald Jenni. He served as composer-in-residence in Rockford, Illinois (1965–7), and later taught at California State University, Fresno (1971–4), and Columbia University (1974–7). Among his many awards are a Fromm Foundation commission, a Guggenheim Fellowship and two NEA grants.

Riley has written two one-act operas, *Rappaccini's Daughter* (1981–4) and *Cats' Concert* (1983), neither of which has been performed. *Rappaccini's Daughter*, to a libretto by Riley and Joseph Pazillo after Nathaniel Hawthorne, concerns the love of a young student in 17th-century Padua for Dr Rappaccini's daughter, Beatrice, whose beauty resembles that of her father's poisonous flowers. The couple's love is used as an experiment by Rappaccini, whose dedication to science has led him beyond moral or humane considerations. The student becomes tainted by the poisonous flowers, and when he tries to give an antidote to Beatrice, she falls dead. The work is atonal but neo-classical in style, tonality being employed at structurally important moments. The vocal writing, though rhythmically complex, often using syncopation and mixed rhythms to approximate real speech, shows an uncanny ability to project the text. *Cats' Concert*, also to a libretto by Pazillo, is a children's opera, a pastiche of spoken dialogue with musical numbers and eclectic in style. Its modest cast requirements make it especially suitable for opera workshops and regional opera theatre.

JAMES P. CASSARO

Rimskaya-Korsakova, Yuliya Lazarevna. *See* VEYSBERG, YULIYA LAZAREVNA.

Rimsky-Korsakov, Nikolay Andreyevich (*b* Tikhvin, 6/18 March 1844; *d* Lyubensk, nr Luga, 8/21 June 1908).

Russian composer and music educator. Of his 15 operas, the largest such body of work composed expressly for the Russian musical stage, most remain in active repertory in his homeland, and one, *The Golden Cockerel*, has become an international classic. In addition, Rimsky-Korsakov was responsible for the original or standard performing editions of important works by Dargomïzhsky (*The Stone Guest*), Musorgsky (*Boris Godunov*, *Khovanshchina*) and Borodin (*Prince Igor*). Taken as a whole, Rimsky-Korsakov's has to be counted the greatest individual contribution towards the establishment of the basic Russian operatic repertory.

1. Background and first opera. 2. Opera and folk tradition. 3. A Wagnerian interlude. 4. Return to opera. 5. Traditionalist paths. 6. Return to folklore. 7. Last operas.

1. BACKGROUND AND FIRST OPERA. Rimsky-Korsakov was born into an old petty-aristocratic family, long distinguished in military and naval affairs. Educated for a career in the family tradition, he graduated as a midshipman from the College of Naval Cadets in St Petersburg in 1862 (his brother Voin, 22 years his senior, was the school's director) and embarked almost immediately on a military cruise that lasted two and a half years and took him by way of the Baltic to England, thence to both Americas and home by way of the Mediterranean.

By the time of this trip Rimsky-Korsakov, who had shown a remarkable aptitude for music at an early age, had been introduced (by his last piano teacher, Théodore Canille) to Balakirev. In characteristic fashion, Balakirev immediately put the talented but untutored 17-year-old to work on a symphony, which the boy took with him on the long voyage but did not complete (he says in his memoirs that he lost interest in music as the cruise wore on). Once back in St Petersburg, however, he again came under Balakirev's spell, joined the latter's regular circle (soon to be known as the 'Mighty Kuchka', later as The Five), and finished the symphony in time for performance on 19/31 December 1865, his public début as a composer. Over the next two years, a combination of sheer talent and Balakirev's inspiring domination got Rimsky-Korsakov (now a commissioned officer and settled into an undemanding sinecure befitting his high social rank) through the task of creating three substantial orchestral works, which established his reputation as a musician. By the end of 1868, the gifted dilettante, who by his own later confession still 'could not decently harmonize a chorale', felt ready to embark on an extremely ambitious opera. He spent the next four years writing it.

The high ideals of the Balakirev circle, Russia's 'Davidsbund' – mirroring in their way the general literary and theatrical climate of the 1860s, a period of liberalism and 'civic' aesthetics – decreed that Rimsky-Korsakov's first opera would be a serious historical drama. For subject he chose a particularly highminded specimen, Lev Mey's *Pskovityanka* ('The Maid of Pskov'), a play that explored the character of Ivan the Terrible and portrayed him (following the theories of Sergey Solov'yov, an influential liberal historian) as a clairvoyantly enlightened despot. The focus on a complex tsar-protagonist obviously parallels that of Musorgsky's exactly contemporaneous *Boris Godunov*; such parallels are many and run deep, the result not only of the two young composers' shared outlook but also of their shared bachelor quarters at the time of writing.

One scene in *The Maid of Pskov* went even further than *Boris Godunov* (in the latter's original version)

towards putting into practice the advanced ideals of dramatic realism that the Mighty Kuchka then preached. In Act 2, the Pskov republican council (the *veche*) meets to consider their options in light of Ivan's threatened invasion. Summoned by a bell, the crowd assemble piecemeal, their confusion musically conveyed by a chorus divided into five groups that parley with mounting intensity until all five are singing (shouting) at once to different words and different themes. Various speakers mount the platform to address the crowd in naturalistic recitative, the crowd responding just as naturalistically with scattered exclamations and mutterings. The end of the scene depicts the secession of a party of young mutineers, whose leader strikes up a recruitment song in mocking farewell to the cautious elders. For this Rimsky-Korsakov appropriated a folksong from Balakirev's recent anthology. The leader, following authentic folk practice, intones the first line as precentor, the gathering party answering responsorially, singing the rough harmony Balakirev had collected in the field. Against this the composer pitted anguished protests from the elders in recitative style, plus continued naturalistic ejaculations from the rest of the chorus, while the *veche* bell continues its tintinnabulations in the orchestra. The resulting montage of almost unretouched folksong, solo and choral recitative and representational orchestral effect makes for a texture that epitomized 'kuchkist' ideals, the more so for its being prompted by the original dramatic text, unmediated by any formal libretto. It was the high water mark for Russian operatic realism and Musorgsky's model for the new final scene ('Kromï') in the second version of *Boris Godunov*. That a virtually untrained composer was able to bring off this breathtaking scene was a tour de force deserving, if anything does, the cachet of genius. (Conversely, it was a project only an untrained composer, in those days, would have ventured.)

It represented, however, something from which Rimsky-Korsakov soon recoiled, with the result that although there are masterpieces among them, and although they contain veritable miracles of harmony and instrumentation, his later operas do not embody conceptions of comparable originality and brilliance. For Rimsky-Korsakov became a sort of 'classicist', concerned more with quality of realization than with conception. As the former became increasingly accomplished, the latter became increasingly conventional.

What brought about the change was a heroic feat of belated self-education, motivated in the first instance by an unexpected invitation, in 1871, to join the faculty of the St Petersburg Conservatory, the very Goliath in opposition to which the Davids of the Kuchka had defined themselves. (Rimsky finally resigned his naval commission in 1873, accepting a nominal post as Inspector of Naval Bands.) As he put in his memoirs, 'having been undeservedly accepted at the Conservatory as a professor, I soon became one of its best and possibly its very best *pupil*'. Tchaikovsky, whom he consulted at this time, wrote to his patron Mme von Meck that 'Korsakov ... is evidently undergoing a crisis now; and how this crisis will end is hard to predict. Either he will become a great master or he will finally founder in contrapuntal tricks'. He did become a great master, and he did periodically founder.

His very first project after finding his academic feet was an unsuccessful revision of *The Maid of Pskov*, in which pedant definitely had the upper hand over master. It was never performed or published, but it was symptomatic. For the rest of his life Rimsky-Korsakov was plagued with neurotic self-doubts, giving rise to an exaggerated work ethic that occasionally led him to what he recognized as 'medium, not to say mediocre' efforts, alternating with periods of creative blockage during which he kept himself in motion by his editorial work and by writing prose, including a valuable orchestration manual as well as his incomparable memoirs *Letopis' moyey muzikal'noy zhizni* ('Chronicle of my Musical Life').

2. OPERA AND FOLK TRADITION. The first new stage piece following the Conservatory appointment was *Mayskaya noch'* ('May Night'), a comic opera after Gogol (composed 1878–9). It too belonged to a genre to which Musorgsky was making a simultaneous contribution (*The Fair at Sorochintsi*), but this time the products were very dissimilar. For one thing, the spirit of Glinka hovers over Rimsky's work more tangibly than in any other opera by a composer of his generation, and it saved him from his 'contrapuntal tricks'. He had just collaborated with Balakirev on an edition of Glinka's works (which involved, among other things, scoring the stage-band music for *Ruslan and Lyudmila*). In its general approach to orchestration – that open-textured, primary-hued idiom that one instantly recognizes as Rimskian (abounding in 'leitmotivic' timbres such as the solo violin for Hanna, the ingénue) – as well as in countless telling details (the combination of piano and harp to represent the hero Levko's bandura, the Farlaf-inspired *buffo* idiom of the Village Head, the Antonida-derived sentimental romance style of the love duet, the polonaise rhythms in the Act 2 trio, the whole-tone harmonies at moments of supernatural horror), the score is a homage to the earlier master, particularly direct in the somewhat archaic but telling use of natural brass.

It was through imitating Glinka that Rimsky-Korsakov truly found himself. Mastering Glinka's extraordinary lightness freed him to wear his new-won learning in *May Night* with delightful nonchalance – for example, in the grotesque fugatos for the Head, the Distiller and the Village Clerk in the farcical second act. There are also some nice touches of parody: a village-band travesty of the *Ruslan* finale in the betrothal celebration at the end of the opera, and an echo (perhaps by now not altogether friendly) of one of Musorgsky's choruses of supplication from the prologue to *Boris Godunov* when the village bailiffs, in Act 2, plead with the Head not to send them out into the dangerous night.

To all of this Rimsky added something all his own: a deliberate cultivation of the ritual aspects of folklore as an avatar of the immemorial Slavonic agrarian religion. The grave khorovods and holiday songs for the women's chorus that form the background to the action in the framing acts are shifted to a timeless plane when they are transferred to the chorus of *rusalki*, the fabled Dnepr water nymphs. Even though the water nymph music in *May Night* is beholden to German prototypes (Weber's *Oberon* in particular), the evocative way it mirrors on a transcendental level the more obviously indigenous ritual music of the human characters strikes an intensely moving and quintessentially Rimskian chord that was to resonate in many later scores and still echoes in some of Stravinsky's 'Russian' music.

The high point of Rimsky's early allegorical manner was reached in 1881 with *Snegurochka* ('The Snow Maiden'), after Ostrovsky's springtime parable. Because of its continuous music and its intricate network of folkloristic and 'fantastic' leitmotifs, Rimsky-Korsakov's opera makes the most of the metaphorical nexus of seasonal cycle, folk ritual and human emotion to which Ostrovsky's artistically transmuted 'pantheistic' folktale gave form. The death of winter and the triumph of the sun – commemorated in the seasonal songs (*kalendarnïye pesni*) through which, as Rimsky noted, 'to this day … the ancient pagan sun-worship lives unconsciously in the people' – is symbolized by the title character's melting 'love-death', the sacrifice through which the frozen land of the Berendeyans is at last redeemed and warmed. And this, in turn, symbolizes the procreative instinct of which human love is the subjective manifestation. The delightful ambiguity is that the symbolism can be construed in either direction: human experience can be viewed as the sentient agency of the eternal cycle; or the seasonal round, and its attendant cast of fanciful characters, may be viewed as the poetically objectified metaphor of a pattern of human experience.

Either way, it is the folk ritual and its concomitant music that mediates between the realm of nature and the realm of humankind. That, rather than simplistic notions of nationalism, was the chief significance of folklore for Rimsky-Korsakov, and what makes his music, at its best, so affecting. In *The Snow Maiden*, the surface events are accompanied by a lofty panoply of seasonal songs and khorovods that cover the whole folk-agrarian calendar from Maslenitsa (the Shrovetide, marking the end of winter) to Kupala (Midsummer, the peak of the sun-god Yarilo's ascendancy), the latter reflected in the name of the character Kupava, the bride of the shepherd Lel' (the Slavonic Eros). In this way, as he had already done to a modest extent in *May Night*, Rimsky-Korsakov 'managed to connect, with a subject I adored, that ceremonial side of folklife which gives expression to the survivals from ancient paganism'.

A special glory of *The Snow Maiden* is its orchestra – 'the Glinka orchestra perfected', as the composer put it, by the use of chromatic brass. Still following Glinka's preference for bright, transparent hues, with much soloistic use of instruments as 'leit-timbres' (e.g. the Snow Maiden's flute and Lel''s clarinet), and still taking over from Glinka such tricks as the use of the piano and harp in tandem to represent the *gusli* (the Russian bardic psaltery), Rimsky managed to achieve much greater warmth and sonority without ever swamping the voices. Some of the orchestral textures – especially the ones alive with nature sounds, like The Bonny Spring's arrival in the prologue or the Snow Maiden's love-ecstasy in Act 4 – are so alluringly memorable (Ravel and Stravinsky certainly remembered them!) as to clinch Rimsky's status as the leading orchestral colourist of the 19th century.

3. A WAGNERIAN INTERLUDE. After *The Snow Maiden* came the biggest creative hiatus in Rimsky-Korsakov's career, his time filled with oppressive teaching duties at three institutions and with editorial work on the legacies of Musorgsky (*d* 1881) and Borodin (*d* 1887). When he returned to composition in 1888 it was at first to orchestral works; his trio of concert warhorses (*Sheherazade*, *Spanish Capriccio* and the *Russian Easter* overture) dates from 1887–8, the exact midpoint of his

career. They were followed by *Mlada*, a mythological opera-ballet based on an aborted project on which four of The Five (sans Balakirev) had briefly worked in 1872. Rimsky was once again attracted to the subject because of its superficial plot and atmospheric parallels with Wagner's *Ring*, first performed in St Petersburg in the season 1889–90, which fascinated Rimsky by its scoring and which he now wished to emulate. Yet however important it may have been in rousing him into operatic action, the Wagnerian fixation was a passing – or, perhaps more accurately, a sporadic – affair with Rimsky-Korsakov, who continued to hold Wagner aesthetically at arm's length; to call it 'the climacteric of Rimsky-Korsakov's creative life' (Abraham, *The New Grove Dictionary*, 1980, xvi, 30) is considerably to exaggerate its impact.

As already implied, what was chiefly Wagnerian in *Mlada* was the scoring. An immense orchestra is required, including triple wind (plus an extra flute), a pit complement of 13 chromatic brass and a stage band of 12 natural horns or tubas for the temple scenes (Acts 2 and 4), plus an assortment of exotic or specially designed instruments on stage for Cleopatra's appearance in Act 3: piccolo clarinets, *timpano piccolo*, eight to ten 'lyres' (little autoharp-like affairs set to produce a diminished 7th chord, glissando) and two sets of brass panpipes (*tsevnitsï*, tuned to play a scale derived from the same diminished 7th chord by interpolating passing notes). In place of the bright, primary-hued sonority of 'the Glinka orchestra perfected', Rimsky-Korsakov now went after the burnished Wagnerian glow, and achieved it by means of multiple doublings, dovetailed voicing, and the use of the augmented brass choir as sonorous 'cushion'.

Yet echoes of the *Ring* were only one element in Rimsky's opulently eclectic mix. The line of descent from *Ruslan and Lyudmila* remained strong, particularly in the evocation of the erotic East, virtually self-parodied in the conjuration of Cleopatra; in the figure of the Czech bard Lumir, who like Glinka's Bayan sings to an orchestrally evoked *gusli* (plus, in *Mlada*, a very high solo double bass representing the bowed *gudok*); and especially in the depiction of the fantastic characters. Like the giant Head in Glinka's opera, the parts of Chernobog and Kashchey are sung by unison choruses, and the evil goddess Morena's musical characterization virtually paraphrases that of Naina. Rimsky enthusiastically kept up his predecessor's exploration of the whole-tone scale and derivative harmonies for eerie effects, and took a significant step further: applying to the diminished 7th chord the kind of figuration applied to the augmented triad within a whole-tone context, Rimsky composed a number of striking passages on a scale of alternating whole tones and semitones (i.e. the scale to which the panpipes are tuned in Act 3; it is now called the octatonic scale). That particular side of Rimsky-Korsakov was especially influential on his younger pupils, including Stravinsky: indeed, the Kashchey music in *The Firebird* leans to the point of virtual plagiarism on the Chernobog-Kashchey episode in *Mlada*.

In *Ruslan and Lyudmila* Glinka had set another precedent: human characters were differentiated from supernatural ones by a contrast in musical style – diatonic (laced with folklore or orientalia) for the humans, chromatic for the others. The antithesis is maintained in *Mlada*, and at a rhythm Glinka never imagined. Particularly striking is the 'Kolo', the festive folkdance

at the end of Act 2, when the Shade of Mlada (a silent role, performed by a ballerina) insinuates herself into the crowd to claim her bridegroom. Each strain of the dance is broken off on an ambiguous deceptive cadence, which acts as a pivot into the voluptuous octatonic-cum-whole-tone world of the immortals. In this dance and elsewhere (e.g. the concluding mazurka-like *redowa* in Act 1), the folk prototypes, in keeping the opera's West Slavonic setting, are Czech and Polish-Ukrainian. The sacerdotal ritual in Act 4, on the other hand, is a masterpiece of neo-Russian stylization, even including a suggestion of folk polyphony.

Only a ballet (and by extension, an opera-ballet) could command the full stage resources of the crown-sponsored Mariinsky. Rimsky-Korsakov counted on a mammoth spectacle and cannily timed his music to accord with it, with the result that for all its powerful sonority, and despite its extravagant richness of colour and texture, *Mlada* makes a protracted and rather insubstantial impression in concert or recorded performance. As Rimsky-Korsakov put it himself in his autobiography, it 'suffers from an underdeveloped dramaturgy, which is an inadequate complement to its folkish and fantastic aspects'. Elsewhere he called it 'cold as ice'. Depressed by its failure (as well as by various family bereavements), he made a second revision of *The Maid of Pskov* that finally satisfied him (1891–2), and having (as he put it) 'closed accounts with the past', forswore composition altogether. He did not touch a piano or commit a note of original music to paper for more than a year.

4. RETURN TO OPERA. It was Tchaikovsky's death late in 1893 that seems to have released Rimsky-Korsakov from his 'neurasthenia' (as his doctors had diagnosed it) and brought on the relatively untroubled creative period that lasted the rest of his life, during which time he became almost exclusively a composer for the stage, completing an opera on average every 18 months.

The first of these 11 operas was based on Gogol's story *Noch' pered rozhdestvom* ('Christmas Eve'), on which Tchaikovsky had also written an opera (*Vakula the Smith*, revised as *Cherevichki*). That it amounted to an exorcism can hardly be doubted, especially since Rimsky so heavily touted the differences between his setting and Tchaikovsky's, priding himself in good old 'kuchkist' fashion on his fidelity to the literary source, for which he professed great reverence (a reverence asserted somewhat peculiarly at the very end of the opera, when the singers step out of character to sing a spirited hymn 'To the Memory of Gogol'). The words are derived wherever possible from Gogol's dialogue, and the opera is instructive from the technical point of view for the way the composer managed to write conventionally rounded musical numbers on Gogol's prose (see, in particular, Oxana's Glinkaesque coloratura aria before the mirror in Act 1).

Yet though Rimsky did not sacrifice the comic elements in the story to the love intrigue as Tchaikovsky had done, his opera departs no less significantly from Gogol – and no less characteristically. As in *May Night*, his other Gogolian opera, but far more overtly, Rimsky-Korsakov placed great emphasis on the fantastic and mythological elements, magnifying them far beyond their original importance. From Alexander Rubets's anthology of Ukrainian folk music he appropriated a whole series of Christmas songs (*kolyadki*), on which he constructed explicit parallels connecting the action of the tale with the pantheistic world of sprites and demons, symbolizing nature. (He also borrowed tunes from Rubets for more conventional purposes, including one – the Village Head's leitmotif – that Musorgsky had used in the folk recitatives of *The Fair at Sorochintsï* (see FAIR AT SOROCHINTSÏ, THE, ex.1).

The old deities Kolyada (whence *kolyadka*) and Ovsen', avatars of the sun-god at the beginning of its annual cycle, are virtual characters in *Christmas Eve*; and – as in *Mlada* with its human, 'fantastic' and 'hellish' circle dances (*kolos*) – earthly existence is mirrored in the timeless dimension by juxtaposing human and 'demonic' *kolyadki*. Most of the supernatural interpolations in *Christmas Eve* are gathered in one big balletic *divertissement* in Act 3 (an obvious echo of *Mlada*), a marvellously imagined and detailed portrayal of Vakula's flight on devil-back to St Petersburg (actually two *divertissements*, for the briefer return trip is also depicted). One orchestral detail deserves special mention: the string glissando of natural harmonics, which Stravinsky claimed to have invented in *The Firebird*.

Rimsky's next opera, *Sadko* (composed 1895–6), marked a turning-point of a rather different kind. It was excluded from the Mariinsky Theatre's repertory on the personal order of Tsar Nikolay II, who told Ivan Vsevolozhsky, Intendant of the Imperial Theatres, to 'find something a bit merrier'. By that time the crown monopoly on theatres had been eased, and Rimsky-Korsakov was able to get *Sadko* staged by the Private Opera Company, owned by the Moscow railway tycoon Savva Mamontov. Itself an opera glorifying a merchant entrepreneur, *Sadko* could not have been a more symbolic choice to inaugurate a relationship between Russia's leading opera composer and her leading entrepreneurial figure in the arts. Over a period of five years, beginning with the *Sadko* première, the Mamontov company was to introduce no fewer than six Rimsky-Korsakov operas, and also – no less important – Rimsky's versions of the operas of Musorgsky. The young Fyodor Shalyapin (who sang the Viking Trader in *Sadko* beginning in 1898) was involved in most of these productions; and it was under Mamontov's auspices that the great bass first made contact with the role of Boris Godunov, in Rimsky's version.

In terms of Rimsky-Korsakov's stylistic development, *Sadko* brought to its peak that time-honoured stylistic dichotomy established by Glinka's *Ruslan and Lyudmila*, whereby the human world is represented by diatonic and folkloristic music and the fantastic by a chromatic idiom fashioned out of virtuoso manipulations of 'artificial' scales and harmonic progressions based on them. The second scene – wherein the title character, a Novgorod minstrel whose musical idiom is founded on that of the Slavonic epics known as *bilinï*, first encounters the Sea King and his daughter, with their scales of alternating tones and semitones – has become a *locus classicus* of the technique.

5. TRADITIONALIST PATHS. At this point Rimsky-Korsakov, while not slackening his new-found creative pace, took an extended break from mythologized folklore. His next opera, the one-act *Motsart i Sal'yeri* ('Mozart and Salieri', composed 1897), was a psychological study in a declamatory style modelled on that of Dargomïzhsky, to whom the opera, both in style and by explicit dedication, was a nostalgic tribute. Then came

two quasi-historical works based, like *The Maid of Pskov*, on dramas by Lev Mey. They, too, thus seem retrospective and nostalgic. The first of them, *Boyarïnya Vera Sheloga* ('The Noblewoman Vera Sheloga', 1898), is another one-act work in declamatory style. A setting of the first act of Mey's *The Maid of Pskov*, it incorporates music from the abortive 1877 revision of Rimsky's first opera and is now usually performed as a prologue to the opera in its second, now standard, revised version. *Tsarskaya nevesta* ('The Tsar's Bride'), which followed in 1899, was an old-fashioned, adamantly conventional (hence anti-'realist') number opera, replete with concerted ensembles and symphonic overture (but for its coda dramaturgically neutral), in which Rimsky was obviously attempting to shake his typecast image as fantastic fabulist as well as distance himself from his iconoclastic 'kuchkist' past. Clearly the product of crisis following the final revision of *The Maid of Pskov*, it implied repudiation of that opera (and of Wagner, too) in favour of the classical operatic mainstream from Mozart to Verdi and indeed Tchaikovsky. The earnestness of Rimsky's project, and its importance for him, may be measured by the music he composed in the late 1890s on the way to *The Tsar's Bride*, which includes (besides *Mozart and Salieri*) an amazing series of 43 romances and duets, all composed in the summer of 1897 in an effort to assimilate the traditional lyric style after a youth misspent in 'declamatory' experimentation.

In this the composer refused to see regression but, on the contrary, the renovation of his style and the validation of his claim to consideration as a major operatic figure on the world stage. His success may be measured by the fact that *The Tsar's Bride* has become Rimsky-Korsakov's most popular opera in his homeland, a staple repertory item in every theatre. It has utterly failed abroad, since it conforms neither to established Western notions of its composer's strengths nor to Western ideas of what 'Russian music' is supposed to be. The few Western critics who have taken note of *The Tsar's Bride* have gone out of their way to insult it. 'One tired-sounding number follows another, and some of it is truly terrible', one enthusiastic devotee of *Sadko* and *Tsar Saltan* wrote of the work; 'Rimsky was trying to go the way of the Romantic historical grand opera, and I doubt he meant a note of it'. These unjustified remarks epitomize the whole paradoxical reception history of Russian opera at home and abroad.

The traditionalist line initiated by *The Tsar's Bride* found continuation in two other operas, which failed however to duplicate the success of the first. *Serviliya* ('Servilia', completed in 1901) – also after Mey, and dedicated to his memory – is set in Rome in Nero's time. *Pan Voyevoda* (completed in 1903) is set in 17th-century Poland for the sake of local colour, but its libretto (by Ilya Tyumenev) is compounded of stock elements, some of them (e.g. the elimination of a love rival by poison) lifted rather transparently from *The Tsar's Bride*, in whose libretto Tyumenev had had a hand. Of greater interest than the opera to which it is appended is the composer's prim performance note to *Servilia* – one of those documents that inform us, by what they interdict, of conditions the composer expected to encounter (hence of standard contemporary practice):

In the performance of his operas the composer does not admit devices, reckoned as dramatic, that lie outside the realm of musical art, as for example: speaking, whispering, laughing, shouting and so on. He demands singing exclusively, with clearly defined pitch whether the music be 'arioso' or declamatory, since he is convinced that only in this way can a truly musical-dramatic effect be achieved.

In the lyrical moments of the opera, those artists on stage who are not occupied with singing must in no way distract the audience from the singing with superfluous acting or gestures, since *an operatic work is above all a musical work*.

The author knows better than anyone else which spots in the opera will seem at first glance to be suitable for cutting. If he did not cut them himself before publication, it is because he considered that to do so would be destructive of the work's artistic form and dramatic meaning. If cuts should appear desirable to others, they may be made only with the author's permission and under his supervision. Otherwise the author does not consent to the production of his work.

The phrase in italics (Rimsky's own) is one that re-appears obsessively during his late period, both in performance notes and in letters, and must again represent the mature composer's aesthetic squeamishness with respect to his own radical past.

6. RETURN TO FOLKLORE. With *Skazka o Tsare Saltane* ('The Tale of Tsar Saltan', composed 1899–1900), Rimsky-Korsakov returned to Russian folklore as the source of his inspiration, but with a difference. Where earlier he had been the musical counterpart of Alexander Afanas'yev, the famous ethnographer who laid the foundations of the Russian 'mythological school' (and whose fundamental work, 'The Slavs' Poetic Outlook on Nature', Rimsky had called his 'pantheistic bible'), the composer now emerged more as a counterpart to the 'neo-nationalist' painters whose work was marking a new departure in Russian art. Many of them – e.g. Viktor Vasnetsov, Mikhail Vrubel and the somewhat younger Ivan Bilibin – designed sets and costumes for Mamontov's Private Russian Opera. (Vrubel's wife, the soprano Nadeshda Zabela, created a number of Rimsky-Korsakov feminine leads, including the Swan-Princess in *Tsar Saltan*.) Neo-nationalist artists sought stylistic and formal inspiration, not just subject matter, in folklore. Similarly, Rimsky now became an inspired musical illustrator of fairy-tales, adapting his musical palette, as the artists did, to a rather garishly alluring colour scheme influenced by the cartoonish peasant woodcuts known as *lubki*. The brash little trumpet tune that introduces every scene in *Tsar Saltan* is a perfect musical translation of that style, functioning in the opera exactly like a *priskazka*, the verbal flourish with which the authentic folktale-spinner would seize his listeners' attention.

With *Kashchey bessmertnïy* ('Kashchey the Death-less', 1902), unexpectedly inspired by a chance perusal of *Siegfried*, Rimsky returned for the last time to the old and somewhat shopworn stylistic dualism of *Ruslan*: icy-evil-supernatural-chromatic versus sunny-humane-diatonic. The new opera's considerable musical interest lies in what was from the beginning its motivation and pretext: the frankly experimental deployment of the chromatic genus to the point where, as the composer put it, 'one can go no further without passing over into hyper-harmony'. Taking off from Act 2 scene i of *Siegfried* (Alberich and Mime at the mouth of Fafner's cave), built throughout over a tonally ambiguous tritone ostinato, Rimsky allowed the tritone a similar stability throughout his opera (until the inevitable resolution to D major, Rimsky's sun-key, at Kashchey's demise). The devilish interval is variously embedded in scales of whole tones or alternating whole tones and semitones, which in turn provided the raw material for a triadic yet tonally suspensive harmonic syntax based on cycles of 3rds in place of 5ths. The result is a remarkably

sustained, ultimately quite un-Wagnerian essay in evocatively frigid but also exceptionally rigid harmonic sequences. While no-one would claim that *Kashchey the Deathless* was one of Rimsky-Korsakov's better operas, it has fascinated historians of early 20th-century music as a Baedeker to the common practice out of which Stravinsky's modernistic idiom (his 'hyper-harmony') emerged.

7. LAST OPERAS. With his next – he thought last – opera, *Skazaniye o nevidimom grade Kitezhe i deve Fevronii* ('The Legend of the Invisible City of Kitezh and the Maiden Fevroniya', composed 1904), Rimsky continued and developed the 'neo-nationalist' trend inaugurated in his work by *The Tale of Tsar Saltan*. The opera is conceived from first to last as a stylization of folk art, both as to sound and as to structure. One telling detail of this conception, which may not be readily apparent as such to non-Russian listeners, can serve as illustration. The finely wrought orchestral texture abounds in overlays of multiple subdivisions of the beat; the frequent 5/8 patterns refer specifically to the metre of the Russian wedding songs that also play, not necessarily at the same time, on the musical surface. Bel'sky's libretto is also a neo-nationalist milestone in its masterly stylization of neo-folkloric and neo-scriptural rhetoric, and, setting it, Rimsky drew on a lifetime of experience in imitating a wide variety of traditional musical genres, now including church chant. The chorus of supplication in Act 2 provided the model for a neo-nationalist folk-ecclesiastical style that survived Rimsky, reaching its peak in Stravinsky's *The Wedding*, which, like many of his 'Russian' works, is specifically beholden to *Kitezh*, the opera on which his teacher was at work during the early period of his tuition (ex.1). (On its third reprise

Ex.1

(a) Rimsky-Korsakov: *Kitezh*, Act 3 scene i

chud - na - ya ne - bes - na - ya tsa - ri - tsa,
['O wondrous Queen of heaven']

(b) Stravinsky: *Svadebka* ('The Wedding') Act 3 (bass voices and pfs I and IV)

Kuz' - ma Dem' - yan___ po se - nyam kho - di___ la
['SS Cosmas and Damian went door to door'] (cf *Kitezh*, Act 2: 'Tï Kuz'ma – Dem'yan, tï svyatoy kuznets, skuy nam *svadebku*' [Cosmas – Damian, holy smith, forge us a wedding!])

the chorus is given a 'westernized', motet-like treatment after the fashion of the little-known functional church music Rimsky had composed during his period of employment at the Imperial Chapel Choir School.)

In its ambitious, syncretic subject matter, its eclectic style and its lofty ethical tone, *Kitezh* was a kind of creative summation or testament. In interviews he gave around the time of the opera, Rimsky tended to deprecate the neo-Russian style he was bringing to a culmination and, so far as he was concerned, exhausting. That he saw the work as a valedictory is strongly suggested by the extraordinary care he took in writing it, and the high critical standards he was pressing on himself. Alternative redactions and rejected drafts fill up a whole supplementary volume in the centenary edition of his collected works. There is no problem of 'versions', however; Rimsky brought the work to what he felt was its definitive form before the first performance, and did not revise it afterwards.

It is unpleasantly ironic that of all Rimsky-Korsakov's operas, only the last, a trifling parody based on Pushkin's mock folktale *Zolotoy petushok* ('The Golden Cockerel', 1909), should be a repertory item in the West; its popularity, which came about as a result of Dyagilev's spectacular and widely copied Paris production of 1914 (thanks to which the opera is still generally called by its French name, *Le coq d'or*), has greatly distorted the reception of Rimsky's work and the evaluation of his achievement. He is generally thought of as a composer who did trivial things superlatively well, whose work – compared as it usually is, invidiously, with Musorgsky's – 'consists of colour, rather than expression', as Calvocoressi put it long ago.

Yet in his finest operas Rimsky-Korsakov did very important things. In the astoundingly precocious *Maid of Pskov* he brought to its very peak the historical-realist genre best known in the West from Musorgsky's work. If Rimsky could not match Musorgsky in psychological penetration that need not condemn him: no one else did, either. It is enough that he wrote the greatest crowd scene in all of Russian opera, which probably means in all of opera. In *The Snow Maiden* he created a pantheistic, animistic musical universe that carries utter conviction, mediating affectingly between reality and myth; the title character's little love-death is among the most touching pages in the repertory. The scene of Fevroniya's spiritual translation in *Kitezh* replays this episode at a heart-rending level of expression. Between them, *Sadko* and *Tsar Saltan* demonstrate the enormous stylistic and poetic range the Russian folk melos could yield in the hands of a genial connoisseur. The fourth act of *The Tsar's Bride* embodies a congruence of grandiose formal means and intense dramatic power to set beside the third act of *Aida*. And of course his unique powers of natural and magical illustration gave rise throughout Rimsky's career to harmonic and instrumental inventions that are truly in a class of their own in the history of Russian music or of world opera; it is only by arbitrary convention that they are, or can be, distinguished from 'expression'.

The trouble has always been the amount of subtext required for full comprehension. Rimsky-Korsakov is a composer who cannot travel light; his work is a semiotician's dream and a critic's nightmare. Unprepared to receive its messages, alien ears perceive mainly its suspiciously decorative packaging and an unacceptably high (but characteristically Slavonic) level of ritualized repetition or sequence. Richard Strauss's reaction to the *Christmas Eve* suite was typical: 'That is all very well, but unfortunately we are no longer children'. Yet to those properly receptive (and that probably means exclusively to Russians), it can seem the most multivalently evocative and transporting music in the world.

See also Christmas Eve; Golden Cockerel, The; Kashchey the Deathless; Legend of the Invisible City of Kitezh and the Maiden Fevroniya, The; Maid of Pskov, The; May Night; Mlada (i); Mlada (ii); Mozart and Salieri; Pan Voyevoda; Sadko; Servilia; Snow Maiden, The; Tale of Tsar Saltan, The; and Tsar's Bride, The.

Edition: N. *Rimsky-Korsakov: Polnoye sobraniye sochineniy* [Collected Works], ed. A. Rimsky-Korsakov and others (Moscow, 1946–70) [RK]

Moscow first performances at Solodovnikov Theatre, St Petersburg first performances at Mariinsky Theatre, unless otherwise stated
* – full score; † – vocal score with pf acc.

title	genre, acts	libretto	first performance	remarks, publication	RK
Pskovityanka [The Maid of Pskov]	3	Rimsky-Korsakov, after L. A. Mey; addl text V. Krestovsky and M. Musorgsky			
1st version			St Petersburg, 1/13 Jan 1873; cond. E. Nápravník	comp. 1868–72 (St Petersburg, 1872)	*1a, b, † 29a
2nd version				comp. 1876–7	
3rd version			St Petersburg, Panayev, 6/18 April 1895, cond. I. Davidov; Moscow, 12/24 Dec 1896, cond. G. Truffi	comp. 1891–2 (St Petersburg, 1892)	*1v, g, † 29b
'standard' version	prol., 3		Moscow, Bol'shoy, 10/23 Oct 1901, cond. I. Al'tani	rev. of 2nd version; incl. prol. Boyarïnya Vera Sheloga; new aria for Act 3 comp. 1898	
Mlada (i)	opera-ballet, 4	V. A. Krïlov		comp. 1872, collab. Borodin, Cui, Musorgsky and Minkus; inc.	
Mayskaya noch' [May Night]	comic op, 3	Rimsky-Korsakov, after N. V. Gogol	St Petersburg, 9/21 Jan 1880, cond. E. Nápravník	comp. 1878–9 (Leipzig, 1893)	*2, † 30

title	genre, acts	libretto	first performance	remarks, publication	RK
Snegurochka [The Snow Maiden]	springtime tale, prol., 4	Rimsky-Korsakov, after A. N. Ostrovsky			
1st version			St Petersburg, 29 Jan/ 10 Feb 1882, cond. E. Nápravník	comp. 1880–81 (St Petersburg, 1881)	
2nd version (slightly abridged)				comp. c1895 (St Petersburg, 1898)	*3, † 31
Mlada (ii)	magical opera-ballet, 4	Rimsky-Korsakov, after Krïlov	St Petersburg, 20 Oct/ 1 Nov 1892, cond. E. Nápravník	comp. 1889–90 (Leipzig, 1891)	*4, † 32
Noch' pered rozhdestvom [Christmas Eve]	carol-come-to-life, 4	Rimsky-Korsakov, after Gogol	St Petersburg, 28 Nov/10 Dec 1895, cond. E. Nápravník	comp. 1894–5	*5, † 33
Sadko	opera-bïlina, 3 or 5 (7 scenes)	Rimsky-Korsakov, V. Stasov, V. Yastrebtsev, N. Shtrup, N. Findeyzen and V. N. Bel'sky	Moscow, 26 Dec 1897/ 7 Jan 1898, cond. E. Esposito	comp. 1895–6 (Leipzig, 1897)	*6, † 34
Bagdadskiy borodobrey [The Barber of Baghdad]	1	Rimsky-Korsakov		sketches, comp. 1895	
Motsart i Sal'yeri [Mozart and Salieri] op.48	1	A. Pushkin	Moscow, 25 Nov/7 Dec 1898, cond. G. Truffi	comp. 1897 (Leipzig, 1898)	*7, † 35
Boyarïnya Vera Sheloga [The Noblewoman Vera Sheloga] op.54	1	Rimsky-Korsakov, after Mey	Moscow, 15/27 Dec 1898	comp. 1898 (St Petersburg, 1898); prol. to 2nd version of Pskovityanka, 1876–7	*8, † 36
Tsarskaya nevesta [The Tsar's Bride]	4	I. F. Tyumenev, after Mey	Moscow, 22 Oct/ 3 Nov 1899, cond. M. Ippolitov-Ivanov	comp. 1898 (Leipzig, 1899); new aria, Act 3, comp. 1899	*9, † 37
Skazka o Tsare Saltane, o sïne ego slavnom i moguchem bogatïre knyaze Gvidone Saltanoviche i o prekrasnoy Tsarevne Lebedi [The Tale of Tsar Saltan, of his Son the Renowned and Mighty Bogatïr Prince Guidon Saltanovich, and of the Beautiful Swan Princess]	prol., 4	Bel'sky, after Pushkin	Moscow, 21 Oct/ 3 Nov 1900, cond. M. Ippolitov-Ivanov	comp. 1899–1900 (St Petersburg, 1901)	*10, † 38
Serviliya [Servilia]	5	Rimsky-Korsakov, after Mey	St Petersburg, 1/ 14 Oct 1902, cond. F. Blumenfeld	comp. 1900–01 (St Petersburg, 1902)	*11, † 39
Kashchey bessmertnïy [Kashchey the Deathless]	autumnal parable, 1 (3 scenes without pause)	Rimsky-Korsakov and S. Rimsky-Korsakov, after Y. M. Petrovsky	Moscow, 12/ 25 Dec 1902, cond. M. Ippolitov-Ivanov	1901–2 (St Petersburg, 1902); conclusion rewritten 1906	*12, † 40
Pan Voyevoda	4	Tyumenev	St Petersburg Conservatory, 3/16 Oct 1904, cond. V. Suk	comp. 1902–3 (St Petersburg, 1904)	*13, † 41
Skazaniye o nevidimom grade Kitezhe i deve Fevronii [Legend of the Invisible City of Kitezh and the Maiden Fevroniya]	4	Bel'sky, after I. S. Meledin, P. I. Mel'nikov and trad. tales	St Petersburg, 7/ 20 Feb 1907, cond. F. Blumenfeld	comp. 1903–4 (Leipzig, 1906)	*14, † 42
Zolotoy petushok [The Golden Cockerel]	prol., 3, epilogue	Bel'sky, after Pushkin	Moscow, 24 Sept/ 7 Oct 1909, cond. E. Cooper	comp. 1906–7 (Moscow, 1908)	*15, † 43
Sten'ka Razin	sketches	Bel'sky		comp. 1905	
Zemlya i nebo [Heaven and Earth]	sketches	Byron		comp. 1905	

GENERAL

N. Rimsky-Korsakov: *Letopis' moyey muzikal'noy zhizni* [Chronicle of my Musical Life] (St Petersburg, 1909; Fr. trans., 1914; Eng. trans., 1924; enlarged 3/1926; Eng. trans., 1942); repr. in *N. Rimsky-Korsakov: Polnoye sobraniye sochineniy: literaturnïye proizvedeniya i perepiska* [Collected Works: Literary Writings and Correspondence], i, ed. A. V. Ossovsky and V. N. Rimsky-Korsakov (Moscow, 1955)

——: *Muzikal'nïye stat'i i zametki 1869–1907* [Articles and Observations on Music, 1869–1907], ed. N. Rimskaya-Korskova (St Petersburg, 1911)

N. van Gilse Van der Pals: *N. A. Rimsky-Korsakow: Opernschaffen nebst Skizzen über Leben und Wirken* (Paris and Leipzig, 1929)

M. Calvocoressi: 'Rimsky-Korsakov's Operas Reconsidered', *MT*, lxxii (1931), 886–8

R. Hofmann: *Un siècle d'opéra russe* (Paris, 1946), chap.8

N. Gilyarovskaya: 'Rimsky-Korsakov i khudozhniki (materialï k stsenicheskoy istorii oper Rimskogo-Korsakova)' [Rimsky-Korsakov and Artists: Documents on the Scenic History of his Operas], *Muzïkal'noye nasledstvo: Rimsky-Korsakov: issledovaniya, materialï, pis'ma* [Musical Heritage: Rimsky-Korsakov: Research Documents, Letters], ed. D. Kabalevsky and others (Moscow, 1954), ii, 261–318

D. Kabalevsky: 'Rimsky-Korsakov i modernizm', *Muzïkal'noye nasledstvo: Rimsky-Korsakov: issledovaniya, materialï, pis'ma* (Moscow, 1954), i, 17–78

A. Kandinsky: 'O muzïkal'nïkh kharakteristikakh v tvorchestve Rimskogo-Korsakova 90kh godov' [On Musical Characterization in Rimsky-Korsakov's Work of the 1890s], ibid, 79–144

A. A. Gozenpud: *N. Rimsky-Korsakov: temï i idei yego opernogo tvorchestva* [Themes and Ideas in his Operas] (Moscow, 1957)

V. V. Yastrebtsev: *Nikolay Andreyevich Rimsky-Korsakov: vospominaniya* [Reminiscences], ed. A. V. Ossovsky (Leningrad, 1959–60; Eng. trans., abridged, 1985)

L. Danilevich: *Posledniye operï N. A. Rimskogo-Korsakova* [Rimsky-Korsakov's Last Operas] (Moscow, 1961)

Yu. A. Kremlyov: *Estetika prirodï v tvorchestve N. A. Rimskogo-Korsakova* [The Aesthetics of Nature in the Works of Rimsky-Korsakov] (Moscow, 1962)

P. Rumyantsev: *Stanislavsky i opera* (Moscow, 1969; Eng. trans., 1975)

S. Yevseyev: *Rimsky-Korsakov i russkaya narodnaya pesnya* [Rimsky-Korsakov and Russian Folksong] (Moscow, 1970)

A. Gozenpud: 'Rimsky-Korsakov v rabote nad opernïm libretto' [Rimsky-Korsakov at Work on an Opera Libretto], *Izbrannïye stat'i* [Selected Articles] (Leningrad, 1971), 128–73

V. Yakovlev: 'N. A. Rimsky-Korsakov i opernïy teatr S. I. Mamontova' [Rimsky-Korsakov and Mamontov's Opera Theatre], *Izbrannïye trudï o muzïke* [Selected Works on Music], ii (Moscow, 1971), 230–74

V. Tsendrovsky: *Uvertyurï i vstupleniya k operam Rimskogo-Korsakova* [The Overtures and Introductions to Rimsky-Korsakov's Operas] (Moscow, 1974)

V. Tsendrovsky and others, eds.: *Operï N. A. Rimskogo-Korsakova: putevoditel'* [A Guide to Rimsky-Korsakov's Operas] (Moscow, 1976)

A. Kandinsky: 'Rimsky-Korsakov v 1890–1900-e godï' [Rimsky-Korsakov in the 1890s and 1900s], *Muzïka XX veka: ocherki* [Music of the 20th Century: Essays], ed. D. Zhitomirsky (Moscow, 1977), i/2, 5–44 [bibliography, 491–4]

——: *Istoriya russkoy muzïki*, ii/2: *N. A. Rimsky-Korsakov* (Moscow, 2/1984)

G. Seaman: *Nikolai Andreevich Rimsky-Korsakov: a Guide to Research* (New York and London, 1988)

INDIVIDUAL OPERAS

The Maid of Pskov and Boyarïnya Vera Sheloga

G. Abraham: 'Rimsky-Korsakov's First Opera', *Studies in Russian Music* (London, 1935), 142–66

Z. Gorodetskaya: *Pskovityanka: opera N. A. Rimskogo-Korsakova* [*The Maid of Pskov*] (Moscow, 1936)

C. Cui: '"Pskovityanka": opera Rimskogo-Korsakova' [*The Maid of Pskov*; orig. pubd 1873], *Izbrannïye stat'i* [Selected Essays], ed. Yu. A. Kremlyov (Leningrad, 1952), 215–24

——: 'Moskovskaya chastnaya russkaya opera: "Boyarïnya Vera Sheloga" Rimskogo-Korsakova' [The Moscow Private Russian Opera: Rimsky-Korsakov's *The Noblewoman Vera Sheloga*], ibid, 497–9

A. Vikhanskaya: 'K istorii "Verï Shelogi"' [Towards a History of *Vera Sheloga*], *SovM* (1958), no.6, pp.42–7

O. Sokolov: 'Leytmotivï operï "Pskovityanka"' [Leitmotifs in *The Maid of Pskov*], *Trudï kafedrï teorii muzïki Moskovskoy konservatorii* [Papers of the Department of Music Theory of the Moscow Conservatory], i (Moscow, 1960), 219–56

G. Abraham: 'Pskovityanka: the Original Version of Rimsky-Korsakov's First Opera', *MQ*, liv (1968), 58–73

A. Kandinsky: 'Obrashcheniye k russkoy klassike' [Treatment of the Russian Classics], *SovM* (1971), no.7, pp.49–55

A. Gozenpud: *Russkiy opernïy teatr XIX veka* [Russian Operatic Theatre of the 19th Century], iii (Leningrad, 1973), chap.3

——: *Russkiy opernïy teatr na rubezhe XIX–XX vekov i F. I.*

Shalyapin 1890–1904 [Russian Operatic Theatre at the Turn of the 20th Century and Shalyapin] (Leningrad, 1974), 219–29

A. Vikhanskaya: 'Neopublikovannaya redaktsiya operï "Pskovityanka" Rimskogo-Korsakova' [An Unpublished Version of *The Maid of Pskov*], *Russkaya i zarubezhnaya muzïkal'naya klassika: voprosï teorii muziki i ispolnitel'stva* [Russian and Foreign Musical Classics: Problems of Music Theory and Practice] (Leningrad, 1974)

L. Polyakova: '"Pskovityanka" i "Vera Sheloga"' [*The Maid of Pskov* and *Vera Sheloga*], *Operï N. A. Rimskogo-Korsakova: putevoditel'* [A Guide to Rimsky-Korsakov's Operas], ed. V. Tsendrovsky and others (Moscow, 1976), 24–64

R. Taruskin: 'The Present in the Past: Russian Opera and Russian Historiography, ca. 1870', *Russian and Soviet Music: Essays for Boris Schwarz* (Ann Arbor, 1984), 74–143

May Night

G. Abraham: 'Rimsky-Korsakov's Gogol Operas', *Studies in Russian Music* (London, 1935), 167–92

C. Cui: '"Mayskaya noch'"', volshebno-komicheskaya opera N. A. Rimskogo-Korsakova' [*May Night*: Rimsky-Korsakov's Magical Comic Opera; orig. pubd 1894], *Izbrannïye stat'i* [Selected Articles], ed. Yu. A. Kremlyov (Leningrad, 1952), 425–35

P. Rumyantsev: *Stanislavsky i opera* (Moscow, 1969), 342–78; (Eng. trans., 1975), 269–303

A. Gozenpud: *Russkiy opernïy teatr XIX veka* [Russian Operatic Theatre of the 19th Century], iii (Leningrad, 1973), chap.13

Z. Finkel'shteyn: '"Mayskaya noch'"', *Operï N. A. Rimskogo-Korsakova: putevoditel'* [A Guide to Rimsky-Korsakov's Operas], ed. V. Tsendrovsky and others (Moscow, 1976), 65–109

A. Velichko: *Mayskaya noch' N. A. Rimskogo-Korsakova* (Moscow, 2/1980)

The Snow Maiden

N. Findeyzen: 'Tematism operï "Snegurochka" N. A. Rimskogo-Korsakova' [The Thematic Structure of *The Snow Maiden*], *RMG*, i (1894), 121–4, 139–45, 157–9, 179–84, 197–200, 219–22

N. Rimsky-Korsakov: '"Snegurochka" – vesennyaya skazka' [*The Snow Maiden*: a Spring Fairy-Tale], in *N. A. Rimsky-Korsakov: Muzïkal'niye stat'i i zametki 1869–1907* [Articles and Observations on Music], ed. N. Rimskaya-Korsakova (St Petersburg, 1911), 181–200 [more complete as 'Razbor "Snegurochki"' [An Analysis of *The Snow Maiden*], in *N. Rimsky-Korsakov: Polnoye sobraniye sochineniy: literaturnïye proizvedeniya i perepiska* [Complete Collected Works: Literary Writings and Correspondence], iv, ed. V. Protopopov (Moscow, 1960), 393–426

L. Kulakovsky: *Snegurochka: opera N. A. Rimskogo-Korsakova* (Moscow, 1933)

G. Abraham: 'Snow Maiden', *Studies in Russian Music* (London, 1935), 193–220

V. Kiselyov: 'A. N. Ostrovsky i N. A. Rimsky-Korsakov (k istorii sozdaniya operï "Snegurochka")' [Ostrovsky and Rimsky-Korsakov: Towards a History of the Creation of *The Snow Maiden*], *A. N. Ostrovsky i russkiye kompozitorï: pis'ma* [Ostrovsky and Russian Composers: Letters], ed. E. Kolosova and V. Filippov (Moscow and Leningrad, 1937), 172–85

C. Cui: '"Snegurochka", vesennyaya skazka Rimskogo-Korsakova' [*The Snow Maiden*: Rimsky-Korsakov's Spring Fairy-Tale; orig. pubd 1898], *Izbrannïye stat'i* [Selected Essays], ed. Yu. A. Kremlyov (Leningrad, 1952), 479–82

I. Prokhorova: *'Snegurochka' N. Rimskogo-Korsakova* (Moscow and Leningrad, 1952)

M. Sabinina: '"Snegurochka" v Bol'shom teatre' [*The Snow Maiden* at the Bol'shoy Theatre], *SovM* (1955), no.3, pp.82–8

E. Nápravník: '"Snegurochka": otzïv' [*The Snow Maiden*: a Review], *E. F. Napravnik: avtobiograficheskiye, tvorcheskiye materialï, dokumentï, pis'ma* [Autobiographical Writings, Materials Relating to his Creative Work, Documents, Letters], ed. L. Kutateladze (Leningrad, 1959), 66–7

A. Kandinsky: 'Rozhdeniye vesenney skazki' [The Birth of a Spring Fairy-Tale], *SovM* (1969), no.3, pp.52–63

B. Asaf'yev: 'Snegurochka', *Simfonicheskiye etyudï* (Leningrad, 1970), 62–6

A. Gozenpud: *Russkiy opernïy teatr XIX veka* [Russian Operatic Theatre of the 19th Century], iii (Leningrad, 1973), 251–64

L. Kulakovsky: 'Snegurochka', *Operï N. A. Rimskogo-Korsakova: putevoditel'* [A Guide to Rimsky-Korsakov's Operas], ed. V. Tsendrovsky and others (Moscow, 1976), 110–44

P. Belïy: 'Snegurochka – nadezhdï i somneniya' [The Snow Maiden: Hopes and Doubts], SovM (1979), no.3, pp.45–9

Mlada

G. Abraham: 'Rimsky-Korsakov's Mlada', On Russian Music (London, 1939), 113–21

V. Rimsky-Korsakov: 'Otkrïtoye pis'mo' [An Open Letter], SovM (1965), no.9, pp.53–4

A. Gozenpud: Russkiy opernïy teatr na rubezhe XIX–XX vekov i F. I. Shalyapin 1890–1904 [Russian Operatic Theatre at the Turn of the 20th Century and Shalyapin] (Leningrad, 1974), chap. 5

D. Alexandrov: '"Mlada" Rimskogo-Korsakova i yeyo problemï' [Mlada and its Problems], SovM (1982), no.3, pp.73–8

S. Savenko: 'Vozrozhdeniye "Mladï", ili znaem li mï klassiku?' [The Revival of Mlada, or Do we know the Classics?], SovM (1989), no.7, pp.30–34

M. Rakhmanova: 'Vokrug "Mladï"' [Concerning Mlada], SovM (1990), no.3, pp.12–20

R. Stevenson: 'Rimsky-Korsakov in the Eastern United States', Inter-American Music Review, xi/1 (1990–91), 117–35

Christmas Eve

V. Ferman: '"Cherevichki" ("Kuznets Vakula") P. I. Chaykovskogo i "Noch' pered Rozhdestvom" N. A. Rimskogo-Korsakova (opït sravneniya opernoy dramaturgii i muzïkal'nogo stilya)' [Tchaikovsky's Cherevichki (Vakula the Smith) and Rimsky-Korsakov's Christmas Eve: a Comparative Study of Operatic Drama and Musical Style], Voprosï muzïkoznaniya [Problems of Musicology], i, ed. A. Ogolevets (1953–4), 205–38

B. Asaf'yev: '"Noch' pered Rozhdestvom" (Bïl'-kolyadka)' [Christmas Eve: a Carol Come to Life], Simfonicheskiye etyudï (Leningrad, 1970), 74–86

A. Gozenpud: Russkiy opernïy teatr na rubezhe XIX–XX vekov i F. I. Shalyapin 1890–1904 [Russian Operatic Theatre at the Turn of the 20th Century and Shalyapin] (Leningrad, 1974), 105–10

P. Taylor: Gogolian Interludes: Gogol's Story 'Christmas Eve' as the Subject of the Operas by Tchaikovsky and Rimsky-Korsakov (London, 1984)

Sadko

'K istorii operï-bïlinï "Sadko" (iz perepiski N. A. Rimskogo-Korsakova i V. V. Stasova)' [Towards a History of Sadko: from the Correspondence of Rimsky-Korsakov and V. V. Stasov], Muzïka (1910), no.4–5, 7–8

G. Abraham: '"Sadko"', Studies in Russian Music (London, 1935), 221–45

C. Cui: '"Sadko", opera-bïlina Rimskogo-Korsakova' [Rimsky-Korsakov's Sadko], Izbrannïye stat'i [Selected Essays], ed. Yu. A. Kremlyov (Leningrad, 1952), 472–9

G. Khubov: '"Sadko", opera Rimskogo-Korsakova v Bol'shom teatre' [Rimsky-Korsakov's Sadko at the Bol'shoy Theatre], O muzïke i muzïkantakh [On Music and Musicians] (Moscow, 1959), 141–6

A. Kandinsky: 'Kogda molchat klassiki' [When the Classics are Silent], SovM (1969), no.6, pp.32–8

B. Asaf'yev: 'Problema grada vidimogo' [The Problem of a Visible City], Simfonicheskiye etyudï (Leningrad, 1970), 86–95

V. Tsukkerman: 'O syuzhete i muzïkal'nom yazïke operï-bïlinï "Sadko"' [On the Subject and Musical Language of Sadko], Muzïkal'no-teoreticheskiye ocherki i etyudï, i (Moscow, 1970), 441–504

A. Gozenpud: Russkiy opernïy teatr na rubezhe XIX–XX vekov i F. I. Shalyapin 1890–1904 [Russian Operatic Theatre at the Turn of the 20th Century and Shalyapin] (Leningrad, 1974), 165–77

V. Tsukkerman: '"Sadko"', Operï N. A. Rimskogo-Korsakova: putevoditel' [A Guide to Rimsky-Korsakov's Operas], ed. V. Tsendrovsky and others (Moscow, 1976), 145–218

Mozart and Salieri

E. Braudo: 'Motsart i Sal'yeri', Orfey, i (Petrograd, 1922), 102–7

C. Cui: 'Moskovskaya chastnaya opera: "Motsart i Sal'yeri"' [The Moscow Private Opera: Mozart and Salieri], Izbrannïye stat'i [Selected Essays], ed. Yu. A. Kremlyov (Leningrad, 1952), 494–7

I. Boelza: Motsart i Sal'yeri, tragediya Pushkina: dramaticheskiye stsenï Rimskogo-Korsakova [Mozart and Salieri, Pushkin's Tragedy: Rimsky-Korsakov's Dramatic Scenes] (Moscow, 1953)

A. Gozenpud: Russkiy opernïy teatr na rubezhe XIX–XX vekov i F. I. Shalyapin 1890–1904 [Russian Operatic Theatre at the Turn of the 20th Century and Shalyapin] (Leningrad, 1974), 191–210

B. Levik: 'Motsart i Sal'yeri', Operï N. A. Rimskogo-Korsakova: putevoditel' [A Guide to Rimsky-Korsakov's Operas], ed. V. Tsendrovsky and others (Moscow, 1976), 219–38

The Tsar's Bride

G. Abraham: 'The Tsar's Bride', Studies in Russian Music (London, 1935), 246–60

I. Tyumenev: 'Vospominaniya o N. A. Rimskom-Korsakove' [Reminiscences about Rimsky-Korsakov], Muzïkal'noye nasledstvo, ii (Moscow, 1954), 177–247

M. Teroganyan: 'Tsarskaya nevesta' N. A. Rimskogo-Korsakova (Moscow, 2/1959)

O. Sobolevskaya: 'Kak stavilas' "Tsarskaya nevesta"?' [How was The Tsar's Bride staged?], SovM (1968), no.8, pp.80–86

P. Rumyantsev: Stanislavsky i opera (Moscow, 1969), 202–71; (Eng. trans., 1975), 152–210

Ya. Vitols: '"Tsarskaya nevesta", opera v tryokh [sic] deystviyakh N. A. Rimskogo-Korsakova' [The Tsar's Bride: an Opera in Three Acts by Rimsky-Korsakov], Vitols: vospominaniya, stat'i, pis'ma [Reminiscences, Essays, Letters], ed. A. Dankevich (Leningrad, 1969), 154–7

A. Gozenpud: Russkiy opernïy teatr na rubezhe XIX–XX vekov i F. I. Shalyapin 1890–1904 [Russian Operatic Theatre at the Turn of the 20th Century and Shalyapin] (Leningrad, 1974), 229–39

V. Bakulin: 'Leytmotivnaya i intonatsionnaya dramaturgiya v opere Rimskogo-Korsakova "Tsarskaya nevesta"' [Leitmotivic and Intonational Dramaturgy in The Tsar's Bride], Voprosï opernoy dramaturgii [Problems of Operatic Drama], ed. Yu. Tyulin (Moscow, 1975), 41–79

C. Osborne: 'Russian Opera', ii, HiFi/MusAm, xxv/1 (1975), 37–46

A. Solovtsov: 'Tsarskaya nevesta', Operï N. A. Rimskogo-Korsakova: putevoditel' [A Guide to Rimsky-Korsakov's Operas], ed. V. Tsendrovsky and others (Moscow, 1976), 239–302

Ye. Ratser: 'Rabota s pevtsami nad muzïkal'nïmi obraztsami Grigoriya Gryaznogo, Lyubashi i Marfï v opere Rimskogo-Korsakova "Tsarskaya nevesta"' [Work with Singers on the Roles of Grigory Gryaznoy, Lyubasha and Marfa in The Tsar's Bride], Muzïkal'no-tvorcheskoye vospriyatiye artistov opernoy stsenï [Musical Perception of Actors on the Operatic Stage], ed. O. Agarkov and L. Yaroslavtsev (Moscow, 1981)

A. Chepalov: '"Slushal i smotrel 'Tsarskuyu nevestu'"' [I have heard and seen The Tsar's Bride], Muzïkal'naya zhizn' (1990), no.23, pp.24–5

The Tale of Tsar Saltan

V. Yastrebtsev: 'O vremeni instrumentovki "Skazki o tsare Saltane" i o narodnïkh temakh, vzyatïkh v ètu operu' [On the Period of the Instrumentation of The Tale of Tsar Saltan and the Folk Themes adopted in this Opera], Muzïka (1913), no.150, pp.623–7

M. Ippolitov-Ivanov: 50 let russkoy muzïki v moikh vospominaniyakh [50 Years of Russian Music in my Reminiscences] (Moscow, 1934), 102ff

G. Abraham: 'Tsar Saltan', On Russian Music (London, 1939), 122–37

O. Frelikh: '"Tsarevna-Lebed"' (iz vospominaniy)' ['The Swan Princess': from Reminiscences], Muzïkal'noye nasledstvo: Rimsky-Korsakov: issledovaniya, materialï, pis'ma [Musical Heritage: Rimsky-Korsakov: Research, Documents, Letters], ed. D. Kabalevsky and others (Moscow, 1954), ii, 348–50

B. Asaf'yev: 'Skazka' [A Fairy-Tale], Simfonicheskiye etyudï (Leningrad, 1970), 95–101

A. Gozenpud: Russkiy opernïy teatr na rubezhe XIX–XX vekov i F. I. Shalyapin 1890–1904 [Russian Operatic Theatre at the Turn of the 20th Century and Shalyapin] (Leningrad, 1974), 239–48

I. Ozeretskovskaya: 'Tsar Saltan', Operï N. A. Rimskogo-Korsakova: putevoditel' [A Guide to Rimsky-Korsakov's Operas], ed. V. Tsendrovsky and others (Moscow, 1976), 303–38

A. Porter: 'Marvels Unfold', New Yorker (18 May 1987), 107–9

Servilia

A. Gozenpud: Russkiy opernïy teatr na rubezhe XIX–XX vekov i F. I. Shalyapin 1890–1904 [Russian Operatic Theatre at the Turn of the 20th Century and Shalyapin] (Leningrad, 1974), 248–53

Kashchey the Deathless

V. Yastrebtsev: '"Kashchey bessmertnïy" (osennyaya skazochka)' [Kashchey the Deathless: a Little Autumn Fairy-Tale], Muzïka (1916), no.253, pp.230–34

M. Gnesin: 'O muzïkal'noy dramaturgii Rimskogo-Korsakova v opere "Kashchey bessmertnïy"' [On the Musical Dramaturgy of Kashchey the Deathless], Mïsli i vospominaniya o N. A. Rimskom-Korsakove [Thoughts and Reminiscences about Rimsky-Korsakov] (Moscow, 1956), 128–60

Yu. Engel: '"Kashchey bessmertnïy" – novaya opera N. A. Rimskogo-Korsakova' [Kashchey the Deathless: a New Opera by

Rimsky-Korsakov], *Glazami sovremennika: izbrannïye stat'i o russkoy muzike 1898–1918* [Through the Eyes of a Contemporary: Selected Essays on Russian Music 1898–1918], ed. I. F. Kunin (Moscow, 1971)

A. Gozenpud: *Russkiy operniy teatr na rubezhe XIX–XX vekov i F. I. Shalyapin 1890–1904* [Russian Operatic Theatre at the Turn of the 20th Century and Shalyapin] (Leningrad, 1974), 255–9

V. Tsendrovsky: 'Kashchey bessmertnïy' [*Kashchey the Deathless*], *Operï N. A. Rimskogo-Korsakova: putevoditel'* [A Guide to Rimsky-Korsakov's Operas], ed. V. Tsendrovsky and others (Moscow, 1976), 339–60

R. Taruskin: 'Chernomor to Kashchei: Harmonic Sorcery; or, Stravinsky's "Angle"', *JAMS*, xxxviii (1985), 72–142

Pan Voyevoda

E. Grosheva: 'Novosibirskiy operniy teatr v Moskve' [Novosibirsk Operatic Theatre Comes to Moscow], *SovM* (1955), no.9, pp.81–8

Yu. Engel: '"Pan Voyevoda" Rimskogo-Korsakova', *Glazami sovremennika: izbrannïye stat'i o russkoy muzike 1898–1918* [Through the Eyes of a Contemporary: Selected Essays on Russian Music 1898–1918], ed. I. F. Kunin (Moscow, 1971), 153–7

A. Gozenpud: *Russkiy operniy teatr na rubezhe XIX–XX vekov i F. I. Shalyapin 1890–1904* [Russian Operatic Theatre at the Turn of the 20th Century and Shalyapin] (Leningrad, 1974), 253–4

The Legend of the Invisible City of Kitezh and the Maiden Fevroniya

B. Schloezer: '"Le dit de la ville invisible de Kitej": essai de psychologie musicale', *ReM*, iv/1–3 (1922), 155–63

G. Abraham: 'Kitezh', *Studies in Russian Music* (London, 1935), 261–89

'Diskussiya v Bol'shom teatre' [A Discussion in the Bol'shoy Theatre], *SovM* (1954), no.4, pp.144–6

A. Lyubimov: 'Beregite opernuyu klassiku' [Take Care of the Operatic Classics], *SovM* (1954), no.5, p.154

G. Orlov: 'K sporam o "Kitezhe"' [On the Arguments about *Kitezh*], *SovM* (1954), no.1, pp.75–80

——: 'Tvorcheskaya evolyutsiya Rimskogo-Korsakova v 90-e i 900-e godï i "Skazaniye o nevidimom grade Kitezhe"' [Rimsky-Korsakov's Creative Evolution in the 1890s and 1900s and *The Legend of the Invisible City of Kitezh*], *Voprosï muzïkoznaniya* [Problems of Musicology], iii, ed. Yu. Keldïsh (Moscow, 1960), 499–538

B. Asaf'yev: 'Skazaniye o nevidimom grade' [The Legend of the Invisible City], *Simfonicheskiye etyudï* (Leningrad, 1970), 101–18

Yu. Engel: '"Skazaniye o nevidimom grade Kitzhe i deve Fevronii"' [*The Legend of the Invisible City of Kitezh and the Maiden Fevroniya*], *Glazami sovremennika: izbrannïye stat'i o russkoy muzike 1898–1918* [Through the Eyes of a Contemporary: Selected Essays on Russian Music 1898–1918], ed. I. F. Kunin (Moscow, 1971), 209–19

B. Pokrovsky: *Opernoye proizvedeniye* [A Work of Opera] (Moscow, 1973)

A. Gozenpud: *Russkiy operniy teatr mezhdu dvukh revolyutsiy 1905–1917* [Russian Operatic Theatre between the Two Revolutions 1905–17] (Leningrad, 1975), 155–90

V. Lapin: '"Skazaniye o nevidimom grade Kitezhe" i russkaya svad'ba' [*The Legend of the Invisible City of Kitezh* and the Russian Wedding], *Voprosï teorii i estetiki muziki* [Problems of Music Theory and Aesthetics], xiv, ed. A. Klimovitsky (Moscow, 1975), 31–8

L. Kershner: 'Skazaniye o nevidimom grade Kitezhe i deve Fevronii' [*The Legend of the Invisible City of Kitezh and the Maiden Fevroniya*], *Operï N. A. Rimskogo-Korsakova: putevoditel'* [A Guide to Rimsky-Korsakov's Operas] ed. V. Tsendrovsky and others (Moscow, 1976), 361–431

A. Korablyova: 'Rol' drevnerusskoy pesennosti v opere N. Rimskogo-Korsakova "Skazaniye o nevidimom grade Kitezhe i deve Fevronii"' [The Role of Old Russian Song in Rimsky-Korsakov's *The Legend of the Invisible City of Kitezh and the Maiden Fevroniya*], *Iz istorii russkoy i sovetskoy muziki*, ed. M. Pekelis and I. Givental (Moscow, 1978), 75–95

V. Kukharsky: 'Postizheniye klassiki' [A Grasp of the Classics], *SovM* (1984), no.6, pp.34–43

M. Rakhmanova: 'K biloy polemike vokrug "Kitezha"' [On Past Controversies about *Kitezh*], *SovM* (1984), no.10, pp.82–90

The Golden Cockerel

E. von Tideböhl: 'Rimsky-Korsakov's Last Opera "Zolotoi petouschok"', *Musical Courier*, lix/2 (1909), 18

N. Zhilayev: 'Ob opere voobshche (po povodu postanovki "Zolotogo petushka")' [On Opera in General (with Regard to the Performance of *The Golden Cockerel*)], *Zolotoye runo*, x (1909), 59–64

A. Rimsky-Korsakov: '"Zolotoy petushok" na Parizhskoy i Londonskoy stsenakh' [*The Golden Cockerel* on the Paris and London Stages], *Apollon*, vi/7 (1914), 46–54

G. Abraham: 'The Golden Cockerel', *Studies in Russian Music* (London, 1935), 290–310

V. Protopopov: 'O muzïkal'nom yazïke "Zolotogo petushka"' [On the Musical Language of *The Golden Cockerel*], *SovM* (1938), no.2, pp.20–31

M. Montagu-Nathan: 'The Origin of The Golden Cockerel', *MR*, xv (1954), 33–8

——: 'King Dodon's Love-Song', *MMR*, lxxxiv (1954), 210–12

A. Kandinsky: 'Zametki o "Zolotom petushke"' [Notes on *The Golden Cockerel*], *SovM* (1958), no.6, pp.24–32

S. Feinberg: 'Rimsky-Korsakov's Suite from *Le Coq d'or*', *MR*, xxx (1969), 47–64

P. Rumyantsev: *Stanislavsky i opera* (Moscow, 1969), 447–60; (Eng. trans., 1975), 364–74

B. Asaf'yev: 'Skomorosh'ye tsarstvo' [The Skomorokh's Kingdom; orig. pubd 1921], *Simfonicheskiye etyudï* (Leningrad, 1970), 109–25

G. Abraham: 'Satire and Symbolism in The Golden Cockerel', *ML*, lii (1971), 46–54; repr. in *Essays on Russian and East European Music* (Oxford, 1985), 83–92

Yu. Engel: '"Zolotoy petushok" (Operniy teatr Zimina)' [*The Golden Cockerel*: Zimin's Opera Theatre], *Glazami sovremennika: izbrannïye stat'i o russkoy muzike 1898–1918* [Through the Eyes of a Contemporary: Selected Essays on Russian Music 1898–1918], ed. I. F. Kunin (Moscow, 1971), 265–74

A. Gozenpud: *Russkiy operniy teatr mezhdu dvukh revolyutsiy 1905–17* [Russian Operatic Theatre between the Two Revolutions 1905–17] (Leningrad, 1975), 233–74

V. Berkov and V. Propotopov: 'Zolotoy petushok' [The Golden Cockerel], *Operï N. A. Rimskogo-Korsakova: putevoditel'* [A Guide to Rimsky-Korsakov's Operas], ed. V. Tsendrovsky and others (Moscow, 1976), 432–76

E. Reilly: 'Rimsky-Korsakov's The Golden Cockerel: a Very Modern Fairy Tale', *Musical Newsletter*, vi/1 (1976), 9–16

A. Kandinsky: 'Visokoye Skazka, ili "vesyoloye predstavleniye"?' [A Lofty Fairy-Tale, or a 'Merry Performance'?], *SovM* (1988), no.10, pp.28–34
RICHARD TARUSKIN

Rinaldi, Alberto (*b* Rome, 6 June 1939). Italian baritone. He studied at the Accademia di S Cecilia in Rome, won the 1963 international competition at Spoleto, and made his début at the festival there as Boccanegra. He was then engaged at principal Italian theatres including La Scala. He sang Guglielmo at the 1967 Aix-en-Provence Festival, and has appeared at the Staatsopern in Munich and Vienna, the Chicago Lyric and San Francisco operas, and in Leningrad and Rio de Janeiro. His British début was in 1973 (with the Edinburgh Festival Opera under Barenboim) as Masetto, which was recorded in 1975, followed by Ford at Glyndebourne in 1980 and Belcore at Covent Garden in 1981. His lyric baritone and keen sense of character are heard to advantage in Mozart and Rossini roles, notably Figaro and Dandini.
NOËL GOODWIN

Rinaldi, Margherita (*b* Turin, 12 Jan 1935). Italian soprano. She studied at Rovigo, winning a competition at Spoleto, where she made her début in 1958 as Lucia. After further study she appeared at Dublin in 1961, as Carolina (*Il matrimonio segreto*) and Gilda, the role of her La Scala (1965) and American (1966, Dallas) débuts. She sang at Chicago, San Francisco, Barcelona, throughout Italy and at Wexford. Her repertory included Mozart (Ilia, Donna Elvira, Fiordiligi), Donizetti (Norina, Adina, Linda, Marie in *La fille du régiment*), Bellini (Giulietta, Amina, Elvira), Verdi (Violetta, Oscar, both Nannetta and Alice Ford) and Strauss

(Sophie and the Marschallin). In 1974 she sang the Marchesa del Poggio in Verdi's *Un giorno di regno* at Bregenz. In 1977 she sang Monteverdi's Poppaea in Turin and Amenaide (*Tancredi*) in Florence. She sang Helena in Britten's *A Midsummer Night's Dream* at Florence (1978). The limpid quality of her voice and its agility combined to make her a fine Bellini interpreter – Amina (*La sonnambula*) was among her most successful roles.   ELIZABETH FORBES

Rinaldo. Opera in three acts by GEORGE FRIDERIC HANDEL to a libretto by GIACOMO ROSSI based on an outline by AARON HILL after TORQUATO TASSO's *Gerusalemme liberata*; London, Queen's Theatre, 24 February 1711 (revised version, London, King's Theatre, 6 April 1731).

Goffredo *captain of the Christian armies*	contralto
Almirena *his daughter, betrothed to Rinaldo*	soprano
Rinaldo *celebrated Christian hero*	mezzo-soprano
Eustazio *brother of Goffredo*	contralto
Argante *Saracen King of Jerusalem*	bass
Armida *Queen of Damascus, enchantress*	soprano
A Christian Magician	bass
A Herald	tenor
A Siren	soprano

Mermaids, spirits, fairies, officers, guards, attendants

Setting Near Jerusalem, during the First Crusade

Rinaldo was not only Handel's first opera for London but also the first Italian opera specifically composed for the London stage; previous examples had been pasticcios or adaptations. It was an immediate public success and (despite mocking notices from Addison and Steele in *The Spectator*) had 15 performances before the close of the 1710–11 season. A strong cast was led by the castrato Nicolini in the title role, and included Isabella Girardeau (Almirena), Elisabetta Pilotti-Schiavonetti (Armida), Valentino Urbani (Eustazio), Francesca Vanini (Goffredo) and her husband Giuseppe Boschi (Argante). There were revivals in 1712, 1713, 1714 and 1717, with many cast changes and consequent revisions. The changes for the first three revivals are difficult to establish because of the absence of printed wordbooks, but the book issued for the 1717 revival indicates several differences from the 1711 version, notably to allow the alto castrato Gaetano Berenstadt to take over the role of Argante; he was given at least three new arias. There was no further revival in London until 1731, when Handel made substantial revisions to the opera, especially in the final act. These were partly to reduce the extravagant scenic demands of the original, and partly to accommodate a much-changed cast, which included the alto castrato Senesino as Rinaldo, the contraltos Antonia Merighi and Francesca Bertolli as Armida and Argante, and the tenor Annibale Pio Fabri as Goffredo.

Rinaldo was performed in a German translation by Barthold Feind in Hamburg in 1715, with revivals in 1723 and 1727. The first performances since the 18th century were given in London in February 1933 by pupils of the Hammersmith Day Continuation School at the Century Theatre, Archer Street, and the 'Venture' Fellowship Centre, Notting Hill. The opera was arranged, translated and conducted by Olive Daunt. The first professional performance was at Halle in June 1954, conducted by Horst-Tanu Margraf, and the first in Britain was by the Handel Opera Society at Sadler's Wells Theatre, London, on 17 May 1961, conducted by Charles Farncombe. It was also the first Handel opera to be seen at the Metropolitan, in a Canadian production with Marilyn Horne in 1984. Chrysander issued two scores of *Rinaldo* in the Händel-Gesellschaft edition, the second (1894), containing both the 1711 and 1731 versions, being a replacement of the first (1874) which contained only the 1711 version. Virtually all the music of 1711 and 1731 is included in the revised volume, though with deficiencies of detail (especially in the stage directions). The additional arias of the revivals in the period 1712–17, of which Chrysander was unaware, are not shown.

Tasso's poem is an epic elaboration of the history of the First Crusade (1096–9) in which Christian forces led by Godfrey of Bouillon (Goffredo; *c*1061–1100) captured Jerusalem from the Saracens. The operatic version treats the poem's material freely, with much emphasis on scenic transformations and other stage effects. The action nominally takes place outside the walls of Jerusalem while the city is under siege by the Christian armies, but some scenes have fantastic settings of no specified location.

ACT 1 Goffredo is reminded that he has promised the knight Rinaldo the hand of his daughter Almirena if the city is captured. A herald announces the appearance of the Saracen king Argante, who emerges from the city to demand a three-day truce, which Goffredo grants. Argante summons the aid of Armida, Queen of Damascus and a sorceress. She appears in a chariot drawn by dragons and proposes to secure victory by seducing Rinaldo away from the Christian camp. Her first action, however, is to abduct Almirena from a beautiful grove in which she and Rinaldo have been exchanging vows of love. Eustazio, Goffredo's brother, advises Rinaldo to consult a local hermit, and Rinaldo vows revenge.

ACT 2 Rinaldo, Goffredo and Eustazio, in search of Almirena, arrive at the shore of a sea in which mermaids are seen playing. A Siren or Spirit tries to entice Rinaldo into a boat. He is at first held back by his companions, but breaks free, boards the boat and sails out of sight. In Armida's enchanted palace, Almirena receives unwelcome attentions from Argante. Armida herself rejoices in Rinaldo's capture. She offers him her love but he scornfully rejects it; she tries to seduce him by taking the form of Almirena, but after initial confusion Rinaldo again avoids her. Argante then resumes his advances to (as he thinks) Almirena, promising to free her from Armida's bondage; but it is the disguised Armida he is addressing. The two part in anger.

ACT 3 By his cave, at the foot of the threatening mountain on which Armida's palace is situated, a Christian Magician – the hermit mentioned by Eustazio – tells Goffredo and Eustazio to ascend the mountain, giving them magic wands to defeat the monsters that defend it. The brothers reach the top and strike the castle gate with the wands, at which the whole mountain vanishes and Goffredo and Eustazio find themselves on a rock amid a turbulent sea, which they descend. The scene changes to the enchanted garden of Armida's palace, where the sorceress is threatening to kill Almirena, but Goffredo and Eustazio arrive in time to save her. The wands cause the garden to disappear and the scene becomes open country outside the walls of Jerusalem. The Christian heroes are reunited and resolve to lead the assault on the city. Argante and Armida, reconciled, review a march of their troops; the Christian forces also march and the two armies engage in battle. The assault, led by Rinaldo, is successful, and Argante and Armida are captured. Rinaldo and Almirena are joyfully reunited. Armida breaks her enchanted wand and resolves to turn Christian. She and Argante are released and they agree to marry.

The changes in the 1731 revivals affect the plot. In Act 2 Armida does not appear in Almirena's form but imitates her voice, and her quarrel with Argante is precipitated by the latter's admiration of Almirena's portrait. Act 3 loses its marches and battle; instead Rinaldo has to contend with the magically generated obstacles of an enchanted grove. Armida and Argante vanish before the final scene on a chariot drawn by dragons, remaining defiantly pagan. The only new music written for this version is the extended accompanied recitative for Rinaldo in which he tackles the magic grove; the other musical changes were created by the incorporation of eight arias from other operas (five from *Lotario*), and by cuts, adaptations or transpositions. In effect the 1731 version is a pasticcio, and, though a tenor Goffredo may be considered an advantage, the characterization is in general enfeebled and much of the brash brilliance of the original is lost.

* * *

In his preface to the libretto Aaron Hill suggested that the earlier Italian operas heard in London had been 'compos'd for Tastes and Voices, different from those who were to sing and hear them on the *English* Stage', and that they lacked 'the Machines and Decorations, which bestow so great a Beauty on their Appearance'. He had therefore 'resolv'd to frame some Dramma, that by different Incidents and Passions, might afford the Musick Scope to vary and display its Excellence, and to fill the Eye with more delightful Prospects, so at once to give Two Senses equal Pleasure'. Handel's music is certainly both varied and excellent, with much resourceful use of woodwind solos and the addition of four trumpets to the score to produce a wide range of instrumental colour; Armida's final aria of Act 2 includes the unusual feature of improvised harpsichord solos. Some of the musical material was taken from works Handel had composed in Italy three or four years earlier, often substantially reworked. Argante's opening aria, 'Sibillar gli angui d'Aletto', taken directly from the part of Polyphemus in the cantata *Aci, Galatea e Polifemo*, is incongruous despite its appropriately bombastic mood, but the other borrowings fit in well. 'Lascia ch'io pianga', Almirena's heartfelt plea for her liberty in Act 2, was originally a seductive song in the allegorical oratorio *Il trionfo del Tempo e del Disinganno*, but the music is far more moving in its new dramatic context.

The dominant character of the opera is Armida, the first of a line of formidable Handelian sorceresses. She gives an immediate impression of fiery passion in her opening cavatina 'Furie terribili'. The mood reappears in the central section of her great lament in Act 2 ('Ah! crudel il pianto mio'), contrasting with the grief-laden Largo of the aria's main section, introduced by plangent solos on oboe and bassoon. Rinaldo makes a lively hero, rescued from conventionality by 'Cara sposa', his own aria of lamentation on the loss of Almirena in Act 1; the fully worked counterpoint of the string accompaniment, with occasional chromatic touches, gives it a remarkable

emotional power. Almirena, despite 'Lascia ch'io pianga', is a slighter figure, but there is great charm in her birdsong aria 'Augelletti', with its solos for sopranino recorder, and in the playful metrical changes of 'Bel piacere' (taken from *Agrippina*). Of the remaining characters only the blustering Argante is specially memorable. The makeweight arias for the ineffective Eustazio are particularly bland, and the character was cut from revivals after 1713.

See also ARMIDA. ANTHONY HICKS

Rinaldo di [da] **Capua** (*b* Capua or Naples, *c*1710; *d* ?Rome, *c*1780). Italian composer, possibly the father of Marcello Bernardini. Burney (1771) described him as:

an old and excellent Neapolitan composer. He is the natural son of a person of very high rank in that county, and at first only studied music as an accomplishment; but being left by his father with only a small fortune, which was soon dissipated, he was forced to make it his profession. He was but seventeen when he composed his first opera at Vienna.

Burney's description of Rinaldo as 'old' in 1771 and his string of operatic successes beginning in 1737 suggest a birthdate around 1710. Presumably the epithet 'di Capua' indicates that Rinaldo was born in the town of this name 30 km north of Naples. Probably he studied privately; his name does not appear on the rolls of the Neapolitan conservatories. Burney (*History*, 1789) cited incomplete training as the reason for the judgment of Rinaldo in La Borde's *Essai*: 'the science of this composer is not equal to his genius'.

Rinaldo made his career in Rome, where he presented his first known opera, *Ciro riconosciuto*, in 1737. In 1738 he scored a notable success with the satirical opera *La commedia in commedia*, repeated in Florence (1741), Venice (1744), London (1748), Munich (1749) and elsewhere. His most celebrated *opera seria*, *Vologeso, re de' Parti*, followed in 1739, and in 1740 his comic opera *La libertà nociva* enjoyed many repetitions. On 18 March 1740 Rinaldo set out for Lisbon, where he had a contract for 1000 scudi per annum; he composed three *opere serie* there but was back in Rome by 1742. Performances in Paris of his comic operas *La donna superba* (an abridged setting of *La commedia in commedia*) and *La zingara* by Eustachio Bambini's troupe figured significantly in the Querelle des Bouffons; the latter work was revived many times in different versions. Rinaldo's last *opera seria*, *Adriano in Siria*, dates from 1758; thereafter he confined himself to comic opera and his productivity declined.

Burney (1789) said Rinaldo 'was living, or rather starving in 1770 at Rome', out of favour despite the recent success of *I finti pazzi per amore*, and (1771) that 'the accumulated produce of his pen, had by a graceless son been sold for waste paper!'. His few surviving operas, from an output of 30 or so, show that Rinaldo's strengths lay in his melodic charm, sense of form and response to a dramatic situation. An innovation he claimed for himself was the use of long ritornellos in accompanied recitative. His preference for thin textures and simple harmonies occasioned La Borde's negative comments concerning his technique, but that was not unusual for the time. Despite Burney's comments (1771) concerning the impossibility of his doing anything really new, Rinaldo seems to have kept pace with his younger contemporaries at least in terms of form, as shown, for instance, in the multi-sectional finale of *La donna vendicativa*. Burney (1789), recalling hearing an aria from *Vologeso*, 'Ombra che pallida', in the London pasticcio *Gianguir* (1742), singled it out along with the preceding accompanied recitative as 'an example of the perfection to which dramatic music was brought in Italy near fifty years ago'.

See also ZINGARA, LA.

first performed in Rome unless otherwise stated

dg – *dramma giocoso*   dm – *dramma per musica*
int – *intermezzo*

Ciro riconosciuto (dm, 3, P. Metastasio), Tordinona, carn. 1737
Untitled comic opera, Valle, 1737
La commedia in commedia (dg, 3, F. Vanneschi, after C. A. Pelli), Valle, 8 Jan 1738; rev. as L'ambizione delusa, Venice, S Cassiano, carn. 1744; abridged as La donna superba (int), Paris, Opéra, 19 Dec 1752, *F-Po*; parodied as La femme orgueilleuse, Paris, 1759 (London, *c*1749)
Vologeso, re de' Parti (dm, 3, G. E. Luccarelli, after A. Zeno: *Lucio Vero*), Torre Argentina, carn. 1739, *D-Dlb*, *US-NH* (*R*1977: IOB, xxxviii)
Farnace (dm, 3, A. M. Lucchini), Venice, S Giovanni Grisostomo, aut. 1739
La libertà nociva (dg, 3, G. Barlocci), Valle, 17 Jan 1740
Catone in Utica (dm, 3, Metastasio), Lisbon, Rua dos Condes, 1740, rev. Milan, Regio, Jan 1748, *P-La*
Didone abbandonata (dm, 3, Metastasio), Lisbon, Rua dos Condes, 1741
Ipermestra (dm, 3), Lisbon, Rua dos Condes, 1741
Le nozze di Don Trifone (int, 2, N. G. Neri), Torre Argentina, carn. 1743
Turno Heredonio Aricino (dm, 3, S. Stampiglia), Capranica, 11 Dec 1743, arias *I-Bborromeo*
Il bravo burlato (int, 2, A. Pavoni), Pallacorda, carn. 1745, rev. as Il capitan Fracasso, Stockholm, 1768, *S-St*
La forza del sangue (int), Pallacorda, 1746
Il bravo e il bello (int), Granari, 1748
Mario in Numidia (dm, 3, G. Tagliazucchi), Dame, Jan 1749
Untitled comic opera, 1750
Il ripiego in amore di Flaminia finta cameriera e Turco (farsetta, 2, A. Lungi), Valle, carn. 1751
Il galoppino (int, 1), Capranica, carn. 1751
Gli impostori (dg, 3), Modena, Ducale, 1751, *I-MOe*
Il cavalier Mignatta (int, 2), Capranica, 1751, *Fc* [6 arias rev. in La zingara]
La forza della pace (int, 2, G. Puccinelli and G. Aureli), Pace, carn. 1752 [also ?1742]
La serva sposa (int, 2), Valle, carn. 1753, aria *Nc*
L'amante deluso (farsetta giocosa, 2, Pavoni), Tordinona, May 1753
La zingara (int, 2), Paris, Opéra, 19 June 1753, *F-Pn*, *I-Fc*, rev. E. Bambini as Il vecchio amante e la zingara (dg, 2), Pesaro, Sole, Jan 1755; as La bohémienne (oc, C.-S. Favart), Paris, Comédie-Italienne (Bourgogne), 28 July 1755, with addns by others, *Mc*; as La bohémienne (comédie, 2), Paris, Foire St Laurent, 14 July 1756, *B-Bc*, *D-B*, *GB-Lbl*, *I-Bc*, *Tn*, *S-St*, *US-Bp*, *Wc*
La chiavarina (int, 2, G. Peruzzini and A. Luigi), Valle, carn. 1754
Attalo (dm, 3, A. Papi [pseud. Cleofante Doriano]), Capranica, Feb 1754
La smorfiosa (int, 2), Valle, carn. 1756; rev. Lucca, Pubblico, 1762
Il capitano napoletano (commedia, 2), Florence, Cocomero, spr. 1756
Adriano in Siria (dm, 3, Metastasio), Torre Argentina, 2 Jan 1758, *P-La*
Le donne ridicole (int, 2, C. Goldoni), Capranica, Jan 1759
Il caffè di campagna (farsetta, 2, P. Chiari), Pace, carn. 1764, *La*
Il passegio in villa (farsetta), Pace, carn. 1765
I finti pazzi per amore (farsetta, 2, T. Mariani), Pace, carn. 1770 [also ?1742], *I-Rdp*
La donna vendicativa, o sia L'erudito spropositato (farsetta, 2, A. Pioli), Pace, carn. 1771 [also *c*1740], *GB-Lbl* (Act 1), *US-Wc*
La Giocondina (comic op), Pace, 1778

Single arias in *A-Wgm*, *B-Bc*, *D-Dlb*, *Mbs*, *MÜp*, *F-Pn*, *GB-Lbl*, *I-Fc*, *Mc*, *Nc*, *US-BE*

BurneyFI; BurneyH
C. d'Orville: *Histoire de l'opéra bouffon*, i (Amsterdam, 1768), 66–72
J.-B. de La Borde: *Essai sur la musique ancienne et moderne* (Paris, 1780)
P. Spitta: 'Rinaldo di Capua', *VMw*, iii (1887), 92–121
E. Celani: 'Musica e musicisti in Roma (1750–1850)', *RMI*, xviii (1911), 1–63
A. Della Corte: *L'opera comica italiana nel '700*, i (Bari, 1923), 81ff
E. Sundström: 'Ett okänt Intermezzo av Rinaldo di Capua', *STMf*, xix (1937), 200-05
F. Walker: '"Tre giorni son che Nina", an Old Controversy Re-opened', *MT*, xc (1949), 432–5
R. L. Bostian: *The Works of Rinaldo di Capua* (diss., U. of North Carolina, 1961)
C. Gallico: 'Rinaldo da Capua: Zingara o Bohémienne?', *Venezia e il melodramma nel settecento: Venice 1973*, i, 425–36
CLAUDIO GALLICO, STEPHEN C. FISHER

Ring des Nibelungen, Der ('The Nibelung's Ring'). *Bühnenfestpiel* ('stage festival play') for three days and a preliminary evening by Richard Wagner (*see* WAGNER family, (1)) to his own libretto; Bayreuth, Festspielhaus, first performance as a cycle: *Das Rheingold*, 13 August 1876; *Die Walküre*, 14 August 1876; *Siegfried*, 16 August 1876; *Götterdämmerung*, 17 August 1876.

Contrary to Wagner's claim that he turned away from historical subjects on discovering the potentialities of myth for his future music dramas, myth and history were interwoven in the *Ring* from the beginning. Not only was he working on his historical drama *Friedrich I*, begun in 1846, as late as 1848–9, but he was also making speculative connections between the stories of the Hohenstaufen emperor and the Nibelung hoard. Those supposed connections were formulated in the essay *Die Wibelungen: Weltgeschichte aus der Sage*. And although it was previously supposed that *Die Wibelungen* preceded the initial prose résumé and libretto for what became the *Ring*, it is now considered more likely that it succeeded them, probably about mid-February 1849 (see Deathridge, Geck and Voss 1986).

The chief sources Wagner drew on for the *Ring* are as follows: the Poetic (or Elder) Edda, the *Völsunga Saga* and the Prose Edda by Snorri Sturluson (all three of which were compiled in Iceland, probably in the first half of the 13th century); *Das Nibelungenlied*, an epic poem written in Middle High German *c*1200; and *Thidreks Saga af Bern*, a prose narrative written *c*1260–70 in Old Norse. Wagner also read copiously around the subject (see Magee 1990) and was indebted to the work of such scholars as Karl Lachmann, Franz Joseph Mone, Ludwig Ettmüller and the Grimm brothers.

Greek drama was also a major influence, not least in its use of mythology, its life-affirming idealism and the religious aura surrounding its performance. The *Oresteia* suggested not only the structure of a trilogy (*Das Rheingold* was merely a 'preliminary evening'), but also the confrontations of pairs of characters, the possibility of linking successive episodes with the themes of guilt and a curse, and perhaps even the leitmotif principle (in Aeschylus's use of recurrent imagery). There are also important parallels between the *Ring* and the *Prometheus* trilogy, especially as reconstructed by its German translator, Johann Gustav Droysen.

Wagner outlined a prose résumé for his drama, dated 4 October 1848, which in his collected writings he called *Der Nibelungen-Mythus: als Entwurf zu einem Drama* (the original manuscript is headed *Der Nibelungensage (Mythus)*). In this résumé the drama centres on Siegfried's death, and, at the conclusion, Brünnhilde purges the guilt of the gods by an act of self-immolation, allowing them to reign in glory instead of perishing. The story at this stage largely follows the order familiar from the finished work, but in autumn

1848 Wagner next compiled a libretto for *Siegfrieds Tod* (originally spelt *Siegfried's Tod*). This created so much back-narration of earlier events, however, that he subsequently, in 1851, wrote *Der junge Siegfried* (originally *Jung-Siegfried*), and finally *Die Walküre* and *Das Rheingold* (1851–2). Returning to revise *Der junge Siegfried* and *Siegfrieds Tod* in the light of the whole cycle, Wagner replaced Siegfried as the central figure by Wotan, and altered the ending so that the gods and Valhalla are all destroyed by fire. *Der junge Siegfried* and *Siegfrieds Tod* were eventually renamed *Siegfried* and *Götterdämmerung*. Thus the librettos of the constituent parts of the *Ring* cycle were written in reverse order, though the original conception was in the 'correct' order, as was the composition of the music.

The principals in the first three cycles given at Bayreuth in August 1876 included: Franz Betz (Wotan/ Wanderer), Amalie Materna (Brünnhilde), Georg Unger (Siegfried), Albert Niemann (Siegmund), Josephine Schefsky (Sieglinde), Karl Hill (Alberich), Friederike Sadler-Grün (Fricka) and Luise Jaide (Erda). The conductor was Hans Richter. The tetralogy was not heard again at Bayreuth until 1896, when it was conducted by Richter, Felix Mottl and Siegfried Wagner. Complete cycles were given in Munich in 1878, Vienna in 1879 and Hamburg in 1880. Following the success of his production in Leipzig in 1878, Angelo Neumann took it on a Europe-wide tour with his travelling theatre, beginning in 1882. The first complete cycle in Britain was given at Her Majesty's, London, in 1882, in German, with Anton Seidl conducting, Emil Scaria as Wotan/ Wanderer and Albert Niemann as Siegmund. Not until 1908 was it given in London in English, in uncut performances under the baton of Hans Richter. The first complete cycle in the USA was given at the Metropolitan in 1889, with Lilli Lehmann as Brünnhilde; the conductor was Seidl.

Notable Wotan/Wanderers have included Van Rooy, Schorr, Bockelmann, Hotter, Adam, McIntyre, Bailey and Morris. Brünnhilde has been sung by Lilli Lehmann, Nordica, Turner, Austral, Leider, Lubin, Flagstad, Varnay, Nilsson, Hunter and Gwyneth Jones. Interpreters of Siegfried have included Jean de Reszke, Melchior, Max Lorenz, Windgassen, Jess Thomas, Suthaus, Alberto Remedios, René Kollo, Jung and Jerusalem. Siegmund has been sung by Niemann, Svanholm, Vinay, James King, Windgassen, Vickers, Alberto Remedios, Peter Hofmann and Jerusalem. Sieglinde has been sung by Lilli Lehmann, Nordica, Ternina, Jeritza, Lotte Lehmann, Flagstad, Varnay, Rysanek, Crespin and Norman. Notable conductors of the *Ring* have included Richter, Mottl, Seidl, Mahler, Nikisch, Bodanzky, Coates, Walter, Beecham, Furtwängler, Solti, Karajan, Goodall, Böhm, Boulez, Colin Davis, Barenboim, Haitink and Levine.

Interpretations of the *Ring*, both literary and dramaturgical, have ranged from those that explore the work's social and political context to those that focus on its imagery and mythological content, denying any political ramifications. Shaw's classic interpretation of the *Ring* (1898) as a socialist allegory has been hugely influential, as has Donington's radically different analysis of the work in terms of Jungian psychology (1963). Taking their cue perhaps from Shaw, a series of radical stagings in the 1970s and 80s attempted to demythologize the work, emphasizing the corruption and debased moral values by which the gods, and in particular Wotan, are tainted. Recent productions have also dwelt on feminist and ecological aspects of the *Ring*.

See also *Götterdämmerung*; *Rheingold, das*; *Siegfried*; and *Walküre, die*.
BARRY MILLINGTON

Rintzler, Marius (*b* Bucharest, 14 March 1932). Romanian bass. He studied in Bucharest, making his début there in 1964 as Don Basilio (*Il barbiere di Siviglia*). He sang the Commendatore at Glyndebourne in 1967, returning for Henry VIII (*Anna Bolena*), Osmin, Mozart's Bartolo, La Roche (*Capriccio*) and Sir Morosus (*Die schweigsame Frau*). Engaged at Düsseldorf for 20 years, he also sang at Geneva, Florence, Brussels, San Francisco, Rio, Dallas, Philadelphia and the Metropolitan; his roles included Leporello, Don Magnifico, Don Geronimo (*Il matrimonio segreto*), Alberich, Ochs and Wesener (*Die Soldaten*). A fine actor with an expressive voice, he sang in the American première of Penderecki's *Die schwarze Maske* at Santa Fe (1988).
ELIZABETH FORBES

Rinuccini, Ottavio (*b* Florence, 20 Jan 1562; *d* Florence, 28 March 1621). Italian librettist. He came of a noble Florentine family prominent in cultural and diplomatic circles since the 13th century. His education was presumably that of a courtier – some classical training and enough exposure to the arts to have made him a lively participator in court entertainments in Florence, for which he began writing verses as early as 1579 (*Maschere d'amazzoni*). The court chronicler Bastiano de' Rossi called him 'a very fine connoisseur' of music, and G. B. Doni suggested that Monteverdi relied on him greatly while setting his libretto for *Arianna*.

Already a member of the Accademia Fiorentina, in 1586 Rinuccini joined another Florentine academy, the Alterati – whose members were particularly interested in dramatic theory and music – and took the name 'Il Sonnacchioso' ('the somnolent one'). There is no evidence to affirm Rinuccini's connection with Giovanni de' Bardi's Camerata, but Bardi (like other musical humanists such as Girolamo Mei and Jacopo Corsi) was also a member of the Accademia degli Alterati and collaborated with Rinuccini on the six *intermedi* of 1589 that he produced for the wedding celebrations of Grand Duke Ferdinando I. The third *intermedio*, which depicts the battle between Apollo and the dragon, later served Rinuccini as the basis for the opening scene of his first operatic text, *Dafne*, which he claimed to have written 'solely to test the power of modern music'. Thus Apollo, god of both music and the sun, by virtue of his power in vanquishing the irrational forces represented by the python, was his first aesthetic spokesman.

During the 1590s Rinuccini was associated with Corsi, who collaborated with Peri in setting *Dafne* to music in the newly invented recitative style. First performed at Corsi's home in 1598 and repeated in the following two years, *Dafne* was the first drama to be sung in its entirety 'in the manner of the ancients'. The innovations claimed by Rinuccini and Peri in their prefaces to *Euridice* (1600) inspired the rival claims of Cavalieri and Caccini, neither of whom, however, had written recitative as such before 1600.

Rinuccini adopted many conventions from the major lyric poets of the day, Tasso, Guarini and Chiabrera. His originality lay in his developing for *Dafne* a consistent and unique kind of verse well suited to Peri's recitative. This verse, a compromise between the blank verse typical of spoken tragedy and the uniform metres and close rhymes of traditional lyrical forms, consists of an irregular alternation of freely rhyming seven- and 11-syllable lines, which, without precluding lyricism, allows for a musical setting designed to imitate the accents of speech. Moreover, by adopting Ovidian plots, which themselves reflect the power of art, and through the Prologue and happy ending of *Euridice*, Rinuccini established a link between the new art form and the tragi-comic genre, defended by Guarini as suitable for the purging of melancholy, rather than of pity and fear, as with the ancients. Thus Rinuccini's librettos must not be seen as unsuccessful imitations of classical tragedy but as highly appropriate vehicles through which 'modern' music might prove its power to move. That he called his next libretto, *Arianna* (1608, set by Monteverdi), a 'tragedia' is more a reflection of its pathetic subject than a generic distinction, for it too follows Ovid and resorts at the end to a 'deus ex machina', with Ariadne being transported to the heavens.

Rinuccini's association with Monteverdi in Mantua also resulted in the *Mascherata dell'ingrate* (1608), which reflects the influence of the French court ballet and his own periodic sojourns in France between 1600 and 1604 as one of Maria de' Medici's courtiers. Also in 1608 *Dafne* was revived in a new setting by Marco da Gagliano, whose Mantuan-based Accademia degli Elevati Rinuccini had joined. However, his last libretto, *Narciso*, dating from about the same period, did not find a willing composer, and he subsequently wrote only a few minor works in the pastoral vein and some sacred verses, in addition to sonnets, *canzoni* and madrigals (including *Zefiro torna* and *Lamento della ninfa*, famous in Monteverdi's settings). His decline as a librettist was due perhaps more than anything else to the gradual shift of operatic activity before his death away from Florence and Mantua to Rome.

*

G. Mazzoni: 'Cenni sul Ottavio Rinuccini, poeta', *Commemorazione della riforma melodrammatica: atti dell'Accademia del R. Istituto musicale di Firenze*, xxxiii (1895)

F. Raccamadoro-Ramelli: *Ottavio Rinuccini* (Fabriano, 1900)

A. Solerti: *Le origini del melodramma* (Turin, 1903)

——: *Gli albori del melodramma* (Milan, 1904–5) [incl. texts of principal works]

——: *Musica, ballo e drammatica alla corte medicea dal 1600 al 1637* (Florence, 1905)

O. G. Sonneck: '*Dafne*, the First Opera: a Chronological Study', *SIMG*, xv (1913–14), 102–10

M. Schild: *Die Musikdramen O. Rinuccinis* (Würzburg, 1933)

C. Calcaterra: *Poesie e canto: studi sulla poesia melica italiana e sulla favola per musica* (Bologna, 1951)

A. A. Abert: *Claudio Monteverdi und das musikalische Drama* (Lippstadt, 1954), 100ff, 105ff

W. V. Porter: 'Peri and Corsi's *Dafne*: Some New Discoveries and Observations', *JAMS*, xviii (1965), 170–96

C. V. Palisca: 'The Alterati of Florence, Pioneers in the Theory of Dramatic Music', *New Looks at Italian Opera: Essays in Honor of Donald J. Grout* (Ithaca, NY, 1968), 9–38

N. Pirrotta: 'Early Opera and Aria', ibid, 39–107

B. R. Hanning: 'Apologia pro Ottavio Rinuccini', *JAMS*, xxvi (1973), 240–62

G. A. Tomlinson: 'Ancora su Ottavio Rinuccini', *JAMS*, xxviii (1975), 351–6

B. Bujić: 'An Early Croat Translation of Rinuccini's "Euridice"', *MZ*, xii (1976), 16–29

F. W. Sternfeld: 'The First Printed Opera Libretto', *ML*, lix (1978), 121–38

F. Angelini: *Il teatro barocco: il seicento* (Bari, 1979), 76–81

B. R. Hanning: 'Glorious Apollo: Poetic and Political Themes in the First Opera', *Renaissance Quarterly*, xxxii (1979), 485–513

F. W. Sternfeld: 'The Birth of Opera: Ovid, Poliziano, and the Lieto fine', *AnMc*, no.19 (1979), 30–51

B. R. Hanning: *Of Poetry and Music's Power: Humanism and the Creation of Opera* (Ann Arbor, 1980)

R. Donington: *The Rise of Opera* (New York, 1981)

G. Tomlinson: 'Madrigal, Monody, and Monteverdi's "via naturale alla immitatione"', *JAMS*, xxxiv (1981), 60–108

T. Carter: 'Jacopo Peri's Euridice (1600): a Contextual Study', *MR*, xliii (1982), 83–103

G. Tomlinson: 'Monteverdi and the Claims of Text: Monteverdi, Rinuccini, and Marino', *Critical Inquiry*, viii (1982), 565–89

N. Pirrotta: 'Monteverdi and the Problems of Opera', *Music and Culture in Italy from the Middle Ages to the Baroque* (Cambridge, MA, and London, 1984), 235–53

R. Katz: *Divining the Powers of Music: Aesthetic Theory and the Origins of Opera* (New York, 1986)

G. Tomlinson: *Monteverdi and the End of the Renaissance* (Berkeley and Los Angeles, 1987)

B. Bujić: '"Figura poetica molto vaga": Structure and Meaning in Rinuccini's *Euridice*', *Early Music History*, x (1991), 29–64

BARBARA R. HANNING

Rio de Janeiro. City in Brazil. It is the country's chief port and former capital. The first opera house was built in 1767, four years after the capital of colonial Brazil was moved to the city from Bahia. The traveller L. A. Bougainville vouched for a repertory of Neapolitan operas, sung by mulattos accompanied by an orchestra directed by a 'hunchbacked priest' named Ventura. During a performance in 1776 of the ballad opera *Os encantos de Medêa* (1735) by the local playwright António José da Silva (1705–39), Ventura's opera house burnt down; it was succeeded by the Teatro de Manuel Luís Ferreira (built by Ferreira, an ex-soldier from Portugal). There, in the 1790s, a troupe headed by the prima donna Joaquina da Conceição Lapa, born in Rio, sang Cimarosa's *L'italiana in Londra* and Millico's *La pietà d'amore*.

A new and brilliant epoch opened in 1808 with the arrival of the Portuguese royal family accompanied by an entourage of singers. The mulatto José Maurício Nunes García was named director of the court chapel by João VI that year, and at his request composed what was to be the first opera by a native of Rio de Janeiro, *Le due gemelle* (score lost). João VI summoned the composer Marcos Portugal from Lisbon in 1811; his theatre works mounted in Rio included *L'oro non compra amore*, given in 1811 at the Teatro Régio (formerly Teatro Manuel Luís Ferreira), *Artaserse*, the allegorical piece *O juramento dos numes*, given at the opening of the Real Teatro de S João in 1813, *Merope* and the serenata *Augurio di felicità, ossia Il trionfo del amore*.

Rossini dominated the repertory at the S João (which burnt down in 1824) and at its successor, the Imperial Teatro S Pedro de Alcântara, inaugurated in December 1824 with *L'inganno felice* sung by imported Italians. When Pedro II (1825–91) was crowned Emperor of Brazil in July 1831, political stability was assured; until his deposition in 1889, Rio de Janeiro was the paramount opera capital of the Americas. A grandson of Emperor Franz I of Austria, Pedro emulated the courts of Europe not only in protecting world-class performers but also in stimulating composers, Brazilian and foreign. Rossini, Bellini, Donizetti, Meyerbeer, Mercadante, Verdi and a host of lesser Italians dominated the repertory (Pacini's *Niccolò de' Lapi*, dedicated to Pedro II, was written for Rio de Janeiro in 1857, though apparently was not performed there), together with Auber, Adam, Boieldieu and Hérold. The S Pedro was destroyed by fire in 1851; it reopened on 18 August

1852 as the Teatro Provisório (renamed Lírico Fluminense in 1854), which burnt down in 1856, to be again reopened under its new name on 3 January 1857. Another theatre, the Teatro Ginásio Dramático, opened on 12 April 1855.

Pedro II chose a national holiday, 25 March 1857, to proclaim the foundation of the Imperial Academia de Música e Opera Nacional. Headed by the Spanish impresario José Amat, the academy on 12 May 1860 became the Empresa de Opera Lírica Nacional. This organization sponsored numerous Brazilian opera singers and the first operas by Brazilians sung in Portuguese: Elías Alvares Lôbo's A noite de São João (1860), Domingos José Ferreira's A côrte de Monaco (1862), Henrique Alves de Mesquita's O vagabundo (1863) and, most important, two operas by Carlos Gomes. After the successful premières of Gomes's A noite do castelo in 1861 and Joana de Flandres in 1863 (both at the Teatro Lírico Fluminense), Pedro sponsored him in Milan for 13 years.

So widely known became Pedro's largesse that in June 1857 Wagner sent him his three operas Der fliegende Holländer, Tannhäuser and Lohengrin. A month earlier he had written to Liszt that the 'Emperor of Brazil has caused me to be invited to go to him in Rio de Janeiro where I am to have everything in plenty'. Before starting to compose Tristan und Isolde later that year he even wrote to the Härtels that he had an excellent 'prospect of producing Tristan in the Italian tongue at Rio de Janeiro'. On 23 August 1871 Pedro met Wagner in Berlin and in 1876 he attended the Bayreuth opening of Das Rheingold. However, not Tristan but Lohengrin became Wagner's first opera produced at Rio de Janeiro, on 19 September 1883 in the Teatro Dom Pedro II (from 1890 the Teatro Lírico). At the same theatre Toscanini made his world début as a conductor, on 30 June 1886 in Aida. During the remainder of the season he conducted 26 performances, including La favorite, Rigoletto, Trovatore, Faust, La Gioconda, Gomes's Salvator Rosa, Thomas's Hamlet, and Les Huguenots.

16 operas by Brazilian composers were mounted at Rio de Janeiro between 1889 and 1937, from Gomes's Lo schiavo to António de Assis Republicano's A natividade de Jesus (for a complete list see Corrêa de Azevedo 1938, pp.87–8). From its opening in 1909, the Teatro Municipal (property of the State of Guanabara) consistently included Brazilian operas in each season, always sung and conducted by Brazilians. Those performed between 1950 and 1986 include Gomes's Il Guarany and Lo schiavo, Nepomuceno's Artemis, Mignone's L'innocente and Guarnieri's Pedro Malazarte.

Thanks to the British Council and the Brazilian Society of English Culture, Peter Grimes had its first Latin American performance at the Teatro Municipal on 27 October 1967, with Britten and Pears present. At its next presentation in 1982 an all-Brazilian cast was conducted by Steuart Bedford. Porgy and Bess arrived at the Municipal on 27 October 1986, and German operas were also given there as visiting companies toured South America, including Der fliegende Holländer, sung in German, on 2 April 1987, when surtitles were used for the first time. During Jacques Pernoo's seventh visit, the 1967 season began with the first staged performance in South America of Honegger's Jeanne d'Arc au bûcher; in 1968 Pernoo triumphed with a staged Damnation de Faust and on 14 April 1972 he conducted the South American première of Milhaud's scenic cantata Saint Louis. In contrast with the early 1950s, when more than 20 operas were given in a season, limited funding in the 1980s usually restricted the Municipal seasons to five operas, each repeated five times. The French version of Gluck's Orfeo ed Euridice, sung in Italian and first staged at the Municipal in 1984, was repeated there in 1987.

*

L. H. Corrêa de Azevedo: Relação das óperas de autores brasileiros (Rio de Janeiro, 1938)

——: 150 anos de música no Brasil, 1800–1950 (Rio de Janeiro, 1956), 59–89, 201–16

Música no Rio de Janeiro imperial 1822–1870: exposição comemorativa do primeiro decênio de Secção de música e arquivo sonora (Rio de Janeiro, 1962)

R. Stevenson: 'Some Portuguese Sources for Early Brazilian Music History', Yearbook: Inter-American Institute for Musical Research, iv (1968), 24–5

B. Kiefer: História da música brasileira dos primórdios ao início do século XX (Porto Alegre, 1976)

R. Stevenson: 'Wagner's Latin American Outreach (to 1900)', Inter-American Music Review, v/2 (1983), 63–85

ROBERT STEVENSON

Riotte, Philipp Jakob (b Wendel, Saar, 16 Aug 1776; d Vienna, 20 Aug 1856). German composer. He was a pupil of Anton André at Offenbach and in 1804 he appeared as pianist and composer at a concert in Frankfurt. In 1805 or 1806 he became music director at Gotha and was subsequently at Danzig (now Gdańsk) and Magdeburg. At the Erfurt Congress in 1808 he directed the French opera performances. He then went to Vienna where he worked at the court opera and then as music director at the Theater an der Wien (1818–21 and 1824–6).

Although Riotte enjoyed success in his lifetime in every musical form then in favour, he was best known for his stage works and keyboard pieces, but the only score to outlive its composer was that written in 1827 for Raimund's Moisasurs Zauberfluch: only the songs survive (they were republished twice in the 1920s), but they are still sometimes used in performances of the play. Some 50 Singspiels and stage scores by Riotte were given in the five principal Viennese theatres between 1809 and 1840, including the parody Staberl als Freischütz, in collaboration with Philipp Röth, which had some 60 performances between 1826 and 1856. Several pantomimes were also particularly successful in their day, notably Horschelt's Der Berggeist, with 76 performances. A large collection of Riotte's works in manuscript is held by the Gesellschaft der Musikfreunde, Vienna.

selective list; first performed in Vienna unless otherwise stated

Pietro und Elmira (grosse Oper, 3), Magdeburg, 1806

Das Grenzstädtchen (Spl, 1, ? A. von Kotzebue), Brunswick, Hof, 1808

Die Brandschatzung, Magdeburg, Schauspielhaus, ?1808

Kasem, oder Die Launen des Glückes (allegorische Operette, 1, A. Klingemann), Wien, 29 June 1818

Azendar (Melodram, 3, F. von Biedenfeld, after Caigniez), An der Wien, 31 July 1819

Die Witwe und ihre Freier (komische Oper, 2, Biedenfeld), An der Wien, 31 July 1820

Mozarts Zauberflöte (Spl), Prague, Landes, 1820

Staberl als Freischütz (Parodie, 3, K. Carl), Munich, Isartor, 4 Dec 1822, collab. P. Röth

Welche ist die beste Frau? (Zauberposse, 2, J. A. Gleich), An der Wien, 16 Aug 1823

Euphemie von Avogara (grosse Oper, 3), Kärntnertor, 3 Oct 1823

Die Gaben des eisernen Königs (Feenmärchen, 3), An der Wien, 24 April 1824

Der kurze Mantel [Act 1] (Volksmärchen, 3, J. G. Seidl), An der Wien, 6 Nov 1824 [Act 2 by Blumenthal, Act 3 by I. von Seyfried]

Nureddin, Prinz von Persien (tragisch-komische Feenoper, 3, F. X. Gewey), An der Wien, 1 Feb 1825

Die Prise Toback, oder Die Vettern als Nebenbuhler (Spl, 1), Kärntnertor, 15 July 1825

Die Drillingsschwestern und der Waldgeist (Zauberposse, 2), Josefstadt, 29 Oct 1825

Das Konzert am Hofe (komische Oper, 2), Josefstadt, 10 Jan 1827 [based on Auber: Le concert à la cour]

Der hölzerne Säbel, oder Die Herrschau (Spl, 1, Kotzebue), An der Wien, 12 July 1827, music by Röth and Riotte

König Richard in Palästina, oder Englands Reichspanier (heroisch-romantisches Schauspiel, 4, J. Lembert, after W. Scott: The Talisman), An der Wien, 18 Aug 1827

Moisasurs Zauberfluch (Zauberspiel, 2, F. Raimund), An der Wien, 25 Sept 1827

Zwei Uhr (Melodram), An der Wien, 25 Oct 1827

Vetter Lukas von Jamaika (komische Oper, 2, after C. D. von Dittersdorf: Hieronymus Knicker), An der Wien, 15 July 1828

Die Waldkönigin, oder Der Giftbecher (Zauberspiel, 3, F. X. Told), Josefstadt, 20 April 1829

Die geschwätzige Stumme von Nussdorf (parodierende Posse, 2, K. Meisl), Leopoldstadt, 27 March 1830

Das Kind des Meeres (Zauberspiel, 2, F. Manussi), Leopoldstadt, 23 April 1831

Fee Rosentritt und Zauberer Sturmschritt (phantastisches Märchen, 2, W. Blum), Leopoldstadt, 2 July 1831

Nina, oder Die Wanderung nach einem Mann (Zauberspiel, 2, J. Schickh), Leopoldstadt, 14 April 1832

Moralis, oder Der Untergang des bösen Zeitgeistes (Zauberspiel, 2, Schickh), Leopoldstadt, 4 Oct 1832

Die Lieb' auf der Alm (Posse, 3, A. Schmidl), Leopoldstadt, 17 Jan 1833

Der Harfenist (Gemälde aus dem Volksleben, 3, Schmidl), Leopoldstadt, 20 April 1833

Liebenau, oder Die Wanderung nach einer Frau (Zauberspiel, 2, Schickh), Leopoldstadt, 12 Sept 1833

Der Sturm, oder Prosperos Geisterinsel (3, J. G. Seidl, after W. Shakespeare: The Tempest), Brno, 20 Sept 1833

Hymens Zauberspruch, oder Die Heiraten nach Geld (Zauberspiel, 2, Schickh), Leopoldstadt, 1 March 1834

Die Lieb' in der Stadt (Posse, 3, Schickh), Leopoldstadt, 19 April 1834

Kupferschmied, Koch und Kappelmacher (Posse, 3, F. Hopp), An der Wien, 5 Feb 1835

Der Postillon von Stade Enzersdorf (parodierende Posse, 3, Gleich), Josefstadt, 18 Jan 1838

Der Kampf der Eilfer mit den Zwölfern (parodierende Posse, 3, Schickh), Josefstadt, 25 April 1840

*

StiegerO; WurzbachL

P. J. Riotte: Autobiographical sketch (MS, 1826, A-Wgm) [with catalogue of works]

Obituary, Neue Wiener Musik-Zeitung, v (1856), 175

F. Hadamowsky: Das Theater in der Wiener Leopoldstadt 1781–1860 (Vienna, 1934)

A. Bauer: 150 Jahre Theater an der Wien (Zürich, 1952)

——: Opern und Operetten in Wien: Verzeichnis ihrer Erstaufführungen von 1629 bis zur Gegenwart (Graz and Cologne, 1955)

——: Das Theater in der Josefstadt zu Wien (Vienna and Munich, 1957)

PETER BRANSCOMBE

Rippon, Michael (b Coventry, 10 Dec 1938). English bass-baritone. He studied at the RAM, singing Gianni Schicchi there in 1962. For the WNO (1967–74) he sang Bartolo (Mozart and Rossini), Leporello and Donald (Billy Budd), and at Glyndebourne (1970–73) his roles included Surin (The Queen of Spades) and the Police Chief (Der Besuch der alten Dame). He has also sung with Opera North, the ENO, the New York City Opera and at Buxton. His repertory ranges from Somnus (Semele), Don Pasquale, Dulcamara and Don Pizarro to the 20th-century works in which he specializes. He sang in the premières of Maxwell Davies's The Martyrdom of St Magnus (1977, Orkney) and The Lighthouse (1980, Edinburgh), and created Antipholus of Ephesus in Andrew Wilson-Dickson's Errors (1980, Leicester) and

Merlin in Hamilton's Lancelot (1985, Arundel). An excellent actor, he sings with impeccable musicianship.

ELIZABETH FORBES

Risack, Rosa Negri. See NEGRI, MARIA ROSA.

Rising of the Moon, The. Opera in three acts by NICHOLAS MAW to a libretto by Beverley Cross; Glyndebourne Festival Opera, 19 July 1970.

The libretto is an original comedy by an experienced playwright; the composer asked for romance rather than farce and for as many women's voices as possible. An English army regiment arrives in County Mayo, Ireland, in 1875. Cornet Beaumont (lyric tenor), a new officer whose interests are music, painting and botany, and who chose the 31st Lancers because he fancied the uniform, agrees to an initiation rite in which he is to smoke three cigars, drink three bottles of champagne and seduce three women before next morning's reveille. Hearing of this, the rebellious Irish contrive in Act 2 to lead Beaumont to the local inn, and involve him first with Lady Eugenie (soprano), wife of the regimental Colonel Lord Jowler (baritone), and next with Elisabeth von Zastrow (mezzo-soprano), wife of a Prussian major (baritone). Beaumont's third conquest is planned to be Atalanta (lyric soprano), the Adjutant's daughter, but the innkeeper's daughter Cathleen (soprano) substitutes herself out of genuine affection. In Act 3 Beaumont produces evidence of his conquests, forcing the regiment to move elsewhere, and is allowed to resign his commission, leaving a desolate Cathleen, while the other Irish celebrate the English discomfiture and withdrawal.

Enclosed within gentle prologue and epilogue arias sung by Brother Timothy (tenor), the one remaining monk in a run-down monastery appropriated for the officers' mess, the opera is fashioned in through-composed acts incorporating musical numbers which provide dramatic repose for developing character or ensemble situations. Maw's well-paced invention flowers readily into lyrical passages, freely atonal in harmonic direction and ornate in texture, allowing clarity of words. Some minor revisions were carried out between 1970 and 1971 at Glyndebourne, where the opera was staged by Colin Graham and conducted in successive years by Raymond Leppard and Myer Fredman. The libretto has been published in English and German, leading to productions at Graz and Bremen in 1978, and Wexford in 1990; in 1986 the opera proved a challenge to student voices in a production at the GSM, London.

NOËL GOODWIN

Rispoli, Salvatore (b Naples, ?c1736–45; d Naples, 1812). Italian composer. He studied with Insanguine and others at the S Onofrio conservatory, Naples, and later taught there. In 1781 he composed the music for Saverio Mattei's cantata on the death of Empress Maria Theresa; in the preface to the libretto Mattei praised Rispoli's abilities and added that through the 'happy disgrace' of not having had the opportunity to compose for the opera house he had avoided its corrupting influence. In 1782–7, however, Rispoli did have five operas, comic, serious and sacred, performed at Milan, Turin and the secondary theatres of Naples, but he never achieved the honour of being asked to compose for S Carlo. Most of his other works were sacred.

Il trionfo de' pupilli oppressi (commedia, P. Mililotti), Naples, Fiorentini, 20 Jan 1782

Nitteti (dramma per musica, P. Metastasio), Turin, Regio, 26 Dec 1782, *P-La*, excerpts *I-Tf*, arias *Gl*, *Mc* and *Tn*
Ipermestra (dramma per musica, Metastasio), Milan, Scala, 26 Dec 1785, *F-Pc*, *P-La* (Acts 1 and 3), aria *I-Mc*
Idalide (dramma per musica, F. Moretti), Turin, Regio, 26 Dec 1786, excerpts *CMbc*, *IBborromeo*, *Tf* and *Tn*
Il trionfo di Davide (dramma sacro), Naples, Fondo, Lent 1787, *Gl*

Arias etc. in *A-Wgm*, *CH-Zz*, *D-Dlb*, *I-Bsf*, *Gl*, *Mc*

*

FétisB; *FlorimoN*; *GerberL*

DENNIS LIBBY (text), JAMES L. JACKMAN (work-list)

Risse, Carl (*b* Dresden, *c*1810; *d* after 1845). German bass. His first engagement was at Leipzig, where he took part in the première of Marschner's *Der Templer und die Jüdin* (1829). Moving to the Dresden Hofoper, he sang there for many years, creating three Wagner roles, Cecco del Vecchio in *Rienzi* (1842), Daland in *Der fliegende Holländer* (1843) and Reinmar von Zweter in *Tannhäuser* (1845). His repertory included Osmin, Sarastro, Marcel (*Les Huguenots*) and Bertram (*Robert le diable*). ELIZABETH FORBES

Ristori, Giovanni Alberto (*b* ?Bologna, 1692; *d* Dresden, 7 Feb 1753). Italian composer. He was the son of Tommaso Ristori, a versatile musician and actor, the director of a travelling company of Italian comedians which, shortly before Giovanni's birth, was in the service of the Saxon elector Johann Georg III at Dresden. But Giovanni's birthplace is variously given as Bologna by La Borde and Gerber, Vienna by a Saxon passport of 1715, and Venice in a score of his cantata *Verdi colli*. His first opera, *Pallide trionfante in Arcadia*, had its première at the Teatro degli Obizzi, Padua, in summer 1713, and in November his *Orlando furioso* was given in the Teatro S Angelo, Venice; both were revived in Venice the following year when, in addition, his *Euristeo* was performed in Venice and Bologna (see Mengelberg) and his *Pigmalione* in Rovigo.

In 1715 Ristori and his wife Maria accompanied his parents to Dresden, but he held no official position there until 1717, when he was appointed composer to the Italian comic theatre managed by his father; at the same time he became director of the *cappella polacca* in Warsaw. Although Lotti was the resident opera composer at Dresden between 1717 and 1719, Ristori had *Cleonice*, his first opera for the court, staged on 15 August 1718. But Italian opera was severely curtailed soon afterwards, and Ristori and his father were among the few Italians not released from service in 1720. Ristori is not known to have composed any music for Dresden between 1718 and 1726, and the revival of *Cleonice* at Verona in 1723 suggests that he may have returned to Italy. The performance in Dresden on 2 September 1726 of his comic opera *Calandro*, sometimes called the first Italian *opera buffa* written in Germany, indicates his presence at the Saxon court. It was followed in 1727 by another Italian comedy, *Un pazzo ne fà cento, ovvero Don Chisciotte*. When *Calandro* was revived in Carnival 1728, Frederick the Great attended a performance and requested a copy of the score.

In 1733 Ristori was demoted to the rank of chamber organist. Gerber's claim that, in 1740, Ristori became Kapellmeister to the court at St Petersburg has not been verified, but he spent some of 1731–2 in Russia in his father's troupe of Italian comedians. A serenata by him was performed in Moscow during summer 1731, and the revival of *Calandro* on 30 November/11 December

is generally accounted the first performance of an Italian opera in Russia. After a short visit to St Petersburg in early 1732, Tommaso Ristori took his company to Poland, but Giovanni left them and went to Dresden to direct his oratorio *La deposizione della croce di nostro Signore* before returning to Warsaw.

Most of the Italian comedians at Dresden were dismissed when the Elector August I died in 1733. When Tommaso, aged 75, was pensioned off, improvised Italian comedy at the Dresden court came to an end, and serious opera, directed by Hasse the new Kapellmeister, dominated the Saxon stage. Ristori was probably in Warsaw between 1734 and August 1736 while the new Saxon elector was securing for himself the Polish throne. Sacred music and occasional secular works of 1735–6 indicate his close association with the court while Hasse was in Italy; he composed cantatas, a coronation opera *Le fate* performed on 10 August 1736, and the *azione scenica Arianna* for the elector's birthday on 7 October 1736.

Ristori probably did not supervise the première of his pasticcio *Didone abbandonata* at Covent Garden, London, on 13 April 1737, but he directed rehearsals and performances of his *Temistocle* and *Adriano in Siria* at S Carlo, Naples, in 1738 and 1739; he must have accompanied the Saxon princess Maria Amalia there following her marriage to Charles III, King of the Two Sicilies, in May 1738. By 1744 he had returned to Dresden, where, in that year, he composed three masses, the quality of which was acknowledged with his appointment as court *Kirchenkomponist* in 1746. In 1750 the elector again rewarded Ristori by renaming him vice-Kapellmeister under Hasse. His last work, a Mass in C, is dated 1752. A revival of *Arianna* at the Dresden court in 1756 is the last known performance of a theatrical work by Ristori in the 18th century.

Despite Mengelberg's excellent study, Ristori's music remains undervalued. His best works are his chamber cantatas and his large sacred pieces, which reveal contrapuntal complexities beyond those of Hasse's works of the 1740s. But he did not match Hasse for breadth or melodic beauty. Only in his intermezzos does Ristori seem to equal his more famous colleague.

drammi per musica unless otherwise stated

Pallide trionfante in Arcadia (dramma pastorale, 3, O. Mandelli), Padua, Obizzi, sum. 1713
Orlando furioso (3, G. Braccioli, after L. Ariosto), Venice, S Angelo, 7 Nov 1713; rev. Venice, 1714, *I-Tn*
Euristeo (3), Venice and Bologna, 1714
Pigmalione (3), Rovigo, 1714, *D-Dlb*
Cleonice (3, A. Constantini), Moritzburg, 15 Aug 1718
Calandro (comic op, 3, S. B. Pallavicino), Dresden, 2 Sept 1726, *Dlb*
Un pazzo ne fà cento, ovvero Don Chisciotte (ob, 3, Pallavicino, after M. de Cervantes), Dresden, 2 Feb 1727, *Dlb*
Le fate (1, Pallavicino), Dresden, Hof, 10 Aug 1736, *Dlb*
Didone abbandonata (pasticcio, 3, P. Metastasio), London, CG, 13 April 1737
Temistocle (3, Metastasio), Naples, S Carlo, 19 Dec 1738, *Dlb*
Adriano in Siria (3, Metastasio), Naples, S Carlo, 19 Dec 1739, *Dlb*, *I-Nc*
Diana vindicata (festa per musica, C. Pasquini), Dresden, 8 Dec 1746
La liberalità di Numa Pompilio (serenata, 1, Pasquini), Dresden, 1746, *D-Dlb*
Trajano (festa di camera, 1, Pasquini), Dresden, 1746
Amore insuperabile (festa di camera, 1, Pasquini), Dresden, 1747
I lamenti di Orfeo (festa di camera, 1, Pasquini), Dresden, 1749
Nicandro (3); Ercole (3): both formerly *Dlb*, lost in World War II

Intermezzos, probably 1st perf. Dresden: Delbo e Dorina; Despina, Simona e Trespolo; Fidelba ed Artabano; Lisandr. e Cast.; Serpilla e Perpello: all *Dlb*

GerberL; GerberNL

J.-B. de La Borde: *Essai sur la musique ancienne et moderne* (Paris, 1780), iii, 228

M. Fürstenau: *Zur Geschichte der Musik und des Theaters am Hofe zu Dresden*, ii (Dresden, 1862), 119–20, 162, 202–3

C. R. Mengelberg: *Giovanni Alberto Ristori* (Leipzig, 1916)

H. Schnoor: *Dresden: vierhundert Jahre deutsche Musikkultur* (Dresden, 1948), 72ff

R.-A. Mooser: *Annales de la musique et des musiciens en Russie an XVIIIme siècle*, i (Geneva, 1948)

B. S. Brook, ed.: *The Breitkopf Thematic Catalogue, 1762–87* (New York, 1966), 174, 178, 332   SVEN HANSELL

Ristorini [Restorini], Antonio Maria (*b* Bologna or Florence; *fl* 1690–1732). Italian tenor. He was the half-brother of Rosaura Mazzanti and husband of Rosa Ungarelli, with whom he enjoyed an international reputation as an interpreter of comic intermezzos. He began as a singer of *opera seria*. Between 1690 and 1710 he appeared in 18 productions in Florence and Venice, including Albinoni's *Griselda* and *Astarto* and works by Gasparini. He also sang in Reggio (1698), Naples (1706) and Parma (1714). By 1716 he had formed a partnership with Ungarelli that was to last for at least 17 years. They performed intermezzos at ten cities in northern Italy and introduced the genre into Germany, Belgium and France. From about 1720 they were frequently styled as 'virtuosi' of the Prince of Hesse-Darmstadt, but they cannot have spent much time at his court in Mantua.

They appear to have made their début at Turin during Carnival 1716 in *Vespetta e Pimpinone*. Three years later, in Venice, they gave the first performance of the revised version of Orlandini's *Il marito giocatore e la moglie bacchettona* (as Serpilla and Bacocco), the most popular intermezzo of the period. Both works were taken to Munich in autumn 1722 and, with others, to Brussels in autumn and winter 1728–9. In 1725, at Pistoia, G. C. Rossi-Melocchi recorded in his diary that they 'succeeded like a wonder of nature unrivalled since the foundation of [the city]' (Troy, 53) and sonnets were dedicated to them; and in Paris in summer 1729 the *Mercure de France* reported that *Il marito giocatore* 'was much applauded by reason of a precise and lively performance, in spite of its slight similarity to our customary [French] operas' (ibid, 56). Their last known appearance was in *Le bourgeois gentilhomme* (as Larinda and Vanesio) at Florence in 1732.

C. E. Troy: *The Comic Intermezzo: a Study in the History of Eighteenth-Century Italian Opera* (Ann Arbor, 1979)

F. Piperno: 'Appunti sulla configurazione sociale e professionale delle "parti buffe" al tempo di Vivaldi', *Antonio Vivaldi: teatro musicale, cultura e società: Venice 1981*, ii, 483–97

COLIN TIMMS

Ristorini, Caterina (*fl* 1757–?85). Italian soprano. She seems to have made her début in Venice, where she sang in 12 operas (1757–9 and 1763–4), including Piccinni's *La buona figliuola maritata*. She may have been the Ristorini who appeared in several operas and concerts in London in 1770–71 (at the King's Theatre) and in 1772–3 (mostly at Covent Garden); her repertory there would have included *La buona figliuola* and Sacchini's *La contadina in corte*. These visits would not have prevented her from singing in Venice in autumn 1771. She appeared in Paisiello's *La frascatana* at Reggio in 1775 and is probably the 'Carolina' Ristorini who performed in that opera, and in *La buona figliuola*, at Pisa in 1775 and 1785. She clearly specialized in works of this kind.

COLIN TIMMS

Ristorini, Giovanni Battista (*fl* 1750–89). Italian tenor. He specialized in *buffo* roles. His first known appearance was in 1750 at Stuttgart, but during the early part of his career his main centre of activity was Venice, where he sang in 11 operas in 1758–9, 1763–4 and 1773. After performances in Reggio (1774), Parma, Modena, Warsaw and Copenhagen he moved to St Petersburg, his base for a decade.

On 13/24 November 1780 he sang in a work in honour of Catherine II, and shortly afterwards he joined the Italian troupe at court as *buffo secondo*. He may be the tenor whom Paisiello described, in a letter of about 1781, as 'comparable à Grimaldi, mais qui remplit encore les rôles de grand comique, et qui chante bien', for in the following year he appeared as Marchese Cicala in Paisiello's *Dal finto il vero*. He left St Petersburg when his contract expired in 1785 but was re-engaged on 21 December/1 January 1787, in which year he apparently sang in two Cimarosa cantatas. He left again in summer 1789 but this time did not return.   COLIN TIMMS

Ristorini, Giuseppe (*b* Bologna; *fl* 1724–44). Italian tenor. The earlier part of his career was devoted to *opera seria*, the later to comic works. His first known appearances were in Venice in 1724 (Albinoni's *Scipione nelle Spagne*) and Florence (1725), but in 1725–6 he sang in four more operas in Venice and two at Turin. During Carnivals 1729, 1731 and 1732 respectively he appeared in Parma (Broschi's *Bradamante nell'isola d'Alcina*) and Florence (Orlandini's *Arsace* and *Ifigenia in Aulide*), and in 1739, also in Florence, he partnered Anna Faini in the intermezzos performed with Arrigoni's *Scipione nelle Spagne*. He sang in three comic operas in Venice and Florence in 1743–4 but then disappears from view.

COLIN TIMMS

Ristorini, Luigi (*fl* 1741–50). Italian singer. Most of his known appearances were in *opera seria*: he sang in Leo's *Demetrio* and in the première of Gennaro Manna's *Tito Manlio* in Rome during Carnival 1742, in Lampugnani's *Ezio* and Hasse's *Demetrio* at Turin in 1747–8 and in similar pieces in Venice (1748) and Florence (1750). He also appeared in comic works at Venice (1743) and Florence (1744) with the tenor Giuseppe Ristorini, to whom he was probably related.

COLIN TIMMS

Risurrezione. *Dramma* in four acts by FRANCO ALFANO to a libretto by Cesare Hanau, after LEV NIKOLAYEVICH TOLSTOY's novel *Voskreseniye*; Turin, Teatro Vittorio Emanuele, 30 November 1904.

In Act 1, the maid Katiusha (soprano), who is secretly in love with Dmitri Nekludov (tenor), confesses for the first time her feelings, and she and Dimitri become lovers. In the second act, set in a railway station in Russia, the pregnant Katiusha is waiting for her lover, only to see him arrive with another woman. Act 3 is set in a prison for prostitutes who are awaiting deportation to Siberia. Dimitri, who had served on the jury during Katiusha's trial, recognizes her and offers to follow her into exile. Act 4, set in a Siberian prison camp, shows the new love between the political prisoner Simonson (baritone) and Katiusha, who refuses Dimitri's hand.

The opera reduces Tolstoy's complex criticism of the political and social problems in Russia to a drama of personal relationships. Alfano's music, quite appropriate for the extended lyrical passages of Acts 1, 3 and

4, failed to provide adequate local colour for the Russian ambience or for the daring novelty of the scenes; it is doubtful whether on the basis of Mascagni's and Catalani's musical language such a characterization could have been at all successful. Apart from some effects in the tradition of the somewhat old-fashioned musical *verismo*, the level of musico-dramatic organization appears considerably inferior to that of other contemporary works.   JÜRGEN MAEHDER

Rita [*Rita, ou Le mari battu* ('Rita, or The Beaten Husband')]. *Opéra comique* in one act by GAETANO DONIZETTI to a libretto by GUSTAVE VAËZ; Paris, Opéra-Comique (Salle Favart), 7 May 1860.

When, one day in June 1841, Donizetti ran into Vaëz, the poet summarized a brief plot which appealed sufficiently to the composer that he asked for a text and set it to music in short order. The complete score, still unperformed, was among the manuscripts left by Donizetti when he died; it was sold to the Parisian music publisher Schoenenberger in about 1855. Another five years elapsed before the comedy had its belated première. It soon lapsed in Paris, but its revival in Italian at the Piccola Scala in 1965 scored a true success. Because of its modest dimensions and well-crafted score the work has been performed frequently since then.

The plot of *Rita* is simple but dramatically effective. An innkeeper, Rita (soprano), is currently married to a timid fellow, Peppe (tenor), who allows her to beat him. Gaspar (baritone) appears; he had been married to her earlier but had struck her and left for Canada. Now he has returned to pick up his marriage certificate so that he will be free to marry again. Peppe is delighted to see a means of escape, but Gaspar insists that they play *morra* to see who wins the wife neither wants. The plot is resolved when Gaspar, having got hold of the marriage certificate, teaches Peppe how to stand up to Rita. The score is unpretentious, yet marked by the musical good taste so central to Donizetti's music; to impose a farcical tone is to endanger the equilibrium of this finely attuned domestic comedy.   WILLIAM ASHBROOK

Ritchie, Margaret [Ritchie, Mabel Willard] (*b* Grimsby, 7 June 1903; *d* Ewelme, Oxon., 7 Feb 1969). English soprano. She studied at the RCM and with Plunket Greene, Agnes Nicholls and Henry Wood, and became known as a concert singer and as a leading soprano of the Intimate Opera Company. In 1944 she joined Sadler's Wells, distinguishing herself especially as Dorabella in *Così fan tutte*. In 1946 she sang Lucia in the first production, at Glyndebourne, of Britten's *Rape of Lucretia*, and in the following year joined the English Opera Group. The part of Miss Wordsworth, the prim and innocent schoolmistress in Britten's *Albert Herring*, displayed to perfection her musical qualities and delightful sense of comedy, and might be called an affectionate portrait of her personality. Her voice, though small, was of pure quality and beautifully produced; she used it with an unfailing sense of style and showed unusual flexibility in the execution of florid passages.

                                    DESMOND SHAWE-TAYLOR

Rites of Passage. Opera by PETER SCULTHORPE to his own libretto; Sydney, Opera House, 27 September 1974.

The first full-length Australian opera to be performed by the Australian Opera company, the work (originally intended to open Sydney Opera House) involves dancers and groups of singers – there are no soloists – who enact a celebration of the nature of the universe. Musically it is made up of two contrasting forms, Rites and Chorales, each with its own group of instrumentalists, singers and position on the stage; there is occasional interaction between the two. The five Rites ('Preparing the Ground', 'Ordeal', 'Interlude', 'Death' and 'Rebirth') are performed by a small instrumental group with mixed chorus whose text, in an Australian aboriginal language, stems from Southern Aranda poems. The six Chorales, on a Latin text from Boethius' *Consolation of Philosophy*, use a significantly larger group of instruments to accompany an SATB chorus and may be performed, together with 'Rebirth', as a concert work. Sculthorpe's music displays Asian influences in both its rhythm and its tonality; small modules are repeated with little development, to hypnotic effect. The result is one of delicately changing modality in which texture is all-important while melodic evolution is repressed.

Much has been written (e.g. Hannan 1978 and 1982) expounding the composer's theories on new opera which fuelled *Rites of Passage*, but in its original production it was perceived as a plotless, near-voiceless display of gesture based on tribal initiation rites, which Sculthorpe interprets in terms of modern man's life crises. Dissatisfied with that initial production and its reception, he has since reworked the piece; subsequent performances have been in concert versions, in evolving forms and with revised scenario.   THÉRÈSE RADIC

Ritorni, Count **Carlo** (*b* Finale, Modena, 6 June 1786; *d* Reggio Emilia, 27 March 1860). Italian writer. He spent most of his life in Reggio Emilia, where he held various civic and administrative posts, including that of mayor from 1856. A devotee of literature, architecture and music, he chronicled the cultural life of the city, notably in the volumes of *Annali del teatro della città di Reggio dal 1807 al 1839* (Bologna, 1826–39), and published an important study of the choreography of Salvatore Viganò (1838). His discussions of all types of opera in two works – *Consigli sull'arte di dirigere gli spettacoli* (Bologna, 1825) and especially his *Ammaestramenti alla composizione d'ogni poema e d'ogni opera appartenente alla musica* (Milan, 1841) – surpass in their detail and coherence the comments of other 19th-century writers and composers and predate the other most informative source of technical information, Abramo Basevi's study of Verdi's operas (1859).

In the *Ammaestramenti*, Ritorni methodically criticized contemporary serious opera and anticipated later stylistic developments in his extensive programme for its reform. A new genre presenting only elevated, heroic subjects – *melotragedia* (for which Bellini's *Norma* served as an archetype) – would improve on contemporary practice by incorporating more continuous organization (even acts consisting of single scenes), by adopting more flexible musical and poetic forms, by expanding the role of the orchestra and by striving towards a closer fusion of musical and textual meaning. As a point of departure, Ritorni articulated numerous Rossinian musical, poetic and dramatic norms, including those involving contrasts between recitative style and lyrical style, distinctions among different types of recitative and types of aria (cavatina, rondò and 'grande scena'), features of the conventional scene forms, the distribution of different types of scenes (arias, duets and ensembles), and the management of singers' workloads.

Though often muddied by inconsistencies, biases and obscure formulations, Ritorni's writings serve present-day scholars by confirming awareness during the 19th century of practices evident in operatic scores, by giving a contemporary rationale for *ottocento* stylistic developments and by providing an invaluable glimpse of attitudes towards Rossinian opera in the era of Bellini and Donizetti.

M. Prati: 'Carlo Ritorni: i suoi scritti e le sue idee sul melodramma', *Bollettino storico reggiano*, no.5 (1972)

P. Fabbri: 'Le memorie teatrali de Carlo Ritorni, rossiniste de 1851', *Bollettino del Centro rossiniano di studi* (1981), 87–128

S. L. Balthazar: 'Ritorni's *Ammaestramenti* and the Conventions of Rossinian melodramma', *Journal of Musicological Research*, vii (1988–9), 281–311

S. L. Balthazar: 'The Rhythm of Text and Music in *Ottocento* Melody: an Empirical Reassessment in Light of Contemporary Treatises', *CMc*, no.49 (1991), 5–28   SCOTT L. BALTHAZAR

Ritorno d'Ulisse in patria, Il ('The Return of Ulysses to his Homeland'). *Dramma per musica* in a prologue and three acts by CLAUDIO MONTEVERDI to a libretto by GIACOMO BADOARO after HOMER's *Odyssey* (books 13–23); Venice, Teatro SS Giovanni e Paolo, 1640.

L'Humana Fragilità [Human Frailty]	soprano
Il Tempo [Time]	bass
La Fortuna [Fortune]	soprano
Amore [Cupid]	soprano
Penelope *Ulysses's wife*	soprano
Ericlea [Eurycleia] *Penelope's old nurse*	mezzo-soprano
Melanto *Penelope's young maid*	soprano
Eurimaco [Eurymachus] *a courtier, Melanto's lover and conspirator with the suitors*	tenor
Nettuno [Neptune]	bass
Giove [Jupiter]	tenor
Ulisse [Ulysses]	tenor
Minerva	soprano
Eumete [Eumaeus] *a swineherd, Ulysses's former servant*	tenor
Iro [Irus] *a parasite*	tenor
Telemaco [Telemachus] *son of Penelope and Ulysses*	tenor
Antinoo [Antinous]	bass
Pisandro [Peisander] ⎫ *Penelope's suitors*	tenor
Anfinomo [Amphinomus] ⎭	alto
Giunone [Juno]	soprano

Phaeacians, celestial beings, sea creatures

Setting   Ithaca, an island in the Ionian Sea, after the Trojan War

This was Monteverdi's first opera for Venice, Badoaro having written the libretto specifically to tempt Monteverdi to display his talents on the Venetian stage. A great success, the opera received ten performances in Venice and was then taken on the road to Bologna, where it was performed at the Teatro Castrovillani, along with another Venetian import from SS Giovanni e Paolo, *La Delia*, by Francesco Manelli on a libretto by Giulio Strozzi. Four of the singers in the Bologna production are known, and they probably also sang in Venice – Giulia Paolelli as Penelope, Maddalena Manelli as Minerva, and her husband Francesco, possibly as Ulysses, and son Costantino. The work was revived in Venice the next year (1641), probably at SS

Giovanni e Paolo, although some sources give S Cassiano as the theatre. The sources include one 17th-century score and at least nine manuscript librettos, most of them 18th-century copies. The numerous and significant differences between the libretto and the score and the stylistic distinctions between *Ritorno* and Monteverdi's other late opera, *L'incoronazione di Poppea*, prompted questions (from Emil Vogel) about the authenticity of the work late in the 19th century, just after the anonymous score was discovered in Vienna. But Robert Haas published it as Monteverdi (DTÖ, lvii, Jg. xxix, 1922), and the attribution, though questioned sporadically since then (most seriously in 1942 by Giacomo Benvenuti but also by Domenico De' Paoli 1945, and Hans Redlich 1949), still stands. The differences between libretto and score are indeed numerous. They include the number of acts (the score has three, the librettos five), and the text and characters of the prologue (they are Fate, Prudence and Fortitude in the librettos). In addition, several scenes in the librettos do not appear in the score, and much dialogue is cut and rearranged. But these differences, rather than casting doubt on Monteverdi's authorship, tend to support it, since he was well known for his editorial intervention in the texts he set. The work has fascinated a number of composers, several of whom edited – or 'translated' – the score for performance: Vincent d'Indy (1925, Paris, probably the first modern revival; published Paris, 1926), Dallapiccola (1942, Maggio Musicale, Florence; published Milan, 1942), and Henze (1985, Salzburg; published Mainz, 1982). Gian Francesco Malipiero's more scholarly edition (*Claudio Monteverdi: Tutte le opere*, xii) appeared in 1930. The work can be said to have entered the operatic mainstream in the early 1970s with performances in Vienna, in an edition by Nikolaus Harnoncourt (1971), and Glyndebourne, in a realization by Raymond Leppard (1972; for illustration *see* BURY, JOHN), both of which were recorded.

PROLOGUE Human Frailty is taunted by Time, Fortune and Cupid who claim, in a final trio, to control man's fate, rendering him weak, poor and confused.

ACT 1.i *A room in the palace* Penelope laments Ulysses's long absence in a passionate monologue, 'Di misera regina', which is one of the musical peaks of the opera. Although largely in recitative, it is structured by two irregularly recurring refrains in arioso style, both of which emphasize the word 'return', and by Eurycleia's periodic interruptions as she echoes her mistress's distress. Monteverdi himself was responsible for creating this piece through skilful cutting and restructuring of Badoaro's exceedingly long and shapeless text. The music consists largely of repeated notes in a low register and descending motion. The largest ascent, a minor 6th, in the refrain 'Tu sol del tuo tornar perdesti il giorno', rises chromatically and laboriously to its highest point over the course of five bars, only to fall back, exhausted, to the lowest note of the line, an octave lower, within a single bar. Penelope leaves the stage even more depressed and without hope than when she entered.

1.ii Melanto and Eurymachus flirt in canzon-etta-style arias (hers, 'Duri e penosi son gli amorosi', comprises two strophes with a refrain, which Monteverdi expands through repetition), and a duet, 'Dolce mia vita sei', built on the descending tetrachord ostinato; their lascivious concerns and melodious style provide a vivid and ironic contrast to Penelope's mournful mood. From this scene we learn that Eurymachus, allied with the deceitful suitors, has urged Melanto to convince Penelope to accept one of them as her husband.

[1.iii Maritime scene with Nereids and Sirens (missing in the score)]

1.iv *An Ithacan seascape* In pantomime, accompanied by a sinfonia of repeated chords, the Phaeacians pass in their ship, disembark with the sleeping Ulysses, and place him close to a naiads' cave with his baggage.

1.v Neptune and Jupiter debate the fate of the Phaeacians, who have disobeyed Neptune's command by returning Ulysses to his homeland. Neptune expresses his anger in martial arpeggios (the *stile concitato*) and furious melismatic passages that exploit the extremes of his bass range. Jupiter approves Neptune's punishment of the Phaeacians.

1.vi The Phaeacians, in their ship, arrogantly sing of man's independence of the gods, whereupon Neptune transforms them and their ship into a rock. In intoning the moral of this story, 'Let the Phaeacians learn today that when heaven is against it, the human journey has no return', Neptune emphasizes once more the keyword of the opera, 'ritorno'.

1.vii Ulysses awakens and, in an extended and wide-ranging recitative monologue, expresses his anguish at being abandoned by the Phaeacians in yet another foreign land.

1.viii Minerva appears disguised as a shepherd, singing a cheerful canzonetta, its two strophes separated by Ulysses's hopeful recitative aside expressing his belief that heaven, in the form of this youth, will help him find his way. During the ensuing conversation, Ulysses learns that he is in Ithaca, that she is Minerva and that the suitors have laid siege to his wife and kingdom, but that Penelope has remained faithful. Minerva advises him to insinuate himself into the court, disguised as an old beggar. Ulysses's music becomes increasingly lyrical as he expresses his joy at the good news, with many passages in triple metre. Minerva's music, on the other hand, becomes exceedingly elaborate once she has revealed her true identity. The scene concludes with a dance-like duet, as a group of naiads hide Ulysses's baggage in their cave.

1.ix Minerva sends Ulysses off to find his old servant, the swineherd Eumaeus, while she leaves for Sparta to bring Telemachus home to help his father reclaim his kingdom from the suitors. Ulysses expresses his happiness in an aria built on the refrain 'O fortunato Ulisse', familiar from the previous scene, where he sang it twice in his joyous dialogue with Minerva. More tentative and impulsive there, it is developed here into a considered, full-blown, two-strophe aria with ritornello. Act 1 of the five-act librettos ends here.

1.x *The palace* Melanto, in her typical, seductive, lyrical style, urges Penelope to choose one of the suitors, punctuating her recitative twice with the brief aria 'Ama dunque'. But the queen is adamant in her refusal. And her musical language, stark recitative within a narrow range, likewise remains as austere as ever: she would not risk increasing her suffering by falling in love again.

1.xi *A woody grove* Eumaeus, driven from court by the suitors, delights in his pastoral existence.

1.xii His reveries are interrupted by Irus, the suitors' parasite, who ridicules the pastoral life. His irregular, stuttering music, with its unpredictable repeti-

tions and metric shifts, contrasts markedly with Eumaeus's noble lyricism. Eumaeus chases him away.

1.xiii As Eumaeus wonders aloud about the fate of his master, Ulysses comes on the scene in his beggar's disguise and assures him that his master is alive and will indeed return. Eumaeus, recognizing that beggars are favoured by the gods but not that this one is his master, offers him shelter and, rejoicing in a brief aria in his characteristically simple, pastoral style ('Come lieto t'accoglio'), leads him away.

ACT 2.i *In Minerva's chariot* Minerva brings Telemachus back to Ithaca. In a brief aria, 'Lieto cammino', he exults in the knowledge that he will soon see his father. He and Minerva sing a brief duet in praise of the gods' power, 'Gli dei possenti', in which the movement of Minerva's chariot is portrayed by the undulating figure setting the words 'navigan' ('navigate') and 'aure' ('breezes').

2.ii *A woody grove* Eumaeus joyfully welcomes Telemachus in his longest lyrical effusion so far, 'O gran figlio d'Ulisse', concluding with an invitation to rejoice in song. The song that materializes is a lyrical duet with the beggar (Ulysses) on a text full of pastoral imagery ('Verdi spiaggie al lieto giorno'), culminating in yet another emphasis on the keyword, 'ritorno'. After a second duet between Eumaeus and the beggar, Telemachus dispatches Eumaeus to the palace to inform Penelope of his imminent arrival.

2.iii Ulysses sheds his disguise and reveals himself to his son, and they join in a duet of reunion, 'O padre sospirato, o figlio desiato', which gains expressive power through a remarkable freedom of rhythm and melody. It concludes in a forceful, unanimous acknowledgment of the power of the gods: 'Mortals can hope for anything, for when heaven is protector, nature can do nothing, and the impossible often occurs'. Then, in a strikingly linear arioso passage, Ulysses sends his son off to his mother, promising to join him soon, but in disguise. Act 2 of the five-act librettos ends here.

2.iv *The palace* Melanto complains to Eurymachus of Penelope's unwillingness to choose a new husband. They, in contrast, will abandon themselves to love. This scene reinforces the moral polarity between fidelity and hedonism set up in Act 1 scenes i–ii.

2.v As if to confirm Melanto's description of her behaviour, in this impressively symmetrical scene Penelope systematically rejects, one after another, the suits of Antinous, Peisander and Amphinomus. Each suitor argues his case individually in recitative and is joined by the other two in a lyrical refrain: 'Ama, dunque, sì, sì'. Penelope's response, 'Non voglio amar', becomes increasingly emphatic each time it recurs. Her tone is predictably adamant and dour. The suitors decide to try to change her mood with singing and dancing.

[2.vi Ballet of Moors (missing in the score)]

2.vii *The palace* Eumaeus informs Penelope that her son will soon arrive, and perhaps also Ulysses. She responds sceptically that unless her stars have changed their course, such rumours can only increase her grief.

2.viii The suitors overhear Eumaeus's message and conspire to murder Telemachus on his arrival, concluding their deliberations with a trio in the *stile concitato*. But an omen appears in the form of an eagle flying over their heads, which frightens them into renouncing their plan and resolving to try once more to move Penelope, this time with promises of gold. They conclude their scene with another trio, this one in the light style of the *giustiniana*, a popular Venetian dance-song. The use of this patently ironic style in conjunction with the suitors does much to undercut the seriousness of their threat to the kingdom and makes problematic the interpretation of the action that follows.

2.ix *A woody grove* In her most florid, Olympian recitative style, Minerva assures Ulysses that when he takes his bow in his hand she will enable him to kill the suitors.

2.x Eumaeus reports to Ulysses the suitors' fearful reaction to the news that he might be alive, to which Ulysses, confident in the knowledge that Minerva is with him, responds with a joyful aria ('Godo anch'io'). They set off for the palace in great anticipation. Act 3 of the five-act librettos ends here.

2.xi *The palace* Telemachus, reunited with his mother, narrates the story of his travels and especially of his encounter with the beautiful Helen, who caused the wars that took his father away to fight. While in Sparta, he reports, a bird flew over his head, which Helen interpreted as an omen that Ulysses would return to slay the suitors and reclaim his kingdom. Telemachus thus reinforces the message Eumaeus has delivered and which Penelope has rejected four scenes earlier.

2.xii All the characters are present in this beautifully constructed scene, the longest in the opera. It builds gradually and inevitably as the beggar comes closer and closer to the centre of the action. First, along with Eumaeus, he is mocked and vilified by the suitors for his lowly appearance; next, the stuttering, blustering Irus challenges him to a fight and is soundly – and pathetically – defeated, a premonition of the climax of the scene yet to come. Welcomed by Penelope for his bravery, the beggar then observes each suitor's vain attempt to woo the queen with lavish gifts. Unaware of Minerva's influence, Penelope surprises herself by agreeing to yield to the one who can string Ulysses's mighty bow. The three trials, each more fatuous than the last, end in ignominious failure. Now the beggar, having earned the right by his bravery, humbly asks a turn, assuring the queen that he does not seek the suitor's prize. All are amazed when he succeeds, whereupon, invoking Jupiter and Minerva, he unleashes his pent-up fury and, screaming for their deaths in the *stile concitato* accompanied by strings, he slays the suitors. Act 4 of the five-act librettos ends here.

ACT 3.i In this strange scene, Irus, alone, relives the suitors' defeat in a stark monologue filled with the literal word-imitations of the text for which Monteverdi was so well known. Recognizing that he cannot survive without the suitors, and crazed with fear and hunger, this comic-turned-pathetic character sees death as the only solution, and commits suicide.

3.ii *A desert* Mercury informs the ghosts of the suitors that they deserved their fate, and they disappear into hell. He then turns to the audience and declares the moral of the tragedy: that death is the end of all things. (Although important for the interpretation of the work, this scene was not set, according to a note in the score, because it was too melancholy.)

3.iii *The palace* Melanto, whose lover Eurymachus perished with the suitors, urges Penelope to recognize the threat posed by the stranger and to react angrily to the bloody slaughter, but she can only continue her lamentation.

3.iv Eumaeus joins them and tells Penelope that the beggar was Ulysses in disguise, but she refuses to believe him.

3.v Telemachus explains that the disguise was provided by Minerva, but Penelope retorts that the gods are merely toying with them and chides Telemachus and Eumaeus for their gullibility.

3.vi *The sea* Minerva elicits Juno's promise to convince Jupiter that Ulysses should be restored to his rightful place, despite Neptune's objection.

3.vii Juno pleads, Jupiter is convinced, Neptune mollified, and a chorus of heavenly and maritime spirits seals the agreement.

3.viii *The palace* In a recitative articulated by a lyrical refrain that recurs three times, each time more insistently, Eurycleia considers whether or not to reveal that she has recognized Ulysses in his bath by the scar on his back.

3.ix Penelope continues obstinately to insist to Telemachus and Eumaeus that she cannot accept the beggar as Ulysses, and they continue to argue with her.

3.x Ulysses, in his true form, joins them to plead his case, but she will not listen. Eurycleia now joins their pleas, adding her knowledge of the scar on his back. But Penelope remains adamant. She yields only when Ulysses describes the cover on her bed, which he alone could have known. In yielding, she releases the lyricism that she has kept in check with her emotions throughout the opera, first in an aria ('Illustratevi o cieli') whose extended phrases are echoed by strings, then in a sensuous final duet with Ulysses.

*   *   *

The opera builds to its inevitable and expected climax with all the sweep of the Greek epic on which it is based. Its expressive power is intensified by the humanity of its characters, each of them individually drawn by the librettist but even more by the composer. Monteverdi's legendary commitment to moving the affections through the portrayal of real human beings finds its fullest realization here and in his final opera. *Il ritorno d'Ulisse in patria*, however, because of its proximity to its classical source, the realism of its musical language, and its cathartic power, may be the last opera of the period legitimately to offer itself as a re-creation of ancient tragedy.

ELLEN ROSAND

Ritter, Alexander [Sascha] (*b* Narva, Estonia, 27 June 1833; *d* Munich, 12 April 1896). German composer. After his father's death the family moved in 1841 to Dresden, where Ritter became acquainted with Bülow, Liszt and Wagner. He studied at the Leipzig Conservatory (1849–51) before taking posts in Weimar and Stettin (Konzertmeister and music director of the city theatre). After periods in Dresden and Schwerin, in 1863 both he and his actress wife (Franziska Wagner, a niece of the composer) were engaged by the theatre in Würzburg, where they remained for the next 19 years.

In 1882 Ritter accepted Bülow's invitation to become second Konzertmeister in the court orchestra at Meiningen. There he met the young Richard Strauss, whom he strongly influenced, encouraging him to grow beyond the conservative compositional style of his early years. Strauss credited Ritter with introducing him to the music of Wagner, Liszt and Berlioz, and the writings of Schopenhauer. When Strauss was engaged in 1886 as third conductor for the Munich court opera he persuaded Ritter also to settle there. On 8 June 1890 Strauss conducted the successful première in Weimar of

Ritter's *Wem die Krone?* (1891, Munich) in a double bill with an earlier opera, *Der faule Hans*, originally performed in Munich on 15 October 1885 (published in Leipzig, 1886). Both works are in one act and to the composer's own texts. As Wagner's nephew by marriage, Ritter frequently joined the Bayreuth circle, even playing more than once in the festival orchestra. Besides the two operas, his compositions include lieder, tone poems and choral works.

S. von Hausegger: 'Alexander Ritter: ein Bild seines Charakters und Schaffens', *Die Musik*, ed. R. Strauss (Berlin, 1907)

W. Schuh, ed.: *Richard Strauss: Betrachtungen und Erinnerungen* (Zürich, 1949, enlarged 2/1957)   GEORGE J. BUELOW

Ritter, Peter (*b* Mannheim, 2 July 1763; *d* Mannheim, 1 Aug 1846). German cellist and composer. After studying composition with G. J. Vogler he obtained in December 1783 a life appointment as cellist in the orchestra of the Mannheim theatre, became its Konzertmeister in 1801 and on 3 November 1803 Kapellmeister of the orchestra of the Grand Duchy of Baden in Mannheim under the director of music Ignaz Fränzl. It was Ritter's duty to direct the operas, which at first he conducted from his raised cello desk. Until his retirement in 1823 he carried out his duties at the Nationaltheater in Mannheim, interrupted only by concert tours. Of Ritter's stage works the most successful was the Singspiel *Der Zitherschläger*, which was praised by Weber on its first performance in Mannheim on 1 April 1810: 'an original German opera … which certainly need not yield to any French work of its kind'. Ritter's Singspiel *Die lustigen Weiber von Windsor* was among the earliest musical settings of the Shakespearean subject.

first performed in Mannheim unless otherwise stated

Der Eremit auf Formentara (2, A. von Kotzebue), National, 14 Dec 1788, *D-Bhm*

Der Sklavenhändler (Spl, 2, C. F. Schwan), National, 11 April 1790 (Mannheim, n.d.)

Die Weihe (prol, G. C. Römer), 1792, *DS*

Die lustigen Weiber von Windsor (Spl, 3, Römer, after W. Shakespeare), National, 4 Nov 1794

Dilara, oder Die schwarze Zauberin (Spl, 2, C. Gozzi), 1798

Das neue Jahr in Famagusta (Spl, 2, C. Brentano), 1804

Salomons Urteil (3, L. C. Caigniez), 1808, *DS*

Marie von Montalban (2, K. Reger), Frankfurt, 1810

Der Zitherschläger (Spl, 1, C. L. Seidel), Stuttgart, 1810 (Bonn, n.d.)

Alexander in Indien (2, P. Metastasio), 1811

Feodore (Spl, 1, Kotzebue), 1811, *DS*

Das Tal von Barzelonetta, oder Die beiden Ermiten (Spl, 1), 1811, *B-Bc*, *D-Mo*

Das Kind des Herkules (pantomime, 1), 1812

Alfred (3, Kotzebue), 1820

Der Mandarin, oder Die gefoppten Chinesen (Spl, 1), Karlsruhe, 1821 (Mannheim, n.d.)

Hoang-Puff, oder Das dreifache Horoskop (Spl, 1), 1822

Bianca (2, Grimm), 1824

Der Talisman (Spl, 1, trans. from Fr.), 1824

Das Grubenlicht (2, L. Beck), 1833

Die Alpenhirtin [mentioned in *EitnerQ*]

Doubtful: Die Geisterburg (Spl, 2, F. Hochkirch), 1799; Der Sturm, oder Die bezauberte Insel (Spl, 2, J. W. Döring, after Shakespeare: *The Tempest*), 1799

*

EitnerQ; *StiegerO*

G. J. Vogler: *Betrachtungen der Mannheimer Tonschule*, ii (Mannheim, 1779)

W. Schulze: *Peter Ritter* (Berlin, 1895)

F. Walter: *Geschichte des Theaters und der Musik am kurpfälzischen Hofe* (Leipzig, 1898)

G. Schmidt: *Peter Ritter* (diss., U. of Munich, 1924)

F. Walter: 'Vom Liebhaberkonzert zur musikalischen Akademie', *150 Jahre Musikalische Akademie des Mannheimer Nationaltheater-Orchesters* (Mannheim, 1929)   ROLAND WÜRTZ

Ritter, Rudolf (*b* Brüx [now Most], 19 Jan 1878; *d* Gaildorf, nr Stuttgart, 3 June 1966). Bohemian tenor. He studied at the Hochschule für Musik in Vienna and sang at the Vienna Volksoper (1910–13), notably in the 1911 première of *Der Kuhreigen* by Kienzl. He sang at the Stuttgart Hofoper from 1913 and toured North America with the German Opera Company (1923–4 and 1929–31); at Chicago in 1923 he sang Mathias in the American première of Kienzl's *Der Evangelimann*. At Bayreuth he sang Siegfried in 1924–5; in 1930 he appeared as Tannhäuser, under Toscanini. Guest appearances took him to South America, Paris, Berlin and Munich. He taught in Stuttgart from 1933.

DAVID CUMMINGS

Ritter-Ciampi, Gabrielle (*b* Paris, 2 Nov 1886; *d* Paimpol, 18 July 1974). French soprano. Her mother (Cécile Ritter-Ciampi) was a principal soprano at the Opéra, her father (Ezio Ciampi) an Italian tenor and later her teacher, while her uncle was the pianist Theodore Ritter. She herself trained first as a pianist and gave some public performances at the age of 16. She then turned to singing and made her début in 1917 as Violetta. She joined the Opéra-Comique two years later, appearing there first as Mozart's Countess Almaviva and as Philine in *Mignon*. She remained with the company for many years, singing Konstanze in their first production of *Die Entführung aus dem Serail* (1937) and creating the leading role of Irène in Reynaldo Hahn's *Le oui des jeunes filles* (1949). She also appeared at the Opéra, at La Scala, in Berlin and at Salzburg in 1932. She was Monte Carlo's first Marschallin in *Der Rosenkavalier* (1926) when 'the perfection of her vocal art and a nobility of bearing' were admired; she also sang there all three main soprano roles in *Les contes d'Hoffmann*. Her impressive versatility, technique and intelligence are evident in many recordings, which also preserve her brightly defined voice and responsive style.

J. B. STEANE

Rivani, Antonio [Ciccolino, Ciecolino] (*b* Florence, first half of 17th century; *d* 1686). Italian soprano castrato. In the service of Cardinal Gian Carlo Medici from at least 1653, he also belonged to the company of the theatre in Via Pergola, Florence, where he sang in comic operas produced each year: Jacopo Melani's *Il potestà di Colognole* (1657), *Il pazzo per forza* (1658) and *Il vecchio burlato* (1659), Domenico Anglesi's *La serva nobile* (1660) and Melani's *Ercole in Tebe* (1661); the last was performed for the marriage of Cosimo III to Marguerite Louise d'Orléans. Rivani was one of the chief contributors to the spread of Italian opera in France. Mazarin's supervisor of court entertainment, Francesco Buti, invited him to Paris for the royal wedding festivities and to contest the fame of Atto and Filippo Melani. He arrived in Paris in summer 1660 and on 19 February 1661 took a leading role in the *Ballet de l'Impatience*, performed before high-ranking courtiers. At the beginning of 1662 he sang Juno in the spectacular *opéra-ballet L'Ercole amante*, with music by Cavalli, libretto by Buti and dances by Lully. After repeat performances he returned to Italy, where he entered the service of Christina of Sweden. He is known to have

Design by Alfonso Rivarola for Act 2 scene iv of G. F. Sances's 'L'Ermiona', performed at the theatre in Prato della Valle, Padua, 11 April 1636

sung in Florence (1662–3), Bologna (1673) and Mantua (1682).

H. Prunières: *L'opéra italien en France avant Lulli* (Paris, 1913)
S. Durante: 'Il cantante', *SOI*, iv (1987), 347–410
P. Besutti: *La corte musicale di Ferdinando Carlo Gonzaga ultimo duca di Mantova: musici, cantanti e teatro d'opera tra il 1665 e il 1707* (Mantua, 1989)   PAOLA BESUTTI

Rivarola [Chenda], **Alfonso** ['Il Chenda'; 'Il Chendi'] (*b* Ferrara, 1591 or 1607; *d* Ferrara, 8 Jan 1640). Italian stage designer, scene painter and architect. He was a pupil and collaborator of Carlo Bononi, and his early style echoed his master's. Count Borso Buonacossi introduced him to scene painting, and he is particularly connected with the architect Giovanni Battista Aleotti. He was responsible for the sets for many theatrical productions. In 1628 Rivarola worked in Parma, preparing, under the supervision of Francesco Guitti, the celebrations for the marriage of Odoardo Farnese and Margherita de' Medici. In 1631 he was in Ferrara for the marriage of Giovanni Francesco Sacchetti and Beatrice Estense Tassoni, and designed an 'academic' theatre in the hall of the castle where the *torneo Bonacossi* and a *favola piscatoria*, *L'Alcina maga*, were performed. In Padua in 1636 he was commissioned by Pio Enea degli Obizzi to design G. F. Sances's *L'Ermiona* (see illustration). The opera included a ballet for female dancers and tourneys on foot and horse, and was performed in a specially erected theatre in Prato della Valle; Rivarola devised machinery and new apparatus. In 1638 in Ferrara at the Piazza Nova, Rivarola designed the sets and machines for *Ferrara trionfonte* (text by Ascanio Pio di Savoia), a festival work dedicated to the Madonna of the Rosary. In the same year also in Ferrara he collaborated with Francesco Giutti on the restoration of the Gran Sala delle Comedie or 'Grande di Corte' for a performance of Michelangelo Rossi's *Andromeda*. It has been suggested by Povoledo that he also worked with Ercole Danesi in 1639 in Venice, designing theatrical machinery for the performance of Manelli's *La Delia o sia la sera sposa di sole* and the production of Manelli and Ferrari's *L'Armida*. Rivarola's last important production was at Bologna in 1639, when he designed the *Torneo Malvasia* in the Palazzo del Podestà. Surviving engravings of the festivities for which he was the designer show that he used the central axis typical of Baroque perspective. Rivarola was important as the inventor and engineer of complex stage machinery, but his chief innovation was the arrangement of the auditorium in tiers of boxes, one above the other.

ES ('Chenda, Alfonso'; E. Povoledo)
C. Cittadella: *Catalogo istorico de' pittori e scultori ferraresi e delle loro opere* (Ferrara, 1738), iii, 193–5
L. Lanzi: *Storia pittorica dell'Italia* (Bassano, 1809), v, 294–5
G. Baruffaldi: *Vite de' pittori e scultori ferraresi* (Ferrara, 1844–6), ii, 188–197
C. Molinari: *Le nozze degli dei: un saggio sul grande spettacolo italiano nel seicento* (Rome, 1968), 87–9, figs. 34–8
F. Mancini, M. T. Muraro and E. Povoledo, eds.: *Illusione e pratica teatrale* (Venice, 1975), 55–6, 60–61 [exhibition catalogue]
A. Frabetti: 'Il Teatro della Sala Grande a Ferrara e i Tornei Aleottiani', *Musei ferraresi*, xii (1982), 183–208
C. Molinari: 'Per una storia di alcuni teatri ferraresi', *Teatri storici dell'Emilia Romagna*, ed. S. M. Bondoni (Bologna, 1982), 116–17
D. Lenzi: 'Teatri ed anfiteatri a Bologna nei secoli XVI e XVII', *Barocco romano e barocco italiano: il teatro, l'effimero, l'allegoria*, ed. M. Fagiolo and M. L. Madonna (Rome, 1985), 174–91   SARA VICINI

Rivoli [Riwoli], **Paulina** (*b* Vilnius, 22 July 1817; *d* Warsaw, 12 Oct 1881). Polish soprano. She studied at the opera school of the Wielki Theatre, Warsaw, where she made her début on 17 June 1837 in *L'italiana in Algeri*. She performed with much success in *Les Huguenots*, *La Juive* and in operas by Weber, Auber, Cimarosa and Moniuszko. She was in Italy in 1851, and in 1858 sang the title role in the première of the revised version of *Halka*. Her lyrical voice was noted for its beauty of timbre.

Her sister, Ludwika Rivoli (*b* Łęczyca, 3 March 1814; *d* Warsaw, 16 Oct 1878), an actress and soprano, sang in Lublin (1832) and Warsaw (1834–51), appearing in *Fra Diavolo*, *Il barbiere di Siviglia*, *Robert le diable*, *Zampa* and various Polish works.

IRENA PONIATOWSKA, ELIZABETH FORBES

Rizzi, Domenico. *See* RICCI, DOMENICO.

Roar, Leif (*b* Copenhagen, 31 Aug 1937). Danish baritone. He studied in Copenhagen, making his début in 1967 at Kiel, then singing the Dutchman at Düsseldorf. In 1969 he sang in the première of Klebe's *Das Märchen von der schönen Lilie* at Schwetzingen. At Salzburg Easter Festival (1973–4) he sang Donner and Kurwenal, and Telramund and Klingsor at Bayreuth (1976–81). He made his Metropolitan début in 1982 as Don Pizarro, and has also appeared at Munich, Stuttgart, Hamburg, La Scala, Brussels and San Francisco, and at Copenhagen, where he has been a member of the company since 1985. His repertory includes Wotan, Escamillo, Don Giovanni, Scarpia, Mandryka, Hindemith's Mathis, Creon, Nick Shadow and Nielsen's Saul.

ELIZABETH FORBES

Roberti, Girolamo Frigimelica. *See* FRIGIMELICA ROBERTI, GIROLAMO.

Robert le diable ('Robert the Devil'). *Grand opéra* in five acts by GIACOMO MEYERBEER to a libretto by EUGÈNE SCRIBE and GERMAIN DELAVIGNE; Paris, Opéra, 21 November 1831.

Robert *a Norman duke*	tenor
Bertram *a friend of Robert*	bass
Alice *a Norman peasant*	soprano
Isabelle *a Sicilian princess*	soprano
Raimbaut *a Norman peasant*	tenor
Alberti *a knight*	bass
A Herald	tenor
Lady-in-waiting to Isabelle	soprano
A Priest	bass
Prince of Granada	silent

Knights, squires, pages, hermits, nuns, peasants, soldiers and celestial voices

Setting Sicily in the Middle Ages

Meyerbeer first turned his attention to an operatic project centred on a half-demonic figure from Norman legend, Robert 'le diable', at the end of 1826 or the beginning of 1827. The director of the Opéra-Comique, Guilbert de Pixérécourt, soon agreed to produce the work and by June 1827 Meyerbeer could report to him that the score was 'well advanced'. The libretto by Scribe and Delavigne had very little to do with a widely disseminated medieval mystery play in which Robert leads a life of debauchery and crime but then, Tannhäuser-like, journeys to Rome to seek papal absolution and subsequently heads an important assault of the forces of Christendom against the Infidel. It did, however, respond to the obvious taste of Opéra-Comique audiences for the supernatural evinced by the recent success of Boieldieu's *La dame blanche*; the figures of Robert and Bertram are also obvious echoes of

Max and Caspar in Weber's *Der Freischütz*, seen as *Robin des bois* on the stage of the Odéon in 1824. Illness and Pixérécourt's abandonment of the Opéra-Comique directorship in the summer of 1827 combined temporarily to deflate Meyerbeer's enthusiasm for the project. Despite the efforts of Pixérécourt's successor to secure the work, Meyerbeer and his collaborators entered into negotiations with the Opéra director, Émile Lubbert, with whom they signed a contract at the end of 1829. This change of destination resulted in a substantial revision of the original project. Not only were the original three acts expanded to five and the spoken dialogue (*de rigueur* at the Opéra-Comique) replaced with recitative, but the plot was adjusted also. The part of Raimbaut was considerably larger in the *opéra comique* project, and his relationship with Alice more developed there. As the two lower-class lovers in the first version, they functioned as a foil to the two aristocrats, Robert and Isabelle. In the opera the first scene of Act 3, showing Raimbaut as recipient of Bertram's demonic largesse, has become merely a comic interlude with no consequence later in the work; indeed, a major structural weakness in the version eventually performed is that Raimbaut inexplicably drops out of the action after this. In the *opéra comique* he reappeared in a scene where he freely spent Bertram's money, and in another where the virtuous Alice forced him to discard his ill-gotten wealth (incomplete drafts of this music are extant). The opera also lengthened through the conversion of certain spoken episodes into complete musical numbers, as well as through the accretion of ballet and spectacle.

Robert le diable was bequeathed by Lubbert to his successor, Louis Véron, who took up the directorship in March 1831. Véron and Meyerbeer followed the advice of the stage director, Duponchel, to replace the ballet first planned as a classical allegory on Olympus with a bacchanale of nuns newly risen from their tombs in a medieval cloister (Act 3). Véron himself suggested that the part of Bertram, scheduled to be performed by the baritone Henri-Bernard Dabadie, was better suited to the great bass Nicolas Levasseur, and Meyerbeer made the necessary changes to the role in summer 1831. The rest of the original cast was just as formidable: Adolphe Nourrit in the title role, Laure Cinti-Damoreau as Isabelle, and Julie Dorus-Gras as Alice. In July 1832 this last role served for the brilliant début of the young Cornélie Falcon, who won the admiration and support of the composer himself. Within three years after its première *Robert le diable* had reached 100 performances on the stage of the Opéra. Its conquest of other stages was no less spectacular: by 1835 it had been seen at 77 houses in ten different countries. Its success secured Meyerbeer's reputation among the pre-eminent opera composers of his day.

ACT 1 *On the shore at Palermo* A group of knights who are to compete in a tournament for the hand of Princess Isabelle begin a multi-sectional introduction with a tribute to wine, women and gambling ('Versez à tasses pleines'). Among them are Robert and his companion Bertram, whose sinister nature is expressed in the dark chromatic music that accompanies his first words. The introduction continues conventionally with a three-strophe ballad sung for Robert by his vassal Raimbaut ('Jadis régnait en Normandie'), which tells of the marriage of a beautiful Norman princess with a demon.

At the mention of the offspring of that union, a certain Robert 'le diable', Raimbaut in the last stanza breaks into breathless declamation above an orchestral version of the melody he had sung previously. Robert indignantly reveals that he is the son in question and orders Raimbaut to be hanged. He commutes the sentence when he learns that Raimbaut is betrothed and, to a reprise of the opening music, savours the prospect of the *droit du seigneur*. Raimbaut's fiancée, Alice, appears; on recognizing her as his foster-sister Robert quells the suggestive insinuations of his comrades, and the introduction closes with a staccato chorus evoking the amusement of the knights at Robert's sudden display of respect for womanly virtue. When they are alone, Alice tells Robert that his mother has died, and in a strophic *romance* ('Va! va! dit-elle') she relays her last words. The strophic structure is again varied: the second stanza begins in a foreign key and is enlivened by orchestral tremolos and sforzandos as Alice refers to maternal warnings about a threatening dark force. She presents Robert with his mother's will, but in his sorrow he asks her to keep it for him. He informs Alice of his separation from his beloved, Princess Isabelle, and she offers to take a letter to her. To a reprise of Raimbaut's ballad she expresses distrust of Bertram but Robert ignores her warning and, encouraged by Bertram, gambles with the other knights, soon losing all his money and even his armour.

ACT 2 *A room in a palace* Isabelle sings of her vanishing prospects of reunion with Robert in the slow section of her entrance aria, 'En vain j'espère'; in a transition she receives his letter and gives expression to her joy in a *cabalette* with a torrent of roulades. When Robert himself appears, Isabelle first playfully mocks her suitor by imitating his words, but the two conclude the first section of their duet ('Avec bonté voyez ma peine') with parallel singing, looking ahead to future happiness. A brass fanfare signals the impending tournament and Isabelle equips Robert with new armour; the martial atmosphere is maintained by triadic vocal lines and dotted rhythms in the *cabalette*. After Isabelle leaves Bertram suddenly appears and contrives to have Robert led away to a neighbouring forest by persuading him that his rival, the Prince of Granada, wishes to engage him in mortal combat there. The entire court gathers to celebrate the marriage of six young couples with a balletic *divertissement*. To the strains of a ceremonial chorus the Prince of Granada enters and asks Isabelle to present him with arms. Another fanfare calls the entire court to the field. Isabelle leads the concluding ensemble with a vigorous triadic melody ('La trompette guerrière'), but in an *a parte* (mirrored by a sudden move to the key of the flattened 6th) she expresses her sorrow that Robert has not appeared.

ACT 3 *A sombre, misty and mountainous country-side* Raimbaut arrives for a rendezvous with Alice, but instead meets Bertram, who promptly gives him a bag of gold. In a Rossinian *duo bouffe* ('Ah! l'honnête homme!') Bertram advises Raimbaut not to throw in his lot with Alice since he will attract many women with his new-found wealth. After Raimbaut leaves, Bertram gloats over this latest conquest and prepares to commune with the spirits of hell in the adjacent cavern. A choral 'Valse infernale' accompanied by brass band is heard from within; above seething passagework in the orchestral strings, Bertram abandons the posture of a diabolical buffoon to express heartfelt attachment for

'*Robert le diable*' (Meyerbeer): painting by François-Gabriel Lépaulle (1804–86) showing the final trio from Act 5, with Nicolas Levasseur (Bertram), Adolphe Nourrit (Robert) and Cornélie Falcon (Alice)

his son, none other than Robert. He enters the cavern to hear a satanic decree about his own destiny. In the meantime Alice arrives, expecting to find Raimbaut. She sings of her love for him in strophic *couplets* ('Quand je quittai la Normandie') that exhibit a naive rustic colour appropriate to her character. Hearing the waltz from the cave, she suspects that evil is afoot and is surprised to hear choral chanting of Robert's name. To a dramatic rescoring of her *couplets* melody, she approaches the cave and learns that Bertram will lose Robert forever if he is unable fully to possess him by midnight. Bertram realizes that Alice has overheard. In the ensuing duet ('Mais Alice, qu'as-tu donc?') he assumes an air of false gallantry (depicted by the leading cello strain), but he soon adopts a menacing stance as he extracts from Alice an assurance that she will not breathe a word of what she knows. When Robert arrives, Bertram tells him of a magic branch at the tomb of Ste Rosalie in an abandoned cloister. With this he will be able to regain Isabelle, but to retrieve it is both a sacrilege and an act of courage. In grand heroic manner, with dotted rhythms, long pedal points and an explosive rise through a 10th to high a'' at the beginning of their duet ('Des chevaliers de ma patrie'), Robert asserts that he will not shrink before the challenge. The mist clears to reveal the cloister in moonlight. Bertram beckons the nuns to rise from their graves (for illustration *see* GRAND OPÉRA, fig.4). When the knight seems to hesitate before his task they hold before him the pleasures of drink, gambling and love. As Robert finally picks the branch, thunder erupts and demons surround him; he clears a path by waving his talisman.

ACT 4 *The apartments of Princess Isabelle* Isabelle's attendants sing of her coming marriage to the Prince of Granada. Alice runs in to inform Isabelle of Robert's situation, but before she can finish several envoys enter, bearing gifts from the Prince, to a restatement of the ceremonial music from the tournament. Robert follows, and through the power of the magic branch induces all except Isabelle to remain frozen in their tracks; the encroachment of inertia upon the assembly is conveyed musically by a gradual augmentation of note values in the Prince's ceremonial chorus. Agitated, Robert does not deny to Isabelle the influence of darker powers, and begs her not to reject him. In a *cavatine* ('Robert, toi que j'aime') she throws herself at his feet, imploring him to repent in a triple reiteration of the memorable refrain, 'Grâce, grâce', the last time fortissimo after two pianissimo renderings. Robert is profoundly moved, breaks the branch, and is captured by Isabelle's attendants who spring back to life in the stretta of the act.

ACT 5 *The entrance to Palermo Cathedral* A group of monks sing in unison of the powerful salutary embrace of the Church ('Malheureux ou coupable'), a strong musical counterweight to the depiction of satanic power before this in the opera. Robert has been extricated from his predicament in the previous act by Bertram, and now he arrives breathless at the cathedral to prevent the marriage of Isabelle to the Prince. During a duet that is set off against a prayer sung in the cathedral, Bertram attempts to have Robert swear in writing that he will be his eternally; hearing the monks from within, Robert hesitates. As a last resort Bertram reveals to Robert that he is his father, but just as Robert is about to succumb to feelings of filial devotion Alice appears bearing news that the party of the Prince has been inexplicably prevented from proceeding up the aisle and that Isabelle awaits him at the altar. Alice then invokes divine help with a pious melody initiated by a threefold rising sequence ('Dieu puissant, ciel propice') and gives Robert his mother's will. Accompanied by a haunting trumpet melody offstage (suggesting a distant voice), Robert reads aloud his mother's warning to beware of the 'rash counsel of the seducer who has ruined me'. Both Alice and Bertram attempt to win over Robert's soul. He continues to vacillate. Midnight sounds and Bertram, his battle lost, is swallowed into the earth. The nave and altar of the cathedral are revealed and, to a chorus of angels and earthly celebrants, Robert is led to Isabelle.

* * *

That *Robert* was the first French opera for which even more money was spent on the sets than on the lavish costumes signals the importance of the *mise en scène* in the emerging genre of French grand opera. The sets were produced in the workshop of P.-L.-C. Ciceri, and the cloister scene of Act 3 became particularly famous in contemporary lithograph reproductions, succinctly communicating the gothic flavour appropriated by the Opéra from boulevard theatres. The abandonment of historical intrigue for more fantastical subject matter somewhat 'popularized' an institution tarred by social exclusiveness. So too did the residue of *opéra comique* in *Robert*, for example the presence of musically distinct 'high' and 'low' pairs of lovers. When Véron took over the directorship of the Opéra, *Robert* as a work (combined with clever business tactics) did much not only to swell the ranks of aristocratic subscribers but also to add an upper bourgeois clientele. Véron was the first to manage the Opéra as a private entrepreneur (albeit with a massive state subsidy) and the enormous commercial success of *Robert* was an important symbol for a government anxious to mediate between free-

enterprise business and more conservative landed interests. A political framework was restored to the librettos of many later grand operas, but the skills of Meyerbeer and Scribe enabled them to retain the kind of kaleidoscopic spectacle developed in *Robert* (and somewhat easier to accomplish there given the supernatural premise of the libretto).

For the playbill for the original production, *see* PARIS, fig.14; *see also* NOURRIT, ADOLPHE. STEVEN HUEBNER

Roberto [Roberti, Ruberti], **Costantino** (*b* Naples, 1700; *d* Naples, 17 March 1773). Italian composer. He studied briefly at the S Maria di Loreto Conservatory, probably under Giovanni Veneziano, *secondo maestro di cappella* from 1716 and one of the pioneers in Neapolitan *opera buffa*, the field that Roberto was to enter. He also took lessons from the master violinist and friend of Alessandro Scarlatti, G. C. Cailò. Subsequently he made his living as a violinist, first in the orchestra of the Teatro di S Bartolomeo, then at the S Carlo after its opening in 1737; he was also a member of the orchestra of the royal chapel. None of his music is known to survive, but his comic operas are of historical interest, for it was just when he was writing, about 1725–35, that in the hands of the librettists Mariani, Saddumene and Federico the form underwent significant morphological changes: the ratio of recitative to set numbers increased, although the latter, while fewer in number, became longer and more elaborate.

all opere buffe performed at Naples

La cantarina [Acts 2 and 3] (A. Piscopo), Fiorentini, carn. 1728 [Act 1 by M. Caballone]
Lo cecisbeo coffeato (T. Mariani), Fiorentini, 1728
Lo conte di Scrignano (Mariani), Fiorentini, 1729, collab. others
La Zita (G. A. Federico), Fiorentini, aut. 1731
Il Filippo (Federico), Nuovo, sum. 1735

*

M. Scherillo: *L'opera buffa napoletana durante il settecento: storia letteraria* (Naples, 1883, 2/1916), 209ff, 214–15
U. Prota-Giurleo: *La grande orchestra del R. teatro San Carlo nel settecento* (Naples, 1927), 7
——: *Nicola Logroscino: 'il dio dell'opera buffa'* (Naples, 1927), 56ff
S. di Giacomo: *I quattri antichi conservatorii musicali di Napoli*, ii (Milan and Naples, 1928), 218–19, 235–6, 239–40
JAMES L. JACKMAN

Roberto Devereux [*Roberto Devereux, ossia Il conte di Essex* ('Robert Devereux, or the Earl of Essex')]. *Tragedia lirica* in three acts by GAETANO DONIZETTI to a libretto by SALVADORE CAMMARANO after François Ancelot's tragedy *Elisabeth d'Angleterre*; Naples, Teatro S Carlo, 28 October 1837.

Donizetti revised the score for its introduction to Paris in December 1838, adding a full-scale overture whose first theme is the melody of *God Save the Queen*. The contrasting second theme is the melody of Roberto's cabaletta in the Tower Scene, 'Bagnato il sen di lagrime', itself another new addition to the score, replacing a different aria at this point. Donizetti also modified the cabaletta of the duet for Elisabetta [Elizabeth] and Roberto [Robert] by giving the tenor a contrasting melody instead of echoing Elizabeth's as he had formerly. Nor were these the last changes Donizetti made to this score. He wrote an alternative G minor *romanza* for Sara [Sarah] in the *introduzione* for Albertazzi, retaining the original text, and for the baritone Barroilhet (the original Nottingham in Naples) he enlarged his role in the French-language version with an expressive cavatina, 'Par toi, Sara'.

Roberto Devereux was very successful for almost three decades as long as there were worthy successors to Ronzi de Begnis, the original singer, to assume the role of Elizabeth. The last of the 19th-century divas to make the role her personal vehicle was Marcella Lotti della Santa. In the 20th century the mantle has fallen on Leyla Gencer, Beverly Sills and Montserrat Caballé.

Act 1 opens with Sarah, Duchess of Nottingham (mezzo-soprano), inconsolable, although the other ladies-in-waiting try to cheer her, while Elizabeth (soprano) eagerly awaits Robert Devereux, Earl of Essex (tenor), but suspects that he is avoiding her. Cecil and Raleigh (basses) urge the queen to charge Essex with treason, but she puts them off. The queen receives Essex, who denies treason. She reminds him of the ring she gave him as a promise of pardon should he be arraigned. But she is hurt by his coolness, and grows increasingly suspicious that he loves another woman. The Duke of Nottingham (baritone) is worried that his wife Sarah is sad and uncommunicative; lately he found her trying to conceal a blue scarf she had been working on. All this he confides to his friend Essex, who is embarrassed, as he is himself in love with Sarah.

Essex goes to see Sarah and reproaches her for marrying Nottingham; she in turn chides him for wearing the queen's ring, which he impulsively tears off and presents to her. In return she gives him the scarf.

In Act 2 the Council has met and condemned Essex to death. Nottingham comes to plead on his friend's behalf; but Raleigh has brought along the scarf, found when Essex's apartment was searched, and at the sight of it Nottingham explodes in a jealous fury, capped only by the rage of the queen. Essex is led off to the Tower.

When Act 3 begins, Sarah has received a letter from Essex begging her to send the ring to Elizabeth. Before she can do so, Nottingham storms in and orders her confined, refusing to heed her protestations of innocence. In the Tower, Essex realizes that he will not be able to clear Sarah's name before his execution. In spite of the indications of Essex's betrayal, Elizabeth wants him to live, but without the ring feels unable to stop the course of events. Too late, Sarah arrives with the ring, followed by Nottingham; the enraged Elizabeth orders their arrest. Oppressed by a vision of Essex's ghost, she presses the ring to her lips, longing to be freed of her role as monarch.

* * *

The portrait of Queen Elizabeth I in *Roberto Devereux* is the most imposing of Donizetti's representations of that character (who also appears in *Elisabetta al castello di Kenilworth* and *Maria Stuarda*), and the role must rank as one of the great acting and singing opportunities in the bel canto repertory. Musically, the score has much to commend it. As in other Donizetti operas, the first act moves in a rather leisurely manner, with a sequence of full *arie di sortita*; the pace accelerates to a dramatic climax in a briefer Act 2; then Act 3, like that of *Lucia*, is a sequence of three powerful scenes.

Particularly impressive are Elizabeth's entrance aria, the duet for Sarah and Essex, the trio-finale to Act 2, the Prison Scene of Essex, and Elizabeth's aria-finale. Everywhere the score shows the sure hand of a composer in control of his materials. The powerful prelude to the Prison Scene recalls the opening of Act 2 of *Fidelio*. Elizabeth's final Larghetto, 'Vivi, ingrato', is a fine example of a melody developing in a long emotional arc

of searing poignancy, and of Donizetti's sensitive response to the expressive colour of the words.

WILLIAM ASHBROOK

Robertson, James (*b* Liverpool, 17 June 1912; *d* Ruabon, North Wales, 18 May 1991). English conductor. After studying at Trinity College, Cambridge, Leipzig Conservatory and the RCM, he joined the music staff of Glyndebourne Festival Opera in 1937 and became chorus master of the Carl Rosa Opera in 1938. On release from wartime service in the RAF, he became musical director of the Sadler's Wells Opera (1946–54), conducting the British premières of *I quatro rusteghi* and Sutermeister's *Romeo und Julia*. Here, and as music director of the Carl Rosa Opera, he played a significant part in the spread of operatic interest in Britain. He was opera adviser to the Théâtre Royale de la Monnaie in Brussels in 1960, and there followed periods in New Zealand, where he was artistic director of the National Opera (1962–3) and conductor (1978–81). He was director of the London Opera Centre (concerned with the training of young singers), 1964–77, and later consultant. KENNETH LOVELAND

Robin, Mado (*b* Yseures-sur-Creuse, nr Tours, 29 Dec 1918; *d* Paris, 10 Dec 1960). French soprano. She studied in Paris, where she made her début at the Opéra in 1945 as Gilda (*Rigoletto*) and also sang the Queen of Night. The following year she sang Lakmé at the Opéra-Comique, followed by Rosina (*Il barbiere di Siviglia*) and Olympia (*Les contes d'Hoffmann*). She appeared at many French regional theatres, in Brussels and in Monte Carlo. In 1953 she returned to the Opéra to sing Konstanze (*Die Entführung*), and in 1954 she sang in San Francisco, as Gilda and Lucia. Her extreme facility for coloratura and very high range were best displayed in roles such as Stravinsky's Nightingale.

ELIZABETH FORBES

Robinson, Anastasia (*b* Italy, *c*1692; *d* Southampton, April 1755). English soprano, later contralto. She studied singing with Sandoni and Lindelheim, and turned professional to support the family when the sight of her father, a portrait painter, failed. She joined the Queen's Theatre opera company in 1714, making her début in the pasticcio *Creso* and singing in *Arminio* and *Ernelinda*. The following season she played Almirena in Handel's *Rinaldo*, sang in the pasticcio *Lucio Vero*, and created Oriana in Handel's *Amadigi*. In 1715–17 she was in Alessandro Scarlatti's *Pirro e Demetrio*, the pasticcios *Clearte* and *Vinceslao*, and revivals of *Rinaldo* and *Amadigi*. Thereafter her voice dropped from soprano to contralto. On the foundation of the Royal Academy of Music she rejoined the opera company and sang in its first three productions, in 1720: Porta's *Numitore*, Handel's *Radamisto* (creating the part of Zenobia) and Roseingrave's arrangement of Domenico Scarlatti's *Narciso*. She sang in all the operas between spring 1721 and summer 1724: the composite *Muzio Scevola* (Irene), Handel's *Floridante* (Elmira), *Ottone* (Matilda), *Flavio* (Teodata) and *Giulio Cesare* (Cornelia), Giovanni Bononcini's *Ciro*, *Crispo*, *Griselda*, *Erminia*, *Farnace* and *Calpurnia*, and Ariosti's *Coriolano*, *Vespasiano* and *Aquilio consolo*. In June 1724 she retired from the stage, having secretly married the elderly Earl of Peterborough two years earlier; he did not acknowledge her publicly until shortly before his death in 1735.

Robinson enjoyed great personal and artistic popularity. She was a woman of culture and social gifts, and a friend of Pope and Bononcini, who gave her lessons in 1723. As a singer she was remarkable for charm and expressiveness rather than virtuosity; the care with which Handel supported and sometimes doubled her parts suggests technical limitations. His richest part for her, Oriana, which offers many openings for pathos, belongs to her soprano period (compass *d'* to *a''*); from 1720 her range diminished (*bb* to *e''*). He gave her a highly emotional part in *Giulio Cesare* and an ironically humorous one in *Flavio*. She disliked playing termagants and found Matilda in *Ottone* as first composed impossible to sing: 'a Patient Grisell by Nature' (an allusion to her success in Bononcini's *Griselda*), she was asked to play 'an abominable Scold'. Afraid to face Handel, she enlisted the help of the diplomat Giuseppe Riva to have it altered – apparently with success, for the aria to which she chiefly objected was replaced. Her letters to Riva in the Campori collection at Modena (*I-MOe*) show an attractive and generous character. She was buried in Bath Abbey.

WINTON DEAN

Robinson, Ann Turner [née Turner] (*d* London, 5 Jan 1741). English soprano, daughter of the composer William Turner. In 1719–20 she sang in Ariosti's cantata *Diana on Mount Latmos* at Drury Lane. She first appeared in opera in the short first season of the Royal Academy of Music (1720) in Porta's *Numitore*, as Polissena in Handel's *Radamisto* and in Domenico Scarlatti's *Narciso*. Her part in *Radamisto* shows that she was a capable singer with some brilliance at the top of her compass (*e'* to *a''*). She was generally announced as 'Mrs Robinson, late Mrs Turner' or 'Mrs Turner Robinson', to distinguish her from Anastasia Robinson. She was probably the Mrs Robinson who sang between the acts at Drury Lane in 1725–6 and played in Carey's pantomime *Apollo and Daphne*. She often sang Handel's arias in concerts, and took part in his first London oratorio performances at the King's Theatre in 1732.

Her daughter (first name unknown) sang in Handel's oratorios in 1744–5 and created Dejanira in *Hercules*.

WINTON DEAN

Robinson, Earl (Hawley) (*b* Seattle, 2 July 1910; *d* Seattle, 20 July 1991). American composer. As a child he studied the piano, violin and viola, and he began composing seriously in his third year at the University of Washington, where he studied with George F. McKay (BM 1933). In 1934 he went to New York, where he joined the Workers Laboratory Theater (later Theater of Action) and the Pierre Degeyter Club and its Composers' Collective. He studied with Hanns Eisler during this period, and also with Aaron Copland at the Downtown (later Metropolitan) Music School. Robinson's energies turned towards writing topical songs and cantatas, often rooted in folk material and his continuing involvement in music as action led naturally to the writing of stage works. The most polished of these, composed between 1951 and 1954 in collaboration with the screenwriter Waldo Salt, is *Sandhog*, a folk opera in three acts, based on the short story *St Columba and the River* by Theodore Dreiser. Another folk opera, about the Armenian folk hero David of Sassoon, was completed in 1978 (and given in abridged form), while Robinson was in residence at California State University, Fresno; it was followed by a children's opera,

Listen for the Dolphin (1982). A music drama, *Song of Atlantis* (1984), has had two concert performances (Santa Barbara and Seattle) with the composer at the piano. Robinson's musicals fall somewhere between his cantatas and operas in terms of seriousness of content and purpose. In general his stage works are continually evolving entities rather than formally fixed structures.

Processional (musical, J. H. Lawson), New York, 1938
Sing for Your Supper (musical, J. Latouche), New York, Adelphi, March 1939
Sandhog (folk op, 3, W. Salt, after T. Dreiser: *St Columba and the River*), New York, Phoenix, Nov 1954, vs (New York, 1956)
One Foot in America (musical, 2, L. Allan, after Y. Suhl), Evanston, IL, 1962
Earl Robinson's America, 1976 (musical, 2, E. Robinson and others), Virginia, MN, May 1980
David of Sassoon (folk op, 3, Robinson), abridged Fresno, CA, Oct 1978
Listen for the Dolphin (children's op, 2, Robinson), Santa Barbara, CA, Garden Street, 12 June 1981
Song of Atlantis (music drama, 2, Robinson), concert perf., Santa Barbara, July 1983
I Been Thinkin' About J. C. (Robinson), Santa Barbara, July 1985

STEVEN E. GILBERT

Robinson, Faye (*b* Houston, 2 Nov 1943). American soprano. She studied at Texas Southern University and with Ellen Faull in New York, making her début there with the City Opera in 1972 as Micaëla. She also sang Liù, Violetta and the Queen of Shemakha (*The Golden Cockerel*) with the company. She appeared with the Washington Civic Opera as Violetta and Gounod's Juliet (1973), and for Opera South in Jackson sang Desdemona (1974) and Adina (*L'elisir d'amore*, 1975). In 1975 she scored a great success at Aix-en-Provence in a double bill of Mozart's *Der Schauspieldirektor* and Pergolesi's *La serva padrona*, and sang the title role in *Lucrezia Borgia* at Houston. She took all three soprano roles in *Les contes d'Hoffmann* in Buenos Aires in 1980, and the following year she sang Konstanze at Frankfurt and Electra (*Idomeneo*) at the Schwetzingen Festival, repeating the latter role in Amsterdam in 1991. She made her Paris Opéra début in 1982 as Gounod's Juliet. Her flexible, silver-toned voice and charming stage presence are as effective in comic roles as in more tragic parts such as Luisa Miller, which she sang at Bordeaux in 1982.

ELIZABETH FORBES

Robinson, (Peter) Forbes (*b* Macclesfield, 21 May 1926; *d* London, 13 May 1987). English bass. He studied at Loughborough College and at the training school of La Scala, joined the Covent Garden Opera in 1954 and made his début that year as Monterone. He took more than 60 roles with the company, the most important being the speaking part of Moses in the British première of Schoenberg's *Moses und Aron* (1965), the title role, which he created, in Tippett's *King Priam* (1962) and Claggart in *Billy Budd*. He also sang frequently with the WNO, notably as Don Giovanni, Boris, Fiesco and Philip II. In 1966 he appeared at the Teatro Colón, Buenos Aires. Robinson had a dark, expressive voice, evenly produced and capable of subtle characterization, especially in such roles as Claggart and Boris.

For illustration see *KING PRIAM*.　　ALAN BLYTH

Robinson, Michael F(inlay) (*b* Gloucester, 3 March 1933). English musicologist. He studied at Oxford, where he took the doctorate with a dissertation on Neapolitan opera (1963). He has taught at Durham University, McGill University, Montreal, and the University of Wales, Cardiff, where he became head of the music department in 1987. Robinson's research, which has centred on Neapolitan opera of the 18th century, is drawn together in his broad survey *Naples and Neapolitan Opera*, where the Neapolitan contribution to operatic history is surveyed and characterized. His earlier book *Opera before Mozart* provides a general picture of the rise of opera in the social and aesthetic circumstances of the 17th and early 18th centuries.

Opera before Mozart (London, 1966, 3/1978)
'Porpora's Operas for London, 1733–1736', *Soundings*, ii (1971–2), 57–87
Naples and Neapolitan Opera (Oxford, 1972; It. trans., 1985)
'Mozart and the *Opera buffa* Tradition', in T. Carter: *W. A. Mozart: 'Le nozze di Figaro'* (Cambridge, 1987), 11–32
A Thematic Catalogue of the Works of Giovanni Paisiello (New York, 1990–)

Robinson, Stanford (*b* Leeds, 5 July 1904; *d* Brighton, 25 Oct 1984). English conductor. He studied at the RCM, where he conducted his first opera performances, and in 1924 joined the BBC as chorus master, remaining a staff conductor until 1966. From 1936 he was responsible for studio opera and for many distinguished broadcasts, including Massenet's *Manon* (1938) with Teyte, Nash and Noble. He was conductor of the BBC Opera Orchestra from 1949 until it became the BBC Concert Orchestra in 1952. After that, Robinson continued to conduct much radio and television opera without being attached to a specific orchestra.

He made his Covent Garden début with *Die Fledermaus* in 1937; he also briefly directed the English Opera Group, and conducted the first London production of Alessandro Scarlatti's *Il trionfo dell'onore* (Fortune Theatre, 1951). From 1946, when he conducted opera and concerts in Budapest, he appeared occasionally abroad; he also made many records, especially with leading singers. His compositions include light orchestral pieces and songs, but his main achievement was in substantially helping to shape the BBC's choral and operatic policy and reputation. He was married to the soprano Lorely Dyer.   ARTHUR JACOBS

Robinson Crusoé ('Robinson Crusoe'). *Opéra comique* in three acts by JACQUES OFFENBACH to a libretto by EUGÈNE CORMON and HECTOR-JONATHAN CRÉMIEUX after Daniel Defoe's novel; Paris, Opéra-Comique (Salle Favart), 23 November 1867.

The action owes as much to the British pantomime version of Defoe as to the novel. Act 1 is set in the Crusoe family home in Bristol and the remainder on the desert island at the mouth of the Orinoco on which Robinson (tenor) lands after sailing away to seek his fortune. There, besides Vendredi [Man Friday] (mezzo-soprano), there appear Robinson's fiancée Edwige (soprano), the family's servants Suzanne (soprano) and Toby (tenor), and a former neighbour, Jim Cocks (baritone), who has become a cannibal chef. The work contains typical Offenbachian farce but, befitting production at the Opéra-Comique, is substantially more operatic. Musical highlights include, in Act 2, Friday's song 'Tamayo, mon frère' and Edwige's waltz song 'Conduisez-moi vers celui que j'adore'. Galli-Marié was the original Man Friday.   ANDREW LAMB

Robin Woman, The. Opera by C. W. Cadman; *see* SHANEWIS.

Robson, Christopher (*b* Falkirk, 9 Dec 1953). Scottish countertenor. He studied with Paul Esswood, making his début in 1979 at Birmingham as Argones (*Sosarme*). He has sung with Kent Opera, Opera Factory (London and Zürich), at Frankfurt and Innsbruck. He made his Covent Garden début in 1988 as Athamas (*Semele*), and has specialized in baroque opera, singing Endymion (*Calisto*), Corindo (Cesti's *Orontea*), Handel's Julius Caesar, Ptolemy and Arsamene (*Xerxes*). His flexible voice is also effective in modern works, and he scored a huge success in the title role of Glass's *Akhnaten* at Houston and with the New York City Opera (1984) and the ENO (1985), for whom he also sang Edgar in Reimann's *Lear* (1989). He sang the voice of Apollo (*Death in Venice*) at Nancy, and Ometti in Casken's *Golem* at Newcastle in 1991.   ELIZABETH FORBES

Robyn, (Johann) Alfred G(eorge) (*b* St Louis, MO, 29 April 1860; *d* New York, 18 Oct 1935). American composer. He was taught by his father, William Robyn (1814–1905), one of the most distinguished pioneers of serious music in the American West. He made his début as a pianist aged nine and a year later became a church organist. He continued to be a regular organist at churches or synagogues until shortly before his death, and was also pianist for the Beethoven Trio. Among his works are a symphony, a symphonic poem, chamber music and art songs. For a time, however, he was best known for his comic operas, of which he wrote 28. These included *Jacinta* (1894), *The Yankee Consul* (1904, to a book by the best of contemporary librettists, Henry Blossom), *The Princess Beggar* (1907), *The Yankee Tourist* (1907) and *All for the Ladies* (1912). Other comic operas of his were mounted regionally. His melodies were attractive and had the youthful verve or innocent lilt so common to the era. But his scores were usually dismissed by the more high-minded critics, one writing off his songs for *The Yankee Consul* as 'bimmity-bang'. When musical styles changed significantly with the coming of World War I, Robyn failed to move with the times. He continued to compose but thereafter his works were produced mostly by semi-professional and amateur groups.   GERALD BORDMAN

Rocca, Lodovico (*b* Turin, 29 Nov 1895; *d* Turin, 25 June 1986). Italian composer. He studied in Turin and under Giacomo Orefice in Milan, and was director of the Turin Conservatory, 1940–66. His fame rests on his third opera, *Il Dibuk*, in relation to which most of his other works – both operatic and non-operatic – may be regarded as preparations, by-products or postscripts. The first two operas, which owe much to Rocca's older Italian contemporaries (notably Puccini and Zandonai), are most interesting where they foreshadow *Il Dibuk* most strongly; the fourth, *Monte Ivnor*, uses an idiom very similar to that of its predecessor, but is less compelling and sometimes self-imitative; *L'uragano* shows signs of more drastic creative decline and comes badly out of inevitable comparisons with Janáček's masterly treatment of the same subject in *Kát'a Kabanová*. *Il Dibuk* is a difficult opera to assess: the music in itself, though resourceful and imaginative, often seems more an eclectic amalgam than a unified whole. Yet the total effect in the theatre proved powerful enough, when the work was new, to win it one of the biggest Italian operatic successes since Puccini's *Turandot*.

See also DIBUK, IL.

La morte di Frine, 1917–20 (1, E. Marco Senea [C. Meano]), Turin radio, 31 May 1936; stage, Milan, Scala, 24 April 1937

In terra di leggenda [La corona di re Gaulo], 1922–3 (3, Meano), concert perf., Milan, Palazzo dell'Arte, 28 Sept 1933; stage, Bergamo, Donizetti, 1 Oct 1936

Il Dibuk, 1928–30 (prol., 3, R. Simoni, after S. Anski: *Tzvishen tzvei Velter*), Milan, Scala, 24 March 1934

Monte Ivnor, 1936–8 (3, Meano, after F. Werfel: *Die vierzig Tage des Musa Dagh*), Rome, Opera, 23 Dec 1939

L'uragano, 1942–51 (3, E. Possenti, after A. N. Ostrovsky: *The Storm*), Milan, Scala, 7 Feb 1952

F. Abbiati: 'Lodovico Rocca e Il Dibuk', *Comoedia* [Milan], xvi/5 (1934), 15–17

G. Rossi-Doria: 'La stagione lirica a Roma: Il Dibuk', *Nuova antologia*, no.383 (1936), 351–2

R. Mariani: 'Musicisti del nostro tempo: Lodovico Rocca', *RaM*, xi (1938), 163–74

L. Colacicchi: 'Lodovico Rocca e *Monte Ivnor*', *Scenario*, ix (1940), 40–41

R. Mariani: 'Ritorno di Rocca', *La Scala*, no.27 (1952), 41–3

G. Gavazzeni: 'Paragrafi su Lodovico Rocca', *La musica e il teatro* (Pisa, 1954), 261–70, esp. 265–7

F. L. Lunghi: 'Lodovico Rocca', *Santa Cecilia*, iii/2 (1954), 54–6

R. Rossellini: 'Lodovico Rocca', *Polemica musicale* (Milan, 1962), 55–7

M. Bruni: *Lodovico Rocca* (Milan, 1963) [Ricordi pamphlet]

J. C. G. Waterhouse: *The Emergence of Modern Italian Music (up to 1940)* (diss., U. of Oxford, 1968), 643–50

G. Vigolo: 'Il temporale eclettico'; 'Il Dibuk', *Mille e una sera all'opera e al concerto* (Florence, 1971), 153–5, 355–7

P. Caputo: 'L'operismo di Lodovico Rocca', *Rassegna musicale Curci*, xxviii/2–3 (1975), 48

G. Pugliaro: 'Lodovico Rocca', *Ghedini e l'attività musicale a Torino tra le due guerre: Turin 1986*, 92–8

G. Landini: 'La vocalità nel melodramma di Lodovico Rocca: aspetti e problemi', ibid, 99–116   JOHN C. G. WATERHOUSE

Roccaforte, Gaetano (*fl* mid-18th century). Italian librettist. He took religious vows and spent most or all of his life in Rome; in his printed librettos he is usually identified as 'Abate Gaetano Roccaforte, romano'. All eight of his known librettos were first performed in Rome. He appears to have acted as resident librettist and impresario at the Teatro Argentina during the 1746 and 1747 opera seasons. Three of his librettos enjoyed some degree of success: *Caio Mario*, *Antigona* and *Tito Manlio* were each set many times. The most successful settings were Galuppi's *Antigona* and Jommelli's *Cajo Mario*, each of which was revived at least a dozen times.

See also CAIO MARIO and TITO MANLIO.

Tito Manlio (os), Manna, 1742 (Jommelli, 1743; Abos, 1751; Latilla, 1755; Cocchi, 1761; P. A. Guglielmi, 1763; Borghi, 1780; Giordani, 1784; Tarchi, 1791); Cajo Mario (os), Jommelli, 1746 (G. Scarlatti, 1755; Piccinni, ?1757; Galuppi, 1764; Scolari, 1765; Anfossi, 1770; C. Monza, 1777; Cimarosa, 1780; Bertoni, 1781; F. Bianchi, 1784; Giordani, 1789); Alcibiade (os), M. Capranica, 1746; Pelopida (os), Abos, 1747 (G. Scarlatti, 1763; Barthelemon, 1766); Antigona (os), Galuppi, 1751 (G. B. Casali, 1752; Latilla, 1753; Bertoni, 1756; G. Scarlatti, 1756; V. Ciampi, 1762; Sales, 1767; G. F. Majo, 1768; Mysliveček, 1774; Mortellari, 1776; Gazzaniga, 1781); Talestri (os), Jommelli, 1751; Sofonisba (os), Galuppi, 1753; Melite riconosciuta (os), Galuppi, 1759 (Tarchi, 1787)   PAUL CAUTHEN

Rochaix, François (*b* Geneva, 2 Aug 1942). Swiss actor and director. He studied at the University of Geneva and was trained as an actor with François Simon and as a director at the Berliner Ensemble, in East Berlin. He worked first as an actor and director at the Atelier de Genève, which he founded in 1963. From 1975 to 1981

he was director of the Théâtre de Carouge. Since 1981 he has been a freelance opera and theatre director. His first important production was *The Turn of the Screw* at Geneva (1981) and his productions since have included *Death in Venice* (Scottish Opera and Geneva, 1983), *La traviata* for Opera North (1985, Leeds), *Der Ring des Nibelungen* (1985–7, Seattle), *Cardillac* (1988, Berne), *Die Meistersinger von Nürnberg* (1989, Seattle) and *Parsifal* (1989, Berne). His work is notable for its narrative clarity and sober neo-classicism.

C. Frochaux: 'Ecrire en Suisse', *L'âge d'homme* (Lausanne, 1973), 36–9

B. Perregaux: 'De l'usage de 3 notions héritées de Brecht', *Silex 7* (Grenoble, 1978), 121–8

A. Clark: 'François Rochaix', *OW* (1985), no.2, pp.21–3
                                                 HUGH CANNING

Rochberg, George (*b* Paterson, NJ, 5 July 1918). American composer. He studied composition at the Mannes School, New York (1939–42) and, after service in World War II, at the Curtis Institute, Philadelphia; his teachers included George Szell and Menotti. In 1948 he joined the faculty of Curtis, remaining there until 1954. After working for Theodore Presser as director of publications, in 1960 became head of the music department at the University of Pennsylvania. He was guest composer at several institutions, and was elected to the American Academy and Institute of Arts and Letters in 1985. *The Aesthetics of Survival: a Composer's View of Twentieth-Century Music*, a collection of his writings, was published in 1984 (edited by William Bolcom). A prolific composer, he has written in most genres.

Rochberg's dramatic works include the seven-act monodrama *Phaedra* (1973–4) and the two-act opera *The Confidence Man* (1982), both to librettos by his wife, Gene Rochberg. *Phaedra* is based on Robert Lowell's version of Racine's tragedy; it is scored for mezzo-soprano and orchestra. The piece was commissioned by the New Music Ensemble and was first performed in Syracuse on 9 January 1976 with Neva Pilgrim as the soloist. *The Confidence Man*, based on Herman Melville's satirical novel, was commissioned by Santa Fe Opera and given its première on 31 July 1982. Couched in the composer's late, neo-romantic idiom, the opera alludes to the styles of various 19th-century composers, while relying heavily on 'realistic' arioso and recitative.

R. H. Kornick: *Recent American Opera: a Production Guide* (New York, 1991), 241–4   AUSTIN CLARKSON

Rochefort, Jean-Baptiste (*b* Paris, 24 June 1746; *d* Paris, 1819). French composer. He was a choirboy at Notre Dame in Paris. In 1775 he joined the orchestra of the Paris Opéra as a double bass player, but left in 1780 to take charge of the French opera at the Landgrave of Hesse's court in Kassel. In 1785 he returned to the Opéra orchestra and shortly afterwards was appointed second conductor; he remained with that institution until 1815. Apart from some chamber music, he composed mainly for the theatre, contributing additional music to other composers' works, arranging a pasticcio, *Descente d'Orphée aux enfers* (1798), and a parody of Anfossi's *L'incognita perseguitata* as *L'inconnue persécutée* (1776). His own works suggest his efficiency in meeting the demands of the ballet-masters rather than any pronounced individuality, although there are moments of originality in some of his major works, and his command of the orchestra is evident. The *ballet-*

héroïque Bacchus et Ariane (1791, Paris) calls for a serpent, an instrument seldom explicitly named in scores of the period. His later works include several pieces of revolutionary sentiment, among them an (unfulfilled) 'prophétie', *La descente en Angleterre*, in which he attempted to depict in music the characteristics of the English and French peoples.

first performed in Paris unless otherwise stated

La corbeille de mariage, ou La force du sang (drame lyrique, 1), Cité, Dec 1775, *F-Pn*

Justine et Landri, ou Le bail à loyer (oc, 1, Le Boutellier), Palais Bourbon, 8 March 1780, *Pn*

Daphnis et Florise (pastorale, 1, Le Boutellier), Kassel, 20 Sept 1782, *Pn*

Ariane (scène lyrique), Opéra, 1788, *Pn*, aria in *Journal hebdomadaire, composé d'airs d'opéra*, no.23 (Paris, 1788)

Toulon soumis (1, Fabre d'Olivet), Opéra, 4 March 1794, *Pn*, *Po*

La descente en Angleterre ('prophétie', 2), Cité, 24 Dec 1797

Others: La cassette (oc, 1), Comédie-Italienne; Dorothée (oc, 1), Montansier; L'esprit de contradiction (oc, 1), Comédie-Italienne; Les noces de Zerbine (oc), Kassel; La pompe funèbre de Crispin (oc), Kassel; L'inconnue persécutée (oc), 14 Dec 1783, Comédie-Italienne [arr. of P. Anfossi: L'incognita perseguita]

Melodramas: Pyrame et Thisbé (Leboeuf), Kassel; L'amour vengé (Parisan), 4 March 1779; Echo et Narcisse, Ambigu-Comique, 1786–9   JULIAN RUSHTON

Rochester. American city, in the state of New York, incorporated in 1834. Touring European musicians appeared in the city from the mid-19th century, and the Columbia Opera Company flourished briefly in the 1880s. After 1900 Rochester became a concert centre in western New York, and by 1921 the hub of musical activity was the Eastman School of Music (part of the University of Rochester), which included the Eastman Theatre (cap. 3100) and Kilbourn Hall (459 seats). In 1922 the Rochester Opera Company (directed by Vladimir Rosing and conducted by Eugene Goossens) developed out of the opera department; its aim was to present contemporary American works as well as standard operas in English translation. It made its professional début at the Eastman Theatre in 1924, later appearing at the Chautauqua Opera Festival and on tour. Renamed the American Opera Company and independent of Eastman's support, it was successful until 1929, when it was dissolved.

The present Opera Theater of Rochester, founded in 1962 by Ruth Rosenberg, presents standard operas with guest artists, local singers and members of the Rochester PO at the Eastman Theatre. The Eastman School of Music Opera Theater, founded in 1947 by Leonard Treash, continues to give full performances under the direction of Richard Pearlman at the Eastman Theatre, Kilbourn Hall and the school's Cutler Union Auditorium (cap. 700). From 1952 to 1976 the Eastman School, together with Monroe County and the New York State Council of the Arts, sponsored an annual Opera Under the Stars Festival at the Highland Park Bowl.   RUTH T. WATANABE

Rochetti, (Gaetano) Filippo (*fl* 1724–after 1750). Italian tenor. He joined Rich's company at Lincoln's Inn Fields as a singer between the acts in 1724, and remained there until the end of 1732, then moved to Rich's new theatre at Covent Garden until 1735. He sang in many pantomimes and afterpieces, with music mostly by Galliard or Pepusch, a revival of Giovanni Bononcini's *Camilla* (1726), Purcell's *Dioclesian* (1731) and a one-act *Telemachus* with music by Alessandro Scarlatti

(1732). He took part in the first public performance of Handel's *Acis and Galatea* in 1731, and in Handel's oratorios at Oxford under the composer in 1733. At Lincoln's Inn Fields in 1734 he played small parts for the Opera of the Nobility in Bononcini's *Astarto* and Porpora's *Enea nel Lazio*. In 1739 he appeared in Pescetti's *Angelica e Medoro* at Covent Garden and sang in a composite Purcell masque. He was a member of Lord Middlesex's company at the New Haymarket in 1740, singing in a pasticcio and in operas by Hasse (*Olimpia in Ebuda*) and Pescetti (*Busiri*), and appeared once at Covent Garden in 1741. He was singing in Edinburgh in the 1750s, having apparently settled permanently in Britain.   WINTON DEAN

Rochois, Marie [Marthe] Le. *See* LE ROCHOIS, MARIE.

Röckel [Roeckel], August (*b* Graz, 1 Dec 1814; *d* Budapest, 18 June 1876). German composer, son of Joseph Röckel. He studied with his father and worked as a répétiteur for his travelling company. He later went on to study in Vienna and Paris, where he was Rossini's assistant at the Théâtre Italien. He became director of music at Bamberg (1838), Weimar (1839–43) and Dresden (1843–9), where he met Wagner. In 1839 he wrote an opera, *Farinelli*, which was later accepted for performance at Dresden, although Röckel withdrew it out of esteem for Wagner's genius. Like Wagner, he was involved in the Dresden Revolution of 1848–9, when he abandoned music and devoted himself entirely to politics. After 13 years in prison (1849–62), he became editor of various newspapers. He is remembered chiefly for his friendship and correspondence with Wagner, whose letters to him throw revealing light on the composer's intentions in the *Ring*.

*

G. Strobel and others, eds.: *Richard Wagner: Sämtliche Briefe*, ii–vii (Leipzig, 1970–89)

S. Spencer and B. Millington, eds.: *Selected Letters of Richard Wagner* (London, 1987)

Röckel [Roeckel], Joseph [Josef] (August) (*b* Neunburg, Upper Palatinate, 28 Aug 1783; *d* Cöthen, 19 Sept 1870). German tenor. Originally intended for the church, he entered the diplomatic service in 1803 and the next year was engaged to sing in Vienna at the Theater an der Wien. On 29 March 1806 he appeared as Florestan in the première of the second version of Beethoven's *Fidelio*. He subsequently taught singing at the Hofoper, where Henriette Sontag was among his pupils. After various travels he went in 1830 to Paris, where he successfully produced German operas with a German company. He remained in Paris until 1832, when he took his company to London and produced *Fidelio*, *Der Freischütz* and other German operas at the King's Theatre with such distinguished singers as Schröder-Devrient and Haizinger. The company was conducted by Hummel, Röckel's brother-in-law. In 1835 he retired from operatic life, and in 1846 went to York as a music teacher; he returned to Germany in 1853.

Rock opera. An operatic work in which the musical idiom is rock and roll. Such works have little direct connection to the opera as traditionally understood. They do not use operatically trained singers; the sound is amplified; some of the more interesting examples were never intended for live performance.

If opera derives from the mainstream of the Western classical music tradition, then 'rock operas' are part of the far larger alternative tradition of music-theatre works stemming from non-Western and vernacular musical cultures. They may eventually join the mainstream; they may borrow, sincerely, cynically or parodistically, the pretensions and cachet of mainstream nomenclature and styles, but for now they remain an outsider phenomenon. Rock itself, born of a marriage of lower-class American black and white musics, was in part a protest not only against standard Tin Pan Alley pop music, but against high art as well (in the words of Chuck Berry's song, 'Roll over, Beethoven, and tell Tchaikovsky the news!').

Rock was based originally on discrete songs, marketed commercially as 'singles'. The first long-playing records in the late 1940s predated rock by some seven years. 'Rock operas' grew out of 'concept albums', LPs with a theme, in the mid-1960s, and hence are really closer to the song cycles of classical tradition than to opera. Nearly all the first examples were British, reflecting the greater tendency on the part of art-school-educated British rockers to aspire to high art in their emulations of the American vernacular.

The Beatles' *Sgt. Pepper's Lonely Hearts Club Band* is often adduced as the first important concept album. It was released in 1967, the year that seemed to mark the emergence of the 'rock opera' in several related guises. Peter Wicke, the (East) German rock historian, cites *The Story of Simon Simonpath: a Science Fiction Pantomime* (1967) by the little-known group Nirvana as the first selfconsciously subtitled rock opera. In the same year The Who released *Tommy*, which made by far the most profound impression of all rock operas among rock fans. On Broadway, 1967 also saw the appearance of Galt MacDermot's *Hair*, which was really a rock-flavoured musical but which established the notion of rock opera in the minds of the adult public.

Rock musicals, including Stephen Schwartz's *Godspell* (1971) and Charlie Smalls's *The Wiz* (1975), conformed far more to the aesthetics of Broadway and the West End than to rock music itself. The most successful exponent of the rock musical has been Andrew Lloyd Webber, especially in his earliest works, *Joseph and the Amazing Technicolor Dreamcoat* (1968; rev. 1972) and *Jesus Christ Superstar* (1971). In later works, such as *Evita* (1978) and *The Phantom of the Opera* (1986), Lloyd Webber used rock music, but his evolution has been towards a neo-romantic eclecticism rather than an extension of the expressive potential of rock *per se*. In classical music, the composer most attuned to the rock musical was Leonard Bernstein. His *Mass* (1971), for which he enlisted Schwartz as co-lyricist, is the most successful American stage work extensively using rock music.

Tommy, performed in concert at the Metropolitan Opera House as part of a tour by The Who in 1969 and made into a flossy film by Ken Russell, was never more than an allegorical song cycle telling of a 'deaf, dumb and blind boy' and his search for spiritual enlightenment. The Who, in particular its chief composer Pete Townshend, followed with an even more explicitly narrative cycle, *Quadrophenia* (1973), which was also made into a movie. Among other English bands, the most interesting was the Kinks, with *Arthur, or the Decline and Fall of the British Empire* (1969), *Soap Opera* (1975) and *Schoolboys in Disgrace* (1975).

As art rock developed grandiose pretensions in the late 1960s and early 70s, all manner of cosmic, album-long meanderings were produced by such continental European bands as Magma, Can and Faust. David Bowie created a powerful series of stage personas with theatrical trappings to match. The most impressive late flowering of this aesthetic came from the English group Pink Floyd, which linked its meditations on the travails of Western society with elaborate rock concert spectacles. The most dazzling, both musically and scenically, was *The Wall* (1979), whose live performances entailed the actual construction of an entire wall, 'brick' by 'brick', at one end of indoor sports arenas. The show was re-created in 1990 to celebrate the breaching of the Berlin wall.

Despite early efforts by Frank Zappa and Captain Beefheart, Americans never developed a comparable genre of overblown art rock with classical aspirations. American 'rock operas' tended more to ruminative, intimate song cycles by the likes of James Taylor, Paul Simon and the country singer Willie Nelson. By the late 1970s, however, classical pretensions along with softer folk-rock had fallen decisively out of favour among the rock intelligentsia, to be replaced by the rude, hard, primordial energies of punk rock. Ideologically, punks were even further removed from any notion of opera than their predecessors. Given the cyclical swings of fashion, however, the British penchant for rock spectacle could not long be suppressed. Post-punk pop ironists such as the Pet Shop Boys eventually reinstated it, as in their lavish 1991 tour staged by the American opera director David Alden.

If rock opera has an artistically significant future, it will almost certainly involve the incorporation of rock's musical gestures into opera or opera's transformation by rock. Rock has already been incorporated organically (the pulsing energy of Philip Glass's *Einstein on the Beach*, *Satyagraha* and *Akhnaten*) and eclectically (the use of rock by composers such as Bernstein and William Bolcom as part of a larger stylistic fabric). But rock is most likely to make a truly creative mark on musical theatre on its own terms. Richard Lester's Beatles films in the mid-1960s, with their jumping, crosscutting metabolism, predated the rock video, which in highly compact form has led to a new, rapidly shifting, non-narrative collage of images laden with violent, sexual or surrealistic connotations. They have already profoundly influenced opera, from the 'cartoon' operas of John Moran in America to the stagings and television productions of Peter Sellars. Electronically manipulated like rock music itself, these videos are a new kind of marriage of picture and sound, of *Wort und Ton*, for a 21st-century era of redefined 'operatic' entertainment.

*

J. Miller, ed.: *The Rolling Stone Illustrated History of Rock & Roll* (New York, 1976, 2/1980)

G. Bordman: *The American Musical Theater: a Chronicle* (New York, 1978)

S. Richards, ed.: *Great Rock Musicals* (New York, 1979)

M. Shore: *The Rolling Stone Book of Rock Videos* (New York, 1984)

P. Wicke: *Rock Pop Jazz Folk: ein Handbuch der populären Musik* (Leipzig, 1985)

M. Walsh: *Andrew Lloyd Webber* (New York, 1989)

JOHN ROCKWELL

Rodde, Anne-Marie (*b* Clermont-Ferrand, 21 Nov 1946). French soprano. She studied at Clermont-Ferrand and in Paris, and made her début as Cupid in Gluck's *Orfeo ed Euridice* (Aix-en-Provence, 1971); in

1972 she sang Yniold in *Pelléas et Mélisande* at Grenoble, and the following year had a conspicuous success in Stravinsky's *The Nightingale* at the Opéra and at Sadler's Wells in London. Her voice, small but of exquisite purity, found its valued place in the revivals of Rameau's operas, notably *Hippolyte et Aricie*, *Les Indes galantes* and *Les Boréades*, which she also sang in Paris and London. Other parts included the Child in *L'enfant et les sortilèges*, Sister Constance in *Dialogues des Carmélites*, Dirce (*Médée*), Zerbinetta and Mélisande. In 1984 she made her North American début as Susanna at Montreal. Her recordings include the Rameau operas and some admirable recitals of French and Italian song.

J. B. STEANE

Rode, Wilhelm (*b* Hanover, 17 Feb 1887; *d* Icking, nr Munich, 2 Sept 1959). German bass-baritone. He studied in Hanover and made his début in 1909 as the Herald in *Lohengrin* at Erfurt. After engagements at Bremerhaven, Breslau and Stuttgart, he joined the Bayerische Staatsoper, Munich (1922–32), and from 1926 sang with the Deutsches Opernhaus, Berlin, where he took part in the premières of Weill's *Die Bürgschaft* and Schreker's *Der Schmied von Gent* (1932). He sang Wotan at Covent Garden (1928), and Count Almaviva and Don Pizarro at Salzburg (1929–32). At the Vienna Staatsoper (1930–33) he sang Scarpia, the four villains in *Les contes d'Hoffmann* and Simon Boccanegra, as well as the Wagner roles for which he was best known. In 1933 he took over as director of the Deutsches Opernhaus following Max von Schillings's death, until 1944. Forced to retire in 1945 owing to his political sympathies, he later sang at Regensburg (1949–51). He had a magnificently resonant and warm-toned voice that was heard to best advantage as Hans Sachs, Wotan, Amfortas and the Dutchman, but he never sang at Bayreuth as he was usually engaged during the summer months at the Munich Festival.

LEO RIEMENS / ELIZABETH FORBES

Rodelinda [Rodelinda, regina de' longobardi] ('Rodelinda, Queen of the Lombards'). Opera in three acts by GEORGE FRIDERIC HANDEL to a libretto by NICOLA FRANCESCO HAYM adapted from ANTONIO SALVI's *Rodelinda, regina de' longobardi* (1710, Florence, Pratolino), after PIERRE CORNEILLE's play *Pertharite, roi des Lombards* (1651, Paris); London, King's Theatre, 13 February 1725.

Rodelinda *Queen of Lombardy, wife of …*	soprano
Bertarido *usurped by …*	alto castrato
Grimoaldo *Duke of Benevento, betrothed to …*	tenor
Eduige *Bertarido's sister*	soprano
Unulfo *a nobleman, counsellor to Grimoaldo, secretly a friend of Bertarido*	alto castrato
Garibaldo *Duke of Turin, rebel to Bertarido, friend of Grimoaldo*	bass
Flavio *son of Rodelinda and Bertarido*	silent

Setting Milan, in the 7th century

Rodelinda was Handel's seventh full-length opera for the Royal Academy of Music. It was produced in the same season as *Tamerlano* and with the same singers: Francesca Cuzzoni (Rodelinda), the castratos Senesino and Andrea Pacini (Bertarido and Unulfo), Francesco

Borosini (Grimoaldo), Anna Vincenza Dotti (Eduige) and Giuseppe Boschi (Garibaldo). The opera was very well received, achieving 14 performances, and was revived with additional arias at the King's Theatre on 18 December 1725 as the second opera of the new season.

Handel gave *Rodelinda* one further revival, on 4 May 1731; cuts and substitutions (the 'new' items all being taken from other operas) make this the weakest of the composer's own versions. A version prepared by Christian Gottlieb Wendt was given in Hamburg on 29 November 1734, with little success, and was repeated in 1735 and 1736. The production at Göttingen on 26 June 1920, in Oskar Hagen's arrangement, was the first revival of a Handel opera in the 20th century (there was a later, more historical revival there in 1953), and was followed by an equally pioneering production in the USA (Smith College, Northampton, MA, 9 May 1931). The first British revival was by the Dartington Hall Opera Group at the Old Vic Theatre on 5 June 1939; it was also given in London by the Handel Opera Society (with Joan Sutherland) on the Handel bicentenary, and by the WNO in 1981. Chrysander's edition generally gives Handel's first performing version of February 1725 as its main text, but inadequately represents the important and often beneficial changes of the December 1725 revival.

The story is based on the account in Paul the Deacon's *Gesta langobardorum* of events in 7th-century Lombardy, and is set in Milan. The Milanese throne, bequeathed to Bertarido by his father, has been usurped by Grimoaldo, Duke of Benevento. In consequence Bertarido was forced to flee to Hungary, leaving behind his wife Rodelinda, his young son Flavio and his sister Eduige, but he has now returned to Milan in disguise, having put out a report of his own death. Grimoaldo, despite being betrothed to Eduige, seeks the love of Rodelinda: marriage to her will confirm his hold on Milan.

ACT 1 *The royal palace* Rodelinda is mourning the supposed death of Bertarido. Grimoaldo offers himself as a new husband and is decisively rejected. Garibaldo, Duke of Turin and a treacherous ally of Grimoaldo, suggests that matters will be helped if Grimoaldo firmly breaks his promise to Eduige. This he does, and Eduige, encouraged by a declaration of love from Garibaldo, determines to see Grimoaldo brought down. Alone, Garibaldo reveals that he is merely using Eduige as a step to the throne, to which, as Bertarido's sister, she has a claim while Flavio remains a minor.

A cypress grove, with the tombs of the Lombardic kings; among the monuments is one to Bertarido Bertarido, in Hungarian dress, appears, wondering what has happened to Rodelinda. He is joined by Unulfo. The two men hide as Rodelinda brings Flavio to see the new monument to his father. Unulfo keeps Bertarido from revealing himself. Garibaldo appears: he takes Flavio hostage and threatens the child with death unless Rodelinda consents to marry Grimoaldo. Rodelinda agrees to accept Grimoaldo to save her son, to the distress of the listening Bertarido; but, as she leaves, she warns Garibaldo that she will demand his head as a gift from her new husband. Grimoaldo arrives and assures Garibaldo of his protection. Unulfo and Bertarido emerge from hiding, baffled by the turn of events. Unulfo tries to comfort Bertarido, but Bertarido remains angry at his wife's apparent treachery.

ACT 2 *A hall in the royal palace* Garibaldo tells Eduige that she has lost Grimoaldo and asks her to marry him instead; her uncertain reply suggests to Garibaldo that she still loves Grimoaldo. Eduige meets Rodelinda and asks her how she can accept Grimoaldo, now as much a traitor to Eduige as to Bertarido; her former love for him has changed to hate. Grimoaldo greets Rodelinda and asks her to confirm that she will marry him. She demands one favour first – not, as expected, the death of Garibaldo, but the death of her son Flavio, murdered before her eyes by Grimoaldo himself: she cannot be the wife of a usurper while remaining the mother of the rightful king. Grimoaldo recoils from such action. Garibaldo sees this as a sign of weakness, and unguardedly reveals to Unulfo his own ambition for the throne.

The countryside Bertarido is wandering distractedly. His laments are overheard by Eduige, who is amazed to find him alive. She learns with pleasure that his only desire is to rescue his wife and son, not to regain the kingdom (to which Eduige still aspires). Unulfo assures Bertarido that Rodelinda has remained faithful and tells him it is time to reveal himself. Bertarido, told by Unulfo that Bertarido is alive, longs to see him again; he arrives and embraces her. Grimoaldo appears: is this, he asks, the chaste Rodelinda in the arms of a lover? Bertarido (whom Grimoaldo has never seen) angrily says who he is; but Rodelinda, fearing for his safety, says he is lying to save her honour. Grimoaldo declares that the man will die anyway and leaves the couple to what they believe will be their final parting.

ACT 3 *The royal palace* Eduige, concerned to save her brother, gives Unulfo a key to the prison. Garibaldo urges Grimoaldo to kill Bertarido without delay, but Grimoaldo wavers.

A prison cell Bertarido bemoans his fate. His thoughts are interrupted by the sound of a sword dropped into his cell. Hearing someone approaching, he assumes he is about to be executed; he lashes out with the sword and wounds the intruder – but it turns out to be Unulfo, and Bertarido is immediately full of remorse. Unulfo tells Bertarido to take off his cloak (now bloodstained) and gives him a change of clothing; they leave by a secret passage. Eduige, Rodelinda and Flavio arrive to rescue Bertarido: they find the bloodstained cloak and assume that Bertarido has been murdered.

The palace garden Bertarido binds up Unulfo's wound and determines to be avenged on Grimoaldo. They hide as Grimoaldo appears, tormented by his crimes; longing for the simpler life of a shepherd, he lies down and sleeps. Garibaldo appears and, taking Grimoaldo's sword from his side, attempts to kill him; but Grimoaldo awakes and Bertarido emerges from hiding and drives Garibaldo off. Bertarido returns, having killed Garibaldo; Rodelinda is amazed to see him alive. Unulfo and Eduige explain that they rescued him. In gratitude Grimoaldo yields the kingdom of Milan to Bertarido and renews his vows to Eduige; she will reign with him in Pavia. All rejoice.

*   *   *

Several qualities combine to give *Rodelinda* its deservedly high reputation among Handel's operas: an unusually coherent story, consistent and credible characters, and music of exceptional power invariably apt to the dramatic situation; only Unulfo's arias are of a decorative nature. Rodelinda's rock-like devotion to her husband makes her an especially sympathetic heroine, and the part allows a wide range of emotions: pathos in the mourning arias of Act 1 ('Ho perduto il caro sposo', 'Ombre piante') and in the prison scene of Act 3 ('Se'l mio duol'), defiance ('Morrai, sì', 'Spietati, io vi giurai'), amorous yearning ('Ritorna, oh caro e dolce mio tesoro') and radiant joy ('Mio caro bene'). Bertarido's arias are no less appealing, his first, 'Dove sei?', having rightfully become one of Handel's most famous. The presence of two villainous characters in the cast contributes significantly to the dramatic tension, the more so because the characters themselves are contrasted: Grimoaldo wracked by doubts and not wholly without honour, Garibaldo darkly cynical. The confrontation scenes are among the most gripping in all Handel's operas, with the final one of Act 2 perhaps taking the palm: the sense of threat generated by Grimoaldo's explosion of vengeful anger in 'Tuo drudo è mio rivale' gives an almost unbearable poignancy to the grave beauty of the closing duet ('Io t'abbraccio') for Rodelinda and Bertarido.   ANTHONY HICKS

Rodgers, Richard (Charles) (*b* Hammels Station, Long Island, NY, 28 June 1902; *d* New York, 30 Dec 1979). American composer. He studied the piano from the age of six; largely self-taught, he learnt to improvise and play by ear. In New York he was attracted to the operettas of Victor Herbert and the early musical comedies of Kern. While at Columbia University (1919–21) and the Institute of Musical Art (1921–3), where he studied with Krehbiel and Goetschius, he began writing music and lyrics for amateur musical productions and conducting some of his shows. In 1918 he met Lorenz Hart (1895–1943); they discussed the need for good poetry in place of the banal lyrics of current popular songs and agreed to collaborate. They wrote Columbia's varsity show *Fly with Me* (1919) and seven songs for *Poor Little Ritz Girl* (1920). Their first success was a revue, the *Garrick Gaieties* (1925). In *Dearest Enemy* (1925) they moved away from the song-and-dance musical format towards the musical play, attempting to integrate song and drama in the context of serious subject matter and characters. Between 1926 and 1930 Rodgers and Hart were among the most popular American songwriters, producing 14 shows (including three for London) and numerous songs for other musicals and revues. They continued to experiment with the musical play; their programme for *Chee-Chee* (1928) announced that the numbers, some brief, were so closely linked with the story that they could not be listed, and in *Present Arms* (1928) Rodgers added transitional music to strengthen the cohesion of the stage action.

In Hollywood (1930–34) Rodgers and Hart wrote songs and background music for films, but with little success. Back in New York, they began writing their own books as well as lyrics, and reverted to musical comedy, but in a more sophisticated form. *On your Toes* (1936) contains Rodgers's first extensive orchestral music for ballet sequences (some choreographed by Balanchine). *Babes in Arms* (1937) is one of their most varied scores; their most daring musical was *Pal Joey* (1940), with a realistic, cynical and immoral story, unsavoury characters and suggestive lyrics ('Bewitched') that shocked audiences used to escapist musical comedy. Hart's death in 1943 ended the collaboration.

The partnership that Rodgers formed with Oscar Hammerstein II in 1943 was even more remarkable. It led to a series of musicals that enjoyed unprecedented artistic, critical and financial success, beginning with *Oklahoma!* (1943), one of the masterpieces of the American musical stage (it has been called the first American vernacular opera). Song, dance and drama are integrated, the play and lyrics dictating the musical techniques; the chorus girls and 'production numbers' of musical comedy are replaced by ballet choreographed by Agnes de Mille and modelled on American square dance. It had 2248 performances on Broadway in five years and has continued to be widely performed. Their works also include *Carousel* (1945) and *Allegro* (1947), musical plays choreographed by de Mille. *Carousel* includes a soliloquy in operatic style and several hit songs; *Allegro*, more of an experimental psychological drama, was less popular. *South Pacific* (1949) also won international acclaim. *The King and I* (1951) and *The Sound of Music* (1959), Rodgers and Hammerstein's last notable successes, furthered the integration of music and plot. After Hammerstein's death Rodgers continued composing, sometimes to his own lyrics, but with less success.

Besides musicals Rodgers wrote ballets, incidental dramatic music and film music. He helped revise many of his musicals for stage revivals and for films. He did much to support musical theatre production and preservation, most prominently by founding in 1965 the Rodgers and Hammerstein Archives of Recorded Sound at the Performing Arts Research Center of the New York Public Library.

With Hart, Rodgers wrote songs largely on the model of Tin Pan Alley, with a limited vocal range, little ornamentation and simple harmonies, though more graceful and imaginative than most popular songs of the time. With Hammerstein, his forms often expanded to meet the demands of the text, sometimes dispensing with the conventional juxtaposition of verse and chorus or the symmetry of four phrases in 32 bars. More than most theatre composers of the 1920s, Rodgers used rhythms derived from popular dances influenced by jazz. Many of his successful songs are graceful and lyrical, their momentum skilfully achieved by the placing of the longer notes and any unusual or colourful chord progressions on the second or third beats of the bar. But some of his livelier songs build up excitement through a held note on the first beat. In the tradition of Broadway, Rodgers relied on orchestrators (particularly Robert Russell Bennett) to prepare his songs for the theatre.

musicals; dates are of first New York performance unless otherwise stated; librettists and lyricists are listed in that order, separated by a semicolon

Poor Little Ritz Girl (G. Campbell and L. Fields; L. Hart), Central, 28 July 1920, collab. S. Romberg
Dearest Enemy (H. Fields; Hart), Knickerbocker, 18 Sept 1925
The Girl Friend (H. Fields; Hart), Vanderbilt, 17 March 1926
Lido Lady (G. Bolton, B. Kalmar, H. Ruby and R. Jeans; Hart), London, Gaiety, 1 Dec 1926
Peggy-Ann (H. Fields; Hart), Vanderbilt, 27 Dec 1926
Betsy (I. Caesar, D. Freedman and W. A. McGuire; Hart), New Amsterdam, 28 Dec 1926
A Connecticut Yankee (H. Fields; Hart), Vanderbilt, 3 Nov 1927
She's my Baby (Bolton, Kalmar and Ruby; Hart), Globe, 3 Jan 1928
Present Arms (H. Fields; Hart), Mansfield, 26 April 1928
Chee-Chee (H. Fields; Hart), Mansfield, 25 Sept 1928
Spring is Here (O. Davis; Hart), Alvin, 11 March 1929
Heads Up! (J. McGowan and P. G. Smith; Hart), Alvin, 11 Nov 1929
Simple Simon (E. Wynn, Bolton and Hart), Ziegfeld, 18 Feb 1930
America's Sweetheart (H. Fields; Hart), Broadhurst, 10 Feb 1931
Jumbo (B. Hecht and C. MacArthur; Hart), Hippodrome, 16 Nov 1935

On your Toes (Rodgers, Hart and G. Abbott; Hart), Imperial, 11 April 1936
Babes in Arms (Rodgers and Hart; Hart), Shubert, 14 April 1937
I'd Rather be Right (G. S. Kaufman and M. Hart; Hart), Alvin, 2 Nov 1937
I Married an Angel (Rodgers and Hart; Hart), Shubert, 11 May 1938
The Boys from Syracuse (Abbott, after W. Shakespeare: *The Comedy of Errors*; Hart), Alvin, 23 Nov 1938
Too Many Girls (G. Marion jr; Hart) Imperial, 18 Oct 1939
Higher and Higher (G. Hurlbut and J. Logan; Hart), Shubert, 4 April 1940
Pal Joey (J. O'Hara; Hart), Barrymore, 25 Dec 1940
By Jupiter (Rodgers and Hart; Hart), Shubert, 2 June 1942
Oklahoma! (O. Hammerstein II, after L. Riggs: *Green Grow the Lilacs*), St James, 31 March 1943
Carousel (Hammerstein), Majestic, 19 April 1945
Allegro (Hammerstein), Majestic, 10 Oct 1947
South Pacific (Logan and Hammerstein, after J. Michener: *Tales of the South Pacific*; Hammerstein), Majestic, 7 April 1949
The King and I (Hammerstein), St James, 29 March 1951
Me and Juliet (Hammerstein), Majestic, 28 May 1953
Pipe Dream (Hammerstein), Shubert, 30 Nov 1955
Flower Drum Song (J. Fields and Hammerstein; Hammerstein), St James, 1 Dec 1958
The Sound of Music (H. Lindsay and R. Crouse; Hammerstein), Lunt-Fontanne, 16 Nov 1959
No Strings (S. Taylor; Rodgers), 54th Street, 15 March 1962
Do I Hear a Waltz? (A. Laurents; S. Sondheim), 46th Street, 18 March 1965
Two by Two (P. Stone; M. Charnin), Imperial, 10 Nov 1970
Rex (S. Yellen; S. Harnick), Lunt-Fontanne, 25 April 1976
I Remember Mama (T. Meehan after T. Van Druten and K. Forbes; Charnin), Majestic, 31 May 1979

*

Fact Book Concerning the Plays of Richard Rodgers and Oscar Hammerstein (New York, 1951, rev. edns 1955–80)
D. Ewen: *Richard Rodgers* (New York, 1957, rev. 2/1963 as *With a Song in his Heart*)
Richard Rodgers Fact Book (New York, 1965; suppl., 1968)
M. Kaye: *Richard Rodgers: a Comparative Analysis of his Songs with Hart and Hammerstein Lyrics* (diss., New York U., 1969)
R. Rodgers: *Musical Stages* (New York, 1975)

RONALD BYRNSIDE, DEANE L. ROOT, GERALD BORDMAN/R

Rodolphe, Jean Joseph [Rudolph, Johann Joseph] (*b* Strasbourg, 14 Oct 1730; *d* Paris, 12 or 18 Aug 1812). Alsatian composer active in France. He was taught counterpoint by Traetta in Parma and continued his studies with Jommelli in Stuttgart, where he composed the ballets *Renaud et Armide* (1761), *Psyche et l'Amour* (1762) and *Médée et Jason* (1763) for Noverre. These were performed alongside *opere serie* by Jommelli. He settled in Paris a few years after the unsuccessful staging of his first *opéra comique*, *Le mariage par capitulation* (1764), which received only one performance. *L'aveugle de Palmire* (1767), another unambitious *opéra comique* in the pastoral style with sentimental overtones, remained in the repertory for slightly longer and was restaged, with a sumptuous *mise-en-scène*, at Fontainebleau in 1776. Grimm, however, criticized the weak libretto and found nothing in the music but 'a string of romances, rondos and couplets without end'. Two further works received premières at court in 1773: *Isménor*, written for the wedding of the Count of Artois (later Charles X) and Marie-Thérèse of Savoy, and *Nanine*, a parody of Monsigny's *Aline, reine de Golconde* (1766).

Le mariage par capitulation (oc, 1, L. H. Dancourt), Paris, Comédie-Italienne, 3 Dec 1764
L'aveugle de Palmire (comédie-pastorale mêlée d'ariettes, 2, Desfontaines [F. G. Fouques], after Mme Riccoboni: *L'aveugle*), Paris, Comédie-Italienne, 5 March 1767, *F-Pc*; (Paris, 1768)
Isménor (ballet-héroïque, 3, Desfontaines), Versailles, 17 Nov 1773

Nanine, sœur de lait de la reine de Golconde (pastorale en ariettes et vaudevilles, 3, Desfontaines or P.-T. Gondot), Fontainebleau, 1773

*

Correspondance littéraire, philosophique et critique par Grimm, Diderot, Raynal, Meister, etc., ed. M. Tourneux (Paris, 1877–82), vii, 281   ELISABETH COOK (text), MICHEL NOIRAY (work-list)

Rodrigo [*Vincer se stesso è la maggior vittoria* ('Conquering Oneself is the Greater Victory')]. Opera in three acts by GEORGE FRIDERIC HANDEL to a libretto anonymously adapted from FRANCESCO SILVANI's *Il duello d'Amore e di Vendetta* (1700, Venice); Florence, Teatro del Cocomero, autumn 1707.

Handel's first opera for Italy was produced by the Academia degl'Infuocati, a group supporting cultural activities under the patronage of Ferdinando de' Medici. The wordbook of the first performance (copies of which were not discovered until 1974) gives its title as *Vincer se stesso è il maggior vittoria*, though Mainwaring in his *Memoirs of ... Handel* (1760) referred to it as *Rodrigo*. Mainwaring stated that the work had been received favourably, but his testimony is uncertain, as he also states that one of the singers was 'Vittoria' (presumably Tarquini), an assertion contradicted by the original cast list. The opera survives today only in the version of Handel's original autograph (except for the opening of Act 1, which is lost). This is not, however, the form in which it was actually performed: the wordbook shows that Handel made substantial revisions before performance, including the insertion of seven new arias. Lacunae in the musical sources prevent this version from being reconstructed.

The discovery in 1983 of previously lost material for Act 3 allowed *Rodrigo* to be revived for the first time in an almost complete version, by the Handel Opera Society at Sadler's Wells Theatre in London on 17 July 1985; the lost recitatives in Act 1 were supplied by the conductor, Charles Farncombe. A shortened version edited by Alan Curtis, not using the new material, had previously been produced at Innsbruck in August 1984. The only printed edition is Chrysander's of 1873, which reproduces the incomplete text of the autograph.

The story, set in Seville, is fictional, though it alludes to real events in the last years of Visigothic rule in Spain, around AD 710. Rodrigo (*d* 711), Duke of Baetica and last of the Visigothic kings, is a historical figure and at least three of the other characters (Giuliano, Florinda and Evanco) have historical counterparts. Rodrigo (soprano castrato) has obtained the kingdom of Aragon by murdering its rightful ruler Vitizza and seizing the throne. Giuliano (tenor), his ally, is away suppressing a rebellion led by Vitizza's son Evanco (soprano castrato). Meanwhile, Rodrigo has seduced Giuliano's sister Florinda (soprano), promising her that he will repudiate his wife Esilena (soprano); but after Florinda bears him a son he breaks his promise.

The opera opens with Florinda railing at Rodrigo for his treachery and resolving to be avenged. Giuliano, ignorant of these events, returns to Seville with Evanco as his prisoner; the rebels have been crushed. When he learns how Rodrigo has dishonoured his sister he decides to avenge her by supporting Evanco's cause. Evanco and Florinda fall in love. Esilena, a mollifying influence throughout, offers to leave Rodrigo and allow Florinda to become queen; but Florinda is determined on Rodrigo's death. Fernando (alto castrato), Rodrigo's general, captures Giuliano by a trick and uses him as a hostage. Giuliano remains defiant and is rescued when the rebel troops storm the walls of Seville and Evanco kills Fernando. Rodrigo is now captured. Florinda is about to kill him when Esilena, carrying Florinda's baby son, intervenes; she pacifies the rebels, and the chastened Rodrigo abdicates. Evanco is granted his father's kingdom of Aragon, with Florinda as his queen. Rodrigo's son by Florinda receives Castile, with Giuliano to rule during the child's minority. Rodrigo goes into humble retreat with Esilena.

*   *   *

In its surviving form, *Rodrigo* shows some points of weakness in characterization and structure: the patient and long-suffering Esilena is nicely contrasted with the fiery Florinda, but the male characters do not come fully to life in the music. There are nevertheless several attractive arias showing Handel's rapidly maturing assimilation of the Italian style.
                                                            ANTHONY HICKS

Rodrigue et Chimène. Unfinished opera in three acts by CLAUDE DEBUSSY to a libretto by Catulle Mendès; Paris, Bibliothèque Nationale, 22 June 1987 (extracts with piano accompaniment in a reconstruction by Richard Langham Smith).

Mendès had completed a libretto for an opera based on the legend of *El Cid* by 1879; it was first announced without mention of a composer. Later Emile Pessard was reported as the intended composer, but it appears that Massenet's *Le Cid* prevented Mendès from proceeding. Over ten years later Mendès approached Debussy, possibly owing to a chance meeting with his father. Debussy began work in 1890 and by 1892 had completed three acts in outline. A short score exists of Acts 1 and 3, while Act 2 was copied out neatly in the form of a vocal score. All contain unfinished passages, and some pages have been lost.

The opera deals with the love between Rodrigue (tenor) and Chimène (soprano), daughter of Don Gomez. Rodrigue's father, Don Diègue (baritone), has been insulted by Don Gomez, and after Rodrigue's two brothers, Hernan (tenor) and Bermudo (tenor), have refused, Rodrigue is called upon to avenge the insult to his father by murdering Gomez. Gomez dies in the arms of Chimène, and a striking chorus of lament, in a pseudo-Renaissance style, ends the second act. In the third act, Chimène is torn between avenging her father and her continuing love for Rodrigue. Eventually Rodrigue is judged but is spared on account of his bravery for the Christian cause.

The epic, realistic text, with its hackneyed imagery, was ultimately unsuited to Debussy's increasingly refined tastes. In several letters he confessed his dissatisfaction with the work, suggesting that he had accepted the collaboration with Mendès partly for the sake of his parents. He was, however, pleased enough with the work to play extracts to Paul Dukas in 1892. Dukas aptly summed up the work in his initial reactions, communicated in a letter to Vincent d'Indy:

Debussy played me extracts from an opera which can't be far from being finished: I think you'd be surprised at the dramatic breadth of some of its scenes ... And I can add that all the episodic scenes are exquisite, having a harmonic finesse which recall his early songs ... The libretto has no interest whatsoever: Parnassian bric-à-brac mixed with fake Spanish barbarism.

The work is important in that it is the only true opera Debussy completed apart from *Pelléas et Mélisande*. Despite the gaps and the extreme difficulty of restoring countless missing accidentals, as well as the lost pages, a staged performance is not entirely beyond the realms of possibility.   RICHARD LANGHAM SMITH

Rodríguez de Hita [Yta], **Antonio** (*b* Valverde, Madrid, ?1724–5; *d* Madrid, 21 Feb 1787). Spanish composer. His precocious talents were rewarded with appointments as organist at the Colegio de Alcalá about the age of 14 and *maestro de capilla* at Palencia Cathedral by 20. In 1757 he published a theory textbook for teachers, *Diapasón instructivo, consonancias físicas y morales: documentos a los profesores de música*, promptly attacked by Roel de los Ríos as falling into what he saw as the false camp of new liberalist Spanish composers. Despite the stir caused by this polemic, Rodríguez secured in 1765 the prestigious post of *maestro de capilla* at the Convento de la Encarnación in Madrid.

Though his output was mainly religious (he wrote nearly 300 such pieces in Latin or Spanish), Rodríguez's most influential works were two racy, down-to-earth zarzuelas written in collaboration with the popular playwright Ramón de la Cruz, *Las segadoras de Vallecas* (1768) and *Las labradoras de Murcia* (1769). Composer and librettist mixed ingredients of Italian *opera buffa* with Spanish regionalistic traditions so effectively that both works proved box-office attractions for a decade. A measure of the difficulties Spanish composers and librettists had to face in pleasing both factions in the protracted 18th-century polemic between neo-classicists and progressives, nationalists and Italianists, may be gauged from the fact that Rodríguez and Ramón, only five months before the première of the first of their two startlingly plebeianized zarzuelas, and again only ten months after the première of the second, wrote two other zarzuelas which set out more to appease hard-line traditionalists and neo-classicists. These were *Briseida*, first performed in 1768 at the home of the Count Aranda and next evening in the Teatro del Príncipe (reputedly the first evening performance in a public theatre in Spain), and *Scipión en Cartagena* (1770). Both drew on the heroic and aristocratic kind of musical drama created by Hidalgo and Calderón in the 17th century as well as on neo-classic literary theory. Ramón de la Cruz stated that *Briseida* was given its first performance before an audience of 'many people of the most educated and elevated classes of the kingdom and ambassadors of foreign courts'. *Briseida* and *Scipión* did indeed draw audiences from the more élite classes, but they were notably less successful with the general public and less influential on subsequent Spanish composers than were the more colourful and folklike *Las segadoras* and *Las labradoras*.

See also LABRADORAS DE MURCIA, LAS.

all zarzuelas in 2 acts, first performed in Madrid

La Briseida (R. de la Cruz), home of Count Aranda, 10 July 1768, Príncipe, 11 July 1768, *E-Mm*
Las segadoras de Vallecas (De la Cruz), Príncipe, 3 Sept 1768
Las labradoras de Murcia (De la Cruz), Príncipe, 16 Sept 1769, *Mm*
Scipión en Cartagena (A. Cordero), Príncipe, 15 July 1770, *Mm*

F. Bonastre: 'Estudio de la obra teórica y práctica del compositor Antonio Rodríguez de Hita', *RdMc*, ii (1979), 47–88
W. M. Bussey: *French and Italian Influence on the Zarzuela 1700–1770* (Ann Arbor, 1980)
A. Martín Moreno: *Historia de la música española, iv: Siglo XVIII* (Madrid, 1985)   JACK SAGE

Rodríguez-Losada Rebellón, Eduardo (*b* La Coruña, 2 March 1886; *d* La Coruña, 2 Nov 1973). Spanish composer. An architect by profession, with functionalist convictions, he was a self-taught composer whose musical ideas were strongly influenced by French and German academic theory. His first comic opera, *El monte de las ánimas*, is an elegant sketch full of modernist charm. Two years later he produced *O Mariscal* with a libretto in Galician, a 'grand opera' based on a late medieval legend of Galician history, interpreted as the vain struggle of a nobleman against the centralist aims of Ferdinand and Isabella. This was followed in 1935 by *¡Ultreya!*, in which the question of nationalism is raised again, with the legend of Santiago, St James the Apostle, being treated as a component of Galician identity.

O Mariscal and *¡Ultreya!* are both in the Wagnerian tradition in their melodic shaping, dense orchestration and harmonic formulae. The use of non-professional singers in *O Mariscal* imposed limitations on the complexity of the vocal writing, to the advantage of the dramatic tension and ensemble scenes, while the use of dialogue in *¡Ultreya!* gives the work a kinship with dramatic epic. Years later Rodríguez-Losada Rebellón embarked on a work of extraordinary complexity, *El gran teatro del mundo*, which could be performed only as a dramatic cantata.

El monte de las ánimas (comic op, 2, N. de Cepeda, after J. J. Casal), La Coruña, 6 June 1927
O Mariscal (3, A. Vilar-Ponte and R. Cabanillas), Vigo, Tamberlick, 31 May 1929
¡Ultreya! (3, A. Cotarelo-Valledor), Madrid, Zarzuela, 12 March 1935

A. Fernández-Cid: *Cien años de teatro musical en España (1875–1975)* (Madrid, 1975)
X. M. Carreira Antelo: 'El compositor Eduardo Rodríguez-Losada Rebellón (1886–1973)', *RdMc*, ix (1986), 97–139
X. M. Carreira: 'El nacionalismo operístico en Galicia', *RdMc*, x (1987), 667–83
—— and others, eds.: *E. Rodríguez-Losada Rebellón: 'O Mariscal'* (forthcoming) [facs. and commentary]   XOAN M. CARREIRA

Rodwell, George (Herbert Bonaparte) (*b* London, 15 Nov 1800; *d* London, 22 Jan 1852). English composer and playwright. He was a pupil of Vincent Novello and Henry Bishop. His brother was proprietor and manager of the Adelphi Theatre, where his first musical stage piece, *Waverley*, was produced in 1824. In March 1825, on his brother's death, he succeeded to the proprietorship. In 1828 he took up a teaching post at the RAM, and in 1836 he was appointed director of the music at Covent Garden Theatre, where his most successful piece, *Teddy the Tiler*, had been produced in 1830. There he assisted in the Covent Garden policy of trying to anticipate the repertory of Drury Lane, as in the case of his version of Auber's *Le cheval de bronze*. He wrote the words of many farces and melodramas: Nicoll lists 21 besides the ones for which he composed music. For many years he persistently advocated the establishment of a national opera. Rodwell's songs, glees and stage pieces enjoyed a good deal of popularity in their day, but they scarcely outlived him, and to modern taste they have only a faint appeal.

all first performed in London

LA – *Adelphi Theatre*   LCG – *Covent Garden*

Waverley, or Sixty Years Since (melodramatic burletta, 3, E. Fitzball, after W. Scott), LA, 11 March 1824
The Songs of the Birds (musical drama, Fitzball), 1826, excerpts pubd
The Flying Dutchman, or The Phantom Ship (nautical burletta, 3, Fitzball), LA, 1 Jan 1827

The Cornish Miners (melodrama, 2, R. B. Peake), Lyceum, 2 July 1827

The Bottle Imp (operatic romance, Peake and Fitzball), Lyceum, 7 July 1828, excerpts pubd

The Mason of Buda (nautical burletta, J. R. Planché, after E. Scribe), LA, 1 Oct 1828; after D.-F.-E. Auber: Le maçon

The Earthquake, or The Spectre of the Nile (operatic spectacle or burletta, 3, Fitzball), LA, 15 Dec 1828, excerpts pubd

The Devil's Elixir, or The Shadowless Man (musical drama, 2, Fitzball, after E. T. A. Hoffmann: Die Elixiere des Teufels), LCG, 20 April 1829, excerpts pubd

The Spring Lock (musical entertainment, Peake), Lyceum, 18 Aug 1829

Teddy the Tiler (farce, Rodwell, after P. le Couvreur), LCG, 8 Feb 1830

The Skeleton Lover (romantic musical drama), LA, 16 July 1830, GB-Lbl

The Black Vulture, or The Wheel of Death (romantic burletta, Fitzball), LA, 4 Oct 1830

The Evil Eye (musical drama, Peake), LA, 18 Aug 1831, excerpts pubd

My Own Lover (operatic farce, Rodwell), Drury Lane, 11 Jan 1832

Don Quixote, the Knight of the Woful Countenance, or The Humours of Sancho Panza (romantic burletta, J. B. Buckstone, after M. de Cervantes: Don Quixote), LA, 7 Jan 1833

The Lord of the Isles, or The Gathering of the Clans (romantic national op, Fitzball, after Scott), Surrey, 20 Nov 1834, vs pubd

The Last Days of Pompeii, or Seventeen Hundred Years Ago (historical burletta, Buckstone, after E. L. Bulwer-Lytton), LA, 15 Dec 1834

The Spirit of the Bell (comic op, 2, J. Kenney), Lyceum, 8 June 1835

Paul Clifford (musical drama, 3, Fitzball, after Bulwer-Lytton), LCG, 28 Oct 1835, excerpts pubd; collab. J. Blewitt

The Bronze Horse, or The Spell of the Cloud King (musical drama, 2, Fitzball, after Scribe), LCG, 14 Dec 1835, vs pubd; after Auber: Le cheval de bronze

Quasimodo, or The Gipsy Girl of Notre Dame (operatic romance, 3, Fitzball, after V. Hugo), LCG, 2 Feb 1836; after C. M. von Weber: Preciosa

The Sexton of Cologne, or The Burgomaster's Daughter (operatic romance, 3, Fitzball) LCG, 13 June 1836

Thalaba the Destroyer, or The Burning Sword, (operatic romance, 3, Fitzball), 1836

Jack Sheppard (drama, Buckstone, after W. H. Ainsworth), LA, 28 Oct 1839

The Seven Maids of Munich, or The Ghost's Tower (musical drama, Rodwell), Princess's, 19 Dec 1846

*

DNB (L. M. Middleton); NicollH

A. Bunn: The Stage (London, 1840), ii, 9–10

E. Fitzball: Thirty-Five Years of a Dramatic Author's Life (London, 1859)

J. S. Curwen: Music at the Queen's Accession (London, 1897)

NICHOLAS TEMPERLEY

Rodziński, Artur (b Spalato [now Split], Dalmatia, 1 Jan 1892; d Boston, 27 Nov 1958). American conductor of Polish descent. In Vienna he studied composition with Schreker and Joseph Marx, and conducting with Franz Schalk, then made his conducting début with Ernani at the Lwów [now L'viv] Opera in 1920. From 1921 he was also active at the Warsaw Opera where he introduced Der Rosenkavalier, Wolf-Ferrari's I gioielli della madonna and Ravel's L'heure espagnole. He later took charge of the opera department of the Curtis Institute before a ten-year engagement with the Cleveland Orchestra led to the American première, in 1935, of Shostakovich's Lady Macbeth of the Mtsensk District. In 1937 he conducted Rose Pauly and the New York PO in a concert performance of Elektra and he later attempted to stage operas in place of regular concerts during his 11-month season with the Chicago SO in 1947–8 (his highly successful Tristan was the occasion of Flagstad's return to the USA after the war). He continued his operatic successes in Italy, conducting the first performance outside Russia of Prokofiev's War and Peace in Florence in May 1953. His last performances, in November 1958, were of Tristan at the Chicago Lyric Opera. As an interpreter, Rodziński was ruggedly energetic, in no way eccentric or even strikingly individual, sometimes fiery, hardly ever poetic or delicate.

MICHAEL STEINBERG